TUFF STUFF®

2006 Standard Catalog of®

FOOTBALL CARDS

9TH EDITION

Collectibles publication partner of the National Football League

Published by

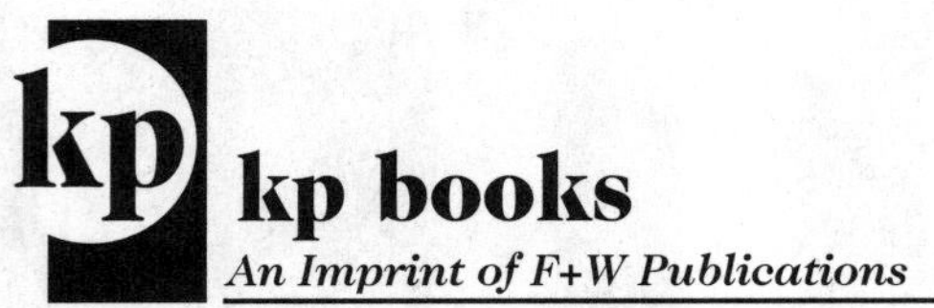

700 East State Street • Iola, WI 54990-0001
715-445-2214 • 888-457-2873

Our toll-free number to place an order or obtain
a free catalog is (800) 258-0929.

Library of Congress Catalog Number: 98642145

ISBN: 0-87349-985-9

Edited by Bert Lehman

Designed by Sally Olson

Printed in the United States of America

TABLE OF CONTENTS

A

B

(CONTINUE ON PAGE 10)

C

D

E

F

G

H

I

J

K

L

M

N

O

P

T

U

V

W

Z

COLLEGE

CANADIAN

WELCOME!

Thank you for purchasing the ninth edition of Standard Catalog of Football Cards.

This book is the most comprehensive annual football card price guide in the industry, complete with listings for more than 550,000 cards and checklists for more than 3,400 sets. The entire *Tuff Stuff* price guide staff contributed to this book, including coordinator Steve Bloedow and staff members Joe Clemens, Bert Lehman.

Krause Publications' Standard Catalog of Baseball Cards is widely accepted in the sports card hobby as the most comprehensive annual price guide, containing current values for over 500,000 cards and checklists of over 9,500 sets. Authored each year by Bob Lemke, the Standard Catalog of Baseball Cards is a standard tool of the trade for the serious baseball card dealer and collector.

Given the outstanding performance of the Standard Catalog of Baseball Cards and the rising popularity of football cards, it was only natural for the price guide staff to extend the successful formula for its baseball catalog to the Standard Catalog of Football Cards.

It is our hope that this book enhances both your collection and your enjoyment of the sports card hobby.

HOW TO USE THIS CATALOG

This catalog has been uniquely designed to serve the needs of beginning and advanced football card collectors. It provides a comprehensive guide to more than 80 years of sports card issues, arranged so that even the novice collector can use it with confidence and ease.

The following explanations summarize the general practices used in preparing this catalog's listings. However, because of specialized requirements which may vary from card set to card set, these explanations should not be considered ironclad, but used as guidelines.

ARRANGEMENT

Because the most important feature in identifying and pricing a sports card is its set of origin, this catalog has been alphabetically arranged according to the name by which the set is most popularly known.

Those sets that were issued for more than one year are then listed chronologically, from earliest to most recent.

Within each set, the cards are listed by their designated card number, or in the absence of card numbers, alphabetically according to the last name of the player pictured.

IDENTIFICATION

While the date and issue of most modern sports cards are well identified on front, back, or both, such has not always been the case. In general, the back of the card is more useful in identifying the set of origin than the front. The issuer or sponsor's name will usually appear on the back since, after all, sports cards were first produced as a promotional item to stimulate sales of other products. As often as not, that issuer's name is the name by which the set is known to collectors and under which it will be found listed in this catalog.

In some difficult cases identifying a sports card's general age, if not specific year of issue, can be fixed by studying the biological or statistical information on the back of the card. The last year mentioned in either the biography or stats is usually the year which preceded the year of issue.

PHOTOGRAPHS

A photograph of the front of at least one representative card from virtually every set listed in this catalog has been incorporated into the listings to aid in identification.

Photographs have been printed in reduced size. The actual size of cards in each set is given in the introductory text preceding its listing, unless the card is the standard size 1-1/2" by 3-1/2".

DATING

The dating of sports cards by year of issue on the front or back of the card itself is a relatively new phenomenon. In most cases, to accurately determine a date of issue for an unidentified card, it must be studied for clues. As mentioned, the biography, career summary or statistics on the back of the card are the best way to pinpoint a year of issue. In most cases, the year of issue will be the year after the last season mentioned on the card.

Luckily for today's collector, earlier generations have done much of the research in determining your year of issue for those cards which bear no clues. The painstaking task of matching players' listed and/or pictured teams against their career records often allowed an issue date to be determined.

In some cases, particular card sets were issued over a period of more than one calendar year, but since they are collected together as a single set, their specific year of issue is not important. Such sets will be listed with their complete known range of issue years.

NUMBERING

While many sports card issues as far back as the early 1900s have contained card numbers assigned by the issuer to facilitate the collecting of a complete set, the practice has by no means been universal. Even today, not every set bears card numbers.

Logically, those sports cards which were numbered by their manufacturer are presented in that numerical order within the listings of this catalog. The many unnumbered issues, however, have been assigned Sports Collectors Digest/Tuff Stuff Price Guide numbers to facilitate their universal identification within the hobby, especially when buying and selling by mail.

In all cases, numbers which have been assigned or which otherwise do not appear on the card through error or by design, are shown in this catalog within parentheses. In virtually all cases, unless a more natural system suggested itself by the unique matter of a particular set, the assignment of Sports Collectors Digest/Tuff Stuff Price Guide numbers by the cataloging staff has been done by alphabetical arrangement of the players' last names or the card's principal title.

Significant collectible variations for any particular card are noted within the listings by the application of a suffix letter within parentheses. In instances of variations, the suffix "a" is assigned to the variation which was created first.

NAMES

The identification of a player by full name on the front of his sports card has been a common practice only since the 1940s. Prior to that, the player's name and team were the usual information found on the card front.

As a general practice, the listings in the Sports Collectors Digest/Tuff Stuff Price Guide present the player's name as it is more commonly known. If the player's name only appears on the back, rather than on the front of the card, the listing corresponds to that designation.

In cases where only the player's last name is given on the card, the cataloging staff has included the first name by which he was most often known for ease of identification.

Cards which contain misspelled first or last names, or even wrong initials, will have included in their listings the incorrect information, with a correction accompanying in parentheses. This extends, also, to cases where the name on the card does not correspond to the player actually pictured.

GRADING

The vast majority of cards in this book were issued between 1981 and 2001 and feature NFL players only. The term "card" is used rather loosely as in this context it is construed to include virtually any series of cardboard or paper product, of whatever size and/or shape, depicting football players. Further, "cards" printed on wood, metal, plastic and other materials are either by their association with other issues or by their compatibility in size with the current 2-1/2" x 3-1/2" card standard also listed here.

Because modern cards are generally not popularly collected in lower grades, cards in this section carry only a Mint (MT) value quote. In general, post-1980 cards which grade Near Mint (NM) will retail at about 75% of the Mint price, while Excellent (EX) condition cards bring 40%.

Here is a more detailed look at grading procedures:

Mint (MT): A perfect card. Well-centered, with parallel borders which appear equal to the naked eye. Four sharp, square corners. No creases, edge dents, surface scratches, paper flaws, loss of luster, yellowing or fading, regardless of age. No imperfectly printed card - out of register, badly cut or ink flawed - or card stained by contact with gum, wax or other substances can be considered truly Mint, even if new out of the pack.

Near Mint (NR MT): A nearly perfect card. At first glance, a Near Mint card appears perfect; upon a closer examination, however, a minor flaw will be discovered. On well-centered cards, three of the four corners must be perfectly sharp; only one corner shows a minor imperfection upon close inspection. A slightly off-center card with one or more borders being noticeably unequal - but still present - would also fit this grade.

Excellent (EX): Corners are still fairly sharp with only moderate wear. Card borders may be off center. No creases. May have very minor gum, wax or product stains, front or back. Surfaces may show slight loss of luster from rubbing across other cards.

Very Good (VG): Show obvious handling. Corners rounded and/or perhaps showing minor creases. Other minor creases may be visible. Surfaces may exhibit loss of luster, but all printing is intact. May show major gum, wax or other packaging stains. No major creases, tape marks or extraneous markings or writing. Exhibit honest wear.

Good (G - generally 50% of the VG price): A well-worn card, but exhibits no intentional damage or abuse. May have major or multiple creases. Corners rounded well beyond the border.

Fair (F - generally 50% of the Good price): Shows excessive wear, along with damage or abuse. Will show all the wear characteristics of a Good card, along with such damage as thumb tack holes in or near margins, evidence of having been taped or pasted, perhaps small tears around the edges, or creases so heavy as to break the cardboard. Backs may show minor added pen or pencil writing, or be missing small bits of paper. Still, basically a complete card.

Poor (P): A card that has been tortured to death. Corners or other areas may be torn off. Card may have been trimmed, show holes from a paper punch or have been used for BB gun practice. Front may have extraneous pen or pencil writing, or other defacement. Major portions of front or back design may be missing. In other words, not a pretty sight.

In addition to these terms, collectors may encounter intermediate grades, such as VG-EX or EX-MT. These cards usually have characteristics of both the lower and higher grades, and are generally priced midway between those two values.

VALUATIONS

Values quoted in this book represent the current retail market and are compiled from recommendations provided and verified through the authors' daily involvement in the publication of the hobby's leading advertising periodicals, as well as the input of specialized consultants.

It should be stressed, however, that this book is intended to serve only as an aid in evaluating cards; actual market conditions are constantly changing. This is especially true of the cards of current players, whose on-field performance during the course of a season can greatly affect the value of their cards - upwards or downward.

Publication of this book is not intended as a solicitation to buy or sell the listed cards by the editors, publishers or contributors.

Again, the values here are retail prices - what a collector can expect to pay when buying a card from a dealer. The wholesale price, that which a collector can expect to receive from a dealer when selling cards, will be significantly lower.

Most dealers operate on a 100 percent mark-up, generally paying about 50 percent of a card's retail value. On some high demand cards, dealers will pay up to 75 percent or even 100 percent or more of retail value, anticipating continued price increases. Conversely, for many low-demand cards, such as common players' cards of recent years, dealers may pay 25 percent or even less of retail.

SETS

Collectors may note that the complete set prices for newer issues quoted in these listings are usually significantly lower than the total of the value of the individual cards which comprise the set. This reflects two factors in the sports card market. First, a seller is often willing to take a lower composite price for a complete set as a "volume discount" and to avoid inventorying a large number of common player or other lower-demand cards.

Second, to a degree, the value of common cards can be said to be inflated as a result of having a built-in overhead charge to justify the dealer's time in sorting cards, carrying them in stock and filling orders. This accounts for the fact that even brand new sports cards, which cost the dealer around 1 cent each when bought in bulk, carry individual price tags of 3 cents or higher.

ERRORS/VARIATIONS

It is often hard for the beginning collector to understand that an error on a sports card, in and of itself, does not usually add premium value to that card. It is usually only when the correcting of an error in the subsequent printing creates a variation that premium value attaches to an error.

Minor errors, such as wrong stats or personal data, create a variation that attaches to an error. Misspellings, inconsistencies, etc. - usually affecting the back of the card - are very common, especially in recent years. Unless a corrected variation was also printed, these errors are not noted in the listings of this book because they are not generally perceived by collectors to have premium value.

On the other hand, major effort had been expended to include the most complete listings ever for collectible variation cards. Many scarce and valuable variations are included in these listings because they are widely collected and often have significant premium value.

COUNTERFEITS/REPRINTS

As the value of sports cards has risen in the past 10-20 years, certain cards and sets have become too expensive for the average collector to obtain. This, along with changes in the technology of color printing, has given rise to increasing numbers of counterfeit and reprint cards.

While both terms describe essentially the same thing - a modern day copy which attempts to duplicate as closely as possible an original sports card - there are differences which are important to the collector.

Generally, a counterfeit is made with the intention of deceiving somebody into believing it is genuine, and thus paying large amounts of money for it. The counterfeiter takes every pain to try to make his fakes look as authentic as possible.

A reprint, on the other hand, while it may have been made to look as close as possible to an original card, is made with the intention of allowing collectors to buy them as substitutes for cards they may never be otherwise able to afford. The big difference is that a reprint is generally marked as such, usually on the back of the card.

In other cases, like the Topps 1952 baseball reprint set, the replicas are printed in a size markedly different from the originals. Collectors should be aware, however, that unscrupulous persons will sometimes cut off or otherwise obliterate the distinguishing word - "Reprint," "Copy" - or modern copyright date on the back of a reprint card in an attempt to pass it as genuine.

A collector's best defense against reprints and counterfeits is to acquire a knowledge of the look and feel of genuine sports cards of various eras and issues.

UNLISTED CARDS

Readers who have cards or sets which are not covered in this edition are invited to correspond with the editor for purposes of adding to the compilation of work now in progress. Address: Tuff Stuff's Standard Catalog of Football Cards, 700 E. State St., Iola, WI 54990. Contributors will be acknowledged in future editions.

COLLECTOR ISSUES

Many cards do not fall under the scope of this catalog because they were issued solely for the collector market. Known as, "collector issues," these cards and sets are distinguished from "legitimate" issues by not having been created as a sales promotional item for another product - bubble gum, soda, snack cakes, dog food, cigarettes, gasoline, etc.

Because of their nature - the person issuing them is always free to print and distribute more if they should ever attain any real value - collector issues are generally regarded as having little or no premium value.

NEW ISSUES

Because new sports cards are being issued all the time, the cataloging of them is an ongoing challenge. Readers are invited to submit news of new issues, especially limited-edition or regionally issued cards, to the editors. Address: Tuff Stuff's Standard Catalog of Football Cards, 700 E. State St., Iola, WI 54990.

ACKNOWLEDGMENTS

The editors wish to thank the many collectors, dealers and hobbyists who helped us compile, list and price the data in this edition.

1987 Ace Fact Pack Chicago Bears

Ace Fact Pack in West Germany printed card sets for 12 National Football League teams. The cards, which have rounded corners, were distributed throughout Great Britain and England. They were designed to look like a deck of playing cards and are unnumbered. There were 33 cards created for each of the 12 teams, which are listed below alphabetically. Twenty-two cards are players; 11 are informational. All but the cards for the Chicago Bears (2-1/2" x 3-1/2") measure 2-1/4" x 3-5/8".

		NM/M
Complete Set (33):		175.00
Common Player:		4.00
(1)	Todd Bell	5.00
(2)	Mark Bortz	4.00
(3)	Kevin Butler	5.00
(4)	Jim Covert	6.00
(5)	Richard Dent	10.00
(6)	Dave Duerson	4.00
(7)	Gary Fencik	5.00
(8)	Willie Gault	8.00
(9)	Dan Hampton	10.00
(10)	Jay Hilgenberg	4.00
(11)	Wilber Marshall	6.00
(12)	Jim McMahon	10.00
(13)	Steve McMichael	6.00
(14)	Emery Moorehead	4.00
(15)	Keith Ortega	4.00
(16)	Walter Payton	70.00
(17)	William Perry	8.00
(18)	Mike Richardson	4.00
(19)	Mike Singletary	10.00
(20)	Matt Suhey	5.00
(21)	Keith Van Horne	4.00
(22)	Otis Wilson	5.00
(23)	Bears Helmet	4.00
(24)	Bears Information	4.00
(25)	Bears Uniform	4.00
(26)	Game Record Holders	4.00
(27)	Season Record Holders	4.00
(28)	Career Record Holders	4.00
(29)	Bears 1967-86	4.00
(30)	1986 Team Statistics	4.00
(31)	All-Time Greats	4.00
(32)	Roll of Honour	4.00
(33)	Soldier Field	4.00

1987 Ace Fact Pack Denver Broncos

Measuring 2-1/4" x 3-5/8", the 33-card set features 22 player cards and 11 organizational cards. The front showcases the team's logo and player's name at the top, with a photo and the player's bio filling the remainder of the card front. The opposite side of the card has a playing card design. The cards are unnumbered. The set was released in Great Britain.

		NM/M
Complete Set (33):		175.00
Common Player:		4.00
(1)	Keith Bishop	4.00
(2)	Bill Bryan	4.00
(3)	Mark Cooper	4.00
(4)	John Elway	90.00
(5)	Steve Foley	5.00
(6)	Mike Harden	4.00
(7)	Rick Hunley	4.00
(8)	Vance Johnson	5.00
(9)	Rulon Jones	5.00
(10)	Rich Karlis	4.00
(11)	Clarence Kay	5.00
(12)	Ken Lanier	5.00
(13)	Karl Mecklenburg	8.00
(14)	Chris Norman	4.00
(15)	Jim Ryan	4.00
(16)	Dennis Smith	5.00
(17)	Dave Studdard	4.00
(18)	Andre Townsend	4.00
(19)	Steve Watson	5.00
(20)	Gerald Wilhite	4.00
(21)	Sammy Winder	5.00
(22)	Louis Wright	5.00
(23)	Team Helmet	4.00
(24)	Team Information	4.00
(25)	Broncos Uniform	4.00
(26)	Game Record Holders	4.00
(27)	Season Record Holders	4.00
(28)	Career Record Holders	4.00
(29)	Record 1967-86	4.00
(30)	Roll of Honour	4.00
(31)	All-Time Greats	4.00
(32)	1986 Team Statistics	4.00
(33)	Denver Mile High Stadium	4.00

1987 Ace Fact Pack Dallas Cowboys

Measuring 2-1/4" x 3-5/8", the 33-card set follows the same design as the Bears and Broncos. The set was released in Great Britain. It has 22 player cards in the set and 11 organizational cards. The cards are unnumbered.

		NM/M
Complete Set (33):		200.00
Common Player:		4.00
(1)	Bill Bates	5.00
(2)	Doug Cosbie	5.00
(3)	Tony Dorsett	25.00
(4)	Michael Downs	4.00
(5)	John Dutton	5.00
(6)	Ron Fellows	4.00
(7)	Mike Hegman	4.00
(8)	Tony Hill	6.00
(9)	Jim Jeffcoat	5.00
(10)	Ed "Too Tall" Jones	12.00
(11)	Crawford Ker	4.00
(12)	Eugene Lockhart	5.00
(13)	Phil Pozderac	4.00
(14)	Tom Rafferty	5.00
(15)	Jeff Rohrer	4.00
(16)	Mike Sherrard	6.00
(17)	Glen Titensor	4.00
(18)	Mark Tuinei	5.00
(19)	Herschel Walker	15.00
(20)	Everson Walls	5.00
(21)	Danny White	8.00
(22)	Randy White	16.00
(23)	Cowboys Helmet	4.00
(24)	Cowboys Information	4.00
(25)	Cowboys Uniform	4.00
(26)	Game Record Holders	4.00
(27)	Season Record Holders	4.00
(28)	Career Record Holders	4.00
(29)	1967-86 Team Record	4.00
(30)	1986 Team Statistics	4.00
(31)	All-Time Greats	4.00
(32)	Roll of Honour	4.00
(33)	Texas Stadium	4.00

1987 Ace Fact Pack Miami Dolphins

Measuring 2-1/4" x 3-5/8", the 33-card set follows the same design as the others. It was released in Great Britain. There are 22 player cards and 11 highlight cards. The cards are unnumbered.

		NM/M
Complete Set (33):		300.00
Common Player:		4.00
(1)	Bob Baumhower	5.00
(2)	Woody Bennett	4.00
(3)	Doug Betters	5.00
(4)	Glenn Blackwood	5.00
(5)	Bud Brown	4.00
(6)	Bob Brudzinski	4.00
(7)	Mark Clayton	7.00
(8)	Mark Duper	7.00
(9)	Roy Foster	4.00
(10)	Jon Giesler	4.00
(11)	Hugh Green	6.00
(12)	Lorenzo Hampton	5.00
(13)	Bruce Hardy	4.00
(14)	William Judson	4.00
(15)	Greg Koch	4.00
(16)	Paul Lankford	4.00
(17)	George Little	4.00
(18)	Dan Marino	175.00
(19)	John Offerdahl	5.00
(20)	Dwight Stephenson	6.00
(21)	Don Strock	5.00
(22)	T.J. Turner	4.00
(23)	Dolphins Helmet	4.00
(24)	Team Information	4.00
(25)	Dolphins Uniform	4.00
(26)	Game Record Holders	4.00
(27)	Season Record Holders	4.00
(28)	Career Record Holders	4.00
(29)	Dolphins 1967-86	4.00
(30)	1986 Team Statistics	4.00
(31)	Dolphin Greats	4.00
(32)	Roll of Honour	4.00
(33)	Joe Robbie Stadium	4.00

1987 Ace Fact Pack San Francisco 49ers

Measuring 2-1/4" x 3-5/8", this 33-card set was released in Great Britain. The design follows the same format of the other teams in the set. There are 22 player cards and 11 highlights cards. The cards are unnumbered.

		NM/M
Complete Set (33):		400.00
Common Player:		4.00
(1)	John Ayers	4.00
(2)	Dwaine Board	4.00
(3)	Michael Carter	6.00
(4)	Dwight Clark	12.00
(5)	Roger Craig	12.00
(6)	Joe Cribbs	5.00
(7)	Randy Cross	5.00
(8)	Riki Ellison	4.00
(9)	Jim Fahnhorst	4.00
(10)	Keith Fahnhorst	4.00
(11)	Russ Francis	5.00
(12)	Don Griffin	5.00
(13)	Ronnie Lott	14.00
(14)	Milt McColl	4.00
(15)	Tim McKyer	5.00
(16)	Joe Montana	175.00
(17)	Bubba Paris	4.00
(18)	Fred Quinlan	4.00
(19)	Jerry Rice	150.00
(20)	Manu Tuiasosopo	4.00
(21)	Keena Turner	6.00
(22)	Carlton Williamson	4.00
(23)	49er Helmet	4.00
(24)	49er Information	4.00
(25)	49er Uniform	4.00
(26)	Game Record Holders	4.00
(27)	Season RecordHolders	4.00
(28)	Career Record Holders	4.00
(29)	49ers History 1967-86	4.00
(30)	1986 Team Statistics	4.00
(31)	All-Time Greats	4.00
(32)	Roll of Honour	4.00
(33)	Candlestick Park	4.00

1987 Ace Fact Pack New York Giants

Measuring 2-1/4" x 3-5/8", the 33-card set follows the same design as the other teams in the series. Released in Great Britain, the set includes 22 player cards and 11 highlight cards. The cards are unnumbered.

		NM/M
Complete Set (33):		150.00
Common Player:		4.00
(1)	Billy Ard	4.00
(2)	Carl Banks	8.00
(3)	Mark Bavaro	5.00
(4)	Brad Benson	4.00
(5)	Harry Carson	8.00
(6)	Maurice Carthon (misspelled Morris)	5.00
(7)	Mark Collins	5.00
(8)	Chris Godfrey	4.00
(9)	Kenny Hill	4.00
(10)	Erik Howard	5.00
(11)	Bobby Johnson	4.00
(12)	Leonard Marshall	6.00
(13)	George Martin	5.00
(14)	Joe Morris	5.00
(15)	Karl Nelson	4.00
(16)	Bart Oates (misspelled Oakes)	5.00
(17)	Gary Reasons	5.00
(18)	Stacy Robinson	4.00
(19)	Phil Simms	20.00
(20)	Lawrence Taylor	30.00
(21)	Herb Welch	4.00
(22)	Perry Williams	4.00
(23)	Giants Helmet	4.00
(24)	Giants Information	4.00
(25)	Giant Uniforms	4.00
(26)	Game Record Holders	4.00
(27)	Season Record Holders	4.00
(28)	Career Record Holders	4.00
(29)	Giants 1967-86	4.00
(30)	1986 Team Statistics	4.00
(31)	All-Time Greats	4.00
(32)	Roll of Honour	4.00
(33)	Giants Stadium	4.00

1987 Ace Fact Pack New York Jets

Measuring 2-1/4" x 3-5/8", the 33-card set follows the same design as the other teams in the series. Released in Great Britain, there are 22 player cards and 11 highlight cards. The cards are unnumbered.

		NM/M
Complete Set (33):		120.00
Common Player:		4.00
(1)	Dan Alexander	4.00
(2)	Tom Baldwin	4.00
(3)	Barry Bennett	4.00
(4)	Russell Carter	5.00
(5)	Kyle Clifton	6.00
(6)	Bob Crable	4.00
(7)	Joe Fields	5.00
(8)	Rusty Guilbeau	4.00
(9)	Harry Hamilton	5.00
(10)	Johnny Hector	7.00
(11)	Jerry Holmes	4.00
(12)	Gordon King	4.00
(13)	Lester Lyles	4.00
(14)	Marty Lyons	5.00
(15)	Kevin McArthur	4.00
(16)	Freeman McNeil	8.00
(17)	Ken O'Brien	7.00
(18)	Tony Paige	6.00
(19)	Mickey Shuler	5.00
(20)	Jim Sweeney	4.00
(21)	Al Toon	8.50
(22)	Wesley Walker	9.50
(23)	Jets Helmet	4.00
(24)	Jets Team Information	4.00
(25)	Jets Uniform	4.00
(26)	Game Record Holders	4.00
(27)	Season Record Holders	4.00
(28)	Career Record Holders	4.00
(29)	1986 Team Statistics	4.00
(30)	Jets 1967-86	4.00
(31)	All-Time Greats	4.00
(32)	Roll of Honour	4.00
(33)	Giants Stadium	4.00

1987 Ace Fact Pack Detroit Lions

Measuring 2-1/4" x 3-5/8", the 33-card set follows the same design as the other teams in the series. Issued in Great Britain, the set includes 22 player cards and 11 highlight cards. The cards are unnumbered.

		NM/M
Complete Set (33):		120.00
Common Player:		4.00
(1)	Carl Bland	4.00
(2)	Lomas Brown	6.00
(3)	Jeff Chadwick	5.00
(4)	Mike Cofer	6.00
(5)	Keith Dorney	4.00
(6)	Keith Ferguson	4.00
(7)	William Gay	6.00
(8)	James Harrell	4.00
(9)	Eric Hipple	5.00
(10)	Garry James	5.00
(11)	Demetrious Johnson	4.00
(12)	James Jones	6.00
(13)	Chuck Long	5.00
(14)	Vernon Maxwell	5.00
(15)	Bruce McNorton	4.00
(16)	Devon Mitchell	4.00
(17)	Steve Lott	4.00
(18)	Eddie Murray	6.00
(19)	Harvey Smith	4.00
(20)	Rich Stenger	4.00
(21)	Eric Williams	4.00
(22)	Jimmy Williams	4.00
(23)	Detroit Lions Helmet	4.00
(24)	Team Information	4.00
(25)	Uniform Design	4.00
(26)	Game Record Holders	4.00
(27)	Season Record Holders	4.00
(28)	Career Record Holders	4.00
(29)	1986 Team Statistics	4.00
(30)	Team Record 1967-86	4.00
(31)	Championship Seasons	4.00
(32)	Pontiac Silverdome	4.00
(33)	All-Time Greats	4.00

1987 Ace Fact Pack Green Bay Packers

Measuring 2-1/4" x 3-5/8", the 33-card set follows the same design as the other teams in the series. Issued in Great Britain, there are 22 player cards and 11 highlight cards. The cards are unnumbered.

		NM/M
Complete Set (33):		120.00
Common Player:		4.00
(1)	John Anderson	6.00
(2)	Robbie Bosco	5.00
(3)	Don Bracken	4.00
(4)	John Cannon	5.00
(5)	Alphonso Carreker	4.00
(6)	Kenneth Davis	8.00
(7)	Al Del Greco	4.00
(8)	Gary Ellerson	4.00
(9)	Gerry Ellis	5.00
(10)	Phillip Epps	6.00
(11)	Ron Hallstrom	4.00
(12)	Mark Lee	5.00
(13)	Bobby Leopold	4.00
(14)	Charles Martin	4.00
(15)	Brian Noble	5.00
(16)	Ken Ruettgers	5.00
(17)	Randy Scott	4.00
(18)	Walter Stanley	5.00
(19)	Ken Stills	4.00
(20)	Keith Uecker	4.00
(21)	Ed West	5.00
(22)	Randy Wright	5.00
(23)	Packer Helmet	4.00
(24)	Packer Information	4.00
(25)	Packer Uniform	4.00
(26)	Game Record Holders	4.00
(27)	Season Record Holders	4.00
(28)	Career Record Holders	4.00
(29)	1967-86 Team Record	4.00
(30)	1986 Team Statistics	4.00
(31)	All-Time Greats	4.00
(32)	Roll of Honour	4.00
(33)	Lambeau Field/Milwaukee County Stadium	4.00

1987 Ace Fact Pack Los Angeles Rams

Measuring 2-1/4" x 3-5/8", the 33-card set follows the same design as the other teams in the series. Issued in Great Britain, it contains 22 player cards and 11 highlight cards, which are unnumbered.

		NM/M
Complete Set (33):		120.00
Common Player:		4.00
(1)	Nolan Cromwell	6.00
(2)	Eric Dickerson	18.00
(3)	Reggie Doss	4.00
(4)	Carl Ekern	4.00
(5)	Henry Ellard	10.00
(6)	Jim Everett	10.00
(7)	Jerry Gray	5.00
(8)	Dennis Harrah	5.00
(9)	David Hull	4.00
(10)	Kevin House	5.00
(11)	LeRoy Irvin	5.00
(12)	Mark Jerue	4.50
(13)	Shawn Miller	4.00
(14)	Tom Newberry	5.00
(15)	Vince Newsome	4.50
(16)	Mel Owens	5.00
(17)	Irv Pankey	4.00
(18)	Doug Reed	5.00
(19)	Doug Smith	5.00
(20)	Jackie Slater	6.00
(21)	Charles White	6.00
(22)	Mike Wilcher	4.00
(23)	Rams Helmet	4.00
(24)	Rams Information	4.50
(25)	Rams Uniform	4.00
(26)	Game Record Holders	4.00
(27)	Season Record Holders	4.00
(28)	Career Record Holders	5.00
(29)	Team Record 1967-86	4.00
(30)	1986 Team Statistics	4.00
(31)	All-Time Greats	4.00
(32)	Rams Roll of Honour	4.50
(33)	Anaheim Stadium	4.00

1987 Ace Fact Pack Washington Redskins

Measuring 2-1/4" x 3-5/8", the 33-card set follows the same design as the other teams in the series. Issued in Great Britain, the set is broken up into 22 player cards and 11 highlight cards, which are unnumbered.

		NM/M
Complete Set (33):		175.00
Common Player:		4.00
(1)	Jeff Bostic	5.00
(2)	Dave Butz	6.00
(3)	Gary Clark	20.00
(4)	Monte Coleman	5.00
(5)	Vernon Dean	4.00
(6)	Clint Didier	5.00
(7)	Darryl Grant	4.00
(8)	Darrell Green	7.50
(9)	Russ Grimm	6.00
(10)	Joe Jacoby	6.00
(11)	Curtis Jordan	4.00
(12)	Dexter Manley	5.00
(13)	Charles Mann	6.00
(14)	Mark May	5.00
(15)	Rich Milot	4.00
(16)	Art Monk	30.00
(17)	Neal Olkewicz	4.00
(18)	George Rogers	8.00
(19)	Jay Schroeder	8.00
(20)	R.C. Thielemann	4.00
(21)	Alvin Walton	4.00
(22)	Don Warren	4.00
(23)	Redskin Helmet	4.00
(24)	Redskin Information	4.00
(25)	Redskin Uniforms	4.00
(26)	Game Record Holders	4.00
(27)	Season Record Holders	4.00
(28)	Career Record Holders	4.00
(29)	Redskins 1867-86	4.00
(30)	1986 Team Statistics	4.00
(31)	All-Time Redskins	4.00
(32)	Roll of Honour	4.00
(33)	Robert F. Kennedy Stadium	4.00

1987 Ace Fact Pack Seattle Seahawks

Measuring 2-1/4" x 3-5/8", the 33-card set follows the same design as the other teams in the series. Issued in Great Britain, the set is broken up into 22 player cards and 11 highlight cards, which are unnumbered.

		NM/M
Complete Set (33):		150.00
Common Player:		4.00
(1)	Edwin Bailey	4.00
(2)	Dave Brown	6.00
(3)	Jeff Bryant	4.00
(4)	Blair Bush	5.00
(5)	Keith Butler	4.00
(6)	Kenny Easley	5.00
(7)	Greg Gaines	4.00
(8)	Jacob Green	6.00
(9)	Norm Johnson	5.00
(10)	Dave Krieg	8.00
(11)	Steve Largent	30.00
(12)	Reggie Kinlaw	4.00
(13)	Ron Mattes	4.00
(14)	Bryan Millard	4.00
(15)	Eugene Robinson	5.00
(16)	Bruce Scholtz	4.00
(17)	Terry Taylor	4.00
(18)	Mike Tice	5.00
(19)	Daryl Turner	5.00
(20)	Curt Warner	7.50
(21)	John L. Williams	12.00
(22)	Fredd Young	5.00
(23)	Seattle Helmet	4.00
(24)	Seahawk Information	4.00
(25)	Seahawk Uniform	4.00
(26)	Game Record Holder	4.00
(27)	Season Record Holders	4.00
(28)	Career Record Holders	4.00
(29)	1977-86 Team Record	4.00
(30)	1986 Team Statistics	4.00
(31)	All-Time Greats	4.00
(32)	Roll of Honour	4.00
(33)	Kingdome	4.00

1989 Action Packed Prototypes

These cards were produced as prototypes before Action Packed released its 1989 30-card test set. The gold-bordered front has a raised color action photo on it; the back has stats, a head shot, notes, a card number and a space for an autograph. These cards, numbered 72 and 101, can be distinguished from the test set by where the card number appears. On these cards, they are on the same side as the mug shot; on the test cards they are on the opposite side.

		NM/M
Complete Set (2):		40.00
Common Player:		20.00
72	Freeman McNeil	20.00
101	Phil Simms	20.00

1989 Action Packed Test

These 30 cards are standard size and were packaged in packs of six. Ten players from the Chicago Bears, New York Giants and Washington Redskins are represented in the set, which was copyrighted by Hi-Pro Marketing of Northbrook, Ill. Each front has a gold-border and a raised color action photo; the back has a head shot, statistics, informational notes, a card number and a space for an autograph.

		NM/M
Complete Set (30):		20.00
Common Player:		.50
Foil Pack (6):		2.50
Foil Wax Box (36):		40.00
1	Neal Anderson	1.00
2	Trace Armstrong	.60
3	Kevin Butler	.50
4	Richard Dent	.75
5	Dennis Gentry	.50
6	Dan Hampton	.75
7	Jay Hilgenberg	.60
8	Thomas Sanders	.60
9	Mike Singletary	.75
10	Mike Tomczak	.75
11	Raul Allegre	.50
12	Ottis Anderson	.75
13	Mark Bavaro	.60
14	Terry Kinard	.50
15	Lionel Manuel	.50
16	Leonard Marshall	.60
17	Dave Meggett	1.00
18	Joe Morris	.75
19	Phil Simms	1.00
20	Lawrence Taylor	1.75
21	Kelvin Bryant	.75
22	Darrell Green	1.00
23	Dexter Manley	.60
24	Charles Mann	.60
25	Wilber Marshall	.60
26	Art Monk	1.50
27	Jamie Morris	.60
28	Tracy Rocker	.60
29	Mark Rypien	2.00
30	Ricky Sanders	1.00

1990 Action Packed

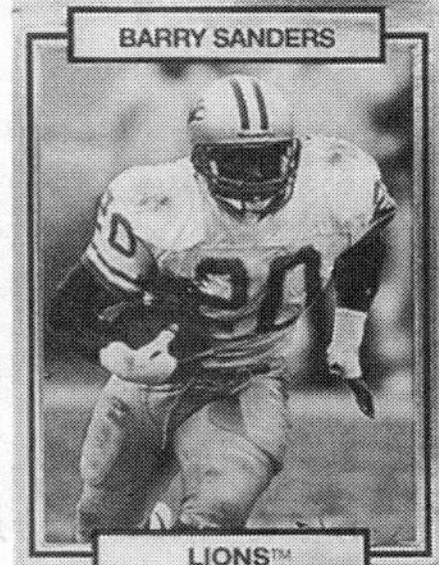

Action Packed was released in two series over the summer, with the first available in June and the second available in August. The total of 280 cards was randomly split up between the two series. In the first series, 126 players were issued; 154 came out in Series II. A factory set was also issued. The cards are embossed, with a gold foil and rounded corners. Special cards included those honoring the retired Reggie Williams and Steve Largent; a card back for Christian Okoye with a phrase written in Nigerian; and a Braille card featuring the retired Jim Plunkett.

		NM/M
Complete Set (280):		20.00
Complete Factory (281):		20.00
Common Player:		.10
Minor Stars:		.20
Series 1 Foil Pack (6):		.50
Series 1 Foil Wax Box (36):		10.00
Series 2 Foil Pack (6):		.50
Series 2 Foil Wax Box (36):		10.00
1	Aundray Bruce	.10
2	Scott Case	.10
3	Tony Casillas	.10
4	Shawn Collins	.10
5	Marcus Cotton	.10
6	Bill Fralic	.10
7	Tim Green	.10
8	Chris Miller	.20
9	Deion Sanders	1.25
10	John Settle	.10
11	Cornelius Bennett	.20
12	Shane Conlan	.10
13	Kent Hill	.10
14	Jim Kelly	.50
15	Mark Kelso	.10
16	Scott Norwood	.10
17	Andre Reed	.20
18	Fred Smerlas	.10
19	Bruce Smith	.20
20	Thurman Thomas	.50
21	Neal Anderson	.20
22	Kevin Butler	.10
23	Richard Dent	.20
24	Dennis Gentry	.10
25	Dan Hampton	.10
26	Jay Hilgenberg	.10
27	Steve McMichael	.10
28	Brad Muster	.10
29	Mike Singletary	.20
30	Mike Tomczak	.10
31	James Brooks	.10
32	Rickey Dixon	.10
33	Boomer Esiason	.20
34	David Fulcher	.10
35	Rodney Holman	.10
36	Tim Krumrie	.10
37	Tim McGee	.10
38	Anthony Munoz	.20
39	Reggie Williams	.10
40	Ickey Woods	.10
41	Thane Gash	.10

42 Mike Johnson .10
43 Bernie Kosar .20
44 Reggie Langhorne .10
45 Clay Matthews .10
46 Eric Metcalf .20
47 Frank Minnifield .10
48 Ozzie Newsome .20
49 Webster Slaughter .10
50 Felix Wright .10
51 Troy Aikman 2.00
52 James Dixon .10
53 Michael Irvin .50
54 Jim Jeffcoat .10
55 Ed Jones .10
56 Eugene Lockhart .10
57 Danny Noonan .10
58 Paul Palmer .10
59 Everson Walls .10
60 Steve Walsh .20
61 Steve Atwater .10
62 Tyrone Braxton .10
63 John Elway 2.00
64 Bobby Humphrey .10
65 Mark Jackson .10
66 Vance Johnson .10
67 Greg Kragen .10
68 Karl Mecklenberg .10
69 Dennis Smith .10
70 David Treadwell .10
71 Jim Arnold .10
72 Jerry Ball .10
73 Bennie Blades .10
74 Mel Gray .10
75 Richard Johnson .10
76 Eddie Murray .10
77 Rodney Peete .10
78 Barry Sanders 5.00
79 Chris Spielman .10
80 Walter Stanley .10
81 Dave Brown .10
82 Brent Fullwood .10
83 Tim Harris .10
84 Johnny Holland .10
85 Don Majkowski .10
86 Tony Mandarich .10
87 Mark Murphy .10
88 Brian Noble .10
89 Ken Ruettgers .10
90 Sterling Sharpe .20
91 Ray Childress .10
92 Ernest Givins .10
93 Alonzo Highsmith .10
94 Drew Hill .10
95 Bruce Matthews .10
96 Bubba McDowell .10
97 Warren Moon .50
98 Mike Munchak .10
99 Allen Pinkett .10
100 Mike Rozier .10
101 Albert Bentley .10
102 Duane Bickett .10
103 Bill Brooks .10
104 Chris Chandler .20
105 Ray Donaldson .10
106 Chris Hinton .10
107 Andre Rison .20
108 Keith Taylor .10
109 Clarence Verdin .10
110 Fredd Young .10
111 Deron Cherry .10
112 Steve DeBerg .10
113 Dino Hackett .10
114 Albert Lewis .10
115 Nick Lowery .10
116 Christian Okoye .10
117 Stephone Paige .10
118 Kevin Ross .10
119 Derrick Thomas .20
120 Mike Webster .10
121 Marcus Allen .20
122 Eddie Anderson .10
123 Steve Beuerlein .20
124 Tim Brown .50
125 Mervyn Fernandez .10
127 Bob Golic .10
128 Bo Jackson .50
129 Howie Long .20
130 Greg Townsend .10
131 Willie Anderson .10
132 Greg Bell .10
133 Robert Delpino .10
134 Henry Ellard .10
135 Jim Everett .20
136 Jerry Gray .10
137 Kevin Greene .20
138 Tom Newberry .10
139 Jackie Slater .10
140 Doug Smith .10
141 Mark Clayton .10
142 Jeff Cross .10
143 Mark Duper .10
144 Ferrell Edmunds .10
145 Jim Jensen .10
146 Dan Marino 3.50
147 John Offerdahl .10
148 Louis Oliver .10
149 Reggie Roby .10
150 Sammie Smith .10
151 Joey Browner .10
152 Anthony Carter .10
153 Chris Doleman .10
154 Steve Jordan .10
155 Carl Lee .10
156 Randall McDaniel .10
157 Keith Millard .10
158 Herschel Walker .20
159 Wade Wilson .10
160 Gary Zimmerman .10
161 Hart Lee Dykes .10
162 Irving Fryar .20
163 Steve Grogan .10
164 Maurice Hurst .10
165 Fred Marion .10
166 Stanley Morgan .10
167 Robert Perryman .10
168 John Stephens .10
169 Andre Tippett .10
170 Brent Williams .10
171 John Fourcade .10
172 Bobby Hebert .20
173 Dalton Hilliard .10
174 Rickey Jackson .10
175 Vaughan Johnson .10
176 Eric Martin .10
177 Robert Massey .10
178 Rueben Mayes .10
179 Sam Mills .10
180 Pat Swilling .10
181 Ottis Anderson .20
182 Carl Banks .10
183 Mark Bavaro .10
184 Mark Collins .10
185 Leonard Marshall .10
186 Dave Meggett .10
187 Gary Reasons .10
188 Phil Simms .20
189 Lawrence Taylor .50
190 Odessa Turner .10
191 Kyle Clifton .10
192 James Hasty .10
193 Johnny Hector .10
194 Jeff Lagemann .10
195 Pat Leahy .10
196 Erik McMillan .10
197 Ken O'Brien .10
198 Mickey Shuler .10
199 Al Toon .10
200 JoJo Townsell .10
201 Eric Allen .10
202 Jerome Brown .10
203 Keith Byars .10
204 Cris Carter 1.00
205 Wes Hopkins .10
206 Keith Jackson .20
207 Seth Joyner .10
208 Mike Quick .10
209 Andre Waters .10
210 Reggie White .50
211 Rich Carmarillo .10
212 Roy Green .10
213 Ken Harvey .10
214 Gary Hogeboom .10
215 Tim McDonald .10
216 Stump Mitchell .10
217 Luis Sharpe .10
218 Vai Sikahema .10
219 J.T. Smith .10
220 Ron Wolfley .10
221 Gary Anderson .10
222 Bubby Brister .10
223 Merril Hoge .10
224 Tunch Ilken .10
225 Louis Lipps .10
226 David Little .10
227 Greg Lloyd .10
228 Dwayne Woodruff .10
229 Rod Woodson .20
230 Tim Worley .10
231 Marion Butts .10
232 Gill Byrd .10
233 Burt Grossman .10
234 Jim McMahon .20
235 Anthony Miller .20
236 Leslie O'Neal .10
237 Gary Plummer .10
238 Billy Ray Smith .10
239 Tim Spencer .10
240 Lee Williams .10
241 Mike Cofer .10
242 Roger Craig .20
243 Charles Haley .10
244 Ronnie Lott .20
245 Guy McIntyre .10
246 Joe Montana 2.50
247 Tom Rathman .10
248 Jerry Rice 2.00
249 John Taylor .20
250 Michael Walter .10
251 Brian Blades .10
252 Jacob Green .10
253 Dave Krieg .10
254 Steve Largent .20
255 Joe Nash .10
256 Rufus Porter .10
257 Eugene Robinson .20
258 Paul Skansi .10
259 Curt Warner .10
260 John L. Williams .10
261 Mark Carrier .10
262 Reuben Davis .10
263 Harry Hamilton .10
264 Bruce Hill .10
265 Donald Igwebuike .10
266 Eugene Marve .10
267 Kevin Murphy .10
268 Mark Robinson .10
269 Lars Tate .10
270 Vinny Testaverde .50
271 Gary Clark .10
272 Monte Coleman .10
273 Darrell Green .20
274 Charles Mann .10
275 Wilbur Marshall .10
276 Art Monk .20
277 Gerald Riggs .10
278 Mark Rypien .20
279 Rickey Sanders .10
280 Alvin Walton .10
NNO Jim Plunkett BR (Braille) 4.00
NNO Checklist .10

1990 Action Packed Rookie Update

Issued in November 1990, the Update set includes each of the 1990 first-round draft choices, rookie prospects, and traded players. Randall Cunningham, who did not appear in the regular 1990 Action Packed set, signed a late contract with the NFL Players Association and does not appear in the Update set. Cards were issued in both wax packs and factory sets.

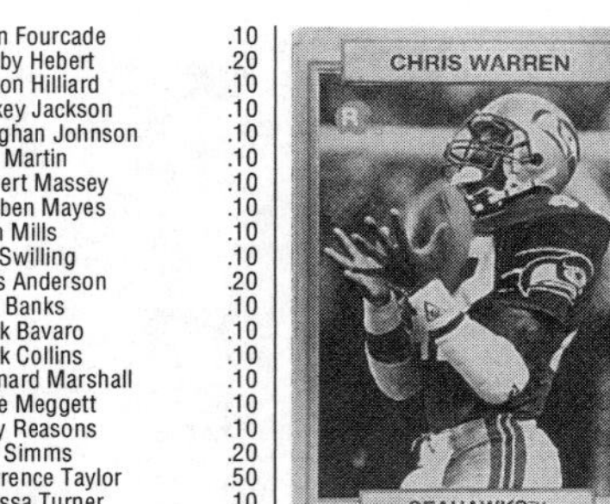

NM/M
Complete Set (84): 15.00
Complete Factory (84): 15.00
Common Player: .10
Minor Stars: .20
Foil Pack (6): 2.00
Foil Box (36): 55.00
1 *Jeff George* 1.00
2 *Richmond Webb* .20
3 *James Williams* .10
4 *Tony Bennett* .20
5 *Darrell Thompson* .10
6 *Steve Broussard* .10
7 *Rodney Hampton* .75
8 *Rob Moore* 3.00
9 *Alton Montgomery* .10
10 *Leroy Butler* .50
11 *Anthony Johnson* .50
12 *Scott Mitchell* 1.00
13 *Mike Fox* .10
14 *Robert Blackmon* .10
15 *Blair Thomas* .10
16 *Tony Stargell* .10
17 *Peter Tom Willis* .10
18 *Harold Green* .20
19 *Bernard Clark* .10
20 *Aaron Wallace* .10
21 *Dennis Brown* .10
22 *Johnny Johnson* .20
23 *Chris Calloway* .50
24 *Walter Wilson* .10
25 *Dexter Carter* .10
26 *Percy Snow* .10
27 *Johnny Bailey* .10
28 *Mike Bellamy* .10
29 *Ben Smith* .10
30 *Mark Carrier* .50
31 *James Francis* .10
32 *Lamar Lathon* .10
33 Bern Brostek .10
34 *Emmitt Smith* 15.00
35 *Andre Collins* .10
36 *Alexander Wright* .10
37 *Fred Barnett* .20
38 *Junior Seau* 3.00
39 *Cortez Kennedy* .50
40 *Terry Wooden* .10
41 *Eric Davis* .10
42 *Fred Washington* .10
43 *Reggie Cobb* .10
44 *Andre Ware* .20
45 *Anthony Smith* .10
46 *Shannon Sharpe* 8.00
47 *Harlon Barnett* .10
48 *Greg McMurty* .10
49 *Stacey Simmons* .10
50 *Calvin Williams* .20
51 *Anthony Thompson* .10
52 *Ricky Proehl* .50
53 *Tony James* .10
54 *Ray Agnew* .10
55 *Tom Hodson* .10
56 *Ron Cox* .10
57 *Leroy Hoard* .10
58 *Eric Green* .50
59 *Barry Foster* .10
60 *Keith McCants* .10
61 *Oliver Barnett* .10
62 *Chris Warren* .10
63 *Pat Terrell* .10
64 *Renaldo Turnbull* .10
65 Chris Chandler .20
66 Everson Walls .10
67 Alonzo Highsmith .10
68 Gary Anderson .20
69 Fred Smerlas .10
70 Jim McMahon .50
71 Curt Warner .20
72 Stanley Morgan .10
73 Dave Waymer .10
74 Billy Joe Tolliver .20
75 Tony Eason .10
76 Max Montoya .10
77 Greg Bell .10
78 Dennis McKinnon .10
79 Raymond Clayborn .10
80 Broderick Thomas .10
81 Timm Rosenbach .10
82 Tim McKyer .10
83 Andre Rison .50
84 Randall Cunningham .75

1990 Action Packed All-Madden

This 58-card set pictures players selected by CBS analyst and former coach John Madden. Cards were released in late February of 1991. Cards were issued in six-card wax packs and in complete sets. The set features Action Packed's first borderless set, previewing the 1991 set. Cards are standard-sized, embossed, and feature Madden's comments about each player on the back.

NM/M
Complete Set (58): 20.00
Common Player: .25
Wax Box: 20.00
1 Joe Montana 3.00
2 Jerry Rice 3.00
3 Charles Haley .40
4 Steve Wisniewski .25
5 Dave Meggett .40
6 Ottis Anderson .40
7 Nate Newton .25
8 Warren Moon 1.00
9 Emmitt Smith 6.00
10 Jackie Slater .25
11 Pepper Johnson .25
12 Lawrence Taylor .75
13 Sterling Sharpe 1.00
14 Sean Landeta .25
15 Richard Dent .40
16 Neal Anderson .50
17 Bruce Matthews .25
18 Matt Millen .25
19 Reggie White .50
20 Greg Townsend .25
21 Troy Aikman 3.00
22 Don Mosebar .25
23 Jeff Zimmerman .25
24 Rod Woodson .50
25 Keith Byars .40
26 Randall Cunningham .75
27 Reyna Thompson .40
28 Marcus Allen .60
29 Gary Clark .50
30 Anthony Carter .40
31 Bubba Paris .25
32 Ronnie Lott .50
33 Erik Howard .25
34 Ernest Givins .25
35 Mike Munchak .25
36 Jim Lachey .25
37 Merril Hoge .25
38 Darrell Green .25
39 Pierce Holt .25
40 Jerome Brown .25
41 William Perry .25
42 Michael Carter .25
43 Keith Jackson .40
44 Kevin Fagan .25
45 Mark Carrier .40
46 Fred Barnett .75
47 Barry Sanders 3.00
48 Pat Swilling, Rickey Jackson .50
49 Sam Mills, Vaughan Johnson .25
50 Jacob Green .25
51 Stan Brock .25
52 Dan Hampton .25
53 Brian Noble .25
54 John Elliott .25
55 Matt Bahr .25
56 Bill Parcells .25
57 Art Shell .25
58 All-Madden Team Trophy .25

1991 Action Packed

Action Packed issued a borderless card with a gold stripe protecting the back seam, both improving on the previous year's design. Cards are arranged in alphabetical order by city and player. Two unnumbered prototype cards were also created, for Randall Cunningham and Emmitt Smith. The cards are labeled on the back as being 1991 prototypes. Cunningham's is valued at $10; Smith's is $15. Eight Braille cards, numbers 281-288, were also produced. The cards, similar in design to the regular issue, feature statistical leaders but have different photos than the players' regular cards. The backs are written in Braille. The Braille cards were only available in factory sets.

NM/M
Complete Set (280): 15.00
Complete Factory (291): 15.00
Common Player: .10
Minor Stars: .20
Pack (6): 1.00
Wax Box (24): 20.00
1 Steve Broussard .10
2 Scott Case .10
3 Brian Jordan .20
4 Darion Conner .10
5 Tim Green .10
6 Chris Miller .20
7 Andre Rison .50
8 Mike Rozier .10
9 Deion Sanders 1.00
10 Jessie Tuggle .10
11 Leonard Smith .10
12 Shane Conlan .10
13 Kent Hull .10
14 Keith McKeller .10
15 James Lofton .20
16 Andre Reed .20
17 Bruce Smith .20
18 Darryl Talley .10
19 Steve Tasker .10
20 Thurman Thomas .50
21 Neal Anderson .10
22 Trace Armstrong .10
23 Mark Bortz .10
24 Mark Carrier (Chi.) .10
25 Wendell Davis .10
26 Richard Dent .10
27 Jim Harbaugh .20
28 Jay Hilgenberg .10
29 Brad Muster .10
30 Mike Singletary .20
31 Harold Green .10
32 James Brooks .10
33 Eddie Brown .10
34 Boomer Esiason .20
35 James Francis .10
36 David Fulcher .10
37 Rodney Holman .10
38 Tim McGee .10
39 Anthony Munoz .10
40 Ickey Woods .10
41 *Rob Burnett* .10
42 Thane Gash .10
43 Mike Johnson .10
44 Brian Brennan .10
45 Reggie Langhorne .10
46 Kevin Mack .10
47 Clay Matthews .10
48 Eric Metcalf .20
49 Anthony Pleasant .10
50 Ozzie Newsome .10
51 Troy Aikman 2.00
52 Issiac Holt .10
53 Michael Irvin .50
54 Jimmie Jones .10
55 Eugene Lockhart .10
56 Kelvin Martin .10
57 Ken Norton Jr. .10
58 Jay Novacek .10
59 Emmitt Smith 4.00
60 Daniel Stubbs .10
61 Steve Atwater .10
62 Michael Brooks .10
63 John Elway 2.00
64 Simon Fletcher .10
65 Bobby Humphrey .10
66 Mark Jackson .10
67 Vance Johnson .10
68 Karl Mecklenburg .10
69 Dennis Smith .10
70 Greg Kragen .10
71 Jerry Ball .10
72 Lomas Brown .10
73 Robert Clark .10
74 Michael Coper .10
75 Mel Gray .10
76 Richard Johnson .10
77 Rodney Peete .20
78 Barry Sanders 4.00
79 Chris Spielman .10
80 Andre Ware .10
81 Matt Brock .10
82 Leroy Butler .10
83 Tim Harris .10
84 Perry Kemp .10
85 Don Majkowski .10
86 Mark Murphy .10
87 Brian Noble .10
88 Sterling Sharpe .20
89 Darrell Thompson .10
90 Ed West .10
91 Ray Childress .10
92 Ernest Givins .10
93 Drew Hill .10
94 Haywood Jeffires .10
95 Richard Johnson .10
96 Sean Jones .10
97 Bruce Matthews .10
98 Warren Moon .20
99 Mike Munchak .10
100 Lorenzo White .10
101 Albert Bentley .10
102 Duane Bickett .10
103 Bill Brooks .10
104 Jeff George .50
105 Jon Hand .10
106 Jeff Herrod .10
107 Jessie Hester .10
108 Mike Prior .10
109 Rohn Stark .10
110 Clarence Verdin .10
111 Steve Deberg .10
112 Dan Saleaumua .10
113 Albert Lewis .10
114 Nick Lowery .10
115 Christian Okoye .10
116 Stephone Paige .10
117 Kevin Ross .10
118 Dino Hackett .10
119 Derrick Thomas .20
120 Barry Word .10
121 Marcus Allen .25
122 Mervyn Fernandez .10
123 Willie Gault .10
124 Bo Jackson .25
125 Terry McDaniel .10
126 Don Mosebar .10
127 Jay Schroeder .10
128 Greg Townsend .10
129 Aaron Wallace .10
130 Steve Wisniewski .10
131 Willie Anderson .10
132 Henry Ellard .10
133 Jim Everett .20
134 Cleveland Gary .10
135 Jerry Gray .10
136 Kevin Greene .10
137 Buford McGee .10
138 Vince Newsome .10
139 Jackie Slater .10
140 Frank Stams .10
141 Jeff Cross .10
142 Mark Duper .10
143 Ferrell Edmunds .10
144 Dan Marino 3.00
145 Louis Oliver .10
146 John Offerdahl .10
147 Tony Paige .10
148 Sammie Smith .10
149 Richmond Webb .10
150 Jarvis Williams .10
151 Joey Browner .10
152 Anthony Carter .10
153 Chris Doleman .10
154 Hassan Jones .10
155 Steve Jordan .10
156 Carl Lee .10
157 Randall McDaniel .10
158 Mike Merriweather .10
159 Herschel Walker .20
160 Wade Wilson .10
161 Ray Agnew .10
162 Bruce Armstrong .10
163 Marv Cook .10
164 Hart Lee Dykes .10
165 Irving Fryar .10
166 Tom Hodson .10
167 Ronnie Lippett .10
168 Fred Marion .10
169 John Stephens .10
170 Brent Williams .10
171 Morten Andersen .10
172 Gene Atkins .10
173 Craig Heyward .10
174 Rickey Jackson .10
175 Vaughan Johnson .10
176 Eric Martin .10
177 Rueben Mayes .10
178 Pat Swilling .10
179 Renaldo Turnbull .10
180 Steve Walsh .10
181 Ottis Anderson .10
182 Rodney Hampton .20
183 Jeff Hostetler .20
184 Pepper Johnson .10
185 Sean Landeta .10
186 Dave Meggett .10
187 Bart Oates .10
188 Phil Simms .10
189 Lawrence Taylor .20
190 Reyna Thompson .10
191 Brad Baxter .10
192 Dennis Byrd .10
193 Kylce Clifton .10
194 James Hasty .10
195 Pat Leahy .10
196 Erik McMillan .10
197 Rob Moore .50
198 Ken O'Brien .10
199 Mark Boyer .10
200 Al Toon .10
201 Fred Barnett .10
202 Jerome Brown .10
203 Keith Byars .10
204 Randall Cunningham .50
205 Wes Hopkins .10
206 Keith Jackson .10
207 Seth Joyner .10
208 Heath Sherman .10
209 Reggie White .50
210 Calvin Williams .10
211 Roy Green .10
212 Ken Harvey .10
213 Luis Sharpe .10
214 Ernie Jones .10
215 Tim McDonald .10
216 Freddie Joe Nunn .10
217 Ricky Proehl .10
218 Timm Rosenbach .10
219 Anthony Thompson .10
220 Lonnie Young .10
221 Gary Anderson .10
222 Bubby Brister .10
223 Eric Green .10
224 Merril Hoge .10
225 Carnell Lake .10
226 Louis Lipps .10
227 David Little .10
228 Greg Lloyd .10
229 Gerald Williams .10
230 Rod Woodson .10
231 Marion Butts .10
232 Gill Byrd .10
233 Burt Grossman .10
234 Courtney Hall .10
235 Ronnie Harmon .10
236 Anthony Miller .10
237 Leslie O'Neal .10
238 Junior Seau .50
239 Billy Joe Tolliver .10
240 Lee Williams .10
241 Dexter Carter .10
242 Kevin Fagan .10
243 Charles Haley .10
244 Brent Jones .10
245 Ronnie Lott .20
246 Guy McIntyre .10
247 Joe Montana 2.50
248 Jerry Rice 2.00
249 John Taylor .10
250 Roger Craig .20
251 Brian Blades .10
252 Derrick Penner .10
253 Nesby Glasgow .10
254 Jacob Green .10
255 Tommy Kane .10
256 Dave Krieg .10
257 Rufus Porter .10
258 Eugene Robinson .10
259 Cortez Kennedy .10
260 John L. Williams .10
261 Gary Anderson .10

262 Mark Carrier .10
263 Steve Christie .10
264 Reggie Cobb .10
265 Paul Gruber .10
266 Wayne Haddix .10
267 Bruce Hill .10
268 Keith McCants .10
269 Vinny Testaverde .50
270 Broderick Thomas .10
271 Earnest Byner .10
272 Gary Clark .10
273 Darrell Green .10
274 Jim Lachey .10
275 Chip Lohmiller .10
276 Charles Mann .10
277 Wilber Marshall .10
278 Art Monk .20
279 Mark Rypien .10
280 Alvin Walton .10
281 Randall Cunningham (Braille) .50
282 Warren Moon (Braille) .20
283 Barry Sanders (Braille) 5.00
284 Thurman Thomas (Braille) .50
285 Jerry Rice (Braille) 2.00
286 Haywood Jeffires (Braille) .20
287 Charles Haley (Braille) .20
288 Derrick Thomas (Braille) .20
289 NFC Logo Card .20
290 AFC Logo Card .20
291 Checklist .10

1991 Action Packed 24K Gold

These cards were randomly issued in foil packs of 1991 Action Packed cards. Cards feature the regular-issue fronts, but the stripe has been done in 24k gold. Cards have also been stamped 24k on the front and are numbered 1G-42G on the back. It's estimated that less than 8,000 were made of each card. Generally, the cards are valued at about 15 times the amount of the corresponding regular Action Packed card.

NM/M
Complete Set (42): 200.00
Common Player: 3.00
Minor Stars: 10.00
1 Andre Rison 4.00
2 Deion Sanders 12.00
3 Andre Reed 3.00
4 Bruce Smith 3.00
5 Thurman Thomas 6.00
6 Neal Anderson 3.00
7 Mark Carrier 3.00
8 Mike Singletary 3.00
9 Boomer Esiason 3.00
10 James Francis 3.00
11 Anthony Munoz 3.00
12 Troy Aikman 20.00
13 Emmitt Smith 35.00
14 John Elway 25.00
15 Bobby Humphrey 3.00
16 Barry Sanders 35.00
17 Don Majikowski 3.00
18 Sterling Sharpe 4.00
19 Warren Moon 6.00
20 Jeff George 4.00
21 Christian Okoye 3.00
22 Derrick Thomas 4.00
23 Barry Word 3.00
24 Marcus Allen 10.00
25 Bo Jackson 10.00
26 Jim Everett 3.00
27 Cleveland Gary 3.00
28 Dan Marino 35.00
29 Herschel Walker 3.00
30 Ottis Anderson 3.00
31 Rodney Hampton 3.00
32 Dave Meggett 3.00
33 Marion Butts 3.00
34 Randall Cunningham 4.00
35 Reggie White 4.00
36 Jerry Rice 25.00
37 Eric Green 3.00
38 Charles Haley 3.00
39 Ronnie Lott 3.00
40 Joe Montana 35.00
41 Vinny Testaverde 4.00
42 Gary Clark 3.00

1991 Action Packed Rookie Update

This set features the first 26 top draft picks among its 74 rookie cards, plus 10 traded and update cards. Each card has an embossed helmet with a white "R" inside to indicate the player is a rookie. The backs are written in red and have the player's collegiate statistics. An Emmitt Smith prototype card was included in each case of 1991 Action Packed Rookie/Update foil or factory set ordered. Special 24K gold cards were also made for the 26 first-round draft draft picks. They were inserted into update packs.

NM/M
Complete Set (84): 15.00
Complete Factory (84): 20.00
Common Player: .05
Minor Stars: .10
Pack (6): 1.25
Wax Box (24): 25.00
1 *Herman Moore* 3.00
2 *Eric Turner* .10
3 *Mike Croel* .10
4 *Alfred Williams* .05
5 *Stanley Richard* .10
6 *Russell Maryland* .25
7 *Pat Harlow* .05
8 *Alvin Harper* .10
9 *Mike Pritchard* .25
10 *Leonard Russell* .25
11 *Jarrod Bunch* .10
12 *Dan McGwire* .10
13 *Bobby Wilson* .05
14 *Vinnie Clark* .05
15 *Kelvin Pritchett* .05
16 *Harvey Williams* .25
17 *Stan Thomas* .05
18 *Todd Marinovich* .10
19 *Antone Davis* .05
20 *Greg Lewis* .05
21 *Brett Favre* 10.00
22 *Wesley Carroll* .05
23 *Ed McCaffrey* 3.00
24 *Reggie Barrett* .05
25 *Chris Zorich* .05
26 *Kenny Walker* .05
27 *Aaron Craver* .05
28 *Browning Nagle* .05
29 *Nick Bell* .05
30 *Anthony Morgan* .05
31 *Jesse Campbell* .05
32 *Eric Bieniemy* .10
33 *Ricky Ervins* .10
34 *Kanavis McGhee* .05
35 *Shawn Moore* .05
36 *Todd Lyght* .10
37 *Eric Swann* .25
38 *Henry Jones* .05
39 *Ted Washington* .05
40 *Charles McRae* .05
41 *Randal Hill* .10
42 *Huey Richardson* .05
43 *Roman Phifer* .05
44 *Ricky Watters* 2.00
45 *Esera Tuaolo* .05
46 *Michael Jackson* .25
47 *Shawn Jefferson* .05
48 *Tim Barnett* .05
49 *Chuck Webb* .05
50 *Moe Gardner* .05
51 *Mo Lewis* .05
52 *Mike Dumas* .05
53 *Jon Vaughn* .05
54 *Jerome Henderson* .05
55 *Harry Colon* .05
56 *David Daniels* .05
57 *Phil Hansen* .05
58 *Ernie Mills* .05
59 *John Kasay* .05
60 *Darren Lewis* .05
61 *James Joseph* .05
62 *Robert Wilson* .05
63 *Lawrence Dawsey* .05
64 *Mike Jones* .05
65 *Dave McCloughan* .05
66 *Erric Pegram* .10
67 *Aeneas Williams* .25
68 *Reggie Johnson* .05
69 *Todd Scott* .05
70 *James Jones* .05
71 *Lamar Rogers* .05
72 *Darryll Lewis* .05
73 *Bryan Cox* .25
74 *Leroy Thompson* .05
75 *Mark Higgs* .05
76 John Friesz .25
77 Tim McKyer .05
78 Roger Craig .10
79 Ronnie Lott .25
80 Steve Young 1.00
81 Percy Snow .05
82 Cornelius Bennett .10
83 Johnny Johnson .10
84 Blair Thomas .05

A player's name in *italic* type indicates a rookie card.

1991 Action Packed Rookie Update 24K Gold

These insert cards were randomly included in 1991 Action Packed Rookie Update foil packs and are devoted to first-round draft picks. Each card front has an embossed color photo, plus gold foil stamping. A "24K" is also stamped on the card to distinguish it as an insert card. The card back is in a horizontal format and includes the player's collegiate statistics, a color mug shot, a panel for an autograph, and a card number. The card is numbered according to the order the player was drafted and uses a "G" suffix.

NM/M
Complete Set (26): 100.00
Common Player: 4.00
Minor Stars: 6.00
1 Russell Maryland 4.00
2 Eric Turner 4.00
3 Mike Croel 4.00
4 Todd Lyght 4.00
5 Eric Swann 6.00
6 Charles McRae 4.00
7 Antone Davis 4.00
8 Stanley Richard 4.00
9 Herman Moore 20.00
10 Pat Harlow 4.00
11 Alvin Harper 4.00
12 Mike Pritchard 4.00
13 Leonard Russell 4.00
14 Huey Richardson 4.00
15 Dan McGwire 4.00
16 Bobby Wilson 4.00
17 Alfred Williams 4.00
18 Vinnie Clark 4.00
19 Kelvin Pritchett 4.00
20 Harvey Williams 5.00
21 Stan Thomas 4.00
22 Randal Hill 4.00
23 Todd Marinovich 4.00
24 Ted Washington 4.00
25 Henry Jones 4.00
26 Jarrod Bunch 4.00

1991 Action Packed NFLPA Awards

1990 NFL award winners are recognized in this 16-card set produced by Action Packed. The cards, similar in design to the regular 1991 issue, were available as a boxed set; 5,000 individually-numbered sets were produced. Each box has the set number on it, plus "NFLPA/MDA Awards Dinner March 12, 1991" inscribed on it. Each card back has the award he won listed under his name.

NM/M
Complete Set (16): 40.00
Common Player: 2.00
1 Jim Lachey 2.00
2 Anthony Munoz 5.00
3 Bruce Smith 6.00
4 Reggie White 6.00
5 Charles Haley 2.00
6 Derrick Thomas 3.00
7 Albert Lewis 2.00
8 Mark Carrier 2.00
9 Reyna Thompson 2.00
10 Steve Tasker 2.00
11 James Francis 2.00
12 Mark Carrier 3.00
13 Johnny Johnson 3.00
14 Eric Green 4.00
15 Warren Moon 6.00
16 Randall Cunningham 6.00

1991 Action Packed Whizzer White Greats

The 25 winners of the Justice Byron "Whizzer" White Humanitarian Award from 1967 to 1991 were pictured in this special Action Packed set issued in conjunction with the 1991 awards banquet in Chicago. The White award is given annually to a single NFL player who serves his team, community and country in the spirit of former NFL player and U.S. Supreme Court Justice Byron White. The card set features Action Packed's 1991 gold standard design with full color, embossed action photos. For the first time, however, the indicia is silver with the award year inscribed in a silver helmet. The card backs feature a color head shot, player biographical information, career and community contributions. A total of 3,500 sets were distributed at the dinner; another 5,000 were made available to collectors through Rotman Productions.

NM/M
Complete Set (25): 25.00
Common Player: .50
1 Bart Starr (1967) 4.00
2 Willie Davis (1968) 2.00
3 Ed Meador (1969) .50
4 Gale Sayers (1970) 4.00
5 Kermit Alexander(1971) .50
6 Ray May (1972) .50
7 Andy Russell (1973) 1.00
8 Floyd Little (1974) 1.00
9 Rocky Bleier (1975) 1.00
10 Jim Hart (1976) 1.00
11 Lyle Alzado (1977) 1.00
12 Archie Manning (1978) 1.00
13 Roger Staubach (1979) 5.00
14 Gene Upshaw (1980) 1.00
15 Ken Houston (1981) 1.00
16 Franco Harris (1982) 2.00
17 Doug Dieken (1983) .50
18 Rolf Benirschke (1984) .50
19 Reggie Williams (1985) .50
20 Nat Moore (1986) .50
21 George Martin (1987) .50
22 Deron Cherry (1988) .50
23 Mike Singletary (1989) 1.00
24 Ozzie Newsome (1990) 1.00
25 Mike Kenn (1991) .50

1991 Action Packed All-Madden

This 52-card set is John Madden's second issue featuring the All-Madden team. The borderless fronts feature embossed color photos with gold and aqua border stripes. Cards, which are standard size, have the Madden logo and team helmet on the front. The back, which is numbered, has stats and a mug shot.

NM/M
Complete Set (52): 25.00
Common Player: .20
Wax Box: 15.00
1 Mark Rypien .40
2 Erik Kramer 1.00
3 Jim McMahon .40
4 Jesse Sapolu .20
5 Jay Hilgenberg .20
6 Howard Ballard .20
7 Lomas Brown .20
8 John Elliott .20
9 Joe Jacoby .20
10 Jim Lachey .20
11 Anthony Munoz .30
12 Nate Newton .20
13 Will Wolford .20
14 Jerry Ball .20
15 Jerome Brown .20
16 William Perry .25
17 Charles Mann .20
18 Clyde Simmons .20
19 Reggie White 1.50
20 Eric Allen .20
21 Darrell Green .25
22 Bennie Blades .20
23 Chuck Cecil .20
24 Rickey Dixon .30
25 David Fulcher .20
26 Ronnie Lott .75
27 Emmitt Smith 6.00
28 Neal Anderson .30
29 Robert Delpino .30
30 Barry Sanders 4.00
31 Thurman Thomas 1.00
32 Cornelius Bennett .35
33 Rickey Jackson .20
34 Seth Joyner .20
35 Wilber Marshall .20
36 Clay Matthews .20
37 Chris Spielman .20
38 Pat Swilling .25
39 Fred Barnett .50
40 Gary Clark .40
41 Michael Irvin 1.50
42 Art Monk .50
43 Jerry Rice 2.50
44 John Taylor .50
45 Tom Waddle .20
46 Kevin Butler .20
47 Bill Bates .20
48 Greg Manusky .20
49 Elvis Patterson .20
50 Steve Tasker .20
51 John Daly 1.00
52 All-Madden Trophy 1.50

1992 Action Packed Prototypes

These standard-size cards are prototypes featuring the basic design for Action Packed's 1992 regular set. Each card has a card number (92) on the back, plus a suffix (A, N or P). The cards made their debut at the 1992 Super Bowl Show in Minneapolis and are labeled on the back as being prototypes.

NM/M
Complete Set (3): 35.00
Common Player: 10.00
A Thurman Thomas 10.00
N Emmitt Smith 15.00
P Barry Sanders 20.00

1992 Action Packed

These standard-size cards feature embossed photos on the front, with gold and red border stripes for AFC players or aqua and gold for NFC players. The cards are numbered alphabetically by team, by player. The set has two subsets - eight Braille cards (#s 281-288) featuring league leaders and two logo cards (#s 289-290). There were 42 24K gold insert cards made, too.

NM/M
Complete Set (280): 30.00
Complete Factory (292): 35.00
Common Player: .15
Minor Stars: .30
Pack (6): 1.00
Wax Box (24): 20.00
1 Steve Broussard .15
2 Michael Haynes .15
3 Tim McKyer .15
4 Chris Miller .30
5 Andre Rison .50
6 Jessie Tuggle .15
7 Mike Pritchard .30
8 Moe Gardner .15
9 Brian Jordan .30
10 Mike Kenn, Chris Hinton .15
11 Steve Tasker .15
12 Cornelius Bennett .30
13 Shane Conlan .15
14 Darryl Talley .15
15 Thurman Thomas .50
16 James Lofton .30
17 Don Beebe .15
18 Jim Ritcher .15
19 Keith McKeller .15
20 Nate Odomes .15
21 Mark Carrier .15
22 Wendell Davis .15
23 Richard Dent .15
24 Jim Harbaugh .30
25 Jay Hilgenberg .15
26 Steve McMichael .15
27 Tom Waddle .15
28 Neal Anderson .15
29 Brad Muster .15
30 Shaun Gayle .15
31 Jim Breech .15
32 James Brooks .15
33 James Francis .15
34 David Fulcher .15
35 Harold Green .15
36 Rodney Holman .15
37 Anthony Munoz .30
38 Tim Krumrie .15
39 Tim McGee .15
40 Eddie Brown .15
41 Kevin Mack .15
42 James Jones .15
43 Vince Newsome .15
44 Ed King .15
45 Eric Metcalf .15
46 Leroy Hoard .30
47 Stephen Braggs .15
48 Clay Matthews .15
49 David Brandon .15
50 Rob Burnett .15
51 Larry Brown .15
52 Alvin Harper .15
53 Michael Irvin .50
54 Ken Norton Jr. .15
55 Jay Novacek .15
56 Emmitt Smith 4.00
57 Tony Tolbert .15
58 Nate Newton .15
59 Steve Beuerlein .15
60 Tony Casillas .15
61 Steve Atwater .15
62 Mike Croel .15
63 Gaston Green .15
64 Mark Jackson .15
65 Greg Kragen .15
66 Karl Mecklenberg .15
67 Dennis Smith .15
68 Steve Sewell .15
69 John Elway 2.00
70 Simon Fletcher .15
71 Mel Gray .15
72 Barry Sanders 4.00
73 Jerry Ball .15
74 Bennie Blades .15
75 Lomas Brown .15
76 Erik Kramer .30
77 Chris Spielman .15
78 Ray Crockett .15
79 Willie Green .15
80 Rodney Peete .15
81 Sterling Sharpe .50
82 Tony Bennett .15
83 Chuck Cecil .15
84 Perry Kemp .15
85 Brian Noble .15
86 Darrell Thompson .15
87 Mike Tomczak .15
88 Vince Workman .15
89 Esera Tuaolo .15
90 Mark Murphy .15
91 William Fuller .15
92 Ernest Givins .15
93 Drew Hill .15
94 Al Smith .15
95 Ray Childress .15
96 Haywood Jeffires .15
97 Cris Dishman .15
98 Warren Moon .50
99 Lamar Lathon .15
100 Mike Munchak, Bruce Matthews .15
101 Bill Brooks .15
102 Duane Bickett .15
103 Eugene Daniel .15
104 Jeff Herrod .15
105 Jessie Hester .15
106 Donnell Thompson .15
107 Anthony Johnson .15
108 Jon Hand .15
109 Rohn Stark .15
110 Clarence Verdin .15
111 Derrick Thomas .50
112 Steve DeBerg .15
113 Deron Cherry .15
114 Chris Martin .15
115 Christian Okoye .15
116 Dan Saleaumua .15
117 Neil Smith .15
118 Barry Word .15
119 Tim Barnett .15
120 Albert Lewis .15
121 Ronnie Lott .30
122 Marcus Allen .50
123 Todd Marinovich .15
124 Nick Bell .15
125 Tim Brown .50
126 Ethan Horton .15
127 Greg Townsend .15
128 Jeff Gossett, Jeff Jaeger .15
129 Scott Davis .15
130 Steve Wisniewski, Don Mosebar .15
131 Kevin Greene .15
132 Roman Phifer .15
133 Tony Zendejas .15
134 Pat Terrell .15
135 Willie Anderson .15
136 Robert Delpino .15
137 Jim Everett .30
138 Larry Kelm .15
139 Todd Lyght .15
140 Henry Ellard .15
141 Mark Clayton .15
142 Jeff Cross .15
143 Mark Duper .15
144 John Offerdahl .15
145 Louis Oliver .15
146 Pete Stoyanovich .15
147 Richmond Webb .15
148 Mark Higgs .15
149 Tony Paige .15
150 Bryan Cox .15
151 Anthony Carter .15
152 Cris Carter 1.00
153 Rich Gannon .15
154 Steve Jordan .15
155 Mike Merriweather .15
156 Henry Thomas .15
157 Herschel Walker .30
158 Randall McDaniel .15
159 Terry Allen .50
160 Joey Browner .15
161 Leonard Russell .30
162 Bruce Armstrong .15
163 Vincent Brown .15
164 Hugh Millen .15
165 Andre Tippett .15
166 Jon Vaughn .15
167 Pat Harlow .15
168 Marv Cook .15
169 Irving Fryar .30
170 Maurice Hurst .15
171 Pat Swilling .15
172 Vince Buck .15
173 Rickey Jackson .15
174 Sam Mills .15
175 Bobby Hebert .15
176 Vaughan Johnson .15
177 Floyd Turner .15
178 Fred McAfee .15
179 Morten Andersen .15
180 Eric Martin .15
181 Rodney Hampton .30
182 Pepper Johnson .15
183 Leonard Russell .15
184 Stephen Baker .15
185 Mark Ingram .15
186 Dave Meggett .15
187 Bart Oates .15
188 Mark Collins .15
189 Myron Guyton .15
190 Jeff Hostetler .30
191 Jeff Lageman .15
192 Brad Baxter .15
193 Mo Lewis .15
194 Chris Burkett .15
195 James Hasty .15
196 Rob Moore .50
197 Kyle Clifton .15
198 Terance Mathis .15
199 Marvin Washington .15

200 Lonnie Young .15
201 Reggie White .50
202 Eric Allen .15
203 Fred Barnett .30
204 Keith Byars .15
205 Seth Joyner .15
206 Clyde Simmons .15
207 Jerome Brown .15
208 Wes Hopkins .15
209 Keith Jackson .15
210 Calvin Williams .15
211 Aeneas Williams .15
212 Ken Harvey .15
213 Ernie Jones .15
214 Freddie Joe Nunn .15
215 Rich Camarillo .15
216 Johnny Johnson .30
217 Tim McDonald .15
218 Eric Swann .15
219 Eric Hill .15
220 Anthony Thompson .15
221 Hardy Nickerson .15
222 Barry Foster .15
223 Louis Lipps .15
224 Greg Lloyd .15
225 Neil O'Donnell .30
226 Jerrol Williams .15
227 Eric Green .15
228 Rod Woodson .15
229 Carnell Lake .15
230 Dwight Stone .15
231 Marion Butts .15
232 John Friesz .30
233 Burt Grossman .15
234 Ronnie Harmon .15
235 Gill Byrd .15
236 Rod Bernstine .15
237 Courtney Hall .15
238 Nate Lewis .15
239 Joe Phillips .15
240 Henry Rolling .15
241 Keith Henderson .15
242 Guy McIntyre .15
243 Bill Romanowski .15
244 Don Griffin .15
245 Dexter Carter .15
246 Charles Haley .30
247 Brent Jones .15
248 John Taylor .15
249 Steve Young 1.50
250 Larry Roberts .15
251 Brian Blades .15
252 Jacob Green .15
253 John Kasay .15
254 Cortez Kennedy .30
255 Rufus Porter .15
256 John L. Williams .15
257 Tommy Kane .15
258 Eugene Robinson .15
259 Terry Wooden .15
260 Chris Warren .50
261 Lawrence Dawsey .15
262 Mark Carrier .15
263 Keith McCants .15
264 Jesse Solomon .15
265 Vinny Testaverde .50
266 Rickey Reynolds .15
267 Broderick Thomas .15
268 Gary Anderson .15
269 Reggie Cobb .15
270 Tony Covington .15
271 Darrell Green .30
272 Charles Mann .15
273 Wilber Marshall .15
274 Gary Clark .15
275 Chip Lohmiller .15
276 Earnest Byner .15
277 Jim Lachey .15
278 Art Monk .30
279 Mark Rypien .30
280 Mark Schlereth .15
281 Mark Rypien (Braille) .15
282 Warren Moon (Braille) .30
283 Emmitt Smith (Braille) 2.00
284 Thurman Thomas (Braille) .30
285 Michael Irvin (Braille) .30
286 Haywood Jeffires (Braille) .15
287 Pat Swilling (Braille) .15
288 Ronnie Lott (Braille) .15
289 NFC logo .15
290 AFC Logo .15

1992 Action Packed 24K Gold

These cards have a color embossed photo on the front, with gold foil stamping and a team helmet. The back has statistics, a mug shot, a biography and a caption which describes the photo on the front. A panel is also included for an autograph. Cards are numbered on the back, using a "G" suffix, and are checklisted alphabetically by team name. Cards were randomly inserted in foil packs. Detroit Lions star Barry Sanders autographed 1,000 of his card (#13G); they were randomly inserted in packs.

NM/M
Complete Set (42): 500.00
Common Player: 7.00
Minor Stars: 14.00
1 Michael Haynes 7.00
2 Chris Miller 7.00
3 Andre Rison 10.00
4 Cornelius Bennett 7.00
5 James Lofton 7.00
6 Thurman Thomas 14.00
7 Neal Anderson 7.00
8 Michael Irvin 20.00
9 Emmitt Smith 75.00
10 Mike Croel 7.00
11 John Elway 50.00
12 Gaston Green 7.00
13 Barry Sanders 75.00
13au Barry Sanders 225.00
14 Sterling Sharpe 10.00
15 Ernest Givins 7.00
16 Drew Hill 7.00
17 Haywood Jeffires 7.00
18 Warren Moon 10.00
19 Christian Okoye 7.00
20 Derrick Thomas 10.00
21 Ronnie Lott 7.00
22 Todd Marinovich 7.00
23 Henry Ellard 7.00
24 Mark Clayton 7.00
25 Herschel Walker 7.00
26 Irving Fryar 7.00
27 Leonard Russell 7.00
28 Pat Swilling 7.00
29 Rodney Hampton 7.00
30 Rob Moore 7.00
31 Seth Joyner 7.00
32 Reggie White 12.00
33 Eric Green 7.00
34 Rod Woodson 7.00
35 Marion Butts 7.00
36 Charles Haley 7.00
37 John Taylor 7.00
38 Steve Young 30.00
39 Earnest Byner 7.00
40 Gary Clark 7.00
41 Art Monk 7.00
42 Mark Rypien 7.00

1992 Action Packed Rookie Update

Twenty-five first-round draft picks are featured in their new teams' uniforms in this 84-card update set, which has 51 rookies in all and 33 NFL stars. The cards have a black-and-gold foil stripe along the side, and a red helmet with an "R" on the front. There were also 35 24K gold insert cards featuring ten NFL quarterbacks and 25 first-round draft picks. A special "Neon Deion Sanders" card, numbered 84N, was also made and features neon fluorescent orange.

NM/M
Complete Set (84): 15.00
Common Player: .15
Minor Stars: .30
Pack (7): 1.00
Wax Box (24): 20.00
1 Steve Emtman .30
2 Quentin Coryatt .30
3 Sean Gilbert .30
4 John Fina .15
5 Alonzo Spellman .30
6 Amp Lee .30
7 Robert Porcher .30
8 Jason Hanson .15
9 Ty Detmer .50
10 Ray Roberts .15
11 Bob Whitfield .15
12 Greg Skrepenak .15
13 Vaughn Dunbar .15
14 Siran Stacy .15
15 Mark D'Onofrio .15
16 Tony Sacca .15
17 Dana Hall .15
18 Courtney Hawkins .30
19 Shane Collins .15
20 Tony Smith .15
21 Rod Smith .15
22 Troy Auzenne .15
23 David Klingler .30
24 Darryl Williams .15
25 Carl Pickens 2.00
26 Ricardo McDonald .15
27 Tommy Vardell .30
28 Kevin Smith .30
29 Rodney Culver .15
30 Jimmy Smith 1.00
31 Robert Jones .15
32 Tommy Maddox .30
33 Shane Dronett .30
34 Terrell Buckley .50
35 Santana Dotson .50
36 Edgar Bennett 1.00
37 Ashley Ambrose .15
38 Dale Carter .50
39 Chester McGlockton .15
40 Steve Israel .15
41 Marc Boutte .15
42 Marco Coleman .30
43 Troy Vincent .30
44 Mark Wheeler .15
45 Darren Perry .15
46 Eugene Chung .15
47 Derek Brown .15
48 Phillippi Sparks .15
49 Johnny Mitchell .30
50 Kurt Barber .15
51 Leon Searcy .15
52 Chris Mims .30
53 Keith Jackson .30
54 Charles Haley .30
55 Dave Krieg .15
56 Dan McGwire .15
57 Phil Simms .30
58 Bobby Humphrey .15
59 Jerry Rice 2.50
60 Joe Montana 3.00
61 Junior Seau .50
62 Leslie O'Neal .15
63 Anthony Miller .30
64 Timm Rosenbach .15
65 Herschel Walker .30
66 Randal Hill .15
67 Randall Cunningham .75
68 Al Toon .15
69 Browning Nagle .15
70 Lawrence Taylor .50
71 Dan Marino 4.00
72 Eric Dickerson .30
73 Harvey Williams .30
74 Jeff George .50
75 Russell Maryland .30
76 Troy Aikman 2.00
77 Michael Dean Perry .30
78 Bernie Kosar .30
79 Boomer Esiason .30
80 Mike Singletary .30
81 Bruce Smith .15
82 Andre Reed .30
83 Jim Kelly .50
84 Deion Sanders 1.00
84N Deion Sanders Neon 4.00

1992 Action Packed Rookie Update 24K Gold

Quarterbacks and first-round draft picks are featured on these insert cards, randomly included in 1992 Action Packed Rookie Update foil packs. Cards have 24K gold foil-stamping on them.

NM/M
Complete Set (35): 450.00
Common Player: 7.00
Minor Stars: 14.00
1 Steve Emtman 7.00
2 Quentin Coryatt 7.00
3 Sean Gilbert 7.00
4 Terrell Buckley 10.00
5 David Klingler 7.00
6 Troy Vincent 7.00
7 Tommy Vardell 7.00
8 Leon Searcy 7.00
9 Marco Coleman 7.00
10 Eugene Chung 7.00
11 Derek Brown 7.00
12 Johnny Mitchell 7.00
13 Chester McGlockton 7.00
14 Kevin Smith 7.00
15 Dana Hall 7.00
16 Tony Smith 7.00
17 Dale Carter 7.00
18 Vaughn Dunbar 7.00
19 Alonzo Spellman 7.00
20 Chris Mims 7.00
21 Robert Jones 7.00
22 Tommy Maddox 25.00
23 Robert Porcher 7.00
24 John Fina 7.00
25 Darryl Williams 7.00
26 Jim Kelly 20.00
27 Randall Cunningham 20.00
28 Dan Marino 60.00
29 Troy Aikman 40.00
30 Boomer Esiason 14.00
31 Bernie Kosar 14.00
32 Jeff George 10.00
33 Phil Simms 14.00
34 Ray Roberts 7.00
35 Bob Whitfield 7.00

1992 Action Packed NFLPA Mackey Awards

These standard-size 24K-gold cards were produced for those who attended the 1992 NFLPA Mackey Awards Banquet. Only 2,000 cards of each player were produced.

NM/M
Complete Set (3): 60.00
(1) John Mackey 10.00
(2) Reggie White 20.00
(3) Jack Kemp 30.00

1992 Action Packed 24K NFLPA MDA Awards

The 1991 NFL Players of the Year are honored in this 16-card set produced by Action Packed for distribution to those who attended the NFLPA/MDA Awards Dinner, March 5, 1992. The sets were packed in a black box and were stamped "Banquet Edition." The cards feature 24K gold stamping. Cards for players from the AFC are red and have the Action Packed logo in the upper left corner. Cards for the NFC players are blue and have the logo in the upper right corner. Only 1,000 sets were produced.

NM/M
Complete Set (16): 100.00
Common Player: 4.00
1 Steve Wisniewski 4.00
2 Jim Lachey 4.00
3 Reggie White 10.00
4 William Fuller 4.00
5 Derrick Thomas 10.00
6 Pat Swilling 8.00
7 Darrell Green 8.00
8 Ronnie Lott 10.00
9 Steve Tasker 4.00
10 Mel Gray 4.00
11 Aeneas Williams 4.00
12 Mike Croel 4.00
13 Leonard Russell 4.00
14 Lawrence Dawsey 4.00
15 Barry Sanders 35.00
16 Thurman Thomas 15.00

1992 Action Packed All-Madden

This third John Madden set includes a card of the famed Madden Cruiser. Cards are standard size and were also made into 24K gold insert versions, too.

NM/M
Complete Set (55): 20.00
Common Player: .15
Wax Box: 18.00
1 Emmitt Smith 6.50
2 Reggie White .75
3 Deion Sanders 1.25
4 Wilber Marshall .15
5 Barry Sanders 3.00
6 Derrick Thomas .50
7 Troy Aikman 3.50
8 Eric Allen .15
9 Cris Carter .15
10 Jerry Rice 2.50
11 Rickey Jackson .15
12 Bubba McDowell .15
13 Jack Del Rio .15
14 Nate Newton .15
15 John Elliott .15
16 Fred Barnett .40
17 Mike Singletary .15
18 Lawrence Taylor .40
19 Bruce Matthews .15
20 Pat Swilling .40
21 Charles Haley .15
22 Andre Rison .50
23 Seth Joyner .15
24 Steve Young 1.75
25 Gary Clark .25
26 Jerry Ball .15
27 Michael Irvin 1.50
28 Haywood Jeffires .30
29 Kevin Ross .15
30 Chris Doleman .15
31 Vai Sikahema .15
32 Ricky Watters 2.00
33 Henry Thomas .15
34 Mike Kenn .15
35 Eric Williams .15
36 Neil Smith .15
37 Mark Schlereth .15
38 Steve Wallace .15
39 Randall McDaniel .15
40 Kurt Gouveia .15
41 Al Noga .15
42 Tom Rathman .15
43 Harris Barton .15
44 Mel Gray .15
45 Keith Byars .15
46 Todd Scott .15
47 Brent Jones .15
48 Audray McMillian .15
49 Ray Childress .15
50 Dennis Smith .15
51 Mark McMillian .15
52 Sean Gilbert .15
53 Pierce Holt .15
54 Daryl Johnston .40
55 Madden Cruiser .50

1993 Action Packed Troy Aikman Promos

The two-card, standard-size set highlights Dallas quarterback Troy Aikman, after he won the MVP award in Super Bowl XXVII. Aikman's name is printed along the left border. The card back has "1993 Prototype" printed over Aikman's statistics. The cards are numbered TA2 and TA3 as they were originally part of an 11-card promo sheet.

NM/M
Complete Set (2): 15.00
Common Player: 8.00
2 Troy Aikman (Running with ball) 8.00
3 Troy Aikman (Pitching the ball) 8.00

1993 Action Packed Emmitt Smith Promos

The five-card, standard-size set features five Emmitt Smith cards to promote the All-Madden Team set. The word "Prototype" is printed on the card back and each card has the prefix "ES." ES1 and ES4 were available at the Super Bowl Card Show in 1993. ES5 was available to members of the Tuff Stuff Buyers Club.

NM/M
Complete Set (5): 40.00
Common Player: 5.00
1 Emmitt Smith (Receiving handoff from quaterback; side view) 5.00
2 Emmitt Smith 10.00
3 Emmitt Smith 10.00
4 Emmitt Smith (Cutting to right to elude tackler; ball cradled in left arm) 5.00
5 Emmitt Smith (Running to right; ball in left arm) 10.00

1993 Action Packed Prototypes

The six-card, standard-size set previewed the 1993 regular series. The player's last name is printed vertically on the card edge in gold foil. The card backs feature "1993 Prototype" and the prefix "FB." The bottom of the back includes a blank space for an autograph.

NM/M
Complete Set (6): 25.00
Common Player: 3.00
1 Emmitt Smith 8.00
2 Thurman Thomas 3.00
3 Steve Young 4.00
4 Barry Sanders 8.00
5 Barry Foster 3.00
6 Warren Moon 4.00

1993 Action Packed

This 204-card set features 162 regular cards and 42 subset cards. The 42 subset cards are three types, each with its own numbering prefix - the "Quarterback Club" (18, with a QB prefix), "Moving Targets" (12, with an MT prefix) and 1,000-yard rushers (12, with an RB prefix). Each of these subset cards also has a 24K gold equivalent, with a G suffix. The Quarterback Club cards were also done in Braille (B suffix) and as Mint versions (500 each). The 1993 Rookie/Update set begins where the regular set ended, excluding subsets, by starting with #163. These cards have a gold, silver and bronze design theme designating the first three rounds of the NFL draft. First-rounders have gold foil accents, seconds have silver, and thirds have bronze. Prominent players who have been traded have also been included in the set; the year they were drafted is on the front of the card. There were six standard-size 1993 prototype cards also produced.

NM/M
Complete Set (222): 75.00
Complete Series 1 (162): 45.00
Complete Series 2 (60): 30.00
Common Player: .15
Minor Stars: .25
Series 1 Pack (6): 2.25
Series 1 Wax Box (24): 45.00
Rook/Up. Pack (8): 2.00
Rook/Up. Wax Box (24): 42.00
1 Michael Haynes .15
2 Chris Miller .15
3 Andre Rison .25
4 Jim Kelly .50
5 Andre Reed .25
6 Thurman Thomas .50
7 Jim Harbaugh .15
8 Harold Green .15
9 David Klingler .25
10 Bernie Kosar .25
11 Troy Aikman 3.00
12 Michael Irvin .50
13 Emmitt Smith 5.00
14 John Elway 1.50
15 Barry Sanders 4.00
16 Brett Favre 5.00
17 Sterling Sharpe .75
18 Ernest Givins .15
19 Haywood Jeffires .15
20 Warren Moon .50
21 Lorenzo White .15
22 Jeff George .50
23 Joe Montana 3.00
24 Jim Everett .25
25 Cleveland Gary .15
26 Dan Marino 4.00
27 Terry Allen .15
28 Rodney Hampton .50
29 Phil Simms .15
30 Fred Barnett .15
31 Randall Cunningham .50
32 Gary Clark .15
33 Barry Foster .15
34 Neil O'Donnell .50
35 Stan Humphries .50
36 Anthony Miller .15
37 Jerry Rice 3.00
38 Ricky Watters .50
39 Steve Young 2.00
40 Chris Warren .40
41 Reggie Cobb .15
42 Mark Rypien .15
43 Deion Sanders 1.50
44 Henry Jones .15
45 Bruce Smith .15
46 Richard Dent .15
47 Tommy Vardell .15
48 Charles Haley .15
49 Ken Norton .15
50 Jay Novacek .15
51 Simon Fletcher .15
52 Pat Swilling .15
53 Tony Bennett .15
54 Reggie White .40
55 Ray Childress .15
56 Quentin Coryatt .15
57 Steve Emtman .15
58 Derrick Thomas .25
59 James Lofton .15
60 Marco Coleman .15
61 Bryan Cox .15
62 Troy Vincent .15
63 Chris Doleman .15
64 Audray McMillian .15
65 Vaughn Dunbar .15
66 Rickey Jackson .15
67 Lawrence Taylor .25
68 Ronnie Lott .15
69 Rob Moore .15
70 Browning Nagle .15
71 Eric Allen .15
72 Tim Harris .15
73 Clyde Simmons .15
74 Steve Beuerlein .15
75 Randal Hill .15
76 Darren Perry .15
77 Rod Woodson .25
78 Marion Butts .15
79 Chris Mims .15
80 Junior Seau .50
81 Cortez Kennedy .15
82 Santana Dotson .15
83 Earnest Byner .15
84 Charles Mann .15
85 Pierce Holt .15
86 Mike Pritchard .15
87 Cornelius Bennett .15
88 Neal Anderson .15
89 Carl Pickens .50
90 Eric Metcalf .15
91 Michael Dean Perry .15
92 Alvin Harper .25
93 Robert Jones .15
94 Steve Atwater .15
95 Rod Bernstine .15
96 Herman Moore 1.00
97 Chris Spielman .15
98 Terrell Buckley .15
99 Dale Carter .15
100 Terry McDaniel .15
101 Tim Brown .25
102 Cleveland Green .15
103 Howie Long .15
104 Todd Marinovich .15
105 Anthony Smith .15
106 Willie Anderson .15
107 Henry Ellard .15
108 Mark Higgs .15

109	Keith Jackson	.15
110	Irving Fryar	.15
111	Cris Carter	.25
112	Leonard Russell	.15
113	Wayne Martin	.15
114	Mark Jackson	.15
115	David Meggett	.15
116	Brad Baxter	.15
117	Boomer Esiason	.15
118	Johnny Johnson	.15
119	Seth Joyner	.15
120	Kevin Greene	.15
121	Ronnie Harmon, Greg Lloyd	.15
122	Brent Jones	.15
123	Amp Lee	.15
124	Tim McDonald	.15
125	Darrell Green	.15
126	Art Monk	.15
127	Tony Smith	.15
128	Bill Brooks	.15
129	Kenneth Davis	.15
130	Donnell Woolford	.15
131	Derrick Fenner	.15
132	Michael Jackson	.15
133	Mark Clayton	.15
134	Al Smith	.15
135	Curtis Duncan, Rodney Culver	.15
137	Harvey Williams	.15
138	Neil Smith	.15
139	Marcus Allen	.25
140	Eric Dickerson	.15
141	Sean Gilbert	.15
142	Shane Conlan	.15
143	Todd Scott	.15
144	Vincent Brown	.15
145	Andre Tippett	.15
146	Jon Vaughn	.15
147	Marv Cook	.15
148	Morten Anderson	.15
149	Sam Mills	.15
150	Mark Collins	.15
151	Heath Sherman	.15
152	Johnny Bailey	.15
153	Eric Green	.15
155	Gill Byrd	.15
156	Leslie O'Neal	.15
157	Rufus Porter	.15
158	Eugene Robinson	.15
159	Broderick Thomas	.15
160	Lawrence Dawsey	.15
161	Anthony Munoz	.15
162	Wilber Marshall	.15
163	*Drew Bledsoe*	8.00
164	*Rick Mirer*	.50
165	*Garrison Hearst*	3.00
166	*Marvin Jones*	.25
167	*John Copeland*	.25
168	*Eric Curry*	.25
169	*Curtis Conway*	2.50
170	*William Roaf*	.25
171	*Lincoln Kennedy*	.15
172	*Jerome Bettis*	3.00
173	*Dan Williams*	.15
174	*Patrick Bates*	.25
175	*Brad Hopkins*	.15
176	*Steve Everitt*	.25
177	*Wayne Simmons*	.15
178	*Tom Carter*	.25
179	*Ernest Dye*	.15
180	*Lester Holmes*	.15
181	*Irv Smith*	.25
182	*Robert Smith*	2.00
183	*Darrien Gordon*	.25
184	*Deon Figures*	.25
185	*Leonard Renfro*	.15
186	*O.J. McDuffie*	1.00
187	*Dana Stubblefield*	.50
188	*Todd Kelly*	.15
189	*Thomas Smith*	.25
190	*George Teague*	.25
191	Wilber Marshall	.15
192	Reggie White	.25
193	*Carlton Gray*	.15
194	*Chris Slade*	.50
195	*Ben Coleman*	.15
196	*Ryan McNeil*	.15
197	*Demetrius DuBose*	.15
198	*Coleman Rudolph*	.15
199	*Tony McGee*	.30
200	*Troy Drayton*	.25
201	*Natrone Means*	.25
202	*Glyn Milburn*	.30
203	*Chad Brown*	.50
204	*Reggie Brooks*	.25
205	*Kevin Williams*	1.00
206	*Micheal Barrow*	.15
207	*Roosevelt Potts*	.25
208	*Victor Bailey*	.25
209	*Qadry Ismail*	1.00
210	*Vincent Brisby*	.40
211	*Billy Joe Hobert*	.40
212	*Lamar Thomas*	.25
213	*Jason Elam*	.15
214	*Andre Hastings*	.40
215	*Terry Kirby*	1.00
216	Joe Montana	3.00
217	*Derrick Lassic*	.25
218	*Mark Brunell*	8.00
219	*Vaughn Hebron*	.25
220	*Troy Brown*	.15
221	*Derek Brown*	.25
222	Raghib Ismail	.25

1993 Action Packed 24K Gold

These cards are identical in format to the regular 1993 Action Packed cards, except they have "24K" written under the Action Packed logo on the card front. The cards use a "G" suffix for numbering; the card number appears on the back. Cards were random inserts in 1993 Action Packed foil packs and feature 24K versions of three insert sets - Quarterback Club (1G-18G), Moving Targets (19G-30G) and 1,000 Yard Rushers (31G-42G), plus 30 others.

		NM/M
Complete Set (72):		500.00
Complete Series 1 (42):		300.00
Complete Series 2 (30):		200.00
Common Player:		5.00
Minor Stars:		10.00
1	Troy Aikman	15.00
2	Randall Cunningham	5.00
3	John Elway	20.00
4	Jim Everett	5.00
5	Brett Favre	40.00
6	Jim Harbaugh	5.00
7	Jeff Hostetler	5.00
8	Jim Kelly	15.00
9	David Klingler	5.00
10	Bernie Kosar	5.00
11	Dan Marino	40.00
12	Chris Miller	5.00
13	Boomer Esiason	5.00
14	Warren Moon	10.00
15	Neil O'Donnell	10.00
16	Mark Rypien	5.00
17	Phil Simms	5.00
18	Steve Young	30.00
19	Fred Barnett	5.00
20	Gary Clark	5.00
21	Mark Clayton	5.00
22	Ernest Givins	5.00
23	Michael Haynes	5.00
24	Michael Irvin	10.00
25	Haywood Jeffires	5.00
26	Anthony Miller	5.00
27	Andre Reed	5.00
28	Jerry Rice	35.00
29	Andre Rison	5.00
30	Sterling Sharpe	10.00
31	Terry Allen	5.00
32	Reggie Cobb	5.00
33	Barry Foster	5.00
34	Cleveland Gary	5.00
35	Harold Green	5.00
36	Rodney Hampton	5.00
37	Barry Sanders	40.00
38	Emmitt Smith	40.00
39	Thurman Thomas	15.00
40	Chris Warren	5.00
41	Ricky Watters	10.00
42	Lorenzo White	5.00
43	Drew Bledsoe	25.00
44	Rick Mirer	5.00
45	Garrison Hearst	10.00
46	Marvin Jones	5.00
47	John Copeland	5.00
48	Eric Curry	5.00
49	Curtis Conway	10.00
50	William Roaf	5.00
51	Lincoln Kennedy	5.00
52	Jerome Bettis	10.00
53	Dan Williams	5.00
54	Patrick Bates	5.00
55	Brad Hopkins	5.00
56	Steve Everitt	5.00
57	Wayne Simmons	5.00
58	Tom Carter	5.00
59	Ernest Dye	5.00
60	Lester Holmes	5.00
61	Irv Smith	5.00
62	Robert Smith	10.00
63	Darrien Gordon	5.00
64	Deon Figures	5.00
65	Leonard Renfro	5.00
66	O.J. McDuffie	5.00
67	Dana Stubblefield	5.00
68	Todd Kelly	5.00
69	Thomas Smith	5.00
70	George Teague	5.00
71	Wilber Marshall	5.00
72	Reggie White	10.00

1993 Action Packed Moving Targets

These 12 cards were random inserts and are numbered with an "MT" prefix. The "Moving Targets" logo appears on each card front, plus a full-bleed embossed photo, along with the player's name in gold foil. The back has a painted football scene, plus a color head shot of the player and career stats. An autograph slot is also included. There were also 24K versions created for these cards; they are random inserts and are numbered with a "G" prefix.

		NM/M
Complete Set (12):		12.00
Common Player:		.50
Minor Stars:		1.00
1	Fred Barnett	.50
2	Gary Clark	.50
3	Mark Clayton	.50
4	Ernest Givins	.50
5	Michael Haynes	.50
6	Michael Irvin	1.00
7	Haywood Jeffires	.50
8	Anthony Miller	.50
9	Andre Reed	.50
10	Jerry Rice	4.00
11	Andre Rison	1.00
12	Sterling Sharpe	1.00

1993 Action Packed Quarterback Club

These subset cards, numbered on the back using a "QB" prefix, were included in 1993 Action Packed boxes at the same rate as the set's regular cards, but 24K versions were randomly inserted in fewer quantities. The gold versions have a "G" suffix after the card number. "Quarterback Club" cards follow the same format as the regular cards, but have the set logo on the front to distinguish them.

		NM/M
Complete Set (18):		20.00
Common Player:		.50
Minor Stars:		1.00
Braille Cards:		2X-3X
1	Troy Aikman	4.00
2	Randall Cunningham	2.00
3	John Elway	3.00
4	Jim Everett	.50
5	Brett Favre	6.00
6	Jim Harbaugh	1.00
7	Jeff Hostetler	.50
8	Jim Kelly	1.00
9	David Klingler	.50
10	Bernie Kosar	.50
11	Dan Marino	6.00
12	Chris Miller	.50
13	Boomer Esiason	.50
14	Warren Moon	1.00
15	Neil O'Donnell	1.00
16	Mark Rypien	.50
17	Phil Simms	.50
18	Steve Young	4.00

1993 Action Packed Quarterback Club Braille

These 18 cards, which each have a "B" suffix after the card number, are identical to their regular version counterparts, except they are done in Braille. They are generally about two or three times more valuable than the regular cards. Cards were random inserts; some were donated to more than 400 schools for the blind.

		NM/M
Complete Set (18):		60.00
Common Player:		1.25
1	Troy Aikman	15.00
2	Randall Cunningham	4.00
3	John Elway	8.00
4	Jim Everett	1.25
5	Brett Favre	10.00
6	Jim Harbaugh	1.25
7	Jeff Hostetler	1.25
8	Jim Kelly	5.00
9	David Klingler	2.00
10	Bernie Kosar	2.00
11	Dan Marino	12.00
12	Chris Miller	1.25
13	Boomer Esiason	3.00
14	Warren Moon	3.50
15	Neil O'Donnell	3.00
16	Mark Rypien	1.25
17	Phil Simms	3.00
18	Steve Young	6.00

1993 Action Packed Rookies Previews

The three-card, standard-size set features Troy Aikman, Brett Favre and Neil O'Donnell. The round the quarterback was drafted in is done in gold (first round), silver (second) or bronze (third) on the card front. The card back has "1993 Prototype" printed with the prefix "RU." The set was available as a topper in select hobby boxes.

		NM/M
Complete Set (3):		6.00
Common Player:		1.00
1	Troy Aikman	2.00
2	Brett Favre	4.00
3	Neil O'Donnell	1.00

1993 Action Packed Rushers

Players who gained 1,000 or more yards rushing during the previous season are featured in this Action Packed insert set. Cards have a "1000 Yard Rushers" logo on the front, plus a full-bleed photo and the player's name in gold foil. Backs have a color head shot of the player and statistics for his team's single-season rushing leaders. Card backs have an autograph slot, and are numbered with an "RB" prefix. There were also 24K versions created of these cards; they are numbered with a "G" suffix and were random inserts.

		NM/M
Complete Set (12):		15.00
Common Player:		.50
Minor Stars:		1.00
1	Terry Allen	.50
2	Reggie Cobb	.50
3	Barry Foster	.50
4	Cleveland Gary	.50
5	Harold Green	.50
6	Rodney Hampton	.50
7	Barry Sanders	4.00
8	Emmitt Smith	6.00
9	Thurman Thomas	1.00
10	Chris Warren	.50
11	Ricky Watters	1.00
12	Lorenzo White	.50

1993 Action Packed NFLPA Awards

Outstanding players from the 1992 NFL season are honored in this 17-card Action Packed set. The cards, issued in a special box, have an embossed front; backs have a head shot, career summary and the position the player was selected as being the best at in 1992. A card number is also on the back. The cards were distributed at the 20th annual NFLPA banquet on March 4, 1993, in Washington, D.C. The District of Columbia's Special Olympics was the beneficiary.

		NM/M
Complete Set (17):		40.00
Common Player:		2.00
1	Randall McDaniel	2.00
2	Bruce Matthews	2.00
3	Richmond Webb	2.00
4	Cortez Kennedy	3.00
5	Clyde Simmons	2.00
6	Wilber Marshall	3.00
7	Junior Seau	8.00
8	Henry Jones	2.00
9	Audray McMillian	2.00
10	Mel Gray	4.00
11	Steve Tasker	2.00
12	Marco Coleman	2.00
13	Santana Dotson	3.00
14	Vaughn Dunbar	2.00
15	Carl Pickens	4.00
16	Barry Foster	2.00
17	Steve Young	10.00

1993 Action Packed All-Madden

This 42-card set marks the 10th Anniversary All-Madden team and features the all-time favorites from the last 10 years as selected by the charismatic broadcaster and former coach, John Madden. Players' names are stamped in gold foil on a stone background. A 12-card insert was also done in a 24K gold equivalent. These cards have the suffix "G" used in their numbering. A five-card Emmitt Smith prototype set was also issued as a promotional for the All-Madden set. The All-Madden logo appears on each card front; the back is labeled as a prototype and is numbered ES1-ES5. Cards ES1 and ES4 were giveaways at the 1993 Super Bowl card show; ES5 was a giveaway to members of the Tuff Stuff Buyers Club.

		NM/M
Complete Set (42):		18.00
Common Player:		.15
1	Troy Aikman	3.00
2	Bill Bates	.15
3	Mark Bavaro	.15
4	Jim Burt	.15
5	Gary Clark	.15
6	Richard Dent	.15
7	Gary Fenciik	.15
8	Darryl Green	.15
9	Roy Green	.15
10	Russ Grimm	.15
11	Charles Haley	.20
12	Dan Hampton	.20
13	Lester Hayes	.15
14	Michael Haynes	.50
15	Jay Hilgenberg	.15
16	Michael Irvin	.50
17	Joe Jacoby	.15
18	Steve Largent	.15
19	Howie Long	.15
20	Ronnie Lott	.25
21	Dan Marino	3.00
22	Jim McMahon	.15
23	Matt Millen	.15
24	Art Monk	.20
25	Joe Montana	2.50
26	Anthony Munoz	.15
27	Nate Newton	.15
28	Walter Payton	.50
29	William Perry	.15
30	Jack Reynolds	.15
31	Jerry Rice	1.50
32	Barry Sanders	3.00
33	Sterling Sharpe	1.00
34	Mike Singletary	.20
35	Jackie Slater	.15
36	Emmitt Smith	4.00
37	Pat Summerall	.25
38	Lawrence Taylor	.40
39	Jeff Van Note	.15
40	Reggie White	.40
41	Otis Wilson	.15
42	Jack Youngblood	.15

1993 Action Packed All-Madden 24K Gold

These 24K gold cards are identical in design to the regular 10th Anniversary All-Madden cards, except they have 24Kt. Gold stamped on the card front in gold foil. They were random inserts in 1993 Action Packed 10th Anniversary All-Madden Team packs and are numbered on the card back using a "G" suffix.

		NM/M
Complete Set (12):		250.00
Common Player:		10.00
1	Troy Aikman	60.00
2	Michael Irvin	25.00
3	Ronnie Lott	10.00
4	Dan Marino	75.00
5	Joe Montana	75.00
6	Walter Payton	30.00
7	Jerry Rice	60.00
8	Barry Sanders	60.00
9	Sterling Sharpe	15.00
10	Emmitt Smith	60.00
11	Lawrence Taylor	10.00
12	Reggie White	15.00

1993 Action Packed Monday Night Football Prototypes

The six-card, standard-size set promoted the Monday Night Football set with highlights from the 1992 season. The date of each game is printed on on each side border while the ABC logo is located in the bottom right corner. Helmets from each team from the Monday Night Game are found on the top corners. The card backs have "1993 Prototype" printed and feature the "MN" prefix.

		NM/M
Complete Set (6):		25.00
Common Player:		3.00
1	Barry Sanders	6.00
2	Steve Young	4.00
3	Emmitt Smith	8.00
4	Thurman Thomas	3.00
5	Barry Foster	3.00
6	Warren Moon	3.00

1993 Action Packed Monday Night Football

The 1993 Monday Night Football schedule is chronicled in this 81-card Action Packed set. The cards preview top players slated to appear in each game, plus ABC's game announcers. Each card gives the date of the game, along with helmets of the two opposing teams participating. A key player from one of the teams is featured on each card front. The back has a mug shot of the player and provides a summary of his performance against that particular opponent. A Monday Night Football trivia fact is also given. Each foil pack also had the chance of obtaining a randomly included gold mint card; there were 250 gold mint cards produced for each card in the set.

		NM/M
Complete Set (81):		22.00
Common Player:		.15
Wax Box:		25.00
1	Michael Irvin	1.25
2	Charles Haley	.15
3	Art Monk	.15
4	Earnest Byner	.15
5	Tom Rathman	.15
6	John Taylor	.30
7	Bernie Kosar	.15
8	Clay Matthews	.15
9	Simon Fletcher	.15
10	John Elway	.50
11	Joe Montana	2.00
12	Derrick Thomas	.40
13	Rod Woodson	.20
14	Gary Anderson	.15
15	Chris Miller	.15
16	Andre Rison	.50
17	Mark Rypien	.25
18	Charles Mann	.15
19	Mark Duper	.15
20	Pete Stoyanovich	.15
21	Warren Moon	.50
22	Lorenzo White	.15
23	Haywood Jeffires	.40
24	Andre Reed	.40
25	Darryl Talley	.15
26	Tim Brown	.15
27	Howie Long	.15
28	Steve Atwater	.15
29	Karl Mecklenberg	.15
30	Chris Doleman	.15
31	Terry Allen	.40
32	Richard Dent	.15
33	Neal Anderson	.15
34	Darrell Green	.15
35	Chip Lohmiller	.15
36	Jim Kelly	.75
37	Cornelius Bennett	.15
38	Brett Favre	3.00
39	Sterling Sharpe	1.00
40	Reggie White	.40
41	Neil Smith	.15
42	Nick Lowery	.15
43	Thurman Thomas	1.50
44	Bruce Smith	.20
45	Barry Foster	.90
46	Neil O'Donnell	.90
47	Rickey Jackson	.15
48	Morten Andersen	.15
49	Brent Jones	.15
50	Ricky Watters	1.50
51	Leslie O'Neil	.15
52	Marion Butts	.15
53	Anthony Miller	.15
54	Jeff George	.25
55	Steve Emtmann	.75

56 Herschel Walker .15
57 Randall Cunningham .50
58 Clyde Simmons .15
59 Emmitt Smith 4.00
60 Ken Norton .15
61 Troy Aikman 2.00
62 Eric Green .15
63 Greg Lloyd .15
64 Bryan Cox .15
65 Mark Higgs .15
66 Phil Simms .15
67 Lawrence Taylor .30
68 Rodney Hampton .75
69 Wayne Martin .15
70 Vaughn Dunbar .15
71 Keith Jackson .15
72 Dan Marino 1.00
73 Junior Seau .50
74 Stan Humphries .15
75 Fred Barnett .40
76 Seth Joyner .15
77 Steve Young 1.00
78 Jerry Rice 1.25
79 Dan Dierdorf .40
80 Frank Gifford .40
81 Al Michaels .40
82 All Three Together .40

1993 Action Packed Monday Night Football Mint

Each 1993 Action Packed Monday Night Football pack had the random chance of including a certificate good for one of 250 gold mint cards produced for each card in the set.

NM/M
Complete Set (78): 1,500
Common Player: 20.00
1 Michael Irvin 30.00
2 Charles Haley 20.00
3 Art Monk 30.00
4 Earnest Byner 20.00
5 Tom Rathman 20.00
6 John Taylor 20.00
7 Bernie Kosar 20.00
8 Clay Matthews 20.00
9 Simon Fletcher 20.00
10 John Elway 50.00
11 Joe Montana 125.00
12 Derrick Thomas 20.00
13 Rod Woodson 20.00
14 Gary Anderson 20.00
15 Chris Miller 20.00
16 Andre Rison 20.00
17 Mark Rypien 20.00
18 Charles Mann 20.00
19 John Offerdahl 20.00
20 Pete Stoyanovich 20.00
21 Warren Moon 40.00
22 Lorenzo White 20.00
23 Haywood Jeffires 20.00
24 Andre Reed 20.00
25 Darryl Talley 20.00
26 Tim Brown 20.00
27 Howie Long 20.00
28 Steve Atwater 20.00
29 Karl Mecklenburg 20.00
30 Chris Doleman 20.00
31 Terry Allen 20.00
32 Richard Dent 20.00
33 Neal Anderson 20.00
34 Darrell Green 20.00
35 Chip Lohmiller 20.00
36 Jim Kelly 60.00
37 Cornelius Bennett 20.00
38 Brett Favre 125.00
39 Sterling Sharpe 30.00
40 Reggie White 30.00
41 Neil Smith 20.00
42 Nick Lowery 20.00
43 Thurman Thomas 60.00
44 Bruce Smith 20.00
45 Barry Foster 20.00
46 Neil O'Donnell 30.00
47 Rickey Jackson 20.00
48 Morten Anderson 20.00
49 Brent Jones 20.00
50 Ricky Watters 40.00
51 Leslie O'Neal 20.00
52 Marion Butts 20.00
53 Anthony Miller 20.00
54 Jeff George 20.00
55 Steve Emtman 20.00
56 Herschel Walker 20.00
57 Randall Cunningham 20.00
58 Clyde Simmons 20.00
59 Emmitt Smith 125.00
60 Ken Norton 20.00
61 Troy Aikman 40.00
62 Eric Green 20.00
63 Greg Lloyd 20.00
64 Bryan Cox 20.00
65 Mark Higgs 20.00
66 Phil Simms 30.00
67 Lawrence Taylor 40.00
68 Rodney Hampton 20.00
69 Wayne Martin 20.00
70 Vaughn Dunbar 20.00
71 Keith Jackson 20.00
72 Dan Marino 125.00
73 Junior Seau 50.00
74 Stan Humphries 20.00
75 Fred Barnett 20.00
76 Seth Joyner 20.00
77 Steve Young 75.00
78 Jerry Rice 100.00

1994 Action Packed Prototypes

These 12 promotional cards preview Action Packed's 1994 design for its regular, subset and insert cards (the type of card is included in the checklist below). Each card is numbered on the back, using one of three different prefixes (FB, MNF or RU). The back is also labeled as a prototype. These cards were given to dealers and to those who attended the Super Bowl 28 card show. A set, which excluded Barry Foster's card, was also produced in its own display frame.

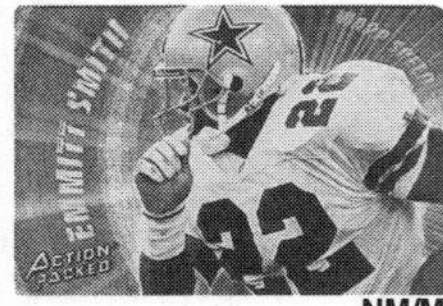

NM/M
Complete Set (12): 40.00
Common Player: 3.00
FB941 Troy Aikman (1994 Action Packed) 10.00
FB942 Jeff Hostetler (Quarterback Challenge) 3.00
FB943 Emmitt Smith (Warp Speed) 12.00
FB944 Jerry Rice (Catching Fire) 7.00
FB945 Barry Foster (Fantasy Forecast Subset) 3.00
MNF941 Steve Young (Monday Night Football) 4.00
MNF942 Steve Young (Monday Night Moment) 4.00
MNF943 Barry Foster (Monday Night Moment) 3.00
RU941 Drew Bledsoe (Rookie Update) 10.00
RU942 Derrick Lassic (Rookie Update) 3.00
RU943 Rick Mirer (Golden Domers) 3.00
RU944 Jerome Bettis (Golden Domers) 4.00

1994 Action Packed

This 120-card set features Action Packed's regular sculptured texture, showing a full-bleed color photo on the card front, along with the player's name burnished in gold. Each card back has a metallic, foil background, a head shot of the player, 1993 statistics and an "Action Note." Insert sets include Quarterback Club, Catching Fire, Warp Speed, and Fantasy Forecast. There were 12 prototype cards made - each one says prototype on the back, and uses either an FB, MNF or RU prefix for the card number.

NM/M
Complete Set (198): 60.00
Complete Series 1 (120): 35.00
Complete Series 2 (78): 25.00
Common Player: .20
Minor Stars: .40
Braille Cards: 2X
Gold Signature Cards: 3X
Inserted 1:1 Retail
Series 1 Pack (8): 2.00
Series 1 Box (24): 25.00
Rook/Update Pack (8): 2.00
Rook/Update Wax Box (24): 25.00
1 Michael Haynes .20
2 Andre Rison .75
3 Mike Pritchard .20
4 Erric Pegram .20
5 Deion Sanders 1.00
6 Jim Kelly .75
7 Andre Reed .40
8 Thurman Thomas .75
9 Bruce Smith .20
10 Cornelius Bennett .20
11 Nate Odomes .20
12 Richard Dent .20
13 Donnell Woolford .20
14 Harold Green .20
15 David Klingler .20
16 Eric Metcalf .20
17 Michael Dean Perry .20
18 Michael Jackson .40
19 Vinny Testaverde .75
20 Troy Aikman 2.50
21 Michael Irvin .75
22 Emmitt Smith 4.00
23 Jay Novacek .20
24 Alvin Harper .40
25 Charles Haley .20
26 John Elway 3.00
27 Shannon Sharpe .40
28 Rod Bernstine .20
29 Simon Fletcher .20
30 Barry Sanders 5.00
31 Herman Moore 1.00
32 Pat Swilling .20
33 Chris Spielman .20
34 Brett Favre 5.00
35 Sterling Sharpe .40
36 Reggie White .75
37 Jackie Harris .20
38 Tony Bennett .20
39 LeRoy Butler .20
40 Warren Moon .75
41 Ernest Givins .20
42 Haywood Jeffires .20
43 Webster Slaughter .20
44 Ray Childress .20
45 Gary Brown .40
46 Jeff George .75
47 Roosevelt Potts .20
48 Quentin Coryatt .20
49 Joe Montana 3.00
50 Derrick Thomas .40
51 Neil Smith .20
52 Marcus Allen .75
53 Willie Davis .20
54 Jerome Bettis 1.00
55 Sean Gilbert .20
56 Chris Miller .20
57 Jeff Hostetler .40
58 Tim Brown .75
59 Anthony Smith .20
60 Greg Townsend .20
61 Terry McDaniel .20
62 Dan Marino 4.00
63 Irving Fryar .20
64 Keith Jackson .20
65 Terry Kirby .20
66 Bryan Cox .20
67 Chris Doleman .20
68 Cris Carter 1.00
69 John Randle .40
70 Drew Bledsoe 3.00
71 Ben Coates .40
72 Vincent Brisby .40
73 Rickey Jackson .20
74 Eric Martin .20
75 Renaldo Turnbull .20
76 Rodney Hampton .40
77 Mike Sherrard .20
78 Phil Simms .40
79 Keith Hamilton .20
80 Rob Moore .75
81 Brad Baxter .20
82 Boomer Esiason .40
83 Johnny Johnson .20
84 Ronnie Lott .40
85 Randall Cunningham .75
86 Herschel Walker .20
87 Eric Allen .20
88 Clyde Simmons .20
89 Seth Joyner .20
90 Calvin Williams .20
91 Garrison Hearst 1.00
92 Steve Beuerlein .20
93 Ricky Proehl .20
94 Ron Moore .20
95 Barry Foster .20
96 Neil O'Donnell .40
97 Eric Green .20
98 Rod Woodson .40
99 Greg Lloyd .20
100 Kevin Greene .20
101 Stan Humphries .40
102 Anthony Miller .20
103 Junior Seau .40
104 Leslie O'Neal .20
105 Ronnie Harmon .20
106 Jerry Rice 2.50
107 Ricky Watters .75
108 Steve Young 2.00
109 Brent Jones .20
110 John Taylor .20
111 Rick Mirer .40
112 Chris Warren .40
113 Cortez Kennedy .20
114 Brian Blades .20
115 Eugene Robinson .20
116 Reggie Cobb .20
117 Hardy Nickerson .20
118 Reggie Brooks .20
119 Darrell Green .20
120 Troy Aikman 2.50
121 *Dan Wilkinson* .40
122 *Marshall Faulk* 7.00
123 *Heath Shuler* .75
124 *Willie McGinest* .40
125 *Trev Alberts* .40
126 *Trent Dilfer* 4.00
127 *Bryant Young* .75
128 *Sam Adams* .40
129 *Antonio Langham* .40
130 *Jamir Miller* .20
131 *John Thierry* .40
132 *Aaron Glenn* .40
133 *Joe Johnson* .20
134 *Bernard Williams* .20
135 *Wayne Gandy* .20
136 *Charles Johnson* .75
137 *DeWayne Washington* .40
138 *Todd Steussie* .40
139 *Tim Bowens* .40
140 *Johnnie Morton* 2.00
141 *Rob Fredrickson* .40
142 *Shante Carver* .40
143 *Thomas Lewis* .40
144 *Greg Hill* .75
145 *Henry Ford* .20
146 *Jeff Burris* .40
147 *William Floyd* .75
148 *Derrick Alexander* .75
149 *Darnay Scott* .50
150 *Isaac Bruce* 6.00
151 *Errict Rhett* 1.00
152 *Kevin Lee* .40
153 *Chuck Levy* .40
154 *David Palmer* .50
155 *Ryan Yarborough* .40
156 *Charlie Garner* 3.00
157 *Mario Bates* .75
158 *Bert Emanuel* .50
159 *Bucky Brooks* .40
160 *Donnell Bennett* .50
161 *Tydus Winans* .40
162 *Andre Coleman* .40
163 *Calvin Jones* .40
164 *LeShon Johnson* .40
165 *Doug Brien* .20
166 *Bam Morris* .75
167 *Lake Dawson* .75
168 *Perry Klein* .40
169 *Doug Nussmeier* .40
170 *Lamont Warren* .20
171 *Gus Frerotte* .50
172 Troy Aikman 1.50
173 Randall Cunningham .40
174 John Elway 1.50
175 Jim Everett .20
176 Drew Bledsoe 1.50
177 Jim Kelly .40
178 Dan Marino 2.00
179 Chris Miller .20
180 Warren Moon .20
181 Rick Mirer .20
182 Jeff Hostetler .20
183 Brett Favre 3.00
184 Steve Young 1.00
185 Anthony Miller .20
186 Michael Haynes .20
187 Mike Pritchard .20
188 Jeff George .40
189 Lewis Tillman .20
190 Ken Norton .20
191 Erik Kramer .20
192 Richard Dent .20
193 Rick Mirer .20
194 Jerome Bettis .40
195 Reggie Brooks .20
196 Tom Carter .20
197 Irv Smith .20
198 Rocket Ismail .20

1994 Action Packed 24K Gold

Action Packed made 24K gold versions for each of its insert sets - Quarterback Club (G1-G20); Catching Fire (G21-G30); and Warp Speed (G31-G42). These Quarterback Club cards feature gold foil fronts rather than in silver like the regular ones.

NM/M
Complete Set (55): 700.00
Complete Series 1 (42): 500.00
Complete Series 2 (13): 200.00
Common Player: 4.00
Minor Stars: 8.00
Inserted 1:96
1 Troy Aikman 20.00
2 Randall Cunningham 10.00
3 John Elway 35.00
4 Boomer Esiason 4.00
5 Jim Everett 4.00
6 Brett Favre 45.00
7 Jerry Rice 30.00
8 Jeff Hostetler 4.00
9 Jim Kelly 10.00
10 David Klingler 4.00
11 Bernie Kosar 4.00
12 Dan Marino 45.00
13 Chris Miller 4.00
14 Warren Moon 10.00
15 Neil O'Donnell 10.00
16 Michael Irvin 10.00
17 Phil Simms 4.00
18 Steve Young 20.00
19 Rick Mirer 10.00
20 Drew Bledsoe 20.00
21 Jerry Rice 30.00
22 Sterling Sharpe 10.00
23 Michael Irvin 10.00
24 Anthony Miller 4.00
25 Tim Brown 10.00
26 Andre Reed 4.00
27 Andre Reed 4.00
28 Herman Moore 6.00
29 Irving Fryar 4.00
30 Shannon Sharpe 10.00
31 Emmitt Smith 35.00
32 Barry Sanders 35.00
33 Thurman Thomas 10.00
34 Jerome Bettis 10.00
35 Barry Foster 4.00
36 Ricky Watters 6.00
37 Rodney Hampton 4.00
38 Chris Warren 4.00
39 Erric Pegram 4.00
40 Reggie Brooks 4.00
41 Marcus Allen 10.00
42 Ron Moore 4.00
43 Troy Aikman 20.00
44 Randall Cunningham 10.00
45 John Elway 25.00
46 Jim Everett 4.00
47 Drew Bledsoe 20.00
48 Jim Kelly 10.00
49 Dan Marino 35.00
50 Chris Miller 4.00
51 Warren Moon 8.00
52 Rick Mirer 4.00
53 Jeff Hostetler 4.00
54 Brett Favre 40.00
55 Steve Young 20.00

1994 Action Packed Catching Fire

The NFL's top 10 wide receivers are featured in this insert set. The "Catching Fire" logo is on the card front, which shows the player surrounded by metallic foil flames. Card backs are numbered with an "R" prefix; except for 24K gold versions which were also created; they are numbered G21-G30.

NM/M
Complete Set (10): 10.00
Common Player: .50
Minor Stars: 1.00
1 Jerry Rice 5.00
2 Sterling Sharpe 1.00
3 Michael Irvin 1.00
4 Andre Rison 1.00
5 Anthony Miller .50
6 Tim Brown 1.00
7 Andre Reed .50
8 Herman Moore 2.00
9 Irving Fryar .50
10 Shannon Sharpe 1.00

1994 Action Packed Fantasy Forecast

This Fantasy Forecast insert set provides a scouting report for 42 top NFL players. Each card front features the player with a football that is covered with heat-sensitive ink. Touching the football reveals how high you should draft the player if you were picking a fantasy football team. Cards are numbered FF1-FF42

NM/M
Complete Set (42): 15.00
Common Player: .25
Minor Stars: .50
1 Rodney Hampton .50
2 Steve Young 1.50
3 Michael Irvin .50
4 Emmitt Smith 3.00
5 Troy Aikman 2.00
6 Jerry Rice 2.00
7 Brett Favre 4.00
8 Jerome Bettis .50
9 Reggie Brooks .25
10 John Elway 2.50
11 Jim Kelly .50
12 Dan Marino 3.00
13 Randall Cunningham .50
14 Sterling Sharpe .50
15 Chris Warren .50
16 Andre Rison .50
17 Mike Pritchard .25
18 Barry Sanders 4.00
19 Marcus Allen .50
20 Thurman Thomas .50
21 Erric Pegram .25
22 Barry Foster .25
23 Anthony Miller .25
24 Shannon Sharpe .50
25 Tim Brown .50
26 Ricky Watters .50
27 Ernest Givins .25
28 Cris Carter .50
29 Willie Davis .25
30 Warren Moon .50
31 Joe Montana 2.50
32 Herman Moore .50
33 Terry Kirby .25
34 Eric Green .25
35 Michael Jackson .25
36 Johnny Johnson .25
37 Calvin Williams .25
38 Michael Haynes .25
39 Irving Fryar .25
40 Gary Brown .25
41 Jeff Hostetler .25
42 Keith Jackson .25

1994 Action Packed Quarterback Challenge

The 12-card, regular-size set was inserted in each retail pack that was available at Foot Action stores. The card fronts feature the quarterback's face - outlined in silver, while the backs include information from the Quarterback Challenge competition. All cards are numbered with the "FA" prefix.

NM/M
Complete Set (12): 15.00
Common Player: .25
Minor Stars: .50
1 Steve Young 2.00
2 John Elway 3.00
3 Troy Aikman 2.50
4 Randall Cunningham .75
5 Warren Moon .50
6 Brett Favre 5.00
7 Rick Mirer .25
8 Drew Bledsoe 3.00
9 Boomer Esiason .25
10 Jeff Hostetler .25
11 Jim Kelly .50
12 Dan Marino 3.50

1994 Action Packed Quarterback Club

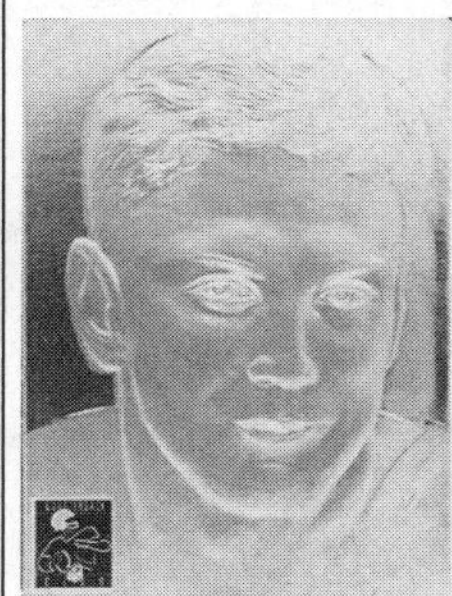

These Action Packed cards are printed with a silver foil front similar to, but far more sturdier and attractive, than Topps 1965 Embossed insert set. Cards were random inserts in 1994 packs and are numbered with a "QB" prefix. They feature the player's embossed portrait on the front. There were also 24K gold versions made for each Quarterback Club card. These cards feature gold foil on the front instead of silver.

NM/M
Complete Set (20): 15.00
Common Player: .25
Minor Stars: .50
1 Troy Aikman 2.50
2 Randall Cunningham .75
3 John Elway 3.00
4 Boomer Esiason .50
5 Jim Everett .25
6 Brett Favre 5.00
7 Jerry Rice 2.50
8 Jeff Hostetler .25
9 Jim Kelly .50
10 David Klingler .25
11 Bernie Kosar .25
12 Dan Marino 3.50
13 Chris Miller .25
14 Warren Moon .50
15 Neil O'Donnell .50
16 Michael Irvin .50
17 Phil Simms .25
18 Steve Young 2.00
19 Rick Mirer .50
20 Drew Bledsoe 3.00

A card number in parenthese ( ) indicates the set is unnumbered.

1994 Action Packed Warp Speed

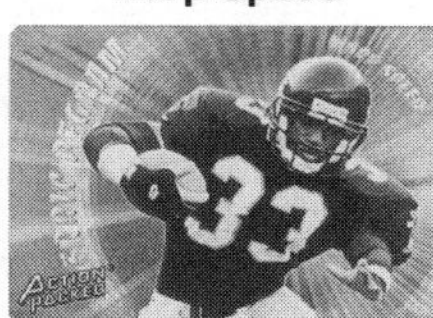

These 1994 Action Packed inserts feature 12 of the NFL's top running backs. Card fronts are printed using a colored foil design and have the "Warp Speed" and player's name in foil, too. Cards are numbered with a "WS" prefix. Gold versions were also made and are numbered G31-G42.

		NM/M
Complete Set (12):		15.00
Common Player:		.25
Minor Stars:		.50
1	Emmitt Smith	4.00
2	Barry Sanders	6.00
3	Thurman Thomas	.50
4	Jerome Bettis	1.00
5	Barry Foster	.25
6	Ricky Watters	.50
7	Rodney Hampton	.50
8	Chris Warren	.25
9	Erric Pegram	.25
10	Reggie Brooks	.25
11	Marcus Allen	.50
12	Ron Moore	.25

1994 Action Packed All-Madden

The 11th Annual All-Madden Team is a 41-card set from Action Packed that showcases Madden's hand-picked All-Pro Team. The fronts have a borderless design and incorporates a band-aid logo, exemplifying the toughness that was required to be selected by Madden. All 41 cards also have a 24kt gold equivalent, of which there is one per every box of the product. Cards were sold in packs of six. Each pack includes a "Smash Mouth" scratch-and-win game card which offers various prizes, including different television sets and 24kt gold cards.

		NM/M
Complete Set (41):		20.00
Common Player:		.15
Wax Box:		35.00
1	Emmitt Smith	4.00
2	Jerome Bettis	1.00
3	Steve Young	2.00
4	Jerry Rice	2.50
5	Richard Dent	.15
6	Junior Seau	.50
7	Harris Barton	.15
8	Steve Wallace	.15
9	Keith Byars	.15
10	Michael Irvin	1.00
11	Joe Montana	2.50
12	Jesse Sapolu	.15
13	Rickey Jackson	.15
14	Ronnie Lott	.50
15	Donnell Woolford	.15
16	Reggie White	1.50
17	John Taylor	.25
18	Bruce Matthews	.15
19	Ron Moore	.15
20	Bill Bates	.15
21	Steve Hendrickson	.15
22	Eric Allen	.25
23	Monte Coleman	.15
24	Mark Collins	.15
25	Barry Sanders	3.00
26	Eric Williams	.15
27	Phil Simms	.25
28	Chris Zorich	.15
29	Troy Aikman	3.00
30	Charles Haley	.15
31	Darrell Green	.15
32	Sean Gilbert	.15
33	Kevin Gogan	.15
34	Rodney Hampton	1.00
35	Chris Doleman	.15
36	Nate Newton	.15
37	Jackie Slater	.15
38	Ricky Watters	1.00
39	LeRoy Butler	.15
40	Gary Clark	.15
41	Sterling Sharpe	.50

1994 Action Packed All-Madden 24k Gold

Each of the 41 cards in the 11th Annual All-Madden Team was created in a 24kt gold version for this parallel set. There was one 24kt gold card in each All-Madden product box.

		NM/M
Complete Set (41):		600.00
Common Player:		10.00
1	Emmitt Smith	90.00
2	Jerome Bettis	20.00
3	Steve Young	40.00
4	Jerry Rice	60.00
5	Richard Dent	10.00
6	Junior Seau	20.00
7	Harris Barton	10.00
8	Steve Wallace	10.00
9	Keith Byars	10.00
10	Michael Irvin	20.00
11	Joe Montana	80.00
12	Jesse Sapolu	10.00
13	Rickey Jackson	10.00
14	Ronnie Lott	20.00
15	Donnell Woolford	10.00
16	Reggie White	35.00
17	John Taylor	25.00
18	Bruce Matthews	10.00
19	Ron Moore	10.00
20	Bill Bates	10.00
21	Steve Hendrickson	10.00
22	Eric Allen	10.00
23	Monte Coleman	10.00
24	Mark Collins	10.00
25	Barry Sanders	70.00
26	Eric Williams	10.00
27	Phil Simms	25.00
28	Chris Zorich	10.00
29	Troy Aikman	60.00
30	Charles Haley	10.00
31	Darrell Green	10.00
32	Sean Gilbert	10.00
33	Kevin Gogan	10.00
34	Rodney Hampton	10.00
35	Chris Doleman	10.00
36	Nate Newton	10.00
37	Jackie Slater	10.00
38	Ricky Watters	20.00
39	LeRoy Butler	10.00
40	Gary Clark	10.00
41	Sterling Sharpe	20.00

1994 Action Packed Monday Night Football

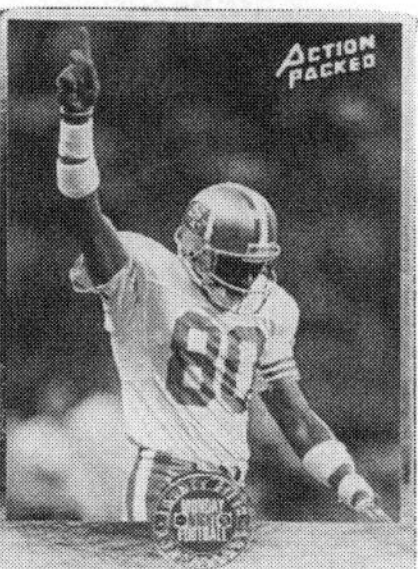

Action Packed released a 71-card, silver foil, football set celebrating 25 years of Monday Night Football. This set includes a randomly inserted .999 pure silver foil insert set and 25 certificates for a sterling silver card with Emmitt Smith, Troy Aikman and Michael Irvin. The card fronts feature a tight shot of each player. The back casts the player in moonlight and discusses specific challenges that player faced in the upcoming Monday night match-up. The set primarily consisted of players expected to shine in 1994 Monday Night match-ups. Also, as part of the 25th anniversary promotion, Action Packed included members of the announcing cast, such as Howard Cosell and Meredith.

		NM/M
Complete Set (71):		25.00
Common Player:		.20
Minor Stars:		.40
Wax Box:		35.00
1	Jeff Hostetler	.20
2	Terry McDaniel	.20
3	Steve Young	2.00
4	Jerry Rice	2.00
5	Donnell Woolford	.20
6	Eric Allen	.20
7	Herschel Walker	.20
8	Barry Sanders	3.00
9	Herman Moore	.75
10	Emmitt Smith	4.00
11	Michael Irvin	1.00
12	John Elway	1.00
13	Jim Kelly	.40
14	Andre Reed	.20
15	Gary Brown	.20
16	Ernest Givins	.20
17	Barry Foster	.20
18	Rod Woodson	.20
19	Warren Moon	.40
20	Cris Carter	.40
21	Rodney Hampton	.20
22	Derrick Thomas	.20
23	Marcus Allen	.40
24	Shannon Sharpe	.20
25	Cody Carlson	.20
26	Haywood Jeffires	.20
27	Randall Cunningham	.20
28	Calvin Williams	.20
29	Brett Favre	2.00
30	Sterling Sharpe	.40
31	Chris Zorich	.20
32	Dante Jones	.20
33	Mike Sherrard	.20
34	Keith Hamilton	.20
35	Charles Haley	.20
36	Thurman Thomas	.40
37	Bruce Smith	.20
38	Greg Lloyd	.20
39	Michael Brooks	.20
40	Jumbo Elliott	.20
41	Ray Childress	.20
42	Bruce Matthews	.20
43	Ricky Watters	.40
44	Brent Jones	.20
45	Morten Andersen	.20
46	Tim Brown	.40
47	Anthony Smith	.20
48	Natrone Means	.60
49	Junior Seau	.40
50	Joe Montana	2.50
51	Neil Smith	.20
52	Dan Marino	4.00
53	Keith Jackson	.20
54	Troy Aikman	1.50
55	Jay Novacek	.20
56	Rickey Jackson	.20
57	John Taylor	.20
58	Tim McDonald	.20
59	John Randle	.20
60	Henry Thomas	.20
61	Prime Time Players	.20
62	The Don & Howard Show	.20
63	The Entertainers	.20
64	I Never Played the Game	.20
65	Monday Night Madness	.20
66	Whoa Nellie	.20
67	Dandy Don Meredith	.20
68	Speaking of Sports	.20
69	Donning a Dierdorf	.20
70	Half-Time Highlights	.20
71	Return to the Field	.20

1994 Action Packed Monday Night Football Silver

Action Packed randomly inserted a 12-card set into its foil packs, called .999 pure silver foil cards. These are comparable to the 24k gold cards randomly inserted into Action Packed's usual gold foil products.

		NM/M
Complete Set (12):		350.00
Common Player:		10.00
1	Steve Young	50.00
2	Jerry Rice	75.00
3	Barry Sanders	75.00
4	Emmitt Smith	75.00
5	John Elway	40.00
6	Jim Kelly	20.00
7	Warren Moon	10.00
8	Randall Cunningham	10.00
9	Brett Favre	75.00
10	Dan Marino	75.00
11	Troy Aikman	40.00
12	Speaking of Sports	10.00

1994 Action Packed Badge of Honor Pins

This set consists of 25 pins measuring 1-1/2" x 1". The front of each pin features a color player portrait with a gold border on a bronze background. The player's last name and Action Packed logo are also on the front. Each box of Action Packed contained three packs of four pins and one of five black pin albums to store five pins. Each pack of pins came in a cardboard holder with the set checklist on the back. A 24K Gold parallel of each pin was created and randomly seeded in packs.

		NM/M
Complete Set (25):		40.00
Common Pin:		.75
*24K Gold Pins:		10X-20X
1	Troy Aikman	3.00
2	Drew Bledsoe	3.00
3	Bubby Brister	.75
4	Randall Cunningham	1.00
5	John Elway	2.00
6	Boomer Esiason	1.00
7	Jim Everett	.75
8	Brett Favre	6.00
9	Jim Harbaugh	.75
10	Jeff Hostetler	.75
11	Michael Irvin	1.50
12	Jim Kelly	1.50
13	David Klingler	.75
14	Bernie Kosar	.75
15	Dan Marino	5.00
16	Chris Miller	.75
17	Rick Mirer	.75
18	Warren Moon	1.00
19	Neil O'Donnell	.50
20	Jerry Rice	3.00
21	Mark Rypien	.75
22	Barry Sanders	4.00
23	Phil Simms	1.00
24	Emmitt Smith	5.00
25	Steve Young	2.00

1994 Action Packed CoaStars

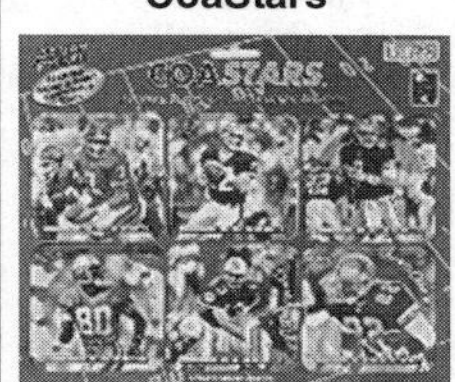

The set of 25 coaster cards were sold in six-card packs. Each coaster has rounded corners and measures 3-1/4" x 3-1/4". The front of the coaster features the player's name and position, while the back has an action shot with 1993 statistics.

		NM/M
Complete Set (25):		25.00
Common Player:		.25
1	Troy Aikman	2.50
2	Drew Bledsoe	2.50
3	Bubby Brister	.25
4	Randall Cunningham	.25
5	John Elway	1.25
6	Boomer Esiason	.40
7	Jim Everett	.40
8	Brett Favre	5.00
9	Jim Harbaugh	.50
10	Jeff Hostetler	.40
11	Michael Irvin	.50
12	Jim Kelly	.50
13	David Klingler	.25
14	Bernie Kosar	.40
15	Dan Marino	5.00
16	Rick Mirer	1.00
17	Chris Miller	.40
18	Warren Moon	.50
19	Neil O'Donnell	.50
20	Jerry Rice	2.50
21	Mark Rypien	.40
22	Barry Sanders	2.50
23	Phil Simms	.40
24	Emmitt Smith	5.00
25	Steve Young	1.50

1994 Action Packed Mammoth

This large set (7-1/2" x 10-1/2") was offered to dealers by Action Packed. Each card has an "MM" prefix on the back and while it is a 25-card set, it's numbered from 1 to 26 as there is no card 25. Series 2 cards of Troy Aikman, Emmitt Smith and Michael Irvin are also included, while three prototypes, including two 24kt gold cards, were randomly inserted. Reportedly, only 25,000 of each base card was produced while less than 2,500 of the Aikman and Smith gold cards were issued.

		NM/M
Complete Set (25):		70.00
Common Player:		2.00
1	Troy Aikman	8.00
2	Drew Bledsoe	8.00
3	Barry Sanders	10.00
4	Chris Miller	2.00
5	Randall Cunningham	2.00
6	John Elway	6.00
7	Boomer Esiason	2.00
8	Jim Everett	2.00
9	Brett Favre	10.00
10	Jim Harbaugh	2.00
11	Jeff Hostetler	2.00
12	Michael Irvin	2.00
13	Jim Kelly	2.00
14	David Klingler	2.00
15	Bernie Kosar	2.00
16	Dan Marino	10.00
17	Rick Mirer	2.00
18	Warren Moon	2.00
19	Neil O'Donnell	2.00
20	Jerry Rice	8.00
21	Mark Rypien	2.00
22	Phil Simms	2.00
23	Emmitt Smith	10.00
24	Steve Young	6.00
26	Bubby Brister	2.00
2MM1	Troy Aikman (Series 2 card numbered MM1-2)	6.00
2MM2	Michael Irvin (Series 2 card numbered MM2-2)	2.00
2MM6	Emmitt Smith (Series 2 card numbered MM6-2)	10.00
P1	Troy Aikman (Prototype Numbered MMP)	6.00
P2	Emmitt Smith (Prototype 24K Gold Numbered MMP1G reportedly 2500 made)	35.00
P3	Troy Aikman (Prototype 24K Gold Numbered MMP2G reportedly 1000 made)	25.00

1995 Action Packed Promos

The four-card, standard-size set was issued as a preview for the 126-card base set. The set included two regular cards, one Armed Forces insert card and one advertisement card. The card fronts are the same as the base set, but the backs have a "Promo" stamp.

		NM/M
Complete Set (4):		10.00
Common Player:		.50
1	Jerry Rice	2.50
2	Emmitt Smith	5.00
AF4	Steve Young	1.75
NNO	Action Packed Ad Card (Armed Forces card)	.50

1995 Action Packed

Action Packed Football returned in 1995 under new ownership, Pinnacle, which repeated the existing embossed technology and added its own improvements. The 126-card set captures game action and candid shots with embossed highlights. All 126 cards were also repeated in a metallized silver foil parallel (Quick Silver) set (one per every six packs). The regular cards feature an action shot on the front, with the player's team helmet in the upper right corner. The player's last name is written in gold foil down the side, with Action Packed and 1995 written below the name. The card back is horizontal, with a mug shot, statistics and a brief career summary included. A panel at the bottom includes his name, biographical information and a team logo. The card number is in the upper right corner. Insert sets include Armed Forces, which are also featured on a parallel Braille set, Rocket Men, G-Force and 24k Gold cards.

		NM/M
Complete Set (126):		25.00
Common Player:		.10
Minor Stars:		.20
Complete Silver Set (126):		
Silver Cards:		3X-6X
Pack (8):		1.25
Wax Box (24):		20.00
1	Jerry Rice	1.50
2	Emmitt Smith	3.00
3	Drew Bledsoe	2.00
4	Ben Coates	.20
5	Jim Everett	.10
6	Warren Moon	.20
7	Herman Moore	.75
8	Deion Sanders	.75
9	Rick Mirer	.20
10	Natrone Means	.50
11	*Jeff Blake*	1.00
12	William Floyd	.20
13	Steve Young	1.00
14	John Elway	.75
15	Brett Favre	3.00
16	Marshall Faulk	.75
17	Heath Shuler	.20
18	Ricky Watters	.50
19	Michael Haynes	.10
20	Troy Aikman	1.25
21	Dan Marino	3.00
22	Bam Morris	.10
23	Marcus Allen	.20
24	Carl Pickens	.20
25	Rodney Hampton	.10
26	Dave Brown	.10
27	Jerome Bettis	.50
28	Jim Kelly	.50
29	Andre Reed	.20
30	Michael Irvin	.50
31	Barry Sanders	3.00
32	Chris Warren	.20
33	Jeff Hostetler	.10
34	Alvin Harper	.10
35	Rob Moore	.20
36	*Steve McNair*	5.00
37	*Rashaan Salaam*	.50
38	*Joey Galloway*	5.00
39	*J.J. Stokes*	2.00
40	*Michael Westbrook*	1.75
41	*Kerry Collins*	2.00
42	*Ki-Jana Carter*	1.00
43	Boomer Esiason	.10
44	Chris Spielman	.10
45	Vinny Testaverde	.20
46	Kevin Williams	.10
47	Ronnie Harmon	.10
48	Fred Barnett	.10
49	Harvey Williams	.10
50	Reggie White	.50
51	Brent Jones	.10
52	Henry Ellard	.10
53	Cris Carter	.50
54	Leroy Hoard	.10
55	Trent Dilfer	.75
56	Desmond Howard	.10
57	Garrison Hearst	.50
58	Lewis Tillman	.10
59	Mark Brunell	1.50
60	Bruce Smith	.10
61	Lake Dawson	.20
62	Bert Emanuel	.20
63	Eric Green	.10
64	Barry Foster	.10
65	Jeff Graham	.10
66	Curtis Conway	.20
67	Herschel Walker	.10
68	Edgar Bennett	.10
69	Mario Bates	.20
70	Irving Fryar	.10
71	Gary Brown	.10
72	Cortez Kennedy	.10
73	John Taylor	.10
74	Jeff George	.50
75	Shannon Sharpe	.50
76	Andre Rison	.50
77	Mike Sherrard	.10
78	Errict Rhett	.20
79	Junior Seau	.50
80	Willie Davis	.10
81	Craig Erickson	.10
82	Torrance Small	.10
83	Randall Cunningham	.50
84	Robert Brooks	.10
85	Terance Mathis	.10
86	Rod Woodson	.20
87	Anthony Miller	.10
88	Stan Humphries	.20
89	Chris Miller	.10
90	Steve Beuerlein	.10
91	Steve Bono	.20
92	Frank Reich	.10
93	Corey Fleming	.10
94	Isaac Bruce	.50
95	Dave Meggett	.10
96	Jackie Harris	.10
97	J.J. Birden	.10
98	Willie Anderson	.10
99	Johnnie Morton	.10
100	Michael Timpson	.10
101	Derek Brown	.10
102	Ricky Ervins	.10
103	*Derrick Alexander*	.50
104	*Dave Barr*	.20
105	*Tony Boselli*	.50
106	*Kyle Brady*	.75
107	*Mark Bruener*	.75
108	*Kevin Carter*	.10
109	Neil O'Donnell	.10
110	Derrick Alexander	.20
111	Charlie Garner	.20
112	Darnay Scott	.20
113	Scott Mitchell	.20
114	Charles Johnson	.20
115	Greg Hill	.20
116	*Ty Law*	.20
117	*Frank Sanders*	1.75
118	*James Stewart Tenn*	2.00
119	*James Stewart Miami*	.50
120	*Kordell Stewart*	6.00
121	*Rob Johnson*	3.00
122	*John Walsh*	.25

123	*Stoney Case*	.50
124	*Tyrone Wheatley*	.50
125	*Sherman Williams*	.50
126	*Ray Zellars*	.50

1995 Action Packed Quick Silver

The 126-card, regular-size set was a parallel release to the 1995 base set, inserted every six packs. The cards have a silver-foil card front while the backs have "Quick Silver" printed.

	NM/M
Common Player:	1.50
Quick Silver Cards:	4X-8X

1995 Action Packed 24K Gold

Twenty-one of the best cards from Action Packed's 1995 regular football set are showcased in this 24K Gold insert set. Inserts, which have special gold foil stamping, could be found one per every 72 packs. They are numbered using a "G" suffix.

		NM/M
Complete Set (21):		350.00
Common Player:		3.00
Minor Stars:		6.00
Inserted 1:72		
1	Jerry Rice	20.00
2	Emmitt Smith	30.00
3	Drew Bledsoe	20.00
4	Warren Moon	3.00
5	Deion Sanders	10.00
6	Natrone Means	3.00
7	Steve Young	15.00
8	John Elway	30.00
9	Brett Favre	35.00
10	Marshall Faulk	15.00
11	Heath Shuler	3.00
12	Troy Aikman	20.00
13	Dan Marino	35.00
14	Jerome Bettis	15.00
15	Jim Kelly	15.00
16	Michael Irvin	15.00
17	Barry Sanders	35.00
18	Steve McNair	25.00
19	Rashaan Salaam	5.00
20	Kerry Collins	15.00
21	Ki-Jana Carter	3.00

1995 Action Packed Armed Forces

These 1995 Action Packed inserts feature 12 of the hottest arms in the NFL Quarterback Club. The cards were randomly included one per every 24 packs. The front is a horizontal design which features a full color raised photo in the center, flanked by the insert set logo and the set logo in the upper corners. The player's name appears in gold below his name, which is adjacent to a team logo in the lower left corner. The card back, numbered using an "AF" prefix, is vertical and includes a close-up shot of the player, plus a brief career summary. A panel along the right side of the card includes an action shot. A parallel Braille version set was also created for the Armed Forces set (1 in 96 packs).

		NM/M
Complete Set (12):		60.00
Common Player:		3.00
Complete Braille Set (12):		150.00
Braille Cards:		1X-2X
1	Drew Bledsoe	10.00
2	Dan Marino	15.00
3	Troy Aikman	10.00
4	Steve Young	10.00
5	Brett Favre	15.00
6	Heath Shuler	3.00
7	Dave Brown	3.00
8	Jeff Blake	3.00
9	John Elway	8.00
10	Rick Mirer	3.00
11	Kerry Collins	5.00
12	Steve McNair	10.00

1995 Action Packed G-Force

Some of the NFL's best running backs are featured on these 1995 Action Packed inserts. The 12 cards, random inserts one per every 24 packs, have a horizontal front format. The card front has two photos on it; one is an action shot, the other is a close-up profile. The player's name, in gold foil, and the insert set logo are on the left side of the card. The back, numbered with a "GF" prefix, contains a color photo and recap of the player's accomplishments in 1994. A panel on the left side has the insert set logo at the top, with the player's name and his yards per carry average underneath.

		NM/M
Complete Set (12):		25.00
Common Player:		2.00
1	Emmitt Smith	10.00
2	Barry Sanders	8.00
3	Marshall Faulk	2.00
4	Natrone Means	2.00
5	Chris Warren	2.00
6	Jerome Bettis	2.00
7	Errict Rhett	2.00
8	Bam Morris	2.00
9	Ki-Jana Carter	2.00
10	Mario Bates	2.00
11	Ricky Watters	2.00
12	Tyrone Wheatley	2.00

1995 Action Packed Rocket Men

These horizontally-designed inserts feature 18 of the NFL's top stars. Cards were random inserts in 1995 Action Packed football, one every 12 jumbo packs. The card front has a color embossed photo with a swirled background. "Rocket Man" is written along the left side of the card, with the player's name and team logo along the bottom, below the photo. The vertical back, numbered using an "RM" prefix, has a panel on the right which includes the player's name, team logo, card number and "Rocket Man." An action photo and a close-up photo are also included on the back, which includes a quote from another player about the "Rocket Man."

		NM/M
Complete Set (18):		125.00
Common Player:		3.00
1	Marshall Faulk	8.00
2	Emmitt Smith	15.00
3	Barry Sanders	12.00
4	Natrone Means	3.00
5	Errict Rhett	3.00
6	Ki-Jana Carter	3.00
7	Tyrone Wheatley	3.00
8	Drew Bledsoe	10.00
9	Dan Marino	15.00
10	Steve Young	10.00
11	Troy Aikman	10.00
12	Brett Favre	15.00
13	Kerry Collins	10.00
14	Steve McNair	10.00
15	Heath Shuler	3.00
16	Jerry Rice	10.00
17	Michael Irvin	3.00
18	Herman Moore	3.00

1995 Action Packed Monday Night Football Promos

The four-card, standard-size set was issued as a preview to the 126-card Monday Night Football set. The set includes two base issues, one Night Flights insert card and one advertisement card. The card fronts are identical to the base set, but the backs have "Promo" printed.

		NM/M
Complete Set (4):		10.00
Common Player:		.50
1	Steve Young	2.00
3A	Troy Aikman	4.00
3B	Drew Bledsoe	4.00
NNO	NMFB Ad Card (Night Flights card)	.50

1995 Action Packed Monday Night Football

Action Packed's 1995 Monday Night Football set contains 26 cards, plus a parallel Highlights set which uses a prismatic foil background. These cards, found one per every six packs, have "Highlights" written in gold foil on the card back. The regular cards feature a full-bleed photo with a raised image of the player. A gold band runs across the top of the card; it includes the player's last name in black, alongside a gold team logo. The Monday Night Football icon appears in the lower right corner. The horizontal card back has a mug shot, statistics, biographical information and a brief player profile. A black band with the various sponsor logos runs across the bottom of the card. Insert sets include Night Flights, 24KT Team and Reverse Angle.

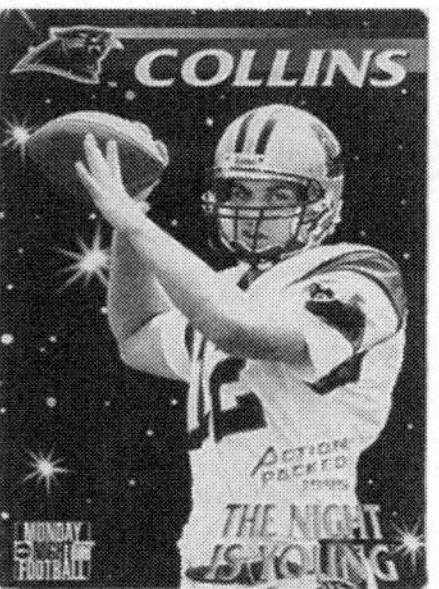

		NM/M
Complete Set (126):		25.00
Common Player:		.10
Minor Stars:		.20
Complete Highlights (126):		100.00
Highlights Cards:		4X
Wax Box:		50.00
1	Jerry Rice	1.00
2	Barry Sanders	2.00
3	Troy Aikman	1.00
4	Jerome Bettis	.40
5	Tim Brown	.20
6	Marcus Allen	.20
7	*Jeff Blake*	2.00
8	Rodney Hampton	.20
9	Reggie White	.20
10	Warren Moon	.20
11	William Floyd	.40
12	Cris Carter	.20
13	Stan Humphries	.20
14	Herschel Walker	.10
15	Dave Brown	.10
16	Jim Everett	.10
17	Mario Bates	.40
18	Terance Mathis	.10
19	Chris Spielman	.10
20	Neil O'Donnell	.20
21	Anthony Miller	.10
22	Steve Bono	.30
23	Henry Ellard	.10
24	Dave Meggett	.10
25	Flipper Anderson	.10
26	Rocket Ismail	.10
27	Leroy Hoard	.10
28	Steve Young	1.00
29	Marshall Faulk	2.00
30	Dan Marino	2.50
31	Errict Rhett	.75
32	Michael Irvin	.20
33	Bam Morris	.20
34	Heath Shuler	.50
35	Jim Kelly	.20
36	Deion Sanders	.50
37	Jeff Hostetler	.20
38	Jeff George	.20
39	Alvin Harper	.10
40	Barry Foster	.10
41	Craig Erickson	.10
42	Vinny Testaverde	.10
43	Andre Reed	.10
44	Eric Green	.10
45	Bruce Smith	.10
46	Frank Reich	.10
47	Shannon Sharpe	.10
48	Chris Miller	.10
49	Darnay Scott	.50
50	Eric Metcalf	.10
51	Mike Sherrard	.10
52	Lorenzo White	.10
53	Scott Mitchell	.20
54	Jay Novacek	.10
55	Emmitt Smith	2.50
56	Drew Bledsoe	1.00
57	Natrone Means	.75
58	John Elway	.50
59	Herman Moore	.30
60	Brett Favre	1.00
61	Ricky Watters	.20
62	Andre Rison	.10
63	Junior Seau	.20
64	Randall Cunningham	.10
65	Chris Warren	.20
66	Garrison Hearst	.10
67	Ben Coates	.10
68	Rick Mirer	.40
69	Johnny Mitchell	.10
70	Trent Dilfer	.40
71	Carl Pickens	.25
72	Craig Heyward	.10
73	Greg Lloyd	.10
74	Boomer Esiason	.10
75	Greg Hill	.30
76	Lewis Tillman	.10
77	Willie Davis	.10
78	Brent Jones	.10
79	Michael Haynes	.10
80	Darryl Johnston	.10
81	Steve Beuerlein	.10
82	*Ki-Jana Carter*	.75
83	*Steve McNair*	4.00
84	*Michael Westbrook*	2.50
85	*Kerry Collins*	4.00
86	*Joey Galloway*	4.00
87	*Kyle Brady*	.40
88	*J.J. Stokes*	3.00
89	*Tyrone Wheatley*	.75
90	*Rashaan Salaam*	3.00
91	*Napoleon Kaufman*	1.50
92	*Frank Sanders*	1.25
93	*Stoney Case*	.50
94	*Todd Collins*	.20
95	*James Stewart*	1.50
96	*Kordell Stewart*	3.00
97	*Joe Aska*	.20
98	*Terrell Fletcher*	.20
99	*Rob Johnson*	1.50
100	Steve Young	.50
101	Jerry Rice	.50
102	Emmitt Smith	1.00
103	Barry Sanders	1.00
104	Marshall Faulk	.50
105	Drew Bledsoe	.50
106	Dan Marino	1.00
107	Troy Aikman	.40
108	John Elway	.30
109	Brett Favre	.50
110	Michael Irvin	.20
111	Heath Shuler	.40
112	Warren Moon	.20
113	Chris Warren	.20
114	Natrone Means	.30
115	Errict Rhett	.75
116	Bam Morris	.20
117	Randall Cunningham	.20
118	Jim Kelly	.20
119	Jeff Hostetler	.10
120	Barry Foster	.10
121	Jim Everett	.10
122	Neil O'Donnell	.10
123	Jerome Bettis	.20
124	Ricky Watters	.20
125	Joe Montana	.75
126	Howard Cosell	.20

1995 Action Packed Monday Night Football Highlights

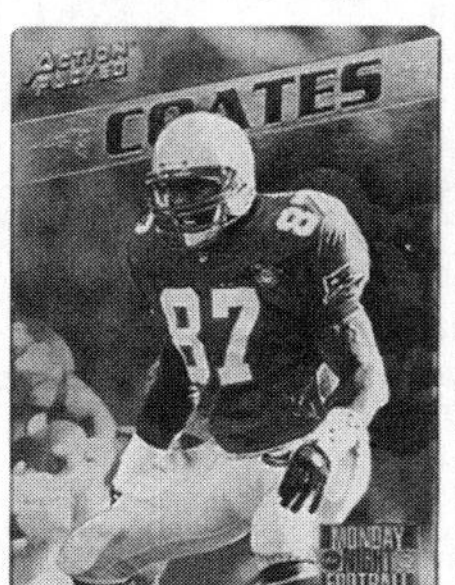

The 126-card, regular-size set was parallel to the 1995 base set and were inserted every six packs. The card fronts feature a silver foil background.

	NM/M
Complete Set (126):	100.00
Common Player:	1.00
Highlight Cards:	4X

1995 Action Packed Monday Night Football 24KT Gold Team

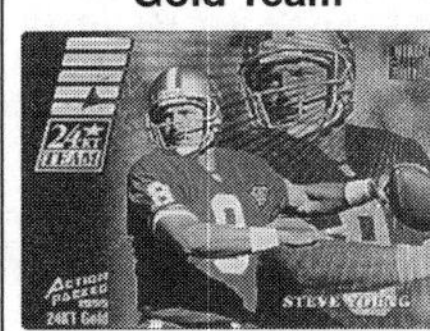

These inserts provide a golden rendition of 12 regular issue cards with micro-etched highlights on rainbow holographic foil with an exclusive gold logo that includes genuine gold leafing. The cards, randomly included in every 72 packs of 1995 Action Packed Monday Night Football, features members of the 24KT Team. Fewer than 2,000 sets were made. The card front is horizontal and includes a smaller photo in the forefront, with a larger image of the same photo in the background. The card back, numbered 1 of 12, etc., has a player photo and brief recap of a game in which the player had a key role. A vertical format is used for the back, which has the appropriate logos in a panel on the right.

		NM/M
Complete Set (12):		250.00
Common Player:		12.00
1	Emmitt Smith	50.00
2	Barry Sanders	50.00
3	Marshall Faulk	30.00
4	Dan Marino	50.00
5	Steve Young	30.00
6	Drew Bledsoe	30.00
7	Troy Aikman	30.00
8	John Elway	40.00
9	Brett Favre	50.00
10	Ki-Jana Carter	12.00
11	Steve McNair	20.00
12	Kerry Collins	20.00

1995 Action Packed Monday Night Football Night Flights

These 1995 Action Packed Monday Night Football inserts feature 12 members of the Quarterback Club on Dufex cards of textured gold foil. Each card front has a colored raised image, with the player's last name running in a gold strip along the left side of the card, which has the MNF logo at its bottom. The Night Flight logo is at the bottom of the card, too. The back is horizontal, with a mug shot, card number (1 of 12, etc.), and 1994 season recap.

		NM/M
Complete Set (12):		50.00
Common Player:		3.00
1	Steve Young	8.00
2	Dan Marino	12.00
3	Drew Bledsoe	8.00
4	Troy Aikman	8.00
5	John Elway	8.00
6	Brett Favre	12.00
7	Heath Shuler	3.00
8	Dave Brown	3.00
9	Steve McNair	8.00
10	Kerry Collins	6.00
11	Warren Moon	3.00
12	Jeff Hostetler	3.00

1995 Action Packed Monday Night Football Reverse Angle

These 18 insert cards could be found one per every 24 hobby packs of 1995 Action Packed Monday Night Football. They feature 18 NFL stars. Fewer than 1,500 sets of Reverse Angle inserts were made. The front has a raised color image, along with the set, insert set and MNF logos, against a metallic background. The player's name runs along the left side of the card. The back has a black panel along the left side, which also has his name and card number (1 of 18, etc.). A photo and brief player profile are also included on the back. Cards were random inserts, one per every 24 hobby packs.

		NM/M
Complete Set (18):		30.00
Common Player:		2.00
1	Emmitt Smith	8.00
2	Barry Sanders	8.00
3	Steve Young	5.00
4	Marshall Faulk	5.00
5	Randall Cunningham	2.00
6	Deion Sanders	2.00
7	John Elway	5.00
8	Brett Favre	8.00
9	William Floyd	2.00
10	Ricky Watters	2.00
11	Ben Coates	2.00
12	Rod Woodson	2.00
13	Marcus Allen	2.00
14	Eric Metcalf	2.00
15	Keith Byars	2.00
16	Jerry Rice	6.00
17	Alvin Harper	2.00
18	Eric Green	2.00

1995 Action Packed Rookies/Stars

Action Packed's 1995 Rookies and Stars set features the NFL's top rookie draft choices, along with a parallel foiled Stargazers set (one card per six packs). The regular cards have a raised full-bleed color photo on the front, with the set name in the upper left corner and the player's team logo in the bottom left corner. The player's name is stamped in gold foil at the bottom. The horizontal back has a photo on two thirds of the card, with a player profile paragraph next to it. A black band at the bottom of the card contains the player's 1994 and career statistics. Insert sets include 24K Gold Team, Bustout, Closing Seconds and Instant Impressions.

		NM/M
Complete Set (105):		25.00
Common Player:		.10
Minor Stars:		.20
Stargazer Cards:		4X-10X
Stargazer Rookies:		2X-4X
Inserted 1:6		
Pack (8):		1.25
Wax Box (24):		20.00
1	Steve Young	1.00
2	Steve Bono	.30
3	Natrone Means	.50
4	Steve Beuerlein	.10
5	Neil O'Donnell	.10
6	Marshall Faulk	1.00
7	Ricky Watters	.20
8	Gary Brown	.10
9	Jeff Hostetler	.10
10	Robert Brooks	.25

11	Johnny Mitchell	.10
12	Barry Sanders	2.00
13	Dave Brown	.10
14	John Elway	2.00
15	Garrison Hearst	.10
16	Jim Everett	.10
17	Michael Irvin	.20
18	Dan Marino	2.50
19	Jeff George	.20
20	Ben Coates	.10
21	Charles Johnson	.30
22	Carl Pickens	.25
23	Deion Sanders	.75
24	Errict Rhett	.75
25	Steve Walsh	.10
26	Bruce Smith	.10
27	Andre Rison	.20
28	Warren Moon	.10
29	Terry Allen	.10
30	Desmond Howard	.10
31	Shannon Sharpe	.10
32	Dave Krieg	.10
33	Bam Morris	.20
34	Rodney Hampton	.10
35	Scott Mitchell	.20
36	Alvin Harper	.10
37	Robert Smith	.10
38	Troy Aikman	1.00
39	William Floyd	.40
40	Randall Cunningham	.10
41	Mario Bates	.30
42	Reggie White	.20
43	Chris Chandler	.10
44	Erik Kramer	.10
45	Emmitt Smith	2.50
46	Irving Fryar	.10
47	*Jeff Blake*	.50
48	Drew Bledsoe	1.50
49	Anthony Miller	.10
50	Marcus Allen	.20
51	Leroy Hoard	.10
52	Stan Humphries	.20
53	Eric Green	.10
54	Herschel Walker	.10
55	Junior Seau	.20
56	Terance Mathis	.10
57	Boomer Esiason	.10
58	Lorenzo White	.10
59	Tim Brown	.20
60	Brett Favre	3.00
61	Craig Erickson	.10
62	Rod Woodson	.10
63	Frank Reich	.10
64	Cris Carter	.20
65	Jerry Rice	1.00
66	Greg Hill	.30
67	Andre Reed	.10
68	Trent Dilfer	.40
69	Eric Metcalf	.10
70	Jim Kelly	.20
71	Herman Moore	.50
72	Vinny Testaverde	.10
73	Jeff Graham	.10
74	Edgar Bennett	.10
75	Jerome Bettis	.30
76	Heath Shuler	.75
77	Chris Warren	.20
78	Reggie Brooks	.10
79	Rick Mirer	.40
80	Chris Miller	.10
81	*Napoleon Kaufman*	1.00
82	*Christian Fauria*	.20
83	*Todd Collins*	.20
84	*J.J. Stokes*	1.00
85	*Mark Bruener*	.40
86	*Frank Sanders*	1.00
87	*Chad May*	.20
88	*Kordell Stewart*	2.00
89	*Ki-Jana Carter*	.50
90	*Curtis Martin*	3.00
91	*Sherman Williams*	.20
92	*Terrell Davis*	8.00
93	*Chris Sanders*	.50
94	*Kyle Brady*	.40
95	*Tyrone Wheatley*	.50
96	*Rodney Thomas*	.50
97	*James Stewart*	1.50
98	*Kerry Collins*	1.00
99	*Rashaan Salaam*	.75
100	*Stoney Case*	.20
101	*Steve McNair*	3.00
102	*Joey Galloway*	100.00
103	*Michael Westbrook*	1.00
104	*Eric Zeier*	.75
105	*Ray Zellars*	.50

1995 Action Packed Rookies & Stars Stargazers

The 105-card, regular-size set was issued as a parallel release to the 1995 Rookies/Stars base set, inserted every six packs. The background of the card fronts contain silver foil while the backs each have a "Stargazers" stamp.

	NM/M
Complete Set (105):	250.00
Common Player:	.75
Stargazers:	4X-10X

1995 Action Packed Rookies/Stars 24K Gold

These 14 cards were the most exclusive of the 1995 Action Packed Rookies & Stars inserts, available at one per every 72 packs. Each card front has a raised color image on it, with part of it against a black background, and most of it against a gold foil panel along the right side of the card. "24 KT Gold Team" is inside the gold panel. The set logo is in the gold in the bottom right corner, opposite the player's name. The horizontal card back has mostly a black background which contains a mug shot and brief summary of the player's accomplishments. A jagged gold panel at the top of the card contains the words "24 KT Gold Team." A card number is in the lower right corner.

		NM/M
Complete Set (14):		350.00
Common Player:		6.00
Minor Stars:		12.00
Inserted 1:72		
1	Steve Young	20.00
2	Brett Favre	50.00
3	Rashaan Salaam	8.00
4	Tyrone Wheatley	6.00
5	Marshall Faulk	20.00
6	Rick Mirer	6.00
7	Troy Aikman	30.00
8	John Elway	40.00
9	Dan Marino	50.00
10	Barry Sanders	50.00
11	Jerry Rice	40.00
12	Emmitt Smith	50.00
13	Michael Irvin	10.00
14	Drew Bledsoe	25.00

1995 Action Packed Rookies/Stars Bustout

These insert cards were available in 12-card jumbo packs of 1995 Action Packed Rookies and Stars. The 12 cards, numbered on the back, feature top NFL running backs. The card front has a raised color photo against a metallic background. The player's name and the set logo are on the left side of the card. The player's name, card number and a team helmet are in a black strip along the left side of the card back; a photo is on the opposite side, along with an example of when the player "busted out" and had a big game.

	NM/M
Complete Set (12):	25.00
Common Player:	1.00
Minor Stars:	2.00
Inserted 1:12	

1	Marshall Faulk	3.00
2	Barry Sanders	10.00
3	Emmitt Smith	10.00
4	Natrone Means	2.00
5	Errict Rhett	1.00
6	Bam Morris	1.00
7	Terry Allen	2.00
8	Rodney Hampton	1.00
9	Ricky Watters	4.00
10	Chris Warren	1.00
11	Jerome Bettis	4.00
12	Gary Brown	1.00

1995 Action Packed Rookies/Stars Closing Seconds

These 12 1995 Action Packed Rookies & Stars inserts feature players who pulled out victories for their teams in the final seconds. A raised color photo is on the front, with a ghosted, rainbow holographic-foiled larger image of the same photo as a background. "Closing Seconds" is written in gold foil. The player's name and set name are in the top corners. The card back has a black panel along the left side which contains a number and accounts of the game he helped win in the final seconds. A photo also appears on the back. Cards were exlusive to hobby packs, one per every 36 packs.

		NM/M
Complete Set (12):		75.00
Common Player:		1.00
Minor Stars:		3.00
Inserted 1:36 Hobby		
1	Dan Marino	12.00
2	Steve Young	8.00
3	Jerry Rice	12.00
4	Emmitt Smith	12.00
5	Barry Sanders	12.00
6	Brett Favre	12.00
7	Drew Bledsoe	8.00
8	Troy Aikman	8.00
9	John Elway	12.00
10	Dave Brown	1.00
11	Warren Moon	6.00
12	Jim Kelly	6.00

1995 Action Packed Rookies/Stars Instant Impressions

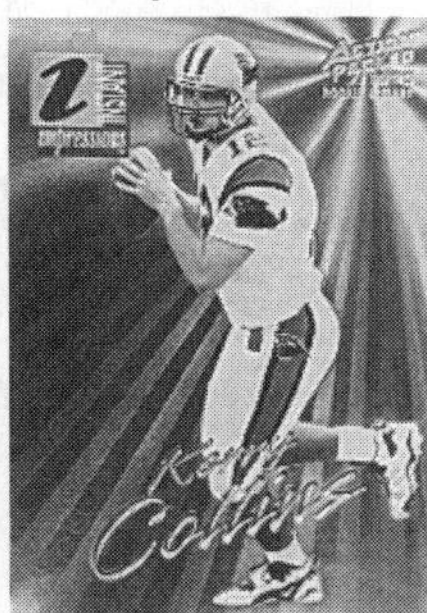

These 1995 Action Packed Rookies & Stars inserts have 12 rookies highlighted on Dufex cards. The front has a raised color image against a strobelight-like background. The set and insert set logos are in the upper corners; the player's name is at the bottom in gold foil. The back has a colored panel on the left side which contains the player's name, position and card number. A smaller horizontal picture is on the right side, with a brief player profile sandwiched between it and the colored panel. Cards were available one per every 24 packs.

	NM/M
Complete Set (12):	40.00
Common Player:	.75
Minor Stars:	2.00
Inserted 1:24	

1	Ki-Jana Carter	2.50
2	Steve McNair	12.00
3	Kerry Collins	5.00
4	Michael Westbrook	2.00
5	Joey Galloway	3.00
6	J.J. Stokes	3.00
7	Rashaan Salaam	1.00
8	Tyrone Wheatley	1.00
9	Eric Zeier	1.00
10	Curtis Martin	8.00
11	Napoleon Kaufman	3.00
12	Kyle Brady	.75

1996 Action Packed Promos

The four-card, regular-size set was released as a preview for the 1996 base set and includes three regular cards and one Studs card. The card fronts are identical to the regular issue cards, but "Promo" is printed on the back.

		NM/M
Complete Set (4):		12.00
Common Player:		1.00
1	Emmitt Smith	4.50
3	Jerry Rice (Studs Card)	6.00
16	Steve Young	2.00
105	Neil O'Donnell	1.00

1996 Action Packed

Action Packed's 1996 football set has 126 regular cards, plus a parallel Artist's Proofs set (one in 24 packs). Each card front has a set logo in the upper left corner, with the player's name, in a black bar, and his team logo stamped in gold foil at the bottom. The full-bleed color action photo on the front uses the company's raised photo format. The card back has a closeup photo of the player on the left, with his name and position below, followed by biographical information and statistics. A colored panel along the right side has a brief player profile. The card number is in the upper left corner. Insert sets include 24k Team, Studs, Sculptor's Proofs, Ball Hog and the Longest Yard.

		NM/M
Complete Set (126):		35.00
Common Player:		.20
Minor Stars:		.40
Comp. Artist's Proof (126):		250.00
Artist's Proof Cards:		5X-10X
Pack (5):		3.00
Wax Box (24):		50.00
1	Emmitt Smith	3.00
2	Dan Marino	3.00
3	Isaac Bruce	.40
4	Eric Zeier	.20
5	Ben Coates	.20
6	Jim Kelly	.20
7	Rodney Hampton	.20
8	Greg Lloyd	.20
9	Reggie White	.20
10	Derrick Thomas	.20
11	Jerry Rice	1.50
12	Drew Bledsoe	1.50
13	Cris Carter	.20
14	Troy Aikman	1.50
15	Steve McNair	1.50
16	Steve Young	1.50
17	Ricky Watters	.20
18	Brett Favre	3.00
19	Michael Westbrook	.40
20	Charles Haley	.20
21	Heath Shuler	.40
22	Tim Brown	.20
23	Kerry Collins	2.00
24	Hugh Douglas	.20
25	Marcus Allen	.40
26	Steve Bono	.20
27	Curtis Martin	3.00
28	Wayne Chrebet	.20
29	Dave Brown	.20
30	James Stewart	.20
31	Chris Sanders	.40
32	Deion Sanders	1.00
33	Rodney Thomas	.40
34	Rashaan Salaam	.40
35	Curtis Conway	.20
36	Harvey Williams	.20
37	William Floyd	.20
38	Carl Pickens	.40
39	Herman Moore	.40
40	Stan Humphries	.20
41	Orlanda Thomas	.20
42	Bert Emanuel	.20
43	Yancey Thigpen	.50
44	Darick Holmes	.40
45	Mario Bates	.20
46	Greg Hill	.20
47	Errict Rhett	.40
48	Erik Kramer	.20
49	Garrison Hearst	.40
50	Jim Everett	.20
51	Barry Sanders	2.50
52	Eric Metcalf	.20
53	Marshall Faulk	1.50
54	Junior Seau	.20
55	Bruce Smith	.20
56	Kordell Stewart	2.00
57	Edgar Bennett	.20
58	Joey Galloway	1.50
59	Jeff Hostetler	.20
60	Frank Sanders	.40
61	John Elway	.75
62	Tyrone Wheatley	.20
63	Jeff George	.20
64	Ken Norton Jr.	.20
65	Bryan Cox	.20
66	Bryce Paup	.20
67	Larry Centers	.20
68	Bernie Parmalee	.20
69	Jeff Graham	.20
70	Rick Mirer	.20
71	Chris Warren	.40
72	Charlie Garner	.20
73	Robert Brooks	.20
74	Jim Harbaugh	.20
75	Tamarick Vanover	.40
76	Napoleon Kaufman	.40
77	Warren Moon	.20
78	Vincent Brisby	.20
79	Ki-Jana Carter	.40
80	Michael Irvin	.40
81	Trent Dilfer	.20
82	Bam Morris	.20
83	Mark Brunell	1.50
84	Jeff Blake	.40
85	Kevin Williams	.20
86	Rod Woodson	.20
87	Andre Reed	.20
88	Erric Pegram	.20
89	Anthony Miller	.20
90	Gus Frerotte	.20
91	Quinn Early	.20
92	Daryl Johnston	.20
93	Tony Martin	.20
94	Terrell Davis	6.00
95	Brent Jones	.20
96	Mark Chmura	.40
97	Kyle Brady	.20
98	J.J. Stokes	.40
99	Rodney Peete	.20
100	Natrone Means	.40
101	Sherman Williams	.20
102	Brian Blades	.20
103	Brett Perriman	.20
104	Antonio Freeman	.20
105	Neil O'Donnell	.20
106	Craig Heyward	.20
107	Derek Loville	.20
108	Jay Novacek	.20
109	Scott Mitchell	.20
110	Bill Brooks	.20
111	Shannon Sharpe	.20
112	Jake Reed	.20
113	Derrick Moore	.20
114	Steve Atwater	.20
115	Darren Woodson	.20
116	Junior Seau	.20
117	Quentin Coryatt	.20
118	Bruce Smith	.20
119	Rod Woodson	.20
120	Charles Haley	.20
121	Derrick Thomas	.20
122	Ken Norton	.20
123	Steve Atwater	.20
124	Greg Lloyd	.20
125	Reggie White	.20
126	Bryan Cox	.20

1996 Action Packed Artist's Proof

The 126-card, regular-size set was issued as a parallel release to the 1996 base set. The cards were inserted every 24 hobby and retail packs and every 30 magazine packs. The cards have "Artist's Proof" printed on the fronts.

		NM/M
Complete Set (126):		250.00
Common Player:		2.00
Artist's Proof Cards:		5X-10X
1	Emmitt Smith	50.00
2	Dan Marino	50.00
3	Isaac Bruce	15.00
11	Jerry Rice	40.00
12	Drew Bledsoe	25.00
14	Troy Aikman	30.00
15	Steve McNair	25.00
16	Steve Young	25.00
18	Brett Favre	50.00
19	Michael Westbrook	5.00
23	Kerry Collins	12.00
27	Curtis Martin	15.00
32	Deion Sanders	15.00
34	Rashaan Salaam	3.00
43	Yancey Thigpen	3.00
47	Errict Rhett	5.00
51	Barry Sanders	45.00
53	Marshall Faulk	25.00
56	Kordell Stewart	10.00
58	Joey Galloway	10.00
61	John Elway	35.00
75	Tamarick Vanover	3.00
84	Jeff Blake	3.00
94	Terrell Davis	25.00
98	J.J. Stokes	6.00

1996 Action Packed 24kt Gold

These insert cards feature the standard raised photo on the front, against a "Prime Frost" background with 24kt gold foil stamping used for the 24kt gold logo. The card back has the number at the top of a panel along the left side of the card. The player's name and position are also in the panel. The right side of the card has a mug shot at the top, along with an action photo. A recap of a memorable game from the previous season is underneath, along with the player's team name. Cards were seeded one per every 72 packs of 1996 Action Packed football.

		NM/M
Complete Set (14):		250.00
Common Player:		5.00
1	Brett Favre	40.00
2	Michael Irvin	5.00
3	Drew Bledsoe	20.00
4	Jerry Rice	35.00
5	Troy Aikman	30.00
6	Dan Marino	40.00
7	Errict Rhett	5.00
8	Curtis Martin	25.00
9	Steve Young	30.00
10	Barry Sanders	35.00
11	Marshall Faulk	30.00
12	Isaac Bruce	10.00
13	John Elway	30.00
14	Emmitt Smith	40.00

1996 Action Packed Ball Hog

This 12-card 1996 Action Packed insert set highlights players who always seem to have the ball in their hands. The cards, seeded one per every 23 packs, use an embossed leather-looking print technology. The card front has a raised action photo against a football background. "Ball Hog" is written along the right side. The brand logo is stamped in gold in the upper left corner; the player's name and his team's name are stamped in gold in the bottom left corner. The back has the player's name written in a panel along the top, with a brief player profile and a player mug shot below.

		NM/M
Complete Set (12):		60.00
Common Player:		2.00
1	Carl Pickens	2.00
2	Terrell Davis	10.00
3	Jerry Rice	12.00

4	Barry Sanders	12.00
5	Marshall Faulk	6.00
6	Isaac Bruce	4.00
7	Michael Irvin	2.00
8	Cris Carter	2.00
9	Rashaan Salaam	2.00
10	Herman Moore	2.00
11	Chris Warren	2.00
12	Emmitt Smith	15.00

1996 Action Packed Jumbo Inserts

These cards were inserted one per retail box as a boxtopper insert. They are a parallel of each player's base set card except they are oversized and numbered differently.

		NM/M
Complete Set (4):		20.00
Common Player:		4.00
1	Emmitt Smith	6.00
2	Drew Bledsoe	4.00
3	Troy Aikman	4.00
4	Brett Favre	8.00

1996 Action Packed Longest Yard

The 12-card, regular-sized set was inserted every 24 magazine packs of 1996 Action Packed.

		NM/M
Complete Set (12):		125.00
Common Player:		3.00
1	Brett Favre	25.00
2	Tamarick Vanover	3.00
3	Joey Galloway	6.00
4	Kerry Collins	10.00
5	Jeff Blake	4.00
6	Jerry Rice	20.00
7	Barry Sanders	20.00
8	Rodney Thomas	3.00
9	Herman Moore	5.00
10	Emmitt Smith	30.00
11	Terrell Davis	20.00
12	Cris Carter	7.00

1996 Action Packed Sculptor's Proof

Sculptor's Proofs inserts are pewter metal-card renditions of 14 players' regular issue cards, except the card numbers on the back correspond to the checklist. These cards were available to consumers through a randomly-inserted redemption card found one per every 192 packs.

		NM/M
Complete Set (14):		500.00
Common Player:		15.00
1	Dan Marino	60.00
2	Deion Sanders	25.00
3	Joey Galloway	20.00
4	Brett Favre	60.00
5	Barry Sanders	60.00
6	Michael Irvin	15.00
7	Drew Bledsoe	40.00
8	Emmitt Smith	60.00
9	Curtis Martin	50.00
10	Steve Young	40.00
11	John Elway	40.00
12	Jerry Rice	50.00
13	Errict Rhett	20.00
14	Troy Aikman	40.00

1996 Action Packed Studs

These 1996 Action Packed insert cards feature six NFL stars and their diamond stud earrings. Studs cards contain a genuine diamond chip and are found one per every 161 packs. There were 1,500 sets produced. Each card front, in a horizontal format, has the set name in the upper right corner in gold foil; the player's name and "Studs" are in gold along the bottom. The card back is also horizontal. An action photo of the player is on the right, with his name, position, team logo and card number in a panel above. The left side of the card has a recap of a memorable game in the player's career, plus his team name in a black strip.

		NM/M
Complete Set (6):		175.00
Common Player:		10.00
Gold parallel		1X
1	Emmitt Smith	100.00
2	Deion Sanders	40.00
3	Jerry Rice	75.00
4	Michael Irvin	10.00
5	Kordell Stewart	25.00
6	Ricky Watters	10.00

1997 Action Packed Promos

This three-card set was issued to promote sales of 1997 Action Packed. It included two base cards and one Studs insert. All three cards contained the words "Promo" in a black box across the back.

		NM/M
Complete Set (3):		5.00
Common Player:		.50
28	Kordell Stewart	1.50
45	Jim Harbaugh	.50
4 of 9	Jerry Rice(Studs)	4.00

1997 Action Packed

The 125-card set features a brown football pebble grain at the bottom of the card front. The player's photo is printed at the top, with the player embossed. The Pinnacle Action Packed logo is at the bottom center, with the player's name printed directly below. The card backs have a player photo with a ghosted photo in the background. The player's bio is listed along the upper right border. The player's name, position and stats are printed at the bottom left. The First Impressions silver-foil parallel of the base set was inserted 1:15 packs, while the Gold Impressions parallel set, which includes gold foil, was seeded 1:44 packs. A 15-card Down "N" Dirty subset was included as part of the base set.

		NM/M
Complete Set (125):		40.00
Common Player:		.10
Minor Stars:		.20
First Impressions:		5X-10X
Gold Impressions:		10X-20X
Pack (5):		3.00
Wax Box (24):		65.00
1	Jerry Rice	2.00
2	Troy Aikman	2.00
3	Ricky Watters	.20
4	Dan Marino	4.00
5	Emmitt Smith	4.00
6	Warren Moon	.20
7	Rashaan Salaam	.50
8	Drew Bledsoe	2.00
9	Eddie George	2.00
10	John Elway	1.25
11	Robert Brooks	.10
12	Scott Mitchell	.10
13	Isaac Bruce	.50
14	Marshall Faulk	.75
15	Steve Bono	.10
16	Barry Sanders	3.00
17	Brett Favre	4.00
18	Curtis Martin	3.00
19	Keyshawn Johnson	.75
20	Dave Brown	.10
21	Frank Sanders	.10
22	Gus Frerotte	.10
23	Eric Metcalf	.10
24	Thurman Thomas	.20
25	Steve Young	1.25
26	Alvin Harper	.10
27	Mark Brunell	2.00
28	Kordell Stewart	2.00
29	Terry Glenn	.30
30	Junior Seau	.20
31	Karim Abdul-Jabbar	.30
32	Jeff Hostetler	.10
33	Rodney Hampton	.10
34	Irving Fryar	.10
35	Cris Carter	.10
36	James Stewart	.10
37	Marcus Allen	.20
38	Napoleon Kaufman	.20
39	Shannon Sharpe	.20
40	LeShon Johnson	.10
41	Tony Banks	.50
42	Lawrence Phillips	.20
43	Kerry Collins	.30
44	Curtis Conway	.10
45	Jim Harbaugh	.10
46	Garrison Hearst	.10
47	Trent Dilfer	.20
48	Terance Mathis	.10
49	Jerome Bettis	.30
50	Chris Sanders	.10
51	Deion Sanders	1.00
52	Herman Moore	.30
53	Elvis Grbac	.10
54	O.J. McDuffie	.10
55	Ben Coates	.10
56	Jim Kelly	.20
57	J.J. Stokes	.10
58	Terrell Davis	3.00
59	Stan Humphries	.10
60	Carl Pickens	.20
61	Neil O'Donnell	.10
62	Edgar Bennett	.10
63	Yancey Thigpen	.10
64	Bert Emanuel	.10
65	Amani Toomer	.10
66	Jeff Blake	.20
67	Eddie Kennison	.75
68	Jason Dunn	.10
69	Rob Moore	.10
70	Andre Rison	.10
71	Vinny Testaverde	.10
72	Henry Ellard	.10
73	Dale Carter	.10
74	Tony Martin	.10
75	Jim Everett	.10
76	Joey Galloway	.50
77	Mike Alstott	.20
78	Kevin Hardy	.10
79	Jake Reed	.10
80	Tim Brown	.10
81	Sean Dawkins	.10
82	Bobby Engram	.10
83	Michael Irvin	.20
84	Rickey Dudley	.20
85	Chris Chandler	.10
86	Keith Jackson	.10
87	Muhsin Muhammad	.20
88	Tamarick Vanover	.20
89	Chris Warren	.10
90	Johnnie Morton	.10
91	Terry Allen	.20
92	Stanley Pritchett	.10
93	Charles Johnson	.10
94	Chris T. Jones	.10
95	Winslow Oliver	.10
96	Anthony Miller	.10
97	Tyrone Wheatley	.10
98	Robert Smith	.10
99	Eric Moulds	.10
100	Hardy Nickerson	.10
101	Derrick Alexander	.10
102	Michael Haynes	.10
103	Jamal Anderson	.20
104	Marvin Harrison	.75
105	Antonio Freeman	.20
106	Dorsey Levens	.20
107	Natrone Means	.20
108	Keenan McCardell	.10
109	Mark Chmura	.10
110	Darren Woodson	.10
111	Brett Favre	2.00
112	Emmitt Smith	2.00
113	Junior Seau	.10
114	Jerry Rice	1.00
115	Barry Sanders	1.50
116	Bruce Smith	.10
117	Troy Aikman	1.00
118	Bryan Cox	.10
119	Zach Thomas	.30
120	Reggie White	.10
121	Ben Coates	.10
122	Jerome Bettis	.10
123	Michael Irvin	.10
124	Quentin Coryatt	.10
125	Checklist	.10

1997 Action Packed First Impressions

This 125-card parallel featured each card from the regular-issue set printed in a silver foil. First Impressions parallels were inserted one per 12 packs.

	NM/M
Complete Set (125):	225.00
First Impression Cards:	2X-6X

1997 Action Packed Gold Impressions

Gold Impressions was a 125-card parallel set to Action Packed that featured the bottom, football-textured part of each base card printed in gold foil. Each card featured a blue "Gold Impressions" logo and they were inserted one per 35 packs.

	NM/M
Complete Set (125):	400.00
Gold Cards:	5X-10X

1997 Action Packed Crash Course

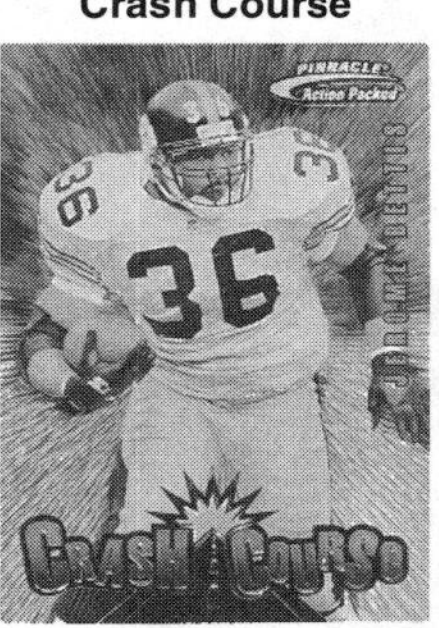

Inserted 1:23 packs, the 18-card set includes the Crash Course logo at the bottom center. The Action Packed logo is in the upper right. The player's name is printed vertically along the upper right side.

		NM/M
Complete Set (18):		100.00
Common Player:		3.00
Minor Stars:		5.00
1	Dan Marino	20.00
2	Troy Aikman	15.00
3	Barry Sanders	20.00
4	Emmitt Smith	20.00
5	Brett Favre	20.00
6	John Elway	15.00
7	Keyshawn Johnson	5.00
8	Jim Harbaugh	3.00
9	Kerry Collins	10.00
10	Karim Abdul-Jabbar	5.00
11	Eddie Kennison	5.00
12	Curtis Martin	15.00
13	Tony Banks	3.00
14	Dorsey Levens	3.00
15	Jerome Bettis	10.00
16	Drew Bledsoe	15.00
17	Marvin Harrison	10.00
18	Jerry Rice	20.00

1997 Action Packed Studs

Numbered as one of 1,500 sets, the nine-card chase set was inserted 1:167 packs. The cards include a real diamond chip in the ears of the player on the card front.

		NM/M
Complete Set (9):		225.00
Common Player:		18.00
1	Deion Sanders	25.00
2	Barry Sanders	60.00
3	Eddie George	35.00
4	Jerry Rice	60.00
5	Kordell Stewart	20.00
6	Emmitt Smith	60.00
7	Terrell Davis	40.00
8	Keyshawn Johnson	18.00
9	Robert Smith	18.00

1997 Action Packed 24K Team

The 15-card chase set was inserted 1:71 packs. The top of the card front has a gold banner, which includes "24KT Gold." The player's name is printed directly below the banner. The player's photo is superimposed over a gold background and silver rays. The Action Packed logo is printed at the bottom center.

		NM/M
Complete Set (15):		325.00
Common Player:		6.00
1	Brett Favre	50.00
2	Steve Young	35.00
3	Terrell Davis	35.00
4	Barry Sanders	45.00
5	Isaac Bruce	10.00
6	Deion Sanders	10.00
7	Dan Marino	50.00
8	Jim Harbaugh	5.00
9	Jerry Rice	35.00
10	John Elway	35.00
11	Herman Moore	10.00
12	Troy Aikman	35.00
13	Emmitt Smith	50.00
14	Drew Bledsoe	35.00
15	Eddie George	20.00

1991 All-World Troy Aikman Promos

The six-card, regular size set used the same Troy Aikman photo, but with different crops and biography versions (English, French and Spanish). Each card is numbered with a "1" and A-F is used to distinguish the cards.

		NM/M
Complete Set (6):		15.00
Common Player:		2.50
1A	Troy Aikman (Green border, English bio)	2.50
1B	Troy Aikman (Green border, French bio)	2.50
1C	Troy Aikman (Green border, Spanish bio)	2.50
1D	Troy Aikman (Speckled border, English bio)	2.50
1E	Troy Aikman (Speckled border, French bio)	2.50
1F	Troy Aikman (Speckled border, Spanish bio)	2.50

1992 All-World

The 1992 All World set, which included 300 regular-size cards, was sold in 12-card packs and 26-card rack packs. The front of each card features an American flag on the top. Two insert sets, Greats/Rookies and Legends/Rookies were randomly inserted in packs, as were autographed cards from Joe Namath, Jim Brown and Desmond Howard. Subsets in the base set included Legends in the Making (LM), and Greats of the Game (GG).

		NM/M
Complete Set (300):		18.00
Common Player:		.05
1	Emmitt Smith (LM)	.75
2	Thurman Thomas (LM)	.10
3	Deion Sanders (LM)	.25
4	Randall Cunningham (LM)	.10
5	Michael Irvin (LM)	.10
6	Bruce Smith (LM)	.10
7	Jeff George (LM)	.10
8	Derrick Thomas (LM)	.10
9	Andre Rison (LM)	.20
10	Troy Aikman (LM)	.40
11	Quentin Coryatt	.25
12	Carl Pickens	.50
13	Steve Emtman	.10
14	Derek Brown (TE)	.10
15	Desmond Howard	.75
16	Troy Vincent	.20
17	David Klingler	.20
18	Vaughn Dunbar	.10
19	Terrell Buckley	.10
20	Jimmy Smith	.50
21	Marquez Pope	.05
22	Kurt Barber	.05
23	Robert Harris	.05
24	Tony Sacca	.10
25	Alonzo Spellman	.20
26	Shane Collins	.05
27	Chris Mims	.20
28	Siran Stacy	.10
29	Edgar Bennett	.40
30	Sean Gilbert	.20
31	Eugene Chung	.05
32	Levon Kirkland	.10
33	Chuck Smith	.05
34	Chester McGlockton	.20
35	Ashley Ambrose	.10
36	Phillippi Sparks	.05
37	Darryl Williams	.10
38	Tracy Scroggins	.10
39	Mike Gaddis	.05
40	Tony Brooks	.05
41	Steve Israel	.05
42	Patrick Rowe	.05
43	Shane Dronett	.05
44	Mike Pawlawski	.05
45	Dale Carter	.20
46	Tyji Armstrong	.05
47	Kevin Smith	.20
48	Courtney Hawkins	.10
49	Marco Coleman	.10
50	Tommy Vardell	.10
51	Ray Ethridge	.05
52	Robert Porcher	.10
53	Todd Collins	.05
54	Robert Jones	.10
55	Tommy Maddox	.10
56	Dana Hall	.10
57	Leon Searcy	.10
58	Robert Brooks	1.00
59	Darren Woodson	.20
60	Jeremy Lincoln	.05
61	Sean Jones	.10
62	Howie Long	.10
63	Rich Gannon	.10
64	Keith Byars	.05
65	John Taylor	.10
66	Burt Grossman	.05
67	Chris Hinton	.05
68	Brad Muster	.05
69	Cris Dishman	.05
70	Russell Maryland	.10
71	Harvey Williams	.20
72	Broderick Thomas	.05
73	Louis Lipps	.05
74	Erik Kramer	.10
75	David Fulcher	.05
76	Andre Tippett	.05
77	Timm Rosenbach	.05
78	Mark Rypien	.10
79	James Lofton	.10
80	Dan Saleaumua	.05
81	John L. Williams	.05
82	Kevin Fagan	.05
83	Flipper Anderson	.05
84	Michael Dean Perry	.10
85	Mark Higgs	.05
86	Pat Swilling	.10
87	Pierce Holt	.05
88	John Elway	.75
89	Bill Brooks	.10
90	Rob Moore	.10
91	Junior Seau	.30
92	Wendell Davis	.05
93	Brian Noble	.05
94	Ernest Givins	.10
95	Phil Simms	.10
96	Eric Dickerson	.20
97	Bennie Blades	.05
98	Gary Anderson (RB)	.05
99	Erric Pegram	.20
100	Hart Lee Dykes	.05
101	Charles Haley	.10
102	Bruce Smith	.20
103	Nick Lowery	.05
104	Webster Slaughter	.05
105	Ray Childress	.10
106	Gene Atkins	.05
107	Bruce Armstrong	.05
108	Anthony Miller	.20
109	Eric Thomas	.05
110	Greg Townsend	.05
111	Anthony Carter	.10
112	James Hasty	.05
113	Chris Miller	.10
114	Sammie Smith	.05
115	Bubby Brister	.10
116	Mark Clayton	.10
117	Richard Johnson	.05
118	Bernie Kosar	.10
119	Lionel Washington	.05
120	Gary Clark	.20
121	Anthony Munoz	.20
122	Brent Jones	.10
123	Thurman Thomas	.20
124	Lee Williams	.05
125	Jessie Hester	.05
126	Andre Ware	.10
127	Patrick Hunter	.05
128	Erik Howard	.05
129	Keith Jackson	.10
130	Troy Aikman	.75
131	Mike Singletary	.10
132	Carnell Lake	.10
133	Jeff Hostetler	.10
134	Alonzo Highsmith	.05
135	Vaughn Johnson	.05
136	Louis Oliver	.05
137	Mel Gray	.10
138	Al Toon	.10
139	Bubba McDowell	.05
140	Ronnie Lott	.10
141	Deion Sanders	.50
142	Jim Harbaugh	.20
143	Gary Zimmerman	.05
144	Ernie Jones	.05
145	Cortez Kennedy	.10
146	Jeff Cross	.05
147	Floyd Turner (UER-Bio says he was drafted in 4th round)	.05
148	Mike Tomczak	.10
149	Lorenzo White	.10
150	Mark Carrier (DB)	.05
151	John Stephens	.05
152	Jerry Rice	.75
153	Jim Kelly	.20
154	Al Smith	.05
155	Duane Bickett	.05
156	Brett Perriman	.20
157	Boomer Esiason	.10
158	Neil Smith	.20
159	Eddie Anderson	.05
160	Browning Nagle	.05
161	John Friesz	.10
162	Robert Delpino	.05
163	Darren Lewis	.05
164	Roger Craig	.10
165	Keith McCants	.05
166	Stephone Paige	.05
167	Steve Broussard	.05
168	Gaston Green	.05
169	Ethan Horton	.05
170	Lewis Billups	.05
171	Mike Merriweather	.05
172	Randall Cunningham	.10
173	Leonard Marshall	.05
174	Jay Novacek	.20
175	Irving Fryar	.10
176	Randal Hill	.05

177 Keith Henderson .05
178 Brad Baxter .10
179 William Fuller .10
180 Leslie O'Neal .10
181 Steve Smith .05
182 Joe Montana (UER-Born 1956, not 1965) .75
183 Eric Green .10
184 Rodney Peete .10
185 Lawrence Dawsey .10
186 Brian Mitchell .10
187 Rickey Jackson .05
188 Christian Okoye .10
189 David Wyman .05
190 Jessie Tuggle .05
191 Ronnie Harmon .10
192 Andre Reed .20
193 Chris Doleman .10
194 Leroy Hoard .10
195 Mark Ingram .05
196 Willie Gault .10
197 Eugene Lockhart .05
198 Jim Everett .10
199 Doug Smith .05
200 Clarence Verdin .05
201 Steve Bono .50
202 Mark Vlasic .05
203 Fred Barnett .20
204 Henry Thomas .05
205 Shaun Gayle .05
206 Rod Bernstine .05
207 Harold Green .10
208 Dan McGwire .05
209 Marv Cook .05
210 Emmitt Smith 1.50
211 Merril Hoge .05
212 Darion Conner .05
213 Mike Sherrard .10
214 Jeff George .25
215 Craig Heyward .10
216 Henry Ellard .10
217 Lawrence Taylor .20
218 Jerry Ball .05
219 Tom Rathman .05
220 Warren Moon .20
221 Ricky Proehl .05
222 Sterling Sharpe .20
223 Earnest Byner .05
224 Jay Schroeder .05
225 Vance Johnson .05
226 Cornelius Bennett .10
227 Ken O'Brien .05
228 Ferrell Edmunds .05
229 Eric Allen .05
230 Derrick Thomas .20
231 Cris Carter .20
232 Jon Vaughn .05
233 Eric Metcalf .20
234 William Perry .10
235 Vinny Testaverde .10
236 Chip Banks .05
237 Brian Blades .10
238 Calvin Williams .10
239 Andre Rison .20
240 Neil O'Donnell .25
241 Michael Irvin .25
242 Gary Plummer .05
243 Nick Bell .05
244 Ray Crockett .05
245 Sam Mills .05
246 Haywood Jeffires .10
247 Steve Young .50
248 Martin Bayless .05
249 Dan Marino 1.50
250 Carl Banks .05
251 Keith McKeller .05
252 Aaron Wallace .05
253 Lamar Lathon .05
254 Derrick Fenner .05
255 Vai Sikahema .05
256 Keith Sims .05
257 Rohn Stark .05
258 Reggie Roby .05
259 Tony Zendejas .05
260 Harris Barton .05
261 Checklist 1-100 .05
262 Checklist 101-200 .05
263 Checklist 201-300 .05
264 Rookies Checklist .05
265 Greats Checklist .05
266 Joe Namath (GG) .10
267 Joe Namath (GG) .10
268 Joe Namath (GG) .10
269 Joe Namath (GG) .10
270 Joe Namath (GG) .10
271 Jim Brown (GG) .10
272 Jim Brown (GG) .10
273 Jim Brown (GG) .10
274 Jim Brown (GG) .10
275 Jim Brown (GG) .10
276 Vince Lombardi (GG) .05
277 Jim Thorpe (GG) .05
278 Tom Fears (GG) .05
279 John Henry Johnson (GG) .05
280 Gale Sayers (GG) .10
281 Willie Brown (GG) .05
282 Doak Walker (GG) .05
283 Dick "Night Train" Lane (GG) .05
284 Otto Graham (GG) .10
285 Hugh McElhenny (GG) .05
286 Roger Staubach (GG) .10
287 Steve Largent (GG) .20
288 Otis Taylor (GG) .05
289 Sam Huff (GG) .05
290 Harold Carmichael (GG) .05
291 Steve Van Buren (GG) .05
292 Gino Marchetti (GG) .05
293 Tony Dorsett (GG) .05
294 Leo Nomellini (GG) .05
295 Jack Lambert (GG) .05
296 Joe Theismann (GG) .05
297 Bobby Layne (GG) .05
298 John Stallworth (GG) .05
299 Paul Hornung (GG) .05
300 Don Maynard (GG) .05

A1 Desmond Howard (AU-Certified autograph) 75.00
A2 Jim Brown (AU-Certified autograph) 125.00
A3 Joe Namath (AU-Certified autograph) 175.00
P1 Desmond Howard (Promo) 3.00
TRI Desmond Howard, Jim Brown, Joe Namath (Triplefolder) 5.00

1992 All-World Greats & Rookies

The 20-card, regular-size set was randomly inserted in the 1992 base set. The set features 15 current (as of 1992) players in color and five older players in black and white. The cards maintain the American flag card fronts, but with gold-foil embossed stars. The card backs lead with the "SG" prefix.

NM/M
Complete Set (20): 12.00
Common Greats: .50
Common Rookies: .25
1 Troy Aikman 3.50
2 Thurman Thomas 1.00
3 Andre Rison .50
4 Emmitt Smith 6.00
5 Derrick Thomas .75
6 Joe Namath .75
7 Jim Brown .75
8 Roger Staubach .50
9 Gale Sayers .50
10 Jim Thorpe .50
11 Quentin Coryatt .50
12 Carl Pickens 3.50
13 Steve Emtman .25
14 Derek Brown (TE) .25
15 Desmond Howard 1.00
16 Troy Vincent .25
17 David Klinger .25
18 Vaughn Dunbar .25
19 Terrell Buckley .25
20 Jimmy Smith .75

1992 All-World Legends & Rookies

The 20-card, standard-size set was randomly inserted in 1992 All-World packs. The first ten cards of the set feature Legends in the Making parallels (with gold stars) while cards 11-20 feature top rookies, also with gold stars on the card front's American flag. The card backs lead with the "L" prefix.

NM/M
Complete Set (20): 20.00
Common Legends: 1.00
Common Rookies: 1.00
1 Emmitt Smith 6.00
2 Thurman Thomas 2.00
3 Deion Sanders 2.00
4 Randall Cunningham 1.00
5 Michael Irvin 1.50
6 Bruce Smith 1.00
7 Jeff George 1.00
8 Derrick Thomas 1.00
9 Andre Rison 1.00
10 Troy Aikman 4.00
11 Quentin Coryatt 1.00
12 Carl Pickens 2.00
13 Steve Emtman 1.00
14 Derek Brown (TE) 1.00
15 Desmond Howard 2.00
16 Troy Vincent 1.00
17 David Klinger 1.00
18 Vaughn Dunbar 1.00
19 Terrell Buckley 1.00
20 Jimmy Smith 1.00

1966 American Oil All-Pro

Released in 1966, the 15/16" x 1-1/8" 20-stamp set could be affixed to an 8-1/2" x 11" collection sheet. American Oil dealers distributed the stamps and collectors could win cash prizes and a 1967 Ford Mustang as a top prize. The stamps feature headshots of top players such as Bob Lilly, Deacon Jones, Alex Karras, Johnny Unitas and Gale Sayers.

NM/M
Complete Set (15): 220.00
Common Player: 10.00
1 Herb Adderley (Winner 5.00)
2 Gary Ballman 10.00
3 Dick Butkus (Winner 250.00)
4 Gary Collins (Winner Car)
5 Willie Davis 20.00
6 Tucker Frederickson 10.00
7 Sam Huff 28.00
8 Charlie Johnson 10.00
9 Deacon Jones 30.00
10 Alex Karras 30.00
11 Bob Lilly 35.00
12 Lenny Moore 35.00
13 Tommy Nobis 20.00
14 Dave Parks 10.00
15 Pete Retzlaff 10.00
16 Frank Ryan 10.00
17 Gale Sayers 45.00
18 Mick Tinglehoff 10.00
19 Johnny Unitas (Winner 25.00)
20 Wayne Walker (Winner 1.00)
NNO Saver Sheet 25.00
--- Envelope 15.00

1968 American Oil Mr. and Mrs.

The 32-card, 2-1/8" x 3-7/16" set featured 16 players and their wives. The cards were distributed by American Oil stations and collectors could win cash or a 1969 Ford. The player card fronts feature a horizontal action shot with the wife cards in domestic-type poses.

NM/M
Complete Set (16): 100.00
Common Player: 5.00
Common Wife: 2.50
1 Kermit Alexander (Winner 100.00)
2 Mrs. Kermit Alexander (Jogging with Family) 2.50
3 Jim Bakken 5.00
4 Mrs. Jim Bakken (Winner 1.00)
5 Gary Collins (Winner 500.00)
6 Mrs. Gary Collins (Enjoying the Outdoors) 2.50
7 Jim Grabowski (Winner 1969 Ford)
8 Mrs. Jim Grabowski (At the Fireside) 2.50
9 Earl Gros (Winner 1.00)
10 Mrs. Earl Gros (At the Park) 2.50
11 Deacon Jones 20.00
12 Mrs. Deacon Jones (Winner 500.00)
13 Billy Lothridge (Winner 10.00)
14 Mrs. Billy Lothridge and Baby Daughter 2.50
15 Tom Matte 10.00
16 Mrs. Tom Matte (Winner 50 cents)
17 Bobby Mitchell (Winner 5.00)
18 Mrs. Bobby Mitchell (At a Backyard Barbecue) 2.50
19 Joe Morrison 10.00
20 Mrs. Joe Morrison (Winner 1969 Ford)
21 Dave Osborn 5.00
22 Mrs. Dave Osborn (Winner 5.00)
23 Dan Reeves (Winner 50 cents)
24 Mrs. Dan Reeves (Enjoying the Children) 2.50
25 Gale Sayers 30.00
26 Mrs. Gale Sayers (Winner 100.00)
27 Norm Snead (Winner 1.00)
28 Mrs. Norm Snead (On the Family Boat) 2.50
29 Steve Stonebreaker 5.00
30 Mrs. Steve Stonebreaker (Winner 10.00)
31 Wayne Walker (Winner 50 cents)
32 Mrs. Wayne Walker (At a Family Picnic) 2.50

1988 Athletes in Action

The 12-card, regular-sized set features six Dallas Cowboys and six Texas Rangers from 1988. The card fronts have a color action shot while the backs contain a player quote, a religious message and the player's favorite Bible verse. The top card in the set is Dallas head coach Tom Landry, featured one year before leaving the Cowboys after 29 years.

NM/M
Complete Set (12): 10.00
Common Player: .50
1 Pete O'Brien .50
2 Scott Fletcher .50
3 Oddibe McDowell .75
4 Steve Buechele .50
5 Jerry Browne .50
6 Larry Parrish .50
7 Tom Landry (CO) 3.00
8 Steve Pelluer .50
9 Gordon Banks .50
10 Bill Bates .75
11 Doug Cosbie .50
12 Herschel Walker 1.50

B

1990 Bandits Smokey

The Fresno Bandits, a semi-pro team, are featured in this 25-card set. The fronts feature a black-and-white player photo with the Smokey the Bear logo in the upper left and the team logo in the bottom right. The card backs have a black-and-white photo of the player with Smokey and a safety message.

NM/M
Complete Set (25): 12.00
Common Player: .50
1 Allan Blades .50
2 Corey Clark .50
3 Darryl Duke .50
4 Heikoti Fakava .50
5 Charles Frazier .50
6 Chris Geile .50
7 Mike Henson .50
8 James Hickey .50
9 Anthony Howard .50
10 Derrick Jinks .50
11 Anthony Jones .50
12 Marvin Jones .50
13 Mike Jones .50
14 Steve Loop .50
15 Thomas Ireland .50
16 Jay Lynch .50
17 Sheldon Martin .50
18 Chuckie McCutchen .50
19 Lance Oberparleiter .50
20 Darrell Rosette .50
21 Fred Sims .50
22 Bryan Turner .50
23 Jim Woods CO .50
24 Rick Zumwalt .50
25 Coaching Staff .50

1959 Bazooka

These cards were found on the backs of Bazooka Bubble Gum boxes in 1959. The unnumbered cards are blank-backed and are checklisted alphabetically. Each card measures 2-13/16" x 4-15/16" and is part of the display box. Intact boxes are worth more than if the cards have been cut out.

NM/M
Complete Set (18): 5,000
Common Player: 150.00
(1) Alan Ameche 190.00
(2) Jon Arnett 150.00
(3) Jim Brown 675.00
(4) Rick Casares 150.00
(5A) Charley Connerly (error, Baltimore Colts) 450.00
(5B) Charley Conerly (correct, New York Giants) 325.00
(6) Howard Ferguson 150.00
(7) Frank Gifford 450.00
(8) Lou Groza 475.00
(9) Bobby Layne 325.00
(10) Eddie LeBaron 200.00
(11) Woodley Lewis 150.00
(12) Ollie Matson 250.00
(13) Joe Perry 250.00
(14) Pete Retzlaff 150.00
(15) Kyle Rote 225.00
(16) Y.A. Tittle 325.00
(17) Tom Tracy 300.00
(18) Johnny Unitas 500.00

1971 Bazooka

These cards were issued on the backs of Bazooka Bubble Gum as panels of three. The panels are 2-5/8" x 5-7/8"; each individual card is 1-15/16" x 2-5/8". The card front has a number, plus a color head shot of the player. The back is blank. Panels generally command a premium price which would be greater than the total of the three players combined. Individual card prices are listed.

NM/M
Complete Set (36): 200.00
Common Player: 3.00
1 Joe Namath 35.00
2 Larry Brown 5.00
3 Bobby Bell 5.00
4 Dick Butkus 15.00
5 Charlie Sanders 3.00
6 Chuck Howley 4.00
7 Gale Gillingham 3.00
8 Leroy Kelly 6.00
9 Floyd Little 6.00
10 Dan Abramowicz 3.50
11 Sonny Jurgensen 15.00
12 Andy Russell 3.00
13 Tommy Nobis 3.00
14 O.J. Simpson 30.00
15 Tom Woodeshick 3.00
16 Roman Gabriel 4.50
17 Claude Humphrey 3.00
18 Merlin Olsen 8.00
19 Daryle Lamonica 4.00
20 Fred Cox 3.00
21 Bart Starr 16.00
22 John Brodie 8.00
23 Jim Nance 3.00
24 Gary Garrison 3.00
25 Fran Tarkenton 17.00
26 Johnny Robinson 3.00
27 Gale Sayers 18.00
28 John Unitas 20.00
29 Jerry LeVias 3.00
30 Virgil Carter 3.00
31 Bill Nelsen 3.00
32 Dave Osborn 3.00
33 Matt Snell 3.00
34 Larry Wilson 6.00
35 Bob Griese 15.00
36 Lance Alworth 8.00

A player's name in *italic* type indicates a rookie card.

1972 Bazooka Official Signals

The 12-card, 6-1/4" x 2-7/8" set was issued by Bazooka on the bottoms of its bubble gum boxes in 1972. The first eight cards define football lingo for juveniles while cards 9-12 describe the responsibilities of the referees.

NM/M
Complete Set (12): 85.00
Common Player: 8.00
1 Football Lingo (Automatic through Bread and Butter Play) 8.00
2 Football Lingo (Broken-Field Runner through Dive) 8.00
3 Football Lingo (Double-Coverage through Interference) 8.00
4 Football Lingo (Game Plan through Lateral Pass) 8.00
5 Football Lingo (Interception through Man-to-Man Coverage) 8.00
6 Football Lingo (Killing the Clock through Punt) 8.00
7 Football Lingo (Belly Series through Quick Whistle) 8.00
8 Football Lingo (Prevent Defense through Primary Receiver) 8.00
9 Officials' Duties (Reveree through Line Judge) 8.00
10 Officials' Duties 8.00
11 Officials' Signals 8.00
12 Officials' Signals 8.00

1976 Bears Coke Discs

The 24 circular-card set was issued in 1976 as part of a local Coca-Cola promotion in Chicago. Each one of the 3-3/8" (diameter) discs feature Chicago Bears players, including a noteworthy disc of Walter Payton, whose rookie Topps card was also issued in 1976. The card front features a headshot with the Coca-Cola logo and a Bears helmet while the back has another Coca-Cola logo with the "Coke adds life to ... halftime fun."

NM/M
Complete Set (24): 60.00
Common Player: 1.50
1 Lionel Antoine 1.50
2 Bob Avellini 3.00
3 Waymond Bryant 1.50
4 Doug Buffone 2.00
5 Wally Chambers 2.00
6A Craig Clemons (Yellow border) 1.50
6B Craig Clemons (Orange border) 1.50
7 Allan Ellis 1.50
8 Roland Harper 2.50
9 Mike Hartenstine 1.50
10 Noah Jackson 2.50
11 Virgil Livers 1.50
12 Jim Osborne 1.50
13 Bob Parsons 1.50
14 Walter Payton 45.00
15 Dan Peiffer 1.50
16A Doug Plank (Yellow border) 3.00
16B Doug Plank (Green border) 3.00
17 Bo Rather 1.50
18 Don Rives 1.50
19 Jeff Sevy 1.50
20 Ron Shanklin 1.50
21 Revie Sorey 1.50
22 Roger Stillwell 1.50

1981 Bears Police

The 24-card, 2-5/8" x 4-1/8" set was released in 1981 and sponsored by the Kiwanis Club, the local law enforcement agency and the Chicago Bears. The card fronts feature an action shot while the backs have a Bears helmet and tips geared toward younger fans.

NM/M
Complete Set (24): 18.50
Common Player: .25
1 Ted Albrecht .25
2 Neil Armstrong CO .40
3 Brian Baschnagel .40
4 Gary Campbell .25
5 Robin Earl .25
6 Allan Ellis .25
7 Vince Evans 1.50
8 Gary Fencik 1.25
9 Dan Hampton 3.75
10 Roland Harper .60
11 Mike Hartenstine .25
12 Tom Hicks .25
13 Noah Jackson .60
14 Dennis Lick .25
15 Jerry Muckensturm .25
16 Dan Neal .25
17 Jim Osborne .25
18 Alan Page 2.75
19 Walter Payton 13.50
20 Doug Plank .40
21 Terry Schmidt .25
22 James Scott .25
23 Revie Sorey .40
24 Rickey Watts .25

1994 Bears 75th Anniversary Sheets

The 10-card, 10-3/4" x 7-5/8" set was inserted into game programs for the 1994 75th anniversary season for the Chicago Bears. Each card in the set could be found on a perforated sheet for the eight regular-season Bears home games and two preseason home games. The card backs feature a WGN AM radio advertisement while the fronts have a light blue face with action shots of past Chicago Hall of Famers.

NM/M
Complete Set (10): 50.00
Common Player: 2.50
1 George Halas OWN/CO (vs. Eagles; 8/5/94) 6.00
2 Doug Atkins, George Connor, George Blanda (vs. Giants; 8/27/94) 2.50
3 Walter Payton (vs. Bucs; 9/4/94) 8.00
4 Dan Fortmann, Mike Ditka, Paddy Driscoll (vs. Vikings; 9/18/94) 5.00
5 Dick Butkus (vs. Bills; 10/2/94) 7.00
6 Bill George, Harold "Red" Grange, Ed Healey (vs. Saints; 10/9/94) 4.00
7 Gale Sayers (vs. Packers; 10/31/94) 7.00
8 Bill Hewitt, Stan Jones, Sid Luckman (vs. Lions; 11/20/94) 3.00
9 Link Lyman, George Musso, George McAfee (vs. Rams; 12/18/94) 2.50
10 Bronko Nagurski, Bulldog Turner, Joe Stydahar, George Trafton (vs. Patriots; 12/24/94) 4.00

1994 Bears Toyota

The two-card, standard-size set was sponsored by Toyota and commemorates October 31, 1994, the day Dick Butkus and Gale Sayers had their jerseys retired by the Bears. The card fronts have a Bears logo in the upper left corner and have a color action shot. The card backs feature a color headshot with a career summary and highlights.

NM/M
Complete Set (2): 16.00
Common Player: 8.00
1 Dick Butkus 8.00
2 Gale Sayers 8.00

1995 Bears Program Sheets

The eight-sheet, 8" x 10" set was inserted in Bears game programs during the 1995 season to commemorate the 10th anniversary of Chicago's Super Bowl XX victory in January of 1986. The fronts contained color action shots of top players including Walter Payton, Jim McMahon and Mike Singletary.

NM/M
Complete Set (8): 40.00
Common Player: 4.00
1 Mike Ditka (9/3/95 vs. Vikings) 6.00
2 Walter Payton (9/11/95 vs. Packers) 8.00
3 Jim McMahon (10/8/95 vs. Panthers) 5.00
4 Mike Singletary, Gary Fencik (10/22/95 vs. Oilers) 5.00
5 Richard Dent (11/5/95 vs. Steelers) 5.00
6 William Perry (11/19/95 vs. Lions) 5.00

7 Otis Wilson (12/17/95 vs. Buccaneers) 4.00
8 Wilber Marshall (12/24/95 vs. Eagles) 4.00

1995 Bears Super Bowl XX 10th Anniversary Kemper

The 20-card, regular-sized set released in 1995, commemorates the Chicago Bears Super Bowl XX win. Issued in conjunction with Kemper Mutual Funds, the fronts feature color action shots with the player's name, position and uniform number along the left border. The card backs have a player closeup with bio statistical information.

NM/M
Complete Set (20): 25.00
Common Player: 1.00
1 Mark Bortz 1.00
2 Kevin Butler 1.00
3 Jim Covert 1.00
4 Richard Dent 1.50
5 Dave Duerson 1.00
6 Gary Fencik 1.00
7 Willie Gault 1.00
8 Dan Hampton 1.00
9 Jay Hilgenberg 1.00
10 Wilber Marshall 1.00
11 Dennis McKinnon 1.00
12 Jim McMahon 2.00
13 Steve McMichael 1.00
14 Walter Payton 4.00
15 William Perry 1.50
16 Mike Singletary 1.50
17 Matt Suhey 1.00
18 Tom Thayer 1.00
19 Keith Van Horne 1.00
20 Otis Wilson 1.00

1995 Bears Super Bowl XX Mont-gomery Ward Cards

The eight-card, regular-sized set was released in conjunction with Montgomery Ward stores and commemorates Chicago's 10th anniversary of a win in Super Bowl XX. The card fronts have a color action shot with a diagonal blue and orange stripe which states the player's name and position. The card backs contain a checklist for the eight cards.

NM/M
Complete Set (8): 12.00
Common Player: 1.00
1 Mike Ditka ('85 Super Bowl) 2.00
2 Kevin Butler 1.00
3 Dan Hampton 1.00
4 Richard Dent 1.50
5 Gary Fencik 1.00
6 Walter Payton 2.50
7 Jim McMahon 1.50
8 Mike Ditka 1.75

1995 Bears Super Bowl XX Mont-gomery Ward Coins

The eight-coin set was released in 1995 in conjunction with Montgomery Ward stores to commemorate Chicago's 10th anniversary of its Super Bowl XX victory. The coins parallel the eight-card set, also released in 1995. The coin fronts depict the player's name and uniform number while the backs have the Super Bowl XX logo.

NM/M
Complete Set (8): 10.00
Common Player: 1.00
1 Kevin Butler 1.00
2 Richard Dent 1.25
3 Mike Ditka CO 1.75
4 Gary Fencik 1.00
5 Dan Hampton 1.00
6 Jim McMahon 1.50
7 Walter Payton 2.50
8 Super Bowl Trophy 1.00

1996 Bears Illinois State Lottery

These cards were Illinois State Lottery scratch-and-win tickets. The tickets feature a color photo of the player. They are usually found scratched.

NM/M
Complete Set (5): 3.00
Common Player: .25
1 Richard Dent .50
2 Mike Ditka 1.00
3 Dan Hampton .50
4 William Perry .25
5 Gale Sayers 1.00

1968 Bengals Team Issue

The Cincinnati Bengals team-issued set consisted of 8-1/2" x 11" cards with a black and white player photo. The player's name and position are below the photo.

NM/M
Complete Set (7): 35.00
Complete Player: 5.00
1 Frank Buncom 5.00
2 Sherrill Headrick 5.00
3 Warren McVea 5.00
4 Fletcher Smith 5.00
5 John Stofa 7.00
6 Dewey Warren 5.00
7 Ernie Wright 7.00

1969 Bengals Tresler Comet

The 20-card, standard-size cards were distributed by Tresler Comet gas stations. The card fronts feature a simulated autograph while the backs contain bio and career highlights. The card backs are not numbered and Bob Johnson's card is unusually higher in value than the other 19 because of its scarcity. Also, future Bengals' coach Sam Wyche is included along with football announcer Bob Trumpy.

NM/M
Complete Set (20): 300.00
Common Player: 5.00
1 Al Beauchamp 5.00
2 Bill Bergey 10.00
3 Royce Berry 5.00
4 Paul Brown CO 35.00
5 Frank Buncom 5.00
6 Greg Cook 10.00
7 Howard Fest SP 25.00
8 Harry Gunner SP 20.00
9 Bobby Hunt 5.00
10 Bob Johnson SP 125.00
11 Charley King 5.00
12 Dale Livingston 5.00
13 Warren McVea SP 25.00
14 Bill Peterson 5.00
15 Jess Phillips 5.00
16 Andy Rice 5.00
17 Bill Staley 5.00
18 Bob Trumpy 20.00
19 Ernie Wright 5.00
20 Sam Wyche 25.00

1960 Bills Team Issue

Issued by the team, this set of 40 black and white 5" x 7" cards were delivered to the 1960 Buffalo Bills season ticketholders. The photos are not numbered and were frequently found autographed.

NM/M
Complete Set (40): 180.00
Common Player: 5.00
1 Bill Atkins 5.00
2 Bob Barrett 5.00
3 Phil Blazer 5.00
4 Bob Brodhead 5.00
5 Dick Brubacher 5.00
6 Bernie Burzinski 5.00
7 Wray Carlton 8.00
8 Don Chelf 5.00
9 Monte Crockett 5.00
10 Bob Dove 5.00
11 Elbert Dubenion 10.00
12 Fred Ford 5.00
13 Dick Gallagher 5.00
14 Darrell Harper 5.00
15 Harvey Johnson 5.00
16 John Johnson 5.00
17 Billy Kinard 5.00
18 Joe Kulbacki 5.00
19 John Laraway 5.00
20 Richie Lucas 10.00
21 Archie Matsos 8.00
22 Richie McCabe 8.00
23 Dan McGrew 5.00
24 Chuck McMurtry 5.00
25 Ed Meyer 5.00
26 Ed Muelhaupt 5.00
27 Tom O'Connell 5.00
28 Harold Olson 5.00
29 Buster Ramsey CO 5.00
30 Floyd Reid 5.00
31 Tom Rychlec 5.00
32 Joe Schaeffer 5.00
33 John Scott 5.00
34 Bob Sedlock 5.00
35 Carl Smith 5.00
36 Jim Sorey 5.00
37 Lavern Torczon 5.00
38 Jim Wagstaff 5.00
39 Ralph Wilson OWN 8.00
40 Mack Yoho 5.00

1963 Bills Jones Dairy

The 40-card, circular cards were available as cardboard cut-outs on milk cartons. The 1" (diameter) discs are frequently found miscut and off-centered and are not numbered.

NM/M
Complete Set (40): 1,000
Common Player: 20.00
1 Ray Abruzzese 20.00
2 Art Baker 20.00
3 Stew Barber 20.00
4 Glenn Bass 20.00
5 Dave Behrman 20.00
6 Al Bemiller 20.00
7 Wray Carlton 20.00
8 Carl Charon 20.00
9 Monte Crockett 20.00
10 Wayne Crow 20.00
11 Tom Day 20.00
12 Elbert Dubenion 25.00
13 Jim Dunaway 20.00
14 Booker Edgerson 20.00
15 Cookie Gilchrist 30.00
16 Dick Hudson 20.00
17 Frank Jackunas 20.00
18 Harry Jacobs 20.00
19 Jack Kemp 375.00
20 Roger Kochman 20.00
21 Daryle Lamonica 85.00
22 Charley Leo 20.00
23 Marv Matuszak 20.00
24 Bill Miller 20.00
25 Leroy Moore 20.00
26 Harold Olson 20.00
27 Herb Paterra 20.00
28 Ken Rice 20.00
29 Henry Rivera 20.00
30 Ed Rutkowski 20.00
31 George Saimes 25.00
32 Tom Sestak 25.00
33 Billy Shaw 25.00
34 Mike Stratton 20.00
35 Gene Sykes 20.00
36 John Tracey 20.00
37 Ernie Warlick 20.00
38 Willie West 20.00
39 Mack Yoho 20.00
40 Sid Youngelman 20.00

1965 Bills Super Duper Markets

The 10-card, 8-1/2" x 11" set was offered as a giveaway from Super Duper food stores in 1965. The fronts contain black and white action (posed) photos and the set is not numbered.

NM/M
Complete Set (10): 180.00
Common Player: 5.00
1 Glenn Bass 5.00
2 Elbert Dubenion 10.00
3 Billy Joe 10.00
4 Jack Kemp 100.00
5 Daryle Lamonica 30.00
6 Tom Sestak 5.00
7 Billy Shaw 10.00
8 Mike Stratton 5.00
9 Ernie Warlick 5.00
10 Team Photo 25.00

1967 Bills Jones-Rich Milk

Through a special mail-in offer, Jones-Rich Milk offered the set of six Buffalo Bills 8-1/2" x 11" cards in 1967.

NM/M
Complete Set (6): 100.00
Common Player: 15.00
1 George (Butch) Byrd 20.00
2 Wray Carlton 20.00
3 Hagood Clarke 15.00
4 Paul Costa 20.00
5 Jim Dunaway 20.00
6 Jack Spikes 20.00

1974 Bills Team Issue

The 12-card, 8-1/2" x 11" photo cards were issued through concession sales at Rich Stadium in Buffalo during the 1974 season.

NM/M
Complete Set (12): 80.00
Common Player: 5.00
1 Jim Braxton 5.00
2 Bob Chandler 8.00
3 Jim Cheyunski 5.00
4 Earl Edwards 5.00
5 Joe Ferguson 12.00
6 Dave Foley 5.00
7 Robert James 5.00
8 Reggie McKenzie 5.00
9 Jerry Patton 5.00
10 Walt Patulski 5.00
11 John Skorupan 5.00
12 O.J. Simpson 30.00

1976 Bills McDonald's

The three-card set was issued by McDonald's in conjunction with WBEN-TV and was given away free with a purchase of a Quarter Pounder hamburger at particpating restaurants. The 8" x 10" color photos included statistical information on the backs.

NM/M
Complete Set (3): 30.00
Common Player: 8.00
1 Bob Chandler 10.00
2 Joe Ferguson 15.00
3 Reggie McKenzie 8.00

1979 Bills Bell's Market

The 11-card, 7-5/8" x 10" photo cards were issued weekly by Bell's Markets during the 1979 season. The cards were printed on thin stock and were not numbered.

NM/M
Complete Set (11): 50.00
Common Player: 4.00
(1) Curtis Brown 4.00
(2) Bob Chandler 5.00
(3) Joe DeLamielleure 4.00
(4) Joe Ferguson 10.00
(5) Reuben Gant 4.00
(6) Dee Hardison 4.00
(7) Frank Lewis 4.00
(8) Reggie McKenzie 5.00
(9) Terry Miller 4.00
(10) Shane Nelson 4.00
(11) Lucius Sanford 4.00

1980 Bills Bell's Market

The 20-card, regular-sized set was issued by Bell's Markets in 1980 and arrived in 20-card packs or two-pack perforation sets. The card fronts contain color shots while the backs have career statistics.

NM/M
Complete Set (20): 9.00
Common Player: .40
1 Curtis Brown .40
2 Shane Nelson .40
3 Jerry Butler .40
4 Joe Ferguson .40
5 Joe Cribbs .40
6 Reggie McKenzie .40
7 Joe Devlin .40
8 Ken Jones .40
9 Steve Freeman .40
10 Mike Kadish .40
11 Jim Haslett .40
12 Isiah Robertson .40
13 Frank Lewis .40
14 Jeff Nixon .40
15 Nick Mike-Mayer .40
16 Jim Ritcher .40
17 Charles Romes .40
18 Fred Smerlas .40
19 Ben Williams .40
20 Roland Hooks .40

1986 Bills Sealtest

The six-card, 3-5/8" x 7-5/8" set was issued on sides of half-gallon Sealtest milk containers. The Freeman and Marve cards were found on vitamin D cartons while the Kelly and Romes cards appeared on lowfat (2%) cartons. The cards featured a black and white player headshot with bio information and stats.

NM/M
Complete Set (6): 30.00
Common Player: 1.50
1 Greg Bell SP 5.00
2 Jerry Butler SP 5.00
3 Steve Freeman 1.50
4 Jim Kelly 20.00
5 Eugene Marve 1.50
6 Charles Romes 1.50

1987 Bills Police

The eight-card, 2-5/8" x 4-1/8" set was sponsored by the Bills, Erie and Niagara County Sheriff's Departments, Louis Rich Turkey products, Claussen Pickles and WBEN radio. The black and white photos on the card fronts were taken by Robert L. Smith, the Bills' official team photographer.

NM/M
Complete Set (8): 8.00
Common Player: .50
1 Marv Levy CO 1.00
2 Bruce Smith 2.00
3 Joe Devlin .50
4 Jim Kelly 3.00
5 Eugene Marve .50
6 Andre Reed 1.00
7 Pete Metzelaars .50
8 John Kidd .50

1988 Bills Police

The eight-card, 2-5/8" x 4-1/8" set was sponsored by the Bills, Erie and Niagara County Sheriff's Departments, Louis Rich Turkey Products and WBEN radio. The fronts feature an action photo while the backs have bio and stat information.

NM/M
Complete Set (8): 5.00
Common Player: .75
1 Steve Tasker 1.50
2 Cornelius Bennett 2.00
3 Shane Conlan .75
4 Mark Kelso .75
5 Will Wolford .75
6 Chris Burkett .75
7 Kent Hull .75
8 Art Still .75

1989 Bills Police

The eight-card, regular-sized set was issued in conjunction with the Bills, Erie County Sheriff's Department and Louis Rich Turkey Products. The card fronts feature an action shot while the backs contain bio and stat information.

NM/M
Complete Set (8): 8.00
Common Player: .75
1 Leon Seals .75
2 Thurman Thomas 4.00
3 Jim Ritcher .75
4 Scott Norwood .75
5 Darryl Talley 1.00
6 Nate Odomes .75
7 Leonard Smith .75
8 Ray Bentley .75

1990 Bills Police

The eight-card, 4" x 6" set was sponsored by Blue Shield of New York. The card fronts feature a color action photo and the card backs contain highlights and career statistics.

NM/M
Complete Set (8): 8.00
Common Player: .50
1 Carlton Bailey .50
2 Kirby Jackson .50
3 Jim Kelly 4.00
4 James Lofton 1.00
5 Keith McKeller .50
6 Mark Pike .50
7 Andre Reed 1.00
8 Jeff Wright .50

1991 Bills Police

The eight-card, regular-sized set was sponsored by Blue Shield of New York. The card fronts feature an action shot and bio information while the backs contain highlights and career statistics.

NM/M
Complete Set (8): 5.00
Common Player: .75
1 Howard Ballard .75
2 Don Beebe 1.50
3 John Davis .75
4 Kenneth Davis 1.00
5 Mark Kelso .75
6 Frank Reich 1.50
7 Butch Rolle .75
8 J.D. Williams .75

1992 Bills Police

The seven-card, 4" x 6" set was sponsored by Blue Shield of New York. The card fronts feature an action photo and bio information while the backs have highlights and stats.

NM/M
Complete Set (7): 5.00
Common Player: .50
1 Carlton Bailey .50
2 Steve Christie .50
3 Shane Conlan .75
4 Phil Hansen .50
5 Henry Jones .75
6 Chris Mohr .50
7 Thurman Thomas 3.00

1994 Bills Police

The six-card, 3" x 5" set was sponsored by the Erie County Sheriff's Office and Coca-Cola. The card fronts feature color action shots with the Bills logo in the lower left corner. The backs feature a headshot with biographical and statistical information with "Tips from the Sheriff."

NM/M
Complete Set (6): 5.00
Common Player: .50
1 Bill Brooks 1.25
2 Kenneth Davis 1.00
3 John Fina .50
4 Phil Hansen .75
5 Pete Metzelaars 1.00
6 Marvcus Patton .75

1995 Bills Police

The six-card, 4" x 6" set was sponsored by the Erie County Sheriff's Office and Coca-Cola. The card fronts feature a color action shot with the Bills logo in the upper left corner. The card backs have a headshot with bio and stat information and a safety tip.

NM/M
Complete Set (6): 5.00
Common Player: .50
1 Jeff Burris .75
2 Joe Ferguson (All-Time Great) 1.50
3 Kent Hull .50
4 Adam Lingner .50
5 Glenn Parker .50
6 Andre Reed 2.50

1996 Bills Police

Coca-Cola and the Erie County Sheriff's Office sponsored this five-card set of the Buffalo Bills. The cards are 4" x 6" and feature a color player photo and the sponsors' logos on the front.

NM/M
Complete Set (5): 4.00
Common Player: .75
24 Kurt Schulz .75
55 Mark Maddox .75
79 Ruben Brown 1.25
94 Mark Pike .75
95 Bryce Paup 1.50

1993-94 Bleachers Troy Aikman Promos

The four-card, standard-size promo set highlights the Dallas Cowboys quarterback in his UCLA uniform. Ten-thousand sets were produced and the card backs feature the same card-front image ghosted behind a text of career highlights. Card #4 was an exclusive promo for the 1994 Houston Tri-Star show and features "Houston 1994" in gold foil.

NM/M
Complete Set (4): 10.00
Common Player: 2.50
1 Troy Aikman (Exclusive promo) 2.50
2 Troy Aikman (UCLA) 2.50
3 Troy Aikman (UCLA) (Comicfest '93) 2.50
4 Troy Aikman (UCLA) (Houston '94) 2.50

1993 Bleachers 23K Troy Aikman

This three-card set is sequentially-numbered to 10,000. The cards feature color photos of Aikman, a facsimile autograph printed in gold foil and golden borders. A promo card with Aikman pictured in his Cowboy uniform was also produced.

NM/M
Complete Set (3): 20.00
Common Player: 5.00
1 Troy Aikman (Oklahoma) 5.00
2 Troy Aikman (UCLA) 5.00
3 Troy Aikman (Cowboys) 5.00
P1 Troy Aikman Promo (Cowboys) 5.00

1994 Bleachers 23K Troy Aikman

The three-card, standard-sized set features the Dallas Cowboys quarterback in collegiate color photos (#1 and #2) and a pro shot with Dallas (#3). The card fronts have a gold-foil border along with his name, team and position in gold on the bottom edge. The card backs are numbered in production "x of 10,000" and in the set "x of 3" and feature a facsimile Aikman autograph.

NM/M
Complete Set (3): 15.00
Common Player: 5.00
1 Troy Aikman (Oklahoma) 5.00
2 Troy Aikman (UCLA) 5.00
3 Troy Aikman 5.00

1995 Bleachers 23K Emmitt Smith

The four-card, regular-sized set features the Dallas Cowboys running back in high school (#1), college (#2) and Dallas (#3). The card fronts feature a gold border while the card backs are numbered in production as "x of 10,000." A promo card, not numbered, featured Smith in his collegiate uniform.

NM/M
Complete Set (3): 30.00
Common Player: 10.00
1 Emmitt Smith (Escambia High School) 10.00
2 Emmitt Smith (Florida Gators) 10.00
3 Emmitt Smith 10.00
NNO Emmitt Smith (Promo) (Escambia High School) 3.00

1983 Blitz Chicago

The eight-sheet, 10" x 8" set featured the United States Football League team. One set contains the coaching staff, including head coach George Allen, while the other seven feature the players. The sheets are unnumbered and the individual photos on the sheets are approximately 2-1/4" x 2-1/2".

NM/M
Complete Set (8): 35.00
Common Player: 4.50
1 George Allen, Joe Haering, Paul Lanham, John Payne, John Teerlink, Dick Walker, Charlie Waller, Ray Wietecha Coaching Staff 4.50
2 Luther Bradley, Eddie Brown, Virgil Livers, Frank Minnifield, Lance Sheilds, Don Schwartz, Maurice Tyler, Ted Walton 4.50
3 Mack Boatner, Frank Collins, Frank Corral, Doug Cozen, Doug Dennison, John Roveto, Jim Stone, Tim Wrightman 4.50
4 Robert Barnes, Bruce Branch, Nick Eyre, Tim Norman, Wally Pesuit, Mark Stevenson, Rob Taylor, Steve Tobin 4.50
5 Junior Ah You, Mark Buben, Bob Cobb, Joe Ehrmann, Kit Lathrop, Karl Lorch, Troy Thomas 4.50
6 Jim Fahnhorst, Joe Federspiel, Doak Field, Bruce Gheesling, Andy Melontree, Ed Smith, Stan White, Kari Yli-Renko 4.50
7 Marcus Anderson, Larry Douglas, Mark May, Pat Schmidt, Lenny Willis, Warren Anderson, Chris Pagnucco, Bruce Allen GM 4.50

1948 Bowman

Considered to be the first true football set of the modern era, the 1948 Bowman set included only players from the National Football League (the first set to do so). Each of the 108 cards measures 2-1/16" x 2-1/2" and shows a player photo on the front with no name or team name. Backs have biographical information. This set was printed on three separate sheets, with the first sheet being plentiful, the second a little scarcer, and the third very difficult to find. So cards numbered 1, 4, 7, 10, etc., are easiest to find; cards numbered 2, 5, 8, 11, etc., are somewhat harder, and those divisble by three (3, 6, 9, 12, etc.) are extremely tough to find. Rookie cards in this set include Hall of Famers Steve Van Buren, Charley Trippi, Sammy Baugh, Bob Waterfield, Bulldog Turner, Alex Wojciechowicz, Pete Pihos, Bill Dudley, George McAfee and Sid Luckman. Other star rookie cards include Johnny Lujack and Charlie Conerly.

NM/M
Complete Set (108): 6,000
Common Player: 30.00
SP Cards: 50.00
1 *Joe Tereshinski* 150.00
2 Larry Olsonoski 30.00
3 *John Lujack* 320.00
4 Ray Poole 30.00
5 Bill DeCorrevont 30.00
6 Paul Briggs 100.00
7 *Steve Van Buren* 150.00
8 *Kenny Washington* 50.00
9 Nolan Luhn 100.00
10 Chris Iversen 30.00
11 Jack Wiley 30.00
12 *Charlie Conerly* 320.00
13 *Hugh Taylor* 30.00
14 Frank Seno 30.00
15 Gil Bouley 100.00
16 *Tommy Thompson* 30.00
17 *Charlie Trippi* 100.00
18 Vince Banonis 100.00
19 Art Faircloth 30.00
20 Clyde Goodnight 30.00
21 Bill Chipley 100.00
22 *Sammy Baugh* 425.00
23 Don Kindt 30.00
24 John Koniszewski 100.00
25 Pat McHugh 30.00
26 *Bob Waterfield* 200.00
27 Tony Compagno 100.00
28 Paul Governali 30.00
29 *Pat Harder* 40.00
30 Vic Lindskog 100.00
31 Salvatore Rosato 30.00
32 John Mastrangelo 30.00
33 Fred Gehrke 100.00
34 Bosh Pritchard 30.00
35 Mike Micka 30.00
36 *Bulldog Turner* 250.00
37 Len Younce 30.00
38 Pat West 30.00
39 Russ Thomas 100.00
40 James Peebles 30.00
41 Bob Skoglund 30.00
42 Wat Stickle 100.00
43 *Whitey Wistert* 30.00
44 *Paul Christman* 45.00
45 Jay Rhodemyre 100.00
46 Skip Minisi 30.00
47 Bob Mann 30.00
48 Mal Kutner 100.00
49 Dick Poillon 30.00
50 Charles Cherundolo 30.00
51 Gerald Cowhig 100.00
52 *Neil Armstrong* 30.00
53 Frak Maznicki 30.00
54 John Sanchez 100.00
55 Frank Reagan 30.00
56 Jim Hardy 30.00
57 John Badaczewski 100.00
58 Robert Nussbaumer 30.00
59 Marvin Pregulman 30.00
60 *Elbert Nickel* 125.00
61 *Alex Wojciechowicz* 75.00
62 Walt Shclinkman 30.00
63 *Pete Pihos* 220.00
64 Joseph Sulaitis 30.00
65 *Mike Holovak* 50.00
66 Cecil Souders 100.00
67 Paul McKee 30.00
68 Bill Moore 30.00
69 Frank Minini 100.00
70 Jack Ferrante 30.00
71 *Leslie Horvath* 40.00
72 Ted Fritsch, Sr. 100.00
73 Tex Coulter 30.00
74 Boley Dancewicz 30.00
75 Dante Mangani 100.00
76 James Hefti 30.00
77 Paul Sarringhaus 30.00
78 Joe Scott 100.00
79 *Bucko Kilroy* 30.00
80 *Bill Dudley* 100.00
81 Marshall Goldberg 100.00
82 John Cannady 30.00
83 Perry Moss 30.00
84 Harold Crisler 100.00
85 Bill Gray 30.00
86 John Clement 30.00
87 Dan Sandifer 100.00
88 Ben Kish 30.00
89 Herbert Banta 30.00
90 Bill Garnaas 100.00
91 Jim White 30.00
92 Frank Barzilauskas 30.00
93 Vic Sears 100.00
94 John Adams 30.00
95 *George McAfee* 100.00
96 Ralph Heywood 100.00
97 Joe Muha 30.00
98 Fred Enke 30.00
99 *Harry Gilmer* 160.00
100 Bill Miklich 30.00
101 Joe Gottlieb 30.00
102 Bud Angsman 100.00
103 Tom Farmer 30.00
104 *Bruce F. Smith* 50.00
105 Bob Cifers 100.00
106 Ernie Steele 30.00
107 *Sid Luckman* 220.00
108 *Buford Ray* 350.00
--- Album 450.00

1950 Bowman

After a one-year absence, Bowman returned to football cards with the first of four straight 144-card sets. As with the '48 Bowman set, cards showed only the player on the front without any identification. Cards again measured 2-1/16" x 2-1/2". Rookie cards in this set include Y.A. Tittle, Lou Groza, Tony Canadeo, Joe Perry, Marion Motley, Otto Graham, Tom Fears, Elroy Hirsch, Dante Lavelli, Tobin Rote and Dub Jones.

NM/M
Complete Set (144): 4,250
Common Player: 30.00
1 Doak Walker 200.00
2 John Greene 30.00
3 Bob Nowasky 30.00
4 Jonathan Jenkins 30.00
5 *Y.A. Tittle* 400.00
6 *Lou Groza* 225.00
7 *Alex Agase* 30.00
8 *Mac Speedie* 35.00
9 *Tony Canadeo* 55.00
10 Larry Craig 30.00
11 Ted Fritsch, Sr. 30.00
12 Joe Goldring 30.00
13 Martin Ruby 30.00
14 George Taliaferro 30.00
15 *Tank Younger* 50.00
16 *Glenn Davis* 150.00
17 Bob Waterfield 75.00
18 Val Jansante 30.00
19 Joe Geri 30.00
20 Jerry Nuzum 30.00
21 Elmer Angsman 30.00
22 Billy Dewell 30.00
23 Steve Van Buren 60.00
24 Cliff Patton 30.00
25 Bosh Pritchard 30.00
26 John Lujack 60.00
27 Sid Luckman 125.00
28 Bulldog Turner 45.00
29 Bill Dudley 45.00
30 Hugh Taylor 30.00
31 George Thomas 30.00
32 Ray Poole 30.00
33 Travis Tidwell 30.00
34 Gail Bruce 30.00
35 *Joe Perry* 200.00
36 *Frankie Albert* 35.00
37 Bobby Layne 200.00
38 Leon Hart 30.00
39 Bob Hoernschemeyer 30.00
40 *Dick Barwegan* 30.00
41 *Adrian Burk* 30.00
42 Barry French 30.00
43 *Marion Motley* 150.00
44 Jim Martin 30.00
45 *Otto Graham* 450.00
46 Al Baldwin 30.00
47 Larry Coutre 30.00
48 John Rauch 30.00
49 Sam Tamburo 30.00
50 Mike Swistowicz 30.00
51 *Tom Fears* 80.00
52 *Elroy Hirsch* 200.00
53 Dick Huffman 30.00
54 Bob Cage 30.00
55 Bob Tinsley 30.00
56 Bill Blackburn 30.00
57 John Cochran 30.00
58 Bill Fischer 30.00
59 Whitey Wistert 30.00
60 Clyde Scott 30.00
61 Walter Barnes 30.00
62 Bob Perina 30.00
63 Bill Wightkin 30.00
64 Bob Goode 30.00
65 Al Demao 30.00
66 Harry Gilmer 30.00
67 Bill Austin 30.00
68 Joe Scott 30.00
69 Tex Coulter 30.00
70 Paul Salata 30.00
71 Emil Sitko 30.00
72 Bill Johnson 30.00
73 *Don Doll* 30.00
74 Dan Sandifer 30.00
75 John Panelli 30.00
76 Bill Leonard 30.00
77 Bob Kelly 30.00
78 *Dante Lavelli* 100.00
79 Tony Adamle 30.00
80 Dick Wildung 30.00
81 *Tobin Rote* 35.00
82 Paul Burris 30.00
83 Lowell Tew 30.00
84 Barney Poole 30.00
85 Fred Naumetz 30.00
86 Dick Hoerner 30.00
87 Bob Reinhard 30.00
88 Howard Hartley 30.00
89 Darrell Hogan 30.00
90 Jerry Shipkey 30.00
91 Frank Tripucka 30.00
92 Garrard Ramsey 30.00
93 Pat Harder 30.00
94 Vic Sears 30.00
95 Tommy Thompson 30.00
96 Bucko Kilroy 30.00
97 George Connor 35.00
98 Fred Morrison 30.00
99 Jim Keane 30.00
100 Sammy Baugh 300.00
101 Harry Ulinski 30.00
102 Frank Spaniel 30.00
103 Charlie Conerly 60.00
104 Dick Hensley 30.00
105 Eddie Price 30.00
106 Ed Carr 30.00
107 Leo Nomellini 60.00
108 Verl Lillywhite 30.00
109 Wallace Triplett 30.00
110 Joe Watson 30.00
111 *Cloyce Box* 30.00
112 Billy Stone 30.00
113 Earl Murray 30.00
114 *Chet Mutryn* 30.00
115 Ken Carpenter 30.00
116 *Lou Rymkus* 30.00
117 *Dub Jones* 30.00
118 Clayton Tonnemaker 30.00
119 Walt Schlinkman 30.00
120 Billy Grimes 30.00
121 *George Ratterman* 30.00
122 Bob Mann 30.00
123 *Buddy Young* 50.00
124 Jack Zilly 30.00
125 Tom Kalmanir 30.00
126 Frank Sinkovitz 30.00
127 Elbert Nickel 30.00
128 *Jim Finks* 45.00
129 Charlie Trippi 45.00
130 Tom Wham 30.00
131 Ventan Yablonski 30.00
132 Chuck Bednarik 75.00
133 Joe Muha 30.00
134 Pete Pihos 45.00
135 Washington Serini 30.00
136 George Gulyanics 30.00
137 Ken Kavanaugh 30.00
138 Howie Livingston 30.00
139 Joe Tereshinski 30.00
140 Jim White 30.00
141 Gene Roberts 30.00
142 William Swiacki 30.00
143 Norm Standlee 30.00
144 *Knox Ramsey* 60.00

1951 Bowman

Bowman's third set was again 144 cards, but cards were increased in size to 2-1/16" x 3-1/8". Cards bear a close similarity to this year's Bowman baseball set on both fronts and backs. Rookies in this set include Norm Van Brocklin, Tom Landry, Arnie Weinmeister, Bill Walsh, Emlen Tunnell, and Ernie Stautner.

NM/M
Complete Set (144): 3,500
Common Player: 30.00
1 *Weldon Humble* 75.00
2 Otto Graham 200.00
3 Mac Speedie 30.00
4 *Norm Van Brocklin* 250.00
5 Woodley Lewis 30.00
6 Tom Fears 35.00
7 George Musacco 30.00
8 George Taliaferro 30.00
9 Barney Poole 30.00
10 Steve Van Buren 60.00
11 Whitey Wistert 30.00
12 Chuck Bednarik 70.00
13 Bulldog Turner 70.00
14 Bob Williams 30.00
15 John Lujack 70.00
16 Roy "Rebel" Steiner 30.00
17 Earl "Jug" Girard 30.00
18 Bill Neal 30.00
19 Travis Tidwell 30.00
20 *Tom Landry* 500.00
21 *Arnie Weinmeister* 90.00
22 Joe Geri 30.00
23 *Bill Walsh* 30.00
24 Fran Rogel 30.00
25 Doak Walker 70.00
26 Leon Hart 30.00
27 Thurman McGraw 30.00
28 Buster Ramsey 30.00
29 Frank Tripucka 30.00
30 Don Paul 30.00
31 Alex Loyd 30.00
32 Y.A. Tittle 120.00
33 Verl Lillywhite 30.00
34 Sammy Baugh 150.00
35 Chuck Drazenovich 30.00
36 Bob Goode 30.00
37 Horace Gillom 30.00
38 Lou Rymkus 30.00
39 Ken Carpenter 30.00
40 Bob Waterfield 75.00
41 Vitamin Smith 30.00
42 Glenn Davis 60.00
43 Dan Edwards 30.00
44 John Rauch 30.00
45 Zollie Toth 30.00
46 Pete Pihos 30.00
47 Russ Craft 30.00
48 Walter Barnes 30.00
49 Fred Morrison 30.00
50 Ray Bray 30.00
51 *Ed Sprinkle* 30.00
52 Floyd Reid 30.00
53 Billy Grimes 30.00
54 Ted Fritsch, Sr. 30.00
55 Al DeRogatis 30.00
56 Charlie Conerly 60.00
57 Jon Baker 30.00
58 Tom McWilliams 30.00
59 Jerry Shipkey 30.00
60 Lynn Chandnois 30.00
61 Don Doll 30.00
62 Lou Creekmur 35.00
63 Bob Hoernschemeyer 30.00
64 Tom Wham 30.00
65 Bill Fischer 30.00
66 Robert Nussbaumer 30.00
67 Gordon Soltau 30.00
68 Visco Grgich 30.00
69 John Strzykalski 30.00
70 Pete Stout 30.00
71 Paul Lipscomb 30.00
72 Harry Gilmer 30.00
73 Dante Lavelli 40.00
74 Dub Jones 30.00
75 Lou Groza 100.00
76 Elroy Hirsch 90.00
77 Tom Kalmanir 30.00
78 Jack Zilly 30.00
79 Bruce Alford 30.00
80 Art Weiner 30.00
81 Brad Ecklund 30.00
82 Bosh Pritchard 30.00
83 John Green 30.00
84 H. Ebert Van Buren 30.00
85 Julie Rykovich 30.00
86 Fred Davis 30.00
87 John Hoffman 30.00
88 Tobin Rote 30.00
89 Paul Burris 30.00
90 Tony Canadeo 30.00
91 *Emlen Tunnell* 125.00
92 Otto Schnellbacher 30.00
93 Ray Poole 30.00
94 Darrell Hogan 30.00
95 Frank Sinkovitz 30.00
96 Ernie Stautner 90.00
97 Elmer Angsman 30.00
98 Jack Jennings 30.00
99 Jerry Groom 30.00
100 John Prchlik 30.00
101 J. Robert Smith 30.00
102 Bobby Layne 140.00
103 Frankie Albert 30.00
104 Gail Bruce 30.00
105 Joe Perry 75.00
106 Leon Heath 30.00
107 Ed Quirk 30.00
108 Hugh Taylor 30.00
109 Marion Motley 100.00
110 Tony Adamle 30.00
111 Alex Agase 30.00
112 Tank Younger 30.00
113 Bob Boyd 30.00
114 Jerry Williams 30.00
115 Joe Goldring 30.00
116 Sherman Howard 30.00
117 John Wozniak 30.00
118 Frank Reagan 30.00
119 Vic Sears 30.00
120 Clyde Scott 30.00
121 George Gulyanics 30.00
122 Bill Wightkin 30.00
123 Chuck Hunsinger 30.00
124 Jack Cloud 30.00
125 Abner Wimberly 30.00
126 Dick Wildung 30.00
127 Eddie Price 30.00
128 Joe Scott 30.00
129 Jerry Nuzum 30.00
130 Jim Finks 40.00
131 Bob Gage 30.00
132 William Swiacki 30.00
133 Joe Watson 30.00
134 Ollie Cline 30.00
135 Jack Lininger 30.00
136 Fran Polsfoot 30.00
137 Charlie Trippi 40.00
138 Ventan Yablonski 30.00
139 Emil Sitko 40.00
140 Leo Nomellini 80.00
141 Norm Standlee 30.00
142 Eddie Saenz 30.00
143 Al Demao 30.00
144 Bill Dudley 75.00

1952 Bowman Large

The player selection in the "Large" set exactly matches Bowman's 1952 "Small" issue. The card size, however, was increased from 2-1/16" x 3-1/8" to 2-1/2" x 3-3/4". A problem surfaced for Bowman while trying to produce the larger set: the company could not fit all the larger cards on one sheet the way it could with the smaller set. So certain cards were pulled. The short-printed cards are those with a factor of nine plus the card immediately following that number. In addition, the second series was issued in lesser quantities than the first. The 1952 Bowman Large set is easily the most valuable football card set ever produced. Card #144, Jim "Buck" Lansford, is practically impossible to find in mint condition, first because it was an odd number on the last sheet, second because it was the last card in the set.

NM/M
Complete Set (144): 12,000
Common Player (1-72): 30.00
Common Player (73-144): 40.00
1 Norm Van Brocklin 425.00
2 Otto Graham 275.00
3 Doak Walker 75.00
4 *Steve Owen* 50.00
5 Frankie Albert 30.00
6 Laurie Niemi 40.00
7 Chuck Hunsinger 40.00
8 Ed Modzelewski 30.00
9 Joe Spencer (SP) 125.00
10 Chuck Bednarik (SP) 350.00
11 Barney Poole 40.00
12 Charlie Trippi 50.00
13 Tom Fears 50.00
14 *Paul Brown* 225.00
15 Leon Hart 30.00
16 *Frank Gifford* 475.00
17 Y.A. Tittle 175.00
18 Charlie Justice (SP) 525.00
19 George Connor (SP) 250.00
20 Lynn Chandnois 40.00
21 *Bill Howton* 50.00
22 Kenneth Snyder 40.00
23 *Gino Marchetti* 200.00
24 John Karras 40.00
25 Tank Younger 50.00
26 Tommy Thompson 40.00
27 *Bob Miller* (SP) 350.00
28 *Kyle Rote* (SP) 225.00
29 *Hugh McElhenny* 200.00
30 Sammy Baugh 350.00
31 Jim Dooley 40.00
32 Ray Matthews 40.00
33 Fred Cone 40.00
34 Al Pollard 40.00
35 Brad Ecklund 40.00
36 *John Lee Hancock* 350.00
37 Elroy Hirsch (SP) 250.00
38 Keever Jankovich 40.00
39 Emlen Tunnell 60.00
40 Steve Dowden 40.00
41 Claude Hipps 40.00
42 Norm Standlee 40.00
43 Dick Todd 40.00
44 Babe Parilli 30.00
45 Steve Van Buren (SP) 300.00
46 *Art Donovan* (SP) 400.00
47 Bill Fischer 40.00
48 *George Halas* 275.00
49 Jerrell Price 40.00
50 *John Sandusky* 50.00
51 Ray Beck 40.00
52 Jim Martin 40.00
53 Joe Back 40.00
54 Glen Christian (SP) 75.00
55 Andy Davis (SP) 75.00
56 Tobin Rote 30.00
57 *Wayne Millner* 70.00
58 Zollie Toth 40.00
59 Jack Jennings 40.00
60 Bill McColl 40.00
61 *Les Richter* 30.00
62 *Walt Michaels* 30.00
63 Charlie Conerly (SP) 500.00
64 Howard Hartley (SP) 125.00
65 Jerome Smith 40.00
66 James Clark 40.00
67 Dick Logan 40.00
68 Wayne Robinson 40.00
69 James Hammond 40.00
70 Gene Schroeder 40.00
71 Tex Coulter 40.00
72 *John Schweder* (SP) 500.00
73 Vitamin Smith (SP) 200.00
74 Joe Campanella 50.00
75 *Joe Kuharich* 50.00
76 Herman Clark 50.00
77 Dan Edwards 50.00
78 Bobby Layne 225.00
79 Bob Hoernschemeyer 50.00
80 John Carr Blount 50.00
81 John Kastan (SP) 200.00
82 *Harry Minarik* (SP) 200.00
83 Joe Perry 80.00
84 Ray Parker 50.00
85 *Andy Robustelli* 175.00
86 Dub Jones 40.00
87 Mal Cook 50.00
88 Billy Stone 50.00
89 George Taliaferro 50.00
90 Thomas Johnson (SP) 200.00
91 Leon Heath (SP) 200.00
92 Pete Pihos 75.00
93 Fred Benners 50.00
94 George Tarasovic 50.00
95 Lawrence Shaw 50.00
96 Bill Wightkin 50.00
97 John Wozniak 50.00
98 Bobby Dillon 50.00
99 *Joe Stydahar* (SP) 575.00
100 Dick Alban (SP) 200.00
101 Arnie Weinmeister 55.00
102 Robert Joe Cross 50.00
103 Don Paul 50.00
104 Buddy Young 50.00
105 Lou Groza 100.00
106 Ray Pelfrey 50.00
107 Maurice Nipp 50.00
108 *Hubert Johnston* 625.00
109 Volney Quinlan (SP) 200.00
110 Jack Simmons 50.00
111 George Ratterman 50.00
112 John Badaczewski 50.00
113 Bill Reichardt 50.00
114 Art Weiner 50.00
115 Keith Flowers 50.00
116 Russ Craft 50.00
117 Jim O'Donahue (SP) 200.00
118 Darrell Hogan (SP) 200.00
119 Frank Ziegler 50.00
120 Deacon Dan Towler 40.00
121 Fred Williams 50.00
122 Jimmy Phelan 50.00
123 Eddie Price 50.00
124 Chet Ostrowski 50.00
125 Leo Nomellini 70.00
126 *Steve Romanik* (SP) 300.00
127 *Ollie Matson* (SP) 300.00
128 Dante Lavelli 75.00
129 *Jack Christiansen* 150.00
130 Dom Moselle 50.00
131 John Rapacz 50.00
132 Chuck Ortman 50.00
133 Bob Williams 50.00
134 Chuck Ulrich 50.00
135 *Gene Ronzani* (SP) 625.00
136 Bert Rechichar (SP) 200.00
137 Bob Waterfield 120.00
138 *Bobby Walston* 40.00
139 Jerry Shipkey 50.00
140 *Yale Lary* 150.00
141 Gordon Soltau 40.00
142 Tom Landry 600.00
143 John Papit 50.00
144 *Jim Lansford* (SP) 3,000

1952 Bowman Small

This set was issued in two sizes, large and small, with the large size being much more scarce and expensive. The Bowman Small set measures 2-1/16" x 3-1/8", and cards feature a flag motif, with flags pointing to the right (two years later, Bowman would use about the same theme, with flags pointing left). This 144-card set features an abundance of rookie cards. They include Steve Owen, Paul Brown, Frank Gifford, Gino Marchetti, Kyle Rote, Hugh McElhenny, George Halas, Wayne Millner, Walt Michaels, Andy Robustelli, Joe Stydahar, Ollie Matson and Yale Lary.

NM/M
Complete Set (144): 5,000
Common Player (1-72): 25.00
Common Player (73-144): 35.00
1 Norm Van Brocklin 240.00
2 Otto Graham 125.00
3 Doak Walker 50.00
4 *Steve Owen* 35.00
5 Frankie Albert 25.00
6 Laurie Niemi 25.00
7 Chuck Hunsinger 25.00
8 Ed Modzelewski 25.00
9 Joe Spencer 25.00
10 Chuck Bednarik 60.00
11 Barney Poole 25.00
12 Charlie Trippi 30.00
13 Tom Fears 30.00
14 *Paul Brown* 125.00
15 Leon Hart 25.00
16 *Frank Gifford* 325.00
17 Y.A. Tittle 80.00
18 Charlie Justice 30.00

19 George Connor 30.00
20 Lynn Chandnois 25.00
21 *Bill Howton* 30.00
22 Kenneth Snyder 25.00
23 *Gino Marchetti* 100.00
24 John Karras 25.00
25 Tank Younger 25.00
26 Tommy Thompson 25.00
27 Bob Miller 25.00
28 *Kyle Rote* 50.00
29 *Hugh McElhenny* 125.00
30 Sammy Baugh 160.00
31 Jim Dooley 25.00
32 Ray Matthews 25.00
33 Fred Cone 25.00
34 Al Pollard 25.00
35 Brad Ecklund 25.00
36 John Lee Hancock 25.00
37 Elroy Hirsch 50.00
38 Keever Jankovich 25.00
39 Emlen Tunnell 35.00
40 Steve Dowden 25.00
41 Claude Hipps 25.00
42 Norm Standlee 25.00
43 Dick Todd 25.00
44 Babe Parilli 25.00
45 Steve Van Buren 45.00
46 *Art Donovan* 150.00
47 Bill Fischer 25.00
48 *George Halas* 150.00
49 Jerrell Price 25.00
50 John Sandusky 25.00
51 Ray Beck 25.00
52 Jim Martin 25.00
53 Joe Back 25.00
54 Glen Christian 25.00
55 Andy Davis 25.00
56 Tobin Rote 35.00
57 *Wayne Millner* 35.00
58 Zollie Toth 25.00
59 Jack Jennings 25.00
60 Bill McColl 25.00
61 *Les Richter* 35.00
62 *Walt Michaels* 35.00
63 Charlie Conerly 50.00
64 Howard Hartley 25.00
65 Jerome Smith 25.00
66 James Clark 25.00
67 Dick Logan 25.00
68 Wayne Robinson 25.00
69 James Hammond 25.00
70 Gene Schroeder 25.00
71 Tex Coulter 25.00
72 John Schweder 25.00
73 Vitamin Smith 35.00
74 Joe Campanella 35.00
75 Joe Kuharich 35.00
76 Herman Clark 35.00
77 Dan Edwards 35.00
78 Bobby Layne 90.00
79 Bob Hoernschemeyer 35.00
80 John Carr Blount 35.00
81 John Kastan 35.00
82 Harry Minarik 35.00
83 Joe Perry 60.00
84 Ray Parker 35.00
85 *Andy Robustelli* 100.00
86 Dub Jones 35.00
87 Mal Cook 35.00
88 Billy Stone 35.00
89 George Taliaferro 35.00
90 Thomas Johnson 35.00
91 Leon Heath 35.00
92 Pete Pihos 40.00
93 Fred Benners 35.00
94 George Tarasovic 35.00
95 Lawrence Shaw 35.00
96 Bill Wightkin 35.00
97 John Wozniak 35.00
98 *Bobby Dillon* 35.00
99 *Joe Stydahar* 40.00
100 Dick Alban 35.00
101 Arnie Weinmeister 35.00
102 Robert Joe Cross 35.00
103 Don Paul 35.00
104 Buddy Young 30.00
105 Lou Groza 50.00
106 Ray Pelfrey 35.00
107 Maurice Nipp 35.00
108 Hubert Johnston 35.00
109 Volney Quinlan 35.00
110 Jack Simmons 35.00
111 George Ratterman 35.00
112 John Badaczewski 35.00
113 Bill Reichardt 35.00
114 Art Weiner 35.00
115 Keith Flowers 35.00
116 Russ Craft 35.00
117 Jim O'Donahue 35.00
118 Darrell Hogan 35.00
119 Frank Ziegler 35.00
120 Deacon Dan Towler 30.00
121 Fred Williams 35.00
122 Jimmy Phelan 35.00
123 Eddie Price 35.00
124 Chet Ostrowski 35.00
125 Leo Nomellini 70.00
126 Steve Romanik 35.00
127 *Ollie Matson* 120.00
128 Dante Lavelli 40.00
129 *Jack Christiansen* 75.00
130 Dom Moselle 35.00
131 John Rapacz 35.00
132 Chuck Ortman 35.00
133 Bob Williams 35.00
134 Chuck Ulrich 35.00
135 *Gene Ronzani* 28.00
136 Bert Rechichar 35.00
137 Bob Waterfield 60.00
138 *Bobby Walston* 30.00
139 Jerry Shipkey 35.00
140 *Yale Lary* 80.00
141 Gordon Soltau 35.00
142 Tom Landry 300.00
143 John Papit 35.00
144 *Jim Lansford* 125.00

1953 Bowman

The "name in a football" theme was one that would next be used by Topps in its 1960 set and again in the 1976 set. Bowman was the only company to issue football cards, but only a 96-card issue was produced (and 24 of those were short-printed).

NM/M
Complete Set (96): 3,200
Common Player: 25.00
SP Cards: 40.00
1 *Eddie LeBaron* 100.00
2 John Dottley 25.00
3 Babe Parilli 25.00
4 Bucko Kilroy 25.00
5 Joe Tereshinski 25.00
6 Doak Walker 50.00
7 Fran Polsfoot 25.00
8 Sisto Averno 25.00
9 Marion Motley 50.00
10 Pat Brady 25.00
11 Norm Van Brocklin 80.00
12 Bill McColl 25.00
13 Jerry Groom 25.00
14 Al Pollard 25.00
15 Dante Lavelli 40.00
16 Eddie Price 25.00
17 Charlie Trippi 40.00
18 Elbert Nickel 25.00
19 George Taliaferro 25.00
20 Charlie Conerly 50.00
21 Bobby Layne 100.00
22 Elroy Hirsch 60.00
23 Jim Finks 35.00
24 Chuck Bednarik 60.00
25 Kyle Rote 30.00
26 Otto Graham 135.00
27 Harry Gilmer 25.00
28 Tobin Rote 25.00
29 Billy Stone 25.00
30 Buddy Young 25.00
31 Leon Hart 25.00
32 Hugh McElhenny 60.00
33 Dale Samuels 25.00
34 Lou Creekmur 25.00
35 Tom Catlin 25.00
36 Tom Fears 40.00
37 George Connor 35.00
38 Bill Walsh 25.00
39 Leo Sanford (SP) 40.00
40 Horace Gillom 25.00
41 John Schweder (SP) 40.00
42 Tom O'Connell 25.00
43 Frank Gifford (SP) 350.00
44 Frank Continetti (SP) 40.00
45 John Olszewski (SP) 40.00
46 Dub Jones 25.00
47 Don Paul (SP) 40.00
48 Gerald Weatherly 25.00
49 Fred Bruney (SP) 40.00
50 Jack Scarbath 25.00
51 John Karras 25.00
52 Al Conway 25.00
53 Emlen Tunnell (SP) 100.00
54 Gern Nagler (SP) 40.00
55 Kenneth Snyder (SP) 40.00
56 Y.A. Tittle 100.00
57 John Rapacz (SP) 40.00
58 Harley Sewell 40.00
59 Don Bingham 25.00
60 Darrell Hogan 25.00
61 Tony Curcillo 25.00
62 *Ray Renfro* (SP) 50.00
63 Leon Heath 25.00
64 Tex Coulter (SP) 40.00
65 Dewayne Douglas 25.00
66 J. Robert Smith (SP) 40.00
67 Bob McChesney (SP) 40.00
68 Dick Alban (SP) 40.00
69 Andy Kozar 25.00
70 Merwin Hodel (SP) 40.00
71 Thurman McGraw 25.00
72 Cliff Anderson 25.00
73 Pete Pihos 40.00
74 Julie Rykovich 25.00
75 John Kreamcheck (SP) 40.00
76 Lynn Chandnois (SP) 25.00
77 Cloyce Box (SP) 40.00
78 Ray Matthews 25.00
79 Bobby Walston 25.00
80 Jim Dooley 25.00
81 Pat Harder (SP) 40.00
82 Jerry Shipkey 25.00
83 Bobby Thomason 25.00
84 Hugh Taylor 25.00
85 George Ratterman 25.00
86 Don Stonesifer 25.00
87 John Williams (SP) 40.00
88 Leo Nomellini 45.00
89 Frank Ziegler 25.00
90 Don Paul 25.00
91 Tom Dublinski 25.00
92 Ken Carpenter 25.00
93 *Ted Marchibroda* 40.00
94 Chuck Drazenovich 25.00
95 Lou Groza (SP) 100.00
96 William Cross (SP) 80.00

1954 Bowman

This 128-card set has a flag motif that points left, almost a reversal of the 1952 theme. Issued in four series of 32 cards, numbers 65-96 are much tougher to find than the other three. Rookies in this set include Doug Atkins, George Blanda, Hawg Hanner and Whizzer White (actually not Whizzer White; see below). There's an error and a variation in this set. The error is on card #125 "Whizzer" White, his rookie card. It shows not the future Supreme Court Justice, but Wilford White. The variation involves #97, Tom Finnan. On the scarcer error version, his name was incorrectly spelled "Finnin." This was corrected.

NM/M
Complete Set (128): 1,600
Common Player (1-64): 6.00
Common Player (65-96): 25.00
Common Player (97-128): 6.00
1 Ray Matthews 25.00
2 John Huzvar 6.00
3 Jack Scarbath 6.00
4 *Doug Atkins* 45.00
5 Bill Stits 6.00
6 Joe Perry 30.00
7 Kyle Rote 12.00
8 Norm Van Brocklin 45.00
9 Pete Pihos 20.00
10 Babe Parilli 10.00
11 *Zeke Bratkowski* 25.00
12 Ollie Matson 25.00
13 Pat Brady 6.00
14 Fred Enke 6.00
15 Harry Ulinski 6.00
16 Bobby Garrett 6.00
17 Bill Bowman 6.00
18 Leo Rucka 6.00
19 John Cannady 6.00
20 Tom Fears 20.00
21 Norm Willey 6.00
22 Floyd Reid 6.00
23 *George Blanda* 180.00
24 Don Doheney 6.00
25 John Schweder 6.00
26 Bert Rechichar 6.00
27 Harry Dowda 6.00
28 John Sandusky 6.00
29 *Les Bingaman* 10.00
30 Joe Arenas 6.00
31 Ray Wietecha 8.00
32 Elroy Hirsch 30.00
33 Harold Giancanelli 6.00
34 Bill Howton 10.00
35 Fred Morrison 6.00
36 Bobby Cavazos 6.00
37 Darrell Hogan 6.00
38 Buddy Young 7.00
39 Charlie Justice 14.00
40 Otto Graham 75.00
41 Doak Walker 25.00
42 Y.A. Tittle 50.00
43 Buford Long 6.00
44 Volney Quinlan 6.00
45 Bobby Thomason 7.00
46 Fred Cone 6.00
47 Gerald Weatherly 6.00
48 Don Stonesifer 6.00
49a Lynn Chandnois ("Chadnois" on back) 6.00
49b Lynn Chandnois (correct) 6.00
50 George Taliaferro 6.00
51 Dick Alban 6.00
52 Lou Groza 25.00
53 Bobby Layne 50.00
54 Hugh McElhenny 30.00
55 Frank Gifford 100.00
56 Leon McLaughlin 6.00
57 Chuck Bednarik 30.00
58 Art Hunter 6.00
59 Bill McColl 6.00
60 Charlie Trippi 25.00
61 *Jim Finks* 10.00
62 Bill Lange 6.00
63 Laurie Niemi 6.00
64 Ray Renfro 6.00
65 Dick Chapman 25.00
66 Bob Hantla 25.00
67 Ralph Starkey 25.00
68 Don Paul 25.00
69 Kenneth Snyder 25.00
70 Tobin Rote 25.00
71 Arthur DeCarlo 25.00
72 Tom Keane 25.00
73 Hugh Taylor 25.00
74 *Warren Lahr* 25.00
75 Jim Neal 25.00
76 Leo Nomellini 50.00
77 Dick Yelvington 25.00
78 Les Richter 25.00
79 Bucko Kilroy 25.00
80 John Martinkovic 25.00
81 *Dale Dodrill* 25.00
82 Ken Jackson 25.00
83 Paul Lipscomb 25.00
84 John Bauer 25.00
85 Lou Creekmur 50.00
86 Eddie Price 25.00
87 Kenneth Farragut 25.00
88 *Dave Hanner* 25.00
89 Don Boll 25.00
90 Chet Hanulak 25.00
91 Thurman McGraw 25.00
92 *Don Heinrich* 25.00
93 Dan McKown 25.00
94 Bob Fleck 25.00
95 Jerry Hilgenberg 25.00
96 Bill Walsh 25.00
97 Tom Finnin 50.00
98 Paul Barry 6.00
99 Harry Jagade 6.00
100 Jack Christiansen 20.00
101 Gordon Soltau 6.00
102a Emlen Tunnel (Tunnell) 25.00
102b Emlen Tunnell(correct) 20.00
103 Stan West 6.00
104 Jerry Williams 6.00
105 Veryl Switzer 6.00
106 Billy Stone 6.00
107 Jerry Watford 6.00
108 Elbert Nickel 6.00
109 Ed Sharkey 6.00
110 Steve Meilinger 6.00
111 Dante Lavelli 20.00
112 Leon Hart 14.00
113 Charlie Conerly 30.00
114 Richard Lemmon 6.00
115 Al Carmichael 6.00
116 George Conner 15.00
117 John Olszewski 6.00
118 Ernie Stautner 20.00
119 Ray Smith 6.00
120 Neil Worden 6.00
121 Jim Dooley 6.00
122 Arnold Galiffa 6.00
123 Kline Gilbert 6.00
124 Bob Hoernschemeyer 6.00
125 *Whizzer White* 15.00
126 Art Spinney 6.00
127 Joe Koch 6.00
128 *John Lattner* 60.00

1955 Bowman

An excellent run of football cards ended after this year when the Bowman Co. released its last set of 160 cards. (Its competitor, Topps Chewing Gum Co., bought it early in 1956). The first 64 cards are relatively easy to find, compared to numbers 65-160. Rookies in this set include Hall of Famers Mike McCormick, Len Ford, John Henry Johnson, Bob St. Clair, Jim Ringo, and Frank Gatski. Other rookies include Pat Summerall and Alan Ameche.

NM/M
Complete Set (160): 1,500
Common Player (1-64): 15.00
Common Player (65-160): 25.00
1 Doak Walker 50.00
2 *Mike McCormack* 30.00
3 John Olszewski 15.00
4 Dorne Dibble 15.00
5 Lindon Crow 15.00
6 Hugh Taylor 15.00
7 Frank Gifford 100.00
8 *Alan Ameche* 50.00
9 Don Stonesifer 15.00
10 Pete Pihos 20.00
11 Bill Austin 15.00
12 Dick Alban 15.00
13 Bobby Walston 15.00
14 *Len Ford* 40.00
15 Jug Girard 15.00
16 Charlie Conerly 30.00
17 Volney Peters 15.00
18 Max Boydston 15.00
19 Leon Hart 20.00
20 Bert Rechichar 15.00
21 Lee Riley 15.00
22 Johnny Carson 15.00
23 Harry Thompson 15.00
24 Ray Wietecha 15.00
25 Ollie Matson 30.00
26 Eddie LeBaron 25.00
27 Jack Simmons 15.00
28 Jack Christiansen 30.00
29 Bucko Kilroy 15.00
30 Tom Keane 15.00
31 Dave Leggett 15.00
32 Norm Van Brocklin 40.00
33 Harlon Hill 25.00
34 Robert Haner 15.00
35 Veryl Switzer 15.00
36 Dick Stanfel 25.00
37 Lou Groza 45.00
38 Tank Younger 15.00
39 Dick Flanagan 15.00
40 Jim Dooley 15.00
41 Ray Collins 15.00
42 *John Henry Johnson* 50.00
43 Tom Fears 15.00
44 Joe Perry 40.00
45 Gene Brito 25.00
46 Bill Johnson 15.00
47 Deacon Dan Towler 25.00
48 Dick Moegle 15.00
49 Kline Gilbert 15.00
50 Les Gobel 15.00
51 Ray Krouse 15.00
52 *Pat Summerall* 75.00
53 *Ed Brown* 25.00
54 Lynn Chandnois 15.00
55 Joe Heap 15.00
56 John Hoffman 15.00
57 Howard Ferguson 15.00
58 Bobby Watkins 15.00
59 Charlie Ane 15.00
60 *Ken MacAfee* 25.00
61 *Ralph Guglielmi* 25.00
62 George Blanda 80.00
63 Kenneth Snyder 15.00
64 Chet Ostrowski 15.00
65 Buddy Young 15.00
66 Gordon Soltau 25.00
67 Eddie Bell 25.00
68 *Ben Agajanian* 25.00
69 Tom Dahms 25.00
70 *Jim Ringo* 50.00
71 Bobby Layne 70.00
72 Y.A. Tittle 70.00
73 Bob Gaona 25.00
74 Tobin Rote 35.00
75 Hugh McElhenny 40.00
76 John Kreamcheck 25.00
77 Al Dorow 25.00
78 Bill Wade 25.00
79 Dale Dodrill 25.00
80 Chuck Drazenovich 25.00
81 *Billy Wilson* 25.00
82 Les Richter 25.00
83 Pat Brady 25.00
84 Bob Hoernschemeyer 25.00
85 Joe Arenas 25.00
86 Len Szafaryn 25.00
87 *Rick Casares* 25.00
88 Leon McLaughlin 25.00
89 Charley Toogood 25.00
90 Tom Bettis 25.00
91 John Sandusky 25.00
92 Bill Wightkin 25.00
93 Darrell Brewster 25.00
94 Marion Campbell 25.00
95 Floyd Reid 25.00
96 Harry Jagade 25.00
97 George Taliaferro 25.00
98 Carleton Massey 25.00
99 Fran Rogel 25.00
100 Alex Sandusky 25.00
101 *Bob St. Clair* 50.00
102 Al Carmichael 25.00
103 Carl Taseff 25.00
104 Leo Nomellini 40.00
105 Tom Scott 25.00
106 Ted Marchibroda 30.00
107 Art Spinney 25.00
108 Wayne Robinson 25.00
109 Jim Ricca 25.00
110 Lou Ferry 25.00
111 Roger Zatkoff 25.00
112 Lou Creekmur 25.00
113 Kenny Konz 25.00
114 Doug Eggers 25.00
115 Bobby Thomason 25.00
116 Bill McPeak 25.00
117 William Brown 25.00
118 Royce Womble 25.00
119 *Frank Gatski* 40.00
120 Jim Finks 25.00
121 Andy Robustelli 40.00
122 Bobby Dillon 25.00
123 Leo Sanford 25.00
124 Elbert Nickel 25.00
125 Wayne Hansen 25.00
126 Buck Lansford 25.00
127 Gern Nagler 25.00
128 Jim Salsbury 25.00
129 Dale Atkeson 25.00
130 John Schweder 25.00
131 Dave Hanner 25.00
132 Eddie Price 25.00
133 Vic Janowicz 35.00
134 Ernie Stautner 35.00
135 James Parmer 25.00
136 Emlen Tunnell 35.00
137 Kyle Rote 30.00
138 Norm Willey 25.00
139 Charlie Trippi 35.00
140 Bill Howton 25.00
141 Bobby Clatterbuck 25.00
142 Bob Boyd 25.00
143 *Bob Toneff* 25.00
144 Jerry Helluin 25.00
145 Adrian Burk 25.00
146 Walt Michaels 25.00
147 Zillie Toth 25.00
148 *Frank Varrichione* 25.00
149 Dick Bielski 25.00
150 George Ratterman 25.00
151 Mike Jarmoluk 25.00
152 Tom Landry 200.00
153 Ray Renfro 25.00
154 Zeke Bratkowski 25.00
155 Jerry Norton 25.00
156 Maurice Bassett 25.00
157 Volney Quinlan 25.00
158 Chuck Bednarik 25.00
159 Don Colo 25.00
160 *L.G. Dupre* 40.00

1991 Bowman

Topps produced this 561-card set in 1991 under the Bowman name. The standard-size cards have color photos on the front, with blue and orange borders. The player's name is in white in a purple stripe at the bottom. The grey backs, in green and black type, have a player profile, biography and statistics. The cards are numbered alphabetically by team, beginning with Atlanta and ending with Washington. Subsets include League Leaders (#s 273-283), Rookie Superstars (#s 1-11), and Road to the Super Bowl (#s 547-557). These 33 subset cards are gold-foil embossed, with one appearing in every pack.

NM/M
Complete Set (561): 10.00
Common Player: .03
Pack: .50
Wax Box (36): 10.00
1 Jeff George (RS) .10
2 Richmond Webb (RS) .03
3 Emmitt Smith (RS) 1.00
4 Mark Carrier (RS) .05
5 Steve Christie (RS) .03
6 Keith Sims (RS) .03
7 Rob Moore (RS) .15
8 Johnny Johnson (RS) .10
9 Eric Green (RS) .03
10 Ben Smith (RS) .03
11 Tory Epps (RS) .03
12 Andre Rison .25
13 Shawn Collins .03
14 Chris Hinton .03
15 Deion Sanders .50
16 Darion Conner .03
17 Michael Haynes .30
18 Chris Miller .03
19 Jessie Tuggle .03
20 Scott Fulhage .03
21 Bill Fralic .03
22 Floyd Dixon .03
23 Oliver Barnett .03
24 Mike Rozier .03
25 Tory Epps .03
26 Tim Green .03
27 Steve Broussard .03
28 Bruce Pickens .03
29 *Mike Pritchard* .50
30 Andre Reed .10
31 Darryl Talley .03
32 Nate Odomes .03
33 Jamie Mueller .03
34 Leon Seals .03
35 Keith McKeller .03
36 Al Edwards .03
37 Butch Rolle .03
38 Jeff Wright .10
39 Will Wolford .03
40 James Williams .03
41 Kent Hull .03
42 James Lofton .03
43 Frank Reich .03
44 Bruce Smith .03
45 Thurman Thomas .50
46 Leonard Smith .03
47 Shane Conlan .03
48 Steve Tasker .03
49 Ray Bentley .03
50 Cornelius Bennett .03
51 Stan Thomas .03
52 Shaun Gayle .03
53 Wendell Davis .10
54 James Thornton .03
55 Mark Carrier .03
56 Richard Dent .03
57 Ron Morris .03
58 Mike Singletary .03
59 Jay Hilgenberg .03
60 Donnell Woolford .03
61 Jim Covert .03
62 Jim Harbaugh .10
63 Neal Anderson .10
64 Brad Muster .03
65 Kevin Butler .03
66 Trace Armstrong .03
67 Ron Cox .03
68 Peter Tom Willis .03
69 Johnny Bailey .03
70 Mark Bortz .03
71 *Chris Zorich* .25
72 Lamar Rogers .03
73 David Grant .03
74 Lewis Billups .03
75 Harold Green .15
76 Ickey Woods .03
77 Eddie Brown .03
78 David Fulcher .03
79 Anthony Munoz .03
80 Carl Zander .03
81 Rodney Holman .03
82 James Brooks .03
83 Tim McGee .03
84 Boomer Esiason .15
85 Leon White .03
86 James Francis .10
87 Mitchell Price .03
88 *Ed King* .10
89 *Eric Turner* .25
90 *Rob Burnett* .10
91 Leroy Hoard .10
92 Kevin Mack .03
93 Thane Gash .03
94 Gregg Rakoczy .03
95 Clay Matthews .03
96 Eric Metcalf .03
97 Stephen Braggs .03
98 Frank Minnifield .03
99 Reggie Langhorne .03
100 Mike Johnson .03
101 Brian Brennan .03
102 Anthony Pleasant .03
103 Godfrey Myles .03
104 *Russell Maryland* .50
105 *James Washington* .10
106 Nate Newton .03
107 Jimmie Jones .03
108 Jay Novacek .15
109 Alexander Wright .10
110 Jack Del Rio .03
111 Jim Jeffcoat .03
112 Mike Saxon .03
113 Troy Aikman 1.00
114 Issiac Holt .03
115 Ken Norton .03
116 Kelvin Martin .03
117 Emmitt Smith 2.00
118 Ken Willis .03
119 Daniel Stubbs .03
120 Michael Irvin .15
121 Danny Noonan .03
122 *Alvin Harper* .50
123 *Reggie Johnson* .10
124 Vance Johnson .03
125 Steve Atwater .03
126 Greg Kragen .03
127 John Elway .40
128 Simon Fletcher .03
129 Wymon Henderson .03
130 Ricky Nattiel .03
131 Shannon Sharpe .10
132 Ron Holmes .03
133 Karl Mecklenburg .03
134 Bobby Humphrey .03

135 Clarence Kay .03
136 Dennis Smith .03
137 Jim Juriga .03
138 Melvin Bratton .03
139 Mark Jackson .03
140 Michael Brooks .03
141 Alton Montgomery .03
142 *Mike Croel* .15
143 Mel Gray .03
144 Michael Cofer .03
145 Jeff Campbell .03
146 Dan Owens .03
147 Robert Clark .03
148 Jim Arnold .03
149 William White .03
150 Rodney Peete .03
151 Jerry Ball .03
152 Bennie Blades .03
153 Barry Sanders 1.50
154 Andre Ware .10
155 Lomas Brown .03
156 Chris Spielman .03
157 Kelvin Pritchett .03
158 *Herman Moore* 3.50
159 Chris Jacke .03
160 Tony Mandarich .03
161 Perry Kemp .03
162 Johnny Holland .03
163 Mark Lee .03
164 Anthony Dilweg .03
165 Scott Stephen .03
166 Ed West .03
167 Mark Murphy .03
168 Darrell Thompson .15
169 James Campen .03
170 Jeff Query .03
171 Brian Noble .03
172 Sterling Sharpe .15
173 Robert Brown .03
174 Tim Harris .03
175 LeRoy Butler .03
176 Don Majkowski .03
177 Vinnie Clark .03
178 Esera Tuaolo .03
179 Lorenzo White .10
180 Warren Moon .25
181 Sean Jones .03
182 Curtis Duncan .03
183 Al Smith .04
184 Richard Johnson .03
185 Tony Jones .03
186 Bubba McDowell .03
187 Bruce Matthews .03
188 Ray Childress .03
189 Haywood Jeffires .25
190 Ernest Givins .03
191 Mike Munchak .03
192 Greg Montgomery .03
193 *Cody Carlson* .30
194 Johnny Meads .03
195 Drew Hill .03
196 Mike Dumas .03
197 *Darryll Lewis* .10
198 Rohn Stark .03
199 Clarence Verdin .03
200 Mike Prior .03
201 Eugene Daniel .03
202 Dean Biasucci .03
203 Jeff Herrod .03
204 Keith Taylor .03
205 Jon Hand .03
206 Pat Beach .03
207 Duane Bickett .03
208 Jessie Hester .03
209 Chip Banks .03
210 Ray Donaldson .03
211 Bill Brooks .03
212 Jeff George .30
213 Tony Siragusa .03
214 Albert Bentley .03
215 Joe Valerio .03
216 Chris Martin .03
217 Christian Okoye .03
218 Stephone Paige .03
219 Percy Snow .03
220 David Scott .03
221 Derrick Thomas .25
222 Todd McNair .03
223 Albert Lewis .03
224 Neil Smith .03
225 Barry Word .10
226 Robb Thomas .03
227 John Alt .03
228 Jonathan Hayes .03
229 Kevin Ross .03
230 Nick Lowery .03
231 Tim Grunhard .03
232 Dan Saleaumua .03
233 Steve DeBerg .03
234 *Harvey Williams* .50
235 *Nick Bell* .15
236 Mervyn Fernandez .03
237 Howie Long .03
238 Marcus Allen .03
239 Eddie Anderson .03
240 Ethan Horton .03
241 Lionel Washington .03
242 Steve Wisniewski .03
243 Bo Jackson .25
244 Greg Townsend .03
245 Jeff Jaeger .03
246 Aaron Wallace .03
247 Garry Lewis .03
248 Steve Smith .03
249 Willie Gault .03
250 Scott Davis .03
251 Jay Schroeder .03
252 Don Mosebar .03
253 *Todd Marinovich* .10
254 Irv Pankey .03
255 Flipper Anderson .03
256 Tom Newberry .03
257 Kevin Greene .03
258 Mike Wilcher .03
259 Bern Brostek .03
260 Buford McGee .03
261 Cleveland Gary .03
262 Jackie Slater .03
263 Henry Ellard .03
264 Alvin Wright .03
265 *Darryl Henley* .10
266 Damone Johnson .03
267 Frank Stams .03
268 Jerry Gray .03
269 Jim Everett .03
270 Pat Terrell .03
271 *Todd Lyght* .15
272 Aaron Cox .03
273 Barry Sanders (LL) .50
274 Jerry Rice (LL) .40
275 Derrick Thomas (LL) .10
276 Mark Carrier (LL) .05
277 Warren Moon (LL) .15
278 Randall Cunningham (LL) .10
279 Nick Lowery (LL) .03
280 Clarence Verdin (LL) .03
281 Thurman Thomas (LL) .25
282 Mike Horan (LL) .03
283 Flipper Anderson (LL) .03
284 John Offerdahl .03
285 Dan Marino 2.00
286 Mark Clayton .03
287 Tony Paige .03
288 Keith Sims .03
289 Jeff Cross .03
290 Pete Stoyanovich .03
291 Ferrell Edmunds .03
292 Reggie Roby .03
293 Louis Oliver .03
294 Jarvis Williams .03
295 Sammie Smith .03
296 Richmond Webb .03
297 J.B. Brown .03
298 Jim Jensen .03
299 Mark Duper .03
300 David Griggs .03
301 *Randal Hill* .35
302 *Aaron Craver* .10
303 Keith Millard .03
304 Steve Jordan .03
305 Anthony Carter .03
306 Mike Merriweather .03
307 *Audray McMillian* .35
308 Randall McDaniel .03
309 Gary Zimmerman .03
310 Carl Lee .03
311 Reggie Rutland .03
312 Hassan Jones .03
313 Kirk Lowdermilk .03
314 Herschel Walker .08
315 Chris Doleman .03
316 Joey Browner .03
317 Wade Wilson .03
318 Henry Thomas .03
319 Rich Gannon .08
320 Al Noga .03
321 *Pat Harlow* .08
322 Bruce Armstrong .03
323 Maurice Hurst .03
324 Brent Williams .03
325 Chris Singleton .03
326 Jason Staurovsky .03
327 Marvin Allen .03
328 Hart Lee Dykes .03
329 Johnny Rembert .03
330 Andre Tippett .03
331 Greg McMurtry .03
332 John Stephens .03
333 Ray Agnew .03
334 Tommy Hodson .03
335 Ronnie Lippett .03
336 Marv Cook .03
337 *Tommy Barnhardt* .08
338 Dalton Hilliard .03
339 Sam Mills .03
340 Morten Andersen .03
341 Stan Brock .03
342 Brett Maxie .03
343 Steve Walsh .03
344 Vaughan Johnson .03
345 Rickey Jackson .03
346 Renaldo Turnbull .03
347 Joel Hilgenberg .03
348 *Toi Cook* .10
349 Robert Massey .03
350 Pat Swilling .03
351 Eric Martin .03
352 Rueben Mayes .03
353 Vince Buck .03
354 Brett Perriman .03
355 *Wesley Carroll* .25
356 *Jarrod Bunch* .10
357 Pepper Johnson .03
358 Dave Meggett .03
359 Mark Collins .03
360 Sean Landeta .03
361 Maurice Carthon .03
362 Mike Fox .03
363 Jeff Hostetler .15
364 Phil Simms .08
365 Leonard Marshall .03
366 Gary Reasons .03
367 Rodney Hampton .50
368 *Greg Jackson* .08
369 Jumbo Elliott .03
370 *Bob Kratch* .08
371 Lawrence Taylor .10
372 Erik Howard .03
373 Carl Banks .03
374 Stephen Baker .03
375 Mark Ingram .03
376 *Browning Nagle* .25
377 Jeff Lageman .03
378 Ken O'Brien .03
379 Al Toon .03
380 Joe Prokop .03
381 Tony Stargell .03
382 Blair Thomas .10
383 Erik McMillan .03
384 Dennis Byrd .03
385 Freeman McNeil .03
386 Brad Baxter .08
387 Mark Boyer .03
388 Terance Mathis .10
389 Jim Sweeney .03
390 Kyle Clifton .03
391 Pat Leahy .03
392 Rob Moore .15
393 James Hasty .03
394 Blaise Bryant .03
395 Jesse Campbell (Error-Photo actually Dan McGwire, see 509 Corrected) .03
396 Keith Jackson .15
397 Jerome Brown .03
398 Keith Byars .03
399 Seth Joyner .03
400 Mike Bellamy .03
401 Fred Barnett .20
402 Reggie Singletary .03
403 Reggie White .15
404 Randall Cunningham .15
405 Byron Evans .03
406 Wes Hopkins .03
407 Ben Smith .03
408 Roger Ruzek .03
409 Eric Allen .03
410 Anthony Toney .03
411 Clyde Simmons .03
412 Andre Waters .03
413 Calvin Williams .15
414 *Eric Swann* .15
415 Eric Hill .03
416 Tim McDonald .03
417 Luis Sharpe .03
418 Ernie Jones .03
419 Ken Harvey .03
420 Ricky Proehl .15
421 Johnny Johnson .25
422 Anthony Bell .03
423 Timm Rosenbach .03
424 Rich Camarillo .03
425 Walter Reeves .03
426 Freddie Joe Nunn .03
427 Anthony Thompson .03
428 Bill Lewis .03
429 *Jim Wahler* .08
430 Cedric Mack .03
431 *Michael Jones* .08
432 Ernie Mills .03
433 Tim Worley .03
434 Greg Lloyd .03
435 Dermontti Dawson .03
436 Louis Lipps .03
437 Eric Green .08
438 Donald Evans .03
439 David Johnson .03
440 Tunch Ilkin .03
441 Bubby Brister .08
442 Chris Calloway .03
443 David Little .03
444 Thomas Everett .03
445 Carnell Lake .03
446 Rod Woodson .05
447 Gary Anderson .03
448 Merril Hoge .03
449 Gerald Williams .03
450 *Eric Moten* .08
451 Marion Butts .05
452 Leslie O'Neal .03
453 Ronnie Harmon .03
454 Gill Byrd .03
455 Junior Seau .25
456 *Nate Lewis* .25
457 Leo Goeas .03
458 Burt Grossman .03
459 Courtney Hall .03
460 Anthony Miller .06
461 Gary Plummer .03
462 Billy Joe Tolliver .03
463 Lee Williams .03
464 Arthur Cox .03
465 John Kidd .03
466 Frank Cornish .03
467 John Carney .03
468 *Eric Bieniemy* .10
469 Don Griffin .03
470 Jerry Rice 1.00
471 Keith DeLong .03
472 John Taylor .10
473 Brent Jones .03
474 Pierce Holt .03
475 Kevin Fagan .03
476 Bill Romanowski .03
477 Dexter Carter .03
478 Guy McIntyre .03
479 Joe Montana 1.00
480 Charles Haley .03
481 Mike Cofer .03
482 Jesse Sapolu .03
483 Eric Davis .03
484 Mike Sherrard .03
485 Steve Young .75
486 Darryl Pollard .03
487 Tom Rathman .03
488 Michael Carter .03
489 *Ricky Watters* 1.50
490 *John Johnson* .08
491 Eugene Robinson .03
492 Andy Heck .03
493 John L. Williams .03
494 Norm Johnson .03
495 David Wyman .03
496 Derrick Fenner .10
497 Rick Donnelly .03
498 Tony Woods .03
499 *Derek Loville* .75
500 Dave Krieg .03
501 Joe Nash .03
502 Brian Blades .03
503 Cortez Kennedy .25
504 Jeff Bryant .03
505 Tommy Kane .03
506 Travis McNeal .03
507 Terry Wooden .03
508 Chris Warren .50
509 *Dan McGwire* (Error-Photo actually Jesse Campbell; see 395 Corrected) .50
510 Mark Robinson .03
511 Ron Hall .03
512 Paul Gruber .03
513 Hary Hamilton .03
514 Keith McCants .03
515 Reggie Cobb .25
516 Steve Christie .03
517 Broderick Thomas .03
518 Mark Carrier .03
519 Vinny Testaverde .10
520 Ricky Reynolds .03
521 Jesse Anderson .03
522 Reuben Davis .03
523 Wayne Haddix .03
524 Gary Anderson .03
525 Bruce Hill .03
526 Kevin Murphy .03
527 *Lawrence Dawsey* .25
528 *Ricky Ervins* .35
529 Charles Mann .03
530 Jim Lachey .03
531 Mark Rypien .10
532 Darrell Green .03
533 Stan Humphries .40
534 Jeff Bostic .03
535 Earnest Byner .03
536 Art Monk .08
537 Don Warren .03
538 Darryl Grant .03
539 Wilber Marshall .03
540 *Kurt Gouveia* .10
541 Markus Koch .03
542 Andre Collins .03
543 Chip Lohmiller .03
544 Alvin Walton .03
545 Gary Clark .10
546 Ricky Sanders .03
547 Redskins vs. Eagles (Gary Clark) .03
548 Bengals vs. Oilers (Cody Carlson) .03
549 Dolphins vs. Chiefs (Mark Clayton) .03
550 Bears vs. Saints (Neal Anderson) .03
551 Bills vs. Dolphins (Thurman Thomas) .10
552 49ers vs. Redskins (Line Play) .03
553 Giants vs. Bears (Ottis Anderson) .03
554 Raiders vs. Bengals (Bo Jackson) .10
555 AFC Championship (Andre Reed) .03
556 NFC Championship (Jeff Hostetler) .03
557 Super Bowl XXV (Ottis Anderson) .03
558 Checklist 1-140 .03
559 Checklist 141-280 .03
560 Checklist 281-420 .03
561 Checklist 421-561 .03

1992 Bowman

SAM MILLS

These standard-size cards have color action photos against a white border. The upper left has a red "B" on a green stripe, while the player's name is at the bottom in an orange-yellow stripe. There are 45 subset cards within the regular set - 28 Team Leader cards, 12 Playoff Star cards and five cards commemorating the longest plays of the 1991 season (punt, kick return, field goal, run and reception). These cards have gold-foil engraved borders and were randomly inserted one per 15-card pack.

	NM/M
Complete Set (573):	75.00
Common Player:	.15
Minor Stars:	.50
Pack (12):	1.75
Wax Box (36):	45.00

1 Reggie White .50
2 Johnny Meads .15
3 Chip Lohmiller .15
4 James Lofton .50
5 Ray Horton .15
6 Rich Moran .15
7 Howard Cross .15
8 Mike Horan .15
9 Erik Kramer .50
10 Steve Wisniewski .15
11 Michael Haynes .15
12 Donald Evans .15
13 Michael Irvin (FOIL) .50
14 Gary Zimmerman .15
15 John Friesz .50
16 Mark Carrier .15
17 Mark Duper .15
18 James Thornton .15
19 Jon Hand .15
20 Sterling Sharpe .50
21 Jacob Green .15
22 Wesley Carroll .15
23 Clay Matthews .15
24 Kevin Greene .50
25 Brad Baxter .15
26 Don Griffin .15
27 Robert Delpino (FOIL SP) .50
28 Lee Johnson .15
29 Jim Wahler .15
30 Leonard Russell .50
31 Eric Moore .15
32 Dino Hackett .15
33 Simon Fletcher .15
34 Al Edwards .15
35 Brad Edwards .15
36 James Joseph .15
37 Rodney Peete .50
38 Ricky Reynolds .15
39 Eddie Anderson .15
40 Ken Clarke .15
41 Tony Bennett (FOIL) .50
42 Larry Brown .15
43 Ray Childress .15
44 Mike Kenn .15
45 Vestee Jackson .15
46 Neil O'Donnell .50
47 Bill Brooks .15
48 Kevin Butler .15
49 Joe Phillips .15
50 Cortez Kennedy .50
51 Rickey Jackson .15
52 Vinnie Clark .15
53 Michael Jackson .50
54 Ernie Jones .15
55 Tom Newberry .15
56 Pat Harlow .15
57 Craig Taylor .15
58 Joe Prokop .15
59 Warren Moon (FOIL SP) 1.00
60 Jeff Lageman .15
61 Neil Smith .50
62 Jim Jeffcoat .15
63 Bill Fralic .15
64 Mark Schlereth .15
65 Keith Byars .15
66 Jeff Hostetler .50
67 Joey Browner .15
68 Bobby Hebert (FOIL SP) .50
69 Keith Sims .15
70 Warren Moon .50
71 *Pio Sagapolutele* .15
72 Cornelius Bennett .50
73 Greg Davis .15
74 Ronnie Harmon .15
75 Ron Hall .15
76 Howie Long .50
77 Greg Lewis .15
78 Carnell Lake .15
79 Ray Crockett .15
80 Tom Waddle .15
81 Vincent Brown .15
82 Bill Brooks (FOIL) .50
83 John L. Williams .15
84 Floyd Turner .15
85 Scott Radecic .15
86 Anthony Munoz .50
87 Lonnie Young .15
88 Dexter Carter .15
89 Tony Zendejas .15
90 Tim Jorden .15
91 LeRoy Butler .50
92 *Richard Brown* .15
93 Erric Pegram .50
94 Sean Landeta .15
95 Clyde Simmons .15
96 Martin Mayhew .15
97 Jarvis Williams .15
98 Barry Word .15
99 John Taylor (FOIL) .50
100 Emmitt Smith 5.00
101 Leon Seals .15
102 Marion Butts .15
103 Mike Merriweather .15
104 Ernest Givins .15
105 Wymon Henderson .15
106 Robert Wilson .15
107 Bobby Hebert .15
108 Terry McDaniel .15
109 Jerry Ball .15
110 John Taylor .15
111 Rob Moore .50
112 Thurman Thomas (FOIL) .75
113 Checklist 1 .15
114 Brian Blades .15
115 Larry Kelm .15
116 James Francis .15
117 Rod Woodson .50
118 Trace Armstrong .15
119 Eugene Daniel .15
120 Andre Tippett .15
121 Chris Jacke .15
122 Jessie Tuggle .15
123 Chris Chandler .40
124 Tim Johnson .15
125 Mark Collins .15
126 Aeneas Williams (FOIL SP) .50
127 James Jones .15
128 George Jamison .15
129 Deron Cherry .15
130 Mark Clayton .15
131 Keith DeLong .15
132 Marcus Allen .50
133 Joe Walter .15
134 Reggie Rutland .15
135 Kent Hull .15
136 Jeff Feagles .15
137 Ronnie Lott (FOIL SP) .75
138 Henry Rolling .15
139 Gary Anderson .15
140 Morten Andersen .50
141 Cris Dishman .15
142 David Treadwell .15
143 Kevin Gogan .15
144 James Hasty .15
145 Robert Delpino .15
146 Patrick Hunter .15
147 Gary Anderson .15
148 Chip Banks .15
149 Dan Fike .15
150 Chris Miller .15
151 Hugh Millen .15
152 Courtney Hall .15
153 Gary Clark .15
154 Michael Brooks .15
155 Jay Hilgenberg .15
156 Tim McDonald .15
157 Andre Tippett (FOIL) .50
158 Doug Riesenberg .15
159 Bill Maas .15
160 Fred Barnett .50
161 Pierce Holt .15
162 Brian Noble .15
163 Harold Green .15
164 Joel Hilgenberg .15
165 Mervyn Fernandez .15
166 John Offerdahl .15
167 Shane Conlan .15
168 Mark Higgs (FOIL SP) .40
169 Bubba McDowell .15
170 Barry Sanders 5.00
171 Larry Roberts .15
172 Herschel Walker .50
173 Steve McMichael .15
174 Kelly Stouffer .15
175 Louis Lipps .15
176 Jim Everett .50
177 Tony Tolbert .15
178 Mike Baab .15
179 Eric Swann .15
180 Emmitt Smith (FOIL SP) 10.00
181 Tim Brown .50
182 Dennis Smith .15
183 Moe Gardner .15
184 Derrick Walker .15
185 Reyna Thompson .15
186 Esera Tuaolo .15
187 Jeff Wright .15
188 Mark Rypien .50
189 Quinn Early .15
190 Christian Okoye .15
191 Keith Jackson .50
192 Doug Smith .15
193 John Elway (FOIL) 6.00
194 Reggie Cobb .15
195 Reggie Roby .15
196 Clarence Verdin .15
197 Jim Breech .15
198 Jim Sweeney .15
199 Marv Cook .15
200 Ronnie Lott .50
201 Mel Gray .15
202 Maury Buford .15
203 Lorenzo Lynch .15
204 Jesse Sapolu .15
205 Steve Jordan .15
206 Don Majkowski .15
207 Flipper Anderson .15
208 Ed King .15
209 Tony Woods .15
210 Ron Heller .15
211 Greg Kragen .15
212 Scott Case .15
213 Tommy Barnhardt .15
214 Charles Mann .15
215 David Griggs .15
216 Kenneth Davis (FOIL SP) .40
217 Lamar Lathon .15
218 Nate Odomes .15
219 Vinny Testaverde .40
220 Rod Bernstine .15
221 Barry Sanders (FOIL) 10.00
222 Carlton Haselrig .15
223 Steve Beuerlein .15
224 John Alt .15
225 Pepper Johnson .15
226 Checklist 2 .15
227 Irv Eatman .15
228 Greg Townsend .15
229 Mark Jackson .15
230 Robert Blackmon .15
231 Terry Allen .50
232 Bennie Blades .15
233 Sam Mills (FOIL) .50
234 Richmond Webb .15
235 Richard Dent .50
236 Alonzo Mitz .15
237 Steve Young 3.00
238 Pat Swilling .15
239 James Campen .15
240 Earnest Byner .15
241 Pat Terrell .15
242 Carwell Gardner .15
243 Charles McRae .15
244 Vince Newsome .15
245 Eric Hill .15
246 Steve Young (FOIL) 4.00
247 Nate Lewis .15
248 William Fuller .15
249 Andre Waters .15
250 Dean Biasucci .15
251 Andre Rison .40
252 Brent Williams .15
253 Todd McNair .15
254 Jeff Davidson .15
255 Art Monk .50
256 Kirk Lowdermilk .15
257 Bob Golic .15
258 Michael Irvin .50
259 Eric Green .15
260 David Fulcher (FOIL) .50
261 Damone Johnson .15
262 Marc Spindler .15
263 Alfred Williams .15
264 Donnie Elder .15
265 Keith McKeller .15
266 *Steve Bono* .50
267 Jumbo Elliott .15
268 Randy Hilliard .15
269 Rufus Porter .15
270 Neal Anderson .15
271 Dalton Hilliard .15
272 Michael Zordich .15
273 Cornelius Bennett (FOIL) .75

274	Louie Aguiar	.15
275	Aaron Craver	.15
276	Tony Bennett	.15
277	Terry Wooden	.15
278	Mike Munchak	.15
279	Chris Hinton	.15
280	John Elway	4.00
281	Randall McDaniel	.15
282	Brad Baxter (FOIL)	.50
283	Wes Hopkins	.15
284	Scott Davis	.15
285	Mark Tuinei	.15
286	Broderick Thompson	.15
287	Henry Ellard	.15
288	Adrian Cooper	.15
289	Don Warren	.15
290	Rodney Hampton	.40
291	Kevin Ross	.15
292	Mark Carrier	.15
293	Ian Beckles	.15
294	Gene Atkins	.15
295	Mark Rypien (FOIL)	.75
296	Eric Metcalf	.50
297	Howard Ballard	.15
298	Nate Newton	.15
299	Dan Owens	.15
300	Tim McGee	.15
301	Greg McMurtry	.15
302	Walter Reeves	.15
303	Jeff Herrod	.15
304	Darren Comeaux	.15
305	Pete Stoyanovich	.15
306	Johnny Holland	.15
307	Jay Novacek	.50
308	Steve Broussard	.15
309	Darrell Green	.50
310	Sam Mills	.15
311	Tim Barnett	.15
312	Steve Atwater	.15
313	Tom Waddle (FOIL)	.50
314	Felix Wright	.15
315	Sean Jones	.15
316	Jim Harbaugh	.40
317	Eric Allen	.15
318	Don Mosebar	.15
319	Rob Taylor	.15
320	Terance Mathis	.40
321	Leroy Hoard	.40
322	Kenneth Davis	.15
323	Guy McIntyre	.15
324	Deron Cherry (FOIL)	.50
325	Tunch Ilkin	.15
326	Willie Green	.50
327	Darryl Henley	.15
328	Shawn Jefferson	.15
329	Greg Jackson	.15
330	John Roper	.15
331	Bill Lewis	.15
332	Rodney Holman	.15
333	Bruce Armstrong	.15
334	Robb Thomas	.15
335	Alvin Harper	.50
336	Brian Jordan	.40
337	Morten Andersen (FOIL)	.75
338	Dermontti Dawson	.15
339	Checklist 3	.15
340	Louis Oliver	.15
341	Paul McJulien	.15
342	Karl Mecklenburg	.15
343	Lawrence Dawsey	.15
344	Kyle Clifton	.15
345	Jeff Bostic	.15
346	Cris Carter	.75
347	Al Smith	.15
348	Mark Kelso	.15
349	Art Monk (FOIL)	.50
350	Michael Carter	.15
351	Ethan Horton	.15
352	Andy Heck	.15
353	Gill Fenerty	.15
354	David Brandon	.15
355	Anthony Johnson	.15
356	Mike Golic	.15
357	Ferrell Edmunds	.15
358	Dennis Gibson	.15
359	Gill Byrd	.15
360	Todd Lyght	.15
361	Jayice Pearson	.15
362	John Rade	.15
363	Keith Van Horne	.15
364	John Kasay	.15
365	Broderick Thomas (FOIL SP)	.40
366	Ken Harvey	.15
367	Rich Gannon	.15
368	Darrell Thompson	.15
369	Jon Vaughn	.15
370	Jesse Solomon	.15
371	Erik McMillan	.15
372	Bruce Matthews	.15
373	Wilber Marshall	.15
374	Brian Blades (FOIL SP)	.40
375	Vance Johnson	.15
376	Eddie Brown	.15
377	Don Beebe	.50
378	Brent Jones	.50
379	Matt Bahr	.15
380	Dwight Stone	.15
381	Tony Casillas	.15
382	Jay Schroeder	.15
383	Byron Evans	.15
384	Dan Saleaumua	.15
385	Wendell Davis	.15
386	Ron Holmes	.15
387	George Thomas	.15
388	Ray Berry	.15
389	Eric Martin	.15
390	Kevin Mack	.15
391	Natu Tuatagaloa	.15
392	Bill Romanowski	.15
393	Nick Bell (FOIL SP)	.40
394	Grant Feasel	.15
395	Eugene Lockhart	.15
396	Lorenzo White	.15
397	Mike Farr	.15
398	Eric Bieniemy	.15
399	Kevin Murphy	.15
400	Luis Sharpe	.15
401	Jessie Tuggle (FOIL SP)	.40
402	Cleveland Gary	.15
403	Tony Mandarich	.50
404	Bryan Cox	.15
405	Marvin Washington	.15
406	Fred Stokes	.15
407	Duane Bickett	.15
408	Leonard Marshall	.15
409	Barry Foster	.15
410	Thurman Thomas	.75
411	Willie Gault	.15
412	Vinson Smith	.15
413	Mark Bortz	.15
414	Johnny Johnson	.15
415	Rodney Hampton (FOIL)	.40
416	Steve Wallace	.15
417	Fuad Reveiz	.15
418	Derrick Thomas	.50
419	*Jackie Harris*	.50
420	Derek Russell	.15
421	David Grant	.15
422	Tommy Kane	.15
423	Stan Brock	.15
424	Haywood Jeffires	.50
425	Broderick Thomas	.15
426	John Kidd	.15
427	Shawn McCarthy (FOIL)	.50
428	Jim Arnold	.15
429	Scott Fulhage	.15
430	Jackie Slater	.15
431	Scott Galbraith	.15
432	Roger Ruzek	.15
433	Irving Fryar	.50
434A	Derrick Thomas (FOIL ERR)	.50
434B	Derrick Thomas (FOIL COR)	.50
435	David Johnson	.15
436	Jim Jensen	.15
437	James Washington	.15
438	Phil Hansen	.15
439	Rohn Stark	.15
440	Jarrod Bunch	.15
441	Todd Marinovich	.15
442	Brett Perriman	.30
443	Eugene Robinson	.50
444	Robert Massey	.15
445	Nick Lowery	.15
446	Rickey Dixon	.15
447	Jim Lachey	.15
448	Johnny Hector (FOIL)	.50
449	Gary Plummer	.15
450	Robert Brown	.15
451	Gaston Green	.15
452	Checklist 4	.15
453	Darion Conner	.15
454	Mike Cofer	.15
455	Craig Heyward	.15
456	Anthony Carter	.15
457	Pat Coleman	.15
458	Jeff Bryant	.15
459	Mark Gunn	.15
460	Stan Thomas	.15
461	Simon Fletcher (FOIL SP)	.40
462	Ray Agnew	.15
463	Jessie Hester	.15
464	Rob Burnett	.15
465	Mike Croel	.15
466	Mike Pitts	.15
467	Darryl Talley	.15
468	Rich Camarillo	.15
469	Reggie White (FOIL)	.75
470	Nick Bell	.15
471	Tracy Hayworth	.15
472	Eric Thomas	.15
473	Paul Gruber	.15
474	David Richards	.15
475	T.J. Turner	.15
476	Mark Ingram	.15
477	Tim Grunhard	.15
478	Marion Butts (FOIL)	.50
479	Tom Rathman	.15
480	Brian Mitchell	.15
481	Bryce Paup	.50
482	Mike Pritchard	.15
483	Ken Norton Jr.	.15
484	Roman Phifer	.15
485	Greg Lloyd	.50
486	Brett Maxie	.15
487	Richard Dent (FOIL SP)	.50
488	Curtis Duncan	.15
489	Chris Burkett	.15
490	Travis McNeal	.15
491	Carl Lee	.15
492	Clarence Kay	.15
493	Tom Thayer	.15
494	Erik Kramer (FOIL SP)	.40
495	Perry Kemp	.15
496	Jeff Jaeger	.15
497	Eric Sanders	.15
498	Burt Grossman	.15
499	Ben Smith	.15
500	Keith McCants	.15
501	John Stephens	.15
502	John Rienstra	.15
503	Jim Ritcher	.15
504	Harris Barton	.15
505	Andre Rison (FOIL SP)	.50
506	Chris Martin	.15
507	Freddie Joe Nunn	.15
508	Mark Higgs	.15
509	Norm Johnson	.15
510	Stephen Baker	.15
511	Ricky Sanders	.15
512	Ray Donaldson	.15
513	David Fulcher	.15
514	Gerald Williams	.15
515	Toi Cook	.15
516	Chris Warren	.30
517	Jeff Gossett	.15
518	Ken Lanier	.15
519	Haywood Jeffires (FOIL SP)	.40
520	Kevin Glover	.15
521	Mo Lewis	.15
522	Bern Brostek	.15
523	*Bo Orlando*	.15
524	Mike Saxon	.15
525	Seth Joyner	.15
526	John Carney	.15
527	Jeff Cross	.15
528	Gary Anderson (FOIL SP)	.40
529	Chuck Cecil	.15
530	Tim Green	.15
531	Kevin Porter	.15
532	Chris Spielman	.15
533	Willie Drewrey	.15
534	Chris Singleton	.15
535	Matt Stover	.15
536	Andre Collins	.15
537	Erik Howard	.15
538	Steve Tasker	.15
539	Anthony Thompson	.15
540	Charles Haley	.50
541	Mike Merriweather (FOIL)	.50
542	Henry Thomas	.15
543	Scott Stephen	.15
544	Bruce Kozerski	.15
545	Tim McKyer	.15
546	Chris Doleman	.15
547	Riki Ellison	.15
548	Mike Prior	.15
549	Dwayne Harper	.15
550	Bubby Brister	.15
551	Dave Meggett	.15
552	Greg Montgomery	.15
553	Kevin Mack (FOIL)	.50
554	Mark Stepnoski	.15
555	Kenny Walker	.15
556	Eric Moten	.15
557	Michael Stewart	.15
558	Calvin Williams	.15
559	Johnny Hector	.15
560	Tony Paige	.15
561	Tim Newton	.15
562	Brad Muster	.15
563	Aeneas Williams	.50
564	Herman Moore	2.00
565	Checklist 5	.15
566	Jerome Henderson	.15
567	Danny Copeland	.15
568	Alexander Wright (FOIL)	.50
569	Tim Harris	.15
570	Jonathan Hayes	.15
571	Tony Jones	.15
572	*Carlton Bailey*	.15
573	Vaughan Johnson	.15

1993 Bowman

The 1993 Bowman set cut back to 423 cards with a numbered subset of 27 special foil-designed cards. These cards feature nine 1993 rookies, nine former #1 draft picks and nine superstars. Each pack of 1993 Bowman contains 14 cards, plus one special foil insert card. The regular cards are glossy and feature full-color photos on premium stock.

		NM/M
Complete Set (423):		40.00
Common Player:		.15
Minor Stars:		.30
Pack (14):		1.50
Wax Box (24):		25.00
1	Troy Aikman	4.00
2	John Parella	.15
3	*Dana Stubblefield*	.40
4	Mark Higgs	.15
5	*Tom Carter*	.30
6	Nate Lewis	.15
7	*Vaughn Hebron*	.30
8	Ernest Givins	.15
9	Vince Buck	.15
10	Levon Kirkland	.15
11	J.J. Birden	.15
12	Steve Jordan	.15
13	Simon Fletcher	.15
14	Willie Green	.15
15	Pepper Johnson	.15
16	Roger Harper	.15
17	Rob Moore	.15
18	David Lang	.15
19	David Klingler	.15
20	*Garrison Hearst*	1.00
21	Anthony Johnson	.15
22	*Eric Curry*	.30
23	Nolan Harrison	.15
24	Earl Dotson	.15
25	Leonard Russell	.15
26	Doug Riesenberg	.15
27	Dwayne Harper	.15
28	Richard Dent	.30
29	*Victor Bailey*	.30
30	Junior Seau	.30
31	Steve Tasker	.15
32	Kurt Gouveia	.15
33	Renaldo Turnbull	.15
34	Dale Carter	.15
35	Russell Maryland	.15
36	Dana Hall	.15
37	Marco Coleman	.15
38	Greg Montgomery	.15
39	*Deon Figures*	.15
40	*Troy Drayton*	.50
41	Eric Metcalf	.15
42	Michael Husted	.15
43	Harry Newsome	.15
44	Kelvin Pritchett	.15
45	Andre Rison	.30
46	*John Copeland*	.30
47	Greg Biekert	.15
48	Johnny Johnson	.15
49	Chuck Cecil	.15
50	*Rick Mirer*	.50
51	Rod Bernstine	.15
52	Steve McMichael	.15
53	*Roosevelt Potts*	.30
54	Mike Sherrard	.15
55	Terrell Buckley	.15
56	Eugene Chung	.15
57	*Kimble Anders*	.30
58	Daryl Johnston	.15
59	Harris Barton	.15
60	Thurman Thomas	.30
61	Eric Martin	.15
62	*Reggie Brooks*	.30
63	Eric Bieniemy	.15
64	John Offerdahl	.15
65	Wilber Marshall	.15
66	Mark Carrier	.15
67	Merril Hoge	.15
68	Cris Carter	.30
69	Marty Thompson	.15
70	Randall Cunningham	.30
71	Winston Moss	.15
72	Doug Pelfrey	.15
73	Jackie Slater	.15
74	Pierce Holt	.15
75	Hardy Nickerson	.15
76	Chris Burkett	.15
77	Michael Brandon	.15
78	Tom Waddle	.15
79	Walter Reeves	.15
80	Lawrence Taylor	.30
81	*Wayne Simmons*	.30
82	Brent Williams	.15
83	Shannon Sharpe	.30
84	Robert Blackmon	.15
85	Keith Jackson	.15
86	A.J. Johnson	.15
87	*Ryan McNeil*	.30
88	Michael Dean Perry	.15
89	*Russell Copeland*	.30
90	Sam Mills	.15
91	Courtney Hall	.15
92	*Gino Torretta*	.30
93	*Artie Smith*	.15
94	David Whitmore	.15
95	Charles Haley	.15
96	Rod Woodson	.15
97	Lorenzo White	.15
98	Tom Scott	.15
99	Tyji Armstrong	.15
100	Boomer Esiason	.30
101	Raghib Ismail	.15
102	Mark Carrier	.15
103	Broderick Thompson	.15
104	Bob Whitfield	.15
105	Ben Coleman	.15
106	Jon Vaughn	.15
107	Marcus Buckley	.15
108	Cleveland Gary	.15
109	Ashley Ambrose	.15
110	Reggie White	.30
111	*Arthur Marshall*	.30
112	Greg McMurtry	.15
113	Mike Johnson	.15
114	Tim McGee	.15
115	John Carney	.15
116	Neil Smith	.15
117	Mark Stepnoski	.15
118	Don Beebe	.15
119	Scott Mitchell	.30
120	Randall McDaniel	.15
121	Chidi Ahanotu	.15
122	Ray Childress	.15
123	*Tony McGee*	.30
124	Marc Boutte	.15
125	Ronnie Lott	.30
126	*Jason Elam*	.30
127	*Martin Harrison*	.30
128	Leonard Renfro	.15
129	Jesse Armstead	.15
130	Quentin Coryatt	.15
131	Luis Sharpe	.15
132	Bill Maas	.15
133	Jesse Solomon	.15
134	Kevin Greene	.30
135	*Derek Brown*	.30
136	Greg Townsend	.15
137	Neal Anderson	.15
138	John Williams	.15
139	*Vincent Brisby*	.50
140	Barry Sanders	6.00
141	Charles Mann	.15
142	Ken Norton	.15
143	Eric Moten	.15
144	John Alt	.15
145	*Dan Footman*	.15
146	Bill Brooks	.15
147	James Thornton	.15
148	Martin Mayhew	.15
149	Andy Harmon	.15
150	Dan Marino	7.00
151	Micheal Barrow	.15
152	Flipper Anderson	.15
153	Jackie Harris	.15
154	Todd Kelly	.15
155	*Dan Williams*	.15
156	Harold Green	.15
157	David Treadwell	.15
158	Chris Doleman	.15
159	Eric Hill	.15
160	*Lincoln Kennedy*	.30
161	Devon McDonald	.15
162	*Natrone Means*	1.00
163	Rick Hamilton	.15
164	Kelvin Martin	.15
165	Jeff Hostetler	.30
166	*Mark Brunell*	7.00
167	Tim Barnett	.15
168	Ray Crockett	.15
169	William Perry	.15
170	Michael Irvin	.30
171	Marvin Washington	.15
172	Irving Fryar	.15
173	Scott Sisson	.15
174	Gary Anderson	.15
175	Bruce Smith	.15
176	Clyde Simmons	.15
177	Russell White	.15
178	*Irv Smith*	.30
179	Mark Wheeler	.15
180	Warren Moon	.30
181	Del Speer	.15
182	Henry Thomas	.15
183	Keith Kartz	.15
184	Ricky Ervins	.15
185	Phil Simms	.30
186	Tim Brown	.30
187	Willis Peguese	.15
188	Rich Moran	.15
189	Robert Jones	.15
190	Craig Heyward	.15
191	Ricky Watters	.30
192	Stan Humphries	.30
193	Larry Webster	.15
194	Brad Baxter	.15
195	Randal Hill	.15
196	Robert Porcher	.15
197	Patrick Robinson	.15
198	Ferrell Edmunds	.15
199	Melvin Jenkins	.15
200	Joe Montana	4.00
201	Marv Cook	.15
202	Henry Ellard	.15
203	Calvin Williams	.15
204	Craig Erickson	.15
205	Steve Atwater	.15
206	Najee Mustafaa	.15
207	Darryl Talley	.15
208	Jarrod Bunch	.15
209	Tim McDonald	.15
210	*Patrick Bates*	.30
211	Sean Jones	.15
212	Leslie O'Neal	.15
213	Mike Golic	.15
214	Mark Clayton	.15
215	Leonard Marshall	.15
216	*Curtis Conway*	1.00
217	*Andre Hastings*	.50
218	Barry Word	.15
219	Will Wolford	.15
220	Desmond Howard	.30
221	Rickey Jackson	.15
222	Alvin Harper	.15
223	William White	.15
224	Steve Broussard	.15
225	Aeneas Williams	.15
226	Michael Brooks	.15
227	Reggie Cobb	.15
228	Derrick Walker	.15
229	Marcus Allen	.30
230	Jerry Ball	.15
231	J.B. Brown	.15
232	Terry McDaniel	.15
233	LeRoy Butler	.15
234	Kyle Clifton	.15
235	Henry Jones	.15
236	Shane Conlan	.15
237	*Michael Bates*	.30
238	Vincent Brown	.15
239	William Fuller	.15
240	Ricardo McDonald	.15
241	Gary Zimmerman	.15
242	Fred Barnett	.15
243	*Elvis Grbac*	1.00
244	Myron Baker	.15
245	Steve Emtman	.15
246	Mike Compton	.15
247	Mark Jackson	.15
248	Santo Stephens	.15
249	Tommie Agee	.15
250	Broderick Thomas	.15
251	Fred Baxter	.15
252	Andre Collins	.15
253	Ernest Dye	.15
254	Raylee Johnson	.15
255	Rickey Dixon	.15
256	Ron Heller	.15
257	Joel Steed	.15
258	Everett Lindsay	.15
259	Tony Smith	.15
260	Sterling Sharpe	.30
261	Tommy Vardell	.15
262	Morten Andersen	.15
263	Eddie Robinson	.15
264	*Jerome Bettis*	3.00
265	Alonzo Spellman	.15
266	Harvey Williams	.15
267	Jason Belser	.15
268	Derek Russell	.15
269	*Derrick Lassic*	.30
270	Steve Young	1.00
271	*Adrien Murrell*	.50
272	Lewis Tillman	.15
273	*O.J. McDuffie*	1.00
274	Marty Carter	.15
275	Ray Seals	.15
276	Earnest Byner	.15
277	Marion Butts	.15
278	Chris Spielman	.15
279	Carl Pickens	.50
280	*Drew Bledsoe*	8.00
281	Mark Kelso	.15
282	Eugene Robinson	.15
283	Eric Allen	.15
284	Ethan Horton	.15
285	Greg Lloyd	.15
286	Anthony Carter	.15
287	Edgar Bennett	.30
288	Bobby Hebert	.15
289	Haywood Jeffires	.15
290	*Glyn Milburn*	.40
291	Bernie Kosar	.15
292	Jumbo Elliott	.15
293	Jessie Hester	.15
294	Brent Jones	.15
295	Carl Banks	.15
296	Brian Washington	.15
297	Steve Beuerlein	.15
298	John Lynch	.15
299	Troy Vincent	.15
300	Emmitt Smith	7.00
301	Chris Zorich	.15
302	Wade Wilson	.15
303	*Darrien Gordon*	.30
304	Fred Stokes	.15
305	Nick Lowery	.15
306	Rodney Peete	.15
307	Chris Warren	.30
308	Herschel Walker	.15
309	Aundray Bruce	.15
310	Barry Foster	.15
311	*George Teague*	.30
312	Darryl Williams	.15
313	*Thomas Smith*	.30
314	Dennis Brown	.15
315	*Marvin Jones*	.30
316	Andre Tippett	.15
317	*Demetrius Dubose*	.15
318	Kirk Lowdermilk	.15
319	Shane Dronett	.15
320	*Terry Kirby*	.40
321	*Qadry Ismail*	.50
322	Lorenzo Lynch	.15
323	Willie Drewrey	.15
324	Jessie Tuggle	.15
325	Leroy Hoard	.15
326	Mark Collins	.15
327	Darrell Green	.15
328	Anthony Miller	.30
329	Brad Muster	.15
330	Jim Kelly	.50
331	Sean Gilbert	.15
332	Tim McKyer	.15
333	Scott Mersereau	.15
334	Willie Davis	.15
335	Brett Favre	10.00
336	Kevin Gogan	.15
337	Jim Harbaugh	.30
338	James Trapp	.15
339	Pete Stoyanovich	.15
340	Jerry Rice	4.00
341	Gary Anderson	.15
342	*Carlton Gray*	.15
343	Dermontti Dawson	.15
344	Ray Buchanan	.15
345	Derrick Fenner	.15
346	Dennis Smith	.15
347	Todd Rucci	.15
348	Seth Joyner	.15
349	Jim McMahon	.30
350	Rodney Hampton	.30
351	Al Smith	.15
352	Steve Everitt	.15
353	Vinnie Clark	.15
354	Eric Swann	.15
355	Brian Mitchell	.15
356	Will Shields	.15
357	Cornelius Bennett	.15
358	*Darrin Smith*	.30
359	Chris Mims	.15
360	Blair Thomas	.15
361	Dennis Gibson	.15
362	Santana Dotson	.15
363	Mark Ingram	.15
364	Don Mosebar	.15
365	Ty Detmer	.30
366	Bob Christian	.15
367	Adrian Hardy	.15
368	Vaughan Johnson	.15
369	Jim Everett	.15
370	Ricky Sanders	.15
371	Jonathan Hayes	.15
372	Bruce Matthews	.15
373	Darren Drozdov	.15
374	Scott Brumfield	.15
375	Cortez Kennedy	.15
376	Tim Harris	.15
377	Neil O'Donnell	.30
378	*Robert Smith*	2.00
379	Mike Caldwell	.15
380	Burt Grossman	.15
381	Corey Miller	.15
382	*Kevin Williams*	.50
383	Ken Harvey	.15
384	*Greg Robinson*	.15
385	Harold Alexander	.15
386	Andre Reed	.30
387	Reggie Langhorne	.15
388	Courtney Hawkins	.15
389	James Hasty	.15
390	Pat Swilling	.15
391	*Chris Slade*	.30
392	Keith Byars	.15
393	Dalton Hilliard	.15
394	David Williams	.15
395	Terry Obee	.15
396	Heath Sherman	.15
397	John Taylor	.15
398	Irv Eatman	.15
399	Johnny Holland	.15
400	John Elway	3.00
401	Clay Matthews	.15
402	Dave Meggett	.15
403	Eric Green	.15
404	Bryan Cox	.15
405	Jay Novacek	.15
406	Kenneth Davis	.15
407	*Lamar Thomas*	.30
408	Lance Gunn	.15
409	Audray McMillian	.15
410	Derrick Thomas	.30
411	Rufus Porter	.15
412	Coleman Rudolph	.15
413	Mark Rypien	.15
414	Duane Bickett	.15
415	Chris Singleton	.15
416	Mitch Lyons	.15
417	Bill Fralic	.15
418	Gary Plummer	.15
419	Ricky Proehl	.15
420	Howie Long	.15

No.	Player	NM/M
421	*Willie Roaf*	.30
422	Checklist 1 of 2	.15
423	Checklist 2 of 2	.15

1994 Bowman

This 360-card set features 116 of this year's draft picks, plus a 30-card rookie subset (#s 215-244). Each card front has a glossy full-color action photo of the player, with a borderless design. Gold-foil stamped yard markers run across the bottom, while the Bowman logo appears in the lower left corner. The player's name is stamped in gold in the opposite corner. The card back has a smaller picture of the player on the left side; statistics are on the right side on top of a football background. The card number is in white in a red triangle in the upper right corner.

		NM/M
Complete Set (390):		60.00
Common Player:		.10
Minor Stars:		.20
Pack (12):		1.75
Wax Box (24):		30.00
1	*Dan Wilkinson*	.20
2	*Marshall Faulk*	20.00
3	*Heath Shuler*	.75
4	*Willie McGinest*	.20
5	*Trent Dilfer*	6.00
6	*Brent Jones*	.20
7	*Sam Adams*	.20
8	*Randy Baldwin*	.20
9	*Jamir Miller*	.20
10	*John Thierry*	.20
11	*Aaron Glenn*	.20
12	*Joe Johnson*	.20
13	*Bernard Williams*	.20
14	*Wayne Gandy*	.20
15	*Aaron Taylor*	.20
16	*Charles Johnson*	.50
17	*Dewayne Washington*	.20
18	Bernie Kosar	.10
19	*Johnnie Morton*	.50
20	*Rob Fredrickson*	.20
21	*Shante Carver*	.20
22	*Thomas Lewis*	.20
23	*Greg Hill*	.75
24	Cris Dishman	.10
25	*Jeff Burris*	.20
26	*Isaac Davis*	.20
27	*Bert Emanuel*	.50
28	*Allen Aldridge*	.20
29	*Kevin Lee*	.20
30	*Chris Brantley*	.20
31	*Rich Braham*	.20
32	Ricky Watters	.20
33	Quentin Coryatt	.10
34	Hardy Nickerson	.10
35	Johnny Johnson	.10
36	Ken Harvey	.10
37	Chris Zorich	.10
38	Chris Warren	.20
39	*David Palmer*	.20
40	Chris Miller	.10
41	Ken Ruettgers	.10
42	*Joe Panos*	.20
43	*Mario Bates*	.30
44	Harry Colon	.10
45	Barry Foster	.10
46	Steve Tasker	.10
47	Richmond Webb	.10
48	*James Folston*	.20
49	Eric Williams	.10
50	Rodney Hampton	.20
51	Derek Russell	.10
52	Greg Montgomery	.10
53	Anthony Phillips	.10
54	Andre Coleman	.10
55	Gary Brown	.10
56	Neil Smith	.10
57	Myron Baker	.10
58	*Sean Dawkins*	.50
59	Marvin Washington	.10
60	Steve Beuerlein	.10
61	*Brentson Buckner*	.20
62	William Gaines	.10
63	*LeShon Johnson*	.20
64	*Errict Rhett*	.50
65	Jim Everett	.10
66	Desmond Howard	.10
67	Jack Del Rio	.10
68	*Isaac Bruce*	15.00
69	*Van Moore*	.20
70	Jim Kelly	.20
71	Leon Lett	.10
72	Greg Robinson	.10
73	*Ryan Yarborough*	.20
74	Terry Wooden	.10
75	Eric Allen	.10
76	Ernest Givins	.10
77	*Marcus Spears*	.20
78	*Thomas Randolph*	.20
79	*Willie Clark*	.20
80	John Elway	3.00
81	*Aubrey Beavers*	.20
82	Jeff Cothran	.10
83	Norm Johnson	.10
84	*Donnell Bennett*	.20
85	Phillippi Sparks	.10
86	Scott Mitchell	.20
87	*Bucky Brooks*	.20
88	Courtney Hawkins	.10
89	Kevin Greene	.10
90	*Doug Nussmeier*	.20
91	Floyd Turner	.10
92	Anthony Newman	.10
93	Vinny Testaverde	.10
94	Ronnie Lott	.10
95	Troy Aikman	2.00
96	John Taylor	.10
97	Henry Ellard	.10
98	Carl Lee	.10
99	Terry McDaniel	.10
100	Joe Montana	3.00
101	David Klingler	.10
102	*Bruce Walker*	.20
103	Rick Cunningham	.10
104	Robert Delpino	.10
105	Mark Ingram	.10
106	Leslie O'Neal	.10
107	Darrell Thompson	.10
108	David Meggett	.10
109	Chris Gardocki	.10
110	Andre Rison	.10
111	Kelvin Martin	.10
112	Marcus Robertson	.10
113	*Jason Gildon*	.20
114	Mel Gray	.10
115	Tommy Vardell	.10
116	Dexter Carter	.10
117	*Scottie Graham*	.20
118	Horace Copeland	.10
119	Cornelius Bennett	.10
120	*Chris Maumalanga*	.20
121	Mo Lewis	.10
122	*Toby Wright*	.20
123	*George Hegamin*	.20
124	Chip Lohmiller	.10
125	*Calvin Jones*	.20
126	*Steve Shine*	.20
127	*Chuck Levy*	.20
128	Sam Mills	.10
129	Terance Mathis	.10
130	Randall Cunningham	.10
131	John Fina	.10
132	Reggie White	.20
133	Tom Waddle	.10
134	Chris Calloway	.10
135	*Kevin Mawae*	.20
136	*Lake Dawson*	.50
137	*Alai Kalaniuhalu*	.20
138	Tom Nalen	.10
139	Cody Carlson	.10
140	Dan Marino	3.00
141	Harris Barton	.10
142	Don Mosebar	.10
143	*Romeo Bandison*	.20
144	Bruce Smith	.10
145	Warren Moon	.20
146	David Lutz	.10
147	Dermontti Dawson	.10
148	Ricky Proehl	.10
149	*Lou Benfatti*	.20
150	Craig Erickson	.10
151	Sean Gilbert	.10
152	*Zefros Moss*	.20
153	*Darnay Scott*	.50
154	Courtney Hall	.10
155	Brian Mitchell	.10
156	*Joe Burch*	.20
157	*Terry Mickens*	.20
158	Jay Novacek	.10
159	Chris Gedney	.10
160	Bruce Matthews	.10
161	*Mario Perry*	.20
162	Vince Buck	.10
163	Michael Bates	.10
164	Willie Davis	.10
165	Mike Pritchard	.10
166	Doug Riesenberg	.10
167	Herschel Walker	.10
168	*Tim Ruddy*	.20
169	*William Floyd*	.50
170	John Randle	.10
171	Winston Moss	.10
172	Thurman Thomas	.20
173	*Eric England*	.20
174	Vincent Brisby	.20
175	Greg Lloyd	.10
176	Paul Gruber	.10
177	*Brad Ottis*	.20
178	George Teague	.10
179	*Willie Jackson*	.20
180	Barry Sanders	3.00
181	Brian Washington	.10
182	Michael Jackson	.10
183	*Jason Mathews*	.20
184	Chester McGlockton	.10
185	*Tydus Winans*	.20
186	Michael Haynes	.10
187	Erik Kramer	.10
188	Chris Doleman	.10
189	Haywood Jeffires	.10
190	*Larry Whigham*	.10
191	Shawn Jefferson	.10
192	Pete Stoyanovich	.10
193	Rod Bernstine	.10
194	William Thomas	.10
195	Marcus Allen	.20
196	Dave Brown	.10
197	*Harold Bishop*	.20
198	Lorenzo Lynch	.10
199	Dwight Stone	.10
200	Jerry Rice	3.00
201	Raghib Ismail	.10
202	LeRoy Butler	.10
203	Glenn Parker	.10
204	Bruce Armstrong	.10
205	Shane Conlan	.10
206	Russell Maryland	.10
207	Herman Moore	.40
208	Eric Martin	.10
209	John Friesz	.10
210	Boomer Esiason	.10
211	Jim Harbaugh	.10
212	Harold Green	.10
213	*Perry Klein*	.20
214	Eric Metcalf	.10
215	Steve Everitt	.10
216	Victor Bailey	.10
217	Lincoln Kennedy	.10
218	Glyn Milburn	.10
219	John Copeland	.10
220	Drew Bledsoe	3.00
221	Kevin Williams	.20
222	Roosevelt Potts	.10
223	Troy Drayton	.10
224	Terry Kirby	.10
225	Ron Moore	.10
226	Tyrone Hughes	.10
227	Wayne Simmons	.10
228	Tony McGee	.10
229	Derek Brown	.10
230	Jason Elam	.10
231	Qadry Ismail	.10
232	O.J. McDuffie	.20
233	Mike Caldwell	.10
234	Reggie Brooks	.10
235	Rick Mirer	.20
236	Steve Tovar	.10
237	Patrick Robinson	.10
238	Tom Carter	.10
239	Ben Coates	.20
240	Jerome Bettis	.75
241	Garrison Hearst	.50
242	Natrone Means	.75
243	Dana Stubblefield	.20
244	William Roaf	.10
245	Cortez Kennedy	.10
246	*Todd Steussie*	.20
247	Pat Coleman	.10
248	David Wyman	.10
249	Jeremy Lincoln	.10
250	Carlester Crumpler	.10
251	Dale Carter	.10
252	Corey Raymond	.10
253	Bryan Cox	.10
254	*Charlie Garner*	2.00
255	Jeff Hostetler	.20
256	Shane Bonham	.10
257	Thomas Everett	.10
258	John Jackson	.10
259	*Terry Irving*	.20
260	*Corey Sawyer*	.20
261	Rob Waldrop	.10
262	Curtis Conway	.30
263	*Winfred Tubbs*	.20
264	Sean Jones	.10
265	James Washington	.10
266	*Lonnie Johnson*	.20
267	Rob Moore	.10
268	Willie Anderson	.10
269	Jon Hand	.10
270	*Joe Patton*	.20
271	Howard Ballard	.10
272	*Fernando Smith*	.20
273	Jessie Tuggle	.10
274	John Alt	.10
275	Corey Miller	.10
276	*Gus Frerotte*	.40
277	Jeff Cross	.10
278	Kevin Smith	.10
279	*Corey Louchiey*	.20
280	Micheal Barrow	.10
281	*Jim Flanigan*	.30
282	Calvin Williams	.10
283	Jeff Jaeger	.10
284	*John Reece*	.20
285	Jason Hanson	.10
286	*Kurt Haws*	.20
287	Eric Davis	.10
288	Maurice Hurst	.10
289	Kirk Lowdermilk	.10
290	Rod Woodson	.10
291	Andre Reed	.10
292	Vince Workman	.10
293	Wayne Martin	.10
294	*Keith Lyle*	.20
295	Brett Favre	5.00
296	*Doug Brien*	.20
297	Junior Seau	.20
298	Randall McDaniel	.10
299	Johnny Mitchell	.10
300	Emmitt Smith	4.00
301	Michael Brooks	.10
302	Steve Jackson	.10
303	Jeff George	.20
304	Irving Fryar	.10
305	Derrick Thomas	.10
306	Dante Jones	.10
307	Darrell Green	.10
308	Mark Bavaro	.10
309	Eugene Robinson	.10
310	Shannon Sharpe	.20
311	Michael Timpson	.10
312	Kevin Mitchell	.10
313	Stevon Moore	.10
314	Eric Swann	.10
315	James Bostic	.10
316	Robert Brooks	.40
317	Pete Pierson	.10
318	Jim Sweeny	.10
319	Anthony Smith	.10
320	Rohn Stark	.10
321	Gary Anderson	.10
322	Robert Porcher	.10
323	Darryl Talley	.10
324	Stan Humphries	.20
325	Shelly Hammonds	.10
326	Jim McMahon	.10
327	Lamont Warren	.10
328	*Chris Penn*	.20
329	Tony Woods	.10
330	*Raymont Harris*	.50
331	*Mitch Davis*	.20
332	Michael Irvin	.20
333	Kent Graham	.10
334	Brian Blades	.10
335	Lomas Brown	.10
336	Willie Drewrey	.10
337	Russell Freeman	.10
338	*Eric Zomalt*	.20
339	Santana Dotson	.10
340	Sterling Sharpe	.20
341	*Ray Crittenden*	.20
342	*Perry Carter*	.20
343	*Austin Robbins*	.20
344	*Mike Wells*	.20
345	Toddrick McIntosh	.10
346	Mark Carrier	.10
347	Eugene Daniel	.10
348	*Tre Johnson*	.20
349	D.J. Johnson	.10
350	Steve Young	1.50
351	Jim Pyne	.10
352	Jocelyn Borgella	.10
353	Pat Carter	.10
354	*Sam Rogers*	.20
355	*Jason Sehorn*	.20
356	Darren Carrington	.10
357	*Lamar Smith*	2.00
358	James Burton	.10
359	Darrin Smith	.10
360	Marco Coleman	.10
361	Webster Slaughter	.10
362	Lewis Tillman	.10
363	David Alexander	.10
364	*Bradford Banta*	.20
365	Erric Pegram	.10
366	Mike Fox	.10
367	Jeff Lageman	.10
368	Kurt Gouveia	.10
369	Tim Brown	.20
370	Seth Joyner	.10
371	Irv Eatman	.10
372	*Dorsey Levens*	2.00
373	Anthony Pleasant	.10
374	Henry Jones	.10
375	Cris Carter	.20
376	Morten Andersen	.10
377	Neil O'Donnell	.10
378	*Tyronne Drakeford*	.20
379	John Carney	.10
380	Vincent Brown	.10
381	J.J. Birden	.10
382	Chris Spielman	.10
383	Mark Bortz	.10
384	Ray Childress	.10
385	Carlton Bailey	.10
386	Charles Haley	.10
387	Shane Dronett	.10
388	Jon Vaughn	.10
389	Checklist 1	.10
390	Checklist 2	.10

1995 Bowman

Bowman's 1995 set features many of the league's top draft picks and emerging young stars among its 357-card lineup. The set features 220 top players, 110 Draft Picks and 27 all-foil Expansion Team theme cards. Two insert sets were also made. Expansion Team cards are showcased utilizing an etched gold foil process with an embossed border (one per 12 packs), while 1st-Round Draft Picks highlights 22 players utilizing gold diffraction foil stamping (one per 12 packs). Each regular card in the set has a color action photo of the player on the right, with a smaller mirror image on a brown-shaded panel on the left. A team logo is in the lower left corner. The player's name is in the lower right corner, with his last name stamped in gold foil. The Bowman logo is in the upper right corner, stamped in red foil. The horizontal card back has biographical info, 1994 game-by-game stats and the player's name on one side; a color photo, team name, position and card number run along the right border.

		NM/M
Complete Set (357):		75.00
Common Player:		.10
Minor Stars:		.20
Expansion Foils (221-247):		.25
First Rounds:		1X-2X
Expansion Golds:		2X-4X
Pack (10):		2.75
Wax Box (24):		45.00
1	*Ki-Jana Carter*	.50
2	*Tony Boselli*	.50
3	*Steve McNair*	6.00
4	*Michael Westbrook*	1.00
5	*Kerry Collins*	4.00
6	*Kevin Carter*	.50
7	*Mike Mamula*	.10
8	*Joey Galloway*	3.00
9	*Kyle Brady*	.50
10	*J.J. Stokes*	1.00
11	*Derrick Alexander*	.10
12	*Warren Sapp*	1.00
13	*Mark Fields*	.10
14	*Ruben Brown*	.10
15	*Ellis Johnson*	.10
16	*Hugh Douglas*	.50
17	*Mike Pelton*	.10
18	*Napoleon Kaufman*	.75
19	*James Stewart*	1.00
20	*Luther Elliss*	.10
21	*Rashaan Salaam*	.40
22	*Tyrone Poole*	.10
23	*Ty Law*	.10
24	*Korey Stringer*	.25
25	*Billy Milner*	.10
26	*Devin Bush*	.10
27	*Mark Bruener*	.75
28	Derrick Brooks	.10
29	Blake Brockermeyer	.10
30	Alundis Brice	.10
31	Trezelle Jenkins	.10
32	*Craig Newsome*	.40
33	Fred Barnett	.10
34	Ray Childress	.10
35	Chris Miller	.10
36	Charles Haley	.10
37	Ray Crittenden	.10
38	Gus Frerotte	.50
39	Jeff George	.20
40	Dan Marino	3.00
41	Shawn Lee	.10
42	Herman Moore	.50
43	Chris Calloway	.10
44	Jeff Graham	.10
45	Ray Buchanan	.10
46	Doug Pelfrey	.10
47	Lake Dawson	.25
48	Glenn Parker	.10
49	Terry McDaniel	.10
50	Rod Woodson	.10
51	Santana Dotson	.10
52	Anthony Miller	.10
53	Bo Orlando	.10
54	David Palmer	.10
55	William Floyd	.50
56	Edgar Bennett	.10
57	*Jeff Blake*	.40
58	Anthony Pleasant	.10
59	Quinn Early	.10
60	Bobby Houston	.10
61	*Terrell Fletcher*	.50
62	Gary Brown	.10
63	Dwayne Sabb	.10
64	Roman Phifer	.10
65	*Sherman Williams*	.50
66	Roosevelt Potts	.10
67	Darnay Scott	.40
68	Charlie Garner	.10
69	Bert Emanuel	.40
70	Herschel Walker	.10
71	Lorenzo Styles	.10
72	Andre Coleman	.10
73	Tyronne Drakeford	.10
74	Jay Novacek	.10
75	Raymont Harris	.10
76	*Tamarick Vanover*	.50
77	Tom Carter	.10
78	Eric Green	.10
79	Patrick Hunter	.10
80	Jeff Hostetler	.20
81	Robert Blackmon	.10
82	Anthony Cook	.10
83	Craig Erickson	.10
84	Glyn Milburn	.10
85	Greg Lloyd	.20
86	Brent Jones	.10
87	Barrett Brooks	.10
88	Alvin Harper	.10
89	Sean Jones	.10
90	Cris Carter	.20
91	Russell Copeland	.10
92	*Frank Sanders*	.50
93	Mo Lewis	.10
94	Michael Haynes	.10
95	Andre Rison	.10
96	Jesse James	.10
97	Stan Humphries	.20
98	James Hasty	.10
99	Ricardo McDonald	.10
100	Jerry Rice	1.50
101	Chris Hudson	.10
102	David Meggett	.10
103	Brian Mitchell	.10
104	Mike Johnson	.10
105	*Kordell Stewart*	2.00
106	Michael Brooks	.10
107	Steve Walsh	.10
108	Eric Metcalf	.10
109	Ricky Watters	.20
110	Brett Favre	3.00
111	Aubrey Beavers	.10
112	Brian Williams	.10
113	Eugene Robinson	.10
114	Matt O'Dwyer	.10
115	Micheal Barrow	.10
116	Raghib Ismail	.10
117	Scott Gragg	.10
118	Leon Lett	.10
119	Reggie Roby	.10
120	Marshall Faulk	1.00
121	Jack Jackson	.10
122	Keith Byars	.10
123	Eric Hill	.10
124	Todd Sauerbrun	.10
125	Dexter Carter	.10
126	Vinny Testaverde	.10
127	Shane Conlan	.10
128	Terrance Shaw	.10
129	William Roaf	.10
130	Jim Kelly	.20
131	Neil O'Donnell	.20
132	Ray McElroy	.10
133	Ed McDaniel	.10
134	Brian Gelzheiser	.10
135	Marcus Allen	.20
136	Carl Pickens	.20
137	Mike Verstegen	.10
138	Chris Mims	.10
139	Darryl Pounds	.10
140	Emmitt Smith	3.00
141	Mike Frederick	.10
142	Henry Ellard	.10
143	Willie McGinest	.10
144	Michael Roan	.10
145	Chris Spielman	.10
146	Darryl Talley	.10
147	Randall Cunningham	.10
148	Andrew Greene	.10
149	George Teague	.10
150	Tyrone Hughes	.10
151	Ron Davis	.10
152	Stevon Moore	.10
153	Merton Hanks	.10
154	Darren Perry	.10
155	Dave Brown	.10
156	Mike Morton	.10
157	Seth Joyner	.10
158	Bryan Cox	.10
159	Corey Fuller	.10
160	John Elway	.50
161	Dewayne Washington	.10
162	Chris Warren	.25
163	Jeff Kopp	.10
164	Sean Dawkins	.10
165	Mark Carrier	.10
166	Andre Hastings	.10
167	Derek West	.10
168	Glenn Montgomery	.10
169	Trent Dilfer	.40
170	*Rob Johnson*	2.00
171	Todd Scott	.10
172	Charles Johnson	.25
173	Kez McCorvey	.10
174	Rob Fredrickson	.10
175	Corey Sawyer	.10
176	Brett Perriman	.20
177	*Ken Dilger*	.40
178	Dana Stubblefield	.10
179	Eric Allen	.10
180	Drew Bledsoe	1.50
181	Tyrone Davis	.10
182	Reggie Brooks	.10
183	Dale Carter	.10
184	William Henderson	.10
185	Reggie White	.20
186	Lorenzo White	.10
187	Leslie O'Neal	.10
188	*Stoney Case*	.50
189	Jeff Burris	.10
190	Leroy Hoard	.10
191	Thomas Randolph	.10
192	*Rodney Thomas*	.40
193	Quentin Coryatt	.10
194	Terry Wooden	.10
195	*David Sloan*	.25
196	Bernie Parmalee	.25
197	*Zack Crockett*	.25
198	Troy Aikman	1.50
199	Bruce Smith	.10
200	*Eric Zeier*	.20
201	Anthony Smith	.10
202	Jake Reed	.10
203	Hardy Nickerson	.10
204	Patrick Riley	.10
205	Bruce Matthews	.10
206	Larry Centers	.10
207	Troy Drayton	.10
208	John Burrough	.10
209	Jason Elam	.10
210	Donnell Woolford	.10
211	Sam Shade	.10
212	Kevin Greene	.10
213	Ronald Moore	.10
214	Shane Hannah	.10
215	Jim Everett	.10
216	Scott Mitchell	.20
217	*Antonio Freeman*	1.00
218	Tony McGee	.10
219	Clay Matthews	.10
220	Neil Smith	.10
221	Mark Williams	.25
222	Derrick Graham	.25
223	Mike Hollis	.25
224	Darion Conner	.25
225	Steve Beuerlein	.25
226	Rod Smith	.25
227	James Williams	.25
228	Bob Christian	.25
229	Jeff Lageman	.25
230	Frank Reich	.25
231	Harry Colon	.25
232	Carlton Bailey	.25
233	Mickey Washington	.25
234	Shawn Bouwens	.25
235	Don Beebe	.25
236	Kelvin Pritchett	.25
237	Tommy Barnhardt	.25
238	Mike Dumas	.25
239	Brett Maxie	.25
240	Desmond Howard	.25
241	Sam Mills	.25
242	Keith Goganious	.25
243	Bubba McDowell	.25
244	Vinnie Clark	.25
245	Lamar Lathon	.25
246	Bryan Barker	.25
247	Darren Carrington	.25
248	Jay Barker	.10
249	Eric Davis	.10
250	Heath Shuler	.40
251	Donta Jones	.10
252	LeRoy Butler	.10
253	Michael Zordich	.10
254	Cortez Kennedy	.10
255	Brian DeMarco	.10
256	Randal Hill	.10
257	Michael Irvin	.50

258 Natrone Means .40
259 Linc Harden .10
260 Jerome Bettis .50
261 Tony Bennett .10
262 Dameian Jeffries .10
263 Cornelius Bennett .10
264 Chris Zorich .10
265 Bobby Taylor .10
266 Terrell Buckley .10
267 Troy Dumas .10
268 Rodney Hampton .10
269 Steve Everitt .10
270 Mel Gray .10
271 Antonio Armstrong .10
272 Jim Harbaugh .10
273 Gary Clark .10
274 Tau Pupua .10
275 Warren Moon .20
276 Corey Croom .10
277 Tony Berti .10
278 Shannon Sharpe .10
279 Boomer Esiason .10
280 Aeneas Williams .10
281 Lethon Flowers .10
282 Derek Brown .10
283 Charlie Williams .10
284 Dan Wilkinson .10
285 Mike Sherrard .10
286 Evan Pilgrim .10
287 Kimble Anders .10
288 Greg Jefferson .10
289 Ken Norton .10
290 Terance Mathis .10
291 Torey Hunter .10
292 Ken Harvey .10
293 Irving Fryar .10
294 Michael Reed .10
295 Andre Reed .10
296 Vencie Glenn .10
297 Corey Swinson .10
298 Harvey Williams .10
299 Willie Davis .10
300 Barry Sanders 3.00
301 *Curtis Martin* 6.00
302 Johnny Mitchell .10
303 Daryl Johnston .10
304 Lorenzo Lynch .10
305 *Christian Fauria* .50
306 Sean Gilbert .10
307 *Ray Zellars* .50
308 William Strong .10
309 Jack Del Rio .10
310 Junior Seau .20
311 Justin Armour .10
312 Eric Bjorson .10
313 Vincent Brown .10
314 Darius Holland .10
315 *Chad May* .50
316 Simon Fletcher .10
317 Roell Preston .10
318 John Thierry .10
319 Orlanda Thomas .10
320 Zach Wiegert .10
321 Derrick Alexander .10
322 Chris Cowart .10
323 *Chris Sanders* .75
324 Robert Brooks .25
325 *Todd Collins* .50
326 Ken Irvin .10
327 Erric Pegram .10
328 Damien Covington .10
329 Brendan Stai .10
330 *James Stewart* .50
331 Jessie Tuggle .10
332 Marco Coleman .10
333 Steve Young 1.50
334 Greg Hill .40
335 Darryl Williams .10
336 Calvin Williams .10
337 Cris Dishman .10
338 Anthony Morgan .10
339 Renaldo Turnbull .10
340 Rick Mirer .50
341 Tim Brown .20
342 Dennis Gibson .10
343 Brad Baxter .10
344 Henry Jones .10
345 Johnny Bailey .10
346 Qadry Ismail .10
347 Richmond Webb .10
348 Robert Jones .10
349 Garrison Hearst .20
350 Errict Rhett .40
351 Steve Atwater .10
352 Joe Cain .10
353 Ben Coates .10
354 Aaron Glenn .10
355 Antonio Langham .10
356 Eugene Daniel .10
357 Tim Bowens .10

1995 Bowman's Best

Ninety veterans, 90 rookies and 15 Mirror Image cards make up the debut set of Bowman's Best Football. Bowman's Best 1995 is divided into three subsets - Black Series (90 veterans), Blue Series (90 rookies) and Mirror Images, which show off one of this year's first-round draft choices on one side and last year's corresponding first-round pick on the other (1 per every four packs). The entire set was also done in a refractor version. Black and Blue Series Refractors could be found one per six packs, while Mirror Images Refactors were seeded one per 36 packs. The Black and Blue Series cards have the same format, except the L-shaped border containing the player's team name and his last name are in the corresponding color. An action photo completes the card front design. The back has an action photo, with biographical information, best skills, best stats and the player's name against the corresponding subset color. Mirror Images cards use a black background for the 1994 first-round picks and a blue background for the 1995 selections. A circle with the overall number the player was drafted at is also included.

NM/M
Complete Set (180): 110.00
Common Player: .50
Minor Stars: 1.00
Refractor Cards: 2X-4X
Refractor Rookies: 1X-3X
Inserted 1:6
Pack (7): 4.50
Wax Box (24): 75.00
V1 Rob Moore .50
V2 Craig Heyward .50
V3 Jim Kelly .50
V4 John Kasay .50
V5 Jeff Graham .50
V6 *Jeff Blake* .50
V7 Antonio Langham .50
V8 Troy Aikman 4.00
V9 Simon Fletcher .50
V10 Barry Sanders 6.00
V11 Edgar Bennett .50
V12 Ray Childress .50
V13 Ray Buchanan .50
V14 Desmond Howard .50
V15 Dale Carter .50
V16 Troy Vincent .50
V17 David Palmer .50
V18 Ben Coates .50
V19 Derek Brown .50
V20 Dave Brown .50
V21 Mo Lewis .50
V22 Harvey Williams .50
V23 Randall Cunningham .50
V24 Kevin Greene .50
V25 Junior Seau .60
V26 Merton Hanks .50
V27 Cortez Kennedy .50
V28 Troy Drayton .50
V29 Hardy Nickerson .50
V30 Brian Mitchell .50
V31 Raymont Harris .50
V32 Keith Goganious .50
V33 Andre Reed .50
V34 Terance Mathis .50
V35 Garrison Hearst .60
V36 Glyn Milburn .50
V37 Emmitt Smith 6.00
V38 Vinny Testaverde .50
V39 Darnay Scott 1.00
V40 Mickey Washington .50
V41 Craig Erickson .50
V42 Chris Chandler .50
V43 Brett Favre 6.00
V44 Scott Mitchell .50
V45 Chris Slade .50
V46 Warren Moon .60
V47 Dan Marino 6.00
V48 Greg Hill .50
V49 Raghib Ismail .50
V50 Bobby Houston .50
V51 Rodney Hampton .50
V52 Jim Everett .50
V53 Rick Mirer .50
V54 Steve Young 3.00
V55 Dennis Gibson .50
V56 Rod Woodson .50
V57 Calvin Williams .50
V58 Tom Carter .50
V59 Trent Dilfer 1.00
V60 Shane Conlan .50
V61 Cornelius Bennett .50
V62 Eric Metcalf .50
V63 Frank Reich .50
V64 Eric Hill .50
V65 Erik Kramer .50
V66 Michael Irvin 1.00
V67 Tony McGee .50
V68 Andre Rison .50
V69 Shannon Sharpe .50
V70 Quentin Coryatt .50
V71 Robert Brooks .60
V72 Steve Beuerlein .50
V73 Herman Moore .60
V74 Jack Del Rio .50
V75 David Meggett .50
V76 Pete Stoyanovich .50
V77 Neil Smith .50
V78 Corey Miller .50
V79 Tim Brown 1.00
V80 Tyrone Hughes .50
V81 Boomer Esiason .50
V82 Natrone Means .60
V83 Chris Warren .60
V84 Byron Morris .50
V85 Jerry Rice 4.00
V86 Michael Zordich .50
V87 Errict Rhett .60
V88 Henry Ellard .50
V89 Chris Miller .50
V90 John Elway 3.00
R1 *Ki-Jana Carter* .60
R2 *Tony Boselli* .50
R3 *Steve McNair* 15.00
R4 *Michael Westbrook* 2.00
R5 *Kerry Collins* 9.00
R6 *Kevin Carter* 1.00
R7 *Mike Mamula* .60
R8 *Joey Galloway* 4.00
R9 *Kyle Brady* .60
R10 *Ray McElroy* .50
R11 *Derrick Alexander* .50
R12 *Warren Sapp* 3.00
R13 *Mark Fields* .50
R14 *Ruben Brown* .50
R15 *Ellis Johnson* .50
R16 *Hugh Douglas* 1.50
R17 *Alundis Brice* .50
R18 *Napoleon Kaufman* 2.00
R19 *James Stewart* 2.00
R20 *Luther Elliss* .50
R21 *Rashaan Salaam* .60
R22 *Tyrone Poole* .50
R23 *Ty Law* .50
R24 *Korey Stringer* 1.00
R25 *Billy Milner* .50
R26 *Roell Preston* .50
R27 *Mark Bruener* .60
R28 *Derrick Brooks* .50
R29 *Blake Brockermeyer* .50
R30 *Mike Frederick* .50
R31 *Trezelle Jenkins* .50
R32 *Craig Newsome* .60
R33 *Matt O'Dwyer* .50
R34 *Terrance Shaw* .50
R35 *Anthony Cook* .50
R36 *Darick Holmes* .60
R37 *Cory Raymer* .50
R38 *Zach Wiegert* .50
R39 *Sam Shade* .50
R40 *Brian DeMarco* .50
R41 *Ron Davis* .50
R42 *Orlanda Thomas* .50
R43 *Derek West* .50
R44 *Ray Zellars* .60
R45 *Todd Collins* .60
R46 *Linc Harden* .50
R47 *Frank Sanders* 2.00
R48 *Ken Dilger* 1.50
R49 *Barrett Robbins* .50
R50 *Bobby Taylor* .50
R51 *Terrell Fletcher* .60
R52 *Jack Jackson* .50
R53 *Jeff Kopp* .50
R54 *Brendan Stai* .50
R55 *Corey Fuller* .50
R56 *Todd Sauerbrun* .50
R57 *Dameian Jeffries* .50
R58 *Troy Dumas* .50
R59 *Charlie Williams* .50
R60 *Kordell Stewart* 2.00
R61 *Jay Barker* .50
R62 *Jesse James* .50
R63 *Shane Hannah* .50
R64 *Rob Johnson* 4.00
R65 *Darius Holland* .50
R66 *William Henderson* .50
R67 *Chris Sanders* 1.00
R68 *Darryl Pounds* .50
R69 *Melvin Tuten* .50
R70 *David Sloan* .50
R71 *Chris Hudson* .50
R72 *William Strong* .50
R73 *Brian Williams* .50
R74 *Curtis Martin* 15.00
R75 *Mike Verstegen* .50
R76 *Justin Armour* .50
R77 *Lorenzo Styles* .50
R78 *Oliver Gibson* .50
R79 *Zack Crockett* .50
R80 *Tau Pupua* .50
R81 *Tamarick Vanover* .60
R82 *Steve McLaughlin* .50
R83 *Sean Harris* .50
R84 *Eric Zeier* .60
R85 *Rodney Young* .50
R86 *Chad May* .60
R87 *Evan Pilgrim* .50
R88 *James Stewart* 1.50
R89 *Torey Hunter* .50
R90 *Antonio Freeman* 2.00

1995 Bowman's Best Refractors

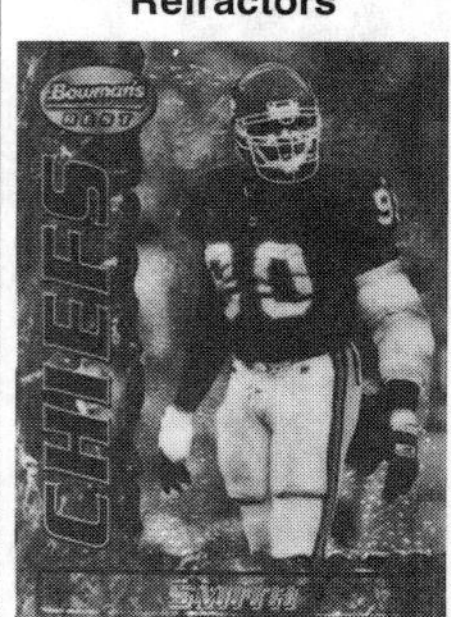

Each of the 195 cards in Bowman's Best football was done in a Refractor version. Black and Blue Series Refractors were seeded one per six packs; Mirror Images Refractors were seeded one per 36 packs. Each Refractor, which has a shiny, rainbow effect, has the same format as its regular counterpart, except it is labeled on the back with the card number as being a Refractor.

NM/M
Common Player: 1.00
Minor Stars: 8.00
Unlisted Cards: 2X-4X
V1 Rob Moore 1.00
V2 Craig Heyward 1.00
V3 Jim Kelly 2.00
V4 John Kasay 1.00
V5 Jeff Graham 1.00
V6 *Jeff Blake* 1.50
V7 Antonio Langham 1.00
V8 Troy Aikman 5.00
V9 Simon Fletcher 1.00
V10 Barry Sanders 12.00
V11 Edgar Bennett 1.00
V12 Ray Childress 1.00
V13 Ray Buchanan 1.00
V14 Desmond Howard 1.00
V15 Dale Carter 1.00
V16 Troy Vincent 1.00
V17 David Palmer 1.00
V18 Ben Coates 1.00
V19 Derek Brown 1.00
V20 Dave Brown 1.00
V21 Mo Lewis 1.00
V22 Harvey Williams 1.00
V23 Randall Cunningham 1.00
V24 Kevin Greene 1.00
V25 Junior Seau 2.00
V26 Merton Hanks 1.00
V27 Cortez Kennedy 1.00
V28 Troy Drayton 1.00
V29 Hardy Nickerson 1.00
V30 Brian Mitchell 1.00
V31 Raymont Harris 1.00
V32 Keith Goganious 1.00
V33 Andre Reed 1.00
V34 Terance Mathis 1.00
V35 Garrison Hearst 2.00
V36 Glyn Milburn 1.00
V37 Emmitt Smith 15.00
V38 Vinny Testaverde 1.00
V39 Darnay Scott 8.00
V40 Mickey Washington 1.00
V41 Craig Erickson 1.00
V42 Chris Chandler 1.00
V43 Brett Favre 15.00
V44 Scott Mitchell 2.00
V45 Chris Slade 1.00
V46 Warren Moon 2.00
V47 Dan Marino 15.00
V48 Greg Hill 1.00
V49 Raghib Ismail 1.00
V50 Bobby Houston 1.00
V51 Rodney Hampton 1.00
V52 Jim Everett 1.00
V53 Rick Mirer 1.00
V54 Steve Young 6.00
V55 Dennis Gibson 1.00
V56 Rod Woodson 1.00
V57 Calvin Williams 1.00
V58 Tom Carter 1.00
V59 Trent Dilfer 2.00
V60 Shane Conlan 1.00
V61 Cornelius Bennett 1.00
V62 Eric Metcalf 1.00
V63 Frank Reich 1.00
V64 Eric Hill 1.00
V65 Erik Kramer 1.00
V66 Michael Irvin 2.00
V67 Tony McGee 1.00
V68 Andre Rison 1.00
V69 Shannon Sharpe 1.00
V70 Quentin Coryatt 1.00
V71 Robert Brooks 2.00
V72 Steve Beuerlein 1.00
V73 Herman Moore 2.00
V74 Jack Del Rio 1.00
V75 David Meggett 1.00
V76 Pete Stoyanovich 1.00
V77 Neil Smith 1.00
V78 Corey Miller 1.00
V79 Tim Brown 2.00
V80 Tyrone Hughes 1.00
V81 Boomer Esiason 1.00
V82 Natrone Means 2.00
V83 Chris Warren 8.00
V84 Byron Morris 1.00
V85 Jerry Rice 12.00
V86 Michael Zordich 1.00
V87 Errict Rhett 2.00
V88 Henry Ellard 1.00
V89 Chris Miller 1.00
V90 John Elway 12.00
R1 *Ki-Jana Carter* 3.00
R2 *Tony Boselli* 3.00
R3 *Steve McNair* 25.00
R4 *Michael Westbrook* 6.00
R5 *Kerry Collins* 14.00
R6 *Kevin Carter* 4.00
R7 *Mike Mamula* 2.00
R8 *Joey Galloway* 10.00
R9 *Kyle Brady* 3.00
R10 *Ray McElroy* 1.00
R11 *Derrick Alexander* 3.00
R12 *Warren Sapp* 8.00
R13 *Mark Fields* 1.00
R14 *Ruben Brown* 1.00
R15 *Ellis Johnson* 1.00
R16 *Hugh Douglas* 1.00
R17 *Alundis Brice* 1.00
R18 *Napoleon Kaufman* 6.00
R19 *James Stewart* 6.00
R20 *Luther Elliss* 1.00
R21 *Rashaan Salaam* 3.00
R22 *Tyrone Poole* 1.00
R23 *Ty Law* 1.00
R24 *Korey Stringer* 3.00
R25 *Billy Milner* 1.00
R26 *Roell Preston* 1.00
R27 *Mark Bruener* 3.00
R28 *Derrick Brooks* 1.00
R29 *Blake Brockermeyer* 1.00
R30 *Mike Frederick* 1.00
R31 *Trezelle Jenkins* 1.00
R32 *Craig Newsome* 3.00
R33 *Matt O'Dwyer* 1.00
R34 *Terrance Shaw* 1.00
R35 *Anthony Cook* 1.00
R36 *Darick Holmes* 3.00
R37 *Cory Raymer* 1.00
R38 *Zach Wiegert* 1.00
R39 *Sam Shade* 1.00
R40 *Brian DeMarco* 1.00
R41 *Ron Davis* 1.00
R42 *Orlanda Thomas* 1.00
R43 *Derek West* 1.00
R44 *Ray Zellars* 1.00
R45 *Todd Collins* 1.00
R46 *Linc Harden* 1.00
R47 *Frank Sanders* 6.00
R48 *Ken Dilger* 3.00
R49 *Barrett Robbins* 1.00
R50 *Bobby Taylor* 1.00
R51 *Terrell Fletcher* 3.00
R52 *Jack Jackson* 1.00
R53 *Jeff Kopp* 1.00
R54 *Brendan Stai* 1.00
R55 *Corey Fuller* 1.00
R56 *Todd Sauerbrun* 1.00
R57 *Dameian Jeffries* 1.00
R58 *Troy Dumas* 1.00
R59 *Charlie Williams* 1.00
R60 *Kordell Stewart* 8.00
R61 *Jay Barker* 1.00
R62 *Jesse James* 1.00
R63 *Shane Hannah* 1.00
R64 *Rob Johnson* 8.00
R65 *Darius Holland* 1.00
R66 *William Henderson* 5.00
R67 *Chris Sanders* 4.00
R68 *Darryl Pounds* 1.00
R69 *Melvin Tuten* 1.00
R70 *David Sloan* 1.00
R71 *Chris Hudson* 1.00
R72 *William Strong* 1.00
R73 *Brian Williams* 1.00
R74 *Curtis Martin* 25.00
R75 *Mike Verstegen* 1.00
R76 *Justin Armour* 1.00
R77 *Lorenzo Styles* 1.00
R78 *Oliver Gibson* 1.00
R79 *Zack Crockett* 3.00
R80 *Tau Pupua* 1.00
R81 *Tamarick Vanover* 3.00
R82 *Steve McLaughlin* 1.00
R83 *Sean Harris* 1.00
R84 *Eric Zeier* 2.00
R85 *Rodney Young* 1.00
R86 *Chad May* 2.00
R87 *Evan Pilgrim* 1.00
R88 *James Stewart* 8.00
R89 *Torey Hunter* 1.00
R90 *Antonio Freeman* 5.00

1995 Bowman's Best Mirror Images

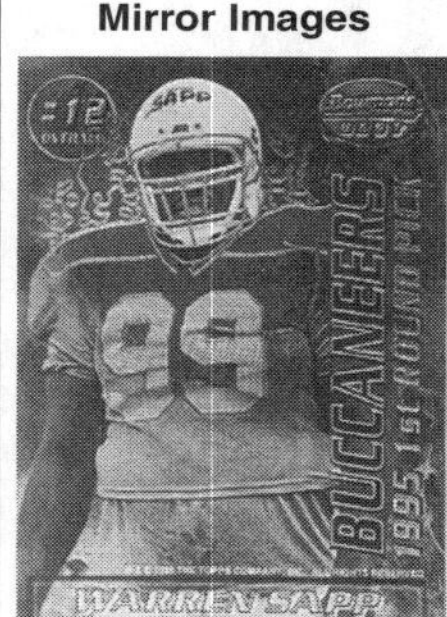

These cards feature one of 1995's first-round draft picks on one side, with the corresponding 1994 pick on the other. The 1994 picks use black for the background; the 1995 picks use blue. A circle with the overall number the player was selected at is also included on both sides. Regular Mirror Images cards were seeded one per four packs of 1995 Bowman's Best football. Mirror Images Refractors were seeded one per 36 packs.

NM/M
Complete Set (15): 35.00
Common Player: 1.00
Minor Stars: 2.00
Inserted 1:4
Refractor Cards: 3X-6X
Inserted 1:36
1 Ki-Jana Carter, Dan Wilkinson 2.00
2 Marshall Faulk, Tony Boselli 2.00
3 Steve McNair, Heath Shuler 8.00
4 Michael Westbrook, Willie McGinest 3.00
5 Kerry Collins, Trev Alberts 3.00
6 Trent Dilfer, Kevin Carter 2.00
7 Mike Mamula, Bryant Young 1.00
8 Joey Galloway, Sam Adams 6.00
9 Kyle Brady, Antonio Langham 1.00
10 J.J. Stokes, Jamir Miller 3.00
11 Derrick Alexander, John Thierry 1.00
12 Warren Sapp, Aaron Glenn 1.00
13 Mark Fields, Joe Johnson 1.00
14 Ruben Brown, Bernard Williams 1.00
15 Ellis Johnson, Wayne Gandy 1.00

1996 Bowman's Best

Bowman's Best contained 135 key veterans on gold designs and 45 1996 NFL draft picks on silver designed cards. All 180 cards are also found in a parallel Refractors and Atomic Refractors insert. The cards show the player in front of a fake field with yard markers running down the length of the card. The player's name and team logo are near the bottom. Bowman's Best had three inserts - Mirror Images, Best Bets and Best Cuts.

NM/M
Complete Set (180): 60.00
Common Player: .25
Minor Stars: .50
Refractors: 1X-3X
Atomic Refractors: 3X-8X
Pack (6): 5.00
Wax Box (24): 85.00
1 Emmitt Smith 6.00
2 Kordell Stewart 2.00
3 Mark Chmura .25
4 Sean Dawkins .25
5 Steve Young 3.00
6 Tamarick Vanover .40
7 Scott Mitchell .25
8 Aaron Hayden .25
9 William Thomas .25
10 Dan Marino 6.00
11 Curtis Conway .25
12 Steve Atwater .25
13 Derrick Brooks .25
14 Rick Mirer .25
15 Mark Brunell 3.00
16 Garrison Hearst .25
17 Eric Turner .25
18 Mark Carrier .25
19 Darnay Scott .25
20 Steve McNair 4.00
21 Jim Everett .25
22 Wayne Chrebet .25
23 Ben Coates .25
24 Harvey Williams .25
25 Michael Westbrook .50
26 Kevin Carter .25
27 Dave Brown .25
28 Jake Reed .25
29 Thurman Thomas .50
30 Jeff George .25
31 Carnell Lake .25
32 J.J. Stokes .50
33 Jay Novacek .25
34 Brett Perriman .25
35 Robert Brooks .25
36 Neil Smith .25
37 Chris Zorich .25
38 Micheal Barrow .25
39 Quentin Coryatt .25
40 Kerry Collins .75
41 Aeneas Williams .25
42 James Stewart .25
43 Warren Moon .25
44 Willie McGinest .25
45 Rodney Hampton .25
46 Jeff Hostetler .25
47 Darrell Green .25
48 Warren Sapp .25
49 Troy Drayton .25
50 Junior Seau .25
51 Mike Mamula .25
52 Antonio Langham .25
53 Eric Metcalf .25
54 Adrian Murrell .25
55 Joey Galloway .50
56 Anthony Miller .25
57 Carl Pickens .25
58 Bruce Smith .25
59 Merton Hanks .25
60 Troy Aikman 3.00
61 Erik Kramer .25
62 Tyrone Poole .25
63 Michael Jackson .25

64 Rob Moore .25
65 Marcus Allen .25
66 Orlando Thomas .25
67 David Meggett .25
68 Trent Dilfer .25
69 Herman Moore .75
70 Brett Favre 8.00
71 Blaine Bishop .25
72 Eric Allen .25
73 Bernie Parmalee .25
74 Kyle Brady .25
75 Terry McDaniel .25
76 Rodney Peete .25
77 Yancey Thigpen .25
78 Stan Humphries .25
79 Craig Heyward .25
80 Rashaan Salaam .75
81 Shannon Sharpe .25
82 Jim Harbaugh .25
83 Vinnie Clark .25
84 Steve Bono .25
85 Drew Bledsoe 3.00
86 Ken Norton .25
87 Brian Mitchell .25
88 Hardy Nickerson .25
89 Todd Lyght .25
90 Barry Sanders 5.00
91 Robert Blackmon .25
92 Larry Centers .25
93 Jim Kelly .25
94 Lamar Lathon .25
95 Cris Carter .25
96 Hugh Douglas .25
97 Michael Strahan .25
98 Lee Woodall .25
99 Michael Irvin .25
100 Marshall Faulk 1.00
101 Terance Mathis .25
102 Eric Zeier .25
103 Marty Carter .25
104 Steve Tovar .25
105 Isaac Bruce 1.00
106 Tony Martin .25
107 Dale Carter .25
108 Terry Kirby .25
109 Tyrone Hughes .25
110 Bryce Paup .25
111 Errict Rhett .75
112 Ricky Watters .50
113 Chris Chandler .25
114 Edgar Bennett .25
115 John Elway 3.00
116 Sam Mills .25
117 Seth Joyner .25
118 Jeff Lageman .25
119 Chris Calloway .25
120 Curtis Martin 4.00
121 Ken Harvey .25
122 Eugene Daniel .25
123 Tim Brown .25
124 Mo Lewis .25
125 Jeff Blake .75
126 Jessie Tuggle .25
127 Vinny Testaverde .25
128 Chris Warren .25
129 Terrell Davis 4.00
130 Greg Lloyd .25
131 Deion Sanders 1.00
132 Derrick Thomas .25
133 Darryll Lewis .25
134 Reggie White .50
135 Jerry Rice 3.00
136 *Tony Banks* .50
137 *Derrick Mayes* .50
138 *Leeland McElroy* .75
139 *Bryan Still* .25
140 *Tim Biakabutuka* .50
141 *Rickey Dudley* .60
142 *Troy James* .25
143 *Lawyer Milloy* .25
144 *Mike Ulufale* .25
145 *Bobby Engram* .75
146 *Willie Anderson* .40
147 *Terrell Owens* 20.00
148 *Jonathan Ogden* .50
149 *Darrius Johnson* .25
150 *Kevin Hardy* .50
151 *Simeon Rice* .50
152 *Alex Molden* .25
153 *Cedric Jones* .25
154 *Duane Clemons* .25
155 *Karim Abdul-Jabbar* .50
156 *Dedric Mathis* .25
157 *John Michels* .25
158 *Winslow Oliver* .25
159 *Stepfret Williams* .25
160 *Eddie Kennison* .50
161 *Marcus Coleman* .25
162 *Tedy Bruschi* .25
163 *Detron Smith* .25
164 *Ray Lewis* 20.00
165 *Marvin Harrison* 20.00
166 *Je'Rod Cherry* .25
167 *Jerris McPhail* .25
168 *Eric Moulds* 10.00
169 *Walt Harris* .50
170 *Eddie George* 15.00
171 *Jermaine Lewis* .50
172 *Jeff Lewis* .75
173 *Ray Mickens* .25
174 *Amani Toomer* 6.00
175 *Zach Thomas* 2.50
176 *Lawrence Phillips* .25
177 *John Mobley* .25
178 *Anthony Dorsett Jr.* .25
179 *DeRon Jenkins* .25
180 *Keyshawn Johnson* 8.00

1996 Bowman's Best Refractors

All 180 cards in Bowman's Best Football had parallel Refractor versions, inserted every 12 packs. The fronts feature a refractive foil, while the backs contain the word "Refractor" within the white card number box.

Refractors: 1X-3X

1996 Bowman's Best Atomic Refractors

All 180 cards in Bowman's Best Football also had Atomic Refractor parallel versions, inserted every 48 packs. Atomic Refractors featured a prismatic refractive foil on the card fronts and the words "Atomic Refractor" on the back within the white card number box.

Atomic Refractors: 5X-10X

1996 Bowman's Best Mirror Images

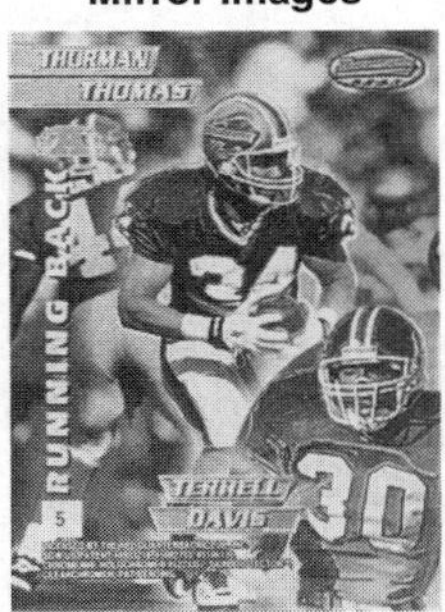

Bowman's Best Mirror Images was a nine-card insert that featured four players per card, with two on each side. Regular versions are seeded every 48 packs, Refractors are found every 96 packs and Atomic Refractors are seeded every 192 packs. Card No. 7 has Jerry Rice on the front with Isaac Bruce with him, but lists running back as their position. This card was an uncorrected error.

NM/M
Complete Set (9): 175.00
Common Player: 6.00
Refractors: 2X
Atomic Refractors: 4X
1a Steve Young, Kerry Collins 25.00
1b Dan Marino, Mark Brunell 35.00
2a Brett Favre, Elvis Grbac 35.00
2b John Elway, Drew Bledsoe 30.00
3a Troy Aikman, Gus Frerotte 20.00
3b Jim Harbaugh, Jeff Blake 8.00
4a Emmitt Smith, Errict Rhett 35.00
4b Chris Warren, Curtis Martin 20.00
5a Barry Sanders, Rashaan Salaam 25.00
5b Thurman Thomas, Terrell Davis 20.00
6a Rodney Hampton, Lawrence Phillips 6.00
6b Marcus Allen, Marshall Faulk 12.00
7a Jerry Rice, I saac Bruce 15.00
7b Tim Brown, Joey Galloway 10.00
8a Cris Carter, Curtis Conway 8.00
8b Carl Pickens, Keyshawn Johnson 8.00
9a Robert Brooks, Michael Westbrook 6.00
9b Anthony Miller, O.J. McDuffie 6.00

1996 Bowman's Best Best Cuts

Bowman's Best Cuts displays 15 of the top players in the NFL on die-cut chromium cards. The player's name runs along the right side, with the majority of the die-cutting on that side. Regular versions are found every 24 packs, Refractors are seeded every 48 packs and Atomic Refractor versions are found every 96 packs.

NM/M
Complete Set (15): 110.00
Common Player: 3.00
Refractors: 2X
Atomic Refractors: 4X
1 Dan Marino 10.00
2 Emmitt Smith 10.00
3 Rashaan Salaam 3.00
4 Herman Moore 5.00
5 Brett Favre 12.00
6 Marshall Faulk 6.00
7 John Elway 8.00
8 Curtis Martin 6.00
9 Deion Sanders 4.00
10 Jerry Rice 10.00
11 Terrell Davis 6.00
12 Kerry Collins 4.00
13 Steve Young 8.00
14 Troy Aikman 10.00
15 Barry Sanders 12.00

1996 Bowman's Best Best Bets

Bowman's Best Bets highlighted nine top rookies on a borderless design with "screws" in all four corners as if the card was in a screw-down holder. Regular versions are seeded every 12 packs, Refractors are found every 48 packs with Atomic Refractors every 96 packs.

NM/M
Complete Set (9): 35.00
Common Player: 2.00
Refractors: 2X
Atomic Refractors: 4X
1 Keyshawn Johnson 5.00
2 Lawrence Phillips 2.00
3 Tim Biakabutuka 2.00
4 Eddie George 10.00
5 John Mobley 2.00
6 Eddie Kennison 2.00
7 Marvin Harrison 10.00
8 Amani Toomer 2.00
9 Bobby Engram 4.00

1997 Bowman's Best

Bowman's Best Football is a 125-card set featuring 95 NFL veterans with a gold design and 30 rookies with a silver design. The base cards also come in Refractor (1:12) and Atomic Refractor (1:24) parallels. The insert sets include Bowman's Best Autographs, Laser Cuts and Mirror Image. Each of the insert cards has a Refractor and Atomic Refractor version. Bowman's Best Football was sold in six-card packs.

NM/M
Complete Set (125): 50.00
Common Player: .25
Minor Stars: .50
Refractor Stars: 2X-4X
Refractor Rookies: 1X-3X
Atomic Ref. Stars: 4X-8X
Atomic Ref. Rookies: 2X-4X
Pack (6): 1.75
Wax Box (24): 30.00
1 Brett Favre 6.00
2 Larry Centers .25
3 Trent Dilfer .50
4 Rodney Hampton .25
5 Wesley Walls .25
6 Jerome Bettis .50
7 Keyshawn Johnson 1.00
8 Keenan McCardell .25
9 Terry Allen .25
10 Troy Aikman 4.00
11 Tony Banks .50
12 Ty Detmer .25
13 Chris Chandler .25
14 Marshall Faulk .50
15 Heath Shuler .25
16 Stan Humphries .25
17 Bryan Cox .25
18 Chris Spielman .25
19 Derrick Thomas .25
20 Steve Young 2.50
21 Desmond Howard .25
22 Jeff Blake .50
23 Michael Jackson .25
24 Cris Carter .25
25 Joey Galloway 1.00
26 Simeon Rice .25
27 Reggie White .50
28 Dave Brown .25
29 Mike Alstott 1.50
30 Emmitt Smith 5.00
31 Anthony Johnson .25
32 Mark Brunell 4.00
33 Ricky Watters .50
34 Terrell Davis 3.00
35 Ben Coates .25
36 Gus Frerotte .25
37 Andre Reed .25
38 Isaac Bruce .50
39 Junior Seau .50
40 Eddie George 3.00
41 Adrian Murrell .50
42 Jake Reed .25
43 Karim Abdul-Jabbar .75
44 Scott Mitchell .25
45 Ki-Jana Carter .25
46 Curtis Conway .50
47 Jim Harbaugh .25
48 Tim Brown .50
49 Mario Bates .25
50 Jerry Rice 4.00
51 Byron Morris .25
52 Marcus Allen .50
53 Errict Rhett .25
54 Steve McNair 3.00
55 Kerry Collins .75
56 Bert Emanuel .25
57 Curtis Martin 4.00
58 Bryce Paup .25
59 Brad Johnson .50
60 John Elway 2.50
61 Natrone Means .50
62 Deion Sanders 2.00
63 Tony Martin .25
64 Michael Westbrook .25
65 Chris Calloway .25
66 Antonio Freeman .50
67 Rick Mirer .25
68 Kent Graham .25
69 O.J. McDuffie .25
70 Barry Sanders 4.00
71 Chris Warren .25
72 Kordell Stewart 1.00
73 Thurman Thomas .50
74 Marvin Harrison 1.00
75 Carl Pickens .25
76 Brent Jones .25
77 Irving Fryar .25
78 Neil O'Donnell .25
79 Elvis Grbac .25
80 Drew Bledsoe 4.00
81 Shannon Sharpe .25
82 Vinny Testaverde .25
83 Chris Sanders .25
84 Herman Moore .50
85 Jeff George .50
86 Bruce Smith .25
87 Robert Smith .25
88 Kevin Hardy .25
89 Kevin Greene .25
90 Dan Marino 5.00
91 Michael Irvin .50
92 Garrison Hearst .25
93 Lake Dawson .25
94 Lawrence Phillips .50
95 Terry Glenn .75
96 *Jake Plummer* 3.00
97 *Byron Hanspard* .50
98 *Bryant Westbrook* .50
99 *Troy Davis* .50
100 *Danny Wuerffel* 1.00
101 *Tony Gonzalez* 2.00
102 *Jim Druckenmiller* .50
103 *Kevin Lockett* .25
104 *Renaldo Wynn* .25
105 *James Farrior* .25
106 *Rae Carruth* .50
107 *Tom Knight* .25
108 *Corey Dillon* 10.00
109 *Kenny Holmes* .25
110 *Orlando Pace* .50
111 *Reidel Anthony* .75
112 *Chad Scott* .25
113 *Antowain Smith* 5.00
114 *David LaFleur* .50
115 *Yatil Green* .50
116 *Darrell Russell* .25
117 *Joey Kent* .40
118 *Darnell Autry* .40
119 *Peter Boulware* .50
120 *Shawn Springs* .25
121 *Ike Hilliard* 3.00
122 *Dwayne Rudd* .25
123 *Reinard Wilson* .25
124 *Michael Booker* .25
125 *Warrick Dunn* 4.00

1997 Bowman's Best Autographs

This 10-card set features autographed versions of 10 base set cards. The cards were inserted 1:131. Refractor (1:1578) and Atomic Refractor (1:4733) parallels are also available.

NM/M
Common Player: 20.00
22 Jeff Blake 20.00
44 Scott Mitchell 20.00
47 Jim Harbaugh 20.00
99 Troy Davis 20.00
102 Jim Druckenmiller 20.00
113 Antowain Smith 30.00
114 David LaFleur 30.00
120 Shawn Springs 20.00
121 Ike Hilliard 30.00
125 Warrick Dunn 45.00

1997 Bowman's Best Cuts

Best Cuts features 20 players on die-cut cards. The top of the cards says Best Cuts and the letters are die-cut. Best Cuts was inserted once per 24 packs. Refractor (1:48) and Atomic Refractor (1:96) parallels were also created. They are numbered with the "BC" prefix.

NM/M
Complete Set (20): 110.00
Common Player: 3.00
Refractors: 2X
Atomic Refractors: 2X-4X
1 Orlando Pace 3.00
2 Eddie George 8.00
3 John Elway 8.00
4 Tony Gonzalez 3.00
5 Brett Favre 12.00
6 Shawn Springs 3.00
7 Warrick Dunn 6.00
8 Troy Aikman 10.00
9 Terry Glenn 6.00
10 Dan Marino 12.00
11 Jake Plummer 6.00
12 Ike Hilliard 4.00
13 Emmitt Smith 12.00
14 Steve Young 8.00
15 Barry Sanders 12.00
16 Jim Druckenmiller 3.00
17 Drew Bledsoe 6.00
18 Antowain Smith 4.00
19 Mark Brunell 6.00
20 Jerry Rice 8.00

1997 Bowman's Best Mirror Images

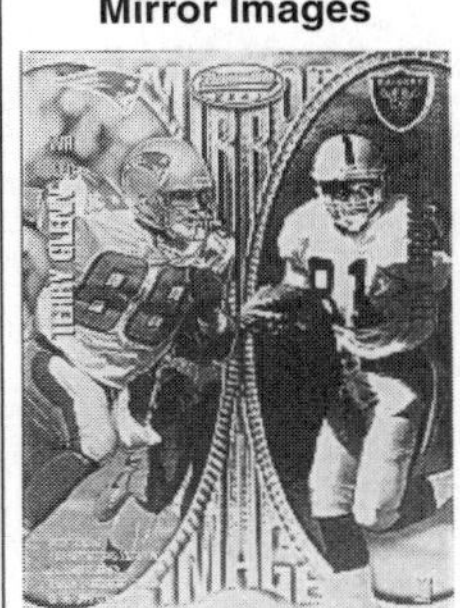

The 10, double-sided cards in Mirror Images showcase four top players from the same position. Two NFC players and two AFC players are featured on each card. The chromium cards (1:48) also had Refractor (1:96) and Atomic Refractor (1:192) parallels. They are numbered with the "MI" prefix.

NM/M
Complete Set (10): 125.00
Common Player: 5.00
Refractors: 2X
Atomic Refractors: 2X-4X
1 Brett Favre, Gus Frerotte, John Elway, Mark Brunell 35.00
2 Steve Young, Tony Banks, Dan Marino, Drew Bledsoe 30.00
3 Troy Aikman, Kerry Collins, Vinny Testaverde, Kordell Stewart 20.00
4 Emmitt Smith, Dorsey Levens, Marcus Allen, Eddie George 30.00
5 Barry Sanders, Errict Rhett, Thurman Thomas, Curtis Martin 25.00
6 Ricky Watters, Jamal Anderson, Chris Warren, Terrell Davis 20.00
7 Jerry Rice, Isaac Bruce, Tony Martin, Marvin Harrison 20.00
8 Herman Moore, Curtis Conway, Tim Brown, Terry Glenn 12.00
9 Michael Irvin, Eddie Kennison, Carl Pickens, Keyshawn Johnson 5.00
10 Wesley Walls, Jason Dunn, Shannon Sharpe, Rickey Dudley 5.00

1998 Bowman

Bowman contained 220 cards, including 150 veterans and 70 rookies. Prospects were featured on a silver and blue design while veterans are shown on a silver and red design. Rookies contain a "Bowman Rookie Card" gold foil stamp. The set is paralleled in Inter-State and Golden Anniversary sets. Three insert sets are included in packs: Bowman Autographs, which come in blue, silver and gold foil versions, Scout's Choice and Bowman Chrome Preview.

NM/M
Complete Set (220): 60.00
Common Player: .25
Minor Stars: .50
Common Rookie: .50
Inter-State Cards: 3X
Inter-State Rookies: 2X
Inserted 1:1
Golden Ann. Stars: 30X-50X
Golden Ann. Rookies: 5X-10X
Inserted 1:180
Production 50 Sets
Pack (10): 4.75
Wax Box (24): 80.00
1 *Peyton Manning* 15.00
2 *Keith Brooking* .50
3 *Duane Starks* .50
4 *Takeo Spikes* .50
5 *Andre Wadsworth* .50
6 *Greg Ellis* .50
7 *Brian Griese* 6.00
8 *Germane Crowell* .60
9 *Jerome Pathon* 1.00
10 *Ryan Leaf* 1.00
11 *Fred Taylor* 8.00
12 *Robert Edwards* 4.00
13 *Grant Wistrom* .50
14 *Robert Holcombe* 1.00
15 *Tim Dwight* 1.00
16 *Jacquez Green* 1.00
17 *Marcus Nash* 1.00
18 *Jason Peter* .50
19 *Anthony Simmons* .50
20 *Curtis Enis* 1.00
21 *John Avery* 1.00
22 *Patrick Johnson* .50
23 *Joe Jurevicius* 2.00
24 *Brian Simmons* 1.00
25 *Kevin Dyson* 3.00
26 *Skip Hicks* 1.00
27 *Hines Ward* 3.00
28 *Tavian Banks* 1.00
29 *Ahman Green* 10.00

30	*Tony Simmons*	.50
31	Charles Johnson	.25
32	Freddie Jones	.25
33	Joey Galloway	.75
34	Tony Banks	.50
35	Jake Plummer	.75
36	Reidel Anthony	.25
37	Steve McNair	.75
38	Michael Westbrook	.50
39	Chris Sanders	.25
40	Isaac Bruce	.50
41	Charlie Garner	.25
42	Wayne Chrebet	.25
43	Michael Strahan	.25
44	Brad Johnson	.50
45	Mike Alstott	.50
46	Tony Gonzalez	.50
47	Johnnie Morton	.25
48	Darnay Scott	.25
49	Rae Carruth	.25
50	Terrell Davis	1.00
51	Jermaine Lewis	.25
52	Frank Sanders	.25
53	Byron Hanspard	.25
54	Gus Frerotte	.25
55	Terry Glenn	.50
56	J.J. Stokes	.50
57	Will Blackwell	.25
58	Keyshawn Johnson	.50
59	Tiki Barber	.50
60	Dorsey Levens	.50
61	Zach Thomas	.25
62	Corey Dillon	1.25
63	Antowain Smith	1.00
64	Michael Sinclair	.25
65	Rod Smith	.25
66	Trent Dilfer	.50
67	Warren Sapp	.25
68	Charles Way	.25
69	Tamarick Vanover	.25
70	Drew Bledsoe	1.50
71	John Mobley	.25
72	Kerry Collins	.50
73	Peter Boulware	.25
74	Simeon Rice	.25
75	Eddie George	1.50
76	Fred Lane	.50
77	Jamal Anderson	.50
78	Antonio Freeman	.75
79	Jason Sehorn	.25
80	Curtis Martin	.75
81	Bobby Hoying	.25
82	Garrison Hearst	.25
83	Glenn Foley	.25
84	Danny Kanell	.25
85	Kordell Stewart	.75
86	O.J. McDuffie	.25
87	Marvin Harrison	.75
88	Bobby Engram	.25
89	Chris Slade	.25
90	Warrick Dunn	1.50
91	Ricky Watters	.50
92	Rickey Dudley	.25
93	Terrell Owens	.50
94	Karim Abdul-Jabbar	.50
95	Napoleon Kaufman	.75
96	Darrell Green	.25
97	Levon Kirkland	.25
98	Jeff George	.50
99	Andre Hastings	.25
100	John Elway	2.00
101	John Randle	.25
102	Andre Rison	.25
103	Keenan McCardell	.25
104	Marshall Faulk	.75
105	Emmitt Smith	3.00
106	Robert Brooks	.25
107	Scott Mitchell	.25
108	Shannon Sharpe	.50
109	Deion Sanders	.75
110	Jerry Rice	2.00
111	Erik Kramer	.25
112	Michael Jackson	.25
113	Aeneas Williams	.25
114	Terry Allen	.25
115	Steve Young	1.25
116	Warren Moon	.50
117	Junior Seau	.50
118	Jerome Bettis	.50
119	Irving Fryar	.25
120	Barry Sanders	4.00
121	Tim Brown	.50
122	Chad Brown	.25
123	Ben Coates	.25
124	Robert Smith	.50
125	Brett Favre	4.00
126	Derrick Thomas	.25
127	Reggie White	.50
128	Troy Aikman	2.00
129	Jeff Blake	.50
130	Mark Brunell	1.50
131	Curtis Conway	.50
132	Wesley Walls	.25
133	Thurman Thomas	.50
134	Chris Chandler	.25
135	Dan Marino	3.00
136	Larry Centers	.25
137	Shawn Jefferson	.25
138	Andre Reed	.25
139	Jake Reed	.25
140	Cris Carter	.50
141	Elvis Grbac	.25
142	Mark Chmura	.50
143	Michael Irvin	.50
144	Carl Pickens	.50
145	Herman Moore	.50
146	Marvin Jones	.25
147	Terance Mathis	.25
148	Rob Moore	.25
149	Bruce Smith	.25
150	Checklist	.25
151	Leslie Shepherd	.25
152	Chris Spielman	.25
153	Tony McGee	.25
154	Kevin Smith	.25
155	Bill Romanowski	.25
156	Stephen Boyd	.25
157	James Stewart	.25
158	Jason Taylor	.25
159	Troy Drayton	.25
160	Mark Fields	.25
161	Jessie Armstead	.25
162	James Jett	.25
163	Bobby Taylor	.25
164	Kimble Anders	.25
165	Jimmy Smith	.25
166	Quentin Coryatt	.25
167	Bryant Westbrook	.25
168	Neil Smith	.25
169	Darren Woodson	.25
170	Ray Buchanan	.25
171	Earl Holmes	.25
172	Ray Lewis	.25
173	Steve Broussard	.25
174	Derrick Brooks	.25
175	Ken Harvey	.25
176	Darryll Lewis	.25
177	Derrick Rodgers	.25
178	James McKnight	.25
179	Cris Dishman	.25
180	Hardy Nickerson	.25
181	*Charles Woodson*	5.00
182	*Randy Moss*	15.00
183	*Stephen Alexander*	.50
184	*Samari Rolle*	.50
185	*Jamie Duncan*	.50
186	*Lance Schulters*	.50
187	*Tony Parrish*	.50
188	*Corey Chavous*	.50
189	*Jammi German*	.50
190	*Sam Cowart*	.50
191	*Donald Hayes*	.50
192	*R.W. McQuarters*	.50
193	*Az-Zahir Hakim*	2.00
194	*Chris Fuamatu-Ma'afala*	1.00
195	*Allen Rossum*	.50
196	*Jon Ritchie*	.50
197	*Blake Spence*	.50
198	*Brian Alford*	.50
199	*Fred Weary*	.50
200	*Rod Rutledge*	.50
201	*Michael Myers*	.50
202	*Rashaan Shehee*	.40
203	*Donovin Darius*	.50
204	*E.G. Green*	.50
205	*Vonnie Holliday*	2.00
206	*Charlie Batch*	2.00
207	*Michael Pittman*	.50
208	*Artrell Hawkins*	.50
209	*Jonathan Quinn*	.50
210	*Kailee Wong*	.50
211	*Deshea Townsend*	.50
212	*Patrick Surtain*	.50
213	*Brian Kelly*	.50
214	*Tebucky Jones*	.50
215	*Pete Gonzalez*	.50
216	*Shaun Williams*	.50
217	*Scott Frost*	.50
218	*Leonard Little*	.50
219	*Alonzo Mayes*	.50
220	*Cordell Taylor*	.50

1998 Bowman Inter-State

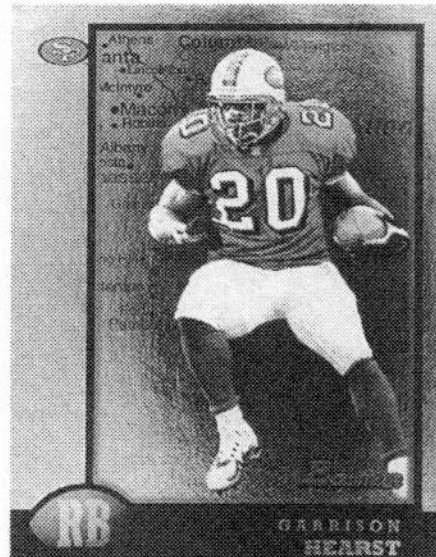

All 220 cards were reprinted in Inter-State parallel versions and seeded one per pack. These are printed on silver foil and included a background map of where the player was born on the front and a vanity plate on the back.

	NM/M
Inter-State Cards:	3X
Inter-State Rookies:	2X

1998 Bowman Blue Autographs

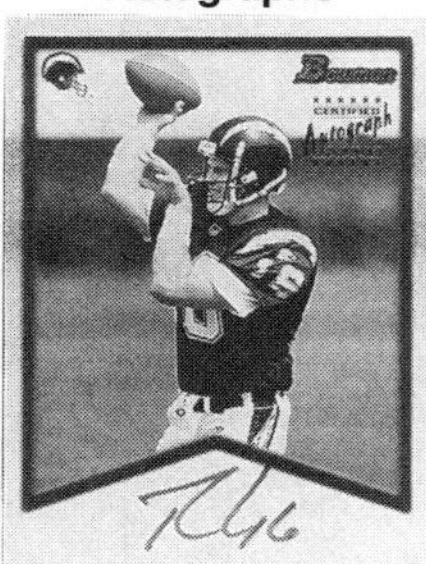

Eleven different players signed cards to be inserted into packs of Bowman. Card rarity was differentiated by blue (1:360 packs), silver (2,401) or gold foil Topps Certified Autograph Issue stamps (1:7,202).

		NM/M
Common Player:		20.00
Inserted 1:360		
Silver Cards:		2X
Inserted 1:2,401		
Gold Cards:		4X
Inserted 1:7,202		
1	Peyton Manning	140.00
2	Andre Wadsworth	20.00
3	Brian Griese	50.00
4	Ryan Leaf	75.00
5	Fred Taylor	75.00
6	Robert Edwards	60.00
7	Randy Moss	150.00
8	Curtis Enis	60.00
9	Kevin Dyson	40.00
10	Charles Woodson	60.00
11	Tim Dwight	40.00

1998 Bowman Chrome Preview

This 10-card insert set previewed the upcoming Bowman Chrome set. It included five veterans and five rookies, with regular versions seeded one per 12 packs and Refractors every 48 packs.

		NM/M
Complete Set (10):		50.00
Common Player:		4.00
Inserted 1:12		
Refractors:		2X
Inserted 1:48		
1	Peyton Manning	20.00
2	Curtis Enis	5.00
3	Charles Woodson	4.00
4	Robert Edwards	6.00
5	Ryan Leaf	7.00
6	Brett Favre	12.00
7	John Elway	6.00
8	Barry Sanders	12.00
9	Kordell Stewart	4.00
10	Terrell Davis	8.00

1998 Bowman Scout's Choice

This 14-card insert set showcased the top rookies according to the Bowman Scouts. Cards featured a borderless, double-etched foil design and were inserted one per 12 packs.

		NM/M
Complete Set (14):		40.00
Common Player:		2.00
Inserted 1:12		
SC1	Peyton Manning	15.00
SC2	John Avery	3.00
SC3	Grant Wistrom	2.00
SC4	Kevin Dyson	3.00
SC5	Andre Wadsworth	3.00
SC6	Joe Jurevicius	2.00
SC7	Charles Woodson	6.00
SC8	Takeo Spikes	2.00
SC9	Fred Taylor	5.00
SC10	Ryan Leaf	8.00
SC11	Robert Edwards	6.00
SC12	Randy Moss	15.00
SC13	Patrick Johnson	2.00
SC14	Curtis Enis	6.00

1998 Bowman's Best

This super-premium set has a 125-card base set that is made up of 100 veterans and 25 rookies. Each veteran card has a gold design, while the rookies are in silver. Each card has a Refractor version that is sequentially numbered to 400 and inserted 1:25 packs. Each player also has a parallel Atomic Refractor version that is numbered to 100 and inserted 1:103 packs.

		NM/M
Complete Set (125):		100.00
Common Player:		.25
Minor Stars:		.50
Common Rookie:		2.00
Inserted 1:2		
Refractor Cards:		8X-16X
Refractor Rookies:		3X-6X
Inserted 1:25		
Production 400 Sets		
Atomic Ref. Cards:		25X-50X
Atomic Ref. Rookies:		10X-20X
Inserted 1:103		
Production 100 Sets		
Pack (6):		4.00
Wax Box (24):		70.00
1	Emmitt Smith	4.00
2	Reggie White	.75
3	Jake Plummer	1.00
4	Ike Hilliard	.25
5	Isaac Bruce	.50
6	Trent Dilfer	.50
7	Ricky Watters	.50
8	Jeff George	.50
9	Wayne Chrebet	.50
10	Brett Favre	6.00
11	Terry Allen	.50
12	Bert Emanuel	.25
13	Andre Reed	.25
14	Andre Rison	.50
15	Jeff Blake	.50
16	Steve McNair	1.50
17	Joey Galloway	1.00
18	Irving Fryar	.25
19	Dorsey Levens	.75
20	Jerry Rice	3.00
21	Kerry Collins	.75
22	Michael Jackson	.25
23	Kordell Stewart	1.00
24	Junior Seau	.50
25	Jimmy Smith	.75
26	Michael Westbrook	.25
27	Eddie George	2.50
28	Cris Carter	1.00
29	Jason Sehorn	.25
30	Warrick Dunn	2.00
31	Garrison Hearst	.75
32	Erik Kramer	.25
33	Chris Chandler	.50
34	Michael Irvin	.50
35	Marshall Faulk	1.00
36	Warren Moon	.50
37	Rickey Dudley	.25
38	Drew Bledsoe	2.50
39	Antowain Smith	1.00
40	Terrell Davis	3.00
41	Gus Frerotte	.25
42	Robert Brooks	.25
43	Tony Banks	.50
44	Terrell Owens	1.50
45	Edgar Bennett	.25
46	Rob Moore	.50
47	J.J. Stokes	.50
48	Yancey Thigpen	.25
49	Elvis Grbac	.25
50	John Elway	3.00
51	Charles Johnson	.25
52	Karim Abdul-Jabbar	.75
53	Carl Pickens	.50
54	Peter Boulware	.25
55	Chris Warren	.25
56	Terance Mathis	.25
57	Andre Hastings	.25
58	Jake Reed	.25
59	Mike Alstott	1.00
60	Mark Brunell	2.50
61	Herman Moore	.75
62	Troy Aikman	3.00
63	Fred Lane	.50
64	Rod Smith	.75
65	Terry Glenn	.75
66	Jerome Bettis	.75
67	Derrick Thomas	.25
68	Marvin Harrison	.50
69	Adrian Murrell	.50
70	Curtis Martin	1.25
71	Bobby Hoying	.25
72	Darrell Green	.25
73	Sean Dawkins	.25
74	Robert Smith	.50
75	Antonio Freeman	.75
76	Scott Mitchell	.25
77	Curtis Conway	.50
78	Rae Carruth	.25
79	Jamal Anderson	1.50
80	Dan Marino	4.00
81	Brad Johnson	1.00
82	Danny Kanell	.25
83	Charlie Garner	.25
84	Rob Johnson	.50
85	Natrone Means	.50
86	Tim Brown	.75
87	Keyshawn Johnson	1.00
88	Ben Coates	.50
89	Derrick Alexander	.25
90	Steve Young	2.00
91	Shannon Sharpe	.50
92	Corey Dillon	1.50
93	Bruce Smith	.25
94	Errict Rhett	.25
95	Jim Harbaugh	.50
96	Napoleon Kaufman	.75
97	Glenn Foley	.50
98	Tony Gonzalez	.25
99	Keenan McCardell	.50
100	Barry Sanders	6.00
101	*Charles Woodson*	6.00
102	*Tim Dwight*	4.00
103	*Marcus Nash*	2.00
104	*Joe Jurevicius*	3.00
105	*Jacquez Green*	2.00
106	*Kevin Dyson*	4.00
107	*Keith Brooking*	1.00
108	*Andre Wadsworth*	1.00
109	*Randy Moss*	15.00
110	*Robert Edwards*	2.00
111	*Patrick Johnson*	1.00
112	*Peyton Manning*	15.00
113	*Duane Starks*	1.00
114	*Grant Wistrom*	1.00
115	*Anthony Simmons*	1.00
116	*Takeo Spikes*	2.00
117	*Tony Simmons*	1.00
118	*Jerome Pathon*	3.00
119	*Ryan Leaf*	1.00
120	*Skip Hicks*	2.00
121	*Curtis Enis*	1.00
122	*Germane Crowell*	1.00
123	*John Avery*	1.00
124	*Hines Ward*	3.00
125	*Fred Taylor*	1.00

1998 Bowman's Best Autographs

Ten players are in this set with each having two different cards. The only difference is the suffix "A" or "B" after the card number. Each of the 20 cards has a "Certified Autograph Issue" stamp on the fronts. Singles are found 1:158 packs, while Refractor versions are 1:840 and Atomic Refractors are 1:2,521.

		NM/M
Complete Set (20):		450.00
Common Player:		15.00
Inserted 1:158		
Refractor Cards:		2X
Inserted 1:840		
Atomic Ref. Cards:		3X
Inserted 1:2,521		
1A	Jake Plummer	40.00
1B	Jake Plummer	40.00
2A	Jason Sehorn	15.00
2B	Jason Sehorn	15.00
3A	Corey Dillon	30.00
3B	Corey Dillon	30.00
4A	Tim Brown	25.00
4B	Tim Brown	25.00
5A	Keenan McCardell	15.00
5B	Keenan McCardell	15.00
6A	Kordell Stewart	25.00
6B	Kordell Stewart	25.00
7A	Peyton Manning	125.00
7B	Peyton Manning	125.00
8A	Danny Kanell	15.00
8B	Danny Kanell	15.00
9A	Fred Taylor	60.00
9B	Fred Taylor	60.00
10A	Curtis Enis	25.00
10B	Curtis Davis	25.00

1998 Bowman's Best Mirror Image Fusion

This insert is made up of 20 double-sided cards that feature two top players at the same position. Singles are found 1:48 packs, while the parallel Refractors are sequentially numbered to 100 and inserted 1:630. Atomic Refractors are numbered to 25 and found 1:2,521.

		NM/M
Complete Set (20):		175.00
Common Player:		4.00
Minor Stars:		8.00
Inserted 1:48		
Refractor Cards:		3X-5X
Inserted 1:630		
Production 100 Sets		
Atomic Ref. Cards:		6X-12X
Inserted 1:2,521		
Production 25 Sets		
MI1	Terrell Davis, John Avery	20.00
MI2	Emmitt Smith, Curtis Enis	30.00
MI3	Barry Sanders, Skip Hicks	25.00
MI4	Eddie George, Robert Edwards	12.00
MI5	Jerome Bettis, Fred Taylor	20.00
MI6	Mark Brunell, Ryan Leaf	20.00
MI7	John Elway, Brian Griese	25.00
MI8	Dan Marino, Peyton Manning	25.00
MI9	Brett Favre, Charlie Batch	30.00
MI10	Drew Bledsoe, Jonathan Quinn	20.00
MI11	Tim Brown, Kevin Dyson	10.00
MI12	Herman Moore, Germane Crowell	10.00
MI13	Joey Galloway, Jerome Pathon	8.00
MI14	Cris Carter, Jacquez Green	12.00
MI15	Jerry Rice, Randy Moss	30.00
MI16	Junior Seau, Takeo Spikes	4.00
MI17	John Randle, Jason Peter	4.00
MI18	Reggie White, Andre Wadsworth	8.00
MI19	Peter Boulware, Anthony Simmons	4.00
MI20	Derrick Thomas, Brian Simmons	4.00

1998 Bowman's Best Performers

This insert showcases the top rookies who came up in '98. Singles were inserted 1:12 packs, while Refractors are numbered to 200 and can be found 1:630. Atomic Refractors are numbered to 50 and found 1:2,521.

		NM/M
Complete Set (10):		35.00
Common Player:		2.00
Inserted 1:12		
Refractor Cards:		2X-4X
Inserted 1:630		
Production 200 Sets		
Atomic Ref. Cards:		5X-10X
Inserted 1:2,521		
Production 50 Sets		
BP1	Peyton Manning	10.00
BP2	Charles Woodson	6.00
BP3	Skip Hicks	4.00
BP4	Andre Wadsworth	2.00
BP5	Randy Moss	15.00
BP6	Marcus Nash	5.00
BP7	Ahman Green	4.00
BP8	Anthony Simmons	2.00
BP9	Tavian Banks	4.00
BP10	Ryan Leaf	2.00

1998 Bowman's Best Super Bowl Show

This 16-card set was available exclusively at the NFL Experience Card Show at Super Bowl XXXII. It features 4" x 5-1/2" Bowman's Best cards, with the Super Bowl logo on the front near the middle. Refractor versions of each of these cards was also available randomly. The cards were obtained by exchanging wrappers of Topps products at the Topps booth.

		NM/M
Complete Set (16):		350.00
Common Player:		8.00
Refractors:		2X
1	Brett Favre	50.00
2	Barry Sanders	40.00
3	Emmitt Smith	50.00
4	John Elway	30.00
5	Tim Brown	8.00
6	Eddie George	20.00
7	Troy Aikman	25.00
8	Drew Bledsoe	20.00
9	Dan Marino	50.00
10	Jerry Rice	30.00
11	Junior Seau	8.00
12	Antowain Smith	10.00
13	Warrick Dunn	10.00
14	Jim Druckenmiller	10.00
15	Terrell Davis	20.00
16	Curtis Martin	20.00

1998 Bowman Chrome

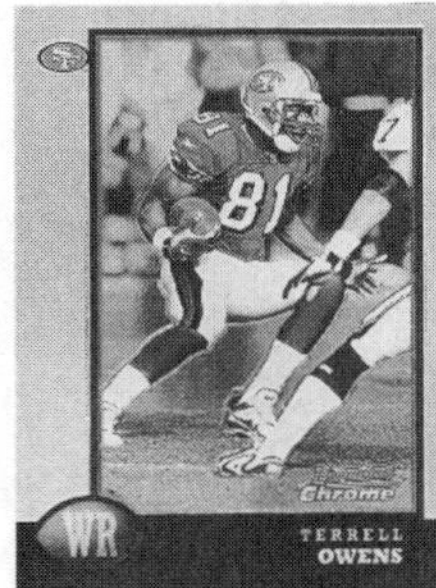

Bowman Chrome football is a 220-card base set that includes 150 veterans and 70 rookies. There are also Refractor parallel cards of every regular card in the set that are randomly inserted 1:12 packs. Rookies are designated with a silver and blue logo design, while the veteran cards are shown with a silver and red design.

		NM/M
Complete Set (220):		135.00
Common Player:		.30
Minor Stars:		.60
Common Rookie:		3.50
Refractor Cards:		3X-6X
Refractor Rookies:		3X
Inserted 1:12		
Inter-State Cards:		3X
Inter-State Rookies:		1.2X
Inserted 1:4		
I.S. Refractor Cards:		5X-10X
I.S. Refractor Rookies:		3X
Inserted 1:24		
Golden Ann. Stars:		30X-60X
Golden Ann. Rookies:		2X-4X
Inserted 1:138		
Production 50 Sets		
Pack (10):		6.75
Wax Box (24):		115.00
1	*Peyton Manning*	35.00
2	*Keith Brooking*	2.00
3	*Duane Starks*	2.00
4	*Takeo Spikes*	7.00
5	*Andre Wadsworth*	2.00
6	*Greg Ellis*	2.00
7	*Brian Griese*	12.00
8	*Germane Crowell*	5.00
9	*Jerome Pathon*	7.00
10	*Ryan Leaf*	2.00
11	*Fred Taylor*	15.00
12	*Robert Edwards*	4.00
13	*Grant Wistrom*	2.00
14	*Robert Holcombe*	2.00
15	*Tim Dwight*	10.00
16	*Jacquez Green*	10.00
17	*Marcus Nash*	4.00
18	*Jason Peter*	2.00
19	*Anthony Simmons*	2.00
20	*Curtis Enis*	2.00
21	*John Avery*	2.00
22	*Patrick Johnson*	2.00
23	*Joe Jurevicius*	7.00
24	*Brian Simmons*	2.00
25	*Kevin Dyson*	10.00
26	*Skip Hicks*	4.00
27	*Hines Ward*	10.00
28	*Tavian Banks*	2.00
29	*Ahman Green*	20.00
30	*Tony Simmons*	2.00
31	Charles Johnson	.30
32	Freddie Jones	.30
33	Joey Galloway	.50
34	Tony Banks	.60
35	Jake Plummer	1.00
36	Reidel Anthony	.30
37	Steve McNair	1.00
38	Michael Westbrook	.60
39	Chris Sanders	.30
40	Isaac Bruce	.60
41	Charlie Garner	.30
42	Wayne Chrebet	.60
43	Michael Strahan	.30
44	Brad Johnson	1.00
45	Mike Alstott	1.00
46	Tony Gonzalez	.60
47	Johnnie Morton	.30
48	Darnay Scott	.30
49	Rae Carruth	.30
50	Terrell Davis	2.00
51	Jermaine Lewis	.30
52	Frank Sanders	.30
53	Byron Hanspard	.30
54	Gus Frerotte	.30
55	Terry Glenn	.60
56	J.J. Stokes	.60
57	Will Blackwell	.30
58	Keyshawn Johnson	1.00
59	Tiki Barber	.60
60	Dorsey Levens	.60
61	Zach Thomas	.30
62	Corey Dillon	1.50
63	Antowain Smith	1.00
64	Michael Sinclair	.30
65	Rod Smith	.60
66	Trent Dilfer	.60
67	Warren Sapp	.30
68	Charles Way	.30
69	Tamarick Vanover	.30
70	Drew Bledsoe	2.50
71	John Mobley	.30
72	Kerry Collins	.60
73	Peter Boulware	.30
74	Simeon Rice	.30
75	Eddie George	2.50
76	Fred Lane	.60
77	Jamal Anderson	1.50
78	Antonio Freeman	.40
79	Jason Sehorn	.30
80	Curtis Martin	1.00
81	Bobby Hoying	.30
82	Garrison Hearst	1.00
83	Glenn Foley	.60
84	Danny Kanell	.30
85	Kordell Stewart	1.00
86	O.J. McDuffie	.30
87	Marvin Harrison	.60
88	Bobby Engram	.30
89	Chris Slade	.30
90	Warrick Dunn	2.00
91	Ricky Watters	.60
92	Rickey Dudley	.30
93	Terrell Owens	1.00
94	Karim Abdul-Jabbar	.60
95	Napoleon Kaufman	.40
96	Darrell Green	.30
97	Levon Kirkland	.30
98	Jeff George	.60
99	Andre Hastings	.30
100	John Elway	3.00
101	John Randle	.30
102	Andre Rison	.30
103	Keenan McCardell	.30
104	Marshall Faulk	1.00
105	Emmitt Smith	4.50
106	Robert Brooks	.30
107	Scott Mitchell	.30
108	Shannon Sharpe	.60
109	Deion Sanders	1.00
110	Jerry Rice	3.00
111	Erik Kramer	.30
112	Michael Jackson	.30
113	Aeneas Williams	.30
114	Terry Allen	.60
115	Steve Young	1.75
116	Warren Moon	.60
117	Junior Seau	.60
118	Jerome Bettis	.60
119	Irving Fryar	.30
120	Barry Sanders	6.00
121	Tim Brown	.60
122	Chad Brown	.30
123	Ben Coates	.30
124	Robert Smith	.60
125	Brett Favre	6.00
126	Derrick Thomas	.30
127	Reggie White	1.00
128	Troy Aikman	3.00
129	Jeff Blake	.60
130	Mark Brunell	2.50
131	Curtis Conway	.60
132	Wesley Walls	.30
133	Thurman Thomas	.60
134	Chris Chandler	.30
135	Dan Marino	4.50
136	Larry Centers	.30
137	Shawn Jefferson	.30
138	Andre Reed	.30
139	Jake Reed	.30
140	Cris Carter	1.00
141	Elvis Grbac	.30
142	Mark Chmura	.60
143	Michael Irvin	.60
144	Carl Pickens	.60
145	Herman Moore	.60
146	Marvin Jones	.30
147	Terance Mathis	.30
148	Rob Moore	.60
149	Bruce Smith	.30
150	Checklist	.30
151	Leslie Shepherd	.30
152	Chris Spielman	.30
153	Tony McGee	.30
154	Kevin Smith	.30
155	Bill Romanowski	.30
156	Stephen Boyd	.30
157	James Stewart	.30
158	Jason Taylor	.30
159	Troy Drayton	.30
160	Mark Fields	.30
161	Jessie Armstead	.30
162	James Jett	.30
163	Bobby Taylor	.30
164	Kimble Anders	.30
165	Jimmy Smith	.60
166	Quentin Coryatt	.30
167	Bryant Westbrook	.30
168	Neil Smith	.30
169	Darren Woodson	.30
170	Ray Buchanan	.30
171	Earl Holmes	.30
172	Ray Lewis	.30
173	Steve Broussard	.30
174	Derrick Brooks	.30
175	Ken Harvey	.30
176	Darryll Lewis	.30
177	Derrick Rodgers	.30
178	James McKnight	.30
179	Cris Dishman	.30
180	Hardy Nickerson	.30
181	*Charles Woodson*	15.00
182	*Randy Moss*	35.00
183	*Stephen Alexander*	6.00
184	*Samari Rolle*	2.00
185	*Jamie Duncan*	2.00
186	*Lance Schulters*	2.00
187	*Tony Parrish*	2.00
188	*Corey Chavous*	2.00
189	*Jammi German*	2.00
190	*Sam Cowart*	3.50
191	*Donald Hayes*	2.00
192	*R.W. McQuarters*	4.00
193	*Az-Zahir Hakim*	10.00
194	*Chris Fuamatu-Ma'afala*	7.00
195	*Allen Rossum*	2.00
196	*Jon Ritchie*	2.00
197	*Blake Spence*	2.00
198	*Brian Alford*	2.00
199	*Fred Weary*	2.00
200	*Rod Rutledge*	2.00
201	*Michael Myers*	2.00
202	*Rashaan Shehee*	2.00
203	*Donovin Darius*	2.00
204	*E.G. Green*	2.00
205	*Vonnie Holliday*	3.00
206	*Charlie Batch*	3.00
207	*Michael Pittman*	4.00
208	*Artrell Hawkins*	2.00
209	*Jonathan Quinn*	2.00
210	*Kailee Wong*	2.00
211	*Deshea Townsend*	2.00
212	*Patrick Surtain*	2.00
213	*Brian Kelly*	2.00
214	*Tebucky Jones*	2.00
215	*Pete Gonzalez*	2.00
216	*Shaun Williams*	2.00
217	*Scott Frost*	2.00
218	*Leonard Little*	2.00
219	*Alonzo Mayes*	2.00
220	*Cordell Taylor*	2.00

1999 Bowman

Bowman Football was a 220-card set that included 70 players who made their first appearance. Each of the rookie cards has the "Rookie Card Logo" on the front of the singles and are printed with a silver and blue logo design. The veterans are shown with a silver and red design. Parallel sets include the Inter-State and Gold singles. Other insert sets include: Autographs (Gold, Silver and Blue), Late Bloomers/Early Risers and Scout's Choice. Nine-card packs had an SRP of $3.00.

		NM/M
Complete Set (220):		50.00
Common Player:		.15
Minor Stars:		.30
Common Rookie:		.75
Pack (10):		2.75
Wax Box (24):		45.00
1	Dan Marino	2.00
2	Michael Westbrook	.30
3	Yancey Thigpen	.15
4	Tony Martin	.15
5	Michael Strahan	.15
6	Dedric Ward	.15
7	Joey Galloway	.50
8	Bobby Engram	.15
9	Frank Sanders	.15
10	Jake Plummer	.75
11	Eddie Kennison	.15
12	Curtis Martin	.50
13	Ryan Leaf	.50
14	Trent Dilfer	.30
15	Tim Biakabutuka	.15
16	Elvis Grbac	.30
17	Charlie Batch	.50
18	Takeo Spikes	.15
19	Tony Banks	.30
20	Doug Flutie	.50
21	Ty Law	.15
22	Isaac Bruce	.30
23	James Jett	.15
24	Kent Graham	.15
25	Derrick Mayes	.30
26	Amani Toomer	.15
27	Ray Lewis	.15
28	Shawn Springs	.15
29	Warren Sapp	.15
30	Jamal Anderson	.50
31	Byron Morris	.15
32	Johnnie Morton	.15
33	Terance Mathis	.15
34	Terrell Davis	1.00
35	John Randle	.15
36	Vinny Testaverde	.30
37	Junior Seau	.30
38	Reidel Anthony	.30
39	Brad Johnson	.50
40	Emmitt Smith	2.00
41	Mo Lewis	.15
42	Terry Glenn	.50
43	Dorsey Levens	.50
44	Thurman Thomas	.30
45	Rob Moore	.30
46	Corey Dillon	.50
47	Jessie Armstead	.15
48	Marshall Faulk	.50
49	Charles Woodson	.50
50	John Elway	2.00
51	Kevin Dyson	.30
52	Tony Simmons	.30
53	Keenan McCardell	.30
54	O.J. Santiago	.15
55	Jermaine Lewis	.30
56	Herman Moore	.50
57	Gary Brown	.15
58	Jim Harbaugh	.30
59	Mike Alstott	.50
60	Brett Favre	3.00
61	Tim Brown	.30
62	Steve McNair	.75
63	Ben Coates	.30
64	Jerome Pathon	.15
65	Ray Buchanan	.15
66	Troy Aikman	1.50
67	Andre Reed	.30
68	Bubby Brister	.30
69	Karim Abdul	.30
70	Peyton Manning	2.00
71	Charles Johnson	.15
72	Natrone Means	.30
73	Michael Sinclair	.15
74	Skip Hicks	.30
75	Derrick Alexander	.15
76	Wayne Chrebet	.30
77	Rod Smith	.30
78	Carl Pickens	.30
79	Adrian Murrell	.30
80	Fred Taylor	1.50
81	Eric Moulds	.50
82	Erik Kramer	.15
83	Marvin Harrison	.50
84	Cris Carter	.50
85	Ike Hilliard	.15
86	Hines Ward	.30
87	Terrell Owens	.50
88	Ricky Proehl	.15
89	Bert Emanuel	.15
90	Randy Moss	3.00
91	Aaron Glenn	.15
92	Robert Smith	.30
93	Andre Hastings	.15
94	Jake Reed	.15
95	Curtis Enis	.50
96	Andre Wadsworth	.30
97	Ed McCaffrey	.50
98	Zach Thomas	.30
99	Kerry Collins	.30
100	Drew Bledsoe	1.25
101	Germane Crowell	.30
102	Bryan Still	.15
103	Chad Brown	.15
104	Jacquez Green	.30
105	Garrison Hearst	.30
106	Napoleon Kaufman	.30
107	Ricky Watters	.30
108	O.J. McDuffie	.30
109	Keyshawn Johnson	.50
110	Jerome Bettis	.50
111	Duce Staley	.30
112	Curtis Conway	.30
113	Chris Chandler	.30
114	Marcus Nash	.30
115	Stephen Alexander	.15
116	Darnay Scott	.15
117	Bruce Smith	.15
118	Priest Holmes	1.00
119	Mark Brunell	1.25
120	Jerry Rice	1.50
121	Randall Cunningham	.50
122	Cameron Cleeland	.30
123	Antonio Freeman	.50
124	Kordell Stewart	.75
125	Jon Kitna	.75
126	Ahman Green	.30
127	Warrick Dunn	.75
128	Robert Brooks	.15
129	Derrick Thomas	.30
130	Steve Young	1.00
131	Peter Boulware	.15
132	Michael Irvin	.30
133	Shannon Sharpe	.30
134	Jimmy Smith	.30
135	John Avery	.30
136	Fred Lane	.15
137	Trent Green	.30
138	Andre Rison	.15
139	Antowain Smith	.30
140	Eddie George	.75
141	Jeff Blake	.30
142	Raghib Ismail	.15
143	Rickey Dudley	.15
144	Courtney Hawkins	.15
145	Mikhael Ricks	.15
146	J.J. Stokes	.30
147	Levon Kirkland	.15
148	Deion Sanders	.50
149	Barry Sanders	2.00
150	Tiki Barber	.15
151	*David Boston*	4.00
152	*Chris McAlister*	.50
153	*Peerless Price*	3.00
154	*D'Wayne Bates*	.50
155	*Cade McNown*	1.00
156	*Akili Smith*	1.00
157	*Kevin Johnson*	2.00
158	*Tim Couch*	4.00
159	*Sedrick Irvin*	1.00
160	*Chris Claiborne*	.50
161	*Edgerrin James*	8.00
162	*Michael Cloud*	.50
163	*Cecil Collins*	2.00
164	*James Johnson*	1.00
165	*Rob Konrad*	1.00
166	*Daunte Culpepper*	8.00
167	*Kevin Faulk*	2.00
168	*Donovan McNabb*	8.00
169	*Troy Edwards*	2.00
170	*Amos Zereoue*	3.00
171	*Karsten Bailey*	1.50
172	*Brock Huard*	1.00
173	*Joe Germaine*	1.00
174	*Torry Holt*	4.00
175	*Shaun King*	2.00
176	*Jevon Kearse*	3.00
177	*Champ Bailey*	2.50
178	*Ebenezer Ekuban*	1.00
179	*Andy Katzenmoyer*	1.00
180	*Antoine Winfield*	1.00
181	*Jermaine Fazande*	.75
182	*Ricky Williams*	3.00
183	*Joel Mackovicka*	.75
184	*Reginald Kelly*	.75
185	*Brandon Stokley*	.75
186	*Shawn Bryson*	.75
187	*Marty Booker*	1.50
188	*Jerry Azumah*	.75
189	*Craig Yeast*	.75
190	*Scott Covington*	.75
191	*Rahim Abdullah*	.75
192	*Darrin Chiaverini*	.75
193	*Dat Nguyen*	1.50
194	*Wane McGarity*	.75
195	*Al Wilson*	.75
196	*Travis McGriff*	.75
197	*Aaron Gibson*	.75
198	*Antwan Edwards*	.75
199	*Aaron Brooks*	8.00
200	*De'Mond Parker*	.75
201	*Dee Miller*	.75
202	*John Tait*	.75
203	*Jim Kleinsasser*	1.50
204	*Michael Bishop*	2.00
205	*Joe Montgomery*	.75
206	*Sean Bennett*	.75
207	*Dameane Douglas*	.75
208	*Na Brown*	.75
209	*Jerame Tuman*	.75
210	*Malcolm Johnson*	.75
211	*Dre' Bly*	.75
212	*Terry Jackson*	.75
213	*Tai Streets*	.75
214	*Autry Denson*	.75
215	*Darnell McDonald*	.75
216	*Charlie Rogers*	.75
217	*Reggie McGrew*	.75
218	*Tony Bryant*	.75
219	*Larry Parker*	.75
220	*Martay Jenkins*	.75

1999 Bowman Gold

This was a 220-card parallel to the base set with the team name stamped in gold foil. Each card was sequentially numbered to 99 and inserted 1:68 packs.

	NM/M
Gold Cards:	6X-10X
Gold Rookies:	2X-5X
Production 99 Sets	

1999 Bowman Interstate

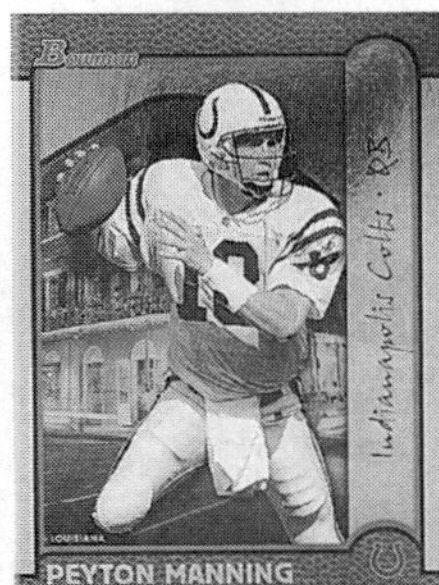

This was a 220-card parallel to the base set. The card fronts have a scenic landmark from the player's home state and the card backs feature a custom-tailored vanity plate from that state. Singles were inserted into every pack.

	NM/M
Interstate Cards:	3X
Interstate Rookies:	1.5X
Inserted 1:1	

1999 Bowman Autographs

The 32-card autograph set was divdided into three sections with the first six cards in Gold and found 1:850 packs. The next 15 cards were printed in Silver and inserted 1:212 packs. The last 11 singles were in Blue and found 1:180 packs.

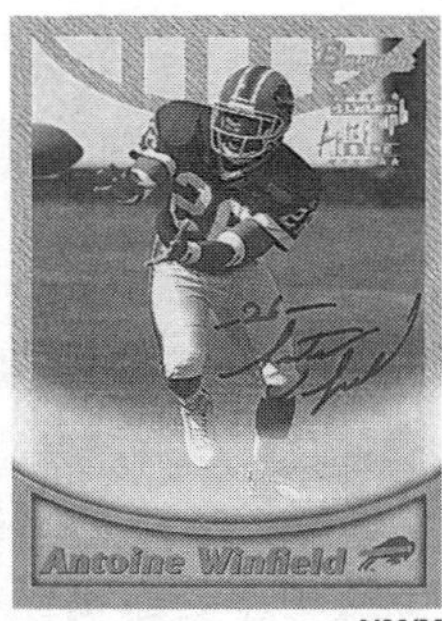

		NM/M
Common Gold (1-6):		75.00
Inserted 1:850		
Common Silver (7-21):		20.00
Inserted 1:212		
Common Blue (22-32):		12.00
Inserted 1:180		
1	Randy Moss G	125.00
2	Akili Smith G	75.00
3	Edgerrin James G	125.00
4	Ricky Williams G	150.00
5	Torry Holt G	75.00
6	Daunte Culpepper G	100.00
7	Donovan McNabb S	85.00
8	Tim Couch S	75.00
9	Champ Bailey S	40.00
10	David Boston S	50.00
11	Chris Claiborne S	20.00
12	Chris McAlister S	20.00
13	Rob Konrad S	20.00
14	Michael Cloud S	20.00
15	Jermaine Fazande S	20.00
16	Brock Huard S	30.00
17	Joe Germaine S	30.00
18	Sedrick Irvin S	40.00
19	Cecil Collins S	80.00
20	Karsten Bailey S	20.00
21	Antoine Winfield S	20.00
22	Cade McNown B	60.00
23	Troy Edwards B	40.00
24	Jevon Kearse B	35.00
25	Andy Katzenmoyer B	20.00
26	Kevin Johnson B	40.00
27	James Johnson B	30.00
28	Kevin Faulk B	30.00
29	Shaun King B	25.00
30	Peerless Price B	30.00
31	D'Wayne Bates B	12.00
32	Amos Zereoue B	30.00

1999 Bowman Late Bloomers/Early Risers

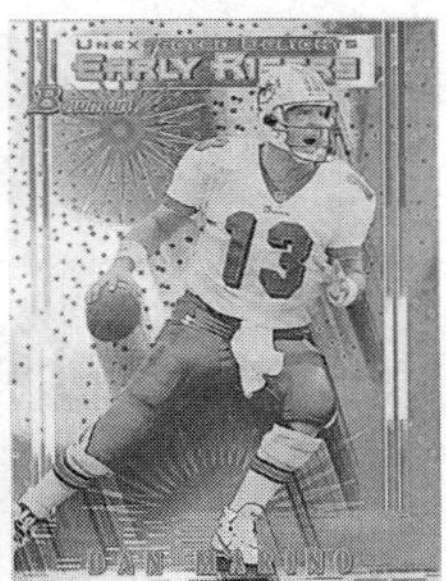

This 10-card set includes five Late Bloomers and five Early Risers. The Late Bloomer theme includes the best late-round selections and the Early Risers include impact players from past NFL Drafts. Singles were found 1:12 packs.

		NM/M
Complete Set (10):		20.00
Common Player:		1.00
Inserted 1:12		
1	Fred Taylor (Early Risers)	3.00
2	Peyton Manning (Early Risers)	4.00
3	Dan Marino (Early Risers)	4.00
4	Barry Sanders (Early Risers)	5.00
5	Randy Moss (Early Risers)	5.00
6	Mark Brunell (Late Bloomers)	2.00
7	Jamal Anderson (Late Bloomers)	1.00
8	Curtis Martin (Late Bloomers)	1.00
9	Wayne Chrebet (Late Bloomers)	1.00
10	Terrell Davis (Late Bloomers)	4.00

1999 Bowman Scout's Choice

This 21-card set included the top rookies from the 1999 Draft.

Each card was borderless and printed on double-etched foil board. Singles were inserted 1:12 packs.

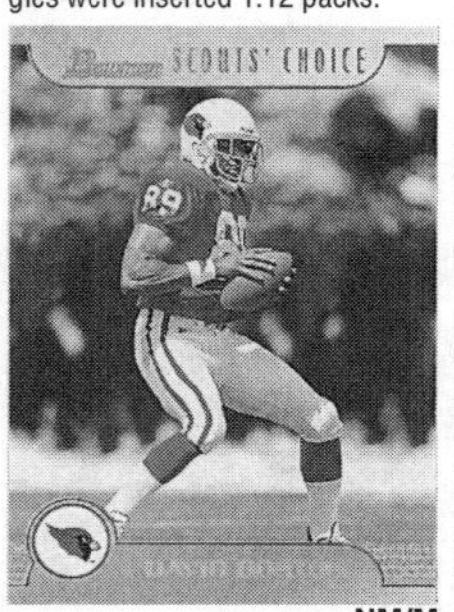

		NM/M
Complete Set (21):		50.00
Common Player:		1.00
Minor Stars:		2.00
Inserted 1:12		
1	David Boston	4.00
2	Champ Bailey	2.50
3	Edgerrin James	10.00
4	Michael Cloud	1.00
5	Kevin Faulk	3.00
6	Troy Edwards	4.00
7	Joe Germaine	2.00
8	Peerless Price	3.00
9	Torry Holt	4.00
10	Rob Konrad	2.00
11	Akili Smith	3.00
12	Daunte Culpepper	6.00
13	D'Wayne Bates	2.00
14	Donovan McNabb	6.00
15	James Johnson	3.00
16	Cade McNown	6.00
17	Kevin Johnson	4.00
18	Ricky Williams	10.00
19	Karsten Bailey	1.00
20	Tim Couch	8.00
21	Shaun King	3.00

1999 Bowman's Best

Bowman's Best Football was a 133-card set that had each single printed on 26-pt. Serillusion stock. The set breakdown was 90 Star Veterans that were printed on gold stock and 10 Best Performance cards. The last 33 cards were rookies and they were printed on silver stock and included the "Bowman's Best Rookie Logo". Rookies were found one-per-pack. Parallel sets included Refractors and Atomic Refractors. Other inserts included: Autographs, Franchise Best, Franchise Favorites, Franchise Favorite Autographs, Future Foundations, Honor Roll, Legacy, Legacy Autographs, Locker Room Autographs and Locker Room Jerseys. Six-card packs had an SRP of $5.00.

		NM/M
Complete Set (133):		100.00
Common Player:		.20
Minor Stars:		.40
Common Rookie:		1.00
Pack (6):		2.50
Wax Box (24):		40.00
1	Randy Moss	3.00
2	Skip Hicks	.40
3	Robert Smith	.75
4	Drew Bledsoe	1.25
5	Tim Brown	.40
6	Marshall Faulk	.75
7	Terance Mathis	.20
8	Sean Dawkins	.20
9	Ed McCaffrey	.50
10	Jamal Anderson	.75
11	Antonio Freeman	.75
12	Terry Kirby	.20
13	Vinny Testaverde	.40
14	Eddie George	1.00
15	Ricky Watters	.50
16	Johnnie Morton	.20
17	Natrone Means	.50
18	Terry Glenn	.75
19	Michael Westbrook	.50
20	Doug Flutie	1.25
21	Jake Plummer	1.25
22	Darnay Scott	.40
23	Andre Rison	.40
24	Jon Kitna	1.00
25	Dan Marino	2.00
26	Ike Hilliard	.20
27	Warrick Dunn	.75
28	Jerome Bettis	.75
29	Curtis Conway	.40
30	Emmitt Smith	2.00
31	Jimmy Smith	.75
32	Isaac Bruce	.75
33	Jerry Rice	2.00
34	Curtis Martin	.75
35	Steve McNair	1.00
36	Jeff Blake	.40
37	Rob Moore	.40
38	Dorsey Levens	.75
39	Terrell Davis	1.00
40	John Elway	2.00
41	Trent Dilfer	.50
42	Joey Galloway	.75
43	Keyshawn Johnson	.75
44	O.J. McDuffie	.40
45	Fred Taylor	1.50
46	Andre Reed	.40
47	Frank Sanders	.40
48	Keenan McCardell	.40
49	Elvis Grbac	.40
50	Barry Sanders	2.00
51	Terrell Owens	.75
52	Trent Green	.50
53	Brad Johnson	.75
54	Rich Gannon	.40
55	Randall Cunningham	.75
56	Tony Martin	.20
57	Rod Smith	.50
58	Eric Moulds	.75
59	Yancey Thigpen	.20
60	Brett Favre	3.00
61	Cris Carter	.75
62	Marvin Harrison	.75
63	Chris Chandler	.40
64	Antowain Smith	.50
65	Carl Pickens	.40
66	Shannon Sharpe	.50
67	Mike Alstott	.75
68	J.J. Stokes	.40
69	Ben Coates	.40
70	Peyton Manning	2.00
71	Duce Staley	.50
72	Michael Irvin	.40
73	Tim Biakabutuka	.40
74	Priest Holmes	1.00
75	Steve Young	1.25
76	Jerome Pathon	.20
77	Wayne Chrebet	.75
78	Bert Emanuel	.20
79	Curtis Enis	.75
80	Mark Brunell	1.25
81	Herman Moore	.75
82	Corey Dillon	.75
83	Jim Harbaugh	.40
84	Gary Brown	.40
85	Kordell Stewart	.75
86	Garrison Hearst	.50
87	Raghib Ismail	.20
88	Charlie Batch	.50
89	Napoleon Kaufman	.75
90	Troy Aikman	1.50
91	Brett Favre	1.50
92	Randy Moss	1.50
93	Terrell Davis	1.00
94	Barry Sanders	1.50
95	Peyton Manning	1.00
96	Troy Edwards	.75
97	Cade McNown	1.00
98	Edgerrin James	4.00
99	Torry Holt	.75
100	Tim Couch	2.00
101	*Chris Claiborne*	1.00
102	*Brock Huard*	1.00
103	*Amos Zereoue*	2.00
104	*Sedrick Irvin*	1.00
105	*Kevin Faulk*	1.00
106	*Ebenezer Ekuban*	1.00
107	*Daunte Culpepper*	8.00
108	*Rob Konrad*	1.00
109	*James Johnson*	1.00
110	*Kurt Warner*	10.00
111	*Mike Cloud*	1.00
112	*Andy Katzenmoyer*	1.00
113	*Jevon Kearse*	2.00
114	*Akili Smith*	2.00
115	*Edgerrin James*	8.00
116	*Cecil Collins*	2.00
117	*Chris McAlister*	1.00
118	*Donovan McNabb*	8.00
119	*Kevin Johnson*	2.00
120	*Torry Holt*	4.00
121	*Antoine Winfield*	1.00
122	*Michael Bishop*	3.00
123	*Joe Germaine*	2.00
124	*David Boston*	4.00
125	*D'Wayne Bates*	2.00
126	*Champ Bailey*	2.50
127	*Cade McNown*	1.00
128	*Shaun King*	2.00
129	*Peerless Price*	3.00
130	*Troy Edwards*	3.00
131	*Karsten Bailey*	1.00
132	*Tim Couch*	3.00
133	*Ricky Williams*	5.00

Values quoted in this guide reflect the retail price of a card—the price a collector can expect to pay when buying a card from a dealer. The wholesale price—that which a collector can expect to receive from a dealer when selling cards—will be significantly lower, depending on desirability and condition.

1999 Bowman's Best Refractors

This was a parallel to the base set except that each single was printed on metalized refractor board. Singles were sequentially numbered to 400 and were inserted 1:17 packs.

	NM/M
Complete Set (133):	550.00
Refractor Cards:	5X-10X
Refractor Rookies:	2X-4X
Inserted 1:17	
Production 400 Sets	

1999 Bowman's Best Atomic Refractors

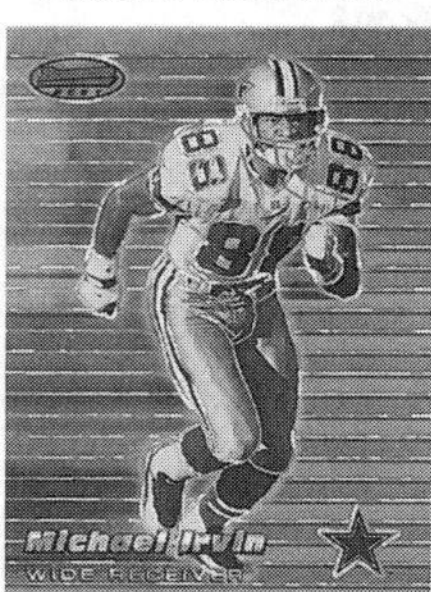

This was a parallel to the base set except that each single was printed on iridescent refractor foil board. Singles were sequentially numbered to 100 and inserted 1:69 packs.

	NM/M
Atomic Cards:	15X-30X
Atomic Rookies:	8X-16X
Inserted 1:69	
Production 100 Sets	

1999 Bowman's Best Autographs

Each of the three autographs in this set include the stamp "Certified Autograph Issue" as well as the Topps-3M authentication sticker on the backs of the cards. The Fred Taylor and Jake Plummer singles were found 1:915 packs and the Randy Moss card was inserted 1:9,129 packs.

		NM/M
Complete Set (3):		220.00
Common Player:		40.00
Inserted 1:915		
Inserted 1:9,129 (Moss)		
1	Fred Taylor	40.00
2	Jake Plummer	40.00
ROY1	Randy Moss	150.00

1999 Bowman's Best Franchise Best

This 9-card insert included the top players in the NFL and pictured them on die-cut cards. Singles were inserted 1:20 packs.

		NM/M
Complete Set (9):		40.00
Common Player:		3.00
Inserted 1:20		
1	Dan Marino	10.00
2	Fred Taylor	4.00
3	Emmitt Smith	10.00
4	Terrell Davis	6.00
5	Brett Favre	15.00
6	Tim Couch	6.00
7	Peyton Manning	15.00
8	Eddie George	3.00
9	Randy Moss	10.00

1999 Bowman's Best Franchise Favorites

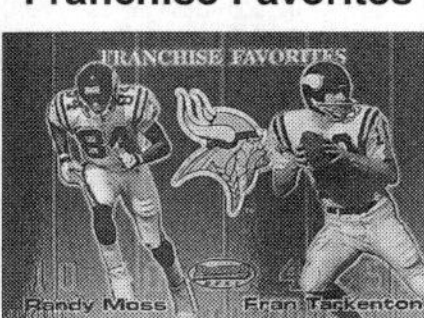

Singles from this insert set include both current and retired stars. Each is printed on prismatic holographic board with two players on each card. Singles were inserted 1:153 packs.

		NM/M
Complete Set (2):		30.00
Common Player:		10.00
Inserted 1:153		
1	Tony Dorsett, Roger Staubach	10.00
2	Randy Moss, Fran Tarkenton	20.00

1999 Bowman's Best Franchise Favorites Autographs

Each of the singles in this 6-card set are autographed and found at different ratios. The odds for the singles are as follows: #1 (1:4,599), #2, 5 (1:1,017) and #3, 4, 6 (1:9,129).

		NM/M
Complete Set (6):		600.00
Common Player:		70.00
Inserted 1:703		
1	Tony Dorsett	70.00
2	Roger Staubach	100.00
3	Tony Dorsett, Roger Staubach	150.00
4	Randy Moss	150.00
5	Fran Tarkenton	70.00
6	Randy Moss, Fran Tarkenton	200.00

1999 Bowman's Best Future Foundations

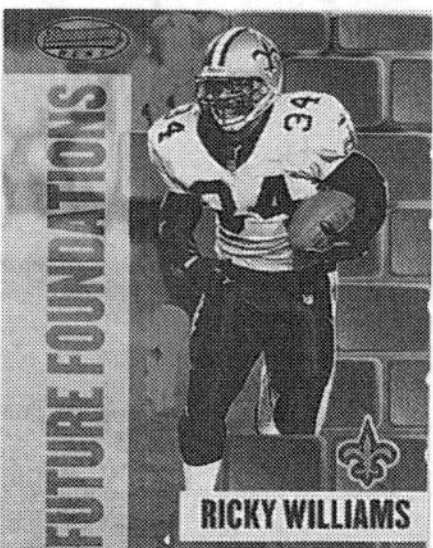

This 18-card insert set included the top rookies from the 1999 NFL Draft. Each card was printed on prismatic holographic stock with a die-cut pattern. Singles were inserted 1:20 packs.

		NM/M
Complete Set (18):		50.00
Common Player:		1.00
Minor Stars:		2.00
Inserted 1:20		
1	Tim Couch	10.00
2	David Boston	3.00
3	Donovan McNabb	5.00
4	Troy Edwards	3.00
5	Ricky Williams	10.00
6	Daunte Culpepper	5.00
7	Torry Holt	3.00
8	Cade McNown	5.00
9	Akili Smith	5.00
10	Edgerrin James	15.00
11	Cecil Collins	3.00
12	Peerless Price	2.00
13	Kevin Johnson	3.00
14	Champ Bailey	2.00
15	Michael Cloud	1.00
16	D'Wayne Bates	1.00
17	Shaun King	5.00
18	James Johnson	2.00

A player's name in *italic* type indicates a rookie card.

1999 Bowman's Best Honor Roll

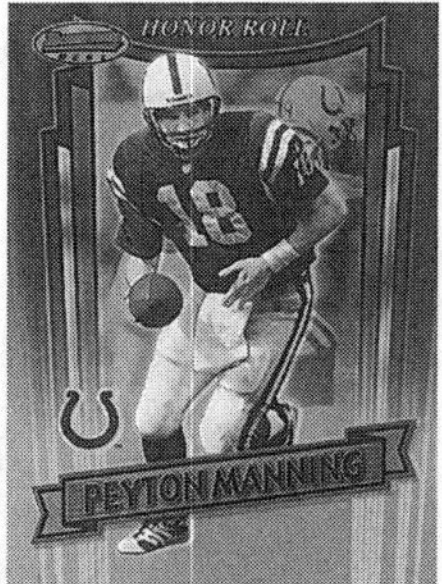

This 8-card insert set included only Heisman winners or first overall Draft Picks. Singles were found 1:40 packs.

		NM/M
Complete Set (8):		35.00
Common Player:		3.00
Inserted 1:40		
1	Peyton Manning	10.00
2	Drew Bledsoe	5.00
3	Doug Flutie	4.00
4	Tim Couch	12.00
5	Charles Woodson	3.00
6	Ricky Williams	12.00
7	Tim Brown	3.00
8	Eddie George	4.00

1999 Bowman's Best Legacy

This 3-card insert set included Texas legends and Heisman Trophy winners. Singles were inserted 1:102 packs.

		NM/M
Complete Set (3):		40.00
Common Player:		10.00
Inserted 1:102		
1	Ricky Williams	15.00
2	Earl Campbell	10.00
3	Ricky Williams, Earl Campbell	15.00

1999 Bowman's Best Legacy Autographs

This was a parallel to the Best Legacy insert. Each single is autographed and includes the "Certified Autograph Issue" stamp on the fronts and the Topps-3M sticker on the backs. Card #1 was found 1:4,599, card #2 was found 1:2,040 and card #3 was found 1:18,108.

		NM/M
Complete Set (3):		425.00
Common Player:		75.00
#1 Inserted 1:4,599		
#2 Inserted 1:2,040		
#3 Inserted 1:18,108		
1	Ricky Williams	150.00
2	Earl Campbell	75.00
3	Ricky Williams, Earl Campbell	250.00

1999 Bowman's Best Rookie Class Photo

This single card included the 1999 NFL Rookie Class with a group shot photo. It was inserted 1:100 packs.

		NM/M
Inserted 1:100		
Refractor:		8X
Inserted 1:7,429		
Production 125 Sets		
Atomic Refractor:		20X
Inserted 1:26,880		
Production 35 Sets		
C1	Rookie Class Photo	12.00

1999 Bowman's Best Rookie Locker Room Autographs

This 5-card insert set included autographs of the top rookies from 1999. Each card included the Topps "Certified Autograph Issue" stamp on the card fronts and the Topps-3M authentication sticker on the backs. Cards #1, 4 & 5 were inserted 1:305 packs and cards #2 & 3 were found 1:915 packs.

		NM/M
Complete Set (5):		300.00
Common Player:		25.00
#1,4,5 Inserted 1:305		
#2,3 Inserted 1:915		
1	Tim Couch	75.00
2	Donovan McNabb	60.00
3	Edgerrin James	125.00
4	David Boston	25.00
5	Torry Holt	25.00

1999 Bowman's Best Rookie Locker Room Jerseys

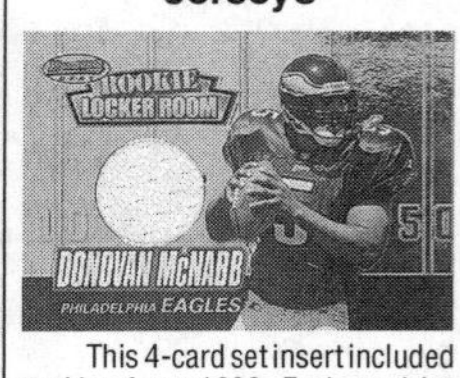

This 4-card set insert included rookies from 1999. Each card included the Topps-3M sticker on the card backs. Some of the singles could only be found through redemption cards. Singles were found 1:229 packs.

		NM/M
Complete Set (4):		150.00
Common Player:		20.00
Inserted 1:229		
1	Kevin Faulk	20.00
2	Donovan McNabb	50.00
3	Ricky Williams	60.00
4	Torry Holt	25.00

1999 Bowman Chrome

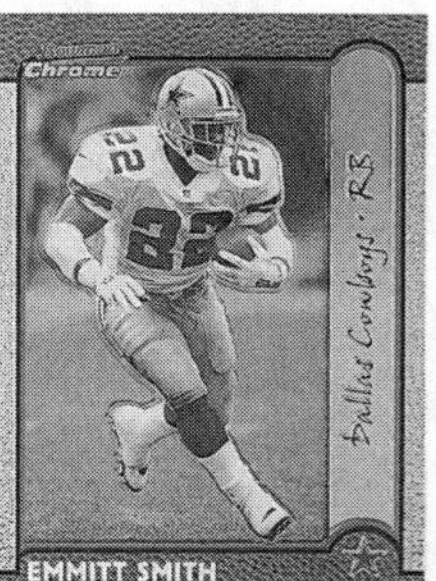

Bowman Chrome Football was a 220-card set that paralleled the regular Bowman issue. The set included 150 veterans and 70 rookies. Each rookie card had the "Bowman Chrome Rookie Card" logo. Parallel sets included: Refractors, Gold, Gold Refractors, Interstate and Interstate Refractors. Other insert sets included: Scout's Choice, Scout's Choice Refractors, Stock in the Game and Stock in the Game Refractors. Four-card packs had an SRP of $3.00.

		NM/M
Complete Set (220):		200.00
Common Player:		.25
Minor Stars:		.50
Common Rookie:		2.00
Pack (4):		5.75
Wax Box (24):		95.00
1	Dan Marino	3.00
2	Michael Westbrook	.50
3	Yancey Thigpen	.50
4	Tony Martin	.25
5	Michael Strahan	.25
6	Dedric Ward	.25
7	Joey Galloway	1.00
8	Bobby Engram	.25
9	Frank Sanders	.50
10	Jake Plummer	.75
11	Eddie Kennison	.25
12	Curtis Martin	1.00
13	Chris Spielman	.25
14	Trent Dilfer	1.00
15	Tim Biakabutuka	.50
16	Elvis Grbac	.50
17	Charlie Batch	.75
18	Takeo Spikes	.25
19	Tony Banks	.75
20	Doug Flutie	.75
21	Ty Law	.25
22	Isaac Bruce	1.00
23	James Jett	.25
24	Kent Graham	.25
25	Derrick Mayes	.50
26	Amani Toomer	.50
27	Ray Lewis	.25
28	Shawn Springs	.25
29	Warren Sapp	.50
30	Jamal Anderson	.75
31	Byron Morris	.25
32	Johnnie Morton	.50
33	Terance Mathis	.25
34	Terrell Davis	1.00
35	John Randle	.50
36	Vinny Testaverde	.75
37	Junior Seau	.75
38	Reidel Anthony	.50
39	Brad Johnson	.75
40	Emmitt Smith	3.00
41	Mo Lewis	.25
42	Terry Glenn	.75
43	Dorsey Levens	.75
44	Thurman Thomas	.75
45	Rob Moore	.50
46	Corey Dillon	1.00

47 Jessie Armstead .25
48 Marshall Faulk 1.00
49 Charles Woodson .50
50 John Elway 3.00
51 Kevin Dyson .50
52 Tony Simmons .50
53 Keenan McCardell .50
54 O.J. Santiago .25
55 Jermaine Lewis .50
56 Herman Moore .50
57 Gary Brown .25
58 Jim Harbaugh .50
59 Mike Alstott 1.00
60 Brett Favre 4.00
61 Tim Brown .75
62 Steve McNair 1.00
63 Ben Coates .50
64 Jerome Pathon .50
65 Ray Buchanan .25
66 Troy Aikman 2.00
67 Andre Reed .50
68 Bubby Brister .50
69 Karim Abdul .50
70 Peyton Manning 3.00
71 Charles Johnson .25
72 Natrone Means .75
73 Michael Sinclair .25
74 Skip Hicks .50
75 Derrick Alexander .25
76 Wayne Chrebet .50
77 Rod Smith .50
78 Carl Pickens .50
79 Adrian Murrell .50
80 Fred Taylor 1.00
81 Eric Moulds .75
82 Erik Kramer .25
83 Marvin Harrison 1.00
84 Cris Carter 1.00
85 Ike Hillard .50
86 Hines Ward .75
87 Terrell Owens 1.00
88 Ricky Proehl .25
89 Bert Emanuel .25
90 Randy Moss 4.00
91 Aaron Glenn .25
92 Robert Smith .75
93 Andre Hastings .25
94 Jake Reed .50
95 Curtis Enis .50
96 Andre Wadsworth .50
97 Ed McCaffrey .75
98 Zach Thomas .50
99 Kerry Collins .50
100 Drew Bledsoe 1.50
101 Germane Crowell .75
102 Bryan Still .25
103 Chad Brown .25
104 Jacquez Green .50
105 Garrison Hearst .50
106 Napoleon Kaufman .50
107 Ricky Watters .50
108 O.J. McDuffie .50
109 Keyshawn Johnson 1.00
110 Jerome Bettis 1.00
111 Duce Staley .50
112 Curtis Conway .50
113 Chris Chandler .50
114 Marcus Nash .50
115 Stephen Alexander .25
116 Darnay Scott .50
117 Bruce Smith .25
118 Priest Holmes 1.50
119 Mark Brunell 1.50
120 Jerry Rice 2.00
121 Randall Cunningham 1.00
122 Cameron Cleeland .50
123 Antonio Freeman .50
124 Kordell Stewart 1.00
125 Jon Kitna .50
126 Ahman Green .50
127 Warrick Dunn 1.00
128 Robert Brooks .25
129 Derrick Thomas .50
130 Steve Young 1.50
131 Peter Boulware .25
132 Michael Irvin .50
133 Shannon Sharpe .50
134 Jimmy Smith .50
135 John Avery .50
136 Fred Lane .50
137 Trent Green .50
138 Andre Rison .50
139 Antowain Smith 1.00
140 Eddie George 1.25
141 Jeff Blake .75
142 Raghib Ismail .25
143 Rickey Dudley .50
144 Courtney Hawkins .25
145 Mikhael Ricks .25
146 J.J. Stokes .50
147 Levon Kirkland .25
148 Deion Sanders 1.00
149 Barry Sanders 3.00
150 Tiki Barber .50
151 *David Boston* 6.00
152 *Chris McAlister* 1.00
153 *Peerless Price* 4.00
154 *D'Wayne Bates* 1.00
155 *Cade McNown* 2.00
156 *Akili Smith* 2.00
157 *Kevin Johnson* 3.00
158 *Tim Couch* 6.00
159 *Sedrick Irvin* 2.00
160 *Chris Claiborne* 1.00
161 *Edgerrin James* 12.00
162 *Michael Cloud* 1.00
163 *Cecil Collins* 2.00
164 *James Johnson* 1.00
165 *Rob Konrad* 2.00
166 *Daunte Culpepper* 12.00
167 *Kevin Faulk* 3.00
168 *Donovan McNabb* 15.00
169 *Troy Edwards* 3.00
170 *Amos Zereoue* 4.00
171 *Karsten Bailey* 3.00
172 *Brock Huard* 2.00
173 *Joe Germaine* 2.00
174 *Torry Holt* 6.00
175 *Shaun King* 2.00
176 *Jevon Kearse* 5.00
177 *Champ Bailey* 3.00
178 *Ebenezer Ekuban* 2.00
179 *Andy Katzenmoyer* 2.00
180 *Antoine Winfield* 1.00
181 *Jermaine Fazande* 1.00
182 *Ricky Williams* 5.00
183 *Joel Mackovicka* 1.00
184 *Reginald Kelly* 1.00
185 *Brandon Stokley* 2.00
186 *L.C. Stevens* 1.00
187 *Marty Booker* 4.00
188 *Jerry Azumah* 1.00
189 *Ted White* 1.00
190 *Scott Covington* 1.00
191 *Tim Alexander* 1.00
192 *Darrin Chiaverini* 1.00
193 *Dat Nguyen* 3.00
194 *Wane McGarity* 2.00
195 *Al Wilson* 1.00
196 *Travis McGriff* 1.00
197 *Stacey Mack* 1.00
198 *Antwan Edwards* 1.00
199 *Aaron Brooks* 12.00
200 *De'Mond Parker* 1.00
201 *Jed Weaver* 1.00
202 *Madre Hill* 1.00
203 *Jim Kleinsasser* 2.00
204 *Michael Bishop* 4.00
205 *Michael Basnight* 1.00
206 *Sean Bennett* 1.00
207 *Dameane Douglas* 1.00
208 *Na Brown* 1.00
209 *Patrick Kerney* 1.00
210 *Malcolm Johnson* 1.00
211 *Dre' Bly* 1.00
212 *Terry Jackson* 2.00
213 *Eugene Baker* 1.00
214 *Autry Denson* 1.00
215 *Darnell McDonald* 1.00
216 *Charlie Rogers* 1.00
217 *Joe Montgomery* 1.00
218 *Cecil Martin* 3.00
219 *Larry Parker* 1.00
220 *Mike Peterson* 1.00

1999 Bowman Chrome Gold

This was a parallel to the base set with each single printed in gold ink. Singles were found 1:24 packs.

NM/M
Complete Set (220): 1,000
Gold Cards: 4X-8X
Gold Rookies: 2X
Inserted 1:24

1999 Bowman Chrome Gold Refractors

This is a parallel to the Gold set except that each card is printed on refractor board. Singles were sequentially numbered to 25 and found 1:253 packs.

NM/M
Complete Set (220): 3,500
Gold Ref. Cards: 35X-70X
Gold Ref. Rookies: 3X-6X
Inserted 1:253
Production 25 Sets

1999 Bowman Chrome Interstate

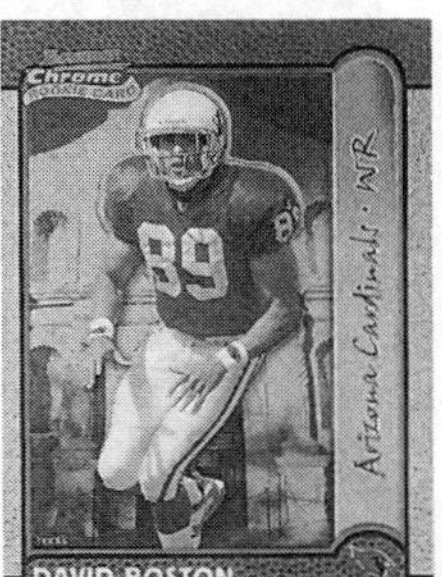

This set was a parallel to the base. The card fronts featured an image that related to that player's home state. The backs had a custom- tailored vanity plate from that state. Singles were found 1:4 packs.

NM/M
Complete Set (220): 450.00
Interstate Cards: 2X-4X
Interstate Rookies: 1.5X
Inserted 1:4

1999 Bowman Chrome Interstate Refractors

This was a parallel to the Interstate insert except that each single is printed on refractor board. Singles were sequentially numbered to 100 and found 1:63 packs.

NM/M
Complete Set (220): 2,200
Interstate Ref. Cards: 15X-30X
Interstate Ref. Rookies: 3X
Inserted 1:63
Production 100 Sets

1999 Bowman Chrome Refractors

This was a parallel to the base set except that each single was printed on refractor board. Singles were found 1:12 packs.

NM/M
Complete Set (220): 800.00
Refractor Cards: 4X-8X
Refractor Rookies: 2X
Inserted 1:12

2000 Bowman Promos

NM/M
Complete Set (6): 3.00
Common Player: .50
PP1 Stephen Davis .50
PP2 Charlie Batch .50
PP3 Patrick Jeffers .50
PP4 Torry Holt 1.00
PP5 Akili Smith .50
PP6 Fred Taylor 1.00

2000 Bowman

NM/M
Complete Set (240): 50.00
Common Player: .10
Minor Stars: .20
Common Europe: .40
Common Rookie: .40
Pack (10): 2.00
Wax Box (24): 35.00
1 Eddie George .60
2 Ike Hilliard .20
3 Terrell Owens .50
4 James Stewart .30
5 Joey Galloway .50
6 Jake Reed .20
7 Derrick Alexander .10
8 Jeff George .30
9 Kerry Collins .20
10 Tony Gonzalez .20
11 Marcus Robinson .30
12 Charles Woodson .30
13 Germane Crowell .20
14 Yancey Thigpen .20
15 Tony Martin .10
16 Frank Sanders .20
17 Napoleon Kaufman .30
18 Jay Fiedler .50
19 Patrick Jeffers .50
20 Steve McNair .50
21 Herman Moore .50
22 Tim Brown .50
23 Olandis Gary .60
24 Corey Dillon .50
25 Warren Sapp .20
26 Curtis Enis .30
27 Vinny Testaverde .30
28 Tim Biakabutuka .20
29 Kevin Johnson .30
30 Charlie Batch .50
31 Jermaine Fazande .20
32 Shaun King .75
33 Errict Rhett .20
34 O.J. McDuffie .20
35 Bruce Smith .10
36 Antonio Freeman .50
37 Tim Couch 1.00
38 Duce Staley .50
39 Jeff Blake .20
40 Jim Harbaugh .20
41 Jeff Graham .10
42 Drew Bledsoe .75
43 Mike Alstott .50
44 Terance Mathis .10
45 Antowain Smith .20
46 Johnnie Morton .20
47 Chris Chandler .20
48 Keith Poole .10
49 Ricky Watters .30
50 Darnay Scott .20
51 Damon Huard .50
52 Peerless Price .30
53 Brian Griese .60
54 Frank Wycheck .10
55 Kevin Dyson .20
56 Junior Seau .20
57 Curtis Conway .20
58 Jamal Anderson .50
59 Jim Miller .10
60 Rob Johnson .20
61 Mark Brunell .75
62 Wayne Chrebet .30
63 James Johnson .20
64 Sean Dawkins .10
65 Stephen Davis .50
66 Daunte Culpepper 1.00
67 Doug Flutie .50
68 Pete Mitchell .10
69 Bill Schroeder .20
70 Terrence Wilkins .50
71 Cade McNown .75
72 Muhsin Muhammad .20
73 E.G. Green .10
74 Edgerrin James 2.00
75 Troy Edwards .30
76 Terry Glenn .50
77 Tony Banks .20
78 Derrick Mayes .20
79 Curtis Martin .50
80 Kordell Stewart .60
81 Amani Toomer .20
82 Dorsey Levens .30
83 Brad Johnson .50
84 Ed McCaffrey .30
85 Charlie Garner .30
86 Brett Favre 2.00
87 J.J. Stokes .20
88 Steve Young .75
89 Jonathon Linton .20
90 Isaac Bruce .50
91 Shawn Jefferson .10
92 Rod Smith .30
93 Champ Bailey .30
94 Ricky Williams 1.00
95 Priest Holmes .75
96 Corey Bradford .20
97 Eric Moulds .50
98 Warrick Dunn .50
99 Jevon Kearse .50
100 Albert Connell .20
101 Az-Zahir Hakim .20
102 Marvin Harrison .50
103 Qadry Ismail .10
104 Oronde Gadsden .20
105 Rob Moore .20
106 Marshall Faulk .50
107 Steve Beuerlein .20
108 Torry Holt .50
109 Donovan McNabb .75
110 Rich Gannon .20
111 Jerome Bettis .50
112 Peyton Manning 2.00
113 Cris Carter .50
114 Jake Plummer .50
115 Kent Graham .10
116 Keenan McCardell .20
117 Tim Dwight .50
118 Fred Taylor .75
119 Jerry Rice 1.25
120 Michael Westbrook .20
121 Kurt Warner 2.00
122 Jimmy Smith .50
123 Emmitt Smith 1.50
124 Terrell Davis 1.00
125 Randy Moss 2.00
126 Akili Smith .50
127 Raghib Ismail .10
128 Jon Kitna .50
129 Elvis Grbac .20
130 Wesley Walls .10
131 Torrance Small .10
132 Tyrone Wheatley .20
133 Carl Pickens .20
134 Zach Thomas .20
135 Jacquez Green .20
136 Robert Smith .50
137 Keyshawn Johnson .50
138 Matthew Hatchette .20
139 Troy Aikman 1.25
140 Charles Johnson .10
141 Terry Battle .40
142 *Pepe Pearson* .40
143 Cory Sauter .40
144 Brian Shay .40
145 *Marcus Crandell* .40
146 Danny Wuerffel .75
147 L.C. Stevens .40
148 Ted White .40
149 *Matt Lytle* .40
150 *Vershan Jackson* .40
151 Mario Bailey .40
152 *Darryl Daniel* .40
153 *Sean Morey* .40
154 *Jim Kubiak* .40
155 *Aaron Stecker* 1.50
156 Damon Dunn .40
157 Kevin Daft .40
158 Corey Thomas .40
159 *Deon Mitchell* .40
160 *Todd Floyd* .40
161 *Norman Miller* .40
162 Jeremaine Copeland .40
163 Michael Blair .40
164 Ron Powlus .75
165 Pat Barnes .75
166 *Dez White* .50
167 *Trung Canidate* 1.00
168 *Thomas Jones* 1.00
169 *Courtney Brown* .50
170 *Jamal Lewis* 3.00
171 *Chris Redman* 1.50
172 *Ron Dayne* 1.00
173 *Chad Pennington* 5.00
174 *Plaxico Burress* 2.00
175 *R. Jay Soward* .50
176 *Travis Taylor* 1.75
177 *Shaun Alexander* 4.00
178 *Brian Urlacher* 4.00
179 *Danny Farmer* 1.00
180 *Tee Martin* 1.25
181 *Sylvester Morris* 1.00
182 *Curtis Keaton* .75
183 *Peter Warrick* 2.00
184 *Anthony Becht* .50
185 *Travis Prentice* 1.50
186 *J.R. Redmond* 1.50
187 *Bubba Franks* 1.50
188 *Ron Dugans* .50
189 *Reuben Droughns* 2.00
190 *Corey Simon* .50
191 *Joe Hamilton* .50
192 *Laveranues Coles* 1.25
193 *Todd Pinkston* 1.00
194 *Jerry Porter* 1.50
195 *Dennis Northcutt* .50
196 *Tim Rattay* 1.00
197 *Giovanni Carmazzi* .50
198 *Mareno Philyaw* .40
199 *Avion Black* .40
200 *Chafie Fields* .40
201 *Rondell Mealey* .75
202 *Troy Walters* .75
203 *Frank Moreau* .50
204 *Vaughn Sanders* .40
205 *Sherrod Gideon* .40
206 *Doug Chapman* .40
207 *Marcus Knight* .40
208 *Jamel White* .75
209 *Windrell Hayes* .40
210 *Reggie Jones* .75
211 *Jarious Jackson* .50
212 *Ronney Jenkins* .40
213 *Quinton Spotwood* .40
214 *Rob Morris* .75
215 *Gari Scott* .40
216 *Kevin Thompson* .40
217 *Trevor Insley* .40
218 *Frank Murphy* .40
219 *Patrick Pass* .75
220 *Mike Anderson* 1.50
221 *Derrius Thompson* .40
222 *John Abraham* .75
223 *Dante Hall* 2.50
224 *Chad Morton* .75
225 *Ahmed Plummer* .75
226 *Julian Peterson* .40
227 *Mike Green* .40
228 *Michael Wiley* .50
229 *Spergon Wynn* .50
230 *Trevor Gaylor* .50
231 *Doug Johnson* 1.00
232 *Marc Bulger* 2.00
233 *Ron Dixon* .50
234 *Aaron Shea* .75
235 *Thomas Hamner* .40
236 *Tom Brady* 8.00
237 *Deltha O'Neal* .75
238 *Todd Husak* .50
239 *Erron Kinney* .40
240 *JaJuan Dawson* .50

2000 Bowman Gold

NM/M
Gold Cards: 5X-10X
Gold Europe Cards: 2X-5X
Gold Rookies: 3X-8X
Inserted 1:60
Production 99 Sets

2000 Bowman ROY Promotion

NM/M
ROY Cards: 5X
Inserted 1:76
170 Jamal Lewis 50.00
172 Ron Dayne 40.00
220 Mike Anderson 40.00

2000 Bowman Autographs

NM/M
Common Player: 6.00
Minor Stars: 12.00
Inserted 1:46
SA Shaun Alexander 40.00
AB Anthony Becht 8.00
CB Courtney Brown 10.00
MB Marc Bulger 40.00
PB Plaxico Burress 40.00
TC Trung Canidate 15.00
GC Giovanni Carmazzi 15.00
LC Laveranues Coles 20.00
RD Ron Dayne 25.00
RDR Reuben Droughns 20.00
RDU Ron Dugans 12.00
DF Danny Farmer 12.00
DFR Daniel "Bubba" Franks 20.00
TG Trevor Gaylor 12.00
JH Joe Hamilton 15.00
TJ Thomas Jones 20.00
CK Curtis Keaton 6.00
JL Jamal Lewis 40.00
TM Tee Martin 15.00
SM Sylvester Morris 12.00
DN Dennis Northcutt 15.00
CP Chad Pennington 60.00
TPI Todd Pinkston 15.00
JP Jerry Porter 40.00
TP Travis Prentice 15.00
TR Tim Rattay 15.00
CR Chris Redman 30.00
JR J.R. Redmond 15.00
CS Corey Simon 12.00
RS R. Jay Soward 12.00
TT Travis Taylor 20.00
BU Brian Urlacher 50.00
PW Peter Warrick 25.00
DW Dez White 12.00

2000 Bowman Bowman's Best Previews

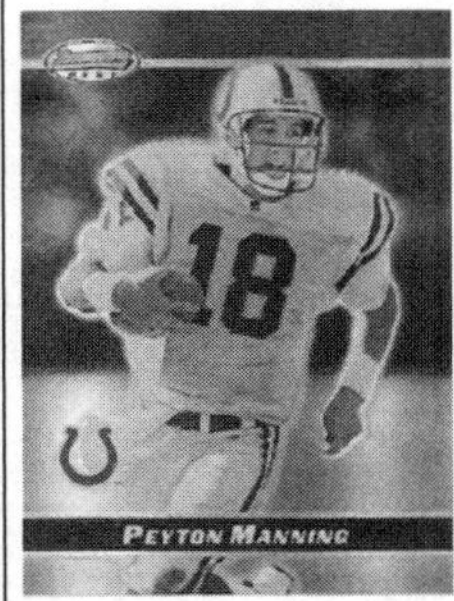

NM/M
Complete Set (10): 25.00
Common Player: 1.50
Inserted 1:24
BBP1 Peyton Manning 6.00
BBP2 Stephen Davis 1.50
BBP3 Marshall Faulk 1.50
BBP4 Marvin Harrison 1.50
BBP5 Brett Favre 6.00
BBP6 Terrell Davis 4.50
BBP7 Eddie George 2.00
BBP8 Kurt Warner 7.00
BBP9 Edgerrin James 6.00
BBP10 Randy Moss 6.00

2000 Bowman Breakthrough Discoveries

NM/M
Complete Set (10): 10.00
Common Player: .50
Minor Stars: 1.00
Inserted 1:12
BD1 Jerry Rice 2.00
BD2 Kurt Warner 4.00
BD3 Wayne Chrebet .50
BD4 Isaac Bruce 1.00
BD5 Steve McNair 1.00
BD6 Shannon Sharpe .50
BD7 Andre Reed .50
BD8 Jimmy Smith 1.00
BD9 Darrell Green .50
BD10 Randy Moss 3.00

2000 Bowman Draft Day Jerseys

NM/M
Complete Set (4): 85.00
Common Player: 15.00
Inserted 1:279
CB Courtney Brown 15.00
TJ Thomas Jones 25.00
CS Chris Samuels 15.00
PW Peter Warrick 20.00

2000 Bowman Road to Success

NM/M
Complete Set (10): 20.00
Common Player: 1.50
Inserted 1:18
R1 Chad Pennington, Randy Moss 5.00
R2 Jamal Lewis, Peyton Manning 5.00

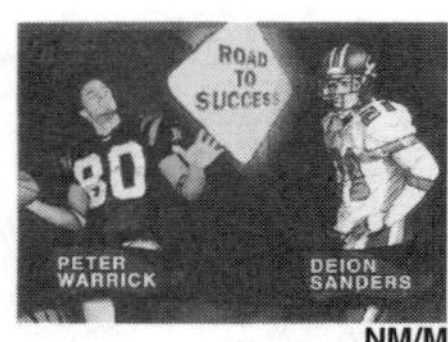

NM/M
R3 R. Jay Soward, Keyshawn Johnson 1.50
R4 Thomas Jones, Germane Crowell 3.00
R5 Giovanni Carmazzi, Wayne Chrebet 2.00
R6 Travis Taylor, Ike Hilliard 2.00
R7 Plaxico Burress, Muhsin Muhammad 3.00
R8 Todd Pinkston, Brett Favre 5.00
R9 Sylvester Morris, Jimmy Smith 2.50
R10 Peter Warrick, Deion Sanders 5.00

2000 Bowman Rookie Rising

NM/M
Complete Set (10): 8.00
Common Player: .50
Minor Stars: 1.00
Inserted 1:12
RR1 Jevon Kearse 1.00
RR2 Edgerrin James 4.00
RR3 Champ Bailey 1.00
RR4 Zach Thomas .50
RR5 Marvin Harrison 1.00
RR6 Kevin Johnson 1.00
RR7 Curtis Martin 1.00
RR8 Jerome Bettis 1.00
RR9 Fred Taylor 1.75
RR10 Terry Glenn 1.00

2000 Bowman Scout's Choice

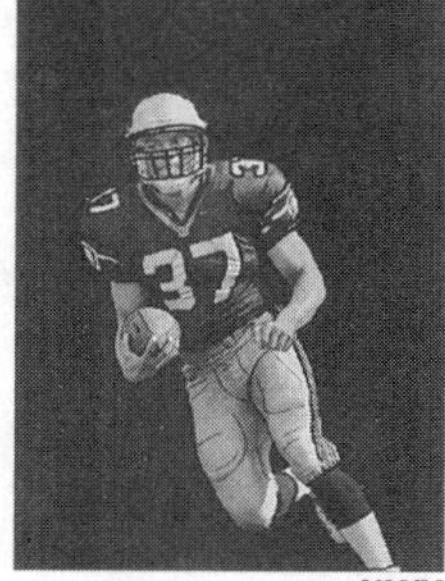

NM/M
Complete Set (20): 35.00
Common Player: 1.50
Inserted 1:18
SC1 Shaun Alexander 4.00
SC2 Bubba Franks 2.00
SC3 Travis Prentice 2.50
SC4 Peter Warrick 2.00
SC5 Plaxico Burress 3.00
SC6 Corey Simon 1.50
SC7 Courtney Brown 1.75
SC8 Tee Martin 2.00
SC9 Brian Urlacher 3.00
SC10 J.R. Redmond 2.00
SC11 Anthony Becht 1.50
SC12 Thomas Jones 2.50
SC13 Giovanni Carmazzi 2.00
SC14 Jamal Lewis 4.00
SC15 Ron Dayne 2.00
SC16 R. Jay Soward 1.50
SC17 Travis Taylor 2.50
SC18 Chad Pennington 6.00
SC19 Sylvester Morris 3.00
SC20 Chris Redman 2.50

Post-1980 cards in Near Mint condition will generally sell for about 75% of the quoted Mint value. Excellent-condition cards bring no more than 40%.

2000 Bowman Chrome

NM/M
Common Player: .25
Minor Stars: .50
Common Europe: 1.00
Common Rookie: .50
Common Rookie SP: 30.00
Inserted 1:134
Pack (4): 3.50
Wax Box (24): 110.00
1 Eddie George 1.00
2 Ike Hilliard .50
3 Terrell Owens .75
4 James Stewart .50
5 Joey Galloway .75
6 Jake Reed .25
7 Derrick Alexander .25
8 Jeff George .50
9 Kerry Collins .50
10 Tony Gonzalez .50
11 Marcus Robinson .75
12 Charles Woodson .50
13 Germane Crowell .75
14 Yancey Thigpen .50
15 Tony Martin .25
16 Frank Sanders .50
17 Napoleon Kaufman .75
18 Jay Fiedler .50
19 Patrick Jeffers .75
20 Steve McNair .75
21 Herman Moore .50
22 Tim Brown .75
23 Olandis Gary .75
24 Corey Dillon .75
25 Warren Sapp .50
26 Curtis Enis .50
27 Vinny Testaverde .50
28 Tim Biakabutuka .50
29 Kevin Johnson .50
30 Charlie Batch .50
31 Jermaine Fazande .50
32 Shaun King .50
33 Errict Rhett .50
34 O.J. McDuffie .50
35 Bruce Smith .50
36 Antonio Freeman .75
37 Tim Couch 1.50
38 Duce Staley .75
39 Jeff Blake .50
40 Jim Harbaugh .50
41 Jeff Graham .25
42 Drew Bledsoe 1.25
43 Mike Alstott .75
44 Terance Mathis .25
45 Antowain Smith .50
46 Johnnie Morton .50
47 Chris Chandler .50
48 Keith Poole .25
49 Ricky Watters .50
50 Darnay Scott .50
51 Damon Huard .50
52 Peerless Price .50
53 Brian Griese 1.00
54 Frank Wycheck .25
55 Kevin Dyson .50
56 Junior Seau .50
57 Curtis Conway .50
58 Jamal Anderson .50
59 Jim Miller .25
60 Rob Johnson .50
61 Mark Brunell 1.25
62 Wayne Chrebet .75
63 James Johnson .50
64 Sean Dawkins .25
65 Stephen Davis .75
66 Daunte Culpepper 1.50
67 Doug Flutie .75
68 Pete Mitchell .25
69 Bill Schroeder .25
70 Terrence Wilkins .50
71 Cade McNown .75
72 Muhsin Muhammad .50
73 E.G. Green .25
74 Edgerrin James 3.00
75 Troy Edwards .50
76 Terry Glenn .75
77 Tony Banks .50
78 Derrick Mayes .50
79 Curtis Martin .75
80 Kordell Stewart .75
81 Amani Toomer .50
82 Dorsey Levens .75
83 Brad Johnson .50
84 Ed McCaffrey .50
85 Charlie Garner .50
86 Brett Favre 3.00
87 J.J. Stokes .50
88 Steve Young 1.25
89 Jonathon Linton .50
90 Isaac Bruce .75
91 Shawn Jefferson .25
92 Rod Smith .75
93 Champ Bailey .50
94 Ricky Williams 1.50
95 Priest Holmes 1.00
96 Corey Bradford .25
97 Eric Moulds .75
98 Warrick Dunn .75
99 Jevon Kearse .75
100 Albert Connell .50
101 Az-Zahir Hakim .50
102 Marvin Harrison .75
103 Qadry Ismail .25
104 Oronde Gadsden .50
105 Rob Moore .50
106 Marshall Faulk .75
107 Steve Beuerlein .50
108 Torry Holt .50
109 Donovan McNabb 1.25
110 Rich Gannon .50
111 Jerome Bettis .75
112 Peyton Manning 2.50
113 Cris Carter .75
114 Jake Plummer .75
115 Kent Graham .25
116 Keenan McCardell .50
117 Tim Dwight .50
118 Fred Taylor .75
119 Jerry Rice 1.75
120 Michael Westbrook .50
121 Kurt Warner 2.00
122 Jimmy Smith .50
123 Emmitt Smith 2.25
124 Terrell Davis 1.50
125 Randy Moss 2.50
126 Akili Smith .75
127 Raghib Ismail .25
128 Jon Kitna .75
129 Elvis Grbac .50
130 Wesley Walls .50
131 Torrance Small .25
132 Tyrone Wheatley .50
133 Carl Pickens .50
134 Zach Thomas .50
135 Jacquez Green .25
136 Robert Smith .75
137 Keyshawn Johnson .75
138 Matthew Hatchette .50
139 Troy Aikman 1.75
140 Charles Johnson .50
141 Terry Battle .40
142 *Pepe Pearson* 1.25
143 Cory Sauter .40
144 Brian Shay .40
145 *Marcus Crandell* .40
146 Danny Wuerffel .40
147 L.C. Stevens .40
148 Ted White .40
149 *Matt Lytle* .40
150 *Vershan Jackson* .40
151 Mario Bailey .40
152 *Darryl Daniel* .40
153 *Sean Morey* .40
154 *Jim Kubiak* .40
155 *Aaron Stecker* 1.00
156 Damon Dunn .40
157 Kevin Daft .40
158 Corey Thomas .40
159 *Deon Mitchell* .40
160 *Todd Floyd* .40
161 *Norman Miller* .40
162 *Jeremaine Copeland* .40
163 *Michael Blair* .40
164 *Ron Powlus* 1.00
165 Pat Barnes 1.00
166 *Dez White* 3.50
167 *Trung Canidate SP* 15.00
168 *Thomas Jones SP* 50.00
169 *Courtney Brown SP* 20.00
170 *Jamal Lewis SP* 60.00
171 *Chris Redman SP* 20.00
172 *Ron Dayne SP* 30.00
173 *Chad Pennington SP* 120.00
174 *Plaxico Burress SP* 60.00
175 *R. Jay Soward SP* 20.00
176 *Travis Taylor SP* 30.00
177 *Shaun Alexander SP* 75.00
178 *Brian Urlacher* 20.00
179 *Danny Farmer* 3.00
180 *Tee Martin SP* 20.00
181 *Sylvester Morris SP* 20.00
182 *Curtis Keaton* 1.00
183 *Peter Warrick SP* 50.00
184 *Anthony Becht* 1.00
185 *Travis Prentice SP* 20.00
186 *J.R. Redmond SP* 20.00
187 *Daniel "Bubba" Franks SP* 30.00
188 *Ron Dugans SP* 20.00
189 *Reuben Droughns* 6.00
190 *Corey Simon* 3.00
191 *Joe Hamilton* 4.00
192 *Laveranues Coles* 5.00
193 *Todd Pinkston SP* 15.00
194 *Jerry Porter SP* 40.00
195 *Dennis Northcutt* 2.00
196 *Tim Rattay* 6.00
197 *Giovanni Carmazzi* 6.00
198 *Mareno Philyaw* .50
199 *Avion Black* .50
200 *Chafie Fields* .50
201 *Rondell Mealey* .75
202 *Troy Walters* .50
203 *Frank Moreau* .50
204 *Vaughn Sanders* .50
205 *Sherrod Gideon* .50
206 *Doug Chapman* .50
207 *Marcus Knight* .50
208 *Jamel White* .50
209 *Windrell Hayes* .50
210 *Reggie Jones* 1.00
211 *Jarious Jackson* 1.00
212 *Ronney Jenkins* .50
213 *Quinton Spotwood* .50
214 *Rob Morris* .50
215 *Gari Scott* .50
216 *Kevin Thompson* .50
217 *Trevor Insley* .50
218 *Frank Murphy* .50
219 *Patrick Pass* .50
220 *Mike Anderson* 8.00
221 *Derrius Thompson* .50
222 *John Abraham* .50
223 *Dante Hall* 8.00
224 *Chad Morton* 1.00
225 *Ahmed Plummer* .50
226 *Julian Peterson* .50
227 *Mike Green* .50
228 *Michael Wiley* .50
229 *Spergon Wynn* 1.00
230 *Trevor Gaylor* .50
231 *Doug Johnson* 1.00
232 *Marc Bulger* 8.00
233 *Ron Dixon* .40
234 *Aaron Shea* .40
235 *Thomas Hamner* .50
236 *Tom Brady* 40.00
237 *Deltha O'Neal* 1.00
238 *Todd Husak* 2.00
239 *Erron Kinney* 1.00
240 *JaJuan Dawson* 2.00
241 Nick Williams .25
242 *Deon Grant* .50
243 *Brad Hoover* 3.00
244 Kamil Loud .25
245 *Rashard Anderson* 1.00
246 *Clint Stoerner* 1.00
247 *Antwain Harris* .50
248 *Jason Webster* .50
249 *Kevin McDougal* .50
250 *Tony Scott* .50
251 *Thabiti Davis* .50
252 *Ian Gold* .50
253 *Sammy Morris* 1.00
254 *Raynoch Thompson* .50
255 Jeremy McDaniel .25
256 *Terrelle Smith* .50
257 *Deon Dyer* .50
258 *Na'il Diggs* 2.00
259 *Brandon Short* .50
260 *Mike Brown* .50
261 *John Engelberger* .50
262 *Rogers Beckett* .50
263 *JaJuan Seider* .50
264 *Desmond Kitchings* .50
265 *Reggie Davis* .50
266 *Corey Moore* .50
267 *Cornelius Griffin* .50
268 *Stockar McDougle* .50
269 *James Williams* .50
270 *Darrell Jackson* 5.00

2000 Bowman Chrome Refractors

Refractor Cards: 2X-4X
Inserted 1:12
Refractor Europe: 3X
Inserted 1:12
Refractor Rookie: 2X-4X
Inserted 1:281
Refractor Rookie SP: 1.5X
Inserted 1:659

2000 Bowman Chrome By Selection

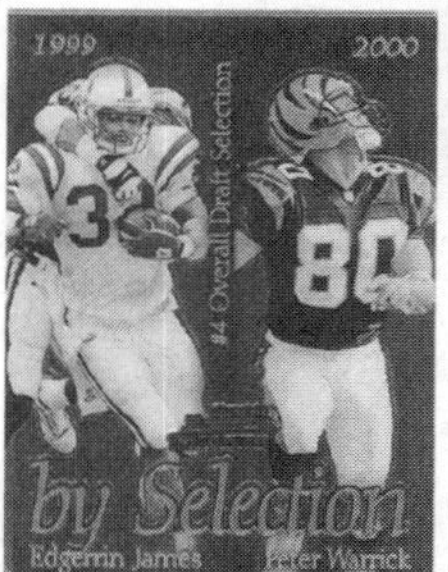

1999
2000
by Selection
Edgerrin James
Peter Warrick

NM/M
Complete Set (10): 30.00
Common Player: 2.00
Inserted 1:24
Refractors: 4X
Inserted 1:240
B1 Troy Aikman, Drew Bledsoe 5.00
B2 Marshall Faulk, Donovan McNabb 3.00
B3 Ricky Williams, Jamal Lewis 10.00
B4 Randy Moss, Sylvester Morris 7.00
B5 Shaun Alexander, Marvin Harrison 4.00
B6 Tim Couch, Peyton Manning 6.00
B7 Edgerrin James, Peter Warrick 7.00
B8 Jimmy Smith, Todd Pinkston 2.00
B9 Steve McNair, Akili Smith 2.00
B10 Plaxico Burress, Joey Galloway 3.50

2000 Bowman Chrome Ground Breakers

NM/M
Complete Set (10): 12.00
Common Player: .75
Minor Stars: 1.50
Inserted 1:12
Refractors: 4X
Inserted 1:120
GB1 Edgerrin James 5.00
GB2 Eddie George 1.75
GB3 Jerome Bettis 1.50
GB4 Fred Taylor 2.00
GB5 Curtis Martin 1.50
GB6 Errict Rhett .75
GB7 Marshall Faulk 1.50
GB8 Karim Abdul .75
GB9 Olandis Gary 1.50
GB10 Terrell Davis 3.00

2000 Bowman Chrome Rookie Autographs

NM/M
Common Player: 80.00
Production 25 Sets
Inserted 1:5,247
168 Thomas Jones 75.00
170 Jamal Lewis 150.00
172 Ron Dayne 75.00
173 Chad Pennington 300.00
175 R. Jay Soward 50.00
177 Shaun Alexander 175.00
181 Sylvester Morris 75.00
183 Peter Warrick 75.00
185 Travis Prentice 50.00

2000 Bowman Chrome Rookie of the Year

NM/M
Complete Set (10): 12.00
Common Player: .75
Minor Stars: 1.50
Inserted 1:Box
R1 Santana Dotson .75
R2 Jerome Bettis 1.50
R3 Marshall Faulk 1.50
R4 Curtis Martin 1.50
R5 Eddie George 2.00
R6 Warrick Dunn 1.50
R7 Charles Woodson .75
R8 Randy Moss 6.00
R9 Jevon Kearse 1.50
R10 Edgerrin James 6.00

2000 Bowman Chrome Scout's Choice Update

NM/M
Complete Set (10): 25.00
Common Player: 2.00
Inserted 1:24
Refractors: 4X
Inserted 1:240
SCU1 Shaun Alexander 4.00
SCU2 Brian Urlacher 5.00
SCU3 Courtney Brown 2.00
SCU4 Jamal Lewis 6.00
SCU5 Sylvester Morris 4.00
SCU6 Plaxico Burress 4.00
SCU7 Ron Dayne 3.00

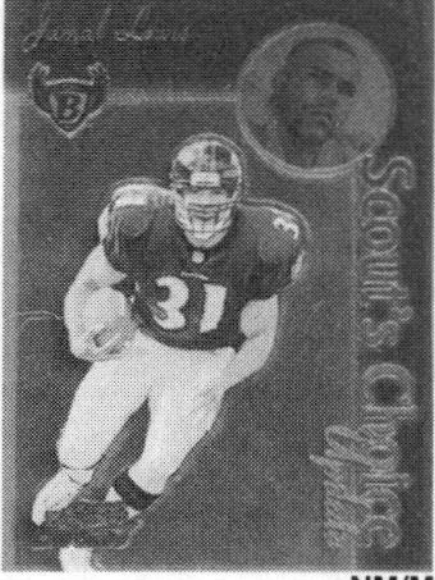

NM/M
SCU8 Thomas Jones 3.00
SCU9 Corey Simon 2.00
SCU10 Travis Taylor 2.50

2000 Bowman Chrome Shattering Performers

NM/M
Complete Set (20): 40.00
Common Player: 1.00
Minor Stars: 2.00
Inserted 1:16
Refractors: 4X
Inserted 1:160
SP1 Kurt Warner 6.00
SP2 Peyton Manning 7.00
SP3 Brian Griese 2.50
SP4 Daunte Culpepper 3.00
SP5 Elvis Grbac 1.00
SP6 Stephen Davis 2.00
SP7 Charlie Garner 1.00
SP8 Mike Anderson 4.00
SP9 Marshall Faulk 2.00
SP10 Robert Smith 2.00
SP11 Tiki Barber 1.00
SP12 Edgerrin James 7.00
SP13 Isaac Bruce 2.00
SP14 Rod Smith 2.00
SP15 Jimmy Smith 2.00
SP16 Torry Holt 2.00
SP17 Keenan McCardell 1.00
SP18 Marcus Robinson 2.00
SP19 Marvin Harrison 2.00
SP20 Randy Moss 7.00

2000 Bowman's Best

NM/M
Complete Set (150): 350.00
Common Player: .15
Minor Stars: .30
Common Rookie: 4.00
Production 1,499 Sets
Inserted 1:11
Pack (5): 2.75
Wax Box (24): 45.00
1 Troy Edwards .30
2 Kurt Warner 2.00
3 Steve McNair .50
4 Terry Glenn .50
5 Charlie Batch .50
6 Patrick Jeffers .50
7 Jake Plummer .50
8 Derrick Alexander .15
9 Joey Galloway .50
10 Tony Banks .30
11 Robert Smith .50
12 Jerry Rice 1.50
13 Jeff Garcia .50
14 Michael Westbrook .30
15 Curtis Conway .30
16 Brian Griese .75

17 Peyton Manning 2.50
18 Daunte Culpepper 1.50
19 Frank Sanders .30
20 Muhsin Muhammad .30
21 Corey Dillon .50
22 Brett Favre 2.50
23 Warrick Dunn .50
24 Tim Brown .50
25 Kerry Collins .30
26 Brad Johnson .50
27 Raghib Ismail .15
28 Jamal Anderson .50
29 Jimmy Smith .50
30 Torry Holt .50
31 Duce Staley .50
32 Drew Bledsoe 1.00
33 Jerome Bettis .50
34 Keyshawn Johnson .50
35 Fred Taylor .50
36 Akili Smith .50
37 Rob Johnson .30
38 Elvis Grbac .30
39 Antonio Freeman .50
40 Curtis Enis .50
41 Terance Mathis .15
42 Terrell Davis 1.00
43 Randy Moss 2.50
44 Jon Kitna .50
45 Curtis Martin .50
46 Terrell Owens .50
47 Robert Smith .50
48 Albert Connell .30
49 Edgerrin James 2.50
50 Tony Gonzalez .30
51 Eric Moulds .50
52 Natrone Means .15
53 Carl Pickens .30
54 Mark Brunell .50
55 Rob Moore .30
56 Marshall Faulk .50
57 Stephen Davis .50
58 Rich Gannon .30
59 Ricky Williams 1.00
60 Emmitt Smith 1.75
61 Germane Crowell .50
62 Doug Flutie .75
63 O.J. McDuffie .15
64 Chris Chandler .30
65 Qadry Ismail .15
66 Tim Couch 1.00
67 James Stewart .30
68 Marvin Harrison .50
69 Cris Carter .50
70 Cade McNown .75
71 Marcus Robinson .50
72 Steve Beuerlein .30
73 Jevon Kearse .50
74 Eddie George .75
75 Donovan McNabb 1.00
76 Jeff Blake .30
77 Wayne Chrebet .50
78 Kordell Stewart .60
79 Steve Young 1.00
80 Mike Alstott .50
81 Ricky Watters .30
82 Charlie Garner .30
83 Troy Aikman 1.50
84 Dorsey Levens .50
85 Ike Hilliard .30
86 Shaun King .50
87 Isaac Bruce .50
88 Tyrone Wheatley .30
89 Amani Toomer .30
90 Ed McCaffrey .50
91 Edgerrin James, Marshall Faulk 1.50
92 Drew Bledsoe, Brad Johnson .50
93 Jimmy Smith, Randy Moss 1.50
94 Eddie George, Stephen Davis .50
95 Mark Brunell, Troy Aikman 1.00
96 Marvin Harrison, Cris Carter .50
97 Curtis Martin, Emmitt Smith 1.25
98 Tim Brown, Isaac Bruce .50
99 Fred Taylor, Ricky Williams 1.00
100 Peyton Manning, Kurt Warner 1.50
101 *Shaun Alexander* 20.00
102 *Thomas Jones* 12.00
103 *Courtney Brown* 4.00
104 *Curtis Keaton* 4.00
105 *Jerry Porter* 12.00
106 *Corey Simon* 4.00
107 *Dez White* 5.00
108 *Jamal Lewis* 20.00
109 *Ron Dayne* 5.00
110 *R. Jay Soward* 4.00
111 *Tee Martin* 6.00
112 *Brian Urlacher* 20.00
113 *Reuben Droughns* 12.00
114 *Travis Taylor* 8.00
115 *Plaxico Burress* 15.00
116 *Chad Pennington* 30.00
117 *Sylvester Morris* 6.00
118 *Ron Dugans* 5.00
119 *Joe Hamilton* 5.00
120 *Chris Redman* 10.00
121 *Trung Canidate* 8.00
122 *J.R. Redmond* 6.00
123 *Danny Farmer* 5.00
124 *Todd Pinkston* 10.00
125 *Dennis Northcutt* 8.00
126 *Laveranues Coles* 12.00
127 *Bubba Franks* 10.00
128 *Travis Prentice* 6.00
129 *Peter Warrick* 12.00
130 *Anthony Becht* 5.00
131 *Ike Charlton* 4.00
132 *Shaun Ellis* 4.00
133 *Sean Morey* 4.00
134 *Sebastian Janikowski* 6.00
135 *Aaron Stecker* 5.00
136 *Ronney Jenkins* 4.00
137 *Jamel White* 4.00
138 *Nick Williams* 4.00
139 *Andy McCullough* 4.00
140 *Kevin Daft* 4.00
141 *Thomas Hamner* 4.00
142 *Tim Rattay* 10.00
143 *Spergon Wynn* 5.00
144 *Brandon Short* 4.00
145 *Chad Morton* 6.00
146 *Gari Scott* 4.00
147 *Frank Murphy* 4.00
148 *James Williams* 4.00
149 *Windrell Hayes* 4.00
150 *Doug Johnson* 8.00

2000 Bowman's Best

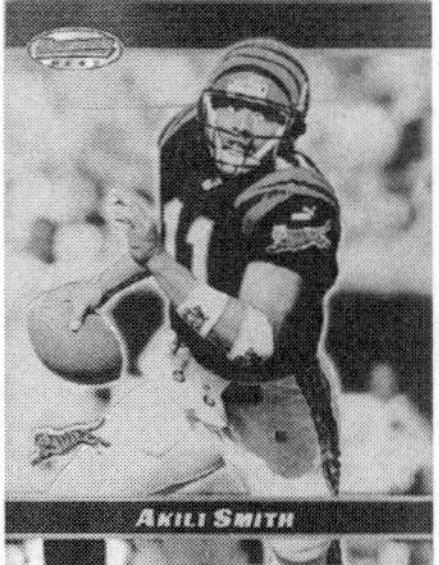

Parallel Cards: 5X-10X
Parallel Rookies: 1.5X
Production 250 Sets
Inserted 1:22

2000 Bowman's Best Autographs

NM/M
Common Player: 100.00
Inserted 1:2,395
JM Joe Montana 200.00
RM Randy Moss 100.00

2000 Bowman's Best Best of the Game Autographs

NM/M
Common Player: 70.00
Inserted 1:837
BG1 Edgerrin James 70.00
BG2 Kurt Warner 100.00

2000 Bowman's Best Bets

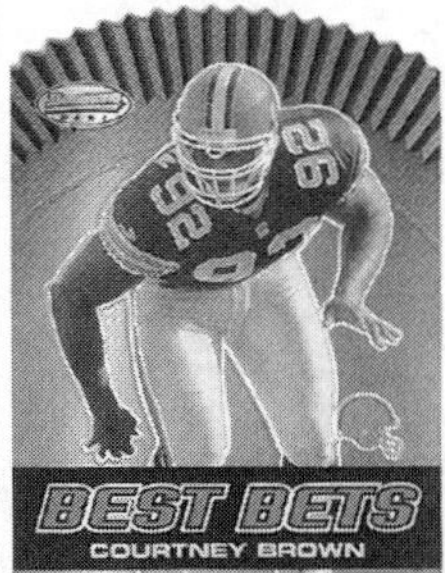

NM/M
Complete Set (13): 18.00
Common Player: .50
Minor Stars: 1.00
Inserted 1:19
B1 Jamal Lewis 3.00
B2 Plaxico Burress 2.00
B3 Chad Pennington 5.00
B4 Sylvester Morris 2.00
B5 Shaun Alexander 2.50
B6 Peter Warrick 2.00
B7 Travis Taylor 1.25
B8 Courtney Brown 1.00
B9 R. Jay Soward 1.00
B10 Ron Dayne 2.00
B11 Jerry Porter 1.00
B12 Curtis Keaton .50
B13 Thomas Jones 1.75

2000 Bowman's Best Franchise 2000

NM/M
Complete Set (20): 30.00
Common Player: .50
Minor Stars: 1.00
Inserted 1:12
F1 Curtis Martin 1.00
F2 Eddie George 1.50
F3 Emmitt Smith 3.00
F4 Stephen Davis 1.00
F5 Cade McNown 1.00
F6 Drew Bledsoe 2.00
F7 Zach Thomas .50
F8 Mark Brunell 2.00
F9 Tim Brown .50
F10 Akili Smith 1.00
F11 Peyton Manning 4.00
F12 Terrell Davis 2.00

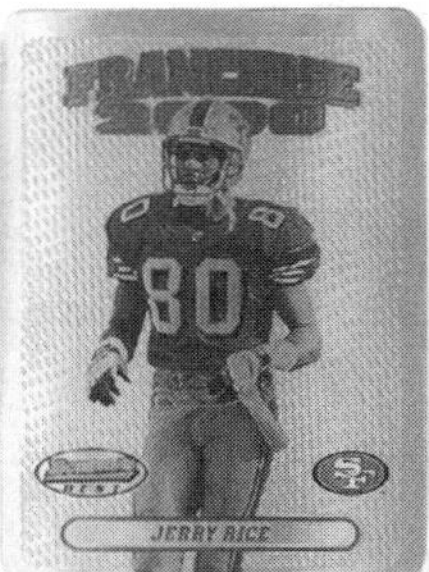

NM/M
F13 Brett Favre 5.00
F14 Randy Moss 4.00
F15 Kurt Warner 3.00
F16 Ricky Williams 2.50
F17 Jerry Rice 2.50
F18 Jake Plummer 1.00
F19 Tim Couch 2.00
F20 Warren Sapp .50

2000 Bowman's Best Pro Bowl Jerseys

NM/M
Complete Set (14): 300.00
Common Player: 10.00
Inserted 1:112
DB Derrick Brooks 10.00
IB Isaac Bruce 15.00
MB Mark Brunell 15.00
SD Stephen Davis 10.00
MF Marshall Faulk 20.00
MH Marvin Harrison 20.00
EJ Edgerrin James 25.00
BJ Brad Johnson 10.00
KJ Keyshawn Johnson 20.00
JK Jevon Kearse 15.00
RM Randy Moss 30.00
JS Jimmy Smith 10.00
KW Kurt Warner 25.00
CW Charles Woodson 10.00

2000 Bowman's Best Rookie Autographs

NM/M
Common Player: 12.00
Inserted 1:83
SA Shaun Alexander 30.00
CB Courtney Brown 30.00
PB Plaxico Burress 30.00
LC Laveranues Coles 18.00
RD Ron Dayne 35.00
RDR Reuben Droughns 20.00
RDU Ron Dugans 12.00
DF Danny Farmer 12.00
JH Joe Hamilton 12.00
TJ Thomas Jones 20.00
JL Jamal Lewis 40.00
TM Tee Martin 15.00
SM Sylvester Morris 30.00
CP Chad Pennington 60.00
TPR Travis Prentice 15.00
JR J.R. Redmond 18.00
RS R. Jay Soward 15.00
BU Brian Urlacher 50.00
PW Peter Warrick 25.00

2000 Bowman's Best Year by Year

NM/M
Complete Set (12): 20.00
Common Player: 1.50
Inserted 1:20
Y1 Peyton Manning, Randy Moss 5.00
Y2 Keyshawn Johnson, Eddie George 2.00
Y3 Tim Brown, Thurman Thomas 1.50
Y4 Drew Bledsoe, Jerome Bettis 2.00
Y5 Edgerrin James, Ricky Williams 5.00
Y6 Troy Aikman, Deion Sanders 3.00
Y7 Isaac Bruce, Marshall Faulk 1.50
Y8 Junior Seau, Emmitt Smith 3.00
Y9 Curtis Martin, Terrell Davis 3.00
Y10 Brad Johnson, Jimmy Smith 1.50
Y11 Brett Favre, Ricky Watters 4.00
Y12 Peter Warrick, Plaxico Burress 3.50

A card number in parenthese ( ) indicates the set is unnumbered.

2000 Bowman Reserve

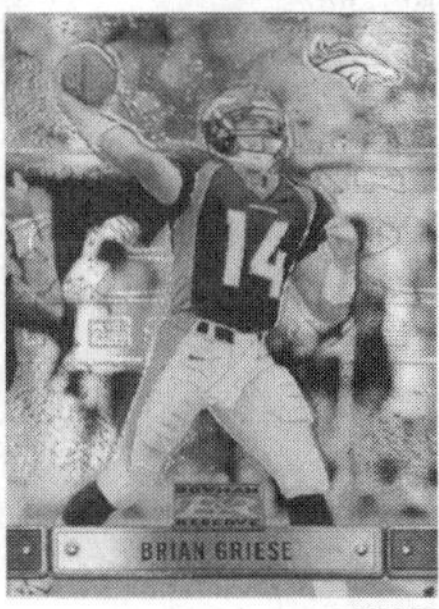

NM/M
Common Player: .30
Minor Stars: .60
Common Rookies: 15.00
Production 999 Sets
Wax Box (10 + Mini Helmet): 125.00
1 *Chad Pennington* 60.00
2 *Shaun Alexander* 40.00
3 *Thomas Jones* 20.00
4 *Courtney Brown* 12.00
5 *Curtis Keaton* 12.00
6 *Jerry Porter* 20.00
7 *Jamal Lewis* 40.00
8 *Ron Dayne* 15.00
9 *R. Jay Soward* 12.00
10 *Tee Martin* 15.00
11 *Travis Taylor* 15.00
12 *Plaxico Burress* 30.00
13 *Giovanni Carmazzi* 12.00
14 *Sylvester Morris* 12.00
15 *Chris Redman* 15.00
16 *Trung Canidate* 15.00
17 *J.R. Redmond* 12.00
18 *Bubba Franks* 15.00
19 *Travis Prentice* 15.00
20 *Peter Warrick* 20.00
21 Frank Sanders .60
22 Edgerrin James 5.00
23 Marcus Robinson .75
24 Mike Alstott .75
25 Jerry Rice 2.50
26 Marshall Faulk 1.00
27 Brad Johnson .75
28 Elvis Grbac .60
29 Wayne Chrebet .75
30 Akili Smith .75
31 Rob Johnson .60
32 Brett Favre 5.00
33 Ricky Williams 2.00
34 Donovan McNabb 2.00
35 Cris Carter .75
36 Ricky Watters .60
37 Steve McNair 1.25
38 Stephen Davis .75
39 Fred Taylor 2.00
40 Raghib Ismail .30
41 Terry Glenn .75
42 Ed McCaffrey .75
43 Patrick Jeffers .75
44 Jake Plummer 1.00
45 Doug Flutie .75
46 Terrell Davis 2.00
47 Marvin Harrison 1.00
48 Amani Toomer .60
49 Tyrone Wheatley .60
50 Charlie Garner 1.00
51 Jevon Kearse 1.00
52 Michael Westbrook 1.00
53 Eddie George 1.50
54 Robert Smith .75
55 Keyshawn Johnson .75
56 Torry Holt .75
57 Jon Kitna .50
58 Curtis Conway .60
59 Jeff Garcia 1.00
60 Randy Moss 5.00
61 Jimmy Smith .75
62 James Stewart .75
63 Troy Aikman 2.50
64 Cade McNown .75
65 Natrone Means .60
66 Jamal Anderson 1.00
67 Warrick Dunn .75
68 Kordell Stewart .75
69 Duce Staley 1.00
70 Rich Gannon .75
71 Curtis Martin 1.00
72 Kerry Collins .60
73 Jeff Blake .60
74 Drew Bledsoe 2.00
75 Kevin Dyson .30
76 Tony Gonzalez 1.00
77 Mark Brunell 2.00
78 Peyton Manning 5.00
79 Dorsey Levens .75
80 Germane Crowell .75
81 Brian Griese .75
82 Steve Beuerlein .60
83 Eric Moulds 1.00
84 Tony Banks .60
85 Chris Chandler .60
86 Isaac Bruce 1.00
87 Terrell Owens 1.00
88 Jerome Bettis .75
89 Daunte Culpepper 2.50
90 Emmitt Smith 3.50
91 Curtis Enis .60
92 Shaun King .75
93 Tim Brown 1.00
94 Antonio Freeman .75
95 Charlie Batch .75
96 Tim Couch 2.50
97 Corey Dillon 1.00
98 Muhsin Muhammad .60
99 Joey Galloway .75
100 Kurt Warner 4.00
101 David Boston 1.00
102 Rod Smith .75
103 Derrick Mayes .30
104 Tony Martin .30
105 Darnay Scott .60
106 Joe Horn .60
107 Troy Edwards .75
108 James Johnson .60
109 Vinny Testaverde .75
110 Qadry Ismail .30
111 Andre Reed .30
112 Zach Thomas .75
113 Ike Hilliard .30
114 Herman Moore .75
115 Kevin Johnson .75
116 Shawn Jefferson .30
117 Terance Mathis .30
118 Peerless Price .75
119 Bert Emanuel .30
120 Terrence Wilkins .75
121 *Mike Anderson* 15.00
122 *Dez White* 15.00
123 *Todd Pinkston* 15.00
124 *Reuben Droughns* 20.00
125 *Danny Farmer* 12.00

2000 Bowman Reserve Autographed Rookie Mini-Helmets

NM/M
Common Helmet: 25.00
Inserted 1:Box
Shaun Alexander 50.00
Mike Anderson 35.00
Courtney Brown SP 35.00
Plaxico Burress 45.00
Trung Canidate 25.00
Giovanni Carmazzi 35.00
Laveranues Coles 35.00
Ron Dayne 35.00
Danny Farmer 25.00
Darrell Jackson 40.00
Thomas Jones 35.00
Jamal Lewis 40.00
Sylvester Morris 40.00
Chad Pennington 75.00
Todd Pinkston 35.00
Travis Prentice 35.00
Chris Redman 45.00
J.R. Redmond 35.00
R. Jay Soward 30.00
Brian Urlacher 75.00
Peter Warrick SP 35.00
Dez White 25.00

2000 Bowman Reserve Autographs

NM/M
Complete Set (7): 130.00
Common Player: 8.00
Inserted 1:Box
GC Germane Crowell 8.00
DC Daunte Culpepper 50.00
TG Tony Gonzalez 8.00
TH Torry Holt 25.00
EJ Edgerrin James 60.00
KJ Kevin Johnson 8.00
MR Marcus Robinson 20.00

2000 Bowman Reserve Pro Bowl Jerseys

NM/M
Complete Set (45): 600.00
Common Player: 8.00
Minor Stars: 15.00
Inserted 1:Box
MA Mike Alstott 25.00
JA Jessie Armstead 8.00

SB Steve Beuerlein 20.00
PB Peter Boulware 8.00
CB Chad Brown 8.00
IB Isaac Bruce 20.00
MB Mark Brunell 25.00
CC Cris Carter 35.00
SD Stephen Davis 25.00
MF Marshall Faulk 30.00
RG Rich Gannon 20.00
SG Sam Gash 8.00
EG Eddie George 35.00
TG Tony Gonzalez 25.00
KH Kevin Hardy 8.00
MH Marvin Harrison 25.00
EJ Edgerrin James 40.00
BJ Brad Johnson 20.00
KJ Keyshawn Johnson 25.00
JK Jevon Kearse 30.00
CK Cortez Kennedy 15.00
CL Carnell Lake 15.00
TL Todd Lyght 8.00
SM Sam Madison 8.00
BM Bruce Matthews 15.00
KM Kevin Mawae 8.00
MM Michael McCrary 8.00
RM Randall McDaniel 8.00
GM Glyn Milburn 8.00
LM Lawyer Milloy 8.00
RM Randy Moss 40.00
HN Hardy Nickerson 8.00
RP Robert Porcher 8.00
WR William Roaf 15.00
DR Darrell Russell 8.00
WS Warren Sapp 15.00
EM Emmitt Smith 50.00
JS Jimmy Smith 20.00
MS Michael Strahan 8.00
TT Tom Tupa 8.00
WW Wesley Walls 15.00
KW Kurt Warner 30.00
CW Charles Woodson 25.00
RW Rod Woodson 15.00
FW Frank Wycheck 15.00

2000 Bowman Reserve Rookie Autographs

NM/M
Complete Set (15): 400.00
Common Player: 10.00
Inserted 1:41 Retail
SA Shaun Alexander 35.00
CB Courtney Brown 12.00
PB Plaxico Burress 25.00
TC Trung Canidate 10.00
RDA Ron Dayne 20.00
TJ Thomas Jones 20.00
JL Jamal Lewis 35.00
SM Sylvester Morris 25.00
CP Chad Pennington 50.00
TPR Travis Prentice 18.00
CR Chris Redman 20.00
JR J.R. Redmond 15.00
RS R. Jay Soward 12.00
PW Peter Warrick 20.00
DW Dez White 10.00

2000 Bowman Reserve Rookie Relic Jerseys

NM/M
Complete Set (2): 25.00
Common Player: 10.00
Randomly Inserted
RDU Ron Dugans 10.00
PW Peter Warrick 15.00

2001 Bowman

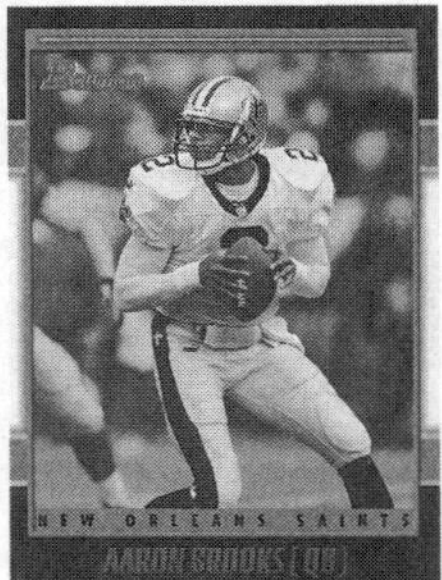

NM/M
Complete Set (275): 70.00
Common Player: .15
Minor Stars: .30
Common Rookie: .50
Pack (10): 3.25
Wax Box (24): 55.00
1 Emmitt Smith 1.25
2 James Stewart .30
3 Jeff Graham .15
4 Keyshawn Johnson .50
5 Stephen Davis .50
6 Chad Lewis .30
7 Drew Bledsoe .60
8 Fred Taylor .60
9 Mike Anderson .75
10 Tony Gonzalez .30
11 Aaron Brooks .50
12 Vinny Testaverde .30
13 Jerome Bettis .50
14 Marshall Faulk .60
15 Jeff Garcia .50
16 Terry Glenn .40
17 Jay Fiedler .40
18 Ahman Green .50
19 Cade McNown .50

20 Rob Johnson .30
21 Jamal Anderson .50
22 Corey Dillon .50
23 Jake Plummer .50
24 Rod Smith .50
25 Trent Green .40
26 Ricky Williams .75
27 Charlie Garner .40
28 Shaun Alexander .50
29 Jeff George .30
30 Torry Holt .50
31 James Thrash .30
32 Rich Gannon .30
33 Ron Dayne .75
34 Dedric Ward .30
35 Edgerrin James 1.25
36 Cris Carter .50
37 Derrick Mason .30
38 Brad Johnson .40
39 Charlie Batch .40
40 Joey Galloway .50
41 James Allen .30
42 Tim Biakabutuka .30
43 Ray Lewis .40
44 David Boston .50
45 Kevin Johnson .40
46 Jimmy Smith .40
47 Joe Horn .30
48 Terrell Owens .50
49 Eddie George .60
50 Brett Favre 2.00
51 Wayne Chrebet .40
52 Hines Ward .30
53 Warrick Dunn .50
54 Matt Hasselbeck .50
55 Tiki Barber .50
56 Lamar Smith .50
57 Tim Couch .60
58 Eric Moulds .50
59 Shawn Jefferson .30
60 Donald Hayes .30
61 Brian Urlacher 1.00
62 Steve McNair .50
63 Kurt Warner 1.50
64 Tim Brown .50
65 Troy Brown .30
66 Albert Connell .30
67 Peyton Manning 1.50
68 Peter Warrick .60
69 Elvis Grbac .40
70 Chris Chandler .30
71 Akili Smith .50
72 Keenan McCardell .30
73 Kerry Collins .40
74 Junior Seau .30
75 Donovan McNabb .75
76 Tony Banks .30
77 Steve Beuerlein .30
78 Daunte Culpepper 1.00
79 Darrell Jackson .30
80 Isaac Bruce .50
81 Tyrone Wheatley .30
82 Derrick Alexander .30
83 Germane Crowell .40
84 Jon Kitna .40
85 Jamal Lewis 1.00
86 Ed McCaffrey .50
87 Mark Brunell .60
88 Jeff Blake .30
89 Duce Staley .50
90 Doug Flutie .60
91 Kordell Stewart .50
92 Randy Moss 1.50
93 Marvin Harrison .50
94 Muhsin Muhammad .30
95 Brian Griese .60
96 Antonio Freeman .40
97 Amani Toomer .30
98 Oronde Gadsden .30
99 Curtis Martin .50
100 Jerry Rice 1.25
101 Michael Pittman .30
102 Shannon Sharpe .30
103 Peerless Price .30
104 Bill Schroeder .30
105 Ike Hilliard .30
106 Freddie Jones .30
107 Tai Streets .30
108 Ricky Watters .40
109 Az-Zahir Hakim .30
110 Jacquez Green .30
111 Bobby Shaw .30
112 Johnnie Morton .30
113 Laveranues Coles .30
114 Chad Pennington 1.00
115 Champ Bailey .40
116 Charles Woodson .40
117 Curtis Conway .30
118 Marcus Robinson .50
119 Michael Westbrook .30
120 Mike Alstott .50
121 Priest Holmes .60
122 Qadry Ismail .30
123 Raghib Ismail .30
124 Shawn Bryson .15
125 Jeff Lewis .30
126 Jeremy McDaniel .15
127 Terance Mathis .30
128 Travis Prentice .30
129 Warren Sapp .30
130 Jevon Kearse .40
131 *George Layne* .75
132 *Correll Buckhalter* 1.50
133 *Tony Stewart* 1.00
134 *Chris Barnes* .50
135 *A.J. Feeley* .75
136 *Margin Hooks* .50
137 *Anthony Henry* .50
138 *Dwight Smith* .50
139 *Torrance Marshall* .50
140 *Gary Baxter* .50
141 *Derek Combs* .50
142 *Marcus Bell* .50
143 *DeLawrence Grant* .50
144 *Jameel Cook* .50
145 *Eric Downing* .50
146 *Marlon McCree* .50
147 *Tay Cody* .50
148 *Mario Monds* .50
149 *Kenny Smith* .50
150 *Sedrick Hodge* .50
151 *Marcus Stroud* .50
152 *Steve Smith* .50
153 *Tyrone Robertson* .50
154 *James Reed* .50
155 *Kris Kocurek* .50
156 *Dan O'Leary* .50
157 *Harold Blackmon* .50
158 *Fred Smoot* 1.00
159 *Billy Baber* .50
160 *Jarrod Cooper* .50
161 *Travis Henry* 2.00
162 *David Terrell* 2.00
163 *Josh Heupel* 1.75
164 *Drew Brees* 4.00
165 *T.J. Houshmandzadeh* .75
166 *Rod Gardner* 2.00
167 *Richard Seymour* .75
168 *Koren Robinson* 2.00
169 *Scotty Anderson* .75
170 *Marques Tuiasosopo* 2.00
171 *John Capel* 1.00
172 *LaMont Jordan* 1.50
173 *James Jackson* 1.75
174 *Bobby Newcombe* 1.00
175 *Anthony Thomas* 3.00
176 *Dan Alexander* 1.00
177 *Quincy Carter* 2.00
178 *Morlon Greenwood* .75
179 *Robert Ferguson* 1.00
180 *Sage Rosenfels* 1.00
181 *Michael Stone* .50
182 *Chris Weinke* 1.00
183 *Travis Minor* 1.00
184 *Gerard Warren* 1.00
185 *Jamar Fletcher* .75
186 *Andre Carter* 1.00
187 *Deuce McAllister* 5.00
188 *Dan Morgan* 1.00
189 *Todd Heap* 1.00
190 *Marvin "Snoop" Minnis* 1.50
191 *Will Allen* .75
192 *Freddie Mitchell* 1.75
193 *Rudi Johnson* 2.50
194 *Kevan Barlow* 2.00
195 *Jamie Winborn* .75
196 *Onomo Ojo* .75
197 *Leonard Davis* .75
198 *Santana Moss* 2.50
199 *Chris Chambers* 2.50
200 *Michael Vick* 8.00
201 *Michael Bennett* 2.50
202 *Mike McMahon* 2.00
203 *Jonathan Carter* .50
204 *Jamal Reynolds* 1.00
205 *Justin Smith* 1.00
206 *Quincy Morgan* 1.75
207 *Chad Johnson* 3.00
208 *Jesse Palmer* 1.00
209 *Reggie Wayne* 2.00
210 *LaDainian Tomlinson* 6.00
211 *Andre King* .75
212 *Richmond Flowers* .50
213 *Derrick Blaylock* .50
214 *Cedrick Wilson* .50
215 *Zeke Moreno* .50
216 *Tommy Polley* .75
217 *Damione Lewis* .50
218 *Aaron Schobel* .50
219 *Alge Crumpler* 1.00
220 *Nate Clements* .75
221 *Quentin McCord* .75
222 *Ken-Yon Rambo* 1.00
223 *Milton Wynn* .50
224 *Derrick Gibson* .50
225 *Chris Taylor* .75
226 *Corey Hall* .50
227 *Vinny Sutherland* 1.00
228 *Kendrell Bell* 1.00
229 *Casey Hampton* .75
230 *Demetric Evans* .50
231 *Brian Allen* .50
232 *Rodney Bailey* .50
233 *Otis Leverette* .50
234 *Ron Edwards* .50
235 *Michael Jameson* .50
236 *Markus Steele* .50
237 *Jimmy Williams* .75
238 *Roger Knight* .50
239 *Randy Garner* .50
240 *Raymond Perryman* .50
241 *Karon Riley* .50
242 *Adam Archuleta* 1.00
243 *Arnold Jackson* .75
244 *Ryan Pickett* .50
245 *Shad Meier* .50
246 *Reggie Germany* 1.00
247 *Justin McCareins* .50
248 *Idrees Bashir* .50
249 *Josh Booty* 1.00
250 *Eddie Berlin* 1.00
251 *Heath Evans* .75
252 *Alex Bannister* 1.00
253 *Corey Alston* .50
254 *Reggie White* 1.00
255 *Orlando Huff* .50
256 *Ken Lucas* .50
257 *Matt Stewart* .50
258 *Cedric Scott* .75
259 *Ronney Daniels* .75
260 *Kevin Kasper* 1.25
261 *Tony Driver* .75
262 *Kyle Vanden Bosch* 1.00
263 *T.J. Turner* .50
264 *Eric Westmoreland* .50
265 *Ronald Flemons* .50
266 *Eric Kelly* .50
267 *Moran Norris* .50
268 *Darnerian McCants* .50
269 *James Boyd* .50
270 *Keith Adams* .50
271 *Brandon Manumaleuna* .50
272 *Dee Brown* .50
273 *Ross Kolodziej* .50
274 *Eddie "Boo" Williams* .50
275 *Patrick Chukwurah* .50

2001 Bowman Gold

NM/M
Gold Cards: 2X-4X
Gold Rookies: 2X
Inserted 1:1

2001 Bowman Autographs

NM/M
Common Player: 8.00
Inserted 1:61
BA-DA Dan Alexander 10.00
BA-KB Kevan Barlow 15.00
BA-MB Michael Bennett 45.00
BA-JB Josh Booty 10.00
BA-DB Drew Brees 50.00
BA-QC Quincy Carter 25.00
BA-CC Chris Chambers 15.00
BA-RG Rod Gardner 20.00
BA-TH Travis Henry 20.00
BA-JH Josh Heupel 12.00
BA-JJ James Jackson 18.00
BA-CJ Chad Johnson 15.00
BA-LJ LaMont Jordan 15.00
BA-TM Travis Minor 12.00
BA-FM Freddie Mitchell 18.00
BA-DM Dan Morgan 10.00
BA-QM Quincy Morgan 20.00
BA-SM Santana Moss 25.00
BA-BN Bobby Newcombe 8.00
BA-JP Jesse Palmer 15.00
BA-KYR Ken-Yon Rambo 10.00
BA-DR David Rivers 8.00
BA-KR Koren Robinson 30.00
BA-DT David Terrell 30.00
BA-AT Anthony Thomas 45.00
BA-LT LaDainian Tomlinson 60.00
BA-MV Michael Vick 85.00
BA-KW Kenyatta Walker 8.00
BA-RW Reggie Wayne 25.00
BA-CW Chris Weinke 30.00

2001 Bowman 1996 Rookies

NM/M
Complete Set (15): 30.00
Common Player: 1.00
Inserted 1:4
BRC1 Eric Moulds 2.50
BRC2 Ray Lewis 3.00
BRC3 Tim Biakabutuka 1.50
BRC4 Eddie George 4.00
BRC5 Marvin Harrison 3.00
BRC6 Joe Horn 2.00
BRC7 Muhsin Muhammad 2.00
BRC8 Mike Alstott 2.50
BRC9 Amani Toomer 2.00
BRC10 Terrell Owens 3.50
BRC11 Keyshawn Johnson 3.00
BRC12 Terry Glenn 1.75
BRC13 Zach Thomas 1.75
BRC14 Stephen Davis 3.00
BRC15 La'Roi Glover 1.00

2001 Bowman Relics

NM/M
RRE-SB Sammy Baugh 25.00
RRE-GM Gino Marchetti 15.00

2001 Bowman Rookie Reprint

NM/M
Complete Set (16): 30.00
Common Player: 1.50
Inserted 1:6
R-AA Alan Ameche 1.50
R-SB Sammy Baugh 4.50
R-CC Charlie Conerly 2.75
R-AD Art Donovan 3.00
R-TF Tom Fears 1.50
R-FG Frank Gifford 5.00
R-OG Otto Graham 3.50
R-LG Lou Groza 3.00
R-EH Elroy Hirsch 3.00
R-BH Bill Howton 1.50
R-SL Sid Luckman 2.75
R-GM Gino Marchetti 2.00
R-YT Y.A. Tittle 4.00
R-ET Emlen Tunnell 1.50
R-BT Bulldog Turner 2.50
R-NV Norm Van Brocklin 3.50

2001 Bowman Senior Bowl/Hula Bowl Relics

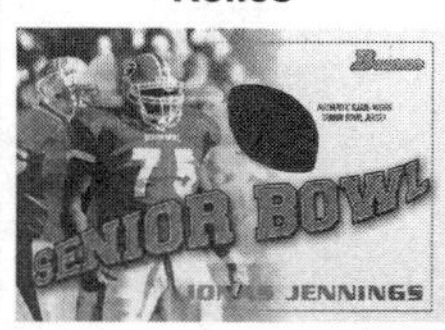

NM/M
Common Player: 5.00
Inserted 1:25
BJ-BA Brian Allen 5.00
BJ-AA Adam Archuleta 10.00
BJ-JB Jeff Backus 7.00
BJ-DB Drew Brees 30.00
BJ-DBU Derrick Burgess 5.00
BJ-JC Jarrod Cooper 5.00
BJ-AC Alge Crumpler 10.00
BJ-TD Tony Dixon 5.00
BJ-MF Mario Fatafehi 8.00
BJ-RG Reggie Germany 10.00
BJ-DG Derrick Gibson 5.00
BJ-JHE Jamie Henderson 5.00
BJ-JH Jabari Holloway 7.00
BJ-SH Steve Hutchinson 8.00
BJ-JJ Jonas Jennings 5.00
BJ-LJ LaMont Jordan 12.00
BJ-BJ Bhawoh Jue 5.00
BJ-KK Kevin Kasper 5.00
BJ-MMC Mike McMahon 12.00
BJ-TM Travis Minor 10.00
BJ-ZM Zeke Moreno 5.00
BJ-LM Leonard Myers 5.00
BJ-BN Bobby Newcombe 5.00
BJ-JP Jesse Palmer 10.00
BJ-SR Sage Rosenfels 12.00
BJ-SS Steve Smith 7.00
BJ-FS Fred Smoot 7.00
BJ-TS Tony Stewart 8.00
BJ-MS Michael Stone 5.00
BJ-CT Chris Taylor 5.00
BJ-LT LaDainian Tomlinson 45.00
BJ-RW Reggie Wayne 15.00
BJ-EW Eric Westmoreland 5.00

2001 Bowman Senior Bowl/Hula Bowl Relics Autographed

NM/M
Common Player: 25.00
Inserted 1:1,780
BJA-DB Drew Brees 80.00
BJA-LJ LaMont Jordan 25.00
BJA-BN Bobby Newcombe 25.00
BJA-JP Jesse Palmer 25.00
BJA-LT LaDainian Tomlinson 125.00
BJA-RW Reggie Wayne 30.00

2001 Bowman's Best

NM/M
Common Player: .15
Minor Stars: .30
Common Rookie JSY: 10.00
Production 999 Sets
Common Rookie (121-170): 3.00
Production 1,499 Sets
Pack (5): 5.00
Box (24): 85.00
1 Jerry Rice 1.50
2 Doug Flutie .75
3 Drew Bledsoe .75
4 Edgerrin James 1.50
5 Muhsin Muhammad .30
6 Charlie Batch .30
7 Marshall Faulk .75
8 Trent Green .30
9 Rich Gannon .50
10 Emmitt Smith 1.50
11 Steve McNair .50
12 Darrell Jackson .30
13 Amani Toomer .30
14 Jimmy Smith .30
15 Kevin Johnson .30
16 Ray Lewis .30
17 Peter Warrick .50
18 Cris Carter .50
19 Jerome Bettis .50
20 Keyshawn Johnson .50
21 Joey Galloway .50
22 Chris Chandler .15
23 Brett Favre 2.50
24 Aaron Brooks .75
25 Kurt Warner 2.00
26 Jeff Graham .15
27 Curtis Martin .50
28 Mike Anderson 1.00
29 Eric Moulds .30
30 David Boston .50
31 Elvis Grbac .30
32 James Stewart .15
33 Randy Moss 2.00
34 Donovan McNabb 1.25
35 Matt Hasselbeck .30
36 Stephen Davis .30
37 Brad Johnson .30
38 Jamal Anderson .30
39 Tim Biakabutuka .15
40 Antonio Freeman .30
41 Mark Brunell .75
42 Tiki Barber .30
43 Charlie Garner .30
44 Eddie George .75
45 Ricky Williams 1.00
46 Rob Johnson .30
47 Jake Plummer .30
48 Peyton Manning 2.00
49 Lamar Smith .30
50 Corey Dillon .30
51 Derrick Alexander .30
52 Troy Brown .30
53 Wayne Chrebet .50
54 Shaun Alexander 1.00
55 Jeff George .15
56 Tim Brown .50
57 Brian Griese .75
58 Cade McNown .15
59 Jamal Lewis .75
60 Germane Crowell .30
61 Junior Seau .30
62 Warrick Dunn .50
63 Isaac Bruce .50
64 Terry Glenn .30
65 Fred Taylor .75
66 Tim Couch .75
67 Akili Smith .15
68 Tony Gonzalez .30
69 Kerry Collins .30
70 James Thrash .30
71 Terrell Owens .50
72 Derrick Mason .30
73 Tyrone Wheatley .30
74 Oronde Gadsden .15
75 Ahman Green .50
76 Jon Kitna .15
77 Tony Banks .15
78 Marvin Harrison .50
79 Daunte Culpepper 1.25
80 Vinny Testaverde .30
81 Chad Lewis .15
82 Torry Holt .50
83 Jeff Garcia .75
84 Rod Smith .30
85 Marcus Robinson .30
86 Keenan McCardell .30
87 Joe Horn .30
88 Kordell Stewart .50
89 Jay Fiedler .30
90 Ed McCaffrey .30
91 Eddie George, Stephen Davis .50
92 Peyton Manning, Jeff Garcia 1.50
93 Rod Smith, Torry Holt .50
94 Edgerrin James, Marshall Faulk 1.00
95 Elvis Grbac, Daunte Culpepper .75
96 Marvin Harrison, Randy Moss 1.50
97 Mike Anderson, Emmitt Smith 1.00
98 Brian Griese, Kurt Warner 1.50
99 Muhsin Muhammad, Ed McCaffrey .30
100 Eric Moulds, Terrell Owens .50
101 *David Terrell JSY* 15.00
102 *Kevan Barlow JSY* 12.00
103 *Quincy Morgan JSY* 10.00
104 *Chris Weinke JSY* 10.00
105 *Josh Heupel JSY* 10.00
106 *Chris Chambers JSY* 20.00
107 *Reggie Wayne JSY* 15.00
108 *Gerard Warren JSY* 10.00
109 *Freddie Mitchell JSY* 15.00
110 *Anthony Thomas JSY* 15.00
111 *Robert Ferguson JSY* 10.00
112 *Deuce McAllister JSY* 25.00
113 *Travis Henry JSY* 12.00
114 *Rod Gardner JSY* 15.00
115 *Michael Bennett JSY* 20.00
116 *Santana Moss JSY* 15.00
117 *Chad Johnson JSY* 20.00
118 *Jesse Palmer JSY* 10.00
119 *James Jackson JSY* 10.00
120 *Dan Morgan JSY* 10.00
121 *Drew Brees* 12.00
122 *Travis Minor* 8.00
123 *Quincy Carter* 15.00
124 *LaDainian Tomlinson* 20.00
125 *Michael Vick* 40.00
126 *Ryan Pickett* 3.00
127 *Mike McMahon* 4.00
128 *Alex Bannister* 3.00
129 *A.J. Feeley* 5.00
130 *Shad Meier* 3.00
131 *Jamie Winborn* 3.00
132 *Fred Smoot* 5.00
133 *Milton Wynn* 3.00
134 *Onomo Ojo* 3.00
135 *Jonathan Carter* 3.00
136 *Todd Heap* 5.00
137 *Bobby Newcombe* 3.00
138 *Tony Stewart* 3.00
139 *Torrance Marshall* 3.00
140 *Jamal Reynolds* 3.00
141 *Jamar Fletcher* 3.00
142 *Richard Seymour* 3.00
143 *Tay Cody* 3.00
144 *Koren Robinson* 8.00
145 *Eddie Berlin* 3.00
146 *Damione Lewis* 3.00
147 *Marques Tuiasosopo* 6.00
148 *Marvin "Snoop" Minnis* 6.00
149 *Chris Barnes* 3.00
150 *Leonard Davis* 3.00
151 *Vinny Sutherland* 5.00
152 *Rudi Johnson* 10.00
153 *Derrick Gibson* 3.00
154 *Dan Alexander* 5.00
155 *Darnerian McCants* 3.00
156 *Adam Archuleta* 5.00
157 *Correll Buckhalter* 6.00
158 *LaMont Jordan* 8.00
159 *Quentin McCord* 3.00
160 *Justin Smith* 3.00
161 *Nate Clements* 3.00
162 *Alge Crumpler* 5.00
163 *Dan O'Leary* 3.00
164 *Sage Rosenfels* 6.00
165 *Andre Carter* 3.00
166 *Marcus Stroud* 3.00
167 *Will Allen* 3.00
168 *Tommy Polley* 3.00
169 *Justin McCareins* 6.00
170 *Josh Booty* 5.00

2001 Bowman's Best Autographs

NM/M
Common Player: 10.00
Inserted 1:23
BB-DA Dan Alexander 10.00
BB-KB Kevan Barlow 15.00
BB-MB Michael Bennett 25.00
BB-DBR Drew Brees 50.00
BB-QC Quincy Carter 20.00
BB-CC Chris Chambers 25.00
BB-SD Stephen Davis 15.00
BB-TD Tim Dwight 10.00
BB-RF Robert Ferguson 10.00
BB-RG Rod Gardner 20.00
BB-DH Donald Hayes 10.00
BB-TH Travis Henry 15.00
BB-JHE Josh Heupel 15.00
BB-JH Joe Horn 10.00
BB-JJ James Jackson 15.00
BB-CJ Chad Johnson 15.00
BB-LJ LaMont Jordan 15.00
BB-JL Jamal Lewis 20.00
BB-FM Freddie Mitchell 20.00
BB-DMO Dan Morgan 10.00
BB-QM Quincy Morgan 15.00
BB-SMO Sammy Morris 10.00
BB-RM Randy Moss 60.00
BB-SM Santana Moss 20.00
BB-EM Eric Moulds 15.00
BB-BN Bobby Newcombe 10.00
BB-TO Terrell Owens 20.00
BB-JP Jesse Palmer 15.00
BB-DR David Rivers 10.00
BB-KR Koren Robinson 25.00
BB-MR Marcus Robinson 15.00
BB-LS Lamar Smith 15.00
BB-TS Tai Streets 10.00
BB-DT David Terrell 25.00
BB-AT Anthony Thomas 30.00
BB-LT LaDainian Tomlinson 40.00
BB-BU Brian Urlacher 10.00
BB-MV Michael Vick 110.00
BB-RW Reggie Wayne 20.00
BB-CW Chris Weinke 20.00
BB-TW Terrence Wilkins 10.00

2001 Bowman's Best Bowman's Best Bets

NM/M
Complete Set (13): 18.00
Common Player: 1.00
Inserted 1:12
BB1 Drew Brees 3.00
BB2 Michael Vick 5.00
BB3 David Terrell 2.50
BB4 Michael Bennett 2.00
BB5 LaDainian Tomlinson 3.00
BB6 Koren Robinson 1.50
BB7 Chris Weinke 1.50

BB8	Rod Gardner	1.50
BB9	Reggie Wayne	1.50
BB10	Deuce McAllister	1.50
BB11	Freddie Mitchell	1.50
BB12	Chad Johnson	1.00
BB13	Santana Moss	1.50

2001 Bowman's Best Franchise Favorites

		NM/M
Common Player:		10.00
Inserted 1:414 H; 1:692 R		
FF-CC	Daunte Culpepper, Cris Carter	30.00
FF-GJ	Eddie George, Edgerrin James	30.00
FF-SG	Jimmy Smith, Tony Gonzalez	10.00
FF-WW	Charles Woodson, Rod Woodson	10.00

2001 Bowman's Best Impact Players

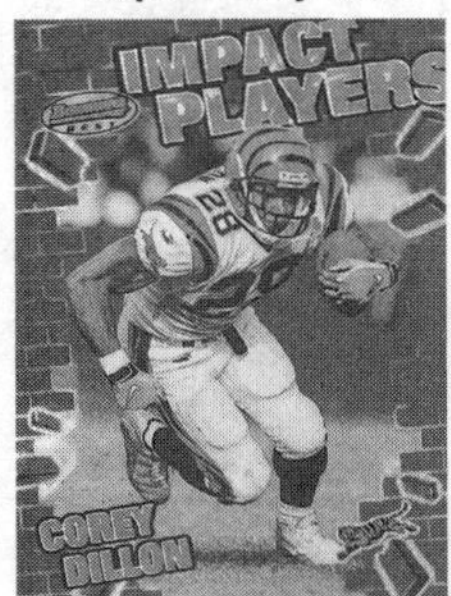

		NM/M
Complete Set (20):		15.00
Common Player:		.50
Inserted 1:4		
IP1	Randy Moss	3.00
IP2	Peyton Manning	3.00
IP3	Eddie George	1.00
IP4	Elvis Grbac	.50
IP5	Marshall Faulk	1.00
IP6	Marvin Harrison	.75
IP7	Tony Gonzalez	.50
IP8	Corey Dillon	.50
IP9	Rod Smith	.50
IP10	Daunte Culpepper	2.00
IP11	Edgerrin James	2.50
IP12	Terrell Owens	.75
IP13	Eric Moulds	.50
IP14	Kurt Warner	3.00
IP15	Donovan McNabb	2.00
IP16	Isaac Bruce	.75
IP17	Jeff Garcia	1.00
IP18	Cris Carter	.50
IP19	Stephen Davis	.50
IP20	Torry Holt	.75

2001 Bowman's Best Rookie Relics

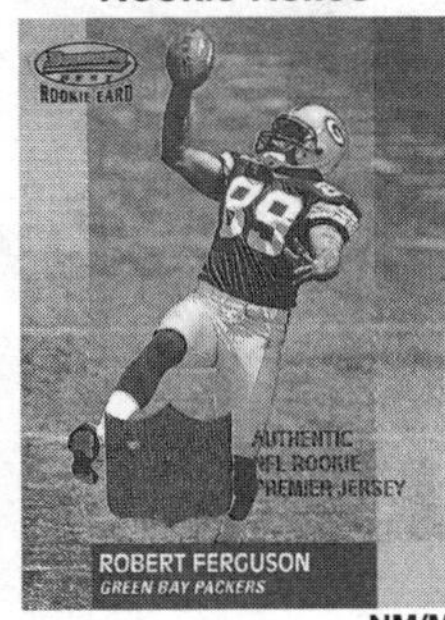

		NM/M
Common Player:		10.00
101	David Terrell	15.00
102	Kevan Barlow	12.00
103	Quincy Morgan	10.00
104	Chris Weinke	15.00
105	Josh Heupel	10.00
106	Chris Chambers	20.00
107	Reggie Wayne	15.00
108	Gerard Warren	10.00
109	Freddie Mitchell	15.00
110	Anthony Thomas	20.00
111	Robert Ferguson	10.00
112	Deuce McAllister	15.00
113	Travis Henry	12.00
114	Rod Gardner	15.00
115	Michael Bennett	20.00
116	Santana Moss	15.00
117	Chad Johnson	10.00
118	Jesse Palmer	10.00
119	James Jackson	10.00
120	Dan Morgan	10.00

2001 Bowman's Best Vintage Best

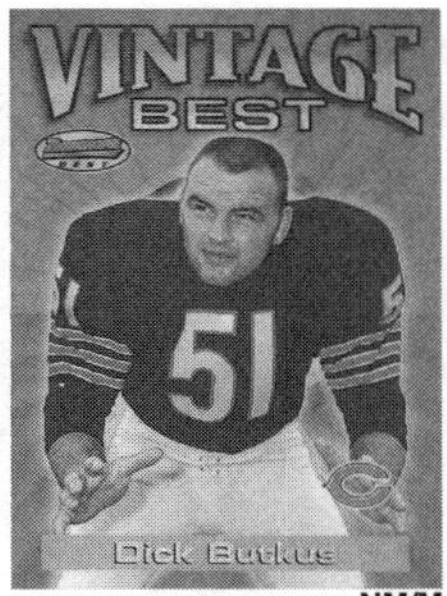

		NM/M
Complete Set (10):		15.00
Common Player:		1.00
Inserted 1:4		
VB JB	Jim Brown	2.00
VB DB	Dick Butkus	1.00
VB ED	Eric Dickerson	2.00
VB FG	Frank Gifford	2.00
VB PH	Paul Hornung	2.00
VB DC	Deacon Jones	3.00
VB JM	Joe Montana	5.00
VB JN	Joe Namath	3.00
VB GS	Gale Sayers	2.00
VB LT	Lawrence Taylor	2.00

2001 Bowman Chrome

		NM/M
Common Player:		.20
Minor Stars:		.40
Common Rookie (111-255):		2.00
Production 1,999 Sets		
Inserted 1:3		
Pack (4):		5.25
Box (24):		65.00
1	Emmitt Smith	2.00
2	James Stewart	.40
3	Jeff Graham	.20
4	Keyshawn Johnson	.75
5	Stephen Davis	.40
6	Chad Lewis	.20
7	Drew Bledsoe	1.00
8	Fred Taylor	.75
9	Mike Anderson	.75
10	Tony Gonzalez	.40
11	Aaron Brooks	.75
12	Vinny Testaverde	.40
13	Jerome Bettis	.40
14	Marshall Faulk	1.00
15	Jeff Garcia	.75
16	Terry Glenn	.40
17	Jay Fiedler	.20
18	Ahman Green	.40
19	Cade McNown	.20
20	Rob Johnson	.20
21	Jamal Anderson	.40
22	Corey Dillon	.40
23	Jake Plummer	.40
24	Rod Smith	.40
25	Trent Green	.20
26	Ricky Williams	1.25
27	Charlie Garner	.20
28	Shaun Alexander	1.25
29	Jeff George	.20
30	Torry Holt	.75
31	James Thrash	.20
32	Rich Gannon	.20
33	Ron Dayne	.40
34	Dedric Ward	.20
35	Edgerrin James	2.00
36	Cris Carter	.40
37	Derrick Mason	.20
38	Brad Johnson	.40
39	Charlie Batch	.20
40	Joey Galloway	.20
41	James Allen	.20
42	Tim Biakabutuka	.20
43	Ray Lewis	.40
44	David Boston	.75
45	Kevin Johnson	.40
46	Jimmy Smith	.40
47	Joe Horn	.20
48	Terrell Owens	.75
49	Eddie George	1.00
50	Brett Favre	3.00
51	Wayne Chrebet	.40
52	Hines Ward	.40
53	Warrick Dunn	.40
54	Matt Hasselbeck	.20
55	Tiki Barber	.40
56	Lamar Smith	.40
57	Tim Couch	1.00
58	Eric Moulds	.40
59	Shawn Jefferson	.20
60	Donald Hayes	.20
61	Brian Urlacher	1.50
62	Steve McNair	.40
63	Kurt Warner	2.50
64	Tim Brown	.40
65	Troy Brown	.20
66	Albert Connell	.20
67	Peyton Manning	2.50
68	Peter Warrick	.75
69	Elvis Grbac	.40
70	Chris Chandler	.20
71	Akili Smith	.40
72	Keenan McCardell	.20
73	Kerry Collins	.40
74	Junior Seau	.40
75	Donovan McNabb	1.50
76	Tony Banks	.20
77	Steve Beuerlein	.20
78	Daunte Culpepper	1.50
79	Darrell Jackson	.20
80	Isaac Bruce	.40
81	Tyrone Wheatley	.20
82	Derrick Alexander	.20
83	Germane Crowell	.40
84	Jon Kitna	.20
85	Jamal Lewis	1.00
86	Ed McCaffrey	.40
87	Mark Brunell	.75
88	Jeff Blake	.40
89	Duce Staley	.40
90	Doug Flutie	.75
91	Kordell Stewart	.75
92	Randy Moss	2.50
93	Marvin Harrison	.75
94	Muhsin Muhammad	.20
95	Brian Griese	1.00
96	Antonio Freeman	.40
97	Amani Toomer	.20
98	Oronde Gadsden	.20
99	Curtis Martin	.40
100	Jerry Rice	2.00
101	Michael Pittman	.20
102	Shannon Sharpe	.40
103	Peerless Price	.20
104	Bill Schroeder	.40
105	Ike Hilliard	.40
106	Freddie Jones	.20
107	Tai Streets	.20
108	Ricky Watters	.40
109	Az-Zahir Hakim	.20
110	Jacquez Green	.20
111	George Layne	2.00
112	Correll Buckhalter	10.00
113	Tony Stewart	2.00
114	Chris Barnes	2.00
115	A.J. Feeley	6.00
116	Margin Hooks	2.00
117	Anthony Henry	6.00
118	Dwight Smith	2.00
119	Torrance Marshall	2.00
120	Gary Baxter	2.00
121	Derek Combs	2.00
122	Marcus Bell	2.00
123	DeLawrence Grant	2.00
124	Jameel Cook	2.00
125	Eric Downing	2.00
126	Marlon McCree	2.00
127	Tay Cody	2.00
128	Mario Monds	2.00
129	Kenny Smith	2.00
130	Sedrick Hodge	2.00
131	Marcus Stroud	2.00
132	Steve Smith	10.00
133	Tyrone Robertson	2.00
134	James Reed	2.00
135	Kris Kocurek	2.00
136	Dan O'Leary	2.00
137	Harold Blackmon	2.00
138	Fred Smoot	2.00
139	Billy Baber	2.00
140	Jarrod Cooper	2.00
141	Travis Henry	12.00
142	David Terrell	10.00
143	Josh Heupel	8.00
144	Drew Brees	15.00
145	T.J. Houshmandzadeh	2.00
146	Rod Gardner	12.00
147	Richard Seymour	4.00
148	Koren Robinson	10.00
149	Scotty Anderson	2.00
150	Marques Tuiasosopo	8.00
151	John Capel	6.00
152	LaMont Jordan	6.00
153	James Jackson	8.00
154	Bobby Newcombe	4.00
155	Anthony Thomas	15.00
156	Dan Alexander	6.00
157	Quincy Carter	10.00
158	Morlon Greenwood	2.00
159	Robert Ferguson	6.00
160	Sage Rosenfels	8.00
161	Michael Stone	2.00
162	Chris Weinke	8.00
163	Travis Minor	8.00
164	Gerard Warren	4.00
165	Jamar Fletcher	4.00
166	Andre Carter	4.00
167	Deuce McAllister	25.00
168	Dan Morgan	4.00
169	Todd Heap	4.00
170	Marvin "Snoop" Minnis	8.00
171	Will Allen	4.00
172	Freddie Mitchell	8.00
173	Rudi Johnson	12.00
174	Kevan Barlow	12.00
175	Jamie Winborn	2.00
176	Onome Ojo	2.00
177	Leonard Davis	4.00
178	Santana Moss	12.00
179	Chris Chambers	15.00
180	Michael Vick	60.00
181	Michael Bennett	15.00
182	Mike McMahon	8.00
183	Jonathan Carter	5.00
184	Jamal Reynolds	2.00
185	Justin Smith	2.00
186	Quincy Morgan	6.00
187	Chad Johnson	15.00
188	Jesse Palmer	8.00
189	Reggie Wayne	15.00
190	LaDainian Tomlinson	30.00
191	Andre King	2.00
192	Richmond Flowers	2.00
193	Derrick Blaylock	5.00
194	Cedrick Wilson	2.00
195	Zeke Moreno	2.00
196	Tommy Polley	2.00
197	Damione Lewis	2.00
198	Aaron Schobel	2.00
199	Alge Crumpler	4.00
200	Nate Clements	4.00
201	Quentin McCord	2.00
202	Ken-Yon Rambo	4.00
203	Milton Wynn	2.00
204	Derrick Gibson	2.00
205	Chris Taylor	2.00
206	Corey Hall	2.00
207	Vinny Sutherland	6.00
208	Kendrell Bell	15.00
209	Casey Hampton	2.00
210	Demetric Evans	2.00
211	Brian Allen	2.00
212	Rodney Bailey	2.00
213	Otis Leverette	2.00
214	Ron Edwards	2.00
215	Michael Jameson	2.00
216	Markus Steele	2.00
217	Jimmy Williams	2.00
218	Roger Knight	2.00
219	Randy Garner	2.00
220	Raymond Perryman	2.00
221	Karon Riley	2.00
222	Adam Archuleta	4.00
223	Arnold Jackson	2.00
224	Ryan Pickett	2.00
225	Shad Meier	2.00
226	Reggie Germany	4.00
227	Justin McCareins	8.00
228	Idrees Bashir	2.00
229	Josh Booty	4.00
230	Eddie Berlin	2.00
231	Heath Evans	2.00
232	Alex Bannister	2.00
233	Corey Alston	2.00
234	Reggie White	2.00
235	Orlando Huff	2.00
236	Ken Lucas	2.00
237	Matt Stewart	2.00
238	Cedric Scott	2.00
239	Ronney Daniels	2.00
240	Kevin Kasper	2.00
241	Tony Driver	2.00
242	Kyle Vanden Bosch	2.00
243	T.J. Turner	2.00
244	Eric Westmoreland	2.00
245	Ronald Flemons	2.00
246	Eric Kelly	2.00
247	Moran Norris	2.00
248	Darnerian McCants	2.00
249	James Boyd	2.00
250	Keith Adams	2.00
251	Brandon Manumaleuna	2.00
252	Dee Brown	2.00
253	Ross Kolodziej	2.00
254	Eddie "Boo" Williams	2.00
255	Patrick Chukwurah	2.00

2001 Bowman Chrome Autographs

		NM/M
Common Player:		12.00
Inserted 1:315		
BC-DA	Dan Alexander	20.00
BC-KB	Kevan Barlow	25.00
BC-MB	Michael Bennett	100.00
BC-DBO	David Boston	25.00
BC-DB	Drew Brees	125.00
BC-QC	Quincy Carter	50.00
BC-CC	Chris Chambers	75.00
BC-RG	Rod Gardner	40.00
BC-RGE	Reggie Germany	20.00
BC-TH	Travis Henry	30.00
BC-JH	Josh Heupel	25.00
BC-JHO	Joe Horn	12.00
BC-JJ	James Jackson	25.00
BC-CJ	Chad Johnson	30.00
BC-LJ	LaMont Jordan	30.00
BC-DM	Derrick Mason	10.00
BC-TM	Travis Minor	25.00
BC-DMO	Dan Morgan	25.00
BC-QM	Quincy Morgan	12.00
BC-SM	Santana Moss	30.00
BC-BN	Bobby Newcombe	20.00
BC-JP	Jesse Palmer	20.00
BC-DT	David Terrell	50.00
BC-AT	Anthony Thomas	100.00
BC-LT	LaDainian Tomlinson	125.00
BC-MV	Michael Vick	250.00
BC-RW	Reggie Wayne	30.00
BC-CW	Chris Weinke	60.00

2001 Bowman Chrome 1996 Bowman Rookie

		NM/M
Complete Set (15):		45.00
Common Player:		2.00
Inserted 1:16		
BRC1	Eric Moulds	4.00
BRC2	Ray Lewis	4.00
BRC3	Tim Biakabutuka	2.00
BRC4	Eddie George	8.00
BRC5	Marvin Harrison	6.00
BRC6	Joe Horn	2.00
BRC7	Muhsin Muhammad	3.00
BRC8	Mike Alstott	4.00
BRC9	Amani Toomer	3.00
BRC10	Terrell Owens	6.00
BRC11	Keyshawn Johnson	6.00
BRC12	Terry Glenn	4.00
BRC13	Zach Thomas	2.00
BRC14	Stephen Davis	4.00
BRC15	La'Roi Glover	2.00

2001 Bowman Chrome Draft Day Relics

		NM/M
Common Player:		10.00
JSY Inserted 1:131		
HAT Inserted 1:2129		
DH-LD	LeonardDavis HAT	10.00
DJ-LD	LeonardDavis SY	10.00
DH-JS	Justin Smith HAT	12.00
DJ-JS	Justin Smith JSY	10.00
DH-DT	David Terrell HAT	20.00
DJ-DT	David Terrell JSY	20.00
DH-LT	LaDainian Tomlinson HAT	60.00
DJ-LT	LaDainian Tomlinson JSY	30.00
DH-MV	Michael Vick HAT	25.00
DJ-MV	Michael Vick JSY	75.00
DH-KW	Kenyatta Walker HAT	15.00
DJ-KW	Kenyatta Walker JSY	10.00

2001 Bowman Chrome Rookie Reprint

		NM/M
Common Player:		2.00
Inserted 1:24		
R-AA	Alan Ameche	4.00
R-SB	Sammy Baugh	6.00
R-CC	Charlie Conerly	2.00
R-AD	Art Donovan	4.00
R-TF	Tom Fears	2.00
R-FG	Frank Gifford	6.00
R-OG	Otto Graham	4.00
R-LG	Lou Groza	4.00
R-EH	Elroy Hirsch	6.00
R-BH	Bill Howton	2.00
R-SL	Sid Luckman	4.00
R-GM	Gino Marchetti	2.00
R-YT	Y.A. Tittle	6.00
R-ET	Emlen Tunnell	2.00
R-BT	Clyde "Bulldog" Turner	2.00
R-NV	Norm Van Brocklin	4.00

2001 Bowman Chrome Senior Bowl/Hula Bowl Relics

		NM/M
Common Player:		10.00
Inserted 1:78		
BCR-BA	Brian Allen	10.00
BCR-JB	Jeff Backus	10.00
BCR-DB	Drew Brees	30.00
BCR-DBU	Derrick Burgess	10.00
BCR-JC	Jarrod Cooper	10.00
BCR-TD	Tony Dixon	10.00
BCR-MF	Mario Fatafehi	10.00
BCR-RG	Reggie Germany	10.00
BCR-JHE	Jamie Henderson	10.00
BCR-JH	Jabari Holloway	10.00
BCR-SH	Steve Hutchinson	10.00
BCR-JJ	Jonas Jennings	10.00
BCR-LJ	LaMont Jordan	15.00
BCR-BJ	Bhawoh Jue	10.00
BCR-KK	Kevin Kasper	15.00
BCR-ZM	Zeke Moreno	10.00
BCR-LM	Leonard Myers	10.00
BCR-JP	Jesse Palmer	15.00
BCR-SS	Steve Smith	12.00
BCR-TS	Tony Stewart	10.00
BCR-MS	Michael Stone	10.00
BCR-RW	Reggie Wayne	15.00
BCR-EW	Eric Westmoreland	10.00

A card number in parenthese ( ) indicates the set is unnumbered.

2002 Bowman

		NM/M
Complete Set (275):		60.00
Common Player:		.25
Unlisted Stars:		.60
Minor Stars:		.50
Common Rookie (111-275):		.75
Minor Rookies:		1.25
Pack (10):		2.25
Wax Box (24):		40.00
1	Emmitt Smith	2.00
2	Drew Brees	1.50
3	Duce Staley	.50
4	Curtis Martin	.50
5	Isaac Bruce	.50
6	Stephen Davis	.50
7	Darrell Jackson	.25
8	James Stewart	.25
9	Tim Couch	1.00
10	Travis Henry	.50
11	Thomas Jones	.25
12	Jamal Lewis	1.00
13	Chris Chambers	.60
14	Jeff Blake	.25
15	Plaxico Burress	.60
16	Michael Pittman	.25
17	Jeff Garcia	.60
18	Tim Brown	.60
19	Kent Graham	.25
20	Shannon Sharpe	.50
21	Corey Dillon	.60
22	Muhsin Muhammad	.50
23	Tony Gonzalez	.50
24	Qadry Ismail	.25
25	Mike McMahon	.60
26	Edgerrin James	1.50
27	Daunte Culpepper	1.25
28	Deuce McAllister	1.00
29	Kerry Collins	.50
30	Eddie George	.60
31	Torry Holt	.50
32	Todd Pinkston	.25
33	Quincy Carter	1.25
34	Rod Smith	.50
35	Michael Vick	2.00
36	Jim Miller	.50
37	Troy Brown	.50
38	Wayne Chrebet	.50
39	Curtis Conway	.50
40	Reidel Anthony	.25
41	Mark Brunell	.60
42	Chris Weinke	.60
43	Eric Moulds	.50
44	Ike Hilliard	.25
45	Jay Fiedler	.50
46	Keyshawn Johnson	.50
47	Rod Gardner	.50
48	Chris Redman	.50
49	James Allen	.25
50	Kordell Stewart	.50
51	Priest Holmes	.60
52	Anthony Thomas	1.50
53	Peter Warrick	.50
54	Jake Plummer	.50
55	Jerry Rice	2.00
56	Joe Horn	.25
57	Derrick Mason	.50
58	Kurt Warner	2.00
59	Antowain Smith	.50
60	Randy Moss	2.00
61	Warrick Dunn	.50
62	Laveranues Coles	.50
63	LaDainian Tomlinson	1.50
64	Michael Westbrook	.25
65	Travis Taylor	.50
66	Brian Griese	.60
67	Bill Schroeder	.25
68	Ahman Green	.60
69	Jimmy Smith	.25
70	Charlie Garner	.50
71	Terrell Owens	.60
72	Brad Johnson	.50
73	James Thrash	.25
74	Marvin Harrison	.50
75	Brett Favre	2.50
76	Raghib Ismail	.25
77	David Boston	.60
78	Jermaine Lewis	.25
79	Aaron Brooks	1.00
80	Shaun Alexander	.60
81	Steve McNair	.60
82	Marshall Faulk	1.25
83	Terrell Davis	1.00
84	Corey Bradford	.25
85	David Terrell	.60
86	Kevin Johnson	.25
87	Jon Kitna	.25
88	Az-Zahir Hakim	.50
89	Drew Bledsoe	1.25
90	Garrison Hearst	.50
91	Doug Flutie	.60
92	Jerome Bettis	.50
93	Vinny Testaverde	.50
94	Tiki Barber	.50
95	Johnnie Morton	.25
96	Lamar Smith	.25

97 Marcus Robinson .50
98 Fred Taylor .50
99 Tom Brady 2.00
100 Peyton Manning 2.00
101 Donovan McNabb 1.25
102 Rich Gannon .50
103 Hines Ward .50
104 Michael Bennett .60
105 Ricky Williams 1.25
106 Germane Crowell .25
107 Joey Galloway .50
108 Amani Toomer .50
109 Trent Green .50
110 Terry Glenn .50
111 Donte Stallworth 2.00
112 Mike Williams .75
113 Kurt Kittner 1.25
114 Josh Reed 1.50
115 Raonall Smith .75
116 David Garrard 1.25
117 Eric Crouch 1.50
118 Bryan Thomas 1.00
119 Levi Jones 1.00
120 Andre Davis 1.50
121 Herb Haygood .75
122 Josh McCown 1.25
123 Quentin Jammer 1.25
124 Cliff Russell 1.00
125 Jeremy Shockey 3.00
126 Jamin Elliott .75
127 Roy Williams 2.50
128 Marquise Walker 1.25
129 Kalimba Edwards .75
130 Daniel Graham 1.25
131 Freddie Milons 1.00
132 Anthony Weaver .75
133 Jake Schifino .75
134 Antonio Bryant 2.00
135 DeShaun Foster 1.50
136 Antwann Randle El 1.50
137 William Green 2.00
138 Edward Reed 1.50
139 Maurice Morris 1.50
140 Joey Harrington 4.00
141 T.J. Duckett 2.00
142 Javon Walker 2.50
143 Albert Haynesworth 1.00
144 Julius Peppers 1.50
145 Clinton Portis 5.00
146 Craig Nall 1.00
147 Ashley Lelie 2.00
148 Donald Reche Caldwell 1.25
149 Rohan Davey 1.50
150 Patrick Ramsey 2.00
151 Jabar Gaffney 1.50
152 Tank Williams .75
153 Ron Johnson 1.00
154 Ladell Betts 1.25
155 Brian Westbrook 2.00
156 Jamar Martin .75
157 Travis Stephens 1.25
158 Tim Carter 1.25
159 Darrell Hill .75
160 Luke Staley 1.25
161 Randy Fasani 1.00
162 Matt Schobel .75
163 Jon McGraw .75
164 Dwight Freeney 1.50
165 Chad Hutchinson 1.00
166 Adrian Peterson 1.00
167 Josh Scobey .75
168 Jonathan Wells 1.50
169 Sam Simmons .75
170 Jerramy Stevens 1.00
171 Jason McAddley .75
172 Ken Simonton .75
173 Chester Taylor .75
174 Brandon Doman .75
175 Javin Hunter .75
176 Eddie Drummond .75
177 Andre Lott .75
178 Travis Fisher .75
179 Jarvis Green .75
180 Ross Tucker .75
181 Lamont Brightful .75
182 Rocky Calmus 1.25
183 Wes Pate .75
184 Lamar Gordon 1.25
185 Terry Jones .75
186 Kyle Johnson .75
187 Daryl Jones .75
188 Tellis Redmon 1.00
189 Howard Green .75
190 Jarrod Baxter .75
191 Delvon Flowers .75
192 Kevin Curtis .75
193 Kelly Campbell 1.50
194 Eddie Freeman .75
195 Atrews Bell .75
196 Omar Easy .75
197 Jeremy Allen .75
198 Andra Davis .75
199 Jack Brewer .75
200 Mike Rumph .75
201 Seth Burford .75
202 Marquand Manuel .75
203 Marques Anderson .75
204 Ben Leber .75
205 Ryan Denney .75
206 Justin Peelle .75
207 Lito Sheppard 1.00
208 Damien Anderson 1.00
209 Lamont Thompson .75
210 David Priestly .75
211 Michael Lewis .75
212 Lee Mays .75
213 Alan Harper .75
214 Verron Haynes .75
215 Chris Hope .75
216 David Thornton .75
217 Derek Ross .75
218 Brett Keisel .75
219 Joseph Jefferson .75
220 Andre Goodman .75
221 Robert Royal .75
222 Sheldon Brown .75
223 DeVeren Johnson .75
224 Rock Cartwright .75
225 Quincy Monk .75
226 Nick Rogers .75
227 Kendall Simmons .75
228 Joe Burns .75
229 Wesly Mallard .75
230 Chris Cash .75
231 David Givens .75
232 John Owens .75
233 Jarrett Ferguson .75
234 Randy McMichael .75
235 Chris Baker .75
236 Rashad Bauman .75
237 Matt Murphy .75
238 LaVar Glover .75
239 Steve Bellisari .75
240 Chad Williams .75
241 Kevin Thomas .75
242 Carlos Hall .75
243 Nick Greisen .75
244 Justin Bannan .75
245 Charles Hill .75
246 Mark Anelli .75
247 Coy Wire .75
248 Darnell Sanders .75
249 Larry Foote .75
250 David Carr 5.00
251 Ricky Williams 1.00
252 Napoleon Harris 1.00
253 Ennis Haywood 1.00
254 Keyuo Craver .75
255 Kahlil Hill .75
256 J.T. O'Sullivan .75
257 Woodrow Dantzler III .75
258 Phillip Buchanon 1.25
259 Charles Grant .75
260 Dusty Bonner .75
261 James Allen .75
262 Ronald Curry 2.00
263 Deion Branch 2.50
264 Larry Ned .25
265 Mel Mitchell .75
266 Kendall Newson .75
267 Shaun Hill .75
268 David Pugh .75
269 Dante Wesley .75
270 Josh Mallard .75
271 Akin Ayodele .75
272 Pete Hunter .75
273 Kevin McCadam .75
274 Jeff Kelly .75
275 John Henderson 1.00

2002 Bowman Gold

Stars: 10X-20X
Rookies: 6X-12X
Production 50 Sets

2002 Bowman Silver

Stars: 3X-6X
Rookies: 2X-4X
Production 250 Sets

2002 Bowman Uncirculated

NM/M
Common Player: 8.00
Random Exchange Card in Packs

2002 Bowman Draft Day Relics

NM/M
Common Player: 10.00
Hats Inserted 1:1850 Hobby
JSY Inserted 1:109 Hobby
DDH-DC David Carr Hat 60.00
DDH-QJ Quentin Jammer Hat 20.00
DDH-BM Bryant McKinnie Hat 15.00
DDH-JP Julius Peppers Hat 25.00
DDH-MW Mike Williams Hat 12.00
DDJ-DC David Carr JSY 30.00
DDJ-QJ Quentin Jammer JSY 10.00
DDJ-BM Bryant McKinnie JSY 10.00
DDJ-JP Julius Peppers JSY 15.00
DDJ-MW MikeWilliams JSY 10.00

2002 Bowman Fabric of the Future Relics

NM/M
Common Player: 8.00
Inserted 1:85
FF-DB Deion Branch 12.00
FF-AB Alex Brown 8.00
FF-KC Kelly Campbell 8.00
FF-DC David Carr 25.00
FF-TC Tim Carter 10.00
FF-WD Woodrow Dantzler III 8.00
FF-DF DeShaun Foster 12.00
FF-EF Eddie Freeman 8.00
FF-LG Lamar Gordon 10.00
FF-HH Herb Haygood 8.00
FF-TJ Terry Jones Jr. 8.00
FF-KK Kurt Kittner 10.00
FF-JM Josh McCown 10.00
FF-TS Travis Stephens 8.00
FF-JW Javon Walker 15.00
FF-JWE Jonathan Wells 10.00
FF-TW Tank Williams 8.00

2002 Bowman Flashback Autos

NM/M
Common Player: 10.00
Inserted 1:412
RFA-CC Chris Chambers 35.00
RFA-BF Brett Favre 200.00
RFA-JG Jeff Garcia 20.00
RFA-LJ LaMont Jordan 10.00
RFA-MR Marcus Robinson 10.00
RFA-BS Bill Schroeder 12.00
RFA-LS Lamar Smith 10.00
RFA-LT LaDainian Tomlinson 25.00

2002 Bowman Flashback Relics

NM/M
Common Player: 8.00
Inserted 1:116
RFR-KB Kevan Barlow 8.00
RFR-RG Rod Gardner 8.00
RFR-CJ Chad Johnson 8.00
RFR-DM Deuce McAllister 15.00
RFR-MMC Mike McMahon 8.00
RFR-MM Marvin "Snoop" Minnis 8.00
RFR-QM Quincy Morgan 8.00
RFR-SM Santana Moss 8.00
RFR-DT David Terrell 8.00
RFR-MV Michael Vick 30.00
RFR-CW Chris Weinke 8.00

2002 Bowman Signs of the Future

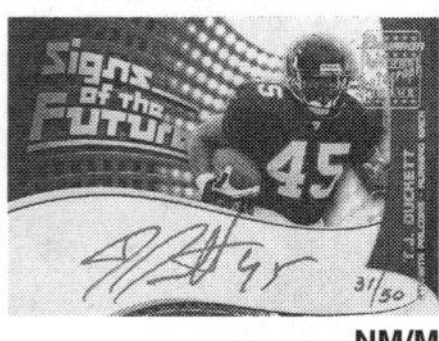

NM/M
Common Player: 10.00
Inserted 1:133
Red Ink versions: 1.5X-3X
Red Production 50 sets
SF-LB Ladell Betts 10.00
SF-AB Antonio Bryant 35.00
SF-DRC Donald Reche Caldwell 15.00
SF-DC David Carr 100.00
SF-TC Tim Carter 15.00
SF-RD Rohan Davey 20.00
SF-TJD T.J. Duckett 40.00
SF-JG Jabar Gaffney 15.00
SF-DG David Garrard 15.00
SF-WG William Green 25.00
SF-JH Joey Harrington 100.00
SF-NH Napoleon Harris 10.00
SF-QJ Quentin Jammer 15.00
SF-JM Josh McCown 15.00
SF-MM Maurice Morris 15.00
SF-AP Adrian Peterson 10.00
SF-PR Patrick Ramsey 20.00
SF-JS Jeremy Shockey 30.00
SF-DS Donte Stallworth 30.00
SF-TS Travis Stephens 15.00
SF-JW Javon Walker 20.00

2002 Bowman Team Topps Autographs

Inserted 1:304
Fred Biletnikoff
Cliff Branch
Jim Brown
Chuck Foreman
John Hannah
Charlie Joiner
Joe Namath
Mike Singletary

2002 Bowman Chrome

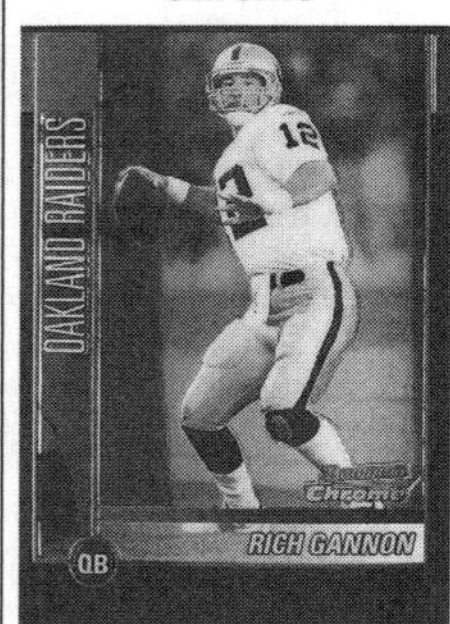

NM/M
Common Player: .25
Unlisted Stars: .75
Minor Stars: .50
Common Rookie (111-220): 1.50
Minor Rookies: 2.00
Common Rookie Auto (221-250): 3.50
Pack (4): 60.00
Wax Box (18):
1 Emmitt Smith 2.50
2 Drew Brees 2.00
3 Duce Staley .50
4 Curtis Martin .75
5 Isaac Bruce .50
6 Stephen Davis .50
7 Darrell Jackson .25
8 James Stewart .25
9 Tim Couch 1.25
10 Travis Henry .50
11 Thomas Jones .25
12 Jamal Lewis 1.25
13 Chris Chambers .75
14 Jeff Blake .25
15 Plaxico Burress .75
16 Michael Pittman .25
17 Jeff Garcia .75
18 Tim Brown .75
19 Kent Graham .25
20 Shannon Sharpe .50
21 Corey Dillon .75
22 Muhsin Muhammad .50
23 Tony Gonzalez .50
24 Qadry Ismail .25
25 Mike McMahon .50
26 Edgerrin James 2.00
27 Daunte Culpepper 1.50
28 Deuce McAllister 1.25
29 Kerry Collins .50
30 Eddie George .75
31 Torry Holt .75
32 Todd Pinkston .25
33 Quincy Carter 1.25
34 Rod Smith .50
35 Michael Vick 2.50
36 Jim Miller .50
37 Troy Brown .50
38 Wayne Chrebet .50
39 Curtis Conway .50
40 Reidel Anthony .25
41 Mark Brunell .75
42 Chris Weinke .25
43 Eric Moulds .50
44 Ike Hilliard .25
45 Jay Fiedler .50
46 Keyshawn Johnson .50
47 Rod Gardner .50
48 Chris Redman .50
49 James Allen .25
50 Kordell Stewart .50
51 Priest Holmes 1.25
52 Anthony Thomas 1.25
53 Peter Warrick .50
54 Jake Plummer .50
55 Jerry Rice 2.50
56 Joe Horn .50
57 Derrick Mason .25
58 Kurt Warner 2.50
59 Antowain Smith .50
60 Randy Moss 2.50
61 Warrick Dunn .50
62 Laveranues Coles .50
63 LaDainian Tomlinson 2.00
64 Michael Westbrook .25
65 Travis Taylor .25
66 Brian Griese .75
67 Bill Schroeder .25
68 Ahman Green .75
69 Jimmy Smith .25
70 Charlie Garner .50
71 Terrell Owens .75
72 Brad Johnson .50
73 James Thrash .25
74 Marvin Harrison .75
75 Brett Favre 3.00
76 Raghib Ismail .25
77 David Boston .75
78 Jermaine Lewis .25
79 Aaron Brooks 1.25
80 Shaun Alexander .75
81 Steve McNair .75
82 Marshall Faulk 1.50
83 Terrell Davis 1.25
84 Corey Bradford .25
85 David Terrell .75
86 Kevin Johnson .50
87 Jon Kitna .25
88 Az-Zahir Hakim .50
89 Drew Bledsoe 1.50
90 Garrison Hearst .50
91 Doug Flutie .75
92 Jerome Bettis .50
93 Vinny Testaverde .25
94 Tiki Barber .50
95 Johnnie Morton .25
96 Lamar Smith .25
97 Marcus Robinson .50
98 Fred Taylor .50
99 Tom Brady 2.50
100 Peyton Manning 2.50
101 Donovan McNabb 1.50
102 Rich Gannon .75
103 Hines Ward .50
104 Michael Bennett .75
105 Ricky Williams 1.50
106 Germane Crowell .25
107 Joey Galloway .50
108 Amani Toomer .50
109 Trent Green .50
110 Terry Glenn .50
111 Donte Stallworth 8.00
112 Mike Williams 2.00
113 Kurt Kittner 5.00
114 Josh Reed 6.00
115 Raonall Smith 2.00
116 David Garrard 3.00
117 Eric Crouch 3.00
118 Levi Jones 2.00
119 Quentin Jammer 3.00
120 Cliff Russell 2.00
121 Jamin Elliott 2.00
122 Roy Williams 10.00
123 Marquise Walker 2.00
124 Kalimba Edwards 2.00
125 Daniel Graham 3.00
126 Anthony Weaver 2.00
127 Antonio Bryant 8.00
128 DeShaun Foster 6.00
129 Antwann Randle El 6.00
130 William Green 8.00
131 Joey Harrington 12.00
132 T.J. Duckett 8.00
133 Javon Walker 10.00
134 Albert Haynesworth 2.00
135 Julius Peppers 6.00
136 Clinton Portis 15.00
137 Ashley Lelie 8.00
138 Donald Reche Caldwell 6.00
139 Rohan Davey 6.00
140 Patrick Ramsey 8.00
141 Ron Johnson 2.00
142 Jamar Martin 2.00
143 Travis Stephens 2.00
144 Darrell Hill 2.00
145 Jon McGraw 2.00
146 Javin Hunter 2.00
147 Eddie Drummond 2.00
148 Andre Lott 2.00
149 Travis Fisher 2.00
150 Lamont Brightful 2.00
151 Rocky Calmus 2.00
152 Wes Pate 2.00
153 Lamar Gordon 5.00
154 Terry Jones 2.00
155 Kyle Johnson 2.00
156 Daryl Jones 2.00
157 Tellis Redmon 2.00
158 Jarrod Baxter 2.00
159 Delvon Flowers 2.00
160 Kelly Campbell 5.00
161 Eddie Freeman 2.00
162 Atrews Bell 2.00
163 Omar Easy 2.00
164 Jeremy Allen 2.00
165 Andra Davis 2.00
166 Mike Rumph 2.00
167 Seth Burford 2.00
168 Marquand Manuel 2.00
169 Marques Anderson 2.00
170 Ben Leber 2.00
171 Ryan Denney 2.00
172 Justin Peelle 2.00
173 Lito Sheppard 2.00
174 Damien Anderson 2.00
175 Lamont Thompson 2.00
176 David Priestly 2.00
177 Michael Lewis 2.00
178 Lee Mays 2.00
179 Alan Harper 2.00
180 Verron Haynes 2.00
181 Chris Hope 2.00
182 Derek Ross 2.00
183 Joseph Jefferson 2.00
184 Carlos Hall 2.00
185 Robert Royal 2.00
186 Sheldon Brown 2.00
187 DeVeren Johnson 2.00
188 Rock Cartwright 2.00
189 Kendall Simmons 2.00
190 Joe Burns 3.00
191 David Givens 6.00
192 John Owens 2.00
193 Jarrett Ferguson 2.00
194 Randy McMichael 8.00
195 Chris Baker 4.00
196 Rashad Bauman 2.00
197 Matt Murphy 2.00
198 Steve Bellisari 2.00
199 Jeff Kelly 2.00
200 Mark Anelli 2.00
201 Darnell Sanders 2.00
202 Coy Wire 2.00
203 Ricky Williams 3.00
204 Napoleon Harris 3.00
205 Ennis Haywood 2.00
206 Keyuo Craver 3.00
207 Kahlil Hill 3.00
208 J.T. O'Sullivan 2.00
209 Woodrow Dantzler III 4.00
210 Phillip Buchanon 4.00
211 Charles Grant 2.00
212 Dusty Bonner 2.00
213 James Allen 4.00
214 Ronald Curry 8.00
215 Deion Branch 10.00
216 Larry Ned 2.00
217 Kendall Newson 2.00
218 Shaun Hill 2.00
219 Akin Ayodele 2.00
220 John Henderson 2.00
221 Andre Davis Auto 25.00
222 Bryan Thomas Auto 12.00
223 Brian Westbrook Auto 40.00
224 Chad Hutchinson Auto 15.00
225 Craig Nall Auto 15.00
226 David Carr Auto 100.00
227 Dwight Freeney Auto 20.00
228 Adrian Peterson Auto 20.00
229 Randy Fasani Auto 10.00
230 Edward Reed Auto 25.00
231 Freddie Milons Auto 10.00
232 Herb Haygood Auto 10.00
233 Jabar Gaffney Auto 25.00
234 Josh McCown Auto 30.00
235 Jeremy Shockey Auto 80.00
236 Jake Schifino Auto 10.00
237 Josh Scobey Auto 10.00
238 Jonathan Wells Auto 15.00
239 Ladell Betts Auto 20.00
240 Luke Staley Auto 15.00
241 Maurice Morris Auto 20.00
242 Matt Schobel Auto 10.00
243 Sam Simmons Auto 10.00
244 Tim Carter Auto 15.00
245 Tank Williams Auto 10.00
246 Jerramy Stevens Auto 15.00
247 Jason McAddley Auto 10.00
248 Ken Simonton Auto 10.00
249 Chester Taylor Auto 15.00
250 Brandon Doman Auto 10.00

2002 Bowman Chrome Refractors

Stars: 2X-4X
Rookies: 1X-2X
Production 500 Sets

2002 Bowman Chrome X-Fractors

Stars: 3X-6X
Rookies/111-220: 2X-4X
Production 250 Sets
Rookie Autos/221-250: 1X-2X
Inserted 1:391

2002 Bowman Chrome Gold Refractors

Stars: 5X-10X
Rookies: 3X-6X
Production 50 Sets

2002 Bowman's Best

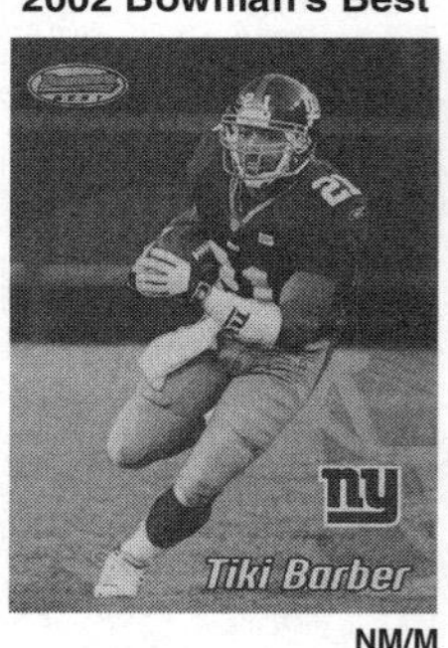

NM/M
Common Player: .25
Unlisted Star: .75
Minor Star: .50
Common Rookie JSY (91-117): 10.00
Common Rookie Auto (118-170): 8.00
Pack (5): 14.00
Wax Box (10): 100.00
1 Peyton Manning 2.00
2 Chris Weinke .40
3 Daunte Culpepper 1.25
4 Deuce McAllister 1.00
5 Duce Staley .40
6 Koren Robinson .25
7 Emmitt Smith 2.00
8 Jamal Lewis 1.00
9 Jake Plummer .50
10 Tim Brown .75
11 LaDainian Tomlinson 1.50
12 Derrick Mason .50
13 Keyshawn Johnson .50
14 Priest Holmes 1.00
15 Marcus Robinson .40
16 Drew Bledsoe 1.25
17 Troy Brown .50
18 Ahman Green .75
19 Edgerrin James 1.50
20 Hines Ward .50
21 Marshall Faulk 1.25
22 Rod Gardner .50
23 Amani Toomer .50
24 Ricky Williams 1.25
25 Peter Warrick .40
26 Ray Lewis .40
27 Warrick Dunn .40
28 Jermaine Lewis .25
29 Mark Brunell .75
30 Randy Moss 2.00

31 Laveranues Coles .50
32 Kordell Stewart .50
33 Darrell Jackson .25
34 Jeff Garcia .75
35 Eddie George .75
36 Tim Dwight .50
37 Trent Green .50
38 Quincy Carter 1.25
39 Mike McMahon .50
40 Corey Dillon .75
41 Corey Bradford .25
42 Aaron Brooks 1.00
43 Todd Pinkston .25
44 Isaac Bruce .50
45 Shane Matthews .25
46 Eric Moulds .50
47 Anthony Thomas 1.25
48 David Boston .75
49 Kevin Johnson .50
50 Brett Favre 2.50
51 Ron Dayne .50
52 Donovan McNabb 1.25
53 Brad Johnson .50
54 Garrison Hearst .50
55 Jimmy Smith .25
56 Muhsin Muhammad .50
57 Michael Vick 2.00
58 Kerry Collins .50
59 Jerome Bettis .50
60 Trent Dilfer .50
61 Torry Holt .75
62 Stephen Davis .50
63 Steve McNair .75
64 Marvin Harrison .75
65 Zach Thomas .40
66 Antowain Smith .50
67 Joe Horn .50
68 Jim Miller .50
69 Travis Taylor .25
70 James Allen .25
71 Tom Brady 2.00
72 Tiki Barber .25
73 Doug Flutie .75
74 Rich Gannon .50
75 Kurt Warner 2.00
76 Michael Pittman .25
77 Curtis Martin .50
78 Plaxico Burress .75
79 Terrell Owens .75
80 Tony Gonzalez .50
81 Michael Bennett .75
82 Brian Griese .75
83 Tim Couch 1.00
84 Shaun Alexander .75
85 Drew Brees 1.50
86 Vinny Testaverde .50
87 Chris Chambers 1.50
88 David Terrell .50
89 Rod Smith .50
90 Jerry Rice 2.00
91 *David Carr* 30.00
92 *Joey Harrington* 25.00
93 *Marquise Walker* 8.00
94 *Ladell Betts* 10.00
95 *David Garrard* 8.00
96 *Antwaan Randle El* 10.00
97 *Antonio Bryant* 10.00
98 *Eric Crouch* 10.00
99 *Tim Carter* 8.00
100 *William Green* 12.00
101 *Rohan Davey* 10.00
102 *Julius Peppers* 15.00
103 *Donte Stallworth* 12.00
104 *Ashley Lelie* 15.00
105 *Jeremy Shockey* 20.00
106 *Javon Walker* 15.00
107 *Patrick Ramsey* 12.00
108 *Roy Williams* 15.00
109 *T.J. Duckett* 12.00
110 *Jabar Gaffney* 10.00
111 *Andre Davis* 10.00
112 *Donald Reche Caldwell* 8.00
113 *Josh McCown* 10.00
114 *Maurice Morris* 10.00
115 *Ron Johnson* 8.00
116 *DeShaun Foster* 10.00
117 *Clinton Portis* 30.00
118 *Aaron Lockett* 8.00
119 *Robert Thomas* 8.00
121 *Atrews Bell* 8.00
122 *Brandon Doman* 8.00
124 *Bryan Thomas* 8.00
125 *Bryant McKinnie* 8.00
126 *Chad Hutchinson* 15.00
127 *Charles Grant* 8.00
128 *Chester Taylor* 8.00
129 *Craig Nall* 10.00
130 *Deion Branch* 20.00
131 *Doug Jolley* 10.00
132 *Dwight Freeney* 12.00
133 *Ed Reed* 12.00
134 *Freddie Milons* 8.00
135 *Herb Haygood* 8.00
136 *J.T. O'Sullivan* 8.00
137 *Jake Schifino* 8.00
138 *Jason McAddley* 8.00
139 *Jeff Kelly* 8.00
140 *Jerramy Stevens* 8.00
141 *John Henderson* 8.00
142 *Jonathan Wells* 10.00
143 *Josh Scobey* 8.00
144 *Kelly Campbell* 10.00
145 *Kahlil Hill* 8.00
146 *Kalimba Edwards* 8.00
147 *Ken Simonton* 8.00
148 *Kurt Kittner* 10.00
149 *Lamar Gordon* 10.00
150 *Leonard Henry* 8.00
151 *Lito Sheppard* 8.00
152 *Luke Staley* 10.00
153 *Matt Schobel* 8.00
154 *Mike Rumph* 8.00
155 *Najeh Davenport* 10.00
156 *Napoleon Harris* 8.00
157 *Phillip Buchanon* 8.00
158 *Quentin Jammer* 12.00
159 *Randy Fasani* 8.00
160 *Ronald Curry* 10.00
161 *Ryan Sims* 8.00
162 *Sam Simmons* 8.00
163 *Seth Burford* 8.00
164 *Tellis Redmon* 8.00
165 *Terry Charles* 8.00
166 *Tracey Wistrom* 8.00
167 *Verron Haynes* 8.00
168 *Wes Pate* 8.00
169 *Wendell Bryant* 8.00
170 *Damien Anderson* 8.00

2002 Bowman's Best Blue

Stars: 2X-4X
Production 300 Sets
Rookies: 1X
Production 399 Sets

2002 Bowman's Best Gold

Stars Production 25 Sets
Rookies: 1.5X-3X
Production 99 Sets

2002 Bowman's Best Red

Stars: 3X-6X
Production 200 Sets
Rookies: 1X-2X
Production 199 Sets

2003 Bowman

NM/M
Complete Set (275): 80.00
Common Player (1-110): .20
Minor Stars: .40
Unlisted Stars: .60
Common Rookie (111-275): .75
Minor Rookies: 1.00
Unlisted Rookies: 1.50
Pack (10): 3.00
Box (24): 50.00
1 Brett Favre 2.00
2 Jeremy Shockey 1.00
3 Fred Taylor .60
4 Rich Gannon .40
5 Joey Galloway .40
6 Ray Lewis .40
7 Jeff Blake .40
8 Stacey Mack .20
9 Matt Hasselbeck .40
10 Laveranues Coles .40
11 Brad Johnson .40
12 Tommy Maddox .60
13 Curtis Martin .60
14 Tom Brady .75
15 Ricky Williams 1.00
16 Stephen Davis .40
17 Chad Johnson .40
18 Joey Harrington 1.25
19 Tony Gonzalez .40
20 Peerless Price .40
21 LaDainian Tomlinson .75
22 James Thrash .40
23 Charlie Garner .40
24 Eddie George .60
25 Terrell Owens .60
26 Brian Urlacher 1.00
27 Eric Moulds .40
28 Emmitt Smith 1.50
29 Tim Couch .60
30 Jake Plummer .40
31 Marvin Harrison .60
32 Chris Chambers .60
33 Tiki Barber .60
34 Kurt Warner .75
35 Michael Pittman .40
36 Kevin Dyson .40
37 Clinton Portis 1.50
38 Peyton Manning 1.00
39 Travis Taylor .40
40 Jeff Garcia .60
41 Patrick Ramsey .60
42 Shaun Alexander .60
43 Joe Horn .40
44 Daunte Culpepper .60
45 Travis Henry .40
46 Brian Finneran .40
47 William Green .60
48 Kordell Stewart .40
49 Reggie Wayne .40
50 Priest Holmes .60
51 Jay Fiedler .40
52 Corey Dillon .60
53 Jamal Lewis .60
54 Mark Brunell .40
55 Santana Moss .40
56 Duce Staley .40
57 Torry Holt .60
58 Rod Gardner .40
59 Kerry Collins .40
60 Randy Moss 1.00
61 Jerry Porter .40
62 Plaxico Burress .60
63 Steve McNair .60
64 Muhsin Muhammad .40
65 Drew Bledsoe .75
66 T.J. Duckett .60
67 Ahman Green .60
68 Rod Smith .40
69 Jimmy Smith .40
70 Trent Green .60
71 Tim Brown .60
72 Jerome Bettis .40
73 Isaac Bruce .40
74 Derrick Mason .40
75 Donovan McNabb .75
76 Deuce McAllister .60
77 Zach Thomas .40
78 Garrison Hearst .40
79 Koren Robinson .40
80 Marshall Faulk .75
81 Keyshawn Johnson .40
82 Jake Delhomme .40
83 Marty Booker .40
84 James Stewart .40
85 Corey Bradford .40
86 Derrius Thompson .40
87 Edgerrin James .75
88 Darrell Jackson .40
89 Hines Ward .40
90 David Boston .60
91 Curtis Conway .40
92 David Patten .20
93 Michael Bennett .60
94 Todd Pinkston .40
95 Jerry Rice 1.50
96 Jon Kitna .40
97 Ed McCaffrey .40
98 Donald Driver .40
99 Anthony Thomas .60
100 Michael Vick 2.00
101 Terry Glenn .40
102 Quincy Morgan .40
103 David Carr 1.50
104 Troy Brown .40
105 Aaron Brooks .60
106 Amani Toomer .40
107 Drew Brees .75
108 Chad Hutchinson .40
109 Warrick Dunn .40
110 Chad Pennington .75
111 *Carson Palmer* 6.00
112 *Brian St. Pierre* 1.50
113 *Keenan Howry* 1.50
114 *Sultan McCullough* 1.00
115 *Terence Newman* 2.50
116 *Kelley Washington* 2.00
117 *Musa Smith* 1.50
118 *Kevin Williams* 1.00
119 *Jordan Gross* 1.00
120 *Lance Briggs* 1.00
121 *Victor Hobson* 1.00
122 *Bryant Johnson* 2.00
123 *Travis Anglin* 1.00
124 *Artose Pinner* 1.50
125 *Willis McGahee* 5.00
126 *Rashean Mathis* 1.00
127 *B.J. Askew* 1.50
128 *Dewayne White* 1.00
129 *Kevin Curtis* 1.00
130 *Tyrone Calico* 2.50
131 *Julian Battle* 1.00
132 *Ricky Manning* 1.00
133 *Corey Redding* 1.00
134 *Michael Haynes* 1.50
135 *Dallas Clark* 1.50
136 *Shaun McDonald* 1.00
137 *Marcus Trufant* 1.00
138 *Kareem Kelly* 1.50
139 Sam Aiken 1.00
140 *Terrell Suggs* 2.00
141 *Gibran Hamdan* 1.00
142 *Bobby Wade* 1.50
143 *Aaron Walker* 1.00
144 *Calvin Pace* 1.00
145 *Quentin Griffin* 4.00
146 *Ken Dorsey* 2.50
147 *Jerome McDougle* 1.50
148 *Earnest Graham* 1.50
149 *Rashad Moore* 1.00
150 *Charles Rogers* 5.00
151 *Cecil Sapp* 1.50
152 *Cato June* 1.00
153 *Ahmaad Galloway* 1.50
154 *William Joseph* 1.50
155 *Anquan Boldin* 3.00
156 *L.J. Smith* 1.50
157 *Antwoine Sanders* .75
158 *Justin Griffith* 1.00
159 *Kevin Garrett* .75
160 *Teyo Johnson* 2.00
161 *Chris Crocker* 1.00
162 *Brad Banks* 1.50
163 *Justin Gage* 1.50
164 *Doug Gabriel* 1.50
165 *Terry Pierce* 1.00
166 *Bradie James* 1.00
167 *Bennie Joppru* 1.50
168 *Malaefou MacKenzie* 2.00
169 *Terrence Edwards* 1.50
170 *E.J. Henderson* 1.00
171 *Tony Romo* 1.50
172 *Dewayne Robertson* 1.50
173 *Dwone Hicks* 1.50
174 *Carl Ford* 1.50
175 *Byron Leftwich* 6.00
176 *Ken Hamlin* 1.00
177 *Domanick Davis* 3.00
178 *Adrian Madise* 1.00
179 *Siddeeq Shabazz* .75
180 *Dave Ragone* 1.50
181 *Mike Seidman* .75
182 *Brooks Bollinger* 1.50
183 *DeAndrew Rubin* .75
184 *Mike Pinkard* .75
185 *Nate Burleson* 1.50
186 *LaBrandon Toefield* 1.50
187 *Angelo Crowell* 1.00
188 *J.R. Tolver* 1.00
189 *Osi Umenyiora* 1.00
190 *Larry Johnson* 4.00
191 *Nick Barnett* 1.50
192 *Brandon Drumm* .75
193 *Rien Long* .75
194 *Zuriel Smith* 1.00
195 *Onterrio Smith* 3.00
196 *Ronald Bellamy* 1.50
197 *Kenny Peterson* 1.00
198 *Charles Tillman* 1.00
199 *Chaun Thompson* .75
200 *Andre Johnson* 4.00
201 *Gerald Hayes* .75
202 *Terrence Holt* 1.00
203 *Ovie Mughelli* .75
204 *Talman Gardner* 1.50
205 *Bethel Johnson* 1.50
206 *Avon Cobourne* 1.50
207 *Brandon Lloyd* 1.50
208 *Andre Woolfolk* 1.50
209 *George Wrighster* 1.00
210 *Justin Fargas* 2.50
211 *Jimmy Kennedy* 1.00
212 *Arnaz Battle* 1.00
213 *Marquel Blackwell* .75
214 *Walter Young* 1.00
215 *Kliff Kingsbury* 1.50
216 *Kawicka Mitchell* 1.00
217 *Drayton Florence* .75
218 *Jeremi Johnson* 1.00
219 *Billy McMullen* 1.50
220 *Lee Suggs* 4.00
221 *David Kircus* 1.00
222 *Roderick Babers* 1.00
223 *Jon Olinger* .75
224 *Ty Warren* 1.00
225 *Kyle Boller* 4.00
226 *Dan Curley* .75
227 *Andrew Pinnock* 1.00
228 *Kirk Farmer* .75
229 *Tully Banta-Cain* 1.00
230 *Alonzo Jackson* 1.00
231 *Anthony Adams* 1.00
232 *Trent Smith* 1.50
233 *Seneca Wallace* 1.50
234 *Shane Walton* 1.00
235 *Chris Brown* 1.50
236 *Daharran Diedrick* 1.50
237 *Juston Wood* 1.00
238 *Mike Doss* 1.00
239 *Visanthe Shiancoe* 1.00
240 *Rex Grossman* 5.00
241 *David Young* .75
242 *Jimmy Wilkerson* .75
243 *Jason Witten* 2.00
244 *Dennis Weathersby* .75
245 *Taylor Jacobs* 1.50
246 *Chris Davis* 1.00
247 *LaTarence Dunbar* 1.00
248 *Eugene Wilson* 1.00
249 *Ryan Hoag* 1.00
250 *Chris Simms* 3.00
251 *Ivan Taylor* 1.00
252 *Brock Forsey* 2.00
253 *Curt Anes* 1.00
254 *Taco Wallace* 1.00
255 *Johnathan Sullivan* 1.00
256 *David Tyree* 1.00
257 *Troy Polamalu* 2.00
258 *Nate Hybl* 1.00
259 *Spencer Nead* 1.00
260 *Boss Bailey* 2.00
261 *LaMarcus McDonald* .75
262 *Casey Moore* .75
263 *Pisa Tinoisamoa* 1.50
264 *Willie Ponder* .75
265 *Donald Lee* 1.00
266 *Nnamdi Asomugha* 1.00
267 *Sammy Davis* 1.50
268 *Joffrey Reynolds* 1.00
269 *Eddie Moore* 1.00
270 *Tony Hollings* 1.50
271 *Nick Maddox* 1.00
272 *Kevin Walter* 1.00
273 *Dan Klecko* 1.00
274 *Antwan Peek* 1.00
275 *Tyler Brayton* 1.00

2003 Bowman Draft Day Selections

NM/M
Common Player: 5.00
Hats Inserted 1:1352
Jersey Inserted 1:79
DH-JK Jimmy Kennedy 6.00
DJ-JK Jimmy Kennedy 5.00
DH-BL Byron Leftwich 25.00
DJ-BL Byron Leftwich 20.00
DH-TN Terence Newman 12.00
DJ-TN Terence Newman 10.00
DH-CP Carson Palmer 20.00
DJ-CP Carson Palmer 15.00
DH-DR Dewayne Robertson 6.00
DJ-DR Dewayne Robertson 5.00
DH-CR Charles Rogers 15.00
DJ-CR Charles Rogers 12.00
DJ-TS Terrell Suggs 8.00

2003 Bowman Fabric of the Future

NM/M
Common Player: 8.00
FA-AB Anquan Boldin 12.00
FA-KB Kyle Boller 15.00
FA-CB Chris Brown 8.00
FA-JF Justin Fargas 10.00
FA-RG Rex Grossman 15.00
FA-TJ Taylor Jacobs 8.00
FA-AJ Andre Johnson 15.00
FA-BJ Bryant Johnson 10.00
FA-LJ Larry Johnson 12.00
FA-TJO Teyo Johnson 10.00
FA-KK Kliff Kingsbury 10.00
FA-BL Byron Leftwich 20.00
FA-WM Willis McGahee 15.00
FA-CP Carson Palmer 20.00
FA-AP Artose Pinner 8.00
FA-DR Dave Ragone 8.00
FA-CR Charles Rogers 15.00
FA-BSP Brian St. Pierre 8.00
FA-OS Onterrio Smith 12.00

2003 Bowman Fabric of the Future Dual

NM/M
Common Player: 15.00
Production 50 Sets
FAD-RJ Charles Rogers, Andre Johnson 40.00
FAD-PL Carson Palmer, Byron Leftwich 60.00
FAD-BG Kyle Boller, Rex Grossman 40.00
FAD-SR Chris Simms, Dave Ragone 15.00
FAD-MJ Willis McGahee, Larry Johnson 30.00

2003 Bowman Franchise Relics

NM/M
Common Player: 6.00
Production 199 Sets
FR-DB Drew Bledsoe 10.00
FR-TB Tim Brown 8.00
FR-DC David Carr 12.00
FR-CD Corey Dillon 8.00
FR-RL Ray Lewis 8.00
FR-DM Deuce McAllister 8.00
FR-SM Steve McNair/99 10.00
FR-CP Chad Pennington 10.00
FR-JS Jimmy Smith 6.00
FR-BU Brian Urlacher 12.00

2003 Bowman Franchise/ Future Relics

FF-LS Ray Lewis, Terrell Suggs
FF-LB Ray Lewis, Kyle Boller
FF-MC Steve McNair, Tyrone Calico
FF-UG Brian Urlacher, Rex Grossman
FF-CJ David Carr, Andre Johnson
FF-SL Jimmy Smith, Byron Leftwich
FF-BM Drew Bledsoe, Willis McGahee
FF-DP Corey Dillon, Carson Palmer
FF-DW Corey Dillon, Kelley Washington
FF-PR Chad Pennington, Dewayne Robertson

2003 Bowman Future Relics

NM/M
Common Player: 8.00
Production 199 Sets
FU-KB Kyle Boller 12.00
FU-TC Tyrone Calico 10.00
FU-RG Rex Grossman 12.00
FU-AJ Andre Johnson 12.00
FU-BL Byron Leftwich 20.00
FU-WM Willis McGahee 12.00
FU-CP Carson Palmer 15.00
FU-DR Dewayne Robertson 8.00
FU-TS Terrell Suggs 10.00
FU-KW Kelley Washington 10.00

2003 Bowman Paydirt Previews

NM/M
Common Player: 6.00
Inserted 1:869
Gold Production 25 Sets
PYP-KB Kyle Boller 15.00
PYP-TC Tyrone Calico 10.00
PYP-JF Justin Fargas 10.00
PYP-TG Talman Gardner 6.00
PYP-TJ Taylor Jacobs 8.00
PYP-BJ Bryant Johnson 8.00
PYP-LJ Larry Johnson 12.00
PYP-CP Carson Palmer 20.00
PYP-DR Dave Ragone 8.00
PYP-CS Chris Simms 10.00

2003 Bowman Pigskin Previews

NM/M
Common Player: 6.00
Inserted 1:869
Gold Production 25 Sets
PGP-KB Kyle Boller 15.00
PGP-TC Tyrone Calico 10.00
PGP-JF Justin Fargas 10.00
PGP-TG Talman Gardner 6.00
PGP-TJ Taylor Jacobs 8.00
PGP-BJ Bryant Johnson 8.00
PGP-LJ Larry Johnson 12.00
PGP-CP Carson Palmer 20.00
PGP-DR Dave Ragone 8.00
PGP-CS Chris Simms 10.00

2003 Bowman Signs of the Future Autographs

NM/M
Common Player: 10.00
SF-SA Sam Aiken 10.00
SF-BB Brad Banks 10.00
SF-MB Marquel Blackwell 10.00
SF-KB Kyle Boller 30.00
SF-CB Chris Brown 15.00
SF-NB Nate Burleson 15.00
SF-TC Tyrone Calico 15.00
SF-AC Avon Cobourne 15.00
SF-KD Ken Dorsey
SF-JF Justin Fargas 12.00
SF-TG Talman Gardner 10.00
SF-EG Earnest Graham 10.00
SF-QG Quentin Griffin 20.00
SF-RG Rex Grossman
SF-TJA Taylor Jacobs 12.00
SF-AJ Andre Johnson 40.00
SF-BJ Bryant Johnson 12.00
SF-LJ Larry Johnson
SF-TJ Teyo Johnson 15.00
SF-KK Kareem Kelly 10.00
SF-RL Reshard Lee 10.00
SF-BL Byron Leftwich
SF-WM Willis McGahee
SF-BM Billy McMullen 10.00
SF-CP Carson Palmer
SF-CR Charles Rogers
SF-CS Chris Simms
SF-BSP Brian St. Pierre
SF-MS Musa Smith 15.00
SF-OS Onterrio Smith 20.00
SF-LS Lee Suggs 15.00
SF-TS Terrell Suggs 12.00
SF-JT Jason Thomas 10.00
SF-LT LaBrandon Toefield 15.00
SF-KW Kelley Washington 15.00

2003 Bowman Signs of the Future Dual Autographs

SFD-RJ Charles Rogers, Andre Johnson
SFD-PL Carson Palmer, Byron Leftwich
SFD-JF Larry Johnson, Justin Fargas
SFD-JW Taylor Jacobs, Kelley Washington
SFD-BG Kyle Boller, Rex Grossman

2003 Bowman Signs of the Future Triple Autographs

SFT-PLB Carson Palmer, Byron Leftwich, Kyle Boller
SFT-JSF Larry Johnson, Onterrio Smith, Justin Fargas
SFT-RJJ Charles Rogers, Andre Johnson, Bryant Johnson

2003 Bowman Chrome

NM/M
Common Player (1-110): .30
Minor Stars: .60
Unlisted Stars: .75
Common Rookie (111-220): 1.50
Minor Rookies: 2.00
Unlisted Rookies: 3.00
Common Rookie AU (221-247): 10.00
Minor Rookie AU: 12.00
Unlisted Rookie AU: 15.00
Pack (4): 3.50
Box (24): 60.00
1 Brett Favre 3.00
2 Jeremy Shockey 1.50
3 Fred Taylor .75
4 Rich Gannon .60
5 Joey Galloway .60
6 Ray Lewis .60
7 Jeff Blake .60
8 Stacey Mack .30
9 Matt Hasselbeck .60
10 Laveranues Coles .60
11 Brad Johnson .60
12 Tommy Maddox .75
13 Curtis Martin .75
14 Tom Brady 1.00
15 Ricky Williams 1.50
16 Stephen Davis .60
17 Chad Johnson .60
18 Joey Harrington 2.00
19 Tony Gonzalez .60
20 Peerless Price .60
21 LaDainian Tomlinson 1.00
22 James Thrash .30
23 Charlie Garner .60
24 Eddie George .75
25 Terrell Owens .75
26 Brian Urlacher 1.00
27 Eric Moulds .60
28 Emmitt Smith 2.50
29 Tim Couch .75
30 Jake Plummer .60
31 Marvin Harrison .75
32 Chris Chambers .75
33 Tiki Barber .60
34 Kurt Warner 1.00
35 Michael Pittman .60
36 Kevin Dyson .30
37 Clinton Portis 2.50
38 Peyton Manning 1.50
39 Travis Taylor .60
40 Jeff Garcia .75
41 Patrick Ramsey .75
42 Shaun Alexander .75
43 Joe Horn .60
44 Daunte Culpepper .75
45 Travis Henry .60
46 Brian Finneran .30
47 William Green .75
48 Kordell Stewart .60
49 Reggie Wayne .60
50 Priest Holmes .75
51 Jay Fiedler .60
52 Corey Dillon .75
53 Jamal Lewis .75

54 Mark Brunell .60
55 Santana Moss .60
56 Duce Staley .60
57 Torry Holt .75
58 Rod Gardner .60
59 Kerry Collins .60
60 Randy Moss 1.50
61 Jerry Porter .60
62 Plaxico Burress .75
63 Steve McNair .75
64 Muhsin Muhammad .30
65 Drew Bledsoe 1.00
66 T.J. Duckett .60
67 Ahman Green .75
68 Rod Smith .60
69 Jimmy Smith .60
70 Trent Green .60
71 Tim Brown .60
72 Jerome Bettis .60
73 Isaac Bruce .60
74 Derrick Mason .60
75 Donovan McNabb 1.00
76 Deuce McAllister .75
77 Zach Thomas .30
78 Garrison Hearst .60
79 Koren Robinson .60
80 Marshall Faulk 1.00
81 Keyshawn Johnson .60
82 Jake Delhomme .60
83 Marty Booker .60
84 James Stewart .30
85 Corey Bradford .30
86 Derrius Thompson .30
87 Edgerrin James 1.00
88 Darrell Jackson .60
89 Hines Ward .60
90 David Boston .75
91 Curtis Conway .60
92 David Patten .30
93 Michael Bennett .75
94 Todd Pinkston .60
95 Jerry Rice 2.50
96 Jon Kitna .60
97 Ed McCaffrey .60
98 Donald Driver .60
99 Anthony Thomas .75
100 Michael Vick 3.00
101 Terry Glenn .60
102 Quincy Morgan .60
103 David Carr 2.00
104 Troy Brown .60
105 Aaron Brooks .60
106 Amani Toomer .60
107 Drew Brees 1.00
108 Chad Hutchinson .60
109 Warrick Dunn .60
110 Chad Pennington 1.00
111 *Brian St. Pierre* 3.00
112 *Keenan Howry* 3.00
113 *Sultan McCullough* 2.00
114 *Terence Newman* 6.00
115 *Kelley Washington* 4.00
116 *Musa Smith* 3.00
117 *Victor Hobson* 2.00
118 *Travis Anglin* 1.50
119 *Artose Pinner* 3.00
120 *Rashean Mathis* 2.00
121 *Dewayne White* 1.50
122 *Kevin Curtis* 2.00
123 *Tyrone Calico* 5.00
124 *Ricky Manning* 2.00
125 *Corey Redding* 2.00
126 *Dallas Clark* 4.00
127 *Marcus Trufant* 3.00
128 *Terrell Suggs* 5.00
129 *Aaron Walker* 2.00
130 *Calvin Pace* 1.50
131 *Ken Dorsey* 5.00
132 *Earnest Graham* 3.00
133 *Cecil Sapp* 3.00
134 *William Joseph* 3.00
135 *Anquan Boldin* 8.00
136 *Justin Griffith* 2.00
137 *Teyo Johnson* 4.00
138 *Chris Crocker* 1.50
139 *Doug Gabriel* 3.00
140 *Terry Pierce* 2.00
141 *Bradie James* 2.00
142 *Terrence Edwards* 3.00
143 *E.J. Henderson* 2.00
144 *Tony Romo* 3.00
145 *Dewayne Robertson* 2.00
146 *Dwone Hicks* 2.00
147 *Carl Ford* 3.00
148 *Ken Hamlin* 3.00
149 *Adrian Madise* 2.00
150 *Siddeeq Shabazz* 1.50
151 *Dave Ragone* 3.00
152 *Mike Seidman* 1.50
153 *DeAndrew Rubin* 1.50
154 *Mike Pinkard* 1.50
155 *Nate Burleson* 3.00
156 *Angelo Crowell* 2.00
157 *J.R. Tolver* 2.00
158 *Osi Umenyiora* 2.00
159 *Nick Barnett* 5.00
160 *Brandon Drumm* 1.50
161 *Rien Long* 1.50
162 *Zuriel Smith* 2.00
163 *Onterrio Smith* 6.00
164 *Kenny Peterson* 2.00
165 *Chaun Thompson* 1.50
166 *Terrence Holt* 2.00
167 *Ovie Mughelli* 1.50
168 *Bethel Johnson* 4.00
169 *Avon Cobourne* 4.00
170 *Andre Woolfolk* 3.00
171 *George Wrighster* 2.00
172 *Justin Fargas* 5.00
173 *Marquel Blackwell* 1.50
174 *Walter Young* 2.00
175 *Kawicka Mitchell* 2.00
176 *Drayton Florence* 1.50
177 *Jeremi Johnson* 2.00
178 *Lee Suggs* 5.00
179 *David Kircus* 2.00
180 *Rex Grossman* 10.00
180A Rex Grossman 75.00
181 *Jon Olinger* 1.50
182 *Dan Curley* 1.50
183 *Andrew Pinnock* 2.00
184 *Kirk Farmer* 1.50
185 *Charles Rogers* 8.00
186 *Alonzo Jackson* 2.00
187 *Trent Smith* 1.50
188 *Seneca Wallace* 3.00
189 *Shane Walton* 2.00
190 *Chris Brown* 4.00
191 *Dahrran Diedrick* 3.00
192 *Juston Wood* 3.00
193 *Mike Doss* 3.00
194 *Visanthe Shiancoe* 1.50
195 *Andre Johnson* 10.00
196 *Dennis Weathersby* 1.50
197 *Chris Davis* 2.00
198 *LaTarence Dunbar* 2.00
199 *Eugene Wilson* 1.50
200 *Ryan Hoag* 2.00
201 *Chris Simms* 6.00
202 *Curt Anes* 1.50
203 *Taco Wallace* 2.00
204 *David Tyree* 2.00
205 *Nate Hybl* 2.00
206 *Willis McGahee* 10.00
207 *Casey Moore* 2.00
208 *Pisa Tinoisamoa* 4.00
209 *Willie Ponder* 1.50
210 *Donald Lee* 2.00
211 *Nnamdi Asomugha* 1.50
212 *Sammy Davis* 2.00
213 *Joffrey Reynolds* 2.00
214 *Eddie Moore* 2.00
215 *Tony Hollings* 3.00
216 *Nick Maddox* 2.00
217 *Kevin Walter* 2.00
218 *Dan Klecko* 3.00
219 *Antwan Peek* 2.00
220 *Tyler Brayton* 2.00
221 *Byron Leftwich* 125.00
222 *Bobby Wade* 12.00
223 *Jerome McDougle* 10.00
224 *Michael Haynes* 10.00
225 *Taylor Jacobs* 12.00
226 *Shaun McDonald* 10.00
227 *Bryant Johnson* 30.00
228 *Talman Gardner* 12.00
229 *Domanick Davis* 40.00
230 *Jason Witten* 20.00
231 *Kyle Boller* 50.00
232 *L.J. Smith* 12.00
233 *Boss Bailey* 15.00
234 *Billy McMullen* 10.00
235 *Larry Johnson* 30.00
236 *Kareem Kelly* 10.00
237 *Carson Palmer* 120.00
238 *Quentin Griffin* 50.00
239 *Kevin Garrett* 10.00
240 *Charles Tillman* 20.00
241 *Arnaz Battle* 10.00
242 *Brooks Bollinger* 12.00
243 *LaBrandon Toefield* 12.00
244 *Sam Aiken* 10.00
245 *Justin Gage* 20.00
246 *Gibran Hamdan* 10.00

2003 Bowman Chrome Refractors

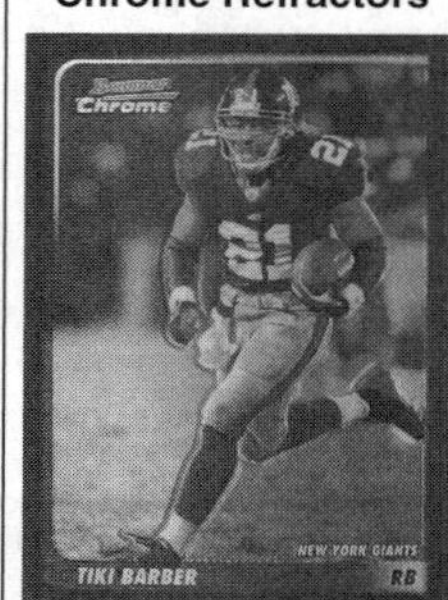

Stars: 2X-4X
Rookies: 1X-2X
Production 500 Sets

2003 Bowman Chrome Gold Refractors

Stars: 6X-12X
Rookies (111-120): 4X-8X
Rookies AU (221-246): 1.5X-3X
Production 50 Sets

2003 Bowman Chrome X-fractors

Stars: 3X-6X
Rookies: 2X-4X
Production 250 Sets

2003 Bowman Chrome Blue Uncirculated Refractors

Rookies (111-220): 2X-4X

2003 Bowman Chrome Red Uncirculated Refractors

Rookies (111-220): 2X-4X
Production 235 Sets
Rookies AU (221-246):
Production 10 Sets

2003 Bowman's Best

NM/M
Common Player (1-80): .50
Minor Stars: 1.00
Unlisted Stars: 1.50
Common Rookie (81-90): 3.00
Common Rookie Jsy (91-115): 5.00
Common Rookie Auto (116-175): 8.00
Pack (5): 12.00
Box (10): 90.00
1 Terrell Owens 1.50
2 Peerless Price 1.00
3 Joey Harrington 3.00
4 Ricky Williams 2.50
5 David Boston 1.50
6 Troy Brown 1.00
7 Deuce McAllister 1.50
8 Marvin Harrison 1.50
9 Ahman Green 1.50
10 Emmitt Smith 4.00
11 Brian Urlacher 2.50
12 Jamal Lewis 1.50
13 Keyshawn Johnson 1.00
14 Kurt Warner 2.50
15 Rod Gardner 1.00
16 Plaxico Burress 1.50
17 Chad Pennington 2.00
18 Jeremy Shockey 3.00
19 Donovan McNabb 2.00
20 T.J. Duckett 1.50
21 Fred Taylor 1.50
22 Daunte Culpepper 1.50
23 Tiki Barber 1.50
24 Brian Griese 1.00
25 Chad Johnson 1.00
26 Julius Peppers 1.00
27 Chad Hutchinson 1.00
28 Eddie George 1.50
29 Torry Holt 1.50
30 Drew Brees 2.00
31 Rich Gannon 1.00
32 Trent Green 1.00
33 Clinton Portis 4.00
34 Tom Brady 2.00
35 Aaron Brooks 1.50
36 Ray Lewis 1.00
37 David Carr 3.00
38 Chris Chambers 1.50
39 Brad Johnson 1.00
40 Tommy Maddox 1.50
41 Curtis Martin 1.50
42 Travis Henry 1.00
43 Brett Favre 5.00
44 Randy Moss 2.50
45 Jimmy Smith 1.00
46 Joey Galloway 1.00
47 Derrick Mason 1.00
48 Darrell Jackson 1.00
49 Curtis Conway 1.00
50 Michael Vick 5.00
51 Rod Smith 1.00
52 Muhsin Muhammad .50
53 Drew Bledsoe 2.00
54 Michael Bennett 1.50
55 Joe Horn 1.00
56 Stephen Davis 1.00
57 Isaac Bruce 1.00
58 Shaun Alexander 1.50
59 Jerry Rice 4.00
60 Peyton Manning 4.00
61 Tony Gonzalez 1.00
62 Jake Plummer 1.00
63 Tim Couch 1.50
64 Marty Booker 1.00
65 Corey Dillon 1.50
66 Steve McNair 1.50
67 Jeff Garcia 1.50
68 Hines Ward 1.00
69 Laveranues Coles 1.00
70 Amani Toomer 1.00
71 Eric Moulds 1.00
72 Donald Driver 1.00
73 Jay Fiedler 1.00
74 Charlie Garner 1.00
75 Priest Holmes 1.50
76 Edgerrin James 2.00
77 Kerry Collins 1.00
78 LaDainian Tomlinson 2.00
79 Mark Brunell 1.00
80 Marshall Faulk 2.00
81 *Lee Suggs* 6.00
82 *William Joseph* 3.00
83 *Brandon Lloyd* 3.00
84 *Nick Barnett* 4.00
85 *Andre Woolfolk* 3.00
86 *Jimmy Kennedy* 3.00
87 *Kliff Kingsbury* 4.00
88 *Andrew Williams* 3.00
89 *Mike Doss* 3.00
90 *Troy Polamalu* 5.00
91 *Bryant Johnson Jsy* 6.00
92 *Justin Fargas Jsy* 10.00
93 *Terence Newman Jsy* 10.00
94 *Brian St. Pierre Jsy* 5.00
95 *Dewayne Robertson Jsy* 5.00
96 *Dave Ragone Jsy* 5.00
97 *Teyo Johnson Jsy* 5.00
98 *Bethel Johnson Jsy* 5.00
99 *Tyrone Calico Jsy* 8.00
100 *Carson Palmer Jsy* 25.00
101 *Marcus Trufant Jsy* 5.00
102 *Nate Burleson Jsy* 6.00
103 *Musa Smith Jsy* 6.00
104 *Anquan Boldin Jsy* 12.00
105 *Chris Simms Jsy* 8.00
106 *Taylor Jacobs Jsy* 5.00
107 *Dallas Clark Jsy* 6.00
108 *Seneca Wallace Jsy* 6.00
109 *Ken Dorsey Jsy* 6.00
110 *Willis McGahee Jsy* 15.00
111 *Chris Brown Jsy* 6.00
112 *Terrell Suggs Jsy* 6.00
113 *Kelley Washington Jsy* 6.00
114 *Onterrio Smith Jsy* 8.00
115 *Rex Grossman Jsy* 15.00
116 *LaBrandon Toefield Auto* 10.00
117 *Sam Aiken Auto* 8.00
118 *Malaefou MacKenzie Auto* 8.00
119 *David Tyree Auto* 8.00
120 *Jerome McDougle Auto* 8.00
121 *Dewayne White Auto* 8.00
122 *Zuriel Smith Auto* 8.00
123 *Shaun McDonald Auto* 8.00
124 *Andre Johnson/199 Auto* 100.00
125 *Ahmaad Galloway Auto* 8.00
126 *Keenan Howry Auto* 10.00
127 *Kareem Kelly Auto* 8.00
128 *Brooks Bollinger Auto* 15.00
129 *Arnaz Battle Auto* 8.00
130 *Adrian Madise Auto* 8.00
131 *LaTarence Dunbar Auto* 8.00
132 *L.J. Smith Auto* 10.00
133 *B.J. Askew* 10.00
134 *Michael Haynes Auto* 10.00
135 *David Kircus Auto* 8.00
136 *Kyle Boller/199 Auto* 60.00
137 *Domanick Davis Auto* 60.00
138 *Osi Umenyiora Auto* 10.00
139 *Bobby Wade Auto* 10.00
140 *Boss Bailey Auto* 12.00
141 *Billy McMullen Auto* 10.00
142 *Doug Gabriel Auto* 10.00
143 *J.R. Tolver Auto* 8.00
144 *Gibran Hamdan Auto* 10.00
145 *Walter Young Auto* 8.00
146 *Carl Ford Auto* 10.00
147 *Andrew Pinnock Auto* 8.00
148 *Byron Leftwich/199 Auto* 175.00
149 *Ty Warren Auto* 10.00
150 *Visanthe Shiancoe Auto* 8.00
151 *Justin Gage Auto* 10.00
152 *Brock Forsey Auto* 25.00
153 *Casey Moore Auto* 8.00
154 *Juston Wood Auto* 8.00
155 *Aaron Walker Auto* 8.00
156 *Trent Smith Auto* 12.00
157 *Travis Anglin Auto* 8.00
158 *Jeremi Johnson Auto* 8.00
159 *Justin Griffith Auto* 8.00
160 *Chris Davis Auto* 8.00
161 *J.T. Wall Auto* 8.00
162 *Larry Johnson/199 Auto* 50.00
163 *Jon Olinger Auto* 8.00
164 *Donald Lee Auto* 8.00
165 *Taco Wallace* 8.00
166 *DeAndrew Rubin Auto* 8.00
167 *Ryan Hoag Auto* 8.00
168 *Kevin Williams Auto* 12.00
169 *Ovie Mughelli Auto* 8.00
170 TBD
171 *Brandon Drumm Auto* 8.00
172 *Brad Banks Auto* 10.00
173 *Talman Gardner Auto* 10.00
174 *Jason Witten Auto* 12.00
175 *Charles Rogers Auto*

2003 Bowman's Best Blue

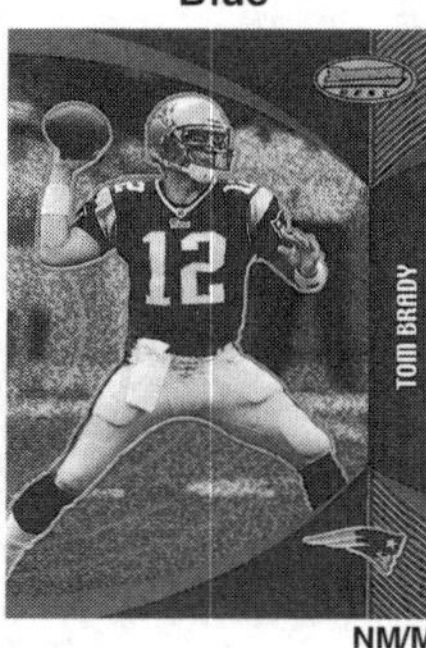

NM/M
Cards (1-90): 1X-2X
Inserted 1:3
Cards (91-115): .5X-1.5X
Inserted 1:12
Cards (116-175): .6X-1.2X
Production 499 Sets
124 Andre Johnson Auto/50
136 Kyle Boller Auto/50
148 Byron Leftwich Auto/50
162 Larry Johnson Auto/50

2003 Bowman's Best Red

Cards (1-110): 3X-6X
Inserted 1:30
Cards (91-115): 1.5X-3X
Inserted 1:110
Cards (116-175): 1.5X-3X
Production 50 Sets
124 Andre Johnson Auto/25
136 Kyle Boller Auto/25
148 Byron Leftwich Auto/25
162 Larry Johnson Auto/25

2003 Bowman's Best Best Coverage Relics

Production 25 Sets
BC-RJ Jerry Rice, Andre Johnson
BC-FB Brett Favre, Kyle Boller
BC-TM LaDainian Tomlinson, Willis McGahee
BC-GJ Eddie George, Larry Johnson
BC-TF Fred Taylor, Justin Fargas
BC-OR Terrell Owens, Charles Rogers
BC-WP Kurt Warner, Carson Palmer
BC-KS Jevon Kearse, Terrell Suggs
BC-JJ Keyshawn Johnson, Bryant Johnson
BC-SJ Jimmy Smith, Taylor Jacobs

2003 Bowman's Best Double Coverage Autographs

NM/M
Common Player: 100.00
Production 50 Sets
DCA-PL Carson Palmer, Byron Leftwich 250.00
DCA-MJ Willis McGahee Larry Johnson 100.00
DCA-BG Kyle Boller Rex Grossman 125.00

2003 Bowman's Best Double Coverage Relics

NM/M
Common Player: 20.00
Production 50 Sets
DCR-PL Carson Palmer, Byron Leftwich 60.00
DCR-RJ Charles Rogers Andre Johnson 40.00
DCR-MJ Willis McGahee Larry Johnson 40.00
DCR-JJ Bryant Johnson Taylor Jacobs 20.00
DCR-BG Kyle Boller Rex Grossman 40.00
DCR-SPK Brian St. Pierre Kliff Kingsbury 25.00
DCR-RW Dave Ragone Seneca Wallace 25.00
DCR-FB Justin Fargas, Chris Brown 25.00
DCR-SS Musa Smith, Onterrio Smith 25.00
DCR-CJ Dallas Clark, Teyo Johnson 20.00
DCR-NT Terence Newman, Marcus Trufant 25.00
DCR-SR Terrell Suggs, Dewayne Robertson 20.00
DCR-BJ Anquan Boldin, Bethel Johnson 25.00
DCR-CW Tyrone Calico, Kelley Washington 20.00
DCR-BC Nate Burleson, Kevin Curtis 20.00

2003 Bowman's Best Single Coverage Autographs

NM/M
Common Player: 20.00
Production 100 Sets
SCA-LC Laveranues Coles 20.00
SCA-DD Donald Driver 25.00
SCA-MH Marvin Harrison 40.00
SCA-TH Travis Henry 20.00
SCA-TM Tommy Maddox 35.00
SCA-MS Michael Strahan 20.00
SCA-JT Jason Taylor 30.00
SCA-HW Hines Ward 35.00

2003 Bowman's Best Single Coverage Relics

NM/M
Common Player: 12.00
Production 100 Sets
SCR-EG Eddie George 12.00
SCR-KJ Keyshawn Johnson 12.00
SCR-JK Jevon Kearse 12.00
SCR-TO Terrell Owens 15.00
SCR-JR Jerry Rice 30.00
SCR-JS Jimmy Smith 12.00
SCR-FT Fred Taylor 12.00
SCR-LT LaDainian Tomlinson 15.00
SCR-KW Kurt Warner 12.00

2003 Bowman's Best Ultimate Coverage Auto Relics

Production 25 Sets
UC-PL Carson Palmer, Byron Leftwich
UC-MJ Willis McGahee, Larry Johnson
UC-BG Kyle Boller, Rex Grossman

2004 Bowman

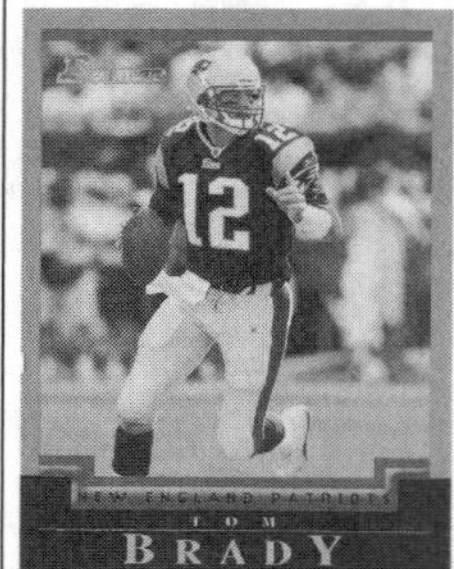

NM/M
Common Player (1-110): .25
Minor Stars: .40
Unlisted Stars: .75
Common Rookie (110-275): .50
Minor Rookies: .75
Unlisted Rookies: 1.00
Pack (10): 4.75
Box (24): 80.00
Jumbo Box: 100.00
1 Brett Favre 2.00
2 Jay Fiedler .40
3 Andre Davis .40
4 Travis Henry .40
5 Jimmy Smith .40
6 Santana Moss .40
7 Correll Buckhalter .40
8 Randy Moss 1.25
9 Edgerrin James 1.00
10 Marc Bulger .75
11 Derrick Mason .40
12 Mark Brunell .40
13 Donte Stallworth .40
14 Deion Branch .40
15 Jake Plummer .40
16 Steve Smith .40
17 Jon Kitna .40
18 Andre Johnson .75
19 A.J. Feeley .40
20 Drew Bledsoe .40
21 Antonio Bryant .40
22 Reggie Wayne .40
23 Thomas Jones .40
24 Alge Crumpler .40
25 Anquan Boldin .75
26 Tim Rattay .40
27 Charlie Garner .40
28 James Thrash .25
29 Koren Robinson .40
30 Terrell Owens .75
31 Amani Toomer .40
32 Kelly Campbell .40
33 Patrick Ramsey .40
34 Plaxico Burress .75
35 Chad Pennington 1.00
36 Fred Taylor .75
37 Domanick Davis .40
38 DeShaun Foster .40
39 T.J. Duckett .40
40 Ahman Green .75
41 Lee Suggs .75
42 Tony Gonzalez .40
43 Rich Gannon .40
44 Kevan Barlow .40
45 Torry Holt .75
46 Aaron Brooks .75

47 Tyrone Calico .40
48 Keenan McCardell .40
49 Hines Ward .40
50 LaDainian Tomlinson 1.00
51 Dante Hall .40
52 Marcus Pollard .25
53 Corey Dillon .40
54 Justin McCareins .40
55 Stephen Davis .40
56 Jeff Garcia .40
57 Ashley Lelie .40
58 Javon Walker .75
59 Kyle Boller .40
60 Chad Johnson .40
61 Anthony Thomas .40
62 Byron Leftwich 1.25
63 David Boston .40
64 Onterrio Smith .40
65 Deuce McAllister .75
66 Antwann Randle El .40
67 Justin Fargas .40
68 Laveranues Coles .40
69 Quincy Morgan .40
70 Priest Holmes 1.00
71 Robert Ferguson .40
72 Charles Rogers .75
73 Drew Brees .75
74 Matt Hasselbeck .40
75 Peyton Manning 1.25
76 Rudi Johnson .40
77 Jake Delhomme .75
78 Tiki Barber .40
79 Brad Johnson .40
80 Steve McNair .75
81 Willis McGahee .75
82 Josh McCown .40
83 Garrison Hearst .40
84 Quincy Carter .40
85 Ricky Williams .75
86 Trent Green .40
87 Curtis Martin .75
88 Jerry Porter .40
89 Brian Westbrook .40
90 Clinton Portis 1.25
91 Eric Moulds .40
92 Marcel Shipp .40
93 Joey Harrington .75
94 David Carr 1.00
95 Marvin Harrison .75
96 Joe Horn .40
97 Chris Chambers .75
98 Darrell Jackson .40
99 Eddie George .75
100 Donovan McNabb 1.00
101 Marshall Faulk 1.00
102 Rex Grossman .75
103 Tai Streets .40
104 Jeremy Shockey .75
105 Jamal Lewis .75
106 Tom Brady 1.25
107 Shaun Alexander .75
108 Carson Palmer 1.00
109 Daunte Culpepper .75
110 Michael Vick 1.50
111 *Eli Manning* 8.00
112 *Kevin Jones* .50
113 *Philip Rivers* 5.00
114 *Ben Roethlisberger* 15.00
115 *Roy Williams* 5.00
116 *Tommie Harris* 1.50
117 *Vontez Duff* 1.00
118 *Karlos Dansby* 1.50
119 *Thomas Tapeh* 1.00
120 *Matt Schaub* 2.50
121 *Dexter Reid* .50
122 *Jonathan Smith* .75
123 *Ricardo Colclough* 1.25
124 *Jeff Dugan* .50
125 *Larry Fitzgerald* 5.00
126 *Gibril Wilson* 1.00
127 *Sean Taylor* 2.50
128 *Marquise Hill* 1.00
129 *Ernest Wilford* 1.25
130 *Cedric Cobbs* 1.25
131 *Rich Gardner* .75
132 *Chris Cooley* .75
133 *Kenechi Udeze* 2.00
134 *John Navarre* 2.00
135 *Ben Troupe* 1.00
136 *Dave Ball* .50
137 *Antwan Odom* 1.25
138 *Stuart Schweigert* 1.00
139 *Derek Abney* 1.00
140 *Keary Colbert* 2.00
141 *Jeris McIntyre* 1.00
142 *Matt Kranchick* 1.00
143 *Rodney Leisle* .50
144 *Vince Wilfork* 2.00
145 *Lee Evans* 2.50
146 *Darnell Dockett* 1.25
147 *Jeremy LeSueur* 1.00
148 Gilbert Gardner 1.00
149 *Amon Gordon* .50
150 *Darius Watts* 2.00
151 *Junior Siavii* 1.00
152 *Igor Olshansky* 1.25
153 *Courtney Watson* 1.25
154 *D.J. Williams* 2.00
155 *Mewelde Moore* 2.00
156 *Teddy Lehman* 1.50
157 *Nathan Vasher* 1.00
158 *Randy Starks* 1.00
159 *Isaac Sopoaga* .50
160 *Drew Henson* 4.00
161 *Erik Coleman* .50
162 *Robert Kent* .75
163 *Jammal Lord* 1.25
164 *Richard Seigler* 1.00
165 *Jeff Smoker* 2.00
166 *Niko Koutouvides* 1.00
167 *Adimchinobe Echemandu* 1.00
168 *Matt Mauck* 1.50
169 *Brandon Miree* 1.00
170 *Dunta Robinson* 1.50
171 *B.J. Symons* 1.50
172 *Courtney Anderson* 1.00
173 *Bruce Perry* 1.25
174 *Shaun Phillips* 1.00
175 *Greg Jones* 2.00
176 *Ryan Krause* 1.00
177 *Charlie Anderson* .50
178 *Tank Johnson* 1.00
179 *Dwan Edwards* .50
180 *Julius Jones* 3.00
181 *Chad Lavalais* .50
182 *Tim Anderson* 1.00
183 *Jarrett Payton* 1.50
184 *Matt Ware* 1.25
185 *DeAngelo Hall* 2.00
186 *Ben Hartsock* 1.25
187 *Bradlee Van Pelt* 1.50
188 *Michael Boulware* 1.25
189 *Keith Smith* 1.00
190 *Michael Jenkins* 1.50
191 *Quincy Wilson* 1.50
192 *Dontarrious Thomas* 1.00
193 *Sloan Thomas* .75
194 *Tony Hargrove* .75
195 *Ben Watson* 1.00
196 *Craig Krenzel* 1.50
197 *Jason Babin* 2.00
198 *Jim Sorgi* 1.00
199 *Triandos Luke* 1.00
200 *Kellen Winslow Jr.* 4.00
201 *Patrick Crayton* 1.25
202 *Michael Waddell* .50
203 *Chris Gamble* 2.00
204 *Josh Harris* 1.25
205 *Devard Darling* 1.50
206 *Shawntae Spencer* 1.00
207 *Will Smith* 1.50
208 *Samie Parker* 1.25
209 *Darrion Scott* 1.00
210 *Chris Perry* 2.50
211 *P.K. Sam* 1.50
212 *Wes Welker* 1.00
213 *Ryan Dinwiddie* 1.00
214 *Rod Davis* .50
215 *Casey Clausen* 2.00
216 *Clarence Moore* 1.00
217 *D.J. Hackett* 1.00
218 *Casey Bramlet* 1.00
219 *Jared Lorenzen* 1.25
220 *Devery Henderson* 1.50
221 *Sean Jones* 1.00
222 *Maurice Mann* 1.00
223 *Jared Allen* .50
224 *Bruce Thornton* .50
225 *Tatum Bell* 2.50
226 *Leon Joe* .75
227 *Tim Euhus* 1.00
228 *John Standeford* 1.00
229 *Reggie Torbor* 1.00
230 *Rashaun Woods* 3.00
231 *Jason Shivers* .50
232 *Jason Peters* 1.50
233 *Ahmad Carroll* 1.50
234 *Jason David* .50
235 *Keyaron Fox* 1.00
236 *Corey Williams* .50
237 *Raheem Orr* .50
238 *Carlos Francis* 1.25
239 *Von Hutchins* 1.00
240 *Marcus Tubbs* 1.50
241 *Daryl Smith* 1.25
242 *Robert Gallery* 2.00
243 *Sean Tufts* 1.00
244 *Marquis Cooper* 1.00
245 *Bernard Berrian* 1.50
246 *Derrick Strait* 2.00
247 *Travis LaBoy* 1.00
248 *Johnnie Morant* 1.50
249 *Caleb Miller* 1.25
250 *Michael Clayton* 2.50
251 *Will Poole* 1.50
252 *Andy Hall* 1.00
253 *Demorrio Williams* 1.00
254 *Chris Thompson* .50
255 *Derrick Hamilton* 1.25
256 *Glenn Earl* 1.00
257 *Jonathan Vilma* 2.00
258 *Donnell Washington* 1.00
259 *Drew Carter* 1.00
260 *Steven Jackson* 4.00
261 *Jamaar Taylor* 1.25
262 *Nate Lawrie* 1.00
263 *Cody Pickett* 1.50
264 *Keiwan Ratliff* 1.25
265 *Luke McCown* 1.50
266 *Jerricho Cotchery* 1.50
267 *Joey Thomas* 1.25
268 *Shawn Andrews* 1.25
269 *Derrick Ward* .50
270 *Reggie Williams* 2.00
271 *Rod Rutherford* 1.25
272 *Michael Turner* 1.25
273 *Michael Gaines* 1.00
274 *Will Allen* 1.25
275 *J.P. Losman* 2.50

2004 Bowman Gold

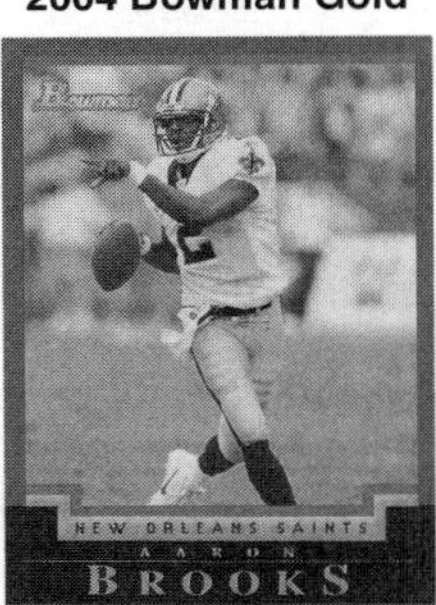

Stars: 1X-2X
Inserted 1:1

2004 Bowman Uncirculated Gold

NM/M

Stars: 3X-6X
Rookies: 4X-8X
Production 165 Sets

2004 Bowman Coaches Autographs

BRPGK Gary Kubiak 12.00
BRCJM Jim Mora Jr. 20.00
BRCMM Mike Mularkey 15.00
BRPSP Sean Payton 15.00

2004 Bowman Draft Day Selections Relics

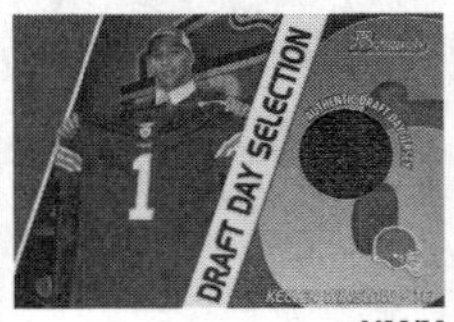

NM/M

DHRG Robert Gallery Hat
DJHRG Robert Gallery JSY/Hat
DJRG Robert Gallery JSY 10.00
DHDH DeAngelo Hall Hat
DJDH DeAngelo Hall JSY 10.00
DJHDH DeAngelo Hall JSY/Hat
DJDEM Eli Manning JSY/JSY/500 50.00
DJEM Eli Manning JSY 25.00
DHBR Ben Roethlisberger Hat
DJBR Ben Roethlisberger JSY 50.00
DJHBR Ben Roethlisberger JSY/Hat
DHRW Roy Williams Hat
DJHRW Roy Williams JSY/Hat
DJRW Roy Williams JSY 15.00
DHKW Kellen Winslow Jr. Hat
DJKW Kellen Winslow Jr. JSY 12.00

2004 Bowman Fabric of the Future

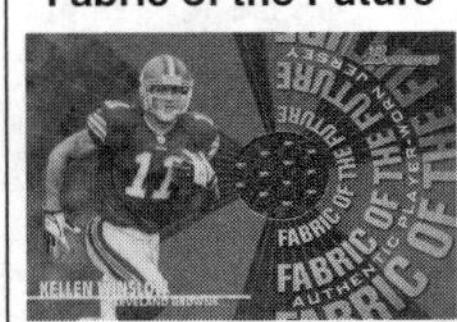

NM/M

Common Player: 8.00
FFTB Tatum Bell 8.00
FFLE Lee Evans 10.00
FFDH DeAngelo Hall 8.00
FFSJ Steven Jackson 10.00
FFMJ Michael Jenkins 8.00
FFKJ Kevin Jones 10.00
FFEM Eli Manning 30.00
FFLM Luke McCown 8.00
FFPR Philip Rivers 12.00
FFDR Dunta Robinson 8.00
FFBR Ben Roethlisberger 50.00
FFBT Ben Troupe 8.00
FFRWI Reggie Williams 8.00
FFRW Roy Williams 12.00
FFKW Kellen Winslow Jr.

2004 Bowman Fabric of the Future Doubles

NM/M

Production 50 Sets
FFDEJ Lee Evans, Michael Jenkins 15.00
FFDHR DeAngelo Hall, Dunta Robinson 10.00
FFDJB Kevin Jones, Tatum Bell 30.00
FFDMW Eli Manning, Reggie Williams 30.00
FFDWT Kellen Winslow Jr., Ben Troupe 20.00

2004 Bowman Fast Forward Jersey Dual

NM/M

Production 199 Sets
FFWBR Tom Brady, Philip Rivers 30.00
FFWCR Daunte Culpepper, Ben Roethlisberger 60.00
FFWFJ Marshall Faulk, Steven Jackson 20.00
FFWHW Torry Holt, Roy Williams 20.00
FFWMM Josh McCown, Luke McCown 10.00

2004 Bowman Rookie Autographs Blue

NM/M

Common Player: 60.00
Red Autos: 1X-2X
111 Eli Manning 150.00
112 Kevin Jones 60.00
113 Philip Rivers 80.00
114 Ben Roethlisberger 300.00
115 Roy Williams 80.00

2004 Bowman Signs of the Future Autographs

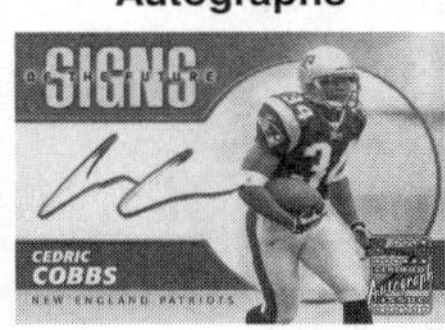

NM/M

Common Player: 8.00
SFTB Tatum Bell 12.00
SFCCL Casey Clausen 8.00
SFMC Michael Clayton 20.00
SFCC Cedric Cobbs 8.00
SFKC Keary Colbert 12.00
SFJC Jerricho Cotchery 8.00
SFLE Lee Evans 15.00
SFJH Josh Harris 8.00
SFMJ Michael Jenkins 10.00
SFGJ Greg Jones 10.00
SFKJ Kevin Jones 30.00
SFJPL J.P. Losman 15.00
SFMM Mewelde Moore 15.00
SFJN John Navarre 10.00
SFCPE Chris Perry 12.00
SFCP Cody Pickett 10.00
SFPR Philip Rivers 40.00
SFMS Matt Schaub 12.00
SFJS Jeff Smoker 12.00
SFEW Ernest Wilford 10.00
SFRWO Rashaun Woods 15.00

2004 Bowman Signs of the Future Autographs Doubles

NM/M

Production 50 Sets
SFDFE Larry Fitzgerald, Lee Evans 80.00
SFDJJ Steven Jackson, Kevin Jones 100.00
SFDLC J.P. Losman, Michael Clayton 60.00
SFDMR Eli Manning, Philip Rivers 150.00

2004 Bowman Chrome

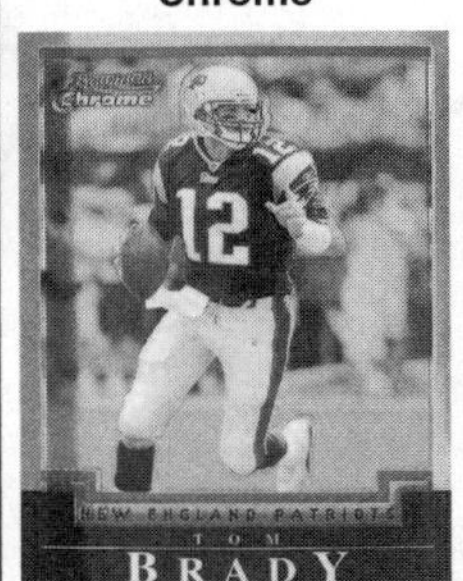

NM/M

Common Player (1-110): .30
Minor Stars: .60
Unlisted Stars: 1.00
Common Rookie (112-220): 2.00
Common Rookie Auto (111, 221-245): 10.00
Pack (4): 8.00
Box (18): 100.00
1 Brett Favre 3.00
2 Jay Fiedler .30
3 Andre Davis .60
4 Travis Henry .60
5 Jimmy Smith .60
6 Santana Moss .60
7 Correll Buckhalter .60
8 Randy Moss 2.00
9 Edgerrin James 1.50
10 Marc Bulger 1.00
11 Derrick Mason .60
12 Mark Brunell .60
13 Donte Stallworth .60
14 Deion Branch .60
15 Jake Plummer .60
16 Steve Smith .60
17 Jon Kitna .60
18 Andre Johnson 1.00
19 A.J. Feeley .60
20 Drew Bledsoe 1.00
21 Antonio Bryant .60
22 Reggie Wayne .60
23 Thomas Jones .60
24 Alge Crumpler .60
25 Anquan Boldin 1.00
26 Tim Rattay .60
27 Charlie Garner .60
28 James Thrash .30
29 Koren Robinson .60
30 Terrell Owens 1.00
31 Amani Toomer .60
32 Kelly Campbell .60
33 Patrick Ramsey 1.00
34 Plaxico Burress 1.00
35 Chad Pennington 1.50
36 Fred Taylor 1.00
37 Domanick Davis 1.00
38 DeShaun Foster .60
39 T.J. Duckett .60
40 Ahman Green 1.00
41 Lee Suggs 1.00
42 Tony Gonzalez .60
43 Rich Gannon .60
44 Kevan Barlow .60
45 Torry Holt .60
46 Aaron Brooks 1.00
47 Tyrone Calico .60
48 Keenan McCardell .60
49 Hines Ward .60
50 LaDainian Tomlinson 1.50
51 Dante Hall .60
52 Marcus Pollard .60
53 Corey Dillon 1.00
54 Justin McCareins .60
55 Stephen Davis .60
56 Jeff Garcia .60
57 Ashley Lelie .60
58 Javon Walker 1.00
59 Kyle Boller .60
60 Chad Johnson .60
61 Anthony Thomas .60
62 Byron Leftwich 2.00
63 David Boston .60
64 Onterrio Smith .60
65 Deuce McAllister 1.00
66 Antwann Randle El .60
67 Justin Fargas .60
68 Laveranues Coles .60
69 Quincy Morgan .60
70 Priest Holmes 1.50
71 Robert Ferguson .60
72 Charles Rogers 1.00
73 Drew Brees 1.00
74 Matt Hasselbeck .60
75 Peyton Manning 2.00
76 Rudi Johnson .60
77 Jake Delhomme 1.00
78 Tiki Barber 1.00
79 Brad Johnson .60
80 Steve McNair 1.00
81 Willis McGahee 1.00
82 Josh McCown .60
83 Garrison Hearst .60
84 Quincy Carter .60
85 Ricky Williams 1.00
86 Trent Green .60
87 Curtis Martin 1.00
88 Jerry Porter .60
89 Brian Westbrook .60
90 Clinton Portis 2.00
91 Eric Moulds .60
92 Marcel Shipp .60
93 Joey Harrington 1.00
94 David Carr 1.50
95 Marvin Harrison 1.00
96 Joe Horn .60
97 Chris Chambers 1.00
98 Darrell Jackson .60
99 Eddie George .60
100 Donovan McNabb 1.50
101 Marshall Faulk 1.50
102 Rex Grossman 1.00
103 Tai Streets .60
104 Jeremy Shockey 1.00
105 Jamal Lewis 1.00
106 Tom Brady 2.00
107 Shaun Alexander 1.00
108 Carson Palmer 1.50
109 Daunte Culpepper 1.00
110 Michael Vick 3.00
111 *Ben Roethlisberger Auto/199* 500.00
112 *Tommie Harris* 4.00
113 *Thomas Tapeh* 2.00
114 *Matt Schaub* 5.00
115 *Jonathan Smith* 2.00
116 *Ricardo Colclough* 3.00
117 *Jeff Dugan* 2.00
118 *Larry Fitzgerald* 10.00
119 *Gibril Wilson* 2.00
120 *Sean Taylor* 5.00
121 *Marquise Hill* 2.50
122 *Cedric Cobbs* 3.00
123 *Rich Gardner* 2.00
124 *Chris Cooley* 2.50
125 *Ben Troupe* 3.00
126 *Antwan Odom* 3.00
127 *Stuart Schweigert* 2.50
128 *Derek Abney* 2.50
129 *Keary Colbert* 4.00
130 *Jeris McIntyre* 2.50
131 *Matt Kranchick* 3.00
132 *Rodney Leisle* 2.00
133 *Vince Wilfork* 4.00
134 *Darnell Dockett* 3.00
135 *Jeremy LeSueur* 2.50
136 *Gilbert Gardner* 2.00
137 *Adrian Gordon* 2.00
138 *Darius Watts* 4.00
139 *Junior Siavii* 3.00
140 *Igor Olshansky* 3.00
141 *Mewelde Moore* 4.00
142 *Nathan Vasher* 3.00
143 *Randy Starks* 2.50
144 *Isaac Sopoaga* 2.00
145 *Drew Henson* 8.00
146 *Erik Coleman* 2.00
147 *Robert Kent* 2.00
148 *Jammal Lord* 3.00
149 *Richard Seigler* 2.00
150 *Niko Koutouvides* 2.50
151 *Brandon Miree* 2.50
152 *Dunta Robinson* 3.00
153 *Courtney Anderson* 2.50
154 *Bruce Perry* 2.50
155 *Shaun Phillips* 2.00
156 *Greg Jones* 4.00
157 *Tank Johnson* 2.50
158 *Dwan Edwards* 2.00
159 *Julius Jones* 10.00
160 *Chad Lavalais* 2.00
161 *Tim Anderson* 3.00
162 *Jarrett Payton* 3.00
163 *Matt Ware* 2.50
164 *DeAngelo Hall* 5.00
165 *Ben Hartsock* 3.00
166 *Keith Smith* 2.00
167 *Michael Jenkins* 4.00
168 *Quincy Wilson* 3.00
169 *Dontarrious Thomas* 3.00
170 *Tony Hargrove* 2.00
171 *Ben Watson* 3.00
172 *Triandos Luke* 3.00
173 *Kellen Winslow Jr.* 5.00
174 *Patrick Crayton* 3.00
175 *Devard Darling* 3.00
176 *Shawntae Spencer* 2.50
177 *Will Smith* 4.00
178 *Darrion Scott* 3.00
179 *Wes Welker* 2.50
180 *Ryan Dinwiddie* 2.00
181 *Rod Davis* 2.00
182 *Casey Clausen* 4.00
183 *Clarence Moore* 3.00
184 *D.J. Hackett* 3.00
185 *Devery Henderson* 3.00
186 *Sean Jones* 2.50
187 *Bruce Thornton* 2.00
188 *Tatum Bell* 6.00
189 *Tim Euhus* 3.00
190 *John Standeford* 2.50
191 *Reggie Torbor* 2.00
192 *Rashaun Woods* 4.00
193 *Jason Shivers* 2.00
194 *Ahmad Carroll* 4.00
195 *Keyaron Fox* 2.00
196 *Von Hutchins* 2.00
197 *Marcus Tubbs* 3.00
198 *Daryl Smith* 3.00
199 *Robert Gallery* 5.00
200 *Marquis Cooper* 2.50
201 *Bernard Berrian* 3.00
202 *Derrick Strait* 3.00
203 *Travis LaBoy* 2.00
204 *Caleb Miller* 2.00
205 *Michael Clayton* 6.00
206 *Will Poole* 3.00
207 *Derrick Hamilton* 2.50
208 *Glenn Earl* 2.00
209 *Donnell Washington* 3.00
210 *Nate Lawrie* 2.00
211 *Keiwan Ratliff* 3.00
212 *Luke McCown* 3.00
213 *Joey Thomas* 2.50
214 *Shawn Andrews* 2.50
215 *Derrick Ward* 2.00
216 *Reggie Williams* 4.00
217 *Rod Rutherford* 3.00
218 *Michael Gaines* 2.50
219 *Will Allen* 3.00
220 *J.P. Losman* 8.00
221 *Roy Williams Auto/199* 150.00
222 *Kevin Jones Auto/199* 125.00
223 *Philip Rivers Auto/199* 125.00
224 *Steven Jackson Auto/199* 125.00
225 *Eli Manning Auto/199* 250.00
226 *Cody Pickett Auto* 12.00
227 *P.K. Sam Auto* 10.00
228 *Maurice Mann Auto* 10.00
229 *Andy Hall Auto* 10.00
230 *Chris Perry Auto* 20.00
231 *Ernest Wilford Auto* 10.00
232 *Kenechi Udeze Auto* 12.00
233 *Michael Boulware Auto* 10.00
234 *B.J. Symons Auto* 12.00
235 *Jared Lorenzen Auto* 10.00
236 *Matt Mauck Auto* 12.00
237 *Carlos Francis Auto* 10.00
238 *Michael Turner Auto* 10.00
239 *Lee Evans Auto* 40.00
240 *Jerricho Cotchery Auto* 12.00
241 *John Navarre Auto* 15.00
242 *Jonathan Vilma Auto* 20.00
243 *Josh Harris Auto* 10.00
244 *Jeff Smoker Auto* 15.00
245 *Jamaar Taylor Auto* 10.00

2004 Bowman Chrome Refractors

Stars: 2X-4X
Rookies: 1X-1.5X
Production 500 Sets

Post-1980 cards in Near Mint condition will generally sell for about 75% of the quoted Mint value. Excellent-condition cards bring no more than 40%.

2004 Bowman Chrome Xfractors

Stars: 3X-6X
Rookies: 1X-2X
Production 250 Sets

2004 Bowman Chrome Red Refractors

NM/M
Rookies (112-220): 1X-2X
112-220 Production 220 Sets
111/221-245 Production 10 Sets

2004 Bowman Chrome Gold Refractors

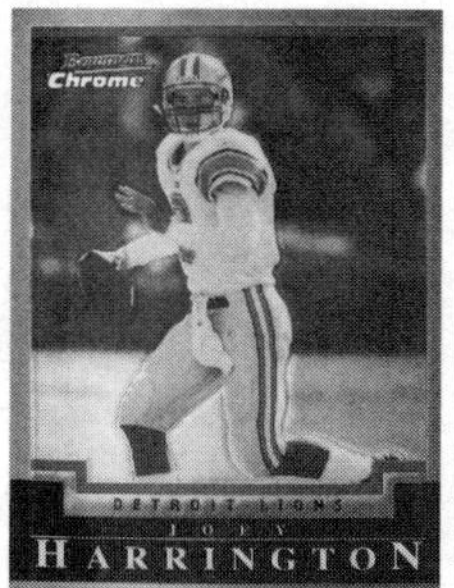

NM/M
Stars: 5X-10X
Rookies: 2X-4X
Rookie Autos: 1X-2X
Production 50 Sets
111 Ben Roethlisberger Auto 800.00
225 Eli Manning Auto 300.00

2004 Bowman Chrome Super Bowl XXXIX Unsigned Draft Pick

NM/M
Common Player: 8.00
111 Ben Roethlisberger 75.00
221 Roy Williams WR 30.00
222 Kevin Jones 25.00
223 Philip Rivers 40.00
224 Steven Jackson 25.00
225 Eli Manning 50.00
226 Cody Pickett 8.00
227 P.K. Sam 10.00
228 Maurice Mann 8.00
229 Andy Hall 8.00
230 Chris Perry 15.00
231 Ernest Wilford 8.00
232 Kenechi Udeze 8.00
233 Michael Boulware 8.00
234 B.J. Symons 8.00
235 Jared Lorenzen 8.00
236 Matt Mauck 8.00
237 Carlos Francis 8.00
238 Michael Turner 8.00
239 Lee Evans 20.00
240 Jerricho Cotchery 10.00
241 John Navarre 10.00
242 Jonathan Vilma 10.00
243 Josh Harris 8.00
244 Jeff Smoker 10.00
245 Jamaar Taylor 8.00

2004 Bowman's Best

NM/M
Common Player (1-80): .40
Minor Stars: .75
Unlisted Stars: 1.50
Common Rookie (81-100): 3.00
Common Rookie Jsy (101-125): 4.00
Common Rookie Auto (126-188): 6.00
Pack (5): 20.00
Box (10): 140.00
1 Brett Favre 5.00
2 Chris Chambers 1.50
3 Kyle Boller .75
4 Brian Urlacher 1.50
5 Marvin Harrison 1.50
6 Matt Hasselbeck 1.50
7 Aaron Brooks 1.50
8 Curtis Martin 1.50

NM/M
9 Keenan McCardell .40
10 Terrell Owens 1.50
11 Terrell Owens .75
12 Garrison Hearst .75
13 Joe Horn .75
14 David Carr 2.00
15 Tom Brady 3.00
16 Shaun Alexander 1.50
17 Tommy Maddox .75
18 Tiki Barber 1.50
19 Trent Green .75
20 Anquan Boldin 1.50
21 Peerless Price .75
22 Jake Delhomme 1.50
23 Eric Moulds .75
24 Quincy Carter .75
25 Steve McNair 1.50
26 Tim Rattay .75
27 Laveranues Coles .75
28 Corey Dillon .75
29 Byron Leftwich 3.00
30 Chad Pennington 2.00
31 Koren Robinson .75
32 Plaxico Burress 1.50
33 Steve Smith .75
34 Warrick Dunn .75
35 Jamal Lewis 1.50
36 Charles Rogers 1.50
37 Tony Gonzalez .75
38 Jake Plummer .75
39 Chad Johnson .75
40 Peyton Manning 3.00
41 Daunte Culpepper 1.50
42 Fred Taylor 1.50
43 Amani Toomer .75
44 Santana Moss .75
45 Deuce McAllister 1.50
46 Rex Grossman 1.50
47 Ray Lewis .75
48 Hines Ward .75
49 Darrell Jackson .75
50 Randy Moss 3.00
51 Carson Palmer 2.00
52 Rod Smith .75
53 Drew Bledsoe 1.50
54 Brad Johnson .75
55 Travis Henry .75
56 Joey Harrington 1.50
57 Edgerrin James 2.00
58 Kurt Warner .75
59 Josh McCown .75
60 Clinton Portis 3.00
61 Brian Westbrook .75
62 Marc Bulger 1.50
63 Charlie Garner .75
64 Torry Holt 1.50
65 LaDainian Tomlinson 2.00
66 Mark Brunell .75
67 Derrick Mason .75
68 Andre Johnson 1.50
69 Keyshawn Johnson .75
70 Ahman Green 1.50
71 Rudi Johnson .75
72 Stephen Davis .75
73 Jeff Garcia .75
74 Michael Strahan .75
75 Michael Vick 4.00
76 Ricky Williams 1.50
77 Domanick Davis 1.50
78 Priest Holmes 2.00
79 Marshall Faulk 2.00
80 Donovan McNabb 2.00
81 *Dunta Robinson* 4.00
82 *Robert Gallery* 5.00
83 *Ben Troupe* 4.00
84 *Antwan Odom* 3.00
85 *Brandon Miree* 3.00
86 *Darnell Dockett* 3.00
87 *Vince Wilfork* 4.00
88 *Randy Starks* 3.00
89 *Chris Cooley* 3.00
90 *Dwan Edwards* 3.00
91 *Patrick Crayton* 3.00
92 *Sean Jones* 3.00
93 *Sean Ryan* 3.00
94 *Chris Gamble* 4.00
95 *Will Smith* 4.00
96 *Sloan Thomas* 3.00
97 *Tim Euhus* 3.00
98 *Tommie Harris* 4.00
99 *Will Poole* 3.00
100 *Karlos Dansby* 3.00
101 *Bernard Berrian Jsy* 5.00
102 *DeAngelo Hall Jsy* 6.00
103 *Mewelde Moore Jsy* 6.00
104 *Rashaun Woods Jsy* 6.00
105 *Reggie Williams Jsy* 6.00
106 *Derrick Hamilton Jsy* 4.00
107 *Kellen Winslow Jr. Jsy* 10.00
108 *Devard Darling Jsy* 5.00
109 *Michael Clayton Jsy* 8.00
110 *Larry Fitzgerald Jsy* 12.00
111 *Greg Jones JSY* 6.00
112 *Chris Perry Jsy* 8.00
113 *Lee Evans Jsy* 8.00
114 *Tatum Bell Jsy* 6.00
115 *Steven Jackson Jsy* 10.00
116 *Matt Schaub Jsy* 8.00
117 *Ben Troupe Jsy* 4.00
118 *Devery Henderson Jsy* 5.00
119 *Ben Watson Jsy* 5.00
120 *J.P. Losman Jsy* 8.00
121 *Keary Colbert Jsy* 6.00
122 *Darius Watts Jsy* 6.00
123 *Cedric Cobbs Jsy* 5.00
124 *Josh McCown Jsy* 6.00
125 *Michael Jenkins Jsy* 5.00
126 *Eli Manning Auto/199* 200.00
127 *Roy Williams Auto/199* 100.00
128 *Kevin Jones Auto/199* 80.00
129 *Philip Rivers Auto/199* 80.00
130 *Ben Roethlisberger Auto/199* 300.00
131 *Carlos Francis Auto* 6.00
132 *Bradlee Van Pelt Auto* 12.00
133 *Michael Turner Auto* 6.00
134 *Kenechi Udeze Auto* 10.00
135 *Jeff Smoker Auto* 12.00
136 *Josh Harris Auto* 6.00
137 *Derrick Strait Auto* 8.00
138 *Jonathan Vilma Auto* 10.00
139 *Triandos Luke Auto* 6.00
140 *Jim Sorgi Auto* 8.00
141 *Ryan Krause Auto* 6.00
142 *Julius Jones Auto* 50.00
143 *Mark Jones Auto* 6.00
144 *P.K. Sam Auto* 8.00
145 *B.J. Symons Auto* 10.00
146 *Adimchinobe Echemandu Auto* 6.00
147 *Casey Bramlet Auto* 6.00
148 *Clarence Moore Auto* 6.00
149 *D.J. Williams Auto* 10.00
150 *Jeris McIntyre Auto* 8.00
151 *Jerricho Cotchery Auto* 8.00
152 *Andy Hall Auto* 6.00
153 *Samie Parker Auto* 8.00
154 *Maurice Mann Auto* 6.00
155 *Jonathan Smith Auto* 6.00
156 *Derrick Ward Auto* 6.00
157 *D.J. Hackett Auto* 8.00
158 *Craig Krenzel Auto* 12.00
159 *Jared Lorenzen Auto* 8.00
160 *Cody Pickett Auto* 10.00
161 *Jamaar Taylor Auto* 8.00
162 *Michael Boulware Auto* 8.00
163 *Matt Mauck Auto* 10.00
164 *John Navarre Auto* 12.00
165 *Ahmad Carroll Auto* 12.00
166 *Bruce Perry Auto* 6.00
167 *Erik Jensen Auto* 6.00
168 *Matt Kranchick Auto* 6.00
169 *Courtney Anderson Auto* 6.00
170 *Nate Lawrie Auto* 6.00
171 *Thomas Tapeh Auto* 6.00
172 *Courtney Watson Auto* 6.00
173 *Drew Carter Auto* 6.00
174 *Ricardo Colclough Auto* 8.00
175 *Dontarrious Thomas Auto* 6.00
176 *Ernest Wilford Auto*
177 *Quincy Wilson Auto* 8.00
178 *Derek Abney Auto* 8.00
179 *Jeff Dugan Auto* 6.00
180 *Ben Hartsock Auto* 8.00
181 *Matt Kegel Auto* 8.00
182 *Derrick Knight Auto* 6.00
183 *Teddy Lehman Auto* 10.00
184 *Johnnie Morant Auto* 8.00
185 *Bob Sanders Auto* 8.00
186 *Michael Gaines Auto* 6.00
187 *Daryl Smith Auto* 6.00
188 *Jason Babin Auto* 12.00

2004 Bowman's Best Green

Stars: 1X-2X
Rookies (81-100): 1.5X
Rookie Jsy (101-125): 1X
Rookie Autos (131-188): 1X
Green Production 499 Sets

2004 Bowman's Best Red

Stars: 3X-6X
Rookies (81-100): 2X-4X
Rookie Jsy (101-125): 1X-2X
Rookie Autos (131-188): 1.5X-3X
Red Production 50 Sets

NM/M

2004 Bowman's Best Best Coverage Jersey Duals

NM/M
Production 25 Sets
BCBF Anquan Boldin, Larry Fitzgerald 40.00
BCBR Tom Brady, Philip Rivers 60.00
BCMM Peyton Manning, Eli Manning 100.00
BCPJ Clinton Portis, Steven Jackson 40.00
BCWJ Ricky Williams, Kevin Jones 20.00

2004 Bowman's Best Double Coverage Autographs

NM/M
Production 50 Sets
DCAJE Steven Jackson, Lee Evans 80.00
DCAMF Eli Manning, Larry Fitzgerald 250.00
DCAPJ Chris Perry, Kevin Jones 80.00
DCARW Philip Rivers, Roy Williams 120.00
DCAWR Reggie Williams, Ben Roethlisberger

2004 Bowman's Best Double Coverage Jerseys

NM/M
Common Player: 12.00
Production 50 Sets
DCEJ Lee Evans, Michael Jenkins 20.00
DCFW Larry Fitzgerald, Reggie Williams 20.00
DCJB Julius Jones, Tatum Bell 30.00
DCJJ Steven Jackson, Kevin Jones 40.00
DCMR Eli Manning, Ben Roethlisberger/25 100.00
DCPJ Chris Perry, Greg Jones 12.00
DCRL Philip Rivers, J.P. Losman 20.00
DCSM Matt Schaub, Luke McCown 12.00
DCWC Roy Williams, Michael Clayton 25.00
DCWW Kellen Winslow Jr., Ben Watson 20.00

2004 Bowman's Best Single Coverage Autographs

NM/M
Production 50 Sets
SCADD Domanick Davis 12.00
SCAAG Ahman Green
SCADH Dante Hall 15.00
SCAPM Peyton Manning 100.00
SCACP Chad Pennington 25.00

2004 Bowman's Best Single Coverage Jerseys

NM/M
Common Player: 10.00
Production 50 Sets
SCCB Champ Bailey 15.00
SCDB Drew Bledsoe 15.00
SCAB Anquan Boldin 12.00
SCTB Tom Brady 20.00
SCCC Chris Chambers 12.00
SCPM Peyton Manning 20.00
SCCP Clinton Portis 15.00
SCKR Koren Robinson 10.00
SCES Emmitt Smith 30.00
SCRW Ricky Williams 12.00

2004 Bowman's Best Ultimate Coverage Jersey Autographs

NM/M
Production 25 Sets
UCFW Larry Fitzgerald, Roy Williams 150.00
UCJP Steven Jackson, Chris Perry 100.00
UCJR Kevin Jones, Ben Roethlisberger
UCMR Eli Manning, Philip Rivers 250.00
UCWE Reggie Williams, Lee Evans

1952 Bread For Health

These early 1950s bread end labels feature 32 NFL players. The cards, which measure 2-3/4" x 2-3/4", were found in loaves of Fisher's Bread (New Jersey, New York and Pennsylvania) and NBC Bread in Michigan. The cards are unnumbered and are blank-backed. A B.E.B. copyright is on the card front, along with an informational note.

NM/M
Complete Set (32): 4,300
Common Player: 90.00
(1) Frankie Albert 120.00
(2) Elmer Angsman 90.00
(3) Dick Barwegen 90.00
(4) Sammy Baugh 350.00
(5) Charley Conerly 200.00
(6) Glenn Davis 150.00
(7) Don Doll 90.00
(8) Tom Fears 150.00
(9) Harry Gilmer 100.00
(10) Otto Graham 350.00
(11) Pat Harder 110.00
(12) Bobby Lane 300.00
(13) Sid Luckman 200.00
(14) Johnny Lujack 175.00
(15) John Panelli 90.00
(16) Barney Poole 90.00
(17) George Ratterman 90.00
(18) Tobin Rote 125.00
(19) Jack Russell 90.00
(20) Lou Rymkus 90.00
(21) Joe Signiago 90.00
(22) Mac Speedie 120.00
(23) Bill Swiacki 90.00
(24) Tommy Thompson 120.00
(25) Y.A. Tittle 300.00
(26) Clayton Tonnemaker 90.00
(27) Charlie Trippi 110.00
(28) Clyde Turner 150.00
(29) Steve Van Buren 150.00
(30) Bill Walsh 90.00
(31) Bob Waterfield 200.00
(32) Jim White 90.00

1992 Breyers Bookmarks

Breyers Bookmarks contained 66 bookmarks measuring 2" x 8". The set was used to promote reading in the city of 11 featured teams. Card fronts feature a cut-out of the player against a yellow background with books. Cards are numbered on the front and arranged in order by teams.

NM/M
Complete Set (66): 150.00
Common Player: 1.50
1 Greg Townsend 1.50
2 Steve Wisniewski 1.50
3 Art Shell (CO) 2.50
4 Jeff Jaeger 1.50
5 Lisa O'Day (Cheerleader) 1.50
6 Los Angeles Raiders (Helmet and SB trophies) 1.50
7 Jerry Rice 12.00
8 Don Griffin 1.50
9 John Taylor 1.50
10 Joe Montana 18.00
11 Mike Walker 1.50
12 San Francisco 49ers (Helmet) 1.50
13 Junior Seau 3.00
14 John Friesz 1.50
15 Ronnie Harmon 1.50
16 Marion Butts 1.50
17 Gill Byrd 1.50
18 San Diego Chargers (Helmet) 1.50
19 Kelly Stouffer 1.50
20 John Kasay 1.50
21 Andy Heck 1.50
22 Jacob Green 1.50
23 Eugene Robinson 1.50
24 Seattle Seahawks (Helmet) 1.50
25 Pat Swilling 1.50
26 Vaughn Johnson 1.50
27 Bobby Hebert 1.50
28 Floyd Turner 1.50
29 Rickey Jackson 1.50
30 New Orleans Saints (Helmet) 1.50
31 Harvey Williams 1.50
32 Derrick Thomas 3.00
33 Bill Maas 1.50
34 Tim Grunhard 1.50
35 Jonathan Hayes 1.50
36 Kansas City Chiefs (Mascot) 1.50
37 Rich Gannon 1.50
38 Tim Irwin 1.50
39 Audray McMillian 1.50
40 Gary Zimmerman 1.50
41 Hassan Jones 1.50
42 Minnesota Vikings (Helmet) 1.50
43 Eric Green 1.50
44 Louis Lipps 1.50
45 Rod Woodson 1.50
46 Merril Hoge 1.50
47 Gary Anderson (RB) 1.50
48 Pittsburgh Steelers (60-Season Emblem) 1.50
49 Anthony Johnson 1.50
50 Bill Brooks 1.50
51 Jeff Herrod 1.50
52 Mike Prior 1.50
53 Jeff George 3.00
54 Ted Marchibroda Indianapolis Colts (CO) 1.50
55 Troy Aikman 12.00
56 Jay Novacek 1.50
57 Emmitt Smith 20.00
58 Michael Irvin 3.00
59 Dorie Braddy (Cheerleader) 1.50
60 Dallas Cowboys (Super Bowl trophy) 1.50
61 Clay Matthews 1.50
62 Tommy Vardell 1.50
63 Eric Turner 1.50
64 Mike Johnson 1.50
65 James Jones 1.50
66 Cleveland Browns (Helmet) 1.50

1990 British Petroleum

This 36-card set featured color fronts and black backs (with either contest rules or advertising). The cards were handed out two at a time in California, with the goal of the game to collect two adjacent numbers (1-2, 3-4). One of the two was difficult to find, with the contest expiring in October of 1991. There were also five instant win cards: Andre Tippett, Freeman McNeil, Clay Matthews, Tim Harris and Deion Sanders. Numbers 1, 3, 6, 8 and 10 had six different possible players.

NM/M
Complete Set (36): 45.00
Common Player: .50
1A John Elway 3.00
1B Boomer Esiason .50
1C Jim Everett .50
1D Bernie Kosar .50
1E Karl Mecklenburg .50
1F Bruce Smith .50
2 Deion Sanders
3A Roger Craig .50
3B Randall Cunningham .50
3C Keith Jackson .50
3D Dan Marino 10.00
3E Freddie Joe Nunn .50
3F Jerry Rice 5.00
3G Vinny Testaverde .50
3H John L. Williams .50
4 Tim Harris
5 Clay Matthews
6A Neal Anderson .50
6B Duane Bickett .50
6C Ronnie Lott .50
6D Anthony Munoz .50
6E Christian Okoye .50
6F Barry Sanders 5.00
7 Freeman McNeil
8A Cornelius Bennett .50
8B Anthony Carter .50
8C Jim Kelly 1.00
8D Louis Lipps .50
8E Phil Simms .50
8F Billy Ray Smith .50
8G Lawrence Taylor 1.00
9 Andre Tippett
10A Bo Jackson 1.50
10B Howie Long .50
10C Don Majkowski .50
10D Art Monk 1.00
10E Warren Moon 1.00
10F Mike Singletary 1.00
10G Al Toon .50
10H Herschel Walker 1.00
10I Reggie White 1.50

1968-70 Broncos

This 53-card set contains black and white photos and black, unnumbered card backs. The cards measure 5" x 7" and include mostly posed shots.

NM/M
Complete Set (53): 130.00
Common Player: 2.00
1 Bob Anderson 4.00
2 Tom Beer 4.00
3 Phil Brady 2.00
4 Sam Brunelli 3.00
5 George Burrell 2.00
6 Carter Campbell 2.00
7 Grady Cavness 3.00
8 Barney Chavous 6.00
9 Dave Costa 3.00
10 Ken Criter (Head shot) 2.00
11 Ken Criter (Head-and-shoulders) 2.00
12 Carl Cunningham 2.00
13 Mike Current (Left-side shot) 4.00
14 Mike Current (Right-side shot) 4.00
15 Joe Dawkins 4.00
16 Al Denson (Offensive end) 4.00
17 Al Denson (Wide receiver) 4.00

18 Wallace Dickey 2.00
19 John Embree 2.00
20 Fred Forsberg 2.00
21 Jack Gehrke 2.00
22 Cornell Gordon 3.00
23 John Grant 2.00
24 Charlie Greer (Head shot) 2.00
25 Charlie Greer (Head-and-shoulders) 2.00
26 Dwight Harrison 2.00
27 Walter Highsmith 2.00
28 Gus Hollomon 2.00
29 Larron Jackson (Left-side shot) 2.00
30 Larron Jackson (Right-side shot) 2.00
31 Calvin Jones 4.00
32 Larry Kaminski (Left-side shot) 2.00
33 Larry Kaminski (Right-side shot) 2.00
34 Bill Laskey 2.00
35 Pete Liske 4.00
36 Fran Lynch 2.00
37 Tom Lyons (Guard on front) 2.00
38 Tommy Lyons (Center on front) 2.00
39 Rex Mirich 2.00
40 Randy Montgomery (Left-side shot) 2.00
41 Randy Montgomery (Right-side shot) 2.00
42 Tom Oberg 2.00
43 Steve Ramsey 6.00
44 Frank Richter 2.00
45 Mike Schnitker 2.00
46 Roger Shoals 2.00
47 Jerry Simmons (Looking toward upper left corner of picture) 4.00
48 Jerry Simmons (Head turned slightly toward right) 4.00
49 Paul Smith (Head shot) 4.00
50 Paul Smith (Head-and-shoulders) 4.00
51 Olen Underwood 2.00
52 Dave Washington 2.00
53 Bob Young 2.00

1980 Broncos Stamps Police

This unnumbered set contains nine different stamps, with each stamp containing two players with a Broncos logo in between. The stamps were given away (one per week) at Albertson's food stores in the Denver area. The set measures 3" x 3" and is tri-sponsored by Albertson's, the Kiwanis Club and local police. There is a poster that the stamps fit on that sold at the time for 99 cents.

NM/M
Complete Set (9): 12.00
Common Player: 1.00
1 Barney Chavous, Rubin Carter 1.00
2 Bernard Jackson, Haven Moses 1.00
3 Tom Jackson, Riley Odoms 3.00
4 Brison Manor, Steve Foley 1.00
5 Claudie Minor, Randy Gradishar 1.00
6 Craig Morton, Tom Glassic 2.00
7 Jim Turner, Bob Swenson 1.00
8 Rick Upchurch, Billy Thompson 1.00
9 Louis Wright, Joe Rizzo 1.00

1982 Broncos Police

Measuring 2-5/8" x 4-1/8", the 15-card set boasts the player's jersey number, name, position, team and Broncos' helmet under a photo. The unnumbered card backs feature Broncos Tips inside a box, which is topped by a Broncos' helmet. The set's sponsor is listed at the bottom center.

NM/M
Complete Set (15): 120.00
Common Player: 2.00
7 Craig Morton 8.00
11 Luke Prestridge 2.00
20 Louis Wright 4.00
24 Rick Parros 2.00
36 Bill Thompson 4.00
41 Rob Lytle 2.00
46 Dave Preston (SP) 5.00
51 Bob Swenson 2.00
53 Randy Gradishar (SP) 30.00
57 Tom Jackson 12.00
60 Paul Howard 2.00
68 Rubin Carter 2.00
79 Barney Chavous (SP) 30.00
80 Rick Upchurch 8.00
88 Riley Odoms (SP) 12.00

A player's name in *italic* type indicates a rookie card.

1984 Broncos KOA

Handed out at Safeway or Dairy Queen stores, this 24-card set was part of the KOA Match 'N Win and KOA/Denver Broncos Silver Anniversary Sweepstakes. Measuring 2" x 4", with a bottom tab measuring 1-1/8", the card fronts showcase a black-and-white photo, with the player's name, number and position inside a banner under the photo. The American Football League and various sponsor logos appear under the photo. The card's tab featured three silver footballs that could be scratched off with a coin. The card backs feature the sweepstakes' rules. Besides the player's jersey number, the cards are unnumbered.

NM/M
Complete Set (24): 90.00
Common Player: 1.00
7 Craig Morton 5.00
11 Bob Anderson (SP) 10.00
12 Charlie Johnson 4.00
15 Jim Turner 2.00
21 Gene Mingo 1.00
22 Fran Lynch 1.00
23 Goose Gonsoulin 2.00
24 Otis Armstrong 4.00
24 Willie Brown 6.00
25 Haven Moses 2.00
36 Billy Thompson 2.00
42 Bill Van Heusen 1.00
44 Floyd Little (SP) 16.00
53 Randy Gradishar (SP) 14.00
71 Claudie Minor (SP) 5.00
72 Sam Brunelli 1.00
74 Mike Current 1.00
75 Eldon Danenhauer 1.00
78 Marv Montgomery 1.00
81 Billy Masters 1.00
82 Bob Scarpitto 1.00
87 Lionel Taylor 2.00
87 Rich Jackson 1.00
88 Riley Odoms 2.00

1987 Broncos Orange Crush

This standard sized nine-card set honors former Denver Broncos players who are featured in the stadium's Ring of Fame. The card fronts feature a black-and-white photo bordered with blue and orange. The Orange Crush logo is on an angle at the top of the card front. The player's number, name, position and years played with the Broncos are printed underneath the photo. The Broncos' Ring of Fame logo is located at the bottom right. The backs feature "1st Annual Collector's Edition Ring of Famer" at the top, with his name, number, position, years played and highlights printed below. The info is packaged inside a box, with the Crush logo appearing at the bottom. The KOA Radio logo is printed at the very bottom of the card back. The cards were handed out for three weeks at 7-11 and Albertsons stores in the Denver area.

NM/M
Complete Set (9): 4.50
Common Player: .50
1 Billy Thompson .50
2 Lionel Taylor .50
3 Goose Gonsoulin .50
4 Paul Smith .50
5 Rich Jackson .50
6 Charlie Johnson .50
7 Floyd Little .75
8 Frank Tripucka .50
9 Gerald Phipps (Owner 1960-1981) .50

1986 Brownell Heisman

Measuring 7-15/16" x 10", the black-and-white cards feature Art Brownell artwork of Heisman Trophy winners. The blank-backed cards are unnumbered. The cards are listed in chronological order. Even though Archie Griffin won the Heisman in both 1974 and 1975, he is featured on only one card. The fronts feature the year the player won the Heisman, plus a short write-up.

NM/M
Complete Set (50): 250.00
Common Player: 5.00
1 Jay Berwanger 4.00
2 Larry Kelley 4.00
3 Clint Frank 4.00
4 Davey O'Brien 4.00
5 Niles Kinnick 10.00
6 Tom Harmon 5.00
7 Bruce Smith 4.00
8 Frank Sinkwich 4.00
9 Angelo Bertelli 4.00
10 Les Horvath 4.00
11 Doc Blanchard 8.00
12 Glenn Davis 8.00
13 Johnny Lujack 12.00
14 Doak Walker 10.00
15 Leon Hart 4.00
16 Vic Janowicz 10.00
17 Dick Kazmaier 4.00
18 Billy Vessels 4.00
19 John Lattner 8.00
20 Alan Ameche 6.00
21 Howard Cassady 5.00
22 Paul Hornung 18.00
23 John David Crow 4.00
24 Pete Dawkins 4.00
25 Billy Cannon 4.00
26 Joe Bellino 4.00
27 Ernie Davis 30.00
28 Terry Baker 4.00
29 Roger Staubach 35.00
30 John Huarte 4.00
31 Mike Garrett 4.00
32 Steve Spurrier 15.00
33 Gary Beban 4.00
34 O.J. Simpson 20.00
35 Steve Owens 5.00
36 Jim Plunkett 10.00
37 Pat Sullivan 4.00
38 Johnny Rodgers 4.00
39 John Cappelletti 4.00
40 Archie Griffin 6.00
41 Tony Dorsett 18.00
42 Earl Campbell 18.00
43 Billy Sims 8.00
44 Charles White 4.00
45 George Rogers 4.00
46 Marcus Allen 10.00
47 Herschel Walker 8.00
48 Mike Rozier 4.00
49 Doug Flutie 8.00
50 Bo Jackson 10.00

1946 Browns Sears

Measuring 2-1/2" x 4", the eight-card set was released by Sears and Roebuck. The set showcases players from the Cleveland Browns' initial season. Card fronts boast a black-and-white photo of the player and a slogan to follow the Browns and shop at Sears. The cards are unnumbered.

NM/M
Complete Set (8): 280.00
Common Player: 35.00
(1) Ernie Blandin 35.00
(2) Jim Daniell 35.00
(3) Fred Evans 35.00
(4) Frank Gatski 50.00
(5) Otto Graham 150.00
(6) Dante Lavelli 75.00
(7) Mel Maceau 35.00
(8) George Young 35.00

1950 Browns Team Issue

Measuring 6-1/2" x 9", the five-card set showcases a black-and-white posed player photo, which is bordered in white. The player's name, printed in cursive, also is on the front of the blank-backed and unnumbered cards.

NM/M
Complete Set (5): 75.00
Common Player: 10.00
1 Frank Gatski 15.00
2 Tommy James 10.00
3 Don Moselle 10.00
4 Marion Motley 30.00
5 Derrell F. Palmer 10.00

1951 Browns White Border

Measuring 6-1/2" x 9", the 25-card team-issued set was anchored by a posed black-and-white photo on the front, bordered in white. The player's name is printed in cursive on the front of the unnumbered and blank-backed cards. The set was housed in an off-white envelope with brown and orange trim. "Cleveland Browns Photographs" is also printed on the envelopes.

NM/M
Complete Set (25): 250.00
Common Player: 5.00
1 Tony Adamle 8.00
2 Alex Agase 8.00
3 Rex Bumgardner 5.00
4 Emerson Cole 5.00
5 Len Ford 12.00
6 Frank Gatski 12.00
7 Horace Gillom 5.00
8 Ken Gorgal 5.00
9 Otto Graham 45.00
10 Forrest Gregg 5.00
11 Lou Groza 20.00
12 Hal Herring 5.00
13 Lin Houston 5.00
14 Weldon Humble 5.00
15 Tommy James 5.00
16 Dub Jones 8.00
17 Warren Lahr 5.00
18 Dante Lavelli 20.00
19 Cliff Lewis 5.00
20 Marion Motley 20.00
21 Lou Rymkus 8.00
22 Mac Speedie 10.00
23 Tommy Thompson 10.00
24 Bill Willis 15.00
25 George Young 15.00

1954-55 Browns White Border

Measuring 8-1/2" x 10", the 20-card set showcases posed player shots on the front, which are bordered in white. The unnumbered and blank-backed cards feature the player's name and position at the bottom inside a white border.

NM/M
Complete Set (20): 125.00
Common Player: 5.00
1 Maurice Bassett 5.00
2 Harold Bradley 5.00
3 Darrell Brewster 5.00
4 Don Colo 5.00
5 Len Ford 10.00
6 Bob Gain 5.00
7 Frank Gatski 10.00
8 Abe Gibron 5.00
9 Tommy James 5.00
10 Dub Jones 7.00
11 Ken Konz 5.00
12 Warren Lahr 5.00
13 Dante Lavelli 15.00
14 Carlton Massey 5.00
15 Mike McCormack 10.00
16 Walt Michaels 5.00
17 Chuck Noll 25.00
18 Don Paul 5.00
19 Ray Renfro 10.00
20 George Ratterman 5.00

1955 Browns Carling Beer

Measuring 8-1/2" x 11-1/2", the 10-card set featured a large black-and-white photo on the front of the white-bordered cards. Carling's Black Label Beer and team name are printed below the photo in black. "DBL 54" is printed in the bottom right corner.

NM/M
Complete Set (10): 250.00
Common Player: 10.00
1 Darrell Brewster 10.00
2 Tom Catlin 10.00
3 Len Ford 20.00
4 Otto Graham 75.00
5 Lou Groza 40.00
6 Kenny Konz 10.00
7 Dante Lavelli 25.00
8 Mike McCormack 20.00
9 Fred Morrison 10.00
10 Chuck Noll 60.00

1955 Browns Color Postcards

These six postcards, which measure 6" x 9", boast a full-bleed color photo on the front. The unnumbered backs have the player's name and team at the top left, with the "place stamp here" box in the upper left and "Giant Post Card" centered on the right. The cards feature rounded corners.

NM/M
Complete Set (6): 140.00
Common Player: 10.00
1 Mo Bassett 10.00
2 Don Colo 10.00
3 Frank Gatski 20.00
4 Lou Groza 70.00
5 Dante Lavelli 40.00
6 George Ratterman 15.00

1959 Browns Carling Beer

Measuring 8-1/2" x 11-1/2", the nine-card set featured a black-and-white posed photo, which was bordered in white. The player's name and position are printed in black inside a white rectangle inside the photo. Printed under the photo are "Carling Black Label Beer" and "The Cleveland Browns." The backs are usually blank, but can be stamped with "Henry M. Barr Studios, Berea, Ohio BE4-1330." The card fronts are numbered in the lower right corner, except for Jim Brown's photo card. The set was also reprinted in the late 1980s on thinner paper and most likely show the Henry M. Barr stamp on the back. Some sources say the Brown photo is only available in the reprint set.

NM/M
Complete Set (9): 130.00
Common Player: 10.00
A Leroy Bolden 10.00
B Vince Costello 10.00
C Galen Fiss 10.00
E Lou Groza 30.00
F Walt Michaels 15.00
G Bobby Mitchell 30.00
J Bob Gain 10.00
K Billy Howton 15.00
NNO Jim Brown (DP) 8.00

1961 Browns Carling Beer

Measuring 8-1/2" x 11-1/2", the 10 black-and-white cards feature posed photos on the front, with the player's name and position printed inside a white rectangle inside the photo. "Carling Back Label Beer" and "The Cleveland Browns" are printed underneath the photo on the card front. The card numbers appear in the lower right corner on the front, while the backs are blank.

NM/M
Complete Set (10): 200.00
Common Player: 10.00
A Milt Plum 20.00
B Mike McCormack 20.00
C Bob Gain 10.00
D John Morrow 10.00
E Jim Brown 80.00
F Bobby Mitchell 35.00
G Bobby Franklin 10.00
H Jim Ray Smith 10.00
K Jim Houston 18.00
L Ray Renfro 15.00

1961 Browns National City Bank

Measuring 2-1/2" x 3-9/16", the 36-card set was released in sheets of six cards. Each sheet was numbered, while each individual card was numbered. The card fronts feature "Quarterback Club Brownie Card 1961 Cleveland Browns" at the top. The posed photos anchor the front, with "issued in 1961 by Cleveland's Oldest Bank National City Bank" printed underneath. The card backs are numbered at the top with a set number and a player (card) number. The player's name, position, bio and write-up are also on the back. The bottom of the card back includes the National City Bank logo.

NM/M
Complete Set (36): 2,000
Common Player: 40.00
1 Mike McCormack 80.00
2 Jim Brown 575.00
3 Leon Clarke 40.00
4 Walt Michaels 40.00
5 Jim Ray Smith 40.00
6 Quarterback Club Membership Card 220.00
7 Len Dawson 225.00
8 John Morrow 40.00
9 Bernie Parrish 40.00
10 Floyd Peters 40.00
11 Paul Wiggin 40.00
12 John Wooten 40.00
13 Ray Renfro 40.00
14 Galen Fiss 40.00
15 Dave Lloyd 40.00
16 Dick Schafrath 40.00
17 Ross Fichtner 40.00
18 Gern Nagler 40.00
19 Rich Kreitling 40.00
20 Duane Putnam 40.00
21 Vince Costello 40.00
22 Jim Shofner 40.00
23 Sam Baker 40.00
24 Bob Gain 40.00
25 Lou Groza 100.00
26 Don Fleming 40.00
27 Tom Watkins 40.00
28 Jim Houston 40.00
29 Larry Stephens 40.00
30 Bobby Mitchell 100.00
31 Bobby Franklin 40.00
32 Charlie Ferguson 40.00
33 Johnny Brewer 40.00
34 Bob Crespino 40.00
35 Milt Plum 40.00
36 Preston Powell 40.00

1961 Browns White Border

Measuring 8-1/2" x 10-1/2", the 20-card set showcased black-and-white photos on the front, with the player's name and position listed inside a white box inside the photo. The fronts are bordered in white. The cards are unnumbered and blank-backed.

NM/M
Complete Set (20): 160.00
Common Player: 5.00
1 Jim Brown 75.00
2 Galen Fiss 5.00
3 Don Fleming 5.00
4 Bobby Franklin 5.00
5 Bob Gain 5.00
6 Jim Houston 5.00
7 Rich Kreitling 5.00
8 Dave Lloyd 5.00
9 Mike McCormack 12.00
10 Bobby Mitchell 16.00
11 John Morrow 5.00
12 Bernie Parrish 5.00
13 Milt Plum 5.00
14 Ray Renfro 5.00
15 Dick Schafrath 5.00
16 Jim Shofner 5.00
17 Jim Ray Smith 5.00
18 Tom Watkins 5.00
19 Paul Wiggin 5.00
20 John Wooten 5.00

1963 Browns White Border

Measuring 7-1/2" x 9-1/2", the 26-card set showcases black-and-white photos on the front. The card backs are blank. Each card is unnumbered.

NM/M
Complete Set (26): 120.00
Common Player: 5.00
1 Johnny Brewer 5.00
2 Monte Clark 5.00
3 Gary Collins 10.00
4 Vince Costello 5.00
5 Bob Crespino 5.00
6 Ross Fichtner 5.00
7 Galen Fiss 5.00
8 Bob Gain 5.00
9 Bill Glass 5.00
10 Ernie Green 10.00
11 Lou Groza 16.00
12 Gene Hickerson 7.00
13 Jim Houston 5.00
14 Tom Hutchinson 5.00
15 Rich Kreitling 5.00
16 Mike Lucci 5.00
17 John Morrow 5.00
18 Jim Ninowski 5.00
19 Frank Parker 5.00
20 Bernie Parrish 5.00
21 Ray Renfro 5.00
22 Dick Schafrath 5.00
23 Jim Shofner 5.00
24 Ken Webb 5.00
25 Paul Wiggin 5.00
26 John Wooten 5.00

1985 Browns Coke/Mr. Hero

Measuring 2-3/4" x 3-1/4", the 48-card set was released on six sheets of eight cards. The card fronts are anchored by a photo, with the player's name and position listed at the bottom center. The player's jersey number is printed in large numerals in the lower left. The unnumbered card backs spotlight the player's name, position, bio and career highlights. Coupons were included on each complete sheet.

NM/M
Complete Set (48): 25.00
Common Player: .50
7 Jeff Gossett (4) .75
9 Matt Bahr (1) .75
16 Paul McDonald (4) .50
18 Gary Danielson (5) .50
19 Bernie Kosar (6) 2.50
20 Don Rogers (4) .50
22 Felix Wright (2) .50
26 Greg Allen (3) .50
27 Al Gross (2) .50
29 Hanford Dixon (5) .50
30 Boyce Green (1) .50
31 Frank Minnifield (1) .50
34 Kevin Mack (3) 1.00
37 Chris Rockins (1) .50
38 Johnny Davis (5) .50
44 Earnest Byner (2) 1.25
47 Larry Braziel (4) .50
50 Tom Cousineau (6) .50
51 Eddie Johnson (2) .50
55 Curtis Weathers (1) .50
56 Chip Banks (6) .75
57 Clay Matthews (5) 1.75
58 Scott Nicolas (1) .50
61 Mike Baab (4) .50
62 George Lilja (5) .50
63 Cody Risien (6) .50
65 Mark Krerowicz (3) .50
68 Robert Jackson (4) .50
69 Dan Fike (2) .50
72 Dave Puzzuoli (1) .50
74 Paul Farren (2) .50
77 Rickey Bolden (3) .50
78 Carl Hairston (2) .50
79 Bob Golic (6) .50
80 Willis Adams (2) .50
81 Harry Holt (3) .50
82 Ozzie Newsome (3) 1.75
83 Fred Banks (3) .50
84 Glen Young (1) .50
85 Clarence Weathers (6) .50
86 Brian Brennan (5) .50
87 Travis Tucker (6) .50

88	Reggie Langhorne (5)	.50
89	John Jefferson (4)	1.00
91	Sam Clancy (4)	.50
96	Reggie Camp (5)	.50
99	Keith Baldwin (6)	.50
NNO	Action Photo (Clay Matthews tackling Eric Dickerson) (3)	1.75

1987 Browns Louis Rich

Louis Rich produced this set to be a promotion in its products. After the cards were printed the promotion was pulled. After the set's cancellation, Oscar Mayer gave collectors who stopped into the Cleveland corporate office a set. The cards measure 5" x 7-1/8".

		NM/M
Complete Set (5):		45.00
Common Player:		5.00
1	Jim Brown, Bobby Mitchell	22.00
2	Otto Graham	15.00
3	Lou Groza	10.00
4	Dante Lavelli (Question Mark)	5.00
5	Marion Motley	5.00

1992 Browns Sunoco

NFL Properties produced this 24-card set as a promotion at Ohio-area Sunoco gas stations. Spotlighting Browns who have been inducted into the Hall of Fame, the player card fronts feature a full-bleed photo. The player's last name is printed in large orange letters at the bottom of the card, with a small Sunoco logo printed over the top of the name. The player card backs feature the player's career highlights and name printed over a ghosted image of the player. Logos for radio stations WMMS and WHK are printed at the bottom of the card backs. Player cards are numbered on the bottom right. The set was sold in three-card cello packs which included a cover card, player card and sweepstakes entry card. Randomly inserted in packs were autographed cards. The cover card fronts had "The Cleveland Browns' Collection" at the top, with a Browns' helmet at the center and the player's name underneath. The cover card backs showcase the sponsors' and Pro Football Hall of Fame logos. Cover card backs are not numbered. In addition, albums were issued to hold the set.

		NM/M
Complete Set (24):		16.00
Common Player (1-12):		.75
Common Cover (1C-12C):		.25
1	Otto Graham (Player card)	2.50
1C	Otto Graham (Cover card)	.25
2	Paul Brown (CO) (Player card)	1.50
2C	Paul Brown (CO) (Cover card)	.25
3	Marion Motley (Player card)	1.25
3C	Marion Motley (Cover card)	.25
4	Jim Brown (Player card)	4.00
4C	Jim Brown (Cover card)	.50
5	Lou Groza (Player card)	1.25
5C	Lou Groza (Cover card)	.25
6	Dante Lavelli (Player card)	1.00
6C	Dante Lavelli (Cover card)	.25
7	Len Ford (Player card)	1.00
7C	Len Ford (Cover card)	.25
8	Bill Willis (Player card)	1.00
8C	Bill Willis (Cover card)	.25
9	Bobby Mitchell (Player card)	1.50
9C	Bobby Mitchell (Cover card)	.25
10	Paul Warfield (Player card)	1.50
10C	Paul Warfield (Cover card)	.25
11	Mike McCormack (Player card)	1.00
11C	Mike McCormack (Cover card)	.25
12	Frank Gatski (Player card)	1.00
12C	Frank Gatski (Cover card)	.25
---	Album	2.50

A player's name in *italic* type indicates a rookie card.

2004 Browns Donruss Playoff National

		NM/M
Common Player:		1.50
1	Kellen Winslow Jr.	8.00
2	Quincy Morgan	2.00
3	Andre Davis	1.50
4	Willie Green	2.00
5	Lee Suggs	3.00
6	Jeff Garcia	3.00
NNO	Kellen Winslow Jr. Silver	8.00

2004 Browns Fleer Tradition National

		NM/M
Common Player:		.75
1	Jeff Garcia	2.00
2	Lee Suggs	2.00
3	Quincy Morgan	1.00
4	William Green	1.25
5	Andre Davis	.75
6	Courtney Brown	1.00
7	Dennis Northcutt	.75
8	Luke McCown	1.00
9	Andra Davis	.75
10	Kellen Winslow Jr.	5.00
NNO	Kellen Winslow Jr. Threads	10.00

1980 Buccaneers Police

Measuring 2-5/8" x 4-1/8", the 56-card set boasts a photo on the front, with the player's name, position and bio underneath on the left. The Bucs' helmet is printed in the lower right. The unnumbered card backs have "Kids and Kops tips from the Buccaneers" at the top. A definition of a football term and a safety tip are included, while the Coca-Cola logo is printed above the various sponsor names at the bottom. Cards including the Paradyne Corp. name on the back are scarce variations, which are valued at two to three times more.

		NM/M
Complete Set (56):		150.00
Common Player:		3.00
1	Ricky Bell	8.00
2	Rick Berns	3.00
3	Tom Blanchard	3.00
4	Scot Brantley	3.00
5	Aaron Brown	3.00
6	Cedric Brown	3.00
7	Mark Cotney	3.00
8	Randy Crowder	3.00
9	Gary Davis	3.00
10	Johnny Davis	3.00
11	Tony Davis	3.00
12	Jerry Eckwood	5.00
13	Chuck Fusina	3.00
14	Jimmie Giles	5.00
15	Isaac Hagins	3.00
16	Charley Hannah	3.00
17	Andy Hawkins	3.00
18	Kevin House	3.00
19	Cecil Johnson	3.00
20	Gordon Jones	3.00
21	Curtis Jordan	3.00
22	Bill Kollar	3.00
23	Jim Leonard	3.00
24	David Lewis	3.00
25	Reggie Lewis	3.00
26	David Logan	3.00
27	Larry Mucker	3.00
28	Jim O'Bradovich	3.00
29	Mike Rae	3.00
30	Dave Reavis	3.00
31	Danny Reece	3.00
32	Greg Roberts	3.00
33	Gene Sanders	3.00
34	Dewey Selmon	5.00
35	Lee Roy Selmon	15.00
36	Ray Snell	3.00
37	Dave Stalls	3.00
38	Norris Thomas	3.00
39	Mike Washington	3.00
40	Doug Williams	10.00
41	Steve Wilson	3.00
42	Richard Wood	3.00
43	George Yarno	3.00
44	Garo Yepremian	6.00
45	Logo Card	3.00
46	Team Photo	5.00
47	Hugh Culverhouse (OWN)	3.00
48	John McKay (CO)	3.00
49	Mascot Capt. Crush	3.00
50	Cheerleaders: Swash-Buc-Lers	3.00
51	Swash-Buc-Lers (Buzz)	3.00
52	Swash-Buc-Lers (Check with me)	3.00
53	Swash-Buc-Lers (Gap Two)	3.00
54	Swash-Buc-Lers (Gas)	3.00
55	Swash-Buc-Lers (Pass Protection)	3.00
56	Swash-Buc-Lers (Post Pattern)	3.00

1982 Buccaneers Shell

Measuring 1-1/2" x 2-1/2", the 32-card set boasts a full-bleed color photo on the front, with a white stripe at the bottom which includes the Buccaneers' helmet on the left, the player's name in the center and Shell logo on the right. The card backs are blank and unnumbered.

		NM/M
Complete Set (32):		30.00
Common Player:		.50
1	Theo Bell	.75
2	Scot Brantley	.75
3	Cedric Brown	.50
4	Bill Capece	.50
5	Neal Colzie	.75
6	Mark Cotney	.50
7	Hugh Culverhouse	.75
8	Jeff Davis	.75
9	Jerry Eckwood	.75
10	Sean Farrell	.75
11	Jimmie Giles	1.00
12	Hugh Green	1.50
13	Charley Hannah	.50
14	Andy Hawkins	.50
15	John Holt	.50
16	Kevin House	1.00
17	Cecil Johnson	.50
18	Gordon Jones	.50
19	David Logan	.75
20	John McKay	1.50
21	James Owens	1.00
22	Greg Roberts	.50
23	Gene Sanders	.50
24	Lee Roy Selmon	4.00
25	Ray Snell	.50
26	Larry Swider	.50
27	Norris Thomas	.50
28	Mike Washington	.50
29	James Wilder	1.50
30	Doug Williams	2.00
31	Steve Wilson	.50
32	Richard Wood	1.00

1984 Buccaneers Police

Measuring 2-5/8" x 4-1/8", the 56-card set boasts a photo on the card front, with the player's name, position and bio on the bottom left. The Bucs' helmet is located in the lower right. The unnumbered card backs have "Kids and Kops tips from the Buccaneers" at the top, with a football term definition and safety tip below it. The various sponsors are listed at the bottom.

		NM/M
Complete Set (56):		65.00
Common Player:		1.00
1	Swash-Buc-Lers	2.00
2	Hugh Culverhouse (OWN)	1.75
3	John McKay (25 Years as Head Coach)	1.50
4	John McKay (CO)	1.50
5	Defensive Action	1.25
6	Fred Acorn	1.00
7	Obed Ariri	1.00
8	Adger Armstrong	1.00
9	Jerry Bell	1.00
10	Theo Bell	2.50
11	Byron Braggs	1.00
12	Scot Brantley	1.00
13	Cedric Brown	1.00
14	Keith Browner	1.50
15	John Cannon	1.00
16	Jay Carroll	1.00
17	Gerald Carter	1.00
18	Melvin Carter	1.00
19	Jeremiah Castille	1.50
20	Mark Cotney	1.00
21	Steve Courson	1.50
22	Jeff Davis	1.00
23	Steve DeBerg	5.00
24	Sean Farrell	1.75
25	Frank Garcia	1.00
26	Jimmie Giles	2.50
27	Hugh Green	3.00
28	Hugh Green (1A)	1.50
29	Randy Grimes	1.00
30	Ron Heller	1.50
31	John Holt	1.00
32	Kevin House	2.00
33	Noah Jackson	2.00
34	Cecil Johnson	1.00
35	Ken Kaplan	1.00
36	Blair Kiel	1.50
37	David Logan	1.50
38	Brison Manor	1.00
39	Michael Morton	1.00
40	James Owens	1.00
41	Beasley Reece	1.50
42	Gene Sanders	1.00
43	Lee Roy Selmon	5.00
44	Lee Roy Selmon (1A)	3.00
45	Danny Spradlin	1.00
46	Kelly Thomas	1.00
47	Norris Thomas	1.00
48	Jack Thompson	1.50
49	Perry Tuttle	1.00
50	Chris Washington	1.00
51	Mike Washington	1.00
52	James Wilder	2.50
53	James Wilder (1A)	1.25
54	Steve Wilson	1.00
44	Mark White	1.00
56	Richard Wood	1.50

1989 Buccaneers Police

Measuring 2-5/8" x 4-1/8", the 10-card set showcases a color action photo at the top, with the player's name, position and team, along with the Bucs' helmet printed inside a box under the photo. The card backs have the Polk County Sheriff's name at the top, with the card number underneath. Located in the center of the card back are the player's name, number, bio, highlights and stats. A safety tip and IMC Fertilizer are listed at the bottom of the card back.

		NM/M
Complete Set (10):		20.00
Common Player:		1.50
1	Vinny Testaverde	6.00
2	Mark Carrier (WR)	4.00
3	Randy Grimes	1.50
4	Paul Gruber	3.00
5	Ron Hall	2.00
6	William Howard	1.50
7	Curt Jarvis	1.50
8	Ervin Randle	1.50
9	Ricky Reynolds	1.50
10	Rob Taylor	1.50

1976 Buckmans Discs

Measuring 3-3/8 inches in diameter, the 20-disc set features a black-and-white headshot of the player on the front, with four stars printed at the top. The player's name is printed on the right side of the photo, with his team name on the left. His position is printed under the photo. A colored border surrounds the disc, except where the stars are at the top. Printed inside the border are the player's bio and "National Football League Players 1976." The unnumbered disc backs have "A collectors and traders item" at the top, with Buckmans and its address and phone number underneath.

		NM/M
Complete Set (20):		45.00
Common Player:		.50
1	Otis Armstrong	1.00
2	Steve Bartkowski	1.00
3	Terry Bradshaw	10.00
4	Doug Buffone	.50
5	Wally Chambers	.50
6	Chuck Foreman	1.00
7	Roman Gabriel	1.00
8	Mel Gray	1.00
9	Franco Harris	7.00
10	James Harris	.50
11	Jim Hart	1.00
12	Gary Huff	.50
13	Billy Kilmer	1.00
14	Terry Metcalf	1.00
15	Jim Otis	.50
16	Jim Plunkett	1.50
17	Greg Pruitt	.50
18	Roger Staubach	10.00
19	Jan Stenerud	1.00
20	Roger Wehrli	.50

C

1960 Cardinals Mayrose Franks

Measuring 2-1/2" x 3-1/2", the 11-card set showcases a black-and-white photo printed over a red background. A box in the upper left includes the Cardinals' logo and card number. The player's name, position and bio are printed under the photo. The card backs describe the Mayrose Franks football contest. The cards are coated in plastic because they were inserted in hot dog and bacon packages. The cards feature rounded corners.

		NM/M
Complete Set (11):		100.00
Common Player:		8.00
1	Don Gillis	8.00
2	Frank Fuller	8.00
3	George Izo	10.00
4	Woodley Lewis	8.00
5	King Hill	12.00
6	John David Crow	16.00
7	Bill Stacy	8.00
8	Ted Bates	8.00
9	Mike McGee	8.00
10	Bobby Joe Conrad	12.00
11	Ken Panfil	8.00

1961 Cardinals Jay Publishing

Measuring 5" x 7", the 12-card set spotlights posed black-and-white photos on the front, while the backs were blank and unnumbered. The set was sold in 12-card packs for 25 cents in 1961.

		NM/M
Complete Set (12):		50.00
Common Player:		5.00
1	Joe Childress	5.00
2	Sam Etcheverry	5.00
3	Ed Henke	5.00
4	Jimmy Hill	5.00
5	Bill Koman	5.00
6	Roland McDole	5.00
7	Mike McGee	5.00
8	Dale Meinert	5.00
9	Jerry Norton	5.00
10	Sonny Randle	5.00
11	Joe Robb	5.00
12	Billy Stacy	5.00

1965 Cardinals Big Red Biographies

Half-gallon milk cartons from St. Louis' Adams Dairy featured these biographies on side panels. When cut from the carton, the panels measure 3-1/16" x 5-9/16". The panels spotlight "Big Red Biographies" in the upper left, with the Cardinals' logo in the upper right. The player's photo is printed on the left center, with his name, number, position and bio listed on the right. His highlights are printed under the photo. "Enjoy Cardinal Football get your tickets now!" and the team's address are printed at the bottom. The card backs are blank.

		NM/M
Complete Set (17):		1,000
Common Player:		50.00
1	Monk Bailey	50.00
2	Jim Bakken	100.00
3	Jim Burson	50.00
4	Willis Crenshaw	50.00
5	Bob DeMarco	50.00
6	Pat Fischer	100.00
7	Billy Gambrell	50.00
8	Ken Gray	75.00
9	Irv Goode	50.00
10	Mike Melinkovich	50.00
11	Bob Reynolds	50.00
12	Marion Rushing	50.00
13	Carl Silvestri	50.00
14	Dave Simmons	50.00
15	Jackie Smith	150.00
16	Bill (Thunder) Thornton	50.00
17	Herschel Turner	50.00

1965 Cardinals Team Issue

Measuring 7-3/8" x 9-3/8", the 10-card set is anchored by a black-and-white photo inside a white border on the front. The player's name, position and team are listed in the white border at the bottom. The unnumbered backs are also blank.

		NM/M
Complete Set (10):		40.00
Common Player:		4.00
1	Don Brumm	4.00
2	Bobby Joe Conrad	5.00
3	Bob DeMarco	4.00
4	Charley Johnson	7.00
5	Ernie McMillan	5.00
6	Dale Meinert	4.00
7	Luke Owens	4.00
8	Sonny Randle	4.00
9	Joe Robb	4.00
10	Jerry Stovall	4.00

1980 Cardinals Police

Measuring 2-5/8" x 4-1/8", the 15-card set showcases the player's name, jersey number, position, bio and team name under the photo. The Cardinals' helmet is printed in the lower left. The card backs feature Cardinal Tips inside a box, with the Cards' helmet at the top of it. The various sponsors are listed, along with their logos, at the bottom of the unnumbered card backs.

		NM/M
Complete Set (15):		16.00
Common Player:		.75
17	Jim Hart	2.00
22	Roger Wehrli	1.00
24	Wayne Morris	.75
32	Ottis Anderson	2.00
33	Theotis Brown	.75
37	Kevin Green	.75
55	Eric Williams	.75
56	Tim Kearney	.75
59	Calvin Favron	.75
68	Terry Stieve	.75
72	Dan Dierdorf	2.50
73	Mike Dawson	.75
82	Bob Pollard	.75
83	Pat Tilley	1.50
85	Mel Gray	2.00

1988 Cardinals Holsum

The standard sized 12-card set showcases the Holsum logo in the upper left, with "1988 Annual Collectors' Edition" in the upper right. The color headshot anchors the front, with the player's name and team listed in a box at the bottom. The backs have the player's facsimile autograph at the top, along with his jersey number, bio and card number. His stats are listed in the center. The NFLPA, MSA and Holsum logos are printed at the bottom of the card backs.

		NM/M
Complete Set (12):		50.00
Common Player:		4.00
1	Roy Green	7.00
2	Stump Mitchell	6.00
3	J.T. Smith	5.00
4	E.J. Junior	5.00
5	Cedric Mack	4.00
6	Curtis Greer	4.00
7	Lonnie Young	4.00
8	David Galloway	4.00
9	Luis Sharpe	4.00
10	Leonard Smith	4.00
11	Ron Wolfley	4.00
12	Earl Ferrell	4.00

1989 Cardinals Holsum

The standard-sized 16-card set showcases the Holsum logo in the upper left, with "1989 Annual Collectors' Edition" in the upper right. The player's name and team are printed inside a stripe underneath the photo. The card backs have the player's name, jersey number, card number, position and bio at the top. His stats are listed in the center, while the NFLPA logo is in the lower left.

		NM/M
Complete Set (16):		6.00
Common Player:		.25
1	Roy Green	1.00
2	J.T. Smith	.50
3	Neil Lomax	1.00
4	Stump Mitchell	.50
5	Vai Sikahema	.25
6	Lonnie Young	.25
7	Robert Awalt	.25
8	Cedric Mack	.25
9	Earl Ferrell	.25
10	Ron Wolfley	.25
11	Bob Clasby	.25
12	Luis Sharpe	.25
13	Steve Alvord	.25
14	David Galloway	.25
15	Freddie Joe Nunn	.25
16	Niko Noga	.25

1989 Cardinals Police

Measuring 2-5/8" x 4-3/16", the 15-card set has a photo bordered in white. The player's name and position are printed under the photo on the left, with his jersey number on the right. The bottom of the card front features the Phoenix Cardinals' logo. The unnumbered card backs feature the Cardinals' logo at the top, with his jersey number, name, position, bio and career highlights listed. The Cardinals rule is printed inside a box. The KTSP-TV and Louis Rich logos also appear at the bottom. The cards are listed here by uniform number. Two cards were distributed each week. Overall, 100,000 of each card was produced.

		NM/M
Complete Set (15):		25.00
Common Player:		1.00
5	Gary Hogeboom	1.25
24	Ron Wolfley	1.00
30	Stump Mitchell	1.25
31	Earl Ferrell	1.00
36	Vai Sikahema	1.00
43	Lonnie Young	1.00
46	Tim McDonald	1.50
65	David Galloway	1.00
67	Luis Sharpe	1.00
70	Derek Kennard (SP)	10.00
79	Bob Clasby	1.00
80	Robert Awalt	1.00
81	Roy Green	1.50
84	J.T. Smith	1.25
85	Jay Novacek	5.00

1990 Cardinals Police

Measuring 2-5/8" x 4-1/4", the 16-card set is bordered in maroon, with the Cardinals' logo in the upper left and NFL shield in upper right. Underneath the photo are the player's name, position and jersey number. The unnumbered card backs feature the Phoenix Cardinals' logo at the top, with the player's number, name, position, bio highlights underneath. The center of the card back has the Cardinal Rule in a box. KTSP, McGruff the Crime Dog and Louis Rich logos are printed at the bottom.

		NM/M
Complete Set (16):		10.00
Common Player:		.25
1	Anthony Bell	.25
2	Joe Bugel (CO)	.50

3	Rich Camarillo	.25
4	Roy Green	1.25
5	Ken Harvey	1.00
6	Eric Hill	1.25
7	Tim McDonald	.50
8	Tootie Robbins	.25
9	Timm Rosenbach	.75
10	Luis Sharpe	.50
11	Vai Sikahema	.50
12	J.T. Smith	.75
13	Lance Smith	.25
14	Jim Wahler	.25
15	Ron Wolfley	.25
16	Lonnie Young	.25

1992 Cardinals Police

The standard-sized 16-card set features a photo on the front that is bordered on the left by a stripe that changes from red to yellow. The NFL shield is in the upper left of the photo, with the player's jersey number and position on a scoreboard in the lower left. The Phoenix Cardinals' logo and player name and number are printed in red and white, respectively, at the bottom right of the photo. The unnumbered card backs have the player's name, jersey number and position at the top, with his bio printed under a stripe. The Cards' logo is ghosted in the center. A red box at the bottom of the card includes a safety tip and sponsor logos.

		NM/M
Complete Set (16):		12.00
Common Player:		.50
1	Joe Bugel (CO)	.75
2	Rich Camarillo	.50
3	Ed Cunningham	.50
4	Greg Davis	.75
5	Ken Harvey	.75
6	Randal Hill	1.50
7	Ernie Jones	.50
8	Mike Jones	.50
9	Tim McDonald	1.00
10	Freddie Joe Nunn	.50
11	Ricky Proehl	1.00
12	Timm Rosenbach	.75
13	Tony Sacca	.75
14	Lance Smith	.50
15	Eric Swann	1.50
16	Aeneas Williams	1.00

1994 Cardinals Police

Collectors believe this set only contains four cards. The card fronts have a maroon and orange border, with a color photo, player name and number. The card backs are unnumbered and carry the player's name, number and bio.

		NM/M
Complete Set (4):		12.00
Common Player:		3.00
1	Greg Davis	3.00
2	Anthony Edwards	3.00
3	Terry Hoage	3.00
4	Aeneas Williams	4.00

1989 CBS Television Announcers

Measuring 2-3/4" x 3-7/8", this 10-card set showcases the 1989 CBS NFL announcers. The card fronts spotlight a color action shot from the announcer's pro career. The photo is bordered in orange and placed over a green and white football field. "Going the extra yard" is printed in red at the top. "NFL on CBS" is located in the bottom right. The horizontal card backs feature a black-and-white head shot of the announcer, with his bio and highlights bordered in red. Approximately 500 sets, which were divided into two five-card series, were given to CBS affiliates.

		NM/M
Complete Set (10):		250.00
Common Player:		10.00
1	Terry Bradshaw	50.00
2	Dick Butkus	45.00
3	Irv Cross	10.00
4	Dan Fouts	25.00
5	Pat Summerall	15.00
6	Gary Fencik	10.00
7	Dan Jiggetts	10.00
8	John Madden	45.00
9	Ken Stabler	35.00
10	Hank Stram	15.00
---	Wrappers	.45

1961 Chargers Golden Tulip

The 22-card, 2" x 3" set was found in bags of Golden Tulip potato chips. The cards featured top players from the San Diego Chargers in black and white with brief bio information also on the card fronts. The back explains how to upgrade to an 8" x 10" photo and win tickets to a Chargers home game. The set was also sponsored by XETV, an independent television station in San Diego.

		NM/M
Complete Set (22):		1,500
Common Player:		40.00
1	Ron Botchan	40.00
2	Howard Clark	40.00
3	Fred Cole	40.00
4	Sam DeLuca	40.00
5	Orlando Ferrante	40.00
6	Charlie Flowers	40.00
7	Dick Harris	40.00
8	Emil Karas	40.00
9	Jack Kemp	550.00
10	Dave Kocourek	40.00
11	Bob Laraba	40.00
12	Paul Lowe	60.00
13	Paul Maguire	70.00
14	Charlie McNeil	40.00
15	Ron Mix	100.00
16	Ron Nery	40.00
17	Don Norton	40.00
18	Volney Peters	40.00
19	Don Rogers	40.00
20	Maury Schleicher	40.00
21	Ernie Wright	40.00
22	Bob Zeman	40.00

1962 Chargers Union Oil

The 14-card, 6" x 8" set, sponsored by Union 76, features black and white player sketches by the artist, "Patrick." The card backs include a player bio and the Union 76 logo.

		NM/M
Complete Set (14):		450.00
Common Player:		8.00
1	Chuck Allen	10.00
2	Lance Alworth	100.00
3	John Hadl	30.00
4	Dick Harris	10.00
5	Bill Hudson	8.00
6	Jack Kemp	225.00
7	Dave Kocourek	10.00
8	Ernie Ladd	25.00
9	Keith Lincoln	18.00
10	Paul Lowe	18.00
11	Charlie McNeil	10.00
12	Ron Mix	25.00
13	Ron Nery	8.00
14	Team Photo	25.00

1966 Chargers White Border

The 50-card, 5-1/2" x 8-1/2" set was issued by the team and features black and white headshots of top players, such as Lance Alworth, with facsimile autographs. With the exception of card No. 16 (George Gross), the card backs are blank.

		NM/M
Complete Set (50):		225.00
Common Player:		3.00
1	Chuck Allen	5.00
2	James Allison	3.00
3	Lance Alworth	30.00
4	Tom Bass	3.00
5	Joe Beauchamp	3.00
6	Frank Buncom	5.00
7	Richard Degen	3.00
8	Steve DeLong	5.00
9	Les Duncan	3.00
10	John Farris	3.00
11	Gene Foster	3.00
12	Willie Frazier	5.00
13	Gary Garrison	5.00
14	Sid Gillman (CO)	10.00
15	Kenny Graham	3.00
16	George Gross	3.00
17	Sam Gruineisen	3.00
18	Walt Hackett (CO)	3.00
19	John Hadl	15.00
20	Dick Harris	5.00
21	Dan Henning	10.00
22	Bob Horton	3.00
23	Harry Johnston (CO)	3.00
24	Howard Kindig	3.00
25	Keith Lincoln	5.00
26	Paul Lowe	5.00
27	Jacque MacKinnon	3.00
28	Joseph Madro (CO)	3.00
29	Ed Mitchell	3.00
30	Bob Mitinger	3.00
31	Ron Mix	10.00
32	Fred Moore	3.00
33	Don Norton	3.00
34	Terry Owen	5.00
35	Bob Petrich	3.00
36	Dave Plump	3.00
37	Rick Redman	3.00
38	Houston Ridge	3.00
39	Pat Shea	3.00
40	Walt Sweeney	5.00
41	Sammy Taylor	3.00
42	Steve Tensi	3.00
43	Herb Travenio	3.00
44	John Travis	3.00
45	Dick Van Raaphorst	3.00
46	Charlie Waller (CO)	3.00
47	Bud Whitehead	3.00
48	Nat Whitmyer	3.00
49	Ernie Wright	3.00
50	Bob Zeman	3.00

1976 Chargers Dean's Photo

The 10-card, 5" x 8" set was sponsored by Dean's Photo Service and featured top Chargers players such as Dan Fouts and Joe Washington. The card fronts are black and white while the Chargers helmet in the lower left corner is in color. The backs are blank.

		NM/M
Complete Set (10):		28.00
Common Player:		2.00
1	Pat Curran	2.00
2	Chris Fletcher	2.00
3	Dan Fouts	12.00
4	Gary Garrison	2.00
5	Louie Kelcher	3.00
6	Joe Washington	3.00
7	Russ Washington	2.00
8	Doug Wilkerson	2.00
9	Don Woods	2.00
10	Schedule Card	2.00

1981 Chargers Police

The 24-card, 2-5/8" x 4-1/8" set was sponsored by San Diego law enforcement, Pepsi and Kiwanis. The card fronts feature an action shot with the player's name and position, along with the Chargers team logo. The backs contain a law enforcement tip. The Fouts and Winslow cards have two versions with different safety tips. The cards are numbered by the player's jersey number.

		NM/M
Complete Set (24):		37.00
Common Player:		.70
6	Rolf Benirschke	1.50
14A	Dan Fouts (After a team...)	10.50
14B	Dan Fouts (Once you've...)	5.25
18	Charlie Joiner	3.00
25	John Cappelletti	1.50
28	Willie Buchanon	.70
29	Mike Williams	.70
43	Bob Gregor	.70
44	Pete Shaw	.70
46	Chuck Muncie	1.50
51	Woodrow Lowe	.70
57	Linden King	.70
59	Cliff Thrift	.70
62	Don Macek	.70
63	Doug Wilkerson	.70
66	Billy Shields	.70
67	Ed White	.70
68	Leroy Jones	.70
70	Russ Washington	.70
74	Louie Kelcher	.70
79	Gary Johnson	.70
80A	Kellen Winslow (Go all out...)	10.50
80B	Kellen Winslow (The length of ...)	5.25
NNO	Don Coryell (CO)	1.50

1982 Chargers Police

The 16-card, 2-5/8" x 4-1/8" set is nearly identical in design with the 1981 Chargers Police set. The card fronts feature a Chargers player with his postion and San Diego helmet. The backs contain a law enforcement tip and are sponsored by San Diego law enforcement, Pepsi and Kiwanis.

		NM/M
Complete Set (16):		45.00
Common Player:		2.00
1	Rolf Benirschke	2.00
2	James Brooks	4.00
3	Wes Chandler	5.00
4	Dan Fouts	10.00
5	Tim Fox	2.00
6	Gary Johnson	2.00
7	Charlie Joiner	8.00
8	Louie Kelcher	2.00
9	Linden King	2.00
10	Bruce Laird	2.00
11	David Lewis	2.00
12	Don Macek	2.00
13	Billy Shields	2.00
14	Eric Sievers	2.00
15	Russ Washington	2.00
16	Kellen Winslow	10.00

1985 Chargers Kodak

The 15-card, 5-1/2" x 8-1/2" set, sponsored by Kodak, features color action shots and San Diego helmet in the lower left corner. The backs contain bio information.

		NM/M
Complete Set (15):		40.00
Common Player:		2.00
1	Carlos Bradley	2.00
2	Wes Chandler	6.00
3	Chuck Ehin	2.00
4	Mike Green	2.00
5	Pete Holohan	2.00
6	Lionel James	2.00
7	Charlie Joiner	12.00
8	Woodrow Lowe	2.00
9	Dennis McKnight	2.00
10	Miles McPherson	2.00
11	Derrie Nelson	2.00
12	Vince Osby	2.00
13	Billy Ray Smith	2.00
14	Danny Walters	2.00
15	Ed White	2.00

1986 Chargers Kodak

The 36-card, 5-1/2" x 8-1/2" set are similar to the 1985 Kodak Chargers cards, but have blank backs. The bio information is featured on the card fronts below the player's name and between the Chargers helmet and the Kodak logo.

		NM/M
Complete Set (36):		45.00
Common Player:		1.00
1	Curtis Adams	1.00
2	Gary Anderson (RB)	3.00
3	Jesse Bendross	1.00
4	Gill Byrd	1.00
5	Sam Claphan	1.00
6	Don Coryell (CO)	2.00
7	Jeffery Dale	1.00
8	Wayne Davis	1.00
9	Jerry Doerger	1.00
10	Chris Faulkner	1.00
11	Mark Fellows	1.00
12	Dan Fouts	8.00
13	Mike Guendling	1.00
14	John Hendy	1.00
15	Mark Hermann	1.00
16	Lionel James	1.00
17	Trumaine Johnson	1.00
18	David King	1.00
19	Linden King	1.00
20	Jim Lachey	2.00
21	Don Macek	1.00
22	Buford McGee	1.00
23	Dennis McKnight	1.00
24	Ralf Mojsiejenko	1.00
25	Ron O'Bard	1.00
26	Fred Robinson	1.00
27	Eric Sievers	1.00
28	Tony Simmons	1.00
29	Billy Ray Smith	1.00
30	Lucious Smith	1.00
31	Alex G. Spanos (PRES)	1.00
32	Tim Spencer	1.00
33	Rich Umphrey	1.00
34	Ed White	1.00
35	Lee Williams	1.00
36	Earl Wilson	1.00

1987 Chargers Junior Coke Tickets

The 12-card, 1-7/8" x 4-1/4" set was issued to members of the Coca-Cola Junior Chargers. The cards are in the form of a ticket, which was exchanged by members for actual game tickets. The card fronts included a color action photo, and had imitation ticket information, such as section, row and seat number. The card backs contain a Chargers logo and a description of how to exchange the coupon for a real ticket.

		NM/M
Complete Set (12):		12.00
Common Player:		1.00
1	Gary Anderson (RB)	1.50
2	Rolf Benirschke	1.00
3	Wes Chandler	1.75
4	Jeffery Dale	1.00
5	Dan Fouts	3.00
6	Pete Holohan	1.00
7	Lionel James	1.00
8	Don Macek	1.00
9	Dennis McKnight	1.00
10	Al Saunders (CO)	1.00
11	Billy Ray Smith	1.00
12	Kellen Winslow	3.00

1987 Chargers Police

The 21-card, 2-5/8" x 4-1/8" set, sponsored by the Chargers, Oscar Meyer and San Diego law enforcement, features top players from the 1987 Chargers squad. Even though the cards are numbered, there was no card No. 13 issued and card Nos. 3 and 17 were pulled during distribution. The card fronts feature an action shot and bio information while the backs have a brief player description with a safety tip.

		NM/M
Complete Set (22):		20.00
Common Player:		.75
1	Alex G. Spanos (OWN)	.75
2	Gary Anderson (RB)	1.00
3	Rolf Benirschke (SP)	5.00
4	Gill Byrd	.75
5	Wes Chandler	1.50
6	Sam Claphan	.75
7	Jeffery Dale	.75
8	Pete Holohan	.75
9	Lionel James	.75
10	Jim Lachey	.75
11	Woodrow Lowe	.75
12	Don Macek	.75
14	Dan Fouts	3.50
15	Eric Sievers	.75
16	Billy Ray Smith	.75
17	Danny Walters (SP)	4.00
18	Lee Williams	.75
19	Kellen Winslow	2.50
20	Al Saunders (CO)	.75
21	Dennis McKnight	.75
22	Chip Banks	.75

1987 Chargers Smokey

The 48-card, 5-1/2" x 8-1/2" sets were issued by the California Forestry Department and fronted color action shots. The card backs contain a safety tip cartoon with Smokey The Bear. Coach Don Coryell's card was pulled after the initial distribution after he was replaced. Also, the cards of Donald Brown, Mike Douglas and Fred Robinson were pulled after they were cut.

		NM/M
Complete Set (48):		100.00
Common Player:		1.00
Common SP:		8.00
1	Curtis Adams	1.00
2	Ty Allert	1.00
3	Gary Anderson (RB)	2.50
4	Rolf Benirschke	2.00
5	Thomas Benson	1.00
6	Donald Brown (SP)	8.00
7	Gill Byrd	1.50
8	Wes Chandler	4.00
9	Sam Claphan	1.00
10	Don Coryell (CO) (SP)	10.00
11	Jeffery Dale	1.00
12	Wayne Davis	1.00
13	Mike Douglass (SP)	8.00
14	Chuck Ehin	1.00
15	James Fitzpatrick	1.00
16	Tom Flick	1.00
17	Dan Fouts	12.00
18	Dee Hardison	1.00
19	Andy Hawkins	1.00
20	John Hendy	1.00
21	Mark Hermann	1.00
22	Pete Holohan	1.00
23	Lionel James	1.50
24	Trumaine Johnson	1.00
25	Charlie Joiner	8.00
26	Gary Kowalski	1.00
27	Jim Lachey	1.50
28	Jim Leonard	1.00
29	Woodrow Lowe	1.00
30	Don Macek	1.00
31	Buford McGee	1.00
32	Dennis McKnight	1.00
33	Ralf Mojsiejenko	1.00
34	Derrie Nelson	1.00
35	Leslie O'Neal	5.00
36	Gary Plummer	1.50
37	Fred Robinson (SP)	8.00
38	Eric Sievers	1.00
39	Billy Ray Smith	1.50
40	Tim Spencer	1.50
41	Kenny Taylor	1.00
42	Terry Unrein	1.00
43	Jeff Walker	1.00
44	Danny Walters	1.00
45	Lee Williams	1.50
46	Earl Wilson	1.00
47	Kellen Winslow	8.00
48	Kevin Wyatt	1.00

1988 Chargers Police

The 12-card, 2-5/8" x 4" set features white and blue borders with color action shots. The card backs have career highlights and safety tips.

		NM/M
Complete Set (12):		12.00
Common Player:		.50
1	Gary Anderson (RB)	.75
2	Rod Bernstine	1.00
3	Gill Byrd	.75
4	Vencie Glenn	.75
5	Lionel James	.75
6	Babe Laufenberg	.75
7	Don Macek	.50
8	Mark Malone	1.00
9	Dennis McKnight	.50
10	Anthony Miller	5.00
11	Billy Ray Smith	.75
12	Lee Williams	.75

1988 Chargers Smokey

The 52-card, 5" x 8" set features color action shots on the card fronts and a forestry safety tip, along with a Smokey The Bear cartoon on the back. Two Alex Spanos cards exist, one stating incorrectly that he purchased the Chargers in 1987, and one stating the correct 1984. Also, 18 of the cards were short printed (Nos. 9, 23, 27, 36, 55, 56, 57, 74, 77, 78, 79, 81, 88, 89, 92, 96 and 98) as some of the players were cut, traded or put on injured reserve.

		NM/M
Complete Set (52):		45.00
Common Player:		.50
2	Ralf Mojsiejenko	.50
9	Mark Hermann (SP)	1.50
10	Vince Abbott	.50
13	Mark Vlasic	.50
14	Dan Fouts	4.00
20	Barry Redden	.50
22	Gill Byrd	.75
23	Danny Walters (SP)	1.50
25	Vencie Glenn	.50
26	Lionel James	.75
27	Daniel Hunter (SP)	1.50
34	Elvis Patterson	.50
36	Mike Davis (SP)	1.50
40	Gary Anderson (RB)	.75
42	Curtis Adams	.50
43	Tim Spencer	.50
44	Martin Bayless	.50
50	Gary Plummer	.50
52	Jeff Jackson	.50
54	Billy Ray Smith	.50
55	Steve Busick (SP)	1.50
56	Chip Banks (SP)	2.00
57	Thomas Benson (SP)	1.50
58	David Brandon	.50
60	Dennis McKnight	.50
61	Ken Dallafior	.50
62	Don Macek	.50
68	Gary Kowalski	.50
69	Les Miller	.50
70	James Fitzpatrick	.50
71	Mike Charles	.50
72	Karl Wilson	.50
74	Jim Lachey (SP)	2.00
75	Joe Phillips	.50
76	Broderick Thompson	.50
77	Sam Claphan (SP)	1.50
78	Chuck Ehin (SP)	1.50
79	Curtis Rouse (SP)	1.50
80	Kellen Winslow	4.00
81	Timmie Ware (SP)	1.50
82	Rod Bernstine	.75
85	Eric Sievers	.50
86	Jamie Holland	.50
88	Pete Holohan (SP)	1.50
89	Wes Chandler (SP)	4.00
92	Dee Hardison (SP)	1.50
94	Randy Kirk	.50
96	Keith Baldwin (SP)	1.50
98	Terry Unrein (SP)	1.50
99	Lee Williams	.50
NNO	Al Saunders (CO)	.50
NNO	Alex G. Spanos (ERR SP Chairman of the Board) (Purchased team 1987)	4.00
NNO	Alex G. Spanos (COR Chairman of the Board) (Purchased team 1984)	.50

1989 Chargers Junior Ralph's Tickets

The 12-card, 1-7/8" x 3-5/8" set was delivered in a perforated sheet which has all 12 cards. The set was sponsored by Ralph's and XTRA and the backs of the cards had coupons to local attractions. The fronts have a color action shot with the coupon description.

		NM/M
Complete Set (12):		10.00
Common Player:		.50
1	Gary Anderson (RB)	.75
2	Gill Byrd	.75
3	Quinn Early	1.50
4	Vencie Glenn	.75
5	Jamie Holland	.50
6	Don Macek	.50
7	Dennis McKnight	.50
8	Anthony Miller	5.00
9	Ralf Mojsiejenko	.50
10	Leslie O'Neal	1.75
11	Billy Ray Smith	.50
12	Lee Williams	.50

1989 Chargers Police

The 12-card, 2-5/8" x 4-3/16" set has white borders with color action shots while the backs have bio information, career highlights and safety messages and are sponsored by Louis Rich. The cards were distributed in two, six-card sheets on Oct. 22 and Nov. 5 at Chargers home games.

		NM/M
Complete Set (12):		10.00
Common Player:		.50
1	Tim Spencer	.50
2	Vencie Glenn	.75
3	Gill Byrd	.75
4	Jim McMahon	1.50
5	David Richards	.50
6	Don Macek	.50
7	Billy Ray Smith	.75
8	Gary Plummer	.75
9	Lee Williams	.50
10	Leslie O'Neal	1.00
11	Anthony Miller	3.00
12	Broderick Thompson	.50

1989 Chargers Smokey

The 48-card, 5" x 8" set has white borders with color action shots while the backs have bio information, career highlights and safety tips.

		NM/M
Complete Set (48):		45.00
Common Player:		1.00
2	Ralf Mojsiejenko	1.00
6	Steve DeLine	1.00
10	Vince Abbott	1.00
13	Mark Vlasic	1.00
16	Mark Malone	1.00
20	Barry Redden	1.00
22	Gill Byrd	1.00
23	Roy Bennett	1.00
25	Vencie Glenn	1.00

26 Lionel James 1.00
30 Sam Seale 1.00
31 Leonard Coleman 1.00
34 Elvis Patterson 1.00
40 Gary Anderson (RB) 1.50
42 Curtis Adams 1.00
43 Tim Spencer 1.00
44 Martin Bayless 1.00
48 Pat Miller 1.00
50 Gary Plummer 1.00
51 Cedric Figaro 1.00
52 Jeff Jackson 1.00
53 Chuck Faucette 1.00
54 Billy Ray Smith 1.00
57 Keith Browner 1.00
58 David Brandon 1.00
59 Ken Woodard 1.00
60 Dennis McKnight 1.00
61 Ken Dallafior 1.00
65 David Richards 1.00
66 Dan Rosado 1.00
69 Les Miller 1.00
70 James Fitzpatrick 1.00
71 Mike Charles 1.00
72 Karl Wilson 1.00
73 Darrick Brilz 1.00
75 Joe Phillips 1.00
76 Broderick Thompson 1.00
82 Rod Bernstine 1.50
83 Anthony Miller 6.00
86 Jamie Holland 1.00
87 Quinn Early 1.50
88 Arthur Cox 1.00
89 Darren Flutie 2.50
91 Leslie O'Neal 2.50
93 Tyrone Keys 1.00
95 Joe Campbell 1.00
97 George Hinkle 1.00
99 Lee Williams 1.00

1990 Chargers Police

The 12-card, 2-5/8" x 4-1/8" set was sponsored by Louis Rich Meats. The card fronts have blue borders with color action shots while the backs have player descriptions and bio information, along with a safety tip.

NM/M
Complete Set (12): 10.00
Common Player: .75
1 Martin Bayless .75
2 Marion Butts 1.25
3 Gill Byrd .75
4 Burt Grossman .75
5 Ronnie Harmon 1.00
6 Anthony Miller 3.00
7 Leslie O'Neal 1.50
8 Joe Phillips .75
9 Gary Plummer .75
10 Billy Ray Smith .75
11 Billy Joe Tolliver 1.00
12 Lee Williams .75

1990 Chargers Smokey

The 36-card, 5" x 8" set was similar to the 1989 set with a fire safety cartoon and brief bio information on the back.

NM/M
Complete Set (36): 30.00
Common Player: .75
11 Billy Joe Tolliver 1.25
13 Mark Vlasic .75
15 David Archer 1.50
20 Darrin Nelson .75
22 Gill Byrd 1.00
24 Lester Lyles .75
25 Vencie Glenn 1.25
30 Sam Seale .75
31 Craig McEwen .75
35 Marion Butts 1.25
43 Tim Spencer .75
44 Martin Bayless .75
46 Joe Caravello .75
50 Gary Plummer .75
51 Cedric Figaro .75
53 Courtney Hall .75
54 Billy Ray Smith 1.00
58 David Brandon .75
59 Ken Woodard .75
60 Dennis McKnight .75
65 David Richards .75
69 Les Miller .75
75 Joe Phillips .75
76 Broderick Thompson .75
78 Joel Patten .75
79 Joey Howard .75
80 Wayne Walker .75
82 Rod Bernstine 1.00
83 Anthony Miller 5.00
85 Andy Parker .75
87 Quinn Early 1.75
88 Arthur Cox .75
91 Leslie O'Neal 1.75
92 Burt Grossman .75
97 George Hinkle .75
99 Lee Williams .75

1991 Chargers Vons

The twelve standard-sized cards were distributed by Vons in three-card sheets (6-5/8" x 3-1/2") with each sheet containing one card, one Junior Chargers Official Membership Card and a Sea World of California discount coupon. The card fronts have a color shot with a white border while the backs have bio and stat information.

NM/M
Complete Set (12): 10.00
Common Player: .75
1 Rod Berstine .75
2 Gill Byrd 1.00
3 Burt Grossman .75
4 Ronnie Harmon 1.00
5 Anthony Miller 2.00
6 Leslie O'Neal 1.50
7 Gary Plummer .75
8 Junior Seau 2.50
9 Billy Ray Smith .75
10 Broderick Thompson .75
11 Billy Joe Tolliver 1.00
12 Lee Williams .75

1992 Chargers Louis Rich

The 52-card, 5" x 8" set, distributed by Louis Rich, had glossy color fronts with the backs containing the Louis Rich logo.

NM/M
Complete Set (52): 30.00
Common Player: .50
1 Sam Anno .50
2 Johnnie Barnes .50
3 Rod Bernstine .75
4 Eric Bieniemy .75
5 Anthony Blaylock .50
6 Brian Brennan .50
7 Marion Butts 1.00
8 Gill Byrd .75
9 John Carney 1.00
10 Darren Carrington .50
11 Robert Claborne .50
12 Floyd Fields .50
13 Donald Frank .50
14 Bob Gagliano .50
15 Leo Goeas .50
16 Burt Grossman .50
17 Courtney Hall .50
18 Delton Hall .50
19 Ronnie Harmon 1.00
20 Steve Hendrickson .50
21 Stan Humphries 3.00
22 Shawn Jefferson 1.00
23 John Kidd .50
24 Shawn Lee .50
25 Nate Lewis .50
26 Eugene Marve .50
27 Deems May .50
28 Anthony Miller 2.00
29 Chris Mims 1.00
30 Eric Moten .50
31 Kevin Murphy .50
32 Pat O'Hara .50
33 Leslie O'Neal 1.50
34 Gary Plummer .50
35 Marquez Pope .50
36 Alfred Pupunu .50
37 Stanley Richard .75
38 David Richards .50
39 Henry Rolling .50
40 Bobby Ross (CO) 1.00
41 Junior Seau 2.50
42 Harry Swayne .75
43 Broderick Thompson .50
44 George Thornton .50
45 Peter Tuipulotu .50
46 Sean Vanhorse .50
47 Derrick Walker .50
48 Reggie E. White .50
49 Curtis Whitley .50
50 Blaise Winter .50
51 Duane Young .50
52 Mike Zandofsky .50

1993 Chargers D.A.R.E

NM/M
Complete Set (30): 4.00
Common Player: .10
1 Sam Anno .10
2 Stan Brock .10
3 Marion Butts .20
4 Gill Byrd .10
5 John Carney .10
6 Darren Carrington .10
7 Brian Davis .10
8 Donald Frank .10
9 John Friesz .10
10 Burt Grossman .10
11 Courtney Hall .10
12 Ronnie Harmon .10
13 Steve Hendrickson .10
14 Stan Humphries .40
15 John Kidd .10
16 Shawn Lee .10
17 Nate Lewis .10
18 Joe Milinichik .10
19 Anthony Miller .10
20 Leslie O'Neal .30
21 Gary Plummer .10
22 Bobby Ross .10
23 Junior Seau 1.00
24 Alex G. Spanos .10
25 Harry Swayne .10
26 Sean Vanhorse .10
27 Derrick Walker .10
28 Jerrol Williams .10
29 Blaise Winter .10
30 Mike Zandofsky .10

1993 Chargers Police

The 32-card, regular-sized set was sponsored by the highway patrol and contained the rookie card of running back Natrone Means. The fronts feature team color borders and the backs have bio information with a safe driving tip appearing in the lower right corner.

NM/M
Complete Set (32): 12.00
Common Player: .25
1 Darrien Gordon .50
2 Natrone Means 3.00
3 John Friesz .75
4 Stan Humphries 1.75
5 Anthony Miller 1.50
6 Marion Butts .75
7 Ronnie Harmon .75
8 Stanley Richard .50
9 Leslie O'Neal 1.00
10 Harry Swayne .25
11 Junior Seau 1.75
12 Courtney Hall .25
13 Gary Plummer .25
14 Eric Moten .25
15 Chris Mims .75
16 Burt Grossman .25
17 Blaise Winter .25
18 Donald Frank .25
19 Sean Vanhorse .25
20 John Carney .50
21 Floyd Fields .25
22 Gill Byrd .50
23 Shawn Jefferson .50
24 Shawn Lee .25
25 Alfred Pupunu .50
26 Marquez Pope .25
27 Darren Carrington .25
28 Duane Young .25
29 Derrick Walker .25
30 Deems May .25
31 Nate Lewis .25
32 Bobby Ross CO, Clarence Tuck (CHP Chief) .75

1994 Chargers Castrol Promos

The six-card, 5" x 8" set was sponsored by Pepboys and Castrol. The card fronts feature a color photo with the backs containing bio information and sponsor logos over the NFL emblem.

NM/M
Complete Set (6): 6.00
Common Player: .50
1 Courtney Hall .50
2 Ronnie Harmon .50
3 Stan Humphries 1.50
4 Natrone Means 2.50
5 Leslie O'Neal 1.00
6 Junior Seau 1.50

1994 Chargers Castrol

The 52-card, 5" x 8" set, as with the Promos set, was sponsored by Pepboys and Castrol with the card fronts containing a color shot. The card backs are similar to the Promos set, with bio information and sponsor logos over the NFL emblem.

NM/M
Complete Set (52): 30.00
Common Player: .50
1 Johnnie Barnes .50
2 Eric Bieniemy .75
3 David Binn .50
4 Stan Brock .50
5 Jeff Brohm .50
6 Lewis Bush .50
7 John Carney 1.00
8 Darren Carrington .50
9 Eric Castle .50
10 Willie Clark .50
11 Joe Cocozzo .50
12 Andre Coleman .75
13 Rodney Culver .75
14 Isaac Davis .50
15 Reuben Davis .50
16 Greg Engel .50
17 Dennis Gilbert .50
18 Gale Gilbert .50
19 Darrien Gordon 1.00
20 David Griggs .50
21 Courtney Hall .50
22 Ronnie Harmon 1.00
23 Dwayne Harper .50
24 Rodney Harrison .50
25 Steve Hendrickson .50
26 Stan Humphries 3.00
27 Shawn Jefferson 1.50
28 Raylee Johnson .50
29 Eric Jonassen .50
30 Aaron Laing .50
31 Shawn Lee .50
32 Deems May .50
33 Natrone Means 3.50
34 Joe Milinichik .50
35 Doug Miller .50
36 Chris Mims 1.00
37 Shannon Mitchell .50
38 Leslie O'Neal 1.50
39 Vaughn Parker .50
40 John Parrella .50
41 Alfred Pupunu .75
42 Stanley Richard .75
43 Junior Seau 3.50
44 Mark Seay 1.75
45 Harry Swayne .50
46 Cornell Thomas .50
47 Sean Vanhorse .50
48 Bryan Wagner .50
49 Reggie E. White .50
50 Curtis Whitley .50
51 Duane Young .50
52 Lonnie Young .50

1994 Chargers Pro Mags/Pro Tags

The 12-card, 2-1/8" x 3-3/8" set (with rounded corners) was issued in 750 boxes that contained six magnets and six "tag" cards. The magnet-card fronts feature the player's name and Super Bowl XXIX logo in gold foil, as do the tag cards which also have a closeup photo and a player profile on the backs.

NM/M
Complete Set (12): 20.00
Common Player: 1.50
1 Stan Humphries 3.00
2 Tony Martin 3.00
3 Natrone Means 4.00
4 Leslie O'Neal 2.00
5 Junior Seau 3.00
6 Mark Seay 1.50
7 Stan Humphries 3.00
8 Tony Martin 3.00
9 Natrone Means 4.00
10 Leslie O'Neal 2.00
11 Junior Seau 3.00
12 Mark Seay 1.50

1964-69 Chiefs Fairmont Dairy

The 19-card, 3-3/8" x 2-3/8" set was available on milk cartons by Fairmont Dairy between the years 1964-69. Most cards are printed in red ink, with some cards printed in black (3-7/16" x 1-9/16"). Although there are 19 cards listed below, there could have been more than that produced in the 1960s. The card fronts feature a player closeup with brief bio information, as well as a Chiefs schedule.

NM/M
Complete Set (19): 1,800
Common Player: 75.00
1 Fred Arbanas (Red printing) 75.00
2 Bobby Bell (Red printing) 175.00
3 Buck Buchanan (Black print) 160.00
4 Chris Burford (Red printing) 75.00
5 Len Dawson (Red printing) 260.00
6 Dave Grayson (Red printing) 75.00
7 Abner Haynes (Red printing) 100.00
8 Sherrill Headrick (Red printing) 100.00
9 Bobby Hunt (Red printing) 75.00
10 Frank Jackson (Red printing) 75.00
11 Curtis McClinton (Red printing) 75.00
12 Bobby Ply (Red printing) 75.00
13 Al Reynolds (Red printing) 75.00
14 Johnny Robinson (Red printing) 125.00
15 Noland Smith 75.00
16 Smokey Stover (Red printing) 75.00
17 Otis Taylor 150.00
18 Jim Tyrer (Red printing) 100.00
19 Jerrel Wilson (Red printing) 75.00

1969 Chiefs Kroger

The eight-card, 8" x 9-3/4" set was sponsored by Kroger and features card fronts with color paintings by artist John Wheeldon. The backs have biographical and statistical information and a brief note about the artist.

NM/M
Complete Set (8): 75.00
Common Player: 5.00
1 Buck Buchanan 10.00
2 Len Dawson 25.00
3 Mike Garrett 10.00
4 Willie Lanier 15.00
5 Jerry Mays 5.00
6 Johnny Robinson 10.00
7 Jan Stenerud 15.00
8 Jim Tyrer 5.00

1971 Chiefs Team Issue

The 10-card, 7" x 10" set features Chiefs players in black and white headshots with white borders. The backs contain bio information and career highlights and limited statistics.

NM/M
Complete Set (10): 45.00
Common Player: 5.00
1 Bobby Bell 10.00
2 Wendell Hayes 5.00
3 Ed Lothamer 5.00
4 Jim Lynch 5.00
5 Jack Rudnay 5.00
6 Sid Smith 5.00
7 Bob Stein 5.00
8 Jan Stenerud 12.00
9 Otis Taylor 10.00
10 Jim Tyrer 5.00

1973-74 Chiefs Team Issue

The 18-card, 5" x 7" set features black and white photos on the card fronts with white borders. The card backs are blank.

NM/M
Complete Set (18): 50.00
Common Player: 3.00
1 Robert Briggs 3.00
2 Larry Brunson 3.00
3 Gary Butler 3.00
4 Dean Carlson 3.00
5 Tom Condon 3.00
6 George Daney 3.00
7 Andy Hamilton 3.00
8 Dave Hill 3.00
9 Jim Kearney 3.00
10 Mike Livingston 3.00
11 Jim Marsalis 3.00
12 Barry Pearson 3.00
13 Francis Peay 3.00
14 Kerry Reardon 3.00
15 Mike Sensibaugh 3.00
16 Bill Thomas 3.00
17 Marvin Upshaw 3.00
18 Clyde Werner 3.00

1979 Chiefs Police

The 10-card, 2-5/8" x 4-1/8" set was issued by Hardee's Restaurants, the Chiefs and the Kansas City Police Department. The card fronts feature an action shot with the backs offering a safety tip.

NM/M
Complete Set (10): 10.00
Common Player: 1.00
1 Bob Grupp 1.00
4 Steve Fuller 1.00
22 Ted McKnight 1.00
24 Gary Green 1.00
26 Gary Barbaro 1.50
32 Tony Reed 1.00
58 Jack Rudnay 1.00
67 Art Still 1.50
73 Bob Simmons 1.00
NNO Marv Levy (CO) 3.00

1980 Chiefs Police

The 10-card, 2-5/8" x 4-1/8" set, sponsored by Frito-Lay, Kiwanis and area law enforcement, features action fronts with "Chiefs Tips" on the backs. The Stenerud card was limited in distribution.

NM/M
Complete Set (10): 12.00
Common Player: 1.00
1 Bob Grupp 1.00
3 Jan Stenerud (SP) 3.00
32 Tony Reed 1.00
53 Whitney Paul 1.00
59 Gary Spani 1.00
67 Art Still 1.75
86 J.T. Smith 1.00
99 Mike Bell 1.00
NNO Defensive Team 1.50
NNO Offensive Team 1.50

1981 Chiefs Police

The 10-card, 2-5/8" x 4-1/8" set, sponsored by Frito-Lay, Kiwanis and local law enforcement, features action shots on the card fronts and "Chiefs Tips" on the backs.

NM/M
Complete Set (10): 4.50
Common Player: .40
1 Warpaint and Carla (Mascots) .40
2 Art Still .60
3 Steve Fuller, Jack Rudnay .60
4 Gary Green .40
5 Tom Condon, Marv Levy (CO) .70
6 J.T. Smith .60
7 Gary Spani, Whitney Paul .40
8 Nick Lowery, Steve Fuller .60
9 Gary Barbaro .40
10 Henry Marshall .40

1982 Chiefs Police

The 10-card, 2-5/8" x 4-1/8" set, sponsored by Frito-Lay, Kiwanis and local law enforcement, features action fronts while the backs contain cartoons in addition to "Chiefs Tips." Some of the card fronts feature two players (card Nos. 1 and 2).

NM/M
Complete Set (10): 6.00
Common Player: .50
1 Bill Kenney, Jack Rudnay .75
2 Steve Fuller, Nick Lowery .75
3 Matt Herkenhoff .50
4 Art Still .75
5 Gary Spani .50
6 James Hadnot .50
7 Mike Bell .50
8 Carol Canfield (Chiefette) .50
9 Gary Green .50
10 Joe Delaney .75

1983 Chiefs Police

The 10-card, 2-5/8" x 4-1/8" set, sponsored by Frito-Lay, KCTV-5, Kiwanis and local law enforcement, features action fronts with "Crime Tip" cartoons on the backs.

NM/M
Complete Set (10): 6.00
Common Player: .50
1 John Mackovic (CO) .75
2 Tom Condon .50
3 Gary Spani .50
4 Carlos Carson .75
5 Brad Budde .50
6 Lloyd Burruss .50
7 Gary Green .50
8 Mike Bell .50
9 Nick Lowery .75
10 Sandi Byrd (Chiefette) .50

1984 Chiefs Police

The 10-card, 2-5/8" x 4-1/8" set, sponsored by Frito-Lay and KCTV, features a "Chiefs Tip" and "Crime Tip" on the card backs.

NM/M
Complete Set (10): 6.00
Common Player: .50
1 John Mackovic (CO) .75
2 Deron Cherry .75
3 Bill Kenney .50
4 Henry Marshall .50
5 Nick Lowery .75
6 Theotis Brown .50
7 Stephone Paige 1.00
8 Gary Spani, Art Still .75
9 Albert Lewis .75
10 Carlos Carson .75

1984 Chiefs QuikTrip

The 16-card, 5" x 7" set was sponsored by QuickTrip and features black and white fronts with blank backs.

NM/M
Complete Set (16): 48.00
Common Player: 2.00
1 Mike Bell 2.00

2 Todd Blackledge 3.00
3 Brad Budde 2.00
4 Lloyd Burruss 2.00
5 Carlos Carson 3.00
6 Gary Green 2.00
7 Anthony Hancock 2.00
8 Eric Harris 2.00
9 Lamar Hunt (OWN) 5.00
10 Bill Kenney 3.00
11 Ken Kremer 2.00
12 Nick Lowery 4.50
13 John Mackovic (CO) 3.00
14 J.T. Smith 3.00
15 Gary Spani 2.00
16 Art Still 3.00

1985 Chiefs Police

The 10-card, 2-5/8" x 4-1/8" set, sponsored by Frito-Lay, KCTV and local law enforcement, features a "Chiefs Tip" and "Crime Tip" on the card backs.

NM/M
Complete Set (10): 6.00
Common Player: .50
1 John Mackovic (CO) .75
2 Herman Heard .50
3 Bill Kenney .75
4 Deron Cherry, Lloyd Burruss .75
5 Jim Arnold .50
6 Kevin Ross .50
7 David Lutz .50
8 Chiefettes Cheerleaders .75
9 Bill Maas .75
10 Art Still 1.00

1986 Chiefs Police

The 10-card, 2-5/8" x 4-1/8" set was sponsored by Frito-Lay, KCTV and local law enforcement and features "Chiefs Tip" and "Crime Tip" on the backs.

NM/M
Complete Set (10): 6.00
Common Player: .50
1 John Mackovic .50
2 Willie Lanier (Hall of Fame) 1.50
3 Stephone Paige 1.00
4 Brad Budde .50
5 Nick Lowery .75
6 Scott Radecic .50
7 Mike Pruitt .50
8 Albert Lewis .75
9 Todd Blackledge .75
10 Deron Cherry 1.25

1987 Chiefs Police

The 10-card, 2-5/8" x 4-1/8" set, sponsored by Frito-Lay, US Sprint, KCTV and local law enforcement, features a "Chiefs Tip" and "Crime Tip" on the backs.

NM/M
Complete Set (10): 5.00
Common Player: .50
1 Frank Gansz (CO) .50
2 Tim Cofield .50
3 Deron Cherry, Albert Lewis .75
4 Chiefs Cheerleaders .50
5 Jeff Smith .50
6 Rick Donnalley .50
7 Lloyd Burruss, Kevin Ross .50
8 Dino Hackett .50
9 Bill Maas .50
10 Carlos Carson .75

1988 Chiefs Police

The 10-card, 2-5/8" x 4-1/8" set was sponsored by Frito-Lay, KCTV, US Sprint and local law enforcement and has "Chiefs Tip" and "Crime Tip" on the backs.

NM/M
Complete Set (10): 6.00
Common Player: .50
1 Frank Gansz (CO) .50
2 Bill Kenney .75
3 Carlos Carson .75
4 Paul Palmer .50
5 Christian Okoye 1.00
6 Mark Adickes .50
7 Bill Maas .50
8 Albert Lewis .75
9 Deron Cherry .75
10 Stephone Paige .75

1989 Chiefs Police

The 10-card, 2-5/8" x 4-1/8" set, sponsored by Western Auto, KCTV and local law enforcement, features a "Chiefs Tip" and "Crime Tip" on the card backs.

NM/M
Complete Set (10): 5.00
Common Player: .50
1 Marty Schottenheimer (CO) 1.00
2 Irv Eatman .50
3 Kevin Ross .50
4 Bill Maas .50
5 Chiefs Cheerleaders .50
6 Carlos Carson .75
7 Steve DeBerg 1.00
8 Jonathan Hayes .50
9 Deron Cherry .75
10 Dino Hackett .50

1997 Chiefs Pocket Schedules

This 22-card set featured a Chiefs player on one side with the Kansas City Chiefs 1997 schedule on the other side. Pocket schedules were distributed in the Kansas City area early in the 1997 season.

NM/M
Complete Set (22): 7.00
Common Player: .25
Marcus Allen 2.00
Kimble Anders .25
Vaughn Booker .25
John Browning .25
Dale Carter .50
Anthony Davis .25
Troy Dumas .25
Donnie Edwards .25
Elvis Grbac 1.00
Tim Grunhard .25
James Hasty .25
Greg Hill .75
Chris Penn .25
Will Shields .25
Tracy Simien .25
Pete Styoyanovich .25
Dave Szott .25
Derrick Thomas 1.00
Reggie Tongue .25
Tamarick Vanover .50
K.C. Wolf .25
Jerome Woods .25

1972 Chiquita NFL Slides

The 13-slide, 3-9/16" x 1-3/4" set features two players on each slide. The slides have a slide image in each of the four corners with a player summary in the middle. The top two images are of the same player, while the bottom two are of the second player. A yellow viewer was also issued.

NM/M
Complete Set (13): 325.00
Common Player: 20.00
1 Joe Greene, Bob Lilly (2) 50.00
3 Bill Bergey, Gary Collins (4) 30.00
5 Walt Sweeney, Bubba Smith (6) 30.00
7 Larry Wilson, Fred Carr (8) 20.00
9 Mac Percival, John Brodie (10) 30.00
11 Lem Barney, Ron Yary (12) 30.00
13 Curt Knight, Alvin Haymond (14) 20.00
15 Floyd Little, Gerry Philbin (16) 30.00
17 Jim Mitchell, Paul Costa (18) 20.00
19 Jake Kupp, Ben Hawkins (20) 20.00
21 Johnny Robinson, George Webster (22) 20.00
23 Mercury Morris, Willie Brown (24) 40.00
25 Ron Johnson, Jon Morris (26) 20.00
NNO Yellow Viewer 30.00

1970 Clark Volpe

The 66-card, 7-1/2" x 9-15/16" set includes cards for eight of the teams in the league in 1970. The Chicago Bears (1-8), Cincinnati Bengals (9-14), Cleveland Browns (15-21), Detroit Lions (22-30), Green Bay Packers (31-39), Kansas City Chiefs (40-48), Minnesota Vikings (49-57) and St. Louis Cardinals (58-66). Cards with the mail tabs measure 7-1/2" x 14" and the backs have mail-in offers for other merchandise while the fronts feature player drawings by artist Nicholas Volpe.

NM/M
Complete Set (66): 325.00
Common Player: 3.00
1 Ron Bull 3.00
2 Dick Butkus 18.00
3 Lee Roy Caffey 3.00
4 Bobby Douglass 6.00
5 Dick Gordon 3.00
6 Bennie McRae 3.00
7 Ed O'Bradovich 3.00
8 George Seals 3.00
9 Bill Bergey 6.00
10 Jess Phillips 3.00
11 Mike Reid 6.00
12 Paul Robinson 6.00
13 Bob Trumpy 8.00
14 Sam Wyche 12.00
15 Erich Barnes 3.00
16 Gary Collins 6.00
17 Gene Hickerson 3.00
18 Jim Houston 3.00
19 Leroy Kelly 12.00
20 Ernie Kellerman 3.00
21 Bill Nelsen 6.00
22 Lem Barney 10.00
23 Mel Farr 6.00
24 Larry Hand 3.00
25 Alex Karras 12.00
26 Mike Lucci 6.00
27 Bill Munson 6.00
28 Charlie Sanders 6.00
29 Tommy Vaughn 3.00
30 Wayne Walker 6.00
31 Lionel Aldridge 3.00
32 Donny Anderson 6.00
33 Ken Bowman 3.00
34 Carroll Dale 6.00
35 Jim Grabowski 6.00
36 Ray Nitschke 15.00
37 Dave Robinson 6.00
38 Travis Williams 6.00
39 Willie Wood 10.00
40 Fred Arbanas 3.00
41 Bobby Bell 10.00
42 Aaron Brown 3.00
43 Buck Buchanan 10.00
44 Len Dawson 16.00
45 Jim Marsalis 3.00
46 Jerry Mays 3.00
47 Johnny Robinson 6.00
48 Jim Tyrer 6.00
49 Bill Brown 6.00
50 Fred Cox 3.00
51 Gary Cuozzo 6.00
52 Carl Eller 10.00
53 Jim Marshall 10.00
54 Dave Osborn 6.00
55 Alan Page 12.00
56 Mick Tingelhoff 6.00
57 Gene Washington 6.00
58 Pete Beathard 6.00
59 John Gilliam 6.00
60 Jim Hart 8.00
61 Johnny Roland 6.00
62 Jackie Smith 10.00
63 Larry Stallings 3.00
64 Roger Wehrli 6.00
65 Dave Williams 3.00
66 Larry Wilson 10.00

1991 Classic Promos

These promotional cards preview Classic's design for its debut set in 1991. The card back only has trademark information, plus the words "For Promotional Purposes Only! Not For Resale." The five cards were also featured together on a 7-1/2" x 7-1/8" promo sheet which was made available to collectors who attended the 12th National Sports Collectors Convention in Anaheim, Calif., in July 1991. Each sheet is serially-numbered (1 of 10,000, etc.) and is labeled on the back as being a promotional sheet.

NM/M
Complete Set (7): 15.00
Common Player (1-5): 1.50
1 Antone Davis 1.50
2A Raghib Rocket Ismail 5.00
2B Raghib Rocket Ismail 5.00
3A Todd Lyght 2.00
3B Todd Lyght 2.00
4 Russell Maryland 2.00
5 Eric Turner 2.00

1991 Classic

Classic's first venture into the football field resulted in this 50-card boxed set released in June. Classic reportedly paid several players for exclusive rights to appear in the set, including Raghib Ismail. No team names or college names are listed on the cards, which have a grey marble-like border on the front, plus the Classic logos. Each back has biographical information, plus a player profile.

NM/M
Complete Set (50): 6.00
Common Player: .05
1 Rocket Ismail .50
2 Russell Maryland .30
3 Eric Turner .30
4 Bruce Pickens .10
5 Mike Croal .10
6 Todd Lyght .10
7 Eric Swann .30
8 Antone Davis .10
9 Stanley Richard .10
10 Pat Harlow .10
11 Alvin Harper .50
12 Mike Pritchard .30
13 Leonard Russell .10
14 Dan McGwire .10
15 Bobby Wilson .10
16 Alfred Williams .10
17 Vinnie Clark .10
18 Kelvin Pritchett .10
19 Harvey Williams .50
20 Stan Thomas .10
21 Randal Hill .25
22 Todd Marinovich .10
23 Henry Jones .05
24 Jarrod Bunch .05
25 Mike Dumas .10
26 Ed King .05
27 Reggie Jackson .05
28 Roman Phifer .10
29 Mike Jones .10
30 Brett Favre 5.00
31 Browning Nagle .10
32 Esera Tualolo .10
33 George Thornton .10
34 Dixon Edwards .10
35 Darryl Lewis .10
36 Eric Bieniemy .20
37 Shane Curry .10
38 Jerome Henderson .10
39 Wesley Carroll .10
40 Nick Bell .10
41 John Flannery .05
42 Ricky Watters 1.00
43 Jeff Graham .50
44 Eric Moten .05
45 Jesse Campbell .05
46 Chris Zorich .20
47 Doug Thomas .05
48 Phil Hansen .05
49 Kanavis McGhee .05
50 Reggie Barrett .10

1992 Classic Promos

The six-card, standard-size set was issued by Classic to preview the upcoming 1992 NFL Draft set. The card fronts contain black borders while the backs have collegiate summaries. The photos on the card fronts of the six promos differ from their card counterparts in the 100-card set.

NM/M
Complete Set (6): 8.00
Common Player: .50
1 Desmond Howard 2.00
2 David Klingler .50
3 Quentin Coryatt .50
4 Carl Pickens 4.00
5 Derek Brown .50
6 Casey Weldon .50

1992 Classic

This set features 100 of the top collegiate players expected to be selected in the NFL draft. The card front has a color glossy photo surrounded by a black border. The player's name and position are at the bottom, along with a set logo. The card back has a summary of the player's collegiate successes and a color mug shot. Statistics, biographical information and a card number are also given. The background is a blurred image of a running back hitting the hole. These cards were sold in foil packs. Cards using the same design and card numbers, but different photos, were also sold in blister packs. There were six promo cards made, previewing the 1992 design but using different photos from the regular cards. Nuances in the card backs are what distinguishes these cards as promos - they are labeled as "For Promotional Purposes Only" and have an ad in place of a career summary.

NM/M
Complete Set (100): 8.00
Common Player: .05
1 Desmond Howard .30
2 David Klingler .20
3 Quentin Coryatt .30
4 Bill Johnson .05
5 Eugene Chung .05
6 Derek Brown .10
7 Carl Pickens 1.50
8 Chris Mims .10
9 Charles Davenport .05
10 Ray Roberts .05
11 Chuck Smith .05
12 Joe Bowden .05
13 Mirko Jurkovic .05
14 Tony Smith .05
15 Ken Swilling .05
16 Greg Skrepenak .05
17 Phillippi Sparks .05
18 Alonzo Spellman .20
19 Bernard Dafney .05
20 Edgar Bennett 1.00
21 Shane Dronett .05
22 Jeremy Lincoln .15
23 Dion Lambert .05
24 Siran Stacy .05
25 Tony Sacca .10
26 Sean Lumpkin .05
27 Tommy Vardell .10
28 Keith Hamilton .05
29 Ashley Ambrose .05
30 Sean Gilbert .75
31 Casey Weldon .20
32 Marc Boutte .05
33 Santana Dotson .05
34 Ronnie West .05
35 Michael Bankston .05
36 Mike Pawlawski .05
37 Dale Carter .10
38 Carlos Snow .05
39 Corey Barlow .05
40 Mark D'Onofrio .05
41 Matt Blundin .05
42 George Rooks .05
43 Patrick Rowe .10
44 Dwight Hollier .05
45 Joel Steed .05
46 Erick Anderson .10
47 Rodney Culver .10
48 Chris Hakel .05
49 Luke Fisher .05
50 Kevin Smith .10
51 Robert Brooks 1.00
52 Bucky Richardson .05
53 Steve Isreal .05
54 Marco Coleman .40
55 Johnny Mitchell .20
56 Scottie Graham .30
57 Keith Goganious .05
58 Tommy Maddox .20
59 Terrell Buckley .20
60 Dana Hall .05
61 Ty Detmer .25
62 Darryl Williams .10
63 Jason Hanson .30
64 Leon Searcy .10
65 Gene McGuire .05
66 Will Furrer .10
67 Darren Woodson .10
68 Tracy Scoggins .10
69 Corey Widmer .05
70 Robert Harris .05
71 Larry Tharpe .05
72 Lance Olberding .05
73 Stacey Dillard .05
74 Anthony Hamlet .05
75 Tommy Jeter .05
76 Mike Evans .05
77 Shane Collins .05
78 Mark Thomas .05
79 Chester McGlockton .10
80 Robert Porcher .10
81 Marquez Pope .10
82 Rico Smith .05
83 Tyrone Williams .05
84 Rod Smith .05
85 Tyrone Legette .05
86 Wayne Hawkins .05
87 Derrick Moore .25
88 Tim Lester .05
89 Calvin Holmes .05
90 Reggie Dwight .05
91 Eddie Robinson .05
92 Robert Jones .05
93 Ricardo McDonald .05
94 Howard Dinkins .05
95 Todd Collins .10
96 Eddie Blake .05
97 Classic Quarterbacks .10
98 Back to Back .10
99 Checklist .05
100 Checklist .05

1992 Classic Draft Blister

These 60 cards feature the top prospects entering the 1992 NFL draft. Each card front has a black border surrounding a glossy color action photo. The player's name and position are at the bottom of the card, along with the Classic logo. The back has a blurred action photo for a background, and gives collegiate statistics and a summary of the player's accomplishments at that level. Bio information, a mug shot, and a card number are also on the back. The cards have the same numbers as those in Classic's regular 100-card main set, but the photos on the front are different. The backgrounds on the backs of these cards also have a richer color tone, too; the regular cards' backgrounds are ghosted. These cards were sold in blister packs.

NM/M
Complete Set (60): 7.00
Common Player: .05
1 Desmond Howard .75
2 David Klingler .75
3 Quentin Coryatt .75
4 Bill Johnson .07
5 Eugene Chung .10
6 Derek Brown .50
7 Carl Pickens .75
8 Chris Mims .30
9 Charles Davenport .12
10 Ray Roberts .10
11 Chuck Smith .10
12 Joe Bowden .07
13 Mirko Jurkovic .05
14 Tony Smith .25
15 Ken Swilling .05
16 Greg Skrepenak .10
17 Phillippi Sparks .07
18 Alonzo Spellman .25
19 Bernard Dafney .07
20 Edgar Bennett .75
21 Shane Dronett .15
22 Jeremy Lincoln .12
23 Dion Lambert .07
24 Siran Stacy .07
25 Tony Sacca .12
26 Sean Lumpkin .07
27 Tommy Vardell .50
28 Keith Hamilton .25
29 Ashley Ambrose .12
30 John Rays .07
31 Casey Weldon .30
32 Marc Boutte .12
33 Santana Dotson .25
34 Ronnie West .05
35 Michael Bankston .10
36 Mike Pawlawski .05
37 Dale Carter .25
38 Carlos Snow .05
39 Corey Barlow .07
40 Mark D'Onofrio .07
41 Matt Blundin .20
42 George Rooks .05
43 Patrick Rowe .07
44 Dwight Hollier .12
45 Joel Steed .07
46 Erick Anderson .10
47 Rodney Culver .15
48 Chris Hakel .07
49 Luke Fisher .05
50 Kevin Smith .25
51 Robert Brooks .12
52 Bucky Richardson .05
53 Steve Israel .05
54 Tyrone Ashley .05
55 Johnny Mitchell .75
56 Scottie Graham .50
57 Keith Goganious .07
58 Tommy Maddox .50
59 Terrell Buckley .30
60 Dana Hall .12

1992 Classic LPs

These gold-foiled stamps were randomly included inside 1992 Classic Draft Picks packs. Approximately 40,000 of each card was produced. Each is numbered on the back using LP 1/10, etc.. The players in the set were projected as top picks in the 1992 NFL draft.

NM/M
Complete Set (10): 10.00
Common Player: .75
1 Desmond Howard 2.00
2 David Klingler 1.25
3 Siran Stacy .75
4 Casey Weldon 1.25
5 Sean Gilbert 1.00
6 Matt Blundin 1.25
7 Tommy Maddox 3.00
8 Derek Brown .75
9 Tony Smith .75
10 Tony Sacca .75

1992 Classic NFL Game

These standard-size cards were included as part of Classic's 1992

NFL football game. The card front has a color action photo framed by rose and dark blue borders. The player's name is also on the front, in a black panel at the bottom, along with a Classic logo, which is at the top. The card back has a player profile, action photo, a card number and five trivia questions. The game included a game board, die, player markers, a scoreboard, rules, and plays which could be used in the game. Two unnumbered cards - Cris Dishman and Andre Ware - had the game's rules on the back.

		NM/M
Complete Set (62):		10.00
Common Player:		.15
1	Steve Atwater	.15
2	Louis Oliver	.15
3	Ronnie Lott	.25
4	Reggie White	.50
5	Cortez Kennedy	.30
6	Derrick Thomas	.40
7	Pat Swilling	.20
8	Cornelius Bennett	.25
9	Mark Rypien	.20
10	Todd Marinovich	.15
11	Steve Young	1.00
12	Warren Moon	.30
13	Mirko Jurkovic	.15
14	Hugh Millen	.15
15	John Friesz	.25
16	John Elway	.75
17	Chris Miller	.25
18	Jim Everett	.25
19	Emmitt Smith	2.00
20	Johnny Johnson	.25
21	Thurman Thomas	.60
22	Leonard Russell	.25
23	Rodney Hampton	.50
24	Marion Butts	.30
25	Neal Anderson	.25
26	Barry Sanders	1.00
27	Dexter Carter	.15
28	Gaston Green	.15
29	Barry Word	.15
30	Eric Bieniemy	.15
31	Nick Bell	.20
32	Reggie Cobb	.15
33	Jay Novacek	.30
34	Keith Jackson	.30
35	Eric Green	.30
36	Lawrence Dawsey	.20
37	Mike Pritchard	.20
38	Michael Haynes	.20
39	James Lofton	.25
40	Art Monk	.25
41	Herman Moore	.40
42	Andre Rison	.40
43	Wendell Davis	.15
44	Sterling Sharpe	.60
45	Fred Barnett	.20
46	Rob Moore	.30
47	Gary Clark	.25
48	Wesley Carroll	.15
49	Michael Irvin	.75
50	John Taylor	.25
51	Robert Brooks	.15
52	Ray Bentley	.15
53	Eric Swann	.20
54	Amp Lee	.20
55	Darryl Williams	.15
56	Wilbur Marshall	.15
57	Siran Stacy	.15
58	Chip Lohmiller	.15
59	Rodney Culver	.15
60	Tommy Vardell	.25
----	Cris Dishman (Rules on back)	.15
----	Andre Ware (Rules on back)	.20

1993 Classic Gold Promos

The two-card, standard-size set was made available to Classic Collectors Club members. The fronts feature color action shots while the backs contain another action photo, biography and player profile. The cards are stamped as "x of 5,000" and are numbered with the "PR" prefix.

		NM/M
Complete Set (2):		7.00
Common Player:		2.00
1	Terry Kirby	2.00
2	Jerome Bettis	5.00

1993 Classic Preview

The one-card, standard size promo was issued as a preview to the base 1993 Classic set. The card, depicting Drew Bledsoe, has the same design as cards in the 1993 base set, although the Bledsoe photo is different from the base card photo.

		NM/M
Complete Set (1):		6.00
Common Player:		6.00
1	Drew Bledsoe	6.00

1993 Classic

These Classic cards feature blue marble-like borders around color action photos. The players name and position are at the bottom of the card in a yellow stripe which contains the set logo. The Classic logo appears in the upper left corner. The back is numbered and is designed in a horizontal manner. Another action photo, collegiate summary, statistics, biographical information and the logo for the team which selected the player in the draft are also included. Inserts within the main set included 1993 Basketball Draft Pick Preview cards, 1,000 cards autographed by Dallas Cowboy quarterback Troy Aikman, 1993 Classic Pro Line Preview cards, and LP cards. Classic also made three types of promo cards - Classic Draft Preview; C3 Presidential Club; and Classic Draft Gold promos. There were 5,000 Gold promos made, each having the words "1 of 5,000" and set logo stamped in gold foil on the front. The back indicates the card is for "Promotional Purposes Only." These cards previewed Classic's gold version set, which parallels its main set. The gold cards were issued in a factory set box and included a certificate of authenticity. There were 5,000 sets made; star gold cards are three to six times more valuable than the regular cards. Drew Bledsoe and Rick Mirer also signed 5,000 of their cards.

		NM/M
Complete Set (100):		8.00
Common Player:		.05
Comp. Gold Set (102):		180.00
Gold Cards:		3X-6X
Drew Bledsoe Auto/5000		75.00
Rick Mirer Auto/5000		45.00
1	Drew Bledsoe	2.00
2	Rick Mirer	.50
3	Garrison Hearst	.75
4	Marvin Jones	.10
5	John Copeland	.10
6	Eric Curry	.10
7	Curtis Conway	.75
8	Willie Roaf	.10
9	Lincoln Kennedy	.10
10	Jerome Bettis	.75
11	Mike Compton	.05
12	John Gerak	.05
13	Will Shields	.10
14	Ben Coleman	.05
15	Ernest Dye	.05
16	Lester Holmes	.05
17	Brad Hopkins	.05
18	Everett Lindsay	.05
19	Todd Rucci	.05
20	Lance Gunn	.05
21	Elvis Grbac	.40
22	Shane Matthews	.10
23	Rudy Harris	.05
24	Rich Anderson	.05
25	Derek Brown	.10
26	Roger Harper	.05
27	Terry Kirby	.30
28	Natrone Means	.50
29	Glyn Milburn	.40
30	Adrian Murrell	.40
31	Lorenzo Neal	.10
32	Roosevelt Potts	.20
33	Kevin Williams	.10
34	Russell Copeland	.10
35	Fred Baxter	.05
36	Troy Drayton	.25
37	Chris Gedney	.10
38	Irv Smith	.10
39	Olanda Truitt	.05
40	Victor Bailey	.20
41	Horace Copeland	.10
42	Ron Dickerson Jr.	.05
43	Willie Harris	.05
44	Tyrone Hughes	.10
45	Qadry Ismail	.25
46	Reggie Brooks	.15
47	Sean LaChapelle	.05
48	O.J. McDuffie	.75
49	Larry Ryans	.05
50	Kenny Shedd	.05
51	Brian Stablein	.05
52	Lamar Thomas	.10
53	Kevin Williams	.75
54	Othello Henderson	.05
55	Kevin Henry	.05
56	Todd Kelly	.05
57	Devon McDonald	.05
58	Michael Strahan	.05
59	Dan Williams	.05
60	Gilbert Brown	.05
61	Mark Caesar	.05
62	Ronnie Dixon	.05
63	John Parrella	.05
64	Leonard Renfro	.05
65	Coleman Rudolph	.05
66	Ronnie Bradford	.05
67	Tom Carter III	.10
68	Deon Figures	.10
69	Derrick Frazier	.05
70	Darrien Gordon	.10
71	Carlton Gray	.10
72	Adrian Hardy	.05
73	Mike Reid	.05
74	Thomas Smith	.05
75	Robert O'Neal	.05
76	Chad Brown	.40
77	Demetrius DuBose	.20
78	Reggie Givens	.05
79	Travis Hill	.05
80	Rich McKenzie	.05
81	Barry Minter	.05
82	Darrin Smith	.10
83	Steve Tovar	.10
84	Patrick Bates	.10
85	Dan Footman	.05
86	Ryan McNeil	.05
87	Danan Hughes	.05
88	Mark Brunell	1.00
89	Ron Moore	.15
90	Antonio London	.10
91	Steve Everitt	.10
92	Wayne Simmons	.20
93	Robert Smith	.50
94	Dana Stubblefield	.30
95	George Teague	.20
96	Carl Simpson	.10
97	Billy Joe Hobert	.20
98	Gino Torretta	.15
99	Checklist No. 1	.05
100	Checklist No. 2	.05
AU1	Troy Aikman Auto/1000	150.00

1993 Classic Draft Stars

1993 Classic Football jumbo packs each contained one of these random inserts. The card front indicates the card is 1 of 20,000 made; the card back uses a DS prefix for the card number. The front has a color full-bleed photo, and foil stamping for the player's name, position and set logo. The card back has biographical information, a mug shot and a congratulatory note indicating the card is one of 20,000 made for each player. The logo of the team which selected the player is also on the card back. A Mirer/Bledsoe jumbo card, available one per every other box, was also produced.

		NM/M
Complete Set (20):		24.00
Common Player:		.50
DS1	Drew Bledsoe	7.00
DS2	Rick Mirer	2.00
DS3	Garrison Hearst	3.00
DS4	Marvin Jones	.50
DS5	John Copeland	.50
DS6	Eric Curry	.50
DS7	Curtis Conway	2.00
DS8	Jerome Bettis	3.00
DS9	Patrick Bates	.50
DS10	Tom Carter	.50
DS11	Irv Smith	.50
DS12	Robert Smith	1.00
DS13	O.J. McDuffie	1.00
DS14	Roosevelt Potts	.75
DS15	Natrone Means	1.00
DS16	Glyn Milburn	.50
DS17	Reggie Brooks	.75
DS18	Kevin Williams	.50
DS19	Qadry Ismail	1.00
DS20	Billy Joe Hobert	.50
----	Drew Bledsoe, Rick Mirer	12.00

1993 Classic LPs

These inserts were randomly included in 1993 Classic football packs. The card front has a blue-gray border which frames a color action photo. The Classic logo is at the top of the card; the player's name, position and set logo are at the bottom in a gold foil stripe. "LP" and "1 of 45,000" are also stamped in gold foil at the bottom. The card back is horizontal and includes another action photo, career summary and card number. The logo of the team which selected the player in the draft is also on the back.

		NM/M
Complete Set (10):		35.00
Common Player:		1.50
1	Drew Bledsoe	12.00
2	Rick Mirer	2.00
3	Garrison Hearst	3.00
4	Marvin Jones	1.50
5	John Copeland	1.50
6	Eric Curry	1.50
7	Curtis Conway	3.00
8	Jerome Bettis	4.00
9	Reggie Brooks	2.00
10	Qadry Ismail	2.00

1993 Classic Superhero Comic

These cards were random inserts in 1993 Classic Football packs. Each card front has a comic-book style drawing of the featured player, as illustrated by artist Neal Adams. The drawing is full-bleed and in color and includes the player's name and position at the bottom in a yellow bar. The card back is numbered with an "SH" prefix and features a ghosted image of the front photo as its background. A second color action photo and career summary are also included. There were 15,000 cards of each player made.

		NM/M
Complete Set (4):		35.00
Common Player:		7.00
1	Troy Aikman	15.00
2	Drew Bledsoe	15.00
3	Rick Mirer	3.00
4	Garrison Hearst	4.00

1993 Classic TONX

The 150-card, 1-5/8" in diameter set features color action shots on the circular fronts with the player's name, team helmet logo and NFL and Classic logos on the back.

		NM/M
Complete Set (150):		12.00
Common Player:		.05
1	Troy Aikman	1.00
2	Eric Allen	.05
3	Terry Allen	.25
4	Morten Anderson	.05
5	Neal Anderson	.05
6	Flipper Anderson	.05
7	Steve Atwater	.05
8	Carl Banks	.05
9	Patrick Bates	.05
10	Cornelius Bennett	.10
11	Rod Bernstine	.05
12	Jerome Bettis	1.00
13	Steve Beuerlein	.05
14	Bennie Blades	.05
15	Brian Blades	.05
16	Drew Bledsoe	3.00
17	Tim Brown	.10
18	Terrell Buckley	.05
19	Marion Butts	.05
20	Mark Carrier (DB)	.05
21	Anthony Carter	.05
22	Cris Carter	.10
23	Dale Carter	.05
24	Ray Childress	.05
25	Gary Clark	.05
26	Reggie Cobb	.05
27	Marco Coleman	.05
28	Curtis Conway	.30
29	John Copeland	.05
30	Quentin Coryatt	.10
31	Randall Cunningham	.10
32	Eric Curry	.05
33	Lawrence Dawsey	.05
34	Chris Doleman	.05
35	Vaughn Dunbar	.05
36	Henry Ellard	.05
37	John Elway	.75
38	Steve Emtman	.05
39	Ricky Ervins	.05
40	Jim Everett	.05
41	Brett Favre	2.00
42	Barry Foster	.05
43	Gary Cleveland	.05
44	Jeff George	.10
45	Sean Gilbert	.05
46	Ernest Givins	.05
47	Harold Green	.05
48	Kevin Greene	.05
49	Paul Gruber	.05
50	Charles Haley	.05
51	Rodney Hampton	.10
52	Jim Harbaugh	.10
53	Ronnie Harmon	.05
54	Michael Haynes	.05
55	Garrison Hearst	.50
56	Randal Hill	.05
57	Merril Hoge	.05
58	Pierce Holt	.05
59	Jeff Hostetler	.05
60	Stan Humphries	.10
61	Michael Irvin	.15
62	Keith Jackson	.05
63	Rickey Jackson	.05
64	Haywood Jeffires	.05
65	Pepper Johnson	.05
66	Brent Jones	.05
67	Marvin Jones	.05
68	Seth Joyner	.05
69	Jim Kelly	.15
70	Cortez Kennedy	.05
71	David Klingler	.05
72	Bernie Kosar	.05
73	Reggie Langhorne	.05
74	Mo Lewis	.05
75	Howie Long	.10
76	Ronnie Lott	.10
77	Charles Mann	.05
78	Dan Marino	2.00
79	Todd Marinovich	.05
80	Eric Martin	.05
81	Clay Matthews	.05
82	Ed McCaffrey	.05
83	O.J. McDuffie	.30
84	Steve McMichael	.05
85	Audray McMillian	.05
86	Greg McMurtry	.05
87	Karl Mecklenburg	.05
88	Dave Meggett	.05
89	Eric Metcalf	.05
90	Anthony Miller	.10
91	Chris Miller	.05
92	Sam Mills	.05
93	Rick Mirer	.50
94	Johnny Mitchell	.05
95	Art Monk	.10
96	Joe Montana	1.00
97	Warren Moon	.15
98	Rob Moore	.05
99	Brad Muster	.05
100	Browning Nagle	.05
101	Ken Norton Jr.	.05
102	Jay Novacek	.05
103	Neil O'Donnell	.10
104	Leslie O'Neal	.05
105	Louis Oliver	.05
106	Rodney Peete	.05
107	Michael Dean Perry	.05
108	Carl Pickens	.30
109	Ricky Proehl	.05
110	Andre Reed	.10
111	Jerry Rice	1.00
112	Andre Rison	.10
113	Leonard Russell	.10
114	Mark Rypien	.05
115	Barry Sanders	1.00
116	Deion Sanders	.50
117	Junior Seau	.10
118	Shannon Sharpe	.10
119	Sterling Sharpe	.10
120	Clyde Simmons	.05
121	Wayne Simmons	.05
122	Phil Simms	.10
123	Bruce Smith	.10
124	Emmitt Smith	2.00
126	Alonzo Spellman	.10
127	Pat Swilling	.05
128	John Taylor	.05
129	Lawrence Taylor	.15
130	Broderick Thomas	.05
131	Derrick Thomas	.10
132	Thurman Thomas	.15
133	Andre Tippett	.05
134	Jessie Tuggle	.05
135	Tommy Vardell	.05
136	Jon Vaughn	.05
137	Clarence Verdin	.05
138	Herschel Walker	.10
139	Andre Ware	.05
140	Chris Warren	.10
141	Ricky Watters	.20
142	Lorenzen White	.05
143	Reggie White	.15
144	Alfred Williams	.05
145	Calvin Williams	.05
146	Harvey Williams	.05
147	John L. Williams	.05
148	Rod Woodson	.15
149	Barry Word	.05
150	Steve Young	.75

1994 Classic Previews

The five-card, standard-size set was issued by Classic to preview its 1994 NFL Draft Pick set. The card fronts feature the same design as the base set with the backs containing a congratulatory message for pulling the card, which was limited to "1 of 1,950" sets. They are numbered with the "PR" prefix.

		NM/M
Complete Set (5):		12.00
Common Player:		2.00
1	Heath Shuler	2.00
2	Trent Dilfer	4.00
3	Dan Wilkinson	2.00
4	David Palmer	2.00
5	Johnnie Morton	3.00

1994 Classic Promos

The three-card, standard-size set previewed the release of the 1994 base set. The card fronts feature the same design as the base set - as do the backs. The cards are numbered with the "PR" prefix.

		NM/M
Complete Set (3):		8.00
Common Player:		4.00
1	Marshall Faulk	5.00
2	Heath Shuler	2.00
3	Heath Shuler	2.00

1994 Classic

This 105-card set features the first licensed cards of 93 NFL rookies. Each card front has a full-bleed color action photo, the player's name and position, the set logo, and a helmet of the team which drafted him. The card back has a ghosted image of the player, except for the player's head, which is full-color. Biographical information, stats, a card number and collegiate summary are also included. The set is limited to just under 10,000 cases. A parallel gold foil card was also made for each card in the set; one card was included in each pack. Other inserts included 1,994 autographed Jerry Rice cards; 9,994 numbered cards honoring Rice's records; sweepstakes Rookie of the Year cards, Classic LPs, Pro Line previews, Basketball previews and Classic Stars. There were also three Classic Draft promo cards produced, using the same design as the main cards also produced, and labeled with a "PR" prefix. The front format is similar to the regular and promo cards, but the back is different; it has a congratulatory message indicating the card is one of five of the 1,950 sets produced.

		NM/M
Complete Set (105):		10.00
Common Player:		.05
Comp. Gold Set (105):		30.00
Gold Cards:		1X-3X
Wax Box:		24.00
1	Heath Shuler	.25
2	Trent Dilfer	.75
3	Marshall Faulk	2.00
4	Errict Rhett	.75
5	Charlie Garner	.40
6	Sam Adams	.10
7	Shante Carver	.10
8	Dwayne Chandler	.05
9	Andre Coleman	.05
10	Carlester Crumpler	.05
11	Charles Johnson	.40
12	David Palmer	.10
13	Dan Wilkinson	.20
14	LeShon Johnson	.10
15	Mario Bates	.50
16	Glenn Foley	.05
17	William Gaines	.05
18	Wayne Gandy	.05
19	Jason Gildon	.05
20	Eric Gant	.05
21	Tre Johnson	.05
22	Calvin Jones	.05
23	Jake Kelchner	.05
24	Perry Klein	.05
25	Chuck Levy	.10
26	Corey Louchiey	.05
27	Chris Maumalanga	.05
28	Jamir Miller	.10
29	Jim Miller	.05
30	Johnnie Morton	.30
31	Doug Nussmeier	.05
32	Vaughn Parker	.05
33	Darnay Scott	.40
34	Fernando Smith	.05
35	Lamar Smith	.75
36	Marcus Spears	.05
37	Irving Spikes	.25
38	Todd Steussie	.10
39	Aaron Taylor	.10
40	John Thierry	.10
41	Dewayne Washington	.05
42	Jason Winrow	.05
43	Ronnie Woolfork	.05
44	Bryant Young	.30
45	Arthur Bussie	.05
46	Derrick Alexander	.25
47	Larry Allen	.05

48	Aubrey Beavers	.05
49	James Bostic	.10
50	Jeff Burris	.05
51	Lindsey Chapman	.05
52	Isaac Davis	.05
53	Lake Dawson	.30
54	Tyronne Drakeford	.05
55	William Floyd	.50
56	Henry Ford	.05
57	Rob Fredrickson	.20
58	Aaron Glenn	.05
59	Shelby Hill	.05
60	Willie Jackson	.20
61	Joe Johnson	.05
62	Aaron Laing	.05
63	Kevin Lee	.05
64	Eric Mahlum	.05
65	Steve Matthews	.05
66	Willie McGinest	.20
67	Kevin Mitchell	.05
68	Bam Morris	.75
69	Thomas Randolph	.05
70	Tony Richardson	.05
71	Corey Sawyer	.05
72	Jason Sehorn	.05
73	Rob Waldrop	.05
74	Jay Walker	.05
75	Bernard Williams	.05
76	Marvin Goodwin	.05
77	Romeo Bandison	.05
78	Bucky Brooks	.05
79	James Folston	.05
80	Donnell Bennett	.05
81	Charlie Ward	.20
82	Antonio Langham	.10
83	Greg Hill	.40
84	Darnay Scott	.10
85	Winfred Tubbs	.05
86	Trev Alberts	.10
87	Tim Bowens	.25
88	Thomas Lewis	.10
89	Allen Aldridge	.05
90	Bert Emanuel	.25
91	Ryan Yarborough	.10
92	Lonnie Johnson	.05
93	Isaac Bruce	1.00
94	Checklist #1	.05
95	Checklist #2	.05
96	Troy Aikman	.25
97	Steve Young	.25
98	Rick Mirer	.15
99	Drew Bledsoe	.40
100	Jerry Rice	.25
101	Heath Shuler	.75
102	Marshall Faulk	1.50
103	Trent Dilfer	.30
104	Dan Wilkerson	.10
105	David Palmer	.10
JR1	Jerry Rice Special	12.00
NNO	Jerry Rice Auto/1994	125.00

1994 Classic Football Gold

This set is a parallel to Classic's main 1994 Draft set; the cards are the same as the regular ones, except the set logo is stamped in gold foil on the card front. One gold card was in each pack.

	NM/M
Complete Set (105):	40.00
Common Player:	.15
Gold Cards:	2X

1994 Classic Draft Stars

These cards feature a full-bleed color action photo on the front, along with the set logo. The player's name, position and helmet of the team which drafted him are at the bottom. The card back has another color photo, part of which is ghosted to allow for the player's name and biographical information.

		NM/M
Complete Set (20):		12.00
Common Player:		.25
1	Trev Alberts	.50
2	Jeff Burris	.25
3	Shante Carver	.25
4	Trent Dilfer	2.00
5	Marshall Faulk	5.00
6	William Floyd	1.50
7	Aaron Glenn	.25
8	Greg Hill	.50
9	Charles Johnson	.50
10	Calvin Jones	.25
11	Antonio Langham	.25
12	Thomas Lewis	.25
13	Willie McGinest	.50
14	Jamir Miller	.25
15	Johnnie Morton	.75
16	David Palmer	.50
17	Darnay Scott	.50
18	Heath Shuler	.50
19	Dan Wilkinson	.50
20	Bryant Young	.75
NNO	Rick Mirer Special	1.00

1994 Classic Picks

These limited-edition cards were randomly included in Classic Draft football packs. Only 20,000 of each card was made, as noted in blue on the card back. The card front features a color action photo against a metallic background. The player's name appears in the upper left corner. The back has a player mug shot, collegiate highlights, and bio notes, all against a ghosted image of the photo on the front. A card number, using an "LP" prefix, is also included. An LP card was in every box.

		NM/M
Complete Set (5):		40.00
Common Player:		4.00
1	Heath Shuler	1.00
2	Trent Dilfer	7.00
3	Johnnie Morton	6.00
4	David Palmer	2.00
5	Marshall Faulk	20.00

1994 Classic ROY Sweepstakes

These 20 sweepstakes cards, issued approximately 5 per case, feature players who were in the running for the NFL's 1994 Rookie of the Year Award. Collectors who obtained a card of the winner could redeem it for an autographed football of the player.

		NM/M
Complete Set (20):		50.00
Common Player:		2.50
1	Trent Dilfer	5.00
2	Mario Bates	2.00
3	Darnay Scott	2.00
4	Johnnie Morton	3.00
5	William Floyd	3.00
6	Errict Rhett	4.00
7	Greg Hill	2.00
8	Lake Dawson	2.00
9	Charlie Garner	5.00
10	Heath Shuler	2.00
11	Derrick Alexander	2.00
12	LeShon Johnson	2.50
13	Kevin Lee	2.50
14	David Palmer	2.50
15	Charles Johnson	2.00
16	Chuck Levy	2.50
17	Calvin Jones	2.50
18	Thomas Lewis	2.50
19	Marshall Faulk	25.00
20	"Field" card	2.50

1994 Classic Game Cards

The 10-card, regular-sized set was inserted in every jumbo pack of 1994 Classic. The card fronts have "Game Card" printed along the left border with a scratch-off section on the back. An unnumbered Drew Bledsoe card was randomly inserted as well, and winning cards could be redeemed for an uncut Gold NFL Draft sheet or a 1994 NFL Draft Day set. The cards are numbered with the "GC" prefix.

		NM/M
Complete Set (10):		10.00
Common Player:		.25
Scratched Cards:		.5X
DB1	Drew Bledsoe Special	12.00
1	Trent Dilfer	.75
2	Marshall Faulk	3.50
3	Heath Shuler	.50
4	Dan Wilkinson	.25
5	Antonio Langham	.25
6	Willie McGinest	.25
7	Greg Hill	.50
8	Trev Alberts	.25
9	Charles Johnson	.50
10	Errict Rhett	2.50

1994 Classic Images

Only 1,994 cases of Classic Images Football were produced, with each card in the 125-card set printed on a specially designed 18-point, micro-lined foil board. The card front has an action shot on a foil background. The player's name is in a stripe at the bottom, with the Images logo in the middle. The card back has stats from the 1993 season and the player's career totals, plus a color photo and card number. Inserts were from two types - All-Pros and All-Pro Prospects cards, and NFL Experience Sneak Preview cards.

		NM/M
Complete Set (125):		40.00
Common Player:		.25
Pack (6):		8.00
Wax Box (24):		75.00
1	Emmitt Smith	4.00
2	Reggie White	.40
3	Michael Haynes	.25
4	Chris Warren	.40
5	Jeff George	.40
6	Sean Gilbert	.25
7	Ricky Watters	.40
8	Eric Metcalf	.25
9	Randall Cunningham	.40
10	Tim Brown	.40
11	*Trent Dilfer*	1.00
12	*Marshall Faulk*	7.00
13	David Klingler	.25
14	Barry Foster	.40
15	John Elway	1.50
16	Joe Montana	4.00
17	Rodney Hampton	.40
18	*Todd Steussie*	.40
19	Bruce Smith	.25
20	Wayne Gandy	.25
21	Anthony Miller	.25
22	Reggie Brooks	.25
23	Johnny Johnson	.25
24	*Byron Morris*	.50
25	Drew Bledsoe	4.00
26	Jeff Hostetler	.25
27	Alvin Harper	.25
28	Cris Carter	.25
29	*Bert Emanuel*	.50
30	*Errict Rhett*	1.00
31	Scott Mitchell	.25
32	Deion Sanders	1.00
33	Lewis Tillman	.25
34	*Tim Bowens*	.75
35	Charles Haley	.25
36	Stan Humphries	.40
37	Haywood Jeffires	.25
38	Andre Reed	.25
39	*Charles Johnson*	.50
40	Ron Moore	.25
41	Jim Everett	.25
42	*Greg Hill*	.50
43	Thurman Thomas	.50
44	*Willie McGinest*	.50
45	*Aaron Glenn*	.40
46	Erric Pegram	.25
47	Terry Kirby	.25
48	Warren Moon	.40
49	Clyde Simmons	.25
50	Eric Turner	.25
51	*Heath Shuler*	.75
52	Rickey Jackson	.25
53	*Johnnie Morton*	1.00
54	*Charlie Garner*	3.00
55	Mark Collins	.25
56	Mike Pritchard	.25
57	*Bryant Young*	1.00
58	*Joe Johnson*	.40
59	Erik Kramer	.25
60	Barry Sanders	3.00
61	Rod Woodson	.40
62	Dave Brown	.25
63	Gary Brown	.25
64	Brett Favre	4.00
65	*Isaac Bruce*	5.00
66	Boomer Esiason	.25
67	Jim Harbaugh	.25
68	Jackie Harris	.25
69	Art Monk	.25
70	*Jamir Miller*	.40
71	Neil O'Donnell	.50
72	Neil Smith	.25
73	Junior Seau	.40
74	*Jerome Bettis*	1.50
75	*Bernard Williams*	.25
76	*Jeff Burris*	.75
77	Henry Ellard	.25
78	Reggie Cobb	.25
79	*Shante Carver*	.40
80	Terry Allen	.25
81	Cortez Kennedy	.25
82	*Trev Alberts*	.50
83	Michael Irvin	.50
84	Herschel Walker	.25
85	Dan Marino	4.00
86	Dave Meggett	.25
87	Herman Moore	.50
88	*Darnay Scott*	.75
89	*Dewayne Washington*	.50
90	*Rob Fredrickson*	.50
91	Rick Mirer	.50
92	*Thomas Lewis*	.75
93	Chris Miller	.25
94	Marion Butts	.25
95	*Sam Adams*	.75
96	Jerry Rice	2.50
97	Ben Coates	.50
98	*David Palmer*	1.00
99	*Antonio Langham*	.50
100	Curtis Conway	.50
101	Derrick Thomas	.40
102	Ken Norton	.25
103	Ronnie Lott	.25
104	Sterling Sharpe	.40
105	Troy Aikman	3.00
106	Shannon Sharpe	.40
107	Natrone Means	.50
108	Derek Brown	.40
109	Dan Wilkinson	.75
110	Andre Rison	.40
111	Quentin Coryatt	.25
112	Cody Carlson	.25
113	*William Floyd*	.75
114	Marcus Allen	.40
115	Steve Young	2.50
116	Jim Kelly	.40
117	*LeShon Johnson*	.50
118	Irving Fryar	.25
119	Carl Pickens	1.00
120	Keith Jackson	.25
121	*John Thierry*	.40
122	Vinny Testaverde	.25
123	*Derrick Alexander*	.50
124	Seth Joyner	.25
125	Checklist	.25
TP1	Drew Bledsoe (NFL EX)	20.00
NNO	Emmitt Smith (NFL EX)	15.00

1994 Classic Images All-Pro

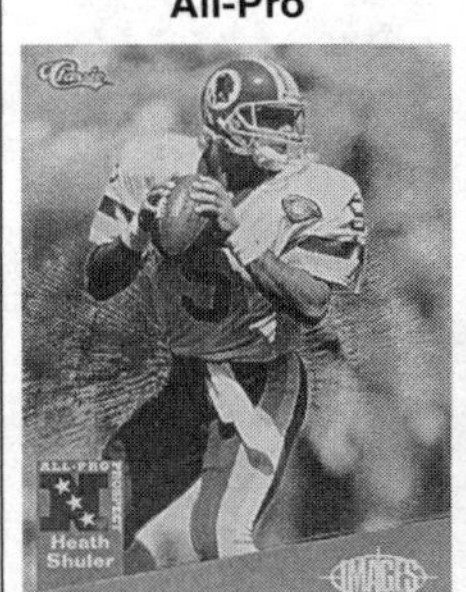

These cards were randomly included in packs of 1994 Classic Images football, either two cards per box or two All-Pro packs per case. Each card in this 25-card set is sequentially numbered up to 2,600. All-Pros have a colored foil stripe across the bottom which includes the Images logo. The player's name, his conference and All-Pro logo are in a box in the lower left corner. The card back has the sequential number, a color action photo, and card number, which uses an "A" prefix.

		NM/M
Complete Set (25):		150.00
Common Player:		2.00
1	Heath Shuler	3.00
2	Steve Young	15.00
3	Trent Dilfer	6.00
4	Troy Aikman	15.00
5	Emmitt Smith	25.00
6	Barry Sanders	25.00
7	Jerome Bettis	6.00
8	Errict Rhett	4.00
9	Jerry Rice	15.00
10	Michael Irvin	4.00
11	Andre Rison	4.00
12	Sterling Sharpe	4.00
13	Reggie White	4.00
14	Rick Mirer	2.00
15	Drew Bledsoe	15.00
16	John Elway	15.00
17	Joe Montana	25.00
18	Dan Marino	25.00
19	Thurman Thomas	6.00
20	Marshall Faulk	12.00
21	Marcus Allen	4.00
22	Charles Johnson	4.00
23	Tim Brown	7.00
24	Anthony Miller	2.00
25	Derrick Thomas	2.00

1994 Classic Images Update

The 10-card, standard-size set was randomly inserted in retail packs of 1995 Classic Images 4-Sport. The cards' numbering starts at No. 126 as an addition to the 1994 Images set.

		NM/M
Complete Set (10):		75.00
Common Player:		4.00
126	Emmitt Smith	15.00
127	Troy Aikman	10.00
128	Steve Young	8.00
129	Deion Sanders	4.00
130	Ben Coates	4.00
131	Natrone Means	4.00
132	Drew Bledsoe	12.00
133	Cris Carter	5.00
134	Marshall Faulk	10.00
135	Errict Rhett	4.00

1994 Classic NFL Experience Promos

The six-card, standard-size set was issued to preview the 100-card 1994 Classic NFL Experience set. The fronts feature full-bleed action shots with "For Promotional Purposes Only" printed on the card backs.

		NM/M
Complete Set (6):		18.00
Common Player:		1.25
1	Troy Aikman	5.00
2	Jerry Rice	5.00
3	Emmitt Smith	10.00
4	Derrick Thomas	1.25
5	Thurman Thomas	2.50
6	Rod Woodson	1.25

1994 Classic NFL Experience

This limited-print 100-card set features the NFL's impact players and highlights 23 top rookies, along with 16 members of the NFL Quarterback Club. Each card front has a borderless color photo of the player, the set logo, and the player's name in a color bar at the bottom. The back has a color photo, a summary of the player's accomplishments during the 1993 season, and a card number. Both sides are UV coated. Classic produced only 1,500 numbered cases, available only through hobby dealers, in conjunction with Super Bowl XXVIII. A 10-card limited-print set of rookies was produced as inserts, as were 1,994 Troy Aikman Super Bowl MVP cards. Six promo cards were also produced to showcase the company's main set. The cards were given away during a Super Bowl card show.

		NM/M
Complete Set (100):		12.00
Common Player:		.06
Pack:		.75
Wax Box (36):		24.00
1	Checklist 1	.06
2	Checklist 2	.06
3	Bobby Hebert	.10
4	Erric Pegram	.25
5	Andre Rison	.30
6	Deion Sanders	.15
7	Cornelius Bennett	.08
8	Jim Kelly	.25
9	Andre Reed	.10
10	Bruce Smith	.10
11	Thurman Thomas	.40
12	Curtis Conway	.30
13	Jim Harbaugh	.06
14	John Copeland	.10
15	David Klingler	.20
16	Carl Pickens	.10
17	Eric Metcalf	.15
18	Vinny Testaverde	.10
19	Eric Turner	.08
20	Tommy Vardell	.08
21	Troy Aikman	1.00
22	Michael Irvin	.45
23	Emmitt Smith	2.00
24	Kevin Williams	.10
25	John Elway	.40
26	Glyn Milburn	.15
27	Shannon Sharpe	.10
28	Herman Moore	.25
29	Rodney Peete	.06
30	Barry Sanders	1.25
31	Pat Swilling	.10
32	Brett Favre	2.00
33	Sterling Sharpe	.10
34	Reggie White	.15
35	Haywood Jeffires	.10
36	Warren Moon	.15
37	Webster Slaughter	.06
38	Lorenzo White	.06
39	Quentin Coryatt	.06
40	Jeff George	.10
41	Roosevelt Potts	.06
42	Marcus Allen	.10
43	Joe Montana	1.25
44	Neil Smith	.08
45	Derrick Thomas	.20
46	Tim Brown	.25
47	Jeff Hostetler	.08
48	Raghib Ismail	.15
49	Anthony Smith	.06
50	Jerome Bettis	.50
51	Jim Everett	.08
52	T.J. Rubley	.06
53	Keith Jackson	.10
54	Terry Kirby	.45
55	Dan Marino	2.00
56	O.J. McDuffie	.25
57	Scott Mitchell	.35
58	Cris Carter	.10
59	Chris Doleman	.08
60	Robert Smith	.10
61	Drew Bledsoe	1.50
62	Vincent Brisby	.45
63	Derek Brown	.20
64	Willie Roaf	.08
65	Irv Smith	.06
66	Renaldo Turnbull	.06
67	Rodney Hampton	.35
68	Phil Simms	.10
69	Lawrence Taylor	.10
70	Boomer Esiason	.06
71	Marvin Jones	.06
72	Ronnie Lott	.10
73	Johnny Mitchell	.06
74	Rob Moore	.10
75	Victor Bailey	.10
76	Randall Cunningham	.10
77	Ken O'Brien	.06
78	Steve Beuerlein	.08
79	Garrison Hearst	.50
80	Ron Moore	.30
81	Ricky Proehl	.08
82	Deon Figures	.06
83	Barry Foster	.20
84	Neil O'Donnell	.12
85	Rod Woodson	.10
86	Natrone Means	.50
87	Anthony Miller	.25
88	Junior Seau	.06
89	Jerry Rice	.75
90	Ricky Watters	.20
91	Steve Young	1.00
92	Brian Blades	.06
93	Cortez Kennedy	.10
94	Rick Mirer	.50
95	Reggie Cobb	.06
96	Eric Curry	.06
97	Craig Erickson	.10
98	Reggie Brooks	.40
99	Desmond Howard	.10
100	Mark Rypien	.06

1994 Classic NFL Experience LPs

This limited-print 10-card set features 10 top NFL prospects. Only 2,400 of each card was produced, and each includes an embossed gold logo of Super Bowl XXVIII on the front. The card front also has a color action photo, the set logo, the player's name and "Classic Rookies" on it. The back, numbered using an "LP" prefix, has another color photo and brief player profile. Cards were random inserts in 1994 Classic NFL Experience packs.

		NM/M
Complete Set (10):		60.00
Common Player:		3.00
Minor Stars:		6.00
1	Jerome Bettis	6.00
2	Drew Bledsoe	25.00
3	Reggie Brooks	3.00
4	Garrison Hearst	5.00
5	Derek Brown	3.00
6	Terry Kirby	6.00
7	Natrone Means	4.00
8	Glyn Milburn	3.00
9	Rick Mirer	4.00
10	Robert Smith	6.00

1995 Classic NFL Rookies

Each of these cards features the 1995 NFL Draft logo and the logo of the team the player was selected by during the draft, along with a full-bleed color action photo on the front. The player's name is in white at the bottom of the card; the Classic logo is in an upper corner. The back has the player's name, position, NFL team name, biographical information and collegiate statistics toward the top; a recap of the player's collegiate accomplishments and a color action photo are on the bottom half. The card number is in the upper left corner in an arrow. Two subsets were also created within the main set - NFL Draft Retro cards and Award Winners. Three parallel sets were also produced - a Silver Series (cards printed on silver foil board; one per pack); a Printer's Proof Series (one per 18 hobby); and a Printer's Proof Silver Series (one in 36 packs). An abbreviated Die-Cut Printer's Proof 1st Round Picks set of the first 32 cards was also made; only 97 sets were made. Only 595 of each regular card appears in a Printer's Proof format, while only 297 of each card was done in a Printer's Proof Silver Series format. Three insert sets were made - Rookie of the Year Redemption, Pro Line Game Breakers and oversized bonus rookie cards. Production of 1995 NFL Classic Rookies was limited to 2,950 hobby and 2,950 retail cases.

		NM/M
Complete Set (110):		15.00
Common Player:		.05
Comp. Silver Set (110):		50.00
Common Silver Player:		.10
Silver Cards:		2X-4X
Comp. Prin. Proof (110):		325.00
Common Prin. Proof:		1.00
Prin. Proof Cards:		3X-8X
Comp. Prin. Proof Sil. (110):		550.00
Common Prin. Proof Sil.:		1.50
Prin. Proof Silvers:		5X-10X
1	Ki-Jana Carter	1.00
2	Tony Boseli	.25
3	Steve McNair	1.00
4	Michael Westbrook	.50
5	Kerry Collins	1.25
6	Kevin Carter	.25
7	Mike Mamula	.25
8	Joseph Galloway	1.25
9	Kyle Brady	.20
10	J.J. Stokes	1.25
11	Derrick Alexander	.25
12	Warren Sapp	.30
13	Mark Fields	.25
14	Ruben Brown	.05
15	Ellis Johnson	.25
16	Hugh Douglas	.40
17	Tyrone Wheatley	.75
18	Napoleon Kaufman	.75
19	James Stewart	.50
20	Luther Elliss	.20
21	Rashaan Salaam	.50
22	Tyrone Poole	.10
23	Ty Law	.10
24	Korey Stringer	.10
25	Billy Milner	.10
26	Devin Bush	.10
27	Mark Bruener	.30
28	Derrick Brooks	.20
29	Blake Brockermeyer	.10
30	Craig Powell	.05
31	Trezelle Jenkins	.10
32	Craig Newsome	.20
33	Thomas Bailey	.05
34	Chad May	.10
35	J.J. Smith	.05
36	Lorenzo Styles	.05
37	Brian Williams	.05
38	Damien Covington	.05
39	Steve Stenstrom	.05
40	Darius Holland	.05
41	Pete Mitchell	.05
42	Todd Collins	.25
43	Kordell Stewart	1.00
44	Eric Zeier	.75
45	Frank Sanders	.50
46	Ben Talley	.05
47	Billy Williams	.05
48	Chris Jones	.05
49	Tamarick Vanover	.50
50	Jimmy Hitchcock	.05
51	Chris Hudson	.05
52	Terrell Fletcher	.20
53	Brent Moss	.05
54	Terrell Davis	1.00
55	Rodney Thomas	.50
56	Larry Jones	.10
57	Ray Zellars	.20
58	David Sloan	.05
59	Brandon Bennett	.05
60	Brian DeMarco	.05
61	Bryan Schwartz	.05
62	Jack Jackson	.05
63	Bobby Taylor	.05
64	Kevin Hickman	.05
65	Matt O'Dwyer	.05
66	Patrick Riley	.05
67	Ki-Jana Carter	.50
68	Kerry Collins	1.25
69	Steve McNair	1.00
70	Tyrone Wheatley	.75
71	Antonio Freeman	.40
72	Clifton Abraham	.05
73	Kez McCorvey	.10
74	Lovell Pinkney	.10
75	Lee DeRamus	.05
76	John Walsh	.10
77	Cory Raymer	.10
78	Corey Fuller	.10
79	Tyrone Davis	.10
80	David Dunn	.10
81	Dana Howard	.05
82	Melvin Johnson	.05
83	Robert Baldwin	.05
84	Curtis Martin	1.50
85	Zack Crockett	.10
86	Jay Barker	.10
87	Christian Fauria	.25
88	Zach Wiegert	.05
89	Barrett Brooks	.05
90	Ken Dilger	.25
91	James Stewart	.20
92	Ed Hervey	.05
93	Torey Hunter	.05
94	Sherman Williams	.40
95	Shawn King	.05
96	Dave Barr	.05
97	Rob Johnson	.10
98	Stoney Case	.25
99	Ki-Jana Carter Checklist 1	.25
100	Steve McNair Checklist 2	.25
101	Rashaan Salaam	.75
102	Kerry Collins	.75
103	Rashaan Salaam	.75
104	Kerry Collins	.75
105	Jay Barker	.10
106	Drew Bledsoe	.50
107	Marshall Faulk	.50
108	Steve Young	.50
109	Troy Aikman	.50
110	Emmitt Smith	.75

1995 Classic NFL Rookies Silver

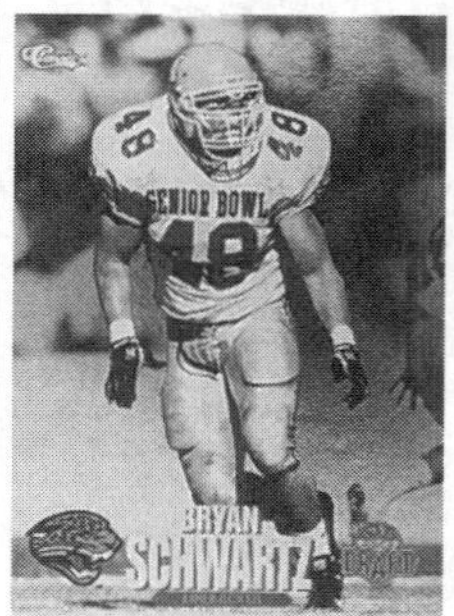

The 110-card, standard-size set is a parallel to the base set and features the same front and back designs as the base set, with the cards being printed on silver-foil stock. The cards were inserted one per pack.

	NM/M
Complete Set (110):	40.00
Common Player:	.10
Silver Cards:	3X

1995 Classic NFL Rookies Printer's Proofs

The 110-card, regular-sized set was a parallel set to the 1995 Classic NFL Rookies set. Limited to 595 each, the cards feature "Printer's Proofs" printed across the front, which are the same fronts as found in the base set. The backs are also identical.

	NM/M
Complete Set (110):	280.00
Common Player:	1.00
Printer's Proofs:	3X-8X

1995 Classic NFL Rookies Printer's Proofs Silver

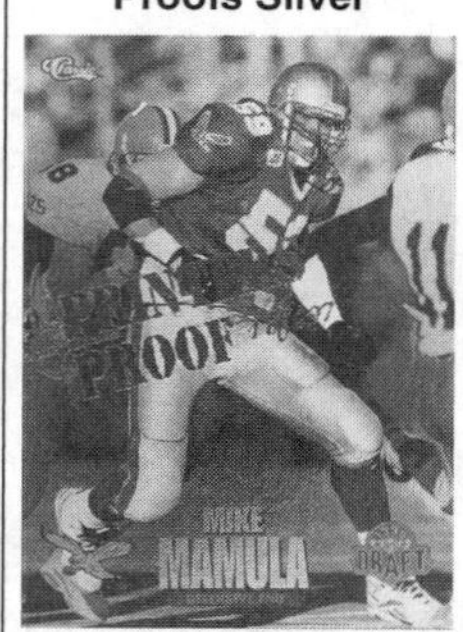

The 110-card, regular-sized set was a parallel set to the Printer's Proofs inserts, with the difference being "Printer's Proofs" is printed in silver foil across the card fronts. Each card was limited to 297 issues.

	NM/M
Complete Set (110):	425.00
Common Player:	1.50
Silver Cards:	5X-10X

1995 Classic NFL Rookies Die Cuts

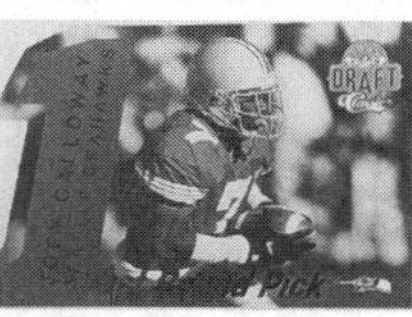

The 32-card, regular-size set featured the 32 players selected in the 1995 NFL Draft's first round. The cards are die cut in the form of a No. 1 and are sequentially numbered to 4,500. Cards in the set were inserted twice per box.

		NM/M
Complete Set (32):		65.00
Common Player:		.50
1	Ki-Jana Carter	2.00
2	Tony Boselli	1.50
3	Steve McNair	10.00
4	Michael Westbrook	4.00
5	Kerry Collins	8.00
6	Kevin Carter	1.00
7	Mike Mamula	1.00
8	Joey Galloway	4.00
9	Kyle Brady	1.00
10	J.J. Stokes	4.00
11	Derrick Alexander	1.00
12	Warren Sapp	1.50
13	Mark Fields	.50
14	Ruben Brown	.50
15	Ellis Johnson	.50
16	Hugh Douglas	1.00
17	Tyrone Wheatley	1.00
18	Napoleon Kaufman	1.00
19	James O. Stewart	2.00
20	Luther Ellis	1.00
21	Rashaan Salaam	1.00
22	Tyrone Poole	1.00
23	Ty Law	1.00
24	Korey Stringer	1.00
25	Billy Miner	.50
26	Devin Bush	.50
27	Mark Bruener	1.00
28	Derrick Brooks	3.00
29	Blake Brockermeyer	.50
30	Craig Powell	.50
31	Trezelle Jenkins	.50
32	Craig Newsome	.50

1995 Classic NFL Rookies Die Cuts Printer's Proofs

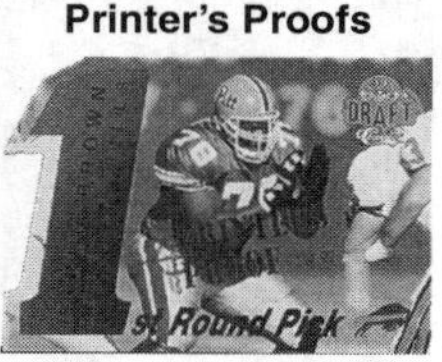

The 32-card, regular-sized set, inserted every hobby case, paralleled the 1995 NFL Rookies Die Cut set with the exception being "Printer's Proofs" printed on the card fronts.

	NM/M
Complete Set (32):	
Common Player:	10.00
Die-Cut Printer's Proofs:	3X-8X

1995 Classic NFL Rookies Die Cuts Silver Signatures

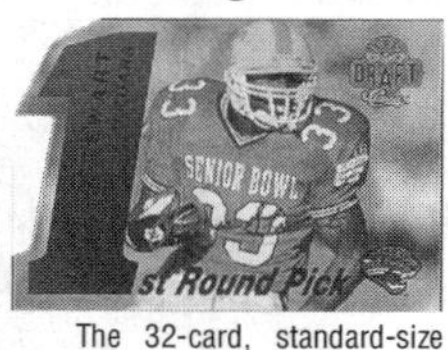

The 32-card, standard-size set paralleled the NFL Rookies set, except for the facsimile autographs stamped on each card front. Cards in the set were inserted every 48 packs and are sequentially numbered to 1,750.

	NM/M
Complete Set (32):	250.00
Common Player:	2.00
Die-Cut Silvers:	2X-3X

1995 Classic NFL Rookies Bonus Card Jumbos NFL Team's

As a special dealer bonus for Classic's 1995 NFL Rookies set, each hobby case of the product contains at least one of these three oversized rookie cards. Each card is sequentially numbered up to 2,500. The front has a photo of the player in his college uniform, with his NFL's team logo in the background. The brand logo is in the upper left corner; the player's name, position and team name are at the bottom. Cards are ticket size, measuring 4-3/4" x 2-1/2". They are printed on micro-lined foil board.

		NM/M
Complete Set (3):		20.00
Common Player:		10.00
1	Ki-Jana Carter	5.00
2	Steve McNair	10.00
3	Kerry Collins	6.00

1995 Classic NFL Rookies Draft Review

The first 14 cards of Draft Review were handed out to the media on NFL Draft Day, and were also later reissued in retail packs of Classic NFL Rookies, every one per three packs. Card No. 14, which was a checklist when first issued, was replaced by an Emmitt Smith card, while the eight additional cards updated team selections. The 14-card set that the media received came with a certificate of authenticity numbered up to 19,995 sets. Since it was not known which team would draft certain players, some are pictured in multiple pro uniforms, and updated in the final eight cards of this 22-card set.

		NM/M
Complete Set (23):		20.00
Common Player:		.25
1	Steve McNair (Oilers)	3.00
2	Steve McNair (Vikings)	1.50
3	Steve McNair (Jaguars)	1.50
4	Ki-Jana Carter (Panthers)	1.00
5	Ki-Jana Carter (Jaguars)	1.00
6	Kerry Collins (Bills)	1.75
7	Kerry Collins (Colts)	1.75
8	Kerry Collins (Cardinals)	1.75
9	John Walsh (Panthers)	.25
10	John Walsh (Vikings)	.25
11	John Walsh (Dolphins)	.25
12	J.J. Stokes (Seahawks)	1.00
13	J.J. Stokes (Rams)	1.00
14A	John Walsh, Steve McNair, Kerry Collins Checklist	1.75
14B	Emmitt Smith	2.50
15	Steve Young	1.00
16	Marshall Faulk	1.00
17	Troy Aikman	1.50
18	Ki-Jana Carter (Bengals)	1.50
19	Kerry Collins (Panthers)	3.50
20	J.J. Stokes (49ers)	1.50
21	Michael Westbrook (Redskins)	1.00
22	Kyle Brady (Jets)	.50

1995 Classic NFL Rookies Instant Energy

The 20-card, standard-sized set was inserted every rack pack of 1995 Classic NFL Rookies. The card fronts feature a color player image over a lightning background with the backs containing another player shot with a profile, also over a lightning background. They cards are numbered with the "IE" prefix.

		NM/M
Complete Set (20):		12.00
Common Player:		.50
1	Ki-Jana Carter	.50
2	Steve McNair	3.00
3	Michael Westbrook	1.00
4	Joey Galloway	1.00
5	Tyrone Wheatley	1.00
6	Napoleon Kaufman	.75
7	Warren Sapp	1.00
8	Kevin Carter	.50
9	Todd Collins	.75
10	Rob Johnson	.50
11	Chad May	.50
12	Mike Mamula	.50
13	Sherman Williams	.50
14	Tony Boselli	.75
15	Kerry Collins	3.00
16	J.J. Stokes	1.50
17	Rashaan Salaam	.50
18	Kordell Stewart	3.00
19	Derrick Brooks	2.00
20	Frank Sanders	1.00

1995 Classic NFL Rookies ROY Redemption

The top 19 offensive players and a field card are featured on these 1995 Classic NFL Rookies inserts. Each card in this set is limited to 2,500 produced and was inserted at a rate of one per every three boxes. Cards depicting the January 1996 NFL Offensive Rookie of the Year are redeemable for a $50 phone card of the player. The card front is horizontal, with "1 of 2,500" and "Rookie of the Year" on it. The back has the contest rules. The cards are numbered with "ROY" prefix.

		NM/M
Complete Set (20):		90.00
Common Player:		3.00
1	Ki-Jana Carter	3.00
2	Tony Boselli	4.00
3	Steve McNair	12.00
4	Michael Westbrook	6.00
5	Kerry Collins	10.00
6	Joseph Galloway	6.00
7	Kyle Brady	2.00
8	J.J. Stokes	6.00
9	Tyrone Wheatley	2.00
10	Napoleon Kaufman	2.00
11	Rashaan Salaam	2.00
12	Kordell Stewart	8.00
13	James Stewart	5.00
14	Frank Sanders	6.00
15	Ray Zellars	2.00
16	Zack Crockett	3.00
17	Tamarick Vanover	2.00
18	Chad May	2.00
19	Eric Zeier	2.00
20	Field Card	10.00

1995 Classic NFL Rookies Rookie Spotlight

The 30-card, standard-size set features a color action shot on the card fronts while the backs contain a color headshot with a player profile. The cards were inserted in every rack pack. The cards are numbered with the "RS" prefix.

		NM/M
Complete Set (30):		20.00
Common Player:		.50
Holographic Cards:		3X-6X
1	Ki-Jana Carter	1.00
2	Steve McNair	3.00
3	Michael Westbrook	1.00
4	Joey Galloway	1.00
5	Tyrone Wheatley	1.00
6	Napoleon Kaufman	1.00
7	Kordell Stewart	2.00
8	Frank Sanders	1.00
9	Zack Crockett	.50
10	Tamarick Vanover	1.00
11	Chad May	.50
12	Eric Zeier	.50
13	Mike Mamula	.50
14	Warren Sapp	1.00
15	Kevin Carter	.50
16	Derrick Brooks	2.00
17	Todd Collins	.50
18	Rob Johnson	.50
19	Chris T. Jones	.50
20	Terrell Fletcher	.50
21	Sherman Williams	.50
22	Tony Boselli	.75
23	Kerry Collins	3.00
24	J.J. Stokes	1.50
25	Rashaan Salaam	1.00
26	James O. Stewart	1.00
27	Rodney Thomas	.50
28	Jack Jackson	.50
29	Lovell Pinkney	.50
30	Ruben Brown	.50

1995 Classic Draft Day Jaguars

The five-card, standard-size set was issued on Draft Day in 1995 to honor the Jacksonville Jaguars first NFL Draft. The card fronts feature color action photos of top 1995 NFL picks in their collegiate uniforms while the backs have the NFL Draft emblem, along with the Jaguars logo. The cards are numbered with the "JJ" prefix.

		NM/M
Complete Set (5):		12.00
Common Player:		2.00
1	Kerry Collins	4.00
2	Steve McNair	5.00
3	Tony Boselli	2.00
4	Kevin Carter	2.00
5	Ki-Jana Carter	1.00

1995 Classic Images Previews

These five micro-lined insert cards preview the design Classic used for its 1995 NFL Images set. Cards were seeded one per every 18 packs of 1995 Classic Pro Line II product.

		NM/M
Complete Set (5):		50.00
Common Player:		8.00
1	Emmitt Smith	20.00
2	Steve Young	8.00
3	Drew Bledsoe	10.00
4	Kerry Collins	6.00
5	Marshall Faulk	8.00

1995 Classic Images Limited/Live

Classic's 1995 NFL Images Limited set has two versions - a hobby version called Limited and a retail version called Live. Both contain 125 cards in the regular issue, with an identical checklist, but slightly different designs. The set showcases top NFL veterans and 35 rookies in their pro uniforms. Limited card fronts have a slightly raised image against a metallic background. The player's team name and position are in the upper right corner, while the Images Limited logo is in the bottom left corner. The player's name runs along the bottom. The card back has the number in the upper left corner, with the player's name running along the left side of the card. A full-bleed color action photo is in the center, with 1994 and career statistics underneath. The Live versions have a slightly raised image with a metallic background. The player's name, team and position are at the bottom. The set icon is in the upper left corner. "Live" repeats itself along the left border. The card back has a photo in the center with a white frame. The player's name and position are underneath, followed by his 1994 and career statistics. The card number is in the upper left corner, while a team logo is in the upper right corner. Images Limited features a 20-card Icons insert set that is printed on fabric. Other insert sets include: DC Images, Silks, NFL Experience Sculpted Previews, Focused and Untouchables.

		NM/M
Complete Set (125):		30.00
Common Player:		.20
Minor Stars:		.40
Pack (6):		3.50
Wax Box (24):		65.00
1	Emmitt Smith	3.00
2	Steve Young	1.00
3	Drew Bledsoe	1.50
4	Dan Marino	3.00
5	John Elway	.75
6	Barry Sanders	2.00
7	Brett Favre	3.00
8	Troy Aikman	1.50
9	Jim Kelly	.40
10	Marshall Faulk	1.00
11	Jerry Rice	1.50
12	Warren Moon	.40
13	Jim Everett	.20
14	Rodney Hampton	.20
15	Jeff Hostetler	.20
16	Errict Rhett	.50
17	Jerome Bettis	.50
18	Byron Morris	.20
19	Randall Cunningham	.20
20	Rick Mirer	.50
21	Natrone Means	.75
22	Jeff George	.40
23	Garrison Hearst	.40
24	Michael Irvin	.75
25	Cris Carter	.40
26	Irving Fryar	.20
27	*Jeff Blake*	.75
28	Bruce Smith	.20
29	Shannon Sharpe	.20
30	Steve Beuerlein	.20
31	Stan Humphries	.40
32	Chris Warren	.40
33	Ben Coates	.20
34	Boomer Esiason	.20
35	Trent Dilfer	.75
36	Chris Miller	.20
37	Dave Brown	.20
38	Herman Moore	.75
39	Anthony Miller	.20
40	Andre Reed	.20
41	Reggie White	.40
42	Darnay Scott	.50
43	Erik Kramer	.20
44	Leroy Hoard	.20
45	Fred Barnett	.20
46	Junior Seau	.40
47	Vinny Testaverde	.20
48	Gus Frerotte	.50
49	William Floyd	.50
50	Mo Lewis	.20
51	Tim Brown	.40
52	Greg Lloyd	.20
53	Chester McGlockton	.20
54	Heath Shuler	.75
55	Rod Woodson	.20
56	Don Beebe	.20
57	Carl Pickens	.40
58	Charles Haley	.20
59	Steve Bono	.50
60	Harvey Williams	.20
61	Greg Hill	.50
62	Eric Metcalf	.20
63	Mario Bates	.50
64	Terry Allen	.20
65	Michael Timpson	.20
66	Mark Stepnoski	.20
67	Jeff Lageman	.20
68	Robert Smith	.20
69	Eric Allen	.20
70	Ricky Watters	.40
71	Derek Loville	.20
72	Bernie Parmalee	.40
73	Bryce Paup	.20
74	Frank Reich	.20
75	Henry Thomas	.20
76	Craig Erickson	.20
77	Eric Green	.20
78	Dave Meggett	.20
79	Deion Sanders	1.00
80	Herschel Walker	.20
81	Andre Rison	.40
82	*Ki-Jana Carter*	.75
83	*Tony Boselli*	.40
84	*Steve McNair*	4.00
85	*Michael Westbrook*	1.00
86	*Kerry Collins*	1.50
87	*Kevin Carter*	.40
88	*Warren Sapp*	.75
89	*Joey Galloway*	1.00
90	*J.J. Stokes*	1.00
91	*Derrick Brooks*	.40
92	*Kyle Brady*	.75
93	*Napoleon Kaufman*	1.00
94	*Tyrone Wheatley*	.75
95	*Mike Mamula*	.40
96	Desmond Howard	.20
97	*James Stewart*	2.00
98	Craig Newsome	.20
99	*Ty Law*	.20
100	Ellis Johnson	.20
101	*Hugh Douglas*	.50
102	*Mark Bruener*	.75
103	*Tyrone Poole*	.20
104	*Luther Elliss*	.20
105	*Mark Fields*	.20
106	*Frank Sanders*	.75
107	*Rashaan Salaam*	.75
108	*Craig Powell*	.20
109	*Sherman Williams*	.40
110	*Chad May*	.40
111	*Rob Johnson*	1.00
112	*Todd Collins*	.40
113	*Terrell Davis*	8.00
114	*Eric Zeier*	.40
115	*Curtis Martin*	4.00
116	*Kordell Stewart*	4.00
117	Troy Vincent	.20
118	*Ray Zellars*	.40
119	Dave Krieg	.20
120	Mike Sherrard	.20
121	Willie Davis	.20
122	Robert Brooks	.40
123	*Chris Sanders*	.75
124	Drew Bledsoe CL	.50
125	Emmitt Smith CL	1.00

1995 Classic Images Limited/Live Die-Cuts

These 1995 NFL Images Limited die-cut cards were seeded one per every 99 packs. The card front has a color action photo on the left side, with the "Images" logo repeated throughout the background. An insert set logo is in the lower left corner. The right side of the card has a black panel with the player's name in it; the panel is die-cut like a puzzle piece. The card back repeats the die-cut design on the left side, with a color action photo on the right against a colored background which has the Images icon throughout it. A white box at the top has numbers which indicate the card is "x of 965" made. The cards are numbered with the "DC" prefix.

		NM/M
Complete Set (30):		350.00
Complete Series 1 (15):		175.00
Complete Series 2 (15):		175.00
Common Player:		7.00
1	Jim Kelly	10.00
2	Kerry Collins	20.00
3	Michael Irvin	10.00
4	Troy Aikman	25.00
5	John Elway	15.00
6	Barry Sanders	35.00
7	Marshall Faulk	10.00
8	James Stewart	7.00
9	Drew Bledsoe	25.00
10	Herman Moore	10.00
11	Bam Morris	7.00
12	Jerry Rice	25.00
13	Joey Galloway	10.00
14	Rick Mirer	7.00
15	Errict Rhett	5.00
16	Rob Moore	3.00
17	Jeff George	3.00
18	Rashaan Salaam	3.00
19	Andre Rison	7.00
20	Emmitt Smith	30.00
21	Brett Favre	30.00
22	Dan Marino	30.00
23	Warren Moon	3.00
24	Dave Brown	3.00
25	Napoleon Kaufman	3.00
26	Natrone Means	3.00
27	Steve Young	12.00
28	Reggie White	8.00
29	Jerome Bettis	10.00
30	Michael Westbrook	6.00

1995 Classic Images Limited/Live Focused

These plastic cards were seeded one per every 24 packs of 1995 NFL Images Limited football. The horizontal front shows two teammates against a background of two wheel cogs. The Images logo is in the upper right corner. A "Focused" icon is in the center of the card at the bottom, sandwiched between the players' names. The card back has ghosted, reversed images of the photos from the front, plus a card number, which is in the upper left corner. The number uses an "F" prefix.

		NM/M
Complete Set (30):		75.00
Common Player:		2.00
1	Erik Kramer, Rashaan Salaam	2.00
2	Frank Reich, Kerry Collins	8.00
3	Jim Kelly, Andre Reed	2.00
4	Jeff George, Craig Heyward	2.00
5	Garrison Hearst, Dave Krieg	2.00
6	Barry Sanders, Herman Moore	10.00
7	John Elway, Shannon Sharpe	7.00
8	Troy Aikman, Emmitt Smith	12.00
9	Andre Rison, Leroy Hoard	2.00
10	Jeff Blake, Carl Pickens	3.00
11	Steve Bono, Willie Davis	2.00
12	James Stewart, Steve Beuerlein	2.00
13	Marshall Faulk, Craig Erickson	10.00
14	Steve McNair, Chris Chandler	7.00
15	Brett Favre, Reggie White	15.00
16	Dave Brown, Rodney Hampton	2.00
17	Jim Everett, Mario Bates	2.00
18	Drew Bledsoe, Ben Coates	12.00
19	Warren Moon, Cris Carter	2.00
20	Dan Marino, Irving Fryar	12.00
21	Stan Humphries, Natrone Means	8.00
22	Bam Morris, Kevin Greene	2.00
23	Randall Cunningham, Ricky Watters	2.00
24	Jeff Hostetler, Tim Brown	2.00
25	Boomer Esiason, Kyle Brady	2.00
26	Terry Allen, Michael Westbrook	2.00
27	Errict Rhett, Trent Dilfer	5.00
28	Jerome Bettis, Kevin Carter	2.00
29	Steve Young, Jerry Rice	8.00
30	Rick Mirer, Joey Galloway	3.00

1995 Classic Images Limited/Live Icons

These 20 cards, numbered on the back using an "I" prefix, are printed on fabric cards which are extremely limited; they are seeded one per every 20 boxes of 1995 Classic NFL Images Limited. The set logo is in the upper right corner; the insert set icon is in the lower right corner, opposite the player's name. A full-bleed fabric action photo comprises the front. The back has the card number in the upper left corner, with a photo on the top half of the card. The player's name is below the photo, at the top of a box which includes a recap of the player's professional accomplishments.

		NM/M
Complete Set (20):		75.00
Common Player:		2.00
1	Jim Kelly	2.00
2	Rashaan Salaam	2.00
3	Andre Rison	2.00
4	Troy Aikman	6.00
5	Emmitt Smith	12.00
6	John Elway	7.00
7	Barry Sanders	12.00
8	Brett Favre	12.00
9	Marshall Faulk	6.00
10	Irving Fryar	2.00
11	Dan Marino	12.00
12	Drew Bledsoe	8.00
13	Rodney Hampton	2.00
14	Ricky Watters	2.00
15	Byron Morris	2.00
16	Natrone Means	7.00
17	Steve Young	6.00
18	Jerry Rice	8.00
19	Errict Rhett	2.00
20	Michael Westbrook	2.00

1995 Classic Images Limited/ Live Sculpted Previews

These five insert cards preview the 1996 Classic NFL Experience Sculpted insert cards. Cards, seeded one per every 24 packs, are numbered using an "NX" prefix. The cards, with a foil background, are die-cut around the top. The team logo is incorporated into the background, with an action photo in the forefront. "Sculpted" is written across the top of the card; the player's name is in the bottom right corner in red foil. The back has the player's name at the top, along with a card number. An action photo is on the right, a recap of the player's 1994 season is on the left.

		NM/M
Complete Set (5):		40.00
Common Player:		2.00
1	Emmitt Smith	15.00
2	Drew Bledsoe	10.00
3	Steve Young	7.00
4	Rashaan Salaam	2.00
5	Marshall Faulk	5.00

1995 Classic Images Limited/Live Silks

These 10 cards were extremely limited; they are seeded one per every 375 packs of 1995 Classic Images Limited/Live football. The card front has a fabric or "silk" action figure cutout of the player against an orange football helmet background. The rest of the card is black, and has a silk set logo in the upper left corner and the player's name in white silk along the bottom. The back, with a number using an "S" prefix in the upper left corner, has an action photo of the player on the right; his name and a summary of his career are on the left. S1-S5 were in Live Images packs; S6-S10 were in Limited packs.

		NM/M
Complete Set (10):		250.00
Complete Series 1 (5):		125.00
Complete Series 2 (5):		140.00
Common Player:		20.00
1	Troy Aikman	40.00
2	Marshall Faulk	30.00
3	Drew Bledsoe	40.00
4	Bam Morris	10.00
5	James Stewart	10.00
6	Emmitt Smith	50.00
7	Steve Young	30.00
8	Rashaan Salaam	5.00
9	Natrone Means	5.00
10	Michael Westbrook	5.00

1995 Classic Images Limited/Live Untouchables

These 25 cards feature some of the NFL's "untouchable" players. Cards were random inserts in 1995 Classic Images Limited/Live packs. The fronts have a large and small photo against a ghosted action background. The player's name and insert set icon are along the left side of the card. A brand logo is in the upper right corner. The back has a photo, stats, career recap, and card number, which uses a "U" prefix.

		NM/M
Complete Set (25):		125.00
Common Player:		2.00
1	Jim Kelly	2.00
2	Kerry Collins	4.00
3	Rashaan Salaam	2.00
4	Troy Aikman	6.00
5	Emmitt Smith	15.00
6	John Elway	6.00
7	Barry Sanders	15.00
8	Reggie White	2.00
9	Steve McNair	6.00
10	Marshall Faulk	8.00
11	Dan Marino	15.00
12	Drew Bledsoe	10.00
13	Ben Coates	2.00
14	Tyrone Wheatley	2.00
15	Chester McGlockton	2.00
16	Ricky Watters	2.00
17	Junior Seau	2.00
18	Natrone Means	2.00
19	Steve Young	6.00
20	Jerry Rice	12.00
21	Rick Mirer	2.00
22	Jerome Bettis	4.00
23	Warren Sapp	2.00
24	Michael Westbrook	2.00
25	Heath Shuler	2.00

1995 Classic NFL Experience

Classic limited production on these cards to 1,995 sequentially-numbered cases. Each card front shows an action shot of the player bordered by his team's colors. His team's name runs along the right side; the player's name is in a small pennant in the lower left corner. The set logo also appears on the card front. The back side has another color photo, a card number and highlights from the first 10 weeks of the 1994 season. Each pack included one gold card, which is part of a parallel set. Other inserts include Throwbacks, 1994 Classic Rookies, a Miami Dolphins commemorative card, an Emmitt Smith "Emmitt Zone" card, and an interactive game card awarding prizes based on the Super Bowl's final score.

		NM/M
Complete Set (110):		10.00
Common Player:		.05
Minor Stars:		.10
Complete Gold Set (110):		35.00
Common Gold Player:		.20
Minor Gold Stars:		.40
Unlisted Gold Stars:		1X-3X
Pack (10):		1.75
Wax Box (24):		35.00
1	Seth Joyner	.05
2	Clyde Simmons	.05
3	Ron Moore	.05
4	Andre Rison	.10
5	Bert Emanuel	.05
6	Jeff George	.10
7	Terance Mathis	.10
8	Jim Kelly	.15
9	Thurman Thomas	.20
10	Andre Reed	.10
11	Bruce Smith	.05
12	Cornelius Bennett	.05
13	Steve Walsh	.05
14	Lewis Tillman	.05
15	Chris Zorich	.05
16	*Jeff Blake*	.40
17	Darnay Scott	.25
18	Dan Wilkinson	.10
19	Eric Metcalf	.05
20	Antonio Langham	.05
21	Pepper Johnson	.05
22	Eric Turner	.05
23	Leroy Hoard	.05
24	Vinny Testaverde	.05
25	Troy Aikman	.75
26	Emmitt Smith	1.00
27	Michael Irvin	.20
28	Alvin Harper	.10
29	Charles Haley	.05
30	John Elway	.25
31	Leonard Russell	.05
32	Shannon Sharpe	.10
33	Herman Moore	.10
34	Barry Sanders	1.00
35	Brett Favre	1.00
36	Sterling Sharpe	.15
37	Reggie White	.10
38	Gary Brown	.05
39	Haywood Jeffires	.05
40	Quentin Coryatt	.05
41	Marshall Faulk	1.00
42	Tony Bennett	.05
43	Joe Montana	1.00
44	Marcus Allen	.10
45	Derrick Thomas	.10
46	Neil Smith	.05
47	Tim Brown	.10
48	Jeff Hostetler	.05
49	Terry McDaniel	.05
50	Jerome Bettis	.30
51	Sean Gilbert	.05
52	Dan Marino	1.50
53	Irving Fryar	.05
54	Keith Jackson	.05
55	Bernie Parmalee	.30
56	Tim Bowens	.05
57	Cris Carter	.10
58	Terry Allen	.05
59	Warren Moon	.15
60	John Randle	.05
61	Jake Reed	.05
62	Drew Bledsoe	1.00
63	Marion Butts	.05
64	Ben Coates	.05
65	Derek Brown	.05
66	Jim Everett	.05
67	Michael Haynes	.05
68	Darion Conner	.05
69	Rodney Hampton	.10
70	Dave Meggett	.05
71	Boomer Esiason	.05
72	Johnny Johnson	.05
73	Ronnie Lott	.05
74	Rob Moore	.05
75	Mo Lewis	.05
76	Randall Cunningham	.10
77	Herschel Walker	.10
78	Charlie Garner	.10
79	Calvin Williams	.05
80	Fred Barnett	.05
81	William Fuller	.05
82	Eric Allen	.05
83	Barry Foster	.10
84	Neil O'Donnell	.05
85	Rod Woodson	.05
86	Kevin Greene	.05
87	Byron Morris	.30
88	Darren Perry	.05
89	Greg Lloyd	.05
90	Steve Young	.40
91	Ricky Watters	.10
92	Jerry Rice	.60
93	Ken Norton	.05
94	Deion Sanders	.50
95	Stan Humphries	.10
96	Natrone Means	.50
97	Junior Seau	.10
98	Leslie O'Neal	.05
99	Chris Mims	.05
100	Rick Mirer	.40
101	Chris Warren	.05
102	Brian Blades	.05
103	Trent Dilfer	.40
104	Errict Rhett	.50
105	Heath Shuler	.50
106	Henry Ellard	.05
107	Ken Harvey	.05
108	Gus Frerotte	.25
109	Checklist 1	.05
110	Checklist 2	.05
MD1	Dan Marino, Don Shula	10.00
NNO	Emmitt Smith Zone 95	40.00

1995 Classic NFL Experience Gold

The 110-card, regular-sized set is a parallel to the 1995 NFL Experience base set, inserted one per hobby pack. The player's name is printed in gold foil on the card fronts, distinguishing it from the base cards.

	NM/M
Complete Set (110):	25.00
Common Player:	.25
Gold Cards:	2X-3X

1995 Classic NFL Experience Rookies

Ten rookies are showcased on these inserts, which were randomly included four per box of product. Each player is displayed on a horizontal design, with a grey border on the top and bottom and a foil embossed Super Bowl XXIX logo.

		NM/M
Complete Set (10):		15.00
Common Player:		1.00
1	Marshall Faulk	6.00
2	Bert Emanuel	1.00
3	Charlie Garner	3.00
4	Errict Rhett	1.00
5	Byron Morris	1.00
6	Heath Shuler	1.00
7	Trent Dilfer	3.00
8	Darnay Scott	2.00
9	Tim Bowens	1.00
10	Antonio Langham	1.00

1995 Classic NFL Experience Super Bowl Game

1995 Classic NFL Experience jumbo packs each had one of 20 of these inserts, based on an interactive game regarding the final score of Super Bowl XXIX. Each card has either an AFC or NFC logo, plus a number (0-9). If the last digit of the final score from the game corresponds with the conference and number of a card found by a collector, he could qualify for an assortment of prizes if he sent the card in by mail by March 6, 1995. The grand prize was to be a trip to Super Bowl XXX in Phoenix in 1996. Game cards submitted to Classic were not returned. The back had the rules and prizes for the game listed.

		NM/M
Complete Set (20):		20.00
Common Player:		.50
0	Marshall Faulk AFC	2.50
1	Natrone Means AFC	1.25
2	Thurman Thomas AFC	.50
3	Joe Montana AFC	2.00
4	John Elway AFC	1.00
5	Rick Mirer AFC	1.00
6	Drew Bledsoe AFC	2.00
7	Dan Marino AFC	3.00
8	Jim Kelly AFC	.50
9	Marcus Allen AFC	.50
0	Troy Aikman NFC	2.00
1	Steve Young NFC	2.00
2	Jerome Bettis NFC	1.00
3	Barry Sanders NFC	2.00
4	Randall Cunningham NFC	.50
5	Andre Rison NFC	.50
6	Jerry Rice NFC	2.00
7	Emmitt Smith NFC	3.00
8	Michael Irvin NFC	1.00
9	Sterling Sharpe NFC	1.00

1995 Classic NFL Experience Throwbacks

These 28 insert cards are printed on parchment to give each card a look and feel of an old-time card. This was done to commemorate the NFL's 75th anniversary. The set features one player from each team in his throwback uniform, bordered by a white frame. A brief history of the NFL franchise and the reason why the team chose that particular uniform are given on the back. The card number uses a "T" prefix. These inserts were included two per box.

		NM/M
Complete Set (28):		60.00
Common Player:		1.00
Minor Stars:		6.00
1	Seth Joyner	1.00
2	Andre Rison	1.00
3	Thurman Thomas	3.00
4	Lewis Tillman	1.00
5	Dan Wilkinson	1.00
6	Eric Metcalf	2.00
7	Emmitt Smith	10.00
8	John Elway	7.00
9	Barry Sanders	10.00
10	Reggie White	3.00
11	Haywood Jeffires	1.00
12	Marshall Faulk	6.00
13	Joe Montana	10.00
14	Jeff Hostetler	1.00
15	Jerome Bettis	3.00
16	Dan Marino	10.00
17	Warren Moon	2.00
18	Drew Bledsoe	8.00
19	Jim Everett	1.00
20	Dave Meggett	1.00
21	Ronnie Lott	1.00
22	Randall Cunningham	2.00
23	Rod Woodson	2.00
24	Natrone Means	2.00
25	Rick Mirer	1.00
26	Steve Young	6.00
27	Trent Dilfer	4.00
28	Henry Ellard	1.00

1996 Classic NFL Draft Day

The 15-card, regular-sized set was distributed by Classic in New York on the 1996 NFL Draft Day. The first nine cards feature the top three players in the draft with three different teams each. The final six cards feature former first-round draft picks.

		NM/M
Complete Set (15):		12.00
Common Player:		.75
1A	Keyshawn Johnson (Jets)	1.00
1B	Keyshawn Johnson (Jaguars)	1.00
1C	Keyshawn Johnson (Redskins)	1.00
2A	Kevin Hardy (Jaguars)	.75
2B	Kevin Hardy (Redskins)	.75
2C	Kevin Hardy (Cardinals)	.75
3A	Terry Glenn (Patriots)	1.00
3B	Terry Glenn (Giants)	1.00
3C	Terry Glenn (Jets)	1.00
4	Eddie George	3.00
5	Emmitt Smith	3.50
6	Troy Aikman	2.00
7	Drew Bledsoe	2.00
8	Kerry Collins	2.00
9	Title Card (Checklist back)	1.00

1996 Classic NFL Rookies

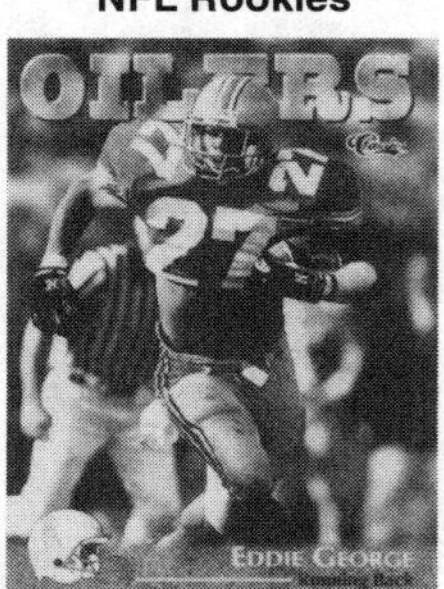

Classic's 1996 NFL Rookies set features top players in the 1996 NFL Draft, including two subsets called All-Americans and NFL Greats. Each card front has a full-bleed color action photo of the player in his college uniform, but his pro team's name is at the top, along with a team helmet at the bottom, next to his name. Backs have a color closeup photo of the player in a square which has his name, team name, position and draft selection number along the four sides. Below the photo is a ghosted body shot from the same closeup shot. A recap of his collegiate accomplishments are on one side; statistics and biographical information are on the other. A card number is in the upper left corner in a blue square. Hobby pack insert cards were Rookie of the Year Interactive, NFL Road Jerseys and Rookie Lasers. Retail pack inserts include Rookie #1 Die-Cuts and NFL Home Jerseys.

		NM/M
Complete Set (100):		10.00
Common Player:		.05
Minor Stars:		.10
1	Keyshawn Johnson	1.50
2	Jonathan Ogden	.20
3	Kevin Hardy	.30
4	Leeland McElroy	.30
5	Terry Glenn	1.00
6	Tim Biakabutuka	.50
7	Tony Brackens	.05
8	Duane Clemons	.10
9	Willie Anderson	.05
10	Karim Abdul-Jabbar	.75
11	Daryl Gardener	.05
12	Simeon Rice	.20
13	Eddie George	2.00
14	Andre Johnson	.05
15	Jon Runyan	.05
16	Jevon Langford	.05
17	Derrick Mayes	.40
18	Stephen Davis	.75
19	Ray Farmer	.05
20	Chris Doering	.10
21	Jimmy Herndon	.05
22	Jerome Woods	.05
23	Scott Greene	.05
24	Jamin Stephens	.05
25	Tommie Frazier	.20
26	Dusty Zeigler	.05
27	Alex Molden	.05
28	Dietrich Jells	.05
29	Brian Roche	.05
30	Danny Kanell	.50
31	Roman Oben	.05
32	Chris Darkins	.20
33	Christian Peter	.05
34	Jeff Hartings	.05
35	Bobby Hoying	.50
36	Steve Taneyhill	.05
37	Lance Johnstone	.05
38	Zach Thomas	.50
39	Donnie Edwards	.05
40	Eric Moulds	1.25
41	Amani Toomer	.40
42	Scott Slutzker	.05
43	Matt Stevens	.05
44	Randall Godfrey	.05
45	Orpheus Roye	.05
46	Jason Odom	.05
47	Jerod Cherry	.05
48	Jeff Lewis	.20
49	Mike Alstott	1.25
50	Tony Banks	.75
51	Stepfret Williams	.20
52	Michael Cheever	.05
53	Bryant Mix	.05
54	James Ritchey	.10
55	Marcus Coleman	.05
56	Sedric Clark	.05
57	Kyle Wachholz	.05
58	Johnny McWilliams	.10
59	Lawyer Milloy	.10
60	Alex Van Dyke	.30
61	Stanley Pritchett	.20
62	Ray Mickens	.10
63	Toraino Singleton	.05
64	Richard Huntley	.20
65	Eddie George	.75
66	Terry Glenn	.25
67	Keyshawn Johnson	.30
68	Jonathan Ogden	.05
69	Tommie Frazier	.10
70	Kevin Hardy	.05
71	Zach Thomas	.10
72	Tony Brackens	.05
73	Lawyer Milloy	.05
74	Leeland McElroy	.10
75	Emmitt Smith	.50
76	Steve McNair	.20
77	Kerry Collins	.10
78	Drew Bledsoe	.25
79	Marshall Faulk	.20
80	Pete Kendall	.05
81	Regan Upshaw	.05
82	Mercury Hayes	.05
83	Dou Innocent	.05
84	DeRon Jenkins	.05
85	Marco Battaglia	.10
86	John Mobley	.10
87	Cedric Jones	.05
88	Marvin Harrison	.50
89	Israel Ifeanyl	.05
90	Reggie Brown	.05
91	Jermain Mayberry	.05
92	Brian Dawkins	.05
93	Tedy Bruschi	.05
94	Terrell Owens	2.00
95	Jermaine Lewis	.50
96	Sean Boyd	.05
97	Phillip Daniels	.05
98	Lawrence Phillips	.30
99	Keyshawn Johnson (Checklist 1)	.50
100	Terry Glenn (Checklist 2)	.25

1996 Classic NFL Rookies Rookie #1 Die-Cuts

Thirty top rookies are featured on these 1996 Classic NFL Rookies inserts, seeded randomly in retail packs. The cards use a metallic stock and are die-cut around the number 1.

		NM/M
Complete Set (30):		150.00
Common Player:		2.00
1	Keyshawn Johnson	10.00
2	Kevin Hardy	2.00
3	Simeon Rice	2.00
4	Jonathan Ogden	2.00
5	Cedric Jones	2.00
6	Lawrence Phillips	2.00
7	Terry Glenn	5.00
8	Tim Biakabutuka	2.00
9	Emmitt Smith	12.00
10	Willie Anderson	2.00
11	Alex Molden	2.00
12	Regan Upshaw	2.00
13	Kerry Collins	10.00
14	Eddie George	30.00
15	John Mobley	2.00
16	Duane Clemons	2.00
17	Reggie Brown	2.00
18	Marshall Faulk	10.00
19	Marvin Harrison	10.00
20	Daryl Gardener	2.00
21	Pete Kendall	2.00
22	Joey Galloway	7.00
23	Jeff Hartings	2.00
24	Eric Moulds	2.00
25	Jermain Mayberry	2.00
26	Steve McNair	12.00
27	Kyle Brady	2.00
28	Jerome Woods	2.00
29	Jamin Stephens	2.00
30	Andre Johnson	2.00

1996 Classic NFL Rookies NFL Home Jerseys

These 30 cards were exclusive inserts to 1996 Classic NFL Rookies retail packs, one per every 15 packs. The card front is horizontal and shows the player in action while he was in college, alongside a home jersey of his new NFL team. Card backs are numbered using an "HJ" prefix.

		NM/M
Complete Set (30):		75.00
Common Player:		3.00
1	Keyshawn Johnson	10.00
2	Kevin Hardy	4.00
3	Jonathan Ogden	3.00
4	Terry Glenn	6.00
5	Tim Biakabutuka	4.00
6	Karim Abdul-Jabbar	4.00
7	Simeon Rice	8.00
8	Eric Moulds	8.00
9	Mike Alstott	7.00
10	Leeland McElroy	4.00
11	Daryl Gardener	3.00
12	Eddie George	17.00
13	Amani Toomer	8.00
14	Johnny McWilliams	3.00
15	Derrick Mayes	3.00
16	Duane Clemons	3.00
17	Chris Darkins	3.00
18	Ray Farmer	3.00
19	Danny Kanell	3.00
20	Bobby Hoying	3.00
21	Zach Thomas	3.00
22	Tony Banks	3.00
23	Alex Van Dyke	3.00
24	Stepfret Williams	3.00
25	Chris Doering	3.00
26	Lance Johnstone	3.00
27	Stephen Davis	3.00
28	Scott Greene	3.00
29	Tony Brackens	3.00
30	Jevon Langford	3.00

1996 Classic NFL Rookies NFL Road Jerseys

Each of these horizontally-designed cards shows the player on the front in his college uniform, but adjacent to a road jersey of the NFL team which drafted him in 1996. The cards were random inserts in 1996 Classic NFL Rookies packs, one per 15 packs. Card backs are numbered using an "RJ" prefix and have a color closeup photo, plus a recap of the player's collegiate accomplishments. Silver foil stamping is used on the front for the player's name and brand logo.

		NM/M
Complete Set (30):		75.00
Common Player:		3.00
1	Keyshawn Johnson	10.00
2	Kevin Hardy	3.00
3	Jonathan Ogden	3.00
4	Terry Glenn	5.00
5	Tim Biakabutuka	4.00
6	Karim Abdul-Jabbar	4.00
7	Simeon Rice	8.00
8	Eric Moulds	8.00
9	Mike Alstott	7.00
10	Leeland McElroy	3.00
11	Daryl Gardener	3.00
12	Eddie George	17.00
13	Amani Toomer	8.00
14	Marvin Harrison	10.00
15	Derrick Mayes	3.00
16	Dietrich Jells	3.00
17	Chris Darkins	3.00
18	Ray Farmer	3.00
19	Danny Kanell	3.00
20	Bobby Hoying	3.00
21	Zach Thomas	3.00
22	Kyle Wachholz	3.00
23	Alex Van Dyke	3.00
24	Stepfret Williams	3.00
25	Chris Doering	3.00
26	Lance Johnstone	3.00
27	Stephen Davis	3.00
28	Scott Greene	3.00
29	Tony Brackens	3.00
30	Jevon Langford	3.00

1996 Classic NFL Rookies Rookie Lasers

Rookie Lasers cards were seeded one per every 100 packs of 1996 Classic NFL Rookies hobby packs. The cards feature 10 of the best rookies and are numbered using an "RL" prefix.

		NM/M
Complete Set (10):		150.00
Common Player:		7.00
1	Keyshawn Johnson	35.00
2	Jonathan Ogden	7.00
3	Eddie George	50.00
4	Terry Glenn	20.00
5	Tommie Frazier	5.00
6	Karim Abdul-Jabbar	5.00
7	Duane Clemons	7.00
8	Leeland McElroy	5.00
9	Tim Biakabutuka	5.00
10	Kevin Hardy	5.00

1996 Classic NFL Rookies Rookie of the Year Contenders

The 10-card, regular-sized set was randomly inserted in retail packs of 1996 Classic NFL. Both the card fronts and backs feature action shots of the players with the player's name appearing in the lower right corner of the fronts. The cards are numbered with the "C" prefix.

		NM/M
Complete Set (10):		35.00
Common Player:		1.50
1	Keyshawn Johnson	10.00
2	Jonathan Ogden	1.50
3	Eddie George	15.00
4	Terry Glenn	4.00
5	Eric Moulds	4.00
6	Karim Abdul-Jabbar	4.00
7	Leeland McElroy	4.00
8	Tim Biakabutuka	4.00
9	Bobby Hoying	3.00
10	Stephen Davis	5.00

1996 Classic NFL Rookies Rookie of the Year Interactive

These interactive insert cards were randomly seeded in hobby packs of 1996 Classic NFL Rookies product. The cards feature 20 leading candidates to win the NFL Offensive Rookie of the Year award. If the player on the card wins, it is redeemable for an autographed collectible of the player. The card front has a full-bleed color action photo, with the player's name towards the bottom of the card. "Rookie of the Year" and "Interactive" are spelled out along the right side of the card. Card backs, numbered using an "ROY" prefix, explain the rules of the redemption program.

		NM/M
Complete Set (20):		75.00
Common Player:		3.00
1	Keyshawn Johnson	15.00
2	Jonathan Ogden	3.00
3	Steve Taneyhill	3.00
4	Leeland McElroy	3.00
5	Terry Glenn	6.00
6	Tim Biakabutuka	6.00
7	Karim Abdul-Jabbar	6.00
8	Eddie George	20.00
9	Johnny McWilliams	3.00
10	Eric Moulds	8.00
11	Bobby Hoying	3.00
12	Chris Darkins	3.00
13	Derrick Mayes	3.00
14	Mike Alstott	3.00
15	Chris Doering	3.00
16	Danny Kanell	3.00
17	Stephen Davis	3.00
18	Amani Toomer	10.00
19	Dietrich Jells	3.00
20	Field Card	5.00

1996 Score Board Laser National Promos

Distributed at the Classic booth at the 1996 National Card Collector's Convention, this five-card set was available separately or in a lucite holder, which was numbered of 300.

		NM/M
Complete Set (5):		25.00
Complete Framed Set (5):		35.00
Common Player:		3.00
1	Kordell Stewart	5.00
2	Troy Aikman	5.00
3	Emmitt Smith	10.00
4	Lawrence Phillips	3.00
5	Keyshawn Johnson	4.00

1996 Score Board NFL Lasers

This 100-card set features some of the NFL's top stars, including seven who have autographed special inserts. The regular card front has a color action photo in it against a metallic background. The left frame of the card is green; the upper right and lower right corners are gold, with NFL Lasers and the player's team name in them. The player's name and position are above the bottom frame. The card back has a card number and the player's name at the top, with biographical information below. The right border has the player's name at the top, with his team name running horizontally toward the bottom. 1995 and career stats are along the bottom. A photo completes the back. The autographed cards, available at a rate of two per case, come in two versions - regular (400 each, one per 150 packs), and die-cuts (100 each, one per 930 packs). The other inserts are Laser Images and Sunday's Heroes.

		NM/M
Complete Set (100):		15.00
Common Player:		.10
Minor Stars:		.20
Wax Box:		40.00
1	Brett Favre	2.50
2	Chris Warren	.10
3	J.J. Stokes	.25
4	Barry Sanders	1.25
5	Ben Coates	.10
6	Bryan Cox	.10
7	Carl Pickens	.10
8	Cris Carter	.10
9	Curtis Martin	2.00
10	Dan Marino	2.50
11	Dave Brown	.10
12	Drew Bledsoe	1.00
13	Edgar Bennett	.10
14	Herman Moore	.30
15	Jeff Blake	.30
16	Jerry Rice	1.25
17	Jim Kelly	.20
18	John Elway	.75
19	Junior Seau	.10
20	Kerry Collins	1.00
21	Kordell Stewart	1.00
22	Leonard Russell	.10
23	Mark Brunell	.50
24	Marshall Faulk	.30
25	Mike Tomczak	.10
26	Reggie White	.20
27	Ricky Watters	.20
28	Rod Woodson	.10
29	Rodney Peete	.10
30	Stan Humphries	.10
31	Steve McNair	.75
32	Terry Allen	.10
33	Thurman Thomas	.20
34	Troy Aikman	1.25
35	Vinny Testaverde	.10
36	Chris T. Jones	.10
37	Deion Sanders	.75
38	Eric Metcalf	.10
39	Erik Kramer	.10
40	Emmitt Smith	2.50
41	Gus Frerotte	.10
42	Jeff George	.10
43	Jerome Bettis	.20
44	Jim Harbaugh	.10
45	Isaac Bruce	.50
46	Jeff Hostetler	.10
47	Ki-Jana Carter	.20
48	Marcus Allen	.20
49	Neil O'Donnell	.10
50	Rashaan Salaam	.40
51	Robert Brooks	.10
52	Steve Bono	.10
53	Scott Mitchell	.10
54	Terrell Davis	1.00
55	Tim Brown	.10
56	Troy Vincent	.10
57	Warren Moon	.10
58	Tony Martin	.10
59	Rodney Hampton	.10
60	Steve Young	1.00
61	Rick Mirer	.10
62	Mark Chmura	.10
63	Larry Centers	.10
64	Ken Dilger	.10
65	Joey Galloway	.50
66	Jim Everett	.10
67	Chris Chandler	.10
68	James Stewart	.10
69	Robert Smith	.10
70	Tamarick Vanover	.50
71	Wayne Chrebet	.10
72	*Keyshawn Johnson*	2.00
73	*Kevin Hardy*	.20
74	*Lawrence Phillips*	.50
75	*Jonathan Ogden*	.20
76	*Terry Glenn*	1.00
77	*Tim Biakabutuka*	1.00
78	*Eddie George*	3.00
79	*Eric Moulds*	1.50

80	*John Mobley*	.10
81	*Amani Toomer*	.20
82	*Marvin Harrison*	2.00
83	*Leeland McElroy*	.30
84	*Rickey Dudley*	.30
85	*Tony Banks*	.50
86	*Zach Thomas*	.75
87	*Alex Molden*	.10
88	*Daryl Gardener*	.10
89	*Jamal Anderson*	3.00
90	*Karim Abdul-Jabbar*	.50
91	*Simeon Rice*	.20
92	*Walt Harris*	.20
93	*Bobby Engram*	.30
94	Kevin Williams	.10
95	Sean Gilbert	.10
96	Kevin Greene	.10
97	Regan Upshaw	.10
98	Marcus Jones	.10
99	Ray Lewis	.30
100	Checklist	.10

1996 Score Board NFL Lasers Laser Images

These cards are seeded one per every 30 packs of 1996 Score Board NFL Lasers. The card front has a color action photo of the player, with a ghosted black laser image of the player in the background, which is metallic. The card has gold foil stamped around three sides as a border; the player's name is also in gold foil on the right side. The Laser Images logo is also on the front. The card back has a color photo of the laser image from the front, with a column down the left side which has a recap of the player's accomplishments and a team logo at the bottom. The card number, using an "I" prefix, is in the upper left corner. The player's name is in a rectangle in the upper right corner. His last name is in scripted letter along the left side of the card.

		NM/M
Complete Set (30):		125.00
Common Player:		1.00
1	Steve Bono	1.00
2	Kerry Collins	10.00
3	Tim Biakabutuka	3.00
4	Rashaan Salaam	1.00
5	Jeff Blake	2.00
6	Emmitt Smith	15.00
7	Troy Aikman	10.00
8	Deion Sanders	5.00
9	John Elway	10.00
10	Herman Moore	1.00
11	Brett Favre	15.00
12	Eddie George	10.00
13	Marvin Harrison	8.00
14	Mark Brunell	6.00
15	Dan Marino	15.00
16	Karim Abdul-Jabbar	4.00
17	Cris Carter	1.00
18	Drew Bledsoe	8.00
19	Curtis Martin	8.00
20	Keyshawn Johnson	6.00
21	Chris T. Jones	1.00
22	Kordell Stewart	4.00
23	Junior Seau	1.00
24	Steve Young	8.00
25	Jerry Rice	10.00
26	Joey Galloway	4.00
27	Lawrence Phillips	1.00
28	Jonathan Ogden	1.00
29	Jim Harbaugh	1.00
30	Neil O'Donnell	1.00

1996 Score Board NFL Lasers Sunday's Heroes

These cards, numbered using an "S" prefix, capture 25 stars on a thicker, embossed surface. Cards were seeded one per every 22 packs of 1996 Score Board NFL Lasers product.

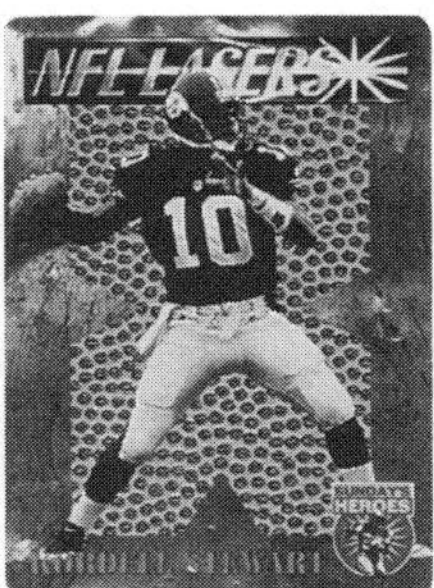

		NM/M
Complete Set (25):		150.00
Common Player:		3.00
1	Tim Brown	4.00
2	Kerry Collins	10.00
3	Tim Biakabutuka	3.00
4	Rashaan Salaam	3.00
5	Jeff Blake	3.00
6	Ki-Jana Carter	3.00
7	Emmitt Smith	20.00
8	Troy Aikman	15.00
9	Deion Sanders	5.00
10	Terrell Davis	15.00
11	Barry Sanders	20.00
12	Brett Favre	20.00
13	Reggie White	4.00
14	Marshall Faulk	10.00
15	Mark Brunell	6.00
16	Kevin Hardy	2.00
17	Dan Marino	20.00
18	Drew Bledsoe	12.00
19	Curtis Martin	12.00
20	Keyshawn Johnson	5.00
21	Kordell Stewart	5.00
22	Steve Young	12.00
23	Jerry Rice	12.00
24	Chris Warren	2.00
25	Karim Abdul-Jabbar	2.00

1996 Score Board NFL Lasers Autographs

Seven players have autographed these 1996 Score Board inserts - Emmitt Smith, Troy Aikman, Keyshawn Johnson, Marshall Faulk, Drew Bledsoe, Steve Young and Kordell Stewart. The cards were available at a rate of two per case, in two different versions. Regular versions (400 each) were seeded one per 150 packs. Die-cut versions (100 each) were seeded one per 930 packs.

	NM/M
Complete Set (7):	400.00
Packs (8):	4.00
Wax Box (24):	40.00
Troy Aikman	100.00
Steve Young	100.00
Kordell Stewart	50.00
Keyshawn Johnson	60.00
Emmitt Smith	150.00
Marshall Faulk	75.00
Drew Bledsoe	75.00

1996 Score Board NFL Lasers Die-Cut Autographs

Also included in packs of NFL Lasers were die-cut versions of each of the seven players. Die-cut versions were limited to only 100 of each.

	NM/M
Complete Set (7):	1,700
Troy Aikman	125.00
Steve Young	100.00
Kordell Stewart	75.00
Keyshawn Johnson	100.00
Emmitt Smith	225.00
Marshall Faulk	100.00
Drew Bledsoe	125.00

1996 Classic NFL Experience

This 125-card 1996 Classic NFL Experience set is geared toward players who participated in the postseason. Each card front has a full-bleed color action photo on glossy stock. The Classic logo is in an upper corner; the player's name and position are in an arch at the bottom. Three-fourths of the card back has a format similar to the design used for the card front, except a number has been added in an upper corner. The bottom fourth of the card has a 1995 recap. Insert sets include: Sculpted, Super Bowl game cards, three oversized bonus cards, Emmitt Zone and The "X." 1996 Classic NFL Experience also continues the Hot Box program. There is an average of one Hot Box every five sealed cases, with each pack in a Hot Box containing 20-percent inserts. Each card in the regular set is also reprinted as part of a Printer's Proof parallel set. Only 499 of each card is printed, with an insert ratio of one per 10 packs.

		NM/M
Complete Set (125):		10.00
Common Player:		.05
Minor Stars:		.10
Comp. Prin. Proof Set (125):		100.00
Prin. Proof Cards:		3X-10X
Pack (10):		2.00
Wax Box (24):		38.00
1	Emmitt Smith	2.00
2	Jerry Rice	1.00
3	Carl Pickens	.15
4	Curtis Conway	.10
5	Isaac Bruce	.10
6	Marshall Faulk	.10
7	Errict Rhett	.10
8	Troy Aikman	.75
9	Jeff Hostetler	.05
10	Dan Marino	2.00
11	Barry Sanders	1.00
12	Drew Bledsoe	.50
13	Ricky Watters	.10
14	Natrone Means	.20
15	Chris Warren	.10
16	Jim Kelly	.10
17	Jeff George	.05
18	Garrison Hearst	.10
19	Brett Favre	2.00
20	John Elway	.50
21	Robert Smith	.05
22	Steve Bono	.10
23	Byron Morris	.20
24	Jim Everett	.05
25	Steve Young	.50
26	Rodney Hampton	.05
27	Terry Allen	.05
28	Chris Chandler	.05
29	Mark Carrier	.05
30	Desmond Howard	.05
31	Erik Kramer	.05
32	Irving Fryar	.05
33	Jeff Blake	.50
34	Vinny Testaverde	.05
35	Stan Humphries	.05
36	Tim Brown	.05
37	Trent Dilfer	.10
38	Jim Harbaugh	.05
39	Warren Moon	.10
40	Ben Coates	.05
41	Boomer Esiason	.05
42	Rodney Peete	.05
43	Gus Frerotte	.10
44	Jerome Bettis	.10
45	Dave Brown	.05
46	William Floyd	.10
47	Andre Rison	.05
48	Robert Brooks	.10
49	Marcus Allen	.10
50	Rick Mirer	.10
51	Alvin Harper	.05
52	Chris Miller	.05
53	Eric Metcalf	.05
54	Dave Krieg	.05
55	Darnay Scott	.10
56	Cris Carter	.05
57	Lake Dawson	.05
58	Haywood Jeffires	.05
59	Herman Moore	.20
60	Michael Irvin	.20
61	Anthony Miller	.05
62	Troy Vincent	.05
63	Jake Reed	.05
64	Michael Haynes	.05
65	Scott Mitchell	.05
66	Roman Phifer	.05
67	Harvey Williams	.05
68	Darren Perry	.05
69	Brian Mitchell	.05
70	Derek Loville	.05
71	Junior Seau	.10
72	Bruce Smith	.05
73	Willie Davis	.05
74	Charles Haley	.05
75	Mike Sherrard	.05
76	Pat Swilling	.05
77	Yancey Thigpen	.25
78	Bryce Paup	.05
79	Eric Green	.05
80	Deion Sanders	.40
81	Mario Bates	.05
82	John Randle	.05
83	Charlie Garner	.05
84	Chris Doleman	.05
85	Robert Porcher	.05
86	Rob Moore	.05
87	Anthony Pleasant	.05
88	Bryan Cox	.05
89	Greg Hill	.05
90	Reggie White	.10
91	Shannon Sharpe	.05
92	Leroy Hoard	.05
93	John Copeland	.05
94	Tony Martin	.05
95	Greg Lloyd	.05
96	Tony Bennett	.05
97	Alonzo Spellman	.05
98	Wayne Martin	.05
99	Craig Heyward	.05
100	Leslie O'Neal	.05
101	Andy Harmon	.05
102	Edgar Bennett	.05
103	Derrick Moore	.05
104	Terrell Davis	.75
105	Kerry Collins	.75
106	Rodney Thomas	.25
107	Mark Brunell	.50
108	Curtis Martin	2.00
109	Tyrone Wheatley	.20
110	Rashaan Salaam	.10
111	Kevin Carter	.10
112	Joey Galloway	.75
113	Mike Mamula	.10
114	Kyle Brady	.10
115	James Stewart	.10
116	Michael Westbrook	.10
117	J.J. Stokes	.10
118	Wayne Chrebet	.10
119	Warren Sapp	.10
120	Hugh Douglas	.05
121	Jim Flanigan	.10
122	Chester McGlockton	.05
123	Shawn Lee	.05
124	Checklist Card 1	.25
125	Checklist Card 2	.25

1996 Classic NFL Experience Printer's Proofs

The 125-card, standard-size set is a parallel set to the 1996 NFL Experience base set, inserted every 20 packs. The card fronts are numbered as "x of 499."

	NM/M
Complete Set (125):	225.00
Common Player:	.75
Printer's Proofs Cards:	3X-10X

1996 Classic NFL Experience Super Bowl Gold/Red

The 125-card, regular-size set is a parallel to the 1996 NFL Experience set. The gold cards are numbered as "x of 799" while the red cards are numbered as "x of 150."

	NM/M
Complete Gold Set (125):	125.00
Common Gold Player:	.50
Gold Cards:	2X-4X
Complete Red Set (125):	550.00
Common Red Player:	2.00
Red Cards:	5X-10X

1996 Classic NFL Experience Class of 1995

This five-card set was included one per every 1996 Classic NFL Experience factory set. Cards are numbered using an "FI" prefix and have the set icon on the card front.

		NM/M
Complete Set (5):		10.00
Common Player:		1.00
1	Steve Young	2.00
2	Emmitt Smith	4.00
3	Deion Sanders	1.50
4	Rashaan Salaam	1.00
5	Kerry Collins	2.00

1996 Classic NFL Experience Emmitt Zone

The five-card, standard-size set was randomly inserted in packs of 1996 NFL Experience. Smith's name is printed down the card front's left border while "Emmitt Zone" appears in the lower right corner. A $5 "Emmitt Zone" phone card was also inserted every 375 Super Bowl packs.

		NM/M
Complete Set (5):		100.00
Common Player:		20.00
1	Emmitt Smith (1990-91 ROY)	20.00
2	Emmitt Smith (1992 NFL Leading Rusher)	20.00
3	Emmitt Smith (1993 3rd NFL Rushing Title)	20.00
4	Emmitt Smith (1994 Leader in League Touchdowns)	20.00
5	Emmitt Smith (1995 Best Season Ever)	20.00

1996 Classic NFL Experience Oversized Bonus Cards

These cards, one of which is randomly placed in each case of 1996 Classic NFL Experience product, complete the company's bonus program for its 1995 NFL-licensed products. The cards feature Emmitt Smith, Michael Westbrook and Reggie White.

		NM/M
Complete Set (15):		15.00
Common Player:		2.00
13	Emmitt Smith	10.00
14	Michael Westbrook	2.00
15	Reggie White	5.00

1996 Classic NFL Experience Super Bowl Die Cut Promos

The 10-card, regular-sized set, given away at the Super Bowl Card Show in Tempe, Ariz., featured players from the NFL Experience Die Cut matched inserts. The card backs contain rules for prize giveaways and "Show Promo." The cards are numbered with the "C" suffix.

		NM/M
Complete Set (10):		25.00
Common Player:		2.00
1	Jim Kelly	3.00
2	Dan Marino	6.00
3	Greg Lloyd	2.00
4	Marcus Allen	3.00
5	Tim Brown	2.00
6	Emmitt Smith	6.00
7	Steve Young	4.00
8	Rashaan Salaam	1.00
9	Brett Favre	6.00
10	Isaac Bruce	3.00

1996 Classic NFL Experience Super Bowl Die Cut Contest

The 20-card, regular-size set features 10 players on two cards each and was inserted in every 12 packs of the Card Show version of 1996 NFL Experience. The cards are numbered 1A through 10A and 1B through 10B. When the cards are put together, they form the Super Bowl XXX logo. The card backs contain rules on how to redeem the cards for a prize.

		NM/M
Complete Set (20):		75.00
Common Player:		2.50
1A	Jim Kelly	5.00
1B	Jim Kelly	5.00
2A	Dan Marino	10.00
2B	Dan Marino	10.00
3A	Greg Lloyd	2.50
3B	Greg Lloyd	2.50
4A	Marcus Allen	4.00
4B	Marcus Allen	4.00
5A	Tim Brown	2.50
5B	Tim Brown	2.50
6A	Emmitt Smith	10.00
6B	Emmitt Smith	10.00
7A	Steve Young	8.00
7B	Steve Young	8.00
8A	Rashaan Salaam	3.00
8B	Rashaan Salaam	3.00
9A	Brett Favre	10.00
9B	Brett Favre	10.00
10A	Isaac Bruce	4.00
10B	Isaac Bruce	4.00

1996 Classic NFL Experience Super Bowl Game Cards

These interactive cards are based on the final score of Super Bowl XXX in 1996. The 20 cards were inserted one per pack of 1996 Classic NFL Experience product; each card has either an AFC or NFC logo, plus a number (0-9). If the last digit of the final score from the game corresponds with the conference and number of a card found by a collector, he could qualify for an assortment of prizes if he sent it in by March 8, 1996. The grand prize was to be a trip to Super Bowl XXXI in 1997 in New Orleans. Game cards submitted to Classic were not returned. Each card front has a silver metallic background, with a color action shot. The Super Bowl XXX logo is in the upper left corner. The player's name and conference logo/card number are at the bottom. The back has a set checklist, list of rules and prizes, and the card number again. The Super Bowl logo repeats itself in the background.

		NM/M
Complete Set (20):		8.00
Common Player:		.75
A0	Drew Bledsoe	1.00
A1	John Elway	1.25
A2	Harvey Williams	.75
A3	Marshall Faulk	1.00
A4	Jim Kelly	.75
A5	Carl Pickens	.75
A6	Stan Humphries	.75
A7	Dan Marino	2.00
A8	Steve Bono	.75
A9	Napoleon Kaufman	.75
N0	Isaac Bruce	1.00
N1	Steve Young	1.00
N2	Michael Westbrook	.50
N3	Troy Aikman	1.00
N4	Barry Sanders	2.00
N5	Rashaan Salaam	.50
N6	Emmitt Smith	3.00
N7	Jerry Rice	2.00
N8	Deion Sanders	1.00
N9	Kerry Collins	1.00

1996 Classic NFL Experience Sculpted

These die-cut foil-board insert cards were seeded one per every 15 packs of 1996 Classic NFL Experience. Cards were limited to 2,400 of each card. The card has a color action photo against a tan background which has the team logo incorporated into it. "Sculpted" is written at the top; the player's name is at the bottom. The card back has a color action photo on one side, with the player's name at the top in his team's primary color. A brief player profile, also using the team color, is given, as is a card number, which uses an "S" prefix.

		NM/M
Complete Set (20):		100.00
Common Player:		2.00
Minor Stars:		3.00
1	Kerry Collins	6.00
2	Jeff Blake	2.00
3	Vinny Testaverde	2.00
4	Emmitt Smith	10.00
5	Troy Aikman	6.00
6	Deion Sanders	4.00
7	John Elway	6.00
8	Barry Sanders	10.00
9	Brett Favre	10.00
10	Marshall Faulk	6.00
11	Steve Bono	2.00
12	Dan Marino	10.00
13	Robert Smith	2.00
14	Drew Bledsoe	6.00
15	Natrone Means	2.00
16	Steve Young	6.00
17	Jerry Rice	6.00
18	Isaac Bruce	3.00
19	Errict Rhett	2.00
20	Michael Westbrook	2.00

1996 Classic NFL Experience X

This 1996 Classic NFL Experience insert set exposes collectors to everything exceptional about the game. Each card is seeded one per every 45 packs; there were only 1,500 of each produced. The card front features a silver stamp, plus a color photo of the player and the set icon, an X. Backs are numbered using an "X" prefix.

		NM/M
Complete Set (10):		175.00
Common Player:		10.00
1	Kerry Collins	15.00
2	Rashaan Salaam	10.00
3	Michael Westbrook	10.00
4	Terrell Davis	20.00
5	Joey Galloway	10.00
6	Deion Sanders	10.00
7	Steve Young	20.00
8	Dan Marino	35.00
9	Drew Bledsoe	20.00
10	Emmitt Smith	35.00

1996 Classic SP Autographs

The eight-card, regular-sized set was available as a mail-in from Score Board Inc. and Scott Paper Company. Each card was originally sold for $7.95 with two UPCs or $10.95 without UPC labels. The autographed cards came with Score Board's certificate of authenticity and the entire set was available for $64.95, or $54.95 with eight UPC labels. The cards are numbered with the "SP" prefix.

		NM/M
Complete Set (8):		60.00
Common Player:		8.00
1	Kyle Brady	8.00
2	Kerry Collins	12.00
3	Ron Jaworski	8.00
4	Napoleon Kaufman	8.00
5	Jim Kiick	8.00
6	Steve McNair	14.00
7	Jim Plunkett	8.00
8	Randy White	8.00

1997 Score Board NFL Experience

The 100-card, regular-sized set was sold in six-card packs. The card fronts feature a color action photo with the player's name and position printed on the bottom edge. The team's logo appears in the lower left corner. The card backs include another photo, a short highlight and a trivia question with answer. The base cards are printed on vintage-style cards. Inserts include Foundations, Teams Of The 90's and NFL Vintage cards.

		NM/M
Complete Set (100):		12.00
Common Player:		.05
Minor Stars:		.10
Pack (6):		1.50
Wax Box (36):		15.00
1	Emmitt Smith	1.50
2	Kordell Stewart	.75
3	Antonio Freeman	.05
4	William Thomas	.05
5	Simeon Rice	.25
6	Drew Bledsoe	.75
7	Elvis Grbac	.05
8	Ken Dilger	.05
9	John Elway	.50
10	Curtis Conway	.05
11	Adrian Murrell	.05
12	Karim Abdul-Jabbar	.25
13	Terry Allen	.05
14	Lawrence Phillips	.50
15	Barry Sanders	1.25
16	Shannon Sharpe	.05
17	Troy Aikman	.75
18	Kevin Greene	.05
19	Cris Carter	.05
20	Jim Kelly	.05
21	Eric Metcalf	.05
22	Joey Galloway	.05
23	Eddie George	1.00
24	Scott Mitchell	.05
25	Neil O'Donnell	.05
26	Ben Coates	.05
27	Andre Reed	.05
28	Michael Jackson	.05
29	Keith Jackson	.05
30	J.J. Stokes	.20
31	Rickey Dudley	.25
32	Ricky Watters	.10
33	Marcus Allen	.10
34	Brett Favre	1.25
35	Kevin Hardy	.05
36	Jim Everett	.05
37	Zach Thomas	.25
38	Lamar Lathon	.05
39	LeShon Johnson	.05
40	Bruce Smith	.05
41	Junior Seau	.05
42	Tony Banks	.50
43	Brian Mitchell	.05
44	Chris T. Jones	.05
45	Ty Detmer	.05
46	Robert Brooks	.05
47	Derrick Thomas	.05
48	Dan Wilkinson	.05
49	Michael Sinclair	.05
50	Dave Brown	.05
51	Carl Pickens	.05
52	Jim Harbaugh	.05
53	Wayne Chrebet	.05
54	Warren Moon	.05
55	Steve Young	.50
56	Sean Gilbert	.05
57	Jerome Bettis	.10
58	Dan Marino	1.50
59	Terrell Davis	.75
60	Mark Brunell	.20
61	Kent Graham	.05
62	Rashaan Salaam	.25
63	Tony Martin	.05
64	Robert Smith	.05
65	Thurman Thomas	.10
66	Marshall Faulk	.40
67	Dale Carter	.05
68	Stan Humphries	.05
69	Isaac Bruce	.40
70	Warren Sapp	.05
71	Kerry Collins	.25
72	Jamal Anderson	.40
73	Chris Chandler	.05
74	Herman Moore	.20
75	Rodney Hampton	.05
76	Tim Brown	.05
77	Keenan McCardell	.05
78	Anthony Miller	.05
79	Jake Reed	.05
80	Earnest Byner	.05
81	Chris Warren	.05
82	Deion Sanders	.50
83	Mike Tomczak	.05
84	Curtis Martin	1.00
85	John Friesz	.05
86	Gus Frerotte	.05
87	Vinny Testaverde	.05
88	Jason Dunn	.05
89	James Stewart	.05
90	Steve Bono	.05
91	Levon Kirkland	.05
92	Merton Hanks	.05
93	Marvin Harrison	.60
94	Reggie Brooks	.05
95	Reggie White	.10
96	Jeff Blake	.30
97	Terry Glenn	.25
98	Jerry Rice	.75
99	Keyshawn Johnson	.75
100	Checklist	.05

1997 Score Board NFL Experience Bayou Country

		NM/M
Complete Set (10):		70.00
Common Player:		2.00
1	Terry Allen	2.00
2	Emmitt Smith	15.00
3	Troy Aikman	10.00
4	Brett Favre	15.00
5	Jerry Rice	10.00
6	Curtis Martin	8.00
7	John Elway	8.00
8	Jerome Bettis	4.00
9	Kevin Greene	2.00
10	Karim Abdul-Jabbar	2.00

1997 Score Board NFL Experience Foundations

The 30-card, regular-sized set was inserted every 12 packs of Score Board's 1997 NFL Experience. The cards feature a key player from each of the league's 30 franchises. The card backs feature another player photo, imaged over a pedestal blueprint, and are numbered with an "F" prefix.

		NM/M
Complete Set (30):		70.00
Common Player:		1.00
1	Ray Lewis	1.00
2	Bruce Smith	1.00
3	Jeff Blake	1.00
4	Terrell Davis	4.00
5	Steve McNair	5.00
6	Marshall Faulk	5.00
7	Mark Brunell	4.00
8	Derrick Thomas	1.00
9	Karim Abdul-Jabbar	1.00
10	Curtis Martin	6.00
11	Keyshawn Johnson	4.00
12	Tim Brown	1.00
13	Kordell Stewart	4.00
14	Junior Seau	1.00
15	Joey Galloway	4.00
16	Simeon Rice	1.00
17	Jessie Tuggle	1.00
18	Kerry Collins	4.00
19	Rashaan Salaam	1.00
20	Emmitt Smith	8.00
21	Barry Sanders	8.00
22	Brett Favre	8.00
23	Cris Carter	1.00
24	Jim Everett	1.00
25	Amani Toomer	1.00
26	Ricky Watters	1.00
27	Tony Banks	1.00
28	Jerry Rice	8.00
29	Warren Sapp	1.00
30	Terry Allen	1.00

1997 Score Board NFL Experience Hard Target

Hard Target cards were distributed at the 1997 NFL Experience in New Orleans. The front of these 5" x 7" cards featured an NFL player and the backs described Score Board's Wrapper Redemption program. A different player was available each day of the show.

		NM/M
Complete Set (5):		12.00
Common Player:		2.00
1	Terrell Davis	3.00
2	Brett Favre	5.00
3	Eddie George	3.00
4	Keyshawn Johnson	2.00
5	Emmitt Smith	5.00

1997 Score Board NFL Experience Season's Heroes

Season's Heroes is a 20-card insert seeded 1:18. Each card features the Super Bowl XXXI logo and football-textured panel on the front. The cards are numbered with the "SH" prefix.

		NM/M
Complete Set (20):		80.00
Common Player:		2.00
1	Gus Frerotte	2.00
2	Terry Allen	2.00
3	Troy Aikman	6.00
4	Emmitt Smith	12.00
5	Ricky Watters	2.00
6	Brett Favre	12.00
7	Reggie White	5.00
8	Steve Young	8.00
9	Jerry Rice	8.00
10	Kevin Greene	2.00
11	Anthony Johnson	2.00
12	Thurman Thomas	5.00
13	Bruce Smith	2.00
14	Jerome Bettis	5.00
15	Rod Woodson	2.00
16	Eddie George	6.00
17	Terrell Davis	6.00
18	John Elway	10.00
19	Drew Bledsoe	8.00
20	Junior Seau	2.00

1997 Score Board NFL Experience Teams of the 90's

The 15-card, regular-sized set highlights players who have starred in Super Bowls of the 1990s. The cards were inserted in every 100 packs of Score Board's 1997 NFL Experience. The cards are die-cut into the shape of an oval ring. The card fronts feature the player over a common Super Bowl ring while the backs have another player shot with a short bio. The cards are numbered with the "T" prefix.

		NM/M
Complete Set (15):		140.00
Common Player:		6.00
1	Emmitt Smith	60.00
2	Bruce Smith	6.00
3	Steve Young	35.00
4	Thurman Thomas	6.00
5	Kordell Stewart	10.00
6	Ricky Watters	6.00
7	Ken Norton	6.00
8	Jeff Hostetler	6.00
9	Jim Kelly	6.00
10	Troy Aikman	20.00
11	Jerry Rice	20.00
12	Mark Rypien	6.00
13	Stan Humphries	6.00
14	Deion Sanders	10.00
15	Andre Reed	6.00

1995 Cleo Quarterback Club Valentines

The eight-card, regular-sized set was available through 38-card boxes of Cleo Valentines. The fronts feature a color action shot with a valentine heart with a catchy message. The set was found in perforated sheets with two rows of two cards each. The backs are blank.

		NM/M
Complete Set (8):		5.00
Common Player:		.25
1	Troy Aikman	1.00
2	John Elway	.50
3	Brett Favre	1.50
4	Jim Kelly	.25
5	Dan Marino	1.50
6	Warren Moon	.25
7	Phil Simms	.25
8	Steve Young	.50

A player's name in *italic* type indicates a rookie card.

1996 Cleo Quarterback Club Valentines

These eight cards were sold in 40-card boxes. The cards are 2-1/2" x 5" (except the Marcus Allen card which measures 3-3/4" x 5"), feature a color photo with a white border and are unnumbered. Each box had two cards on the bottom which are identical to cards in the set.

		NM/M
Complete Set (10):		2.50
Common Player:		.15
1	Troy Aikman	.40
2	Marcus Allen	.15
3	Drew Bledsoe	.40
4	John Elway	.30
5	Jim Kelly	.25
6A	Junior Seau (Valentine)	.15
6B	Junior Seau (box bottom card)	.25
7A	Emmitt Smith (Valentine)	.60
7B	Emmitt Smith (box bottom card)	.75
8	Steve Young	.30

1981 Coke

Players from seven NFL teams are represented in this 84-card set produced by Topps for Coca-Cola. Each card is numbered from 1-11 within its own team, but has been checklisted below using #s 1-77, plus seven unnumbered header cards (one for each team). The Coca-Cola logo appears on both sides of the card, making it identifiable from the regular 1981 Topps card, which the set is patterned after.

		NM/M
Complete Set (77):		37.00
Common Player:		.15
(1)	Raymond Butler	.30
(2)	Roger Carr	.25
(3)	Curtis Dickey	.30
(4)	Nesby Glasgow	.15
(5)	Bert Jones	.70
(6)	Bruce Laird	.15
(7)	Greg Landry	.30
(8)	Reese McCall	.15
(9)	Don McCauley	.15
(10)	Herb Orvis	.15
(11)	Ed Simonini	.15
(12)	Pat Donovan	.15
(13)	Tony Dorsett	2.00
(14)	Billy Joe DuPree	.30
(15)	Tony Hill	.30
(16)	Ed "Too Tall" Jones	.60
(17)	Harvey Martin	.25
(18)	Robert Newhouse	.25
(19)	Drew Pearson	.30
(20)	Charlie Waters	.25
(21)	Danny White	.50
(22)	Randy White	1.25
(23)	Mike Barber	.25
(24)	Elvin Bethea	.25
(25)	Gregg Bingham	.15
(26)	Robert Brazile	.25
(27)	Ken Burrough	.25
(28)	Rob Carpenter	.25
(29)	Leon Gray	.25
(30)	Vernon Perry	.15
(31)	Mike Renfro	.25
(32)	Carl Roaches	.25
(33)	Morris Towns	.15
(34)	Harry Carson	.60
(35)	Mike Dennis	.15
(36)	Mike Friede	.15
(37)	Earnest Gray	.15
(38)	Dave Jennings	.25
(39)	Gary Jeter	.25
(40)	George Martin	.25
(41)	Roy Simmons	.15
(42)	Phil Simms	2.00
(43)	Billy Taylor	.15
(44)	Brad Van Pelt	.25
(45)	Ottis Anderson	1.25
(46)	Rush Brown	.15
(47)	Theotis Brown	.25
(48)	Dan Dierdorf	.60
(49)	Mel Gray	.25
(50)	Ken Greene	.15
(51)	Jim Hart	.40
(52)	Doug Marsh	.15
(53)	Wayne Morris	.15
(54)	Pat Tilley	.15
(55)	Roger Wehrli	.25
(56)	Rolf Bernirschke	.25
(57)	Fred Dean	.25
(58)	Dan Fouts	.90
(59)	John Jefferson	.30
(60)	Gary Johnson	.25
(61)	Charlie Joiner	.60
(62)	Louie Kelcher	.25
(63)	Chuck Muncie	.25
(64)	Doug Wilkerson	.15
(65)	Clarence Williams	.15
(66)	Kellen Winslow	1.25
(67)	Coy Bacon	.15
(68)	Wilbur Jackson	.15
(69)	Karl Lorch	.15
(70)	Rich Milot	.15
(71)	Art Monk	3.75
(72)	Mark Moseley	.25
(73)	Mike Nelms	.25
(74)	Lemar Parrish	.25
(75)	Joe Theismann	.90
(76)	Ricky Thompson	.15
(77)	Joe Washington	.25

1993 Coke Monsters of the Gridiron

The 30-card, standard-size set, sponsored by Coca-Cola, was available as a complete set at the Super Bowl Card Show in Atlanta. The card fronts feature players in uniforms, but with scary monster makeup. The card backs contain career highlights with the player's scary monster nickname. The set was available to the first 10,000 collectors who redeemed 10 1993 NFL-licensed trading card wrappers.

		NM/M
Complete Set (30):		20.00
Common Player:		.25
1	Title Card (Checklist)	.50
2	Cornelius Bennett (Big Bear)	.25
3	Terrell Buckley (Tiger)	.25
4	Tony Casillas (Conde (Count))	.25
5	Reggie Cobb (Crossbones)	.25
6	Marco Coleman (Cobra)	.25
7	Shane Conlan (Conlan the Barbarian)	.25
8	Randall Cunningham (Rocket Man)	.50
9	Chris Doleman (Dr. Doomsday)	.25
10	Steve Emtman (Beast-Man)	.25
11	Harold Green (Slime)	.25
12	Michael Haynes (Moonlight Flyer)	.25
13	Garrison Hearst (Hearse)	2.00
14	Craig Heyward (Iron Head)	.25
15	Rickey Jackson (The Jackal)	.25
16	Joe Jacoby (Frankenstein)	.25
17	Sean Jones (Ghost)	.25
18	Cortez Kennedy (Tez Rex)	.25
19	Howie Long (Howlin')	.75
20	Ronnie Lott (The Rattler)	.75
21	Karl Mecklenburg (Midnight Marauder)	.25
22	Neil O'Donnell (Knight Raider)	.50
23	Tom Rathman (Psycho)	.25
24	Junior Seau (Stealth)	1.00
25	Emmitt Smith (Lone Star Sheriff)	10.00
26	Pat Swilling (Chillin')	.25
27	Lawrence Taylor (Six Gun)	.75
28	Derrick Thomas (Attack Cat)	.75
29	Andre Tippett (Andre the Terrible)	.25
30	Eric Turner (Bad Bone)	.25

1994 Coke Monsters of the Gridiron

Coca-Cola and Classic teamed up for the promotion and distribution of Monsters of the Gridiron, which is a 30-card set featuring one player from each team transformed into a bizarre, supernatural creature. Two cards were inserted into specially marked multi-packs of Coca-Cola Classic, diet Coke, caffeine-free diet Coke and Sprite. The two additional cards feature a logo of the expansion Panthers and Jaguars. Classic used this promotion to launch its new line of pins, called PINHEADS. These pins were also offered in a parallel set to the cards.

		NM/M
Complete Set (30):		12.00
Common Player:		.25
(1)	Eric "The Red" Swann	.25
(2)	Jessie " Tarantula" Tuggle	.25
(3)	Cornelius "Big Bear" Bennett	.25

(4) Team mascot (Panther) .25
(5) Chris "Zorro" Zorich .25
(6) Dan Wilkinson .50
(7) Eric "Bad Bone" Turner .25
(8) Emmitt "Lone Star Sheriff" Smith 3.50
(9) Steve "The Bandit" Atwater .25
(10) Pat "Chillin" Swilling .25
(11) Sean "Ghost" Jones .25
(12) Ray "Scarecrow" Childress .25
(13) Marshall "The Missile" Faulk 3.00
(14) Team mascot (Jaguar) .25
(15) Derrick "Attack Cat" Thomas .50
(16) Chester "Renegade Raider" McGlockton .25
(17) Shane "The Barbarian" Conlan .25
(18) Marco "Cobra" Coleman .25
(19) John "Runaway Train" Randle .25
(20) Bruce "The Pile Driver" Armstrong .25
(21) Renaldo "Raging" Turnbull .25
(22) John "Jumbo" Elliot .25
(23) Ronnie "The Rattler" Lott .50
(24) Randall "Rocket Man" Cunningham .25
(25) Neil "Knight Rider" O'Donnell .25
(26) Junior "Stealth" Seau .50
(27) Ken "Commando" Norton Jr. .25
(28) Cortez "Tez Rex" Kennedy .25
(29) Hardy "Hyena" Nickerson .25
(30) Ken "Jackhammer" Harvey .25

1994 Collector's Choice

Upper Deck's Collector's Choice set was issued in one 384-card series, marking this brand's football debut. Each card has a color action photo on the front with a white frame. The set logo is in the upper left corner; a position icon is in the lower right corner. The player's name and team is in white letters along the bottom of the card. The card back has another photo, player profile, stats and a card number. All cards are UV coated and have the Upper Deck security hologram. Subsets within the main set include: 1994 Rookie Class, Images of '93, Traditions of Excellence, and Expansion cards. Two parallel sets to the main issue were also produced - silver-foil cards, one per pack, and gold-foil cards, one every 35 packs. Instant win "Crash the Game" cards were also made as random inserts. A Joe Montana prototype card was also produced to preview the regular set's design. The back, numbered 19, is somewhat different; the card back has a ghosted picture for its background and only has statistics.

NM/M
Complete Set (384): 25.00
Common Player: .05
Minor Stars: .10
Silver Cards: 3X
Silver Rookies: 2X
Inserted 1:1
Gold Cards: 5X-15X
Gold Rookies: 3X-8X
Inserted 1:36
Pack (12): 1.00
Wax Box (36): 30.00
1 *Antonio Langham* .50
2 *Aaron Glenn* .25
3 *Sam Adams* .25
4 *DeWayne Washington* .20
5 *Dan Wilkinson* .40
6 *Bryant Young* .50
7 *Aaron Taylor* .10
8 *Willie McGinest* .50
9 *Trev Alberts* .25
10 *Jamir Miller* .25
11 John Thierry .20
12 *Heath Shuler* .25
13 *Trent Dilfer* 2.00
14 *Marshall Faulk* 4.00
15 *Greg Hill* .50
16 *William Floyd* .30
17 *Chuck Levy* .25
18 *Charlie Gardner* 1.50
19 *Mario Bates* .20
20 *Donnell Bennett* .25
21 *LeShon Johnson* .40
22 *Calvin Jones* .25
23 *Darnay Scott* .50
24 *Charles Johnson* .50
25 *Johnnie Morton* .50
26 *Shante Carver* .15
27 *Derrick Alexander* .50
28 *David Palmer* .50
29 *Ryan Yarborough* .25
30 *Errict Rhett* .75
31 James Washington .05
32 Sterling Sharpe .10
33 Drew Bledsoe .50
34 Eric Allen .10
35 Jerome Bettis .30
36 Joe Montana .50
37 John Carney .05
38 Emmitt Smith 1.00
39 Chris Warren .05
40 Reggie Brooks .05
41 Gary Brown .05
42 Tim Brown .10
43 Erric Pegram .05
44 Ron Moore .10
45 Jerry Rice .50
46 Ricky Watters .10
47 Joe Montana .75
48 Reggie Brooks .05
49 Rick Mirer .50
50 Raghib Ismail .10
51 Curtis Conway .10
52 Junior Seau .10
53 Mark Carrier .05
54 Ronnie Lott .05
55 Marcus Allen .10
56 Michael Irvin .15
57 Bennie Blades .10
58 Randal Hill .05
59 Brian Blades .05
60 Russell Maryland .05
61 Jim Kelly .15
62 Arthur Marshall .05
63 Webster Slaughter .05
64 Dave Krieg .05
65 Steve Jordan .05
66 Neil O'Donnell .10
67 Andre Reed .10
68 Mike Croel .05
69 Al Smith .05
70 Joe Montana 1.00
71 Randall McDaniel .05
72 Greg Lloyd .05
73 Thomas Smith .05
74 Glyn Milburn .10
75 Lorenzo White .05
76 Neil Smith .05
77 John Randle .05
78 Rod Woodson .10
79 Russell Maryland .05
80 Rodney Peete .05
81 Jackie Harris .05
82 James Jett .05
83 Rodney Hampton .10
84 Bill Romanowski .05
85 Ken Norton Jr. .05
86 Barry Sanders 1.25
87 Johnny Holland .05
88 Terry McDaniel .05
89 Greg Jackson .05
90 Dana Stubblefield .10
91 Jay Novacek .05
92 Chris Spielman .05
93 Ken Ruettgers .05
94 Greg Robinson .05
95 Mark Jackson .05
96 John Taylor .10
97 Roger Harper .05
98 Jerry Ball .05
99 Keith Byars .05
100 Morten Andersen .05
101 Eric Allen .05
102 Marion Butts .05
103 Michael Haynes .05
104 Rob Burnett .05
105 Marco Coleman .05
106 Derek Brown .10
107 Andy Harmon .05
108 Darren Carrington .05
109 Bobby Hebert .05
110 Mark Carrier .05
111 Bryan Cox .05
112 Toi Cook .05
113 Tim Harris .05
114 John Friesz .05
115 Neal Anderson .05
116 Jerome Bettis .50
117 Bruce Armstrong .05
118 Brad Baxter .05
119 Johnny Bailey .05
120 Brian Blades .05
121 Mark Carrier .05
122 Shane Conlan .05
123 Drew Bledsoe 1.00
124 Chris Burkett .05
125 Steve Beuerlein .05
126 Ferrell Edmunds .05
127 Curtis Conway .10
128 Troy Drayton .05
129 Vincent Brown .05
130 Boomer Esiason .05
131 Larry Centers .05
132 Carlton Gray .05
133 Chris Miller .05
134 Eric Metcalf .05
135 Mark Higgs .05
136 Tyrone Hughes .05
137 Randall Cunningham .10
138 Ronnie Harmon .05
139 Andre Rison .10
140 Eric Turner .05
141 Terry Kirby .05
142 Eric Martin .05
143 Seth Joyner .05
144 Stan Humphries .10
145 Deion Sanders .50
146 Vinny Testaverde .05
147 Dan Marino 1.50
148 Renaldo Turnbull .05
149 Herschel Walker .05
150 Anthony Miller .10
151 Richard Dent .05
152 Jim Everett .05
153 Ben Coates .20
154 Jeff Lageman .05
155 Garrison Hearst .50
156 Kelvin Martin .05
157 Dante Jones .05
158 Sean Gilbert .05
159 Leonard Russell .05
160 Ronnie Lott .05
161 Randal Hill .05
162 Rick Mirer .50
163 Alonzo Spellman .05
164 Todd Lyght .05
165 Chris Slade .05
166 Johnny Mitchell .05
167 Ron Moore .20
168 Eugene Robinson .05
169 Chris Hinton .05
170 Dan Footman .05
171 Keith Jackson .05
172 Ricky Jackson .05
173 Heath Sherman .05
174 Chris Mims .05
175 Erric Pegram .05
176 Leroy Hoard .05
177 O.J. McDuffie .20
178 Wayne Martin .05
179 Clyde Simmons .05
180 Leslie O'Neal .05
181 Mike Pritchard .05
182 Michael Jackson .05
183 Scott Mitchell .10
184 Lorenzo Neal .05
185 William Thomas .05
186 Junior Seau .20
187 Chris Gedney .05
188 Tim Lester .05
189 Sam Gash .05
190 Johnny Johnson .05
191 Chuck Cecil .05
192 Cortez Kennedy .10
193 Jim Harbaugh .05
194 Roman Phifer .05
195 Pat Harlow .05
196 Rob Moore .05
197 Gary Clark .05
198 John Vaughn .05
199 Craig Heyward .05
200 Michael Stewart .05
201 Greg McCurty .05
202 Brian Washington .05
203 Ken Harvey .05
204 Chris Warren .05
205 Bruce Smith .05
206 Tom Rouen .05
207 Cris Dishman .05
208 Keith Cash .05
209 Carlos Jenkins .05
210 Levon Kirkland .05
211 Pete Metzelaars .05
212 Shannon Sharpe .10
213 Cody Carlson .05
214 Derrick Thomas .10
215 Emmitt Smith 1.50
216 Robert Porcher .05
217 Sterling Sharpe .20
218 Anthony Smith .05
219 Mike Sherrard .05
220 Tom Rathman .05
221 Nate Newton .05
222 Pat Swilling .05
223 George Teague .05
224 Greg Townsend .05
225 Eric Guliford .20
226 Leroy Thompson .05
227 Thurman Thomas .20
228 Dan Williams .05
229 Bubba McDowell .05
230 Tracy Simien .05
231 *Scottie Graham* .25
232 Eric Green .05
233 Phil Simms .05
234 Ricky Watters .10
235 Kevin Williams .40
236 Brett Perriman .05
237 Reggie White .10
238 Steve Wisniewski .05
239 Mark Collins .05
240 Steve Young .50
241 Steve Tovar .05
242 Jason Belser .05
243 Ray Seals .05
244 Earnest Byner .05
245 Ricky Proehl .05
246 Rich Miano .05
247 Alfred Williams .05
248 Ray Buchanan .05
249 Hardy Nickerson .05
250 Brad Edwards .05
251 Jerrol Williams .05
252 Marvin Washington .05
253 Tony McGhee .05
254 Jeff George .10
255 Ron Hall .05
256 Tim Johnson .05
257 Willie Roaf .05
258 Andre Tippett .05
259 Richardo McDonald .05
260 Jeff Herrod .05
261 Demetrius Dubose .05
262 Ricky Sanders .05
263 John L. Williams .05
264 John Lynch .05
265 Lance Gurn .05
266 Jessie Hester .05
267 Mark Wheeler .05
268 Chip Lohmiller .05
269 Eric Swann .05
270 Byron Evans .05
271 Gary Plummer .05
272 Roger Duffy .05
273 Irv Smith .05
274 Todd Collins .05
275 Robert Blackmon .05
276 Reggie Roby .05
277 Russell Copeland .05
278 Simon Fletcher .05
279 Ernest Givins .05
280 Tim Barnett .05
281 Chris Doleman .05
282 Jeff Graham .05
283 Kenneth Davis .05
284 Vance Johnson .05
285 Haywood Jeffires .05
286 Todd McNair .05
287 Daryl Johnston .05
288 Ryan McNeil .05
289 Terrell Buckley .05
290 Ethan Horton .05
291 Corey Miller .05
292 Marc Logan .05
293 *Lincoln Coleman* .10
294 Derrick Moore .05
295 Leroy Butler .05
296 Jeff Hostetler .05
297 Qadry Ismail .10
298 Andre Hastings .05
299 Henry Jones .05
300 John Elway .50
301 Warren Moon .15
302 Willie Davis .05
303 Vencie Glenn .05
304 Kevin Green .05
305 Marcus Buckley .05
306 Tim McDonald .05
307 Michael Irvin .30
308 Herman Moore .20
309 Brett Favre 2.00
310 Raghib Ismail .10
311 Jerrod Bunch .05
312 Don Beebe .05
313 Steve Atwater .05
314 Gary Brown .05
315 Marcus Allen .10
316 Terry Allen .05
317 Chad Brown .05
318 Cornelius Bennett .05
319 Rod Bernstine .05
320 Greg Montgomery .05
321 Kimble Anders .05
322 Charles Haley .05
323 Mel Gray .05
324 Edgar Bennett .05
325 Eddie Anderson .05
326 Derek Brown .05
327 Steve Bono .10
328 Alvin Harper .10
329 Willie Green .05
330 Robert Brooks .05
331 Patrick Bates .05
332 Anthony Carter .05
333 Barry Foster .10
334 Bill Brooks .05
335 Jason Elam .05
336 Ray Childress .05
337 J.J. Birden .05
338 Cris Carter .10
339 Deion Figures .10
340 Carlton Bailey .05
341 Brent Jones .05
342 Troy Aikman 1.00
343 Rodney Holman .05
344 Tony Bennett .05
345 Tim Brown .10
346 Michael Brooks .05
347 Martin Harrison .05
348 Jerry Rice 1.00
349 John Copeland .05
350 Kerry Cash .05
351 Reggie Cobb .05
352 Brian Mitchell .05
353 Derrick Fenner .05
354 Roosevelt Potts .05
355 Courtney Hawkins .05
356 Carl Banks .05
357 Harold Green .05
358 Steve Emtman .05
359 Santana Dotson .05
360 Reggie Greeks .10
361 Terry Obee .05
362 David Klingler .05
363 Quentin Coryatt .05
364 Craig Erickson .05
365 Desmond Howard .05
366 Carl Pickens .05
367 Lawrence Dawsey .05
368 Henry Ellard .05
369 Shaun Gayle .05
370 David Lang .05
371 Anthony Johnson .05
372 *Darnell Walker* .10
373 Pepper Johnson .05
374 Kurt Gouveia .05
375 Louis Oliver .05
376 Lincoln Kennedy .05
377 Anthony Pleasant .05
378 Irving Fryar .05
379 Carolina Panthers .25
380 Jacksonville Jaguars .25
381 Checklist .05
382 Checklist .05
383 Checklist .05
384 Checklist .05

1994 Collector's Choice Silver

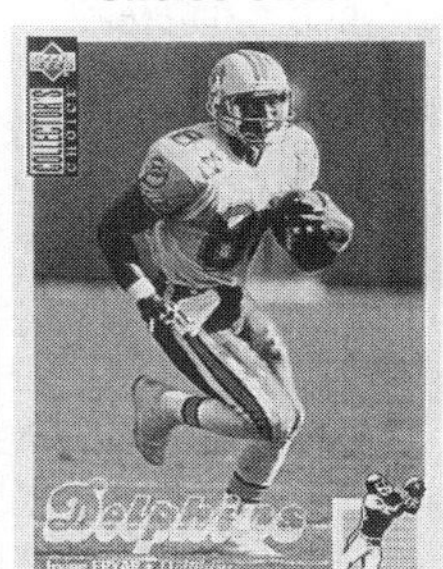

The 384-card, standard-sized set, parallel to the 1994 Collector's Choice base set, was available one per hobby pack, two per retail pack and three per jumbo pack. Unlike the base set, the Silver set has the team's name on the card front in silver foil.

NM/M
Complete Set (384): 75.00
Common Player: .20
Silver Cards: 2X-4X

1994 Collector's Choice Gold

This 384-card set features each card in the base set, but includes a gold border around the card and the team name is printed in gold foil. Gold parallel cards were seeded every 35 packs of Collector's Choice.

NM/M
Complete Set (384): 1,500
Common Player: 2.00
Minor Stars: 4.00
Unlisted Stars: 5X-15X

1994 Collector's Choice Crash the Game

These instant-win sweepstakes cards were randomly inserted in 1994 Upper Deck Collector's Choice packs, one every 36th pack. More than 300,000 prizes were to be given away, including a grand prize of a $10,000 football card and memorabilia shopping spree at Upper Deck and Upper Deck Authenticated, plus an afternoon with Joe Montana.

NM/M
Complete Set (30): 40.00
Common Player: 1.00
Minor Stars: 2.00
Bronze Cards: .2X
Silver Cards: .3X
Gold Cards: .5X
1 Steve Young 2.50
2 Troy Aikman 3.00
3 Rick Mirer 1.00
4 Trent Dilfer 2.00
5 Dan Marino 4.00
6 John Elway 4.00
7 Heath Shuler 1.00
8 Joe Montana 4.00
9 Drew Bledsoe 3.00
10 Warren Moon 1.00
11 Marshall Faulk 3.00
12 Thurman Thomas 1.00
13 Barry Foster 1.00
14 Gary Brown 1.00
15 Emmitt Smith 4.00
16 Barry Sanders 4.00
17 Rodney Hampton 1.00
18 Jerome Bettis 2.00
19 Ricky Watters 1.00
20 Ron Moore 1.00
21 Jerry Rice 3.00
22 Andre Rison 1.00
23 Michael Irvin 1.00
24 Sterling Sharpe 2.00
25 Shannon Sharpe 1.00
26 Darnay Scott 1.00
27 Andre Reed 1.00
28 Tim Brown 1.00
29 Charles Johnson 1.00
30 Irving Fryar 1.00

1994 Collector's Choice Then and Now

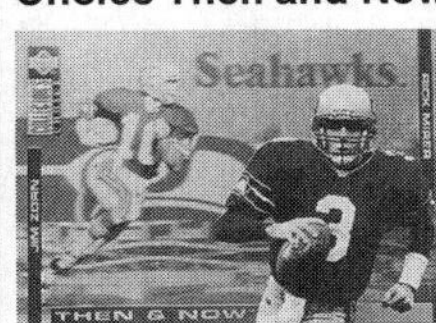

The eight-card, regular-sized set was available to collectors by sending in a redemption card. The horizontal card fronts feature a current top player with a former great in a holographic image. The backs feature color shots of each player with highlights of each player.

NM/M
Complete Set (8): 10.00
Common Player: .50
1 Eric Dickerson, Jerome Bettis 1.00
2 Fred Biletnikoff, Tim Brown .50
3 Len Dawson, Joe Montana 2.00
4 Joe Montana, Steve Young 3.00
5 Bob Griese, Dan Marino 3.00
6 Jim Zorn, Rick Mirer .50
NNO Joe Montana Header Card 2.00
NNO Then/Now Exch. Card .50
NNO Eric Dickerson Checklist .50

1994-95 Collector's Choice Crash Super Bowl XXIX

The eight-card, standard-sized set, produced specifically for Super Bowl XXIX, were available at the NFL Experience card show in Miami, as well as other media outlets. The set features four players from the San Diego Chargers and four from the San Francisco 49ers. If a player featured in the set scored a touchdown in the Super Bowl, the card was redeemable for a special nine-card set.

NM/M
Complete Set (9): 12.00
Common Player: .50
1 Steve Young (WIN) 3.00
2 Jerry Rice (WIN) 4.00
3 Brent Jones .50
4 Ricky Watters (WIN) 1.00
5 Stan Humphries (WIN) 1.00
6 Natrone Means (WIN) 1.50
7 Ronnie Harmon .50
8 Tony Martin (WIN) .50
NNO Header Card .50

1995 Collector's Choice

Upper Deck's 1995 Collector's Choice 348-card set includes 296 regular cards, plus 30 1995 Rookie Class and 20 Did You Know cards. Each regular card front has a color photo with a white frame. The brand logo is in the upper left corner; the player's name, team name and position are at the bottom. The card back has that information at the top, along with biographical information and a card number. The middle of the card has another action photo, with statistics and a brief summary of the player's accomplishments. Two parallel sets were also created - Players Club, which uses a silver stamp (one card every pack) and Platinum Players Club, which reproduces each card on silver-foil paper (one in 35 packs). Other inserts include eight of 20 Joe Montana Trilogy cards, and You Crash the Game cards. Once again, Collector's Choice features Crash Packs, which contain all types of insert cards. These packs are inserted one per 144 packs.

NM/M
Complete Set (348): 25.00
Common Player: .05
Minor Stars: .10
Marino Chronicles (10): 15.00
Montana Chronicles (10): 15.00
1:1 Special Retail
Player Club Cards: 2X
Inserted 1:1
PC Platinum Cards: 6X-10X
PC Platinum Rookies: 3X-5X
Inserted 1:35
Pack (12): .75
Wax Box (36): 20.00
1 *Ki-Jana Carter* .30
2 *Tony Boselli* .10
3 *Steve McNair* 2.50
4 *Michael Westbrook* 1.00
5 *Kerry Collins* 2.00
6 *Kevin Carter* .10
7 *Mike Mamula* .10
8 *Joey Galloway* 2.00

9 *Kyle Brady* .40
10 *J.J. Stokes* 1.00
11 *Derrick Alexander* .20
12 *Warren Sapp* .50
13 *Mark Fields* .10
14 *Tyrone Wheatley* .30
15 *Napoleon Kaufman* .50
16 *James Stewart* .75
17 *Luther Elliss* .10
18 *Rashaan Salaam* .30
19 *Ty Law* .10
20 *Mark Bruener* .20
21 *Derrick Brooks* .10
22 *Christian Fauria* .10
23 *Ray Zellars* .10
24 *Todd Collins* .10
25 *Sherman Williams* .10
26 *Frank Sanders* 1.00
27 *Rodney Thomas* .10
28 *Rob Johnson* 1.25
29 *Steve Stenstrom* .20
30 *James Stewart* .10
31 Barry Sanders 1.00
32 Marshall Faulk .20
33 Darnay Scott .10
34 Joe Montana .50
35 Michael Irvin .10
36 Jerry Rice .50
37 Errict Rhett .20
38 Drew Bledsoe .50
39 Dan Marino .75
40 Terance Mathis .10
41 Natrone Means .20
42 Tim Brown .10
43 Steve Young .40
44 Mel Gray .05
45 Jerome Bettis .20
46 Aeneas Williams .05
47 Charlie Gardner .05
48 Deion Sanders .20
49 Ken Harvey .05
50 Emmitt Smith .75
51 Andre Reed .10
52 Sean Dawkins .15
53 Irving Fryar .05
54 Vincent Brisby .05
55 Rob Moore .05
56 Carl Pickens .05
57 Vinny Testaverde .05
58 Webster Slaughter .05
59 Eric Green .05
60 Anthony Miller .05
61 Lake Dawson .20
62 Tim Brown .25
63 Stan Humphries .10
64 Rick Mirer .40
65 Gary Clark .05
66 Troy Aikman 1.00
67 Mike Sherrard .05
68 Fred Barnett .05
69 Henry Ellard .05
70 Terry Allen .05
71 Jeff Graham .05
72 Herman Moore .10
73 Brett Favre 2.00
74 Trent Dilfer .40
75 Derek Brown .05
76 Andre Rison .10
77 Willie Anderson .05
78 Jerry Rice 1.00
79 Thurman Thomas .20
80 Marshall Faulk .75
81 O.J. McDuffie .05
82 Ben Coates .05
83 Johnny Mitchell .05
84 Darnay Scott .40
85 Derrick Alexander .20
86 Micheal Barrow .05
87 Charles Johnson .20
88 John Elway 1.00
89 Willie Davis .05
90 James Jett .05
91 Mark Seay .05
92 Brian Blades .05
93 Ricky Proehl .05
94 Charles Haley .05
95 Cris Calloway .05
96 Calvin Williams .05
97 Ethan Horton .05
98 Cris Carter .10
99 Curtis Conway .05
100 Lomas Brown .05
101 Edgar Bennett .05
102 Craig Erickson .05
103 Jim Everett .05
104 Terance Mathis .05
105 Wayne Gandy .05
106 Brent Jones .05
107 Bruce Smith .05
108 Roosevelt Potts .05
109 Dan Marino 1.50
110 Michael Timpson .05
111 Boomer Esiason .05
112 David Klingler .05
113 Eric Metcalf .05
114 Lorenzo White .05
115 Neil O'Donnell .10
116 Shannon Sharpe .10
117 Joe Montana 1.00
118 Jeff Hostetler .10
119 Ronnie Harmon .05
120 Chris Warren .10
121 Randal Hill .05
122 Alvin Harper .10
123 Dave Brown .05
124 Randall Cunningham .10
125 Heath Shuler .50
126 Jake Reed .05
127 Donnell Woolford .05
128 Scott Mitchell .05
129 Reggie White .10
130 Lawrence Dawsey .05
131 Michael Haynes .05
132 Bert Emanuel .20
133 Troy Drayton .05
134 Merton Hanks .05
135 Jim Kelly .10
136 Tony Bennett .05
137 Terry Kirby .05
138 Drew Bledsoe 1.00
139 Johnny Johnson .05
140 Dan Wilkinson .05
141 Leroy Hoard .05
142 Gary Brown .05
143 Barry Foster .05
144 Shane Dronett .05
145 Marcus Allen .10
146 Harvey Williams .05
147 Tony Martin .05
148 Rod Stephens .05
149 Ronald Moore .05
150 Michael Irvin .20
151 Rodney Hampton .05
152 Herschel Walker .05
153 Reggie Brooks .05
154 Qadry Ismail .05
155 Chris Zorich .05
156 Barry Sanders 2.00
157 Sean Jones .05
158 Errict Rhett .10
159 Tyrone Hughes .05
160 Jeff George .10
161 Chris Miller .05
162 Steve Young .75
163 Cornelius Bennett .05
164 Trev Alberts .05
165 Marco Coleman .05
166 Marion Butts .05
167 Aaron Glenn .05
168 James Francis .05
169 Eric Turner .05
170 Darryll Lewis .05
171 John L. Williams .05
172 Simon Fletcher .05
173 Neil Smith .05
174 Chester McGlockton .05
175 Natrone Means .40
176 Michael Sinclair .05
177 Larry Centers .05
178 Daryl Johnston .05
179 Dave Meggett .05
180 Greg Jackson .05
181 Ken Harvey .05
182 Warren Moon .10
183 Steve Walsh .05
184 Chris Spielman .05
185 Bryce Paup .05
186 Courtney Hawkins .05
187 Willie Roaf .05
188 Chris Doleman .05
189 Jerome Bettis .40
190 Ricky Watters .10
191 Henry Jones .05
192 Quentin Coryatt .05
193 Bryan Cox .05
194 Kevin Turner .05
195 Siupeli Malamala .05
196 Louis Oliver .05
197 Rob Burnett .05
198 Cris Dishman .05
199 Bam Morris .40
200 Ray Crockett .05
201 Jon Vaughn .05
202 Nolan Harrison .05
203 Leslie O'Neal .05
204 Sam Adams .05
205 Eric Swann .05
206 Jay Novacek .05
207 Keith Hamilton .05
208 Charlie Garner .05
209 Tom Carter .05
210 Henry Thomas .05
211 Lewis Tillman .05
212 Pat Swilling .05
213 Terrell Buckley .05
214 Hardy Nickerson .05
215 Mario Bates .20
216 D.J. Johnson .05
217 Robert Young .05
218 Dana Stubblefield .05
219 Jeff Burris .05
220 Floyd Turner .05
221 Troy Vincent .05
222 Willie McGinest .05
223 James Hasty .05
224 *Jeff Blake* .50
225 Stevon Moore .05
226 Ernest Givins .05
227 Greg Lloyd .05
228 Steve Atwater .05
229 Dale Carter .05
230 Terry McDaniels .05
231 John Carney .05
232 Cortez Kennedy .05
233 Clyde Simmons .05
234 Emmitt Smith 1.50
235 Thomas Lewis .05
236 William Fuller .05
237 Ricky Ervins .05
238 John Randle .05
239 John Thierry .05
240 Mel Gray .05
241 George Teague .05
242 Charles Wilson .05
243 Joe Johnson .05
244 Chuck Smith .05
245 Sean Gilbert .05
246 Bryant Young .05
247 Bucky Brooks .05
248 Ray Buchanan .05
249 Tim Bowens .05
250 Vincent Brown .05
251 Marcus Turner .05
252 Derrick Fenner .05
253 Antonio Langham .05
254 Cody Carlson .05
255 Kevin Greene .05
256 Leonard Russell .05
257 Donnell Bennett .05
258 Raghib Ismail .05
259 Alfred Pupunu .20
260 Eugene Robinson .05
261 Seth Joyner .05
262 Darren Woodson .05
263 Phillipi Sparks .05
264 Andy Harmon .05
265 Brian Mitchell .05
266 Fuad Reveiz .05
267 Mark Carrier .05
268 Johnnie Morton .05
269 LeShon Johnson .05
270 Eric Curry .05
271 Quinn Early .05
272 Elbert Shelley .05
273 Roman Phifer .05
274 Ken Norton .05
275 Steve Tasker .05
276 Jim Harbaugh .05
277 Aubrey Beavers .05
278 Chris Slade .05
279 Mo Lewis .05
280 Alfred Williams .05
281 Michael Dean Perry .05
282 Marcus Robertson .05
283 Rod Woodson .10
284 Glyn Milburn .05
285 Greg Hill .25
286 Rob Fredrickson .05
287 Junior Seau .10
288 Rick Tuten .05
289 Aeneas Williams .05
290 Darrin Smith .05
291 John Booty .05
292 Eric Allen .05
293 Reggie Roby .05
294 David Palmer .05
295 Trace Armstrong .05
296 Dave Krieg .05
297 Robert Brooks .05
298 Brad Culpepper .05
299 Wayne Martin .05
300 Craig Heyward .05
301 Isaac Bruce .15
302 Deion Sanders .40
303 Matt Darby .05
304 Kirk Lowdermilk .05
305 Bernie Parmalee .20
306 Leroy Thompson .05
307 Ronnie Lott .05
308 Steve Tovar .05
309 Michael Jackson .05
310 Al Smith .05
311 Chad Brown .05
312 Elijah Alexander .05
313 Kimble Anders .05
314 Anthony Smith .05
315 Andre Coleman .05
316 Terry Wooden .05
317 Garrison Hearst .10
318 Russell Maryland .05
319 Michael Brooks .05
320 Bernard Williams .05
321 Andre Collins .05
322 DeWayne Washington .05
323 Raymont Harris .15
324 Brett Perriman .05
325 LeRoy Butler .05
326 Santana Dotson .05
327 Irv Smith .05
328 Ron George .05
329 Marquez Pope .05
330 William Floyd .25
331 Mickey Washington .05
332 Keith Goganious .05
333 Derek Brown .05
334 Steve Beuerlein .05
335 Reggie Cobb .05
336 Jeff Lageman .05
337 Kelvin Martin .05
338 Darren Carrington .05
339 Mark Carrier .05
340 Willie Green .05
341 Frank Reich .05
342 Don Beebe .05
343 Lamar Lathon .05
344 Tim McKyer .05
345 Pete Metzelaars .05
346 Vernon Turner .05
347 Checklist 1-174 .05
348 Checklist 175-348 .05

1995 Collector's Choice Player's Club

The 348-card, regular-size parallel set was inserted in each pack of 1995 Collector's Choice. The card fronts have a silver border with a silver "Player's Club" logo.

	NM/M
Complete Set (348):	45.00
Common Player:	.20
Player's Club Cards:	2X

1995 Collector's Choice Player's Club Platinum

The 348-card, regular-sized parallel set was inserted every 35 packs of Collector's Choice. The card fronts feature a silver "Platinum Player's Club" logo, as well as a silver border.

	NM/M
Complete Set (348):	750.00
Common Player:	1.00
Player's Club Platinum:	3X-8X

1995 Collector's Choice Crash The Game

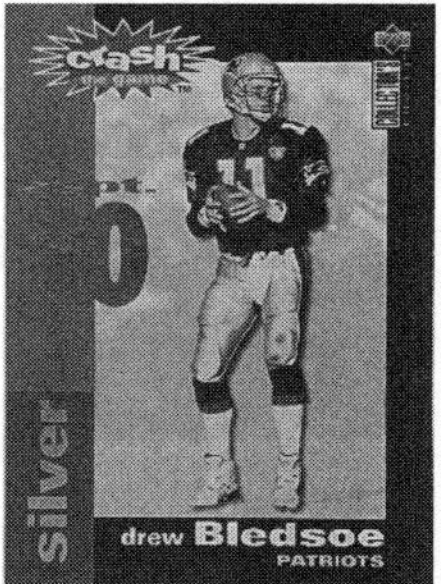

These 30 cards feature an action photo of a player, with a silver or gold foil date stamped into the design. If the player pictured scored a touchdown during his team's game on the date on the card front, a collector could redeem the card for a complete 30-card set. Odds of finding a silver version were one per every five packs; gold cards were inserted one per every 50 packs. The back of the card is numbered using a "C" prefix and includes the rules of the game.

	NM/M
Complete Silver Set (90):	60.00
Common Player:	.25
Minor Stars:	.50
Inserted 1:5	
Gold Cards:	3X
Inserted 1:50	
Silver Red. Cards:	.5X
Gold Red. Cards:	2X

1 Dan Marino 2.00
2 John Elway 2.00
3 Kerry Collins .50
4 Stan Humphries .25
5 Steve Young 1.00
6 Brett Favre 2.50
7 Troy Aikman 1.25
8 Warren Moon .50
9 Drew Bledsoe 1.25
10 Steve McNair 1.00
11 Chris Warren .25
12 Natrone Means .50
13 Thurman Thomas .50
14 Barry Sanders 2.50
15 Emmitt Smith 2.00
16 Jerome Bettis .50
17 Ki-Jana Carter .50
18 Napoleon Kaufman .50
19 Marshall Faulk .75
20 Errict Rhett .25
21 Cris Carter .75
22 Jerry Rice 1.25
23 Tim Brown .50
24 Andre Reed .25
25 Andre Rison .50
26 Ben Coates .25
27 Michael Irvin .50
28 Terance Mathis .25
29 Michael Westbrook .50
30 Herman Moore .50

1995 Collector's Choice Marino Chronicles

The 10-card, regular-sized set was inserted in specially marked retail packs and features Marino highlight cards. The card fronts feature an aqua border with "Marino" in gold foil. The cards are numbered with the "DM" prefix.

	NM/M
Complete Set (10):	10.00
Common Player:	1.25

1 Dan Marino (Rookie of the Year) 1.25
2 Dan Marino (5000 Yards Passing) 1.25
3 Dan Marino (48 TD Passes) 1.25
4 Dan Marino (Super Bowl XIX) 1.25
5 Dan Marino (30,000 Yards Passing) 1.25
6 Dan Marino (4000 Yard Season) 1.25
7 Dan Marino (40,000 Yards Passing) 1.25
8 Dan Marino (Marino's Back) 1.25
9 Dan Marino (300th TD Pass) 1.25
10 Dan Marino (More Records to Fall) 1.25

1995 Collector's Choice Montana Trilogy

Eight of 20 Joe Montana Trilogy cards were included in packs of 1995 Upper Deck Collector's Choice football cards. These cards are numbered 1-8, using an "MT" prefix. Cards recap Montana's career, and were included one per every 12 packs. A Montana Trilogy header card was also produced.

	NM/M
Complete Set (9):	30.00
Common Player:	4.00
Header Card:	5.00

1 1977 NCAA Champs 4.00
2 1978 Cotton Bowl 4.00
3 The 1978 NFL Draft 4.00
4 The Catch 4.00
5 Super Bowl XVI 4.00
6 Super Bowl XVI MVP 4.00
7 Super Bowl XIX 4.00
8 Super Bowl XIX MVP 4.00
CCH Trilogy Header 5.00

1995 Collector's Choice Update

The 1995 Upper Deck Collector's Choice set has 225 cards, including 103 regular player cards (featuring free agents, traded players and rookies in the uniforms of their new teams), 60 "Rookie Collection" cards (picturing first-year players in their NFL uniforms), 30 cards featuring players from the expansion team Carolina Panthers and Jacksonville Jaguars, two checklists and 30 "The Key" cards (describing what NFL teams do to stop "key" players on each team). The set is numbered U1-U225. Gold and silver parallel sets were made for two of the subsets; silver Rookie Collection cards are found one per three packs, while gold versions are one in every 35. Silver "The Key" cards are seeded one per every five packs, while gold ones are one per every 52. Also included as inserts are Stick-Ums, restickable stickers the size of a trading card which picture top stars, rookies and team helmets. Each one has either four mini-stickers on it, a large "superstar" sticker, or one with three players and a team helmet. One of these 90 cards was seeded in every pack of 1995 Upper Deck Collector's Choice Update product. Six different Stick-Ums sticker booklets were also available through a wrapper mail-in offer. A new version of the "You Crash the Game" interactive cards were redesigned for the playoffs. "You Crash the Playoffs" cards were randomly inserted every 18th pack; if the player on the card scored a touchdown during the playoffs the card could be redeemed for various prizes.

	NM/M
Complete Set (225):	20.00
Common Player:	.05
Minor Stars:	.10
Silver Cards:	2X
Inserted 1:3	
Gold Cards:	3X-8X
Gold Rookies:	2X-4X
Inserted 1:35	
Pack (10):	1.25
Wax Box (36):	35.00

1 Roell Preston .05
2 Lorenzo Styles .05
3 Todd Collins .10
4 *Darick Holmes* .75
5 Justin Armour .10
6 Tony Cline .05
7 Tyrone Poole .05
8 Kerry Collins .50
9 Sean Harris .05
10 Steve Stenstrom .05
11 Rashaan Salaam .30
12 Ki-Jana Carter .30
13 Craig Powell .05
14 *Eric Zeier* .50
15 Ernest Hunter .05
16 Sherman Williams .10
17 *Terrell Davis* 5.00
18 Luther Elliss .05
19 Craig Newsome .05
20 Steve McNair 1.00
21 *Chris Sanders* .30
22 Rodney Thomas .30
23 Ellis Johnson .05
24 *Ken Dilger* .40
25 *Zack Crockett* .20
26 Tony Boselli .10
27 Rob Johnson 1.00
28 James O. Stewart .20
29 Pete Mitchell .05
30 *Tamarick Vanover* .20
31 Napoleon Kaufman .50
32 Kevin Carter .05
33 Steve McLaughlin .05
34 Lovell Pinkney .05
35 James A. Stewart .05
36 *Chad May* .30
37 Derrick Alexander .05
38 *Curtis Martin* 2.50
39 Will Moore .05
40 Ty Law .05
41 Ray Zellars .05
42 Mark Fields .05
43 Tyrone Wheatley .30
44 Kyle Brady .05
45 Mike Mamula .05
46 Bobby Taylor .05
47 *Chris Jones* .30
48 Frank Sanders .50
49 *Stoney Case* .25
50 Mark Bruener .05
51 *Kordell Stewart* 2.00
52 Jimmy Oliver .05
53 Terrance Shaw .05
54 *Terrell Fletcher* .30
55 J.J. Stokes .50
56 Christian Fauria .05
57 Joey Galloway 1.00
58 Warren Sapp .05
59 Derrick Brooks .05
60 Michael Westbrook .50
61 Emmitt Smith .75
62 Barry Sanders 1.00
63 Marshall Faulk .30
64 Troy Aikman .50
65 Steve Young .40
66 Junior Seau .10
67 John Elway .50
68 Dan Marino .75
69 Drew Bledsoe .50
70 Errict Rhett .30
71 Natrone Means .10
72 Deion Sanders .30
73 Brett Favre 2.00
74 Cris Carter .25
75 Ben Coates .05
76 Jerome Bettis .20
77 Reggie White .20
78 Stan Humphries .05
79 Michael Westbrook .30
80 Steve McNair .75
81 Kevin Greene .05
82 Joey Galloway .50
83 Napoleon Kaufman .75
84 Jerry Rice .50
85 Andre Rison .05
86 Eric Metcalf .05
87 Kerry Collins .20
88 Chris Warren .10
89 Irving Fryar .05
90 Michael Irvin .10
91 Don Beebe .05
92 Pete Metzelaars .05
93 Mark Carrier .05
94 Frank Reich .05
95 Randy Baldwin .05
96 Bob Christian .05
97 John Kasay .05
98 Lamar Lathon .05
99 Sam Mills .05
100 Carlton Bailey .05
101 Darrion Conner .05
102 Blake Brockermeyer .05
103 Gerald Williams .05
104 Willie Green .05
105 Derrick Graham .05
106 Desmond Howard .05
107 Harry Colon .05
108 Steve Beuerlein .05
109 Reggie Cobb .05
110 Jeff Lageman .05
111 Mark Brunell 1.00
112 Darren Carrington .05
113 Brian DeMarco .05
114 Ernest Givins .05
115 LeShia Maston .05
116 Willie Jackson .05
117 Keith Goganious .05
118 Kelvin Pritchett .05
119 Ryan Christopherson .05
120 Brian Schwartz .05
121 Dave Kreig .05
122 Darryl Talley .05
123 Bryce Paup .05
124 Anthony Johnson .05
125 Eric Bieniemy .05
126 Andre Rison .05
127 Rodney Peete .05
128 Aaron Craver .05
129 Henry Thomas .05
130 *Antonio Freeman* .50
131 Chris Chandler .05
132 Craig Erickson .05
133 Roell Preston .05
134 Brian Washington .05
135 Eric Green .05
136 Broderick Thomas .05
137 Dave Meggett .05
138 Eric Allen .05
139 Herschel Walker .05
140 Dexter Carter .05
141 Kerry Cash .05
142 Kelvin Martin .05
143 Eric Pegram .05
144 Bo Orlando .05
145 Ricky Ervins .05
146 John Friesz .05
147 Alexander Wright .05
148 Alvin Harper .05
149 Gus Frerotte .25
150 Duval Love .05
151 Eric Metcalf .05
152 Ruben Brown .05
153 Marty Carter .05
154 James Joseph .05
155 Steve Emtman .05
156 Wade Wilson .05
157 Britt Hager .05
158 Mark Schlereth .05
159 Corey Scheliger .05

160 Mark Ingram .05
161 Mark Stepnoski .05
162 Willie Anderson .05
163 Donta Jones .05
164 James Hasty .05
165 Gary Clark .05
166 David Sloan .05
167 Jeff Dallenbach .05
168 Rufus Porter .05
169 Mike Croel .05
170 Charles Wilson .05
171 Pat Swilling .05
172 Kurt Gouveia .05
173 Norm Johnson .05
174 Shawn Gayle .05
175 Marquez Pope .05
176 Tyrone Stowe .05
177 Anthony Parker .05
178 Kenneth Gant .05
179 James Washington .05
180 Rob Moore .05
181 Alundis Brice .05
182 Lamont Warren .05
183 Michael Timpson .05
184 Lorenzo White .05
185 Charlie Williams .05
186 Ed McCaffrey .05
187 James Jones .05
188 Derrick Fenner .05
189 Mel Gray .05
190 James Williams .05
191 Jeff Criswell .05
192 Randal Hill .05
193 Terry Allen .05
194 Joel Smeenge .05
195 Ricky Watters .10
196 Don Sasa .05
197 Steve Bono .10
198 Steve Broussard .05
199 Carlos Jenkins .05
200 Reggie Roby .05
201 Stanley Richard .05
202 Vince Workman .05
203 Eric Guliford .05
204 Lionel Washington .05
205 Brian Williams .05
206 Ronnie Lott .05
207 Corey Harris .05
208 Harlon Barnett .05
209 Bubby Brister .05
210 Darren Bennett .05
211 Winston Moss .05
212 Leonard Russell .05
213 Ronald Davis .05
214 Curtis Whitley .05
215 Webster Slaughter .05
216 Korey Stringer .05
217 Don Davey .05
218 Mark Rypien .05
219 Chad Cota .05
220 Tim Ruddy .05
221 Corey Fuller .05
222 Mike Dumas .05
223 Eddie Murray .05
224 Checklist .05
225 Checklist .05

1995 Collector's Choice Update Silver

The 90-card, regular-sized set was inserted every three packs of Collector's Choice Update and paralleled the first 90 cards of the set with the card name in silver foil.

NM/M

Common Player: .15
Silver Cards: 1.5X-2X

1995 Collector's Choice Update Gold

The 90-card, regular-size set was inserted every 35 packs of Collector's Choice Update and paralleled the first 90 cards of the Update set.

NM/M

Common Player: 1.50
Gold Cards: 3X-8X

1995 Collector's Choice Update Crash the Playoffs

Upper Deck's "You Crash the Game" interactive cards were redesigned for the 1995 Upper Deck Collector's Choice Update set to spotlight the playoffs. Called "You Crash the Playoffs," the cards allow fans holding the cards to redeem them for special card sets if any of the players pictured on the cards is involved in a scoring play during the playoffs (catching or throwing a touchdown pass, running for one). Each card pictures five players at one position (either quarterback, running back or wide receiver) for each division. The winning cards were redeemable for a 20-card set which highlights the playoffs and Super Bowl XXX. Two versions were made - silver (good for a silver set; one in five packs), or gold (good for a gold set; one in 50 packs). The cards are numbered with the "CP" prefix.

NM/M

Complete Set (18): 20.00
Common Player: .50
Minor Stars: 1.00
Inserted 1:5
Gold Cards: 3X
Inserted 1:50
1 AFC East QB 3.00
2 AFC Central QB 1.50
3 AFC West QB 2.00
4 NFC East QB 1.50
5 NFC Central QB 3.00
6 NFC West QB 1.50
7 AFC East RB 2.50
8 AFC Central RB .50
9 AFC West RB 3.00
10 NFC East RB 1.00
11 NFC Central RB .50
12 NFC West RB .50
13 AFC West WR .50
14 AFC Central WR .50
15 AFC West WR 1.00
16 NFC East WR 1.00
17 NFC Central WR 3.00
18 NFC West WR 1.50

1995 Collector's Choice Update Post Season Heroics

The 20-card, standard-size set was available by redeeming a winning Collector's Choice Update Crash The Playoffs silver or gold card. The cards are similar to the base set cards with "Post Season Heroics" printed along the card fronts in silver or gold foil.

NM/M

Complete Set (20): 10.00
Common Player: .25
Minor Stars: .50
Gold Cards: 3X
1 Stan Humphries .25
2 Natrone Means .50
3 Tony Martin .25
4 Neil O'Donnell .25
5 Byron "Bam" Morris .25
6 Charles Johnson .25
7 Jim Harbaugh .50
8 Darick Holmes .50
9 Sean Dawkins .25
10 Steve Young 1.50
11 Craig Heyward .25
12 Jerry Rice 2.00
13 Brett Favre 4.00
14 Edgar Bennett .25
15 Robert Brooks .50
16 Troy Aikman 2.00
17 Emmitt Smith 3.00
18 Michael Irvin .50
19 Byron "Bam" Morris .25
20 Larry Brown .25

1995 Collector's Choice Update Stick-Ums

These 1995 Upper Deck Collector's Choice inserts were seeded one per every pack. The 90 restickable stickers are the size of a trading card and picture some of the NFL's biggest stars and top rookies, plus team helmets. Cards have either four mini-stickers on it, one large full-size superstar sticker, or three players and a team helmet sticker. Six different Stick-Ums booklets (one for each division) were also made to display the stickers. Each booklet, which contains team trivia and important dates in team history, were available as a mail-in offer for $2 and two Collector's Choice Update foil wrappers.

NM/M

Complete Set (90): 10.00
Common Player: .10
Minor Stars: .20
Inserted 1:1
1 Jeff George .20
2 Kerry Collins .20
3 Jerome Bettis .20
4 Mario Bates .10
5 Steve Young .50
6 Rashaan Salaam .20
7 Barry Sanders 1.00
8 Brett Favre 1.00
9 Warren Moon .20
10 Errict Rhett .20
11 Emmitt Smith .75
12 Rodney Hampton .20
13 Ricky Watters .20
14 Garrison Hearst .20
15 Michael Westbrook .20
16 Jim Kelly .20
17 Marshall Faulk .30
18 Dan Marino .75
19 Drew Bledsoe .50
20 Kyle Brady .10
21 Ki-Jana Carter .10
22 Andre Rison .20
23 Steve McNair .50
24 James O. Stewart .20
25 Bam Morris .10
26 John Elway .75
27 Marcus Allen .20
28 Tim Brown .20
29 Natrone Means .20
30 Chris Warren .20
31 Terance Mathis, Mark Carrier, Chris Miller, Jim Everett .10
32 Bert Emanuel, Pete Metzelaars, Isaac Bruce, Dana Stubblefield .20
33 Chris Doleman, Frank Reich, Derek Brown, Jerry Rice .30
34 Jessie Tuggle, Roman Phifer, Tyrone Hughes, Bryant Young .30
35 Sam Mills, Kevin Carter, Michael Haynes, Brent Jones .10
36 Eric Metcalf, Tyrone Poole, Lovell Pinkney Falcons .10
37 Morten Andersen, John Kasay, Troy Drayton Panthers .10
38 Sean Gilbert, Mark Fields, J.J. Stokes Vikings .10
39 Darion Conner, Willie Roaf, Ken Norton Saints .10
40 Craig Heyward, Renaldo Turnbull, William Floyd 49ers .10
41 Raymont Harris, Herman Moore, Edgar Bennett, Cris Carter .10
42 Jeff Graham, Henry Thomas, Reggie White, Trent Dilfer .10
43 Curtis Conway, Scott Mitchell, Scottie Graham, Alvin Harper .10
44 Steve Walsh, Sean Jones, Qadry Ismail, Hardy Nickerson .10
45 John Randle, Mark Carrier, Chris Spielman, John Jurkovic .10
46 John Thierry, Luther Elliss, LeRoy Butler Bears .10
47 Johnnie Morton, Robert Brooks, Jake Reed Lions .10
48 LeShon Johnson, DeWayne Washington, Jackie Harris Packers .10
49 Donnell Woolford, James A. Stewart, Eric Curry Vikings .10
50 Mark Carrier, Chris Spielman, Warren Sapp Buccaneers .10
51 Troy Aikman, Mike Sherrard, Fred Barnett, Dave Kreig .30
52 Michael Irvin, Chris Calloway, Calvin Williams, Henry Ellard .10
53 Sherman Williams, Dave Brown, Rob Moore, Heath Shuler .10
54 Charles Haley, Randall Cunningham, Eric Swann, Ken Harvey .10
55 Thomas Lewis, Charlie Garner, Clyde Simmons, Tom Carter .10
56 Tyrone Wheatley, Bobby Taylor, Daryl Johnston Cowboys .10
57 Mike Croel, Byron Evans, Aeneas Williams Giants .10
58 Mike Mamula, Larry Centers, Brian Mitchell Eagles .10
59 Jay Novacek, Frank Sanders, Terry Allen Cardinals .10
60 Deion Sanders, Herschel Walker, Sterling Palmer Redskins .20
61 Henry Jones, Craig Erickson, Terry Kirby, Ben Coates .10
62 Andre Reed, Willie Anderson, Irving Fryar, Johnny Mitchell .10
63 Russell Copeland, Sean Dawkins, Vincent Brisby, Boomer Esiason .10
64 Bruce Smith, O.J. McDuffie, Willie McGinest, Ryan Yarborough .10
65 Roosevelt Potts, Keith Byars, Curtis Martin, Brad Baxter .75
66 Cornelius Bennett, Ray Buchanan, Marco Coleman Bills .10
67 Quentin Coryatt, Bryan Cox, Chris Slade Colts .10
68 Eric Green, Ty Law, Marvin Washington Dolphins .10
69 Todd Collins, Vincent Brown, Ronald Moore Patriots .10
70 Jeff Burris, Floyd Turner, Aaron Glenn Jets .10
71 Carl Pickens, Vinny Testaverde, Haywood Jeffires, Desmond Howard .10
72 Darnay Scott, Eric Turner, Gary Brown, Neil O'Donnell .10
73 David Klingler, Leroy Hoard, Tony Boselli, Charles Johnson .10
74 Steve Tovar, Al Smith, Derek Brown, John L. Williams .10
75 Lorenzo White, Rodney Thomas, Steve Beuerlein, Kevin Greene .10
76 Jeff Blake, Derrick Alexander, Ray Childress Bengals .10
77 Eric Zeier, Mel Gray, Reggie Cobb Browns .10
78 Todd McNair, Jeff Lageman, Greg Lloyd Oilers .10
79 Dan Wilkinson, Rob Johnson, Rod Woodson Jaguars .30
80 Eric Bieniemy, Antonio Langham, Mark Bruener Steelers .10
81 Shannon Sharpe, Willie Davis, Jeff Hostetler, Stan Humphries .10
82 Rod Bernstine, Ronnie Lott, Harvey Williams, Rick Mirer .10
83 Anthony Miller, Neil Smith, Junior Seau, Brian Blades .10
84 Mike Pritchard, Napoleon Kaufman, Leslie O'Neal, Sam Adams .20
85 Greg Hill, Raghib Ismail, Alfred Pupunu, Cortez Kennedy .10
86 Steve Atwater, Tamarick Vanover, Chester McGlockton Broncos .10
87 Steve Bono, Rob Fredrickson, Tony Martin Chiefs .10
88 Terry McDaniel, Jimmy Oliver, Christian Fauria Raiders .10
89 Glyn Milburn, John Carney, Joey Galloway Chargers .20
90 Simon Fletcher, Keith Cash, Eugene Robinson Seahawks .10

1996 Collector's Choice

Upper Deck's 1996 Collector's Choice Series I contains 375 cards - broken down into 294 regular cards, 45 Rookie Class cards, two checklists and 34 Season to Remember cards. Each regular card front has a color action photo on it, with a brand logo in the upper right corner. The left side of the card has a team color-coded panel with the player's name and team helmet at the bottom; the top portion, which is black, has the player's position in it. The card back has biographical information at the top, along with a card number. A color action photo is underneath, followed by statistics and a football quiz. The right side of the card has a color-coded panel with the player's name at the bottom and the player's team name and position at the top. Insert sets created are MVPs (in gold and silver versions) and You Crash the Game redemption cards. Play Action Stick-Ums also return from the previous year's Update set. These re-stickable die-cut stickers allow collectors to create a football scene. The set consists of 30 NFL athletes and is seeded one per every three packs.

NM/M

Complete Set (375): 20.00
Common Player: .05
Minor Stars: .10
Pack (14): 1.00
Wax Box (40): 25.00
1 *Keyshawn Johnson* 1.50
2 *Kevin Hardy* .10
3 *Simeon Rice* .10
4 *Jonathan Ogden* .10
5 *Cedric Jones* .05
6 *Lawrence Phillips* .25
7 *Tim Biakabutuka* .50
8 *Terry Glenn* .50
9 *Rickey Dudley* .50
10 *Regan Upshaw* .05
11 *Walt Harris* .05
12 *Eddie George* 3.00
13 *John Mobley* .05
14 *Duane Clemons* .05
15 *Marvin Harrison* 2.00
16 *Daryl Gardener* .05
17 *Pete Kendall* .05
18 *Marcus Jones* .05
19 *Eric Moulds* 1.50
20 *Ray Lewis* .50
21 *Alex Van Dyke* .10
22 *Leeland McElroy* .20
23 *Mike Alstott* 1.50
24 *Lawyer Milloy* .05
25 *Marco Battaglia* .05
26 *Je'Rod Cherry* .05
27 *Israel Ifeanyl* .05
28 *Bobby Engram* .50
29 *Jason Dunn* .25
30 *Derrick Mayes* .75
31 *Stepfret Williams* .25
32 *Bobby Hoying* .75
33 *Karim Abdul-Jabbar* .50
34 *Danny Kanell* .50
35 *Chris Darkins* .10
36 *Charlie Jones* .05
37 *Tedy Bruschi* .05
38 *Stanley Pritchett* .05
39 *Donnie Edwards* .05
40 *Jeff Lewis* .50
41 *Stephen Davis* 1.00
42 *Winslow Oliver* .05
43 *Mercury Hayes* .05
44 *Jon Runyan* .05
45 *Steve Taneyhill* .05
46 Eric Metcalf .05
47 Bryce Paup .05
48 Kerry Collins .40
49 Rashaan Salaam .25
50 Carl Pickens .05
51 Emmitt Smith 1.00
52 Michael Irvin .05
53 Troy Aikman .50
54 Terrell Davis .30
55 John Elway .15
56 Herman Moore .05
57 Brett Favre .50
58 Rodney Thomas .05
59 Jim Harbaugh .05
60 Mark Brunell .25
61 Marcus Allen .05
62 Tamarick Vanover .15
63 Steve Bono .05
64 Dan Marino 1.00
65 Warren Moon .05
66 Curtis Martin .75
67 Tyrone Hughes .05
68 Rodney Hampton .05
69 Hugh Douglas .05
70 Tim Brown .05
71 Ricky Watters .05
72 Kordell Stewart .30
73 Andre Coleman .05
74 Jerry Rice .50
75 Joey Galloway .30
76 Isaac Bruce .40
77 Errict Rhett .40
78 Michael Westbrook .25
79 Brian Mitchell .05
80 Aeneas Williams .05
81 Andre Reed .05
82 Brett Maxie .05
83 Jim Flanigan .05
84 Jeff Blake .30
85 Mike Frederick .05
86 Michael Irvin .10
87 Aaron Craver .05
88 Barry Sanders 1.00
89 Keith Jackson .05
90 Chris Sanders .25
91 Marshall Faulk .75
92 Bryan Schwartz .05
93 Tamarick Vanover .20
94 Troy Vincent .05
95 Robert Smith .05
96 Drew Bledsoe .75
97 Quinn Early .05
98 Wayne Chrebet .05
99 Tim Brown .05
100 Charlie Garner .05
101 Yancey Thigpen .30
102 Isaac Bruce .75
103 Natrone Means .10
104 Jerry Rice 1.00
105 Chris Warren .10
106 Errict Rhett .50
107 Heath Shuler .40
108 Eric Swann .05
109 Jeff George .10
110 Steve Tasker .05
111 Sam Mills .05
112 Jeff Graham .05
113 Carl Pickens .10
114 Vinny Testaverde .05
115 Emmitt Smith 2.00
116 John Elway .25
117 Henry Thomas .05
118 Leroy Butler .05
119 Blaine Bishop .05
120 Floyd Turner .05
121 Jeff Lageman .05
122 Kimble Anders .05
123 Bryan Cox .05
124 Qadry Ismail .05
125 Ted Johnson .05
126 Wesley Walls .05
127 Rodney Hampton .05
128 Adrian Murrell .05
129 Daryl Hobbs .05
130 Ricky Watters .10
131 Carnell Lake .05
132 Toby Wright .05
133 Darren Bennett .05
134 J.J. Stokes .50
135 Eugene Robinson .05
136 Eric Curry .05
137 Tom Carter .05
138 Dave Krieg .05
139 Eric Metcalf .05
140 Bill Brooks .05
141 Pete Metzelaars .05
142 Kevin Butler .05
143 John Copeland .05
144 Keenan McCardell .05
145 Larry Brown .05
146 Jason Elam .05
147 Willie Clay .05
148 Robert Brooks .05
149 Chris Chandler .05
150 Quentin Coryatt .05
151 Pete Mitchell .05
152 Martin Bayless .05
153 Pete Stoyanovich .05
154 Cris Carter .10
155 Jimmy Hitchcock .05
156 Mario Bates .05
157 Mike Sherrard .05
158 Boomer Esiason .05
159 Chester McGlockton .05
160 Bobby Taylor .05
161 Kordell Stewart .60
162 Kevin Carter .05
163 Junior Seau .10
164 Derek Loville .05
165 Brian Blades .05
166 Jackie Harris .05
167 Michael Westbrook .50
168 Rob Moore .05
169 Jessie Tuggle .05
170 Darick Holmes .05
171 Tim McKyer .05
172 Erik Kramer .05
173 Harold Green .05
174 Stevon Moore .05
175 Deion Sanders .40
176 Anthony Miller .05
177 Herman Moore .20
178 Brett Favre 2.00
179 Rodney Thomas .30
180 Ken Dilger .05
181 Mark Brunell .50
182 Marcus Allen .10
183 Dan Marino 2.00
184 John Randle .05
185 Ben Coates .05
186 Tyrone Hughes .05
187 Dave Brown .05
188 Johnny Mitchell .05
189 Harvey Williams .05
190 Andy Harmon .05
191 Kevin Greene .05
192 D'Marco Farr .05
193 Andre Coleman .05
194 Bryant Young .05
195 Rick Mirer .05
196 Horace Copeland .05
197 Leslie Shepherd .05
198 Jamir Miller .05
199 Bert Emanuel .05
200 Steve Christie .05
201 Kerry Collins .75
202 Rashaan Salaam .50
203 Steve Tovar .05
204 Michael Jackson .05
205 Kevin Williams .05
206 Glyn Milburn .05
207 Johnnie Morton .05
208 Antonio Freeman .05
209 Cris Dishman .05
210 Ellis Johnson .05
211 Cedric Tillman .05
212 Steve Bono .10
213 Eric Green .05
214 David Palmer .05
215 Vincent Brisby .05
216 Michael Haynes .05
217 Chris Calloway .05
218 Kyle Brady .05
219 Terry McDaniel .05
220 Calvin Williams .05
221 Greg Lloyd .05
222 Jerome Bettis .05
223 Stan Humphries .05
224 Lee Woodall .05
225 Robert Blackmon .05
226 Warren Sapp .05
227 Brian Mitchell .05
228 Garrison Hearst .05
229 Terance Mathis .05
230 Bryce Paup .05
231 Derrick Moore .05
232 Curtis Conway .05
233 Darnay Scott .05
234 Andre Rison .05
235 Jay Novacek .05
236 Terrell Davis .60
237 David Sloan .05
238 Reggie White .05
239 Todd McNair .05
240 Ray Buchanan .05
241 Steve Beuerlein .05
242 Dan Saleaumua .05
243 Bernie Parmalee .05
244 Warren Moon .05
245 Ty Law .05
246 Torrance Small .05
247 Philippi Sparks .05
248 Mo Lewis .05
249 Jeff Hostetler .05
250 Rodney Peete .05
251 Bam Morris .05
252 Chris Miller .05
253 Tony Martin .05
254 Eric Davis .05
255 Joey Galloway .60
256 Derrick Brooks .05
257 Ken Harvey .05
258 Frank Sanders .10
259 Morten Andersen .05
260 Marlon Kerner .05
261 Mark Carrier .05
262 Mark Carrier .05
263 Tony McGee .05
264 Eric Zeier .05
265 Darren Woodson .05
266 Shannon Sharpe .05
267 Brett Perriman .05
268 Edgar Bennett .05
269 Darryll Lewis .05
270 Jim Harbaugh .05
271 Desmond Howard .05
272 Derrick Thomas .05
273 Irving Fryar .05
274 Jake Reed .05
275 Curtis Martin 1.50
276 Eric Allen .05
277 Thomas Lewis .05
278 Hugh Douglas .05
279 Pat Swilling .05
280 William Thomas .05
281 Norm Johnson .05
282 Roman Phifer .05
283 Chris Mims .05
284 Steve Young 1.00
285 Cortez Kennedy .05
286 Trent Dilfer .05
287 Terry Allen .05
288 Clyde Simmons .05
289 Craig Heyward .05
290 Jim Kelly .05
291 Tyrone Poole .05
292 Chris Zorich .05
293 Dan Wilkinson .05
294 Antonio Langham .05
295 Troy Aikman 1.00
296 Steve Atwater .05

297	Scott Mitchell	.05
298	Mark Chmura	.20
299	Steve McNair	.50
300	Tony Bennett	.05
301	Willie Jackson	.05
302	Neil Smith	.05
303	Terry Kirby	.05
304	Orlanda Thomas	.05
305	Willie McGinest	.05
306	Wayne Martin	.05
307	Michael Brooks	.05
308	Marvin Washington	.05
309	Nolan Harrison	.05
310	William Fuller	.05
311	Willie Williams	.05
312	Troy Drayton	.05
313	Shawn Lee	.05
314	Ken Norton	.05
315	Terry Wooden	.05
316	Hardy Nickerson	.05
317	Gus Frerotte	.05
318	Oscar McBride	.05
319	Merton Hanks	.05
320	Justin Armour	.05
321	Willie Green	.05
322	Roger Jones	.05
323	Leroy Hoard	.05
324	Chris Boniol	.05
325	Jason Hanson	.05
326	Sean Jones	.05
327	Roosevelt Potts	.05
328	Greg Hill	.05
329	O.J. McDuffie	.05
330	Amp Lee	.05
331	Chris Slade	.05
332	Jim Everett	.05
333	Tyrone Wheatley	.10
334	Charles Wilson	.05
335	Napoleon Kaufman	.10
336	Fred Barnett	.05
337	Neil O'Donnell	.05
338	Sean Gilbert	.05
339	*Aaron Hayden*	.30
340	Brent Jones	.05
341	Christian Fauria	.05
342	Alvin Harper	.05
343	Henry Ellard	.05
344	Willie Davis	.05
345	Charles Haley	.05
346	Chris Jacke	.05
347	Allen Aldridge	.05
348	Jeff Herrod	.05
349	Raghib Ismail	.05
350	Leslie O'Neal	.05
351	Marquez Pope	.05
352	Brock Marion	.05
353	Ernie Mills	.05
354	Larry Centers	.05
355	Chris Doleman	.05
356	Bruce Smith	.05
357	John Kasay	.05
358	Donnell Woolford	.05
359	David Dunn	.05
360	Eric Turner	.05
361	Sherman Williams	.05
362	Chris Spielman	.05
363	Craig Newsome	.05
364	Sean Dawkins	.05
365	James O. Stewart	.05
366	Dale Carter	.05
367	Marco Coleman	.05
368	Dave Meggett	.05
369	Irv Smith	.05
370	Mike Mamula	.05
371	Erric Pegram	.05
372	Dana Stubblefield	.05
373	Terrance Shaw	.05
374	Jerry Rice CL	.25
375	Dan Marino CL	.25

1996 Collector's Choice A Cut Above

This 10-card set was seeded one per special retail pack and included 10 different players.

		NM/M
Complete Set (10):		10.00
Common Player:		.20
Minor Stars:		.40
Inserted 1:1 Special Retail		
1	Terrell Davis	2.00
2	Tim Biakabutuka	.20
3	Drew Bledsoe	1.00
4	Emmitt Smith	1.50
5	Marshall Faulk	.40
6	Brett Favre	2.00
7	Keyshawn Johnson	.75
8	Deion Sanders	.40
9	Curtis Martin	1.00
10	Jerry Rice	1.00

1996 Collector's Choice Crash The Game

These inserts were available in 1996 Upper Deck Collector's Choice packs. If the player on the card throws for, runs for or catches a touchdown pass on the date specified, that card is redeemable for an exclusive Light F/X card of that player. Two versions were made - silver (one per five packs) and gold (one per 50). The basic card front design has a color action photo in the center, with the brand logo in the upper left corner. The player's name, team name and position are in the upper right corner. The bottom has a black panel which has the set icon in silver foil, along with the game date for the contest. The back, numbered using a "CG" prefix, has the rules of the redemption program.

		NM/M
Complete Set (90):		50.00
Common Player:		.50
Minor Stars:		1.00
Gold Cards:		2X-4X
Comp. Gold Redemption (22):		225.00
Gold Redemptions:		3X-5X
Comp. Silver Redemption (22):		75.00
Silver Redemptions:		1.5X-2X
1	Dan Marino	4.00
2	John Elway	3.00
3	Jeff Blake	1.00
4	Drew Bledsoe	2.00
5	Steve Young	2.00
6	Brett Favre	4.00
7	Jim Kelly	1.00
8	Scott Mitchell	.50
9	Jeff George	.50
10	Erik Kramer	.50
11	Jerry Rice	2.00
12	Michael Irvin	.50
13	Joey Galloway	1.00
14	Cris Carter	.50
15	Carl Pickens	.50
16	Herman Moore	.50
17	Isaac Bruce	1.00
18	Tim Brown	.50
19	Keyshawn Johnson	1.00
20	Terry Glenn	1.00
21	Emmitt Smith	3.00
22	Rodney Hampton	.50
23	Chris Warren	.50
24	Marshall Faulk	2.00
25	Curtis Martin	2.00
26	Barry Sanders	3.00
27	Rashaan Salaam	.50
28	Leeland McElroy	1.00
29	Tim Biakabutuka	.40
30	Lawrence Phillips	.40

1996 Collector's Choice Crash The Game Gold

You Crash the Game Golds ran parallel to the 90 cards in the silver version, but were inserted one per 50 packs. As the name indicates, gold versions are gold foil stamped instead of the silver foil used on regular versions. Similar to the rules for silver versions, if the player on the gold version throws for, runs for or catches a touchdown pass on the date specified, that card is redeemable for a gold Light F/X card of that player. Thirty different players are featured in this insert, with each having three specified dates.

	NM/M
Complete Set (90):	300.00
Gold Cards:	2X-4X
Gold Redemptions:	3X-5X

1996 Collector's Choice Cut Above Dan Marino

This 10-card insert features Miami Dolphins quarterback Dan Marino and highlights different moments in his Hall of Fame career. One Marino A Cut Above insert was found in each special retail pack of Collector's Choice Series I. The cards are numbered with the "CA" prefix.

		NM/M
Complete Set (10):		15.00
Common Player:		1.50
1	Dan Marino	1.50
2	Dan Marino	1.50
3	Dan Marino	1.50
4	Dan Marino	1.50
5	Dan Marino	1.50
6	Dan Marino	1.50
7	Dan Marino	1.50
8	Dan Marino	1.50
9	Dan Marino	1.50
10	Dan Marino	1.50

1996 Collector's Choice Jumbos

This nine-card set consists of enlarged versions (3-1/2" x 5") of the players' Season to Remember subset cards from the regular 1996 Collector's Choice set. The cards were inserted one per retail blister pack, which also included a team set and a foil pack of 1996 Collector's Choice.

		NM/M
Complete Set (9):		20.00
Common Player:		1.00
48	Kerry Collins	2.00
49	Rashaan Salaam	1.00
51	Emmitt Smith	4.00
57	Brett Favre	4.00
60	Mark Brunell	2.00
64	Dan Marino	4.00
70	Tim Brown	1.00
72	Kordell Stewart	1.00
74	Jerry Rice	3.00

1996 Collector's Choice MVPs

This set highlights the MVP and co-MVP of each NFL team in two different versions - gold or silver. The card has a marble-like background for the front, in either gold or silver. A player color photo is in the center. MVP is stamped into the upper left corner; the player's name is stamped in the lower left corner. A brand logo is in the upper right corner, while a circle towards the bottom has the player's position and team name inside it. Part of the circle's diameter is stamped in silver dots; the other is in the same color used to shadow the frame around the picture on the front. The back has biographical information, 1995 stats and a card number, which uses an "M" prefix. Gold versions were seeded one every 35 packs of 1996 Upper Deck Collector's Choice product; silver cards were in every pack.

		NM/M
Complete Set (45):		12.00
Common Player:		.20
Minor Stars:		.40
Gold Cards:		2X-5X
1	Larry Centers	.20
2	Jeff George	.20
3	Jim Kelly	.20
4	Bryce Paup	.20
5	Kerry Collins	.50
6	Erik Kramer	.20
7	Rashaan Salaam	.75
8	Jeff Blake	.75
9	Carl Pickens	.20
10	Vinny Testaverde	.20
11	Michael Irvin	.40
12	Emmitt Smith	2.00
13	John Elway	.50
14	Terrell Davis	1.00
15	Herman Moore	.40
16	Barry Sanders	1.50
17	Brett Favre	2.00
18	Edgar Bennett	.20
19	Rodney Thomas	.40
20	Jim Harbaugh	.20
21	Marshall Faulk	.75
22	Mark Brunell	1.00
23	Steve Bono	.20
24	Marcus Allen	.20
25	Dan Marino	2.00
26	Bryan Cox	.20
27	Cris Carter	.20
28	Drew Bledsoe	1.00
29	Curtis Martin	1.50
30	Jim Everett	.20
31	Rodney Hampton	.20
32	Adrian Murrell	.20
33	Tim Brown	.20
34	Rodney Peete	.20
35	Ricky Watters	.20
36	Yancey Thigpen	.75
37	Greg Lloyd	.20
38	Isaac Bruce	.75
39	Tony Martin	.20
40	Junior Seau	.20
41	Steve Young	1.00
42	Jerry Rice	1.00
43	Chris Warren	.40
44	Errict Rhett	.40
45	Brian Mitchell	.20

A player's name in *italic* type indicates a rookie card.

1996 Collector's Choice MVP Golds

This insert paralleled the MVP set, and is inserted every 35 packs of Series I. While regular versions are printed on silver foil, MVP Gold are printed on gold foil.

Gold Cards:	2X-5X

1996 Collector's Choice Stick-Ums

Stick-Ums featured 30 top NFL players on re-stickable, die-cut stickers. The stickers offer removable players, names, footballs, referees, yardage markers and play calls. One Stick-Ums insert is found in every three packs of Series I. The cards are numbered with the "S" prefix.

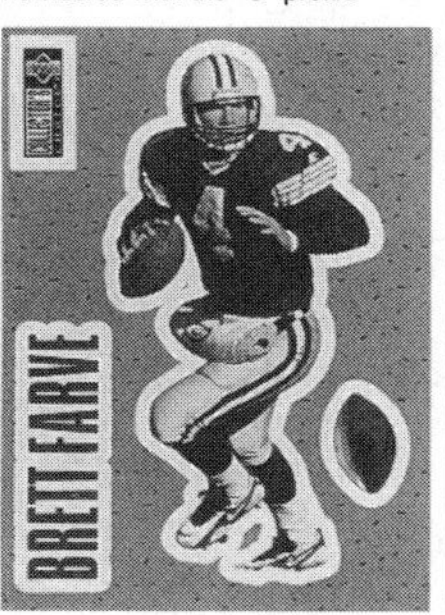

		NM/M
Complete Set (30):		10.00
Common Player:		.25
Minor Stars:		.50
1	Dan Marino	2.00
2	Mike Mamula	.25
3	Errict Rhett	.25
4	Drew Bledsoe	1.00
5	Anthony Smith	.25
6	Brett Favre	2.00
7	Morten Andersen	.25
8	Deion Sanders	.75
9	Jeff George	.25
10	Erik Kramer	.25
11	Jerry Rice	1.00
12	Michael Irvin	.50
13	Greg Lloyd	.25
14	Cris Carter	.25
15	Ken Norton	.25
16	Natrone Means	.50
17	Robert Brooks	.50
18	Action Words-Bomb	.25
19	Kordell Stewart	1.00
20	Referee	.25
21	Emmitt Smith	2.00
22	Reggie White	.50
23	Eric Metcalf	.25
24	Jesse Sapolu	.25
25	Curtis Martin	1.50
26	Neil Smith	.25
27	Junior Seau	.25
28	Action Words-TD	.25
29	Accessories-Yardmarkers	.25
30	Terry McDaniel	.25

1996 Collector's Choice Update

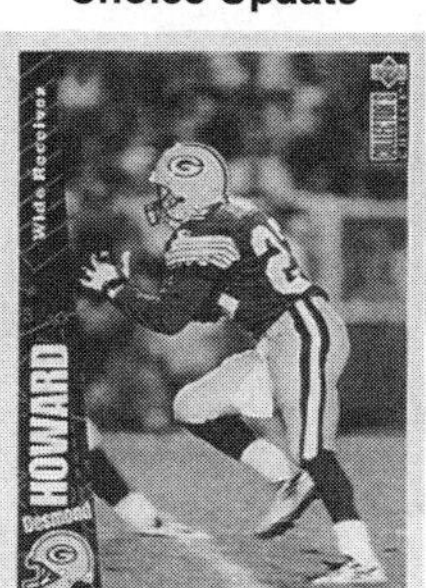

The 200-card, regular-sized set was issued as an update to the 375-card Collector's Choice set in 1996. The Update set included a 60-card rookies subset and 30 Franchise Play Makers subset. The base card fronts included the player's team colors along the left border with the player's position and team helmet. Inserts included were Play Action Stick-Ums, Play Action Stick-Ums Base Cards, Record-Breaking Trio, You Make The Play and Meet The Stars Trivia Game Cards.

		NM/M
Complete Set (200):		15.00
Common Player:		.05
Minor Stars:		.10
Pack (12):		1.00
Wax Box (36):		20.00
1	*Zack Thomas*	.75
2	Simeon Rice	.10
3	Jonathan Ogden	.05
4	Eric Moulds	.20
5	Tim Biakabutuka	.20
6	Walt Harris	.10
7	Willie Anderson	.05
8	Rickey Whittle	.05
9	John Mobley	.05
10	Reggie Brown	.05
11	John Michels	.05
12	Eddie George	1.00
13	Marvin Harrison	1.00
14	Kevin Hardy	.10
15	Kavika Pittman	.05
16	Daryl Gardener	.05
17	Duane Clemons	.05
18	Terry Glenn	.75
19	Alex Molden	.05
20	Cedric Jones	.05
21	Keyshawn Johnson	.60
22	Rickey Dudley	.20
23	Jason Dunn	.05
24	Jermain Stephens	.05
25	Lawrence Phillips	.60
26	Bryan Still	.05
27	Isreal Ifeanyi	.05
28	Pete Kendall	.05
29	Regan Upshaw	.05
30	Andre Johnson	.05
31	Leeland McElroy	.20
32	Ray Lewis	.25
33	Sean Moran	.05
34	*Mushin Muhammad*	.50
35	Bobby Engram	.20
36	Marco Battaglia	.05
37	Stepfret Williams	.05
38	Jeff Lewis	.05
39	Derrick Mayes	.05
40	Reggie Tongue	.05
41	Tory James	.05
42	*Tony Banks*	.75
43	Tedy Bruschi	.05
44	Mike Alstott	.50
45	Anthony Dorsett Jr.	.05
46	*Tony Brackens*	.30
47	Bryant Mix	.05
48	Karim Abdul-Jabbar	.75
49	Moe Williams	.05
50	Lawyer Milloy	.05
51	Je'Rod Cherry	.05
52	*Amani Toomer*	.30
53	Alex Van Dyke	.20
54	Lance Johnstone	.05
55	Bobby Hoying	.05
56	John Wittman	.05
57	*Eddie Kennison*	.50
58	Brian Roche	.05
59	*Terrell Owens*	2.50
60	Stephen Davis	1.25
61	Jeff George	.05
62	Darick Holmes	.05
63	Kerry Collins	.40
64	Rashaan Salaam	.05
65	Jeff Blake	.20
66	Emmitt Smith	.75
67	Troy Aikman	.40
68	John Elway	.30
69	Terrell Davis	.50
70	Barry Sanders	1.00
71	Herman Moore	.05
72	Brett Favre	.75
73	Robert Brooks	.05
74	Steve McNair	.20
75	Marshall Faulk	.20
76	Marcus Allen	.05
77	Dan Marino	.75
78	Warren Moon	.05
79	Drew Bledsoe	.40
80	Curtis Martin	.50
81	Mario Bates	.05
82	Tim Brown	.05
83	Charlie Garner	.05
84	Kordell Stewart	.40
85	Isaac Bruce	.20
86	Tony Martin	.05
87	Jerry Rice	.40
88	J.J. Stokes	.05
89	Joey Galloway	.20
90	Errict Rhett	.15
91	Mike Pritchard	.05
92	Jerome Bettis	.10
93	Winslow Oliver	.05
94	David Klingler	.05
95	Lawrence Dawsey	.05
96	Charlie Jones	.05
97	Dave Krieg	.05
98	Chris Spielman	.05
99	Stanley Pritchett	.05
100	Sean Gilbert	.05
101	Tommy Vardell	.05
102	DeRon Jenkins	.05
103	Larry Bowie	.05
104	Kyle Wachholz	.05
105	Brady Smith	.05
106	Steve Walsh	.05
107	Wesley Walls	.05
108	Kevin Ross	.05
109	Willie Clay	.05
110	Olanda Truitt	.05
111	Calvin Williams	.05
112	Chris Doleman	.05
113	Irving Fryar	.05
114	Jimmy Spencer	.05
115	Reggie Barlow	.05
116	Reggie Brown	.05
117	Dixon Edwards	.05
118	Haywood Jeffires	.05
119	Santana Dotson	.05
120	Herschel Walker	.05
121	Darryl Williams	.05
122	Bryan Cox	.05
123	Lamar Thomas	.05
124	Hendrick Lusk	.05
125	Jahine Arnold	.05
126	Boomer Esiason	.05
127	Willie Davis	.05
128	Pete Stoyanovich	.05
129	Bill Romanowski	.05
130	Tim McKyer	.05
131	Patrick Sapp	.05
132	Natrone Means	.05
133	Quinn Early	.05
134	Leslie O'Neal	.05
135	Mark Seay	.05
136	Pete Metzelaars	.05
137	Jay Leuwenberg	.05
138	Buster Owens	.05
139	Todd McNair	.05
140	Eugene Robinson	.05
141	Sean Salisbury	.05
142	Eugene Robinson	.05
143	Jerris McPhail	.05
144	Ray Farmer	.05
145	Garrison Hearst	.05
146	Leonard Russell	.05
147	Ray Barker	.05
148	Larry Brown	.05
159	Webster Slaughter	.05
150	Roman Oben	.05
151	LeShon Johnson	.05
152	Patrick Bates	.05
153	Iheanyi Uwaezuoke	.05
154	Scott Slutzker	.05
155	John Jurkovic	.05
156	Brian Milne	.05
157	Mike Sherrard	.05
158	Neil O'Donnell	.05
159	Roger Harper	.05
160	Desmond Howard	.05
161	Alfred Williams	.05
162	Ronnie Harmon	.05
163	Sammie Burroughs	.05
164	Keenan McCardell	.05
165	Shane Dronett	.05
166	Jeff Graham	.05
167	Bill Brooks	.05
168	Shawn Jefferson	.05
169	Detron Smith	.05
170	Danny Kanell	.05
171	Jevon Langford	.05
172	Russell Maryland	.05
173	Scott Milanovich	.05
174	Eric Davis	.05
175	Ernie Conwell	.05
176	Kurt Gouveia	.05
177	Andre Rison	.05
178	Harold Green	.05
179	Frank Reich	.05
180	Glyn Milburn	.05
181	Nilo Silvan	.05
182	Cornelius Bennett	.05
183	Freddie Solomon	.05
184	Pat Terrell	.05
185	Miles Mecik	.05
186	Bo Orlando	.05
187	Kelvin Martin	.05
188	Todd Kinchen	.05
189	Reggie Brooks	.05
190	Steve Beuerlein	.05
191	Marco Coleman	.05
192	Johnnie Johnson	.05
193	Dedric Mathis	.05
194	Leon Searcy	.05
195	Kevin Greene	.05
196	Daniel Stubbs	.05
197	Ray Mickens	.05
198	Devin Wyman	.05
199	Lorenzo Lynch	.05
200	Checklist	.20

1996 Collector's Choice Update Record Breaking Trio

The four-card, regular-sized, die-cut set was inserted every 100 packs of Collector's Choice 1996 Update. The cards feature Joe Montana, Dan Marino, Jerry Rice and a fourth card including all three. The cards are numbered with the "RS" prefix.

		NM/M
Complete Set (4):		30.00
Common Player:		8.00
1	Joe Montana	10.00
2	Dan Marino	10.00
3	Jerry Rice	8.00
4	Joe Montana, Dan Marino, Jerry Rice	12.00

1996 Collector's Choice Update You Make The Play

You Make the Play is an interactive card deck that allows collectors to play a football game through cards. The deck contains 90 cards and is found at a rate of one per pack.

		NM/M
Complete Set (90):		20.00
Common Player:		.10
Minor Stars:		.20
1	Norm Johnson	.10
2	Jerry Rice	1.00

		NM/M
3	Dan Marino	2.00
4	Marshall Faulk	.30
5	Neil Smith	.10
6	Herman Moore	.20
7	Brett Favre	2.00
8	Curtis Martin	1.50
9	Reggie White	.20
10	Cris Carter	.10
11	Rick Tuten	.10
12	Steve Young	.75
13	Barry Sanders	2.00
14	Deion Sanders	.50
15	Isaac Bruce	.30
16	Troy Aikman	1.00
17	Emmitt Smith	2.00
18	Junior Seau	.10
19	Joey Galloway	.30
20	Drew Bledsoe	1.00
21	Jason Elam	.10
22	Edgar Bennett	.10
23	Greg Lloyd	.10
24	Tamarick Vanover	.20
25	John Elway	.75
26	Larry Centers	.10
27	Derrick Thomas	.10
28	Michael Irvin	.20
29	Jeff George	.10
30	Thurman Thomas	.20
31	Darren Bennett	.10
32	Ken Norton	.10
33	Carl Pickens	.10
34	Jeff Blake	.20
35	Craig Heyward	.10
36	Aeneas Williams	.10
37	Terance Mathis	.10
38	Jim Kelly	.20
39	Marcus Allen	.20
40	Tim McDonald	.10
41	Jason Hanson	.10
42	Scott Mitchell	.10
43	Tim Brown	.10
44	Kordell Stewart	1.00
45	Eric Metcalf	.10
46	Norm Johnson	.10
47	Jerry Rice	1.00
48	Dan Marino	2.00
49	Marshall Faulk	.30
50	Neil Smith	.10
51	Herman Moore	.30
52	Brett Favre	2.00
53	Curtis Martin	1.50
54	Reggie White	.20
55	Cris Carter	.10
56	Rick Tuten	.10
57	Steve Young	.75
58	Barry Sanders	2.00
59	Deion Sanders	.50
60	Isaac Bruce	.30
61	Troy Aikman	1.00
62	Emmitt Smith	2.00
63	Junior Seau	.20
64	Joey Galloway	.30
65	Drew Bledsoe	1.00
66	Jason Elam	.10
67	Edgar Bennett	.10
68	Greg Lloyd	.10
69	Tamarick Vanover	.20
70	John Elway	.75
71	Larry Centers	.10
72	Derrick Thomas	.10
73	Michael Irvin	.20
74	Jeff George	.10
75	Thurman Thomas	.20
76	Darren Bennett	.10
77	Ken Norton	.10
78	Carl Pickens	.10
79	Jeff Blake	.20
80	Craig Heyward	.10
81	Aeneas Williams	.10
82	Terance Mathis	.10
83	Jim Kelly	.20
84	Marcus Allen	.20
85	Tim McDonald	.10
86	Jason Hanson	.10
87	Scott Mitchell	.10
88	Tim Brown	.10
89	Kordell Stewart	1.00
90	Eric Metcalf	.10

1996 Collector's Choice Update Stick-Ums

The 30-card Stick-Ums set was inserted every four packs of Collector's Choice 1996 Update. The regular-sized set came with peel-off stickers of the player, team helmet and name. Thirty base cards were also inserted every four packs. The base cards feature a white outline of the corresponding player and contain clues as to which player's sticker goes with which base card. The cards are numbered with the "S" prefix.

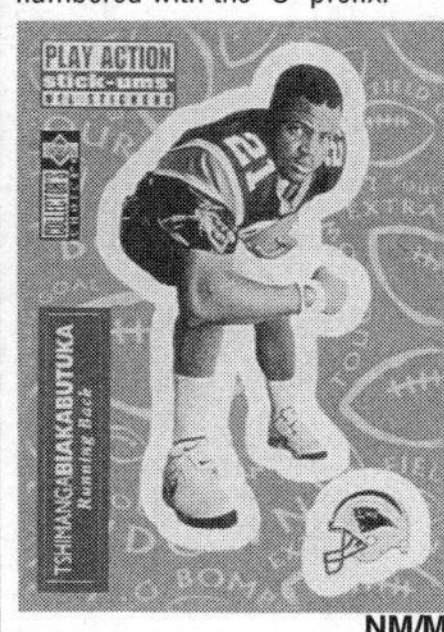

		NM/M
Complete Set (30):		15.00
Common Player:		.25
Minor Stars:		.50
Mystery Base Cards:		.5X
1	Jeff George	.25
2	Darren Bennett	.25
3	Marcus Allen	.50
4	Brett Favre	2.00
5	Carl Pickens	.25
6	Troy Aikman	1.00
7	John Elway	.75
8	Steve Young	.75
9	Norm Johnson	.25
10	Kordell Stewart	.50
11	Drew Bledsoe	1.00
12	Jim Kelly	.50
13	Dan Marino	2.00
14	Joey Galloway	.50
15	Lawrence Phillips	.50
16	Reggie White	.50
17	Kevin Hardy	.25
18	Isaac Bruce	.50
19	Keyshawn Johnson	.50
20	Barry Sanders	1.50
21	Deion Sanders	.75
22	Emmitt Smith	2.00
23	Chris Warren	.25
24	Tim Biakabutuka	.50
25	Terry Glenn	1.00
26	Marshall Faulk	.50
27	Tamarick Vanover	.25
28	Curtis Martin	1.50
29	Terrell Davis	1.50
30	Jerry Rice	1.00

1996 Collector's Choice Update Stick-Ums Mystery Base

Each Stick-Ums card in Collector's Choice Update has a corresponding Mystery Base card. It is printed on cardboard stock like regular-issue cards and have a background of an action shot, with a white space where the player is supposed to be. The sticker is supposed to be used with the Mystery Base base to complete the football action scene. One Mystery Base card is included in every four packs of Collector's Choice Update.

	NM/M
Complete Set (30):	7.50
Mystery Base Cards:	.5X

1996 Collector's Choice Packers

This 90-card set was exclusively available in ShopKo stores and contained all Green Bay Packers including current players and all-time greats. The set featured several different subsets, including A Season to Remember and Legends of the Green and Gold. The regular-issue set contained the first 69 cards, while the final 21 cards, called Leaders of the Pack, is considered an insert set. The cards are numbered with the "GB" prefix.

		NM/M
Complete Set (69):		14.00
Common Player:		.10
1	Brett Favre	1.50
2	Mark Chmura	.25
3	Edgar Bennett	.25
4	Robert Brooks	.50
5	Antonio Freeman	.25
6	Travis Jervey	.10
7	Craig Newsome	.10
8	Reggie White	.75
9	Sean Jones	.10
10	LeRoy Butler	.10
11	Chris Jacke	.10
12	Derrick Mayes	.10
13	Chris Darkins	.10
14	Anthony Morgan	.10
15	Terry Mickens	.10
16	Dorsey Levens	.40
17	Jim McMahon	.10
18	Craig Hendricks	.10
19	George Koonce	.10
20	William Henderson	.10
21	Doug Evans	.10
22	Mike Prior	.10
23	Wayne Simmons	.10
24	Darius Holland	.10
25	Gilbert Brown	.10
26	Aaron Taylor	.10
27	Frank Winters	.10
28	Ken Ruettgers	.10
29	Earl Dotson	.10
30	Eugene Robinson	.10
31	Brett Favre (Season to Remember)	1.50
32	Brett Favre (Season to Remember)	1.50
33	Brett Favre (Season to Remember)	1.50
34	Edgar Bennett (Season to Remember)	.25
35	Edgar Bennett (Season to Remember)	.25
36	Robert Brooks (Season to Remember)	.50
37	Robert Brooks (Season to Remember)	.50
38	Mark Chmura (Season to Remember)	.25
39	Mark Chmura (Season to Remember)	.25
40	LeRoy Butler (Season to Remember)	.10
41	LeRoy Butler (Season to Remember)	.10
42	Craig Newsome (Season to Remember)	.10
43	Craig Newsome (Season to Remember)	.10
44	Reggie White (Season to Remember)	.75
45	Reggie White (Season to Remember)	.75
46	Sean Jones (Season to Remember)	.10
47	Sean Jones (Season to Remember)	.10
48	Antonio Freeman (Season to Remember)	.25
49	Chris Jacke (Season to Remember)	.10
50	Offensive Line (Season to Remember)	.10
51	Forrest Gregg (Legends of the Green & Gold)	.10
52	Paul Hornung (Legends of the Green & Gold)	.50
53	Jim Taylor (Legends of the Green & Gold)	.10
54	Vince Lombardi (Legends of the Green & Gold)	.50
55	Ray Nitschke (Legends of the Green & Gold)	.30
56	Willie Wood (Legends of the Green & Gold)	.10
57	Don Hutson (Legends of the Green & Gold)	.10
58	Don Majkowski (Legends of the Green & Gold)	.10
59	Bryce Paup (Legends of the Green & Gold)	.10
60	Sterling Sharpe (Legends of the Green & Gold)	.40
61	Ted Hendricks (Legends of the Green & Gold)	.10
62	Lynn Dickey (Legends of the Green & Gold)	.10
63	James Lofton (Legends of the Green & Gold)	.20
64	Brett Favre (Legends of the Green & Gold)	1.50
65	Edgar Bennett (Legends of the Green & Gold)	.25
66	Reggie White (Legends of the Green & Gold)	.75
67	John Jurkovic (Legends of the Green & Gold)	.20
68	Mike Holmgren (Legends of the Green & Gold)	.30
69	Ron Wolf (Legends of the Green & Gold)	.20

1996 Collector's Choice Leaders of the Pack

Leaders of the Pack consisted of the final 21 cards of the Collector's Choice Packers set that was exclusively available at ShopKo stores. Although it's numbered consecutively with the regular-issue set, it was considered an insert and seeded one per pack. The cards are identified by a thick gold-foil border across the top with the words "Leaders of the Pack." In addition, a color shot of the featured player is shown over a black-and-white dotted background, with a bold yellow strip at the bottom that contains the player's name.

		NM/M
Complete Set (21):		8.00
Common Player:		.15
70	Forrest Gregg	.15
71	Paul Hornung	1.50
72	Jim Taylor	.15
73	Ray Nitschke	.15
74	Willie Wood	.15
75	Don Hutson	.15
76	Sterling Sharpe	1.25
77	Don Majkowski	.15
78	Ted Hendricks	.15
79	Lynn Dickey	.15
80	James Lofton	.50
81	Brett Favre	4.50
82	Edgar Bennett	.75
83	Robert Brooks	1.50
84	Mark Chmura	.75
85	Reggie White	2.50
86	Sean Jones	.15
87	Chris Jacke	.15
88	LeRoy Butler	.15
89	Craig Newsome	.15
90	Checklist	.25

1997 Collector's Choice

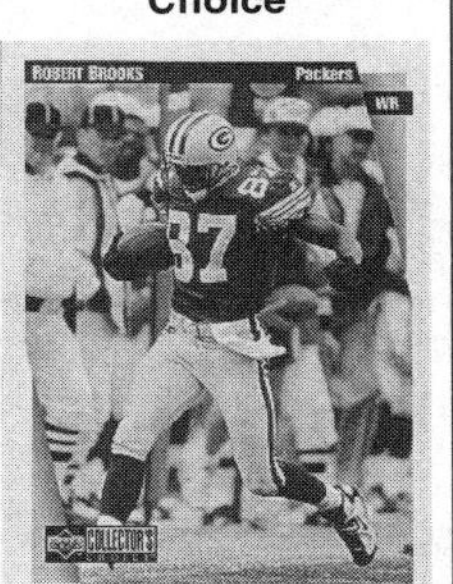

The 565-card set features white borders on the front. The player's name and team are printed inside a stripe at the top, while his position is located inside a rectangle at the upper right. The Collector's Choice logo is printed in the lower left on the front. The backs have a photo on the left, with the player's bio, "Did you know?" and stats along the right side. The cards feature a dual numbering system that helps collectors put players from their favorite team together. Series I also features a 45-card Rookie Class subset and a 40-card Names of the Game subset. Series II includes Checklist/Collector Info cards, 30 NFL Mini Standees and the StarQuest insert.

		NM/M
Complete Set (565):		35.00
Complete Series 1 (310):		25.00
Complete Series 2 (255):		15.00
Common Player:		.05
Minor Stars:		.10
Ser 1, 2 Pack (14):		1.30
Ser 1, 2 Wax Box (36):		35.00
1	*Orlando Pace*	.25
2	*Darrell Russell*	.05
3	*Shawn Springs*	.25
4	*Peter Boulware*	.05
5	*Bryant Westbrook*	.10
6	*Tom Knight*	.05
7	*Ike Hilliard*	.50
8	*James Farrior*	.05
9	*Chris Naeole*	.05
10	*Michael Booker*	.05
11	*Warrick Dunn*	1.00
12	*Tony Gonzalez*	1.00
13	*Reinard Wilson*	.05
14	*Yatil Green*	.75
15	*Reidel Anthony*	.50
16	*Kenard Lang*	.05
17	*Kenny Holmes*	.05
18	*Tarik Glenn*	.05
19	*Dwayne Rudd*	.05
20	*Renaldo Wynn*	.05
21	*David LaFleur*	.20
22	*Antowain Smith*	1.00
23	*Jim Druckenmiller*	.75
24	*Rae Carruth*	.50
25	*Jared Tomich*	.05
26	*Chris Canty*	.05
27	*Jake Plummer*	1.50
28	*Troy Davis*	.50
29	*Sedrick Shaw*	.50
30	*Jamie Sharper*	.05
31	*Tiki Barber*	1.50
32	*Byron Hanspard*	.75
33	*Darnell Autry*	.50
34	*Corey Dillon*	3.00
35	*Joey Kent*	.30
36	*Nathan Davis*	.05
37	*Will Blackwell*	.30
38	*Kim Herring*	.05
39	*Pat Barnes*	.30
40	*Kevin Lockett*	.20
41	*Trevor Pryce*	.05
42	*Matt Russell*	.05
43	*Greg Jones*	.05
44	*Antonio Anderson*	.05
45	*George Jones*	.10
46	Steve Young	.20
47	Jerry Rice	.35
48	Curtis Conway	.05
49	Jeff Blake	.05
50	Carl Pickens	.05
51	Bruce Smith	.05
52	John Elway	.20
53	Terrell Davis	.50
54	Shannon Sharpe	.05
55	Junior Seau	.05
56	Darren Bennett	.05
57	Jim Harbaugh	.05
58	Marshall Faulk	.05
59	Emmitt Smith	.75
60	Troy Aikman	.35
61	Deion Sanders	.20
62	Dan Marino	.75
63	Ricky Watters	.05
64	Mark Brunell	.35
65	Keenan McCardell	.05
66	Keyshawn Johnson	.20
67	Barry Sanders	.50
68	Herman Moore	.05
69	Eddie George	.50
70	Steve McNair	.25
71	Brett Favre	1.00
72	Reggie White	.05
73	Edgar Bennett	.05
74	Kerry Collins	.35
75	Kevin Greene	.05
76	Drew Bledsoe	.35
77	Terry Glenn	.40
78	Curtis Martin	.50
79	Jeff Hostetler	.05
80	Napoleon Kaufman	.05
81	Isaac Bruce	.05
82	Terry Allen	.05
83	Joey Galloway	.05
84	Kordell Stewart	.20
85	Jerome Bettis	.05
86	Dana Stubblefield	.05
87	Merton Hanks	.05
88	Terrell Owens	.50
89	Brent Jones	.05
90	Ken Norton Jr.	.05
91	Jerry Rice	.75
92	Terry Kirby	.05
93	Bryant Young	.05
94	Raymont Harris	.05
95	Jeff Jaeger	.05
96	Curtis Conway	.10
97	Walt Harris	.05
98	Bobby Engram	.10
99	Donnell Woolford	.05
100	Rashaan Salaam	.10
101	Jeff Blake	.10
102	Tony McGee	.05
103	Ashley Ambrose	.05
104	Dan Wilkinson	.05
105	Jevon Langford	.05
106	Darnay Scott	.05
107	David Dunn	.05
108	Eric Moulds	.05
109	Darrick Holmes	.05
110	Thurman Thomas	.10
111	Quinn Early	.05
112	Jim Kelly	.10
113	Bryce Paup	.05
114	Bruce Smith	.05
115	Todd Collins	.05
116	Tory James	.05
117	Anthony Miller	.05
118	Terrell Davis	.50
119	Tyrone Braxton	.05
120	John Mobley	.05
121	Bill Romanowski	.05
122	Vaughn Hebron	.05
123	Mike Alstott	.15
124	Errict Rhett	.10
125	Trent Dilfer	.10
126	Courtney Hawkins	.05
127	Hardy Nickerson	.05
128	Donnie Abraham	.05
129	Regan Upshaw	.05
130	Kent Graham	.05
131	Rob Moore	.05
132	Simeon Rice	.05
133	LeShon Johnson	.05
134	Frank Sanders	.05
135	Leeland McElroy	.05
136	Seth Joyner	.05
137	Andre Coleman	.05
138	Stan Humphries	.05
139	Charlie Jones	.05
140	Junior Seau	.10
141	Rodney Harrison	.05
142	Darrien Gordon	.05
143	Terrell Fletcher	.05
144	Tamarick Vanover	.10
145	Greg Hill	.05
146	Marcus Allen	.10
147	Lake Dawson	.05
148	Dale Carter	.05
149	Kimble Anders	.05
150	Chris Penn	.05
151	Sean Dawkins	.05
152	Ken Dilger	.05
153	Marvin Harrison	.40
154	Jeff Herrod	.05
155	Jim Harbaugh	.05
156	Cary Blanchard	.05
157	Aaron Bailey	.05
158	Deion Sanders	.40
159	Jim Schwantz	.05
160	Michael Irvin	.10
161	Herschel Walker	.05
162	Emmitt Smith	1.00
163	Chris Boniol	.05
164	Eric Bjornson	.05
165	Karim Abdul-Jabbar	.60
166	O.J. McDuffie	.05
167	Troy Drayton	.05
168	Zach Thomas	.40
169	Irving Spikes	.05
170	Shane Burton	.05
171	Stanley Pritchett	.05
172	Ty Detmer	.05
173	Chris T. Jones	.05
174	Troy Vincent	.05
175	Brian Dawkins	.05
176	Irving Fryar	.05
177	Charlie Garner	.05
178	Bobby Taylor	.05
179	Jamal Anderson	.10
180	Terance Mathis	.05
181	Craig Heyward	.05
182	Cornelius Bennett	.05
183	Jessie Tuggle	.05
184	Devin Bush	.05
185	Dave Brown	.05
186	Danny Kanell	.05
187	Rodney Hampton	.05
188	Tyrone Wheatley	.05
189	Amani Toomer	.05
190	Phillipi Sparks	.05
191	Thomas Lewis	.05
192	Jimmy Smith	.05
193	Pete Mitchell	.05
194	Natrone Means	.10
195	Mark Brunell	.75
196	Kevin Hardy	.05
197	Tony Brackens	.05
198	Aaron Beasley	.05
199	Chris Hudson	.05
200	Wayne Chrebet	.05
201	Keyshawn Johnson	.40
202	Adrian Murrell	.05
203	Neil O'Donnell	.05
204	Hugh Douglas	.05
205	Mo Lewis	.05
206	Glenn Foley	.05
207	Aaron Glenn	.05
208	Johnnie Morton	.05
209	Reggie Brown	.05
210	Barry Sanders	1.00
211	Glyn Milburn	.05
212	Bennie Blades	.05
213	Steve McNair	.40
214	Frank Wycheck	.05
215	Chris Sanders	.05
216	Blaine Bishop	.05
217	Willie Davis	.05
218	Darryll Lewis	.05
219	Marcus Robertson	.05
220	Robert Brooks	.10
221	Antonio Freeman	.30
222	Keith Jackson (Retired)	.05
223	Mark Chmura	.05
224	Brett Favre	1.75
225	Sean Jones	.05
226	Reggie White	.10
227	LeRoy Butler	.05
228	Craig Newsome	.05
229	Wesley Walls	.05
230	Mark Carrier	.05
231	Muhsin Muhammad	.05
232	John Kasay	.05
233	Anthony Johnson	.05
234	Kerry Collins	.75
235	Kevin Greene	.05
236	Sam Mills	.05
237	Ben Coates	.05
238	Terry Glenn	.75
239	Willie McGinest	.05
240	Ted Johnson	.05
241	Lawyer Milloy	.05
242	Drew Bledsoe	.75
243	Willie Clay	.05
244	Chris Slade	.05
245	Tim Brown	.05
246	Daryl Hobbs	.05
247	Rickey Dudley	.05
248	Joe Aska	.05
249	Chester McGlockton	.05
250	Rob Fredrickson	.05
251	Terry McDaniel	.05
252	Tony Banks	.25
253	Lawrence Phillips	.10
254	Isaac Bruce	.15
255	Eddie Kennison	.25
256	Kevin Carter	.05
257	Roman Phifer	.05
258	Keith Lyle	.05
259	Vinny Testaverde	.05
260	Derrick Alexander	.05
261	Ray Lewis	.05
262	Jermaine Lewis	.05
263	Bam Morris	.05
264	Stevon Moore	.05
265	Antonio Langham	.05
266	Brian Mitchell	.05
267	Henry Ellard	.05
268	Leslie Shepherd	.05
269	Michael Westbrook	.05
270	Jamie Asher	.05
271	Ken Harvey	.05
272	Gus Frerotte	.05
273	Michael Haynes	.05

274 Ray Zellars .05
275 Jim Everett .05
276 Tyrone Hughes (Bears) .05
277 Joe Johnson .05
278 Eric Allen .05
279 Brady Smith .05
280 Mario Bates .05
281 Torrance Small .05
282 John Friesz .05
283 Brian Blades .05
284 Chris Warren .05
285 Joey Galloway .25
286 Michael Sinclair .05
287 Lamar Smith .05
288 Mike Pritchard .05
289 Jerome Bettis .10
290 Charles Johnson .05
291 Mike Tomczak .05
292 Levon Kirkland .05
293 Carnell Lake .05
294 Eric Pegram .05
295 Kordell Stewart .50
296 Greg Lloyd .05
297 Dixon Edwards .05
298 Cris Carter .05
299 Brad Johnson .05
300 Qadry Ismail .05
301 John Randle .05
302 Orlando Thomas .05
303 DeWayne Washington .05
304 Jake Reed .05
305 Derrick Alexander .05
306 Eddie George .75
307 Dan Marino 1.50
308 Curtis Martin .75
309 Troy Aikman .75
310 Marcus Allen .10
311 Jim Druckenmiller .40
312 Greg Clark .05
313 Darnell Autry .30
314 Reinard Wilson .05
315 Corey Dillon 1.50
316 Antowain Smith .75
317 Trevor Pryce .05
318 Warrick Dunn 1.00
319 Reidel Anthony .75
320 Jake Plummer 1.00
321 Tom Knight .05
322 Freddie Jones .10
323 Tony Gonzalez .30
324 Pat Barnes .30
325 Kevin Lockett .05
326 Tarik Glenn .05
327 David LaFleur .30
328 Antonio Anderson .05
329 Yatil Green .40
330 Jason Taylor .05
331 Brian Manning .05
332 Michael Booker .05
333 Byron Hanspard .40
334 Ike Hilliard .40
335 Tiki Barber .50
336 Renaldo Wynn .05
337 Damon Jones .05
338 James Farrior .05
339 Dedric Ward .05
340 Bryant Westbrook .05
341 Matt Russell .05
342 Joey Kent .05
343 Kenny Holmes .05
344 Darren Sharper .05
345 Rae Carruth .40
346 Chris Canty .05
347 Darrell Russell .05
348 Orlando Pace .05
349 Peter Boulware .05
350 *Danny Wuerffel* .75
351 Troy Davis .40
352 Shawn Springs .05
353 Walter Jones .05
354 Will Blackwell .05
355 Dwayne Rudd .05
356 Cardinals .05
357 Falcons .05
358 Ravens .05
359 Bills .05
360 Panthers .05
361 Bears .05
362 Bengals .05
363 Cowboys .05
364 Broncos .05
365 Lions .05
366 Packers .05
367 Oilers .05
368 Colts .05
369 Jaguars .05
370 Chiefs .05
371 Dolphins .05
372 Vikings .05
373 Patriots .05
374 Saints .05
375 Jets .05
376 Giants .05
377 Raiders .05
378 Eagles .05
379 Steelers .05
380 Chargers .05
381 49ers .05
382 Seahawks .05
383 Rams .05
384 Buccaneers .05
385 Redskins .05
386 William Floyd .05
387 Steve Young .75
388 Lee Woodall .05
389 J.J. Stokes .05
390 Marc Edwards .05
391 Rod Woodson .05
392 Jim Schwantz .05
393 Garrison Hearst .05
394 Rick Mirer .05
395 Alonzo Spellman .05
396 Tom Carter .05
397 Bryan Cox .05
398 John Allred .05
399 Ricky Proehl .05
400 Tyrone Hughes .05
401 Carl Pickens .05
402 Tremain Mack .05
403 Boomer Esiason .05
404 Ki-Jana Carter .05
405 Steve Tovar .05
406 Billy Joe Hobert .05
407 Andre Reed .05
408 Marcellus Wiley .05
409 Steve Tasker .05
410 Chris Spielman .05
411 Alfred Williams .05
412 John Elway .75
413 Shannon Sharpe .05
414 Steve Atwater .05
415 Neil Smith .05
416 Darrien Gordon .05
417 Jeff Lewis .05
418 Flipper Anderson .05
419 Willie Green .05
420 Jackie Harris .05
421 Steve Walsh .05
422 Anthony Parker .05
423 Ronde Barber .05
424 Warren Sapp .05
425 Aeneas Williams .05
426 Larry Centers .05
427 Eric Swann .05
428 Kevin Williams .05
429 Darren Bennett .05
430 Tony Martin .05
431 John Carney .05
432 Jim Everett .05
433 William Fuller .05
434 Latario Rachel .05
435 Erric Pegram .05
436 Eric Metcalf .05
437 Jerome Woods .05
438 Derrick Thomas .05
439 Elvis Grbac .05
440 Terry Wooden .05
441 Andre Rison .05
442 Brett Perriman .05
443 Roosevelt Potts .05
444 Robert Blackman .05
445 Carlton Gray .05
446 Chris Gardocki .05
447 Marshall Faulk .10
448 Sammie Burroughs .05
449 Quentin Coryatt .05
450 Troy Aikman 1.00
451 Daryl Johnston .05
452 Tony Tolbert .05
453 Brock Marion .05
454 Billy Davis .05
455 Dexter Coakley .05
456 Anthony Miller .05
457 Dan Marino 2.00
458 Jerris McPhail .05
459 Terrell Buckley .05
460 Daryl Gardener .05
461 George Teague .05
462 Qadry Ismail .05
463 Fred Barnett .05
464 Darrin Smith .05
465 Michael Timpson .05
466 Jon Harris .05
467 Jason Dunn .05
468 Bobby Hoying .05
469 Ricky Watters .10
470 Derrick Witherspoon .05
471 Chris Chandler .05
472 Ray Buchanan .05
473 Michael Haynes .05
474 Nathan Davis .05
475 Morten Andersen .05
476 Bert Emanuel .05
477 Chris Calloway .05
478 Jason Sehorn .05
479 John Jurkovic .05
480 Keenan McCardell .05
481 James O. Stewart .05
482 Rob Johnson .05
483 Mike Logan .05
484 Deon Figures .05
485 Kyle Brady .05
486 Alex Van Dyke .05
487 Jeff Graham .05
488 Jason Hanson .05
489 Herman Moore .10
490 Scott Mitchell .05
491 Tommy Vardell .05
492 *Derrick Mason* 1.00
493 Rodney Thomas .05
494 Ronnie Harmon .05
495 Eddie George 1.00
496 Edgar Bennett .05
497 William Henderson .05
498 Dorsey Levens .10
499 Gilbert Brown .05
500 Steve Bono .05
501 Derrick Mayes .05
502 *Fred Lane* .50
503 Ernie Mills .05
504 Tshimanga Biakabutuka .05
505 Michael Bates .05
506 Winslow Oliver .05
507 Ty Law .05
508 Shawn Jefferson .05
509 Vincent Brisby .05
510 Henry Thomas .05
511 Tedy Bruschi .05
512 Curtis Martin .75
513 Jeff George .05
514 Desmond Howard .05
515 Napoleon Kaufman .10
516 Kenny Shedd .05
517 Russell Maryland .05
518 Lance Johnstone .05
519 Chad Levitt .05
520 Dexter McLeon .05
521 Craig Heyward .05
522 Ryan McNeil .05
523 Mark Rypien .05
524 Mike Jones .05
525 Jamie Sharper .05
526 Tony Siragusa .05
527 Michael Jackson .05
528 Floyd Turner .05
529 Eric Green .05
530 Michael McCrary .05
531 Jay Graham .05
532 Terry Allen .05
533 Sean Gilbert .05
534 Scott Turner .05
535 Cris Dishman .05
536 Jeff Hostetler .05
537 Chris Mims .05
538 Alvin Harper .05
539 Daryl Hobbs .05
540 Wayne Martin .05
541 Heath Shuler .05
542 Andre Hastings .05
543 Jared Tomich .05
544 Nicky Savoie .05
545 Cortez Kennedy .05
546 Warren Moon .05
547 Chad Brown .05
548 Willie Williams .05
549 Bennie Blades .05
550 Darren Perry .05
551 Mark Bruener .05
552 Yancey Thigpen .05
553 Courtney Hawkins .05
554 Chad Scott .05
555 George Jones .05
556 Robert Tate .05
557 Torrian Gray .05
558 Robert Griffith .05
559 Leroy Hoard .05
560 Robert Smith .05
561 Randall Cunningham .05
562 Darrell Russell CL .05
563 Troy Aikman CL .25
564 Dan Marino CL .40
565 Jim Druckenmiller CL .25

1997 Collector's Choice Crash the Game

This 30-card chase set was inserted 1:5 packs. If the player featured on the front scored on the date shown on the card, the collector won a redemption card of the player. This insert appeared only in Series I.

NM/M

Complete Set (30): 25.00
Common Player: .50
Minor Stars: 1.00
Each player has three cards with 3 different dates.
1 Troy Aikman 1.50
2 Dan Marino 2.00
3 Steve Young 1.25
4 Brett Favre 2.50
5 Drew Bledsoe 1.50
6 Jeff Blake .50
7 Mark Brunell 1.00
8 John Elway 1.25
9 Vinny Testaverde .50
10 Steve McNair 1.25
11 Jerry Rice 2.00
12 Terry Glenn .50
13 Michael Jackson .50
14 Tony Martin .50
15 Isaac Bruce 1.00
16 Cris Carter 1.00
17 Shannon Sharpe .50
18 Rae Carruth .50
19 Ike Hilliard .50
20 Yatil Green .75
21 Terry Allen .50
22 Emmitt Smith 2.00
23 Karim Abdul-Jabbar .50
24 Barry Sanders 1.50
25 Terrell Davis 1.50
26 Jerome Bettis 1.00
27 Ricky Watters 1.00
28 Curtis Martin 1.25
29 Byron Hanspard .50
30 Warrick Dunn .50

1997 Collector's Choice Mini-Standee

Inserted 1:5, the 30-card Mini Standee insert appeared in Series II. The cards can be folded into a football shaped stand-up card. The cards are numbered with the "ST" prefix.

NM/M

Complete Set (30): 25.00
Common Player: .25
Minor Stars: .50
1 Jerry Rice 1.50
2 Rashaan Salaam .25
3 Jeff Blake .50
4 Antowain Smith .50
5 John Elway 1.25

NM/M

6 Errict Rhett .25
7 Jake Plummer .50
8 Junior Seau .25
9 Marcus Allen .50
10 Marvin Harrison .50
11 Emmitt Smith 3.00
12 Dan Marino 3.00
13 Ricky Watters .50
14 Jamal Anderson .25
15 Rodney Hampton .25
16 Mark Brunell 1.00
17 Keyshawn Johnson .50
18 Barry Sanders 2.00
19 Eddie George 1.00
20 Brett Favre 3.50
21 Kerry Collins 1.00
22 Drew Bledsoe 1.50
23 Napoleon Kaufman .50
24 Tony Banks .50
25 Vinny Testaverde .25
26 Terry Allen .25
27 Mario Bates .25
28 Joey Galloway .50
29 Jerome Bettis .50
30 Robert Smith .25

1997 Collector's Choice Star Quest

StarQuest is a four-tiered insert available in Series II. The tiers are indicated by the number of stars on the card - one per tier. Tier one includes 45 cards and were inserted 1:1. Tier two includes 20 cards inserted 1:21. The 15 tier three cards were inserted 1:71. Tier four had 10 cards and was inserted 1:145. The insert set totaled 90 cards, featuring the top players in the game. The cards are numbered with the "SQ" prefix.

NM/M

Complete Set (90): 250.00
Common Player (1-45): .25
Common Player (46-65): 1.00
Common Player (66-80): 2.00
Common Player (81-90): 4.00
1 Frank Sanders .25
2 Jamal Anderson .50
3 Bam Morris .25
4 Thurman Thomas .50
5 Muhsin Muhammad .25
6 Bobby Engram .25
7 Carl Pickens .25
8 Deion Sanders .75
9 Shannon Sharpe .25
10 Herman Moore .50
11 Robert Brooks .25
12 Steve McNair 1.50
13 Marshall Faulk .50
14 Keenan McCardell .25
15 Tamarick Vanover .25
16 Fred Barnett .25
17 Orlanda Thomas .25
18 Drew Bledsoe 1.50
19 Mario Bates .25
20 Keyshawn Johnson .50
21 Rodney Hampton .25
22 Darrell Russell .25
23 Irving Fryar .25
24 Charles Johnson .25
25 Stan Humphries .25
26 Terrell Owens .50
27 Chris Warren .25
28 Isaac Bruce .50
29 Warrick Dunn 1.50
30 Gus Frerotte .25
31 Raghib Ismail .25
32 Natrone Means .50
33 Chris Sanders .25
34 Vinny Testaverde .25
35 Ken Norton .25
36 Kevin Greene .25
37 Marcus Allen .50
38 Zach Thomas .25
39 Derrick Thomas .25
40 Tyrone Wheatley .25
41 Dorsey Levens .50
42 Darnay Scott .25
43 Scott Mitchell .25
44 Marvin Harrison .50
45 Eddie Kennison .50
46 Jake Reed 1.00
47 Andre Reed 1.00
48 Neil Smith 1.00
49 Anthony Johnson .50
50 Napoleon Kaufman .50
51 Terance Mathis .50
52 Tony Martin .50
53 Adrian Murrell .50
54 Bryant Westbrook 1.00
55 Errict Rhett 1.00
56 Kerry Collins 3.00
57 Curtis Conway 1.00
58 Eric Swann 1.00
59 Michael Jackson 1.00
60 Ty Detmer 1.00
61 Michael Irvin 2.00
62 Andre Coleman 1.00
63 Brian Mitchell 1.00
64 Tony Banks 2.00
65 Eddie George 4.00
66 Kordell Stewart 3.00
67 Greg Hill 2.00
68 Karim Abdul-Jabbar 2.00
69 Cris Carter 3.00
70 Terry Glenn 8.00
71 Emmitt Smith 25.00
72 Jim Harbaugh 5.00
73 Jeff Blake 3.00
74 Rashaan Salaam 2.00
75 Ricky Watters 5.00
76 Joey Galloway 5.00
77 Junior Seau 5.00
78 Dave Brown 2.00
79 Tim Brown 8.00
80 Troy Aikman 12.00
81 Dan Marino 25.00
82 Brett Favre 25.00
83 John Elway 20.00
84 Steve Young 15.00
85 Mark Brunell 15.00
86 Barry Sanders 20.00
87 Jerome Bettis 4.00
88 Terrell Davis 20.00
89 Curtis Martin 20.00
90 Jerry Rice 35.00

1997 Collector's Choice Stick-Ums

Inserted 1:3 packs in Series I, these 30 stickers featured a photo of the player on the front, the Stick-Ums logo, his name and team helmet which could be peeled off. The sticker number is printed on the upper left of the back. Directions on how to use the stickers are on the left of the back, while the checklist is on the right. Each of the stickers' numbers included an "S" prefix.

NM/M

Complete Set (30): 15.00
Common Player: .25
Minor Stars: .50
1 Kerry Collins .75
2 Troy Aikman 1.25
3 Steve Young .75
4 Ricky Watters .50
5 Cris Carter .25
6 Terry Allen .25
7 Bobby Engram .50
8 Simeon Rice .25
9 Mike Alstott .25
10 Rodney Hampton .25
11 Eddie Kennison .50
12 Jamal Anderson .50
13 Jim Everett .25
14 Curtis Martin 1.25
15 Keenan McCardell .25
16 Kordell Stewart 1.00
17 John Elway .75
18 Terrell Davis 1.25
19 Thurman Thomas .50
20 Marshall Faulk .50
21 Marcus Allen .50
22 Tony Martin .25
23 Dan Marino 2.00
24 Karim Abdul-Jabbar .50
25 Carl Pickens .25
26 Eddie George 1.00
27 Joey Galloway .50
28 Napoleon Kaufman .25
29 Vinny Testaverde .25
30 Keyshawn Johnson .50

1997 Collector's Choice Turf Champions

The 90-card chase set was broken up into four tiers. Tier one and two both contain 30 cards, while Tier three has 20. Tier four includes 10. The Tiers were inserted as follows: one (every pack), two (1:21), three (1:71) and four (1:145). The holofoil cards have a green-marble border at the top and bottom. The Collector's Choice logo is in the upper left, with the Turf Champions' logo in the lower left. The player's name, position and team are listed at the bottom center. The backs, which are numbered with a "TC" prefix, have the player's highlights printed over a green area on the left, with his achievement printed vertically in the center. The right has a photo and quote. Turf Champions appeared in Series I.

NM/M

Complete Set (90): 300.00
Common Player (1-30): .20
Inserted 1:1
Common Player (31-60): 1.00
Inserted 1:21
Common Player (61-80): 3.00
Inserted 1:71
Common Player (81-90): 4.00
Inserted 1:145
1 Kerry Collins .50
2 Scott Mitchell .20
3 Jim Schwantz .20
4 Orlando Pace .40
5 Troy Davis .40
6 Vinny Testaverde .50
7 Raghib Ismail .20
8 Henry Ellard .20
9 Kevin Turner .20
10 Bobby Engram .20
11 Keyshawn Johnson .75
12 Trent Dilfer .50
13 Elvis Grbac .40
14 Trev Alberts .20
15 Kevin Hardy .20
16 Warren Sapp .40
17 Chris Hudson .20
18 Antonio Langham .20
19 Jonathan Ogden .20
20 Bruce Smith .40
21 Marcus Allen .50
22 Desmond Howard .20
23 Eric Metcalf .20
24 Terance Mathis .20
25 LeShon Johnson .20
26 Kevin Greene .20
27 Alex Van Dyke .20
28 Jeff Jaeger .20
29 Jason Elam .20
30 Thomas Lewis .20
31 Rick Mirer .75
32 Warren Moon 1.00
33 Jim Kelly 1.00
34 Junior Seau 1.00
35 Jeff Hostetler .50
36 Neil O'Donnell .50
37 Jeff Blake 1.00
38 Kordell Stewart 2.00
39 Terry Glenn 1.00
40 Simeon Rice 1.00
41 Jimmy Smith 1.00
42 Natrone Means .50
43 Tony Martin .50
44 Charles Johnson .50
45 Napoleon Kaufman .50
46 Dale Carter .50
47 Brett Perriman .50
48 Cortez Kennedy 1.00
49 Bryce Paup .50
50 Greg Lloyd 1.00
51 Bryant Young 1.00
52 Steve McNair 6.00
53 Garrison Hearst 4.00
54 John Copeland .50
55 Eric Curry .50
56 Reggie White 2.00
57 Rod Woodson 2.00
58 Andre Rison 1.00
59 Herschel Walker 2.00
60 John Kasay 1.00
61 Emmitt Smith 25.00
62 Dan Marino 25.00
63 Michael Irvin 6.00
64 Drew Bledsoe 10.00
65 Mark Brunell 10.00

66 Jim Harbaugh 5.00
67 Herman Moore 5.00
68 Rashaan Salaam 2.00
69 Ty Detmer 2.00
70 Cris Carter 4.00
71 Chris Warren 2.00
72 Thurman Thomas 5.00
73 Ricky Watters 5.00
74 Tim Brown 10.00
75 Marshall Faulk 15.00
76 Jerome Bettis 10.00
77 Karim Abdul-Jabbar 1.00
78 Deion Sanders 5.00
79 Ben Coates 3.00
80 Andre Reed 3.00
81 Brett Favre 35.00
82 Terrell Davis 20.00
83 Troy Aikman 20.00
84 Carl Pickens 6.00
85 Barry Sanders 25.00
86 Jerry Rice 20.00
87 Curtis Martin 15.00
88 Steve Young 15.00
89 Eddie George 15.00
90 John Elway 25.00

1992 Collector's Edge Prototypes

Two different versions of this six-card prototype set were issued. One version had a removable piece of paper glued to the card back, while the other version was not sticky. The paper-covered backs are tougher to find. Edge produced 8,000 of each card. The card fronts are bordered in black, with a color photo. The Edge '92 logo is in the upper left. The player's name and position are in the lower left. The player's team's helmet is located on the lower right of the card back. The backs have a player headshot at the top, with his name, position, team, bio and stats listed below. The cards are numbered in the upper right with a "prototype" suffix.

NM/M
Complete Set (6): 25.00
Common Player: 2.00
1 Jim Kelly 3.00
2 Randall Cunningham 4.00
3 Warren Moon 2.00
4 John Elway 10.00
5 Dan Marino 10.00
6 Bernie Kosar 2.00

1992 Collector's Edge

Each card in this 175-card set is individually numbered from 1-100,000. The standard-size cards are printed on a plastic stock and feature color action shots with black borders. A team helmet is on the lower right-hand corner. Backs, which have the card front image ghosted through, have a mug shot, statistics and a biography. John Elway and Ken O'Brien autographed 2,500 cards which were randomly inserted in factory sets and foil packs. Rookie/Update cards begin with #176 and are considered a second series. There were also 2,500 Ronnie Lott autographed cards in the series, plus 20,000 cards each for Terrell Buckley and Tommy Maddox.

NM/M
Complete Set (250): 20.00
Complete Series 1 (175): 15.00
Complete Series 2 (75): 10.00
Common Player: .10
Minor Stars: .20
Elway Auto: 100.00
Lott Auto: 40.00
O'Brien Auto: 20.00
Series 1 Pack (6): .75
Series 1 Wax Box (24): 15.00
Rookie/Update Pack (6): .75
Rookie/Update Wax Box (24): 15.00
1 Chris Miller .10
2 Steve Broussard .10
3 Mike Pritchard .20
4 Tim Green .10
5 Andre Rison .30
6 Deion Sanders .50
7 Jim Kelly .50
8 James Lofton .10
9 Andre Reed .10
10 Bruce Smith .10
11 Thurman Thomas .50
12 Cornelius Bennett .10
13 Jim Harbaugh .10
14 William Perry .10
15 Mike Singletary .10
16 Mark Carrier .10
17 Kevin Butler .10
18 Tom Waddle .10
19 Boomer Esiason .20
20 David Fulcher .10
21 Anthony Munoz .10
22 Tim McGee .10
23 Harold Green .10
24 Rickey Dixon .10
25 Bernie Kosar .10
26 Michael Dean Perry .10
27 Mike Baab .10
28 Brian Brennan .10
29 Michael Jackson .20
30 Eric Metcalf .10
31 Troy Aikman 2.00
32 Emmitt Smith 4.00
33 Michael Irvin .50
34 Jay Novacek .10
35 Issiac Holt .10
36 Ken Norton .10
37 John Elway 1.25
38 Gaston Green .10
39 Charles Dimry .10
40 Vance Johnson .10
41 Dennis Smith .10
42 David Treadwell .10
43 Michael Young .10
44 Bennie Blades .10
45 Mel Gray .10
46 Andre Ware .10
47 Rodney Peete .10
48 *Toby Caston* .10
49 Herman Moore .75
50 Brian Noble .10
51 Sterling Sharpe .50
52 Mike Tomczak .10
53 Vinnie Clark .10
54 Tony Mandarich .10
55 Ed West .10
56 Warren Moon .30
57 Ray Childress .10
58 Haywood Jeffires .10
59 Al Smith .10
60 Cris Dishman .10
61 Ernest Givins .10
62 Richard Johnson .10
63 Eric Dickerson .10
64 Jessie Hester .10
65 Robin Stark .10
66 Clarence Verdin .10
67 Dean Biasucci .10
68 Duane Bickett .10
69 Jeff George .30
70 Christian Okoye .10
71 Derrick Thomas .30
72 Stephone Paige .10
73 Dan Saleaumua .10
74 Deron Cherry .10
75 Kevin Ross .10
76 Barry Word .10
77 Ronnie Lott .10
78 Greg Townsend .10
79 Willie Gault .10
80 Howie Long .10
81 Winston Moss .10
82 Steve Smith .10
83 Jay Schroeder .10
84 Jim Everett .20
85 Willie Anderson .10
86 Henry Ellard .10
87 Tony Zendejas .10
88 Robert Delpino .10
89 Pat Terrel .10
90 Dan Marino 5.00
91 Mark Clayton .10
92 Jim Jensen .10
93 Reggie Roby .10
94 Sammie Smith .10
95 Tony Martin .10
96 Jeff Cross .10
97 Anthony Carter .10
98 Chris Doleman .10
99 Wade Wilson .10
100 Cris Carter .20
101 Mike Meriweather .10
102 Gary Zimmerman .10
103 Chris Singleton .10
104 Bruce Armstrong .10
105 Marv Cook .10
106 Andre Tippet .10
107 Tom Hodson .10
108 Greg McMurtry .10
109 Jon Vaughn .10
110 Vaughan Johnson .10
111 Craig Heyward .10
112 Floyd Turner .10
113 Pat Swilling .10
114 Ricky Jackson .10
115 Steve Walsh .10
116 Phil Simms .10
117 Carl Banks .10
118 Mark Ingram .10
119 Bart Oates .10
120 Lawrence Taylor .20
121 Jeff Hostetler .30
122 Rob Moore .20
123 Ken O'Brien .10
124 Bill Pickel .10
125 Irv Eatman .10
126 Browning Nagle .10
127 Al Toon .10
128 Randall Cunningham .20
129 Eric Allen .10
130 Mike Golic .10
131 Fred Barnett .10
132 Keith Byars .10
133 Calvin Williams .10
134 Randal Hill .10
135 Ricky Proehl .10
136 Lance Smith .10
137 Ernie Jones .10
138 Timm Rosenbach .10
139 Anthony Thompson .10
140 Bubby Brister .10
141 Merril Hoge .10
142 Louis Lipps .10
143 Eric Green .10
144 Gary Anderson .10
145 Neil O'Donnell .40
146 Rod Bernstine .10
147 John Friesz .10
148 Anthony Miller .10
149 Junior Seau .50
150 Leslie O'Neal .10
151 Nate Lewis .10
152 Steve Young 2.00
153 Kevin Fagan .10
154 Charles Haley .10
155 Tom Rathman .10
156 Jerry Rice 3.00
157 John Taylor .10
158 Brian Blades .10
159 Patrick Hunter .10
160 Cortez Kennedy .20
161 Vann McElroy .10
162 Dan McGwire .10
163 John L. Williams .10
164 Gary Anderson .10
165 Broderick Thomas .10
166 Vinny Testaverde .20
167 Lawrence Dawsey .10
168 Paul Gruber .10
169 Keith McCants .10
170 Mark Rypien .10
171 Gary Clark .10
172 Earnest Byner .10
173 Brian Mitchell .10
174 Monte Coleman .10
175 Joe Jacoby .10
176 *Tommy Vardell* .20
177 *Troy Vincent* .25
178 *Robert Jones* .20
179 *Marc Boutte* .10
180 *Marco Coleman* .30
181 *Chris Mims* .50
182 Tony Casillas .10
183 *Shane Dronett* .20
184 *Sean Gilbert* .40
185 *Siran Stacy* .10
186 *Tommy Maddox* 2.00
187 Steve Israel .10
188 Brad Muster .10
189 *Shane Collins* .20
190 *Terrell Buckley* .25
191 *Eugene Chung* .10
192 *Leon Searcy* .20
193 *Chuck Smith* .10
194 *Patrick Rowe* .20
195 *Bill Johnson* .10
196 *Gerald Dixon* .10
197 *Robert Porcher* .25
198 *Tracy Scroggins* .40
199 *Jason Hanson* .30
200 *Corey Harris* .20
201 *Eddie Robinson* .20
202 *Steve Emtman* .30
203 *Ashley Ambrose* .20
204 *Greg Skrepenak* .20
205 *Todd Collins* .20
206 *Derek Brown* .25
207 *Kurt Barber* .20
208 *Tony Sacca* .20
209 *Mark Wheeler* .20
210 *Kevin Smith* .30
211 *John Fina* .10
212 *Johnny Mitchell* .50
213 *Dale Carter* .30
214 *Bobby Spitulski* .10
215 *Phillippi Sparks* .10
216 *Levon Kirkland* .10
217 Mike Sherrard .10
218 *Marquez Pope* .10
219 *Courtney Hawkins* .30
220 *Tyji Armstrong* .20
221 Keith Jackson .20
222 *Clayton Holmes* .10
223 *Quentin Coryatt* .30
224 *Troy Auzenne* .10
225 *David Klingler* .25
226 *Darryl Williams* .25
227 *Carl Pickens* 1.50
228 *Jimmy Smith* 2.00
229 *Chester McGlockton* .50
230 *Robert Brooks* .75
231 *Alonzo Spellman* .50
232 *Darren Woodson* .30
233 Lewis Billups .10
234 *Edgar Bennett* .75
235 *Vaughn Dunbar* .20
236 *Steve Bono* .75
237 Clarence Kay .10
238 Chris Hinton .10
239 Jimmie Jones .10
240 Vai Sikahema .10
241 Russell Maryland .10
242 Neal Anderson .10
243 Charles Mann .10
244 Hugh Millen .10
245 Roger Craig .10
246 Rich Gannon .10
247 Ricky Ervins .10
248 Leonard Marshall .10
249 Eric Dickerson .20
250 Joe Montana 3.00

1992 Collector's Edge Special

Produced to promote Tuff Stuff's Buyer's Club, one of the four cards was inserted in all copies of the November 1992 magazine. Over 250,000 cards were issued of the first card. The other three cards were printed in quantities of approximately 40,000 each. One of each of the three cards were given as a bonus with each paid membership. The Elway card was also printed as "Proto 1," "John Elway Dealerships" and "Elway Foundation." Reportedly, less than 50,000 of these cards were issued. The card fronts have a dark blue border, with a color photo, the player's name and position in the lower left and his team's helmet in the lower right. The card backs are numbered with a "TS" prefix for the Buyer's Club. "Proto 1" is numbered as such, while the Elway Foundation and Elway Dealerships are not numbered. The card backs have a headshot, player's name, bio, position and stats. The card number is in the upper right.

NM/M
Complete Set (4): 12.00
Common Player: 2.00
1 John Elway 3.00
2 Ronnie Lott 4.00
3 Jim Everett 2.00
4 Bernie Kosar 2.00
PROT1 John Elway 10.00
NNO Elway Foundation 30.00
NNO Elway Dealerships 25.00

1993 Collector's Edge Prototype

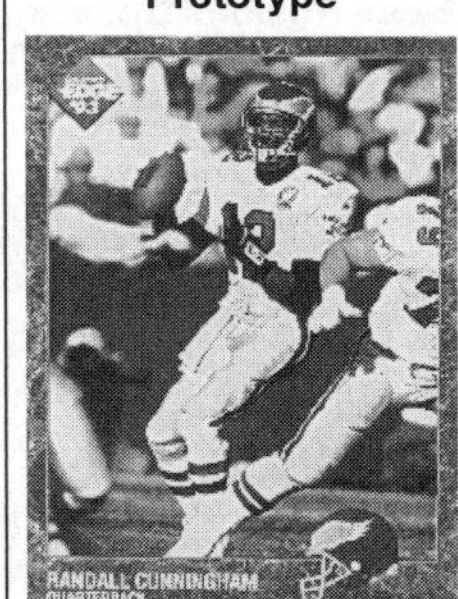

These cards, which promote the 1993 Collector's Edge set, are numbered from 1 to 40,000 on the back. Each card front has a blue marble-like border and an action photo. The back uses a green marble-like border and also indicates that the card is a "Proto." In addition to these cards, there were 8-1/2" x 11" versions of these cards made, too. They, however, are not numbered and were included in dealer cases. They are generally two to four times more valuable than the smaller versions.

NM/M
Complete Set (6): 15.00
Common Player: 4.00
1 John Elway 5.00
2 Derrick Thomas 2.00
3 Randall Cunningham 2.00
4 Thurman Thomas 3.00
5 Warren Moon 2.00
6 Barry Sanders 5.00

1993 Collector's Edge RU Prototypes

Blue-marble borders highlight the front of this five-card Rookie/Update set. The Edge logo is in the upper left, with his name and position in the lower left. His team's helmet is printed in the lower right. The card backs have the player's headshot on the upper left, with his team's logo, name, team, position, jersey number and card number, prefixed with "RU." The card's serial number is printed in the center above the player's bio and stats.

NM/M
Complete Set (5): 6.00
Common Player: 1.00
1 Garrison Hearst 1.50
2 Reggie White 2.00
3 Boomer Esiason 1.00
4 Rod Bernstine 1.00
5 Dana Stubblefield 1.50

1993 Collector's Edge

The second set from Collector's Edge uses the same features features as its first set in 1992 - the cards are plastic and are each individually numbered from 1-100,000. The fronts have an action photo with against a blue marble background. A team helmet is at the bottom of the card, while the Collector's Edge logo is at the top. The backs have statistics, a career summary and a mug shot. Rookie/Update cards are numbered from #251-325. Ten John Elway prism inserts were randomly included in packs; E1-E5 were in late packs, while S1-S5 were in early packs. Twenty-five Collector's Edge Rookies FX cards were randomly inserted in Rookie/Update packs and are numbered with an "FX" prefix. Five Collector's Edge checklists were also made and were randomly inserted in regular packs. Six promo cards were also made featuring Elway, Derrick Thomas, Randall Cunningham, Thurman Thomas, Warren Moon and Barry Sanders. There were 40,000 cards produced for each player.

NM/M
Complete Set (325): 20.00
Complete Series 1 (250): 10.00
Complete Series 2 (75): 10.00
Common Player: .05
Minor Stars: .10
Comp. Checklists (5): 2.00
John Elway Auto. 75.00
Series 1 Pack (6): .75
Series 1 Wax Box (24): 13.00
Rookie/Up. Pack (6): .90
Rookie/Up. Wax Box (24): 16.00
1 Atlanta Team .05
2 Michael Haynes .05
3 Chris Miller .05
4 Mike Pritchard .05
5 Andre Rison .10
6 Deion Sanders .50
7 Chuck Smith .05
8 Drew Hill .05
9 Bobby Hebert .05
10 Buffalo Team .05
11 Matt Darby .05
12 John Fina .05
13 Jim Kelly .15
14 *Marvcus Patton* .10
15 Andre Reed .10
16 Thurman Thomas .15
17 James Lofton .05
18 Bruce Smith .05
19 Chicago Team .05
20 Neal Anderson .05
21 Troy Auzenne .05
22 Jim Harbaugh .05
23 Alonzo Spellman .05
24 Tom Waddle .05
25 Darren Lewis .05
26 Wendell Davis .05
27 Will Furrer .05
28 Cincinnati Team .05
29 David Klingler .15
30 Ricardo McDonald .05
31 Carl Pickens .40
32 Harold Green .05
33 Anthony Munoz .05
34 Darryl Williams .05
35 Cleveland Team .05
36 Michael Jackson .05
37 Pio Sagapolutele .05
38 Tommy Vardell .05
39 Bernie Kosar .05
40 Michael Dean Perry .05
41 Bill Johnson .05
42 Vinny Testaverde .05
43 Dallas team .05
44 Troy Aikman .75
45 Alvin Harper .20
46 Michael Irvin .10
47 Russell Maryland .05
48 Emmitt Smith 2.00
49 Kenneth Gant .05
50 Jay Novacek .05
51 Robert Jones .05
52 Clayton Holomes .05
53 Denver Team .05
54 Mike Croel .05
55 Shane Dronett .05
56 Kenny Walker .05
57 Tommy Maddox .05
58 Dennis Smith .05
59 John Elway .40
60 Karl Mecklenberg .05
61 Steve Atwater .05
62 Vance Johnson .05
63 Detroit team .05
64 Barry Sanders 1.25
65 Andre Ware .05
66 Pat Swilling .05
67 Jason Hanson .05
68 Willie Green .05
69 Herman Moore .50
70 Rodney Peete .05
71 Erik Kramer .10
72 Robert Porcher .05
73 Green Bay team .05
74 Terrell Buckley .10
75 Reggie White .10
76 Brett Favre 2.00
77 Don Majkowski .05
78 Edgar Bennett .10
79 Ty Detmer .05
80 Sanjay Beach .05
81 Sterling Sharpe .10
82 Houston team .05
83 Gary Brown .10
84 Ernest Givins .05
85 Haywood Jeffires .05
86 Corey Harris .05
87 Warren Moon .15
88 Eddie Robinson .05
89 Lorenzo White .05
90 Bo Orlando .05
91 Indianapolis team .05
92 Quentin Coryatt .05
93 Steve Emtman .05
94 Jeff George .10
95 Jessie Hester .05
96 Rohn Stark .05
97 Ashley Ambrose .05
98 John Baylor .05
99 Kansas City team .05
100 Tim Barnett .05
101 Derrick Thomas .10
102 Barry Word .05
103 Dale Carter .05
104 Jayice Pearson .05
105 Tracy Simien .05
106 Harvey Williams .15
107 Dave Krieg .05
108 Christian Okoye .05
109 Joe Montana 1.00
110 Miami team .05
111 J.B. Brown .05
112 Marco Coleman .05
113 Dan Marino 2.00
114 Mark Clayton .05
115 Mark Higgs .05
116 Bryan Cox .05
117 Chuck Klingbeil .05
118 Troy Vincent .10
119 Keith Jackson .10
120 Bruce Alexander .05
121 Minnesota team .05
122 Terry Allen .10
123 Rich Gannon .05
124 Todd Scott .05
125 Cris Carter .10
126 Sean Salisbury .05
127 Jack Del Rio .05
128 Chris Doleman .05
129 Anthony Carter .05
130 New England team .05
131 Eugene Chung .05
132 Todd Collins .05
133 Tom Hodson .05
134 Leonard Russell .05
135 Jon Vaughn .05
136 Andre Tippet .05
137 New Orleans team .05
138 Wesley Carroll .05
139 Richard Cooper .05
140 Vaughn Dunbar .05
141 Fred McAfee .05
142 Torrance Small .05
143 Steve Walsh .05
144 Vaughan Johnson .05
145 New York Giants team .05
146 Jarrod Bunch .05
147 Phil Simms .05
148 Carl Banks .05
149 Lawrence Taylor .10
150 Rodney Hampton .10
151 Phillippi Sparks .05
152 Derek Brown .05
153 New York Jets team .05
154 Boomer Esiason .10
155 Johnny Mitchell .05
156 Rob Moore .05
157 Ronnie Lott .05
158 Browning Nagle .05
159 Johnny Johnson .05
160 Dwayne White .05
161 Blair Thomas .05
162 Philadelphia team .05
163 Randall Cunningham .10
164 Fred Barnett .05
165 Siran Stacy .05
166 Keith Byars .05
167 Calvin Williams .05
168 Jeff Sydner .05
169 Tommy Jeter .05
170 Andre Waters .05
171 Phoenix team .05
172 Steve Beuerlein .10
173 Randal Hill .05
174 Timm Rosenbach .05

175	Ed Cunningham	.05
176	Walter Reeves	.05
177	Michael Zordich	.05
178	Gary Clark	.05
179	Ken Harvey	.05
180	Pittsburgh team	.05
181	Barry Foster	.10
182	Neil O'Donnell	.15
183	Leon Searcy	.05
184	Bubby Brister	.05
185	Merril Hoge	.05
186	Joel Steed	.05
187	Los Angeles Raiders team	.05
188	Nick Bell	.05
189	Eric Dickerson	.05
190	Nolan Harrison	.05
191	Todd Marinovich	.05
192	Greg Skrepenak	.05
193	Howie Long	.05
194	Jay Schroeder	.05
195	Chester McGlockton	.05
196	Los Angeles Rams team	.05
197	Jim Everett	.05
198	Sean Gilbert	.05
199	Steve Israel	.05
200	Marc Boutte	.05
201	Joe Milinichik	.05
202	Henry Ellard	.05
203	Jackie Slater	.05
204	San Diego team	.05
205	Eric Bieniemy	.05
206	Marion Butts	.05
207	Nate Lewis	.05
208	Junior Seau	.15
209	Steve Hendrickson	.05
210	Chris Mims	.05
211	Harry Swayne	.05
212	Marquez Pope	.05
213	Donald Frank	.05
214	Anthony Miller	.05
215	Seattle team	.05
216	Cortez Kennedy	.10
217	Dan McGwire	.05
218	Kelly Stouffer	.05
219	Chris Warren	.20
220	Brian Blades	.05
221	Rod Stephens	.05
222	San Francisco team	.05
223	Jerry Rice	1.00
224	Ricky Watters	.20
225	Steve Young	1.00
226	Tom Rathman	.05
227	Dana Hall	.05
228	Amp Lee	.10
229	Brian Bollinger	.05
230	Keith DeLong	.05
231	John Taylor	.05
232	Tampa Bay Team	.05
233	Tyji Armstrong	.05
234	Lawrence Dawsey	.05
235	Mark Wheeler	.05
236	Vince Workman	.05
237	Reggie Cobb	.05
238	Tony Mayberry	.05
239	Marty Carter	.05
240	Courtney Hawkins	.05
241	Ray Seals	.05
242	Mark Carrier	.05
243	Washington Team	.05
244	Mark Rypien	.05
245	Ricky Ervins	.05
246	Gerald Riggs	.05
247	Art Monk	.10
248	Mark Schlereth	.05
249	Monte Coleman	.05
250	Wilber Marshall	.05
251	*Ben Coleman*	.05
252	*Curtis Conway*	.75
253	*Ernest Dye*	.05
254	*Todd Kelly*	.05
255	*Patrick Bates*	.10
256	*George Teague*	.10
257	*Mark Brunell*	2.00
258	*Adrian Hardy*	.05
259	*Dana Stubblefield*	.50
260	*William Roaf*	.10
261	*Irv Smith*	.10
262	*Drew Bledsoe*	3.00
263	*Dan Williams*	.10
264	Jerry Ball	.05
265	Mark Clayton	.05
266	John Stephens	.05
267	Reggie White	.10
268	Jeff Hostetler	.10
269	Boomer Esiason	.05
270	Wade Wilson	.05
271	Steve Beuerlein	.05
272	Tim McDonald	.05
273	Craig Heyward	.05
274	Everson Walls	.05
275	Stan Humphries	.10
276	Carl Banks	.05
277	Brad Muster	.05
278	Tim Harris	.05
279	Gary Clark	.05
280	Joe Milinichik	.05
281	Leonard Marshall	.05
282	Joe Montana	1.00
283	Rod Bernstine	.05
284	Mark Carrier	.05
285	Michael Brooks	.05
286	*Marvin Jones*	.10
287	*John Copeland*	.20
288	*Eric Curry*	.10
289	*Steve Everitt*	.10
290	*Tom Carter*	.10
291	*Deon Figures*	.15
292	*Leonard Renfro*	.10
293	*Thomas Smith*	.10
294	*Carlton Gray*	.10
295	*Demetrius DeBose*	.10
296	*Coleman Rudolph*	.05
297	*John Parrella*	.05
298	*Glyn Milburn*	.30
299	*Reggie Brooks*	.20
300	*Garrison Hearst*	1.00
301	John Elway	.40
302	*Brad Hopkins*	.05
303	*Darrien Gordon*	.20
304	*Robert Smith*	.60
305	*Chris Slade*	.25
306	*Ryan McNeil*	.10
307	*Micheal Barrow*	.10
308	*Roosevelt Potts*	.10
309	*Qadry Ismail*	.50
310	*Reggie Freeman*	.05
311	*Vincent Brisby*	.30
312	*Rick Mirer*	.30
313	*Billy Joe Hobert*	.25
314	*Natrone Means*	.50
315	Gary Zimmerman	.05
316	Bobby Hebert	.05
317	Don Beebe	.05
318	Wilber Marshall	.05
319	Marcus Allen	.10
320	Ronnie Lott	.05
321	Ricky Sanders	.05
322	Charles Mann	.05
323	Simon Fletcher	.05
324	Johnny Johnson	.05
325	Gary Plummer	.05
326	Carolina Panthers	12.00

1993 Collector's Edge Elway Prisms

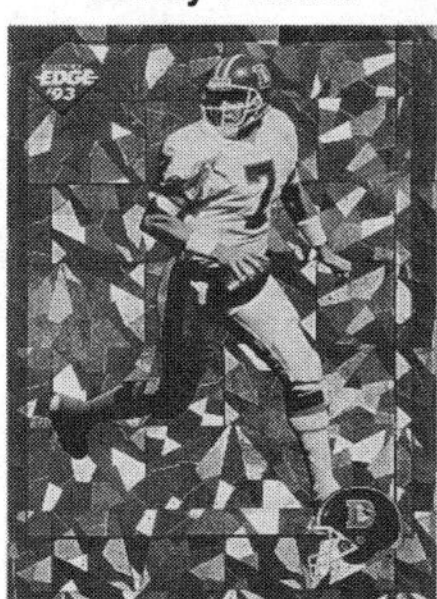

This five-card chase set was randomly seeded in 1993 Collector's Edge packs. The cards are bordered with blue prism foil. The photo of Elway is placed over a silver prism background. The Edge logo is in the upper left, while the Broncos' helmet is in the lower right. The card backs have an action shot at the top, with the card's serial number underneath it. Elway's highlights are printed inside a box in the center of the card. The cards are numbered with an "E" prefix. Two versions of each card were produced. Those cards with the "S" prefix were inserted in early packs, and tougher to locate. The "E" prefix cards were inserted in later runs. The backgrounds are different on the different versions of cards. Five "S" prefix cards were included with each box of All-Star Collection Manager software from Taurus Technologies. Approximately 500 sets were produced for this offer. Elway's best two-minute marches are featured in this Two-Minute Warning set.

		NM/M
Complete Set (5):		5.00
Common Player:		1.00
E1	John Elway (Both arms outstretched)	1.00
E2	John Elway (Passing, orange jersey)	1.00
E3	John Elway (Running, orange jersey)	1.00
E4	John Elway (Passing, white jersey)	1.00
E5	John Elway (Running, white jersey)	1.00
S1	John Elway (Both arms outstretched)	3.00
S2	John Elway (Passing, orange jersey)	3.00
S3	John Elway (Running, orange jersey)	3.00
S4	John Elway (Passing, white jersey)	3.00
S5	John Elway (Running, white jersey)	3.00
PRO1	John Elway (AU/3000)	80.00

1993 Collector's Edge Rookies FX

These inserts, randomly available in 1993 Collector's Edge Rookie Update foil packs, feature top rookies. Each card is clear plastic and features a color action photo within a maroon border. A team helmet, in the lower right corner, and player's name, in white letters in the upper right, are also given on the card front. A card number, using an "F/X" prefix, is also on the front. The card back is clear; the reverse image from the front photo can be seen. Cards with gold backgrounds also exist; they are generally about 10 to 20 times more valuable than the regular inserts.

		NM/M
Complete Set (25):		15.00
Common Player:		.25
Minor Stars:		.50
Comp. Gold Set (25):		50.00
Gold Stars:		2X-5X
1	Garrison Hearst	1.00
2	Glyn Milburn	.50
3	Demetrius Debose	.25
4	Joe Montana	3.00
5	Thomas Smith	.25
6	Mark Clayton	.25
7	Curtis Conway	1.00
8	Drew Bledsoe	3.00
9	Todd Kelly	.25
10	Stan Humphries	.75
11	John Elway	1.50
12	Troy Aikman	3.00
13	Marion Butts	.25
14	Alvin Harper	.50
15	Drew Hill	.25
16	Michael Irvin	.50
17	Warren Moon	.50
18	Andre Reed	.25
19	Andre Rison	.50
20	Emmitt Smith	3.00
21	Thurman Thomas	.75
22	Ricky Watters	.75
23	Calvin Williams	.25
24	Steve Young	1.50
25	Howie Long	.25

1994 Collector's Edge Boss Rookies Update Promos

Printed on green plastic stock, the six-card set promoted the upcoming series. The cards have a photo of the player superimposed over the clear background. The player's name, position and Edge logo are included inside a stripe near the bottom of the card. The card number is located on the upper right of the card front. The cards are prefixed with either a "P" or "SHR." The card backs have the player's bio inside the stripe, along with the various logos.

		NM/M
Complete Set (6):		8.00
Common Player:		.50
1	Trent Dilfer	1.00
2	Marshall Faulk	3.00
3	Heath Shuler	1.00
4	Errict Rhett	1.00
5	Johnnie Morton	1.00
6	Charlie Garner	1.00

1994 Collector's Edge

Once again, Collector's Edge has used plastic for its card stock for this 200-card set. Each card front has a full-color action shot, framed by a thin black border. The set logo appears in the upper right corner. The player's name and a team logo appear in a panel at the bottom of the card. Each card back has a player mug shot and statistics at the top of the page, with a stadium shot underneath. A serial number and card number are also on the back. A parallel 1st Day Production set was also created; these cards have a gold-foil stamp for the logo. Insert cards were Boss Squad, F/X player and F/X gold checklist cards, and Boss Rookies.

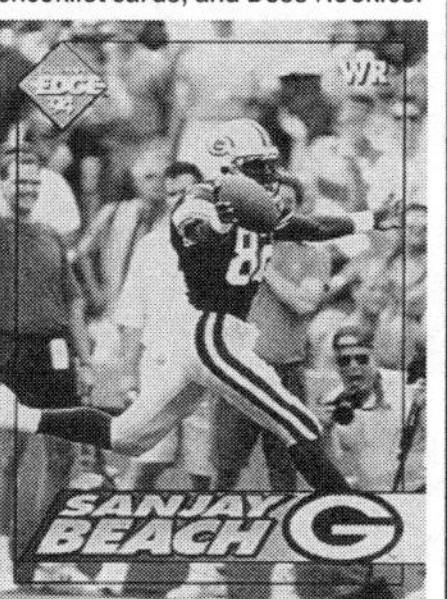

		NM/M
Complete Set (200):		17.00
Common Player:		.10
Gold Set (200):		35.00
Gold Cards:		2X
Retail Pack (6):		1.50
Retail Wax Box (24):		30.00
Silver/Pop Warner Pack (6):		1.75
Silver/Pop Warner Wax Box (36):		50.00
Gold Pack (7):		2.50
Gold Wax Box (36):		70.00
1	Mike Pritchard	.12
2	Erric Pegram	.10
3	Michael Haynes	.12
4	Bobby Hebert	.10
5	Deion Sanders	.75
6	Andre Rison	.20
7	Don Beebe	.10
8	Mark Kelso	.10
9	Darryl Talley	.10
10	Cornelius Bennett	.10
11	Jim Kelly	.40
12	Andre Reed	.15
13	Bruce Smith	.10
14	Thurman Thomas	.50
15	Craig Heyward	.10
16	Chris Zorich	.10
17	Alonzo Spellman	.10
18	Tom Waddle	.10
19	Neal Anderson	.10
20	Kevin Butler	.10
21	Curtis Conway	.30
22	Richard Dent	.10
23	Jim Harbaugh	.10
24	Derrick Fenner	.10
25	Harold Green	.10
26	David Klingler	.10
27	Daniel Stubbs	.10
28	Alfred Williams	.10
29	John Copeland	.10
30	Mark Carrier	.10
31	Michael Jackson	.10
32	Eric Metcalf	.10
33	Vinny Testaverde	.10
34	Tommy Vardell	.10
35	Alvin Harper	.12
36	Ken Norton	.10
37	Tony Casillas	.10
38	Leon Lett	.10
39	Jay Novacek	.10
40	Kevin Smith	.10
41	Troy Aikman	1.00
42	Michael Irvin	.50
43	Russell Maryland	.10
44	Emmitt Smith	2.00
45	Robert Delpino	.10
46	Simon Fletcher	.10
47	Greg Kragen	.10
48	Arthur Marshall	.10
49	Steve Atwater	.10
50	Rod Bernstine	.10
51	John Elway	1.00
52	Glyn Milburn	.20
53	Shannon Sharpe	.10
54	Bennie Blades	.10
55	Mel Gray	.10
56	Herman Moore	.15
57	Pat Swilling	.10
58	Chris Spielman	.10
59	Rodney Peete	.10
60	Andre Ware	.10
61	Brett Perriman	.10
62	Erik Kramer	.10
63	Barry Sanders	1.25
64	Mark Clayton	.10
65	Chris Jacke	.10
66	Terrell Buckley	.10
67	Ty Detmer	.10
68	Sanjay Beach	.10
69	Brian Noble	.10
70	Edgar Bennett	.10
71	Brett Favre	2.00
72	Sterling Sharpe	.55
73	Reggie White	.12
74	Ernest Givins	.10
75	Al Del Greco	.10
76	Chris Dishman	.10
77	Curtis Duncan	.10
78	Webster Slaughter	.10
79	Spencer Tillman	.10
80	Warren Moon	.10
81	Wilber Marshall	.10
82	Haywood Jeffires	.10
83	Lorenzo White	.10
84	Gary Brown	.10
85	Reggie Langhorne	.10
86	Dean Biasucci	.10
87	Steve Emtman	.10
88	Jessie Hester	.10
89	Quentin Coryatt	.10
90	Roosevelt Potts	.10
91	Jeff George	.10
92	Nick Lowery	.10
93	Willie Davis	.10
94	Joe Montana	1.00
95	Neil Smith	.10
96	Marcus Allen	.15
97	Derrick Thomas	.12
98	Greg Townsend	.10
99	Willie Gault	.10
100	Ethan Horton	.10
101	Jeff Hostetler	.10
102	Tim Brown	.12
103	Raghib Ismail	.25
104	Shane Conlan	.10
105	Henry Ellard	.10
106	T.J. Rubley	.15
107	Sean Gilbert	.10
108	Troy Drayton	.20
109	Jerome Bettis	.50
110	Terry Kirby	.15
111	Mark Ingram	.10
112	John Offerdahl	.10
113	Louis Oliver	.10
114	Irving Fryar	.10
115	Dan Marino	2.00
116	Keith Jackson	.10
117	O.J. McDuffie	.40
118	Jim McMahon	.10
119	Sean Salisbury	.10
120	Randell McDaniel	.10
121	Jack Del Rio	.10
122	Cris Carter	.10
123	Chris Doleman	.10
124	John Randle	.10
125	Vincent Brisby	.20
126	Greg McMurtry	.10
127	Drew Bledsoe	1.00
128	Leonard Russell	.10
129	Michael Brooks	.10
130	Mark Jackson	.10
131	Pepper Johnson	.10
132	Doug Riesenberg	.10
133	Phil Simms	.10
134	Rodney Hampton	.35
135	Leonard Marshall	.10
136	Rob Moore	.10
137	Chris Burkett	.10
138	Boomer Esiason	.10
139	Johnny Johnson	.10
140	Ronnie Lott	.10
141	Brad Muster	.10
142	Renaldo Turnbull	.10
143	William Roaf	.20
144	Ricky Jackson	.10
145	Morton Anderson	.10
146	Vaughn Dunbar	.10
147	Wade Wilson	.10
148	Eric Martin	.10
149	Seth Joyner	.10
150	Calvin Williams	.10
151	Vai Sikahema	.10
152	Herschel Walker	.10
153	Eric Allen	.10
154	Fred Barnett	.10
155	Randall Cunningham	.25
156	Steve Beurlein	.10
157	Gary Clark	.10
158	Anthony Edwards	.10
159	Randall Hill	.10
160	Freddie Joe Nunn	.10
161	Garrison Hearst	.50
162	Ricky Proehl	.10
163	Eric Green	.10
164	Levon Kirkland	.10
165	Joel Steed	.10
166	Deon Figures	.15
167	Leroy Thompson	.10
168	Barry Foster	.35
169	Neil O'Donnell	.10
170	Junior Seau	.10
171	Leslie O'Neil	.10
172	Stan Humphries	.10
173	Marion Butts	.10
174	Anthony Miller	.10
175	Natrone Means	.50
176	Odessa Turner	.10
177	Dana Stubblefield	.25
178	John Taylor	.10
179	Ricky Watters	.15
180	Steve Young	1.00
181	Jerry Rice	1.00
182	Tom Rathman	.10
183	Brian Blades	.10
184	Patrick Hunter	.10
185	Rick Mirer	.20
186	Chris Warren	.12
187	Cortez Kennedy	.12
188	Reggie Cobb	.10
189	Craig Erickson	.10
190	Hardy Nickerson	.10
191	Lawrence Dawsey	.10
192	Broderick Thomas	.10
193	Ricky Sanders	.10
194	Carl Banks	.10
195	Ricky Ervins	.10
196	Darrell Green	.10
197	Mark Rypien	.10
198	Desmond Howard	.15
199	Art Monk	.10
200	Reggie Brooks	.10

1994 Collector's Edge Silver

Randomly inserted into packs, this 200-card set was a parallel to the 1994 Edge base set. The card fronts have a silver-foil stamp on the front. The card backs resemble the base card backs.

	NM/M
Complete Set (200):	25.00
Common Player:	.10
Silver Cards:	1X

1994 Collector's Edge Gold

A parallel of the regular Collector's Edge set, the 200-card set features a gold-foil "First Day" logo on the front of the card. The backs resemble the base card backs.

	NM/M
Complete Set (200):	45.00
Common Player:	.15
Gold Cards:	2X

1994 Collector's Edge Pop Warner

This 200-card set was produced as a fund-raiser for Pop Warner football teams. The cards were available from participating dealers and Pop Warner players. Edge printed 1,000 cases of the product. An updated 25-card Boss Rookie chase set, printed on Edge-Glo card stock, was randomly seeded.

	NM/M
Complete Set (200):	25.00
Common Player:	.10
Pop Warner Cards:	1X

1994 Collector's Edge Pop Warner 22K Gold

The 200-card set was a parallel to the Edge Pop Warner base cards. The cards showcase the Pop Warner logo and a gold-foil helmet (with 22K printed under the helmet) on the card fronts.

	NM/M
Complete Set (200):	100.00
Common Player:	.40
Pop Warner 22K Cards:	2X-4X

1994 Collector's Edge Boss Rookies

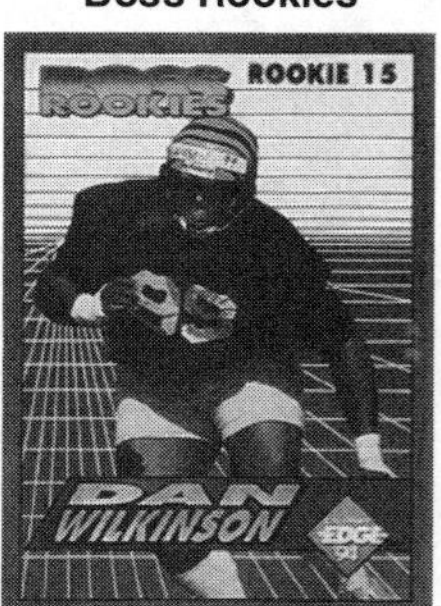

Top rookies are featured on these insert cards, which were randomly included in 1994 Collector's Edge packs. The cards are similar to the format used by the Boss Squad insert cards; "Boss Rookies" is written in the upper left corner and the card number, Rookie 1, etc., is in the upper right corner. The player's name, position and Collector's Edge logo are at the bottom of the card. The back of the card shows a reverse image of the photo on the front.

		NM/M
Complete Set (19):		15.00
Common Player:		.25
Minor Stars:		.50
Inserted 1:2		
1	Isaac Bruce	1.75
2	Jeff Burris	.25
3	Shante Carver	.25
4	Lake Dawson	.50
5	Bert Emanuel	.75
6	William Floyd	.75
7	Wayne Gandy	.25
8	Aaron Glenn	.25
9	Chris Maumalanga	.25
10	David Palmer	.50
11	Errict Rhett	.75

12 Heath Shuler .75
13 DeWayne Washington .25
14 Bryant Young .50
15 Dan Wilkinson .25
16 Rob Frederickson .25
17 Calvin Jones .25
18 James Folston .25
19 Marshall Faulk 4.00

1994 Collector's Edge Boss Rookies Update

Randomly seeded in 1994 Pop Warner packs, this 25-card set was printed on Edge-Glo green plastic. The card fronts feature a purple Pop Warner logo in the upper left corner.

NM/M
Complete Set (25): 12.00
Common Player: .75
Minor Stars: 1.50
Diamond Cards: 2X
Green Cards: 1X
Inserted 1:3 Pop Warner
1 Trent Dilfer 2.00
2 Jeff Burris .75
3 Shante Carver .75
4 Lake Dawson .50
5 Bert Emanuel 1.00
6 Marshall Faulk 4.00
7 William Floyd 1.00
8 Charlie Garner 1.50
9 Rob Fredrickson .75
10 Wayne Gandy .75
11 Aaron Glenn .75
12 Greg Hill .50
13 Isaac Bruce 3.00
14 Charles Johnson .50
15 Johnnie Morton .50
16 Calvin Jones .75
17 Tim Bowens .75
18 David Palmer .75
19 Errict Rhett 1.00
20 Darnay Scott 1.00
21 Heath Shuler .75
22 John Thierry .75
23 Bernard Williams .75
24 Dan Wilkinson .75
25 Bryant Young 1.00
NNO Diamond Exch. Expired 1.50

1994 Collector's Edge Boss Squad Promos

Previewing the 1994 Edge Boss Squad insert, this six-card transparent plastic promo set showcases a cutout photo of a player over a background of lines which make a 3-D effect. The player's name, position and Edge logo are printed inside a stripe near the bottom of the front of the card. The card number is printed on the top right of the card front, prefixed by "Boss." The set was released on two uncut sheets.

NM/M
Complete Set (6): 10.00
Common Player: 1.00
1 Marshall Faulk 4.00
2 Jerome Bettis 2.50
3 Erric Pegram 1.25
4 Sterling Sharpe 1.25
5 Shannon Sharpe 1.25
6 Leonard Russell 1.00

1994 Collector's Edge Boss Squad

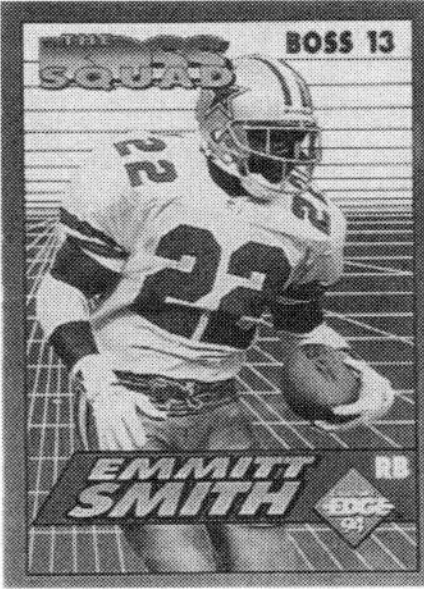

This transparent set features eight top quarterbacks, running backs and receivers for this insert set titled Boss Squad. If the player on the card finished the 1994 season in first or second place in statistics for that position, the card could be redeemed for prizes. Receptions were used for receivers, rushing yards were used for running backs, and quarterback ratings were used for quarterbacks. Cards are numbered with a "Boss" prefix. The card back shows a reversed image of the photo on the front.

NM/M
Complete Set (24): 15.00
Common Player: .50
Minor Stars: 1.00
Inserted 1:2
Silver Cards: 1X
Inserted 1:2 Pop Warner
Bronze EQII Cards: 1X
Gold Helmet Cards: 1X
1 John Elway 2.00
2 Joe Montana 2.50
3 Vinny Testaverde 1.00
4 Boomer Esiason .50
5 Steve Young 1.50
6 Troy Aikman 2.00
7 Phil Simms .50
8 Bobby Hebert .50
9 Thurman Thomas 1.00
10 Leonard Russell .50
11 Chris Warren .50
12 Gary Brown .50
13 Emmitt Smith 3.00
14 Jerome Bettis 1.00
15 Erric Pegram .50
16 Barry Sanders 3.00
17 Reggie Langhorne .50
18 Anthony Miller .50
19 Shannon Sharpe 1.00
20 Tim Brown 1.00
21 Sterling Sharpe 1.00
22 Jerry Rice 2.00
23 Michael Irvin .50
24 Andre Rison .50

1994 Collector's Edge EdgeQuest

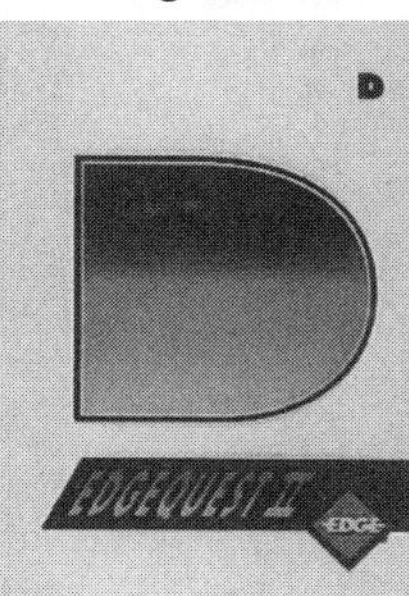

Randomly seeded in packs and offered as a dealer promotion, the nine-card set showcased a letter on the front, with EdgeQuest II printed inside a bar near the bottom of the card. The "Q" card was released in smaller numbers in packs. The cards were redeemable for prizes. Card backs include the rules of the contest. The identical cards with a clear background were inserted into Pop Warner packs.

NM/M
Complete Set (10): 4.00
Comm. Pack Insert (A/B/D/U): .40
Comm. Box Insert (E/G/O/S): .40
Clear Cards: 1X
A Letter A .40
B Letter B .40
D Letter D .40
E Letter E .40
G Letter G .40
O Letter O .40
Q Letter Q (SP)(Expired) 1.00
S Letter S .40
U Letter U .40
WC Clear Star Wild Card 1.00

1994 Collector's Edge FX

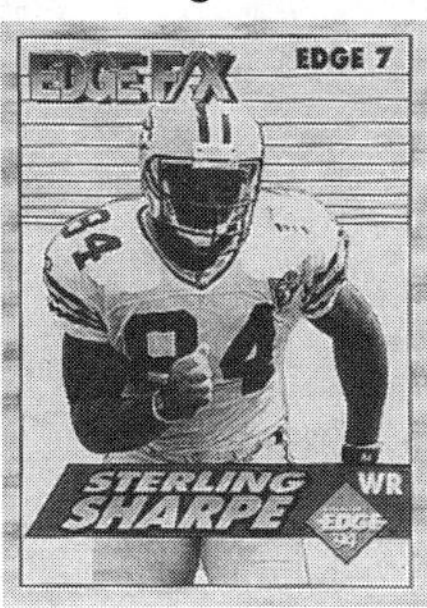

Two versions of these insert cards were made - a regular F/X card and a gold version. Seven top players are featured on these cards, which were random inserts.

NM/M
Complete Set (7): 20.00
Common Player: .75
Minor Stars: 1.50
Inserted 1:7 Gold
Gold Shield Cards: 2X
Inserted 1:200 Gold
White Back Cards: 1X
Inserted 1:7 Retail
Silver Shield Cards: 5X
Inserted 1:200 Retail
Silver Back Cards: .5X
Inserted 1:7 Silver
Gold Back Cards: 3X
Inserted 1:200 Silver
Silver Letter Cards: 1X
Inserted 1:7 Pop Warner
Gold Letter Cards: 2X
Inserted 1:200 Pop Warner
Red Letter Cards: 1X
1 John Elway 5.00
2 Joe Montana 5.00
3 Troy Aikman 4.00
4 Emmitt Smith 6.00
5 Jerome Bettis 1.50
6 Anthony Miller .75
7 Sterling Sharpe 1.50

1994 Collector's Edge Excalibur Elway Promos

This three-card set previewed the 1994 Excalibur set. Each of the cards featured John Elway. The Excalibur logo is printed in silver foil at the top, with his name and position printed in silver foil at the bottom to the right of the Edge logo. The backs have his headshot inside a shield design on the left, which also includes his position and jersey number. The shield in the right corner has his name, the Broncos' logo and card number "of 3" prefixed by "SL." A quote about Elway from Dick Butkus is included above his stats. The card's serial number is printed under the stats.

NM/M
Complete Set (3): 15.00
Common Player: 5.00
1 John Elway 5.00
2 John Elway (Looking to pass) 5.00
3 John Elway (Running with football) 5.00

1994 Excalibur

This 75-card NFL All-Star set involves a medieval theme and features the company's unique plastic cards. Each card front has a full-bleed action photo and silver foil on the front for the player's name and position. The card back has a statement about the player by Hall of Famer Dick Butkus. The set's theme is based on Excalibur, the sword pulled from the stone in the legend of King Arthur. A player mug shot also appears on the card back, along with a medieval shield containing his name. A knight is ghosted in the background. All of the teams in the NFL are represented in the set, except for the Minnesota Vikings. Insert cards randomly included in Excalibur packs are: EdgeQuest cards, Excalibur FX, and Excalibur Knights of the NFL.

NM/M
Complete Set (75): 30.00
Common Player: .25
Minor Stars: .50
Pack (6): 4.00
Wax Box (24): 100.00
1 Bobby Hebert .25
2 Deion Sanders .50
3 Andre Rison .75
4 Cornelius Bennett .25
5 Jim Kelly .75
6 Andre Reed .50
7 Bruce Smith .25
8 Thurman Thomas .75
9 Curtis Conway .50
10 Richard Dent .25
11 Jim Harbaugh .25
12 Troy Aikman 2.50
13 Michael Irvin .75
14 Russell Maryland .25
15 Emmitt Smith 4.00
16 Steve Atwater .25
17 Rod Bernstine .25
18 John Elway 3.00
19 Glyn Milburn .25
20 Shannon Sharpe .75
21 Barry Sanders 3.00
22 Edgar Bennett .25
23 Brett Favre 4.00
24 Sterling Sharpe .75
25 Reggie White .75
26 Warren Moon .50
27 Wilber Marshall .25
28 Haywood Jeffires .25
29 Lorenzo White .25
30 Quentin Coryatt .25
31 Roosevelt Potts .25
32 Jeff George .75
33 Joe Montana 3.00
34 Neil Smith .25
35 Marcus Allen .75
36 Derrick Thomas .50
37 Jeff Hostetler .25
38 Tim Brown .75
39 Raghib Ismail .25
40 Howie Long .25
41 Jerome Bettis 1.00
42 Dan Marino 3.00
43 Keith Jackson .25
44 O.J. McDuffie .50
45 Drew Bledsoe 2.00
46 Leonard Russell .25
47 Wade Wilson .25
48 Eric Martin .25
49 Phil Simms .50
50 Lawrence Taylor .75
51 Rodney Hampton .50
52 Boomer Esiason .50
53 Johnny Johnson .25
54 Ronnie Lott .50
55 Fred Barnett .25
56 Leroy Thompson .25
57 Barry Foster .50
58 Neil O'Donnell .50
59 Stan Humphries .50
60 Marion Butts .25
61 Anthony Miller .25
62 Natrone Means .50
63 Dana Stubblefield .50
64 John Taylor .25
65 Ricky Watters .75
66 Steve Young 2.00
67 Jerry Rice 2.50
68 Tom Rathman .25
69 Rick Mirer .50
70 Chris Warren .50
71 Cortez Kennedy .25
72 Mark Rypien .25
73 Desmond Howard .25
74 Art Monk .50
75 Reggie Brooks .25

1994 Excalibur 22K

These 22K gold cards feature a color photo on the front against a background with a knight in shining armor. A gold sword appears at the top of the card; the player's name and position are at the bottom. The card back has a knight with a sword and shield as a background. The player's name and a team logo are in the forefront. Cards were random inserts in 1994 Collector's Edge foil packs. The set is titled Knights of the NFL.

NM/M
Complete Set (25): 50.00
Common Player: .75
Minor Stars: 1.50
Inserted 1:2
1 Troy Aikman 2.00
2 Michael Irvin 1.00
3 Emmitt Smith 4.00
4 Edgar Bennett .75
5 Brett Favre 4.00
6 Sterling Sharpe 1.00
7 Rodney Hampton .75
8 Jerome Bettis 1.50
9 Jerry Rice 3.00
10 Steve Young 2.00
11 Ricky Watters .75
12 Thurman Thomas .75
13 John Elway 3.00
14 Shannon Sharpe 1.50
15 Joe Montana 4.00
16 Marcus Allen 1.00
17 Tim Brown 1.50
18 Raghib Ismail .75
19 Barry Foster .75
20 Natrone Means .50
21 Rick Mirer .50
22 Dan Marino 4.00
23 AFC Card .75
24 NFC Card .75
25 Excalibur card .75

1994 Collector's Edge Excalibur EdgeQuest

Designed as a contest, this nine-card set was both inserted into packs and provided to dealers as a premium. The card fronts featured a letter and "EdgeQuest" at the bottom. The letter X was inserted in smaller quantities and was issued in both gold-foil and silver-foil versions. The letters C, E, L and U were printed as case promos for dealers. If a collector spelled out "Excalibur" with the cards, they could redeem the cards for a prize. A single card could be exchanged for a promo card. A gold version of "Excalibur" could be redeemed for an uncut sheet of 22K Gold insert cards. The card backs have the rules for the contest.

NM/M
Complete Set (9): 5.00
Common Insert (A/B/I/R) .50
Common Dealer (C/E/L/U) .50
A Letter A .50
B Letter B .50
C Letter C .50
E Letter E .50
I Letter I .50
L Letter L .50
R Letter R .50
U Letter U .50
X Letter X SP Expired 2.00

1994 Excalibur FX

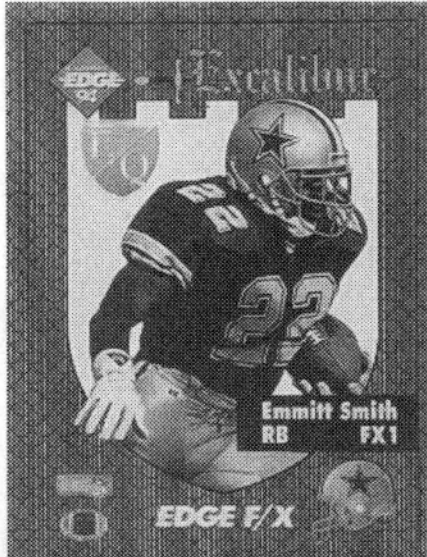

These acetate cards were random inserts in 1994 foil packs. The front has a photo of a player inside a shield. His name, team helmet, position and card number are in the bottom right corner. Cards are numbered on the front using an "FX" prefix. Special gold versions of each card were also made and are generally eight to 10 times more valuable than the regular inserts.

NM/M
Complete Set (7): 30.00
Common Player: 1.00
Minor Stars: 2.00
Inserted 1:7
FX Gold Shield Cards: 4X
Inserted 1:170
EQ Gold Shield Cards: 1X
EQ Silver Shield Cards: 1X
1 Emmitt Smith 10.00
2 Rodney Hampton 1.00
3 Jerome Bettis 2.00
4 Steve Young 1.00
5 Rick Mirer 2.00
6 John Elway 8.00
7 Troy Aikman 7.00

1994 Collector's Edge Excalibur Redemption

These nine EdgeQuest insert redemption cards were randomly included in 1994 Collector's Edge Excalibur packs. Each of the nine cards is numbered using a letter from the word EXCALIBUR, not a number. The object of the game is to get each different letter insert, to spell out Excalibur. Those who obtained all nine cards could redeem them for an F/X subset or uncut press sheet. Individual cards could be redeemed for a Collector's Edge prototype card. The A, B, I, R and X cards were randomly inserted into every ninth foil pack. The C, E, L and U cards were given to dealers who purchased a case of the Excalibur cards.

NM/M
Complete Set (9): 4.50
Common Player: 4.50
1 Dealer promo 4.50
2 Foil Pack Insert 4.50
3 Dealer promo 4.50
4 Foil Pack Insert 4.50
5 Dealer promo 4.50
6 Foil Pack Insert 4.50
7 Foil Pack Insert 4.50
8 Dealer promo 4.50
9 Foil Pack Insert 4.50

1995 Collector's Edge Junior Seau Promos

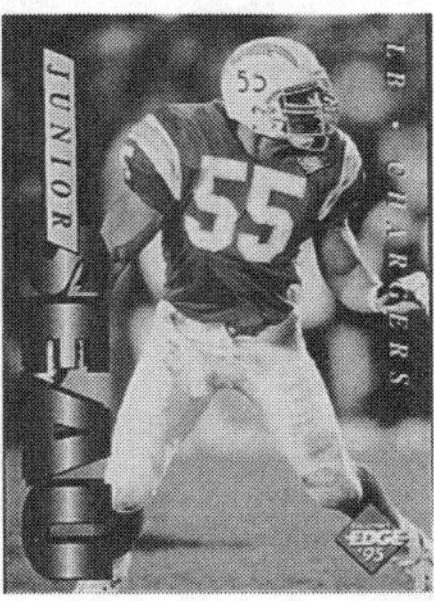

Each card in the five-card set showcased a full-bleed photo of Seau on the front, with his last name running along the left border of the card. "Seau" is printed in large letters, while "Junior" is in a stripe. The card backs feature a head shot, the player's name, team, position, bio and stats. The cards are numbered "/5," with a promo prefix. "Promo '95" is printed in a white stripe along the right side of the card back.

NM/M
Complete Set (5): 5.00
Common Player: 1.00
1 Rookie Season 1990 1.00
2 Second Season 1991 1.00
3 Third Season 1992 1.00
4 Fourth Season 1993 1.00
5 Super Bowl Season 1994 1.00

1995 Collector's Edge

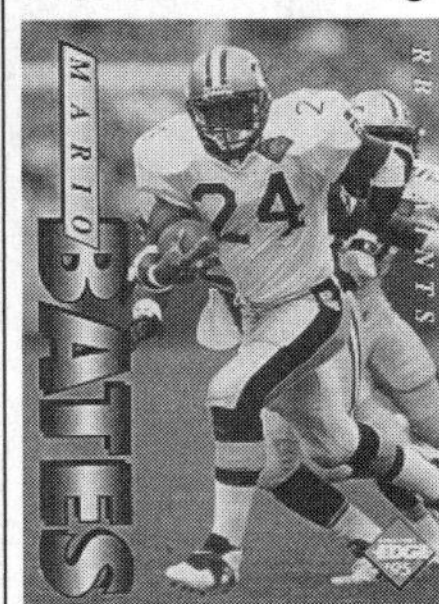

The 1995 Collector's Edge football set is a 200-card retail set, with a Black Label hobby version also issued. The main cards in the set have a full-bleed color photo on the front, with the player's name along the left side and his position and team nickname along the right side. The horizontal back has a mug shot of the player in the upper right corner, and a ghosted image of him with his stats and biographical information superimposed over them. Two parallel sets were also made - a die-cut version (one per every 24 packs) and a gold foil-based set (one per every 20 packs). Insert sets include TimeWarp Matchups, Rookies, EdgeTech, and EdgeQuest 12th Man cards. Retail cards have the same card numbers as the hobby versions, but different photos and designs are used, plus a Black Label logo is foil-stamped into the hobby cards. This set has the same insert sets as the hobby brand does.

NM/M
Complete Set (205): 15.00
Common Player: .10

Minor Stars: .20
Comp. Gold Set (205): 15.00
Gold Cards Equal Value
Comp. Die Cut Set (205): 140.00
Die Cuts: 2X-4X
Comp. Black Label Set (205): 25.00
Black Label Cards: 1X-1.5X
Comp. BL Silv. Die Cut (205): 250.00
Silv. Die Cut Cards: 2X-4X
Comp. BL 22K Gold (205): 2,200
BL 22K Gold Cards: 8X-20X
Comp. EdgeQuest 12th Man (7): 15.00
Common EdgeQuest: 2.50
Hobby Pack (6): 1.25
Hobby Wax Box (36): 40.00
Retail Pack (6): 1.25
Retail Wax Box (24): 30.00
1 Anthony Edwards .10
2 Garrison Hearst .20
3 Seth Joyner .10
4 Dave Krieg .10
5 Chuck Levy .10
6 Rob Moore .10
7 J.J. Birden .10
8 Jeff George .20
9 Craig Heyward .10
10 Norm Johnson .10
11 Terance Mathis .10
12 Eric Metcalf .10
13 Chuck Smith .10
14 Darryl Talley .10
15 Cornelius Bennett .10
16 Steve Christie .10
17 Kenneth Davis .10
18 Phil Hansen .10
19 Jim Kelly .20
20 Bryce Paup .10
21 Andre Reed .10
22 Bruce Smith .10
23 Eric Ball .10
24 Don Beebe .10
25 Mark Carrier .10
26 Tim McKyer .10
27 Pete Metzelaars .10
28 Sam Mills .10
29 Jack Trudeau .10
30 Mark Carrier .10
31 Curtis Conway .10
32 Eric Kramer .10
33 Lewis Tillman .10
34 Michael Timpson .10
35 Steve Walsh .10
36 Chris Zorich .10
37 *Jeff Blake* .50
38 Harold Green .10
39 David Klinger .10
40 Carl Pickens .20
41 Tom Waddle .10
42 Dan Wilkinson .10
43 Leroy Hoard .10
44 Michael Jackson .10
45 Antonio Langham .10
46 Andre Rison .20
47 Vinny Testaverde .10
48 Eric Turner .10
49 Tommy Vardell .10
50 Troy Aikman .75
51 Charles Haley .10
52 Michael Irvin .25
53 Daryl Johnston .10
54 Leon Lett .10
55 Jay Novacek .10
56 Emmitt Smith 1.50
57 Kevin Williams .10
58 Steve Atwater .10
59 John Elway .30
60 Simon Fletcher .10
61 Glyn Milburn .10
62 Anthony Miller .10
63 Leonard Russell .10
64 Shannon Sharpe .10
65 Scott Mitchell .10
66 Herman Moore .20
67 Johnnie Morton .10
68 Brett Perriman .10
69 Barry Sanders 1.25
70 Edgar Bennett .10
71 Brett Favre 1.50
72 Mark Ingram .10
73 Chris Jacke .10
74 Guy McIntyre .10
75 Reggie White .20
76 Gary Brown .10
77 Ernest Givins .10
78 Mel Gray .10
79 Haywood Jeffires .10
80 Webster Slaughter .10
81 Craig Erickson .10
82 Marshall Faulk 1.00
83 Jim Harbaugh .10
84 Roosevelt Potts .10
85 Floyd Turner .10
86 Steve Beuerlein .10
87 Reggie Cobb .10
88 Jeff Lageman .10
89 Mazio Royster .10
90 Marcus Allen .20
91 Steve Bono .20
92 Willie Davis .10
93 Lake Dawson .25
94 Ronnie Lott .10
95 Eric Martin .10
96 Chris Penn .10
97 Tim Brown .20
98 Derrick Fenner .10
99 Rob Fredrickson .10
100 Nolan Harrison .10
101 Jeff Hostetler .10
102 Raghib Ismail .10
103 James Jett .10
104 Chester McGlockton .10
105 Anthony Smith .10
106 Harvey Williams .10
107 Jerome Bettis .25
108 Troy Drayton .10
109 Chris Miller .10
110 Robert Young .10
111 Keith Byars .10
112 Gary Clark .10
113 Bryan Cox .10
114 Jeff Cross .10
115 Irving Fryar .10
116 Randall Hill .10
117 Terry Kirby .10
118 Dan Marino 1.50
119 O.J. McDuffie .10
120 Bernie Parmalee .25
121 Terry Allen .10
122 Cris Carter .20
123 Qadry Ismail .10
124 Warren Moon .25
125 John Randle .10
126 Jake Reed .10
127 Fuad Reveiz .10
128 Broderick Thomas .10
129 Drew Bledsoe 1.00
130 Vincent Brisby .10
131 Ben Coates .10
132 David Meggett .10
133 Chris Slade .10
134 Leroy Thompson .10
135 Eric Allen .10
136 Mario Bates .30
137 Quinn Early .10
138 Jim Everett .10
139 Michael Haynes .10
140 Torrance Small .10
141 Dave Brown .10
142 Chris Calloway .10
143 Keith Hamilton .10
144 Rodney Hampton .10
145 Mike Sherrard .10
146 David Treadwell .10
147 Herschel Walker .10
148 Boomer Esiason .10
149 Erik Howard .10
150 Johnny Johnson .10
151 Mo Lewis .10
152 Johnny Mitchell .10
153 Fred Barnett .10
154 Randall Cunningham .20
155 William Fuller .10
156 Charlie Garner .10
157 Greg Jackson .10
158 Ricky Watters .20
159 Calvin Williams .10
160 Barry Foster .10
161 Kevin Greene .10
162 Greg Lloyd .10
163 Bam Morris .40
164 Neil O'Donnell .10
165 Erric Pegram .10
166 John L. Williams .10
167 Rod Woodson .10
168 John Carney .10
169 Stan Humphries .20
170 Natrone Means .40
171 Chris Mims .10
172 Leslie O'Neal .10
173 Alfred Pupunu .20
174 Junior Seau .20
175 Mark Seay .10
176 William Floyd .40
177 Jerry Rice .75
178 Deion Sanders .40
179 Dana Stubblefield .10
180 John Taylor .10
181 Steve Young .50
182 Bryant Young .10
183 Brian Blades .10
184 Cortez Kennedy .10
185 Kelvin Martin .10
186 Rick Mirer .30
187 Ricky Proehl .10
188 Michael Sinclair .10
189 Chris Warren .10
190 Trent Dilfer .40
191 Alvin Harper .10
192 Jackie Harris .10
193 Hardy Nickerson .10
194 Errict Rhett .75
195 Reggie Roby .10
196 Henry Ellard .10
197 Ricky Ervins .10
198 Darrell Green .10
199 Brian Mitchell .10
200 Heath Shuler .50

1995 Collector's Edge Die Cuts

These 205 die-cut cards were a parallel to the base cards in the regular set. The top of each card was die-cut. The Edge logo is printed in silver foil on card fronts.

NM/M
Common Player: .30
Die Cut Cards: 2X-4X

1995 Collector's Edge Gold Logo

Randomly inserted into hobby and retail packs, the 205-card set was a parallel to the base cards. The card fronts each showcase a gold-foil Edge logo at the bottom right.

NM/M
Complete Set (205): 18.00
Common Player: .05
Gold Cards: 1X

1995 Collector's Edge 22K Gold

Randomly inserted into retail packs, the 205-card set was a parallel to the base set. Each card front has a gold-foil 22K logo on it.

NM/M
Common Player: 3.00
22K Gold Cards: 10X-30X

1995 Collector's Edge EdgeTech

This insert set features 36 of the premier players in the game on cards with a prismatic background. Cards came in four versions - 22k Gold and Circular Prisms (in Edge packs) and Quantum and Die-Cuts (in Black Label packs).

NM/M
Complete Set (36): 35.00
Common Player: .50
Black Label Same Price
Comp. 22K Gold Set (36):
22K Gold Cards: 1X-3X
Comp. Quantum Set (36):
Quantum Cards: 2X-4X
Comp. Quantum Die Cut (36):
Quantum Die Cuts: 3X-5X
Comp. Circular Prisms (36):
Circular Prisms: Half Value
1 Dan Marino 6.00
2 Steve Young 4.00
3 Rick Mirer .50
4 Emmitt Smith 6.00
5 John Elway 4.00
6 Neil O'Donnell .50
7 Marshall Faulk 3.00
8 Deion Sanders 2.00
9 Terance Mathis .50
10 Kevin Greene .50
11 Ricky Watters 2.00
12 Tim Brown 1.50
13 Antonio Langham .50
14 Lake Dawson .50
15 Jay Novacek 1.00
16 Herman Moore 1.00
17 Mark Seay .50
18 Bernie Parmalee .50
19 Drew Bledsoe 3.00
20 Troy Aikman 4.00
21 Brett Favre 6.00
22 Jerry Rice 4.00
23 Barry Sanders 6.00
24 Heath Shuler .50
25 Errict Rhett .50
26 Cris Carter 1.00
27 Jerome Bettis 2.00
28 Reggie White 2.00
29 Chris Warren .50
30 Ben Coates 1.00
31 Bryant Young .50
32 Mel Gray 1.00
33 Darryl Talley .50
34 Mike Sherrard .50
35 William Floyd 1.00
36 Alvin Harper .75

1995 Collector's Edge Rookies

These 1995 Collector's Edge inserts come in three versions - two in the retail packs, including a gold version, and one in the hobby Black Label packs. The cards feature 25 of the top 1995 NFL draft picks. The front has a photo of the player in his college uniform, along with a set logo in the upper right corner. The horizontal card back has a closeup shot of the player, biographical information, and a synopsis of the player's selection in the draft.

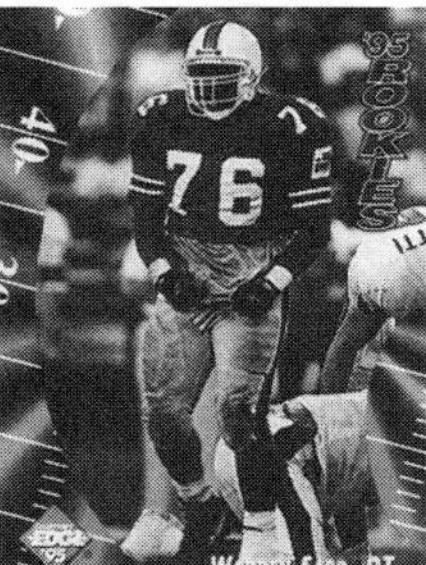

NM/M
Complete Set (24): 15.00
Common Player: .50
Minor Stars: 1.00
22K Gold Cards: 2X-4X
Black Label Same Price
1 Derrick Alexander .50
2 Tony Boselli 1.00
3 Ki-Jana Carter 1.00
4 Kevin Carter .50
5 Kerry Collins 3.00
6 Steve McNair 4.00
7 Billy Milner .50
8 Rashaan Salaam .75
9 Warren Sapp 1.00
10 James Stewart .50
11 J.J. Stokes 1.00
12 Bobby Taylor .50
13 Tyrone Wheatley .50
14 Derrick Brooks .50
15 Reuben Brown .50
16 Mark Bruener .50
17 Joey Galloway 1.00
18 Napolean Kaufman .50
19 Ty Law .50
20 Craig Newsome .50
21 Kordell Stewart 2.00
22 Korey Stringer .50
23 Zach Weigert .50
24 Michael Westbrook .75

1995 Collector's Edge TimeWarp

These 1995 Collector's Edge inserts feature one star from today matched up against a former NFL star in game action, through the magic of computers. Three versions were made - two for Edge retail packs, including a gold version, and one for the hobby Black Label packs. Card fronts have a TimeWarp logo in the upper right corner, and show the two players competing against each other. The card back has mug shots of each player, with biographical information underneath. A quote from Hall of Fame linebacker Dick Butkus, the company's spokesman, is also given regarding the matchup.

NM/M
Complete Set (20): 40.00
Common Player: 2.50
Minor Stars: 5.00
22K Gold Cards: 2X-4X
Black Label Same Price
1 Emmitt Smith, Dick Butkus 8.00
2 Troy Aikman, Gino Marchetti 6.00
3 Natrone Means, Ray Nitschke 2.00
4 Chris Zorich, Steve Van Buren 1.00
5 Barry Sanders, Deacon Jones 6.00
6 Kevin Greene, Paul Hornung 2.50
7 Charles Haley, Len Dawson 2.00
8 Marshall Faulk, Willie Lanier 4.00
9 Ronnie Lott, Gale Sayers 4.00
10 Cris Carter, Jack Ham 2.00
11 Junior Seau, Gale Sayers 2.50
12 Reggie White, Otto Graham 2.50
13 Leslie O'Neil, Y.A. Tittle 1.00
14 Drew Bledsoe, Ted Hendricks 5.00
15 Heath Shuler, Bob Lilly 2.00
16 Ricky Watters, Daryle Lamonica 1.00
17 Marshall Faulk, Dick Butkus 5.00
18 Deion Sanders, Raymond Berry 3.00
19 Steve Young, Jack Youngblood 4.00
20 Bruce Smith, Sammy Baugh 2.00
NNO Checklist 1.00
TW1 Gale Sayers, Junior Seau, Dick Butkus 2.00

1995 Collector's Edge TimeWarp Jumbos

Measuring 8 x 10 inches, the 42-card set has full-bleed photos on the front, with Time Warp in the upper right. The Time Warp logo also is in the lower right, with an Edge logo in the lower left. The cards resemble the regular sized Time Warp cards which were inserted into 1995 Collector's Edge. The backs have headshots of each featured player, along with the Time Warp logo, at the top. Each player's bio appears under the photo. A Dick Butkus quote appears in the lower center of the back. Overall, 5,000 of each card were issued and given to hobby dealers. Signed editions of each card were produced and autographed by a Hall of Famer. The cards were also offered through a 1996 Edge retail pack mail-in offer for $3.95 each with 12 wrappers.

NM/M
Common Player: 2.00
1 Dick Butkus, Emmitt Smith 10.00
2 Dick Butkus, Emmitt Smith 10.00
3 Gino Marchetti, Troy Aikman 6.00
4 Gino Marchetti, Troy Aikman 6.00
5 Ray Nitschke, Natrone Means 4.00
6 Ray Nitschke, Natrone Means 4.00
7 Steve Van Buren, Chris Zorich 2.00
8 Steve Van Buren, Chris Zorich 2.00
9 Deacon Jones, Barry Sanders 8.00
10 Deacon Jones, Barry Sanders 8.00
11 Paul Hornung, Kevin Greene 3.00
12 Paul Hornung, Kevin Greene 3.00
13 Len Dawson, Charles Haley 2.00
14 Len Dawson, Charles Haley 2.00
15 Willie Lanier, Marshall Faulk 6.00
16 Willie Lanier, Marshall Faulk 6.00
17 Gale Sayers, Ronnie Lott 6.00
18 Gale Sayers, Ronnie Lott 6.00
19 Jack Ham, Cris Carter 2.00
20 Jack Ham, Cris Carter 2.00
21 Gale Sayers, Junior Seau 6.00
22 Gale Sayers, Junior Seau 6.00
23 Otto Graham, Reggie White 4.00
24 Otto Graham, Reggie White 4.00
25 Y.A. Tittle, Leslie O'Neal 3.00
26 Y.A. Tittle, Leslie O'Neal 3.00
27 Daryle Lamonica, Ricky Watters 2.00
28 Daryle Lamonica, Ricky Watters 2.00
29 Dick Butkus, Marshall Faulk 6.00
30 Dick Butkus, Marshall Faulk 6.00
31 Raymond Berry, Deion Sanders 6.00
32 Raymond Berry, Deion Sanders 6.00
33 Jack Youngblood, Steve Young 4.00
34 Jack Youngblood, Steve Young 4.00
35 Sammy Baugh, Bruce Smith 3.00
36 Sammy Baugh, Bruce Smith 3.00
37 Ted Hendricks, Dan Marino 10.00
38 Bob Lilly, Dan Marino 10.00
39 Ted Hendricks, Drew Bledsoe 5.00
40 Bob Lilly, Heath Shuler 2.00
41 Dick Butkus, Jeff Blake 3.00
42 Dick Butkus, Michael Westbrook 3.00

1995 Collector's Edge TimeWarp Sunday Ticket

Offered for $19.95 per set through a mail order offer, the five-card set had a full-bleed photo on the front, with the Edge logo in the upper left and NFL Sunday Ticket logo in the lower right. The card backs resemble the Time Warp Jumbo backs, except the background has a prism effect. Overall, 2,500 sets were produced.

NM/M
Complete Set (5): 15.00
Common Player: 2.00
1 Paul Hornung, Chris Zorich 2.00
2 Gale Sayers, Kevin Greene 2.00
3 Ted Hendricks, Ricky Watters 3.00
4 Sammy Baugh, Bruce Smith 3.00
5 Dick Butkus, Marshall Faulk 7.00

1995 Collector's Edge 12th Man Redemption

This redemption set was available through 1995 Black Label and retail version packs. If a collector compiled all the cards which spelled "12th Man," they could exchange them plus $19.95 for this complete 25-card set. The cards carry a 1996 copyright date, but are part of the 1995 set. The card fronts feature a cutout photo of the player over a multi-colored background, with "12th Man" printed at the top of the card. The card backs include a headshot, player name, bio and highlight. The card number is printed in the upper right.

NM/M
Complete Set (25): 15.00
Common Player: .30
Comp. Letters Set (7): 2.50
1 Dan Marino 4.00
2 Jeff Blake .50
3 Steve Bono .50
4 Brett Favre 4.00
5 Steve Young 3.00
6 Scott Mitchell .50
7 Chris Warren .50
8 Marshall Faulk 2.00
9 Byron "Bam" Morris .30
10 Emmitt Smith 4.00
11 Barry Sanders 4.00
12 Rashaan Salaam .50
13 Carl Pickens .50
14 Anthony Miller .30
15 Tim Brown 1.00
16 Jerry Rice 3.00
17 Herman Moore .50
18 Isaac Bruce 1.00
19 Ben Coates .50
20 Shannon Sharpe 1.00
21 Alfred Pupunu .30
22 Jackie Harris .30
23 Jay Novacek .30
24 Brent Jones .30
25 Checklist .30

1995 Collector's Edge Black Label

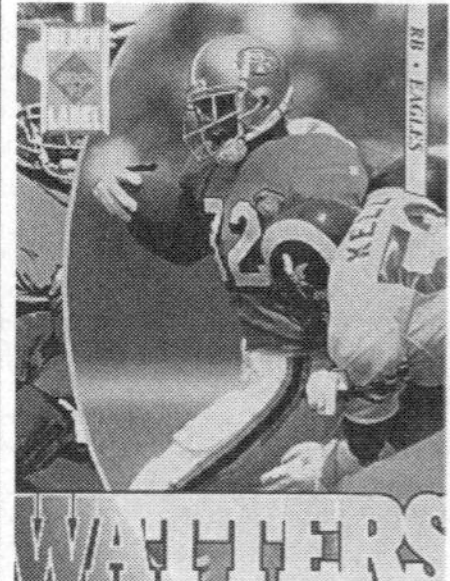

This was the hobby version of the Collector's Edge set. The 205-card set was sold in six-card packs. The card fronts spotlight a full-bleed photo, with the player's last name at the bottom. The Black Label logo is printed in the top left. Showcased on the horizontal card backs are the player's headshot and an action photo in the background. The player's bio and stats are on the back, too.

	NM/M
Complete Set (205):	25.00
Common Player:	.05
Black Label Cards:	1X
Pack (6):	1.00
Wax Box (36):	30.00

1995 Collector's Edge Black Label 22K Gold

This parallel of the base set featured the Black Label logo in gold foil, along with a 22K logo, on the front of each card in the 205-card set.

	NM/M
Common Player:	3.00
BL 22K Gold Cards:	8X-20X

1995 Collector's Edge Black Label Silver Die Cuts

Randomly seeded one per 24 packs, the 205-card set was a parallel of the base set. Each front showcased a Black Label logo in silver foil. The top of each card was die-cut.

	NM/M
Common Player:	.50
Silver Die Cuts:	3X-5X

1995 Excalibur

1995 Collector's Edge Excalibur was issued in two 75-card series - I, called the Sword, and II, called the Stone. The regular cards have a full-bleed color action photo on the front, with a Collector's Edge logo in the upper left corner. The player's name is in silver foil along the right side of the card, with a silver-foiled sword next to it. The card back indicates at the top which series the card is from and includes a mug shot of the player. Each player is addressed as "Sir" and has his statistics from 1991-1994 listed, along with a team logo. Each card was also reprinted in a die-cut version resembling a castle (one in every nine packs). Insert sets in both series include Rookie Roundtable and Knights of the NFL. Sword Challengers Draft Day Redemption cards were exclusive to Series I packs, while DragonSlayers could be found only in Series II packs. EdgeTech cards in Series I were continued in Series II, but were called TekTech and had a different design. "Stone" and "Sword" game cards were also randomly included in their respective series' packs.

		NM/M
Comp. Series 1 (75):		15.00
Comp. Series 2 (75):		15.00
Common Player:		.20
Minor Stars:		.40
Die Cut Cards:		1X-3X
Inserted 1:9		
Series 1 Pack (7):		2.00
Series 1 Wax Box (36):		50.00
Series 2 Pack (7):		2.00
Series 2 Wax Box (36):		50.00
1	Gary Clark	.20
2	Randall Hill	.20
3	Anthony Edwards	.20
4	Terrance Mathis	.40
5	Erric Pegram	.40
6	Jeff George	.40
7	Pete Metzelaars	.20
8	Jim Kelly	.40
9	Andre Reed	.20
10	Lewis Tillman	.20
11	Curtis Conway	.50
12	Steve Walsh	.20
13	Derrick Fenner	.20
14	Harold Green	.20
15	Michael Jackson	.20
16	Eric Metcalf	.20
17	Antonio Langham	.20
18	Troy Aikman	2.00
19	Alvin Harper	.40
20	Jay Novacek	.20
21	John Elway	3.00
22	Glyn Milburn	.20
23	Steve Atwater	.20
24	Mel Gray	.20
25	Herman Moore	.75
26	Scott Mitchell	.40
27	Guy McIntyre	.20
28	Edgar Bennett	.20
29	Sterling Sharpe	.40
30	Gary Brown	.20
31	Haywood Jeffires	.20
32	Marshall Faulk	.75
33	Roosevelt Potts	.20
34	Marcus Allen	.40
35	Willie Davis	.20
36	Lake Dawson	.75
37	Jeff Hostetler	.20
38	Raghib Ismail	.20
39	Troy Drayton	.20
40	Jerome Bettis	.75
41	Dan Marino	4.00
42	Mark Ingram	.20
43	O.J. McDuffie	.20
44	Warren Moon	.40
45	Qadry Ismail	.20
46	Jake Reed	.20
47	Ben Coates	.20
48	Vincent Brisby	.20
49	Michael Timpson	.20
50	Brad Daluiso	.20
51	Rodney Hampton	.20
52	Chris Calloway	.20
53	Rob Moore	.20
54	Boomer Esiason	.20
55	Michael Haynes	.20
56	Vaughn Dunbar	.20
57	Calvin Williams	.20
58	Herschel Walker	.20
59	Charlie Garner	.20
60	Neil O'Donnell	.40
61	Deon Figures	.20
62	Bam Morris	1.50
63	Junior Seau	.40
64	Leslie O'Neil	.20
65	Natrone Means	.50
66	Jerry Rice	2.00
67	Deion Sanders	.50
68	William Floyd	.50
69	Chris Warren	.40
70	Cortez Kennedy	.20
71	Hardy Nickerson	.20
72	Craig Erickson	.20
73	Heath Shuler	.50
74	Reggie Brooks	.20
75	Henry Ellard	.20
76	Garrison Hearst	.20
77	Steve Beuerlein	.20
78	Seth Joyner	.20
79	Andre Rison	.20
80	Norm Johnson	.20
81	Craig Hayword	.20
82	Thurman Thomas	.40
83	Kenny Davis	.20
84	Bruce Smith	.20
85	Tom Waddle	.20
86	Erik Kramer	.20
87	Alonzo Spellman	.20
88	Dan Wilkinson	.20
89	*Jeff Blake*	.50
90	Vinny Testaverde	.20
91	Tommy Vardell	.20
92	Mark Carrier	.20
93	Emmitt Smith	3.00
94	Michael Irvin	.75
95	Daryl Johnston	.20
96	Shannon Sharpe	.20
97	Anthony Miller	.20
98	Leonard Russell	.20
99	Barry Sanders	3.00
100	Brett Perriman	.40
101	Johnnie Morton	.20
102	Brett Favre	3.00
103	Bryce Paup	.40
104	Jackie Harris	.20
105	Ernest Givins	.20
106	Webster Slaughter	.20
107	Jim Harbaugh	.40
108	Joe Montana	3.00
109	J.J. Birden	.20
110	Tim Burnett	.20
111	James Jett	.20
112	Tim Brown	.40
113	Rob Fredrickson	.20
114	Chris Miller	.20
115	Bernie Parmalee	.50
116	Terry Kirby	.20
117	Keith Jackson	.20
118	Irving Fryer	.20
119	Terry Allen	.20
120	Cris Carter	.40
121	Fuad Reveiz	.20
122	Drew Bledsoe	2.00
123	Greg McMurtry	.20
124	Dave Brown	.20
125	David Meggett	.20
126	Johnnie Johnson	.20
127	Ronnie Lott	.20
128	Johnny Mitchell	.20
129	Eric Martin	.20
130	Jim Everett	.20
131	Randall Cunningham	.20
132	Fred Barnett	.20
133	Eric Allen	.20
134	Barry Foster	.20
135	Kevin Greene	.20
136	Eric Green	.20
137	Stan Humphries	.40
138	Mark Seay	.20
139	*Alfred Pupunu*	.50
140	Steve Young	2.00
141	John Taylor	.20
142	Ricky Watters	.50
143	Brian Blades	.20
144	Rick Mirer	.75
145	Cortez Kennedy	.20
146	Errict Rhett	.50
147	Trent Dilfer	.75
148	Brian Mitchell	.20
149	Ricky Ervins	.20
150	Desmond Howard	.20

1995 Excalibur Die Cuts

This 150-card set paralleled the base Excalibur set, and was inserted in packs at a rate of one per nine. Similar to the Excalibur set in 1995, this die-cut set was issued in two, 75-card series.

	NM/M
Common Sword Card (1-75):	3.00
Common Stone Card (76-150):	3.00
Die Cuts:	1X-3X

1995 Excalibur 22K Gold

This 22K Knights of the NFL insert set was issued in two 25-card subsets; cards 1-25 were randomly included one per every 35 packs of Excalibur Series I product, while #s 26-50 were in Excalibur Series II packs at the same ratio. In addition to the regular versions, there were also limited editions of each card created in a prism format. The card front has "Excalibur 22K" stamped in gold foil at the top, with a colorful swirly-patterned background. The card back has a shield with the player's name and team logo in it, also against a background of a knight holding a football.

		NM/M
Common Player:		2.00
Prism Cards:		2X-3X
1	Steve Young	8.00
2	Barry Sanders	15.00
3	John Elway	12.00
4	Warren Moon	2.00
5	Chris Warren	2.00
6	Jim Kelly	6.00
7	Troy Aikman	12.00
8	Jerome Bettis	4.00
9	Marcus Allen	4.00
10	William Floyd	2.00
11	Terance Mathis	2.00
12	Antonio Langham	2.00
13	Sterling Sharpe	6.00
14	Leonard Russell	2.00
15	Drew Bledsoe	12.00
16	Rodney Hampton	2.00
17	Herschel Walker	2.00
18	Jim Everett	2.00
19	Eric Allen	2.00
20	Junior Seau	6.00
21	Natrone Means	4.00
22	Deion Sanders	6.00
23	Charlie Garner	2.00
24	Marshall Faulk	12.00
25	Ben Coates	2.00
26	Emmitt Smith	20.00
27	Jerry Rice	15.00
28	Stan Humphries	2.00
29	Joe Montana	20.00
30	Thurman Thomas	5.00
31	Eric Metcalf	2.00
32	Jay Novacek	2.00
33	Brett Favre	25.00
34	Dan Marino	25.00
35	Bam Morris	4.00
36	Heath Shuler	2.00
37	Trent Dilfer	6.00
38	Errict Rhett	4.00
39	Herman Moore	4.00
40	Terry Allen	2.00
41	Cris Carter	6.00
42	Ronnie Lott	2.00
43	Randall Cunningham	2.00
44	Barry Foster	2.00
45	John Taylor	2.00
46	Rick Mirer	2.00
47	Jerry Rice	15.00
48	Michael Irvin	5.00
49	Ricky Watters	4.00
50	Andre Rison	2.00

1995 Excalibur Challengers Draft Day Rookie Redemption

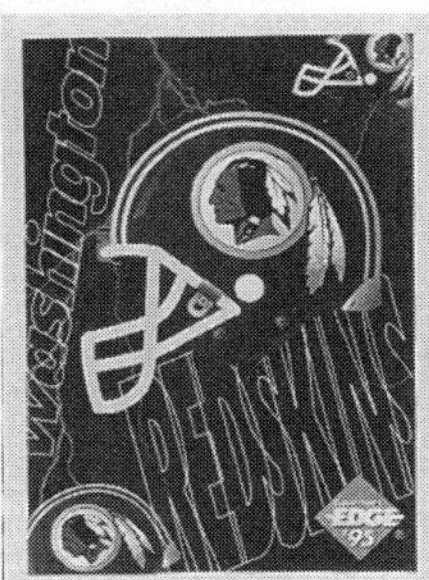

Each of these 1995 Collector's Edge Excalibur Series I Sword inserts could be exchanged for a card of its respective team's top draft choice. Cards were seeded one per every four Series I packs. The front shows the team's helmet three times; a larger one dominates the center of the card, while smaller ones appear in the upper right and lower left corners. The team name is printed into the background, too. The card back states the rules of the redemption program.

		NM/M
Complete Set (31):		20.00
Common Player:		.40
Minor Stars:		1.00
Gold Cards:		2X
1	Derrick Alexander	.40
2	Tony Boselli	.50
3	Kyle Brady	.40
4	Mark Bruener	.40
5	Jamie Brown	.40
6	Ruben Brown	.40
7	Devin Bush	.40
8	Kevin Carter	.40
9	Ki-Jana Carter	1.00
10	Kerry Collins	3.00
11	Kordell Stewart	4.00
12	Mark Fields	.40
13	Joey Galloway	3.00
14	Trezelle Jenkins	.40
15	Ellis Johnson	.40
16	Napoleon Kaufman	1.00
17	Ty Law	1.00
18	Mike Mamula	.40
19	Steve McNair	4.00
20	Billy Milner	.40
21	Craig Newsome	.40
22	Craig Powell	.40
23	Rashaan Salaam	.40
24	Frank Sanders	1.00
25	Warren Sapp	2.00
26	Terrance Shaw	.40
27	J.J. Stokes	2.00
28	Michael Westbrook	1.00
29	Tyrone Wheatley	1.00
30	Sherman Williams	.50
31	Cover Card	.40

1995 Excalibur Dragon Slayers

These 1995 Collector's Edge Excalibur Series II inserts were made by members of the art departments of hobby price guide editors, so each card has a different design. Fourteen players were spotlighted on the cards, which were random inserts one per every 12 packs.

		NM/M
Complete Set (14):		25.00
Common Player:		.75
Minor Stars:		1.50
1	Troy Aikman	2.00
2	Jerome Bettis	1.50
3	Ricky Watters	1.50
4	Barry Sanders	6.00
5	Emmitt Smith	8.00
6	Marshall Faulk	4.00
7	Drew Bledsoe	4.00
8	Errict Rhett	1.50
9	Joe Montana	5.00
10	Junior Seau	2.00
11	Deion Sanders	1.50
12	Bam Morris	.75
13	Jerry Rice	4.00
14	Natrone Means	1.00

1995 Excalibur EdgeQuest

Designed as an insert and a dealer promotion, the set was printed on clear acetate. The fronts have a large letter and EdgeQuest at the bottom. Collectors who spelled "Sword" or "Stone" with the cards could redeem them for prizes. The D, R and W cards were in Sword packs. The E, N and T cards were in Stone packs. The S and O cards were given to hobby dealers. "Sword" cards could be exchanged for a Rookie Roundtable set, while "Stone" cards could be exchanged for a Challengers Rookie set.

		NM/M
Complete Set (9):		5.00
Common Box Insert (O/S):		.40
Common Sword Insert (D/R/W):		.40
Common Stone Insert (E/N/T):		.40
1	Letter D	.40
2	Letter E	.40
3	Letter N	.40
4	Letter T	.40
5	Letter O	.40
6	Letter R	.40
7	Letter S	.40
8	Letter W	.40
9	Ampersand	1.50

1995 Excalibur EdgeTech

These 1995 Collector's Edge Excalibur Series I inserts were the rarest, seeded one per every 75 packs. The cards are continued as a TekTech series in Excalibur Series II packs, starting with #13, but the designs remain different.

		NM/M
Complete Set (12):		100.00
Common Player:		3.00
Minor Stars:		5.00
1	Emmitt Smith	25.00
2	Errict Rhett	5.00
3	Steve Young	15.00
4	Jerry Rice	20.00
5	Ben Coates	3.00
6	Marcus Allen	5.00
7	John Elway	20.00
8	Keith Jackson	3.00
9	Garrison Hearst	5.00
10	Natrone Means	5.00
11	Michael Haynes	3.00
12	Bam Morris	5.00

A player's name in *italic* type indicates a rookie card.

1995 Excalibur Rookie Roundtable

These 25 inserts, featuring the top sophomores heading into the 1995 season, were issued in both 1995 Collector's Edge Excalibur series packs. Cards 1-13 were seeded one per every nine packs in Series I; cards 14-25 were in every ninth Series II pack. The card front has the Rookie Roundtable banner stamped in silver foil in the upper left corner; the player's name is along the bottom. The card back has a mug shot of the player, with biographical information beside it, plus his 1994 statistics and a quote from Hall of Fame linebacker Dick Butkus, the company's spokesman. The player's team helmet is in the upper right corner.

		NM/M
Complete Set (25):		15.00
Comp. Series 1 (13):		8.00
Comp. Series 2 (12):		15.00
Common Player:		.75
1	Sam Adams	.75
2	Joe Johnson	.75
3	Tim Bowens	.75
4	Bryant Young	.75
5	Aubrey Beavers	.75
6	Willie McGinnest	.75
7	Rob Fredrickson	.75
8	Lee Woodall	.75
9	Antonio Langham	.75
10	DeWayne Washington	.75
11	Darryl Morrison	.75
12	Keith Lyle	.75
13	Antonio Langham	.75
14	Darnay Scott	1.00
15	Derrick Alexander	.75
16	Todd Steussie	.75
17	Larry Allen	.75
18	Anthony Redmon	.75
19	Joe Panos	.75
20	Kevin Mawae	.75
21	Andrew Jordan	.75
22	Heath Shuler	1.00
23	Marshall Faulk	4.00
24	Errict Rhett	1.00
25	Marshall Faulk	8.00

1995 Excalibur TekTech

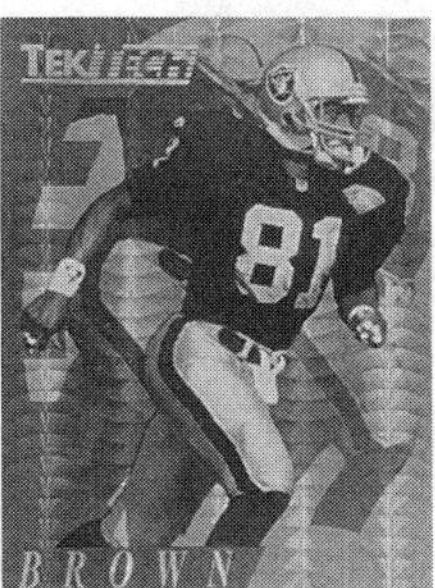

Like the Series I inserts, these cards were seeded one per 75 packs of 1995 Collector's Edge Excalibur Series II packs. The cards pick up where the first series left off, at #13, but have different designs from that series. The card front has a prism-like background, which contains ghosted images of the player in the background. The back has a mug shot of the player, with his name running down the left side of the card. Brief biographical information is underneath the photo.

		NM/M
Complete Set (12):		50.00
Common Player:		1.00
Minor Stars:		2.00
1	Ricky Watters	2.00
2	Rick Mirer	1.00
3	Drew Bledsoe	8.00

4	Barry Sanders	20.00
5	Junior Seau	1.00
6	Dan Marino	25.00
7	Edgar Bennett	1.00
8	Haywood Jeffires	1.00
9	Deion Sanders	3.00
10	Tim Brown	1.00
11	Jerome Bettis	3.00
12	Marshall Faulk	5.00

1995 Collector's Edge Instant Replay

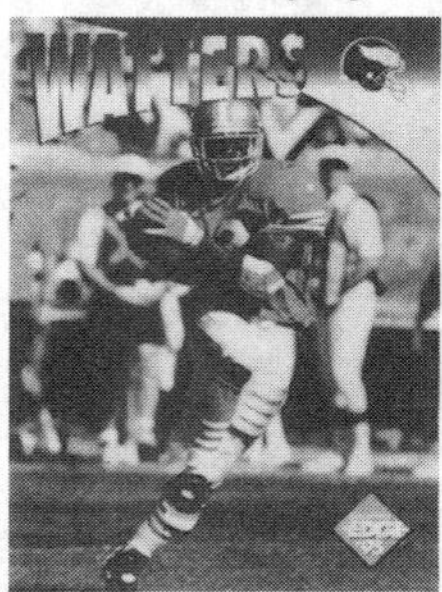

The 51-card set showcased the player's last name and team helmet at the top of the card fronts. The Edge logo is in the lower right. The card backs have the player's name, team, position and jersey number, along with a head shot, at the top. His bio is printed underneath. A quote is printed about the player's team logo background. Logos included on the back are Team NFL, Pop Warner and Edge. There is a Prism parallel of the set, which were seeded one per two packs. A Micro Mini set, an eight-card set of Black Label base cards, were found one per 14 packs. Each card showcased 50 mini-cards with 25 on each side.

		NM/M
Complete Set (51):		15.00
Common Player:		.05
Minor Stars:		.10
Prism Cards:		2X
Inserted 1:2		
Pack (8):		2.00
Wax Box (20):		20.00
1	Jeff George	.10
2	Eric Metcalf	.05
3	Jim Kelly	.20
4	Jeff Blake	.20
5	Andre Rison	.10
6	Troy Aikman	.75
7	Michael Irvin	.10
8	Emmitt Smith	1.00
9	John Elway	1.00
10	*Terrell Davis*	4.00
11	Herman Moore	.20
12	Barry Sanders	1.50
13	Brett Favre	1.50
14	Marshall Faulk	.30
15	Steve Beuerlein	.05
16	Steve Bono	.10
17	Tim Brown	.10
18	Jeff Hostetler	.05
19	Jerome Bettis	.20
20	Dan Marino	1.00
21	Cris Carter	.20
22	Drew Bledsoe	.75
23	Ben Coates	.10
24	Randall Cunningham	.20
25	Terry Kirby	.05
26	Ricky Watters	.10
27	Kyle Brady	.05
28	Byron "Bam" Morris	.05
29	Neil O'Donnell	.10
30	Natrone Means	.20
31	Junior Seau	.10
32	William Floyd	.10
33	Jerry Rice	.75
34	Deion Sanders	.40
35	Steve Young	.50
36	Rick Mirer	.10
37	Chris Warren	.10
38	Trent Dilfer	.20
39	Errict Rhett	.10
40	Heath Shuler	.10
41	*Ki-Jana Carter*	.10
42	*Kerry Collins*	.75
43	*Steve McNair*	2.00
44	*Rashaan Salaam*	.20
45	*James O. Stewart*	.20
46	*J.J. Stokes*	.50
47	*Tyrone Wheatley*	.20
48	*Joey Galloway*	1.00
49	*Napoleon Kaufman*	.75
50	*Michael Westbrook*	.75
NNO	Checklist	.05

1995 Collector's Edge Instant Replay Edge Tech Die Cuts

Randomly seeded one per four regular retail packs and one per special retail pack, the 13-card set showcased a die-cut in the shape of a helmet on the top of the card. The player's name is printed at the bottom of the card. A helmet also appears in the background. The card backs have "EdgeTech" at the top, with the player's headshot inside a circle. The player's name and bio are inside a stripe underneath his picture.

		NM/M
Complete Set (13):		10.00
Common Player:		.25
1	Troy Aikman	1.50
2	Drew Bledsoe	1.50
3	Tim Brown	.50
4	Ben Coates	.25
5	Marshall Faulk	.75
6	William Floyd	.25
7	Dan Marino	3.00
8	Errict Rhett	1.00
9	Deion Sanders	1.25
10	Emmitt Smith	3.00
11	Ricky Watters	.50
12	Steve Young	1.25
NNO	Checklist	.25

1995 Collector's Edge Instant Replay Quantum Motion

Cards Nos. 1-10 of the 22-card set were seeded one per 12 packs, while the remaining 11 cards were offered through a mail-in redemption. Card Nos. 1-10 include game action on the lenticular card fronts, with "Quantum Motion" printed at the bottom. The card backs have a headshot in the upper left, with the player's team's helmet on the right. The player's name and highlights are listed inside a box in the center of the card. The cards are numbered "of 21."

		NM/M
Complete Set (22):		25.00
Complete Series 1 (11):		20.00
Complete Series 2 (11):		15.00
Common Player:		.50
1	Troy Aikman	3.00
2	Drew Bledsoe	3.00
3	Marshall Faulk	3.00
4	Michael Irvin	2.00
5	Dan Marino	5.00
6	Jerry Rice	4.00
7	Rod Smith	.50
8	Emmitt Smith	5.00
9	Michael Westbrook	.50
10	Steve Young	2.00
11	Erik Kramer	.50
12	Jeff Blake	.50
13	Eric Metcalf	.50
14	Steve Bono	.50
15	Carl Pickens	.50
16	Isaac Bruce	2.00
17	Errict Rhett	.50
18	Kerry Collins	3.00
19	Rashaan Salaam	.50
20	Gus Frerotte	.50
21	Terry Kirby	.50
NNO	Checklist	.50

1996 Collector's Edge Promos

This six-card set gave a sampling of the Collector's Edge set for 1996. It included three regular-issue cards and a sampling of inserts that resemble that of the regular-issue series.

		NM/M
Complete Set (4):		2.50
Common Player:		.25
P1	Errict Rhett	.50
P2	Junior Seau	.75
P3	Terry Kirby	.50
NNO	Cover Card	.25

1996 Collector's Edge

1996 Collector's Edge Series I football has 240 cards, consisting of veterans and rookies. Each regular card is also reprinted as part of a parallel Holofoil set, found one per every six packs. Three insert sets were also made - Quantum, Ripped and Too Cool Rookies.

		NM/M
Complete Set (240):		20.00
Common Player:		.05
Minor Stars:		.10
Comp. Die Cut Set (240):		
Die Cut Cards:		1.5X-3X
Comp. Holofoil Set (240):		
Holofoil Cards:		5X-8X
Comp. Draft Redemp. (30):		
Common Draft:		1.00
Pack (6):		1.25
Wax Box (24):		30.00
1	Larry Centers	.05
2	Garrison Hearst	.10
3	Dave Krieg	.05
4	Rob Moore	.05
5	Frank Sanders	.05
6	Eric Swann	.05
7	Morten Andersen	.05
8	Chris Doleman	.05
9	Bert Emanuel	.05
10	Jeff George	.10
11	Craig Heyward	.05
12	Terance Mathis	.05
13	Clay Matthews	.05
14	Eric Metcalf	.05
15	Bill Brooks	.05
16	Todd Collins	.05
17	Russell Copeland	.05
18	Jim Kelly	.10
19	Bryce Paup	.05
20	Andre Reed	.05
21	Bruce Smith	.05
22	Mark Carrier	.05
23	Kerry Collins	.30
24	Willie Green	.05
25	Eric Guliford	.05
26	Brett Maxie	.05
27	Tim McKyer	.05
28	Derrick Moore	.05
29	Curtis Conway	.05
30	Jim Flanigan	.05
31	Jeff Graham	.05
32	Robert Green	.05
33	Erik Kramer	.05
34	Rashaan Salaam	.50
35	Alonzo Spellman	.05
36	Donnell Woolford	.05
37	Chris Zorich	.05
38	Eric Bieniemy	.05
39	Jeff Blake	.50
40	Ki-Jana Carter	.25
41	John Copeland	.05
42	Harold Green	.05
43	Tony McGee	.05
44	Carl Pickens	.10
45	Darnay Scott	.05
46	Bracey Walker	.05
47	Dan Wilkinson	.05
48	Rob Burnett	.05
49	Leroy Hoard	.05
50	Earnest Hunter	.05
51	Michael Jackson	.05
52	Stevon Moore	.05
53	Anthony Pleasant	.05
54	Andre Rison	.05
55	Vinny Testaverde	.05
56	Eric Zeier	.05
57	Troy Aikman	1.00
58	Bill Bates	.05
59	Shante Carver	.05
60	Michael Irvin	.10
61	Daryl Johnston	.05
62	Jay Novacek	.05
63	Deion Sanders	.50
64	Emmitt Smith	2.00
65	Sherman Williams	.05
66	Terrell Davis	.50
67	John Elway	.50
68	Ed McCaffrey	.05
69	Glyn Milburn	.05
70	Anthony Miller	.05
71	Michael Dean Perry	.05
72	Shannon Sharpe	.05
73	Willie Clay	.05
74	Scott Mitchell	.05
75	Herman Moore	.25
76	Johnnie Morton	.05
77	Brett Perriman	.05
78	Barry Sanders	1.25
79	Tracy Scroggins	.05
80	Edgar Bennett	.05
81	Robert Brooks	.10
82	Brett Favre	2.00
83	Dorsey Levens	.10
84	Craig Newsome	.05
85	Wayne Simmons	.05
86	Reggie White	.10
87	Chris Chandler	.05
88	Anthony Cook	.05
89	Mel Gray	.05
90	Haywood Jeffires	.05
91	Darryll Lewis	.05
92	Steve McNair	.50
93	Todd McNair	.05
94	Rodney Thomas	.20
95	Trev Alberts	.05
96	Tony Bennett	.05
97	Quentin Coryatt	.05
98	Sean Dawkins	.05
99	Ken Dilger	.05
100	Marshall Faulk	.75
101	Jim Harbaugh	.05
102	Ronald Humphrey	.05
103	Floyd Turner	.05
104	Steve Beuerlein	.05
105	Tony Boselli	.05
106	Mark Brunell	.75
107	Willie Jackson	.05
108	Jeff Lageman	.05
109	James Stewart	.05
110	Cedric Tillman	.05
111	Marcus Allen	.05
112	Kimble Anders	.05
113	Steve Bono	.05
114	Dale Carter	.05
115	Willie Davis	.05
116	Lake Dawson	.05
117	Dan Saleaumua	.05
118	Neil Smith	.05
119	Derrick Thomas	.05
120	Tamarick Vanover	.30
121	Marco Coleman	.05
122	Bryan Cox	.05
123	Steve Emtman	.05
124	Irving Fryar	.05
125	Eric Green	.05
126	Terry Kirby	.05
127	Dan Marino	2.00
128	O.J. McDuffie	.05
129	Bernie Parmalee	.05
130	Troy Vincent	.05
131	Cris Carter	.05
132	Jack Del Rio	.05
133	Qadry Ismail	.05
134	Amp Lee	.05
135	Warren Moon	.05
136	John Randle	.05
137	Jake Reed	.05
138	Robert Smith	.05
139	Drew Bledsoe	.75
140	Vincent Brisby	.05
141	Ben Coates	.05
142	Curtis Martin	1.50
143	David Meggett	.05
144	Will Moore	.05
145	Chris Slade	.05
146	Mario Bates	.05
147	Quinn Early	.05
148	Jim Everett	.05
149	Michael Haynes	.05
150	Tyrone Hughes	.05
151	Wayne Martin	.05
152	Renaldo Turnbull	.05
153	Dave Brown	.05
154	Chris Calloway	.05
155	Rodney Hampton	.05
156	Mike Sherrard	.05
157	Michael Strahan	.05
158	Herschel Walker	.05
159	Tyrone Wheatley	.05
160	Kyle Brady	.05
161	Wayne Chrebet	.05
162	Hugh Douglas	.05
163	Adrian Murrell	.05
164	Todd Scott	.05
165	Charles Wilson	.05
166	Tim Brown	.05
167	Aundray Bruce	.05
168	Andrew Glover	.05
169	Jeff Hostetler	.05
170	Napoleon Kaufman	.05
171	Terry McDaniel	.05
172	Chester McGlockton	.05
173	Pat Swilling	.05
174	Harvey Williams	.05
175	Fred Barnett	.05
176	Randall Cunningham	.05
177	William Fuller	.05
178	Charlie Garner	.05
179	Andy Harmon	.05
180	Rodney Peete	.05
181	Ricky Watters	.05
182	Calvin Williams	.05
183	Chad Brown	.05
184	Kevin Greene	.05
185	Greg Lloyd	.05
186	Bam Morris	.05
187	Neil O'Donnell	.05
188	Eric Pegram	.05
189	Kordell Stewart	.75
190	Yancey Thigpen	.25
191	Rod Woodson	.05
192	Darren Bennett	.05
193	Ronnie Harmon	.05
194	Stan Humphries	.05
195	Tony Martin	.05
196	Natrone Means	.05
197	Leslie O'Neil	.05
198	Junior Seau	.10
199	Mark Seay	.05
200	William Floyd	.05
201	Merton Hanks	.05
202	Brent Jones	.05
203	Derek Loville	.05
204	Ken Norton Jr.	.05
205	Gary Plummer	.05
206	Jerry Rice	1.00
207	J.J. Stokes	.30
208	Dana Stubblefield	.05
209	John Taylor	.05
210	Bryant Young	.05
211	Steve Young	.75
212	Brian Blades	.05
213	Joey Galloway	.50
214	Carlton Gray	.05
215	Cortez Kennedy	.05
216	Rick Mirer	.05
217	Chris Warren	.10
218	Jerome Bettis	.05
219	Isaac Bruce	.40
220	Troy Drayton	.05
221	D'Marco Farr	.05
222	Sean Gilbert	.05
223	Chris Miller	.05
224	Roman Phifer	.05
225	Trent Dilfer	.05
226	Santana Dotson	.05
227	Alvin Harper	.05
228	Jackie Harris	.05
229	John Lynch	.05
230	Hardy Nickerson	.05
231	Errict Rhett	.50
232	Warren Sapp	.05
233	Terry Allen	.05
234	Henry Ellard	.05
235	Gus Frerotte	.05
236	Ken Harvey	.05
237	Brian Mitchell	.05
238	Heath Shuler	.20
239	James Washington	.05
240	Michael Westbrook	.30

1996 Collector's Edge Die Cuts

Randomly seeded one per retail pack, the die-cut had a pink front, with a front that was similar to base set cards, except for the die-cut.

	NM/M
Complete Set (240):	50.00
Common Player:	.25
Die-Cut Cards:	2X-4X

1996 Collector's Edge Holofoil

Seeded one per 48 retail, hobby or Cowboybilia packs, the 240-card set was a parallel to the Edge base cards.

	NM/M
Common Player:	2.00
Holofoil Cards:	5X-10X

1996 Collector's Edge All-Stars

This 13-card set (includes a checklist) was done on plastic stock and features two photos of the player on the front.

		NM/M
Complete Set (13):		15.00
Common Player:		.60
1	Junior Seau	1.00
2	Drew Bledsoe	3.00
3	Marshall Faulk	3.00
4	John Elway	4.00
5	Jerry Rice	4.00
6	Errict Rhett	.60
7	Jerome Bettis	.60
8	Deion Sanders	1.00
9	Byron "Bam" Morris	.60
10	Cris Carter	1.00
11	Terrell Davis	3.00
12	Terance Mathis	.60
---	Checklist Card	1.00

1996 Collector's Edge Big Easy

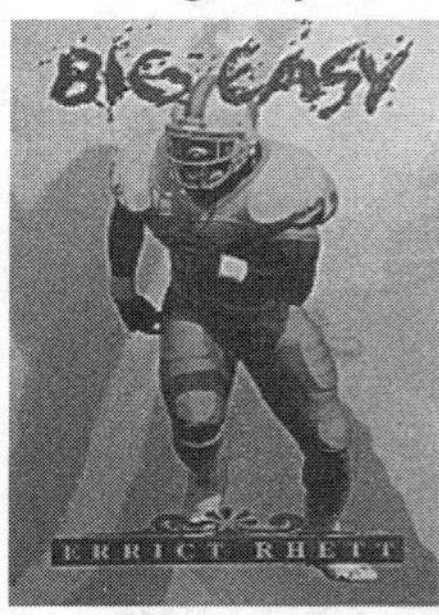

Big Easy cards were inserted in various 1996 Collector's Edge packs. Each card is numbered one of 2,000. A gold foil parallel was released through mail order. Each card in the parallel is numbered one of 3,100.

		NM/M
Complete Set (19):		50.00
Common Player:		1.00
1	Kerry Collins	2.00
2	Rashaan Salaam	1.00
3	Troy Aikman	6.00
4	Deion Sanders	2.00
5	Emmitt Smith	10.00
6	Terrell Davis	6.00
7	Barry Sanders	10.00
8	Brett Favre	10.00
9	Marshall Faulk	6.00
10	Tamarick Vanover	2.00
11	Dan Marino	10.00
12	Drew Bledsoe	6.00
13	Curtis Martin	6.00
14	J.J. Stokes	2.00
15	Joey Galloway	2.00
16	Isaac Bruce	2.00
17	Errict Rhett	1.00
18	Carl Pickens	1.00
---	Checklist Card	1.00

1996 Collector's Edge Draft Day Redemption

This 30-card set features one 1996 draft pick from each NFL team. One card could be obtained via that team's redemption card. The redemption cards were inserted 1:8.

		NM/M
Complete Set (30):		60.00
Common Player:		1.00
Trade Cards:		.10
1	Simeon Rice	1.00
2	Richard Huntley	1.00
3	Jonathan Ogden	1.00
4	Eric Moulds	4.00
5	Tim Biakabutuka	1.00
6	Walt Harris	1.00
7	Marco Battaglia	1.00
8	Stepfret Williams	1.00
9	John Mobley	1.00
10	Reggie Brown LB	1.00
11	Derrick Mayes	1.00
12	Eddie George	6.00
13	Marvin Harrison	5.00
14	Kevin Hardy	1.00
15	Jerome Woods	1.00
16	Karim Abdul-Jabbar	1.00
17	Duane Clemons	1.00
18	Terry Glenn	3.00
19	Ricky Whittle	1.00
20	Amani Toomer	1.00
21	Keyshawn Johnson	5.00
22	Rickey Dudley	2.00
23	Bobby Hoying	1.00
24	Jahine Arnold	1.00
25	Tony Banks	2.00
26	Bryan Still	1.00
27	Terrell Owens	5.00
28	Reggie Brown RB	1.00
29	Mike Alstott	4.00
30	Stephen Davis	4.00

1996 Collector's Edge Proteges

The cards in this 12-card insert feature an established star on one side and a young player with similar skills on the other. They were inserted 1:164 in 1996 Collector's Edge packs.

		NM/M
Complete Set (13):		75.00
Common Player:		3.00
1	Eric Metcalf, Joey Galloway	5.00
2	Herman Moore, Michael Westbrook	5.00
3	Emmitt Smith, Errict Rhett	12.00
4	Kordell Stewart, John Elway	10.00
5	Terrell Davis, Marshall Faulk	12.00
6	Rashaan Salaam, Marcus Allen	5.00
7	Dan Marino, Drew Bledsoe	15.00
8	Brett Favre, Kerry Collins	15.00
9	Tim Brown, Isaac Bruce	6.00
10	Cris Carter, Chris Sanders	3.00
11	Curtis Martin, Chris Warren	6.00
12	Tamarick Vanover, Brian Mitchell	3.00
---	Checklist Card	2.00
P1	Rashaan Salaam Promo, Terry Kirby Promo	2.00

1996 Collector's Edge Ripped

These 1996 Collector's Edge Series I inserts feature 36 of the NFL's top stars. Cards were seeded one per 18 packs of Series I product.

		NM/M
Complete Set (36):		40.00
Complete Hobby (18):		20.00
Complete Retail (18):		20.00
Common Player:		1.00
1	Jeff Blake	1.00
2	Steve Bono	1.00
3	Terrell Davis	3.00
4	John Elway	4.00
5	Marshall Faulk	3.00
6	Brett Favre	6.00
7	Jeff Hostetler	1.00
8	Erik Kramer	1.00
9	Dan Marino	6.00
10	Natrone Means	1.00
11	Eric Metcalf	1.00
12	Anthony Miller	1.00
13	Herman Moore	1.00
14	Errict Rhett	1.00
15	Andre Rison	1.00
16	Barry Sanders	5.00
17	Yancey Thigpen	1.00
18	Michael Westbrook	1.00
19	Troy Aikman	4.00
20	Drew Bledsoe	4.00
21	Tim Brown	1.00
22	Mark Brunell	3.00
23	Cris Carter	1.00
24	Kerry Collins	3.00
25	Joey Galloway	1.00
26	Michael Irvin	1.00
27	Terry Kirby	1.00
28	Curtis Martin	4.00
29	Carl Pickens	1.00
30	Jerry Rice	4.00
31	Rashaan Salaam	1.00
32	Deion Sanders	2.00
33	Emmitt Smith	6.00
34	Kordell Stewart	2.00
35	Ricky Watters	1.00
36	Steve Young	3.00

1996 Collector's Edge Too Cool Rookies

The NFL's top 25 rookies from 1995 are featured on these 1996 Collector's Edge Series I inserts. Cards were seeded one per every 25 packs of Series I product.

		NM/M
Complete Set (25):		40.00
Common Player:		.75
1	Tony Boselli	.75
2	Kyle Brady	.75
3	Ki-Jana Carter	1.00
4	Kerry Collins	3.00
5	Todd Collins	.75
6	Terrell Davis	6.00
7	Hugh Douglas	.75
8	Joey Galloway	3.00
9	Darius Holland	.75
10	Napoleon Kaufman	.75
11	Mike Mamula	.75
12	Curtis Martin	6.00
13	Steve McNair	6.00
14	Billy Milner	.75
15	Rashaan Salaam	1.00
16	Frank Sanders	.75
17	Warren Sapp	1.50
18	James Stewart	.75
19	Kordell Stewart	3.00
20	J.J. Stokes	2.00
21	Tamarick Vanover	1.00
22	Michael Westbrook	1.00
23	Tyrone Wheatley	.75
24	Sherman Williams	.75
25	Eric Zeier	.75

1996 Collector's Edge Quantum

These 24 cards were seeded one per 36 packs of 1996 Collector's Edge Series I football. The cards change images; NFL stars are shown in their current pro team's uniform and also in their college uniforms.

		NM/M
Complete Set (24):		125.00
Common Player:		2.00
1	Troy Aikman	10.00
2	Jeff Blake	3.00
3	Drew Bledsoe	10.00
4	Steve Bono	2.00
5	Tim Brown	4.00
6	Isaac Bruce	4.00
7	Mark Brunell	6.00
8	Kerry Collins	6.00
9	Marshall Faulk	8.00
10	Brett Favre	15.00
11	Jeff George	2.00
12	Terry Kirby	2.00
13	Dan Marino	15.00
14	Natrone Means	2.00
15	Carl Pickens	2.00
16	Errict Rhett	2.00
17	Rashaan Salaam	2.00
18	Deion Sanders	4.00
19	Barry Sanders	15.00
20	Emmitt Smith	15.00
21	Kordell Stewart	4.00
22	Yancey Thigpen	2.00
23	Michael Westbrook	2.00
24	Steve Young	6.00

1996 Collector's Edge Advantage Promos

This three-card promo set featured one regular-issue card (EA1), one Role Models insert (RM1) and one Edge Video (PR1). The cards detailed what the Edge Advantage set for 1996 would look like.

		NM/M
Complete Set (3):		3.00
Common Player:		1.00
EA1	Jeff Blake	1.00
PR1	Rashaan Salaam	1.00
RM1	Michael Westbrook	1.00

1996 Collector's Edge Advantage

Collector's Edge's 1996 Advantage set includes 150 cards, including 25 cards of rookies in their NFL uniforms. Each card front and back is gold foil stamped and embossed, with the rookie cards featuring extra foil stamping. The base set is also paralleled by Perfect Play Holofoil inserts; these cards, seeded one per two packs, use prism art technology. Five other insert sets were also produced - Role Models, Edge Video, Crystal Cuts, Game Ball and Super Bowl Game Ball. Portions of the proceeds made from the sale of this product were donated to the Pop Warner Football program.

		NM/M
Complete Set (150):		25.00
Common Player:		.10
Minor Stars:		.20
Foil Cards:		1X-3X
Pack (6):		1.50
Wax Box (24):		40.00
1	Drew Bledsoe	1.00
2	Chris Warren	.10
3	*Eddie George*	3.50
4	Barry Sanders	1.75
5	Scott Mitchell	.10
6	Carl Pickens	.10
7	Tim Brown	.10
8	John Elway	.75
9	Michael Westbrook	.20
10	Cris Carter	.10
11	Troy Aikman	1.25
12	Ben Coates	.10
13	Brett Favre	2.50
14	Marshall Faulk	.40
15	Steve Young	1.00
16	Terrell Davis	2.00
17	*Keyshawn Johnson*	2.00
18	Mario Bates	.10
19	Steve McNair	.75
20	Kerry Collins	.30
21	Natrone Means	.10
22	Kordell Stewart	.75
23	Jeff George	.10
24	Rick Mirer	.10
25	Herman Moore	.20
26	Rodney Peete	.10
27	Isaac Bruce	.50
28	Errict Rhett	.20
29	Jerry Rice	1.25
30	Rashaan Salaam	.50
31	Eric Metcalf	.10
32	Jim Kelly	.20
33	Jerome Bettis	.20
34	Deion Sanders	.75
35	J.J. Stokes	.20
36	Neil O'Donnell	.10
37	Marcus Allen	.20
38	Thurman Thomas	.20
39	Dan Marino	2.50
40	*Rickey Dudley*	.75
41	Napoleon Kaufman	.10
42	Kyle Brady	.10
43	Emmitt Smith	2.50
44	Tyrone Wheatley	.10
45	Jeff Blake	.20
46	Reggie White	.20
47	Joey Galloway	.50
48	Antonio Langham	.10
49	Craig Heyward	.10
50	Curtis Martin	1.75
51	*Karim Abdul-Jabbar*	.50
52	Antonio Freeman	.10
53	Ki-Jana Carter	.20
54	Willie Davis	.10
55	Jim Everett	.10
56	Gus Frerotte	.10
57	Daryl Gardener	.10
58	Charles Haley	.10
59	Michael Irvin	.20
60	Keith Jackson	.10
61	Cortez Kennedy	.10
62	Greg Lloyd	.10
63	Tony Martin	.10
64	Ken Norton Jr.	.10
65	Leslie O'Neal	.10
66	Bryce Paup	.10
67	Jake Reed	.10
68	Frank Sanders	.10
69	Vinny Testaverde	.10
70	Regan Upshaw	.10
71	Tamarick Vanover	.50
72	Walt Harris	.10
73	John Randle	.10
74	Ricky Watters	.20
75	Terry Allen	.10
76	Edgar Bennett	.10
77	Larry Centers	.10
78	Chris Penn	.10
79	*Bobby Engram*	.75
80	Irving Fryar	.10
81	Charlie Garner	.10
82	Rodney Hampton	.10
83	Michael Jackson	.10
84	O.J. McDuffie	.10
85	Shannon Sharpe	.10
86	Aaron Hayden	.10
87	*Mushin Muhammad*	1.00
88	Rodney Woodson	.10
89	Levon Kirkland	.10
90	Chad Brown	.10
91	Junior Seau	.10
92	Terry Kirby	.10
93	*Zach Thomas*	1.00
94	Harvey Williams	.10
95	Robert Brooks	.10
96	Darrell Green	.10
97	Chester McGlockton	.10
98	Neil Smith	.10
99	Eric Swann	.10
100	*Mike Alstott*	1.50
101	*Tim Biakabutuka*	.50
102	Mark Brunell	1.00
103	Chris Doleman	.10
104	Sean Gilbert	.10
105	Jim Harbaugh	.10
106	Chris T. Jones	.10
107	Tyrone Hughes	.10
108	*Amani Toomer*	.40
109	Larry Brown	.10
110	Kevin Greene	.10
111	John Mobley	.10
112	*Danny Kanell*	.75
113	*Kevin Hardy*	.40
114	Brett Perriman	.10
115	*Simeon Rice*	.40
116	Chris Sanders	.10
117	Dave Brown	.10
118	Bryan Cox	.10
119	Yancey Thigpen	.10
120	Terance Mathis	.10
121	Warren Moon	.10
122	Derrick Thomas	.10
123	Trent Dilfer	.10
124	*Terry Glenn*	1.00
125	Jeff Hostetler	.10
126	*Leeland McElroy*	.50
127	Hardy Nickerson	.10
128	Steve Bono	.10
129	Stanley Pritchett	.10
130	Dana Stubblefield	.10
131	Andre Coleman	.10
132	Anthony Miller	.10
133	Stan Humphries	.10
134	Robert Smith	.10
135	Curtis Conway	.10
136	Derrick Holmes	.10
137	Pat Swilling	.10
138	Andre Rison	.10
139	Erik Kramer	.10
140	Jason Dunn	.10
141	Torrance Small	.10
142	Cedric Jones	.10
143	Derek Loville	.10
144	Brian Mitchell	.10
145	*Eric Moulds*	2.00
146	James Stewart	.10
147	Bruce Smith	.10
148	Keenan McCardell	.10
149	Warren Sapp	.10
150	*Marvin Harrison*	3.00

1996 Collector's Edge Advantage Perfect Play Holofoil

Perfect Play Holofoil cards put a prismatic finish on all 150 cards in the Advantage set. These parallel cards were inserted every two packs.

Holofoil Cards:	1X-3X

1996 Collector's Edge Advantage Game Ball

These 1996 Collector's Edge Advantage inserts feature a medallion cut from an authentic game-used NFL football, with highlights of the game in which the ball was used. The card front has a color photo on it, plus foil stamping. The background of the card has a football field, with smaller color photos along the left side. Each card back contains a statement of authentication for the ball and game in which it was used. The cards are limited to 400 individually dual-numbered cards, seeded one per 72 packs.

		NM/M
Common Player:		10.00
1	Kordell Stewart	35.00
2	Emmitt Smith	75.00
3	Brett Favre	75.00
4	Steve Young	35.00
5	Barry Sanders	75.00
6	John Elway	40.00
7	Drew Bledsoe	35.00
8	Dan Marino	75.00
9	Keyshawn Johnson	20.00
10	Eddie George	35.00
11	Kevin Hardy	10.00
12	Terry Glenn	15.00
13	Michael Westbrook	10.00
14	Joey Galloway	15.00
15	John Mobley	10.00
16	Curtis Martin	25.00
17	Rashaan Salaam	10.00
18	J.J. Stokes	10.00
19	Kerry Collins	25.00
20	Deion Sanders	20.00
21	Shannon Sharpe	10.00
22	Terry Allen	10.00
23	Rickey Watters	10.00
24	Marshall Faulk	25.00
25	Tim Biakabutaka	10.00
26	Troy Aikman	35.00
27	Jerry Rice	45.00
28	Chris Warren	10.00
29	Jeff Blake	10.00
30	Carl Pickens	10.00
31	Isaac Bruce	15.00
32	Terrell Davis	35.00
33	Mark Brunell	25.00
34	Karim Abdul-Jabbar	10.00
35	Herman Moore	10.00
36	Cris Carter	10.00

1996 Collector's Edge Advantage Super Bowl Game Ball

Collector's Edge obtained several footballs from the Super Bowl to create these 1996 inserts. Each card has a medallion cut from an authentic NFL Super Bowl game-used ball, with highlights of the game in which the ball was used. The 36 cards were limited to 200 individually-numbered cards each, with odds of one per 164 packs.

		NM/M
Common Player:		6.00
1	Emmitt Smith	75.00
2	Troy Aikman	60.00
3	Michael Irvin	30.00
4	Deion Sanders	40.00
5	John Elway	60.00
6	Dan Marino	75.00
7	Marcus Allen	35.00
8	Kordell Stewart	25.00
9	Steve Young	40.00
10	Ricky Watters	15.00
11	Jerry Rice	60.00
12	Jim Kelly	25.00
13	Thurman Thomas	25.00
14	Bruce Smith	6.00
15	Stan Humphries	6.00
16	Junior Seau	15.00
17	Natrone Means	6.00
18	Neil O'Donnell	6.00
19	Rod Woodson	6.00
20	Andre Reed	6.00
21	Jeff Hostetler	6.00
22	Dave Meggett	6.00
23	Greg Lloyd	6.00
24	Kevin Green	6.00
25	Yancey Thigpen	6.00
26	Charles Haley	6.00
27	Bam Morris	6.00
28	Alvin Harper	6.00
29	Ken Norton Jr.	6.00
30	William Floyd	6.00
31	Leslie O'Neal	6.00
32	Jay Novacek	6.00
33	Irvin Fryar	6.00
34	Leon Lett	6.00
35	Tony Martin	6.00
36	Mark Collins	6.00

1996 Collector's Edge Advantage Role Models

These 1996 Collector's Edge Advantage inserts were seeded one per 12 packs. Each card front has an action shot on it, on a die-cut, embossed metallized card. A smaller photo is in the background of the card front, which has the Collector's Edge logo stamped in gold foil.

		NM/M
Complete Set (12):		25.00
Common Player:		1.00
1	John Elway	3.00
2	Dan Marino	6.00
3	Jerry Rice	4.00
4	Emmitt Smith	6.00
5	Chris Warren	1.00
6	Tim Brown	1.00
7	Jeff George	1.00
8	Tyrone Wheatley	1.00
9	Steve Bono	1.00
10	Kerry Collins	2.00
11	Jerome Bettis	2.00
12	Steve Beuerlein	1.00

1996 Collector's Edge Advantage Edge Video

These 1996 Collector's Edge Advantage inserts depict real game action with an overlaid photograph. The card front has a stand-out player shot with a state-of-the-art "Edge Video" background showing actual in-motion footage. The cards, each limited to 1,200, were seeded one per 36 packs.

		NM/M
Complete Set (25):		120.00
Common Player:		2.00
1	Brett Favre	15.00
2	Keyshawn Johnson	5.00
3	Deion Sanders	5.00
4	Marcus Allen	2.00
5	Rashaan Salaam	2.00
6	Thurman Thomas	2.00
7	Emmitt Smith	15.00
8	Isaac Bruce	4.00
9	Michael Westbrook	2.00
10	Cris Carter	2.00
11	Marshall Faulk	6.00
12	Jerry Rice	12.00
13	Tim Brown	4.00
14	Steve Young	8.00
15	Eric Metcalf	2.00
16	Chris Warren	2.00
17	Drew Bledsoe	6.00
18	Barry Sanders	12.00
19	Herman Moore	2.00
20	Rodney Peete	2.00
21	Troy Aikman	10.00
22	Jerome Bettis	2.00
23	Errict Rhett	2.00
24	Dan Marino	15.00
25	Natrone Means	2.00

1996 Collector's Edge Advantage Crystal Cuts

These 1996 Collector's Edge Advantage die-cut inserts are printed on clear plastic stock. The cards, dual numbered up to 5,000, were seeded one per eight packs. The card front has a color photo on it, with a background which makes the card look like a filmstrip. The player's name, position, number and team name are in gold foil and form a circle at the bottom of the card. The Collector's Edge logo is stamped in gold foil in the middle.

		NM/M
Complete Set (25):		65.00
Common Player:		1.00
1	Barry Sanders	5.00
2	Eddie George	4.00
3	Curtis Martin	4.00
4	J.J. Stokes	2.00
5	Kyle Brady	1.00
6	Chris Warren	1.00
7	Jerry Rice	5.00
8	Ben Coates	1.00
9	Terrell Davis	4.00
10	Marcus Allen	1.00
11	John Elway	5.00
12	Joey Galloway	2.00
13	Dan Marino	6.00
14	Napoleon Kaufman	1.00
15	Emmitt Smith	6.00
16	Eric Metcalf	1.00
17	Kerry Collins	3.00
18	Troy Aikman	5.00
19	Rickey Dudley	1.00
20	Steve McNair	3.00
21	Steve Young	4.00
22	Isaac Bruce	2.00
23	Kordell Stewart	2.00
24	LeShon Johnson	1.00
25	Scott Mitchell	1.00

1996 Collector's Edge Cowboybilia

Each of the 25 cards, except Troy Aikman, were signed by the featured player. They were seeded one per 2.5 packs in Cowboybilia. Other packs included a certificate for signed Cowboys items like jerseys, helmets, photos, footballs and pennants. In addition, 24K Prism parallel cards of Deion Sanders, Troy Aikman, Emmitt Smith and Michael Irvin were seeded four per case (one of each player per case). A Roger Staubach/Drew Pearson autographed Hail Mary card was found one per 192 packs. The cards are numbered with the "DC" prefix.

		NM/M
Complete Set (25):		450.00
Common Player:		8.00
1	Chris Boniol (4000)	8.00
2	John Jett (4000)	8.00
3	Sherman Williams (4000)	8.00
4	Chad Hennings (4000)	8.00
5	Larry Allen (4000)	10.00
6	Jason Garrett (4000)	8.00
7	Tony Tolbert (4000)	8.00
8	Kevin Williams (4000)	20.00
9	Mark Tuinei (4000)	8.00
10	Larry Brown (4000)	10.00
11	Kevin Smith (4000)	10.00
12	Darrin Smith (4000)	8.00
13	Robert Jones (4000)	8.00
14	Nate Newton (4000)	12.00
15	Darren Woodson (4000)	12.00
16	Leon Lett (4000)	12.00
17	Russell Maryland(4000)	10.00
18	Eric Williams (4000)	12.00
19	Bill Bates (4000)	12.00
20	Daryl Johnston (2300)	20.00
21	Jay Novacek (2300)	20.00
22	Charles Haley (2300)	20.00
23	Troy Aikman (600 all cards unsigned)	18.00
24	Michael Irvin (500)	60.00
25	Emmitt Smith (500)	175.00
NNO	Roger Staubach, Drew Pearson (Hail Mary Pass numbered of 1000)	200.00

1996 Collector's Edge Cowboybilia 24K Holofoil

Randomly seeded one per 48 1995 Edge Cowboybilia packs, the four cards parallel the players' 1995 Edge Holofoil card. The Cowboybilia 24K Holofoil cards have a 24K logo and are numbered with the "CB" prefix.

		NM/M
Complete Set (4):		100.00
Common Player:		15.00
57	Troy Aikman	25.00
60	Michael Irvin	115.00
63	Deion Sanders	15.00
64	Emmitt Smith	60.00

1996 Collector's Edge President's Reserve Promos

The 1996 Edge President's Reserve set was hyped by this six-card set, which included one card from each of the upcoming set's regular and chase sets. The cards each are numbered with the "PR" prefix.

		NM/M
Complete Set (6):		7.00
Common Player:		.50
1	Jeff Blake, Errict Rhett (Running Mates)	2.50
2	Dick Butkus, Steve Bono (TimeWarp)	2.50
3	Philadelphia Eagles (Candidates Rookie Redemption)	.50
4	Rashaan Salaam (New Regime)	1.00
5	Junior Seau (Base Brand)	.50
6	Michael Westbrook (Air Force One)	1.00

1996 Collector's Edge President's Reserve

1996 Collector's Edge President's Reserve Series I contains 200 cards. The cards replace the Excalibur series of the previous year. There were only 20,000 boxes made (1,000 cases). Boxes could be purchased by invitation only, with collectors being limited to one box and dealers to two. Consumers who were invited to purchase the product were to order through an authorized President's Reserve dealer, who displays a marker in his store shop window. The cards are plastic, with gold foil used for the brand name, player's name and card trimmings and borders. An action photo is set against a color square. The card back uses that square as a box for biographical and statistical information about the player, plus a mug shot. Insert sets include: Air Force One; New Regime; Tan, Rested and Ready (Pro Bowl '96); Running Mates; Time Warp; and Candidates rookie redemption cards. These cards have a team logo on the front, with the team's colors as a background. The insert set and President's Reserve logos are also on the front. The back has the rules, which indicate the card can be returned for a set of "long shot" cards of players signed by the corresponding team pictured on the front. These cards, included in every fourth pack, were limited to 6,000 each.

		NM/M
Complete Set (400):		60.00
Complete Series 1 (200):		35.00
Complete Series 2 (200):		25.00
Common Player:		.15
Minor Stars:		.50
Comp. Candidates (30):		40.00
Candidates Cards:		4.00
Series 1 or 2 Pack (6):		3.00
Series 1 or 2 Wax Box (32):		75.00
1	Larry Centers	.15
2	Frank Sanders	.50
3	Clyde Simmons	.15
4	Eric Swann	.15
5	Morten Andersen	.15
6	Lester Archambeau	.15
7	J.J. Birden	.15
8	Bert Emanuel	.50
9	Jumpy Geathers	.15
10	Jeff George	.50
11	Craig Heyward	.15
12	Bill Brooks	.15
13	Steve Christie	.15
14	Todd Collins	.50
15	Darick Holmes	.50
16	Andre Reed	.15
17	Bryce Paup	.15
18	Bruce Smith	.15
19	Blake Brockermeyer	.15
20	Mark Carrier	.15
21	Kerry Collins	.75
22	Darion Conner	.15
23	Eric Guliford	.15
24	Lamar Lathon	.15
25	Derrick Moore	.15
26	Frank Reich	.15
27	Kevin Butler	.15
28	Tony Carter	.15
29	Curtis Conway	.50
30	Robert Green	.15
31	Jay Leeuwenburg	.15
32	Alonzo Spellman	.15
33	Chris Zorich	.15
34	Eric Bieniemy	.15
35	Jeff Blake	.50
36	Tony McGee	.15
37	Carl Pickens	.50
38	Rob Burnett	.15
39	Earnest Byner	.15
40	Michael Jackson	.15
41	Antonio Langham	.15
42	Anthony Pleasant	.15
43	Vinny Testaverde	.15
44	Troy Aikman	3.00
45	Larry Allen	.15
46	Bill Bates	.15
47	Chris Boniol	.15
48	Charles Haley	.15
49	Michael Irvin	.50
50	Robert Jones	.15
51	Leon Lett	.15
52	Russell Maryland	.15
53	Nate Newton	.15
54	Deion Sanders	2.00
55	Sherman Williams	.50
56	Darren Woodson	.15
57	Aaron Craver	.15
58	Terrell Davis	3.50
59	Jason Elam	.15
60	Simon Fletcher	.15
61	Anthony Miller	.15
62	Shannon Sharpe	.15
63	Tracy Scroggins	.15
64	Antonio London	.15
65	Scott Mitchell	.15
66	Johnnie Morton	.15
67	Barry Sanders	3.00
68	Edgar Bennett	.15
69	Mark Chmura	.15
70	Brett Favre	4.00
71	Mark Ingram	.15
72	Dorsey Levens	.50
73	Wayne Simmons	.15
74	Gary Brown	.15
75	Anthony Cook	.15
76	Al Del Greco	.15
77	Haywood Jeffires	.15
78	Steve McNair	3.00
79	Rodney Thomas	.50
80	Trev Alberts	.15
81	Quentin Coryatt	.15
82	Ken Dilger	.15
83	Jim Harbaugh	.15
84	Floyd Turner	.15
85	Lamont Warren	.15
86	Steve Beuerlein	.15
87	Mark Brunell	1.50
88	Eugene Chung	.15
89	Jeff Lageman	.15
90	Willie Jackson	.15
91	Kimble Anders	.15
92	Steve Bono	.50
93	Derrick Thomas	.15
94	Willie Davis	.15
95	Greg Hill	.15
96	Neil Smith	.15
97	Tamarick Vanover	.50
98	James Hasty	.15
99	Gary Clark	.15
100	Marco Coleman	.15
101	Steve Emtman	.15
102	Irving Fryar	.15
103	Randal Hill	.15
104	Terry Kirby	.15
105	Dan Marino	4.00
106	Cris Carter	.15
107	Jack Del Rio	.15
108	David Palmer	.15
109	Jake Reed	.15
110	Robert Smith	.15
111	Korey Stringer	.15
112	Orlanda Thomas	.15
113	Drew Bledsoe	3.00
114	Vincent Brisby	.15
115	Ted Johnson	.15
116	Curtis Martin	3.00
117	Chris Slade	.15
118	Jim Dombrowski	.15
119	Vaughn Dunbar	.15
120	Quinn Early	.15
121	Wesley Walls	.15
122	Wayne Martin	.15
123	Irv Smith	.15
124	Torrance Small	.15
125	Dave Brown	.15
126	Chris Calloway	.15
127	John Elliott	.15
128	Rodney Hampton	.15
129	Tyrone Wheatley	.50
130	Kyle Brady	.15
131	Hugh Douglas	.15
132	Todd Scott	.15
133	Adrian Murrell	.15
134	Wayne Chrebet	.15
135	Aundray Bruce	.15
136	Andrew Glover	.15
137	*Daryl Hobbs*	.50
138	Napoleon Kaufman	.50
139	Chester McGlockton	.15
140	Rob Fredrickson	.15
141	Guy McIntyre	.15
142	Bobby Taylor	.15
143	Fred Barnett	.15
144	William Fuller	.15
145	Rodney Peete	.15
146	Daniel Stubbs	.15
147	Charlie Garner	.15
148	Myron Bell	.15
149	Rod Woodson	.15
150	Charles Johnson	.15
151	Ernie Mills	.15
152	Levon Kirkland	.15
153	Carnell Lake	.15
154	Kevin Greene	.15
155	Neil O'Donnell	.50
156	Erric Pegram	.15
157	Ray Seals	.15
158	Willie Williams	.15
159	Kordell Stewart	2.00
160	Yancey Thigpen	.50
161	Darren Bennett	.15
162	Andre Coleman	.15
163	*Aaron Hayden*	.30
164	Tony Martin	.15
165	Chris Mims	.15
166	Shawn Lee	.15
167	Junior Seau	.50
168	Merton Hanks	.15
169	Rickey Jackson	.15
170	Derek Loville	.15
171	Gary Plummer	.15
172	J.J. Stokes	.50
173	John Taylor	.15
174	Bryant Young	.15
175	Antonio Edwards	.15
176	Joey Galloway	.50
177	Carlton Gary	.15
178	Rick Mirer	.15
179	Winston Moss	.15
180	Jerome Bettis	.15
181	Troy Drayton	.15
182	Wayne Gandy	.15
183	Sean Gilbert	.15
184	Jessie Hester	.15
185	Sean Landeta	.15
186	Roman Phifer	.15
187	Alberto White	.15
188	Santana Dotson	.15
189	Jerry Ellison	.15
190	Jackie Harris	.15
191	Courtney Hawkins	.15
192	Horace Copeland	.15
193	Hardy Nickerson	.15
194	Warren Sapp	.15
195	Terry Allen	.15
196	Henry Ellard	.15
197	Gus Frerotte	.50
198	John Gesek	.15
199	Jim Lachey	.15
200	Brian Mitchell	.15
201	Garrison Hearst	.15
202	Dave Krieg	.15
203	Rob Moore	.15
204	Aeneas Williams	.15
205	Chris Doleman	.15
206	Terance Mathis	.15
207	Clay Matthews	.15
208	Eric Metcalf	.15
209	Jessie Tuggle	.15
210	Cornelius Bennett	.15
211	Ruben Brown	.15
212	Russell Copeland	.15
213	Phil Hansen	.15
214	Jim Kelly	.50
215	Don Beebe	.15
216	Willie Green	.15
217	Howard Griffith	.15
218	John Kasay	.15
219	Brett Maxie	.15
220	Tim McKyer	.15
221	Sam Mills	.15
222	Jim Flanigan	.15
223	Jeff Graham	.15
224	Erik Kramer	.15
225	Rashaan Salaam	.50
226	Steve Walsh	.15
227	Donnell Woolford	.15
228	Ki-Jana Carter	.50
229	John Copeland	.15
230	Harold Green	.15
231	Doug Pelfrey	.15
232	Darney Scott	.15
233	Bracey Walker	.15
234	Dan Wilkinson	.15
235	Leroy Hoard	.15
236	Earnest Hunter	.15
237	Keenan McCardell	.15
238	Steven Moore	.15
239	Andre Rison	.15
240	Eric Zeier	.50
241	Larry Brown	.15
242	Shante Carver	.15
243	Chad Hennings	.15
244	John Jett	.15
245	Daryl Johnston	.15
246	Derek Kennard	.15
247	Brock Marion	.15
248	Jay Novacek	.15
249	Emmitt Smith	4.00
250	Tony Tolbert	.15
251	Mark Tuinei	.15
252	Eric Williams	.15
253	Kevin Williams	.15
254	John Elway	2.00
255	Ed McCaffrey	.15
256	Glyn Milburn	.15
257	Michael Dean Perry	.15
258	Mike Pritchard	.15
259	Willie Clay	.15
260	Jason Hanson	.15
261	Herman Moore	.75
262	Brett Perriman	.15
263	Lomas Brown	.15
264	Chris Spielman	.15
265	Henry Thomas	.15
266	Robert Brooks	.15
267	Sean Jones	.15
268	John Jurkovic	.15
269	Anthony Morgan	.15
270	Craig Newsome	.15
271	Reggie White	.15
272	Chris Chandler	.15
273	Mel Gray	.15
274	Darryll Lewis	.15
275	Bruce Matthews	.15
276	Todd McNair	.15
277	Chris Sanders	.40
278	Mark Stepnoski	.15
279	Ashley Ambrose	.15
280	Tony Bennett	.15
281	Zack Crockett	.15
282	Sean Dawkins	.15
283	Marshall Faulk	2.00
284	Ronald Humphrey	.15
285	Tony Siragusa	.15
286	Roosevelt Potts	.15
287	Bryan Barker	.15
288	Tony Boselli	.15
289	Keith Goganious	.15
290	Desmond Howard	.15
291	Jeff Lageman	.15
292	Corey Mayfield	.15
293	James Stewart	.15
294	Cedric Tillman	.15
295	Marcus Allen	.50
296	Dale Carter	.15
297	Lake Dawson	.15
298	Darren Mickell	.15
299	Dan Saleaumua	.15
300	Webster Slaughter	.15
301	Keith Cash	.15
302	Bryan Cox	.15
303	Jeff Cross	.15
304	Eric Green	.15
305	O.J. McDuffie	.15
306	Bernie Parmalee	.15
307	Billy Milner	.15
308	Pete Stoyanovich	.15
309	Troy Vincent	.15
310	Qadry Ismail	.15
311	Amp Lee	.15
312	Warren Moon	.50
313	Scottie Graham	.15
314	John Randle	.15
315	Fuad Reveiz	.15
316	Broderick Thomas	.15
317	Ben Coates	.15
318	Willie McGinest	.15
319	David Meggett	.15
320	Will Moore	.15
321	Dave Wohlabaugh	.15
322	Mario Bates	.15
323	Jim Everett	.15
324	Tyrone Hughes	.15
325	William Roaf	.15
326	Renaldo Turnbull	.15
327	Michael Haynes	.15
328	Mike Sherrard	.15
329	Michael Strahan	.15
330	Herschel Walker	.15
331	Charles Wilson	.15
332	Otis Smith	.15
333	Mo Lewis	.15
334	Marvin Washington	.15
335	Tim Brown	.15
336	Greg Skrepenak	.15
337	Kevin Gogan	.15
338	Jeff Hostetler	.15
339	Terry McDaniel	.15
340	Anthony Smith	.15
341	Pat Swilling	.15
342	Harvey Williams	.15
343	Tom Hutton	.15
344	Mike Mamula	.15
345	Randall Cunningham	.15
346	Ricky Watters	.15
347	Andy Harmon	.15
348	William Thomas	.15
349	Calvin Williams	.15
350	Mark Breunner	.15
351	Dermonte Dawson	.15
352	Greg Lloyd	.15
353	Norm Johnson	.15
354	Bam Morris	.15
355	Thomas Newberry	.15
356	Darren Perry	.15
357	Rohn Stark	.15
358	Joel Steed	.15
359	Brenden Stal	.15
360	Justin Strzelczyk	.15
361	Leon Searcy	.15
362	Chad Brown	.15
363	John Carney	.15
364	Rodney Culver	.15
365	Ronnie Harmon	.15
366	Stan Humphries	.15
367	Leslie O'Neal	.15
368	Natrone Means	.75
369	Mark Seay	.15
370	William Floyd	.15
371	Brent Jones	.15
372	Tim McDonald	.15
373	Ken Norton Jr.	.15
374	Jerry Rice	3.00
375	Dana Stubblefield	.15
376	Steve Young	2.00
377	Brian Blades	.15
378	Cortez Kennedy	.15
379	Michael Sinclair	.15
380	Lamar Smith	.15
381	Chris Warren	.50
382	Johnny Bailey	.15
383	Isaac Bruce	.50
384	Kevin Carter	.15
385	Shane Conlan	.15
386	D'Marco Farr	.15
387	Todd Kinchen	.15
388	Chris Miller	.15
389	Lonnie Marts	.15
390	Trent Dilfer	.15
391	Alvin Harper	.15
392	John Lynch	.15
393	Errict Rhett	.50
394	Darnell Stephens	.15
395	Ken Harvey	.15
396	Eddie Murray	.15
397	Heath Shuler	.50
398	Matt Turk	.15
399	Michael Westbrook	.50
400	James Washington	.15

1996 Collector's Edge President's Reserve Air Force One

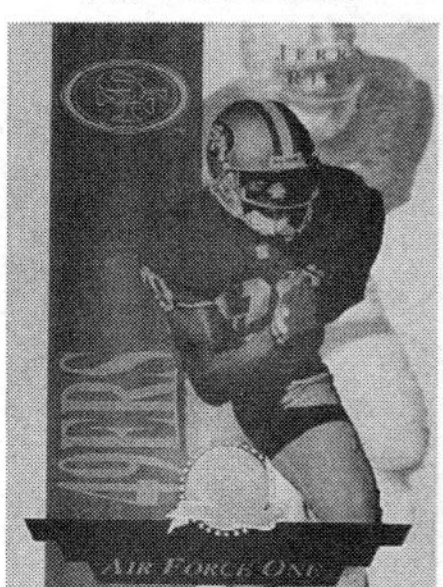

These 18 cards, randomly inserted into 1996 Collector's Edge President's Reserve packs, feature top wide receivers and quarterbacks in the NFL. Cards were seeded one per 16 packs. The card front has a color action photo, with the set icon at the bottom. The player's team logo is in the upper left corner, with the team name running down the side. The player's name is in the upper right corner. The back has a color action photo, plus a color panel on one side which includes the player's name, team logo, biographical information, a card number and recap of the player's achievements. There were only 2,500 of each card made.

		NM/M
Complete Set (36):		150.00
Complete Series 1 (18):		150.00
Complete Series 2 (18):		75.00
Common Player:		1.00
Jumbo Cards:		1.5X
1	Brett Favre	15.00
2	Neil O'Donnell	1.00
3	Steve Young	8.00
4	Dan Marino	15.00
5	Kerry Collins	6.00
6	Scott Mitchell	1.00
7	Deion Sanders	4.00
8	Cris Carter	1.00
9	Tim Brown	4.00
10	Joey Galloway	5.00
11	Robert Brooks	1.00
12	Tony Martin	1.00
13	Michael Westbrook	3.00
14	Eric Metcalf	1.00
15	Vincent Brisby	1.00
16	Anthony Miller	1.00
17	J.J. Stokes	2.00
18	Kordell Stewart	3.00
19	Troy Aikman	10.00
20	Drew Bledsoe	8.00
21	Jeff Blake	2.00
22	John Elway	12.00
23	Jim Harbaugh	1.00
24	Erik Kramer	1.00
25	Herman Moore	1.00
26	Carl Pickens	1.00
27	Michael Irvin	2.00
28	Jerry Rice	12.00
29	Isaac Bruce	1.00
30	Yancey Thigpen	1.00
31	Brett Perriman	1.00
32	Ben Coates	1.00
33	Jay Novacek	1.00
34	Tamarick Vanover	1.00
35	Terrell Davis	8.00
36	Jeff Graham	1.00

A player's name in *italic* type indicates a rookie card.

1996 Collector's Edge P.R. Candidates Top Picks

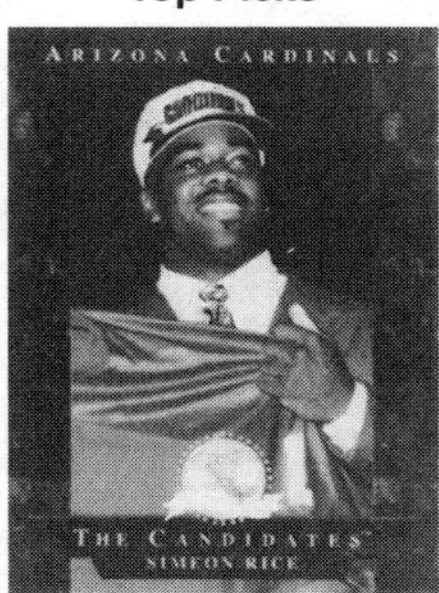

This 30-card set was available through the mail in exchange for team logo cards, which were inserted one per four President's Reserve Series II packs. Overall, 6,000 of each card was produced. According to the company, eight of these 30 cards were completed in time to be inserted directly into packs, including Simeon Rice, Tim Biakabutuka, Jonathan Ogden, John Mobley, Eddie George, Keyshawn Johnson, Daryl Gardener and Kevin Hardy. The card fronts feature the rookie on draft day holding his new team jersey, while the backs feature the rookie in college action and information about the draft pick.

		NM/M
Complete Set (30):		60.00
Common Player:		1.00
Minor Stars:		2.00
1	Simeon Rice	2.00
2	Shannon Brown	1.00
3	Willie Anderson	1.00
4	Tim Biakabutuka	1.00
5	Eric Moulds	2.00
6	Kavika Pittman	1.00
7	Jonathan Ogden	1.00
8	Reggie Brown	1.00
9	John Mobley	1.00
10	John Michels	1.00
11	Walt Harris	1.00
12	Eddie George	4.00
13	Marvin Harrison	4.00
14	Kevin Hardy	1.00
15	Jerome Woods	1.00
16	Duane Clemons	1.00
17	Daryl Gardener	1.00
18	Terry Glenn	2.00
19	Alex Molden	1.00
20	Cedric Jones	1.00
21	Rickey Dudley	2.00
22	Keyshawn Johnson	5.00
23	Jermaine Mayberry	1.00
24	Jermain Stephens	1.00
25	Lawrence Phillips	1.00
26	Bryan Still	1.00
27	Isreal Ifeanyi	1.00
28	Pete Kendall	1.00
29	Regan Upshaw	1.00
30	Andre Johnson	1.00

1996 Collector's Edge P.R. Candidates Long Shots

This 30-card set was available through the mail in exchange for redemption cards which were inserted one per four packs in President's Reserve Series I. According to the company, 6,000 of each card was produced. The cards feature an action shot of the rookie in the NFL, while the backs feature the rookie in college action and information about the draft pick.

		NM/M
Complete Set (30):		35.00
Common Player:		.75
Minor Stars:		2.00
1	Leeland McElroy	.75
2	Richard Huntley	.75
3	Ray Lewis	2.00
4	Sean Moran	.75
5	Muhsin Muhammad	4.00
6	Bobby Engram	2.00
7	Marco Battaglia	.75
8	Stepfret Williams	.75
9	Jeff Lewis	.75
10	Ryan Stewart	.75
11	Derrick Mayes	1.00
12	Terry Killens	.75
13	Scott Slutzker	.75
14	Reggie Barlow	.75
15	Joe Horn	1.00
16	Karim Abdul-Jabbar	1.00
17	Moe Williams	.75
18	Kantroy Barber	.75
19	Je'Rod Cherry	.75
20	Amani Toomer	4.00
21	Alex Van Dyke	.75
22	Tim Hall	.75
23	Bobby Hoying	1.00
24	Jahine Arnold	.75
25	Tony Banks	1.00
26	Freddie Bradley	.75
27	Stephen Pitts	.75
28	Reggie Brown	.75
29	Mike Alstott	6.00
30	Stephen Davis	4.00

1996 Collector's Edge President's Reserve New Regime

These 1996 Collector's Edge President's Reserve cards were seeded one per every five packs. There were 12,000 cards produced for each of the 12 players in the set. The card front is die-cut around the words "New Regime," which appear along the left side of the card. The player's name, position, team name and set logo appear on the right, with a ghosted closeup shot of the player in the background. A set icon is stamped in gold foil in the lower right corner. An action photo is in the center of the card. The card back has a closeup shot of the player, with 1995 and career stats under it. To the right is biographical information, a brief player profile, plus the limited-edition number of 12,000.

		NM/M
Complete Set (24):		40.00
Complete Series 1 (12):		30.00
Complete Series 2 (12):		30.00
Common Player:		.50
Minor Stars:		1.00
1	Tamarick Vanover	1.00
2	Kerry Collins	4.00
3	J.J. Stokes	1.00
4	Napoleon Kaufman	1.00
5	Steve McNair	6.00
6	Todd Collins	.50
7	Frank Sanders	1.00
8	Warren Sapp	2.00
9	Tony Boselli	.50
10	Curtis Martin	6.00
11	Ki-Jana Carter	1.00
12	Zack Crockett	.50
13	Joey Galloway	2.00
14	Terrell Davis	6.00
15	Chris Sanders	1.00
16	Rashaan Salaam	1.00
17	Michael Westbrook	2.00
18	Hugh Douglas	.50
19	Eric Zeier	.50
20	Kordell Stewart	4.00
21	Ted Johnson	.50
22	Ken Dilger	.50
23	Derrick Holmes	1.00
24	Wayne Chrebet	.50

1996 Collector's Edge President's Reserve Honor Guard

This set was a bonus redemption from President's Reserve. Collectors could redeem wrappers for a Jumbo Running Mates card and receive one Honor Guard card as a bonus. Each Honor Guard card is numbered one of 1,000 with an "HG" prefix.

		NM/M
Complete Set (30):		60.00
Common Player:		1.00
1	Troy Aikman	3.00
2	Michael Irvin	1.00
3	Emmitt Smith	5.00
4	Brett Favre	5.00
5	Steve Young	3.00
6	Tim Brown	2.50
7	Errict Rhett	1.00
8	Curtis Martin	3.00
9	Carl Pickens	1.00
10	Herman Moore	1.00
11	Robert Brooks	1.00
12	Michael Westbrook	1.00
13	Leon Lett	1.00
14	Russell Maryland	1.00
15	Eric Swann	1.00
16	John Elway	4.00
17	Barry Sanders	5.00
18	Dan Marino	5.00
19	Drew Bledsoe	4.00
20	Jerry Rice	4.00
21	Deion Sanders	2.00
22	Rashaan Salaam	1.00
23	Marshall Faulk	2.50
24	Napoleon Kaufman	1.00
25	Ki-Jana Carter	1.00
26	Cris Carter	1.00
27	Joey Galloway	1.00
28	Eric Metcalf	1.00
29	Derrick Thomas	1.00
30	Bruce Smith	1.00

1996 Collector's Edge President's Reserve Running Mates

These double-sided inserts feature two teammates per card. Cards, limited to 2,000 each, were randomly inserted into every 33rd pack of 1996 Collector's Edge President's Reserve. The cards match up a top NFL quarterback with a top running back from his team on the opposite side.

		NM/M
Complete Set (24):		200.00
Complete Series 1 (12):		100.00
Complete Series 2 (12):		100.00
Common Player:		2.00
Minor Stars:		5.00
1	Troy Aikman, Emmitt Smith	25.00
2	Jim Harbaugh, Marshall Faulk	8.00
3	John Elway, Terrell Davis	25.00
4	Stan Humphries, Natrone Means	4.00
5	Erik Kramer, Rashaan Salaam	2.00
6	Chris Miller, Jerome Bettis	4.00
7	Trent Dilfer, Errict Rhett	4.00
8	Jeff George, Craig Heyward	2.00
9	Gus Frerotte, Terry Allen	2.00
10	Drew Bledsoe, Curtis Martin	20.00
11	Jeff Blake, Ki-Jana Carter	4.00
12	Rick Mirer, Chris Warren	2.00
13	Brett Favre, Edgar Bennett	25.00
14	Neil O'Donnell, Bam Morris	2.00
15	Scott Mitchell, Barry Sanders	20.00
16	Steve Young, Derek Loville	15.00
17	Warren Moon, Robert Smith	2.00
18	Heath Shuler, Brian Mitchell	2.00
19	Rodney Peete, Ricky Watters	2.00
20	Kerry Collins, Derrick Moore	15.00
21	Dan Marino, Terry Kirby	25.00
22	Steve Bono, Marcus Allen	6.00
23	Jim Kelly, Darick Holmes	8.00
24	Kordell Stewart, Eric Pegram	6.00

1996 Collector's Edge President's Reserve Pro Bowl '96

These cards feature participants in the 1996 Pro Bowl. Cards were seeded one per eight packs of 1996 Collector's Edge President's Reserve packs. The metallic card front has palm trees in the background, with the player in the center wearing his Pro Bowl uniform. The President's Reserve logo is stamped in gold at the bottom of the card. The player's name is written in a rectangle at the bottom which is flanked on each side by the appropriate football conference logo. The back has biographical information and a brief player profile on the left side, with 1995 and career stats below. A player close-up shot is on the right, along with the limited-edition number (1 of 7,500).

		NM/M
Complete Set (24):		40.00
Complete Series 1 (12):		20.00
Complete Series 2 (12):		20.00
Common Player:		.75
1	Jeff Blake	.75
2	Jim Harbaugh	.75
3	Brett Favre	6.00
4	Steve Young	4.00
5	Emmitt Smith	6.00
6	Ricky Watters	.75
7	Michael Irvin	.75
8	Carl Pickens	.75
9	Tim Brown	2.00
10	Anthony Miller	.75
11	Darren Bennett	.75
12	Yancey Thigpen	.75
13	Bryce Paup	.75
14	Warren Moon	1.00
15	Barry Sanders	6.00
16	Herman Moore	1.00
17	Cris Carter	.75
18	Chris Warren	.75
19	Marshall Faulk	3.00
20	Curtis Martin	4.00
21	Ben Coates	.75
22	Brent Jones	.75
23	Shannon Sharpe	.75
24	Brian Mitchell	.75
25	Ken Harvey	.75

1996 Collector's Edge President's Reserve TimeWarp

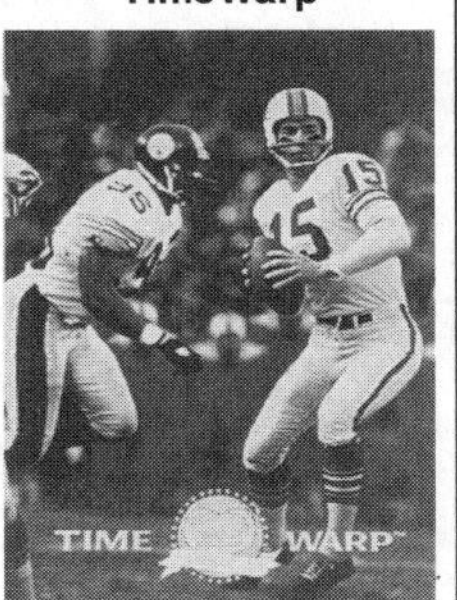

These cards feature a former NFL star matched up against a current NFL star, whose picture is superimposed into an action scene of the former star. The matchups are different from those produced last year. These cards were inserted one every 64th 1996 Collector's Edge President's Reserve pack and were limited in production to 2,000 each.

		NM/M
Complete Set (12):		100.00
Complete Series 1 (6):		50.00
Complete Series 2 (6):		50.00
Common Player:		2.00
1	Jack Kemp, Greg Lloyd	2.00
2	Sonny Jurgensen, Marshall Faulk	6.00
3	Fran Tarkenton, Bryce Paup	2.00
4	Roger Staubach, Emmitt Smith	15.00
5	Jack Lambert, Curtis Martin	10.00
6	Jack Youngblood, Brett Favre	15.00
7	Fran Tarkenton, Reggie White	3.00
8	Art Donovan, Steve Bono	2.00
9	Bobby Mitchell, Troy Aikman	12.00
10	Larry Csonka, Kordell Stewart	6.00
11	Dick Butkus, Deion Sanders	6.00
12	Deacon Jones, Dan Marino	15.00

1997 Collector's Edge Excalibur

The 150-card base set appears in two versions. The base set includes a space-motif Excalibur dragon in the top corner, with the tail filling the bottom right of the card. The premium parallel set featured a gold-foil stamped dragon. The backs have the player's headshot on the left over an outer space background. An Excalibur medallion is pictured in the upper right, along with the card number, player's name and bio. His stats appear in six sword blades near the bottom of the card back.

		NM/M
Complete Set (150):		15.00
Common Player:		.10
Minor Stars:		.20
Pack (6):		2.00
Wax Box (24):		40.00
1	Larry Centers	.10
2	Leeland McElroy	.20
3	Simeon Rice	.10
4	Eric Swann	.10
5	Jamal Anderson	.30
6	Bert Emanuel	.10
7	Eric Metcalf	.10
8	Ray Lewis	.10
9	Derrick Alexander	.10
10	Michael Jackson	.10
11	Vinny Testaverde	.10
12	Todd Collins	.20
13	Jim Kelly	.20
14	Eric Moulds	.10
15	Andre Reed	.10
16	Bruce Smith	.10
17	Thurman Thomas	.20
18	Tim Biakabutuka	.20
19	Kerry Collins	.30
20	Kevin Greene	.10
21	Anthony Johnson	.10
22	Lamar Lathon	.10
23	Muhsin Muhammad	.10
24	Curtis Conway	.20
25	Bryan Cox	.10
26	Walt Harris	.10
27	Erik Kramer	.10
28	Rick Mirer	.10
29	Rashaan Salaam	.20
30	Jeff Blake	.30
31	Ki-Jana Carter	.20
32	Carl Pickens	.20
33	Troy Aikman	1.50
34	Michael Irvin	.20
35	Daryl Johnston	.10
36	Emmitt Smith	2.50
37	Broderick Thomas	.10
38	Terrell Davis	1.50
39	John Elway	1.00
40	Anthony Miller	.10
41	John Mobley	.10
42	Shannon Sharpe	.10
43	Neil Smith	.10
44	Scott Mitchell	.10
45	Herman Moore	.30
46	Brett Perriman	.10
47	Barry Sanders	2.50
48	Edgar Bennett	.10
49	Robert Brooks	.20
50	Brett Favre	3.00
51	Antonio Freeman	.30
52	Dorsey Levens	.20
53	Reggie White	.20
54	Eddie George	1.75
55	Darryll Lewis	.10
56	Steve McNair	1.25
57	Chris Sanders	.10
58	Marshall Faulk	.20
59	Jim Harbaugh	.10
60	Marvin Harrison	.75
61	Jimmy Smith	.10
62	Tony Brackens	.10
63	Mark Brunell	.75
64	Kevin Hardy	.10
65	Keenan McCardell	.10
66	Natrone Means	.20
67	Marcus Allen	.20
68	Elvis Grbac	.10
69	Derrick Thomas	.10
70	Tamarick Vanover	.10
71	Karim Abdul-Jabbar	.30
72	Terrell Buckley	.10
73	Irving Fryar	.10
74	Dan Marino	2.50
75	O.J. McDuffie	.10
76	Zach Thomas	.50
77	Terry Kirby	.10
78	Cris Carter	.20
79	Brad Johnson	.10
80	John Randle	.10
81	Jake Reed	.10
82	Robert Smith	.10
83	Drew Bledsoe	1.50
84	Ben Coates	.10
85	Terry Glenn	.30
86	Ty Law	.10
87	Curtis Martin	1.50
88	Willie McGinest	.10
89	Mario Bates	.10
90	Jim Everett	.10
91	Wayne Martin	.10
92	Heath Shuler	.10
93	Torrance Small	.10
94	Ray Zellars	.10
95	Dave Brown	.10
96	Jason Sehorn	.10
97	Amani Toomer	.10
98	Tyrone Wheatley	.10
99	Hugh Douglas	.10
100	Aaron Glenn	.10
101	Jeff Graham	.10
102	Keyshawn Johnson	.75
103	Adrian Murrell	.10
104	Neil O'Donnell	.10
105	Tim Brown	.10
106	Jeff George	.10
107	Jeff Hostetler	.10
108	Napoleon Kaufman	.20
109	Chester McGlockton	.10
110	Fred Barnett	.10
111	Ty Detmer	.10
112	Chris T. Jones	.10
113	Ricky Watters	.20
114	Bobby Engram	.10
115	Jerome Bettis	.20
116	Charles Johnson	.10
117	Greg Lloyd	.10
118	Kordell Stewart	.75
119	Yancey Thigpen	.10
120	Rod Woodson	.10
121	Stan Humphries	.10
122	Tony Martin	.10
123	Leonard Russell	.10
124	Junior Seau	.10
125	Chad Brown	.10
126	John Friesz	.10
127	Joey Galloway	.40
128	Cortez Kennedy	.10
129	Warren Moon	.10
130	Chris Warren	.10
131	Garrison Hearst	.10
132	Terrell Owens	1.00
133	Jerry Rice	1.50
134	Dana Stubblefield	.10
135	Bryant Young	.10
136	Steve Young	1.00
137	Tony Banks	.75
138	Isaac Bruce	.30
139	Eddie Kennison	.75
140	Keith Lyle	.10
141	Lawrence Phillips	.20
142	Mike Alstott	.20
143	Hardy Nickerson	.10
144	Errict Rhett	.20
145	Warren Sapp	.10
146	Gus Frerotte	.10
147	Sean Gilbert	.10
148	Ken Harvey	.10
149	Terry Allen	.10
150	Michael Westbrook	.20

1997 Collector's Edge Excalibur 22K Knights

The 25-card set includes a player photo superimposed over a foil background on the card front. The player's name is printed in gold foil at the top, while the "Excalibur 22k" logo is printed at the bottom center. The backs have the player's name printed vertically along the left border of the card. The player's head shot appears in the center, with his bio in the lower right. Edge produced 2,000 of each card. The cards were inserted 1:20 packs. A 22k Black Magnum Knights parallel version, which includes a prism logo printed above the Excalibur 22k logo on the card front, was inserted 1:75 packs in super premium boxes.

		NM/M
Complete Set (25):		125.00
Common Player:		1.00
Magnum Cards:		2X-3X
Supreme Edge Cards:		5X
Production 50 Sets		
1	Troy Aikman	8.00
2	John Elway	8.00
3	Brett Favre	12.00
4	Dan Marino	12.00
5	Barry Sanders	12.00
6	Emmitt Smith	12.00
7	Mark Brunell	6.00
8	Jerry Rice	10.00
9	Terrell Davis	6.00
10	Natrone Means	1.00
11	Joey Galloway	2.00
12	Keyshawn Johnson	1.00
13	Curtis Martin	5.00
14	Herman Moore	1.00
15	Eddie George	5.00
16	Terry Glenn	2.00
17	Steve McNair	4.00
18	Marshall Faulk	1.00

19	Ricky Watters	1.00
20	Karim Abdul-Jabbar	1.00
21	Gus Frerotte	1.00
22	Terry Allen	1.00
23	Andre Reed	1.00
24	Jerome Bettis	1.00
25	Tim Brown	2.00

1997 Collector's Edge Excalibur Crusaders

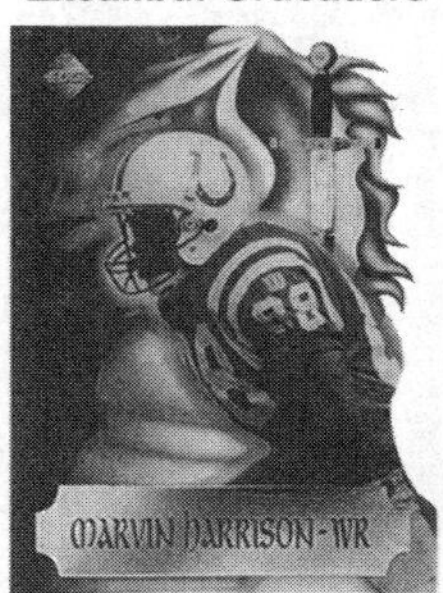

The 25 acetate die-cut cards have the player's photo superimposed over a chess piece background on the front. The Edge logo is printed in the upper left, with an Excalibur sword printed in the background on the right side. The player's name is printed inside a gold-foil "plaque" at the bottom of the front. The chess piece is printed in purple in the background. The backs are a reverse of the front, with the card number inside a diamond in the upper right. The card's individual number is printed at the bottom center. Edge produced 750 of each card.

		NM/M
Complete Set (25):		100.00
Common Player:		1.00
1	Brett Favre	20.00
2	Mark Brunell	8.00
3	Jim Kelly	8.00
4	Michael Westbrook	1.00
5	Emmitt Smith	20.00
6	Marshall Faulk	10.00
7	Kerry Collins	6.00
8	Jeff Hostetler	1.00
9	Rashaan Salaam	1.00
10	Garrison Hearst	1.00
11	Tamarick Vanover	1.00
12	Rodney Hampton	1.00
13	Leeland McElroy	1.00
14	Tony Banks	1.00
15	Deion Sanders	3.00
16	Errict Rhett	1.00
17	Thurman Thomas	4.00
18	Chris Warren	1.00
19	Andre Reed	1.00
20	Napoleon Kaufman	1.00
21	Terry Allen	1.00
22	Carl Pickens	1.00
23	Marvin Harrison	4.00
24	Lawrence Phillips	1.00
25	Troy Aikman	12.00

1997 Collector's Edge Excalibur Game Gear

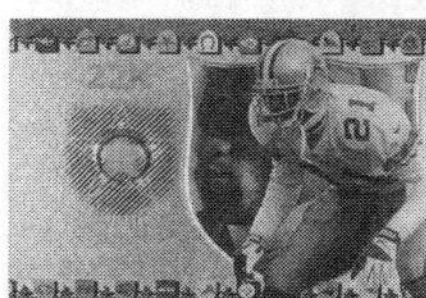

The 19 Game Gear chase cards are hard to miss, as they are as thick as six base cards. The fronts include a photo of the player along with a circular piece of the player's game-used helmet. Edge produced 500 of each card, which were inserted one per 60 packs. Autographed Game Gear cards were inserted one per 350 packs.

		NM/M
Common Player:		6.00
1	Brett Favre	60.00
2	Mark Brunell	25.00
3	Barry Sanders	60.00
4	John Elway	40.00
5	Emmitt Smith	60.00
6	Drew Bledsoe	25.00
7	Troy Aikman	35.00
8	Dan Marino	60.00
9	Eddie George	25.00
10	Terry Glenn	10.00
11	Keyshawn Johnson	15.00
12	Terrell Davis	25.00
13	Curtis Martin	25.00
14	Steve McNair	25.00
15	Muhsin Muhammad	12.00
16	Antonio Freeman	10.00
17	Ricky Watters	6.00
18	Jerome Bettis	6.00
19	Herman Moore	6.00
20	Isaac Bruce	12.00
21	Deion Sanders	12.00
22	Cris Carter	6.00
23	Tim Biakabutuka	6.00
24	Karim Abdul-Jabbar	6.00
25	Mike Alstott	12.00

1997 Collector's Edge Excalibur Gridiron Sorcerers

Featuring the top 25 players from the 1997 draft, these chase cards include a photo superimposed over a purple background filled with lightning. "1997 NFL Draft" is printed at the top of the front, with the player's team helmet printed at the top center. His name appears across the bottom of the front. The backs have the team name at the top, with the logo in the background on the left. The card number is in the top right. The player's name and bio is printed in the lower left, with his photo appearing on the right center. The card's individual number is printed at the bottom right. Edge produced 1,000 of each card.

		NM/M
Complete Set (25):		60.00
Common Player:		.75
1	Orlando Pace	.75
2	Peter Boulware	.75
3	Darrell Russell	.75
4	Shawn Springs	.75
5	Yatil Green	.75
6	Jim Druckenmiller	1.00
7	Bryant Westbrook	.75
8	Dwayne Rudd	.75
9	David LaFleur	.75
10	Rae Carruth	.75
11	Corey Dillon	8.00
12	Antowain Smith	6.00
13	Tiki Barber	6.00
14	Marcus Harris	.75
15	Warrick Dunn	6.00
16	Chris Canty	.75
17	Tony Gonzalez	5.00
18	Danny Wuerffel	1.00
19	Ike Hilliard	2.00
20	James Farrior	.75
21	Reidel Anthony	1.00
22	Jake Plummer	5.00
23	Troy Davis	1.00
24	Pat Barnes	1.00
25	Darnell Autry	1.00

1997 Collector's Edge Excalibur Gridiron Wizards

Similar to the Gridiron Sorcerers, this 25-card set included the top players from the 1997 draft. Like the Sorcerers cards, the Wizard cards were inserted one per 20 packs, the only difference being the Wizard cards were seeded in super premium boxes and the Sorcerers cards were inserted in premium packs.

		NM/M
Complete Set (25):		140.00
Common Player:		1.00
1	Orlando Pace	2.00
2	Peter Boulware	1.00
3	Darrell Russell	1.00
4	Shawn Springs	1.00
5	Yatil Green	1.00
6	Jim Druckenmiller	1.00
7	Bryant Westbrook	1.00
8	Dwayne Rudd	1.00
9	David LaFleur	1.00
10	Rae Carruth	1.00
11	Corey Dillon	8.00
12	Antowain Smith	6.00
13	Tiki Barber	6.00
14	Marcus Harris	1.00
15	Warrick Dunn	6.00
16	Chris Canty	1.00
17	Tony Gonzalez	4.00
18	Danny Wuerffel	1.00
19	Ike Hilliard	2.00
20	James Farrior	1.00
21	Reidel Anthony	1.00
22	Jake Plummer	6.00
23	Troy Davis	1.00
24	Pat Barnes	1.00
25	Darnell Autry	1.00

1997 Collector's Edge Excalibur Marauders

The 25-card set featured 50 players, as two appeared on each double-front card. The player's photo is superimposed over a blue lenticular background, which featured vertical black lines moving from side-to-side. The team's logo appears in the upper left inside a shield, while the team name and his position are printed in gold foil in the upper right. The player's last name is printed inside a gold-foil stripe in the upper right. The appropriate logos appear in the lower left, while "Marauders" and the card number are printed in the lower right in dark blue. The cards were inserted in one of 20 super premium packs.

		NM/M
Complete Set (25):		100.00
Common Player:		1.00
Supreme Edge Cards:		5X
Production 50 Sets		
1	Antonio Freeman, Tony Banks	4.00
2	Heath Shuler, Tim Biakabutuka	1.00
3	Brett Favre, Eddie Kennison	12.00
4	Marcus Allen, Todd Collins	1.00
5	Dan Marino, Shannon Sharpe	12.00
6	Desmond Howard, Napoleon Kaufman	2.00
7	Dorsey Levens, Muhsin Muhammad	3.00
8	Drew Bledsoe, Mike Alstott	6.00
9	Emmitt Smith, Michael Westbrook	12.00
10	Heath Shuler, Marvin Harrison	3.00
11	Jeff Blake, Marshall Faulk	3.00
12	Jeff George, Lawrence Phillips	1.00
13	Tony Martin, Edgar Bennett	1.00
14	Jerry Rice, Karim Abdul-Jabbar	6.00
15	Jim Harbaugh, Terrell Owens	4.00
16	John Elway, Isaac Bruce	12.00
17	Dave Brown, Eric Metcalf	1.00
18	Junior Seau, Eddie Kennison	4.00
19	Mark Brunell, Eddie George	10.00
20	Cris Carter, Deion Sanders	6.00
21	Steve Young, Eric Moulds	8.00
22	Ben Coates, Chris Warren	1.00
23	Robert Brooks, Carl Pickens	1.00
24	Tim Brown, Bobby Engram	3.00
25	Troy Aikman, Ben Coates	10.00

1997 Collector's Edge Excalibur Overlords

The 25-card set, which is printed on acetate, features a die-cut design in the shape of a dragon. The player's photo is superimposed over a orange and red dragon in the background on the front. The player's last name is printed in large capital letters at the bottom, with his first name printed in white in small letters. The team's logo is printed to the left of the player's name on the front. The backs have the player's headshot in the left center, with the team logo, his name and bio to the right of the photo. The top and bottom of the back have a brick design. The card's individual number appears at the bottom right. Edge produced 750 of each card.

		NM/M
Complete Set (25):		140.00
Common Player:		2.00
Minor Stars:		8.00
Inserted 1:30		
Production 750 Sets		
Castle Cards:		1X
Production 750 Sets		
1	Jeff Blake	1.00
2	Mark Brunell	8.00
3	Bobby Engram	2.00
4	Joey Galloway	4.00
5	Eddie Kennison	2.00
6	Terrell Davis	12.00
7	Joey Galloway	4.00
8	Hardy Nickerson	2.00
9	Errict Rhett	2.00
10	Emmitt Smith	15.00
11	Kordell Stewart	6.00
12	Steve Young	10.00
13	Marcus Allen	8.00
14	Edgar Bennett	2.00
15	Robert Brooks	2.00
16	Kerry Collins	6.00
17	Todd Collins	2.00
18	Brett Favre	15.00
19	Gus Frerotte	2.00
20	Elvis Grbac	2.00
21	Jeff Hostetler	2.00
22	Tony Martin	2.00
23	Terrell Owens	8.00
24	Dorsey Levens	3.00
25	Thurman Thomas	5.00

1997 Collector's Edge Extreme

Extreme includes a 180-card base set. Three different parallel sets were made. Extreme Base Parallel I (1:2) parallels 108 base cards with a flat silver foil stamp. Extreme Base Parallel II (1:12) adds a gold foil stamp to 36 base cards redone on a silver card. Base Parallel III (1:36) parallels the other 36 base cards with a diamond etched foil stamp on a silver, die-cut card. The inserts include Force, Finesse, Fury, Forerunners and Gamegear Quads.

		NM/M
Complete Set (180):		30.00
Common Player:		.10
Minor Stars:		.20
Pack (6):		1.50
Wax Box (36):		40.00
1	Larry Centers	.10
2	Leeland McElroy	.10
3	*Jake Plummer*	2.00
4	Simeon Rice	.10
5	Eric Swann	.10
6	Jamal Anderson	.20
7	Bert Emanuel	.10
8	*Byron Hanspard*	.75
9	Derrick Alexander	.10
10	Peter Boulware	.10
11	Michael Jackson	.10
12	Ray Lewis	.10
13	Vinny Testaverde	.10
14	Todd Collins	.10
15	Eric Moulds	.10
16	Bryce Paup	.10
17	Andre Reed	.10
18	Bruce Smith	.10
19	*Antowain Smith*	1.25
20	Chris Spielman	.10
21	Thurman Thomas	.20
22	Tim Biakabutuka	.10
23	*Rae Carruth*	.75
24	Kerry Collins	.30
25	Anthony Johnson	.10
26	Lamar Lathon	.10
27	Muhsin Muhammad	.10
28	*Darnell Autry*	.50
29	Curtis Conway	.10
30	Bryan Cox	.10
31	Bobby Engram	.10
32	Walt Harris	.10
33	Erik Kramer	.10
34	Rashaan Salaam	.10
35	Jeff Blake	.20
36	Ki-Jana Carter	.10
37	*Corey Dillon*	2.50
38	Carl Pickens	.20
39	Troy Aikman	1.00
40	Dexter Coakley	.10
41	Michael Irvin	.20
42	Daryl Johnston	.10
43	*David LaFleur*	.50
44	Anthony Miller	.10
45	Deion Sanders	.50
46	Emmitt Smith	2.00
47	Broderick Thomas	.10
48	Terrell Davis	1.00
49	John Elway	.75
50	John Mobley	.10
51	Shannon Sharpe	.10
52	Neil Smith	.10
53	Checklist	.10
54	Scott Mitchell	.10
55	Herman Moore	.20
56	Barry Sanders	1.25
57	Edgar Bennett	.10
58	Robert Brooks	.20
59	Mark Chmura	.20
60	Brett Favre	2.25
61	Antonio Freeman	.20
62	Dorsey Levens	.20
63	Reggie White	.20
64	Eddie George	1.50
65	Darryll Lewis	.10
66	Steve McNair	.75
67	Chris Sanders	.10
68	Marshall Faulk	.20
69	Jim Harbaugh	.10
70	Marvin Harrison	.20
71	Tony Brackens	.10
72	Mark Brunell	1.00
73	Kevin Hardy	.10
74	Rob Johnson	.20
75	Keenan McCardell	.10
76	Natrone Means	.20
77	Jimmy Smith	.10
78	Marcus Allen	.20
79	*Pat Barnes*	.50
80	*Tony Gonzalez*	1.00
81	Elvis Grbac	.10
82	Brett Perriman	.10
83	Andre Rison	.10
84	Derrick Thomas	.10
85	Tamarick Vanover	.10
86	Karim Abdul-Jabbar	.50
87	Fred Barnett	.10
88	Terrell Buckley	.10
89	*Yatil Green*	.40
90	Dan Marino	2.00
91	O.J. McDuffie	.10
92	Jason Taylor	.10
93	Zach Thomas	.20
94	Cris Carter	.10
95	Brad Johnson	.20
96	John Randle	.10
97	Jake Reed	.10
98	Robert Smith	.10
99	Drew Bledsoe	1.00
100	Chris Canty	.10
101	Ben Coates	.10
102	Terry Glenn	.30
103	Ty Law	.10
104	Curtis Martin	1.00
105	Willie McGinest	.10
106	*Troy Davis*	.30
107	Wayne Martin	.10
108	Heath Shuler	.10
109	*Danny Wuerffel*	.75
110	Ray Zellars	.10
111	*Tiki Barber*	1.00
112	Dave Brown	.10
113	Checklist	.10
114	*Ike Hilliard*	.75
115	Jason Sehorn	.10
116	Amani Toomer	.10
117	Tyrone Wheatley	.10
118	Hugh Douglas	.10
119	Aaron Glenn	.10
120	Jeff Graham	.10
121	Keyshawn Johnson	.20
122	Adrian Murrell	.20
123	Neil O'Donnell	.10
124	Tim Brown	.10
125	Jeff George	.10
126	Desmond Howard	.10
127	Napoleon Kaufman	.20
128	Chester McGlockton	.10
129	Darrell Russell	.10
130	Ty Detmer	.10
131	Irving Fryar	.10
132	Chris T. Jones	.10
133	Ricky Watters	.20
134	Jerome Bettis	.20
135	Charles Johnson	.10
136	George Jones	.10
137	Greg Lloyd	.10
138	Kordell Stewart	.75
139	Yancey Thigpen	.10
140	Jim Everett	.10
141	Stan Humphries	.10
142	Tony Martin	.10
143	Eric Metcalf	.10
144	Junior Seau	.10
145	*Jim Druckenmiller*	.50
146	Kevin Greene	.10
147	Garrison Hearst	.10
148	Terry Kirby	.10
149	Terrell Owens	.50
150	Jerry Rice	1.00
151	Dana Stubblefield	.10
152	Rod Woodson	.10
153	Bryant Young	.10
154	Steve Young	.50
155	Chad Brown	.10
156	John Friesz	.10
157	Joey Galloway	.20
158	Cortez Kennedy	.10
159	Warren Moon	.10
160	*Shawn Springs*	.20
161	Chris Warren	.10
162	Tony Banks	.50
163	Isaac Bruce	.20
164	Eddie Kennison	.20
165	Keith Lyle	.10
166	*Orlando Pace*	.20
167	Lawrence Phillips	.10
168	Checklist	.10
169	Mike Alstott	.50
170	*Reidel Anthony*	1.00
171	*Warrick Dunn*	1.25
172	Hardy Nickerson	.10
173	Errict Rhett	.10
174	Warren Sapp	.10
175	Terry Allen	.10
176	Gus Frerotte	.10
177	Sean Gilbert	.10
178	Ken Harvey	.10
179	Jeff Hostetler	.10
180	Michael Westbrook	.10

1997 Collector's Edge Extreme Foil

Collector's Edge ran three parallel sets to its Extreme set. The first parallel simply included a silver foil stripe up the left side and contained all 180 cards with an insert rate of one per two packs. The second parallel contained only 36 of the cards and featured a gold and silver strip on the left side, with the rest of the card done with a silver finish. These gold parallels are inserted every 12 packs. The third parallel level included a gold, silver and blue foil strip up the left side and was die-cut around the entire perimeter. The card fronts also featured a silver finish, with the cards inserted one per 36 packs. All three levels were numbered on the back with a "P" prefix.

Silver Cards:	1X-2X
Gold Cards:	1X-3X
Die-Cut Stars:	4X-8X
Die-Cut Rookies:	2X-4X

1997 Collector's Edge Extreme Finesse

This 19-card insert is done on frosted, clear, foil-stamped cards. The cards were inserted 1:60 packs of Extreme.

		NM/M
Complete Set (25):		200.00
Common Player:		2.00
Minor Stars:		4.00
1	Troy Aikman	12.00
2	Marcus Allen	6.00
3	Ben Coates	2.00
4	Tony Banks	2.00
5	Jeff Blake	2.00
6	Tim Brown	4.00
7	Mark Brunell	8.00
8	Todd Collins	2.00
9	Terrell Davis	10.00
10	Jim Druckenmiller	2.00
11	John Elway	12.00
12	Marshall Faulk	8.00

13	Brett Favre	15.00
14	Antonio Freeman	2.00
15	Joey Galloway	3.00
16	Eddie George	8.00
17	Terry Glenn	4.00
18	Marvin Harrison	6.00
19	Garrison Hearst	4.00
20	Warrick Dunn	6.00
21	Muhsin Muhammad	4.00
22	Jerry Rice	12.00
23	Barry Sanders	15.00
24	Emmitt Smith	15.00
25	Shawn Springs	2.00

1997 Collector's Edge Extreme Force

Force features 26 players on silver cards with flow etched designs. Force was inserted 1:8 packs of Extreme.

		NM/M
Complete Set (25):		25.00
Common Player:		.50
Minor Stars:		1.00
1	Marcus Allen	1.00
2	Chris Canty	.50
3	Jerome Bettis	1.00
4	Carl Pickens	.50
5	Drew Bledsoe	3.00
6	Robert Brooks	.50
7	Shannon Sharpe	.50
8	Tim Brown	.50
9	Mark Brunell	2.00
10	Ben Coates	.50
11	Todd Collins	.50
12	Terrell Davis	3.00
13	John Elway	4.00
14	Brett Favre	5.00
15	Antonio Freeman	1.00
16	Joey Galloway	1.00
17	Warrick Dunn	2.00
18	Terry Glenn	1.00
19	Marvin Harrison	1.00
20	Dan Marino	5.00
21	Jerry Rice	4.00
22	Junior Seau	.50
23	Tony Banks	1.00
24	Emmitt Smith	5.00
25	Napoleon Kaufman	1.00

1997 Collector's Edge Extreme Forerunners

This 25-card redemption subset was made on clear two-way view cards with a large head shot on the back visible from the front. Gold foil was also added to the cards. The cards were available by redemption through instant win cards, of which 250 were made.

		NM/M
Complete Set (25):		150.00
Common Player:		1.00
Minor Stars:		3.00
1	Karim Abdul-Jabbar	2.00
2	Marcus Allen	3.00
3	Jerome Bettis	3.00
4	Drew Bledsoe	8.00
5	Robert Brooks	2.00
6	Mark Brunell	6.00
7	Todd Collins	1.00
8	Terrell Davis	8.00
9	John Elway	12.00
10	Brett Favre	15.00
11	Joey Galloway	4.00
12	Eddie George	8.00
13	Terry Glenn	4.00
14	Marvin Harrison	6.00
15	Keyshawn Johnson	5.00
16	Rob Johnson	5.00
17	Eddie Kennison	2.00
18	Dorsey Levens	2.00
19	Dan Marino	15.00
20	Steve McNair	8.00
21	Terrell Owens	6.00
22	Carl Pickens	3.00
23	Jerry Rice	12.00
24	Emmitt Smith	15.00
25	Kordell Stewart	5.00

1997 Collector's Edge Extreme Fury

Fury is an 18-card insert with top players featured on a Deep Metal card with chromium finish. Fury was inserted 1:48 packs of Extreme.

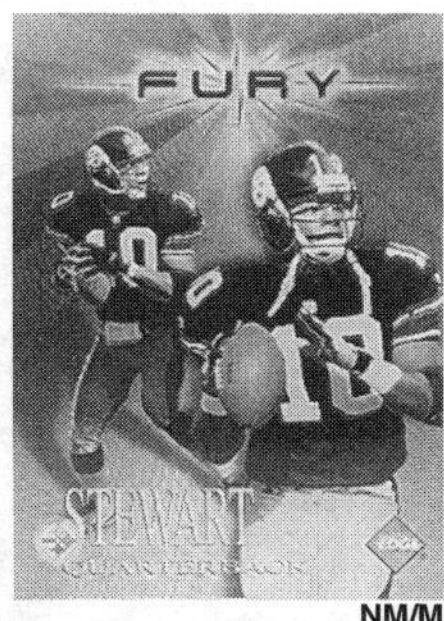

		NM/M
Complete Set (18):		100.00
Common Player:		1.00
Minor Stars:		3.00
1	Jerome Bettis	3.00
2	Terry Glenn	3.00
3	Drew Bledsoe	6.00
4	Mark Brunell	6.00
5	Terrell Davis	6.00
6	Troy Davis	2.00
7	Marshall Faulk	6.00
8	Brett Favre	12.00
9	Antonio Freeman	2.00
10	Joey Galloway	4.00
11	Eddie George	8.00
12	Eddie Kennison	2.00
13	Errict Rhett	1.00
14	Rashaan Salaam	1.00
15	Emmitt Smith	12.00
16	Kordell Stewart	4.00
17	Danny Wuerffel	2.00
18	Steve Young	8.00

1997 Collector's Edge Masters

The 270 standard-sized cards include 240 player cards and 30 team flag cards. The fronts have a player photo superimposed over a background of etched foil that is in a "burst" design. The player's last name is printed in gold at the top center, while the Edge Masters' logo is located at the bottom center and printed in gold. The card backs have the player's headshot in the upper left, with the card number in the upper right. The player's name and bio runs vertically along the right side of the back. The stats are printed horizontally inside stripes along the left side of the back. All of the information is printed over a teal ghosted image of a Wilson football.

		NM/M
Complete Set (270):		25.00
Common Player:		.05
Minor Stars:		.10
Pack (6):		2.00
Wax Box (24):		45.00
1	Arizona Cardinals	.05
2	Larry Centers	.05
3	Rob Moore	.05
4	Frank Sanders	.05
5	Eric Swann	.05
6	Atlanta Falcons	.05
7	Morten Andersen	.05
8	Bert Emanuel	.05
9	Jeff George	.05
10	Craig Heyward	.05
11	Terance Mathis	.05
12	Clay Matthews	.05
13	Eric Metcalf	.05
14	Baltimore Ravens	.05
15	Rob Burnett	.05
16	Leroy Hoard	.05
17	Earnest Hunter	.05
18	Michael Jackson	.05
19	Stevon Moore	.05
20	Anthony Pleasant	.05
21	Vinny Testaverde	.05
22	Eric Zeier	.05
23	Buffalo Bills	.05
24	Todd Collins	.05
25	Russell Copeland	.05
26	Quinn Early	.05
27	Jim Kelly	.10
28	Bryce Paup	.05
29	Andre Reed	.05
30	Bruce Smith	.05
31	Carolina Panthers	.05
32	Steve Beuerlein	.05
33	Mark Carrier	.05
34	Kerry Collins	.30
35	Willie Green	.05
36	Kevin Greene	.05
37	Eric Guliford	.05
38	Brett Maxie	.05
39	Tim McKyer	.05
40	Derrick Moore	.05
41	Chicago Bears	.05
42	Curtis Conway	.05
43	Bryan Cox	.05
44	Jim Flanigan	.05
45	Robert Green	.05
46	Erik Kramer	.05
47	Dave Krieg	.05
48	Rashaan Salaam	.10
49	Alonzo Spellman	.05
50	Donnell Woolford	.05
51	Chris Zorich	.05
52	Cincinnati Bengals	.05
53	Eric Bieniemy	.05
54	Jeff Blake	.20
55	Ki-Jana Carter	.05
56	John Copeland	.05
57	Garrison Hearst	.05
58	Tony McGee	.05
59	Carl Pickens	.05
60	Darnay Scott	.05
61	Bracey Walker	.05
62	Dan Wilkinson	.05
63	Dallas Cowboys	.05
64	Troy Aikman	1.00
65	Bill Bates	.05
66	Shante Carver	.05
67	Michael Irvin	.10
68	Daryl Johnston	.05
69	Jay Novacek	.05
70	Deion Sanders	.50
71	Emmitt Smith	2.00
72	Herschel Walker	.05
73	Sherman Williams	.05
74	Denver Broncos	.05
75	Terrell Davis	1.50
76	John Elway	.75
77	Ed McCaffrey	.05
78	Anthony Miller	.05
79	Michael Dean Perry	.05
80	Shannon Sharpe	.05
81	Mike Sherrard	.05
82	Detroit Lions	.05
83	Scott Mitchell	.05
84	Glyn Milburn	.05
85	Herman Moore	.20
86	Johnnie Morton	.05
87	Brett Perriman	.05
88	Barry Sanders	2.00
89	Tracy Scroggins	.05
90	Green Bay Packers	.05
91	Edgar Bennett	.05
92	Robert Brooks	.05
93	Santana Dotson	.05
94	Brett Favre	2.00
95	Dorsey Levens	.10
96	Craig Newsome	.05
97	Wayne Simmons	.05
98	Reggie White	.10
99	Houston Oilers	.05
100	Chris Chandler	.05
101	Anthony Cook	.05
102	Willie Davis	.05
103	Mel Gray	.05
104	Ronnie Harmon	.05
105	Darryll Lewis	.05
106	Steve McNair	1.00
107	Todd McNair	.05
108	Rodney Thomas	.05
109	Indianapolis Colts	.05
110	Trev Alberts	.05
111	Tony Bennett	.05
112	Quentin Coryatt	.05
113	Sean Dawkins	.05
114	Ken Dilger	.05
115	Marshall Faulk	.25
116	Jim Harbaugh	.05
117	Ronald Humphrey	.05
118	Floyd Turner	.05
119	Jacksonville Jaguars	.05
120	Tony Boselli	.05
121	Mark Brunell	1.00
122	Willie Jackson	.05
123	Jeff Lageman	.05
124	Natrone Means	.05
125	Andre Rison	.05
126	James Stewart	.05
127	Cedric Tillman	.05
128	Kansas City Chiefs	.05
129	Marcus Allen	.10
130	Kimble Anders	.05
131	Steve Bono	.05
132	Dale Carter	.05
133	Lake Dawson	.05
134	Dan Salesaumua	.05
135	Neil Smith	.05
136	Derrick Thomas	.05
137	Tamarick Vanover	.15
138	Miami Dolphins	.05
139	Fred Barnett	.05
140	Steve Emtman	.05
141	Eric Green	.05
142	Dan Marino	2.00
143	O.J. McDuffie	.05
144	Bernie Parmalee	.05
145	Minnesota Vikings	.05
146	Cris Carter	.05
147	Jack Del Rio	.05
148	Qadry Ismail	.05
149	Amp Lee	.05
150	Warren Moon	.05
151	John Randle	.05
152	Jake Reed	.05
153	Robert Smith	.05
154	New England Patriots	.05
155	Drew Bledsoe	1.00
156	Vincent Brisby	.05
157	Willie Clay	.05
158	Ben Coates	.05
159	Curtis Martin	1.50
160	Dave Meggett	.05
161	Will Moore	.05
162	Chris Slade	.05
163	New Orleans Saints	.05
164	Mario Bates	.05
165	Jim Everett	.05
166	Michael Haynes	.05
167	Tyrone Hughes	.05
168	Haywood Jeffires	.05
169	Wayne Martin	.05
170	Renaldo Turnbull	.05
171	New York Giants	.05
172	Dave Brown	.05
173	Chris Calloway	.05
174	Rodney Hampton	.05
175	Michael Strahan	.05
176	Tyrone Wheatley	.05
177	New York Jets	.05
178	Kyle Brady	.05
179	Wayne Chrebet	.05
180	Hugh Douglas	.05
181	Jeff Graham	.05
182	Adrian Murrell	.05
183	Neil O'Donnell	.05
184	Oakland Raiders	.05
185	Tim Brown	.05
186	Aundray Bruce	.05
187	Andrew Glover	.05
188	Jeff Hostetler	.05
189	Napoleon Kaufman	.05
190	Terry McDaniel	.05
191	Chester McGlockton	.05
192	Pat Swilling	.05
193	Harvey Williams	.05
194	Philadelphia Eagles	.05
195	Randall Cunningham	.05
196	Irving Fryar	.05
197	William Fuller	.05
198	Charlie Garner	.05
199	Andy Harmon	.05
200	Rodney Peete	.05
201	Mark Seay	.05
202	Troy Vincent	.05
203	Ricky Watters	.10
204	Calvin Williams	.05
205	Pittsburgh Steelers	.05
206	Jerome Bettis	.10
207	Chad Brown	.05
208	Greg Lloyd	.05
209	Bam Morris	.05
210	Erric Pegram	.05
211	Kordell Stewart	.50
212	Yancey Thigpen	.05
213	Rod Woodson	.05
214	San Diego Chargers	.05
215	Darren Bennett	.05
216	Marco Coleman	.05
217	Stan Humphries	.05
218	Tony Martin	.05
219	Junior Seau	.05
220	San Francisco 49ers	.05
221	Chris Doleman	.05
222	William Floyd	.05
223	Merton Hanks	.05
224	Brent Jones	.05
225	Terry Kirby	.05
226	Derek Loville	.05
227	Ken Norton Jr.	.05
228	Gary Plummer	.05
229	Jerry Rice	1.00
230	J.J. Stokes	.10
231	Dana Stubblefield	.05
232	John Taylor	.05
233	Bryant Young	.05
234	Steve Young	.75
235	Seattle Seahawks	.05
236	Brian Blades	.05
237	Joey Galloway	.30
238	Carlton Gray	.05
239	Cortez Kennedy	.05
240	Rick Mirer	.05
241	Chris Warren	.05
242	St. Louis Rams	.05
243	Isaac Bruce	.20
244	Troy Drayton	.05
245	D'Marco Farr	.05
246	Harold Green	.05
247	Chris Miller	.05
248	Leslie O'Neal	.05
249	Roman Phifer	.05
250	Tampa Bay Buccaneers	.05
251	Trent Dilfer	.10
252	Alvin Harper	.05
253	Jackie Harris	.05
254	John Lynch	.05
255	Hardy Nickerson	.05
256	Errict Rhett	.20
257	Warren Sapp	.05
258	Todd Scott	.05
259	Charles Wilson	.05
260	Washington Redskins	.05
261	Terry Allen	.05
262	Bill Brooks	.05
263	Henry Ellard	.05
264	Gus Frerotte	.05
265	Sean Gilbert	.05
266	Ken Harvey	.05
267	Brian Mitchell	.05
268	Heath Shuler	.05
269	James Washington	.05
270	Michael Westbrook	.10

1997 Collector's Edge Masters '96 Rookies

Inserted in retail packs, this chase set included a color photo of the player in the top center of the front. The photo is surrounded by holographic foil, with the Rookie Year '96 logo printed in the upper right. Printed at the bottom of the front is "'96 Rookies." The player's name is printed in yellow at the top center of the card. The backs have the player's name printed in yellow in the top center, followed by the team logo, his bio and stats. The card number is printed in the upper right. Each card is serial numbered, which is located along the left of the back. All the information on the back is printed over a ghosted image of a football player. Overall, 2,000 of each card was produced by Edge.

		NM/M
Complete Set (25):		45.00
Common Player:		1.00
1	Simeon Rice	1.00
2	Jonathan Ogden	1.00
3	Eric Moulds	2.00
4	Tim Biakabutuka	1.00
5	Walt Harris	1.00
6	John Mobley	1.00
7	Reggie Brown	1.00
8	Derrick Mayes	1.00
9	Eddie George	6.00
10	Marvin Harrison	4.00
11	Kevin Hardy	1.00
12	Jerome Woods	1.00
13	Karim Abdul-Jabbar	2.00
14	Duane Clemons	1.00
15	Terry Glenn	3.00
16	Rickey Whittle	1.00
17	Amani Toomer	3.00
18	Keyshawn Johnson	5.00
19	Rickey Dudley	1.00
20	Bobby Hoying	1.00
21	Eddie Kennison	1.00
22	Bryan Still	1.00
23	Terrell Owens	5.00
24	Reggie Brown	1.00
25	Mike Alstott	3.00

1997 Collector's Edge Masters Crucibles

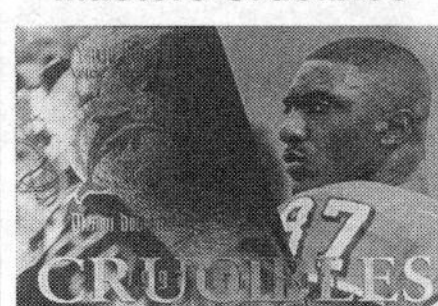

Inserted one per six hobby packs, the chase set includes a color photo of the player on the right. The left side of the front is printed in holographic foil, with a "rolled over" effect in the center. The player's name and position are in the upper left, while the team logo is in the center left and the team name printed directly underneath. "Crucibles" is printed in large capital letters along the bottom front, with "1997 NFL Draft" printed in red over "Crucibles." The backs have the player's write-up along the left and right, with his name, team helmet and bio printed in the center over a ghosted gray background. The card's serial number is printed in the lower right. Edge produced 3,000 of each card in the chase set.

		NM/M
Complete Set (25):		40.00
Common Player:		.75
Minor Stars:		1.50
1	Jake Plummer	1.00
2	Byron Hanspard	.75
3	Peter Boulware	.75
4	Jay Graham	.75
5	Antowain Smith	3.00
6	Rae Carruth	.75
7	Darnell Autry	.75
8	Corey Dillion	5.00
9	Bryant Westbrook	2.00
10	Joey Kent	.75
11	Kevin Lockett	.75
12	Pat Barnes	.75
13	Tony Gonzalez	3.00
14	Yatil Green	.75
15	Danny Wuerffel	1.00
16	Troy Davis	.75
17	Tiki Barber	4.00
18	Ike Hilliard	4.00
19	Darrell Russell	.75
20	Leon Johnson	.75
21	Jim Druckenmiller	1.00
22	Shawn Springs	.75
23	Orlando Pace	2.00
24	Warrick Dunn	6.00
25	Reidel Anthony	2.00

1997 Collector's Edge Masters Night Games

Inserted one per 20 packs, the 25-card chase set features a color photo of the player superimposed over a black and brown computer-generated background. The player's name is printed in gold foil at the top, while the Night Games' logo is printed at the bottom center. The backs have the player's name running vertically along the left. The player's bio runs vertically along the right border. The card number is in the upper right. A color photo of the player is located at the bottom center printed over a colored ghosted image of the player. The card's serial number is printed in the lower right. Edge produced 1,500 of each card in the chase set. A Prism parallel set was inserted 1:60 packs. Edge produced 250 of each Prism card.

		NM/M
Complete Set (25):		100.00
Common Player:		1.00
1	Terry Glenn	3.00
2	Eddie George	6.00
3	Ricky Watters	2.00
4	Barry Sanders	10.00
5	Curtis Martin	8.00
6	Brett Favre	12.00
7	Emmitt Smith	12.00
8	John Elway	8.00
9	Keyshawn Johnson	4.00
10	Kordell Stewart	4.00
11	Drew Bledsoe	6.00
12	Kerry Collins	4.00
13	Terrell Davis	8.00
14	Karim Abdul-Jabbar	1.00
15	Jerome Bettis	2.00
16	Antonio Freeman	1.00
17	Dorsey Levens	1.00
18	Herman Moore	1.00
19	Jerry Rice	10.00
20	Mark Brunell	5.00
21	Mike Alstott	1.00
22	Napoleon Kaufman	1.00
23	Terry Allen	1.00
24	Tony Banks	1.00
25	Vinny Testaverde	1.00

1997 Collector's Edge Masters Nitro-Hobby

This chase set was split between hobby and retail packs. The fronts resemble the base cards with a player photo superimposed over an etched-foil background. The player's name is printed in gold at the top, while a gold-foil burst is printed at bottom of the card and includes the Nitro logo and the player's outstanding stat. The backs are identical to the base cards.

		NM/M
Complete Set (18):		20.00
Common Player:		.75
2	Larry Centers	.75
24	Todd Collins	.75
34	Kerry Collins	1.25
59	Carl Pickens	.75
71	Emmitt Smith	5.00
76	John Elway	1.50
88	Barry Sanders	6.00
116	Jim Harbaugh	.75
121	Mark Brunell	2.50
137	Tamarick Vanover	.75
159	Curtis Martin	3.50
189	Napoleon Kaufman	.75
206	Jerome Bettis	1.00
211	Kordell Stewart	2.00
229	Jerry Rice	2.50
237	Joey Galloway	1.25
243	Isaac Bruce	1.25
264	Gus Frerotte	.75

A player's name in *italic* type indicates a rookie card.

1997 Collector's Edge Masters Nitro-Retail

This chase set was split between hobby and retail packs. The fronts are identical to the base cards, except for a gold-foil "burst" at the bottom of the card front. The Nitro logo and outstanding player stats are printed inside the burst. The backs are identical to the base cards.

		NM/M
Complete Set (18):		20.00
Common Player:		.75
18	Michael Jackson	.75
30	Bruce Smith	.75
36	Kevin Green	.75
64	Troy Aikman	2.50
75	Terrell Davis	3.50
85	Herman Moore	1.25
94	Brett Favre	5.00
98	Reggie White	1.00
106	Steve McNair	2.50
126	Derrick Thomas	.75
142	Dan Marino	5.00
155	Drew Bledsoe	2.50
167	Tyrone Huges	.75
203	Ricky Watters	.75
207	Chad Brown	.75
218	Tony Martin	.75
234	Steve Young	1.50
261	Terry Allen	.75

1997 Collector's Edge Masters Playoff Game Ball

Inserted one per 72 packs, the 19-card set features two player photos on the front. The horizontal cards have a gold-foil background at the top, with the NFC or AFC logo in the top center. The two teams which matched up in the playoff game are printed in black over the logo. A piece of a game-used ball from the contest is embedded into the card in the bottom center. The bottom half of the card front has a Wilson football background. The player's names are printed over their respective photos in the lower corners of the front. The backs have a photo of each of the players, their names, game summary, score and date. All of the information is printed over a football background. Edge produced 250 of each of the cards in the chase set.

		NM/M
Common Player:		10.00
1	Natrone Means, Thurman Thomas	12.00
2	Tony Boselli, Bruce Smith	10.00
3	Jerome Bettis, Marshall Faulk	25.00
4	Kordell Stewart, Jim Harbaugh	15.00
5	Natrone Means, Terrell Davis	25.00
6	Mark Brunell, John Elway	60.00
7	Curtis Martin, Jerome Bettis	40.00
8	Drew Bledsoe, Mark Brunell	60.00
9	Terry Glenn, Keenan McCardell	15.00
10	Troy Aikman, Brad Johnson	40.00
11	Steve Young, Ty Detmer	15.00
12	Jerry Rice, Irving Fryer	35.00
13	Dorsey Levens, Terry Kirby	10.00
14	Brett Favre, Steve Young	60.00
15	Andre Rison, Jerry Rice	40.00
16	Reggie White, Ken Norton Jr.	10.00
17	Kerry Collins, Troy Aikman	40.00
18	Kerry Collins, Brett Favre	65.00
19	Kevin Green, Reggie White	15.00

1997 Collector's Edge Masters Radical Rivals

The 12-card set features two players on each card, one on each side. A player photo is superimposed over a background of the two players' teams' helmets. The player's name and team are printed at the top in gold, while "Radical Rivals" and the card number are printed vertically along the left. The card's serial number is printed along the left border on one side of the card. Edge produced 1,000 of each card. The cards were inserted one per 30 hobby packs.

		NM/M
Complete Set (12):		130.00
Common Player:		2.00
1	Emmitt Smith, Eddie George	25.00
2	Brett Favre, Kerry Collins	25.00
3	Jerry Rice, Antonio Freeman	12.00
4	Ricky Watters, Napoleon Kaufman	2.00
5	Herman Moore, Keyshawn Johnson	6.00
6	Dan Marino, John Elway	25.00
7	Jerome Bettis, Karim Abdul-Jabbar	10.00
8	Isaac Bruce, Carl Pickens	2.00
9	Barry Sanders, Terry Allen	25.00
10	Terry Glenn, Joey Galloway	10.00
11	Mark Brunell, Steve Young	12.00
12	Terrell Davis, Curtis Martin	18.00

1997 Collector's Edge Masters Ripped

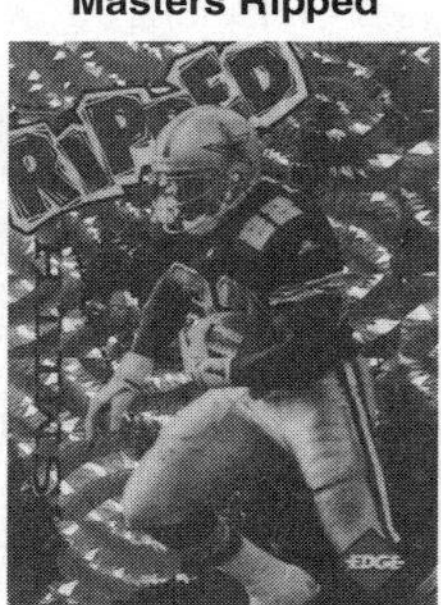

This retail-only chase set continues where the 1996 Ripped set left off, beginning with No. 19. The card fronts have the "Ripped" logo in the upper left, with the player's name printed vertically in black along the lower left border. A color photo of the player is superimposed over a background of red and blue prism-effect foil. The Edge logo is in the lower right of the front. The backs have the card number in gold in the upper right, with a quote about the player from Dick Butkus printed at the top. The player's head shot is printed in the right center, with the team's helmet and player's name, team, position and number printed to the left.

		NM/M
Complete Set (18):		150.00
Common Player:		3.00
19	Troy Aikman	15.00
20	Drew Bledsoe	15.00
21	Tim Brown	3.00
22	Mark Brunell	15.00
23	Cris Carter	6.00
24	Kerry Collins	5.00
25	Barry Sanders	20.00
26	Michael Irvin	3.00
27	Jeff Hostetler	3.00
28	Curtis Martin	20.00
29	Carl Pickens	3.00
30	Marshall Faulk	6.00
31	Rashaan Salaam	6.00
32	Deion Sanders	8.00
33	Emmitt Smith	30.00
34	Kordell Stewart	10.00
35	Ricky Watters	3.00
36	Steve Young	10.00

1997 Collector's Edge Masters Super Bowl XXXI Game Ball

Included with each card in this chase set was a circular piece of a game-used football from Super Bowl XXXI. Featured on the fronts are photos of one New England player and one Green Bay player (one on each side of the front). The Super Bowl XXXI logo appears in the top center in gold foil. The football piece is embedded in the card in the lower center of the front. The players' names are printed in the bottom corners. The Superdome is printed in the background of the lower part of the front. The backs have the player photos over the Super Bowl logo on the left. On the right over gold foil are the players' names, game score, date, game summary and team logos. Edge produced 250 of each card. One card was inserted per 350 packs.

		NM/M
Complete Set (6):		475.00
Common Player:		30.00
1	Brett Favre, Drew Bledsoe	300.00
2	Dorsey Levens, Curtis Martin	125.00
3	Desmond Howard, Dave Meggett	30.00
4	Antonio Freeman, Terry Glenn	100.00
5	Keith Jackson, Ben Coates	30.00
6	Reggie White, Willie McGinest	30.00

1998 Collector's Edge Advantage

Edge Advantage was a 180-card set that included three different parallel sets and five insert sets. The base cards contain the words "Advantage '98" written in script across the top, with the player's name, team logo and position in the bottom left corner. An action shot of the player is on the left part of the card with a close-up head shot on the right side, with all of this over another closer shot of the player in the background. Advantage also has a silver parallel (one per two packs) that has the front in a silver foil, a gold parallel (one per six) that has the front printed on gold foil and a 50-point stock parallel (one per pack) with the words "Advantage '98" printed in gold foil. Advantage Football included five insert sets: Livin' Large, Memorable Moments, Personal Victory, Prime Connection and Showtime.

		NM/M
Complete Set (200):		60.00
Common Player:		.25
Minor Stars:		.50
Gold Cards:		5X
50-Point Cards:		3X
Silver Cards:		4X
Pack (6):		6.00
Wax Box (18):		50.00
1	Larry Centers	.25
2	Kent Graham	.25
3	LaShon Johnson	.25
4	Leeland McElroy	.25
5	Jake Plummer	1.00
6	Jamal Anderson	.50
7	Chris Chandler	.25
8	Bert Emanuel	.25
9	Byron Hanspard	.50
10	O.J. Santiago	.25
11	Derrick Alexander	.25
12	Peter Boulware	.25
13	Eric Green	.25
14	Michael Jackson	.25
15	Bam Morris	.25
16	Vinny Testaverde	.25
17	Todd Collins	.25
18	Quinn Early	.25
19	Jim Kelly	.50
20	Andre Reed	.25
21	Antowain Smith	1.00
22	Steve Tasker	.25
23	Thurman Thomas	.50
24	Steve Beuerlein	.25
25	Rae Carruth	.50
26	Kerry Collins	.50
27	Anthony Johnson	.25
28	Ernie Mills	.25
29	Wesley Walls	.25
30	Curtis Conway	.50
31	Bobby Engram	.25
32	Raymont Harris	.25
33	Erik Kramer	.25
34	Rick Mirer	.25
35	Darnay Scott	.25
36	Tony McGee	.25
37	Jeff Blake	.50
38	Corey Dillon	2.00
39	Carl Pickens	.25
40	Troy Aikman	2.50
41	Billy Davis	.25
42	David LaFleur	.50
43	Anthony Miller	.25
44	Emmitt Smith	4.00
45	Herschel Walker	.25
46	Sherman Williams	.25
47	Flipper Anderson	.25
48	Terrell Davis	2.50
49	Jason Elam	.25
50	John Elway	2.00
51	Darrien Gordon	.25
52	Ed McCaffrey	.25
53	Shannon Sharpe	.25
54	Neil Smith	.25
55	Rod Smith	.25
56	Maa Tanuvasa	.25
57	Glyn Milburn	.25
58	Scott Mitchell	.25
59	Herman Moore	.50
60	Johnnie Morton	.25
61	Barry Sanders	3.00
62	Tommy Vardell	.25
63	Bryant Westbrook	.25
64	Robert Brooks	.25
65	Mark Chmura	.25
66	Brett Favre	4.00
67	Antonio Freeman	.50
68	Dorsey Levens	.50
69	*Bill Schroeder*	1.00
70	Marshall Faulk	.50
71	Jim Harbaugh	.50
72	Marvin Harrison	.50
73	Derek Brown	.25
74	Mark Brunell	1.00
75	Rob Johnson	.50
76	Keenan McCardell	.25
77	Natrone Means	.50
78	Jimmy Smith	.25
79	James Stewart	.25
80	Marcus Allen	.50
81	Pat Barnes	.50
82	Tony Gonzalez	.50
83	Elvis Grbac	.25
84	Greg Hill	.25
85	Kevin Lockett	.25
86	Andre Rison	.25
87	Karim Abdul-Jabbar	.50
88	Fred Barnett	.25
89	Troy Drayton	.25
90	Dan Marino	4.00
91	Irving Spikes	.25
92	Cris Carter	.25
93	Matthew Hatchette	.25
94	Brad Johnson	.50
95	Jake Reed	.25
96	Robert Smith	.25
97	Drew Bledsoe	2.50
98	Keith Byars	.25
99	Ben Coates	.25
100	Terry Glenn	.50
101	Shawn Jefferson	.25
102	Curtis Martin	2.00
103	Dave Meggett	.25
104	Troy Davis	.50
105	Danny Wuerffel	.50
106	Ray Zellers	.25
107	Tiki Barber	1.25
108	Rodney Hampton	.25
109	Ike Hilliard	.50
110	Danny Kanell	.25
111	Tyrone Wheatley	.25
112	Kyle Brady	.25
113	Wayne Chrebet	.25
114	Aaron Glenn	.25
115	Jeff Graham	.25
116	Keyshawn Johnson	.50
117	Adrian Murrell	.50
118	Neil O'Donnell	.25
119	Heath Shuler	.25
120	Tim Brown	.50
121	Rickey Dudley	.25
122	Jeff George	.50
123	Desmond Howard	.25
124	James Jett	.25
125	Napoleon Kaufman	.50
126	Chad Levitt	.25
127	Darrell Russell	.25
128	Ty Detmer	.25
129	Irving Fryar	.25
130	Charlie Garner	.25
131	Kevin Turner	.25
132	Ricky Watters	.50
133	Jerome Bettis	.50
134	Will Blackwell	.25
135	Mark Bruener	.25
136	Charles Johnson	.25
137	George Jones	.25
138	Kordell Stewart	1.00
139	Yancey Thigpen	.25
140	Gary Brown	.25
141	Jim Everett	.25
142	Terrell Fletcher	.25
143	Stan Humphries	.25
144	Freddie Jones	.25
145	Tony Martin	.25
146	Jim Druckenmiller	.50
147	Garrison Hearst	.25
148	Brent Jones	.25
149	Terrell Owens	.50
150	Jerry Rice	2.50
151	J.J. Stokes	.25
152	Steve Young	1.50
153	Steve Broussard	.25
154	Joey Galloway	.50
155	Jon Kitna	.25
156	Warren Moon	.50
157	Shawn Springs	.25
158	Chris Warren	.25
159	Tony Banks	.50
160	Isaac Bruce	.50
161	Eddie Kennison	.50
162	Orlando Pace	.25
163	Lawrence Phillips	.25
164	Mike Alstott	.50
165	Reidel Anthony	.50
166	Horace Copeland	.25
167	Trent Dilfer	.50
168	Warrick Dunn	1.00
169	Hardy Nickerson	.25
170	Karl Williams	.25
171	Eddie George	2.50
172	Ronnie Harmon	.25
173	Joey Kent	.25
174	Steve McNair	2.00
175	Chris Sanders	.25
176	Terry Allen	.25
177	Jamie Asher	.25
178	Stephen Davis	.25
179	Gus Frerotte	.25
180	Leslie Shepherd	.25
181	*Victor Reilly*	.50
182	*Curtis Enis*	.50
183	*Brian Griese*	3.00
184	*Eric Brown*	.50
185	*Jacquez Green*	1.00
186	*Andre Wadsworth*	.75
187	*Ryan Leaf*	.50
188	*Rashaan Shehee*	.75
189	*Peyton Manning*	8.00
190	*Flozell Adams*	.50
191	*Fred Taylor*	3.00
192	*Charlie Batch*	1.00
193	*Kevin Dyson*	1.50
194	*Charles Woodson*	2.00
195	*Ahman Green*	6.00
196	*Randy Moss*	6.00
197	*Robert Edwards*	.75
198	*Reidel Anthony*	1.00
199	*Jerome Pathon*	.75
200	*Samari Rolle*	.50

1998 Collector's Edge Advantage Gold

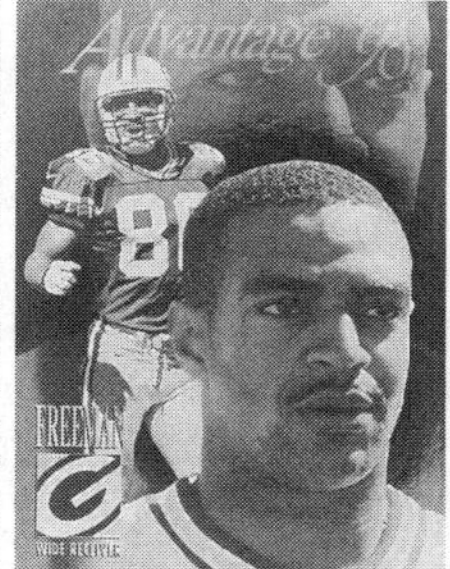

The 180-card Advantage base set has a lacquered gold parallel version. The cards were inserted one per six packs.

Gold Cards: 3X

1998 Collector's Edge Advantage 50-Point

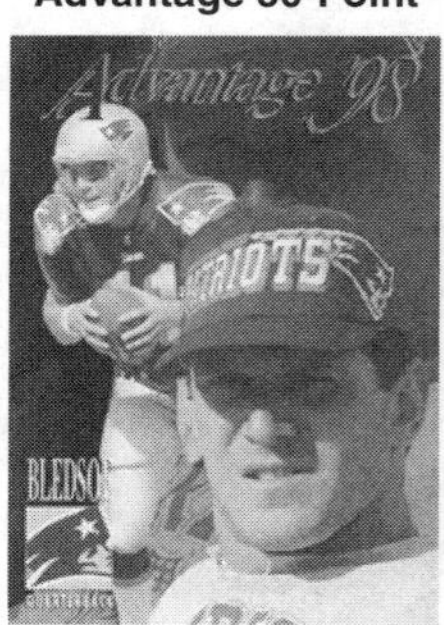

This parallel of the 180-card Advantage base set was printed on 50-point card stock and seeded one per pack.

50-Point Cards: 2X

1998 Collector's Edge Advantage Silver

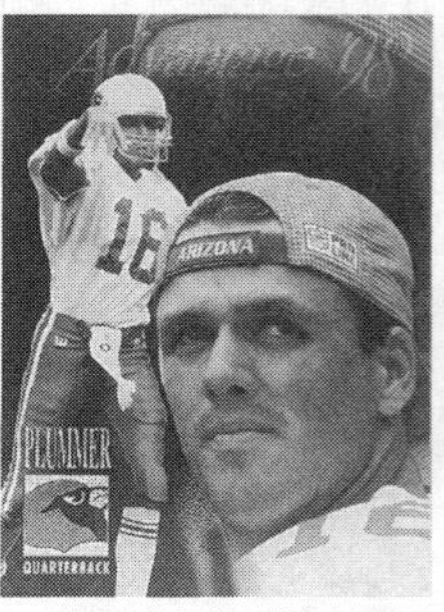

A parallel of the 180-card Advantage base set was printed on embossed silver stock and inserted 1:2.

Silver Cards: 2X

1998 Collector's Edge Advantage Livin' Large

Livin' Large was a 22-card insert that was printed on plastic with a die-cut out of the top of the card. Inserted every 12 packs, these inserts featured a head shot of the player, with a football over his head with the insert name inside. The player's name, position and team logo was printed across the bottom, with the background colors related to that team. Holofoil versions of each card were also printed with a stated print run of 100 sets.

		NM/M
Complete Set (22):		125.00
Common Player:		1.00
Minor Stars:		2.00
Holofoil Cards:		3X-5X
1	Leeland McElroy	1.00
2	Jamal Anderson	2.00
3	Antowain Smith	4.00
4	Emmitt Smith	10.00
5	John Elway	8.00
6	Barry Sanders	10.00
7	Elvis Grbac	1.00
8	Dan Marino	10.00
9	Cris Carter	1.00
10	Drew Bledsoe	6.00
11	Curtis Martin	6.00
12	Troy Davis	1.00
13	Ike Hilliard	3.00
14	Adrian Murrell	1.00
15	Tim Brown	3.00
16	Kordell Stewart	4.00
17	Jerry Rice	8.00
18	Tony Banks	1.00
19	Mike Alstott	3.00
20	Trent Dilfer	3.00
21	Eddie George	6.00
22	Steve McNair	6.00

1998 Collector's Edge Advantage Personal Victory

This six-card set was also individually numbered to 200 on the back and contained a piece of a game-used ball on the front. The front has three shots of the player - one on each side of a large gold foil "V" and another inside the "V." The player's name is stamped across the bottom, with the piece of game ball above it with the words "Personal Victory" over the game ball. A dull finish is used on the back of the card along with a shot of the game in which the featured player achieved his personal victory.

NM/M
Common Player: 60.00
1 John Elway 125.00
2 Barry Sanders 125.00
3 Brett Favre 150.00
4 Mark Brunell 60.00
5 Drew Bledsoe 75.00
6 Jerry Rice 125.00

1998 Collector's Edge Advantage Prime Connection

Prime Connection spotlights the top tandems of 25 NFL teams on a double-sided, metallic looking card. Each side has an action shot of a player on the right side, with the player's name, position and team on the left side, along with the Prime Connection's logo in the upper left corner. The cards are numbered on both sides in the upper right corner and were inserted every 36 packs of Advantage.

NM/M
Complete Set (25): 250.00
Common Player: 2.00
1 LeShon Johnson, Leeland McElroy 2.00
2 Peter Boulware, Michael Jackson 2.00
3 Andre Reed, Antowain Smith 6.00
4 Rae Carruth, Anthony Johnson 2.00
5 Herschel Walker, Emmitt Smith 20.00
6 Terrell Davis, John Elway 20.00
7 Ed McCaffrey, Shannon Sharpe 4.00
8 Herman Moore, Barry Sanders 20.00
9 Brett Favre, Antonio Freeman 25.00
10 Mark Brunell, James Stewart 10.00
11 Marcus Allen, Elvis Grbac 6.00
12 Karim Abdul-Jabbar, Dan Marino 25.00
13 Drew Bledsoe, Ben Coates 15.00
14 Terry Glenn, Curtis Martin 12.00
15 Troy Davis, Danny Wuerffel 2.00
16 Ike Hilliard, Danny Kanell 4.00
17 Aaron Glenn, Adrian Murrell 2.00
18 Tim Brown, Napoleon Kaufman 8.00
19 Mark Bruener, Jerome Bettis 6.00
20 Jim Druckenmiller, Terrell Owens 6.00
21 Garrison Hearst, Steve Young 8.00
22 Tony Banks, Eddie Kennison 2.00
23 Mike Alstott, Reidel Anthony 6.00
24 Hardy Nickerson, Warrick Dunn 8.00
25 Eddie George, Steve McNair 15.00

1998 Collector's Edge Advantage Showtime

This 23-card insert set was seeded one per 18 packs of Advantage Football. Card fronts featured an action shot of the player, with his name written across the bottom. The background was printed in team colors and was supposed to look like jersey material, with the player's position in large letters behind him. Holofoil versions of these cards also exist and were limited in print run to 100 sets.

NM/M
Complete Set (23): 125.00
Common Player: 1.00
Minor Stars: 2.00
Holofoils: 2X-4X
1 LeShon Johnson 1.00
2 Peter Boulware 1.00
3 Jim Kelly 3.00
4 Rae Carruth 1.00
5 Kerry Collins 5.00
6 Troy Aikman 8.00
7 Terrell Davis 8.00
8 Shannon Sharpe 1.00
9 Brett Favre 15.00
10 Mark Brunell 6.00
11 Keenan McCardell 1.00
12 Marcus Allen 4.00
13 Terry Glenn 4.00
14 Danny Wuerffel 2.00
15 Danny Kanell 1.00
16 Aaron Glenn 1.00
17 Napoleon Kaufman 1.00
18 Mark Bruener 1.00
19 Jim Druckenmiller 1.00
20 Terrell Owens 6.00
21 Steve Young 8.00
22 Reidel Anthony 2.00
23 Warrick Dunn 6.00

1998 Collector's Edge First Place

Singles from this base set feature large action shots of each of the 250 players in this set. Each single has a parallel 50-Point card that are found one per pack. Also, each player has a 50-Point Silver issue that is sequentially numbered to 125 and found 1:24 packs.

NM/M
Complete Set (250): 40.00
Common Player: .10
Minor Stars: .20
50-Point Cards: 2X-4X
50-Point Rookies: 2X
Inserted 1:1
50-Point Gold Cards: 5X-10X
50-Point Gold Rookies: 3X-5X
Inserted 1:24
Production 125 Sets
Pack (6): 2.50
Wax Box (24): 50.00
1 Karim Abdul-Jabbar .50
2 *Flozell Adams* .50
3 Troy Aikman 1.50
4 Robert Smith .20
5 *Stephen Alexander* 1.00
6 *Harold Shaw* .50
7 Marcus Allen .20
8 Terry Allen .20
9 Mike Alstott .50
10 Jamal Anderson .50
11 Reidel Anthony .20
12 Jamie Asher .10
13 Darnell Autry .10
14 *Phil Savoy* .50
15 *Jon Ritchie* .30
16 Tony Banks .20
17 Tiki Barber .20
18 Pat Barnes .20
19 *Charlie Batch* .50
20 *Mikhael Ricks* .50
21 Jerome Bettis .20
22 Tim Biakabutuka .10
23 *Roosevelt Blackmon* .50
24 Jeff Blake .20
25 Drew Bledsoe 1.50
26 Tony Boselli .10
27 Peter Boulware .10
28 Tony Brackens .10
29 *Corey Bradford* 2.00
30 *Michael Pittman* 1.00
31 *Keith Brooking* .40
32 Robert Brooks .10
33 Derrick Brooks .10
34 *Ken Oxendine* .40
35 *R.W. McQuarters* .75
36 Tim Brown .20
37 Chad Brown .10
38 Isaac Bruce .20
39 Mark Brunell 1.50
40 Chris Canty .10
41 Mark Carrier .10
42 Rae Carruth .10
43 Ki-Jana Carter .10
44 Cris Carter .20
45 Larry Centers .10
46 *Corey Chavous* .50
47 Mark Chmura .10
48 *Cameron Cleeland* .20
49 Dexter Coakley .10
50 Ben Coates .10
51 *Jonathon Linton* .30
52 Todd Collins .10
53 Kerry Collins .20
54 *Tebucky Jones* .50
55 Curtis Conway .20
56 *Sam Cowart* .50
57 Bryan Cox .10
58 Randall Cunningham .50
59 Terrell Davis 2.00
60 Troy Davis .10
61 *Patrick Johnson* .50
62 Trent Dilfer .20
63 *Vonnie Holliday* .40
64 Corey Dillon 1.00
65 Hugh Douglas .10
66 Jim Druckenmiller .20
67 Warrick Dunn 1.50
68 *Robert Edwards* 1.00
69 *Greg Ellis* .40
70 John Elway 1.50
71 Bert Emanuel .10
72 Bobby Engram .10
73 *Curtis Enis* 1.00
74 Marshall Faulk .50
75 Brett Favre 3.00
76 Doug Flutie .50
77 Glenn Foley .10
78 Antonio Freeman .50
79 Gus Frerotte .10
80 John Friesz .10
81 Irving Fryar .10
82 Joey Galloway .50
83 Rich Gannon .10
84 Charlie Garner .10
85 Jeff George .20
86 Eddie George 1.25
87 Sean Gilbert .10
88 Terry Glenn .20
89 Aaron Glenn .10
90 Tony Gonzalez .10
91 Jeff Graham .10
92 Elvis Grbac .10
93 *Jacquez Green* 2.00
94 Kevin Greene .10
95 *Brian Griese* 3.00
96 Byron Hanspard .10
97 Jim Harbaugh .10
98 Kevin Hardy .10
99 Walt Harris .10
100 Marvin Harrison .20
101 Rodney Harrison .10
102 Jeff Hartings .10
103 Ken Harvey .10
104 Garrison Hearst .20
105 Ike Hilliard .10
106 Jeff Hostetler .10
107 Bobby Hoying .20
108 Michael Jackson .10
109 Anthony Johnson .10
110 Brad Johnson .50
111 Keyshawn Johnson .20
112 Charles Johnson .10
113 Daryl Johnston .10
114 Chris Jones .10
115 George Jones .10
116 *Donald Hayes* .40
117 Danny Kanell .10
118 Napoleon Kaufman .50
119 Cortez Kennedy .10
120 Eddie Kennison .20
121 Levon Kirkland .10
122 Jon Kitna .10
123 Erik Kramer .10
124 David LaFleur .10
125 Lamar Lathon .10
126 Ty Law .10
127 *Ryan Leaf* .40
128 Dorsey Levens .20
129 Ray Lewis .10
130 Darryll Lewis .10
131 *Matt Hasselbeck* 40.00
132 Greg Lloyd .10
133 Kevin Lockett .10
134 Keith Lyle .10
135 *Peyton Manning* 8.00
136 Dan Marino 2.00
137 Wayne Martin .10
138 *Ahman Green* 6.00
139 Tony Martin .10
140 *E.G. Green* .40
141 Derrick Mayes .10
142 Ed McCaffrey .20
143 Keenan McCardell .10
144 O.J. McDuffie .10
145 Leeland McElroy .10
146 Willie McGinest .10
147 Chester McGlockton .10
148 Steve McNair .50
149 Natrone Means .20
150 Eric Metcalf .10
151 Anthony Miller .10
152 Rick Mirer .10
153 Scott Mitchell .10
154 John Mobley .10
155 Warren Moon .50
156 Herman Moore .50
157 *Randy Moss* 6.00
158 Eric Moulds .20
159 Muhsin Muhammad .10
160 Adrian Murrell .10
161 *Marcus Nash* 1.00
162 Hardy Nickerson .10
163 Ken Norton .10
164 Neil O'Donnell .10
165 Terrell Owens .50
166 Orlando Pace .10
167 *Jammi German* .40
168 Erric Pegram .10
169 *Jason Peter* .50
170 Carl Pickens .20
171 Jake Plummer .75
172 John Randle .10
173 Andre Reed .10
174 Jake Reed .10
175 Errict Rhett .10
176 Simeon Rice .10
177 Jerry Rice 1.50
178 Andre Rison .20
179 Darrell Russell .10
180 Rashaan Salaam .10
181 Deion Sanders .50
182 Barry Sanders 3.00
183 Chris Sanders .10
184 Warren Sapp .10
185 Junior Seau .20
186 Jason Sehorn .10
187 Shannon Sharpe .20
188 Sedrick Shaw .10
189 Heath Shuler .10
190 *Chris Floyd* .50
191 *Terry Fair* .40
192 *Kevin Dyson* 2.00
193 Torrance Small .10
194 Antowain Smith .75
195 Bruce Smith .10
196 *Tarik Smith* .50
197 Emmitt Smith 2.00
198 Neil Smith .10
199 Jimmy Smith .20
200 Chris Spielman .10
201 Danny Wuerffel .10
202 Irving Spikes .10
203 Shawn Springs .10
204 *Duane Starks* .50
205 Kordell Stewart .60
206 J.J. Stokes .20
207 Eric Swann .10
208 Steve Tasker .10
209 *Tim Dwight* 2.00
210 Jason Taylor .10
211 Vinny Testaverde .20
212 Thurman Thomas .20
213 Broderick Thomas .10
214 Derrick Thomas .10
215 Zach Thomas .10
216 *Germane Crowell* .50
217 Amani Toomer .10
218 Tamarick Vanover .10
219 Ross Verba .10
220 *Andre Wadsworth* .50
221 Ray Zellars .10
222 Chris Warren .10
223 Steve Young 1.00
224 Tyrone Wheatley .10
225 Reggie White .50
226 *John Avery* 1.00
227 *Charles Woodson* 2.00
228 *Takeo Spikes* 1.50
229 Bryant Young .10
230 *Tavian Banks* .50
231 *Fred Beasley* .50
232 *Chris Ruhman* .50

1998 Collector's Edge First Place Game Gear Jersey

Jerseys present at the NFL Draft Day Ceremonies and worn during the pre-season were used to make these cards. Singles were found 1:480 packs.

NM/M
Complete Set (2): 110.00
Common Player: 10.00
Inserted 1:480
1 Peyton Manning 100.00
2 Ryan Leaf 10.00

1998 Collector's Edge First Place Peyton Manning

Edge produced a five-card insert of Manning and inserted them 1:24 packs.

NM/M
Complete Set (5): 40.00
Common Player: 8.00
Inserted 1:24

1998 Collector's Edge First Place Rookie Ink

This set features autographed cards from the top 1998 rookies. Cards are enhanced with silver foil and each card back contains a certificate of authenticity. Singles are signed in blue ink and are found 1:24 packs. Red signatures also exist and are limited to 50 of each.

NM/M
Common Player: 8.00
Inserted 1:24
Red Signatures: 2X
Production 50 Sets
1 Brian Griese 45.00
2 Adrian Murrell 12.00
3 Marvin Harrison 25.00
4 Tavian Banks 8.00
5 Mike Alstott 18.00
6 Joe Jurevicius 12.00
7 Tim Dwight 18.00
8 Derrick Mayes 12.00
9 Kevin Greene 8.00
10 Marcus Nash 12.00
11 Charlie Batch 12.00
12 Cris Carter 25.00
13 Randy Moss 150.00
14 Tiki Barber 20.00
15 Ahman Green 50.00
16 Terrell Owens 20.00
17 Jim Druckenmiller 8.00
18 Reidel Anthony 8.00
19 Jacquez Green 12.00
20 Skip Hicks 12.00
21 Terry Allen 12.00
22 Fred Lane 8.00
23 Robert Holcombe 8.00
24 Jeremy Newberry 8.00
25 Fred Taylor 40.00
26 Mark Bruener 8.00
27 Hines Ward 20.00
28 Stephen Davis 20.00
29 Justin Armour 8.00
30 Peyton Manning 125.00
31 Ryan Leaf 12.00

1998 Collector's Edge First Place Rookie Markers

Each single in this 30-card set has a special embossed foil icon that recognizes the player's draft pick number. Singles were inserted 1:24 packs.

NM/M
Complete Set (30): 75.00
Common Player: 1.00
Minor Stars: 2.00
Inserted 1:24
1 Michael Pittman 1.00
2 Andre Wadsworth 1.00
3 Keith Brooking 1.00
4 Patrick Johnson 1.00
5 Jonathon Linton 1.00
6 Donald Hayes 1.00
7 Mark Chmura 1.00
8 Terry Allen 1.00
9 Brian Griese 8.00
10 Marcus Nash 2.00
11 Germane Crowell 2.00
12 Roosevelt Blackmon 1.00
13 Peyton Manning 20.00
14 Tavian Banks 2.00
15 Fred Taylor 15.00
16 Jim Druckenmiller 1.00
17 John Avery 2.00
18 Randy Moss 20.00
19 Robert Edwards 4.00
20 Cameron Cleeland 2.00
21 Joe Jurevicius 3.00
22 Charles Woodson 4.00
23 Terry Allen 1.00
24 Ryan Leaf 1.00
25 Chris Ruhman 1.00
26 Ahman Green 8.00
27 Jerome Pathon 4.00
28 Jacquez Green 3.00
29 Kevin Dyson 4.00
30 Skip Hicks 2.00

1998 Collector's Edge First Place Ryan Leaf

Edge produced a five-card insert set of Leaf and inserted them 1:24 packs.

NM/M
Complete Set (5): 5.00
Common Player: 1.00
Inserted 1:24

1998 Collector's Edge First Place Successors

Only the top players in the NFL are in this 25-card set. Singles are featured on mirror silver with gold foil. Cards were inserted 1:8 packs.

NM/M
Complete Set (25): 35.00
Common Player: .50
Minor Stars: 1.00
Inserted 1:8
1 Troy Aikman 4.00
2 Jerome Bettis 2.00
3 Drew Bledsoe 4.00
4 Tim Brown 2.00
5 Mark Brunell 2.00
6 Cris Carter 2.00
7 Terrell Davis 4.00
8 Robert Edwards 1.00
9 John Elway 5.00
10 Brett Favre 6.00
11 Eddie George 2.00
12 Brian Griese 2.00
13 Napoleon Kaufman .50
14 Ryan Leaf .50
15 Dorsey Levens .50
16 Peyton Manning 6.00
17 Dan Marino 5.00
18 Jim Druckenmiller .50
19 Herman Moore 1.00
20 Randy Moss 6.00
21 Jake Plummer 1.00
22 Barry Sanders 5.00
23 Emmitt Smith 5.00
24 Rod Smith .50
25 Fred Taylor 3.00

1998 Collector's Edge First Place Triple Threat

Three different levels to this 40-card insert. The first being Bronze that are found 1:12 packs. The next level is Silver that are inserted 1:24. The toughest is the Gold which are inserted 1:36.

NM/M
Complete Set (40): 100.00
Common Bronze: .75
Inserted 1:12
Common Silver: 1.25
Inserted 1:24
Common Gold: 2.00
Inserted 1:36
1 Robert Brooks .75
2 Troy Aikman 4.00
3 Randy Moss 10.00
4 Tim Brown 1.50
5 Brad Johnson 1.00
6 Kevin Dyson 2.00
7 Mark Chmura .75
8 Joey Galloway 2.00
9 Eddie George 3.00
10 Napoleon Kaufman .75
11 Dan Marino 6.00
12 Ed McCaffrey 3.00
13 Herman Moore 2.00
14 Carl Pickens .75
15 Emmitt Smith 6.00
16 Drew Bledsoe 4.00
17 Andre Wadsworth 1.00
18 Charles Woodson 2.00
19 Terrell Davis 5.00
20 Yancey Thigpen 1.00
21 Drew Bledsoe 4.00
22 Keith Brooking 1.00
23 Mark Brunell 3.00
24 Terrell Davis 5.00
25 Antonio Freeman 1.00
26 Peyton Manning 6.00
27 Jerry Rice 3.00
28 Takeo Spikes 1.00
29 Danny Wuerffel .75
30 Jerome Bettis 2.00
31 Cris Carter 2.00
32 Jim Druckenmiller 1.00
33 Warrick Dunn 3.00
34 John Elway 6.00
35 Brett Favre 6.00
36 Ryan Leaf 1.00
37 Dorsey Levens 1.00
38 Terrell Owens 2.00
39 Barry Sanders 6.00
40 Kordell Stewart 2.00

1998 Collector's Edge First Place Triumph

Each Triumph card is printed on clear acetate stock with a large action shot in the foreground with a head shot in the background. The 25 different singles were inserted 1:12 packs.

NM/M
Complete Set (25): 45.00
Common Player: .75
Inserted 1:12
1 Troy Aikman 3.00
2 Jerome Bettis .75
3 Drew Bledsoe 3.00
4 Tim Brown 2.00
5 Mark Brunell 2.00
6 Cris Carter .75
7 Terrell Davis 3.00
8 Jim Druckenmiller .75
9 Robert Edwards 1.00
10 John Elway 4.00
11 Brett Favre 5.00
12 Eddie George 3.00
13 Brian Griese 2.00
14 Napoleon Kaufman .75
15 Ryan Leaf 1.00
16 Dorsey Levens .75
17 Peyton Manning 6.00
18 Dan Marino 5.00
19 Herman Moore .75
20 Randy Moss 6.00
21 Jake Plummer 1.00
22 Barry Sanders 5.00
23 Emmitt Smith 5.00
24 Rod Smith .75
25 Fred Taylor 2.00

1998 Collector's Edge Masters

This is the first super-premium product that Edge has released. Every card in this set is sequentially numbered to 5,000, with double-thick parallel levels. The first being the 50-Point cards that are numbered to 3,000 and inserted one-per-pack. The 50-Point Gold singles are numbered to 150 and inserted 1:20 packs. HoloGold cards are numbered to 10 and found 1:300 packs.

NM/M
Complete Set (199): 150.00
Common Player: .25
Minor Stars: .50
Common Rookie: .50
Production 5,000 Sets
50-Point Cards: 1.5X
Inserted 1:1
Production 3,000 Sets
50-Point Gold Cards: 3X-5X
50-Point Gold Rookies: 2X-4X
Inserted 1:20
Production 150 Sets
Hologold Cards: 10X-25X
Hologold Rookies: 4X-8X
Inserted 1:300
Production 10 Sets
Pack (3): 3.00
Wax Box (20): 50.00
1 Rob Moore .50
2 Adrian Murrell .25
3 Jake Plummer 2.00
4 *Michael Pittman* 1.50
5 Frank Sanders .50

6 *Andre Wadsworth* 1.00
7 Jamal Anderson 1.00
8 Chris Chandler .50
9 *Tim Dwight* 3.00
10 Tony Martin .25
11 Terance Mathis .25
12 *Ken Oxendine* .50
13 Jim Harbaugh .50
14 *Priest Holmes* 25.00
15 Michael Jackson .25
16 *Pat Johnson* .50
17 Jermaine Lewis .25
18 Eric Zeier .25
19 Doug Flutie 1.00
20 Rob Johnson .50
21 Eric Moulds 1.00
22 Andre Reed .50
23 Antowain Smith 1.00
24 Bruce Smith .25
25 Thurman Thomas .50
26 Steve Beuerlein .25
27 Kevin Greene .25
29 Raghib Ismail .25
30 Fred Lane .25
31 Muhsin Muhammad .25
32 Edgar Bennett .25
33 Curtis Conway .50
34 Bobby Engram .25
35 *Curtis Enis* 2.00
36 Erik Kramer .25
37 Chris Penn .25
38 Jeff Blake .50
39 Corey Dillon 2.00
40 Neil O'Donnell .25
41 Carl Pickens .50
42 Darnay Scott .25
43 *Damon Gibson* .50
44 Troy Aikman 3.00
45 Billy Davis .25
46 Michael Irvin .50
47 Ernie Mills .25
48 Deion Sanders 1.00
49 Emmitt Smith 4.50
50 Chris Warren .50
51 Bubby Brister .25
52 Terrell Davis 4.50
53 John Elway 4.50
54 *Brian Griese* 5.00
55 Ed McCaffrey .75
56 *Marcus Nash* 1.00
57 Shannon Sharpe .50
58 Rod Smith .50
59 *Charlie Batch* 1.00
60 *Germane Crowell* 1.00
61 Scott Mitchell .25
62 Johnnie Morton .25
63 Herman Moore .75
64 Barry Sanders 5.00
65 Robert Brooks .25
66 Brett Favre 5.00
67 Antonio Freeman 1.00
68 Raymont Harris .25
69 Dorsey Levens 1.00
70 Reggie White 1.00
71 Marshall Faulk 1.00
72 Marvin Harrison .50
73 *Peyton Manning* 15.00
74 *Jerome Pathon* 3.00
75 *Tavian Banks* 1.00
76 Mark Brunell 1.00
77 Keenan McCardell .25
78 Jimmy Smith .75
79 *Fred Taylor* 5.00
80 Derrick Alexander .25
81 Donnell Bennett .25
82 Rich Gannon .25
83 Elvis Grbac .50
84 Andre Rison .50
85 *Rashaan Shehee* .50
86 Karim Abdul .75
87 *John Avery* 1.00
88 *Oronde Gadsden* 1.00
89 Dan Marino 4.50
90 O.J. McDuffie .50
91 Zach Thomas .50
92 Cris Carter 1.00
93 Randall Cunningham 1.00
94 Brad Johnson .75
95 *Randy Moss* 12.00
96 Jake Reed .25
97 Robert Smith .50
98 Drew Bledsoe 3.00
99 Ben Coates .50
100 *Robert Edwards* 2.00
101 Terry Glenn .75
102 Shawn Jefferson .25
103 Ty Law .25
104 *Cameron Cleeland* .50
105 Kerry Collins .50
106 Sean Dawkins .25
107 Andre Hastings .25
108 Lamar Smith .25
109 Danny Wuerffel .25
110 Gary Brown .25
111 Chris Calloway .25
112 Ike Hilliard .25
113 *Joe Jurevicius* 3.00
114 Danny Kanell .25
115 Wayne Chrebet .75
116 Glenn Foley .50
117 Keyshawn Johnson 1.00
118 Leon Johnson .25
119 Curtis Martin 1.00
120 Vinny Testaverde .50
121 Tim Brown .50
122 Jeff George .50
123 James Jett .25
124 Napoleon Kaufman .50
125 *Charles Woodson* 3.00
126 Irving Fryar .25
127 Jeff Graham .25
128 Bobby Hoying .25
129 Duce Staley .25
130 Jerome Bettis .75
131 *Chris Fuamatu-Ma'afala* 2.00
132 Courtney Hawkins .25
133 Charles Johnson .25
134 Kordell Stewart 1.00
135 *Hines Ward* 3.00
136 Tony Banks .50
137 Isaac Bruce .50
138 *Robert Holcombe* 1.00
139 Eddie Kennison .50
140 *Ryan Leaf* 1.00
141 Natrone Means .50
142 *Mikhael Ricks* .50
143 Junior Seau .50
144 Bryan Still .25
145 Garrison Hearst .75
146 *R.W. McQuarters* 1.00
147 Terrell Owens 1.00
148 Jerry Rice 3.00
149 J.J. Stokes .50
150 Steve Young 2.00
151 Joey Galloway 1.00
152 *Ahman Green* 12.00
153 Warren Moon .50
154 Shawn Springs .25
155 Ricky Watters .50
156 Mike Alstott .50
157 Reidel Anthony .50
158 Trent Dilfer .50
159 Warrick Dunn 1.00
160 *Jacquez Green* 2.00
161 *Kevin Dyson* 3.00
162 Eddie George 2.00
163 Steve McNair 1.00
164 Yancy Thigpen .25
165 Frank Wycheck .50
166 Terry Allen .50
167 Gus Frerotte .25
168 Trent Green .50
169 *Skip Hicks* 1.00
170 Michael Westbrook .50
171 Jamal Anderson .50
172 Carl Pickens .25
173 Deion Sanders .50
174 Emmitt Smith 2.00
175 Terrell Davis 2.00
176 John Elway 2.00
177 Charlie Batch 1.00
178 Herman Moore .25
179 Barry Sanders 3.00
180 Brett Favre 3.00
181 Antonio Freeman .50
182 Marshall Faulk .50
183 Peyton Manning 6.00
184 Mark Brunell 1.50
185 Dan Marino 2.00
186 Randy Moss 6.00
187 Drew Bledsoe 1.50
188 Robert Edwards 1.00
189 Curtis Martin .50
190 Charles Woodson 1.00
191 Jerome Bettis .25
192 Robert Holcombe .50
193 Ryan Leaf .50
194 Natrone Means .50
195 Jerry Rice 1.50
196 Steve Young 1.00
197 Warrick Dunn 1.00
198 Eddie George 1.00
199 Peyton Manning CL 4.00
200 Ryan Leaf CL .50

1998 Collector's Edge Masters Legends

This 30-card set includes the top players from '98. Each card is sequentially numbered to 2,500 and inserted 1:8 packs.

NM/M
Complete Set (30): 40.00
Common Player: .50
Minor Stars: 1.00
Inserted 1:8
Production 2,500 Sets
1 Jake Plummer 1.00
2 Doug Flutie 1.00
3 Corey Dillon 3.00
4 Carl Pickens .50
5 Troy Aikman 3.00
6 Deion Sanders 1.00
7 Emmitt Smith 5.00
8 Terrell Davis 4.00
9 John Elway 4.00
10 Herman Moore 1.00
11 Barry Sanders 5.00
12 Brett Favre 5.00
13 Antonio Freeman 1.00
14 Marshall Faulk 3.00
15 Mark Brunell 2.00
16 Dan Marino 5.00
17 Cris Carter 1.00
18 Drew Bledsoe 3.00
19 Keyshawn Johnson 1.00
20 Curtis Martin 2.00
21 Napoleon Kaufman .50
22 Jerome Bettis 1.00
23 Kordell Stewart 1.00
24 Natrone Means .50
25 Jerry Rice 4.00
26 Steve Young 3.00
27 Joey Galloway 1.00
28 Warrick Dunn 1.00
29 Eddie George 1.00
30 Terry Allen .50

1998 Collector's Edge Masters Main Event

Main Event singles are sequentially numbered to 2,000 and inserted 1:16 packs.

NM/M
Complete Set (20): 75.00
Common Player: .75
Minor Stars: 2.00
Inserted 1:16
Production 2,000 Sets
1 Troy Aikman 3.00
2 Jamal Anderson 2.00
3 Charlie Batch 1.00
4 Jerome Bettis 1.00
5 Mark Brunell 2.00
6 Terrell Davis 4.00
7 Warrick Dunn 2.00
8 Robert Edwards 1.00
9 John Elway 5.00
10 Brett Favre 6.00
11 Doug Flutie 2.00
12 Eddie George 2.00
13 Dan Marino 5.00
14 Curtis Martin 2.00
15 Randy Moss 10.00
16 Carl Pickens .75
17 Jake Plummer 1.00
18 Barry Sanders 6.00
19 Emmitt Smith 6.00
20 Fred Taylor 8.00

1998 Collector's Edge Masters Rookie Masters

This 30-card set is made up of the top rookies from the class of '98. Each card is sequentially numbered to 2,500 and inserted 1:8 packs.

NM/M
Complete Set (30): 50.00
Common Player: .75
Minor Stars: 1.50
Inserted 1:8
Production 2,500 Sets
1 Peyton Manning 15.00
2 Ryan Leaf 1.00
3 Charlie Batch 1.00
4 Brian Griese 5.00
5 Randy Moss 15.00
6 Jacquez Green 2.00
7 Kevin Dyson 4.00
8 Mikhael Ricks 1.00
9 Jerome Pathon 2.00
10 Joe Jurevicius 3.00
11 Germane Crowell 2.00
12 Tim Dwight 3.00
13 Pat Johnson 1.00
14 Hines Ward 3.00
15 Marcus Nash 1.00
16 Damon Gibson .75
17 Robert Edwards 2.00
18 Robert Holcombe 1.00
19 Tavian Banks 1.00
20 Fred Taylor 8.00
21 Skip Hicks 2.00
22 Curtis Enis 1.00
23 Ahman Green 6.00
24 John Avery 1.00
25 Chris Fuamatu-Ma'afala 2.00
26 Rashaan Shehee .75
27 Cameron Cleeland 1.00
28 Charles Woodson 3.00
29 R.W. McQuarters 1.00
30 Andre Wadsworth 1.00

1998 Collector's Edge Masters Sentinels

This 10-card set is made up of the top 10 most collectible superstars in the NFL. Each card is sequentially numbered to 500 and found 1:120 packs.

NM/M
Complete Set (10): 125.00
Common Player: 10.00
Inserted 1:120
Production 500 Sets
1 John Elway 15.00
2 Brett Favre 20.00
3 Barry Sanders 20.00
4 Terrell Davis 15.00
5 Dan Marino 20.00
6 Emmitt Smith 20.00
7 Randy Moss 25.00
8 Peyton Manning 25.00
9 Robert Edwards 10.00
10 Fred Taylor 15.00

1998 Collector's Edge Masters Super Masters

We have the checklist at 23 players for a complete set. Ten of the players also have signed versions of their insert card. Insert odds are 1:10 packs for the regular insert and the Autographs vary.

NM/M
Common Player: 1.50
Minor Stars: 3.00
Inserted 1:10
Production 2,000 Sets
Troy Aikman 8.00
Edgar Bennett 1.50
Robert Brooks 1.50
Dwight Clark 3.00
Dwight Clark AUTO 15.00
Roger Craig 3.00
Roger Craig AUTO 15.00
Terrell Davis 12.00
Len Dawson 3.00
Len Dawson AUTO 40.00
John Elway 12.00
Brett Favre 16.00
Antonio Freeman 3.00
Jack Ham 3.00
Jack Ham AUTO 15.00
Michael Irvin 3.00
Butch Johnson AUTO 10.00
Drew Pearson 3.00
Drew Pearson AUTO 15.00
Jerry Rice 8.00
Deion Sanders 3.00
Shannon Sharpe 3.00
Emmitt Smith 12.00
Rod Smith 3.00
John Stallworth 3.00
John Stallworth AUTO 15.00
Bart Starr 10.00
Bart Starr AUTO 225.00
Johnny Unitas 8.00
Johnny Unitas AUTO 225.00
Steve Young 5.00
Reggie White 3.00

1998 Collector's Edge Odyssey

The base set is made up of 250 cards and is broken down into four tiers or quarters. The first 150 cards are from the 1st Quarter subset. Cards 151-200 are 2nd Quarter and are inserted 1:1.5 packs. Cards 201-230 are 3rd Quarter and are found 1:3 packs. Cards 231-250 are the 4th Quarter singles and are the toughest to find at 1:18 packs.

NM/M
Complete Set (250): 250.00
Common 1st Quarter: .10
Minor Stars: .20
Common Rookie: .50
Common 2nd Quarter: .25
Inserted 1:1.5
Common 3rd Quarter: .50
Inserted 1:3
Common 4th Quarter: 1.00
Inserted 1:18
Pack: 3.00
Wax Box (24): 55.00
1 Terance Mathis .10
2 Tony Martin .10
3 Chris Chandler .20
4 Jamal Anderson .50
5 Jake Plummer .75
6 Adrian Murrell .10
7 Rob Moore .10
8 Frank Sanders .10
9 Larry Centers .10
10 *Andre Wadsworth* .50
11 Jim Harbaugh .20
12 Errict Rhett .10
13 Jermaine Lewis .10
14 Michael Jackson .10
15 Eric Zeier .10
16 Rob Johnson .20
17 Antowain Smith .50
18 Andre Reed .10
19 Bruce Smith .10
20 Doug Flutie .50
21 Thurman Thomas .20
22 Kerry Collins .20
23 Fred Lane .20
24 Muhsin Mohammed .10
25 Rae Carruth .10
26 Raghib Islmail .10
27 Kevin Greene .10
28 *Curtis Enis* .50
29 Curtis Conway .20
30 Erik Kramer .10
31 Edgar Bennett .20
32 Neil O'Donnell .20
33 Jeff Blake .20
34 Carl Pickens .20
35 Corey Dillon .50
36 Troy Aikman 1.00
37 Jason Garrett .10
38 Emmitt Smith 1.50
39 Deion Sanders .50
40 Michael Irvin .20
41 Chris Warren .20
42 John Elway 1.00
43 Terrell Davis 1.50
44 Shannon Sharpe .20
45 Rod Smith .10
46 *Marcus Nash* 1.00
47 *Brian Griese* 4.00
48 Barry Sanders 2.00
49 Herman Moore .20
50 Scott Mitchell .10
51 Johnnie Morton .10
52 *Rashaan Shehee* .10
53 *Charlie Batch* 1.00
54 Brett Favre 2.00
55 Dorsey Levens .20
56 Antonio Freeman .50
57 Reggie White .50
58 Robert Brooks .10
59 Raymont Harris .10
60 *Peyton Manning* 8.00
61 Marshall Faulk .50
62 *Jerome Pathon* 1.00
63 Marvin Harrison .20
64 Mark Brunell .75
65 *Fred Taylor* 4.00
66 Jimmy Smith .20
67 James Stewart .20
68 Keenan McCardell .10
69 Andre Rison .10
70 Elvis Grbac .10
71 Donnell Bennett .10
72 Rich Gannon .10
73 Derrick Thomas .10
74 Dan Marino 1.50
75 Karim Abdul-Jabbar .10
76 *John Avery* 1.00
77 O.J. McDuffie .10
78 *Oronde Gadsden* .50
79 Zach Thomas .20
80 *Randy Moss* 6.00
81 Cris Carter .50
82 Jake Reed .10
83 Robert Smith .20
84 Brad Johnson .50
85 Drew Bledsoe 1.00
86 *Robert Edwards* 1.00
87 Terry Glenn .50
88 Troy Brown .10
89 Shawn Jefferson .10
90 Danny Wuerffel .10
91 Dana Stubblefield .10
92 Derrick Alexander .10
93 Ray Zellars .10
94 Andre Hastings .10
95 Danny Kanell .10
96 Tiki Barber .10
97 Ike Hilliard .10
98 Charles Way .10
99 Chris Calloway .10
100 Curtis Martin .50
101 Glenn Foley .20
102 Vinny Testaverde .20
103 Keyshawn Johnson .50
104 Wayne Chrebet .50
105 Leon Johnson .10
106 Jeff George .20
107 *Charles Woodson* 3.00
108 Tim Brown .20
109 James Jett .10
110 Napoleon Kaufman .50
111 Charlie Garner .10
112 Bobby Hoying .10
113 Duce Staley .75
114 Irving Fryar .10
115 Kordell Stewart .75
116 Jerome Bettis .50
117 Charles Johnson .10
118 Randall Cunningham .50
119 Courtney Hawkins .10
120 Tony Banks .50
121 Isaac Bruce .50
122 *Robert Holcombe* 1.00
123 Greg Hill .10
124 *Ryan Leaf* .50
125 *Mikhael Ricks* .50
126 Natrone Means .50
127 Junior Seau .20
128 Jerry Rice 1.00
129 Terrell Owens .75
130 Garrison Hearst .20
131 Steve Young .75
132 J.J. Stokes .20
133 Warren Moon .20
134 Joey Galloway .50
135 Ricky Watters .20
136 *Ahman Green* 6.00
137 Trent Dilfer .20
138 Mike Alstott .50
139 Warrick Dunn .75
140 Reidel Anthony .20
141 *Jacquez Green* 1.00
142 Steve McNair .50
143 Eddie George .75
144 Yancey Thigpen .20
145 *Kevin Dyson* 2.00
146 Trent Green .20
147 Gus Frerotte .10
148 Terry Allen .20
149 Michael Westbrook .20
150 Jim Druckenmiller .20
151 Jake Plummer .75
152 Adrian Murrell .50
153 Rob Johnson .50
154 Antowain Smith .75
155 Kerry Collins .50
156 Curtis Enis .75
157 Carl Pickens .50
158 Corey Dillon 1.00
159 Troy Aikman 1.50
160 Emmitt Smith 2.00
161 Deion Sanders .50
162 Michael Irvin .50
163 John Elway 1.50
164 Terrell Davis 2.00
165 Shannon Sharpe .50
166 Rod Smith .50
167 Barry Sanders 3.00
168 Herman Moore .50
169 Brett Favre 3.00
170 Dorsey Levens .50
171 Antonio Freeman .75
172 Peyton Manning 8.00
173 Marshall Faulk .50
174 Mark Brunell 1.00
175 Fred Taylor 5.00
176 Dan Marino 2.00
177 Randy Moss 8.00
178 Cris Carter .50
179 Drew Bledsoe 1.00
180 Robert Edwards 1.00
181 Curtis Martin .50
182 Napoleon Kaufman .50
183 Kordell Stewart 1.00
184 Jerome Bettis .50
185 Tony Banks .50
186 Isaac Bruce .50
187 Ryan Leaf 1.00
188 Natrone Means .50
189 Jerry Rice 1.50
190 Terrell Owens .75
191 Garrison Hearst .50
192 Steve Young .75
193 Warren Moon .50
194 Joey Galloway .50
195 Trent Dilfer .50
196 Mike Alstott .50
197 Warrick Dunn 1.50
198 Steve McNair .75
199 Eddie George 1.00
200 Terry Allen .50
201 Jake Plummer 1.00
202 Curtis Enis 1.00
203 Carl Pickens .75
204 Corey Dillon 1.00
205 Troy Aikman 2.00
206 Emmitt Smith 3.00
207 John Elway 2.00
208 Terrell Davis 3.00
209 Barry Sanders 4.00
210 Brett Favre 4.00
211 Antonio Freeman .75
212 Peyton Manning 10.00
213 Mark Brunell 1.50
214 Fred Taylor 6.00
215 Dan Marino 3.00
216 Randy Moss 10.00
217 Drew Bledsoe 1.50
218 Robert Edwards 2.00
219 Curtis Martin .75
220 Kordell Stewart .75
221 Jerome Bettis .75
222 Tony Banks .75
223 Ryan Leaf 1.00
224 Jerry Rice 2.00
225 Steve Young 1.00
226 Warren Moon .75
227 Trent Dilfer .75
228 Warrick Dunn 1.00
229 Steve McNair 1.00
230 Eddie George 1.50
231 Curtis Enis 1.00
232 Carl Pickens 3.00
233 Troy Aikman 6.00
234 Emmitt Smith 8.00
235 John Elway 6.00
236 Terrell Davis 6.00
237 Barry Sanders 8.00
238 Brett Favre 8.00
239 Peyton Manning 15.00
240 Fred Taylor 10.00
241 Dan Marino 8.00
242 Randy Moss 15.00
243 Drew Bledsoe 5.00
244 Kordell Stewart 1.00
245 Jerome Bettis 3.00
246 Ryan Leaf 1.00
247 Jerry Rice 6.00
248 Steve Young 4.00
249 Warren Moon 3.00
250 Eddie George 5.00

1998 Collector's Edge Odyssey Galvanized

Each base card has a parallel Galvanized single that is also tiered four ways. Each single has the letter "G" on the back and has a foil front. Cards 1-150 were inserted 1:3 packs, Cards 151-200 were found 1:15 packs, 201-230 at 1:29 and 231-250 at 1:59.

1st Quarter Cards: 2X
1st Quarter Rookies: 1.5X
Inserted 1:3
2nd Quarter Cards: 3X
2nd Quarter Rookies: 2X
Inserted 1:15
3rd Quarter Cards: 2X
3rd Quarter Rookies: 1.5X
Inserted 1:29
4th Quarter Cards: 3X
4th Quarter Rookies: 2X
Inserted 1:144

1998 Collector's Edge Odyssey HoloGold

HoloGold is the second parallel set to the base and is also tiered four different ways. These singles have the letter "H" on the backs and also have foil fronts. Cards 1-150 are numbered to 150 and inserted 1:34 packs, cards 151-200 are numbered to 50 and found 1:307, cards 201-230 are limited to 30 and found 1:840 and the last tier are cards numbered 231-250 with a production run of 20 and inserted 1:1,920.

1st Quarter Cards: 8X-15X
1st Quarter Rookies: 3X-5X
Inserted 1:34
Production 150 Sets

Values quoted in this guide reflect the retail price of a card—the price a collector can expect to pay when buying a card from a dealer. The wholesale price—that which a collector can expect to receive from a dealer when selling cards—will be significantly lower, depending on desirability and condition.

1998 Collector's Edge Odyssey Leading Edge

Leading Edge features 30 of the NFL's top stars in an attractive foil set. Singles were inserted 1:7 packs.

NM/M
Complete Set (30): 35.00
Common Player: .50
Inserted 1:7
1 Jake Plummer 1.00
2 Rob Johnson .50
3 Curtis Enis 1.00
4 Carl Pickens .50
5 Troy Aikman 2.00
6 Emmitt Smith 4.50
7 John Elway 3.00
8 Terrell Davis 2.00
9 Shannon Sharpe .50
10 Barry Sanders 4.00
11 Brett Favre 5.00
12 Antonio Freeman 1.50
13 Peyton Manning 6.00
14 Marshall Faulk 1.50
15 Mark Brunell 2.00
16 Dan Marino 4.50
17 Randy Moss 6.00
18 Cris Carter 1.50
19 Robert Edwards 2.00
20 Curtis Martin 1.50
21 Ryan Leaf 1.00
22 Terrell Owens 1.50
23 Garrison Hearst .50
24 Steve Young 1.50
25 Joey Galloway 1.50
26 Mike Alstott 1.50
27 Warrick Dunn 1.00
28 Eddie George 2.50
29 Kevin Dyson 2.00
30 Terry Allen .50

1998 Collector's Edge Odyssey Prodigies

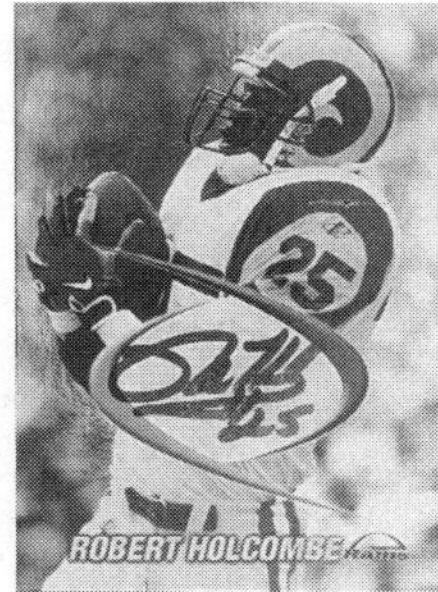

The Prodigies insert is made up of autographs from young talent and rookies from '98. Singles were inserted 1:24 packs. A parallel of Red Signatures exist with most signing between 50 to 80.

NM/M
Common Player: 5.00
Minor Stars: 10.00
Inserted 1:24
John Avery 5.00
Tavian Banks 5.00
Charlie Batch 15.00
Blaine Bishop 5.00
Robert Brooks 15.00
Tim Brown 50.00
Mark Brunell 60.00
Wayne Chrebet 30.00
Jim Druckenmiller 10.00
Robert Edwards 10.00
Doug Flutie 25.00
Glenn Foley 5.00
Oronde Gadsden 10.00
Joey Galloway 20.00
Garrison Hearst 20.00
Robert Holcombe 5.00
Joey Kent 5.00
Jon Kitna 10.00
Herman Moore 30.00
Randy Moss 125.00
Terrell Owens 30.00
Mikhael Ricks 5.00
Rashaan Shehee 5.00
Antowain Smith 20.00
Emmitt Smith 150.00
Robert Smith 20.00
Rod Smith 20.00
J.J. Stokes 20.00
Fred Taylor 40.00
Derrick Thomas 15.00
Chris Warren 5.00
Eric Zeier 5.00

1998 Collector's Edge Odyssey S.L. Edge

Super Limited Edge singles includes 12 of the game's most collectible superstars and were found 1:99 packs.

NM/M
Complete Set (12): 150.00
Common Player: 5.00
Inserted 1:99
1 Emmitt Smith 25.00
2 Deion Sanders 8.00
3 John Elway 20.00
4 Brett Favre 25.00
5 Antonio Freeman 5.00
6 Peyton Manning 20.00
7 Mark Brunell 10.00
8 Dan Marino 25.00
9 Randy Moss 25.00
10 Joey Galloway 5.00
11 Mike Alstott 5.00
12 Eddie George 10.00

1998 Collector's Edge Supreme

Supreme Season Review consists of a 200-card base set, with 170 veterans and 30 redmeption cards for the top draft pick from each NFL team. The player's name and Collector's Edge logo are printed in gold foil on the front. The base set is paralleled by Gold Ingots. Inserts include Markers, T-3 Triple Threat and Pro Signatures Authentic. Two 1-of-1 inserts were also created: Memorable Moments and the 200-card Personal Collection, which features photos from Super Bowl XXXII.

NM/M
Complete Set (200): 50.00
Common Player: .20
Minor Stars: .40
Comp. Gold Ingot (200):
Gold Ingot Cards: 2X-4X
Gold Ingot Rookies: 2X
Pack (6): 4.00
Wax Box (24): 60.00
1 Larry Centers .20
2 Jake Plummer 1.00
3 Simeon Rice .20
4 Arizona Draft Pick .20
4A *Andre Wadsworth* .50
4B *Michael Pittman* 2.00
5 Jamal Anderson .40
6 Bert Emanuel .20
7 Byron Hanspard .40
8 Atlanta Draft Pick .20
8A *Jammi German* .50
8B *Keith Brooking* .50
9 Derrick Alexander .20
10 Peter Boulware .20
11 Michael Jackson .20
12 Ray Lewis .20
13 Vinny Testaverde .40
14 Baltimore Draft Pick .20
14A *Duane Starks* .50
14B *Patrick Johnson* .50
15 Todd Collins .20
16 Jim Kelly .40
17 Andre Reed .20
18 Antowain Smith 1.00
19 Bruce Smith .20
20 Thurman Thomas .40
21 Buffalo Draft Pick .20
21A *Jonathan Linton* 1.00
22 Tim Biakabutuka .20
23 Rae Carruth .40
24 Kerry Collins .40
25 Anthony Johnson .20
26 Lamar Lathon .20
27 Carolina Draft Pick .20
27A *Jason Peters* .50
27B *Donald Hayes* .50
28 Curtis Conway .40
29 Bryan Cox .20
30 Bobby Engram .20
31 Erik Kramer .20
32 Rick Mirer .20
33 Rashaan Salaam .40
34 Chicago Draft Pick .20
34A *Curtis Enis* .50
35 Jeff Blake .40
36 Ki-Jana Carter .20
37 Corey Dillon 1.50
38 Carl Pickens .40
39 Cincinnati Draft Pick .20
39A *Takeo Spikes* 1.00
39B *Brian Simmons* .50
40 Troy Aikman 2.00
41 Daryl Johnston .20
42 David LaFleur .40
43 Anthony Miller .20
44 Deion Sanders 1.00
45 Emmitt Smith 3.00
46 Broderick Thomas .20
47 Dallas Draft Pick .20
47A *Greg Ellis* .50
48 Terrell Davis 2.00
49 John Elway 2.00
50 Ed McCaffrey .20
51 John Mobley .20
52 Bill Romanowski .20
53 Shannon Sharpe .20
54 Neil Smith .20
55 Rod Smith .20
56 Maa Tanuvasa .20
57 Denver Draft Pick .20
57A *Marcus Nash* 1.50
57B *Brian Griese* 4.00
58 Scott Mitchell .20
59 Herman Moore .40
60 Barry Sanders 3.00
61 Detroit Draft Pick .20
61A *Jamal Alexander* .50
61B *Chris Liwienski* .50
61C *Terry Fair* .50
61D *Germane Crowell* .50
61E *Charlie Batch* .75
62 Robert Brooks .40
63 Mark Chmura .20
64 Brett Favre 4.00
65 Antonio Freeman .40
66 Dorsey Levens .40
67 Derrick Mayes .20
68 Ross Verba .20
69 Reggie White .40
70 Green Bay Draft Pick .20
70A *Vonnie Holliday* .50
70B *Roosevelt Blackmon* .50
71 Marshall Faulk .40
72 Jim Harbaugh .40
73 Marvin Harrison .40
74 Indianapolis Draft Pick .20
74A *E.G. Green* .50
74B *Peyton Manning* 10.00
75 Tony Brackens .20
76 Mark Brunell 2.00
77 Rob Johnson .40
78 Keenan McCardell .20
79 Natrone Means .40
80 Jimmy Smith .20
81 Jacksonville Draft Pick .20
81A *Tavian Banks* .50
82 Marcus Allen .40
83 Tony Gonzalez .40
84 Elvis Grbac .20
85 Derrick Thomas .20
86 Tamarick Vanover .20
87 Kansas City Draft Pick .20
87A *Rashaan Shehee* .50
88 Karim Abdul-Jabbar .40
89 Fred Barnett .20
90 Dan Marino 3.00
91 O.J. McDuffie .20
92 Brett Perriman .20
93 Irving Spikes .20
94 Zach Thomas .20
95 Miami Draft Pick .20
95A *John Avery* .50
96 Cris Carter .20
97 Brad Johnson .40
98 John Randle .20
99 Jake Reed .20
100 Robert Smith .20
101 Minnesota Draft Pick .20
101A *Randy Moss* 8.00
102 Drew Bledsoe 2.00
103 Chris Canty .20
104 Ben Coates .20
105 Terry Glenn .40
106 Curtis Martin 1.50
107 Willie McGinest .20
108 Sedrick Shaw .20
109 New England Draft Pick .20
109A *Chris Floyd* 1.00
109B *Tebucky Jones* .50
109C *Harold Shaw* .50
110 Mario Bates .20
111 Heath Shuler .20
112 Danny Wuerffel .40
113 New Orleans Draft Pick .20
113A *Cameron Cleeland* .50
114 Ray Zellars .20
115 Tiki Barber .40
116 Dave Brown .20
117 Ike Hilliard .40
118 Danny Kanell .20
119 Jason Sehorn .20
120 Amani Toomer .20
121 New York Giants Draft Pick .20
121A *Shaun Williams* .50
121B *Joe Jurevicius* 2.00
121C *Brian Alford* .50
122 Wayne Chrebet .20
123 Hugh Douglas .20
124 Jeff Graham .20
125 Keyshawn Johnson .40
126 Adrian Murrell .40
127 Neil O'Donnell .20
128 New York Jets Draft Pick .20
128A *Scott Frost* .50
129 Tim Brown .40
130 Jeff George .40
131 Desmond Howard .20
132 Napoleon Kaufman .40
133 Darrell Russell .20
134 Oakland Draft Pick .20
134A *Charles Woodson* 3.00
135 Ty Detmer .20
136 Irving Fryar .20
137 Bobby Hoying .40
138 Chris T. Jones .20
139 Ricky Watters .40
140 Philadelphia Draft Pick .20
140A *Allen Rossum* .50
141 Jerome Bettis .40
142 Charles Johnson .20
143 George Jones .20
144 Greg Lloyd .20
145 Kordell Stewart 1.00
146 Yancey Thigpen .20
147 Pittsburgh Draft Pick .20
147A *Chris Fuamatu-Ma'afala* 2.00
148 Stan Humphries .20
149 Tony Martin .20
150 Eric Metcalf .20
151 Junior Seau .40
152 San Diego Draft Pick .20
152A *Ryan Leaf* .75
153 Jim Druckenmiller .40
154 William Floyd .40
155 Kevin Greene .20
156 Garrison Hearst .20
157 Ken Norton .20
158 Terrell Owens .40
159 Jerry Rice 2.00
160 J.J. Stokes .20
161 Dana Stubblefield .20
162 Rod Woodson .20
163 Bryant Young .20
164 Steve Young 1.00
165 San Francisco Draft Pick .20
165A *Fred Beasley* .50
165B *R.W. McQuarters* 1.00
165C *Chris Ruhman* .50
166 Steve Broussard .20
167 Chad Brown .20
168 Joey Galloway .40
169 Jon Kitna .20
170 Warren Moon .40
171 Chris Warren .20
172 Seattle Draft Pick .20
172A *Ahman Green* 8.00
173 Tony Banks .40
174 Isaac Bruce .40
175 Eddie Kennison .40
176 Keith Lyle .20
177 Lawrence Phillips .20
178 St. Louis Draft Pick .20
178A *Robert Holcombe* 1.50
179 Mike Alstott .40
180 Anthony Reidel .40
181 Trent Dilfer .40
182 Warrick Dunn 2.00
183 Hardy Nickerson .20
184 Errict Rhett .20
185 Warren Sapp .20
186 Tampa Bay Draft Pick .20
186A *Jacquez Green* 2.00
187 Eddie George 2.00
188 Darryll Lewis .20
189 Steve McNair 1.00
190 Chris Sanders .20
191 Tennessee Draft Pick .20
191A *Kevin Dyson* 2.00
192 Terry Allen .40
193 Jamie Asher .20
194 Stephen Davis .20
195 Gus Frerotte .40
196 Sean Gilbert .20
197 Ken Harvey .20
198 Jeff Hostetler .20
199 Michael Westbrook .20
200 *Stephen Alexander* Washington Draft Pick .20
200A *Stephen Alexander* 1.50
200B *Mike Sellers* .50

1998 Collector's Edge Supreme Gold Ingots

Gold Ingots is a full parallel of the Supreme Season Review base set. The cards are printed on 48-point card stock and have "Gold Ingots" printed in gold foil on the front.

NM/M
Gold Ingots Cards: 2X-4X
Gold Ingots Rookies: 2X

1998 Collector's Edge Supreme Markers

Markers is a 30-card insert seeded one per 24 packs. The cards are printed on 48-point stock. The player's last name, position and team are listed at the top. An embossed gold-foil logo denotes which statistical "marker" the player has acheived.

NM/M
Complete Set (30): 150.00
Common Player: 1.00
Minor Stars: 3.00
1 Jamal Anderson 3.00
2 Corey Dillon 5.00
3 Emmitt Smith 12.00
4 Terrell Davis 8.00
5 John Elway 10.00
6 Rod Smith 1.00
7 Herman Moore 2.00
8 Barry Sanders 12.00
9 Robert Brooks 1.00
10 Brett Favre 15.00
11 Antonio Freeman 2.00
12 Dorsey Levens 2.00
13 Marshall Faulk 5.00
14 Mark Brunell 4.00
15 Karim Abdul-Jabbar 1.00
16 Dan Marino 15.00
17 Cris Carter 1.00
18 Drew Bledsoe 8.00
19 Curtis Martin 8.00
20 Adrian Murrell 1.00
21 Tim Brown 3.00
22 Jeff George 1.00
23 Napoleon Kaufman 1.00
24 Jerome Bettis 3.00
25 Kordell Stewart 3.00
26 Yancey Thigpen 1.00
27 Garrison Hearst 1.00
28 Steve Young 8.00
29 Joey Galloway 3.00
30 Eddie George 5.00

1998 Collector's Edge Supreme Pro Signatures Authentic

Seven players signed cards for the Pro Signatures Authentic insert (1:800). Collector's Edge also obtained rookie draft-day jerseys and put swatches on Draft Day Jersey cards.

NM/M
Common Player: 50.00
TA Troy Aikman 250.00
DH Desmond Howard 50.00
JR Jerry Rice 300.00
MA Marcus Allen 100.00
TD Terrell Davis 200.00
RL Ryan Leaf 50.00
PM Peyton Manning 150.00

1998 Collector's Edge Supreme T-3 Triple Threat

T-3 Triple Threat is a 30-card insert. The set features 10 quarterbacks (1:36), 10 running backs (1:24) and 10 wide receivers (1:12). The front has a color player image which is repeated on the left and right. The team's logo is in the upper right and the player's name and T-3 logo are at the bottom.

NM/M
Complete Set (29): 125.00
Common WR: .50
Common RB: 1.00
Common QB: 2.00
Card #18 Never Issued
1 Rae Carruth .50
2 Carl Pickens 1.00
3 Troy Aikman 5.00
4 Emmitt Smith 8.00
5 Terrell Davis 5.00
6 John Elway 6.00
7 Herman Moore 1.00
8 Barry Sanders 8.00
9 Robert Brooks 1.00
10 Brett Favre 10.00
11 Antonio Freeman 1.00
12 Dorsey Levens 1.00
13 Rob Johnson 2.00
14 Jerry Rice 8.00
15 Dan Marino 10.00
16 Cris Carter 1.00
17 Drew Bledsoe 5.00
19 Adrian Murrell 1.00
20 Tim Brown 2.50
21 Napoleon Kaufman 1.00
22 Jerome Bettis 1.50
23 Kordell Stewart 3.00
24 Joey Galloway 2.00
25 Jim Druckenmiller 2.00
26 Terrell Owens 2.50
27 Jake Plummer 2.00
28 Warrick Dunn 3.00
29 Eddie George 4.00
30 Steve McNair 6.00

1999 Collector's Edge Advantage

Edge Advantage is a 190-card set that is made up of 150 veterans, 38 draft pick rookies and 2 checklists. Each card has three different parallels that include Gold Ingot, Galvanized and HoloGold. Other inserts in the product include Rookie Autographs, Jumpstarters, Memorable Moments, Overture, Prime Connection, Shockwaves and Showtime.

NM/M
Complete Set (190): 40.00
Common Player: .15
Minor Stars: .30
Common Rookie: .50
Pack (8): 3.00
Wax Box (24): 50.00
1 Larry Centers .15
2 Rob Moore .30
3 Adrian Murrell .15
4 Jake Plummer 1.25
5 Frank Sanders .15
6 Jamal Anderson .50
7 Chris Chandler .30
8 Tim Dwight .50
9 Tony Martin .15
10 Terance Mathis .15
11 O.J. Santiago .15
12 Jim Harbaugh .30
13 Priest Holmes .75
14 Jermaine Lewis .30
15 Rod Woodson .15
16 Eric Zeier .15
17 Doug Flutie .75
18 Sam Gash .15
19 Rob Johnson .30
20 Eric Moulds .50
21 Andre Reed .30
22 Antowain Smith .50
23 Bruce Smith .15
24 Thurman Thomas .30
25 Steve Beuerlein .15
26 Kevin Greene .15
27 Raghib Ismail .15
28 Fred Lane .15
29 Muhsin Muhammad .15
30 Edgar Bennett .15
31 Curtis Conway .30
32 Bobby Engram .15
33 Curtis Enis .50
34 Erik Kramer .15
35 Jeff Blake .30
36 Corey Dillon .75
37 Neil O'Donnell .30
38 Carl Pickens .30
39 Takeo Spikes .15
40 Troy Aikman 1.25
41 Billy Davis .15
42 Michael Irvin .30
43 Deion Sanders .50
44 Emmitt Smith 1.75
45 Darren Woodson .15
46 Bubby Brister .30
47 Terrell Davis 1.75
48 John Elway 1.75
49 Ed McCaffrey .30
50 Bill Romanowski .15
51 Shannon Sharpe .30
52 Rod Smith .30
53 Charlie Batch 1.00
54 Germane Crowell .30
55 Herman Moore .50
56 Johnnie Morton .15
57 Barry Sanders 2.50
58 Robert Brooks .15
59 Brett Favre 2.50

60 Antonio Freeman .50
61 Darick Holmes .15
62 Dorsey Levens .50
63 Roell Preston .15
64 Marshall Faulk .50
65 E.G. Green .15
66 Marvin Harrison .30
67 Peyton Manning 2.00
68 Jerome Pathon .15
69 Mark Brunell 1.00
70 Kevin Hardy .15
71 Keenan McCardell .15
72 Jimmy Smith .30
73 Fred Taylor 1.25
74 Alvis Whitted .15
75 Kimble Anders .15
76 Donnell Bennett .15
77 Rich Gannon .15
78 Elvis Grbac .15
79 Bam Morris .15
80 Andre Rison .30
81 Karim Abdul .30
82 John Avery .30
83 Oronde Gadsden .30
84 Sam Madison .15
85 Dan Marino 1.75
86 O.J. McDuffie .30
87 Zach Thomas .30
88 Cris Carter .50
89 Randall Cunningham .50
90 Brad Johnson .50
91 Randy Moss 3.00
92 John Randle .30
93 Jake Reed .15
94 Robert Smith .50
95 Drew Bledsoe 1.00
96 Ben Coates .30
97 Robert Edwards .50
98 Terry Glenn .50
99 Ty Law .15
100 Cam Cleeland .30
101 Kerry Collins .30
102 Gary Brown .15
103 Kent Graham .15
104 Ike Hilliard .30
105 Joe Jurevicius .30
106 Danny Kanell .15
107 Wayne Chrebet .50
108 Aaron Glenn .15
109 Keyshawn Johnson .50
110 Curtis Martin .50
111 Vinny Testaverde .30
112 Tim Brown .30
113 Jeff George .30
114 James Jett .15
115 Napoleon Kaufman .50
116 Charles Woodson .50
117 Koy Detmer .15
118 Duce Staley .15
119 Jerome Bettis .50
120 Charles Johnson .15
121 Kordell Stewart .75
122 Tony Banks .30
123 Isaac Bruce .30
124 June Henley .15
125 Ryan Leaf .15
126 Natrone Means .50
127 Mikhael Ricks .15
128 Craig Whelihan .15
129 Garrison Hearst .30
130 Terrell Owens .75
131 Jerry Rice 1.25
132 J.J. Stokes .30
133 Steve Young 1.00
134 Joey Galloway .50
135 Ahman Green .30
136 Jon Kitna .75
137 Ricky Watters .30
138 Mike Alstott .50
139 Reidel Anthony .30
140 Trent Dilfer .30
141 Warrick Dunn .75
142 Jacquez Green .30
143 Kevin Dyson .30
144 Eddie George .75
145 Steve McNair .75
146 Yancy Thigpen .30
147 Terry Allen .30
148 Trent Green .50
149 Skip Hicks .30
150 Michael Westbrook .30
151 *Rahim Abdullah* .50
152 *Champ Bailey* 2.00
153 *Marlon Barnes* .50
154 *D'Wayne Bates* 1.00
155 *Michael Bishop* 2.00
156 *Dre' Bly* .50
157 *David Boston* 4.00
158 *Chris Claiborne* .50
159 *Tim Couch* 4.00
160 *Daunte Culpepper* 8.00
161 *Autrey Denson* .50
162 *Jared DeVries* .50
163 *Troy Edwards* 1.00
164 *Kris Farris* .50
165 *Kevin Faulk* 1.00
166 *Martin Gramatica* 1.50
167 *Torry Holt* 4.00
168 *Brock Huard* 2.00
169 *Sedrick Irvin* 1.75
170 *Edgerrin James* 8.00
171 *James Johnson* .50
172 *Kevin Johnson* 2.00
173 *Andy Katzenmoyer* 1.50
174 *Jevon Kearse* 2.00
175 *Shaun King* 1.00
176 *Rob Konrad* 1.00
177 *Chris McAlister* .50
178 *Darnell McDonald* .50
179 *Donovan McNabb* 8.00
180 *Cade McNown* 2.50
181 *Dat Nguyen* 1.50
182 *Peerless Price* 3.00
183 *Akili Smith* 1.00
184 *Tai Streets* 1.00
185 *Cuncho Brown* .50
186 *Ricky Williams* 8.00
187 *Craig Yeast* .50
188 *Amos Zereoue* 2.00
189 Checklist .15
190 Checklist .15

1999 Collector's Edge Advantage Galvanized

Galvanized singles are printed on silver foil board with gold foil stamping. Each has a Galvanized stamp on the front and are sequentially numbered on the back. Veterans are numbered to 500 and rookies to 200.

NM/M
Galvanized Cards: 3X-5X
Production 500 Sets
Galvanized Rookies: 2X-4X
Production 200 Sets

1999 Collector's Edge Advantage Gold Ingot

Each Gold Ingot single is identical to the base card except for the foil is in gold rather than silver and each has a Gold Ingot stamp on the fronts of the cards. It is a parallel to the base and singles were inserted 1:1 packs.

Gold Ingot Cards: 2X
Gold Ingot Rookies: 1.5X
Inserted 1:1

1999 Collector's Edge Advantage Holo Gold

HoloGold singles are printed on holographic foil board with veterans numbered to 50 and rookies to 20.

NM/M
HoloGold Cards: 10X-20X
Production 50 Sets
HoloGold Rookies: 5X-10X
Production 20 Sets

1999 Collector's Edge Advantage Jumpstarters

Each of the singles in this set are printed on clear acetate and offer commentary of each player from Peyton Manning. Each card was sequentially numbered to 500.

NM/M
Complete Set (10): 40.00
Common Player: 1.00
Production 500 Sets
1 Champ Bailey 2.00
2 David Boston 5.00
3 Tim Couch 12.00
4 Daunte Culpepper 12.00
5 Torry Holt 8.00
6 Donovan McNabb 12.00
7 Cade McNown 2.00
8 Peerless Price 7.00
9 Brock Huard 1.00
10 Ricky Williams 15.00

1999 Collector's Edge Advantage Memorable Moments

Each card in this set highlights a memorable moment from 1998. Each is printed on silver foil and they were found 1:24 packs.

NM/M
Complete Set (10): 40.00
Common Player: 2.00
Inserted 1:24
1 Terrell Davis 6.00
2 Randy Moss 10.00
3 Peyton Manning 10.00
4 Emmitt Smith 10.00
5 Keyshawn Johnson 2.00
6 Dan Marino 10.00
7 John Elway 6.00
8 Doug Flutie 2.00
9 Jerry Rice 6.00
10 Steve Young 4.00

1999 Collector's Edge Advantage Overture

Ten of the NFL's superstars are featured in this foil set with gold foil stamping. Singles were inserted 1:24 packs.

NM/M
Complete Set (10): 60.00
Common Player: 2.00
Inserted 1:24
1 Jamal Anderson 3.00
2 Terrell Davis 6.00
3 John Elway 6.00
4 Brett Favre 8.00
5 Peyton Manning 8.00
6 Dan Marino 8.00
7 Randy Moss 8.00
8 Jerry Rice 6.00
9 Barry Sanders 8.00
10 Emmitt Smith 8.00

1999 Collector's Edge Advantage Preview Set

NM/M
Complete Set (10): 6.00
Common Player: .50
JA Jamal Anderson .50
MB Mark Brunell .50
TD Terrell Davis 1.00
RE Robert Edwards .50
DF Doug Flutie .50
GH Garrison Hearst .50
PM Peyton Manning 2.00
DM Dan Marino 3.00
CM Curtis Martin 1.00
RM Randy Moss 2.00

1999 Collector's Edge Advantage Prime Connection

Current and future NFL stars were included in this 20-card set. Singles were inserted 1:4 packs.

NM/M
Complete Set (20): 35.00
Common Player: .75
Minor Stars: 3.00
Inserted 1:4
1 Ricky Williams 8.00
2 Fred Taylor 4.00
3 Tim Couch 6.00
4 Peyton Manning 4.00
5 Daunte Culpepper 4.00
6 Drew Bledsoe 2.00
7 Torry Holt 2.00
8 Keyshawn Johnson .75
9 Champ Bailey .75
10 Charles Woodson .75
11 Brock Huard .75
12 Jake Plummer 1.00
13 Donovan McNabb 5.00
14 Steve Young 2.00
15 Edgerrin James 7.00
16 Jamal Anderson 1.00
17 Cade McNown 1.00
18 Mark Brunell 2.00
19 Peerless Price 3.50
20 Randy Moss 5.00

1999 Collector's Edge Advantage Rookie Autographs

Each of the autographs are printed on holographic foil board with the signature found on the fronts of each card. Singles were inserted on average of 1:24 packs.

NM/M
Common Player: 6.00
Minor Stars: 12.00
Inserted 1:24
151 Rahim Abdullah 6.00
152 Champ Bailey 15.00
153 Marlon Barnes 6.00
154 D'Wayne Bates 6.00
155 Michael Bishop 20.00
156 Dre' Bly 6.00
157 David Boston 30.00
158 Cuncho Brown 6.00
159 Chris Claiborne 6.00
160 Tim Couch 50.00
161 Daunte Culpepper 50.00
162 Autry Denson 6.00
163 Jared DeVries 6.00
164 Troy Edwards 20.00
165 Kris Farris 6.00
166 Kevin Faulk 12.00
167 Martin Gramatica 6.00
168 Torry Holt 25.00
169 Brock Huard 15.00
170 Sedrick Irvin 6.00
171 Edgerrin James 60.00
172 James Johnson 15.00
173 Kevin Johnson 15.00
174 Andy Katzenmoyer 15.00
175 Jevon Kearse 18.00
176 Shaun King 15.00
177 Rob Konrad 12.00
178 Chris McAlister 6.00
179 Darnell McDonald 6.00
180 Donovan McNabb 50.00
181 Cade McNown 15.00
182 Dat Nguyen 12.00
183 Peerless Price 30.00
184 Akili Smith 12.00
185 Tai Streets 12.00
186 Ricky Williams 60.00
187 Craig Yeast 6.00
188 Amos Zereoue 20.00

1999 Collector's Edge Advantage Shockwaves

This 20-card set was printed on foil board with gold foil stamping. They were inserted 1:12 packs.

NM/M
Complete Set (20): 60.00
Common Player: 2.00
Inserted 1:12
1 Jamal Anderson 2.00
2 Jake Plummer 3.00
3 Eric Moulds 2.00
4 Troy Aikman 5.00
5 Emmitt Smith 8.00
6 Marshall Faulk 2.00
7 Jerome Bettis 2.00
8 Barry Sanders 8.00
9 Brett Favre 8.00
10 Peyton Manning 8.00
11 Mark Brunell 3.00
12 Fred Taylor 3.00
13 Randall Cunningham 2.00
14 Randy Moss 8.00
15 Drew Bledsoe 4.00
16 Keyshawn Johnson 2.00
17 Curtis Martin 2.00
18 Steve Young 3.00
19 Warrick Dunn 2.00
20 Eddie George 3.00

1999 Collector's Edge Advantage Showtime

Each of the 15 cards in this insert are printed on clear acetate with gold foil stamping. Each was sequentially numbered to 500.

NM/M
Complete Set (15): 60.00
Common Player: 2.00
Production 500 Sets
1 Troy Aikman 6.00
2 Jamal Anderson 2.00
3 Mark Brunell 3.00
4 Terrell Davis 6.00
5 Warrick Dunn 2.00
6 Brett Favre 8.00
7 Doug Flutie 2.00
8 Eddie George 3.00
9 Keyshawn Johnson 2.00
10 Peyton Manning 8.00
11 Dan Marino 6.00
12 Randy Moss 8.00
13 Jake Plummer 2.00
14 Jerry Rice 6.00
15 Barry Sanders 8.00

1999 Collector's Edge First Place

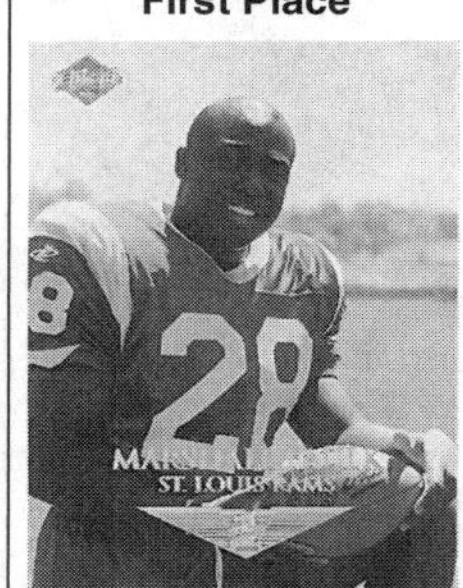

First Place Football was a 200-card set printed on 20-pt. stock. The set included 148 veterans, 50 rookies and 2 checklists. The Kurt Warner #201 was added late to the print run and each was hand-numbered to 500. Parallel sets included Galvanized, Gold Ingot and HoloGold. Other insert sets included: Adrenalin, Excalibur, Future Legends, Loud & Proud, Pro Signature Authentics, Rookie Game Gear and Successors. SRP was $3.99 for 12-card packs.

NM/M
Complete Set (200): 40.00
Common Player: .15
Minor Stars: .30
Common Rookie: .50
Pack (12): 2.00
Wax Box (24): 40.00
1 Adrian Murrell .15
2 Rob Moore .30
3 Jake Plummer .75
4 Simeon Rice .15
5 Frank Sanders .15
6 Jamal Anderson .75
7 Chris Calloway .15
8 Chris Chandler .30
9 Tim Dwight .75
10 Terance Mathis .15
11 Jessie Tuggle .15
12 Tony Banks .30
13 Priest Holmes .50
14 Jermaine Lewis .15
15 Scott Mitchell .15
16 Doug Flutie .50
17 Eric Moulds .75
18 Andre Reed .30
19 Antowain Smith .50
20 Bruce Smith .15
21 Thurman Thomas .30
22 Steve Beuerlein .30
23 Tim Biakabutuka .30
24 Kevin Greene .15
25 Muhsin Muhammad .30
26 Edgar Bennett .15
27 Curtis Conway .30
28 Bobby Engram .15
29 Curtis Enis .75
30 Erik Kramer .15
31 Jeff Blake .30
32 Corey Dillon .75
33 Carl Pickens .30
34 Darnay Scott .30
35 Takeo Spikes .15
36 Ty Detmer .15
37 Terry Kirby .15
38 Leslie Shepherd .15
39 Chris Spielman .15
40 Troy Aikman 1.50
41 Michael Irvin .30
42 Raghib Ismail .15
43 Ernie Mills .15
44 Deion Sanders .75
45 Emmitt Smith 2.00
46 Chris Warren .15
47 Bubby Brister .30
48 Terrell Davis 2.00
49 Brian Griese 1.25
50 Ed McCaffrey .50
51 Shannon Sharpe .30
52 Rod Smith .50
53 Charlie Batch .50
54 Terry Fair .15
55 Herman Moore .75
56 Johnnie Morton .15
57 Barry Sanders 3.00
58 Robert Brooks .15
59 Brett Favre 3.00
60 Mark Chmura .30
61 Antonio Freeman .75
62 Dorsey Levens .75
63 Derrick Mayes .30
64 Marvin Harrison .75
65 Peyton Manning 2.00
66 Jerome Pathon .15
67 Mark Brunell 1.25
68 Keenan McCardell .30
69 Jimmy Smith .75
70 Fred Taylor 1.50
71 Derrick Alexander .15
72 Kimble Anders .15
73 Elvis Grbac .30
74 Warren Moon .30
75 Bam Morris .15
76 Andre Rison .30
77 Karim Abdul .30
78 Dan Marino 2.00
79 Tony Martin .15
80 O.J. McDuffie .30
81 Zach Thomas .30
82 Cris Carter .75
83 Randall Cunningham .75
84 Jeff George .75
85 Randy Moss 3.00
86 Jake Reed .30
87 Robert Smith .75
88 Drew Bledsoe 1.25
89 Ben Coates .30
90 Terry Glenn .75
91 Ty Law .15
92 Shawn Jefferson .15
93 Cameron Cleeland .30
94 Andre Hastings .15
95 Billy Joe Hobert .15
96 Eddie Kennison .15
97 Gary Brown .15
98 Kerry Collins .30
99 Kent Graham .15
100 Ike Hilliard .30
101 Joe Jurevicius .15
102 Wayne Chrebet .75
103 Aaron Glenn .15
104 Keyshawn Johnson .75
105 Mo Lewis .15
106 Curtis Martin .75
107 Vinny Testaverde .50
108 Tim Brown .30
109 Rich Gannon .30
110 James Jett .15
111 Napoleon Kaufman .75
112 Charles Woodson .75
113 Koy Detmer .15
114 Charles Johnson .15
115 Duce Staley .50
116 Jerome Bettis .75
117 Courtney Hawkins .15
118 Levon Kirkland .15
119 Kordell Stewart .75
120 Isaac Bruce .75
121 Marshall Faulk .75
122 Trent Green .50
123 Amp Lee .15
124 Jim Harbaugh .30
125 Charlie Jones .15
126 Freddie Jones .30
127 Ryan Leaf .75
128 Natrone Means .50
129 Junior Seau .30
130 Garrison Hearst .50
131 Terrell Owens .75
132 Jerry Rice 1.50
133 J.J. Stokes .30
134 Steve Young 1.00
135 Joey Galloway .75
136 Jon Kitna .75
137 Ricky Watters .50
138 Mike Alstott .75
139 Reidel Anthony .30
140 Trent Dilfer .50
141 Warrick Dunn .75
142 Kevin Dyson .30
143 Eddie George 1.00
144 Steve McNair 1.00
145 Frank Wycheck .30
146 Skip Hicks .30
147 Brad Johnson .50
148 Michael Westbrook .30
149 Checklist .15
150 Checklist .15
151 *David Boston* 2.50

152 *Patrick Kerney* .50
153 *Chris McAlister* .50
154 *Peerless Price* 2.00
155 *Antoine Winfield* .50
156 *D'Wayne Bates* .50
157 *Cade McNown* 1.00
158 *Akili Smith* 1.00
159 *Rahim Abdullah* .50
160 *Tim Couch* 5.00
161 *Kevin Johnson* 2.00
162 *Ebenezer Ekuban* .50
163 *Dat Nguyen* .50
164 *Al Wilson* .50
165 *Chris Claiborne* .50
166 *Sedrick Irvin* .50
167 *Antwan Edwards* .50
168 *Aaron Brooks* 5.00
169 *De'Mond Parker* .50
170 *Edgerrin James* 5.00
171 *Fernando Bryant* .50
172 *Michael Cloud* .50
173 *John Tait* .50
174 *Cecil Collins* 1.00
175 *J.J. Johnson* .50
176 *Rob Konrad* 1.00
177 *Daunte Culpepper* 5.00
178 *Jim Kleinsasser* 1.00
179 *Dimitrius Underwood* .50
180 *Michael Bishop* 1.75
181 *Kevin Faulk* 1.75
182 *Andy Katzenmoyer* 1.00
183 *Ricky Williams* 2.00
184 *Joe Montgomery* .50
185 *Donovan McNabb* 5.00
186 *Troy Edwards* 2.00
187 *Amos Zereoue* 1.50
188 *Joe Germaine* .50
189 *Torry Holt* 2.50
190 *Jermaine Fazande* .50
191 *Reggie McGrew* .50
192 *Karsten Bailey* 1.00
193 *Lamar King* .50
194 *Autry Denson* .50
195 *Martin Gramatica* 1.00
196 *Shaun King* 1.00
197 *Darnell McDonald* .50
198 *Anthony McFarland* .50
199 *Jevon Kearse* 2.00
200 *Champ Bailey* 1.50
201 *Kurt Warner/500* 100.00
201P Kurt Warner Parallel 12.00

1999 Collector's Edge First Place Galvanized

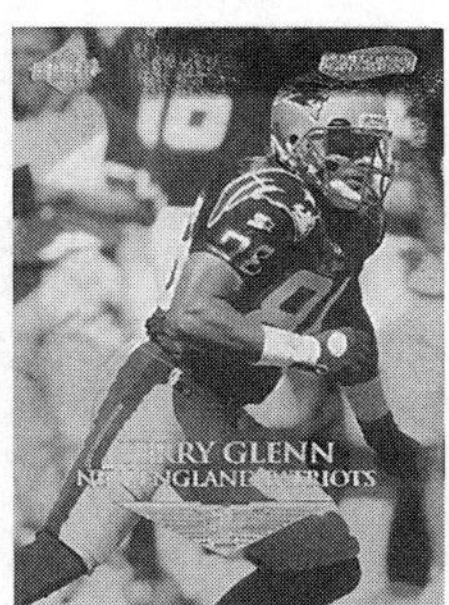

This was a 200-card parallel to the base set. Each single had the Galvanized stamp on the front of the card. Veterans were sequentially numbered to 500 and rookies to 100.

Galvanized Cards: 2X-4X
Production 500 Sets
Galvanized Rookies: 3X-5X
Production 100 Sets

1999 Collector's Edge First Place Gold Ingot

This was a 200-card parallel to the base set. Each single had the Gold Ingot stamp on the front of the card. Singles were found one-per-pack.

NM/M
Gold Ingot Cards: 2X
Gold Ingot Rookies: 1.5X
Inserted 1:1

1999 Collector's Edge First Place HoloGold

This was a 200-card parallel to the base set. Each single had the HoloGold stamp on the front of the card. Veterans were sequentially numbered to 50 and rookies to 10.

NM/M
HoloGold Cards: 10X-20X
Production 50 Sets
HoloGold Rookies: No Pricing
Production 10 Sets

1999 Collector's Edge First Place Adrenalin

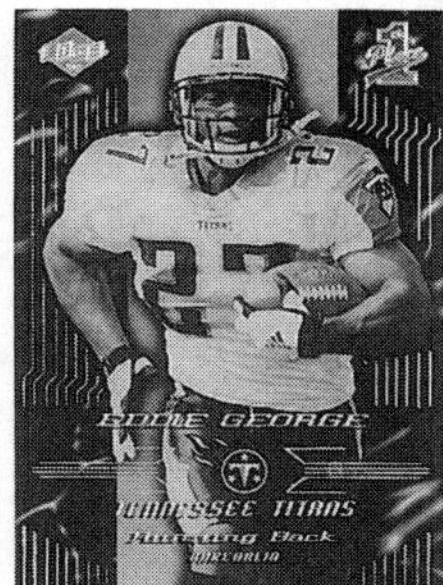

This 20-card insert set included high impact players. Each single was sequentially numbered to 1,000 and printed on clear vinyl stock.

NM/M
Complete Set (20): 50.00
Common Player: 2.00
Production 1,000 Sets
1 Jake Plummer 2.00
2 Jamal Anderson 2.00
3 Eric Moulds 2.00
4 Emmitt Smith 6.00
5 Terrell Davis 4.00
6 Barry Sanders 6.00
7 Brett Favre 6.00
8 Antonio Freeman 2.00
9 Peyton Manning 6.00
10 Mark Brunell 3.00
11 Fred Taylor 4.00
12 Dan Marino 6.00
13 Cris Carter 2.00
14 Randy Moss 6.00
15 Keyshawn Johnson 2.00
16 Curtis Martin 2.00
17 Jerome Bettis 2.00
18 Terrell Owens 2.00
19 Joey Galloway 2.00
20 Eddie George 2.00

1999 Collector's Edge First Place Excalibur

Excalibur was a 25-card set that was a cross-brand program. Singles were found in First Place, Odyssey and Masters. Nine of the singles appeared in First Place and were found 1:24 packs.

NM/M
Complete Set (9): 25.00
Common Player: 2.00
Inserted 1:24
2 Torry Holt 2.00
5 Edgerrin James 6.00
6 Brett Favre 6.00
13 Peyton Manning 6.00
17 Randy Moss 6.00
19 Terrell Davis 4.00
20 Mark Brunell 2.00
22 Eddie George 2.00
24 Doug Flutie 2.00

1999 Collector's Edge First Place Future Legends

This 20-card insert set included all of the top rookies from 1999. Singles were found 1:6 packs.

NM/M
Complete Set (20): 25.00
Common Player: .50
Minor Stars: 1.00
Inserted 1:6
1 Tim Couch 6.00
2 Donovan McNabb 5.00
3 Akili Smith 2.00
4 Edgerrin James 6.00
5 Ricky Williams 7.00
6 Torry Holt 3.00
7 Champ Bailey 1.50
8 David Boston 3.00
9 Daunte Culpepper 5.00
10 Cade McNown 1.00
11 Troy Edwards 1.00
12 Chris Claiborne .50
13 Jevon Kearse 1.00
14 Shaun King 1.00
15 Kevin Faulk 1.00
16 James Johnson 1.00
17 Peerless Price 3.00
18 Kevin Johnson 1.00
19 Brock Huard 1.00
20 Joe Germaine .50

1999 Collector's Edge First Place Loud and Proud

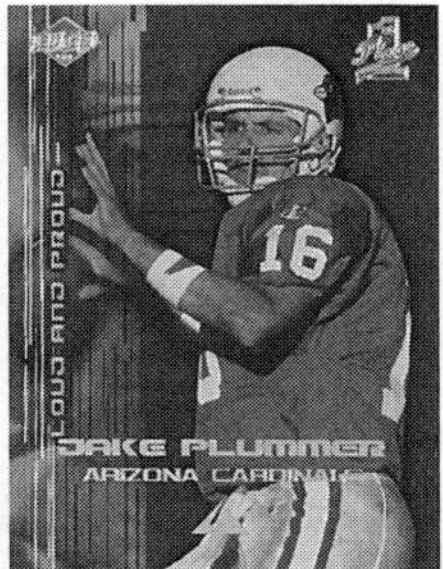

This 20-card insert set included the top stars in the NFL. Singles were found 1:12 packs.

NM/M
Common Player: 1.00
Inserted 1:12
1 Jamal Anderson 1.00
2 Emmitt Smith 4.00
3 Terrell Davis 3.00
4 Barry Sanders 4.00
5 Fred Taylor 2.00
6 Randy Moss 4.00
7 Antonio Freeman 1.00
8 Curtis Martin 1.00
9 Terrell Owens 1.00
10 Eddie George 1.00
11 Dan Marino 4.00
12 Brett Favre 4.00
13 Jerry Rice 3.00
14 Steve Young 2.00
15 Doug Flutie 1.00
16 Jake Plummer 1.00
17 Troy Aikman 3.00
18 Mark Brunell 1.00
19 Jon Kitna 1.00
20 Charlie Batch 1.00

1999 Collector's Edge First Place Pro Signatures

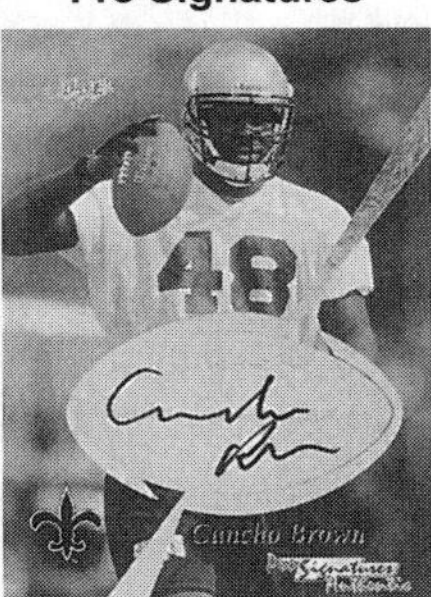

This 29-card insert set included autographed cards from both rookies and veterans. Singles were found 1:24 packs. A parallel Blue version was made with each single sequentially numbered to 40. A Red version was also made with each single numbered to 10.

NM/M
Complete Set (29): 425.00
Common Player: 6.00
Minor Stars: 12.00
Inserted 1:24
Blue Cards: 3X
Production 40 Sets
Red Cards:
Production 10 Sets
Rahim Abdullah 6.00
Kimble Anders 6.00
Dre' Bly 6.00
David Boston 25.00
Cuncho Brown 6.00
Gary Brown 6.00
Ray Buchanan 6.00
Tim Couch 45.00
Autry Denson 6.00
Jared DeVries 6.00
Bobby Engram 6.00
Terry Fair 6.00
Kevin Faulk 12.00
Joey Galloway 20.00
Rich Gannon 25.00
Marvin Harrison 30.00
Andre Hastings 6.00
Courtney Hawkins 6.00
Brock Huard 12.00
Edgerrin James 60.00
Shaun King 12.00
Chris McAlister 6.00
Keenan McCardell 12.00
Dat Nguyen 12.00
Andre Reed 12.00
Jimmy Smith 20.00
Akili Smith 12.00
Duce Staley 20.00
Craig Yeast 6.00

1999 Collector's Edge First Place Rookie Game Gear

This 10-card insert set included only rookies from 1999. Each single was sequentially numbered to 500.

NM/M
Common: 10.00
Production 500 Sets
1 Tim Couch 40.00
2 Donovan McNabb 30.00
3 Akili Smith 15.00
4 Daunte Culpepper 30.00
5 Ricky Williams 50.00
6 Kevin Johnson 20.00
7 Cade McNown 10.00
8 Torry Holt 20.00
9 Champ Bailey 10.00
10 David Boston 20.00

1999 Collector's Edge First Place Successors

This 15-card insert set included a top rookie and a top NFL star from the same position and matched them up on the same card. Singles were found 1:12 packs.

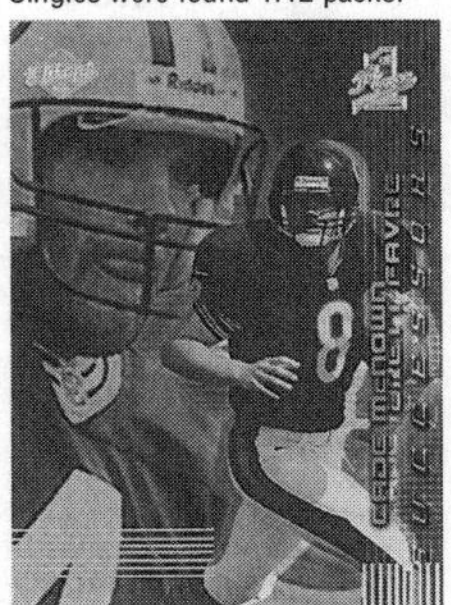

NM/M
Complete Set (15): 35.00
Common Player: 1.00
Minor Stars: 2.00
Inserted 1:12
1 David Boston, Cris Carter 4.00
2 Peerless Price, Eric Moulds 3.00
3 Cade McNown, Brett Favre 6.00
4 Akili Smith, Charlie Batch 1.00
5 Tim Couch, Peyton Manning 5.00
6 Keyshawn Johnson, Joey Galloway 2.00
7 Edgerrin James, Emmitt Smith 6.00
8 James Johnson, Curtis Martin 1.00
9 Daunte Culpepper, Dan Marino 6.00
10 Kevin Faulk, Barry Sanders 5.00
11 Ricky Williams, Marshall Faulk 6.00
12 Donovan McNabb, Steve Young 5.00
13 Troy Edwards, Kevin Johnson 1.00
14 Torry Holt, Jerry Rice 4.00
15 Shaun King, Jake Plummer 1.00

1999 Collector's Edge Fury

Edge Fury is a 200-card set with 148 veteran players, two checklists and 50 seeded rookies found one-per-pack. The product includes three parallel sets with Gold Ingot, Galvanized and HoloGold inserts. Other inserts include: Extreme Team, Fast and Furious, Forerunners, Game Ball, Heir Force and Xplosive.

NM/M
Complete Set (200): 40.00
Common Player: .15
Minor Stars: .30
Common Rookie: .50
Inserted 1:1
Pack (10): 2.00
Wax Box (24): 40.00
1 Checklist .15
2 Checklist .15
3 Karim Abdul .30
4 Troy Aikman 1.50
5 Derrick Alexander .15
6 Mike Alstott .50
7 Jamal Anderson .50
8 Reidel Anthony .30
9 Tiki Barber .15
10 Charlie Batch .40
11 Edgar Bennett .15
12 Jerome Bettis .50
13 Steve Beuerlein .15
14 Tim Biakabutuka .30
15 Jeff Blake .30
16 Drew Bledsoe 1.00
17 Bubby Brister .30
18 Robert Brooks .15
19 Gary Brown .15
20 Tim Brown .30
21 Isaac Bruce .30
22 Mark Brunell 1.00
23 Chris Calloway .15
24 Cris Carter .50
25 Larry Centers .15
26 Chris Chandler .30
27 Wayne Chrebet .50
28 Cam Cleeland .30
29 Kerry Collins .30
30 Curtis Conway .30
31 Germane Crowell .30
32 Randall Cunningham .50
33 Terrell Davis 2.00
34 Koy Detmer .15
35 Ty Detmer .30
36 Trent Dilfer .50
37 Corey Dillon .50
38 Warrick Dunn .75
39 Tim Dwight .50
40 Kevin Dyson .30
41 John Elway 2.00
42 Bobby Engram .15
43 Curtis Enis .50
44 Terry Fair .15
45 Marshall Faulk .50
46 Brett Favre 3.00
47 Doug Flutie .75
48 Antonio Freeman .50
49 Joey Galloway .50
50 Rich Gannon .15
51 Eddie George .75
52 Jeff George .30
53 Terry Glenn .50
54 Elvis Grbac .15
55 Ahman Green .30
56 Jacquez Green .30
57 Trent Green .50
58 Kevin Greene .15
59 Brian Griese 1.00
60 Az-Zahir Hakim .30
61 Jim Harbaugh .30
62 Marvin Harrison .30
63 Courtney Hawkins .15
64 Garrison Hearst .50
65 Ike Hilliard .30
66 Billy Joe Hobert .15
67 Priest Holmes .50
68 Michael Irvin .30
69 Raghib Ismail .15
70 Shawn Jefferson .15
71 James Jett .15
72 Brad Johnson .50
73 Charles Johnson .15
74 Keyshawn Johnson .50
75 Pat Johnson .15
76 Joe Jurevicius .15
77 Napoleon Kaufman .50
78 Eddie Kennison .30
79 Terry Kirby .15
80 Jon Kitna .75
81 Erik Kramer .15
82 Fred Lane .15
83 Ty Law .15
84 Ryan Leaf .75
85 Amp Lee .15
86 Dorsey Levens .50
87 Jermaine Lewis .30
88 Sam Madison .15
89 Peyton Manning 2.00
90 Dan Marino 2.00
91 Curtis Martin .75
92 Tony Martin .15
93 Terance Mathis .15
94 Ed McCaffrey .30
95 Keenan McCardell .15
96 O.J. McDuffie .30
97 Steve McNair .75
98 Natrone Means .30
99 Herman Moore .50
100 Rob Moore .30
101 Bam Morris .30
102 Johnnie Morton .15
103 Randy Moss 3.00
104 Eric Moulds .50
105 Muhsin Muhammad .15
106 Adrian Murrell .30
107 Terrell Owens .50
108 Jerome Pathon .15
109 Carl Pickens .30
110 Jake Plummer 1.25
111 Andre Reed .15
112 Jake Reed .15
113 Jerry Rice 1.50
114 Mikhael Ricks .15
115 Andre Rison .30
116 Barry Sanders 3.00
117 Deion Sanders .50
118 Frank Sanders .30
119 O.J. Santiago .15
120 Darnay Scott .15
121 Junior Seau .30
122 Shannon Sharpe .30
123 Leslie Shepherd .15
124 Antowain Smith .50
125 Bruce Smith .15
126 Emmitt Smith 2.00
127 Jimmy Smith .30
128 Robert Smith .50
129 Rod Smith .30
130 Chris Spielman .15
131 Takeo Spikes .15
132 Duce Staley .30
133 Kordell Stewart .75
134 Bryan Still .15
135 J.J. Stokes .30
136 Fred Taylor 1.50
137 Vinny Testaverde .30
138 Yancey Thigpen .30
139 Thurman Thomas .30
140 Zach Thomas .30
141 Amani Toomer .15
142 Hines Ward .30
143 Chris Warren .30
144 Ricky Watters .30
145 Michael Westbrook .30
146 Alvis Whitted .15
147 Charles Woodson .50
148 Rod Woodson .15
149 Frank Wycheck .15
150 Steve Young 1.00
151 *Rabih Abdullah* .50
152 *Champ Bailey* 2.00
153 *D'Wayne Bates* 1.00
154 *Michael Bishop* 2.00
155 *Dre' Bly* .50
156 *David Boston* 3.00
157 *Fernando Bryant* .50
158 *Chris Claiborne* .50
159 *Mike Cloud* 1.00
160 *Cecil Collins* .50
161 *Tim Couch* 3.00
162 *Daunte Culpepper* 6.00
163 *Antwan Edwards* 1.00
164 *Troy Edwards* 2.00
165 *Ebenezer Ekuban* .50
166 *Kevin Faulk* 1.00
167 *Joe Germaine* .50
168 *Aaron Gibson* .50
169 *Martin Gramatica* 1.00
170 *Torry Holt* 3.00
171 *Brock Huard* 1.00
172 *Sedrick Irvin* .50
173 *Edgerrin James* 6.00
174 *James Johnson* 1.50
175 *Kevin Johnson* 2.00
176 *Andy Katzenmoyer* 1.00
177 *Jevon Kearse* 2.50
178 *Patrick Kerney* .50
179 *Lamar King* .50
180 *Shaun King* 1.00
181 *Jim Kleinsasser* 1.00
182 *Rob Konrad* 1.00
183 *Chris McAlister* .50
184 *Anthony McFarland* .50
185 *Karsten Bailey* .50
186 *Donovan McNabb* 6.00
187 *Cade McNown* 1.00
188 *Joe Montgomery* .50
189 *Dat Nguyen* 1.00
190 *Luke Petitgout* .50
191 *Peerless Price* 2.50
192 *Akili Smith* 1.00
193 *Matt Stinchcomb* .50
194 *John Tait* .50
195 *Jermaine Fazande* .50
196 *Ricky Williams* 6.00
197 *Al Wilson* .50
198 *Antoine Winfield* .50
199 *Damien Woody* .50
200 *Amos Zereoue* 1.50

A player's name in *italic* type indicates a rookie card.

1999 Collector's Edge Fury Galvanized

This 200-card parallel is identical to the Gold Ingot parallel except for the Galvanized stamp on the front of the card in silver and each card is sequentially numbered on the back. Veterans are numbered to 500 and rookies to 100.

	NM/M
Galvanized Cards:	2X-4X
Production 500 Sets	
Galvanized Rookies:	3X-5X
Production 100 Sets	

1999 Collector's Edge Fury Gold Ingot

This is a 200-card parallel to the base set that was inserted 1:1 packs. The photo is the same as the base except for it's printed on foil board and the foil on the front is gold rather than silver. Each also has a Gold Ingot gold stamp on the fronts of the cards.

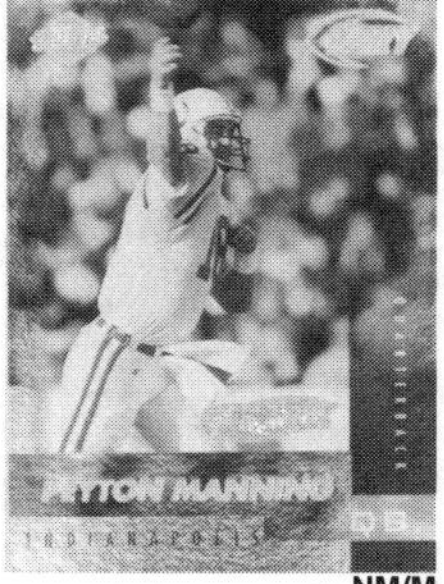

	NM/M
Gold Ingot Cards:	2X
Gold Ingot Rookies:	1.5X
Inserted 1:1	

1999 Collector's Edge Fury HoloGold

Each card in this 200-card parallel set are printed on prismatic silver foil board. Each card front has the HoloGold stamp in gold foil. Veterans are printed to 50 and rookies to 10.

	NM/M
HoloGold Cards:	15X-30X
Production 50 Sets	
HoloGold Rookies:	
Production 10 Sets	

1999 Collector's Edge Fury Extreme Team

Each card in this 10-card set is printed on micro-etched gold holographic foil board. Singles were inserted 1:24 packs.

		NM/M
Complete Set (10):		30.00
Common Player:		2.00
Inserted 1:24		
1	Keyshawn Johnson	2.00
2	Emmitt Smith	6.00
3	John Elway	5.00
4	Terrell Davis	5.00
5	Barry Sanders	6.00
6	Brett Favre	6.00
7	Peyton Manning	6.00
8	Fred Taylor	4.00
9	Dan Marino	6.00
10	Randy Moss	6.00

1999 Collector's Edge Fury Fast and Furious

This 25-card insert is sequentially numbered to 500 and is printed on plastic card stock with gold foil stamping.

		NM/M
Complete Set (25):		60.00
Common Player:		1.00
Minor Stars:		2.00
Production 500 Sets		
1	Jake Plummer	2.00
2	Jamal Anderson	2.00
3	Eric Moulds	2.00
4	Curtis Enis	1.00
5	Emmitt Smith	6.00
6	Deion Sanders	2.00
7	Terrell Davis	5.00
8	Barry Sanders	6.00
9	Herman Moore	2.00
10	Charlie Batch	1.00
11	Marshall Faulk	4.00
12	Mark Brunell	3.00
13	Fred Taylor	3.00
14	Randy Moss	6.00
15	Cris Carter	2.00
16	Robert Edwards	1.00
17	Keyshawn Johnson	2.00
18	Curtis Martin	3.00
19	Charles Woodson	2.00
20	Jerome Bettis	2.00
21	Kordell Stewart	2.00
22	Steve Young	3.00
23	Jerry Rice	5.00
24	Warrick Dunn	2.00
25	Eddie George	3.00

1999 Collector's Edge Fury Forerunners

This 15-card set includes the top running backs in the NFL. Each card is printed on holographic foil board with gold foil stamping. Singles were inserted 1:8 packs.

		NM/M
Complete Set (15):		20.00
Common Player:		.50
Minor Stars:		1.00
Inserted 1:8		
1	Jamal Anderson	1.00
2	Curtis Enis	.50
3	Corey Dillon	2.00
4	Emmitt Smith	5.00
5	Barry Sanders	5.00
6	Terrell Davis	3.00
7	Marshall Faulk	2.00
8	Fred Taylor	3.00
9	Robert Smith	2.00
10	Curtis Martin	2.00
11	Jerome Bettis	2.00
12	Garrison Hearst	2.00
13	Warrick Dunn	2.00
14	Eddie George	2.00
15	Ricky Watters	1.00

A card number in parenthese ( ) indicates the set is unnumbered.

1999 Collector's Edge Fury Game Ball

Each card in this 43-card set includes a piece of a game-used football that the player used. Singles were found 1:24 packs.

	NM/M
Common Player:	6.00
Minor Stars:	12.00
Inserted 1:24	
Troy Aikman	25.00
Mike Alstott	12.00
Charlie Batch	12.00
Jerome Bettis	12.00
Mark Brunell	20.00
Cris Carter	12.00
Terrell Davis	40.00
Corey Dillon	12.00
Warrick Dunn	15.00
John Elway	40.00
Curtis Enis	12.00
Marshall Faulk	12.00
Brett Favre	50.00
Antonio Freeman	12.00
Joey Galloway	12.00
Eddie George	15.00
Garrison Hearst	12.00
Michael Irvin	6.00
Rob Johnson	12.00
Napoleon Kaufman	6.00
Ryan Leaf	6.00
Dorsey Levens	12.00
Peyton Manning	40.00
Curtis Martin	12.00
Steve McNair	15.00
Natrone Means	6.00
Warren Moon	12.00
Herman Moore	12.00
Randy Moss	40.00
Adrian Murrell	6.00
Terrell Owens	12.00
Carl Pickens	6.00
Jake Plummer	15.00
Jerry Rice	25.00
Barry Sanders	40.00
Deion Sanders	12.00
Shannon Sharpe	6.00
Antowain Smith	12.00
Emmitt Smith	40.00
Rod Smith	6.00
Kordell Stewart	12.00
Fred Taylor	15.00
Steve Young	20.00

1999 Collector's Edge Fury Heir Force

This 20-card set includes the top rookies and were inserted 1:6 packs. Each card was printed on holographic foil board with gold foil stamping.

		NM/M
Complete Set (20):		25.00
Common Player:		.50
Inserted 1:6		
1	Rahim Abdullah	.50
2	Champ Bailey	2.00
3	D'Wayne Bates	.50
4	Michael Bishop	1.00
5	David Boston	3.00
6	Chris Claiborne	.50
7	Tim Couch	6.00
8	Daunte Culpepper	6.00
9	Kevin Faulk	3.00
10	Torry Holt	2.50
11	Brock Huard	1.00
12	Edgerrin James	8.00
13	Andy Katzenmoyer	1.50
14	Shaun King	1.00
15	Rob Konrad	.50
16	Donovan McNabb	6.00
17	Cade McNown	1.00
18	Peerless Price	3.00
19	Akili Smith	2.00
20	Ricky Williams	8.00

1999 Collector's Edge Fury Preview Set

		NM/M
Complete Set (10):		6.00
Common Player:		.50
JA	Jamal Anderson	.50
JB	Jerome Bettis	1.00
CC	Cris Carter	1.00
TD	Terrell Davis	2.00
WD	Warrick Dunn	.50
RE	Robert Edwards	.50
BF	Brett Favre	3.00
PM	Peyton Manning	2.00
DM	Dan Marino	3.00
RM	Randy Moss	2.00

1999 Collector's Edge Fury X-Plosive

Each card is printed on explosive micro-etched holofoil with foil stamping. Singles from this 20-card set were found 1:12 packs.

		NM/M
Complete Set (20):		60.00
Common Player:		1.00
Minor Stars:		2.00
Inserted 1:12		
1	Jake Plummer	2.00
2	Doug Flutie	2.00
3	Eric Moulds	3.00
4	Troy Aikman	5.00
5	John Elway	6.00
6	Charlie Batch	2.00
7	Herman Moore	3.00
8	Brett Favre	8.00
9	Antonio Freeman	3.00
10	Peyton Manning	8.00
11	Mark Brunell	3.00
12	Dan Marino	8.00
13	Randy Moss	8.00
14	Drew Bledsoe	4.00
15	Keyshawn Johnson	3.00
16	Vinny Testaverde	1.00
17	Kordell Stewart	2.00
18	Terrell Owens	3.00
19	Jerry Rice	5.00
20	Steve Young	4.00

1999 Collector's Edge Masters

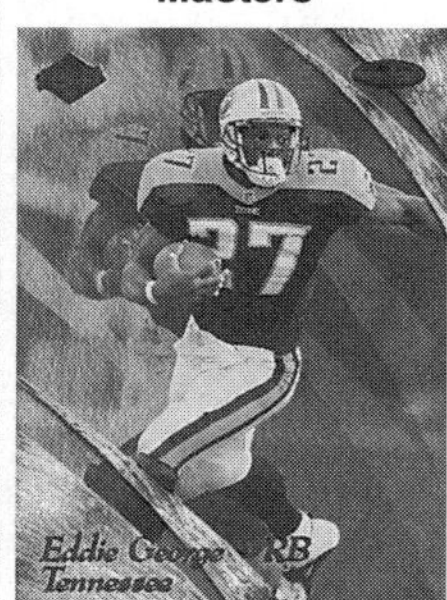

Edge Masters was a 200-card set that had every single card sequentially numbered. Veterans were numbered to 5,000 and rookies to 2,000. Each card was printed on micro-etched holographic foil board. Two parallel sets were issued as HoloSilver and HoloGold. Insert sets included Excalibur, Master Legends, Main Event, Majestic, Pro Signature Authentics, Quest, Rookie Masters and Sentinels. Three-card packs had an SRP of $5.59.

		NM/M
Complete Set (200):		325.00
Common Player:		.25
Minor Stars:		.50
Production 5,000 Sets		
Common Rookie:		1.00
Production 2,000 Sets		
Pack (3):		3.00
Wax Box (20):		50.00
1	*David Boston*	10.00
2	*Marc Cody*	1.00
3	*Chris Griesen*	1.00
4	*Joel Makovicka*	1.00
5	Adrian Murrell	.25
6	Jake Plummer	1.00
7	Frank Sanders	.50
8	Jamal Anderson	1.00
9	Chris Chandler	.50
10	*Reggie Kelly*	1.00
11	*Patrick Kerney*	1.00
12	Terance Mathis	.25
13	*Jeff Paulk*	1.00
14	Stoney Case	.50
15	Qadry Ismail	.25
16	*Chris McAlister*	1.00
17	Errict Rhett	.50
18	*Brandon Stokley*	1.00
19	Doug Flutie	1.50
20	*Kamil Loud*	1.00
21	Eric Moulds	1.00
22	*Peerless Price*	8.00
23	Andre Reed	.50
24	Antowain Smith	1.00
25	*Antoine Winfield*	1.00
26	Steve Beuerlein	.50
27	Tim Biakabutuka	.50
28	*Dameyune Craig*	1.00
29	*Patrick Jeffers*	2.00
30	Muhsin Muhammad	.50
31	*D'Wayne Bates*	2.00
32	*Marty Booker*	3.00
33	Bobby Engram	.25
34	Curtis Enis	.50
35	*Ty Hallock*	1.00
36	Shane Matthews	.40
37	*Cade McNown*	2.00
38	Marcus Robinson	2.00
39	*Scott Covington*	1.00
40	Corey Dillon	1.00
41	*Damon Griffin*	1.00
42	Carl Pickens	.50
43	Darnay Scott	.50
44	*Akili Smith*	3.00
45	*Craig Yeast*	1.00
46	*Darrin Chiaverini*	1.00
47	*Tim Couch*	10.00
48	*Phil Dawson*	1.00
49	*Kevin Johnson*	4.00
50	Terry Kirby	.25
51	*Wali Ranier*	1.00
52	Troy Aikman	2.00
53	*Ebenezer Ekuban*	1.00
54	Michael Irvin	.50
55	Raghib Ismail	.25
56	*Wane McGarity*	1.00
57	*Dat Nguyen*	4.00
58	Deion Sanders	1.00
59	Emmitt Smith	3.00
60	Byron Chamberlain	.50
61	*Andre Cooper*	1.00
62	Terrell Davis	3.00
63	*Olandis Gary*	6.00
64	Brian Griese	2.00
65	Ed McCaffrey	.50
66	*Travis McGriff*	1.00
67	Shannon Sharpe	.50
68	Rod Smith	.50
69	*Al Wilson*	1.00
70	Charlie Batch	.50
71	*Chris Claiborne*	2.00
72	Germane Crowell	.50
73	Greg Hill	.25
74	*Sedrick Irvin*	1.00
75	Herman Moore	.50
76	Johnnie Morton	.25
77	Barry Sanders	4.00
78	*Aaron Brooks*	20.00
79	*Antwan Edwards*	1.00
80	Brett Favre	4.00
81	Antonio Freeman	.50
82	Dorsey Levens	.50
83	Bill Schroeder	.25
84	E.G. Green	.25
85	Marvin Harrison	1.00
86	*Edgerrin James*	20.00
87	Peyton Manning	3.00
88	Mark Brunell	1.50
89	Jay Fiedler	.50
90	Keenan McCardell	.50
91	Jimmy Smith	1.00
92	James Stewart	.50
93	Fred Taylor	2.00
94	Derrick Alexander	.25
95	*Michael Cloud*	1.00
96	Elvis Grbac	.50
97	Bam Morris	.25
98	Andre Rison	.50
99	*Cecil Collins*	1.00
100	Damon Huard	.50
101	*J.J. Johnson*	1.00
102	*Rob Konrad*	1.00
103	Dan Marino	3.00
104	O.J. McDuffie	.50
105	Cris Carter	.50
106	*Daunte Culpepper*	20.00
107	Randall Cunningham	1.00
108	Jeff George	.50
109	*Jim Kleinsasser*	2.00
110	Randy Moss	3.00
111	Robert Smith	.50
112	Terry Allen	.50
113	*Michael Bishop*	3.00
114	Drew Bledsoe	1.50
115	*Kevin Faulk*	2.00
116	Terry Glenn	1.00
117	*Andy Katzenmoyer*	2.00
118	Billy Joe Hobert	.25
119	Eddie Kennison	.25
120	*Ricky Williams*	20.00
121	Tiki Barber	.50
122	*Sean Bennett*	1.00
123	Gary Brown	.25
124	Kent Graham	.25
125	Ike Hilliard	.25
126	*Joe Montgomery*	1.00
127	Amani Toomer	.50
128	Wayne Chrebet	.50
129	Keyshawn Johnson	.50
130	Curtis Martin	1.00
131	*Ray Lucas*	2.00
132	Vinny Testaverde	.50
133	Tim Brown	2.00
134	*Tony Bryant*	1.00
135	*Scott Driesbach*	1.00
136	Rich Gannon	.75
137	Tyrone Wheatley	.50
138	Charles Woodson	1.00
139	*Na Brown*	1.00
140	Charles Johnson	.25
141	*Cecil Martin*	2.00
142	*Donovan McNabb*	20.00
143	Doug Pederson	.25
144	Duce Staley	1.00
145	Jerome Bettis	1.00
146	*Kris Brown*	1.00
147	*Troy Edwards*	2.00
148	Kordell Stewart	.75
149	Hines Ward	.50
150	*Amos Zereoue*	3.00
151	*Dre' Bly*	1.00
152	Isaac Bruce	1.00
153	Marshall Faulk	1.00
154	*Joe Germaine*	1.00
155	Az-Zahir Hakim	.50
156	*Torry Holt*	10.00
157	*Kurt Warner*	15.00
158	*Justin Watson*	1.00
159	*Jermaine Fazande*	1.00
160	Jeff Graham	.25
161	Jim Harbaugh	.50
162	*Steve Heiden*	1.00
163	Erik Kramer	.25
164	Natrone Means	.50
165	Mikhael Ricks	.50
166	Junior Seau	.50
167	*Jeff Garcia*	20.00
168	Charlie Garner	.50
169	*Terry Jackson*	1.00
170	Terrell Owens	1.00
171	Jerry Rice	2.00
172	Steve Young	1.25
173	*Karsten Bailey*	1.00
174	Joey Galloway	1.00
175	*Brock Huard*	2.00
176	Jon Kitna	1.00
177	Derrick Mayes	.50
178	*Charlie Rogers*	1.00
179	Ricky Watters	.50
180	*Rabih Abdullah*	1.00
181	Mike Alstott	1.00
182	Reidel Anthony	.50
183	Trent Dilfer	.50
184	Warrick Dunn	1.00
185	*Martin Gramatica*	2.00
186	*Shaun King*	4.00
187	*Darnell McDonald*	1.00
188	*Yo Murphy*	1.00
189	*Kevin Daft*	1.00
190	Kevin Dyson	.50
191	Eddie George	1.25
192	*Jevon Kearse*	4.00
193	Steve McNair	1.25
194	Yancey Thigpen	.50
195	*Champ Bailey*	4.00
196	Albert Connell	.50
197	Stephen Davis	1.00
198	Skip Hicks	.50
199	Brad Johnson	1.00
200	Michael Westbrook	.50

1999 Collector's Edge Masters HoloSilver

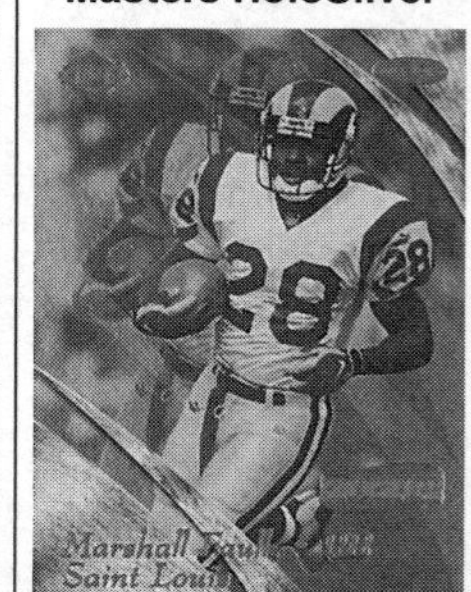

This was a 200-card parallel to the base set. Each card was sequentially numbered to 3,500.

HoloSilver Cards:	2X
HoloSilver Rookies(2,000): 50%	
HoloSilver Rookies(5,000): 75%	
Production 3,500 Sets	

1999 Collector's Edge Masters HoloGold

This was a 200-card parallel to the base set. Each single was sequentially numbered to 25.

HoloGold Cards:	10X-25X
HoloGold Rookies:	2X-4X
Production 25 Sets	

1999 Collector's Edge Masters Excalibur

Excalibur was a 25-card set that was a cross-brand program. Singles were found in First Place, Odyssey and Masters. Eight of the singles were inserted into Masters and were sequentially numbered to 5,000.

		NM/M
Complete Set (8):		25.00
Common Player:		2.00
Production 5,000 Sets		
3	Dan Marino	5.00
6	Champ Bailey	2.00
9	Barry Sanders	5.00
10	Brett Favre	5.00
12	Tim Couch	4.00
14	Akili Smith	2.00
18	Steve Young	4.00
21	Curtis Martin	2.00

1999 Collector's Edge Masters Main Event

This 10-card insert set included the key matchups from the 1999 NFL season. Each card included two players whose teams went head-to-head in big games. Each single was printed on clear plastic and was sequentially numbered to 1,000.

		NM/M
Complete Set (10):		25.00
Common Player:		2.00
Production 1,000 Sets		
1	Randy Moss, Jamal Anderson	8.00
2	Mark Brunell, Eddie George	4.00
3	Terrell Davis, Cecil Collins	4.00
4	Rocket Ismail, Stephen Davis	2.00
5	Troy Edwards, Kevin Johnson	3.00
6	Antonio Freeman, Charlie Batch	2.00
7	Terry Glenn, Marvin Harrison	4.00
8	Keyshawn Johnson, Doug Flutie	4.00
9	Cade McNown, Ricky Williams	8.00
10	Steve Young, Marshall Faulk	6.00

1999 Collector's Edge Masters Majestic

This 30-card insert set included the most popular and collectible stars and featured them on a clear vinyl card. Singles were sequentially numbered to 3,000.

		NM/M
Complete Set (30):		50.00
Common Player:		1.00
Minor Stars:		2.00
Production 3,000 Sets		
1	Jake Plummer	2.00
2	David Boston	4.00
3	Doug Flutie	2.00
4	Eric Moulds	2.00
5	Peerless Price	3.00
6	Tim Biakabutuka	1.00
7	Troy Aikman	4.00
8	Olandis Gary	2.00
9	Brian Griese	3.00
10	Charlie Batch	1.00
11	Antonio Freeman	1.00
12	Peyton Manning	5.00
13	Edgerrin James	6.00
14	Marvin Harrison	2.00
15	Fred Taylor	2.00
16	Daunte Culpepper	5.00
17	Terry Glenn	2.00
18	Keyshawn Johnson	2.00
19	Curtis Martin	2.00
20	Donovan McNabb	5.00
21	Kordell Stewart	2.00
22	Torry Holt	4.00
23	Marshall Faulk	2.00
24	Kurt Warner	12.00
25	Jerry Rice	5.00
26	Jon Kitna	2.50
27	Eddie George	3.00
28	Champ Bailey	2.00
29	Brad Johnson	2.00
30	Stephen Davis	2.00

1999 Collector's Edge Masters Master Legends

This 20-card insert set included the best players in football and pictured them on a clear card. Singles were sequentially numbered to 3,000.

		NM/M
Complete Set (20):		60.00
Common Player:		2.00
Production 1,000 Sets		
1	Doug Flutie	2.00
2	Troy Aikman	5.00
3	Emmitt Smith	6.00
4	Terrell Davis	4.00
5	Charlie Batch	1.00
6	Barry Sanders	6.00
7	Brett Favre	6.00
8	Antonio Freeman	2.00
9	Peyton Manning	6.00
10	Mark Brunell	3.00
11	Fred Taylor	3.00
12	Dan Marino	6.00
13	Randy Moss	6.00
14	Drew Bledsoe	4.00
15	Kurt Warner	8.00
16	Marshall Faulk	2.00
17	Steve Young	6.00
18	Jerry Rice	6.00
19	Jon Kitna	2.00
20	Eddie George	3.00

1999 Collector's Edge Masters Pro Signature Authentics

This 3-card insert set included some of the top names in the NFL. Each single was numbered to 500. The Manning 1B was a mail-in redemption and was numbered to 445.

		NM/M
Complete Set (3):		300.00
Common Player:		40.00
Production 500 Sets		
--	Stephen Davis	40.00
1A	Peyton Manning 500	100.00
1B	Peyton Manning 445	125.00
--	Kurt Warner	75.00

1999 Collector's Edge Masters Quest

This 20-card insert set included players who had the Super Bowl in their sights. Each single had a vinyl background and was sequentially numbered to 3,000.

		NM/M
Complete Set (20):		25.00
Common Player:		1.00
Minor Stars:		2.00
Production 3,000 Sets		
1	Jake Plummer	1.00
2	Eric Moulds	2.00
3	Curtis Enis	1.00
4	Emmitt Smith	5.00
5	Brian Griese	3.00
6	Dorsey Levens	1.00
7	Marvin Harrison	2.00
8	Mark Brunell	2.00
9	Fred Taylor	2.00
10	Cris Carter	1.00
11	Terry Glenn	1.00
12	Keyshawn Johnson	2.00
13	Isaac Bruce	2.00
14	Terrell Owens	2.00
15	Jon Kitna	1.00
16	Natrone Means	1.00
17	Warrick Dunn	1.00
18	Steve McNair	2.00
19	Brad Johnson	1.00
20	Stephen Davis	2.00

1999 Collector's Edge Masters Rookie Masters

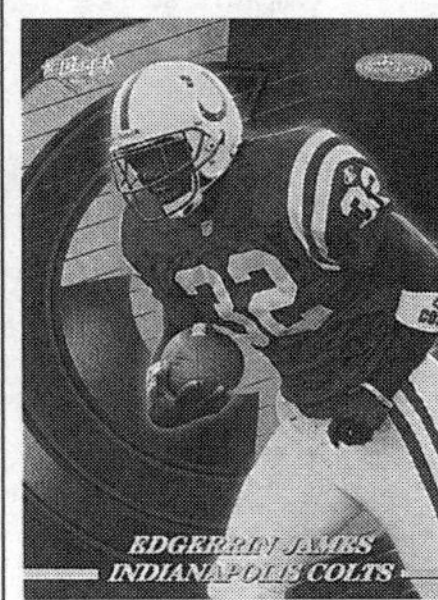

This 30-card insert set included the hottest rookies from the 1999 Draft. Each single was sequentially numbered to 3,000.

		NM/M
Complete Set (30):		40.00
Common Player:		1.00
Minor Stars:		2.00
Production 3,000 Sets		
1	David Boston	3.00
2	Chris McAlister	1.00
3	Peerless Price	3.00
4	D'Wayne Bates	1.00
5	Cade McNown	2.00
6	Akili Smith	2.00
7	Tim Couch	6.00
8	Kevin Johnson	3.00
9	Wane McGarity	1.00
10	Chris Claiborne	1.00
11	Sedrick Irvin	2.00
12	Edgerrin James	8.00
13	Michael Cloud	2.00
14	Cecil Collins	2.00
15	J.J. Johnson	1.00
16	Rob Konrad	2.00
17	Daunte Culpepper	6.00
18	Kevin Faulk	2.00
19	Andy Katzenmoyer	2.00
20	Ricky Williams	10.00
21	Donovan McNabb	6.00
22	Troy Edwards	4.00
23	Amos Zereoue	2.00
24	Joe Germaine	2.00
25	Torry Holt	4.00
26	Karsten Bailey	2.00
27	Brock Huard	2.50
28	Shaun King	2.00
29	Jevon Kearse	4.00
30	Champ Bailey	2.50

1999 Collector's Edge Masters Sentinels

This 20-card set included the 10 hottest veterans and the 10 hottest rookies from 1999. Each single was sequentially numbered to 500.

		NM/M
Complete Set (20):		150.00
Common Player:		3.00
Production 500 Sets		
1	Troy Aikman	8.00
2	Emmitt Smith	12.00
3	Terrell Davis	8.00
4	Barry Sanders	12.00
5	Brett Favre	12.00
6	Peyton Manning	10.00
7	Dan Marino	12.00
8	Randy Moss	12.00
9	Drew Bledsoe	6.00
10	Isaac Bruce	3.00
11	Kurt Warner	12.00
12	David Boston	3.00
13	Cade McNown	3.00
14	Akili Smith	3.00
15	Tim Couch	8.00
16	Edgerrin James	8.00
17	Ricky Williams	12.00
18	Donovan McNabb	8.00
19	Troy Edwards	3.00
20	Torry Holt	5.00

1999 Collector's Edge Odyssey

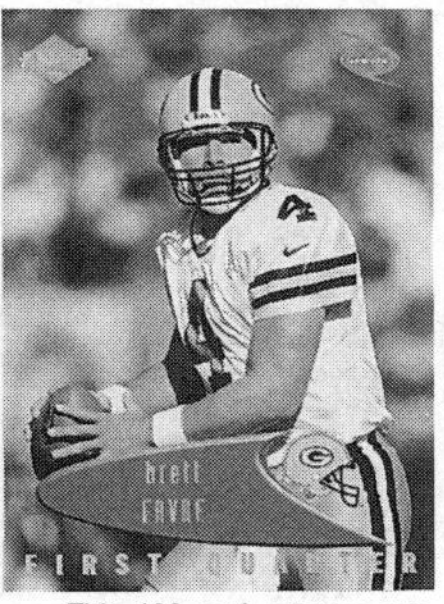

This 193-card set was supposed to be a 195-card set, but cards #21 and #55 were never produced. The first 150 cards were 1st Quarter singles. Cards #151-170 were 2nd Quarter singles and were inserted 1:4 packs. Cards #171-185 were 3rd Quarter singles and they were found 1:8 packs. Cards #186-195 were 4th Quarter singles and they were found 1:24 packs. Insert sets included: Two Minute Warning, Overtime, Cut 'n' Ripped, Cutting Edge, Excalibur, End Zone, Game Gear, Old School, Pro Signature Authentics and Super Limited Edge. Ten-card packs had an SRP of $3.99.

		NM/M
Complete Set (193):		125.00
Common Player:		.15
Minor Stars:		.30
Common Rookie:		.50
Common Player (151-170):		1.00
Inserted 1:4		
Common Player (171-185):		2.50
Inserted 1:8		
Common Player (186-195):		5.00
Inserted 1:24		
#21 and 55 never produced		
Wax Box:		45.00
1	Checklist	.15
2	Checklist	.15
3	*David Boston*	1.75
4	Rob Moore	.30
5	Adrian Murrell	.30
6	Jake Plummer	.50
7	Frank Sanders	.30
8	Jamal Anderson	.50
9	Chris Calloway	.15
10	Chris Chandler	.30
11	Tim Dwight	.50
12	Terance Mathis	.15
13	Tony Banks	.30
14	Priest Holmes	.50
15	Jermaine Lewis	.15
16	*Chris McAlister*	.50
17	Scott Mitchell	.15
18	Doug Flutie	.75
19	Eric Moulds	.50
20	*Peerless Price*	1.25
22	Antowain Smith	.50
23	*Antoine Winfield*	.50
24	Steve Beuerlein	.30
25	Tim Biakabutuka	.30
26	Rae Carruth	.15
27	Muhsin Muhammad	.30
28	*D'Wayne Bates*	.50
29	Bobby Engram	.15
30	Curtis Enis	.50
31	Shane Matthews	.30
32	*Cade McNown*	1.50
33	Jeff Blake	.30
34	Corey Dillon	.50
35	Carl Pickens	.30
36	Darnay Scott	.30
37	*Akili Smith*	1.00
38	*Tim Couch*	2.50
39	*Kevin Johnson*	2.00
40	Terry Kirby	.15
41	Leslie Shepherd	.15
42	Troy Aikman	1.25
43	Michael Irvin	.30
44	Raghib Ismail	.15
45	Deion Sanders	.50
46	Emmitt Smith	1.75
47	Bubby Brister	.30
48	Terrell Davis	1.75
49	Brian Griese	1.00
50	Ed McCaffrey	.50
51	Shannon Sharpe	.30
52	Rod Smith	.50
53	Charlie Batch	.75
54	*Chris Claiborne*	.50
56	Herman Moore	.50
57	Johnnie Morton	.15
58	Ron Rivers	.15
59	Brett Favre	2.50
60	Mark Chmura	.30
61	Antonio Freeman	.50
62	Dorsey Levens	.50
63	E.G. Green	.15
64	Marvin Harrison	.50
65	*Edgerrin James*	6.00
66	Peyton Manning	1.75
67	Mark Brunell	1.00
68	Keenan McCardell	.30
69	Jimmy Smith	.50
70	Fred Taylor	1.25
71	Derrick Alexander	.15
72	Kimble Anders	.15
73	*Michael Cloud*	.50
74	Elvis Grbac	.30
75	Andre Rison	.30
76	Karim Abdul	.30
77	*Cecil Collins*	1.00
78	*J.J. Johnson*	.50
79	*Rob Konrad*	.50
80	Dan Marino	1.75
81	O.J. McDuffie	.30
82	Cris Carter	.50
83	*Daunte Culpepper*	5.00
84	Randall Cunningham	.50
85	Randy Moss	2.50
86	Jake Reed	.30
87	Robert Smith	.50
88	Terry Allen	.30
89	Drew Bledsoe	1.00
90	Ben Coates	.30
91	*Kevin Faulk*	1.25
92	Terry Glenn	.50
93	*Andy Katzenmoyer*	.50
94	Cameron Cleeland	.30
95	Billy Joe Hobert	.15
96	Eddie Kennison	.15
97	*Ricky Williams*	5.00
98	*Sean Bennett*	.75
99	Gary Brown	.15
100	Kerry Collins	.30
101	Kent Graham	.15
102	Ike Hilliard	.15
103	Wayne Chrebet	.50
104	Keyshawn Johnson	.50
105	Curtis Martin	.50
106	Rick Mirer	.30
107	Tim Brown	.30
108	Rich Gannon	.30
109	Napoleon Kaufman	.50
110	Charles Woodson	.50
111	Charles Johnson	.15
112	*Donovan McNabb*	5.00
113	Doug Pederson	.15
114	Duce Staley	.50
115	Jerome Bettis	.50
116	*Troy Edwards*	1.75
117	Kordell Stewart	.50
118	*Amos Zereoue*	.75
119	Isaac Bruce	.50
120	Marshall Faulk	.50
121	*Joe Germaine*	.50
122	*Torry Holt*	1.75
123	*Kurt Warner*	6.00
124	Jim Harbaugh	.30
125	Erik Kramer	.15
126	Natrone Means	.30
127	Junior Seau	.30
128	Terrell Owens	.50
129	Lawrence Phillips	.30
130	Jerry Rice	1.25
131	J.J. Stokes	.30
132	Steve Young	.75
133	*Karsten Bailey*	.50
134	Joey Galloway	.50
135	*Brock Huard*	1.25
136	Jon Kitna	.50
137	Ricky Watters	.30
138	Reidel Anthony	.30
139	Trent Dilfer	.30
140	Warrick Dunn	.50
141	*Shaun King*	1.00
142	*Jevon Kearse*	2.00
143	Kevin Dyson	.30
144	Eddie George	.75
145	Steve McNair	.75
146	*Champ Bailey*	1.25
147	Stephen Davis	.50
148	Skip Hicks	.30
149	Brad Johnson	.50
150	Michael Westbrook	.30
151	Chris McAlister	1.00
152	Peerless Price	1.75
153	Antoine Winfield	.50
154	D'Wayne Bates	.50
155	Kevin Johnson	1.00
156	Chris Claiborne	.50
157	Sedrick Irvin	.50
158	Michael Cloud	.50
159	Cecil Collins	1.00
160	J.J. Johnson	.50
161	Rob Konrad	.50
162	Daunte Culpepper	3.50
163	Andy Katzenmoyer	1.00
164	Amos Zereoue	1.00
165	Joe Germaine	.50
166	Karsten Bailey	.50
167	Brock Huard	.50
168	Shaun King	1.00
169	Jevon Kearse	2.50
170	Champ Bailey	1.50
171	Jake Plummer	1.00
172	Doug Flutie	.75
173	Troy Aikman	3.00
174	Emmitt Smith	4.00
175	Terrell Davis	3.00
176	Barry Sanders	5.00
177	Brett Favre	5.00
178	Peyton Manning	4.00
179	Mark Brunell	2.50
180	Fred Taylor	2.00
181	Dan Marino	5.00
182	Randy Moss	4.00
183	Drew Bledsoe	2.50
184	Jerry Rice	5.00
185	Steve Young	2.50
186	David Boston	6.00
187	Cade McNown	2.00
188	Akili Smith	2.00
189	Tim Couch	8.00
190	Edgerrin James	15.00
191	Kevin Faulk	5.00
192	Ricky Williams	15.00
193	Donovan McNabb	15.00
194	Troy Edwards	3.00
195	Torry Holt	8.00

1999 Collector's Edge Odyssey Two Minute Warning

This insert was a 45-card partial parallel to the base set. Cards #151-170 were sequentially numbered to 600. Cards #171-185 were numbered to 300 and cards #186-195 were numbered to 100.

	NM/M
Common Player (151-170):	3.50
Rookies:	4X
Production 600 Sets	
Common Player (171-185):	7.50
Stars:	3X
Production 300 Sets	
Common Player (186-195):	20.00
Rookies:	4X
Production 100 Sets	

1999 Collector's Edge Odyssey Overtime

This was a 45-card partial set parallel to the base set. Cards #151-170 were sequentially numbered to 60. Cards #171-185 were numbered to 30 and cards #186-195 were numbered to 10.

	NM/M
Common Player (151-170):	25.00
Rookies:	5X-8X
Production 60 Sets	
Common Player (171-185):	75.00
Stars:	5X-10X
Production 30 Sets	
Common Player (186-195):	100.00
Rookies:	3X-8X
Production 10 Sets	

1999 Collector's Edge Odyssey Cut 'n' Ripped

This 15-card insert set included the top rookies from the 1999 class. Each was photographed in the weight room and singles were found 1:12 packs.

		NM/M
Complete Set (15):		15.00
Common Player:		.50
Inserted 1:12		
1	Chris McAlister	.50
2	Kevin Johnson	1.00
3	Chris Claiborne	.50
4	Sedrick Irvin	.50
5	Edgerrin James	4.00
6	Michael Cloud	.50
7	J.J. Johnson	.50
8	Rob Konrad	.50
9	Daunte Culpepper	4.00
10	Andy Katzenmoyer	.50
11	Amos Zereoue	.50

12	Torry Holt	2.00
13	Shaun King	1.00
14	Jevon Kearse	2.00
15	Champ Bailey	1.50

1999 Collector's Edge Odyssey Cutting Edge

This 10-card set had each single printed on holographic foil with foil stamping. Singles were found 1:18 packs.

		NM/M
Complete Set (10):		20.00
Common Player:		1.00
Inserted 1:18		
1	Akili Smith	1.00
2	Tim Couch	4.00
3	Brian Griese	2.00
4	Charlie Batch	1.00
5	Brett Favre	5.00
6	Peyton Manning	4.00
7	Mark Brunell	1.00
8	Dan Marino	5.00
9	Drew Bledsoe	1.00
10	Steve Young	1.00

1999 Collector's Edge Odyssey End Zone

This 20-card insert set included the top players in the NFL. Singles were inserted 1:9 packs.

		NM/M
Complete Set (20):		20.00
Common Player:		.50
Minor Stars:		2.00
Inserted 1:9		
1	Jamal Anderson	1.00
2	Priest Holmes	2.00
3	Doug Flutie	1.00
4	Eric Moulds	2.00
5	Charlie Batch	1.00
6	Barry Sanders	5.00
7	Antonio Freeman	2.00
8	Fred Taylor	2.00
9	Cris Carter	2.00
10	Randy Moss	5.00
11	Keyshawn Johnson	2.00
12	Curtis Martin	2.00
13	Vinny Testaverde	.50
14	Kordell Stewart	1.00
15	Jerry Rice	4.00
16	Terrell Owens	2.00
17	Jon Kitna	1.00
18	Warrick Dunn	1.00
19	Eddie George	2.50
20	Steve McNair	2.50

1999 Collector's Edge Odyssey Excalibur

Excalibur was a 25-card set that was a cross-brand program. Singles were inserted into First Place, Odyssey and Masters. Eight of the singles were found in Odyssey at 1:24 packs.

		NM/M
Complete Set (8):		20.00
Common Player:		2.00
Inserted 1:24		
2	Cade McNown	2.00
5	David Boston	3.00
7	Daunte Culpepper	6.00
8	Troy Edwards	2.00

		NM/M
11	Donovan McNabb	7.00
15	Ricky Williams	10.00
20	Troy Aikman	4.00
25	Emmitt Smith	5.00

1999 Collector's Edge Odyssey Game Gear

This 8-card insert set included a swatch of a game-used football. Each card is sequentially numbered and odds were 1:360 packs.

		NM/M
Common Player:		10.00
Inserted 1:360		
1	Terrell Davis 500	30.00
2	Curtis Enis 338	10.00
3	Marshall Faulk 247	30.00
4	Brian Griese 500	25.00
5	Skip Hicks 315	10.00
6	Randy Moss 415	35.00
7	Lawrence Phillips 406	10.00
8	Fred Taylor 85	30.00

1999 Collector's Edge Odyssey Old School

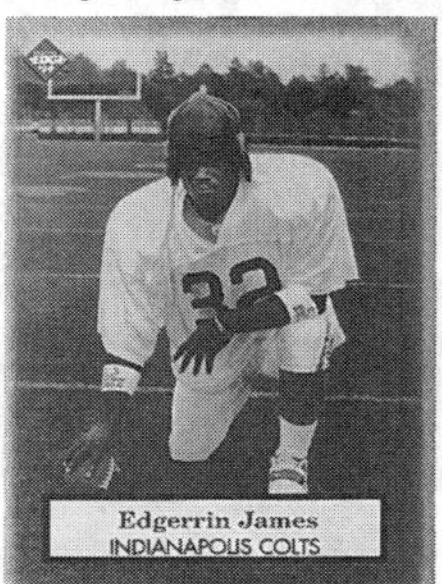

Each card in this 25-card set is in black and white and has an Old School theme to it. Players are photographed in throwback jerseys, leather helmets and in Heisman-style poses. Singles were inserted 1:8 packs.

		NM/M
Complete Set (25):		25.00
Common Player:		.50
Minor Stars:		1.00
Inserted 1:8		
1	David Boston	2.00
2	Chris McAlister	.50
3	Peerless Price	2.00
4	D'Wayne Bates	.50
5	Cade McNown	1.00
6	Akili Smith	1.00
7	Tim Couch	5.00
8	Kevin Johnson	2.00
9	Chris Claiborne	.50
10	Sedrick Irvin	.50
11	Edgerrin James	6.00
12	Michael Cloud	.50
13	J.J. Johnson	1.00
14	Rob Konrad	.50
15	Daunte Culpepper	4.00
16	Kevin Faulk	2.00
17	Donovan McNabb	5.00
18	Troy Edwards	2.00
19	Amos Zereoue	2.00
20	Joe Germaine	1.00
21	Torry Holt	2.00
22	Karsten Bailey	1.00
23	Shaun King	1.00
24	Jevon Kearse	2.00
25	Champ Bailey	2.00

1999 Collector's Edge Odyssey Pro Signature Authentics

This 18-card set included autographs from the rookies of 1999. Each player had signed a different amount of cards and each was sequentially numbered. They were inserted 1:36 packs.

		NM/M
Complete Set (18):		425.00
Common Player:		8.00
Minor Stars:		16.00
Inserted 1:36		
DB	D'Wayne Bates 1450	8.00
MB	Michael Bishop 2200	16.00

		NM/M
CC	Chris Claiborne 1120	8.00
DC	Daunte Culpepper 450	45.00
JD	Jared DeVries 290	8.00
JG	Jeff Garcia 2110	25.00
MG	Martin Gramatica 1950	16.00
TH	Torry Holt 1115	25.00
BH	Brock Huard 350	12.00
SI	Sedrick Irvin 1240	8.00
EJ	Edgerrin James 435	75.00
KJ	Kevin Johnson 1920	25.00
SK	Shaun King 920	20.00
RK	Rob Konrad 1420	8.00
DM	Darnell McDonald 2435	8.00
PP	Peerless Price 825	20.00
AS	Akili Smith 111	20.00
AZ	Amos Zereoue 1450	8.00

1999 Collector's Edge Odyssey Super Limited Edge

This 30-card insert set included football's biggest stars and featured them on a clear, vinyl card with foil stamping. Each single was sequentially numbered to 1,000.

		NM/M
Complete Set (30):		60.00
Common Player:		2.00
Production 1,000 Sets		
1	Jake Plummer	2.00
2	Jamal Anderson	2.00
3	Doug Flutie	2.00
4	Eric Moulds	2.00
5	Troy Aikman	5.00
6	Emmitt Smith	8.00
7	Terrell Davis	5.00
8	Charlie Batch	2.00
9	Herman Moore	2.00
10	Barry Sanders	8.00
11	Brett Favre	8.00
12	Antonio Freeman	2.00
13	Dorsey Levens	2.00
14	Peyton Manning	8.00
15	Mark Brunell	3.00
16	Fred Taylor	4.00
17	Dan Marino	8.00
18	Cris Carter	2.00
19	Randall Cunningham	2.00
20	Randy Moss	8.00
21	Drew Bledsoe	4.00
22	Ricky Williams	8.00
23	Keyshawn Johnson	2.00
24	Curtis Martin	2.00
25	Jerome Bettis	2.00
26	Jerry Rice	6.00
27	Terrell Owens	2.00
28	Jon Kitna	2.00
29	Eddie George	4.00
30	Steve Young	4.00

1999 Collector's Edge Supreme

The 170-card base set includes 40 rookie cards. A few errors in the set with two different Tim Couch cards #141. The error is the rarest to find without stats on the back. The corrected versions are numbered TC and include stats. Michael Wiley was suppose to be #166, but chose to stay in college and they had to be pulled from the set. Some still found their way into packs. The #166B Edgerrin James Trade card was inserted late and tough to find. Two parallel sets with Gold Ingot and Galvanized. Other inserts include: Future, Homecoming, Markers, PSA 10 Redemptions, Route XXXIII, Supremacy and T3.

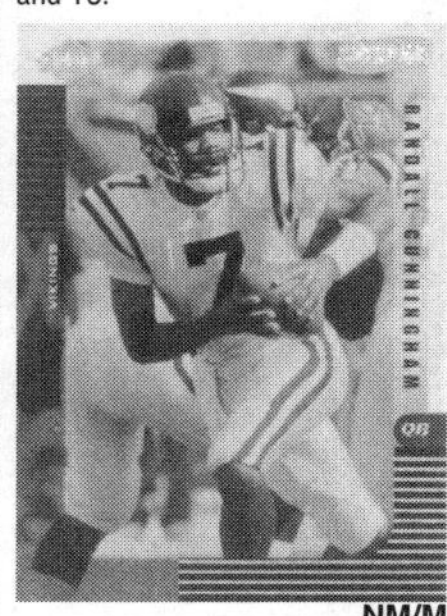

		NM/M
Complete Set (170):		80.00
Common Player:		.20
Minor Stars:		.40
Common Rookie:		1.00
Card #166A not part of set price		
Gold Ingot Cards:		2X
Gold Ingot Rookies:		1X
Inserted 1:1		
Galvanized Cards:		2X-4X
Production 500 Sets		
Galvanized Rookies:		3X
Production 250 Sets		
Pack (8):		3.00
Wax Box (24):		65.00
1	Randy Moss CL	1.50
2	Peyton Manning CL	.75
3	Rob Moore	.40
4	Adrian Murrell	.20
5	Jake Plummer	.75
6	Andre Wadsworth	.20
7	Jamal Anderson	.75
8	Chris Chandler	.40
9	Tony Martin	.20
10	Terance Mathis	.20
11	Jim Harbaugh	.40
12	Priest Holmes	.75
13	Jermaine Lewis	.20
14	Eric Zeier	.20
15	Doug Flutie	.75
16	Eric Moulds	.75
17	Andre Reed	.40
18	Antowain Smith	.75
19	Steve Beuerlein	.20
20	Kevin Greene	.20
21	Raghib Ismail	.20
22	Fred Lane	.20
23	Edgar Bennett	.20
24	Curtis Conway	.40
25	Curtis Enis	.75
26	Erik Kramer	.20
27	Corey Dillon	.75
28	Neil O'Donnell	.20
29	Carl Pickens	.40
30	Darnay Scott	.20
31	Troy Aikman	1.50
32	Michael Irvin	.40
33	Deion Sanders	.75
34	Emmitt Smith	2.00
35	Chris Warren	.40
36	Terrell Davis	2.00
37	John Elway	2.00
38	Ed McCaffrey	.75
39	Shannon Sharpe	.40
40	Rod Smith	.40
41	Charlie Batch	.50
42	Herman Moore	.40
43	Johnnie Morton	.20
44	Barry Sanders	3.00
45	Robert Brooks	.20
46	Brett Favre	3.00
47	Antonio Freeman	.75
48	Darick Holmes	.20
49	Dorsey Levens	.75
50	Reggie White	.40
51	Marshall Faulk	.75
52	Marvin Harrison	.40
53	Peyton Manning	2.50
54	Jerome Pathon	.40
55	Tavian Banks	.40
56	Mark Brunell	1.25
57	Keenan McCardell	.20
58	Fred Taylor	1.00
59	Derrick Alexander	.20
60	Donnell Bennett	.20
61	Rich Gannon	.20
62	Andre Rison	.40
63	Karim Abdul	.40
64	John Avery	.40
65	Oronde Gadsden	.40
66	Dan Marino	2.00
67	O.J. McDuffie	.20
68	Cris Carter	.75
69	Randall Cunningham	.75
70	Brad Johnson	.40
71	Randy Moss	3.00
72	Jake Reed	.20
73	Robert Smith	.40
74	Drew Bledsoe	1.25
75	Ben Coates	.40
76	Robert Edwards	.75
77	Terry Glenn	.40
78	Cameron Cleeland	.40
79	Kerry Collins	.40
80	Sean Dawkins	.20
81	Lamar Smith	.20
82	Gary Brown	.20
83	Chris Calloway	.20
84	Ike Hilliard	.20
85	Danny Kanell	.20
86	Wayne Chrebet	.75
87	Keyshawn Johnson	.75
88	Curtis Martin	.75
89	Vinny Testaverde	.40
90	Tim Brown	.40
91	Jeff George	.40
92	Napoleon Kaufman	.75
93	Charles Woodson	.75
94	Irving Fryar	.20
95	Bobby Hoying	.20
96	Duce Staley	.20
97	Jerome Bettis	.40
98	Courtney Hawkins	.20
99	Charles Johnson	.20
100	Kordell Stewart	.50
101	Hines Ward	.40
102	Tony Banks	.40
103	Isaac Bruce	.40
104	Robert Holcombe	.40
105	Ryan Leaf	.40
106	Natrone Means	.40
107	Mikhael Ricks	.40
108	Junior Seau	.40
109	Garrison Hearst	.40
110	Terrell Owens	.75
111	Jerry Rice	1.50
112	J.J. Stokes	.40
113	Steve Young	1.00
114	Joey Galloway	.75
115	Jon Kitna	.40
116	Warren Moon	.40
117	Ricky Watters	.40
118	Mike Alstott	.40
119	Reidel Anthony	.40
120	Warrick Dunn	.50
121	Trent Dilfer	.40
122	Jacquez Green	.40
123	Kevin Dyson	.40
124	Eddie George	1.00
125	Steve McNair	.75
126	Frank Wycheck	.20
127	Terry Allen	.40
128	Trent Green	.40
129	Skip Hicks	.40
130	Michael Westbrook	.20
131	*Rahim Abdullah*	.50
132	*Champ Bailey*	2.00
133	*Marlon Barnes*	.50
134	*D'Wayne Bates*	.50
135	*Michael Bishop*	2.00
136	*Dre' Bly*	.50
137	*David Boston*	2.50
138	*Cuncho Brown*	.50
139	*Na Brown*	.50
140	*Tony Bryant*	.50
141	*Tim Couch ERROR*	40.00
141TC	*Tim Couch*	10.00
142	*Chris Claiborne*	2.00
143	*Daunte Culpepper*	5.00
144	*Jared DeVries*	.50
145	*Troy Edwards*	1.00
146	*Kris Farris*	.50
147	*Kevin Faulk*	1.00
148	*Joe Germaine*	.50
149	*Aaron Gibson*	.50
150	*Torry Holt*	2.50
151	*Brock Huard*	1.00
152	*Sedrick Irvin*	.50
153	*James Johnson*	.50
154	*Kevin Johnson*	1.00
155	*Andy Katzenmoyer*	.50
156	*Jevon Kearse*	2.00
157	*Shaun King*	1.00
158	*Rob Konrad*	.50
159	*Chris McAlister*	.50
160	*Darnell McDonald*	.50
161	*Donovan McNabb*	5.00
162	*Cade McNown*	1.00
163	*Peerless Price*	2.00
164	*Akili Smith*	1.00
165	*Matt Stinchcomb*	.50
166A	Michael Wiley	40.00
166B	*Edgerrin James Trade*	25.00
167	*Ricky Williams*	5.00
168	*Antoine Winfield*	.50
169	*Craig Yeast*	.50
170	*Amos Zereoue*	2.00

1999 Collector's Edge Supreme Galvanized

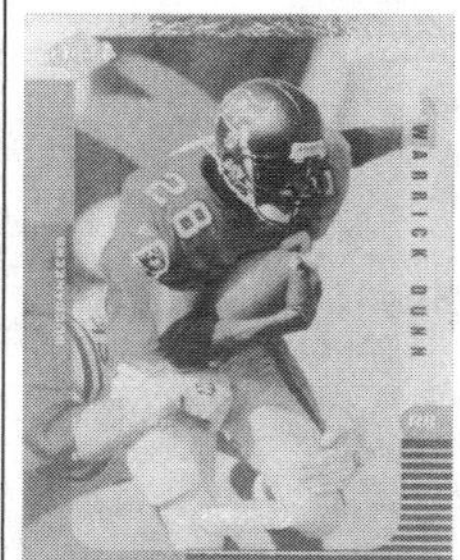

This 169-card set is a parallel to the base minus the cards of Michael Wiley and Edgerrin James #166. Each card is printed on silver foil board and is sequentially numbered. Veterans are printed to 500 and rookies to 250.

Galvanized Cards:	2X-4X
Production 500 Sets	
Galvanized Rookies:	3X
Production 250 Sets	

1999 Collector's Edge Supreme Gold Ingot

The 169-card set is a parallel to the base minus the Michael Wiley and Edgerrin James cards #166. The cards are the same as the base except for the foil is in gold and the Gold Ingot stamp on the fronts. They were inserted one-per-pack.

Gold Ingot Cards:	2X
Gold Ingot Rookies:	1X
Inserted 1:1	

1999 Collector's Edge Supreme Future

Each card in this 10-card set is printed on micro-etched foil board and was inserted 1:24 packs.

		NM/M
Complete Set (10):		40.00
Common Player:		1.00
Inserted 1:24		
1	Ricky Williams	12.00
2	Tim Couch	8.00
3	Daunte Culpepper	8.00
4	Torry Holt	3.00
5	Edgerrin James	10.00
6	Brock Huard	2.00
7	Donovan McNabb	8.00
8	Joe Germaine	1.00
9	Cade McNown	1.00
10	Michael Bishop	2.00

1999 Collector's Edge Supreme Homecoming

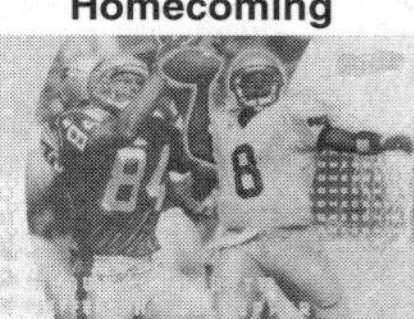

Each card in this 20-card set includes two players on the front who went to the same college. A rookie from the 1999 draft and a veteran. Singles were inserted 1:12 packs.

		NM/M
Complete Set (20):		35.00
Common Player:		1.50
Inserted 1:12		
1	Ricky Williams, Priest Holmes	12.00
2	Andy Katzenmoyer, Eddie George	3.00
3	Daunte Culpepper, Shawn Jefferson	5.00
4	Torry Holt, Erik Kramer	2.00
5	Edgerrin James, Vinny Testaverde	4.00
6	Chris Claiborne, Junior Seau	1.50
7	Brock Huard, Mark Brunell	2.00
8	Champ Bailey, Terrell Davis	4.00
9	Donovan McNabb, Rob Moore	6.00
10	David Boston, Joey Galloway	3.00
11	Cade McNown, Troy Aikman	3.00
12	Kevin Faulk, Eddie Kennison	1.50
13	Sedrick Irvin, Andre Rison	1.50
14	Rob Konrad, Darryl Johnston	1.50

15	Amos Zereoue, Adrian Murrell	1.50
16	Peerless Price, Peyton Manning	6.00
17	Kevin Johnson, Marvin Harrison	3.00
18	Jevon Kearse, Emmitt Smith	5.00
19	Antoine Winfield, Shawn Springs	1.50
20	Tony Bryant, Andre Wadsworth	1.50

1999 Collector's Edge Supreme Markers

The cards are printed on clear vinyl stock with foil stamping. The set features 15 NFL stars and focuses on record-setting performances and milestones reached in the 1998 NFL season. They were sequentially numbered to 5,000.

		NM/M
Complete Set (15):		35.00
Common Player:		1.00
Minor Stars:		2.00
Production 5,000 Sets		
1	Terrell Davis	3.00
2	John Elway	4.00
3	Dan Marino	5.00
4	Peyton Manning	4.00
5	Barry Sanders	5.00
6	Emmitt Smith	5.00
7	Randy Moss	5.00
8	Jake Plummer	2.00
9	Cris Carter	1.00
10	Brett Favre	5.00
11	Drew Bledsoe	3.00
12	Charlie Batch	1.00
13	Curtis Martin	1.00
14	Mark Brunell	2.00
15	Jamal Anderson	1.00

1999 Collector's Edge Supreme Preview Set

		NM/M
Complete Set (10):		8.00
Common Player:		.50
JA	Jamal Anderson	.50
CB	Charlie Batch	.50
MB	Mark Brunell	.50
TD	Terrell Davis	1.00
RE	Robert Edwards	.50
KJ	Keyshawn Johnson	.50
PM	Peyton Manning	2.00
RM	Randy Moss	2.00
BS	Barry Sanders	3.00
ES	Emmitt Smith	3.00

1999 Collector's Edge Supreme PSA 10 Redemptions

Each card in this set was a redemption card for the player that was on it. You could then redeem it for a PSA 10 graded rookie of that player. The redemption cards were limited to 1,999.

		NM/M
Complete Set (3):		175.00
Common Player:		50.00
Production 1,999 Sets		
1	Ricky Williams	75.00
2	Tim Couch	50.00
3	Daunte Culpepper	60.00

1999 Collector's Edge Supreme Route XXXIII

This set includes the top stars from the 1998 NFL playoffs. Each player in the 10-card set is sequentially numbered to 1,000.

		NM/M
Complete Set (10):		65.00
Common Player:		4.00
Production 1,000 Sets		
1	Randy Moss	15.00
2	Jamal Anderson	4.00
3	Jake Plummer	4.00
4	Steve Young	6.00
5	Fred Taylor	6.00
6	Dan Marino	12.00
7	Keyshawn Johnson	4.00
8	Curtis Martin	6.00
9	John Elway	12.00
10	Terrell Davis	10.00

1999 Collector's Edge Supreme Supremacy

This set features 5 players from Super Bowl XXXIII. Each is printed on foil board with foil stamping and is sequentially numbered to 500.

		NM/M
Complete Set (5):		40.00
Common Player:		6.00
Production 500 Sets		
1	John Elway	15.00
2	Terrell Davis	12.00
3	Ed McCaffrey	6.00
4	Jamal Anderson	6.00
5	Chris Chandler	6.00

1999 Collector's Edge Supreme T3

This 30-card set is tiered into three levels with 10 wide receivers (foil board with bronze foil stamping), running backs (foil board with silver foil stamping) and quarterbacks (foil board with gold foil stamping). The receivers were the easiest to find at 1:8, running backs at 1:12 and the quarterbacks the toughest to get at 1:24.

		NM/M
Complete Set (30):		75.00
Common WR:		1.00
Inserted 1:8		
Common RB:		2.00
Inserted 1:12		
Common QB:		3.00
Inserted 1:24		
1	Doug Flutie (QB)	3.00
2	Troy Aikman (QB)	6.00
3	John Elway (QB)	8.00
4	Jake Plummer (QB)	3.00
5	Brett Favre (QB)	8.00
6	Mark Brunell (QB)	4.00
7	Peyton Manning (QB)	8.00
8	Dan Marino (QB)	8.00
9	Drew Bledsoe (QB)	6.00
10	Steve Young (QB)	4.00
11	Jamal Anderson (RB)	2.00
12	Emmitt Smith (RB)	6.00
13	Terrell Davis (RB)	5.00
14	Barry Sanders (RB)	6.00
15	Robert Smith (RB)	2.50
16	Robert Edwards (RB)	2.00
17	Curtis Martin (RB)	3.00
18	Jerome Bettis (RB)	2.50
19	Fred Taylor (RB)	4.00
20	Eddie George (RB)	3.00
21	Michael Irvin (WR)	1.50
22	Eric Moulds (WR)	2.00
23	Herman Moore (WR)	1.50
24	Reidel Anthony (WR)	1.50
25	Randy Moss (WR)	6.00
26	Cris Carter (WR)	1.50
27	Keyshawn Johnson (WR)	2.00
28	Jacquez Green (WR)	1.00
29	Jerry Rice (WR)	5.00
30	Terrell Owens (WR)	3.00

1999 Collector's Edge Triumph

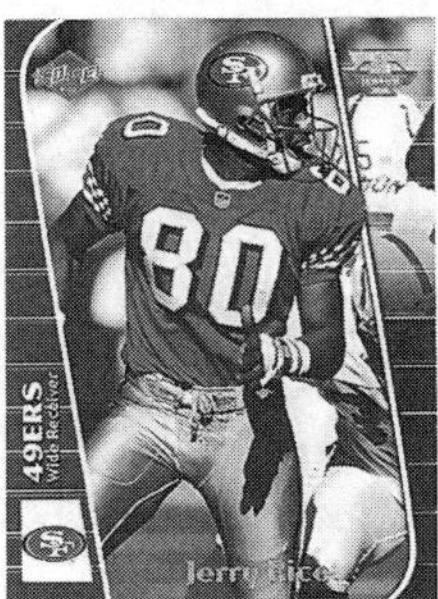

Triumph was a 180-card set that included 40 rookie cards found one-per-pack. Insert sets included: Commissioner's Choice, Fantasy Team, Future Fantasy Team, Heir Supply, K-Klub Y3K, Pack Warriors and Signed, Sealed, Delivered. Packs contained eight cards.

		NM/M
Complete Set (180):		40.00
Common Player:		.15
Minor Stars:		.30
Common Rookie:		.50
Inserted 1:1		
Pack (8):		2.00
Wax Box (32):		55.00
1	Jamal Anderson	.50
2	Jerome Bettis	.50
3	Terrell Davis	1.00
4	Corey Dillon	.50
5	Warrick Dunn	.50
6	Marshall Faulk	.50
7	Eddie George	.75
8	Garrison Hearst	.30
9	Skip Hicks	.30
10	Napoleon Kaufman	.50
11	Dorsey Levens	.50
12	Curtis Martin	.50
13	Natrone Means	.30
14	Adrian Murrell	.30
15	Barry Sanders	2.50
16	Antowain Smith	.50
17	Emmitt Smith	2.50
18	Robert Smith	.50
19	Fred Taylor	1.00
20	Ricky Watters	.30
21	Cameron Cleeland	.30
22	Ben Coates	.30
23	Shannon Sharpe	.30
24	Frank Wycheck	.15
25	Derrick Alexander	.15
26	Reidel Anthony	.30
27	Robert Brooks	.15
28	Tim Brown	.30
29	Cris Carter	.50
30	Wayne Chrebet	.50
31	Curtis Conway	.30
32	Tim Dwight	.50
33	Kevin Dyson	.30
34	Antonio Freeman	.50
35	Joey Galloway	.50
36	Terry Glenn	.50
37	Marvin Harrison	.50
38	Ike Hilliard	.30
39	Michael Irvin	.30
40	Keyshawn Johnson	.50
41	Jermaine Lewis	.15
42	Terance Mathis	.15
43	Ed McCaffrey	.50
44	Keenan McCardell	.30
45	O.J. McDuffie	.30
46	Herman Moore	.50
47	Rob Moore	.30
48	Randy Moss	2.50
49	Eric Moulds	.50
50	Muhsin Muhammad	.30
51	Terrell Owens	.50
52	Jerome Pathon	.15
53	Carl Pickens	.30
54	Andre Reed	.30
55	Jake Reed	.30
56	Jerry Rice	1.25
57	Andre Rison	.30
58	Jimmy Smith	.50
59	Rod Smith	.50
60	Michael Westbrook	.30
61	Morten Andersen	.15
62	Gary Anderson	.15
63	Doug Brien	.15
64	Chris Boniol	.15
65	John Carney	.15
66	Steve Christie	.15
67	Richie Cunningham	.15
68	Brad Daluiso	.15
69	Al Del Greco	.15
70	Jason Elam	.15
71	John Hall	.15
72	Jason Hanson	.15
73	Mike Hollis	.15
74	Norm Johnson	.15
75	Olindo Mare	.15
76	Doug Pelfrey	.15
77	Wade Richey	.15
78	Pete Stoyanovich	.15
79	Mike Vanderjagt	.15
80	Adam Vinatieri	.15
81	Ray Buchanan	.15
82	Jim Flanigan	.15
83	Darrell Green	.15
84	Kevin Greene	.15
85	Ty Law	.15
86	Ken Norton Jr.	.15
87	John Randle	.15
88	Bill Romanowski	.15
89	Deion Sanders	.50
90	Junior Seau	.30
91	Michael Sinclair	.15
92	Bruce Smith	.15
93	Takeo Spikes	.15
94	Michael Strahan	.15
95	Derrick Thomas	.30
96	Zach Thomas	.30
97	Andre Wadsworth	.15
98	Charles Woodson	.50
99	Checklist	.15
100	Checklist	.15
101	Troy Aikman	1.25
102	Tony Banks	.30
103	Charlie Batch	.75
104	Steve Beuerlein	.30
105	Jeff Blake	.30
106	Drew Bledsoe	1.00
107	Bubby Brister	.30
108	Mark Brunell	1.00
109	Chris Chandler	.30
110	Kerry Collins	.30
111	Randall Cunningham	.50
112	Koy Detmer	.15
113	Ty Detmer	.15
114	Trent Dilfer	.30
115	John Elway	1.75
116	Brett Favre	2.50
117	Doug Flutie	.75
118	Rich Gannon	.30
119	*Jeff Garcia*	6.00
120	Jeff George	.30
121	Kent Graham	.15
122	Elvis Grbac	.30
123	Brian Griese	1.00
124	Trent Green	.30
125	Jim Harbaugh	.30
126	Billy Joe Hobert	.15
127	Brad Johnson	.50
128	Rob Johnson	.30
129	Jon Kitna	.50
130	Erik Kramer	.15
131	Ryan Leaf	.50
132	Peyton Manning	1.75
133	Dan Marino	1.75
134	Steve McNair	.75
135	Scott Mitchell	.15
136	Warren Moon	.30
137	Jake Plummer	1.00
138	Kordell Stewart	.50
139	Vinny Testaverde	.30
140	Steve Young	.75
141	*Champ Bailey*	2.00
142	*Karsten Bailey*	.50
143	*D'Wayne Bates*	.50
144	*David Boston*	3.00
145	*Cuncho Brown*	.50
146	*Dat Nguyen*	.50
147	*Chris Claiborne*	.50
148	*Michael Cloud*	.50
149	*Cecil Collins*	1.00
150	*Tim Couch*	3.00
151	*Daunte Culpepper*	6.00
152	*Autry Denson*	.50
153	*Troy Edwards*	2.00
154	*Ebenezer Ekuban*	.50
155	*Kevin Faulk*	1.00
156	*Jermaine Fazande*	.50
157	*Joe Germaine*	.50
158	*Martin Gramatica*	1.00
159	*Torry Holt*	3.00
160	*Brock Huard*	1.00
161	*Sedrick Irvin*	.50
162	*Edgerrin James*	6.00
163	*James Johnson*	1.00
164	*Kevin Johnson*	2.00
165	*Andy Katzenmoyer*	.60
166	*Jevon Kearse*	2.00
167	*Patrick Kerney*	.50
168	*Shaun King*	1.00
169	*Jim Kleinsasser*	1.00
170	*Rob Konrad*	.50
171	*Chris McAlister*	.50
172	*Donovan McNabb*	6.00
173	*Cade McNown*	1.00
174	*Joe Montgomery*	.50
175	*Peerless Price*	2.50
176	*Akili Smith*	1.00
177	*Ricky Williams*	6.00
178	*Larry Parker*	.50
179	*Antoine Winfield*	.50
180	*Amos Zereoue*	1.00

1999 Collector's Edge Triumph Commissioner's Choice

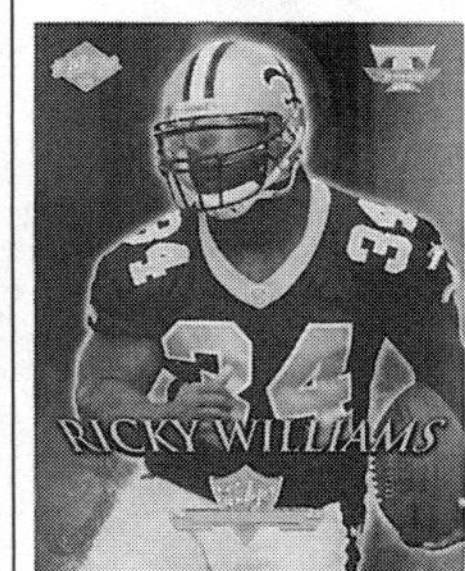

This 10-card insert set included the top rookies from the 1999 Draft. Singles were inserted 1:15 packs. A parallel Gold version was also made and each card was sequentially numbered to 500.

		NM/M
Complete Set (10):		35.00
Common Player:		2.00
Inserted 1:15		
Gold Cards:		2X
Production 500 Sets		
1	Tim Couch	6.00
2	Donovan McNabb	7.00
3	Cade McNown	2.00
4	Daunte Culpepper	7.00
5	Akili Smith	2.00
6	Ricky Williams	8.00
7	Edgerrin James	8.00
8	Torry Holt	3.50
9	David Boston	3.50
10	Champ Bailey	2.00

1999 Collector's Edge Triumph Fantasy Team

This 10-card insert set included the top players in the NFL and inserted them 1:10 packs.

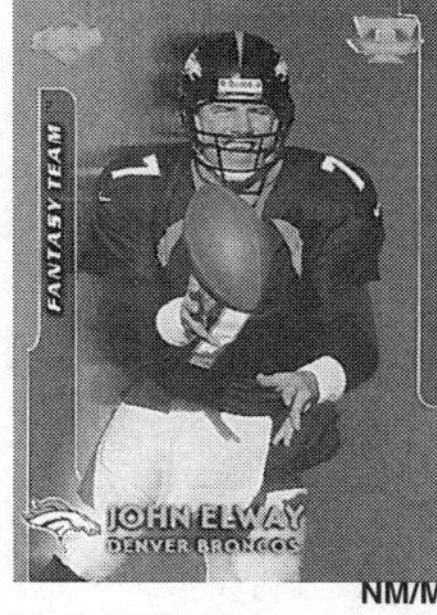

		NM/M
Complete Set (10):		25.00
Common Player:		2.00
Inserted 1:10		
1	Terrell Davis	3.00
2	John Elway	4.00
3	Brett Favre	6.00
4	Peyton Manning	6.00
5	Dan Marino	6.00
6	Randy Moss	6.00
7	Jake Plummer	2.00
8	Barry Sanders	6.00
9	Emmitt Smith	6.00
10	Fred Taylor	2.00

1999 Collector's Edge Triumph Future Fantasy Team

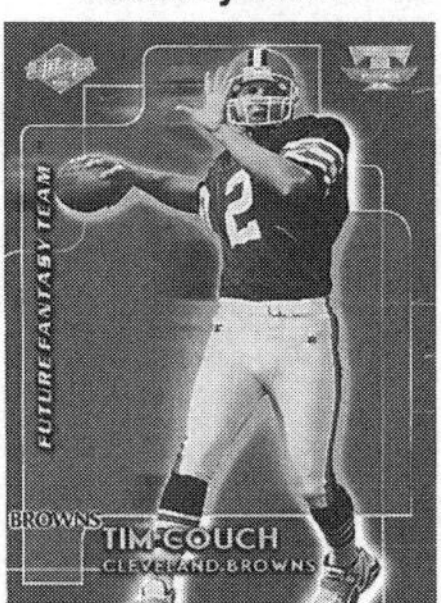

This 20-card insert set included the top rookies from 1999. Singles were inserted 1:6 packs.

		NM/M
Complete Set (20):		30.00
Common Player:		1.00
Inserted 1:6		
1	Champ Bailey	1.50
2	D'Wayne Bates	1.00
3	David Boston	2.00
4	Tim Couch	4.00
5	Daunte Culpepper	5.00
6	Troy Edwards	2.00
7	Kevin Faulk	1.50
8	Torry Holt	2.00
9	Brock Huard	1.50
10	Sedrick Irvin	1.50
11	Edgerrin James	6.00
12	James Johnson	1.50
13	Kevin Johnson	2.00
14	Rob Konrad	1.00
15	Donovan McNabb	6.00
16	Cade McNown	1.00
17	Peerless Price	3.00
18	Akili Smith	1.00
19	Ricky Williams	8.00
20	Amos Zereoue	1.50

1999 Collector's Edge Triumph Heir Supply

This 15-card insert set included the top rookies from the 1999 Draft. Singles were inserted 1:3 packs.

		NM/M
Complete Set (15):		20.00
Common Player:		.75
Minor Stars:		1.50
Inserted 1:3		
1	Ricky Williams	4.00
2	Tim Couch	3.00
3	Cade McNown	1.00
4	Donovan McNabb	3.00
5	Akili Smith	1.00
6	Daunte Culpepper	3.00
7	Torry Holt	2.00
8	Edgerrin James	4.00
9	David Boston	2.00
10	Troy Edwards	2.00
11	Peerless Price	2.00
12	Champ Bailey	1.50
13	D'Wayne Bates	.75
14	Kevin Faulk	.75
15	Amos Zereoue	.75

1999 Collector's Edge Triumph K-Klub Y3K

This 50-card insert set included both young and veteran players. Singles were sequentially numbered to 1,000.

		NM/M
Complete Set (50):		60.00
Common Player:		1.00
Minor Stars:		2.00
Production 1,000 Sets		
1	Kareem Abdul-Jabbar	1.00
2	Jamal Anderson	2.00
3	Jerome Bettis	2.00
4	Isaac Bruce	2.00
5	Cris Carter	2.00
6	Terrell Davis	4.00
7	Corey Dillon	2.00
8	Warrick Dunn	2.00
9	Curtis Enis	1.00
10	Marshall Faulk	3.00
11	Antonio Freeman	1.00
12	Joey Galloway	1.00
13	Eddie George	3.00
14	Terry Glenn	1.00
15	Garrison Hearst	1.00
16	Keyshawn Johnson	2.00
17	Napoleon Kaufman	1.00
18	Curtis Martin	3.00
19	Rob Moore	1.00
20	Herman Moore	1.00
21	Eric Moulds	2.00
22	Randy Moss	5.00
23	Adrian Murrell	1.00
24	Carl Pickens	1.00
25	Jerry Rice	4.00
26	Barry Sanders	5.00
27	Antowain Smith	1.00
28	Emmitt Smith	5.00
29	Fred Taylor	3.00
30	Ricky Watters	1.00
31	Troy Aikman	4.00
32	Charlie Batch	1.00
33	Drew Bledsoe	3.00
34	Mark Brunell	2.00
35	Chris Chandler	1.00
36	Randall Cunningham	2.00
37	Trent Dilfer	1.00
38	John Elway	4.00
39	Brett Favre	5.00
40	Doug Flutie	2.00
41	Brad Johnson	1.00
42	Jon Kitna	1.00
43	Ryan Leaf	1.00
44	Peyton Manning	5.00
45	Dan Marino	5.00
46	Steve McNair	3.00
47	Jake Plummer	2.00
48	Kordell Stewart	2.00
49	Vinny Testaverde	1.00
50	Steve Young	3.00

1999 Collector's Edge Triumph Pack Warriors

This 15-card insert set included veteran players. Singles were inserted 1:4 packs.

		NM/M
Complete Set (15):		20.00
Common Player:		1.00
Inserted 1:4		
1	Jamal Anderson	1.00
2	Jake Plummer	1.00
3	Emmitt Smith	3.00
4	Troy Aikman	2.00
5	Terrell Davis	2.00
6	John Elway	3.00

7	Barry Sanders	3.00
8	Brett Favre	3.00
9	Peyton Manning	3.00
10	Randy Moss	3.00
11	Dan Marino	3.00
12	Keyshawn Johnson	1.00
13	Fred Taylor	2.00
14	Jerry Rice	2.00
15	Jerome Bettis	1.00

1999 Collector's Edge Triumph Preview Set

		NM/M
Complete Set (20):		10.00
Common Player:		.50
CB	Champ Bailey	.50
DB	David Boston	1.00
CC	Chris Claiborne	.50
TC	Tim Couch	1.00
DC	Daunte Culpepper	2.00
TE	Troy Edwards	.50
KF	Kevin Faulk	.50
JF	Jermaine Fazande	.50
JG	Joe Germaine	.50
TH	Torry Holt	1.00
SI	Sedrick Irvin	.50
EJ	Edgerrin James	2.00
JJ	James Johnson	.50
AK	Andy Katzenmoyer	.50
DM	Donovan McNabb	2.00
CM	Cade McNown	.50
JM	Joe Montgomery	.50
AS	Akili Smith	.50
AW	Antoine Winfield	.50
AZ	Amos Zereoue	.50

1999 Collector's Edge Triumph Signed, Sealed, Delivered

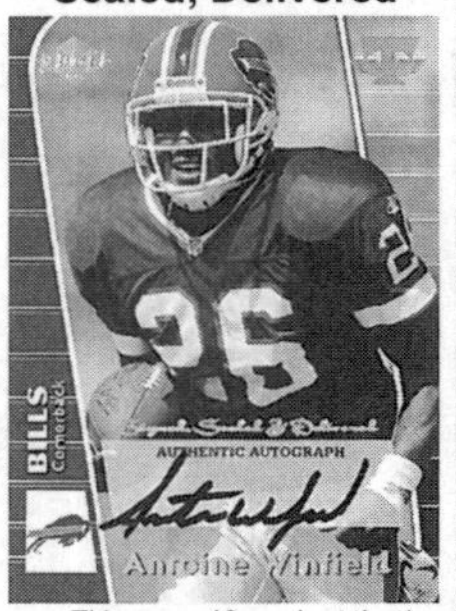

This was a 40-card set that included autographs from the top rookies of 1999. Singles were inserted 1:32 packs. A parallel Blue version was issued and each was sequentially numbered to 40. A parallel Red version was also made and each of those singles was numbered to 10.

	NM/M
Common Player:	5.00
Minor Stars:	10.00
Inserted 1:32	
Blue Cards:	4X
Production 40 Sets	
Red Cards:	
Production 10 Sets	
Champ Bailey	15.00
Karsten Bailey	10.00
D'Wayne Bates	10.00
David Boston	20.00
Cuncho Brown	5.00
Dat Nguyen	5.00
Chris Claiborne	5.00
Michael Cloud	5.00
Cecil Collins	15.00
Tim Couch	40.00
Daunte Culpepper	40.00
Autry Denson	10.00
Troy Edwards	20.00
Ebenezer Ekuban	5.00
Kevin Faulk	15.00
Jermaine Fazande	5.00
Joe Germaine	5.00
Martin Gramatica	10.00
Torry Holt	20.00
Brock Huard	10.00
Sedrick Irvin	5.00
Edgerrin James	50.00
James Johnson	15.00
Kevin Johnson	20.00
Andy Katzenmoyer	10.00
Jevon Kearse	20.00
Patrick Kerney	5.00
Shaun King	15.00
Jim Kleinsasser	10.00
Rob Konrad	10.00
Chris McAlister	10.00
Donovan McNabb	40.00
Cade McNown	15.00
Joe Montgomery	5.00
Peerless Price	25.00
Akili Smith	15.00
Ricky Williams	60.00
Larry Parker	5.00
Antoine Winfield	5.00
Amos Zereoue	10.00

Post-1980 cards in Near Mint condition will generally sell for about 75% of the quoted Mint value. Excellent-condition cards bring no more than 40%.

2000 Collector's Edge Graded

		NM/M
Complete Set (148):		60.00
Common Player:		.25
Minor Stars:		.50
Common Rookie:		1.25
Pack (10 + PSA Graded Card):		10.00
Wax Box (12):		100.00
Cards #93 & 110 Never Released		
1	Marcus Robinson	1.00
2	Adrian Murrell	.25
3	Qadry Ismail	.25
4	Tim Biakabutuka	.50
5	Jamal Anderson	.50
6	Dorsey Levens	.50
7	Robert Smith	.50
8	Tony Banks	.50
9	Yancey Thigpen	.50
10	Elvis Grbac	.50
11	Sedrick Irvin	.50
12	Rob Johnson	.50
13	Frank Sanders	.50
14	Rich Gannon	.50
15	Steve Beuerlein	.50
16	James Stewart	.50
17	Ricky Watters	.50
18	Curtis Enis	.75
19	Eddie Kennison	.50
20	Kerry Collins	.50
21	Ray Lucas	.75
22	Carl Pickens	.75
23	Natrone Means	.50
24	Daunte Culpepper	1.75
25	Karim Abdul	.50
26	David Boston	1.00
27	Raghib Ismail	.25
28	Jacquez Green	.50
29	Kevin Dyson	.50
30	Chris Chandler	.50
31	Brian Griese	1.25
32	Charlie Garner	.50
33	Wayne Chrebet	.75
34	Mike Alstott	.50
35	Germane Crowell	.50
36	Michael Cloud	.25
37	Antowain Smith	.25
38	Jeff George	.75
39	Antonio Freeman	.40
40	Champ Bailey	.75
41	Terrence Wilkins	.50
42	Junior Seau	.50
43	Jimmy Smith	.50
44	Greg Hill	.25
45	Tyrone Wheatley	.50
46	Tony Gonzalez	.75
47	Rod Smith	.75
48	Damon Huard	.50
49	Jerome Bettis	.50
50	Cris Carter	.50
51	Darnay Scott	.50
52	Ike Hilliard	.25
53	Errict Rhett	.50
54	Tim Brown	.75
55	Terry Glenn	.40
56	Jeff Blake	.50
57	Terance Mathis	.25
58	Duce Staley	.50
59	Amani Toomer	.25
60	Terry Allen	.25
61	Corey Dillon	1.00
62	Kordell Stewart	.50
63	Az-Zahir Hakim	.50
64	Jim Harbaugh	.50
65	Bill Schroeder	.25
66	O.J. McDuffie	.50
67	Keenan McCardell	.50
68	Terrell Owens	1.00
69	Joey Galloway	.50
70	Derrick Alexander	.25
71	Ed McCaffrey	.75
72	Reidel Anthony	.50
73	Michael Irvin	.50
74	Herman Moore	.50
75	Joe Montgomery	.25
76	Muhsin Muhammad	.50
77	Charles Johnson	.25
78	Michael Westbrook	.50
79	Jevon Kearse	1.00
80	*Courtney Brown*	1.00
81	*Shaun Alexander*	4.00
82	*R. Jay Soward*	1.00
83	*Sylvester Morris*	1.00
84	*Giovanni Carmazzi*	1.00
85	*J.R. Redmond*	2.00
86	*Sherrod Gideon*	1.00
87	*Tee Martin*	2.00
88	*Dennis Northcutt*	1.00
89	*Troy Walters*	1.00
90	*Joe Hamilton*	2.00
91	*Reuben Droughns*	1.00
92	*Trung Canidate*	2.00
94	*Tim Rattay*	1.00
95	*Jerry Porter*	3.00
96	*Michael Wiley*	1.00
97	*Anthony Lucas*	1.00
98	*Danny Farmer*	1.25
99	*Travis Prentice*	1.00
100	*Dez White*	2.50
101	*Chad Pennington*	10.00
102	*Chris Redman*	2.00
103	*Thomas Jones*	3.00
104	*Ron Dayne*	2.00
105	*Jamal Lewis*	5.00
106	*Shyrone Stith*	1.00
107	*Peter Warrick*	2.00
108	*Plaxico Burress*	5.00
109	*Travis Taylor*	4.00
111	Terrell Davis	2.00
112	Dan Marino	3.00
113	Brad Johnson	1.00
114	Isaac Bruce	1.00
115	Eric Moulds	1.00
116	Olandis Gary	.50
117	Drew Bledsoe	1.50
118	Steve Young	1.50
119	Keyshawn Johnson	.75
120	Emmitt Smith	3.00
121	Warrick Dunn	.50
122	Doug Flutie	.50
123	Troy Edwards	1.00
124	Brett Favre	3.00
125	Charlie Batch	.50
126	Curtis Martin	1.00
127	Stephen Davis	1.00
128	Troy Aikman	2.50
129	Fred Taylor	1.50
130	Jerry Rice	2.50
131	Jon Kitna	.50
132	Steve McNair	1.00
133	Jake Plummer	.50
134	Donovan McNabb	1.50
135	Ricky Williams	2.50
136	Torry Holt	1.00
137	J.J. Johnson	.50
138	Kevin Johnson	1.00
139	Akili Smith	.50
140	Cade McNown	.50
141	Eddie George	1.25
142	Shaun King	.50
143	Marshall Faulk	1.00
144	Kurt Warner	3.00
145	Randy Moss	3.00
146	Mark Brunell	1.00
147	Marvin Harrison	1.00
148	Edgerrin James	2.00
149	Tim Couch	2.00
150	Peyton Manning	3.00
E1	Doug Flutie	2.00
E2	Cade McNown	2.00
E3	Akili Smith	2.00
E4	Tim Couch	5.00
E5	Kevin Johnson	2.00
E6	Troy Aikman	4.00
E7	Emmitt Smith	6.00
E8	Terrell Davis	4.00
E9	Brett Favre	6.00
E10	Marvin Harrison	2.00
E11	Edgerrin James	4.00
E12	Peyton Manning	6.00
E13	Mark Brunell	2.00
E14	Dan Marino	6.00
E15	Randy Moss	6.00
E16	Drew Bledsoe	4.00
E17	Ricky Williams	5.00
E18	Keyshawn Johnson	2.00
E19	Curtis Martin	2.00
E20	Donovan McNabb	4.00
E21	Marshall Faulk	2.00
E22	Torry Holt	2.00
E23	Kurt Warner	5.00
E24	Jerry Rice	5.00
E25	Steve Young	4.00
E26	Jon Kitna	2.00
E27	Shaun King	2.00
E28	Eddie George	3.00
E29	Stephen Davis	2.00
E30	Brad Johnson	2.00
E31	Chad Pennington	8.00
E32	Chris Redman	3.00
E33	Tim Rattay	3.00
E34	Tee Martin	4.00
E35	Thomas Jones	5.00
E36	Ron Dayne	5.00
E37	Jamal Lewis	6.00
E38	J.R. Redmond	4.00
E39	Travis Prentice	5.00
E40	Shaun Alexander	6.00
E41	Michael Wiley	2.00
E42	Quinton Spotwood	2.00
E43	Peter Warrick	5.00
E44	Plaxico Burress	6.00
E45	Travis Taylor	5.00
E46	Troy Walters	2.00
E47	R. Jay Soward	2.00
E48	Dez White	2.00
E50	Courtney Brown	2.00

2000 Collector's Edge Graded Brilliant

		NM/M
Common Gem Mint:		40.00
Common Mint:		20.00
Production 500 Sets		
101	Chad Pennington Gem	200.00
101	Chad Pennington Mint	100.00
102	Chris Redman Gem	60.00
102	Chris Redman Mint	30.00
103	Thomas Jones Gem	100.00
103	Thomas Jones Mint	50.00
104	Ron Dayne Gem	200.00
104	Ron Dayne Mint	100.00
105	Jamal Lewis Gem	100.00
105	Jamal Lewis Mint	50.00
106	Shyrone Stith Gem	50.00
106	Shyrone Stith Mint	25.00
107	Peter Warrick Gem	200.00
107	Peter Warrick Mint	100.00
108	Plaxico Burress Gem	150.00
108	Plaxico Burress Mint	75.00
109	Travis Taylor Gem	70.00
109	Travis Taylor Mint	35.00
111	Terrell Davis Gem	70.00
111	Terrell Davis Mint	35.00
112	Dan Marino Gem	70.00
112	Dan Marino Mint	35.00
113	Brad Johnson Gem	40.00
113	Brad Johnson Mint	20.00
114	Isaac Bruce Gem	40.00
114	Isaac Bruce Mint	20.00
115	Eric Moulds Gem	40.00
115	Eric Moulds Mint	20.00
116	Olandis Gary Gem	40.00
116	Olandis Gary Mint	20.00
117	Drew Bledsoe Gem	50.00
117	Drew Bledsoe Mint	25.00
118	Steve Young Gem	50.00
118	Steve Young Mint	25.00
119	Keyshawn Johnson Gem	40.00
119	Keyshawn Johnson Mint	20.00
120	Emmitt Smith Gem	70.00
120	Emmitt Smith Mint	35.00
121	Warrick Dunn Gem	40.00
121	Warrick Dunn Mint	20.00
122	Doug Flutie Gem	50.00
122	Doug Flutie Mint	25.00
123	Troy Edwards Gem	40.00
123	Troy Edwards Mint	20.00
124	Brett Favre Gem	80.00
124	Brett Favre Mint	40.00
125	Charlie Batch Gem	40.00
125	Charlie Batch Mint	20.00
126	Curtis Martin Gem	40.00
126	Curtis Martin Mint	20.00
127	Stephen Davis Gem	40.00
127	Stephen Davis Mint	20.00
128	Troy Aikman Gem	60.00
128	Troy Aikman Mint	30.00
129	Fred Taylor Gem	50.00
129	Fred Taylor Mint	25.00
130	Jerry Rice Gem	60.00
130	Jerry Rice Mint	30.00
131	Jon Kitna Gem	40.00
131	Jon Kitna Mint	20.00
132	Steve McNair Gem	40.00
132	Steve McNair Mint	20.00
133	Jake Plummer Gem	40.00
133	Jake Plummer Mint	20.00
134	Donovan McNabb Gem	50.00
134	Donovan McNabb Mint	25.00
135	Ricky Williams Gem	60.00
135	Ricky Williams Mint	30.00
136	Torry Holt Gem	40.00
136	Torry Holt Mint	20.00
137	J.J. Johnson Gem	40.00
137	J.J. Johnson Mint	20.00
138	Kevin Johnson Gem	40.00
138	Kevin Johnson Mint	20.00
139	Akili Smith Gem	40.00
139	Akili Smith Mint	20.00
140	Cade McNown Gem	50.00
140	Cade McNown Mint	25.00
141	Eddie George Gem	40.00
141	Eddie George Mint	20.00
142	Shaun King Gem	50.00
142	Shaun King Mint	25.00
143	Marshall Faulk Gem	40.00
143	Marshall Faulk Mint	20.00
144	Kurt Warner Gem	100.00
144	Kurt Warner Mint	50.00
145	Randy Moss Gem	80.00
145	Randy Moss Mint	40.00
146	Mark Brunell Gem	50.00
146	Mark Brunell Mint	25.00
147	Marvin Harrison Gem	40.00
147	Marvin Harrison Mint	20.00
148	Edgerrin James Gem	80.00
148	Edgerrin James Mint	40.00
149	Tim Couch Gem	60.00
149	Tim Couch Mint	30.00
150	Peyton Manning Gem	80.00
150	Peyton Manning Mint	40.00

2000 Collector's Edge Graded Edge Gems

		NM/M
Common Player:		2.00
Production 500 Sets		
E1	Doug Flutie	2.00
E2	Cade McNown	2.00
E3	Akili Smith	2.00
E4	Tim Couch	5.00
E5	Kevin Johnson	2.00
E6	Troy Aikman	4.00
E7	Emmitt Smith	6.00
E8	Terrell Davis	4.00
E9	Brett Favre	6.00
E10	Marvin Harrison	2.00
E11	Edgerrin James	4.00
E12	Peyton Manning	6.00
E13	Mark Brunell	2.00
E14	Dan Marino	6.00
E15	Randy Moss	6.00
E16	Drew Bledsoe	4.00
E17	Ricky Williams	5.00
E18	Keyshawn Johnson	2.00
E19	Curtis Martin	2.00
E20	Donovan McNabb	4.00
E21	Marshall Faulk	2.00
E22	Torry Holt	2.00
E23	Kurt Warner	5.00
E24	Jerry Rice	5.00
E25	Steve Young	4.00
E26	Jon Kitna	2.00
E27	Shaun King	2.00
E28	Eddie George	3.00
E29	Stephen Davis	2.00
E30	Brad Johnson	2.00
E31	Chad Pennington	8.00
E32	Chris Redman	3.00
E33	Tim Rattay	3.00
E34	Tee Martin	4.00
E35	Thomas Jones	5.00
E36	Ron Dayne	5.00
E37	Jamal Lewis	6.00
E38	J.R. Redmond	4.00
E39	Travis Prentice	5.00
E40	Shaun Alexander	6.00
E41	Michael Wiley	2.00
E42	Quinton Spotwood	2.00
E43	Peter Warrick	5.00
E44	Plaxico Burress	6.00
E45	Travis Taylor	5.00
E46	Troy Walters	2.00
E47	R. Jay Soward	2.00
E48	Dez White	2.00
E50	Courtney Brown	2.00

2000 Collector's Edge Graded Golden Edge

		NM/M
Complete Set (49):		75.00
Common Player:		1.00
Minor Stars:		2.50
Production 2,000 Sets		
GE1	Jake Plummer	1.00
GE2	Qadry Ismail	1.00
GE3	Doug Flutie	1.00
GE4	Muhsin Muhammad	1.00
GE5	Cade McNown	1.00
GE6	Marcus Robinson	1.00
GE7	Akili Smith	1.00
GE8	Tim Couch	3.00
GE9	Kevin Johnson	2.00
GE10	Troy Aikman	4.00
GE11	Emmitt Smith	5.00
GE12	Terrell Davis	4.00
GE13	Charlie Batch	1.00
GE14	Brett Favre	5.00
GE15	Marvin Harrison	2.50
GE16	Edgerrin James	4.00
GE17	Peyton Manning	5.00
GE18	Mark Brunell	2.00
GE19	Fred Taylor	3.00
GE20	Dan Marino	5.00
GE21	Randy Moss	5.00
GE22	Drew Bledsoe	3.00
GE23	Ricky Williams	4.00
GE24	Curtis Martin	2.00
GE25	Donovan McNabb	3.00
GE26	Isaac Bruce	2.50
GE27	Marshall Faulk	2.50
GE28	Torry Holt	2.50
GE29	Kurt Warner	4.00
GE30	Jerry Rice	4.00
GE31	Jon Kitna	1.00
GE32	Eddie George	3.00
GE33	Steve McNair	2.00
GE34	Stephen Davis	2.00
GE35	Brad Johnson	1.00
GE36	Travis Prentice	3.00
GE37	Dez White	2.00
GE38	Chad Pennington	6.00
GE39	Chris Redman	2.00
GE40	Thomas Jones	3.00
GE41	Ron Dayne	2.00
GE42	Jamal Lewis	4.00
GE43	Shyrone Stith	1.00
GE44	Peter Warrick	2.00
GE45	Plaxico Burress	6.00
GE46	Travis Taylor	4.00
GE48	Shaun Alexander	5.00
GE49	R. Jay Soward	2.00
GE50	Sylvester Morris	2.00

2000 Collector's Edge Graded Impeccable

		NM/M
Complete Set (20):		45.00
Common Player:		1.00
Production 2,000 Sets		
I1	Cade McNown	1.00
I2	Tim Couch	3.00
I3	Troy Aikman	4.00
I4	Emmitt Smith	5.00
I5	Terrell Davis	4.00
I6	Brett Favre	5.00
I7	Edgerrin James	4.00
I8	Peyton Manning	5.00
I9	Mark Brunell	2.00
I10	Fred Taylor	2.00
I11	Dan Marino	5.00
I12	Randy Moss	5.00
I13	Drew Bledsoe	3.00
I14	Ricky Williams	4.00
I15	Curtis Martin	1.00
I16	Marshall Faulk	1.00
I17	Kurt Warner	4.00
I18	Eddie George	2.00
I19	Steve McNair	1.00
I20	Stephen Brown	1.00

2000 Collector's Edge Graded Making the Grade

		NM/M
Complete Set (29):		45.00
Common Player:		1.00
Production 2,000 Sets		
M1	Shaun Alexander	4.00
M2	R. Jay Soward	1.00
M3	Sylvester Morris	2.00
M4	Giovanni Carmazzi	1.00
M5	J.R. Redmond	2.00
M6	Bubba Franks	1.00
M7	Tee Martin	2.00
M8	Dennis Northcutt	1.00
M9	Troy Walters	1.00
M10	Joe Hamilton	2.00
M11	Reuben Droughns	1.00
M12	Trung Canidate	1.00
M13	Laveranues Coles	3.00
M14	Tim Rattay	1.00
M15	Jerry Porter	4.00
M16	Ron Dugans	1.00
M17	Anthony Becht	1.00
M18	Danny Farmer	1.00
M19	Travis Prentice	4.00
M20	Dez White	3.00
M21	Chad Pennington	8.00
M22	Chris Redman	2.00
M23	Thomas Jones	5.00
M24	Ron Dayne	3.00
M25	Jamal Lewis	5.00
M26	Todd Pinkston	3.00
M27	Peter Warrick	3.00
M28	Plaxico Burress	6.00
M29	Travis Taylor	4.00

2000 Collector's Edge Graded Rookie Leatherbacks

		NM/M
Common Player:		150.00
Production 12 Sets		
SA	Shaun Alexander	350.00
AB	Anthony Becht	150.00
PB	Plaxico Burress	450.00
TC	Trung Canidate	200.00
LC	Laveranues Coles	200.00
RD	Ron Dayne	600.00
RD	Reuben Droughns	150.00
RD	Ron Dugans	200.00
DF	Danny Farmer	150.00
BF	Bubba Franks	200.00
JH	Joe Hamilton	225.00
TJ	Thomas Jones	350.00
CK	Curtis Keaton	150.00
JL	Jamal Lewis	350.00
TM	Tee Martin	250.00
SM	Sylvester Morris	300.00
DN	Dennis Northcutt	225.00
CP	Chad Pennington	450.00
TP	Todd Pinkston	200.00
JP	Jerry Porter	200.00
TP	Travis Prentice	300.00
CR	Chris Redman	275.00
JR	J.R. Redmond	275.00
CS	Corey Simon	150.00
RS	R. Jay Soward	225.00
TT	Travis Taylor	300.00
BU	Brian Urlacher	275.00
PW	Peter Warrick	600.00
DW	Dez White	200.00

2000 Collector's Edge Graded Uncirculated

		NM/M
Common Gem Mint:		12.00
Common Mint:		6.00
Production 5,000 Sets		
101	Chad Pennington Gem	50.00
101	Chad Pennington Mint	25.00
102	Chris Redman Gem	25.00
102	Chris Redman Mint	12.00
103	Thomas Jones Gem	40.00
103	Thomas Jones Mint	20.00
104	Ron Dayne Gem	60.00
104	Ron Dayne Mint	30.00
105	Jamal Lewis Gem	40.00
105	Jamal Lewis Mint	20.00
106	Shyrone Stith Gem	15.00

106 Shyrone Stith Mint 8.00
107 Peter Warrick Gem 60.00
107 Peter Warrick Mint 30.00
108 Plaxico Burress Gem 50.00
108 Plaxico Burress Mint 25.00
109 Travis Taylor Gem 30.00
109 Travis Taylor Mint 15.00
111 Terrell Davis Gem 30.00
111 Terrell Davis Mint 15.00
112 Dan Marino Gem 30.00
112 Dan Marino Mint 15.00
113 Brad Johnson Gem 12.00
113 Brad Johnson Mint 6.00
114 Isaac Bruce Gem 12.00
114 Isaac Bruce Mint 6.00
115 Eric Moulds Gem 12.00
115 Eric Moulds Mint 6.00
116 Olandis Gary Gem 12.00
116 Olandis Gary Mint 6.00
117 Drew Bledsoe Gem 20.00
117 Drew Bledsoe Mint 10.00
118 Steve Young Gem 20.00
118 Steve Young Mint 10.00
119 Keyshawn Johnson Gem 12.00
119 Keyshawn Johnson Mint 6.00
120 Emmitt Smith Gem 30.00
120 Emmitt Smith Mint 15.00
121 Warrick Dunn Gem 12.00
121 Warrick Dunn Mint 6.00
122 Doug Flutie Gem 20.00
122 Doug Flutie Mint 10.00
123 Troy Edwards Gem 12.00
123 Troy Edwards Mint 6.00
124 Brett Favre Gem 40.00
124 Brett Favre Mint 20.00
125 Charlie Batch Gem 12.00
125 Charlie Batch Mint 6.00
126 Curtis Martin Gem 12.00
126 Curtis Martin Mint 6.00
127 Stephen Davis Gem 12.00
127 Stephen Davis Mint 6.00
128 Troy Aikman Gem 25.00
128 Troy Aikman Mint 12.00
129 Fred Taylor Gem 20.00
129 Fred Taylor Mint 10.00
130 Jerry Rice Gem 25.00
130 Jerry Rice Mint 12.00
131 Jon Kitna Gem 12.00
131 Jon Kitna Mint 6.00
132 Steve McNair Gem 12.00
132 Steve McNair Mint 6.00
133 Jake Plummer Gem 12.00
133 Jake Plummer Mint 6.00
134 Donovan McNabb Gem 16.00
134 Donovan McNabb Mint 8.00
135 Ricky Williams Gem 30.00
135 Ricky Williams Mint 15.00
136 Torry Holt Gem 12.00
136 Torry Holt Mint 6.00
137 J.J. Johnson Gem 12.00
137 J.J. Johnson Mint 6.00
138 Kevin Johnson Gem 12.00
138 Kevin Johnson Mint 6.00
139 Akili Smith Gem 12.00
139 Akili Smith Mint 6.00
140 Cade McNown Gem 16.00
140 Cade McNown Mint 8.00
141 Eddie George Gem 16.00
141 Eddie George Mint 8.00
142 Shaun King Gem 16.00
142 Shaun King Mint 8.00
143 Marshall Faulk Gem 12.00
143 Marshall Faulk Mint 6.00
144 Kurt Warner Gem 40.00
144 Kurt Warner Mint 20.00
145 Randy Moss Gem 40.00
145 Randy Moss Mint 20.00
146 Mark Brunell Gem 20.00
146 Mark Brunell Mint 10.00
147 Marvin Harrison Gem 12.00
147 Marvin Harrison Mint 6.00
148 Edgerrin James Gem 40.00
148 Edgerrin James Mint 20.00
149 Tim Couch Gem 30.00
149 Tim Couch Mint 15.00
150 Peyton Manning Gem 40.00
150 Peyton Manning Mint 20.00

2000 Collector's Edge Masters

NM/M
Common Player: .50
Minor Stars: 1.00
Production 2,000 Sets
Common Rookies: 2.00
Production 1,000 Sets
Retail Box (3 packs + 2 PSA): 35.00
1 David Boston 1.50
2 Michael Pittman .50
3 Jake Plummer .75
4 Frank Sanders .50
5 Jamal Anderson 1.00
6 Chris Chandler .50
7 Tim Dwight .75
8 Shawn Jefferson .50
9 Terance Mathis .50
10 Tony Banks .50
11 Trent Dilfer .50
12 Priest Holmes 2.00
13 Qadry Ismail .50
14 Jermaine Lewis .50
15 Shannon Sharpe 1.00
16 Doug Flutie .75
17 Rob Johnson .50
18 Jeremy McDaniel .50
19 Eric Moulds 1.50
20 Peerless Price 2.00
21 Antowain Smith 1.00
22 Steve Beuerlein .50
23 Tim Biakabutuka .50
24 Dialleo Burks .50
25 Dameyune Craig .50
26 Donald Hayes .50
27 Patrick Jeffers .75
28 Muhsin Muhammad 1.00
29 Reggie White .50
30 Bobby Engram .50
31 Curtis Enis .50
32 Eddie Kennison .50
33 Cade McNown .50
34 Marcus Robinson 1.00
35 Corey Dillon 1.50
36 James Hundon .50
37 Scott Mitchell .50
38 Tony McGee .50
39 Akili Smith .50
40 Craig Yeast .50
41 Darrin Chiaverini .50
42 Tim Couch 2.00
43 Kevin Johnson .75
44 Errict Rhett .50
45 Troy Aikman 3.50
46 Randall Cunningham .50
47 Joey Galloway .75
48 Raghib Ismail .50
49 James McKnight .50
50 Dat Nguyen .50
51 Emmitt Smith 4.00
52 Chris Warren .50
53 Robert Brooks .50
54 Terrell Davis 3.00
55 Gus Frerotte .50
56 Olandis Gary .50
57 Brian Griese 1.00
58 Ed McCaffrey 1.00
59 Rod Smith 1.00
60 Charlie Batch .50
61 Germane Crowell .50
62 Sedrick Irvin .50
63 Herman Moore .50
64 Johnnie Morton 1.00
65 James Stewart 1.00
66 Corey Bradford .50
67 Brett Favre 3.00
68 Antonio Freeman .50
69 Matt Hasselbeck .50
70 Dorsey Levens .50
71 Bill Schroeder .50
72 Ken Dilger .50
73 E.G. Green .50
74 Marvin Harrison 1.50
75 Edgerrin James 3.00
76 Peyton Manning 3.00
77 Jerome Pathon .50
78 Terrence Wilkins .50
79 Kyle Brady .50
80 Mark Brunell 1.00
81 Kevin Hardy .50
82 Stacey Mack .50
83 Keenan McCardell .50
84 Jimmy Smith 1.00
85 Fred Taylor 1.00
86 Derrick Alexander .50
87 Michael Cloud .50
88 Tony Gonzalez 1.00
89 Elvis Grbac .50
90 Kevin Lockett .50
91 Tony Richardson .50
92 Jay Fiedler .75
93 Oronde Gadsden .50
94 Damon Huard .50
95 Rob Konrad .50
96 J.J. Johnson .50
97 Tony Martin .50
98 O.J. McDuffie .50
99 Lamar Smith .50
100 Thurman Thomas .75
101 Todd Bouman .50
102 Bubby Brister .50
103 Cris Carter 1.00
104 Daunte Culpepper 2.00
105 Matthew Hatchette .50
106 Randy Moss 3.00
107 Robert Smith 1.00
108 Moe Williams .50
109 Michael Bishop 1.00
110 Drew Bledsoe 2.00
111 Troy Brown .50
112 Kevin Faulk .50
113 Terry Glenn .75
114 Andy Katzenmoyer .50
115 Tony Simmons .50
116 Jeff Blake .50
117 Aaron Brooks 2.00
118 Jake Delhomme .50
119 Joe Horn 1.00
120 Jake Reed .50
121 Ricky Williams 3.00
122 Tiki Barber 1.00
123 Kerry Collins 1.00
124 Ike Hilliard 1.00
125 Amani Toomer 1.00
126 Wayne Chrebet 1.00
127 Ray Lucas .50
128 Curtis Martin 1.50
129 Vinny Testaverde .50
130 Dedric Ward .50
131 Tim Brown 1.00
132 Rickey Dudley .50
133 Rich Gannon 1.00
134 James Jett .50
135 Napoleon Kaufman .50
136 Tyrone Wheatley .50
137 Charles Woodson 1.00
138 Charles Johnson .50
139 Donovan McNabb 2.00
140 Torrance Small .50
141 Duce Staley 1.00
142 Jerome Bettis 1.00
143 Troy Edwards 1.00
144 Kent Graham .50
145 Richard Huntley .50
146 Kordell Stewart 1.00
147 Amos Zereoue .75
148 Isaac Bruce 1.00
149 Kevin Carter .50
150 Marshall Faulk 1.50
151 Trent Green 1.00
152 Az-Zahir Hakim 1.00
153 Robert Holcombe .50
154 Torry Holt 1.50
155 Kurt Warner 3.00
156 Kenny Bynum .50
157 Robert Chancey .50
158 Curtis Conway 1.00
159 Jermaine Fazande .50
160 Jeff Graham .50
161 Jim Harbaugh .50
162 Ryan Leaf .50
163 Junior Seau 1.00
164 Jeff Garcia 1.50
165 Charlie Garner 1.00
166 Terrell Owens 1.50
167 Jerry Rice 3.00
168 J.J. Stokes 1.00
169 Karsten Bailey .50
170 Sean Dawkins .50
171 Brock Huard .50
172 Jon Kitna .50
173 Derrick Mayes .50
174 Ricky Watters 1.00
175 Rabih Abdullah .50
176 Mike Alstott 1.00
177 Reidel Anthony .50
178 Warrick Dunn 1.00
179 Jacquez Green .50
180 Keyshawn Johnson 1.00
181 Shaun King .75
182 Warren Sapp 1.00
183 Kevin Dyson .50
184 Eddie George 1.75
185 Jevon Kearse 1.50
186 Steve McNair 1.50
187 Neil O'Donnell .50
188 Carl Pickens 1.00
189 Yancey Thigpen .50
190 Frank Wycheck .50
191 Champ Bailey 1.00
192 Larry Centers .50
193 Albert Connell .50
194 Stephen Davis 1.00
195 Jeff George .50
196 Brad Johnson .50
197 Deion Sanders .75
198 Bruce Smith .50
199 James Thrash .50
200 Michael Westbrook .50
201 *Thomas Jones* 3.00
202 *Jamal Lewis* 10.00
203 *Chris Redman* 4.00
204 *Travis Taylor* 5.00
205 *Avion Black* 2.00
206 *Kwame Cavil* 2.00
207 *Sammy Morris* 3.00
208 *Brian Urlacher* 20.00
209 *Dez White* 3.00
210 *Ron Dugans* 3.00
211 *Danny Farmer* 3.00
212 *Curtis Keaton* 2.00
213 *Peter Warrick* 4.00
214 *Courtney Brown* 4.00
215 *JaJuan Dawson* 2.00
216 *Dennis Northcutt* 2.00
217 *Travis Prentice* 4.00
218 *Spergon Wynn* 2.00
219 *Michael Wiley* 2.00
220 *Mike Anderson* 8.00
221 *Chris Cole* 2.00
222 *Deltha O'Neal* 2.00
223 *Reuben Droughns* 2.00
224 *Bubba Franks* 3.00
225 *Charles Lee* 2.00
226 *Rob Morris* 2.00
227 *R. Jay Soward* 3.00
228 *Shyrone Stith* 2.00
229 *Frank Moreau* 3.00
230 *Sylvester Morris* 4.00
231 *J.R. Redmond* 5.00
232 *Chad Morton* 3.00
233 *Ron Dayne* 4.00
234 *Ron Dixon* 4.00
235 *Anthony Becht* 3.00
236 *Laveranues Coles* 4.00
237 *Chad Pennington* 25.00
238 *Sebastian Janikowski* 4.00
239 *Jerry Porter* 6.00
240 *Todd Pinkston* 3.00
241 *Gari Scott* 2.00
242 *Corey Simon* 3.00
243 *Plaxico Burress* 12.00
244 *Tee Martin* 4.00
245 *Trung Canidate* 3.00
246 *Trevor Gaylor* 3.00
247 *Giovanni Carmazzi* 4.00
248 *Tim Rattay* 4.00
249 *Shaun Alexander* 10.00
250 *Joe Hamilton* 4.00

2000 Collector's Edge Masters HoloGold

HoloGold Cards: 3X-6X
HoloGold Rookies: 2X
Production 50 Sets

2000 Collector's Edge Masters HoloSilver

HoloSilver Cards: 2X
HoloSilver Rookies: 75%
Production 1,000 Sets

2000 Collector's Edge Masters Domain

NM/M
Complete Set (20): 15.00
Common Player: .75
Minor Stars: 1.50
Production 5,000 Sets
D1 Qadry Ismail .75
D2 Muhsin Muhammad .75
D3 Marcus Robinson 1.00
D4 Akili Smith 1.00
D5 Tim Couch 3.00
D6 Kevin Johnson 1.50
D7 Troy Aikman 4.50
D8 Brian Griese 2.00
D9 James Stewart .75
D10 Dorsey Levens 1.00
D11 Marvin Harrison 1.50
D12 Cris Carter 1.50
D13 Daunte Culpepper 3.00
D14 Donovan McNabb 3.00
D15 Duce Staley 1.50
D16 Isaac Bruce 1.50
D17 Torry Holt 1.50
D18 Kurt Warner 3.00
D19 Jeff Garcia 1.50
D20 Jerry Rice 4.00

2000 Collector's Edge Masters Future Masters

NM/M
Complete Set (30): 40.00
Common Player: 1.00
Minor Stars: 2.00
Production 2,000 Sets
FM1 Thomas Jones 3.00
FM2 Jamal Lewis 6.00
FM3 Chris Redman 4.00
FM4 Travis Taylor 2.50
FM5 Brian Urlacher 8.00
FM6 Dez White 2.00
FM7 Ron Dugans 2.00
FM8 Danny Farmer 2.00
FM9 Curtis Keaton 1.00
FM10 Peter Warrick 2.00
FM11 Courtney Brown 2.00
FM12 JaJuan Dawson 2.00
FM13 Dennis Northcutt 2.00
FM14 Travis Prentice 3.00
FM15 Spergon Wynn 2.00
FM16 Reuben Droughns 2.00
FM17 R. Jay Soward 2.00
FM18 J.R. Redmond 2.50
FM19 Ron Dayne 2.00
FM20 Anthony Becht 2.00
FM21 Laveranues Coles 2.50
FM22 Chad Pennington 10.00
FM23 Jerry Porter 2.00
FM24 Todd Pinkston 2.00
FM25 Plaxico Burress 4.50
FM26 Tee Martin 2.50
FM27 Trung Canidate 2.00
FM28 Giovanni Carmazzi 2.50
FM29 Tim Rattay 2.50
FM30 Joe Hamilton 2.00

2000 Collector's Edge Masters Game Gear Leatherbacks

NM/M
Common Player: 150.00
Production 12 Sets
TC Tim Couch 300.00
DC Daunte Culpepper 325.00
RD Ron Dayne 450.00
EJ Edgerrin James 400.00
PM Peyton Manning 400.00
SM Sylvester Morris 250.00
RM Randy Moss 400.00
TT Travis Taylor 150.00
KW Kurt Warner 450.00
PW Peter Warrick 400.00

2000 Collector's Edge Masters Hasta La Vista

NM/M
Complete Set (20): 35.00
Common Player: 1.00
Minor Stars: 2.00
Production 2,000 Sets
H1 Eric Moulds 3.00
H2 Cade McNown 1.00
H3 Emmitt Smith 5.00
H4 Terrell Davis 4.00
H5 Charlie Batch 1.00
H6 Marvin Harrison 2.00
H7 Edgerrin James 4.00
H8 Peyton Manning 5.00
H9 Mark Brunell 3.00
H10 Fred Taylor 2.00
H11 Daunte Culpepper 3.00
H12 Torry Holt 1.00
H13 Marshall Faulk 3.00
H14 Kurt Warner 4.00
H15 Ryan Leaf 1.00
H16 Keyshawn Johnson 2.00
H17 Shaun King 1.00
H18 Steve McNair 3.00
H19 Stephen Davis 2.00
H20 Brad Johnson 1.00

2000 Collector's Edge Masters K-Klub

NM/M
Complete Set (50): 35.00
Common Player: .75
Minor Stars: 1.50
Production 3,000 Sets
K1 David Boston 1.50
K2 Frank Sanders .75
K3 Jamal Anderson 1.00
K4 Terance Mathis .75
K5 Qadry Ismail .75
K6 Eric Moulds 1.00
K7 Antowain Smith 1.00
K8 Patrick Jeffers .75
K9 Muhsin Muhammad .75
K10 Curtis Enis .75
K11 Marcus Robinson 1.00
K12 Corey Dillon 1.50
K13 Kevin Johnson 1.50
K14 Joey Galloway 1.00
K15 Raghib Ismail .75
K16 Emmitt Smith 4.00
K17 Olandis Gary 1.00
K18 Ed McCaffrey 1.50
K19 Germane Crowell .75
K20 Herman Moore .75
K21 Antonio Freeman .75
K22 Dorsey Levens 1.00
K23 Marvin Harrison 1.50
K24 Edgerrin James 4.00
K25 Keenan McCardell .75
K26 Jimmy Smith 1.50
K27 Fred Taylor 2.00
K28 Cris Carter 1.00
K29 Randy Moss 5.00
K30 Robert Smith 1.50
K31 Terry Glenn 1.00
K32 Ricky Williams 4.00
K33 Curtis Martin 1.50
K34 Tim Brown 1.50
K35 Duce Staley 1.50
K36 Jerome Bettis 1.50
K37 Isaac Bruce 1.50
K38 Marshall Faulk 1.50
K39 Torry Holt 1.50
K40 Charlie Garner .75
K41 Terrell Owens 1.50
K42 Ricky Watters .75
K43 Warrick Dunn 1.50
K44 Keyshawn Johnson 1.50
K45 Kevin Dyson .75
K46 Eddie George 1.75
K47 Carl Pickens .75
K48 Albert Connell .75
K49 Stephen Davis 1.50
K50 Michael Westbrook 1.50

2000 Collector's Edge Masters Legends

NM/M
Complete Set (30): 25.00
Common Player: .50
Minor Stars: 1.00
Production 5,000 Sets
ML1 Jake Plummer .50
ML2 Eric Moulds 1.00
ML3 Cade McNown .50
ML4 Marcus Robinson 1.00
ML5 Akili Smith .50
ML6 Tim Couch 2.00
ML7 Troy Aikman 2.00
ML8 Emmitt Smith 3.00
ML9 Terrell Davis 2.00
ML10 Brett Favre 3.00
ML11 Antonio Freeman .50
ML12 Dorsey Levens .50
ML13 Mark Brunell 1.00
ML14 Fred Taylor 1.00
ML15 Cris Carter .75
ML16 Randy Moss 3.00
ML17 Drew Bledsoe 2.00
ML18 Curtis Martin 1.00
ML19 Donovan McNabb 2.00
ML20 Ricky Williams 2.50
ML21 Jerome Bettis 1.00
ML22 Isaac Bruce 1.00
ML23 Marshall Faulk 1.00
ML24 Jerry Rice 2.50
ML25 Jon Kitna .50
ML26 Keyshawn Johnson 1.00
ML27 Shaun King .50
ML28 Steve McNair 1.00
ML29 Stephen Davis 1.00
ML30 Brad Johnson .50

2000 Collector's Edge Masters Majestic

NM/M
Complete Set (30): 30.00
Common Player: .50
Minor Stars: 1.00
Production 5,000 Sets
M1 Thomas Jones 2.00
M2 Jamal Lewis 4.00
M3 Travis Taylor 2.00
M4 Brian Urlacher 5.00
M5 Dez White 1.00
M6 Danny Farmer 1.00
M7 Curtis Keaton .50
M8 Peter Warrick 2.00
M9 Courtney Brown 1.50
M10 JaJuan Dawson .50
M11 Spergon Wynn .50
M12 Michael Wiley .50
M13 Reuben Droughns .50
M14 Bubba Franks 1.00
M15 Rob Morris .50
M16 Sylvester Morris 1.00
M17 Ron Dayne 2.00
M18 Ron Dixon .50
M19 Anthony Becht .50
M20 Chad Pennington 6.00
M21 Sebastian Janikowski 1.00
M22 Todd Pinkston 1.00
M23 Corey Simon 1.00
M24 Plaxico Burress 3.50
M25 Tee Martin 1.00
M26 Trevor Gaylor .50
M27 Giovanni Carmazzi .50
M28 Tim Rattay .50
M29 Shaun Alexander 4.00
M30 Joe Hamilton 1.50

2000 Collector's Edge Masters Rookie Masters

NM/M
Complete Set (30): 45.00
Common Player: 1.00
Minor Stars: 2.00
Production 2,000 Sets
MR1 Thomas Jones 3.00
MR2 Jamal Lewis 4.00
MR3 Chris Redman 2.00
MR4 Travis Taylor 2.00
MR5 Dez White 2.00
MR6 Ron Dugans 1.00
MR7 Curtis Keaton 1.00
MR8 Peter Warrick 2.00
MR9 Brian Urlacher 6.00
MR10 JaJuan Dawson 1.00
MR11 Dennis Northcutt 1.00
MR12 Travis Prentice 2.50
MR13 Spergon Wynn 1.00
MR14 Reuben Droughns 1.00
MR15 Bubba Franks 2.00
MR16 Sylvester Morris 2.00
MR17 J.R. Redmond 2.50
MR18 Ron Dayne 2.00
MR19 Anthony Becht 1.00
MR20 Laveranues Coles 2.00
MR21 Chad Pennington 8.00
MR22 Jerry Porter 3.00
MR23 Todd Pinkston 2.00
MR24 Plaxico Burress 3.50
MR25 Tee Martin 2.00
MR26 Trung Canidate 1.00
MR27 Giovanni Carmazzi 1.00
MR28 Tim Rattay 2.00
MR29 Shaun Alexander 4.00
MR30 Joe Hamilton 2.00

2000 Collector's Edge Masters Rookie Sentinels

NM/M
Complete Set (30): 70.00
Common Player: 1.00
Minor Stars: 3.00
Production 1,000 Sets
RS1 Thomas Jones 3.00
RS2 Jamal Lewis 6.00
RS3 Chris Redman 3.00
RS4 Travis Taylor 3.50
RS5 Ron Dugans 1.00
RS6 Peter Warrick 2.00
RS7 Courtney Brown 3.00
RS8 Dennis Northcutt 2.00
RS9 Travis Prentice 4.00
RS10 Bubba Franks 3.00
RS11 R. Jay Soward 2.00
RS12 Sylvester Morris 3.00
RS13 J.R. Redmond 3.50
RS14 Ron Dayne 3.00
RS15 Laveranues Coles 4.00
RS16 Chad Pennington 10.00
RS17 Jerry Porter 3.00
RS18 Plaxico Burress 5.00
RS19 Trung Canidate 3.00
RS20 Shaun Alexander 5.00
RS21 Mike Anderson 4.00
RS22 Danny Farmer 3.00
RS23 Brian Urlacher 7.50
RS24 Michael Wiley 1.00
RS25 Rob Morris 1.00
RS26 Corey Simon 1.00
RS27 Sebastian Janikowski 3.00
RS28 Sammy Morris 3.00
RS29 Keith Bulluck 1.00
RS30 Frank Moreau 1.00

2000 Collector's Edge Masters Sentinels

NM/M
Complete Set (20): 50.00
Common Player: 2.00
Production 1,000 Sets
S1 Jake Plummer 2.00
S2 Eric Moulds 2.00
S3 Cade McNown 2.00
S4 Akili Smith 2.00
S5 Tim Couch 4.00
S6 Kevin Johnson 2.00
S7 Troy Aikman 5.00
S8 Terrell Davis 5.00
S9 Brett Favre 6.00
S10 Edgerrin James 5.00
S11 Peyton Manning 6.00
S12 Daunte Culpepper 5.00
S13 Randy Moss 6.00
S14 Curtis Martin 2.00
S15 Donovan McNabb 4.00
S16 Ricky Williams 6.00
S17 Kurt Warner 5.00
S18 Jon Kitna 2.00
S19 Eddie George 4.00
S20 Brad Johnson 2.00

2000 Collector's Edge Odyssey

NM/M
Common Player: .15
Minor Stars: .30
Common Rookie: 3.50
Production 999 Sets
Common Survivor/Last Man Standing: 1.50
Production 2,500 Sets
Pack (5): 2.00
Wax Box (20): 35.00
1 David Boston .50
2 Jake Plummer .50
3 Frank Sanders .30
4 Jamal Anderson .50
5 Chris Chandler .30
6 Terance Mathis .15

		NM/M
7	Tony Banks	.30
8	Qadry Ismail	.15
9	Doug Flutie	.75
10	Rob Johnson	.30
11	Eric Moulds	.50
12	Peerless Price	.50
13	Antowain Smith	.30
14	Steve Beuerlein	.30
15	Tim Biakabutuka	.30
16	Muhsin Muhammad	.30
17	Curtis Enis	.50
18	Cade McNown	.75
19	Marcus Robinson	.50
20	Corey Dillon	.50
21	Akili Smith	.50
22	Tim Couch	1.00
23	Kevin Johnson	.50
24	Errict Rhett	.30
25	Troy Aikman	1.25
26	Joey Galloway	.50
27	Raghib Ismail	.15
28	Emmitt Smith	2.00
29	Terrell Davis	1.75
30	Olandis Gary	.60
31	Brian Griese	.75
32	Ed McCaffrey	.50
33	Charlie Batch	.50
34	Germane Crowell	.30
35	Herman Moore	.30
36	James Stewart	.30
37	Brett Favre	2.50
38	Antonio Freeman	.50
39	Dorsey Levens	.50
40	Marvin Harrison	.50
41	Edgerrin James	2.00
42	Peyton Manning	2.50
43	Terrence Wilkins	.50
44	Mark Brunell	1.00
45	Keenan McCardell	.30
46	Jimmy Smith	.50
47	Fred Taylor	1.00
48	Michael Cloud	.15
49	Tony Gonzalez	.30
50	Elvis Grbac	.30
51	Damon Huard	.50
52	J.J. Johnson	.30
53	Tony Martin	.15
54	Cris Carter	.50
55	Daunte Culpepper	1.25
56	Randy Moss	2.00
57	Robert Smith	.50
58	Drew Bledsoe	1.00
59	Terry Glenn	.50
60	Jeff Blake	.30
61	Ricky Williams	1.25
62	Kerry Collins	.30
63	Ike Hilliard	.30
64	Amani Toomer	.30
65	Wayne Chrebet	.50
66	Curtis Martin	.50
67	Vinny Testaverde	.30
68	Tim Brown	.50
69	Rich Gannon	.30
70	Donovan McNabb	1.00
71	Duce Staley	.50
72	Jerome Bettis	.50
73	Troy Edwards	.30
74	Kordell Stewart	.60
75	Isaac Bruce	.50
76	Marshall Faulk	.50
77	Torry Holt	.50
78	Kurt Warner	2.00
79	Jermaine Fazande	.30
80	Jim Harbaugh	.30
81	Jeff Garcia	.50
82	Charlie Garner	.30
83	Terrell Owens	.30
84	Jerry Rice	1.25
85	Jon Kitna	.50
86	Derrick Mayes	.50
87	Ricky Watters	.50
88	Mike Alstott	.50
89	Warrick Dunn	.50
90	Keyshawn Johnson	.50
91	Shaun King	.50
92	Kevin Dyson	.30
93	Eddie George	.75
94	Jevon Kearse	.50
95	Steve McNair	.50
96	Carl Pickens	.30
97	Champ Bailey	.30
98	Stephen Davis	.50
99	Brad Johnson	.50
100	Michael Westbrook	.30
101	*Thomas Jones*	5.00
102	*Doug Johnson*	3.00
103	*Mareno Philyaw*	2.00
104	*Jamal Lewis*	15.00
105	*Chris Redman*	6.00
106	*Travis Taylor*	6.00
107	*Kwame Cavil*	2.00
108	*Sammy Morris*	4.00
109	*Frank Murphy*	2.00
110	*Brian Urlacher*	20.00
111	*Dez White*	3.00
112	*Ron Dugans*	2.00
113	*Curtis Keaton*	2.00
114	*Peter Warrick*	5.00
115	*Courtney Brown*	6.00
116	*JaJuan Dawson*	3.00
117	*Dennis Northcutt*	3.00
118	*Travis Prentice*	6.00
119	*Michael Wiley*	3.00
120	*Mike Anderson*	15.00
121	*Chris Cole*	3.00
122	*Jarious Jackson*	3.00
123	*Deltha O'Neal*	3.00
124	*Reuben Droughns*	3.00
125	*Bubba Franks*	6.00
126	*Anthony Lucas*	3.50
127	*Rondell Mealey*	2.00
128	*Rob Morris*	2.00
129	*R. Jay Soward*	4.00
130	*Shyrone Stith*	3.00
131	*Frank Moreau*	3.00
132	*Sylvester Morris*	6.00
133	*Doug Chapman*	3.00
134	*J.R. Redmond*	6.00
135	*Marc Bulger*	10.00
136	*Sherrod Gideon*	3.50
137	*Terrelle Smith*	3.00
138	*Ron Dayne*	6.00
139	*Anthony Becht*	3.00
140	*Laveranues Coles*	10.00
141	*Shaun Ellis*	2.00
142	*Chad Pennington*	25.00
143	*Sebastian Janikowski*	5.00
144	*Jerry Porter*	7.00
145	*Todd Pinkston*	6.00
146	*Gari Scott*	3.00
147	*Corey Simon*	3.00
148	*Plaxico Burress*	20.00
149	*Danny Farmer*	5.00
150	*Tee Martin*	6.00
151	*Trung Canidate*	5.00
152	*Trevor Gaylor*	3.00
153	*Giovanni Carmazzi*	5.00
154	*John Engelberger*	3.50
155	*Ahmed Plummer*	6.00
156	*Tim Rattay*	4.00
157	*Shaun Alexander*	15.00
158	*Joe Hamilton*	5.00
159	*Keith Bulluck*	3.50
160	*Todd Husak*	3.00
161	Cade McNown	2.00
162	Tim Couch	3.00
163	Terrell Davis	4.00
164	Brett Favre	5.00
165	Edgerrin James	4.00
166	Peyton Manning	5.00
167	Daunte Culpepper	3.00
168	Randy Moss	5.00
169	Ricky Williams	4.00
170	Kurt Warner	4.00
171	Cade McNown	2.00
172	Akili Smith	1.50
173	Tim Couch	3.00
174	Troy Aikman	3.50
175	Emmitt Smith	5.00
176	Terrell Davis	4.00
177	Brett Favre	5.00
178	Edgerrin James	4.00
179	Peyton Manning	5.00
180	Mark Brunell	2.50
181	Daunte Culpepper	3.00
182	Randy Moss	5.00
183	Drew Bledsoe	2.50
184	Ricky Williams	4.00
185	Donovan McNabb	2.00
186	Torry Holt	1.50
187	Kurt Warner	4.00
188	Shaun King	2.00
189	Eddie George	1.75
190	Steve McNair	1.50

2000 Collector's Edge Odyssey Hologold Rookies

Hologold Rookies:	1X
Production 500 Sets	

2000 Collector's Edge Odyssey GameGear

		NM/M
Common Player:		10.00
SA	Shaun Alexander	60.00
AB	Anthony Becht	10.00
PB	Plaxico Burress	75.00
TC	Trung Canidate	10.00
LC	Laveranues Coles	60.00
RD	Ron Dayne	25.00
RD	Reuben Droughns	10.00
RD	Ron Dugans	10.00
DF	Danny Farmer	10.00
BF	Bubba Franks	25.00
JH	Joe Hamilton	10.00
TJ	Thomas Jones	40.00
CK	Curtis Keaton	25.00
JL	Jamal Lewis	40.00
TM	Tee Martin	25.00
SM	Sylvester Morris	25.00
DN	Dennis Northcutt	10.00
CP	Chad Pennington	100.00
TP	Todd Pinkston	10.00
JP	Jerry Porter	40.00
TP	Travis Prentice	10.00
CR	Chris Redman	25.00
JR	J.R. Redmond	10.00
CS	Corey Simon	10.00
RS	R. Jay Soward	10.00
TT	Travis Taylor	30.00
BU	Brian Urlacher	80.00
PW	Peter Warrick	25.00
DW	Dez White	25.00

2000 Collector's Edge Odyssey Old School

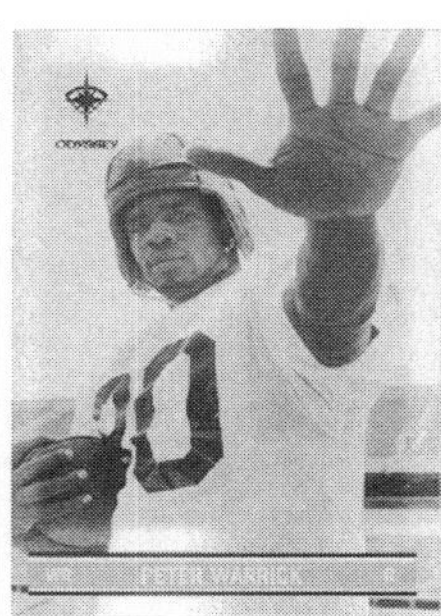

		NM/M
Complete Set (30):		20.00
Common Player:		.50
Minor Stars:		1.00
Inserted 1:6		
OS1	Thomas Jones	1.00
OS2	Jamal Lewis	3.00
OS3	Chris Redman	1.75
OS4	Travis Taylor	1.50
OS5	Brian Urlacher	4.00
OS6	Dez White	1.00
OS7	Ron Dugans	1.00
OS8	Curtis Keaton	.50
OS9	Peter Warrick	1.00
OS10	Courtney Brown	1.25
OS11	Dennis Northcutt	1.25
OS12	Travis Prentice	1.50
OS13	Reuben Droughns	1.00
OS14	Bubba Franks	1.25
OS15	R. Jay Soward	1.00
OS16	Sylvester Morris	1.50
OS17	J.R. Redmond	1.25
OS18	Ron Dayne	2.00
OS19	Anthony Becht	1.00
OS20	Laveranues Coles	1.25
OS21	Chad Pennington	6.00
OS22	Jerry Porter	1.00
OS23	Todd Pinkston	1.00
OS24	Corey Simon	1.00
OS25	Plaxico Burress	2.50
OS26	Danny Farmer	1.00
OS27	Tee Martin	1.25
OS28	Trung Canidate	1.00
OS29	Shaun Alexander	3.00
OS30	Joe Hamilton	1.25

2000 Collector's Edge Odyssey Restaurant Quality

		NM/M
Complete Set (10):		15.00
Common Player:		1.50
Inserted 1:20		
RQ1	Thomas Jones	2.00
RQ2	Jamal Lewis	3.00
RQ3	Travis Taylor	2.00
RQ4	Peter Warrick	2.00
RQ5	Bubba Franks	1.50
RQ6	Sylvester Morris	2.00
RQ7	Ron Dayne	2.00
RQ8	Chad Pennington	5.00
RQ9	Plaxico Burress	3.00
RQ10	Shaun Alexander	3.50

2000 Collector's Edge Odyssey Rookie Ink

		NM/M
Common Player:		10.00
Inserted 1:99		
PB	Plaxico Burress	40.00
TC	Trung Canidate	10.00
LC	Laveranues Coles	20.00
TJ	Thomas Jones	30.00
CK	Curtis Keaton	10.00
JL	Jamal Lewis	45.00
SM	Sylvester Morris	35.00
DN	Dennis Northcutt	10.00
CP	Chad Pennington	75.00
TP	Todd Pinkston	10.00
TP	Travis Prentice	25.00
CR	Chris Redman	35.00
JR	J.R. Redmond	30.00
TT	Travis Taylor	30.00
BU	Brian Urlacher	60.00

2000 Collector's Edge Odyssey Tight

		NM/M
Complete Set (30):		30.00
Common Player:		.75
Minor Stars:		1.50
Inserted 1:10		
T1	Thomas Jones	2.00
T2	Jamal Lewis	4.00
T3	Chris Redman	3.00
T4	Travis Taylor	2.50
T5	Brian Urlacher	5.00
T6	Dez White	1.50
T7	Ron Dugans	1.50
T8	Curtis Keaton	.75
T9	Peter Warrick	2.00
T10	Courtney Brown	1.75
T11	Dennis Northcutt	1.75
T12	Travis Prentice	2.50
T13	Reuben Droughns	1.50
T14	Bubba Franks	1.75
T15	R. Jay Soward	1.50
T16	Sylvester Morris	2.50
T17	J.R. Redmond	2.00
T18	Ron Dayne	2.00
T19	Anthony Becht	1.50
T20	Laveranues Coles	1.75
T21	Chad Pennington	6.00
T22	Jerry Porter	1.50
T23	Todd Pinkston	1.50
T24	Corey Simon	1.50
T25	Plaxico Burress	3.50
T26	Danny Farmer	1.50
T27	Tee Martin	2.00
T28	Trung Canidate	1.50
T29	Shaun Alexander	4.00
T30	Joe Hamilton	1.75

2000 Collector's Edge Odyssey Wasssuppp

		NM/M
Complete Set (20):		20.00
Common Player:		1.00
Inserted 1:10		
W1	Thomas Jones	2.00
W2	Jamal Lewis	4.00
W3	Travis Taylor	1.50
W4	Ron Dugans	1.00
W5	Peter Warrick	2.00
W6	Dez White	1.00
W7	Dennis Northcutt	1.25
W8	Travis Prentice	1.50
W9	Bubba Franks	1.50
W10	R. Jay Soward	1.00
W11	Sylvester Morris	1.75
W12	J.R. Redmond	1.50
W13	Ron Dayne	2.00
W14	Laveranues Coles	1.25
W15	Chad Pennington	5.00
W16	Jerry Porter	1.00
W17	Todd Pinkston	1.00
W18	Plaxico Burress	3.00
W19	Danny Farmer	1.00
W20	Shaun Alexander	3.00

2000 Collector's Edge Supreme

		NM/M
Complete Set (190):		125.00
Common Player:		.10
Minor Stars:		.20
Common Rookie:		4.00
Production 2,000 Sets		
Pack (10):		2.00
Wax Box (24):		40.00
1	David Boston	.50
2	Adrian Murrell	.20
3	Michael Pittman	.10
4	Jake Plummer	.50
5	Frank Sanders	.10
6	Jamal Anderson	.30
7	Chris Chandler	.20
8	Terance Mathis	.10
9	Justin Armour	.10
10	Tony Banks	.20
11	Qadry Ismail	.10
12	Errict Rhett	.20
13	Doug Flutie	.75
14	Eric Moulds	.50
15	Peerless Price	.50
16	Andre Reed	.20
17	Antowain Smith	.30
18	Steve Beuerlein	.20
19	Tim Biakabutuka	.20
20	Muhsin Muhammad	.20
21	Wesley Walls	.20
22	Bobby Engram	.10
23	Curtis Enis	.30
24	Shane Matthews	.10
25	Cade McNown	.75
26	Jim Miller	.10
27	Marcus Robinson	.50
28	Corey Dillon	.50
29	Carl Pickens	.20
30	Darnay Scott	.20
31	Akili Smith	.75
32	Karim Abdul	.20
33	Tim Couch	1.25
34	Kevin Johnson	.50
35	Troy Aikman	1.25
36	Michael Irvin	.20
37	Raghib Ismail	.10
38	Deion Sanders	.30
39	Emmitt Smith	2.00
40	Terrell Davis	1.00
41	Olandis Gary	.75
42	Brian Griese	.50
43	Ed McCaffrey	.20
44	Rod Smith	.20
45	Charlie Batch	.50
46	Germane Crowell	.20
47	Greg Hill	.10
48	Sedrick Irvin	.10
49	Herman Moore	.30
50	Johnnie Morton	.10
51	Corey Bradford	.20
52	Brett Favre	2.50
53	Antonio Freeman	.30
54	Dorsey Levens	.30
55	Bill Schroeder	.10
56	E.G. Green	.10
57	Marvin Harrison	.50
58	Edgerrin James	2.00
59	Peyton Manning	2.00
60	Terrence Wilkins	.10
61	Mark Brunell	.75
62	Keenan McCardell	.20
63	Jimmy Smith	.30
64	James Stewart	.20
65	Fred Taylor	.75
66	Derrick Alexander	.10
67	Donnell Bennett	.10
68	Michael Cloud	.10
69	Tony Gonzalez	.30
70	Elvis Grbac	.20
71	Damon Huard	.20
72	J.J. Johnson	.10
73	Rob Konrad	.10
74	Dan Marino	2.50
75	Tony Martin	.10
76	O.J. McDuffie	.20
77	Cris Carter	.50
78	Daunte Culpepper	.75
79	Jeff George	.50
80	Randy Moss	2.00
81	Robert Smith	.30
82	Terry Allen	.20
83	Drew Bledsoe	.75
84	Kevin Faulk	.30
85	Terry Glenn	.30
86	Shawn Jefferson	.10
87	Billy Joe Hobert	.10
88	Eddie Kennison	.20
89	Billy Joe Tolliver	.10
90	Ricky Williams	1.25
91	Tiki Barber	.20
92	Gary Brown	.10
93	Kent Graham	.10
94	Ike Hilliard	.20
95	Amani Toomer	.20
96	Wayne Chrebet	.30
97	Keyshawn Johnson	.50
98	Ray Lucas	.30
99	Curtis Martin	.50
100	Vinny Testaverde	.30
101	Tim Brown	.30
102	Rich Gannon	.20
103	James Jett	.10
104	Napoleon Kaufman	.30
105	Tyrone Wheatley	.20
106	Charles Johnson	.10
107	Donovan McNabb	.75
108	Duce Staley	.30
109	Jerome Bettis	.30
110	Troy Edwards	.50
111	Kordell Stewart	.50
112	Hines Ward	.20
113	Isaac Bruce	.50
114	Marshall Faulk	.50
115	Az-Zahir Hakim	.20
116	Torry Holt	.50
117	Kurt Warner	2.00
118	Jeff Graham	.10
119	Jim Harbaugh	.20
120	Freddie Jones	.10
121	Natrone Means	.20
122	Junior Seau	.20
123	Jeff Garcia	.50
124	Charlie Garner	.20
125	Terrell Owens	.50
126	Jerry Rice	1.25
127	Steve Young	.75
128	Sean Dawkins	.10
129	Joey Galloway	.50
130	Jon Kitna	.50
131	Derrick Mayes	.30
132	Ricky Watters	.20
133	Mike Alstott	.50
134	Reidel Anthony	.20
135	Trent Dilfer	.20
136	Warrick Dunn	.50
137	Jacquez Green	.20
138	Shaun King	.75
139	Kevin Dyson	.20
140	Eddie George	.50
141	Jevon Kearse	.50
142	Steve McNair	.50
143	Yancey Thigpen	.20
144	Champ Bailey	.30
145	Albert Connell	.20
146	Stephen Davis	.50
147	Brad Johnson	.50
148	Michael Westbrook	.30
149	Checklist	.10
150	Checklist	.10
151	Redemption	8.00
152	*Peter Warrick*	6.00
153	*Chad Pennington*	25.00
154	*Courtney Brown*	8.00
155	*Thomas Jones*	6.00
156	*Chris Redman*	6.00
157	*R. Jay Soward*	6.00
158	*Jamal Lewis*	12.00
159	*Shaun Alexander*	15.00
160	*Travis Taylor*	8.00
161	*Ron Dayne*	8.00
162	*Travis Prentice*	6.00
163	*Plaxico Burress*	12.50
164	*J.R. Redmond*	8.00
165	*Sherrod Gideon*	4.00
166	*Dez White*	6.00
167	*Chafie Fields*	4.00
168	*Brandon Short*	8.00
169	*Reuben Droughns*	6.00
170	*Trung Canidate*	6.00
171	Redemption	8.00
172	Redemption	8.00
173	*Shyrone Stith*	4.00
174	*Michael Wiley*	6.00
175	*Bubba Franks*	8.00
176	*Tom Brady*	25.00
177	*Anthony Lucas*	4.00
178	*Danny Farmer*	6.00
179	*Rob Morris*	4.00
180	*Dennis Northcutt*	8.00
181	*Troy Walters*	6.00
182	*Giovanni Carmazzi*	8.00
183	*Tee Martin*	8.00
184	*Joe Hamilton*	6.00
185	*Tim Rattay*	8.00
186	*Sebastian Janikowski*	6.00
187	*Na'il Diggs*	4.00
188	*Todd Husak*	4.00
189	*Jerry Porter*	12.00
190	Redemption	25.00

2000 Collector's Edge Supreme Hologold

	NM/M
Hologold Cards:	3X-5X
Production 200 Sets	
Hologold Rookies:	
Production 20 Sets	

2000 Collector's Edge Supreme Edge Tech

		NM/M
Common Player:		3.00
Production 100 Sets		
ET1	Doug Flutie	5.00
ET2	Cade McNown	5.00
ET3	Akili Smith	5.00
ET4	Tim Couch	8.00
ET5	Kevin Johnson	3.00
ET6	Troy Aikman	10.00
ET7	Emmitt Smith	15.00
ET8	Terrell Davis	12.00
ET9	Brett Favre	15.00
ET10	Marvin Harrison	6.00
ET11	Edgerrin James	12.00
ET12	Peyton Manning	15.00
ET13	Mark Brunell	6.00
ET14	Dan Marino	15.00
ET15	Randy Moss	15.00
ET16	Drew Bledsoe	10.00
ET17	Ricky Williams	12.00
ET18	Keyshawn Johnson	3.00
ET19	Curtis Martin	3.00
ET20	Donovan McNabb	10.00
ET21	Marshall Faulk	3.00
ET22	Torry Holt	3.00
ET23	Kurt Warner	15.00
ET24	Jerry Rice	12.00
ET25	Steve Young	10.00
ET26	Jon Kitna	3.00
ET27	Shaun King	3.00
ET28	Eddie George	6.00
ET29	Stephen Davis	3.00
ET30	Brad Johnson	3.00
ET31	Chad Pennington	35.00
ET32	Chris Redman	12.00
ET33	Tim Rattay	6.00
ET34	Tee Martin	8.00
ET35	Thomas Jones	10.00
ET36	Ron Dayne	10.00
ET37	Jamal Lewis	15.00
ET38	J.R. Redmond	12.00
ET39	Travis Prentice	10.00
ET40	Shaun Alexander	20.00
ET41	Michael Wiley	6.00
ET42	Shyrone Stith	3.00
ET43	Peter Warrick	10.00
ET44	Plaxico Burress	25.00
ET45	Travis Taylor	15.00
ET46	Jerry Porter	15.00

ET47 R. Jay Soward 6.00
ET48 Dez White 8.00
ET50 Courtney Brown 20.00

2000 Collector's Edge Supreme Future

NM/M
Common Player: 6.00
Production 100 Sets
SF1 Peter Warrick 12.00
SF2 Plaxico Burress 30.00
SF3 R. Jay Soward 6.00
SF4 Ron Dayne 12.00
SF5 Thomas Jones 20.00
SF6 Shaun Alexander 25.00
SF7 Chad Pennington 40.00
SF8 Chris Redman 15.00
SF9 Travis Prentice 6.00

2000 Collector's Edge Supreme Monday Knights

NM/M
Complete Set (20): 20.00
Common Player: 1.00
Inserted 1:8
MK1 Jake Plummer 1.00
MK2 Doug Flutie 1.00
MK3 Cade McNown 1.00
MK4 Akili Smith 1.00
MK5 Tim Couch 2.50
MK6 Kevin Johnson 1.00
MK7 Troy Aikman 2.50
MK8 Emmitt Smith 3.50
MK9 Terrell Davis 3.00
MK10 Charlie Batch 1.00
MK11 Brett Favre 4.00
MK12 Cris Carter 1.00
MK13 Drew Bledsoe 2.00
MK14 Ricky Williams 2.50
MK15 Curtis Martin 1.00
MK16 Jerry Rice 2.50
MK17 Jon Kitna 1.00
MK18 Shaun King 1.00
MK19 Eddie George 1.25
MK20 Brad Johnson 1.00

2000 Collector's Edge Supreme Pro Signature Authentics

NM/M
Common Player: 10.00
TC Tim Couch 40.00
JJ J.J. Johnson 10.00
DM Darnell McDonald 10.00
PM Peyton Manning 60.00
CM Cade McNown 15.00
RM Randy Moss 100.00
RW Ricky Williams 100.00

2000 Collector's Edge Supreme PSA Redemption

NM/M
Common Player: 25.00
Production 100 Sets
1 Peter Warrick 30.00
2 Plaxico Burress 60.00
3 R. Jay Soward 25.00
4 Ron Dayne 25.00
5 Thomas Jones 35.00
6 Shaun Alexander 60.00
7 Chad Pennington 100.00
8 Chris Redman 40.00
9 Travis Prentice 25.00
10 TBA 25.00

2000 Collector's Edge Supreme Route XXXIV

NM/M
Complete Set (10): 15.00
Common Player: 1.00
Inserted 1:16
R1 Peyton Manning 3.00
R2 Edgerrin James 2.00
R3 Warrick Dunn 1.00
R4 Dan Marino 3.50
R5 Steve McNair 1.00
R6 Mark Brunell 1.50
R7 Kurt Warner 3.00
R8 Marshall Faulk 1.00
R9 Randy Moss 3.00
R10 Stephen Davis 1.00

2000 Collector's Edge Supreme Team

NM/M
Complete Set (20): 25.00
Common Player: 1.00
Inserted 1:8
ST1 Peyton Manning 3.00
ST2 Kurt Warner 3.00
ST3 Tim Couch 2.00
ST4 Cade McNown 1.50
ST5 Akili Smith 1.00
ST6 Donovan McNabb 1.50
ST7 Edgerrin James 2.00
ST8 Stephen Davis 1.00
ST9 Mark Brunell 1.50
ST10 Brett Favre 4.00
ST11 Marvin Harrison 1.00
ST12 Isaac Bruce 1.00
ST13 Terrell Davis 3.00
ST14 Ricky Williams 2.50
ST15 Keyshawn Johnson 1.00
ST16 Randy Moss 4.00
ST17 Kevin Johnson 1.00
ST18 Torry Holt 1.00
ST19 Dan Marino 4.00
ST20 Troy Aikman 2.50

2000 Collector's Edge T-3

NM/M
Common Player: .15
Minor Stars: .30
Common Rookie: 3.00
Production 999 Sets
Pack (5): 3.00
Wax Box (20): 50.00
1 David Boston .50
2 Rob Moore .30
3 Michael Pittman .15
4 Jake Plummer .50
5 Frank Sanders .30
6 Jamal Anderson .50
7 Chris Chandler .30
8 Tim Dwight .50
9 Shawn Jefferson .15
10 Terance Mathis .15
11 Tony Banks .30
12 Priest Holmes .50
13 Qadry Ismail .15
14 Shannon Sharpe .30
15 Doug Flutie .75
16 Rob Johnson .30
17 Eric Moulds .50
18 Peerless Price .50
19 Antowain Smith .30
20 Steve Beuerlein .30
21 Tim Biakabutuka .30
22 Muhsin Muhammad .30
23 Patrick Jeffers .50
24 Wesley Walls .15
25 Bobby Engram .15
26 Curtis Enis .30
27 Cade McNown .50
28 Marcus Robinson .50
29 Corey Dillon .50
30 Carl Pickens .30
31 Darnay Scott .30
32 Akili Smith .50
33 Tim Couch 1.50
34 Kevin Johnson .50
35 Errict Rhett .30
36 Troy Aikman 1.25
37 Joey Galloway .50
38 Raghib Ismail .15
39 Emmitt Smith 1.75
40 Chris Warren .15
41 Terrell Davis 1.75
42 Olandis Gary .60
43 Brian Griese .75
44 Ed McCaffrey .30
45 Rod Smith .30
46 Charlie Batch .50
47 Germane Crowell .50
48 Sedrick Irvin .15
49 Herman Moore .50
50 Johnnie Morton .30
51 James Stewart .30
52 Brett Favre 2.50
53 Antonio Freeman .50
54 Dorsey Levens .50
55 Bill Schroeder .30
56 Ken Dilger .15
57 Marvin Harrison .50
58 Edgerrin James 2.00
59 Peyton Manning 2.00
60 Terrence Wilkins .30
61 Mark Brunell 1.00
62 Keenan McCardell .30
63 Jimmy Smith .50
64 Fred Taylor 1.00
65 Derrick Alexander .15
66 Donnell Bennett .15
67 Michael Cloud .15
68 Tony Gonzalez .30
69 Elvis Grbac .30
70 Tony Richardson .15
71 Damon Huard .30
72 J.J. Johnson .30
73 Rob Konrad .15
74 Tony Martin .15
75 O.J. McDuffie .30
76 Cris Carter .50
77 Daunte Culpepper 1.25
78 Randy Moss 2.00
79 Robert Smith .50
80 Drew Bledsoe 1.00
81 Kevin Faulk .50
82 Terry Glenn .50
83 Willie McGinest .15
84 Tony Simmons .15
85 Jeff Blake .30
86 Jake Reed .15
87 Ricky Williams 1.50
88 Kerry Collins .30
89 Ike Hilliard .15
90 Joe Montgomery .15
91 Amani Toomer .15
92 Wayne Chrebet .30
93 Ray Lucas .30
94 Curtis Martin .50
95 Vinny Testaverde .50
96 Tim Brown .30
97 Rich Gannon .30
98 James Jett .15
99 Napoleon Kaufman .30
100 Tyrone Wheatley .30
101 Charles Woodson .30
102 Charles Johnson .15
103 Donovan McNabb 1.00
104 Duce Staley .50
105 Jerome Bettis .50
106 Troy Edwards .50
107 Kent Graham .15
108 Kordell Stewart .50
109 Hines Ward .30
110 Isaac Bruce .50
111 Kevin Carter .15
112 Marshall Faulk .50
113 Trent Green .30
114 Az-Zahir Hakim .30
115 Torry Holt .50
116 Kurt Warner 3.00
117 Curtis Conway .30
118 Jermaine Fazande .30
119 Jeff Graham .15
120 Jim Harbaugh .30
121 Junior Seau .30
122 Jeff Garcia .50
123 Charlie Garner .30
124 Garrison Hearst .30
125 Terrell Owens .50
126 Jerry Rice 1.25
127 Steve Young 1.00
128 Sean Dawkins .15
129 Jon Kitna .50
130 Derrick Mayes .30
131 Ricky Watters .30
132 Mike Alstott .50
133 Warrick Dunn .50
134 Jacquez Green .30
135 Keyshawn Johnson .50
136 Shaun King 1.00
137 Warren Sapp .30
138 Kevin Dyson .30
139 Eddie George .75
140 Jevon Kearse .50
141 Steve McNair .60
142 Yancey Thigpen .30
143 Frank Wycheck .15
144 Champ Bailey .30
145 Larry Centers .15
146 Albert Connell .30
147 Stephen Davis .50
148 Jeff George .50
149 Brad Johnson .50
150 Michael Westbrook .30
151 *Thomas Jones* 12.00
152 *Doug Johnson* 3.00
153 *Mareno Philyaw* 3.00
154 *Jamal Lewis* 20.00
155 *Chris Redman* 12.00
156 *Travis Taylor* 12.00
157 *Kwame Cavil* 3.00
158 *Sammy Morris* 6.00
159 *Deon Grant* 3.00
160 *Frank Murphy* 3.00
161 *Brian Urlacher* 40.00
162 *Dez White* 12.00
163 *Ron Dugans* 3.00
164 *Curtis Keaton* 3.00
165 *Peter Warrick* 12.00
166 *Courtney Brown* 6.00
167 *JaJuan Dawson* 3.00
168 *Dennis Northcutt* 3.00
169 *Travis Prentice* 8.00
170 *Michael Wiley* 3.00
171 *Mike Anderson* 35.00
172 *Chris Cole* 3.00
173 *Jarious Jackson* 3.00
174 *Deltha O'Neal* 3.00
175 *Reuben Droughns* 3.00
176 *Na'il Diggs* 3.00
177 *Bubba Franks* 6.00
178 *Anthony Lucas* 3.00
179 *Rondell Mealey* 3.00
180 *Dan Kendra* 3.00
181 *Rob Morris* 4.00
182 *R. Jay Soward* 4.00
183 *Shyrone Stith* 3.00
184 *Frank Moreau* 3.00
185 *Sylvester Morris* 12.00
186 *Deon Dyer* 3.00
187 *Quinton Spotwood* 3.00
188 *Doug Chapman* 3.00
189 *Troy Walters* 3.00
190 *J.R. Redmond* 10.00
191 *Marc Bulger* 15.00
192 *Sherrod Gideon* 3.00
193 *Darren Howard* 3.00
194 *Chad Morton* 3.00
195 *Terrelle Smith* 3.00
196 *Ron Dayne* 12.00
197 *John Abraham* 3.00
198 *Anthony Becht* 3.00
199 *Laveranues Coles* 20.00
200 *Shaun Ellis* 6.00
201 *Chad Pennington* 65.00
202 *Sebastian Janikowski* 6.00
203 *Jerry Porter* 15.00
204 *Todd Pinkston* 12.00
205 *Corey Simon* 3.00
206 *Plaxico Burress* 35.00
207 *Danny Farmer* 10.00
208 *Tee Martin* 12.00
209 *Hank Poteat* 6.00
210 *Trung Canidate* 10.00
211 *Jacoby Shepherd* 3.00
212 *Trevor Gaylor* 3.00
213 *Giovanni Carmazzi* 3.00
214 *John Engelberger* 3.00
215 *Chafie Fields* 3.00
216 *Julian Peterson* 3.00
217 *Ahmed Plummer* 3.00
218 *Tim Rattay* 4.00
219 *Paul Smith* 3.00
220 *Shaun Alexander* 25.00
221 *Joe Hamilton* 5.00
222 *Keith Bulluck* 3.00
223 *Erron Kinney* 3.00
224 *Todd Husak* 4.00
225 *Chris Samuels* 3.00

2000 Collector's Edge T-3 HoloPlatinum

Platinum Cards: 2X-4X
Platinum Rookies: 1X
Production 500 Sets

2000 Collector's Edge T-3 HoloRed

Red Cards: 3X-5X
Red Rookies: 2X
Production 50 Sets

2000 Collector's Edge T-3 Adrenaline

NM/M
Complete Set (20): 15.00
Common Player: 1.00
Inserted 1:10
A1 Doug Flutie 1.00
A2 Troy Aikman 2.00
A3 Emmitt Smith 3.00
A4 Terrell Davis 2.00
A5 Brett Favre 3.00
A6 Mark Brunell 1.00
A7 Fred Taylor 2.00
A8 Daunte Culpepper 2.00
A9 Drew Bledsoe 2.00
A10 Donovan McNabb 1.50
A11 Troy Edwards 1.00
A12 Isaac Bruce 1.00
A13 Marshall Faulk 1.00
A14 Jerry Rice 2.50
A15 Jon Kitna 1.00
A16 Shaun King 1.00
A17 Keyshawn Johnson 1.00
A18 Eddie George 1.50
A19 Steve McNair 1.00
A20 Stephen Davis 1.00

2000 Collector's Edge T-3 EdgeQuest

NM/M
Complete Set (25): 40.00
Common Player: 1.00
Production 1,000 Sets
EQ1 Marcus Robinson 1.00
EQ2 Kevin Johnson 1.00
EQ3 Randy Moss 5.00
EQ4 Troy Edwards 1.00
EQ5 Torry Holt 1.00
EQ6 Keyshawn Johnson 1.00
EQ7 Emmitt Smith 5.00
EQ8 Terrell Davis 4.00
EQ9 Edgerrin James 4.00
EQ10 Fred Taylor 3.00
EQ11 Ricky Williams 4.00
EQ12 Curtis Martin 1.00
EQ13 Marshall Faulk 1.00
EQ14 Eddie George 3.00
EQ15 Stephen Davis 1.00
EQ16 Cade McNown 1.00
EQ17 Akili Smith 1.00
EQ18 Tim Couch 3.00
EQ19 Brett Favre 5.00
EQ20 Peyton Manning 5.00
EQ21 Daunte Culpepper 4.00
EQ22 Donovan McNabb 3.50
EQ23 Kurt Warner 4.00
EQ24 Jon Kitna 1.00
EQ25 Shaun King 1.00

2000 Collector's Edge T-3 Future Legends

NM/M
Complete Set (20): 30.00
Common Player: 1.00
Inserted 1:10
FL1 Thomas Jones 2.00
FL2 Jamal Lewis 3.00
FL3 Travis Taylor 2.50
FL4 Peter Warrick 2.00
FL5 Ron Dayne 2.00
FL6 Chad Pennington 5.00
FL7 Plaxico Burress 4.00
FL8 Bubba Franks 1.50
FL9 Shaun Alexander 4.00
FL10 Sylvester Morris 3.00
FL11 Laveranues Coles 2.00
FL12 Jerry Porter 2.00
FL13 Todd Pinkston 1.00
FL14 Dennis Northcutt 1.50
FL15 Travis Prentice 2.50
FL16 R. Jay Soward 1.50
FL17 Chris Redman 2.50
FL18 Trung Canidate 1.00
FL19 Dez White 1.00
FL20 J.R. Redmond 2.00

2000 Collector's Edge T-3 Heir Force

NM/M
Complete Set (30): 45.00
Common Player: 1.00
Production 1,000 Sets
HF1 Thomas Jones 3.00
HF2 Jamal Lewis 4.00
HF3 Chris Redman 2.00
HF4 Travis Taylor 3.00
HF5 Brian Urlacher 5.00
HF6 Dez White 3.00
HF7 Ron Dugans 1.00
HF8 Curtis Keaton 1.00
HF9 Peter Warrick 2.00
HF10 Courtney Brown 2.00
HF11 Dennis Northcutt 2.00
HF12 Travis Prentice 3.00
HF13 Reuben Droughns 1.00
HF14 Bubba Franks 2.00
HF15 R. Jay Soward 2.00
HF16 Sylvester Morris 2.00
HF17 J.R. Redmond 2.00
HF18 Ron Dayne 2.00
HF19 Anthony Becht 1.00
HF20 Laveranues Coles 3.00
HF21 Chad Pennington 10.00
HF22 Jerry Porter 3.00
HF23 Todd Pinkston 2.00
HF24 Corey Simon 2.00
HF25 Plaxico Burress 6.00
HF26 Danny Farmer 1.00
HF27 Tee Martin 3.00
HF28 Trung Canidate 1.00
HF29 Shaun Alexander 8.00
HF30 Joe Hamilton 3.00

2000 Collector's Edge T-3 JerseyBacks

NM/M
Common Player: 150.00
Production 20 Sets
GG1 Thomas Jones 350.00
GG2 Jamal Lewis 350.00
GG3 Travis Taylor 250.00
GG4 Peter Warrick 500.00
GG5 R. Jay Soward 150.00
GG6 Sylvester Morris 300.00
GG7 Ron Dayne 500.00
GG8 Chad Pennington 400.00
GG9 Plaxico Burress 400.00
GG10 Shaun Alexander 350.00

2000 Collector's Edge T-3 LeatherBacks

NM/M
Common Player: 150.00
Production 12 Sets
GG1 Cade McNown 200.00
GG2 Marcus Robinson 150.00
GG3 Akili Smith 175.00
GG4 Tim Couch 300.00
GG5 Troy Aikman 325.00
GG6 Emmitt Smith 350.00
GG7 Terrell Davis 350.00
GG8 Brett Favre 450.00
GG9 Edgerrin James 450.00
GG10 Peyton Manning 450.00
GG11 Randy Moss 450.00
GG12 Ricky Williams 300.00
GG13 Donovan McNabb 200.00
GG14 Torry Holt 150.00
GG15 Kurt Warner 450.00
GG16 Jon Kitna 150.00
GG17 Shaun King 200.00
GG18 Eddie George 175.00
GG19 Steve McNair 150.00
GG20 Stephen Davis 150.00

2000 Collector's Edge T-3 Overture

NM/M
Complete Set (10): 15.00
Common Player: 1.50
Inserted 1:20
O1 Cade McNown 1.00
O2 Akili Smith 1.00
O3 Tim Couch 2.00
O4 Edgerrin James 3.00
O5 Peyton Manning 4.00
O6 Daunte Culpepper 2.50
O7 Randy Moss 4.00
O8 Ricky Williams 3.00
O9 Torry Holt 1.50
O10 Kurt Warner 3.00

2000 Collector's Edge T-3 Personal Collection

SA Shaun Alexander
AB Anthony Becht
PB Plaxico Burress
TC Trung Canidate
LC Laveranues Coles
RD Ron Dayne
RD Reuben Droughns
RD Ron Dugans
DF Danny Farmer
BF Bubba Franks
JH Joe Hamilton
TJ Thomas Jones
CK Curtis Keaton
JL Jamal Lewis
TM Tee Martin
SM Sylvester Morris
DN Dennis Northcutt
CP Chad Pennington
TP Todd Pinkston
JP Jerry Porter
TP Travis Prentice
CR Chris Redman
JR J.R. Redmond
CS Corey Simon
RS R. Jay Soward
TT Travis Taylor
BU Brian Urlacher
PW Peter Warrick
DW Dez White

2000 Collector's Edge T-3 Rookie Excalibur

NM/M
Complete Set (20): 40.00
Common Player: 1.00
Production 1,000 Sets
RE1 Thomas Jones 2.00
RE2 Jamal Lewis 4.00
RE3 Chris Redman 2.00
RE4 Travis Taylor 3.00
RE5 Dez White 1.00
RE6 Peter Warrick 2.00
RE7 Dennis Northcutt 1.00
RE8 Travis Prentice 2.00
RE9 R. Jay Soward 2.00
RE10 Sylvester Morris 2.00
RE11 Ron Dayne 2.00
RE12 Chad Pennington 10.00
RE13 Laveranues Coles 4.00
RE14 Jerry Porter 4.00
RE15 Todd Pinkston 2.00
RE16 Plaxico Burress 8.00
RE17 Trung Canidate 1.00
RE18 Bubba Franks 3.00
RE19 Shaun Alexander 8.00
RE20 J.R. Redmond 4.00

2000 Collector's Edge T-3 Rookie Ink

NM/M
Complete Set (9): 275.00
Common Player: 10.00
Inserted 1:99
Blue Cards: 1X-3X
Production 24-40 Sets
Red Cards: 4X
Production 10 Sets
Plaxico Burress 440 60.00
Giovanni Carmazzi 1455 20.00
Thomas Jones 915 35.00
Jamal Lewis 485 60.00
Sylvester Morris 1000 30.00
Chad Pennington 470 70.00
Chris Redman 480 35.00
J.R. Redmond 1610 10.00
R. Jay Soward 1350 15.00

1961 Colts Jay Publishing

Measuring 5" x 7", the 12-card set showcases black-and-white posed photos on the front. The 12 cards were included in a package and sold for 25 cents. The backs are blank and unnumbered.

NM/M
Complete Set (12): 80.00
Common Player: 5.00
1 Raymond Berry 14.00
2 Art Donovan 12.00
3 Weeb Ewbank (CO) 5.00
4 Alex Hawkins 5.00
5 Gino Marchetti 10.00
6 Lenny Moore 12.00
7 Jim Mutscheller 5.00
8 Steve Myhra 5.00
9 Jimmy Orr 5.00
10 Jim Parker 7.00
11 Joe Perry 10.00
12 Johnny Unitas 25.00

1967 Colts Johnny Pro

Measuring 4-1/8" x 2-7/8", each player punchout featured a color photo, with the player's name, number and position inside a white box near the bottom. By inserting the punchout into a stand, which was included with each punchout, the player punchout stood upright. The punchouts are unnumbered.

		NM/M
Complete Set (41):		750.00
Common Player:		15.00
1	Sam Ball	15.00
2	Raymond Berry	40.00
3	Bob Boyd	15.00
4	Ordell Braase	15.00
5	Barry Brown	15.00
6	Bill Curry	20.00
7	Mike Curtis	20.00
8	Norman Davis	15.00
9	Jim Detwiler	15.00
10	Dennis Gaubatz	15.00
11	Alvin Haymond	15.00
12	Jerry Hill	15.00
13	Roy Hilton	15.00
14	David Lee	15.00
15	Jerry Logan	15.00
16	Tony Lorick	15.00
17	Lenny Lyles	15.00
18	John Mackey	30.00
19	Tom Matte	20.00
20	Lou Michaels	15.00
21	Fred Miller	15.00
22	Lenny Moore	40.00
23	Jimmy Orr	20.00
24	Jim Parker	30.00
25	Ray Perkins	20.00
26	Glenn Ressler	15.00
27	Willie Richardson	20.00
28	Don Shinnick	15.00
29	Billy Ray Smith	20.00
30	Bubba Smith	40.00
31	Charlie Stukes	15.00
32	Andy Stynchula	15.00
33	Dan Sullivan	15.00
34	Dick Szymanski	15.00
35	Johnny Unitas	75.00
36	Bob Vogel	15.00
37	Rick Volk	20.00
38	Bob Wade	15.00
39	Jim Ward	15.00
40	Jim Welch	15.00
41	Butch Wilson	15.00

1978 Colts Team Issue

Measuring 5" x 7", the 28-photo set featured a player photo on the front, with the player's name, team and position listed under the photo. The blank backs are also unnumbered.

		NM/M
Complete Set (28):		45.00
Common Player:		1.50
1	Mack Alston	2.00
2	Ron Baker	1.50
3	Mike Barnes	1.50
4	Tim Baylor	1.50
5	Randy Burke	1.50
6	Glenn Doughty	2.00
7	Joe Ehrmann	2.00
8	Wade Griffin	1.50
9	Don Hardeman	1.50
10	Dwight Harrison	1.50
11	Ken Huff	1.50
12	Marshall Johnson	1.50
13	Bert Jones	8.00
14	Bruce Laird	1.50
15	Roosevelt Leaks	2.50
16	David Lee	1.50
17	Ron Lee	1.50
18	Toni Linhart	1.50
19	Derrel Luce	1.50
20	Reese McCall	1.50
21	Ken Mendenhall	1.50
22	Don Morrison	1.50
23	Lloyd Mumphord	1.50
24	Calvin O'Neal	1.50
25	Robert Pratt	1.50
26	Mike Siani	1.50
27	Bill Troup	1.50
28	Stan White	1.50

1985 Colts Kroger

Measuring 5-1/2" x 8-1/2", the 17-photo set spotlighted a large photo on the front, with the Colts' helmet, player name, position, number and Kroger logo underneath from left to right. The card backs have the Indianapolis Colts at the top, with the player's name, position, number and bio underneath. The NFL logo and Kroger logos are also printed on the backs. The cards are unnumbered.

		NM/M
Complete Set (17):		30.00
Common Player:		1.00
1	Karl Baldischwiler	1.00
2	Pat Beach	1.00
3	Albert Bentley	2.00
4	Duane Bickett	3.00
5	Matt Bouza	1.00
6	Nesby Glasgow	1.00
7	Chris Hinton	2.00
8	Lamonte Hunley	1.00
9	Barry Krauss	1.00
10	Orlando Lowry	1.00
11	Tate Randle	1.00
12	Tim Sherwin	1.00
13	Ron Solt	1.00
14	Rohn Stark	1.50
15	Ben Utt	1.00
16	Brad White	1.00
17	Anthony Young	1.50

1988 Colts Police

Measuring 2-5/8" x 4-1/8", the eight-card set boasts a large photo, with the photo credit, player's name, number, position and bio beneath it. The Colts' helmet and name are at the bottom of the card front. The card backs feature two cartoon drawings -- one is a Colts Tip, while the other is a Crime Stoppers Tip. The card backs are numbered "of 8." Oscar Mayer and WTHR-TV logos are printed at the bottom of the card backs.

		NM/M
Complete Set (8):		8.00
Common Player:		1.00
1	Eric Dickerson	3.00
2	Barry Krauss	1.00
3	Bill Brooks	1.50
4	Duane Bickett	1.00
5	Chris Hinton	1.00
6	Eugene Daniel	1.00
7	Jack Trudeau	1.00
8	Ron Meyer (CO)	1.00

1989 Colts Police

Measuring 2-5/8" x 4-1/8", the nine-card set showcases a photo on the front, with a photo credit, player's name, number, position, bio, Colts' helmet and "Indianapolis Colts" printed beneath the photo. The card backs feature two cartoon drawings — one being a Colts Tip and the other a Crime Stoppers Tip. The cards are numbered. The Indiana Law Enforcement, Louis Rich and WTHR logos are at the bottom of the card backs.

		NM/M
Complete Set (9):		8.00
Common Player:		.50
1	Colts Team Card	.50
2	Dean Biasucci	.50
3	Andre Rison	1.75
4	Chris Chandler	1.25
5	O'Brien Alston	.50
6	Ray Donaldson	.75
7	Donnell Thompson	.50
8	Fredd Young	.50
9	Eric Dickerson	1.50

1990 Colts Police

Measuring 2-5/8" x 4-1/8", the eight-card set features a large photo on the front, with a photo credit, player's name, position, bio, Colts' helmet and "Indianapolis Colts" printed underneath. The card backs have a Colts Tip and a Crime Stoppers Tip. The Indiana Law Enforcement, Louis Rich and WTHR logos are printed at the bottom of the card backs.

		NM/M
Complete Set (8):		6.00
Common Player:		.50
1	Harvey Armstrong	.50
2	Pat Beach	.50
3	Albert Bentley	.75
4	Kevin Call	.50
5	Jeff George	3.00
6	Mike Prior	.50
7	Rohn Stark	.50
8	Clarence Verdin	.50

1991 Colts Police

Measuring 2-5/8" x 4-1/4", the eight-card set showcases a photo on the front, with a photo credit, player's name, Colts' helmet, "Indianapolis Colts" and Indiana Law Enforcement logo beneath it. The card backs feature the player's name, number, position and bio at the top and Colts quiz in the center. An anti-drug message, WTHR and Coke logos are printed at the bottom. The cards are numbered in the lower right corner.

		NM/M
Complete Set (8):		5.00
Common Player:		.75
1	Jeff George	1.75
2	Jack Trudeau	1.00
3	Jeff Herrod	.75
4	Eric Dickerson	1.50
5	Bill Brooks	1.25
6	Jon Hand	.75
7	Keith Taylor	.75
8	Randy Dixon	.75

1994 Costacos Brothers Poster Cards

Measuring 4-1/4" x 6-1/4", the 12 mini-poster cards were packaged in cello packs. A cardboard sleeve in the packs pictured the set on the front, while the back was numbered of 25,000. The poster was bordered in white on the front, while the backs have the standard postcard look, with the team's logo in the center. The cards are numbered at the bottom center.

		NM/M
Complete Set (12):		15.00
Common Player:		.50
1	Troy Aikman (Strong Arm of the Law)	2.00
2	Barry Sanders (The Silver Streak)	2.00
3	Steve Young (Run and Gun)	1.00
4	Rick Mirer (Natural Wonder)	.75
5	John Elway (The Rifleman)	1.00
6	Dan Marino (Tropical Storm)	3.00
7	Drew Bledsoe (Patriot Games)	2.00
8	Emmitt Smith (Catch 22)	3.00
9	Warren Moon (Moonshine)	.50
10	Jerry Rice (Elite)	2.00
11	Michael Irvin (Playmaker)	.50
12	Jim Kelly (Machine Gun Kelly)	.50

1992 Courtside Draft Pix Promos

These eight cards were produced to preview Courtside's 1992 Draft Pix set. The cards are similar in design to those in the regular set, but are labeled on the back as being "Promotion - Not For Sale." A card number appears on the back; two #20 cards were made. Some of the cards were given away at card shows and may be stamped on the back in red indicating what show they were given away at.

		NM/M
Complete Set (8):		8.00
Common Player:		1.00
20A	Tony Brooks	1.00
20B	Amp Lee	1.00
22	Terrell Buckley	1.00
30	Tommy Vardell	1.00
40	Carl Pickens	3.00
44	Quentin Coryatt	1.00
50	Mike Gaddis	1.00
60	Steve Emtman	1.00

1992 Courtside

Courtside's 1992 set had an abundance of insert cards, each of which had a limited print run. The main set's cards are glossy and have a color action photo on the front. A gold stripe at the bottom of the card has the player's name and position inside. The card back has another photo on the top half, with biographical and collegiate statistics under the picture. A card number and the set's logo are also on the back. Special bronze, silver and gold foil versions were also made for each regular card; they were random inserts in limited quantities and command higher prices. There were also autographed cards inserted into the packs; these cards also command premium values, based on the value of the player's regular card. Short printed insert cards were also randomly included in packs. These cards, five each for Award Winners and All-Americans, are numbered using an "AW" or "AA" prefix. In addition, there were 50,000 Steve Emtman foilgram cards randomly inserted in packs.

		NM/M
Complete Set (140):		6.00
Common Player:		.05
Bronze Cards:		2X
Silver Cards:		2X
Gold Cards:		2X
Common Autograph:		4.00
Autograph Cards:		15X-30X
1	Steve Emtman	.10
2	Quentin Coryatt	.30
3	Ken Swilling	.10
4	Jay Leeuwenburg	.05
5	Mazio Royster	.05
6	Matt Veatch	.05
7	Scott Lockwood	.05
8	Todd Collins	.05
9	Gene McGuire	.05
10	Dale Carter	.10
11	Michael Bankston	.05
12	Jeremy Lincoln	.10
13	Troy Auzenne	.05
14	Rod Smith	.05
15	Andy Kelly	.05
16	Chris Holder	.05
17	Rico Smith	.05
18	Chris Pedersen	.05
19	Brian Treggs	.05
20	Eugene Chung	.05
21	Joel Steed	.05
22	Ricardo McDonald	.05
23	Nate Turner	.05
24	Sean Lumpkin	.05
25	Ty Detmer	.25
26	Matt Darby	.05
27	Michael Warfield	.05
28	Tracy Scroggins	.10
29	Carl Pickens	1.50
30	Chris Mims	.10
31	Mark D'Onofrio	.05
32	Dwight Hollier	.05
33	Siupeli Malamala	.05
34	Mark Barsotti	.05
35	Charles Davenport	.05
36	Brian Bollinger	.05
37	Willie McClendon	.05
38	Calvin Holmes	.05
39	Phillippi Sparks	.05
40	Darryl Williams	.05
41	Greg Skrepenak	.05
42	Larry Webster	.05
43	Dion Lambert	.05
44	Sam Gash	.10
45	Patrick Rowe	.05
46	Scottie Graham	.15
47	Darian Hagan	.05
48	Arthur Marshall	.05
49	Amp Lee	.25
50	Tommy Vardell	.10
51	Robert Porcher	.10
52	Reggie Dwight	.05
53	Torrance Small	.05
54	Ronnie West	.05
55	Tony Brooks	.05
56	Anthony McDowell	.05
57	Chris Haskel	.05
58	Ed Cunningham	.05
59	Ashley Ambrose	.05
60	Alonzo Spellman	.15
61	Harold Heath	.05
62	Ron Lopez	.05
63	Bill Johnson	.05
64	Kent Graham	.05
65	Aaron Pierce	.05
66	Bucky Richardson	.05
67	Todd Kinchen	.10
68	Ken Ealy	.05
69	Carlos Snow	.05
70	Dana Hall	.05
71	Matt Rodgers	.05
72	Howard Dinkins	.05
73	Tim Lester	.05
74	Mark Chmura	.75
75	Johnny Mitchell	.25
76	Mirko Jurkovic	.05
77	Anthony Lynn	.05
78	Roosevelt Collins	.05
79	Tony Sands	.05
80	Kevin Smith	.05
81	Tony Brown	.05
82	Bobby Fuller	.05
83	Darryl Ashmore	.05
84	Tyrone Legette	.05
85	Mike Gaddis	.05
86	Gerald Dixon	.05
87	T.J. Rubley	.05
88	Mark Thomas	.05
89	Corey Widmer	.05
90	Robert Jones	.05
91	Eddie Robinson	.05
92	Rob Tomlinson	.05
93	Russ Campbell	.05
94	Keith Goganious	.05
95	Rod Moore	.05
96	Jerry Ostroski	.05
97	Tyji Armstrong	.10
98	Ronald Humphrey	.05
99	Corey Harris	.05
100	Terrell Buckley	.15
101	Cal Dixon	.05
102	Tyrone Williams	.05
103	Joe Bowden	.05
104	Santana Dotson	.10
105	Jeff Blake	1.50
106	Erick Anderson	.05
107	Steve Israel	.05
108	Chad Roghair	.05
109	Todd Harrison	.05
110	Chester McGlockton	.10
111	Marquez Pope	.10
112	George Rooks	.05
113	Dion Johnson	.05
114	Tim Simpson	.05
115	Chris Walsh	.05
116	Marc Boutte	.05
117	Jamie Gill	.05
118	Willie Clay	.05
119	Tim Paulk	.05
120	Ray Roberts	.05
121	Jeff Thomason	.05
122	Leodis Flowers	.05
123	Robert Brooks	.75
124	Jeff Ellis	.05
125	John Fina	.05
126	Michael Smith	.05
127	Mike Saunders	.05
128	John Brown III	.05
129	Reggie Yarbrough	.05
130	Leon Searcy	.05
131	Marcus Woods	.05
132	Shane Collins	.05
133	Chuck Smith	.05
134	Keith Hamilton	.05
135	Rodney Blackshear	.05
136	Corey Barlow	.05
137	Robert Harris	.05
138	Tony Smith	.05
139	Checklist 1	.05
140	Checklist 2	.05

1992 Courtside Foilgrams

1992 Courtside Draft Pix wrappers offered these foilgram cards as a mail-in offer; collectors could receive one by sending in 10 wrappers. There were 15,000 foilgram cards produced for each card; which is numbered #1 of 5 limited edition foilgram cards.

		NM/M
Complete Set (5):		5.00
Common Player:		1.00
1	Steve Emtman	1.00
2	Tommy Vardell	1.25
3	Terrell Buckley	1.25
4	Ty Detmer	1.00
5	Amp Lee	1.00

1992 Courtside Inserts

These short-printed foilgram cards, random inserts in 1992 Courtside Draft Pix foil cases, feature glossy color action photos on the front, bordered with a white frame. Five Award Winners and Five All-Americans are featured in the set; the football logo on the card front indicates if the player is an Award Winner or All-American. The card back, which features a color photo on one side and player profile on the other, also distinguishes which type of card it is by using a corresponding "AW" or "AA" prefix for the card number.

		NM/M
Complete Set (10):		10.00
Common Player:		.50
Award Winners		
1	Steve Emtman Outland Trophy	2.00
2	Ty Detmer '90 Heisman Trophy	3.00
3	Steve Emtman Lombardi Award	2.00
4	Terrell Buckley Jim Thorpe Award	2.00
5	Erick Anderson Dick Butkus Award	.50
All-America		
1	Carl Pickens	4.00
2	Dale Carter	2.00
3	Tommy Vardell	2.00
4	Amp Lee	2.00
5	Leon Searcy	.50

1993 Courtside Sean Dawkins

Indiana Colts first-round draft pick Sean Dawkins is featured in this five-card insert set. There were 20,000 sets produced; the complete set value below does not include an autographed card. Dawkins signed 5,000 cards, which were randomly inserted within the sets. Each card front has a color action photo against a blurred background. Gold foil stamping is used to incorporate the player's name, a football and "Draft Pix" into the design. A promotional card was also produced, similar to card #3, except it has "Promotional - Not For Sale" and "Authentic Signature" written on the card front.

		NM/M
Complete Set (5):		5.00
Common Player:		1.00
1	Sean Dawkins (Ball cradles in right arm, running up field)	1.00
2	Sean Dawkins (Hands outstretched to catch ball)	1.00
3	Sean Dawkins (Being handchecked by cornerback)	1.00
4	Sean Dawkins (Kneeling pose)	1.00
5	Sean Dawkins (Dressed in tuxedo)	1.00
----	Sean Dawkins (AU 5000) (certified autograph)	15.00

1993 Courtside Russell White

Los Angeles Rams' third-round draft pick Russell White is featured in this five-card insert set. Each card front has a full-bleed color, glossy action photo against a blurred background. Gold foil is used to incorporate the player's name, Draft Pix and football logo into the design of the card. The card back has a color photo of the player, plus either statistics, biographical or player profile information, or highlights. A card number is also included. There were 20,000 sets produced. White autographed 5,000 cards, which were randomly inserted within the set. (The complete set price does not include an autographed card.) Promo cards were also issued for #s 3-5. They can be distinguished from the regular cards by the words "Promotional - Not For Sale," which appear on the card front, and the words "Authentic Signature," which also appear on the front.

		NM/M
Complete Set (5):		5.00
Common White:		1.00
1	Russell White (Running almost straight head)	1.00
2	Russell White (Running toward the right)	1.00
3	Russell White (Running toward defensive player number 78)	1.00
4	Russell White (Running upfield; side view)	1.00
5	Russell White (Dressed in tuxedo)	1.00
----	Russell White (AU/5000) (certified autograph)	12.00

1969 Cowboys Team Issue

Measuring 7" x 10", the card fronts showcase color action shots of players. The photos have black rounded-corner borders. The player's name and team are printed below the photo. The unnumbered backs are blank.

		NM/M
Complete Set (5):		35.00
Common Player:		5.00
1	Walt Garrison	5.00
2	Lee Roy Jordan	7.00
3	Bob Lilly	10.00
4	Dave Manders	5.00
5	Mel Renfro	8.00

1971 Cowboys Team Issue

Measuring 5" x 6-1/2", the 40-card set showcases black-and-white posed shots on the front, bordered in white. The player's name and team are printed below the photo. The cards are unnumbered and have blank backs.

		NM/M
Complete Set (40):		150.00
Common Player:		2.00
1	Herb Adderley	5.00
2	Lance Alworth	12.00
3	George Andrie	2.00
4	Mike Clark	2.00
5	Larry Cole	2.00
6	Mike Ditka	16.00
7	Dave Edwards	2.00
8	John Fitzgerald	2.00

9	Toni Fritsch	2.00
10	Walt Garrison	2.00
11	Cornell Green	2.00
12	Bill Gregory	2.00
13	Cliff Harris	3.00
14	Bob Hayes	6.00
15	Calvin Hill	5.00
16	Chuck Howley	3.00
17	Lee Roy Jordan	4.00
18	D.D. Lewis	2.00
19	Bob Lilly	10.00
20	Tony Liscio	2.00
21	Dave Manders	2.00
22	Craig Morton	5.00
23	Ralph Neely	2.00
24	John Niland	2.00
25	Jethro Pugh	2.00
26	Dan Reeves	12.00
27	Mel Renfro	8.00
28	Gloster Richardson	2.00
29	Tody Smith	2.00
30	Roger Staubach	30.00
31	Don Talbert	2.00
32	Duane Thomas	2.00
33	Isaac Thomas	2.00
34	Pat Toomay	2.00
35	Billy Truax	2.00
36	Rodney Wallace	2.00
37	Mark Washington	2.00
38	Charlie Waters	3.00
39	Claxton Welch	2.00
40	Ron Widby	2.00

1972 Cowboys Team Issue

Measuring 4-1/4" x 5-1/2", the 13-card set showcases black-and-white photos on the front, bordered in white. The player's name is printed underneath the photo. The cards are unnumbered and have blank backs.

		NM/M
Complete Set (13):		50.00
Common Player:		2.00
1	Herb Adderley	4.00
2	Mike Ditka	15.00
3	Toni Fritsch	2.00
4	Walt Garrison	2.00
5	Cornell Green	2.00
6	Cliff Harris	3.00
7	Bob Hayes	6.00
8	Calvin Hill	5.00
9	Robert Newhouse	2.00
10	Billy Parks	2.00
11	Mel Renfro	6.00
12	Dan Reeves	10.00
13	Charlie Waters	3.00

1979 Cowboys Police

Measuring 2-5/8" x 4-1/8", the 15-card set showcases a player photo on the front, with a photo credit, player's name, number, position and team listed below. The Cowboys logo is in the lower left. The card backs have Cowboys Tips in a box, with the Cowboys' helmet at the top. The sponsors are listed at the bottom of the card back. D.D. Lewis replaced Thomas "Hollywood" Henderson during the season, which means lesser amounts were printed of both cards.

		NM/M
Complete Set (15):		25.00
Common Player:		.50
12	Roger Staubach	6.00
33	Tony Dorsett	4.00
41	Charlie Waters	.75
43	Cliff Harris	.50
44	Robert Newhouse	.50
50	D.D. Lewis (SP)	2.00
53	Bob Breunig	.50
54	Randy White	2.00
56	Thomas Henderson (SP)	2.00
67	Pat Donovan	.50
79	Harvey Martin	.50
80	Tony Hill	.50
88	Drew Pearson	1.00
89	Billy Joe DuPree	.50
NNO	Tom Landry (CO)	2.50

1980 Cowboys Police

Measuring 2-5/8" x 4-1/8", the 14-card set is anchored by a large photo on the front, with the player's name, number, position and team printed under the photo. A photo credit is also listed beneath the photo. The Cowboys' helmet is printed in the lower left, while a Kiwanis logo is located in the lower right. The card backs feature Cowboys Tips inside a box, which features the Cowboys' helmet at the top. The sponsor names are printed at the bottom of the card backs. The cards are numbered by the player's jersey numbers.

		NM/M
Complete Set (14):		10.00
Common Player:		.50
1	Rafael Septien	1.00
11	Danny White	2.00
25	Aaron Kyle	.50
26	Preston Pearson	1.00
31	Benny Barnes	.75
35	Scott Laidlaw	.50
42	Randy Hughes	.50
62	John Fitzgerald	.75
63	Larry Cole	.75
64	Tom Rafferty	.75
68	Herbert Scott	.50
70	Rayfield Wright	.75
78	John Dutton	.75
87	Jay Saldi	.75

1981 Cowboys Police

Measuring 2-5/8" x 4-1/8", the 14-card set showcases a photo on the front, with a photo credit, player's name, jersey number, position and team printed beneath the photo. The Cowboys' helmet is in the lower left corner, while the Kiwanis' logo is in the lower right. The card backs feature Cowboys Tips inside a box with the Cowboys helmet at the top. The cards are numbered with the player's jersey number.

		NM/M
Complete Set (14):		7.50
Common Player:		.40
18	Glenn Carano	.60
20	Ron Springs	.70
23	James Jones	.40
26	Michael Downs	.60
32	Dennis Thurman	.60
45	Steve Wilson	.40
51	Anthony Dickerson	.40
52	Robert Shaw	.40
58	Mike Hegman	.40
59	Guy Brown	.40
61	Jim Cooper	.40
72	Ed "Too Tall" Jones	1.50
84	Doug Cosbie	.70
86	Butch Johnson	.70

1981 Cowboys Thousand Oaks Police

Measuring 2-5/8" x 4-1/8", the 14-card set is anchored by a photo on the front. A photo credit, player's name, jersey number, position and team are printed below the photo. The Cowboys' helmet is in the lower left, while a sponsor's logo is in the lower right. The card backs feature Cowboys Tips inside a box, with the Cowboys' helmet at the top. The sponsors, including the Thousand Oaks Police Dept., are listed at the bottom of the card backs.

		NM/M
Complete Set (14):		31.50
Common Player:		1.25
11	Danny White	3.00
31	Benny Barnes	1.25
33	Tony Dorsett	6.00
41	Charlie Waters	1.25
42	Randy Hughes	1.25
44	Robert Newhouse	1.50
54	Randy White	4.50
55	D.D. Lewis	1.25
78	John Dutton	1.25
79	Harvey Martin	2.25
80	Tony Hill	2.25
88	Drew Pearson	3.00
89	Billy Joe DuPree	1.50
NNO	Tom Landry (CO)	5.25

1982 Cowboys Carrollton Park

Measuring 3" x 4", the six-card set showcases a large photo on the front, with "Carrollton Park Mall" printed below it inside a white border. The card backs spotlight the card's number at the top inside a circle. The player's name, position and stats are printed below the number. The Cowboys' 1982-83 scheduled takes up the bottom 2/3 of the card back. The set is also available in uncut sheets.

		NM/M
Complete Set (6):		5.00
Common Player:		.50
1	Roger Staubach	2.00
2	Danny White	.75
3	Tony Dorsett	1.00
4	Randy White	.75
5	Charlie Waters	.50
6	Billy Joe DuPree	.50

1983 Cowboys Police

Measuring 2-5/8" x 4-1/8", the 28-card set is anchored by a large photo on the front, with a photo credit, player's name, number, position and team printed underneath the photo. The Cowboys' helmet is printed in the lower right, while the Kiwanis' logo is in the lower right. The card backs have Cowboys Tips inside a box, with the Cowboys' helmet at the top. The sponsors are listed at the bottom of the card back.

		NM/M
Complete Set (28):		25.00
Common Player:		.50
1	Rafael Septien	.50
11	Danny White	1.50
20	Ron Springs	.50
24	Everson Walls	.50
26	Michael Downs	.50
30	Timmy Newsome	.50
32	Dennis Thurman	.50
33	Tony Dorsett	3.00
47	Dexter Clinkscale	.50
53	Bob Breunig	.50
54	Randy White	3.00
65	Kurt Petersen	.50
67	Pat Donovan	.50
70	Howard Richards	.50
72	Ed "Too Tall" Jones	2.00
78	John Dutton	.50
79	Harvey Martin	1.00
80	Tony Hill	.75
83	Doug Donley	.50
84	Doug Cosbie	.50
86	Butch Johnson	.50
88	Drew Pearson	1.75
89	Billy Joe DuPree	.50
NNO	Tom Landry (CO)	2.00
NNO	Melinda May (CHEER)	.50
NNO	Dana Presley (CHEER)	.50
NNO	Judy Trammell (CHEER)	.50
NNO	Toni Washington (CHEER)	.50

1985 Cowboys Frito Lay

Measuring 4" x 5-1/2", this 41 card set is anchored on the front by a large black-and-white photo. The player's name, jersey number, position and bio are listed beneath the photo on the front. The Cowboys' helmet is printed in the lower left, with the Frito Lay logo in the lower right. The backs are unnumbered and blank.

		NM/M
Complete Set (41):		50.00
Common Player:		1.00
1	Vince Albritton	1.00
2	Brian Baldinger	1.00
3	Dexter Clinkscale	1.00
4	Jim Cooper	1.00
5	Fred Cornwell	1.00
6	Doug Crosbie	1.50
7	Steve DeOssie	1.00
8	John Dutton	1.00
9	Ricky Easmon	1.00
10	Ron Fellows	1.00
11	Leon Gonzalez	1.00
12	Gary Hogeboom	1.50
13	Jim Jeffcoat	2.50
14	Ed "Too Tall" Jones	3.00
15	James Jones	1.00
16	Crawford Ker	1.00
17	Robert Lavette	1.00
18	Eugene Lockhart	1.00
19	Timmy Newsome	1.00
20	Drew Pearson (ACO)	2.00
21	Steve Pelluer	1.50
22	Jesse Penn	1.00
23	Kurt Petersen	1.00
24	Karl Powe	1.00
25	Phil Pozderac	1.00
26	Tom Rafferty	1.00
27	Mike Renfro	1.00
28	Howard Richards	1.00
29	Jeff Rohrer	1.00
30	Mike Saxon	1.00
31	Victor Scott	1.00
32	Rafael Septien	1.00
33	Don Smerek	1.00
34	Roger Staubach	10.00
35	Broderick Thompson	1.00
36	Dennis Thurman	1.00
37	Glen Titensor	1.00
38	Mark Tuinei	1.50
39	Everson Walls	1.50
40	John Williams	1.00
41	Team Photo	3.00

1994 Cowboys ProLine Live Kroger Stickers

Each sticker measures 3-5/8 inches and is part of a three-sticker strip which measures 2-1/2" x 12". The sticker fronts showcase the same design as the 1994 Pro Line card series, with the player's name printed in large letters at the bottom of the sticker and his team printed inside a stripe beneath his name. The Classic Pro Line logo is located in the upper right corner. The sticker backs feature $1 off Fuji Film coupons or a team poster sweepstakes form. The strips were sold at Kroger stores for 99 cents for seven weeks. The sticker strips are numbered by their respective weeks.

		NM/M
Complete Set (7):		5.00
Common Player:		.50
1	Troy Aikman, Darren Woodson, Eric Williams	1.50
2	Emmitt Smith, James Washington, Mark Stepnoski	2.00
3	Michael Irvin, Kenneth Gant, Tony Tolbert	.75
4	Daryl Johnston, Kevin Williams WR, Leon Lett	.50
5	Nate Newton, Shante Carver, Charles Haley	.50
6	Russell Maryland, Mark Tuinei, Kevin Smith	.50
7	Alvin Harper, Willie Jackson, Jay Novacek	.50

1976 Crane Discs

These circular cards measure 3-3/8" in diameter and were produced by Michael Schechter Associates, as noted by the MSA letters on the card back. Each card front has a black- and-white mug shot of a player, along with his team, name and position. The card has a colored border with the word "Crane" at the top, representing Crane Potato Chips, which offered the cards as a mail-in offer. The Crane logo appears on the card back, but there are a few other sponsors which may also appear on the back; these are slightly more valuable than their Crane counterparts. The cards are unnumbered.

		NM/M
Complete Set (30):		15.00
Common Player:		.10
(1)	Ken Anderson	.50
(2)	Otis Armstrong	.15
(3)	Steve Bartkowski	.35
(4)	Terry Bradshaw	2.00
(5)	John Brockington	.25
(6)	Doug Buffone	.10
(7)	Wally Chambers	.10
(8)	Isaac Curtis	.25
(9)	Chuck Foreman	.20
(10)	Roman Gabriel	.75
(11)	Mel Gray	.15
(12)	Joe Greene	.65
(13)	James Harris	.25
(14)	Jim Hart	.25
(15)	Billy Kilmer	.25
(16)	Greg Landry	.25
(17)	Ed Marinaro	.50
(18)	Lawrence McCutcheon	.25
(19)	Terry Metcalf	.15
(20)	Lydell Mitchell	.25
(21)	Jim Otis	.15
(22)	Alan Page	.35
(23)	Walter Payton	10.00
(24)	Greg Pruitt	.40
(25)	Charlie Sanders	.25
(26)	Ron Shanklin	.25
(27)	Roger Staubach	2.00
(28)	Jan Stenerud	.40
(29)	Charley Taylor	.40
(30)	Roger Wehrli	.25

1992 Crown Pro Dogtags Fb

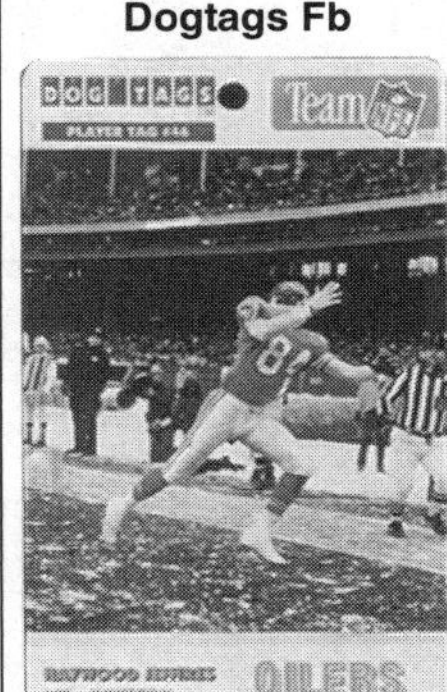

Measuring 2-1/8" x 3-3/8", the 81 dog tags were manufactured by Chris Martin Enterprises Inc., which later became Crown Pro. Produced of plastic, the tags are similar to credit cards. The tag fronts include a color photo in the center, with the "Dog Tags," NFL logo and tag number inside a white border at the top. The player's name, position and team, along with the team's logo, are printed inside a white border at the bottom. The backs have the player's name, headshot, bio, highlights and a team logo area that could be autographed. The top center of each tag had a hole in it, which allowed collectors to wear the tags on a chain. The team tags were horizontal and featured a photo of the team's stadium on the front. The rookie tags resemble the regular tags, however, they have a gold-foil border at the top. An Emmitt Smith promo tag was also released and it has "promo tag" printed on the back. Chris Martin autographed tags were also produced.

		NM/M
Complete Set (81):		70.00
Common Player:		.50
1	Atlanta Falcons	.50
2	Buffalo Bills	.50
3	Chicago Bears	.50
4	Cincinnati Bengals	.50
5	Cleveland Browns	.50
6	Dallas Cowboys	.50
7	Denver Broncos	.50
8	Detroit Lions	.50
9	Green Bay Packers	.50
10	Houston Oilers	.50
11	Indianapolis Colts	.50
12	Kansas City Chiefs	.50
13	Los Angeles Raiders	.50
14	Los Angeles Rams	.50
15	Miami Dolphins	.50
16	Minnesota Vikings	.50
17	New England Patriots	.50
18	New Orleans Saints	.50
19	New York Giants	.50
20	New York Jets	.50
21	Philadelphia Eagles	.50
22	Phoenix Cardinals	.50
23	Pittsburgh Steelers	.50
24	San Diego Chargers	.50
25	San Francisco 49ers	.50
26	Seattle Seahawks	.50
27	Tampa Bay Buccaneers	.50
28	Washington Redskins	.50
29A	Chris Martin (Reg.)	1.00
29B	Chris Martin (Gold)	2.00
29AU	Chris Martin (Autograph)	10.00
30	Dan Marino	10.00
31	Chris Miller	.50
32	Deion Sanders	3.00
33	Jim Kelly	1.00
34	Thurman Thomas	1.00
35	Jim Harbaugh	1.00
36	Mike Singletary	.50
37	Boomer Esiason	.50
38	Anthony Munoz	.50
39	Bernie Kosar	.50
40	Troy Aikman	5.00
41	Michael Irvin	2.00
42	Emmitt Smith	10.00
43	John Elway	3.00
44	Rodney Peete	.50
45	Sterling Sharpe	1.00
46	Haywood Jeffires	.50
47	Warren Moon	1.00
48	Jeff George	1.00
49	Christian Okoye	.50
50	Derrick Thomas	1.00
51	Howie Long	.50
52	Ronnie Lott	.50
53	Jim Everett	.50
54	Mark Clayton	.50
55	Anthony Carter	.50
56A	Chris Doleman	.50
56B	Chris Doleman (Autograph)	.50
57	Andre Tippett	.50
58A	Pat Swilling	.50
58B	Pat Swilling (Autograph)	.50
59	Jeff Hostetler	.50
60	Lawrence Taylor	1.00
61	Robert Moore	.50
62	Ken O'Brien	.50
63	Keith Byars	.50
64	Randall Cunningham	.50
65	Keith Byars	.50
66	Timm Rosenbach	.50
67	Bubby Brister	.50
68	John Friesz	1.00
69	Jerry Rice	5.00
70	Steve Young	4.00
71	Dan McGwire	.50
72	Broderick Thomas	.50
73	Vinny Testaverde	1.00
74	Gary Clark	.50
75	Mark Rypien	.50

1993 Crown Pro Dogtags Fb

Measuring 2-1/8" x 3-3/8", the tags were produced by Chris Martin Enterprises, which later became Crown Pro. The 138-plastic tag set featured a full-bleed photo on the front with "1993" gold-foil stamped in the upper left and the Dog Tags logo printed in the upper right. The player's name is printed in white inside a stripe in the lower right. The tag backs have the number in the upper left, with the player's headshot, name, number, bio, highlights and stats listed along the right side. An autograph strip is located along the left border. Overall, 50,000 of each tag was produced. Tag Nos. 48 and 138 were not printed for the set. Originally, the tags were sold in packs, however, complete team sets were sold later in the season. Atlanta and the Raiders were not distributed as team sets. In addition, 25,000 Joe Montana bonus tags were available through a mail-in offer. A contest offered collectors the chance to win a 14K gold bead chain or a seven-point diamond tag.

		NM/M
Complete Set (140):		80.00
Common Player:		.50
1	Atlanta Falcons	.50
2	Buffalo Bills	.50
3	Chicago Bears	.50
4	Cincinnati Bengals	.50
5	Cleveland Browns	.50
6	Dallas Cowboys	.50
7	Denver Broncos	.50
8	Detroit Lions	.50
9	Green Bay Packers	.50
10	Houston Oilers	.50
11	Indianapolis Colts	.50
12	Kansas City Chiefs	.50
13	Los Angeles Raiders	.50
14	Los Angeles Rams	.50
15	Miami Dolphins	.50
16	Minnesota Vikins	.50
17	New England Patriots	.50
18	New Orleans Saints	.50
19	New York Giants	.50
20	New York Jets	.50
21	Philadelphia Eagles	.50
22	Phoenix Cardinals	.50
23	Pittsburgh Steelers	.50
24	San Diego Chargers	.50
25	San Francisco 49ers	.50
26	Seattle Seahawks	.50
27	Tampa Bay Buccaneers	.50
28	Washington Redskins	.50
29	Steve Broussard	.50
30	Chris Miller	.50
31	Andre Rison	1.00
32	Deion Sanders	3.00
33	Cornelius Bennett	.50
34	Jim Kelly	1.00
35	Bruce Smith	.50
36	Thurman Thomas	1.00
37	Neal Anderson	.50
38	Mark Carrier	.50
39	Jim Harbaugh	1.00
40	Alonzo Spellman	1.00
41	David Fulcher	.50
42	Harold Green	.50
43	David Klingler	.50
44	Carl Pickens	2.00
45	Bernie Kosar	.50
46	Clay Matthews	.50
47	Eric Metcalf	.50
49	Troy Aikman	4.00
50	Michael Irvin	2.00
51	Russell Maryland	.50
52	Emmitt Smith	8.00
53	Steve Atwater	.50
54	John Elway	3.00
55	Tommy Maddox	.50
56	Shannon Sharpe	1.00
57	Herman Moore	2.00
58	Rodney Peete	.50
59	Barry Sanders	4.00
60	Andre Ware	.50
61	Terrell Buckley	.50
62	Brett Favre	10.00
63	Sterling Sharpe	1.00
64	Reggie White	2.00
65	Ray Childress	.50
66	Haywood Jeffires	.50
67	Warren Moon	1.00
68	Lorenzo White	.50
69	Duane Bickett	.50
70	Quentin Coryatt	.50
71	Steve Emtman	.50
72	Jeff George	.50
73	Dale Carter	.50
74	Neil Smith	.50
75	Derrick Thomas	1.00
76	Harvey Williams	.50
77	Eric Dickerson	.50
78	Howie Long	.50
79	Todd Marinovich	.50
80	Alexander Wright	.50
81A	Flipper Anderson	.50

81B	Flipper Anderson (Autograph)	.50
82A	Jim Everett	.50
82B	Jim Everett (Autograph)	.50
83	Cleveland Gary	.50
84A	Chris Martin	.50
84B	Chris Martin (Autograph)	.50
85	Irving Fryer	.50
86	Keith Jackson	.50
87	Dan Marino	8.00
88	Louis Oliver	.50
89	Terry Allen	2.00
90	Anthony Carter	.50
91	Chris Doleman	.50
92	Rich Gannon	.50
93	Eugene Chung	.50
94	Marv Cook	.50
95	Leonard Russell	.50
96	Andre Tippett	.50
97	Morten Anderson	.50
98	Vaughn Dunbar	.50
99	Rickey Jackson	.50
100	Sam Mills	.50
101	Derek Brown	.50
102	Lawrence Taylor	1.00
103	Rodney Hampton	1.00
104	Phil Simms	.50
105	Johnny Mitchell	.50
106	Rob Moore	.50
107	Blair Thomas	.50
108	Browning Nagle	.50
109	Eric Allen	.50
110	Fred Barnett	.50
111	Randall Cunningham	.50
112	Herschel Walker	.50
113	Chris Chandler	.50
114	Randal Hill	.50
115	Ricky Proehl	.50
116	Eric Swann	.50
117	Barry Foster	.50
118	Eric Green	.50
119	Neil O'Donnell	.50
120	Rod Woodson	.50
121	Marion Butts	.50
122	Stan Humphries	.50
123	Anthony Miller	.50
124	Junior Seau	1.00
125	Amp Lee	.50
126	Jerry Rice	4.00
127	Ricky Watters	2.00
128	Steve Young	3.00
129	Brian Blades	.50
130	Cortez Kennedy	.50
131	Dan McGwire	.50
132	John L. Williams	.50
133	Reggie Cobb	.50
134	Steve Deberg	.50
135	Keith McCants	.50
136	Broderick Thomas	.50
137	Earnest Byner	.50
138	Mark Rypien	.50
140	Ricky Sanders	.50

1994-95 Crown Pro Tags Fb

While the first two sets of these tags were known as Dog Tags, this 168-card issue was called Pro Tags, and was sold in six-card packs. Like Dog Tags, this set was made of plastic and measured 2-1/8" x 3-3/8". Autographed tags were available of Jerome Bettis, J.J. Birden, Dale Carter, Keith Cash, Willie Davis, Sean Gilbert, Chris Martin, Roman Phifer, Todd Lyght and Neil Smith. Pro Tags offered a chance to receive six AFC or six NFC Super Rookie Pro Tags for three proofs of purchase and $10.99 per set, or all 12 for five proofs of purchase and $15.99. The set also exists in a Super Bowl XXIX version, with no premium in price.

		NM/M
Complete Set (168):		70.00
Common Player:		.50
1	Steve Beuerlein	.50
2	Chuck Cecil	.50
3	Randal Hill	.50
4	Garrison Hearst	.50
5	Ricky Proehl	.50
6	Eric Swann	.50
7	Jeff George	.50
8	Drew Hill	.50
9	Eric Pegram	.50
10	Andre Rison	.50
11	Deion Sanders	1.50
12	Jessie Tuggle	.50
13	Cornelius Bennett	.50
14	Kenneth Davis	.50
15	Jim Kelly	1.00
16	Andre Reed	.50
17	Darryl Talley	.50
18	Steve Tasker	.50
19	Trace Armstrong	.50
20	Curtis Conway	1.00
21	Dante Jones	.50
22	Donnell Woolford	.50
23	Tim Worley	.50
24	Chris Zorich	.50
25	Derrick Fenner	.50
26	Harold Green	.50
27	David Klingler	.50
28	Tony McGee	.50
29	Carl Pickens	1.00
30	Jeff Query	.50
31	Mark Carrier	.50
32	Michael Jackson	.50
33	Eric Metcalf	.50
34	Michael Dean Perry	.50
35	Vinny Testaverde	.50
36	Tommy Vardell	.50
37	Troy Aikman	3.00
38	Alvin Harper	.50
39	Michael Irvin	1.00
40	Russell Maryland	.50
41	Jay Novacek	.50
42	Emmitt Smith	6.00
43	Rod Bernstine	.50
44	Mike Croel	.50
45	John Elway	1.50
46	Glyn Milburn	.50
47	Shannon Sharpe	.50
48	Dennis Smith	.50
49	Jason Hanson	.50
50	Herman Moore	1.00
51	Brett Perriman	.50
52	Barry Sanders	3.00
53	Chris Spielman	.50
54	Pat Swilling	.50
55	Edgar Bennett	.50
56	Terrell Buckley	.50
57	Brett Favre	8.00
58	Chris Jacke	.50
59	Sterling Sharpe	1.00
60	Reggie White	1.00
61	Gary Brown	.50
62	Cody Carlson	.50
63	Ernest Givins	.50
64	Haywood Jeffires	.50
65	Bruce Matthews	.50
66	Webster Slaughter	.50
67	Jason Belser	.50
68	Roosevelt Potts	.50
69	Rodney Culver	.50
70	Jim Harbaugh	1.00
71	Scott Radecic	.50
72	Kerry Cash	.50
73	Marcus Allen	1.00
74	J.J. Birden	.50
75	Dale Carter	.50
76	Keith Cash	.50
77	Willie Davis	.50
78	Neil Smith	.50
79	Eddie Anderson	.50
80	Tim Brown	1.00
81	Jeff Hostetler	.50
82	Raghib Ismail	.50
83	James Jett	.50
84	Terry McDaniel	.50
85	Willie Anderson	.50
86	Jerome Bettis	1.50
87	Todd Drayton	.50
88	Sean Gilbert	.50
89	Todd Lyght	.50
90	Chris Martin	.50
91	Keith Byars	.50
92	Bryan Cox	.50
93	Irving Fryar	.50
94	Terry Kirby	.50
95	Dan Marino	6.00
96	O.J. McDuffie	.50
97	Terry Allen	.50
98	Cris Carter	.50
99	Qadry Ismail	.50
100	Randall McDaniel	.50
101	Warren Moon	1.00
102	Robert Smith	1.00
103	Drew Bledsoe	3.00
104	Vincent Brisby	.50
105	Vincent Brown	.50
106	Marv Cook	.50
107	Leonard Russell	.50
108	Reyna Thompson	.50
109	Morten Andersen	.50
110	Quinn Early	.50
111	Tyrone Hughes	.50
112	Sam Mills	.50
113	William Roaf	.50
114	Renaldo Turnbull	.50
115	Stephen Baker	.50
116	John Elliott	.50
117	Rodney Hampton	.50
118	Mark Jackson	.50
119	David Meggett	.50
120	Kenyon Rasheed	.50
121	Brad Baxter	.50
122	Boomer Esiason	.50
123	Johnny Johnson	.50
124	Ronnie Lott	.50
125	Johnny Mitchell	.50
126	Rob Moore	.50
127	Fred Barnett	.50
128	Mark Bavaro	.50
129	Bubby Brister	.50
130	Randall Cunningham	.50
131	Tim Harris	.50
132	Herschel Walker	.50
133	Gary Anderson	.50
134	Barry Foster	.50
135	Kevin Greene	.50
136	Greg Lloyd	.50
137	Neil O'Donnell	.50
138	Rod Woodson	.50
139	Eric Bieniemy	.50
140	Ronnie Harmon	.50
141	Stan Humphries	.50
142	Natrone Means	1.50
143	Leslie O'Neal	.50
144	Junior Seau	1.00
145	Tim McDonald	.50
146	Jerry Rice	3.00
147	Dana Stubblefield	.50
148	John Taylor	.50
149	Ricky Watters	1.00
150	Steve Young	2.00
151	Brian Blades	.50
152	Cortez Kennedy	.50
153	Rick Mirer	.50
154	Rufus Porter	.50
155	Eugene Robinson	.50
156	Chris Warren	.50
157	Santana Dotson	.50
158	Craig Erickson	.50
159	Hardy Nickerson	.50
160	Dan Stryzinski	.50
161	Charles Wilson	.50
162	Thomas Everett	.50
163	Reggie Brooks	.50
164	Darryl Green	.50
165	Ricky Ervins	.50
166	John Friesz	.50
167	Brian Mitchell	.50
168	Sterling Palmer	.50

1994-95 Crown Pro Mags Fb

This 168-magnet set was sold in five-magnet packs that included a team magnet. It included 140 players and 28 team magnets, which all measure 2-1/8" x 3-3/8". A Warren Moon magnet was also available by mailing in a redemption card and three proofs of purchase along with $6. The magnets display the player's name at the bottom in team colors, with the team name running up the right side. A parallel Super Bowl XXIX set was also issued, but carries no premium in price. The player magnets are numbered on the front, but the team magnets were unnumbered and checklisted in alphabetical order. In addition, a Troy Aikman promo magnet is also listed below.

		NM/M
Complete Set (140):		75.00
Common Player:		.50
1	Rod Bernstine	.50
2	John Elway	2.00
3	Glyn Milburn	.50
4	Shannon Sharpe	.50
5	Dennis Smith	.50
6	Cody Carlson	.50
7	Ernest Givins	.50
8	Haywood Jeffires	.50
9	Bruce Matthews	.50
10	Webster Slaughter	.50
11	O.J. McDuffie	1.00
12	Keith Byars	.50
13	Bryan Cox	.50
14	Irving Fryar	.50
15	Dan Marino	6.00
16	Barry Foster	.50
17	Kevin Greene	1.00
18	Greg Lloyd	1.00
19	Neil O'Donnell	.50
20	Rod Woodson	.50
21	Steve Beuerlein	.50
22	Chuck Cecil	.50
23	Randal Hill	.50
24	Ricky Proehl	.50
25	Eric Swann	.50
26	Troy Aikman	3.00
27	Emmitt Smith	6.00
28	Michael Irvin	1.00
29	Russell Maryland	.50
30	Jay Novacek	.50
31	Jerome Bettis	2.00
32	Sean Gilbert	.50
33	Todd Lyght	.50
34	Chris Martin	.50
35	Roman Phifer	.50
36	Neal Anderson	.50
37	Quinn Early	.50
38	Rickey Jackson	.50
39	Sam Mills	.50
40	William Roaf	.50
41	Cornelius Bennett	.50
42	Jim Kelly	1.00
43	Kenneth Davis	.50
44	Darryl Tallfy	.50
45	Andre Reed	.50
46	Cris Carter	1.00
47	Warren Moon	1.00
48	Terry Allen	1.00
49	Raghib Ismail	.50
50	Robert Smith	1.00
51	Eric Pegram	.50
52	Andre Rison	1.00
53	Deion Sanders	2.00
54	Jessie Tuggle	.50
55	Jeff George	.50
56	Brian Blades	.50
57	Rick Mirer	1.00
58	Cortez Kennedy	.50
59	Chris Warren	1.00
60	Eugene Robinson	.50
61	Reggie Brooks	.50
62	Ricky Ervins	.50
63	Brian Mitchell	.50
64	Ricky Sanders	.50
65	Sterling Palmer	.50
66	Tim Brown	1.00
67	Jeff Hostetler	.50
68	Raghib Ismail	.50
69	Terry McDaniel	.50
70	James Jett	.50
71	Sterling Sharpe	1.00
72	Brett Favre	8.00
73	Reggie White	1.00
74	Terrell Buckley	.50
75	Edgar Bennett	.50
76	Jerry Rice	3.00
77	Steve Young	2.00
78	Ricky Watters	1.00
79	Dana Stubblefield	1.00
80	John Taylor	.50
81	Ronnie Harmon	.50
82	Stan Humphries	.50
83	Natrone Means	1.50
84	Junior Seau	1.00
85	Eric Bieniemy	.50
86	Dean Biasucci	.50
87	Jim Harbaugh	1.00
88	Roosevelt Potts	.50
89	Scott Radecic	.50
90	Rohn Stark	.50
91	Eric Metcalf	.50
92	Michael Dean Perry	.50
93	Vinny Testaverde	.50
94	Mark Carrier	.50
95	Michael Jackson	.50
96	Marcus Allen	1.00
97	Dale Carter	.50
98	Neil Smith	.50
99	J.J. Birden	.50
100	Willie Davis	.50
101	Rodney Hampton	.50
102	Mark Jackson	.50
103	David Meggett	.50
104	John Elliott	.50
105	Kenyon Rasheed	.50
106	Boomer Esiason	.50
107	Johnny Johnson	.50
108	Johnny Mitchell	.50
109	Brad Baxter	.50
110	Ronnie Lott	.50
111	Derrick Fenner	.50
112	David Klingler	.50
113	Bruce Pickens	.50
114	Harold Green	.50
115	Jeff Query	.50
116	Leonard Russell	.50
117	Drew Bledsoe	3.00
118	Marv Cook	.50
119	Vincent Brisby	.50
120	Vincent Brown	.50
121	Trace Armstrong	.50
122	Curtis Conway	1.00
123	Dante Jones	.50
124	Tim Worley	.50
125	Chris Zorich	.50
126	Ron Moore	.50
127	Barry Sanders	3.00
128	Pat Swilling	.50
129	Brett Perriman	.50
130	Chris Spielman	.50
131	Keith Byars	.50
132	Fred Barnett	.50
133	Randall Cunningham	.50
134	Herschel Walker	.50
135	Bubby Brister	.50
136	Craig Erickson	.50
137	Hardy Nickerson	.50
138	Demetrius Dubose	.50
139	Dan Stryzinski	.50
140	Charles Wilson	.50

1995 Crown Pro Magnets Fb

This 150-card set was produced by Chris Martin Enterprises and was sold in five-card packs. The magnets are grouped alphabetically according to team below. There were three insert sets available, called By The Zone, Classics and Die-cuts, as well as a Superhero Jumbos redemption set.

		NM/M
Complete Set (150):		70.00
Common Player:		.50
1	Larry Centers	.50
2	Garrison Hearst	1.00
3	Seth Joyner	.50
4	Ron Moore	.50
5	Eric Swann	.50
6	Chris Doleman	.50
7	Jeff George	.50
8	Craig Heyward	.50
9	Terrance Mathis	.50
10	Jessie Tuggle	.50
11	Cornelius Bennett	.50
12	Jim Kelly	1.00
13	Andre Reed	.50
14	Bruce Smith	.50
15	Darryl Talley	.50
16	Trace Armstrong	.50
17	Dante Jones	.50
18	Steve Walsh	.50
19	Donnell Woolford	.50
20	Tim Worley	.50
21	Jeff Blake	2.00
22	Harold Green	.50
23	Carl Pickens	1.00
24	Danny Scott	1.00
25	Dan Wilkinson	.50
26	Derrick Alexander	.50
27	Leroy Hoard	.50
28	Antonio Langham	.50
29	Vinny Testaverde	.50
30	Eric Turner	.50
31	Troy Aikman	2.00
32	Michael Irvin	1.00
33	Daryl Johnston	.50
34	Russell Maryland	.50
35	Emmitt Smith	4.00
36	Rod Bernstine	.50
37	John Elway	1.50
38	Anthony Miller	.50
39	Glyn Milburn	.50
40	Shannon Sharpe	.50
41	Scott Mitchell	1.00
42	Herman Moore	1.00
43	Brett Perriman	.50
44	Barry Sanders	2.00
45	Chris Spielman	.50
46	Edgar Bennett	.50
47	Robert Brooks	.50
48	Brett Favre	6.00
49	Sean Jones	.50
50	Reggie White	1.00
51	Gary Brown	.50
52	Cody Carlson	.50
53	Ernest Givins	.50
54	Haywood Jeffires	.50
55	Bruce Matthews	.50
56	Quentin Coryatt	.50
57	Steve Emtman	.50
58	Marshall Faulk	1.50
59	Jim Harbaugh	1.00
60	Roosevelt Potts	.50
61	Marcus Allen	1.00
62	Steve Bono	.50
63	Willie Davis	.50
64	Lake Dawson	.50
65	Neil Smith	.50
66	Tim Brown	.50
67	Jeff Hostetler	.50
68	Raghib Ismail	.50
69	James Jett	.50
70	Harvey Williams	.50
71	Jerome Bettis	1.00
72	Troy Drayton	.50
73	Wayne Gandy	.50
74	Sean Gilbert	.50
75	Todd Lyght	.50
76	Tim Bowens	.50
77	Bryan Cox	.50
78	Irving Fryar	.50
79	Dan Marino	4.00
80	Bernie Parmalee	.50
81	Terry Allen	1.00
82	Cris Carter	.50
83	Qadry Ismail	.50
84	Warren Moon	1.00
85	John Randle	.50
86	Bruce Armstrong	.50
87	Drew Bledsoe	2.00
88	Vincent Brisby	.50
89	Marion Butts	.50
90	Ben Coates	.50
91	Morten Andersen	.50
92	Quinn Early	.50
93	Jim Everett	.50
94	Tyrone Hughes	.50
95	Renaldo Turnbull	.50
96	Michael Brooks	.50
97	Dave Brown	.50
98	John Elliott	.50
99	Rodney Hampton	.50
100	Mike Sherrard	.50
101	Boomer Esiason	.50
102	Johnny Johnson	.50
103	Nick Lowery	.50
104	Johnny Mitchell	.50
105	Aaron Glenn	.50
106	Fred Barnett	.50
107	Bubby Brister	.50
108	Randall Cunningham	.50
109	Charlie Garner	.50
110	Calvin Williams	.50
111	Byron "Bam" Morris	.50
112	Barry Foster	.50
113	Kevin Greene	.50
114	Neil O'Donnell	.50
115	Rod Woodson	.50
116	Ronnie Harmon	.50
117	Stan Humphries	.50
118	Tony Martin	.50
119	Natrone Means	1.00
120	Junior Seau	1.00
121	William Floyd	1.00
122	Jerry Rice	2.00
123	Deion Sanders	1.50
124	Dana Stubblefield	.50
125	Steve Young	1.50
126	Brian Blades	.50
127	Cortez Kennedy	.50
128	Rick Mirer	.50
129	Eugene Robinson	.50
130	Chris Warren	.50
131	Trent Dilfer	1.00
132	Santana Dotson	.50
133	Craig Erickson	.50
134	Thomas Everett	.50
135	Errict Rhett	1.00
136	Reggie Brooks	.50
137	Ricky Ervins	.50
138	Darryl Green	.50
139	Brian Mitchell	.50
140	Heath Shuler	1.00
141	Frank Ricci	.50
142	Tim McKyer	.50
143	Tyrone Poole	.50
144	Derrick Lassic	.50
145	Bob Christian	.50
146	Steve Beuerlein	.50
147	Cedric Tillman	.50
148	Reggie Cobb	.50
149	Eugene Chung	.50
150	Desmond Howard	.50

1995 Crown Pro Magnets In The Zone Fb

By the Zone was a 12-card magnet insert in 1995 Pro Mags. The magnets feature a borderless color action shot of a player, and were inserted every three packs.

		NM/M
Complete Set (12):		15.00
Common Player:		.75
1	Troy Aikman	2.00
2	Drew Bledsoe	2.00
3	John Elway	1.50
4	Brett Favre	4.00
5	Jeff Hostetler	.75
6	Stan Humphries	.75
7	Dan Marino	4.00
8	Jim Kelly	.75
9	Warren Moon	.75
10	Neil O'Donnell	.75
11	Rick Mirer	.75
12	Steve Young	1.50

1995 Crown Pro Magnets Magnetic Classics Fb

Classics features 12 players in front of a column background with the team logo. Classics were inserted into every three packs of 1995 Pro Mags.

		NM/M
Complete Set (12):		15.00
Common Player:		.75
1	Barry Sanders	2.00
2	Deion Sanders	1.50
3	Dan Marino	4.00
4	Drew Bledsoe	2.00
5	Marcus Allen	.75
6	Jerome Bettis	1.00
7	John Elway	1.50
8	Jerry Rice	2.00
9	Emmitt Smith	4.00
10	Steve Young	1.50
11	Troy Aikman	2.00
12	Marshall Faulk	1.00

1995 Crown Pro Mags Rookies

This 12-magnet set features players taken in the 1994 NFL Draft. The magnets measure 2-1/8" x 3-3/8" and include a color photo and the player's name printed in gold foil.

		NM/M
Complete Set (12):		12.00
Common Player:		.75
1	Trent Dilfer	1.50
2	Heath Shuler	1.00
3	John Thierry	.75
4	Wayne Gandy	.75
5	Errict Rhett	1.00

6	David Palmer	1.00
7	Andre Coleman	.75
8	Lake Dawson	1.00
9	Marshall Faulk	1.50
10	Dan Wilkinson	.75
11	Greg Hill	1.00
12	Willie McGinest	1.00

1995 Crown Pro Superhero Jumbos

Chris Martin Enterprises offered this three oversized magnet set through the mail. With details on 1995 Pro Mag packs, collectors received the set for $6. Each card, measuring 3-3/4" x 7", features fantasy art of either Jerome Bettis, John Elway or Warren Moon.

		NM/M
Complete Set (3):		20.00
Common Player:		6.00
1	Jerome Bettis	7.00
2	John Elway	8.00
3	Warren Moon	6.00

1995 Crown Pro Mags Teams

Each magnet in this set features three top players from an NFL team and the embossed team logo. The unnumbered magnets were originally released as a promo set.

		NM/M
Complete Set (5):		20.00
Common Player:		3.00
1	Junior Seau, Stan Humphries, Natrone Means Chargers	3.00
2	Michael Irvin, Troy Aikman, Emmitt Smith Cowboys	6.00
3	Dan Marino, O.J. McDuffie, Bernie Parmalee Dolphins	6.00
4	Ricky Watters, Steve Young, Jerry Rice 49ers	5.00
5	Barry Foster, Neil O'Donnell, Rod Woodson Steelers	3.00

1995 Crown Pro Stamps

This 140-stamp set was sold in 12-stamp sheets. The stamps measure 1-1/2" x 2".

		NM/M
Complete Set (140):		40.00
Common Player:		.25
1	Steve Young DP	.50
2	Jerry Rice	1.00
3	Deion Sanders	.75
4	Dana Stubblefield	.25
5	William Floyd	.40
6	Troy Aikman DP	.75
7	Michael Irvin	.50
8	Emmitt Smith DP	1.50
9	Russell Maryland	.25
10	Daryl Johnston	.40
11	Dan Marino DP	1.50
12	Bernie Parmalee	.25
13	Tim Bowens	.25
14	Irving Fryar	.25
15	Bryan Cox	.25
16	Drew Bledsoe	1.00
17	Bruce Armstrong	.25
18	Vincent Brisby	.25
19	Marion Butts	.25
20	Ben Coates	.25
21	Dave Brown	.25
22	Michael Brooks	.25
23	Jumbo Elliott	.25
24	Rodney Hampton	.25
25	Mike Sherrard	.25
26	Jeff Hostetler	.25
27	Tim Brown	.60
28	Rocket Ismail	.25
29	James Jett	.25
30	Harvey Williams	.25
31	Heath Shuler	.50
32	Reggie Brooks	.25
33	Ricky Ervins	.25
34	Darrell Green UER (Darryl on front)	.25
35	Brian Mitchell	.25
36	Trace Armstrong	.25
37	Dante Jones	.25
38	Steve Walsh	.25
39	Donnell Woolford	.25
40	Tim Worley	.25
41	Boomer Esiason	.25
42	Aaron Glenn	.25
43	Johnny Johnson	.25
44	Nick Lowery	.25
45	Johnny Mitchell	.25
46	Neil O'Donnell	.25
47	Barry Foster	.25
48	Byron "Bam" Morris	.25
49	Rod Woodson	.25
50	Kevin Greene	.25
51	Randall Cunningham	.25
52	Bubby Brister	.25
53	Fred Barnett	.25
54	Charlie Garner	.25
55	Calvin Williams	.25
56	Brett Favre	2.00
57	Reggie White	.60
58	Edgar Bennett	.25
59	Robert Brooks	.25
60	Sean Jones	.25
61	Ronnie Harmon	.25
62	Stan Humphries	.25
63	Natrone Means	.60
64	Tony Martin	.25
65	Junior Seau	.25
66	John Elway	.75
67	Glyn Milburn	.25
68	Rod Bernstine	.25
69	Anthony Miller	.25
70	Shannon Sharpe	.60
71	Barry Sanders	1.00
72	Scott Mitchell	.40
73	Herman Moore	.60
74	Brett Perriman	.40
75	Chris Spielman	.40
76	Marcus Allen	.60
77	Steve Bono	.40
78	Willie Davis	.25
79	Lake Dawson	.25
80	Neil Smith	.25
81	Vinny Testaverde	.60
82	Eric Turner	.25
83	Antonio Langham	.25
84	Leroy Hoard	.25
85	Derrick Alexander WR	.25
86	Jim Kelly	.60
87	Cornelius Bennett	.25
88	Andre Reed	.25
89	Bruce Smith	.25
90	Darryl Talley	.25
91	Warren Moon	.60
92	Qadry Ismail	.25
93	Terry Allen	.60
94	Cris Carter	.60
95	John Randle	.25
96	Jeff George	.60
97	Chris Doleman	.25
98	Craig Heyward	.25
99	Terance Mathis	.25
100	Jessie Tuggle	.25
101	Jerome Bettis	.60
102	Sean Gilbert	.25
103	Troy Drayton	.25
104	Wayne Gandy	.25
105	Todd Lyght	.25
106	Jeff Blake	.75
107	Harold Green	.25
108	Carl Pickens	.60
109	Dan Wilkinson	.25
110	Darnay Scott	.40
111	Cody Carlson	.25
112	Gary Brown	.25
113	Ernest Givins	.25
114	Haywood Jeffires	.25
115	Bruce Matthews	.25
116	Jim Everett	.25
117	Morten Andersen	.25
118	Quinn Early	.25
119	Tyrone Hughes	.25
120	Renaldo Turnbull	.25
121	Larry Centers	.25
122	Garrison Hearst	.60
123	Seth Joyner	.25
124	Ronald Moore	.25
125	Eric Swann	.25
126	Rick Mirer	.60
127	Chris Warren	.40
128	Brian Blades	.25
129	Cortez Kennedy	.25
130	Eugene Robinson	.25
131	Marshall Faulk	.60
132	Quentin Coryatt	.25
133	Jim Harbaugh	.60
134	Roosevelt Potts	.25
135	Steve Emtman	.25
136	Trent Dilfer	.60
137	Santana Dotson	.25
138	Errict Rhett	.60
139	Thomas Everett	.25
140	Craig Erickson	.25

1996 Crown Pro Retail Mags

Not to be confused with the 1996 Pro Magnets, this 12-magnet set was sold in one-magnet cello packs. A cut-out action photo of the player is placed over a team-colored foil background. "Compacted" ghosted images of the action shot are also included in the foil background. The player's name is printed in gold foil along the left side of the magnet. The team logo is in foil in the lower left, while a larger team logo is located in the lower right. The magnet's number is printed in gold foil in the lower right. A 1996 Chris Martin Enterprises copyright tag line is printed at the bottom of the magnet in black. The backs are blank.

		NM/M
Complete Set (12):		30.00
Common Player:		1.00
1	Tim Brown	1.00
2	John Elway	4.00
3	Marshall Faulk	2.00
4	Dan Marino	6.00
5	Curtis Martin	3.00
6	Rashaan Salaam	1.00
7	Barry Sanders	6.00
8	Emmitt Smith	6.00
9	Neil Smith	1.00
10	Reggie White	2.00
11	Rod Woodson	1.00
12	Steve Young	3.00

1996 Crown Pro Magnets Fb

The 100-card set features a cut-out action photo of a player placed over a team-colored foil background. A marble-type 3-D box is behind the cut-out photo. The player's name is in gold-foil along the left side, with the team's logo in gold-foil near the bottom right. The fronts include the magnet number in the lower left in gold-foil. The team name is printed in all capital letters at the top right of the magnet. The Pro Magnets logo is in the upper left. NFL and NFL Players Inc. logos, along with the Chris Martin Enterprises tag line, are printed at the bottom. The backs are blank.

		NM/M
Complete Set (100):		70.00
Common Player:		.50
1	Troy Aikman	2.00
2	Michael Irvin	1.00
3	Emmitt Smith	4.00
4	Deion Sanders	1.50
5	Jay Novacek	.50
6	Jerry Rice	2.00
7	Steve Young	1.50
8	J.J. Stokes	.50
9	William Floyd	.50
10	Merton Hanks	.50
11	Greg Lloyd	.50
12	Rod Woodson	.50
13	Kordell Stewart	3.00
14	Yancey Thigpen	.50
15	Charles Johnson	.50
16	Richmond Webb	.50
17	Eric Green	.50
18	Bernie Parmalee	.50
19	Dan Marino	4.00
20	O.J. McDuffie	.50
21	Brett Favre	5.00
22	Reggie White	1.00
23	Robert Brooks	.50
24	Edgar Bennett	.50
25	Marcus Allen	1.00
26	Tamarick Vanover	1.00
27	Lake Dawson	.50
28	Neil Smith	.50
29	Steve Bono	.50
30	Harvey Williams	.50
31	Tim Brown	.50
32	Jeff Hostetler	.50
33	Drew Bledsoe	2.00
34	Vincent Brisby	.50
35	Curtis Martin	3.00
36	Rashaan Salaam	1.00
37	Erik Kramer	.50
38	Curtis Conway	1.00
39	Kerry Collins	2.00
40	Sam Mills	.50
41	Mark Carrier	.50
42	Dave Brown	.50
43	Rodney Hampton	.50
44	Tyrone Wheatley	.50
45	Vinny Testaverde	.50
46	Andre Rison	.50
47	Eric Turner	.50
48	Michael Jackson	.50
49	Mark Brunell	1.50
50	Jeff Lageman	.50
51	Roman Phifer	.50
52	Isaac Bruce	1.00
53	Rodney Peete	.50
54	Ricky Watters	1.00
55	Calvin Williams	.50
56	Warren Moon	.50
57	Cris Carter	.50
58	David Palmer	.50
59	Scott Mitchell	.50
60	Barry Sanders	2.00
61	Herman Moore	1.00
62	Brett Perriman	.50
63	Jim Kelly	.50
64	Bruce Smith	.50
65	Bryce Paup	.50
66	Junior Seau	1.00
67	Stan Humphries	.50
68	Andre Coleman	.50
69	Tony Martin	.50
70	Terry Allen	.50
71	Heath Shuler	.50
72	John Elway	1.50
73	Terrell Davis	2.00
74	Mike Pritchard	.50
75	Neil O'Donnell	.50
76	Kyle Brady	.50
77	Jim Harbaugh	.50
78	Marshall Faulk	1.00
79	Zack Crockett	.50
80	Quentin Coryatt	.50
81	Jeff George	.50
82	Morten Anderson	.50
83	Eric Metcalf	.50
84	Joey Galloway	1.00
85	Rick Mirer	.50
86	Chris Warren	.50
87	Ray Zellars	.50
88	Eric Allen	.50
89	Jim Everett	.50
90	Jeff Blake	1.00
91	Carl Pickens	.50
92	Ki-Jana Carter	.50
93	Larry Centers	.50
94	Garrison Hearst	.50
95	Trent Dilfer	.50
96	Errict Rhett	1.00
97	Hardy Nickerson	.50
98	Alvin Harper	.50
99	Steve McNair	2.00
100	Haywood Jeffires	.50

1996 Crown Pro Destination All-Pro Fb

This six-magnet set was randomly inserted one per four Pro Magnets packs. The magnets have a cut-out action photo of the player placed over an etched-foil background, which is red and silver for the AFC and blue and silver for the NFC Pro Bowlers. A ghosted image of the player is included in the background at the upper left. The Pro Magnets logo is in the upper right. The AFC or NFC Pro Bowl logo, along with the player's name, are printed in gold foil at the bottom center of the magnet. The magnets are numbered in the lower left with a prefix of "PB". The backs are blank.

		NM/M
Complete Set (6):		20.00
Common Player:		1.00
1	Jim Harbaugh	1.00
2	Curtis Martin	3.00
3	Yancey Thigpen	1.00
4	Brett Favre	8.00
5	Jerry Rice	4.00
6	Barry Sanders	6.00

1996 Crown Pro Die-Cuts

This 16-magnet set includes a cut-out action shot of the player placed over a die-cut background of the team's logo and player name. The player's first name is printed in gold foil over the top left portion of his last name, which is printed in team colors. "Die-Cut Magnets" is printed in gold foil to the right of the NFL and NFL Players Inc. logos at the bottom. The team's logo is printed in team colors over the upper right portion of the player's last name. A 1996 Chris Martin Enterprises Inc. copyright tag line is printed in black at the bottom center of the magnets. The magnets were sold in one-magnet cello packs.

		NM/M
Complete Set (16):		50.00
Common Player:		1.00
1	Troy Aikman	4.00
2	Deion Sanders	3.00
3	Emmitt Smith	6.00
4	Jerry Rice	4.00
5	Steve Young	3.00
6	Kordell Stewart	4.00
7	Dan Marino	6.00
8	Brett Favre	8.00
9	Marcus Allen	2.00
10	Drew Bledsoe	4.00
11	Barry Sanders	6.00
12	Marshall Faulk	2.00
13	John Elway	4.00
14	Rashaan Salaam	1.00
15	Jeff Hostetler	1.00
16	Keyshawn Johnson	1.00

A player's name in *italic* type indicates a rookie card.

1996 Crown Pro Draft Day Future Stars Fb

This six-card chase set included NFL rookies on randomly inserted magnets. The magnets are the same size as the other magnets in the Pro Magnets set.

		NM/M
Complete Set (6):		15.00
Common Player:		1.00
1	Kevin Hardy	1.00
2	Eddie George	8.00
3	Keyshawn Johnson	5.00
4	Tim Biakabutuka	1.00
5	Lawrence Phillips	3.00
6	Alex Molden	1.00

1996 Crown Pro Stamps

This 144-stamp set is similar to the 1995 series. They are the same size and utilize the same design and many of the same player photos. They were also sold in 12-stamp packs.

		NM/M
Complete Set (144):		35.00
Common Player:		.25
1	Steve Young	.75
2	Jerry Rice	1.00
3	Merton Hanks	.25
4	J.J. Stokes	.40
5	William Floyd	.40
6	Troy Aikman	1.00
7	Michael Irvin	.50
8	Emmitt Smith	2.00
9	Deion Sanders	.60
10	Daryl Johnston	.40
11	Dan Marino	2.00
12	Bernie Parmalee	.25
13	O.J. McDuffie	.40
14	Richmond Webb	.25
15	Eric Green	.25
16	Drew Bledsoe	1.00
17	Bruce Armstrong	.25
18	Dave Meggett	.25
19	Curtis Martin	1.00
20	Ben Coates	.40
21	Dave Brown	.25
22	Michael Brooks	.25
23	Tyrone Wheatley	.40
24	Rodney Hampton	.40
25	Jeff Hostetler	.25
26	Tim Brown	.50
27	Rocket Ismail	.40
28	James Jett	.25
29	Harvey Williams	.40
30	Heath Shuler	.50
31	Michael Westbrook	.50
32	Terry Allen	.50
33	Darrell Green	.40
34	Brian Mitchell	.25
35	Rashaan Salaam	.50
36	Erik Kramer UER 37	.25
37	Donnell Woolford	.25
38	Alonzo Spellman	.25
39	Kyle Brady	.40
40	Aaron Glenn	.25
41	Adrian Murrell	.40
42	Nick Lowery	.25
43	Charles Johnson	.40
44	Kordell Stewart	1.00
45	Yancey Thigpen	.40
46	Rod Woodson	.40
47	Greg Lloyd	.50
48	Randall Cunningham	.40
49	Rodney Peete	.25
50	Ricky Watters	.50
51	Charlie Garner	.25
52	Calvin Williams	.25
53	Brett Favre	2.50
54	Reggie White	.50
55	Edgar Bennett	.40
56	Robert Brooks	.50
57	Sean Jones	.25
58	Ronnie Harmon	.25
59	Stan Humphries	.40
60	Andre Coleman	.25
61	Tony Martin	.40
62	Junior Seau	.50
63	John Elway	.50
64	Mike Pritchard	.25
65	Terrell Davis	1.00
66	Anthony Miller	.40
67	Shannon Sharpe	.50
68	Barry Sanders	1.25
69	Scott Mitchell	.40
70	Herman Moore	.50
71	Brett Perriman	.40
72	Johnnie Morton	.40
73	Marcus Allen	.50
74	Steve Bono	.40
75	Tamarick Vanover	.25
76	Lake Dawson	.25
77	Neil Smith	.25
78	Vinny Testaverde	.40
79	Eric Turner	.25
80	Michael Jackson	.40
81	Leroy Hoard	.25
82	Andre Rison	.50
83	Jim Kelly	.50
84	Carwell Gardner	.25
85	Andre Reed	.40
86	Bruce Smith	.50
87	Bryce Paup	.40
88	Warren Moon	.50
89	Qadry Ismail	.40
90	Robert Smith	.40
91	Cris Carter	.50
92	David Palmer	.25
93	Jeff George	.50
94	Morten Andersen	.25
95	Craig Heyward	.25
96	Eric Metcalf	.40
97	Jessie Tuggle	.25
98	Roman Phifer	.25
99	Todd Lyght	.25
100	Troy Drayton	.25
101	Isaac Bruce	.50
102	Sean Gilbert	.25
103	Jeff Blake	.60
104	Harold Green	.25
105	Carl Pickens	.50
106	Dan Wilkinson	.25
107	Ki-Jana Carter	.40
108	Steve McNair	.75
109	Gary Brown	.25
110	Haywood Jeffires	.25
111	Bruce Matthews	.25
112	Jim Everett	.25
113	Mario Bates	.25
114	Ray Zellars	.25
115	Tyrone Hughes	.25
116	Eric Allen	.25
117	Larry Centers	.40
118	Garrison Hearst	.50
119	Aeneas Williams	.25
120	Rob Moore	.25
121	Neil O'Donnell	.40
122	Rick Mirer	.25
123	Chris Warren	.40
124	Eric Swann	.25
125	Cortez Kennedy	.25
126	Joey Galloway	.50
127	Marshall Faulk	.50
128	Quentin Coryatt	.25
129	Jim Harbaugh	.50
130	Trev Alberts	.25
131	Zack Crockett	.25
132	Trent Dilfer	.40
133	Hardy Nickerson	.25
134	Errict Rhett	.50
135	Alvin Harper	.25
136	Sam Mills	.25
137	Tyrone Poole	.40
138	Kerry Collins	.75
139	Bob Christian	.25
140	Randy Baldwin	.25
141	Steve Beuerlein	.25
142	Mark Brunell	1.00
143	Tony Boselli	.40
144	Jeff Lageman	.25

1986 DairyPak Cartons

These cards were sponsored by various brands of milk across the country in 1986; different colors (purple, green, lavender, aqua, orange, red, light blue, dark blue, black and brown) were used for different sponsors. Each card is perforated and features a black-and-white head shot of the player, plus a facsimilie autograph and card number. Cards which have been cut from the milk carton measure 3-1/4" x 4-7/16", but generally are more valuable if they are left intact as a complete carton. The set was not licensed by the NFL, so no team logos are shown; the NFLPA, however, licensed the set. Below each card was an offer to receive a 24" x 32" poster featuring the 24 cards.

		NM/M
Complete Set (24):		65.00
Common Player:		1.25
1	Joe Montana	10.00
2	Marcus Allen	3.00
3	Art Monk	2.00
4	Mike Quick	1.25
5	John Elway	5.00
6	Eric Hipple	1.25
7	Louis Lipps	1.25
8	Dan Fouts	2.00
9	Phil Simms	2.00
10	Mike Rozier	1.25
11	Greg Bell	1.25
12	Ottis Anderson	1.50
13	Dave Krieg	1.75
14	Anthony Carter	1.25
15	Freeman McNeil	1.25
16	Doug Cosbie	1.25
17	James Lofton	6.00
18	Dan Marino	8.00
19	James Wilder	1.25
20	Cris Collinsworth	1.50

21 Eric Dickerson 4.00
22 Walter Payton 6.00
23 Ozzie Newsome 2.00
24 Chris Hinton 1.25

1971-72 Dell

This 48-player set, which measures 8-1/4" x 10-3/4", from the 1971-72 Dell Pro Football Guide includes a center insert that unfolds to show 48 color photos. The photos, bordered in black and yellow, each measure 1-3/4" x 3". The player's name and team name are located inside a rectangle under the photo. The backs boast action photos, which are bordered in black and white. The football guide includes bios on each of the players offered in the set. The photos are not numbered. A complete set which is still intact in the guides are valued at 25 percent over what is listed here.

NM/M

Complete Set (48): 100.00
Common Player: 1.00
1 Dan Abramowicz 1.00
2 Herb Adderley 2.00
3 Lem Barney 1.00
4 Bobby Bell 1.00
5 George Blanda 3.00
6 Terry Bradshaw 15.00
7 John Brodie 2.00
8 Larry Brown 1.00
9 Dick Butkus 10.00
10 Fred Carr 1.00
11 Virgil Carter 1.00
12 Mike Curtis 1.00
13 Len Dawson 2.50
14 Carl Eller 1.00
15 Mel Farr 1.00
16 Roman Gabriel 1.50
17 Gary Garrison 1.00
18 Dick Gordon 1.00
19 Bob Griese 5.00
20 Bob Hayes 1.50
21 Rich Jackson 1.00
22 Charlie Johnson 1.00
23 Ron Johnson 1.00
24 Deacon Jones 2.50
25 Sonny Jurgensen 2.50
26 Leroy Kelly 1.50
27 Daryle Lamonica 1.50
28 MacArthur Lane 1.00
29 Willie Lanier 1.50
30 Bob Lilly 3.00
31 Floyd Little 1.00
32 Mike Lucci 1.00
33 Don Maynard 2.50
34 Joe Namath 16.00
35 Tommy Nobis 1.50
36 Merlin Olsen 3.00
37 Alan Page 2.00
38 Gerry Philbin 1.00
39 Jim Plunkett 2.00
40 Tim Rossovich 1.00
41 Gale Sayers 10.00
42 Dennis Shaw 1.00
43 O.J. Simpson 14.00
44 Fran Tarkenton 7.00
45 Johnny Unitas 12.00
46 Paul Warfield 3.00
47 Gene Washington 1.00
48 Larry Wilson 1.50

1933 Diamond Matchbooks Silver

With covers measuring 1-1/2" x 4-1/2" when folded out, the 95-matchbook set has a photo of the player over a pink or green background, bordered in silver. Prices listed here are with the matches removed. The player's name and team are listed at the bottom of the cover fronts. The cover backs showcase the player's name and highlights inside a box. The matchbooks are not numbered. Matchbooks with the matches intact are worth 1-1/2 to 2 times more than what is listed.

NM/M

Complete Set (95): 1,100
Common Player: 50.00
1 All-American Board of Football Seal 50.00
2 Gene Alford 50.00
3 Marger Apsit 50.00
4 Morris "Red" Badgro 60.00
5 Cliff Battles 70.00
6 Morris (Maury) Bodenger 50.00
7 Jimmy Bowdoin 50.00
8 John Boylan 50.00
9 Hank Bruder 50.00
10 Carl Brumbaugh 60.00
11 Bill Buckler 50.00
12 Jerome Buckley 50.00
13 Dale Burnett 50.00
14 Ernie Caddel 50.00
15 Red Cagle 50.00
16 Glen Campbell 50.00
17 John Cannella 50.00
18 Zuck Carlson 50.00
19 George Christensen 60.00
20 Stu Clancy 50.00
21 Paul (Rip) Collins 50.00
22 John F. Connell 50.00
23 George Corbett 50.00
24 Orien Crow 50.00
25 Ed Danowski 50.00
26 Sylvester (Red) Davis 50.00
27 John Isola 50.00
28 John Doehring 50.00
29 Glen Edwards 60.00
30 Earl Elser 50.00
31 Ox Emerson 50.00
32 Tiny Feather 50.00
33 Ray Flaherty 20.00
34 Ike Frankian 50.00
35 Harold "Red" Grange 500.00
36 Len Grant 50.00
37 Ace Gutowsky 50.00
38 Mel Hein 60.00
39 Arnie Herber 60.00
40 Bill Hewitt 60.00
41 Herman Hickman 50.00
42 Clarke Hinkle 75.00
43 Cal Hubbard 75.00
44 George Hurley 50.00
45 Herman Hussey 50.00
46 Cecil (Tex) Irvin 50.00
47 Luke Johnson 50.00
48 Bruce Jones 50.00
49 Tom Jones 50.00
50 Thacker Kay 50.00
51 John Kelly 50.00
52 Joe (Doc) Kopcha 50.00
53 Joe Kurth 50.00
54 Milo Lubratevich 50.00
55 Father Lumpkin 50.00
56 Jim MacMurdo 50.00
57 Joe Maniaci 50.00
58 Jack McBride 50.00
59 Ookie Miller 50.00
60 Granville Mitchell 50.00
61 Keith Molesworth 50.00
62 Bob Monnett 50.00
63 Hap Moran 50.00
64 Bill Morgan 50.00
65 Maynard (Doc) Morrison 50.00
66 Mathew Murray 50.00
67 Jim Musick 50.00
68 Bronko Nagurski 750.00
69 Dick Nesbitt 50.00
70 Harry Newman 50.00
71 Steve Owen 60.00
72 Bill (Red) Owen 50.00
73 Andy Pavlicovic 50.00
74 Bert Pearson 50.00
75 William Pendergast 50.00
76 Jerry Pepper 50.00
77 Stan Piawlock 50.00
78 Ernie Pinckert 50.00
79 Glenn Presnell 50.00
80 Jess Quatse 50.00
81 Hank Reese 50.00
82 Dick Richards 50.00
83 Tony Sarausky 50.00
84 Elmer (Dutch) Schaake 50.00
85 John Schneller 50.00
86 Johnny Sisk 50.00
87 Mike Steponovich 50.00
88 Ken Strong 100.00
89 Charles Tackwell 50.00
90 Harry Thayer 60.00
91 Walt Uzdavinis 50.00
92 John Welch 50.00
93 William Whelan 50.00
94 Fay (Mule) Wilson 50.00
95 Frank (Babe) Wright 50.00

1934 Diamond Matchbooks

Measuring 1-1/2" x 4-1/2", each matchbook showcases four different colored borders, including blue, red, tan and green. Many players have each of the four color combinations. Other players have one or two variations of borders. The player's name and team are printed above the photo on the front. The backs spotlight the player's name and highlights. This set features "The Diamond Match Co., N.Y.C" above the striking strip on the matchbook backs. As a note, the 1935 matchbooks resemble this set, but do not have the "Diamond Match" tag line at the bottom. The books are unnumbered. If matches are intact in the book, they are worth 1-1/2 times more.

NM/M

Complete Set (121): 4,000
Common Player: 25.00
1 Arvo Antilla 25.00
2 Morris "Red" Badgro 40.00
3 Norbert Bartell 25.00
4 Cliff Battles 25.00
5 Chuck Bennis 25.00
6 Jack Beynon 25.00
7 Morris (Maury) Bodenger 25.00
8 John Bond 25.00
9 John Brown 25.00
10 Carl Brumbaugh 25.00
11 Dale Burnett 25.00
12 Ernie Caddel 25.00
13 Red Cagle 25.00
14 Glen Campbell 25.00
15 John Cannella 25.00
16 Joe Carter 25.00
17 Les Caywood 25.00
18 George (Buck) Chapman 25.00
19 Frank Christensen 25.00
20 Stu Clancy 25.00
21 Algy Clark 25.00
22 Paul (Rip) Collins 25.00
23 Jack Connell 25.00
24 Orien Crow 25.00
25 Lone Star Dietz (CO) 25.00
26 John Doehring 25.00
27 Glen Edwards 50.00
28 Ox Emerson 25.00
29 Tiny Feather 25.00
30 Ray Flaherty 50.00
31 Frank Froschauer 25.00
32 Chuck Galbreath 25.00
33 Elbert (Red) Gragg 25.00
34 Harold "Red" Grange 500.00
35 Cy Grant 25.00
36 Len Grant 25.00
37 Ross Grant 25.00
38 Jack Griffith 25.00
39 Ed Gryboski 25.00
40 Ace Gutowsky 25.00
41 Thomas (Swede) Hanson 25.00
42 Mel Hein 25.00
43 Warren Heller 25.00
44 Bill Hewitt 50.00
45 Cecil (Tex) Irvin 25.00
46 Frank Johnson 25.00
47 Jack Johnson 25.00
48 Bob Jones 25.00
49 Tom Jones 25.00
50 Carl Jorgensen 25.00
51 John Karcis 25.00
52 Eddie Kawal 25.00
53 John Kelly 25.00
54 George Kenneally 25.00
55 Walt Kiesling 50.00
56 Jack Knapper 25.00
57 Frank Knox 25.00
58 Joe (Doc) Kopcha 25.00
59 Joe Kresky 25.00
60 Joe Laws 25.00
61 Russ Lay 25.00
62 Biff Lee 25.00
63 Gil LeFebvre 25.00
64 Jim Leonard 25.00
65 Les Lindberg 25.00
66 John Lipski 25.00
67 Milo Lubratevich 25.00
68 Father Lumpkin 25.00
69 Jim MacMurdo 25.00
70 Ed Matesic 25.00
71 Dave McCollough 25.00
72 John McKnight 25.00
73 Johnny "Blood" McNally 100.00
74 Al Minot 25.00
75 Keith Molesworth 25.00
76 Jim Mooney 25.00
77 Leroy Moorehead 25.00
78 Bill Morgan 25.00
79 Bob Moser 25.00
80 Lee Mulleneaux 25.00
81 George Munday 25.00
82 George Musso 50.00
83 Harry Newman 25.00
84 Al Norgard 25.00
85 John (Cap) Oehler 25.00
86 Charlie Opper 25.00
87 Bill (Red) Owen 25.00
88 Steve Owen 20.00
89 Bert Pearson 25.00
90 Tom Perkinson 25.00
91 Mace Pike 25.00
92 Joe Pilconis 25.00
93 Lew Pope 25.00
94 Crain Portman 25.00
95 Glenn Presnell 25.00
96 Jess Quatse 25.00
97 Clare Randolph 25.00
98 Hank Reese 25.00
99 Paul Riblett 25.00
100 Dick Richards 25.00
101 Jack Roberts 25.00
102 John Rogers 25.00
103 Gene Ronzani 25.00
104 John Schueller 25.00
105 Bob Rowe 25.00
106 Alolph Schwammel 25.00
107 Earl (Red) Seick 25.00
108 Allen Shi 25.00
109 Ben Smith 25.00
110 Ken Strong 75.00
111 Elmer Taber 25.00
112 Charles Tackwell 25.00
113 Ray Tesser 25.00
114 John (Stumpy) Thomason 25.00
115 Charlie Turbyville 25.00
116 Claude Urevig 25.00
117 John (Harp) Vaughan 25.00
118 Henry Wagnon 25.00
119 John West 25.00
120 Lee Woodruff 25.00
121 Jim Zyntell 25.00

1934 Diamond Matchbooks College Rivals

The 12-matchbook set honors a college rivalry with text about the recent history of the games. Bordered in black or tan, matchbooks could be found in either variation. Matchbooks which still have the matches intact are worth 1-1/2 times more than what is listed here.

NM/M

Complete Set (12): 150.00
Common Player: 20.00
1 Alabama vs. Fordham 1933 20.00
2 Army vs. Navy start to finish 20.00
3 lose by a 13-6 score 20.00
4 Bulldog Alumni and followers 20.00
5 in atoning for this one defeat 20.00
6 victory for Lafayette 20.00
7 Michigan vs. Ohio State Champions 20.00
8 leader of men, Knute Rockne 35.00
9 Penn vs. Cornell pass 20.00
10 USC vs. Notre Dame year 35.00
11 Yale vs. Harvard Harvard 20.00
12 Yale vs. Princeton scoring 27 20.00

1935 Diamond Matchbooks

In 1935, three different colored borders were used for this set, including tan, green and red. However, this time players were only printed with one color border. Resembling the 1934 set, this set can be identified by the "Made in U.S.A./The Diamond Match Co., N.Y.C." tag line. The unnumbered matchbooks measure 1-1/2" x 4-1/2". The player photo is not bordered and a player position is not listed. Matchbooks with the matches intact are valued at 1-1/2 times the values listed here.

NM/M

Complete Set (96): 2,000
Common Player: 20.00
1 Alf Anderson 20.00
2 Alec Ashford 20.00
3 Gene Augusterfer 20.00
4 Morris "Red" Badgro 20.00
5 Cliff Battles 50.00
6 Harry Benson 20.00
7 Tony Blazine 20.00
8 John Bond 20.00
9 Maurice (Mule) Bray 20.00
10 Dale Burnett 20.00
11 Charles (Cocky) Bush 20.00
12 Ernie Caddel 20.00
13 Zuck Carlson 20.00
14 Joe Carter 20.00
15 Cy Casper 20.00
16 Paul Causey 20.00
17 Frank Christensen 20.00
18 Stu Clancy 20.00
19 Earl "Dutch" Clark 75.00
20 Paul (Rip) Collins 20.00
21 Dave Cook (Chicago Cardinals) 20.00
22 Fred Crawford 20.00
23 Paul Cuba 20.00
24 Harry Ebding 20.00
25 Glen Edwards 20.00
26 Marvin (Swede) Ellstrom 20.00
27 Beattie Feathers 20.00
28 Ray Flaherty 20.00
29 John Gildea 20.00
30 Tom Graham 20.00
31 Len Grant 20.00
32 Maurice Green 20.00
33 Norman Greeney 20.00
34 Ace Gutowsky 20.00
35 Julius Hall 20.00
36 Thomas (Swede) Hanson 20.00
37 Charles Harold 20.00
38 Tom Haywood 20.00
39 Mel Hein 20.00
40 Bill Hewitt 20.00
41 Cecil (Tex) Irvin 20.00
42 Frank Johnson 20.00
43 Jack Johnson 20.00
44 Luke Johnson 20.00
45 Tom Jones 20.00
46 Carl Jorgensen 20.00
47 George Kenneally 20.00
48 Roger Kirkman 20.00
49 Frank Knox 20.00
50 Joe (Doc) Kopcha 20.00
51 Rick Lackman 20.00
52 Jim Leonard 20.00
53 Joe (Hunk) Malkovich 20.00
54 Ed Manske 20.00
55 Bernie Masterson 20.00
56 James McMillen 20.00
57 Mike Mikulak 20.00
58 Ookie Miller 20.00
59 Milford (Dub) Miller 20.00
60 Al Minot 20.00
61 Buster Mitchell 20.00
62 Bill Morgan 20.00
63 George Musso 20.00
64 Harry Newman 20.00
65 Al Nichelini 20.00
66 Bill (Red) Owen 20.00
67 Steve Owen 30.00
68 Max Padlow 20.00
69 Hal Pangle 20.00
70 Melvin Pittman 20.00
71 William Pollock 20.00
72 Glenn Presnell 20.00
73 George Rado 20.00
74 Clare Randolph 20.00
75 Hank Reese 20.00
76 Ray Richards 20.00
77 Doug Russell 20.00
78 Sandy Sandberg 20.00
79 John Schneller 20.00
80 Michael Sebastian 20.00
81 Allen Shi 20.00
82 Johnny Sisk 20.00
83 Phil Sarboe 20.00
84 James Stacy 20.00
85 Ed Storm 20.00
86 Ken Strong 50.00
87 Art Strutt 20.00
88 Frank Sullivan 20.00
89 Charles Treadaway 20.00
90 John Turley 20.00
91 Claude Urevig 20.00
92 Charles Vaughan 20.00
93 Izzy Weinstock 20.00
94 Henry Wiesenbaugh 20.00
95 Joe Zeller 20.00
96 Vince Zizak 20.00

1935 Diamond Matchbooks College Rivals

With all the variations available, this set goes from 12 matchbooks to 36. Covers include highlights on recent games in the rivalry. The Diamond name is printed in tan with a double-lined company name or the Diamond name is printed on a single line with a tan or black border. Matchbooks with the matches intact are valued at 1-1/2 times more than what is listed here.

NM/M

Complete Set (12): 100.00
Common Player: 10.00
1 Alabama vs. Fordham once championship 10.00
2 Army vs. Navy over the Cadets since 1921 10.00
3 the gamely fighting "Rams" 10.00
4 Georgia vs. Georgia Tech 7-0 defeat 10.00
5 Holy Cross vs. Boston College defeat 10.00
6 in a 13-7 victory for Lehigh 10.00
7 Michigan vs. Ohio State tory for State 10.00
8 Notre Dame vs. Army Cadets 12-6 12.00
9 Penn vs. Cornell from start to finish 10.00
10 carries of Elmer Layden 12.00
11 Yale vs. Harvard set back 10.00
12 Yale vs. Princeton ed still led 7-0 10.00

1936 Diamond Matchbooks

Chicago Bears and Philadelphia Eagles players were featured in this matchbook set. The matchbooks, when folded out, measure 1-1/2" x 4-1/2". The words were printed in black or brown, while borders were in three different colors, tan, red and green. Ray Nolting is the lone exception to the rule, as matchbooks featuring him were printed with black and brown ink. The front of the books include a player picture, his name and team. The backs showcase his name and his highlights. With the different variations available, a complete set totals 96 matchbooks, which are unnumbered. Books with matches intact are worth 1-1/2 times more than what is listed here.

NM/M

Complete Set (47): 1,000
Common Player: 15.00
1 Carl Brumbaugh 15.00
2 Zuck Carlson 15.00
3 George Corbett (last line - Sigma Alpha Epsilon.) 15.00
4 John Doehring (last line - is a bachelor.) 15.00
5 Beattie Feathers (first line - ...will be 28 years) 25.00
6 Dan Fortmann (first line - ...April 11, 1916, at) 25.00
7 George Grosvenor 15.00
8 Bill Hewitt 15.00
9 Luke Johnson 15.00
10 William Karr (first line - ...in Ripley,) 15.00
11 Eddie Kawal 15.00
12 Jack Manders (last line - 200, Height 6 ft. 1 in.) 15.00
13 Bernie Masterson (last line - Alpha Epsilon, Single.) 15.00
14 Eddie Michaels 15.00
15 Ookie Miller 15.00
16 Keith Molesworth (last line - 5 ft. 9 1/2 in. Weight 168.) 15.00
17 George Musso (last line - Science degree, Is single.) 50.00
18 Bronko Nagurski 400.00
19 Ray Nolting (first line - ...three years of Cin-) 15.00
20 Vernon Oech 15.00
21 William Pollock 15.00
22 Gene Ronzani (last line - is married.) 15.00
23 Ted Rosequist 15.00
24 Johnny Sisk 15.00
25 Joe Stydahar (last line - is single.) 25.00
26 Frank Sullivan (first line - ...Loyola U.) (New) 15.00
27 Russell Thompson (last line - Sigma Nu fraternity.) 15.00
28 Milt Trost (last line - is single.) 15.00
29 Joe Zeller (last line - and is single, Sigma Nu.) 15.00
30 Bill Brian 15.00
31 Art Buss 15.00
32 Joe Carter 15.00
33 Thomas (Swede) Hanson 15.00
34 Don Jackson 15.00
35 John Kusko 15.00
36 Jim Leonard 15.00
37 Jim MacMurdo 15.00
38 Ed Manske 15.00
39 George McPherson 15.00
40 George Mulligan 15.00
41 Joe Pilconis 15.00
42 Hank Reese 15.00
43 Jim Russell 15.00
44 Dave Smukler 15.00
45 Pete Stevens 15.00
46 John Thomason 15.00
47 Vince Zizak 15.00

1937 Diamond Matchbooks

This time only Chicago Bears players were featured. Measuring 1-1/2" x 4-1/2" when folded out, the matchbooks resemble the 1936 set, however, this 1937 set has a smaller type size. With text printed in gray or black, the 24-matchbook set showcases three different colored borders - red, green and tan. The cover fronts feature a player photo, with his name and team printed above the photo. The backs of the matchbooks have the player's name and highlights inside a box. Matchbooks with the matches intact are valued at 1-1/2 times the prices listed here.

NM/M

Complete Set (24): 450.00
Common Player: 12.00
1 Frank Bausch 12.00
2 Delbert Bjork 12.00
3 William Conkright 12.00
4 George Corbett (last line - ion.) 12.00
5 John Doehring (last line - baseball.) 12.00
6 Beattie Feathers (first line - ...turned 29 years) 25.00
7 Dan Fortmann (first line - April 11, 1916, in) 30.00
8 Harrison Francis 12.00
9 Henry Hammond 12.00
10 William Karr (first line - in Ripley, W.) 12.00
11 Jack Manders (last line - height 6 ft. 1 in.) 12.00
12 Ed Manske 12.00
13 Bernie Masterson (last line - single.) 25.00
14 Keith Molesworth (last line - 9 1/2 in. Weight 168.) 25.00
15 George Musso (last line - married.) 40.00
16 Ray Nolting (first line - ... three years for) 12.00
17 Richard Plasman 12.00
18 Gene Ronzani (last line - married.) 20.00
19 Joe Stydahar (last line - ing. Is single.) 35.00
20 Frank Sullivan (first line - Loyola U. New) 12.00
21 Russell Thompson (last line - year.) 12.00
22 Milt Trost (last line - pounds. Is single.) 12.00
23 George Wilson 12.00
24 Joe Zeller (last line - Nu.) 12.00

1938 Diamond Matchbooks

Showcasing players from the Chicago Bears and Detroit Lions, the 24-matchbook set measures 1-1/2" x 4-1/2" when folded out. They are bordered in silver. The player's highlights feature different colored backgrounds for the two teams - Bears have red backgrounds, while the Lions have blue. No variations are known for this set. The unnumbered matchbooks are listed alphabetically. As always, matchbooks with the matches intact are valued at 1-1/2 times the values listed here.

		NM/M
Complete Set (24):		450.00
Common Player:		15.00
1	Delbert Bjork	15.00
2	Raymond Buivid	15.00
3	Gary Famiglietti	2.50
4	Dan Fortmann	15.00
5	Bert Johnson	15.00
6	Jack Manders	20.00
7	Joe Maniaci	25.00
8	Lester McDonald	15.00
9	Frank Sullivan	15.00
10	Robert Swisher	15.00
11	Russell Thompson	15.00
12	Gus Zarnas	15.00
13	Ernie Caddel	25.00
14	Lloyd Cardwell	15.00
15	Earl "Dutch" Clark	50.00
16	Jack Johnson	15.00
17	Ed Klewicki	15.00
18	James McDonald	15.00
19	James (Monk) Moscrip	15.00
20	Maurice (Babe) Patt	15.00
21	Bob Reynolds	15.00
22	Kent Ryan	15.00
23	Fred Vanzo	15.00
24	Alex Wojciechowicz	50.00

1967 Dolphins Royal Castle

Measuring 3" x 4-3/8", the 27-card set was released by Royal Castle restaurants in South Florida. The fronts showcase a large black-and-white photo, with his facsimile signature under the photo in a white area. The card fronts are bordered in orange. Each card back includes the player's name, position and bio, along with the Royal Castle and Miami Dolphins' logos. A 28th card in the set, featuring George Wilson Jr., may have also been produced.

		NM/M
Complete Set (27):		2,700
Common Player:		25.00
Common Player (SP):		100.00
1	Joe Auer (SP)	100.00
2	Tom Beier	25.00
3	Mel Branch	25.00
4	Jon Brittenum	35.00
5	George Chesser	25.00
6	Edward Cooke	25.00
7	Frank Emanuel (SP)	125.00
8	Tom Erlandson (SP)	100.00
9	Norm Evans (SP)	150.00
10	Bob Griese (SP)	800.00
11	Abner Haynes (SP)	175.00
12	Jerry Hopkins (SP)	100.00
13	Frank Jackson	25.00
14	Billy Joe	25.00
15	Wahoo McDaniel	150.00
16	Robert Neff	25.00
17	Billy Neighbors	25.00
18	Rick Norton	25.00
19	Bob Petrich	25.00
20	Jim Riley	25.00
21	John Stofa (SP)	150.00
22	Lavern Torczon	25.00
23	Howard Twilley	80.00
24	Jimmy Warren (SP)	100.00
25	Richard Westmoreland	25.00
26	Maxie Williams (SP)	150.00
27	George Wilson, Sr. (SP) (Head Coach)	150.00

1974 Dolphins All-Pro Graphics

Measuring 8-1/4" x 10-3/4", the 10-photo set showcases color action shots on the front, surrounded by a white border. The player's name, position and team are printed in the top left corner. The unnumbered photos have blank backs.

		NM/M
Complete Set (10):		100.00
Common Player:		5.00
1	Dick Anderson	8.00
2	Nick Buoniconti	14.00
3	Larry Csonka	18.00
4	Manny Fernandez	6.00
5	Bob Griese	25.00
6	Jim Kiick	8.00
7	Earl Morrall	12.00
8	Mercury Morris	8.00
9	Jake Scott	6.00
10	Garo Yepremian	5.00

1980 Dolphins Police

Measuring 2-5/8" x 4-1/8", the 16-card set features a photo on the front, with the player's name and position under the photo. The Kiwanis logo appears in the lower right. The unnumbered card backs feature Miami Dolphins Tips inside a box, which has the Dolphins' logo at the top. Sponsors are listed at the bottom of the card backs.

		NM/M
Complete Set (16):		75.00
Common Player:		2.50
5	Uwe Von Schamann	2.50
10	Don Strock	5.00
12	Bob Griese	12.00
22	Tony Nathan	5.00
24	Delvin Williams	5.00
25	Tim Foley	4.00
50	Larry Gordon	2.50
58	Kim Bokamper	2.50
64	Ed Newman	2.50
66	Larry Little (SP)	20.00
67	Bob Kuechenberg	5.00
73	Bob Baumhower	4.00
77	A.J. Duhe	5.00
82	Duriel Harris	4.00
89	Nat Moore	5.00
NNO	Don Shula (CO)	15.00

1981 Dolphins Police

Measuring 2-5/8" x 4-1/8", the 16-card set features a photo, with the player's name, number, position and bio under the photo. The Dolphins and Kiwanis logos appear on the lower left and right, respectively. The card backs, numbered in the upper left corner, have Dolphins Tips in a box, with the Dolphins logo at the top. The sponsors are listed at the bottom of the card backs.

		NM/M
Complete Set (16):		18.50
Common Player:		.70
1	Duriel Harris	.70
2	Bob Kuechenberg	.70
3	Don Bessillieu	.70
4	Gerald Small	.70
5	David Woodley	1.25
6	Don McNeal	.70
7	Nat Moore	1.50
8	A.J. Duhe	1.25
9	Glenn Blackwood	.70
10	Don Strock	1.50
11	Doug Betters	.70
12	George Roberts	.70
13	Bob Baumhower	1.25
14	Kim Bokamper	.70
15	Tony Nathan	1.50
16	Don Shula (CO)	4.50

1982 Dolphins Police

Measuring 2-5/8" x 4-1/8", the 16-card set is anchored by a color photo on the front, with the player's name and number in the upper left corner. His position and college are located in a stripe above the photo. The Kiwanis logo is in the lower right. The card fronts are bordered in orange and aqua. The card backs, numbered in the lower right, showcase Dolphins Tips inside a box, with the Dolphins logo in the upper right. The sponsors names are listed in the lower left.

		NM/M
Complete Set (16):		25.00
Common Player:		1.00
1	Don Shula (CO) (SP)	10.00
2	Uwe Von Schamann (SP)	5.00
3	Jimmy Cefalo	1.50
4	Andra Franklin	1.50
5	Larry Gordon	1.00
6	Nat Moore	1.75
7	Bob Baumhower	1.25
8	A.J. Duhe	1.25
9	Tony Nathan	1.75
10	Glenn Blackwood	1.00
11	Don Strock	2.00
12	David Woodley	1.25
13	Kim Bokamper	1.00
14	Bob Kuechenberg	1.25
15	Duriel Harris	1.25
16	Ed Newman	1.00

1983 Dolphins Police

Measuring 2-5/8" x 4-1/8", the 16-card set is anchored by a photo on the front, with the player's name in the upper left and his position near the bottom of the photo. The cards are bordered in aqua and orange. The card backs, numbered in the lower right, feature Dolphins Tips, with the Dolphins logo in the upper right. The sponsors are listed at the bottom of the card back. The Kiwanis and Burger King logos both are printed inside the photo on the front of the cards.

		NM/M
Complete Set (16):		15.00
Common Player:		.50
1	Earnie Rhone	.50
2	Andra Franklin	.75
3	Eric Laakso	.50
4	Joe Rose	.50
5	David Woodley	1.00
6	Uwe Von Schamann	.50
7	Eddie Hill	.50
8	Bruce Hardy	.50
9	Woody Bennett	.50
10	Fulton Walker	.50
11	Lyle Blackwood	.50
12	A.J. Duhe	.75
13	Bob Baumhower	.75
14	Duriel Harris	.50
15	Bob Brudzinski	.50
16	Don Shula (CO)	3.00

1984 Dolphins Police

Measuring 2-5/8" x 4-1/8", the 17-card set is anchored by a photo on the front, with the player's number and name in the upper left and his position at the bottom center. Sponsor logos are printed in the two lower corners. The card backs, which are unnumbered, have a "Dolphins Say" safety tip, with the Dolphins logo in the upper right. The sponsors are listed at the bottom of the card backs. The Mark Clayton card was added to the set after it was released.

		NM/M
Complete Set (17):		30.00
Common Player:		.50
1	Bob Baumhower	.75
2	Doug Betters	.50
3	Glenn Blackwood	.50
4	Kim Bokamper	.50
5	Dolfan Denny (Mascot)	.50
6	A.J. Duhe	.75
7	Mark Duper	1.75
8	Jim Jensen	.50
9	Dan Marino	25.00
10	Don McNeal	.50
11	Nat Moore	1.00
12	Tony Nathan	1.00
13	Ed Newman	.50
14	Don Shula (CO)	2.00
15	Dwight Stephenson	.75
16	Fulton Walker	.50
17	Mark Clayton (SP)	4.00

1985 Dolphins Police

Measuring 2-5/8" x 4-1/8", the 16-card set is anchored by a large photo on the front, with the player's name, number and position listed at the bottom center. The Dolphins and Kiwanis logos are in the lower left and right, respectively. The card backs, which are numbered in the lower right, have a "Dolphins Say" safety tip, with the Dolphins logo in the upper right. The sponsors are printed at the bottom of the card backs.

		NM/M
Complete Set (16):		20.00
Common Player:		.50
1	William Judson	.50
2	Fulton Walker	.50
3	Mark Clayton	1.25
4	Lyle & Glenn Blackwood, Glenn Blackwood (Bruise Brothers)	.50
5	Dan Marino	12.00
6	Reggie Roby	.75
7	Doug Betters	.50
8	Jay Brophy	.50
9	Dolfan Denny (Mascot)	.50
10	Kim Bokamper	.50
11	Mark Duper	1.00
12	Nat Moore	.75
13	Mike Kozlowski	.50
14	Don Shula (CO)	1.50
15	Don McNeal	.50
16	Tony Nathan	.75

1986 Dolphins Police

Measuring 2-5/8" x 4-1/8", the 16-card set is anchored by a large photo on the front, with the player's name printed inside a stripe on the right, his number printed inside a helmet in the lower left and his position located inside a stripe in the lower right. Anon Anew and the Kiwanis logos are printed in the lower right, too. The card backs, which are numbered in the lower right, have a "Dolphins Say" safety tip, along with the sponsors names.

		NM/M
Complete Set (16):		15.00
Common Player:		.50
1	Dwight Stephenson	.75
2	Bob Baumhower	.50
3	Dolfan Denny (Mascot)	.50
4	Don Shula (CO)	1.50
5	Dan Marino	8.00
6	Tony Nathan	.75
7	Mark Duper	1.00
8	John Offerdahl	1.00
9	Fuad Reveiz	.50
10	Hugh Green	.50
11	Lorenzo Hampton	.50
12	Mark Clayton	1.50
13	Nat Moore	.75
14	Bob Brudzinski	.50
15	Reggie Roby	.50
16	T.J. Turner	.50

1987 Dolphins Holsum

The cards in this Miami Dolphins' set were available in Holsum Bread packages. The fronts have a color photo inside a green border and the backs feature basic player information.

		NM/M
Complete Set (22):		60.00
Common Player:		2.00
1	Bob Baumhower	3.00
2	Mark Brown	2.00
3	Mark Clayton	6.00
4	Mark Duper	4.00
5	Roy Foster	2.00
6	Hugh Green	3.00
7	Lorenzo Hampton	2.00
8	William Judson	2.00
9	George Little	2.00
10	Dan Marino	40.00
11	Nat Moore	3.00
12	Tony Nathan	3.00
13	John Offerdahl	4.00
14	James Pruitt	2.00
15	Fuad Reveiz	2.00
16	Dwight Stephenson	3.00
17	Glenn Blackwood	2.00
18	Bruce Hardy	2.00
19	Reggie Roby	2.00
20	Bob Brudzinski	2.00
21	Ron Jaworski	3.00
22	T.J. Turner	2.00

1987 Dolphins Police

Measuring 2-5/8" x 4-1/8", the 16-card set resembles the 1986 set in design. This time, however, the player's name is printed in a stripe on the left, with his position printed inside a stripe under the photo. The player's number is located inside a helmet on the lower right. The Kiwanis and Fair Oaks Hospital logos appear in the lower left. The card backs, which are numbered in the lower right, have a "Dolphins Say" safety message and the sponsors listed.

		NM/M
Complete Set (16):		20.00
Common Player:		.50
1	Joe Robbie (OWN)	.50
2	Glenn Blackwood	.50
3	Mark Duper	1.00
4	Fuad Reveiz	.50
5	Dolfan Denny (Mascot)	.50
6	Dwight Stephenson (SP)	5.00
7	Hugh Green	.50
8	Larry Csonka (All-Time Great)	3.00
9	Bud Brown	.50
10	Don Shula (CO)	1.50
11	T.J. Turner	.50
12	Reggie Roby	.50
13	Dan Marino	10.00
14	John Offerdahl	.75
15	Bruce Hardy	.50
16	Lorenzo Hampton	.50

1988 Dolphins Holsum

The standard sized cards in this 12-card set showcase the Holsum logo in the upper left corner, with "1988 Annual Collectors' Edition" printed in the upper right. The player's name and team are printed inside a rectangle at the bottom of the card, beneath the player's photo. The card backs, numbered "of 12," have the player's facsimile autograph at the top and his number, bio and stats printed underneath inside a box. Cards were available in specially marked packages of Holsum Bread.

		NM/M
Complete Set (12):		30.00
Common Player:		1.50
1	Mark Clayton	3.00
2	Dwight Stephenson	2.00
3	Mark Duper	2.00
4	John Offerdahl	2.00
5	Dan Marino	20.00
6	T.J. Turner	1.50
7	Lorenzo Hampton	1.50
8	Bruce Hardy	1.50
9	Fuad Reveiz	1.50
10	Reggie Roby	1.50
11	William Judson	1.50
12	Bob Brudzinski	1.50

1995 Dolphins Chevron Pin Cards

Each 3" x 5" card in this eight-card set featured a pin at the bottom. The unnumbered cards were part of a Chevron promotion. The card fronts have the player's name and position at the top, with his photo and Dolphins logo underneath. The Chevron logo is next to the pin at the bottom of the card. The card backs have the player's name, number, bio, highlights and a checklist.

		NM/M
Complete Set (8):		20.00
Common Player:		2.00
1	Miami Dolphins	2.00
2	Dan Marino	10.00
3	Bryan Cox	2.00
4	Troy Vincent	2.00
5	Irving Fryar	2.00
6	Eric Green	2.00
7	Team '95	2.00
8	Hall of Famers	3.00

1996 Dolphins AT&T Set

Fans who attended the Miami Dolphins home season finale were rewarded for their fan appreciation by receiving a photo album card set of the team, sponsored by AT&T. The booklet features Zach Thomas, Dan Marino and the team picture on the cover. The 24-card perforated set, which is standard size, has the player's name vertically along the left side and position along the bottom. The player's number and Dolphins logo appear along the side of the position. The AT&T logo is printed in the top left corner. The backs feature a color profile, as well as personal and career stats. The cards are numbered with the player's jersey numbers.

		NM/M
Complete Set (24):		15.00
Common Player:		.25
---	Jimmy Johnson	1.00
13	Dan Marino	6.00
17	Jason Kidd	.25
22	Shawn Wooden	.25
25	Louis Oliver	.25
27	Terrell Buckley	.50
33	Karim Abdul-Jabbar	2.00
36	Stanley Pritchett	.25
38	Calvin Jackson	.25
50	Dwight Hollier	.25
54	Zach Thomas	1.00
55	Chris Singleton	.25
61	Tim Ruddy	.25
62	Chris Gray	.25
69	Keith Sims	.25
76	James Brown	.25
78	Richmond Webb	.25
80	Fred Barnett	.50
81	O.J. McDuffie	1.00
84	Troy Drayton	.50
92	Daryl Gardner	.25
93	Trace Armstrong	.25
95	Tim Bowens	.25
96	Daniel Stubbs	.25

1996 Dolphins Miami Subs Cards/Coins

The Dolphins and Miami Subs Restaurants produced this 9-card, 9-coin set. The cards front features a color player photo and the backs have the card set checklist. The coins have the player's likeness on one side and the Dolphins logo on the other. The coins are unnumbered. A cardboard holder featuring five Dolphins was produced to hold the set.

		NM/M
Complete Set (18):		20.00
Complete Card Set (9):		10.00
Complete Coin Set (9):		10.00
Common Card (CA1-CA9):		.75
Common Coin (CO1-CO9):		.75
CA1	Dan Marino	6.00
CA2	Larry Csonka	1.50
CA3	Pete Stoyanovich	.75
CA4	Paul Warfield	1.50
CA5	Bernie Kosar	.75
CA6	Mark Clayton	.75
CA7	Fred Barnett	.75
CA8	Nat Moore	1.00
CA9	Don Shula, George Allen Super Bowl VII	2.00
CO1	Fred Barnett	.75
CO2	Mark Clayton	.75
CO3	Larry Csonka	1.50
CO4	Bernie Kosar	.75
CO5	Dan Marino	6.00
CO6	Nat Moore	1.00
CO7	Pete Stoyanovich	.75
CO8	Paul Warfield	1.50
CO9	Super Bowl VII Trophy gold coin	1.25
---	Dan Marino, Jimmy Johnson, Bernie Kosar, Mark Clayton, Fred Barnett,Pete Stoyanovic h Display Holder	1.50

1997 Dolphins Score

1	Dan Marino	
2	Troy Drayton	
3	O.J. McDuffie	
4	Karim Abdul-Jabbar	
5	Terrell Buckley	
6	Stanley Pritchett	
7	Jerris McPhail	
8	Fred Barnett	
9	Zach Thomas	
10	Daryl Gardener	
11	Tim Bowens	
12	Shawn Wooden	
13	Richmond Webb	
14	Lamar Thomas	
15	Craig Erickson	

1991 Domino's Quarterbacks

Upper Deck produced 50-card sets of NFL Quarterback cards in conjunction with a national promotion kicked off during the Aug. 3 NBC telecast of "NFL Quarterback Challenge". The set was sponsored by Dominos, sold in foil packs and feature 32 active quarterbacks, 14 retired quarterbacks and three multi-player cards. Cards were produced especially for this promotion and were distributed through the 5,000 Domino's stores across the country. Each franchise initially received 2,500 packs or two cases of 1,250. Stores could order additional packs in cases of 1,250 or 500. Stores could also order sets.

		NM/M
Complete Set (50):		6.00
Common Player:		.05
1	Chris Miller	.05
2	Jim Kelly	.20
3	Jim Harbaugh	.10
4	Boomer Esiason	.10
5	Bernie Kosar	.10
6	Troy Aikman	1.00
7	John Elway	.50
8	Rodney Peete	.05
9	Andre Ware	.05
10	Anthony Dilweg	.05
11	Warren Moon	.10
12	Jeff George	.10
13	Jim Everett	.05
14	Jay Schroeder	.05
15	Wade Wilson	.05
16	Dan Marino	1.50
17	Phil Simms	.05
18	Jeff Hostetler	.05
19	Ken O'Brien	.05
20	Timm Rosenbach	.05
21	Bubby Brister	.05
22	Steve DeBerg	.05
23	Randall Cunningham	.10
24	Steve Walsh	.10
25	Billy Joe Tolliver	.05
26	Steve Young	.50
27	Dave Krieg	.05
28	Dan McGwire	.05
29	Vinny Testaverde	.10
30	Stan Humphries	.10
31	Mark Rypien	.05
32	Terry Bradshaw	.75
33	John Brodie	.10
34	Len Dawson	.10
35	Dan Fouts	.25
36	Otto Graham	.50
37	Bob Griese	.25
38	Sonny Jurgensen	.20
39	Daryle Lamonica	.20
40	Archie Manning	.20
41	Jim Plunkett	.10
42	Bart Starr	.40
43	Roger Staubach	.75
44	Joe Theismann	.25
45	Y.A. Tittle	.20
46	Johnny Unitas	.50
47	Troy Aikman, Roger Staubach Cowboy Gunslingers	.75
48	Bubby Brister, Terry Bradshaw Cajun Connection	.30
49	Dan Marino, Bob Griese Dolphin Duo	.75
50	Checklist Card	.05

1995 Donruss Red Zone

Cards for this game were available in both 80-card starter decks and 12-card booster packs. The 336-card set has the game logo in red on the backs of the cards. The cards were unnumbered.

NM/M
Complete Set (336): 225.00
Common DP Player: .05
Common Player: .30
Common SP Player: 1.00
1 Michael Bankston .30
2 Larry Centers .30
3 Ben Coleman (DP) .05
4 Ed Cunningham (DP) .05
5 Garrison Hearst .75
6 Eric Hill .30
7 Lorenzo Lynch (DP) .05
8 Clyde Simmons (DP) .05
9 Eric Swann .30
10 Aeneas Williams (SP) 1.50
11 Chris Doleman .30
12 Bert Emanuel (DP) .30
13 Roman Fortin (DP) .05
14 Jeff George (SP) 1.00
15 Craig Heyward (DP) .05
16 D.J. Johnson (SP) 1.00
17 Terance Mathis (SP) 2.00
18 Clay Matthews (DP) .05
19 Kevin Ross (DP) .05
20 Jessie Tuggle (DP) .05
21 Bob Whitfield (SP) 1.00
22 Cornelius Bennett (SP) 1.50
23 Russell Copeland (DP) .05
24 John Fina (SP) 1.00
25 Carwell Gardner (DP) .05
26 Henry Jones (DP) .05
27 Jim Kelly (SP) 3.00
28 Mark Maddox (DP) .05
29 Glenn Parker .30
30 Andre Reed (SP) 2.00
31 Bruce Smith (SP) 2.00
32 Thomas Smith (DP) .05
33 Joe Cain (DP) .05
34 Mark Carrier .30
35 Curtis Conway (DP) .30
36 Al Fontenot (DP) .05
37 Jeff Graham (DP) .05
38 Raymont Harris (DP) .05
39 Andy Heck .30
40 Erik Kramer (DP) .10
41 Vinson Smith .30
42 Lewis Tillman (DP) .05
43 Steve Walsh .30
44 James Williams (DP) .05
45 Donnell Woolford (SP) 1.00
46 Mike Brim (DP) .05
47 Tony McGee (DP) .05
48 Carl Pickens 1.00
49 Keith Rucker (DP) .05
50 Darnay Scott (SP) 2.00
51 Dan Wilkinson (DP) .10
52 Darryl Williams (DP) .05
53 Derrick Alexander (WR) .50
54 Carl Banks (DP) .05
55 Rob Burnett (SP) 1.00
56 Earnest Byner .30
57 Steve Everitt (DP) .05
58 Leroy Hoard (SP) 1.50
59 Michael Jackson (DP) .10
60 Pepper Johnson .30
61 Tony Jones .30
62 Antonio Langham .30
63 Anthony Pleasant (DP) .05
64 Vinny Testaverde (DP) .10
65 Eric Turner (SP) 1.50
66 Tommy Vardell .30
67 Troy Aikman (SP) 6.00
68 Larry Brown .30
69 Dixon Edwards (DP) .05
70 Charles Haley (SP) 2.00
71 Michael Irvin (SP) 3.00
72 Daryl Johnston (DP) .10
73 Leon Lett .30
74 Nate Newton .30
75 Jay Novacek (SP) 2.00
76 Darrin Smith .30
77 Kevin Smith .30
78 Tony Tolbert (DP) .05
79 Mark Tuinei (SP) 1.50
80 Kevin Williams (DP) .10
81 Darren Woodson .30
82 Elijah Alexander .30
83 Steve Atwater .30
84 Rod Bernstine (SP) 1.50
85 Ray Crockett .30
86 Shane Dronett (DP) .05
87 John Elway (SP) 8.00
88 Simon Fletcher .30
89 Brian Habib (DP) .05
90 Glyn Milburn .30
91 Anthony Miller (SP) 3.00
92 Mike Pritchard (DP) .10
93 Shannon Sharpe .60
94 Gary Zimmerman (DP) .05
95 Bennie Blades .30
96 Lomas Brown (SP) 1.50
97 Mike Johnson (DP) .05
98 Robert Massey (DP) .05
99 Scott Mitchell (DP) .10
100 Herman Moore (SP) 2.00
101 Brett Perriman .60
102 Barry Sanders (SP) 6.00
103 Tracy Scroggins (DP) .05
104 Chris Spielman .30
105 Doug Widell (SP) 1.50
106 Edgar Bennett (SP) 1.00
107 LeRoy Butler (DP) .05
108 Harry Galbreath (DP) .05
109 Sean Jones (SP) 1.00
110 George Koonce (DP) .05
111 Anthony Morgan (DP) .05
112 Ken Ruettgers (DP) .05
113 Fred Strickland (DP) .05
114 George Teague .30
115 Reggie White (SP) 2.00
116 Micheal Barrow .30
117 Blaine Bishop (DP) .05
118 Gary Brown .30
119 Ray Childress .30
120 Kenny Davidson (SP) 1.00
121 Cris Dishman (SP) 1.50
122 Brad Hopkins (SP) 1.00
123 Haywood Jeffires (DP) .05
124 Eddie Robinson (DP) .05
125 Al Smith (DP) .05
126 David Williams (SP) 1.00
127 Tony Bennett (SP) 1.50
128 Ray Buchanan (SP) 1.00
129 Quentin Coryatt (DP) .05
130 Eugene Daniel (DP) .05
131 Sean Dawkins (DP) .05
132 Marshall Faulk (SP) 5.00
133 Jim Harbaugh .60
134 Jeff Herrod (DP) .05
135 Kirk Lowdermilk (DP) .05
136 Tony Siragusa (DP) .05
137 Floyd Turner (DP) .05
138 Will Wolford (SP) 1.50
139 Marcus Allen .75
140 Kimble Anders (SP) 1.00
141 Steve Bono (DP) .40
142 Dale Carter (DP) .05
143 Mark Collins (DP) .05
144 Willie Davis .30
145 Lake Dawson (DP) .20
146 Tim Grunhard (DP) .05
147 Greg Hill (DP) .10
148 George Jamison (DP) .05
149 Darren Mickell (DP) .05
150 Will Shields (DP) .05
151 Tracy Simien (DP) .05
152 Neil Smith (SP) 1.00
153 Tim Bowens (DP) .05
154 J.B. Brown (DP) .05
155 Keith Byars .30
156 Bryan Cox .30
157 Jeff Cross .30
158 Irving Fryar (SP) 1.00
159 Ron Heller .30
160 Terry Kirby (SP) 1.50
161 Dan Marino (SP) 6.00
162 O.J. McDuffie .60
163 Bernie Parmalee (DP) .05
164 Chris Singleton (DP) .05
165 Troy Vincent (SP) 1.50
166 Richmond Webb (SP) 1.50
167 Roy Barker (DP) .05
168 Cris Carter (DP) .10
169 Jack Del Rio (SP) 1.50
170 Chris Hinton (DP) .05
171 Qadry Ismail .60
172 Amp Lee .30
173 Ed McDaniel .30
174 Randall McDaniel (DP) .05
175 Warren Moon (SP) 1.00
176 John Randle (SP) 1.00
177 Jake Reed (DP) .10
178 Robert Smith (DP) .10
179 Todd Steussie (DP) .05
180 DeWayne Washington (DP) .05
181 Bruce Armstrong (DP) .05
182 Drew Bledsoe 3.00
183 Vincent Brisby (DP) .05
184 Vincent Brown (DP) .05
185 Ben Coates (SP) 2.00
186 Sam Gash (DP) .05
187 Myron Guyton (DP) .05
188 Maurice Hurst (SP) 1.00
189 Mike Jones (DP) .05
190 Bob Kratch (DP) .05
191 Chris Slade (SP) 1.00
192 Derek Brown (DP) .05
193 Vince Buck (DP) .05
194 Jim Dombrowski (DP) .05
195 Quinn Early (DP) .05
196 Jim Everett .30
197 Michael Haynes (DP) .05
198 Wayne Martin (SP) 1.00
199 Lorenzo Neal (DP) .05
200 William Roaf (SP) 1.50
201 Irv Smith (DP) .05
202 Jimmy Spencer (DP) .05
203 Winfred Tubbs (DP) .05
204 Renaldo Turnbull (SP) 1.00
205 Michael Brooks (DP) .05
206 Dave Brown (DP) .05
207 Chris Calloway .30
208 Jesse Campbell (DP) .05
209 John Elliott (DP) .05
210 Keith Hamilton (DP) .05
211 Rodney Hampton (DP) .10
212 Corey Miller (DP) .05
213 Doug Riesenberg (DP) .05
214 Mike Sherrard .30
215 Phillippi Sparks .30
216 Michael Strahan (DP) .05
217 Richie Anderson (DP) .05
218 Brad Baxter (DP) .05
219 Tony Casillas (DP) .05
220 Roger Duffy .30
221 Boomer Esiason (DP) .10
222 Aaron Glenn (DP) .05
223 Bobby Houston (DP) .05
224 Mo Lewis (SP) 1.50
225 Siupeli Malamala (DP) .05
226 Johnny Mitchell (DP) .05
227 Eddie Anderson (DP) .05
228 Jerry Ball (DP) .05
229 Greg Biekert .30
230 Tim Brown (SP) 3.00
231 Rob Fredrickson (DP) .05
232 Nolan Harrison .30
233 Jeff Hostetler (DP) .10
234 Rocket Ismail (SP) 2.00
235 Terry McDaniel (SP) 1.00
236 Chester McGlockton (SP) 1.00
237 Don Mosebar .30
238 Anthony Smith .30
239 Harvey Williams (DP) .05
240 Steve Wisniewski (DP) .05
241 Fred Barnett .30
242 Randall Cunningham .30
243 William Fuller (SP) 1.00
244 Charlie Garner .30
245 Vaughn Hebron (DP) .05
246 Lester Holmes .30
247 Greg Jackson (SP) 1.00
248 Bill Romanowski (DP) .05
249 William Thomas (SP) 1.00
250 Bernard Williams .30
251 Calvin Williams (DP) .05
252 Michael Zordich (SP) 1.00
253 Chad Brown (SP) 2.00
254 Dermontti Dawson (DP) .05
255 Kevin Greene (SP) 3.00
256 Charles Johnson .60
257 Carnell Lake .30
258 Greg Lloyd (SP) 3.00
259 Neil O'Donnell (DP) .10
260 Ray Seals (DP) .05
261 Leon Searcy (SP) 1.00
262 Yancey Thigpen (DP) 1.00
263 John L. Williams (DP) .05
264 Rod Woodson (SP) 3.00
265 Stan Brock .30
266 Courtney Hall .30
267 Ronnie Harmon .30
268 Dwayne Harper (DP) .05
269 Rodney Harrison (DP) .05
270 Stan Humphries (DP) .20
271 Shawn Jefferson .30
272 Shawn Lee .30
273 Tony Martin .75
274 Natrone Means (SP) 1.00
275 Chris Mims (SP) 1.00
276 Leslie O'Neal (SP) 1.00
277 Junior Seau (SP) 3.00
278 Mark Seay (DP) .10
279 Harry Swayne (DP) .05
280 Eric Davis .30
281 William Floyd .75
282 Merton Hanks (SP) 1.00
283 Brent Jones .30
284 Tim McDonald (DP) .05
285 Ken Norton (SP) 1.00
286 Gary Plummer (DP) .05
287 Jerry Rice (SP) 6.00
288 Dana Stubblefield (SP) 1.00
289 John Taylor (SP) 1.50
290 Bryant Young (DP) .10
291 Steve Young (SP) 5.00
292 Steve Wallace (SP) 1.00
293 Sam Adams (DP) .05
294 Robert Blackmon (DP) .05
295 Jeff Blackshear (DP) .05
296 Brian Blades .30
297 Howard Ballard (SP) 1.00
298 Cortez Kennedy (DP) .05
299 Rick Mirer .75
300 Eugene Robinson (DP) .05
301 Chris Warren (SP) 1.00
302 Terry Wooden (SP) 1.00
303 Johnny Bailey .30
304 Isaac Bruce (DP) .75
305 Shane Conlan (DP) .05
306 Troy Drayton (DP) .05
307 Sean Gilbert (DP) .05
308 Leo Goeas (DP) .05
309 Jessie Hester .30
310 Clarence Jones .30
311 Todd Lyght .30
312 Chris Miller (DP) .05
313 Toby Wright (DP) .05
314 Robert Young (DP) .05
315 Eric Curry (DP) .05
316 Trent Dilfer .75
317 Thomas Everett (DP) .05
318 Paul Gruber (DP) .05
319 Jackie Harris (DP) .05
320 Courtney Hawkins (DP) .05
321 Lonnie Marts (DP) .05
322 Tony Mayberry (DP) .05
323 Martin Mayhew (DP) .05
324 Hardy Nickerson (DP) .05
325 Errict Rhett (DP) .50
326 Reggie Brooks (DP) .05
327 Tom Carter (DP) .05
328 Henry Ellard (SP) 1.50
329 Darrell Green (SP) 1.50
330 Ken Harvey (SP) 1.00
331 James Jenkins (DP) .05
332 Tim Johnson (DP) .05
333 Jim Lachey .30
334 Brian Mitchell .30
335 Heath Shuler 1.00
336 Tony Woods (DP) .05

1996 Donruss

This 250-card set marks the debut of Donruss football cards. The base brand includes 10 Rated Rookies, a subset made popular in the Donruss baseball sets. Each card front has a full-bleed color action photo, with a banner at the top in the team's primary color containing the player's name. The Donruss logo is stamped in silver in the upper left corner. A football, using team colors, is at the bottom of the card, with the position along the top and the team name below. A star in the middle of the football contains a team logo. The horizontal back has the player's position in the upper left corner, with the player's name running in a team-colored banner along the top. Career totals and stats from 1995 are below this information, followed by a brief recap of the player's accomplishments underneath. The background is a team logo. The right side of the card has a number in the upper corner, with a photograph below. Biographical information is in a stripe along the bottom. There were 240 of the cards also produced as a parallel Press Proof set. Each card, numbered 1 of 2,000, has a helmet die-cut in it. The Donruss logo is stamped in gold foil, which is also used for the words "First 2,000 Printed" and "Press Proof" toward the bottom. Insert sets include Hit List, Stop Action, What If?, Will to Win and Silver and Gold Elite cards.

NM/M
Complete Set (240): 20.00
Common Player: .05
Minor Stars: .10
Gold Press Proof Cards: 5X-10X
Hobby Pack (11): 1.50
Hobby Wax Box (18): 20.00
Retail Pack (16): 1.75
Retail Wax Box (24): 30.00
Magazine Pack (5): 1.25
Magazine Wax Box (48): 40.00
1 Barry Sanders 1.25
2 Flipper Anderson .05
3 Ben Coates .05
4 Rob Johnson .05
5 Rodney Hampton .05
6 Desmond Howard .05
7 Craig Heyward .05
8 Alvin Harper .05
9 Todd Collins .05
10 Ken Norton Jr. .05
11 Stan Humphries .05
12 Aeneas Williams .05
13 Jeff Hostetler .05
14 Frank Sanders .05
15 J.J. Birden .05
16 Bryce Paup .05
17 Bill Brooks .05
18 Kevin Williams .05
19 Boomer Esiason .05
20 O.J. McDuffie .05
21 Eric Swann .05
22 Neil Smith .05
23 Charlie Garner .05
24 Greg Lloyd .05
25 Willie Jackson .05
26 Shawn Jefferson .05
27 Rodney Peete .05
28 Michael Westbrook .50
29 J.J. Stokes .50
30 Troy Aikman 1.00
31 Sean Dawkins .05
32 Larry Centers .05
33 Herschel Walker .05
34 Stoney Case .05
35 Kevin Greene .05
36 Quinn Early .05
37 Fred Barnett .05
38 Andre Coleman .05
39 Mark Chmura .25
40 Adrian Murrell .05
41 Roosevelt Potts .05
42 Jay Novacek .05
43 Derrick Alexander .05
44 Ken Dilger .05
45 Rob Moore .05
46 Cris Carter .05
47 Jeff Blake .50
48 Derek Loville .05
49 Tyrone Wheatley .05
50 Terrell Fletcher .05
51 Sherman Williams .05
52 Justin Armour .05
53 Kordell Stewart 1.00
54 Tim Brown .05
55 Kevin Carter .05
56 Andre Rison .05
57 James Stewart .05
58 Brent Jones .05
59 Erik Kramer .05
60 Floyd Turner .05
61 Ricky Watters .05
62 Hardy Nickerson .05
63 Aaron Craver .05
64 Dave Krieg .05
65 Warren Moon .05
66 Wayne Chrebet .05
67 Napoleon Kaufman .10
68 Terance Mathis .05
69 Chad May .05
70 Andre Reed .05
71 Reggie White .10
72 Brett Favre 2.00
73 Chris Zorich .05
74 Kerry Collins .30
75 Herman Moore .30
76 Yancey Thigpen .50
77 Glenn Foley .05
78 Quentin Coryatt .05
79 Terry Kirby .05
80 Edgar Bennett .05
81 Mark Brunell .75
82 Heath Shuler .05
83 Gus Frerotte .05
84 Deion Sanders .50
85 Calvin Williams .05
86 Junior Seau .10
87 Jim Kelly .10
88 Daryl Johnston .05
89 Irving Fryar .05
90 Brian Blades .05
91 Willie Davis .05
92 Jerome Bettis .10
93 Marcus Allen .10
94 Jeff Graham .05
95 Rick Mirer .05
96 Harvey Williams .05
97 Steve Atwater .05
98 Carl Pickens .10
99 Darick Holmes .05
100 Bruce Smith .05
101 Vinny Testaverde .05
102 Thurman Thomas .10
103 Drew Bledsoe .75
104 Bernie Parmalee .05
105 Greg Hill .05
106 Steve McNair .50
107 Andre Hastings .05
108 Eric Metcalf .05
109 Kimble Anders .05
110 Steve Tasker .05
111 Mark Carrier .05
112 Jerry Rice 1.00
113 Joey Galloway .75
114 Robert Smith .05
115 Hugh Douglas .05
116 Willie McGinest .05
117 Terrell Davis .75
118 Cortez Kennedy .05
119 Marshall Faulk .50
120 Michael Haynes .05
121 Isaac Bruce .50
122 Brian Mitchell .05
123 Bryan Cox .05
124 Tamarick Vanover .50
125 William Floyd .05
126 Chris Chandler .05
127 Carnell Lake .05
128 Aaron Bailey .05
129 Darnay Scott .20
130 Darren Woodson .05
131 Ernie Mills .05
132 Charles Haley .05
133 Rocket Ismail .05
134 Bert Emanuel .05
135 Lake Dawson .05
136 Jake Reed .05
137 Dave Brown .05
138 Steve Bono .05
139 Terry Allen .05
140 Errict Rhett .20
141 Rod Woodson .05
142 Charles Johnson .05
143 Emmitt Smith 2.00
144 Ki-Jana Carter .40
145 Garrison Hearst .05
146 Rashaan Salaam .50
147 Tony Boselli .05
148 Derrick Thomas .05
149 Mark Seay .05
150 Derrick Alexander .05
151 Christian Fauria .05
152 Aaron Hayden .05
153 Chris Warren .10
154 Dave Meggett .05
155 Jeff George .10
156 Jackie Harris .05
157 Michael Irvin .10
158 Scott Mitchell .05
159 Trent Dilfer .05
160 Kyle Brady .05
161 Dan Marino 2.00
162 Curtis Martin 1.50
163 Mario Bates .05
164 Erric Pegram .05
165 Eric Zeier .05
166 Rodney Thomas .05
167 Neil O'Donnell .05
168 Warren Sapp .05
169 Jim Harbaugh .10
170 Henry Ellard .05
171 Anthony Miller .05
172 Derrick Moore .05
173 John Elway .50
174 Vincent Brisby .05
175 Antonio Freeman .05
176 Chris Sanders .30
177 Steve Young .75
178 Shannon Sharpe .05
179 Brett Perriman .05
180 Orlando Thomas .05
181 Eric Bjornson .05
182 Natrone Means .05
183 Jim Everett .05
184 Curtis Conway .05
185 Robert Brooks .10
186 Tony Martin .05
187 Mark Carrier .05
188 LeShon Johnson .05
189 Bernie Kosar .05
190 Ray Zellars .05
191 Steve Walsh .05
192 Craig Erickson .05
193 Tommy Maddox .05
194 Leslie O'Neal .05
195 Harold Green .05
196 Steve Beuerlein .05
197 Ron Moore .05
198 Leslie Shepherd .05
199 Leroy Hoard .05
200 Michael Jackson .05
201 Will Moore .05
202 Ricky Ervins .05
203 Keith Jennings .05
204 Eric Green .05
205 Mark Rypien .05
206 Torrance Small .05
207 Sean Gilbert .05
208 *Mike Alstott* 1.50
209 Willie Anderson .05
210 Alex Molden .05
211 Jonathan Ogden .05
212 Stepfret Williams .05
213 *Jeff Lewis* .50
214 Regan Upshaw .05
215 Daryl Gardener .05
216 *Danny Kanell* .50
217 John Mobley .05
218 Reggie Brown .05
219 *Mushin Muhammad* .75
220 *Kevin Hardy* .25
221 *Stanley Pritchett* .40
222 Cedric Jones .05
223 Marco Battaglia .05
224 Duane Clemons .05
225 Jerald Moore .05
226 *Simeon Rice* .30
227 Chris Darkins .10
228 *Bobby Hoying* .50
229 *Stephen Davis* 2.00
230 *Walt Harris* .30
231 Jermain Mayberry .05
232 Tony Brackens .05
233 *Eric Moulds* 2.00
234 *Alex Van Dyke* .50
235 *Marvin Harrison* 4.00
236 *Rickey Dudley* .50
237 *Terrell Owens* 3.00
238 Jerry Rice CL Checklist .25
239 Dan Marino CL Checklist .30
240 Checklist .05

1996 Donruss Press Proofs

Press Proofs paralleled the 240-card regular-issue set, and included the words "Press Proof" in gold foil on the front of the card, along with a die-cut. Each Gold Press Proof was numbered 1 of 2,000.

NM/M
Complete Set (240): 300.00
Press Proof Cards: 3X-5X

1996 Donruss Elite

Donruss' initial football set continues the legacy of an Elite insert set, which debuted in the company's baseball line in 1991. Ten of the NFL's premiere running backs are featured on two versions of the foil-enhanced card - Silver Elite and Gold Elite. The Silver cards are limited to 10,000 each; the Gold ones are sequentially numbered to 2,000. The card front uses the corresponding color for the foiled borders around the picture, plus the Donruss and Elite logos. The card back uses the appropriate color for the background, which has a scripted Elite "E" and a short player profile on the left side. The right side has a color photo with a team logo underneath. The card number is along the top of the card.

		NM/M
Complete Set (20):		60.00
Common Player:		1.00
Comp. Gold Set (20):		
Gold Cards:		2X
1	Emmitt Smith	10.00
2	Barry Sanders	10.00
3	Marshall Faulk	3.00
4	Curtis Martin	5.00
5	Junior Seau	1.00
6	Troy Aikman	6.00
7	Steve Young	6.00
8	Dan Marino	10.00
9	Brett Favre	10.00
10	John Elway	10.00
11	Kerry Collins	2.00
12	Drew Bledsoe	6.00
13	Jerry Rice	8.00
14	Keyshawn Johnson	6.00
15	Deion Sanders	3.00
16	Isaac Bruce	3.00
17	Rashaan Salaam	1.00
18	Tim Biakabutuka	1.00
19	Lawrence Phillips	1.00
20	Robert Brooks	1.00

1996 Donruss Elite Gold

Donruss Elite Golds run parallel with the Elite Silvers, but are numbered up to 2,000. In this insert, the silver foil is replaced by gold foil.

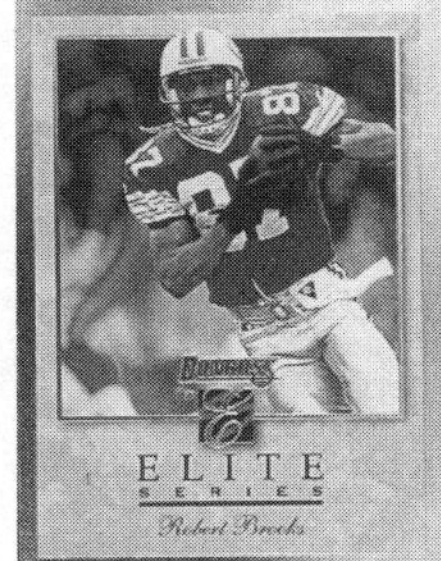

	NM/M
Gold Cards:	2X

1996 Donruss Hit List

These 1996 Donruss insert cards feature the NFL's most physical players on cards which use silver holographic foil and die-cutting for the design. The front has a color photo, with a holographic background. "Hit List" is written at the top of the card; Donruss and the player's team name are below the photo. The sides of the card are die-cut, with foiled rivets in them. The card back has a color photo on it, with most of it, except for the player's face, ghosted as the background. The player's face is in full color, highlighted by a sunburst around it. There's a paragraph below which details a moment when the player survived, or delivered, a devastating hit. A serial number appears in a white rectangle along the bottom. The card number is in the upper right corner.

		NM/M
Complete Set (20):		60.00
Common Player:		.50
1	Bruce Smith	.50
2	Barry Sanders	6.00
3	Kevin Hardy	.50
4	Greg Lloyd	.50
5	Brett Favre	6.00
6	Emmitt Smith	6.00
7	Kerry Collins	1.00
8	Ken Norton Jr.	.50
9	Steve Atwater	.50
10	Curtis Martin	4.00
11	Chris Warren	.50
12	Steve Young	4.00
13	Marshall Faulk	2.00
14	Junior Seau	.50
15	Lawrence Phillips	.50
16	Troy Aikman	4.00
17	Jerry Rice	5.00
18	Dan Marino	6.00
19	Reggie White	1.00
20	John Elway	6.00

1996 Donruss Rated Rookies

In a concept first made popular with its baseball line, Donruss has issued this 10-card insert set honoring 10 of the top NFL newcomers.

		NM/M
Complete Set (10):		20.00
Common Player:		1.00
1	Keyshawn Johnson	3.00
2	Terry Glenn	3.00
3	Tim Biakabutuka	2.00
4	Bobby Engram	1.00
5	Leeland McElroy	1.00
6	Eddie George	5.00
7	Lawrence Phillips	1.00
8	Derrick Mayes	1.00
9	Karim Abdul-Jabbar	1.00
10	Eddie Kennison	2.00

1996 Donruss What If?

These 1996 Donruss inserts go back in time to chronicle the NFL's top talents with a post-dated rookie card. Each card uses rookie photography, with a design that fits the era that the player entered the league. Each card also has a sequential serial number. Cards were in hobby packs only.

		NM/M
Complete Set (10):		60.00
Common Player:		2.00
1	Troy Aikman	6.00
2	Jerry Rice	6.00
3	Barry Sanders	8.00
4	Drew Bledsoe	5.00
5	Deion Sanders	2.00
6	Brett Favre	8.00
7	Dan Marino	8.00
8	Steve Young	7.00
9	Emmitt Smith	8.00
10	John Elway	6.00

1996 Donruss Stop Action

1996 Donruss football magazine packs have these Stop Action inserts, which feature some of the best action photos in the sport. Each shot is enhanced by holographic foil and die-cutting. Each card is serial numbered to 5,000.

		NM/M
Complete Set (10):		50.00
Common Player:		1.00
1	Deion Sanders	2.00
2	Troy Aikman	6.00
3	Brett Favre	8.00
4	Steve Young	4.00
5	Joey Galloway	1.00
6	Dan Marino	8.00
7	Jerry Rice	6.00
8	Emmitt Smith	8.00
9	Isaac Bruce	3.00
10	Barry Sanders	8.00

1996 Donruss Will to Win

These inserts are exclusive to 1996 Donruss retail packs only. The cards, having sequential numbering to 5,000, are one of the scarcest inserts in the product. They feature some of the NFL's grittiest competitors.

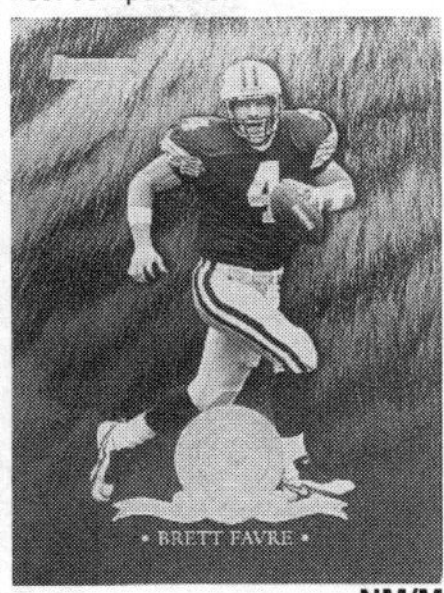

		NM/M
Complete Set (10):		50.00
Common Player:		1.00
1	Emmitt Smith	8.00
2	Brett Favre	8.00
3	Curtis Martin	4.00
4	Jerry Rice	6.00
5	Barry Sanders	8.00
6	Errict Rhett	1.00
7	Troy Aikman	6.00
8	Dan Marino	8.00
9	Steve Young	4.00
10	John Elway	6.00

1997 Donruss

The 230-card set features a full-bleed photo on the front. The Donruss logo is in the upper left. The team name is printed vertically in the lower left, while the team logo and player position are in the lower left corner. The player's name is to the right of the team logo. The base set is paralleled with a Press Proofs set, which are numbered "1 of 1,500," and Press Proofs - First 500, which are numbered "1 of 500" and die-cut with gold foil.

		NM/M
Complete Set (230):		20.00
Common Player:		.05
Minor Stars:		.10
Silvers:		5X-8X
Golds:		8X-15X
Pack (10):		1.25
Wax Box (24):		20.00
1	Dan Marino	1.50
2	Brett Favre	1.75
3	Emmitt Smith	1.50
4	Eddie George	1.25
5	Karim Abdul-Jabbar	.50
6	Terrell Davis	1.00
7	Curtis Martin	1.00
8	Drew Bledsoe	.75
9	Jerry Rice	.75
10	Troy Aikman	.75
11	Barry Sanders	1.25
12	Mark Brunell	.75
13	Kerry Collins	.30
14	Steve Young	.50
15	Kordell Stewart	.75
16	Eddie Kennison	.40
17	Terry Glenn	.75
18	John Elway	.50
19	Joey Galloway	.30
20	Deion Sanders	.40
21	Keyshawn Johnson	.40
22	Lawrence Phillips	.10
23	Ricky Watters	.10
24	Marvin Harrison	.40
25	Bobby Engram	.10
26	Marshall Faulk	.10
27	Carl Pickens	.10
28	Isaac Bruce	.15
29	Herman Moore	.15
30	Jerome Bettis	.10
31	Rashaan Salaam	.10
32	Errict Rhett	.10
33	Tim Biakabutuka	.10
34	Robert Brooks	.10
35	Antonio Freeman	.30
36	Steve McNair	.50
37	Jeff Blake	.10
38	Tony Banks	.30
39	Terrell Owens	.50
40	Eric Moulds	.05
41	Leeland McElroy	.10
42	Chris Sanders	.05
43	Thurman Thomas	.10
44	Bruce Smith	.05
45	Reggie White	.10
46	Chris Warren	.05
47	J.J. Stokes	.05
48	Ben Coates	.05
49	Tim Brown	.05
50	Marcus Allen	.10
51	Michael Irvin	.10
52	William Floyd	.05
53	Ken Dilger	.05
54	Bobby Taylor	.05
55	Keenan McCardell	.05
56	Raymont Harris	.05
57	Keith Byars	.05
58	O.J. McDuffie	.05
59	Robert Smith	.05
60	Bert Emanuel	.05
61	Rick Mirer	.05
62	Vinny Testaverde	.05
63	Kyle Brady	.05
64	Mark Bruener	.05
65	Neil O'Donnell	.05
66	Anthony Johnson	.05
67	Ken Norton	.05
68	Warren Sapp	.05
69	Amani Toomer	.05
70	Simeon Rice	.05
71	Kevin Hardy	.05
72	Junior Seau	.05
73	Neil Smith	.05
74	LeShon Johnson	.05
75	Quinn Early	.05
76	Andre Reed	.05
77	Jake Reed	.05
78	Elvis Grbac	.05
79	Tyrone Wheatley	.05
80	Adrian Murrell	.05
81	Fred Barnett	.05
82	Darrell Green	.05
83	Stan Humphries	.05
84	Troy Drayton	.05
85	Steve Atwater	.05
86	Quentin Coryatt	.05
87	Dan Wilkinson	.05
88	Scott Mitchell	.05
89	Willie McGinest	.05
90	Kevin Smith	.05
91	Gus Frerotte	.05
92	Bam Morris	.05
93	Darick Holmes	.05
94	Zach Thomas	.20
95	Tom Carter	.05
96	Cortez Kennedy	.05
97	Kevin Williams	.05
98	Michael Haynes	.05
99	Lamont Warren	.05
100	Jeff Graham	.05
101	Alex Van Dyke	.05
102	Jim Everett	.05
103	Chris Chandler	.05
104	Qadry Ismail	.05
105	Ray Zellars	.05
106	Chris T. Jones	.05
107	Charlie Garner	.05
108	Bobby Hoying	.05
109	Mark Chmura	.05
110	Cris Carter	.05
111	Darnay Scott	.05
112	Anthony Miller	.05
113	Desmond Howard	.05
114	Terance Mathis	.05
115	Rodney Hampton	.05
116	Napoleon Kaufman	.05
117	Jim Harbaugh	.05
118	Shannon Sharpe	.05
119	Irving Fryar	.05
120	Garrison Hearst	.05
121	Terry Allen	.05
122	Larry Centers	.05
123	Sean Dawkins	.05
124	Jeff George	.05
125	Tony Martin	.05
126	Mike Alstott	.10
127	Rickey Dudley	.05
128	Kevin Carter	.05
129	Derrick Alexander	.05
130	Greg Lloyd	.05
131	Bryce Paup	.05
132	Derrick Thomas	.05
133	Greg Hill	.05
134	Jamal Anderson	.05
135	Curtis Conway	.05
136	Frank Sanders	.05
137	Brett Perriman	.05
138	Edgar Bennett	.05
139	Wayne Chrebet	.05
140	Natrone Means	.05
141	Eric Metcalf	.05
142	Trent Dilfer	.05
143	Terry Kirby	.05
144	Johnnie Morton	.05
145	Dale Carter	.05
146	Michael Westbrook	.05
147	Stanley Pritchett	.05
148	Todd Collins	.05
149	Tamarick Vanover	.05
150	Kevin Greene	.05
151	Lamar Lathon	.05
152	Muhsin Muhammad	.05
153	Dorsey Levens	.10
154	Rod Woodson	.05
155	Brent Jones	.05
156	Michael Jackson	.05
157	Shawn Jefferson	.05
158	Kimble Anders	.05
159	Sean Gilbert	.05
160	Carnell Lake	.05
161	Darren Woodson	.05
162	Dave Meggett	.05
163	Henry Ellard	.05
164	Eric Swann	.05
165	Tony Boselli	.05
166	Daryl Johnston	.05
167	Willie Jackson	.05
168	Wesley Walls	.05
169	Mario Bates	.05
170	Lake Dawson	.05
171	Mike Mamula	.05
172	Ed McCaffrey	.05
173	Tony Brackens	.05
174	Craig Heyward	.05
175	Harvey Williams	.05
176	Dave Brown	.05
177	Aaron Glenn	.05
178	Jeff Hostetler	.05
179	Alvin Harper	.05
180	Ty Detmer	.05
181	James Jett	.05
182	James Stewart	.05
183	Warren Moon	.05
184	Herschel Walker	.05
185	Ki-Jana Carter	.05
186	Leslie O'Neal	.05
187	Danny Kanell	.05
188	Eric Bjornson	.05
189	Alex Molden	.05
190	Bryant Young	.05
191	Merton Hanks	.05
192	Heath Shuler	.05
193	Brian Blades	.05
194	Steve Bono	.05
195	Wayne Simmons	.05
196	*Warrick Dunn*	1.25
197	*Peter Boulware*	.10
198	*David LaFleur*	.50
199	*Shawn Springs*	.40
200	*Reidel Anthony*	.50
201	*Jim Druckenmiller*	.50
202	*Orlando Pace*	.40
203	*Yatil Green*	.50
204	*Bryant Westbrook*	.10
205	*Tiki Barber*	2.00
206	*James Farrior*	.10
207	*Rae Carruth*	.25
208	*Danny Wuerffel*	.50
209	*Corey Dillon*	3.00
210	*Ike Hilliard*	1.00
211	*Tony Gonzalez*	1.00
212	*Antowain Smith*	1.25
213	*Pat Barnes*	.50
214	*Troy Davis*	.50
215	*Byron Hanspard*	.50
216	*Joey Kent*	.40
217	*Jake Plummer*	1.00
218	*Kenny Holmes*	.10
219	*Darnell Autry*	.25
220	*Darrell Russell*	.10
221	*Walter Jones*	.10
222	*Dwayne Rudd*	.10
223	*Tom Knight*	.10
224	*Kevin Lockett*	.20
225	*Will Blackwell*	.20
226	Dan Marino CL	.75
227	Brett Favre CL	1.00
228	Emmitt Smith CL	.75
229	Barry Sanders CL	.50
230	Jerry Rice CL	.30

1997 Donruss Press Proof Silvers

Silver Press Proofs were a parallel set to the 230-card Donruss set in 1997. Silver Press Proofs have silver foil added to the front in streaks throughout the card, which originate from the bottom left corner. The words "Press Proof" are printed up the right side in silver foil. Card backs contain a "1 of 1,500" line printed just below the player's name.

Silver Cards:	3X-8X

1997 Donruss Press Proof Golds

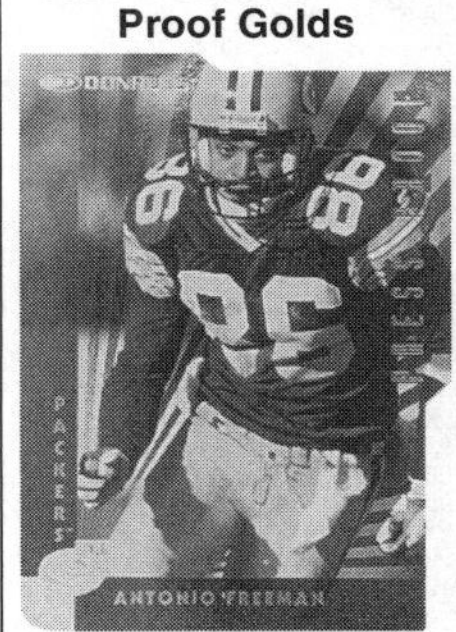

Gold Press Proofs were a parallel to the 230-card Donruss set in 1997. Gold Press Proofs were die-cut across the top and right side and had rounded corners in the bottom left corner. Fronts featured gold foil streaks across the front that originated in the bottom left corner. The words "Press Proof" are printed in gold up the right side of the card, while the backs are numbered "1 of 500" under the player's name.

Gold Cards:	8X-15X

1997 Donruss Elite

The 20-card chase set is featured on Silver and Gold foil cards. The Silver Elite is numbered to 5,000, while the Gold version was produced in an edition of 2,000 sets.

		NM/M
Complete Set (20):		125.00
Common Player:		3.00
Minor Stars:		5.00
Production 5,000 Sets		
Gold Cards:		2X
Production 2,000 Sets		
1	Emmitt Smith	15.00
2	Dan Marino	15.00
3	Brett Favre	15.00
4	Curtis Martin	6.00
5	Terrell Davis	8.00
6	Barry Sanders	12.00
7	Drew Bledsoe	8.00
8	Mark Brunell	8.00
9	Troy Aikman	8.00
10	Jerry Rice	12.00
11	Steve McNair	8.00
12	Kerry Collins	8.00
13	John Elway	12.00
14	Eddie George	6.00
15	Karim Abdul-Jabbar	4.00
16	Kordell Stewart	6.00
17	Jerome Bettis	3.00
18	Terry Glenn	6.00
19	Errict Rhett	3.00
20	Carl Pickens	3.00

1997 Donruss Legends of the Fall

The 10-card chase set is numbered to 10,000 and features artwork from artist Dan Gardiner. The first 500 of the cards were printed directly on actual canvas.

		NM/M
Complete Set (10):		60.00
Common Player:		3.00
Canvas Cards:		1X-3X
1	Troy Aikman	8.00
2	Barry Sanders	12.00
3	John Elway	10.00
4	Dan Marino	12.00
5	Emmitt Smith	12.00
6	Jerry Rice	10.00
7	Deion Sanders	4.00
8	Brett Favre	12.00
9	Marcus Allen	3.00
10	Steve Young	6.00

1997 Donruss Passing Grade

The 16-card hobby-exclusive set is styled like a report card. The die-cut insert showcases the talents of the top quarterbacks. It utilizes a card-within-a-card design with red-foil stamping. Each football shaped, die-cut card came in its own envelope. The cards are numbered to 3,000.

NM/M
Complete Set (16): 75.00
Common Player: 2.00
Minor Stars: 8.00
Production 3,000 Sets
1 Steve Young 6.00
2 Drew Bledsoe 6.00
3 Mark Brunell 6.00
4 Kerry Collins 4.00
5 Steve McNair 5.00
6 John Elway 10.00
7 Ty Detmer 2.00
8 Jeff Blake 2.00
9 Dan Marino 14.00
10 Kordell Stewart 4.00
11 Tony Banks 4.00
12 Brett Favre 14.00
13 Gus Frerotte 2.00
14 Troy Aikman 12.00
15 Jeff George 2.00
16 Brad Johnson 4.00

1997 Donruss Rated Rookies

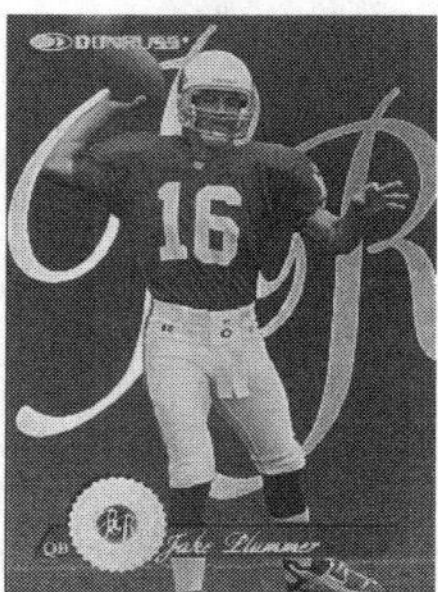

The 10-card chase set features a rookie player, with the Rated Rookies logo in the lower left corner. The set was paralleled by a Medalist micro-etched, all foil set with gold-foil holographic stamping.

NM/M
Complete Set (10): 25.00
Common Player: 1.00
Medalist Cards: 2X-5X
1 Ike Hilliard 4.00
2 Warrick Dunn 5.00
3 Yatil Green 1.00
4 Jim Druckenmiller 1.00
5 Rae Carruth 1.00
6 Antowain Smith 4.00
7 Tiki Barber 4.00
8 Byron Hanspard 1.00
9 Reidel Anthony 2.00
10 Jake Plummer 5.00

1997 Donruss Zoning Commission

The 20-card retail-exclusive set is printed on micro-etched, holographic foil card stock, with gold-foil stamping. The cards are numbered to 5,000.

NM/M
Complete Set (20): 100.00
Common Player: 2.00
Minor Stars: 5.00
1 Brett Favre 20.00
2 Jerry Rice 15.00
3 Jerome Bettis 5.00
4 Troy Aikman 15.00
5 Drew Bledsoe 12.00
6 Natrone Means 2.00
7 Steve Young 12.00
8 John Elway 12.00
9 Barry Sanders 15.00
10 Emmitt Smith 15.00
11 Curtis Martin 6.00
12 Terry Allen 2.00
13 Dan Marino 15.00
14 Mark Brunell 6.00
15 Terry Glenn 2.00
16 Herman Moore 2.00
17 Ricky Watters 2.00
18 Terrell Davis 8.00
19 Isaac Bruce 6.00
20 Curtis Conway 2.00

1997 Donruss Preferred

The inaugural issue of Donruss Preferred Football contained 150 cards which were divided into four different tiers, with 80 Bronze, 40 Silver, 20 Gold and 10 Platinum cards. The cards are printed on all-foil, micro-etched surfaces and contain an action shot of the player, with his name and team across the bottom and "Donruss Preferred" and the word bronze, silver, gold or platinum across the top. There is also a white star in each corner of the card within the color border. Preferred also had a Cut to the Chase parallel set, as well as Chain Reaction, Staremaster and Precious Metals insert sets. Another interesting facet of this product is that it arrived in collectible tins, of which, there were 24 different players featured. The tins were packed into larger Hobby Master Tins for hobby accounts and came in boxes to retail accounts.

NM/M
Complete Set (150): 425.00
Complete Bronze (80): 35.00
Common Bronze: .25
Minor Bronze Star: .50
Common Silver: 2.00
Minor Silver Star: 4.00
Inserted 1:5
Common Gold: 4.00
Minor Gold Star: 8.00
Inserted 1:17
Common Platinum: 10.00
1 Emmitt Smith P 30.00
2 Steve Young G 10.00
3 Cris Carter S 4.00
4 Tim Biakabutuka B .25
5 Brett Favre P 30.00
6 Troy Aikman G 12.00
7 Eddie Kennison S 2.00
8 Ben Coates B .25
9 Dan Marino P 30.00
10 Deion Sanders G 8.00
11 Curtis Conway S 2.00
12 Jeff George S 2.00
13 Barry Sanders P 30.00
14 Kerry Collins G 8.00
15 Marvin Harrison S 4.00
16 Bobby Engram B .25
17 Jerry Rice P 20.00
18 Kordell Stewart G 10.00
19 Tony Banks S 4.00
20 Jim Harbaugh B .25
21 Mark Brunell P 15.00
22 Steve McNair G 10.00
23 Terrell Owens S 8.00
24 Raymont Harris B .25
25 Curtis Martin P 12.00
26 Karim Abdul-Jabbar G 4.00
27 Joey Galloway S 4.00
28 Bobby Hoying B .25
29 Terrell Davis P 30.00
30 Terry Glenn G 8.00
31 Antonio Freeman S 4.00
32 Brad Johnson B 1.00
33 Drew Bledsoe P 15.00
34 John Elway G 25.00
35 Herman Moore G 8.00
36 Robert Brooks S 2.00
37 Rod Smith B .50
38 Eddie George P 15.00
39 Keyshawn Johnson G 8.00
40 Greg Hill S 2.00
41 Scott Mitchell B .25
42 Muhsin Muhammad B .75
43 Isaac Bruce G 10.00
44 Jeff Blake S 4.00
45 Neil O'Donnell B .25
46 Jimmy Smith B .75
47 Jerome Bettis G 8.00
48 Terry Allen S 2.00
49 Andre Reed B .50
50 Frank Sanders B .50
51 Tim Brown G 8.00
52 Thurman Thomas S 4.00
53 Heath Shuler B .25
54 Vinny Testaverde B .75
55 Marcus Allen S 4.00
56 Napoleon Kaufman B .75
57 Derrick Alexander B .25
58 Carl Pickens G 4.00
59 Marshall Faulk S 5.00
60 Mike Alstott B 1.00
61 Jamal Anderson B 2.00
62 Ricky Watters G 8.00
63 Dorsey Levens S 4.00
64 Todd Collins B .25
65 Trent Dilfer B .50
66 Natrone Means S 4.00
67 Gus Frerotte B .25
68 Irving Fryar B .25
69 Adrian Murrell S 2.00
70 Rodney Hampton B .25
71 Garrison Hearst B .50
72 Reggie White S 4.00
73 Anthony Johnson B .25
74 Tony Martin B .25
75 Chris Sanders S 2.00
76 O.J. McDuffie B .50
77 Leeland McElroy B .25
78 Ki-Jana Carter S 2.00
79 Anthony Miller B .25
80 Johnnie Morton B .25
81 Robert Smith S 4.00
82 Brett Perriman B .25
83 Errict Rhett B .50
84 Michael Irvin S 4.00
85 Darnay Scott B .50
86 Shannon Sharpe B .50
87 Lawrence Phillips S 2.00
88 Bruce Smith B .25
89 James Stewart B 1.00
90 J.J. Stokes B .50
91 Chris Warren B .25
92 Daryl Johnston B .25
93 Andre Rison B .50
94 Rashaan Salaam B .50
95 Amani Toomer B .50
96 *Warrick Dunn G* 20.00
97 *Tiki Barber S* 8.00
98 *Peter Boulware B* 1.00
99 *Ike Hilliard G* 12.00
100 *Antowain Smith S* 8.00
101 *Yatil Green S* 2.00
102 *Tony Gonzalez B* 5.00
103 *Reidel Anthony G* 12.00
104 *Troy Davis S* 2.00
105 *Rae Carruth S* 2.00
106 *David LaFleur B* 1.00
107 *Jim Druckenmiller G* 10.00
108 *Joey Kent S* 2.00
109 *Byron Hanspard S* 5.00
110 *Darrell Russell B* 1.00
111 *Danny Wuerffel S* 4.00
112 *Jake Plummer S* 15.00
113 *Jay Graham B* 1.00
114 *Corey Dillon S* 12.00
115 *Orlando Pace B* 1.00
116 *Pat Barnes S* 4.00
117 *Shawn Springs B* 1.00
118 Troy Aikman B (National Treasures) 2.00
119 Drew Bledsoe B (National Treasures) 2.00
120 Mark Brunell B (National Treasures) 2.00
121 Kerry Collins B (National Treasures) .50
122 Terrell Davis B (National Treasures) 3.00
123 Jerome Bettis B (National Treasures) .50
124 Brett Favre B (National Treasures) 4.00
125 Eddie George B (National Treasures) 2.00
126 Terry Glenn B (National Treasures) .50
127 Karim Abdul-Jabbar B (National Treasures) .25
128 Keyshawn Johnson B (National Treasures) .50
129 Dan Marino B (National Treasures) 4.00
130 Curtis Martin B (National Treasures) 1.00
131 Natrone Means B (National Treasures) .25
132 Herman Moore S (National Treasures) 2.00
133 Jerry Rice B (National Treasures) 2.00
134 Barry Sanders B (National Treasures) 4.00
135 Deion Sanders B (National Treasures) .50
136 Emmitt Smith B (National Treasures) 3.00
137 Kordell Stewart B (National Treasures) 1.00
138 Steve Young B (National Treasures) 1.50
139 Carl Pickens S (National Treasures) 2.00
140 Isaac Bruce S (National Treasures) 3.00
141 Steve McNair S (National Treasures) 5.00
142 John Elway S (National Treasures) 8.00
143 Cris Carter B (National Treasures) .50
144 Tim Brown B (National Treasures) .50
145 Ricky Watters S (National Treasures) .50
146 Robert Brooks B (National Treasures) .25
147 Jeff Blake B (National Treasures) .25
148 Tiki Barber CL B .50
149 Jim Druckenmiller CLB .50
150 Warrick Dunn CL B 1.00

1997 Donruss Preferred Tins

Each pack of Donruss Preferred arrived for sale in a collectible tin, with 24 different players each featured on their own tin. The 24 tins arrived in five different varieties: smaller blue pack tins were the "base" tins; silver pack tins were in hobby exclusive boxes and were numbered to 1,200; gold pack tins were also available in hobby box tins and numbered to 300; blue box tins were hobby exclusive and contained 24 smaller tins - these were numbered to 1,200 and essentially the same as the smaller blue tins except in size; and gold box tins, which were parallel to the larger blue box tins, but printed in gold and numbered to 300. The larger box tins were only available to hobby accounts. Retail accounts received the tins packed in cardboard boxes.

NM/M
Complete Blue Pack (24): 20.00
Common Pack: .25
Complete Silver Pack (24):
Silver Pack Tins: 2X-5X
Complete Blue Box (24):
Blue Box Tins: 1X-3X
Complete Gold Pack (24):
Gold Pack Tins: 3X-8X
Complete Gold Box (24):
Gold Box Tins: 3X-6X
1 Mark Brunell 1.00
2 Karim Abdul-Jabbar .50
3 Terry Glenn .75
4 Brett Favre 2.00
5 Troy Aikman 1.00
6 Eddie George 1.50
7 John Elway .75
8 Steve Young .75
9 Terrell Davis 1.00
10 Kordell Stewart 1.00
11 Drew Bledsoe 1.00
12 Kerry Collins .75
13 Dan Marino 2.00
14 Tim Brown .25
15 Carl Pickens .25
16 Warrick Dunn 1.50
17 Herman Moore .25
18 Curtis Martin .75
19 Ike Hilliard .50
20 Barry Sanders 1.25
21 Deion Sanders .50
22 Emmitt Smith 2.00
23 Keyshawn Johnson .25
24 Jerry Rice 1.00

1997 Donruss Preferred Chain Reaction

This 24-card insert set captured 12 different offensive teammates on die-cut cards that linked together in order to display them side by side. The insert was printed on thick plastic stock with holographic treatments and sequentially numbered to 3,000.

NM/M
Complete Set (24): 150.00
Common Player: 2.00
Minor Stars: 5.00
1a Dan Marino 15.00
1b Karim Abdul-Jabbar 2.00
2a Troy Aikman 12.00
2b Emmitt Smith 15.00
3a Steve McNair 6.00
3b Eddie George 6.00
4a Brett Favre 15.00
4b Robert Brooks 2.00
5a John Elway 12.00
5b Terrell Davis 8.00
6a Drew Bledsoe 8.00
6b Curtis Martin 8.00
7a Steve Young 10.00
7b Jerry Rice 12.00
8a Mark Brunell 6.00
8b Natrone Means 2.00
9a Barry Sanders 15.00
9b Herman Moore 2.00
10a Kordell Stewart 5.00
10b Jerome Bettis 5.00
11a Jeff Blake 2.00
11b Carl Pickens 2.00
12a Lawrence Phillips 2.00
12b Isaac Bruce 5.00

1997 Donruss Preferred Cut To The Chase

Cut to the Chase paralleled the full 150-card set from Donruss Preferred. The base set was fractured into different colors corresponding to the base set and was also die-cut around the perimeter. Cut to the Chase bronze cards are one per seven packs, silvers are one per 63, golds are one per 189 and platinums are one per 756.

NM/M
Complete Set (150): 2,500
Complete Bronze (80): 300.00
Bronze Stars: 4X-8X
Bronze Rookies: 2X-4X
Complete Silver (40): 500.00
Silver Stars: 2X-4X
Silver Rookies: 1X-2X
Complete Gold (20): 600.00
Gold Cards: 1X-2X
Complete Platinum (10): 1,100
Platinum Cards: 2X-3X

1997 Donruss Preferred Precious Metals

Precious Metals was a 15-card partial parallel set that was printed on actual silver, gold or platinum corresponding to which color subset the base card was from. Only 100 individually numbered Precious Metals sets were produced.

NM/M
Common Player: 25.00
1 Drew Bledsoe 75.00
2 Curtis Martin 75.00
3 Troy Aikman 100.00
4 Eddie George 60.00
5 Warrick Dunn 50.00
6 Brett Favre 150.00
7 John Elway 100.00
8 Barry Sanders 150.00
9 Emmitt Smith 150.00
10 Terrell Davis 75.00
11 Mark Brunell 60.00
12 Jerry Rice 100.00
13 Dan Marino 150.00
14 Terry Glenn 25.00
15 Tiki Barber 25.00

1997 Donruss Preferred Staremasters

These horizontal cards were printed on all-foil card stock with holographic foil stamping. Card fronts featured two close-up photos of the player, with one in full color and the other within the foil background. There were 1,500 sequentially numbered sets of Staremaster produced.

NM/M
Complete Set (24): 300.00
Common Player: 2.00
Minor Stars: 5.00
1 Tim Brown 5.00
2 Mark Brunell 8.00
3 Kerry Collins 8.00
4 Brett Favre 30.00
5 Eddie George 15.00
6 Terry Glenn 8.00
7 Dan Marino 30.00
8 Curtis Martin 12.00
9 Jerry Rice 25.00
10 Barry Sanders 30.00
11 Deion Sanders 6.00
12 Emmitt Smith 30.00
13 Drew Bledsoe 12.00
14 Troy Aikman 25.00
15 Tiki Barber 6.00
16 Terrell Davis 20.00
17 Karim Abdul-Jabbar 4.00
18 Warrick Dunn 8.00
19 John Elway 20.00
20 Yatil Green 5.00
21 Ike Hilliard 6.00
22 Kordell Stewart 8.00
23 Ricky Watters 2.00
24 Steve Young 20.00

1997 Studio

1997 Studio Football is a special Quarterback Club edition. The 36-card base set features the NFL Quarterback Club stars on 8x10 cards. Each player is captured in full-color portrait photography. The base set features 24 Studio Portraits and 12 Class of Distinction cards. Class of Distinction highlights 12 of the stars in an action shot. The parallel sets include Silver Portrait Proof (individually numbered to 4,000) and Gold Portrait Proof (numbered to 1,000). The insert sets were Red Zone Masterpieces and Stained Glass Stars.

NM/M
Complete Set (36): 40.00
Common Player: .50
Minor Stars: 1.00
Silver Proof Cards: 1X-3X
Gold Proof Cards: 3X-5X
Pack (2): 3.00
Wax Box (18): 45.00
1 Troy Aikman 3.00
2 Tony Banks 1.00
3 Jeff Blake 1.00
4 Drew Bledsoe 3.00
5 Mark Brunell 3.00
6 Kerry Collins 1.00
7 Trent Dilfer 1.00
8 John Elway 2.00
9 Brett Favre 6.00
10 Gus Frerotte .50
11 Jeff George .50
12 Neil O'Donnell .50
13 Jim Harbaugh .50
14 Michael Irvin 1.00
15 Dan Marino 5.00
16 Steve McNair 2.00
17 Rick Mirer .50
18 Jerry Rice 3.00
19 Barry Sanders 3.00
20 Junior Seau .50
21 Heath Shuler .50
22 Emmitt Smith 5.00
23 Kordell Stewart 3.00
24 Steve Young 2.00
25 Troy Aikman (Class of Distinction) 1.50
26 Drew Bledsoe (Class of Distinction) 1.50
27 Mark Brunell (Class of Distinction) 1.50
28 Kerry Collins (Class of Distinction) 1.00
29 John Elway (Class of Distinction) 1.00
30 Brett Favre (Class of Distinction) 3.00
31 Dan Marino (Class of Distinction) 2.50
32 Jerry Rice (Class of Distinction) 1.50
33 Barry Sanders (Class of Distinction) 2.00
34 Emmitt Smith (Class of Distinction) 2.50
35 Kordell Stewart (Class of Distinction) 1.50
36 Steve Young (Class of Distinction) 1.00

1997 Studio Portrait Proofs

Portrait Proofs was a 36-card parallel set to Studio Football, and arrived in gold and silver versions. The cards were identified by gold or silver prismatic foil running up both the left and right side of the card, and corresponding "Silver Press Proof" or "Gold Press Proof" written in silver or gold foil across the bottom. Gold Press Proofs were limited to 1,000 sets, while Silver Press Proofs were limited to 3,500 sets.

1997 Studio Red Zone Masterpiece

Red Zone Masterpieces features the 24 players in the base set on a canvas material card. Each card is individually numbered to 3,500.

NM/M
Complete Set (24): 125.00
Common Player: 2.00
Minor Stars: 4.00
1 Troy Aikman 10.00
2 Tony Banks 10.00
3 Jeff Blake 2.00
4 Drew Bledsoe 10.00
5 Mark Brunell 6.00
6 Kerry Collins 6.00
7 Trent Dilfer 4.00
8 John Elway 12.00
9 Brett Favre 15.00
10 Gus Frerotte 2.00
11 Jeff George 2.00
12 Elvis Grbac 2.00
13 Neil O'Donnell 2.00
14 Michael Irvin 4.00
15 Dan Marino 15.00
16 Steve McNair 6.00
17 Rick Mirer 2.00
18 Jerry Rice 12.00
19 Barry Sanders 15.00
20 Warren Moon 2.00
21 Heath Shuler 2.00
22 Emmitt Smith 15.00
23 Kordell Stewart 4.00
24 Steve Young 8.00

1997 Studio Stained Glass Stars

This 24-card insert features the QB Club stars on a die-cut plastic 8x10 card. Multi-color ink is used to give the appearance of stained glass. Stained Glass Stars are numbered to 1,000.

NM/M
Complete Set (24): 250.00
Common Player: 3.00
Minor Stars: 6.00
1 Troy Aikman 15.00
2 Tony Banks 3.00
3 Jeff Blake 3.00
4 Drew Bledsoe 15.00
5 Mark Brunell 10.00
6 Kerry Collins 6.00
7 Trent Dilfer 6.00
8 John Elway 15.00
9 Brett Favre 20.00
10 Gus Frerotte 3.00
11 Jeff George 3.00
12 Elvis Grbac 3.00
13 Jim Harbaugh 3.00
14 Michael Irvin 5.00
15 Dan Marino 20.00
16 Steve McNair 6.00
17 Rick Mirer 3.00
18 Jerry Rice 15.00
19 Barry Sanders 20.00
20 Junior Seau 3.00
21 Vinny Testaverde 3.00
22 Emmitt Smith 20.00
23 Kordell Stewart 6.00
24 Steve Young 12.00

1999 Donruss

This was a 200-card set that included 50 different rookie cards that were inserted 1:4 packs. Parallel sets included Career Stat Line and Season Stat Line. Other insert sets included: All-Time Gridiron Kings, All-Time Gridiron Kings Autographs, Elite Inserts, Executive Producers, Fan Club, Gridiron Kings, Private Signings, Rated

Rookies, Rookie Gridiron Kings, Zoning Commission and Zoning Commission Red. Packs contained seven cards.

		NM/M
Complete Set (200):		125.00
Common Player:		.15
Minor Stars:		.30
Common Rookie:		1.00
Inserted 1:4		
Pack (7):		1.75
Wax Box (24):		30.00
1	Jake Plummer	.75
2	Rob Moore	.30
3	Adrian Murrell	.15
4	Frank Sanders	.15
5	Jamal Anderson	.50
6	Tim Dwight	.50
7	Terance Mathis	.15
8	Chris Chandler	.30
9	Byron Hanspard	.15
10	Priest Holmes	.50
11	Jermaine Lewis	.15
12	Errict Rhett	.15
13	Doug Flutie	.75
14	Eric Moulds	.50
15	Antowain Smith	.50
16	Thurman Thomas	.30
17	Andre Reed	.30
18	Bruce Smith	.15
19	Tim Biakabutuka	.30
20	Rae Carruth	.15
21	Muhsin Muhammad	.30
22	Curtis Enis	.50
23	Curtis Conway	.30
24	Bobby Engram	.15
25	Corey Dillon	.50
26	Carl Pickens	.30
27	Jeff Blake	.30
28	Darnay Scott	.30
29	Ty Detmer	.15
30	Leslie Shepherd	.15
31	Emmitt Smith	1.50
32	Troy Aikman	1.00
33	Michael Irvin	.30
34	Deion Sanders	.50
35	Raghib Ismail	.15
36	John Elway	1.50
37	Terrell Davis	1.00
38	Ed McCaffrey	.50
39	Shannon Sharpe	.30
40	Rod Smith	.30
41	Bubby Brister	.30
42	Brian Griese	1.00
43	Barry Sanders	2.00
44	Charlie Batch	.75
45	Herman Moore	.50
46	Germane Crowell	.30
47	Johnnie Morton	.15
48	Ron Rivers	.15
49	Brett Favre	2.00
50	Antonio Freeman	.50
51	Dorsey Levens	.50
52	Mark Chmura	.30
53	Corey Bradford	.30
54	Bill Schroeder	.30
55	Peyton Manning	1.50
56	Marvin Harrison	.50
57	E.G. Green	.15
58	Fred Taylor	1.00
59	Mark Brunell	.75
60	Tavian Banks	.30
61	Jimmy Smith	.50
62	Keenan McCardell	.30
63	Warren Moon	.30
64	Derrick Alexander	.15
65	Bam Morris	.15
66	Elvis Grbac	.30
67	Andre Rison	.30
68	Dan Marino	1.50
69	Karim Abdul	.30
70	O.J. McDuffie	.30
71	Tony Martin	.15
72	Randy Moss	2.00
73	Cris Carter	.50
74	Randall Cunningham	.50
75	Robert Smith	.50
76	Jeff George	.50
77	Jake Reed	.30
78	Terry Allen	.30
79	Drew Bledsoe	.75
80	Terry Glenn	.50
81	Ben Coates	.30
82	Tony Simmons	.30
83	Cameron Cleeland	.30
84	Eddie Kennison	.15
85	Kerry Collins	.30
86	Ike Hilliard	.30
87	Gary Brown	.15
88	Joe Jurevicius	.15
89	Kent Graham	.15
90	Wayne Chrebet	.50
91	Keyshawn Johnson	.50
92	Curtis Martin	.50
93	Vinny Testaverde	.30
94	Tim Brown	.30
95	Napoleon Kaufman	.50
96	Charles Woodson	.50
97	Tyrone Wheatley	.30
98	Rich Gannon	.15
99	Charles Johnson	.15
100	Duce Staley	.50
101	Kordell Stewart	.50
102	Jerome Bettis	.50
103	Hines Ward	.30
104	Ryan Leaf	.30
105	Natrone Means	.30
106	Jim Harbaugh	.30
107	Junior Seau	.30
108	Mikhael Ricks	.15
109	Jerry Rice	1.00
110	Steve Young	.75
111	Garrison Hearst	.50
112	Terrell Owens	.75
113	Lawrence Phillips	.30
114	J.J. Stokes	.30
115	Sean Dawkins	.15
116	Derrick Mayes	.30
117	Joey Galloway	.50
118	Jon Kitna	.50
119	Ahman Green	.30
120	Ricky Watters	.30
121	Isaac Bruce	.50
122	Marshall Faulk	.50
123	Az-Zahir Hakim	.30
124	Warrick Dunn	.50
125	Mike Alstott	.50
126	Trent Dilfer	.30
127	Reidel Anthony	.30
128	Jacquez Green	.30
129	Warren Sapp	.15
130	Eddie George	.60
131	Steve McNair	.60
132	Kevin Dyson	.30
133	Yancey Thigpen	.30
134	Frank Wycheck	.15
135	Stephen Davis	.50
136	Brad Johnson	.50
137	Skip Hicks	.30
138	Michael Westbrook	.30
139	Darrell Green	.15
140	Albert Connell	.15
141	*Tim Couch*	3.00
142	*Donovan McNabb*	6.00
143	*Akili Smith*	2.00
144	*Edgerrin James*	6.00
145	*Ricky Williams*	3.00
146	*Torry Holt*	3.00
147	*Champ Bailey*	2.00
148	*David Boston*	3.00
149	*Andy Katzenmoyer*	2.00
150	*Chris McAlister*	2.00
151	*Daunte Culpepper*	6.00
152	*Cade McNown*	2.00
153	*Troy Edwards*	2.00
154	*Kevin Johnson*	2.00
155	*James Johnson*	2.00
156	*Rob Konrad*	2.00
157	*Jim Kleinsasser*	2.00
158	*Kevin Faulk*	2.00
159	*Joe Montgomery*	2.00
160	*Shaun King*	2.00
161	*Peerless Price*	2.50
162	*Michael Cloud*	2.00
163	*Jermaine Fazande*	2.00
164	*D'Wayne Bates*	2.00
165	*Brock Huard*	2.00
166	*Marty Booker*	2.00
167	*Karsten Bailey*	2.00
168	*Shawn Bryson*	1.50
169	*Jeff Paulk*	2.00
170	*Travis McGriff*	2.00
171	*Amos Zereoue*	2.00
172	*Craig Yeast*	1.50
173	*Joe Germaine*	2.00
174	*Dameane Douglas*	1.50
175	*Brandon Stokley*	1.50
176	*Larry Parker*	1.50
177	*Joel Makovicka*	2.00
178	*Wane McGarity*	1.50
179	*Na Brown*	1.50
180	*Cecil Collins*	2.00
181	*Nick Williams*	1.50
182	*Charlie Rogers*	1.50
183	*Darrin Chiaverini*	2.00
184	*Terry Jackson*	2.00
185	*De'Mond Parker*	2.00
186	*Sedrick Irvin*	2.00
187	*Mar Tay Jenkins*	2.00
188	*Kurt Warner*	5.00
189	*Michael Bishop*	2.00
190	*Sean Bennett*	2.00
191	Jamal Anderson CL	.30
192	Eric Moulds CL	.30
193	Terrell Davis CL	.75
194	John Elway CL	.75
195	Barry Sanders CL	1.00
196	Peyton Manning CL	.75
197	Fred Taylor CL	.50
198	Dan Marino CL	.75
199	Randy Moss CL	1.00
200	Terrell Owens CL	.30

1999 Donruss All-Time Gridiron Kings

This insert included five NFL legends. Each card was sequentially numbered to 1,000 and accented with bronze foil. The first 500 of each card was printed on canvas and was autographed.

		NM/M
Complete Set (5):		45.00
Common Player:		6.00
Production 1,000 Sets		
1	Bart Starr	10.00
2	Johnny Unitas	10.00
3	Earl Campbell	6.00
4	Walter Payton	20.00
5	Jim Brown	20.00

1999 Donruss All-Time Gridiron Kings Autographs

This was a parallel to the All-Time Gridiron Kings insert. Each of these singles was printed on canvas and was autographed. Each single was sequentially numbered to 500.

		NM/M
Complete Set (5):		600.00
Common Player:		60.00
Production 500 Sets		
1	Bart Starr	125.00
2	Johnny Unitas	125.00
3	Earl Campbell	60.00
4	Walter Payton	250.00
5	Jim Brown	150.00

1999 Donruss Elite Inserts

This 20-card insert set included the NFL's cream of the crop and featured them on foil board with micro-etching and silver foil stamping. Each card was sequentially numbered to 2,500.

		NM/M
Complete Set (20):		85.00
Common Player:		2.00
Production 2,500 Sets		
1	Cris Carter	2.00
2	Jerry Rice	6.00
3	Mark Brunell	4.00
4	Brett Favre	10.00
5	Keyshawn Johnson	2.00
6	Eddie George	3.00
7	John Elway	8.00
8	Troy Aikman	6.00
9	Marshall Faulk	2.00
10	Antonio Freeman	2.00
11	Drew Bledsoe	4.00
12	Steve Young	3.00
13	Dan Marino	8.00
14	Emmitt Smith	8.00
15	Fred Taylor	6.00
16	Jake Plummer	4.00
17	Terrell Davis	8.00
18	Peyton Manning	8.00
19	Randy Moss	10.00
20	Barry Sanders	10.00

1999 Donruss Executive Producers

This 45-card insert set included the top producers at quarterback, running back and wide receiver and highlighted each position on a different colored, holographic foil board. Each card was sequentially numbered to the player's specific 1998 stat.

		NM/M
Complete Set (45):		125.00
Common Player:		2.00
1	Dan Marino 3497	5.00
2	John Elway 2806	7.00
3	Kordell Stewart 2560	2.00
4	Troy Aikman 2330	5.00
5	Steve Young 4170	2.00
6	Doug Flutie 2711	3.00
7	Drew Bledsoe 3633	2.00
8	Jon Kitna 1177	3.00
9	Steve McNair 3228	2.00
10	Mark Brunell 2601	3.00
11	Randall Cunningham 3704	2.00
12	Jake Plummer 3737	3.00
13	Charlie Batch 2178	3.00
14	Peyton Manning 3739	5.00
15	Brett Favre 4212	6.00
16	Terrell Davis 2008	5.00
17	Fred Taylor 1223	5.00
18	Eddie George 1294	2.00
19	Corey Dillon 1130	2.00
20	Jamal Anderson 1846	2.00
21	Curtis Martin 1287	2.00
22	Dorsey Levens 378	3.00
23	Karim Abdul 960	2.00
24	Curtis Enis 497	3.00
25	Mike Alstott 846	2.00
26	Natrone Means 883	2.00
27	Jerome Bettis 1185	2.00
28	Warrick Dunn 1026	2.00
29	Emmitt Smith 1332	6.00
30	Barry Sanders 1491	10.00
31	Jerry Rice 1157	6.00
32	Randy Moss 1313	10.00
33	Keyshawn Johnson 1131	2.00
34	Isaac Bruce 457	3.00
35	Antonio Freeman 1424	2.00
36	Eric Moulds 1368	2.00
37	Tim Dwight 94	12.00
38	Herman Moore 983	2.00
39	Tim Brown 1012	2.00
40	Marshall Faulk 1319	2.00
41	Terry Glenn 792	2.00
42	Joey Galloway 1047	2.00
43	Carl Pickens 1023	2.00
44	Terrell Owens 1097	2.00
45	Cris Carter 1011	2.00

1999 Donruss Fan Club

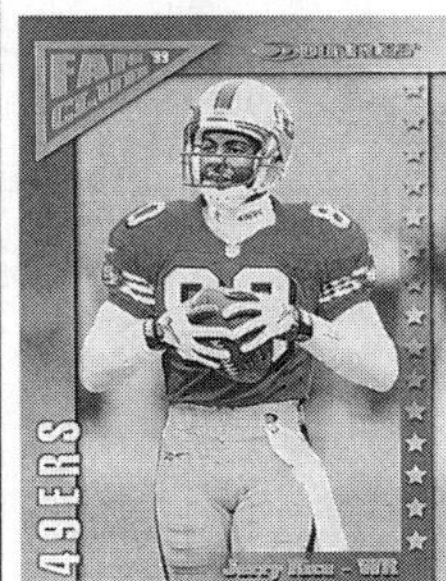

This 20-card insert set included players who were fan favorites. Each single was sequentially numbered to 5,000.

		NM/M
Complete Set (20):		40.00
Common Player:		1.00
Minor Stars:		2.00
Production 5,000 Sets		
1	Troy Aikman	4.00
2	Ricky Williams	6.00
3	Jerry Rice	5.00
4	Brett Favre	6.00
5	Terrell Davis	4.00
6	Doug Flutie	3.00
7	John Elway	5.00
8	Steve Young	3.00
9	Steve McNair	2.00
10	Kordell Stewart	2.00
11	Drew Bledsoe	3.00
12	Donovan McNabb	4.00
13	Dan Marino	6.00
14	Cade McNown	5.00
15	Vinny Testaverde	1.00
16	Jake Plummer	3.00
17	Randall Cunningham	2.00
18	Peyton Manning	5.00
19	Keyshawn Johnson	2.00
20	Barry Sanders	6.00

1999 Donruss Gridiron Kings

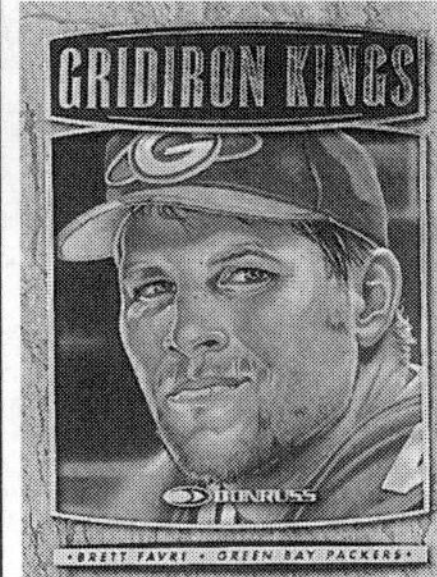

This 20-card insert set showcased artwork of each player. Singles were sequentially numbered to 5,000. A parallel Canvas version was also made with each of those singles numbered to 500.

		NM/M
Complete Set (20):		60.00
Common Player:		2.00
Production 5,000 Sets		
Canvas Cards:		3X
Production 500 Sets		
1	Randy Moss	8.00
2	Fred Taylor	4.00
3	Doug Flutie	2.00
4	Brett Favre	8.00
5	Mark Brunell	3.00
6	Troy Aikman	5.00
7	John Elway	6.00
8	Jerry Rice	6.00
9	Drew Bledsoe	4.00
10	Eddie George	2.00
11	Randall Cunningham	2.00
12	Emmitt Smith	6.00
13	Dan Marino	6.00
14	Jake Plummer	2.00
15	Jamal Anderson	2.00
16	Terrell Davis	4.00
17	Steve Young	3.00
18	Peyton Manning	5.00
19	Jerome Bettis	2.00
20	Barry Sanders	6.00

1999 Donruss Private Signings

This 32-card insert set included autographs from some of the top players in the NFL. More than 10,000 autographs were randomly inserted into packs. The print runs were between 50 and 600, depending on the player.

		NM/M
Complete Set (32):		1,200
Common Player:		12.50
Minor Stars:		25.00
1	Terrell Davis	75.00
2	Cris Carter	30.00
3	Thurman Thomas	25.00
4	Derrick Thomas	12.50
5	Priest Holmes	20.00
6	Corey Dillon	25.00
7	Antonio Freeman	25.00
8	Duce Staley	12.50
9	Jerome Bettis	12.50
10	Natrone Means	12.50
11	Mike Alstott	30.00
12	Eddie George	45.00
13	Terrell Owens	25.00
14	Curtis Enis	25.00
15	Wesley Walls	12.50
16	Neil Smith	12.50
17	Doug Flutie	45.00
18	Tim Brown	25.00
19	Randy Moss	125.00
20	Ricky Williams	100.00
21	Skip Hicks	12.50
22	Isaac Bruce	30.00
23	Barry Sanders	125.00
24	Fred Taylor	50.00
25	Steve Young	50.00
26	Vinny Testaverde	12.50
27	Randall Cunningham	25.00
28	Jake Plummer	50.00
29	Jerry Rice	100.00
30	Eric Moulds	25.00
31	Kordell Stewart	30.00
32	Brian Griese	35.00

1999 Donruss Rated Rookies

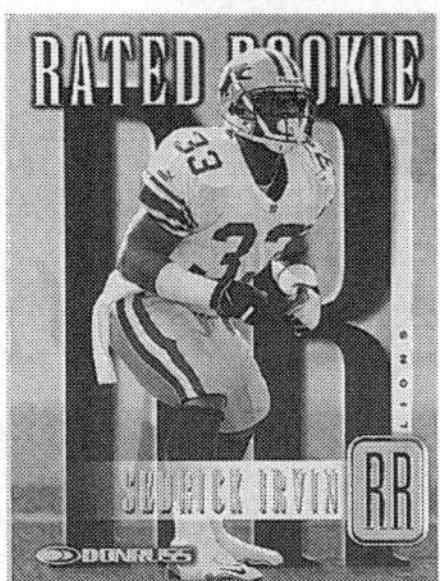

This 20-card insert set included rookies from 1999 and featured them on silver foil board. Each was sequentially numbered to 5,000. A parallel Medalist version was made in which the first 250 singles were sequentially numbered. Each was printed with gold foil instead of silver.

		NM/M
Complete Set (20):		60.00
Common Player:		2.00
Production 5,000 Sets		
Medalists Cards:		3X
Production 250 Sets		
1	Tim Couch	8.00
2	Peerless Price	4.00
3	Ricky Williams	10.00
4	Torry Holt	5.00
5	Champ Bailey	3.00
6	Rob Konrad	2.00
7	Donovan McNabb	8.00
8	Edgerrin James	8.00
9	David Boston	5.00
10	Akili Smith	2.00
11	Cecil Collins	2.00
12	Troy Edwards	3.00
13	Daunte Culpepper	8.00
14	Kevin Faulk	3.00
15	Kevin Johnson	3.00
16	Cade McNown	2.00
17	Shaun King	2.00
18	Brock Huard	2.00
19	James Johnson	2.00
20	Sedrick Irvin	2.00

1999 Donruss Rookie Gridiron Kings

This 10-card insert set included the top rookies from 1999. Each was sequentially numbered to 5,000 and included gold foil on the front of each card. The first 500 singles were printed on canvas stock.

		NM/M
Complete Set (10):		45.00
Common Player:		2.00
Production 5,000 Sets		
Canvas Cards:		3X
Production 500 Sets		

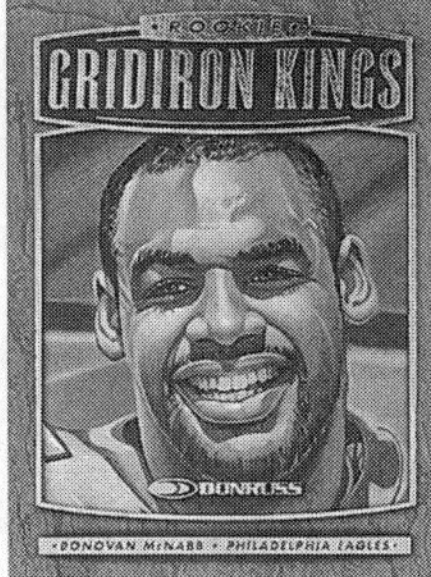

		NM/M
1	Ricky Williams	10.00
2	Donovan McNabb	8.00
3	Daunte Culpepper	8.00
4	Edgerrin James	8.00
5	David Boston	5.00
6	Champ Bailey	2.00
7	Torry Holt	4.00
8	Cade McNown	2.00
9	Akili Smith	2.00
10	Tim Couch	6.00

1999 Donruss Zoning Commission

This 25-card insert set included star players who patrol the end zone. Each die-cut single was sequentially numbered to 1,000. A parallel Red version was made in which each single was sequentially numbered to the player's 1998 touchdown total.

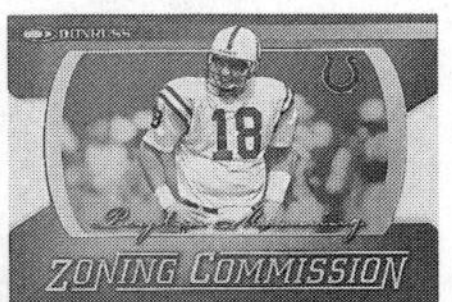

		NM/M
Complete Set (25):		50.00
Common Player:		1.00
Production 1,000 Sets		
1	Eric Moulds	1.00
2	Steve Young	2.00
3	Brad Johnson	1.00
4	Peyton Manning	6.00
5	Randy Moss	6.00
6	Brett Favre	6.00
7	Emmitt Smith	6.00
8	Mark Brunell	2.00
9	Keyshawn Johnson	1.00
10	Dan Marino	6.00
11	Eddie George	1.00
12	Drew Bledsoe	3.00
13	Terrell Davis	4.00
14	Terrell Owens	1.00
15	Barry Sanders	6.00
16	Curtis Martin	1.00
17	John Elway	5.00
18	Jake Plummer	2.00
19	Jerry Rice	5.00
20	Fred Taylor	4.00
21	Antonio Freeman	1.00
22	Marshall Faulk	1.00
23	Dorsey Levens	1.00
24	Steve McNair	1.00
25	Cris Carter	1.00

1999 Donruss Elite

This is a 200-card base set that includes 40 rookies. Cards #1-100 are printed on 20 point foil board with a foil stamped logo in red and full UV coating on both sides. They were inserted four-per-pack. Cards #101-200 are also printed on 20 point foil board with full UV coating and platinum blue tint on each side. They are found one-per-pack. Inserts include Common Threads, Field of Vision, Passing the Torch, Power Formulas and Primary Colors.

		NM/M
Complete Set (200):		175.00
Common Player (1-100):		.25

Minor Stars (1-100): .50
Common Player (101-200): .50
Minor Stars (101-200): 1.00
Common Rookie (161-200): 1.00
#101-200 Inserted 1:1
Pack (5): 7.50
Wax Box (18): 95.00

1 Warren Moon .50
2 Terry Allen .50
3 Jeff George .50
4 Brett Favre 3.00
5 Rob Moore .50
6 Bubby Brister .25
7 John Elway 2.50
8 Troy Aikman 1.50
9 Steve McNair .75
10 Charlie Batch 1.00
11 Elvis Grbac .25
12 Trent Dilfer .50
13 Kerry Collins .50
14 Neil O'Donnell .25
15 Tony Simmons .50
16 Ryan Leaf 1.00
17 Bobby Hoying .25
18 Marvin Harrison .50
19 Keyshawn Johnson .75
20 Cris Carter .75
21 Deion Sanders .75
22 Emmitt Smith 2.50
23 Antowain Smith .75
24 Terry Fair .50
25 Robert Holcombe .50
26 Napoleon Kaufman .75
27 Eddie George 1.00
28 Corey Dillon .75
29 Adrian Murrell .25
30 Charles Way .25
31 Amp Lee .25
32 Ricky Watters .50
33 Gary Brown .25
34 Thurman Thomas .50
35 Patrick Johnson .25
36 Jerome Bettis .75
37 Muhsin Muhammad .25
38 Kimble Anders .25
39 Curtis Enis .75
40 Mike Alstott .75
41 Charles Johnson .25
42 Chris Warren .25
43 Tony Banks .50
44 Leroy Hoard .25
45 Chris Fuamatu-Ma'afala .25
46 Michael Irvin .75
47 Robert Edwards .75
48 Hines Ward .50
49 Trent Green .50
50 Eric Zeier .25
51 Sean Dawkins .25
52 Yancey Thigpen .25
53 Jacquez Green .50
54 Zach Thomas .50
55 Junior Seau .50
56 Darnay Scott .25
57 Kent Graham .25
58 O.J. Santiago .25
59 Tony Gonzalez .25
60 Ty Detmer .25
61 Albert Connell .25
62 James Jett .25
63 Bert Emanuel .25
64 Derrick Alexander .25
65 Wesley Walls .25
66 Jake Reed .25
67 Randall Cunningham .75
68 Leslie Shepherd .25
69 Mark Chmura .25
70 Bobby Engram .25
71 Rickey Dudley .25
72 Darick Holmes .25
73 Andre Reed .50
74 Az-Zahir Hakim .50
75 Cameron Cleeland .25
76 Lamar Thomas .25
77 Oronde Gadsden .50
78 Ben Coates .50
79 Bruce Smith .25
80 Jerry Rice 1.50
81 Tim Brown .50
82 Michael Westbrook .50
83 J.J. Stokes .50
84 Shannon Sharpe .50
85 Reidel Anthony .25
86 Antonio Freeman .75
87 Keenan McCardell .50
88 Terry Glenn .75
89 Andre Rison .50
90 Neil Smith .25
91 Terrance Mathis .25
92 Raghib Ismail .25
93 Bam Morris .25
94 Ike Hillard .25
95 Eddie Kennison .25
96 Tavian Banks .50
97 Yatil Green .25
98 Frank Wycheck .25
99 Warren Sapp .25
100 Germane Crowell 1.00
101 Curtis Martin 2.00
102 John Avery 1.00
103 Eric Moulds 2.00
104 Randy Moss 8.00
105 Terrell Owens 2.00
106 Vinny Testaverde 1.00
107 Doug Flutie 2.50
108 Mark Brunell 3.00
109 Isaac Bruce 1.00
110 Kordell Stewart 2.50
111 Drew Bledsoe 3.00
112 Chris Chandler .50
113 Dan Marino 6.00
114 Brian Griese 4.00
115 Carl Pickens .50
116 Jake Plummer 4.00
117 Natrone Means 1.00
118 Peyton Manning 8.00
119 Garrison Hearst 1.00
120 Barry Sanders 8.00
121 Steve Young 3.00
122 Rashaan Shehee .50
123 Ed McCaffrey 1.50
124 Charles Woodson 2.00
125 Dorsey Levens 1.50
126 Robert Smith 1.50
127 Greg Hill .50
128 Fred Taylor 5.00
129 Marcus Nash 1.00
130 Terrell Davis 6.00
131 Ahman Green 1.00
132 Jamal Anderson 2.00
133 Karim Abdul 1.00
134 Jermaine Lewis .50
135 Jerome Pathon .50
136 Brad Johnson 1.00
137 Herman Moore 1.50
138 Tim Dwight 2.00
139 Johnnie Morton .50
140 Marshall Faulk 2.00
141 Frank Sanders 1.00
142 Kevin Dyson 1.00
143 Curtis Conway 1.00
144 Derrick Mayes .50
145 O.J. McDuffie 1.00
146 Joe Jurevicius .50
147 Jon Kitna 2.00
148 Joey Galloway 1.50
149 Jimmy Smith 1.00
150 Skip Hicks 1.00
151 Rod Smith 1.00
152 Duce Staley .50
153 James O. Stewart .50
154 Rob Johnson 1.00
155 Mikhael Ricks .50
156 Wayne Chrebet 1.50
157 Robert Brooks .50
158 Tim Biakabutuka .50
159 Priest Holmes 2.00
160 Warrick Dunn 2.00
161 *Champ Bailey* 2.00
162 *D'Wayne Bates* 1.00
163 *Michael Bishop* 2.00
164 *David Boston* 6.00
165 *Na Brown* 1.00
166 *Chris Claiborne* 1.00
167 *Joe Montgomery* 1.00
168 *Mike Cloud* 1.00
169 *Travis McGriff* 1.00
170 *Tim Couch* 5.00
171 *Daunte Culpepper* 12.00
172 *Autry Denson* 1.00
173 *Jermaine Fazande* 1.00
174 *Troy Edwards* 2.00
175 *Kevin Faulk* 2.00
176 *Dee Miller* 1.00
177 *Brock Huard* 2.00
178 *Torry Holt* 6.00
179 *Sedrick Irvin* 1.00
180 *Edgerrin James* 12.00
181 *Joe Germaine* 1.00
182 *James Johnson* 1.00
183 *Kevin Johnson* 4.00
184 *Andy Katzenmoyer* 2.00
185 *Jevon Kearse* 4.00
186 *Shaun King* 2.00
187 *Rob Konrad* 1.00
188 *Jim Kleinsasser* 2.00
189 *Chris McAlister* 1.00
190 *Donovan McNabb* 12.00
191 *Cade McNown* 2.00
192 *De'Mond Parker* 1.00
193 *Craig Yeast* 1.00
194 *Shawn Bryson* 1.00
195 *Peerless Price* 5.00
196 *Darnell McDonald* 1.00
197 *Akili Smith* 2.00
198 *Tai Streets* 2.00
199 *Ricky Williams* 10.00
200 *Amos Zereoue* 6.00

1999 Donruss Elite Common Threads

Each card is printed on conventional board with foil and game-used jersey swatches. Twelve players are featured with six cards with one player on it and the other six are combo cards. Each is sequentially numbered to 150.

NM/M
Common Player: 50.00
Production 150 Sets
1 Randy Moss, Randall Cunningham 125.00
2 Randy Moss 100.00
3 Randall Cunningham 50.00
4 John Elway, Terrell Davis 150.00
5 John Elway 100.00
6 Terrell Davis 75.00
7 Jerry Rice, Steve Young 125.00
8 Jerry Rice 75.00
9 Steve Young 50.00
10 Mark Brunell, Fred Taylor 75.00
11 Mark Brunell 50.00
12 Fred Taylor 50.00
13 Kordell Stewart, Jerome Bettis 75.00
14 Kordell Stewart 50.00
15 Jerome Bettis 50.00
16 Dan Marino, Karim Abdul 125.00
17 Dan Marino 100.00
18 Karim Abdul 50.00

1999 Donruss Elite Field of Vision

Each card is printed on clear plastic with holo-foil stamping. Twelve players are featured on three seperate cards, with each representing a section of the playing field (left-middle-right). Each card is then sequentially numbered to the yards the player gained in that area of the field in 1998.

NM/M
Common Player: 2.00
Production #'d to a Season Stat
1A Dan Marino 1712 6.00
1B Dan Marino 834 8.00
1C Dan Marino 951 8.00
2A Emmitt Smith 640 8.00
2B Emmitt Smith 202 10.00
2C Emmitt Smith 490 8.00
3A Jake Plummer 1165 2.00
3B Jake Plummer 624 4.00
3C Jake Plummer 1948 2.00
4A Brett Favre 1408 8.00
4B Brett Favre 983 8.00
4C Brett Favre 1820 8.00
5A Fred Taylor 486 6.00
5B Fred Taylor 400 6.00
5C Fred Taylor 337 6.00
6A Drew Bledsoe 1355 4.00
6B Drew Bledsoe 689 6.00
6C Drew Bledsoe 1589 4.00
7A Terrell Davis 1283 6.00
7B Terrell Davis 306 8.00
7C Terrell Davis 419 8.00
8A Jerry Rice 611 6.00
8B Jerry Rice 234 10.00
8C Jerry Rice 312 8.00
9A Randy Moss 639 8.00
9B Randy Moss 16
9C Randy Moss 658 8.00
10A John Elway 1320 6.00
10B John Elway 615 8.00
10C John Elway 871 6.00
11A Peyton Manning 1141 6.00
11B Peyton Manning 1020 6.00
11C Peyton Manning 1578 6.00
12A Barry Sanders 556 6.00
12B Barry Sanders 373 8.00
12C Barry Sanders 562 6.00

1999 Donruss Elite Field of Vision Die Cuts

This is similar to the Field of Vision cards except each card is die-cut and sequentially numbered to the number of attempts, receptions or completions of that particular player.

NM/M
Common Player: 8.00
Production #'d to a Season Stat
1A Dan Marino 164 10.00
1B Dan Marino 56 14.00
1C Dan Marino 90 12.00
2A Emmitt Smith 158 10.00
2B Emmitt Smith 64 12.00
2C Emmitt Smith 97 12.00
3A Jake Plummer 89 6.00
3B Jake Plummer 44 8.00
3C Jake Plummer 191 6.00
4A Brett Favre 112 12.00
4B Brett Favre 67 14.00
4C Brett Favre 168 12.00
5A Fred Taylor 103 6.00
5B Fred Taylor 79 8.00
5C Fred Taylor 82 8.00
6A Drew Bledsoe 90 10.00
6B Drew Bledsoe 48 12.00
6C Drew Bledsoe 125 8.00
7A Terrell Davis 217 8.00
7B Terrell Davis 66 12.00
7C Terrell Davis 109 10.00
8A Jerry Rice 50 12.00
8B Jerry Rice 11
8C Jerry Rice 21
9A Randy Moss 34 20.00
9B Randy Moss 2
9C Randy Moss 33 14.00
10A John Elway 98 10.00
10B John Elway 35 15.00
10C John Elway 77 12.00
11A Peyton Manning 110 12.00
11B Peyton Manning 79 14.00
11C Peyton Manning 137 12.00
12A Barry Sanders 137 12.00
12B Barry Sanders 83 14.00
12C Barry Sanders 123 12.00

1999 Donruss Elite Passing the Torch

Each card is printed with holo-foil board on the front and back with UV coating on both sides and sequentially numbered to 1,500. Twelve players were used with each having an individual card as well as six cards pairing two players together. The first 100 of each card are autographed.

NM/M
Complete Set (18): 125.00
Common Player: 5.00
Production 1,500 Sets
1 Johnny Unitas, Peyton Manning 12.00
2 Johnny Unitas 8.00
3 Peyton Manning 10.00
4 Walter Payton, Barry Sanders 15.00
5 Walter Payton 10.00
6 Barry Sanders 10.00
7 Earl Campbell, Ricky Williams 12.00
8 Earl Campbell 5.00
9 Ricky Williams 12.00
10 Jim Brown, Terrell Davis 10.00
11 Jim Brown 8.00
12 Terrell Davis 10.00
13 Emmitt Smith, Fred Taylor 15.00
14 Emmitt Smith 10.00
15 Fred Taylor 8.00
16 Cris Carter, Randy Moss 15.00
17 Cris Carter 5.00
18 Randy Moss 12.00

1999 Donruss Elite Passing the Torch Autographs

This is the same as the regular Passing the Torch cards except for each one of these are autographed. They are each sequentially numbered to 100.

NM/M
Complete Set (18): 5,000
Common Player: 85.00
Production 100 Sets
1 Johnny Unitas, Peyton Manning 400.00
2 Johnny Unitas 150.00
3 Peyton Manning 200.00
4 Walter Payton, Barry Sanders 600.00
5 Walter Payton 250.00
6 Barry Sanders 250.00
7 Earl Campbell, Ricky Williams 250.00
8 Earl Campbell 100.00
9 Ricky Williams 250.00
10 Jim Brown, Terrell Davis 200.00
11 Jim Brown 200.00
12 Terrell Davis 150.00
13 Emmitt Smith, Fred Taylor 350.00
14 Emmitt Smith 200.00
15 Fred Taylor 50.00
16 Cris Carter, Randy Moss 200.00
17 Cris Carter 85.00
18 Randy Moss 200.00

1999 Donruss Elite Power Formulas

This 30-card set spotlights the NFL's most powerful players and the statistical formulas behind their greatness. Each is sequentially numbered to 3,500.

NM/M
Complete Set (30): 70.00
Common Player: 1.00
Minor Stars: 4.00
Production 3,500 Sets
1 Randy Moss 10.00
2 Terrell Davis 6.00
3 Brett Favre 12.00
4 Dan Marino 10.00
5 Barry Sanders 10.00
6 Peyton Manning 8.00
7 John Elway 8.00
8 Fred Taylor 4.00
9 Emmitt Smith 10.00
10 Steve Young 4.00
11 Jerry Rice 6.00
12 Jake Plummer 2.00
13 Kordell Stewart 2.00
14 Mark Brunell 2.00
15 Drew Bledsoe 5.00
16 Eddie George 2.00
17 Troy Aikman 4.00
18 Warrick Dunn 2.00
19 Keyshawn Johnson 2.00
20 Jamal Anderson 2.00
21 Randall Cunningham 2.00
22 Doug Flutie 2.00
23 Jerome Bettis 2.00
24 Garrison Hearst 2.00
25 Curtis Martin 3.00
26 Corey Dillon 3.00
27 Antowain Smith 2.00
28 Antonio Freeman 2.00
29 Terrell Owens 3.00
30 Carl Pickens 1.00

1999 Donruss Elite Primary Colors

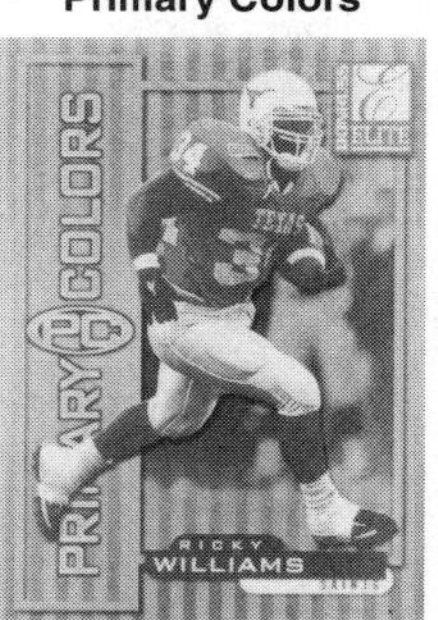

The 40-card set is printed on holo-foil board and is sequentially numbered to 1,875. This insert has five different parallel sets with a Blue (#'d to 950), Red (#'d to 25), Blue Die-Cut (#'d to 50), Red Die-Cut (#'d to 75) and a Yellow Die-Cut (#'d to 25) version.

NM/M
Complete Set (40): 125.00
Common Yellow: 2.00
Production 1,875 Sets
Blue Cards: 1.5X
Production 950 Sets
Red Cards: 8X-15X
Red Rookies: 3X-8X
Production 25 Sets
Blue Die-Cut Cards: 3X-10X
Blue Die-Cut Rookies: 2X-5X
Production 50 Sets
Red Die-Cut Cards: 3X-8X
Red Die-Cut Rookies: 2X-3X
Production 75 Sets
Yellow Die-Cut Cards: 8X-15X
Yellow Die-Cut Rookies: 3X-8X
Production 25 Sets
1 Herman Moore 2.00
2 Marshall Faulk 2.00
3 Dorsey Levens 2.00
4 Napoleon Kaufman 2.00
5 Jamal Anderson 2.00
6 Edgerrin James 6.00
7 Troy Aikman 6.00
8 Cris Carter 2.00
9 Eddie George 4.00
10 Donovan McNabb 10.00
11 Drew Bledsoe 5.00
12 Daunte Culpepper 8.00
13 Mark Brunell 5.00
14 Corey Dillon 2.00
15 Kordell Stewart 2.00
16 Curtis Martin 2.00
17 Jake Plummer 2.00
18 Charlie Batch 2.00
19 Jerry Rice 6.00
20 Antonio Freeman 2.00
21 Steve Young 4.00
22 Steve McNair 2.00
23 Emmitt Smith 8.00
24 Terrell Owens 2.00
25 Fred Taylor 6.00
26 Joey Galloway 2.00
27 John Elway 8.00
28 Ryan Leaf 2.00
29 Barry Sanders 10.00
30 Ricky Williams 14.00
31 Dan Marino 8.00
32 Tim Couch 10.00
33 Brett Favre 12.00
34 Eric Moulds 2.00
35 Peyton Manning 8.00
36 Deion Sanders 2.00
37 Terrell Davis 8.00
38 Tim Brown 2.00
39 Randy Moss 10.00
40 Mike Alstott 2.00

1999 Donruss Preferred QBC

This was a 120-card set that was divided into four levels. The first 45 cards were in Bronze and cards #46-#80 were in Silver and found one-per-pack. Cards #81-#105 were in Gold and inserted 1:4 packs and cards #106-#120 were Platinum singles and found 1:8 packs. The set featured all 44 members of the Quarterback Club. Insert sets included: Power (parallel), Autographs, Chain Reaction, Hard Hats, Materials, National Treasures, Passing Grade, Precious Metals, Staremasters and X-Ponential Power. SRP was $3.99 for four-card packs.

NM/M
Complete Set (120): 150.00
Common Bronze: .15
Minor Stars Bronze: .30
Common Silver: .50
Minor Stars Silver: 1.00
Inserted 1:1
Common Gold: 1.00
Minor Stars Gold: 2.00
Inserted 1:4
Common Platinum: 2.50
Inserted 1:8
Pack (4): 3.00
Wax Box (20): 60.00
1 Troy Aikman B 1.50
2 Tony Banks B .30
3 Jeff Blake B .30
4 Drew Bledsoe B 1.00
5 Bubby Brister B .15
6 Chris Chandler B .15
7 Kerry Collins B .30
8 Randall Cunningham B .50
9 Terrell Davis B 2.00
10 Trent Dilfer B .30
11 John Elway B 2.00
12 Boomer Esiason B .30
13 Jim Everett B .15
14 Brett Favre B 3.00
15 Doug Flutie B .75
16 Gus Frerotte B .15
17 Jeff George B .50
18 Elvis Grbac B .15
19 Jim Harbaugh B .30
20 Michael Irvin B .30
21 Brad Johnson B .50
22 Keyshawn Johnson B .50
23 Danny Kanell B .15
24 Jim Kelly B .50
25 Bernie Kosar B .15
26 Erik Kramer B .15
27 Ryan Leaf B .50
28 Peyton Manning B 2.00
29 Dan Marino B 2.00
30 *Donovan McNabb B* 4.00
31 Steve McNair B .50
32 *Cade McNown B* 2.50
33 Scott Mitchell B .15
34 Warren Moon B .30
35 Neil O'Donnell B .15
36 Jake Plummer B 1.50
37 Jerry Rice B 1.50
38 Barry Sanders B 3.00
39 Junior Seau B .30
40 Phil Simms B .30
41 Kordell Stewart B .50
42 Vinny Testaverde B .30
43 *Ricky Williams B* 8.00
44 Steve Young B .75
45 Dan Marino, Brett Favre, John Elway B 2.00
46 Troy Aikman S 2.50
47 Tony Banks S .50
48 Drew Bledsoe S 1.75
49 Bubby Brister S .50
50 Chris Chandler S .50
51 Kerry Collins S .50
52 Randall Cunningham S 1.00
53 Terrell Davis S 3.50
54 Trent Dilfer S 1.00
55 John Elway S 3.50
56 Boomer Esiason S 1.00

57	Brett Favre S	5.00
58	Doug Flutie S	1.50
59	Elvis Grbac S	.50
60	Jim Harbaugh S	.50
61	Michael Irvin S	1.00
62	Brad Johnson S	1.00
63	Keyshawn Johnson S	1.00
64	Jim Kelly S	1.00
65	Ryan Leaf S	1.00
66	Peyton Manning S	3.50
67	Dan Marino S	3.50
68	Donovan McNabb S	6.00
69	Steve McNair S	1.25
70	Cade McNown S	6.00
71	Warren Moon S	1.00
72	Jake Plummer S	2.50
73	Jerry Rice S	2.50
74	Barry Sanders S	5.00
75	Junior Seau S	1.00
76	Phil Simms S	1.00
77	Kordell Stewart S	1.25
78	Vinny Testaverde S	1.00
79	Ricky Williams S	12.00
80	Steve Young S	1.75
81	Troy Aikman G	4.00
82	Drew Bledsoe G	3.00
83	Bubby Brister G	1.00
84	Chris Chandler G	1.00
85	Randall Cunningham G	2.00
86	Terrell Davis G	6.00
87	John Elway G	6.00
88	Brett Favre G	8.00
89	Doug Flutie G	2.50
90	Brad Johnson G	2.00
91	Keyshawn Johnson G	2.00
92	Ryan Leaf G	2.00
93	Peyton Manning G	6.00
94	Dan Marino G	6.00
95	Donovan McNabb G	12.00
96	Steve McNair G	2.00
97	Cade McNown G	3.00
98	Warren Moon G	2.00
99	Jake Plummer G	4.00
100	Jerry Rice G	4.00
101	Barry Sanders G	8.00
102	Kordell Stewart G	2.00
103	Vinny Testaverde G	2.00
104	Ricky Williams G	25.00
105	Steve Young G	2.50
106	Troy Aikman P	8.00
107	Drew Bledsoe P	6.00
108	Terrell Davis P	10.00
109	John Elway P	10.00
110	Brett Favre P	15.00
111	Keyshawn Johnson P	2.50
112	Peyton Manning P	10.00
113	Dan Marino P	10.00
114	Donovan McNabb P	15.00
115	Cade McNown P	3.00
116	Jake Plummer P	2.00
117	Jerry Rice P	8.00
118	Barry Sanders P	15.00
119	Kordell Stewart P	2.50
120	Ricky Williams P	30.00

1999 Donruss Preferred QBC Power

This was a 120-card parallel to the base set. Each single was printed on holographic-foil board. The Bronze singles were numbered to 500, Silver singles to 300, Gold singles to 150 and Platinum singles to 50.

	NM/M
Bronze Cards:	3X-6X
Bronze Rookies:	3X
Production 500 Sets	
Silver Cards:	3X-6X
Silver Rookies:	3X
Production 300 Sets	
Gold Cards:	3X-6X
Gold Rookies:	3X
Production 150 Sets	
Platinum Cards:	4X-8X
Platinum Rookies:	4X
Production 50 Sets	

1999 Donruss Preferred QBC Autographs

This was a 15-card insert set that included autographs of the top players in the NFL. Cards were randomly inserted into packs.

		NM/M
Complete Set (15):		850.00
Common Player:		25.00
1	Steve Young 700	50.00
2	Ricky Williams 700	125.00
3	Jerry Rice 350	100.00
4	Jake Plummer 700	70.00
5	Peyton Manning 650	100.00
6	Michael Irvin 500	35.00
7	Dan Marino 600	125.00
8	Randall Cunningham 700	40.00
9	Troy Aikman 600	85.00
10	Terrell Davis 500	90.00
11	Vinny Testaverde 700	25.00
12	Chris Chandler 600	25.00
13	Bubby Brister 500	25.00
14	Steve McNair 700	50.00
15	Kordell Stewart 700	50.00

1999 Donruss Preferred QBC Chain Reaction

This was a 20-card insert set that included players who know how to move the chains. Each single was sequentially numbered to 5,000 and was printed on prismatic-foil board stock.

		NM/M
Complete Set (20):		65.00
Common Player:		1.00
Minor Stars:		2.00
Production 5,000 Sets		
1A	Terrell Davis	5.00
1B	Ricky Williams	10.00
2A	Donovan McNabb	5.00
2B	Cade McNown	2.00
3A	Brett Favre	10.00
3B	Barry Sanders	10.00
4A	Jerry Rice	5.00
4B	Steve Young	3.00
5A	John Elway	7.00
5B	Chris Chandler	1.00
6A	Dan Marino	7.00
6B	Drew Bledsoe	4.00
7A	Keyshawn Johnson	2.00
7B	Vinny Testaverde	2.00
8A	Warren Moon	2.00
8B	Steve McNair	2.00
9A	Jake Plummer	2.00
9B	Kordell Stewart	2.00
10A	Troy Aikman	5.00
10B	Peyton Manning	7.00

1999 Donruss Preferred QBC Hard Hats

This was a 30-card insert set that pictured each player on a helmet-shaped die-cut card. Each single was printed on clear plastic and was sequentially numbered to 3,000.

		NM/M
Complete Set (30):		65.00
Common Player:		1.00
Minor Stars:		2.00
Production 3,000 Sets		
1	Brett Favre	8.00
2	Keyshawn Johnson	3.00
3	John Elway	6.00
4	Drew Bledsoe	5.00
5	Chris Chandler	1.00
6	Terrell Davis	6.00
7	Ryan Leaf	1.00
8	Ricky Williams	8.00
9	Cade McNown	2.00
10	Barry Sanders	8.00
11	Donovan McNabb	8.00
12	Peyton Manning	8.00
13	Troy Aikman	6.00
14	Steve Young	4.00
15	Vinny Testaverde	1.00
16	Dan Marino	8.00
17	Steve McNair	3.00
18	Kordell Stewart	2.00
19	Michael Irvin	3.00
20	Jake Plummer	2.00
21	Jerry Rice	6.00
22	Brad Johnson	3.00
23	Phil Simms	2.00
24	Jim Kelly	3.00
25	Trent Dilfer	2.00
26	Kerry Collins	1.00
27	Warren Moon	2.00
28	Bubby Brister	1.00
29	Randall Cunningham	2.00
30	Doug Flutie	2.00

1999 Donruss Preferred QBC Materials

This was a 21-card insert set that included either a piece of game-used helmet, jersey or cleats. Jersey and cleat singles were numbered to 300 and helmet singles were numbered to 120. Singles were randomly inserted into packs.

		NM/M
Common Player:		25.00
#13 never produced		
1	Dan Marino Jersey 300	75.00
2	John Elway Jersey 300	60.00
3	Drew Bledsoe Jersey 300	50.00
4	Jake Plummer Jersey 300	25.00
5A	Doug Flutie White Jersey 150	30.00
5B	Doug Flutie Blue Jersey 150	30.00
6	Peyton Manning Jersey 300	75.00
7A	Jerry Rice White Jersey 150	75.00
7B	Jerry Rice Red Jersey 150	75.00
8	Brett Favre Jersey 300	100.00
9	Jim Kelly Jersey 300	25.00
10	Barry Sanders Jersey 300	100.00
11	Keyshawn Johnson Shoes 200	25.00
12	Brett Favre Shoes 100	125.00
14	Troy Aikman Shoes 300	75.00
15	Terrell Davis Shoes 300	60.00
16	Dan Marino Helmets 125	125.00
17	Troy Aikman Helmets 125	75.00
18	Brett Favre Helmets 125	125.00
19	Jerry Rice Helmets 125	100.00
20	Terrell Davis Helmets 125	75.00

1999 Donruss Preferred QBC National Treasures

This 44-card insert set included the top stars in the NFL. Each single was sequentially numbered to 2,000.

		NM/M
Complete Set (44):		80.00
Common Player:		1.00
Minor Stars:		3.00
Production 2,000 Sets		
1	Jake Plummer	2.00
2	Chris Chandler	1.00
3	Danny Kanell	1.00
4	Tony Banks	1.00
5	Scott Mitchell	1.00
6	Doug Flutie	2.00
7	Jim Kelly	3.00
8	Erik Kramer	1.00
9	Cade McNown	2.00
10	Jim Blake	2.00
11	Boomer Esiason	3.00
12	Bernie Kosar	1.00
13	Troy Aikman	6.00
14	Michael Irvin	3.00
15	Bubby Brister	1.00
16	Terrell Davis	6.00
17	John Elway	8.00
18	Gus Frerotte	1.00
19	Barry Sanders	10.00
20	Brett Favre	10.00
21	Peyton Manning	8.00
22	Elvis Grbac	1.00
23	Warren Moon	3.00
24	Dan Marino	10.00
25	Randall Cunningham	3.00
26	Jeff George	2.00
27	Drew Bledsoe	6.00
28	Ricky Williams	10.00
29	Kerry Collins	2.00
30	Phil Simms	1.00
31	Keyshawn Johnson	1.00
32	Vinny Testaverde	1.00
33	Donovan McNabb	6.00
34	Kordell Stewart	2.00
35	Jim Harbaugh	1.00
36	Ryan Leaf	1.00
37	Junior Seau	2.00
38	Jerry Rice	6.00
39	Steve Young	4.00
40	Jim Everett	1.00
41	Trent Dilfer	2.00
42	Steve McNair	4.00
43	Brad Johnson	2.00
44	Neil O'Donnell	1.00

1999 Donruss Preferred QBC Passing Grade

This 20-card insert set included the top Quarterbacks in the NFL. Each single was a two-piece card that included a football-shaped die-cut inside a conventional card envelope. Each was sequentially numbered to 1,500.

		NM/M
Complete Set (20):		80.00
Common Player:		1.00
Minor Stars:		2.00
Production 1,500 Sets		
1	Steve Young	6.00
2	Dan Marino	10.00
3	Kordell Stewart	2.00
4	Trent Dilfer	2.00
5	Doug Flutie	2.00
6	Vinny Testaverde	2.00
7	Donovan McNabb	6.00
8	Brad Johnson	2.00
9	Troy Aikman	6.00
10	Brett Favre	10.00
11	Steve McNair	5.00
12	Peyton Manning	8.00
13	John Elway	8.00
14	Chris Chandler	1.00
15	Randall Cunningham	2.00
16	Cade McNown	2.00
17	Ryan Leaf	1.00
18	Drew Bledsoe	6.00
19	Jake Plummer	2.00
20	Warren Moon	2.00

1999 Donruss Preferred QBC Staremasters

This was a 20-card insert set that included the most intense players in the game today. Each single was sequentially numbered to 1,000.

		NM/M
Complete Set (20):		125.00
Common Player:		2.00
Minor Stars:		4.00
Production 1,000 Sets		
1	Jake Plummer	3.00
2	Doug Flutie	3.00
3	Cade McNown	3.00
4	Troy Aikman	8.00
5	Michael Irvin	2.00
6	Terrell Davis	10.00
7	John Elway	12.00
8	Barry Sanders	15.00
9	Brett Favre	15.00
10	Peyton Manning	10.00
11	Dan Marino	15.00
12	Randall Cunningham	3.00
13	Drew Bledsoe	6.00
14	Ricky Williams	12.00
15	Keyshawn Johnson	3.00
16	Donovan McNabb	8.00
17	Kordell Stewart	3.00
18	Ryan Leaf	2.00
19	Steve Young	8.00
20	Jerry Rice	10.00

1999 Donruss Preferred QBC X-Ponential Power

This 20-card insert set matched fellow stars from the same position. Each was printed on die-cut plastic with foil highlights and each was numbered to 2,500.

		NM/M
Complete Set (20):		80.00
Common Player:		2.00
Production 2,500 Sets		
1A	Troy Aikman	6.00
1B	Cade McNown	2.00
2A	Kordell Stewart	2.00
2B	Steve McNair	2.00
3A	Donovan McNabb	6.00
3B	Ricky Williams	10.00
4A	Barry Sanders	10.00
4B	Terrell Davis	6.00
5A	Dan Marino	10.00
5B	Peyton Manning	8.00
6A	Jerry Rice	8.00
6B	Keyshawn Johnson	2.00
7A	Doug Flutie	2.00
7B	Jim Kelly	2.00
8A	Brett Favre	10.00
8B	Steve Young	6.00
9A	Drew Bledsoe	6.00
9B	Ryan Leaf	2.00
10A	John Elway	8.00
10B	Jake Plummer	2.00

2000 Donruss

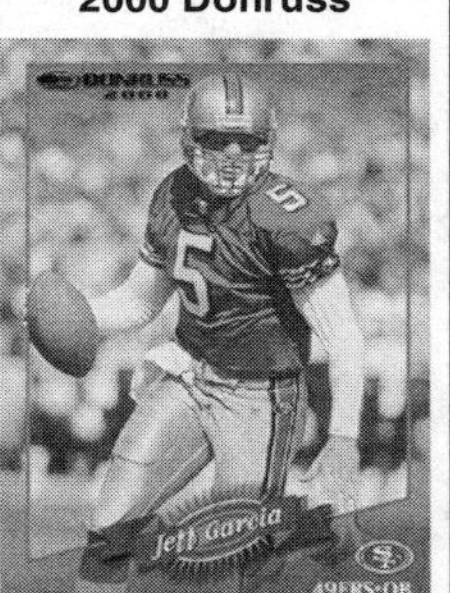

		NM/M
Complete Set (250):		550.00
Common Player:		.15
Minor Stars:		.30
Common Rookie:		3.00
Production 1,325 Sets		
Pack (16):		2.75
Wax Box (18):		50.00
1	Jake Plummer	.50
2	Frank Sanders	.30
3	Rob Moore	.30
4	David Boston	.50
5	Tim Dwight	.50
6	Jamal Anderson	.50
7	Chris Chandler	.30
8	Terance Mathis	.15
9	Tony Banks	.15
10	Jermaine Lewis	.15
11	Shannon Sharpe	.30
12	Trent Dilfer	.30
13	Qadry Ismail	.15
14	Eric Moulds	.50
15	Doug Flutie	.75
16	Antowain Smith	.30
17	Jonathon Linton	.30
18	Peerless Price	.50
19	Rob Johnson	.30
20	Natrone Means	.30
21	Muhsin Muhammad	.30
22	Wesley Walls	.30
23	Tim Biakabutuka	.30
24	Steve Beuerlein	.30
25	Patrick Jeffers	.50
26	Curtis Enis	.30
27	Cade McNown	.50
28	Bobby Engram	.15
29	Marcus Robinson	.50
30	Marty Booker	.15
31	Corey Dillon	.50
32	Darnay Scott	.30
33	Carl Pickens	.30
34	Akili Smith	.50
35	Michael Basnight	.15
36	Tim Couch	1.00
37	Kevin Johnson	.50
38	Karim Abdul	.15
39	Errict Rhett	.30
40	Darrin Chiaverini	.15
41	Emmitt Smith	1.50
42	Troy Aikman	1.25
43	Joey Galloway	.50
44	Randall Cunningham	.30
45	Michael Irvin	.30
46	Raghib Ismail	.15
47	Jason Tucker	.30
48	Terrell Davis	1.00
49	John Elway	1.50
50	Olandis Gary	.50
51	Ed McCaffrey	.30
52	Rod Smith	.50
53	Brian Griese	.75
54	Charlie Batch	.50
55	Barry Sanders	1.75
56	Herman Moore	.50
57	Johnnie Morton	.30
58	Germane Crowell	.50
59	James Stewart	.30
60	Brett Favre	2.50
61	Dorsey Levens	.50
62	Antonio Freeman	.50
63	Corey Bradford	.15
64	Bill Schroeder	.15
65	E.G. Green	.30
66	Peyton Manning	2.00
67	Edgerrin James	2.00
68	Marvin Harrison	.50
69	Terrence Wilkins	.50
70	Mark Brunell	.75
71	Fred Taylor	.75
72	Keenan McCardell	.30
73	Jimmy Smith	.50
74	Warren Moon	.30
75	Elvis Grbac	.30
76	Tony Gonzalez	.30
77	Dan Marino	1.50
78	O.J. McDuffie	.30
79	Tony Martin	.15
80	James Johnson	.30
81	Thurman Thomas	.30
82	Randy Moss	2.00
83	Daunte Culpepper	1.00
84	Cris Carter	.50
85	Robert Smith	.50
86	John Randle	.30
87	Drew Bledsoe	.75
88	Terry Glenn	.50
89	Kevin Faulk	.30
90	Ricky Williams	1.00
91	Jeff Blake	.30
92	Jake Reed	.30
93	Amani Toomer	.30
94	Kerry Collins	.30
95	Tiki Barber	.30
96	Ike Hilliard	.30
97	Curtis Martin	.50
98	Vinny Testaverde	.30
99	Wayne Chrebet	.30
100	Ray Lucas	.30
101	Charles Woodson	.50
102	Napoleon Kaufman	.50
103	Tim Brown	.50
104	Tyrone Wheatley	.30
105	Rich Gannon	.30
106	Duce Staley	.50
107	Donovan McNabb	.75
108	Amos Zereoue	.30
109	Kordell Stewart	.50
110	Jerome Bettis	.50
111	Troy Edwards	.30
112	Ryan Leaf	.30
113	Junior Seau	.30
114	Jim Harbaugh	.30
115	Jermaine Fazande	.30
116	Curtis Conway	.30
117	Steve Young	.75
118	Jerry Rice	1.25
119	Terrell Owens	.50
120	Charlie Garner	.30
121	Jeff Garcia	.50
122	Jon Kitna	.50
123	Derrick Mayes	.30
124	Ricky Watters	.30
125	Kurt Warner	2.50
126	Marshall Faulk	.50
127	Torry Holt	.50
128	Az-Zahir Hakim	.30
129	Isaac Bruce	.50
130	Mike Alstott	.50
131	Warrick Dunn	.50
132	Shaun King	.50
133	Keyshawn Johnson	.50
134	Jacquez Green	.30
135	Reidel Anthony	.30
136	Warren Sapp	.30
137	Eddie George	.75
138	Steve McNair	.50
139	Yancey Thigpen	.30
140	Kevin Dyson	.30
141	Frank Wycheck	.30
142	Jevon Kearse	.50
143	Stephen Davis	.50
144	Skip Hicks	.30
145	Brad Johnson	.50
146	Bruce Smith	.30
147	Michael Westbrook	.30
148	Albert Connell	.30
149	Jeff George	.30
150	Deion Sanders	.50
151	*Courtney Brown*	2.00
152	*Corey Simon*	1.00
153	*Brian Urlacher*	10.00
154	*Shaun Ellis*	2.00
155	*John Abraham*	2.00
156	*Deltha O'Neal*	2.00
157	*Ahmed Plummer*	2.00
158	*Chris Hovan*	4.00
159	*Rob Morris*	2.00
160	*Keith Bulluck*	2.00
161	*Darren Howard*	2.00
162	*John Engelberger*	2.00
163	*Raynoch Thompson*	2.00
164	*Cornelius Griffin*	2.00
165	*William Bartee*	2.00
166	*Fred Robbins*	2.00
167	*Micheal Boireau*	2.00
168	*Brandon Short*	2.00
169	*Jacoby Shepherd*	2.00
170	*Peter Warrick*	6.00
171	*Jamal Lewis*	12.00
172	*Thomas Jones*	6.00
173	*Plaxico Burress*	8.00
174	*Travis Taylor*	6.00
175	*Ron Dayne*	4.00
176	*Bubba Franks*	5.00
177	*Sebastian Janikowski*	4.00
178	*Chad Pennington*	20.00
179	*Shaun Alexander*	15.00
180	*Sylvester Morris*	3.00
181	*Anthony Becht*	2.00
182	*R. Jay Soward*	2.00
183	*Trung Canidate*	4.00
184	*Dennis Northcutt*	2.00
185	*Todd Pinkston*	5.00
186	*Jerry Porter*	6.00
187	*Travis Prentice*	4.00
188	*Giovanni Carmazzi*	2.00
189	*Ron Dugans*	2.00
190	*Erron Kinney*	2.00
191	*Dez White*	5.00
192	*Chris Cole*	2.00
193	*Ron Dixon*	2.00
194	*Chris Redman*	5.00
195	*J.R. Redmond*	4.00
196	*Laveranues Coles*	6.00
197	*JaJuan Dawson*	2.00
198	*Darrell Jackson*	6.00
199	*Reuben Droughns*	6.00
200	*Doug Chapman*	2.00
201	*Terrelle Smith*	2.00
202	*Curtis Keaton*	2.00
203	*Gari Scott*	2.00
204	*Danny Farmer*	4.00
205	*Hank Poteat*	2.00
206	*Ben Kelly*	2.00
207	*Corey Moore*	2.00
208	*Na'il Diggs*	3.00
209	*Aaron Shea*	2.00
210	*Trevor Gaylor*	2.00
211	*Julian Peterson*	2.00
212	*Frank Moreau*	2.00
213	*Deon Dyer*	2.00
214	*Avion Black*	2.00
215	*Paul Smith*	2.00
216	*Michael Wiley*	3.00
217	*Dante Hall*	10.00
218	*Mike Brown*	2.00
219	*Sammy Morris*	3.00
220	*Billy Volek*	2.00
221	*Tee Martin*	4.00
222	*Troy Walters*	2.00
223	*Chad Morton*	4.00
224	*Erik Flowers*	2.00
225	*Ronney Jenkins*	3.00
226	*Thomas Hamner*	2.00
227	*Mareno Philyaw*	2.00
228	*James Williams*	2.00
229	*Mike Anderson*	5.00
230	*Tom Brady*	40.00
231	*Mike Green*	2.00
232	*Todd Husak*	4.00
233	*Tim Rattay*	6.00
234	*Jarious Jackson*	5.00
235	*Joe Hamilton*	5.00
236	*Shyrone Stith*	2.00
237	*Rondell Mealey*	2.00
238	*Demario Brown*	2.00
239	*Chris Coleman*	3.00
240	*Dwayne Goodrich*	2.00
241	*Drew Haddad*	2.00
242	*Doug Johnson*	2.00
243	*Windrell Hayes*	2.00
244	*Charles Lee*	2.00
245	*Kevin McDougal*	2.00
246	*Spergon Wynn*	4.00
247	*Shockmain Davis*	2.00
248	*Jamel White*	2.00
249	*Bashir Yamini*	2.00
250	*Kwame Cavil*	2.00

2000 Donruss Stat Line Career

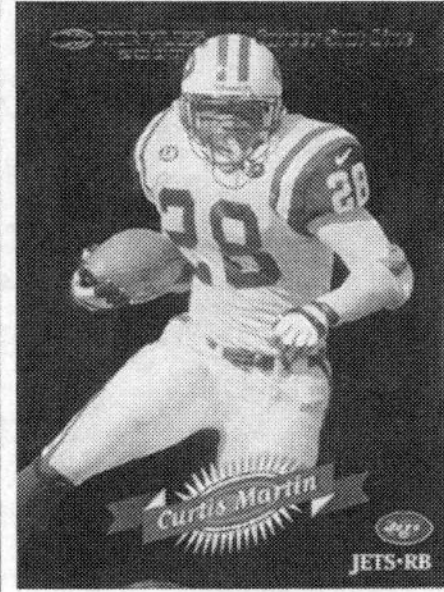

		NM/M
Common Player (131-300):		2.50
Common Player (65-130):		5.00
Common Player (30-64):		12.00
Common Player (10-29):		25.00
Production to a career stat.		
Inserted 1:25		
1	Jake Plummer 129	6.00
2	Frank Sanders 70	10.00
3	Rob Moore 153	2.50
4	David Boston 62	25.00
5	Tim Dwight 80	10.00
6	Jamal Anderson 47	25.00
7	Chris Chandler 300	5.00
8	Terance Mathis 81	5.00
9	Tony Banks 80	10.00
10	Jermaine Lewis 96	5.00
11	Shannon Sharpe 44	12.00
12	Trent Dilfer 70	10.00
13	Qadry Ismail 186	2.50
14	Eric Moulds 84	12.00
15	Doug Flutie 205	7.00
16	Antowain Smith 22	25.00
17	Jonathon Linton 250	5.00

18 Peerless Price 45 12.00
19 Rob Johnson 65 5.00
20 Natrone Means 72 5.00
21 Muhsin Muhammad 216 5.00
22 Wesley Walls 42 12.00
23 Tim Biakabutuka 67 5.00
24 Steve Beurlein 120 10.00
25 Patrick Jeffers 84 10.00
26 Curtis Enis 51 12.00
27 Cade McNown 235 6.00
28 Bobby Engram 230 2.50
29 Marcus Robinson 80 12.00
30 Marty Booker 57 12.00
31 Corey Dillon 71 12.00
32 Darnay Scott 93 5.00
33 Carl Pickens 63 12.00
34 Akili Smith 153 6.00
35 Michael Basnight 62 12.00
36 Tim Couch 15 85.00
37 Kevin Johnson 66 10.00
38 Karim Abdul 33 12.00
39 Errict Rhett 52 12.00
40 Darrin Chiaverini 44 12.00
41 Emmitt Smith 155 25.00
42 Troy Aikman 158 20.00
43 Randall Cunningham 95 12.00
44 Joey Galloway 283 5.00
45 Michael Irvin 65 10.00
46 Raghib Ismail 76 5.00
47 Jason Tucker 90 5.00
48 Terrell Davis 58 50.00
49 John Elway 300 20.00
50 Olandis Gary 276 7.00
51 Ed McCaffrey 78 10.00
52 Rod Smith 257 5.00
53 Brian Griese 262 6.00
54 Charlie Batch 98 10.00
55 Barry Sanders 99 45.00
56 Herman Moore 93 5.00
57 Johnnie Morton 98 5.00
58 Germane Crowell 106 5.00
59 James Stewart 119 5.00
60 Brett Favre 129 45.00
61 Dorsey Levens 52 12.00
62 Antonio Freeman 42 12.00
63 Corey Bradford 74 5.00
64 Bill Schroeder 74 5.00
65 E.G. Green 50 12.00
66 Peyton Manning 52 70.00
67 Edgerrin James 72 60.00
68 Marvin Harrison 61 15.00
69 Terrence Wilkins 42 12.00
70 Mark Brunell 297 6.00
71 Fred Taylor 78 12.00
72 Keenan McCardell 99 5.00
73 Jimmy Smith 28 25.00
74 Warren Moon 290 5.00
75 Elvis Grbac 260 5.00
76 Tony Gonzalez 168 5.00
77 Dan Marino 240 20.00
78 O.J. McDuffie 2 50.00
79 Tony Martin 99 5.00
80 James Johnson 100 5.00
81 Thurman Thomas 74 10.00
82 Randy Moss 28 75.00
83 Daunte Culpepper 6 125.00
84 Cris Carter 93 15.00
85 Robert Smith 78 10.00
86 John Randle 105 8.00
87 Drew Bledsoe 147 12.00
88 Terry Glenn 86 10.00
89 Kevin Faulk 98 10.00
90 Ricky Williams 253 10.00
91 Jeff Blake 88 10.00
92 Jake Reed 82 10.00
93 Amani Toomer 101 5.00
94 Kerry Collins 149 5.00
95 Tiki Barber 250 5.00
96 Ike Hilliard 125 5.00
97 Curtis Martin 70 12.00
98 Vinny Testaverde 205 5.00
99 Wayne Chrebet 21 30.00
100 Ray Lucas 279 5.00
101 Charles Woodson 6 40.00
102 Napoleon Kaufman 83 10.00
103 Tim Brown 176 5.00
104 Tyrone Wheatley 21 25.00
105 Rich Gannon 90 5.00
106 Duce Staley 64 25.00
107 Donovan McNabb 216 8.00
108 Amos Zereoue 48 12.00
109 Kordell Stewart 279 5.00
110 Jerome Bettis 41 12.00
111 Troy Edwards 234 5.00
112 Ryan Leaf 245 5.00
113 Junior Seau 224 2.50
114 Jim Harbaugh 139 2.50
115 Jermaine Fazande 54 12.00
116 Curtis Conway 85 5.00
117 Steve Young 96 20.00
118 Jerry Rice 180 15.00
119 Terrell Owens 222 5.00
120 Charlie Garner 23 25.00
121 Jeff Garcia 225 6.00
122 Jon Kitna 132 5.00
123 Derrick Mayes 116 5.00
124 Ricky Watters 123 10.00
125 Kurt Warner 41 50.00
126 Marshall Faulk 63 25.00
127 Torry Holt 63 15.00
128 Az-Zahir Hakim 75 5.00
129 Isaac Bruce 41 25.00
130 Mike Alstott 137 5.00
131 Warrick Dunn 76 10.00
132 Shaun King 89 10.00
133 Keyshawn Johnson 31 25.00
134 Jacquez Green 53 12.00
135 Reidel Anthony 79 5.00
136 Warren Sapp 160 5.00
137 Eddie George 114 12.00
138 Steve McNair 292 6.00
139 Yancey Thigpen 298 2.50
140 Kevin Dyson 75 5.00
141 Frank Wycheck 42 12.00
142 Jevon Kearse 48 20.00
143 Stephen Davis 22 30.00
144 Skip Hicks 200 2.50
145 Brad Johnson 82 10.00
146 Bruce Smith 281 5.00
147 Michael Westbrook 211 5.00
148 Albert Connell 99 5.00
149 Jeff George 147 5.00
150 Deion Sanders 21 35.00
151 Courtney Brown 106 12.00
152 Corey Simon 14 50.00
153 Brian Urlacher 3 175.00
154 Shaun Ellis 12 25.00
155 John Abraham 60 20.00
156 Deltha O'Neal 5 50.00
157 Ahmed Plummer 14 30.00
158 Chris Hovan 148 5.00
159 Rob Morris 223 5.00
160 Keith Bulluck 3 45.00
161 Darren Howard 84 5.00
162 John Engelberger 26 25.00
163 Raynoch Thompson 4 45.00
164 Cornelius Griffin 6 45.00
165 William Bartee 41 20.00
166 Fred Robbins 132 5.00
167 Micheal Boireau 62 15.00
168 Deon Grant 14 30.00
169 Jacoby Shepherd 2 50.00
170 Peter Warrick 31 25.00
171 Jamal Lewis 17 100.00
172 Thomas Jones 36 60.00
173 Plaxico Burress 131 20.00
174 Travis Taylor 15 65.00
175 Ron Dayne 63 25.00
176 Bubba Franks 77 25.00
177 Sebastian Janikowski 66 12.00
178 Chad Pennington 123 75.00
179 Shaun Alexander 41 60.00
180 Sylvester Morris 34 30.00
181 Anthony Becht 11 30.00
182 R. Jay Soward 179 6.00
183 Trung Canidate 25 40.00
184 Dennis Northcutt 225 8.00
185 Todd Pinkston 22 35.00
186 Jerry Porter 38 25.00
187 Travis Prentice 73 30.00
188 Giovanni Carmazzi 71 25.00
189 Ron Dugans 105 10.00
190 Erron Kinney 5 30.00
191 Dez White 14 35.00
192 Chris Cole 8 30.00
193 Ron Dixon 89 20.00
194 Chris Redman 84 35.00
195 J.R. Redmond 28 60.00
196 Laveranues Coles 7 65.00
197 JaJuan Dawson 29 35.00
198 Darrell Jackson 97 30.00
199 Reuben Droughns 19 30.00
200 Doug Chapman 55 15.00
201 Terrelle Smith 126 8.00
202 Curtis Keaton 33 25.00
203 Gari Scott 18 30.00
204 Danny Farmer 159 7.00
205 Hank Poteat 10 30.00
206 Ben Kelly 11 30.00
207 Corey Moore 166 6.00
208 Na'il Diggs 18 30.00
209 Aaron Shea 27 25.00
210 Trevor Gaylor 128 6.00
211 Anthony Lucas 134 5.00
212 Frank Moreau 233 5.00
213 Deon Dyer 9 35.00
214 Avion Black 11 35.00
215 Paul Smith 16 30.00
216 Michael Wiley 27 35.00
217 Dante Hall 22 30.00
218 Muneer Moore 144 5.00
219 Sammy Morris 169 12.00
220 James Whalen 120 5.00
221 Tee Martin 32 50.00
222 Troy Walters 244 5.00
223 Chad Morton 24 40.00
224 Marc Bulger 59 15.00
225 Frank Murphy 8 35.00
226 Thomas Hamner 21 30.00
227 Mareno Philyaw 59 15.00
228 James Williams 17 30.00
229 Mike Anderson 22 50.00
230 Tom Brady 298 30.00
231 Sherrod Gideon 193 2.50
232 Todd Husak 41 25.00
233 Tim Rattay 112 25.00
234 Jarious Jackson 34 25.00
235 Joe Hamilton 203 8.00
236 Shyrone Stith 21 30.00
237 Rondell Mealey 29 30.00
238 Demario Brown 37 15.00
239 Chris Coleman 122 10.00
240 Chafie Fields 8 35.00
241 Drew Haddad 240 5.00
242 Doug Johnson 62 20.00
243 Windrell Hayes 176 5.00
244 Charles Lee 162 5.00
245 Marcus Knight 82 8.00
246 Spergon Wynn 24 40.00
247 Leon Murray 56 15.00
248 Quinton Spotwood 105 10.00
249 Bashir Yamini 10 35.00
250 Kwame Cavil 174 5.00

2000 Donruss Stat Line Season

NM/M
Common Player (80-175): 4.00
Common Player (45-79): 7.00
Common Player (20-44): 18.00
Common Player (10-19): 25.00
Production to a 1999 season stat.
Inserted 1:192
1 Jake Plummer 57 8.00
2 Frank Sanders 79 7.00
3 Rob Moore 37 10.00
4 David Boston 53 15.00
5 Tim Dwight 80 8.00
6 Jamal Anderson 32 25.00
7 Chris Chandler 42 8.00
8 Terance Mathis 98 4.00
9 Tony Banks 24 8.00
10 Jermaine Lewis 57 7.00
11 Shannon Sharpe 86 4.00
12 Trent Dilfer 25 30.00
13 Qadry Ismail 3 50.00
14 Eric Moulds 10 50.00
15 Doug Flutie 50 8.00
16 Antowain Smith 30 18.00
17 Jonathon Linton 96 4.00
18 Peerless Price 62 7.00
19 Rob Johnson 32 8.00
20 Natrone Means 79 7.00
21 Muhsin Muhammad 11 35.00
22 Wesley Walls 96 4.00
23 Tim Biakabutuka 31 8.00
24 Steve Beurlein 5 45.00
25 Patrick Jeffers 8 45.00
26 Curtis Enis 79 7.00
27 Cade McNown 4 60.00
28 Bobby Engram 13 25.00
29 Marcus Robinson 3 85.00
30 Marty Booker 19 25.00
31 Corey Dillon 3 85.00
32 Darnay Scott 8 35.00
33 Carl Pickens 7 35.00
34 Akili Smith 42 8.00
35 Michael Basnight 62 7.00
36 Tim Couch 46 15.00
37 Kevin Johnson 90 8.00
38 Karim Abdul 84 4.00
39 Errict Rhett 27 8.00
40 Darrin Chiaverini 10 25.00
41 Emmitt Smith 9 125.00
42 Troy Aikman 5 125.00
43 Randall Cunningham 47 10.00
44 Joey Galloway 15 35.00
45 Michael Irvin 3 45.00
46 Raghib Ismail 8 30.00
47 Jason Tucker 27 20.00
48 Terrell Davis 67 45.00
49 John Elway 26 150.00
50 Olandis Gary 95 10.00
51 Ed McCaffrey 3 45.00
52 Rod Smith 9 40.00
53 Brian Griese 3 80.00
54 Charlie Batch 74 10.00
55 Barry Sanders 8 150.00
56 Herman Moore 16 35.00
57 Johnnie Morton 10 30.00
58 Germane Crowell 99 8.00
59 James Stewart 30 18.00
60 Brett Favre 50 85.00
61 Dorsey Levens 99 8.00
62 Antonio Freeman 8 40.00
63 Corey Bradford 94 4.00
64 Bill Schroeder 93 4.00
65 E.G. Green 21 18.00
66 Peyton Manning 54 70.00
67 Edgerrin James 3 200.00
68 Marvin Harrison 14 35.00
69 Terrence Wilkins 81 8.00
70 Mark Brunell 3 85.00
71 Fred Taylor 27 30.00
72 Keenan McCardell 9 25.00
73 Jimmy Smith 14 30.00
74 Warren Moon 20 20.00
75 Elvis Grbac 49 10.00
76 Tony Gonzalez 90 10.00
77 Dan Marino 52 40.00
78 O.J. McDuffie 85 4.00
79 Tony Martin 10 30.00
80 James Johnson 86 4.00
81 Thurman Thomas 36 18.00
82 Randy Moss 12 150.00
83 Daunte Culpepper 3 275.00
84 Cris Carter 3 80.00
85 Robert Smith 70 15.00
86 John Randle 27 18.00
87 Drew Bledsoe 49 30.00
88 Terry Glenn 13 25.00
89 Kevin Faulk 43 18.00
90 Ricky Williams 99 30.00
91 Jeff Blake 4 50.00
92 Jake Reed 50 7.00
93 Amani Toomer 99 4.00
94 Kerry Collins 51 7.00
95 Tiki Barber 66 10.00
96 Ike Hilliard 8 35.00
97 Curtis Martin 38 20.00
98 Vinny Testaverde 15 25.00
99 Wayne Chrebet 88 10.00
100 Ray Lucas 4 50.00
101 Charles Woodson 52 10.00
102 Napoleon Kaufman 76 10.00
103 Tim Brown 11 35.00
104 Tyrone Wheatley 66 10.00
105 Rich Gannon 4 50.00
106 Duce Staley 93 8.00
107 Donovan McNabb 3 85.00
108 Amos Zereoue 17 25.00
109 Kordell Stewart 32 20.00
110 Jerome Bettis 99 8.00
111 Troy Edwards 86 10.00
112 Ryan Leaf 2 70.00
113 Junior Seau 75 10.00
114 Jim Harbaugh 46 15.00
115 Jermaine Fazande 30 20.00
116 Curtis Conway 9 30.00
117 Steve Young 45 35.00
118 Jerry Rice 9 100.00
119 Terrell Owens 9 50.00
120 Charlie Garner 53 10.00
121 Jeff Garcia 11 45.00
122 Jon Kitna 3 60.00
123 Derrick Mayes 7 50.00
124 Ricky Watters 99 8.00
125 Kurt Warner 5 175.00
126 Marshall Faulk 7 70.00
127 Torry Holt 87 10.00
128 Az-Zahir Hakim 4 35.00
129 Isaac Bruce 4 50.00
130 Mike Alstott 4 50.00
131 Warrick Dunn 11 40.00
132 Shaun King 23 30.00
133 Keyshawn Johnson 11 40.00
134 Jacquez Green 96 4.00
135 Reidel Anthony 94 4.00
136 Warren Sapp 12 30.00
137 Eddie George 31 20.00
138 Steve McNair 5 60.00
139 Yancey Thigpen 84 4.00
140 Kevin Dyson 79 7.00
141 Frank Wycheck 87 4.00
142 Jevon Kearse 14 10.00
143 Stephen Davis 6 60.00
144 Skip Hicks 52 7.00
145 Brad Johnson 32 25.00
146 Bruce Smith 3 50.00
147 Michael Westbrook 5 50.00
148 Albert Connell 97 4.00
149 Jeff George 45 10.00
150 Deion Sanders 3 60.00
151 Courtney Brown 16 60.00
152 Corey Simon 59 25.00
153 Brian Urlacher 90 40.00
154 Shaun Ellis 30 20.00
155 John Abraham 6 35.00
156 Deltha O'Neal 9 35.00
157 Ahmed Plummer 48 5.00
158 Chris Hovan 11 35.00
159 Rob Morris 6 45.00
160 Keith Bulluck 90 5.00
161 Darren Howard 2 50.00
162 John Engelberger 31 20.00
163 Raynoch Thompson 49 12.00
164 Cornelius Griffin 30 25.00
165 William Bartee 1 60.00
166 Fred Robbins 5 45.00
167 Micheal Boireau 3 45.00
168 Deon Grant 49 15.00
169 Jacoby Shepherd 12 30.00
170 Peter Warrick 71 8.00
171 Jamal Lewis 15 250.00
172 Thomas Jones 16 150.00
173 Plaxico Burress 12 150.00
174 Travis Taylor 34 45.00
175 Ron Dayne 19 45.00
176 Bubba Franks 5 65.00
177 Sebastian Janikowski 54 15.00
178 Chad Pennington 38 85.00
179 Shaun Alexander 19 125.00
180 Sylvester Morris 69 45.00
181 Anthony Becht 35 25.00
182 R. Jay Soward 4 50.00
183 Trung Canidate 11 45.00
184 Dennis Northcutt 8 50.00
185 Todd Pinkston 48 25.00
186 Jerry Porter 4 50.00
187 Travis Prentice 17 75.00
188 Giovanni Carmazzi 11 60.00
189 Ron Dugans 3 55.00
190 Erron Kinney 16 40.00
191 Dez White 44 25.00
192 Chris Cole 22 30.00
193 Ron Dixon 19 60.00
194 Chris Redman 29 85.00
195 J.R. Redmond 78 25.00
196 Laveranues Coles 12 75.00
197 JaJuan Dawson 78 10.00
198 Darrell Jackson 9 45.00
199 Reuben Droughns 10 35.00
200 Doug Chapman 12 35.00
201 Terrelle Smith 22 25.00
202 Curtis Keaton 20 25.00
203 Gari Scott 30 20.00
204 Danny Farmer 3 50.00
205 Hank Poteat 31 20.00
206 Ben Kelly 27 20.00
207 Corey Moore 60 15.00
208 Na'il Diggs 64 15.00
209 Aaron Shea 31 20.00
210 Trevor Gaylor 11 35.00
211 Anthony Lucas 5 40.00
212 Frank Moreau 17 40.00
213 Deon Dyer 73 10.00
214 Avion Black 47 15.00
215 Paul Smith 12 30.00
216 Michael Wiley 10 45.00
217 Dante Hall 53 7.00
218 Muneer Moore 7 40.00
219 Sammy Morris 3 65.00
220 James Whalen 10 30.00
221 Tee Martin 12 65.00
222 Troy Walters 10 35.00
223 Chad Morton 15 40.00
224 Marc Bulger 145 12.00
225 Frank Murphy 11 35.00
226 Thomas Hamner 10 35.00
227 Mareno Philyaw 4 45.00
228 James Williams 47 12.00
229 Mike Anderson 10 100.00
230 Tom Brady 20 30.00
231 Sherrod Gideon 7 35.00
232 Todd Husak 18 40.00
233 Tim Rattay 32 50.00
234 Jarious Jackson 17 45.00
235 Joe Hamilton 29 45.00
236 Shyrone Stith 13 45.00
237 Rondell Mealey 8 40.00
238 Demario Brown 14 35.00
239 Chris Coleman 41 20.00
240 Chafie Fields 39 20.00
241 Drew Haddad 6 35.00
242 Doug Johnson 20 35.00
243 Windrell Hayes 4 35.00
244 Charles Lee 5 35.00
245 Marcus Knight 36 20.00
246 Spergon Wynn 14 30.00
247 Leon Murray 18 25.00
248 Quinton Spotwood 3 40.00
249 Bashir Yamini 31 20.00
250 Kwame Cavil 6 35.00

2000 Donruss All-Time Gridiron Kings

NM/M
Complete Set (10): 25.00
Common Player: 2.00
Production 2,500 Sets
Studio Autographs: 12X
Fouts Autograph never released.
Production 250 Sets
1 Joe Montana 8.00
2 Terry Bradshaw 7.00
3 Fran Tarkenton 6.00
4 Dan Fouts 5.00
5 Sammy Baugh 4.00
6 Eric Dickerson 2.00
7 Bob Griese 5.00
8 Ken Stabler 5.00
9 Joe Namath 8.00
10 Lawrence Taylor 4.00

2000 Donruss Dominators

NM/M
Complete Set (60): 30.00
Common Player: .50
Minor Stars: 1.00
Production 5,000 Sets
1 Jake Plummer 1.00
2 Tim Couch 1.50
3 Emmitt Smith 2.50
4 Troy Aikman 2.00
5 John Elway 2.50
6 Terrell Davis 2.50
7 Charlie Batch 1.00
8 Barry Sanders 2.50
9 Brett Favre 3.50
10 Peyton Manning 3.00
11 Edgerrin James 3.00
12 Mark Brunell 1.50
13 Fred Tayor 1.25
14 Dan Marino 2.50
15 Randy Moss 3.00
16 Drew Bledsoe 1.50
17 Ricky Williams 1.75
18 Jerry Rice 2.00
19 Steve Young 1.50
20 Kurt Warner 3.50
21 Eddie George 1.25
22 Jamal Anderson 1.00
23 Eric Moulds 1.00
24 Cade McNown 1.00
25 Corey Dillon 1.00
26 Kevin Johnson .50
27 Joey Galloway 1.00
28 Olandis Gary 1.00
29 Dorsey Levens 1.00
30 Antonio Freeman 1.00
31 Marvin Harrison 1.00
32 Daunte Culpepper 1.75
33 Cris Carter 1.00
34 Robert Smith 1.00
35 Curtis Martin 1.00
36 Tim Brown 1.00
37 Duce Staley 1.00
38 Donovan McNabb 1.25
39 Jerome Bettis 1.00
40 Terrell Owens 1.00
41 Jon Kitna 1.00
42 Marshall Faulk 1.25
43 Warrick Dunn 1.00
44 Shaun King 1.00
45 Keyshawn Johnson 1.00
46 Steve McNair 1.00
47 Stephen Davis 1.00
48 Brad Johnson .50
49 Muhsin Muhammad .50
50 Marcus Robinson 1.00
51 Akili Smith 1.00
52 Brian Griese 1.25
53 Germane Crowell 1.00
54 Jimmy Smith 1.00
55 Ricky Watters 1.00
56 Isaac Bruce 1.00
57 Warren Sapp .50
58 Jevon Kearse 1.00
59 Michael Westbrook 1.00
60 Ed McCaffrey 1.00

2000 Donruss Elite Series

NM/M
Complete Set (40): 60.00
Common Player: .75
Minor Stars: 1.50
Production 2,500 Sets
1 Jake Plummer 1.50
2 Emmitt Smith 5.00
3 Tim Couch 2.50
4 Troy Aikman 4.00
5 John Elway 5.00
6 Terrell Davis 5.00
7 Barry Sanders 5.00
8 Brett Favre 7.00
9 Peyton Manning 5.00
10 Mark Brunell 2.50
11 Edgerrin James 5.00
12 Fred Taylor 2.00
13 Dan Marino 5.00
14 Randy Moss 5.00
15 Drew Bledsoe 2.50
16 Ricky Williams 3.00
17 Jerry Rice 4.00
18 Steve Young 2.50
19 Kurt Warner 7.00
20 Eddie George 2.00
21 Deion Sanders 1.50
22 Cade McNown 1.50
23 Joey Galloway 1.50
24 Dorsey Levens 1.50
25 Antonio Freeman 1.50
26 Marvin Harrison 1.50
27 Daunte Culpepper 3.00
28 Cris Carter 1.50
29 Curtis Martin 1.50
30 Tim Brown 1.50
31 Donovan McNabb 2.00
32 Jerome Bettis 1.50
33 Marshall Faulk 1.75
34 Jon Kitna 1.50
35 Keyshawn Johnson 1.50
36 Steve McNair 1.50
37 Stephen Davis 1.50
38 Jimmy Smith 1.50
39 Brad Johnson .75
40 Isaac Bruce 1.50

2000 Donruss Gridiron Kings

NM/M
Complete Set (10): 35.00
Common Player: 3.00
Production 2,500 Sets
Studio Cards: 5X
Production 250 Sets
Studio Autographs: 30X
Production 50 Sets
1 Emmitt Smith 5.00
2 John Elway 5.00
3 Barry Sanders 5.00
4 Brett Favre 7.00
5 Peyton Manning 5.00
6 Dan Marino 5.00
7 Randy Moss 5.00
8 Jerry Rice 4.00
9 Steve Young 3.00
10 Kurt Warner 7.00

2000 Donruss Jersey King Autographs

NM/M
Complete Set (10): 2,000
Common Player: 85.00
Production 50 Sets
1 John Elway 200.00
2 Barry Sanders 225.00
3 Dan Marino 250.00
4 Jerry Rice 200.00
5 Kurt Warner 225.00
6 Joe Montana 300.00
7 Terry Bradshaw 200.00
8 Fran Tarkenton 175.00
9 Eric Dickerson 85.00
10 Joe Namath 200.00

Post-1980 cards in Near Mint condition will generally sell for about 75% of the quoted Mint value. Excellent-condition cards bring no more than 40%.

2000 Donruss Rated Rookies

NM/M
Complete Set (40): 40.00
Common Player: 1.00
Minor Stars: 2.00
Production 2,500 Sets
Medalist Cards: 5X
Production 100 Sets
1 Peter Warrick 2.00
2 Jamal Lewis 6.00
3 Thomas Jones 3.00
4 Plaxico Burress 4.00
5 Travis Taylor 2.50
6 Ron Dayne 2.00
7 Bubba Franks 2.00
8 Chad Pennington 8.00
9 Shaun Alexander 5.00
10 Sylvester Morris 4.00
11 R. Jay Soward 2.00
12 Trung Canidate 1.00
13 Dennis Northcutt 2.00
14 Todd Pinkston 2.00
15 Jerry Porter 2.00
16 Travis Prentice 2.50
17 Giovanni Carmazzi 2.00
18 Ron Dugans 2.00
19 Dez White 2.00
20 Chris Cole 1.00
21 Ron Dixon 2.50
22 Chris Redman 3.00
23 J.R. Redmond 2.50
24 Laveranues Coles 2.50
25 JaJuan Dawson 2.00
26 Darrell Jackson 2.50
27 Reuben Droughns 1.00
28 Doug Chapman 1.00
29 Curtis Keaton 1.00
30 Gari Scott 1.00
31 Danny Farmer 1.00
32 Trevor Gaylor 1.00
33 Anthony Lucas 1.00
34 Frank Moreau 2.00
35 Avion Black 1.00
36 Michael Wiley 1.00
37 Dante Hall 5.00
38 Tim Rattay 2.00
39 Tee Martin 2.00
40 Courtney Brown 2.00

2000 Donruss Rookie Gridiron Kings

NM/M
Complete Set (10): 20.00
Common Player: 2.00
Production 2,500 Sets
Studio Cards: 4X
Production 250 Sets
Studio Autographs: 15X
Production 50 Sets
1 Peter Warrick 2.00
2 Jamal Lewis 6.00
3 Thomas Jones 3.00
4 Plaxico Burress 4.00
5 Travis Taylor 2.00
6 Ron Dayne 2.00
7 Chad Pennington 8.00
8 Shaun Alexander 5.00
9 Sylvester Morris 2.00
10 Chris Redman 2.00

2000 Donruss Signature Series Red

NM/M
Common Player: 10.00
1 Troy Aikman 25 100.00
2 Tony Banks 325 10.00
3 Jeff Blake 125 15.00
4 Drew Bledsoe 35 50.00
5 Isaac Bruce 25 25.00
6 Trung Canidate 75 15.00
7 Giovanni Carmazzi 175 15.00
8 Kwame Cavil 375 10.00
9 Doug Chapman 375 10.00
10 Laveranues Coles 175 20.00
11 Kerry Collins 125 15.00
12 Albert Connell 750 10.00
13 Tim Couch 25 40.00
14 Germane Crowell 350 10.00
15 Daunte Culpepper 375 40.00
16 Reuben Droughns 375 10.00
17 Ron Dugans 175 15.00
18 Tim Dwight 350 15.00
19 Troy Edwards 350 10.00
20 Kevin Faulk 750 10.00
21 Danny Farmer 175 15.00
22 Marshall Faulk 25 60.00
23 Jermaine Fazande 750 10.00
24 Antonio Freeman 175 15.00
25 Charlie Garner 750 10.00
26 Olandis Gary 350 15.00
27 Trevor Gaylor 175 10.00
28 Eddie George 25 50.00
29 Marvin Harrison 75 25.00
30 Torry Holt 75 25.00
31 Darrell Jackson 175 20.00
32 Edgerrin James 25 75.00
33 Patrick Jeffers 750 10.00
34 Brad Johnson 25 30.00
35 Kevin Johnson 350 10.00
36 Curtis Martin 75 25.00
37 Tee Martin 275 15.00
38 Derrick Mayes 750 10.00
39 Cade McNown 75 35.00
40 Sylvester Morris 125 30.00
41 Randy Moss 75 100.00
42 Eric Moulds 100 20.00
43 Dennis Northcutt 175 15.00
44 Todd Pinkston 175 15.00
45 Jake Plummer 25 25.00
46 Jerry Porter 175 15.00
47 Travis Prentice 175 20.00
48 Tim Rattay 375 20.00
49 J.R. Redmond 175 15.00
50 Corey Simon 175 15.00
51 Akili Smith 75 10.00
52 Antowain Smith 75 15.00
53 Jimmy Smith 75 15.00
54 R. Jay Soward 175 15.00
55 Shyrone Stith 175 10.00
56 Fred Taylor 75 45.00
57 Thurman Thomas 75 20.00
58 Kurt Warner 75 60.00
59 Ricky Williams 25 50.00
60 Tyrone Wheatley 350 10.00

2000 Donruss Signature Series Blue

NM/M
Common Player: 12.50
Production 100 Sets
2 Tony Banks 12.50
3 Jeff Blake 12.50
7 Giovanni Carmazzi 20.00
8 Kwame Cavil 12.50
9 Doug Chapman 12.50
10 Laveranues Coles 25.00
11 Kerry Collins 12.50
12 Albert Connell 12.50
14 Germane Crowell 12.50
15 Daunte Culpepper 65.00
16 Reuben Droughns 12.50
17 Ron Dugans 20.00
18 Tim Dwight 20.00
19 Troy Edwards 12.50
20 Kevin Faulk 12.50
21 Danny Farmer 12.50
23 Jermaine Fazande 12.50
24 Antonio Freeman 20.00
25 Charlie Garner 12.50
26 Olandis Gary 20.00
27 Trevor Gaylor 12.50
31 Darrell Jackson 25.00
33 Patrick Jeffers 15.00
35 Kevin Johnson 15.00
37 Tee Martin 20.00
38 Derrick Mayes 12.50
40 Sylvester Morris 40.00
43 Dennis Northcutt 20.00
44 Todd Pinkston 20.00
46 Jerry Porter 20.00
47 Travis Prentice 30.00
48 Tim Rattay 25.00
49 J.R. Redmond 25.00
50 Corey Simon 25.00
54 R. Jay Soward 20.00
55 Shyrone Stith 12.50
60 Tyrone Wheatley 12.50

2000 Donruss Signature Series Gold

NM/M
Common Player: 20.00
Production 25 Sets
1 Troy Aikman 100.00
2 Tony Banks 20.00
3 Jeff Blake 20.00
4 Drew Bledsoe 60.00
5 Isaac Bruce 25.00
6 Trung Canidate 25.00
7 Giovanni Carmazzi 35.00
8 Kwame Cavil 20.00
9 Doug Chapman 20.00
10 Laveranues Coles 40.00
11 Kerry Collins 20.00
12 Albert Connell 20.00
13 Tim Couch 50.00
14 Germane Crowell 25.00
15 Daunte Culpepper 80.00
16 Reuben Droughns 20.00
17 Ron Dugans 20.00
18 Tim Dwight 40.00
19 Troy Edwards 20.00
20 Kevin Faulk 20.00
21 Danny Farmer 20.00
22 Marshall Faulk 45.00
23 Jermaine Fazande 20.00
24 Antonio Freeman 40.00
25 Charlie Garner 20.00
26 Olandis Gary 40.00
27 Trevor Gaylor 20.00
28 Eddie George 50.00
29 Marvin Harrison 40.00
30 Torry Holt 35.00
31 Darrell Jackson 40.00
32 Edgerrin James 100.00
33 Patrick Jeffers 35.00
34 Brad Johnson 30.00
35 Kevin Johnson 30.00
36 Curtis Martin 30.00
37 Tee Martin 30.00
38 Derrick Mayes 20.00
39 Cade McNown 35.00
40 Sylvester Morris 50.00
41 Randy Moss 100.00
42 Eric Moulds 30.00
43 Dennis Northcutt 25.00
44 Todd Pinkston 25.00
45 Jake Plummer 35.00
46 Jerry Porter 35.00
47 Travis Prentice 45.00
48 Tim Rattay 35.00
49 J.R. Redmond 30.00
50 Corey Simon 35.00
51 Akili Smith 30.00
52 Antowain Smith 25.00
53 Jimmy Smith 30.00
54 R. Jay Soward 30.00
55 Shyrone Stith 25.00
56 Fred Taylor 50.00
57 Thurman Thomas 35.00
58 Kurt Warner 75.00
59 Ricky Williams 50.00
60 Tyrone Wheatley 20.00

2000 Donruss Zoning Commission

NM/M
Complete Set (60): 85.00
Common Player: 1.00
Minor Stars: 2.00
Production 1,000 Sets
1 Jake Plummer 2.00
2 Tim Couch 3.00
3 Emmitt Smith 6.00
4 Troy Aikman 5.00
5 Charlie Batch 2.00
6 Brett Favre 8.00
7 Peyton Manning 8.00
8 Edgerrin James 8.00
9 Mark Brunell 3.00
10 Fred Taylor 2.50
11 Dan Marino 8.00
12 Randy Moss 8.00
13 Drew Bledsoe 3.00
14 Ricky Williams 4.00
15 Jerry Rice 5.00
16 Steve Young 3.00
17 Kurt Warner 6.00
18 Eddie George 2.50
19 Eric Moulds 2.00
20 Doug Flutie 2.50
21 Antowain Smith 1.00
22 Cade McNown 2.00
23 Corey Dillon 2.00
24 Kevin Johnson 1.00
25 Joey Galloway 2.00
26 Olandis Gary 2.00
27 Dorsey Levens 2.00
28 Antonio Freeman 2.00
29 Marvin Harrison 2.00
30 Cris Carter 2.00
31 Robert Smith 2.00
32 Curtis Martin 2.00
33 Tim Brown 2.00
34 Duce Staley 2.00
35 Donovan McNabb 2.50
36 Kordell Stewart 2.00
37 Jerome Bettis 2.00
38 Terrell Owens 2.00
39 Jon Kitna 2.00
40 Marshall Faulk 2.50
41 Torry Holt 2.00
42 Mike Alstott 2.00
43 Shaun King 2.50
44 Keyshawn Johnson 2.00
45 Steve McNair 2.00
46 Stephen Davis 2.00
47 Brad Johnson 1.00
48 Qadry Ismail 1.00
49 Muhsin Muhammad 1.00
50 Patrick Jeffers 2.00
51 Marcus Robinson 2.00
52 Akili Smith 2.00
53 Germane Crowell 2.00
54 James Stewart 2.00
55 Jimmy Smith 2.00
56 Amani Toomer 1.00
57 Charlie Garner 2.00
58 Isaac Bruce 2.00
59 Albert Connell 1.00
60 Jeff George 2.00

2000 Donruss Zoning Commission Red

NM/M
Common Player: 20.00
Minor Stars: 40.00
Production to 1999 TD total.
1 Jake Plummer 9 40.00
2 Tim Couch 15 65.00
3 Emmitt Smith 11 120.00
4 Troy Aikman 17 100.00
5 Charlie Batch 13 40.00
6 Brett Favre 22 125.00
7 Peyton Manning 26 100.00
8 Edgerrin James 13 125.00
9 Mark Brunell 14 65.00
10 Fred Taylor 6 65.00
11 Dan Marino 12 150.00
12 Randy Moss 11 130.00
13 Drew Bledsoe 19 65.00
14 Ricky Williams 2 100.00
15 Jerry Rice 5 125.00
16 Steve Young 3 75.00
17 Kurt Warner 41 70.00
18 Eddie George 9 65.00
19 Eric Moulds 7 50.00
20 Doug Flutie 19 50.00
21 Antowain Smith 6 40.00
22 Cade McNown 8 50.00
23 Corey Dillon 5 50.00
24 Kevin Johnson 8 50.00
25 Joey Galloway 1 80.00
26 Olandis Gary 7 50.00
27 Dorsey Levens 9 50.00
28 Antonio Freeman 6 50.00
29 Marvin Harrison 12 40.00
30 Cris Carter 13 40.00
31 Robert Smith 2 50.00
32 Curtis Martin 5 50.00
33 Tim Brown 6 50.00
34 Duce Staley 4 60.00
35 Donovan McNabb 8 80.00
36 Kordell Stewart 6 60.00
37 Jerome Bettis 7 50.00
38 Terrell Owens 4 50.00
39 Jon Kitna 23 20.00
40 Marshall Faulk 7 60.00
41 Torry Holt 6 50.00
42 Mike Alstott 7 50.00
43 Shaun King 7 50.00
44 Keyshawn Johnson 8 50.00
45 Steve McNair 12 50.00
46 Stephen Davis 17 40.00
47 Brad Johnson 24 40.00
48 Qadry Ismail 6 40.00
49 Muhsin Muhammad 8 40.00
50 Patrick Jeffers 12 50.00
51 Marcus Robinson 9 50.00
52 Akili Smith 2 60.00
53 Germane Crowell 7 50.00
54 James Stewart 13 40.00
55 Jimmy Smith 6 50.00
56 Amani Toomer 6 50.00
57 Charlie Garner 4 50.00
58 Isaac Bruce 12 50.00
59 Albert Connell 7 40.00
60 Jeff George 23 20.00

2000 Donruss Elite

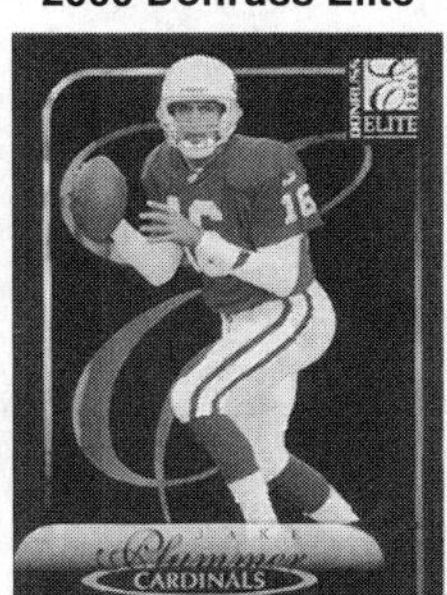

NM/M
Complete Set (200): 500.00
Common Player: .20
Minor Stars: .40
Common Player (101-125): 1.00
Minor Stars (101-125): 2.00
Common Rookie: 4.00
Production 2,000 Sets
Pack (5): 6.25
Wax Box (18): 80.00
1 Jake Plummer .60
2 David Boston .75
3 Rob Moore .40
4 Chris Chandler .40
5 Tim Dwight .75
6 Terance Mathis .20
7 Jamal Anderson .75
8 Priest Holmes .75
9 Tony Banks .40
10 Shannon Sharpe .40
11 Qadry Ismail .20
12 Eric Moulds .75
13 Doug Flutie .50
14 Antowain Smith .40
15 Peerless Price .50
16 Muhsin Muhammad .40
17 Tim Biakabutuka .40
18 Patrick Jeffers .75
19 Steve Beuerlein .75
20 Wesley Walls .40
21 Curtis Enis .40
22 Marcus Robinson .75
23 Carl Pickens .40
24 Corey Dillon .50
25 Akili Smith .50
26 Darnay Scott .50
27 Kevin Johnson .75
28 Errict Rhett .40
29 Emmitt Smith 2.00
30 Deion Sanders .75
31 Troy Aikman 1.50
32 Joey Galloway .75
33 Michael Irvin .40
34 Raghib Ismail .20
35 Jason Tucker .75
36 Ed McCaffrey .50
37 Rod Smith .50
38 Brian Griese 1.00
39 Terrell Davis 1.00
40 Olandis Gary .50
41 Charlie Batch .75
42 Johnnie Morton .20
43 Herman Moore .50
44 James Stewart .50
45 Dorsey Levens .50
46 Antonio Freeman .50
47 Brett Favre 3.00
48 Bill Schroeder .20
49 Peyton Manning 2.00
50 Keenan McCardell .40
51 Fred Taylor 1.25
52 Jimmy Smith .50
53 Elvis Grbac .40
54 Tony Gonzalez .50
55 Derrick Alexander .20
56 Dan Marino 2.00
57 Tony Martin .20
58 James Johnson .20
59 Damon Huard .40
60 Thurman Thomas .40
61 Robert Smith .50
62 Randall Cunningham .50
63 Jeff George .50
64 Terry Glenn .50
65 Drew Bledsoe 1.00
66 Jeff Blake .40
67 Amani Toomer .40
68 Kerry Collins .40
69 Joe Montgomery .20
70 Vinny Testaverde .40
71 Ray Lucas .40
72 Keyshawn Johnson .75
73 Wayne Chrebet .50
74 Napoleon Kaufman .50
75 Tim Brown .50
76 Rich Gannon .40
77 Duce Staley .75
78 Kordell Stewart .75
79 Jerome Bettis .50
80 Troy Edwards .75
81 Natrone Means .40
82 Curtis Conway .40
83 Jim Harbaugh .40
84 Junior Seau .40
85 Jermaine Fazande .40
86 Terrell Owens .75
87 Charlie Garner .40
88 Steve Young 1.00
89 Jeff Garcia .50
90 Derrick Mayes .40
91 Ricky Watters .40
92 Az-Zahir Hakim .40
93 Torry Holt .75
94 Warren Sapp .40
95 Mike Alstott .75
96 Warrick Dunn .75
97 Kevin Dyson .40
98 Bruce Smith .20
99 Albert Connell .40
100 Michael Westbrook 1.00
101 Cade McNown 1.00
102 Tim Couch 2.00
103 John Elway 3.00
104 Barry Sanders 6.00
105 Germane Crowell 1.00
106 Marvin Harrison 2.00
107 Edgerrin James 4.00
108 Mark Brunell 3.00
109 Randy Moss 6.00
110 Cris Carter 2.00
111 Daunte Culpepper 3.00
112 Ricky Williams 3.00
113 Curtis Martin 2.00
114 Donovan McNabb 3.00
115 Jerry Rice 4.00
116 Jon Kitna 2.00
117 Isaac Bruce 2.00
118 Marshall Faulk 2.00
119 Kurt Warner 3.00
120 Shaun King 3.00
121 Eddie George 2.00
122 Steve McNair 2.00
123 Jevon Kearse 2.00
124 Stephen Davis 2.00
125 Brad Johnson 2.00
126 *Mike Anderson* 2.00
127 *Peter Warrick* 2.00
128 *Courtney Brown* 3.00
129 *Plaxico Burress* 8.00
130 *Corey Simon* 4.00
131 *Thomas Jones* 6.00
132 *Travis Taylor* 2.00
133 *Shaun Alexander* 12.00
134 *Deon Grant* 4.00
135 *Chris Redman* 5.00
136 *Chad Pennington* 20.00
137 *Jamal Lewis* 12.00
138 *Brian Urlacher* 10.00
139 *Keith Bulluck* 5.00
140 *Bubba Franks* 6.00
141 *Dez White* 5.00
142 *Na'il Diggs* 4.00
143 *Ahmed Plummer* 4.00
144 *Ron Dayne* 5.00
145 *Shaun Ellis* 4.00
146 *Sylvester Morris* 4.00
147 *Delthea O'Neal* 4.00
148 *Raynoch Thompson* 4.00
149 *R. Jay Soward* 4.00
150 *Mario Edwards* 4.00
151 *John Engelberger* 4.00
152 Redemption 4.00
153 *Sherrod Gideon* 4.00
154 *John Abraham* 4.00
155 Redemption 4.00
156 *Travis Prentice* 4.00
157 *Darrell Jackson* 6.00
158 *Giovanni Carmazzi* 4.00
159 *Anthony Lucas* 4.00
160 *Danny Farmer* 4.00
161 *Dennis Northcutt* 4.00
162 *Troy Walters* 4.00
163 *Laveranues Coles* 6.00
164 *Tee Martin* 5.00
165 *J.R. Redmond* 4.00
166 *Tim Rattay* 6.00
167 *Jerry Porter* 6.00
168 *Sebastian Janikowski* 4.00
169 *Michael Wiley* 4.00
170 *Reuben Droughns* 8.00
171 *Trung Canidate* 5.00
172 *Shyrone Stith* 4.00
173 *Chris Hovan* 4.00
174 Redemption Card 4.00
175 Redemption Card 4.00
176 *Trevor Gaylor* 4.00
177 *Chris Cole* 4.00
178 *Hank Poteat* 4.00
179 *Darren Howard* 4.00
180 *Rob Morris* 4.00
181 Redemption Card 4.00
182 *Marc Bulger* 10.00
183 *Tom Brady* 40.00
184 *Todd Husak* 4.00
185 *Gari Scott* 4.00
186 *Erron Kinney* 4.00
187 Redemption Card 4.00
188 *Sammy Morris* 5.00
189 *Rondell Mealey* 4.00
190 Redemption Card 4.00
191 *Ron Dugans* 4.00
192 *Deon Dyer* 4.00
193 *Fred Robbins* 4.00
194 Redemption Card 4.00
195 *Mareno Philyaw* 4.00
196 Redemption Card 4.00
197 *Jarious Jackson* 4.00
198 *Anthony Becht* 4.00
199 *Joe Hamilton* 4.00
200 *Todd Pinkston* 6.00

2000 Donruss Elite Aspirations

NM/M
Common Player 65-99: 5.00
Common Player 45-64: 10.00
Common Player 20-29: 15.00
Common Player 10-19: 20.00
Cards #'d 9 And Under Not Priced 4.00
1 Jake Plummer 84 15.00
2 David Boston 11 40.00
3 Rob Moore 15 20.00
4 Chris Chandler 88 10.00
5 Tim Dwight 17 40.00
6 Terance Mathis 19 20.00
7 Jamal Anderson 68 15.00
8 Priest Holmes 67 15.00
9 Tony Banks 88 10.00
10 Shannon Sharpe 16 40.00
11 Qadry Ismail 13 20.00
12 Eric Moulds 20 45.00
13 Doug Flutie 93 20.00
14 Antowain Smith 77 10.00
15 Peerless Price 19 35.00
16 Muhsin Muhammad 13 35.00
17 Tim Biakabutuka 79 10.00
18 Patrick Jeffers 17 40.00
19 Steve Beuerlein 93 5.00
20 Wesley Walls 15 20.00
21 Curtis Enis 56 20.00
22 Marcus Robinson 12 50.00
23 Carl Pickens 19 35.00
24 Corey Dillon 72 10.00
25 Akili Smith 89 12.00
26 Darnay Scott 14 30.00
27 Kevin Johnson 14 50.00
28 Errict Rhett 68 5.00
29 Emmitt Smith 78 60.00
30 Deion Sanders 79 10.00
31 Troy Aikman 92 40.00
32 Joey Galloway 16 35.00
33 Michael Irvin 12 30.00
34 Raghib Ismail 19 20.00
35 Jason Tucker 13 35.00
36 Ed McCaffrey 13 35.00
37 Rod Smith 20 25.00
38 Brian Griese 86 20.00
39 Terrell Davis 70 60.00
40 Olandis Gary 78 12.00
41 Charlie Batch 90 12.00
42 Johnnie Morton 13 25.00
43 Herman Moore 16 35.00
44 James Stewart 67 10.00
45 Dorsey Levens 75 10.00
46 Antonio Freeman 14 45.00
47 Brett Favre 96 70.00
48 Bill Schroeder 16 20.00
49 Peyton Manning 82 60.00
50 Keenan McCardell 13 30.00
51 Fred Taylor 72 35.00
52 Jimmy Smith 18 35.00
53 Elvis Grbac 82 5.00
54 Tony Gonzalez 12 35.00
55 Derrick Alexander 18 20.00
56 Dan Marino 87 60.00
57 Tony Martin 20 30.00
58 James Johnson 68 5.00
59 Damon Huard 89 12.00
60 Thurman Thomas 66 10.00
61 Robert Smith 74 10.00
62 Randall Cunningham 93 12.00
63 Jeff George 97 12.00
64 Terry Glenn 12 50.00
65 Drew Bledsoe 89 25.00
66 Jeff Blake 92 10.00
67 Amani Toomer 19 20.00
68 Kerry Collins 95 5.00
69 Joe Montgomery 75 5.00
70 Vinny Testaverde 84 5.00
71 Ray Lucas 94 10.00
72 Keyshawn Johnson 81 10.00
73 Wayne Chrebet 20 25.00
74 Napoleon Kaufman 74 10.00
75 Tim Brown 19 40.00
76 Rich Gannon 88 5.00
77 Duce Staley 78 10.00
78 Kordell Stewart 90 12.00
79 Jerome Bettis 64 15.00
80 Troy Edwards 19 40.00
81 Natrone Means 80 10.00
82 Curtis Conway 20 30.00

83 Jim Harbaugh 96 5.00
84 Junior Seau 45 10.00
85 Jermaine Fazande 65 10.00
86 Terrell Owens 19 40.00
87 Charlie Garner 75 5.00
88 Steve Young 92 25.00
89 Jeff Garcia 95 10.00
90 Derrick Mayes 13 30.00
91 Ricky Watters 68 10.00
92 Az-Zahir Hakim 19 35.00
93 Torry Holt 12 45.00
94 Warren Sapp 1
95 Mike Alstott 60 15.00
96 Warrick Dunn 72 12.00
97 Kevin Dyson 13 30.00
98 Bruce Smith 22 20.00
99 Albert Connell 17 30.00
100 Michael Westbrook 18 30.00
101 Cade McNown 92 20.00
102 Tim Couch 98 30.00
103 John Elway 93 60.00
104 Barry Sanders 80 70.00
105 Germane Crowell 18 30.00
106 Marvin Harrison 12 45.00
107 Edgerrin James 68 60.00
108 Mark Brunell 92 25.00
109 Randy Moss 16 150.00
110 Cris Carter 20 45.00
111 Daunte Culpepper 88 20.00
112 Ricky Williams 66 40.00
113 Curtis Martin 72 10.00
114 Donovan McNabb 95 20.00
115 Jerry Rice 20 125.00
116 Jon Kitna 93 12.00
117 Isaac Bruce 20 50.00
118 Marshall Faulk 72 12.00
119 Kurt Warner 87 85.00
120 Shaun King 90 20.00
121 Eddie George 73 25.00
122 Steve McNair 91 15.00
123 Jevon Kearse 10 50.00
124 Stephen Davis 52 15.00
125 Brad Johnson 86 10.00
127 Peter Warrick 91 120.00
128 Courtney Brown 14 100.00
129 Plaxico Burress 96 75.00
130 Corey Simon 47 30.00
131 Thomas Jones 94 60.00
132 Travis Taylor 81 40.00
133 Shaun Alexander 63 50.00
134 Deon Grant 93 15.00
135 Chris Redman 93 30.00
136 Chad Pennington 90 85.00
137 Jamal Lewis 69 75.00
138 Brian Urlacher 56 45.00
139 Keith Bulluck 67 20.00
140 Bubba Franks 12 75.00
141 Dez White 78 25.00
142 Na'il Diggs 68 20.00
143 Ahmed Plummer 81 15.00
144 Ron Dayne 67 120.00
145 Shaun Ellis 7
146 Sylvester Morris 15 100.00
147 Delthea O'Neal 92 15.00
148 Raynoch Thompson 54 20.00
149 R. Jay Soward 82 35.00
150 Mario Edwards 85 10.00
151 John Engelberger 4
153 Sherrod Gideon 89 15.00
154 John Abraham 5
156 Travis Prentice 59 40.00
157 Darrell Jackson 91 20.00
158 Giovanni Carmazzi 81 45.00
159 Anthony Lucas 20 45.00
160 Danny Farmer 13 40.00
161 Dennis Northcutt 92 25.00
162 Troy Walters 95 20.00
163 Laveranues Coles 93 20.00
164 Tee Martin 83 30.00
165 J.R. Redmond 79 40.00
166 Tim Rattay 87 25.00
167 Jerry Porter 99 30.00
168 Sebastian Janikowski 62 20.00
169 Michael Wiley 95 25.00
170 Reuben Droughns 78 25.00
171 Trung Canidate 70 25.00
172 Shyrone Stith 62 25.00
173 Chris Hovan 5
176 Trevor Gaylor 91 12.00
177 Chris Cole 20 40.00
178 Hank Poteat 69 20.00
179 Darren Howard 51 20.00
180 Rob Morris 56 20.00
182 Marc Bulger 90 15.00
183 Tom Brady 90 75.00
184 Todd Husak 93 20.00
185 Gari Scott 14 35.00
186 Erron Kinney 12 35.00
188 Sammy Morris 95 20.00
189 Rondell Mealey 93 20.00
191 Ron Dugans 20 50.00
192 Deon Dyer 62 20.00
193 Fred Robbins 10 40.00
195 Mareno Philyaw 92 12.00
197 Jarious Jackson 93 25.00
198 Anthony Becht 18 35.00
199 Joe Hamilton 86 25.00
200 Todd Pinkston 20 50.00

Values quoted in this guide reflect the retail price of a card—the price a collector can expect to pay when buying a card from a dealer. The wholesale price—that which a collector can expect to receive from a dealer when selling cards—will be significantly lower, depending on desirability and condition.

2000 Donruss Elite Rookie Die Cuts

Die Cut Cards: 1.5X

2000 Donruss Elite Status

NM/M
Common Player 65-99: 5.00
Common Player 20-64: 10.00
Common Player 10-19: 30.00
Cards #'d 9 And Under Not Priced 2.00
1 Jake Plummer 16 60.00
2 David Boston 89 12.00
3 Rob Moore 85 5.00
4 Chris Chandler 12 30.00
5 Tim Dwight 83 10.00
6 Terance Mathis 81 5.00
7 Jamal Anderson 32 30.00
8 Priest Holmes 33 35.00
9 Tony Banks 12 30.00
10 Shannon Sharpe 84 10.00
11 Qadry Ismail 87 5.00
12 Eric Moulds 80 12.00
13 Doug Flutie 7
14 Antowain Smith 23 40.00
15 Peerless Price 81 10.00
16 Muhsin Muhammad 87 10.00
17 Tim Biakabutuka 21 20.00
18 Patrick Jeffers 83 12.00
19 Steve Beuerlein 7
20 Wesley Walls 85 8.00
21 Curtis Enis 44 30.00
22 Marcus Robinson 88 12.00
23 Carl Pickens 81 8.00
24 Corey Dillon 28 40.00
25 Akili Smith 11 65.00
26 Darnay Scott 86 5.00
27 Kevin Johnson 86 10.00
28 Errict Rhett 32 15.00
29 Emmitt Smith 22 120.00
30 Deion Sanders 21 40.00
31 Troy Aikman 8
32 Joey Galloway 84 10.00
33 Michael Irvin 88 10.00
34 Raghib Ismail 81 5.00
35 Jason Tucker 87 8.00
36 Ed McCaffrey 87 10.00
37 Rod Smith 80 8.00
38 Brian Griese 14 70.00
39 Terrell Davis 30 85.00
40 Olandis Gary 22 40.00
41 Charlie Batch 10 65.00
42 Johnnie Morton 87 5.00
43 Herman Moore 84 10.00
44 James Stewart 33 20.00
45 Dorsey Levens 25 30.00
46 Antonio Freeman 86 10.00
47 Brett Favre 4
48 Bill Schroeder 84 5.00
49 Peyton Manning 18 200.00
50 Keenan McCardell 87 5.00
51 Fred Taylor 28 75.00
52 Jimmy Smith 82 10.00
53 Elvis Grbac 18 30.00
54 Tony Gonzalez 88 8.00
55 Derrick Alexander 82 5.00
56 Dan Marino 13 225.00
57 Tony Martin 80 5.00
58 James Johnson 32 15.00
59 Damon Huard 11 50.00
60 Thurman Thomas 34 25.00
61 Robert Smith 26 25.00
62 Randall Cunningham 7
63 Jeff George 3
64 Terry Glenn 88 10.00
65 Drew Bledsoe 11 120.00
66 Jeff Blake 8
67 Amani Toomer 81 5.00
68 Kerry Collins 5
69 Joe Montgomery 25 15.00
70 Vinny Testaverde 16 45.00
71 Ray Lucas 6
72 Keyshawn Johnson 19 60.00
73 Wayne Chrebet 80 10.00
74 Napoleon Kaufman 26 35.00
75 Tim Brown 81 8.00
76 Rich Gannon 12 30.00
77 Duce Staley 22 40.00
78 Kordell Stewart 10 60.00
79 Jerome Bettis 36 20.00
80 Troy Edwards 81 10.00
81 Natrone Means 20 20.00
82 Curtis Conway 80 5.00
83 Jim Harbaugh 4
84 Junior Seau 55 10.00
85 Jermaine Fazande 35 20.00
86 Terrell Owens 81 10.00
87 Charlie Garner 25 15.00
88 Steve Young 8
89 Jeff Garcia 5
90 Derrick Mayes 87 8.00
91 Ricky Watters 32 25.00
92 Az-Zahir Hakim 81 5.00
93 Torry Holt 88 10.00
94 Warren Sapp 99 5.00
95 Mike Alstott 40 25.00
96 Warrick Dunn 28 25.00
97 Kevin Dyson 87 8.00
98 Bruce Smith 78 5.00
99 Albert Connell 83 5.00
100 Michael Westbrook 82 10.00
101 Cade McNown 8
102 Tim Couch 2
103 John Elway 7
104 Barry Sanders 20 175.00
105 Germane Crowell 82 8.00
106 Marvin Harrison 88 10.00
107 Edgerrin James 32 125.00
108 Mark Brunell 8
109 Randy Moss 84 60.00
110 Cris Carter 80 10.00
111 Daunte Culpepper 12 85.00
112 Ricky Williams 34 70.00
113 Curtis Martin 28 25.00
114 Donovan McNabb 5
115 Jerry Rice 80 45.00
116 Jon Kitna 7
117 Isaac Bruce 80 10.00
118 Marshall Faulk 28 45.00
119 Kurt Warner 13 300.00
120 Shaun King 10 50.00
121 Eddie George 27 35.00
122 Steve McNair 9
123 Jevon Kearse 90 12.00
124 Stephen Davis 48 20.00
125 Brad Johnson 14 45.00
127 Peter Warrick 9
128 Courtney Brown 86 35.00
129 Plaxico Burress 4
130 Corey Simon 83 25.00
131 Thomas Jones 6
132 Travis Taylor 19 125.00
133 Shaun Alexander 37 125.00
134 Deon Grant 7
135 Chris Redman 7
136 Chad Pennington 10 300.00
137 Jamal Lewis 31 150.00
138 Brian Urlacher 44 50.00
139 Keith Bulluck 33 40.00
140 Bubba Franks 88 30.00
141 Dez White 22 60.00
142 Na'il Diggs 32 25.00
143 Ahmed Plummer 19 45.00
144 Ron Dayne 33 250.00
145 Shaun Ellis 93 12.00
146 Sylvester Morris 85 30.00
147 Delthea O'Neal 8
148 Raynoch Thompson 46 25.00
149 R. Jay Soward 18 85.00
150 Mario Edwards 15 50.00
151 John Engelberger 96 10.00
153 Sherrod Gideon 11 50.00
154 John Abraham 95 15.00
156 Travis Prentice 41 60.00
157 Darrell Jackson 9
158 Giovanni Carmazzi 19 125.00
159 Anthony Lucas 80 20.00
160 Danny Farmer 87 20.00
161 Dennis Northcutt 8
162 Troy Walters 5
163 Laveranues Coles 7
164 Tee Martin 17 85.00
165 J.R. Redmond 21 85.00
166 Tim Rattay 13 80.00
167 Jerry Porter 1
168 Sebastian Janikowski 38 25.00
169 Michael Wiley 5
170 Reuben Droughns 22 50.00
171 Trung Canidate 30 40.00
172 Shyrone Stith 38 25.00
173 Chris Hovan 95 12.00
175 Mark Roman 8
177 Chris Cole 80 12.00
178 Hank Poteat 31 25.00
179 Darren Howard 49 25.00
180 Rob Morris 44 15.00
182 Marc Bulger 10 45.00
183 Tom Brady 10 300.00
184 Todd Husak 7
185 Gari Scott 86 15.00
186 Erron Kinney 88 15.00
188 Sammy Morris 5
189 Rondell Mealey 7
191 Ron Dugans 80 15.00
192 Deon Dyer 38 25.00
193 Fred Robbins 90 10.00
195 Mareno Philyaw 8
197 Jarious Jackson 7
198 Anthony Becht 82 15.00
199 Joe Hamilton 14 60.00
200 Todd Pinkston 80 20.00

A card number in parenthese ( ) indicates the set is unnumbered.

2000 Donruss Elite Craftsmen

NM/M
Complete Set (40): 60.00
Common Player: 1.50
Production 2,500 Sets
Master Cards: 2X-5X
Production 50 Sets
C1 Dan Marino 5.00
C2 Edgerrin James 5.00
C3 Peyton Manning 5.00
C4 Drew Bledsoe 2.50
C5 Doug Flutie 2.00
C6 Curtis Martin 1.50
C7 Eddie George 2.00
C8 Steve McNair 2.00
C9 Fred Taylor 2.50
C10 Mark Brunell 2.50
C11 Tim Couch 3.00
C12 Corey Dillon 1.50
C13 Terrell Davis 4.00
C14 Jon Kitna 1.50
C15 Emmitt Smith 4.00
C16 Troy Aikman 3.50
C17 Stephen Davis 1.50
C18 Brad Johnson 1.50
C19 Jake Plummer 2.00
C20 Brett Favre 6.00
C21 Barry Sanders 6.00
C22 Marshall Faulk 1.50
C23 Kurt Warner 8.00
C24 Ricky Williams 3.00
C25 Steve Young 2.50
C26 Randy Moss 6.00
C27 John Elway 5.00
C28 Jerry Rice 3.50
C29 Tim Brown 1.50
C30 Cris Carter 1.50
C31 Antonio Freeman 1.50
C32 Joey Galloway 1.50
C33 Terry Glenn 1.50
C34 Marvin Harrison 1.50
C35 Keyshawn Johnson 1.50
C36 Eric Moulds 1.50
C37 Isaac Bruce 1.50
C38 Peter Warrick 3.00
C39 Plaxico Burress 8.00
C40 Thomas Jones 7.00

2000 Donruss Elite Down and Distance

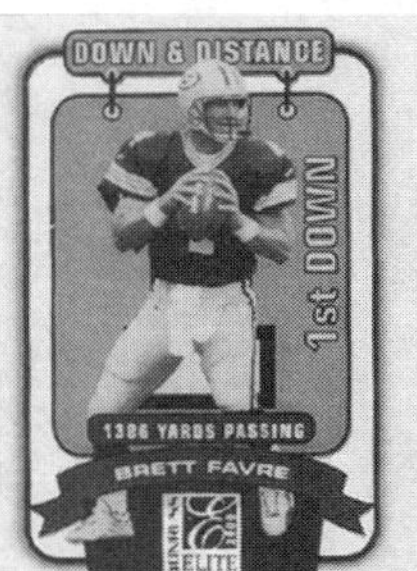

NM/M
Common Player: 5.00
Production #'d To A Season Stat
Cards #'d 9 And Under Not Priced
1A Randy Moss 611 10.00
1B Randy Moss 493 15.00
1C Randy Moss 263 20.00
1D Randy Moss 46 45.00
2A Brett Favre 1386 10.00
2B Brett Favre 1543 10.00
2C Brett Favre 1139 15.00
2D Brett Favre 23 90.00
3A Dan Marino 1023 10.00
3B Dan Marino 855 15.00
3C Dan Marino 505 20.00
3D Dan Marino 65 60.00
4A Peyton Manning 1857 10.00
4B Peyton Manning 1219 15.00
4C Peyton Manning 1029 15.00
4D Peyton Manning 30 60.00
5A Emmitt Smith 832 10.00
5B Emmitt Smith 506 15.00
5C Emmitt Smith 55 40.00
5D Emmitt Smith 4
6A Jerry Rice 391 15.00
6B Jerry Rice 238 20.00
6C Jerry Rice 176 25.00
6D Jerry Rice 25 60.00
7A Mark Brunell 1066 5.00
7B Mark Brunell 1112 5.00
7C Mark Brunell 878 5.00
7D Mark Brunell 4
8A Eddie George 716 5.00
8B Eddie George 487 7.00
8C Eddie George 98 15.00
8D Eddie George 3
9A Marshall Faulk 762 5.00
9B Marshall Faulk 512 6.00
9C Marshall Faulk 101 10.00
9D Marshall Faulk 6
10A Kurt Warner 1682 12.00
10B Kurt Warner 1336 15.00
10C Kurt Warner 1307 15.00
10D Kurt Warner 28 60.00
11A Edgerrin James 894 12.00
11B Edgerrin James 531 15.00
11C Edgerrin James 126 30.00
11D Edgerrin James 2
12A Tim Couch 940 10.00
12B Tim Couch 908 10.00
12C Tim Couch 564 15.00
12D Tim Couch 35 50.00

2000 Donruss Elite Down and Distance Die-Cuts

NM/M
Common Player: 7.00
Production #'d To A Season Stat
Cards #'d 9 And Under Not Priced
1A Randy Moss 34 85.00
1B Randy Moss 30 85.00
1C Randy Moss 14 125.00
1D Randy Moss 2
2A Brett Favre 133 35.00
2B Brett Favre 119 35.00
2C Brett Favre 88 45.00
2D Brett Favre 1
3A Dan Marino 82 40.00
3B Dan Marino 77 40.00
3C Dan Marino 42 50.00
3D Dan Marino 3
4A Peyton Manning 121 25.00
4B Peyton Manning 118 25.00
4C Peyton Manning 91 30.00
4D Peyton Manning 3
5A Emmitt Smith 175 20.00
5B Emmitt Smith 121 20.00
5C Emmitt Smith 29 75.00
5D Emmitt Smith 4
6A Jerry Rice 24 65.00
6B Jerry Rice 24 65.00
6C Jerry Rice 16 85.00
6D Jerry Rice 3
7A Mark Brunell 81 15.00
7B Mark Brunell 100 10.00
7C Mark Brunell 77 15.00
7D Mark Brunell 1
8A Eddie George 171 7.00
8B Eddie George 119 10.00
8C Eddie George 29 30.00
8D Eddie George 1
9A Marshall Faulk 138 7.00
9B Marshall Faulk 94 10.00
9C Marshall Faulk 20 25.00
9D Marshall Faulk 1
10A Kurt Warner 129 45.00
10B Kurt Warner 106 45.00
10C Kurt Warner 87 55.00
10D Kurt Warner 3
11A Edgerrin James 220 20.00
11B Edgerrin James 130 30.00
11C Edgerrin James 17 150.00
11D Edgerrin James 2
12A Tim Couch 83 25.00
12B Tim Couch 81 25.00
12C Tim Couch 56 35.00
12D Tim Couch 3

2000 Donruss Elite Passing the Torch

NM/M
Complete Set (18): 200.00
Common Player: 5.00
#1-#12 Production 1,500 Sets
#13-#18 Production 500 Sets
PT1 Jerry Rice 7.00
PT2 Randy Moss 12.00
PT3 Dan Marino 10.00
PT4 Kurt Warner 15.00
PT5 Joe Montana 15.00
PT6 Steve Young 5.00
PT7 Bart Starr 10.00
PT8 Brett Favre 12.00
PT9 Roger Staubach 10.00
PT10 Troy Aikman 8.00
PT11 Gale Sayers 8.00
PT12 Edgerrin James 12.00
PT13 Jerry Rice, Randy Moss 12.00
PT14 Dan Marino, Kurt Warner 20.00
PT15 Joe Montana, Steve Young 20.00
PT16 Bart Starr, Brett Favre 15.00
PT17 Roger Staubach, Troy Aikman 12.00
PT18 Gale Sayers, Edgerrin James 15.00

2000 Donruss Elite Passing the Torch Autographs

NM/M
Common Player: 50.00
#1-#12 Production 150 Sets
#13-#18 Production 50 Sets
PT1 Jerry Rice 125.00
PT2 Randy Moss 150.00
PT3 Dan Marino 175.00
PT4 Kurt Warner 100.00
PT5 Joe Montana 250.00
PT6 Steve Young 100.00
PT7 Bart Starr 125.00
PT8 Brett Favre 250.00
PT9 Roger Staubach 150.00
PT10 Troy Aikman 125.00
PT11 Gale Sayers 50.00
PT12 Edgerrin James 100.00
PT13 Jerry Rice, Randy Moss 250.00
PT14 Dan Marino, Kurt Warner 300.00
PT15 Joe Montana, Steve Young 450.00
PT16 Bart Starr, Brett Favre 400.00
PT17 Roger Staubach, Troy Aikman 225.00
PT18 Gale Sayers, Edgerrin James 225.00

2000 Donruss Elite Throwback Threads

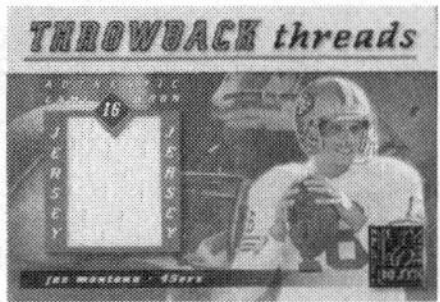

NM/M
Common Player: 50.00
Single Jerseys Production #'d To 100
Dual Jerseys Production #'d To 50
TT1 Joe Namath AUTO 200.00
TT2 Dan Marino 100.00
TT3 Walter Payton 175.00
TT4 Barry Sanders 150.00
TT5 Joe Montana 50 200.00
TT5A Joe Montana AUTO 50 450.00
TT6 Steve Young 75.00
TT7 Eric Dickerson 50 50.00
TT7A Eric Dickerson AUTO 50 100.00
TT8 Edgerrin James 75.00
TT9 Johnny Unitas 75 100.00
TT10 Peyton Manning 100.00
TT11 Bart Starr 125.00
TT12 Brett Favre 100.00
TT13 Terry Bradshaw 50 100.00
TT13A Terry Bradshaw AUTO 50 200.00
TT14 Kurt Warner 60.00
TT15 Dan Fouts 50 50.00
TT15A Dan Fouts AUTO 50 100.00
TT16 Drew Bledsoe 60.00
TT17 Earl Campbell 75 100.00
TT17A Earl Campbell AUTO 25 200.00
TT18 Eddie George 50.00
TT19 Jim Brown 125.00
TT20 Terrell Davis 60.00
TT21 Marcus Allen 60.00
TT22 Emmitt Smith 125.00
TT23 Bob Griese 75 75.00
TT24 Brian Griese 75.00
TT25 Don Meredith AUTO 150.00
TT26 Troy Aikman 100.00
TT27 Ken Stabler 75 50.00
TT27A Ken Stabler AUTO 25 200.00
TT28 Jake Plummer 50.00
TT29 Fran Tarkenton 75 60.00
TT29A Fran Tarkenton AUTO 25 200.00
TT30 Mark Brunell 50.00
TT31 Joe Namath, Dan Marino AUTO 700.00
TT32 Walter Payton, Barry Sanders 350.00
TT33 Joe Montana, Steve Young 350.00
TT34 Eric Dickerson, Edgerrin James 150.00
TT35 Johnny Unitas, Peyton Manning 300.00

TT36	Bart Starr, Brett Favre	300.00
TT37	Terry Bradshaw, Kurt Warner	150.00
TT38	Dan Fouts, Drew Bledsoe	75.00
TT39	Earl Campbell, Eddie George	100.00
TT40	Jim Brown, Terrell Davis	200.00
TT41	Marcus Allen, Emmitt Smith	175.00
TT42	Bob Griese, Brian Griese	100.00
TT43	Don Meredith, Troy Aikman AUTO	225.00
TT44	Ken Stabler, Jake Plummer	100.00
TT45	Fran Tarkenton, Mark Brunell	100.00

2000 Donruss Elite Turn of the Century

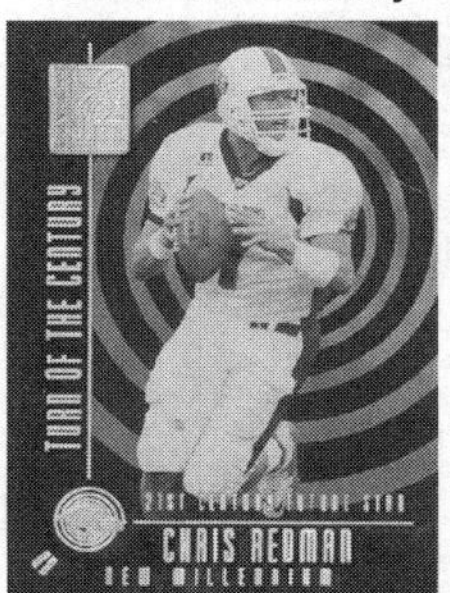

		NM/M
Complete Set (60):		150.00
Common Player:		1.50
Minor Stars:		3.00
Production 1,000 Sets		
Die Cut Cards:		8X-16X
Production 21 Sets		
TC1	Dan Marino	10.00
TC2	Edgerrin James	8.00
TC3	Peyton Manning	10.00
TC4	Drew Bledsoe	5.00
TC5	Doug Flutie	3.50
TC6	Curtis Martin	3.00
TC7	Eddie George	3.00
TC8	Steve McNair	3.00
TC9	Fred Taylor	3.50
TC10	Mark Brunell	3.50
TC11	Tim Couch	4.00
TC12	Peter Warrick	3.00
TC13	Terrell Davis	6.00
TC14	Jon Kitna	3.00
TC15	Emmitt Smith	8.00
TC16	Troy Aikman	6.00
TC17	Stephen Davis	3.00
TC18	Brad Johnson	3.00
TC19	Jake Plummer	3.00
TC20	Brett Favre	10.00
TC21	Barry Sanders	10.00
TC22	Marshall Faulk	3.00
TC23	Kurt Warner	6.00
TC24	Ricky Williams	6.00
TC25	Steve Young	4.00
TC26	Randy Moss	10.00
TC27	John Elway	8.00
TC28	Jerry Rice	6.00
TC29	Plaxico Burress	10.00
TC30	Cris Carter	3.00
TC31	Antonio Freeman	1.50
TC32	Thomas Jones	4.00
TC33	Travis Taylor	6.00
TC34	Marvin Harrison	3.00
TC35	Keyshawn Johnson	3.00
TC36	Shaun Alexander	5.00
TC37	Isaac Bruce	3.00
TC38	Ricky Watters	1.50
TC39	Ron Dayne	3.00
TC40	Brian Griese	3.50
TC41	Charlie Batch	3.00
TC42	Jamal Lewis	4.00
TC43	Jamal Anderson	3.00
TC44	Dorsey Levens	3.00
TC45	Chris Redman	5.00
TC46	Robert Smith	1.50
TC47	Chad Pennington	10.00
TC48	Terrell Owens	3.00
TC49	Deion Sanders	3.00
TC50	Duce Staley	3.00
TC51	Dez White	4.00
TC52	Jimmy Smith	3.00
TC53	Cade McNown	2.00
TC54	Daunte Culpepper	4.00
TC55	Akili Smith	2.00
TC56	Torry Holt	3.00
TC57	Kevin Johnson	3.00
TC58	Shaun King	2.00
TC59	Olandis Gary	2.00
TC60	Donovan McNabb	4.00

2000 Donruss Preferred

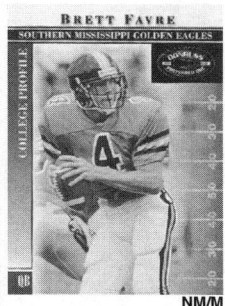

		NM/M
Complete Set (100):		20.00
Common Player:		.20
Minor Stars:		.40
Pack (4 plus Graded):		16.00
Wax Box (10):		140.00
1	Jake Plummer	.40
2	Chris Chandler	.20
3	Trent Dilfer	.20
4	Doug Flutie	.50
5	Cade McNown	.40
6	Michael Irvin	.40
7	Troy Aikman	1.00
8	Terrell Davis	1.00
9	John Elway	1.50
10	Brett Favre	1.50
11	Peyton Manning	1.25
12	Warren Moon	.20
13	Randall Cunningham	.20
14	Drew Bledsoe	.60
15	Ricky Williams	.75
16	Kerry Collins	.20
17	Vinny Testaverde	.20
18	Donovan McNabb	.60
19	Jim Harbaugh	.20
20	Jerry Rice	1.00
21	Steve Young	.60
22	Keyshawn Johnson	.40
23	Neil O'Donnell	.20
24	Steve McNair	.50
25	Brad Johnson	.40
26	Jeff George	.40
27	Dan Marino	1.50
28	Jim Kelly	.40
29	Barry Sanders	1.50
30	Phil Simms	.20
31	Gus Frerotte	.20
32	Elvis Grbac	.40
33	Jeff Blake	.20
34	Kordell Stewart	.40
35	Tony Banks	.20
36	Doug Flutie	.50
37	Cade McNown	.40
38	Troy Aikman	1.00
39	Terrell Davis	1.00
40	John Elway	1.50
41	Brett Favre	1.50
42	Peyton Manning	1.25
43	Drew Bledsoe	.60
44	Ricky Williams	.75
45	Kerry Collins	.20
46	Vinny Testaverde	.20
47	Donovan McNabb	.60
48	Kordell Stewart	.40
49	Ryan Leaf	.20
50	Jerry Rice	1.00
51	Steve Young	.60
52	Keyshawn Johnson	.40
53	Steve McNair	.40
54	Jeff George	.40
55	Dan Marino	1.50
56	Jim Kelly	.40
57	Barry Sanders	1.50
58	Bernie Kosar	.20
59	Chris Chandler	.20
60	Jim Everett	.20
61	Jake Plummer	.40
62	Cade McNown	.40
63	Troy Aikman	1.00
64	Ricky Williams	.75
65	Donovan McNabb	.60
66	Steve Young	.60
67	Brad Johnson	.40
68	Kerry Collins	.20
69	Ryan Leaf	.20
70	Drew Bledsoe	.60
71	Jake Plummer	.40
72	Chris Chandler	.20
73	Michael Irvin	.40
74	Troy Aikman	1.00
75	Terrell Davis	1.25
76	John Elway	1.50
77	Brett Favre	1.50
78	Peyton Manning	1.25
79	Drew Bledsoe	.60
80	Junior Seau	.20
81	Jerry Rice	1.00
82	Steve Young	.60
83	Keyshawn Johnson	.40
84	Steve McNair	.40
85	Brad Johnson	.40
86	Dan Marino	1.50
87	Jim Kelly	.40
88	Barry Sanders	1.50
89	Phil Simms	.20
90	Boomer Esiason	.20
91	Jake Plummer	.40
92	Chris Chandler	.20
93	Bubby Brister	.20
94	Cade McNown	.40
95	Jim Harbaugh	.20
96	Peyton Manning	1.25
97	Donovan McNabb	.60
98	Jim Kelly	.40
99	Brad Johnson	.40
100	Kordell Stewart	.40

2000 Donruss Preferred Graded Series

		NM/M
Common BGS 9.5:		12.00
Common BGS 9:		8.00
Common BGS 8.5:		5.00
Common BGS 8:		5.00
1	Jake Plummer 9.5	15.00
1	Jake Plummer 9.0	10.00
1	Jake Plummer 8.5	6.00
1	Jake Plummer 8.0	6.00
2	Chris Chandler 9.5	12.00
2	Chris Chandler 9.0	8.00
2	Chris Chandler 8.5	5.00
2	Chris Chandler 8.0	5.00
3	Trent Dilfer 9.5	12.00
3	Trent Dilfer 9.0	8.00
3	Trent Dilfer 8.5	5.00
3	Trent Dilfer 8.0	5.00
4	Doug Flutie 9.5	15.00
4	Doug Flutie 9.0	10.00
4	Doug Flutie 8.5	6.00
4	Doug Flutie 8.0	6.00
5	Cade McNown 9.5	12.00
5	Cade McNown 9.0	8.00
5	Cade McNown 8.5	5.00
5	Cade McNown 8.0	5.00
6	Michael Irvin 9.5	12.00
6	Michael Irvin 9.0	8.00
6	Michael Irvin 8.5	5.00
6	Michael Irvin 8.0	5.00
7	Troy Aikman 9.5	20.00
7	Troy Aikman 9.0	13.00
7	Troy Aikman 8.5	8.00
7	Troy Aikman 8.0	8.00
8	Terrell Davis 9.5	25.00
8	Terrell Davis 9.0	15.00
8	Terrell Davis 8.5	10.00
8	Terrell Davis 8.0	10.00
9	John Elway 9.5	25.00
9	John Elway 9.0	15.00
9	John Elway 8.5	10.00
9	John Elway 8.0	10.00
10	Brett Favre 9.5	35.00
10	Brett Favre 9.0	18.00
10	Brett Favre 8.5	12.00
10	Brett Favre 8.0	12.00
11	Peyton Manning 9.5	25.00
11	Peyton Manning 9.0	15.00
11	Peyton Manning 8.5	10.00
11	Peyton Manning 8.0	10.00
12	Warren Moon 9.5	12.00
12	Warren Moon 9.0	8.00
12	Warren Moon 8.5	5.00
12	Warren Moon 8.0	5.00
13	Randall Cunningham 9.5	12.00
13	Randall Cunningham9.0	8.00
13	Randall Cunningham8.5	5.00
13	Randall Cunningham 8.0	5.00
14	Drew Bledsoe 9.5	15.00
14	Drew Bledsoe 9.0	10.00
14	Drew Bledsoe 8.5	6.00
14	Drew Bledsoe 8.0	6.00
15	Ricky Williams 9.5	20.00
15	Ricky Williams 9.0	12.00
15	Ricky Williams 8.5	8.00
15	Ricky Williams 8.0	8.00
16	Kerry Collins 9.5	12.00
16	Kerry Collins 9.0	8.00
16	Kerry Collins 8.5	5.00
17	Vinny Testaverde 9.5	12.00
17	Vinny Testaverde 9.0	8.00
17	Vinny Testaverde 8.5	5.00
17	Vinny Testaverde 8.0	5.00
18	Donovan McNabb 9.5	20.00
18	Donovan McNabb 9.0	10.00
18	Donovan McNabb 8.5	6.00
18	Donovan McNabb 8.0	6.00
18	Donovan McNabb 7.5	6.00
19	Jim Harbaugh 9.5	12.00
19	Jim Harbaugh 9.0	8.00
19	Jim Harbaugh 8.5	5.00
19	Jim Harbaugh 8.0	5.00
20	Jerry Rice 9.5	20.00
20	Jerry Rice 9.0	12.00
20	Jerry Rice 8.5	8.00
20	Jerry Rice 8.0	8.00
20	Jerry Rice 7.5	7.00
21	Steve Young 9.5	15.00
21	Steve Young 9.0	10.00
21	Steve Young 8.5	6.00
21	Steve Young 8.0	6.00
22	Keyshawn Johnson 9.5	12.00
22	Keyshawn Johnson 9.0	8.00
22	Keyshawn Johnson 8.5	5.00
22	Keyshawn Johnson 8.0	5.00
23	Neil O'Donnell 9.5	12.00
23	Neil O'Donnell 9.0	8.00
23	Neil O'Donnell 8.5	5.00
23	Neil O'Donnell 8.0	5.00
24	Steve McNair 9.5	12.00
24	Steve McNair 9.0	8.00
24	Steve McNair 8.5	5.00
24	Steve McNair 8.0	5.00
25	Brad Johnson 9.0	12.00
25	Brad Johnson 8.5	8.00
25	Brad Johnson 8.0	5.00
26	Jeff George 9.5	12.00
26	Jeff George 9.0	8.00
26	Jeff George 8.5	5.00
26	Jeff George 8.0	5.00
27	Dan Marino 9.5	25.00
27	Dan Marino 9.0	15.00
27	Dan Marino 8.5	10.00
27	Dan Marino 8.0	10.00
28	Jim Kelly 9.5	12.00
28	Jim Kelly 9.0	8.00
28	Jim Kelly 8.5	5.00
28	Jim Kelly 8.0	5.00
29	Barry Sanders 9.5	25.00
29	Barry Sanders 9.0	15.00
29	Barry Sanders 8.5	10.00
29	Barry Sanders 8.0	10.00
30	Phil Simms 9.5	12.00
30	Phil Simms 9.0	8.00
30	Phil Simms 8.5	5.00
30	Phil Simms 8.0	5.00
31	Gus Frerotte 9.5	12.00
31	Gus Frerotte 9.0	8.00
31	Gus Frerotte 8.5	5.00
31	Gus Frerotte 8.0	5.00
32	Elvis Grbac 9.0	8.00
32	Elvis Grbac 8.5	5.00
32	Elvis Grbac 8.0	5.00
33	Jeff Blake 9.5	12.00
33	Jeff Blake 9.0	8.00
33	Jeff Blake 8.5	5.00
33	Jeff Blake 8.0	5.00
34	Kordell Stewart 9.5	12.00
34	Kordell Stewart 9.0	8.00
34	Kordell Stewart 8.5	5.00
34	Kordell Stewart 8.0	5.00
34	Kordell Stewart 7.5	5.00
35	Tony Banks 9.5	12.00
35	Tony Banks 9.0	8.00
35	Tony Banks 8.5	5.00
35	Tony Banks 8.0	5.00
36	Doug Flutie 9.5	15.00
36	Doug Flutie 9.0	10.00
36	Doug Flutie 8.5	6.00
36	Doug Flutie 8.0	6.00
37	Cade McNown 9.5	12.00
37	Cade McNown 9.0	8.00
37	Cade McNown 8.5	5.00
37	Cade McNown 8.0	5.00
38	Troy Aikman 9.5	20.00
38	Troy Aikman 9.0	12.00
38	Troy Aikman 8.5	8.00
38	Troy Aikman 8.0	8.00
39	Terrell Davis 9.5	25.00
39	Terrell Davis 9.0	15.00
39	Terrell Davis 8.5	10.00
39	Terrell Davis 8.0	10.00
40	John Elway 9.5	25.00
40	John Elway 9.0	15.00
40	John Elway 8.5	10.00
40	John Elway 8.0	10.00
41	Brett Favre 9.5	35.00
41	Brett Favre 9.0	18.00
41	Brett Favre 8.5	12.00
41	Brett Favre 8.0	12.00
41	Brett Favre 7.5	10.00
42	Peyton Manning 9.5	25.00
42	Peyton Manning 9.0	15.00
42	Peyton Manning 8.5	10.00
42	Peyton Manning 8.0	10.00
43	Drew Bledsoe 9.5	15.00
43	Drew Bledsoe 9.0	10.00
43	Drew Bledsoe 8.5	6.00
43	Drew Bledsoe 8.0	6.00
44	Ricky Williams 9.5	20.00
44	Ricky Williams 9.0	12.00
44	Ricky Williams 8.5	8.00
44	Ricky Williams 8.0	8.00
45	Kerry Collins 9.5	12.00
45	Kerry Collins 9.0	8.00
45	Kerry Collins 8.5	5.00
45	Kerry Collins 8.0	5.00
46	Vinny Testaverde 9.5	12.00
46	Vinny Testaverde 9.0	8.00
46	Vinny Testaverde 8.5	5.00
46	Vinny Testaverde 8.0	5.00
47	Donovan McNabb 9.5	20.00
47	Donovan McNabb 9.0	10.00
47	Donovan McNabb 8.5	6.00
47	Donovan McNabb 8.0	6.00
48	Kordell Stewart 9.5	12.00
48	Kordell Stewart 9.0	8.00
48	Kordell Stewart 8.5	5.00
48	Kordell Stewart 8.0	5.00
49	Ryan Leaf 9.5	12.00
49	Ryan Leaf 9.0	8.00
49	Ryan Leaf 8.5	5.00
50	Jerry Rice 9.5	20.00
50	Jerry Rice 9.0	12.00
50	Jerry Rice 8.5	8.00
50	Jerry Rice 8.0	8.00
51	Steve Young 9.5	15.00
51	Steve Young 9.0	10.00
51	Steve Young 8.5	6.00
51	Steve Young 8.0	6.00
52	Keyshawn Johnson 9.5	12.00
52	Keyshawn Johnson 9.0	8.00
52	Keyshawn Johnson 8.5	5.00
52	Keyshawn Johnson 8.0	5.00
53	Steve McNair 9.5	12.00
53	Steve McNair 9.0	8.00
53	Steve McNair 8.5	5.00
53	Steve McNair 8.0	5.00
54	Jeff George 9.5	12.00
54	Jeff George 9.0	8.00
54	Jeff George 8.5	5.00
55	Dan Marino 9.5	25.00
55	Dan Marino 9.0	15.00
55	Dan Marino 8.5	10.00
55	Dan Marino 8.0	10.00
56	Jim Kelly 9.5	12.00
56	Jim Kelly 9.0	8.00
56	Jim Kelly 8.5	5.00
56	Jim Kelly 8.0	5.00
57	Barry Sanders 9.5	25.00
57	Barry Sanders 9.0	15.00
57	Barry Sanders 8.5	10.00
57	Barry Sanders 8.0	10.00
58	Bernie Kosar 9.5	12.00
58	Bernie Kosar 9.0	8.00
58	Bernie Kosar 8.5	5.00
58	Bernie Kosar 8.0	5.00
59	Chris Chandler 9.5	12.00
59	Chris Chandler 9.0	8.00
59	Chris Chandler 8.5	5.00
59	Chris Chandler 8.0	5.00
60	Jim Everett 9.5	12.00
60	Jim Everett 9.0	8.00
60	Jim Everett 8.5	5.00
60	Jim Everett 8.0	5.00
61	Jake Plummer 9.5	15.00
61	Jake Plummer 9.0	10.00
61	Jake Plummer 8.5	6.00
61	Jake Plummer 8.0	6.00
62	Cade McNown 9.5	12.00
62	Cade McNown 9.0	8.00
62	Cade McNown 8.5	5.00
62	Cade McNown 8.0	5.00
62	Cade McNown 7.5	5.00
63	Troy Aikman 9.5	20.00
63	Troy Aikman 9.0	12.00
63	Troy Aikman 8.5	8.00
63	Troy Aikman 8.0	8.00
64	Ricky Williams 9.5	20.00
64	Ricky Williams 9.0	12.00
64	Ricky Williams 8.5	8.00
64	Ricky Williams 8.0	8.00
65	Donovan McNabb 9.5	20.00
65	Donovan McNabb 9.0	10.00
65	Donovan McNabb 8.5	6.00
66	Steve Young 9.5	15.00
66	Steve Young 9.0	10.00
66	Steve Young 8.5	6.00
66	Steve Young 8.0	6.00
67	Brad Johnson 9.5	12.00
67	Brad Johnson 9.0	8.00
67	Brad Johnson 8.5	5.00
67	Brad Johnson 8.0	5.00
68	Kerry Collins 9.0	8.00
68	Kerry Collins 8.5	5.00
68	Kerry Collins 8.0	5.00
69	Ryan Leaf 9.5	12.00
69	Ryan Leaf 9.0	8.00
69	Ryan Leaf 8.5	5.00
69	Ryan Leaf 8.0	5.00
70	Drew Bledsoe 9.5	15.00
70	Drew Bledsoe 9.0	10.00
70	Drew Bledsoe 8.5	6.00
70	Drew Bledsoe 8.0	6.00
71	Jake Plummer 9.5	15.00
71	Jake Plummer 9.0	10.00
71	Jake Plummer 8.5	6.00
71	Jake Plummer 8.0	6.00
72	Chris Chandler 9.5	12.00
72	Chris Chandler 9.0	8.00
72	Chris Chandler 8.5	5.00
72	Chris Chandler 8.0	5.00
73	Michael Irvin 9.5	12.00
73	Michael Irvin 9.0	8.00
73	Michael Irvin 8.5	5.00
73	Michael Irvin 8.0	5.00
74	Troy Aikman 9.5	20.00
74	Troy Aikman 9.0	12.00
74	Troy Aikman 8.5	8.00
74	Troy Aikman 8.0	8.00
75	Terrell Davis 9.5	25.00
75	Terrell Davis 9.0	15.00
75	Terrell Davis 8.5	10.00
75	Terrell Davis 8.0	10.00
76	John Elway 9.5	25.00
76	John Elway 9.0	15.00
76	John Elway 8.5	10.00
77	Brett Favre 9.5	35.00
77	Brett Favre 9.0	18.00
77	Brett Favre 8.5	12.00
77	Brett Favre 8.0	12.00
78	Peyton Manning 9.5	15.00
78	Peyton Manning 9.0	10.00
78	Peyton Manning 8.5	7.00
78	Peyton Manning 8.0	7.00
79	Drew Bledsoe 9.5	15.00
79	Drew Bledsoe 9.0	10.00
79	Drew Bledsoe 8.5	6.00
79	Drew Bledsoe 8.0	6.00
80	Junior Seau 9.5	12.00
80	Junior Seau 9.0	8.00
80	Junior Seau 8.5	5.00
80	Junior Seau 8.0	5.00
81	Jerry Rice 9.5	20.00
81	Jerry Rice 9.0	12.00
81	Jerry Rice 8.5	8.00
81	Jerry Rice 8.0	8.00
82	Steve Young 9.5	15.00
82	Steve Young 9.0	10.00
82	Steve Young 8.5	6.00
82	Steve Young 8.0	6.00
82	Steve Young 7.5	6.00
83	Keyshawn Johnson 9.5	12.00
83	Keyshawn Johnson 9.0	8.00
83	Keyshawn Johnson 8.5	5.00
83	Keyshawn Johnson 8.0	5.00
84	Steve McNair 9.5	12.00
84	Steve McNair 9.0	8.00
84	Steve McNair 8.5	5.00
84	Steve McNair 8.0	5.00
85	Brad Johnson 9.5	12.00
85	Brad Johnson 9.0	8.00
85	Brad Johnson 8.5	5.00
85	Brad Johnson 8.0	5.00
86	Dan Marino 9.5	25.00
86	Dan Marino 9.0	15.00
86	Dan Marino 8.5	10.00
86	Dan Marino 8.0	10.00
87	Jim Kelly 9.5	12.00
87	Jim Kelly 9.0	8.00
87	Jim Kelly 8.5	5.00
87	Jim Kelly 8.0	5.00
88	Barry Sanders 9.5	25.00
88	Barry Sanders 9.0	15.00
88	Barry Sanders 8.5	10.00
88	Barry Sanders 8.0	10.00
89	Phil Simms 9.5	12.00
89	Phil Simms 9.0	8.00
89	Phil Simms 8.5	5.00
89	Phil Simms 8.0	5.00
90	Boomer Esiason 9.5	12.00
90	Boomer Esiason 9.0	8.00
90	Boomer Esiason 8.5	5.00
90	Boomer Esiason 8.0	5.00
91	Jake Plummer 9.5	15.00
91	Jake Plummer 9.0	10.00
91	Jake Plummer 8.5	6.00
91	Jake Plummer 8.0	6.00
92	Chris Chandler 9.5	12.00
92	Chris Chandler 9.0	8.00
92	Chris Chandler 8.5	5.00
92	Chris Chandler 8.0	5.00
93	Bubby Brister 9.5	12.00
93	Bubby Brister 9.0	8.00
93	Bubby Brister 8.5	5.00
93	Bubby Brister 8.0	5.00
94	Cade McNown 9.5	15.00
94	Cade McNown 9.0	10.00
94	Cade McNown 8.5	6.00
94	Cade McNown 8.0	6.00
95	Jim Harbaugh 9.5	12.00
95	Jim Harbaugh 9.0	8.00
95	Jim Harbaugh 8.5	5.00
95	Jim Harbaugh 8.0	5.00
96	Peyton Manning 9.5	25.00
96	Peyton Manning 9.0	15.00
96	Peyton Manning 8.5	10.00
96	Peyton Manning 8.0	10.00
97	Donovan McNabb 9.5	20.00
97	Donovan McNabb 9.0	10.00
97	Donovan McNabb 8.5	7.00
97	Donovan McNabb 8.0	7.00
98	Jim Kelly 9.5	15.00
98	Jim Kelly 9.0	10.00
98	Jim Kelly 8.5	6.00
98	Jim Kelly 8.0	6.00
99	Brad Johnson 9.5	12.00
99	Brad Johnson 9.0	8.00
99	Brad Johnson 8.5	5.00
99	Brad Johnson 8.0	5.00
100	Kordell Stewart 9.5	15.00
100	Kordell Stewart 9.0	10.00
100	Kordell Stewart 8.5	6.00
100	Kordell Stewart 8.0	6.00
101	Rob Johnson 9.5	12.00
101	Rob Johnson 9.0	8.00
101	Rob Johnson 8.5	5.00
101	Rob Johnson 8.0	5.00
102	Jevon Kearse 9.5	12.00
102	Jevon Kearse 9.0	8.00
102	Jevon Kearse 8.5	5.00
103	Rich Gannon 9.5	12.00
103	Rich Gannon 9.0	8.00
103	Rich Gannon 8.5	5.00
103	Rich Gannon 8.0	5.00

2000 Donruss Preferred Power

#1-20 Power:	3X-6X
Production 750 Sets	
#21-40 Power:	4X-8X
Production 500 Sets	
#41-60 Power:	5X-10X
Production 300 Sets	
#61-80 Power:	6X-12X
Production 150 Sets	
#81-103 Power:	15X-30X
Production 50 Sets	

2000 Donruss Preferred Materials

		NM/M
Common Player 125:		40.00
Common Player 300:		20.00
Inserted 1:34		
1	Jerry Rice H 125	120.00
2	John Elway H 125	150.00
3	Doug Flutie H 125	60.00
4	Barry Sanders H 125	125.00
5	Dan Marino P 250	100.00
6	Jerry Rice P 250	75.00
7	Steve McNair S 50	60.00
9	Peyton Manning S 125	100.00
10	Steve Young S 125	50.00
11	John Elway S 125	125.00
12	Dan Marino S 125	125.00
14	Kordell Stewart	20.00
15	Brett Favre S 125	120.00
16	Barry Sanders S 125	120.00
17	Randall Cunningham	20.00
18	Bernie Kosar	20.00
19	Boomer Esiason	20.00
20	Brett Favre J 100	120.00
21	Barry Sanders J 200	75.00
22	Cade McNown	20.00
23	Dan Marino J 300	75.00
24	Drew Bledsoe J 100	50.00
25	Doug Flutie Wh. J 300	25.00
26	Doug Flutie Bl. J 300	25.00
27	Donovan McNabb J 300	30.00
28	Jerry Rice J 300	50.00
29	Jim Harbaugh	20.00
30	Jim Kelly	40.00
31	John Elway J 100	100.00
32	Jake Plummer	20.00
33	Junior Seau	20.00
34	Kordell Stewart	30.00
35	Phil Simms	30.00
36	Peyton Manning J 100	100.00
37	Randall Cunningham	20.00
38	Ricky Williams Wh. J 100	60.00
39	Ricky Williams Bl. J 100	60.00
40	Steve McNair J 100	45.00
41	Steve Young J 300	30.00
42	Troy Aikman J 100	85.00
43	Vinny Testaverde	20.00
44	Warren Moon	20.00

2000 Donruss Preferred National Treasures

		NM/M
Complete Set (41):		75.00
Common Player:		1.50
Minor Stars:		3.00
Inserted 1:8		
Production 1,000 Sets		
1	Warren Moon	1.50
2	Steve Young	4.00
3	Jeff Blake	1.50
4	Brett Favre	12.00
5	Donovan McNabb	3.50
6	Bubby Brister	1.50
7	John Elway	8.00
8	Troy Aikman	6.00
9	Steve McNair	3.00
10	Kordell Stewart	3.00
11	Drew Bledsoe	4.00
12	Chris Chandler	1.50

NM/M
13 Dan Marino 8.00
14 Brad Johnson 1.50
15 Jim Kelly 3.00
16 Jake Plummer 3.00
17 Boomer Esiason 1.50
18 Peyton Manning 10.00
19 Keyshawn Johnson 3.00
20 Barry Sanders 10.00
21 Bernie Kosar 1.50
22 Cade McNown 3.00
23 Elvis Grbac 1.50
24 Junior Seau 1.50
25 Phil Simms 3.00
26 Jim Everett 1.50
27 Vinny Testaverde 3.00
28 Jerry Rice 6.00
29 Terrell Davis 8.00
30 Ryan Leaf 3.00
31 Neil O'Donnell 1.50
32 Ricky Williams 5.00
33 Michael Irvin 3.00
34 Jim Harbaugh 1.50
36 Jeff George 3.00
36 Gus Frerotte 1.50
37 Doug Flutie 3.50
38 Trent Dilfer 3.00
39 Randall Cunningham 3.00
40 Kerry Collins 3.00
41 Tony Banks 1.50

2000 Donruss Preferred Pass Time

NM/M
Complete Set (20): 70.00
Common Player: 2.50
Inserted 1:31
Production 500 Sets
1 John Elway 12.00
2 Jim Kelly 5.00
3 Steve McNair 2.50
4 Doug Flutie 5.00
5 Dan Marino 12.00
6 Brett Favre 15.00
7 Cade McNown 4.00
8 Elvis Grbac 2.50
9 Vinny Testaverde 2.50
10 Kordell Stewart 4.00
11 Donovan McNabb 5.00
12 Jake Plummer 4.00
13 Troy Aikman 8.00
14 Chris Chandler 2.50
15 Kerry Collins 2.50
16 Peyton Manning 10.00
17 Steve Young 5.00
18 Brad Johnson 2.50
19 Jeff Blake 2.50
20 Drew Bledsoe 5.00

2001 Donruss Classics

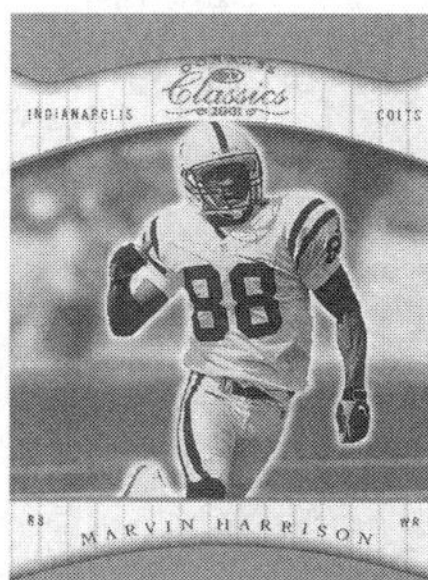

NM/M
Complete Set (200): 350.00
Common Player: .15
Minor Stars: .30
Common Rookie: 4.00
Production 475 Sets
Common Legends: 1.00
Production 1,425 Sets
Pack: 7.50
Wax Box(18): 95.00
1 David Boston .50
2 Jake Plummer .50
3 Thomas Jones .30
4 Jamal Anderson .50
5 Chris Redman .30
6 Elvis Grbac .30
7 Jamal Lewis 1.50
8 Qadry Ismail .30
9 Ray Lewis .50
10 Shannon Sharpe .30
11 Travis Taylor .30
12 Eric Moulds .50
13 Rob Johnson .30
14 Muhsin Muhammad .50
15 Brian Urlacher 1.25
16 Cade McNown .50
17 Marcus Robinson .50
18 Akili Smith .30
19 Corey Dillon .50
20 Peter Warrick .75
21 Courtney Brown .30
22 Tim Couch .75
23 Emmitt Smith 1.50
24 Brian Griese .60
25 Ed McCaffrey .50
26 Olandis Gary .50
27 Mike Anderson 1.50
28 Rod Smith .50
29 Terrell Davis 1.25
30 Charlie Batch .50
31 James Stewart .30
32 Ahman Green .50
33 Antonio Freeman .40
34 Brett Favre 2.50
35 Edgerrin James 1.50
36 Marvin Harrison .50
37 Peyton Manning 2.00
38 Fred Taylor .75
39 Jimmy Smith .40
40 Keenan McCardell .50
41 Mark Brunell .75
42 Sylvester Morris .50
43 Tony Gonzalez .30
44 Zach Thomas .30
45 Jay Fiedler .50
46 Lamar Smith .50
47 Cris Carter .50
48 Daunte Culpepper 1.25
49 Randy Moss 2.00
50 Drew Bledsoe .75
51 Terry Glenn .40
52 Aaron Brooks .50
53 Joe Horn .30
54 Ricky Williams 1.00
55 Amani Toomer .30
56 Ike Hilliard .30
57 Kerry Collins .30
58 Ron Dayne 1.00
59 Tiki Barber .50
60 Chad Pennington .50
61 Curtis Martin .50
62 Laveranues Coles .30
63 Vinny Testaverde .30
64 Wayne Chrebet .50
65 Charles Woodson .50
66 Rich Gannon .40
67 Tim Brown .40
68 Tyrone Wheatley .30
69 Corey Simon .30
70 Donovan McNabb 1.00
71 Duce Staley .50
72 Jerome Bettis .50
73 Plaxico Burress .50
74 Doug Flutie .75
75 Junior Seau .40
76 Jeff Garcia .50
77 Jerry Rice 1.50
78 Giovanni Carmazzi .30
79 Terrell Owens .50
80 Darrell Jackson .30
81 Ricky Watters .40
82 Shaun Alexander .50
83 Isaac Bruce .50
84 Kurt Warner 2.00
85 Marshall Faulk .75
86 Torry Holt .50
87 Brad Johnson .40
88 Keyshawn Johnson .50
89 Mike Alstott .50
90 Shaun King .50
91 Warren Sapp .40
92 Warrick Dunn .50
93 Eddie George .75
94 Jevon Kearse .50
95 Steve McNair .50
96 Jeff George .30
97 Stephen Davis .50
98 Charlie Garner .40
99 Trent Dilfer .40
100 Troy Aikman 1.25
101 *Michael Vick* 50.00
102 *Drew Brees* 20.00
103 *Chris Weinke* 8.00
104 *Mike McMahon* 10.00
105 *Jesse Palmer* 8.00
106 *Quincy Carter* 12.00
107 *Josh Heupel* 8.00
108 *Tim Hasselbeck* 8.00
109 *LaDainian Tomlinson* 40.00
110 *Deuce McAllister* 30.00
111 *Michael Bennett* 20.00
112 *Anthony Thomas* 20.00
113 *LaMont Jordan* 10.00
114 *Travis Henry* 15.00
115 *Kevan Barlow* 12.00
116 *Travis Minor* 10.00
117 *Rudi Johnson* 15.00
118 *David Allen* 5.00
119 *Heath Evans* 4.00
120 *Moran Norris* 4.00
121 *David Terrell* 12.00
122 *Koren Robinson* 12.00
123 *Rod Gardner* 15.00
124 *Santana Moss* 15.00
125 *Freddie Mitchell* 12.00
126 *Reggie Wayne* 15.00
127 *Quincy Morgan* 10.00
128 *Chad Johnson* 20.00
129 *Robert Ferguson* 8.00
130 *Chris Chambers* 20.00
131 *Marvin "Snoop" Minnis* 8.00
132 *Eddie Berlin* 4.00
133 *Alex Bannister* 4.00
134 *Todd Heap* 10.00
135 *Alge Crumpler* 7.00
136 *Justin Smith* 4.00
137 *Andre Carter* 4.00
138 *Jamal Reynolds* 4.00
139 *Richard Seymour* 4.00
140 *Marcus Stroud* 4.00
141 *Casey Hampton* 4.00
142 *Gerard Warren* 4.00
143 *Torrance Marshall* 4.00
144 *Brian Allen* 4.00
145 *Morlon Greenwood* 4.00
146 *Keith Adams* 4.00
147 *Will Allen* 4.00
148 *Nate Clements* 4.00
149 *Adam Archuleta* 5.00
150 *Hakim Akbar* 4.00
151 James Lofton 1.00
152 Jim Kelly 2.00
154 Mike Singletary 1.50
155 Boomer Esiason 1.25
156 Charlie Joiner 1.00
157 Ken Anderson 1.50
158 Y.A. Tittle 2.00
159 Jim Brown 3.50
160 Otto Graham 2.00
161 Ozzie Newsome 1.25
162 Drew Pearson 1.50
163 Lance Alworth 1.50
164 Roger Staubach 4.00
165 Tony Dorsett 2.00
166 John Elway 5.00
167 Barry Sanders 3.50
168 Bart Starr 4.00
169 Paul Hornung 2.00
171 Warren Moon 1.50
172 Johnny Unitas 3.00
173 Deacon Jones 1.50
174 Eric Dickerson 1.50
175 Bob Griese 2.00
176 Dan Marino 5.00
177 Larry Csonka 1.75
178 Paul Warfield 1.75
179 Fran Tarkenton 2.50
180 Archie Manning 1.50
181 Frank Gifford 3.00
182 Lawrence Taylor 1.50
183 Dan Fouts 2.00
184 Don Maynard 1.50
185 Joe Namath 4.00
186 Fred Biletnikoff 2.00
187 Marcus Allen 2.00
188 Jim Plunkett 1.50
189 Franco Harris 2.00
190 Terry Bradshaw 4.00
191 Joe Montana 7.00
192 Roger Craig 1.50
193 Steve Young 2.50
194 Dwight Clark 1.00
195 Steve Largent 2.00
196 Art Monk 1.50
197 Charley Taylor 1.50
198 Joe Theismann 2.00
199 Sammy Baugh 2.00
200 Sonny Jurgensen 2.00

2001 Donruss Classics Combos

NM/M
Common Player: 30.00
Dual Cards #'d to 100
Quad Cards #'d to 25
1 Walter Payton, Gale Sayers 75 175.00
1A Walter Payton, Gale Sayers AUTO 25
2 Cade McNown, Jim McMahon 100.00
3 Roger Staubach, Tony Dorsett 75.00
4 Troy Aikman, Emmitt Smith 75.00
5 Terry Bradshaw, Franco Harris 75.00
6 Jack Ham, Joe Greene 100.00
7 Joe Montana, Jerry Rice 150.00
8 Steve Young, Terrell Owens 50.00
9 Jim Kelly, Thurman Thomas 50.00
10 Doug Flutie, Eric Moulds 50.00
11 Joe Namath, Don Maynard 100.00
12 Vinny Testaverde, Curtis Martin 25.00
13 Deacon Jones, Fred Dryer 50.00
14 Kurt Warner, Isaac Bruce 50.00
15 Joe Montana, Marcus Allen 100.00
16 Tony Gonzalez, Sylvester Morris 25.00
17 Phil Simms, Lawrence Taylor 100.00
18 Kerry Collins, Ron Dayne 25.00
19 Jim Plunkett, George Blanda 50.00
20 Ken Stabler, Daryle Lamonica 100.00
21 Earl Campbell, Warren Moon 50.00
22 Eddie George, Steve McNair 50.00
23 Dan Marino, John Elway 100.00
24 Brian Griese, Jay Fiedler 50.00
25 Barry Sanders, Eric Dickerson 50.00
26 Marshall Faulk, Terrell Davis 50.00
27 Peyton Manning, Edgerrin James 50.00
28 Mark Brunell, Fred Taylor 50.00
29 Daunte Culpepper, Randy Moss 75.00
30 Brett Favre, Antonio Freeman 50.00
31 Walter Payton, Gale Sayers, Cade McNown, Jim McMahon
32 Roger Staubach, Tony Dorsett, Troy Aikman, Emmitt Smith
33 Terry Bradshaw, Franco Harris, Jack Ham, Joe Greene
34 Joe Montana, Jerry Rice, Steve Young, Terrell Owens
35 Jim Kelly, Thurman Thomas, Doug Flutie, Eric Moulds
36 Joe Namath, Don Maynard, Vinny Testaverde, Curtis Martin
37 Deacon Jones, Fred Dryer, Kurt Warner, Isaac Bruce
38 Joe Montana, Marcus Allen, Tony Gonzalez, Sylvester Morris
39 Phil Simms, Lawrence Taylor, Kerry Collins, Ron Dayne
40 Jim Plunkett, George Blanda, Ken Stabler, Daryle Lamonica
41 Earl Campbell, Warren Moon, Eddie George, Steve McNair
42 Dan Marino, John Elway, Jay Fiedler, Brian Griese
43 Barry Sanders, Eric Dickerson, Marshall Faulk, Terrell Davis
44 Peyton Manning, Edgerrin James, Mark Brunell, Fred Taylor
45 Daunte Culpepper, Randy Moss, Brett Favre, Antonio Freeman

2001 Donruss Classics Classic Combos Autos

1 Gale Sayers
2 Jim McMahon
6 Jack Ham, Joe Greene
11 Joe Namath
13 Deacon Jones, Fred Dryer
17 Phil Simms
20 Ken Stabler, Daryle Lamonica

2001 Donruss Classics Hash Marks

NM/M
Complete Set (25): 280.00
Common Player: 15.00
Inserted 1:box
1 Jamal Lewis 20.00
2 Jim Kelly 20.00
3 Archie Griffin 15.00
4 Walter Payton 35.00
5 Emmitt Smith 25.00
6 Troy Aikman 20.00
7 John Elway 30.00
8 Barry Sanders 25.00
9 Bart Starr 20.00
10 Brett Favre 30.00
11 Reggie White 15.00
12 Edgerrin James 25.00
13 Dan Marino 30.00
14 Fran Tarkenton 15.00
15 Cris Carter 15.00
16 Cris Collinsworth 15.00
17 Fred Biletnikoff 15.00
18 George Blanda 15.00
19 Donovan McNabb 20.00
20 Jerry Rice 25.00
21 Steve Young 18.00
22 Steve Largent 15.00
23 Marshall Faulk 18.00
24 Eddie George 18.00
25 Joe Theismann 15.00

2001 Donruss Classics Hash Marks Autographs

NM/M
2 Jim Kelly 50.00
3 Archie Griffin 10.00
7 John Elway 100.00
8 Barry Sanders 100.00
9 Bart Starr 100.00
14 Fran Tarkenton 100.00
16 Cris Collinsworth 10.00
18 George Blanda 25.00

2001 Donruss Classics Significant Signatures

NM/M
Common Player: 12.00
Inserted 1:18
101 Michael Vick 25 550.00
102 Drew Brees 60.00
103 Chris Weinke 25.00
104 Mike McMahon 20.00
105 Jesse Palmer 15.00
106 Quincy Carter 20.00
107 Josh Heupel 20.00
108 Tim Hasselbeck 15.00
109 LaDainian Tomlinson 100.00
110 Deuce McAllister 25 35.00
111 Michael Bennett 45.00
112 Anthony Thomas 40.00
113 LaMont Jordan 15.00
114 Travis Henry 30.00
115 Kevan Barlow 25.00
116 Travis Minor 15.00
117 Rudi Johnson 15.00
118 David Allen 12.00
119 Heath Evans 12.00
120 Moran Norris 12.00
121 David Terrell 25 40.00
122 Koren Robinson 25 30.00
123 Rod Gardner 25 30.00
124 Santana Moss 30.00
125 Freddie Mitchell 25.00
126 Reggie Wayne 25.00
127 Quincy Morgan 25.00
128 Chad Johnson 20.00
129 Robert Ferguson 15.00
130 Chris Chambers 20.00
131 Marvin "Snoop" Minnis 20.00
132 Eddie Berlin 15.00
133 Alex Bannister 15.00
134 Todd Heap 15.00
135 Alge Crumpler 15.00
136 Justin Smith 12.00
137 Andre Carter 15.00
138 Jamal Reynolds 15.00
139 Richard Seymour 12.00
140 Marcus Stroud 12.00
141 Casey Hampton 12.00
142 Gerald Warren 20.00
143 Torrance Marshall 12.00
144 Brian Allen 12.00
145 Morlon Greenwood 12.00
146 Keith Adams 12.00
147 Will Allen 15.00
148 Nate Clements 12.00
149 Adam Archuleta 18.00
150 Hakim Akbar 12.00
151 James Lofton 15.00
152 Jim Kelly 45.00
153 Gale Sayers 35.00
154 Mike Singletary 15.00
155 Boomer Esiason 18.00
156 Charlie Joiner 12.00
157 Ken Anderson 15.00
158 Y.A. Tittle 18.00
159 Jim Brown 60.00
160 Otto Graham 20.00
161 Ozzie Newsome 12.00
162 Drew Pearson 12.00
163 Lance Alworth 30.00
164 Roger Staubach 50.00
165 Tony Dorsett 40.00
166 John Elway 50 150.00
167 Barry Sanders 125.00
168 Bart Starr 100.00
169 Paul Hornung 30.00
170 Earl Campbell 25.00
171 Warren Moon 25.00
172 Johnny Unitas 50.00
173 Deacon Jones 15.00
174 Eric Dickerson 25.00
175 Bob Griese 40.00
176 Dan Marino 50 150.00
177 Larry Csonka 35.00
178 Paul Warfield 15.00
179 Fran Tarkenton 25.00
180 Archie Manning 18.00
181 Frank Gifford 30.00
182 Lawrence Taylor 25.00
183 Dan Fouts 20.00
184 Don Maynard 15.00
185 Joe Namath 85.00
186 Fred Biletnikoff 20.00
187 Marcus Allen 35.00
188 Jim Plunkett 15.00
189 Franco Harris 25.00
190 Terry Bradshaw 65.00
191 Joe Montana 125.00
192 Roger Craig 12.00
193 Steve Young 35.00
194 Dwight Clark 15.00
195 Steve Largent 20.00
196 Art Monk 15.00
197 Charlie Taylor 12.00
198 Joe Theismann 20.00
199 Sammy Baugh 25.00
200 Sonny Jurgensen 25.00

2001 Donruss Classics Stadium Stars

NM/M
Complete Set (25): 225.00
Common Player: 10.00
Inserted 1:18
Card #12 Never Released
1 Johnny Unitas 20.00
2 Raymond Berry 10.00
3 Jamal Lewis 15.00
4 Ray Lewis 10.00
5 Eddie George 12.00
6 Jim Brown 25.00
7 Ozzie Newsome 10.00
8 Paul Warfield 10.00
9 Tim Couch 12.00
10 John Elway 25.00
11 Rocky Bleier 12.00
13 Jack Lambert 18.00
14 John Stallworth 15.00
15 Bernie Kosar 12.00
16 Jerome Bettis 12.00
17 Emmitt Smith 20.00
18 Troy Aikman 15.00
19 Barry Sanders 20.00
20 Brett Favre 25.00
21 Donovan McNabb 15.00
22 Corey Dillon 12.00
23 Jerry Rice 18.00
24 Steve Young 12.00
25 Dan Marino 25.00

2001 Donruss Classics Stadium Stars Autographs

NM/M
Common Player: 25.00
Randomly Inserted
1 Johnny Unitas 125.00
2 Raymond Berry 25.00
6 Jim Brown 75.00
7 Ozzie Newsome 25.00
8 Paul Warfield 25.00
11 Rocky Bleier 25.00
13 Jack Lambert 75.00
14 John Stallworth 25.00
24 Steve Young 60.00

2001 Donruss Classics Team Colors

NM/M
Complete Set (50): 550.00
Common Player: 10.00
Inserted 1:18
1 John Elway 65.00
2 Brian Griese 20.00
3 Terrell Davis 30.00
4 Olandis Gary 10.00
5 Rod Smith 10.00
6 Ed McCaffrey 10.00
7 Allen Aldridge, Bill Romanowski, John Mobley, Keith Traylor, Neil Smith, Trevor Pryce 25.00
8 Dan Neil, Gary Zimmerman, Mark Schlereth 20.00
9 Kurt Warner 35.00
10 Marshall Faulk 20.00
11 Isaac Bruce 18.00
12 London Fletcher, Mike Jones, Todd Lyght 20.00
13 Az-Zahir Hakim, Isaac Bruce, Torry Holt 40.00
14 Marshall Faulk, Justin Watson, Robert Holcombe 30.00
15 Eddie George PANTS 20.00
16 Eddie George 20.00
17 Jevon Kearse PANTS 15.00
18 Jevon Kearse 15.00
19 Steve McNair 12.00
20 Brett Favre 35.00
21 Antonio Freeman 10.00
22 Dorsey Levens 10.00
23 LeRoy Butler 10.00
24 Daunte Culpepper 25.00
25 Warren Moon 15.00
26 Cris Carter, Jake Reed, Randy Moss 50.00
27 Mark Brunell 15.00
28 Fred Taylor 15.00
29 Jimmy Smith, Keenan McCardell, R. Jay Soward 20.00
30 Hardy Nickerson 10.00
31 Tony Boselli 10.00
32 Troy Aikman 30.00
33 Emmitt Smith 45.00
34 Daryl Johnston 20.00
35 Deion Sanders 25.00
36 Bill Bates 15.00
37 Michael Irvin 20.00
38 Barry Sanders 50.00
39 Sedrick Irvin 10.00
40 Charlie Batch 12.00
41 Herman Moore 10.00
42 Johnnie Morton 10.00
43 Donovan McNabb 10.00
44 Irving Fryar 10.00
45 Charles Johnson 10.00
46 Duce Staley 12.00
47 Curtis Martin 15.00
48 Bryan Cox 10.00
49 Vinny Testaverde 10.00
50 Ray Lucas, Keyshawn Johnson, Wayne Chrebet 20.00

2001 Donruss Classics Team Colors Autos

NM/M
Common Player: 20.00
9 Kurt Warner 75.00
25 Warren Moon 20.00

34	Daryl Johnston	20.00
36	Bill Bates	20.00
44	Irving Fryar	20.00

2001 Donruss Classics Timeless Treasures

		NM/M
Common Player:		25.00
Inserted 1:340		
1	Mike Anderson	30.00
2	Frenchy Fuqua	25.00
3	Corey Dillon	25.00
4	Jamal Lewis	25.00
5	Drew Bledsoe	35.00

2001 Donruss Classics Timeless Tributes

TT Cards:	6X-12X
TT Rookies:	2X
Production 100 Sets	

2001 Donruss Elite

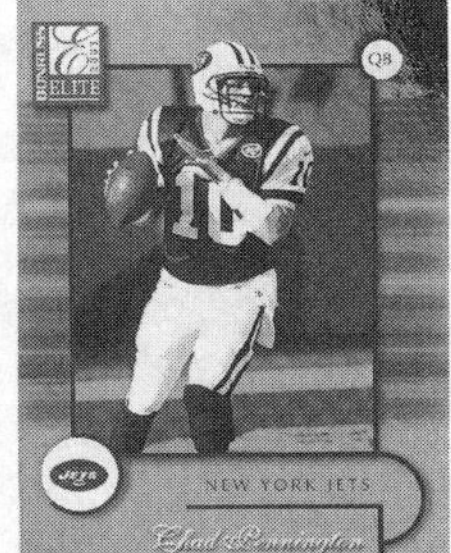

		NM/M
Common Player:		.15
Minor Stars:		.30
Common Rookie:		7.00
Production 500 Sets		
Rookie Autographs:		2X
First 50 Rookies Signed		
Pack (5):		6.75
Wax Box (18):		85.00
1	David Boston	.50
2	Jake Plummer	.50
3	Thomas Jones	.50
4	Chris Redman	.50
5	Jamal Anderson	.50
6	Jamal Lewis	1.50
7	Shannon Sharpe	.30
8	Travis Taylor	.50
9	Trent Dilfer	.30
10	Doug Flutie	.50
11	Eric Moulds	.50
12	Rob Johnson	.30
13	Muhsin Muhammad	.30
14	Steve Beuerlein	.30
15	Brian Urlacher	1.00
16	Cade McNown	.50
17	Marcus Robinson	.50
18	Akili Smith	.50
19	Corey Dillon	.50
20	Peter Warrick	1.00
21	Kevin Johnson	.30
22	Tim Couch	.75
23	Emmitt Smith	1.50
24	Troy Aikman	1.00
25	Brian Griese	.60
26	John Elway	1.75
27	Mike Anderson	1.50
28	Rod Smith	.30
29	Terrell Davis	1.25
30	Barry Sanders	1.75
31	Charlie Batch	.50
32	James Stewart	.50
33	Ahman Green	.50
34	Antonio Freeman	.50
35	Brett Favre	2.00
36	Edgerrin James	1.50
37	Marvin Harrison	.50
38	Peyton Manning	1.50
39	Fred Taylor	.75
40	Jimmy Smith	.50
41	Keenan McCardell	.30
42	Mark Brunell	.75
43	Derrick Alexander	.15
44	Elvis Grbac	.30
45	Sylvester Morris	.50
46	Tony Gonzalez	.30
47	Dan Marino	1.75
48	Jay Fiedler	.50
49	Lamar Smith	.50
50	Oronde Gadsden	.30
51	Cris Carter	.50
52	Daunte Culpepper	1.00
53	Randy Moss	1.50
54	Robert Smith	.30
55	Drew Bledsoe	.75
56	Terry Glenn	.50
57	Aaron Brooks	.75
58	Joe Horn	.30
59	Ricky Williams	.75
60	Amani Toomer	.30
61	Ike Hilliard	.30
62	Kerry Collins	.30
63	Ron Dayne	1.00
64	Tiki Barber	.30
65	Chad Pennington	1.00
66	Curtis Martin	.50
67	Vinny Testaverde	.50
68	Wayne Chrebet	.50
69	Rich Gannon	.50
70	Tim Brown	.30
71	Tyrone Wheatley	.30
72	Donovan McNabb	.75
73	Jerome Bettis	.50
74	Plaxico Burress	.50
75	Junior Seau	.30
76	Charlie Garner	.30
77	Jeff Garcia	.50
78	Jerry Rice	1.25
79	Terrell Owens	.50
80	Darrell Jackson	.30
81	Ricky Watters	.30
82	Shaun Alexander	.50
83	Isaac Bruce	.50
84	Kurt Warner	1.50
85	Marshall Faulk	.60
86	Torry Holt	.50
87	Trent Green	.50
88	Keyshawn Johnson	.50
89	Shaun King	.50
90	Warren Sapp	.30
91	Warrick Dunn	.50
92	Eddie George	.60
93	Jevon Kearse	.50
94	Steve McNair	.50
95	Albert Connell	.30
96	Jeff George	.50
97	Brad Johnson	.50
98	Bruce Smith	.15
99	Michael Westbrook	.30
100	Stephen Davis	.50
101	*Michael Vick*	80.00
102	*Drew Brees*	20.00
103	*Chris Weinke*	10.00
104	*Sage Rosenfels*	10.00
105	*Josh Heupel*	10.00
106	*Tony Driver*	10.00
107	*Ben Leard*	10.00
108	*Marques Tuiasosopo*	12.00
109	*Tim Hasselbeck*	10.00
110	*Mike McMahon*	10.00
111	*Deuce McAllister*	30.00
112	*LaMont Jordan*	12.00
113	*LaDainian Tomlinson*	40.00
114	*James Jackson*	12.00
115	*Anthony Thomas*	15.00
116	*Travis Henry*	15.00
117	*DeAngelo Evans*	7.00
118	*Travis Minor*	12.00
119	*Rudi Johnson*	15.00
120	*Michael Bennett*	25.00
121	*Kevan Barlow*	15.00
122	*Dan Alexander*	10.00
123	*David Allen*	10.00
124	*Correll Buckhalter*	15.00
125	*David Rivers*	10.00
126	*Reggie White*	12.00
127	*Moran Norris*	7.00
128	*Ja'Mar Toombs*	10.00
129	*Jason McKinley*	10.00
130	*Scotty Anderson*	10.00
131	*Dustin McClintock*	12.00
132	*Heath Evans*	10.00
133	*David Terrell*	12.00
134	*Santana Moss*	12.00
135	*Rod Gardner*	12.00
136	*Quincy Morgan*	10.00
137	*Freddie Mitchell*	10.00
138	*Boo Williams*	7.00
139	*Reggie Wayne*	12.00
140	*Ronney Daniels*	7.00
141	*Bobby Newcombe*	12.00
142	*Reggie Germany 250*	12.00
143	*Jesse Palmer*	12.00
144	*Robert Ferguson*	10.00
145	*Ken-Yon Rambo*	10.00
146	*Alex Bannister*	10.00
147	*Koren Robinson*	12.00
148	*Chad Johnson*	15.00
149	*Chris Chambers*	25.00
150	*Javon Green*	7.00
151	*Marvin "Snoop" Minnis*	10.00
152	*Vinny Sutherland*	12.00
153	*Cedrick Wilson*	10.00
154	*John Capel 250*	12.00
155	*T.J. Houshmandzadeh*	10.00
156	*Todd Heap*	15.00
157	*Alge Crumpler*	12.00
158	*Jabari Holloway*	10.00
159	*Marcellus Rivers*	7.00
160	*Rashon Burns*	7.00
161	*Tony Stewart*	12.00
162	*Jevaris Johnson*	7.00
163	*Jamal Reynolds*	7.00
164	*Andre Carter*	12.00
165	*David Warren*	7.00
166	*Justin Smith*	7.00
167	*Josh Booty*	12.00
168	*Karon Riley*	7.00
169	*Cedric Scott*	7.00
170	*Kenny Smith*	7.00
171	*Richard Seymour*	7.00
172	*Willie Howard*	7.00
173	*Marcus Stroud*	7.00
175	*Damione Lewis*	7.00
176	*Casey Hampton*	7.00
177	*Ennis Davis*	7.00
178	*Gerard Warren*	7.00
179	*Tommy Polley*	7.00
180	*Kendrell Bell 250*	50.00
181	*Dan Morgan*	12.00
182	*Morlon Greenwood*	7.00
183	*Quinton Caver*	7.00
184	*Keith Adams*	7.00
185	*Brian Allen*	7.00
186	*Carlos Polk*	7.00
187	*Torrance Marshall*	7.00
188	*Jamie Winborn*	7.00
189	*Jamar Fletcher*	7.00
190	*Ken Lucas*	7.00
191	*Fred Smoot*	7.00
192	*Nate Clements*	7.00
193	*Will Allen*	7.00
194	*Willie Middlebrooks*	7.00
195	*Gary Baxter*	7.00
196	*Derrick Gibson*	7.00
197	*Robert Carswell*	7.00
198	*Hakim Akbar*	7.00
199	*Adam Archuleta*	12.00

2001 Donruss Elite Aspirations

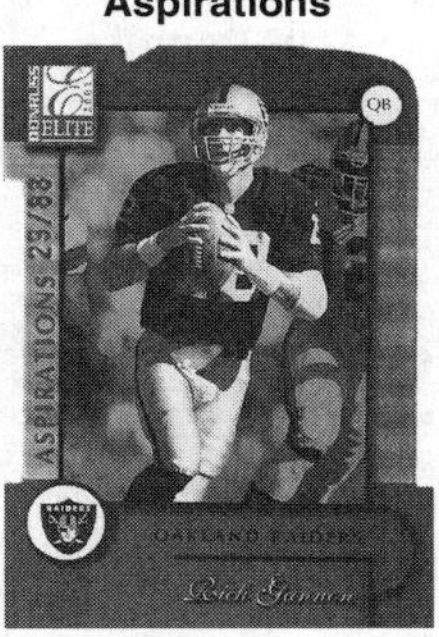

Cards #'d 80-99:	10X-20X
Rookies #'d 80-99:	1X
Cards #'d 65-79:	15X-30X
Rookies #'d 65-79:	1.2X
Cards #'d 45-64:	20X-40X
Rookies #'d 45-64:	1.5X
Cards #'d 30-44:	30X-60X
Rookies #'d 30-44:	2X
Stars #'d 20-29:	50X-100X
Rookies #'d 20-29:	2.5X
Stars #'d 10-19:	60X-120X
Rookies #'d 10-19:	3X

2001 Donruss Elite Status

Stars #'d 80-99:	10X-20X
Rookies #'d 80-99:	1X
Stars #'d 65-79:	15X-30X
Rookies #'d 65-79:	1.2X
Stars #'d 45-64:	20X-40X
Rookies #'d 45-64:	1.5X
Stars #'d 30-44:	30X-60X
Rookies #'d 30-44:	2X
Stars #'d 20-29:	50X-100X
Rookies #'d 20-29:	2.5X
Stars #'d 10-19:	60X-120X
Rookies #'d 10-19:	3X

2001 Donruss Elite Face to Face

		NM/M
Common Player:		20.00
Single Masks #'d to 100		
Double Masks #'d to 50		
1	John Elway	125.00
2	Dan Marino	125.00
3	Brett Favre	125.00
4	Barry Sanders	100.00
5	Marshall Faulk	50.00
6	Edgerrin James	100.00
7	Troy Aikman	80.00
8	Steve Young	60.00
9	Terrell Davis	80.00
10	Jamal Anderson	20.00
11	Tim Brown	40.00
12	Jerry Rice	80.00
13	Isaac Bruce	30.00
14	Torry Holt	30.00
15	Warren Sapp	20.00
16	Jerome Bettis	25.00
17	Fred Taylor	35.00
18	Ray Lewis	30.00
19	Eddie George	50.00
20	Ryan Leaf	20.00
21	Peyton Manning	100.00
22	Phil Simms	35.00
24	Keyshawn Johnson	30.00
27	Wayne Chrebet	30.00
28	Shaun King	30.00
29	Donovan McNabb	60.00
30	Dan Marino, John Elway	300.00
31	Brett Favre, Barry Sanders	250.00
32	Edgerrin James, Marshall Faulk	125.00
33	Troy Aikman, Steve Young	100.00
34	Jamal Anderson, Terrell Davis	75.00
35	Jerry Rice, Tim Brown	120.00
36	Isaac Bruce, Torry Holt	50.00
37	Warren Sapp, Reggie White	40.00
38	Fred Taylor, Jerome Bettis	60.00
39	Ray Lewis, Eddie George	60.00
40	Peyton Manning, Ryan Leaf	100.00
41	Phil Simms, Lawrence Taylor	45.00
42	Joe Montana, Marcus Allen	150.00
43	Wayne Chrebet, Keyshawn Johnson	40.00
44	Donovan McNabb, Shaun King	100.00
45		

2001 Donruss Elite Passing the Torch

		NM/M
Complete Set (24):		100.00
Common Player:		3.00
Single Player #'d to 1,000		
Double Player #'d to 500		
1	John Elway	10.00
2	Brian Griese	3.50
3	Dick Butkus	8.00
4	Brian Urlacher	4.00
5	Fran Tarkenton	5.00
6	Daunte Culpepper	5.00
7	Jim Brown	5.00
8	Jamal Lewis	6.00
9	Larry Csonka	4.00
10	Ron Dayne	4.00
11	Tony Dorsett	3.50
12	Emmitt Smith	6.00
13	Eric Dickerson	3.00
14	Marshall Faulk	3.00
15	Joe Namath	8.00
16	Chad Pennington	4.00
17	John Elway, Brian Griese	20.00
18	Brian Urlacher, Dick Butkus	20.00
19	Fran Tarkenton, Daunte Culpepper	10.00
20	Jamal Lewis, Jim Brown	12.00
21	Larry Csonka, Ron Dayne	7.00
22	Tony Dorsett, Emmitt Smith	12.00
23	Marshall Faulk, Eric Dickerson	6.00
24	Chad Pennington, Joe Namath	15.00

2001 Donruss Elite Passing the Torch Autographs

		NM/M
Common Player:		40.00
Single Player #'d to 100		
Double Player #'d to 50		
1	John Elway	150.00
2	Brian Griese	75.00
3	Dick Butkus	100.00
4	Brian Urlacher	85.00
5	Fran Tarkenton	60.00
6	Daunte Culpepper	85.00
7	Jim Brown	125.00
8	Jamal Lewis	85.00
9	Larry Csonka	75.00
10	Ron Dayne	60.00
11	Tony Dorsett	75.00
12	Emmitt Smith	175.00
13	Eric Dickerson	40.00
14	Marshall Faulk	75.00
15	Joe Namath	150.00
16	Chad Pennington	100.00
17	John Elway, Brian Griese	225.00
18	Brian Urlacher, Dick Butkus	150.00
19	Fran Tarkenton, Daunte Culpepper	180.00
20	Jamal Lewis, Jim Brown	200.00
21	Larry Csonka, Ron Dayne	125.00
22	Tony Dorsett, Emmitt Smith	200.00
23	Marshall Faulk, Eric Dickerson	100.00
24	Chad Pennington, Joe Namath	300.00

2001 Donruss Elite Primary Colors

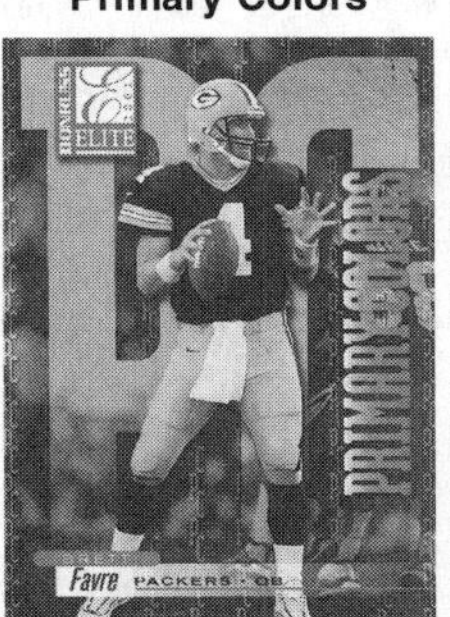

		NM/M
Complete Set (40):		100.00
Common Player:		1.50
Production 975 Sets		
Red Die-Cut Cards:		6X-12X
Production 25 Sets		
Blue Cards:		2X
Production 200 Sets		
Blue Die Cut Cards:		4X-8X
Production 50 Sets		
Yellow Cards:		6X-12X
Production 25 Sets		
Yellow Die Cut Cards:		3X-6X
Production 75 Sets		
1	Peyton Manning	6.00
2	Edgerrin James	6.00
3	Marvin Harrison	2.00
4	Curtis Martin	2.00
5	Eric Moulds	1.50
6	Dan Marino	7.00
7	Drew Bledsoe	2.50
8	Drew Brees	8.00
9	Jamal Lewis	5.00
10	Michael Vick	18.00
11	Eddie George	2.00
12	Steve McNair	1.50
13	Jerome Bettis	1.50
14	Koren Robinson	5.00
15	Mark Brunell	2.50
16	Fred Taylor	2.50
17	Michael Bennett	7.00
18	David Terrell	7.00
19	Brian Griese	2.00
20	Mike Anderson	5.00
21	John Elway	7.00
22	Terrell Owens	2.00
23	Rudi Johnson	2.50
24	Larry Rice	5.00
25	Ricky Williams	3.00
26	Aaron Brooks	2.00
27	Kurt Warner	7.00
28	Marshall Faulk	2.50
29	Isaac Bruce	2.00
30	Brett Favre	8.00
31	Santana Moss	7.00
32	Daunte Culpepper	4.00
33	Randy Moss	6.00
34	Cris Carter	2.00
35	Barry Sanders	6.00
36	Emmitt Smith	5.00
37	Stephen Davis	1.50
38	Ron Dayne	3.00
39	Donovan McNabb	3.00
40	Deuce McAllister	6.00

2001 Donruss Elite Prime Numbers

1	Dan Marino
2	John Elway
3	Mike Anderson
4	Randy Moss
5	Daunte Culpepper
6	Kurt Warner
7	Jerry Rice
8	Edgerrin James
9	Peyton Manning
10	Brett Favre

2001 Donruss Elite Throwback Threads

		NM/M
Common Player:		25.00
Single Jerseys #'d to 100:		
Double Jerseys #'d to 50:		
1	Art Monk	45.00
2	Joe Theismann	45.00
3	Jim Kelly	75.00
4	Thurman Thomas	25.00
5	Joe Namath	125.00
6	Don Maynard	25.00
7	Bob Griese	40.00
8	Larry Csonka	60.00
9	Joe Montana	125.00
10	Jerry Rice	85.00
11	Raymond Berry	25.00
12	Marvin Harrison	40.00
13	Warren Moon	35.00
14	Steve McNair	25.00
15	Terrell Davis	70.00
16	Mike Anderson	60.00
17	Frank Gifford	50.00
18	Ron Dayne	25.00
19	Walter Payton	150.00
20	Gale Sayers	60.00
21	Terry Bradshaw	100.00
22	Lynn Swann	50.00
23	Troy Aikman	80.00
24	Emmitt Smith	100.00
25	Fran Tarkenton	60.00
26	Daunte Culpepper	60.00
27	John Elway	100.00
28	Brian Griese	50.00
29	Eric Dickerson	25.00
30	Marshall Faulk	50.00
31	Joe Theismann, Art Monk	85.00
32	Thurman Thomas, Jim Kelly	100.00
33	Don Maynard, Joe Namath	120.00
34	Larry Csonka, Bob Griese	100.00
35	Jerry Rice, Joe Montana	250.00
36	Marvin Harrison, Raymond Berry	50.00
37	Warren Moon, Steve McNair	75.00
38	Terrell Davis, Mike Anderson	100.00
39	Ron Dayne, Frank Gifford	75.00
40	Walter Payton, Gale Sayers	225.00
41	Terry Bradshaw, Franco Harris	175.00
42	Troy Aikman, Emmitt Smith	200.00
43	Fran Tarkenton, Daunte Culpepper	175.00
44	John Elway, Brian Griese	180.00
45	Eric Dickerson, Marshall Faulk	100.00

2001 Donruss Elite Title Waves

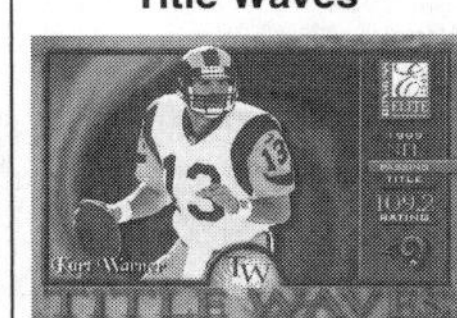

		NM/M
Complete Set (30):		60.00
Common Player:		1.50
Numbered To Stat		
Holofoil Cards:		4X-8X
Production 100 Sets		
1	Kurt Warner 1999	5.00
2	Dan Marino 1994	5.00
3	Brett Favre 1995	6.00
4	Peyton Manning 2000	5.00
5	John Elway 1996	5.00
6	Steve Young 1997	2.50
7	Barry Sanders 1997	4.00
8	Emmitt Smith 1993	4.00
9	Terrell Davis 1998	3.50
10	Edgerrin James 2000	4.00
11	Stephen Davis 1999	1.50
12	Curtis Martin 1995	1.50
13	Marvin Harrison 1999	1.50
14	Antonio Freeman 1998	1.50
15	Jerry Rice 1995	3.00
16	Randy Moss 1999	5.00
17	Tim Brown 1997	1.50
18	Isaac Bruce 1996	1.50
19	Ricky Williams 2000	2.50
20	Peyton Manning 1999	5.00
21	Eddie George 2000	2.00
22	Barry Sanders 1993	4.00
23	Daunte Culpepper 2000	3.00
24	Dan Marino 1994	5.00
25	John Elway 1999	5.00
26	Marshall Faulk 2000	2.00
27	Brett Favre 1997	6.00
28	Steve Young 1995	2.50
29	Troy Aikman 1993	3.00
30	Jerry Rice 1990	3.00

2002 Donruss

		NM/M
Complete Set (300):		200.00
Common Player:		.15
Unlisted Stars:		.75
Minor Stars:		.60
Common Rookie (201-300):		1.50
Minor Rookies:		2.00
Pack (5):		2.25
Wax Box (24):		40.00
1	Jake Plummer	.60
2	David Boston	.75
3	MarTay Jenkins	.15
4	Thomas Jenkins	.15
5	Frank Sanders	.15
6	Shawn Jefferson	.15

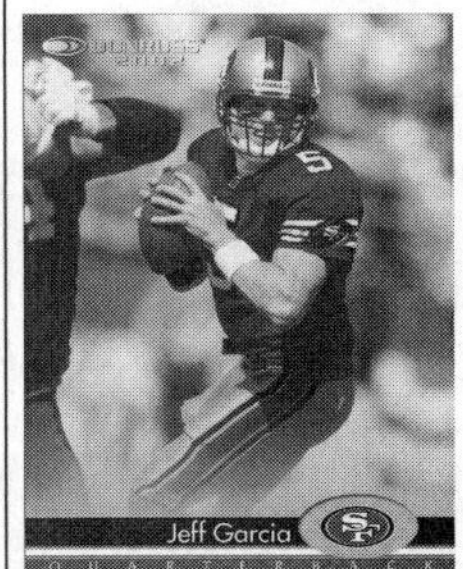

7	Alge Crumpler	.40
8	Michael Vick	2.50
9	Jamal Anderson	.40
10	Warrick Dunn	.40
11	Peter Boulware	.15
12	Jamal Lewis	1.25
13	Jeff Blake	.15
14	Travis Taylor	.15
15	Ray Lewis	.60
16	Todd Heap	.15
17	Nate Clements	.15
18	Alex Van Pelt	.15
19	Reggie Germany	.15
20	Larry Centers	.15
21	Eric Moulds	.60
22	Travis Henry	.60
23	Wesley Walls	.15
24	Steve Smith	.15
25	Lamar Smith	.60
26	Patrick Jeffers	.15
27	Chris Weinke	.60
28	Muhsin Muhammad	.60
29	Marcus Robinson	.60
30	Jim Miller	.60
31	Anthony Thomas	2.00
32	David Terrell	.75
33	Brian Urlacher	2.00
34	Marty Booker	.15
35	Darnay Scott	.15
36	Jon Kitna	.15
37	Chad Johnson	.15
38	T.J. Houshmandzadeh	.15
39	Corey Dillon	.75
40	Peter Warrick	.60
41	Gerard Warren	.15
42	Anthony Henry	.15
43	Quincy Morgan	.50
44	JaJuan Dawson	.15
45	Tim Couch	1.25
46	Kevin Johnson	.15
47	James Jackson	.60
48	La'Roi Glover	.15
49	Anthony Wright	.15
50	Raghib Ismail	.15
51	Troy Hambrick	.15
52	Emmitt Smith	2.50
53	Quincy Carter	1.50
54	Joey Galloway	.60
55	Shannon Sharpe	.60
56	Kevin Kasper	.15
57	Olandis Gary	.15
58	Brian Griese	.75
59	Rod Smith	.60

60 Terrell Davis 1.25
61 Ed McCaffrey .60
62 Mike Anderson 1.25
63 Bill Schroeder .15
64 Scotty Anderson .15
65 Mike McMahon .75
66 James Stewart .40
67 Az-Zahir Hakim .15
68 Germane Crowell .15
69 Kabeer Gbaja-Biamila .15
70 LeRoy Butler .60
71 Antonio Freeman .60
72 Bubba Franks .40
73 Brett Favre 3.00
74 Ahman Green .75
75 Terry Glenn .60
76 Jamie Sharper .15
77 Tony Simmons .15
78 James Allen .40
79 Terrence Wilkins .15
80 Dominic Rhodes .40
81 Qadry Ismail .40
82 Peyton Manning 2.50
83 Edgerrin James 2.00
84 Marvin Harrison .60
85 Reggie Wayne .60
86 Fred Taylor .60
87 Elvis Joseph .15
88 Mark Brunell .75
89 Keenan McCardell .60
90 Jimmy Smith .60
91 Kyle Brady .15
92 Derrick Alexander .15
93 Johnnie Morton .40
94 Trent Green .60
95 Priest Holmes .75
96 Tony Gonzalez .60
97 Marvin "Snoop" Minnis .60
98 Travis Minor .60
99 Oronde Gadsden .15
100 Jay Fiedler .60
101 Chris Chambers .75
102 Ricky Williams 1.50
103 Zach Thomas .60
104 Byron Chamberlain .15
105 Todd Bouman .15
106 Daunte Culpepper 1.50
107 Michael Bennett .75
108 Randy Moss 2.50
109 Cris Carter .60
110 David Patten .15
111 Donald Hayes .40
112 Tom Brady 2.50
113 Antowain Smith .60
114 Troy Brown .40
115 Drew Bledsoe 1.50
116 Bryan Cox .15
117 Eddie "Boo" Williams .15
118 Aaron Brooks 1.25
119 Deuce McAllister 1.25
120 Joe Horn .15
121 Amani Toomer .40
122 Ron Dayne .60
123 Kerry Collins .60
124 Ike Hilliard .40
125 Tiki Barber .60
126 Michael Strahan .60
127 Chad Pennington .60
128 Santana Moss .60
129 LaMont Jordan .60
130 Curtis Martin .60
131 Wayne Chrebet .60
132 Laveranues Coles .60
133 Vinny Testaverde .60
134 Charles Woodson .60
135 Tyrone Wheatley .15
136 Jerry Porter .15
137 Rich Gannon .60
138 Charlie Garner .60
139 Tim Brown .75
140 Jerry Rice 2.50
141 James Thrash .15
142 Todd Pinkston .60
143 A.J. Feeley .15
144 Donovan McNabb 1.50
145 Duce Staley .60
146 Freddie Mitchell .60
147 Correll Buckhalter .40
148 Casey Hampton .15
149 Hines Ward .60
150 Chris Fuamatu-Ma'afala .15
151 Jerome Bettis .60
152 Kordell Stewart .60
153 Plaxico Burress .75
154 Kendrell Bell .60
155 Trevor Gaylor .15
156 Curtis Conway .40
157 Doug Flutie .75
158 Drew Brees 2.00
159 LaDainian Tomlinson 2.00
160 Junior Seau .60
161 Bryant Young .15
162 Andre Carter .15
163 Eric Johnson .15
164 Jeff Garcia .75
165 Garrison Hearst .60
166 Terrell Owens .75
167 Kevan Barlow .60
168 Levon Kirkland .15
169 Ricky Watters .60
170 Trent Dilfer .60
171 Shaun Alexander .75
172 Koren Robinson .60
173 Darrell Jackson .15
174 Adam Archuleta .15
175 Aeneas Williams .15
176 Trung Canidate .40
177 Kurt Warner 2.50
178 Marshall Faulk 1.50
179 Torry Holt .60
180 Isaac Bruce .60
181 John Lynch .15
182 Joe Jurevicius .40
183 Brad Johnson .60
184 Rob Johnson .60
185 Keyshawn Johnson .60
186 Mike Alstott .60
187 Warren Sapp .60
188 Drew Bennett .15
189 Frank Wycheck .15
190 Kevin Dyson .60
191 Steve McNair .75
192 Eddie George .75
193 Jevon Kearse .60
194 Derrick Mason .60
195 Champ Bailey .40
196 Darrell Green .40
197 Bruce Smith .60
198 Jacquez Green .60
199 Stephen Davis .60
200 Rod Gardner .60
201 *David Carr* 10.00
202 *Joey Harrington* 10.00
203 *Patrick Ramsey* 3.00
204 *Kurt Kittner* 2.50
205 *Rohan Davey* 3.00
206 *Josh McCown* 2.50
207 *David Garrard* 1.50
208 *Randy Fasani* 1.50
209 *Atrews Bell* 1.00
210 *Brandon Doman* 1.00
211 *Eric Crouch* 3.00
212 *Woodrow Dantzler III* 1.00
213 *Chad Hutchinson* 2.00
214 *Zak Kustok* 2.00
215 *Ronald Curry* 2.50
216 *William Green* 4.00
217 *T.J. Duckett* 5.00
218 *Clinton Portis* 10.00
219 *DeShaun Foster* 3.00
220 *Lamar Gordon* 2.50
221 *Jonathan Wells* 3.00
222 *Adrian Peterson* 2.50
223 *Ladell Betts* 2.50
224 *Maurice Morris* 3.00
225 *Brian Westbrook* 5.00
226 *Luke Staley* 2.50
227 *Travis Stephens* 2.50
228 *Craig Nall* 2.00
229 *Chester Taylor* 2.00
230 *Ken Simonton* 2.00
231 *Verron Haynes* 2.00
232 *Tellis Redmon* 2.00
233 *J.T. O'Sullivan* 2.00
234 *Major Applewhite* 2.00
235 *Ricky Williams* 2.00
236 *James Mungro* 2.00
237 *Josh Scobey* 2.00
238 *Najeh Davenport* 3.00
239 *Dicenzo Miller* 2.00
240 *Ennis Haywood* 2.00
241 *Jabar Gaffney* 3.00
242 *Antonio Bryant* 4.00
243 *Donte Stallworth* 5.00
244 *Josh Reed* 3.00
245 *Ashley Lelie* 5.00
246 *Donald Reche Caldwell* 2.50
247 *Marquise Walker* 2.50
248 *Javon Walker* 5.00
249 *Andre Davis* 3.00
250 *Antwaan Randle El* 4.00
251 *Kelly Campbell* 2.00
252 *Cliff Russell* 2.00
253 *Kahlil Hill* 2.00
254 *Ron Johnson* 2.00
255 *Deion Branch* 3.00
256 *Brian Poli-Dixon* 2.00
257 *Freddie Milons* 2.00
258 *Lee Mays* 2.00
259 *Tim Carter* 2.00
260 *Terry Charles* 2.00
261 *Jamar Martin* 2.00
262 *Jason McAddley* 2.00
263 *Chris Hope* 2.00
264 *Howard Green* 2.00
265 *Jeremy Shockey* 6.00
266 *Daniel Graham* 2.50
267 *Eddie Freeman* 2.00
268 *Julius Peppers* 4.00
269 *Kalimba Edwards* 2.00
270 *Dwight Freeney* 2.00
271 *Dennis Johnson* 2.00
272 *Alex Brown* 2.00
273 *Bryan Thomas* 2.00
274 *Bryan Fletcher* 2.00
275 *Will Overstreet* 2.00
276 *Ryan Denney* 2.00
277 *Charles Grant* 2.00
278 *John Henderson* 2.00
279 *Albert Haynesworth* 2.00
280 *Wendell Bryant* 2.00
281 *Ryan Sims* 2.00
282 *Anthony Weaver* 2.00
283 *Larry Tripplett* 2.00
284 *Alan Harper* 2.00
285 *Napoleon Harris* 2.00
286 *Robert Thomas* 2.00
287 *Levar Fisher* 2.00
288 *Andra Davis* 2.00
289 *Quentin Jammer* 2.50
290 *Phillip Buchanon* 2.50
291 *Keyuo Craver* 2.00
292 *Lito Sheppard* 2.00
293 *Rocky Calmus* 2.00
294 *Mike Rumph* 2.00
295 *Mike Echols* 2.00
296 *Joseph Jefferson* 2.00
297 *Roy Williams* 4.00
298 *Edward Reed* 2.00
299 *Michael Lewis* 2.00
300 *Eddie Drummond* 2.00

2002 Donruss Statline Career

NM/M
Stars/300-430: 2X-4X
Rookies/300-430: 1X
Stars/200-299: 3X-6X
Rookies/200-299: 2X
Stars/100-199: 6X-12X
Rookies/100-199: 2X-4X
Stars/50-99: 10X-20X
Rookies/50-99: 4X-8X
Stars/25-50: 15X-30X
Rookies/25-50: 5X-10X

2002 Donruss Statline Season

Stars/300-430: 2X-4X
Rookies/300-430: 1X
Stars/200-299: 3X-6X
Rookies/200-299: 2X
Stars/100-199: 6X-12X
Rookies/100-199: 2X-4X
Stars/50-99: 10X-20X
Rookies/50-99: 4X-8X
Stars/25-50: 15X-30X
Rookies/25-50: 5X-10X

2002 Donruss All-Time Gridiron Kings

NM/M
Common Player: 2.00
Production 2000 sets
Studio version: 1.5X-3X
Production 250 sets
1 Dan Marino 6.00
2 Jim Kelly 3.00
3 Earl Campbell 2.00
4 John Elway 6.00
5 Dick Butkus 4.00
6 Troy Aikman 4.00
7 Barry Sanders 5.00
8 Roger Staubach 5.00
9 John Riggins 4.00
10 Steve Young 3.00

2002 Donruss Elite Series

NM/M
Common Player: 4.00
Production 1500 sets
1 Brett Favre 8.00
2 Kordell Stewart 4.00
3 Jevon Kearse 4.00
4 Ahman Green 4.00
5 Anthony Thomas 4.00
6 Cris Carter 4.00
7 Tim Brown 4.00
8 Ray Lewis 4.00
9 Aaron Brooks 4.00
10 Isaac Bruce 4.00
11 Chris Chambers 4.00
12 David Boston 4.00
13 Jimmy Smith 4.00
14 Brian Urlacher 6.00
15 Edgerrin James 4.00
16 Dan Marino 8.00
17 Barry Sanders 8.00
18 Steve Young 4.00
19 Troy Aikman 6.00
20 Thurman Thomas 4.00

2002 Donruss Elite Series Signatures

NM/M
Common Player: 15.00
Production 50 sets
1 Brett Favre 150.00
2 Kordell Stewart 25.00
3 Jevon Kearse 30.00
4 Ahman Green 50.00
5 Anthony Thomas 25.00
6 Cris Carter 40.00
7 Tim Brown 40.00
8 Ray Lewis 50.00
9 Aaron Brooks 25.00
10 Isaac Bruce 40.00
11 Chris Chambers 25.00
12 David Boston 25.00
13 Jimmy Smith 25.00
14 Brian Urlacher 75.00
15 Edgerrin James 60.00
16 Dan Marino 200.00
17 Barry Sanders 100.00
18 Steve Young 75.00
19 Troy Aikman 100.00
20 Thurman Thomas 40.00

2002 Donruss Executive Producers

NM/M
Common Player: 2.00
Production 1000 sets
1 Randy Moss 3.00
2 Emmitt Smith 3.00
3 Kurt Warner 3.00
4 Jerry Rice 3.00
5 Edgerrin James 2.00
6 Anthony Thomas 2.00
7 Jerome Bettis 2.00
8 Daunte Culpepper 2.00
9 Brian Griese 2.00
10 Steve McNair 2.00
11 Marshall Faulk 2.00
12 Ahman Green 2.00
13 Peyton Manning 3.00
14 Shaun Alexander 2.00
15 Donovan McNabb 2.00
16 Jeff Garcia 2.00
17 Eddie George 2.00
18 Tim Brown 2.00
19 Brett Favre 5.00
20 Curtis Martin 2.00

2002 Donruss Gridiron Kings Inserts

NM/M
Common Player: 2.00
Production 2000 sets
Studio versions: 2X-4X
Production 250 sets
1 Emmitt Smith 3.00
2 Jerome Bettis 2.00
3 Jerry Rice 3.00
4 Brett Favre 4.00
5 Tom Brady 3.00
6 Anthony Thomas 2.00
7 Kurt Warner 3.00
8 Daunte Culpepper 2.00
9 Brian Griese 2.00
10 Cris Carter 2.00
11 Peyton Manning 3.00
12 Donovan McNabb 2.00
13 LaDainian Tomlinson 2.00
14 Eddie George 2.00
15 Edgerrin James 2.00
16 Randy Moss 3.00
17 Tim Brown 2.00
18 Brian Urlacher 3.00
19 Marshall Faulk 2.00
20 Michael Vick 3.00

2002 Donruss Jersey Kings

NM/M
Common Player: 15.00
Production 125 sets
Studio versions: 1.5X-3X
Production 25 sets
1 Emmitt Smith 60.00
2 Jerome Bettis 20.00
3 Jerry Rice 40.00
4 Brett Favre 50.00
5 Tom Brady 30.00
6 Anthony Thomas 25.00
7 Kurt Warner 25.00
8 Daunte Culpepper 30.00
9 Brian Griese 25.00
10 Cris Carter 30.00
11 Peyton Manning 35.00
12 Donovan McNabb 25.00
13 LaDainian Tomlinson 20.00
14 Eddie George 15.00
15 Edgerrin James 30.00
16 Randy Moss 30.00
17 Tim Brown 25.00
18 Brian Urlacher 30.00
19 Marshall Faulk 30.00
20 Michael Vick 40.00

2002 Donruss Leather Kings

NM/M
Common Player: 10.00
Production 250 sets
Studio versions: 1.5X-3X
Production 25 sets
1 Emmitt Smith 40.00
2 Jerome Bettis 15.00
3 Jerry Rice 30.00
4 Brett Favre 40.00
5 Tom Brady 30.00
6 Anthony Thomas 15.00
7 Kurt Warner 20.00
8 Daunte Culpepper 20.00
9 Brian Griese 15.00
10 Cris Carter 15.00
11 Peyton Manning 30.00
12 Donovan McNabb 20.00
13 LaDainian Tomlinson 15.00
14 Eddie George 10.00
15 Edgerrin James 20.00
16 Randy Moss 25.00
17 Tim Brown 15.00
18 Brian Urlacher 20.00
19 Marshall Faulk 20.00
20 Michael Vick 30.00

2002 Donruss Private Signings

NM/M
1 Adrian Peterson 20.00
2 Alex Brown 10.00
3 Andra Davis 10.00
4 Andre Davis 35.00
5 Andre Lott 15.00
6 Antonio Bryant 35.00
7 Brian Poli-Dixon 15.00
8 Bryant McKinnie 25.00
9 Chad Hutchinson 15.00
10 Chester Taylor 15.00
11 Clinton Portis/50 100.00
12 Cortlen Johnson 15.00
13 Damien Anderson 10.00
14 David Carr/50 100.00
15 David Garrard 20.00
16 Demontray Carter 15.00
17 Dwight Freeney 20.00
18 Ed Reed 15.00
19 Eric Crouch/63 40.00
20 Freddie Milons 12.00
21 Javon Walker No Auto 25.00
22 Ron Johnson 15.00
23 Jerramy Stevens/50 25.00
24 Joey Harrington/75 80.00
25 Josh Reed/50 30.00
26 Julius Peppers/15 80.00
27 Kalimba Edwards 15.00
28 Kelly Campbell 15.00
29 Ken Simonton 15.00
30 Keyua Craver 15.00
31 Kurt Kittner/50 25.00
32 Lito Sheppard 10.00
33 Luke Staley 15.00
34 Maurice Morris 25.00
35 Najeh Davenport 15.00
36 Quentin Jammer 25.00
37 Donald Reche Caldwell/50 25.00
38 Rocky Calmus 15.00
39 Tavon Mason 10.00
40 Woodrow Dantzler/25 30.00
41 John Riggins 60.00
42 Deuce McAllister/50 50.00
43 Drew Brees/50 50.00
44 Edgerrin James/27 75.00
45 Emmitt Smith/25 200.00
46 Kurt Warner/35 50.00
47 Marshall Faulk/50 50.00
48 Quincy Carter/50 40.00
49 Tim Brown/50 40.00
50 Brett Favre/25 200.00

2002 Donruss Rookie Year Materials

NM/M
Common Player: 15.00
Production 100 sets
1 John Riggins 50.00
2 Joe Montana 200.00
3 Randy Moss 50.00
4 Ricky Williams 40.00
5 Tim Couch 25.00
6 Peyton Manning 50.00
7 Mark Brunell 25.00
8 Keyshawn Johnson 25.00
9 LaDainian Tomlinson 30.00
10 Michael Vick 60.00

2002 Donruss Rookie Year Materials Numbers

NM/M
Common Player: 40.00
1 John Riggins/44 100.00
2 Joe Montana/16
3 Randy Moss/84 50.00
4 Ricky Williams/34 60.00
5 Tim Couch/2
6 Peyton Manning/18
7 Mark Brunell/8
8 Keyshawn Johnson/19
9 LaDainian Tomlinson/21 40.00
10 Michael Vick/7

2002 Donruss Zoning Commission

NM/M
Complete Set (8): 25.00
Common Player: 3.00
Production 500 sets
1 Marshall Faulk 4.00
2 Terrell Owens 3.00
3 Shaun Alexander 4.00
4 Marvin Harrison 3.00
5 Antowain Smith 3.00
6 Kurt Warner 5.00
7 Jeff Garcia 3.00
8 Brett Favre 5.00

2002 Donruss Classics

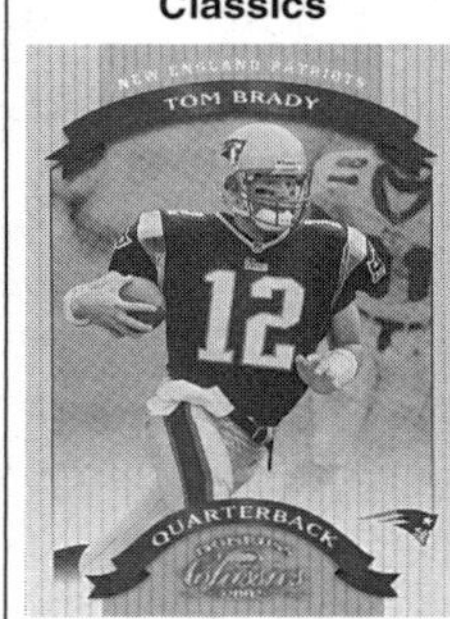

NM/M
Common Player: .25
#'s 1-100 veterans
#'s 101-150 Retired players
#'s 151-200 Rookies
Timeless Tribute parallel 2X to 4X
Production 150 veterans, 100 others
Pack (6): 8.00
Wax Box (18): 105.00
1 David Boston 1.25
2 Jake Plummer .75
3 Jamal Anderson .25
4 Michael Vick 4.00
5 Chris Weinke .75
6 Muhsin Muhammad .75
7 Steve Smith .25
8 Anthony Thomas 3.00
9 David Terrell 1.25
10 Brian Urlacher 3.00
11 Marty Booker .25
12 Quincy Carter 2.50
13 Emmitt Smith 4.00
14 Mike McMahon 1.25
15 James Stewart .75
16 Brett Favre 5.00
17 Ahman Green 1.25
18 Antonio Freeman .75
19 Michael Bennett 1.25
20 Randy Moss 4.00
21 Cris Carter .75
22 Daunte Culpepper 2.50
23 Aaron Brooks 2.00
24 Ricky Williams 2.50
25 Deuce McAllister 2.00
26 Kerry Collins .75
27 Michael Strahan .75
28 Donovan McNabb 2.50
29 Duce Staley .75
30 Freddie Mitchell .75
31 Correll Buckhalter .25
32 Jeff Garcia 1.25
33 Terrell Owens 1.25
34 Garrison Hearst .75
35 Marshall Faulk 2.50
36 Isaac Bruce .75
37 Kurt Warner 3.00
38 Torry Holt .75
39 Brad Johnson .75
40 Keyshawn Johnson .75
41 Mike Alstott .75
42 Warrick Dunn .75
43 Stephen Davis .75
44 Rod Gardner .75
45 Bruce Smith .60
46 Elvis Grbac .60
47 Ray Lewis .75
48 Jamal Lewis 2.00
49 Rob Johnson .75
50 Eric Moulds .75
51 Travis Henry .75
52 Corey Dillon 1.25
53 Peter Warrick .75
54 Tim Couch 2.00
55 James Jackson .75
56 Kevin Johnson .50
57 Brian Griese 1.25
58 Terrell Davis 2.00
59 Rod Smith .75
60 Mike Anderson 2.00
61 Peyton Manning 4.00
62 Marvin Harrison .75
63 Edgerrin James 3.00
64 Dominic Rhodes .25
65 Mark Brunell 1.25
66 Fred Taylor .50
67 Jimmy Smith .50
68 Tony Gonzalez .50
69 Trent Green .50
70 Priest Holmes .25
71 Marvin "Snoop" Minnis .25
72 Jay Fiedler .25
73 Lamar Smith .25
74 Chris Chambers 2.00
75 Tom Brady 5.00
76 Drew Bledsoe 1.00
77 Antowain Smith .25
78 Troy Brown .25
79 Vinny Testaverde .25
80 Curtis Martin .75
81 Wayne Chrebet .25
82 Laveranues Coles .25
83 Tim Brown .75
84 Jerry Rice 3.00
85 Rich Gannon .50
86 Charlie Garner .25
87 Kordell Stewart .50
88 Jerome Bettis .50
89 Kendrell Bell .25
90 Plaxico Burress 1.00
91 Drew Brees 2.00
92 LaDainian Tomlinson 2.00
93 Doug Flutie 1.00
94 Shaun Alexander 1.00
95 Matt Hasselbeck .25
96 Koren Robinson .50
97 Steve McNair .50
98 Eddie George .50
99 Derrick Mason .25
100 Jevon Kearse .40
101 Joe Montana 2.00
102 Joe Namath 1.00
103 Warren Moon .25
104 Dan Marino 1.00
105 Steve Bartkowski .25
106 John Elway 1.00
107 Troy Aikman 1.00
108 Steve Young .25
109 Terry Bradshaw 1.00
110 Bart Starr 1.00
111 Bert Jones .25
112 Craig Morton .25
113 Bob Griese 1.00
114 Dan Fouts .25
115 Phil Simms .25
116 Jim McMahon 1.00
117 Joe Theismann .25
118 Ken Stabler .25
119 Johnny Unitas 1.00
120 Roger Staubach 1.00
121 Len Dawson .25
122 Tony Dorsett .75
123 Gale Sayers 1.00
124 Jim Kelly .75
125 Herschel Walker .25
126 John Riggins 1.00
127 Eric Dickerson 1.00
128 Franco Harris 1.00
129 Earl Campbell 1.00
130 Thurman Thomas .25
131 Barry Sanders 1.00
132 Marcus Allen .25
134 Natrone Means .25
135 Steve Largent .25
136 Don Maynard .25
137 Henry Ellard .25
138 Sterling Sharpe 1.00
139 Art Monk 1.00
140 Andre Reed .25
141 Raymond Berry .25
142 Ozzie Newsome .25
143 William Perry .25
144 Deacon Jones .25
145 Howie Long .25
146 L.C. Greenwood .25
147 Ronnie Lott .25
148 Dick Butkus 1.00
149 Fran Tarkenton 1.00
150 Mike Singletary .25
151 *David Carr* 25.00
152 *Joey Harrington* 20.00
153 *Patrick Ramsey* 12.00
154 *Kurt Kittner* 6.00
155 *DeShaun Foster* 8.00
156 *William Green* 8.00
157 *Clinton Portis* 25.00
158 *T.J. Duckett* 12.00
159 *Cliff Russell* 5.00
160 *Antonio Bryant* 8.00
161 *Donte Stallworth* 12.00
162 *Donald Reche Caldwell* 8.00
163 *Jabar Gaffney* 8.00
164 *Ashley Lelie* 12.00
165 *Andre Davis* 8.00
166 *Josh Reed* 8.00
167 *Ron Johnson* 6.00
168 *Kelly Campbell* 5.00
169 *Javon Walker* 15.00
170 *Antwaan Randle El* 8.00
171 *Marquise Walker* 8.00
172 *Jeremy Shockey* 15.00
173 *Jerramy Stephens* 5.00

174	*Daniel Graham*	8.00
175	*Julius Peppers*	15.00
176	*Kalimba Edwards*	5.00
177	*Alex Brown*	5.00
178	*Will Overstreet*	5.00
179	*Dwight Freeney*	5.00
180	*John Henderson*	5.00
181	*Ryan Sims*	5.00
182	*Albert Haynesworth*	5.00
183	*Wendell Bryant*	5.00
184	*Anthony Weaver*	5.00
185	*Napoleon Harris*	5.00
186	*Robert Thomas*	5.00
187	*Quentin Jammer*	8.00
188	*Ed Reed*	5.00
189	*Roy Williams*	10.00
190	*Phillip Buchanon*	8.00
191	*Lito Sheppard*	6.00
192	*Mike Rumph*	5.00
193	*Keyuo Craver*	5.00
194	*Randy Fasani*	5.00
195	*Rohan Davey*	5.00
196	*Chad Hutchinson*	5.00
197	*Eric Crouch*	8.00
198	*Lamar Gordon*	8.00
199	*Brian Westbrook*	12.00
200	*Adrian Peterson*	8.00

2002 Donruss Classics Timeless Tributes

Stars: 4X-8X
Retired Stars: 2X-4X
Rookies: 1X-2X
1-100 Production 150 Sets
101-200 Production 100 Sets

2002 Donruss Classics Classic Materials

		NM/M
	Common Player:	20.00
	Autographs Unpriced Due to Scarcity	
1	Bart Starr/50	150.00
2	William Perry/100	20.00
3	L.C. Greenwood/100	20.00
4	Len Dawson/100	20.00
5	Terry Bradshaw/100	50.00
6	Bob Griese/100	50.00
7	Ken Stabler/150	30.00
8	Steve Largent/250	30.00
9	Earl Campbell/150	30.00
10	Warren Moon/300	25.00
11	Fran Tarkenton/250	50.00
12	Barry Sanders/100	50.00
13	Dan Marino/250	75.00
14	John Elway/250	75.00
15	Marcus Allen/300	50.00
16	Ozzie Newsome/300	20.00
17	Howie Long/300	30.00
18	Deacon Jones/300	20.00
19	Jerry Rice/250	35.00
20	Bert Jones/300	20.00
21	Brett Favre, Sterling Sharpe/100	125.00
22	Johnny Unitas, Raymond Berry/100	75.00
23	Emmitt Smith, Herschel Walker/100	125.00
24	Steve Young, Joe Montana/100	200.00
25	Joe Theismann, Art Monk/100	50.00
26	Joe Namath, Don Maynard/100	100.00
27	Eric Dickerson, Henry Ellard/100	25.00
28	Jim Kelly, Andre Reed/100	50.00
29	Walter Payton, Gale Sayers, Anthony Thomas/50	250.00
30	Roger Staubach, Craig Morton, Troy Aikman/50	150.00
31	Dick Butkus, Mike Singletary, Brian Urlacher/50	300.00

2002 Donruss Classics Classic Pigskin

		NM/M
	Common Player:	50.00
	Production 250 sets	
	Doubles Production 25 Sets	
1	Jerry Rice	60.00
2	Joe Montana	100.00
3	Troy Aikman	50.00
4	Emmitt Smith	75.00
5	Ray Lewis	50.00
6	Jamal Lewis	50.00

2002 Donruss Classics New Millennium Classics

		NM/M
	Common Player:	2.00
	Production 400 or 500 sets	
1	Ahman Green	2.00
2	Brian Griese	2.00
3	Chris Chambers	4.00
4	Curtis Martin	2.00
5	Daunte Culpepper	3.00
6	Edgerrin James	4.00
7	Emmitt Smith	5.00
8	Kurt Warner	5.00
9	Marshall Faulk	2.00
10	Randy Moss	4.00
11	Antonio Freeman	2.00
12	Charles Woodson	2.00
13	Corey Dillon	2.00
14	Cris Carter	2.00
15	David Boston	2.00
16	Donovan McNabb	2.00
17	Drew Bledsoe	2.00
18	Champ Bailey	2.00
19	Eric Moulds	2.00
20	Germane Crowell	2.00
21	Jake Plummer	2.00
22	Jeff Garcia	2.00
23	Jerome Bettis	2.00
24	Jevon Kearse	2.00
25	Keyshawn Johnson	2.00
26	Kordell Stewart	2.00
27	Warren Sapp	2.00
28	Marvin Harrison	2.00
29	Zach Thomas	3.00
30	Rod Smith	2.00
31	Steve McNair	2.00
32	Terrell Owens	2.00

2002 Donruss Classics Past and Present

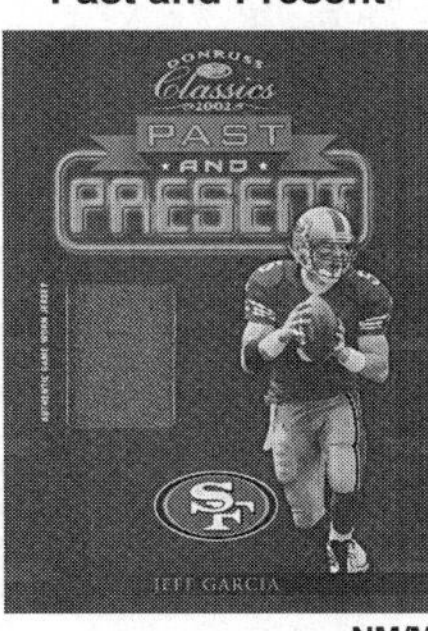

		NM/M
	Production 400 singles, 100 doubles	
	Autograph Production 25 Sets	
1	Donovan McNabb	15.00
2	Kurt Warner	20.00
3	Mark Brunell	15.00
4	Jeff Garcia	15.00
5	Brett Favre	45.00
6	LaDainian Tomlinson	15.00
7	Jamal Anderson	15.00
8	Mike Anderson	15.00
9	Terrell Davis	15.00
10	Ricky Watters	40.00
11	Stephen Davis	15.00
12	Eddie George	15.00
13	Marshall Faulk	25.00
14	Edgerrin James	20.00
15	Jerome Bettis	15.00
16	Emmitt Smith	50.00
17	Tony Dorsett	15.00
19	Thurman Thomas	15.00
20	Marcus Allen	20.00
21	Earl Campbell, Franco Harris	50.00
22	Eric Dickerson, Barry Sanders	65.00
23	Gale Sayers, John Riggins	75.00
24	Dan Marino, John Elway	150.00
25	Troy Aikman, Steve Young	40.00

2002 Donruss Classics Significant Signatures

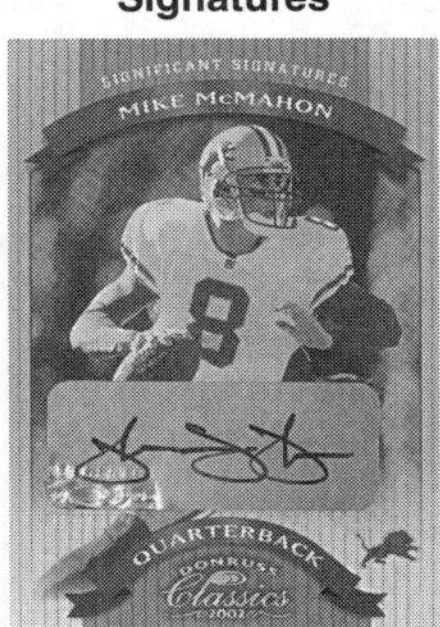

		NM/M
1	David Boston/50	25.00
5	Chris Weinke/100	25.00
8	Anthony Thomas/150	25.00
9	David Terrell/100	25.00
10	Brian Urlacher/224	60.00
12	Quincy Carter/250	30.00
14	Mike McMahon/250	20.00
16	Brett Favre/25	400.00
17	Ahman Green/50	75.00
19	Michael Bennett/150	30.00
22	Daunte Culpepper/50	40.00
23	Aaron Brooks/150	25.00
24	Ricky Williams/35	100.00
25	Deuce McAllister/150	30.00
26	Kerry Collins/142	20.00
27	Michael Strahan/50	25.00
31	Correll Buckhalter/250	15.00
32	Jeff Garcia/25	60.00
33	Terrell Owens/100	25.00
35	Marshall Faulk/25	200.00
36	Isaac Bruce/125	25.00
37	Kurt Warner/40	60.00
38	Torry Holt/150	25.00
43	Stephen Davis/100	20.00
44	Rod Gardner/25	50.00
46	Elvis Grbac/75	15.00
47	Ray Lewis/100	40.00
48	Jamal Lewis/100	25.00
50	Eric Moulds/150	15.00
51	Travis Henry No Auto/100	15.00
53	Peter Warrick/100	20.00
55	James Jackson/200	15.00
58	Terrell Davis/50	50.00
60	Mike Anderson/75	15.00
62	Marvin Harrison/75	40.00
63	Edgerrin James/50	60.00
65	Mark Brunell/75	25.00
67	Jimmy Smith/150	15.00
68	Tony Gonzalez/75	25.00
71	Snoop Minnis No Auto/200	15.00
74	Chris Chambers/75	25.00
76	Drew Bledsoe/75	75.00
79	Vinny Testaverde/100	20.00
82	Laveranues Coles/200	20.00
83	Tim Brown/75	40.00
87	Kordell Stewart/50	30.00
91	Drew Brees/150	25.00
96	Koren Robinson/200	15.00
100	Jevon Kearse/100	20.00
101	Joe Montana/100	150.00
102	Joe Namath/50	125.00
104	Dan Marino/25	400.00
105	Steve Bartkowski/97	15.00
106	John Elway/25	350.00
107	Troy Aikman/40	100.00
108	Steve Young/50	75.00
109	Terry Bradshaw/78	75.00
110	Bart Starr/40	125.00
111	Bert Jones/243	20.00
112	Craig Morton/250	25.00
113	Bob Griese/50	50.00
114	Dan Fouts/25	100.00
115	Phil Simms/50	50.00
116	Jim McMahon/66	60.00
117	Joe Theismann/93	30.00
118	Ken Stabler/63	60.00
119	Johnny Unitas/75	125.00
120	Roger Staubach/55	75.00
121	Len Dawson/50	40.00
122	Tony Dorsett/50	50.00
123	Gale Sayers/25	100.00
125	Herschel Walker/50	30.00
126	John Riggins/125	50.00
127	Eric Dickerson/25	100.00
128	Franco Harris/25	100.00
129	Earl Campbell/50	50.00
130	Thurman Thomas/150	25.00
131	Barry Sanders/50	125.00
132	Marcus Allen/25	125.00
134	Natrone Means/170	15.00
135	Steve Largent/20	
136	Don Maynard/112	15.00
137	Henry Ellard/20	
138	Sterling Sharpe/116	25.00
139	Art Monk/25	
140	Andre Reed/117	20.00
141	Raymond Berry/68	20.00
142	Ozzie Newsome/43	30.00
143	William Perry/75	25.00
144	Deacon Jones/50	25.00
145	Howie Long/25	60.00
146	L.C. Greenwood/75	50.00
147	Ronnie Lott/75	30.00
148	Dick Butkus/24	75.00
149	Fran Tarkenton/50	50.00
150	Mike Singletary/50	40.00
151	David Carr/50	150.00
152	Joey Harrington/50	150.00
156	William Green/43	50.00
157	Clinton Portis/150	125.00
160	Antonio Bryant/100	50.00
161	Donte Stallworth/33	100.00
164	Ashley Lelie/100	75.00
165	Andre Davis/150	30.00
166	Josh Reed/75	50.00
168	Kelly Campbell/150	15.00
176	Kalimba Edwards/250	15.00
177	Alex Brown/250	15.00
181	Ryan Sims No Auto/250	15.00
186	Robert Thomas/250	15.00
189	Roy Williams/150	60.00
192	Mike Rumph/200	15.00
200	Adrian Peterson/200	20.00

2002 Donruss Classics Timeless Treasures

		NM/M
	Common Player:	20.00
1	Harold "Red" Grange/25	
2	Jim Thorpe/100	200.00
3	Brett Favre/375	50.00
4	Terrell Davis/375	20.00
5	Barry Sanders/300	30.00
6	Jerry Rice/375	30.00

2002 Donruss Elite

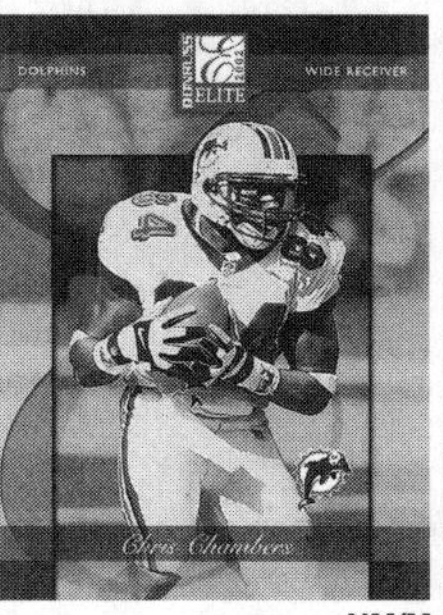

		NM/M
	Minor Stars	.40
	Unlisted Stars:	.60
	Common Rookie (101-200):	5.00
	Minor Rookies:	6.00
	Production 400 Sets	
	Pack (5)	5.75
	Wax Box (20)	100.00
1	Elvis Grbac	.20
2	Jamal Lewis	.20
3	Ray Lewis	.20
4	Travis Henry	.20
5	Eric Moulds	.20
6	Corey Dillon	.40
7	Peter Warrick	.40
8	Tim Couch	1.00
9	James Jackson	.40
10	Kevin Johnson	.20
11	Mike Anderson	.20
12	Terrell Davis	1.25
13	Brian Griese	1.00
14	Rod Smith	.20
15	Marvin Harrison	.40
16	Reggie Wayne	.20
17	Dominic Rhodes	.20
18	Edgerrin James	2.00
19	Mark Brunell	1.00
20	Keenan McCardell	.20
21	Jimmy Smith	.20
22	Tony Gonzalez	.20
23	Trent Green	.40
24	Priest Holmes	.40
25	Marvin "Snoop" Minnis	1.00
26	Chris Chambers	2.00
27	Jay Fiedler	.20
28	Travis Minor	.20
29	Lamar Smith	.20
30	Tom Brady	2.00
31	Troy Brown	.20
32	Antowain Smith	.20
33	Laveranues Coles	.20
34	Curtis Martin	.40
35	Vinny Testaverde	.20
36	Wayne Chrebet	.20
37	Tim Brown	.40
38	Rich Gannon	.20
39	Jerry Rice	2.00
40	Charlie Garner	.40
41	Jerome Bettis	.40
42	Plaxico Burress	.75
43	Kordell Stewart	.40
44	Kendrell Bell	.20
45	Doug Flutie	.75
46	LaDainian Tomlinson	2.00
47	Junior Seau	.40
48	Drew Brees	2.00
49	Shaun Alexander	1.25
50	Koren Robinson	.20
51	Ricky Watters	.20
52	Eddie George	1.00
53	Derrick Mason	.20
54	Steve McNair	.75
55	David Boston	1.00
56	Jake Plummer	.20
57	Chris Chandler	.20
58	Jamal Anderson	.20
59	Michael Vick	2.50
60	Wesley Walls	.20
61	Chris Weinke	2.00
62	David Terrell	2.00
63	Anthony Thomas	2.50
64	Brian Urlacher	2.00
65	Quincy Carter	1.00
66	Raghib Ismail	.20
67	Emmitt Smith	2.00
68	James Stewart	.40
69	Germane Crowell	.20
70	Mike McMahon	.20
71	Brett Favre	3.00
72	Ahman Green	.75
73	Antonio Freeman	.20
74	Michael Bennett	2.00
75	Cris Carter	.20
76	Daunte Culpepper	1.25
77	Randy Moss	2.50
78	Aaron Brooks	.40
79	Deuce McAllister	2.00
80	Ricky Williams	.75
81	Kerry Collins	.20
82	Ron Dayne	.40
83	Amani Toomer	.20
84	Correll Buckhalter	.20
85	James Thrash	.20
86	Freddie Mitchell	.75
87	Duce Staley	.40
88	Jeff Garcia	.20
89	Garrison Hearst	.20
90	Terrell Owens	.75
91	Isaac Bruce	.60
92	Marshall Faulk	1.25
93	Torry Holt	.20
94	Kurt Warner	2.00
95	Mike Alstott	.20
96	Brad Johnson	.20
97	Keyshawn Johnson	.40
98	Stephen Davis	.75
99	Rod Gardner	.75
100	Tony Banks	.20
101	*David Carr*	50.00
102	*Joey Harrington*	40.00
103	*Rohan Davey*	10.00
104	*Chad Hutchinson*	10.00
105	*Patrick Ramsey*	25.00
106	*Kurt Kittner*	15.00
107	*Eric Crouch*	12.00
108	*David Garrard*	8.00
109	*Ronald Curry*	15.00
110	*Zak Kustok*	5.00
111	*Woodrow Dantzler III*	5.00
112	*Wes Pate*	5.00
113	*Brian Westbrook*	20.00
114	*Josh McCown*	20.00
115	*Travis Stephens*	8.00
116	*Luke Staley*	6.00
117	*William Green*	20.00
118	*Clinton Portis*	60.00
119	*DeShaun Foster*	15.00
120	*Verron Haynes*	5.00
121	*T.J. Duckett*	25.00
122	*Antwoine Womack*	5.00
123	*Leonard Henry*	8.00
124	*Lamar Gordon*	10.00
125	*Adrian Peterson*	10.00
126	*Chester Taylor*	5.00
127	*Damien Anderson*	8.00
128	*Maurice Morris*	15.00
129	*Ricky Williams*	6.00
130	*Terry Charles*	5.00
131	*Demontray Carter*	5.00
132	*Jason McAddley*	5.00
133	*Ladell Betts*	15.00
134	*Cortlen Johnson*	5.00
135	*James Mungro*	8.00
136	*Atrews Bell*	5.00
137	*Josh Scobey*	5.00
138	*Justin Peelle*	5.00
139	*Najeh Davenport*	10.00
140	*Josh Reed*	20.00
141	*Marquise Walker*	8.00
142	*Jabar Gaffney*	20.00
143	*Antwann Randle El*	20.00
144	*Ashley Lelie*	40.00
145	*Tavon Mason*	5.00
146	*Antonio Bryant*	25.00
147	*Javon Walker*	30.00
148	*Kelly Campbell*	8.00
149	*Ron Johnson*	5.00
150	*Andre Davis*	20.00
151	*Cliff Russell*	5.00
152	*Donald Reche Caldwell*	8.00
153	*Kyle Johnson*	5.00
154	*Freddie Milons*	5.00
155	*Brian Poli-Dixon*	6.00
156	*David Thornton*	5.00
157	*Bryan Thomas*	5.00
158	*Kahlil Hill*	5.00
159	*Deion Branch*	25.00
160	*Akin Ayodele*	5.00
161	*Donte Stallworth*	40.00
162	*Tim Carter*	5.00
163	*Kenyon Coleman*	5.00
164	*Jeremy Shockey*	40.00
165	*Eddie Freeman*	5.00
166	*Tracey Wistrom*	8.00
167	*Daniel Graham*	8.00
168	*Julius Peppers*	25.00
169	*Alex Brown*	8.00
170	*Dwight Freeney*	15.00
171	*Kalimba Edwards*	5.00
172	*Dennis Johnson*	5.00
173	*Travis Fisher*	8.00
174	*John Henderson*	10.00
175	*Anthony Weaver*	5.00
176	*Ryan Sims*	10.00
177	*Alan Harper*	5.00
178	*Larry Tripplett*	5.00
179	*Wendell Bryant*	8.00
180	*Albert Haynesworth*	10.00
181	*Levar Fisher*	5.00
182	*Andra Davis*	5.00
183	*Joseph Jefferson*	5.00
184	*Lamont Thompson*	5.00
185	*Robert Thomas*	5.00
186	*Michael Lewis*	5.00
187	*Rocky Calmus*	10.00
188	*Napoleon Harris*	10.00
189	*Lito Sheppard*	8.00
190	*Quentin Jammer*	10.00
191	*Roy Williams*	30.00
192	*Marques Anderson*	6.00
193	*Chris Hope*	5.00
194	*Raonall Smith*	5.00
195	*Mike Rumph*	5.00
196	*James Allen*	8.00
197	*Ed Reed*	20.00
198	*Mike Williams*	10.00
199	*Phillip Buchanon*	12.00
200	*Bryant McKinnie*	5.00

2002 Donruss Elite Aspirations

Stars/60-99: 10X-20X
Rookies/60-99: 1X
Stars/30-59: 15X-30X
Rookies/30-59: 1.5X
Stars/20-29: 25X-50X
Rookies/20-29: 1.5X-3X

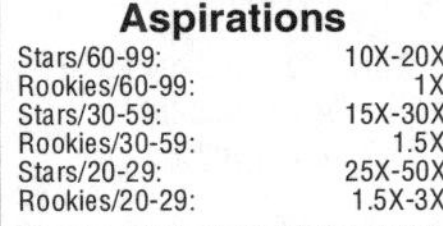
Values quoted in this guide reflect the retail price of a card—the price a collector can expect to pay when buying a card from a dealer. The wholesale price—that which a collector can expect to receive from a dealer when selling cards—will be significantly lower, depending on desirability and condition.

2002 Donruss Elite Status

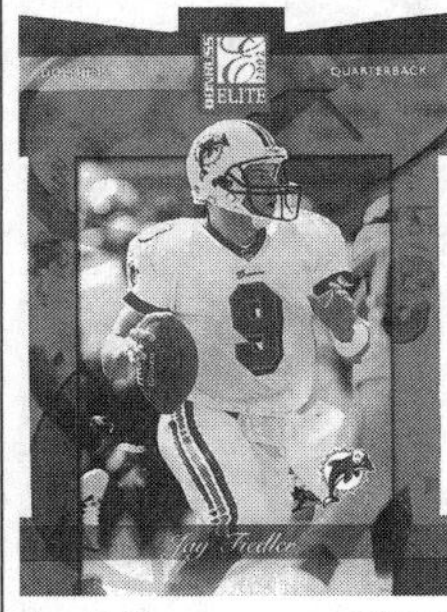

Stars/60-99: 10X-15X
Rookies/60-99: 1X
Stars/30-59: 10X-20X
Rookies/30-59: 1.5X
Stars/20-29: 25X-50X
Rookies/20-29: 1.5X-3X

2002 Donruss Elite Back to the Future

		NM/M
	Common Player:	2.00
	Single Production 800 Sets	
	Double Production 400 Sets	
1	Walter Payton	4.00
2	Anthony Thomas	4.00
3	Bernie Kosar	5.00
4	James Jackson	2.00
5	Troy Aikman	3.00
6	Quincy Carter	2.00
7	Steve Bartkowski	2.00
8	Michael Vick	4.00
9	Natrone Means	2.00
10	LaDainian Tomlinson	4.00
11	Earl Campbell	2.00
12	Eddie George	2.00
13	Eric Dickerson	2.00
14	Edgerrin James	4.00
15	John Elway	3.00
16	Brian Griese	2.00
17	Anthony Thomas, Walter Payton	10.00
18	Bernie Kosar, James Jackson	8.00
19	Troy Aikman, Quincy Carter	8.00
20	Steve Bartkowski, Michael Vick	10.00
21	LaDainian Tomlinson, Natrone Means	10.00
22	Earl Campbell, Eddie George	8.00
23	Eric Dickerson, Edgerrin James	10.00
24	Brian Griese, John Elway	10.00

2002 Donruss Elite Back to the Future Threads

		NM/M
	Common Player:	12.00
	Single Production 75 Sets	
	Double Production 25 Sets	
1	Walter Payton	125.00
2	Anthony Thomas	12.00
3	Bernie Kosar	25.00
4	James Jackson	12.00
5	Troy Aikman	40.00
6	Quincy Carter	15.00
7	Steve Bartkowski	12.00
8	Michael Vick	80.00
9	Natrone Means	15.00
10	LaDainian Tomlinson	30.00
11	Earl Campbell	40.00
12	Eddie George	15.00
13	Eric Dickerson	30.00
14	Edgerrin James	25.00
15	John Elway	60.00
16	Brian Griese	12.00
17	Anthony Thomas, Walter Payton	200.00
18	Bernie Kosar, James Jackson	40.00
19	Troy Aikman, Quincy Carter	100.00
20	Steve Bartkowski, Michael Vick	100.00
21	LaDainian Tomlinson, Natrone Means	80.00
22	Earl Campbell, Eddie George	80.00
23	Eric Dickerson, Edgerrin James	125.00
24	Brian Griese, John Elway	200.00

2002 Donruss Elite College Ties

NM/M
Common Player: 2.00
Production 1600 sets
1 Marquise Walker, David Terrell 5.00
2 Travis Stephens, Travis Henry 2.00
3 David Carr, Trent Dilfer 10.00
4 Jevon Kearse, Alex Brown 2.00
5 Ahman Green, Eric Crouch 8.00
6 Edgerrin James, Clinton Portis 5.00
7 Plaxico Burress, T.J. Duckett 5.00
8 Marvin "Snoop" Minnis, Jevon Walker 5.00
9 Kevin Dyson, Cliff Russell 2.00
10 Andre Davis, Michael Vick 5.00
11 Ken Simonton, Chad Johnson 2.00
12 Freddie Mitchell, DeShaun Foster 5.00
13 Marvin Harrison, Qadry Ismail 2.00
14 Quincy Carter, Kendrell Bell 2.00
15 Brian Griese, Tom Brady 4.00
16 Tim Brown, Jerome Bettis 2.00
17 Cris Carter, Eddie George 2.00
18 Drew Brees, Mike Alstott 3.00
19 Kevan Barlow, Curtis Martin 2.00
20 Priest Holmes, Ricky Williams 2.00
21 Jamal Lewis, Charlie Garner 2.00
22 Junior Seau, Keyshawn Johnson 2.00
23 Corey Dillon, Mark Brunell 2.00
24 Emmitt Smith, Fred Taylor 3.00
25 Edgerrin James, James Jackson 3.00

2002 Donruss Elite Face 2 Face

NM/M
Common Player: 15.00
Production 350 sets
1 Eddie George, Zach Thomas 15.00
2 Darrell Green, Michael Irvin 15.00
3 Mike Anderson, Junior Seau 15.00
4 Jake Plummer, Jason Sehorn 15.00
5 Mark Brunell, Jevon Kearse 15.00
6 Randy Moss, Brett Favre 100.00
7 Ray Lewis, Kerry Collins 15.00
8 Kurt Warner, Steve McNair 50.00
9 Steve Young, John Elway 60.00
10 Jerry Rice, Cris Carter 50.00
11 Daunte Culpepper, Tim Couch 50.00
12 Barry Sanders, Dan Marino 60.00
13 LaDainian Tomlinson, Michael Vick 50.00
14 Warren Moon, Troy Aikman 25.00
15 Curtis Martin, Lamar Smith 15.00

2002 Donruss Elite Passing the Torch

NM/M
Common Player: 2.00
Singles Production 800 Sets
Doubles Production 400 Sets
1 Thurman Thomas 2.00
2 Travis Henry 2.00
3 Gale Sayers 3.00
4 Anthony Thomas 4.00
5 Dan Fouts 2.00
6 Drew Brees 4.00
7 Bernie Kosar 2.00
8 Tim Couch 3.00
9 Steve Young 2.00
10 Jeff Garcia 2.00
11 Ricky Watters 2.00
12 Shaun Alexander 2.00
13 Herschel Walker 3.00
14 Michael Bennett 3.00
15 Jerry Rice 3.00
16 Terrell Owens 2.00
17 Travis Henry, Thurman Thomas 4.00
18 Gale Sayers, Anthony Thomas 6.00
19 Drew Brees, Dan Fouts 4.00
20 Bernie Kosar, Tim Couch 4.00
21 Jeff Garcia, Steve Young 5.00
22 Ricky Watters, Shaun Alexander 4.00
23 Herschel Walker, Michael Bennett 5.00
24 Jerry Rice, Terrell Owens 5.00

2002 Donruss Elite Passing the Torch Autos

NM/M
Common Player: 25.00
Single Production 100 Sets
Double Production 50 Sets
1 Thurman Thomas 40.00
2 Travis Henry 25.00
3 Gale Sayers 60.00
4 Anthony Thomas 30.00
5 Dan Fouts 40.00
6 Drew Brees 40.00
7 Bernie Kosar 30.00
8 Tim Couch 30.00
9 Steve Young 60.00
10 Jeff Garcia 40.00
11 Ricky Watters 30.00
12 Shaun Alexander 30.00
13 Herschel Walker 40.00
14 Michael Bennett 30.00
15 Jerry Rice 100.00
16 Terrell Owens 50.00
17 Travis Henry, Thurman Thomas 60.00
18 Gale Sayers, Anthony Thomas 100.00
19 Drew Brees, Dan Fouts 100.00
20 Bernie Kosar, Tim Couch 60.00
21 Jeff Garcia, Steve Young 125.00
22 Ricky Watters, Shaun Alexander 80.00
23 Herschel Walker, Michael Bennett 80.00
24 Jerry Rice, Terrell Owens 200.00

2002 Donruss Elite Prime Numbers

NM/M
Common Player: 2.00
Production 1600 sets
1 Zach Thomas, Brian Urlacher 3.00
2 Jake Plummer, Chris Weinke 2.00
3 Steve McNair, Drew Brees 3.00
4 Jeff Garcia, Kerry Collins 2.00
5 Emmitt Smith, Duce Staley 3.00
6 Eddie George, Ron Dayne 2.00
7 Marshall Faulk, Curtis Martin 2.00
8 Chris Chambers, Randy Moss 4.00
9 Terrell Owens, Tim Brown 2.00
10 Isaac Bruce, Jerry Rice 3.00

2002 Donruss Elite Recollection Collection

NM/M
Common Player: 40.00
Jeff Garcia/25 60.00
Jeff Garcia/75 40.00

2002 Donruss Elite Throwback Threads

NM/M
Common Player: 30.00
Single Production 75 Sets
Double Production 25 Sets
Unpriced Autos Numbered to 25 Sets
1 Jim Thorpe 300.00

NM/M
2 Harold "Red" Grange 300.00
3 Bart Starr 100.00
4 Brett Favre 100.00
5 Joe Namath 100.00
6 John Riggins 80.00
7 Dan Marino 100.00
8 Bob Griese 30.00
9 Roger Staubach 60.00
10 Troy Aikman 40.00
11 Bernie Kosar 30.00
12 Ozzie Newsome 30.00
13 John Elway 80.00
14 Craig Morton 30.00
15 Jim McMahon 60.00
16 Walter Payton 125.00
17 Franco Harris 50.00
18 Jerome Bettis 30.00
19 Brian Urlacher 50.00
20 Dick Butkus 100.00
21 Harold "Red" Grange, Jim Thorpe 1,200
22 Bart Starr, Brett Favre 300.00
23 John Riggins, Joe Namath 300.00
24 Bob Griese, Dan Marino 250.00
25 Troy Aikman, Roger Staubach 200.00
26 Ozzie Newsome, Bernie Kosar 60.00
27 John Elway, Craig Morton 200.00
28 Walter Payton, Jim McMahon 250.00
29 Franco Harris, Jerome Bettis 125.00
30 Brian Urlacher, Dick Butkus 200.00

2002 Donruss Elite Turn of the Century Autos

NM/M
Common Player: 20.00
Production 40 Sets
101 David Carr 200.00
102 Joey Harrington 150.00
103 Rohan Davey 40.00
106 Kurt Kittner 30.00
107 Eric Crouch 60.00
111 Woody Dantzler 30.00
115 Travis Stephens 20.00
116 Luke Staley 20.00
117 William Green 60.00
118 Clinton Portis 200.00
119 DeShaun Foster 80.00
121 T.J. Duckett 80.00
125 Adrian Peterson 30.00
127 Damien Anderson 20.00
128 Maurice Morris 40.00
131 Demontray Carter 20.00
134 Cortlen Johnson 20.00
139 Najeh Davenport 30.00
140 Josh Reed 80.00
141 Marquise Walker 20.00
142 Jabar Gaffney 30.00
143 Antwann Randle El 100.00
144 Ashley Lelie 100.00
146 Antonio Bryant 80.00
147 Javon Walker 80.00
148 Kelly Campbell 30.00
149 Ron Johnson 20.00
150 Andre Davis 60.00
152 Reche Caldwell 30.00
154 Freddie Milons 20.00
155 Brian Poli-Dixon 20.00
161 Donte Stallworth 125.00
164 Jeremy Shockey 150.00
167 Daniel Graham 30.00
168 Julius Peppers 80.00
169 Alex Brown 20.00
170 Dwight Freeney 40.00
171 Kalimba Edwards 20.00
174 John Henderson 20.00
176 Ryan Sims No Auto 20.00
179 Wendell Bryant 30.00
181 Levar Fisher 20.00
182 Andra Davis 20.00
185 Robert Thomas 20.00
187 Rocky Calmus 20.00
189 Lito Sheppard 20.00
190 Quentin Jammer 40.00
191 Roy Williams 100.00
195 Mike Rumph 20.00
199 Phillip Buchanon No Auto 30.00

2002 Donruss Gridiron Kings

NM/M
Common Player: .40
Unlisted Stars: 1.25
Minor Stars: .75
Common Rookie (101-150): 1.50
Minor Rookies: 2.50
Pack (4): 2.25
Wax Box (24): 40.00
1 David Boston 1.25
2 Jake Plummer .75
3 Michael Vick 4.00
4 Warrick Dunn .75
5 Jamal Lewis 2.00

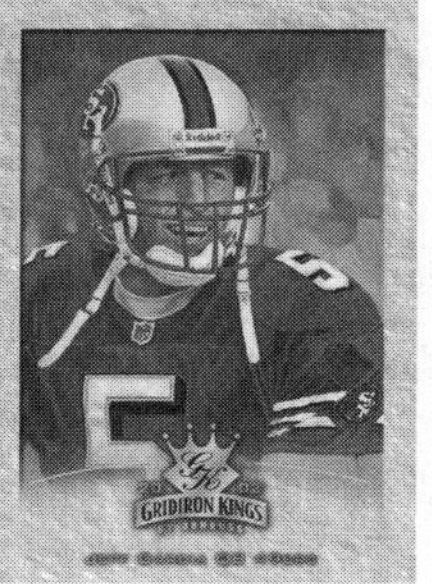

NM/M
6 Ray Lewis .75
7 Drew Bledsoe 2.50
8 Travis Henry .75
9 Eric Moulds .75
10 Chris Weinke 1.25
11 Lamar Smith .75
12 Anthony Thomas 3.00
13 Chris Chandler .75
14 Brian Urlacher 3.00
15 Corey Dillon 1.25
16 Peter Warrick .75
17 Tim Couch 2.00
18 James Jackson .75
19 Kevin Johnson .40
20 Quincy Carter 2.50
21 Emmitt Smith 4.00
22 Joey Galloway .75
23 Brian Griese 1.25
24 Terrell Davis 2.00
25 Ed McCaffrey .75
26 Rod Smith .75
27 Mike McMahon 1.25
28 Az-Zahir Hakim .75
29 Germane Crowell .40
30 Brett Favre 5.00
31 Terry Glenn .75
32 Ahman Green 1.25
33 James Allen .40
34 Tony Simmons .40
35 Peyton Manning 4.00
36 Edgerrin James 3.00
37 Marvin Harrison .75
38 Dominic Rhodes .40
39 Mark Brunell 1.25
40 Jimmy Smith .40
41 Keenan McCardell .40
42 Fred Taylor .40
43 Priest Holmes 1.25
44 Marvin "Snoop" Minnis .75
45 Trent Green .75
46 Tony Gonzalez .75
47 Chris Chambers 1.25
48 Ricky Williams 2.50
49 Jay Fiedler .75
50 Zach Thomas .75
51 Randy Moss 4.00
52 Cris Carter .75
53 Daunte Culpepper 2.50
54 Michael Bennett 1.25
55 Tom Brady 5.00
56 Antowain Smith .75
57 Troy Brown 1.25
58 Aaron Brooks 2.00
59 Deuce McAllister 2.00
60 Joe Horn .40
61 Kerry Collins .75
62 Ron Dayne .75
63 Michael Strahan .75
64 Vinny Testaverde .75
65 Curtis Martin .75
66 Wayne Chrebet .75
67 Rich Gannon .75
68 Tim Brown 1.25
69 Jerry Rice 4.00
70 Charlie Garner .75
71 Donovan McNabb 2.50
72 Duce Staley .75
73 Freddie Mitchell .75
74 Kordell Stewart .75
75 Jerome Bettis .75
76 Plaxico Burress 1.25
77 Kendrell Bell .75
78 LaDainian Tomlinson 3.00
79 Drew Brees 3.00
80 Doug Flutie 1.25
81 Junior Seau .75
82 Jeff Garcia 1.25
83 Terrell Owens 1.25
84 Garrison Hearst .75
85 Trent Dilfer .75
86 Shaun Alexander 1.25
87 Koren Robinson .75
88 Marshall Faulk 2.50
89 Kurt Warner 3.00
90 Torry Holt .75
91 Isaac Bruce .75
92 Brad Johnson .75
93 Keyshawn Johnson .75
94 Mike Alstott .75
95 Warren Sapp .75
96 Steve McNair 1.25
97 Eddie George 1.25
98 Jevon Kearse .75
99 Stephen Davis .75
100 Rod Gardner .75
101 *David Carr* 12.00
102 *Joey Harrington* 10.00
103 *Patrick Ramsey* 5.00
104 *Josh McCown* 2.50
105 *David Garrard* 1.50
106 *Rohan Davey* 3.00
107 *Randy Fasani* 1.50
108 *Kurt Kittner* 2.50
109 *William Green* 4.00
110 *T.J. Duckett* 5.00
111 *DeShaun Foster* 3.00
112 *Clinton Portis* 15.00
113 *Maurice Morris* 3.00
114 *Ladell Betts* 2.50
115 *Lamar Gordon* 2.50
116 *Brian Westbrook* 5.00
117 *Jonathan Wells* 3.00
118 *Travis Stephens* 2.50
119 *Josh Scobey* 1.50
120 *Donte Stallworth* 5.00
121 *Ashley Lelie* 5.00
122 *Javon Walker* 8.00
123 *Jabar Gaffney* 3.00
124 *Josh Reed* 3.00
125 *Tim Carter* 2.50
126 *Andre Davis* 3.00
127 *Donald Reche Caldwell* 2.50
128 *Antwann Randle El* 4.00
129 *Antonio Bryant* 4.00
130 *Deion Branch* 4.00
131 *Marquise Walker* 2.50
132 *Cliff Russell* 1.50
133 *Eric Crouch* 3.00
134 *Ron Johnson* 1.50
135 *Terry Charles* 1.50
136 *Jeremy Shockey* 6.00
137 *Daniel Graham* 2.50
138 *Julius Peppers* 4.00
139 *Dwight Freeney* 1.50
140 *Ryan Sims* 1.50
141 *John Henderson* 1.50
142 *Wendell Bryant* 1.50
143 *Albert Haynesworth* 1.50
144 *Quentin Jammer* 2.50
145 *Phillip Buchanon* 2.50
146 *Lito Sheppard* 1.50
147 *Roy Williams* 4.00
148 *Ed Reed* 1.50
149 *Napoleon Harris* 1.50
150 *Mike Williams* 1.50
151 Art Monk 1.00
152 Barry Sanders 4.00
153 Bob Griese 1.00
154 Dan Marino 4.00
155 Dick Butkus 2.00
156 Earl Campbell 2.00
157 Eric Dickerson 1.00
158 Fran Tarkenton 1.00
159 Franco Harris 1.00
160 Herschel Walker 1.00
161 Joe Montana 4.00
162 Ronnie Lott 1.00
163 Joe Theismann 1.00
164 John Elway 3.00
165 John Riggins 2.00
166 Ken Stabler 1.00
167 Len Dawson 1.00
168 Marcus Allen 1.00
169 Mike Singletary 1.00
170 Roger Staubach 2.00
171 Walter Payton 5.00
172 Steve Largent 1.00
173 Terry Bradshaw 2.00
174 Thurman Thomas 1.00
175 Tony Dorsett 1.00

2002 Donruss Gridiron Kings Bronze

Stars: 1.5X-3X
Rookies: 1X
Retired Stars: 1.5X
Inserted 1:6

2002 Donruss Gridiron Kings Gold

Stars: 5X-10X
Rookies: 2X-4X
Retired Stars: 3X-6X
Production 100 Sets

2002 Donruss Gridiron Kings Silver

Stars: 2X-4X
Rookies: 2X
Retired Stars: 1.5X-3X
Production 400 Sets

2002 Donruss Gridiron Kings Heritage Collection

NM/M
Common Player: 3.00
Inserted 1:23
1 Art Monk 3.00
2 Barry Sanders 10.00
3 Bob Griese 3.00
4 Dan Marino 10.00
5 Dick Butkus 6.00
6 Earl Campbell 4.00
7 Eric Dickerson 3.00
8 Fran Tarkenton 3.00
9 Franco Harris 4.00
10 Herschel Walker 4.00
11 Joe Montana 15.00
12 Ronnie Lott 4.00
13 Joe Theismann 3.00
14 John Elway 10.00
15 John Riggins 4.00
16 Ken Stabler 3.00
17 Len Dawson 3.00
18 Marcus Allen 4.00
19 Mike Singletary 3.00
20 Roger Staubach 6.00
21 Walter Payton 10.00
22 Steve Largent 3.00
23 Terry Bradshaw 4.00
24 Thurman Thomas 3.00
25 Tony Dorsett 4.00

A player's name in *italic* type indicates a rookie card.

2002 Donruss Gridiron Kings DK Originals

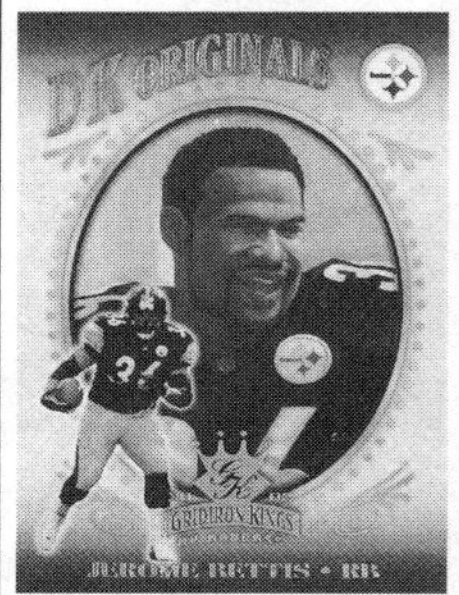

NM/M
Common Player: 4.00
Production 1000 sets
1 Emmitt Smith 10.00
2 Brett Favre 12.00
3 Shaun Alexander 4.00
4 Tom Brady 10.00
5 Chris Chambers 4.00
6 Mark Brunell 4.00
7 Jeff Garcia 4.00
8 Marvin Harrison 4.00
9 Ahman Green 4.00
10 LaDainian Tomlinson 6.00
11 Brian Griese 4.00
12 Jerome Bettis 4.00
13 Quincy Carter 6.00
14 Tim Couch 4.00
15 Donovan McNabb 6.00
16 Corey Dillon 4.00
17 Chris Weinke 4.00
18 Rich Gannon 4.00
19 Drew Bledsoe 8.00
20 Terrell Davis 4.00
21 Travis Henry 4.00
22 Curtis Martin 4.00
23 Aaron Brooks 4.00
24 Ray Lewis 6.00
25 Michael Vick 6.00

2002 Donruss Gridiron Kings Donruss 1894

NM/M
Common Player: 2.00
Production 1000 sets
1 Anthony Thomas 4.00
2 Randy Moss 6.00
3 Tom Brady 6.00
4 Jerry Rice 6.00
5 Jerome Bettis 2.00
6 Junior Seau 2.00
7 Emmitt Smith 6.00
8 Marshall Faulk 2.00
9 Eddie George 2.00
10 Barry Sanders 6.00
11 Kurt Warner 4.00
12 Peyton Manning 4.00
13 Dan Marino 15.00
14 Ricky Williams 3.00
15 Dick Butkus 10.00
16 Brett Favre 15.00
17 Earl Campbell 4.00
18 Zach Thomas 4.00
19 John Elway 10.00
20 Edgerrin James 4.00
21 Joey Harrington 8.00
22 William Green 6.00
23 Donte Stallworth 6.00
24 Roy Williams 6.00
25 Brian Urlacher 8.00

2002 Donruss Gridiron Kings Gridiron Cut Collection

NM/M
Common Player: 6.00
GC1 Art Monk Auto/219 50.00
GC2 Barry Sanders Auto/83 150.00
GC3 Bob Griese Auto/50 100.00
GC4 Dick Butkus Auto/125 60.00
GC5 Earl Campbell Auto/50 60.00
GC6 Eric Dickerson Auto/50 60.00

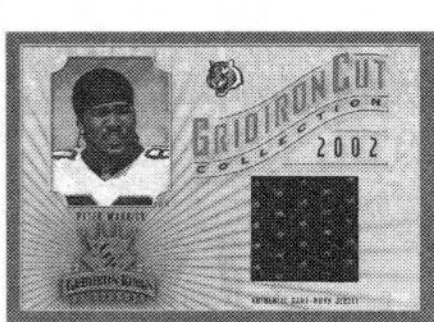

NM/M
GC7 Fran Tarkenton Auto/50 125.00
GC8 Franco Harris Auto/50 125.00
GC9 Herschel Walker Auto/50 60.00
GC10 Joe Montana Auto/50 300.00
GC11 Ronnie Lott Auto/82 60.00
GC12 Joe Theismann Auto/50 40.00
GC13 John Riggins Auto/50 80.00
GC14 Ken Stabler Auto/50 100.00
GC15 Len Dawson Auto/50 100.00
GC16 Marcus Allen Auto/50 80.00
GC17 Mike Singletary Auto/50 80.00
GC18 Roger Staubach Auto/83 125.00
GC19 Steve Largent Auto/50 125.00
GC20 Terry Bradshaw Auto/160 100.00
GC21 Thurman Thomas Auto/400 25.00
GC22 Tony Dorsett Auto/50 100.00
GC23 Brian Urlacher Auto/197 60.00
GC24 Chris Weinke Auto/300 15.00
GC25 David Boston Auto/266 15.00
GC26 Deuce McAllister Auto/310 30.00
GC27 Drew Brees Auto/400 20.00
GC28 Zach Thomas Auto/400 20.00
GC29 Quincy Carter Auto/400 25.00
GC30 Ray Lewis Auto/245 25.00
GC31 Terrell Owens Auto/200 25.00
GC32 Garrison Hearst Auto/400 15.00
GC33 DeShaun Foster Auto 20.00
GC34 Dwight Freeney Auto/400 15.00
GC35 Lito Sheppard Auto/400 15.00
GC36 Reche Caldwell Auto/350 20.00
GC37 Rohan Davey Auto/350 12.00
GC38 Maurice Morris Auto/382 12.00
GC39 Phillip Buchanon No Auto 8.00
GC40 Travis Stephens Auto/400 10.00
GC41 Dan Marino Jsy/400 40.00
GC42 John Elway Jsy/400 40.00
GC43 Daunte Culpepper Jsy/400 12.00
GC44 Kordell Stewart Jsy/400 10.00
GC45 Steve McNair Jsy/400 12.00
GC46 Jeff Garcia Jsy/400 10.00
GC47 Kurt Warner Jsy/400 10.00
GC48 Jake Plummer Jsy/400 8.00
GC49 Donovan McNabb Jsy/400 20.00
GC50 Tim Couch Jsy/400 8.00
GC51 Rich Gannon Jsy/400 8.00
GC52 Quincy Carter Jsy/400 10.00
GC53 Tom Brady Jsy/400 25.00
GC54 Brian Griese Jsy/400 8.00
GC55 Mark Brunell Jsy/400 8.00
GC56 Brett Favre Jsy/400 40.00
GC57 Peyton Manning Jsy/400 25.00
GC58 Emmitt Smith Jsy/400 30.00
GC59 Mike Alstott Jsy/400 8.00
GC60 Jerome Bettis Jsy/400 8.00
GC61 Marshall Faulk Jsy/400 15.00
GC62 LaDainian Tomlinson Jsy/400 20.00
GC63 Terrell DavisJsy/400 12.00
GC64 Antowain Smith Jsy/400 8.00
GC65 Fred Taylor Jsy/400 10.00
GC66 Edgerrin James Jsy/400 15.00
GC67 Ron Dayne Jsy/400 8.00
GC68 Curtis Martin Jsy/400 10.00
GC69 Stephen Davis Jsy/400 8.00
GC70 Walter Payton Jsy/400 60.00
GC71 Freddie Mitchell Jsy/400 8.00
GC72 Cris Carter Jsy/400 10.00
GC73 David Boston Jsy/400 10.00
GC74 Tony Gonzalez Jsy/400 20.00
GC75 Marvin Harrison Jsy/400 12.00
GC76 Torry Holt Jsy/400 12.00
GC77 Jerry Rice Jsy/400 25.00
GC78 Randy MossJsy/400 25.00
GC79 Jimmy Smith Jsy/400 8.00
GC80 Ed McCaffrey Jsy/400 8.00
GC81 Eric Moulds Jsy/400 12.00
GC82 Keyshawn Johnson Jsy/400 8.00
GC83 Isaac Bruce Jsy/400 12.00
GC84 Tim Brown Jsy/400 10.00
GC85 Peter Warrick Jsy/400 10.00
GC86 Zach Thomas Jsy/400 10.00
GC87 Warren Sapp Jsy/400 8.00
GC88 Junior Seau Jsy/400 8.00
GC89 Jevon Kearse Jsy/400 8.00
GC90 Ray Lewis Jsy/400 12.00
GC91 Donovan McNabb FB/550 10.00
GC92 Eddie George FB/550 6.00
GC93 Curtis Martin FB/550 6.00
GC94 Anthony Thomas FB/550 10.00
GC95 Jeff Garcia FB/550 6.00
GC96 Shaun Alexander FB/550 6.00
GC97 Rod Smith FB/550 6.00
GC98 Aaron Brooks FB/550 8.00
GC99 Peyton Manning FB/550 15.00
GC100 Brett Favre FB/550 25.00
GC101 David Carr Jsy/400 30.00
GC102 Joey Harrington Jsy/400 20.00
GC103 William Green Jsy/400 15.00
GC104 T.J. Duckett Jsy/400 15.00
GC105 Clinton Portis Jsy/400 30.00
GC106 DeShaun FosterJsy/400 12.00
GC107 Donte Stallworth Jsy/400 20.00
GC108 Ashley Lelie Jsy/400 20.00
GC109 Antwann Randle El Jsy/400 15.00
GC110 Jeremy Shockey Jsy/400 25.00

2002 Donruss Gridiron Kings Team Duos

NM/M
Common Player: 5.00
Inserted 1:72
1 Anthony Thomas, Brian Urlacher 10.00
2 Peyton Manning, Edgerrin James 10.00
3 Ricky Williams, Zach Thomas 8.00
4 Daunte Culpepper, Randy Moss 10.00
5 David Carr, Jabar Gaffney 15.00
6 Terry Bradshaw, Franco Harris 8.00
7 Kurt Warner, Marshall Faulk 8.00
8 Roger Staubach, Tony Dorsett 8.00
9 Steve McNair, Eddie George 5.00
10 Jerry Rice, Tim Brown 8.00

2002 Donruss Gridiron Kings National Promos

NM/M
Complete Set (6): 20.00
Common Player: 1.00
N1 Anthony Thomas 1.00
N2 Brian Urlacher 3.00
N3 Brett Favre 5.00
N4 Tom Brady 3.00
N5 Jeff Garcia 2.00
N6 Joey Harrington 12.00

2003 Donruss Kickoff Magazine

NM/M
Complete Set (16): 6.00
Common Player: .35
1 Marcellus Wiley .25
2 Sam Adams .50
3 Eddie George 2.00
4 Jeff Garcia 1.00
5 Keith Brooking .25
6 Drew Bledsoe 2.00
7 Edgerrin James 2.00
8 Zach Thomas .50
9 Shaun O'Hara .25
10 Tiki Barber .50
11 Ronde Barber .25
12 Ricky Williams 2.00
13 Hines Ward 1.00
14 Eddie Mason .25
15 Billy Conaty .25
16 Gerald McBurrows .25

2003 Donruss Classic

NM/M
Common Player: .20
Unlisted Star: .75
Minor Star: .50
Cards 101-150 numbered to 1000
Common Rookie (151-250): 3.00
Cards 151-250 numbered to 900
Pack (7): 7.00
Wax Box (18): 80.00
1 Jake Plummer .40
2 Marcel Shipp .20
3 David Boston .60
4 Michael Vick 2.50
5 T.J. Duckett .50
6 Warrick Dunn .40
7 Ray Lewis .50
8 Jamal Lewis .50
9 Todd Heap .30
10 Drew Bledsoe 1.25
11 Travis Henry .50
12 Peerless Price .60
13 Eric Moulds .60
14 Julius Peppers .60
15 Steve Smith .20
16 Lamar Smith .20
17 Anthony Thomas .50
18 Marty Booker .20
19 Brian Urlacher 1.50
20 Corey Dillon .40
21 Chad Johnson .40
22 Tim Couch 1.00
23 William Green .50
24 Quincy Morgan .20
25 Chad Hutchinson .20
26 Emmitt Smith 2.00
27 Antonio Bryant .60
28 Roy Williams .75
29 Brian Griese .50
30 Clinton Portis 2.00
31 Rod Smith .40
32 Ashley Lelie 1.00
33 Joey Harrington 1.50
34 James Stewart .20
35 Bill Schroeder .20
36 Brett Favre 2.50
37 Ahman Green .75
38 Donald Driver .50
39 David Carr 1.50
40 Jonathan Wells .50
41 Corey Bradford .20
42 Peyton Manning 2.00
43 Edgerrin James 1.25
44 Marvin Harrison .60
45 Mark Brunell .60
46 Fred Taylor .50
47 Jimmy Smith .20
48 Trent Green .40
49 Priest Holmes 1.00
50 Tony Gonzalez .40
51 Ricky Williams 1.25
52 Chris Chambers .50
53 Zach Thomas .20
54 Daunte Culpepper 1.25
55 Michael Bennett .50
56 Randy Moss 2.00
57 Tom Brady 1.25
58 Antowain Smith .20
59 Troy Brown .40
60 Aaron Brooks 1.00
61 Deuce McAllister 1.00
62 Donte Stallworth 1.00
63 Kerry Collins .40
64 Jeremy Shockey 1.50
65 Amani Toomer .40
66 Chad Pennington 1.00
67 Curtis Martin .60
68 Laveranues Coles .50
69 Rich Gannon .50
70 Charlie Garner .50
71 Jerry Rice 2.00
72 Tim Brown .75
73 Donovan McNabb 1.25
74 Duce Staley .20
75 Todd Pinkston .20
76 Tommy Maddox .75
77 Jerome Bettis .60
78 Plaxico Burress .75
79 Hines Ward .75
80 Drew Brees 1.25
81 LaDainian Tomlinson 1.50
82 Junior Seau .50
83 Jeff Garcia .50
84 Garrison Hearst .20
85 Terrell Owens .75
86 Matt Hasselbeck .20
87 Shaun Alexander .75
88 Koren Robinson .40
89 Kurt Warner 1.50
90 Marshall Faulk 1.25
91 Isaac Bruce .75
92 Brad Johnson .50
93 Mike Alstott .50
94 Keyshawn Johnson .50
95 Steve McNair .75
96 Eddie George .75
97 Derrick Mason .50
98 Patrick Ramsey .75
99 Stephen Davis .50
100 Rod Gardner .50
101 Archie Manning .50
102 Bo Jackson 1.00
103 Bob Griese .50
104 Bob Lilly .50
105 Craig James .20
106 Cliff Branch .20
107 Dan Fouts .20
108 Daryl Johnston .20
109 Daryle Lamonica .20
110 Dick Butkus 1.00
111 Don Maynard .20
112 Ed "Too Tall" Jones .20
113 Franco Harris 1.00
114 Frank Gifford 1.00
115 Fred Biletnikoff .20
116 Gale Sayers 1.50
117 George Blanda .50
118 Herman Edwards .20
119 Herschel Walker .20
120 Jack Ham .20
121 Jack Tatum .20
122 Jack Youngblood .20
123 James Lofton .20
124 Jay Novacek .20
125 Jim Brown 1.50
126 Jim McMahon/100 15.00
127 Jim Plunkett .20
128 Jimmy Johnson/100 5.00
129 Joe Green .50
130 Joe Montana 6.00
131 John Riggins .50
132 John Stallworth .20
133 John Taylor .20
134 Ken Stabler .50
135 L.C. Greenwood .20
136 Lance Alworth .50
137 Mel Blount .20
138 Mike Ditka/100 5.00
139 Paul Hornung 1.00
140 Randy White .20
141 Raymond Berry .20
142 Roger Craig .20
143 Roger Staubach 1.00
144 Ron Jaworski .20
145 Sammy Baugh .20
146 Sonny Jurgensen .20
147 Steve Young .75
148 Ted Hendricks .20
149 Thurman Thomas .20
150 Tom Jackson .20
151 *Brian St. Pierre* 4.00
152 *Byron Leftwich* 25.00
153 *Carson Palmer* 20.00
154 *Chris Simms* 10.00
155 *Dave Ragone* 8.00
156 *Ken Dorsey* 8.00
157 *Kliff Kingsbury* 6.00
158 *Kyle Boller* 12.00
159 *Rex Grossman* 15.00
160 *Seneca Wallace* 6.00
161 *Jason Gesser* 5.00
162 *Artose Pinner* 5.00
163 *Avon Cobourne* 5.00
164 *Cecil Sapp* 5.00
165 *Chris Brown* 10.00
166 *Derek Watson* 4.00
167 *Domanick Davis* 12.00
168 *Dwone Hicks* 3.00
169 *Earnest Graham* 4.00
170 *Justin Fargas* 8.00
171 *Larry Johnson* 12.00
172 *Lee Suggs* 12.00
173 *Musa Smith* 6.00
174 *Onterrio Smith* 12.00
175 *Quentin Griffin* 15.00
176 *Willis McGahee* 15.00
177 *Sultan McCullough* 5.00
178 *LaBrandon Toefield* 5.00
179 *B.J. Askew* 5.00
180 *Andre Johnson* 15.00
181 *Anquan Boldin* 15.00
182 *Arnaz Battle* 5.00
183 *Bethel Johnson* 5.00
184 *Billy McMullen* 5.00
185 *Bobby Wade* 5.00
186 *Brandon Lloyd* 5.00
187 *Bryant Johnson* 8.00
188 *Charles Rogers* 15.00
189 *Doug Gabriel* 4.00
190 *Justin Gage* 5.00
191 *Kareem Kelly* 5.00
192 *Kelley Washington* 6.00
193 *Kevin Curtis* 5.00
194 *Nate Burleson* 5.00
195 *Sam Aiken* 3.00
196 *Shaun McDonald* 5.00
197 *Talman Gardner* 5.00
198 *Taylor Jacobs* 6.00
199 *Terrence Edwards* 5.00
200 *Tyrone Calico* 10.00
201 *Walter Young* 5.00
202 *Ryan Hoag/100* 8.00
203 *Paul Arnold* 3.00
204 *Bennie Joppru* 6.00
205 *Dallas Clark* 8.00
206 *George Wrighster* 3.00
207 *Jason Witten* 8.00
208 *Mike Pinkard* 4.00
209 *Robert Johnson* 4.00
210 *Teyo Johnson* 5.00
211 *Calvin Pace* 5.00
212 *Chris Kelsay* 4.00
213 *Corey Redding* 4.00
214 *Dewayne Robertson* 5.00
215 *Dewayne White* 4.00
216 *Jerome McDougle* 5.00
217 *Kenny Peterson* 4.00
218 *Kindal Moorehead* 4.00
219 *Michael Haynes* 5.00
220 *Terrell Suggs* 8.00
221 *Tully Banta-Cain* 3.00
222 *Jimmy Kennedy* 5.00
223 *Johnathan Sullivan* 3.00
224 *Kevin Williams* 4.00
225 Nick Eason/100 6.00
226 *Rien Long* 4.00
227 *Ty Warren* 4.00
228 *William Joseph* 6.00
229 *Boss Bailey* 6.00
230 *Bradie James* 3.00
231 *Victor Hobson* 3.00
232 *Clifton Smith* 3.00
233 *E.J. Henderson/100* 8.00
234 Gerald Hayes/100 8.00
235 *LaMarcus McDonald* 3.00
236 *Nick Barnett* 8.00
237 *Terry Pierce* 3.00
238 *Andre Woolfolk* 5.00
239 *Dennis Weathersby* 3.00
240 *Drayton Florence* 3.00
241 *Eugene Wilson* 3.00
242 *Marcus Trufant* 6.00
243 *Rashean Mathis* 3.00
244 *Ricky Manning Jr.* 4.00
245 Sammy Davis/100 6.00
246 *Terence Newman* 8.00
247 *Julian Battle* 4.00
248 *Ken Hamlin* 4.00
249 *Mike Doss* 5.00
250 *Troy Polamalu* 5.00

2003 Donruss Classic Timeless Tributes

Stars (1-100): 4X-8X
Stars (101-150): 1.5X-3X
1-150 Production 150 Sets
Rookies (151-250): 1X-2X
151-250 Production 100 Sets

2003 Donruss Classic Classic Materials

NM/M
Common Player: 10.00
CM1 Alan Page/100 30.00
CM2 Andre Reed/400 10.00
CM3 Art Monk/400 12.00
CM4 Bart Starr/50 75.00
CM5 Earl Campbell/300 15.00
CM6 Eric Dickerson/400 12.00
CM7 Irving Fryar/400 10.00
CM8 Jim Kelly/400 25.00
CM9 Larry Csonka/100 20.00
CM10 Leonard Marshall/100
CM11 Marcus Allen/400 12.00
CM12 Ray Nitschke/50 50.00
CM13 Terry Bradshaw/300 30.00
CM14 Tony Dorsett/100 30.00
CM15 Troy Aikman/300 30.00
CM16 Barry Sanders/200 40.00
CM17 Craig James/400 10.00
CM18 Dan Fouts/300 12.00
CM19 Dan Marino/400 30.00
CM20 Darryl Johnston/400 10.00
CM21 Frank Gifford/100 15.00
CM22 Steve Young/400 15.00
CM23 Herman Edwards/400 10.00
CM24 Jack Youngblood/100 15.00
CM25 Jim Brown/50 75.00
CM26 Warren Moon/400 12.00
CM27 Jimmy Johnson/400 10.00
CM28 Randy White/125 12.00
CM29 Ron Jaworski/100 20.00
CM30 Cris Carter/400 12.00
CM31 Dick Butkus, Walter Payton/100 100.00
CM32 Jim McMahon, Gale Sayers/100 50.00
CM33 Earl Campbell, Warren Moon/100 25.00
CM34 Franco Harris, Terry Bradshaw/100 60.00
CM35 Daryle Lamonica, Fred Biletnikoff/100 30.00
CM36 Ted Hendricks, Jack Tatum/100 30.00
CM37 Troy Aikman, Jay Novacek/100 40.00
CM38 Roger Staubach, Tony Dorsett/100 50.00
CM39 Johnny Unitas, Raymond Berry/100 80.00
CM40 Peyton Manning, Edgerrin James/100 40.00
CM41 Dick Butkus, Walter Payton, Gale Sayers, Jim McMahon 10 EXCH
CM42 Earl Campbell, Franco Harris, Terry Bradshaw, Warren Moon/10
CM43 Daryle Lamonica, Fred Biletnikoff, Jack Tatum, Ted Hendricks/10
CM44 Troy Aikman, Jay Novacek, Tony Dorsett, Roger Staubach/10
CM45 Johnny Unitas, Raymond Berry, Peyton Manning, Craig James/10

2003 Donruss Classic Classic Materials AU

NM/M
Common Player: 20.00
Production to varying quantities
1 Alan Page/100 50.00
2 Andre Reed/50 30.00
3 Art Monk/50 65.00
4 Bart Starr/35 250.00
5 Earl Campbell/50 50.00
6 Eric Dickerson/50 60.00
7 Irving Fryar/100 20.00
8 Jim Kelly/50 85.00
9 Larry Csonka/65 40.00
10 Leonard Marshall/100 30.00
11 Marcus Allen/50 40.00
12 Ray Nitschke/50
13 Terry Bradshaw/50 150.00
14 Tony Dorsett/50 100.00
15 Troy Aikman/75 100.00

2003 Donruss Classic Classic Pigskin

NM/M
Common Player: 12.00
Production 250 sets
Double Production 25 Sets
1 Marcus Allen 20.00
2 John Elway 40.00
3 Jim Kelly 25.00
4 Emmitt Smith 50.00
5 Trent Dilfer 12.00
6 Tom Brady 20.00

2003 Donruss Classic Dress Code

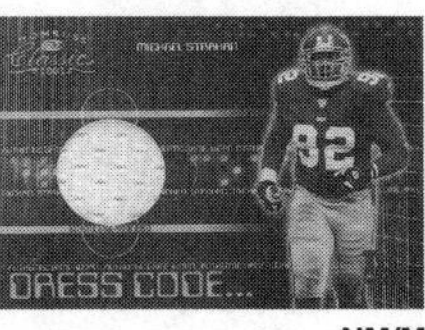

NM/M
Common Player: 5.00
Production 550 sets
1 Dennis Northcutt 5.00
2 Jason Taylor 10.00
3 Donovan McNabb 8.00
4 Jerome Bettis 6.00
5 Joey Harrington 10.00
6 Duce Staley 5.00
7 Keyshawn Johnson 7.00
8 Kurt Warner 5.00
9 Santana Moss 5.00
10 Marvin Harrison 5.00
11 Michael Strahan 5.00
12 Mike Alstott 6.00
13 Rod Gardner 8.00
14 Rod Smith 8.00
15 Stephen Davis 5.00
16 Charles Woodson 8.00
17 Eric Moulds 5.00
18 Jeff Garcia 8.00
19 Anthony Thomas 5.00

2003 Donruss Classic Membership

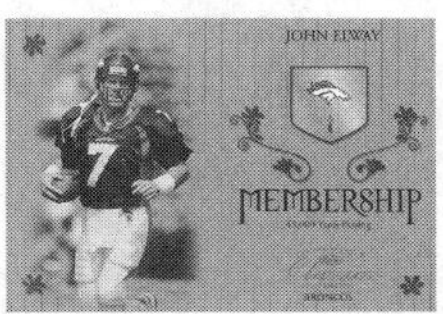

NM/M
Common Player: 1.00
Production 1500 sets
1 Warren Moon 1.00
2 Dan Marino 4.00
3 John Elway 3.00
4 Jerry Rice 3.00
5 Cris Carter 1.00
6 Tim Brown 1.50
7 Emmitt Smith 4.00
8 John Riggins 2.00
9 Priest Holmes 1.50
10 Lawrence Taylor 1.00
12 Bruce Smith 1.00
13 Jerry Rice 3.00
14 Emmitt Smith 3.00
15 Marcus Allen 1.00
16 Walter Payton 4.00
17 Emmitt Smith 3.00
18 Barry Sanders 3.00
19 Eric Dickerson 1.00
20 Tony Dorsett 1.00

2003 Donruss Classic Membership VIP

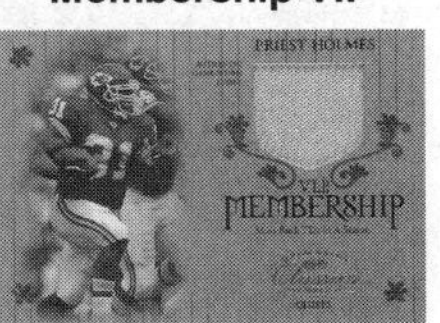

NM/M
Common Player: 10.00
1 Warren Moon/400 15.00
2 Dan Marino/250 45.00
3 John Elway/250 45.00
4 Jerry Rice/250 20.00
5 Cris Carter/200 10.00
6 Tim Brown/200 12.00
7 Emmitt Smith/75 35.00
8 John Riggins/100 25.00
9 Priest Holmes/100 12.00
10 Lawrence Taylor/200 10.00
11 Reggie White/300 10.00
12 Bruce Smith/400 10.00
13 Jerry Rice/75 35.00
14 Emmitt Smith/100 35.00
15 Marcus Allen/150 25.00
16 Walter Payton/100 65.00
17 Emmitt Smith/250 25.00
18 Barry Sanders/200 30.00
19 Eric Dickerson/250 12.00
20 Tony Dorsett/100 15.00

2003 Donruss Classic Membership VIP AU

NM/M
Common Player: 40.00
1 Warren Moon/50 40.00
2 Dan Marino/50 200.00
3 John Elway/15

10 Lawrence Taylor/50 100.00
11 Reggie White/50 50.00
18 Barry Sanders/50 200.00

2003 Donruss Classic Significant Signatures

NM/M
Common Player: 10.00
Numbered to various quantities
4 Michael Vick/25
8 Jamal Lewis/25
13 Eric Moulds/50 20.00
17 Anthony Thomas/25 40.00
18 Marty Booker/50 20.00
19 Brian Urlacher/25 100.00
20 Corey Dillon/25 15.00
30 Clinton Portis/25
31 Rod Smith/50 25.00
33 Joey Harrington/25
36 Brett Favre/15
37 Ahman Green/25
38 Donald Driver/50 35.00
39 David Carr/15
44 Marvin Harrison/25
47 Jimmy Smith/50
49 Priest Holmes/25
52 Chris Chambers/25 35.00
53 Zach Thomas/25
56 Randy Moss/25 100.00
58 Antowain Smith/25 15.00
62 Donte Stallworth/25 25.00
66 Chad Pennington/25 25.00
68 Laveranues Coles/50
76 Tommy Maddox/50 40.00
83 Jeff Garcia/25 40.00
84 Garrison Hearst/25 15.00
85 Terrell Owens/25
89 Kurt Warner/50 50.00
91 Isaac Bruce/25 20.00
93 Mike Alstott/25
95 Steve McNair/25
97 Derrick Mason/25
101 Archie Manning/150 25.00
102 Bo Jackson/100 100.00
103 Bob Griese/100 25.00
104 Bob Lilly/200 20.00
105 Craig James/200 15.00
106 Cliff Branch/200 15.00
107 Dan Fouts/100 15.00
108 Daryl Johnston/200 15.00
109 Daryle Lamonica/150 20.00
110 Dick Butkus/100 80.00
111 Don Maynard/100 10.00
112 Ed "Too Tall" Jones/200 15.00
113 Franco Harris/100
114 Frank Gifford/100 20.00
115 Fred Biletnikoff/100 20.00
116 Gale Sayers/100 35.00
117 George Blanda/100 30.00
118 Herman Edwards/150 15.00
119 Herschel Walker/200 20.00
120 Jack Ham/150 20.00
121 Jack Tatum/150 30.00
122 Jack Youngblood/150 20.00
123 James Lofton/100 15.00
124 Jay Novacek/200 25.00
125 Jim Brown/250 65.00
127 Jim Plunkett/200 20.00
128 Jimmy Johnson/100 50.00
129 Joe Green/100 30.00
130 Joe Montana/225 125.00
131 John Riggins/200 35.00
132 John Stallworth/250 25.00
133 John Taylor/250 15.00
134 Ken Stabler/150 30.00
135 L.C. Greenwood/150 30.00
136 Lance Alworth/150 25.00
137 Mel Blount/253 20.00
138 Mike Ditka/100 50.00
139 Paul Hornung/200 25.00
140 Randy White/200 20.00
141 Raymond Berry/150 15.00
142 Roger Craig/150 15.00
143 Roger Staubach/117 50.00
144 Ron Jaworski/150 15.00
145 Sammy Baugh/200 35.00
146 Sonny Jurgensen/150 20.00
147 Steve Young/100 35.00
148 Ted Hendricks/150 20.00
149 Thurman Thomas/150 10.00
150 Tom Jackson/250 12.00
152 Byron Leftwich/100 85.00
153 Carson Palmer/100 125.00
154 Chris Simms/125 30.00
155 Dave Ragone/200 15.00
164 Cecil Sapp/225 10.00
176 Willis McGahee/125 45.00
189 Doug Gabriel/250 12.00
190 Justin Gage/220 12.00
204 Bennie Joppru/200 12.00
210 Teyo Johnson/250 12.00
214 Dewayne Robertson/250 12.00
215 Dewayne White/250 12.00
216 Jerome McDougle/250 12.00
217 Kenny Peterson/300 12.00
223 Johnathan Sullivan/300
224 Kevin Williams/250 12.00
226 Rien Long/250 8.00
228 William Joseph/250 12.00
233 E.J. Henderson/200 12.00
239 Dennis Weathersby/250 8.00
242 Marcus Trufant/250 20.00
246 Terence Newman/250 45.00
249 Mike Doss/200 12.00

2003 Donruss Classic Timeless Triples

NM/M
Common Player: 30.00
1 Doak Walker, Jim Thorpe, Harold "Red" Grange/50 500.00
2 Jim Kelly, Thurman Thomas, Andre Reed/150 60.00
3 Troy Aikman, Emmitt Smith, Darryl Johnston/100 100.00
4 Joe Montana, John Taylor, Jerry Rice/150 120.00
5 Dan Marino, Bob Griese, Jay Fiedler/100 150.00
6 Terrell Davis, Mike Anderson, Clinton Portis/50 50.00
7 Fred Biletnikoff, Jerry Rice, Tim Brown/100 100.00
8 Kurt Warner, Marshall Faulk, Isaac Bruce/100 30.00
9 Joe Greene, Mel Blount, L.C. Greenwood/100 80.00
10 Steve McNair, Eddie George, Derrick Mason/100 30.00

2003 Donruss Elite

NM/M
Common Player: .20
Unlisted Star: .60
Minor Star: .40
Common Rookie (101-200): 6.00
Minor Rookie: 8.00
Pack (5): 5.00
Wax Box (24): 90.00
1 Jamal Lewis .40
2 Ray Lewis .40
3 Todd Heap .20
4 Drew Bledsoe 1.00
5 Travis Henry .50
6 Eric Moulds .50
7 Peerless Price .60
8 Jon Kitna .20
9 Corey Dillon .60
10 Chad Johnson .20
11 Tim Couch .75
12 William Green .60
13 Andre Davis .60
14 Brian Griese .60
15 Ashley Lelie .60
16 Clinton Portis 1.50
17 Rod Smith .40
18 David Carr 1.25
19 Jonathan Wells .50
20 Jabar Gaffney .20
21 Peyton Manning 1.50
22 Edgerrin James 1.00
23 Marvin Harrison .60
24 Mark Brunell .60
25 Jimmy Smith .40
26 Fred Taylor .40
27 Priest Holmes .75
28 Trent Green .40
29 Tony Gonzalez .40
30 Chris Chambers .40
31 Zach Thomas .40
32 Ricky Williams 1.00
33 Tom Brady 1.50
34 Antowain Smith .20
35 Troy Brown .40
36 Chad Pennington .75
37 Curtis Martin .60
38 Laveranues Coles .40
39 Tim Brown .60
40 Rich Gannon .60
41 Jerry Rice 1.50
42 Charlie Garner .40
43 Antwann Randle El 1.00
44 Plaxico Burress .60
45 Tommy Maddox .60
46 Jerome Bettis .40
47 Drew Brees 1.00
48 LaDainian Tomlinson 1.25
49 Junior Seau .40
50 Eddie George .60
51 Steve McNair .60
52 Derrick Mason .40
53 David Boston .40
54 Jake Plummer .40
55 Marcel Shipp .20
56 Michael Vick 2.00
57 T.J. Duckett .60
58 Warrick Dunn .40
59 Julius Peppers .50
60 Steve Smith .30
61 Muhsin Muhammad .40
62 Anthony Thomas .40
63 Brian Urlacher 1.25
64 Marty Booker .40
65 Chad Hutchinson .20
66 Antonio Bryant .60
67 Emmitt Smith 1.50
68 Joey Harrington 1.25
69 Germane Crowell .20
70 James Stewart .20
71 Brett Favre 2.00
72 Donald Driver .50
73 Ahman Green .60
74 Randy Moss 1.50
75 Michael Bennett .50
76 Daunte Culpepper 1.00
77 Aaron Brooks .75
78 Deuce McAllister .75
79 Donte Stallworth .50
80 Tiki Barber .40
81 Jeremy Shockey 1.25
82 Kerry Collins .40
83 Donovan McNabb 1.00
84 James Thrash .20
85 Duce Staley .20
86 Jeff Garcia .40
87 Terrell Owens .50
88 Garrison Hearst .40
89 Shaun Alexander .60
90 Darrell Jackson .20
91 Koren Robinson .20
92 Marshall Faulk 1.00
93 Kurt Warner 1.25
94 Isaac Bruce .40
95 Keyshawn Johnson .40
96 Brad Johnson .20
97 Warren Sapp .40
98 Patrick Ramsey .40
99 Rod Gardner .20
100 Stephen Davis .40
101 *Brian St. Pierre* 6.00
102 *Byron Leftwich* 50.00
103 *Carson Palmer* 35.00
104 *Chris Simms* 20.00
105 *Dave Ragone* 15.00
106 *Ken Dorsey* 15.00
107 *Kliff Kingsbury* 8.00
108 *Kyle Boller* 20.00
109 *Rex Grossman* 30.00
110 *Seneca Wallace* 10.00
111 *Jason Gesser* 8.00
112 *Artose Pinner* 8.00
113 *Avon Cobourne* 8.00
114 *Cecil Sapp* 6.00
115 *Chris Brown* 15.00
116 *Derek Watson* 6.00
117 *Domanick Davis* 20.00
118 *Dwone Hicks/100* 20.00
119 *Earnest Graham* 8.00
120 *Justin Fargas* 12.00
121 *Larry Johnson* 25.00
122 *Lee Suggs* 25.00
123 *Musa Smith* 8.00
124 *Onterrio Smith* 15.00
125 *Quentin Griffin* 20.00
126 *Willis McGahee* 25.00
127 *Sultan McCullough* 6.00
128 *LaBrandon Toefield* 6.00
129 *B.J. Askew* 6.00
130 *Andre Johnson* 30.00
131 *Anquan Boldin* 30.00
132 *Arnaz Battle* 8.00
133 *Bethel Johnson* 12.00
134 *Billy McMullen* 6.00
135 *Bobby Wade* 6.00
136 *Brandon Lloyd* 8.00
137 *Bryant Johnson* 15.00
138 *Charles Rogers* 20.00
139 *Doug Gabriel* 8.00
140 *Justin Gage* 8.00
141 *Kareem Kelly* 8.00
142 *Kelley Washington* 10.00
143 *Kevin Curtis* 6.00
144 *Nate Burleson* 6.00
145 *Sam Aiken* 6.00
146 *Shaun McDonald* 6.00
147 *Talman Gardner* 8.00
148 *Taylor Jacobs* 10.00
149 *Terrence Edwards* 6.00
150 *Tyrone Calico* 12.00
151 *Walter Young* 6.00
152 *Ryan Hoag/100* 10.00
153 *Paul Arnold/100* 10.00
154 *Bennie Joppru* 10.00
155 *Dallas Clark* 12.00
156 *George Wrighster* 6.00
157 *Jason Witten* 12.00
158 *Mike Pinkard* 6.00
159 *Robert Johnson/100* 8.00
160 *Teyo Johnson* 8.00
161 *Andrew Williams* 6.00
162 *Chris Kelsay* 6.00
163 *Corey Redding* 6.00
164 *Dewayne Robertson* 8.00
165 *Dewayne White* 8.00
166 *Jerome McDougle* 8.00
167 *Kenny Peterson* 6.00
168 *Kindal Moorehead* 6.00
169 *Michael Haynes* 10.00
170 *Terrell Suggs* 15.00
171 *Tully Banta-Cain* 6.00
172 *Jimmy Kennedy* 8.00
173 *Jonathon Sullivan* 8.00
174 *Kevin Williams* 8.00
175 *Nick Eason/100* 10.00
176 *Rien Long* 8.00
177 *Ty Warren* 6.00
178 *William Joseph* 10.00
179 *Boss Bailey* 10.00
180 *Bradie James* 6.00
181 *Victor Hobson* 6.00
182 *Clifton Smith/100* 10.00
183 *E.J. Henderson/100* 15.00
184 *Gerald Hayes/100* 10.00
185 *LaMarcus McDonald/100* 10.00
186 *Nick Barnett* 12.00
187 *Terry Pierce* 6.00
188 *Andre Woolfolk* 6.00
189 *Dennis Weathersby* 6.00
190 *Drayton Florence/100* 10.00
191 *Eugene Wilson* 6.00
192 *Marcus Trufant* 10.00
193 *Rashean Mathis* 6.00
194 *Ricky Manning Jr.* 6.00
195 *Sammy Davis/100* 10.00
196 *Terence Newman* 15.00
197 *Julian Battle* 6.00
198 *Ken Hamlin* 6.00
199 *Mike Doss* 8.00
200 *Troy Polamalu/100* 25.00

2003 Donruss Elite Aspirations

Stars/60-99: 10X-20X
Rookies/60-99: 1X
Stars/30-59: 15X-30X
Rookies/30-59: 1.5X
Stars/20-29: 25X-50X
Rookies/20-29: 1.5X-3X

2003 Donruss Elite Status

Stars/60-99: 10X-20X
Rookies/60-99: 1X
Stars/30-59: 15X-30X
Rookies/30-59: 1.5X
Stars/20-29: 25X-50X
Rookies/20-29: 1.5X-3X

2003 Donruss Elite Back to the Future

NM/M
Common Player: 1.00
1-12 Production 1000 Sets
13-18 Production 500 Sets
1 Drew Brees 2.00
2 Dan Fouts 3.00
3 Marvin Harrison 3.00
4 Raymond Berry 2.00
5 Rod Gardner 2.00
6 Art Monk 3.00
7 Daunte Culpepper 3.00
8 Warren Moon 3.00
9 Kerry Collins 2.00
10 Frank Gifford 3.00
11 Tom Brady 5.00
12 Drew Bledsoe 4.00
13 Dan Fouts 3.00
14 Marvin Harrison, Raymond Berry 4.00
15 Art Monk, Rod Gardner 4.00
16 Daunte Culpepper, Warren Moon 6.00
17 Frank Gifford, Kerry Collins 6.00
18 Drew Bledsoe, Tom Brady 8.00

2003 Donruss Elite Back to the Future Threads

NM/M
Common Player: 10.00
1-12 Production 250 Sets
13-18 Production 100 Sets
1 Drew Brees 10.00
2 Dan Fouts 15.00
3 Marvin Harrison 12.00
4 Raymond Berry 20.00
5 Rod Gardner 10.00
6 Art Monk 20.00
7 Daunte Culpepper 12.00
8 Warren Moon 20.00
9 Kerry Collins 10.00
10 Frank Gifford 20.00
11 Tom Brady 20.00
12 Drew Bledsoe 15.00
13 Dan Fouts, Drew Brees 25.00
14 Marvin Harrison, Raymond Berry 25.00
15 Art Monk, Rod Gardner 25.00
16 Daunte Culpepper, Warren Moon 30.00
17 Frank Gifford, Kerry Collins 30.00
18 Drew Bledsoe, Tom Brady 40.00

2003 Donruss Elite College Ties

NM/M
Common Player: 1.00
Production 2000 sets
1 Chris Simms, Ricky Williams 2.50
2 Byron Leftwich, Chad Pennington 3.00
3 Carson Palmer, Keyshawn Johnson 3.00
4 Dave Ragone, Deion Branch 1.50
5 Drew Bledsoe, Jason Gesser 1.50
6 Jeremy Shockey, Ken Dorsey 2.50
7 Lee Suggs, Michael Vick 3.00
8 Clinton Portis, Willis McGahee 3.00
9 Emmitt Smith, Rex Grossman 2.50
10 Charlie Rogers, Plaxico Burress 2.50
11 Andre Johnson, Santana Moss 1.50
12 Kerry Collins, Larry Johnson 1.50
13 Donte Stallworth, Kelley Washington 1.00
14 Warren Sapp, William Joseph 1.00
15 Mike Doss, Nate Clements 1.00

2003 Donruss Elite Masks of Steel

NM/M
Common Player: 8.00
1-25 Production 400 Sets
26-30 Production 50 Sets
31-35 Production 25 Sets
1 Michael Vick 20.00
2 Marvin Harrison 10.00
3 Jeff Garcia 10.00
4 Eddie George 8.00
5 Tom Brady 15.00
6 Jerry Rice 15.00
7 Aaron Brooks 10.00
8 Chris Chambers 8.00
9 Kordell Stewart 8.00
10 Koren Robinson 8.00
11 Quincy Morgan 8.00
12 Deuce McAllister 10.00
13 LaDainian Tomlinson 10.00
14 Travis Henry 8.00
15 Mark Brunell 8.00
16 Quincy Carter 10.00
17 Chad Johnson 8.00
18 Chad Pennington 12.00
19 Drew Brees 8.00
20 Santana Moss 8.00
21 Kevan Barlow 8.00
22 Reggie Wayne 8.00
23 Anthony Thomas 8.00
24 Todd Heap 8.00
25 Michael Bennett 8.00
26 Aaron Brooks, Michael Vick 40.00
27 Anthony Thomas, Eddie George 15.00
28 Deuce McAllister, Travis Henry 15.00
29 Jeff Garcia, Jerry Rice 40.00
30 Drew Brees, LaDainian Tomlinson 20.00
31 Drew Brees, Mark Brunell
32 Michael Bennett, Travis Henry
33 Chris Chambers, Jerry Rice
34 Deuce McAllister, Eddie George, LaDainian Tomlinson
35 Aaron Brooks, Jeff Garcia, Michael Vick

2003 Donruss Elite Passing the Torch

NM/M
Common Player: 2.00
1-20 Production 1000 Sets
21-27 Production 500 Sets
Cards 17,18,29 Not Issued
1 David Carr 4.00
2 Warren Moon 3.00
3 Patrick Ramsey 2.00
4 Joe Theismann 2.00
5 Clinton Portis 4.00
6 Terrell Davis 2.00
7 Roy Williams 2.00
8 Deion Sanders 3.00
9 Deuce McAllister 2.00
10 Ricky Williams 3.00
11 Drew Bledsoe 2.00
12 Jim Kelly 3.00
13 Jerome Bettis 2.00
14 Franco Harris 2.00
15 Priest Holmes 3.00
16 Marcus Allen 3.00
19 Kendrell Bell 2.00
20 Jack Lambert 3.00
21 David Carr, Warren Moon 5.00
22 Joe Theismann, Patrick Ramsey 5.00
23 Clinton Portis, Terrell Davis 6.00
24 Roy Williams, Deion Sanders 3.00
25 Deuce McAllister, Ricky Williams 5.00
26 Drew Bledsoe, Jim Kelly 8.00
27 Franco Harris, Jerome Bettis 6.00
28 Marcus Allen, Priest Holmes 5.00
30 Jack Lambert, Kendrell Bell 5.00

2003 Donruss Elite Passing the Torch Autographs

NM/M
Common Player: 25.00
1-20 Production 100 Sets
21-27 Production 50 Sets
Cards 17,18,29 Not Issued
1 David Carr 60.00
2 Warren Moon 40.00
3 Patrick Ramsey 25.00
4 Joe Theismann 40.00
5 Clinton Portis 50.00
6 Terrell Davis 25.00
7 Roy Williams 40.00
8 Deion Sanders 100.00
9 Deuce McAllister 40.00
10 Ricky Williams 60.00
11 Drew Bledsoe 50.00
12 Jim Kelly 80.00
13 Jerome Bettis 25.00
14 Franco Harris 50.00
15 Priest Holmes 50.00
16 Marcus Allen 40.00
19 Kendrell Bell 30.00
20 Jack Lambert 60.00
21 David Carr, Warren Moon 100.00
22 Joe Theismann, Patrick Ramsey 100.00
23 Clinton Portis, Terrell Davis 100.00
24 Roy Williams, Deion Sanders 125.00
25 Deuce McAllister, Ricky Williams 125.00
26 Drew Bledsoe, Jim Kelly 150.00
27 Franco Harris, Jerome Bettis 100.00
28 Marcus Allen, Priest Holmes 100.00
30 Jack Lambert, Kendrell Bell 100.00

2003 Donruss Elite Prime Patches

NM/M
Common Player: 25.00
Production 50 sets
1 Emmitt Smith 75.00
2 William Green 20.00
3 Travis Henry 20.00
4 Tim Brown 30.00
5 Steve McNair 20.00
6 Jerry Rice 60.00
7 Michael Vick 75.00
8 Jamal Lewis 30.00
9 Brett Favre 75.00
10 Randy Moss 50.00
11 Joey Harrington 30.00
12 Peyton Manning 50.00
13 Garrison Hearst 20.00
14 Junior Seau 20.00
15 Priest Holmes 40.00
16 Deuce McAllister 30.00
17 Terrell Owens 30.00
18 LaDainian Tomlinson 30.00
19 Donovan McNabb 40.00
20 Eddie George 25.00

2003 Donruss Elite Pro Bowl Standouts

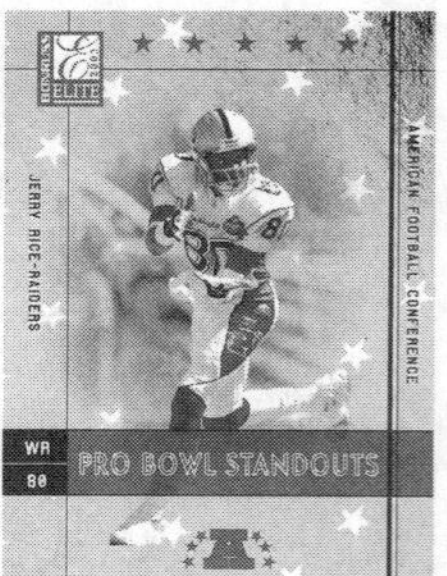

NM/M
Common Player: 1.00
Production 2002 sets
1 Donovan McNabb 2.00
2 Mike Alstott 1.00
3 Jeff Garcia 1.00
4 Deuce McAllister 1.00
5 Michael Bennett 1.00
6 Marshall Faulk 1.50
7 Jeremy Shockey 2.00
8 Terrell Owens 1.00
9 Joe Horn 1.00
10 Brian Urlacher 1.00
11 Rich Gannon 1.00
12 Drew Bledsoe 1.25
13 Peyton Manning 1.50
14 Ricky Williams 1.50

15 Travis Henry 1.00
16 LaDainian Tomlinson 1.25
17 Marvin Harrison 1.00
18 Jerry Rice 2.00
19 Eric Moulds 1.00
20 Zach Thomas 1.00

2003 Donruss Elite Throwback Threads

NM/M
Common Player: 10.00
1-30 Production 250 Sets
31-45 Production 75 Sets
1 Joe Montana 40.00
2 Jeff Garcia 10.00
3 Walter Payton 50.00
4 Harold "Red" Grange 100.00
5 Jim Kelly 30.00
6 Thurman Thomas 10.00
7 Jim Brown 50.00
8 Jim Thorpe 120.00
9 Bob Griese 20.00
10 Larry Csonka 20.00
11 Barry Sanders 30.00
12 Doak Walker 60.00
13 Warren Moon 10.00
14 Earl Campbell 20.00
15 Eric Dickerson 20.00
16 Marshall Faulk 20.00
17 Joe Theismann 20.00
18 John Riggins 25.00
19 Fred Biletnikoff 15.00
20 Jerry Rice 30.00
21 Joe Greene 30.00
22 L.C. Greenwood 25.00
23 Sterling Sharpe 15.00
24 James Lofton 10.00
25 Tony Dorsett 25.00
26 Emmitt Smith 40.00
27 Bart Starr 30.00
28 Ray Nitschke 30.00
29 Sonny Jurgensen 15.00
30 Charley Taylor 12.00
31 Joe Montana, Jeff Garcia 60.00
32 Harold "Red" Grange, Walter Payton 250.00
33 Jim Kelly, Thurman Thomas 40.00
34 Jim Brown, Jim Thorpe 250.00
35 Bob Griese, Larry Csonka 50.00
36 Barry Sanders, Doak Walker 100.00
37 Earl Campbell, Warren Moon 40.00
38 Eric Dickerson, Marshall Faulk 40.00
39 Joe Theismann, John Riggins 60.00
40 Fred Biletnikoff, Jerry Rice 80.00
41 Joe Greene, L.C. Greenwood 40.00
42 James Lofton, Sterling Sharpe 30.00
43 Emmitt Smith, Tony Dorsett 100.00
44 Bart Starr, Ray Nitschke 100.00
45 Charley Taylor, Sonny Jurgensen 40.00

2003 Donruss Elite Throwback Threads Autographs

Production 25 Sets
1 Joe Montana
7 Jim Brown
9 Bob Griese
10 Larry Csonka
11 Barry Sanders
14 Earl Campbell
18 John Riggins
23 Sterling Sharpe

2003 Donruss Elite Turn of the Century Autographs

NM/M
Common Player: 20.00
Production 125 sets
101 Brian St. Pierre 30.00
102 Byron Leftwich 200.00
103 Carson Palmer 150.00
104 Chris Simms 50.00
105 Dave Ragone 30.00
108 Kyle Boller 60.00
109 Rex Grossman 80.00
112 Artose Pinner 25.00
114 Cecil Sapp 25.00
115 Chris Brown 40.00
120 Justin Fargas 40.00
121 Larry Johnson 40.00
122 Lee Suggs 80.00
123 Musa Smith 30.00
124 Onterrio Smith 80.00
126 Willis McGahee 80.00
130 Andre Johnson 100.00
136 Brandon Lloyd 25.00
137 Bryant Johnson 40.00
138 Charles Rogers 60.00
139 Doug Gabriel 20.00
140 Justin Gage 40.00
142 Kelley Washington 40.00
143 Kevin Curtis 20.00
145 Sam Aiken 20.00
148 Taylor Jacobs 25.00
149 Terrence Edwards 20.00
150 Tyrone Calico 50.00
154 Bennie Joppru 20.00
155 Dallas Clark 30.00
157 Jason Witten 40.00
158 Mike Pinkard 20.00
160 Teyo Johnson 30.00
162 Chris Kelsay 20.00
164 Dewayne Robertson 25.00
165 Dewayne White 20.00
166 Jerome McDougal 20.00
167 Kenny Peterson 20.00
170 Terrell Suggs 40.00
172 Jimmy Kennedy 20.00
173 Jonathon Sullivan 20.00
174 Kevin Williams 20.00
176 Rien Long 20.00
178 William Joseph 20.00
179 Boss Bailey 40.00
183 *E.J. Henderson* 30.00
189 Dennis Weathersby 20.00
192 Marcus Trufant 30.00
196 Terence Newman 60.00
199 Mike Doss 30.00

2003 Donruss Gridiron Kings

NM/M
Complete Set (175): 200.00
Common Player (1-100): .40
Minor Stars: .75
Unlisted Stars: 1.00
Common Rookie (101-150): 2.00
Minor Rookies: 3.00
Unlisted Rookies: 4.00
Common Retire (151-175): 2.00
Pack (5): 3.25
Box (24): 55.00
1 David Boston 1.00
2 Marcel Shipp .40
3 Jake Plummer .75
4 Michael Vick 4.00
5 T.J. Duckett 1.00
6 Warrick Dunn .75
7 Ray Lewis .75
8 Jamal Lewis 1.00
9 Todd Heap .75
10 Drew Bledsoe 1.50
11 Eric Moulds .75
12 Travis Henry .75
13 Julius Peppers .75
14 Steve Smith .40
15 Muhsin Muhammad .40
16 Anthony Thomas .75
17 David Terrell .75
18 Brian Urlacher 2.00
19 Corey Dillon 1.00
20 Chad Johnson .75
21 William Green 1.00
22 Tim Couch 1.00
23 Quincy Morgan .75
24 Roy Williams 1.00
25 Emmitt Smith 3.00
26 Antonio Bryant .75
27 Clinton Portis 3.00
28 Ashley Lelie .75
29 Rod Smith .75
30 Brian Griese .75
31 Joey Harrington 2.50
32 James Stewart .75
33 Az-Zahir Hakim .40
34 Brett Favre 4.00
35 Ahman Green 1.00
36 Donald Driver .75
37 Javon Walker .75
38 David Carr 2.50
39 Jabar Gaffney .75
40 Jonathan Wells .40
41 Edgerrin James 1.50
42 Marvin Harrison 1.00
43 Peyton Manning 2.00
44 Mark Brunell .75
45 Jimmy Smith .75
46 Fred Taylor 1.00
47 Priest Holmes 1.00
48 Tony Gonzalez .75
49 Trent Green .75
50 Jay Fiedler .75
51 Chris Chambers .75
52 Zach Thomas .40
53 Ricky Williams 2.00
54 Randy Moss 2.00
55 Daunte Culpepper 1.00
56 Michael Bennett 1.00
57 Tom Brady 2.00
58 Deion Branch .40
59 Antowain Smith .40
60 Donte Stallworth 1.00
61 Deuce McAllister 1.00
62 Aaron Brooks 1.00
63 Kerry Collins 1.00
64 Jeremy Shockey 2.00
65 Tiki Barber .75
66 Curtis Martin 1.00
67 Chad Pennington 1.50
68 Santana Moss .75
69 Jerry Rice 3.00
70 Rich Gannon .75
71 Tim Brown .75
72 Charlie Garner .75
73 Donovan McNabb 1.50
74 Duce Staley .75
75 Antonio Freeman .75
76 Tommy Maddox 1.00
77 Jerome Bettis .75
78 Antwann Randle El .75
79 Plaxico Burress 1.00
80 LaDainian Tomlinson 1.50
81 Junior Seau .75
82 Drew Brees 1.50
83 Terrell Owens 1.00
84 Jeff Garcia 1.00
85 Garrison Hearst .75
86 Koren Robinson .75
87 Shaun Alexander 1.00
88 Trent Dilfer .40
89 Marshall Faulk 1.50
90 Kurt Warner 1.50
91 Isaac Bruce .75
92 Brad Johnson .75
93 Keyshawn Johnson 1.00
94 Warren Sapp .75
95 Steve McNair 1.00
96 Derrick Mason .75
97 Eddie George 1.00
98 Bruce Smith .40
99 Rod Gardner .75
100 Patrick Ramsey 1.00
101 *Carson Palmer* 15.00
102 *Byron Leftwich* 15.00
103 *Kyle Boller* 8.00
104 *Chris Simms* 6.00
105 *Dave Ragone* 3.00
106 *Rex Grossman* 12.00
107 *Brian St. Pierre* 3.00
108 *Kliff Kingsbury* 3.00
109 *Seneca Wallace* 3.00
110 *Larry Johnson* 8.00
111 *Lee Suggs* 4.00
112 *Justin Fargas* 5.00
113 *Onterrio Smith* 5.00
114 *Willis McGahee* 10.00
115 *Chris Brown* 6.00
116 *Musa Smith* 3.00
117 *Artose Pinner* 3.00
118 *Domanick Davis* 6.00
119 *Charles Rogers* 8.00
120 *Andre Johnson* 8.00
121 *Taylor Jacobs* 3.00
122 *Bryant Johnson* 4.00
123 *Kelley Washington* 4.00
124 *Brandon Lloyd* 3.00
125 *Tyrone Calico* 4.00
126 *Kevin Curtis* 2.00
127 *Bethel Johnson* 4.00
128 *Anquan Boldin* 6.00
129 *Nate Burleson* 4.00
130 *Jason Witten* 4.00
131 *Bennie Joppru* 2.00
132 *Teyo Johnson* 4.00
133 *Dallas Clark* 6.00
134 *Terrell Suggs* 4.00
135 *Chris Kelsay* 3.00
136 *Jerome McDougle* 3.00
137 *Michael Haynes* 3.00
138 *Calvin Pace* 2.00
139 *Jimmy Kennedy* 2.00
140 *Kevin Williams* 2.00
141 *Dewayne Robertson* 3.00
142 *William Joseph* 3.00
143 *Johnathan Sullivan* 2.00
144 *Boss Bailey* 4.00
145 *E.J. Henderson* 3.00
146 *Terence Newman* 5.00
147 *Marcus Trufant* 3.00
148 *Andre Woolfolk* 3.00
149 *Troy Polamalu* 5.00
150 *Mike Doss* 3.00
151 Andre Reed 2.00
152 Bo Jackson 3.00
153 Dan Marino 5.00
154 Deacon Jones 2.00
155 Deion Sanders 3.00
156 Doak Walker 2.00
157 Don Maynard 2.00
158 Frank Gifford 2.00
159 Fred Biletnikoff 2.00
160 Gale Sayers 2.00
161 Jack Lambert 2.00
162 Jim Brown 3.00
163 Jim Kelly 3.00
164 Joe Greene 2.00
165 Joe Montana 6.00
166 John Elway 5.00
167 John Riggins 2.00
168 Johnny Unitas 3.00
169 Larry Csonka 2.00
170 Lawrence Taylor 2.00
171 Mike Ditka 2.00
172 Ozzie Newsome 2.00
173 Harold "Red" Grange 2.00
174 Troy Aikman 3.00
175 Warren Moon 2.00

2003 Donruss Gridiron Kings Bronze

Veterans: 1X-2X
Rookies: 1X
Retired: 1.5X
Inserted 1:6

2003 Donruss Gridiron Kings Gold

Veterans: 5X-10X
Rookies: 2X-4X
Retired: 4X-8X
Production 75 Sets

2003 Donruss Gridiron Kings Silver

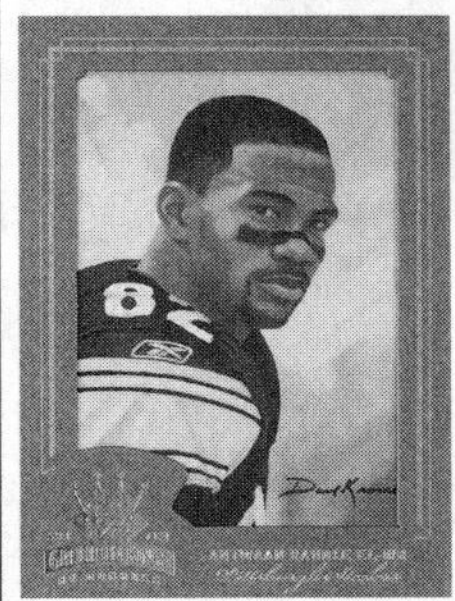

Veterans: 2X-4X
Rookies: 1.5X
Retired: 1.5X-3X
Production 150 Sets

2003 Donruss Gridiron Kings Base Royal Expectations

NM/M
Common Player: 2.00
Inserted 1:23
Materials versions: 2X-4X
Inserted 1:52
1 Andre Johnson 4.00
2 Byron Leftwich 6.00
3 Carson Palmer 6.00
4 Bryant Johnson 2.00
5 Chris Brown 2.00
6 Dallas Clark 2.00
7 Justin Fargas 2.50
8 Kelley Washington 2.00
9 Kyle Boller 4.00
10 Larry Johnson 4.00
11 Willis McGahee 5.00
12 Terence Newman 2.50
13 Rex Grossman 5.00
14 Taylor Jacobs 2.00
15 Terrell Suggs 2.50

2003 Donruss Gridiron Kings Donruss 1894

NM/M
Common Player: 2.00
Production 600 Sets
26 Michael Vick 10.00
27 Drew Bledsoe 4.00
28 Julius Peppers 2.00

29 Clinton Portis 8.00
30 Ahman Green 3.00
31 David Carr 6.00
32 Marvin Harrison 3.00
33 Priest Holmes 3.00
34 Michael Bennett 3.00
35 Deuce McAllister 3.00
36 Jeremy Shockey 5.00
37 Chad Pennington 4.00
38 Rich Gannon 2.00
39 Donovan McNabb 4.00
40 LaDainian Tomlinson 4.00
41 Jeff Garcia 3.00
42 Steve McNair 3.00
43 Doak Walker 2.00
44 Jim Brown 4.00
45 Jim Kelly 3.00
46 Joe Montana 10.00
47 Carson Palmer 8.00
48 Byron Leftwich 8.00
49 Charles Rogers 6.00
50 Andre Johnson 5.00

2003 Donruss Gridiron Kings GK Evolution

NM/M
Common Player: 2.00
Inserted 1:23
1 Michael Vick 8.00
2 Travis Henry 2.00
3 Emmitt Smith 6.00
4 Clinton Portis 6.00
5 Joey Harrington 5.00
6 Brett Favre 8.00
7 David Carr 5.00
8 Peyton Manning 4.00
9 Priest Holmes 2.50
10 Ricky Williams 3.00
11 Randy Moss 4.00
12 Deuce McAllister 2.50
13 Jeremy Shockey 4.00
14 Chad Pennington 3.00
15 Jerry Rice 6.00
16 Donovan McNabb 3.00
17 Plaxico Burress 2.50
18 LaDainian Tomlinson 3.00
19 Terrell Owens 2.50
20 Shaun Alexander 2.50
21 Marshall Faulk 3.00
22 Warren Sapp 2.00
23 Eddie George 2.50
24 Dan Marino 8.00
25 John Elway 8.00

2003 Donruss Gridiron Kings Gridiron Cut Collection

NM/M
Common Player: 8.00
Cards 1-40 Auto
Cards 41-80 Jsy
Cards 81-90 Leather
Cards 81-90 Auto/Jsy
1 Andre Reed/200 20.00
2 Bo Jackson/100 100.00
3 Dan Marino/25 8.00
4 Deacon Jones/100 20.00
5 Deion Sanders/25 8.00
6 Don Maynard/100 30.00
7 Frank Gifford/100 30.00

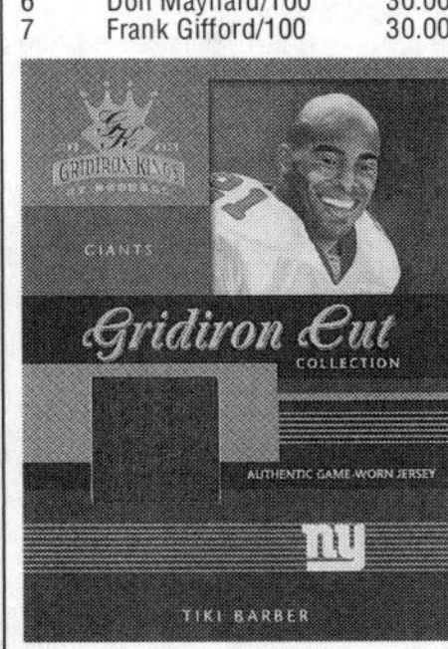

8 Fred Biletnikoff/100 30.00
9 Gale Sayers/100 50.00
10 Jack Lambert/150 80.00
11 Jim Brown/50 8.00
12 Jim Kelly/25 150.00
13 Joe Greene/150 50.00
14 Joe Montana/50 8.00
15 John Elway/24 8.00
16 John Riggins/50 60.00
17 Johnny Unitas/40 8.00
18 Larry Csonka/100 30.00
19 Lawrence Taylor/100 50.00
20 Mike Ditka/100 40.00
21 Ozzie Newsome/100 20.00
22 Troy Aikman/25 8.00
23 Warren Moon/100 40.00
24 Artose Pinner/100 20.00
25 Bennie Joppru/250 15.00
26 Boss Bailey/250 20.00
27 Brian St. Pierre/250 15.00
28 Bryant Johnson/150 20.00
29 Jimmy Kennedy/250 15.00
30 Chris Kelsay/250 15.00
31 Dallas Clark/250 20.00
32 Dewayne Robertson/250 15.00
33 Brandon Lloyd/250 20.00
34 Kelley Washington/107 20.00
35 Lee Suggs/250 20.00
37 Onterrio Smith/150 30.00
38 Terrell Suggs/100 25.00
39 Tyrone Calico/150 30.00
40 Carson Palmer/25 150.00
41 David Boston/475 10.00
42 T.J. Duckett/275 8.00
43 Jamal Lewis/375 10.00
44 Eric Moulds/375 8.00
45 Travis Henry/375 8.00
46 David Terrell/375 8.00
47 Anthony Thomas/375 8.00
48 Corey Dillon/475 8.00
49 Tim Couch/475 8.00
50 Emmitt Smith/375 20.00
51 Antonio Bryant/375 8.00
52 Clinton Portis/275 12.00
53 Joey Harrington/375 12.00
54 Brett Favre/275 25.00
55 Javon Walker/475 8.00
56 Edgerrin James/375 10.00
57 Peyton Manning/375 12.00
58 Fred Taylor/475 8.00
59 Priest Holmes/375 15.00
60 Trent Green/475 8.00
61 Ricky Williams/275 12.00
62 Randy Moss/275 12.00
63 Jeremy Shockey/375 12.00
64 Tiki Barber/475 8.00
65 Santana Moss/375 8.00
66 Curtis Martin/375 8.00
67 Rich Gannon/275 8.00
68 Donovan McNabb/475 12.00
69 Duce Staley/475 8.00
70 Jerome Bettis/475 8.00
71 Antwann Randle El/375 8.00
72 LaDainian Tomlinson/375 10.00
73 Junior Seau/475 8.00
74 Terrell Owens/375 8.00
75 Jeff Garcia/275 8.00
76 Marshall Faulk/275 10.00
77 Kurt Warner/375 8.00
78 Warren Sapp/375 8.00
79 Troy Aikman/225 20.00
80 Joe Montana/225 40.00
81 LaDainian Tomlinson/275 10.00
82 Jeremy Shockey/275 12.00
83 Antonio Bryant/275 8.00
84 Marshall Faulk/275 12.00
85 Jerry Rice/275 20.00
86 Joey Harrington/275 12.00
87 Jeff Garcia/275 8.00
88 Marvin Harrison/275 8.00
89 Rod Smith/275 8.00
90 Charlie Garner/275 8.00
91 Deacon Jones/50 40.00
92 Don Maynard/50 50.00
93 Fred Biletnikoff/50 50.00
94 Jim Brown/50 150.00
95 Jim Kelly/50 80.00
96 Joe Montana/50 200.00
97 John Riggins/50 60.00
98 Ozzie Newsome/50 40.00
99 Warren Moon/50 80.00
100 Kurt Warner/50 60.00

2003 Donruss Gridiron Kings Heritage Collection

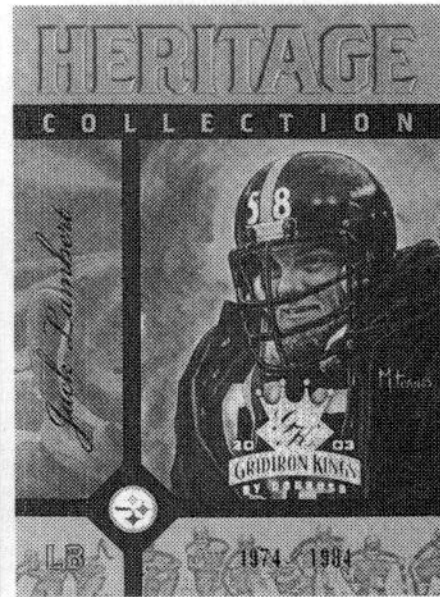

NM/M
Common Player: 2.00
Inserted 1:23
1 Andre Reed 2.00
2 Bo Jackson 5.00
3 Dan Marino 8.00
4 Deacon Jones 2.00
5 Deion Sanders 4.00
6 Doak Walker 2.00
7 Don Maynard 2.00
8 Frank Gifford 2.00
9 Fred Biletnikoff 2.00
10 Gale Sayers 3.00
11 Jack Lambert 3.00
12 Jim Brown 5.00
13 Jim Kelly 4.00
14 Joe Greene 3.00
15 Joe Montana 10.00
16 John Elway 8.00
17 John Riggins 3.00

18 Johnny Unitas 5.00
19 Larry Csonka 2.00
20 Lawrence Taylor 3.00
21 Mike Ditka 2.00
22 Ozzie Newsome 2.00
23 Harold "Red" Grange 2.00
24 Troy Aikman 5.00
25 Warren Moon 2.00

2003 Donruss Gridiron Kings Team Timeline

NM/M
Common Player: 3.00
Production 600 Sets
1 Dan Marino, Jay Fiedler 10.00
2 Deion Sanders, Roy Williams 4.00
3 Doak Walker, Joey Harrington 4.00
4 Fred Biletnikoff, Tim Brown 3.00
5 Gale Sayers, Anthony Thomas 3.00
6 Jim Brown, William Green 5.00
7 Joe Montana, Jeff Garcia 10.00
8 Johnny Unitas, Peyton Manning 6.00
9 Larry Csonka, Ricky Williams 4.00
10 Warren Moon, David Carr 4.00

2003 Donruss Gridiron Kings Team Timeline Materials

NM/M
Common Player: 20.00
Production 100 Sets
1 Dan Marino, Jay Fiedler 60.00
2 Deion Sanders, Roy Williams 30.00
3 Doak Walker, Joey Harrington 40.00
4 Fred Biletnikoff, Tim Brown 20.00
5 Gale Sayers, Anthony Thomas 30.00
6 Jim Brown, William Green 30.00
7 Joe Montana, Jeff Garcia 80.00
8 Johnny Unitas, Peyton Manning 60.00
9 Larry Csonka, Ricky Williams 30.00
10 Warren Moon, David Carr 30.00

2004 Donruss Classics

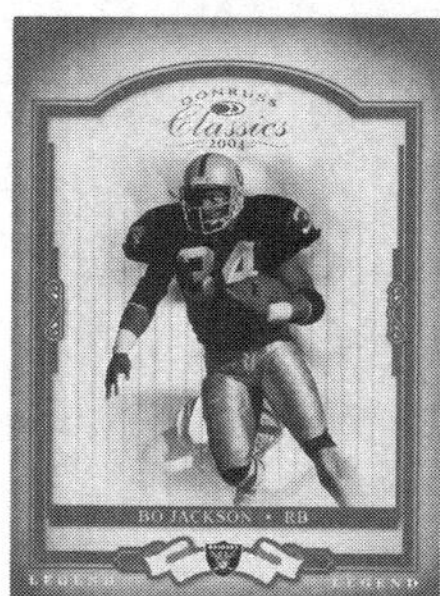

NM/M
Common Player (1-100): .25
Minor Stars (1-100): .50
Unlisted Stars (1-100): .75
Common Legend (101-150): 1.00
Production 2,000 Sets
Common Rookie (151-175): 3.00
Production 1,850 Sets
Common Rookie (176-200): 4.00
Production 1,250 Sets
Common Rookie (201-225): 5.00
Production 925 Sets
Common Rookie (226-250): 6.00
Production 500 Sets
Pack: 7.00
Box (18): 90.00
1 Anquan Boldin .75
2 Emmitt Smith 2.00
3 Michael Vick 2.00
4 Peerless Price .50
5 Warrick Dunn .25
6 Jamal Lewis .75
7 Kyle Boller .75
8 Terrell Suggs .25
9 Todd Heap .50
10 Drew Bledsoe .75
11 Travis Henry .25
12 DeShaun Foster .25
13 Jake Delhomme .75
14 Stephen Davis .50
15 Steve Smith .25
16 Anthony Thomas .50
17 Brian Urlacher .75
18 Rex Grossman .75
19 Chad Johnson .50
20 Carson Palmer 1.00
21 Rudi Johnson .50
22 Andre Davis .50
23 Lee Suggs .25
24 Quincy Carter .75
25 Roy Williams .50
26 Clinton Portis 1.50
27 Jake Plummer .50
28 Rod Smith .25
29 Charles Rogers .75
30 Joey Harrington .75
31 Ahman Green .75
32 Brett Favre 2.50
33 Javon Walker .50
34 Andre Johnson .75
35 David Carr 1.00
36 Domanick Davis .75
37 Edgerrin James 1.00
38 Marvin Harrison .75
39 Peyton Manning 1.50
40 Reggie Wayne .25
41 Byron Leftwich 1.50
42 Fred Taylor .75
43 Jimmy Smith .25
44 Priest Holmes 1.00
45 Dante Hall .25
46 Tony Gonzalez .50
47 Trent Green .25
48 Chris Chambers .75
49 Ricky Williams .75
50 Zach Thomas .25
51 Daunte Culpepper .75
52 Michael Bennett .75
53 Randy Moss 1.50
54 Deion Branch .25
55 Adam Vinatieri .25
56 Tedy Bruschi .25
57 Tom Brady 1.50
58 Aaron Brooks .75
59 Deuce McAllister .75
60 Donte Stallworth .50
61 Joe Horn .25
62 Jeremy Shockey .75
63 Kerry Collins .25
64 Michael Strahan .25
65 Tiki Barber .25
66 Chad Pennington 1.00
67 Curtis Martin .75
68 Santana Moss .25
69 Jerry Rice 2.00
70 Charles Woodson .25
71 Rod Woodson .25
72 Tim Brown .75
73 Brian Westbrook .25
74 Correll Buckhalter .25
75 Donovan McNabb 1.00
76 Antwaan Randle El .50
77 Hines Ward .50
78 Kendrell Bell .25
79 David Boston .50
80 Drew Brees .50
81 LaDainian Tomlinson 1.00
82 Jeff Garcia .75
83 Kevan Barlow .25
84 Terrell Owens .75
85 Koren Robinson .25
86 Matt Hasselbeck .50
87 Shaun Alexander .75
88 Isaac Bruce .50
89 Marc Bulger .50
90 Marshall Faulk 1.00
91 Torry Holt .75
92 Brad Johnson .25
93 Keenan McCardell .25
94 Keyshawn Johnson .50
95 Derrick Mason .25
96 Eddie George .75
97 Steve McNair .75
98 LaVar Arrington .50
99 Laveranues Coles .50
100 Patrick Ramsey .50
101 Archie Manning 2.00
102 Bart Starr 5.00
103 Bo Jackson 3.00
104 Bob Griese 2.50
105 Christian Okoye 1.00
106 Darryl Johnston 1.00
107 Deacon Jones 2.00
108 Deion Sanders 3.00
109 Dick Butkus 3.00
110 Lynn Swann 3.00
111 Don Maynard 2.00
112 Don Shula 2.00
113 Franco Harris 3.00
114 Fred Biletnikoff 2.00
115 Gale Sayers 3.00
116 George Blanda 2.50
117 Herman Edwards 1.00
118 Herschel Walker 2.00
119 Jack Lambert 2.50
120 James Lofton 1.00
121 Jim Plunkett 1.00
122 Jim Thorpe 2.50
123 Joe Greene 2.50
124 John Riggins 2.50
125 L.C. Greenwood 2.00
126 Larry Csonka 2.50
127 Leroy Kelly 1.00
128 Walter Payton 8.00
129 Marcus Allen 3.00
130 Mark Bavaro 1.00
131 Mel Blount 1.00
132 Michael Irvin 2.50
133 Mike Ditka 2.00
134 Mike Singletary 2.00
135 Ozzie Newsome 2.00
136 Paul Hornung 2.50
137 Paul Warfield 2.00
138 Randall Cunningham 2.00
139 Ray Nitschke 2.00
140 Reggie White 2.00
141 Richard Dent 1.00
142 Sammy Baugh 2.00
143 Sonny Jurgensen 2.00
144 Sterling Sharpe 2.00
145 Steve Largent 2.00
146 Terrell Davis 2.00
147 Terry Bradshaw 5.00
148 Thurman Thomas 1.00
149 Tony Dorsett 2.50
150 Warren Moon 2.00
151 *John Navarre* 5.00
152 *Derek Abney* 3.00
153 *Ryan Dinwiddie* 3.00
154 *Bruce Perry/100* 25.00
155 *Adimchinobe Echemandu* 3.00
156 *Troy Fleming* 3.00
157 *Brandon Miree* 3.00
158 *Jarrett Payton* 6.00
159 *Ben Hartsock* 3.00
160 *Chris Cooley* 3.00
161 *Derrick Ward* 3.00
162 *Triandos Luke* 3.00
163 *Clarence Moore* 3.00
164 *D.J. Hackett* 3.00
165 *Mark Jones* 3.00
166 *Sloan Thomas* 3.00
167 *Jamaar Taylor* 3.00
168 *Casey Bramlet* 4.00
169 *Drew Carter* 3.00
170 *Antwan Odom* 4.00
171 *Marquise Hill* 3.00
172 *Ricardo Colclough* 3.00
173 *Keith Smith* 3.00
174 *Joey Thomas* 3.00
175 *Stuart Schweigert* 3.00
176 *Cody Pickett* 6.00
177 *B.J. Symons* 5.00
178 *Matt Mauck* 6.00
179 *Bradlee Van Pelt* 6.00
180 *Jim Sorgi* 4.00
181 *Ernest Wilford* 5.00
182 *Bernard Berrian* 6.00
183 *Darius Watts* 6.00
184 *Derrick Hamilton* 5.00
185 *Jerricho Cotchery* 4.00
186 *Jeris McIntyre* 4.00
187 *Carlos Francis* 4.00
188 *Maurice Mann* 4.00
189 *Randy Starks* 4.00
190 *Darnell Dockett* 4.00
191 *Marcus Tubbs* 4.00
192 *Daryl Smith* 4.00
193 *Karlos Dansby* 4.00
194 *Michael Boulware* 4.00
195 *Teddy Lehman* 6.00
196 *Will Poole* 4.00
197 *Derrick Strait* 5.00
198 *Ahmad Carroll* 4.00
199 *Jeremy LeSueur* 4.00
200 *Bob Sanders* 4.00
201 *J.P. Losman* 12.00
202 *Matt Schaub* 6.00
203 *Josh Harris* 5.00
204 *Luke McCown* 6.00
205 *Quincy Wilson* 5.00
206 *Michael Turner* 5.00
207 *Mewelde Moore* 5.00
208 *Cedric Cobbs* 6.00
209 *Ben Watson* 5.00
210 *Michael Jenkins* 8.00
211 *Devery Henderson* 6.00
212 *Johnnie Morant* 5.00
213 *Keary Colbert* 6.00
214 *Devard Darling* 6.00
215 *P.K. Sam* 8.00
216 *Samie Parker* 5.00
217 *Jason Babin* 5.00
218 *Tommie Harris* 8.00
219 *Vince Wilfork* 8.00
220 *Jonathan Vilma* 8.00
221 *D.J. Williams* 8.00
222 *Chris Gamble* 5.00
223 *Matt Ware* 5.00
224 *Shawntae Spencer* 5.00
225 *Sean Jones* 5.00
226 *Drew Henson* 12.00
227 *Ben Roethlisberger* 50.00
228 *Eli Manning* 30.00
229 *Philip Rivers* 25.00
230 *Steven Jackson* 15.00
231 *Kevin Jones* 15.00
232 *Chris Perry* 10.00
233 *Greg Jones* 8.00
234 *Tatum Bell* 10.00
235 *Jeff Smoker* 8.00
236 *Julius Jones* 15.00
237 *Kellen Winslow Jr.* 12.00
238 *Ben Troupe* 6.00
239 *Larry Fitzgerald* 20.00
240 *Craig Krenzel* 6.00
241 *Roy Williams* 20.00
242 *Reggie Williams* 12.00
243 *Michael Clayton* 12.00
244 *Lee Evans* 12.00
245 *Rashaun Woods* 12.00
246 *Kenechi Udeze* 6.00
247 *Will Smith* 6.00
248 *DeAngelo Hall* 10.00
249 *Dunta Robinson* 6.00
250 *Sean Taylor* 12.00

A card number in parenthese ( ) indicates the set is unnumbered.

2004 Donruss Classics Classic

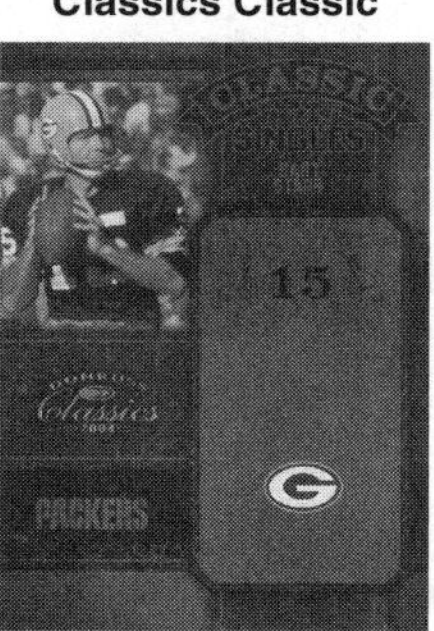

NM/M
Common Single (1-30): 3.00
Production 1,000 Sets
Common Combo (31-45): 5.00
Production 750 Sets
Common Triple (46-50): 8.00
Production 500 Sets
CS-1 Barry Sanders 8.00
CS-2 Bart Starr 8.00
CS-3 Bob Griese 3.00
CS-4 Dan Marino 10.00
CS-5 Doak Walker 3.00
CS-6 Don Shula 3.00
CS-7 Emmitt Smith 6.00
CS-8 Franco Harris 4.00
CS-9 Jerry Rice 6.00
CS-10 Jim Brown 4.00
CS-11 Jim Kelly 5.00
CS-12 Jim Thorpe 4.00
CS-13 Joe Montana 10.00
CS-14 Joe Namath 5.00
CS-15 John Elway 10.00
CS-16 John Riggins 4.00
CS-17 Johnny Unitas 6.00
CS-19 Lawrence Taylor 4.00
CS-20 Mark Bavaro 3.00
CS-21 Michael Irvin 4.00
CS-22 Mike Singletary 3.00
CS-23 Paul Warfield 3.00
CS-24 Ray Nitschke 3.00
CS-25 Roger Staubach 5.00
CS-26 Terrell Davis 3.00
CS-27 Terry Bradshaw 6.00
CS-28 Tom Brady 5.00
CS-29 Troy Aikman 5.00
CS-30 Walter Payton 12.00
CS-31 Bart Starr, Ray Nitschke 10.00
CS-32 Bob Griese, Dan Marino 12.00
CS-33 Walter Payton, Mike Singletary 15.00
CS-34 Doak Walker, Barry Sanders 10.00
CS-35 Don Shula, Johnny Unitas 8.00
CS-36 Roger Staubach, Troy Aikman 6.00
CS-37 Michael Irvin, Emmitt Smith 8.00
CS-38 Joe Montana, Jerry Rice 12.00
CS-39 Jim Brown, Paul Warfield 5.00
CS-40 Jim Kelly, Thurman Thomas 6.00
CS-41 Joe Namath, John Riggins 6.00
CS-42 John Elway, Terrell Davis 12.00
CS-43 Lawrence Taylor, Mark Bavaro 5.00
CS-44 Terry Bradshaw, Franco Harris 8.00
CS-45 Doak Walker, Jim Thorpe 5.00
CS-46 Dan Marino, John Elway, Jim Kelly 15.00
CS-47 Johnny Unitas, Joe Namath, Bart Starr 12.00
CS-48 Walter Payton, Barry Sanders, Emmitt Smith 18.00
CS-49 Jim Thorpe, Doak Walker, Jim Brown 8.00
CS-50 Troy Aikman, Joe Montana, Tom Brady 15.00

2004 Donruss Classics Classic Game-Used Jersey

NM/M
Common Single (1-30): 12.00
Production 150 Sets
Common Combo (31-45): 40.00
Production 75 Sets
Common Triple (46-50): 125.00
Production 25 Sets
CS-1 Barry Sanders 30.00
CS-2 Bart Starr 40.00
CS-3 Bob Griese 12.00
CS-4 Dan Marino 30.00
CS-5 Doak Walker 12.00
CS-6 Don Shula 15.00
CS-7 Emmitt Smith 25.00
CS-8 Franco Harris 20.00
CS-9 Jerry Rice 20.00
CS-10 Jim Brown 20.00
CS-11 Jim Kelly 12.00
CS-12 Jim Thorpe 100.00
CS-13 Joe Montana 30.00
CS-14 Joe Namath 25.00
CS-15 John Elway 30.00
CS-16 John Riggins 15.00
CS-17 Johnny Unitas 50.00
CS-18 Larry Csonka 15.00
CS-19 Larry Taylor 15.00
CS-20 Mark Bavaro 12.00
CS-21 Michael Irvin 12.00
CS-22 Mike Singletary 20.00
CS-23 Paul Warfield 20.00
CS-24 Ray Nitschke 30.00
CS-25 Roger Staubach 30.00
CS-26 Terrell Davis 12.00
CS-27 Terry Bradshaw 30.00
CS-28 Tom Brady 15.00
CS-29 Troy Aikman 20.00
CS-30 Walter Payton 50.00
CC-31 Bart Starr, Ray Nitschke 75.00
CC-32 Bob Griese, Dan Marino 80.00
CC-33 Walter Payton, Mike Singletary 100.00
CC-34 Doak Walker, Barry Sanders 50.00
CC-35 Don Shula, Johnny Unitas 60.00
CC-36 Roger Staubach, Troy Aikman 50.00
CC-37 Michael Irvin, Emmitt Smith 40.00
CC-38 Joe Montana, Jerry Rice 80.00
CC-39 Jim Brown, Paul Warfield 40.00
CC-40 Jim Kelly, Thurman Thomas 40.00
CC-41 Joe Namath John Riggins 60.00
CC-42 John Elway, Terrell Davis 40.00
CC-43 Lawrence Taylor, Mark Bavaro 40.00
CC-44 Terry Bradshaw, Franco Harris 50.00
CC-45 Doak Walker, Jim Thorpe 100.00
CT-46 Dan Marino, John Elway, Jim Kelly 125.00
CT-47 Johnny Unitas, Joe Namath, Bart Starr 125.00
CT-48 Walter Payton, Barry Sanders, Emmitt Smith 300.00
CT-49 Jim Thorpe, Doak Walker, Jim Brown 200.00
CT-50 Troy Aikman, Joe Montana, Tom Brady 200.00

2004 Donruss Classics Classic Pigskin

NM/M
Common Player: 15.00
Production 250 Sets
Laces: 2X-5X
Production 25 Sets
CP-1 Roger Staubach 30.00
CP-2 Lawrence Taylor 15.00
CP-3 Joe Montana 50.00
CP-4 Emmitt Smith 25.00
CP-5 Troy Aikman 20.00
CP-6 Tom Brady 20.00

2004 Donruss Classics Dress Code Jersey

NM/M
Common Player: 6.00
Production 250 Sets
DC-1 Aaron Brooks 8.00
DC-2 Ahman Green 8.00
DC-3 Brian Urlacher 10.00
DC-4 Byron Leftwich 12.00
DC-5 Chad Johnson 6.00
DC-6 Chris Chambers 6.00
DC-7 Curtis Martin 6.00
DC-8 Daunte Culpepper 8.00
DC-9 David Carr 10.00
DC-10 Donovan McNabb 10.00
DC-11 Drew Bledsoe 8.00
DC-12 Drew Brees 6.00
DC-13 Eddie George 6.00
DC-14 Isaac Bruce 6.00
DC-15 Jake Plummer 6.00
DC-16 Jeff Garcia 6.00
DC-17 Jerome Bettis 6.00
DC-18 Jevon Kearse 6.00
DC-19 Joey Harrington 6.00
DC-20 Kurt Warner 6.00
DC-21 LaVar Arrington 20.00
DC-22 Laveranues Coles 6.00
DC-23 Marc Bulger 6.00
DC-24 Stephen Davis 6.00
DC-25 Terrell Owens 8.00

2004 Donruss Classics Legendary Materials G-U Jersey

NM/M
Common Player: 12.00
Production 100 Sets
Prime Game-Used Jersey: No Pricing
Production 5 Sets
LP-1 Barry Sanders 30.00
LP-2 Bart Starr 40.00
LP-3 Bruce Smith 12.00
LP-4 Dan Marino 30.00
LP-5 Deion Sanders 15.00
LP-6 Earl Campbell 20.00
LP-7 Franco Harris 20.00
LP-8 Fred Biletnikoff 20.00
LP-9 Jim Brown 25.00
LP-10 Joe Montana 40.00
LP-11 Joe Namath 30.00
LP-12 Johnny Unitas 50.00
LP-13 Larry Csonka 15.00
LP-14 Lawrence Taylor 15.00
LP-15 Mark Bavaro 12.00
LP-16 Mike Singletary 15.00
LP-17 Ozzie Newsome 15.00
LP-18 Sterling Sharpe 15.00
LP-19 Steve Largent 25.00
LP-20 Terry Bradshaw 30.00
LP-21 Thurman Thomas 12.00
LP-22 Walter Payton 60.00
LP-23 Warren Moon 15.00
LP-24 Jim Thorpe 100.00
LP-25 Reggie White 20.00

2004 Donruss Classics Legendary Players

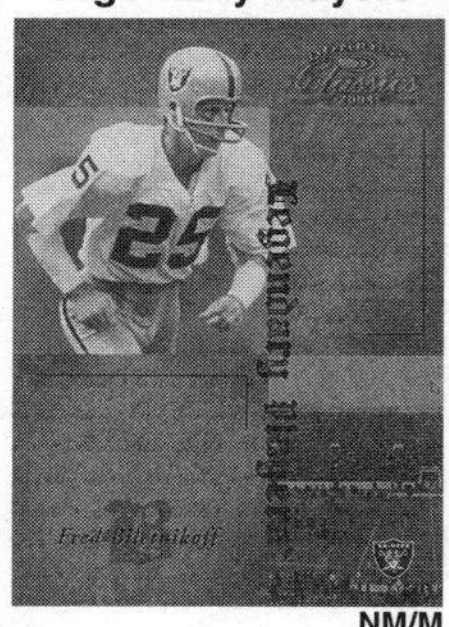

NM/M
Common Player: 3.00
Production 1,000 Sets
LP-1 Barry Sanders 8.00
LP-2 Bart Starr 8.00
LP-3 Bruce Smith 3.00
LP-4 Dan Marino 10.00
LP-5 Deion Sanders 4.00
LP-6 Earl Campbell 3.00
LP-7 Franco Harris 4.00
LP-8 Fred Biletnikoff 3.00
LP-9 Jim Brown 4.00
LP-10 Joe Montana 10.00
LP-11 Joe Namath 5.00
LP-12 Johnny Unitas 6.00
LP-14 Lawrence Taylor 4.00
LP-15 Mark Bavaro 3.00
LP-16 Mike Singletary 3.00
LP-17 Ozzie Newsome 3.00
LP-18 Sterling Sharpe 3.00
LP-19 Steve Largent 4.00
LP-20 Terry Bradshaw 6.00
LP-21 Thurman Thomas 3.00
LP-22 Walter Payton 12.00
LP-23 Warren Moon 3.00
LP-24 Jim Thorpe 4.00
LP-25 Reggie White 3.00

2004 Donruss Classics Membership

NM/M
Common Player: 3.00
Production 1,000 Sets
M-1 Anquan Boldin 3.00
M-2 Barry Sanders 8.00
M-3 Brett Favre 8.00
M-4 Chad Pennington 4.00
M-5 Clinton Portis 5.00
M-6 Dan Marino 10.00
M-7 Earl Campbell 3.00
M-8 Jamal Lewis 3.00
M-9 Jim Brown 5.00
M-10 Jim Kelly 5.00
M-11 Joe Montana 10.00
M-12 Joe Namath 5.00
M-13 John Elway 10.00
M-14 Johnny Unitas 6.00
M-15 LaDainian Tomlinson 4.00
M-16 Lawrence Taylor 4.00
M-17 Marcus Allen 5.00
M-18 Marshall Faulk 4.00
M-19 Michael Vick 6.00
M-20 Peyton Manning 5.00
M-21 Ricky Williams 3.00
M-22 Roger Staubach 5.00
M-23 Steve McNair 3.00
M-24 Tom Brady 5.00
M-25 Troy Aikman 5.00

2004 Donruss Classics Sideline Generals

NM/M
Common Player: 3.00
Production 2,000 Sets
SG-1 Barry Switzer, Jimmy Johnson 5.00
SG-2 Bill Walsh, Bill Belichick 5.00
SG-3 Chuck Noll, Bill Cowher 5.00
SG-4 Don Shula, Tony Dungy 3.00
SG-5 Dick Vermeil, Andy Reid 3.00

2004 Donruss Classics Sideline Generals Signatures

NM/M

Production 250 Sets
SG-1 Barry Switzer, Jimmy Johnson 75.00
SG-2 Bill Walsh, Bill Belichick 60.00
SG-3 Chuck Noll, Bill Cowher 120.00
SG-4 Don Shula, Tony Dungy 40.00
SG-5 Dick Vermeil, Andy Reid 60.00

2004 Donruss Classics Significant Signatures Red

NM/M

Common Player: 20.00
Numbered to varying quantities
7 Kyle Boller/50 20.00
9 Todd Heap/50 25.00
15 Steve Smith 25.00
21 Rudi Johnson 25.00
33 Javon Walker/50 25.00
36 Domanick Davis 25.00
45 Dante Hall/25
48 Chris Chambers/25
55 Adam Vinatieri/75 25.00
68 Santana Moss 20.00
95 Derrick Mason/90 20.00
99 Laveranues Coles/25
101 Archie Manning/75 30.00
103 Bo Jackson/50 125.00
105 Christian Okoye 30.00
106 Daryl Johnston 25.00
107 Deacon Jones 20.00
110 Lynn Swann/62 125.00
111 Don Maynard 20.00
114 Fred Biletnikoff 20.00
116 George Blanda/84 30.00
117 Herman Edwards 20.00
118 Herschel Walker 30.00
120 James Lofton 20.00
121 Jim Plunkett 25.00
123 Joe Greene/75 40.00
124 John Riggins 60.00
125 L.C. Greenwood 30.00
126 Larry Csonka/11
127 Leroy Kelly 20.00
130 Mark Bavaro/50 30.00
131 *Mel Blount* 30.00
133 Mike Ditka/75 50.00
136 Paul Hornung 30.00
137 Paul Warfield 30.00
138 Randall Cunningham 25.00
141 Richard Dent/50 20.00
142 Sammy Baugh 40.00
143 Sonny Jurgensen 30.00
144 Sterling Sharpe/66 40.00
145 Steve Largent/75 40.00
148 Thurman Thomas 20.00
150 Warren Moon/50 25.00
164 D.J. Hackett 20.00
182 Bernard Berrian 25.00
184 Derrick Hamilton 25.00
185 Jerricho Cotchery 25.00
207 Mewelde Moore 25.00
208 Cedric Cobbs 25.00
211 Devery Henderson/75 25.00
212 Johnnie Morant 25.00
213 Keary Colbert 25.00
215 P.K. Sam 25.00
233 Greg Jones/75 30.00

2004 Donruss Classics Significant Signatures Green

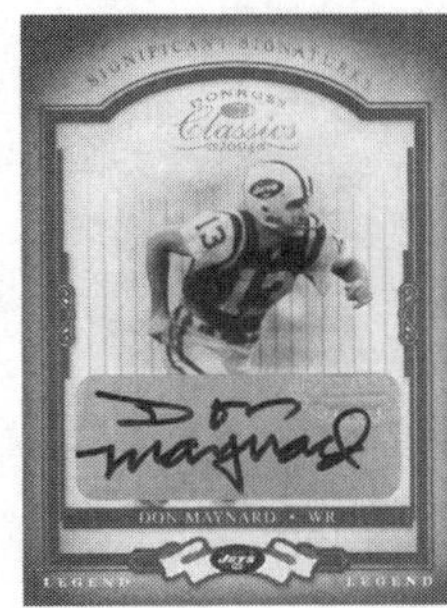

NM/M

Common Player: 20.00
Production 75 Sets
7 Kyle Boller 20.00
9 Todd Heap 25.00
15 Steve Smith 30.00
21 Rudi Johnson 30.00
33 Javon Walker 25.00
36 Domanick Davis 30.00
45 Dante Hall 30.00
55 Adam Vinatieri 25.00
68 Santana Moss 25.00
78 Kendrell Bell 30.00
95 Derrick Mason 25.00
99 Laveranues Coles 25.00
100 Patrick Ramsey 25.00
101 Archie Manning 30.00
104 Brian Griese 30.00
105 Christian Okoye 40.00
106 Daryl Johnston 30.00
107 Deacon Jones 25.00
109 Dick Butkus 50.00
110 Lynn Swann 125.00
111 Don Maynard 25.00
112 Don Shula 25.00
113 Franco Harris 40.00
114 Fred Biletnikoff 25.00
116 George Blanda 30.00
117 Herman Edwards 25.00
118 Herschel Walker 40.00
119 Jack Lambert 50.00
120 James Lofton 25.00
121 *Jim Plunkett* 30.00
123 Joe Greene 40.00
124 John Riggins 60.00
125 L.C. Greenwood 40.00
127 Leroy Kelly 25.00
129 Marcus Allen 40.00
130 Mark Bavaro 30.00
131 Mel Blount 40.00
132 Michael Irvin 40.00
133 Mike Ditka 50.00
134 Mike Singletary 30.00
135 Ozzie Newsome 30.00
136 Paul Hornung 40.00
137 Paul Warfield 40.00
138 Randall Cunningham 30.00
140 Reggie White 40.00
141 Richard Dent 25.00
142 Sammy Baugh 50.00
143 Sonny Jurgensen 40.00
144 Sterling Sharpe 40.00
145 Steve Largent 40.00
146 Terrell Davis 30.00
148 Thurman Thomas 25.00
150 Warren Moon 25.00
164 D.J. Hackett 25.00
172 Ricardo Colclough 30.00
182 Bernard Berrian 30.00
184 Derrick Hamilton 30.00
185 Jerricho Cotchery 30.00
205 Quincy Wilson 30.00
207 Mewelde Moore 30.00
208 Cedric Cobbs 30.00
210 Michael Jenkins 30.00
211 Devery Henderson 25.00
212 Johnnie Morant 30.00
213 Keary Colbert 30.00
214 Devard Darling 30.00
215 P.K. Sam 30.00
218 Tommie Harris 30.00
219 Vince Wilfork 30.00
221 D.J. Williams 30.00
229 Philip Rivers 75.00
233 Greg Jones 40.00
234 Tatum Bell 50.00
236 Julius Jones 60.00
244 Lee Evans 60.00

2004 Donruss Classics Significant Signatures Platinum

No Pricing
Production 25 Sets

2004 Donruss Classics Team Colors Away Jersey

NM/M

Common Player: 10.00
Production 150 Sets
Home Jersey: .75X-1.5X
Production 75 Sets
Prime Jersey: 1.5X-3X
Production 25 Sets
TC-1 Anquan Boldin 10.00
TC-2 Barry Sanders 25.00
TC-3 Brian Urlacher 10.00
TC-4 Daunte Culpepper 10.00
TC-5 Deuce McAllister 10.00
TC-6 Donovan McNabb 12.00
TC-7 Drew Bledsoe 10.00
TC-8 Earl Campbell 12.00
TC-9 Edgerrin James 12.00
TC-10 Jeremy Shockey 10.00
TC-11 Jerry Rice 20.00
TC-12 Jim Kelly 15.00
TC-13 Brett Favre 25.00
TC-14 John Elway 30.00
TC-15 Kurt Warner 10.00
TC-16 LaDainian Tomlinson 12.00
TC-17 Marshall Faulk 12.00
TC-18 Marvin Harrison 10.00
TC-19 Peyton Manning 15.00
TC-20 Plaxico Burress 10.00
TC-21 Priest Holmes 12.00
TC-22 Randy Moss 15.00
TC-23 Steve McNair 10.00
TC-24 Torry Holt 10.00
TC-25 Walter Payton 40.00

2004 Donruss Classics Timeless Tributes Green

Current (1-100): 8X-20X
Legends (101-150): 3X-6X
Rookies (151-175): 2X-4X
Rookies (176-200): 1.5X-3X
Rookies (201-225): 1.5X-3X
Rookies (226-250): 1X-2.5X
Production 50 Sets

A player's name in *italic* type indicates a rookie card.

2004 Donruss Classics Timeless Tributes Red

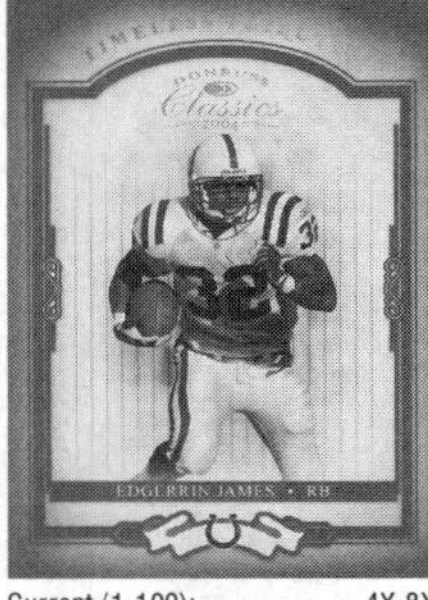

Current (1-100): 4X-8X
Legends (101-150): 1.5X-3X
Rookies (151-175): 1X-2X
Rookies (176-200): .75X-1.5X
Rookies (201-225): .75X-1.5X
Rookies (226-250): .5X-1.25X
Production 100 Sets

2004 Donruss Classics Timeless Tributes Platinum

No Pricing
Production 1 Set

2004 Donruss Classics Timeless Triples Game-Used Jersey

NM/M

Common Player: 50.00
Production 100 Sets
Triples Game-Used
Prime: No Pricing
Production 10 Sets
TT-1 Fred Biletnikoff, Jim Plunkett, Marcus Allen 50.00
TT-2 Dick Butkus, Walter Payton, Mike Singletary 125.00
TT-3 Terry Bradshaw, Franco Harris, Lynn Swann 100.00
TT-4 Bart Starr, Ray Nitschke, Brett Favre 120.00
TT-5 Bob Griese, Larry Csonka, Dan Marino 80.00
TT-6 Don Shula, Johnny Unitas, Peyton Manning 80.00
TT-7 Joe Montana, Jerry Rice, Terrell Owens 100.00
TT-8 Troy Aikman, Emmitt Smith, Michael Irvin 80.00
TT-9 Jim Brown, Paul Warfield, Leroy Kelly 60.00
TT-10 Joe Namath, John Riggins, Don Maynard 60.00
TT-11 John Elway, Terrell Davis, Rod Smith 75.00
TT-12 Jim Kelly, Bruce Smith, Thurman Thomas 50.00
TT-13 Joe Greene, L.C. Greenwood, Mel Blount 50.00
TT-14 Roger Staubach, Tony Dorsett, Deion Sanders 50.00

2004 Donruss Classics VIP Membership Game-Used Jersey

NM/M

Common Player: 8.00
Production 250 Sets
M-1 Anquan Boldin 8.00
M-2 Barry Sanders 25.00
M-2 Barry Sanders/25 Auto
M-3 Brett Favre 20.00
M-4 Chad Pennington 10.00
M-5 Clinton Portis 12.00
M-6 Dan Marino 25.00
M-6 Dan Marino/25 Auto
M-7 Earl Campbell 10.00
M-7 Earl Campbell/25 Auto
M-8 Jamal Lewis 8.00
M-9 Jim Brown 15.00
M-9 Jim Brown/50 Auto
M-10 Jim Kelly 12.00
M-10 Jim Kelly/25 Auto
M-11 Joe Montana 30.00
M-11 Joe Montana/25 Auto
M-12 Joe Namath 20.00
M-12 Joe Namath/25 Auto
M-13 John Elway 25.00
M-13 John Elway/25 Auto
M-14 Johnny Unitas 25.00
M-15 LaDainian Tomlinson 10.00
M-16 Lawrence Taylor 15.00
M-16 Lawrence Taylor/25 Auto
M-17 Marcus Allen 20.00
M-18 Marshall Faulk 10.00
M-19 Michael Vick 15.00
M-20 Peyton Manning 12.00
M-21 Ricky Williams 8.00
M-22 Roger Staubach 20.00
M-22 Roger Staubach/25 Auto
M-23 Steve McNair 8.00
M-24 Tom Brady 12.00
M-25 Troy Aikman 20.00
M-25 Troy Aikman/25 Auto

2004 Donruss Elite

NM/M

Common Player (1-100): .40
Minor Stars: .60
Unlisted Stars: 1.00
Common Rookie (101-200): 4.00
Production 500 Sets
Pack (5): 7.50
Box (20): 105.00
1 Emmitt Smith 2.50
2 Anquan Boldin 1.00
3 Michael Vick 2.50
4 Peerless Price .60
5 T.J. Duckett .60
6 Warrick Dunn .60
7 Jamal Lewis 1.00
8 Kyle Boller 1.00
9 Todd Heap .40
10 Ray Lewis .60
11 Drew Bledsoe 1.00
12 Eric Moulds .60
13 Travis Henry .60
14 Jake Delhomme .60
15 Stephen Davis .60
16 Steve Smith .60
17 Anthony Thomas .60
18 Brian Urlacher 1.00
19 Rex Grossman 1.00
20 Chad Johnson .60
21 Carson Palmer 1.50
22 Rudi Johnson .60
23 Peter Warrick .60
24 Andre Davis .60
25 Tim Couch .60
26 Quincy Carter .60
27 Roy Williams .60
28 Terence Newman .60
29 Clinton Portis 2.00
30 Jake Plummer .60
31 Rod Smith .60
32 Charles Rogers 1.00
33 Joey Harrington 1.00
34 Ahman Green 1.00
35 Brett Favre 3.00
36 Javon Walker .60
37 Andre Johnson 1.00
38 David Carr 1.50
39 Domanick Davis .60
40 Edgerrin James 1.50
41 Marvin Harrison 1.00
42 Peyton Manning 2.00
43 Reggie Wayne .60
44 Byron Leftwich 2.00
45 Fred Taylor 1.00
46 Jimmy Smith .60
47 Priest Holmes 1.50
48 Tony Gonzalez .60
49 Trent Green .60
50 Chris Chambers .60
51 Ricky Williams 1.50
52 Zach Thomas .60
53 Daunte Culpepper 1.00
54 Michael Bennett 1.00
55 Moe Williams .40
56 Randy Moss 2.00
57 Deion Branch .60
58 Tom Brady 2.00
59 Tedy Bruschi .40
60 Aaron Brooks 1.00
61 Deuce McAllister 1.00
62 Joe Horn .60
63 Jeremy Shockey 1.00
64 Kerry Collins .60
65 Michael Strahan .60
66 Tiki Barber .60
67 Chad Pennington 1.00
68 Curtis Martin 1.00
69 Santana Moss .60
70 Jerry Porter .60
71 Jerry Rice 2.50
72 Tim Brown 1.00
73 Brian Westbrook .60
74 Correll Buckhalter .60
75 Donovan McNabb 1.50
76 Hines Ward 1.00
77 Kendrell Bell .60
78 Plaxico Burress 1.00
79 David Boston .60
80 Drew Brees .60
81 LaDainian Tomlinson 1.50
82 Jeff Garcia 1.00
83 Kevan Barlow 6.00
84 Terrell Owens 1.00
85 Koren Robinson .60
86 Matt Hasselbeck .60
87 Shaun Alexander 1.00
88 Isaac Bruce .60
89 Marc Bulger .60
90 Marshall Faulk 1.50
91 Torry Holt 1.00
92 Brad Johnson .60
93 Derrick Brooks .60
94 Keenan McCardell .40
95 Derrick Mason .60
96 Eddie George .60
97 Steve McNair 1.00
98 Jevon Kearse .60
99 Laveranues Coles .60
100 Patrick Ramsey .60
101 *Adimchinobe Echemandu* 4.00
102 *Ahmad Carroll* 8.00
103 *Antwan Odom* 6.00
104 *B.J. Johnson* 6.00
105 *Ben Roethlisberger* 75.00
106 *Ben Troupe* 6.00
107 *Ben Watson* 6.00
108 *Bernard Berrian* 8.00
109 *Bob Sanders* 6.00
110 *Brandon Everage* 6.00
111 *Brandon Miree* 5.00
112 *Carlos Francis* 5.00
113 *Cedric Cobbs* 8.00
114 *Chad Lavalais* 5.00
115 *Chris Collins* 5.00
116 *Chris Gamble* 8.00
117 *Chris Perry* 12.00
118 *Cody Pickett* 6.00
119 *Craig Krenzel* 6.00
120 *D.J. Hackett* 5.00
121 *D.J. Williams* 8.00
122 *Darius Watts* 8.00
123 *Darnell Dockett* 5.00
124 *DeAngelo Hall* 10.00
125 *Derek Abney* 6.00
126 *Derrick Hamilton* 5.00
127 *Derrick Strait* 8.00
128 *Devard Darling* 6.00
129 *Devery Henderson* 6.00
130 *Dontarrious Thomas* 5.00
131 *Drew Henson* 20.00
132 *Dunta Robinson* 6.00
133 *Dwan Edwards* 4.00
134 *Eli Manning* 50.00
135 *Ernest Wilford* 6.00
136 *Fred Russell* 6.00
137 *Greg Jones* 8.00
138 *Igor Olshansky* 4.00
139 *J.P. Losman* 12.00
140 *Jared Lorenzen* 6.00
141 *Jarrett Payton* 10.00
142 *Jason Babin* 6.00
143 *Jason Fife* 6.00
144 *Jeff Smoker* 8.00
145 *Jeremy LeSueur* 4.00
146 *Jerricho Cotchery* 6.00
147 *John Navarre* 8.00
148 *John Standeford* 4.00
149 *Johnnie Morant* 6.00
150 *Jonathan Vilma* 8.00
151 *Josh Davis* 6.00
152 *Josh Harris* 6.00
153 *Julius Jones* 25.00
154 *Justin Jenkins* 4.00
155 *Karlos Dansby* 6.00
156 *Keary Colbert* 8.00
157 *Keith Smith* 4.00
158 *Keiwan Ratliff* 6.00
159 *Kellen Winslow Jr.* 12.00
160 *Kendrick Starling* 4.00
161 *Kenechi Udeze* 8.00
162 *Kevin Jones* 20.00
163 *Larry Fitzgerald* 25.00
164 *Lee Evans* 12.00
165 *Luke McCown* 8.00
166 *Marquise Hill* 6.00
167 *Matt Schaub* 8.00
168 *Matt Ware* 6.00
169 *Matt Mauck* 8.00
170 *Maurice Mann* 6.00
171 *Mewelde Moore* 6.00
172 *Michael Boulware* 6.00
173 *Michael Clayton* 12.00
174 *Michael Jenkins* 10.00
175 *Michael Turner* 4.00
176 *B.J. Symons* 6.00
177 *Nathan Vasher* 4.00
178 *P.K. Sam* 8.00
179 *Philip Rivers* 25.00
180 *Quincy Wilson* 8.00
181 *Ran Carthon* 6.00
182 *Randy Starks* 4.00
183 *Rashaun Woods* 12.00
184 *Reggie Williams* 10.00
185 *Ricardo Colclough* 6.00
186 *Robert Kent* 4.00
187 *Roy Williams* 25.00
188 *Samie Parker* 6.00
189 *Scott Rislov* 6.00
190 *Sean Jones* 6.00
191 *Sean Taylor* 20.00
192 *Steven Jackson* 20.00
193 *Stuart Schweigert* 4.00
194 *Tatum Bell* 12.00
195 *Teddy Lehman* 8.00
196 *Tommie Harris* 8.00
197 *Troy Fleming* 4.00
198 *Vince Wilfork* 8.00
199 *Will Poole* 6.00
200 *Will Smith* 8.00

2004 Donruss Elite Aspirations

Stars/60-99: 5X-10X
Rookies/60-99: 1X-2X
Stars/30-59: 6X-12X
Rookies/30-59: 1.5X-3X
Stars/20-29: 10X-20X
Rookies/20-29: 2X-4X

2004 Donruss Elite Status

Stars/60-99: 5X-10X
Rookies/60-99: 1X-2X
Stars/30-59: 6X-12X
Rookies/30-59: 1.5X-3X
Stars/20-29: 10X-20X
Rookies/20-29: 2X-4X

2004 Donruss Elite Career Best

NM/M

Common Player: 3.00
Production 1500 Sets
CB-1 Barry Sanders 5.00
CB-2 Brett Favre 6.00
CB-3 Chad Pennington 3.00
CB-4 Clinton Portis 3.00
CB-5 Dan Marino 6.00
CB-6 Priest Holmes 3.00
CB-7 Deuce McAllister 3.00
CB-8 Jerry Rice 5.00
CB-9 John Elway 6.00
CB-10 Marshall Faulk 3.00
CB-11 Emmitt Smith 5.00
CB-12 Marvin Harrison 3.00
CB-13 Peyton Manning 4.00
CB-14 Ricky Williams 3.00
CB-15 Steve McNair 3.00

2004 Donruss Elite Career Best Materials

NM/M

Common Player: 8.00
Production 250 Sets
Prime: 2X-4X
Prime Production 25 Sets
Year: 1X-1.5X
Year Production 84-103
CB-1 Barry Sanders 25.00
CB-2 Brett Favre 20.00
CB-3 Chad Pennington 8.00
CB-4 Clinton Portis 10.00
CB-5 Dan Marino 30.00
CB-6 Priest Holmes 10.00
CB-7 Deuce McAllister 8.00
CB-8 Jerry Rice 15.00
CB-9 John Elway 25.00
CB-10 Marshall Faulk 8.00
CB-11 Emmitt Smith 20.00
CB-12 Marvin Harrison 8.00
CB-13 Peyton Manning 12.00
CB-14 Ricky Williams 10.00
CB-15 Steve McNair 8.00

2004 Donruss Elite College Ties

NM/M

Common Player: 2.00
Production 2000 Sets
CT-1 Deuce McAllister, Eli Manning 6.00
CT-2 Torry Holt, Philip Rivers 5.00
CT-3 Patrick Ramsey, J.P. Losman 3.00
CT-4 Chad Johnson, Steven Jackson 4.00
CT-5 Michael Vick, Kevin Jones 5.00
CT-6 Ricky Williams, Roy Williams 4.00
CT-7 Corey Dillon, Reggie Williams 2.00
CT-8 Domanick Davis, Michael Clayton 2.00
CT-9 Jeremy Shockey, Kellen Winslow Jr. 4.00
CT-10 Anthony Thomas, Chris Perry 3.00
CT-11 Antonio Bryant, Larry Fitzgerald 4.00
CT-12 Eddie George, Michael Jenkins 2.00
CT-13 Warrick Dunn, Greg Jones 2.00
CT-14 Michael Bennett, Lee Evans 2.00
CT-15 Jerry Porter, Quincy Wilson 2.00

2004 Donruss Elite Elite Series

NM/M

Common Player: 2.00
Production 750 Sets
ES-1 Aaron Brooks 2.00
ES-2 Ahman Green 4.00
ES-3 Anquan Boldin 4.00
ES-4 Brett Favre 10.00
ES-5 Brian Urlacher 4.00
ES-6 Byron Leftwich 6.00
ES-7 Chad Johnson 2.00
ES-8 Chad Pennington 4.00
ES-9 Chris Chambers 2.00
ES-10 Clinton Portis 5.00
ES-11 David Carr 5.00
ES-12 Deuce McAllister 4.00
ES-13 Drew Bledsoe 4.00
ES-14 Edgerrin James 4.00
ES-15 Jamal Lewis 4.00
ES-16 Jerry Rice 8.00
ES-17 Jimmy Smith 2.00
ES-18 LaDainian Tomlinson 4.00
ES-19 Michael Vick 8.00
ES-20 Donovan McNabb 5.00
ES-21 Peyton Manning 6.00
ES-22 Priest Holmes 4.00
ES-23 Randy Moss 5.00
ES-24 Ricky Williams 4.00
ES-25 Steve McNair 4.00
ES-26 Terrell Owens 4.00
ES-27 Tom Brady 6.00
ES-28 Emmitt Smith 8.00
ES-29 Daunte Culpepper 4.00
ES-30 Joey Harrington 4.00

2004 Donruss Elite Elite Series Jerseys Bronze

NM/M

Common Players: 6.00
Bronze Production 250 Sets
Silver: 1X
Silver Production 150 Sets
Gold: 2X-4X
Gold Production 25 Sets
Platinum Production 10 Sets
ES-1 Aaron Brooks 6.00
ES-2 Ahman Green 8.00
ES-3 Anquan Boldin 8.00
ES-4 Brett Favre 20.00
ES-5 Brian Urlacher 10.00
ES-6 Byron Leftwich 10.00
ES-7 Chad Johnson 6.00
ES-8 Chad Pennington 8.00
ES-9 Chris Chambers 6.00
ES-10 Clinton Portis 10.00
ES-11 David Carr 8.00
ES-12 Deuce McAllister 8.00
ES-13 Drew Bledsoe 8.00
ES-14 Edgerrin James 8.00
ES-15 Jamal Lewis 8.00
ES-16 Jerry Rice 15.00

ES-17	Jimmy Smith	6.00
ES-18	LaDainian Tomlinson	8.00
ES-19	Michael Vick	15.00
ES-20	Donovan McNabb	8.00
ES-21	Peyton Manning	12.00
ES-22	Priest Holmes	10.00
ES-23	Randy Moss	10.00
ES-24	Ricky Williams	10.00
ES-25	Steve McNair	8.00
ES-26	Terrell Owens	8.00
ES-27	Tom Brady	12.00
ES-28	Emmitt Smith	20.00
ES-29	Daunte Culpepper	8.00
ES-30	Joey Harrington	8.00

2004 Donruss Elite Face to Face

		NM/M
Common Player:		10.00
Production 125 Sets		
FF-1	Jim Kelly, Troy Aikman	20.00
FF-2	Brett Favre, Randy Moss	40.00
FF-3	Ricky Williams, Deuce McAllister	15.00
FF-4	Brian Urlacher, Michael Bennett	20.00
FF-5	John Elway, Dan Marino	60.00
FF-6	Zach Thomas, Travis Henry	10.00
FF-7	Peyton Manning, Champ Bailey	15.00
FF-8	Marshall Faulk, Shaun Alexander	15.00
FF-9	Barry Sanders, Mike Singletary	25.00
FF-10	Emmitt Smith, Terrell Owens	25.00
FF-11	Priest Holmes, Rich Gannon	15.00
FF-12	Peyton Manning, Steve McNair	15.00
FF-13	Jeremy Shockey, Todd Heap	12.00
FF-14	Chad Pennington, Tom Brady	25.00
FF-15	Chad Johnson, Marvin Harrison	12.00
FF-16	Jeff Garcia, Marc Bulger	12.00
FF-17	Ray Lewis, Eddie George	12.00
FF-18	Torry Holt, Koren Robinson	12.00
FF-19	Jerry Rice	30.00
FF-20	Matt Hasselbeck, Anquan Boldin	12.00
FF-21	Jake Plummer, Trent Green	12.00
FF-22	Chris Chambers, Santana Moss	12.00
FF-23	Peter Warrick, Ed Reed	12.00
FF-24	Kevin Faulk, Corey Dillon	10.00
FF-25	Ahman Green, Duce Staley	15.00

2004 Donruss Elite Gridiron Gear Bronze

		NM/M
Common Player:		5.00
Bronze Production 250 Sets		
Silver:		1X
Silver Production 150 Sets		
Gold:		2X-4X
Gold Production 25 Sets		
Platinum Production 10 Sets		
GG-1	Ashley Lelie	5.00
GG-2	Chris Chambers	5.00
GG-3	Correll Buckhalter	5.00
GG-4	Donovan McNabb	8.00
GG-5	Drew Brees	6.00
GG-6	Fred Taylor	6.00
GG-7	Hines Ward	6.00
GG-8	Isaac Bruce	6.00
GG-9	Jeff Garcia	6.00
GG-10	Jerome Bettis	6.00
GG-11	Jevon Kearse	6.00
GG-12	Jimmy Smith	6.00
GG-13	Joey Harrington	8.00
GG-14	Josh Reed	5.00
GG-15	LaDainian Tomlinson	8.00
GG-16	Marc Bulger	6.00
GG-17	Steve McNair	8.00
GG-18	Peyton Manning	12.00
GG-19	Randy Moss	10.00
GG-20	Santana Moss	6.00
GG-21	Tim Brown	6.00
GG-22	Dan Marino	30.00
GG-23	John Elway	25.00
GG-24	Barry Sanders	25.00
GG-25	Troy Aikman	15.00

2004 Donruss Elite Lineage

		NM/M
Common Player:		2.00
Inserted 1:24		
L-1	Aaron Brooks, Michael Vick	6.00
L-2	Ronde Barber, Tiki Barber	2.00
L-3	Archie Manning, Eli Manning, Peyton Manning	10.00
L-4	Chad Johnson, Keyshawn Johnson	3.00
L-5	Anthony Dorsett, Tony Dorsett	3.00

2004 Donruss Elite Lineage Autographs

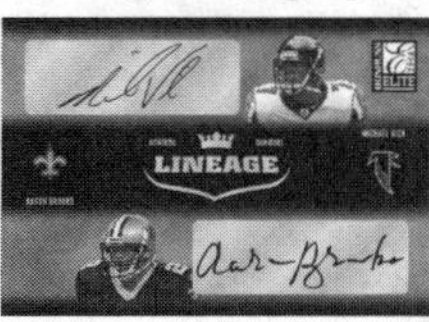

		NM/M
Common Player:		30.00
Production 100 Sets		
L-1	Aaron Brooks, Michael Vick	125.00
L-2	Ronde Barber, Tiki Barber	30.00
L-3	Archie Manning, Eli Manning, Peyton Manning	600.00
L-4	Chad Johnson, Keyshawn Johnson	40.00
L-5	Anthony Dorsett, Tony Dorsett	50.00

2004 Donruss Elite Passing the Torch

		NM/M
Common Player:		2.00
1-20 Production 1000 Sets		
21-30 Production 500 Sets		
PT-1	Earl Campbell	3.00
PT-2	Domanick Davis	2.00
PT-3	Ricky Williams	4.00
PT-4	Larry Csonka	3.00
PT-5	John Elway	8.00
PT-6	Jake Plummer	2.00
PT-7	Mike Singletary	3.00
PT-8	Brian Urlacher	3.00
PT-9	Drew Bledsoe	3.00
PT-10	Tom Brady	5.00
PT-11	Paul Hornung	3.00
PT-12	Ahman Green	4.00
PT-13	Randall Cunningham	2.00
PT-14	Donovan McNabb	4.00
PT-15	Christian Okoye	2.00
PT-16	Priest Holmes	4.00
PT-17	Warren Moon	3.00
PT-18	Steve McNair	3.00
PT-19	Archie Manning	3.00
PT-20	Eli Manning	10.00
PT-21	Domanick Davis, Earl Campbell	5.00
PT-22	Larry Csonka, Ricky Williams	5.00
PT-23	Jake Plummer, John Elway	12.00
PT-24	Brian Urlacher, Mike Singletary	8.00
PT-25	Drew Bledsoe, Tom Brady	8.00
PT-26	Ahman Green, Paul Hornung	6.00
PT-27	Donovan McNabb, Randall Cunningham	6.00
PT-28	Christian Okoye, Priest Holmes	6.00
PT-29	Steve McNair, Warren Moon	6.00
PT-30	Archie Manning, Eli Manning	15.00

2004 Donruss Elite Passing the Torch Autographs

		NM/M
Common Player:		25.00
1-20 Production 100 Sets		
21-30 Production 50 Sets		
PT-1	Earl Campbell	50.00
PT-2	Domanick Davis	25.00
PT-3	Ricky Williams	50.00
PT-4	Larry Csonka	40.00
PT-5	John Elway	125.00
PT-6	Jake Plummer	30.00
PT-7	Mike Singletary	40.00
PT-8	Brian Urlacher	50.00
PT-9	Drew Bledsoe	30.00
PT-10	Tom Brady	100.00
PT-11	Paul Hornung	40.00
PT-12	Ahman Green	40.00
PT-13	Randall Cunningham	30.00
PT-14	Donovan McNabb	40.00
PT-15	Christian Okoye	25.00
PT-16	Priest Holmes	40.00
PT-17	Warren Moon	30.00
PT-18	Steve McNair	40.00
PT-19	Archie Manning	40.00
PT-20	Eli Manning	150.00
PT-21	Domanick Davis, Earl Campbell	60.00
PT-22	Larry Csonka, Ricky Williams	80.00
PT-23	Jake Plummer, John Elway	250.00
PT-24	Brian Urlacher, Mike Singletary	100.00
PT-25	Drew Bledsoe, Tom Brady	150.00
PT-26	Ahman Green, Paul Hornung	100.00
PT-27	Donovan McNabb, Randall Cunningham	150.00
PT-28	Christian Okoye, Priest Holmes	60.00
PT-29	Steve McNair, Warren Moon	50.00
PT-30	Archie Manning, Eli Manning	300.00

2004 Donruss Elite Throwback Threads

		NM/M
1-30 Production 150 Sets		
31-45 Production 75 Sets		
TT-1	Mark Bavaro	10.00
TT-2	Jeremy Shockey	10.00
TT-3	Tony Dorsett	15.00
TT-4	Clinton Portis	12.00
TT-5	Lynn Swann	40.00
TT-6	Hines Ward	8.00
TT-7	Larry Csonka	20.00
TT-8	Ricky Williams	12.00
TT-9	Troy Aikman	30.00
TT-10	Quincy Carter	8.00
TT-11	Jim Kelly	25.00
TT-12	Drew Bledsoe	10.00
TT-13	Mike Singletary	25.00
TT-14	Brian Urlacher	10.00
TT-15	Warren Moon	15.00
TT-16	David Carr	10.00
TT-17	Thurman Thomas	15.00
TT-18	Travis Henry	8.00
TT-19	Marcus Allen	20.00
TT-20	Priest Holmes	12.00
TT-21	Randall Cunningham	15.00
TT-22	Donovan McNabb	10.00
TT-23	Joe Namath	40.00
TT-24	Chad Pennington	10.00
TT-25	Jim Brown	40.00
TT-26	Jamal Lewis	10.00
TT-27	Walter Payton	50.00
TT-28	LaDainian Tomlinson	10.00
TT-29	Johnny Unitas	50.00
TT-30	Peyton Manning	15.00
TT-31	Mark Bavaro, Jeremy Shockey	20.00
TT-32	Tony Dorsett, Clinton Portis	25.00
TT-33	Lynn Swann, Hines Ward	50.00
TT-34	Larry Csonka, Ricky Williams	25.00
TT-35	Troy Aikman, Quincy Carter	30.00
TT-36	Jim Kelly, Drew Bledsoe	25.00
TT-37	Mike Singletary, Brian Urlacher	30.00
TT-38	Warren Moon, David Carr	25.00
TT-39	Thurman Thomas, Travis Henry	25.00
TT-40	Marcus Allen, Priest Holmes	25.00
TT-41	Randall Cunningham, Donovan McNabb	25.00
TT-42	Joe Namath, Chad Pennington	50.00
TT-43	Jim Brown, Jamal Lewis	40.00
TT-44	Walter Payton, LaDainian Tomlinson	80.00
TT-45	Johnny Unitas, Peyton Manning	50.00

2004 Donruss Elite Throwback Threads Prime

Prime 1-30:		1.5X-3X
Prime 31-45:		1X-2X
Prime Production 25 Sets		
TT-1	Mark Bavaro Auto	
TT-3	Tony Dorsett Auto	
TT-6	Hines Ward Auto	
TT-10	Quincy Carter Auto	
TT-13	Mike Singletary Auto	
TT-17	Thurman Thomas Auto	
TT-21	Randall Cunningham Auto	
TT-22	Donovan McNabb Auto	
TT-23	Joe Namath Auto	

2004 Donruss Elite Turn of the Century Autographs

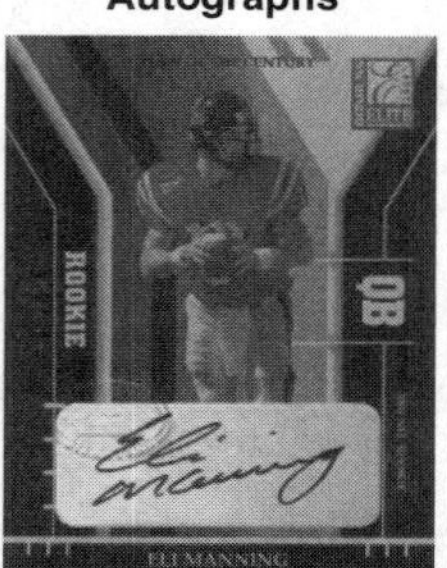

		NM/M
Common Player:		20.00
Production 125 Sets		
102	Ahmad Carroll	30.00
105	Ben Roethlisberger	250.00
108	Bernard Berrian	30.00
113	Cedric Cobbs	30.00
116	Chris Gamble	30.00
117	Chris Perry	40.00
120	D.J. Hackett	20.00
121	D.J. Williams	30.00
122	Darius Watts	30.00
124	DeAngelo Hall	40.00
126	Derrick Hamilton	20.00
128	Devard Darling	25.00
129	Devery Henderson	25.00
131	Drew Henson	100.00
132	Dunta Robinson	25.00
134	Eli Manning	200.00
135	Ernest Wilford	25.00
137	Greg Jones	30.00
139	J.P. Losman	50.00
146	Jerricho Cotchery	25.00
149	Johnnie Morant	20.00
150	Jonathan Vilma	30.00
152	Josh Harris	20.00
153	Julius Jones	60.00
156	Keary Colbert	30.00
159	Kellen Winslow Jr.	60.00
161	Kenechi Udeze	30.00
162	Kevin Jones	80.00
163	Larry Fitzgerald	100.00
164	Lee Evans	40.00
165	Luke McCown	30.00
167	Matt Schaub	30.00
171	Mewelde Moore	25.00
173	Michael Clayton	40.00
174	Michael Jenkins	40.00
175	Michael Turner	20.00
178	P.K. Sam	25.00
179	Philip Rivers	100.00
180	Quincy Wilson	30.00
183	Rashaun Woods	50.00
184	Reggie Williams	40.00
185	Ricardo Colclough	30.00
187	Roy Williams	80.00
188	Samie Parker	20.00
191	Sean Taylor	80.00
192	Steven Jackson	80.00
194	Tatum Bell	60.00
196	Tommie Harris	30.00
198	Vince Wilfork	30.00
200	Will Smith	25.00

E

1959 Eagles Jay Publishing

Measuring 5" x 7", the 12-card set is anchored by a black-and-white photo on the front, with the player's name and team printed in the white border underneath. The cards are blank-backed and unnumbered. The set was originally sold in 12-card packs for 25 cents.

		NM/M
Complete Set (12):		75.00
Common Player:		5.00
1	Bill Barnes	5.00
2	Chuck Bednarik	10.00
3	Tom Brookshier	5.00
4	Marion Campbell	5.00
5	Ted Dean	5.00
6	Tommy McDonald	8.00
7	Clarence Peaks	5.00
8	Pete Retzlaff	5.00
9	Jesse Richardson	5.00
10	Norm Van Brocklin	15.00
11	Bobby Walston	5.00
12	Chuck Weber	5.00

1960 Eagles White Border

Measuring 5" x 7", the 11-card set is anchored by a black-and-white photo on the front, wth the player's name and team printed in the white border underneath. The cards are blank-backed and unnumbered.

		NM/M
Complete Set (11):		50.00
Common Player:		5.00
1	Maxie Baughan	7.00
2	Chuck Bednarik	10.00
3	Don Burroughs	5.00
4	Jimmy Carr	5.00
5	Howard Keys	5.00
6	Ed Khayat	5.00
7	Jim McCusker	5.00
8	John Nocera	5.00
9	Nick Skorich	5.00
10	J.D. Smith	5.00
11	John Wittenborn	5.00

1961 Eagles Jay Publishing

Measuring 5" x 7", the 12-card set is anchored by a black-and-white photo on the front, with his name and team printed underneath in a white border. The backs are blank and unnumbered. Originally, the set was sold in packs for 25 cents.

		NM/M
Complete Set (12):		50.00
Common Player:		5.00
1	Maxie Baughan	7.00
2	Jim McCusker	5.00
3	Tommy McDonald	7.00
4	Bob Pellegrini	5.00
5	Pete Retzlaff	5.00
6	Jesse Richardson	5.00
7	Joe Robb	5.00
8	Theron Sapp	5.00
9	J.D. Smith	5.00
10	Bobby Walston	5.00
11	Jerry Williams (ACO)	5.00
12	John Wittenborn	5.00

A player's name in *italic* type indicates a rookie card.

1971 Eagles Team Issue

Measuring 4-1/4" x 5-1/2", the 16-card set showcases a posed black-and-white photo on the front, with the player's name and team printed inside the white border at the bottom of the card. The cards are unnumbered and the backs are blank.

		NM/M
Complete Set (16):		45.00
Common Player:		3.00
1	Gary Ballman	3.00
2	Lee Bouggess	3.00
3	Kent Kramer	3.00
4	Tom McNeill	3.00
5	Mark Nordquist	3.00
6	Ron Porter	3.00
7	Steve Preece	3.00
8	Tim Rossovich (Facing right edge of card)	3.00
9	Tim Rossovich (Facing left edge of card)	3.00
10	Jim Skaggs	3.00
11	Norm Snead	5.00
12	Jim Thrower	3.00
13	Mel Tom	3.00
14	Jim Ward	3.00
15	Adrian Young	3.00
16	Don Zimmerman	3.00

1983 Eagles Frito Lay

Measuring 4-1/4" x 5-1/2", the 37-card set is anchored by an action photo on the front, with the player's facsimile autograph on the photo. The player's name, position and Frito Lay logo are printed inside the white border under the photo. The top white margin features the "Philadelphia Eagles" and their logo on the card front. The set is unnumbered. The backs of Harold Carmichael, Max Runager and Jerry Sisemore's cards are done in a postcard format, while the others are blank.

		NM/M
Complete Set (37):		45.00
Common Player:		1.00
1	Harvey Armstrong	1.00
2	Ron Baker	1.00
3	Greg Brown	1.00
4	Marion Campbell (CO)	1.00
5	Harold Carmichael	3.00
6	Ken Clarke	1.00
7	Dennis DeVaughn	1.00
8	Herman Edwards	1.00
9	Ray Ellis	1.00
10	Major Everett	1.50
11	Anthony Griggs	1.00
12	Michael Haddix	1.50
13	Perry Harrington	1.00
14	Dennis Harrison	1.00
15	Wes Hopkins	1.50
16	Ron Jaworski	4.00
17	Ron Johnson	1.00
18	Vyto Kab	1.00
19	Steve Kenney	1.00
20	Dean Miraldi	1.00
21	Leonard Mitchell	1.00
22	Wilbert Montgomery	4.00
23	Hubie Oliver	1.00
24	Joe Pisarcik	1.50
25	Mike Quick	2.00
26	Jerry Robinson	1.50
27	Max Runager	1.00
28	Buddy Ryan (CO)	4.00
29	Lawrence Sampleton	1.00
30	Jody Schulz	1.00
31	Jerry Sisemore	1.00
32	John Spagnola	1.50
33	Reggie Wilkes	1.00
34	Mike Williams	1.00
35	Tony Woodruff	1.00
36	Glen Young	1.00
37	Roynell Young	1.00

1984 Eagles Police

Measuring 2-5/8" x 4-1/8", this eight-card set is anchored on the front with a photo, with the player's name, number, position, team and Eagles' logo inside a box at the bottom. The backs have the card number, player's name, number, position, bio, safety tip and sponsors.

		NM/M
Complete Set (8):		6.00
Common Player:		.50
1	Mike Quick	1.00
2	Dennis Harrison	.50
3	Jerry Robinson	.75
4	Wilbert Montgomery	1.50
5	Herman Edwards	.50
6	Kenny Jackson	1.00
7	Anthony Griggs	.50
8	Ron Jaworski	1.75

1985 Eagles Police

Measuring 2-5/8" x 4-1/8", the 16-card set is identical on the front to the 1984 set, with the large photo and the player's name, number, position, team and Eagles' logo in a box at the bottom. The backs have the card number, player's name, number, bio, highlights and a safety tip. The sponsors are listed at the bottom of the card back.

		NM/M
Complete Set (16):		6.00
Common Player:		.50
1	Ken Clarke	.50
2	Roynell Young	.50
3	Ray Ellis	.50
4	Ron Baker	.50
5	John Spagnola	.50
6	Reggie Wilkes	.50
7	Ron Jaworski	1.00
8	Steve Kenney	.50
9	Paul McFadden	.50
10	Mike Quick	1.00
11	Hubie Oliver	.50
12	Greg Brown	.50
13	Anthony Griggs	.50
14	Michael Haddix	.50
15	Kenny Jackson	.75
16	Vyto Kab	.50

1985 Eagles Team Issue

Measuring 2-15/16" x 3-7/8", the 53-card set is anchored by a glossy color photo on the front, with the player's name, position and number in the white margin under the photo. The backs have the player's name, position and number at the top, with his career highlights located inside a box. The cards are unnumbered.

		NM/M
Complete Set (53):		50.00
Common Player:		1.00
1	Harvey Armstrong	1.00
2	Ron Baker	1.00
3	Norman Braman (PRES)	1.00
4	Greg Brown	1.00
5	Marion Campbell (CO)	1.00
6	Jeff Christensen	1.00
7	Ken Clarke	1.00
8	Evan Cooper	1.00
9	Byron Darby	1.00
10	Mark Dennard	1.00
11	Herman Edwards	1.00
12	Ray Ellis	1.00
13	Major Everett	1.00
14	Gerry Feehery	1.00
15	Elbert Foules	1.00
16	Gregg Garrity	1.00
17	Anthony Griggs	1.00
18	Michael Haddix	1.00
19	Andre Hardy	1.00
20	Dennis Harrison	1.00
21	Joe Hayes	1.00
22	Melvin Hoover	1.00
23	Wes Hopkins	1.50
24	Mike Horan	1.00
25	Kenny Jackson	1.50
26	Ron Jaworski	4.00
27	Vyto Kab	1.00
28	Steve Kenney	1.00
29	Rich Kraynak	1.00
30	Dean May	1.00
31	Paul McFadden	1.00
32	Dean Miraldi	1.00
33	Leonard Mitchell	1.00
34	Wilbert Montgomery	3.00
35	Hubie Oliver	1.00
36	Mike Quick	2.00
37	Mike Reichenbach	1.00
38	Jerry Robinson	1.00
39	Rusty Russell	1.00
40	Lawrence Sampleton	1.00
41	Jody Schulz	1.00
42	John Spagnola	1.50
43	Tom Strauthers	1.00
44	Andre Waters	2.00
45	Reggie Wilkes	1.00
46	Joel Williams	1.00
47	Michael Williams	1.00
48	Brenard Wilson	1.00
49	Tony Woodruff	1.00
50	Roynell Young	1.00
51	Logo Card (Eagle holding football on both sides)	1.50
52	1985 Schedule Card (Both sides)	1.50
53	Title Card 1985-86 (Eagles' Helmet)	1.50

1986 Eagles Frito Lay

The cards in this set are 4-1/4" x 5-1/2". They can be distinguished from other Eagles Frito Lay sets by the Frito Lay logo in the lower right and the 3/8" borders on the sides. The cards are blank-backed and unnumbered.

		NM/M
Complete Set (7):		12.00
Common Player:		1.00
1	Wes Hopkins	1.50
2	Ron Jaworski	4.00
3	Ron Johnson WR	1.00
4	Mike Quick	2.00
5	Buddy Ryan CO	4.00
6	Tom Strauthers	1.00
7	Andre Waters	1.50

1986 Eagles Police

Measuring 2-5/8" x 4-1/8", the 16-card set is anchored by a large photo on the front, with the player's name, number, position, team and Eagles' logo in a box at the bottom. The backs have the card number, player's name, number, bio, position, highlights, safety tip and sponsors. The Eagles' and Frito Lay logos are also shown on the backs.

NM/M
Complete Set (16): 10.00
Common Player: .50
1 Greg Brown .50
2 Reggie White 3.50
3 John Spagnola .50
4 Mike Quick .75
5 Ken Clarke .50
6 Ken Reeves .50
7 Mike Reichenbach .50
8 Wes Hopkins .75
9 Roynell Young .50
10 Randall Cunningham 3.00
11 Paul McFadden .50
12 Matt Cavanaugh .50
13 Ron Jaworski 1.00
14 Byron Darby .50
15 Andre Waters .75
16 Buddy Ryan (CO) 1.00

1987 Eagles Police

Measuring 2-3/4" x 4-1/8", the 12-card set includes a photo on the front, along with the player's name, bio and position. The Eagles' helmet is printed in the bottom center. The backs have "Tips from the Eagles" printed at the top, with the New Jersey police force logos printed directly underneath. A safety tip is also included on the unnumbered backs, which feature the sponsor names at the bottom. Overall, 10,000 sets were handed out by New Jersey police officers.

NM/M
Complete Set (12): 60.00
Common Player: 3.00
1 Ron Baker 3.00
2 Keith Byars 7.00
3 Ken Clarke 3.00
4 Randall Cunningham 12.00
5 Paul McFadden 3.00
6 Mike Quick 5.00
7 Mike Reichenbach 3.00
8 Buddy Ryan (CO) 7.00
9 John Spagnola 3.00
10 Anthony Toney 5.00
11 Andre Waters 5.00
12 Reggie White 16.00

1988 Eagles Police

Measuring 2-3/4" x 4-1/8", the 12-card set is anchored on the front by a large photo. "Philadelphia Eagles" and two Eagles' helmets printed in each corner are at the top of the card fronts. Under the photo are the player's name, number, height, position and weight. The unnumbered backs feature "Tips from the Eagles" at the top, with the New Jersey police logos located directly underneath. The McGruff the Crime Dog logo is printed at the bottom, along with the sponsors.

NM/M
Complete Set (12): 60.00
Common Player: 3.00
1 Jerome Brown 5.00
2 Keith Byars 5.00
3 Randall Cunningham 8.00
4 Matt Darwin 3.00
5 Keith Jackson 8.00
6 Seth Joyner 5.00
7 Mike Quick 4.00
8 Buddy Ryan (CO) 6.00
9 Clyde Simmons 5.00
10 John Teltschik 3.00
11 Anthony Toney 4.00
12 Reggie White 10.00

1989 Eagles Daily News

Measuring 5-9/16" x 4-1/4", the 24-card set features the Eagles logo in the upper left corner, with "Philadelphia Eagles" on the right side above the photo on the card front. Beneath the photo are the player's name and position, along with McDonald's, KYW radio and the Philadelphia News logos. The unnumbered cards have blank backs.

NM/M
Complete Set (24): 25.00
Common Player: 1.00
1 Eric Allen 2.00
2 Jerome Brown 2.00
3 Keith Byars 2.00
4 Cris Carter (UER) (Name misspelled Chris on front) 5.00
5 Randall Cunningham 3.00
6 Matt Darwin 1.00
7 Gerry Feehery 1.00
8 Ron Heller 1.00
9A Terry Hoage (Solid color jersey) 1.00
9B Terry Hoage (With white collar or undershirt) 1.00
10 Wes Hopkins 1.50
11 Keith Jackson 3.00
12 Seth Joyner 2.00
13 Mike Pitts 1.00
14 Mike Quick 1.50
15 Mike Reichenbach 1.00
16 Clyde Simmons 2.00
17 John Spagnola 1.00
18 Junior Tautalatasi 1.00
19 John Teltschik 1.00
20 Anthony Toney 1.00
21 Andre Waters 1.50
22 Reggie White 6.00
23 Luis Zendejas 1.00

1989 Eagles Police

Measuring 8-1/2" x 11", the nine-card set is anchored by a photo on the front, with the player's name and bio underneath the photo between the New Jersey State Police Crime Prevention Resource Center and Security Savings Bank logos. The unnumbered backs have "Alcohol and Other Drugs: Facts and Myths" and five questions and answers. The team logo and sponsors' logos are on the back. This set was released after the season.

NM/M
Complete Set (9): 50.00
Common Player: 3.00
1 Cris Carter 15.00
2 Gregg Garrity 3.00
3 Mike Golic 4.00
4 Keith Jackson 7.00
5 Clyde Simmons 6.00
6 John Teltschik 3.00
7 Anthony Toney 3.00
8 Andre Waters 4.00
9 Luis Zendejas 3.00

1989 Eagles Smokey

Measuring 3" x 5", the 49-card set features a full-bleed photo on the front, with the player's name, number and position in the lower right. The unnumbered card backs have the player's name, number, position and bio at the top, with a Smokey the Bear cartoon underneath. The Eagles' and sponsor logos appear at the bottom of the card backs. Some cards were produced with two versions, which can be differentiated by the home and away jerseys.

NM/M
Complete Set (49): 125.00
Common Player: 1.50
6 Matt Cavanaugh 2.00
8 Luis Zendejas 1.50
9 Don McPherson 2.00
10 John Teltschik 1.50
12A Randall Cunningham (White jersey) 8.00
12B Randall Cunningham (Green jersey) 8.00
20 Andre Waters 3.00
21 Eric Allen 3.00
25 Anthony Toney 2.00
33 William Frizzell 1.50
34 Terry Hoage 1.50
35 Mark Konecny 1.50
41 Keith Byars 3.00
42 Eric Everett 1.50
43 Roynell Young 1.50
46 Izel Jenkins 1.50
48 Wes Hopkins 2.00
50 Dave Rimington 1.50
52 Todd Bell 1.50
53 Dwayne Jiles 1.50
55 Mike Reichenbach 1.50
56 Byron Evans 1.50
58 Ty Allert 1.50
59 Seth Joyner 3.00
61 Ben Tamburello 1.50
63 Ron Baker 1.50
66 Ken Reeves 1.50
68 Reggie Singletary 1.50
72 David Alexander 1.50
73 Ron Heller 1.50
74 Mike Pitts 1.50
78 Matt Darwin 1.50
80 Cris Carter 8.00
81 Kenny Jackson 2.00
82A Mike Quick (White jersey) 2.50
82B Mike Quick (Green jersey) 2.50
83 Jimmie Giles 1.50
85 Ron Johnson 1.50
86 Gregg Garrity 1.50
88 Keith Jackson 5.00
89 David Little 2.00
90 Mike Golic 2.00
91 Scott Curtis 1.50
92 Reggie White 14.00
96 Clyde Simmons 3.00
97 John Klingel 1.50
99 Jerome Brown 4.00
NNO Buddy Ryan (CO) (Wearing white cap) 7.00
NNO Buddy Ryan (CO) (Wearing green cap) 7.00

1990 Eagles Police

Measuring 2-5/8" x 4-1/8", the 12-card set has "Philadelphia Eagles" and two Eagles' helmets at the top of the card fronts above the photo. Beneath the photo are the player's name, position and bio. The unnumbered card backs have "Tips from the Eagles" and sponsor logos at the top, with a tip and McGruff the Crime Dog logo at the bottom.

NM/M
Complete Set (12): 30.00
Common Player: 2.00
1 David Alexander 2.00
2 Eric Allen 3.00
3 Randall Cunningham 5.00
4 Keith Byars 3.00
5 James Feagles 2.00
6 Mike Golic 3.00
7 Keith Jackson 4.00
8 Rich Kotite (CO) 3.00
9 Roger Ruzek 2.00
10 Mickey Shuler 3.00
11 Clyde Simmons 4.00
12 Reggie White 8.00

1990 Eagles Sealtest

Measuring 2" x 8", the set of six bookmarks showcases the Sealtest logo at the top, with "The Reading Team" inside a scoreboard above the player photo. The Eagles' logo, player name, number, bio and highlights are printed inside a box at the bottom of the card. The backs are unnumbered and contain the sponsor logos and give information on two books that are available at the public library. This set is identical to the the 1990 Knudsen 49ers and Chargers sets.

NM/M
Complete Set (6): 15.00
Common Player: 2.50
1 David Alexander 2.50
2 Eric Allen 3.50
3 Keith Byars 3.50
4 Randall Cunningham 4.00
5 Mike Pitts 2.50
6 Mike Quick 3.50

1991 Enor Pro Football HOF Promos

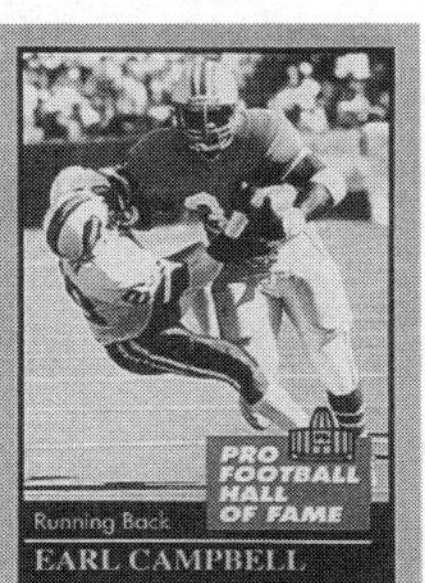

PRO FOOTBALL HALL OF FAME
Running Back
EARL CAMPBELL

The six standard-sized cards were produced to show what the 1991 Enor set would look like. The cards are identical to the regular cards, except for the differences in numbering and color tones. To tell these cards apart from the regular cards, look at the Team NFL logo on the back. If the NFL logo is black and white it is a promo card. If it is red, white and blue, it is a card from the regular series.

NM/M
Complete Set (6): 8.00
Common Player: 1.00
1 Pro Football Hall of Fame (Building) (Regular issue card number is also 1) 1.00
2 Earl Campbell (Regular issue card number is 23) 3.50
3 John Hannah (Regular issue card number is 57) 1.00
4 Stan Jones (Regular issue card number is 74) 1.00
5 Jan Stenerud (Regular issue card number is 131) 1.00
6 Tex Schramm ADM (Regular issue card number is 127) 1.00

1991 Enor Pro Football Hall of Fame

Photos from the NFL's files were used for the card fronts for this 160-card set, which features a blend of color and black-and-white photos bordered by black and gold frames. The Pro Football Hall of Fame logo also appears on the card front, in a purple square. The player's name and position are in the lower left corner in a black panel. The card back has a photo of the Hall of Fame on the bottom half, along with a card number. Biographical information, a career summary and the year of induction comprise the rest of the back. Special cards randomly inserted in packs allowed the holder to redeem them for a special Hall of Fame card album and free admission to the museum. Six different promo cards were also produced for the set. The cards, which are numbered on the back, do not match the numbers assigned to their counterparts in the regular set. Also, the cards have a different shade of color and the NFL logo on the back is black-and-white, not in color like those on the regular cards.

NM/M
Complete Set (160): 12.00
Common Player: .10
1 Pro Football Hall of Fame .15
1A Pro Football Hall of Fame (Canton, OH) .15
2 Herb Adderley .15
3 Lance Alworth .20
4 Doug Atkins .15
5 Morris "Red" Badgro .10
6 Cliff Battles .15
7 Sammy Baugh .60
8 Chuck Bednarik .25
9A Bert Bell (FOUND/OWN) (Factory set version in coat and tie) .20
9B Bert Bell (FOUND/OWN) (Wax pack version in Steelers tee shirt) .20
10 Bobby Bell .10
11 Raymond Berry .30
12 Charles W. Bidwill (OWN) .10
13 Fred Biletnikoff .25
14 George Blanda .30
15 Mel Blount .20
16 Terry Bradshaw .75
17 Jim Brown .75
18 Paul Brown (CO/OWN/FOUND) .20
19 Roosevelt Brown .10
20 Willie Brown .15
21 Buck Buchanan .15
22 Dick Butkus .50
23 Earl Campbell .75
24 Tony Canadeo .10
25 Joe Carr (PRES) .10
26 Guy Chamberlin .10
27 Jack Christiansen .10
28 Earl "Dutch" Clark .15
29 George Connor .15
30 Jimmy Conzelman .10
31 Larry Csonka .30
32 Willie Davis .10
33 Len Dawson .25
34 Mike Ditka .50
35 Art Donovan .25
36 John (Paddy) Driscoll .10
37 Billy Dudley .15
38 Turk Edwards .10
39 Weeb Ewbank (CO) .10
40 Tom Fears .10
41 Ray Flaherty (CO) .10
42 Len Ford .10
43 Dan Fortmann .10
44 Frank Gatski .10
45 Bill George .10
46 Frank Gifford .50
47 Sid Gillman (CO) .10
48 Otto Graham .50
49 Harold "Red" Grange .50
50 Joe Greene .20
51 Forrest Gregg .15
52 Bob Griese .30
53 Lou Groza .20
54 Joe Guyon .10
55 George Halas (CO/OWN/FOUND) .30
56 Jack Ham .25
57 John Hannah .10
58 Franco Harris .30
59 Ed Healey .10
60 Mel Hein .10
61 Ted Hendricks .15
62 Pete (Fats) Henry .10
63 Arnie Herber .10
64 Bill Hewitt .10
65 Clarke Hinkle .10
66 Elroy Hirsch .20
67 Ken Houston .15
68 Cal Hubbard .10
69 Sam Huff .20
70 Lamar Hunt (OWN/FOUND) .10
71 Don Hutson .20
72 John Henry Johnson .15
73 Deacon Jones .25
74 Stan Jones .15
75 Sonny Jurgensen .25
76 Walt Kiesling .10
77 Frank "Bruiser" Kinard .10
78 Earl (Curly) Lambeau (CO/FOUND/OWN) .25
79 Jack Lambert .30
80 Tom Landry (CO) .30
81 Dick "Night Train" Lane .15
82 Jim Langer .10
83 Willie Lanier .15
84 Yale Lary .10
85 Dante Lavelli .15
86 Bobby Layne .50
87 Tuffy Leemans .10
88 Bob Lilly .25
89 Sid Luckman .25
90 William Roy Lyman .10
91 Tim Mara (FOUND/OWN) .10
92 Gino Marchetti .20
93 Geo. Preston Marshall (FOUND/OWN) .10
94 Don Maynard .20
95 George McAfee .10
96 Mike McCormack .10
97 Johnny "Blood" McNally .10
98 Mike Michalske .10
99 Wayne Millner .10
100 Bobby Mitchell .20
101 Ron Mix .15
102 Lenny Moore .20
103 Marion Motley (See also 130) .20
104 George Musso .10
105 Bronko Nagurski .30
106 Earle "Greasy" Neale (CO) .10
107 Ernie Nevers .10
108 Ray Nitschke .25
109 Leo Nomellini .15
110 Merlin Olsen .25
111 Jim Otto .20
112 Steve Owen (CO) .10
113 Alan Page .15
114 Clarence (Ace) Parker .10
115 Jim Parker .10
116 1958 NFL Championship .10
117 Pete Pihos .10
118 Hugh (Shorty) Ray (OFF) .10
119 Dan Reeves (OWN) .10
120 Jim Ringo .10
121 Andy Robustelli .15
122 Art Rooney (FOUND/ADM) .15
123 Pete Rozelle (COMM) .20
124 Bob St. Clair .15
125 Gale Sayers .50
126 Joe Schmidt .15
127 Tex Schramm (ADM) .15
128 Art Shell .20
129 Roger Staubach .75
130 Ernie Stautner (UER) (Numbered as 103) .20
131 Jan Stenerud .15
132 Ken Strong .15
133 Joe Stydahar .10
134 Fran Tarkenton .30
135 Charley Taylor .15
136 Jim Taylor .15
137 Jim Thorpe .50
138 Y.A. Tittle .40
139 George Trafton .10
140 Charlie Trippi .10
141 Emlen Tunnell .10
142 Clyde "Bulldog" Turner .20
143 Johnny Unitas .50
144 Gene Upshaw .15
145 Norm Van Brocklin .20
146 Steve Van Buren .20
147 Doak Walker .20
148 Paul Warfield .20
149 Bob Waterfield .20
150 Arnie Weinmeister .10
151 Bill Willis .10
152 Larry Wilson .10
153 Alex Wojciechowicz .10
154 Willie Wood .15
155 Enshrinement Day HOF Induction Ceremony .10
156 Enshrinee Mementos Room .10
157 Checklist 1 - The Beginning .10
158 Checklist 2 - The Early Years .10
159 Checklist 3 - The Modern Era .10
160A Checklist 4 - Evolution of Uniform (includes #133-160) .10

1994 Enor Pro Football HOF

Having the identical design as the 1991 set, these six cards were inserted into ProGard protective sheet boxes. The cards are unnumbered. They feature each of the players and coach who were inducted into the Hall of Fame in 1994.

NM/M
Complete Set (6): 4.00
Common Player: .40
1 Tony Dorsett 1.25
2 Bud Grant (CO) .40
3 Jim Johnson .40
4 Leroy Kelly .40
5 Jackie Smith .40
6 Randy White .75

1995 Enor Pro Football HOF

The company re-released its 1991 Hall of Fame series in a factory set in 1995. This includes the first 159 cards from the 1991 set, in addition to 21 new cards, which feature a 1995 copyright date. The original cards still carry the 1991 copyright. Card No. 160 carries a "B" suffix.

NM/M
Complete Set (21): 8.00
Common Player: .25
160B Checklist 4 - Evolution of Uniform (includes #133-180) .25
161 Lem Barney .25
162 Al Davis .40
163 John Mackey .25
164 John Riggins .50
165 Dan Fouts .50
166 Larry Little .25
167 Chuck Noll .50
168 Bill Walsh .50
169 Tony Dorsett 1.00
170 Bud Grant .25
171 Jimmy Johnson .25
172 Leroy Kelly .25
173 Jackie Smith .25
174 Randy White .50
175 O.J. Simpson 1.00
176 Jim Finks .25
177 Hank Jordan .25
178 Steve Largent .75
179 Lee Roy Selmon .25
180 Kellen Winslow .40

1969 Eskimo Pie

These 2-1/2" x 3" panels each feature two mug shot stickers of American Football League players. The panels are in color but are unnumbered. Card 14 (Len Dawson/Jim Otto) has the players' names reversed under their pictures. The bottom half of each panel explains that these cards were also on other Eskimo "take home cartons."

NM/M
Complete Set (15): 850.00
Common Player: 50.00
(1) Lance Alworth, John Charles 95.00
(2) Al Atkinson, George Goeddeke 50.00
(3) Marlin Briscoe, Billy Shaw 50.00
(4) Gino Cappelletti, Dale Livingston 50.00
(5) Eric Crabtree, Jim Dunaway 50.00
(6) Ben Davidson, Bob Griese 130.00
(7) Hewritt Dixon, Pete Beathard 60.00
(8) Mike Garrett, Bob Hunt 50.00
(9) Daryle Lamonica, Willie Frazier 60.00
(10) Jim Lynch, John Hadl 60.00
(11) Kent McCloughan, Tom Regner 50.00
(12) Jim Nance, Billy Neighbors 50.00
(13) Rick Norton, Paul Costa 50.00
(14) Jim Otto, Len Dawson (Names reversed) 125.00
(15) Matt Snell, Dick Post 50.00

1995 ESPN/Sports Illustrated

NM/M
Complete Set (6): 4.00
Common Player: .50
Chris Berman .50
Art Donovan 1.00
Tom Jackson .50
Chris Mortenson .50
Sterling Sharpe 1.00
Joe Theismann 1.00

1997 E-X2000

E-X2000 consists of a 60-card base set with one parallel and four inserts. The base cards feature "SkyView" technology, with a die-cut image over a transparent window. The Essential Credentials parallel set consists of less than 100 numbered sets. The inserts include A Cut Above, Fleet of Foot, Star Date 2000 and Autographics.

NM/M
Complete Set (60): 50.00
Common Player: .40
Minor Stars: .75
Credential Cards: 3X-5X
Credential Rookies: 2X-4X
Pack (2): 2.50
Wax Box (24): 40.00
1 *Jake Plummer* 3.00
2 Jamal Anderson .75

3 *Rae Carruth* 1.00
4 Kerry Collins 1.00
5 *Darnell Autry* 1.00
6 Rashaan Salaam .75
7 Troy Aikman 4.00
8 Deion Sanders 1.00
9 Emmitt Smith 6.00
10 Herman Moore .75
11 Barry Sanders 6.00
12 Mark Chmura .75
13 Brett Favre 7.00
14 Antonio Freeman .75
15 Reggie White .75
16 Cris Carter .40
17 Brad Johnson .40
18 *Troy Davis* .75
19 *Danny Wuerffel* 1.00
20 Dave Brown .40
21 *Ike Hilliard* 2.00
22 Ty Detmer .40
23 Ricky Watters .75
24 Tony Banks 1.00
25 Eddie Kennison 1.00
26 *Jim Druckenmiller* 1.00
27 Jerry Rice 4.00
28 Steve Young 2.00
29 Trent Dilfer .75
30 *Warrick Dunn* 3.00
31 Terry Allen .40
32 Gus Frerotte .40
33 Vinny Testaverde .40
34 *Antowain Smith* 3.00
35 Thurman Thomas .75
36 Jeff Blake .75
37 Carl Pickens .40
38 Terrell Davis 2.00
39 John Elway 3.00
40 Eddie George 3.00
41 Steve McNair 2.00
42 Marshall Faulk .75
43 Marvin Harrison 2.50
44 Mark Brunell 2.00
45 Marcus Allen .75
46 Elvis Grbac .40
47 Karim Abdul-Jabbar 1.00
48 Dan Marino 6.00
49 Drew Bledsoe 3.00
50 Terry Glenn 1.00
51 Curtis Martin 3.00
52 Keyshawn Johnson 1.00
53 Tim Brown .40
54 Jeff George .40
55 Jerome Bettis .75
56 Kordell Stewart 1.00
57 Stan Humphries .40
58 Junior Seau .75
59 Joey Galloway .75
60 Chris Warren .40

1997 E-X2000 Essential Credentials

Essential Credentials paralleled the 60-card E-X2000 set, but was reprinted with silver holofoil around the border. The cards contained the words "Essential Credentials" across the top and were numbered to 100 sets on the back.

Essential Credential Cards: 3X-5X
Essential Credential Rookies: 2X-4X
Production 100 Sets

1997 E-X2000 Essential Creditials

NM/M
Complete Set (60): 100.00
Common Player: .40
Minor Stars: .75
Credential Cards: 3X-5X
Credential Rookies: 2X-4X
Wax Box: 100.00

1997 E-X2000 A Cut Above

This 10-card insert features players on cards die-cut to look like saw blades. A Cut Above cards were inserted 1:288.

NM/M
Common Player: 15.00
1 Barry Sanders 50.00
2 Brett Favre 60.00
3 Dan Marino 50.00
4 Eddie George 25.00
5 Emmitt Smith 50.00
6 Jerry Rice 35.00
7 Joey Galloway 15.00
8 John Elway 40.00
9 Mark Brunell 20.00
10 Terrell Davis 25.00

1997 E-X2000 Fleet of Foot

The cards in this 20-card insert are die-cut to look like football cleats. They were inserted 1:20.

NM/M
Complete Set (20): 100.00
Common Player: 1.00
1 Antonio Freeman 1.00
2 Barry Sanders 12.00
3 Carl Pickens 1.00
4 Chris Warren 1.00
5 Curtis Martin 6.00
6 Deion Sanders 4.00
7 Emmitt Smith 12.00
8 Jerry Rice 10.00
9 Joey Galloway 2.00
10 Karim Abdul-Jabbar 2.00
11 Kordell Stewart 4.00
12 Lawrence Phillips 1.00
13 Mark Brunell 4.00
14 Marvin Harrison 5.00
15 Rae Carruth 1.00
16 Ricky Watters 2.00
17 Steve Young 8.00
18 Terrell Davis 8.00
19 Terry Glenn 4.00
20 Shawn Springs 1.00

1997 E-X2000 Star Date 2000

This 15-card insert features young stars of the NFL. The cards were inserted 1:9.

NM/M
Complete Set (15): 20.00
Common Player: 1.00
1 Curtis Martin 3.00
2 Darnell Autry 1.00
3 Darrell Russell 1.00
4 Eddie Kennison 1.00
5 Jim Druckenmiller 1.00
6 Karim Abdul-Jabbar 1.00
7 Kerry Collins 3.00
8 Keyshawn Johnson 3.00
9 Marvin Harrison 4.00
10 Orlando Pace 1.00
11 Pat Barnes 1.00
12 Reidel Anthony 1.00
13 Tim Biakabutuka 1.00
14 Warrick Dunn 3.00
15 Yatil Green 1.00

1998 E-X2001

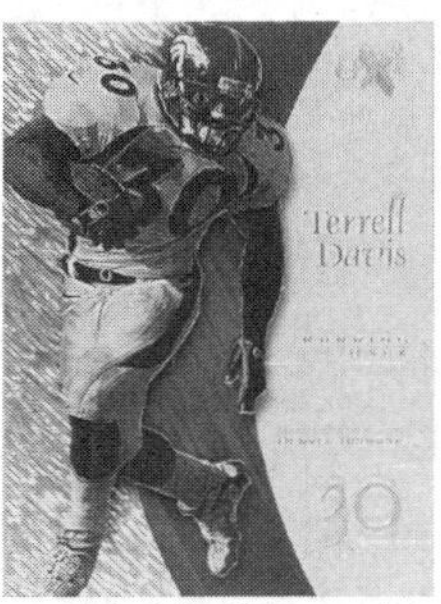

Each of the 60 base cards in this set are holographic and gold-foil stamped with player-specific die-cuts mounted on durable, see-thru plastic stock exposed along a large portion of the card. The Essential Credentials Now parallel cards differ from the base set in color, holo-foil and scarcity. Each card is sequentially numbered according to the player's card number in the base set. Card #1 has only one single and card #60 has cards numbered to 60. The Essential Credentials Future is similar to the Now set except in color, holo-foil and the sequentially numbering is opposite the player's card number. For example, card #1 has 60 cards and card #60 only has one.

NM/M
Complete Set (60): 40.00
Common Player: .30
Minor Stars: .60
Pack (2): 4.00
Wax Box (24): 70.00
1 Kordell Stewart 2.00
2 Steve Young 2.50
3 Mark Brunell 2.00
4 Brett Favre 6.00
5 Barry Sanders 6.00
6 Warrick Dunn 3.00
7 Jerry Rice 4.00
8 Dan Marino 6.00
9 Emmitt Smith 6.00
10 John Elway 4.00
11 Eddie George 3.00
12 Jake Plummer 1.00
13 Terrell Davis 3.00
14 Curtis Martin 2.50
15 Troy Aikman 4.00
16 Terry Glenn 1.00
17 Mike Alstott 1.00
18 Drew Bledsoe 3.00
19 Keyshawn Johnson .30
20 Dorsey Levens .30
21 Elvis Grbac .30
22 Ricky Watters 1.00
23 Robert Smith 1.00
24 Trent Dilfer 1.00
25 Joey Galloway 1.00
26 Rob Moore .30
27 Steve McNair 1.50
28 Jim Harbaugh .30
29 Troy Davis .30
30 Rob Johnson 1.00
31 Shannon Sharpe .30
32 Jerome Bettis 1.00
33 Tim Brown .30
34 Kerry Collins 1.00
35 Garrison Hearst .30
36 Antonio Freeman .30
37 Charlie Garner .30
38 Glenn Foley .30
39 Yatil Green .30
40 Tiki Barber .30
41 Bobby Hoying .30
42 Corey Dillon 2.00
43 Antowain Smith 1.50
44 *Robert Edwards* 3.00
45 *Jammi German* .50
46 *Ahman Green* 15.00
47 *Hines Ward* 8.00
48 *Skip Hicks* 4.00
49 *Brian Griese* 8.00
50 *Charlie Batch* 4.00
51 *Jacquez Green* 4.00
52 *John Avery* 4.00
53 *Kevin Dyson* 4.00
54 *Peyton Manning* 20.00
55 *Randy Moss* 15.00
56 *Ryan Leaf* 3.00
57 *Curtis Enis* 3.00
58 *Charles Woodson* 5.00
59 *Robert Holcombe* 4.00
60 *Fred Taylor* 8.00

1998 E-X2001 Essential Credentials Future

NM/M
Complete Set (60): 125.00
Common Player: .30
Minor Stars: .60
Too uncommon to price
1 Kordell Stewart (60) 3.00
2 Steve Young (59) 2.50
3 Mark Brunell (58) 3.00
4 Brett Favre (57) 8.00
5 Barry Sanders (56) 8.00
6 Warrick Dunn (55) 3.00
7 Jerry Rice (54) 4.00
8 Dan Marino (53) 6.00
9 Emmitt Smith (52) 6.00
10 John Elway (51) 4.00
11 Eddie George (50) 3.00
12 Jake Plummer (49) 3.00
13 Terrell Davis (48) 6.00
14 Curtis Martin (47) 2.50
15 Troy Aikman (46) 4.00
16 Terry Glenn (45) 1.00
17 Mike Alstott (44) 1.00
18 Drew Bledsoe (43) 3.00
19 Keyshawn Johnson (42) .50
20 Dorsey Levens (41) .50
21 Elvis Grbac (40) .50
22 Ricky Watters (39) 1.00
23 Robert Smith (38) 1.00
24 Trent Dilfer (37) 1.00
25 Joey Galloway (36) 1.00
26 Rob Moore (35) .50
27 Steve McNair (34) 1.50
28 Jim Harbaugh (33) .50
29 Troy Davis (32) .50
30 Rob Johnson (31) 1.00
31 Shannon Sharpe (30) .50
32 Jerome Bettis (29) 1.00
33 Tim Brown (28) .50
34 Kerry Collins (27) 1.00
35 Garrison Hearst (26) .50
36 Antonio Freeman (25) 1.00
37 Charlie Garner (24) .50
38 Glenn Foley (23) .50
39 Yatil Green (22) .50
40 Tiki Barber (21) .50
41 Bobby Hoying (20) .50
42 Corey Dillon (19) 2.00
43 Antowain Smith (18) 1.50
44 *Robert Edwards (17)* 10.00
45 *Jammi German (16)* 2.00
46 *Ahman Green (15)* 6.00
47 *Hines Ward (14)* 5.00
48 *Skip Hicks (13)* 4.00
49 *Brian Griese (12)* 6.00
50 *Charlie Batch (11)* 12.00
51 *Jacquez Green (10)* 6.00
52 *John Avery (9)* 6.00
53 *Kevin Dyson (8)* 6.00
54 *Peyton Manning (7)* 600.00
55 *Randy Moss (6)* 40.00
56 *Ryan Leaf (5)* 12.00
57 *Curtis Enis (4)* 10.00
58 *Charles Woodson (3)* 10.00
59 *Robert Holcombe (2)* 6.00
60 *Fred Taylor (1)* 18.00

1998 E-X2001 Essential Credentials Now

NM/M
Complete Set (60): 125.00
Common Player: .30
Minor Stars: .60
Too uncommon to price
1 Kordell Stewart (1) 3.00
2 Steve Young (2) 2.50
3 Mark Brunell (3) 3.00
4 Brett Favre (4) 8.00
5 Barry Sanders (5) 8.00
6 Warrick Dunn (6) 3.00
7 Jerry Rice (7) 4.00
8 Dan Marino (8) 6.00
9 Emmitt Smith (9) 6.00
10 John Elway (10) 4.00
11 Eddie George (11) 3.00
12 Jake Plummer (12) 3.00
13 Terrell Davis (13) 6.00
14 Curtis Martin (14) 2.50
15 Troy Aikman (15) 4.00
16 Terry Glenn (16) 1.00
17 Mike Alstott (17) 1.00
18 Drew Bledsoe (18) 3.00
19 Keyshawn Johnson (19) .50
20 Dorsey Levens (20) .50
21 Elvis Grbac (21) .50
22 Ricky Watters (22) 1.00
23 Robert Smith (23) 1.00
24 Trent Dilfer (24) 1.00
25 Joey Galloway (25) 1.00
26 Rob Moore (26) .50
27 Steve McNair (27) 1.50
28 Jim Harbaugh (28) .50
29 Troy Davis (29) .50
30 Rob Johnson (30) 1.00
31 Shannon Sharpe (31) .50
32 Jerome Bettis (32) 1.00
33 Jim Brown (33) .50
34 Kerry Collins (34) 1.00
35 Garrison Hearst (35) .50
36 Antonio Freeman (36) 1.00
37 Charlie Garner (37) .50
38 Glenn Foley (38) .50
39 Yatil Green (39) .50
40 Tiki Barber (40) .50
41 Bobby Hoying (41) .50
42 Corey Dillon (42) 2.00
43 Antowain Smith (43) 1.50
44 *Robert Edwards (44)* 10.00
45 *Jammi German (45)* 2.00
46 *Ahman Green (46)* 6.00
47 *Hines Ward (47)* 5.00
48 *Skip Hicks (48)* 4.00
49 *Brian Griese (49)* 6.00
50 *Charlie Batch (50)* 12.00
51 *Jacquez Green (51)* 6.00
52 *John Avery (52)* 6.00
53 *Kevin Dyson (53)* 6.00
54 *Peyton Manning (54)* 250.00
55 *Randy Moss (55)* 400.00
56 *Ryan Leaf (56)* 12.00
57 *Curtis Enis (57)* 10.00
58 *Charles Woodson (58)* 10.00
59 *Robert Holcombe (59)* 6.00
60 *Fred Taylor (60)* 18.00

1998 E-X2001 Destination Honolulu

Hawaiian culture is celebrated on these wooden inserts, with five different statuesque die-cuts. Singles were inserted 1:720 packs.

NM/M
Common Player: 10.00
Inserted 1:720
1 Peyton Manning 50.00
2 Terrell Davis 40.00
3 Corey Dillon 40.00
4 Eddie George 50.00
5 Emmitt Smith 75.00
6 Warrick Dunn 40.00
7 Brett Favre 75.00
8 Antowain Smith 20.00
9 Barry Sanders 75.00
10 Ryan Leaf 10.00

1998 E-X2001 Helmet Heroes

Each single is die-cut around the helmet at the top of the cards. These team color-coded, thick plastic inserts featured some of the NFL's most dynamic players. They were found 1:24 packs.

NM/M
Complete Set (20): 80.00
Common Player: 1.00
Inserted 1:24
1 Barry Sanders 12.00
2 Emmitt Smith 12.00
3 Brett Favre 12.00
4 Mark Brunell 4.00
5 Jerry Rice 8.00
6 Steve Young 6.00
7 Warrick Dunn 2.00
8 Kordell Stewart 2.00
9 John Elway 10.00
10 Troy Aikman 8.00
11 Dan Marino 12.00
12 Curtis Martin 4.00
13 Dorsey Levens 1.00
14 Jake Plummer 2.00
15 Corey Dillon 4.00
16 Yancey Thigpen 1.00
17 Randy Moss 12.00
18 Curtis Enis 1.00
19 Charles Woodson 3.00
20 Fred Taylor 6.00

1998 E-X2001 Star Date 2001

The idea behind this set was to include the stars of tomorrow on a thick, plastic stock with flecks of foil running through it and highlighted with etched silver foil stamping. Singles were inserted 1:12 packs.

NM/M
Complete Set (15): 40.00
Common Player: 1.00

NM/M
Minor Stars: 2.00
Inserted 1:12
1 Randy Moss 10.00
2 Fred Taylor 4.00
3 Corey Dillon 4.00
4 Jake Plummer 2.00
5 Antowain Smith 2.00
6 Wilmont Perry 1.00
7 Donald Hayes 1.00
8 Tavian Banks 1.00
9 John Dutton 1.00
10 Kevin Dyson 2.00
11 Germane Crowell 1.00
12 Bobby Hoying 1.00
13 Jerome Pathon 1.00
14 Ryan Leaf 1.00
15 Peyton Manning 10.00

1999 E-X Century

This was a 90-card set that included 30 rookie cards found 1:4 packs. Each base card was printed on clear plastic stock with holographic foil stamping. Parallel sets included Essential Credentials Future and Essential Credentials Now. Other inserts included: Authen-Kicks, Autographics, Bright Lites and E-Xtraordinary. SRP was $5.99 for three-card packs.

NM/M
Complete Set (90): 160.00
Common Player: .25
Minor Stars: .50
Common Rookie: 1.50
Inserted 1:4
Pack (3): 4.00
Wax Box (24): 70.00
1 Keyshawn Johnson 1.00
2 Natrone Means .50
3 Antonio Freeman .40
4 Muhsin Muhammad .50
5 Curtis Martin 1.00
6 Chris Chandler .50
7 Priest Holmes 1.00
8 Vinny Testaverde .50
9 Tim Brown .50
10 Eddie George 1.25
11 Brad Johnson 1.00
12 Mike Alstott 1.00
13 Dorsey Levens .40
14 Jamal Anderson .40
15 Herman Moore .40
16 Brett Favre 4.00
17 John Elway 3.00
18 Steve Young 1.50
19 Warrick Dunn 1.00
20 Fred Taylor 2.00
21 Charlie Batch .40
22 Jimmy Smith .50
23 Steve McNair 1.25
24 Jerry Rice 2.00
25 Dan Marino 3.00
26 Jake Plummer 1.00
27 Marshall Faulk 1.00
28 Garrison Hearst .50
29 Terrell Davis 2.00
30 Barry Sanders 3.00
31 Carl Pickens .50
32 Jerome Bettis 1.00
33 Scott Mitchell .25
34 Duce Staley .75
35 Robert Smith .40
36 Wayne Chrebet .40
37 Steve Beuerlein .50
38 Elvis Grbac .50
39 Troy Aikman 2.00
40 Emmitt Smith 3.00
41 Joey Galloway 1.00
42 Ryan Leaf .40
43 Skip Hicks .50
44 Cris Carter 1.00
45 Shannon Sharpe .50
46 Mark Brunell 1.50
47 Kerry Collins .50
48 Corey Dillon 1.00
49 Kordell Stewart 1.25
50 Randy Moss 4.00
51 Jon Kitna .40
52 Deion Sanders 1.00
53 Rod Smith .50
54 Drew Bledsoe 1.50
55 Terrell Owens 1.00
56 Napoleon Kaufman .40
57 Trent Green 1.00
58 Ricky Watters 1.00
59 Randall Cunningham .40
60 Peyton Manning 3.00
61 *Tim Couch* 8.00
62 *Amos Zereoue* 5.00
63 *Cade McNown* 2.00
64 *Donovan McNabb* 15.00
65 *Ricky Williams* 12.00
66 *Daunte Culpepper* 15.00
67 *Troy Edwards* 4.00
68 *Peerless Price* 6.00
69 *Edgerrin James* 15.00
70 *Champ Bailey* 4.00
71 *Akili Smith* 4.00
72 *Kevin Johnson* 2.00
73 *Cecil Collins* 2.00
74 *David Boston* 8.00
75 *Torry Holt* 8.00
76 *J.J. Johnson* 2.00
77 *Na Brown* 1.50
78 *Rob Konrad* 3.00
79 *Michael Cloud* 2.00
80 *Craig Yeast* 1.50
81 *Brock Huard* 2.00
82 *Chris McAlister* 2.00
83 *Shaun King* 2.00
84 *Dee Miller* 1.50
85 *Joe Germaine* 2.00
86 *D'Wayne Bates* 2.00
87 *Kevin Faulk* 2.00
88 *Antoine Winfield* 2.00
89 *Reggie Kelly* 1.50
90 *Antwan Edwards* 1.50

1999 E-X Century Essential Credentials Future

This was a 90-card parallel set that was sequentially numbered opposite of the player's card number.

NM/M
Cards numbered from 30-90 10X to 40X
Cards numbered from 10-29 5X to10X
Under 9 too uncommon to price

1999 E-X Century Essential Credentials Now

This was a 90-card parallel set that was sequentially numbered to the player's card number.

NM/M
Minor Stars: 15.00
Rookies numbered from 45-90 2X to 5X
Stars numbered from 20-70 10X to 40X
Under 20 too uncommon to price

1999 E-X Century Authen-Kicks

This 12-card insert included swatches of game-worn shoes. Each player hand-numbered their cards with each to a different amount. Singles were randomly inserted.

NM/M
Common Player: 10.00
1 Travis McGriff 235 10.00
2 Trent Green 190 10.00
3 Brock Huard 280 10.00
4 Randall Cunningham 290 25.00
5 Donovan McNabb 210 50.00
6 Torry Holt 285 35.00
7 Joe Germaine 280 10.00
8 Cade McNown 260 15.00
9 Doug Flutie 215 15.00
10 O.J. McDuffie 285 10.00
11 Ricky Williams 215 60.00
12 Dan Marino 285 50.00

1999 E-X Century Bright Lights

This was a 20-card insert that included the game's best and pictured them on a green plastic stock with a glowing star background. Singles were found 1:24 packs. A parallel Orange version was also issued.

NM/M
Complete Set (20): 60.00
Common Player: 1.00
Inserted 1:24
1 Randy Moss 8.00
2 Tim Couch 6.00
3 Eddie George 3.00
4 Brett Favre 8.00
5 Steve Young 4.00
6 Barry Sanders 8.00
7 Troy Aikman 6.00
8 Jake Plummer 2.00
9 Edgerrin James 8.00

		NM/M
10	Terrell Davis	4.00
11	Warrick Dunn	1.00
12	Jerry Rice	6.00
13	Fred Taylor	4.00
14	Mark Brunell	2.00
15	Emmitt Smith	8.00
16	Ricky Williams	8.00
17	Charlie Batch	1.00
18	Jamal Anderson	1.00
19	Peyton Manning	6.00
20	Dan Marino	8.00

1999 E-X Century E-Xtraordinary

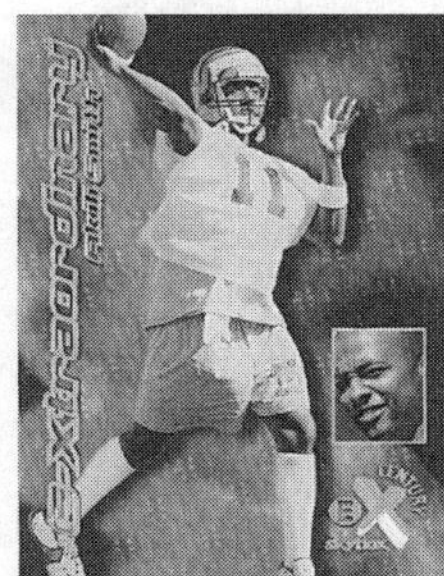

This 15-card insert included the top young players in the game and pictured them on lenticular stock with a team color coded background. Singles were inserted 1:9 packs.

		NM/M
Complete Set (15):		40.00
Common Player:		1.00
Inserted 1:9		
1	Ricky Williams	6.00
2	Corey Dillon	1.00
3	Charlie Batch	1.00
4	Terrell Davis	4.00
5	Edgerrin James	6.00
6	Jake Plummer	1.00
7	Tim Couch	5.00
8	Warrick Dunn	1.00
9	Akili Smith	1.00
10	Randy Moss	6.00
11	Cade McNown	1.00
12	Fred Taylor	3.00
13	Donovan McNabb	5.00
14	Torry Holt	3.00
15	Peyton Manning	6.00

2000 E-X

		NM/M
Complete Set (150):		450.00
Common Player:		.20
Minor Stars:		.40
Common Rookie:		1.00
Production 1,500 Sets		
Pack (5):		4.75
Wax Box (24):		80.00
1	Tim Couch	1.00
2	Daunte Culpepper	1.25
3	Jake Reed	.40
4	Donovan McNabb	1.00
5	Terry Glenn	.50
6	Vinny Testaverde	.40
7	Michael Westbrook	.40
8	Errict Rhett	.40
9	Joey Galloway	.50
10	O.J. McDuffie	.20
11	Rob Johnson	.40
12	Warren Sapp	.40
13	Brian Griese	.75
14	Derrick Mayes	.40
15	Ike Hilliard	.20
16	Kevin Dyson	.40
17	Shannon Sharpe	.40
18	Cade McNown	.75
19	Damon Huard	.50
20	James Stewart	.40
21	Kevin Johnson	.50
22	Muhsin Muhammad	.40
23	Shaun King	1.00
24	Corey Dillon	.50
25	Fred Taylor	.75
26	Peyton Manning	2.50
27	Steve McNair	.50
28	Tim Brown	.50
29	Brad Johnson	.50
30	Edgerrin James	2.50
31	Germane Crowell	.40
32	Kordell Stewart	.50
33	Randy Moss	2.50
34	Tony Banks	.40
35	Akili Smith	.50
36	Charlie Batch	.50
37	Duce Staley	.50
38	Jerome Bettis	.50
39	Rich Gannon	.40
40	Steve Young	1.00
41	Tony Gonzalez	.40
42	Curtis Martin	.50
43	Eddie George	.75
44	Marshall Faulk	.50
45	Troy Edwards	.40
46	Curtis Enis	.40
47	Jake Plummer	.50
48	Jon Kitna	.50
49	Qadry Ismail	.20
50	Terrell Davis	1.00
51	Troy Aikman	1.25
52	Elvis Grbac	.40
53	Jeff Blake	.40
54	Kurt Warner	2.50
55	Ricky Watters	.40
56	Torry Holt	.50
57	Brett Favre	2.50
58	Chris Chandler	.40
59	Eric Moulds	.50
60	Jimmy Smith	.50
61	Ricky Williams	1.00
62	Antonio Freeman	.50
63	Curtis Conway	.40
64	Emmitt Smith	1.75
65	Kerry Collins	.40
66	Marvin Harrison	.50
67	Tyrone Wheatley	.40
68	Charlie Garner	.40
69	Derrick Alexander	.20
70	Jamal Anderson	.50
71	Mike Alstott	.50
72	Ryan Leaf	.50
73	Tim Biakabutuka	.40
74	Amani Toomer	.20
75	Dorsey Levens	.50
76	Frank Sanders	.40
77	Junior Seau	.40
78	Steve Beuerlein	.40
79	Wayne Chrebet	.50
80	Carl Pickens	.40
81	Drew Bledsoe	1.00
82	Isaac Bruce	.50
83	Marcus Robinson	.50
84	Stephen Davis	.50
85	Cris Carter	.50
86	Ed McCaffrey	.50
87	Jerry Rice	1.25
88	Mark Brunell	1.00
89	Peerless Price	.40
90	Terance Mathis	.20
91	Tony Martin	.20
92	Jevon Kearse	.50
93	Robert Smith	.50
94	Rob Moore	.20
95	Charles Johnson	.20
96	Doug Flutie	.75
97	Sean Dawkins	.20
98	Keenan McCardell	.20
99	Bill Schroeder	.20
100	Rod Smith	.40
101	*Peter Warrick*	15.00
102	*Corey Simon*	1.00
103	*Danny Farmer*	2.00
104	*Jamal Lewis*	20.00
105	*Jerry Porter*	12.00
106	*Joe Hamilton*	2.00
107	*Marc Bulger*	15.00
108	*R. Jay Soward*	2.00
109	*Ron Dugans*	1.00
110	*Shaun Alexander*	20.00
111	*Travis Prentice*	5.00
112	*Anthony Becht*	1.00
113	*Bubba Franks*	10.00
114	*Chris Redman*	5.00
115	*Dennis Northcutt*	2.00
116	*Dez White*	5.00
117	*Gari Scott*	1.00
118	*Mareno Philyaw*	1.00
119	*Ron Dayne*	3.00
120	*Shyrone Stith*	1.00
121	*Tee Martin*	5.00
122	*Tom Brady*	55.00
123	*Trung Canidate*	5.00
124	*Chad Pennington*	40.00
125	*Chris Cole*	1.00
126	*Courtney Brown*	2.00
127	*Doug Chapman*	1.00
128	*Giovanni Carmazzi*	2.00
129	*J.R. Redmond*	5.00
130	*Michael Wiley*	1.00
131	*Reuben Droughns*	10.00
132	*Terrelle Smith*	1.00
133	*Thomas Jones*	10.00
134	*Travis Taylor*	4.00
135	*Anthony Lucas*	1.00
136	*Curtis Keaton*	1.00
137	*Frank Moreau*	1.00
138	*Darrell Jackson*	10.00
139	*Laveranues Coles*	12.00
140	*Brian Urlacher*	25.00
141	*Plaxico Burress*	20.00
142	*Sammy Morris*	4.00
143	*Sylvester Morris*	4.00
144	*Tim Rattay*	12.00
145	*Todd Pinkston*	10.00
146	*Troy Walters*	2.00
147	*Sebastian Janikowski*	6.00
148	*JaJuan Dawson*	2.00
149	*Trevor Gaylor*	1.00
150	*Rondell Mealey*	1.00

2000 E-X Essential Credentials

	NM/M
Essential Credential Cards:	15X-30X
Production 50 Sets	
Essential Credential Rookies:	2X-4X
Production 25 Sets	

2000 E-X E-Xceptional Red

		NM/M
Complete Set (15):		25.00
Common Player:		1.00
Minor Stars:		2.00
Inserted 1:12		
Green Cards:		2X-4X
Inserted 1:288		
Blue Cards:		3X-5X
Production 100 Sets		
1	Kurt Warner	3.00
2	Peyton Manning	4.00
3	Brett Favre	4.00
4	Tim Couch	2.50
5	Keyshawn Johnson	1.00
6	Mark Brunell	2.00
7	Eddie George	2.00
8	Edgerrin James	4.00
9	Ricky Williams	2.50
10	Randy Moss	4.00
11	Jamal Lewis	5.00
12	Emmitt Smith	3.00
13	Thomas Jones	3.00
14	Fred Taylor	2.00
15	Chad Pennington	6.00

2000 E-X E-Xciting

		NM/M
Complete Set (10):		25.00
Common Player:		2.00
Inserted 1:24		
1	Fred Taylor	3.00
2	Troy Aikman	4.00
3	Edgerrin James	4.00
4	Brett Favre	6.00
5	Peyton Manning	5.00
6	Emmitt Smith	5.00
7	Randy Moss	6.00
8	Kurt Warner	4.00
9	Marshall Faulk	2.00
10	Peter Warrick	2.00

2000 E-X E-Xplosive

		NM/M
Complete Set (20):		25.00
Common Player:		1.00
Inserted 1:8		
1	Kurt Warner	3.00
2	Marvin Harrison	2.00
3	Ricky Williams	2.50
4	Eddie George	1.50
5	Emmitt Smith	4.00
6	Troy Aikman	2.50
7	Randy Moss	4.00
8	Edgerrin James	3.00
9	Keyshawn Johnson	1.00
10	Tim Couch	2.00
11	Fred Taylor	1.75
12	Brett Favre	4.00
13	Peyton Manning	4.00
14	Donovan McNabb	1.50
15	Ron Dayne	1.00
16	Jake Plummer	1.00
17	Marshall Faulk	1.00
18	Travis Taylor	2.00
19	Terrell Davis	3.00
20	Shaun Alexander	3.50

2000 E-X Generation E-X

		NM/M
Complete Set (15):		15.00
Common Player:		.50
Minor Stars:		1.00
Inserted 1:4		
1	Peter Warrick	1.00
2	Plaxico Burress	1.75
3	R. Jay Soward	1.00
4	Shaun Alexander	2.50
5	Chad Pennington	4.00
6	Giovanni Carmazzi	1.00
7	Thomas Jones	1.50
8	Todd Pinkston	.50
9	Chris Redman	1.50
10	Jamal Lewis	2.00
11	Ron Dayne	1.00
12	Dez White	.50
13	J.R. Redmond	1.25
14	Sylvester Morris	1.75
15	Travis Taylor	1.25

2000 E-X NFL Debut Postmarks

		NM/M
Complete Set (15):		300.00
Common Player:		15.00
Inserted 1:288		
1	Peter Warrick	10.00
2	Travis Taylor	25.00
3	Thomas Jones	20.00
4	Ron Dayne	10.00
5	Plaxico Burress	35.00
6	Sylvester Morris	15.00
7	Todd Pinkston	12.00
8	Jamal Lewis	20.00
9	Shaun Alexander	30.00
10	J.R. Redmond	12.00
11	Dennis Northcutt	10.00
12	Bubba Franks	15.00
13	R. Jay Soward	15.00
14	Jerry Porter	15.00
15	Chad Pennington	45.00

2001 Fleer E-X

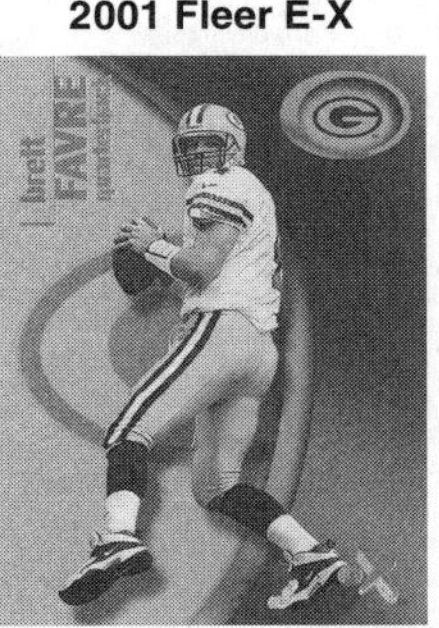

		NM/M
Common Player:		.20
Minor Stars:		.40
Common Rookie:		5.00
Pack (4):		4.00
Wax Box (24):		70.00
1	Jamal Anderson	.50
2	Tim Couch	.75
3	Jeff Garcia	.50
4	Brett Favre	2.75
5	Donovan McNabb	1.00
6	Kerry Collins	.40
7	Doug Flutie	.50
8	Steve McNair	.50
9	Kordell Stewart	.50
10	Daunte Culpepper	1.25
11	Rich Gannon	.40
12	Kurt Warner	2.00
13	Brian Griese	.60
14	Brad Johnson	.40
15	Jake Plummer	.50
16	Mark Brunell	.60
17	Peyton Manning	2.00
18	Keyshawn Johnson	.50
19	Derrick Alexander	.20
20	Emmitt Smith	1.75
21	Rob Johnson	.40
22	Aaron Brooks	.50
23	Charlie Garner	.50
24	Lamar Smith	.40
25	Eddie George	.60
26	Marshall Faulk	.75
27	Tiki Barber	.40
28	Terrell Davis	1.50
29	Jamal Lewis	1.50
30	Edgerrin James	2.00
31	Duce Staley	.50
32	Ricky Williams	1.00
33	Dorsey Levens	.40
34	Jerome Bettis	.50
35	Ron Dayne	1.25
36	Mike Anderson	1.25
37	Peter Warrick	.50
38	Mike Alstott	.50
39	Fred Taylor	.60
40	Curtis Martin	.50
41	Warrick Dunn	.50
42	Vinny Testaverde	.40
43	Stephen Davis	.50
44	Ahman Green	.50
45	James Stewart	.40
46	Ricky Watters	.40
47	Ray Lewis	.40
48	Thomas Jones	.40
49	Zach Thomas	.40
50	Junior Seau	.40
51	Brian Urlacher	1.25
52	Isaac Bruce	.50
53	Corey Dillon	.50
54	Cris Carter	.50
55	Terrell Owens	.50
56	Drew Bledsoe	.60
57	Torry Holt	.50
58	Charlie Batch	.50
59	Germane Crowell	.40
60	Jimmy Smith	.40
61	Tim Biakabutuka	.30
62	Jay Fiedler	.40
63	Joey Galloway	.40
64	Michael Westbrook	.30
65	Shaun Alexander	.50
66	Matt Hasselbeck	.40
67	Elvis Grbac	.40
68	Derrick Mason	.40
69	Trent Green	.40
70	Wayne Chrebet	.40
71	Rod Smith	.50
72	Jerry Rice	1.50
73	Tim Brown	.50
74	Shannon Sharpe	.40
75	Joe Horn	.40
76	Randy Moss	2.00
77	Amani Toomer	.30
78	Antonio Freeman	.40
79	Ed McCaffrey	.40
80	Marvin Harrison	.50
81	Muhsin Muhammad	.30
82	Chad Pennington	1.00
83	Kevin Johnson	.40
84	Tony Gonzalez	.40
85	Terry Glenn	.40
86	David Boston	.50
87	Jevon Kearse	.40
88	Marcus Robinson	.50
89	Warren Sapp	.30
90	Eric Moulds	.50
91	*Andre Carter 1250*	8.00
92	*Kevan Barlow 1250*	12.00
93	*Michael Bennett 1000*	25.00
94	*Josh Booty 1500*	4.00
95	*Drew Brees 1000*	20.00
96	*Correll Buckhalter 1500*	15.00
97	*Quincy Carter 1250*	15.00
98	*Chris Chambers1000*	20.00
99	*Nick Goings 1500*	8.00
100	*Kevin Kasper 1500*	8.00
101	*Dave Dickenson 1500*	12.00
102	*Robert Ferguson 1250*	8.00
103	*Jamar Fletcher 1500*	5.00
104	*Rod Gardner 1250*	15.00
105	*Justin McCareins 1250*	10.00
106	*Jason Brookins1500*	12.00
107	*Todd Heap 1500*	8.00
108	*Travis Henry 1000*	18.00
109	*Gerard Warren 1500*	8.00
110	*James Jackson 1250*	8.00
111	*Chad Johnson 1250*	20.00
112	*Rudi Johnson 1500*	15.00
113	*LaMont Jordan 1250*	10.00
114	*Deuce McAllister 1250*	20.00
115	*Mike McMahon 1250*	10.00
116	*Marvin "Snoop" Minnis 1000*	8.00
117	*Travis Minor 1500*	8.00
118	*Freddie Mitchell 1000*	8.00
119	*Quincy Morgan 1250*	12.00
120	*Santana Moss 1250*	15.00
121	*Cedrick Wilson 1500*	5.00
122	*Jesse Palmer 1500*	8.00
123	*Ken-Yon Rambo 1500*	5.00
124	*Jamal Reynolds 1500*	5.00
125	*Koren Robinson 1250*	10.00
126	*Sage Rosenfels 1500*	10.00
127	*Dan Morgan 1250*	7.00
128	*Justin Smith 1500*	7.00
129	*Fred Smoot 1500*	7.00
130	*Vinny Sutherland 1500*	8.00
131	*David Terrell 1000*	20.00
132	*Anthony Thomas 1250*	20.00
133	*LaDainian Tomlinson 1000*	40.00
134	*Dan Alexander 1500*	8.00
135	*Marques Tuiasosopo 1250*	15.00
136	*Michael Vick 1000*	60.00
137	*Steve Smith 1250*	5.00
138	*Reggie Wayne 1250*	12.00
139	*Chris Weinke 1000*	10.00
140	*Alex Bannister 1250*	7.00

2001 Fleer E-X Essential Credentials

Ess.Cred. Cards:	6X-12X
Production 299 Sets	
Ess.Cred. Rookies:	5X
Production 29 Sets	

2001 Fleer E-X Behind the Numbers

		NM/M
Common Player:		10.00
Minor Stars:		15.00
Inserted 1:24		
1BN	Mike Alstott	15.00
2BN	Mark Brunell	15.00
3BN	Cris Carter	15.00
4BN	Daunte Culpepper	20.00
5BN	Stephen Davis	10.00
6BN	Terrell Davis	25.00
7BN	Ron Dayne	18.00
8BN	Corey Dillon	15.00
9BN	Marshall Faulk	20.00
10BN	Brett Favre	35.00
11BN	Eddie George	20.00
12BN	Brian Griese	18.00
13BN	Marvin Harrison	15.00
14BN	Edgerrin James	25.00
15BN	Curtis Martin	10.00
16BN	Donovan McNabb	20.00
17BN	Randy Moss	30.00
18BN	Emmitt Smith	35.00
19BN	Fred Taylor	18.00
20BN	Ricky Williams	20.00
21BN	Jamal Anderson	12.00
22BN	Tim Brown	12.00
23BN	Isaac Bruce	15.00
24BN	Antonio Freeman	12.00
25BN	Jeff Garcia	15.00

2001 Fleer E-X Constant Threads

		NM/M
Common Player:		10.00
Minor Stars:		15.00
Inserted 1:40		
1CT	Tim Brown	12.00
2CT	Mark Brunell	16.00
3CT	Germane Crowell	10.00
4CT	Tim Dwight	10.00
5CT	Torry Holt	15.00
6CT	Dan Marino	40.00
7CT	Fred Taylor	16.00
8CT	Edgerrin James	25.00
9CT	Kevin Johnson	10.00
10CT	Herman Moore	10.00
11CT	Eddie George	25.00
12CT	Steve McNair	10.00
13CT	Jake Plummer	15.00
14CT	Brett Favre	30.00
15CT	Jerry Rice	25.00
16CT	Brad Johnson	10.00
17CT	Doug Flutie	10.00

2001 Fleer E-X Turf Team

		NM/M
Common Player:		15.00
Inserted 1:240		
1TT	Jake Plummer	15.00
2TT	Troy Aikman	40.00
3TT	Stephen Davis	15.00
4TT	Duce Staley	15.00
5TT	Peyton Manning	45.00
6TT	Edgerrin James	30.00
7TT	Marvin Harrison	20.00
8TT	Drew Bledsoe	20.00
9TT	Kurt Warner	25.00
10TT	Torry Holt	15.00
11TT	Marshall Faulk	25.00
12TT	Ron Dayne	20.00
13TT	Donovan McNabb	25.00
14TT	Emmitt Smith	40.00
15TT	Eddie George	20.00
16TT	Steve McNair	15.00
17TT	Keyshawn Johnson	15.00
18TT	Peter Warrick	20.00
19TT	Corey Dillon	20.00
20TT	Jamal Anderson	15.00

2004 E-X

		NM/M
Common Player (1-40):		2.00
Minor Stars (1-40):		3.00
Unlisted Stars (1-40):		4.00
Common Unsigned Rookie (41-65):		3.00
Minor Unsigned Rookie (41-65):		5.00
Unsigned Rookie Production 500 Sets		
Pack(7):		225.00
1	Travis Henry	2.00
2	Deion Sanders	4.00
3	Donovan McNabb	5.00
4	LaDainian Tomlinson	5.00
5	Shaun Alexander	4.00
6	Daunte Culpepper	4.00
7	Peyton Manning	6.00
8	Deuce McAllister	4.00
9	Marshall Faulk	5.00
10	Jamal Lewis	4.00
11	Chad Pennington	5.00
12	Clinton Portis	6.00
13	Brett Favre	10.00
14	Anquan Boldin	4.00
15	Priest Holmes	5.00
16	Brian Urlacher	4.00
17	David Carr	5.00
18	Joey Harrington	4.00
19	Tom Brady	6.00
20	Michael Vick	8.00
21	Jerry Rice	8.00
22	Mike Alstott	2.00
23	Keyshawn Johnson	3.00
24	Jeremy Shockey	4.00
25	Stephen Davis	3.00
26	Kevan Barlow	2.00
27	Carson Palmer	5.00
28	Steve McNair	4.00
29	Jake Plummer	3.00
30	Jeff Garcia	4.00
31	Byron Leftwich	6.00
32	Hines Ward	3.00
33	Randy Moss	6.00
34	Marvin Harrison	4.00
35	Terrell Owens	4.00
36	Ahman Green	4.00
37	Edgerrin James	5.00
38	Emmitt Smith	8.00
39	Torry Holt	4.00
40	Drew Bledsoe	4.00
41	*Eli Manning Jsy AU/100*	
42	*Philip Rivers Jsy AU/90*	80.00
43	*Larry Fitzgerald*	15.00
44	*Roy Williams Jsy AU/100*	80.00
45	*Drew Henson Jsy AU/95*	40.00
46	*Ben Roethlisberger Jsy AU/100*	300.00
47	*Kevin Jones Jsy AU/100*	

48 *Kellen Winslow Jr.* 5.00
49 *Chris Perry* 8.00
50 *Reggie Williams Jsy AU/100* 40.00
51 *Steven Jackson* 10.00
52 *Rashaun Woods* 6.00
53 *Tatum Bell* 8.00
54 *J.P. Losman* 12.00
55 *Sean Taylor* 6.00
56 *Michael Clayton Jsy AU/80* 60.00
57 *Lee Evans* 8.00
58 *Julius Jones* 30.00
59 *Jonathan Vilma* 5.00
60 *Michael Jenkins Jsy AU/96* 30.00
61 *Greg Jones* 5.00
62 *Will Smith* 3.00
63 *Ernest Wilford* 3.00
64 *Quincy Wilson* 3.00
65 *Cody Pickett* 3.00

2004 E-X Essential Credentials Future

Cards 1-25: .75X-2X
Cards 26-40: 2X-4X
Cards 41-65: No Pricing
Production 65-1 Sets

2004 E-X Essential Credentials Now

NM/M
Cards 41-65: 1X-2X
Cards 25-40: 2X-5X
Cards 1-24: No Pricing
Production 1-65 Sets
41 Eli Manning/41 75.00
42 Philip Rivers/42 60.00
44 Roy Williams WR/44 60.00
45 Drew Henson/45 40.00
46 Ben Roethlisberger/46 125.00
47 Kevin Jones/47 60.00
50 Reggie Williams/50 30.00
56 Michael Clayton/56 30.00
60 Michael Jenkins/60 25.00

2004 E-X Rookie Die Cuts

Rookies: .5X-1X
Production 500 Sets

2004 E-X Clearly Authentics Jersey Autographs

NM/M
Common Player: 20.00
CASA Shaun Alexander/2
CAAB1 Anquan Boldin/100 25.00
CAAB2 Anquan Boldin/23
CAJD Jake Delhomme
CABF1 Brett Favre/90 250.00
CABF2 Brett Favre/13
CAAG Ahman Green/85 50.00
CAJH1 Joey Harrington/36 50.00
CAJH2 Joey Harrington/95 40.00
CASJ1 Steven Jackson/100 80.00
CASJ2 StevenJackson/45 100.00
CAEJ1 Edgerrin James/100 50.00
CAEJ2 Edgerrin James/52
CAAJ Andre Johnson
CACJ1 Chad Johnson/65 25.00
CACJ2 Chad Johnson/4
CABL1 Byron Leftwich/100 50.00
CABL2 Byron Leftwich/77 60.00
CAJL Jamal Lewis
CAPM Peyton Manning
CADM1 Deuce McAllister/100 20.00
CADM2 Deuce McAllister/88 30.00
CADM3 Donovan McNabb Exch 60.00
CASM1 Santana Moss/90 20.00
CASM2 Santana Moss/21
CACP1 Chad Pennington Exch
CACP2 Chris Perry Exch 20.00
CAMV Michael Vick Exch
CAKW Kellen Winslow Jr./90 40.00

2004 E-X Clearly Authentics Patch Black

NM/M
Common Player: 20.00
Sequentially #'d to indicated quantity
Gold: .5X-1.25X
Production 50 Sets
Pewter: .5X-1.25X
Production 44 Sets
Tan: No Pricing
Production 22 Sets
Bronze: No Pricing
Production 11 Sets
Burgundy: No Pricing
Production 13 Sets
Turquoise: No Pricing
Production 4 to 15 Sets
Royal: No Pricing
Production 8 Sets
CASA Shaun Alexander/90 20.00
CAAB Anquan Boldin/81 20.00
CATB Tom Brady/90 40.00
CADC David Carr/65 25.00
CADC2 Daunte Culpepper/90 20.00
CAJD Jake Delhomme/90 20.00
CAMF Marshall Faulk/90 25.00
CABF Brett Favre/90 50.00
CALF Larry Fitzgerald/90 25.00
CAJG Jeff Garcia
CAAG Ahman Green/75 20.00
CAJH Joey Harrington/90 20.00
CAMH Marvin Harrison/88 20.00
CADH Drew Henson/90 25.00
CAPH Priest Holmes/90 25.00
CATH Torry Holt/81 20.00
CAEJ Edgerrin James/75 25.00
CACJ Chad Johnson/85 20.00
CABL Byron Leftwich/90 25.00
CAJL Jamal Lewis/90 20.00
CARL Ray Lewis/90 20.00
CAEM Eli Manning/90 40.00
CAPM Peyton Manning 30.00
CADM Deuce McAllister/80 20.00
CADM2 Donovan McNabb/90 25.00
CASM Steve McNair/50 20.00
CARM Randy Moss/84 30.00
CATO Terrell Owens/81 20.00
CACP Carson Palmer/90 25.00
CACP3 Chad Pennington/90 25.00
CACP2 Clinton Portis/75 25.00
CAJR Jerry Rice/80 40.00
CAPR Philip Rivers/50 50.00
CABR Ben Roethlisberger/90 75.00
CADS Deion Sanders/65 30.00
CAJS Jeremy Shockey/80 20.00
CAES Emmitt Smith/90 40.00
CALT LaDainian Tomlinson/90 25.00
CABU Brian Urlacher/90 20.00
CAMV Michael Vick/90 40.00

2004 E-X Clearly Authentics Signature Pewter

NM/M
Sequentially Numbered
Burgundy: No Pricing
Production 5 Sets
Emerald: No Pricing
Production 1 Set
CASA Shaun Alexander/30
CAAB Anquan Boldin/41 30.00
CAJD Jake Delhomme/46
CABF Brett Favre
CAAG Ahman Green/60 40.00
CAJH Joey Harrington/74 30.00
CASJ Steven Jackson/56 100.00
CAEJ Edgerrin James/59 50.00
CAAJ Andre Johnson/39
CACJ Chad Johnson/39 40.00
CABL Byron Leftwich/68
CAJL Jamal Lewis/26
CAPM Peyton Manning
CADM Deuce McAllister/20
CADM3 Donovan McNabb
CASM Santana Moss/54 25.00
CACP Chad Pennington/18
CAMV Michael Vick/104 100.00
CAKW Kellen Winslow Jr./65 75.00

2004 E-X Clearly Authentics Signature Tan

NM/M
Sequentially Numbered
CASA Shaun Alexander/37 40.00
CAAB Anquan Boldin/81
CAJD Jake Delhomme/17
CABF Brett Favre/4
CAAG Ahman Green/30 60.00
CAJH Joey Harrington/3
CASJ Steven Jackson/39 125.00
CAEJ Edgerrin James/32 60.00
CAAJ Andre Johnson
CACJ Chad Johnson/85 30.00
CABL Byron Leftwich
CAJL Jamal Lewis
CAPM Peyton Manning/18
CADM Deuce McAllister/26 30.00
CADM3 Donovan McNabb
CASM Santana Moss/83 20.00
CACP Chad Pennington
CAMV Michael Vick
CAKW Kellen Winslow Jr./80 60.00

2004 E-X Check Mates

No Pricing
Production 25 Sets
Troy Aikman, Michael Irvin
Donovan McNabb, Michael Vick
Joe Montana, Steve Young
Eli Manning, Peyton Manning
Tony Dorsett, Roger Staubach
John Elway, Dan Marino
Jim Kelly, Steve Largent

2004 E-X Classic ConnEXions Doubles

No Pricing
Production 22 Sets
Emerald: No Pricing
Production 1 Set
1 Deion Sanders, Michael Irvin
2 Thurman Thomas, Jim Kelly
3 Troy Aikman, Steve Young
4 Sterling Sharpe, Shannon Sharpe
5 Dan Marino, John Elway
6 Jack Lambert, Mike Singletary
7 Walter Payton, Barry Sanders
8 Joe Montana, Joe Namath
9 Steve Largent, Shaun Alexander
10 Jim Plunkett, Rich Gannon
11 Franco Harris, Tony Dorsett
12 Fran Tarkenton, Daunte Culpepper
13 Paul Hornung, Bart Starr
14 Troy Aikman, Emmitt Smith
15 Jay Novacek, Michael Irvin
16 Thurman Thomas, Barry Sanders
17 Joe Montana, Steve Young
18 Mike Singletary, Walter Payton
19 Jim Kelly, Troy Aikman
20 Shannon Sharpe, John Elway

2004 E-X Classic ConnEXions Triples

No Pricing
Production 13 Sets
Emerald: No Pricing
Production 1 Set
1 Michael Irvin, Troy Aikman, Emmitt Smith
2 Steve Young, Joe Montana, Jerry Rice
3 Joe Montana, John Elway, Dan Marino
4 Walter Payton, Barry Sanders, Emmitt Smith
5 Jack Lambert, Mike Singletary, Lawrence Taylor
6 Paul Hornung, Bart Starr, Brett Favre
7 Sterling Sharpe, Michael Irvin, Jerry Rice
8 Brett Favre, Sterling Sharpe, Reggie White
9 Reggie White, Lawrence Taylor, Deion Sanders
10 Troy Aikman, Steve Young, John Elway

2004 E-X Signings of the Times

NM/M
Common Player: 15.00
TA Troy Aikman/100 75.00
BB Boss Bailey/300 15.00
CB Champ Bailey/300 20.00
TB Tiki Barber/200 30.00
JB Jim Brown/100 80.00
TB Troy Brown/350 30.00
CC Chris Chambers/52 25.00
JD Jake Delhomme/250 20.00
RG Rex Grossman/52 40.00
JM Luke McCown/250 15.00
AO Adewale Ogunleye/56 20.00
JR John Riggins 40.00
BS Billy Sims/255 20.00
SS Steve Smith 15.00
BW Brian Westbrook/50 80.00

2004 E-X Signings of the Times Half Century

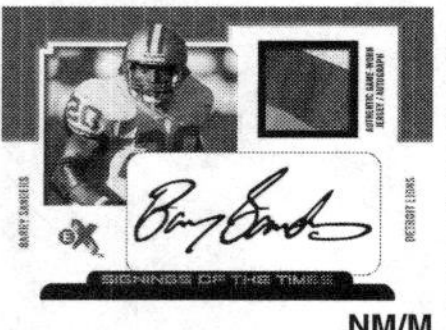

NM/M
Production 50 Sets
Quarter Century: .75X-2X
Production 25 Sets
Emerald: No Pricing
Production 1 Set
TA Troy Aikman 100.00
MA Marcus Allen
EC Earl Campbell
TC Tony Dorsett
MI Michael Irvin
JK Jim Kelly 75.00
SL Steve Largent/48 50.00
JM Joe Montana
BS Barry Sanders
RS Roger Staubach 125.00
FT Fran Tarkenton
SY Steve Young

1948-52 Exhibit W468 Football

The 59-card set, which measures 3-1/4" x 5-3/8", was released by the Exhibit Supply Co. of Chicago in 1948-52. The thick cards were sold in vending machines. The cards, which have blank backs, were originally in black and white. In the following years they were released in sepia, blue, yellow and red. The cards that are colored carry a 3-4 times higher value than the black-and-white and sepia cards. Released in three groups of 32 in 1948, 1950 and 1951, the 1951 set is the easiest to find of the three. The 1951 cards were also reissued in sepia tone in 1952 and possibly 1953. A checklist card was produced in 1950. It was printed in black-and-white and green. It resembles the Bednarik card, however, it lists the 32 players from the 1950 set on the front. In addition, nine-card ad displays were produced, and feature the Bednarik checklist. In 1948, the words "Made in USA" measure 5/8 inch on the card. Also, 11 of the 1948 cards were single prints (Comp, Jacobs, Cifers, Horvath, Mastrangelo, LeForce, Johnson, Pritko, Wedemeyer, Coulter and Schlinkman). In 1950, the single-print cards were Bednarik, Hoerner, Davis, Perry, Ruby and Justice. When the 1950 cards went into a second printing, 11 new cards were issued to replace the original 11 single prints. On the new cards, "Made in USA" measures 7/16 of an inch. The 1951 printing featured only 16 cards, with the six single-print cards from 1950 and 10 cards from 1948 shelved. The 1951 cards feature "Made in USA" in 1/2-inch high letters.

NM/M
Complete Set (59): 4,000
Common Player DP: 10.00
Common Player: 40.00
Common Player SP48: 175.00
Common Player SP50: 50.00
1 Frankie Albert (DP) (48/50/51/52) 10.00
2 Dick Barwegan (DP) (51/52) 10.00
3 Sammy Baugh (DP) (48/50/51/52) 45.00
4 Chuck Bednarik (SP50) 125.00
5 Tony Canadeo (DP) (51/52) 15.00
6 Paul Christman (48/50) 40.00
7 Bob Cifers (SP48) 175.00
8 Irv Comp (SP48) 175.00
9 Charley Conerly (DP) (48/50/51/52) 20.00
10 George Connor (DP) (51/52) 15.00
11 Dewitt Coulter (SP50) 175.00
12 Glenn Davis (SP50) 100.00
13 Glenn Dobbs (48/50) 40.00
14 John Dottley (DP) (51/52) 10.00
15 Bill Dudley (48/50) 50.00
16 Tom Fears (DP) (51/52) 15.00
17 Joe Geri (DP) (51/52) 10.00
18 Otto Graham (DP) (48/50/51/52) 50.00
19 Pat Harder (48/50) 40.00
20 Elroy Hirsch (DP) (51/52) 20.00
21 Dick Hoerner (SP50) 60.00
22 Bob Hoernschemeyer (DP) (51/52) 10.00
23 Les Horvath (SP48) 200.00
24 Jack Jacobs (SP48) 175.00
25 Nate Johnson (SP48) 175.00
26 Charlie Justice (SP50) 75.00
27 Bobby Layne (DP) (48/50/51/52) 35.00
28 Clyde LeForce (SP48) 175.00
29 Sid Luckman (48/50) 75.00
30 John Lujack (48/50) 60.00
31 Bill McColl (DP) (51/52) 175.00
32 Ollie Matson (DP) (51/52) 20.00
33 Bill McColl (DP) (51/52) 10.00
34 Fred Morrison (DP) (50/51/52) 10.00
35 Marion Motley (DP) (48/50/51/52) 20.00
36 Chuck Ortmann (DP) (51/52) 10.00
37 Joe Perry (SP50) 100.00
38 Pete Pihos (48/50) 50.00
39 Steve Pritko (SP48) 175.00
40 George Ratterman (DP) (48/50/51/52) 10.00
41 Jay Rhodemyre (DP) (51/52) 10.00
42 Martin Ruby (SP50) 75.00
43 Julie Rykovich (DP) (51/52) 10.00
44 Walt Schlinkman (SP48) 185.00
45 Emil (Red) Sitko (DP) (51/52) 10.00
46 Vitamin Smith (DP) (50/51/52) 10.00
47 Norm Standlee (48/50) 40.00
48 George Taliaferro (DP) (50/51/52) 10.00
49 Y.A. Tittle (HOR) (48/50) 75.00
50 Charley Trippi (DP) (48/50/51/52) 15.00
51 Frank Tripucka (DP) (48/50/51/52) 12.00
52 Emlen Tunnell (DP) (51/52) 15.00
53 Bulldog Turner (DP) (48/50/51/52) 15.00
54 Steve Van Buren (48/50) 60.00
55 Bob Waterfield (DP) (48/50/51/52) 25.00
56 Herm Wedemeyer (SP48) 500.00
57 Bob Williams (DP) (51/52) 10.00
58 Claude Buddy Young (DP) (passing) (48/50/51/52) 10.00
59 Tank Younger (DP) (50/51/52) 10.00
NNO Chuck Bednarik Checklist Card SP50 500.00

A card number in parenthese ( ) indicates the set is unnumbered.

F

1990 FACT Pro Set Cincinnati

Produced for 29 schools in the Cincinnati school district, the set was used as an educational tool for grade school students. The promotion ran for 15 straight weeks, with 25-card cello packs handed out to the students. The card fronts are identical to 1990 Pro Set Series I cards, while the backs have math, grammar and science questions. The card backs carry the card numbers in the lower right. The missing numbers from the first series are 338, 376 and 377.

NM/M
Complete Set (375): 550.00
Common Player: 1.00
1 Barry Sanders (W1) 25.00
2 Joe Montana (W1) 20.00
3 Lindy Infante Coach of the Year (W1) (UER) (missing Coach next to Packers) 1.00
4 Warren Moon Man of the Year (W1) (UER) (missing R symbol) 2.00
5 Keith Millard Defensive Player of the Year (W1) 1.00
6 Derrick Thomas Defensive Rookie of the Year (W1) (UER) (no 1989 on front banner of card) 2.00
7 Ottis Anderson Comeback Player of the Year (W1) 1.50
8 Joe Montana Passing Leader (W2) 20.00
9 Christian Okoye Rushing Leader (W2) 1.00
10 Thurman Thomas Total Yardage Leader (W2) 3.00
11 Mike Cofer Kick Scoring Leader (W2) 1.00
12 Dalton Hilliard TD Scoring Leader (W2) (UER) (O.J. Simpson not listed in stats, but is mentioned in text) 1.00
13 Sterling Sharpe Receiving Leader (W2) 3.00
14 Rich Camarillo Punting Leader (W3) 1.00
15 Walter Stanley Punt Return Leader (W3) 1.00
16 Rod Woodson Kickoff Return Leader (W3) 2.00
17 Felix Wright Interception Leader (W3) 1.00
18 Chris Doleman Sack Leader (W3) 1.00
19 Andre Ware Heisman Trophy (W3) 1.00
20 Mohammed Elewonibi Outland Trophy (W4) 1.00
21 Percy Snow Lombardi Award (W4) 1.00
22 Anthony Thompson Maxwell Award (W4) 1.00
23 Buck Buchanan 1990 HOF Selection (W4) (Sacking Bart Starr) 1.00
24 Bob Griese 1990 HOF Selection (W4) 1.50
25 Franco Harris 1990 HOF Selection (W5) 1.50
26 Ted Hendricks 1990 HOF Selection (W4) 1.00
27 Jack Lambert 1990 HOF Selection (W5) 1.00
28 Tom Landry 1990 HOF Selection (W5) 1.50
29 Bob St. Clair 1990 HOF Selection (W5) 1.00
30 Aundray Bruce (W5) (UER) (Stats say Falcons) 1.00
31 Tony Casillas (W5) (UER) (Stats say Falcons) 1.00
32 Shawn Collins (W5) 1.00
33 Marcus Cotton (W6) 1.00
34 Bill Fralic (W6) 1.00
35 Chris Miller (W6) 1.50
36 Deion Sanders (W6) (UER) (Stats say Falcons) 14.00
37 John Settle (W6) 1.00
38 Jerry Glanville (CO) (W6) 1.00
39 Cornelius Bennett (W7) 1.50
40 Jim Kelly (W7) 3.00
41 Mark Kelso (W7) (UER) (No fumble rec. in '88; mentioned in '89) 1.00
42 Scott Norwood (W7) 1.00
43 Nate Odomes (W7) 1.50
44 Scott Radecic (W7) 1.00
45 Jim Ritcher (W8) 1.00
46 Leonard Smith (W8) 1.00
47 Darryl Talley (W8) 1.00
48 Marv Levy (CO) (W8) 1.00
49 Neal Anderson (W8) 1.00
50 Kevin Butler (W8) 1.00
51 Jim Covert (W9) 1.00
52 Richard Dent (W9) 1.00
53 Jay Hilgenberg (W9) 1.00
54 Steve McMichael (W9) 1.00
55 Ron Morris (W9) 1.00
56 John Roper (W9) 1.00
57 Mike Singletary (W9) 1.50
58 Keith Van Horne (W10) 1.00
59 Mike Ditka (CO) (W10) 3.00
60 Lewis Billups (W10) 1.00
61 Eddie Brown (W10) 1.00
62 Jason Buck (W10) 1.00
63 Rickey Dixon (W10) 1.00
64 Tim McGee (W11) 1.00
65 Eric Thomas (W11) 1.00
66 Ickey Woods (W11) 1.00
67 Carl Zander (W11) 1.00
68 Sam Wyche (CO) (W11) 1.00
69 Paul Farren (W11) 1.00
70 Thane Gash (W12) 1.00
71 David Grayson (W12) 1.00
72 Bernie Kosar (W12) 1.50
73 Reggie Langhorne (W12) 1.00
74 Eric Metcalf (W12) 2.00
75 Ozzie Newsome (W12) 1.50
76 Felix Wright (W13) 1.00
77 Bud Carson (CO) (W13) 1.00
78 Troy Aikman (W13) 25.00
79 Michael Irvin (W13) 4.00
80 Jim Jeffcoat (W13) 1.00
81 Crawford Ker (W13) 1.00
82 Eugene Lockhart (W13) 1.00
83 Kelvin Martin (W14) 1.50
84 Ken Norton Jr. 1.50
85 Jimmy Johnson (CO) (W14) 2.00
86 Steve Atwater (W14) 1.00
87 Tyrone Braxton (W14) 1.00
88 John Elway (W14) 14.00
89 Simon Fletcher (W15) 1.00
90 Ron Holmes (W15) 1.00
91 Bobby Humphrey (W15) 1.00
92 Vance Johnson (W15) 1.00
93 Ricky Nattiel (W15) 1.00
94 Dan Reeves (CO) (W15) 1.50
95 Jim Arnold (W1) 1.00
96 Jerry Ball (W1) 1.00
97 Bennie Blades (W1) 1.00
98 Lomas Brown (W1) 1.00
99 Michael Cofer (W1) 1.00
100 Richard Johnson (W4) 1.00
101 Eddie Murray (W4) 1.00
102 Barry Sanders (W2) 25.00
103 Chris Spielman (W2) 1.00
104 William White (W2) 1.50
105 Eric Williams (W2) 1.00
106 Wayne Fontes (CO) (W3) (UER) (Says born in MO, actually born in MA) 1.00
107 Brent Fullwood (W3) 1.00
108 Ron Hallstrom (W3) 1.00
109 Tim Harris (W8) 1.00
110 Johnny Holland (W8) 1.00
111 Perry Kemp (W8) 1.00
112 Don Majkowski (W9) 1.00
113 Mark Murphy (W9) 1.00
114 Sterling Sharpe (W9) 4.00
115 Ed West (W9) 1.50
116 Lindy Infante (CO) (W9) 1.00
117 Steve Brown (W9) 1.00
118 Ray Childress (W10) 1.00
119 Ernest Givins (W10) 1.50
120 John Grimsley (W10) 1.00
121 Alonzo Highsmith (W10) 1.00
122 Drew Hill (W10) 1.50
123 Bubba McDowell (W10) 1.50
124 Dean Steinkuhler (W10) 1.00
125 Lorenzo White (W11) 1.00
126 Tony Zendejas (W11) 1.00
127 Jack Pardee (CO) (W11) 1.00
128 Albert Bentley (W11) 1.00
129 Dean Biasucci (W11) 1.00
130 Duane Bickett (W11) 1.00
131 Bill Brooks (W12) 1.50
132 Jon Hand (W12) 1.00
133 Mike Prior (W12) 1.00
134 Andre Rison (W12) 2.00
135 Rohn Stark (W12) 1.00
136 Donnell Thompson (W12) 1.00
137 Clarence Verdin (W13) 1.00
138 Fredd Young (W13) 1.00
139 Ron Meyer (CO) (W14) 1.00
140 John Alt (W14) 1.00
141 Steve DeBerg (W14) 1.50
142 Irv Eatman (W1) 1.00
143 Dino Hackett (W2) 1.00
144 Nick Lowery (W2) 1.00
145 Bill Maas (W2) 1.00
146 Stephone Paige (W5) 1.00
147 Neil Smith (W3) 2.00
148 Marty Schottenheimer (CO) (W3) 1.00
149 Steve Beuerlein (W3) 1.00
150 Tim Brown (W4) 3.00
151 Mike Dyal (W4) 1.00
152 Mervyn Fernandez (W4) 1.00
153 Willie Gault (W4) 1.00
154 Bob Golic (W5) 1.00
155 Bo Jackson (W5) 3.00
156 Don Mosebar (W5) 1.00
157 Steve Smith (W5) 1.00
158 Greg Townsend (W5) 1.00
159 Bruce Wilkerson (W6) 1.00
160 Steve Wisniewski (W6) (Blocking for Bo Jackson) 1.00
161 Art Shell (CO) (W6) 2.00
162 Flipper Anderson (W6) 1.00
163 Greg Bell (W6) (UER) (Stats have 5 catches, should be 9) 1.00
164 Henry Ellard (W6) 1.50
165 Jim Everett (W6) 1.50
166 Jerry Gray (W7) 1.00
167 Kevin Greene (W7) 2.00
168 Pete Holohan (W13) 1.00
169 Larry Kelm (W13) 1.00
170 Tom Newberry (W13) 1.00
171 Vince Newsome (W13) 1.00
172 Irv Pankey (W14) 1.00
173 Jackie Slater (W14) 1.00
174 Fred Strickland (W14) 1.00

175 Mike Wilcher (W14) (UER) (Fumble rec. number different from 1989 Pro Set card) 1.00
176 John Robinson (CO) (W7) (UER) (Stats say Rams, should says L.A. Rams) 1.00
177 Mark Clayton (W7) 1.50
178 Roy Foster (W7) 1.00
179 Harry Galbreath (W7) 1.00
180 Jim C. Jensen (W8) 1.00
181 Dan Marino (W15) 35.00
182 Louis Oliver (W15) 1.00
183 Sammie Smith (W15) 1.00
184 Brian Sochia (W15) 1.00
185 Don Shula (CO) (W15) 1.50
186 Joey Browner (W8) 1.00
187 Anthony Carter (W15) 1.50
188 Chris Doleman (W8) 1.00
189 Steve Jordan (W4) 1.00
190 Carl Lee (W4) 1.00
191 Randall McDaniel (W5) 1.00
192 Mike Merriweather (W5) 1.00
193 Keith Millard (W14) 1.00
194 Al Noga (W12) 1.00
195 Scott Studwell (W5) 1.00
196 Henry Thomas (W12) 1.50
197 Herschel Walker (W5) 1.50
198 Wade Wilson (W5) 1.50
199 Gary Zimmerman (W5) 1.00
200 Jerry Burns (CO) (W6) 1.00
201 Vincent Brown (W6) 1.50
202 Hart Lee Dykes (W14) 1.00
203 Sean Farrell (W6) 1.00
204 Fred Marion (W6) 1.00
205 Stanley Morgan (W15) (UER) (Text says he reached 10,000 yards fastest; 3 players did it in 10 seasons) 1.50
206 Eric Sievers (W6) 1.00
207 John Stephens (W15) 1.00
208 Andre Tippett (W15) 1.00
209 Rod Rust (CO) (W15) 1.00
210 Morten Andersen (W6) 1.00
211 Brad Edelman (W12) 1.00
212 John Fourcade (W12) 1.00
213 Dalton Hilliard (W13) 1.00
214 Rickey Jackson (W13) (Forcing Jim Kelly fumble) 1.00
215 Vaughan Johnson (W13) 1.00
216 Eric Martin (W13) 1.50
217 Sam Mills (W7) 1.00
218 Pat Swilling (W7) (UER) (Total fumble recoveries listed as 4, should be 5) 1.50
219 Frank Warren (W7) 1.00
220 Jim Wilks (W7) 1.00
221 Jim Mora (CO) (W7) 1.00
222 Raul Allegre (W2) 1.00
223 Carl Banks (W1) 1.00
224 John Elliott (W1) 1.00
225 Erik Howard (W7) 1.00
226 Pepper Johnson (W2) 1.00
227 Leonard Marshall (W7) (UER) (In Super Bowl XXI, George Martin had the safety) 1.00
228 Dave Meggett (W2) 1.50
229 Bart Oates (W3) 1.00
230 Phil Simms (W8) 1.50
231 Lawrence Taylor(W8) 2.00
232 Bill Parcells (CO) (W8) 1.50
233 Troy Benson (W8) 1.00
234 Kyle Clifton (W8) (UER) (Born: Onley, should be Olney) 1.00
235 Johnny Hector (W8) 1.00
236 Jeff Lageman (W9) 1.50
237 Pat Leahy (W9) 1.00
238 Freeman McNeil (W9) 1.00
239 Ken O'Brien (W9) 1.00
240 Al Toon (W9) 1.50
241 Jo Jo Townsell 1.00
242 Bruce Coslet (CO) (W10) 1.00
243 Eric Allen (W10) 1.00
244 Jerome Brown (W10) 1.50
245 Keith Byars (W10) 1.50
246 Cris Carter (W13) 4.00
247 Randall Cunningham (W13) 2.00
248 Keith Jackson (W14) 1.50
249 Mike Quick (W14) 1.50
250 Clyde Simmons (W14) 1.50
251 Andre Waters (W14) 1.00
252 Reggie White (W15) 2.00
253 Buddy Ryan(CO) (W15) 1.00
254 Rich Camarillo (W15) 1.00
255 Earl Ferrell (W10) (No mention of retirement on card front) 1.00
256 Roy Green (W10) 1.00
257 Ken Harvey (W3) 1.00
258 Ernie Jones 1.00
259 Tim McDonald (W11) 1.00
260 Timm Rosenbach (W11) (UER) (Born '67, should be '66) 1.50
261 Luis Sharpe (W3) 1.00
262 Vai Sikahema (W3) 1.00
263 J.T. Smith (W1) 1.00
264 Ron Wolfley (W1) (UER) (Born Blaisdel, should be Blasdel) 1.00
265 Joe Bugel (CO) (W11) 1.00
266 Gary Anderson (W11) 1.00
267 Bubby Brister (W1) 1.00
268 Merril Hoge (W11) 1.00
269 Carnell Lake (W2) 1.00
270 Louis Lipps (W11) 1.00
271 David Little (W3) 1.00
272 Greg Lloyd (W3) 2.00
273 Keith Willis (W11) 1.00
274 Tim Worley (W3) 1.00
275 Chuck Noll (CO) (W4) 1.50
276 Marion Butts (W4) 1.00
277 Gill Byrd (W2) 1.00
278 Vencie Glenn (W2) (UER) (Sack total should be 2, not 2.5) 1.00
279 Burt Grossman (W4) 1.00
280 Gary Plummer (W4) 1.00
281 Bill Ray Smith (W12) 1.00
282 Billy Joe Tolliver (W12) 1.00
283 Dan Henning (CO) (W1) 1.00
284 Harris Barton (W1) 1.00
285 Michael Carter (W1) 1.00
286 Mike Cofer (W1) 1.00
287 Roger Craig (W1) 1.50
288 Don Griffin (W1) 1.00
289 Charles Haley (W2) 1.50
290 Pierce Holt (W2) 1.00
291 Ronnie Lott (W2) 1.50
292 Guy McIntyre (W2) 1.00
293 Joe Montana (W2) 20.00
294 Tom Rathman (W2) 1.50
295 Jerry Rice (W3) 20.00
296 Jesse Sapolu (W3) 1.00
297 John Taylor (W3) 1.50
298 Michael Walter (W3) 1.00
299 George Seifert (CO) (W3) 2.00
300 Jeff Bryant (W3) 1.00
301 Jacob Green (W4) 1.00
302 Norm Johnson (UER) (W4) (Card shop not in Garden Grove, should say Fullerton) 1.00
303 Bryan Millard (W4) 1.00
304 Joe Nash (W4) 1.00
305 Eugene Robinson (W4) 1.00
306 John L. Williams (W14) 1.00
307 Dave Wyman (W14) (NFL EXP is in caps, inconsisten with rest of the set) 1.00
308 Chuck Knox (CO) (W14) 1.00
309 Mark Carrier (C14) 1.50
310 Paul Gruber (W14) 1.00
311 Harry Hamilton (W15) 1.00
312 Bruce Hill (W15) 1.00
313 Donald Igwebuike (W15) 1.00
314 Kevin Murphy (W15) 1.00
315 Ervin Randle (W12) 1.00
316 Mark Robinson (W12) 1.00
317 Lars Tate (W12) 1.00
318 Vinny Testaverde (W12) 2.00
319 Ray Perkins (CO) (W12) 1.00
320 Earnest Byner (W12) 1.00
321 Gary Clark (W12) (Randall Cunningham looking on from sidelines) 2.00
322 Darryl Grant (W13) 1.00
323 Darrell Green (W13) 1.00
324 Jim Lachey (W13) 1.00
325 Charles Mann (W13) 1.00
326 Wilber Marshall (W13) 1.00
327 Ralf Mojsiejenko (W13) 1.00
328 Art Monk (W15) 2.00
329 Gerald Riggs (W15) 1.00
330 Mark Rypien (W14) 1.00
331 Ricky Sanders (W14) 1.00
332 Alvin Walton (W4) 1.00
333 Joe Gibbs (CO) (W5) 2.00
334 Aloha Stadium (W5) (Site of Pro Bowl) 1.00
335 Brian Blades (PB) (W5) 1.50
336 James Brooks (PB) (W5) 1.00
337 Shane Conlan (PB) (W5) 1.00
339 Ray Donaldson (PB) (W5) 1.00
340 Ferrell Edmunds (PB) (W6) 1.00
341 Boomer Esiason (PB) (W6) 1.50
342 David Fulcher (PB) (W6) 1.00
343 Chris Hinton (PB) (W6) 1.00
344 Rodney Holman (PB) (W6) 1.00
345 Kent Hull (PB) (W6) 1.00
346 Tunch Ilkin (PB) (W7) 1.00
347 Mike Johnson (PB) (W7) 1.00
348 Greg Kragen (PB) (W7) 1.00
349 Dave Krieg (PB) (W7) 1.00
350 Albert Lewis (PB) (W7) 1.00
351 Howie Long (PB) (W7) 1.50
352 Bruce Matthews (PB) (W8) 1.00
353 Clay Matthews (PB) (W8) 1.00
354 Erik McMillan (PB) (W8) 1.00
355 Karl Mecklenburg (PB) (W8) 1.00
356 Anthony Miller (PB) (W8) 2.00
357 Frank Minnifield (PB) (W8) 1.00
358 Max Montoya (PB) (W8) 1.00
359 Warren Moon (PB) (W10) 2.00
360 Mike Munchak (PB) (W9) 1.00
361 Anthony Munoz (PB) (W9) 1.00
362 John Offerdahl (PB) (W9) 1.00
363 Christian Okoye (PB) (W9) 1.00
364 Leslie O'Neal (PB) (W9) 1.00
365 Rufus Porter (PB) (W9) (UER) (TM logo missing) 1.00
366 Andre Reed (PB) (W10) 1.50
367 Johnny Rembert (PB) (W10) 1.00
368 Reggie Roby (PB) (W10) 1.00
369 Kevin Ross (PB) (W10) 1.00
370 Webster Slaughter (PB) (W10) 1.00
371 Bruce Smith (PB) (W11) 1.50
372 Dennis Smith (PB) (W11) 1.00
373 Derrick Thomas (PB) (W11) 2.00
374 Thurman Thomas (PB) (W11) 2.00
375 David Treadwell (PB) (W11) 1.00
376 Lee Williams (PB) (W11) 1.00

1991 FACT Pro Set Mobil

Each of the NFL cities received these cards, sponsored by Mobil Oil and Pro Set, to use as an educational tool for fourth grade students. The cards are identical to the 1990 Pro Set Series I cards, while the backs have questions for the students. Six different sets were issued throughout the program, each with a header card.

NM/M
Complete Set (108): 130.00
Common Player: .75
3 Joe Montana (S1) 10.00
5 Mike Singletary (S2) 1.00
12 Jay Novacek (S3) 1.50
20 Ottis Anderson (S2) 1.00
40 Tim Brown (S1) 1.50
44 Herschel Walker (S1) 1.00
59 Eric Dorsey (S3) .75
60 John Elliott (S1) .75
63 Jeff Hostetler (S2) 1.00
69 Eric Moore (S4) .75
70 Bart Oates (S3) .75
71 Gary Reasons (S4) .75
75 Shane Conlan (S3) .75
78 Jim Kelly (S4) 2.50
84 Darryl Talley (S4) .75
90 Marv Levy (CO) (S1) .75
94 Tim Green (S2) .75
99 Jerry Glanville (CO) (S3) .75
101 Mark Carrier (S3) .75
104 Jim Harbaugh (S6) 1.50
105 Brad Muster (S4) .75
107 Keith Van Horne (S6) .75
111 Boomer Esiason (S1) 1.00
116 Anthony Munoz (S2) 1.00
117 Sam Wyche (CO) (S4) .75
118 Paul Farren (S6) .75
119 Thane Gash (S3) .75
122 Clay Matthews (S2) .75
123 Eric Metcalf (S6) 1.25
127 Tommie Agee (S6) .75
128 Troy Aikman (S6) 12.00
132 Michael Irvin (S6) 3.00
134 Daniel Stubbs (S6) .75
136 Steve Atwater (S1) .75
138 John Elway (S2) 8.00
141 Mark Jackson (S6) .75
142 Karl Mecklenburg (S3) .75
143 Doug Widell (S2) .75
153 Wayne Fontes (CO) (S2) .75
156 Don Majkowski (S1) .75
157 Tony Mandarich (S6) .75
158 Mark Murphy (S6) .75
161 Sterling Sharpe (S4) 2.00
162 Lindy Infante (CO) (S3) .75
163 Ray Childress (S6) .75
166 Bruce Matthews (S3) .75
167 Warren Moon (S6) 2.50
168 Mike Munchak (S4) .75
169 Al Smith (S6) .75
174 Bill Brooks (S1) 1.00
179 Clarence Verdin (S3) .75
182 Steve DeBerg (S1) 1.00
185 Christian Okoye (S3) .75
189 Marty Schottenheimer (CO) (S1) .75
191 Howie Long (S2) 1.00
194 Steve Smith (S4) .75
196 Lionel Washington (S6) .75
198 Art Shell (CO) (S3) 1.00
203 Buford McGee (S2) .75
204 Tom Newberry (S6) .75
205 Frank Stams (S1) .75
210 Dan Marino (S4) 18.00
212 John Offerdahl (S1) .75
216 Don Shula (S4) 1.00
217 Darrell Fullington (S6) .75
218 Tim Irwin (S2) .75
219 Mike Merriweather (S3) .75
231 Ed Reynolds (S3) .75
238 Robert Massey (S4) .75
246 James Hasty (S1) .75
247 Erik McMillan (S2) .75
249 Ken O'Brien (S4) .75
260 Andre Waters (S2) .75
270 Joe Bugel (CO) (S2) .75
271 Gary Anderson (S1) .75
272 Dermontti Dawson (S4) .75
275 Tunch Ilkin (S2) .75
282 Gill Byrd (S4) .75
290 Michael Carter (S2) .75
292 Pierce Holt (S3) .75
297 George Seifert (CO) (S1) 1.25
306 Chuck Knox (CO) (S3) .75
310 Harry Hamilton (S4) .75
321 Martin Mayhew (S4) .75
322 Mark Rypien (S1) .75
NNO Title Card - Stay Fit (S1) .75
NNO Title Card - Eat Smart (S2) .75
NNO Title Card - Stay Off Drugs (S3) .75
NNO Title Card - Stay In Tune (S4) .75
NNO Title Card - Stay True to Yourself (S5) .75
NNO Title Card - Stay In School (S6) .75
NNO Title Card - Stay In School (S6) .75

1992 FACT NFL Properties

The 18-card set was produced by NFL Properties. It showcases a photo of the player, with the NFL shield and "It's A Fact" printed at the top and a slogan at the bottom. The card is bordered in black at the top and bottom. The backs include a quote, with "Think about it..." printed in the lower right. The card number is printed in a black stripe in the lower right.

NM/M
Complete Set (18): 35.00
Common Player: 1.00
1 Warren Moon Crack Kills 1.50
2 Boomer Esiason Think Before You Drink 1.00
3 Troy Aikman Play It Straight 8.00
4 Anthony Munoz Quedate en la Escuela 1.00
5 Charles Mann Steroids Destroy 1.00
6 Earnest Byner Never Give Up 1.00
7 Joe Jacoby Don't Pollute 1.00
8 Howie Long Aids Kills 1.00
9 Dan Marino School's The Ticket 12.00
10 Mike Singletary Be The Best 1.50
11 Cornelius Bennett Chill 1.00
12 Chris Doleman Turn It Off 1.00
13 Jim Harbaugh Eat To Win 1.50
14 Chris Hinton Say It Don't Spray It 1.00
15 Nick Lowery Heal The Planet 1.00
16 Rodney Peete Respect The Law 1.00
17 Pat Swilling Vote 1.00
18 Jim Everett Study 1.00

1993 FACT Fleer Shell

Fleer, Shell Oil and Russell Athletic sponsored this 108-card set. The cards were used as educational materials for teachers throughout the country. A set of 18 cards were released each month. The card fronts were identical to the regular 1993 Fleer cards. The backs, however, featured educational questions and player bios.

NM/M
Complete Set (108): 50.00
Common Player: .25
1 Stay in School - Scorecard .25
2 Andre Rison .50
3 Jim Kelly .50
4 Mark Carrier (DB) .25
5 David Fulcher .25
6 Eric Metcalf .25
7 Emmitt Smith 5.00
8 John Elway 2.00
9 Rodney Peete .25
10 Brett Favre 5.00
11 Warren Moon Houson Oilers .50
12 Reggie Langhorne .25
13 Christian Okoye .25
14 Nick Bell .25
15 Jim Everett .25
16 Dan Marino 5.00
17 Chris Doleman .25
18 Leonard Russell .25
19 Stay Fit - Scoreboard .25
20 Sam Mills .25
21 Rodney Hampton .50
22 Rob Moore .25
23 Seth Joyner .25
24 Chris Chandler .25
25 Barry Foster .25
26 Stan Humphries .50
27 Steve Young 2.00
28 Cortez Kennedy .25
29 Reggie Cobb .25
30 Mark Rypien .25
31 Michael Haynes .25
32 Thurman Thomas .50
33 Tom Waddle .25
34 Harold Green .25
35 Tommy Vardell .25
36 Michael Irvin .50
37 Eat Smart - Scorecard .25
38 Mike Croel .25
39 Barry Sanders 3.00
40 Sterling Sharpe .50
41 Haywood Jeffires .25
42 Duane Bickett .25
43 Nick Lowery .25
44 Greg Townsend .25
45 Todd Lyght .25
46 Richmond Webb .25
47 Cris Carter .50
48 Marv Cook .25
49 Vaughan Johnson .25
50 Pepper Johnson .25
51 Kyle Clifton .25
52 Fred Barnett .25
53 Ken Harvey .25
54 Rod Woodson .50
55 Stay In Tune - Scorecard .25
56 Marion Butts .25
57 Ricky Watters .50
58 Brian Blades .25
59 Broderick Thomas .25
60 Charles Mann .25
61 Chris Hinton .25
62 Cornelius Bennett .25
63 Jim Harbaugh .50
64 Tim Krumrie .25
65 Bernie Kosar .25
66 Troy Aikman 3.00
67 Shannon Sharpe .50
68 Chris Spielman .25
69 Brian Noble .25
70 Curtis Duncan .25
71 Quentin Coryatt .50
72 Derrick Thomas .50
73 Stay Off Drugs - Scorecard .25
74 Tim Brown .50
75 Jackie Slater .25
76 Keith Jackson .25
77 Terry Allen .50
78 Andre Tippett .25
79 Morten Andersen .25
80 Phil Simms .25
81 Jeff Lageman .25
82 Randall Cunningham .25
83 Randal Hill .25
84 Neil O'Donnell .50
85 Gill Byrd .25
86 John Taylor .25
87 Eugene Robinson .25
88 Paul Gruber .25
89 Andre Collins .25
90 Chris Miller .25
91 Stay True To Yourself - Scorecard .25
92 Andre Reed .50
93 Richard Dent .25
94 David Klingler .25
95 Jay Novacek .50
96 Steve Atwater .25
97 Bennie Blades .25
98 Terrell Buckley .25
99 Ray Childress .25
100 Harvey Williams .25
101 Howie Long .25
102 Lawrence Taylor .50
103 Johnny Mitchell .25
104 Carnell Lake .25
105 Junior Seau .50
106 Kevin Fagan .25
107 Lawrence Dawsey .25
108 Art Monk .50

1994 FACT Fleer Shell

This 108-card set was sponsored by Fleer and Shell Oil. The educational sets were broken up into six 18-card subsets which showcased 17 player cards and one header card. The fronts feature the same design as the 1994 Fleer set. The card backs include a head shot and an action photo, with questions printed over the top. The card number is printed in the lower left corner, with the player's name and facsimile autograph in the upper left.

NM/M
Complete Set (108): 35.00
Common Player: .10
1 Cover Card - Stay In School .10
2 Steve Beuerlein .10
3 Erric Pegram .10
4 Darryl Talley .10
5 Tom Waddle .10
6 Darryl Williams .10
7 Tony Jones .10
8 Jay Novacek .20
9 Simon Fletcher .10
10 Jason Hanson .10
11 Reggie White .30
12 Ernest Givins .10
13 Kerry Cash .10
14 Joe Montana 1.75
15 Anthony Smith .10
16 Jackie Slater .10
17 Terry Kirby .10
18 John Randle .10
19 Cover Card - Stay Fit .10
20 Drew Bledsoe 1.75
21 Vaughan Johnson .10
22 Greg Jackson .10
23 Rob Moore .10
24 Byron Evans .10
25 Rod Woodson .20
26 Junior Seau .20
27 Steve Young 1.25
28 Cortez Kennedy .10
29 Paul Gruber .10
30 Darrell Green .10
31 Tyronne Stowe .10
32 Pierce Holt .10
33 Steve Tasker .10
34 Chris Zorich .10
35 Ricardo McDonald .10
36 Mark Carrier (WR) .10
37 Cover Card - Eat Smart .10
38 Emmitt Smith 3.50
39 Shannon Sharpe .20
40 Chris Spielman .10
41 Ken Ruettgers .10
42 Bubba McDowell .10
43 Rohn Stark .10
44 Derrick Thomas .20
45 Tim Brown .20
46 Shane Conlan .10
47 Marco Coleman .10
48 Steve Jordan .10
49 Ben Coates .20
50 Willie Roaf .10
51 Carlton Bailey .10
52 Ronnie Lott .20
53 Eric Allen .10
54 Dermontti Dawson .10
55 Cover Card - Stay In Tune .10
56 Ronnie Harmon .10
57 Dana Stubblefield .20
58 Rick Mirer .30
59 Santana Dotson .10
60 Jim Lachey .10
61 Ricky Proehl .10
61 Jessie Tuggle .10
63 Jim Kelly .20
64 Mark Carrier (DB) .10
65 David Klingler .10
66 Eric Turner .10
67 Darrin Smith .10
68 Glyn Milburn .20
69 Herman Moore .30
70 Sterling Sharpe .20
71 Ray Childress .10
72 Quentin Coryatt .10
73 Cover Card - Stay Off Drugs .10
74 Marcus Allen .20
75 Jeff Hostetler .10
76 Jerome Bettis .40
77 Richmond Webb .10
78 Randall McDaniel .10
79 Maurice Hurst .10
80 Morten Andersen .10
81 Dave Meggett .10
82 Brian Washington .10
83 Randall Cunningham .10
84 Kevin Greene .20
85 Leslie O'Neal .10
86 Tim McDonald .10
87 Eugene Robinson .10
88 Hardy Nickerson .10
89 Chip Lohmiller .10
90 Jeff George .20
91 Cover Card - Stay True To Yourself .10
92 Cornelius Bennett .10
93 Erik Kramer .10
94 Tommy Vardell .10
95 Troy Aikman 1.75
96 John Elway 1.25
97 Barry Sanders 1.75
98 Dan Saleaumua .10
99 Dan Marino 3.50
100 Jack Del Rio .10
101 Bruce Armstrong .10
102 Renaldo Turnbull .10
103 Phil Simms .10
104 Boomer Esiason .10
105 Fred Barnett .10
106 Greg Lloyd .20
107 John Carney .10
108 Jerry Rice 1.75

1994 FACT NFL Properties

The 18-card NFL Properties set has the NFL shield and "It's A Fact" printed at the top and a slogan at the bottom. The top and bottom are bordered with a black stripe. The backs include a quote, with "Think About It..." printed in the bottom right. The card number is located in a black stripe in the lower right.

NM/M
Complete Set (18): 30.00
Common Player: .75
1 Troy Aikman Play It Straight 4.00
2 Cornelius Bennett Chill .75
3 Lesley Visser Aim High (ANN) .75
4 Junior Seau Eat Smart 1.50
5 Chris Hinton Clean Up Your Act .75
6 Howie Long Plan Ahead 1.00
7 Nick Lowery Heal The Planet .75
8 Tony Casillas Guns Are For Foods .75
9 Dan Marino School's The Ticket 7.00
10 Warren Moon Make A Difference 1.25
11 Rod Bernstine Jim Kelly - We're the Same Inside .75
12 Rohn Stark Smoking Is Stupid .75
13 Michael Irvin Respect The Law 1.00
14 Steve Young Education Works 3.00
15 Bart Oates Kids Deserve Love .75
16 Erik Kramer Be Fit! .75
17 Emmitt Smith Don't Quit 7.00
18 Steve Beuerlein Think .75

1994 FACT NFL Properties Artex

The three-card set carries the same design as the NFL Properties set, except it is numbered 1-3 and the Artex logo is printed on the back. The cards were distributed through K-Mart.

NM/M
Complete Set (3): 7.00
Common Player: 1.50
1 Troy Aikman Play It Straight 1.50

2	Dan Marino School's The Ticket	3.00
3	Emmitt Smith Don't Quit	3.00

1995 FACT Fleer Shell

The 108-card set, sponsored by Fleer and Shell Oil, was used as an educational tool by elementary school teachers. The set was broken up into six subsets of 18 cards each. The card fronts are identical to the 1995 Fleer set, while the backs carry the same design, except for educational questions instead of player stats.

		NM/M
Complete Set (108):		20.00
Common Player:		.10
1	Cover Card - Stay In School	.10
2	Seth Joyner	.10
3	J.J. Birden	.10
4	Jim Kelly	.20
5	Pete Metzelaars	.10
6	Joe Cain	.10
7	Carl Pickens	.20
8	Leroy Hoard	.10
9	Troy Aikman	1.50
10	Steve Atwater	.10
11	Bennie Blades	.10
12	Brett Favre	3.00
13	Mel Gray	.10
14	Tony Bennett	.10
15	Steve Beuerlein	.10
16	Marcus Allen	.20
17	Tim Brown	.20
18	Tim Bowens	.10
19	Cover Card - Stay Fit	.10
20	Jack Del Rio	.10
21	Drew Bledsoe	1.50
22	Jim Everett	.10
23	Michael Brooks	.10
24	Tony Casillas	.10
25	Fred Barnett	.10
26	Kevin Greene	.10
27	Jerome Bettis	.40
28	John Carney	.10
29	Ken Norton	.10
30	Cortez Kennedy	.10
31	Alvin Harper	.10
32	Henry Ellard	.10
33	Aeneas Williams	.10
34	Jeff George	.20
35	Bryce Paup	.20
36	Sam Mills	.10
37	Cover Card - Eat Smart	.10
38	Mark Carrier	.10
39	Darnay Scott	.20
40	Pepper Johnson	.10
41	Michael Irvin	.20
42	John Elway	1.00
43	Herman Moore	.30
44	John Jurkovic	.10
45	Al Smith	.10
46	Steve Emtman	.10
47	Darren Carrington	.10
48	Kimble Anders	.10
49	Jeff Hostetler	.10
50	Eric Green	.10
51	Cris Carter	.20
52	Ben Coates	.10
53	Michael Haynes	.10
55	Dave Brown Cover Card - Stay In Tune	.10
56	Boomer Esiason	.10
57	Randall Cunningham	.10
58	Byron "Bam" Morris	.10
59	Sean Gilbert	.10
60	Stan Humphries	.20
61	Jerry Rice	1.50
62	Rick Mirer	.40
63	Hardy Nickerson	.10
64	Ricky Ervins	.10
65	Eric Swann	.10
66	Craig Heyward	.10
67	Andre Reed	.10
68	Frank Reich	.10
69	Steve Walsh	.10
70	Dan Wilkinson	.10
71	Vinny Testaverde	.10
72	Russell Maryland	.10
73	Cover Card - Stay Off Drugs	.10
74	Shannon Sharpe	.10
75	Brett Perriman	.10
76	Reggie White	.25
77	Mark Stepnoski	.10
78	Marshall Faulk	.75
79	Reggie Cobb	.10
80	Lake Dawson	.10
81	Rocket Ismail	.10
82	Dan Marino	3.00
83	Warren Moon	.20
84	Willie McGinest	.10
85	William Roaf	.10
86	Rodney Hampton	.20
87	Marvin Washington	.10
88	Charlie Garner	.10
89	Neil O'Donnell	.20
90	Todd Lyght	.10
91	Cover Card - Stay True To Yourself	.10
92	Natrone Means	.40
93	Deion Sanders	1.00
94	Chris Warren	.20
95	Errict Rhett	1.00
96	Ken Harvey	.10
97	Bruce Smith	.10
98	Chris Zorich	.10
99	Eric Turner	.10
100	Emmitt Smith	3.00
101	Barry Sanders	1.50
102	Neil Smith	.10
103	Chester McGlockton	.10
104	Fuad Reveiz	.10
105	Thomas Lewis	.10
106	Rod Woodson	.10
107	Junior Seau	.20
108	Steve Young	1.00

1995 FACT NFL Properties

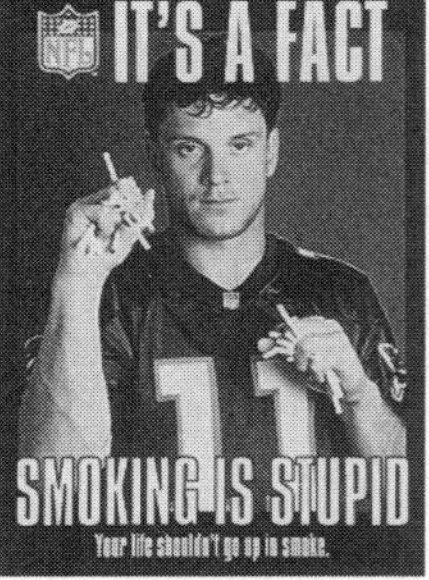

Produced by NFL Properties, the 18-card set had the NFL shield and "It's A Fact" printed at the top on the card fronts. A slogan was printed at the bottom. The card fronts are bordered with black stripes on the top and bottom. The backs have a quote and "Think About It..." printed in the lower right. The card number is printed in a black stripe on the bottom right.

		NM/M
Complete Set (18):		20.00
Common Player:		.50
1	Troy Aikman	2.50
2	Rocket Ismail, Qadry Ismail	.75
3	Robin Roberts	.50
4	Junior Seau	1.00
5	Chris Hinton	.50
6	Sean Jones	.50
7	Thurman Thomas	1.00
8	Neil Smith	.50
9	Dan Marino	5.00
10	Reggie Williams	.50
11	Rod Bernstine, Jim Kelly	1.00
12	Drew Bledsoe	2.50
13	Michael Irvin	1.00
14	Steve Young	1.75
15	Jerry Rice	2.50
16	Herschel Walker	.75
17	Emmitt Smith	5.00
18	Barry Sanders	2.50

1968 Falcons Team Issue

Measuring 7-1/2" x 9-1/2", the fronts feature a black-and-white photo, with the player's name and team printed in the white border at the bottom. The only card not using a posed action photo is Bob Berry's, which features a portrait. The cards are unnumbered and the backs are blank.

		NM/M
Complete Set (14):		65.00
Common Player:		4.00
1	Bob Berry	4.00
2	Carlton Dabney	4.00
3	Bob Etter	4.00
4	Bill Harris	4.00
5	Ralph Heck	4.00
6	Claude Humphrey	4.00
7	Randy Johnson	4.00
8	George Kunz (White jersey 78)	6.00
9	George Kunz (Dark jersey 75)	6.00
10	Errol Linden	4.00
11	Billy Lothridge	4.00
12	Ken Reaves	4.00
13	Jerry Shay	4.00
14	Tommy Nobis	15.00

1978 Falcons Kinnett Dairies

Measuring 4-1/4" x 6", this six-card set showcases four black-and-white player head shots on the front. The Kinnett logo appears in the middle left, while "Atlanta Player Cards" and the NFLPA logo are printed to the right. The unnumbered cards have blank backs.

		NM/M
Complete Set (6):		35.00
Common Player:		5.00
1	William Andrews, Jeff Yeates, Wilson Faumuina, Phil McKinnely	5.00
2	Warren Bryant, R.C. Thielemann, Steve Bartkowski, Frank Reed	10.00
3	Wallace Francis, Jim Mitchell, Jeff Van Note, Ray Easterling	5.00
4	Dewey McClain, Billy Ryckman, Paul Ryczek, Bubba Bean	5.00
5	Robert Pennywell, Dave Scott, Jim Bailey, John James	5.00
6	Haskel Stanback, Rick Byas, Mike Esposito, Tom Moriarty	5.00

1980 Falcons Police

Measuring 2-5/8" x 4-1/8", the 30-card set boasts a player photo on the front, with the Falcons' logo in the upper left and the player's name, number, position and bio under the photo on the left. Below the photo on the right is the Falcons' logo. The unnumbered card backs include "Tips from the Falcons" at the top, with the Atlanta Police Athletic League and Atlanta Jaycees logos underneath. A safety tip is printed in the center of the card, with the Coca-Cola logo at the bottom center of the card back.

		NM/M
Complete Set (30):		30.00
Common Player:		.90
1	William Andrews	3.75
2	Steve Bartkowski	7.50
3	Bubba Bean	2.00
4	Warren Bryant	.90
5	Rick Byas	.90
6	Lynn Cain	2.25
7	Buddy Curry	.90
8	Edgar Fields	.90
9	Wallace Francis	2.75
10	Alfred Jackson	2.25
11	John James	.90
12	Alfred Jenkins	3.00
13	Kenny Johnson	.90
14	Mike Kenn	2.25
15	Fulton Kuykendall	1.50
16	Rolland Lawrence	1.50
17	Tim Mazzetti	.90
18	Dewey McLean	.90
19	Jeff Merrow	1.50
20	Junior Miller	2.25
21	Tom Pridemore	.90
22	Frank Reed	.90
23	Al Richardson	.90
24	Dave Scott	.90
25	Don Smith	.90
26	Reggie Smith	.90
27	R.C. Thielemann	1.50
28	Jeff Van Note	2.25
29	Joel Williams	.90
30	Jeff Yeates	.90

1981 Falcons Police

Measuring 2-5/8" x 4-1/8", the 30-card set is anchored with a large photo on the front. The Atlanta Police Athletic League logo is printed in the upper left of the card front, while "NFC Western Division Champions 1980" is located in the upper right. Beneath the photo are the player's name, number, position, bio and Falcons' logo. The unnumbered card backs boast a Coca-Cola logo in the upper left and a Chevron logo in the upper right. The player's name and a highlight are printed in the center of the back, with a safety tip located beneath it. Photo and printing credits appear on the bottom of the card backs.

		NM/M
Complete Set (30):		9.00
Common Player:		.40
6	John James	.40
10	Steve Bartkowski	2.25
16	Reggie Smith	.40
18	Mick Luckhurst	.40
21	Lynn Cain	.70
23	Bobby Butler	.40
27	Tom Pridemore	.40
30	Scott Woerner	.40
31	William Andrews	.90
36	Bob Glazebrook	.40
37	Kenny Johnson	.40
50	Buddy Curry	.40
51	Jim Laughlin	.40
54	Fulton Kuykendall	.40
56	Al Richardson	.40
57	Jeff Van Note	.40
58	Joel Williams	.40
65	Don Smith	.40
66	Warren Bryant	.40
68	R.C. Thielemann	.40
70	Dave Scott	.40
74	Wilson Faumuina	.40
75	Jeff Merrow	.40
78	Mike Kenn	.40
79	Jeff Yeates	.40
80	Junior Miller	.40
84	Alfred Jenkins	.70
85	Alfred Jackson	.40
89	Wallace Francis	.70
NNO	Leeman Bennett (CO)	.40

1993 FCA Super Bowl

Showcased on the front of these six standard-sized cards is the Fellowship of Christian Athletes' logo in the upper left, with "professional football" located along the left border. The player photo, which is bordered in a screen that goes from light blue to dark blue, is featured on the left side of the card, with the player's name and position printed on the bottom right. The card backs, which are numbered in the upper right, have a player headshot in the upper left, with his name and bio printed along the right. A Christian message from the player is printed in yellow in the center. The FCA's toll-free number is printed at the bottom right.

		NM/M
Complete Set (6):		8.00
Common Player:		.75
1	Alfred Anderson	.75
2	Bob Lilly	1.50
3	Tom Landry (CO)	2.00
4	Brent Jones	1.00
5	Bruce Matthews	.75
6	Title Card	.75

1992 Finest

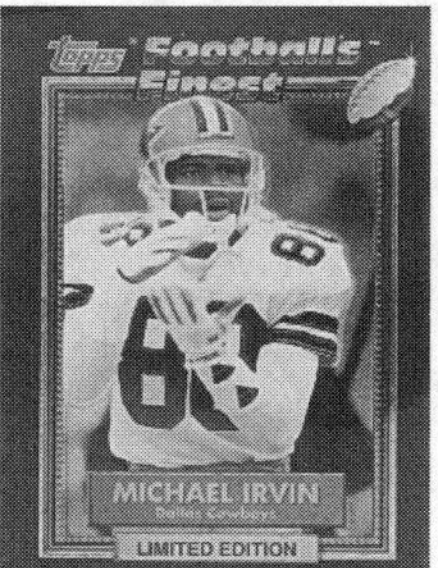

Produced in a print run of 3,000 cases, with 20 sets per case, the 44-card set showcases a player photo in foil on the front of the card, with the Topps Football's Finest logo at the top. The player's name and team are listed under the photo in a blue rectangle. "Limited Edition" is printed inside a gold stripe at the bottom. The 33 veteran cards are bordered in blue, gold and black. The 11 rookie cards are bordered in gold and red. The card backs have "Topps Football's Finest" at the top, with the player's name printed in large letters, overlapping a football helmet on the left. The cards are numbered "of 44" and feature the player's bio and position at the bottom.

		NM/M
Complete Set (45):		25.00
Common Player:		.25
1	Neal Anderson	.25
2	Cornelius Bennett	.25
3	Marion Butts	.25
4	Anthony Carter	.25
5	Mike Croel	.25
6	John Elway	10.00
7	Jim Everett	.25
8	Ernest Givins	.25
9	Rodney Hampton	.50
10	Alvin Harper	.50
11	Michael Irvin	.75
12	Rickey Jackson	.25
13	Seth Joyner	.25
14	James Lofton	.25
15	Ronnie Lott	.50
16	Eric Metcalf	.25
17	Chris Miller	.25
18	Art Monk	.50
19	Warren Moon	.50
20	Rob Moore	.25
21	Anthony Munoz	.25
22	Christian Okoye	.25
23	Andre Rison	.50
24	Leonard Russell	.25
25	Mark Rypien	.25
26	Barry Sanders	10.00
27	Emmitt Smith	10.00
28	Pat Swilling	.25
29	John Taylor	.25
30	Derrick Thomas	1.00
31	Thurman Thomas	1.00
32	Reggie White	1.00
33	Rod Woodson	.25
34	Edgar Bennett	.50
35	Terrell Buckley	.25
36	Keith Hamilton	.25
37	Amp Lee	.25
38	Ricardo McDonald	.25
39	Chris Mims	.25
40	Robert Porcher	.25
41	Leon Searcy	.25
42	Siran Stacy	.25
43	Tommy Vardell	.25
44	Bob Whitfield	.25
NNO	Checklist	.25

1994 Finest

Topps created its 1994 Finest set using its chromium technology to give the cards a high-tech metallic look. Each front has a full-color player action shot, with a color bar at the bottom which has his name; the Topps Finest logo is at the top of the card. The back is horizontal. One side has a full-color photo bordered by a picture frame. Stats, biographical information and a summary of the player's finest moment in football are on the opposite side. A parallel set featuring refracting foil cards for each regular card was also made. These refractors were randomly inserted into every ninth pack. In addition, super size versions of 37 specially-designed rookie cards from the main were made in a 4" x 6" format. One of these cards was put into every 24-count box of packs. One in every six of these cards is enhanced with refracting foil.

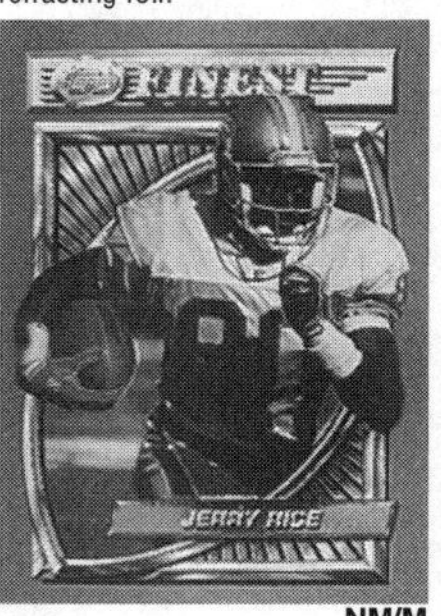

		NM/M
Complete Set (220):		40.00
Common Player:		.50
Minor Stars:		1.00
Refractor Cards:		3X-5X
Pack (6):		3.00
Wax Box (24):		50.00
1	Emmitt Smith	6.00
2	Calvin Williams	.50
3	Mark Collins	.50
4	Steve McMichael	.50
5	Jim Kelly	1.00
6	Michael Dean Perry	.50
7	Wayne Simmons	.50
8	Raghib Ismail	.50
9	Mark Rypien	.50
10	Brian Blades	.50
11	Barry Word	.50
12	Jerry Rice	6.00
13	Derrick Fenner	.50
14	Karl Mecklenburg	.50
15	Reggie Cobb	.50
16	Eric Swann	.50
17	Neil Smith	.50
18	Barry Foster	.50
19	Willie Roaf	.50
20	Troy Drayton	.50
21	Warren Moon	1.00
22	Richmond Webb	.50
23	Anthony Miller	.50
24	Chris Slade	.50
25	Mel Gray	.50
26	Ronnie Lott	.50
27	Andre Rison	1.00
28	Jeff George	.50
29	John Copeland	.50
30	Derrick Thomas	.50
31	Sterling Sharpe	1.00
32	Chris Doleman	.50
33	Monte Coleman	.50
34	Mark Bavaro	.50
35	Kevin Williams	.50
36	Eric Metcalf	.50
37	Brent Jones	.50
38	Steve Tasker	.50
39	Dave Meggett	.50
40	Howie Long	.50
41	Rick Mirer	.50
42	Jerome Bettis	2.00
43	Marion Butts	.50
44	Barry Sanders	6.00
45	Jason Elam	.50
46	Broderick Thomas	.50
47	Derek Brown	.50
48	Lorenzo White	.50
49	Neil O'Donnell	.50
50	Chris Burkett	.50
51	John Offerdahl	.50
52	Rohn Stark	.50
53	Neal Anderson	.50
54	Steve Beuerlein	.50
55	Bruce Armstrong	.50
56	Lincoln Kennedy	.50
57	Darrell Green	.50
58	Ricardo McDonald	.50
59	Chris Warren	.50
60	Mark Jackson	.50
61	Pepper Johnson	.50
62	Chris Spielman	.50
63	Marcus Allen	1.00
64	Jim Everett	.50
65	Greg Townsend	.50
66	Cris Carter	1.00
67	Don Beebe	.50
68	Reggie Langhorne	.50
69	Randall Cunningham	.50
70	Johnny Holland	.50
71	Morten Andersen	.50
72	Leonard Marshall	.50
73	Keith Jackson	.50
74	Leslie O'Neal	.50
75	Hardy Nickerson	.50
76	Dan Williams	.50
77	Steve Young	4.00
78	Deon Figures	.50
79	Michael Irvin	.75
80	Luis Sharpe	.50
81	Andre Tippett	.50
82	Ricky Sanders	.50
83	Erric Pegram	.50
84	Albert Lewis	.50
85	Anthony Blaylock	.50
86	Pat Swilling	.50
87	Duane Bickett	.50
88	Myron Guyton	.50
89	Clay Matthews	.50
90	Jim McMahon	.50
91	Bruce Smith	.50
92	Reggie White	1.00
93	Shannon Sharpe	.50
94	Rickey Jackson	.50
95	Ronnie Harmon	.50
96	Terry McDaniel	.50
97	Bryan Cox	.50
98	Webster Slaughter	.50
99	Boomer Esiason	.50
100	Tim Krumrie	.50
101	Cortez Kennedy	.50
102	Henry Ellard	.50
103	Clyde Simmons	.50
104	Craig Erickson	.50
105	Eric Green	.50
106	Gary Clark	.50
107	Jay Novacek	.50
108	Dana Stubblefield	.50
109	Mike Johnson	.50
110	Ray Crockett	.50
111	Leonard Russell	.50
112	Robert Smith	2.00
113	Art Monk	1.00
114	Ray Childress	.50
115	O.J. McDuffie	.75
116	Tim Brown	.50
117	Kevin Ross	.50
118	Richard Dent	.50
119	John Elway	6.00
120	James Hasty	.50
121	Gary Plummer	.50
122	Pierce Holt	.50
123	Eric Martin	.50
124	Brett Favre	6.00
125	Cornelius Bennett	.50
126	Jessie Hester	.50
127	Lewis Tillman	.50
128	Quadry Ismail	.50
129	Jay Schroeder	.50
130	Curtis Conway	1.00
131	Santana Dotson	.50
132	Nick Lowery	.50
133	Lomas Brown	.50
134	Reggie Roby	.50
135	John L. Williams	.50
136	Vinny Testaverde	.50
137	Seth Joyner	.50
138	Ethan Horton	.50
139	Jackie Slater	.50
140	Rod Bernstine	.50
141	Rob Moore	.50
142	Dan Marino	6.00
143	Ken Harvey	.50
144	Ernest Givins	.50
145	Russell Maryland	.50
146	Drew Bledsoe	6.00
147	Kevin Greene	.50
148	Bobby Hebert	.50
149	Junior Seau	1.00
150	Tim McDonald	.50
151	Thurman Thomas	1.00
152	Phil Simms	.50
153	Terrell Buckley	.50
154	Sam Mills	.50
155	Anthony Carter	.50
156	Kelvin Martin	.50
157	Shane Conlan	.50
158	Irving Fryar	.50
159	Demetrius DuBose	.50
160	David Klingler	.50
161	Herman Moore	.75
162	Jeff Hostetler	.50
163	Tommy Vardell	.50
164	Craig Heyward	.50
165	Wilber Marshall	.50
166	Quentin Coryatt	.50
167	Glyn Milburn	1.00
168	Fred Barnett	.50
169	Charles Haley	.50
170	Carl Banks	.50
171	Ricky Proehl	.50
172	Joe Montana	6.00
173	Johnny Mitchell	.50
174	Andre Reed	1.00
175	Marco Coleman	.50
176	Vaughan Johnson	.50
177	Carl Pickens	1.00
178	Dwight Stone	.50
179	Ricky Watters	1.00
180	Michael Haynes	.50
181	Roger Craig	.50
182	Cleveland Gary	.50
183	Steve Emtman	.50
184	Patrick Bates	.50
185	Mark Carrier	.50
186	Brad Hopkins	.50
187	Dennis Smith	.50
188	Natrone Means	.50
189	Michael Jackson	.50
190	Ken Norton	.50
191	Carlton Gray	.50
192	Edgar Bennett	.50
193	Lawrence Taylor	1.00
194	Marv Cook	.50
195	Eric Curry	.50
196	Victor Bailey	.50
197	Ryan McNeil	.50
198	Rod Woodson	1.00
199	Ernest Byner	.50
200	Marvin Jones	.50
201	Thomas Smith	.50
202	Troy Aikman	4.00
203	Audray McMillian	.50
204	Wade Wilson	.50

205	George Teague	.50
206	Deion Sanders	1.00
207	Will Shields	.50
208	John Taylor	.50
209	Jim Harbaugh	.50
210	Micheal Barrow	.50
211	Harold Green	.50
212	Steve Everitt	.50
213	Flipper Anderson	.50
214	Rodney Hampton	.50
215	Steve Atwater	.50
216	James Trapp	.50
217	Terry Kirby	.50
218	Garrison Hearst	1.00
219	Jeff Bryant	.50
220	Roosevelt Potts	.50

1994 Finest Refractors

Refractors paralleled the 220-card regular-issue set with a holographic, rainbow finish on each card. Refractors were inserted every nine packs of Finest.

		NM/M
Unlisted Stars:		3X-5X
1	Emmitt Smith	85.00
2	Calvin Williams	4.00
3	Mark Collins	4.00
4	Steve McMichael	4.00
5	Jim Kelly	10.00
6	Michael Dean Perry	4.00
7	Wayne Simmons	4.00
8	Raghib Ismail	4.00
9	Mark Rypien	4.00
10	Brian Blades	4.00
11	Barry Word	4.00
12	Jerry Rice	50.00
13	Derrick Fenner	4.00
14	Karl Mecklenburg	4.00
15	Reggie Cobb	4.00
16	Eric Swann	4.00
17	Neil Smith	4.00
18	Barry Foster	4.00
19	Willie Roaf	4.00
20	Troy Drayton	4.00
21	Warren Moon	8.00
22	Richmond Webb	4.00
23	Anthony Miller	4.00
24	Chris Slade	4.00
25	Mel Gray	4.00
26	Ronnie Lott	4.00
27	Andre Rison	8.00
28	Jeff George	8.00
29	John Copeland	4.00
30	Derrick Thomas	8.00
31	Sterling Sharpe	8.00
32	Chris Doleman	4.00
33	Monte Coleman	4.00
34	Mark Bavaro	4.00
35	Kevin Williams	10.00
36	Eric Metcalf	4.00
37	Brent Jones	4.00
38	Steve Tasker	4.00
39	Dave Meggett	4.00
40	Howie Long	4.00
41	Rick Mirer	8.00
42	Jerome Bettis	25.00
43	Marion Butts	4.00
44	Barry Sanders	100.00
45	Jason Elam	4.00
46	Broderick Thomas	4.00
47	Derek Brown	4.00
48	Lorenzo White	4.00
49	Neil O'Donnell	8.00
50	Chris Burkett	4.00
51	John Offerdahl	4.00
52	Rohn Stark	4.00
53	Neal Anderson	4.00
54	Steve Beuerlein	4.00
55	Bruce Armstrong	4.00
56	Lincoln Kennedy	4.00
57	Darrell Green	4.00
58	Ricardo McDonald	4.00
59	Chris Warren	8.00
60	Mark Jackson	4.00
61	Pepper Johnson	4.00
62	Chris Spielman	4.00
63	Marcus Allen	10.00
64	Jim Everett	4.00
65	Greg Townsend	4.00
66	Cris Carter	8.00
67	Don Beebe	4.00
68	Reggie Langhorne	4.00
69	Randall Cunningham	4.00
70	Johnny Holland	4.00
71	Morten Andersen	4.00
72	Leonard Marshall	4.00
73	Keith Jackson	4.00
74	Leslie O'Neal	4.00
75	Hardy Nickerson	4.00
76	Dan Williams	4.00
77	Steve Young	40.00
78	Deon Figures	4.00
79	Michael Irvin	10.00
80	Luis Sharpe	4.00
81	Andre Tippett	4.00
82	Ricky Sanders	4.00
83	Erric Pegram	4.00
84	Albert Lewis	4.00
85	Anthony Blaylock	4.00
86	Pat Swilling	4.00
87	Duane Bickett	4.00
88	Myron Guyton	4.00
89	Clay Matthews	4.00
90	Jim McMahon	4.00
91	Bruce Smith	4.00
92	Reggie White	10.00
93	Shannon Sharpe	4.00
94	Rickey Jackson	4.00
95	Ronnie Harmon	4.00
96	Terry McDaniel	4.00
97	Bryan Cox	4.00
98	Webster Slaughter	4.00
99	Boomer Esiason	4.00
100	Tim Krumrie	4.00
101	Cortez Kennedy	4.00
102	Henry Ellard	4.00
103	Clyde Simmons	4.00
104	Craig Erickson	4.00
105	Eric Green	4.00
106	Gary Clark	4.00
107	Jay Novacek	4.00
108	Dana Stubblefield	8.00
109	Mike Johnson	4.00
110	Ray Crockett	4.00
111	Leonard Russell	4.00
112	Robert Smith	30.00
113	Art Monk	8.00
114	Ray Childress	4.00
115	O.J. McDuffie	8.00
116	Tim Brown	8.00
117	Kevin Ross	4.00
118	Richard Dent	4.00
119	John Elway	80.00
120	James Hasty	4.00
121	Gary Plummer	4.00
122	Pierce Holt	4.00
123	Eric Martin	4.00
124	Brett Favre	100.00
125	Cornelius Bennett	4.00
126	Jessie Hester	4.00
127	Lewis Tillman	4.00
128	Qadry Ismail	4.00
129	Jay Schroeder	4.00
130	Curtis Conway	30.00
131	Santana Dotson	4.00
132	Nick Lowery	4.00
133	Lomas Brown	4.00
134	Reggie Roby	4.00
135	John L. Williams	4.00
136	Vinny Testaverde	4.00
137	Seth Joyner	4.00
138	Ethan Horton	4.00
139	Jackie Slater	4.00
140	Rod Bernstine	4.00
141	Rob Moore	4.00
142	Dan Marino	85.00
143	Ken Harvey	4.00
144	Ernest Givins	4.00
145	Russell Maryland	4.00
146	Drew Bledsoe	60.00
147	Kevin Greene	4.00
148	Bobby Hebert	4.00
149	Junior Seau	8.00
150	Tim McDonald	4.00
151	Thurman Thomas	10.00
152	Phil Simms	4.00
153	Terrell Buckley	4.00
154	Sam Mills	4.00
155	Anthony Carter	4.00
156	Kelvin Martin	4.00
157	Shane Conlan	4.00
158	Irving Fryar	4.00
159	Demetrius DuBose	4.00
160	David Klingler	4.00
161	Herman Moore	10.00
162	Jeff Hostetler	8.00
163	Tommy Vardell	4.00
164	Craig Heyward	4.00
165	Wilber Marshall	4.00
166	Quentin Coryatt	4.00
167	Glyn Milburn	4.00
168	Fred Barnett	4.00
169	Charles Haley	4.00
170	Carl Banks	4.00
171	Ricky Proehl	4.00
172	Joe Montana	100.00
173	Johnny Mitchell	4.00
174	Andre Reed	8.00
175	Marco Coleman	4.00
176	Vaughan Johnson	4.00
177	Carl Pickens	10.00
178	Dwight Stone	4.00
179	Ricky Watters	8.00
180	Michael Haynes	4.00
181	Roger Craig	4.00
182	Cleveland Gary	4.00
183	Steve Emtman	4.00
184	Patrick Bates	4.00
185	Mark Carrier	4.00
186	Brad Hopkins	4.00
187	Dennis Smith	4.00
188	Natrone Means	25.00
189	Michael Jackson	4.00
190	Ken Norton	4.00
191	Carlton Gray	4.00
192	Edgar Bennett	4.00
193	Lawrence Taylor	8.00
194	Marv Cook	4.00
195	Eric Curry	4.00
196	Victor Bailey	4.00
197	Ryan McNeil	4.00
198	Rod Woodson	8.00
199	Ernest Byner	4.00
200	Marvin Jones	4.00
201	Thomas Smith	4.00
202	Troy Aikman	50.00
203	Audray McMillian	4.00
204	Wade Wilson	4.00
205	George Teague	4.00
206	Deion Sanders	25.00
207	Will Shields	4.00
208	John Taylor	4.00
209	Jim Harbaugh	8.00
210	Micheal Barrow	4.00
211	Harold Green	4.00
212	Steve Everitt	4.00
213	Flipper Anderson	4.00
214	Rodney Hampton	8.00
215	Steve Atwater	4.00
216	James Trapp	4.00
217	Terry Kirby	4.00
218	Garrison Hearst	25.00
219	Jeff Bryant	4.00
220	Roosevelt Potts	4.00

1994 Finest Rookie Jumbos

The Finest Rookie Jumbos set has 37 rookies with identical cards from the regular set; however, the jumbos measure 4-1/2" x 6". These oversized cards were found at a rate of one per 24-count box.

		NM/M
Complete Set (37):		75.00
Common Player:		1.00
Minor Stars:		2.00
1:Box		
7	Wayne Simmons	1.00
19	Willie Roaf	1.00
20	Troy Drayton	1.00
24	Chris Slade	1.00
29	John Copeland	1.00
35	Kevin Williams	2.00
41	Rick Mirer	2.00
42	Jerome Bettis	5.00
45	Jason Elam	1.00
47	Derek Brown (RB)	1.00
56	Lincoln Kennedy	1.00
78	Deon Figures	1.00
108	Dana Stubblefield	1.00
112	Robert Smith	4.00
115	O.J. McDuffie	5.00
128	Qadry Ismail	1.00
130	Curtis Conway	5.00
146	Drew Bledsoe	20.00
159	Demetrius DuBose	1.00
167	Glyn Milburn	1.00
184	Patrick Bates	1.00
186	Brad Hopkins	1.00
188	Natrone Means	1.00
191	Carlton Gray	1.00
195	Eric Curry	1.00
196	Victor Bailey	1.00
197	Ryan McNeil	1.00
200	Marvin Jones	1.00
201	Thomas Smith	1.00
205	George Teague	1.00
207	Will Shields	1.00
210	Micheal Barrow	1.00
212	Steve Everitt	1.00
216	James Trapp	1.00
217	Terry Kirby	3.00
218	Garrison Hearst	5.00
220	Roosevelt Potts	1.00

1995 Finest

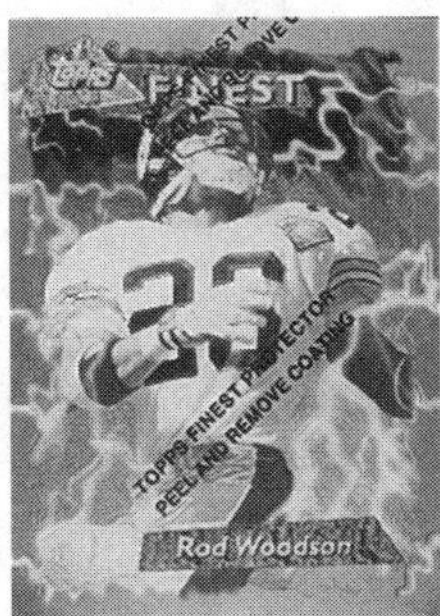

The regular issue 1995 Topps Finest set was released in two series - Series I had 165 cards, while Series II had 110. Each card comes with the standard Finest Protector, a peel-off laminate, to assure its Mint condition out of the pack. A 1994 Draft Picks subset was included in Series I; it features a different design from the regular cards. A 275-card parallel set of Finest Refractor cards was also made; cards were seeded one per every 12 packs. Series I inserts, titled Fan Favorites, feature impact players on clear cut cards. Series II inserts were Boosters, numbered B166-B187.

		NM/M
Complete Set (275):		50.00
Complete Series 1 (165):		20.00
Complete Series 2 (110):		40.00
Common Player:		.25
Minor Stars:		1.00
Series 1 Pack (7):		1.50
Series 1 Wax Box (24):		25.00
Series 2 Pack (7):		2.35
Series 2 Wax Box (24):		40.00
1	Natrone Means	.25
2	David Meggett	.25
3	*Tim Bowens*	.25
4	Jay Novacek	.25
5	Michael Jackson	.25
6	Eric Allen	.25
7	Neil Smith	.25
8	Chris Gardocki	.25
9	*Jeff Burris*	.25
10	Warren Moon	1.00
11	Gary Anderson	.25
12	*Bert Emanuel*	.25
13	Rick Tuten	.25
14	Steve Wallace	.25
15	Marion Butts	.25
16	*Johnnie Morton*	1.50
17	Art Monk	1.00
18	*Wayne Gandy*	.25
19	Quentin Coryatt	.25
20	Richmond Webb	.25
21	*Errict Rhett*	1.00
22	*Joe Johnson*	.25
23	Gary Brown	.25
24	Jeff Hostetler	.25
25	Larry Centers	.25
26	Tom Carter	.25
27	Steve Atwater	.25
28	Doug Pelfrey	.25
29	Bryce Paup	.25
30	Eric Williams	.25
31	Henry Jones	.25
32	Stanley Richard	.25
33	Marcus Allen	1.00
34	*Antonio Langham*	.25
35	Lewis Tillman	.25
36	*Thomas Randolph*	.25
37	*Byron Morris*	.25
38	*David Palmer*	1.00
39	Ricky Watters	1.00
40	Brett Perriman	.25
41	Will Wolford	.25
42	Burt Grossman	.25
43	Vincent Brisby	.25
44	Ronnie Lott	.25
45	Brian Blades	.25
46	Brent Jones	.25
47	Anthony Newman	.25
48	William Roaf	.25
49	Paul Gruber	.25
50	Jeff George	.25
51	*Jamir Miller*	.25
52	Anthony Miller	.25
53	Darrell Green	.25
54	Steve Wisniewski	.25
55	*Dan Wilkinson*	.25
56	Brett Favre	4.00
57	Leslie O'Neal	.25
58	Keith Byars	.25
59	James Washington	.25
60	Andre Reed	.25
61	Ken Norton	.25
62	John Randle	.25
63	*Lake Dawson*	.25
64	Greg Montgomery	.25
65	Erric Pegram	.25
66	Steve Everitt	.25
67	*Chris Brantley*	.25
68	Rod Woodson	.25
69	Eugene Robinson	.25
70	Dave Brown	.25
71	Ricky Reynolds	.25
72	Rohn Stark	.25
73	Randal Hill	.25
74	Brian Washington	.25
75	*Heath Shuler*	.25
76	Darion Conner	.25
77	Terry McDaniel	.25
78	Al Del Greco	.25
79	*Allen Aldridge*	.25
80	Trace Armstrong	.25
81	*Darnay Scott*	.25
82	Charlie Garner	1.00
83	*Harold Bishop*	.25
84	Reggie White	1.00
85	Shawn Jefferson	.25
86	Irving Spikes	.25
87	Mel Gray	.25
88	D.J. Johnson	.25
89	Daryl Johnston	.25
90	Joe Montana	4.00
91	Michael Strahan	.25
92	Robert Blackmon	.25
93	*Ryan Yarborough*	.25
94	Terry Allen	.25
95	Michael Haynes	.25
96	Jim Harbaugh	.25
97	Micheal Barrow	.25
98	*John Thierry*	.25
99	Seth Joyner	.25
100	Deion Sanders	1.00
101	Eric Turner	.25
102	*LeShon Johnson*	.25
103	John Copeland	.25
104	Cornelius Bennett	.25
105	Sean Gilbert	.25
106	Herschel Walker	.25
107	Henry Ellard	.25
108	Neil O'Donnell	.25
109	Charles Wilson	.25
110	*Willie McGinest*	1.00
111	Tim Brown	1.00
112	Simon Fletcher	.25
113	Broderick Thomas	.25
114	Tom Waddle	.25
115	Jessie Tuggle	.25
116	Maurice Hurst	.25
117	*Aubrey Beavers*	.25
118	*Donnell Bennett*	.25
119	*Shante Carver*	.25
120	Eric Metcalf	.25
121	John Carney	.25
122	*Thomas Lewis*	.25
123	Johnny Mitchell	.25
124	Trent Dilfer	2.00
125	Marshall Faulk	2.00
126	Ernest Givins	.25
127	Aeneas Williams	.25
128	*Bucky Brooks*	.25
129	*Todd Steussie*	.25
130	Randall Cunningham	.25
131	Reggie Brooks	.25
132	Morten Andersen	.25
133	James Jett	.25
134	George Teague	.25
135	John Taylor	.25
136	*Charles Johnson*	.60
137	Isaac Bruce	2.00
138	Jason Elam	.25
139	Carl Pickens	1.00
140	Chris Warren	.25
141	Bruce Armstrong	.25
142	Mark Carrier	.25
143	Irving Fryar	.25
144	*Van Malone*	.25
145	Charles Haley	.25
146	Chris Calloway	.25
147	J.J. Birden	.25
148	Tony Bennett	.25
149	Lincoln Kennedy	.25
150	Stan Humphries	.25
151	Hardy Nickerson	.25
152	Randall McDaniel	.25
153	Marcus Robertson	.25
154	Ronald Moore	.25
155	Thurman Thomas	1.00
156	Tommy Vardell	.25
157	Ken Ruettgers	.25
158	*Rob Frederickson*	.25
159	Johnny Bailey	.25
160	Greg Lloyd	.25
161	David Alexander	.25
162	*Kevin Mawae*	.25
163	Derek Brown	.25
164	*William Floyd*	.60
165	*Aaron Glenn*	.60
166	*Joey Galloway*	5.00
167	Troy Drayton	.25
168	Dermontti Dawson	.25
169	Ronald Moore	.25
170	Dan Marino	4.00
171	Dennis Gibson	.25
172	Raymont Harris	.25
173	Shannon Sharpe	.25
174	Kevin Williams	.25
175	Jim Everett	.25
176	Raghib Ismail	.25
177	Mark Fields	.25
178	George Koonce	.25
179	Chris Hudson	.25
180	Jerry Rice	3.00
181	DeWayne Washington	.25
182	Dale Carter	.25
183	Pete Stoyanovich	.25
184	Blake Brockermeyer	.25
185	Troy Aikman	3.00
186	*Jeff Blake*	.60
187	Troy Vincent	.25
188	Lamar Lathon	.25
189	*Tony Boselli*	.60
190	Emmitt Smith	4.00
191	Bobby Houston	.25
192	Edgar Bennett	.25
193	Derrick Brooks	.25
194	Ricky Proehl	.25
195	Rodney Hampton	.25
196	Dave Krieg	.25
197	Vinny Testaverde	.25
198	Erik Kramer	.25
199	Ben Coates	.25
200	Steve Young	3.00
201	Glyn Milburn	.25
202	Bryan Cox	.25
203	Luther Elliss	.25
204	Mark McMillian	.25
205	Jerome Bettis	1.00
206	Craig Heyward	.25
207	Ray Buchanan	.25
208	Kimble Anders	.25
209	Kevin Greene	.25
210	Eric Allen	.25
211	Ricardo McDonald	.25
212	Ruben Brown	.25
213	Harvey Williams	.25
214	Broderick Thomas	.25
215	Frank Reich	.25
216	*Frank Sanders*	2.00
217	Craig Newsome	.25
218	Merton Hanks	.25
219	Chris Miller	.25
220	John Elway	3.00
221	Ernest Givins	.25
222	Boomer Esiason	.25
223	Reggie Roby	.25
224	Qadry Ismail	.25
225	*Ki-Jana Carter*	1.00
226	Leon Lett	.25
227	Eric Hill	.25
228	Scott Mitchell	.25
229	Craig Erickson	.25
230	Drew Bledsoe	3.00
231	Sean Landeta	.25
232	Barrett Brooks	.25
233	Brian Mitchell	.25
234	Tyrone Poole	.25
235	Desmond Howard	.25
236	Wayne Simmons	.25
237	*Michael Westbrook*	2.00
238	Quinn Early	.25
239	Willie Davis	.25
240	*Rashaan Salaam*	.60
241	Devin Bush	.25
242	Dana Stubblefield	.25
243	Dexter Carter	.25
244	Shane Conlan	.25
245	Keith Elias	.25
246	Robert Brooks	.60
247	Garrison Hearst	1.00
248	*Eric Zeier*	1.00
249	Nate Newton	.25
250	Barry Sanders	4.00
251	David Meggett	.25
252	Courtney Hawkins	.25
253	Cortez Kennedy	.25
254	Mario Bates	.60
255	Junior Seau	.75
256	Brian Washington	.25
257	Darius Holland	.25
258	Jeff Graham	.25
259	Rob Moore	.25
260	Andre Rison	.25
261	*Kerry Collins*	8.00
262	Roosevelt Potts	.25
263	Cris Carter	1.00
264	*Curtis Martin*	10.00
265	Rick Mirer	.25
266	Mo Lewis	.25
267	Mike Sherrard	.25
268	Herman Moore	.60
269	Eric Metcalf	.25
270	Ray Childress	.25
271	Chris Slade	.25
272	Michael Irvin	.60
273	Jim Kelly	1.00
274	Terance Mathis	.25
275	LeRoy Butler	.25

1995 Finest Refractors

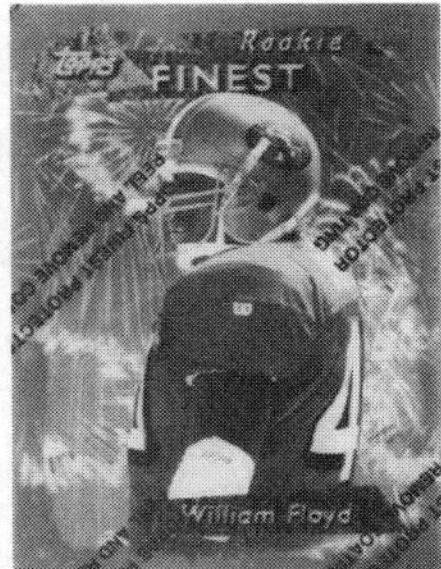

These cards were randomly inserted into Series I and II packs of 1995 Topps Finest, one per every 12 packs. The cards, a parallel set to the regular issue, have a shiny, rainbow effect when viewed.

		NM/M
Unlisted Stars:		2X-6X
1	Natrone Means	15.00
2	David Meggett	3.00
3	Tim Bowens	6.00
4	Jay Novacek	3.00
5	Michael Jackson	3.00
6	Eric Allen	3.00
7	Neil Smith	3.00
8	Chris Gardocki	3.00
9	Jeff Burris	6.00
10	Warren Moon	6.00
11	Gary Anderson	3.00
12	Bert Emanuel	25.00
13	Rick Tuten	3.00
14	Steve Wallace	3.00
15	Marion Butts	3.00
16	Johnnie Morton	10.00
17	Art Monk	6.00
18	Wayne Gandy	3.00
19	Quentin Coryatt	3.00
20	Richmond Webb	3.00
21	Errict Rhett	10.00
22	Joe Johnson	3.00
23	Gary Brown	3.00
24	Jeff Hostetler	3.00
25	Larry Centers	3.00
26	Tom Carter	3.00
27	Steve Atwater	3.00
28	Doug Pelfrey	3.00
29	Bryce Paup	3.00
30	Eric Williams	3.00
31	Henry Jones	3.00
32	Stanley Richard	3.00
33	Marcus Allen	6.00
34	Antonio Langham	6.00
35	Lewis Tillman	3.00
36	Thomas Randolph	3.00
37	Byron Morris	10.00
38	David Palmer	6.00
39	Ricky Watters	6.00
40	Brett Perriman	3.00
41	Will Wolford	3.00
42	Burt Grossman	3.00
43	Vincent Brisby	3.00
44	Ronnie Lott	3.00
45	Brian Blades	3.00
46	Brent Jones	3.00
47	Anthony Newman	3.00
48	William Roaf	3.00
49	Paul Gruber	3.00
50	Jeff George	6.00
51	Jamir Miller	6.00
52	Anthony Miller	3.00
53	Darrell Green	3.00
54	Steve Wisniewski	3.00
55	Dan Wilkinson	6.00
56	Brett Favre	100.00
57	Leslie O'Neal	3.00
58	Keith Byars	3.00
59	James Washington	3.00
60	Andre Reed	3.00

61	Ken Norton	3.00
62	John Randle	3.00
63	Lake Dawson	10.00
64	Greg Montgomery	3.00
65	Erric Pegram	3.00
66	Steve Everitt	3.00
67	Chris Brantley	3.00
68	Rod Woodson	6.00
69	Eugene Robinson	3.00
70	Dave Brown	3.00
71	Ricky Reynolds	3.00
72	Rohn Stark	3.00
73	Randal Hill	3.00
74	Brian Washington	3.00
75	Heath Shuler	15.00
76	Darion Conner	3.00
77	Terry McDaniel	3.00
78	Al Del Greco	3.00
79	Allen Aldridge	3.00
80	Trace Armstrong	3.00
81	Darnay Scott	10.00
82	Charlie Garner	20.00
83	Harold Bishop	3.00
84	Reggie White	6.00
85	Shawn Jefferson	3.00
86	Irving Spikes	6.00
87	Mel Gray	3.00
88	D.J. Johnson	3.00
89	Daryl Johnston	3.00
90	Joe Montana	75.00
91	Michael Strahan	3.00
92	Robert Blackmon	3.00
93	Ryan Yarborough	3.00
94	Terry Allen	3.00
95	Michael Haynes	3.00
96	Jim Harbaugh	3.00
97	Micheal Barrow	3.00
98	John Thierry	3.00
99	Seth Joyner	3.00
100	Deion Sanders	40.00
101	Eric Turner	3.00
102	LeShon Johnson	6.00
103	John Copeland	3.00
104	Cornelius Bennett	3.00
105	Sean Gilbert	3.00
106	Herschel Walker	3.00
107	Henry Ellard	3.00
108	Neil O'Donnell	6.00
109	Charles Wilson	3.00
110	Willie McGinest	6.00
111	Tim Brown	6.00
112	Simon Fletcher	3.00
113	Broderick Thomas	3.00
114	Tom Waddle	3.00
115	Jessie Tuggle	3.00
116	Maurice Hurst	3.00
117	Aubrey Beavers	3.00
118	Donnell Bennett	3.00
119	Shante Carver	3.00
120	Eric Metcalf	3.00
121	John Carney	3.00
122	Thomas Lewis	3.00
123	Johnny Mitchell	3.00
124	Trent Dilfer	30.00
125	Marshall Faulk	40.00
126	Ernest Givins	3.00
127	Aeneas Williams	3.00
128	Bucky Brooks	6.00
129	Todd Steussie	6.00
130	Randall Cunningham	6.00
131	Reggie Brooks	3.00
132	Morten Andersen	3.00
133	James Jett	3.00
134	George Teague	3.00
135	John Taylor	3.00
136	Charles Johnson	15.00
137	Isaac Bruce	35.00
138	Jason Elam	3.00
139	Carl Pickens	6.00
140	Chris Warren	6.00
141	Bruce Armstrong	3.00
142	Mark Carrier	3.00
143	Irving Fryar	3.00
144	Van Malone	3.00
145	Charles Haley	3.00
146	Chris Calloway	3.00
147	J.J. Birden	3.00
148	Tony Bennett	3.00
149	Lincoln Kennedy	3.00
150	Stan Humphries	6.00
151	Hardy Nickerson	3.00
152	Randall McDaniel	3.00
153	Marcus Robertson	3.00
154	Ronald Moore	3.00
155	Thurman Thomas	6.00
156	Tommy Vardell	3.00
157	Ken Ruettgers	3.00
158	Rob Frederickson	3.00
159	Johnny Bailey	3.00
160	Greg Lloyd	3.00
161	David Alexander	3.00
162	Kevin Mawae	3.00
163	Derek Brown	3.00
164	William Floyd	8.00
165	Aaron Glenn	6.00
166	Joey Galloway	75.00
167	Troy Drayton	3.00
168	Dermontti Dawson	3.00
169	Ronald Moore	3.00
170	Dan Marino	85.00
171	Dennis Gibson	3.00
172	Raymont Harris	3.00
173	Shannon Sharpe	3.00
174	Kevin Williams	3.00
175	Jim Everett	3.00
176	Raghib Ismail	3.00
177	Mark Fields	3.00
178	George Koonce	3.00
179	Chris Hudson	3.00
180	Jerry Rice	60.00
181	DeWayne Washington	3.00
182	Dale Carter	3.00
183	Pete Stoyanovich	3.00
184	Blake Brockermeyer	3.00
185	Troy Aikman	60.00
186	Jeff Blake	8.00
187	Troy Vincent	3.00
188	Lamar Lathon	3.00
189	Tony Boselli	6.00
190	Emmitt Smith	85.00
191	Bobby Houston	3.00
192	Edgar Bennett	3.00
193	Derrick Brooks	3.00
194	Ricky Proehl	3.00
195	Rodney Hampton	3.00
196	Dave Krieg	3.00
197	Vinny Testaverde	3.00
198	Erik Kramer	3.00
199	Ben Coates	3.00
200	Steve Young	45.00
201	Glyn Milburn	3.00
202	Bryan Cox	3.00
203	Luther Elliss	3.00
204	Mark McMillian	3.00
205	Jerome Bettis	25.00
206	Craig Heyward	3.00
207	Ray Buchanan	3.00
208	Kimble Anders	3.00
209	Kevin Greene	3.00
210	Eric Allen	3.00
211	Ricardo McDonald	3.00
212	Ruben Brown	3.00
213	Harvey Williams	3.00
214	Broderick Thomas	3.00
215	Frank Reich	3.00
216	Frank Sanders	25.00
217	Craig Newsome	3.00
218	Merton Hanks	3.00
219	Chris Miller	3.00
220	John Elway	60.00
221	Ernest Givins	3.00
222	Boomer Esiason	3.00
223	Reggie Roby	3.00
224	Qadry Ismail	3.00
225	Ki-Jana Carter	20.00
226	Leon Lett	3.00
227	Eric Hill	3.00
228	Scott Mitchell	3.00
229	Craig Erickson	3.00
230	Drew Bledsoe	60.00
231	Sean Landeta	3.00
232	Barrett Brooks	3.00
233	Brian Mitchell	3.00
234	Tyrone Poole	3.00
235	Desmond Howard	3.00
236	Wayne Simmons	3.00
237	Michael Westbrook	20.00
238	Quinn Early	3.00
239	Willie Davis	3.00
240	Rashaan Salaam	15.00
241	Devin Bush	3.00
242	Dana Stubblefield	3.00
243	Dexter Carter	3.00
244	Shane Conlan	3.00
245	Keith Elias	3.00
246	Robert Brooks	8.00
247	Garrison Hearst	15.00
248	Eric Zeier	20.00
249	Nate Newton	3.00
250	Barry Sanders	100.00
251	David Meggett	3.00
252	Courtney Hawkins	3.00
253	Cortez Kennedy	3.00
254	Mario Bates	8.00
255	Junior Seau	6.00
256	Brian Washington	3.00
257	Darius Holland	3.00
258	Jeff Graham	3.00
259	Rob Moore	3.00
260	Andre Rison	3.00
261	Kerry Collins	30.00
262	Roosevelt Potts	3.00
263	Cris Carter	3.00
264	Curtis Martin	100.00
265	Rick Mirer	10.00
266	Mo Lewis	3.00
267	Mike Sherrard	3.00
268	Herman Moore	15.00
269	Eric Metcalf	3.00
270	Ray Childress	3.00
271	Chris Slade	3.00
272	Michael Irvin	15.00
273	Jim Kelly	6.00
274	Terance Mathis	3.00
275	LeRoy Butler	3.00

1995 Finest Fan Favorite

These cards, random inserts in 1995 Topps Finest football packs, feature impact players on clear cut cards. The back, numbered using an "FF" prefix, has biographical information and a list of where the player played in college and in the NFL. Cards were included in every 12th pack.

		NM/M
Complete Set (25):		75.00
Common Player:		1.00
Minor Stars:		2.00
1	Drew Bledsoe	5.00
2	Jerome Bettis	3.00
3	Rick Mirer	1.00
4	Andre Rison	1.00
5	Troy Aikman	5.00
6	Cortez Kennedy	1.00
7	Emmitt Smith	8.00
8	Sterling Sharpe	2.00
9	Junior Seau	2.00
10	Michael Irvin	2.00
11	Jim Kelly	3.00
12	Steve Young	4.00
13	John Elway	8.00
14	Jerry Rice	6.00
15	Barry Sanders	8.00
16	Dan Marino	8.00
17	Dan Wilkinson	1.00
18	Reggie White	2.00
19	Deion Sanders	2.00
20	Willie McGinest	1.00
21	Stan Humphries	1.00
22	Heath Shuler	1.00
23	Natrone Means	1.00
24	Warren Moon	2.00
25	Marshall Faulk	3.00

1995 Topps Finest Landmark

This four-card set was available only through Topps direct mailers ($99 plus shipping), and utilizes Finest technology on metal cards overlaid on a four-ounce ingot of solid bronze.

		NM/M
Complete Set (4):		170.00
Common Player:		25.00
1	Troy Aikman	40.00
2	Jerry Rice	40.00
3	Emmitt Smith	70.00
4	Steve Young	25.00

1995-96 Topps Finest Pro Bowl Jumbos

This 22-card set was distributed at the 1996 NFL Experience Pro Bowl show in Hawaii, and is almost identical to the 1995 Finest cards, except for its 4" x 5-5/8" measurement. The only difference is in addition to the cards' original number, each also carries a new 1-22 card number. A larger, poster-sized Steve Young card was also produced for promotional purposes and for distribution at the Pro Bowl show. Parallel Refractor versions are also available, but with a reduced print run.

		NM/M
Complete Set (22):		40.00
Common Player:		.50
Refractors		3X to 8X
1	Troy Aikman	4.00
2	Tim Brown	2.00
3	Cris Carter	2.00
4	Marshall Faulk	3.00
5	Brett Favre	6.00
6	Merton Hanks	.50
7	Michael Irvin	2.00
8	Greg Lloyd	.50
9	Dan Marino	6.00
10	Curtis Martin	4.00
11	Herman Moore	3.00
12	Terry McDaniel	.50
13	Ken Norton	.50
14	Bryce Paup	.50
15	John Randle	.50
16	Jerry Rice	5.00
17	Barry Sanders	6.00
18	Junior Seau	3.00
19	Steve Young	3.00
20	Reggie White	2.00
21	Chris Warren	1.00
22	Emmitt Smith	6.00
P1	Steve Young (20" by 14" poster Promo)	12.00

1995-96 Topps Finest Pro Bowl Jumbos Refractors

Refractor versions of the Pro Bowl Jumbo Refractors were also available at the 1996 NFL Experience Show in Hawaii. Odds for the Refractor versions are not known.

		NM/M
1	Troy Aikman	30.00
2	Tim Brown	15.00
3	Cris Carter	12.00
4	Marshall Faulk	20.00
5	Brett Favre	50.00
6	Merton Hanks	5.00
7	Michael Irvin	15.00
8	Greg Lloyd	10.00
9	Dan Marino	50.00
10	Curtis Martin	40.00
11	Herman Moore	12.00
12	Terry McDaniel	10.00
13	Ken Norton	10.00
14	Bryce Paup	8.00
15	John Randle	12.00
16	Jerry Rice	45.00
17	Barry Sanders	50.00
18	Junior Seau	20.00
19	Steve Young	35.00
20	Reggie White	20.00
21	Chris Warren	10.00
22	Emmitt Smith	50.00

1996 Finest

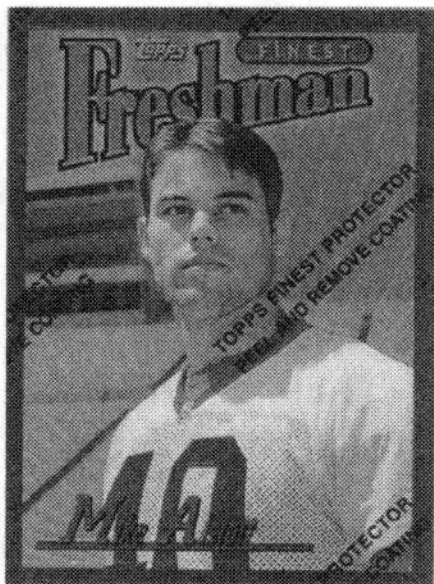

Topps' 1996 Finest football has 359 cards, split into five different subsets - 113 Destroyers, 43 Future, 34 Freshman, 115 Playmakers and 52 Sterling cards. Cards are numbered within the regular issue set from 1-359, and also within the subset, using a "D", "F", "P" or "S" prefix. Within the regular issue set there are three types of cards. There are 220 common cards, 91 uncommon cards (one per every four packs) and 47 rare cards (one per every 24 packs). Commons have a bronze border, uncommons have a silver border, and rares have a gold border. Refractors of every card were also made. Commons are seeded one per every 12 packs, uncommons are one per every 48, and rares are one every 288. Fewer than 150 Refractor sets were produced.

		NM/M
Complete Set (359):		550.00
Comp. Bronze Ser.1 (110):		40.00
Comp. Bronze Ser.2 (110):		50.00
Common Bronze Player:		.25
Common Silver Player:		2.00
Common Gold Player:		4.00
Series 1 Pack (6):		2.00
Series 1 Wax Box (24):		40.00
Series 2 Pack (6):		3.00
Series 2 Wax Box (24):		50.00
Refractors		2X to10X
1	Kordell Stewart G	8.00
2	Jay Novacek	.25
3	Ray Buchanan	.25
4	Brett Favre S	15.00
5	Phil Hansen	.25
6	Mike Mamula	.25
7	Kimble Anders G	3.00
8	Merton Hanks G	3.00
9	Bernie Parmalee	.25
10	Herman Moore	1.50
11	Shawn Jefferson	.25
12	Chris Doleman	.25
13	Erik Kramer	.25
14	Chester McGlockton S	2.00
15	Orlando Thomas	.25
16	Terrell Davis	4.00
17	Rick Mirer G	4.00
18	Roman Phifer	.25
19	Trent Dilfer	.50
20	Tyrone Hughes S	1.00
21	Darnay Scott	.50
22	Steve McNair	3.00
23	Lamar Lathon	.25
24	Ty Law S	2.00
25	Brian Mitchell S	2.00
26	Thomas Randolph	.25
27	Michael Jackson	.25
28	Seth Joyner	.25
29	Jeff Lageman	.25
30	Darryl Williams	.25
31	Darren Woodson S	2.00
32	Erric Pegram	.25
33	Craig Newsome G	3.00
34	Sean Dawkins	.25
35	Brian Mitchell S	2.00
36	Bryce Paup G	3.00
37	Dana Stubblefield S	2.00
38	Dan Saleaumua	.25
39	Henry Thomas	.25
40	Dan Marino G	25.00
41	Kerry Collins S	4.00
42	Andre Coleman G	2.00
43	Pat Swilling	.25
44	Marty Carter	.25
45	Anthony Miller	.25
46	Orlando Thomas S	2.00
47	Kevin Carter G	3.00
48	Chris Warren	.50
49	Derek Brown	.25
50	Jerry Rice S	10.00
51	Blaine Bishop	.25
52	Jake Reed	.25
53	Willie McGinest S	2.00
54	Blake Brockermeyer S	2.00
55	Vencie Glenn	.25
56	Michael Westbrook S	2.00
57	Garrison Hearst S	4.00
58	Derrick Alexander	.25
59	Kyle Brady S	2.00
60	Mark Brunell G	10.00
61	David Palmer G	2.00
62	Tim Brown S	4.00
63	Jeff Graham S	2.00
64	Jessie Tuggle	.25
65	Terrance Shaw	.25
66	David Sloan	.25
67	Dan Marino S	15.00
68	Brent Jones	.25
69	Tamarick Vanover S	2.00
70	William Thomas	.25
71	Robert Smith	.25
72	Wayne Simmons	.25
73	Jim Harbaugh	.50
74	Daryl Johnston S	2.00
75	Carnell Lake G	2.00
76	Wayne Chrebet	.25
77	Chris Hudson	.25
78	Frank Sanders S	2.00
79	Stevon Moore	.25
80	Chris Calloway	.25
81	Tom Carter	.25
82	David Meggett	.25
83	Sam Mills	.25
84	Darryll Lewis S	2.00
85	Carl Pickens S	4.00
86	Renaldo Turnbull	.25
87	Derrick Brooks	.25
88	Jerome Bettis S	4.00
89	Eugene Robinson	.25
90	Terrell Davis S	10.00
91	Rodney Thomas	2.00
92	Dan Wilkinson	.25
93	Mark Fields	.25
94	Warren Sapp	.25
95	Curtis Martin	3.00
96	Joey Galloway G	6.00
97	Ray Crockett	.25
98	Ed McDaniel	.25
99	Napoleon Kaufman S	2.00
100	Rashaan Salaam S	1.00
101	Craig Heyward	.25
102	Ellis Johnson	.25
103	Barry Sanders S	15.00
104	O.J. McDuffie	.25
105	J.J. Stokes	2.50
106	Mo Lewis	.25
107	Tony Boselli S	2.00
108	Rob Moore	.25
109	Eric Zeier S	2.00
110	Tyrone Wheatley	.50
111	Ken Harvey	.25
112	Melvin Tuten G	2.00
113	Willie Green	.25
114	Willie Davis	.25
115	Andy Harmon	.25
116	Bruce Smith S	2.00
117	Bryan Cox	.25
118	Zack Crockett S	2.00
119	Bert Emanuel	.25
120	Greg Lloyd	.25
121	Aaron Glenn G	3.00
122	Willie Jackson	.25
123	Lorenzo Lynch	.25
124	Pepper Johnson	.25
125	Joey Galloway S	4.00
126	Heath Shuler S	1.00
127	Curtis Martin S	10.00
128	Tyrone Poole	.25
129	Neil Smith	.25
130	Eddie Robinson	.25
131	Bryce Paup	.25
132	Brett Favre G	30.00
133	Ken Dilger G	2.00
134	Troy Aikman	4.00
135	Greg Lloyd S	2.00
136	Chris Sanders	2.00
137	Marshall Faulk S	10.00
138	Jim Everett	.25
139	Frank Sanders	.50
140	Barry Sanders G	25.00
141	Cortez Kennedy	.25
142	Glyn Milburn G	2.00
143	Derrick Alexander	.25
144	Rob Fredrickson	.25
145	Chris Zorich	.25
146	Devin Bush	.25
147	Tyrone Poole S	2.00
148	Brett Perriman G	3.00
149	Troy Vincent	.25
150	J.J. Stokes S	3.00
151	Deion Sanders	2.00
152	James Stewart	.25
153	Drew Bledsoe S	10.00
154	Terry McDaniel S	2.00
155	Terrell Fletcher S	2.00
156	Lawrence Dawsey	.25
157	Robert Brooks	.50
158	Rashaan Salaam	.50
159	Dave Brown S	2.00
160	Kerry Collins G	10.00
161	Tim Brown	.50
162	Brendan Stai	.25
163	Sean Gilbert	.25
164	Lee Woodall G	2.00
165	Jim Harbaugh S	1.00
166	Larry Brown S	1.00
167	Neil Smith S	1.00
168	Herman Moore S	2.00
169	Calvin Williams	.25
170	Deion Sanders S	3.00
171	Ruben Brown	.25
172	Eric Green	.25
173	Marshall Faulk G	15.00
174	Mark Chmura S	4.00
175	Jerry Rice	4.00
176	Bruce Smith	.25
177	Mark Bruener	.25
178	Troy Aikman G	20.00
179	Lamont Warren	.25
180	Tamarick Vanover	.50
181	Chris Warren S	1.00
182	Scott Mitchell	.25
183	Robert Brooks S	1.00
184	Steve McNair S	10.00
185	Kordell Stewart S	3.00
186	Terry Wooden	.25
187	Ken Norton	.25
188	Jeff Herrod	.25
189	Charlie Garner S	2.00
190	Drew Bledsoe G	20.00
191	Checklist	.25
192	Gus Frerotte	.25
193	Michael Irvin G	5.00
194	Brett Maxie	.25
195	Harvey Williams S	1.00
196	Warren Moon G	8.00
197	Jeff George S	2.00
198	*Eddie Kennison*	2.00
199	Ricky Watters S	4.00
200	Steve Young G	15.00
201	Marcus Jones	.25
202	Terry Allen	.50
203	Leroy Hoard	.25
204	Steve Bono S	2.00
205	Reggie White	.50
206	Larry Centers	.25
207	*Alex Van Dyke G*	2.00
208	Vincent Brisby	.25
209	Michael Timpson	.25
210	Jeff Blake S	2.00
211	John Mobley	.25
212	Clay Matthews	.25
213	Shannon Sharpe	.25
214	Tony Bennett	.25
215	Phillippi Sparks S	1.00
216	Mickey Washington	.25
217	Fred Barnett	.25
218	Michael Haynes	.25
219	Stan Humphries	.25
220	Cris Carter G	6.00
221	Winston Moss	.25
222	*Tim Biakabutuka*	2.00
223	*Leeland McElroy*	1.50
224	Vinnie Clark	.25
225	*Keyshawn Johnson*	5.00
226	William Floyd S	2.00
227	Troy Drayton S	1.00
228	Tony Woods	.25
229	Rodney Hampton S	2.00
230	John Elway G	20.00
231	Anthony Pleasant	.25
232	Jeff George	.25
233	Curtis Conway	.50
234	Charles Haley G	3.00
235	*Jeff Lewis*	2.50
236	Edgar Bennett	.25
237	Regan Upshaw	.25
238	William Fuller	.25
239	Duane Clemons S	2.00
240	Jim Kelly G	12.00
241	Willie Anderson	.25
242	Derrick Thomas	.25
243	*Marvin Harrison*	10.00
244	Darion Conner	.25
245	Antonio Langham	.25
246	Rodney Peete	.25
247	Tim McDonald	.25
248	Robert Jones	.25
249	Curtis Conway S	2.00
250	Rodney Hampton G	5.00
251	Mark Carrier	.25
252	Steve Grant	.25
253	John Mobley S	2.00
254	Jeff Hostetler	.25
255	Darrell Green	.25
256	Errict Rhett G	6.00
257	*Alex Molden G*	2.00
258	Chris Slade S	1.00
259	Derrick Thomas S	2.00
260	*Kevin Hardy G*	2.00
261	Eric Swann	.25
262	Eric Metcalf S	2.00
263	Irv Smith	.25
264	Tim McKyer	.25
265	Emmitt Smith S	15.00
266	Sean Jones	.25
267	Bryant Young G	5.00
268	Jeff Blake G	5.00
269	Jeff Hostetler S	2.00
270	*Keyshawn Johnson G*	10.00
271	Yancey Thigpen	1.00
272	Thurman Thomas S	4.00
273	Quentin Coryatt	.25
274	Hardy Nickerson	.25
275	Ricardo McDonald	.25
276	Steve Atwater S	2.00
277	Robert Blackmon	.25
278	Junior Seau G	10.00
279	Alonzo Spellman	.25
280	Isaac Bruce S	4.00
281	*Rickey Dudley*	3.00
282	Joe Cain	.25
283	Neil O'Donnell S	2.00
284	John Randle	.25
285	Terry Kirby G	5.00
286	Vinny Testaverde	.25
287	Jim Kelly S	4.00
288	*Lawrence Phillips S*	2.00
289	Henry Jones	.25
290	*Simeon Rice*	1.50
291	Terance Mathis S	2.00
292	Errict Rhett S	3.00
293	Hugh Douglas G	4.00
294	Santo Stephens S	2.00
295	Leslie O'Neal	.25
296	Reggie White G	10.00
297	Greg Hill	.25
298	Elvis Grbac G	5.00
299	*Walt Harris S*	1.00
300	Emmitt Smith G	25.00
301	Eric Metcalf	.25
302	Jamir Miller S	2.00
303	Jerome Woods	.25
304	Ben Coates S	2.00
305	Marcus Allen S	4.00
306	Anthony Smith	.25
307	Darren Perry	.25
308	*Jonathan Ogden S*	2.00
309	Ricky Watters G	6.00
310	John Elway S	12.00
311	James Hasty	.25
312	Cris Carter	.50
313	Irving Fryar S	2.00
314	*Lawrence Phillips*	1.00
315	Junior Seau S	4.00
316	*Alex Molden S*	1.50
317	Aeneas Williams	.25
318	Eric Hill	.25
319	*Kevin Hardy*	1.50
320	Steve Young S	10.00
321	Chris Chandler	.25

322 Raghib Ismail .25
323 Anthony Parker .25
324 John Thierry .25
325 Micheal Barrow .25
326 Henry Ford .25
327 Aaron Hayden .25
328 Terance Mathis .25
329 Kirk Pointer .25
330 *Ray Mickens* .75
331 Jermaine Mayberry .25
332 Mario Bates .25
333 Carlton Gray .25
334 Derek Loville .25
335 *Mike Alstott* 4.00
336 Eric Guliford .25
337 Marvcus Patton .25
338 *Terrell Owens* 10.00
339 Lance Johnstone .25
340 Lake Dawson .25
341 Winslow Oliver .25
342 Adrian Murrell .25
343 Jason Belser .25
344 Brian Dawkins .25
345 Reggie Brown .25
346 Shaun Gayle .25
347 *Tony Brackens* 1.00
348 Thomas Lewis .25
349 Kelvin Pritchett .25
350 *Bobby Engram* 3.00
351 Moe Williams .25
352 Thomas Smith .25
353 Dexter Carter .25
354 Qadry Ismail .25
355 Marco Battaglia .25
356 Levon Kirkland .25
357 Eric Allen .25
358 *Bobby Hoying* 2.50
359 Checklist .25

1996 Finest Refractors

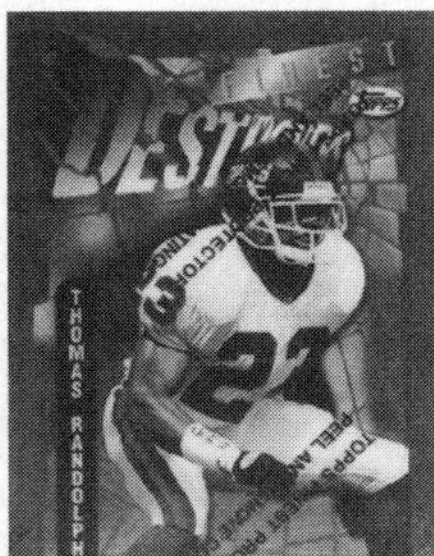

Each card in Topps' 1996 Finest set has a Refractor card made for it, as labeled on the back. Commons are seeded one per every 12 packs, uncommons are one every 48, and rares are one every 288 packs. Fewer than 150 rare Refractor sets were produced.

NM/M
Refractors 5X to10X

1997 Finest

The 175-card Series I set has a numbering format that features card No. 1-100 labeled as Common, cards No. 101-150 as Uncommon and No. 151-175 as Rare. Each card also has a different number corresponding to its theme. The Finest themes are Masters, Bulldozers, Hitmen, Dynamos and Field Generals. The numbering box on each card back indicates both sets of numbers, and which type of card it is, either Common, Uncommon or Rare. The card's theme is printed at the top of each card. Uncommon cards were seeded 1:4 packs, while Rare cards were inserted 1:24. Embossed Uncommon cards were seeded 1:16, while Embossed Die-Cut Rare cards were inserted 1:96. Embossed Die-Cut Rare cards were found 1:96. Series II was numbered 176-350. It consisted of 100 commons, 50 uncommons and 25 rares. The themes in Series II were Champions, Dominators, Impact, Masters and Stalwarts. Insertion rates for Series II were identical to Series I.

NM/M
Complete Set (350): 600.00
Comp. Bronze Ser.1 (100): 30.00
Comp. Bronze Ser.2 (100): 60.00
Common Bronze Player: .25
Embossed Silvers: 2X
Embossed Die-Cut Golds: 1.5X
Series 1 Pack (6): 1.75
Series 1 Wax Box (24): 30.00
Series 2 Pack (6): 2.75
Series 2 Wax Box (24): 45.00
1 Mark Brunell 1.00
2 Chris Slade .25
3 Chris Doleman .25
4 Chris Hudson .25
5 Karim Abdul-Jabbar .50
6 Darren Perry .25
7 Daryl Johnston .25
8 Rob Moore .25
9 Robert Smith .25
10 Terry Allen .25
11 Jason Dunn .25
12 Henry Thomas .25
13 Rod Stephens .25
14 Ray Mickens .25
15 Ty Detmer .25
16 Fred Barnett .25
17 Derrick Alexander .25
18 Marcus Robertson .25
19 Robert Blackmon .25
20 Isaac Bruce .75
21 Chester McGlockton .25
22 Stan Humphries .25
23 Lonnie Marts .25
24 Jason Sehorn .25
25 Bobby Engram .25
26 Brett Perriman .25
27 Stevon Moore .25
28 Jamal Anderson 1.00
29 Wayne Martin .25
30 Michael Irvin .50
31 Thomas Smith .25
32 Tony Brackens .25
33 Eric Davis .25
34 James Stewart .25
35 Ki-Jana Carter .25
36 Ken Norton .25
37 William Thomas .25
38 Tim Brown .25
39 Lawrence Phillips .50
40 Ricky Watters .50
41 Tony Bennett .25
42 Jesse Armstead .25
43 Trent Dilfer .25
44 Rodney Hampton .25
45 Sam Mills .25
46 Rodney Harrison .25
47 Rob Fredrickson .25
48 Eric Hill .25
49 Bennie Blades .25
50 Eddie George 2.00
51 Dave Brown .25
52 Raymont Harris .25
53 Steve Tovar .25
54 Thurman Thomas .50
55 Leeland McElroy .25
56 Brian Mitchell .25
57 Eric Allen .25
58 Vinny Testaverde .25
59 Marvin Washington .25
60 Junior Seau .25
61 Bert Emanuel .25
62 Kevin Carter .25
63 Mark Carrier .25
64 Andre Coleman .25
65 Chris Warren .25
66 Aeneas Williams .25
67 Eugene Robinson .25
68 Darren Woodson .25
69 Anthony Johnson .25
70 Terry Glenn 1.00
71 Troy Vincent .25
72 John Copeland .25
73 Warren Sapp .25
74 Bobby Hebert .25
75 Jeff Hostetler .25
76 Willie Davis .25
77 Mickey Washington .25
78 Cortez Kennedy .25
79 Michael Strahan .25
80 Jerome Bettis .50
81 Andre Hastings .25
82 Simeon Rice .25
83 Cornelius Bennett .25
84 Napoleon Kaufman .50
85 Jim Harbaugh .25
86 Aaron Hayden .25
87 Gus Frerotte .25
88 Jeff Blake .50
89 Anthony Miller .25
90 Deion Sanders 1.00
91 Curtis Conway .25
92 William Floyd .25
93 Eric Moulds .25
94 Mel Gray .25
95 Andre Rison .25
96 Eugene Daniel .25
97 Jason Belser .25
98 Mike Mamula .25
99 Jim Everett .25
100 Checklist .25
101 Drew Bledsoe S 4.00
102 Shannon Sharpe S 2.00
103 Ken Harvey S 2.00
104 Isaac Bruce S 2.00
105 Terry Allen S 2.00
106 Lawyer Milloy S 2.00
107 Ashley Ambrose S 2.00
108 Alfred Williams S 2.00
109 Hugh Douglas S 2.00
110 Junior Seau S 2.00
111 Kordell Stewart S 2.00
112 Adrian Murrell S 2.00
113 Byron Morris S 2.00
114 Terrell Buckley S 2.00
115 Dan Marino S 8.00
116 Willie Clay S 2.00
117 Neil Smith S 2.00
118 Blaine Bishop S 2.00
119 John Mobley S 2.00
120 Herman Moore S 3.00
121 Keyshawn Johnson S 2.00
122 Boomer Esiason S 2.00
123 Marshall Faulk S 3.00
124 Keith Jackson S 2.00
125 Ricky Watters S 3.00
126 Carl Pickens S 3.00
127 Cris Carter S 2.00
128 Mike Alstott S 2.00
129 Simeon Rice S 2.00
130 Troy Aikman S 6.00
131 Tamarick Vanover S 3.00
132 Marquez Pope S 2.00
133 Winslow Oliver S 2.00
134 Edgar Bennett S 2.00
135 David Meggett S 2.00
136 Marcus Allen S 3.00
137 Jerry Rice S 8.00
138 Steve Atwater S 2.00
139 Tim McDonald S 2.00
140 Barry Sanders S 8.00
141 Eddie George S 4.00
142 Wesley Walls S 2.00
143 Jerome Bettis S 2.00
144 Kevin Greene S 2.00
145 Terrell Davis S 4.00
146 Gus Frerotte S 2.00
147 Joey Galloway S 2.00
148 Vinny Testaverde S 2.00
149 Hardy Nickerson S 2.00
150 Brett Favre S 10.00
151 Desmond Howard G 2.00
152 Keyshawn Johnson G 4.00
153 Tony Banks G 2.00
154 Chris Spielman G 2.00
155 Reggie White G 4.00
156 Zach Thomas G 4.00
157 Carl Pickens G 4.00
158 Karim Abdul-Jabbar G 2.00
159 Chad Brown G 2.00
160 Kerry Collins G 4.00
161 Marvin Harrison G 6.00
162 Steve Young G 10.00
163 Deion Sanders G 6.00
164 Trent Dilfer G 4.00
165 Barry Sanders G 25.00
166 Cris Carter G 4.00
167 Keenan McCardell G 4.00
168 Terry Glenn G 4.00
169 Emmitt Smith G 25.00
170 John Elway G 20.00
171 Jerry Rice G 20.00
172 Troy Aikman G 20.00
173 Curtis Martin G 20.00
174 Darrell Green G 4.00
175 Mark Brunell G 10.00
176 *Corey Dillon* 12.00
177 Tyrone Poole .25
178 Anthony Pleasant .25
179 Frank Sanders .25
180 Troy Aikman 4.00
181 Bill Romanowski .25
182 Ty Law .25
183 Orlando Thomas .25
184 Quentin Coryatt .25
185 Kenny Holmes .25
186 Bryant Young .25
187 Michael Sinclair .25
188 Mike Tomczak .25
189 Bobby Taylor .25
190 Brett Favre 5.00
191 Kent Graham .25
192 Jessie Tuggle .25
193 Jimmy Smith .25
194 Greg Hill .25
195 *Yatil Green* 2.00
196 Mark Fields .25
197 Phillippi Sparks .25
198 Aaron Glenn .25
199 Pat Swilling .25
200 Barry Sanders 5.00
201 Mark Chmura .50
202 Marco Coleman .25
203 Merton Hanks .25
204 Brian Blades .25
205 Errict Rhett .50
206 Henry Ellard .25
207 Andre Reed .25
208 Bryan Cox .25
209 Darnay Scott .25
210 John Elway 3.00
211 Glyn Milburn .25
212 Don Beebe .25
213 Kevin Lockett .25
214 Dorsey Levens .50
215 Kordell Stewart 1.00
216 Larry Centers .25
217 Cris Carter .50
218 Willie McGinest .25
219 Renaldo Wynn .25
220 Jerry Rice 3.00
221 *Reidel Anthony* 2.00
222 Mark Carrier .25
223 Quinn Early .25
224 Chris Sanders .25
225 *Shawn Springs* .50
226 Kevin Smith .25
227 Ben Coates .25
228 Tyrone Wheatley .25
229 Antonio Freeman 1.50
230 Dan Marino 5.00
231 Dwayne Rudd .25
232 Leslie O'Neal .25
233 Brent Jones .25
234 *Jake Plummer* 6.00
235 Kerry Collins 2.00
236 Rashaan Salaam .50
237 Tyrone Braxton .25
238 Herman Moore .50
239 Keyshawn Johnson .50
240 Drew Bledsoe 4.00
241 Rickey Dudley .25
242 *Antowain Smith* 6.00
243 Jeff Lageman .25
244 Chris T. Jones .25
245 Steve Young 3.00
246 Eddie Robinson .25
247 Chad Cota .25
248 Michael Jackson .25
249 Robert Porcher .25
250 Reggie White .50
251 Carnell Lake .25
252 Chris Calloway .25
253 Terance Mathis .25
254 Carl Pickens .50
255 Curtis Martin 3.00
256 Jeff Graham .25
257 Regan Upshaw .25
258 Sean Gilbert .25
259 *Will Blackwell* .50
260 Emmitt Smith 5.00
261 *Reinard Wilson* .50
262 *Darrell Russell* .50
263 Wayne Chrebet .25
264 Kevin Hardy .25
265 Shannon Sharpe .25
266 Harvey Williams .25
267 John Randle .25
268 Tim Bowens .25
269 *Tony Gonzalez* 6.00
270 *Warrick Dunn* 6.00
271 Sean Dawkins .25
272 Darryll Lewis .25
273 Alonzo Spellman .25
274 Mark Collins .25
275 Checklist 2 .25
276 *Pat Barnes S* 1.00
277 Dana Stubblefield S 1.00
278 Dan Wilkinson S 2.00
279 Bryce Paup S 2.00
280 Kerry Collins S 4.00
281 Derrick Brooks S 2.00
282 Walter Jones S 2.00
283 Terry McDaniel S 2.00
284 James Farrior S 2.00
285 Curtis Martin S 6.00
286 O.J. McDuffie S 2.00
287 Natrone Means S 2.00
288 *Bryant Westbrook S* 3.00
289 *Peter Boulware S* 3.00
290 Emmitt Smith S 10.00
291 *Joey Kent S* 1.00
292 Eddie Kennison S 2.00
293 LeRoy Butler S 2.00
294 Dale Carter S 2.00
295 *Jim Druckenmiller S* 2.00
296 *Byron Hanspard S* 1.00
297 Jeff Blake S 2.00
298 Levon Kirkland S 2.00
299 Michael Westbrook S 2.00
300 John Elway S 8.00
301 Lamar Lathon S 2.00
302 Ray Lewis S 2.00
303 Steve McNair S 6.00
304 *Shawn Springs S* 1.00
305 Karim Abdul-Jabbar S 1.00
306 *Orlando Pace S* 3.00
307 Scott Mitchell S 2.00
308 Walt Harris S 1.00
309 Bruce Smith S 2.00
310 Reggie White S 3.00
311 Eric Swann S 2.00
312 Derrick Thomas S 2.00
313 Tony Martin S 2.00
314 Darrell Russell S 2.00
315 Mark Brunell S 6.00
316 Trent Dilfer S 3.00
317 Irving Fryar S 2.00
318 Amani Toomer S 2.00
319 Jake Reed S 2.00
320 Steve Young S 8.00
321 *Troy Davis S* 4.00
322 Jim Harbaugh S 2.00
323 Neil O'Donnell S 2.00
324 Terry Glenn S 2.00
325 Deion Sanders S 2.00
326 Gus Frerotte G 2.00
327 Tom Knight G 1.00
328 *Peter Boulware G* 2.00
329 Jerome Bettis G 6.00
330 *Orlando Pace G* 6.00
331 *Darnell Autry G* 3.00
332 *Ike Hilliard G* 15.00
333 *David LaFleur G* 2.00
334 Jim Harbaugh G 3.00
335 Eddie George G 10.00
336 Vinny Testaverde G 3.00
337 Terry Allen G 3.00
338 *Jim Druckenmiller G* 4.00
339 Ricky Watters G 5.00
340 Brett Favre G 30.00
341 Simeon Rice G 4.00
342 Shannon Sharpe G 7.50
343 Kordell Stewart G 8.00
344 Isaac Bruce G 8.00
345 Drew Bledsoe G 10.00
346 Jeff Blake G 3.00
347 Herman Moore G 3.00
348 Junior Seau G 5.00
349 *Rae Carruth G* 2.00
350 Dan Marino G 30.00

1997 Finest Refractors

Each of the 350 base cards has a parallel Refractor. Refractor Common cards were inserted 1:12 packs, while Refractor Uncommon were seeded 1:48. Refractor Rare could be found 1:288 packs. In addition, Refractors of the Embossed and Embossed Die-Cut cards were also randomly seeded. An Embossed Uncommon Refractor was inserted 1:192 packs, while an Embossed Die-Cut Refractor was seeded 1:1,152 packs.

NM/M
Common Bronze Player: 3.00
Common Silver Player: 10.00
Embossed Silver Refractors: 2X
Common Gold Player: 40.00
Embossed DC Gold Refractors: 2X

1998 Finest

Finest was issued in two, 150-card series in 1998, with 150 in Series I and 120 in Series II. Each card was available in a Protector (base cards), No-Protector (1:2 packs), Protector Refractor (1:12) and No-Protector Refractor (1:24) version. An interesting twist to the releases was that the 30 rookies (121-150) were available in Protector and No-Protector Refractor versions in Series I, but the No-Protector and Protector Refractor versions were only issued in Series II packs. Series I inserts were: Double-Sided Mystery Finest, Centurions, Undergrads and Jumbos, while Series II inserts included Mystery Finest, Stadium Stars, Future's Finest, Jumbos (base cards), Jumbo Stadium Stars and Jumbo Mystery.

NM/M
Complete Set (270): 75.00
Complete Series 1 (150): 60.00
Complete Series 2 (120): 40.00
Common Player: .25
Minor Stars: .50
Common Rookie: 1.50
Refractor Cards: 3X-5X
Refractor Rookies: 2X-4X
Inserted 1:12
No-Protector Cards: 2X-4X
No-Protector Rookies: 2X
Inserted 1:2
NP Refractor Cards: 5X-10X
NP Refractor Rookies: 3X-6X
Inserted 1:24
Series 1 Pack (6): 4.75
Series 1 Wax Box (24): 80.00
Series 2 Pack (6): 2.00
Series 2 Wax Box (24): 35.00
1 John Elway 3.00
2 Terance Mathis .25
3 Jermaine Lewis .25
4 Fred Lane .50
5 Bryan Cox .25
6 David Dunn .25
7 Dexter Coakley .25
8 Carl Pickens .50
9 Antonio Freeman .75
10 Herman Moore .75
11 Kevin Hardy .25
12 Tony Gonzalez .50
13 O.J. McDuffie .50
14 David Palmer .25
15 Lawyer Milloy .25
16 Danny Kanell .25
17 Randal Hill .25
18 Keyshawn Johnson .75
19 Charlie Garner .25
20 Mark Brunell 1.00
21 Donnell Woolford .25
22 Freddie Jones .25
23 Ken Norton .25
24 Tony Banks .50
25 Isaac Bruce .50
26 Willie Davis .25
27 Cris Dishman .25
28 Aeneas Williams .25
29 Michael Booker .25
30 Cris Carter .75
31 Michael McCrary .25
32 Eric Moulds .50
33 Rae Carruth .25
34 Bobby Engram .25
35 Jeff Blake .50
36 Deion Sanders 1.00
37 Rod Smith .50
38 Bryant Westbrook .25
39 Mark Chmura .50
40 Tim Brown .50
41 Bobby Taylor .25
42 James Stewart .25
43 Kimble Anders .25
44 Karim Abdul-Jabbar .75
45 Willie McGinest .25
46 Jessie Armstead .25
47 Aaron Glenn .25
48 Greg Lloyd .25
49 Stephen Davis .25
50 Jerome Bettis .75
51 Warren Sapp .25
52 Horace Copeland .25
53 Chad Brown .25
54 Chris Canty .25
55 Robert Smith .50
56 Pete Mitchell .25
57 Aaron Bailey .25
58 Robert Porcher .25
59 John Mobley .25
60 Tony Martin .25
61 Michael Irvin .50
62 Charles Way .25
63 Raymont Harris .25
64 Chuck Smith .25
65 Larry Centers .25
66 Greg Hill .25
67 Kenny Holmes .25
68 John Lynch .25
69 Michael Sinclair .25
70 Steve Young 1.50
71 Michael Strahan .25
72 Levon Kirkland .25
73 Rickey Dudley .25
74 Marcus Allen .50
75 John Randle .25
76 Erik Kramer .25
77 Neil Smith .25
78 Byron Hanspard .50
79 Quinn Early .25
80 Warren Moon .50
81 William Thomas .25
82 Ben Coates .25
83 Lake Dawson .25
84 Steve McNair 1.00
85 Gus Frerotte .25
86 Rodney Harrison .25
87 Reggie White .75
88 Derrick Thomas .25
89 Dale Carter .25
90 Warrick Dunn 1.00
91 Will Blackwell .25
92 Troy Vincent .25
93 Johnnie Morton .25
94 David LaFleur .25
95 Tony McGee .25
96 Lonnie Johnson .25
97 Thurman Thomas .50
98 Chris Chandler .50
99 Jamal Anderson 1.00
100 Checklist .25
101 Marshall Faulk 1.00
102 Chris Calloway .25
103 Chris Spielman .25
104 Zach Thomas .50
105 Jeff George .50
106 Darrell Russell .25
107 Darryll Lewis .25
108 Reidel Anthony .50
109 Terrell Owens 1.00
110 Rob Moore .50
111 Darrell Green .25
112 Merton Hanks .25
113 Shawn Jefferson .25
114 Chris Sanders .25
115 Scott Mitchell .50
116 Vaughn Hebron .25
117 Ed McCaffrey .50
118 Bruce Smith .25
119 Peter Boulware .25
120 Brett Favre 5.00
121 *Peyton Manning* 15.00
122 *Brian Griese* 6.00
123 *Tavian Banks* 2.00
124 *Duane Starks* 1.50
125 *Robert Holcombe* 2.00
126 *Brian Simmons* 1.50
127 *Skip Hicks* 2.00
128 *Keith Brooking* 1.50
129 *Ahman Green* 12.00
130 *Jerome Pathon* 3.00
131 *Curtis Enis* 2.00
132 *Grant Wistrom* 2.00
133 *Germane Crowell* 2.00
134 *Jacquez Green* 3.00
135 *Randy Moss* 12.00
136 *Jason Peter* 2.00
137 *John Avery* 2.00
138 *Takeo Spikes* 2.00
139 *Patrick Johnson* 2.00
140 *Andre Wadsworth* 2.00
141 *Fred Taylor* 6.00
142 *Charles Woodson* 4.00
143 *Marcus Nash* 3.00
144 *Robert Edwards* 3.00
145 *Kevin Dyson* 3.00
146 *Joe Jurevicius* 3.00
147 *Anthony Simmons* 2.00
148 *Hines Ward* 6.00
149 *Greg Ellis* 2.00
150 *Ryan Leaf* 2.00
151 Jerry Rice 2.50
152 Tony Martin .25
153 Billy Joe Hobert .25
154 Rob Johnson .50
155 Shannon Sharpe .50
156 Bert Emanuel .25
157 Eric Metcalf .25
158 Natrone Means .75
159 Derrick Alexander .25
160 Emmitt Smith 3.50
161 Jeff Burris .25
162 Chris Warren .25
163 Corey Fuller .25
164 Courtney Hawkins .25
165 James McKnight .25
166 Shawn Springs .25
167 Wayne Martin .25
168 Michael Westbrook .25
169 Michael Jackson .25
170 Dan Marino 3.50
171 Amp Lee .25
172 James Jett .25
173 Ty Law .25
174 Kerry Collins .50
175 Robert Brooks .50
176 Blaine Bishop .25
177 Stephen Boyd .25
178 Keyshawn Johnson .75

179	Deon Figures	.25
180	Allen Aldridge	.25
181	Corey Miller	.25
182	Chad Lewis	.25
183	Derrick Rodgers	.25
184	Troy Drayton	.25
185	Darren Woodson	.25
186	Ken Dilger	.25
187	Elvis Grbac	.50
188	Terrell Fletcher	.25
189	Frank Sanders	.25
190	Curtis Martin	1.00
191	Derrick Brooks	.25
192	Darrien Gordon	.25
193	Andre Reed	.50
194	Darnay Scott	.25
195	Curtis Conway	.50
196	Tim McDonald	.25
197	Sean Dawkins	.25
198	Napoleon Kaufman	1.00
199	Willie Clay	.25
200	Terrell Davis	3.00
201	Wesley Walls	.25
202	Santana Dotson	.25
203	Frank Wycheck	.25
204	Wayne Chrebet	.75
205	Andre Rison	.50
206	Jason Sehorn	.25
207	Jessie Tuggle	.25
208	Kevin Turner	.25
209	Jason Taylor	.25
210	Yancey Thigpen	.25
211	Jake Reed	.50
212	Carnell Lake	.25
213	Joey Galloway	.75
214	Andre Hastings	.25
215	Terry Allen	.50
216	Jim Harbaugh	.50
217	Tony Banks	.50
218	Greg Clark	.25
219	Corey Dillon	1.25
220	Troy Aikman	2.50
221	Antowain Smith	1.00
222	Steve Atwater	.25
223	Trent Dilfer	.75
224	Junior Seau	.50
225	Garrison Hearst	.75
226	Eric Allen	.25
227	Chad Cota	.25
228	Vinny Testaverde	.50
229	Chris T. Jones	.25
230	Drew Bledsoe	2.00
231	Charles Johnson	.25
232	Jake Plummer	1.00
233	Errict Rhett	.25
234	Doug Evans	.25
235	Phillippi Sparks	.25
236	Ashley Ambrose	.25
237	Bryan Cox	.25
238	Kevin Smith	.25
239	Hardy Nickerson	.25
240	Terry Glenn	.75
241	Lee Woodall	.25
242	Andre Coleman	.25
243	Michael Bates	.25
244	Mark Fields	.25
245	Eddie Kennison	.50
246	Dana Stubblefield	.25
247	Bobby Hoying	.50
248	Mo Lewis	.25
249	Derrick Mayes	.25
250	Eddie George	2.00
251	Mike Alstott	1.00
252	J.J. Stokes	.50
253	Adrian Murrell	.50
254	Kevin Greene	.25
255	LeRoy Butler	.25
256	Glenn Foley	.50
257	Jimmy Smith	.50
258	Tiki Barber	.25
259	Irving Fryar	.25
260	Ricky Watters	.50
261	Jeff Graham	.25
262	Kordell Stewart	1.00
263	Rod Woodson	.25
264	Leslie Shepherd	.25
265	Ryan McNeil	.25
266	Ike Hilliard	.25
267	Keenan McCardell	.50
268	Marvin Harrison	.75
269	Dorsey Levens	.75
270	Barry Sanders	5.00

1998 Finest Refractors

Both Protector and No-Protector versions had parallel Refractor versions for all 270 cards. Protector Refractors were inserted one per 12 packs and had only the front of the card with a Refractor finish, while No-Protector Refractors were inserted one per 24 packs and were basically a double-sided Refractor. No-Protector Refractor versions of the 30 rookies (121-150) were inserted into Series I packs, while Protector Refractor versions were only in Series II packs.

Refractors: 3X-5X

1998 Finest Centurions

This 20-card insert set was found in packs of Series I. Regular versions were numbered to 500, while Refractors were numbered to only 75. Centurions inserts were numbered with a "C" prefix.

		NM/M
Complete Set (20):		300.00
Common Player:		5.00
Minor Stars:		10.00
Inserted 1:125		
Production 500 Sets		
Refractors:		2X
Inserted 1:831		
Production 75 Sets		
C1	Brett Favre	50.00
C2	Eddie George	20.00
C3	Antonio Freeman	10.00
C4	Napoleon Kaufman	5.00
C5	Terrell Davis	25.00
C6	Keyshawn Johnson	24.00
C7	Peter Boulware	5.00
C8	Mike Alstott	10.00
C9	Jake Plummer	10.00
C10	Mark Brunell	20.00
C11	Marvin Harrison	15.00
C12	Antowain Smith	10.00
C13	Dorsey Levens	10.00
C14	Terry Glenn	10.00
C15	Warrick Dunn	15.00
C16	Joey Galloway	10.00
C17	Steve McNair	20.00
C18	Corey Dillon	20.00
C19	Drew Bledsoe	25.00
C20	Kordell Stewart	15.00

1998 Finest Future's Finest

This insert set features 20 players taking America's game into the next century. Singles were sequentially numbered to 500 and inserted 1:83 packs. Each card also had a parallel Refractor that was numbered to 75 and found 1:557 packs.

		NM/M
Complete Set (20):		150.00
Common Player:		4.00
Minor Stars:		8.00
Inserted 1:83		
Production 500 Sets		
Refractors:		2X-3X
Inserted 1:557		
Production 75 Sets		
F1	Peyton Manning	20.00
F2	Napoleon Kaufman	4.00
F3	Jake Plummer	8.00
F4	Terry Glenn	4.00
F5	Ryan Leaf	4.00
F6	Drew Bledsoe	15.00
F7	Dorsey Levens	8.00
F8	Andre Wadsworth	4.00
F9	Joey Galloway	8.00
F10	Curtis Enis	4.00
F11	Warrick Dunn	8.00
F12	Kordell Stewart	8.00
F13	Randy Moss	25.00
F14	Robert Edwards	4.00
F15	Eddie George	8.00
F16	Fred Taylor	15.00
F17	Corey Dillon	10.00
F18	Brett Favre	30.00
F19	Kevin Dyson	8.00
F20	Terrell Davis	20.00

1998 Finest Jumbos 1

Eight different Jumbo Finest cards were inserted as box toppers in both Series I and II. The 16-card set was inserted 1:3 boxes (1:2 hobby collector boxes), with Refractors every 12 boxes (1:6 hobby collector boxes).

		NM/M
Complete Set (8):		60.00
Common Player:		3.00
Inserted 1:3 Boxes		
Refractors:		2X
Inserted 1:12 Boxes		
1	John Elway	10.00
2	Peyton Manning	15.00
3	Mark Brunell	8.00
4	Curtis Enis	3.00
5	Jerome Bettis	3.00
6	Ryan Leaf	3.00
7	Warrick Dunn	5.00
8	Brett Favre	20.00

1998 Finest Jumbos 2

Eight different Jumbo Finest cards were inserted as box toppers in both Series I and II. The 16-card set was inserted 1:3 boxes (1:2 hobby collector boxes), with Refractors every 12 boxes (1:6 hobby collector boxes).

		NM/M
Complete Set (7):		50.00
Common Player:		3.00
Inserted 1:3 Boxes		
Refractors:		2X
Inserted 1:12 Boxes		
151	Jerry Rice	12.00
160	Emmitt Smith	15.00
170	Dan Marino	15.00
213	Joey Galloway	3.00
230	Drew Bledsoe	8.00
250	Eddie George	8.00
270	Barry Sanders	15.00

1998 Finest Mystery Finest 1

Twenty different players were displayed either with one of three other players on the back, or by themselves on both sides in Mystery Finest. Each side has a Finest Opaque protector and is numbered with a "M" prefix. Regular versions are seeded one per 36 packs, while Refractors are found every 144 packs.

		NM/M
Common Player:		4.00
Inserted 1:36		
Refractor Set (50):		1,650
Refractors:		1.5X
Inserted 1:144		
M1	Brett Favre, Mark Brunell	25.00
M2	Brett Favre, Jake Plummer	25.00
M3	Brett Favre, Steve Young	25.00
M4	Brett Favre, Brett Favre	30.00
M5	Mark Brunell, Steve Young	15.00
M6	Mark Brunell, Mark Brunell	10.00
M7	Jake Plummer, Mark Brunell	10.00
M8	Jake Plummer, Jake Plummer	10.00
M9	Steve Young, Jake Plummer	15.00
M10	Steve Young, Steve Young	15.00
M11	John Elway, Drew Bledsoe	20.00
M12	John Elway, Troy Aikman	25.00
M13	John Elway, Dan Marino	30.00
M14	John Elway, John Elway	25.00
M15	Drew Bledsoe, Troy Aikman	20.00
M16	Drew Bledsoe, Drew Bledsoe	15.00
M17	Troy Aikman, Dan Marino	25.00
M18	Troy Aikman, Troy Aikman	15.00
M19	Dan Marino, Drew Bledsoe	30.00
M20	Dan Marino, Dan Marino	30.00
M21	Kordell Stewart, Corey Dillon	10.00
M22	Kordell Stewart, Tim Brown	10.00
M23	Kordell Stewart, Barry Sanders	20.00
M24	Kordell Stewart, Kordell Stewart	10.00
M25	Corey Dillon, Tim Brown	10.00
M26	Corey Dillon, Corey Dillon	10.00
M27	Tim Brown, Barry Sanders	25.00
M28	Tim Brown, Tim Brown	10.00
M29	Barry Sanders, Corey Dillon	20.00
M30	Barry Sanders, Barry Sanders	25.00
M31	Terrell Davis, Emmitt Smith	25.00
M32	Terrell Davis, Jerome Bettis	20.00
M33	Terrell Davis, Eddie George	20.00
M34	Terrell Davis, Terrell Davis	20.00
M35	Emmitt Smith, Eddie George	25.00
M36	Emmitt Smith, Emmitt Smith	25.00
M37	Jerome Bettis, Emmitt Smith	25.00
M38	Jerome Bettis, Jerome Bettis	4.00
M39	Eddie George, Jerome Bettis	10.00
M40	Eddie George, Eddie George	10.00
M41	Herman Moore, Jerry Rice	15.00
M42	Herman Moore, Herman Moore	4.00
M43	Warrick Dunn, Herman Moore	10.00
M44	Warrick Dunn, Jerry Rice	15.00
M45	Warrick Dunn, Dorsey Levens	5.00
M46	Warrick Dunn, Warrick Dunn	5.00
M47	Jerry Rice, Dorsey Levens	15.00
M48	Jerry Rice, Jerry Rice	20.00
M49	Dorsey Levens, Herman Moore	4.00
M50	Dorsey Levens, Dorsey Levens	4.00

1998 Finest Mystery Finest 2

Twenty different players were displayed either with one of three other players on the back, or by themselves on both sides in Mystery Finest. Each side has a Finest Opaque protector and is numbered with an "M" prefix. Regular versions are seeded one per 36 packs, while Refractors are found every 144 packs.

		NM/M
Common Player:		3.00
Inserted 1:36		
Refractors:		1.5X
Inserted 1:144		
M1	Brett Favre, Dan Marino	20.00
M2	Brett Favre, Peyton Manning	20.00
M3	Brett Favre, Ryan Leaf	15.00
M4	Dan Marino, Peyton Manning	20.00
M5	Dan Marino, Ryan Leaf	15.00
M6	Peyton Manning, Ryan Leaf	12.00
M7	Barry Sanders, Emmitt Smith	20.00
M8	Barry Sanders, Curtis Enis	15.00
M9	Barry Sanders, Fred Taylor	15.00
M10	Emmitt Smith, Curtis Enis	15.00
M11	Emmitt Smith, Fred Taylor	15.00
M12	Curtis Enis, Fred Taylor	10.00
M13	John Elway, Jerry Rice	20.00
M14	John Elway, Randy Moss	20.00
M15	John Elway, Charles Woodson	15.00
M16	Jerry Rice, Randy Moss	25.00
M17	Jerry Rice, Charles Woodson	15.00
M18	Randy Moss, Charles Woodson	20.00
M19	Terrell Davis, Kordell Stewart	15.00
M20	Terrell Davis, Ricky Watters	15.00
M21	Terrell Davis, Kevin Dyson	10.00
M22	Kordell Stewart, Ricky Watters	8.00
M23	Kordell Stewart, Kevin Dyson	8.00
M24	Ricky Watters, Kevin Dyson	3.00
M25	Warrick Dunn, Eddie George	8.00
M26	Warrick Dunn, Curtis Martin	8.00
M27	Warrick Dunn, Robert Edwards	8.00
M28	Eddie George, Curtis Martin	12.00
M29	Eddie George, Robert Edwards	8.00
M30	Curtis Martin, Robert Edwards	8.00
M31	Peyton Manning, Peyton Manning	15.00
M32	Ryan Leaf, Ryan Leaf	3.00
M33	Curtis Enis, Curtis Enis	3.00
M34	Fred Taylor, Fred Taylor	5.00
M35	Randy Moss, Randy Moss	20.00
M36	Charles Woodson, Charles Woodson	6.00
M37	Ricky Watters, Ricky Watters	3.00
M38	Kevin Dyson, Kevin Dyson	4.00
M39	Curtis Martin, Curtis Martin	6.00
M40	Robert Edwards, Robert Edwards	4.00

1998 Finest Mystery Finest Jumbos 2

These singles measured 3-1/2" x 5", were inserted as box toppers and found 1:4 boxes. Refractor versions for each single were also produced and found 1:17 boxes.

		NM/M
Complete Set (3):		50.00
Common Player:		15.00
Inserted 1:4 Boxes		
Refractors:		2X
Inserted 1:17 Boxes		
M3	Brett Favre, Ryan Leaf	15.00
M8	Barry Sanders, Curtis Enis	15.00
M16	Jerry Rice, Randy Moss	30.00

1998 Finest Stadium Stars

Only 20 of the top players in the game were included in this 1:45 pack insert. Each single has the letter "S" prefixed to the card number.

		NM/M
Complete Set (20):		75.00
Common Player:		2.00
Inserted 1:45		
S1	Barry Sanders	20.00
S2	Steve Young	10.00
S3	Emmitt Smith	20.00
S4	Mark Brunell	6.00
S5	Curtis Martin	2.00
S6	Kordell Stewart	3.00
S7	Jerry Rice	10.00
S8	Warrick Dunn	4.00
S9	Peyton Manning	15.00
S10	Brett Favre	20.00
S11	Terrell Davis	12.00
S12	Cris Carter	2.00
S13	Herman Moore	2.00
S14	Troy Aikman	12.00
S15	Tim Brown	5.00
S16	Dan Marino	20.00
S17	Drew Bledsoe	10.00
S18	Jerome Bettis	2.00
S19	Ryan Leaf	2.00
S20	John Elway	15.00

1998 Finest Stadium Stars Jumbos

These cards were inserted as box toppers at 1:12 boxes. Each single measures 3-1/2" x 5".

		NM/M
Complete Set (6):		50.00
Common Player:		2.00
Inserted 1:12 Boxes		
9	Peyton Manning	20.00
10	Brett Favre	20.00
11	Terrell Davis	15.00
18	Jerome Bettis	2.00
19	Ryan Leaf	2.00
20	John Elway	12.00

Values quoted in this guide reflect the retail price of a card—the price a collector can expect to pay when buying a card from a dealer. The wholesale price—that which a collector can expect to receive from a dealer when selling cards—will be significantly lower, depending on desirability and condition.

1998 Finest Undergrads

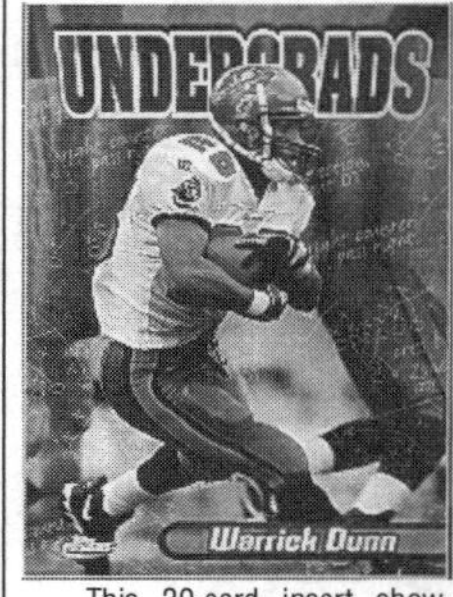

This 20-card insert showcased top rookies and second-year players. Undergrads were numbered with a "U" prefix and inserted one per 72 packs, with Refractor versions one per 216 packs.

		NM/M
Complete Set (20):		75.00
Common Player:		3.00
Inserted 1:72		
Refractors:		1.5X
Inserted 1:216		
U1	Warrick Dunn	6.00
U2	Tony Gonzalez	3.00
U3	Antowain Smith	6.00
U4	Jake Plummer	10.00
U5	Peter Boulware	3.00
U6	Derrick Rodgers	3.00
U7	Freddie Jones	3.00
U8	Reidel Anthony	4.00
U9	Bryant Westbrook	3.00
U10	Corey Dillon	15.00
U11	Curtis Enis	3.00
U12	Andre Wadsworth	3.00
U13	Fred Taylor	15.00
U14	Greg Ellis	3.00
U15	Ryan Leaf	3.00
U16	Robert Edwards	8.00
U17	Germane Crowell	4.00
U18	Brian Griese	12.00
U19	Kevin Dyson	10.00
U20	Peyton Manning	25.00

1999 Finest

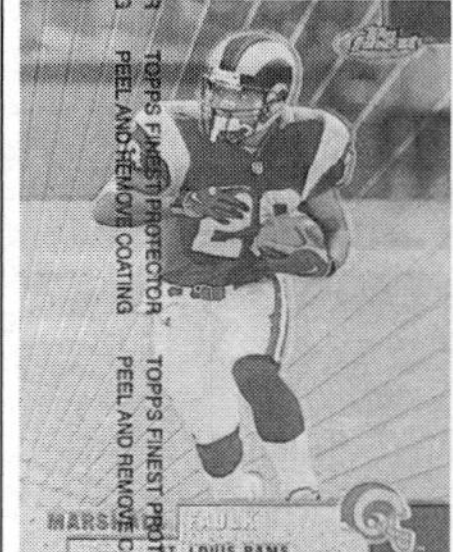

This was a 175-card set that included 51 bonus base cards found 1:1. The bonus cards were divided into three subsets: Rookies, Gems and Sensations. Each base card was printed on 27-point stock. Two parallel sets were issued with Refractors and Gold Refractors. Other inserts included: Double Team, Future's Finest, Leading Indicators, Main Attractions, Prominent Figures, Salute and Team Finest. SRP was $5.00 for six-card packs.

		NM/M
Complete Set (175):		75.00
Common Player:		.25
Minor Stars:		.50
Common Rookie:		2.00
Inserted 1:1		
Pack (6):		3.00
Wax Box (24):		50.00
1	Peyton Manning	3.00
2	Priest Holmes	.75
3	Kordell Stewart	1.00
4	Shannon Sharpe	.50
5	Andre Rison	.50
6	Rickey Dudley	.25
7	Duce Staley	.50
8	Randall Cunningham	.75
9	Warrick Dunn	1.00
10	Dan Marino	3.00
11	Kevin Greene	.25
12	Garrison Hearst	.50
13	Eric Moulds	.75
14	Marvin Harrison	1.00
15	Eddie George	1.00
16	Vinny Testaverde	.50
17	Darrell Green	.25
18	Derrick Thomas	.25
19	Chris Chandler	.50
20	Troy Aikman	2.00
21	Terance Mathis	.25
22	Terrell Owens	.75

23 Junior Seau .50
24 Cris Carter .75
25 Fred Taylor 2.00
26 Adrian Murrell .25
27 Terry Glenn .75
28 Rod Smith .50
29 Darnay Scott .50
30 Brett Favre 4.00
31 Cameron Cleeland .50
32 Ricky Watters .50
33 Derrick Alexander .25
34 Bruce Smith .25
35 Steve McNair 1.00
36 Wayne Chrebet .75
37 Herman Moore .75
38 Bert Emanuel .25
39 Michael Irvin .50
40 Steve Young 1.50
41 Napoleon Kaufman .75
42 Tim Biakabutuka .25
43 Isaac Bruce .75
44 J.J. Stokes .50
45 Antonio Freeman .75
46 John Randle .25
47 Frank Sanders .50
48 O.J. McDuffie .25
49 Keenan McCardell .25
50 Randy Moss 4.00
51 Ed McCaffrey .75
52 Yancey Thigpen .50
53 Curtis Conway .50
54 Mike Alstott .50
55 Deion Sanders 1.00
56 Dorsey Levens .75
57 Joey Galloway .75
58 Natrone Means .50
59 Tim Brown .50
60 Jerry Rice 2.00
61 Robert Smith .75
62 Carl Pickens .50
63 Ben Coates .50
64 Jerome Bettis .75
65 Corey Dillon .75
66 Curtis Martin .75
67 Jimmy Smith .50
68 Keyshawn Johnson .75
69 Charlie Batch 1.25
70 Jamal Anderson .75
71 Mark Brunell 1.50
72 Antowain Smith .75
73 Aeneas Williams .25
74 Wesley Walls .25
75 Jake Plummer 2.00
76 Oronde Gadsden .50
77 Gary Brown .25
78 Peter Boulware .25
79 Stephen Alexander .25
80 Barry Sanders 4.00
81 Warren Sapp .25
82 Michael Sinclair .25
83 Freddie Jones .25
84 Ike Hilliard .25
85 Jake Reed .25
86 Tim Dwight .75
87 Johnnie Morton .25
88 Robert Brooks .25
89 Frank Wycheck .25
90 Emmitt Smith 3.00
91 Ricky Proehl .25
92 James Jett .25
93 Karim Abdul .50
94 Mark Chmura .50
95 Andre Reed .50
96 Michael Westbrook .50
97 Michael Strahan .25
98 Chad Brown .25
99 Trent Dilfer .50
100 Terrell Davis 2.00
101 Aaron Glenn .25
102 Skip Hicks .50
103 Tony Gonzalez .50
104 Ty Law .25
105 Jermaine Lewis .50
106 Ray Lewis .25
107 Zach Thomas .50
108 Reidel Anthony .25
109 Levon Kirkland .25
110 Drew Bledsoe 2.00
111 Bobby Engram .25
112 Jerome Pathon .25
113 Muhsin Muhammed .50
114 Vonnie Holliday .50
115 Bill Romanowski .25
116 Marshall Faulk 1.00
117 Jessie Armstead .25
118 Mo Lewis .25
119 Charles Woodson 1.00
120 Doug Flutie .75
121 Jon Kitna 1.00
122 Courtney Hawkins .25
123 Stephen Boyd .25
124 John Elway 3.00
125 Barry Sanders Gems 4.00
126 Brett Favre Gems 4.00
127 Curtis Martin Gems .75
128 Dan Marino Gems 3.00
129 Eddie George Gems 1.00
130 Emmitt Smith Gems 3.00
131 Jamal Anderson Gems .75
132 Jerry Rice Gems 2.00
133 John Elway Gems 3.00
134 Terrell Davis Gems 3.00
135 Troy Aikman Gems 2.00
136 Skip Hicks Sensations .75
137 Charles Woodson Sensations .75
138 Charlie Batch Sensations 1.25
139 Curtis Enis Sensations .75
140 Fred Taylor Sensations 2.00
141 Jake Plummer Sensations 2.00
142 Peyton Manning Sensations 3.00
143 Randy Moss Sensations 4.00
144 Corey Dillon Sensations 1.00
145 Priest Holmes Sensations .75
146 Warrick Dunn Sensations .75
147 *Jevon Kearse* 3.00
148 *Chris Claiborne* 2.00
149 *Akili Smith* 2.00
150 *Brock Huard* 2.00
151 *Daunte Culpepper* 10.00
152 *Edgerrin James* 12.00
153 *Cecil Collins* 2.00
154 *Kevin Faulk* 3.00
155 *Amos Zereoue* 3.00
156 *James Johnson* 3.00
157 *Sedrick Irvin* 3.00
158 *Ricky Williams* 5.00
159 *Michael Cloud* 2.00
160 *Chris McAlister* 2.00
161 *Rob Konrad* 3.00
162 *Champ Bailey* 3.00
163 *Ebenezer Ekuban* 2.00
164 *Tim Couch* 5.00
165 *Cade McNown* 2.00
166 *Donovan McNabb* 10.00
167 *Joe Germaine* 2.00
168 *Shaun King* 3.00
169 *Peerless Price* 4.00
170 *Kevin Johnson* 2.00
171 *Troy Edwards* 3.00
172 *Karsten Bailey* 2.00
173 *David Boston* 5.00
174 *D'Wayne Bates* 2.00
175 *Torry Holt* 5.00

1999 Finest Refractors

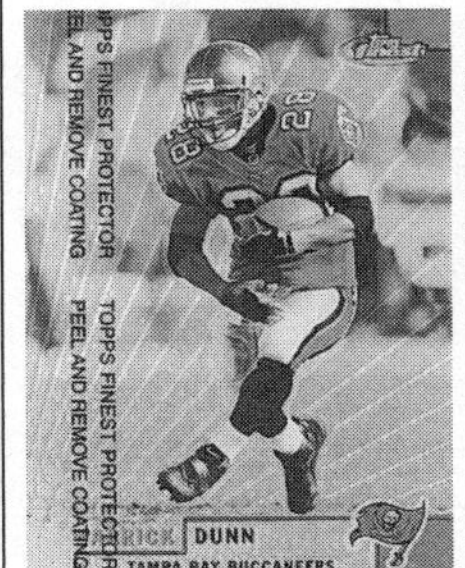

This was a 175-card set that paralleled the base set. Each of these singles used the Refractor technology on the fronts of the cards. Singles were found 1:12 packs.

Refractor Cards: 3X-8X
Refractor Gems/Sensations: 3X-6X
Refractor Rookies: 2X-4X
Inserted 1:12

1999 Finest Gold Refractors

This was a 175-card parallel to the base set. Each single was die cut and printed with a gold background. They were found 1:72 packs and were sequentially numbered to 100.

	NM/M
Refractor Cards:	8X-20X
Refractor Gems/Sensations:	5X-10X
Refractor Rookies:	5X-10X
Inserted 1:72	
Production 100 Sets	

1999 Finest Double Team

This seven-card insert set included a pair of teammates on the same card and pictured each on the fronts of the cards. Singles were inserted 1:50 packs. Partial Refractor versions were also issued with half the card a Refractor and the other half normal. They were also found 1:50 packs. A complete Refractor version was issued and found 1:150 packs.

	NM/M
Complete Set (7):	15.00
Common Player:	2.00
Inserted 1:50	
Dual Refractors:	2X
Inserted 1:150	
1 Akili Smith, Carl Pickens	3.00
2 Cade McNown, Curtis Enis	3.00
3 Doug Flutie, Eric Moulds	5.00
4 Mark Brunell, Fred Taylor	5.00
5 Kordell Stewart, Jerome Bettis	2.00
6 Jon Kitna, Joey Galloway	2.00
7 Warrick Dunn, Mike Alstott	2.00

1999 Finest Future's Finest

This 10-card insert set included the top rookies from 1999. Singles were inserted 1:253 packs and sequentially numbered to 500. A parallel Refractor version was also released. Each of those singles was sequentially numbered to 100 and found 1:1,262 packs.

	NM/M
Complete Set (10):	75.00
Common Player:	5.00
Inserted 1:253	
Production 500 Sets	
Refractors:	3X
Inserted 1:1,264	
Production 100 Sets	
1 Akili Smith	5.00
2 Cade McNown	5.00
3 Champ Bailey	5.00
4 Daunte Culpepper	20.00
5 David Boston	15.00
6 Donovan McNabb	20.00
7 Edgerrin James	20.00
8 Ricky Williams	25.00
9 Tim Couch	15.00
10 Torry Holt	15.00

1999 Finest Leading Indicators

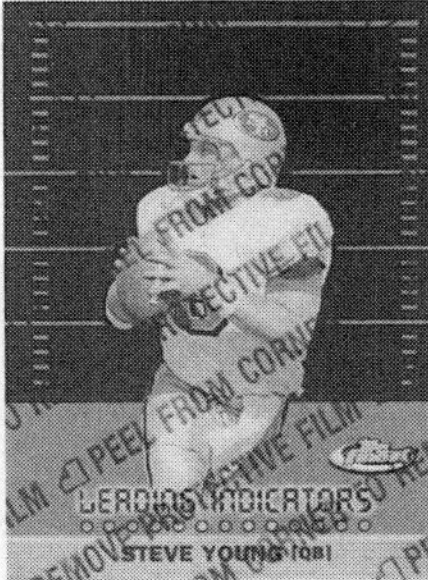

Each of the singles in this 10-card set utilized an innovative, heat-sensitive, thermal ink technology with each star in this insert set. Collectors touched points of the field behind each player image and the player's statistics appeared. Singles were inserted 1:30 packs.

	NM/M
Complete Set (10):	30.00
Common Player:	1.00
Minor Stars:	4.00
Inserted 1:30	
1 Jamal Anderson	2.00
2 Doug Flutie	2.00
3 Drew Bledsoe	4.00
4 Eddie George	2.00
5 Emmitt Smith	5.00
6 John Elway	5.00
7 Keyshawn Johnson	2.00
8 Steve Young	4.00
9 Terrell Owens	2.00
10 Vinny Testaverde	1.00

1999 Finest Main Attractions

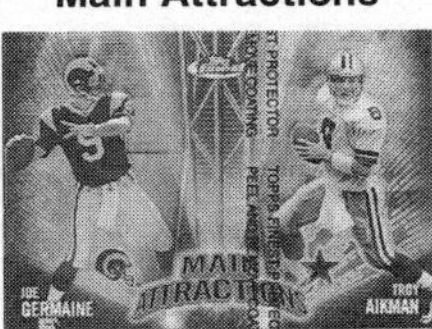

This seven-card insert set included 14 different players with two per card. Singles were found 1:50 packs. A parallel version with half the card a Refractor and the other a non-Refractor was issued at 1:50 packs. The Refractor version with the whole card as a Refractor was issued 1:150 packs.

	NM/M
Complete Set (7):	25.00
Common Player:	2.00
Inserted 1:50	
Dual Refractors:	2X
Inserted 1:150	
1 Champ Bailey, Deion Sanders	2.00
2 Daunte Culpepper, Steve McNair	5.00
3 Donovan McNabb, Kordell Stewart	5.00
4 Edgerrin James, Marshall Faulk	8.00
5 Kevin Faulk, Warrick Dunn	2.00
6 Joe Germaine, Troy Aikman	4.00
7 Rob Konrad, Mike Alstott	2.00

1999 Finest Prominent Figures

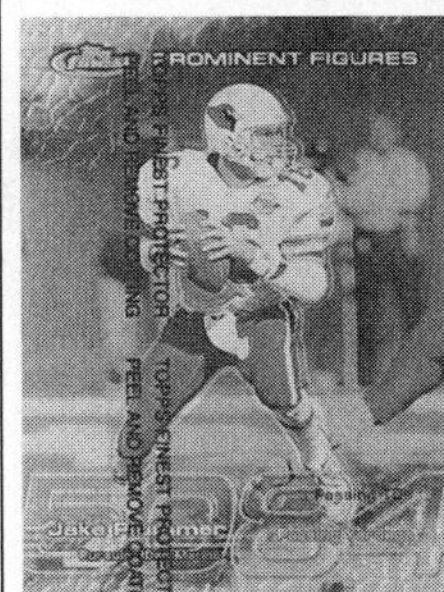

This 60-card insert set included players who were chasing records and the set was divided into six statistical categories. Each of these singles was sequentially numbered to the all-time single season record. Passing Yards were numbered to 5,084 and inserted 1:25 packs. Touchdown Passes were numbered to 48 and inserted 1:2,634. Rushing Yards were numbered to 2,105 and found 1:60 packs. Rushing Touchdowns were numbered to 25 and inserted 1:5,099. Receiving Yards were numbered to 1,848 and found 1:68 packs. Touchdown Receptions were numbered to 22 and found 1:5,779.

	NM/M
Common QB (1-10):	1.00
Inserted 1:25	
Production 5,084 Sets	
Common QB (11-20):	25.00
Inserted 1:2,634	
Production 48 Sets	
Common RB (21-30):	50.00
Inserted 1:5,099	
Production 25 Sets	
Common RB (31-40):	5.00
Inserted 1:60	
Production 2,105 Sets	
Common WR (41-50):	50.00
Inserted 1:5,779	
Production 22 Sets	
Common WR (51-60):	3.00
Inserted 1:68	
Production 1,848 Sets	
1 Brett Favre	10.00
2 Dan Marino	7.00
3 Drew Bledsoe	4.00
4 Jake Plummer	5.00
5 Mark Brunell	4.00
6 Peyton Manning	7.00
7 Randall Cunningham	2.00
8 Steve Young	3.00
9 Tim Couch	15.00
10 Vinny Testaverde	1.00
11 Brett Favre	120.00
12 Dan Marino	120.00
13 Drew Bledsoe	50.00
14 Jake Plummer	75.00
15 Mark Brunell	50.00
16 Peyton Manning	120.00
17 Randall Cunningham	35.00
18 Steve Young	50.00
19 Tim Couch	75.00
20 Vinny Testaverde	25.00
21 Barry Sanders	120.00
22 Curtis Martin	50.00
23 Eddie George	75.00
24 Emmitt Smith	120.00
25 Fred Taylor	75.00
26 Garrison Hearst	50.00
27 Jamal Anderson	50.00
28 Marshall Faulk	50.00
29 Ricky Williams	150.00
30 Terrell Davis	75.00
31 Barry Sanders	20.00
32 Curtis Martin	5.00
33 Eddie George	6.00
34 Emmitt Smith	15.00
35 Fred Taylor	10.00
36 Garrison Hearst	5.00
37 Jamal Anderson	5.00
38 Marshall Faulk	5.00
39 Ricky Williams	30.00
40 Terrell Davis	15.00
41 Antonio Freeman	50.00
42 David Boston	75.00
43 Cris Carter	50.00
44 Jerry Rice	100.00
45 Joey Galloway	50.00
46 Keyshawn Johnson	50.00
47 Randy Moss	125.00
48 Terrell Owens	50.00
49 Tim Brown	50.00
50 Torry Holt	50.00
51 Antonio Freeman	4.00
52 David Boston	8.00
53 Eric Moulds	4.00
54 Jerry Rice	10.00
55 Joey Galloway	4.00
56 Keyshawn Johnson	4.00
57 Randy Moss	20.00
58 Terrell Owens	4.00
59 Jimmy Smith	3.00
60 Torry Holt	8.00

1999 Finest Salute

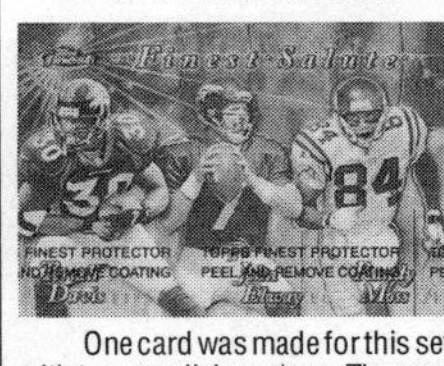

One card was made for this set with two parallel versions. The card included the three 1998 season award winners with the NFL Rookie of the Year Randy Moss, NFL MVP Terrell Davis and Super Bowl XXXII MVP John Elway. The single was found 1:53 packs. A parallel Refractor was made and inserted 1:1,900 packs. Also, a parallel Gold Refractor was found 1:12,384 packs and was sequentially numbered to 100.

	NM/M
Complete Set (3):	275.00
Inserted 1:53	
Refractor Inserted 1:1,900	
Gold Ref. Inserted 1:12,384	
Production 100 Sets	
Terrell Davis, John Elway, Randy Moss	10.00
Terrell Davis, John Elway, Randy Moss GR	250.00
Terrell Davis, John Elway, Randy Moss REF	75.00

1999 Finest Team Finest

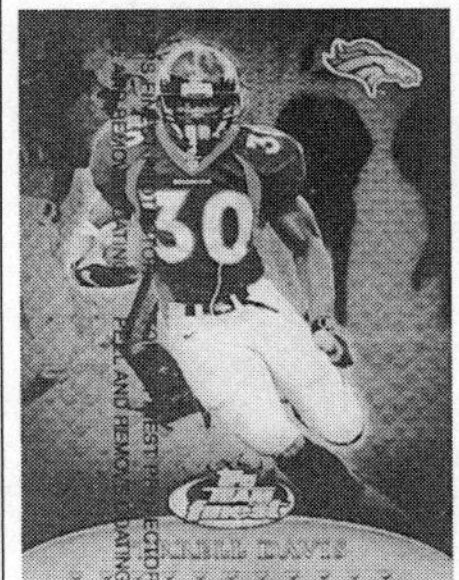

This was a 10-card set that included top NFL stars and pictured them on a prismatic card. The base set was in Blue, inserted 1:84 packs and numbered to 1,500. A Gold parallel was made and inserted 1:57 packs and numbered to 250. A Red version was issued at 1:29 packs and numbered to 500. Each had a parallel Refractor version. The Blue singles were found 1:843 packs and numbered to 150. The Red singles were inserted 1:285 packs and numbered to 50. While the Gold singles were issued 1:573 packs and numbered to 25.

	NM/M
Complete Set (10):	100.00
Common Player:	5.00
Inserted 1:84	
Production 1,500 Sets	
Blue Refractors:	4X
Inserted 1:843	
Production 150 Sets	
Gold Cards:	3X
Inserted 1:57	
Production 250 Sets	
Gold Refractors:	8X-16X
Inserted 1:573	
Production 25 Sets	
Red Cards:	2X
Inserted 1:29	
Production 500 Sets	
Red Refractors:	4X-8X
Inserted 1:285	
Production 50 Sets	
1 Barry Sanders	15.00
2 Brett Favre	15.00
3 Dan Marino	12.00
4 Drew Bledsoe	7.00
5 Jamal Anderson	5.00
6 John Elway	12.00
7 Peyton Manning	12.00
8 Randy Moss	15.00
9 Terrell Davis	12.00
10 Troy Aikman	8.00

2000 Finest

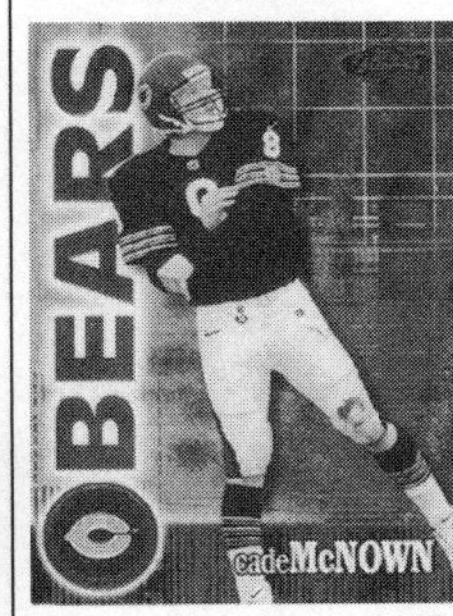

	NM/M
Complete Set (205):	450.00
Common Player:	.15
Minor Stars:	.30
Common Rookie:	6.00
Production 2,400 Sets	
Inserted 1:11	
Common Inherent Fire:	2.00
Inserted 1:8	
Common Gems:	2.00
Inserted 1:24	
Pack (5):	3.25
Wax Box (24):	65.00
1 Tim Dwight	.50
2 Cade McNown	.50
3 Drew Bledsoe	1.00
4 Torry Holt	.50
5 Derrick Mayes	.30
6 Vinny Testaverde	.50
7 Patrick Jeffers	.50
8 Dorsey Levens	.50
9 James Johnson	.30
10 Champ Bailey	.30
11 Jeff George	.50
12 Shawn Jefferson	.15
13 Terrence Wilkins	.50
14 J.J. Stokes	.15
15 Doug Flutie	.75
16 Corey Dillon	.50
17 Rod Smith	.30
18 Jimmy Smith	.50
19 Amani Toomer	.15
20 Curtis Conway	.15
21 Brad Johnson	.50
22 Edgerrin James	2.50
23 Derrick Alexander	.15
24 Terrell Owens	.50
25 Kurt Warner	2.00
26 Frank Sanders	.30
27 Tony Banks	.30
28 Troy Aikman	1.25
29 Curtis Enis	.30
30 Eddie George	.75
31 Bill Schroeder	.15
32 Kent Graham	.15
33 Mike Alstott	.50
34 Steve Young	1.00
35 Jacquez Green	.30
36 Frank Wycheck	.15
37 Kerry Collins	.30
38 Stephen Davis	.50
39 Tony Gonzalez	.30
40 Tyrone Wheatley	.30
41 Brett Favre	2.50
42 Joey Galloway	.50
43 Terrell Davis	1.00
44 Marvin Harrison	.50
45 Zach Thomas	.30
46 Jerry Rice	1.25
47 Keyshawn Johnson	.50
48 Rob Johnson	.30
49 Raghib Ismail	.15
50 Elvis Grbac	.30
51 Warrick Dunn	.50
52 Jevon Kearse	.60
53 Albert Connell	.30
54 Muhsin Muhammad	.30
55 Carl Pickens	.30
56 Peyton Manning	2.00
57 Daunte Culpepper	1.25
58 Ike Hilliard	.15
59 Steve McNair	.50
60 Sean Dawkins	.15
61 Steve Beuerlein	.30
62 Priest Holmes	.50
63 Jim Harbaugh	.30
64 Germane Crowell	.50
65 Cris Carter	.50
66 Jamal Anderson	.50
67 Kevin Johnson	.50
68 Herman Moore	.30
69 Ricky Williams	1.00
70 Rich Gannon	.30
71 Isaac Bruce	.50
72 Peerless Price	.50
73 Az-Zahir Hakim	.30
74 Mark Brunell	1.00
75 Rob Moore	.30
76 Antowain Smith	.30
77 Tim Biakabutuka	.30
78 Ed McCaffrey	.30
79 Tony Martin	.15

80 Marcus Robinson .50
81 Kevin Dyson .30
82 Wesley Walls .30
83 Chris Chandler .30
84 Keenan McCardell .30
85 Napoleon Kaufman .30
86 Emmitt Smith 1.75
87 James Stewart .30
88 Tim Brown .30
89 Ricky Watters .30
90 Johnnie Morton .15
91 Jake Plummer .50
92 Olandis Gary .60
93 Jerome Bettis .50
94 Terry Glenn .50
95 Kordell Stewart .50
96 Charlie Garner .30
97 Yancey Thigpen .15
98 Michael Westbrook .30
99 Bobby Engram .15
100 Eric Moulds .50
101 Darnay Scott .30
102 Antonio Freeman .50
103 Wayne Chrebet .30
104 Akili Smith .50
105 Jeff Blake .30
106 Curtis Martin .50
107 Errict Rhett .30
108 Damon Huard .50
109 Jeff Graham .15
110 Terance Mathis .15
111 Jon Kitna .50
112 Tim Couch 1.50
113 Fred Taylor 1.00
114 Qadry Ismail .15
115 Donovan McNabb 1.00
116 Charles Johnson .15
117 Troy Edwards .50
118 Shaun King .40
119 Charlie Batch .50
120 Robert Smith .50
121 Marshall Faulk .50
122 Brian Griese .75
123 O.J. McDuffie .30
124 Randy Moss 2.00
125 Duce Staley .50
126 *Peter Warrick* 12.00
127 *Dez White* 3.00
128 *Ron Dayne* 3.00
129 *J.R. Redmond* 6.00
130 *Thomas Jones* 10.00
131 *Plaxico Burress* 15.00
132 *Reuben Droughns* 12.00
133 *Shaun Alexander* 20.00
134 *Ron Dugans* 2.00
135 *Travis Prentice* 6.00
136 *Joe Hamilton* 4.00
137 *Curtis Keaton* 2.00
138 *Chris Redman* 6.00
139 *Chad Pennington* 30.00
140 *Travis Taylor* 10.00
141 *Bubba Franks* 10.00
142 *Dennis Northcutt* 3.00
143 *Jerry Porter* 12.00
144 *Sylvester Morris* 6.00
145 *Anthony Becht* 3.00
146 *Trung Canidate* 5.00
147 *Jamal Lewis* 20.00
148 *R. Jay Soward* 3.00
149 *Tee Martin* 4.00
150 *Courtney Brown* 4.00
151 *Brian Urlacher* 20.00
152 *Danny Farmer* 6.00
153 *Laveranues Coles* 12.00
154 *Todd Pinkston* 10.00
155 *Corey Simon* 4.00
156 *Spergon Wynn* 3.00
157 *Tim Rattay* 10.00
158 *Todd Husak* 3.00
159 *Aaron Shea* 3.00
160 *Giovanni Carmazzi* 3.00
161 *Trevor Gaylor* 3.00
162 *JuJuan Dawson* 3.00
163 *Jarious Jackson* 3.00
164 *Chris Samuels* 3.00
165 *Rob Morris* 3.00
166 Peter Warrick, Randy Moss 6.00
167 Randy Moss, Peter Warrick 6.00
168 Travis Prentice, Stephen Davis 2.00
169 Stephen Davis, Travis Prentice 2.00
170 Chris Redman, Kurt Warner 5.00
171 Kurt Warner, Chris Redman 5.00
172 Sylvester Morris, Jimmy Smith 2.00
173 Jimmy Smith, Sylvester Morris 2.00
174 Chad Pennington, Peyton Manning 5.00
175 Peyton Manning, Chad Pennington 5.00
176 R. Jay Soward, Marvin Harrison 2.00
177 Marvin Harrison, R. Jay Soward 2.00
178 Ron Dayne, Jamal Anderson 4.00
179 Jamal Anderson, Ron Dayne 4.00
180 Shaun Alexander, Eddie George 3.00
181 Eddie George, Shaun Alexander 3.00
182 Courtney Brown, Bruce Smith 2.00
183 Bruce Smith, Courtney Brown 2.00
184 Jamal Lewis, Edgerrin James 5.00
185 Edgerrin James, Jamal Lewis 5.00
186 Trung Canidate, Emmitt Smith 3.00
187 Emmitt Smith, Trung Canidate 3.00
188 Travis Taylor, Cris Carter 2.00
189 Cris Carter, Travis Taylor 2.00
190 Curtis Keaton, Marshall Faulk 2.00
191 Marshall Faulk, Curtis Keaton 2.00
192 Plaxico Burress, Jerry Rice 3.00
193 Jerry Rice, Plaxico Burress 3.00
194 Thomas Jones, Terrell Davis 3.00
195 Terrell Davis, Thomas Jones 3.00
196 Peyton Manning 5.00
197 Randy Moss 5.00
198 Terrell Davis 3.00
199 Marshall Faulk 2.00
200 Edgerrin James 6.00
201 Emmitt Smith 4.00
202 Ricky Williams 3.00
203 Kurt Warner 7.00
204 Eddie George 2.00
205 Brett Favre 6.00

2000 Finest Gold Refractors

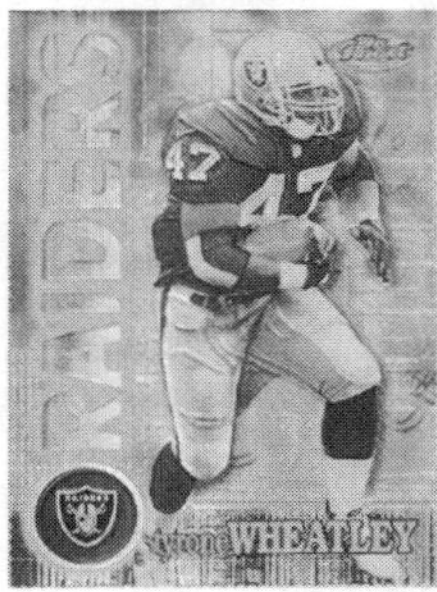

NM/M
Gold Ref. Cards: 10X-20X
Production #1-125 300 Sets
Gold Ref. Rookies: 3X
Production 200 Sets
Inserted 1:132
Gold Ref. Inherent Fire: 8X-16X
Production 100 Sets
Inserted 1:365
Gold Ref. Gems: 10X-20X
Production 50 Sets
Inserted 1:2,372

2000 Finest Moments

NM/M
Complete Set (25): 25.00
Common Player: .50
Minor Stars: 1.00
Inserted 1:8
Refractor Cards: 2X
Inserted 1:18
1 Bart Starr 2.00
2 Phil Simms 1.00
3 John Elway 6.00
4 Dan Marino 6.00
5 Kellen Winslow 1.00
6 Franco Harris 2.00
7 Stephen Davis 1.00
8 Isaac Bruce 1.00
9 Edgerrin James 5.00
10 Marshall Faulk 1.00
11 Patrick Jeffers 1.00
12 Kurt Warner 6.00
13 Joe Montana 10.00
14 Kevin Carter .50
15 Andre Reed .50
16 Torry Holt 1.00
17 Frank Wycheck, Kevin Dyson 1.00
18 Jason Elam .50
19 Mike Jones .50
20 Cade McNown 2.00
21 Germane Crowell 1.00
22 Bruce Matthews .50
23 Champ Bailey 1.00
24 Qadry Ismail .50
25 Tony Brackens .50

A card number in parenthese ( ) indicates the set is unnumbered.

2000 Finest Moments Refractor Autographs

NM/M
Common Player: 15.00
Minor Stars: 30.00
Inserted 1:48
1 Bart Starr 150.00
2 Phil Simms 30.00
3 John Elway 175.00
4 Dan Marino 175.00
5 Kellen Winslow 30.00
6 Franco Harris 50.00
7 Stephen Davis 30.00
8 Isaac Bruce 30.00
9 Edgerrin James 100.00
10 Marshall Faulk 30.00
11 Patrick Jeffers 30.00
12 Kurt Warner 100.00
13 Joe Montana 300.00
14 Kevin Carter 15.00
15 Andre Reed 15.00
16 Torry Holt 30.00
17 Frank Wycheck, Kevin Dyson 30.00
18 Jason Elam 15.00
19 Mike Jones 15.00
20 Cade McNown 15.00
21 Germane Crowell 30.00
22 Bruce Matthews 15.00
23 Champ Bailey 30.00
24 Qadry Ismail 15.00
25 Tony Brackens 15.00

2000 Finest Moments Jumbos

NM/M
Complete Set (7): 30.00
Common Player: 2.00
Inserted 1:Box
1 Bart Starr 6.00
2 Phil Simms 2.00
3 John Elway 8.00
4 Dan Marino 8.00
5 Edgerrin James 6.00
6 Marshall Faulk 2.00
7 Joe Montana 10.00

2000 Finest NFL Europe's Finest

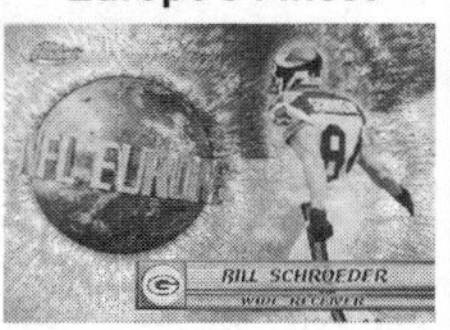

NM/M
Complete Set (10): 12.00
Common Player: 1.00
Inserted 1:24
1 Kurt Warner 7.00
2 Bill Schroeder 1.50
3 Andy McCullough 1.00
4 Dameyune Craig 1.00
5 Marcus Robinson 2.00
6 La'Roi Glover 1.00
7 Damon Huard 2.00
8 Brad Johnson 2.00
9 Jake Delhomme 1.50
10 Jon Kitna 1.50

2000 Finest Out of the Blue

NM/M
Complete Set (15): 25.00
Common Player: .75
Minor Stars: 1.50
Inserted 1:24
1 Kurt Warner 7.00
2 Patrick Jeffers 1.50
3 Stephen Davis 1.50
4 Amani Toomer .75
5 Marcus Robinson 1.50
6 Tyrone Wheatley .75
7 Kevin Johnson 1.50
8 Tony Gonzalez .75
9 Olandis Gary 1.50
10 Brad Johnson 1.50
11 Germane Crowell 1.50
12 Ricky Williams 3.50
13 Edgerrin James 6.00
14 Tim Couch 3.50
15 Steve Beuerlein .75

2000 Finest Pro Bowl Jerseys

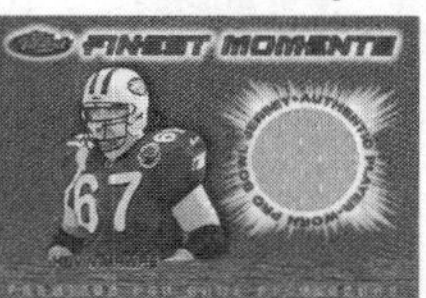

NM/M
Common Player: 10.00
Minor Stars: 20.00
Inserted 1:77
MB Mitch Berger 10.00
SB Steve Beuerlein 10.00
SB Stephen Boyd 10.00
TB Tony Brackens 10.00
KC Kevin Carter 10.00
DC Dexter Coakley 10.00
SD Stephen Davis 20.00
BD Brian Dawkins 10.00
CD Corey Dillon 25.00
LE Luther Elliss 10.00
RG Rich Gannon 40.00
TG Tony Gonzalez 20.00
KH Kevin Hardy 10.00
MH Marvin Harrison 40.00
EJ Edgerrin James 45.00
BJ Brad Johnson 10.00
TJ Tre' Johnson 10.00
JK Jevon Kearse 15.00
TL Todd Lyght 10.00
TM Tremain Mack 10.00
SM Sam Madison 10.00
OM Olindo Mare 10.00
KM Kevin Mawae 10.00
MM Muhsin Muhammad 20.00
OP Orlando Pace 10.00
TP Trevor Pryce 10.00
LS Lance Schulters 10.00
LS Leon Searcy 10.00
DS David Sloan 10.00
DS Detron Smith 10.00
ZT Zach Thomas 10.00
TT Tom Tupa 10.00
KW Kurt Warner 50.00

2000 Finest Superstars

NM/M
Complete Set (15): 25.00
Common Player: 1.00
Inserted 1:16
1 Dan Marino 4.00
2 Eddie George 1.50
3 Marshall Faulk 1.00
4 Stephen Davis 1.00
5 Jerry Rice 2.50
6 Emmitt Smith 3.00
7 Terrell Davis 3.00
8 Jimmy Smith 1.00
9 Cris Carter 1.00
10 Troy Aikman 2.50
11 Curtis Martin 1.00
12 Brett Favre 5.00
13 Kurt Warner 4.00
14 Marvin Harrison 1.00
15 Steve Young 1.75

2000 Finest Super Bowl XXXIV

Complete Set (12):
1 Brett Favre
2 Marvin Harrison
3 Marshall Faulk
4 Randy Moss
5 Kurt Warner
6 Stephen Davis
7 Peyton Manning
8 Edgerrin James
9 Drew Bledsoe
10 Emmitt Smith
11 Terrell Davis
12 Brad Johnson

2001 Finest

NM/M
Complete Set (140): 300.00
Common Player: .25
Minor Stars: .50
Common Rookie: 5.00
Production 1,000 Sets
Inserted 1:4
Wax Box (10): 130.00
1 Eddie George 1.25
2 Jay Fiedler 1.00
3 Peter Warrick .50
4 Vinny Testaverde .50
5 Charles Johnson .25
6 Ahman Green .75
7 Isaac Bruce 1.00
8 Junior Seau .50
9 Daunte Culpepper 2.00
10 Ike Hilliard .50
11 Tony Banks .50
12 Steve Beuerlein .50
13 Jamal Anderson 1.00
14 Tyrone Wheatley .50
15 Sylvester Morris .75
16 Edgerrin James 2.50
17 Shaun King 1.00
18 Terrell Owens 1.00
19 Donovan McNabb 1.50
20 Cade McNown 1.00
21 Elvis Grbac .75
22 James Stewart .75
23 Joe Horn .75
24 Randy Moss 3.00
25 Matt Hasselbeck .75
26 Jerome Bettis 1.00
27 Bill Schroeder .50
28 Jake Plummer 1.00
29 Rod Smith 1.00
30 Akili Smith .50
31 Jimmy Smith .75
32 Oronde Gadsden .50
33 Kerry Collins .75
34 Warrick Dunn 1.00
35 Jeff Graham .25
36 Ray Lewis .75
37 Joey Galloway 1.00
38 Tim Brown 1.00
39 Derrick Alexander .25
40 Jerry Rice 2.50
41 Muhsin Muhammad 1.00
42 Shawn Jefferson .50
43 Curtis Martin 1.00
44 Terry Glenn .75
45 Marvin Harrison 1.00
46 Mike Anderson 2.50
47 Stephen Davis 1.00
48 Chad Lewis .75
49 Fred Taylor 1.25
50 Corey Dillon 1.00
51 Charlie Batch 1.00
52 Kevin Johnson .75
53 Brett Favre 4.00
54 Marshall Faulk 1.25
55 Kordell Stewart 1.00
56 Steve McNair 1.00
57 Jeff Blake .50
58 Eric Moulds 1.00
59 Emmitt Smith 2.50
60 David Boston 1.00
61 Cris Carter 1.00
62 Peyton Manning 3.00
63 Keyshawn Johnson 1.00
64 Doug Flutie 1.25
65 Drew Bledsoe 1.25
66 Ricky Williams 1.50
67 Keenan McCardell .50
68 Brian Urlacher 2.00
69 Jamal Lewis 1.00
70 Ed McCaffrey 1.00
71 Antonio Freeman .50
72 Darrell Jackson .75
73 Jeff George .75
74 Chris Chandler .50
75 Germane Crowell .75
76 Tim Biakabutuka .75
77 Jon Kitna .75
78 Troy Brown .50
79 Lamar Smith .50
80 Derrick Mason .75
81 Hines Ward .50
82 Mark Brunell 1.25
83 Trent Dilfer .75
84 Tim Couch 1.25
85 Donald Hayes .50
86 Amani Toomer .50
87 Tony Gonzalez .75
88 Rich Gannon .75
89 Rob Johnson .50
90 Torry Holt 1.00
91 Jeff Garcia 1.00
92 Kurt Warner 3.00
93 Aaron Brooks 1.00
94 Brian Griese 1.25
95 James Allen .75
96 Wayne Chrebet 1.00
97 Tiki Barber 1.00
98 Brad Johnson .75
99 Ricky Watters .75
100 Charlie Garner .75
101 *Andre Carter* 2.00
102 *Dan Morgan* 3.00
103 *Gerard Warren* 2.00
104 *Jesse Palmer* 4.00
105 *Josh Heupel* 5.00
106 *Justin Smith* 2.00
107 *LaMont Jordan* 5.00
108 *Leonard Davis* 2.00
109 *Marques Tuiasosopo* 10.00
110 *Marvin "Snoop" Minnis* 8.00
111 *Quincy Carter* 10.00
112 *Quincy Morgan* 12.00
113 *Richard Seymour* 3.00
114 *Rudi Johnson* 15.00
115 *Sage Rosenfels* 10.00
116 *Todd Heap* 8.00
117 *Travis Minor* 8.00
118 *Will Allen* 5.00
119 *Jamal Reynolds* 4.00
120 *Scotty Anderson* 5.00
121 *Anthony Thomas* 12.00
122 *Chad Johnson* 20.00
123 *Chris Chambers* 20.00
124 *Chris Weinke* 10.00
125 *David Terrell* 10.00
126 *Deuce McAllister* 25.00
127 *Drew Brees* 20.00
128 *Freddie Mitchell* 10.00
129 *James Jackson* 8.00
130 *Kevan Barlow* 12.00
131 *Koren Robinson* 10.00
132 *LaDainian Tomlinson* 30.00
133 *Michael Bennett* 15.00
134 *Michael Vick* 50.00
135 *Mike McMahon* 10.00
136 *Reggie Wayne* 15.00
137 *Robert Ferguson* 8.00
138 *Rod Gardner* 15.00
139 *Santana Moss* 15.00
140 *Travis Henry* 12.00

2001 Finest Refractor Autographs

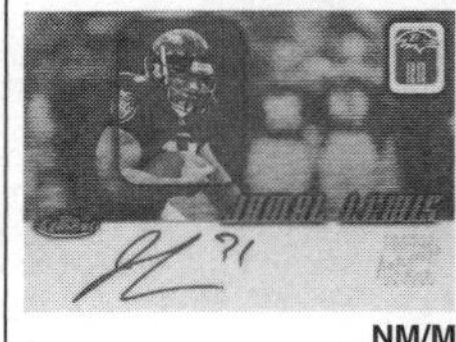

NM/M
Common Player: 8.00
Inserted 1:5
FA-DA Dan Alexander 8.00
FA-MB Michael Bennett 45.00
FA-AB Aaron Brooks 20.00
FA-DC Daunte Culpepper 45.00
FA-JG Jeff Garcia 20.00
FA-EG Eddie George 30.00
FA-DH Donald Hayes 8.00
FA-TH Travis Henry 15.00
FA-JH Joe Horn 8.00
FA-JJ James Jackson 15.00
FA-EJ Edgerrin James 60.00
FA-JL Jamal Lewis 25.00
FA-TM Travis Minor 12.00
FA-SCM Sammy Morris 8.00
FA-SM Sylvester Morris 10.00
FA-SMO Santana Moss 20.00
FA-EM Eric Moulds 12.00
FA-BN Bobby Newcombe 8.00
FA-MR Marcus Robinson 10.00
FA-BS Bill Schroeder 15.00
FA-ES Emmitt Smith 110.00
FA-JS Jimmy Smith 10.00
FA-LS Lamar Smith 12.00
FA-CW Chris Weinke 40.00

2001 Finest Jersey Relics

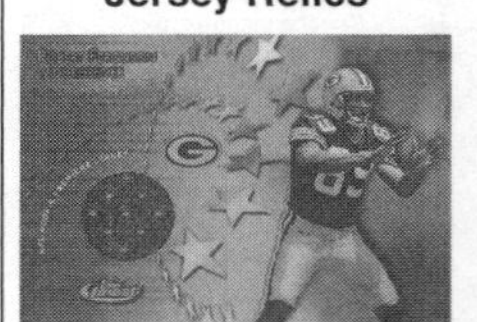

NM/M
Common Player: 10.00
Inserted 1:5
RPJ-KB Kevan Barlow 12.00
RPJ-AC Andre Carter 10.00
RPJ-LD Leonard Davis 10.00
RPJ-RF Robert Ferguson 10.00
RPJ-RG Rod Gardner 12.00
RPJ-TH Todd Heap 10.00
RPJ-CJ Chad Johnson 10.00
RPJ-RJ Rudi Johnson 12.00
RPJ-MM Mike McMahon 10.00
RPJ-MMI Marvin "Snoop" Minnis 12.00
RPJ-TM Travis Minor 10.00
RPJ-SM Santana Moss 15.00
RPJ-JP Jesse Palmer 10.00
RPJ-KR Koren Robinson 12.00
RPJ-SR Sage Rosenfels 10.00
RPJ-JS Justin Smith 10.00
RPJ-AT Anthony Thomas 20.00
RPJ-MT Marques Tuiasosopo 12.00
RPJ-RW Reggie Wayne 12.00
RPJ-CW Chris Weinke 12.00

2001 Finest Moments Relics

NM/M
Complete Set (10): 120.00
Common Player: 10.00
Inserted 1:176
FMR-DA Dan Alexander 10.00
FMR-KB Kevan Barlow 15.00
FMR-DC Daunte Culpepper 20.00
FMR-RG Rich Gannon 15.00
FMR-RGA Rod Gardner 15.00
FMR-EJ Edgerrin James 30.00
FMR-CJ Chad Johnson 10.00
FMR-LJ LaMont Jordan 12.00
FMR-LT LaDainian Tomlinson 50.00
FMR-RW Reggie Wayne 15.00

2001 Finest Moments Refractor Autographs

NM/M
Common Player: 15.00
Inserted 1:160
FMA-DC Daunte Culpepper 45.00
FMA-JG Jeff Garcia 25.00
FMA-EM Eric Moulds 15.00
FMA-MV Michael Vick 200.00
FMA-CW Chris Weinke 35.00

2001 Finest Stadium Throwback Relics

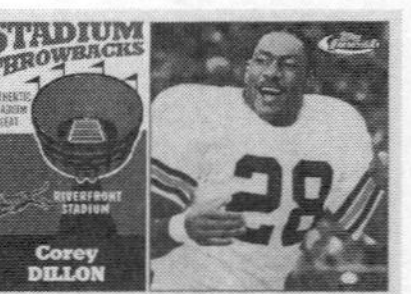

NM/M
Complete Set (20): 185.00
Common Player: 10.00
Inserted 1:10
FS DB Drew Brees 25.00
FS CC Cris Carter 12.00
FS TC Tim Couch 15.00
FS DC Daunte Culpepper 15.00
FS CD Corey Dillon 12.00
FS MF Marshall Faulk 15.00
FS BF Brett Favre 25.00
FS RG Rod Gardner 10.00
FS TG Tony Gonzalez 10.00
FS MH Marvin Harrison 12.00
FS EJ Edgerrin James 25.00
FS PM Peyton Manning 25.00
FS DM Donovan McNabb 15.00
FS MM Marvin "Snoop" Minnis 10.00
FS RM Randy Moss 25.00
FS KR Koren Robinson 10.00
FS LT LaDainian Tomlinson 30.00
FS KW Kurt Warner 30.00

2001 Finest Team Topps Legends

Complete Set (8):
TTR10 Chuck Foreman
TTF16 Cliff Branch
TTR15 Mike Singletary
TTR22 Barry Sanders
TTR18 Fred Biletnikoff
TTF14 Charlie Joiner
TTF4 Tommy McDonald
TTR5 John Hannah

2002 Finest

NM/M
Common Player: .40
Unlisted Stars: .75
Minor Stars: .50
Common veteran relic (63-76): 10.00
Group A 1:5 Group B 1:17
Common Rookie (77-114): 2.00
Common Rookie Autos (115-136): 15.00
Production 1200 Sets
Pack (5): 20.00
Wax Box (18) Mini(6): 275.00
1 Peyton Manning 2.50
2 Troy Brown .60
3 Curtis Martin .40
4 Kordell Stewart .40
5 Michael Pittman .40
6 Rod Gardner .50
7 Germane Crowell .40
8 Terrell Davis 1.25
9 Eric Moulds .40
10 Jake Plummer .40
11 Tony Gonzalez .40
12 Ricky Williams 1.50
13 Deuce McAllister 1.25
14 Jerry Rice 2.50
15 Torry Holt .40
16 Michael Vick 2.50
17 David Terrell .75
18 Terry Glenn .75
19 Mark Brunell .75
20 Vinny Testaverde .40
21 Jerome Bettis .60
22 Randy Moss 2.50
23 Marvin Harrison .60
24 Chris Weinke .60
25 Tiki Barber .40
26 Corey Bradford .40
27 David Boston .75
28 Emmitt Smith 2.50
29 Santana Moss .40
30 Brian Griese .40
31 Priest Holmes .75
32 Rich Gannon .75
33 Antowain Smith .40
34 Marcus Robinson .40
35 Warrick Dunn .40
36 Daunte Culpepper 1.50
37 Shaun Alexander .75
38 Kurt Warner 2.50
39 Quincy Carter 1.50
40 Ray Lewis .40
41 Aaron Brooks 1.25
42 Plaxico Burress .75
43 Jamal Lewis 1.25
44 Ahman Green .75
45 Rod Smith .50
46 Tim Couch 1.25
47 Muhsin Muhammad .50
48 Drew Bledsoe 1.50
49 Anthony Thomas 2.00
50 Tom Brady 2.50
51 Trent Green .50
52 Charlie Garner .50
53 Darrell Jackson .40
54 Mike McMahon .75
55 Donovan McNabb 1.50
56 Fred Taylor .50
57 Corey Dillon .75
58 Keyshawn Johnson .40
59 Drew Brees 2.00
60 Steve McNair .75
61 Jimmy Smith .40
62 Terrell Owens .75
63 Eddie George 15.00
64 Jeff Garcia 15.00
65 LaDainian Tomlinson 10.00
66 Cris Carter 10.00
67 Chris Chambers 10.00
68 Brian Urlacher 20.00
69 Tim Brown 15.00
70 Marshall Faulk 10.00
71 Stephen Davis 10.00
72 Jevon Kearse 15.00
73 Edgerrin James 12.00
74 Mike Anderson 15.00
75 Warren Sapp 10.00
76 Brett Favre 30.00
77 *Julius Peppers* 6.00
78 *Tim Carter* 3.00
79 *Travis Stephens* 4.00
80 *Jabar Gaffney* 5.00
81 *Cliff Russell* 3.00
82 *Donald Reche Caldwell* 4.00
83 *Maurice Morris* 5.00
84 *Antwann Randle El* 6.00
85 *Ladell Betts* 4.00
86 *Daniel Graham* 5.00
87 *Jeremy Shockey* 12.00
88 *Mike Williams* 3.00
89 *Josh McCown* 5.00
90 *Rohan Davey* 5.00
91 *David Garrard* 4.00
92 *Dwight Freeney* 5.00
93 *Leonard Henry* 3.00
94 *Albert Haynesworth* 3.00
95 *Herb Haygood* 3.00
96 *Kurt Kittner* 6.00
97 *Jason McAddley* 3.00
98 *Bryan Thomas* 3.00
99 *Wendell Bryant* 3.00
100 *Mike Rumph* 3.00
101 *Chad Hutchinson* 5.00
102 *Brian Westbrook* 6.00
103 *Deion Branch* 8.00
104 *John Henderson* 3.00
105 *Jerramy Stevens* 3.00
106 *Tracey Wistrom* 3.00
107 *Phillip Buchanon* 4.00
108 *Matt Schobel* 3.00
109 *Edward Reed* 5.00
110 *Randy Fasani* 3.00
111 *Josh Scobey* 3.00
112 *Luke Staley* 4.00
113 *Anthony Weaver* 3.00
114 *Kyle Johnson* 3.00
115 *David Carr* 100.00
116 *Joey Harrington* 80.00
117 *Donte Stallworth* 30.00
118 *Ashley Lelie* 30.00
119 *Patrick Ramsey* 30.00
120 *William Green* 30.00
121 *Josh Reed* 30.00
122 *Clinton Portis* 120.00
123 *Antonio Bryant* 30.00
124 *Javon Walker* 40.00
125 *Roy Williams* 40.00
126 *Marquise Walker* 20.00
127 *Quentin Jammer* 20.00
128 *DeShaun Foster* 30.00
129 *Andre Davis* 30.00
130 *Ron Johnson* 20.00
131 *Lamar Gordon* 20.00
132 *T.J. Duckett/300* 60.00
133 *Freddie Milons* 20.00
134 *Eric Crouch* 20.00
135 *Adrian Peterson* 20.00
136 *Damien Anderson* 15.00

2002 Finest Refractors

Stars (1-62): 3X-6X
63-76 JSY: 1X-1.5X
Rookies (77-114): 1.5X-3X
1-114 Production 250 Sets
Rookie Auto (115-136): 1X-1.5X
115-136 Production 175 Sets

2002 Finest Gold Refractors

Gold Production 25 Sets

2002 Finest Xfractors

Production 20 Sets

2002 Finest Team Topps Autographs

Group A 1:866 Group B 1:215 Group C 1:29
Cliff Branch 10.00
Jim Brown 40.00
Charlie Joiner 10.00
Joe Namath
Mike Singletary 10.00

2003 Finest

NM/M
Common Player (1-60): .50
Minor Stars: .75
Unlisted Stars: 1.00
Common Rookie (61-100): 1.50
Minor Rookies: 2.00
Unlisted Rookies: 2.50
Common Jsy (101-118): 8.00
Common Rookie AU: 10.00
Production 999 Sets
Pack (5): 6.50
Mini Box (6): 35.00
Box (3 Mini Boxes): 85.00
1 Chad Pennington 1.50
2 Tommy Maddox 1.00
3 Brett Favre 4.00
4 Eric Moulds .75
5 Randy Moss 2.00
6 Duce Staley .75
7 Derrick Mason .75
8 Shaun Alexander 1.00
9 Peyton Manning 2.00
10 Kerry Collins .75
11 Joe Horn .50
12 Laveranues Coles .75
13 Marty Booker .50
14 Emmitt Smith 3.00
15 Edgerrin James 1.50
16 Aaron Brooks 1.00
17 Curtis Martin 1.00
18 Hines Ward .75
19 Rod Smith .50
20 Priest Holmes 1.00
21 Jerry Rice 3.00
22 Peerless Price .75
23 Mark Brunell .75
24 Trent Green .75
25 David Boston 1.00
26 Chris Chambers 1.00
27 Marshall Faulk 1.50
28 Fred Taylor 1.00
29 Tim Couch 1.00
30 Amani Toomer .75
31 Travis Henry .75
32 Jeff Blake .75
33 Troy Brown .50
34 Charlie Garner .75
35 Tom Brady 2.00
36 Warrick Dunn .75
37 Plaxico Burress 1.00
38 Marvin Harrison 1.00
39 Clinton Portis 3.00
40 Deuce McAllister 1.00
41 Matt Hasselbeck .75
42 Jeff Garcia 1.00
43 David Carr 2.50
44 Ahman Green 1.00
45 Eddie George 1.00
46 Drew Brees 1.50
47 Tiki Barber 1.00
48 Jay Fiedler .75
49 Curtis Conway .75
50 Steve McNair 1.00
51 Donald Driver .75
52 Jake Plummer .75
53 Jamal Lewis 1.00
54 Corey Dillon 1.00
55 Stephen Davis .75
56 Terrell Owens 1.00
57 Torry Holt 1.00
58 Chad Johnson .75
59 Chad Hutchinson .75
60 Kurt Warner 1.50
61 *Troy Polamalu* 4.00
62 *Eugene Wilson* 2.00
63 *Juston Wood* 2.00
64 *Anquan Boldin* 5.00
65 *Doug Gabriel* 2.00
66 *Domanick Davis* 5.00
67 *J.R. Tolver* 2.00
68 *Jerome McDougle* 2.00
69 *Keenan Howry* 2.50
70 *Teyo Johnson* 3.00
71 *Bethel Johnson* 2.50
72 *Ken Hamlin* 2.00
73 *L.J. Smith* 2.50
74 *Rashean Mathis* 1.50
75 *Arnaz Battle* 2.00
76 *B.J. Askew* 2.50
77 *Mike Doss* 2.50
78 *Kevin Curtis* 2.00
79 *Terence Newman* 4.00
80 *Shaun McDonald* 1.50
81 *Kevin Williams* 2.00
82 *Nate Burleson* 2.50
83 *Tyrone Calico* 4.00
84 *Dewayne White* 1.50
85 *Marcus Trufant* 2.50
86 *Nick Barnett* 3.00
87 *Bennie Joppru* 2.50
88 *Andre Woolfolk* 2.00
89 *Billy McMullen* 2.00
90 *Boss Bailey* 3.00
91 *William Joseph* 2.00
92 *Michael Haynes* 1.50
93 *Dewayne Robertson* 2.00
94 *LaTarence Dunbar* 2.00
95 *David Tyree* 2.00
96 *Walter Young* 1.50
97 *E.J. Henderson* 2.00
98 *Ty Warren* 2.00
99 *Zuriel Smith* 2.00
100 *Brock Forsey* 3.00
101 Ricky Williams 12.00
102 Drew Bledsoe 12.00
103 Joey Harrington 15.00
104 Tim Brown 10.00
105 Brian Urlacher 15.00
106 Zach Thomas 10.00
107 Jeremy Shockey 15.00
108 Michael Strahan 10.00
109 Jason Taylor 15.00
110 Donovan McNabb 15.00
111 LaDainian Tomlinson 12.00
112 Rich Gannon 10.00
113 Brad Johnson 10.00
114 Daunte Culpepper 12.00
115 Michael Vick 20.00
116 Jimmy Smith 8.00
117 Keyshawn Johnson 10.00
118 Keith Brooking 8.00
119 *Carson Palmer AU/399* 100.00
120 *Byron Leftwich AU/399* 120.00
121 *Chris Simms AU/399* 40.00
122 *Kyle Boller AU/399* 60.00
123 *Justin Fargas AU* 20.00
124 *Seneca Wallace AU* 12.00
125 *Larry Johnson AU* 30.00
126 *Kareem Kelly AU* 10.00
127 *Willis McGahee AU/399* 60.00
128 *Kelley Washington AU* 15.00
129 *Brian St. Pierre AU* 12.00
130 *Kliff Kingsbury AU* 12.00
131 *Ken Dorsey AU* 20.00
132 *Bryant Johnson AU* 15.00
133 *Dallas Clark AU* 15.00
134 *Chris Brown AU* 40.00
135 *Taylor Jacobs AU* 12.00
136 *Artose Pinner AU* 12.00
137 *Lee Suggs AU* 40.00
138 *LaBrandon Toefield AU* 12.00
139 *Jason Witten AU* 15.00
140 *Brad Banks AU* 12.00
141 *Earnest Graham AU* 12.00
142 *Bobby Wade AU* 12.00
143 *Talman Gardner AU* 10.00
144 *Justin Gage AU* 15.00
145 *Sam Aiken AU* 10.00
146 *Musa Smith AU* 12.00
147 *Terrell Suggs AU* 15.00
148 *Brandon Lloyd AU* 12.00
149 *Onterrio Smith AU* 25.00
150 *Rex Grossman AU* 50.00

2003 Finest Refractors

Cards 1-60: 2X-4X
Rookies 61-100: 2X-4X
Jsy 101-118: 1X
Rookies AU/999: 1X-2X
Rookies AU/399: 1.5X
Production 199 Sets

2003 Finest Gold Refractors

Cards 1-60: 5X-10X
Rookies 61-100: 4X-8X
Jsy 101-118: 1.5X
Rookies AU/999: 1.5X-3X
Rookies AU/399: 2X
Production 50 Sets

2003 Finest Xfractors

Cards 1-60: 2X-4X
Rookies 61-100: 2X-4X
Production 175 Sets
Jsy 101-118: 1.5X
Rookies AU/999: 1.5X-3X
Rookies AU/399: 2X
Production 50 Sets

2004 Finest

NM/M
Common Player (1-60): .30
Minor Stars: .60
Unlisted Stars: 1.00
Common Rookie (61-100): 1.00
Common JSY (101-107): 5.00
Common Rookie (108-134): 8.00
Rookie Auto/999 Inserted 1:12
Rookie Auto/399 Inserted 1:120
Xfractors Production 5 Sets
Printing Plates Production 1 Set
Pack (5): 10.00
Box (18): 140.00
1 Steve McNair 1.00
2 Corey Dillon 1.00
3 Joey Harrington 1.00
4 Travis Henry .60
5 Donovan McNabb 1.50
6 Jamal Lewis 1.00
7 Jeff Garcia .60
8 Fred Taylor 1.00
9 Aaron Brooks 1.00
10 Marc Bulger 1.00
11 Keenan McCardell .30
12 David Carr 1.50
13 Charles Rogers 1.00
14 Ray Lewis .60
15 Priest Holmes 1.50
16 Curtis Martin 1.00
17 Plaxico Burress 1.00
18 Shaun Alexander 1.00
19 Brad Johnson .30
20 Marvin Harrison 1.00
21 Rod Smith .30
22 Jake Delhomme 1.00
23 Santana Moss .60
24 Trent Green .60
25 Michael Vick 2.50
26 Tim Rattay .30
27 Chris Chambers 1.00
28 Robert Ferguson .30
29 Tiki Barber .60
30 Terrell Owens 1.00
31 Marshall Faulk 1.50
32 Quincy Carter .60
33 Stephen Davis .60
34 Josh McCown .60
35 Jeremy Shockey 1.00
36 Tommy Maddox .30
37 Derrick Mason .60
38 Kerry Collins .60
39 Jimmy Smith .60
40 Chad Pennington 1.50
41 Domanick Davis .60
42 Darrell Jackson .60
43 Steve Smith .60
44 Drew Bledsoe 1.00
45 Deuce McAllister 1.00
46 Jerry Porter .60
47 Peerless Price .60
48 Eric Moulds .60
49 Garrison Hearst .60
50 Brett Favre 3.00
51 Amani Toomer .60
52 Andre Johnson 1.00
53 Edgerrin James 1.50
54 Rex Grossman 1.00
55 Daunte Culpepper 1.00
56 Tony Gonzalez .60
57 Byron Leftwich 2.00
58 Mark Brunell .60
59 Laveranues Coles .60
60 Matt Hasselbeck .60
61 *Chris Gamble* 2.00
62 *Michael Turner* 1.00
63 *Julius Jones* 5.00
64 *Dunta Robinson* 2.00
65 *Sean Taylor* 2.50
66 *Ahmad Carroll* 2.00
67 *Derrick Strait* 2.00
68 *Dontarrious Thomas* 1.00
69 *Jason Babin* 2.00
70 *Reggie Williams* 2.00
71 *Dwan Edwards* 1.00
72 *Rashaun Woods* 2.50
73 *Ricardo Colclough* 1.50
74 *Will Smith* 1.50
75 *Kellen Winslow Jr.* 3.00
76 *Roy Williams* 6.00
77 *B.J. Symons* 1.50
78 *Carlos Francis* 1.00
79 *Triandos Luke* 1.00
80 *Drew Henson* 4.00
81 *Keiwan Ratliff* 1.00
82 *Will Poole* 1.50
83 *Tommie Harris* 2.00
84 *Steven Jackson* 5.00
85 *Greg Jones* 2.00
86 *Vince Wilfork* 2.00
87 *DeAngelo Hall* 2.50
88 *Daryl Smith* 1.50
89 *Teddy Lehman* 2.00
90 *Casey Bramlet* 1.00
91 *Marcus Tubbs* 1.00
92 *Andy Hall* 1.00
93 *Jim Sorgi* 1.50
94 *Kenechi Udeze* 2.00
95 *Darius Watts* 2.00
96 *Tank Johnson* 1.00
97 *Matt Mauck* 2.00
98 *Bradlee Van Pelt* 2.00
99 *D.J. Williams* 2.00
100 *Larry Fitzgerald* 6.00
101 Peyton Manning JSY 10.00
102 Clinton Portis JSY 6.00
103 Chad Johnson JSY 5.00
104 Randy Moss JSY 8.00
105 Tom Brady JSY 10.00
106 LaDainian Tomlinson JSY 6.00
107 Ahman Green JSY 6.00
108 *Ben Roethlisberger Auto/399* 300.00
109 *Philip Rivers Auto/399* 75.00
110 *Eli Manning Auto/399* 150.00
111 *Kevin Jones Auto* 60.00
112 *Bernard Berrian Auto* 10.00
113 *Jeff Smoker Auto* 15.00
114 *Mewelde Moore Auto* 15.00
115 *Michael Clayton Auto* 30.00
116 *Jonathan Vilma Auto* 12.00
117 *Johnnie Morant Auto* 10.00
118 *Devard Darling Auto* 8.00
119 *Cedric Cobbs Auto* 10.00
120 *Chris Perry Auto* 25.00
121 *Ernest Wilford Auto* 10.00
122 *Michael Jenkins Auto* 10.00
123 *Jerricho Cotchery Auto* 10.00
124 *P.K. Sam Auto* 10.00
125 *Tatum Bell Auto* 25.00
126 *Derrick Hamilton Auto* 8.00
127 *Luke McCown Auto* 10.00
128 *Devery Henderson Auto* 10.00
129 *Craig Krenzel Auto* 15.00
130 *J.P. Losman Auto* 25.00
131 *Lee Evans Auto* 25.00
132 *Matt Schaub Auto* 20.00
133 *Robert Gallery Auto* 15.00
134 *Keary Colbert Auto* 15.00

2004 Finest Refractors

NM/M
Stars: 3X-6X
Rookies (61-100): 1.5X-3X
1-100 Production 199 Sets
Stars JSY (101-107): 1X
Inserted 1:168
Rookie Autos (108-134): 1.5X
108-134 Production 199 Sets
108 Ben Roethlisberger Auto 400.00
109 Philip Rivers Auto 80.00
110 Eli Manning Auto 200.00
120 Chris Perry Auto 30.00

2004 Finest Refractors Gold

NM/M
Stars: 5X-10X
Rookies (61-100): 3X-6X
1-100 Production 50 Sets
Stars JSY (101-107): 1.5X-3X
Inserted 1:684
Rookie Autos (108-134): 1.5X-3X
108-134 Production 50 Sets
108 Ben Roethlisberger Auto 750.00
109 Philip Rivers Auto 120.00
110 Eli Manning Auto 400.00
120 Chris Perry Auto 60.00

1995 Flair

Each of the regular 220 cards in this set features a player on a horizontal card with a foil-etched background. Two photos appear on each front - one is a mug shot of the player without his helmet on, the other is an action photo. The Flair logo is stamped in gold at the top of the card; the player's name and team name are stamped at the bottom. The player's initials are scripted in silver foil at the bottom. The card back has a full-bleed action photo, with the player's name and team helmet stamped in the center in gold foil. The player's statistics are also listed. Insert sets include Hot Numbers, TD Power and Wave of the Future.

NM/M
Complete Set (220): 20.00
Common Player: .20
Minor Stars: .40
Pack (11): 1.00
Pack (9): 1.00
Wax Box (36): 22.00
1 Larry Centers .20
2 Garrison Hearst .50
3 Seth Joyner .20
4 Dave Krieg .20
5 Rob Moore .20
6 *Frank Sanders* 1.00
7 Eric Swann .20
8 Devin Bush .20
9 Chris Coleman .20
10 Bert Emanuel .50
11 Jeff George .25
12 Craig Heyward .20
13 Terance Mathis .20
14 Eric Metcalf .20
15 Cornelius Bennett .20
16 Jeff Burris .20
17 *Todd Collins* .50
18 Russell Copeland .20
19 Jim Kelly .75
20 Andre Reed .40
21 Bruce Smith .40
22 Don Beebe .20
23 Mark Carrier .20
24 *Kerry Collins* 2.50
25 Barry Foster .20
26 Pete Metzelaars .20
27 Tyrone Poole .20
28 Frank Reich .20
29 Curtis Conway .40
30 Chris Gedney .20
31 Jeff Graham .20
32 Raymont Harris .20
33 Erik Kramer .20
34 *Rashaan Salaam* .50
35 Lewis Tillman .20
36 Michael Timpson .20
37 *Jeff Blake* 1.00
38 *Ki-Jana Carter* .75
39 Tony McGee .20
40 Carl Pickens .40
41 Corey Sawyer .20
42 Darnay Scott .40
43 Dan Wilkinson .20
44 Derrick Alexander .40
45 Leroy Hoard .20
46 Michael Jackson .20
47 Antonio Langham .20
48 Andre Rison .40
49 Vinny Testaverde .75
50 Eric Turner .20
51 Troy Aikman 2.00
52 Charles Haley .20
53 Michael Irvin .40
54 Daryl Johnston .20
55 Leon Lett .20
56 Jay Novacek .20
57 Emmitt Smith 4.00
58 Kevin Williams .20
59 Steve Atwater .20
60 Rod Bernstine .20
61 John Elway 3.00
62 Glyn Milburn .20
63 Anthony Miller .20
64 Mike Pritchard .20
65 Shannon Sharpe .40
66 Scott Mitchell .40
67 Herman Moore .75
68 Johnnie Morton .20
69 Brett Perriman .20
70 Barry Sanders 4.00
71 Chris Spielman .20
72 Edgar Bennett .20
73 Robert Brooks .40
74 Brett Favre 4.00
75 LeShon Johnson .20
76 Sean Jones .20
77 George Teague .20
78 Reggie White .50
79 Micheal Barrow .20
80 Gary Brown .20
81 Mel Gray .20
82 Haywood Jeffires .20
83 *Steve McNair* 5.00
84 *Rodney Thomas* .40
85 Trev Alberts .20
86 Flipper Anderson .20
87 Tony Bennett .20
88 Quentin Coryatt .20
89 Sean Dawkins .20
90 Craig Erickson .20
91 Marshall Faulk 2.00
92 Steve Beuerlein .40
93 *Tony Boselli* .75
94 Reggie Cobb .20
95 Ernest Givens .20
96 Desmond Howard .20
97 Jeff Lageman .20
98 *James Stewart* 3.00
99 Marcus Allen .50
100 Steve Bono .40
101 Dale Carter .20
102 Willie Davis .20
103 Lake Dawson .40
104 Greg Hill .40
105 Neil Smith .20
106 Tim Bowens .20
107 Bryan Cox .20
108 Irving Fryar .20
109 Eric Green .20
110 Terry Kirby .20
111 Dan Marino 3.00

112	O.J. McDuffie	.40
113	Bernie Parmalee	.20
114	Derrick Alexander	.20
115	Cris Carter	.75
116	Qadry Ismail	.40
117	Warren Moon	.40
118	Jake Reed	.20
119	Robert Smith	.75
120	DeWayne Washington	.20
121	Drew Bledsoe	2.00
122	Vincent Brisby	.20
123	Ben Coates	.40
124	*Curtis Martin*	4.00
125	Willie McGinest	.20
126	Dave Meggett	.20
127	Chris Slade	.20
128	Eric Allen	.20
129	Mario Bates	.40
130	Jim Everett	.40
131	Michael Haynes	.20
132	Tyrone Hughes	.20
133	Renaldo Turnbull	.20
134	*Ray Zellars*	.40
135	Michael Brooks	.20
136	Dave Brown	.20
137	Rodney Hampton	.20
138	Thomas Lewis	.20
139	Mike Sherrard	.20
140	Herschel Walker	.40
141	*Tyrone Wheatley*	1.00
142	*Kyle Brady*	.75
143	Boomer Esiason	.40
144	Aaron Glenn	.20
145	Mo Lewis	.20
146	Johnny Mitchell	.20
147	Ronald Moore	.20
148	*Joe Aska*	.40
149	Tim Brown	.75
150	Jeff Hostetler	.20
151	Raghib Ismail	.20
152	*Napoleon Kaufman*	1.00
153	Chester McGlockton	.20
154	Harvey Williams	.20
155	Fred Barnett	.20
156	Randall Cunningham	.75
157	Charlie Garner	.50
158	*Mike Mamula*	.40
159	Kevin Turner	.20
160	Ricky Watters	.75
161	Calvin Williams	.20
162	*Mark Bruener*	.75
163	Kevin Greene	.20
164	Charles Johnson	.50
165	Greg Lloyd	.20
166	Bam Morris	.40
167	Neil O'Donnell	.40
168	*Kordell Stewart*	1.00
169	John L. Williams	.20
170	Rod Woodson	.20
171	Jerome Bettis	.75
172	Isaac Bruce	1.50
173	*Kevin Carter*	.50
174	Troy Drayton	.20
175	Sean Gilbert	.20
176	Carlos Jenkins	.20
177	Todd Lyght	.20
178	Chris Miller	.20
179	Andre Coleman	.20
180	Stan Humphries	.40
181	Shawn Jefferson	.20
182	Natrone Means	.40
183	Leslie O'Neal	.20
184	Junior Seau	.40
185	Mark Seay	.20
186	William Floyd	.40
187	Merton Hanks	.20
188	Brent Jones	.20
189	Ken Norton	.20
190	Jerry Rice	2.00
191	Deion Sanders	1.00
192	*J.J. Stokes*	1.00
193	Dana Stubblefield	.20
194	Steve Young	1.50
195	Sam Adams	.20
196	Brian Blades	.20
197	*Joey Galloway*	2.50
198	Cortez Kennedy	.20
199	Rick Mirer	.40
200	Chris Warren	.40
201	Derrick Brooks	.20
202	Lawrence Dawsey	.20
203	Trent Dilfer	.40
204	Alvin Harper	.20
205	Jackie Harris	.20
206	Courtney Hawkins	.20
207	Hardy Nickerson	.20
208	Errict Rhett	.50
209	*Warren Sapp*	1.00
210	Terry Allen	.40
211	Tom Carter	.20
212	Henry Ellard	.20
213	Darrell Green	.20
214	Brian Mitchell	.20
215	Heath Shuler	.40
216	*Michael Westbrook*	2.00
217	Tydus Winans	.20
218	Checklist	.20
219	Checklist	.20
220	Checklist	.20

1995 Flair Hot Numbers

These 1995 Fleer Flair inserts feature 10 top statistical leaders for the 1994-95 season. Cards, numbered 1 of 10, etc., were were randomly included one per every six packs. The card front has gold foil stamping for the player's name, position and Flair and insert set logos. The key numbers from the player's season statistics are in the background of the card. The horizontal back has another photo of the player, with a box next to it containing a brief summary of his accomplishments. Gold foil stamping is used for his name, team name and "Hot Numbers," which are at the top of the box.

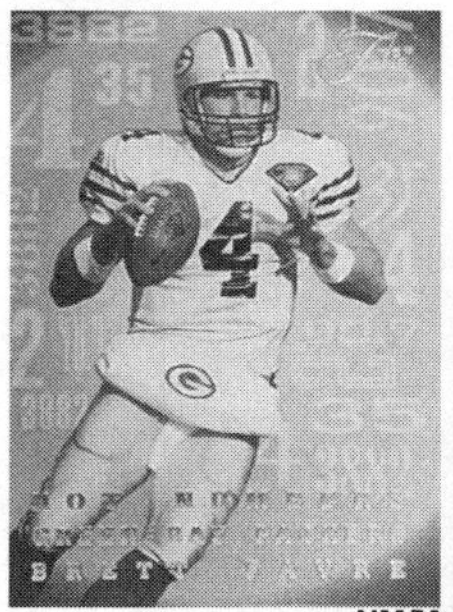

		NM/M
Complete Set (10):		20.00
Common Player:		1.00
1	Jeff Blake	2.00
2	Drew Bledsoe	5.00
3	Tim Brown	1.00
4	Ben Coates	1.00
5	Trent Difler	2.00
6	Brett Favre	7.00
7	Dan Marino	7.00
8	Bam Morris	1.00
9	Ricky Watters	2.00
10	Steve Young	5.00

1995 Flair TD Power

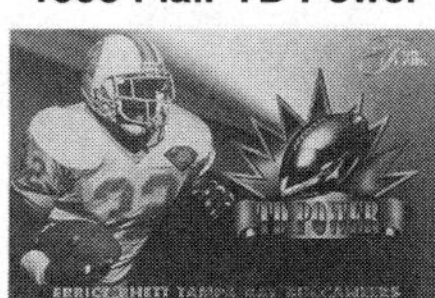

These horizontally-designed insert cards could be found one per every 12 packs of 1995 Fleer Flair. The cards feature 10 of the top touchdown scorers from the previous season. The TD Power logo appears on the front, along with a player action photo and the Flair logo, which is stamped in gold. The player's name and team name are stamped in gold and are at the bottom of the card. The card back has another photo on one side, with a box containing a brief player profile. The insert set logo is included inside the box, at the top. Cards are numbered 1 of 10, etc.

		NM/M
Complete Set (10):		20.00
Common Player:		1.00
1	Marshall Faulk	3.00
2	William Floyd	1.00
3	Natrone Means	1.00
4	Bam Morris	1.00
5	Errict Rhett	1.00
6	Jerry Rice	5.00
7	Andre Rison	1.00
8	Barry Sanders	6.00
9	Emmitt Smith	6.00
10	Chris Warren	1.00

1995 Flair Wave of the Future

These 1995 Fleer Flair insert cards, randomly included one per every 37 packs, feature nine top rookies. The cards, which use gold foil stamping on the front, offer a unique die-cut that is actually cut around the player's face. The back, numbered 1 of 9, etc., also uses gold foil stamping and includes another action photo. A brief summary of the player's collegiate accomplishments, plus his potential as a pro, is also given.

		NM/M
Complete Set (9):		50.00
Common Player:		3.00
1	Kyle Brady	3.00
2	Ki-Jana Carter	3.00
3	Kerry Collins	10.00
4	Joey Galloway	10.00
5	Steve McNair	20.00
6	Rashaan Salaam	3.00
7	James Stewart	5.00
8	Michael Westbrook	5.00
9	Tyrone Wheatley	3.00

1997 Flair Showcase

Flair Showcase NFL is a 360-card set featuring 120 players. Each player has three base cards: Style, Grace and Showcase. The fronts feature distinct action and headshots with a holographic foil background on 24 pt card stock. The backs have another photo and complete career statistics. The basic card types have a tiered insertion ratio. Two parallel sets were issued: Legacy, with less than 100 cards per player, and the one-of-a-kind Legacy Masterpiece. Four insert sets were included: Wave of the Future, Hot Hands, Midas Touch and Then & Now.

		NM/M
Common Style (A1-A120):		.25
Common Grace (B1-B120):		.50
Comp. Showcase Set (120):		1,500
Common Showcase (C1-C120):		2.00
Pack (5):		3.00
Wax Box (24):		45.00
A1	Jerry Rice STY	4.00
A2	Mark Brunell STY	4.00
A3	Eddie Kennison STY	.50
A4	Brett Favre STY	8.00
A5	Karim Abdul-Jabbar STY	.75
A6	*David LaFleur STY*	1.50
A7	John Elway STY	3.00
A8	Troy Aikman STY	4.00
A9	Steve McNair STY	3.00
A10	Kordell Stewart STY	4.00
A11	Drew Bledsoe STY	4.00
A12	Kerry Collins STY	.50
A13	Dan Marino STY	6.00
A14	Steve Young STY	3.00
A15	Marvin Harrison STY	1.00
A16	Lawrence Phillips STY	.50
A17	Jeff Blake STY	.50
A18	*Yatil Green STY*	1.50
A19	*Jake Plummer STY*	4.00
A20	Barry Sanders STY	4.00
A21	Deion Sanders STY	2.50
A22	Emmitt Smith STY	6.00
A23	*Rae Carruth STY*	2.00
A24	Chris Warren STY	.25
A25	Terry Glenn STY	1.00
A26	*Jim Druckenmiller STY*	4.00
A27	Eddie George STY	5.00
A28	Curtis Martin STY	4.00
A29	*Warrick Dunn STY*	4.00
A30	Terrell Davis STY	4.00
A31	Rashaan Salaam STY	.25
A32	Marcus Allen STY	.50
A33	Jeff George STY	.50
A34	Thurman Thomas STY	.50
A35	Keyshawn Johnson STY	1.00
A36	Jerome Bettis STY	.50
A37	Larry Centers STY	.25
A38	Tony Banks STY	1.00
A39	Marshall Faulk STY	.50
A40	Mike Alstott STY	.50
A41	Elvis Grbac STY	.25
A42	Errict Rhett STY	.50
A43	Edgar Bennett STY	.25
A44	Jim Harbaugh STY	.25
A45	Antonio Freeman STY	1.00
A46	*Tiki Barber STY*	4.00
A47	Tim Biakabutuka STY	.25
A48	Joey Galloway STY	.50
A49	*Tony Gonzalez STY*	1.50
A50	Keenan McCardell STY	.25
A51	Darnay Scott STY	.25
A52	Brad Johnson STY	.25
A53	Herman Moore STY	.50
A54	*Reidel Anthony STY*	3.00
A55	Junior Seau STY	.50
A56	Ricky Watters STY	.50
A57	Amani Toomer STY	.25
A58	Andre Reed STY	.25
A59	*Antowain Smith STY*	5.00
A60	*Ike Hilliard STY*	2.50
A61	*Byron Hanspard STY*	1.50
A62	Robert Smith STY	.25
A63	Gus Frerotte STY	.25
A64	Charles Way STY	.25
A65	Trent Dilfer STY	.50
A66	Adrian Murrell STY	.50
A67	Stan Humphries STY	.25
A68	Robert Brooks STY	.25
A69	Jamal Anderson STY	.50
A70	Natrone Means STY	.50
A71	John Friesz STY	.25
A72	Ki-Jana Carter STY	.25
A73	Marc Edwards STY	.25
A74	Michael Westbrook STY	.25
A75	Neil O'Donnell STY	.25
A76	Scott Mitchell STY	.25
A77	Wesley Walls STY	.25
A78	Bruce Smith STY	.25
A79	*Corey Dillon STY*	7.00
A80	Wayne Chrebet STY	.25
A81	Tony Martin STY	.25
A82	Jimmy Smith STY	.25
A83	Terry Allen STY	.25
A84	Shannon Sharpe STY	.25
A85	Derrick Alexander STY	.25
A86	Garrison Hearst STY	.25
A87	Tamarick Vanover STY	.25
A88	Michael Irvin STY	.50
A89	Mark Chmura STY	.50
A90	Bert Emanuel STY	.25
A91	Eric Metcalf STY	.25
A92	Reggie White STY	.50
A93	Carl Pickens STY	.25
A94	Chris Sanders STY	.25
A95	Frank Sanders STY	.25
A96	Desmond Howard STY	.25
A97	Michael Jackson STY	.25
A98	Tim Brown STY	.50
A99	O.J. McDuffie STY	.25
A100	Mario Bates STY	.25
A101	Warren Moon STY	.25
A102	Curtis Conway STY	.25
A103	Irving Fryar STY	.25
A104	Isaac Bruce STY	.50
A105	Cris Carter STY	.50
A106	Chris Chandler STY	.25
A107	Charles Johnson STY	.25
A108	Kevin Lockett STY	.25
A109	Rob Moore STY	.25
A110	Napoleon Kaufman STY	.75
A111	Henry Ellard STY	.25
A112	Vinny Testaverde STY	.25
A113	Rick Mirer STY	.25
A114	Ty Detmer STY	.25
A115	Todd Collins STY	.25
A116	Jake Reed STY	.25
A117	Dave Brown STY	.25
A118	*Dedric Ward STY*	1.50
A119	Heath Shuler STY	.25
A120	Ben Coates STY	.25
B1	Jerry Rice GRA	6.00
B2	Mark Brunell GRA	6.00
B3	Eddie Kennison GRA	1.00
B4	Brett Favre GRA	12.00
B5	Karim Abdul-Jabbar GRA	1.50
B6	David LaFleur GRA	2.00
B7	John Elway GRA	4.50
B8	Troy Aikman GRA	6.00
B9	Steve McNair GRA	4.50
B10	Kordell Stewart GRA	6.00
B11	Drew Bledsoe GRA	6.00
B12	Kerry Collins GRA	1.50
B13	Dan Marino GRA	9.00
B14	Steve Young GRA	4.50
B15	Marvin Harrison GRA	2.00
B16	Lawrence Phillips GRA	.75
B17	Jeff Blake GRA	.75
B18	Yatil Green GRA	2.50
B19	Jake Plummer GRA	10.00
B20	Barry Sanders GRA	6.00
B21	Deion Sanders GRA	4.00
B22	Emmitt Smith GRA	9.00
B23	Rae Carruth GRA	3.00
B24	Chris Warren GRA	.50
B25	Terry Glenn GRA	2.50
B26	Jim Druckenmiller GRA	6.00
B27	Eddie George GRA	7.50
B28	Curtis Martin GRA	6.00
B29	Warrick Dunn GRA	5.00
B30	Terrell Davis GRA	6.00
B31	Rashaan Salaam GRA	.50
B32	Marcus Allen GRA	.75
B33	Jeff George GRA	.75
B34	Thurman Thomas GRA	.75
B35	Keyshawn Johnson GRA	2.00
B36	Jerome Bettis GRA	.75
B37	Larry Centers GRA	.50
B38	Tony Banks GRA	2.00
B39	Marshall Faulk GRA	.75
B40	Mike Alstott GRA	.75
B41	Elvis Grbac GRA	.50
B42	Errict Rhett GRA	.75
B43	Edgar Bennett GRA	.50
B44	Jim Harbaugh GRA	.50
B45	Antonio Freeman GRA	1.50
B46	Tiki Barber GRA	4.50
B47	Tim Biakabutuka GRA	.50
B48	Joey Galloway GRA	.75
B49	Tony Gonzalez GRA	2.00
B50	Keenan McCardell GRA	.50
B51	Darnay Scott GRA	.50
B52	Brad Johnson GRA	.50
B53	Herman Moore GRA	.75
B54	Reidel Anthony GRA	4.50
B55	Junior Seau GRA	.75
B56	Ricky Watters GRA	.75
B57	Amani Toomer GRA	.50
B58	Andre Reed GRA	.50
B59	Antowain Smith GRA	8.00
B60	Ike Hilliard GRA	4.00
B61	Byron Hanspard GRA	1.50
B62	Robert Smith GRA	.50
B63	Gus Frerotte GRA	.50
B64	Charles Way GRA	.50
B65	Trent Dilfer GRA	.75
B66	Adrian Murrell GRA	.75
B67	Stan Humphries GRA	.50
B68	Robert Brooks GRA	.50
B69	Jamal Anderson GRA	.75
B70	Natrone Means GRA	.75
B71	John Friesz GRA	.50
B72	Ki-Jana Carter GRA	.50
B73	Marc Edwards GRA	.50
B74	Michael Westbrook GRA	.50
B75	Neil O'Donnell GRA	.50
B76	Scott Mitchell GRA	.50
B77	Wesley Walls GRA	.50
B78	Bruce Smith GRA	.50
B79	Corey Dillon GRA	8.00
B80	Wayne Chrebet GRA	.50
B81	Tony Martin GRA	.50
B82	Jimmy Smith GRA	.50
B83	Terry Allen GRA	.50
B84	Shannon Sharpe GRA	.50
B85	Derrick Alexander GRA	.50
B86	Garrison Hearst GRA	.50
B87	Tamarick Vanover GRA	.50
B88	Michael Irvin GRA	.75
B89	Mark Chmura GRA	.75
B90	Bert Emanuel GRA	.50
B91	Eric Metcalf GRA	.50
B92	Reggie White GRA	.75
B93	Carl Pickens GRA	.50
B94	Chris Sanders GRA	.50
B95	Frank Sanders GRA	.50
B96	Desmond Howard GRA	.50
B97	Michael Jackson GRA	.50
B98	Tim Brown GRA	.75
B99	O.J. McDuffie GRA	.50
B100	Mario Bates GRA	.50
B101	Warren Moon GRA	.50
B102	Curtis Conway GRA	.50
B103	Irving Fryar GRA	.50
B104	Isaac Bruce GRA	.75
B105	Cris Carter GRA	.75
B106	Chris Chandler GRA	.50
B107	Charles Johnson GRA	.50
B108	Kevin Lockett GRA	.50
B109	Rob Moore GRA	.50
B110	Napoleon Kaufman GRA	1.00
B111	Henry Ellard GRA	.50
B112	Vinny Testaverde GRA	.50
B113	Rick Mirer GRA	.50
B114	Ty Detmer GRA	.50
B115	Todd Collins GRA	.50
B116	Jake Reed GRA	.50
B117	Dave Brown GRA	.50
B118	Dedric Ward GRA	.50
B119	Heath Shuler GRA	.50
B120	Ben Coates GRA	.50
C1	Jerry Rice SHOW	40.00
C2	Mark Brunell SHOW	30.00
C3	Eddie Kennison SHOW	6.00
C4	Brett Favre SHOW	60.00
C5	Karim Abdul-Jabbar SHOW	6.00
C6	David LaFleur SHOW	2.00
C7	John Elway SHOW	50.00
C8	Troy Aikman SHOW	50.00
C9	Steve McNair SHOW	30.00
C10	Kordell Stewart SHOW	15.00
C11	Drew Bledsoe SHOW	30.00
C12	Kerry Collins SHOW	6.00
C13	Dan Marino SHOW	60.00
C14	Steve Young SHOW	40.00
C15	Marvin Harrison SHOW	8.00
C16	Lawrence Phillips SHOW	2.00
C17	Jeff Blake SHOW	4.00
C18	Yatil Green SHOW	2.00
C19	Jake Plummer SHOW	15.00
C20	Barry Sanders SHOW	50.00
C21	Deion Sanders SHOW	15.00
C22	Emmitt Smith SHOW	60.00
C23	Rae Carruth SHOW	2.00
C24	Chris Warren SHOW	2.00
C25	Terry Glenn SHOW	8.00
C26	Jim Druckenmiller SHOW	4.00
C27	Eddie George SHOW	30.00
C28	Curtis Martin SHOW	30.00
C29	Warrick Dunn SHOW	20.00
C30	Terrell Davis SHOW	30.00
C31	Rashaan Salaam SHOW	2.00
C32	Marcus Allen SHOW	6.00
C33	Jeff George SHOW	6.00
C34	Thurman Thomas SHOW	6.00
C35	Keyshawn Johnson SHOW	8.00
C36	Jerome Bettis SHOW	6.00
C37	Larry Centers SHOW	2.00
C38	Tony Banks SHOW	6.00
C39	Marshall Faulk SHOW	6.00
C40	Mike Alstott SHOW	7.50
C41	Elvis Grbac SHOW	2.00
C42	Errict Rhett SHOW	4.00
C43	Edgar Bennett SHOW	2.00
C44	Jim Harbaugh SHOW	2.00
C45	Antonio Freeman SHOW	8.00
C46	Tiki Barber SHOW	25.00
C47	Tim Biakabutuka SHOW	2.00
C48	Joey Galloway SHOW	7.50
C49	Tony Gonzalez SHOW	15.00
C50	Keenan McCardell SHOW	2.00
C51	Darnay Scott SHOW	2.00
C52	Brad Johnson SHOW	2.00
C53	Herman Moore SHOW	7.50
C54	Reidel Anthony SHOW	6.00
C55	Junior Seau SHOW	4.00
C56	Ricky Watters SHOW	4.00
C57	Amani Toomer SHOW	2.00
C58	Andre Reed SHOW	2.00
C59	Antowain Smith SHOW	25.00
C60	Ike Hilliard SHOW	25.00
C61	Byron Hanspard SHOW	6.00
C62	Robert Smith SHOW	2.00
C63	Gus Frerotte SHOW	2.00
C64	Charles Way SHOW	2.00
C65	Trent Dilfer SHOW	6.00
C66	Adrian Murrell SHOW	4.00
C67	Stan Humphries SHOW	2.00
C68	Robert Brooks SHOW	2.00
C69	Jamal Anderson SHOW	7.50
C70	Natrone Means SHOW	6.00
C71	John Friesz SHOW	2.00
C72	Ki-Jana Carter SHOW	2.00
C73	Marc Edwards SHOW	2.00
C74	Michael Westbrook SHOW	2.00
C75	Neil O'Donnell SHOW	2.00
C76	Scott Mitchell SHOW	2.00
C77	Wesley Walls SHOW	2.00
C78	Bruce Smith SHOW	2.00
C79	Corey Dillon SHOW	30.00
C80	Wayne Chrebet SHOW	2.00
C81	Tony Martin SHOW	2.00
C82	Jimmy Smith SHOW	2.00
C83	Terry Allen SHOW	2.00
C84	Shannon Sharpe SHOW	2.00
C85	Derrick Alexander SHOW	2.00
C86	Garrison Hearst SHOW	2.00
C87	Tamarick Vanover SHOW	2.00
C88	Michael Irvin SHOW	5.00
C89	Mark Chmura SHOW	4.00
C90	Bert Emanuel SHOW	2.00
C91	Eric Metcalf SHOW	2.00
C92	Reggie White SHOW	5.00
C93	Carl Pickens SHOW	2.00
C94	Chris Sanders SHOW	2.00
C95	Frank Sanders SHOW	2.00
C96	Desmond Howard SHOW	2.00
C97	Michael Jackson SHOW	2.00
C98	Tim Brown SHOW	4.00
C99	O.J. McDuffie SHOW	2.00
C100	Mario Bates SHOW	2.00
C101	Warren Moon SHOW	2.00
C102	Curtis Conway SHOW	2.00
C103	Irving Fryar SHOW	2.00
C104	Isaac Bruce SHOW	4.00
C105	Cris Carter SHOW	4.00
C106	Chris Chandler SHOW	2.00
C107	Charles Johnson SHOW	2.00
C108	Kevin Lockett SHOW	2.00
C109	Rob Moore SHOW	2.00
C110	Napoleon Kaufman SHOW	6.00
C111	Henry Ellard SHOW	2.00
C112	Vinny Testaverde SHOW	2.00
C113	Rick Mirer SHOW	2.00
C114	Ty Detmer SHOW	2.00
C115	Todd Collins SHOW	2.00
C116	Jake Reed SHOW	2.00
C117	Dave Brown SHOW	2.00
C118	Dedric Ward SHOW	2.00
C119	Heath Shuler SHOW	2.00
C120	Ben Coates SHOW	2.00

1997 Flair Showcase Legacy

Legacy parallels the 360-base cards in Flair Showcase. The cards feature blue-foil stamping and are sequentially numbered to 100. The backs are done in matte finish. The Legacy Masterpiece versions are a one-of-one parallel of each base card. The cards are stamped to signify their distinctness.

	NM/M
Common Player:	10.00
Minor Stars:	20.00
Production 100 Sets	
Legacy	5X to 20X

1997 Flair Showcase Hot Hands

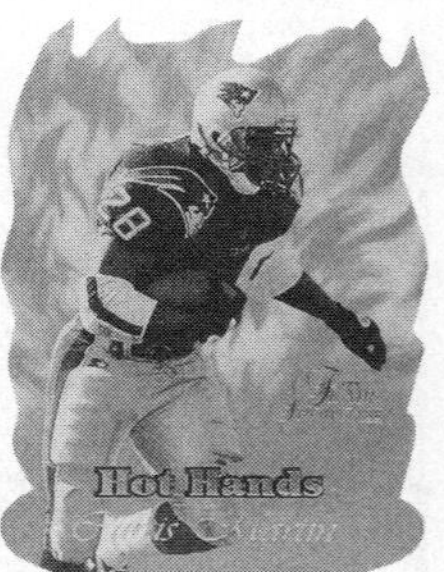

Hot Hands is a 12-card insert featuring some of the top players in the NFL. The cards are die-cut in the shape of flames and have a fiery background. They are inserted once in every 90 packs. The cards are numbered with the "HH" prefix.

		NM/M
Complete Set (12):		200.00
Common Player:		5.00
1	Kerry Collins	20.00
2	Emmitt Smith	40.00

3	Terrell Davis	30.00
4	Brett Favre	50.00
5	Eddie George	20.00
6	Marvin Harrison	10.00
7	Mark Brunell	20.00
8	Dan Marino	50.00
9	Curtis Martin	30.00
10	Terry Glenn	10.00
11	Keyshawn Johnson	10.00
12	Jerry Rice	40.00

1997 Flair Showcase Midas Touch

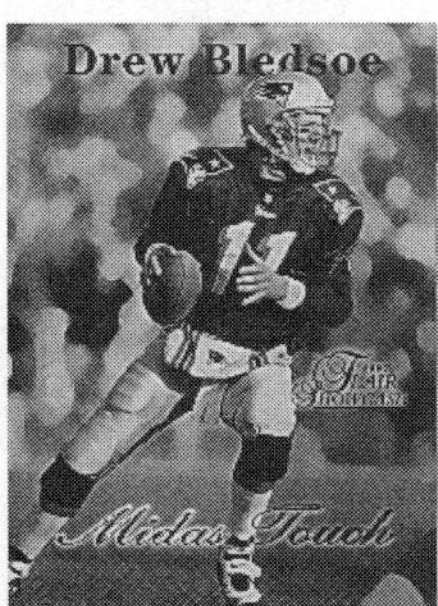

Midas Touch is a 12-card insert featuring superstars with a "golden touch." The cards have a gold-colored background and were inserted once in every 20 packs. The cards are numbered with the "MT" prefix.

		NM/M
Complete Set (12):		60.00
Common Player:		1.00
Minor Stars:		2.00
1	Troy Aikman	12.00
2	John Elway	12.00
3	Barry Sanders	15.00
4	Marshall Faulk	6.00
5	Karim Abdul-Jabbar	2.00
6	Drew Bledsoe	12.00
7	Ricky Watters	6.00
8	Kordell Stewart	4.00
9	Tony Martin	1.00
10	Steve Young	12.00
11	Joey Galloway	1.00
12	Isaac Bruce	6.00

1997 Flair Showcase Now & Then

A four-card insert set, Then & Now features 12 NFL players as they looked when they entered the league. Each card highlights a particular draft year and three of the top players who were picked. The cards were inserted once in every 288 packs. The cards are numbered with the "NT" prefix.

		NM/M
Complete Set (4):		150.00
Common Player:		40.00
1	Marino, Elway, D. Green (1983)	60.00
2	Aikman, B. Sanders, D. Sanders (1989)	40.00
3	E. Smith, C. Warren, J. Seau (1990)	60.00
4	Favre, H. Moore, R. Watters (1991)	60.00

1997 Flair Showcase Wave of the Future

Wave of the Future showcases 25 top rookies entering the 1997 season. The fronts and backs feature a tidal wave design. Inserted once in every four packs. The cards are numbered with the "WF" prefix.

		NM/M
Complete Set (25):		20.00
Common Player:		1.00
Minor Stars:		2.00
1	Mike Adams	1.00
2	John Allred	1.00
3	Pat Barnes	2.00
4	Kenny Bynum	1.00
5	Will Blackwell	2.00
6	Peter Boulware	2.00
7	Greg Clark	2.00
8	Troy Davis	2.00
9	Albert Connell	2.00
10	Jay Graham	2.00
11	Leon Johnson	1.00
12	Damon Jones	1.00
13	Freddie Jones	3.00
14	George Jones	2.00
15	Chad Levitt	1.00
16	Joey Kent	2.00
17	Danny Wuerffel	2.00
18	Orlando Pace	2.00
19	Darnell Autry	1.00
20	Sedrick Shaw	2.00
21	Shawn Springs	2.00
22	Duce Staley	4.00
23	Darrell Russell	2.00
24	Bryant Westbrook	2.00
25	Antowuan Wyatt	1.00

1998 Flair Showcase Row 3

Row 3 is made up of 80 base cards with four different tiers. Cards 1-20 were inserted 1:0.9 packs, cards 21-40 at 1:1.1, cards 41-60 at 1:1.4 and cards 61-80 at 1:1.8.

		NM/M
Complete Set (80):		75.00
Common Player:		.25
Minor Stars:		.50
Common Rookie:		1.00
1-20 Inserted 1:0.9		
21-40 Inserted 1:1.1		
41-60 Inserted 1:1.4		
61-80 Inserted 1:1.8		
Pack (5):		3.50
Wax Box (24):		60.00
1	Brett Favre	3.00
2	Emmitt Smith	2.00
3	*Peyton Manning*	8.00
4	Mark Brunell	1.00
5	*Randy Moss*	8.00
6	Jerry Rice	1.50
7	John Elway	1.50
8	Troy Aikman	1.50
9	Warrick Dunn	1.00
10	Kordell Stewart	1.00
11	Drew Bledsoe	1.00
12	Eddie George	1.00
13	Dan Marino	2.00
14	Antowain Smith	.75
15	*Curtis Enis*	1.50
16	Jake Plummer	1.00
17	Steve Young	1.00
18	*Ryan Leaf*	1.00
19	Terrell Davis	2.00
20	Barry Sanders	3.00
21	Corey Dillon	1.00
22	*Fred Taylor*	3.00
23	Herman Moore	.50
24	Marshall Faulk	.75
25	*John Avery*	2.00
26	Terry Glenn	.50
27	Keyshawn Johnson	.50
28	*Charles Woodson*	2.00
29	Garrison Hearst	.50
30	Steve McNair	.75
31	Deion Sanders	.75
32	*Robert Holcombe*	1.00
33	Jerome Bettis	.50
34	*Robert Edwards*	2.00
35	*Skip Hicks*	2.00
36	*Marcus Nash*	2.00
37	Fred Lane	.25
38	*Kevin Dyson*	2.00
39	Dorsey Levens	.50
40	*Jacquez Green*	1.50
41	Shannon Sharpe	.50
42	Michael Irvin	.75
43	Jim Harbaugh	.25
44	Curtis Martin	.75
45	Bobby Hoying	.25
46	Trent Dilfer	.50
47	Yancey Thigpen	.25
48	Warren Moon	.50
49	Danny Kanell	.25
50	Rob Johnson	.50
51	Carl Pickens	.50
52	Scott Mitchell	.25
53	Tim Brown	.50
54	Tony Banks	.50
55	Jamal Anderson	1.00
56	Kerry Collins	.50
57	Elvis Grbac	.25
58	Mike Alstott	.75
59	Glenn Foley	.25
60	Brad Johnson	.75
61	Robert Brooks	.25
62	Irving Fryar	.25
63	Natrone Means	.40
64	Rae Carruth	.25
65	Isaac Bruce	.75
66	Andre Rison	.50
67	Jeff George	.50
68	Charles Way	.25
69	Derrick Alexander	.25
70	Michael Jackson	.25
71	Rob Moore	.50
72	Ricky Watters	.50
73	Curtis Conway	.50
74	Antonio Freeman	.50
75	Jimmy Smith	.75
76	Troy Davis	.25
77	Robert Smith	.50
78	Terry Allen	.50
79	Joey Galloway	1.25
80	Charles Johnson	.25

1998 Flair Showcase Row 2

Row 2 is set up the same way that Row 3 is with 80 base cards and four tiers. It has different insert odds with cards 1-20 found 1:3 packs, cards 21-40 at 1:2.5 packs, cards 41-60 at 1:4 packs and cards 61-80 at 1:3.4 packs.

	NM/M
Complete Set (80):	150.00
Common Player:	.50
Minor Stars:	1.00
Common Rookie:	1.50
1-20 Inserted 1:3	
21-40 Inserted 1:2.5	
41-60 Inserted 1:4	
61-80 Inserted 1:3.4	
1X to 2X Row 3	

1998 Flair Showcase Row 1

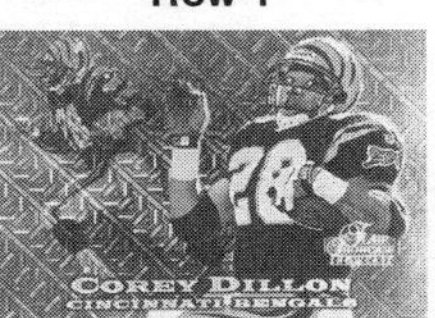

Row 1 singles are much tougher to find than the previous Row 3 and 2 because of tougher insert odds. Same setup with 80 cards and four tiers. Cards 1-20 were inserted 1:16 packs, cards 21-40 at 1:24, cards 41-60 at 1:6 and the last tier of cards 61-80 at 1:9.6.

	NM/M
Complete Set (80):	600.00
Common Player:	1.50
Minor Stars:	3.00
Common Rookie:	4.00
1-20 Inserted 1:16	
21-40 Inserted 1:24	
41-60 Inserted 1:6	
61-80 Inserted 1:9.6	
2X to 5X Row 3	

1998 Flair Showcase Row 0

The Row 0 set is made up of 80 cards and is tiered at four different levels. The first level includes cards 1-20 and each is sequentially numbered to 250. The next level includes cards 21-40 and are numbered to 500. Cards 41-60 are numbered to 1,000 and the last level of cards 61-80 are numbered to 2,000.

	NM/M
Complete Set (80):	3,500
Common Player (1-20):	7.00
Production 250 Sets	
Common Player (21-40):	5.00
Production 500 Sets	
Common Player (41-60):	3.00
Production 1000 Sets	
Common Player (61-80):	2.00
Production 2000 Sets	
6X to 20X Row 3	

1998 Flair Showcase Legacy

Each of the 320 cards in this set has a parallel Legacy card. Each card has a foil front and is sequentially numbered to 100.

	NM/M
Common Player:	15.00
Minor Stars:	30.00
Production 100 Sets	
Each Player Has Four Different Cards	
6X to 20X Row 3	

1998 Flair Showcase Feature Film

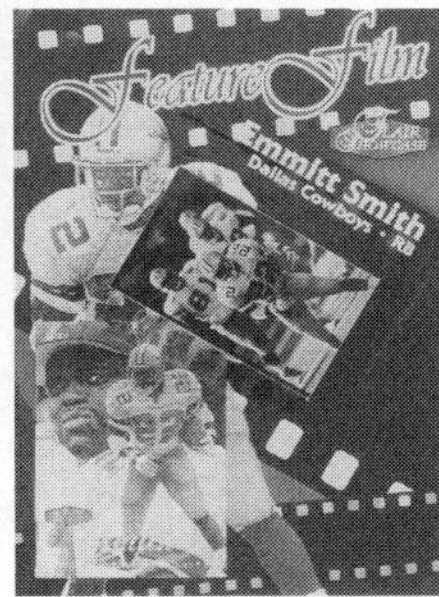

Each card in this set has an actual slide from the Showcase set mounted on it. Singles were inserted 1:60 packs.

		NM/M
Complete Set (10):		150.00
Common Player:		5.00
Inserted 1:60		
1	Terrell Davis	25.00
2	Brett Favre	40.00
3	Antowain Smith	5.00
4	Emmitt Smith	35.00
5	Dan Marino	35.00
6	Kordell Stewart	10.00
7	Warrick Dunn	10.00
8	Barry Sanders	35.00
9	Peyton Manning	30.00
10	Ryan Leaf	5.00

1999 Flair Showcase

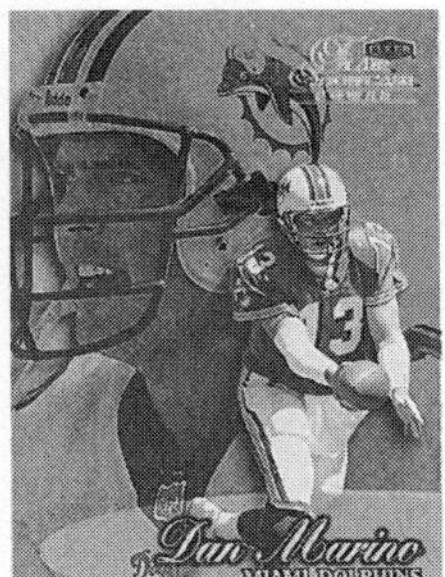

This was a 192-card set that included three levels of scarcity. The Power subset included 32 veterans, the Passion subset was made up of 64 veterans and the Showcase subset included the last 96 cards with 21 of them being rookies and 11 of them being veterans, sequentially numbered to 1,999. Two parallel sets were issued with the Legacy Collection and Masterpieces. Other inserts included: Class of '99, Feel the Game, First Rounders and Shrine Time. SRP was $4.99 for five-card packs.

		NM/M
Complete Set (192):		500.00
Common Player:		.25
Minor Stars:		.50
Common Rookie:		2.00
Production 1,999 Sets		
Pack (5):		5.00
Wax Box (24):		90.00
1	Troy Aikman	2.00
2	Jamal Anderson	.75
3	Charlie Batch	1.25
4	Jerome Bettis	.75
5	Drew Bledsoe	1.50
6	Mark Brunell	1.50
7	Randall Cunningham	.75
8	Terrell Davis	2.00
9	Corey Dillon	.75
10	Warrick Dunn	.75
11	Curtis Enis	.75
12	Marshall Faulk	.75
13	Brett Favre	4.00
14	Doug Flutie	1.25
15	Eddie George	1.00
16	Brian Griese	1.50
17	Keyshawn Johnson	.75
18	Peyton Manning	3.00
19	Dan Marino	3.00
20	Curtis Martin	.75
21	Steve McNair	1.00
22	Randy Moss	3.00
23	Terrell Owens	.75
24	Jake Plummer	1.50
25	Jerry Rice	2.00
26	Barry Sanders	3.00
27	Antowain Smith	.75
28	Emmitt Smith	3.00
29	Kordell Stewart	.75
30	J.J. Stokes	.50
31	Fred Taylor	2.00
32	Steve Young	1.25
33	Troy Aikman	2.00
34	Mike Alstott	.75
35	Jamal Anderson	.75
36	Charlie Batch	1.25
37	Jerome Bettis	.75
38	Drew Bledsoe	1.50
39	Mark Brunell	1.50
40	Cris Carter	.75
41	Mark Chmura	.50
42	Wayne Chrebet	.75
43	Kerry Collins	.50
44	Randall Cunningham	.75
45	Terrell Davis	2.00
46	Trent Dilfer	.50
47	Corey Dillon	.75
48	Warrick Dunn	.75
49	Kevin Dyson	.25
50	Curtis Enis	.75
51	Marshall Faulk	.75
52	Brett Favre	4.00
53	Doug Flutie	1.25
54	Antonio Freeman	.75
55	Eddie George	1.00
56	Terry Glenn	.75
57	Tony Gonzalez	.50
58	Elvis Grbac	.50
59	Jacquez Green	.50
60	Brian Griese	1.50
61	Marvin Harrison	.75
62	Garrison Hearst	.50
63	Skip Hicks	.50
64	Priest Holmes	.75
65	Michael Irvin	.50
66	Brad Johnson	.75
67	Keyshawn Johnson	.75
68	Napoleon Kaufman	.75
69	Dorsey Levens	.75
70	Peyton Manning	3.00
71	Dan Marino	3.00
72	Curtis Martin	.75
73	Ed McCaffrey	.75
74	Keenan McCardell	.50
75	O.J. McDuffie	.25
76	Steve McNair	1.00
77	Scott Mitchell	.25
78	Randy Moss	3.00
79	Eric Moulds	.75
80	Terrell Owens	.75
81	Lawrence Phillips	.25
82	Jake Plummer	1.50
83	Jerry Rice	2.00
84	Andre Rison	.50
85	Barry Sanders	3.00
86	Shannon Sharpe	.75
87	Antowain Smith	.75
88	Emmitt Smith	3.00
89	Rod Smith	.75
90	Duce Staley	.75
91	Kordell Stewart	.75
92	J.J. Stokes	.50
93	Fred Taylor	3.00
94	Vinny Testaverde	.50
95	Ricky Watters	.50
96	Steve Young	1.25
97	Mike Alstott	.75
98	Jamal Anderson	.75
99	Charlie Batch	.50
100	Jerome Bettis	.75
101	Tim Biakabutuka	.50
102	Drew Bledsoe	1.50
103	Tim Brown	.50
104	Mark Brunell	1.25
105	Cris Carter	.75
106	Chris Chandler	.50
107	Mark Chmura	.50
108	Wayne Chrebet	.75
109	Ben Coates	.50
110	Kerry Collins	.50
111	Randall Cunningham	.75
112	Trent Dilfer	.50
113	Corey Dillon	.75
114	Warrick Dunn	.75
115	Kevin Dyson	.25
116	Curtis Enis	.75
117	Marshall Faulk	.75
118	Doug Flutie	1.25
119	Antonio Freeman	.75
120	Joey Galloway	.75
121	Rich Gannon	.50
122	Eddie George	1.00
123	Terry Glenn	.75
124	Tony Gonzalez	.50
125	Elvis Grbac	.50
126	Jacquez Green	.50
127	Brian Griese	1.50
128	Marvin Harrison	.75
129	Garrison Hearst	.50
130	Skip Hicks	.50
131	Priest Holmes	.75
132	Michael Irvin	.50
133	Brad Johnson	.75
134	Napoleon Kaufman	.75
135	Terry Kirby	.25
136	Dorsey Levens	.75
137	Curtis Martin	.75
138	Ed McCaffrey	.75
139	Keenan McCardell	.50
140	O.J. McDuffie	.25
141	Steve McNair	1.00
142	Natrone Means	.50
143	Scott Mitchell	.25
144	Herman Moore	.75
145	Eric Moulds	.75
146	Terrell Owens	.75
147	Lawrence Phillips	.25
148	Jerry Rice	2.00
149	Andre Rison	.50
150	Deion Sanders	.50
151	Shannon Sharpe	.50
152	Antowain Smith	.75
153	Rod Smith	.75
154	Duce Staley	.75
155	Kordell Stewart	.75
156	J.J. Stokes	.50
157	Vinny Testaverde	.50
158	Yancey Thigpen	.25
159	Ricky Watters	.50
160	Steve Young	1.25
161	Troy Aikman SP	10.00
162	*Champ Bailey*	10.00
163	*Karsten Bailey*	2.00
164	*D'Wayne Bates*	2.00
165	*David Boston*	10.00
166	*Michael Cloud*	2.00
167	*Cecil Collins*	5.00
168	*Tim Couch*	20.00
169	*Daunte Culpepper*	50.00
170	Terrell Davis SP	15.00
171	*Troy Edwards*	5.00
172	*Kevin Faulk*	10.00
173	Brett Favre SP	20.00
174	*Torry Holt*	25.00
175	*Sedrick Irvin*	5.00
176	*Edgerrin James*	50.00
177	*J.J. Johnson*	5.00
178	*Kevin Johnson*	5.00
179	Keyshawn Johnson SP	5.00
180	Peyton Manning SP	15.00
181	Dan Marino SP	15.00
182	*Donovan McNabb*	50.00
183	*Cade McNown*	5.00
184	*Joe Montgomery*	5.00
185	Randy Moss SP	20.00
186	Jake Plummer SP	5.00
187	*Peerless Price*	20.00
188	Barry Sanders SP	20.00
189	*Akili Smith*	5.00
190	Emmitt Smith SP	15.00
191	Fred Taylor SP	15.00
192	*Ricky Williams*	50.00

1999 Flair Showcase Legacy Collection

This was a 192-card parallel to the base set. Each single was sequentially numbered to 99.

	NM/M
Legacy Cards:	5X-10X
Legacy Rookies:	1.5X
Production 99 Sets	

1999 Flair Showcase Class of '99

This 15-card insert set included the top rookies from 1999. Each was sequentially numbered to 500.

		NM/M
Complete Set (15):		150.00
Common Player:		5.00
Production 500 Sets		
1	Tim Couch	20.00
2	Donovan McNabb	25.00
3	Akili Smith	5.00
4	Cade McNown	5.00
5	Daunte Culpepper	25.00
6	Ricky Williams	30.00
7	Edgerrin James	30.00
8	Kevin Faulk	12.00
9	Torry Holt	15.00
10	David Boston	15.00
11	Sedrick Irvin	5.00
12	Peerless Price	12.00
13	Joe Germaine	5.00
14	Brock Huard	5.00
15	Shaun King	5.00

1999 Flair Showcase Feel The Game

This 10-card insert set contained pieces of game-used gloves, shorts, jerseys or shoes. Each single was hand-numbered and inserted 1:168 packs.

NM/M
Complete Set (10): 800.00
Common Player: 25.00
Cecil Collins shoes 25.00
Sean Dawkins shoes 25.00
Marshall Faulk jersey 75.00
Brett Favre jersey 125.00
Torry Holt shoes 50.00
Edgerrin James gloves 100.00
Peyton Manning jersey 100.00
Dan Marino jersey 125.00
Jake Plummer shoes 60.00
Antowain Smith shorts 50.00

1999 Flair Showcase First Rounders

This 10-card set included the top skilled position players selected in the 1999 NFL Draft. Singles were inserted 1:10 packs.

NM/M
Complete Set (10): 25.00
Common Player: 2.50
Inserted 1:10
1 Tim Couch 5.00
2 Donovan McNabb 5.00
3 Akili Smith 2.00
4 Cade McNown 2.00
5 Daunte Culpepper 5.00
6 David Boston 2.50
7 Torry Holt 2.50
8 Ricky Williams 6.00
9 Edgerrin James 6.00
10 Troy Edwards 2.50

1999 Flair Showcase Shrine Time

This 15-card insert set included players who could be on their way to the Hall of Fame. Each single was sequentially numbered to 1,500.

NM/M
Complete Set (15): 60.00
Common Player: 2.00
Production 1,500 Sets
1 Peyton Manning 8.00
2 Fred Taylor 4.00
3 Terrell Owens 2.00
4 Charlie Batch 2.00
5 Jerry Rice 8.00
6 Randy Moss 12.00
7 Warrick Dunn 2.00
8 Mark Brunell 6.00
9 Emmitt Smith 12.00
10 Eddie George 5.00
11 Barry Sanders 12.00
12 Terrell Davis 6.00
13 Dan Marino 12.00
14 Troy Aikman 8.00
15 Brett Favre 12.00

2002 Flair

NM/M
Common Player: .25
Unlisted Stars: .60
Minor Stars: .50
Common Rookie (101-135): 3.00
Minor Rookies: 5.00
Pack (5): 4.25
Wax Box (20): 60.00
1 Jeff Garcia .60
2 Jevon Kearse .50
3 Chris Weinke .60
4 Ray Lewis .50

NM/M
5 Donovan McNabb 1.50
6 Tiki Barber .50
7 Rich Gannon .50
8 Jamal Anderson .50
9 Curtis Martin .50
10 Darrell Jackson .25
11 Ricky Williams 1.50
12 Drew Brees 2.00
13 Mark Brunell .60
14 Johnnie Morton .50
15 Quincy Carter 1.50
16 Brian Urlacher 2.00
17 Peerless Price .50
18 Drew Bledsoe 1.50
19 Aaron Brooks 1.25
20 Derrick Mason .50
21 Charlie Garner .50
22 Mike Alstott .50
23 Freddie Mitchell .50
24 Isaac Bruce .50
25 Hines Ward .50
26 Doug Flutie .60
27 Terrell Owens .60
28 Peyton Manning 2.50
29 Ron Dayne .50
30 Peter Warrick .50
31 Randy Moss 2.50
32 Priest Holmes .60
33 Joey Galloway .50
34 Jimmy Smith .25
35 Marvin Harrison .50
36 Junior Seau .50
37 Zach Thomas .50
38 Antowain Smith .50
39 Marty Booker .50
40 Deuce McAllister 1.25
41 Rod Smith .50
42 Michael Westbrook .25
43 Antonio Freeman .25
44 Kerry Collins .50
45 Koren Robinson .50
46 Jamal Lewis 1.25
47 Duce Staley .50
48 Jerome Bettis .50
49 David Terrell .50
50 Daunte Culpepper 1.50
51 Tim Couch 1.25
52 Brian Griese .60
53 Marshall Faulk 1.50
54 Brad Johnson .50
55 Eddie George .60
56 Kurt Warner 2.50
57 Steve McNair .60
58 Stephen Davis .50
59 Corey Dillon .60
60 Troy Brown .60
61 Warrick Dunn .50
62 Ed McCaffrey .50
63 Amani Toomer .50
64 Rod Gardner .50
65 Mike McMahon .60
66 Wayne Chrebet .50
67 Jake Plummer .50
68 Edgerrin James 2.00
69 Eric Moulds .50
70 Tony Gonzalez .50
71 Marcus Robinson .25
72 Muhsin Muhammad .50
73 Trent Dilfer .50
74 Kevin Johnson .50
75 Fred Taylor .50
76 Terrell Davis 1.25
77 Emmitt Smith 2.50
78 Az-Zahir Hakim .50
79 Tim Brown .60
80 Jerry Rice 2.50
81 Warren Sapp .50
82 Michael Strahan .50
83 Garrison Hearst .50
84 David Boston .60
85 Michael Vick 2.50
86 Anthony Thomas 2.00
87 Ahman Green .75
88 Chris Chambers .60
89 Tom Brady 2.50
90 Plaxico Burress .60
91 LaDainian Tomlinson 2.00
92 Shaun Alexander .60
93 Torry Holt .50
94 Kordell Stewart .50
95 Chad Pennington .50
96 Chris Redman .50
97 Kendrell Bell .50
98 Michael Bennett .60
99 Joe Horn .50
100 Brett Favre 3.50
101 *David Carr* 25.00
102 *Joey Harrington* 15.00
103 *Ashley Lelie* 12.00
104 *Javon Walker* 12.00
105 *Donald Reche Caldwell* 5.00
106 *Andre Davis* 10.00
107 *William Green* 10.00
108 *Antonio Bryant* 10.00
109 *Clinton Portis* 25.00
110 *Luke Staley* 5.00
111 *Josh Reed* 8.00
112 *Ron Johnson* 3.00
113 *Lamar Gordon* 5.00
114 *Cliff Russell* 3.00
115 *Eric Crouch* 8.00
116 *Ladell Betts* 8.00
117 *Patrick Ramsey* 12.00
118 *Adrian Peterson* 6.00
119 *DeShaun Foster* 8.00
120 *Tim Carter* 3.00
121 *Jabar Gaffney* 8.00
122 *T.J. Duckett* 10.00
123 *Julius Peppers* 10.00
124 *Rohan Davey* 6.00
125 *Antwann Randle El* 10.00
126 *Jeremy Shockey* 15.00
127 *Donte Stallworth* 12.00
128 *Marquise Walker* 3.00
129 *Brian Westbrook* 8.00
130 *Randy Fasani* 3.00
131 *Jonathan Wells* 5.00
132 *Travis Stephens* 3.00
133 *Daniel Graham* 5.00
134 *Maurice Morris* 8.00
135 *David Garrard* 5.00

2002 Flair Collection

Stars: 2X-4X
Production 200 Sets
Rookies: 1.5X-3X
Production 50 Sets

2002 Flair Franchise Favorites

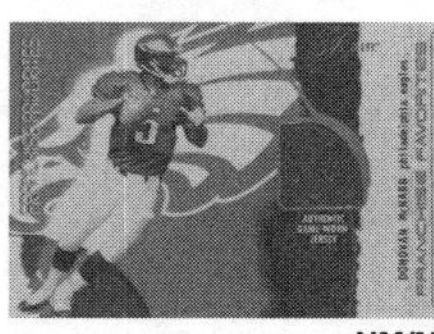

NM/M
Common Player: 2.00
Inserted 1:4
1FF Donovan McNabb 3.00
2FF Tim Brown 2.00
3FF Michael Vick 3.00
4FF Peerless Price 2.00
5FF Anthony Thomas 2.00
6FF Corey Dillon 2.00
7FF Emmitt Smith 3.00
8FF Brett Favre 4.00
9FF Edgerrin James 2.00
10FF Fred Taylor 2.00
11FF Tony Gonzalez 2.00
12FF Daunte Culpepper 2.00
13FF Tom Brady 3.00
14FF Deuce McAllister 2.00
15FF Jerome Bettis 2.00
16FF LaDainian Tomlinson 2.00
17FF Kurt Warner 2.00
18FF Eddie George 2.00

2002 Flair Franchise Favorites Jerseys

NM/M
Inserted 1:10
Donovan McNabb 15.00
Tim Brown
Michael Vick 20.00
Peerless Price
Anthony Thomas 15.00
Corey Dillon 10.00
Emmitt Smith
Brett Favre 25.00
Edgerrin James 15.00
Fred Taylor 15.00
Tony Gonzalez
Daunte Culpepper 20.00
Tom Brady
Deuce McAllister
Jerome Bettis 10.00
LaDainian Tomlinson 20.00
Kurt Warner 15.00
Eddie George 15.00

2002 Flair Franchise Tools

NM/M
Common Player: 15.00
Inserted 1:40
1FT Joey Harrington 50.00
2FT Cliff Russell 15.00
3FT David Garrard 15.00
4FT Ashley Lelie 25.00
5FT Javon Walker 25.00
6FT Andre Davis 20.00
7FT Jabar Gaffney 15.00
8FT Ron Johnson 15.00
9FT Tim Carter 15.00
10FT DeShaun Foster 15.00
11FT Clinton Portis 40.00
12FT Travis Stephens 15.00
13FT Ladell Betts 15.00
14FT Antwann Randle El 25.00
15FT Maurice Morris 20.00
16FT Rohan Davey 15.00
17FT Jeremy Shockey 30.00
18FT Donte Stallworth 20.00
19FT Patrick Ramsey 15.00
20FT T.J. Duckett 35.00

2002 Flair Hot Numbers

Prodction 100 sets
Ricky Williams
Marvin Harrison
Brian Urlacher
Terrell Davis
Randy Moss
Fred Taylor
Aaron Brooks
Jerry Rice
Curtis Martin
Kordell Stewart
Doug Flutie
Steve McNair
Marshall Faulk
Jeff Garcia
Brian Griese
Isaac Bruce
Drew Bledsoe
Rich Gannon

2002 Flair Jersey Heights

NM/M
Common Player: 2.00
Inserted 1:10
1JH Ricky Williams 3.00
2JH Marvin Harrison 2.00
3JH Brian Urlacher 3.00
4JH Terrell Davis 2.00
5JH Randy Moss 3.00
6JH Fred Taylor 2.00
7JH Aaron Brooks 2.00
8JH Jerry Rice 3.00
9JH Curtis Martin 2.00
10JH Kordell Stewart 2.00
11JH Doug Flutie 2.00
12JH Steve McNair 2.00
13JH Marshall Faulk 3.00
14JH Jeff Garcia 2.00
15JH Brian Griese 2.00
16JH Isaac Bruce 2.00
17JH Drew Bledsoe 3.00
18JH Rich Gannon 3.00

2002 Flair Jersey Heights Jerseys

NM/M
Inserted 1:18
Ricky Williams
Marvin Harrison
Brian Urlacher 30.00
Terrell Davis
Randy Moss 25.00
Fred Taylor
Aaron Brooks 15.00
Jerry Rice
Curtis Martin
Kordell Stewart 15.00
Doug Flutie 15.00
Steve McNair 15.00
Marshall Faulk
Jeff Garcia
Brian Griese
Isaac Bruce 20.00
Drew Bledsoe 20.00
Rich Gannon 20.00

2002 Flair Sweet Swatch Autographs

NM/M
Oversized Box toppers
1SSAU Kurt Warner 75.00
2SSAU Jeff Garcia 35.00
3SSAU Donovan McNabb
4SSAU Joe Montana 150.00
5SSAU Chad Pennington 35.00

2002 Flair Sweet Swatch Memorabilia

NM/M
Oversized Box Toppers
2SSGU Ahman Green 25.00
3SSGU Brett Favre 40.00
4SSGU Corey Dillon
5SSGU Curtis Martin 10.00
6SSGU Daunte Culpepper 15.00
7SSGU Donovan McNabb
8SSGU Eddie George 15.00
9SSGU Edgerrin James 25.00
10SSGU Jake Plummer
11SSGU Kurt Warner 20.00
12SSGU LaDainian Tomlinson
13SSGU Marvin Harrison
14SSGU Michael Vick 45.00
15SSGU Jeff Garcia
16SSGU Steve McNair
17SSGU Tim Brown
18SSGU Tim Couch 20.00
19SSGU Torry Holt 15.00
20SSGU Terrell Owens 20.00

2003 Flair

NM/M
Common Player: .25
Minor Star: .50
Unlisted Star: .75
Common Rookie (91-130): 6.00
Production 500 Sets
Pack (5): 3.50
Wax Box (20): 50.00
1 Jamal Lewis .25
2 Aaron Brooks 1.25
3 Joey Harrington 2.00
4 Brett Favre 3.00
5 Donovan McNabb 1.50
6 Marcel Shipp .25
7 Michael Vick 3.00
8 David Carr 2.00
9 Tommy Maddox .75
10 Drew Brees 1.50
11 Chad Pennington 1.25
12 Drew Bledsoe 1.50
13 Rich Gannon .75
14 Kurt Warner 2.00
15 Brian Griese .60
16 William Green .75
17 Jake Plummer .75
18 Eric Moulds .25
19 Peyton Manning 2.50
20 Keyshawn Johnson .50
21 Travis Henry .25
22 Tiki Barber .50
23 Emmitt Smith 2.50
24 Michael Bennett .50
25 Curtis Martin .75
26 Donald Driver .50
27 Clinton Portis 2.00
28 Eddie George .75
29 Marshall Faulk 1.50
30 Jeremy Shockey 2.00
31 Ahman Green .75
32 Priest Holmes 1.25
33 Edgerrin James 1.50
34 Plaxico Burress .75
35 Ricky Williams 1.50
36 Anthony Thomas .50
37 Jerome Bettis .50
38 Shaun Alexander .75
39 Fred Taylor .50
40 Isaac Bruce .50
41 Mike Alstott .50
42 Peerless Price .75
43 Corey Dillon .50
44 Amani Toomer .50
45 Warrick Dunn .25
46 Tim Brown .50
47 Deuce McAllister 1.25
48 Terrell Owens .75
49 Stephen Davis .25
50 Torry Holt .50
51 Duce Staley .25
52 Jimmy Smith .50
53 Ray Lewis .50
54 Brian Urlacher 2.00
55 Zach Thomas .75
56 Joey Galloway .75
57 LaDainian Tomlinson 2.00
58 Chris Chambers .75
59 Ronde Barber .25
60 Randy Moss 2.50
61 Tom Brady 2.00
62 Jerry Porter .75
63 Patrick Ramsey .50
64 Derrick Mason .25
65 Daunte Culpepper 1.50
66 Marty Booker .50
67 Steve McNair .75
68 Hines Ward .50
69 Matt Hasselbeck .25
70 Joe Horn .50
71 Mark Brunell .75
72 Laveranues Coles .75
73 Chad Hutchinson .50
74 Tony Gonzalez .50
75 Jeff Garcia .75
76 Kendrell Bell .75
77 Kerry Collins .50
78 Warren Sapp .50
79 Tim Couch 1.25
80 Jerry Rice 2.50
81 Koren Robinson .50
82 Antwaun Randle El 1.50
83 Donte Stallworth 1.25
84 Shannon Sharpe .50
85 Chad Johnson .50
86 Todd Heap .25
87 Rod Gardner .50
88 Marvin Harrison .75
89 David Boston .75
90 Julius Peppers .75
91 *Byron Leftwich* 40.00
92 *Terrell Suggs* 15.00
93 *Kelley Washington* 10.00
94 *Brandon Lloyd* 10.00
95 *Kliff Kingsbury* 8.00
96 *Willis McGahee* 25.00
97 *Terence Newman* 15.00
98 *Bryant Johnson* 15.00
99 *Musa Smith* 8.00
100 *Ken Dorsey* 15.00
101 *Larry Johnson* 20.00
102 *Dewayne Robertson* 6.00
103 *Onterrio Smith* 15.00
104 *Tyrone Calico* 15.00
105 *Kareem Kelly* 6.00
106 *Chris Brown* 20.00
107 *Andrew Pinnock* 6.00
108 *Taylor Jacobs* 10.00
109 *Dallas Clark* 10.00
110 *Marcus Trufant* 6.00
111 *Charles Rogers* 20.00
112 *Lee Suggs* 30.00
113 *Rex Grossman* 30.00
114 *Doug Gabriel* 6.00
115 *Arnaz Battle* 8.00
116 *William Joseph* 10.00
117 *Justin Fargas* 12.00
118 *Anquan Boldin* 25.00
119 *Teyo Johnson* 8.00
120 *Bobby Wade* 8.00
121 *Brian St. Pierre* 6.00
122 *Carson Palmer* 35.00
123 *Kyle Boller* 20.00
124 *Andre Johnson* 25.00
125 *Dave Ragone* 15.00
126 *Chris Simms* 15.00
127 *Seneca Wallace* 10.00
128 *Justin Gage* 6.00
129 *LaBrandon Toefield* 6.00
130 *Talman Gardner* 8.00

2003 Flair Collection

Stars: 4X-8X
Rookies: 1X-1.2X
Production 125 Sets

2003 Flair A Cut Above

NM/M
Common Player: 6.00
Production 500 sets
Final Cut versions: 1.5X-3X
Final Cut Production 50 Sets
ACA-MA Mike Alstott 10.00
ACA-DB Drew Bledsoe 10.00
ACA-TB Tim Brown 8.00
ACA-IB Isaac Bruce 6.00
ACA-DC Daunte Culpepper 8.00
ACA-MF Marshall Faulk 6.00
ACA-JH Joe Horn 6.00
ACA-EJ Edgerrin James 8.00
ACA-KJ Keyshawn Johnson 6.00
ACA-PP Peerless Price 6.00

2003 Flair Canton Calling

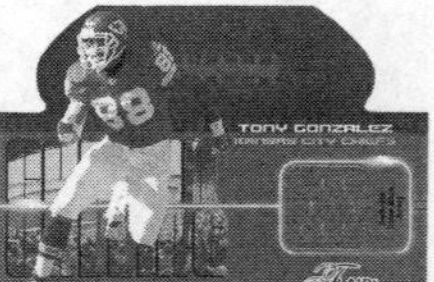

NM/M
Common Player: 8.00
Inserted 1:20
Patch Version 1X-1.5X
Patch Production 150 sets
CC-CC Cris Carter 10.00
CC-CD Corey Dillon 8.00
CC-MF Marshall Faulk 12.00
CC-BF Brett Favre 25.00
CC-TG Tony Gonzalez 8.00
CC-RL Ray Lewis 8.00
CC-CM Curtis Martin 10.00
CC-EM Ed McCaffrey 8.00
CC-RM Randy Moss 12.00
CC-TO Terrell Owens 10.00
CC-ES Emmitt Smith 20.00
CC-JR Jerry Rice 15.00
CC-JS Junior Seau 8.00
CC-KW Kurt Warner 8.00
CC-RW Rod Woodson 8.00

2003 Flair Sweet Swatch Autographs

NM/M
Common Player: 50.00
Production 175 Sets
Gold Production 25 Sets
Masterpiece Production 1 Set
SSAG-TB Tom Brady 75.00
SSAG-WM Willis McGahee 50.00
SSAG-LT LaDainian Tomlinson 50.00

2003 Flair Sweet Swatch Jerseys

NM/M
Common Player: 6.00
Production 200 sets
Patch Production 25 Sets
SSJR-KB Kendrell Bell 8.00
SSJR-MB Michael Bennett 8.00
SSJR-DB Drew Brees 6.00
SSJR-AB Aaron Brooks 8.00
SSJR-DC David Carr 15.00
SSJR-TG Tony Gonzalez 8.00
SSJR-JH Joey Harrington 12.00
SSJR-MH Marvin Harrison 10.00
SSJR-PH Priest Holmes 15.00
SSJR-PM Peyton Manning 15.00
SSRJ-CM Curtis Martin 8.00
SSJR-DM Deuce McAllister 8.00
SSJR-RM Randy Moss 15.00
SSJR-CP Chad Pennington 12.00
SSJR-PP Peerless Price 6.00
SSJR-ES Emmitt Smith 30.00
SSJR-LT LaDainian Tomlinson 10.00
SSJR-MV Michael Vick 20.00
SSJR-HW Hines Ward 8.00
SSJR-RW Ricky Williams 15.00

2003 Flair Sweet Swatch Jerseys Jumbos

NM/M
Common Player: 8.00
SSJE-MB Michael Bennett/208 8.00
SSJE-DB Drew Brees/518 8.00
SSJE-AB Aaron Brooks/293 8.00
SSJE-DC David Carr/352 15.00
SSJE-TG Tony Gonzalez/455 6.00
SSJE-JH Joey Harrington/455 15.00
SSJE-MH Marvin Harrison/520 8.00
SSJE-PH Priest Holmes/455 10.00
SSJE-PM Peyton Manning/483 15.00
SSJE-CM Curtis Martin/377 8.00
SSJE-DM Deuce McAllister/256 8.00
SSJE-RM Randy Moss/264 15.00
NSJE-CP Chad Pennington/368 12.00
SSJE-PP Peerless Price/416 8.00
SSJE-ES Emmitt Smith/263 25.00
SSJE-LT LaDainian Tomlinson/520 8.00
SSJE-MV Michael Vick/455 25.00
SSJE-HW Hines Ward/180 8.00
SSJE-RW Ricky Williams/275 15.00

2003 Fleer Flair Sweet Swatch Jerseys Dual Jumbos

Production 25 Sets
ES/RW Emmitt Smith, Ricky Williams
PM/MH Peyton Manning, Marvin Harrison
DB/LT Drew Brees, LaDainian Tomlinson
MV/PP Michael Vick, Peerless Price
PH/TG Priest Holmes, Tony Gonzalez
DC/JH David Carr, Joey Harrington
KB/HW Kendrell Bell, Hines Ward
RM/MB Randy Moss, Michael Bennett
DM/AB Deuce McAllister, Aaron Brooks
CP/CM Chad Pennington, Curtis Martin

2003 Fleer Flair Sweet Swatch Patches Jumbos

NM/M
Common Player: 20.00
SSPE-MB Michael Bennett/120 20.00
SSPE-DB Drew Brees/146 25.00
SSPE-AB Aaron Brooks/83 25.00
SSPE-DC David Carr/61 50.00
SSPE-TG Tony Gonzalez/146 20.00
SSPE-JH Joey Harrington/115 25.00
SSPE-MH Marvin Harrison/116 25.00
SSPE-PH Priest Holmes/146 30.00
SSPE-PM Peyton Manning/116 30.00
SSPE-CM Curtis Martin/120 25.00
SSPE-DM Deuce McAllister/108 25.00
SSPE-RM Randy Moss/165 30.00
SSPE-CP Chad Pennington/165 30.00
SSPE-PP Peerless Price/88 20.00
SSPE-ES Emmitt Smith/144 60.00
SSPE-LT LaDainian Tomlinson/116 25.00
SSPE-MV Michael Vick/86 50.00
SSPE-HW Hines Ward/95 20.00
SSPE-RW Ricky Williams/116 30.00

A player's name in *italic* type indicates a rookie card.

2003 Fleer Flair Sunday Showdown

NM/M
Common Player: 8.00
Production 500 Sets
Patches: 1X-2X
Patch Production 100 Sets
SSDB Drew Bledsoe 10.00
SSCC Chris Chambers 6.00
SSRG Rich Gannon 6.00
SSEG Eddie George 6.00
SSAG Ahman Green 10.00
SSWG William Green 6.00
SSMH Marvin Harrison Pants 8.00
SSJL Jamal Lewis 8.00
SSDM Deuce McAllister 8.00
SSDM Donovan McNabb 12.00
SSSM Steve McNair 8.00
SSJP Julius Peppers 6.00
SSCP Clinton Portis 12.00
SSJS Jeremy Shockey 10.00
SSFT Fred Taylor 6.00
SSBU Brian Urlacher 12.00

2003 Fleer Flair Sunday Showdown Dual Patches

NM/M
Common Player: 15.00
Production 50 sets
SS-MADC Mike Alstott, Deuce McAllister 25.00
SS-CCMH Chris Chambers, Marvin Harrison 25.00
SS-EGFT Eddie George, Fred Taylor 25.00
SS-AGBU Ahman Green, Brian Urlacher 40.00
SS-JLWG Jamal Lewis, William Green 25.00
SS-DMJS Donovan McNabb, Jeremy Shockey 40.00
SS-SMPM Steve McNair, Peyton Manning 50.00
SS-JHDC Joey Harrington, Daunte Culpepper 40.00

2004 Fleer Flair

NM/M
Common Player (1-60): .50
Minor Stars (1-60): .75
Unlisted Stars (1-60): 1.50

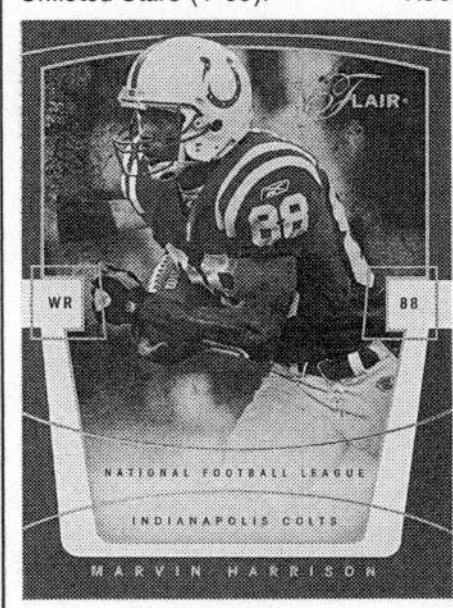

Common Rookie (61-85): 4.00
Rookie Production 799 Sets
Box (1): 125.00
1 Clinton Portis 3.00
2 Deuce McAllister 1.50
3 Marshall Faulk 2.00
4 Tom Brady 3.00
5 Ahman Green 1.50
6 LaDainian Tomlinson 2.00
7 Lee Suggs .50
8 Amani Toomer .75
9 Priest Holmes 2.00
10 Peerless Price .75
11 Warren Sapp .50
12 Andre Davis .75
13 Chad Pennington 2.00
14 Quincy Carter 1.50
15 Santana Moss .50
16 Antonio Bryant .75
17 Jerry Porter .50
18 Laveranues Coles .75
19 Daunte Culpepper 1.50
20 Stephen Davis .75
21 Rich Gannon .75
22 Chad Johnson .75
23 Ashley Lelie .50
24 Ray Lewis .75
25 Joey Harrington 1.50
26 Brian Westbrook .50
27 Marvin Harrison 1.50
28 Torry Holt 1.50
29 Kevan Barlow .50
30 Peyton Manning 3.00
31 Andre Johnson 1.50
32 Steve Smith .50
33 Troy Brown .50
34 Brian Urlacher 1.50
35 Anquan Boldin 1.50
36 Matt Hasselbeck .75
37 Edgerrin James 2.00
38 Dante Hall .50
39 Brad Johnson .50
40 Jamal Lewis 1.50
41 Rudi Johnson .75
42 Michael Strahan .50
43 Donovan McNabb 2.00
44 Steve McNair 1.50
45 Ricky Williams 2.00
46 Jake Delhomme 1.50
47 Patrick Ramsey .75
48 Randy Moss 3.00
49 David Carr 2.00
50 Jeff Garcia 1.50
51 Shaun Alexander 1.50
52 Byron Leftwich 3.00
53 Michael Vick 4.00
54 Brett Favre 5.00
55 Hines Ward .75
56 Chris Chambers 1.50
57 Eddie George 1.50
58 Eric Moulds .50
59 Plaxico Burress 1.50
60 Charles Rogers 1.50
61 *Eli Manning* 30.00
62 *Larry Fitzgerald* 15.00
63 *Chris Perry* 8.00
64 *Ben Roethlisberger* 40.00
65 *Roy Williams* 15.00
66 *Kellen Winslow Jr.* 10.00
67 *Steven Jackson* 12.00
68 *Kevin Jones* 15.00
69 *Reggie Williams* 8.00
70 *Michael Clayton* 8.00
71 *Rashaun Woods* 8.00
72 *Ben Troupe* 4.00
73 *Greg Jones* 5.00
74 *J.P. Losman* 8.00
75 *Philip Rivers* 15.00
76 *Michael Jenkins* 6.00
77 *Darius Watts* 4.00
78 *Michael Turner* 4.00
79 *Lee Evans* 8.00
80 *Drew Henson* 12.00
81 *Luke McCown* 5.00
82 *Julius Jones* 12.00
83 *Bernard Berrian* 4.00
84 *Keary Colbert* 4.00
85 *Tatum Bell* 6.00

2004 Fleer Flair Collection Row 1

Stars (1-60): 2X-5X
Rookies (61-85): 1X-3X

2004 Fleer Flair Collection Row 2

No Pricing
Production 1 Set

2004 Fleer Flair Auto. Collection Fleer Crown Panels

NM/M
.75X-1.5X Regular Panel Price
Parchment Panels: 1X-3X
Production 25 Sets
No parchment card for Henson, Perry, Jenkins, Losman, J. Jones, Bell, Carr, Delhomme
Masterpiece: No Pricing
Production 1 Set
No Masterpiece card for Jenkins, Losman, J. Jones, Bell, Carr, Delhomme
AC-DHE Drew Henson 60.00
AC-CP Chris Perry 30.00
AC-KW Kellen Winslow Jr. 50.00

2004 Fleer Flair Autograph Collection Regular Panels

NM/M
Common Player: 15.00
Production To Indicated Quantity
AC-TB Tatum Bell/150 30.00
AC-DC David Carr/150 25.00
AC-MC Michael Clayton/150 30.00
AC-JD Jake Delhomme/150 25.00
AC-LE Lee Evans/220 20.00
AC-LF Larry Fitzgerald/82 125.00
AC-RG Rex Grossman/150 25.00
AC-DHA Dante Hall/150 20.00
AC-SJ Steven Jackson/150 40.00
AC-MJ Michael Jenkins/150 25.00
AC-JJ Julius Jones/150 50.00
AC-KJ Kevin Jones/150 50.00
AC-AL Ashley Lelie/150 15.00
AC-JL J.P. Losman/150 40.00
AC-EM Eli Manning/200 125.00
AC-WM Willis McGahee/175 30.00
AC-JP Julius Peppers/150 30.00
AC-PRA Patrick Ramsey/158 20.00
AC-PRI Philip Rivers/350 50.00
AC-BR Ben Roethlisberger /250 100.00
AC-DS Donte Stallworth/150 15.00
AC-JW Javon Walker/150 20.00
AC-REW Reggie Williams/350 25.00
AC-ROW Roy Williams WR/150 40.00
AC-RAW Rashaun Woods/350 25.00

2004 Fleer Flair Cuts and Glory Jersey

NM/M
Common Player: 25.00
Production 100 Sets
Level II: .75X-2X
Production 50 Sets
Kyle Boller & David Carr Level II cards not priced. 9 Boller & 10 Carr cards produced
Patch: No Pricing
Production 15 Sets

NM/M
Masterpiece: No Pricing
Producton 1 Set
CAG-AB Anquan Boldin 30.00
CAG-KB Kyle Boller 25.00
CAG-DC David Carr 50.00
CAG-JD Jake Delhomme 40.00
CAG-MF Marshall Faulk 60.00
CAG-DF DeShaun Foster 25.00
CAG-AG Ahman Green 50.00
CAG-MH Matt Hasselbeck 30.00
CAG-BL Byron Leftwich 50.00
CAG-DM Donovan McNabb 60.00
CAG-SM Santana Moss 25.00
CAG-CP Chad Pennington 40.00
CAG-WS Warren Sapp 30.00
CAG-BW Brian Westbrook 25.00

2004 Fleer Flair Gridiron Cuts Single Blue

NM/M
Common Player: 6.00
Production 200 Sets
Green: .5X-1X
Inserted In Retail Packs
Red: .75X-1.25X
Production 150 Sets
Silver: 1X-3X
Production 75 Sets
Die-Cut: 2X-5X
Production 25 Sets
Purple: No Pricing
Production 1 Set
GC-SA Shaun Alexander 8.00
GC-TB Tom Brady 15.00
GC-DC David Carr 10.00
GC-DC2 Daunte Culpepper 8.00
GC-MF Marshall Faulk 10.00
GC-BF Brett Favre 20.00
GC-AG Ahman Green 8.00
GC-JH Joey Harrington 6.00
GC-MH Matt Hasselbeck 6.00
GC-TH Torry Holt 6.00
GC-AJ Andre Johnson 6.00
GC-JL Jamal Lewis 8.00
GC-PM Peyton Manning 12.00
GC-DM Deuce McAllister 8.00
GC-DM2 Donovan McNabb 10.00
GC-SM Steve McNair 6.00
GC-RM Randy Moss 12.00
GC-CR Charles Rogers 6.00
GC-ES Emmitt Smith 12.00
GC-LT LaDainian Tomlinson 10.00

2004 Fleer Flair Gridiron Cuts Dual

No Pricing
Production 10 Sets
RM-BL Randy Moss, Byron Leftwich
BF-AG Brett Favre, Ahman Green
DM-MH Donovan McNabb, Marvin Harrison
JH-CR Joey Harrington, Charles Rogers
DM-LT Deuce McAllister, LaDainian Tomlinson
DC-AJ David Carr, Andre Johnson
TB-PM Tom Brady, Peyton Manning
TH-MF Torry Holt,Marshall Faulk
RM-DC Randy Moss, Daunte Culpepper
MH-PM Marvin Harrison, Peyton Manning

2004 Fleer Flair Hot Numbers

NM/M
Common Player: 2.00
Production 500 Sets
Retail Only
Gold: Numbered To Player's Jersey #
#75-99: 1X-3X
#25-74: 1X-5X
Less Than 25: No Pricing
1HN Peyton Manning 10.00
2HN Brett Favre 15.00
3HN Shaun Alexander 4.00
4HN Charles Rogers 4.00
5HN Jamal Lewis 4.00
6HN Clinton Portis 10.00
7HN Jeremy Shockey 4.00
8HN Daunte Culpepper 4.00
9HN Jake Delhomme 4.00
10HN Tom Brady 10.00
11HN Quincy Carter 4.00
12HN Donovan McNabb 6.00
13HN Byron Leftwich 10.00
14HN Santana Moss 2.00
15HN Marvin Harrison 4.00
16HN Randy Moss 10.00
17HN Laveranues Coles 2.00
18HN Andre Johnson 4.00
19HN Marshall Faulk 6.00
20HN Edgerrin James 6.00
21HN Ray Lewis 2.00
22HN Joey Harrington 4.00
23HN David Carr 6.00
24HN Ahman Green 4.00
25HN Torry Holt 4.00

2004 Fleer Flair Hot Numbers Game Used Blue

NM/M
Hot Numbers Blue
Common Player: 6.00
Production 200 Sets
Green: .5X-1X
Inserted In Retail Packs
Red: .75X-1.25X
Production 150 Sets
Silver: 1X-3X
Production 75 Sets
Gold: Numbered To Player's Jersey #
#75-99: 1X-3X
#25-74: 1X-5X
Less Than 25: No Pricing
Die-Cut: 2X-5X
Production 25 Sets
Purple: No Pricing
Production 1 Set
HN-SA Shaun Alexander 8.00
HN-TB Tom Brady 20.00
HN-PB Plaxico Burress 6.00
HN-DC David Carr 10.00
HN-QC Quincy Carter 6.00
HN-DC Daunte Culpepper 8.00
HN-JD Jake Delhomme 8.00
HN-MF Marshall Faulk 10.00
HN-BF Brett Favre 20.00
HN-AG Ahman Green 10.00
HN-JH Joey Harrington 6.00
HN-MH Marvin Harrison 8.00
HN-PH Priest Holmes 12.00
HN-TH Torry Holt 6.00
HN-EJ Edgerrin James 8.00
HN-AJ Andre Johnson 6.00
HN-CJ Chad Johnson 8.00
HN-BL Byron Leftwich 10.00
HN-JL Jamal Lewis 8.00
HN-RL Ray Lewis 6.00
HN-PM Peyton Manning 12.00
HN-DM Donovan McNabb 10.00
HN-CP Chad Pennington 10.00
HN-JP Jerry Porter 6.00
HN-CR Charles Rogers 6.00
HN-WS Warren Sapp 6.00
HN-JS Jeremy Shockey 8.00
HN-LT LaDainian Tomlinson 10.00
HN-BU Brian Urlacher 10.00
HN-RW Roy Williams 6.00

2004 Fleer Flair Lettermen

No Pricing
Numbered To Number Of Letters In Player's Last Name
1 Edgerrin James/5
2 Shaun Alexander/9
3 Tom Brady/5
4 Donovan McNabb/6
5 Emmitt Smith/5
6 Joey Harrington/10
7 Matt Hasselbeck/10
8 Priest Holmes/6
9 Brett Favre/5
10 Daunte Culpepper/9
11 Deuce McAllister/10
12 Jerry Rice/4
13 Jeremy Shockey/7
14 LaDainian Tomlinson/9
15 Michael Vick/4

2004 Fleer Flair Power Swatch Blue

NM/M
Common Player: 6.00
Production 200 Sets
Red: .75X-1.25X
Production 150 Sets
Silver: 1X-3X
Production 75 Sets
Gold: Numbered To Player's Jersey #
#75-99: 1X-3X
#25-74: 1X-5X
Less Than 25: No Pricing
Die-Cut: 2X-5X
Production 25 Sets
Production 25 Sets
Purple: No Pricing
Production 1 Set
PS-AB Anquan Boldin 6.00
PS-ST Stephen Davis 8.00
PS-MF Marshall Faulk 10.00
PS-RG Rex Grossman 6.00
PS-MH Marvin Harrison 8.00
PS-PH Priest Holmes 10.00
PS-EJ Edgerrin James 8.00
PS-AJ Andre Johnson 6.00
PS-CJ Chad Johnson 6.00
PS-BL Byron Leftwich 8.00
PS-DM Donovan McNabb 10.00
PS-RM Randy Moss 12.00
PS-JS Jeremy Shockey 6.00
PS-MV Michael Vick 15.00
PS-RW Ricky Williams 10.00

2004 Fleer Flair SIGnificant Cuts

NM/M
Common Player: 30.00
Production To Indicated Quantity
SIG-SA Shaun Alexander/100 30.00
SIG-JE John Elway/50 125.00
SIG-JH Joey Harrington/50 40.00
SIG-BL Byron Leftwich/25 75.00
SIG-JL Jamal Lewis/50
SIG-PM Peyton Manning/75 60.00
SIG-DM Dan Marino/50
SIG-DM Deuce McAllister/100 30.00
SIG-DM2 Donovan McNabb/100 40.00
SIG-JM Joe Montana/50
SIG-CP Chad Pennington/25
SIG-BS Barry Sanders/50 125.00
SIG-AV Adam Vinatieri/58 80.00
SIG-BW Brian Westbrook/25

1960 Fleer

Fleer's first venture into football depicted cards of players from the newly-formed American Football League. Outside of George Blanda, Sammy Baugh and several rookie cards detailed below, the set basically features a lot of no-names, many of whom appeared on their only card with this issue. It's not surprising that this set includes the most rookie cards of any other set issued since football cards were issued. (Not coincidentally, Topps' 1984 USFL set ranks second because of the amount of rookies who played in that league.) Rookie cards in this set include Sid Gillman (as a coach - this was his only card), Lou Saban (only card), Hank Stram (only card until Pro Set announcer cards), Abner Haynes, and Ron Mix. The card that carries the set is Jack Kemp's rookie card.

NM/M
Complete Set (132): 750.00
Common Player: 3.00
Wax Pack (6): 225.00
1 *Harvey White* 20.00
2 Tom "Corky" Tharp 3.00
3 Dan McGrew 3.00
4 Bob White 3.25
5 Dick Jamieson 3.00
6 Sam Salerno 3.00
7 *Sid Gillman* 20.00
8 Ben Preston 3.00
9 George Blanch 3.00
10 Bob Stransky 3.00
11 Fran Curci 3.00
12 George Shirkey 3.00
13 Paul Larson 3.00
14 John Stolte 3.00
15 *Serafino Frazio* 3.50
16 Tom Dimitroff 3.00
17 *Elbert Dubenion* 7.50
18 Hogan Wharton 3.00
19 Tom O'Connell 3.00
20 Sammy Baugh 40.00
21 Tony Sardisco 3.00
22 Alan Cann 3.00
23 Mike Hudock 3.00
24 Bill Atkins 3.00
25 Charlie Jackson 3.00
26 Frank Tripucka 4.00
27 Tony Teresa 3.00
28 Joe Amstutz 3.00
29 Bob Fee 3.00
30 Jim Baldwin 3.00
31 Jim Yates 3.00
32 Don Flynn 3.00
33 Ken Adamson 3.00
34 Ron Drzewiexki 3.00
35 J.W. Slack 3.00
36 Bob Yates 3.00
37 Gary Cobb 3.00
38 *Jacky Lee* 4.00
39 *Jack Spikes* 3.50
40 Jim Padgett 3.00
41 Jack Larsheid 3.00
42 Bob Reifsnyder 3.00
43 Fran Rogel 3.00
44 Ray Moss 3.00
45 Tony Banfield 3.25
46 George Herring 3.00

47	Willie Smith	3.00
48	Buddy Allen	3.00
49	Bill Brown	3.00
50	Ken Ford	3.00
51	Billy Kinard	3.00
52	Buddy Mayfield	3.00
53	Bill Krisher	3.25
54	Frank Bernardi	3.00
55	*Lou Saban*	3.50
56	Gene Cockrell	3.00
57	Sam Sanders	3.00
58	George Blanda	40.00
59	*Sherrill Headrick*	5.50
60	Carl Larpenter	3.00
61	Gene Prebola	3.00
62	Dick Chorovich	3.00
63	Bob McNamara	3.00
64	Tom Saidock	3.00
65	Willie Evans	3.00
66	*Billy Cannon*	16.00
67	Sam McCord	3.00
68	Mike Simmons	3.00
69	*Jim Swink*	3.50
70	Don Hitt	3.00
71	Gerhard Schwedes	3.00
72	Thurlow Cooper	3.00
73	*Abner Haynes*	16.00
74	Billy Shoemaker	3.00
75	Marv Lasater	3.00
76	*Paul Lowe*	15.00
77	Bruce Hartman	3.00
78	Blanche Martin	3.00
79	Gene Grabosky	3.00
80	Lou Rymkus	3.00
81	*Chris Burford*	5.50
82	Don Allen	3.00
83	Bob Nelson	3.00
84	Jim Woodard	3.00
85	Tom Rychlec	3.00
86	Bob Cox	3.00
87	Jerry Cornelison	3.00
88	Jack Work	3.00
89	Sam DeLuca	3.00
90	Rommie Loudd	3.00
91	Teddy Edmondson	3.00
92	Buster Ramsey	3.00
93	Doug Asad	3.00
94	Jimmy Harris	3.00
95	Lary Cundiff	3.00
96	*Richie Lucas*	3.50
97	Don Norwood	3.00
98	*Larry Grantham*	4.00
99	*Bill Mathis*	4.00
100	*Mel Branch*	4.00
101	Marvin Terrell	3.00
102	Charlie Flowers	3.25
103	John McMullan	3.00
104	Charlie Kaaihue	3.00
105	Joe Schaffer	3.00
106	Al Day	3.00
107	Johnny Carson	3.00
108	Alan Goldstein	3.00
109	Doug Cline	3.00
110	Al Carmichael	3.00
111	Bob Dee	3.00
112	John Bredice	3.00
113	Don Floyd	3.00
114	Ronnie Cain	3.00
115	Stan Flowers	3.00
116	*Hank Stram*	45.00
117	Bob Dougherty	3.00
118	*Ron Mix*	35.00
120	Elvin Caldwell	3.00
121	Bill Kimber	3.00
122	Jim Matheny	3.00
123	*Curley Johnson*	3.00
124	*Jack Kemp*	250.00
125	Ed Denk	3.00
126	Jerry McFarland	3.00
127	Dan Lamphear	3.00
128	*Paul Maguire*	16.00
129	Ray Collins	3.00
130	*Ron Burton*	5.00
131	Eddie Erdelatz	3.00
132	*Ron Beagle*	16.00

1960 Fleer Decals

This group of eight American Football League inserts was inserted in wax packs of Fleer football. The decals, which measure about 1-1/2" x 3-1/2", depict the logo of each AFL team. The decals were unnumbered.

		NM/M
Complete Set (8):		50.00
Common Team:		4.00
1	Boston Patriots	4.00
2	Buffalo Bills	5.00
3	Dallas Texans	5.00
4	Denver Broncos	5.00
5	Houston Oilers	5.00
6	Los Angeles Chargers	4.00
7	New York Titans	5.00
8	Oakland Raiders	5.00

1960 Fleer College Pennant Decals

This 19-decal set was also inserted into packs of 1960 Fleer Football along with the AFL Team Decals. These decals measured approximately 2-1/4" x 3" and included two colleges per card.

		NM/M
Complete Set (19):		180.00
Common Player:		8.00
1	Alabama/Yale	10.00
2	Army/Mississippi	8.00
3	California/Indiana	8.00
4	Duke/Notre Dame	18.00
5	Florida St./Kentucky	10.00
6	Georgia/Oklahoma	10.00
7	Houston/Iowa	8.00
8	Idaho St./Penn.	8.00
9	Iowa St./Penn State	14.00
10	Kansas/UCLA	12.00
11	Marquette/ New Mexico	8.00
12	Maryland/Missouri	8.00
13	Miss.South./ N.Carolina	8.00
14	Navy/Stanford	10.00
15	Nebraska/Purdue	12.00
16	Pittsburgh/Utah	8.00
17	SMU/West Virginia	8.00
18	So.Carolina/USC	10.00
19	Wake Forest/ Wisconsin	10.00

1961 Fleer

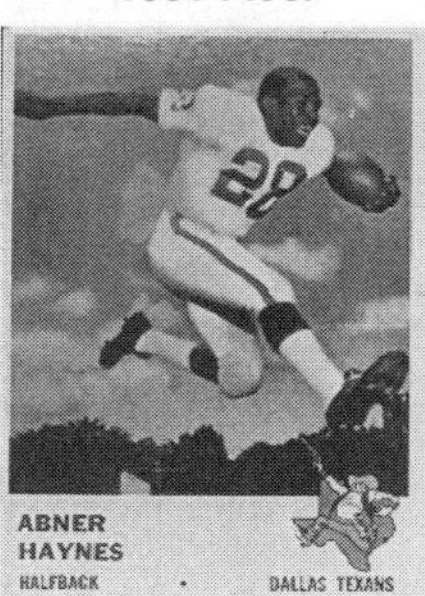

This 220-card set by Fleer - its biggest of the four it produced was the last to include NFL players (future sets would include only AFL players). Cards 1-132 showcase NFL players; 133-up depict AFLers. Cards are again grouped alphabetically by city name. A number of cards in this set are short-printed, and are indicated by (SP) in the following checklist. Rookies in the '61 Fleer issue include Don Meredith, Tom Flores, Don Maynard, and Jim Otto. Second-year cards include Night Train Lane (his rookie card was in '57), Forrest Gregg, Jerry Kramer, Jack Kemp and Ron Mix. (Key: SP meads short-printed).

		NM/M
Complete Set (220):		1,600
Common Player (1-132):		3.50
Common Player (133-220):		5.50
Series 1 Wax Pack (5):		215.00
Series 2 Wax Pack (5):		250.00
1	Ed Brown	12.00
2	Rick Casares	3.50
3	Willie Galimore	5.50
4	Jim Dooley	3.50
5	Harlon Hill	3.50
6	Stan Jones	5.00
7	J.C. Caroline	3.50
8	Joe Fortunato	3.50
9	Doug Atkins	6.25
10	Milt Plum	3.50
11	Jim Brown	150.00
12	Bobby Mitchell	8.00
13	Ray Renfro	3.50
14	Gern Nagler	3.50
15	Jim Shofner	3.50
16	Vince Costello	3.50
17	Galen Fiss	3.50
18	Walt Michaels	3.50
19	Bob Gain	3.50
20	Mal Hammack	3.50
21	Frank Mestnick	3.50
22	Bobby Joe Conrad	3.50
23	John David Crow	4.00
24	*Sonny Randle*	4.00
25	Don Gillis	3.50
26	Jerry Norton	3.50
27	Bill Stacy	3.50
28	Leo Sugar	3.50
29	Frank Fuller	3.50
30	John Unitas	70.00
31	Alan Ameche	8.00
32	Lenny Moore	12.00
33	Raymond Berry	12.00
34	Jim Mutscheller	3.50
35	Jim Parker	6.50
36	Bill Pellington	3.50
37	Gino Marchetti	6.00
38	Gene Lipscomb	5.50
39	Art Donovan	12.00
40	Eddie LeBaron	4.00
41	*Don Meredith*	150.00
42	Don McIlhenny	3.50
43	L.G. Dupre	3.50
44	Fred Dugan	3.50
45	Bill Howton	3.50
46	Duane Putnam	3.50
47	Gene Cronin	3.50
48	Jerry Tubbs	3.50
49	Clarence Peaks	3.50
50	*Ted Dean*	4.00
51	Tommy McDonald	3.50
52	Bill Barnes	3.50
53	Pete Retzlaff	3.50
54	Bobby Walston	3.50
55	Chuck Bednarik	12.00
56	Maxie Baughan	5.50
57	Bob Pellegrini	3.50
58	Jesse Richardson	3.50
59	*John Brodie*	50.00
60	J.D. Smith	3.50
61	*Ray Norton*	3.50
62	Monty Stickles	3.50
63	Bob St. Clair	5.00
64	Dave Baker	3.50
65	Abe Woodson	3.50
66	Matt Hazeltine	3.50
67	Leo Nomellini	7.00
68	Charley Conerly	13.00
69	Kyle Rote	5.50
70	Jack Stroud	3.50
71	Roosevelt Brown	5.00
72	Jim Patton	3.50
73	Erich Barnes	3.50
74	Sam Huff	12.00
75	Andy Robustelli	6.00
76	Dick Modzelewski	3.50
77	Roosevelt Grier	4.00
78	Earl Morrall	4.50
79	Jim Ninowski	3.50
80	*Nick Pietrosante*	4.00
81	Howard Cassady	3.50
82	Jim Gibbons	3.50
83	*Gail Cogdill*	3.50
84	Dick "Night Train" Lane	6.00
85	Yale Lary	6.00
86	Joe Schmidt	6.50
87	Darris McCord	3.50
88	Bart Starr	50.00
89	Jim Taylor	30.00
90	Paul Hornung	45.00
91	*Tom Moore*	5.00
92	*Boyd Dowler*	8.00
93	Max McGee	3.50
94	*Forrest Gregg*	8.50
95	Jerry Kramer	7.50
96	Jim Ringo	6.50
97	Bill Forester	3.50
98	Frank Ryan	3.50
99	Ollie Matson	9.50
100	Jon Arnett	3.50
101	*Dick Bass*	4.00
102	Jim Phillips	3.50
103	Del Shofner	3.50
104	Art Hunter	3.50
105	Lindon Crow	3.50
106	Les Richter	4.00
107	Lou Michaels	3.50
108	Ralph Guglielmi	4.00
109	Don Bosseler	3.50
110	John Olszewski	3.50
111	Bill Anderson	3.50
112	Joe Walton	4.00
113	Jim Schrader	3.50
114	Gary Glick	3.50
115	Ralph Felton	3.50
116	Bob Toneff	3.50
117	Bobby Layne	25.00
118	John Henry Johnson	8.00
119	Tom Tracy	3.50
120	*Jimmy Orr*	6.50
121	John Nisby	3.50
122	Dean Derby	3.50
123	John Reger	3.50
124	George Tarsovic	3.50
125	Ernie Stautner	6.00
126	George Shaw	3.50
127	Hugh McElhenny	9.00
128	Dick Haley	3.50
129	Dave Middleton	3.50
130	Perry Richards	3.50
131	Gene Johnson	3.50
132	Don Joyce	3.50
133	John "Chuck" Green	5.50
134	*Wray Carlton*	5.50
135	Richie Lucas	5.50
136	Elbert Dubenion	5.50
137	Tom Rychlec (SP)	5.50
138	Mark Yoho (SP)	5.50
139	Phil Blazer (SP)	5.50
140	Dan McGrew (SP)	5.50
141	Bill Atkins	5.50
142	*Archie Matsos*	5.50
143	Gene Grabosky	5.50
144	Frank Tripucka	6.00
145	Al Carmichael (SP)	6.00
146	Bob McNamara (SP)	6.00
147	*Lionel Taylor* (SP)	12.00
148	Eldon Danenhauer (SP)	6.00
149	Willie Smith	5.50
150	Carl Larpenter	5.50
151	Ken Adamson	5.50
152	*Goose Gonsoulin*	5.50
153	Joe Young (SP)	4.00
154	Gordy Molz (SP)	4.00
155	Jack Kemp (SP)	230.00
156	Charlie Flowers (SP)	6.00
157	Paul Lowe	7.00
158	Don Norton	5.50
159	Howard Clark	5.50
160	Paul Maguire	15.00
161	*Ernie Wright* (SP)	6.00
162	Ron Mix (SP)	16.00
163	Fred Cole (SP)	6.00
164	Jim Sears (SP)	6.00
165	Volney Peters	5.50
166	George Blanda	45.00
167	Jacky Lee	5.50
168	Bob White	5.50
169	Doug Cline (SP)	6.00
170	Dave Smith (SP)	6.00
171	Billy Cannon (SP)	8.00
172	Bill Groman (SP)	6.00
173	Al Jamison	5.50
174	Jim Norton	5.50
175	Dennit Morris	5.50
176	Don Floyd	5.50
177	Butch Songin (SP)	6.00
178	Billy Lott (SP)	6.00
179	Ron Burton (SP)	6.00
180	Jim Colchough (SP)	6.00
181	Charley Leo	5.50
182	Walt Cudzik	5.50
183	Fred Bruney	5.50
184	Ross O'Hanley	5.50
185	Tony Sardisco (SP)	6.00
186	Harry Jacobs (SP)	6.00
187	Bob Dee (SP)	6.00
188	*Tom Flores* (SP)	35.00
189	Jack Larsheid	5.50
190	Dick Christy	5.50
191	Alan Miller	5.50
192	Jim Smith	5.50
193	Gerald Burch (SP)	6.00
194	Gene Prebola (SP)	6.00
195	Alan Goldstein (SP)	6.00
196	Don Manoukian (SP)	6.00
197	*Jim Otto*	60.00
198	Wayne Crow	5.50
199	*Cotton Davidson*	5.50
200	*Randy Duncan*	5.50
201	Jack Spikes (SP)	6.00
202	*Johnny Robinson* (SP)	12.00
203	Abner Haynes (SP)	6.00
204	Chris Burford (SP)	6.00
205	Bill Krisher	5.50
206	Marvin Terrell	5.50
207	Jimmy Harris	5.50
208	Mel Branch (SP)	6.00
209	Paul Miller (SP)	6.00
210	Al Dorow (SP)	6.00
211	Dick Jamieson (SP)	6.00
212	Pete Hart	5.50
213	Bill Shockley	5.50
214	Dewey Bohling	5.50
215	*Don Maynard*	90.00
216	Bob Mischak	5.50
217	Mike Hudock (SP)	6.00
218	Bob Reifsnyder (SP)	6.00
219	Tom Saidock (SP)	6.00
220	Sid Youngelman (SP)	22.00

1961 Fleer Magic Message Blue Inserts

These 40 cards, which pose a trivia question on the front, instruct collectors to turn and wet the card to determine the answer. A line drawing also appears on the front, as does a card number, which is located in the lower right corner. Along the bottom of the card is a tag line which indicates the cards were printed by Business Service of Long Island, N.Y. The blank-backed cards, measuring 3" x 2-1/8", were inserts in 1961 Fleer football packs.

		NM/M
Complete Set (40):		125.00
Common Player:		4.00
1	First Sugar Bowl game	4.00
2	Point-A-Minute team	4.00
3	Gloomy Gil	4.00
4	College record for years coached	4.00
5	Two Platoon System	4.00
6	The only Sudden Death playoff	4.00
7	Sudden Death playoff	4.00
8	Longest field goal	4.00
9	Colorado All-American	5.00
10	Michigan All-American sportscaster	5.00
11	First North-South game	4.00
12	First Army-Navy game	4.00
13	Outfielder/All-American back	5.00
14	All-American Mr. Inside & Mr. Outside	5.00
15	The Thundering Herd	4.00
16	First NFL Championship playoff	4.00
17	Record for field goals dropkicked	4.00
18	Longest college winning streak	4.00
19	First collegian drafted	4.00
20	First team to use the huddle	4.00
21	The first Intercollegiate Champion	4.00
22	The first broadcast	4.00
23	The longest field goal	4.00
24	The tackling dummy	4.00
25	Greatest player in the half-century	5.00
26	The most touchdowns in a game	4.00
27	Who ran the wrong way?	4.00
28	The first college field goal	4.00
29	The first All-American team	4.00
30	The forward pass	4.00
31	The first college to use numbers	4.00
32	The first professional football game	4.00
33	Where is the Football Hall of Fame?	4.00
34	The Four Horsemen	5.00
35	The first Rose Bowl	4.00
36	Record for forward passes in a prof gam	4.00
37	Galloping Ghost	5.00
38	Rose Bowl in California	4.00
39	Seven Blocks of Granite	4.00
40	First game in the U.S.	4.00

1962 Fleer

Fleer's third of four early '60s sets included only AFL players this time around. Cards are again grouped by team, alphabetically by city. The only rookie card of note in this set is Gino Cappelletti; second-year cards in this issue are Don Maynard, Tom Flores and Jim Otto.

		NM/M
Complete Set (88):		800.00
Common Player:		6.00
Wax Pack (6):		400.00
1	Billy Lott	16.00
2	Ron Burton	7.00
3	*Gino Cappelletti*	17.00
4	Babe Parilli	7.00
5	Jim Colclough	6.00
6	Tony Sardisco	6.00
7	Walt Cudzik	6.00
8	Bob Dee	6.00
9	Tommy Addison	6.50
10	Harry Jacobs	6.00
11	Ross O'Hanley	6.00
12	Art Baker	6.00
13	John "Chuck" Green	6.00
14	Elbert Dubenion	3.00
15	Tom Rychlec	6.00
16	*Billy Shaw*	8.50
17	Ken Rice	6.00
18	Bill Atkins	6.00
19	Richie Lucas	6.00
20	Archie Matsos	6.00
21	Lavern Torczon	6.00
22	Warren Rabb	6.00
23	Jack Spikes	6.00
24	Cotton Davidson	6.00
25	*Abner Haynes*	9.00
26	Jimmy Saxton	6.00
27	Chris Burford	6.00
28	Bill Miller	6.00
29	Sherrill Headrick	6.00
30	*E.J. Holub*	9.50
31	*Jerry Mays*	9.00
32	Mel Branch	6.00
33	Paul Rochester	6.00
34	Frank Tripucka	8.00
35	Gene Mingo	6.00
36	Lionel Taylor	9.50
37	Ken Adamson	6.00
38	Eldon Danenhauer	6.00
39	Goose Gonsoulin	6.00
40	Gordy Holz	6.00
41	Bud McFadin	6.00
42	Jim Stinnette	6.00
43	Bob Hudson	6.00
44	George Herring	6.00
45	*Charley Tolar*	7.50
46	George Blanda	55.00
47	Billy Cannon	10.00
48	*Charlie Hennigan*	16.00
49	Bill Groman	6.00
50	Al Jamison	6.00
51	Tony Banfield	6.00
52	Jim Norton	6.00
53	Dennit Morris	6.00
54	Don Floyd	6.00
55	Ed Husmann	6.00
56	Robert Brooks	6.00
57	Al Dorow	6.00
58	Dick Christy	6.00
59	Don Maynard	35.00
60	Art Powell	10.00
61	Mike Hudock	6.00
62	Bill Mathis	6.00
63	Butch Songin	6.00
64	Larry Grantham	6.50
65	Nick Mumley	6.00
66	Tom Saidock	6.00
67	Alan Miller	6.00
68	Tom Flores	10.00
69	Bob Coolbaugh	6.00
70	George Fleming	6.00
71	*Wayne Hawkins*	6.00
72	Jim Otto	25.00
73	Wayne Crow	6.00
74	*Fred Willamson*	20.00
75	Tom Lauderback	6.00
76	Volney Peters	6.00
77	Charley Powell	6.00
78	Don Norton	6.00
79	Jack Kemp	250.00
80	Paul Lowe	9.00
81	Dave Kocourek	6.00
82	Ron Mix	13.00
83	Ernie Wright	6.00
84	Dick Harris	6.00
85	Bill Hudson	6.00
86	*Ernie Ladd*	30.00
87	Earl Faison	7.00
88	*Ron Nery*	16.00

1963 Fleer

After a four-year run, this 89-card set (88 player cards plus an unnumbered checklist) was the company's football farewell. (Fleer printed football "Teams in Action" sets in the '70s and '80s that featured NFL offenses and defenses, but apparently was unable to obtain a contract allowing the production of individual player cards. The 1963 Fleer football set showcases three of the most sought-after and rarest cards of the '60s - the checklist card (almost impossible to find in Mint condition), and cards #6 (Charles Long) and #64 (Bob Dougherty). The latter two cards were short-printed; it's believed both were pulled to make room for the checklist. The set includes AFL players only. Rookies featured in the set are Nick Buoniconti, Cookie Gilchrist, Keith Lincoln, Len Dawson and Lance Alworth. Gino Cappelletti's second-year card is in the set as well. (Key: SP means short-printed).

		NM/M
Complete Set (88):		2,000
Common Player:		8.00
Checklist:		400.00
Wax Pack (5):		450.00
1	*Larry Garron*	24.00
2	Babe Parilli	9.00
3	Ron Burton	8.00
4	Jim Colclough	8.00
5	Gino Cappelletti	11.00
6	*Charles Long* (SP)	180.00
7	*Bill Neighbors*	10.00
8	Dick Felt	8.00
9	Tommy Addison	8.00
10	*Nick Buoniconti*	75.00
11	Larry Eisenhauer	10.00
12	Bill Mathis	8.00
13	*Lee Grosscup*	10.00
14	Dick Christy	8.00
15	Don Maynard	45.00
16	*Alex Kroll*	8.00
17	Bob Mischak	8.00
18	Dainard Paulson	8.00
19	Lee Riley	8.00
20	Larry Grantham	8.00
21	Hubert Bobo	8.00
22	Nick Mumley	8.00
23	*Cookie Gilchrist*	40.00
24	Jack Kemp	250.00
25	Wray Carlton	8.00
26	Elbert Dubenion	8.00
27	Ernie Warlick	8.00
28	Billy Shaw	8.00
29	Ken Rice	8.00
30	Booker Edgerson	8.00
31	Ray Abbruzzese	8.00
32	Mike Stratton	9.00
33	Tom Sestak	10.00
34	Charlie Tolar	8.00
35	Dave Smith	8.00
36	George Blanda	55.00
37	Billy Cannon	9.00
38	Charlie Hennegan	13.00
39	*Bob Talamini*	10.00
40	Jim Norton	8.00
41	Tony Banfield	8.00
42	Doug Cline	8.00
43	Don Floyd	8.00
44	Ed Husmann	8.00
45	*Curtis McClinton*	12.00
46	Jack Spikes	8.00
47	*Len Dawson*	250.00
48	Abner Haynes	10.00
49	Chris Burford	8.00
50	*Fred Arbanas*	12.00
51	Johnny Robinson	9.00
52	E.J. Holub	8.00
53	Sherrill Headrick	8.00
54	Mel Branch	8.00
55	Jerry Mays	8.00
56	Cotton Davidson	8.00
57	*Clem Daniels*	15.00
58	Bo Roberson	8.00
59	Art Powell	10.00
60	Bob Coolbaugh	8.00
61	Wayne Hawkins	8.00
62	Jim Otto	30.00
63	Fred Williamson	9.00
64	Bob Dougherty (SP)	230.00
65	Dalva Allen	8.00
66	Chuck McMutry	8.00
67	Gerry McDougall	8.00
68	Tobin Rote	9.00
69	Paul Lowe	10.00
70	*Keith Lincoln*	25.00
71	Dave Kocourek	8.00
72	*Lance Alworth*	250.00
73	Ron Mix	22.00
74	*Charles McNeil*	10.00
75	Emil Karas	8.00
76	Ernie Ladd	15.00
77	Earl Faison	8.00
78	Jim Stinnette	8.00
79	Frank Tripucka	9.50
80	Don Stone	8.00
81	Bob Scarpitto	8.00
82	Lionel Taylor	10.50
83	Jerry Tarr	8.00
84	Eldon Danehauer	8.00
85	Goose Gonsoulin	8.00
86	Jim Fraser	8.00
87	Chuck Gavin	10.00
88	Bud McFadin	20.00

1972 Fleer Quiz

This 28-card set was issued at a rate of one per pack with Fleer cloth team patches. Cards measure 2-1/2" x 4" and feature three questions about players and events, with answers upside down. Each card has the words "Official Football Quiz" across the top, a card number in the lower right hand corner and a blank back.

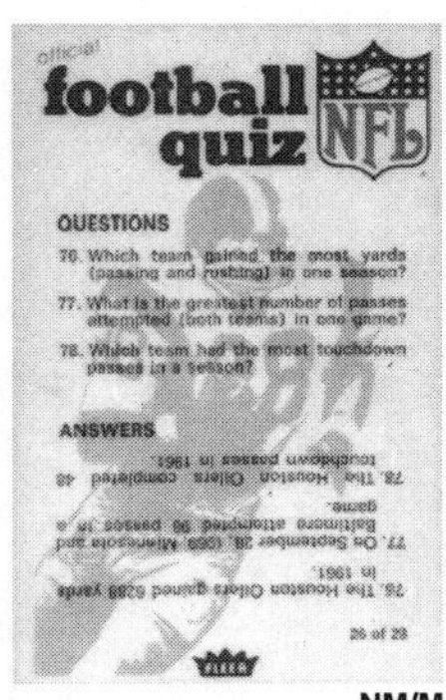

official
football quiz
NFL
QUESTIONS
76. Which team gained the most yards (passing and rushing) in one season?
77. What is the greatest number of passes attempted (both teams) in one game?
78. Which team had the most touchdown passes in a season?
ANSWERS
26 of 29

NM/M
Complete Set (28): 45.00
Common Player: 2.50
1 Questions 1-3 2.50
2 Questions 4-6 2.50
3 Questions 7-9 2.50
4 Questions 10-12 2.50
5 Questions 13-15 2.50
6 Questions 16-18 2.50
7 Questions 19-21 2.50
8 Questions 22-24 2.50
9 Questions 25-27 2.50
10 Questions 28-30 2.50
11 Questions 31-33 2.50
12 Questions 34-36 2.50
13 Questions 37-39 2.50
14 Questions 40-42 2.50
15 Questions 43-45 2.50
16 Questions 46-48 2.50
17 Questions 49-51 2.50
18 Questions 52-54 2.50
19 Questions 55-57 2.50
20 Questions 58-60 2.50
21 Questions 61-63 2.50
22 Questions 64-66 2.50
23 Questions 67-69 2.50
24 Questions 70-72 2.50
25 Questions 73-75 2.50
26 Questions 76-78 2.50
27 Questions 79-81 2.50
28 Questions 82-84 2.50

1973 Fleer Pro Bowl Scouting Report

The 14-card, blank backed set explains the ideal responsibilities and assignments of each player on an NFL team. These unnumbered cards were found at a rate of one per pack with two cloth football logos from 1972.

NM/M
Complete Set (14): 35.00
Common Player: 3.00
1 Center 3.00
2 Cornerback 3.00
3 Defensive End 3.00
4 Defensive Tackle 3.00
5 Guard 3.00
6 Kicker 3.00
7 Linebacker 3.00
8 Offensive Tackle 3.00
9 Punter 3.00
10 Quarterback 3.00
11 Running Back 3.00
12 Safety 3.00
13 Tight End 3.00
14 Wide Receiver 3.00

1974 Fleer Big Signs

The 1974 version of Big Signs is generally considered a Series II issue, but is credited to 1968 in roman numerals on the back. The cards measure 7-3/4" x 11-1/2" and have blank backs that are unnumbered. The 1974 set was issued in a brown box, while the fronts contain generic, faceless color drawings. Two 26-card Big Signs sets were produced by Fleer that carry a 1968 copyright on them, but one released in 1970 with this series releasing in 1974. The former version was issued in a green box and contains the team name in small letters across the top, while the 1974 version has the team name in bold letters across the card bottom.

NM/M
Complete Set (26): 45.00
Common Player: 2.50
1 Atlanta Falcons 2.50
2 Baltimore Colts 2.50
3 Buffalo Bills 2.50
4 Chicago Bears 4.00
5 Cincinnati Bengals 2.50
6 Cleveland Browns 2.50
7 Dallas Cowboys 4.00
8 Denver Broncos 2.50
9 Detroit Lions 2.50
10 Green Bay Packers 4.00
11 Houston Oilers 2.50
12 Kansas City Chiefs 2.50
13 Los Angeles Rams 2.50
14 Miami Dolphins 4.00
15 Minnesota Vikings 2.50
16 New England Patriots 2.50
17 New Orleans Saints 2.50
18 New York Giants 2.50
19 New York Jets 2.50
20 Oakland Raiders 4.00
21 Philadelphia Eagles 2.50
22 Pittsburgh Steelers 4.00
23 St. Louis Cardinals 2.50
24 San Diego Chargers 2.50
25 San Francisco 49ers 4.00
26 Washington Redskins 4.00

1974 Fleer Hall of Fame

These cards were issued one per pack, along with two cloth stickers featuring team logos. Each card front has a black- and-white player action photo, with a set logo and "The Immortal Role" at the bottom of the card. The cards, which are unnumbered, are listed below alphabetically and feature 50 players who have been enshrined in the Pro Football Hall of Fame in Canton, Ohio. The Hall of Fame logo appears on the back of the card, along with biographical information about the player. Each card measures 2-1/2" x 4".

NM/M
Complete Set (50): 50.00
Common Player: 1.00
(1) Cliff Battles 1.00
(2) Sammy Baugh 1.50
(3) Chuck Bednarik 1.00
(4) Bert Bell 1.00
(5) Paul Brown 1.00
(6) Joe Carr 1.00
(7) Guy Chamberlin 1.00
(8) Earl "Dutch" Clark 1.00
(9) Jimmy Conzelman 1.00
(10) Art Donovan 1.00
(11) John (Paddy) Driscoll 1.00
(12) Billy Dudley 1.00
(13) Dan Fortmann 1.00
(14) Otto Graham 1.00
(15) Harold "Red" Grange 2.00
(16) George Halas 1.00
(17) Mel Hein 1.00
(18) Fats Henry 1.25
(19) Bill Hewitt 1.00
(20) Clarke Hinkle 1.25
(21) Elroy (Crazylegs) Hirsch 1.00
(22) Robert "Cal" Hubbard 1.00
(23) Lamar Hunt 1.00
(24) Don Hutson 1.00
(25) Earl (Curly) Lambeau 1.25
(26) Bobby Layne 1.00
(27) Vince Lombardi 2.00
(28) Sid Luckman 1.00
(29) Gino Marchetti 1.25
(30) Ollie Matson 1.00
(31) George McAfee 1.00
(32) Hugh McElhenny 1.00
(33) Johnny "Blood" McNally 1.00
(34) Marion Motley 1.00
(35) Bronko Nagurski 1.50
(36) Ernie Nevers 1.00
(37) Leo Nomellini 1.25
(38) Steve Owen 1.00
(39) Joe Perry 1.00
(40) Pete Pihos 1.25
(41) Andy Robustelli 1.00
(42) Ken Strong 1.00
(43) Jim Thorpe 2.00
(44) Y.A. Tittle 1.00
(45) Charlie Trippi 1.00
(46) Emlen Tunnell 1.25
(47) Clyde "Bulldog" Turner 1.00
(48) Norm Van Brocklin 1.00
(49) Steve Van Buren 1.00
(50) Bob Waterfield 1.25

1975 Fleer Hall of Fame

These 84 cards, which feature players who have been inducted into the Football Hall of Fame, can be distinguished from the 1974 cards by the card numbers which appear on the card backs. Fifty of the cards in the set are similar to the 1974 cards, except the fronts have brown borders, not white ones like the 1974 cards have. Each card measures 2-1/2" x 4". They were issued in wax packs along with cloth team logo stickers.

NM/M
Complete Set (84): 30.00
Common Player: .35
1 Jim Thorpe 1.00
2 Cliff Battles .35
3 Bronko Nagurski .75
4 Harold "Red" Grange 1.00
5 Guy Chamberlin .35
6 Joe Carr .35
7 George Halas .50
8 Jimmy Conzelman .35
9 George McAfee .35
10 Clarke Hinkle .35
11 John Driscoll .35
12 Mel Hein .35
13 Johnny McNally .35
14 Earl Clark .35
15 Steve Owen .35
16 Bill Hewitt .35
17 Robert Hubbard .35
18 Don Hutson .50
19 Ernie Nevers .50
20 Dan Fortmann .35
21 Ken Strong .35
22 Chuck Bednarik .50
23 Bert Bell .35
24 Paul Brown .50
25 Art Donovan .50
26 Bill Dudley .35
27 Otto Graham 1.00
28 Fats Henry .35
29 Elroy Hirsch .50
30 Lamar Hunt .50
31 Earl Lambeau .75
32 Vince Lombardi .75
33 Sid Luckman .75
34 Gino Marchetti .50
35 Ollie Matson .50
36 Hugh McElhenny .50
37 Marion Motley .50
38 Leo Nomellini .35
39 Joe Perry .50
40 Andy Robustelli .35
41 Pete Pihos .35
42 Y.A. Tittle .50
43 Charlie Trippi .35
44 Emlen Tunnell .35
45 Clyde Turner .35
46 Norm Van Brocklin .50
47 Steve Van Buren .50
48 Bob Waterfield .75
49 Bobby Layne .50
50 Sammy Baugh 1.00
51 Joe Guyon .35
52 William Roy Lyman .35
53 George Trafton .35
54 Albert G. Edwards .35
55 Ed Healey .35
56 Mike Michalske .35
57 Alex Wojciechowicz .35
58 Dante Lavelli .35
59 George Connor .35
60 Wayne Millner .35
61 Jack Christiansen .35
62 Roosevelt Brown .35
63 Joe Stydahar .35
64 Ernie Stautner .50
65 Jim Parker .50
66 Raymond Berry .50
67 George Preston Marshall .35
68 Clarence Parker .50
69 Earle Neale .35
70 Tim Mara .35
71 Hugh Ray .35
72 Tom Fears .50
73 Arnie Herber .35
74 Walt Kiesling .35
75 Frank Kinard .35
76 Tony Canadeo .35
77 Bill George .35
78 Art Rooney .50
79 Joe Schmidt .50
80 Dan Reeves .35
81 Lou Groza .50
82 Charles W. Bidwill .35
83 Lenny Moore .50
84 Dick "Night Train" Lane .50

1976 Fleer Team Action

Beginning in 1976, and continuing through 1988, Fleer produced a series of "Team Action" cards showing football action shots but not identifying the individual players. All cards measure the standard 2-1/2" x 3-1/2". Because the sets did not contain individual player cards they have held little interest for collectors, and very few cards have any premium value. Generally, only the cards priced above common price are those with recognizable superstars prominently displayed in the action scene. The various years of issue can be determined by the border color on the front and the copyright date on the back. Sets from 1976 through 1984 and 1987 and 1988 feature an odd-numbered offensive card and an even-numbered defensive card for each NFL team. The backs list statistics from the previous year. In 1985 and 1986 each team had a third "In Action" card added - the backs of which show team schedules for the upcoming season. All sets (except 1988) are essentially numbered to correspond to team-city alphabetical order. The 1976 set is actually comprised of 66 stickercards and is quite scarce. For each subsequent year (up through 1980) the number of cards in the set was increased by one, adding a card for the most recent Super Bowl. Beginning in 1981, all sets were enlarged to 88 cards. Fleer's initial set in 1976 has two cards per team, plus 10 Super Bowl cards. The cards were issued in four-card wax packs, without inserts. It includes a Jack Lambert "rookie", a Joe Namath (not found in Topps) and the only team action card of O.J. Simpson.

NM/M
Complete Set (66): 375.00
Common Card: 5.00
Common SB Card: 7.50
1 Baltimore Colts (High Scorers) 5.25
2 Baltimore Colts (Effective Tackle) 5.00
3 Buffalo Bills (Perfect Blocking) 5.00
4 Buffalo Bills (The Sack) 5.00
5 Cincinnati Bengals (Being Hit Behind The Runner) 5.00
6 Franco Harris Cincinnati Bengals (A Little Help) 9.00
7 Cleveland Browns (Blocking Tight End) 5.00
8 Cleveland Browns (Stopping the Double Threat) 5.00
9 Denver Broncos (The Swing Pass) 5.00
10 Denver Broncos (The Gang Tackle) 5.00
11 Dan Pastorini Houston Oilers (Short Zone Flooded) 6.00
12 Franco Harris Houston Oilers (Run Stoppers) 9.00
13 Kansas City Chiefs (Off On the Ball) 5.00
14 Kansas City Chiefs (Forcing the Scramble) 5.00
15 Bob Griese Miami Dolphins (Pass Protection) 10.00
16 Miami Dolphins (Natural Turf) 6.00
17 New England Patriots (Quicker Than the Eye) 5.00
18 New England Patriots (The Rugby Touch) 5.00
19 John Riggins, Joe Namath New York Jets (They Run, Too) 16.50
20 O.J. Simpson New York Jets (The Buck Stops Here) 15.00
21 Oakland Raiders (A Strong Offense) 6.00
22 Oakland Raiders (High and Low) 6.00
23 Terry Bradshaw, Franco Harris, Rocky Bleier Pittsburgh Steelers (The Pitch-Out) 14.00
24 Jack Lambert Pittsburgh Steelers (The Takeaway) 15.00
25 San Diego Chargers (Run to Daylight) 5.00
26 San Diego Chargers (The Swarm) 5.00
27 Tampa Bay Buccaneers (Stadium) 5.00
28 Tampa Bay Bucaneers (Buccaneers Uniform) 5.00
29 Atlanta Falcons (A Key Block) 5.00
30 Robert Newhouse Atlanta Falcons (Breakthrough) 5.00
31 Chicago Bears (An Inside Look) 5.00
32 Chicago Bears (Defensive Emphasis) 5.00
33 Robert Newhouse Dallas Cowboys (Eight-Yard Burst) 6.00
34 Dallas Cowboys (The Big Return) 6.00
35 Detroit Lions (Power Sweep) 5.00
36 Detroit Lions (A Tough Defense) 5.00
37 Green Bay Packers (Tearaway Gain) 5.00
38 Green Bay Packers (Good Support) 5.00
39 Los Angeles Rams 5.00
40 Los Angeles Rams (Low-Point Defense) 5.00
41 Fran Tarkenton, Chuck Foreman Minnesota Vikings (The Running Guards) 10.00
42 Minnesota Vikings (A Stingy Defense) 5.00
43 New York Giants (The Quick Opener) 5.00
44 New York Giants (Defending a Tradition) 5.00
45 Archie Manning New Orleans Saints (Head for the Hole) 6.00
46 New Orleans Saints (The Contain Man) 5.00
47 Philadelphia Eagles (Line Signals) 5.00
48 Philadelphia Eagles (Don't Take Sides) 5.00
49 San Francisco 49ers (The Clues) 5.00
50 San Francisco 49ers (Goal-Line Stand) 5.00
51 Jim Hart St. Louis Cardinals (Nonskid Handoff) 6.00
52 St. Louis Cardinals (Strong Pursuit) 5.00
53 Seattle Seahawks (Stadium) 5.25
54 Seattle Seahawks (Uniform) 5.25
55 Billy Kilmer Washington Redskins (A Fancy Passing) 6.00
56 Chris Hanburger Washington Redskins (Let's Go Defense) 5.00
57 Jim Taylor Super Bowl I (Green Bay vs. Kansas City) 7.50
58 Ben Davidson Super Bowl II (Green Bay vs. Oakland) 7.50
59 Super Bowl III (New York vs. Baltimore) 7.50
60 Super Bowl IV (Kansas City vs. Minnesota) 7.50
61 Super Bowl V (Baltimore vs. Dallas) 7.50
62 Roger Staubach, Walt Garrison Super Bowl VI (Dallas vs. Miami) 16.00
63 Larry Csonka Super Bowl VII (Miami vs. Washington) 9.50
64 Larry Csonka Super Bowl VIII (Miami vs. Minnesota) 9.50
65 Super Bowl IX (Pittsburgh vs. Minnesota) 7.50
66 Terry Bradshaw, Franco Harris Super Bowl X (Pittsburgh vs. Dallas) 19.00

1977 Fleer Team Action

The 1977 set Fleer set has white borders and is complete at 67 cards, two for each NFL team and one for each Super Bowl. Odd-numbered cards picture offensive teams; defensive squads are on even-numbered cards. The set features Joe Namath (not found in 1977 Topps) and two different first-year Fleer Walter Payton cards. The packs had four cards and four team logo stickers.

NM/M
Complete Set (67): 80.00
Common Card: 1.00
Common SB Card: 1.50
1 Bert Jones Baltimore Colts (The Easy Chair) 1.75
2 Baltimore Colts (A Handy Solution) 1.00
3 Buffalo Bills (Blocking Tight End) 1.00
4 Buffalo Bills (Search and Destroy) 1.00
5 Ken Anderson Cincinnati Bengals (Cutting on a Rug) 1.50
6 Cincinnati Bengals (Strength in the Middle) 1.00
7 Brian Sipe Cleveland Browns(Snap, Drop, Set) 1.25
8 Cleveland Browns (High and Low) 1.00
9 Denver Broncos (Green Light) 1.25
10 Denver Broncos (Help From Behind) 1.25
11 Houston Oilers (Room to Move) 1.00
12 Houston Oilers (For The Defense) 1.00
13 Kansas City Chiefs (Chance to Motor) 1.00
14 Kansas City Chiefs (From the Ground Up) 1.00
15 Miami Dolphins (Eye of the Storm) 1.25
16 Miami Dolphins (When Man Takes Flight) 1.25
17 New England Patriots (Turning the Corner) 1.00
18 New England Patriots (A Matter of Inches) 1.00
19 Joe Namath New York Jets (Keeping Him Clean) 7.25
20 New York Jets (Plugging the Leaks) 1.00
21 Oakland Raiders (On Solid Ground) 1.25
22 Oakland Raiders (3-4 and Shut the Door) 1.25
23 Rocky Bleier Pittsburgh Steelers (Daylight Saving Time) 1.25
24 Pittsburgh Steelers (A Controlled Swarm) 1.25
25 Dan Fouts San Diego Chargers (Youth on the Move) 3.75
26 San Diego Chargers (A Rude Housewarming) 1.00
27 Jim Zorn Seattle Seahawks (Play Action Pass) 2.00
28 Seattle Seahawks (Birds of Prey) 1.25
29 Atlanta Falcons (Ad-Libbing on Defense) 1.00
30 Atlanta Falcons (A Futile Chase) 1.00
31 Walter Payton Chicago Bears (Follow Me) 6.75
32 Chicago Bears (A Nose for the Ball) 1.00
33 Dallas Cowboys (The Plunge) 1.25
34 Ed "Too Tall" Jones Dallas Cowboys (Unassisted Sack) 3.00
35 Detroit Lions (Motor City Might) 1.00
36 Detroit Lions (Block Party) 1.00
37 Green Bay Packers (Another Era) 1.00
38 Walter Payton Green Bay Packers (Face-to-Face) 6.50
39 Los Angeles Rams (Personal Escort) 1.00
40 Los Angeles Rams (A Closed Case) 1.00
41 Minnesota Vikings (Nothing Fancy) 1.00
42 Minnesota Vikings (Lending a Hand) 1.00
43 New Orleans Saints (Ample Protection) 1.00
44 New Orleans Saints (Well-Timed Contact) 1.00
45 New York Giants (Quick Pitch) 1.00
46 New York Giants (In a Pinch) 1.00
47 Philadelphia Eagles (When to Fly) 1.00
48 Philadelphia Eagles (Swooping Defense) 1.00
49 Jim Hart St. Louis Cardinals (Speed Outside) 1.25
50 St. Louis Cardinals (The Circle Tightens) 1.00
51 Gene Washington San Francisco 49ers (Sideline Route) 1.25
52 San Francisco 49ers (The Gold Rush) 1.00
53 Tampa Bay Buccaneers (A Rare Occasion) 1.00
54 Tampa Bay Buccaneers (Expansion Blues) 1.00
55 Joe Theismann Washington Redskins (Splitting the Seam) 2.75
56 Washington Redskins (The Hands of Time) 1.00
57 Super Bowl I (Green Bay vs. Kansas City) 1.50
58 Super Bowl II (Green Bay vs. Oakland) 1.50
59 Tom Matte Super Bowl III (New York vs. Baltimore) 1.50
60 Super Bowl IV (Kansas City vs. Minnesota) 1.50
61 Super Bowl V (Baltimore vs. Dallas) 1.50
62 Walt Garrison, Roger Staubach Super Bowl VI (Dallas vs. Miami) 4.25
63 Larry Csonka Super Bowl VII (Miami vs. Washington) 2.25
64 Larry Csonka Super Bowl VIII (Miami vs. Minnesota) 2.25
65 Super Bowl IX (Pittsburgh vs. Minnesota) 1.50
66 Terry Bradshaw, Franco Harris Super Bowl X (Pittsburgh vs. Dallas) 3.75
67 Ken Stabler Super Bowl XI (Oakland vs. Minnesota) 3.75

1978 Fleer Team Action

The 1978 Fleer set contains 68 cards, two for each team and for each Super Bowl. The borders are yellow. Fleer continued with its odd-for-offense and even-for-defense numbering scheme. The set is highlighted by a Tony Dorsett "rookie" card. Seven cards and four team logo stickers were in each pack.

NM/M
Complete Set (68): 50.00
Common Card: .55
Common SB Card: .70
1 Atlanta Falcons (Sticking to Basics) .60
2 Atlanta Falcons (In Pursuit) .55
3 New England Colts (Foward Plunge) .55
4 New England Colts (Stacking It Up) .55
5 Buffalo Bills (Daylight Breakers) .55
6 Buffalo Bills (Swarming Defense) .55
7 Walter Payton Chicago Bears (Up the Middle) 6.75
8 Chicago Bears (Rejuvenated Defense) .55
9 Ken Anderson Cincinnati Bengals (Poise and Execution) 1.25
10 Cincinnati Bengals (Down-to-Earth) .55
11 Greg Pruitt Cleveland Browns (Breakaway) .80
12 Ken Anderson Cleveland Browns (Red Dogs) 1.00
13 Dorsett Dallas Cowboys (Up and Over) 7.50

14 Dallas Cowboys (Doomsday II) .75
15 Denver Broncos (Mile-Hile Offense) .75
16 Walter Payton Denver Broncos (Orange Crush) 5.25
17 Detroit Lions (End-Around) .55
18 Detroit Lions (Special Teams) .55
19 Green Bay Packers (Running Strong) .55
20 Green Bay Packers (Tearin' em Down) .55
21 Houston Oilers (Goal-Line Drive) .55
22 Houston Oilers (Interception) .55
23 Ed Podolak Kansas City Chiefs (Running Wide) .60
24 Kansas City Chiefs (Armed Defense) .55
25 Los Angeles Rams (Rushing Power) .55
26 Los Angeles Rams (Backing the Line) .55
27 Bob Griese Miami Dolphins (Protective Pocket) 2.50
28 Miami Dolphins (Life in the Pit) .75
29 Chuck Foreman Minnesota Vikings (Storm Breakers) .80
30 Minnesota Vikings (Blocking the Kick) .55
31 New England Patriots (Clearing the Way) .55
32 New England Patriots (One-on-One) .55
33 New Orleans Saints (Extra Yardage) .55
34 New Orleans Saints (Drag-Down Defense) .55
35 New York Giants (Ready, Aim, Fire) .55
36 New York Giants (Meeting of Minds) .55
37 New York Jets (Take-Off) .55
38 New York Jets (Ambush) .55
39 Oakland Raiders (Power 31 Left) .75
40 Oakland Raiders (Welcoming Committee) .75
41 Philadelphia Eagles (Taking Flight) .55
42 Philadelphia Eagles (Soaring High) .55
43 Pittsburgh Steelers (Ironclad Offense) .75
44 Jack Lambert Pittsburgh Steelers (Curtain Closes) 2.00
45 St. Louis Cardinals (A Good Bet) .55
46 St. Louis Cardinals (Gang Tackle) .55
47 San Diego Chargers (Circus Catch) .55
48 San Diego Chargers (Charge) .55
49 San Francisco 49ers (Follow the Block) .55
50 San Francisco 49ers (Goal-Line Stand) .55
51 Seattle Seahawks (Finding Daylight) .60
52 Seattle Seahawks (Rushing the Pass) .60
53 Tampa Bay Buccaneers (Play Action) .55
54 Tampa Bay Buccaneers (Youth on the Move) .55
55 Washington Redskins (Renegade Runners) .55
56 Washington Redskins (Dual Action) .55
57 Bart Starr Super Bowl I (Green Bay vs. Kansas City) 2.25
58 Super Bowl II (Green Bay vs. Oakland) .70
59 Super Bowl III (New York vs. Baltimore) .70
60 Super Bowl IV (Kansas City vs. Minnesota) .70
61 Super Bowl V (Baltimore vs. Dallas) .70
62 Super Bowl VI (Dallas vs. Miami) .70
63 Super Bowl VII (Miami vs. Washington) .70
64 Larry Csonka Super Bowl VIII (Miami vs. Minnesota) 1.75
65 Terry Bradshaw,Franco Harris Super Bowl IX (Pittsburgh vs. Minnesota) 3.00
66 Super Bowl X (Pittsburgh vs. Dallas) .70
67 Ken Stabler Super Bowl XI (Oakland vs. Minnesota) 2.00
68 Roger Staubach,Tony Dorsett Super Bowl XII (Dallas vs. Denver) 5.75

1979 Fleer Team Action

The 1979 white-bordered set contains 69 cards, two for each team plus one for each Super Bowl. The cards are numbered to correspond to team-city alphabetical order, followed by a chronological series of all 13 Super Bowls. An odd-offensive and even-defensive numbering format is used again. Earl Campbell's rookie card is the set's most significant. Packs were distributed with seven cards and three logo stickers.

	NM/M
Complete Set (69):	40.00
Common Card:	.50
Common SB Card:	.60

1 Atlanta Falcons (What's Up Front Counts) .80
2 Atlanta Falcons (Following the Bouncing Ball) .50
3 Baltimore Colts (Big Enough to Drive a Truck Through) .50
4 Baltimore Colts (When the Defense Becomes the Offense) .50
5 Buffalo Bills (Full Steam Ahead) .50
6 Buffalo Bills (Three's a Crowd) .50
7 Chicago Bears (Moving Out as One) .50
8 Chicago Bears (Stack' Em Up) .50
9 Cincinnati Bengals (Out in the Open Field) .50
10 Cincinnati Bengals (Sandwiched) .50
11 Cleveland Browns (Protective Pocket) .50
12 Cleveland Browns (Shake Rattle and Roll) .50
13 Tony Dorsett Dallas Cowboys Paving the Way) 3.75
14 Dallas Cowboys (The Right Place at the Right Time) .65
15 Denver Broncos (A Stable of Runners) .65
16 Denver Broncos (Orange Crush) .65
17 Detroit Lions (Through the Line) .50
18 Detroit Lions (Tracked Down) .50
19 Green Bay Packers (Power Play) .50
20 Green Bay Packers (Four-To-One Odds) .50
21 Earl Campbell Houston Oilers (Offensive Gusher) 7.00
22 Houston Oilers (Gotcha) .50
23 Kansas Chiefs (Get Wings) .50
24 Kansas City Chiefs (Ambushed) .50
25 Los Angeles Rams (Men in the Middle) .50
26 Los Angeles Rams (Nowhere To Go But Down) .50
27 Miami Dolphins (Escort Service) .65
28 Miami Dolphins (All For One) .65
29 Minnesota Vikings (Up and Over) .50
30 Minnesota Vikings (The Purple Gang) .50
31 New England Patriots (Prepare For Takeoff) .50
32 New England Patriots (Dept. of Defense) .50
33 Archie Manning New Orleans Saints (Bombs Away) .85
34 New Orleans Saints (Duel in the Dome) .50
35 New York Giants (Battle of the Line of Scrimmage) .50
36 New York Giants (Piled Up) .50
37 New York Jets (Hitting the Hole) .50
38 New York Jets (Making Sure) .50
39 Ken Stabler Oakland Raiders (Left-Handed Strength) 2.00
40 Oakland Raiders (Black Sunday) .85
41 Philadelphia Eagles (Ready Aim Fire) .50
42 Philadelphia Eagles (Closing In) .50
43 Pittsburgh Steelers (Anchor Man) .65
44 Pittsburgh Steelers (The Steel Curtain) .85
45 Jim Hart St. Louis Cardinals (High Altitude Bomber) .85
46 St. Louis Cardinals (Three On One) .50
47 San Diego Chargers (Charge) .50
48 San Diego Chargers (Special Teams Shot) .50
49 San Francisco 49ers (In For the Score) .50
50 San Francisco 49ers (Nothing But Red Shirts) .50
51 Seattle Seahawks (North-South Runner) .65
52 Seattle Seahawks (The Sting) .65
53 Tampa Bay Buccaneers (Hitting Paydirt) .50
54 Tmpa Bay Buccaneers (Making' Em Pay the Price) .50
55 Washington Redskins (On the Warpath) .50
56 Washington Redskins (Drawing a Crowd) .50
57 Jim Taylor Super Bowl I (Green Bay vs. Kansas City) .85
58 Bart Starr Super Bowl II (Green Bay vs. Oakland) 2.00
59 Super Bowl III (New York vs. Baltimore) .65
60 Super Bowl IV (Kansas City vs. Minnesota) .65
61 Super Bowl V (Baltimore vs. Dallas) .65
62 Bob Griese, Bob Lilly Super Bowl VI (Dallas vs. Miami) 2.00
63 Super Bowl VII (Miami vs. Washington) .65
64 Bob Griese, Larry Csonka Super Bowl VIII (Miami vs. Minnesota) 2.00
65 Terry Bradshaw, Franco Harris Super Bowl IX (Pittsburgh vs. Minnesota) 3.00
66 Super Bowl X (Pittsburgh vs. Dallas) .65
67 Super Bowl XI (Oakland vs. Minnesota) .65
68 Super Bowl XII (Dallas vs. Denver) .65
69 Super Bowl XIII (Pittsburgh vs Dallas) 1.25

1980 Fleer Team Action

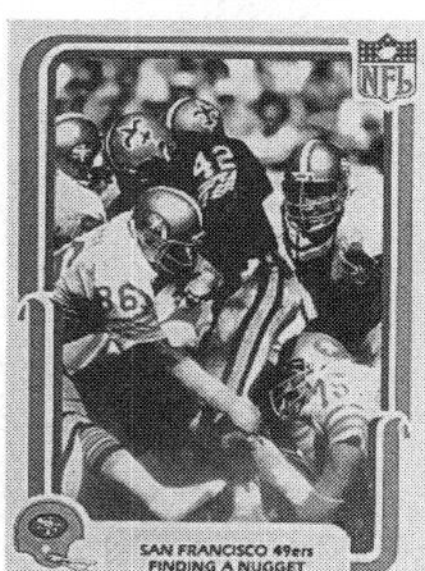

The 1980 Fleer set has white borders and is complete at 70 cards, two for each NFL team and one for each Super Bowl. The cards are numbered to correspond to team-city alphabetical order. Odds are offensive cards, evens are defensive plays. The last 14 picture Super Bowl action. A key card in the set is the Phil Simms "rookie" card. Seven cards and three logo stickers were in each pack.

	NM/M
Complete Set (70):	38.00
Common Card:	.40
Common SB Card:	.50

1 Atlanta Falcons (Getting the Extra Yards) .70
2 Atlanta Falcons (Falcons Get Their Prey) .40
3 Baltimore Colts (Looking for Daylight) .45
4 Baltimore Colts (Ready If Needed) .40
5 Buffalo Bills (You Block For Me, I'll Block For You) .40
6 Buffalo Bills (Stand 'Em Up and Push 'Em Back) .40
7 Walter Payton Chicago Bears(Coming Through) 4.00
8 Chicago Bears (Four On One) .40
9 Cincinnati Bengals (Power Running) .40
10 Cincinnati Bengals (Out Of Running Room) .40
11 Ozzie Newsome Cleveland Browns (End Around) 2.00
12 Cleveland Browns (Rubber Band Defense) .40
13 Tony Dorsett Dallas Cowboys (Point of Attack) 3.00
14 Bob Breunig Dallas Cowboys (Man in the Middle) .60
15 Denver Broncos (Strong and Steady) .45
16 Denver Broncos (Orange Power) .45
17 Detroit Lions (On the March) .40
18 Detroit Lions (The Silver Rush) .40
19 Green Bay Packers (Getting Underway) .40
20 Green Bay Packers (The Best Offense is a Good Defense) .40
21 Houston Oilers (Airborne) .40
22 Houston Oilers (Search and Destroy) .40
23 Kansas City Chiefs (Blazing the Trail) .40
24 Kansas City Chiefs (Making Sure) .40
25 Los Angeles Rams (One Good Turn Deserves Another) .40
26 Los Angeles Rams (Shedding the Block) .40
27 Miami Dolphins (Sweeping the Flanks) .50
28 Miami Dolphins (Keep 'Em Busy) .50
29 Minnesota Vikings (One Man To Beat) .40
30 Minnesota Vikings (Purple People Eaters II) .40
31 New England Patriots (Hitting the Hole) .40
32 New England Patriots (Getting to the Ball) .40
33 New Orleans Saints (Splitting the Defenders) .40
34 Joe Theismann New Orleans Saints (Don't Let Him Get Outside) 1.00
35 Phil Simms New York Giants (Audible) 4.00
36 New York Giants (Wrong Side Up) .40
37 New York Jets (Make Him Miss) .40
38 Mark Gastineau New York Jets (The Only Way To Play) .45
39 Oakland Raiders (Pulling Out All the Stops) .60
40 Oakland Raiders (Right On) .60
41 Philadelphia Eagles (Not Pretty, But Still Points) .40
42 Philadelphia Eagles (Applying the Clamps) .40
43 Franco Harris Pittsburgh Steelers (All Systems Go) 1.75
44 Pittsburgh Steelers (Still the Steal Curtain) .70
45 Ottis Anderson St. Louis Cardinals (On the Move) 2.00
46 St. Louis Cardinals (Long Gone) .40
47 San Diego Chargers (Short-Range Success) .40
48 San Diego Chargers (Pursuit) .40
49 San Francisco 49ers (Getting Field Position) .40
50 San Francisco 49ers (Finding a Nugget) .40
51 Seattle Seahawks (They'll Try Anything Once) .45
52 Seattle Seahawks (Paying the Price) .45
53 Tampa Bay Buccaneers (Coming of Age) .40
54 Walter Payton Tampa Bay Buccaneers (3-4 Shut the Door) 3.00
55 Washington Redskins (Wide Open) .40
56 Washington Redskins (Rude Reception) .40
57 Super Bowl I (Green Bay vs. Kansas City) .50
58 Bart Starr Super Bowl II (Green Bay vs. Oakland) 1.75
59 Joe Namath Super Bowl III (New York vs. Baltimore) 3.75
60 Super Bowl IV (Kansas City vs. Minnesota) .50
61 Super Bowl V (Baltimore vs. Dallas) .50
62 Roger Staubach Super Bowl VI (Dallas vs. Miami) 3.00
63 Super Bowl VII (Miami vs. Washington) .50
64 Super Bowl VIII (Miami vs. Minnesota) .50
65 Terry Bradshaw, Rocky Bleier Super Bowl IX (Pittsburgh vs. Minnesota) 1.75
66 Jack Lambert Super Bowl X (Pittsburgh vs. Dallas) .70
67 Chuck Foreman Super Bowl XI (Oakland vs. Minnesota) .60
68 Super Bowl XII (Dallas vs. Denver) .50
69 Terry Bradshaw Super Bowl XIII (Pittsburgh vs. Dallas) 2.00
70 Franco Harris Super Bowl XIV (Pittsburgh vs. Los Angeles) 2.00

1981 Fleer Team Action

The 1981 Fleer football set is complete at 88 cards, including two cards for each team, one for each Super Bowl, plus a series of extra cards at the end to round out the set. The front borders are white, while the backs are designed around a red, white and blue color scheme. Once again, Fleer used its alphabetical, offense/defense numbering scheme. Packs were marketed with eight cards and three logo stickers.

	NM/M
Complete Set (88):	20.00
Common Card:	.25
Common SB Card:	.25

1 Atlanta Falcons (Out In the Open) .45
2 Atlanta Falcons (Grits Blitz) .25
3 Baltimore Colts (Sprung Through the Line) .25
4 Baltimore Colts (Human Pyramid) .25
5 Buffalo Bills (Buffalo Bills' Wild West Show) .25
6 Buffalo Bills (Buffaloed) .25
7 Walter Payton Chicago Bears (About to Hit Paydirt) 2.25
8 Chicago Bears (Bear Trap) .25
9 Pete Johnson Cincinnati Bengals (Behind the Wall) .25
10 Cincinnati Bengals (Black Cloud) .25
11 Mike Pruitt Cleveland Browns (Point of Attack) .35
12 Rocky Bleier Cleveland Browns (The Only Way to Go is Down) .40
13 Ron Springs Dallas Cowboys (Big O in Big D) .35
14 Dallas Cowboys (Headed Off at the Pass) .35
15 Craig Morton Dallas Cowboys (Man Versus Elements) .25
16 Denver Broncos (The Old High-Low Treatment) .25
17 Billy Sims Detroit Lions (Play Action) .70
18 Detroit Lions (Into the Lions' Den) .25
19 Green Bay Packers (A Packer Packs the Pigskin) .25
20 Green Bay Packers (Sandwiched) .25
21 Houston Oilers (Wait A Minute) .25
22 Houston Oilers (3-4 Shut the Door) .25
23 Kansas City Chiefs (On the Ball) .25
24 Kansas City Chiefs (Seeing Red) .25
25 Los Angeles Rams (The Point of Attack) .25
26 Los Angeles Rams (Get Your Hands Up) .25
27 David Woodley Miami Dolphins (Plenty of Time) .35
28 Miami Dolphins (Pursuit) .25
29 Minnesota Vikings (Tough Yardage) .25
30 Pete Johnson Minnesota Vikings (Purple Avalanche) .25
31 New England Patriots (In High Gear) .25
32 Ken Stabler New England Patriots (Keep 'Em Covered) 1.25
33 Archie Manning New Orleans Saints (Setting Up) .35
34 New Orleans Saints (Air Ball) .25
35 New York Giants (Off Tackle) .25
36 New York Giants (In the Land of the Giants) .25
37 Richard Todd New York Jets (Cleared for Launching) .25
38 New York Jets (Airborne) .25
39 Oakland Raiders (Off and Running) .35
40 Oakland Raiders (Block that Kick) .35
41 Philadelphia Eagles (About to Take Flight) .25
42 Robert Newhouse Philadelphia Eagles (Birds of Prey) .35
43 Franco Harris Pittsburgh Steelers (Here Comes the Infantry) .90
44 Pittsburgh Steelers (Like a Steel Trap) .25
45 St. Louis Cardinals (Run to Daylight) .25
46 St. Louis Cardinals (Stacked Up and Up) .25
47 San Diego Chargers (Straight-Ahead Power) .25
48 San Diego Chargers (Stonewalled) .25
49 San Francisco 49ers (Follow the Leader) .25
50 San Francisco 49ers (Search and Destroy) .25
51 Seattle Seahawks (Short-Range Success) .25
52 Seattle Seahawks (Take Down) .25
53 Jerry Eckwood Tampa Bay Buccaneers (Orange Blossom Special) .25
54 Tampa Bay Buccaneers (Tropical Storm Buc) .25
55 Washington Redskins (Alone for a Moment) .25
56 Washington Redskins (Ambushed) .25
57 Jim Taylor Super Bowl I (Green Bay vs. Kansas City) .40
58 Super Bowl II (Green Bay vs. Oakland) .25
59 Super Bowl III (New York vs. Baltimore) .25
60 Super Bowl IV (Kansas City vs. Minnesota) .25
61 Super Bowl V (Baltimore vs. Dallas) .25
62 Super Bowl VI (Dallas vs. Miami) .25
63 Super Bowl VII (Miami vs. Washington) .25
64 Larry Csonka Super Bowl VIII (Miami vs. Minnesota) .70
65 Franco Harris Super Bowl IX (Pittsburgh vs. Minnesota) .70
66 Franco Harris Super Bowl X (Pittsburgh vs. Dallas) .25
67 Kenny Stabler Super Bowl XI (Oakland vs. Minnesota) 1.25
68 Roger Staubach, Tony Dorsett Super Bowl XII (Dallas vs. Denver) 1.75
69 Roger Staubach, Tony Dorsett Super Bowl XIII (Pittsburgh vs. Dallas) 1.75
70 Franco Harris Super Bowl XIV (Pittsburgh vs. Los Angeles) .70
71 Jim Plunkett Super Bowl XV (Oakland vs. Philadelphia) .40
72 Chuck Noll Steeler Training Camp .40
73 Practice Makes Perfect .25
74 Airborn Carrier .25
75 The National Anthem Chargers .25
76 Filling Up .25
77 Terry Bradshaw (Away in Time) 1.50
78 Flat Out .25
79 Halftime (Band playing) .25
80 Warm Ups Patriots .25
81 Getting to the Bottom of It .25
82 Souvenir (Crowd) .25
83 A Game of Inches (Officials measuring) .25
84 The Overview .25
85 The Dropback .25
86 Pregame Huddle (Washington Redskins) .25
87 Every Way But Loose .25
88 Mudders .40

1982 Fleer Team Action

The 1982 Fleer set is again complete at 88 cards, but is slightly more valuable than other Fleer sets from this period, because it contains a couple of cards featuring Joe Montana. The same numbering scheme is used, but 16 NFL Team Highlight cards are included and added at the end. Seven cards and three logo stickers were in each pack.

	NM/M
Complete Set (88):	45.00
Common Card:	.25
Common SB Card:	.30

1 Atlanta Falcons (Running to Daylight) .50
2 Atlanta Falcons (Airborne Falcons) .25

3 Mark Gastineau, Bert Jones Baltimore Colts (Plenty of Time to Throw) .45
4 Baltimore Colts (Lassoing the Opponent) .25
5 Joe Ferguson Buffalo Bills (Point of Attack) .45
6 Buffalo Bills (Capturing the Enemy) .25
7 Walter Payton Chicago Bears (Three on One) 2.50
8 Chicago Bears (Stretched Out) .25
9 Pete Johnson Cincinnati Bengals (About to Hit Paydirt) .30
10 Cincinnati Bengals (Tiger-Striped Attack) .25
11 Brian Sipe Cleveland Browns (Reading the Field) .45
12 Cleveland Browns (Covered From All Angles) .25
13 Tony Dorsett Dallas Cowboys (Blocking Convoy) 1.50
14 Dallas Cowboys (Encircled) .45
15 Craig Morton Denver Broncos (Springing into Action) .45
16 Denver Broncos (High and Low) .30
17 Detroit Lions (Setting Up the Screen Pass) .25
18 Doug Williams Detroit Lions (Poised and Ready to Attack) .30
19 Green Bay Packers (Flying Through the Air) .25
20 Green Bay Packers (Hitting the Pack) .25
21 Earl Campbell Houston Oilers (Waiting for the Hole to Open) 3.25
22 Houston Oilers (Biting the Dust) .25
23 Kansas City Chiefs (Going in Untouched) .25
24 Kansas City Chiefs (No Place to Go) .25
25 Wendell Tyler Los Angeles Rams (Getting to the Outside) .30
26 John Riggins Los Angeles Rams (Double Team, Double Trouble) .70
27 Tony Nathan Miami Dolphins (Cutting Back Against the Grain) .45
28 Miami Dolphins (Taking Two Down) .30
29 Minnesota Vikings (Running Inside for Tough Yardage) .25
30 Minnesota Vikings (Bowling Over the Oppenent) .25
31 New England Patriots (Leaping for the First Down) .25
32 New England Patriots (Gang Tackling) .25
33 New Orleans Saints (Breaking Into the Clear) .45
34 New Orleans Saints (Double Jeopardy) .25
35 New York Giants (Getting Ready to Hit the Opening) .25
36 Tony Dorsett New York Giants (Negative Yardage) 1.25
37 Freeman McNeil New York Jets (Off to the Races) 1.00
38 New York Jets (Sandwiched) .25
39 Marc Wilson Oakland Raiders (Throwing the Down and Out) .45
40 Oakland Raiders (The Second Wave is on the Way) .45
41 Ron Jaworski Philadelphia Eagles (Blasting Up the Middle) .45
42 Carl Hairston, John Riggins Philadelphia Eagles (Triple Teaming) .70
43 Pittsburgh Steelers (Stretching for the Score) .30
44 Pittsburgh Steelers (Rising Above the Crowd) .30
45 Jim Hart St. Louis Cardinals (Sweeping to the Right) .45
46 St. Louis Cardinals (No Plave to go but Down) .25
47 San Diego Chargers (Looking for Someone to Block) .25
48 San Diego Chargers (Being in the Right Place) .25
49 Joe Montana San Francisco 49ers (Giving Second Effort) 17.50
50 Steve Bartkowski San Francisco 49ers (In Your Face) .50
51 Jack Lambert Seattle Seahawks (Nothing But Open Space) .70
52 Brian Sipe Seattle Seahawks (Attacking From the Blind Side) .45
53 Doug Williams Tampa Bay Buccaneers (Everyone in Motion) .30
54 Tampa Bay Buccaneers (Ring Around the Running Back) .25
55 Joe Theismann Washington Redskins (Knocking Them Down One-By-One) .70
56 Washington Redskins (Coming From All Directions) .25
57 Jim Taylor Super Bowl I (Green Bay vs. Kansas City) .50
58 Super Bowl II (Green Bay vs. Oakland) .25
59 Super Bowl III (New York vs. Baltimore) .25
60 Super Bowl IV (Kansas City vs. Minnesota) .25
61 Super Bowl V (Baltimore vs. Dallas) .25
62 Bob Griese, Bob Lilly Super Bowl VI (Dallas vs. Miami) .80
63 Larry Csonka Super Bowl VII (Miami vs. Washington) .70
64 Larry Csonka, Paul Warfield Super Bowl VIII (Miami vs. Minnesota) 1.00
65 Super Bowl IX (Pittsburgh vs.Minnesota) .25
66 Roger Staubach Super Bowl X (Pittsburgh vs. Dallas) 2.00
67 Mark Van Eeghen Super Bowl XI (Oakland vs. Minnesota) .30
68 Roger Staubach Super Bowl XII (Dallas vs. Denver) 2.00
69 Lynn Swann Super Bowl XIII (Pittsburgh vs. Dallas) 1.00
70 Super Bowl XIV (Pittsburgh vs. Los Angeles) .25
71 Jim Plunkett Super Bowl XV (Oakland vs. Philadelphia) .45
72 Dwight Clark Super Bowl XVI (San Francisco vs. Cincinnati) .85
73 Joe Montana NFL Team Highlights (Pro Bowl) 12.00
74 Ken Anderson, Anthony Munoz NFL Team Highlights (Pro Bowl) 2.50
75 NFL Team Highlights (Aloha Stadium) .75
76 NFL Team Highlights (On the Field Meeting) .25
77 Joe Theismann NFL Team Highlights (First Down) .70
78 Jerry Markbright NFL Team Highlights (The Man in Charge) .25
79 NFL Team Highlights (Coming Onto the Field) .25
80 NFL Team Highlights (In the Huddle) .30
81 NFL Team Highlights (Lying In Wait) .25
82 NFL Team Highlights (Celebration) .25
83 NFL Team Highlights (Men in Motion) .25
84 NFL Team Highlights (Shotgun Formation) .25
85 NFL Team Highlights (Training Camp) .25
86 Bill Walsh NFL Team Highlights (Halftime Instructions) .75
87 Rolf Bernirschke NFL Team Highlights (Field Goal Attempt) .30
88 NFL Team Highlights (Free Kick) .50

1983 Fleer Team Action

The 1983 Fleer football set is again complete at 88 cards, including two cards for each team, one for each Super Bowl, plus a series of "Highlights" cards at the end of the set. There is a numbering error in the set that was not corrected. The card depicting Super Bowl X, which should have been card number "66," was erroneously numbered "67," meaning there are two cards numbered "67" in the set and no card numbered "66." Collectors should be aware that the premium value attached to the Super Bowl X card is beacuse it pictures Terry Bradshaw, and not because of the numbering error. The set follows all of Fleer's usual numbering formats. A Jim McMahon "rookie" card highlights the set. Packs had seven cards and three logo stickers.

NM/M
Complete Set (88): 26.00
Common Card: .25
Common SB Card: .30
1 Ronnie Lott Atlanta Falcons (Breaking Away to Daylight) 2.50
2 Atlanta Falcons (Piles Up) .25
3 Baltimore Colts (Cutting Back to Daylight) .25
4 Joe Ferguson Baltimore Colts (Pressuring the QB) .30
5 Buffalo Bills (Moving to the Outside) .30
6 Buffalo Bills (Buffalo Stampede) .25
7 Jim McMahon, Walter Payton Chicago Bears (Ready to Let it Fly) 2.25
8 Chicago Bears (Jump Ball) .25
9 Cincinnati Bengals (Hurdling Into Open) .25
10 Cincinnati Bengals (Hands Up) .25
11 Mike Pruitt Cleveland Browns (An Open Field Ahead) .30
12 Cleveland Browns (Reacting to the Ball Carrier) .25
13 Tony Dorsett Dallas Cowboys (Mid-Air Ballet) 1.50
14 Dallas Cowboys (3, 2, 1 Takeoff) .30
15 Denver Broncos (Clear Sailing) .30
16 Denver Broncos (Stacking Up Offense) .30
17 Detroit Lions (Hitting the Wall) .25
18 Detroit Lions (Snapping into Action) .25
19 Ed "Too Tall" Jones Green Bay Packers (Fingertip Control) .60
20 Green Bay Packers (QB Sack) .25
21 Houston Oilers (Sweeping to Outside) .25
22 Freeman McNeil Houston Oilers (Halting Forward Progress) .45
23 Kansas City Chiefs (Waiting for the Key Block) .25
24 John Hannah Kansas City Chiefs (Going Head to Head) .50
25 Jim Plunkett Los Angeles Raiders (Bowms Away) .45
26 Los Angeles Raiders (Caged Bengal) .45
27 Los Angeles Rams (Clearing Out Middle) .25
28 Los Angeles Rams (One on One Tackle) .25
29 Miami Dolphins (Skating Through Hole) .30
30 Miami Dolphins (Follow the Bouncing Ball) .30
31 Tommy Kramer Minnesota Vikings (Dropping into Pocket) .30
32 Minnesota Vikings (Attacking from All Angles) .25
33 New England Patriots (Touchdown) .25
34 Walter Payton New England Patriots (Pouncing Patroits) 2.00
35 New Orleans Saints (Only One Man to Beat) .25
36 Tony Dorsett New Orleans Saints (Closing In) 1.25
37 New York Giants (Setting Up to Pass) .25
38 New York Giants (In Pursuit) .25
39 New York Jets (Just Enough Room) .25
40 New York Jets (Warpping Up Runner) .25
41 Ron Jarowski, Harry Carson Philadelphia Eagles (Play Action Fakers) .30
42 Archie Manning Philadelphia Eagles (Step Away From Sack) .45
43 Franco Harris, Terry Bradshaw Pittsburgh Steelers (Exploding Through a Hole) 1.50
44 Jack Lambert Pittsburgh Steelers (Outnumbered) .60
45 St. Louis Cardinals (Keeping His Balance) .25
46 St. Louis Cardinals (Waiting for the Reinforcements) .25
47 San Diego Chargers (Supercharged Charger) .25
48 San Diego Chargers (Triple Team Tackle) .25
49 San Francisco 49ers (There's No Stopping Him Now) .25
50 San Francisco 49ers (Heading 'Em Off at the Pass) .30
51 Jim Zorn Seattle Seahawks (Calling the Signals) .45
52 Seattle Seahawks (The Hands Have it) .30
53 Tampa Bay Buccaneers (Off to the Races) .25
54 Tampa Bay Buccaneers (Buccaneer Sandwich) .25
55 Washington Redskins (Looking for Daylight) .25
56 Washington Redskins (Smothering the Ball Carrier) .25
57 Jim Taylor Super Bowl I (Green Bay vs. Kansas City) .60
58 Super Bowl II (Green Bay vs. Oakland) .30
59 Super Bowl III (New York vs. Baltimore) .30
60 Super Bowl IV (Kansas City vs. Minnesota) .30
61 Johnny Unitas Super Bowl V (Baltimore vs. Dallas) 1.50
62 Bob Griese, Bob Lilly Super Bowl VI (Dallas vs. Miami) .75
63 Manny Fernandez Super Bowl VII (Miami vs. Washington) .30
64 Larry Csonka Super Bowl VIII (Miami vs. Minnesota) .60
65 Franco Harris Super Bowl IX (Pittsburgh vs. Minnesota) 1.00
66 Terry Bradshaw Super Bowl X (Pittsburgh vs. Dallas) 1.75
67 Super Bowl XI (Oakland vs. Minnesota) .45
68 Super Bowl XII (Dallas vs. Denver) .30
69 Terry Bradshaw Super Bowl XIII (Pittsburgh vs. Dallas) 1.50
70 Vince Ferragamo Super Bowl XIV (Pittsburgh vs. Los Angeles) .30
71 Super Bowl XV (Oakland vs. Philadelphia) .30
72 Super Bowl XVI (San Francisco vs. Cincinnati) .30
73 John Riggins Super Bowl XVII (Washington vs. Miami) .60
74 Dan Fouts NFL Team Highlights (Pro Bowl) 1.00
75 NFL Team Highlights (Super Bowl XVII Spectacular) .30
76 NFL Team Highlights (Tampa Stadium: Super Bowl XVIII) .30
77 NFL Team Highlights (Up, Up, and Away) .30
78 Steve Bartkowski NFL Team Highlights (Sideline Conference) .30
79 Mike Lansford NFL Team Highlights (Barefoot Follow-Through) .30
80 NFL Team Highlights (Fourth and Long) .30
81 NFL Team Highlights (Blocked Punt) .30
82 NFL Team Highlights (Fumble) .30
83 NFL Team Highlights (National Anthem) .30
84 Tony Franklin NFL Team Highlights (Concentrating on the Ball) .30
85 NFL Team Highlights (Splashing Around) .30
86 NFL Team Highlights (Loading in Shotgun) .30
87 NFL Team Highlights (Taking the Snap) .30
88 NFL Team Highlights (Line of Scrimmage) .45

1984 Fleer Team Action

The 1984 Fleer football set is again complete at 88 cards, using Fleer's typical numbering arrangement. However, the newly-relocated Indianapolis Colts are placed in Baltimore's usual position. A series of 18 Super Bowl and 14 NFL Team Highlight cards are included. The most signigicant cards are two of Earl Campbell, which are not found in the 1984 Topps set, a first-year Marcus Allen, and a Howie Long "rookie." Seven cards and three logo stickers were in each pack. Cards green borders.

NM/M
Complete Set (88): 23.50
Common Card: .25
1 Atlanta Falcons .50
2 Atlanta Falcons (Gang Tackle) .25
3 Indianapolis Colts (About to Break Free) .25
4 Indianapolis Colts (Cutting Off All the Angles) .25
5 Buffalo Bills (Cracking the First Line of Defense) .25
6 Buffalo Bills (Getting Help from a Friend) .25
7 Jim McMahon, Walter Payton Chicago Bears (Over the Top) 1.75
8 Chicago Bears (You Grab Him High I'll Grab Him Low) .25
9 Cincinnati Bengals (Skipping Through an Opening) .25
10 Joe Ferguson Cincinnati Bengals (Saying Hello to a QB) .40
11 Greg Pruitt Cleveland Browns (Free Sailing into the End Zone) .40
12 Cleveland Browns (Making Sure of the Tackle) .25
13 Danny White Dallas Cowboys .50
14 Ed "Too Tall" Jones Dallas Cowboys (Cowboy's Corral) .60
15 Denver Broncos (Sprinting into the Open) .40
16 Curt Warner Denver Broncos (Ready to Pounce) .50
17 Billy Sims Detroit Lions (Lion on the Prowl) .50
18 John Riggins Detroit Lions (Stacking Up the Ball Carrier) .60
19 Green Bay Packers (Waiting for the Hole to Open) .25
20 Green Bay Packers (Packing Up Your Opponent) .25
21 Earl Campbell Houston Oilers (Nothing but Open Spaces Ahead) 2.50
22 Houston Oilers (Meeting Him Head On) .25
23 Kansas City Chiefs (Going Outside for Extra Yardage) .25
24 Kansas City Chiefs (A Running Back in Trouble) .25
25 Marcus Allen Los Angeles Raiders (No Defenders in Sight) 2.75
26 Howie Long,John Riggins Los Angeles Raiders (Rampaging Raiders) 2.25
27 Los Angeles Rams (Making the Cut) .25
28 Los Angeles Rams (Caught From Behind) .25
29 Miami Dolphins (Sliding Down the Line) .40
30 Miami Dolphins (Making Sure) .40
31 Minnesota Vikings (Stretching For Touchdown) .25
32 Minnesota Vikings (Hitting the Wall) .25
33 Steve Grogan New England Patriots (Straight Up the Middle) .50
34 Earl Campbell New England Patriots (Come Here an Give Me a Hug) 2.00
35 New Orleans Saints (One Defender to Beat) .25
36 New Orleans Saints (Saints Sandwich) .25
37 New York Giants (A Six Point Landing) .25
38 New York Giants (Leaping to the Aid of a Teammate) .25
39 New York Jets (Galloping Through Untouched) .25
40 New York Jets (Capturing the Enemy) .25
41 Philadelphia Eagles (One More Block and He's Gone) .25
42 Philadelphoa Ealges (Meeting an Oppenent With Open Arms) .25
43 Pittsburgh Steelers (The Play Begins to Develop) .40
44 Pittsburgh Steelers (Rally Around the Ball Carrier) .40
45 St. Louis Cardinals (Sprinting Around the Corner) .25
46 St. Louis Cardinals (Overmatched) .25
47 San Diego Chargers (Up, Up and Away) .25
48 San Diego Chargers (Engulfing the Oppenent) .25
49 Wendell Tyler San Francisco 49ers (Tunneling Up the Middle) .40
50 John Riggins San Francisco 49ers (Nowhere to Go but Down) .60
51 Jim Zorn Seattle Seahawks (Letting the Ball Fly) .50
52 Seattle Seahawks (Handing Out Some Punishment) .40
53 Tampa Bay Buccaneers (When He Hits the Ground He's Gone) .25
54 Tampa Bay Buccaneers (One Leg Takedown) .25
55 John Riggins Washington Redskins (Plenty of Room to Run) .60
56 Washington Redskins (Squashing the Oppenent) .25
57 Jim Taylor Super Bowl I (Green Bay vs. Kansas City) .60
58 Bart Starr Super Bowl II (Green Bay vs. Oakland) .80
59 Super Bowl III (New York vs. Baltimore) .25
60 Super Bowl IV (Kansas City vs. Minnesota) .25
61 Earl Morrall Super Bowl V (Baltimore vs. Dallas) .75
62 Roger Staubach Super Bowl VI (Dallas vs. Miami) 1.50
63 Jim Kiick, Bob Griese Super Bowl VII (Miami vs. Washington) .50
64 Larry Csonka Super Bowl VIII (Miami vs. Minnesota) .75
65 Terry Bradshaw Super Bowl IX (Pittsburgh vs. Minnesota) 1.25
66 Franco Harris Super Bowl X (Pittsburgh vs. Dallas) .75
67 Super Bowl XI (Oakland vs. Minnesota) .25
68 Tony Dorsett Super Bowl XII (Dallas vs. Denver) 1.00
69 Franco Harris Super Bowl XIII (Pittsburgh vs. Dallas) .75
70 Franco Harris Super Bowl XIV (Pittsburgh vs. Los Angeles) .75
71 Jim Plunkett Super Bowl XV (Oakland vs. Philadelphia) .40
72 Super Bowl XVI (San Francisco vs. Cincinnati) .25
73 Super Bowl XVII (Washington vs. Miami) .25
74 Howie Long Super Bowl XVIII (Los Angeles vs. Washington) 1.75
75 NFL Team Highlights (Official's Conference) .25
76 NFL Team Highlights (Leaping for the Ball Carrier) .25
77 Jim Plunkett NFL Team Highlights (Setting Up in the Passing Pocket) .40
78 NFL Team Highlights (Field Goal Block) .25
79 Steve Grogan NFL Team Highlights (Stopped for No Gain) .40
80 NFL Team Highlights (Double Team Block) .25
81 NFL Team Highlights (Kickoff) .25
82 NFL Team Highlights (Punt Block) .25
83 NFL Team Highlights (Coaches Signals) .25
84 NFL Team Highlights (Training Camp) .25
85 Dwight Stephenson NFL Team Highlights (Fumble) .50
86 NFL Team Highlights (1984 AFC-NFC Pro Bowl) .25
87 NFL Team Highlights (Cheerleaders) .50
88 Joe Theismann NFL Team Highlights (In the Huddle) .80

1985 Fleer Team Action

Fleer changed its format slightly for its 1985 set. The set is still complete at 88 cards, but there are three cards for each team this year and fewer Super Bowl cards. The "In Action" cards for each team have a team schedule. Three cards for Super Bowl XIX and a 1985 Pro Bowl card are also included. A first-year Fleer Dan Marino card and a Warren Moon "rookie" card highlight the set. Packs had 15 cards and one logo sticker.

NM/M
Complete Set (88): 30.00
Common Card: .25
1 Atlanta Falcons (Nothing But Open Spaces Ahead) .50
2 Atlanta Falcons (Leveling Ball Carrier) .25

3 Joe Theismann, John Riggins Atlanta Falcons (Flying Falcon) .60
4 Buffalo Bills (Ducking Under the Pressure) .25
5 Buffalo Bills (Swallowing Up the Oppenent) .25
6 Buffalo Bills (Avoiding Late Hits) .25
7 Walter Payton Chicago Bears (Picking His Spot) 1.50
8 Chicago Bears (C'Mon Guys, Give Me Some Room to Breathe) .25
9 Richard Dent Chicago Bears (Just Hanging Around in Case They're Needed) 2.25
10 Cincinnati Bengals (Struggling for Every Extra Yard) .25
11 Cincinnati Bengals (Making Opponent Pay) .25
12 Cincinnati Bengals (Just Out of the Reach of the Defender) .25
13 Cleveland Browns (Plenty of Time to Fire the Ball) .25
14 Cleveland Browns (Hitting the Wall) .25
15 Cleveland Browns (Look What We Found) .25
16 Tony Dorsett, Wilbur Marshall Dallas Cowboys (Waiting for the Right Moment to Burst Upfield) 1.25
17 Walter Payton, Ed "Too Tall" Jones Dallas Cowboys (Sorry Buddy, This is the End of the Line) 1.50
18 Ed "Too Tall" Jones Dallas Cowboys (Following Through for Three Points) .60
19 Denver Broncos (Blasting Up the Middle) .40
20 Denver Broncos (Finishing Off the Tackle) .40
21 Denver Broncos (About to Hit Paydirt) .40
22 Dexter Manley Detroit Lions (Waiting to Throw Until the Last Second) .40
23 Detroit Lions (Double Trouble on the Tackle) .25
24 Detroit Lions (Quick Pitch) .25
25 Steve McMichael Green Bay Packers (Unleashing the Long Bomb) .90
26 Marcus Allen Green Bay Packers (Encircling the Ball Carrier) 1.50
27 Green Bay Packers (Piggy-Back Ride) .25
28 Warren Moon, Earl Campbell Houston Oilers (Retreating into the Pocket) 5.75
29 Houston Oilers (Punishing the Enemy) .25
30 Houston Oilers (No Chance to Block This One) .25
31 Indianapolis Colts (Getting Ready to Let It Fly) .25
32 Indianapolis Colts (Pushing the Ball Carrier Backward) .25
33 Indianapolis Colts (Nowhere to Go) .25
34 Kansas City Chiefs (Cutting Back for Extra Yardage) .25
35 Kansas City Chiefs (Reaching for the Deflection) .25
36 Kansas City Chiefs (Rising to the Occasion) .25
37 Howie Long Los Angeles Raiders (Hurdling into the Open Field) .40
38 Los Angeles Raiders (No Place to Go) .25
39 Los Angeles Raiders (Standing Tall in the Pocket) .25
40 Eric Dickerson Los Angeles Rams (One More Barrier and He's Off to the Races) 1.50
41 Los Angeles Rams (Driving a Shoulder into the Opponent) .25
42 Los Angeles Rams (The Kickoff) .25
43 Tony Nathan Miami Dolphins (Sidestepping Trouble) .50
44 Miami Dolphins (Hold On, We're Coming) .40
45 Dan Marino Miami Dolphins (The Release Point) 7.25
46 Tommy Kramer Minnesota Vikings (Putting as Much as He Has into the Pass) .40
47 Minnesota Vikings (Gang Tackling) .25
48 Minnesota Vikings (You're Not Getting Away From Me This Time) .25
49 Tony Eason New England Patriots (Throwing on the Run) .40
50 New England Patriots (The Only Place to Go is Down) .25
51 New England Patriots (Standing the Ball Carrier Up) .25
52 New Orleans Saints (Going Up the Middle) .25
53 New Orleans Saints (Putting Everything They've Got into the Tackle) .25
54 New Orleans Saints (Getting Off the Ground to Block the Kick) .25
55 New York Giants (Over the Top) .25
56 New York Giants (Rallying Around the Opposition) .25
57 Phil Simms New York Giants (The Huddle) .60
58 New York Jets (Following His Blockers) .25
59 New York Jets (This is as Far as You Go) .25
60 New York Jets (Looking Over the Defense) .25
61 Philadelphia Eagles (Going Through the Opening Untouched) .25
62 Philadelphia Eagles (Squashing the Enemy) .25
63 Philadelphia Eagles (There's No Room Here, So Let's Go Outside) .25
64 Pittsburgh Steelers (Sprinting Around the End) .40
65 Pittsburgh Steelers (Mismatch) .40
66 Pittsburgh Steelers (About to Be Thrown Back) .40
67 St. Louis Cardinals (In for Six) .25
68 St. Louis Cardinals (Piling Ip the Ball Carrier) .25
69 Joe Theismann St. Louis Cardinals (Causing the Fumble) .75
70 San Diego Chargers (Plenty of Open Space Ahead) .25
71 San Diego Chargers (Ready to Be Swallowed Up) .25
72 San Diego Chargers (A Quarterback in Serious Trouble) .25
73 San Francisco 49ers (Reading the Hole and Exploding Through) .25
74 San Francisco 49ers (Burying the Opponent) .25
75 Joe Montana, Russ Francis San Francisco 49ers (Waiting to Throw Until His Receiver Breaks Free) 4.25
76 Dave Krieg Seattle Seahawks (Getting Just Enough Time to Pass) .50
77 Craig James Seattle Seahawks (Capturing the Enemy) .50
78 Seattle Seahawks (It's Going to be a Fottrace Now) .40
79 Tampa Bay Buccaneers (Heading Outside Away From Trouble) .25
80 Tampa Bay Buccaneers (One-On-One Tackle) .25
81 Eric Dickerson Tampa Bay Buccaneers (A Buccaneers Sandwich) 1.25
82 John Riggins Washington Redskins (Just Enough Room to Get Through) .60
83 Washington Redskins (Wrapping Up the Opponent) .25
84 Mark Moseley Washington Redskins (Field-Goal Attempt) .40
85 Roger Craig Super Bowl XIX (San Francisco vs. Miami) .90
86 Joe Montana Super Bowl XIX (San Francisco vs. Miami) 3.75
87 Tony Nathan Super Bowl XIX (San Francisco vs. Miami) .40
88 1985 Pro Bowl .50

1986 Fleer Team Action

The 1986 Fleer football set is again complete at 88 cards and is organized in an identical fashion to the previous year's set. These cards, which have a light blue border, include three for Super Bowl XX and a 1986 Pro Bowl card. Other highlights include a first-year Fleer John Elway, a Bernie Kosar "rookie" and a pre-Topps Keith Byars "rookie." Packs had seven cards and three logo stickers.

NM/M

Complete Set (88): 23.00
Common Card: .25
1 Atlanta Falcons (Preparing to Make Cut) .50
2 Atlanta Falcons (Everybody Gets Into the Act) .25
3 Atlanta Falcons (Where Do You Think You're Going) .25
4 Buffalo Bills (Turning On the After-Burners) .25
5 Buffalo Bills (Running Into a Wall of Blue) .25
6 Buffalo Bills (Up and Over) .25
7 Jim McMahon, Walter Payton Chicago Bears (Pocket Forms Around Passer) 1.25
8 Richard Dent, Dan Hampton Chicago Bears (Monsters of the Midway II) 1.00
9 Mike Singletary Chicago Bears (Blitz in a Blizzard) .85
10 Dave Rimington, Anthony Munoz Cincinnati Bengals (Plowing Trough Defense) .60
11 Cincinnati Bengals (Zeroing in for the Hit) .25
12 Marcus Allen Cincinnati Bengals (Oh, No You Don't) 1.25
13 Bernie Kosar, Kevin Mack Cleveland Browns (Looking for a Hole to Develop) 2.25
14 Cleveland Browns (Buried by the Browns) .25
15 Cleveland Browns (Another Runner Pounded Into the Turf) .25
16 Tony Dorsett Dallas Cowboys (Hole You Could Drive Truck Through) .85
17 Dallas Cowboys (We've Got You Surrounded) .50
18 Randy White Dallas Cowboys (Giving the Referee Some Help) .75
19 John Elway Denver Broncos (The Blockers Spring into Action) 3.75
20 Denver Broncos (The Orange Crush Shows Its Stuff) .50
21 Denver Broncos (A Stampede to Block the Kick) .40
22 Detroit Lions (A Runner's Eye View of the Situation) .25
23 Detroit Lions (Leveling the Ball Carrier) .25
24 Detroit Lions (Going All Out to Get the Quarterback) .25
25 Green Bay Packers (Sweeping Around the Corner) .25
26 Green Bay Packers (Not Afraid to Go Head to Head) .25
27 Green Bay Packers (Taking the Snap) .25
28 Houston Oilers (Plunging for That Extra Yard) .25
29 Houston Oilers (Tightening the Vise) .25
30 Houston Oilers (Launching a Field Goal) .25
31 Indianapolis Colts (Galloping Out of an Arm-Tackle) .25
32 Indianapolis Colts (Ball is Knocked Loose) .25
33 Indianapolis Colts (Busting Out of the Backfield) .25
34 Kansas City Chiefs (About to Head Upfield) .25
35 Kansas City Chiefs (One the Warpath) .25
36 Kansas City Chiefs (Getting the Point Across) .25
37 Los Angeles Raiders (Looks Like Clear Sailing Ahead) .40
38 Los Angeles Raiders (Surrounded by Unfriendly Faces) .40
39 Los Angeles Raiders (Vaulting for Six Points) .40
40 Eric Dickerson Los Angeles Rams (Breaking into an Open Field) .85
41 Los Angeles Rams (Swept Away by a Wave of Rams) .25
42 Los Angeles Rams (Alertly Scooping Up a Fumble) .25
43 Miami Dolphins (Clearing a Path for the Running Bacj) .40
44 Miami Dolphins (Teaching a Painful Lesson) .40
45 Miami Dolphins (Trying for a Piece of the Ball) .40
46 Tommy Kramer Minnesota Vikings (All Day to Throw) .50
47 Walter Payton Minnesota Vikings (The Moment Before Impact) 1.00
48 Minnesota Vikings (Leaving the Competition Behind) .25
49 New England Patriots (Solid Line of Blockers) .25
50 New England Patriots (Surprise Attack From the Rear) .25
51 New England Patriots (Getting a Grip on the Opponent) .25
52 New Orleans Saints (Look Out, I'm Coming Through) .25
53 New Orleans Saints (A Furious Assault) .25
54 New Orleans Saints (Line of Scrimmage) .25
55 Phil Simms, Joe Morris New York Giants (Pass Play Develops) .75
56 New York Giants (Putting Squeeze on Offense) .25
57 New York Giants (Using a Great Block to Turn Corner) .25
58 New York Jets (The Runner Spots Lane) .25
59 New York Jets (About to Deliver a Headache) .25
60 New York Jets (Flying Formation) .25
61 Keith Byars Philadelphia Eagles (Slipping a Tackle) 1.50
62 Philadelphia Ealges (Airborne Eagles Break Up Pass) .25
63 Ron Jaworski Philadelphia Eagles (Connecting On Toss Over Middle) .50
64 Pittsburgh Steelers (Letting Big Guy Lead the Way) .25
65 Pittsburgh Steelers (Converging From Every Direction) .25
66 Gary Anderson Pittsburgh Steelers (All Eyes are on the Football) .40
67 Neil Lomax, Jim Burt St. Louis Cardinals (Calmly Dropping Back to Pass) .40
68 St. Louis Cardinals (Applying Some Bruises) .25
69 St. Louis Cardinals (Looking for Yardage on Interception Return) .25
70 San Diego Chargers (Human Cannonball) .50
71 Dave Krieg San Diego Chargers (Another One Bites the Dust) .50
72 San Diego Chargers (A Clean Steel by the Defense) .25
73 Joe Montana San Francisco 49ers (Looking for Safe Passage) 4.00
74 San Francisco 49ers (An Uplifting Experience) .25
75 Danny White San Francisco 49ers (In Hot Pursuit) .50
76 Seattle Seahawks (Perparing for Collision) .40
77 Seattle Seahawks (A Group Effort) .40
78 Dan Fouts Seattle Seahawks (Forcing a Hurried Throw) .75
79 Tamps Bay Buccaneers (Protecting Quarterback at All Costs) .25
80 Tampa Bay Buccaneers (Dishing Out Some Punishment) .25
81 Tampa Bay Buccaneers (No Trespassing) .25
82 Washington Redskins (Squaring Off in the Trenches) .25
83 Danny White Washington Redskins (Pouncing on the Passer) .50
84 Washington Redskins (Two Hits Are Better Than One) .25
85 Walter Payton Super Bowl XX (Chicago vs. New England) 1.25
86 Jim McMahon Super Bowl XX (Chicago vs. New England) .75
87 Super Bowl XX (Chicago vs. New England) .40
88 Marcus Allen Pro Bowl 1986 1.50

1987 Fleer Team Action

Again complete at 88 cards, the 1987 Fleer football set contains two cards for each team, one card representing each Super Bowl and eight cards depicting the previous season's playoff games. The cards have a yellow and black border. The set features a first-year Fleer Steve Young and two pre-Topps Bo Jackson "rookies." Each pack had seven cards and three logo stickers.

NM/M

Complete Set (88): 21.50
Common Card: .20
1 Atlanta Falcons (A Clear View Downfield) .45
2 Roger Craig Atlanta Falcons (Pouncing on a Runner) .45
3 Buffalo Bills (Buffalo Stampede) .20
4 Buffalo Bills (Double Bill) .20
5 Walter Payton Chicago Bears (Stay Out of Our Way) 1.00
6 Dan Hampton Chicago Bears (Quarterback's Nightmare) .45
7 Eddie Brown Cincinnati Bengals (Irresistible Force) .45
8 Cincinnati Bengals (Bengals on the Prowl) .20
9 Cleveland Browns (Following the Lead Blocker) .20
10 Cleveland Browns (Block That Kick) .20
11 Dallas Cowboys (Next Stop...End Zone) .30
12 Dallas Cowboys (Ride 'Em Cowboys) .30
13 John Elway Denver Broncos (Pitchout in Progress) 2.25
14 Denver Broncos (Broncos' Busters) .30
15 Detroit Lions (Off to the Races) .20
16 Detroit Lions (Entering the Lions' Den) .20
17 Green Bay Packers (Setting the Wheels in Motion) .20
18 Green Bay Packers (Stack of Packers) .20
19 Houston Oilers (Making a Cut at the Line of Scrimmage) .20
20 Houston Oilers (Hit Parade) .20
21 Indianapolis Colts (The Horses Up Front) .20
22 Indianapolis Colts (Stopping the Runner in His Tracks) .20
23 Kansas City Chiefs (It's A Snap) .20
24 Bo Jackson Kansas City Chiefs (Nowhere to Hide) 1.50
25 Bo Jackson Los Angeles Raiders (Looking For Daylight) 2.00
26 Los Angeles Raiders (Wrapped Up by Raiders) .30
27 Jim Everett Los Angeles Rams (Movers and Shakers) 2.00
28 Los Angeles Rams (In the Quarterback's Face) .20
29 Miami Dolphins (Full Speed Ahead) .30
30 Miami Dolphins (Acrobatic Interception) .30
31 Tommy Kramer Minnesota Vikings (Solid Line of Protection) .30
32 Minnesota Vikings (Bearing a Heavy Load) .20
33 Craig James New England Patriots (The Blockers Fan Out) .45
34 New England Patriots (Converging Linebackers) .20
35 Dalton Hilliard, Jim Burt New Orleans Saints (Saints Go Diving In) .45
36 New Orleans Saints (Crash Course) .20
37 Phil Simms New York Giants (Armed and Dangerous) .45
38 Lawrence Taylor New York Giants (A Giant-sized Hit) .75
39 Ken O'Brien New York Jets (Jets Prepare for Takeoff) .30
40 New York Jets (Showing No Mercy) .20
41 Philadelphia Eagles (Taking It Straight Up the Middle) .20
42 Reggie White Philadelphia Eagles (The Strong Arm of the Defense) 1.25
43 Pittsburgh Steelers (Double-Team Trouble) .20
44 Pittsburgh Steelers (Caught in a Steel Trap) .20
45 St. Louis Cardinals (The Kick is Up and... It's Good) .20
46 St. Louis Cardinals (Seeing Red) .20
47 San Diego Chargers (Blast Off) .20
48 Todd Christensen San Diego Chargers (Lightning Strikes) .45
49 San Francisco 49ers (The Rush Is On) .75
50 San Francisco 49ers (Shoulder to Shoulder) .20
51 Curt Warner Seattle Seahawks (Not a Defender in Sight) .30
52 Seattle Seahawks (Hard Knocks) .20
53 Steve Young Tampa Bay Bucaneers (Rolling Out Against the Grain) 3.75
54 Tampa Bay Buccaneers (Crunch Time) .20
55 Jay Schroeder Washington Redskins (Getting the Drop on the Defense) .45
56 Washington Redskins (The Blitz Claims Another Victim) .20
57 AFC Championship Game (Denver vs. Cleveland) .20
58 AFC Divisional Playoff (Cleveland vs. New York Jets) .20
59 Andre Tippett AFC Divisional Playoff (Denver vs. New England) .30
60 AFC Wild Card Game (New York Jets vs. Kansas City) .20
61 Lawrence Taylor NFC Championship (New York Giants vs. Washington) .60
62 William Perry NFC Divisional Playoff (Chicago vs. Washington) .30
63 Joe Morris NFC Divisional Playoff (New York Giants vs. San Francisco) .30
64 Eric Dickerson NFC Wild Card Game (Washington vs. Los Angeles Rams) .65
65 Super Bowl I (Green Bay vs. Kansas City) .30
66 Bart Starr Super Bowl II (Green Bay vs. Oakland) .50
67 Matt Snell Super Bowl III (New York vs. Baltimore) .30
68 Super Bowl IV (Kansas City vs. Minnesota) .20
69 Duane Thomas Super Bowl V (Baltimore vs. Dallas) .45
70 Roger Staubach Super Bowl VI (Dallas vs. Miami) .85
71 Bob Griese, Jim Kiick Super Bowl VII (Miami vs. Washington) .60
72 Larry Csonka Super Bowl VIII (Miami vs. Minnesota) .60
73 Fran Tarkenton Super Bowl IX (Pittsburgh vs. Minnesota) .75
74 Franco Harris Super Bowl X (Pittsburgh vs. Dallas) .75
75 Chuck Foreman Super Bowl XI (Oakland vs. Minnesota) .30
76 Tony Dorsett Super Bowl XII (Dallas vs. Denver) .60
77 Terry Bradshaw Super Bowl XIII (Pittsburgh vs. Dallas) 1.00
78 Cullen Bryant Super Bowl XIV (Pittsburgh vs. Los Angeles) .30
79 Jim Plunkett Super Bowl XV (Oakland vs. Philadelphia) .30
80 Super Bowl XVI (San Francisco vs. Cincinnati) .20
81 Super Bowl XVII (Washington vs. Miami) .20
82 Super Bowl XVIII (Los Angeles vs. Washington) .20
83 R. Craig, Joe Montana Super Bowl XIX (San Francisco vs. Miami) 2.50
84 Wilber Marshall, Richard Dent Super Bowl XX (Chicago vs. New England) .45
85 Lawrence Taylor Super Bowl XXI (New York vs. Denver) .70
86 Phil Simms Super Bowl XXI (New York vs. Denver) .45
87 Lawrence Taylor, Carl Banks Super Bowl XXI (Giants erupt in 3rd, Score 17 Points) .50
88 Super Bowl XXI (Giants Outrun Broncos by only 27 yards) .50

1988 Fleer Team Action

The final Fleer Team Action set contained 88 cards, including two for each team, 11 Super Bowl cards, special playoff cards and a few league-leader cards at the end of the set. The set was basically structured alphabetically by team nicknames within each conference. There are three subsets: Super Bowls of the Decade (#s 57-67); Playoff Games (#s 68-75) and "League Leading Teams" (#s 76-88). Other highlights are two cards each for Dan Marino, Joe Montana, John Elway and Bo Jackson. Cards were sold in packs of seven, plus three logo stickers.

NM/M

Complete Set (88): 18.50
Common Card: .18
1 Boomer Esiason Cincinnati Bengals (A Great Wall) .80
2 Cincinnati Bengals (Stacking the Odds) .18
3 Jim Kelly Buffalo Bills (Play-Action) 1.25
4 Buffalo Bills (Buffalo Soldiers) .18
5 John Elway Denver Broncos (Sneak Attack) 1.25
6 Denver Broncos (Crushing the Opposition) .18
7 Bernie Kosar, Kevin Mack Cleveland Browns (On the Run) .50
8 Eric Dickerson Cleveland Browns (Dogs' Day) .65
9 Gary Anderson San Diego Chargers (A Bolt of Blue) .25
10 San Diego Chargers (That's a Wrap) .18
11 Kansas City Chiefs (Last Line of Offense) .18
12 Kansas City Chiefs (Hard-Hitting in the Heartland) .18

13 Indianapolis Colts (An Eye to the End Zone) .18
14 Indianapolis Colts (Free Ball) .18
15 Dan Marino Miami Dolphins (Miami Scoring Machine) 2.00
16 Miami Dolphins (No Mercy) .25
17 Ken O'Brien New York Jets (On a Roll) .25
18 New York Jets (Jets Win a Dogfight) .18
19 Warren Moon Houston Oilers (Well-Oiled Machine) .85
20 Houston Oilers (Hard Shoulder) .18
21 Craig James New England Patriots (A Clean Sweep) .25
22 Bo Jackson New England Patriots (A Fall in New England) 1.00
23 Bo Jackson Los Angeles Raiders (Rush Hour in Los Angeles) 1.50
24 Howie Long Los Angeles Raiders (Cut Me Some Slack) .30
25 Curt Warner Seattle Seahawks (Follow the Leader) .25
26 Brian Bosworth Seattle Seahawks (Pain, But No Gain) .30
27 Pittsburgh Steelers (Life in the Fast Lane) .18
28 Pittsburgh Steelers (No Exit) .18
29 Chicago Bears (Bearly Audible) .18
30 Chicago Bears (Here, Kitty, Kitty) .18
31 Vinny Testaverde Tampa Bay Buccaneers (Letting Loose) 1.00
32 Tampa Bay Buccaneers (In the Grasp) .18
33 Neil Lomax St. Louis Cardinals (You've Gotta Hand it to Him) .25
34 Roger Craig St. Louis Cardinals (Stack of Cards) .35
35 Herschel Walker Dallas Cowboys (Take it Away) .50
36 Randy White Dallas Cowboys (Howdy, Partner) .40
37 Randall Cunningham Philadelphia Eagles (Eagle in Flight) 1.25
38 Reggie White Philadelphia Eagles (Buffalo Sandwich) .75
39 Atlanta Falcons (Rumbling Runner) .18
40 Atlanta Falcons (The Brink of Disaster) .18
41 Roger Craig San Francisco 49ers (Move Aside) .40
42 Ronnie Lott San Francisco 49ers (Bullies By the Bay) .50
43 Phil Simms New York Giants (Firing a Fastball) .40
44 New York Giants (A Giant Headache) .18
45 Detroit Lions (Charge Up the Middle) .18
46 Detroit Lions (Rocking and Rolling in Motown) .18
47 Carl Lee Green Bay Packers (Gaining Attitude) .18
48 Green Bay Packers (This Play is a Hit) .18
49 Jim Everett Los Angeles Rams (Rams Lock Horns) .40
50 Los Angeles Rams (Greetings from L.A.) .18
51 Washington Redskins (Capital Gains) .18
52 Washington Redskins (No More Mr. Nice Guy) .18
53 New Orleans Saints (Roamin' in the Dome) .18
54 New Orleans Saints (He'll Feel This One Tomorrow) .18
55 Wade Wilson Minnesota Vikings (Passing Fancy) .45
56 Minnesota Vikings (A Vikings' Siege) .18
57 Timmy Smith Super Bowl XXII (Washington vs. Denver) .25
58 Timmy Smith Super Bowl Checklist .25
59 John Elway Super Bowl Checklist 1.00
60 Lawrence Taylor, Carl Banks Super Bowl XXI (New York vs. Denver) .75
61 Walter Payton Super Bowl XX (Chicago vs. New England) .75
62 Roger Craig Super Bowl XIX (San Francisco vs. Miami) .30
63 Marcus Allen Super Bowl XVIII (Los Angeles Raiders vs. Washington) .50
64 Super Bowl XVII (Washington vs. Miami) .18
65 Joe Montana Super Bowl XVI (San Francisco vs. Cincinnati) 1.75
66 Jim Plunkett Super Bowl XV (Oakland vs. Philadelphia) .25
67 Super Bowl XIV (Pittsburgh vs. Los Angeles Rams) .18
68 NFC Championship (Washington vs. Minnesota) .18
69 John Elway AFC Championship (Denver vs. Cleveland) 1.00
70 Joe Montana NFC Playoff Game (Minnesota vs. San Francisco) 1.75
71 NFC Playoff Game (Washington vs. Chicago) .18
72 Ozzie Newsome, Kevin Mack AFC Playoff Game (Cleveland vs. Indianapolis) .30
73 AFC Playoff Game (Denver vs. Houston) .18
74 NFC Wild Card Game (Minnesota vs. New Orleans) .18
75 AFC Wild Card Game (Houston vs. Seattle) .18
76 Roger Craig League Leading Team Rushing (San Francisco 49ers) .25
77 Dan Marino League Leading Team Passing (Miami Dolphins) 1.50
78 League Leading Team Interceptions (New Orleans Saints) .18
79 League Leading Team Fumble Recovery (Philadelphia Eagles) .18
80 Richard Dent League Leading Team Sacks (Chicago Bears) .40
81 Kickoff Reurns (Buffalo Bills) .18
82 Punt Returns (New York Jets) .18
83 League Leading Teams Punt Returns (St. Louis Cardinals) .18
84 League Leading Team Kickoff Returns (Atlanta Falcons) .18
85 League Leading Team Fewest Fumbles (Pittsburgh Steelers) .18
86 Bernie Kosar League Leading Team Fewest Interceptions (Cleveland Browns) .50
87 Allowed (Indianapolis Colts) .18
88 Henry Ellard League Leading Team TD's on Returns (Los Angeles Rams) .40

1990 Fleer

The 1990 "Premier Edition" football card series, Fleer's first player card issue since 1963, was issued in mid-June. Cards were available in 15- and 43-count packs and 45-count three-pack strips. The cards carry full-color printing on the fronts and backs. Card fronts show full-figure action photography, while backs highlight a head shot, stats and text. The 25 cards in the All-Pro subset are different than the other Premier Edition cards. The All-Pro cards contain two photos on each card front - a large facial close-up and a smaller full-figure shot against a silver background. Special metallic links are used for graphic design effect. Jeff George, Andre Ware, Blair Thomas and Percy Snow are featured within the set as first-round draft choices by their respective teams. With the introduction of this football card set, Fleer was the only manufacturer offering a full line of football, baseball and basketball cards.

	NM/M
Complete Set (400):	7.00
Common Player:	.03
Wax Pack (15):	.50
Wax Box (36):	10.00

1 Harris Barton .03
2 Chet Brooks .03
3 Michael Carter .03
4 Mike Cofer .03
5 Roger Craig .03
6 *Kevin Fagan* .06
7 Charles Haley .03
8 *Pierce Holt* .15
9 Ronnie Lott .03
10 Joe Montana (stats reversed on back) 1.00
11 Bubba Paris .03
12 Tom Rathman .03
13 Jerry Rice .75
14 John Taylor .20
15 Keena Turner .03
16 Mike Walter .03
17 Steve Young .75
18 Steve Atwater .03
19 Tyrone Braxton .03
20 *Michael Brooks* .15
21 John Elway .50
22 Simon Fletcher .03
23 Bobby Humphrey .03
24 Mark Jackson .03
25 Vance Johnson .03
26 Greg Kragen .03
27 Ken Lanier .03
28 Karl Mecklenburg .03
29 Orson Mobley .03
30 Steve Sewell .03
31 Dennis Smith .03
32 David Treadwell .03
33 Willie Anderson .03
34 Greg Bell .03
35 Henry Ellard .03
36 Jim Everett .03
37 Jerry Gray .03
38 Kevin Greene .03
39 Pete Holohan .03
40 LeRoy Irvin .03
41 Mike Lansford .03
42 *Buford McGee* .08
43 Tom Newberry .03
44 Vince Newsome .03
45 Jackie Slater .03
46 Mike Wilcher .03
47 Matt Bahr .03
48 Brian Brennan .03
49 Thane Gash .03
50 Mike Johnson .03
51 Bernie Kosar .03
52 Reggie Langhorne .03
53 Tim Manoa .03
54 Clay Matthews .03
55 Eric Metcalf .08
56 Frank Minnifield .03
57 Gregg Rakoczy .03
58 Webster Slaughter .03
59 Bryan Wagner .03
60 Felix Wright .03
61 Raul Allegre .03
62 Ottis Anderson .03
63 Carl Banks .03
64 Mark Bavaro .03
65 Maurice Carthon .03
66 Mark Collins .03
67 *Jeff Hostetler* .50
68 Erik Howard .03
69 Pepper Johnson .03
70 Sean Landeta .03
71 Lionel Manuel .03
72 Leonard Marshall .03
73 Dave Meggett .08
74 Bart Oates .03
75 Doug Riesenberg .03
76 Phil Simms .10
77 Lawrence Taylor .10
78 Eric Allen .03
79 Jerome Brown .03
80 Keith Byars .03
81 Cris Carter .30
82 Randall Cunningham, Byron Evans (error) .20
83 Ron Heller, Byron Evans (error) .10
84 Ron Heller .03
85 Terry Hoage .03
86 Keith Jackson .20
87 Seth Joyner .03
88 Mike Quick .03
89 Mike Schad .03
90 Clyde Simmons .03
91 John Teltschik .03
92 Anthony Toney .03
93 Reggie White .15
94 Ray Berry .03
95 Joey Browner .03
96 Anthony Carter .03
97 Chris Doleman .03
98 Rick Fenney .03
99 *Rich Gannon* 1.50
100 Hassan Jones .03
101 Steve Jordan .03
102 Rich Karlis .03
103 *Andre Ware* .20
104 Kirk Lowdermilk .03
105 Keith Millard .03
106 Scott Studwell .03
107 Herschel Walker .03
108 Wade Wilson .03
109 Gary Zimmerman .03
110 Don Beebe .10
111 Cornelius Bennett .03
112 Shane Conlan .03
113 Jim Kelly .20
114 Scott Norwood .03
115 Mark Kelso .03
116 Larry Kinnebrew .03
117 Pete Metzelaars .03
118 Scott Radecic .03
119 Andre Reed .20
120 Jim Richter .03
121 Bruce Smith .03
122 Leonard Smith .03
123 Art Still .03
124 Thurman Thomas .50
125 Steve Brown .03
126 Ray Childress .03
127 Ernest Givins .03
128 John Grimsley .03
129 Alonzo Highsmith .03
130 Drew Hill .03
131 Bruce Matthews .03
132 Johnny Meads .03
133 Warren Moon .20
134 Mike Munchak .03
135 Mike Rozier .03
136 Dean Steinkuhler .03
137 Lorenzo White .15
138 Tony Zendejas .03
139 Gary Anderson .03
140 Bubby Brister .08
141 Thomas Everett .03
142 Derek Hill .03
143 Merril Hoge .03
144 Tim Johnson .03
145 Louis Lipps .03
146 David Little .03
147 Greg Lloyd .03
148 Mike Mularkey .03
149 John Rienstra .03
150 Gerald Williams .08
151 Keith Willis .03
152 Rod Woodson .10
153 Tim Worley .03
154 Gary Clark .10
155 Darryl Grant .03
156 Darrell Green .03
157 Joe Jacoby .03
158 Jim Lachey .03
159 Chip Lohmiller .03
160 Charles Mann .03
161 Wilber Marshall .03
162 Mark May .03
163 Ralf Mojsiejenko .03
164 Art Monk .06
165 Gerald Riggs .03
166 Mark Rypien .15
167 Ricky Sanders .03
168 Don Warren .03
169 Robert Brown .03
170 Blair Bush .03
171 Brent Fullwood .03
172 Tim Harris .03
173 Chris Jacke .03
174 Perry Kemp .03
175 Don Majkowski .03
176 Tony Mandarich .03
177 Mark Murphy .03
178 Brian Noble .03
179 Ken Ruettgers .03
180 Sterling Sharpe .20
181 Ed West .03
182 Keith Woodside .03
183 Morten Andersen .03
184 Stan Brock .03
185 *Jim Dombrowski* .10
186 John Fourcade .03
187 Bobby Hebert .10
188 Craig Heyward .03
189 Dalton Hilliard .03
190 Rickey Jackson .03
191 Buford Jordan .03
192 Eric Martin .03
193 Robert Massey .03
194 Sam Mills .03
195 Pat Swilling .03
196 Jim Wilks .03
197 *John Alt* .10
198 Walker Lee Ashley .03
199 Steve DeBerg .03
200 Leonard Griffin .03
201 Albert Lewis .03
202 Nick Lowery .03
203 Bill Maas .03
204 Pete Mandley .03
205 *Chris Martin* .10
206 Christian Okoye .03
207 Stephone Paige .03
208 *Kevin Porter* .10
209 Derrick Thomas .20
210 Lewis Billups .03
211 James Brooks .03
212 Jason Buck .03
213 *Rickey Dixon* .10
214 Boomer Esiason .10
215 David Fulcher .03
216 Rodney Holman .03
217 Lee Johnson .03
218 Tim Krumrie .03
219 Tim McGee .03
220 Anthony Munoz .03
221 Bruce Reimers .03
222 Leon White .03
223 Ickey Woods .03
224 Harvey Armstrong .03
225 Michael Ball .03
226 Chip Banks .03
227 Pat Beach .03
228 Duane Bickett .03
229 Bill Brooks .03
230 Jon Hand .03
231 Andre Rison .25
232 Rohn Stark .03
233 Donnell Thompson .03
234 Jack Trudeau .03
235 Clarence Verdin .03
236 Mark Clayton .03
237 Jeff Cross .03
238 *Jeff Dellenbach* .10
239 Mark Duper .03
240 Ferrell Edmunds .03
241 Hugh Green .03
242 E.J. Junior .03
243 Marc Logan .03
244 Dan Marino 1.00
245 John Offerdahl .03
246 Reggie Roby .03
247 Sammie Smith .03
248 Pete Stoyanovich .03
249 Marcus Allen .08
250 *Eddie Anderson* .10
251 Steve Beuerlein .15
252 Mike Dyal .03
253 Mervyn Fernandez .03
254 Bob Golic .03
255 Mike Harden .03
256 Bo Jackson .40
257 Howie Long .03
258 Don Mosebar .03
259 Jay Schroeder .03
260 Steve Smith .03
261 Greg Townsend .03
262 Lionel Washington .03
263 Brian Blades .10
264 Jeff Bryant .03
265 Grant Feasel .03
266 Jacob Green .03
267 James Jefferson .03
268 Norm Johnson .03
269 Dave Krieg .03
270 Travis McNeal .03
271 Joe Nash .03
272 Rufus Porter .03
273 Kelly Stouffer .03
274 John L. Williams .03
275 Jim Arnold .03
276 Jerry Ball .03
277 Bennie Blades .03
278 Lomas Brown .03
279 Mike Cofer .03
280 Bob Gagliano .03
281 Richard Johnson .03
282 Eddie Murray .03
283 Rodney Peete .10
284 Barry Sanders 1.25
285 Eric Sanders .03
286 Chris Spielman .03
287 *Eric Williams* .10
288 Neal Anderson .08
289 Kevin Butler (placekicker/PK placekicker/P punter/P punter/PK) .08
290 Jim Covert .03
291 Richard Dent .03
292 Dennis Gentry .03
293 Jim Harbaugh .15
294 Jay Hilgenberg .03
295 Vestee Jackson .03
296 Steve McMichael .03
297 Ron Morris .03
298 Brad Muster .03
299 Mike Singletary .03
300 James Thornton .03
301 Mike Tomczak .03
302 Keith Van Horne .03
303 Chris Bahr .03
304 *Martin Bayless* .10
305 Marion Butts .10
306 Gill Byrd .03
307 Arthur Cox .03
308 Burt Grossman .03
309 Jamie Holland .03
310 Jim McMahon .03
311 Anthony Miller .30
312 Leslie O'Neal .03
313 Billy Ray Smith .03
314 Tim Spencer .03
315 *Broderick Thompson* .10
316 Lee Williams .03
317 Bruce Armstrong .03
318 Tim Goad .03
319 Steve Grogan .03
320 Roland James .03
321 Cedric Jones .03
322 Fred Marion .03
323 Stanley Morgan .03
324 Robert Perryman .03
325 Johnny Rembert .03
326 Ed Reynolds .03
327 Kenneth Sims .03
328 John Stephens .03
329 *Danny Villa* .06
330 Robert Awalt .03
331 Anthony Bell .03
332 Rich Camarillo .03
333 Earl Ferrell .03
334 Roy Green .03
335 Gary Hogeboom .03
336 Cedric Mack .03
337 Freddie Joe Nunn .03
338 Luis Sharpe .03
339 Vai Sikahema .03
340 J.T. Smith .03
341 *Tom Tupa* .08
342 *Percy Snow* .10
343 Mark Carrier (TB) .03
344 Randy Grimes .03
345 Paul Gruber .03
346 Ron Hall .03
347 *Jeff George* 1.25
348 Bruce Hill .03
349 William Howard .03
350 Donald Igwebuike .03
351 *Chris Mohr* .08
352 *Winston Moss* .08
353 Ricky Reynolds .03
354 Mark Robinson .03
355 Lars Tate .03
356 Vinny Testaverde .10
357 Broderick Thomas .03
358 Troy Benson .03
359 *Jeff Criswell* .10
360 Tony Eason .03
361 James Hasty .03
362 Johnny Hector .03
363 Bobby Humphery .03
364 Pat Leahy .03
365 Erik McMillan .03
366 Freeman McNeil .03
367 Ken O'Brien .03
368 Ron Stallworth .03
369 Al Toon .03
370 *Blair Thomas* .15
371 Aundray Bruce .03
372 Tony Casillas .03
373 Shawn Collins .03
374 Evan Cooper .03
375 Bill Fralic .03
376 Scott Fulhage .03
377 Mike Gann .03
378 Ron Heller .03
379 Keith Jones .03
380 Mike Kenn .03
381 Chris Miller .10
382 Deion Sanders .35
383 John Settle .03
384 Troy Aikman .75
385 Bill Bates .03
386 Willie Broughton .03
387 Steve Folsom .03
388 Ray Horton .03
389 Michael Irvin .25
390 Jim Jeffcoat .03
391 Eugene Lockhart .03
392 *Kelvin Martin* .15
393 Nate Newton .03
394 Mike Saxon .03
395 Derrick Shepard .03
396 Steve Walsh .03
397 Joe Montana, Jerry Rice .70
398 Checklist .03
399 Checklist .03
400 Checklist .03

1990 Fleer All-Pro

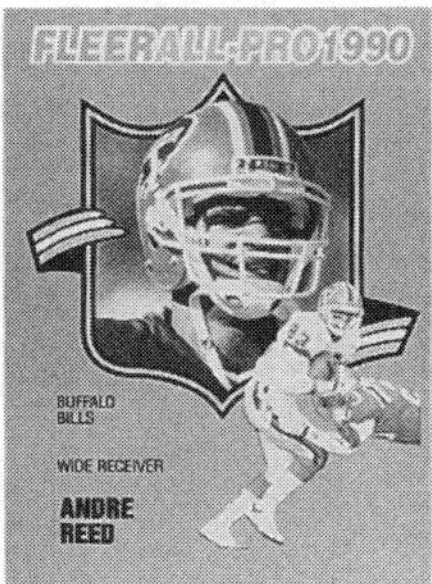

These silver cards were distributed randomly in Fleer wax and cello packs. Cards were prone to damage, since the silver coating easily suffered scratches and dings. Cards were issued approximately one to every six to 10 packs.

	NM/M
Complete Set (25):	7.50
Common Player:	.25

1 Joe Montana 3.00
2 Jerry Rice 2.00
3 Keith Jackson .50
4 Barry Sanders 3.00
5 Christian Okoye .25
6 Tom Newberry .25
7 Jim Covert .25
8 Anthony Munoz .25
9 Mike Munchak .25
10 Jay Hilgenberg .25
11 Chris Doleman .25
12 Keith Millard .25
13 Derrick Thomas 1.00
14 Lawrence Taylor .75
15 Karl Mecklenburg .25
16 Reggie White .60
17 Tim Harris .25
18 David Fulcher .25
19 Ronnie Lott .50
20 Eric Allen .25
21 Steve Atwater .25
22 Rich Camarillo .25
23 Morten Anderson .25
24 Andre Reed 1.00
25 Rod Woodson .50

1990 Fleer Stars 'n Stripes

Issued in eight-card boxes by the Asher Candy Co., a subsidiary of Fleer, these cards were considered by the parent company to be little more than a test set. Collation was bad, and the set was riddled with basic errors. The first edition of Stars 'N Stripes features 80 players from the 1990 Pro Bowl plus 10 college stars selected in the first round of the 1990 NFL draft. All 90 cards carry full-color printing on both sides, with action photography on the front and a head shot of the player on the back. Pro Bowlers are shown in their all-conference uniforms while first-round picks are shown in collegiate action. Front borders have red, white and blue striping. Each package is shrink-wrapped. A full checklist is on the back of each pack.

	NM/M
Complete Set (90):	15.00
Common Player:	.05

1 Warren Moon .35
2 Reggie Roby .05
3 David Treadwell .05
4 Dave Krieg .05

5 James Brooks .20
6 Erik McMillan .05
7 Rod Woodson .10
8 Albert Lewis .05
9 Kevin Ross .05
10 Frank Minnifield .05
11 David Fulcher .07
12 Thurman Thomas .75
13 Christian Okoye .25
14 Dennis Smith .05
15 Johnny Rembert .05
16 Ray Donaldson .05
17 John Offerdahl .15
18 Clay Matthews .05
19 Shane Conlan .10
20 Derrick Thomas .30
21 Tunch Ilken .05
22 Mike Munchak .07
23 Max Montoya .05
24 Kent Hull .07
25 Greg Kragen .05
26 Bruce Matthews .70
27 Howie Long .10
28 Chris Hinton .10
29 Anthony Munoz .10
30 Bruce Smith .20
31 Ferrell Edmunds .05
32 Rodney Holman .05
33 Andre Reed .50
34 Webster Slaughter .05
35 Anthony Miller .20
36 Brian Blades .10
37 Leslie O'Neal .10
38 Rufus Porter .10
39 Lee Williams .05
40 Ed Murray .05
41 Mark Rypien .20
42 Randall Cunningham .35
43 Rich Camarillo .05
44 Barry Sanders 2.50
45 Dalton Hilliard .10
46 Eric Allen .10
47 Brent Fullwood .05
48 Ron Wolfley .05
49 Jerry Gray .05
50 Dave Meggett .50
51 Roger Craig .35
52 Carl Lee .10
53 Ronnie Lott .20
54 Tim McDonald .05
55 Joey Browner .10
56 Mike Singletary .20
57 Vaughan Johnson .05
58 Chris Spielman .05
59 Doug Smith .05
60 Lawrence Taylor .50
61 Chris Doleman .10
62 Guy McIntyre .05
63 Jay Hilgenberg .07
64 Randall McDaniel .05
65 Gary Zimmerman .05
66 Luis Sharpe .05
67 Charles Mann .05
68 Keith Millard .10
69 Jackie Slater .05
70 Bill Fralic .05
71 Henry Ellard .10
72 Jerry Rice .65
73 Steve Jordan .05
74 Sterling Sharpe .50
75 Keith Jackson .25
76 Mark Carrier (TB) .10
77 Kevin Greene .10
78 Reggie White .20
79 Jerry Ball .10
80 Tim Harris .10
81 Jeff George 1.00
82 Blair Thomas .40
83 Cortez Kennedy .75
84 Junior Seau .75
85 Mark Carrier .40
86 Andre Ware .40
87 Chris Singleton .50
88 Percy Snow .75
89 Steve Broussard .90
90 Rodney Hampton .50

1990 Fleer Update

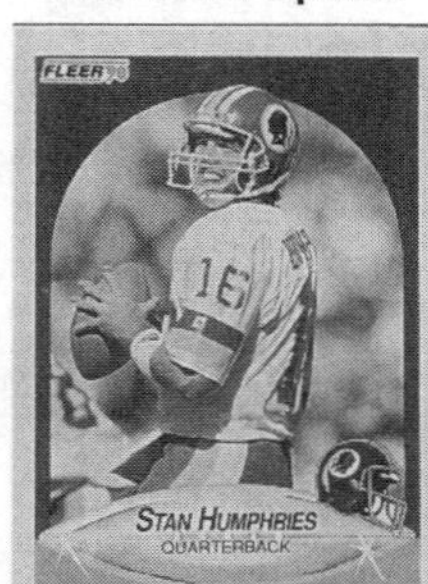

Fleer's 1990 update football set of 120 cards was sold to hobby shops in boxed form. Cards are arranged alphabetically by teams and are the same style as 1990 Fleer football.

NM/M
Complete Set (120): 30.00
Common Player: .10
Minor Stars: .20
1 Albert Bentley .10
2 Dean Biasucci .10
3 Ray Donaldson .10
4 Jeff George .50
5 *Ray Agnew* .10
6 Greg McMurtry .10
7 *Chris Singleton* .10
8 *James Francis* .10
9 *Harold Green* .20
10 John Elliott .10
11 *Rodney Hampton* .75
12 Gary Reasons .10
13 *Lewis Tillman* .20
14 Everson Walls .10
15 *David Alexander* .10
16 Jim McMahon .20
17 *Ben Smith* .10
18 Andre Waters .10
19 *Calvin Williams* .20
20 Earnest Byner .10
21 *Andre Collins* .10
22 Russ Grimm .10
23 *Stan Humphries* .50
24 *Martin Mayhew* .10
25 *Barry Foster* .20
26 *Eric Green* .30
27 Tunch Ilkin .10
28 Hardy Nickerson .10
29 Jerrol Williams .10
30 Mike Baab .10
31 *Leroy Hoard* .50
32 Eddie Johnson .10
33 William Fuller .10
34 *Haywood Jeffires* .30
35 *Don Maggs* .10
36 Allen Pinkett .10
37 Robert Awalt .10
38 Dennis McKinnon .10
39 *Ken Norton Jr.* .30
40 *Emmitt Smith* 20.00
41 *Alexander Wright* .20
42 Eric Hill .10
43 *Johnny Johnson* .20
44 Timm Rosenbach .10
45 *Anthony Thompson* .20
46 *Dexter Carter* .20
47 Eric Davis .10
48 Keith DeLong .10
49 *Brent Jones* .30
50 *Darryl Pollard* .10
51 *Steve Wallace* .10
52 *Bern Brostek* .10
53 Aaron Cox .10
54 Cleveland Gary .10
55 *Fred Strickland* .20
56 *Pat Terrell* .10
57 Steve Broussard .10
58 Scott Case .10
59 *Brian Jordan* .30
60 Andre Rison .30
61 Kevin Haverdink .10
62 Reuben Mayes .10
63 Steve Walsh .20
64 Greg Bell .10
65 Tim Brown .30
66 Willie Gault .10
67 *Vance Mueller* .10
68 Bill Pickel .10
69 Aaron Wallace .10
70 Glenn Parker .10
71 Frank Reich .20
72 *Leon Seals* .10
73 Darryl Talley .10
74 *Brad Baxter* .10
75 Jeff Causwell .10
76 Jeff Lageman .10
77 *Rob Moore* 3.00
78 Blair Thomas .20
79 Louis Oliver .10
80 Tony Paige .10
81 *Richmond Webb* .20
82 *Robert Blackmon* .10
83 *Derrick Fenner* .20
84 Andy Heck .10
85 *Cortez Kennedy* .30
86 *Terry Wooden* .10
87 Jeff Donaldson .10
88 *Tim Grunhard* .10
89 Emile Harry .10
90 *Dan Saleaumua* .20
91 Percy Snow .10
92 Andre Ware .20
93 *Darrell Fullington* .10
94 Mike Merriweather .10
95 Henry Thomas .10
96 Robert Brown .10
97 *Leroy Butler* .10
98 Anthony Dilweg .10
99 *Darrel Thompson* .10
100 Keith Woodside .10
101 Gary Plummer .10
102 *Junior Seau* 4.00
103 Billy Joe Tolliver .20
104 Mark Vlasic .10
105 Gary Anderson .10
106 *Ian Beckles* .10
107 *Reggie Cobb* .20
108 *Keith McCants* .20
109 *Mark Bortz* .10
110 Maury Buford .10
111 *Mark Carrier* .20
112 Dan Hampton .10
113 William Perry .10
114 Ron Rivera .10
115 Lemuel Stinson .10
116 *Melvin Bratton* .10
117 *Gary Kubiak* .10
118 *Alton Montgomery* .10
119 Ricky Nattiel .10
120 Checklist .10

1991 Fleer

Fleer's second football set expanded by 32 cards. The issues again included randomly-packed all-star cards. New features included a league leaders subset, a hitters subset, and Pro Visions and All-Pros randomly-packed insert sets.

NM/M
Complete Set (432): 6.00
Common Player: .03
Pack (14): .40
Wax Box (36): 8.00
1 Shane Conlan .07
2 John Davis .03
3 Kent Hull .05
4 James Lofton .10
5 Keith McKeller .07
6 Scott Norwood .03
7 Nate Odomes .03
8 Andre Reed .20
9 Jim Ritcher .03
10 Leon Seals .03
11 Bruce Smith .15
12 Leonard Smith .07
13 Steve Tasker .05
14 Thurman Thomas .40
15 Lewis Billups .03
16 James Brooks .15
17 Eddie Brown .07
18 Carl Carter .03
19 Boomer Esiason .15
20 James Francis .10
21 David Fulcher .10
22 Harold Green .15
23 Rodney Holman .07
24 Bruce Kozerski .03
25 Tim McGee .07
26 Anthony Munoz .07
27 Bruce Reimers .03
28 Ickey Woods .10
29 Carl Zander .10
30 Mike Baab .03
31 Brian Brennan .05
32 Rob Burnett .03
33 Paul Farren .03
34 Thane Gash .03
35 David Grayson .03
36 Mike Johnson .03
37 Reggie Langhorne .05
38 Kevin Mack .05
39 Eric Metcalf .07
40 Frank Minnifield .03
41 Gregg Rakoczy .03
42 Felix Wright .03
43 Steve Atwater .07
44 Michael Brooks .03
45 John Elway .35
46 Simon Fletcher .03
47 Bobby Humphrey .20
48 Mark Jackson .05
49 Keith Kartz .03
50 Clarence Kay .03
51 Greg Kragen .03
52 Karl Mecklenburg .10
53 Warren Powers .03
54 Dennis Smith .05
55 Jim Szymanski .03
56 David Treadwell .03
57 Michael Young .03
58 Ray Childress .05
59 Curtis Duncan .05
60 William Fuller .03
61 Ernest Givins .07
62 Drew Hill .10
63 Haywood Jeffires .15
64 Richard Johnson .03
65 Sean Jones .03
66 Don Maggs .03
67 Bruce Matthews .05
68 Johnny Meads .03
69 Greg Montgomery .03
70 Warren Moon .20
71 Mike Munchak .05
72 Allen Pinkett .05
73 Lorenzo White .07
74 Pat Beach .03
75 Albert Bentley .05
76 Dean Biasucci .03
77 Duane Bickett .03
78 Bill Brooks .05
79 Sam Clancy .03
80 Ray Donaldson .03
81 Jeff George .30
82 Alan Grant .03
83 Jessie Hester .03
84 Jeff Herrod .03
85 Rohn Stark .03
86 Jack Trudeau .03
87 Clarence Verdin .05
88 John Alt .03
89 Steve DeBerg .15
90 Tim Grunhard .03
91 Dino Hackett .03
92 Jonathan Hayes .03
93 Albert Lewis .07
94 Nick Lowery .03
95 Bill Maas .03
96 Christian Okoye .15
97 Stephone Paige .07
98 Kevin Porter .03
99 David Szott .03
100 Derrick Thomas .25
101 Barry Word .20
102 Marcus Allen .15
103 Tom Benson .03
104 Tim Brown .07
105 Riki Ellison .03
106 Mervyn Fernandez .07
107 Willie Gault .07
108 Bob Golic .03
109 Ethan Horton .03
110 Bo Jackson .35
111 Howie Long .10
112 Don Mosebar .03
113 Jerry Robinson .03
114 Jay Schroeder .10
115 Steve Smith .05
116 Greg Townsend .05
117 Steve Wisniewski .05
118 Mark Clayton .07
119 Mark Duper .07
120 Ferrell Edmunds .03
121 Hugh Green .03
122 David Griggs .03
123 Jim Jensen .03
124 Dan Marino .75
125 Tim McKyer .03
126 John Offerdahl .07
127 Louis Oliver .05
128 Tony Paige .03
129 Reggie Roby .03
130 Keith Sims .03
131 Sammie Smith .10
132 Pete Stoyanovich .03
133 Richmond Webb .07
134 Bruce Armstrong .05
135 Vincent Brown .03
136 Hart Lee Dykes .05
137 Irving Fryar .05
138 Tim Goad .03
139 Tom Hodson .10
140 Maurice Hurst .03
141 Ronnie Lippett .03
142 Greg McMurtry .03
143 Ed Reynold .03
144 John Stephens .10
145 Andre Tippett .05
146 Danny Villa .03
147 Brad Baxter .15
148 Kyle Clifton .03
149 Jeff Criswell .03
150 James Hasty .03
151 Jeff Lageman .03
152 Pat Leahy .03
153 Rob Moore .20
154 Al Toon .10
155 Gary Anderson .03
156 Bubby Brister .15
157 Chris Calloway .03
158 Donald Evans .03
159 Eric Green .15
160 Bryan Hinkle .03
161 Merril Hoge .07
162 Tunch Ilkin .03
163 Louis Lipps .05
164 David Little .05
165 Mike Mularkey .03
166 Gerald Williams .03
167 Warren Williams .03
168 Rod Woodson .10
169 Tim Worley .07
170 Martin Bayless .03
171 Marion Butts .20
172 Gill Byrd .03
173 Frank Cornish .03
174 Arthur Cox .03
175 Burt Grossman .07
176 Anthony Miller .15
177 Leslie O'Neal .07
178 Gary Plummer .03
179 Junior Seau .25
180 Billy Joe Tolliver .03
181 Derrick Walker .03
182 Lee Williams .07
183 Robert Blackmon .03
184 Brian Blades .10
185 Grant Feasel .03
186 Derrick Fenner .25
187 Andy Heck .03
188 Norm Johnson .03
189 Tommy Kane .10
190 Cortez Kennedy .20
191 Dave Krieg .10
192 Travis McNeal .03
193 Eugene Robinson .03
194 Chris Warren .50
195 John L. Williams .10
196 Steve Broussard .10
197 Scott Case .03
198 Shawn Collins .05
199 Darion Conner .03
200 Tory Epps .03
201 Bill Fralic .05
202 Michael Haynes .25
203 Chris Hinton .05
204 Keith Jones .03
205 Brian Jordan .05
206 Mike Kenn .03
207 Chris Miller .15
208 Andre Rison .25
209 Mike Rozier .07
210 Deion Sanders .25
211 Gary Wilkins .03
212 Neal Anderson .20
213 Trace Armstrong .05
214 Mark Bortz .05
215 Kevin Butler .03
216 Mark Carrier .10
217 Wendell Davis .07
218 Richard Dent .07
219 Dennis Gentry .03
220 Jim Harbaugh .15
221 Jay Hilgenberg .05
222 Steve McMichael .05
223 Ron Morris .05
224 Brad Muster .05
225 Mike Singletary .07
226 James Thornton .03
227 Tommie Agee .03
228 Troy Aikman 1.50
229 Jack Del Rio .03
230 Issiac Holt .03
231 Ray Horton .03
232 Jim Jeffcoat .03
233 Eugene Lockhart .03
234 Kelvin Martin .07
235 Nate Newton .03
236 Mike Saxon .03
237 Emmitt Smith 2.00
238 Danny Stubbs .03
239 Jim Arnold .03
240 Jerry Ball .05
241 Benny Blades .03
242 Lomas Brown .03
243 Robert Clark .05
244 Mike Cofer .03
245 Mel Gray .03
246 Rodney Peete .15
247 Barry Sanders 1.25
248 Andre Ware .15
249 *Matt Brock* .05
250 Robert Brown .03
251 Anthony Dilweg .03
252 Johnny Holland .03
253 Tim Harris .07
254 Chris Jacke .03
255 Perry Kemp .05
256 Don Majkowski .15
257 Tony Mandarich .05
258 Mark Murphy .03
259 Brian Noble .03
260 Jeff Query .05
261 Sterling Sharpe .10
262 Ed West .05
263 Keith Woodside .03
264 Willie Anderson .10
265 Aaron Cox .05
266 Henry Ellard .07
267 Jim Everett .15
268 Cleveland Gary .07
269 Kevin Greene .07
270 Pete Holohan .03
271 Mike Lansford .03
272 Duval Love .03
273 Buford McGee .05
274 Tom Newberry .05
275 Jackie Slater .05
276 Frank Stams .03
277 Alfred Anderson .05
278 Joey Browner .07
279 Anthony Carter .07
280 Chris Doleman .10
281 Rick Fenney .05
282 Rich Gannon .07
283 Hassan Jones .05
284 Steve Jordan .05
285 Carl Lee .05
286 Randall McDaniel .05
287 Keith Millard .10
288 Herschel Walker .15
289 Wade Wilson .05
290 Gary Zimmerman .05
291 Morten Andersen .05
292 Jim Dombrowski .03
293 Gill Fenerty .07
294 Craig Heyward .07
295 Dalton Hilliard .10
296 Rickey Jackson .05
297 Vaughan Johnson .05
298 Eric Martin .05
299 Robert Massey .05
300 Rueben Mayes .05
301 Sam Mills .05
302 Brett Perriman .03
303 Pat Swilling .05
304 Steve Walsh .10
305 Ottis Anderson .03
306 Matt Bahr .03
307 Mark Bavaro .03
308 Maurice Carthon .03
309 Mark Collins .03
310 John Elliott .03
311 Rodney Hampton .10
312 Jeff Hostetler .10
313 Erik Howard .10
314 Pepper Johnson .03
315 Sean Landeta .03
316 Dave Meggett .03
317 Bart Oates .03
318 Phil Simms .08
319 Lawrence Taylor .10
320 Reyna Thompson .03
321 Everson Walls .03
322 Eric Allen .03
323 Fred Barnett .15
324 Jerome Brown .03
325 Keith Byars .03
326 Randall Cunningham .10
327 Byran Evans .03
328 Ron Heller .03
329 Keith Jackson .06
330 Seth Joyner .03
331 Heath Sherman .03
332 Clyde Simmons .03
333 Ben Smith .03
334 Anthony Toney .03
335 Andre Waters .03
336 Reggie White .15
337 Calvin Williams .20
338 Anthony Bell .03
339 Rich Camarillo .03
340 Roy Green .03
341 Tim Jorden .03
342 Cedric Mack .03
343 Dexter Manley .03
344 Freddie Joe Nunn .03
345 Ricky Proehl .03
346 Tootie Robbins .03
347 Timm Rosenbach .10
348 Luis Sharpe .03
349 Vai Sikahema .03
350 Anthony Thompson .03
351 Lonnie Young .03
352 Dexter Carter .03
353 Mike Cofer .03
354 Kevin Fagan .03
355 Don Griffin .03
356 Charles Haley .03
357 Pierce Holt .03
358 Brent Jones .03
359 Guy McIntyre .03
360 Joe Montana 1.00
361 Darryl Pollard .03
362 Tom Rathman .03
363 Jerry Rice .75
364 Bill Romanowski .03
365 John Taylor .10
366 Steve Wallace .03
367 Steve Young .40
368 Gary Anderson .03
369 Ian Beckles .03
370 Mark Carrier (TB) .03
371 Reggie Cobb .25
372 Reuben Davis .03
373 Randy Grimes .03
374 Wayne Haddix .03
375 Ron Hall .03
376 Harry Hamilton .03
377 Bruce Hill .03
378 Keith McCants .03
379 Bruce Perkins .03
380 Vinny Testaverde .10
381 Broderick Thomas .04
382 Jeff Bostic .03
383 Earnest Byner .03
384 Gary Clark .06
385 Darryl Grant .03
386 Darrell Green .05
387 Stan Humphries .35
388 Jim Lachey .03
389 Charles Mann .03
390 Wilber Marshall .03
391 Art Monk .06
392 Gerald Riggs .03
393 Mark Rypien .15
394 Ricky Sanders .03
395 Don Warren .03
396 Bruce Smith (H) .03
397 Reggie White (H) .08
398 Lawrence Taylor (H) .08
399 David Fulcher (H) .03
400 Derrick Thomas (H) .08
401 Mark Carrier (H) .05
402 Mike Singletary (H) .05
403 Charles Haley (H) .04
404 Jeff Cross (H) .03
405 Leslie O'Neal (H) .03
406 Tim Harris (H) .03
407 Steve Atwater (H) .03
408 Joe Montana (LL) .50
409 Randall Cunningham (LL) .08
410 Warren Moon (LL) .08
411 Andre Rison (LL) .08
412 Haywood Jeffires (LL) .06
413 Stephone Paige (LL) .03
414 Phil Simms (LL) .08
415 Barry Sanders (LL) .50
416 Bo Jackson (LL) .20
417 Thurman Thomas (LL) .20
418 Emmitt Smith (LL) 1.00
419 John L. Williams (LL) .03
420 *Nick Bell* (R) .10
422 *Eric Bienemy* .10
423 *Russell Maryland* .45
424 *Derek Russel* .20
425 Chris Smith .08
426 *Michael Stonebreaker* .08
427 Patrick Tyrance .04
428 Kenny Walker .08
429 Checklist 1 .03
430 Checklist 2 .03
431 Checklist 3 .03
432 Checklist 4 .03

1991 Fleer All-Pro

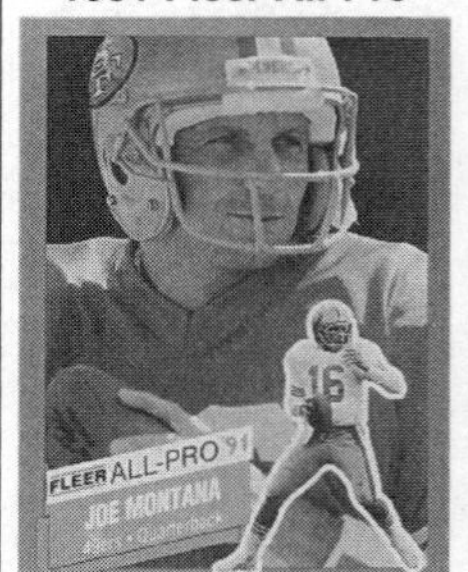

These standard-size cards were random inserts in 1991 Fleer football packs. The card front has a full-color portrait and a smaller picture of the player in action. Card backs contain the card number and a career summary.

NM/M
Complete Set (26): 5.00
Common Player: .10
1 Andre Reed .35
2 Bobby Humphrey .10
3 Kent Hull .10
4 Mark Bortz .10
5 Bruce Smith .10
6 Greg Townsend .10
7 Ray Childress .10
8 Andre Rison .40
9 Barry Sanders 1.50
10 Bo Jackson .50
11 Neal Anderson .10
12 Keith Jackson .30
13 Derrick Thomas .40
14 John Offerdahl .10
15 Lawrence Taylor .40
16 Darrell Green .10
17 Mark Carrier .10
18 David Fulcher .10

19	Joe Montana	1.00
20	Jerry Rice	1.50
21	Charles Haley	.10
22	Mike Singletary	.10
23	Nick Lowery	.10
24	Jim Lachey	.10
25	Anthony Munoz	.10
26	Thurman Thomas	1.00

1991 Fleer Pro Visions

These 1991 Fleer inserts feature artwork from artist Terry Smith. The cards are similar to Fleer's baseball Pro Vision counterparts. The card front has a drawing of the player and his name at the bottom. The back, numbered 1 of 10, etc., has a career summary.

		NM/M
Complete Set (10):		5.00
Common Player:		.25
1	Joe Montana	1.00
2	Barry Sanders	1.50
3	Lawrence Taylor	.40
4	Mike Singletary	.25
5	Dan Marino	2.00
6	Bo Jackson	.50
7	Randall Cunningham	.40
8	Bruce Smith	.25
9	Derrick Thomas	.50
10	Howie Long	.25

1991 Fleer Stars 'n Stripes

This 140-card set was produced by Fleer in conjunction with Asher Candy, which sold the set with cherry-flavored candy sticks. Each card front has a color action photo, with the set logo in the upper left corner. The card back has biographical information, statistics and a card number, plus a circle which contains a player mug shot.

		NM/M
Complete Set (140):		14.00
Common Player:		.10
1	Shane Conlan	.15
2	Kent Hull	.10
3	Andre Reed	.35
4	Bruce Smith	.30
5	Thurman Thomas	.75
6	James Brooks	.15
7	Boomer Esiason	.35
8	David Fulcher	.10
9	Rodney Holman	.10
10	Anthony Munoz	.15
11	Reggie Langhorne	.10
12	Clay Matthews	.10
13	Eric Metcalf	.20
14	Gregg Rakoczy	.10
15	Steve Atwater	.15
16	John Elway	.50
17	Bobby Humphrey	.15
18	Karl Mecklenburg	.15
19	Dennis Smith	.10
20	Ray Childress	.15
21	Ernest Givins	.20
22	Haywood Jeffires	.25
23	Warren Moon	.60
24	Mike Munchak	.10
25	Albert Bentley	.10
26	Jeff George	.25
27	Rohn Stark	.10
28	Clarence Verdin	.10
29	Albert Lewis	.10
30	Nick Lowery	.10
31	Christian Okoye	.10
32	Stephone Paige	.10
33	Derrick Thomas	.25
34	Barry Word	.10
35	Albert Lewis	.50
36	Howie Long	.15
37	Greg Townsend	.10
38	Steve Wisniewski	.10
39	Mark Clayton	.10
40	Dan Marino	1.50
41	John Offerdahl	.10
42	Richmond Webb	.10
43	Irving Fryar	.15
44	Ed Reynolds	.10
45	John Stephens	.10
46	Rob Moore	.25
47	Ken O'Brien	.15
48	Al Toon	.20
49	Bubby Brister	.20
50	Eric Green	.15
51	Merril Hoge	.10
52	David Little	.10
53	Rod Woodson	.20
54	Marion Butts	.15
55	Leslie O'Neal	.10
56	Junior Seau	.25
57	Billy Joe Tolliver	.15
58	Cortez Kennedy	.20
59	Dave Krieg	.15
60	John L. Williams	.10
61	Steve Broussard	.10
62	Bill Fralic	.15
63	Andre Rison	.35
64	Neal Anderson	.15
65	Mark Carrier	.15
66	Richard Dent	.15
67	Jim Harbaugh	.15
68	Mike Singletary	.20
69	Troy Aikman	2.00
70	Emmitt Smith	3.00
71	Mel Gray	.10
72	Rodney Peete	.20
73	Barry Sanders	2.00
74	Tim Harris	.15
75	Perry Kemp	.10
76	Sterling Sharpe	.40
77	Henry Ellard	.15
78	Jim Everett	.20
79	Kevin Greene	.15
80	Jackie Slater	.15
81	Joey Browner	.15
82	Chris Doleman	.15
83	Steve Jordan	.10
84	Carl Lee	.10
85	Herschel Walker	.25
86	Morten Andersen	.15
87	Dalton Hilliard	.10
88	Vaughan Johnson	.10
89	Steve Walsh	.15
90	Ottis Anderson	.15
91	John Elliott	.10
92	Rodney Hampton	.50
93	Sean Landeta	.10
94	Dave Meggett	.15
95	Phil Simms	.25
96	Lawrence Taylor	.35
97	Randall Cunningham	.25
98	Keith Jackson	.20
99	Seth Joyner	.15
100	Reggie White	.35
101	Roy Green	.15
102	Johnny Johnson	.20
103	Ricky Proehl	.15
104	Tootie Robbins	.10
105	Kevin Fagan	.10
106	Charles Haley	.15
107	Guy McIntyre	.10
108	Joe Montana	3.00
109	Tom Rathman	.15
110	Jerry Rice	1.50
111	John Taylor	.20
112	Wayne Haddix	.10
113	Vinny Testaverde	.15
114	Earnest Byner	.15
115	Gary Clark	.20
116	Darrell Green	.15
117	Jim Lachey	.10
118	Art Monk	.25
119	Mark Rypien	.20
120	Nick Bell	.15
121	Eric Bieniemy	.10
122	Jarrod Bunch	.15
123	Aaron Craver	.10
124	Lawrence Dawsey	.25
125	Mike Dumas	.10
126	Jeff Graham	.15
127	Paul Justin	.10
128	Darryll Lewis	.15
129	Todd Marinovich	.15
130	Russell Maryland	.20
131	Kanavis McGhee	.10
132	Ernie Mills	.10
133	Herman Moore	.20
134	Godfrey Myles	.15
135	Browning Nagle	.15
136	Esera Tuaolo	.10
137	Mark Vander Poel	.10
138	Harvey Williams	.15
139	Chris Zorich	.15
140	Checklist Card	.10

1992 Fleer Prototypes

These standard-size cards were distributed as two- and three-card panels to promote Fleer's 1992 cards. Each card back clearly identifies it as a prototype card; "1992 Pre-Production Sample" is written on the card back. Otherwise, the cards are identical in design to the regular 1992 Fleer cards.

		NM/M
Complete Set (6):		10.00
Common Player:		1.00
93	Mike Croel	1.00
191	Tim Brown	1.50
428	Mark Rypien	1.50
435	Terrell Buckley	1.00
457	Barry Sanders (LL)	3.00
475	Emmitt Smith (PV)	4.00

1992 Fleer

Fleer increased its 1992 set to 480 cards and this time used a glossy format. The player's name, position and team logo are at the bottom, along with "Fleer 92". The back has a close-up shot, with career stats and a biography. The cards are numbered alphabetically by team, beginning with Atlanta and ending with Washington. Subsets include Prospects (#s 432-451), League Leaders (#s 452-470), Pro-Visions (#s 471-476) and checklists (#s 477-480). Insert sets include All-Pro (24 cards, in wax packs), Mark Rypien (12, in wax, rack and cellos), Rookie Sensations (20, in cello packs) and Team Leaders (24, in rack packs).

		NM/M
Complete Set (480):		8.00
Common Player:		.03
Pack (17):		.40
Wax Box (36):		12.00
1	Steve Broussard	.03
2	Rick Bryan	.03
3	Scott Case	.03
4	Tony Epps	.03
5	Bill Fralic	.03
6	Moe Gardner	.03
7	Michael Haynes	.25
8	Chris Hinton	.03
9	Brian Jordan	.03
10	Mike Kenn	.03
11	Tim McKyer	.03
12	Chris Miller	.03
13	Erric Pegram	.20
14	Mike Pritchard	.20
15	Andre Rison	.25
16	Jessie Tuggle	.03
17	Carlton Bailey	.03
18	Howard Ballard	.03
19	Don Beebe	.03
20	Cornelius Bennett	.03
21	Shane Conlan	.03
22	Kent Hull	.03
23	Mark Kelso	.03
24	James Lofton	.03
25	Keith McKeller	.03
26	Scott Norwood	.03
27	Nate Odomes	.03
28	Frank Reich	.03
29	Jim Ritcher	.03
30	Leon Seals	.03
31	Darryl Talley	.03
32	Steve Tasker	.03
33	Thurman Thomas	.50
34	Will Wolford	.03
35	Neal Anderson	.10
36	Trace Armstrong	.03
37	Mark Carrier	.03
38	Richard Dent	.03
39	Shaun Gayle	.03
40	Jim Harbaugh	.03
41	Jay Hilgenberg	.03
42	Darren Lewis	.03
43	Steve McMichael	.03
44	Brad Muster	.03
45	William Perry	.03
46	John Roper	.03
47	Lemuel Stinson	.03
48	Stan Thomas	.03
49	Keith Van Horne	.03
50	Tom Waddle	.10
51	Donnell Woolford	.03
52	Chris Zorich	.10
53	Eddie Brown	.03
54	James Francis	.03
55	David Fulcher	.03
56	David Grant	.03
57	Harold Green	.03
58	Rodney Holman	.03
59	Lee Johnson	.03
60	Tim Krumrie	.03
61	Anthony Munoz	.03
62	*Joe Walter*	.10
63	Mike Baab	.03
64	Stephen Braggs	.04
65	*Richard Brown*	.10
66	Dan Fike	.03
67	*Scott Galbraith*	.10
68	*Randy Hilliard*	.10
69	Michael Jackson	.15
70	Tony Jones	.03
71	Ed King	.03
72	Kevin Mack	.03
73	Clay Matthews	.03
74	Eric Metcalf	.03
75	Vince Newsome	.03
76	John Rienstra	.03
77	Steve Beuerlein	.15
78	Larry Brown	.03
79	Tony Casillas	.03
80	Alvin Harper	.10
81	Issiac Holt	.03
82	Ray Horton	.03
83	Michael Irvin	.40
84	Daryl Johnston	.08
85	Kelvin Martin	.03
86	Nate Newton	.03
87	Ken Norton	.03
88	Jay Novacek	.15
89	Emmitt Smith	2.00
90	Vinson Smith	.03
91	Mark Stepnoski	.03
92	Steve Atwater	.03
93	Mike Croel	.03
94	John Elway	.50
95	Simon Fletcher	.03
96	Gaston Green	.03
97	Mark Jackson	.03
98	Keith Kartz	.03
99	Greg Kragen	.03
100	Greg Lewis	.03
101	Karl Mecklenburg	.03
102	Derek Russell	.15
103	Steve Sewell	.03
104	Dennis Smith	.03
105	David Treadwell	.03
106	Kenny Walker	.03
107	Doug Widell	.03
108	Michael Young	.03
109	Jerry Ball	.03
110	Bennie Blades	.03
111	Lomas Brown	.03
112	*Scott Conover*	.10
113	Ray Crockett	.03
114	Mike Farr	.03
115	Mel Gray	.03
116	Willie Green	.15
117	*Tracy Hayworth*	.15
118	Erik Kramer	.03
119	Herman Moore	.50
120	Dan Owens	.03
121	Rodney Peete	.03
122	Brett Perriman	.03
123	Barry Sanders	1.25
124	Chris Spielman	.03
125	Marc Spindler	.03
126	Tony Bennett	.03
127	Matt Brock	.03
128	LeRoy Butler	.06
129	Johnny Holland	.03
130	Perry Kemp	.03
131	Don Majkowski	.03
132	Mark Murphy	.03
133	Brian Noble	.03
134	Bryce Paup	.03
135	Sterling Sharpe	.10
136	Scott Stephen	.03
137	Darrell Thompson	.03
138	Mike Tomczak	.03
139	Esera Tuaolo	.03
140	Keith Woodside	.03
141	Ray Childress	.03
142	Cris Dishman	.03
143	Curtis Duncan	.03
144	John Flannery	.03
145	William Fuller	.03
146	Ernest Givins	.03
147	Haywood Jeffires	.15
148	Sean Jones	.03
149	Lamar Lathon	.03
150	Bruce Matthews	.03
151	Bubba McDowell	.03
152	Johnny Meads	.03
153	Warren Moon	.20
154	Mike Munchak	.03
155	Al Smith	.03
156	Doug Smith	.03
157	Lorenzo White	.03
158	Michael Ball	.03
159	Chip Banks	.03
160	Duane Bickett	.03
161	Bill Brooks	.03
162	Ken Clark	.03
163	Jon Hand	.03
164	Jeff Herrod	.03
165	Jessie Hester	.03
166	Scott Radecic	.03
167	Rohn Stark	.03
168	Clarence Verdin	.03
169	John Alt	.03
170	Tim Barnett	.03
171	Tim Grunhard	.03
172	Dino Hackett	.03
173	Jonathan Hayes	.03
174	Bill Maas	.03
175	Chris Martin	.03
176	Christian Okoye	.03
177	Stephone Paige	.03
178	*Jayice Pearson*	.10
179	Kevin Porter	.03
180	Kevin Ross	.03
181	Dan Saleaumua	.03
182	*Tracy Simien*	.10
183	Neil Smith	.03
184	Derrick Thomas	.15
185	Robb Thomas	.03
186	Mark Vlasic	.03
187	Barry Word	.15
188	Marcus Allen	.08
189	Eddie Anderson	.03
190	Nick Bell	.10
191	Tim Brown	.10
192	Scott Davis	.03
193	Riki Ellison	.03
194	Mervyn Fernandez	.03
195	Willie Gault	.03
196	Jeff Gossett	.03
197	Ethan Horton	.03
198	Jeff Jaeger	.03
199	Howie Long	.03
200	Ronnie Lott	.03
201	Todd Marinovich	.10
202	Don Mosebar	.03
203	Jay Schroeder	.03
204	Greg Townsend	.03
205	Lionel Washington	.03
206	Steve Wisniewski	.03
207	Flipper Anderson	.03
208	Bern Brostek	.03
209	Robert Delpino	.03
210	Henry Ellard	.03
211	Jim Everett	.03
212	Cleveland Gary	.03
213	Kevin Greene	.03
214	Darryl Henely	.03
215	Damone Johnson	.03
216	Larry Kelm	.03
217	Todd Lyght	.03
218	Jackie Slater	.03
219	Michael Stewart	.03
220	Pat Terrell	.03
221	Robert Young	.03
222	Mark Clayton	.03
223	Bryan Cox	.03
224	Aaron Craver	.03
225	Jeff Cross	.03
226	Mark Duper	.03
227	Harry Galbreath	.03
228	David Griggs	.03
229	Mark Higgs	.15
230	Vestee Jackson	.03
231	John Offerdahl	.03
232	Louis Oliver	.03
233	Tony Paige	.03
234	Reggie Roby	.03
235	Sammie Smith	.03
236	Pete Stoyanovich	.03
237	Richmond Webb	.03
238	Terry Allen	.20
239	Ray Berry	.03
240	Joey Browner	.03
241	Anthony Carter	.03
242	Cris Carter	.03
243	Chris Doleman	.03
244	Rich Gannon	.10
245	Tim Irwin	.03
246	Steve Jordan	.03
247	Carl Lee	.03
248	Randall Cunningham	.03
249	Mike Merriweather	.03
250	Harry Newsome	.03
251	John Randle	.03
252	Henry Thomas	.03
253	Herschel Walker	.03
254	Ray Agnew	.03
255	Bruce Armstrong	.03
256	Vincent Brown	.03
257	Marv Cook	.03
258	Irving Fryar	.03
259	Pat Harlow	.03
260	Tommy Hodson	.03
261	Maurice Hurst	.03
262	Ronnie Lippett	.03
263	Eugene Lockhart	.03
264	Greg McMurty	.03
265	Hugh Millen	.03
266	Leonard Russell	.25
267	Andre Tippett	.03
268	Brent Williams	.03
269	Morten Andersen	.03
270	Gene Atkins	.03
271	Wesley Carroll	.03
272	Jim Dombrowski	.03
273	Quinn Early	.03
274	Gill Fenerty	.03
275	Bobby Hebert	.03
276	Joel Hilgenberg	.03
277	Rickey Jackson	.03
278	Vaughan Johnson	.03
279	Eric Martin	.03
280	Brett Maxie	.03
281	*Fred McAfee*	.10
282	Sam Mills	.03
283	Pat Swilling	.03
284	Floyd Turner	.03
285	Steve Walsh	.03
286	Frank Warren	.03
287	Stephen Baker	.03
288	Maurice Carthon	.03
289	Mark Collins	.03
290	John Elliott	.03
291	Myron Guyton	.03
292	Rodney Hampton	.10
293	Jeff Hostetler	.10
294	Mark Ingram	.03
295	Pepper Johnson	.03
296	Sean Landeta	.03
297	Leonard Marshall	.03
298	Dave Meggett	.03
299	Bart Oates	.03
300	Phil Simms	.10
301	Reyna Thompson	.03
302	Lewis Tillman	.03
303	Brad Baxter	.03
304	Kyle Clifton	.03
305	James Hasty	.03
306	Joe Kelly	.03
307	Jeff Lageman	.03
308	Mo Lewis	.03
309	Erik McMillan	.03
310	Rob Moore	.10
311	Tony Stargell	.03
312	Jim Sweeney	.03
313	Marvin Washington	.03
314	Lonnie Young	.03
315	Eric Allen	.03
316	Fred Barnett	.10
317	Jerome Brown	.03
318	Keith Byars	.03
319	Wes Hopkins	.03
320	Keith Jackson	.10
321	James Joseph	.03
322	Seth Joyner	.03
323	Jeff Kemp	.03
324	Roger Ruzek	.03
325	Clyde Simmons	.03
326	William Thomas	.03
327	Reggie White	.15
328	Calvin Williams	.15
329	Rich Camarillo	.03
330	Ken Harvey	.03
331	Eric Hill	.03
332	Johnny Johnson	.15
333	Ernie Johnson	.03
334	Tim Jorden	.03
335	Tim McDonald	.03
336	Freddie Joe Nunn	.03
337	Luis Sharpe	.03
338	Eric Swann	.03
339	Aeneas Williams	.03
340	Gary Anderson	.03
341	Bubby Brsiter	.03
342	Adrian Cooper	.03
343	Barry Foster	.10
344	Eric Green	.03
345	Bryan Hinkle	.03
346	Tunch Ilkin	.03
347	Carnell Lake	.03
348	Louis Lipps	.03
349	David Little	.03
350	Greg Lloyd	.03
351	Neil O'Donnell	.25
352	Dwight Stone	.03
353	Rod Woodson	.03
354	Rod Bernstine	.03
355	Eric Bieniemy	.03
356	Marion Butts	.03
357	Gill Byrd	.03
358	John Friesz	.03
359	Burt Grossman	.03
360	Courtney Hall	.03
361	Ronnie Harmon	.03
362	Shawn Jefferson	.03
363	Nate Lewis	.03
364	*Craig McEwen*	.10
365	Eric Moten	.03
366	Joe Phillips	.03
367	Gary Plummer	.03
368	Henry Rolling	.03
369	Broderick Thompson	.03
370	Harris Barton	.03
371	*Steve Bono*	1.00
372	Todd Bowles	.03
373	Dexter Carter	.03
374	Michael Carter	.03
375	Mike Cofer	.03
376	Keith DeLong	.03
377	Charles Haley	.03
378	Menton Hanks	.03
379	Tim Harris	.03
380	Brent Jones	.03
381	Guy McIntyre	.03
382	Tom Rathman	.03
383	Bill Romanowski	.03
384	Jesse Sapolu	.03
385	John Taylor	.03
386	Steve Young	1.00
387	Robert Blackmon	.03
388	Brian Blades	.03
389	Jacob Green	.03
390	Dwayne Harper	.03
391	Andy Heck	.03
392	Tommy Kane	.03
393	John Kasay	.03
394	Cortez Kennedy	.15
395	Bryan Millard	.03
396	Rufus Porter	.03
397	Eugene Robinson	.03
398	John L. Williams	.03
399	Terry Wooden	.03
400	Gary Anderson	.03
401	Ian Beckles	.03
402	Mark Carrier	.03
403	Reggie Cobb	.15
404	Lawrence Dawsey	.03
405	Ron Hall	.03
406	Keith McCants	.03
407	Charles McRae	.03
408	Tim Newton	.03
409	Jesse Solomon	.03
410	Vinny Testaverde	.03
411	Broderick Thomas	.03
412	Robert Wilson	.03
413	Jeff Bostic	.03
414	Earnest Byner	.03
415	Gary Clark	.03
416	Andre Collins	.03
417	Brad Edwards	.03
418	Kurt Gouveia	.03
419	Darrell Green	.03
420	Joe Jacoby	.03
421	Jim Lachey	.03
422	Chip Lohmiller	.03
423	Charles Mann	.03
424	Wilber Marshall	.03
425	*Ron Middleton*	.10
426	Brian Mitchell	.03
427	Art Monk	.03
428	Mark Rypien	.10
429	Ricky Sanders	.03
430	*Mark Schlereth*	.10
431	Fred Stokes	.03
432	*Edgar Bennett*	.75
433	*Brian Bollinger*	.08
434	*Joe Bowden*	.08
435	*Terrell Buckley*	.35
436	*Willie Clay*	.10
437	Steve Gordon	.03
438	*Keith Hamilton*	.10
439	Carlos Huerta	.03
440	Matt LaBounty	.03
441	*Amp Lee*	.40
442	*Ricardo McDonald*	.10
443	*Chris Mims*	.20
444	*Michael Mooney*	.10
445	*Patrick Rowe*	.10
446	*Leon Searcy*	.10
447	*Siran Stacy*	.10
448	*Kevin Turner*	.15
449	*Tommy Vardell*	.30
450	*Bob Whitfield*	.10
451	*Darryl Williams*	.10
452	Thurman Thomas (LL)	.25
453	Emmitt Smith (LL)	1.00
454	Haywood Jeffires (LL)	.08
455	Michael Irvin (LL)	.20
456	Mark Clayton (LL)	.03
457	Barry Sanders (LL)	.50
458	Pete Stoyanovich (LL)	.03
459	Chip Lohmiller (LL)	.03
460	William Fuller (LL)	.03
461	Pat Swilling (LL)	.03
462	Ronnie Lott (LL)	.03
463	Ray Crockett (LL)	.03
464	Tim McKyer (LL)	.03
465	Aeneas Williams (LL)	.03
466	Rod Woodson (LL)	.03
467	Mel Gray (LL)	.03
468	Nate Lewis (LL)	.03
469	Steve Young (LL)	.03
470	Reggie Roby (LL)	.03
471	John Elway (PV)	.10
472	Ronnie Lott (PV)	.03
473	Art Monk (PV)	.03
474	Warren Moon (PV)	.10
475	Emmitt Smith (PV)	1.00
476	Thurman Thomas (PV)	.20
477	Checklist Card	.03
478	Checklist Card	.03
479	Checklist Card	.03
480	Checklist Card	.03

1992 Fleer All-Pro

These 24 inserts were randomly included in 1992 Fleer wax packs. The card front has a red-white-and-blue NFL emblem with a cutout player photo superimposed on it. The card background is blue. The player's name and position are also given in gold foil letters. The back has a pink background with a career summary and color portrait. Cards are numbered 1 of 24, etc.

		NM/M
Complete Set (24):		7.00
Common Player:		.25
1	Marv Cook	.25
2	Mike Kenn	.25
3	Steve Wisniewski	.25
4	Jim Ritcher	.25
5	Jim Lachey	.25
6	Michael Irvin	.75
7	Andre Rison	.50
8	Thurman Thomas	.75
9	Barry Sanders	3.00
10	Bruce Matthews	.25
11	Mark Rypien	.25
12	Jeff Jaeger	.25
13	Reggie White	.75
14	Clyde Simmons	.25
15	Pat Swilling	.25
16	Sam Mills	.25
17	Ray Childress	.25
18	Jerry Ball	.25
19	Derrick Thomas	.50
20	Darrell Green	.25
21	Ronnie Lott	.50
22	Steve Atwater	.25
23	Mark Carrier	.25
24	Jeff Gossett	.25

1992 Fleer Rookie Sensations

These 20 cards, featuring some of the NFL's top rookies in 1991, were random inserts in Fleer cello packs. Each card front is designed like a football field, containing a player photo which slants to the left with shadow borders on the left and bottom. "Rookie Sensations" appears at the top of the card, highlighted by gold foil stripes simulating the flight of a football. The player's name is in gold foil at the bottom. The back, which is designed similar to the front, has a career summary and card number.

		NM/M
Complete Set (20):		12.00
Common Player:		.50
Minor Stars:		1.00
1	Moe Gardner	.50
2	Mike Pritchard	1.00
3	Stan Thomas	.50
4	Larry Brown	.50
5	Todd Lyght	1.00
6	James Joseph	.50
7	Aeneas Williams	3.00
8	Michael Jackson	1.00
9	Ed King	.50
10	Mike Croel	.50
11	Kenny Walker	.50
12	Tim Barnett	.50
13	Nick Bell	.50
14	Todd Marinovich	.50
15	Leonard Russell	.50
16	Pat Harlow	.50
17	Mo Lewis	.50
18	John Kasay	.50
19	Lawrence Dawsey	.50
20	Charles McRae	.50

1992 Fleer Mark Rypien

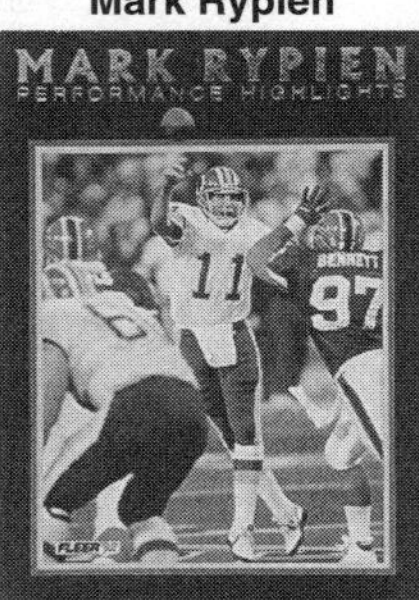

Mark Rypien is featured in this 15-card "Performance Highlight" insert set. Cards were randomly included in 1992 Fleer Football packs. Each card front has a dark blue background with a player action photo outlined in the team's colors. Rypien's name and "Performance Highlights" are in gold-foil lettering at the top. Each back has a summary of a different stage of Rypien's career. Cards are numbered on the back. Rypien, the MVP of Super Bowl XXVI, autographed more than 2,000 cards, which were then randomly inserted. Collectors could also get three extra Rypien cards by mailing in 10 Fleer pack proofs of purchase. These cards are numbered 13-15.

		NM/M
Complete Set (12):		4.00
Common Rypien:		.40
1	Mark Rypien A Matter of Faith	.40
2	Mark Rypien Mr. Everything	.40
3	Mark Rypien Great Expectations	.40
4	Mark Rypien Hill and Valleys	.40
5	Mark Rypien Breakout Season	.40
6	Mark Rypien The End of the Beginning	.40
7	Mark Rypien BowledOver	.40
8	Mark Rypien Watching and Waiting	.40
9	Mark Rypien QB Controversy	.40
10	Mark Rypien Redemption	.40
11	Mark Rypien Pain and Pressure	.40
12	Mark Rypien Jubilation	.40

1992 Fleer Team Leaders

These 24 inserts were randomly included in 1992 Fleer rack packs. Each color photo on the front has a black border. The player's name, position, team and "Team Leader" logo are at the bottom of the card in green foil lettering. Each back has a player portrait in an oval frame in the upper left corner, plus a career summary. The background is grayish-blue. A card number is also included on the card back.

		NM/M
Complete Set (24):		50.00
Common Player:		1.50
Minor Stars:		3.00
1	Chris Miller	1.50
2	Neal Anderson	1.50
3	Emmitt Smith	8.00
4	Chris Spielman	1.50
5	Brian Noble	1.50
6	Jim Everett	3.00
7	Joey Browner	1.50
8	Sam Mills	1.50
9	Rodney Hampton	3.00
10	Reggie White	4.00
11	Tim McDonald	1.50
12	Charles Haley	3.00
13	Mark Rypien	1.50
14	Cornelius Bennett	1.50
15	Clay Matthews	1.50
16	John Elway	6.00
17	Warren Moon	3.00
18	Derrick Thomas	3.00
19	Greg Townsend	1.50
20	Bruce Armstrong	1.50
21	Brad Baxter	1.50
22	Rod Woodson	1.50
23	Marion Butts	1.50
24	Rufus Porter	1.50

1992 Fleer GameDay Draft Day Promos

These 2-1/2" x 4-11/16" cards feature six players who were projected to be top selections in the 1992 NFL draft. Some of the players have more than one card, to cover various draft day scenarios. The card front has a full-color action photo with a white border. The player's name, team name and Game-Day logo are at the bottom of the card. The back has a mug shot of the player, plus a summary of his collegiate accomplishments. Each card has an NFL Draft logo, and the same card number, #1. NFL Properties produced the set. An ad in a May 1992 issue of USA Today offered the 13-card set for $50. Proceeds went to NFL Charities. Dealers and members of the hobby press also received promo sets.

		NM/M
Complete Set (13):		15.00
Common Player:		1.00
1	Quentin Coryatt (Los Angeles Rams)	1.00
2	Vaughn Dunbar (Atlanta Falcons)	1.00
3	Vaughn Dunbar (San Francisco 49ers)	1.00
4	Vaughn Dunbar (Seattle Seahawks)	1.00
5	Steve Emtman (Indianapolis Colts)	1.00
6	Steve Emtman (Los Angeles Rams)	1.00
7	Desmond Howard (Indianapolis Colts)	2.00
8	Desmond Howard (Washington Redskins)	2.00
9	David Klingler (Kansas City Chiefs)	1.00
10	David Klingler (New York Giants)	1.00
11	Troy Vincen (Cincinnati Bengals)	1.00
12	Troy Vincent (Indianapolis Colts)	1.00
13	Troy Vincent (Green Bay Packers)	1.00

1992 Fleer GameDay

GameDay's debut set features 500 cards with color action photos against a black-and-white background. Each card is bordered with the player's corresponding team color, and team colors are used for the player's name and GameDay, which are printed at the bottom. Card backs are printed horizontally, and contain a close-up photo, biography, statistics and career highlights. The numbered card backs feature the player's name, team name, position and team logo in his team's colors. What distinguishes these cards from other sets is the size - they are 2-1/2" x 4-11/16", which makes them the same size as Topps' 1965 football issue.

		NM/M
Complete Set (500):		25.00
Common Player:		.10
Wax Box:		20.00
1	Jim Kelly	.75
2	Mark Ingram	.12
3	Travis McNeal	.10
4	Ricky Ervins	.20
5	Joe Montana	3.50
6	Broderick Thompson	.10
7	Darion Conner	.10
8	Jim Harbaugh	.15
9	Harvey Williams	.35
10	Chip Banks	.10
11	Henry Thomas	.10
12	*Derek Brown*	.20
13	James Joseph	.15
14	Kevin Fagan	.10
15	*Chuck Klingbell*	.20
16	Harlon Barnett	.10
17	Jim Price	.10
18	*Terrell Buckley*	.40
19	*Paul McJulien*	.15
20	James Hasty	.10
21	James Francis	.12
22	Andre Tippett	.12
23	John Elway	1.00
24	Eric Dickerson	.40
25	James Jefferson	.10
26	Danny Noonan	.10
27	Warren Moon	.40
28	Gene Atkins	.10
29	Jessie Hester	.10
30	*Mike Mooney, Kevin Smith, Ron Humphrey, Tracy Boyd*	.25
31	*Toby Caston*	.15
32	*Howard Dinkins*	.15
33	*James Patton*	.15
34	Walter Reeves	.10
35	*Johnny Mitchell*	1.25
36	*Michael Brim*	.20
37	Irving Fryar	.12
38	Lewis Billups	.10
39	*Alonzo Spellman*	.50
40	John Friesz	.12
41	Patrick Hunter	.10
42	Reuben Davis	.10
43	*Tom Myslinski, Shawn Harper, Mark Thomas, Mike Frier*	.15
44	*Siran Stacy*	.15
45	Stephone Paige	.12
46	*Eddie Robinson*	.15
47	*Tracy Scroggins*	.35
48	*David Klingler*	.50
49a	Deion Sanders	.75
49b	Deion Sanders (Last line of card says plays outfield)	.40
50	Tom Waddle	.20
51	Gary Anderson	.12
52	Kevin Butler	.10
53	Bruce Smith	.12
54	Steve Sewell	.10
55	Wesley Walls	.10
56	Lawrence Taylor	.20
57	Mike Merriweather	.12
58	Roman Phifer	.10
59	Shaun Gayle	.10
60	*Marc Boutte*	.15
61	*Tony Mayberry*	.15
62	Antone Davis (Card has 9th pick in 91 draft, was 8th)	.10
63	Rod Bernstine	.12
64	*Shane Collins*	.25
65	Martin Bayless	.10
66	*Corey Harris*	.15
67	*Jason Hanson*	.25
68	*John Fina*	.15
69	Cornelius Bennett	.12
70	Mark Bortz	.10
71	Gary Anderson	.10
72	*Paul Siever*	.20
73	Flipper Anderson	.12
74	*Shane Dronett*	.30
75	Brian Noble	.10
76	Tim Green	.10
77	Percy Snow	.10
78	Greg McMurty	.10
79	*Dana Hall*	.30
80	*Tyji Armstrong*	.20
81	Gary Clark	.25
82	*Steve Emtman*	.30
83	Eric Moore	.10
84	Brent Jones	.12
85	*Ray Seals*	.20
86	James Jones	.10
87	Jeff Hostetler	.25
88	Keith Jackson	.15
89	Gary Plummer	.10
90	Robert Blackmon	.10
91	*Larry Tharpe, Mike Brandon, Anthony Hamlet, Mike Pawlawski*	.15
92	*Greg Skrepenak*	.20
93	Kevin Call	.10
94	Clarence Kay	.10
95	William Fuller	.10
96	*Troy Auzenne*	.15
97	*Carl Pickens*	1.00
98	Lorenzo White	.25
99	Doug Smith	.10
100	*Dale Carter*	.40
101	*Fred McAfee*	.20
102	Jack Del Rio	.10
103	*Vaugn Dunbar*	.20
104	J.J. Birden	.12
105	Harris Barton	.10
106	*Ray Ethridge*	.15
107	John Gesek	.10
108	Mike Singletary	.12
109	Mark Rypien	.15
110	Robb Thomas	.10
111	Joe Kelly	.10
112	Ben Smith	.10
113	Neil O'Donnell	.50
114	John L. Williams	.12
115	Mike Sherrard	.12
116	*Chad Hennings*	.15
117	Henry Ellard	.12
118	Jay Hilgenberg	.12
119	Charles Dimry	.10
120	*Chuck Smith*	.15
121	Brian Mitchell	.12
122	Eric Allen	.12
123	Nate Lewis	.20
124	Kevin Ross	.12
125	*Jimmy Smith*	1.00
126	*Kevin Smith*	.60
127	*Larry Webster*	.25
128	Marv Cook	.12
129	Calvin Williams	.10
130	*Harry Swayne*	.15
131	Jimmie Jones	.10
132	Ethan Horton	.10
133	*Chris Mims*	.20
134	Derrick Thomas	.20
135	*Gerald Dixon*	.25
136	Gary Zimmerman	.10
137	*Robert Jones*	.20
138	Steve Broussard	.12
139	David Wyman	.10
140	Ian Beckles	.10
141	*Steve Bono*	2.00
142	Cris Carter	.10
143	Anthony Cater	.12
144	Greg Townsend	.12
145	Al Smith	.10
146	*Troy Vincent*	.25
147	Jessie Tuggle	.10
148	David Fulcher	.10
149	Johnny Rembert	.10
150	Ernie Jones	.10
151	Mark Royals	.10
152	Jeff Bryant	.10
153	Vai Sikahema	.12
154	Tony Woods	.10
155	*Joe Bowden, Doug Rigby, Marcus Dowdell, Ostell Miles*	.15
156	Mark Carrier	.12
157	Joe Nash	.10
158	Keith Van Horne	.10
159	Kelvin Martin	.12
160	Peter Tom Willis	.12
161	Richard Johnson	.10
162	Louis Oliver	.12
163	Nick Lowery	.12
164	Ricky Proehl	.12
165	Terance Mathis	.10
166	Keith Sims	.10
167	E.J. Junior	.10
168	Scott Mersereau	.10
169	Tom Rathman	.12
170	*Robert Harris*	.15
171	*Ashley Ambrose*	.15
172	David Treadwell	.10
173	Mark Green	.10
174	*Clayton Holmes*	.15
175	*Tony Sacca*	.25
176	Wes Hopkins	.10
177	*Mark Wheeler*	.15
178	Robert Clark	.10
179	Eugene Daniel	.10
180	Rob Burnett	.10
181	Al Edwards	.10
182	Clarence Verdin	.10
183	Tom Newberry	.10
184	Mike Jones	.10
185	Roy Foster	.10
186	Leslie O'Neal	.12
187	Izel Jenkins	.10
188	*Willie Clay, Ty Detmer, Mike Evans, Ed McDaniel*	1.00
189	Mike Tomczak	.12
190	*Leonard Wheeler*	.15
191	Gaston Green	.15
192	Maury Buford	.10
193	*Jeremy Lincoln*	.15
194	*Todd Collins*	.15
195	Billy Ray Smith	.10
196	Renaldo Turnbull	.10
197	Michael Carter	.10
198	*Rod Milstead, Dion Lambert, Hesham Ismail, Reggie E. White*	.15
199	Shawn Collins	.10
200	Issiac Holt	.10
201	Irv Eatman	.10
202	Anthony Thompson	.12
203	*Chester McGlockton*	.25
204	*Greg Biggs, Chris Crooms, Ephesians Bartley, Curtis Whitley*	.15
205	*James Brown*	.15
206	Marvin Washington	.10
207	*Richard Cooper*	.15
208	Jim C. Jensen	.10
209	Sam Seale	.10
210	Andre Reed	.15
211	Thane Gash	.10
212	Randal Hill	.20
213	Brad Baxter	.12
214	Michael Cofer	.10
215	Ray Crockett	.10
216	Tony Mandarich	.10
217	Warren Williams	.10
218	Erik Kramer	.25
219	Bubby Brister	.12
220	Steve Young	1.50
221	Jeff George	.35
222	James Washington	.10
223	*Bruce Alexander*	.15
224	Broderick Thomas	.12
225	Bern Brostek	.10
226	Brian Blades	.12
227	Troy Aikman	4.00
228	Aaron Wallace	.10
229	*Tommy Jeter*	.15
230	Russell Maryland	.30
231	Charles Haley	.12
232	James Lofton	.20
233	William White	.10
234	Tim McGee	.10
235	Haywood Jeffires	.15
236	Charles Mann	.12
237	Robert Lyles	.10
238	Rohn Stark	.10
239	Jim Morrissey	.10
240	Mel Gray	.12
241	Barry Word	.20
242	*Dave Widell*	.15
243	*Sean Gilbert*	.40
244	*Tommy Maddox*	.50
245	Bernie Kosar	.15
246	John Roper	.10
247	Mark Higgs	.20
248	Rob Moore	.20
249	Dan Fike	.10
250	Dan Saleaumua	.10
251	Tim Krumrie	.10
252	Tony Casillas	.10
253	*Jayice Pearson*	.12
254	Dan Marino	4.00
255	Tony Marty	.10
256	Mike Fox	.10
257	*Courtney Hawkins*	.75
258	Leonard Marshall	.12
259	Willie Gault	.12
260	Al Toon	.12
261	Browning Nagle	.20
262	Ronnie Lott	.12
263	Sean Jones	.10
264	Ernest Givins	.20
265	Ray Donaldson	.10
266	Vaughan Johnson	.12
267	Tom Hodson	.12
268	Chris Doleman	.12
269	Pat Swilling	.10
270	Merril Hoge	.12
271	Bill Maas	.10
272	Sterling Sharpe	1.00
273	Mitchell Price	.10
274	*Richard Brown*	.15
275	Randall Cunningham	.25
276	Chris Martin	.10
277	Courtney Hall	.10
278	Michael Walter	.10
279	*Ricardo McDonald, David Wilson, Sean Lumpkin, Tony Brooks*	.10
280	Bill Brooks	.12
281	Jay Schroeder	.12
282	John Stephens	.12
283	William Perry	.12
284	Floyd Turner	.10
285	Carnell Lake	.10
286	*Joel Steed*	.15
287	Vinnie Clark	.10
288	Ken Norton	.12
289	Eric Thomas	.10
290	Derrick Fenner	.12
291	*Tony Smith*	.20
292	Eric Metcalf	.12
293	Roger Craig	.12
294	*Leon Searcy*	.15
295	*Tyrone Legette*	.15
296	Rob Taylor	.10
297	Eric Williams	.10
298	David Little	.10
299	Wayne Martin	.10
300	Eric Martin	.12
301	Jim Everett	.20
302	Michael Dean Perry	.20
303	*Dwayne White*	.12
304	Greg Lloyd	.10
305	Ricky Reynolds	.10
306	Anthony Smith	.10
307	Robert Delpino	.12
308	Ken Clark	.10
309	Chris Jacke	.10
310	*Reggie Dwight, Anthony McCoy, Craig Thompson, Klaus Wilmsmeyer*	.15
311	Doug Widell	.10
312	Sammie Smith	.12
313	Ken O'Brien	.12
314	Timm Rosenbach	.10
315	Jesse Sapolu	.10
316	Ronnie Harmon	.10
317	Bill Pickel	.10
318	Lonnie Young	.10
319	Chris Burkett	.10
320	Ervin Randle	.10
321	Ed West	.10
322	Tom Thayer	.10
323	Keith McKeller	.10
324	Webster Slaughter	.12
325	Duane Bickett	.10
326	Howie Long	.12
327	Sam Mills	.12
328	Mike Golic	.10
329	Bruce Armstrong	.10
330	Pat Terrell	.10
331	Mike Pritchard	.45
332	Audray McMillian	.10
333	*Marquez Pope*	.12
334	Pierce Holt	.10
335	Erik Howard	.10
336	Jerry Rice	2.25
337	Vinny Testaverde	.12
338	Bart Oates	.10
339	*Nolan Harrison*	.12
340	Chris Goode	.10
341	Ken Ruettgers	.10
342	Brad Muster	.12
343	Paul Farren	.10
344	*Corey Miller*	.20
345	Brian Washington	.10
346	Jim Sweeney	.10
347	Keith McCants	.10
348	Louis Lipps	.12
349	Keith Byars	.12
350	Steve Walsh	.12
351	Jeff Jaeger	.10
352	Christian Okoye	.12
353	Cris Dishman	.12

354 Keith Kartz .10
355 Harold Green .10
356 *Richard Shelton* .15
357 Jacob Green .12
358 Al Noga .10
359 Dean Biasucci .10
360 Jeff Herrod .10
361 Bennie Blades .10
362 Mark Vlasic .12
363 Chris Miller .15
364 Bubba McDowell .10
365 *Tyrone Stowe* .15
366 Jon Vaughn .15
367 Winston Moss .10
368 *Levon Kirkland* .15
369 Ted Washington .10
370 Cortez Kennedy .25
371 Jeff Feagles .10
372 Aundray Bruce .10
373 Michael Irvin .30
374 Lemuel Stinson .10
375 Billy Joe Tolliver .12
376 Anthony Munoz .12
377 Nate Newton .10
378 Steve Smith .12
379 *Eugene Chung* .15
380 Bryan Hinkle .10
381 Dan McGwire .30
382 Jeff Cross .10
383 Ferrell Edmunds .10
384 Craig Heyward .12
385 Shannon Sharpe .50
386 Anthony Miller .12
387 Eugene Lockhart .10
388 Darryl Henley .10
389 LeRoy Butler .10
390 Scott Fulhage .10
391 Andre Ware .35
392 Lionel Washington .10
393 Rick Fenney .10
394 John Taylor .20
395 Chris Singleton .10
396 Monte Coleman .10
397 Brett Perriman .12
398 Hugh Millen .35
399 Dennis Gentry .10
400 Eddie Anderson .10
401 *Lance Olberding, Eddie Miller, Dwayne Sabb, Corey Widmer* .15
402 Brent Williams .10
403 Tony Zendejas .10
404 Donnell Woolford .10
405 Boomer Esiason .20
406 Gill Fenerty .12
407 *Kurt Barber* .12
408 William Thomas .10
409 Keith Henderson .10
410 Paul Gruber .12
411 Alfred Oglesby .10
412 Wendell Davis .20
413 *Robert Brooks* 2.00
414 Ken Willis .10
415 Aaron Cox .10
416 Thurman Thomas .50
417 Alton Montgomery .10
418 Mike Prior .10
419 Albert Bentley .10
420 John Randle .10
421 Dermontti Dawson .10
422 *Phillippi Sparks* .15
423 Michael Jackson .30
424 Carl Banks .12
425 Chris Zorich .10
426 Dwight Stone .10
427 Bryan Millard .10
428 Neal Anderson .20
429 Michael Haynes .15
430 Michael Young .10
431 Dennis Byrd .12
432 Fred Barnett .15
433 Junior Seau .50
434 Mark Clayton .12
435 *Marco Coleman* .50
436 Lee Williams .12
437 Stan Thomas .10
438 Lawrence Dawsey .15
439 *Tommy Vardell* .60
440 *Steve Israel* .20
441 Ray Childress .12
442 *Darren Woodson* .20
443 Lamar Lathon .10
444 Reggie Roby .10
445 Eric Green .12
446 Mark Carrier .12
447 Kevin Walker .10
448 Vince Workman .20
449 Leonard Griffin .10
450 *Robert Porcher* .40
451 Hart Lee Dykes .10
452 *Thomas McLemore* .15
453 *Jamie Dukes* .15
454 Bill Romanowski .10
455 Deron Cherry .10
456 Burt Grossman .10
457 Lance Smith .10
458 Jay Novacek .15
459 Erric Pegram .20
460 Reggie Rutland .10
461 Rickey Jackson .12
462 Dennis Brown .10
463 Neil Smith .12
464 Rich Gannon .15
465 Herman Moore 1.00
466 Rodney Peete .25
467 Alvin Harper .50
468 Andre Rison .50
469 Rufus Porter .10
470 Robert Wilson .10
471 Phil Simms .15
472 Art Monk .15
473 Mike Tice .10
474 *Quentin Coryatt* .60
475 Chris Hinton .10
476 Vance Johnson .12
477 Kyle Clifton .10
478 Garth Jax .10
479 Ray Agnew .10
480 *Patrick Rowe* .15
481 Joe Jacoby .10
482 Bruce Pickens .10
483 Keith DeLong .10
484 Eric Swann .12
485 Steve McMichael .12
486 Leroy Hoard .12
487 Rickey Dixon .10
488 Robert Perryman .10
489 *Darryl Williams* .30
490 Emmitt Smith 6.00
491 Dino Hackett .10
492 Earnest Byner .12
493 *Bucky Richardson, Bernard Dafney, Anthony Davis, Tony Brown* .50
494 *Bill Johnson* .20
495 *Darryl Ashmore, Joe Campbell, Kelvin Harris, Tim Lester* .15
496 Nick Bell .20
497 Jerry Ball .12
498 *Edgar Bennett, Mark Chmura, Chris Holder, Mazio Royster* 4.00
499 Steve Christie .10
500 Kenneth Davis .12

1992 Fleer GameDay Box Tops

Display boxes from 1992 GameDay featured four different box tops, all of which have blank backs and are unnumbered. Although most photos are different than the player's card in the regular-issue set, Randall Cunningham is on all four tops.

NM/M
Complete Set (4): 2.00
Common Player: .50
1 Randall Cunningham, Anthony Munoz, Earnest Byner, Jim Everett .50
2 Haywood Jeffires, Randall Cunningham, Mark Carrier, Vinny Testaverde .50
3 Howie Long, Thurman Thomas, Randall Cunningham, Jerry Rice .75
4 Christian Okoye, Pat Swilling, Steve Emtman, Randall Cunningham .50

1992 Fleer GameDay National

Persons attending the 13th National Sports Card Convention in Atlanta, Ga., were given this 46-card set, which was contained in a black vinyl binder. The convention logo is printed on the card back, thereby distinguishing the card from GameDay's regular cards. The card front has a color action photo against a black-and-white background. The back has a card number, biographical information, stats and a mug shot. Each card measures 2-1/2" x 4-11/16".

NM/M
Complete Set (46): 40.00
Common Player: 1.00
1 Deion Sanders 2.50
2 Jim Kelly 2.00
3 Jim Harbaugh 1.25
4 Boomer Esiason 1.50
5 Bernie Kosar 1.50
6 Troy Aikman 7.00
7 John Elway 3.00
8 Rodney Peete 1.00
9 Sterling Sharpe 2.50
10 Warren Moon 2.00
11 Jeff George 2.00
12 Derrick Thomas 2.00
13 Howie Long 1.25
14 Jim Everett 1.50
15 Dan Marino 5.00
16 Chris Doleman 1.00
17 Irving Fryar 1.25
18 Pat Swilling 1.25
19 Lawrence Taylor 2.00
20 Ken O'Brien 1.00
21 Randall Cunningham 2.00
22 Timm Rosenbach 1.00
23 Bubby Brister 1.25
24 John Friesz 2.00
25 Joe Montana 6.00
26 Dan McGwire 1.00
27 Vinny Testaverde 1.25
28 Mark Rypien 1.25
29 Ronnie Lott 2.00
30 Marco Coleman 1.50
31 Rob Moore 2.00
32 Bill Pickel 1.00
33 Brad Baxter 1.25
34 Steve Broussard 1.00
35 Darion Conner 1.00
36 Chris Hinton 1.00
37 Erric Pegram 1.25
38 Jessie Tuggle 1.00
39 Billy Joe Tolliver 1.00
40 David Klingler 2.00
41 Michael Irvin 3.00
42 Emmitt Smith 8.00
43 Quentin Coryatt 1.50
44 Steve Emtman 1.25
45 Deron Cherry 1.00
46 Ricky Ervins 1.00

1992-93 Fleer GameDay Gamebreakers

This 14-card set previewed the 1993 GameDay design and was available at the Super Bowl show. According to the checklist card, there are 5,000 sets produced.

NM/M
Complete Set (14): 7.00
Common Player: .20
1 Marco Coleman .20
2 Bill Cowher (CO) .20
3 John Elway 1.50
4 Barry Foster .20
5 Cortez Kennedy .20
6 James Lofton .30
7 Art Monk .30
8 Jerry Rice 2.00
9 Sterling Sharpe .40
10 Emmitt Smith 4.00
11 Thurman Thomas .50
12 Gino Torretta .20
13 Steve Young 1.75
14 Checklist Card .20

1992-93 Fleer GameDay SB Program

This six-card set was available through 1993 Super Bowl programs (one card per program). The cards are unnumbered and preview the 1993 GameDay set.

NM/M
Complete Set (6): 10.00
Common Player: 1.00
1 Troy Aikman 5.00
2 Terry Allen 1.75
3 Ray Childress 1.00
4 Marco Coleman 1.00
5 Barry Foster 1.00
6 Sterling Sharpe 1.50

1993 Fleer

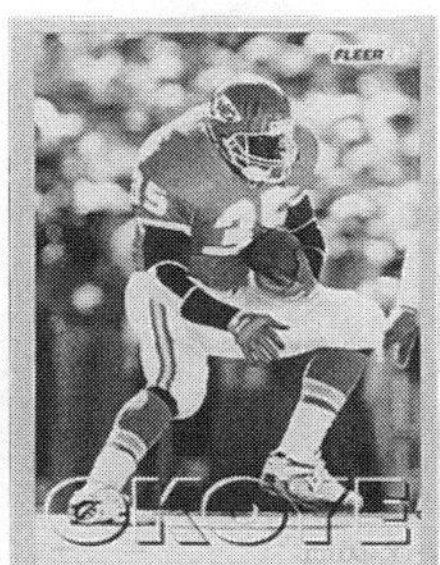

This 500-card set features color action photos and UV coating. The card front has a silver metallic border. The player's name is at the bottom in an embossed, transparent lettering. His team and position are at the lower right. The back has a color-coded panel which includes a close-up photo, stats, profile, biography and team logo. Subsets include Award Winners (#s 236-240, 253-257), League Leaders (#s 241-243, 258-262) and Pro Visions (#s 246-248, 263-264). Insert sets include NFL Prospects (30 cards, randomly in foil packs), All-Pro (25, in foil), Rookie Sensations (20, in jumbo packs), Team Leaders (5, in foil) and Steve Young (10, in foil). A nine-card promo sheet was also produced. It measures 7-1/2" x 10-1/2" and previews the 1993 Fleer card design. The nine players are: Steve Young, Kenny Walker, Chip Lohmiller, Kevin Greene, Craig Heyward, Ernie Jones, Emmitt Smith, Keith Byars and a promotional Fleer card.

NM/M
Complete Set (500): 20.00
Common Player: .05
Minor Stars: .10
Pack (15): .75
Wax Box (36): 21.00
1 Dan Saleaumua .05
2 Bryan Cox .05
3 Dermontti Dawson .05
4 Michael Jackson .05
5 Calvin Williams .05
6 Terry McDaniel .05
7 Jack Del Rio .05
9 Ernie Jones .05
10 Brad Muster .05
11 Harold Green .05
12 Eric Bieniemy .05
13 Eric Dorsey .05
14 Fred Barnett .05
15 Cleveland Gary .05
16 Darion Conner .05
17 Jerry Ball .05
18 Tony Casillas .05
19 Brian Blades .05
20 Tony Bennett .05
21 Reggie Cobb .05
22 Kurt Gouveia .05
23 Greg McMurty .05
24 Kyle Clifton .05
25 Trace Armstrong .05
26 Terry Allen .05
27 Steve Bono .50
28 Barry Word .05
29 Mark Duper .05
30 Nate Newton .05
31 Will Wolford .05
32 Curtis Duncan .05
33 Nick Bell .05
34 Don Beebe .05
36 Rich Camarillo .05
37 Wade Wilson .05
38 John Taylor .05
39 Marion Butts .05
40 Rodney Hampton .10
41 Seth Joyner .05
42 Wilber Marshall .05
43 Bobby Hebert .05
44 Bennie Blades .05
45 Thomas Everett .05
46 Ricky Sanders .05
47 Matt Brock .05
48 Lawrence Dawsey .05
49 Brad Edwards .05
50 Vincent Brown .05
51 Jeff Lageman .05
52 Mark Carrier .05
53 Cris Carter .50
54 Brent Jones .05
55 Barry Foster .05
56 Derrick Thomas .10
57 Scott Zolak .05
58 Mark Stepnoski .05
59 Eric Metcalf .05
60 Al Smith .05
61 Ronnie Harmon .05
62 Cornelius Bennett .05
64 Chris Chandler .05
65 Toi Cook .05
66 Tim Krumrie .05
67 Gill Byrd .05
68 Mark Jackson .05
69 Tim Harris .05
70 Shane Conlan .05
71 Moe Gardner .05
72 Lomas Brown .05
73 Charles Haley .05
74 Mark Rypien .05
75 LeRoy Butler .05
76 Steve DeBerg .05
77 Darrell Green .05
78 Marv Cook .05
79 Chris Burkett .05
80 Richard Dent .05
81 Roger Craig .05
82 Amp Lee .05
83 Eric Green .05
84 Willie Davis .05
85 Mark Higgs .05
86 Carlton Haselrig .05
87 Tommy Vardell .05
88 Haywood Jeffires .05
89 Tim Brown .10
90 Randall McDaniel .05
91 John Elway 1.00
92 Ken Harvey .05
93 Joel Hilgenberg .05
94 Steve Wallace .05
95 Stan Humphries .10
96 Greg Jackson .05
97 Clyde Simmons .05
98 Jim Everett .05
99 Michael Hayes .05
100 Mel Gray .05
101 Alvin Harper .10
102 Art Monk .10
103 Brett Favre 2.00
104 Keith McCants .05
105 Charles Mann .05
106 Leonard Russell .05
107 Mo Lewis .05
108 Shaun Gayle .05
109 Chris Doleman .05
110 Tim McDonald .05
111 Louis Oliver .05
112 Greg Lloyd .10
113 Chip Banks .05
114 Sean Jones .05
115 Ethan Horton .05
116 Kenneth Davis .05
118 Johnny Johnson .05
119 Vaughan Johnson .05
120 Derrick Fenner .05
121 Nate Lewis .05
122 Pepper Johnson .05
123 Heath Sherman .05
124 Darryl Henley .05
125 Pierce Holt .05
126 Herman Moore .50
127 Michael Irvin .30
128 Tommy Kane .05
129 Jackie Harris .05
130 Hardy Nickerson .05
131 Chip Lohmiller .05
132 Andre Tippett .05
133 Leonard Marshall .05
134 Craig Heyward .05
135 Anthony Carter .05
136 Tom Rathman .05
137 Lorenzo White .05
138 Nick Lowery .05
139 John Offerdahl .05
140 Neil O'Donnell .10
141 Clarence Verdin .05
142 Ernest Givins .05
143 Todd Marinovich .05
144 Jeff Wright .05
146 Freddie Joe Nunn .05
147 William Perry .05
148 Daniel Stubbs .05
149 Morten Anderson .05
150 David Meggett .05
151 Andre Waters .05
152 Todd Lyght .05
153 Chris Miller .05
154 Rodney Peete .05
155 Jim Jeffcoat .05
156 Cortez Kennedy .05
157 Johnny Holland .05
158 Ricky Reynolds .05
159 Kevin Greene .05
160 Jeff Herrod .05
161 Bruce Matthews .05
162 Anthony Smith .05
163 Henry Jones .05
164 Rob Burnett .05
165 Eric Swann .05
166 Tom Waddle .05
167 Alfred Williams .05
168 *Darren Carrington* .05
169 Mike Sherrard .05
170 Frank Reich .05
171 *Anthony Newman* .05
172 Mike Pritchard .05
173 Andre Ware .05
174 Daryl Johnston .05
175 Rufus Porter .05
176 Reggie White .10
177 *Charles Mincy* .05
178 Pete Stoyanovich .05
179 Rod Woodson .10
180 Anthony Johnson .05
181 Cody Carlson .05
182 Gaston Green .05
183 Audray McMillian .05
184 Mike Johnson .05
185 Aeneas Williams .05
186 Jarrod Bunch .05
188 Quinn Early .05
189 James Hasty .05
190 Daryl Talley .05
191 Jon Vaughn .05
192 Andre Rison .10
193 Kelvin Pritchett .05
194 Ken Norton .05
195 Chris Warren .25
196 Sterling Sharpe .10
197 Christian Okoye .05
198 Richmond Webb .05
199 James Francis .05
200 Reggie Langhorne .05
201 J.J. Birden .05
202 Aaron Wallace .05
203 Henry Thomas .05
204 Clay Matthews .05
205 Robert Massey .05
206 Donnell Woolford .05
207 Ricky Watters .20
208 Wayne Martin .05
209 Rob Moore .05
210 Steve Tasker .05
211 Jackie Slater .05
212 Steve Young 1.00
213 Barry Sanders 1.25
214 Jay Novacek .05
215 Eugene Robinson .05
216 Duane Bickett .05
217 Broderick Thomas .05
218 David Fulcher .05
219 Rohn Stark .05
220 Warren Moon .10
221 Steve Wisniewski .05
222 Nate Odomes .05
224 Byron Evans .05
225 Mark Collins .05
227 Sam Mills .05
228 Marvin Washington .05
229 Thurman Thomas .15
230 Brent Williams .05
231 Jesse Tuggle .05
232 Chris Spielman .05
233 Emmitt Smith 2.00
234 John L. Williams .05
235 Jeff Cross .05
236 Chris Doleman .05
237 John Elway (AW) .20
238 Barry Foster (AW) .05
239 Cortez Kennedy (AW) .05
240 Steve Young (AW) .50
241 Barry Foster (LL) .05
242 Warren Moon (LL) .05
243 Sterling Sharpe (LL) .05
244 Emmitt Smith (LL) 1.00
245 Thurman Thomas (LL) .10
246 Michael Irvin (PV) .15
247 Steve Young (PV) .50
248 Barry Foster (PV) .05
249 Checklist .05
250 Checklist .05
251 Checklist .05
252 Checklist .05
253 Troy Aikman (AW) .40
254 Jason Hanson (AW) .05
255 Carl Pickens (AW) .20
256 Santana Doleman .05
257 Dale Carter .05
258 Clyde Simmons .05
259 Audray McMillian .05
260 Henry Jones .05
261 Deion Sanders .20
262 Haywood Foster .05
263 Deion Sanders .20
264 Andre Reed .05
265 Vince Workman .05
266 Robert Brown .05
267 Ray Agnew .05
268 Ronnie Lott .05
269 Wesley Carroll .05
270 John Randle .05
271 Rodney Culver .05
272 David Alexander .05
273 Troy Aikman 1.00
274 Bernie Kosar .05
275 Scott Case .05
276 Dan McGwire .05
277 John Alt .05
278 Dan Marino 2.00
279 Santana Dotson .05
280 Johnny Mitchell .05
281 Alonzo Spellman .05
282 Adrian Cooper .05
283 Gary Clark .05
285 Eric Martin .05
286 Jesse Solomon .05
287 Carl Banks .05
288 Harris Barton .05
289 Jim Harbaugh .10
290 Bubba McDowell .05
291 *Anthony McDowell* .05
292 Terrell Buckley .05
293 Bruce Armstrong .05
294 Kurt Barber .05
295 Reginald Jones .05
296 Steve Jordan .05
297 Kerry Cash .05
298 Ray Crockett .05
299 Keith Byars .05
300 Russell Maryland .05
301 Johnny Bailey .05
302 Vinnie Clark .05
303 Terry Wooden .05
304 Harvey Williams .05
305 Marco Coleman .05
306 Mark Wheeler .05
307 Greg Townsend .05
308 Tim McGee .05
309 Donald Evans .05
310 Randal Hill .05
312 Dalton Hilliard .05
313 Howard Ballard .05
314 Phil Simms .05
315 Jerry Rice 1.00
316 Courtney Hall .05
317 Darren Lewis .05
318 Greg Montgomery .05
319 Paul Gruber .05
320 *George Koonce* .05
321 Eugene Chung .05
322 Mike Brim .05
323 Patrick Hunter .05
324 Todd Scott .05
325 Steve Emtman .05
326 *Andy Harmon* .05
327 Larry Brown .05
328 Chuck Cecil .05
329 Tim McKyer .05
330 Jeff Bryant .05
331 Tim Barnett .05
332 Irving Fryar .05
333 Tyji Armstrong .05
334 Brad Baxter .05
335 Shane Collins .05
336 Jeff Graham .05
337 Ricky Proehl .05
338 Tommy Maddox .05
339 Jim Dombrowski .05
340 Bill Brooks .05
341 *Dave Brown* .30
342 Eric Davis .05
345 Mike Munchak .05
346 Ron Hall .05
347 Brian Noble .05
348 Chris Singleton .05
349 Boomer Esiason .05
350 Ray Roberts .05
351 Gary Zimmerman .05
352 Quentin Coryatt .05
353 Willie Green .05
354 Randall Cunningham .05
355 Kevin Smith .05
356 Michael Dean Perry .05
357 Tim Green .05
358 Dwayne Harper .05
359 Dale Carter .05
360 Keith Jackson .05
361 Martin Mayhew .05
362 Brian Washington .05
363 Earnest Byner .05
364 David Johnson .05
365 Timm Rosenbach .05
367 Vaughn Dunbar .05
368 Phil Hansen .05
369 Mike Fox .05
370 Dana Hall .05
371 Junior Seau .10
373 Eddie Robinson .05
374 *Milton Mack* .05
375 Mike Prior .05
376 Jerome Henderson .05
377 Scott Mersereau .05
378 Neal Anderson .05
379 Harry Newsome .05
380 John Baylor .05
381 Bill Fralic .05
382 Mark Bavaro .05
383 Robert Jones .05
384 Tyronne Stowe .05
385 Deion Sanders .50
386 Robert Blackman .05
387 Neil Smith .05
388 Mark Ingram .05
389 Mark Carrier .05
390 Browning Nagle .05
391 Ricky Evans .05
392 Carnell Lake .05
393 Luis Sharpe .05
395 Tommy Barnhardt .05
396 Mark Kelso .05
397 *Kent Graham* .10
398 Bill Romanowski .05
399 Anthony Miller .05
400 John Roper .05
401 Lamar Rogers .05
402 Troy Auzenne .05
403 Webster Slaughter .05
404 David Brandon .05
405 Chris Hinton .05
406 Andy Heck .05
407 Tracy Simien .05
408 Troy Vincent .05
409 Jason Hanson .05
410 *Rod Jones* .05
411 Al Noga .05
412 Ernie Mills .05
413 Willie Gault .05
414 Henry Ellard .05
415 Rickey Jackson .05

416	Bruce Smith	.05
417	Derek Brown	.05
418	Kevin Fagan	.05
419	Gary Plummer	.05
420	Wendell Davis	.05
421	Craig Thompson	.05
422	Wes Hopkins	.05
423	Ray Childress	.05
424	Pat Harlow	.05
425	Howie Long	.05
427	Sean Salisbury	.05
428	*Dwight Hollier*	.05
429	Brett Perriman	.10
430	Donald Hollas	.05
431	Jim Lachey	.05
432	Darren Perry	.05
433	Lionel Washington	.05
434	Sean Gilbert	.05
435	Gene Atkins	.05
436	Jim Kelly	.15
437	Ed McCaffrey	.05
438	Don Griffin	.05
439	Jerrol Williams	.05
440	Bryce Paup	.10
441	Darryl Williams	.05
442	Vai Sikahema	.05
443	Cris Dishman	.05
444	Kevin Mack	.05
445	Winston Moss	.05
447	Mike Merriweather	.05
448	Tony Paige	.05
449	Robert Porcher	.05
450	Ricardo McDonald	.05
451	Danny Copeland	.05
452	Tony Tolbert	.05
453	Eric Dickerson	.05
454	Willie Anderson	.05
455	Dave Krieg	.05
456	*Brad Lamb*	.05
457	Bart Oates	.05
458	Guy McIntyre	.05
459	Stanley Richard	.05
460	Edgar Bennett	.05
461	Pat Carter	.05
462	Eric Allen	.05
463	William Fuller	.05
464	James Jones	.05
465	Chester McGlockton	.05
467	Tim Grunhard	.05
468	Jarvis Williams	.05
469	Tracy Scroggins	.05
470	David Klingler	.05
471	Andre Collins	.05
472	Eric Williams	.05
473	Eddie Anderson	.05
474	Marc Boutte	.05
475	Joe Montana	1.00
476	Andre Reed	.10
477	Lawrence Taylor	.10
478	Jeff George	.15
479	Chris Mims	.05
480	Ken Ruettgers	.05
481	Roman Phifer	.05
482	William Thomas	.05
483	Lamar Lathon	.05
484	Vinny Testaverde	.05
485	Mike Kenn	.05
487	Chris Martin	.05
488	Maurice Hurst	.05
489	Pat Swilling	.05
490	Carl Pickens	.75
491	Tony Smith	.05
492	James Washington	.05
493	Jeff Hostetler	.10
494	Jeff Chadwick	.05
495	Kevin Ross	.05
496	Jim Ritcher	.05
497	Jessie Hester	.05
498	Burt Grossman	.05
499	Keith Van Horne	.05
500	Gerald Robinson	.05

1993 Fleer All-Pros

Twenty-five of the NFL's best are featured on these cards, which were randomly inserted into 1993 Fleer foil packs. Each card front is horizontal with white borders and features a color photo of the player superimposed against a black-and-white action photo. The "All-Pro" logo and player's name are in gold foil at the bottom. Each card back is numbered and includes a career summary on a background of team color-coded panels.

		NM/M
Complete Set (25):		20.00
Common Player:		1.00
Minor Stars:		2.00
1	Steve Atwater	1.00
2	Rich Camarillo	1.00
3	Ray Childress	1.00
4	Chris Doleman	1.00
5	Barry Foster	1.00
6	Henry Jones	1.00
7	Cortez Kennedy	1.00
8	Nick Lowery	1.00
9	Wilber Marshall	1.00
10	Bruce Matthews	1.00
11	Randall McDaniel	1.00
12	Audray McMillian	1.00
13	Sam Mills	1.00
14	Jay Novacek	1.00
15	Jerry Rice	8.00
16	Junior Seau	2.00
17	Sterling Sharpe	2.00
18	Clyde Simmons	1.00
19	Emmitt Smith	8.00
20	Derrick Thomas	2.00
21	Steve Wallace	1.00
22	Richmond Webb	1.00
23	Steve Wisniewski	1.00
24	Rod Woodson	1.00
25	Steve Young	6.00

1993 Fleer Prospects

Thirty players from the 1993 NFL draft are featured on these cards, which were randomly inserted in 1993 Fleer foil packs. Each card front has a color cut-out photo of the player on a gold background with blue borders. The "1993 NFL Prospect" logo, player's name, round he was drafted in and team name are in gold foil on the front, too. The back has a close-up shot and a career summary, plus a card number.

		NM/M
Complete Set (30):		40.00
Common Player:		1.50
1	Drew Bledsoe	12.00
2	Garrison Hearst	5.00
3	John Copeland	1.50
4	Eric Curry	1.50
5	Curtis Conway	5.00
6	Lincoln Kennedy	1.50
7	Jerome Bettis	5.00
8	Patrick Bates	1.50
9	Brad Hopkins	1.50
10	Tom Carter	1.50
11	Irv Smith	1.50
12	Robert Smith	2.00
13	Deon Figures	1.50
14	Leonard Renfro	1.50
15	O.J. McDuffie	4.00
16	Dana Stubblefield	1.50
17	Todd Kelly	1.50
18	George Teague	1.50
19	Demetrius DeBose	1.50
20	Coleman Rudolph	1.50
21	Carlton Gray	1.50
22	Troy Drayton	1.50
23	Natrone Means	2.00
24	Qadry Ismail	4.00
25	Gino Torretta	1.50
26	Carl Simpson	1.50
27	Glyn Milburn	1.50
28	Chad Brown	1.50
29	Reggie Brooks	1.50
30	Billy Joe Hobert	1.50

1993 Fleer Rookie Sensations

These cards feature 20 of the NFL's top players beginning their NFL careers. The cards have the player's name and "Rookie Sensations" logo in gold foil on the front. The backs have a player profile and card number, 1 of 20, etc. Cards were random inserts in 1993 Fleer football jumbo packs.

		NM/M
Complete Set (20):		30.00
Common Player:		1.00
1	Dale Carter	1.00
2	Eugene Chung	1.00
3	Marco Coleman	1.00
4	Quentin Coryatt	2.00
5	Santana Dotson	2.00
6	Vaughn Dunbar	1.00
7	Steve Emtman	1.00
8	Sean Gilbert	2.00
9	Dana Hall	1.00
10	Jason Hanson	1.00
11	Robert Jones	1.00
12	David Klingler	1.00
13	Amp Lee	2.00
14	Troy Auzenne	1.00
15	Ricardo McDonald	1.00
16	Chris Mims	1.00
17	Johnny Mitchell	2.00
18	Carl Pickens	5.00
19	Darren Perry	1.00
20	Troy Vincent	3.00

1993 Fleer Team Leaders

Five premiere players in the NFL are featured in this insert set; cards were randomly inserted into 1993 Fleer foil packs. The card front features a player action photo against a blue background with lightning streaks. "Team Leader" and the player's name are in gold foil at the bottom. The backs have a blue background with gold border and contain another color photo and career summary, plus a card number (1 of 5 etc.).

		NM/M
Complete Set (5):		20.00
Common Player:		2.00
1	Brett Favre	10.00
2	Derrick Thomas	2.00
3	Steve Young	6.00
4	John Elway	8.00
5	Cortez Kennedy	2.00

1993 Fleer Steve Young

The NFL's 1992 MVP, Steve Young, is featured in this "Performance Highlights" issue from Fleer. Each card front has an action photo with a white border, plus the set and player's name stamped in gold foil. The back has a close-up shot and player profile against a red background with white borders. The cards are numbered on the backs. Cards 11-13 were available through Fleer through a mail-in offer only, for 10 wrappers and $1. Young also signed more than 2,000 cards, which were randomly inserted.

	NM/M
Complete Set (10):	10.00
Common Young:	1.00
Autograph:	120.00
Mail-In Young (11-13):	2.00

1993 Fleer Fruit of the Loom

Specially-marked packages of Fruit of the Loom underwear contained six of these cards, which were produced by Fleer. The cards are similar in design to Fleer's regular 1993 set, except a Fruit of the Loom logo appears on the card front. The photos are the same, but the card number, which is on the back, indicates the card is x of 50, etc.

		NM/M
Complete Set (50):		100.00
Common Player:		.40
1	Andre Rison	1.00
2	Deion Sanders	2.00
3	Neal Anderson	1.00
4	Jim Harbaugh	1.00
5	Bernie Kosar	2.50
6	Eric Metcalf	1.00
7	John Elway	5.00
8	Karl Mecklenburg	.40
9	Sterling Sharpe	2.00
10	Reggie White (Traded to Green Bay Packers)	4.00
11	Steve Emtman	2.00
12	Jeff George	2.00
13	Willie Gault	2.00
14	Jim Kelly	5.00
15	Thurman Thomas	5.00
16	Harold Green	.40
17	Carl Pickens	.40
18	Troy Aikman	8.00
19	Emmitt Smith	10.00
20	Barry Sanders	10.00
21	Pat Swilling (Traded to Detroit Lions)	1.00
22	Haywood Jeffires	1.00
23	Warren Moon	2.00
24	Derrick Thomas	1.00
25	Christian Okoye	1.00
26	Flipper Anderson	.40
27	Jim Everett	2.00
28	Keith Jackson	2.50
29	Dan Marino	10.00
30	Andre Tippett	.40
31	Lawrence Taylor	2.50
32	Randall Cunningham	2.50
33	Barry Foster	1.00
34	Rod Woodson	2.00
35	Jerry Rice	8.00
36	Steve Young	6.00
37	Reggie Cobb	.40
38	Roger Craig	2.00
39	Chris Doleman	.40
40	Morten Andersen	.40
41	Dalton Hilliard	.40
42	Ronnie Lott (Traded to New York Jets)	2.50
43	Chris Chandler	.40
44	Stan Humphries	1.00
45	Junior Seau	4.00
46	Brian Blades	.40
47	Cortez Kennedy	1.00
48	Wilber Marshall	.40
49	Art Monk	2.50
50	Checklist Card	.40

1993 Fleer GameDay

GameDay used the same format as its 1992 debut set - oversized cards which measure 2-1/2" x 4-11/16" - but cut back the number of cards by 20. However, the 1993 set included three insert sets - "GameBreakers" (20 cards of impact players), "Rookie Standouts" (16 of the top 1993 NFL draft picks), and "Second-Year Stars" (16 of the game's top sophomores). All three types were randomly inserted in packs.

		NM/M
Complete Set (480):		25.00
Common Player:		.10
Minor Stars:		.20
Wax Box:		35.00
1	Troy Aikman	2.00
2	Terry Allen	.10
3	Ray Childress	.10
4	Marco Coleman	.10
5	Barry Foster	.20
6	Sterling Sharpe	.30
7	Steve McMichael	.10
8	Steve Young	2.00
9	Derrick Thomas	.20
10	John Elway	1.00
11	*Drew Bledsoe*	7.00
12	Jim Kelly	.30
13	Dan Marino	3.00
14	Mo Lewis	.10
15	David Klingler	.20
16	Darrell Green	.10
17	James Francis	.10
18	*John Copeland*	.30
19	Terry McDaniel	.10
20	Barry Sanders	2.00
21	Deion Sanders	1.00
22	Emmitt Smith	4.00
23	Marion Butts	.10
24	Darryl Talley	.10
25	Randall Cunningham	.20
26	Rod Woodson	.20
27	Terrell Buckley	.10
28	Michael Haynes	.10
29	Tony Jones	.10
30	Santana Dotson	.10
31	Lomas Brown	.10
32	Eric Metcalf	.10
33	Morten Andersen	.10
34	Reggie Cobb	.10
35	Ferrell Edmunds	.10
36	Joe Montana	3.00
37	Ken Harvey	.10
38	Rodney Hampton	.30
39	Kurt Gouveia	.10
40	Ken Norton	.10
41	Frank Reich	.10
42	Kevin Greene	.10
43	Cleveland Gary	.10
44	Maurice Hurst	.10
45	Troy Vincent	.10
46	*Eric Curry*	.30
47	*Curtis Conway*	1.25
48	Christian Okoye	.10
49	Tunch Ilkin	.10
50	Michael Irvin	.50
51	Bart Oates	.10
52	Pepper Johnson	.10
53	Vaughan Johnson	.10
54	Lawrence Taylor	.20
55	Junior Seau	.40
56	Michael Brooks	.10
57	Neal Anderson	.10
58	D.J. Johnson	.10
59	Seth Joyner	.10
60	Marvin Washington	.10
61	Ernest Givins	.10
62	*Jaime Feilds*	.10
63	Vincent Brown	.10
64	Randall McDaniel	.10
65	Tommy Maddox	.10
66	*Steve Everitt*	.30
67	Brian Noble	.10
68	Bryce Paup	.10
69	Brad Baxter	.10
70	*Demetrius DuBose*	.20
71	Duane Bickett	.10
72	Mark Rypien	.10
73	Harris Barton	.10
74	Bruce Matthews	.10
75	Irving Fryar	.10
76	Steve Wisniewski	.10
77	*Will Shields*	.10
78	*Tom Carter*	.40
79	Steve Emtman	.10
80	Jerry Rice	2.00
81	Art Monk	.20
82	Tony Tolbert	.10
83	Johnny Mitchell	.10
84	*Deon Figures*	.30
85	Marv Cook	.10
86	Darion Conner	.10
87	Ricky Proehl	.10
88	Tony Bennett	.10
89	Jay Schroeder	.10
90	Neil Smith	.10
91	Jarvis Williams	.10
92	James Hasty	.10
93	Anthony Miller	.20
94	*Thomas Smith*	.20
95	Richard Dent	.10
96	Henry Jones	.10
97	Renaldo Turnbull	.10
98	Jason Hanson	.10
99	Cortez Kennedy	.20
100	Brett Favre	3.00
101	Anthony Carter	.10
102	Cris Carter	.20
103	*Dana Stubblefield*	1.00
104	Nick Bell	.10
105	Marcus Allen	.20
106	Neil O'Donnell	.40
107	Steve DeBerg	.10
108	Leonard Russell	.10
109	Ethan Horton	.10
110	William Perry	.10
111	Don Griffin	.10
112	Clarence Verdin	.10
113	Amp Lee	.10
114	Earnest Byner	.10
115	Ricky Reynolds	.10
116	Tom Waddle	.10
117	Robert Jones	.10
118	Willie Davis	.10
119	Chris Miller	.10
120	Drew Hill	.10
121	Warren Moon	.30
122	Willie Anderson	.10
123	*George Teague*	.30
124	John L. Williams	.10
125	Ed McCaffrey	.10
126	Eric Green	.10
127	Scott Mersereau	.10
128	Charles Mann	.10
129	Todd Lyght	.10
130	Rodney Culver	.10
131	Richmond Webb	.10
132	*John Parrella*	.10
133	*Reggie Brooks*	.50
134	*Lincoln Kennedy*	.20
135	Tim Johnson	.10
136	Robert Massey	.10
137	Keith Jackson	.20
138	Alfred Williams	.10
139	Leroy Hoard	.10
140	Jessie Tuggle	.10
141	Chris Mims	.10
142	Herschel Walker	.10
143	Clyde Simmons	.10
144	Dana Hall	.10
145	Nate Newton	.10
146	Dennis Smith	.10
147	Rich Camarillo	.10
148	Chris Spielman	.10
149	Jim Dombrowski	.10
150	Steve Beuerlein	.10
151	Mark Clayton	.10
152	Lee Williams	.10
153	*Robert Smith*	1.50
154	Greg Jackson	.10
155	Jay Hilgenberg	.10
156	Howard Ballard	.10
157	*Mike Compton*	.10
158	Brent Williams	.10
159	Tommy Kane	.10
160	Barry Word	.10
161	Darren Lewis	.10
162	Steve Atwater	.10
163	Gary Clark	.10
164	Donnell Woolford	.10
165	Henry Thomas	.10
166	Tim Brown	.25
167	Andre Ware	.10
168	Jackie Harris	.20
169	Browning Nagle	.10
170	Chris Singleton	.10
171	Ronnie Lott	.10
172	Leonard Marshall	.10
173	Dale Carter	.10
174	Bruce Armstrong	.10
175	Tommy Vardell	.10
176	Bubba McDowell	.10
177	*Patrick Bates*	.20
178	Tyji Armstrong	.10
179	Keith Sims	.10
180	Boomer Esiason	.20
181	Ricky Watters	.40
182	Keith Sims	.10
183	Burt Grossman	.10
184	Richard Cooper	.10
185	Marc Boutte	.10
186	Shane Conlan	.10
187	Luis Sharpe	.10
188	*O.J. McDuffie*	2.00
189	Harvey Williams	.10
190	Blair Thomas	.10
191	Charles Haley	.10
192	Chip Lohmiller	.10
193	Vinny Testaverde	.20
194	Desmond Howard	.20
195	Johnny Johnson	.10
196	Bennie Blades	.10
197	Jeff Wright	.10
198	Cody Carlson	.10
199	*Micheal Barrow*	.10
200	Pat Swilling	.10
201	*Willie Roaf*	.25
202	Mike Walter	.10
203	Kevin Fagan	.10
204	Nate Odomes	.10
205	Michael Dean Perry	.10
206	Bruce Pickens	.10
207	Mel Gray	.10
208	Jack Trudeau	.10
209	Ricky Sanders	.10
210	Bobby Hebert	.10
211	Craig Heyward	.10
212	Eric Bieniemy	.10
213	Andre Rison	.20
214	Bernie Kosar	.10
215	*Lester Holmes*	.10
216	*Marcus Buckley*	.20
217	Tony Casillas	.10
218	Cornelius Bennett	.10
219	Kyle Clifton	.10
220	Kirk Lowdermilk	.10
221	Leon Searcy	.10
222	Gary Anderson	.10
223	Tim Barnett	.10
224	Gene Atkins	.10
225	Jeff Cross	.10
226	*Darrin Smith*	.25
227	Rohn Stark	.10
228	Chris Warren	.50
229	Eric Allen	.10
230	*Wayne Simmons*	.10
231	Al Smith	.10
232	*Reggie Rivers*	.10
233	Kevin Smith	.10
234	Vince Workman	.10
235	Thurman Thomas	.30
236	*Kevin Williams*	1.50
237	Dan McGwire	.10
238	Greg Lloyd	.10
239	*Ray Buchanan*	.25
240	Shannon Sharpe	.20
241	Ricardo McDonald	.10
242	Aaron Wallace	.10
243	Chris Hinton	.10
244	Bill Romanowski	.10
245	Randal Hill	.10
246	Ray Agnew	.10
247	*Todd Kelly*	.10
248	John Stephens	.10
249	Sean Sailsbury	.10
250	Roger Craig	.10
251	Dave Krieg	.10
252	Brian Blades	.10
253	Jerrod Bunch	.10
254	Phil Simms	.10
255	Keith Van Horne	.10
256	Jim Price	.10
257	*Garrison Hearst*	3.00
258	Derrick Walker	.10
259	Mike Pritchard	.10
260	*Leonard Renfro*	.10
261	Rodney Peete	.10
262	Jeff Bryant	.10
263	Dermontti Dawson	.10
264	Greg McMurty	.10
265	Wendell Davis	.10
266	Kerry Cash	.10
267	Jackie Slater	.10
268	Sam Mills	.10
269	Carlton Bailey	.10
270	Mark Wheeler	.10
271	Darren Perry	.10
272	Todd Scott	.10
273	John Holland	.10
274	Mike Croel	.10
275	Shane Dronett	.10
276	Andre Collins	.10
277	Eric Swann	.10
278	Jessie Hester	.10
279	Bryan Cox	.10
280	Mark Jackson	.10
281	Thomas Everett	.10
282	James Lofton	.10
283	Carl Pickens	1.00
284	Mark Carrier (Cleve)	.10
285	Heath Sherman	.10
286	Chris Burkett	.10
287	*Coleman Rudolph*	.10
288	Todd Marinovich	.10
289	Nate Lewis	.10
290	Fred Barnett	.10
291	Jim Lachey	.10
292	Jerry Ball	.10
293	Jeff George	.50
294	William Fuller	.10
295	Courtney Hawkins	.10
296	Kelvin Martin	.10
297	Trace Armstrong	.10
298	Carl Banks	.10
299	*Terry Kirby*	.75
301	John Offerdahl	.10
302	Wilber Marshall	.10
303	Guy McIntyre	.10
304	Steve Wallace	.10
305	*Chris Slade*	.50
306	*Anthony Newman*	.10
307	Chip Banks	.10
308	*Carlton Gray*	.10
309	Wayne Martin	.10
310	Tom Rathman	.10
311	Shaun Gayle	.10
312	*Billy Joe Hobert*	.50
313	Matt Brock	.10
314	*Arthur Marshall*	.25
315	Wade Wilson	.10
316	Michael Jackson	.10
317	Bruce Kozerski	.10
318	Reggie Langhorne	.10
319	Jerrol Williams	.10

320 Aeneas Williams .10
321 *Tony McGee* .50
322 *Carl Simpson* .10
323 Russell Maryland .10
324 Nick Lowery .10
325 Steve Tasker .10
326 Alvin Harper .40
327 Haywood Jeffires .10
328 Hardy Nickerson .10
329 Alonzo Spellman .10
330 Eric Dickerson .10
331 Scott Zolak .10
332 Darryl Henley .10
333 Daniel Stubbs .10
334 Andy Heck .10
335 Mark May .10
336 *Roosevelt Potts* .25
337 Erik Howard .10
338 Sean Gilbert .10
339 *Jerome Bettis* 3.00
340 *Darren Carrington* .20
341 Gill Byrd .10
342 John Friesz .10
343 *Roger Harper* .10
344 Fred Stokes .10
345 Stanley Richard .10
346 Johnny Bailey .10
347 David Wyman .10
348 Merril Hoge .10
349 Brett Perriman .10
350 Kelvin Pritchett .10
351 Rod Bernstine .10
352 Jim Ritcher .10
353 Mark Stepnoski .10
354 Jeff Lageman .10
355 *Darrin Gordon* .50
356 Don Mosebar .10
357 Simon Fletcher .10
358 *Charles Mincy* .20
359 Ron Hall .10
360 Brent Jones .10
361 Byron Evans .10
362 *Dan Footman* .20
363 Mark Higgs .10
364 Brian Washington .10
365 *Brad Hopkins* .10
366 Tracy Simien .10
367 Derrick Fenner .10
368 Lorenzo White .10
369 *Marvin Jones* .25
370 Chris Doleman .10
371 Jeff Harrod .10
372 Jim Harbaugh .10
373 Jim Jeffcoat .10
374 *Michael Strahan* .10
375 Ricky Ervins .10
376 Joel Hilgenberg .10
377 Curtis Duncan .10
378 *Glyn Milburn* .75
379 Jack Del Rio .10
380 Eric Martin .10
381 David Meggett .10
382 Jeff Hostetler .20
383 Greg Townsend .10
384 Brad Muster .10
385 *Irv Smith* .50
386 Chris Jacke .10
387 *Ernest Dye* .20
388 Henry Ellard .10
389 John Taylor .10
390 Chris Chandler .10
391 *Larry Centers* .50
392 Henry Rolling .10
393 Dan Saleaumua .10
394 Moe Gardner .10
395 Darryl Williams .10
396 Paul Gruber .10
397 Dwayne Harper .10
398 Pat Harlow .10
399 Rickey Jackson .10
400 Quentin Coryatt .10
401 Steve Jordan .10
402 *Rick Mirer* .75
403 Howard Cross .10
404 Mike Johnson .10
405 Broderick Thomas .10
406 Stan Humphries .40
407 Ronnie Harmon .10
408 *Andy Harmon* .10
409 *Troy Drayton* .75
410 *Dan Williams* .10
411 Mark Bavaro .10
412 Bruce Smith .10
413 *Elbert Shelley* .20
414 Tim McGee .10
415 Tim Harris .10
416 Rob Moore .10
417 Rob Burnett .10
418 Howie Long .10
419 Chuck Cecil .10
420 Carl Lee .10
421 Anthony Smith .10
422 Jeff Graham .20
423 Clay Matthews .10
424 Jay Novacek .10
425 Phil Hansen .10
426 *Andre Hastings* .75
427 Toi Cook .10
428 Rufus Porter .10
429 Mike Pitts .10
430 Eddie Robinson .10
431 Herman Moore 1.00
432 Erik Kramer .10
433 Mark Carrier (Chi.) .10
434 *Natrone Means* 1.00
435 Carnell Lake .10
436 Carlton Haselrig .10
437 John Randle .10
438 Louis Oliver .10
439 Ray Roberts .10
440 Leslie O'Neal .10
441 Reggie White .25
442 Dalton Hilliard .10
443 Tim Krumrie .10
444 Leroy Butler .10
445 Greg Kragen .10
446 Anthony Johnson .10
447 Aydrey McMillian .10
448 Lawrence Dawsey .10
449 Pierce Holt .10
450 Brad Edwards .10
451 J.J. Birden .10
452 Mike Munchak .10
453 Tracy Scroggins .10
454 Mike Tomczak .10
455 Harold Green .10
456 Vaughn Dunbar .10
457 Calvin Williams .10
458 Pete Stoyanovich .10
459 Willie Gault .10
460 Ken Ruettgers .10
461 Eugene Robinson .10
462 Larry Brown .10
463 *Antonio London* .10
464 Andre Reed .10
465 Daryl Johnston .10
466 Karl Mecklenburg .10
467 David Lang .10
468 Bill Brooks .10
469 Jim Everett .20
470 *Qadry Ismail* 1.00
471 Vai Sikahema .10
472 Andre Tippett .10
473 Eugene Chung .10
474 Cris Dishman .10
475 Tim McDonald .10
476 Freddie Joe Nunn .10
477 Checklist #1 .10
478 Checklist #2 .10
479 Checklist #3 .10
480 Checklist #4 .10

1993 Fleer GameDay Game Breakers

These 2-1/2" x 4-3/4" cards were randomly inserted in 1993 GameDay packs. Twenty top offensive players are represented. The card front has a color action photo against a black-and-white game action photo, with a black border. The player's and set's name are stamped in gold foil at the bottom. Each back has a closeup picture of the player, his name, his jersey number and a recap of his 1992 season. The backs are borderless and are numbered 1 of 20, etc.

NM/M
Complete Set (20): 20.00
Common Player: .50
Minor Stars: 1.00
1 Troy Aikman 3.00
2 Brett Favre 4.00
3 Steve Young 3.00
4 Dan Marino 4.00
5 Joe Montana 4.00
6 Jim Kelly 1.00
7 Emmitt Smith 4.00
8 Ricky Watters 1.00
9 Barry Foster .50
10 Barry Sanders 4.00
11 Michael Irvin 1.50
12 Thurman Thomas 1.00
13 Sterling Sharpe 1.00
14 Jerry Rice 4.00
15 Andre Rison .50
16 Deion Sanders 2.00
17 Harold Green .50
18 Lorenzo White .50
19 Terry Allen .50
20 Haywood Jeffires .50

1993 Fleer GameDay Rookie Standouts

These cards are devoted to the top 16 players chosen in the 1993 NFL Draft. Cards, which measure 2-1/2" x 4-3/4", were random inserts in 1993 GameDay packs. Each card front is dark blue and features a color action photo against a black-and-white action background. The player's and set's name are stamped in gold foil at the bottom. The card back, numbered 1 of 16, etc., is white and includes the player's name and uniform number, plus a color photo and recap of his 1992 season.

NM/M
Complete Set (16): 25.00
Common Player: .50
Minor Stars: 1.00
1 Drew Bledsoe 7.00
2 Rick Mirer 3.00
3 Garrison Hearst 3.00
4 Jerome Bettis 4.00
5 Marvin Jones .50
6 Reggie Brooks .50
7 O.J. McDuffie 2.00
8 Qadry Ismail 1.00
9 Glyn Milburn 1.00
10 Andre Hastings .50
11 Curtis Conway 2.00
12 Eric Curry .50
13 John Copeland .50
14 Kevin Williams 2.00
15 Patrick Bates .50
16 Lincoln Kennedy .50

1993 Fleer GameDay Second-Year Stars

Sixteen top rookies from the 1992 NFL season are featured on these cards, which were random inserts in 1993 GameDay packs. Each card is 2-1/2" x 4-3/4" and has a green-bordered front which includes a color action photo against a black-and-white action background. The set's and player's name are stamped in gold foil at the bottom. The back has a shot of the player, his name and jersey number and a recap of his 1992 season. Each is numbered 1 of 16, etc.

NM/M
Complete Set (16): 10.00
Common Player: .25
1 Carl Pickens 2.00
2 David Klingler .50
3 Santana Dotson .25
4 Chris Mims .25
5 Steve Emtman .25
6 Marco Coleman .25
7 Robert Jones .25
8 Dale Carter .25
9 Troy Vincent .25
10 Tracy Scroggins .25
11 Vaughn Dunbar .25
12 Quentin Coryatt .25
13 Dana Hall .25
14 Terrell Buckley .25
15 Tommy Vardell .25
16 Johnny Mitchell .25

1994 Fleer

Fleer's 1994 set includes 474 player cards and six checklist cards. There were also 137 different insert cards produced; one was randomly included in every pack. The regular cards have a color-enhanced photo and gold-foil stamped player signature on the front, plus his team logo, position and name. Card backs have two large photos with a screened-back action shot and a closeup player portrait. Insert cards have full-bleed photos; the regular cards have a white frame around the photo on the card front.

NM/M
Complete Set (480): 20.00
Common Player: .05
Minor Stars: .10
Pack (15): 1.00
Wax Box (36): 20.00
1 Michael Bankston .05
2 Steve Beuerlein .05
3 John Booty .05
4 Rich Camarillo .05
5 Chuck Cecil .05
6 Larry Centers .10
7 Gary Clark .05
8 Garrison Hearst .50
9 Eric Hill .05
10 Randal Hill .05
11 Ron Moore .10
12 Ricky Proehl .05
13 Luis Sharpe .05
14 Clyde Simmons .05
15 Tyronne Stowe .05
16 Eric Swann .05
17 Aeneas Williams .05
18 Darion Conner .05
19 Moe Gardner .05
20 Jumpy Geathers .05
21 Jeff George .10
22 Roger Harper .05
23 Bobby Hebert .10
24 Pierce Holt .05
25 David Johnson .05
26 Mike Kenn .05
27 Lincoln Kennedy .05
28 Erric Pegram .05
29 Mike Pritchard .10
30 Andre Rison .15
31 Deion Sanders .40
32 Tony Smith .05
33 Jesse Solomon .05
34 Jessie Tuggle .05
35 Don Beebe .05
36 Cornelius Bennett .05
37 Bill Brooks .05
38 Kenneth Davis .05
39 John Fina .05
40 Phil Hansen .05
41 Kent Hull .05
42 Henry Jones .05
43 Jim Kelly .15
44 Pete Metzelaars .05
45 Marvcus Patton .05
46 Andre Reed .10
47 Frank Reich .05
48 Bruce Smith .05
49 Thomas Smith .05
50 Darryl Talley .05
51 Steve Tasker .05
52 Thurman Thomas .20
53 Jeff Wright .05
54 Neal Anderson .05
55 Trace Armstrong .05
56 Troy Auzenne .05
57 Joe Cain .15
58 Mark Carrier .05
59 Curtis Conway .10
60 Richard Dent .05
61 Shaun Gayle .05
62 Andy Heck .05
63 Dante Jones .05
64 Erik Kramer .05
65 Steve McMichael .05
66 Terry Obee .05
67 Vinson Smith .05
68 Alonzo Spellman .05
69 Tom Waddle .05
70 Donnell Woolford .05
71 Tim Worley .05
72 Chris Zorich .05
73 Mike Brim .05
74 John Copeland .05
75 Derrick Fenner .05
76 James Francis .05
77 Harold Green .05
78 Rod Jones .05
79 David Klingler .10
80 Bruce Kozerski .05
81 Tim Krumrie .05
82 Ricardo McDonald .05
83 Tim McGee .05
84 Tony McGee .05
85 Louis Oliver .05
86 Carl Pickens .30
87 Jeff Query .05
88 Daniel Stubbs .05
89 Steve Tovar .05
90 Alfred Williams .05
91 Darryl Williams .05
92 Rob Burnett .05
93 Mark Carrier .05
94 Leroy Hoard .05
95 Michael Jackson .05
96 Mike Johnson .05
97 Pepper Johnson .05
98 Tony Jones .05
99 Clay Matthews .05
100 Eric Metcalf .05
101 Stevon Moore .05
102 Michael Dean Perry .05
103 Anthony Pleasant .05
104 Vinny Testaverde .10
105 Eric Turner .05
106 Tommy Vardell .05
107 Troy Aikman .75
108 Larry Brown .05
109 Dixon Edwards .05
110 Charles Haley .05
111 Alvin Harper .15
112 Michael Irvin .25
113 Jim Jeffcoat .05
114 Daryl Johnston .05
115 Leon Lett .05
116 Russell Maryland .05
117 Nate Newton .05
118 Ken Norton Jr. .05
119 Jay Novacek .05
120 Darrin Smith .05
121 Emmitt Smith 2.00
122 Kevin Smith .05
123 Mark Stepnoski .05
124 Tony Tolbert .05
125 Eric Williams .05
126 Kevin Williams .40
127 Darren Woodson .05
128 Steve Atwater .05
129 Rod Bernstine .05
130 Ray Crockett .05
131 Mike Croel .05
132 Robert Delpino .05
133 Shane Dronett .05
134 Jason Elam .05
135 John Elway .40
136 Simon Fletcher .05
137 Greg Kragen .05
138 Karl Mecklenburg .05
139 Glyn Milburn .10
140 Anthony Miller .10
141 Derek Russell .05
142 Shannon Sharpe .10
143 Dennis Smith .05
144 Dan Williams .05
145 Gary Zimmerman .05
146 Bennie Blades .05
147 Lomas Brown .05
148 Bill Fralic .05
149 Mel Gray .05
150 Willie Green .05
151 Jason Hanson .05
152 Robert Massey .05
153 Ryn McNeil .05
154 Scott Mitchell .15
155 Derrick Moore .05
156 Herman Moore .30
157 Brett Perriman .05
158 Robert Porcher .05
159 Kelvin Pritchett .05
160 Barry Sanders 1.25
161 Tracy Scroggins .05
162 Chris Spielman .05
163 Pat Swilling .05
164 Edgar Bennett .05
165 Robert Brooks .05
166 Terrell Buckley .05
167 LeRoy Butler .05
168 Brett Favre 2.00
169 Harry Galbreath .05
170 Jackie Harris .05
171 Johnny Holland .05
172 Chris Jacke .05
173 George Koonce .05
174 Bryce Paup .05
175 Ken Ruettgers .05
176 Sterling Sharpe .15
177 Wayne Simmons .05
178 George Teague .05
179 Darrell Thompson .05
180 Reggie White .15
181 Gary Brown .05
182 Cody Carlson .10
183 Ray Childress .05
184 Cris Dishman .05
185 Ernest Givins .05
186 Haywood Jeffires .05
187 Sean Jones .05
188 Lamar Lathon .05
189 Bruce Matthews .05
190 Bubba McDowell .05
191 Glenn Montgomery .05
192 Greg Montgomery .05
193 Warren Moon .15
194 Bo Orlando .05
195 Marcus Robertson .05
196 Eddie Robinson .05
197 Webster Slaughter .05
198 Lorenzo White .05
199 John Baylor .05
200 Jason Belser .05
201 Tony Bennett .05
202 Dean Biasucci .05
203 Ray Buchanan .05
204 Kerry Cash .05
205 Quentin Coryatt .05
206 Eugene Daniel .05
207 Steve Emtman .05
208 Jon Hand .05
209 Jim Harbaugh .05
210 Jeff Herrod .05
211 Anthony Johnson .05
212 Roosevelt Potts .05
213 Rohn Stark .05
214 Will Wolford .05
215 Marcus Allen .10
216 John Alt .05
217 Kimble Anders .05
218 J.J. Birden .05
219 Dale Carter .05
220 Keith Cash .05
221 Tony Casillas .05
222 Willie Davis .05
223 Tim Grunhard .05
224 Nick Lowery .05
225 Charles Mincy .05
226 Joe Montana 1.50
227 Dan Saleaumua .05
228 Travy Simien .05
229 Neil Smith .05
230 Derrick Thomas .10
231 Eddie Anderson .05
232 Tim Brown .10
233 Nolan Harrison .05
234 Jeff Hostetler .10
235 Raghib Ismail .10
236 Jeff Jaeger .05
237 James Jett .05
238 Joe Kelly .05
239 Albert Lewis .05
240 Terry McDaniel .05
241 Chester McGlockton .05
242 Winston Moss .05
243 Gerald Perry .05
244 Greg Robinson .05
245 Anthony Smith .05
246 Steve Smith .05
247 Greg Townsend .05
248 Lionel Washington .05
249 Steve Wisniewski .05
250 Alexander Wright .05
251 Willie Anderson .05
252 Jerome Bettis .50
253 Marc Boutte .05
254 Shane Conlan .05
255 Troy Drayton .20
256 Henry Ellard .05
257 Sean Gilbert .10
258 Nate Lewis .05
259 Todd Lyght .05
260 Chris Miller .10
261 Anthony Newman .05
262 Roman Phifer .05
263 Henry Rolling .05
264 T.J. Rubley .05
265 Jackie Slater .05
266 Fred Stokes .05
267 Robert Young .05
268 Gene Atkins .05
269 J.B. Brown .05
270 Keith Byars .05
271 Marco Coleman .05
272 Bryan Cox .05
273 Jeff Cross .05
274 Irving Fryar .05
275 Mark Higgs .05
276 Dwight Hollier .05
277 Mark Ingram .05
278 Keith Jackson .05
279 Terry Kirby .10
280 Bernie Kosar .05
281 Dan Marino 2.00
282 O.J. McDuffie .20
283 Keith Sims .05
284 Pete Stoyanovich .05
285 Troy Vincent .05
286 Richmond Webb .05
287 Terry Allen .05
288 Anthony Carter .05
289 Cris Carter .10
290 Jack Del Rio .05
291 Chris Doleman .05
292 Vencie Glenn .05
293 Scottie Graham .20
294 Chris Hinton .05
295 Qadry Ismail .10
296 Carlos Jenkins .05
297 Steve Jordan .05
298 Carl Lee .05
299 Randall McDaniel .05
300 John Randle .05
301 Todd Scott .05
302 Robert Smith .15
303 Fred Strickland .05
304 Henry Thomas .05
305 Bruce Armstrong .05
306 Harlon Barnett .05
307 Drew Bledsoe 1.25
308 Vincent Brown .05
309 Ben Coates .20
310 Todd Collins .05
311 Myron Guyton .05
312 Pat Harlow .05
313 Maurice Hurst .05
314 Leonard Russell .05
315 Chris Slade .10
316 Michael Thompson .05
317 Andre Tippett .05
318 Morten Andersen .05
319 Derek Brown .05
320 Vince Buck .05
321 Toi Cook .05
322 Quinn Early .05
323 Jim Everett .10
324 Michael Haynes .05
325 Tyrone Hughes .05
326 Rickey Jackson .05
327 Vaughan Johnson .05
328 Eric Martin .05
329 Wayne Martin .05
330 Sam Mills .05
331 William Roaf .05
332 Irv Smith .05
333 Keith Taylor .05
334 Renaldo Turnbull .05
335 Carlton Bailey .05
336 Michael Brooks .05
337 Jarrod Bunch .05
338 Chris Calloway .05
339 Mark Collins .05
340 Howard Cross .05
341 Stacey Dillard .05
342 John Elliot .05
343 Rodney Hampton .10
344 Greg Jackson .05
345 Mark Jackson .05
346 David Meggett .05
347 Corey Miller .05
348 Mike Sherrard .05
349 Phil Simms .05
350 Lewis Tillman .05
351 Brad Baxter .05
352 Kyle Clifton .05
353 Boomer Esiason .10
354 James Hasty .05
355 Bobby Houston .05
356 Johnny Johnson .05
357 Jeff Lageman .05
358 Mo Lewis .05
359 Ronnie Lott .05
360 Leonard Marshall .05
361 Johnny Mitchell .05
362 Rob Moore .05
363 Eric Thomas .05
364 Brian Washington .05
365 Marvin Washington .05
366 Eric Allen .05
367 Fred Barnett .05
368 Bubby Brister .05
369 Randall Cunningham .15
370 Byron Evans .05
371 William Fuller .05
372 Andy Harmon .05
373 Seth Joyner .05
374 William Perry .05
375 Leonard Renfro .05
376 Heath Sherman .05
377 Ben Smith .05
378 William Thomas .05
379 Herschel Walker .05
380 Calvin Williams .05
381 Chad Brown .10
382 Dermontti Dawson .05
383 Deon Figures .05
384 Barry Foster .10
385 Jeff Graham .05
386 Eric Green .05
387 Kevin Greene .05
388 Carlton Haselrig .05
389 Levon Kirkland .05
390 Carnell Lake .05
391 Greg Lloyd .05
392 Neil O'Donnell .10
393 Darren Perry .05
394 Dwight Stone .05
395 Leroy Thompson .05
396 Rod Woodson .10
397 Marion Butts .05
398 John Carney .05
399 Darren Carrington .05
400 Burt Grossman .05
401 Courtney Hall .05
402 Ronnie Harmon .05
403 Stan Humphries .20
404 Shawn Jefferson .05
405 Vance Johnson .05
406 Chris Mims .05

407	Leslie O'Neal	.05
408	Stanley Richard	.05
409	Junior Seau	.15
410	Harris Barton	.05
411	Dennis Brown	.05
412	Eric Davis	.05
413	Merton Hanks	.05
414	John Johnson	.05
415	Brent Jones	.05
416	Marc Logan	.05
417	Tim McDonald	.05
418	Gary Plummer	.05
419	Tom Rathman	.05
420	Jerry Rice	1.00
421	Bill Romanowski	.05
422	Jesse Sapolu	.05
423	Dana Stubblefield	.10
424	John Taylor	.05
425	Steve Wallace	.05
426	Ted Washington	.05
427	Ricky Watters	.10
428	Troy Wilson	.05
429	Steve Young	1.00
430	Howard Ballard	.05
431	Michael Bates	.05
432	Robert Blackmon	.05
433	Brian Blades	.05
434	Ferrell Edmunds	.05
435	Carlton Gray	.05
436	Patrick Hunter	.05
437	Cortez Kennedy	.10
438	Kelvin Martin	.05
439	Rick Mirer	.10
440	Nate Odomes	.05
441	Ray Roberts	.05
442	Eugene Robinson	.05
443	Rod Stephens	.05
444	Chris Warren	.10
445	John L. Williams	.05
446	Terry Wooden	.05
447	Marty Carter	.05
448	Reggie Cobb	.05
449	Lawrence Dawsey	.05
450	Santana Dotson	.05
451	Craig Erickson	.05
452	Thomas Everett	.05
453	Paul Gruber	.05
454	Courtney Hawkins	.05
455	Martin Mayhew	.05
456	Hardy Nickerson	.05
457	Ricky Reynolds	.05
458	Vince Workman	.05
459	Reggie Brooks	.10
460	Earnest Byner	.05
461	Andre Collins	.05
462	Brad Edwards	.05
463	Kurt Gouveia	.05
464	Darrell Green	.05
465	Ken Harvey	.05
466	Ethan Horton	.05
467	A.J. Johnson	.05
468	Tim Johnson	.05
469	Jim Lachey	.05
470	Chip Lohmiller	.05
471	Art Monk	.10
472	Sterling Palmer	.05
473	Mark Rypien	.05
474	Ricky Sanders	.05
475	Checklist	.05
476	Checklist	.05
477	Checklist	.05
478	Checklist	.05
479	Checklist	.05
480	Checklist	.05

1994 Fleer All-Pros

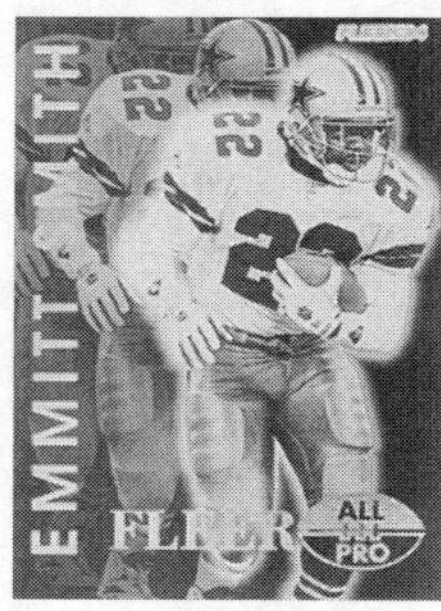

Fleer selected the top players from each conference for this 24-card insert set. Cards, which were randomly inserted in packs, feature borderless color action photos on the front, with ghosted images behind the main picture. The player's name is in gold foil running vertical on the left side of the card. The back is borderless and includes a career summary and a photo of the player with a glowing aura about him. Cards are numbered 1 of 24, etc.

		NM/M
Complete Set (24):		15.00
Common Player:		.25
Minor Stars:		.50
1	Troy Aikman	2.00
2	Eric Allen	.25
3	Jerome Bettis	1.00
4	Barry Foster	.50
5	Michael Irvin	.50
6	Cortez Kennedy	.50
7	Joe Montana	3.00
8	Hardy Nickerson	.25
9	Jerry Rice	3.00
10	Andre Rison	.50
11	Barry Sanders	3.00
12	Deion Sanders	1.00
13	Junior Seau	.50
14	Shannon Sharpe	.50
15	Sterling Sharpe	.50
16	Bruce Smith	.25
17	Emmitt Smith	3.00
18	Neil Smith	.25
19	Derrick Thomas	.50
20	Thurman Thomas	.50
21	Renaldo Turnbull	.25
22	Reggie White	.50
23	Rod Woodson	.50
24	Steve Young	2.00

1994 Fleer Award Winners

Five award-winning performers from the 1993 season are featured on these insert cards randomly available in 1994 packs. Each card front has a smaller cutout photo of the player against a larger black-and-white closeup photo. The player's name is in gold foil in the lower left corner; the set logo is to the right. The backs have a background which fades from black to white and features a color action photo. A color-screened box contains a summary of the player's career. The cards are numbered 1 of 5, etc. The Super Bowl MVP, AFC and NFC Offensive Rookies of the Year, the NFL Defensive Player of the Year, and the NFL Rookie of the Year are represented in the set.

		NM/M
Complete Set (5):		4.00
Common Player:		.25
1	Jerome Bettis	1.00
2	Rick Mirer	.50
3	Deion Sanders	1.00
4	Emmitt Smith	2.00
5	Dana Stubblefield	.25

1994 Fleer Jerome Bettis

This 12-card set is devoted to former Notre Dame and Los Angeles Rams running back Jerome Bettis, a Rookie of the Year. Each card has a color action photo on the front against an abstract background. A player head shot and Bettis' name are stamped in gold foil at the bottom. The horizontal back includes a color photo, career highlights and a card number. Three cards in the set could be obtained only through the mail for ten 1994 Fleer Football wrappers and $1.50.

		NM/M
Complete Set (12):		6.00
Common Bettis:		.50
Mail-In Bettis (13-15):		1.00

1994 Fleer League Leaders

The top quarterbacks, running backs and receivers from 1993 are featured in this 10-card insert set devoted to statistical leaders. The card front has a color photo of the player emerging from a blurred background. The "League Leader" logo and player's name are on the front, while the back has a small color photo and a summary of the player's 1993 accomplishments. Cards were randomly inserted in Fleer packs.

		NM/M
Complete Set (10):		10.00
Common Player:		.50
1	Marcus Allen	.50
2	Tim Brown	.50
3	John Elway	1.50
4	Tyrone Huges	.50
5	Jerry Rice	2.50
6	Sterling Sharpe	.50
7	Emmitt Smith	4.00
8	Neil Smith	.50
9	Thurman Thomas	.50
10	Steve Young	2.00

1994 Fleer Living Legends

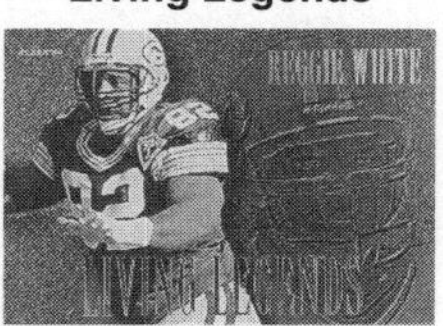

Six legendary active players are featured in this insert set; cards were randomly inserted in 1994 packs. The horizontally-arranged card front uses a metallic design for the photo, while the player's and set's name are stamped in foil. The card back is numbered 1 of 6, etc., and has a color photo and career highlights.

		NM/M
Complete Set (6):		50.00
Common Player:		5.00
1	Marcus Allen	5.00
2	John Elway	10.00
3	Joe Montana	15.00
4	Jerry Rice	15.00
5	Emmitt Smith	15.00
6	Reggie White	5.00

1994 Fleer Pro-Vision

This set continues Fleer's tradition of using artwork on the card fronts. The player is featured against a background with a landmark from his team's city. The backs, numbered 1 of 9, etc., have a career summary. Cards were standard size (2-1/2" x 3-1/2") and were random inserts in Fleer packs, but jumbo versions were also made for each card. One nine-card jumbo set was included in every hobby case. Jumbo cards are generally worth two to four times more than the standard-size cards.

		NM/M
Complete Set (9):		5.00
Common Player:		.25
Minor Stars:		.50
1	Rodney Hampton	.50
2	Ricky Watters	.50
3	Rick Mirer	.50
4	Brett Favre	3.00
5	Troy Aikman	1.25
6	Jerome Bettis	.50
7	Joe Montana	2.00
8	Cornelius Bennett	.25
9	Rod Woodson	.25

1994 Fleer Prospects

This insert set features 25 top collegiate prospects who have a chance to shine in the NFL. The card front shows the player in his collegiate uniform, superimposed against a background of a steel mill. The backs have a card number (1 of 25, etc.), a photo and a summary of the player's collegiate achievements.

		NM/M
Complete Set (25):		30.00
Common Player:		.50
Minor Stars:		1.00
1	Sam Adams	.50
2	Trev Alberts	.50
3	Derrick Alexander	2.00
4	Mario Bates	1.00
5	Jeff Buris	.50
6	Shante Carver	.50
7	Marshall Faulk	6.00
8	William Floyd	3.00
9	Rob Fredrickson	.50
10	Wayne Gandy	.50
11	Charlie Garner	1.00
12	Aaron Glenn	.50
13	Charles Johnson	2.00
14	Joe Johnson	.50
15	Tre Johnson	.50
16	Antonio Langham	1.00
17	Chuck Levy	1.00
18	Willie McGinest	1.00
19	David Palmer	1.00
20	Errict Rhett	4.00
21	Jason Sehorn	.50
22	Heath Shuler	1.00
23	Charlie Ward	1.00
24	DeWayne Washington	.50
25	Bryant Young	1.00

1994 Fleer Rookie Exchange

This 12-card Rookie Exchange set featured the same design as the 1994 Fleer set and was available by sending in a Rookie Exchange card found in packs.

		NM/M
Complete Set (12):		40.00
Common Player:		1.00
Minor Stars:		2.00
1	Derrick Alexander	3.50
2	Trent Dilfer	6.00
3	Marshall Faulk	25.00
4	Charlie Garner	7.00
5	Greg Hill	1.00
6	Charles Johnson	4.00
7	Antonio Langham	1.00
8	Willie McGinest	1.00
9	Heath Shuler	4.00
10	DeWayne Washington	1.00
11	Dan Wilkinson	2.00
12	Bryant Young	2.00
NNO	Rookie Exchange Exp.	1.00

1994 Fleer Rookie Sensations

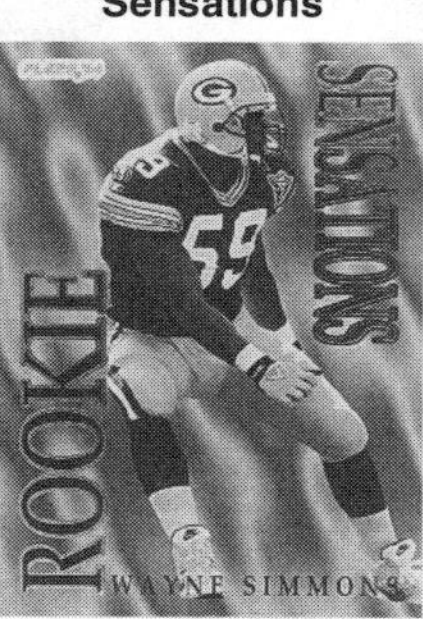

These cards were randomly inserted in 1994 21-card jumbo packs. Players who were rookies during the 1993 NFL season are featured. The card front shows a picture of the player against a wavy background design that is primarily in his team's dominant color. The back also features his team's colors, with a smaller photo and biography. The set name is stamped in foil on the card front; the back has the card number, 1 of 20, etc.

		NM/M
Complete Set (20):		75.00
Common Player:		2.00
1	Jerome Bettis	10.00
2	Drew Bledsoe	30.00
3	Reggie Brooks	5.00
4	Tom Carter	2.00
5	John Copeland	2.00
6	Jason Elam	4.00
7	Garrison Hearst	6.00
8	Tyrone Hughes	2.00
9	James Jett	3.00
10	Lincoln Kennedy	3.00
11	Terry Kirby	5.00
12	Glyn Milburn	2.00
13	Rick Mirer	2.00
14	Ron Moore	2.00
15	William Roaf	3.00
16	Wayne Simmons	2.00
17	Chris Slade	2.00
18	Darrin Smith	2.00
19	Dana Stubblefield	3.00
20	George Teague	2.00

1994 Fleer Scoring Machines

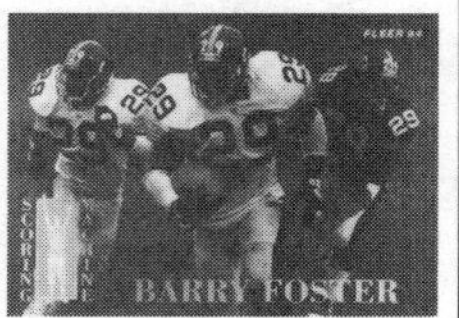

These cards, inserted only in 15-card 1994 Fleer packs, feature some of the leading point producers in the NFL who play running back, quarterback and receiver. Card fronts have three photos of the player, plus his name and set logo stamped in foil. The back has a color photo and career summary, plus a card number (1of 10, etc.).

		NM/M
Complete Set (20):		75.00
Common Player:		3.00
1	Marcus Allen	3.00
2	Natrone Means	3.00
3	Jerome Bettis	5.00
4	Tim Brown	5.00
5	Barry Foster	3.00
6	Rodney Hampton	3.00
7	Michael Irvin	3.00
8	Nick Lowery	3.00
9	Dan Marino	15.00
10	Joe Montana	15.00
11	Warren Moon	3.00
12	Andre Rison	3.00
13	Jerry Rice	15.00
14	Andre Rison	3.00
15	Barry Sanders	15.00
16	Shannon Sharpe	3.00
17	Sterling Sharpe	3.00
18	Emmitt Smith	15.00
19	Thurman Thomas	3.00
20	Ricky Watters	3.00

1994 Fleer GameDay

NFL GameDay from Fleer feature an all-new design in a super-sized format. The cards are 35 percent larger than a normal card, measuring 4-11/16" x 2-1/2". UV coating and team color-coding are used on the cards, which feature "up-close-and-personal" photos on the fronts. Card backs have another player photo, with statistics and a player profile. Four insert sets were also made: GameBreakers, 2nd Year Stars, Rookie Standouts, and Flashing Stars.

		NM/M
Complete Set (420):		20.00
Common Player:		.10
Wax Box:		20.00
1	Michael Bankston	.10
2	Steve Beuerlein	.10
3	Gary Clark	.10
4	Garrison Hearst	1.00
5	Eric Hill	.10
6	Randal Hill	.10
7	Seth Joyner	.10
8	Jim McMahon	.10
9	*Jamir Miller*	.40
10	Ron Moore	.45
11	Ricky Proehl	.10
12	Luis Sharpe	.10
13	Clyde Simmons	.10
14	Eric Swann	.10
15	Aeneas Williams	.10
16	Chris Doleman	.10
17	*Bert Emanuel*	1.50
18	Moe Gardner	.10
19	Jeff George	.10
20	Roger Harper	.10
21	Pierce Holt	.10
22	Lincoln Kennedy	.12
23	Erric Pegram	.10
24	Andre Rison	.20
25	Deion Sanders	1.00
26	Tony Smith	.10
27	Jessie Tuggle	.10
28	Don Beebe	.10
29	Cornelius Bennett	.10
30	Bill Brooks	.10
31	*Bucky Brooks*	.50
32	*Jeff Burris*	.75
33	Kenneth Davis	.10
34	Phil Hansen	.10
35	Kent Hull	.10
36	Henry Jones	.10
37	Jim Kelly	.30
38	Pete Metzelaars	.10
39	Marvcus Patton	.10
40	Andre Reed	.10
41	Bruce Smith	.10
42	Thomas Smith	.10
43	Darryl Talley	.10
44	Steve Tasker	.10
45	Thurman Thomas	.45
46	Jeff Wright	.10
47	Trace Armstrong	.10
48	Joe Cain	.10
49	Mark Carrier	.10
50	Curtis Conway	.25
51	Shaun Gayle	.10
52	Dante Jones	.10
53	Erik Kramer	.10
54	Terry Obee	.10
55	Vinson Smith	.10
56	Alonzo Spellman	.10
57	*John Thierry*	.35
58	Tom Waddle	.10
59	Donnell Woolford	.10
60	Tim Worley	.10
61	Chris Zorich	.10
62	Mike Brim	.10
63	John Copeland	.10
64	Derrick Fenner	.10
65	James Francis	.10
66	Harold Green	.10
67	David Klingler	.10
68	Ricardo McDonald	.10
69	Tony McGee	.10
70	Carl Pickens	.10
71	Jeff Query	.10
72	*Darnay Scott*	1.00
73	Steve Tovar	.10
74	*Dan Wilkinson*	.60
75	Alfred Williams	.10
76	Darryl Williams	.10
77	*Derrick Alexander*	.50
78	Rob Burnett	.10
79	Steve Everitt	.10
80	Michael Jackson	.10
81	Pepper Johnson	.10
82	Tony Jones	.10
83	*Antonio Langham*	.60
84	Eric Metcalf	.10
85	Stevon Moore	.10
86	Michael Dean Perry	.10
87	Anthony Pleasant	.10
88	Vinny Testaverde	.10
89	Eric Turner	.12
90	Tommy Vardell	.10
91	Troy Aikman	2.75
92	Larry Brown	.10
93	*Shante Carver*	.25
94	Charles Haley	.10
95	Alvin Harper	.10
96	Michael Irvin	.50
97	Daryl Johnston	.10
98	Leon Lett	.10
99	Russell Maryland	.10
100	Nate Newton	.10
101	Jay Novacek	.10
102	Darrin Smith	.10
103	Emmitt Smith	3.00
104	Kevin Smith	.10
105	Mark Stepnoski	.10
106	Tony Tolbert	.10
107	Eric Williams	.10
108	Kevin Williams	.25
109	Darren Woodson	.10
110	*Allen Aldridge*	.25
111	Steve Atwater	.10
112	Rod Bernstine	.10
113	Ray Crockett	.10
114	Mike Croel	.10
115	Robert Delpino	.10
116	Shane Dronett	.10
117	Jason Elam	.10
118	John Elway	1.00
119	Simon Fletcher	.10
120	Glyn Milburn	.30
121	Anthony Miller	.10
122	Mike Pritchard	.10
123	Shannon Sharpe	.10
124	Dan Williams	.10

125	Bennie Blades	.10
126	Lomas Brown	.10
127	Anthony Carter	.10
128	Mel Gray	.10
129	Jason Hanson	.10
130	Robert Massey	.10
131	Ryan McNeil	.10
132	Scott Mitchell	.15
133	Herman Moore	1.00
134	*Johnnie Morton*	.90
135	Brett Perriman	.10
136	Robert Porcher	.10
137	Barry Sanders	1.50
138	Tracy Scroggins	.10
139	Chris Spielman	.10
140	Pat Swilling	.10
141	Edgar Bennett	.10
142	Robert Brooks	.10
143	Terrell Buckley	.10
144	LeRoy Butler	.10
145	Reggie Cobb	.10
146	Curtis Duncan	.10
147	Brett Favre	2.00
148	Sean Jones	.10
149	George Koonce	.10
150	Ken Ruettgers	.10
151	Sterling Sharpe	.50
152	Wayne Simmons	.10
153	*Aaron Taylor*	.25
154	George Teague	.10
155	Reggie White	.10
156	Micheal Barrow	.10
157	Gary Brown	.10
158	Rich Camarillo	.10
159	Cody Carlson	.10
160	Ray Childress	.10
161	Cris Dishman	.10
162	*Henry Ford*	.30
163	Ernest Givins	.10
164	Steve Jackson	.10
165	Haywood Jeffires	.10
166	Bruce Matthews	.10
167	Bubba McDowell	.10
168	Marcus Robertson	.10
169	Eddie Robinson	.10
170	Webster Slaughter	.10
171	*Trev Alberts*	.50
172	Tony Bennett	.10
173	Ray Buchanan	.10
174	Kerry Cash	.10
175	Quentin Coryatt	.10
176	Eugene Daniel	.10
177	*Sean Dawkins*	1.00
178	Steve Emtman	.10
179	*Marshall Faulk*	6.00
180	John Hand	.10
181	Jim Harbaugh	.10
182	Jeff Herrod	.10
183	Roosevelt Potts	.20
184	Rohn Stark	.10
185	Marcus Allen	.10
186	*Donnell Bennett*	.45
187	J.J. Birden	.10
188	Dale Carter	.10
189	Mark Collins	.10
190	Willie Davis	.10
191	*Lake Dawson*	1.50
192	Tim Grunhard	.10
193	*Greg Hill*	.50
194	Joe Montana	2.50
195	Tracy Simion	.10
196	Neil Smith	.10
197	Derrick Thomas	.15
198	Tim Brown	.10
199	*James Folston*	.25
200	*Rob Fredrickson*	.25
201	Nolan Harrison	.10
202	Jeff Hostetler	.10
203	Raghib Ismail	.25
204	Jeff Jaeger	.10
205	James Jett	.20
206	Terry McDaniel	.10
207	Chester McGlockton	.10
208	Winston Moss	.10
209	Tom Rathman	.10
210	Anthony Smith	.10
211	Harvey Williams	.10
212	Steve Wisniewski	.10
213	Alexander Wright	.10
214	Willie Anderson	.10
215	Jerome Bettis	1.00
216	*Isaac Bruce*	4.00
217	Troy Drayton	.20
218	*Wayne Gandy*	.20
219	Sean Gilbert	.15
220	Nate Lewis	.10
221	Todd Lyght	.10
222	Chris Miller	.10
223	Anthony Newman	.10
224	Roman Phifer	.10
225	Henry Rolling	.10
226	Jackie Slater	.10
227	Fred Stokes	.10
228	Gene Atkins	.10
229	*Aubrey Beavers*	.30
230	*Tim Bowens*	.30
231	J.B. Brown	.10
232	Keith Byars	.10
233	Marco Coleman	.10
234	Bryan Cox	.10
235	Jeff Cross	.10
236	Irving Fryar	.10
237	Mark Ingram	.10
238	Keith Jackson	.10
239	Terry Kirby	.25
240	Dan Marino	1.25
241	Michael Stewart	.10
242	Troy Vincent	.10
243	Richmond Webb	.10
244	Terry Allen	.12
245	Cris Carter	.12
246	Jack Del Rio	.10
247	Vencie Glenn	.10
248	Chris Hinton	.10
249	Qadry Ismail	.25
250	Carlos Jenkins	.10
251	Randall McDaniel	.10
252	Warren Moon	.10
253	*David Palmer*	.50
254	John Randle	.10
255	Jake Reed	.10
256	Todd Scott	.10
257	*Todd Steussie*	.25
258	Henry Thomas	.10
259	*DeWayne Washington*	.25
260	Bruce Armstrong	.10
261	Drew Bledsoe	2.00
262	Vincent Brisby	.20
263	Vincent Brown	.10
264	Marion Butts	.10
265	Ben Coates	.20
266	Pat Harlow	.10
267	Maurice Hurst	.10
268	*Willie McGinest*	.75
269	Chris Slade	.10
270	Michael Timpson	.10
271	Morten Andersen	.10
272	*Mario Bates*	1.00
273	Derek Brown	.25
274	Quinn Early	.10
275	Jim Everett	.10
276	Michael Haynes	.10
277	Tyrone Hughes	.10
278	*Joe Johnson*	.25
279	Eric Martin	.10
280	Wayne Martin	.10
281	Sam Mills	.10
282	William Roaf	.15
283	Irv Smith	.10
284	Renaldo Turnbull	.10
285	Carlton Bailey	.10
286	Michael Brooks	.10
287	*Dave Brown*	.30
288	Jarrod Bunch	.10
289	Howard Cross	.10
290	John Elliott	.10
291	Keith Hamilton	.10
292	Rodney Hampton	.40
293	Mark Jackson	.10
294	*Thomas Lewis*	.80
295	David Meggett	.10
296	Corey Miller	.10
297	Mike Sherrard	.10
298	Brad Baxter	.10
299	Kyle Clifton	.10
300	Boomer Esiason	.10
301	*Aaron Glenn*	.25
302	James Hasty	.10
303	Johnny Johnson	.10
304	Jeff Lageman	.10
305	Mo Lewis	.10
306	Ronnie Lott	.10
307	Johnny Mitchell	.10
308	Art Monk	.10
309	Rob Moore	.10
310	Brian Washington	.10
311	Marvin Washington	.10
312	*Ryan Yarborough*	.45
313	Eric Allen	.10
314	Victor Bailey	.10
315	Fred Barnett	.10
316	Mark Bavaro	.10
317	Randall Cunningham	.20
318	Byron Evans	.10
319	William Fuller	.10
320	*Charlie Garner*	1.50
321	Andy Harmon	.10
322	Vaughn Hebron	.10
323	Mark McMillan	.10
324	Bill Romanowski	.10
325	William Thomas	.10
326	Greg Townsend	.10
327	Herschel Walker	.10
328	*Bernard Williams*	.25
329	Calvin Williams	.10
330	Dermontti Dawson	.10
331	Deon Figures	.10
332	Barry Foster	.25
333	Eric Green	.10
334	Kevin Greene	.10
335	Carlton Haselrig	.10
336	*Charles Johnson*	1.00
337	Levon Kirkland	.10
338	Carnell Lake	.10
339	Greg Lloyd	.10
340	Neil O'Donnell	.10
341	Darren Perry	.10
342	Dwight Stone	.10
343	John L. Williams	.10
344	Rod Woodson	.10
345	John Carney	.10
346	Darren Carrington	.10
347	*Isaac Davis*	.25
348	Courtney Hall	.10
349	Ronnie Harmon	.10
350	Dwayne Harper	.10
351	Stan Humphries	.10
352	Shawn Jefferson	.10
353	Vance Johnson	.10
354	Natrone Means	.75
355	Chris Mims	.10
356	Leslie O'Neal	.10
357	Stanley Richard	.10
358	Junior Seau	.12
359	Harris Barton	.10
360	Eric Davis	.10
361	Richard Dent	.10
362	*William Floyd*	1.00
363	Merton Hanks	.10
364	Brent Jones	.10
365	Marc Logan	.10
366	Tim McDonald	.10
367	Ken Norton	.10
368	Jerry Rice	1.00
369	Jesse Sapolu	.10
370	Dana Stubblefield	.15
371	John Taylor	.10
372	Ricky Watters	.10
373	*Bryant Young*	.50
374	Steve Young	1.50
375	*Sam Adams*	.35
376	Michael Bates	.10
377	Robert Blackmon	.10
378	Brian Blades	.10
379	Ferrell Edmunds	.10
380	John Kasay	.10
381	Cortez Kennedy	.10
382	Kelvin Martin	.10
383	Rick Mirer	.75
384	Rufus Porter	.10
385	Eugene Robinson	.10
386	Rod Stephens	.10
387	Chris Warren	.10
388	Marty Carter	.10
389	Horace Copeland	.10
390	Eric Curry	.10
391	Lawrence Dawsey	.10
392	*Trent Dilfer*	1.00
393	Santana Dotson	.10
394	Craig Erickson	.10
395	Thomas Everett	.10
396	Paul Gruber	.10
397	Jackie Harris	.10
398	Courtney Hawkins	.10
399	Martin Mayhew	.10
400	Hardy Nickerson	.10
401	*Errict Rhett*	2.00
402	Vince Workman	.10
403	Reggie Brooks	.75
404	Tom Carter	.10
405	Andre Collins	.10
406	Henry Ellard	.10
407	Kurt Gouveia	.10
408	Darrell Green	.10
409	Ken Harvey	.10
410	Ethan Horton	.15
411	Desmond Howard	.10
412	Jim Lachey	.10
413	Sterling Palmer	.10
414	*Heath Shuler*	1.00
415	Tyronne Stowe	.10
416	Tony Woods	.10
417	Checklist	.10
418	Checklist	.10
419	Checklist	.10
420	Checklist	.10

1994 Fleer GameDay Flashing Stars

These cards, the scarcest of all inserts in the 1994 Fleer GameDay set, were randomly included in 1994 packs. The set features four of the NFL's outstanding younger players on 100 percent etched foil. Card backs, numbered 1 of 4, etc., include information about the player and a color photo of the player. Each card measures 4-11/16" x 2-1/2."

		NM/M
Complete Set (4):		60.00
Common Player:		5.00
1	Jerome Bettis	5.00
2	Rick Mirer	5.00
3	Jerry Rice	10.00
4	Emmitt Smith	15.00

1994 Fleer GameDay Game Breakers

Top running backs, quarterbacks and receivers who can break the game wide open are featured in this 1994 GameDay insert set. The cards, which measure 4-11/16" x 2-1/2" inches, were random inserts in GameDay packs. The card front has a large sepia-toned photo, along with a smaller, color photo of the same picture. The player's name and GameDay logo are stamped in gold foil; "Gamebreaker" is written across the card front in different type sizes and styles. The card back has a color photo against a sepia background, with a card number, too (1 of 16, etc.). A summary of the player's career is also given.

		NM/M
Complete Set (16):		15.00
Common Player:		.50
1	Troy Aikman	3.00
2	Marcus Allen	.50
3	Tim Brown	.50
4	John Elway	1.50
5	Michael Irvin	.75
6	Dan Marino	4.00
7	Joe Montana	4.00
8	Jerry Rice	4.00
9	Andre Rison	.50
10	Barry Sanders	4.00
11	Deion Sanders	1.00
12	Sterling Sharpe	.75
13	Emmitt Smith	4.00
14	Thurman Thomas	.75
15	Rod Woodson	.50
16	Steve Young	2.00

1994 Fleer GameDay Rookie Standouts

Sixteen "can't-miss" rookies are featured on these cards, which were randomly inserted in 1994 Fleer GameDay packs. The card front shows a color action photo of the player on a 3-D embossed design. Unlike the other inserts in this set, the "Rookie Standouts" insert set does not use any foil stamping. The card back has a player mug shot and provides a scouting report on the player as he enters his first year in the NFL. Cards are numbered 1 of 16, etc., and measure 4-11/16" x 2-1/2."

		NM/M
Complete Set (16):		15.00
Common Player:		.40
1	Sam Adams	.40
2	Trev Alberts	.40
3	Lake Dawson	.40
4	Trent Dilfer	1.00
5	Marshall Faulk	4.00
6	Aaron Glenn	1.00
7	Charles Johnson	1.00
8	Willie McGinest	1.25
9	Jamir Miller	.40
10	Johnnie Morton	2.00
11	David Palmer	1.00
12	Errict Rhett	3.00
13	Heath Shuler	1.00
14	John Thierry	.40
15	Dan Wilkinson	.40
16	Bryant Young	1.00

1994 Fleer GameDay Second-Year Stars

These cards, randomly inserted in 1994 Fleer GameDay packs, feature 16 of the top rookies in 1993 who are beginning their second year in the NFL in 1994. The "GameDay," the set name and player name are stamped in gold foil on the card front. A small action shot appears against a larger, full-bleed profile shot, which has a swirl effect to it. The card back also has a swirl effect, which is used to present information about the player's first NFL season. Cards, numbered 1 of 16, etc., have an action photo on the back. Cards are 35 percent larger than a standard size card; they measure 4-11/16" x 2-1/2".

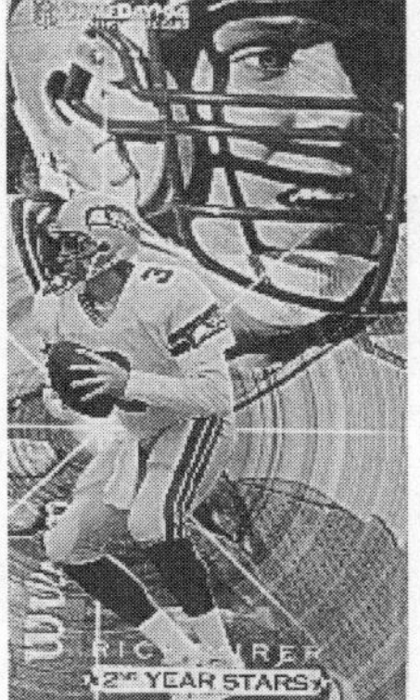

		NM/M
Complete Set (16):		15.00
Common Player:		.50
1	Jerome Bettis	2.00
2	Drew Bledsoe	5.00
3	Reggie Brooks	1.00
4	Tom Carter	.60
5	Eric Curry	.60
6	Steve Everitt	.60
7	Tyrone Hughes	.50
8	James Jett	1.50
9	Terry Kirby	1.00
10	Natrone Means	1.00
11	Rick Mirer	1.00
12	Ron Moore	1.00
13	William Roaf	.50
14	Chris Slade	.50
15	Darrin Smith	.60
16	Dana Stubblefield	1.00

1995 Fleer

Fleer's 1995 set includes 400 cards, using the "Different by Design" concept it has used for baseball issues; different styles are used for different divisions. Several insert sets were randomly included in packs: Pro-Visions (1 in 6 packs); Rookie Sensations (1 in 3 17-card packs); Aerial Attack (1 in 37); Gridiron Leaders (1 in 4); TD Sensations (1 in 3 11- card packs); NFL Prospects (1 in 6); and Flair Preview (1 in each pack). Fleer products were sold in 11-card and 17-card packs. The cards are numbered alphabetically by team names, with the players numbered alphabetically within the team subsets.

		NM/M
Complete Set (400):		20.00
Common Player:		.75
Minor Stars:		.10
Wax Box:		15.00
1	Michael Bankston	.05
2	Larry Centers	.05
3	Gary Clark	.05
4	Eric Hill	.05
5	Seth Joyner	.05
6	Dave Krieg	.05
7	Lorenzo Lynch	.05
8	Jamir Miller	.05
9	Ron Moore	.05
10	Ricky Proehl	.05
11	Clyde Simmons	.05
12	Eric Swann	.05
13	Aeneas Williams	.05
14	J.J. Birden	.05
15	Chris Doleman	.05
16	Bert Emanuel	.20
17	Jumpy Geathers	.05
18	Jeff George	.10
19	Roger Harper	.05
20	Craig Heyward	.05
21	Pierce Holt	.05
22	D.J. Johnson	.05
23	Terance Mathis	.05
24	Clay Mathews	.05
25	Andre Rison	.10
26	Chuck Smith	.05
27	Jessie Tuggle	.05
28	Cornelius Bennett	.05
29	Bucky Brooks	.05
30	Jeff Burris	.05
31	Russell Copeland	.05
32	Matt Darby	.05
33	Phil Hansen	.05
34	Henry Jones	.05
35	Jim Kelly	.10
36	Mark Maddox	.10
37	Bryce Paup	.05
38	Andre Reed	.10
39	Bruce Smith	.05
40	Darryl Talley	.05
41	Dewell Brewer	.10
42	Mike Fox	.05
43	Eric Guliford	.05
44	Lamar Lathon	.05
45	Pete Metzelaars	.05
46	Sam Mills	.05
47	Frank Reich	.05
48	Rod Smith	.05
49	Jack Trudeau	.05
50	Trace Armstrong	.05
51	Joe Cain	.05
52	Mark Carrier	.05
53	Curtis Conway	.05
54	Shaun Gayle	.05
55	Jeff Graham	.05
56	Raymont Harris	.15
57	Erik Kramer	.05
58	Lewis Tillman	.05
59	Tom Waddle	.05
60	Steve Walsh	.05
61	Donnell Woolford	.05
62	Chris Zorich	.05
63	*Jeff Blake*	.50
64	Mike Brim	.05
65	Steve Broussard	.05
66	James Francis	.05
67	Ricardo McDonald	.05
68	Tony McGee	.05
69	Carl Pickens	.05
70	Darnay Scott	.40
71	Steve Tovar	.05
72	Dan Wilkinson	.05
73	Alfred Williams	.05
74	Darryl Williams	.05
75	Derrick Alexander	.20
76	Randy Baldwin	.05
77	Carl Banks	.05
78	Rob Burnett	.05
79	Steve Everitt	.05
80	Leroy Hoard	.05
81	Michael Jackson	.05
82	Pepper Johnson	.05
83	Tony Jones	.05
84	Antonio Langham	.05
85	Eric Metcalf	.05
86	Stevon Moore	.05
87	Anthony Pleasant	.05
88	Vinny Testaverde	.05
89	Eric Turner	.05
90	Troy Aikman	.60
91	Charles Haley	.05
92	Michael Irvin	.20
93	Daryl Johnston	.05
94	Robert Jones	.05
95	Leon Lett	.05
96	Russell Maryland	.05
97	Nate Newton	.05
98	Jay Novacek	.05
99	Darrin Smith	.05
100	Emmitt Smith	1.50
101	Kevin Smith	.05
102	Eric Williams	.05
103	Kevin Williams	.05
104	Darren Woodson	.05
105	Elijah Alexander	.05
106	Steve Atwater	.05
107	Ray Crockett	.05
108	Shane Dronett	.05
109	Jason Elam	.05
110	John Elway	.25
111	Simon Fletcher	.05
112	Glyn Milburn	.05
113	Anthony Miller	.05
114	Michael Dean Perry	.05
115	Mike Pritchard	.05
116	Derek Russell	.05
117	Leonard Russell	.05
118	Shannon Sharpe	.05
119	Gary Zimmerman	.05
120	Bennie Blades	.05
121	Lomas Brown	.05
122	Willie Clay	.05
123	Mike Johnson	.05
124	Robert Massey	.05
125	Scott Mitchell	.05
126	Herman Moore	.05
127	Brett Perriman	.05
128	Robert Porcher	.05
129	Barry Sanders	1.25
130	Chris Spielman	.05
131	Henry Thomas	.05
132	Edgar Bennett	.05
133	Robert Brooks	.05
134	LeRoy Butler	.05
135	Brett Favre	1.50
136	Sean Jones	.05
137	John Jurkovic	.05
138	George Koonce	.05
139	Wayne Simmons	.05
140	George Teague	.05
141	Reggie White	.10
142	Micheal Barrow	.05
143	Gary Brown	.05
144	Cody Carlson	.05
145	Ray Childress	.05
146	Cris Dishman	.05
147	Ernest Givins	.05
148	Mel Gray	.05
149	Darryl Lewis	.05
150	Bruce Matthews	.05
151	Marcus Robertson	.05
152	Webster Slaughter	.05
153	Al Smith	.05
154	Mark Stepnoski	.05

155 Trev Alberts .05
156 Willie Anderson .05
157 Jason Belser .05
158 Tony Bennett .05
159 Ray Buchanan .05
160 Quentin Coryatt .05
161 Sean Dawkins .15
162 Steve Emtman .05
163 Marshall Faulk 1.00
164 Steve Grant .05
165 Jim Harbaugh .05
166 Jeff Herrod .05
167 Tony Siragusa .05
168 Steve Beuerlein .05
169 Darren Carrington .05
170 Reggie Cobb .05
171 Kelvin Martin .05
172 Kelvin Pritchett .05
173 Joel Smeenge .05
174 James Williams .05
175 Marcus Allen .10
176 Kimble Anders .05
177 Dale Carter .05
178 Mark Collins .05
179 Willie Davis .05
180 Lake Dawson .20
181 Greg Hill .20
182 Darren Mickell .05
183 Joe Montana 1.00
184 Tracy Simien .05
185 Neil Smith .05
186 William White .05
187 Greg Biekert .05
188 Tim Brown .10
189 Rob Fredrickson .05
190 *Andrew Glover* .10
191 Nolan Harrison .05
192 Jeff Hostetler .05
193 Raghib Ismail .05
194 Terry McDaniel .05
195 Chester McGlockton .05
196 Winston Moss .05
197 Anthony Smith .05
198 Harvey Williams .05
199 Steve Wisniewski .05
200 Johnny Bailey .05
201 Jerome Bettis .25
202 Isaac Bruce .50
203 Shane Conlan .05
204 Troy Drayton .05
205 Sean Gilbert .05
206 Jessie Hester .05
207 Jimmie Jones .05
208 Todd Lyght .05
209 Chris Miller .05
210 Roman Phifer .05
211 Marquez Pope .05
212 Robert Young .05
213 Gene Atkins .05
214 Aubrey Beavers .05
215 Tim Bowens .05
216 Bryan Cox .05
217 Jeff Cross .05
218 Irving Fryar .05
219 Eric Green .05
220 Mark Ingram .05
221 Terry Kirby .05
222 Dan Marino 1.50
223 O.J. McDuffie .05
224 Bernie Parmalee .25
225 Keith Sims .05
226 Irving Spikes .10
227 Michael Stewart .05
228 Troy Vincent .05
229 Richmond Webb .05
230 Terry Allen .05
231 Cris Carter .10
232 Jack Del Rio .05
233 Vencie Glenn .05
234 Qadry Ismail .05
235 Carlos Jenkins .05
236 Ed McDaniel .05
237 Randall McDaniel .05
238 Warren Moon .10
239 Anthony Parker .05
240 John Randle .05
241 Jake Reed .05
242 Fuad Reveiz .05
243 Broderick Thomas .05
244 DeWayne Washington .05
245 Bruce Armstrong .05
246 Drew Bledsoe 1.00
247 Vincent Brisby .05
248 Vincent Brown .05
249 Marion Butts .05
250 Ben Coates .05
251 Tim Goad .05
252 Myron Guyton .05
253 Maurice Hurst .05
254 Mike Jones .05
255 Willie McGinest .05
256 David Meggett .05
257 Ricky Reynolds .05
258 Chris Slade .05
259 Michael Timpson .05
260 Mario Bates .20
261 Derek Brown .05
262 Darion Connor .05
263 Quinn Early .05
264 Jim Everett .05
265 Michael Haynes .05
266 Tyrone Hughes .05
267 Joe Johnson .05
268 Wayne Martin .05
269 William Roaf .05
270 Irv Smith .05
271 Jimmy Spencer .05
272 Winfred Tubbs .05
273 Renaldo Turnbull .05
274 Michael Brooks .05
275 Dave Brown .05
276 Chris Calloway .05
277 Jesse Campbell .05
278 Howard Cross .05
279 John Elliott .05
280 Keith Hamilton .05
281 Rodney Hampton .05
282 Thomas Lewis .05
283 Thomas Randolph .05
284 Mike Sherrard .05
285 Michael Strahan .05
286 Brad Baxter .05
287 Tony Casillas .05
288 Kyle Clifton .05
289 Boomer Esiason .05
290 Aaron Glenn .05
291 Bobby Houston .05
292 Johnny Johnson .05
293 Jeff Lageman .05
294 Mo Lewis .05
295 Johnny Mitchell .05
296 Rob Moore .05
297 Marcus Turner .05
298 Marvin Washington .05
299 Eric Allen .05
300 Fred Barnett .05
301 Randall Cunningham .10
302 Byron Evans .05
303 William Fuller .05
304 Charlie Garner .10
305 Andy Harmon .05
306 Greg Jackson .05
307 Bill Romanowski .05
308 William Thomas .05
309 Herschel Walker .10
310 Calvin Williams .05
311 Michael Zordich .05
312 Chad Brown .05
313 Dermontti Dawson .05
314 Barry Foster .10
315 Kevin Greene .05
316 Charles Johnson .20
317 Levon Kirkland .05
318 Carnell Lake .05
319 Greg Lloyd .05
320 Bam Morris .40
321 Neil O'Donnell .10
322 Darren Perry .05
323 Ray Seals .05
324 John L. Williams .05
325 Rod Woodson .05
326 John Carney .05
327 Andre Coleman .05
328 Courtney Hall .05
329 Ronnie Harmon .05
330 Dwayne Harper .05
331 Stan Humphries .10
332 Shawn Jefferson .05
333 Tony Martin .05
334 Natrone Means .40
335 Chris Mims .05
336 Leslie O'Neal .05
337 Alfred Pupunu .15
338 Junior Seau .10
339 Mark Seay .05
340 Eric Davis .05
341 William Floyd .25
342 Merton Hanks .05
343 Rickey Jackson .05
344 Brent Jones .05
345 Tim McDonald .05
346 Ken Norton .05
347 Gary Plummer .05
348 Jerry Rice .50
349 Deion Sanders .50
350 Jesse Sapolu .05
351 Dana Stubblefield .05
352 John Taylor .05
353 Steve Wallace .05
354 Ricky Watters .10
355 Lee Woodall .05
356 Bryant Young .05
357 Steve Young .40
358 Sam Adams .05
359 Howard Ballard .05
360 Robert Blackmon .05
361 Brian Blades .05
362 Carlton Gray .05
363 Cortez Kennedy .05
364 Rick Mirer .35
365 Eugene Robinson .05
366 Chris Warren .05
367 Terry Wooden .05
368 Brad Culpepper .05
369 Lawrence Dawsey .05
370 Trent Dilfer .40
371 Santana Dotson .05
372 Craig Erickson .05
373 Thomas Everett .05
374 Paul Gruber .05
375 Alvin Harper .05
376 Jackie Harris .05
377 Courtney Hawkins .05
378 Martin Mayhew .05
379 Hardy Nickerson .05
380 Errict Rhett .50
381 Charles Wilson .05
382 Reggie Brooks .05
383 Tom Carter .05
384 Andre Collins .05
385 Henry Ellard .05
386 Ricky Ervins .05
387 Darrell Green .05
388 Ken Harvey .05
389 Brian Mitchell .05
390 Stanley Richard .05
391 Heath Shuler .50
392 Rod Stephens .05
393 Tyronne Stowe .05
394 Tydus Winans .05
395 Tony Woods .05
396 Checklist .05
397 Checklist .05
398 Checklist .05
399 Checklist .05
400 Checklist .05

1995 Fleer Aerial Attack

This 6-card insert set features two top NFL quarterbacks and four top wide receivers. Cards, which were included one per every 37 packs, use 100 percent foil-etched designs, with an "Aerial Attack" football logo on the front. An action photo is also featured, against a background of footballs. The card back is numbered 1 of 6, etc.

NM/M
Complete Set (6): 20.00
Common Player: 3.00
1 Tim Brown 3.00
2 Dan Marino 8.00
3 Joe Montana 8.00
4 Jerry Rice 6.00
5 Andre Rison 3.00
6 Sterling Sharpe 3.00

1995 Fleer Flair Preview

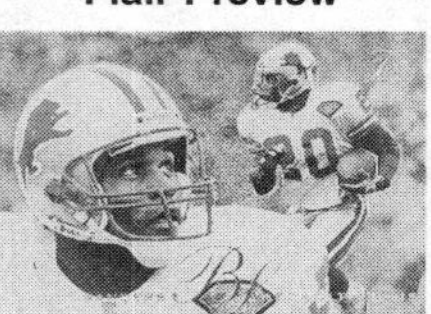

Every pack of 1995 Fleer football included one of these 1995 Fleer Flair preview cards, showcasing the company's 100 percent etched-foil Flair product. The card front uses a horizontal format, with a player mug shot and an action shot. The player's initials are stamped in silver in a scripted typeface. The card back, numbered 1 of 30, etc., has a brief summary of the player's 1994 season. It also indicates the card backs of the regular Flair set will feature statistics and a player photo on them. Cards are glossy poly-laminated and are double in thickness.

NM/M
Complete Set (30): 20.00
Common Player: .25
Minor Stars: .50
1 Aeneas Williams .25
2 Jeff George .50
3 Andre Reed .25
4 Kerry Collins .50
5 Mark Carrier .25
6 Jeff Blake .50
7 Leroy Hoard .25
8 Emmitt Smith 3.00
9 Shannon Sharpe .50
10 Barry Sanders 2.50
11 Reggie White .50
12 Bruce Matthews .25
13 Marshall Faulk 2.00
14 Tony Boselli .75
15 Joe Montana 2.00
16 Tim Brown .25
17 Jerome Bettis .75
18 Dan Marino 3.00
19 Cris Carter .50
20 Drew Bledsoe 2.00
21 William Roaf .25
22 Rodney Hampton .25
23 Rob Moore .25
24 Fred Barnett .25
25 Rod Woodson .25
26 Natrone Means 1.50
27 Jerry Rice 1.75
28 Chris Warren .50
29 Errict Rhett .75
30 Henry Ellard .25

1995 Fleer Gridiron Leaders

Ten of the NFL's top statistical leaders from 1994 are shown on these 1995 Fleer insert cards. Cards were randomly included one per every four packs. The card front has the player photo against a grid-like background, with "Gridiron Leader" running along the left side. The back has another color photo and a summary of the player's 1994 accomplishments, plus the categories he led the league in. Cards are numbered 1 of 10, etc.

NM/M
Complete Set (10): 8.00
Common Player: .25
Minor Stars: .50
1 Cris Carter .50
2 Ben Coates .25
3 Marshall Faulk .50
4 Jerry Rice 1.00
5 Barry Sanders 1.50
6 Deion Sanders .75
7 Emmitt Smith 2.00
8 Eric Turner .25
9 Chris Warren .25
10 Steve Young 1.00

1995 Fleer Prospects

Twenty of the top 1995 NFL draft picks with promising futures are featured on these 1995 insert cards. Cards, numbered on the back 1 of 20, etc., feature a color action photo of the player on the front; he is wearing his collegiate uniform. The background is a metallic-like burst. The player's name and the "NFL Prospects" logo are in gold. The card back has another photo of the player, plus a summary of the player's collegiate achievements.

NM/M
Complete Set (20): 30.00
Common Player: .50
Minor Stars: 1.00
1 Tony Boselli .75
2 Kyle Brady 1.00
3 Ruben Brown .50
4 Kevin Carter 1.00
5 Ki-Jana Carter 1.00
6 Kerry Collins 2.00
7 Luther Elliss .50
8 Jimmy Hitchcock .50
9 Jack Jackson .50
10 Ellis Johnson .50
11 Rob Johnson 2.00
12 Steve McNair 5.00
13 Rashaan Salaam 1.00
14 Warren Sapp 1.00
15 J.J. Stokes 2.00
16 Bobby Taylor .50
17 John Walsh .50
18 Michael Westbrook 1.50
19 Tyrone Wheatley 1.00
20 Sherman Williams 1.00

1995 Fleer Pro-Visions

These six 1995 Fleer insert cards feature the usual artwork design which has been used for previous Pro Visions sets. Cards were randomly included one per every six packs. The fronts of the six cards combine to form an interlocking design. Card backs, numbered 1 of 6, etc., have a summary of the player's career, but no photo or artwork.

NM/M
Complete Set (6): 5.00
Common Player: .25
1 Natrone Means .50
2 Sterling Sharpe .25
3 Ken Norton .25
4 Drew Bledsoe 1.00
5 Marshall Faulk 1.00
6 Tim Brown .50

1995 Fleer Rookie Sensations

Twenty top rookies from 1994 are featured on these insert cards, included one per every three 17-card packs. The card front has a color action photo, with the player's name and "Rookie Sensations" running down the side of the card. Card backs are numbered 1 of 20, etc.

NM/M
Complete Set (20): 25.00
Common Player: 1.00
Minor Stars: 2.00
1 Derrick Alexander 1.00
2 Mario Bates 1.00
3 Tim Bowens 1.00
4 Lake Dawson 1.00
5 Bert Emanuel 2.00
6 Marshall Faulk 10.00
7 William Floyd 2.00
8 Rob Frederickson 1.00
9 Greg Hill 1.00
10 Charles Johnson 2.00
11 Antonio Langham 2.00
12 Willie McGinest 2.00
13 Bam Morris 2.00
14 Errict Rhett 2.00
15 Darnay Scott 2.00
16 Heath Shuler 2.00
17 DeWayne Washington 1.00
18 Dan Wilkinson 1.00
19 Lee Woodall 1.00
20 Bryant Young 2.00

1995 Fleer TD Sensations

Ten top NFL scorers are featured on these 1995 Fleer insert cards, issued one per every three 11-card packs. Card fronts have a color action photo, with the "TD Sensation" logo stamped in green and gold. The player's name is also in gold. The card back has another color photo, plus a brief player profile running down one side of the card. Cards are numbered 1 of 10, etc..

NM/M
Complete Set (10): 8.00
Common Player: .25
Minor Stars: .50
1 Marshall Faulk 1.00
2 Dan Marino 2.00
3 Natrone Means .50
4 Herman Moore .25
5 Jerry Rice 1.00
6 Sterling Sharpe .25
7 Emmitt Smith 2.00
8 Chris Warren .25
9 Ricky Watters .50
10 Steve Young 1.00

1995 Fleer Bettis/ Mirer Sheet

These sheets feature 10 cards of Jerome Bettis on one side and 10 cards of Rick Mirer on the other and were distributed at the Super Bowl show in Miami. The sheets could be purchased for five wrappers and $1. There were also 400 sheets signed by one of the players that were sold for $25.

NM/M
Complete Set (1): 2.50
1 Jerome Bettis, Rick Mirer 2.50

1995 Fleer Shell

This 10-card set was produced by Fleer and issued by Shell in its "Drive for the Super Bowl XXX" sweepstakes. The cards are standard sized and were originally attached to a rub-off tab card of equal size and divided by a perforated line.

NM/M
Complete Set (10): 10.00
Common Player: 1.00
1 Super Bowl XXIII (Joe Montana's drive) 1.50
2 1967 NFL Championship (Bart Starr's TD) 1.00
3 1986 AFC Championship (The Drive, Mark Jackson) 1.00
4 Super Bowl XIII (Steeler's drive, Terry Bradshaw) 1.00
5 1975 NFC Divisional Playoffs (Cowboy's drive, Doug Dennison featured) 1.00
6 1968 AFL Championship (Jet's drive) 1.00
7 1981 NFC Championship (49ers team shot) 1.00
8 1983 NFC Championship (Redskin's drive, John Riggins' TD) 1.00
9 1969 AFL Divisional Playoffs (Len Dawson in huddle) 1.00
10 Super Bowl V (Colts' field goal, Bob Lilly and Mel Renfro pictured) 1.00

1996 Fleer

Fleer's 1996 football card set contains 200 cards, many of which are from subsets in the main set. The best players from the 1996 draft are featured on 40 cards, while the top 20 from 1995 have their own subset. Key match-ups for 1996's biggest games, as selected by Pro Football Weekly, are spotlighted on 17 other subset cards. Pro Football Weekly writers have also written the card backs. Each basic card design includes a "Greatest Game" note on the front, plus career statistics, basic statistics and the player's "Triangle Numbers" - his height, weight and time in the 40-yard dash. Six insert sets were created - Rookie Sensations, Breakthrough, RAC Pack, Statistically Speaking, Rookie Write Up and Signature Series. The Signature Series cards are autographed cards by Eddie George, Leeland McElroy and Tim Biakabutuka. Fleer also offered Rookie Sensation Hot Packs, which contained specially-marked versions of all 11 cards from that insert set. These packs were seeded one per every 960 packs.

NM/M
Complete Set (200): 20.00
Common Player: .05
Minor Stars: .10
Pack (11): 1.50
Wax Box (24): 34.00
1 Garrison Hearst .10
2 Rob Moore .05
3 Frank Sanders .05
4 Eric Swann .05
5 Aeneas Williams .05
6 Jeff George .10
7 Craig Heyward .05
8 Terance Mathis .05
9 Eric Metcalf .05
10 Michael Jackson .05
11 Andre Rison .05
12 Vinny Testaverde .05
13 Eric Turner .05
14 Darick Holmes .05
15 Jim Kelly .10
16 Bryce Paup .05
17 Bruce Smith .05
18 Thurman Thomas .10
19 Kerry Collins .30
20 Lamar Lathon .05
21 Derrick Moore .05
22 Tyrone Poole .05
23 Curtis Conway .05
24 Bryan Cox .05
25 Erik Kramer .05
26 Rashaan Salaam .60
27 Jeff Blake .60
28 Ki-Jana Carter .25
29 Carl Pickens .10
30 Darnay Scott .05
31 Troy Aikman 1.00
32 Charles Haley .05
33 Michael Irvin .10
34 Daryl Johnston .05
35 Jay Novacek .05
36 Deion Sanders .60
37 Emmitt Smith 2.00
38 Steve Atwater .05
39 Terrell Davis .60
40 John Elway .50
41 Anthony Miller .05
42 Shannon Sharpe .05
43 Scott Mitchell .05
44 Herman Moore .30
45 Johnnie Morton .05
46 Brett Perriman .05
47 Barry Sanders 1.00
48 Edgar Bennett .05
49 Robert Brooks .05
50 Mark Chmura .30
51 Brett Favre 2.00
52 Reggie White .10
53 Mel Gray .05
54 Steve McNair .60
55 Chris Sanders .30
56 Rodney Thomas .05
57 Quentin Coryatt .05
58 Sean Dawkins .05
59 Ken Dilger .05
60 Marshall Faulk .75
61 Jim Harbaugh .05
62 Tony Boselli .05
63 Mark Brunell .50
64 Natrone Means .10
65 James Stewart .05
66 Marcus Allen .05
67 Steve Bono .05
68 Neil Smith .05
69 Derrick Thomas .05
70 Tamarick Vanover .60
71 Fred Barnett .05
72 Eric Green .05
73 Dan Marino 2.00
74 O.J. McDuffie .05
75 Bernie Parmalee .05
76 Cris Carter .05
77 Qadry Ismail .05
78 Warren Moon .05
79 Jake Reed .05
80 Robert Smith .05
81 Drew Bledsoe .75
82 Vincent Brisby .05
83 Ben Coates .05
84 Curtis Martin 1.50
85 David Meggett .05
86 Mario Bates .05
87 Jim Everett .05
88 Michael Haynes .05
89 Renaldo Turnbull .05
90 Dave Brown .05
91 Rodney Hampton .05
92 Thomas Lewis .05
93 Tyrone Wheatley .05
94 Kyle Brady .05
95 Hugh Douglas .05
96 Aaron Glenn .05
97 Jeff Graham .05
98 Adrian Murrell .05
99 Neil O'Donnell .05
100 Tim Brown .05
101 Jeff Hostetler .05
102 Napoleon Kaufman .30
103 Chester McGlockton .05
104 Harvey Williams .05
105 William Fuller .05
106 Charlie Garner .05
107 Ricky Watters .05
108 Calvin Williams .05
109 Jerome Bettis .05
110 Greg Lloyd .05
111 Bam Morris .05
112 Kordell Stewart 1.00
113 Yancey Thigpen .40
114 Rod Woodson .05
115 Isaac Bruce .50
116 Troy Drayton .05
117 Leslie O'Neal .05
118 Steve Walsh .05
119 Marco Coleman .05
120 Aaron Hayden .05
121 Stan Humphries .05
122 Junior Seau .10
123 William Floyd .05
124 Brent Jones .05
125 Ken Norton .05
126 Jerry Rice 1.00
127 J.J. Stokes .10
128 Steve Young .75
129 Brian Blades .05
130 Joey Galloway .60
131 Rick Mirer .05
132 Chris Warren .10
133 Trent Dilfer .05
134 Alvin Harper .05
135 Hardy Nickerson .05
136 Errict Rhett .50
137 Terry Allen .05
138 Henry Ellard .05
139 Heath Shuler .30
140 Michael Westbrook .10
141 *Karim Abdul-Jabbar* .50
142 *Mike Alstott* 1.00
143 *Marco Battaglia* .05
144 *Tim Biakabutuka* .75
145 *Tony Brackens* .05
146 *Duane Clemons* .05
147 *Ernie Conwell* .05
148 *Chris Darkins* .25
149 *Stephen Davis* 3.00
150 *Brian Dawkins* .05
151 *Rickey Dudley* .50
152 *Jason Dunn* .05
153 *Bobby Engram* .50
154 *Daryl Gardener* .05
155 *Eddie George* 3.00
156 *Terry Glenn* 1.50
157 *Kevin Hardy* .40
158 *Walt Harris* .05
159 *Marvin Harrison* 4.00
160 *Bobby Hoying* .50
161 *Keyshawn Johnson* 2.00
162 *Cedric Jones* .05
163 *Marcus Jones* .05
164 *Eddie Kennison* .30
165 *Ray Lewis* 2.00
166 *Derrick Mayes* .75
167 *Leeland McElroy* .20
168 *Johnny McWilliams* .05
169 *John Mobley* .05
170 *Alex Molden* .05
171 *Eric Moulds* 1.50
172 *Muhsin Muhammad* .75
173 *Jonathan Ogden* .05
174 *Lawrence Phillips* .50
175 *Stanley Pritchett* .25
176 *Simeon Rice* .30
177 *Bryan Still* .05
178 *Amani Toomer* .50
179 *Regan Upshaw* .05
180 *Alex Van Dyke* .25
181 Minnesota/Detroit (PFW Weekly Matchups) .05
182 Oakland/Kansas City (PFW Weekly Matchups) .05
183 Buffalo/Pittsburgh (PFW Weekly Matchups) .05
184 Atlanta/San Francisco (PFW Weekly Matchups) .05
185 Carolina/Jacksonville (PFW Weekly Matchups) .05
186 Philadelphia/Dallas (PFW Weekly Matchups) .05
187 Green Bay/Chicago (PFW Weekly Matchups) .05
188 Pittsburgh/Kansas City (PFW Weekly Matchups) .05
189 Cincinnati/Pittsburgh (PFW Weekly Matchups) .05
190 Dallas/Miami (PFW Weekly Matchups) .05
191 Denver/Oakland (PFW Weekly Matchups) .05
192 Kansas City/Minnesota (PFW Weekly Matchups) .05
193 San Diego/Indianapolis (PFW Weekly Matchups) .05
194 Dallas/San Francisco (PFW Weekly Matchups) .05
195 Miami/Oakland (PFW Weekly Matchups) .05
196 San Francisco/Pittsburgh (PFW Weekly Matchups) .05
197 Kansas City/Buffalo (PFW Weekly Matchups) .05
198 Checklist .05
199 Checklist .05
200 Checklist .05

1996 Fleer Rookie Sensations

Eleven of the NFL's top rookies entering the 1996 season are featured on these 1996 Fleer football plastic card inserts. The cards were seeded one per every 72 packs. Each front has an action photo on it, with the player's name and a team logo in the upper right corner. The Fleer logo is at the bottom of the card, with the Rookie Sensations logo in the bottom left corner. The card back has a card number (1 of 11, etc.) in the upper right corner; the set's logo is also at the top. A brief career write-up is in the middle, with a Pro Football Weekly logo and the player's name and position underneath. Special Rookie Sensation Hot Packs were also created; these packs contained all 11 cards, each with a special Hot Packs logo on it. Hot Packs were seeded one per every 960 packs.

NM/M
Complete Set (11): 60.00
Common Player: 6.00
Comp. Hot Pack Set (11): 60.00
Hot Pack Cards: Half Price
1 Karim Abdul-Jabbar 3.00
2 Tim Biakabutuka 3.00
3 Rickey Dudley 3.00
4 Eddie George 15.00
5 Terry Glenn 5.00
6 Kevin Hardy 3.00
7 Marvin Harrison 12.00
8 Keyshawn Johnson 10.00
9 Jon Ogden 3.00
10 Lawrence Phillips 3.00
11 Simeon Rice 6.00

1996 Fleer Rookie Sensations Hot Packs

This 11-card insert parallels the Rookie Sensations insert, but was found as a complete set in every 960 packs of Fleer Football. The cards are exactly like regular Rookie Sensations, except for a red foil Hot Packs logo on the front.

NM/M
Complete Set (11): 75.00
Hot Pack Cards: 50%

1996 Fleer Rookie Signatures

Three top rookie running backs have autographed cards for this 1996 Fleer insert set. The cards were seeded one per every 288 hobby packs only.

NM/M
Complete Set (3): 100.00
Common Player: 10.00
Inserted 1:288 Hobby
Blue Signatures: 1.5X
A1 Tim Biakabutuka 20.00
A2 Eddie George 70.00
A3 Leeland McElroy 10.00

1996 Fleer Breakthroughs

These players were chosen by Pro Football Weekly to have career seasons in 1996, including rookies who are predicted to have breakthrough campaigns in their first NFL season. The cards, seeded one per every three packs of 1996 Fleer football product, feature a 100% etched foil design for the card front. The Fleer logo and player's name and "Breakthrough" are stamped in gold foil. The horizontal back has the card number in a circle in the upper left corner next to a Pro Football Weekly logo. The player's name, team name, position and a team logo are underneath, followed by a brief write-up about the player's career accomplishments. A photo is on the right half of the card.

NM/M
Complete Set (24): 25.00
Common Player: .50
1 Tim Bowens .50
2 Kyle Brady .50
3 Devin Bush .50
4 Kevin Carter .50
5 Ki-Jana Carter .50
6 Kerry Collins 3.00
7 Trent Dilfer .50
8 Ken Dilger .50
9 Joey Galloway 2.00
10 Aaron Hayden .50
11 Napoleon Kaufman .50
12 Craig Newsome .50
13 Tyrone Poole .50
14 Jake Reed .50
15 Rashaan Salaam .50
16 Chris Sanders .50
17 Frank Sanders .50
18 Kordell Stewart 5.00
19 J.J. Stokes .50
20 Bobby Taylor .50
21 Orlando Thomas .50
22 Michael Timpson .50
23 Tamarick Vanover .50
24 Michael Westbrook .50

1996 Fleer RAC Pack

These 10 cards showcase receivers who rack up yards after the catch (Run After Catch yards). The cards, seeded one every 18th pack of 1996 Fleer product, feature an etched foil and color-foil stamped design for the card front's background (a football field design) and set/brand logos and player's name. The horizontal back has a bull's-eye in the upper left corner, with a player photo against it. The player's name, Pro Football Weekly logo and an explanation of the player's run-after-catch skills are on the opposite side.

NM/M
Complete Set (10): 15.00
Common Player: 1.00
1 Robert Brooks 1.00
2 Tim Brown 1.00
3 Isaac Bruce 4.00
4 Cris Carter 1.00
5 Curtis Conway 1.00
6 Michael Irvin 2.00
7 Eric Metcalf 1.00
8 Herman Moore 3.00
9 Carl Pickens 2.00
10 Jerry Rice 6.00

1996 Fleer Statistically Speaking

The NFL's statistical standouts are featured on these plastic cards using hot colors. These 1996 Fleer inserts are some of the tougher to find; they are seeded one per every 37 packs. Each card front has an action photo against a box filled with stats. The set's logo and player's name are along the bottom of the card. The background is a ghosted action scene. The horizontal back has a photo of the player on one side, against a ghosted action background which also contains a stat box. The card number (1 of 20, etc.) is in the upper left corner. The right side has a colored panel which has his name, position, team logo, Pro Football Weekly logo and a write-up of his accomplishments.

NM/M
Complete Set (20): 40.00
Common Player: 1.50
1 Troy Aikman 6.00
2 Larry Centers 1.50
3 Ben Coates 1.50
4 Brett Favre 10.00
5 Joey Galloway 3.00
6 Rodney Hampton 1.50
7 Dan Marino 10.00
8 Curtis Martin 6.00
9 Anthony Miller 1.50
10 Brian Mitchell 1.50
11 Herman Moore 1.50
12 Errict Rhett 1.50
13 Rashaan Salaam 1.50
14 Barry Sanders 10.00
15 Deion Sanders 2.00
16 Emmitt Smith 10.00
17 Kordell Stewart 2.00
18 Chris Warren 1.50
19 Ricky Watters 1.50
20 Steve Young 6.00

1996 Fleer Rookie Write-Ups

These hobby-exclusive insert cards feature 10 rookies entering the 1996 NFL season with scouting reports similar to those of previous rookies. Cards were inserted at a ratio of one per every 12 packs of 1996 Fleer hobby packs. The card front has a black band at the top with the player's name stamped in gold foil. His position and the set/brand logos are also stamped in gold. The middle of the card has an action shot of the player, against a written scouting report. The back has the player's name at the top, along with a card number (1 of 10, etc.). The background is white, with a brief write-up of the player and a colored/ghosted photo on it. The Pro Football Weekly Logo is also on the back.

NM/M
Complete Set (10): 20.00
Common Player: 1.50
1 Tim Biakabutuka 1.50
2 Rickey Dudley 1.50
3 Eddie George 5.00
4 Terry Glenn 2.00
5 Kevin Hardy 1.50
6 Marvin Harrison 4.00
7 Keyshawn Johnson 3.00
8 Leeland McElroy 1.50
9 Lawrence Phillips 1.50
10 Simeon Rice 1.50

1997 Fleer

The 450-card set includes 415 player cards, five checklists and 30 Something Special subset cards. The matte-finish cards have full-bleed photos on the front, with his last name in large block letters at the bottom. His first name is printed in small letters above, while his team and position appear directly below the player's last name. The backs have the name in the upper left, with the card number in the upper right. Rounding out the backs are a player head shot, team name and logo, highlights, bio and career stats. Two parallels are randomly seeded in hobby packs. Crystal Collection cards were seeded 1:2, while Tiffany Collection cards were 1:20.

NM/M
Complete Set (450): 40.00
Common Player: .05
Minor Stars: .10
Crystal Collection: 2X-4X
Tiffany Collection: 15X-30X
Pack (10): 1.50
Wax Box (36): 45.00
1 Mark Brunell 1.00
2 Andre Reed .05
3 Darrell Green .05
4 Mario Bates .05
5 Eddie George 1.50
6 Cris Carter .05
7 Terrell Owens 1.00
8 Bill Romanowski .05
9 Isaac Bruce .20
10 Eric Curry .05
11 Danny Kanell .05
12 Ki-Jana Carter .10
13 Antonio Freeman .30
14 Ricky Watters .10
15 Ty Law .05
16 Alonzo Spellman .05
17 Kordell Stewart .75
18 Jerry Rice 1.00
19 Derrick Alexander .05
20 Barry Sanders 2.00
21 Keyshawn Johnson .75
22 Emmitt Smith 2.00
23 Ricky Proehl .05
24 Daryl Gardner .05
25 Dan Saleaumua .05
26 Kevin Greene .05
27 Junior Seau .10
28 Randall McDaniel .05
29 Marshall Faulk .25
30 Lorenzo Lynch .05
31 Terance Mathis .05
32 Warren Sapp .05
33 Chris Sanders .05
34 Tom Carter .05
35 Aeneas Williams .05
36 Lawrence Phillips .10
37 John Elway .75
38 Stanley Richard .05
39 Darryl Williams .05
40 Phillippi Sparks .05
41 Tedy Bruschi .05
42 Merton Hanks .05
43 Ray Lewis .05
44 Eric Williams .05
45 Jason Gildon .05
46 George Koonce .05
47 Louis Oliver .05
48 Muhsin Muhammad .30
49 Daryl Hobbs .05
50 Terry Glenn 1.25
51 Marvin Harrison .75
52 Brian Dawkins .05
53 Dale Carter .05
54 Alex Molden .05
55 Raymont Harris .05
56 Jeff Burris .05
57 Don Beebe .05
58 Jamir Miller .05
59 Carl Pickens .10
60 Antonio London .05
61 Courtney Hall .05
62 Derrick Brooks .05
63 Chris Boniol .05
64 Jeff Lageman .05
65 Roy Barker .05
66 Devin Bush .05
67 Aaron Glenn .05
68 Wayne Simmons .05
69 Steve Atwater .05
70 Jimmie Jones .05
71 Mark Carrier .05
72 Chris Chandler .05
73 Andy Harmon .05
74 John Friesz .05
75 Karim Abdul-Jabbar 1.00
76 Levon Kirkland .05
77 Torrance Small .05
78 Harvey Williams .05
79 Chris Calloway .05
80 Vinny Testaverde .05
81 Bryant Young .05
82 Ray Buchanan .05
83 Robert Smith .05
84 Robert Brooks .10
85 Ray Crockett .05
86 Bennie Blades .05
87 Mark Carrier .05
88 Mike Tomczak .05
89 Darick Holmes .05

90	Drew Bledsoe	1.00
91	Darren Woodson	.05
92	Dan Wilkinson	.05
93	Charles Way	.05
94	Ray Farmer	.05
95	Marcus Allen	.10
96	Marco Coleman	.05
97	Zach Thomas	.30
98	Wesley Walls	.05
99	Frank Wycheck	.05
100	Troy Aikman	1.00
101	Clyde Simmons	.05
102	Courtney Hawkins	.05
103	Chuck Smith	.05
104	Neil O'Donnell	.05
105	Kevin Carter	.05
106	Chris Slade	.05
107	Jessie Armstead	.05
108	Sean Dawkins	.05
109	Robert Blackmon	.05
110	Kevin Smith	.05
111	Lonnie Johnson	.05
112	Craig Newsome	.05
113	Jonathan Ogden	.05
114	Chris Zorich	.05
115	Tim Brown	.05
116	Fred Barnett	.05
117	Michael Haynes	.05
118	Eric Hill	.05
119	Ronnie Harmon	.05
120	Sean Gilbert	.05
121	Derrick Alexander	.05
122	Derrick Thomas	.10
123	Tyrone Wheatley	.10
124	Cortez Kennedy	.05
125	Jeff George	.05
126	Chad Cota	.05
127	Gary Zimmerman	.05
128	Johnnie Morton	.05
129	Chad Brown	.05
130	Marvcus Patton	.05
131	James Stewart	.05
132	Terry Kirby	.05
133	Chris Mims	.05
134	William Thomas	.05
135	Steve Tasker	.05
136	Jason Belser	.05
137	Bryan Cox	.05
138	Jessie Tuggle	.05
139	Ashley Ambrose	.05
140	Mark Chmura	.05
141	Jeff Hostetler	.05
142	Rich Owens	.05
143	Willie Davis	.05
144	Hardy Nickerson	.05
145	Curtis Martin	1.25
146	Ken Norton	.05
147	Victor Green	.05
148	Anthony Miller	.05
149	John Kasay	.05
150	O.J. McDuffie	.05
151	Darren Perry	.05
152	Luther Elliss	.05
153	Greg Hill	.05
154	John Randle	.05
155	Stephen Grant	.05
156	Leon Lett	.05
157	Darrien Gordon	.05
158	Ray Zellars	.05
159	Michael Jackson	.05
160	Leslie O'Neal	.05
161	Bruce Smith	.05
162	Santana Dotson	.05
163	Bobby Hebert	.05
164	Keith Hamilton	.05
165	Tony Boselli	.05
166	Alfred Williams	.05
167	Ty Detmer	.05
168	Chester McGlockton	.05
169	William Floyd	.05
170	Bruce Matthews	.05
171	Simeon Rice	.05
172	Scott Mitchell	.05
173	Ricardo McDonald	.05
174	Tyrone Poole	.05
175	Greg Lloyd	.05
176	Bruce Armstrong	.05
177	Erik Kramer	.05
178	Kimble Anders	.05
179	Lamar Smith	.05
180	Tony Tolbert	.05
181	Joe Aska	.05
182	Eric Allen	.05
183	Eric Turner	.05
184	Brad Johnson	.05
185	Tony Martin	.05
186	Mike Mamula	.05
187	Irving Spikes	.05
188	Keith Jackson	.05
189	Carlton Bailey	.05
190	Tyrone Braxton	.05
191	Chad Bratzke	.05
192	Adrian Murrell	.05
193	Roman Phifer	.05
194	Todd Collins	.05
195	Chris Warren	.05
196	Kevin Hardy	.05
197	Rick Mirer	.10
198	Cornelius Bennett	.05
199	Jimmy Hitchcock	.05
200	Michael Irvin	.10
201	Quentin Coryatt	.05
202	Reggie White	.10
203	Larry Centers	.05
204	Rodney Thomas	.05
205	Dana Stubblefield	.05
206	Rod Woodson	.05
207	Rhett Hall	.05
208	Steve Tovar	.05
209	Michael Westbrook	.10
210	Steve Wisniewski	.05
211	Carlester Crumpler	.05
212	Elvis Grbac	.10
213	Tim Bowens	.05
214	Kevin Porcher	.05
215	John Carney	.05
216	Anthony Newman	.05
217	Ernest Byner	.05
218	DeWayne Washington	.05
219	Willie Green	.05
220	Terry Allen	.10
221	William Fuller	.05
222	Al Del Greco	.05
223	Trent Dilfer	.10
224	Michael Dean Perry	.05
225	Larry Allen	.05
226	Mark Bruener	.05
227	Clay Matthews	.05
228	Ruben Brown	.05
229	Edgar Bennett	.05
230	Neil Smith	.05
231	Ken Harvey	.05
232	Kyle Brady	.05
233	Corey Miller	.05
234	Tony Siragusa	.05
235	Todd Sauerbrun	.05
236	Daniel Stubbs	.05
237	Robb Thomas	.05
238	Jimmy Smith	.05
239	Marquez Pope	.05
240	Tim Biakabutuka	.10
241	Jamie Asher	.05
242	Steve McNair	.75
243	Harold Green	.05
244	Frank Sanders	.05
245	Joe Johnson	.05
246	Eric Bieniemy	.05
247	Kevin Turner	.05
248	Rickey Dudley	.10
249	Orlando Thomas	.05
250	Dan Marino	2.00
251	Deion Sanders	.50
252	Dan Williams	.05
253	Sam Gash	.05
254	Lonnie Marts	.05
255	Mo Lewis	.05
256	Charles Johnson	.05
257	Chris Jacke	.05
258	Keenan McCardell	.05
259	Donnell Woolford	.05
260	Terrance Shaw	.05
261	Jason Dunn	.05
262	Willie McGinest	.05
263	Ken Dilger	.05
264	Keith Lyle	.05
265	Antonio Langham	.05
266	Carlton Gray	.05
267	LeShon Johnson	.05
268	Thurman Thomas	.10
269	Jesse Campbell	.05
270	Carnell Lake	.05
271	Cris Dishman	.05
272	Kevin Williams	.05
273	Troy Brown	.05
274	William Roaf	.05
275	Terrell Davis	1.25
276	Herman Moore	.20
277	Walt Harris	.05
278	Mark Collins	.05
279	Bert Emanuel	.05
280	Qadry Ismail	.05
281	Phil Hansen	.05
282	Steve Young	.75
283	Michael Sinclair	.05
284	Jeff Graham	.05
285	Sam Mills	.05
286	Terry McDaniel	.05
287	Eugene Robinson	.05
288	Tony Bennett	.05
289	Daryl Johnston	.05
290	Eric Swann	.05
291	Bam Morris	.05
292	Thomas Lewis	.05
293	Terrell Fletcher	.05
294	Gus Frerotte	.05
295	Stanley Pritchett	.05
296	Mike Alstott	.10
297	Will Shields	.05
298	Errict Rhett	.10
299	Garrison Hearst	.05
300	Kerry Collins	.25
301	Darryll Lewis	.05
302	Chris T. Jones	.05
303	Yancey Thigpen	.05
304	Jackie Harris	.05
305	Steve Christie	.05
306	Gilbert Brown	.05
307	Terry Wooden	.05
308	Pete Mitchell	.05
309	Tim McDonald	.05
310	Jake Reed	.05
311	Ed McCaffrey	.05
312	Chris Doleman	.05
313	Eric Metcalf	.05
314	Ricky Reynolds	.05
315	David Sloan	.05
316	Marvin Washington	.05
317	Herschel Walker	.05
318	Michael Timpson	.05
319	Blaine Bishop	.05
320	Irv Smith	.05
321	Seth Joyner	.05
322	Terrell Buckley	.05
323	Michael Strahan	.05
324	Sam Adams	.05
325	Leslie Shepherd	.05
326	James Jett	.05
327	Anthony Pleasant	.05
328	Lee Woodall	.05
329	Shannon Sharpe	.05
330	Jamal Anderson	.20
331	Andre Hastings	.05
332	Troy Vincent	.05
333	Sean LaChapelle	.05
334	Winslow Oliver	.05
335	Sean Jones	.05
336	Darnay Scott	.05
337	Todd Lyght	.05
338	Leonard Russell	.05
339	Nate Newton	.05
340	Zack Crockett	.05
341	Amp Lee	.05
342	Bobby Engram	.05
343	Mike Hollis	.05
344	Rodney Hampton	.05
345	Mel Gray	.05
346	Van Malone	.05
347	Aaron Craver	.05
348	Jim Everett	.05
349	Trace Armstrong	.05
350	Pat Swilling	.05
351	Brent Jones	.05
352	Chris Spielman	.05
353	Brett Perriman	.05
354	Brian Kinchen	.05
355	Joey Galloway	.30
356	Henry Ellard	.05
357	Ben Coates	.05
358	Dorsey Levens	.20
359	Charlie Garner	.05
360	Erric Pegram	.05
361	Anthony Johnson	.05
362	Rashaan Salaam	.10
363	Jeff Blake	.20
364	Kent Graham	.05
365	Broderick Thomas	.05
366	Richmond Webb	.05
367	Alfred Pupunu	.05
368	Mark Stepnoski	.05
369	David Dunn	.05
370	Bobby Houston	.05
371	Anthony Parker	.05
372	Quinn Early	.05
373	LeRoy Butler	.05
374	Kurt Gouveia	.05
375	Greg Biekert	.05
376	Jim Harbaugh	.05
377	Eric Bjornson	.05
378	Craig Heyward	.05
379	Steve Bono	.05
380	Tony Banks	.30
381	John Mobley	.05
382	Irving Fryar	.05
383	Dermontti Dawson	.05
384	Eric Davis	.05
385	Natrone Means	.10
386	Jason Sehorn	.05
387	Michael McCrary	.05
388	Corwin Brown	.05
389	Kevin Glover	.05
390	Jerris McPhail	.05
391	Bobby Taylor	.05
392	Tony McGee	.05
393	Curtis Conway	.05
394	Napoleon Kaufman	.05
395	Brian Blades	.05
396	Richard Dent	.05
397	Dave Brown	.05
398	Stan Humphries	.05
399	Stevon Moore	.05
400	Brett Favre	2.00
401	Jerome Bettis	.10
402	Darrin Smith	.05
403	Chris Penn	.05
404	Rob Moore	.05
405	Micheal Barrow	.05
406	Tony Brackens	.05
407	Wayne Martin	.05
408	Warren Moon	.05
409	Jason Elam	.05
410	J.J. Birden	.05
411	Hugh Douglas	.05
412	Lamar Lathon	.05
413	John Kidd	.05
414	Bryce Paup	.05
415	Shawn Jefferson	.05
416	Leeland McElroy	.10
417	Elbert Shelley	.05
418	Jermaine Lewis	.05
419	Eric Moulds	.10
420	Michael Bates	.05
421	John Mangum	.05
422	Corey Sawyer	.05
423	Jim Schwantz	.05
424	Rod Smith	.05
425	Glyn Milburn	.05
426	Desmond Howard	.10
427	John Henry Mills	.05
428	Cary Blanchard	.05
429	Chris Hudson	.05
430	Tamarick Vanover	.10
431	Kirby Dar Dar	.05
432	David Palmer	.05
433	Dave Meggett	.05
434	Tyrone Hughes	.05
435	Amani Toomer	.10
436	Wayne Chrebet	.05
437	Carl Kidd	.05
438	Derrick Witherspoon	.05
439	Jahine Arnold	.05
440	Andre Coleman	.05
441	Jeff Wilkins	.05
442	Jay Bellamy	.05
443	Eddie Kennison	.50
444	Nilo Silvan	.05
445	Brian Mitchell	.05
446	Checklist	.05
447	Checklist	.05
448	Checklist	.05
449	Checklist	.05
450	Checklist	.05

1997 Fleer Crystal Silver

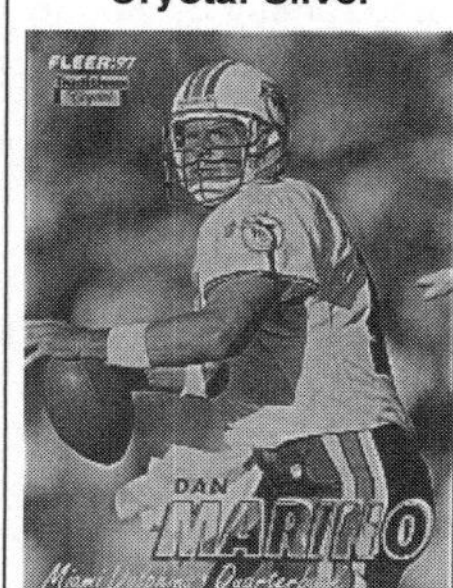

This set paralleled the 445 cards included in Fleer Football (minus five checklist cards) and was seeded one per pack. Each card was distinguished by a "Traditions Crystal" logo on one of the upper corners. This parallel also contained a glossy finish, whereas the base cards had a matte finish, and silver foil instead of the gold foil used on the base cards.

	NM/M
Complete Set (445):	160.00
Crystal Silver Cards:	2X-4X

1997 Fleer Tiffany Blue

This parallel reprinted 445 cards from Fleer Football and was seeded one per 20 packs. The fronts featured a glossy silver finish versus the matte finish on the base cards, and featured blue foil stamping on the front versus gold foil on the base cards. Card fronts also had a "Traditions Tiffany" logo in either top corner.

	NM/M
Tiffany Blue Cards:	8X-15X

1997 Fleer All-Pro

This 24-card set was inserted 1:36 retail packs. All-Pros from the previous season were commemorated.

		NM/M
Complete Set (24):		75.00
Common Player:		2.00
Minor Stars:		4.00
1	Troy Aikman	6.00
2	Larry Allen	2.00
3	Drew Bledsoe	6.00
4	Terrell Davis	6.00
5	Dermontti Dawson	2.00
6	John Elway	8.00
7	Brett Favre	10.00
8	Herman Moore	4.00
9	Jerry Rice	8.00
10	Barry Sanders	10.00
11	Shannon Sharpe	2.00
12	Eric Williams	2.00
13	Ashley Ambrose	2.00
14	Chad Brown	2.00
15	LeRoy Butler	2.00
16	Kevin Greene	2.00
17	Sam Mills	2.00
18	John Randle	2.00
19	Deion Sanders	3.00
20	Junior Seau	4.00
21	Bruce Smith	2.00
22	Alfred Williams	2.00
23	Darren Woodson	2.00
24	Bryant Young	2.00

1997 Fleer Decade of Excellence

Inserted 1:36 hobby packs, this 12-card set featured photography from 10 years prior. Ten percent of the cards were printed with holographic foil and were inserted 1:360 hobby packs.

		NM/M
Complete Set (12):		30.00
Common Player:		1.50
1	Marcus Allen	3.00
2	Cris Carter	3.00
3	John Elway	6.00
4	Irving Fryar	1.50
5	Darrell Green	1.50
6	Dan Marino	8.00
7	Jerry Rice	6.00
8	Bruce Smith	1.50
9	Herschel Walker	1.50
10	Reggie White	3.00
11	Rod Woodson	1.50
12	Steve Young	4.00

1997 Fleer Game Breakers

Inserted 1:2 retail packs, this 20-card set showcased players who have the ability to break a game open. A Game Breakers Supreme parallel was inserted 1:18 of all pack types.

		NM/M
Complete Set (20):		20.00
Common Player:		.30
Minor Stars:		.60
Supreme Cards:		2X-4X
1	Troy Aikman	2.50
2	Jerome Bettis	.60
3	Drew Bledsoe	2.50
4	Isaac Bruce	.75
5	Mark Brunell	2.50
6	Kerry Collins	2.00
7	Terrell Davis	2.50
8	Marshall Faulk	.30
9	Antonio Freeman	.60
10	Joey Galloway	1.00
11	Terry Glenn	.75
12	Desmond Howard	.30
13	Keyshawn Johnson	1.00
14	Eddie Kennison	1.00
15	Curtis Martin	2.50
16	Herman Moore	.30
17	Lawrence Phillips	.60
18	Barry Sanders	3.00
19	Shannon Sharpe	.30
20	Emmitt Smith	5.00

1997 Fleer Million Dollar Moments

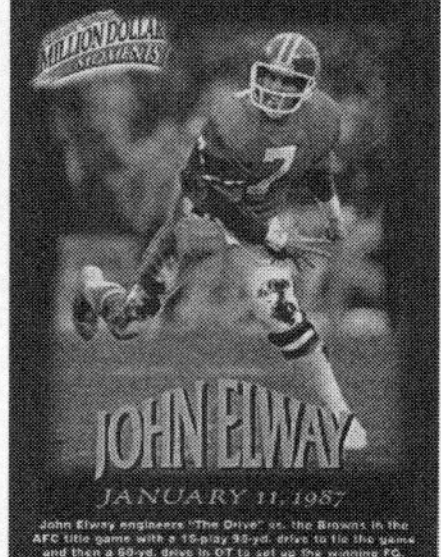

The 50-card set was part of a season-long multi-sport promotion which was available in all 1997 packs of Fleer, Fleer Ultra and Flair Showcase football products released after June, 1997. Each pack contained one of 50 different Million Dollar Moments cards. The fronts of the cards had the Million Dollar Moments logo in the upper left. The player's name, date of his highlight and highlight are included at the bottom front. The backs include the contest details. Cards numbered 1-45 are common, while 46-50 are difficult to find. Those who collected cards 1-45 plus any one of 46-49 won up to a $1,000 shopping spree. The grand prize of $1 million was awarded to the collector of all 50 cards. To reward collectors who complete the "common" 45-card set, Fleer offered the opportunity to redeem the 45-card set (with $5.99 for shipping) for a complete parallel 50-card set.

		NM/M
Complete Set (45):		5.00
Common Player:		.05
Minor Stars:		.10
1	Checklist	.05
2	Troy Aikman	.50
3	Sid Luckman	.10
4	Barry Sanders	.50
5	Tom Fears	.05
6	Reggie White	.10
7	Lou Groza	.05
8	John Elway	.35
9	Raymond Berry	.05
10	Marcus Allen	.10
11	Paul Hornung	.10
12	Herschel Walker	.05
13	Norm Van Brocklin	.05
14	Bruce Smith	.05
15	Billy Wade	.05
16	Andre Reed	.05
17	Gale Sayers	.10
18	Terrell Davis	.50
19	Jim Bakken	.05
20	Marshall Faulk	.10
21	Tom Dempsey	.05
22	Dan Marino	1.00
23	Garo Yepremian	.05
24	Jerry Rice	.50
25	Herman Edwards	.05
26	Derrick Thomas	.05
27	Kellen Winslow	.05
28	Steve Young	.35
29	Tony Dorsett	.10
30	Desmond Howard	.05
31	Roger Craig	.05
32	Drew Bledsoe	.50
33	Doug Williams	.05
34	Jerome Bettis	.10
35	Bobby Layne	.05
36	Junior Seau	.10
37	Roman Gabriel	.05
38	Cris Carter	.10
39	Drew Pearson	.05
40	Warren Moon	.05
41	Wesley Walker	.05
42	Ricky Watters	.10
43	Carl Eller	.05
44	Kordell Stewart	.50
45	John Mackey	.05
46	Thurman Thomas	
47	Ken Stabler	
48	Emmitt Smith	
49	Jim Brown	
50	Eddie George	

1997 Fleer Prospects

The 10-card set was inserted 1:6 packs. It featured the top prospects from the 1997 NFL Draft.

		NM/M
Complete Set (10):		10.00
Common Player:		.75
1	Peter Boulware	.75
2	Rae Carruth	.75
3	Jim Druckenmiller	1.00
4	Warrick Dunn	4.00
5	Tony Gonzalez	1.50
6	Yatil Green	2.00
7	Ike Hilliard	4.00
8	Orlando Pace	1.50
9	Darrell Russell	.75
10	Shawn Springs	.75

1997 Fleer Rookie Sensations

Inserted 1:4 packs, the 20-card set focused on rookies who had positive impacts on their team in 1996.

		NM/M
Complete Set (20):		20.00
Common Player:		.50
Minor Stars:		1.00
1	Karim Abdul-Jabbar	1.00
2	Mike Alstott	1.00
3	Tony Banks	2.00
4	Tony Brackens	.50
5	Rickey Dudley	.50
6	Bobby Engram	.50
7	Eddie George	5.00
8	Terry Glenn	2.00
9	Kevin Hardy	.50
10	Marvin Harrison	2.00
11	Keyshawn Johnson	2.00
12	Eddie Kennison	1.00
13	Jermaine Lewis	.50
14	Ray Lewis	.50
15	John Mobley	.50
16	Eric Moulds	.50
17	Jonathan Ogden	.50
18	Lawrence Phillips	.50
19	Simeon Rice	.50
20	Zach Thomas	1.50

1997 Fleer Thrill Seekers

Inserted 1:288 packs, the 12-card set looks at players known for making the big play.

		NM/M
Complete Set (12):		200.00
Common Player:		10.00
1	Karim Abdul-Jabbar	10.00
2	Jerome Bettis	10.00
3	Terrell Davis	30.00
4	John Elway	35.00
5	Brett Favre	50.00
6	Eddie George	20.00
7	Terry Glenn	10.00
8	Keyshawn Johnson	15.00
9	Dan Marino	50.00
10	Curtis Martin	20.00
11	Deion Sanders	15.00
12	Emmitt Smith	50.00

1997 Fleer Goudey

Goudey included 150 cards that adopted the old-time look of the Goudey brand from the 1930s.

The cards measure 2-3/8" x 2-7/8", with player pictures appearing as illustrations. Backs include a player synopsis "old-time" text. Also included in the regular-issue set were cards of Chuck Bednarik and Y.A. Tittle, as well as two checklists and a History of Goudey card. Insert sets found in Goudey were Gridiron Greats (parallel set), Heads Up, Concrete Chuck Bednarik Says, Y.A.Tittle Says and Pigskin 2000.

		NM/M
Complete Set (150):		18.00
Common Player:		.05
Minor Stars:		.10
Pack (10):		1.50
Wax Box (36):		45.00
1	Michael Jackson	.05
2	Ray Lewis	.05
3	Vinny Testaverde	.05
4	Eric Turner	.05
5	Jim Kelly	.10
6	Bryce Paup	.05
7	Andre Reed	.05
8	Bruce Smith	.05
9	Thurman Thomas	.10
10	Jeff Blake	.10
11	Ki-Jana Carter	.10
12	Carl Pickens	.05
13	Darnay Scott	.05
14	Terrell Davis	1.25
15	John Elway	.75
16	Anthony Miller	.05
17	John Mobley	.05
18	Shannon Sharpe	.05
19	Chris Chandler	.05
20	Eddie George	1.50
21	Steve McNair	.50
22	Chris Sanders	.05
23	Quentin Coryatt	.05
24	Sean Dawkins	.05
25	Ken Dilger	.05
26	Marshall Faulk	.30
27	Jim Harbaugh	.05
28	Marvin Harrison	.75
29	Tony Brackens	.05
30	Mark Brunell	1.00
31	Kevin Hardy	.10
32	Keenan McCardell	.05
33	James Stewart	.05
34	Marcus Allen	.10
35	Steve Bono	.05
36	Dale Carter	.05
37	Neil Smith	.05
38	Derrick Thomas	.05
39	Tamarick Vanover	.10
40	Karim Abdul-Jabbar	.25
41	Dan Marino	2.00
42	O.J. McDuffie	.05
43	Stanley Pritchett	.05
44	Zach Thomas	.50
45	Drew Bledsoe	1.00
46	Ben Coates	.05
47	Terry Glenn	.25
48	Shawn Jefferson	.05
49	Curtis Martin	1.50
50	David Meggett	.05
51	Hugh Douglas	.05
52	Keyshawn Johnson	.75
53	Adrian Murrell	.05
54	Tim Brown	.05
55	Rickey Dudley	.10
56	Jeff Hostetler	.05
57	Napoleon Kaufman	.05
58	Chester McGlockton	.05
59	Jerome Bettis	.10
60	Andre Hastings	.05
61	Greg Lloyd	.05
62	Kordell Stewart	1.00
63	Yancey Thigpen	.05
64	Rod Woodson	.05
65	Andre Coleman	.05
66	Stan Humphries	.05
67	Tony Martin	.05
68	Leonard Russell	.05
69	Junior Seau	.05
70	Brian Blades	.05
71	Joey Galloway	.50
72	Chris Warren	.05
73	Larry Centers	.05
74	Leeland McElroy	.10
75	Simeon Rice	.10
76	Frank Sanders	.05
77	Eric Swann	.05
78	Jamal Anderson	.40
79	Bert Emanuel	.05
80	Terance Mathis	.05
81	Eric Metcalf	.05
82	Tim Biakabutuka	.40
83	Kerry Collins	.25
84	Kevin Greene	.05
85	Muhsin Muhammad	.10
86	Wesley Walls	.05
87	Curtis Conway	.05
88	Bryan Cox	.05
89	Walt Harris	.05
90	Erik Kramer	.05
91	Rashaan Salaam	.10
92	Troy Aikman	1.00
93	Michael Irvin	.10
94	Daryl Johnston	.05
95	Leon Lett	.05
96	Deion Sanders	.50
97	Emmitt Smith	2.00
98	Scott Mitchell	.05
99	Herman Moore	.10
100	Johnnie Morton	.05
101	Brett Perriman	.05
102	Barry Sanders	1.25
103	Edgar Bennett	.05
104	Robert Brooks	.05
105	Brett Favre	2.00
106	Antonio Freeman	.05
107	Keith Jackson	.05
108	Reggie White	.10
109	Cris Carter	.05
110	Warren Moon	.10
111	John Randle	.05
112	Jake Reed	.05
113	Robert Smith	.05
114	Jim Everett	.05
115	Michael Haynes	.05
116	Alex Molden	.05
117	Ray Zellars	.05
118	Chris Calloway	.05
119	Rodney Hampton	.05
120	Phillippi Sparks	.05
121	Amani Toomer	.10
122	Ty Detmer	.05
123	Jason Dunn	.05
124	Irving Fryar	.05
125	Chris T. Jones	.05
126	Ricky Watters	.10
127	Tony Banks	.25
128	Isaac Bruce	.25
129	Eddie Kennison	.20
130	Lawrence Phillips	.10
131	Merton Hanks	.05
132	Terry Kirby	.05
133	Ken Norton	.05
134	Jerry Rice	1.00
135	J.J. Stokes	.10
136	Steve Young	.75
137	Alvin Harper	.05
138	Jackie Harris	.05
139	Hardy Nickerson	.05
140	Errict Rhett	.20
141	Terry Allen	.05
142	Henry Ellard	.05
143	Gus Frerotte	.05
144	Brian Mitchell	.05
145	Michael Westbrook	.10
146	Chuck Bednarik	.10
147	Y.A. Tittle	.10
148	Checklist	.05
149	Checklist	.05
150	Checklist	.05

1997 Fleer Goudey Gridiron Greats

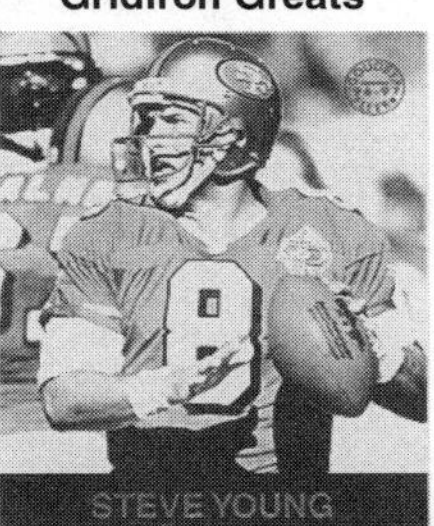

Gridiron Greats was a 147-card parallel set (150 minus the two checklists and one History of Goudey card) that was found at a rate of one per three packs in Goudey Football. Each card contains a solid black strip across the bottom with the player's name in red foil. Unlike the regular-issue cards, these are actual photos instead of illustrations.

	NM/M
Complete Set (147):	100.00
Gridiron Greats Cards:	3X-6X

1997 Fleer Goudey Heads Up

Heads Up contained 20 players in a cartoon format, with the player's head larger and in color, compared to the small black and white body. The player's last name runs up the left side in white letters. Heads Up cards were found in every 30 hobby packs and every 36 retail packs.

		NM/M
Complete Set (20):		60.00
Common Player:		1.00
1	Troy Aikman	6.00
2	Marcus Allen	2.00
3	Tim Biakabutuka	1.00
4	Robert Brooks	1.00
5	Isaac Bruce	3.00
6	Kerry Collins	3.00
7	Terrell Davis	6.00
8	Brett Favre	10.00
9	Terry Glenn	2.00
10	Rodney Hampton	1.00
11	Michael Irvin	2.00
12	Chris T. Jones	1.00
13	Carl Pickens	1.00
14	Barry Sanders	8.00
15	Kordell Stewart	2.00
16	Thurman Thomas	1.00
17	Tamarick Vanover	1.00
18	Chris Warren	1.00
19	Ricky Watters	1.00
20	Steve Young	6.00

1997 Fleer Goudey Pigskin 2000

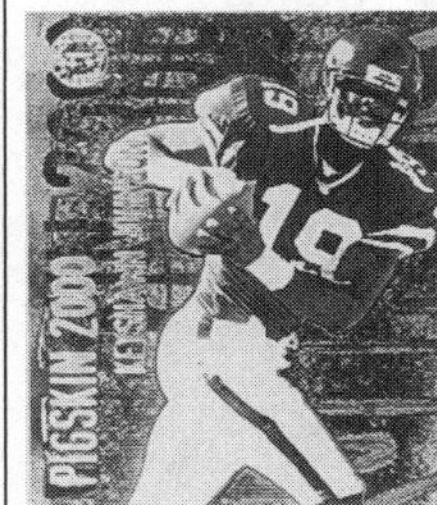

Pigskin 2000 was a 15-card foil-etched insert that highlighted some of the NFL's elite. The insert name and player's name are included in gold foil along the left side, with the Fleer Goudey logo in the top left corner. Pigskin 2000 cards are found every 360 hobby packs.

		NM/M
Complete Set (15):		125.00
Common Player:		5.00
1	Karim Abdul-Jabbar	5.00
2	Jeff Blake	5.00
3	Drew Bledsoe	20.00
4	Robert Brooks	5.00
5	Terrell Davis	25.00
6	Marshall Faulk	20.00
7	Joey Galloway	8.00
8	Eddie George	20.00
9	Terry Glenn	8.00
10	Keyshawn Johnson	15.00
11	Chris T. Jones	5.00
12	Curtis Martin	20.00
13	Steve McNair	25.00
14	Lawrence Phillips	5.00
15	Kordell Stewart	15.00

1997 Fleer Goudey Tittle Says

Y.A. Tittle Says shows 20 of the top offensive stars, with Tittle providing insight on each card back. Each card has a color photo of the player over a color background with the insert's name scattered across it. They were found every 72 hobby and every 85 retail packs.

		NM/M
Complete Set (20):		75.00
Common Player:		4.00
1	Karim Abdul-Jabbar	4.00
2	Jerome Bettis	4.00
3	Tim Brown	6.00
4	Isaac Bruce	8.00
5	Cris Carter	4.00
6	Curtis Conway	4.00
7	John Elway	12.00
8	Marshall Faulk	10.00
9	Brett Favre	20.00
10	Joey Galloway	4.00
11	Eddie George	12.00
12	Keyshawn Johnson	8.00
13	Dan Marino	20.00
14	Curtis Martin	12.00
15	Herman Moore	4.00
16	Jerry Rice	15.00
17	Barry Sanders	20.00
18	Emmitt Smith	20.00
19	Thurman Thomas	4.00
20	Ricky Watters	4.00

1997 Fleer Goudey Bednarik Says

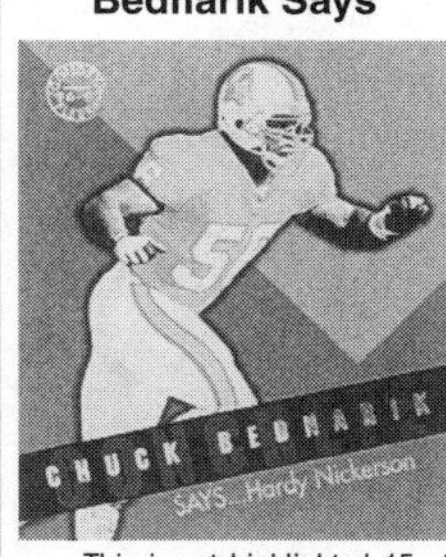

This insert highlighted 15 of the top defensive players in the league, with Bednarik's assessment of each player on the card back. Cards in this insert are identified by a large solid block pattern in the back featuring the team's colors, with a black strip near the bottom with the words "Concrete Chuck Bednarik" in it. These inserts were found every 60 hobby packs and every 72 retail packs.

		NM/M
Complete Set (15):		40.00
Common Player:		1.00
1	Kevin Greene	1.00
2	Ray Lewis	2.00
3	Greg Lloyd	1.00
4	Chester McGlockton	1.00
5	Hardy Nickerson	1.00
6	Bryce Paup	1.00
7	Simeon Rice	1.00
8	Deion Sanders	5.00
9	Junior Seau	1.00
10	Bruce Smith	2.00
11	Derrick Thomas	1.00
12	Zach Thomas	4.00
13	Eric Turner	1.00
14	Reggie White	4.00
15	Rod Woodson	1.00

1997 Fleer Goudey II

Goudey Series II is a 150-card set. It contians 145 player cards, all of which feature "Gale Sayers Says" on the backs. There are also two checklist cards and a three card Gale Sayers subset (1:9). The parallel sets are Gridiron Greats (1:3) and Goudey Greats (numbered to 150). Sayers has autographed 40 of each subset card and each card #40 of the Goudey Greats parallel set. The insert sets included Rookie Classics, Glory Days, Vintage Goudey, Big Time Backs and Million Dollar Moments.

		NM/M
Complete Set (150):		25.00
Common Player:		.05
Minor Stars:		.10
Gridiron Greats:		2X-4X
Goudey Greats Cards:		20X-40X
Goudey Greats Rookies:		10X-20X
Pack (8):		1.00
Wax Box (36):		35.00
1	Gale Sayers	1.25
2	Vinny Testaverde	.05
3	Jeff George	.10
4	Brett Favre	2.25
5	Eddie Kennison	.50
6	Ken Norton	.05
7	John Elway	.75
8	Troy Aikman	1.00
9	Steve McNair	.75
10	Kordell Stewart	1.00
11	Drew Bledsoe	1.00
12	Kerry Collins	.25
13	Dan Marino	2.00
14	Brad Johnson	.05
15	Todd Collins	.05
16	Ki-Jana Carter	.10
17	*Pat Barnes*	.50
18	Aeneas Williams	.05
19	Keyshawn Johnson	.20
20	Barry Sanders	1.25
21	*Tiki Barber*	1.00
22	Emmitt Smith	2.00
23	Kevin Hardy	.05
24	Mario Bates	.05
25	Ricky Watters	.10
26	Chris Canty	.05
27	Eddie George	1.50
28	Curtis Martin	1.00
29	Adrian Murrell	.10
30	Terrell Davis	1.00
31	Rashaan Salaam	.10
32	Marcus Allen	.10
33	Karim Abdul-Jabbar	.50
34	Thurman Thomas	.10
35	Marvin Harrison	.50
36	Jerome Bettis	.10
37	Larry Centers	.05
38	Stan Humphries	.05
39	Lawrence Phillips	.10
40	Gale Sayers	1.25
41	Henry Ellard	.05
42	Chris Warren	.05
43	Robert Brooks	.10
44	*Sedrick Shaw*	.50
45	Muhsin Muhammad	.05
46	Napoleon Kaufman	.20
47	*Reidel Anthony*	1.00
48	Jamal Anderson	.10
49	Scott Mitchell	.05
50	Mark Brunell	1.00
51	William Thomas	.05
52	Bryan Cox	.05
53	Carl Pickens	.10
54	Chris Spielman	.05
55	Junior Seau	.10
56	Hardy Nickerson	.05
57	*Dwayne Rudd*	.10
58	*Peter Boulware*	.10
59	*Jim Druckenmiller*	2.00
60	Michael Westbrook	.05
61	*Shawn Springs*	.25
62	Zach Thomas	.10
63	*David LaFleur*	.50
64	*Darrell Russell*	.10
65	*Jake Plummer*	1.50
66	Tim Biakabutuka	.10
67	Tyrone Wheatley	.05
68	Elvis Grbac	.05
69	Antonio Freeman	.30
70	Wayne Chrebet	.05
71	*Walter Jones*	.10
72	Marshall Faulk	.10
73	Jason Dunn	.05
74	Darnay Scott	.05
75	Errict Rhett	.10
76	*Orlando Pace*	.25
77	Natrone Means	.10
78	Bruce Smith	.05
79	Jamie Sharper	.05
80	Jerry Rice	1.00
81	Tim Brown	.10
82	Brian Mitchell	.05
83	Andre Reed	.05
84	Herman Moore	.10
85	Rob Moore	.05
86	*Rae Carruth*	.75
87	Bert Emanuel	.05
88	Michael Irvin	.10
89	Mark Chmura	.10
90	Tony Brackens	.05
91	Kevin Greene	.05
92	Reggie White	.10
93	Derrick Thomas	.05
94	*Troy Davis*	.25
95	Greg Lloyd	.05
96	Cortez Kennedy	.05
97	Simeon Rice	.05
98	Terrell Owens	.50
99	Hugh Douglas	.05
100	Terry Glenn	.25
101	Jim Harbaugh	.05
102	Shannon Sharpe	.05
103	*Joey Kent*	.30
104	Jeff Blake	.05
105	Terry Allen	.05
106	Cris Carter	.05
107	Amani Toomer	.05
108	Derrick Alexander	.05
109	*Darnell Autry*	.50
110	Irving Fryar	.05
111	*Bryant Westbrook*	.10
112	Tony Banks	.50
113	Michael Booker	.05
114	*Yatil Green*	.40
115	*James Farrior*	.10
116	*Warrick Dunn*	1.50
117	Greg Hill	.05
118	Tony Martin	.05
119	Chris Sanders	.05
120	Charles Johnson	.05
121	John Mobley	.05
122	Keenan McCardell	.05
123	Willie McGinest	.05
124	O.J. McDuffie	.05
125	Deion Sanders	.50
126	Curtis Conway	.05
127	Desmond Howard	.05
128	Johnnie Morton	.05
129	*Ike Hilliard*	1.00
130	Gus Frerotte	.05
131	*Tom Knight*	.10
132	Sean Dawkins	.05
133	Isaac Bruce	.10
134	Wesley Walls	.05
135	*Danny Wuerffel*	1.00
136	*Tony Gonzalez*	.50
137	Ben Coates	.05
138	Joey Galloway	.10
139	Michael Jackson	.05
140	Steve Young	.50
141	*Corey Dillon*	2.00
142	Jake Reed	.05
143	Edgar Bennett	.05
144	Ty Detmer	.05
145	Darrell Green	.05
146	*Antowain Smith*	1.50
147	Mike Alstott	.10
148	Checklist	.05
149	Checklist	.05
150	Gale Sayers (Commemorative Card)	1.25

1997 Fleer Goudey II Big Time Backs

This 10-card insert features top quarterbacks and running backs on a die-cut, embossed card designed as a clipboard. The cards were inserted 1:72.

		NM/M
Complete Set (10):		150.00
Common Player:		3.00
1	Karim Abdul-Jabbar	3.00
2	Marcus Allen	3.00
3	Jerome Bettis	3.00
4	Terrell Davis	15.00
5	Brett Favre	30.00
6	Eddie George	20.00
7	Dan Marino	25.00
8	Curtis Martin	15.00
9	Barry Sanders	30.00
10	Emmitt Smith	25.00

1997 Fleer Goudey II Glory Days

This 18-card insert features top players on an embossed card. Glory Days was inserted once per 18 retail packs.

		NM/M
Complete Set (15):		40.00
Common Player:		2.00
1	Troy Aikman	5.00
2	Isaac Bruce	2.00
3	Mark Brunell	3.00
4	Cris Carter	2.00
5	Joey Galloway	2.00
6	Terry Glenn	2.00
7	Marvin Harrison	4.00
8	Dan Marino	8.00
9	Deion Sanders	2.00
10	Shannon Sharpe	2.00
11	Emmitt Smith	8.00
12	Bruce Smith	2.00
13	Kordell Stewart	2.00
14	Ricky Watters	2.00
15	Reggie White	2.00

1997 Fleer Goudey II Rookie Classics

This 20-card insert features top 1997 rookies on a die-cut card. The first down marker is die-cut on the right side of the card. This set was inserted 1:3.

		NM/M
Complete Set (20):		18.00
Common Player:		.25
1	Reidel Anthony	1.50
2	Pat Barnes	.50
3	Peter Boulware	.25
4	Rae Carruth	.75
5	Troy Davis	.50
6	Corey Dillon	2.50
7	Jim Druckenmiller	1.00
8	Warrick Dunn	2.00
9	Tony Gonzalez	.75
10	Yatil Green	.50
11	Ike Hilliard	1.00

12	Walter Jones	.25
13	David LaFleur	.75
14	Orlando Pace	.50
15	Jake Plummer	3.00
16	Darrell Russell	.25
17	Antowain Smith	2.00
18	Shawn Springs	.25
19	Bryant Westbrook	.25
20	Danny Wuerffel	1.00

1997 Fleer Goudey II Vintage Goudey

This 15-card insert features players who are throwbacks to old-time football. The players are featured on cards die-cut into a football shape. This set also contained redemption cards for an original 1933 Sport Kings Football card of Red Grange, Jim Thorpe and Knute Rockne. This set was inserted 1:36 in hobby packs.

		NM/M
Complete Set (15):		75.00
Common Player:		4.00
1	Karim Abdul-Jabbar	4.00
2	Kerry Collins	6.00
3	Terrell Davis	8.00
4	John Elway	8.00
5	Brett Favre	25.00
6	Eddie George	6.00
7	Terry Glenn	4.00
8	Keyshawn Johnson	4.00
9	Curtis Martin	6.00
10	Herman Moore	4.00
11	Jerry Rice	8.00
12	Barry Sanders	12.00
13	Deion Sanders	5.00
14	Zach Thomas	4.00
15	Steve Young	8.00

1998 Fleer

Fleer scrapped its matte finish and produced Tradtion in 1998. This 250-card set, including 247 player cards and three checklists, is printed on a borderless design with the player's name, position and team printed across the bottom in gold foil. Tradition arrived with a parallel set called Heritage, which was numbered to 125 sets, and four different inserts, including Big Numbers, Rookie Sensations, Red Zone Rockers and Playmakers Theatre.

		NM/M
Complete Set (250):		45.00
Common Player:		.15
Minor Stars:		.30
Heritage Cards:		12X-25X
Heritage Rookies:		5X-12X
Production 125 Sets		
Pack (10):		1.75
Wax Box (36):		55.00
1	Brett Favre	3.00
2	Barry Sanders	2.50
3	John Elway	1.50
4	Emmitt Smith	2.50
5	Dan Marino	2.50
6	Eddie George	1.50
7	Jerry Rice	1.50
8	Jake Plummer	1.50
9	Joey Galloway	.30
10	Mike Alstott	.50
11	Brian Mitchell	.15
12	Keyshawn Johnson	.30
13	Jerald Moore	.15
14	Randal Hill	.15
15	Byron Hanspard	.15
16	Jeff George	.30
17	Terry Glenn	.30
18	Jerome Bettis	.30
19	Curtis Conway	.30
20	Fred Lane	.30
21	Isaac Bruce	.30
22	Tiki Barber	.30
23	Bobby Hoying	.15
24	Marcus Allen	.30
25	Dana Stubblefield	.15
26	Peter Boulware	.15
27	John Randle	.15
28	Jason Sehorn	.15
29	Rod Smith	.30
30	Michael Sinclair	.15
31	Marshall Faulk	.30
32	Karl Williams	.15
33	Kordell Stewart	1.50
34	Corey Dillon	1.00
35	Bryant Young	.15
36	Charlie Garner	.15
37	Andre Reed	.15
38	Ray Buchanan	.15
39	Brett Perriman	.15
40	Leon Lett	.15
41	Keenan McCardell	.15
42	Eric Swann	.15
43	Leslie Shepherd	.15
44	Curtis Martin	1.00
45	Andre Rison	.30
46	Keith Lyle	.15
47	Rae Carruth	.15
48	William Henderson	.15
49	Sean Dawkins	.15
50	Terrell Davis	1.00
51	Tim Brown	.30
52	Willie McGinest	.15
53	Jermaine Lewis	.15
54	Ricky Watters	.30
55	Freddie Jones	.15
56	Robert Smith	.30
57	Reidel Anthony	.15
58	James Stewart	.15
59	Earl Holmes	.15
60	Dale Carter	.15
61	Michael Irvin	.30
62	Jason Taylor	.15
63	Eric Metcalf	.15
64	LeRoy Butler	.15
65	Jamal Anderson	.30
66	Jamie Asher	.15
67	Chris Sanders	.15
68	Warren Sapp	.15
69	Ray Zellars	.15
70	Carl Pickens	.30
71	Garrison Hearst	.15
72	Eddie Kennison	.30
73	John Mobley	.15
74	Rob Johnson	.30
75	William Thomas	.15
76	Drew Bledsoe	1.50
77	Micheal Barrow	.15
78	Jim Harbaugh	.30
79	Terry McDaniel	.15
80	Johnnie Morton	.15
81	Danny Kanell	.15
82	Larry Centers	.15
83	Courtney Hawkins	.15
84	Tony Brackens	.15
85	Tony Gonzalez	.15
86	Aaron Glenn	.15
87	Cris Carter	.30
88	Chuck Smith	.15
89	Tamarick Vanover	.15
90	Karim Abdul-Jabbar	.30
91	Bryant Westbrook	.15
92	Mike Pritchard	.15
93	Darren Woodson	.15
94	Wesley Walls	.15
95	Tony Banks	.30
96	Michael Westbrook	.15
97	Shannon Sharpe	.30
98	Jeff Blake	.30
99	Terrell Owens	.30
100	Warrick Dunn	1.50
101	Levon Kirkland	.15
102	Frank Wycheck	.15
103	Gus Frerotte	.15
104	Simeon Rice	.15
105	Shawn Jefferson	.15
106	Irving Fryar	.15
107	Michael McCrary	.15
108	Robert Brooks	.15
109	Chris Chandler	.15
110	Junior Seau	.30
111	O.J. McDuffie	.15
112	Glenn Foley	.15
113	Darryl Williams	.15
114	Elvis Grbac	.15
115	Napoleon Kaufman	.50
116	Anthony Miller	.15
117	Troy Davis	.15
118	Charles Way	.15
119	Scott Mitchell	.15
120	Ken Harvey	.15
121	Tyrone Hughes	.15
122	Mark Brunell	1.25
123	David Palmer	.15
124	Rob Moore	.15
125	Kerry Collins	.75
126	Will Blackwell	.15
127	Ray Crockett	.15
128	Leslie O'Neal	.15
129	Antowain Smith	.75
130	Carlester Crumpler	.15
131	Michael Jackson	.15
132	Trent Dilfer	.30
133	Dan Williams	.15
134	Dorsey Levens	.30
135	Ty Law	.15
136	Rickey Dudley	.15
137	Jessie Tuggle	.15
138	Darrien Gordon	.15
139	Kevin Turner	.15
140	Willie Davis	.15
141	Zach Thomas	.15
142	Tony McGee	.15
143	Dexter Coakley	.15
144	Troy Brown	.15
145	Leeland McElroy	.15
146	Michael Strahan	.15
147	Ken Dilger	.15
148	Bryce Paup	.15
149	Herman Moore	.30
150	Reggie White	.30
151	DeWayne Washington	.15
152	Natrone Means	.30
153	Ben Coates	.15
154	Bert Emanuel	.15
155	Steve Young	1.00
156	Jimmy Smith	.15
157	Darrell Green	.15
158	Troy Aikman	1.50
159	Greg Hill	.15
160	Raymont Harris	.15
161	Troy Drayton	.15
162	Stevon Moore	.15
163	Warren Moon	.30
164	Wayne Martin	.15
165	Jason Gildon	.15
166	Chris Calloway	.15
167	Aeneas Williams	.15
168	Michael Bates	.15
169	Hugh Douglas	.15
170	Brad Johnson	.30
171	Bruce Smith	.15
172	Neil Smith	.15
173	James McKnight	.15
174	Robert Porcher	.15
175	Merton Hanks	.15
176	Ki-Jana Carter	.15
177	Mo Lewis	.15
178	Chester McGlockton	.15
179	Zack Crockett	.15
180	Derrick Thomas	.15
181	J.J. Stokes	.15
182	Derrick Rodgers	.15
183	Daryl Johnston	.15
184	Chris Penn	.15
185	Steve Atwater	.15
186	Amp Lee	.15
187	Frank Sanders	.15
188	Chris Slade	.15
189	Mark Chmura	.30
190	Kimble Anders	.15
191	Charles Johnson	.15
192	William Floyd	.15
193	Jay Graham	.15
194	Hardy Nickerson	.15
195	Terry Allen	.15
196	James Jett	.15
197	Jessie Armstead	.15
198	Yancey Thigpen	.15
199	Terance Mathis	.15
200	Steve McNair	.75
201	Wayne Chrebet	.15
202	Jamir Miller	.15
203	Duce Staley	.15
204	Deion Sanders	.75
205	Carnell Lake	.15
206	Ed McCaffrey	.15
207	Shawn Springs	.15
208	Tony Martin	.15
209	Jerris McPhail	.15
210	Darnay Scott	.15
211	Jake Reed	.15
212	Adrian Murrell	.30
213	Quinn Early	.15
214	Marvin Harrison	.30
215	Ryan McNeil	.15
216	Derrick Alexander	.15
217	Ray Lewis	.15
218	Antonio Freeman	.30
219	Dwayne Rudd	.15
220	Muhsin Muhammad	.15
221	Kevin Hardy	.15
222	Andre Hastings	.15
223	*John Avery*	2.00
224	*Keith Brooking*	1.00
225	*Kevin Dyson*	1.50
226	*Robert Edwards*	2.50
227	*Greg Ellis*	.15
228	*Curtis Enis*	2.00
229	*Terry Fair*	1.00
230	*Ahman Green*	6.00
231	*Jacquez Green*	2.00
232	*Brian Griese*	3.00
233	*Skip Hicks*	2.00
234	*Ryan Leaf*	2.00
235	*Peyton Manning*	8.00
236	*R.W. McQuarters*	.15
237	*Randy Moss*	6.00
238	*Marcus Nash*	2.00
239	*Anthony Simmons*	.50
240	*Brian Simmons*	1.00
241	*Takeo Spikes*	1.00
242	*Duane Starks*	.15
243	*Fred Taylor*	3.00
244	*Andre Wadsworth*	1.00
245	*Shaun Williams*	.15
246	*Grant Wistrom*	1.00
247	*Charles Woodson*	2.50
248	Checklist	.15
249	Checklist	.15
250	Checklist	.15

1998 Fleer Heritage

This parallel set was exclusive to hobby packs and was sequentially numbered to 125 sets. Heritage cards added a special foil treatment on the front and sequential numbering on the back.

Heritage Cards:	12X-25X
Heritage Rookies:	5X-10X

1998 Fleer Big Numbers

Big Numbers was a nine-card interactive set featuring top players at each skill position, with nine total players each featured on 11 different versions (0-9 and a wild card). The goal was to collect four cards, whereby the overprinted numbers, when combined, make out the players total yards through all games of Dec. 1, 1998. Winners were eligible to enter a contest for a chance to win a trip to the 2000 Pro Bowl. Big Numbers inserts were seeded one per four packs.

		NM/M
Common Player:		.25
BN1	Tim Brown	.25
BN2	Cris Carter	.25
BN3	Terrell Davis	1.00
BN4	John Elway	1.00
BN5	Brett Favre	2.00
BN6	Eddie George	1.00
BN7	Dorsey Levens	.50
BN8	Herman Moore	.50
BN9	Steve Young	.75

1998 Fleer Playmakers Theatre

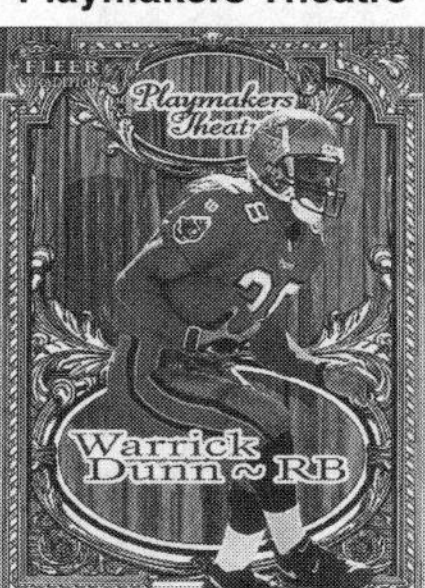

This 15-card insert set included the game's elite players on silver holofoil and sculpture embossing. Playmakers Theatre cards were sequentially numbered to 100 sets.

		NM/M
Complete Set (15):		400.00
Common Player:		20.00
Production 100 Sets		
PT1	Terrell Davis	70.00
PT2	Corey Dillon	60.00
PT3	Warrick Dunn	30.00
PT4	John Elway	100.00
PT5	Brett Favre	125.00
PT6	Antonio Freeman	20.00
PT7	Joey Galloway	20.00
PT8	Eddie George	40.00
PT9	Terry Glenn	20.00
PT10	Dan Marino	125.00
PT11	Curtis Martin	40.00
PT12	Jake Plummer	30.00
PT13	Barry Sanders	125.00
PT14	Deion Sanders	30.00
PT15	Kordell Stewart	25.00

1998 Fleer Red Zone Rockers

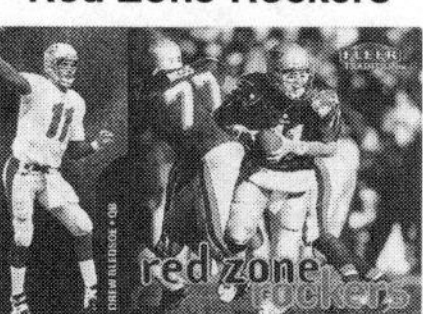

Red Zone Rockers were printed on a horizontal red laser holofoil and inserted one per 32 packs. The insert included 10 players who are best in the clutch.

		NM/M
Complete Set (10):		30.00
Common Player:		2.00
RZ1	Jerome Bettis	2.00
RZ2	Drew Bledsoe	5.00
RZ3	Mark Brunell	3.00
RZ4	Corey Dillon	4.00
RZ5	Joey Galloway	2.00
RZ6	Keyshawn Johnson	2.00
RZ7	Dorsey Levens	2.00
RZ8	Dan Marino	6.00
RZ9	Barry Sanders	6.00
RZ10	Emmitt Smith	6.00

1998 Fleer Rookie Sensations

This 15-card insert displayed the top rookies in 1998. Cards were embossed with spot UV coating and inserted one per 16 packs.

		NM/M
Complete Set (15):		40.00
Common Player:		2.00
RS1	John Avery	2.00
RS2	Keith Brooking	2.00
RS3	Kevin Dyson	4.00
RS4	Robert Edwards	2.00
RS5	Greg Ellis	2.00
RS6	Curtis Enis	2.00
RS7	Terry Fair	2.00
RS8	Ryan Leaf	2.00
RS9	Peyton Manning	15.00
RS10	Randy Moss	15.00
RS11	Marcus Nash	3.00
RS12	Fred Taylor	7.00
RS13	Andre Wadsworth	2.00
RS14	Grant Wistrom	2.00
RS15	Charles Woodson	5.00

1998 Fleer Brilliants

This was the premier issue of Brilliants by Fleer. The 150-card set is made up of 100 veterans and 50 rookies (inserted 1:2 packs). The product also included three parallel sets. The easiest being the Brilliant Blues with veterans found 1:3 packs and the rookies 1:6. Each single from this series has a blue background with the letter "B" prefix on the card number. The Brilliant Golds have a sparkling gold background on super bright mirror foil and the letter "G" prefix on the card number. Each single is sequentially numbered to 99. The rarest parallel is the 24-Karat Gold set. Each single has a sparkling gold background on rainbow holographic reflective mirror foil with an actual 24-kt. gold logo. Each single is sequentially numbered to 24.

		NM/M
Complete Set (150):		125.00
Common Player:		.15
Minor Stars:		.30
Common Rookie:		3.00
Inserted 1:2		
Blue Veterans:		2X-3X
Inserted 1:3		
Blue Rookies:		1.2X
Inserted 1:6		
Brilliant Gold Cards:		10X-20X
Brilliant Gold Rookies:		3X-5X
Production 99 Sets		
24-Karat Gold Cards:		20X-40X
24-Karat Gold Rookies:		5X-10X
Production 24 Sets		
Pack (5):		3.00
Wax Box (24):		60.00
1	John Elway	3.00
2	Curtis Conway	.30
3	Danny Wuerffel	.15
4	Emmitt Smith	4.50
5	Marvin Harrison	.30
6	Antowain Smith	.75
7	James Stewart	.15
8	Junior Seau	.30
9	Herman Moore	.50
10	Drew Bledsoe	2.00
11	Rae Carruth	.15
12	Trent Dilfer	.30
13	Derrick Alexander	.15
14	Ike Hilliard	.15
15	Bruce Smith	.15
16	Warren Moon	.30
17	Jermaine Lewis	.15
18	Mike Alstott	.50
19	Robert Brooks	.15
20	Jerome Bettis	.50
21	Brett Favre	6.00
22	Garrison Hearst	.50
23	Neil O'Donnell	.15
24	Joey Galloway	.50
25	Barry Sanders	5.00
26	Donnell Bennett	.15
27	Jamal Anderson	.75
28	Isaac Bruce	.30
29	Chris Chandler	.30
30	Kordell Stewart	2.00
31	Corey Dillon	1.75
32	Troy Aikman	3.00
33	Frank Sanders	.15
34	Cris Carter	.50
35	Greg Hill	.15
36	Tony Martin	.15
37	Shannon Sharpe	.30
38	Wayne Chrebet	.30
39	Trent Green	.30
40	Warrick Dunn	2.00
41	Michael Irvin	.30
42	Eddie George	2.00
43	Carl Pickens	.30
44	Wesley Walls	.15
45	Steve McNair	.75
46	Bert Emanuel	.15
47	Terry Glenn	.30
48	Elvis Grbac	.15
49	Charles Way	.15
50	Steve Young	1.75
51	Deion Sanders	.75
52	Keyshawn Johnson	.50
53	Kerry Collins	.30
54	O.J. McDuffie	.15
55	Ricky Watters	.30
56	Scott Mitchell	.15
57	Antonio Freeman	.50
58	Jake Plummer	2.00
59	Andre Reed	.15
60	Jerry Rice	3.00
61	Dorsey Levens	.50
62	Eddie Kennison	.30
63	Marshall Faulk	.50
64	Michael Jackson	.15
65	Karim Abdul-Jabbar	.30
66	Andre Rison	.15
67	Glenn Foley	.30
68	Jake Reed	.15
69	Tony Banks	.30
70	Dan Marino	4.50
71	Bryan Still	.15
72	Tim Brown	.30
73	Charles Johnson	.30
74	Jeff George	.30
75	Jimmy Smith	.30
76	Ben Coates	.30
77	Rob Moore	.15
78	Johnnie Morton	.15
79	Peter Boulware	.15
80	Curtis Martin	.75
81	James McKnight	.15
82	Danny Kanell	.15
83	Brad Johnson	.30
84	Amani Toomer	.15
85	Terry Allen	.30
86	Rod Smith	.30
87	Keenan McCardell	.30
88	Leslie Shepherd	.15
89	Irving Fryar	.15
90	Terrell Davis	2.00
91	Robert Smith	.50
92	Duce Staley	.15
93	Rickey Dudley	.15
94	Bobby Hoying	.15
95	Terrell Owens	.75
96	Fred Lane	.30
97	Natrone Means	.30
98	Yancey Thigpen	.15
99	Reggie White	.50
100	Mark Brunell	2.00
101	*Ahman Green*	15.00
102	*Skip Hicks*	4.00
103	*Hines Ward*	6.00
104	*Marcus Nash*	4.00
105	*Terry Hardy*	3.00
106	*Patrick Johnson*	4.00
107	*Tremayne Stephens*	3.00
108	*Joe Jurevicius*	4.00
109	*Moses Moreno*	4.00
110	*Charles Woodson*	4.00
111	*Kevin Dyson*	4.00
112	*Alvis Whitted*	3.00
113	*Michael Pittman*	3.00
114	*Stephen Alexander*	4.00
115	*Tavian Banks*	4.00
116	*John Avery*	4.00
117	*Keith Brooking*	3.00
118	*Jerome Pathon*	4.00
119	*Terry Fair*	4.00
120	*Peyton Manning*	20.00
121	*R.W. McQuarters*	4.00
122	*Charlie Batch*	3.00
123	*Jonathan Quinn*	4.00
124	*Chris Fuamatu-Ma'afala*	4.00
125	*Jacquez Green*	4.00
126	*Germane Crowell*	3.00
127	*Oronde Gadsden*	4.00
128	*Koy Detmer*	4.00
129	*Robert Holcombe*	5.00
130	*Curtis Enis*	3.00
131	*Brian Griese*	10.00
132	*Tony Simmons*	4.00
133	*Vonnie Holliday*	4.00
134	*Alonzo Mayes*	3.00
135	*Jon Ritchie*	4.00
136	*Robert Edwards*	4.00
137	*Mike Vanderjagt*	3.00
138	*Jonathon Linton*	3.00
139	*Fred Taylor*	6.00
140	*Randy Moss*	15.00
141	*Rod Rutledge*	3.00
142	*Andre Wadsworth*	4.00
143	*Rashaan Shehee*	4.00
144	*Shaun Williams*	3.00
145	*Mikhael Ricks*	3.00
146	*Wade Richey*	3.00
147	*Carlos King*	3.00
148	*Tim Dwight*	4.00
149	*Scott Frost*	4.00
150	*Ryan Leaf*	4.00

1998 Fleer Brilliants Illuminators

Each card in this 15-card set has the players team color in super bright mirror foil on the front. Singles can be found 1:10 packs.

		NM/M
Complete Set (15):		40.00
Common Player:		1.50
Minor Stars:		3.00
Inserted 1:10		
1	Robert Edwards	2.00
2	Fred Taylor	5.00
3	Kordell Stewart	3.00
4	Troy Aikman	6.00
5	Curtis Enis	2.00
6	Drew Bledsoe	6.00
7	Curtis Martin	4.00
8	Joey Galloway	3.00
9	Jerome Bettis	3.00
10	Glenn Foley	1.50
11	Karim Abdul-Jabbar	2.00
12	Jake Plummer	3.00
13	Jerry Rice	8.00
14	Charlie Batch	2.00
15	Jacquez Green	2.00

1998 Fleer Brilliants Shining Stars

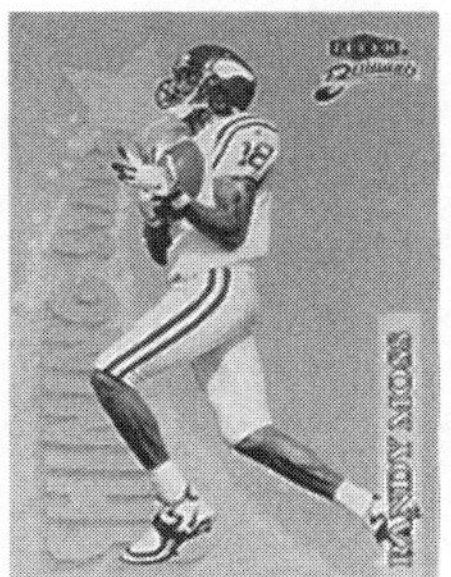

Singles in this insert are two-sided with super bright mirror foil and includes the top 15 players from the NFL. Singles were inserted 1:20 packs. A parallel version called Pulsars can also be found 1:400 packs.

		NM/M
Complete Set (15):		75.00
Common Player:		2.00
Inserted 1:20		
Pulsar Cards:		5X-10X
Inserted 1:400		
1	Terrell Davis	10.00
2	Emmitt Smith	15.00
3	Barry Sanders	15.00
4	Mark Brunell	5.00
5	Brett Favre	15.00
6	Ryan Leaf	2.00
7	Randy Moss	15.00
8	Warrick Dunn	3.00
9	Peyton Manning	12.00
10	Corey Dillon	4.00
11	Dan Marino	15.00
12	Keyshawn Johnson	2.00
13	John Elway	10.00
14	Eddie George	8.00
15	Antowain Smith	5.00

1999 Fleer

The 300-card set includes 50 unseeded rookies. The card fronts include the player's name and conference logo in blue foil for the NFC and red for the AFC. Inserts include: Trophy Case, Aerial Assault, Rookie Sensations, Under Pressure and Unsung Heroes.

		NM/M
Complete Set (300):		30.00
Common Player:		.10
Minor Stars:		.20
Common Rookie:		.40
Pack (10):		1.50
Wax Box (36):		40.00
1	Randy Moss	2.00
2	Peyton Manning	1.50
3	Barry Sanders	2.00
4	Terrell Davis	1.50
5	Brett Favre	2.50
6	Fred Taylor	1.00
7	Jake Plummer	.75
8	John Elway	1.50
9	Emmitt Smith	1.50
10	Kerry Collins	.20
11	Peter Boulware	.10
12	Jamal Anderson	.50
13	Doug Flutie	.50
14	Michael Bates	.10
15	Corey Dillon	.50
16	Curtis Conway	.20
17	Ty Detmer	.20
18	Robert Brooks	.10
19	Dale Carter	.10
20	Charlie Batch	.75
21	Ken Dilger	.10
22	Troy Aikman	1.00
23	Tavian Banks	.20
24	Cris Carter	.50
25	Derrick Alexander	.10
26	Chris Bordano	.10
27	Karim Abdul	.30
28	Jessie Armstead	.10
29	Drew Bledsoe	.75
30	Brian Dawkins	.10
31	Wayne Chrebet	.50
32	Garrison Hearst	.30
33	Eric Allen	.10
34	Tony Banks	.20
35	Jerome Bettis	.50
36	Stephen Alexander	.10
37	Rodney Harrison	.10
38	Mike Alstott	.50
39	Chad Brown	.10
40	Johnny McWilliams	.10
41	Kevin Dyson	.20
42	Keith Brooking	.10
43	Jim Harbaugh	.20
44	Bobby Engram	.10
45	John Holecek	.10
46	Steve Beuerlein	.10
47	Tony McGee	.10
48	Greg Ellis	.10
49	Corey Fuller	.10
50	Stephen Boyd	.10
51	Marshall Faulk	.50
52	Leroy Butler	.10
53	Reggie Barlow	.10
54	Randall Cunningham	.50
55	Aeneas Williams	.10
56	Kimble Anders	.10
57	Cameron Cleeland	.20
58	John Avery	.20
59	Gary Brown	.10
60	Ben Coates	.20
61	Koy Detmer	.10
62	Bryan Cox	.10
63	Edgar Bennett	.10
64	Tim Brown	.20
65	Isaac Bruce	.30
66	Eddie George	.75
67	Reidel Anthony	.20
68	Charlie Jones	.10
69	Terry Allen	.20
70	Joey Galloway	.50
71	Jamir Miller	.10
72	Will Blackwell	.10
73	Ray Buchanan	.10
74	Priest Holmes	.50
75	Michael Irvin	.20
76	Jonathon Linton	.10
77	Curtis Enis	.50
78	Neil O'Donnell	.20
79	Tim Biakabutuka	.20
80	Terry Kirby	.10
81	Germane Crowell	.20
82	Jason Elam	.10
83	Mark Chmura	.20
84	Marvin Harrison	.30
85	Jimmy Hitchcock	.10
86	Tony Brackens	.10
87	Sean Dawkins	.10
88	Tony Gonzalez	.20
89	Kent Graham	.10
90	Oronde Gadsden	.20
91	Hugh Douglas	.10
92	Robert Edwards	.30
93	R.W. McQuarters	.10
94	Aaron Glenn	.10
95	Kevin Carter	.10
96	Rickey Dudley	.10
97	Derrick Brooks	.10
98	Mark Bruener	.10
99	Darrell Green	.10
100	Jessie Tuggle	.10
101	Freddie Jones	.10
102	Rob Moore	.20
103	Ahman Green	.20
104	Chris Chandler	.20
105	Steve McNair	.50
106	Kevin Greene	.10
107	Jermaine Lewis	.20
108	Erik Kramer	.10
109	Eric Moulds	.50
110	Terry Fair	.10
111	Carl Pickens	.20
112	La'Roi Glover	.10
113	Chris Spielman	.10
114	Leroy Hoard	.10
115	Mark Brunell	.75
116	*Patrick Jeffers*	1.00
117	Elvis Grbac	.20
118	Ike Hilliard	.20
119	Sam Madison	.10
120	Terrell Owens	.50
121	Rich Gannon	.10
122	Skip Hicks	.50
123	Eric Green	.10
124	Trent Dilfer	.50
125	Terry Glenn	.30
126	Trent Green	.50
127	Charles Johnson	.10
128	Adrian Murrell	.20
129	Jason Gildon	.10
130	Tim Dwight	.50
131	Ryan Leaf	.50
132	Raghib Ismail	.10
133	Jon Kitna	.50
134	Alonzo Mayes	.10
135	Yancey Thigpen	.20
136	David LaFleur	.10
137	Ray Lewis	.10
138	Herman Moore	.50
139	Brian Griese	.30
140	Antonio Freeman	.50
141	Darnay Scott	.10
142	Ed McDaniel	.10
143	Andre Reed	.10
144	Andre Hastings	.10
145	Chris Warren	.10
146	Kevin Hardy	.10
147	Joe Jurevicius	.10
148	Jerome Pathon	.10
149	Duce Staley	.20
150	Dan Marino	1.50
151	Jerry Rice	1.00
152	Bam Morris	.20
153	Az-Zahir Hakim	.20
154	Ty Law	.10
155	Warrick Dunn	.50
156	Keyshawn Johnson	.50
157	Brian Mitchell	.10
158	James Jett	.10
159	Fred Lane	.10
160	Courtney Hawkins	.10
161	Andre Wadsworth	.20
162	Natrone Means	.30
163	Andrew Glover	.10
164	Anthony Simmons	.10
165	Leon Lett	.10
166	Frank Wycheck	.10
167	Barry Minter	.10
168	Michael McCrary	.10
169	Johnnie Morton	.10
170	Jay Riemersma	.10
171	Vonnie Holliday	.20
172	Brian Simmons	.10
173	Joe Johnson	.10
174	Ed McCaffrey	.30
175	Jason Sehorn	.10
176	Keenan McCardell	.10
177	Bobby Taylor	.10
178	Andre Rison	.20
179	Greg Hill	.10
180	O.J. McDuffie	.20
181	Darren Woodson	.10
182	Willie McGinest	.10
183	J.J. Stokes	.20
184	Leon Johnson	.10
185	Bert Emanuel	.10
186	Napoleon Kaufman	.50
187	Leslie Shepherd	.10
188	Levon Kirkland	.10
189	Simeon Rice	.10
190	Mikhael Ricks	.10
191	Robert Smith	.50
192	Michael Sinclair	.10
193	Muhsin Muhammad	.10
194	Duane Starks	.10
195	Terance Mathis	.10
196	Antowain Smith	.50
197	Tony Parrish	.10
198	Takeo Spikes	.10
199	Ernie Mills	.10
200	John Mobley	.10
201	Robert Porcher	.10
202	Pete Mitchell	.10
203	Darick Holmes	.10
204	Derrick Thomas	.20
205	David Palmer	.10
206	Jason Taylor	.10
207	Sammy Knight	.10
208	Dwayne Rudd	.10
209	Lawyer Milloy	.10
210	Michael Strahan	.10
211	Mo Lewis	.10
212	William Thomas	.10
213	Darrell Russell	.10
214	Brad Johnson	.50
215	Kordell Stewart	.50
216	Robert Holcombe	.20
217	Junior Seau	.20
218	Jacquez Green	.20
219	Shawn Springs	.10
220	Michael Westbrook	.20
221	Rod Woodson	.10
222	Frank Sanders	.20
223	Bruce Smith	.10
224	Eugene Robinson	.10
225	Bill Romanowski	.10
226	Wesley Walls	.10
227	Jimmy Smith	.20
228	Deion Sanders	.50
229	Lamar Thomas	.10
230	Dorsey Levens	.50
231	Tony Simmons	.20
232	John Randle	.10
233	Curtis Martin	.50
234	Bryant Young	.10
235	Charles Woodson	.50
236	Charles Way	.10
237	Zack Thomas	.20
238	Ricky Proehl	.10
239	Ricky Watters	.20
240	Hardy Nickerson	.10
241	Shannon Sharpe	.20
242	O.J. Santiago	.10
243	Vinny Testaverde	.20
244	Preston Roell	.10
245	James Stewart	.10
246	Jake Reed	.10
247	Steve Young	.75
248	Shaun Williams	.10
249	Rod Smith	.20
250	Warren Sapp	.10
251	*Champ Bailey*	1.50
252	*Karsten Bailey*	.40
253	*D'Wayne Bates*	.75
254	*Michael Bishop*	1.50
255	*David Boston*	2.50
256	*Na Brown*	.40
257	*Fernando Bryant*	.40
258	*Shawn Bryson*	.40
259	*Darrin Chiaverini*	.40
260	*Chris Claiborne*	.50
261	*Mike Cloud*	.40
262	*Cecil Collins*	1.00
263	*Tim Couch*	2.50
264	*Scott Covington*	.40
265	*Daunte Culpepper*	5.00
266	*Antwan Edwards*	.40
267	*Troy Edwards*	1.50
268	*Ebenezer Ekuban*	.75
269	*Kevin Faulk*	2.00
270	*Jermaine Fazande*	.40
271	*Joe Germaine*	1.25
272	*Martin Gramatica*	.40
273	*Torry Holt*	2.50
274	*Brock Huard*	.75
275	*Sedrick Irvin*	.75
276	*Sheldon Jackson*	.40
277	*Edgerrin James*	5.00
278	*James Johnson*	1.00
279	*Kevin Johnson*	1.50
280	*Malcolm Johnson*	.40
281	*Andy Katzenmoyer*	1.00
282	*Jevon Kearse*	2.00
283	*Patrick Kerney*	.40
284	*Shaun King*	1.00
285	*Jim Kleinsasser*	.40
286	*Rob Konrad*	.75
287	*Chris McAlister*	.75
288	*Donovan McNabb*	5.00
289	*Cade McNown*	1.00
290	*Dee Miller*	.40
291	*Joe Montgomery*	1.00
292	*De'Mond Parker*	.40
293	*Peerless Price*	2.00
294	*Akili Smith*	1.00
295	*Justin Swift*	.40
296	*Jerame Tuman*	.40
297	*Ricky Williams*	5.00
298	*Antoine Winfield*	.75
299	*Craig Yeast*	.40
300	*Amos Zereoue*	2.00

1999 Fleer Trophy Case

Trophy Case Cards:	100X-200X
Trophy Case Rookies:	20X-40X
Production 20 Sets	

1999 Fleer Aerial Assault

Each card is printed on plastic with silver holofoil featuring the NFL's top throwers and their targets. The 15 different singles were inserted 1:24 packs.

		NM/M
Complete Set (15):		50.00
Common Player:		1.00
Minor Stars:		2.00
Inserted 1:24		
1	Troy Aikman	4.00
2	Jamal Anderson	1.00
3	Charlie Batch	1.00
4	Mark Brunell	3.00
5	Terrell Davis	5.00
6	John Elway	7.00
7	Brett Favre	8.00
8	Keyshawn Johnson	2.00
9	Jon Kitna	1.00
10	Peyton Manning	5.00
11	Dan Marino	7.00
12	Randy Moss	7.00
13	Eric Moulds	1.00
14	Jake Plummer	2.00
15	Jerry Rice	6.00

1999 Fleer Fresh Ink

	NM/M
Complete Set (14):	750.00
Common Player:	25.00
Production 200 Sets	
Champ Bailey	40.00
David Boston	60.00
Chris Claiborne	25.00
Torry Holt	60.00
Edgerrin James	125.00
James Johnson	35.00
Kevin Johnson	60.00
Jevon Kearse	50.00
Shaun King	50.00
Rob Konrad	25.00
Donovan McNabb	100.00
Cade McNown	100.00
Akili Smith	75.00
Ricky Williams	175.00

1999 Fleer Rookie Sensations

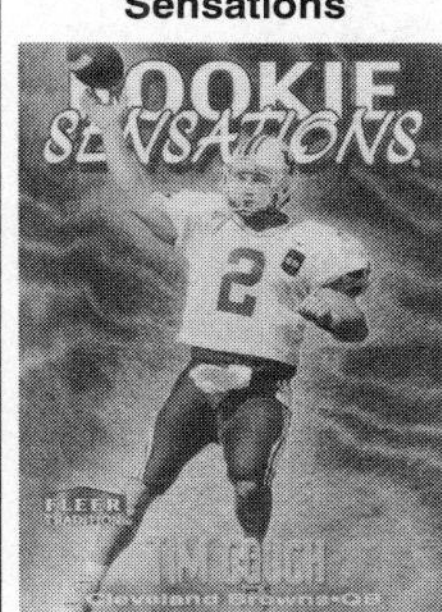

Rookies from the 1999 season are featured against team color backgrounds and glistening on silver foil fronts. The 20 different singles can be found 1:6 packs.

		NM/M
Complete Set (20):		40.00
Common Player:		1.00
Inserted 1:6		
1	Champ Bailey	2.00
2	Michael Bishop	2.50
3	David Boston	3.00
4	Chris Claiborne	1.00
5	Tim Couch	4.00
6	Daunte Culpepper	4.00
7	Troy Edwards	3.00
8	Kevin Faulk	3.00
9	Torry Holt	3.00
10	Brock Huard	2.00
11	Edgerrin James	5.00
12	Kevin Johnson	2.00
13	Shaun King	2.00
14	Rob Konrad	1.00
15	Chris McAlister	1.00
16	Donovan McNabb	4.00
17	Cade McNown	2.00
18	Peerless Price	2.50
19	Akili Smith	1.00
20	Ricky Williams	5.00

1999 Fleer Under Pressure

This 15-card set spotlights a sculpture embossed player image on patterned holofoil. Each is die-cut and found 1:96 packs.

		NM/M
Complete Set (15):		125.00
Common Player:		3.00
Inserted 1:96		
1	Charlie Batch	3.00
2	Terrell Davis	15.00
3	Warrick Dunn	6.00
4	John Elway	20.00
5	Brett Favre	25.00
6	Keyshawn Johnson	3.00
7	Peyton Manning	20.00
8	Dan Marino	25.00
9	Curtis Martin	12.00
10	Randy Moss	25.00
11	Jake Plummer	6.00
12	Barry Sanders	25.00
13	Emmitt Smith	25.00
14	Fred Taylor	10.00
15	Charles Woodson	3.00

1999 Fleer Unsung Heroes

This 30-card set picks one under-recognized star from each team and highlights him on card-board. Singles were inserted 1:3 packs.

		NM/M
Complete Set (30):		7.00
Common Player:		.25
Minor Stars:		.50
Inserted 1:3		
1	Tommy Bennett	.25
2	Lester Archambeau	.25
3	James Jones	.25
4	Phil Hansen	.25
5	Anthony Johnson	.25
6	Bobby Engram	.25
7	Eric Bienemy	.25
8	Daryl Johnston	.25
9	Maa Tanuvasa	.25
10	Stephen Boyd	.25
11	Adam Timmerman	.25
12	Ken Dilger	.25
13	Bryan Barker	.25
14	Rich Gannon	.25
15	O.J. Brigance	.25
16	Jeff Christy	.25
17	Shawn Jefferson	.25
18	Aaron Craver	.25
19	Chris Calloway	.25
20	Pepper Johnson	.25
21	Greg Biekert	.25
22	Duce Staley	.50
23	Courtney Hawkins	.25
24	Rodney Harrison	.25
25	Ray Brown	.25
26	Jon Kitna	.50
27	D'Marco Farr	.25
28	Brad Culpepper	.25
29	Steve Jackson	.25
30	Brian Mitchell	.25

1999 Fleer Focus

This 175-card set included 75 rookie cards found at four different levels. The 10 defensive rookies were found 1:4 packs. The 25 wide receiver rookies were sequentially numbered to 3,850. The 25 running backs were numbered to 2,500 and the 15 quarterbacks were numbered to 2,250. The Stealth insert was a parallel to the base and each was sequentially numbered to 300. Other inserts include: Feel the Game, Fresh Ink, Glimmer Men, Reflexions, Sparklers and Wondrous. SRP was $2.99 for five-card packs.

		NM/M
Complete Set (175):		200.00
Common Player:		.20
Minor Stars:		.40
Common Rookie (101-110):		.50
Inserted 1:4		
Common Rookie (111-135):		1.00
Production 3,850 Sets		
Common Rookie (136-160):		1.00
Production 2,500 Sets		
Common Rookie (161-175):		1.50
Production 2,250 Sets		
Pack (5):		3.00
Wax Box (24):		65.00
1	Randy Moss	2.00
2	Andre Rison	.40
3	Ed McCaffrey	.50
4	Jerry Rice	2.00
5	Tim Biakabutuka	.40
6	Wayne Chrebet	.75
7	Deion Sanders	.75
8	Ricky Watters	.50
9	Skip Hicks	.40
10	Charlie Batch	1.25
11	Joey Galloway	.75
12	Stephen Alexander	.20
13	Curtis Conway	.40
14	Garrison Hearst	.40
15	Kerry Collins	.40
16	Cris Carter	.75
17	Eddie George	1.00
18	Eric Moulds	.75
19	Vinny Testaverde	.40
20	Curtis Enis	.75
21	Gary Brown	.20
22	Junior Seau	.40
23	Kevin Dyson	.40
24	Jeff Blake	.40
25	Herman Moore	.75
26	Natrone Means	.50
27	Terry Glenn	.75
28	Fred Taylor	1.00
29	Ben Coates	.40
30	Corey Dillon	.75
31	Eddie Kennison	.20
32	Bam Morris	.20
33	Doug Pederson	.20
34	Jamal Anderson	.75
35	Michael Westbrook	.50
36	Peyton Manning	2.00
37	Carl Pickens	.40
38	Drew Bledsoe	1.50
39	Jim Harbaugh	.40
40	*Kurt Warner*	8.00
41	Mark Chmura	.40
42	Hines Ward	.40
43	Terry Kirby	.20

#	Player	Price
44	Brett Favre	4.00
45	Kordell Stewart	.75
46	Leslie Shepherd	.20
47	Marshall Faulk	.75
48	Troy Aikman	2.00
49	Isaac Bruce	.75
50	Michael Irvin	.40
51	Robert Smith	.75
52	Dorsey Levens	.75
53	Duce Staley	.50
54	Jake Plummer	1.50
55	Adrian Murrell	.40
56	Antonio Freeman	.75
57	Jerome Bettis	.75
58	Elvis Grbac	.40
59	Keyshawn Johnson	.75
60	Steve Beuerlein	.40
61	Yancey Thigpen	.20
62	Doug Flutie	.75
63	Jacquez Green	.40
64	Jimmy Smith	.75
65	Tim Brown	.50
66	Jason Sehorn	.20
67	Muhsin Muhammad	.40
68	Shannon Sharpe	.40
69	Terrell Owens	.75
70	Keenan McCardell	.40
71	Rich Gannon	.40
72	Scott Mitchell	.20
73	Warrick Dunn	.75
74	Brad Johnson	.75
75	Charles Johnson	.20
76	Chris Chandler	.40
77	Marcus Pollard	.20
78	Mike Alstott	.75
79	Bubby Brister	.40
80	Jon Kitna	1.00
81	Randall Cunningham	.75
82	Antowain Smith	.75
83	Curtis Martin	.75
84	Steve McNair	1.00
85	Tony Gonzalez	.40
86	O.J. McDuffie	.40
87	Steve Young	1.25
88	Terrell Davis	2.00
89	Mark Brunell	1.50
90	Napoleon Kaufman	.75
91	Priest Holmes	.75
92	Trent Dilfer	.50
93	Brian Griese	1.50
94	J.J. Stokes	.40
95	Karim Abdul	.40
96	Barry Sanders	3.00
97	Dan Marino	3.00
98	Emmitt Smith	3.00
99	Marvin Harrison	.75
100	Rod Smith	.50
101	*Champ Bailey*	2.00
102	*Fernando Bryant*	2.00
103	*Chris Claiborne*	2.00
104	*Antwan Edwards*	2.00
105	*Martin Gramatica*	1.00
106	*Andy Katzenmoyer*	2.50
107	*Jevon Kearse*	5.00
108	*Chris McAlister*	2.00
109	*Al Wilson*	2.00
110	*Antoine Winfield*	2.00
111	*Karsten Bailey*	4.00
112	*D'Wayne Bates*	4.00
113	*Marty Booker*	4.00
114	*David Boston*	12.00
115	*Na Brown*	3.00
116	*Desmond Clark*	3.00
117	*Dameane Douglas*	3.00
118	*Donald Driver*	20.00
119	*Troy Edwards*	4.00
120	*Torry Holt*	12.00
121	*Kevin Johnson*	1.00
122	*Reggie Kelly*	1.00
123	*Jim Kleinsasser*	2.00
124	*Jeremy McDaniel*	1.00
125	*Darnell McDonald*	1.00
126	*Travis McGriff*	1.00
127	*Billy Miller*	1.00
128	*Dee Miller*	1.00
129	*Peerless Price*	10.00
130	*Troy Smith*	1.00
131	*Brandon Stokley*	1.00
132	*Wane McGarity*	1.00
133	*Mark Campbell*	1.00
134	*Jerame Tuman*	1.00
135	*Craig Yeast*	1.00
136	*Jerry Azumah*	1.00
137	*Marlon Barnes*	1.00
138	*Michael Basnight*	1.00
139	*Shawn Bryson*	1.00
140	*Michael Cloud*	1.00
141	*Cecil Collins*	3.00
142	*Autry Denson*	1.00
143	*Kevin Faulk*	3.00
144	*Jermaine Fazande*	1.00
145	*Jim Finn*	1.00
146	*Madre Hill*	1.00
147	*Sedrick Irvin*	2.00
148	*Terry Jackson*	1.00
149	*Edgerrin James*	25.00
150	*J.J. Johnson*	2.00
151	*Rob Konrad*	2.00
152	*Joel Makovicka*	1.00
153	*Cecil Martin*	2.00
154	*Joe Montgomery*	1.00
155	*Demonn Parker*	1.00
156	*Sirr Parker*	1.00
157	*Jeff Paulk*	1.00
158	*Nick Williams*	1.00
159	*Ricky Williams*	20.00
160	*Amos Zereoue*	4.00
161	*Michael Bishop*	4.00
162	*Aaron Brooks*	25.00
163	*Tim Couch*	10.00
164	*Scott Covington*	4.00
165	*Daunte Culpepper*	25.00
166	*Kevin Daft*	2.00
167	*Joe Germaine*	2.00
168	*Chris Greisen*	2.00
169	*Brock Huard*	3.00
170	*Shaun King*	3.00
171	*Cory Sauter*	2.00
172	*Donovan McNabb*	25.00
173	*Cade McNown*	4.00
174	*Chad Plummer*	2.00
175	*Akili Smith*	4.00

1999 Fleer Focus Stealth

This was a 175-card parallel to the base set. Each single was sequentially numbered to 300.

	NM/M
Stealth Cards:	3X-5X
Stealth Rookies:	2X
Production 300 Sets	

1999 Fleer Focus Feel the Game

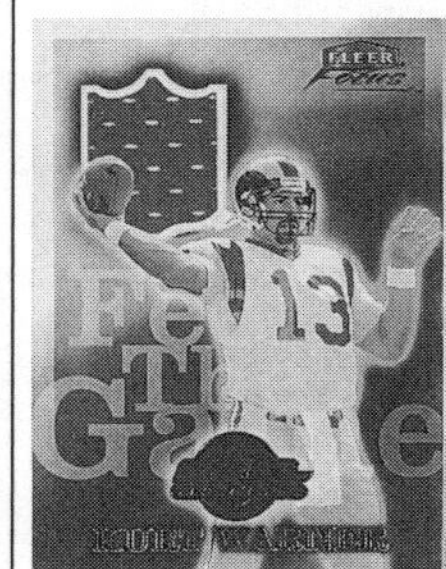

This 10-card insert set included pieces of game-used jerseys except for the Brett Favre single which included a piece of game-worn shoes. Singles were inserted 1:192 packs.

		NM/M
Common Player:		20.00
Inserted 1:192		
1	Vinny Testaverde	20.00
2	Mark Brunell	35.00
3	Brett Favre Shoes	125.00
4	Fred Taylor	35.00
5	Jeff Blake	20.00
6	Emmitt Smith	100.00
7	Joe Germaine	20.00
8	Cecil Collins	25.00
9	Charles Woodson	35.00
10	Kurt Warner	50.00

1999 Fleer Focus Fresh Ink

This 37-card insert set included autographs of both veterans and rookies. Each single was hand-numbered and found 1:48 packs.

	NM/M
Complete Set (37):	1,250
Common Player:	10.00
Minor Stars:	20.00
Inserted 1:48	
Reidel Anthony	10.00
Charlie Batch	15.00
Jeff Blake	10.00
Darrin Chiaverini	10.00
Wayne Chrebet	20.00
Daunte Culpepper	45.00
Terrell Davis	75.00
Koy Detmer	10.00
Corey Dillon	30.00
Troy Edwards	30.00
Doug Flutie	40.00
Eddie George	30.00
Trent Green	10.00
Marvin Harrison	25.00
Torry Holt	30.00
Sedrick Irvin	20.00
Edgerrin James	75.00
Brad Johnson	20.00
Charles Johnson	10.00
Jon Kitna	30.00
Jim Kleinsasser	10.00
Peyton Manning	120.00
O.J. McDuffie	10.00
Travis McGriff	10.00
Donovan McNabb	45.00
Cade McNown	15.00
Joe Montgomery	20.00
Randy Moss	125.00
Jake Plummer	25.00
Akili Smith	25.00
Antowain Smith	20.00
Duce Staley	20.00
Brandon Stokley	10.00
Fred Taylor	50.00
Vinny Testaverde	20.00
Ricky Williams	150.00
Steve Young	50.00

1999 Fleer Focus Glimmer Men

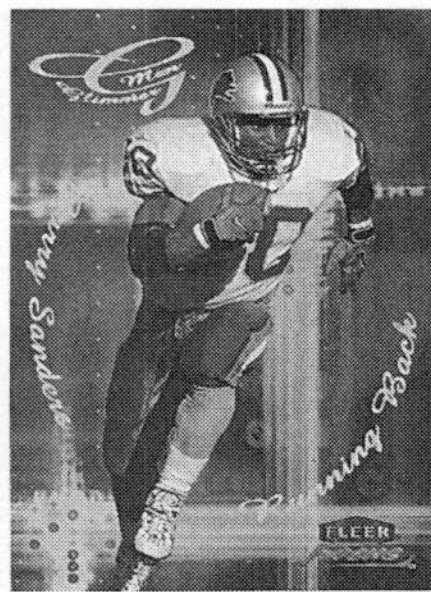

This 10-card insert set included stars from the NFL and were printed with silver and gold foil. Singles were inserted 1:20 packs.

		NM/M
Complete Set (10):		30.00
Common Player:		2.00
Inserted 1:20		
1	Tim Couch	4.00
2	Barry Sanders	6.00
3	Terrell Davis	4.00
4	Dan Marino	6.00
5	Troy Aikman	4.00
6	Brett Favre	6.00
7	Randy Moss	6.00
8	Emmitt Smith	6.00
9	Edgerrin James	4.00
10	Fred Taylor	2.00

1999 Fleer Focus Reflexions

This 10-card insert set was a parallel to the Glimmer Men insert. Each single was sequentially numbered to 100.

		NM/M
Complete Set (10):		250.00
Common Player:		20.00
Production 100 Sets		
1	Tim Couch	35.00
2	Barry Sanders	50.00
3	Terrell Davis	35.00
4	Dan Marino	35.00
5	Troy Aikman	25.00
6	Brett Favre	50.00
7	Randy Moss	35.00
8	Emmitt Smith	35.00
9	Edgerrin James	45.00
10	Fred Taylor	20.00

1999 Fleer Focus Sparklers

This 15-card insert set highlighted the top rookies from 1999. Singles were found 1:10 packs.

		NM/M
Complete Set (15):		20.00
Common Player:		1.00
Inserted 1:10		
1	Tim Couch	4.00
2	Donovan McNabb	4.00
3	Akili Smith	2.00
4	Cade McNown	1.00
5	Daunte Culpepper	4.00
6	Ricky Williams	5.00
7	Edgerrin James	5.00
8	Kevin Faulk	1.00
9	Torry Holt	2.00
10	David Boston	3.00
11	Sedrick Irvin	1.00
12	Peerless Price	3.00
13	Troy Edwards	1.00
14	Brock Huard	1.00
15	Shaun King	1.00

1999 Fleer Focus Wondrous

This was a 20-card insert set that pictured each star on silver holo foil with gold foil stamping. Singles were found 1:20 packs.

		NM/M
Complete Set (20):		40.00
Common Player:		1.00
Inserted 1:20		
1	Peyton Manning	5.00
2	Fred Taylor	3.00
3	Tim Couch	4.00
4	Charlie Batch	1.00
5	Jerry Rice	4.00
6	Randy Moss	5.00
7	Warrick Dunn	1.00
8	Mark Brunell	2.00
9	Emmitt Smith	5.00
10	Eddie George	1.00
11	Brian Griese	2.00
12	Terrell Davis	4.00
13	Dan Marino	5.00
14	Ricky Williams	5.00
15	Brett Favre	5.00
16	Jake Plummer	1.00
17	Troy Aikman	3.00
18	Drew Bledsoe	3.00
19	Edgerrin James	4.00
20	Cade McNown	1.00

1999 Fleer Mystique

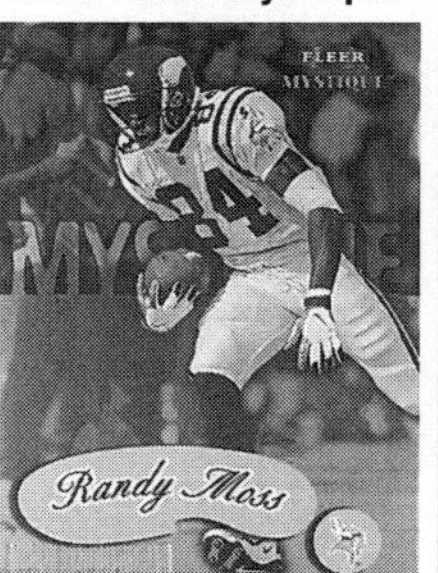

The 160-card set included 50 short-printed rookie cards that were sequentially numbered to 2,999 and 10 veteran stars numbered to 2,500. Parallel sets of Gold and Masterpieces were made for the first 100 cards in the base set. Other insert sets included: Feel the Game, Fresh Ink, NFL 2000, Potential and Star Power. SRP was $4.99 for four-card packs.

		NM/M
Complete Set (160):		450.00
Common Player:		.25
Minor Stars:		.50
Common SP (1-100):		1.50
Common Rookie:		2.00
Production 2,999 Sets		
Common Player (151-160):		2.00
Production 2,500 Sets		
Pack (4):		4.00
Wax Box (24):		90.00
1	Terrell Davis SP	2.00
2	Jerome Bettis SP	1.50
3	J.J. Stokes	.50
4	Frank Wycheck	.25
5	O.J. McDuffie	.25
6	Johnnie Morton	.25
7	Marshall Faulk SP	1.50
8	Ryan Leaf	.75
9	Sean Dawkins	.25
10	Brett Favre SP	6.00
11	Steve Young SP	2.50
12	Jimmy Smith	.75
13	Isaac Bruce	.75
14	Trent Dilfer	.50
15	Brian Mitchell	.25
16	Kordell Stewart SP	1.50
17	Herman Moore	.75
18	Troy Aikman SP	3.00
19	Cris Carter	.75
20	Barry Sanders SP	6.00
21	Tony Gonzalez	.50
22	Skip Hicks	.50
23	Steve McNair SP	1.50
24	Brad Johnson	.75
25	Mark Chmura	.50
26	Randall Cunningham SP	1.50
27	Jerry Rice SP	3.00
28	Jamie Asher	.25
29	Brian Griese SP	2.50
30	Peyton Manning SP	4.00
31	Keith Poole	.25
32	Wayne Chrebet	.75
33	Rich Gannon	.50
34	Michael Irvin	.50
35	Yancey Thigpen	.50
36	Corey Dillon	.75
37	Steve Beurlein	.50
38	Terry Kirby	.25
39	Jacquez Green	.50
40	Mark Brunell SP	2.50
41	Rickey Dudley	.50
42	Shannon Sharpe	.75
43	Andre Rison	.50
44	Chris Chandler	.50
45	Fred Taylor SP	3.00
46	Kerry Collins	.50
47	Antowain Smith SP	1.50
48	Wesley Walls	.50
49	Rob Moore	.50
50	Dan Marino SP	4.00
51	Robert Smith	.75
52	Keenan McCardell	.50
53	Joey Galloway	.75
54	Fred Lane	.50
55	Napoleon Kaufman	.75
56	Curtis Martin	.75
57	Rod Smith	.75
58	Curtis Conway	.50
59	Kevin Dyson	.25
60	Warrick Dunn SP	1.50
61	Ahman Green	.50
62	Duce Staley	.75
63	Emmitt Smith SP	4.00
64	Adrian Murrell	.25
65	Dorsey Levens	.75
66	Drew Bledsoe SP	2.50
67	Ed McCaffery	.75
68	Natrone Means	.50
69	Deion Sanders	.50
70	Keyshawn Johnson SP	1.50
71	Antonio Freeman	.75
72	James Stewart	.50
73	Ben Coates	.50
74	Priest Holmes	.75
75	Jake Reed	.50
76	Mike Alstott	.75
77	Vinny Testaverde	.50
78	Ricky Watters	.50
79	Garrison Hearst	.50
80	Junior Seau	.50
81	Tim Brown	.50
82	Jamal Anderson	.75
83	Robert Brooks	.25
84	Marc Edwards	.25
85	Curtis Enis	.75
86	Doug Flutie	.50
87	Terry Glenn	.75
88	Charlie Batch SP	2.00
89	Marvin Harrison	.75
90	Jake Plummer SP	3.00
91	Terrell Owens	.75
92	Scott Mitchell	.25
93	Tim Dwight	.75
94	Eddie George SP	1.50
95	Ike Hilliard	.50
96	Robert Holcombe	.25
97	Charles Johnson	.25
98	Eric Moulds	.75
99	Michael Westbrook	.75
100	Randy Moss SP	6.00
101	*Tim Couch*	12.00
102	*Donovan McNabb*	30.00
103	*Akili Smith*	3.00
104	*Cade McNown*	3.00
105	*Daunte Culpepper*	30.00
106	*Ricky Williams*	20.00
107	*Edgerrin James*	30.00
108	*Kevin Faulk*	4.00
109	*Torry Holt*	15.00
110	*David Boston*	15.00
111	*Chris Claiborne*	2.00
112	*Mike Cloud*	2.00
113	*Joe Germaine*	2.00
114	*Cecil Collins*	4.00
115	*Tim Alexander*	2.00
116	*Brandon Stokley*	2.00
117	*Lamarr Glenn*	2.00
118	*Shawn Bryson*	2.00
119	*Jeff Paulk*	2.00
120	*Kevin Johnson*	8.00
121	*Charlie Rogers*	2.00
122	*Joe Montgomery*	2.00
123	*Travis McGriff*	2.00
124	*Dee Miller*	2.00
125	*Rob Konrad*	3.00
126	*Peerless Price*	12.00
127	*D'Wayne Bates*	4.00
128	*Craig Yeast*	2.00
129	*Malcolm Johnson*	2.00
130	*Brock Huard*	4.00
131	*Sedrick Irvin*	3.00
132	*Troy Smith*	2.00
133	*Troy Edwards*	6.00
134	*Al Wilson*	2.00
135	*Terry Jackson*	3.00
136	*Dameane Douglas*	2.00
137	*Amos Zereoue*	8.00
138	*Shaun King*	4.00
139	*James Johnson*	2.00
140	*Jermaine Fazande*	2.00
141	*Autry Denson*	3.00
142	*Darren Hall*	2.00
143	*Na Brown*	2.00
144	*Mike Lucky*	2.00
145	*Karsten Bailey*	4.00
146	*Kevin Daft*	2.00
147	*Sean Bennett*	2.00
148	*Madre Hill*	2.00
149	*Michael Bishop*	6.00
150	*Scott Covington*	2.00
151	Randy Moss STAR	20.00
152	Fred Taylor STAR	10.00
153	Brett Favre STAR	20.00
154	Dan Marino STAR	15.00
155	Terrell Davis STAR	15.00
156	Barry Sanders STAR	20.00
157	Emmitt Smith STAR	15.00
158	Jake Plummer STAR	3.00
159	Warrick Dunn STAR	3.00
160	Troy Aikman STAR	10.00

1999 Fleer Mystique Gold

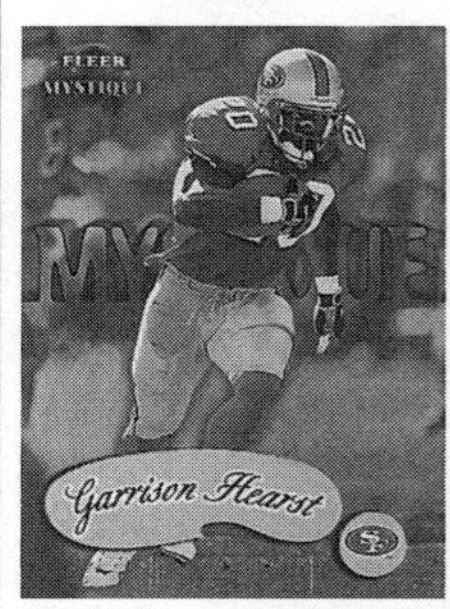

This was a parallel to the first 100 cards in the set. The name is in gold foil rather than silver as in the base set. Singles were randomly inserted.

	NM/M
Gold Cards:	2X-4X

1999 Fleer Mystique Feel The Game

This 10-card insert set featured a piece of game-used memorabilia. Each single was hand-numbered and randomly inserted.

	NM/M
Common Player:	10.00
Terrell Davis jersey 510	40.00
Charles Johnson shoes 325	10.00
Jon Kitna shorts 640	10.00
Dorsey Levens jersey 515	15.00
Dan Marino socks 220	80.00
Curtis Martin jersey 690	35.00
Johnnie Morton jersey 580	10.00
Randy Moss jersey 510	50.00
Brandon Stokley gloves 85	15.00
Steve Young jersey 580	35.00

1999 Fleer Mystique Fresh Ink

This 30-card insert set ncluded autographs of both veterans and rookies. Each single was hand-numbered and randomly inserted.

		NM/M
Common Player:		10.00
Minor Stars:		20.00
1	Charlie Batch 250	15.00
2	Mark Brunell 45	50.00
3	Shawn Bryson 650	10.00
4	Cecil Collins 725	35.00
5	Daunte Culpepper 300	60.00
6	Randall Cunningham 200	35.00
7	Terrell Davis 50	100.00
8	Sean Dawkins 700	10.00
9	Corey Dillon 250	30.00
10	Dameane Douglas 750	10.00
11	Tim Dwight 725	20.00
12	Troy Edwards 200	50.00
13	Doug Flutie 250	50.00
14	Eddie George 250	35.00
15	Joe Germaine 575	10.00
16	Trent Green 350	20.00
17	Torry Holt 350	40.00
18	Brock Huard 700	20.00
19	Edgerrin James 150	100.00
20	Brad Johnson 300	25.00
21	Jon Kitna 350	40.00
22	Peyton Manning250	150.00
23	Randy Moss 150	150.00
24	Doug Peterson 750	10.00
25	Jake Plummer 300	25.00
26	Peerless Price 675	40.00
27	Akili Smith 100	20.00
28	Antowain Smith 150	45.00
29	Emmitt Smith 125	150.00
30	Ricky Williams 150	100.00

1999 Fleer Mystique NFL 2000

This 10-card insert set included players who are ready for superstardom. Each single was sequentially numbered to 999.

		NM/M
Complete Set (10):		30.00
Common Player:		1.00
Production 999 Sets		
1	Peyton Manning	10.00
2	Ryan Leaf	1.00
3	Charlie Batch	1.00
4	Fred Taylor	4.00
5	Keyshawn Johnson	3.00
6	J.J. Stokes	1.00
7	Jake Plummer	2.00
8	Brian Griese	3.00
9	Antowain Smith	3.00
10	Jamal Anderson	5.00

1999 Fleer Mystique Pro-Tential

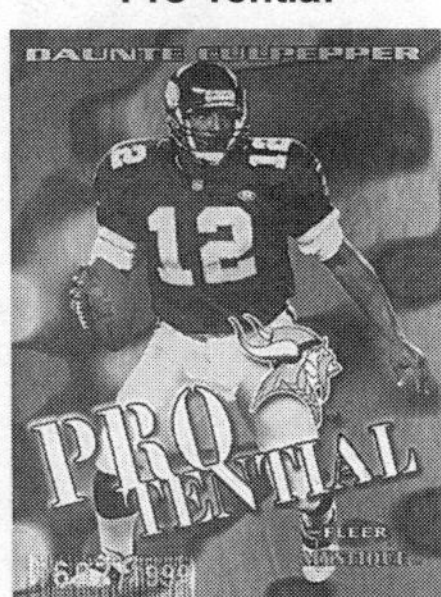

This 10-card insert set included the top rookies from 1999. Each of these singles was sequentially numbered to 1,999.

		NM/M
Complete Set (10):		35.00
Common Player:		2.00
Production 1,999 Sets		
1	Tim Couch	8.00
2	Donovan McNabb	10.00
3	Akili Smith	3.00
4	Cade McNown	3.00
5	Daunte Culpepper	8.00
6	Ricky Williams	10.00
7	Edgerrin James	10.00
8	Kevin Faulk	2.00
9	Torry Holt	4.00
10	David Boston	5.00

1999 Fleer Mystique Star Power

This 10-card insert set included the superstars from the NFL and featured them on a plastic card with a full silver-metallic holofoil background. Each single was sequentially numbered to 100.

		NM/M
Complete Set (10):		200.00
Common Player:		10.00
Production 100 Sets		
1	Randy Moss	40.00
2	Warrick Dunn	10.00
3	Mark Brunell	15.00
4	Emmitt Smith	40.00
5	Eddie George	10.00
6	Barry Sanders	40.00
7	Terrell Davis	30.00
8	Dan Marino	40.00
9	Troy Aikman	30.00
10	Brett Favre	40.00

2000 Fleer

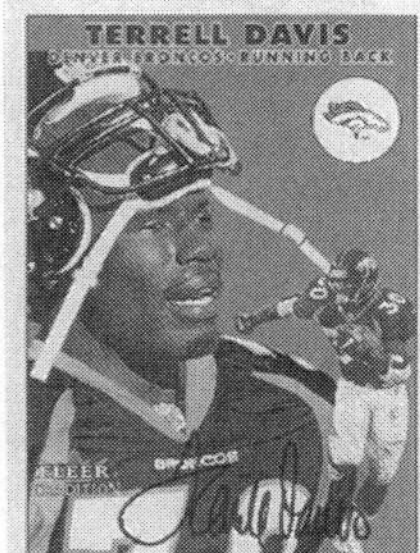

		NM/M
Complete Set (400):		40.00
Common Player:		.10
Minor Stars:		.20
Common Rookie:		.30
Pack (10):		1.50
Wax Box (36):		35.00
1	Kevin Johnson	.30
2	Chris Chandler	.20
3	Peerless Price	.30
4	Andre Rison	.20
5	Curtis Enis	.20
6	Tim Couch	1.00
7	Brian Dawkins	.10
8	Akili Smith	.40
9	Kevin Faulk	.30
10	Joey Galloway	.40
11	Bill Romanowski	.10
12	Charlie Batch	.40
13	Terrence Wilkins	.30
14	Kevin Hardy	.10
15	Cade McNown	.75
16	Elvis Grbac	.20
17	Cris Carter	.40
18	Willie McGinest	.10
19	Michael Bishop	.30
20	Lee Woodall	.10
21	Jake Reed	.20
22	Bryan Cox	.10
23	Chris Sanders	.10
24	Tavian Banks	.20
25	Levon Kirkland	.10
26	James Hundon	.10
27	Junior Seau	.20
28	Darren Woodson	.10
29	Kevin Carter	.10
30	Joe Jurevicius	.10
31	John Lynch	.10
32	Steve McNair	.40
33	Jake Plummer	.40
34	Antonio Freeman	.40
35	Peter Boulware	.10
36	Brad Johnson	.40
37	Bobby Engram	.10
38	David Boston	.40
39	Jason Tucker	.20
40	Troy Brown	.10
41	Brian Griese	.50
42	Dorsey Levens	.40
43	Cornelius Bennett	.10
44	Donovan McNabb	.75
45	Rob Johnson	.30
46	Robert Smith	.40
47	Stanley Pritchett	.10
48	Tedy Bruschi	.10
49	Dan Marino	1.25
50	Amani Toomer	.20
51	Aaron Glenn	.10
52	Rickey Dudley	.20
53	Tim Brown	.30
54	Jim Harbaugh	.20
55	Terrell Owens	.40
56	Jason Sehorn	.10
57	Cortez Kennedy	.10
58	London Fletcher	.10
59	Simeon Rice	.10
60	Shaun King	.75
61	Stephen Davis	.40
62	Andre Wadsworth	.10
63	Kyle Brady	.10
64	Priest Holmes	.30
65	Patrick Jeffers	.40
66	Barry Minter	.10
67	Curtis Martin	.40
68	Darrin Chiaverini	.10
69	Robert Thomas	.10
70	Samari Rolle	.10
71	Robert Porcher	.10
72	Jerry Rice	1.00
73	Bill Schroeder	.20
74	Chad Bratzke	.10
75	Tony Brackens	.10
76	O.J. McDuffie	.20
77	John Randle	.20
78	Michael Pittman	.20
79	Drew Bledsoe	.75
80	Ike Hilliard	.20
81	Victor Green	.10
82	Duce Staley	.40
83	Bruce Smith	.10
84	Amos Zereoue	.20
85	Charlie Garner	.30
86	Shawn Springs	.10
87	Kurt Warner	1.00
88	Eddie George	.50
89	Michael Westbrook	.30
90	Dexter Coakley	.10
91	Rob Moore	.20
92	Duane Starks	.10
93	Steve Beuerlein	.20
94	Marty Booker	.10
95	Karim Abdul	.10
96	Troy Aikman	1.00
97	Germane Crowell	.40
98	Matt Hasselbeck	.20
99	E.G. Green	.10
100	Mark Brunell	.75
101	Tony Martin	.10
102	Darrell Green	.10
103	Ricky Williams	1.00
104	Michael Strahan	.10
105	Vinny Testaverde	.30
106	Charles Johnson	.10
107	Hines Ward	.30
108	Bryant Young	.10
109	Mo Lewis	.10
110	Greg Clark	.10
111	Jon Kitna	.30
112	Jacquez Green	.20
113	Kevin Dyson	.20
114	Stephen Alexander	.10
115	Cameron Cleeland	.20
116	Keith Poole	.10
117	Az-Zahir Hakim	.20
118	Tim Dwight	.30
119	Corey Bradford	.20
120	Carlos Emmons	.10
121	Trent Dilfer	.20
122	Lance Schulters	.10
123	Byron Hanspard	.10
124	Tim Biakabutuka	.20
125	Eddie Kennison	.10
126	Terry Kirby	.10
127	Mike McKenzie	.10
128	Fred Beasley	.10
129	Chad Brown	.10
130	Terrell Davis	1.00
131	Herman Moore	.30
132	Vonnie Holliday	.10
133	Jim Miller	.10
134	Peyton Manning	1.25
135	Derrick Alexander	.10
136	Oronde Gadsden	.20
137	Robert Griffith	.10
138	Troy Edwards	.30
139	Damon Huard	.40
140	Jessie Armstead	.10
141	Charles Woodson	.30
142	Troy Vincent	.10
143	Natrone Means	.20
144	Jeff Garcia	.50
145	Terry Glenn	.40
146	Marshall Faulk	.40
147	Patrick Johnson	.20
148	Frank Wycheck	.10
149	Champ Bailey	.30
150	Jamal Anderson	.40
151	Doug Flutie	.50
152	Michael Bates	.10
153	Corey Dillon	.40
154	Keith McKenzie	.10
155	Orpheus Roye	.10
156	Olandis Gary	.50
157	Johnnie Morton	.20
158	Brett Favre	1.50
159	Adrian Murrell	.20
160	Fred Taylor	.60
161	Tony Gonzalez	.30
162	Zach Thomas	.30
163	Randy Moss	1.25
164	Marcus Robinson	.40
165	Tiki Barber	.30
166	Rich Gannon	.30
167	Jeremiah Trotter	.10
168	Jermaine Fazande	.20
169	Steve Young	.75
170	Isaac Bruce	.40
171	Warrick Dunn	.40
172	Yancey Thigpen	.20
173	Rod Smith	.30
174	Albert Connell	.20
175	Freddie Jones	.20
176	Terance Mathis	.10
177	Eric Moulds	.40
178	Brian Mitchell	.10
179	Wesley Walls	.20
180	Carl Pickens	.20
181	Errict Rhett	.20
182	Madre Hill	.10
183	Jason Elam	.10
184	Greg Ellis	.10
185	David Sloan	.10
186	Edgerrin James	1.50
187	Jimmy Smith	.40
188	Tony Richardson	.10
189	James Hasty	.10
190	Sam Madison	.10
191	Tony Simmons	.10
192	Andre Hastings	.10
193	Keyshawn Johnson	.40
194	Na Brown	.10
195	Napoleon Kaufman	.30
196	Torrance Small	.10
197	Curtis Conway	.20
198	Jeff Graham	.10
199	Jason Hanson	.10
200	Derrick Mayes	.20
201	Torry Holt	.40
202	Warren Sapp	.20
203	Kimble Anders	.10
204	Blaine Bishop	.10
205	Leroy Hoard	.10
206	Larry Centers	.10
207	O.J. Santiago	.10
208	Antowain Smith	.20
209	Chuck Smith	.10
210	Takeo Spikes	.10
211	Raghib Ismail	.10
212	Ed McCaffrey	.30
213	Karsten Bailey	.10
214	Terry Fair	.10
215	Ken Dilger	.10
216	Jamie Martin	.10
217	Cris Dishman	.10
218	Jay Fiedler	.40
219	Lawyer Milloy	.10
220	*Jake Delhomme*	2.00
221	Wayne Chrebet	.30
222	Darrell Russell	.10
223	Christian Fauria	.10
224	Jerome Bettis	.40
225	Ryan Leaf	.40
226	Ricky Watters	.30
227	Keenan McCardell	.20
228	Grant Wistrom	.10
229	Jevon Kearse	.40
230	Frank Sanders	.20
231	Shannon Sharpe	.20
232	Jonathon Linton	.20
233	Alonzo Mayes	.10
234	Jason Garrett	.10
235	Kordell Stewart	.40
236	David LaFleur	.10
237	Kenny Bynum	.10
238	Byron Chamberlain	.10
239	Tyrone Davis	.10
240	Jerome Pathon	.10
241	Alvis Whitted	.10
242	Kevin Lockett	.10
243	Matthew Hatchette	.20
244	Rod Woodson	.10
245	Joe Horn	.20
246	Ronnie Powell	.10
247	Dedric Ward	.10
248	J.J. Johnson	.10
249	James Jett	.10
250	*Bobby Shaw*	.50
251	J.J. Stokes	.20
252	Paul Shields	.10
253	Sean Dawkins	.10
254	Hardy Nickerson	.10
255	Stephen Boyd	.10
256	Chris Warren	.20
257	Kerry Collins	.30
258	Isaac Byrd	.10
259	Bobby Hoying	.20
260	Daunte Culpepper	.75
261	Moe Williams	.10
262	Kamil Loud	.10
263	Derrick Brooks	.10
264	Jay Riemersma	.20
265	Ray Lucas	.30
266	Jason Gildon	.10
267	James Stewart	.30
268	Marcellus Wiley	.10
269	Craig Yeast	.10
270	Michael Basnight	.10
271	Tyrone Wheatley	.30
272	Martin Gramatica	.10
273	Phillip Daniels	.10
274	Richard Huntley	.20
275	Muhsin Muhammad	.30
276	Todd Lyght	.10
277	Carlester Crumpler	.10
278	Jeff Lewis	.10
279	Jeff George	.40
280	Jeff Blake	.30
281	Mike McCrary	.10
282	Shawn Jefferson	.10
283	Mark Bruener	.10
284	Donnie Abraham	.10
285	Yatil Green	.10
286	Jermaine Lewis	.20
287	Rob Fredrickson	.10
288	Thurman Thomas	.20
289	Kent Graham	.10
290	Darnay Scott	.30
291	Tony Graziani	.10
292	Qadry Ismail	.10
293	Aeneas Williams	.10
294	Marvin Harrison	.40
295	Jimmy Hitchcock	.10
296	Bob Christian	.10
297	Pete Mitchell	.10
298	Mike Alstott	.40
299	Emmitt Smith	1.25
300	Trevor Pryce	.10
301	Tony Banks	.20
302	Mikhael Ricks	.10
303	Randall Cunningham	.30
304	*Thomas Jones*	2.00
305	*Mark Simoneau*	.30
306	*Jamal Lewis*	3.00
307	*Kwame Cavil*	.30
308	*Rashard Anderson*	.30
309	*Brian Urlacher*	2.50
310	*Peter Warrick*	2.00
311	*Courtney Brown*	1.00
312	*Michael Wiley*	.75
313	*Chris Cole*	.50
314	*Reuben Droughns*	2.00
315	*Bubba Franks*	1.00
316	*Rob Morris*	.30
317	*R. Jay Soward*	1.00
318	*Sylvester Morris*	1.50
319	*Ben Kelly*	.30
320	*Doug Chapman*	.30
321	*J.R. Redmond*	1.25
322	*Darren Howard*	.30
323	*Ron Dayne*	1.00
324	*Chad Pennington*	5.00
325	*Jerry Porter*	2.00
326	*Corey Simon*	.50
327	*Plaxico Burress*	2.50
328	*Trung Canidate*	.75
329	*Rogers Beckett*	.30
330	*Giovanni Carmazzi*	1.00
331	*Shaun Alexander*	3.00
332	*Joe Hamilton*	.75
333	*Keith Bulluck*	.30
334	*Todd Husak*	.50
335	*Raynoch Thompson, Darwin Walker*	.30
336	*Anthony Midget, Mareno Philyaw*	.30
337	*Travis Taylor, Chris Redman*	1.25
338	*Avion Black, ammy Morris*	1.00
339	*Deon Grant, Alvin McKinley*	.30
340	*Dez White, Frank Murphy*	.75
341	*Ron Dugans, Curtis Keaton*	.75
342	*Dennis Northcutt, Travis Prentice*	1.25
343	*Dwayne Goodrich, Orantes Grant*	.30
344	*Deltha O'Neal, Ian Gold*	.30
345	*Stockar McDougle, Barrett Green*	.30
346	*Na'il Diggs, Anthony Lucas*	.30
347	*Marcus Washington, Dan Kendra*	.30
348	*T.J. Slaughter, Shyrone Stith*	.50
349	*William Bartee, Frank Moreau*	.50
350	*Deon Dyer, Todd Wade*	.30
351	*Chris Hovan, Troy Walters*	.30
352	*David Stachelski, Tom Brady*	5.00
353	*Terrelle Smith, Marc Bulger*	.30
354	*Ron Dixon, Cornelius Griffin*	.75
355	*Laveranues Coles, Anthony Becht*	2.00
356	*Sebastian Janikowski, Shane Lechler*	.75
357	*Todd Pinkston, Gari Scott*	.75
358	*Danny Farmer, Tee Martin*	1.00
359	*Jacoby Shepherd, Brian Young*	.30
360	*Trevor Gaylor, JaJuan Seider*	.50
361	*Chafie Fields, Tim Rattay*	2.00
362	*Darrell Jackson, James Williams*	2.00
363	*Nate Webster, James Whalen*	.30
364	*Erron Kinney, Chris Coleman*	.30
365	*Chris Samuels, Leon Murray*	.50
366	Arizona Cardinals Team	.20
367	Atlanta Falcons Team	.10
368	Baltimore Ravens Team	.10
369	Buffalo Bills Team	.20
370	Carolina Panthers Team	.10
371	Chicago Bears Team	.20
372	Cincinnati Bengals Team	.20
373	Cleveland Browns Team	.20
374	Dallas Cowboys Team	.50
375	Denver Broncos Team	.10
376	Detroit Lions Team	.10
377	Green Bay Packers Team	.10
378	Indianapolis Colts Team	.75
379	Jacksonville Jaguars Team	.10
380	Kansas City ChiefsTeam	.10
381	Miami Dolphins Team	.50
382	Minnesota Vikings Team	.10
383	New England Patriots Team	.30
384	New Orleans Saints Team	.10
385	New York Giants Team	.10
386	New York Jets Team	.20
387	Oakland Raiders Team	.10
388	Philadelphia Eagles Team	.20
389	Pittsburgh Steelers Team	.10
390	St. Louis Rams Team	.20
391	San Diego Chargers Team	.10
392	San Francisco 49ers Team	.10
393	Seattle Seahawks Team	.10
394	Tampa Bay Buccaneers Team	.10
395	Tennessee Titans Team	.20
396	Washington Redskins Team	.20
397	Tim Couch CL	.50
398	Peyton Manning CL	.75
399	Kurt Warner CL	.75
400	Randy Moss CL	.75

2000 Fleer Autographics

		NM/M
Common Player:		10.00
Minor Stars:		20.00
Inserted 1:144		
Silver Cards:		1.2X
Production 250 Sets		
1	Shaun Alexander	45.00
2	Mike Alstott	20.00
3	Charlie Batch	20.00
4	Donnell Bennett	10.00
5	Peter Boulware	10.00
6	Tom Brady	75.00
7	Isaac Bruce	25.00
8	Marc Bulger	35.00
9	Trung Canidate	20.00
10	Giovanni Carmazzi	20.00
11	Darren Chiaverini	10.00
12	Laveranues Coles	20.00
13	Tim Couch	40.00
14	Daunte Culpepper	45.00
15	Stephen Davis	25.00
16	Jake Delhomme	20.00
17	Corey Dillon	25.00
18	Reuben Droughns	12.00
19	Deon Dyer	10.00
20	Kevin Dyson	10.00
21	Kevin Faulk	10.00
22	Jay Fiedler	20.00
23	Bubba Franks	25.00
24	Jason Garrett	10.00
25	Trevor Gaylor	10.00
26	Jeff Graham	10.00
27	Az-Zahir Hakim	20.00
28	Joe Hamilton	20.00
29	Tony Hartley	10.00
30	Priest Holmes	35.00
31	Raghib Ismail	10.00
32	Edgerrin James	85.00
33	Thomas Jones	35.00
34	Keyshawn Johnson	25.00
35	Curtis Keaton	10.00
36	Dorsey Levens	20.00
37	Curtis Martin	20.00
38	Derrick Mayes	10.00
39	O.J. McDuffie	10.00
40	Cade McNown	25.00
41	Johnnie Morton	10.00
42	Randy Moss Silver	100.00
43	Eric Moulds	25.00
44	Dennis Northcutt	20.00
45	Terrell Owens	25.00
46	Mareno Philyaw	10.00
47	Peerless Price	20.00
48	Chris Redman	45.00
49	J.R. Redmond	35.00
51	Warren Sapp	20.00
52	Gari Scott	10.00
53	Jason Sehorn	10.00
54	Akili Smith	25.00
55	Quinton Spotwood	10.00
56	Duce Staley	25.00
57	Michael Strahan	10.00
58	Amani Toomer	10.00
59	Peter Warrick	25.00
60	Tyrone Wheatley	20.00

2000 Fleer Genuine Coverage Nostalgic

		NM/M
Complete Set (9):		220.00
Common Player:		20.00
Inserted 1:360		
1	Chad Pennington	50.00
2	Ron Dayne	35.00
3	Plaxico Burress	40.00
4	Brian Urlacher	45.00
5	Bubba Franks	25.00
6	Jerry Porter	15.00
7	Trung Canidate	20.00
8	Dez White	25.00
9	Courtney Brown	25.00

2000 Fleer Rookie Retro

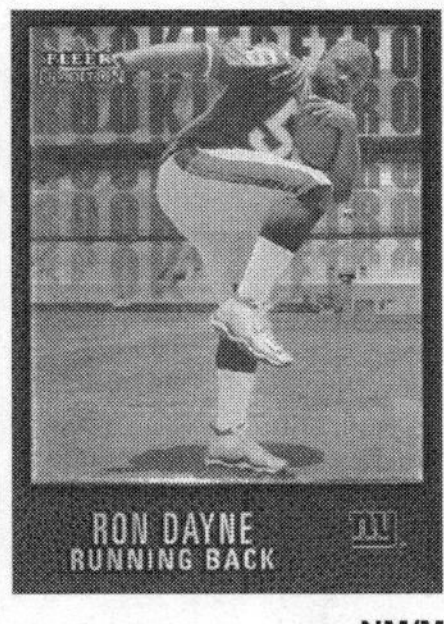

		NM/M
Complete Set (10):		25.00
Common Player:		2.00
Inserted 1:36		
1	Chad Pennington	8.00
2	Ron Dayne	4.00
3	Plaxico Burress	6.00
4	Brian Urlacher	6.00
5	Bubba Franks	3.00
6	Jerry Porter	4.00
7	Trung Canidate	2.00
8	Dez White	2.00
9	Courtney Brown	3.00
10	Shaun Alexander	5.00

2000 Fleer Throwbacks

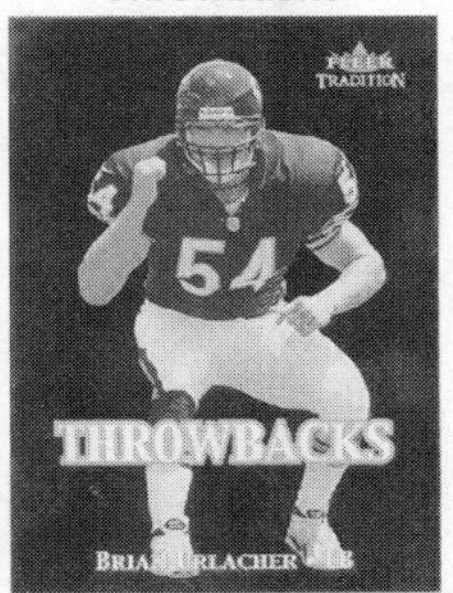

		NM/M
Complete Set (20):		10.00
Common Player:		.25
Minor Stars:		.50
Inserted 1:3		
1	Troy Aikman	1.00
2	Junior Seau	.25
3	Ron Dayne	1.00
4	Steve Young	.75
5	Wesley Walls	.25
6	Duce Staley	.50
7	Brian Urlacher	.75
8	Jerome Bettis	.50
9	Marshall Faulk	.50
10	Doug Flutie	.75
11	Brett Favre	2.00
12	Warren Sapp	.50
13	Charlie Batch	.50
14	Mike Alstott	.50
15	Cade McNown	.75
16	Jon Kitna	.50
17	Emmitt Smith	1.50
18	Tony Gonzalez	.50
19	Zach Thomas	.25
20	Cris Carter	.50

2000 Fleer Tradition of Excellence

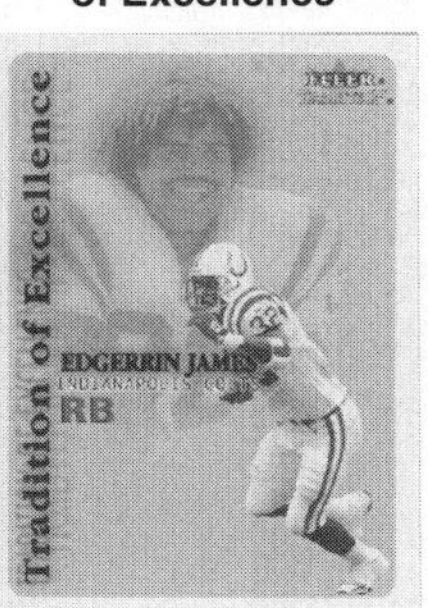

		NM/M
Complete Set (20):		25.00
Common Player:		.75
Inserted 1:9		
1	Brett Favre	4.00
2	Randy Moss	4.00
3	Tim Couch	2.00
4	Peter Warrick	2.00
5	Ron Dayne	2.00
6	Kurt Warner	3.00
7	Jevon Kearse	.75
8	Ricky Williams	2.00
9	Keyshawn Johnson	.75

10 Emmitt Smith 2.50
11 Donovan McNabb 1.50
12 Jamal Lewis 2.00
13 Jerry Rice 2.00
14 Eddie George 1.25
15 Peyton Manning 3.00
16 Stephen Davis .75
17 Thomas Jones 2.00
18 Plaxico Burress 3.00
19 Troy Aikman 2.00
20 Edgerrin James 2.00

2000 Fleer Whole Ten Yards

NM/M
Complete Set (15): 25.00
Common Player: 1.00
Inserted 1:18
1 Edgerrin James 4.00
2 Stephen Davis 1.00
3 Kurt Warner 4.00
4 Keyshawn Johnson 1.00
5 Mark Brunell 2.00
6 Peyton Manning 4.00
7 Emmitt Smith 3.50
8 Peter Warrick 2.00
9 Brett Favre 5.00
10 Marshall Faulk 1.00
11 Fred Taylor 1.75
12 Shaun Alexander 4.00
13 Terrell Davis 3.00
14 Eddie George 1.25
15 Randy Moss 4.00

2000 Fleer Focus

NM/M
Complete Set (260): 350.00
Common Player: .15
Minor Stars: .30
Common Rookie (201-211): 1.00
Production 3,999 Sets
Common Rookie (212-233): 2.00
Production 1,999 Sets
Common Rookie (234-250): 1.00
Production 2,499 Sets
Common Rookie (251-260): 2.00
Production 2,999 Sets
Pack (10): 2.75
Wax Box (24): 45.00
1 Tim Couch 1.25
2 Germane Crowell .30
3 Curtis Martin .50
4 Samari Rolle .15
5 Brian Griese .50
6 Kerry Collins .30
7 Jevon Kearse .50
8 Raghib Ismail .15
9 Cameron Cleeland .30
10 Warrick Dunn .50
11 Carl Pickens .30
12 Cris Carter .50
13 Mike Pritchard .15
14 Corey Dillon .50
15 Randy Moss 2.00
16 Derrick Mayes .30
17 Marcus Robinson .50
18 Thurman Thomas .30
19 J.J. Stokes .15
20 Muhsin Muhammad .30
21 Derrick Alexander .15
22 Curtis Conway .15
23 Qadry Ismail .15
24 Ken Dilger .15
25 Troy Edwards .50
26 Shawn Jefferson .15
27 Terrence Wilkins .30
28 Duce Staley .50
29 Aeneas Williams .15
30 Antonio Freeman .50
31 Tim Brown .30
32 Darrell Green .15
33 Herman Moore .30
34 Vinny Testaverde .30
35 Yancey Thigpen .15
36 Emmitt Smith 1.50
37 Ricky Williams 1.00
38 Keyshawn Johnson .15
39 Eddie Kennison .15
40 Zach Thomas .30
41 Shawn Springs .15
42 Wesley Walls .15
43 Andre Rison .15
44 Jerry Rice 1.25
45 Rob Johnson .30
46 Keenan McCardell .30
47 Ryan Leaf .50
48 Mike McCrary .15
49 Marvin Harrison .50
50 Donovan McNabb 1.00
51 Curtis Enis .15
52 Tony Martin .15
53 Jeff Garcia .15
54 Tim Biakabutuka .30
55 Tony Gonzalez .30
56 Jim Harbaugh .15
57 Peerless Price .50
58 Fred Taylor .75
59 Kordell Stewart .50
60 Chris Chandler .30
61 Bill Schroeder .15
62 Charles Woodson .30
63 Terance Mathis .15
64 Brett Favre 2.00
65 Rickey Dudley .15
66 Rob Moore .30
67 Charlie Batch .50
68 Wayne Chrebet .30
69 Jeff George .30
70 Olandis Gary .50
71 Amani Toomer .30
72 Kevin Dyson .30
73 Darrin Chiaverini .15
74 Willie McGinest .15
75 Ricky Proehl .15
76 Craig Yeast .15
77 Dwayne Rudd .15
78 Marshall Faulk .50
79 Bobby Engram .15
80 Jay Fiedler .50
81 Jon Kitna .50
82 Patrick Jeffers .50
83 J.J. Johnson .30
84 Charlie Garner .30
85 Eric Moulds .50
86 Mark Brunell .75
87 Richard Huntley .30
88 Frank Sanders .15
89 Robert Porcher .15
90 Aaron Glenn .15
91 Stephen Davis .50
92 Ed McCaffrey .30
93 Pete Mitchell .15
94 Frank Wycheck .15
95 David LaFleur .15
96 *Jake Delhomme* 1.50
97 John Lynch .15
98 Michael Pittman .15
99 Andy Katzenmoyer .15
100 Isaac Bruce .50
101 Terry Kirby .15
102 Kevin Faulk .30
103 Kevin Carter .15
104 Darnay Scott .30
105 Robert Smith .50
106 Brian Mitchell .15
107 Shane Matthews .15
108 O.J. McDuffie .30
109 Bryant Young .15
110 Jay Riemersma .15
111 Elvis Grbac .30
112 Jermaine Fazande .30
113 Johnathon Linton .30
114 Kyle Brady .15
115 Junior Seau .30
116 Shannon Sharpe .30
117 Jerome Pathon .15
118 Jerome Bettis .50
119 O.J. Santiago .15
120 Ahman Green .15
121 Troy Vincent .15
122 David Boston .50
123 James Stewart .30
124 Ray Lucas .50
125 Brad Johnson .50
126 Rod Smith .30
127 Joe Jurevicius .15
128 Eddie George .60
129 Darren Woodson .15
130 Jake Reed .15
131 Mike Alstott .50
132 Leslie Shepherd .15
133 Terry Glenn .50
134 Az-Zahir Hakim .30
135 Alonzo Mayes .15
136 Sam Madison .15
137 Ricky Watters .30
138 Antowain Smith .50
139 Jimmy Smith .50
140 Hines Ward .15
141 Priest Holmes .50
142 Edgerrin James 2.00
143 Charles Johnson .15
144 Jamal Anderson .50
145 Dorsey Levens .50
146 Rich Gannon .30
147 Champ Bailey .30
148 Bill Romanowski .15
149 Jason Sehorn .15
150 Steve McNair .50
151 Jermaine Lewis .15
152 Cornelius Bennett .15
153 Torrance Small .15
154 Tim Dwight .50
155 Corey Bradford .15
156 Napoleon Kaufman .50
157 Jake Plummer .50
158 David Sloan .15
159 Dedric Ward .15
160 Michael Westbrook .30
161 Terrell Davis 1.00
162 Ike Hilliard .30
163 Derrick Brooks .15
164 Greg Ellis .15
165 Keith Poole .15
166 Jacquez Green .30
167 Joey Galloway .50
168 Lawyer Milloy .15
169 Warren Sapp .15
170 Takeo Spikes .15
171 John Randle .15
172 Torry Holt .50
173 Cade McNown .75
174 Damon Huard .30
175 Terrell Owens .50
176 Steve Beuerlein .30
177 Tony Richardson .15
178 Jeff Graham .15
179 Doug Flutie .50
180 Kevin Hardy .15
181 Mark Bruener .15
182 Tony Banks .30
183 Peyton Manning 1.75
184 Hugh Douglas .15
185 Simeon Rice .15
186 Terry Fair .15
187 James Jett .15
188 Albert Connell .30
189 Troy Aikman 1.25
190 Jeff Blake .30
191 Shaun King .75
192 Kevin Johnson .50
193 Drew Bledsoe .75
194 Kurt Warner 1.50
195 Akili Smith .50
196 Daunte Culpepper .75
197 Sean Dawkins .15
198 Natrone Means .30
199 Kimble Anders .15
200 Steve Young .75
201 *Courtney Brown* 4.00
202 *Chris Samuels* 1.00
203 *Corey Simon* 1.00
204 *Deon Grant* 1.00
205 *Darren Howard* 1.00
206 *Rob Morris* 1.00
207 *Ahmed Plummer* 3.00
208 *Anthony Becht* 1.00
209 *Brian Urlacher* 10.00
210 *Shaun Ellis* 1.00
211 *Bubba Franks* 5.00
212 *Plaxico Burress* 10.00
213 *R. Jay Soward* 4.00
214 *Dez White* 6.00
215 *Peter Warrick* 8.00
216 *Jerry Porter* 8.00
217 *Ron Dugans* 4.00
218 *Laveranues Coles* 8.00
219 *Travis Taylor* 6.00
220 *Anthony Lucas* 4.00
221 *Sylvester Morris* 5.00
222 *Dennis Northcutt* 6.00
223 *Chafie Fields* 1.00
224 *Danny Farmer* 5.00
225 *Chris Cole* 1.00
226 *Sherrod Gideon* 2.00
227 *Todd Pinkston* 8.00
228 *Gari Scott* 2.00
229 *Darrell Jackson* 8.00
230 *JaJuan Dawson* 4.00
231 *Trevor Gaylor* 2.00
232 *Bashir Yamini* 2.00
233 *Quinton Spotwood* 2.00
234 *Michael Wiley* 2.00
235 *Ron Dayne* 4.00
236 *Thomas Jones* 8.00
237 *Jamal Lewis* 12.00
238 *Travis Prentice* 5.00
239 *J.R. Redmond* 5.00
240 *Trung Canidate* 6.00
241 *Shaun Alexander* 12.00
242 *Frank Murphy* 2.00
243 *Shyrone Stith* 2.00
244 *Rondell Mealey* 2.00
245 *Terrelle Smith* 2.00
246 *Reuben Droughns* 6.00
247 *Chad Morton* 6.00
248 *Mike Anderson* 10.00
249 *Paul Smith* 2.00
250 *Curtis Keaton* 2.00
251 *Jarious Jackson* 5.00
252 *Marc Bulger* 10.00
253 *Tee Martin* 5.00
254 *Todd Husak* 5.00
255 *Joe Hamilton* 6.00
256 *Doug Johnson* 5.00
257 *Giovanni Carmazzi* 4.00
258 *Chris Redman* 5.00
259 *Tim Rattay* 6.00
260 *Chad Pennington* 20.00

2000 Fleer Focus Autographics

NM/M
Common Player: 10.00
Minor Stars: 20.00
Inserted 1:72
Silver Cards: 1.2X
Production 250 Sets
1 Troy Aikman 60.00
2 Shaun Alexander 50.00
3 Mike Alstott 25.00
4 Kimble Anders 10.00
5 Tim Biakabutuka 10.00
6 Peter Boulware 10.00
7 Trung Canidate 20.00
8 Giovanni Carmazzi 15.00
9 Darren Chiaverini 10.00
10 Germane Crowell 10.00
11 Stephen Davis 25.00
12 Jake Delhomme 20.00
13 Reuben Droughns 25.00
14 Kevin Dyson 10.00
15 Marshall Faulk 30.00
16 Jay Fiedler 20.00
17 Bubba Franks 25.00
18 Jeff Garcia 25.00
19 Olandis Gary 30.00
20 Sherrod Gideon 10.00
21 Tony Graziani 10.00
22 Marvin Harrison 30.00
23 Priest Holmes 35.00
24 Torry Holt 20.00
25 Damon Huard 20.00
26 Darrell Jackson 20.00
27 Edgerrin James 85.00
28 Jon Kitna 20.00
29 Marcus Knight 10.00
30 Dorsey Levens 20.00
31 Tee Martin 25.00
32 Shane Matthews 20.00
33 O.J. McDuffie 10.00
34 Cade McNown 30.00
35 Rondell Mealey 20.00
36 Sylvester Morris 25.00
37 Johnnie Morton 10.00
38 Dennis Northcutt 20.00
39 Chad Pennington 60.00
40 Travis Prentice 25.00
41 Peerless Price 25.00
42 Jon Ritchie 10.00
43 Marcus Robinson 25.00
44 Warren Sapp 10.00
45 Jason Sehorn 10.00
46 Jimmy Smith 20.00
47 Rod Smith 20.00
48 Amani Toomer 10.00
49 Troy Walters 10.00
50 Kurt Warner 75.00
51 Peter Warrick 25.00
52 Dez White 20.00

2000 Fleer Focus Feel the Game

NM/M
Common Player: 20.00
Inserted 1:144
1 Troy Aikman Blue 50.00
2 Tim Brown 20.00
3 Curtis Conway Jersey 20.00
4 Curtis Conway Pants 20.00
5 Germane Crowell 25.00
6 Terrell Davis 65.00
7 Kevin Dyson Jersey 20.00
8 Kevin Dyson Pants 20.00
9 Curtis Enis Pants 25.00
10 Antonio Freeman 25.00
11 Eddie George Jersey 45.00
12 Eddie George Pants 45.00
13 Edgerrin James 75.00
14 Rob Johnson 25.00
15 Jevon Kearse 30.00
16 Peyton Manning 75.00
17 Terance Mathis 20.00
18 Steve McNair Jersey 40.00
19 Steve McNair Pants 40.00
20 Cade McNown Pants 50.00
21 Herman Moore 20.00
22 Johnnie Morton White 20.00
23 Marcus Robinson Pants 40.00
24 Deion Sanders 35.00
25 Emmitt Smith Blue 75.00

2000 Fleer Focus Good Hands

NM/M
Complete Set (15): 25.00
Common Player: .75
Minor Stars: 1.50
Inserted 1:18
1 Keyshawn Johnson 1.50
2 Joey Galloway 1.50
3 Jerry Rice 4.00
4 Cris Carter 1.50
5 Randy Moss 6.00
6 Marvin Harrison 1.50
7 Marcus Robinson 1.50
8 Edgerrin James 5.00
9 Tim Brown .75
10 Jimmy Smith 1.50
11 Isaac Bruce 1.50
12 Peter Warrick 2.00
13 Marshall Faulk 1.50
14 Germane Crowell .75
15 Plaxico Burress 5.00

2000 Fleer Focus Good Hands TD Edition

NM/M
Numbered to 1999 TD total
Cards numbered under 10 not priced
1 Keyshawn Johnson 8
2 Joey Galloway 1
3 Jerry Rice 5
4 Cris Carter 15 50.00
5 Randy Moss 12 75.00
6 Marvin Harrison 12 50.00
7 Marcus Robinson 9
8 Edgerrin James 17 75.00
9 Tim Brown 6
10 Jimmy Smith 6
11 Isaac Bruce 12 50.00
12 Peter Warrick 12 50.00
13 Marshall Faulk 12 50.00
14 Germane Crowell 7
15 Plaxico Burress 12 75.00

2000 Fleer Focus Last Man Standing

NM/M
Complete Set (25): 40.00
Common Player: 1.50
Inserted 1:12
1 Tim Couch 3.00
2 Randy Moss 5.00
3 Akili Smith 1.50
4 Peyton Manning 5.00
5 Kurt Warner 4.00
6 Ricky Williams 3.00

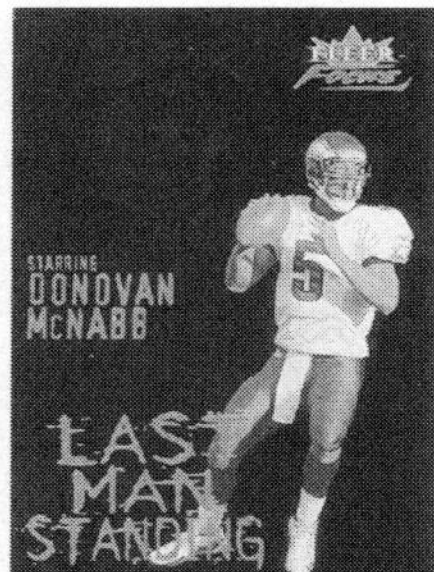

NM/M
7 Edgerrin James 4.00
8 Eddie George 2.00
9 Emmitt Smith 4.00
10 Terrell Davis 3.00
11 Brett Favre 5.00
12 Brian Griese 2.00
13 Donovan McNabb 2.00
14 Charlie Batch 1.50
15 Shaun King 1.50
16 Marshall Faulk 1.50
17 Jake Plummer 1.50
18 Cade McNown 2.00
19 Jerry Rice 4.00
20 Troy Aikman 3.00
21 Keyshawn Johnson 1.50
22 Peter Warrick 2.00
23 Ron Dayne 2.00
24 Mark Brunell 2.50
25 Fred Taylor 3.00

2000 Fleer Focus Last Man Standing TD Edition

NM/M
Numbered to 1999 TD total
Cards numbered under 10 not priced
1 Tim Couch 16 75.00
2 Randy Moss 12 125.00
3 Akili Smith 3
4 Peyton Manning 28 100.00
5 Kurt Warner 42 85.00
6 Ricky Williams 2
7 Edgerrin James 17 125.00
8 Eddie George 13 60.00
9 Emmitt Smith 13 100.00
10 Terrell Davis 2
11 Brett Favre 22 125.00
12 Brian Griese 16 50.00
13 Donovan McNabb 18 50.00
14 Charlie Batch 15 50.00
15 Shaun King 7
16 Marshall Faulk 12 50.00
17 Jake Plummer 11 50.00
18 Cade McNown 8
19 Jerry Rice 5
20 Troy Aikman 18 90.00
21 Keyshawn Johnson 8
22 Peter Warrick 12 150.00
23 Ron Dayne 20 125.00
24 Mark Brunell 15 60.00
25 Fred Taylor 6

2000 Fleer Focus Sparklers

NM/M
Complete Set (15): 30.00
Common Player: 1.00
Inserted 1:6
1 Chad Pennington 5.00
2 Ron Dayne 2.00
3 Shaun Alexander 3.00
4 Plaxico Burress 4.00
5 Peter Warrick 2.00
6 Thomas Jones 3.00
7 Chris Redman 2.00
8 Sylvester Morris 1.50
9 J.R. Redmond 1.50
10 Dez White 1.00
11 Jamal Lewis 3.00
12 Travis Taylor 2.00
13 R. Jay Soward 1.00
14 Todd Pinkston 1.00
15 Dennis Northcutt 1.00

2000 Fleer Focus Sparklers TD Edition

NM/M
Numbered to 1999 TD total
Cards numbered under 10 not priced
1 Chad Pennington 40 75.00
2 Ron Dayne 20 40.00
3 Shaun Alexander 26 65.00
4 Plaxico Burress 12 125.00
5 Peter Warrick 12 50.00
6 Thomas Jones 18 40.00
7 Chris Redman 32 30.00
8 Sylvester Morris 13 40.00
9 J.R. Redmond 13 40.00
10 Dez White 5
11 Jamal Lewis 8
12 Travis Taylor 6
13 R. Jay Soward 5
14 Todd Pinkston 11 25.00
15 Dennis Northcutt 8

2000 Fleer Focus Star Studded

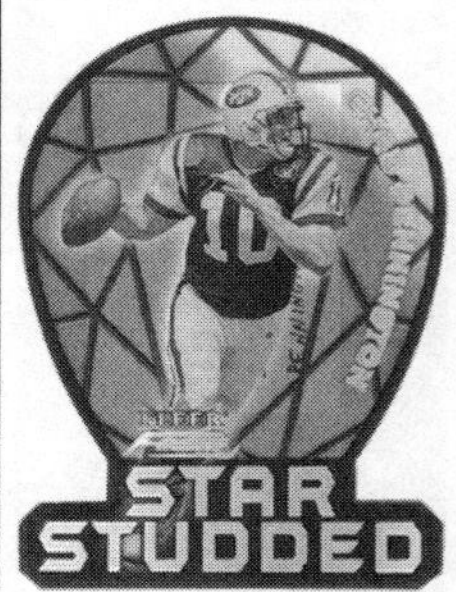

NM/M
Complete Set (25): 125.00
Common Player: 3.00
Inserted 1:24
1 Peyton Manning 6.00
2 Fred Taylor 4.00
3 Tim Couch 4.00
4 Charlie Batch 2.00
5 Jerry Rice 6.00
6 Randy Moss 6.00
7 Ron Dayne 3.00
8 Mark Brunell 3.00
9 Emmitt Smith 6.00
10 Thomas Jones 3.00
11 Brian Griese 2.00
12 Terrell Davis 5.00
13 Brad Johnson 3.00
14 Ricky Williams 5.00
15 Brett Favre 6.00
16 Jake Plummer 2.00
17 Troy Aikman 4.00
18 Drew Bledsoe 3.00
19 Edgerrin James 4.00
20 Steve McNair 3.00
21 Doug Flutie 2.00
22 Chad Pennington 8.00
23 Jamal Lewis 5.00
24 Plaxico Burress 6.00
25 Kurt Warner 4.00

2000 Fleer Focus Star Studded TD Edition

NM/M
Numbered to 1999 TD total
Cards numbered under 10 not priced
1 Peyton Manning 28 100.00
2 Fred Taylor 6
3 Tim Couch 16 85.00
4 Charlie Batch 15 50.00
5 Jerry Rice 5
6 Randy Moss 12 125.00
7 Ron Dayne 20 125.00
8 Mark Brunell 15 60.00
9 Emmitt Smith 13 100.00
10 Thomas Jones 18 75.00
11 Brian Griese 16 50.00
12 Terrell Davis 2
13 Brad Johnson 26 40.00
14 Ricky Williams 2
15 Brett Favre 22 125.00
16 Jake Plummer 11 50.00
17 Troy Aikman 18 90.00
18 Drew Bledsoe 19 60.00
19 Edgerrin James 17 125.00
20 Steve McNair 20 40.00
21 Doug Flutie 20 45.00
22 Chad Pennington 40 75.00
23 Jamal Lewis 8
24 Plaxico Burress 12 125.00
25 Kurt Warner 42 60.00

2000 Fleer Gamers

NM/M
Complete Set (145): 75.00
Common Player: .15
Minor Stars: .30
Common Rookie: 1.00
Inserted 1:8

Pack (5): 2.00
Wax Box (24): 35.00
1 Edgerrin James 2.50
2 Tim Couch 1.50
3 Cris Carter .50
4 Rich Gannon .30
5 Akili Smith .50
6 Muhsin Muhammad .30
7 Dorsey Levens .50
8 Dedric Ward .30
9 Jevon Kearse .50
10 Peerless Price .30
11 Mike Alstott .50
12 Michael Strahan .15
13 Stephen Davis .50
14 Rob Moore .30
15 James Stewart .30
16 Robert Smith .50
17 Napoleon Kaufman .30
18 Peyton Manning 2.00
19 Keyshawn Johnson .50
20 Tony Martin .15
21 Jermaine Fazande .30
22 Jamal Anderson .50
23 Ed McCaffrey .30
24 Drew Bledsoe 1.00
25 Duce Staley .50
26 Warrick Dunn .50
27 Chris Chandler .30
28 Olandis Gary .60
29 Terry Glenn .50
30 Donovan McNabb 1.00
31 Torry Holt .50
32 Tim Dwight .30
33 Terrell Davis 1.00
34 Tony Simmons .15
35 Jerome Bettis .50
36 Az-Zahir Hakim .30
37 Darrin Chiaverini .30
38 Fred Taylor .75
39 Jon Kitna .30
40 Tony Banks .30
41 Brian Griese .75
42 Jeff Blake .30
43 Kordell Stewart .50
44 Isaac Bruce .50
45 Shannon Sharpe .30
46 Raghib Ismail .15
47 Ricky Williams 1.00
48 Marshall Faulk .50
49 Qadry Ismail .15
50 Joey Galloway .50
51 Jake Reed .15
52 Kurt Warner 3.00
53 Cade McNown 1.00
54 Herman Moore .30
55 Curtis Martin .50
56 Steve McNair .50
57 Tim Biakabutuka .30
58 Brett Favre 2.50
59 Wayne Chrebet .30
60 Eddie George .75
61 Troy Aikman 1.25
62 Jimmy Smith .50
63 Derrick Mayes .30
64 Emmitt Smith 1.75
65 Mark Brunell .50
66 Ricky Watters .30
67 Marcus Robinson .50
68 Randy Moss 2.50
69 Troy Edwards .50
70 Carl Pickens .30
71 Damon Huard .50
72 Mikhael Ricks .15
73 David Boston .50
74 Charlie Batch .50
75 Randall Cunningham .50
76 Tim Brown .30
77 Shaun King .50
78 Darnay Scott .30
79 Derrick Alexander .15
80 Steve Young 1.00
81 Kevin Johnson .50
82 Elvis Grbac .30
83 Tai Streets .30
84 Steve Beuerlein .30
85 Antonio Freeman .50
86 Vinny Testaverde .30
87 Brad Johnson .50
88 Curtis Enis .30
89 Jay Fiedler .50
90 Junior Seau .30
91 Eric Moulds .50
92 Jake Plummer .50
93 Amani Toomer .15
94 Champ Bailey .30
95 Germane Crowell .50
96 Tony Gonzalez .30
97 Jerry Rice 1.25
98 Rob Johnson .30
99 Marvin Harrison .50
100 Kerry Collins .30
101 *Thomas Jones* 4.00
102 *Jarious Jackson* 3.00
103 *R. Jay Soward* 2.00
104 *Trung Canidate* 3.00
105 *Travis Taylor* 3.00
106 *Giovanni Carmazzi* 2.00
107 *Jerry Porter* 4.00
108 *Chris Redman* 3.00
109 *Tee Martin* 2.00
110 *Dez White* 3.00
111 *Danny Farmer* 2.50
112 *Brian Urlacher* 5.00
113 *Reuben Droughns* 4.00
114 *Marc Bulger* 5.00
115 *Peter Warrick* 4.00
116 *Plaxico Burress* 5.00
117 *Ron Dugans* 2.00
118 *Gari Scott* 1.00
119 *Curtis Keaton* 1.00
120 *Corey Simon* 1.00
121 *Rob Morris* 1.00
122 *Chad Morton* 2.50
123 *Hank Poteat* 1.00
124 *Ahmed Plummer* 1.00
125 *Bashir Yamini* 1.00
126 *J.R. Redmond* 3.00
127 *Travis Prentice* 3.00
128 *Todd Pinkston* 3.00
129 *Courtney Brown* 2.00
130 *Laveranues Coles* 4.00
131 *Jamal Lewis* 6.00
132 *Tim Rattay* 2.00
133 *Anthony Becht* 1.00
134 *Chris Cole* 1.00
135 *Ron Dayne* 3.00
136 *Sylvester Morris* 2.00
137 *Joe Hamilton* 3.00
138 *Dennis Northcutt* 2.00
139 *Doug Johnson* 2.50
140 *Shyrone Stith* 1.00
141 *Darrell Jackson* 4.00
142 *Michael Wiley* 2.00
143 *Chad Pennington* 10.00
144 *Bubba Franks* 4.00
145 *Shaun Alexander* 6.00

2000 Fleer Gamers Extra

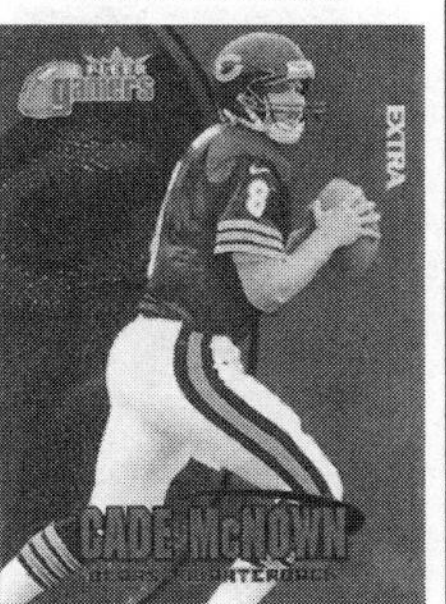

NM/M
Extra Cards: 2X-4X
Inserted 1:8
Extra Rookies: 2X
Inserted 1:24

2000 Fleer Gamers Autographics

NM/M
Common Player: 10.00
Minor Stars: 20.00
Inserted 1:287
Silver Cards: 1.2X
Production 250 Sets
1 Shaun Alexander 45.00
2 Charlie Batch 20.00
3 Drew Bledsoe 35.00
4 Tim Brown 20.00
5 Isaac Bruce 25.00
6 Giovanni Carmazzi 35.00
7 Laveranues Coles 20.00
8 Tim Couch 55.00
9 Ron Dayne 35.00
10 Danny Farmer 10.00
11 Bubba Franks 20.00
12 Tony Gonzalez 20.00
13 Thomas Jones 35.00
14 Cade McNown 35.00
15 Dennis Northcutt 20.00
16 J.R. Redmond 25.00
17 Peter Warrick 35.00

2000 Fleer Gamers Change the Game

NM/M
Complete Set (15): 40.00
Common Player: 2.00
Inserted 1:24
1 Kurt Warner 4.00
2 Brett Favre 6.00
3 Eddie George 3.00
4 Keyshawn Johnson 2.00
5 Randy Moss 5.00
6 Tim Couch 3.00
7 Ricky Williams 4.00
8 Peyton Manning 5.00
9 Terrell Davis 4.00
10 Troy Aikman 4.00
11 Fred Taylor 3.50
12 Cade McNown 2.00
13 Edgerrin James 4.00
14 Peter Warrick 2.00
15 Jamal Lewis 3.00

2000 Fleer Gamers Contact Sport

NM/M
Complete Set (20): 20.00
Common Player: 1.00
Inserted 1:4
1 Peter Warrick 2.00
2 Jamal Lewis 3.00
3 Thomas Jones 3.00
4 Plaxico Burress 3.00
5 Travis Taylor 2.00
6 Ron Dayne 1.00
7 Bubba Franks 1.50
8 Chad Pennington 6.00
9 Shaun Alexander 3.00
10 Sylvester Morris 2.50
11 R. Jay Soward 1.00
12 Trung Canidate 1.00
13 Dennis Northcutt 1.00
14 Todd Pinkston 1.00
15 Jerry Porter 1.00
16 Travis Prentice 2.00
17 Courtney Brown 1.50
18 Ron Dugans 1.00
19 Dez White 1.00
20 Chris Redman 2.00

2000 Fleer Gamers Uniformity

NM/M
Common Player: 8.00
Inserted 1:44
1 Kurt Warner 30.00
2 Az-Zahir Hakim 8.00
3 Marshall Faulk 25.00
4 Bruce Smith 8.00
5 Curtis Enis 8.00
6 Mark Brunell 20.00
7 Troy Aikman 30.00
8 Emmitt Smith 65.00
9 Ed McCaffrey 20.00
10 Jerry Rice 55.00
11 Stephen Davis 20.00
12 Tim Brown 25.00
13 Randall Cunningham 20.00
14 Steve Young 35.00
15 John Lynch 8.00
16 Isaac Bruce 20.00
17 Torry Holt 20.00
18 Jake Plummer 20.00
19 David Boston 30.00
20 Charlie Batch 20.00
21 Germane Crowell 20.00
22 Herman Moore 25.00
23 Johnnie Morton 8.00
24 Peyton Manning 45.00
25 Edgerrin James 35.00
26 Marvin Harrison 25.00
27 Tim Couch 25.00
28 Kevin Johnson 25.00
29 Rob Moore 8.00
30 Frank Sanders 8.00
31 Chris Chandler 8.00
32 Jamal Anderson 20.00
33 Tim Dwight 15.00
34 Terry Kirby 8.00

2000 Fleer Gamers Yard Chargers

NM/M
Complete Set (15): 50.00
Common Player: 1.50
#1-5 Inserted 1:9
#6-10 Inserted 1:24
#11-15 Inserted 1:144
1 Marvin Harrison 1.50
2 Randy Moss 3.00
3 Keyshawn Johnson 1.50
4 Tim Brown 1.50
5 Jerry Rice 2.00
6 Terrell Davis 3.00
7 Emmitt Smith 4.50
8 Eddie George 2.50
9 Edgerrin James 3.00
10 Marshall Faulk 2.00
11 Tim Couch 12.00
12 Kurt Warner 10.00
13 Peyton Manning 12.00
14 Brett Favre 15.00
15 Troy Aikman 12.00

2000 Fleer Glossy

NM/M
Complete Set (400): 40.00
Complete Factory Set: 40.00
Factory set includes cards #1-400, 5 rookies (#401-450) & Threads card.
Common Player: .25
Minor Stars: .50
Common Rookie (#304-365): 1.00
Common Rookie (#401-450): 1.00
Production for Rookies (#401-450)
750 Sets
Total of 7,500 Factory Sets Released
1 Kevin Johnson .75
2 Chris Chandler .50
3 Peerless Price .75
4 Andre Rison .50
5 Curtis Enis .50
6 Tim Couch 1.50

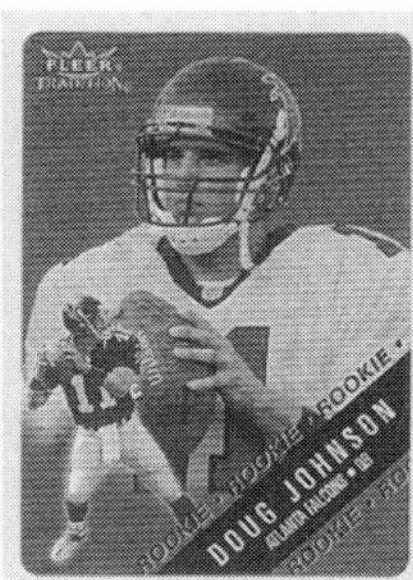

NM/M
7 Brian Dawkins .25
8 Akili Smith .75
9 Kevin Faulk .50
10 Joey Galloway .75
11 Bill Romanowski .25
12 Charlie Batch .75
13 Terrence Wilkins .50
14 Kevin Hardy .25
15 Cade McNown .75
16 Elvis Grbac .50
17 Cris Carter .75
18 Willie McGinest .25
19 Michael Bishop .75
20 Lee Woodall .25
21 Jake Reed .50
22 Bryan Cox .25
23 Chris Sanders .25
24 Tavian Banks .50
25 Levon Kirkland .25
26 James Hundon .25
27 Junior Seau .50
28 Darren Woodson .25
29 Kevin Carter .25
30 Joe Jurevicius .50
31 John Lynch .25
32 Steve McNair .75
33 Jake Plummer .75
34 Antonio Freeman .75
35 Peter Boulware .25
36 Brad Johnson .75
37 Bobby Engram .25
38 David Boston .75
39 Jason Tucker .50
40 Troy Brown .25
41 Brian Griese 1.00
42 Dorsey Levens .75
43 Cornelius Bennett .25
44 Donovan McNabb 1.25
45 Rob Johnson .75
46 Robert Smith .75
47 Stanley Pritchett .25
48 Tedy Bruschi .25
49 Dan Marino 2.50
50 Amani Toomer .25
51 Aaron Glenn .25
52 Rickey Dudley .25
53 Tim Brown .75
54 Jim Harbaugh .50
55 Terrell Owens .75
56 Jason Sehorn .25
57 Cortez Kennedy .25
58 London Fletcher .25
59 Simeon Rice .25
60 Shaun King 1.25
61 Stephen Davis .75
62 Andre Wadsworth .25
63 Kyle Brady .25
64 Priest Holmes .75
65 Patrick Jeffers .75
66 Barry Minter .25
67 Curtis Martin .75
68 Darrin Chiaverini .25
69 Robert Thomas .25
70 Samari Rolle .25
71 Robert Porcher .25
72 Jerry Rice 1.75
73 Bill Schroeder .50
74 Chad Bratzke .25
75 Tony Brackens .25
76 O.J. McDuffie .50
77 John Randle .25
78 Michael Pittman .50
79 Drew Bledsoe 1.25
80 Ike Hilliard .50
81 Victor Green .25
82 Duce Staley .75
83 Bruce Smith .50
84 Amos Zereoue .50
85 Charlie Garner .50
86 Shawn Springs .25
87 Kurt Warner 2.00
88 Eddie George .75
89 Michael Westbrook .50
90 Dexter Coakley .25
91 Rob Moore .50
92 Duane Starks .25
93 Steve Beuerlein .50
94 Marty Booker .25
95 Karim Abdul .25
96 Troy Aikman 1.75
97 Germane Crowell .75
98 Matt Hasselbeck .50
99 E.G. Green .50
100 Mark Brunell 1.25
101 Tony Martin .25
102 Darrell Green .25
103 Ricky Williams 1.00
104 Michael Strahan .25
105 Vinny Testaverde .75
106 Charles Johnson .50
107 Hines Ward .50
108 Bryant Young .25
109 Mo Lewis .25
110 Greg Clark .25
111 Jon Kitna .75
112 Jacquez Green .50
113 Kevin Dyson .50
114 Stephen Alexander .25
115 Cameron Cleeland .50
116 Keith Poole .25
117 Az-Zahir Hakim .50
118 Tim Dwight .75
119 Corey Bradford .50
120 Carlos Emmons .25
121 Trent Dilfer .50
122 Lance Schulters .25
123 Byron Hanspard .50
124 Tim Biakabutuka .50
125 Eddie Kennison .50
126 Terry Kirby .25
127 Mike McKenzie .25
128 Fred Beasley .25
129 Chad Brown .25
130 Terrell Davis 1.50
131 Herman Moore .75
132 Vonnie Holliday .25
133 Jim Miller .25
134 Peyton Manning 3.00
135 Derrick Alexander .25
136 Oronde Gadsden .50
137 Robert Griffith .25
138 Troy Edwards .50
139 Damon Huard .50
140 Jessie Armstead .25
141 Charles Woodson .75
142 Troy Vincent .25
143 Natrone Means .50
144 Jeff Garcia .75
145 Terry Glenn .75
146 Marshall Faulk 1.00
147 Patrick Johnson .50
148 Frank Wycheck .25
149 Champ Bailey .50
150 Jamal Anderson .75
151 Doug Flutie 1.00
152 Michael Bates .25
153 Corey Dillon 1.00
154 Keith McKenzie .25
155 Orpheus Roye .25
156 Olandis Gary .75
157 Johnnie Morton .50
158 Brett Favre 3.50
159 Adrian Murrell .25
160 Fred Taylor 1.25
161 Tony Gonzalez .75
162 Zach Thomas .50
163 Randy Moss 3.00
164 Marcus Robinson .75
165 Tiki Barber .75
166 Rich Gannon .50
167 Jeremiah Trotter .25
168 Jermaine Fazande .50
169 Steve Young 1.25
170 Isaac Bruce .75
171 Warrick Dunn .75
172 Yancey Thigpen .50
173 Rod Smith .75
174 Albert Connell .50
175 Freddie Jones .50
176 Terance Mathis .25
177 Eric Moulds .75
178 Brian Mitchell .25
179 Wesley Walls .50
180 Carl Pickens .50
181 Errict Rhett .50
182 Madre Hill .25
183 Jason Elam .25
184 Greg Ellis .25
185 David Sloan .25
186 Edgerrin James 3.00
187 Jimmy Smith .75
188 Tony Richardson .50
189 James Hasty .25
190 Sam Madison .25
191 Tony Simmons .50
192 Andre Hastings .25
193 Keyshawn Johnson .75
194 Na Brown .50
195 Napoleon Kaufman .75
196 Torrance Small .25
197 Curtis Conway .50
198 Jeff Graham .25
199 Jason Hanson .25
200 Derrick Mayes .50
201 Torry Holt .75
202 Warren Sapp .50
203 Kimble Anders .25
204 Blaine Bishop .25
205 Leroy Hoard .25
206 Larry Centers .25
207 O.J. Santiago .25
208 Antowain Smith .50
209 Chuck Smith .25
210 Takeo Spikes .25
211 Raghib Ismail .25
212 Ed McCaffrey .75
213 Karsten Bailey .25
214 Terry Fair .25
215 Ken Dilger .25
216 Jamie Martin .25
217 Cris Dishman .25
218 Jay Fiedler .75
219 Lawyer Milloy .25
220 *Jake Delhomme* 4.00
221 Wayne Chrebet .75
222 Darrell Russell .25
223 Christian Fauria .25
224 Jerome Bettis .75
225 Ryan Leaf .75
226 Ricky Watters .75
227 Keenan McCardell .50
228 Grant Wistrom .25
229 Jevon Kearse .75
230 Frank Sanders .50
231 Shannon Sharpe .50
232 Jonathon Linton .50
233 Alonzo Mayes .25
234 Jason Garrett .25
235 Kordell Stewart .75
236 David LaFleur .25
237 Kenny Bynum .25
238 Byron Chamberlain .25
239 Tyrone Davis .25
240 Jerome Pathon .25
241 Alvis Whitted .25
242 Kevin Lockett .25
243 Matthew Hatchette .50
244 Rod Woodson .25
245 Joe Horn .75
246 Ronnie Powell .25
247 Dedric Ward .50
248 J.J. Johnson .50
249 James Jett .25
250 *Bobby Shaw* 1.50
251 J.J. Stokes .50
252 Paul Shields .25
253 Sean Dawkins .25
254 Hardy Nickerson .25
255 Stephen Boyd .25
256 Chris Warren .50
257 Kerry Collins .75
258 Isaac Byrd .25
259 Bobby Hoying .50
260 Daunte Culpepper 1.75
261 Moe Williams .25
262 Kamil Loud .25
263 Derrick Brooks .25
264 Jay Riemersma .50
265 Ray Lucas .50
266 Jason Gildon .25
267 James Stewart .50
268 Marcellus Wiley .25
269 Craig Yeast .25
270 Michael Basnight .25
271 Tyrone Wheatley .50
272 Martin Gramatica .50
273 Phillip Daniels .25
274 Richard Huntley .50
275 Muhsin Muhammad .50
276 Todd Lyght .25
277 Carlester Crumpler .25
278 Jeff Lewis .50
279 Jeff George .50
280 Jeff Blake .50
281 Mike McCrary .25
282 Shawn Jefferson .25
283 Mark Bruener .25
284 Donnie Abraham .25
285 Yatil Green .25
286 Jermaine Lewis .50
287 Rob Fredrickson .25
288 Thurman Thomas .50
289 Kent Graham .25
290 Darnay Scott .50
291 Tony Graziani .50
292 Qadry Ismail .25
293 Aeneas Williams .25
294 Marvin Harrison .75
295 Jimmy Hitchcock .25
296 Bob Christian .25
297 Pete Mitchell .25
298 Mike Alstott .75
299 Emmitt Smith 2.50
300 Trevor Pryce .25
301 Tony Banks .50
302 Mikhael Ricks .25
303 Randall Cunningham .50
304 *Thomas Jones* 3.00
305 *Mark Simoneau* 1.00
306 *Jamal Lewis* 6.00
307 *Kwame Cavil* 1.00
308 *Rashard Anderson* 1.50
309 *Brian Urlacher* 5.00
310 *Peter Warrick* 4.00
311 *Courtney Brown* 1.50
312 *Michael Wiley* 1.00
313 *Chris Cole* 1.00
314 *Reuben Droughns* 2.00
315 *Bubba Franks* 1.50
316 *Rob Morris* 1.00
317 *R. Jay Soward* 1.50
318 *Sylvester Morris* 1.50
319 *Ben Kelly* 1.00
320 *Doug Chapman* 1.00
321 *J.R. Redmond* 2.00
322 *Darren Howard* 1.00
323 *Ron Dayne* 2.00
324 *Chad Pennington* 10.00
325 *Jerry Porter* 1.50
326 *Corey Simon* 1.50
327 *Plaxico Burress* 5.00
328 *Trung Canidate* 1.50
329 *Rogers Beckett* 1.00
330 *Giovanni Carmazzi* 1.50
331 *Shaun Alexander* 6.00
332 *Joe Hamilton* 1.50
333 *Keith Bulluck* 1.00
334 *Todd Husak* 1.50
335 *Raynoch Thompson, Darwin Walker* 1.00
336 *Anthony Midget, Mareno Philyaw* 1.00
337 *Travis Taylor, Chris Redman* 3.00
338 *Avion Black, Sammy Morris* 2.50
339 *Deon Grant, Alvin McKinley* 1.00
340 *Dez White, Frank Murphy* 1.00
341 *Ron Dugans, Curtis Keaton* 1.50
342 *Dennis Northcutt, Travis Prentice* 2.50
343 *Dwayne Goodrich, Orantes Grant* 1.00
344 *Deltha O'Neal, Ian Gold* 1.00
345 *Stockar McDougle, Barrett Green* 1.00
346 *Na'il Diggs, Anthony Lucas* 1.00
347 *Marcus Washington, Dan Kendra* 1.00
348 *T.J. Slaughter, Shyrone Stith* 1.50
349 *William Bartee, Frank Moreau* 1.50
350 *Deon Dyer, Todd Wade* 1.00

No.	Player	Price
351	*Chris Hovan, Troy Walters*	1.50
352	*David Stachelski, Tom Brady*	10.00
353	*Terrelle Smith, Marc Bulger*	1.00
354	*Ron Dixon, Cornelius Griffin*	2.00
355	*Laveranues Coles, Anthony Becht*	2.00
356	*Sebastian Janikowski, Shane Lechler*	1.50
357	*Todd Pinkston, Gari Scott*	1.50
358	*Danny Farmer, Tee Martin*	1.50
359	*Jacoby Shepherd, Brian Young*	1.00
360	*Trevor Gaylor, JaJuan Seider*	1.50
361	*Chafie Fields, Tim Rattay*	1.50
362	*Darrell Jackson, James Williams*	2.00
363	*Nate Webster, James Whalen*	1.00
364	*Erron Kinney, Chris Coleman*	1.00
365	*Chris Samuels, Leon Murray*	1.00
366	Arizona Cardinals Team	.50
367	Atlanta Falcons Team	.25
368	Baltimore Ravens Team	.50
369	Buffalo Bills Team	.50
370	Carolina Panthers Team	.25
371	Chicago Bears Team	.50
372	Cincinnati Bengals Team	.50
373	Cleveland Browns Team	.75
374	Dallas Cowboys Team	1.50
375	Denver Broncos Team	.50
376	Detroit Lions Team	.25
377	Green Bay Packers Team	.50
378	Indianapolis Colts Team	1.50
379	Jacksonville Jaguars Team	.50
380	Kansas City Chiefs Team	.25
381	Miami Dolphins Team	1.50
382	Minnesota Vikings Team	.50
383	New England Patriots Team	.50
384	New Orleans Saints Team	.75
385	New York Giants Team	.25
386	New York Jets Team	.25
387	Oakland Raiders Team	.25
388	Philadelphia Eagles Team	.50
389	Pittsburgh Steelers Team	.25
390	St. Louis Rams Team	.50
391	San Diego Chargers Team	.25
392	San Francisco 49ers Team	.50
393	Seattle Seahawks Team	.25
394	Tampa Bay Buccaneers Team	.25
395	Tennessee Titans Team	.50
396	Washington Redskins Team	.25
397	Tim Couch CL	.75
398	Peyton Manning CL	1.50
399	Kurt Warner CL	1.50
400	Randy Moss CL	1.50
401	*JaJuan Dawson*	2.50
402	*Mike Anderson*	15.00
403	*Windrell Hayes*	1.00
404	*Shockmain Davis*	1.00
405	*Dante Hall*	20.00
406	*Charles Lee*	1.00
407	*Maurice Smith*	2.00
408	*Obafemi Ayanbadejo*	1.00
409	Travis Taylor	3.00
410	Dez White	3.00
411	Sammy Morris	3.00
412	Darrell Jackson	3.00
413	Todd Pinkston	3.00
414	Ron Dixon	2.00
415	Frank Moreau	1.00
416	James Williams	1.00
417	*Lenzie Jackson*	1.00
418	*Chad Morton*	3.00
419	*Matt Lytle*	1.00
420	Travis Prentice	3.00
421	Laveranues Coles	4.00
422	*Clint Stoerner*	2.00
423	*KaRon Coleman*	1.00
424	Ron Dugans	1.00
425	Dennis Northcutt	2.00
426	*Herbert Goodman*	1.00
427	*Dane Looker*	1.00
428	*Mike Brown*	2.00
429	*Derrius Thompson*	1.00
430	Danny Farmer	3.00
431	*Bashir Yamini*	1.00
432	Trevor Gaylor	1.00
433	*Erron Kinney*	1.00
434	*James Hodgins*	1.00
435	*Aaron Shea*	1.00
436	*Patrick Pass*	1.00
437	Terrelle Smith	1.00
438	Avion Black	1.00
439	Deltha O'Neal	2.00
440	Chris Coleman	2.00
441	*Reggie Jones*	2.00
442	Shyrone Stith	1.00
443	*Aaron Stecker*	2.00
444	Chris Redman	3.00
445	Curtis Keaton	1.00
446	*Jamel White*	2.00
447	Troy Walters	1.00
448	Spergon Wynn	2.00
449	*Ronney Jenkins*	1.00
450	*Doug Johnson*	2.00

2000 Fleer Glossy Traditional Threads

NM/M

Common Player: 15.00
Inserted 1:Factory Set

No.	Player	Price
1	Troy Aikman 140	40.00
2	Jamal Anderson 225	15.00
3	Charlie Batch 55	20.00
4	Drew Bledsoe 325	20.00
5	David Boston 55	25.00
6	Tim Brown 81	20.00
7	Mark Brunell 700	18.00
8	Chris Chandler 12	30.00
9	Tim Couch 430	25.00
10	Germane Crowell 82	20.00
11	Stephen Davis 155	20.00
12	Terrell Davis 100	40.00
13	Ron Dayne 27	35.00
14	Curtis Enis 44	35.00
15	Marshall Faulk 275	30.00
16	Brett Favre 585	50.00
17	Doug Flutie 7	60.00
18	Antonio Freeman 86	20.00
19	Brian Griese 165	30.00
20	Marvin Harrison 250	20.00
21	Torry Holt 55	35.00
22	Edgerrin James 285	60.00
23	Dorsey Levens 25	45.00
24	Peyton Manning 345	60.00
25	Dan Marino 14	100.00
26	Curtis Martin 90	25.00
27	Steve McNair 200	20.00
28	Herman Moore 15	45.00
29	Johnnie Morton 25	35.00
30	Jake Plummer 250	25.00
31	Junior Seau 55	35.00
32	Antowain Smith 26	25.00
33	Emmitt Smith 750	45.00
34	Rod Smith 25	35.00
35	Fred Taylor 325	30.00
36	Vinny Testaverde 225	15.00
37	Amani Toomer 25	30.00
38	Kurt Warner 700	50.00
39	Charles Woodson 24	35.00
40	Steve Young 125	35.00

2000 Fleer Greats of the Game

NM/M

Complete Set (130): 250.00
Common Player: .15
Minor Stars: .30
Common Rookie: 2.00
Production 1,500 Sets
Cards #131-134 are Redemptions
Production 500 Sets
Pack (5): 5.00
Wax Box (24): 100.00

No.	Player	Price
1	Terry Bradshaw	2.50
2	Paul Hornung	.50
3	Tony Dorsett	.50
4	L.C. Greenwood	.15
5	Ozzie Newsome	.30
6	Michael Irvin	.30
7	Art Donovan	.30
8	Don Maynard	.30
9	Bobby Mitchell	.15
10	Bob Lilly	.15
11	Earl Morrall	.15
12	Harvey Martin	.15
13	Dan Fouts	.50
14	Joe Theismann	.30
15	Roger Staubach	2.50
16	Otto Graham	.50
17	Cliff Branch	.30
18	Sonny Jurgensen	.30
19	Eric Dickerson	.30
20	Lee Roy Selmon	.15
21	Roger Craig	.30
22	Raymond Berry	.15
23	Bob Hayes	.30
24	Steve Largent	.50
25	Lenny Moore	.15
26	Chuck Bednarik	.15
27	Ken Stabler	2.00
28	William Perry	.30
29	Joe Greene	.30
30	Joe Namath	2.50
31	Jim Kelly	.50
32	Steve Young	.75
33	Randy White	.30
34	Lawrence Taylor	.30
35	Franco Harris	.50
36	Marcus Allen	.50
37	Mike Singletary	.30
38	Fran Tarkenton	1.00
39	Mel Renfro	.15
40	Len Dawson	.50
41	Carl Eller	.15
42	Chuck Foreman	.15
43	Gino Marchetti	.15
44	Jim Marshall	.15
45	Jack Ham	.15
46	Mercury Morris	.15
47	Anthony Munoz	.15
48	Herschel Walker	.30
49	Drew Pearson	.15
50	John Elway	2.50
51	George Blanda	.30
52	Earl Campbell	.50
53	Bart Starr	2.00
54	Dan Marino	2.50
55	Johnny Unitas	2.00
56	Sammy Baugh	.50
57	Steve Van Buren	.15
58	Mel Blount	.15
59	Fred Biletnikoff	.30
60	John Brodie	.15
61	Daryle Lamonica	.15
62	James Lofton	.30
63	Ronnie Lott	.30
64	Gale Sayers	1.00
65	Art Monk	.30
66	Jim Plunkett	.30
67	Charlie Joiner	.30
68	Deacon Jones	.30
69	Paul Warfield	.50
70	Jim Otto	.15
71	Billy Kilmer	.15
72	Archie Manning	.30
73	Alex Karras	.30
74	Tom Matte	.15
75	Jay Novacek	.15
76	Charley Taylor	.15
77	Sam Huff	.15
78	Jack Lambert	.15
79	Mike Ditka	1.00
80	Frank Gifford	.75
81	Jim Thorpe	.50
82	Walter Payton	3.00
83	Doak Walker	.15
84	Sid Luckman	.15
85	Bronko Nagurski	.50
86	Alan Ameche	.15
87	Merlin Olsen	.30
88	Dick Butkus	1.00
89	Elroy Hirsch	.30
90	Max McGee	.30
91	Ray Nitschke	.50
92	Phil Simms	.30
93	Vince Lombardi	1.50
94	Tom Landry	1.00
95	Bill Walsh	.30
96	Mike Ditka	.75
97	Jimmy Johnson	.30
98	Chuck Noll	.15
99	Dan Reeves	.30
100	Don Shula	.50
101	*Peter Warrick*	12.00
102	*Thomas Jones*	10.00
103	*Jamal Lewis*	20.00
104	*Chad Pennington*	30.00
105	*Chris Redman*	5.00
106	*Ron Dayne*	5.00
107	*Trung Canidate*	8.00
108	*Shaun Alexander*	20.00
109	*Plaxico Burress*	15.00
110	*J.R. Redmond*	6.00
111	*Travis Taylor*	5.00
112	*Dez White*	8.00
113	*Todd Pinkston*	8.00
114	*Laveranues Coles*	12.00
115	*Dennis Northcutt*	5.00
116	*Jerry Porter*	10.00
117	*R. Jay Soward*	6.00
118	*Sylvester Morris*	5.00
119	*Ron Dugans*	5.00
120	*Travis Prentice*	6.00
121	*Tee Martin*	6.00
122	*James Williams*	5.00
123	*Trevor Gaylor*	6.00
124	*Shyrone Stith*	3.00
125	*Frank Moreau*	2.00
126	*Kwame Cavil*	2.00
127	*Ron Dixon*	3.00
128	*Darrell Jackson*	12.00
129	*Sammy Morris*	3.00
130	*JuJuan Dawson*	2.00
131	*Doug Johnson*	20.00
132	*Brian Urlacher*	60.00
133	*Brad Hoover*	20.00
134	*Mike Anderson AUTO*	30.00

2000 Fleer Greats of the Game Autographs

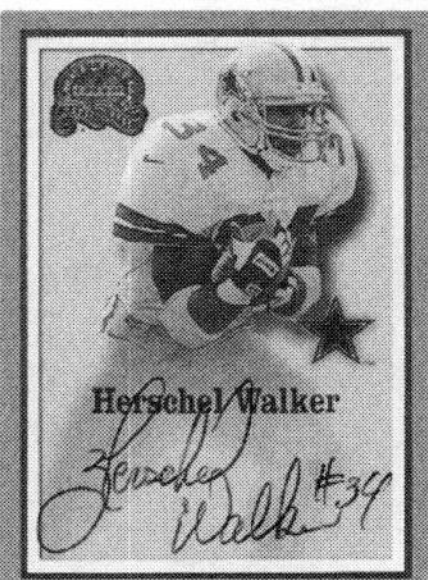

NM/M

Common Player: 10.00
Minor Stars: 20.00
Inserted 1:24

No.	Player	Price
1	Marcus Allen	25.00
2	Sammy Baugh	100.00
3	Chuck Bednarik	10.00
4	Raymond Berry	10.00
5	Fred Biletnikoff	20.00
6	George Blanda	30.00
7	Mel Blount	20.00
8	Terry Bradshaw	100.00
9	Cliff Branch	20.00
10	John Brodie	150.00
11	Earl Campbell	40.00
12	Roger Craig	20.00
13	Len Dawson	25.00
14	Eric Dickerson	20.00
15	Mike Ditka	60.00
16	Mike Ditka CC	60.00
17	Art Donovan	20.00
18	Tony Dorsett	50.00
19	Carl Eller	50.00
20	John Elway	125.00
21	Chuck Foreman	20.00
22	Dan Fouts	20.00
23	Frank Gifford	75.00
24	Otto Graham	30.00
25	Joe Greene	40.00
26	L.C. Greenwood	20.00
27	Jack Ham	20.00
28	Franco Harris	50.00
29	Bob Hayes	30.00
30	Paul Hornung	50.00
31	Sam Huff	20.00
32	Michael Irvin	50.00
33	Jimmy Johnson	75.00
34	Charlie Joiner	10.00
35	Deacon Jones	25.00
36	Sonny Jurgensen	40.00
37	Alex Karras	30.00
38	Jim Kelly	50.00
39	Billy Kilmer	25.00
40	Jack Lambert	50.00
41	Daryle Lamonica	25.00
42	Steve Largent	30.00
43	Bob Lilly	20.00
44	James Lofton	20.00
45	Ronnie Lott	25.00
46	Archie Manning	30.00
47	Gino Marchetti	20.00
48	Dan Marino	150.00
49	Jim Marshall	25.00
50	Harvey Martin	20.00
51	Tom Matte	10.00
52	Don Maynard	20.00
53	Bobby Mitchell	10.00
54	Art Monk	60.00
55	Lenny Moore	10.00
56	Earl Morrall	10.00
57	Mercury Morris	20.00
58	Anthony Munoz	20.00
59	Joe Namath	85.00
60	Ozzie Newsome	20.00
61	Chuck Noll	75.00
62	Jay Novacek	20.00
63	Jim Otto	20.00
64	Drew Pearson	20.00
65	William Perry	20.00
66	Jim Plunkett	30.00
67	Dan Reeves	35.00
68	Mel Renfro	10.00
69	Gale Sayers	40.00
70	Lee Roy Selmon	10.00
71	Don Shula	75.00
72	Mike Singletary	20.00
73	Ken Stabler	30.00
74	Bart Starr	150.00
75	Roger Staubach	100.00
76	Fran Tarkenton	50.00
77	Charley Taylor	10.00
78	Lawrence Taylor	75.00
79	Joe Theismann	30.00
80	Johnny Unitas	150.00
81	Steve Van Buren	100.00
82	Herschel Walker	30.00
83	Bill Walsh	75.00
84	Paul Warfield	20.00
85	Randy White	20.00
86	Steve Young	60.00

2000 Fleer Greats of the Game Cowboys Clippings

NM/M

Complete Set (9): 600.00
Common Player: 25.00
Inserted 1:72
Card #3 Bob Hayes was never issued

No.	Player	Price
CCL1	Troy Aikman	50.00
CCL2	Tony Dorsett	50.00
CCL4	Michael Irvin	25.00
CCL5	Tom Landry SP	225.00
CCL6	Bob Lilly	25.00
CCL7	Harvey Martin Shoes	75.00
CCL8	Jay Novacek	25.00
CCL9	Mel Renfro	25.00
CCL10	Roger Staubach	60.00

2000 Fleer Greats of the Game Feel The Game Classics

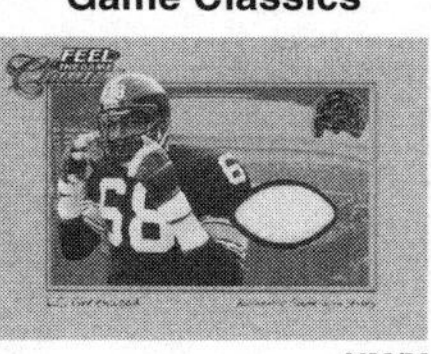

NM/M

Common Player: 25.00
Inserted 1:36

No.	Player	Price
1	Marcus Allen	25.00
2	Fred Biletnikoff	25.00
3	Terry Bradshaw	50.00
4	Eric Dickerson	25.00
5	John Elway	50.00
6	L.C. Greenwood Jersey	25.00
7	L.C. Greenwood Shoe	35.00
8	Paul Hornung Pants	35.00
9	Jim Kelly	35.00
10	James Lofton	25.00
11	Ronnie Lott	25.00
12	Dan Marino White	50.00
13	Dan Marino Teal	50.00
14	Joe Namath	50.00
15	Walter Payton	75.00
16	Jim Plunkett Black	25.00
17	Jim Plunkett White	25.00
18	Mike Singletary	25.00
19	Bart Starr Pants	50.00
20	Fran Tarkenton	35.00
21	Lawrence Taylor	35.00
22	Johnny Unitas	50.00
23	Steve Young	30.00

2000 Fleer Greats of the Game Retrospection Collection

NM/M

Complete Set (10): 18.00
Common Player: 1.00
Inserted 1:6

No.	Player	Price
RC1	Terry Bradshaw	3.00
RC2	John Elway	3.00
RC3	Roger Staubach	2.50
RC4	Franco Harris	1.00
RC5	Paul Hornung	1.00
RC6	Dan Marino	3.00
RC7	Fran Tarkenton	1.50
RC8	Joe Namath	3.00
RC9	Walter Payton	4.00
RC10	Jim Thorpe	1.00

2000 Fleer Mystique

NM/M

Complete Set (145): 225.00
Common Player: .25
Minor Stars: .50
Common Rookie: 1.00
Production 2,000 Sets
Pack (5): 3.00
Wax Box (20): 40.00

No.	Player	Price
1	Tim Couch	1.50
2	Edgerrin James	2.50
3	Terrell Davis	1.50
4	Eddie George	1.00
5	Jevon Kearse	.75
6	Mike Alstott	.75
7	Tony Martin	.25
8	Jermaine Fazande	.50
9	Akili Smith	.75
10	Damon Huard	.75
11	Kordell Stewart	.75
12	Peyton Manning	3.50
13	Michael Westbrook	.50
14	Tim Biakabutuka	.50
15	Curtis Martin	.75
16	Shaun King	1.25
17	Jamal Anderson	.75
18	Terry Allen	.50
19	Sean Dawkins	.25
20	Muhsin Muhammad	.50
21	Vinny Testaverde	.75
22	Warren Sapp	.25
23	Wesley Walls	.50
24	Mark Brunell	1.25
25	Tim Brown	.75
26	Kevin Dyson	.50
27	Curtis Enis	.50
28	Keenan McCardell	.50
29	Rich Gannon	.50
30	Jermaine Lewis	.25
31	Johnnie Morton	.50
32	Kerry Collins	.50
33	Az-Zahir Hakim	.50
34	Cade McNown	1.00
35	Jimmy Smith	.75
36	Tyrone Wheatley	.50
37	Marcus Robinson	.75
38	Fred Taylor	1.25
39	Donovan McNabb	1.50
40	Steve McNair	.75
41	Corey Dillon	.75
42	Tony Gonzalez	.50
43	Duce Staley	.75
44	Albert Connell	.50
45	Isaac Bruce	.75
46	Troy Aikman	1.75
47	Charlie Garner	.50
48	Kevin Johnson	.50
49	Cris Carter	.75
50	Ryan Leaf	.75
51	Doug Flutie	1.00
52	Brett Favre	3.50
53	Joe Montgomery	.25
54	Torry Holt	.75
55	Jonathon Linton	.50
56	Antonio Freeman	.75
57	Amani Toomer	.50
58	Kurt Warner	2.50
59	Jake Plummer	1.00
60	Rob Johnson	.50
61	Randy Moss	3.50
62	Jerry Rice	1.75
63	Chris Chandler	.50
64	Joey Galloway	.75
65	Olandis Gary	1.00
66	Drew Bledsoe	1.25
67	Steve Beuerlein	.50
68	Marvin Harrison	.75
69	Keyshawn Johnson	.75
70	Warrick Dunn	.75
71	Tim Dwight	.75
72	Brian Griese	1.00
73	Terry Glenn	.75
74	Jon Kitna	.75
75	Qadry Ismail	.25
76	Germane Crowell	.75
77	Ricky Williams	1.00
78	Marshall Faulk	.75
79	Karim Abdul	.25
80	J.J. Johnson	.50
81	Hines Ward	.50
82	Frank Sanders	.50
83	Emmitt Smith	2.50
84	Robert Smith	.75
85	Steve Young	1.25
86	Darnay Scott	.50
87	Tamarick Vanover	.25
88	Troy Edwards	.75
89	Brad Johnson	.75
90	Tony Banks	.50
91	Charlie Batch	.75
92	Jeff Blake	.50
93	Ricky Watters	.50
94	Carl Pickens	.50
95	Elvis Grbac	.50
96	Jerome Bettis	.75
97	Eric Moulds	.75
98	Dorsey Levens	.75
99	Wayne Chrebet	.75
100	Stephen Davis	.75
101	*Shaun Alexander*	12.00
102	*Sebastian Janikowski*	4.00
103	*Tom Brady*	30.00
104	*Courtney Brown*	4.00
105	*Marc Bulger*	10.00
106	*Plaxico Burress*	10.00
107	*Trung Canidate*	4.00
108	*Giovanni Carmazzi*	2.00
109	*Trevor Gaylor*	2.00
110	*Laveranues Coles*	8.00
111	*Ron Dayne*	3.00
112	*Reuben Droughns*	6.00
113	*Danny Farmer*	4.00
114	*Chafie Fields*	1.00
115	*Bubba Franks*	6.00
116	*Sherrod Gideon*	1.00
117	*Joe Hamilton*	4.00
118	*Chris Cole*	1.00
119	*Darrell Jackson*	8.00
120	*Thomas Jones*	6.00
121	*Jamal Lewis*	12.00
122	*Anthony Lucas*	2.50
123	*Tee Martin*	4.00
124	*Frank Murphy*	1.00
125	*Rondell Mealey*	1.00
126	*Sylvester Morris*	2.00
127	*Dennis Northcutt*	2.00
128	*Chad Pennington*	20.00
129	*Travis Prentice*	5.00
130	*Tim Rattay*	6.00
131	*Chris Redman*	2.00
132	*J.R. Redmond*	2.00
133	*R. Jay Soward*	5.00
134	*Quinton Spotwood*	1.00
135	*Shyrone Stith*	1.00
136	*Travis Taylor*	5.00
137	*Troy Walters*	2.00
138	*Peter Warrick*	8.00
139	*Dez White*	3.00
140	*Michael Wiley*	2.00
141	*Jerry Porter*	8.00
142	*Mareno Philyaw*	1.00
143	*Anthony Becht*	1.00
144	*JaJuan Dawson*	2.00
145	*Ron Dugans*	1.00

2000 Fleer Mystique Gold

Gold Cards: 2X-4X
Gold Rookies: 1.5X
Inserted 1:20

2000 Fleer Mystique Big Buzz

NM/M

Complete Set (10): 15.00
Common Player: 1.50
Inserted 1:10

No.	Player	Price
1	Peter Warrick	2.00
2	Shaun Alexander	3.00

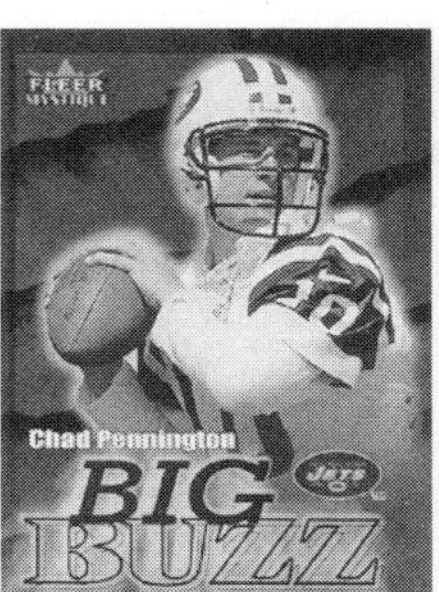

3 Ron Dayne 2.00
NM/M
4 Joe Hamilton 1.50
5 Thomas Jones 2.00
6 Jamal Lewis 5.00
7 Chad Pennington 5.00
8 Tim Rattay 1.75
9 Chris Redman 2.00
10 Plaxico Burress 2.50

2000 Fleer Mystique Canton Calling

NM/M
Complete Set (10): 25.00
Common Player: 1.00
Minor Stars: 2.00
Inserted 1:20
1 Jerry Rice 4.00
2 Troy Aikman 4.00
3 Dan Marino 5.00
4 Brett Favre 5.00
5 Peyton Manning 4.00
6 Emmitt Smith 5.00
7 Randy Moss 4.00
8 Marvin Harrison 2.00
9 Marshall Faulk 2.00
10 Thurman Thomas 1.00

2000 Fleer Mystique Destination Tampa

NM/M
Complete Set (10): 15.00
Common Player: 1.00
Inserted 1:10
1 Kurt Warner 3.00
2 Peyton Manning 4.00
3 Brett Favre 4.00
4 Tim Couch 1.75
5 Keyshawn Johnson 1.00
6 Mark Brunell 1.50
7 Eddie George 1.25
8 Edgerrin James 3.00
9 Ricky Williams 2.00
10 Randy Moss 4.00

2000 Fleer Mystique Numbers Game

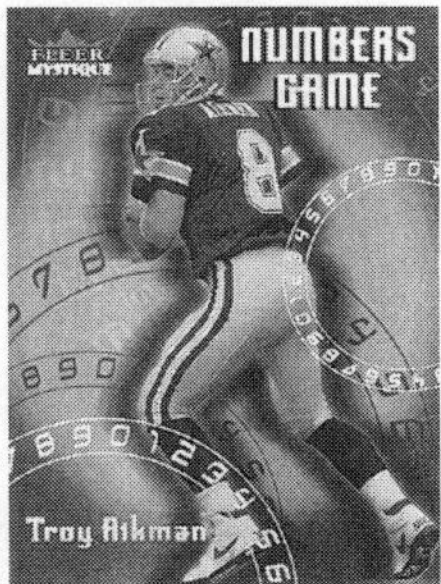

NM/M
Complete Set (10): 35.00
Common Player: 3.00
Inserted 1:40
Red Zone cards: 4X
Production 100 Sets
1 Kurt Warner 5.00
2 Peyton Manning 6.00
3 Keyshawn Johnson 3.00
4 Terrell Davis 4.00
5 Brett Favre 6.00
6 Jevon Kearse 3.00
7 Troy Aikman 5.00
8 Edgerrin James 5.00
9 Eddie George 4.00
10 Marshall Faulk 3.00

2000 Fleer Mystique Running Men

NM/M
Complete Set (20): 15.00
Common Player: .50
Minor Stars: 1.00
Inserted 1:5
1 Antowain Smith 1.00
2 Corey Dillon 1.00
3 Terrell Davis 2.00
4 Edgerrin James 2.00
5 Fred Taylor 1.50
6 Kevin Faulk .50
7 Jerome Bettis 1.00
8 Ricky Watters 1.00
9 Eddie George 1.25
10 Jamal Anderson 1.00
11 Tim Biakabutuka .50
12 Curtis Enis .50
13 Emmitt Smith 2.50

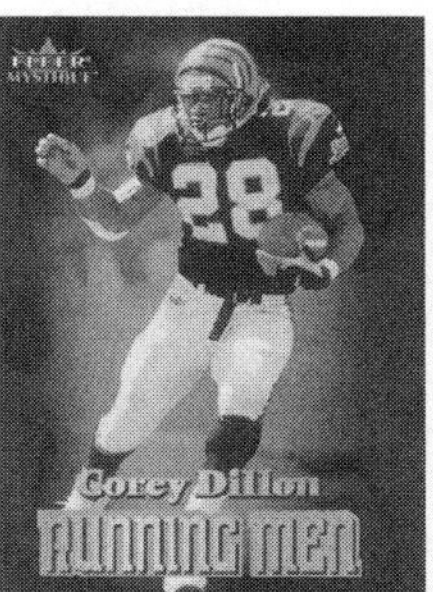

14 James Stewart .50
NM/M
15 Dorsey Levens 1.00
16 Robert Smith 1.00
17 Duce Staley 1.00
18 Marshall Faulk 1.00
19 Stephen Davis 1.00
20 Mike Alstott 1.00

2000 Fleer Showcase

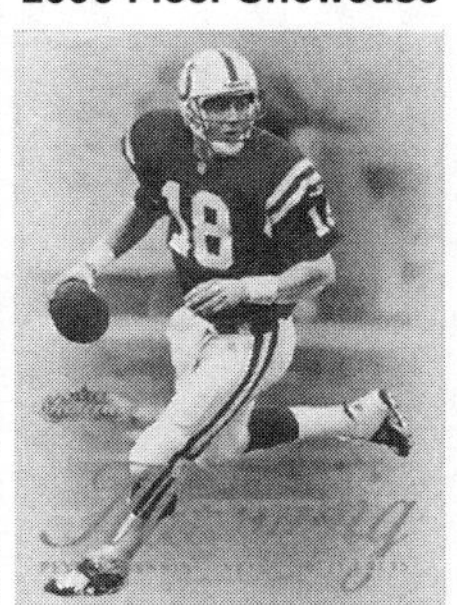

NM/M
Complete Set (160): 300.00
Common Player: .15
Minor Stars: .30
Common Rookie (101-120): 3.00
Production 1,000 Sets
Common Rookie (121-160): 2.00
Production 2,000 Sets
Pack (5): 3.50
Wax Box (24): 60.00
1 Tim Couch 1.25
2 Deion Sanders .50
3 Darnay Scott .30
4 Brett Favre 2.50
5 Mark Brunell 1.00
6 Randy Moss 2.00
7 Tyrone Wheatley .30
8 Isaac Bruce .50
9 Eddie George .75
10 Troy Aikman 1.50
11 Charlie Batch .50
12 Marvin Harrison .50
13 Terry Glenn .50
14 Charles Johnson .15
15 Jerry Rice 1.50
16 Kurt Warner 2.00
17 Kevin Johnson .50
18 Jay Fiedler .50
19 Vinny Testaverde .50
20 Curtis Enis .50
21 Elvis Grbac .30
22 Kordell Stewart .50
23 Jamal Anderson .50
24 Dorsey Levens .50
25 Derrick Mayes .30
26 Marcus Robinson .50
27 Cam Cleeland .30
28 Charlie Garner .30
29 Germane Crowell .50
30 Cade McNown .75
31 Tony Gonzalez .30
32 Shaun King 1.00
33 Wayne Chrebet .50
34 Muhsin Muhammad .30
35 Olandis Gary .50
36 Ray Lewis .15
37 Terrell Davis 1.00
38 Steve Beuerlein .30
39 James Stewart .30
40 Jon Kitna .50
41 Tim Biakabutuka .30
42 Ryan Leaf .50
43 Mike Alstott .50
44 Yancey Thigpen .30
45 Champ Bailey .50
46 Peerless Price .50
47 Ken Dilger .15
48 Derrick Alexander .15
49 Drew Bledsoe 1.00
50 Jerome Bettis .50
51 Jermaine Fazande .30
52 Joey Galloway .50
53 Jeff Blake .30
54 Emmitt Smith 1.75
55 Ricky Williams 1.00
56 Marshall Faulk .50
57 Stephen Davis .50
58 Rob Johnson .30
59 Brian Griese .75
60 Damon Huard .50
61 Jevon Kearse .50
62 Doug Flutie .75
63 Curtis Martin .50
64 Torry Holt .50
65 David Boston .50
66 Cris Carter .50
67 Jason Sehorn .15
68 Keyshawn Johnson .50
69 Chris Chandler .30
70 Antonio Freeman .50
71 Kerry Collins .30
72 Akili Smith .50
73 Troy Edwards .50
74 Tim Dwight .50
75 Donovan McNabb 1.50
76 Tony Banks .30
77 Ed McCaffrey .50
78 Errict Rhett .30
79 Fred Taylor 1.00
80 Terrell Owens .50
81 Steve McNair .60
82 Rob Moore .30
83 Jimmy Smith .50
84 Daunte Culpepper 1.25
85 Carl Pickens .30
86 Moses Moreno .15
87 Brad Johnson .50
88 Jake Plummer .50
89 Edgerrin James 2.50
90 Zach Thomas .30
91 Rich Gannon .30
92 Warrick Dunn .50
93 Shannon Sharpe .30
94 Peyton Manning 2.00
95 Keenan McCardell .30
96 Tony Simmons .15
97 Duce Staley .50
98 Corey Dillon .50
99 Tim Brown .50
100 Ricky Watters .30
101 *Peter Warrick* 12.00
102 *Shaun Alexander* 20.00
103 *Anthony Becht* 2.00
104 *Courtney Brown* 5.00
105 *Plaxico Burress* 15.00
106 *Trung Canidate* 8.00
107 *Giovanni Carmazzi* 3.00
108 *Laveranues Coles* 12.00
109 *Ron Dayne* 5.00
110 *Reuben Droughns* 6.00
111 *Danny Farmer* 4.00
112 *Bubba Franks* 10.00
113 *Thomas Jones* 10.00
114 *Jamal Lewis* 20.00
115 *Sylvester Morris* 5.00
116 *Chad Pennington* 30.00
117 *Travis Prentice* 6.00
118 *J.R. Redmond* 6.00
119 *R. Jay Soward* 5.00
120 *Dez White* 8.00
121 *Sebastian Janikowski* 6.00
122 *Todd Pinkston* 8.00
123 *Spergon Wynn* 5.00
124 *Ron Dugans* 3.00
125 *Joe Hamilton* 6.00
126 *Curtis Keaton* 3.00
127 *Tee Martin* 6.00
128 *Dennis Northcutt* 3.00
129 *Corey Simon* 3.00
130 *Chris Redman* 6.00
131 *Brian Urlacher* 15.00
132 *Travis Taylor* 8.00
133 *Michael Wiley* 6.00
134 *Tim Rattay* 8.00
135 *Jerry Porter* 10.00
136 *Tom Brady* 40.00
137 *Deon Dyer* 2.00
138 *Mareno Philyaw* 2.00
139 *Shaun Ellis* 2.00
140 *John Abraham* 2.00
141 *Ahmed Plummer* 2.00
142 *Chris Hovan* 5.00
143 *Rob Morris* 3.00
144 *Keith Bulluck* 2.00
145 *JaJuan Dawson* 3.00
146 *Chris Cole* 2.00
147 *Chafie Fields* 2.00
148 *Darrell Jackson* 12.00
149 *Marcus Knight* 2.00
150 *Gari Scott* 2.00
151 *Kwame Cavil* 2.00
152 *Frank Moreau* 2.00
153 *Doug Chapman* 2.00
154 *Erron Kinney* 2.00
155 *Ron Dixon* 3.00
156 *Ben Kelly* 2.00
157 *Bashir Yamini* 2.00
158 *Anthony Lucas* 3.00
159 *Avion Black* 2.00
160 *Ian Gold* 2.00

2000 Fleer Showcase Legacy

Legacy Cards: 25X-50X
Legacy Rookies (#101-120): 2.5X
Legacy Rookies (#121-160): 4X-8X
Production 20 Sets

2000 Fleer Showcase Rookie Showcase Firsts

#1-20 Firsts: 1X
#21-60 Firsts: 2X
Production 250 Sets

2000 Fleer Showcase Autographics

NM/M
Common Player: 10.00
Minor Stars: 20.00
Inserted 1:24
Silver Cards: 1.2X
Production 250 Sets
1 Champ Bailey 20.00
2 Donnell Bennett 10.00
3 Jerome Bettis 20.00
4 Drew Bledsoe 40.00
5 David Boston 20.00
6 Tom Brady 75.00
7 Trung Canidate 10.00
8 Giovanni Carmazzi 30.00
9 Darren Chiaverini 10.00
10 Laveranues Coles 20.00
11 Kerry Collins 20.00
12 Daunte Culpepper 65.00
13 Stephen Davis 25.00
14 Ron Dayne 35.00
15 Corey Dillon 25.00
16 Tim Dwight 10.00
17 Deon Dyer 10.00
18 Kevin Dyson 10.00
19 Danny Farmer 20.00
20 Kevin Faulk 10.00
21 Marshall Faulk 25.00
22 Christian Fauria 10.00
23 Olandis Gary 25.00
24 Trevor Gaylor 10.00
25 Tony Gonzalez 20.00
26 Az-Zahir Hakim 20.00
27 Joe Hamilton 20.00
28 Marvin Harrison 25.00
29 Priest Holmes 20.00
30 Torry Holt 20.00
31 Damon Huard 20.00
32 Raghib Ismail 10.00
33 Patrick Jeffers 20.00
34 Curtis Keaton 10.00
35 Curtis Martin 25.00
36 Tee Martin 25.00
37 Shane Matthews 10.00
38 Derrick Mayes 10.00
39 Ed McCaffrey 20.00
40 Cade McNown 25.00
41 Herman Moore 20.00
42 Sylvester Morris 30.00
43 Johnnie Morton 10.00
45 Muhsin Muhammad 10.00
46 Dennis Northcutt 20.00
47 Terrell Owens 25.00
48 Chad Pennington 75.00
49 Jake Plummer 25.00
50 Travis Prentice 20.00
51 Peerless Price 20.00
52 John Randle 10.00
53 Tim Rattay 20.00
54 Chris Redmond 45.00
55 Jay Riemersma 10.00
56 Marcus Robinson 20.00
57 Warren Sapp 20.00
58 Gari Scott 10.00
59 Jason Sehorn 10.00
60 Shannon Sharpe 20.00
61 David Sloan 10.00
62 Akili Smith 25.00
63 Rod Smith 20.00
64 R. Jay Soward 10.00
65 Shawn Springs 10.00
66 Duce Staley 25.00
67 Kordell Stewart 25.00
68 Michael Strahan 10.00
69 Amani Toomer 10.00
70 Kurt Warner 50.00
71 Peter Warrick 25.00
72 Tyrone Wheatley 20.00
73 Frank Wycheck 10.00

2000 Fleer Showcase Air to the Throne

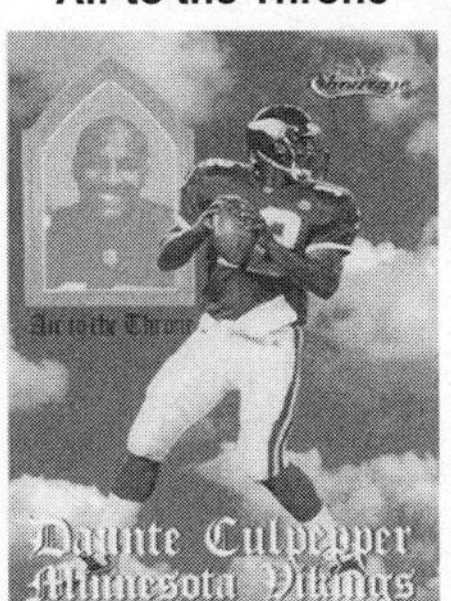

NM/M
Complete Set (10): 12.00
Common Player: 1.00
Inserted 1:10
1 Peyton Manning 5.00
2 Charlie Batch 1.00
3 Giovanni Carmazzi 1.50
4 Brian Griese 1.50
5 Daunte Culpepper 2.50
6 Steve McNair 1.50
7 Brad Johnson 1.00
8 Rob Johnson 1.00
9 Cade McNown 1.50
10 Chad Pennington 5.00

2000 Fleer Showcase Feel the Game

NM/M
Common Player: 15.00
Inserted 1:72
Gold Cards: 2X
Production 50 Sets
1 Troy Aikman 50.00
2 Jamal Anderson 20.00
3 David Boston 20.00
4 Curtis Conway 15.00
5 Tim Couch 30.00
6 Germane Crowell 20.00
7 Kevin Dyson 15.00
8 Curtis Enis Pants 20.00
9 Brett Favre 60.00
10 Eddie George 40.00
11 Rob Johnson 15.00
12 Jevon Kearse 30.00
13 Peyton Manning 50.00
14 Steve McNair 40.00
15 Rob Moore 15.00
16 Johnnie Morton 15.00
17 Jake Plummer 25.00
18 Jerry Rice 50.00
19 Deion Sanders 25.00
20 Frank Sanders 15.00
21 Emmitt Smith 50.00
22 Jimmy Smith 20.00
23 J.J. Stokes 15.00
24 Fred Taylor 35.00
25 Kurt Warner Pants 50.00
26 Charles Woodson 15.00

2000 Fleer Showcase License to Skill

NM/M
Complete Set (10): 20.00
Common Player: 2.00
Inserted 1:20
1 Tim Couch 3.00
2 Keyshawn Johnson 2.00
3 Peyton Manning 5.00
4 Brett Favre 7.00
5 Terrell Davis 4.00
6 Cade McNown 2.00
7 Marvin Harrison 2.00
8 Eddie George 2.50
9 Randy Moss 5.00
10 Emmitt Smith 6.00

2000 Fleer Showcase Mission Possible

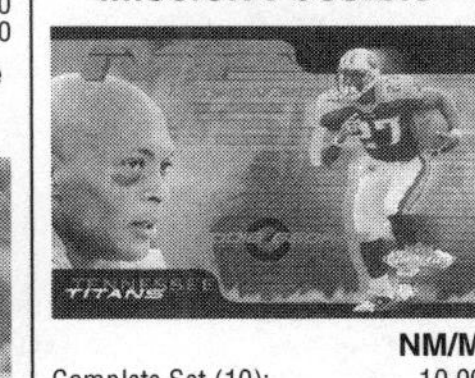

NM/M
Complete Set (10): 10.00
Common Player: .50
Inserted 1:5
1 Tim Couch 1.25
2 Brett Favre 3.00
3 Ricky Williams 1.50
4 Akili Smith .75
5 Shaun King .75
6 Marvin Harrison .75
7 Vinny Testaverde .50
8 Terrell Davis 2.00
9 Edgerrin James 3.00
10 Eddie George 1.00

2000 Fleer Showcase Next

NM/M
Complete Set (20): 15.00
Common Player: .50
Inserted 1:2.5
1 Peter Warrick 1.00
2 Bubba Franks .75
3 Jamal Lewis 3.00
4 Anthony Becht .50
5 R. Jay Soward .75
6 Courtney Brown .75
7 Plaxico Burress 2.00
8 Trung Canidate .50
9 Chris Redman 1.50
10 Laveranues Coles 2.00
11 Ron Dayne 1.00
12 Reuben Droughns .50
13 Danny Farmer .50
14 Travis Prentice 1.50
15 Dez White .50
16 Shaun Alexander 2.50
17 Thomas Jones 1.50
18 J.R. Redmond 1.00
19 Sylvester Morris 2.00
20 Chad Pennington 4.00

2000 Fleer Showcase Season Pass

1 Peyton Manning
2 Peter Warrick
3 Marshall Faulk
4 Ron Dayne
5 Keyshawn Johnson
6 Marvin Harrison

2000 Fleer Showcase Super Natural

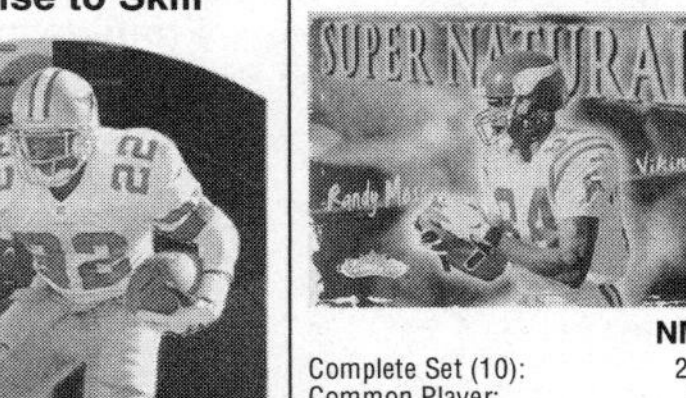

NM/M
Complete Set (10): 25.00
Common Player: 2.00
Inserted 1:20
1 Randy Moss 5.00
2 Marshall Faulk 2.00
3 Edgerrin James 4.00
4 Terrell Davis 4.00
5 Kurt Warner 4.00
6 Fred Taylor 3.00
7 Peyton Manning 5.00
8 Brett Favre 6.00
9 Brad Johnson 2.00
10 Warrick Dunn 2.00

2000 Fleer Showcase Touch Football

NM/M
Common Player: 8.00
Inserted 1:150
1 Trung Canidate 8.00
2 Thomas Jones 25.00
3 Curtis Keaton 8.00
4 Anthony Becht 8.00
5 Courtney Brown 12.00
6 Chris Redman 25.00
7 Dennis Northcutt 8.00
8 Sylvester Morris 30.00
9 Shaun Alexander 40.00
10 Todd Pinkston 10.00
11 Danny Farmer 10.00
12 Dez White 10.00
13 Laveranues Coles 12.00
14 R. Jay Soward 12.00
15 Jamal Lewis 40.00
16 J.R. Redmond 16.00
17 Travis Taylor 16.00
18 Plaxico Burress 30.00
19 Peter Warrick 20.00
20 Joe Hamilton 12.00
21 Ron Dugans 8.00
22 Tee Martin 12.00
23 Brian Urlacher 40.00
24 Ron Dayne 20.00
25 Travis Prentice 20.00
26 Chad Pennington 50.00
27 Bubba Franks 12.00
28 Reuben Droughns 8.00
29 Corey Simon 10.00
30 Jerry Porter 10.00

2001 Fleer Authority

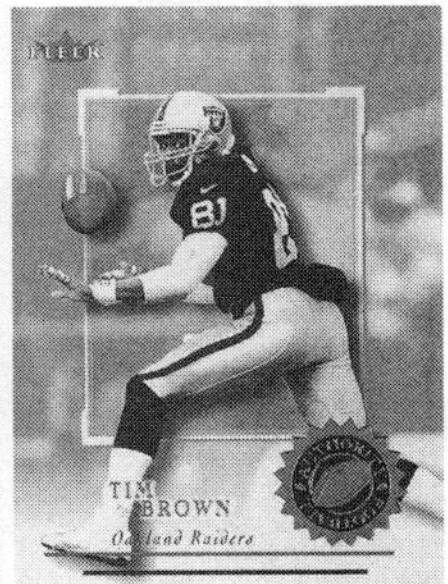

NM/M
Common Player: .15
Minor Stars: .30
Common Rookie: 3.00
Production 1,350 Sets
Pack (5): 3.50
Box (20): 50.00
1 Brian Urlacher 1.25

2 James Stewart .30
3 Lamar Smith .30
4 Curtis Martin .40
5 Shannon Sharpe .30
6 Germane Crowell .15
7 Daunte Culpepper 1.25
8 Charlie Garner .30
9 Jake Plummer .40
10 Eric Moulds .40
11 Brett Favre 2.50
12 Robert Smith .15
13 Tim Brown .50
14 David Boston .60
15 Cade McNown .15
16 Ahman Green .60
17 Terry Glenn .30
18 Wayne Chrebet .30
19 Jamal Lewis 1.25
20 Peter Warrick .50
21 Peyton Manning 2.00
22 Ricky Williams 1.00
23 Donovan McNabb 1.25
24 Isaac Bruce .60
25 Tim Couch .75
26 Marvin Harrison .60
27 Kerry Collins .30
28 Kordell Stewart .50
29 Keyshawn Johnson .50
30 Kevin Johnson .30
31 Mark Brunell .75
32 Ron Dayne .40
33 Doug Flutie .75
34 Warrick Dunn .30
35 Emmitt Smith 1.50
36 Jimmy Smith .30
37 Amani Toomer .15
38 Chad Pennington .60
39 Steve McNair .50
40 Brian Griese .75
41 Derrick Alexander .30
42 Vinny Testaverde .40
43 Terrell Owens .60
44 Derrick Mason .30
45 Mike Anderson 1.00
46 Michael Westbrook .30
47 Rich Gannon .50
48 Shaun Alexander 1.00
49 Jevon Kearse .30
50 Ed McCaffrey .30
51 Tony Gonzalez .30
52 Tyrone Wheatley .15
53 Kurt Warner 2.00
54 Stephen Davis .40
55 Rod Smith .50
56 Deion Sanders .50
57 Brad Johnson .50
58 Ike Hilliard .15
59 Trent Green .40
60 Terrell Davis 1.25
61 Warren Sapp .30
62 Marshall Faulk .75
63 Tiki Barber .30
64 Keenan McCardell .15
65 Joey Galloway .30
66 Frank Wycheck .15
67 Ricky Watters .30
68 Joe Horn .15
69 Fred Taylor .75
70 Troy Aikman 1.25
71 Mike Alstott .40
72 Matt Hasselbeck .40
73 Aaron Brooks .75
74 Terrence Wilkins .15
75 Travis Prentice .15
76 Eddie George .75
77 Jeff Garcia .50
78 Randy Moss 2.00
79 Edgerrin James 1.50
80 Corey Dillon .50
81 Torry Holt .60
82 Todd Pinkston .30
83 Drew Bledsoe .75
84 Antonio Freeman .50
85 Marcus Robinson .40
86 Muhsin Muhammad .15
87 Junior Seau .30
88 Zach Thomas .15
89 Dorsey Levens .30
90 Tim Biakabutuka .30
91 Elvis Grbac .50
92 Jerome Bettis .50
93 Cris Carter .50
94 Jerry Rice 1.50
95 Rob Johnson .30
96 Thomas Jones .15
97 Duce Staley .30
98 Ray Lucas .15
99 Charlie Batch .15
100 Jamal Anderson .30
101 *Michael Vick* 30.00
102 *Drew Brees* 12.00
103 *Andre Carter* 3.00
104 *David Terrell* 10.00
105 *Koren Robinson* 10.00
106 *Rod Gardner* 10.00
107 *Santana Moss* 10.00
108 *Deuce McCallister* 12.00
109 *Freddie Mitchell* 8.00
110 *Michael Bennett* 12.00
111 *Reggie Wayne* 10.00
112 *Todd Heap* 5.00
113 *LaDainian Tomlinson* 20.00
114 *Chad Johnson* 10.00
115 *Anthony Thomas* 10.00
116 *Robert Ferguson* 5.00
117 *LaMont Jordan* 5.00
118 *Chris Chambers* 10.00
119 *Travis Henry* 8.00
120 *Marques Tuiasosopo* 10.00
121 *James Jackson* 6.00
122 *Heath Evans* 3.00
123 *Travis Minor* 6.00
124 *Rudi Johnson* 10.00
125 *Chris Weinke* 10.00
126 *Sage Rosenfels* 6.00
127 *Fred Smoot* 4.00
128 *Correll Buckhalter* 8.00
129 *Justin McCareins* 6.00
130 *Jesse Palmer* 6.00
131 *Scotty Anderson* 4.00
132 *Kevan Barlow* 10.00
133 *John Capel* 4.00
134 *Mike McMahon* 8.00
135 *Marvin "Snoop" Minnis* 5.00
136 *Quincy Morgan* 6.00
137 *Vinny Sutherland* 5.00
138 *Dan Alexander* 5.00
139 *Cedrick Wilson* 4.00
140 *Josh Booty* 4.00
141 *Bobby Newcombe* 4.00
142 *Josh Heupel* 6.00
143 *Ken-Yon Rambo* 5.00
144 *Eddie Berlin* 3.00
145 *Reggie Germany* 4.00
146 *Quincy Carter* 8.00
147 *Steve Smith* 8.00
148 *Dan Morgan* 3.00
149 *Chris Barnes* 4.00
150 *Alex Bannister* 4.00
151 *A.J. Feeley* 4.00
152 *Jason Brookins* 5.00
153 *Kevin Kasper* 5.00
154 *Nick Goings* 4.00
155 *Gerard Warren* 3.00

2001 Fleer Authority Prominence 75

Veterans: 10X-20X
Rookies: 3X
Production 75 Sets

2001 Fleer Authority Prominence 125

Veterans: 6X-12X
Production 125 Sets

2001 Fleer Authority Autographs

NM/M
Common Player: 8.00
1 Shaun Alexander 15.00
2 Drew Brees 25.00
3 Isaac Bruce 15.00
4 Chris Chambers 25.00
5 Wayne Chrebet 8.00
6 Daunte Culpepper 75.00
7 Stephen Davis 10.00
8 Corey Dillon 10.00
9 Marshall Faulk 75.00
10 Eddie George 60.00
11 Travis Henry 8.00
12 Josh Heupel 8.00
13 Torry Holt 10.00
14 Edgerrin James 60.00
15 Jamal Lewis 15.00
16 Donovan McNabb 30.00
17 Travis Minor 8.00
18 Quincy Morgan 10.00
19 Randy Moss 100.00
20 Santana Moss 25.00
21 Ken-Yon Rambo 10.00
22 Koren Robinson 10.00
23 Sage Rosenfels 10.00
24 Jimmy Smith 10.00
25 Duce Staley 10.00
26 David Terrell 10.00
27 Anthony Thomas 25.00
28 LaDainian Tomlinson 40.00
29 Marques Tuiasosopo 10.00
30 Michael Vick 150.00
31 Chris Weinke 15.00

2001 Fleer Authority Authority Figures

NM/M
Complete Set (20): 35.00
Common Player: 1.00
Production 1,750 Sets
1AF Michael Vick, Jamal Anderson 6.00
2AF Drew Brees, Doug Flutie 2.00
3AF David Terrell, Marcus Robinson 3.00
4AF Koren Robinson, Matt Hasselbeck 1.00
5AF Rod Gardner, Stephen Davis 1.00
6AF Santana Moss, Wayne Chrebet 1.00
7AF Deuce McAllister, Ricky Williams 3.00
8AF Dan Morgan, Brian Urlacher 2.00
9AF Reggie Wayne, Marvin Harrison 2.00
10AF Marques Tuiasosopo, Tim Brown 2.00
11AF Freddie Mitchell, Donovan McNabb 2.00
12AF Quincy Morgan, Tim Couch 1.00
13AF Chad Johnson, Peter Warrick 1.00
14AF Robert Ferguson, Brett Favre 5.00
15AF Josh Heupel, Chris Weinke 2.00
16AF Anthony Thomas, Cade McNown 4.00
17AF Quincy Carter, Emmitt Smith 3.00
18AF Kevan Barlow, Jeff Garcia 1.00
19AF James Jackson, Edgerrin James 2.00
20AF Michael Bennett, Randy Moss 4.00

2001 Fleer Authority Goal Line Gear

NM/M
Complete Set (30):
Common Player: 8.00
1 David Boston 12.00
2 Mark Brunell 8.00
3 Tim Couch 12.00
4 Marshall Faulk 12.00
5 Eddie George 8.00
6 Torry Holt 8.00
7 Edgerrin James 15.00
8 Kevin Johnson 8.00
9 Thomas Jones 8.00
10 Jevon Kearse 8.00
11 Donovan McNabb 15.00
12 Steve McNair 12.00
13 Cade McNown 8.00
14 Emmitt Smith 35.00
15 Duce Staley 8.00
16 Fred Taylor 12.00
17 Brian Urlacher 25.00
18 Kurt Warner 15.00
20 Rich Gannon 15.00
21 Warrick Dunn 12.00
22 R. Jay Soward 8.00
23 Junior Seau 15.00
24 Brett Favre 40.00
25 Dez White 8.00
26 Ron Dayne 8.00
27 Marvin Harrison 12.00
28 Warren Sapp 8.00
29 Chad Pennington 35.00
30 Jake Plummer 8.00

2001 Fleer Authority Seal of Approval

NM/M
Complete Set (15): 60.00
Common Player: 3.00
Inserted 1:80
1SA Donovan McNabb 6.00
2SA Emmitt Smith 12.00
3SA Edgerrin James 8.00
4SA Brett Favre 15.00
5SA Michael Vick 15.00
6SA Daunte Culpepper 6.00
7SA Eddie George 3.00
8SA LaDainian Tomlinson 10.00
9SA Jamal Lewis 6.00
10SA Marshall Faulk 3.00
11SA Peyton Manning 10.00
12SA Randy Moss 10.00
13SA Ricky Williams 4.00
14SA Fred Taylor 3.00
15SA Kurt Warner 6.00

2001 Fleer Authority We're No. 1

NM/M
Complete Set (14): 30.00
Common Player: 1.50
Inserted 1:20
Troy Aikman 5.00
Drew Bledsoe 3.00
Terry Bradshaw 5.00
Earl Campbell 3.00
Tim Couch 3.00
John Elway 8.00
Irving Fryar 1.50
Paul Hornung 3.00
Bo Jackson 4.00
Keyshawn Johnson 2.00
Jim Plunkett 3.00
George Rogers 1.50
Billy Sims 2.00
Michael Vick 8.00

2001 Fleer Authority We're No. 1 Autographs

NM/M
Troy Aikman 50.00
Drew Bledsoe 30.00
Terry Bradshaw 100.00
Earl Campbell 40.00
Irving Fryar 25.00
Paul Hornung 30.00
Bo Jackson 75.00
Jim Plunkett 25.00
George Rogers 25.00
Michael Vick 175.00

2001 Fleer Authority We're No. 1 Jerseys

NM/M
Common Player: 20.00
Inserted 1:100
Drew Bledsoe 20.00
Terry Bradshaw 40.00
Tim Couch 20.00
John Elway 50.00
Bo Jackson 40.00
Jim Plunkett 20.00

2001 Fleer Focus

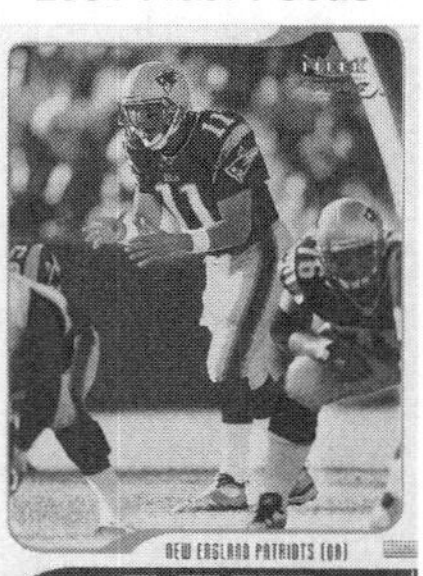

NM/M
Common Player: .15
Minor Stars: .30
Common Rookie: 2.50
Production 1,850 Sets
Pack (8): 3.25
Wax Box (24): 55.00
1 Marshall Faulk .60
2 Randy Moss 1.50
3 Cade McNown .50
4 Jeff Graham .15
5 Donovan McNabb .75
6 Shannon Sharpe .30
7 Todd Pinkston .30
8 Terrence Wilkins .30
9 Michael Strahan .30
10 Rich Gannon .30
11 Germane Crowell .30
12 Warren Sapp .30
13 La'Roi Glover .15
14 Peter Warrick .60
15 Shaun Alexander .50
16 Ray Lucas .30
17 Muhsin Muhammad .30
18 Curtis Conway .30
19 R. Jay Soward .30
20 Jamal Lewis 1.25
21 Tony Gonzalez .30
22 Bill Schroeder .30
23 Frank Sanders .30
24 Charles Woodson .30
25 Johnnie Morton .30
26 Frank Wycheck .15
27 Ron Dayne .75
28 Travis Prentice .30
29 Isaac Bruce .50
30 Drew Bledsoe .60
31 James Allen .30
32 Matt Hasselbeck .50
33 Zach Thomas .30
34 Shawn Bryson .15
35 Jerry Rice 1.00
36 Michael Cloud .15
37 Sammy Morris .30
38 Corey Simon .15
39 Peyton Manning 1.50
40 Thomas Jones .30
41 Tyrone Wheatley .30
42 Herman Moore .30
43 Jeff George .30
44 Kerry Collins .30
45 Raghib Ismail .30
46 Andre Rison .30
47 David Sloan .30
48 Michael Westbrook .15
49 Ron Dixon .15
50 Randall Cunningham .30
51 Keyshawn Johnson .50
52 Aaron Brooks .60
53 Corey Dillon .50
54 John Randle .50
55 Cris Carter .50
56 Donald Hayes .30
57 Hines Ward .30
58 Edgerrin James 1.25
59 Terance Mathis .15
60 Doug Johnson .30
61 Rod Smith .50
62 Kevin Dyson .30
63 Amani Toomer .30
64 Courtney Brown .50
65 Mike Alstott .50
66 Kevin Faulk .30
67 Shane Matthews .30
68 Ricky Watters .30
69 Peter Boulware .15
70 Tim Biakabutuka .30
71 Troy Aikman 1.00
72 Keenan McCardell .30
73 Priest Holmes .30
74 Duce Staley .50
75 Antonio Freeman .50
76 David Boston .50
77 Chad Pennington .50
78 Brian Griese .60
79 Stephen Davis .50
80 Curtis Martin .50
81 Tony Banks .30
82 Warrick Dunn .30
83 Willie McGinest .15
84 Marty Booker .30
85 James Williams .15
86 Oronde Gadsden .30
87 Patrick Jeffers .30
88 Junior Seau .30
89 Frank Moreau .15
90 Ray Lewis .50
91 Doug Flutie .60
92 Jimmy Smith .30
93 Qadry Ismail .30
94 Jeremiah Trotter .15
95 Dorsey Levens .30
96 Michael Pittman .30
97 Wayne Chrebet .50
98 Mike Anderson 1.25
99 Derrick Mason .30
100 Jason Sehorn .15
101 Kevin Johnson .50
102 Terrell Owens .50
103 Lamar Smith .50
104 Eric Moulds .50
105 Jerome Bettis .50
106 Marvin Harrison .50
107 Shawn Jefferson .15
108 Rickey Dudley .30
109 James Stewart .50
110 Bruce Smith .30
111 Matthew Hatchette .15
112 Emmitt Smith 1.25
113 Steve McNair .50
114 Ricky Williams .75
115 Tim Couch .60
116 Darrell Jackson .50
117 Doug Chapman .30
118 Jeff Lewis .30
119 Freddie Jones .30
120 Sylvester Morris .50
121 Elvis Grbac .50
122 Plaxico Burress .50
123 Marcus Pollard .15
124 Chris Chandler .30
125 James Thrash .30
126 Brett Favre 2.00
127 Jake Plummer .50
128 Vinny Testaverde .30
129 Terrell Davis 1.00
130 Jevon Kearse .50
131 Albert Connell .30
132 Dennis Northcutt .30
133 Az-Zahir Hakim .30
134 J.R. Redmond .30
135 Marcus Robinson .50
136 Eddie George .60
137 Ike Hilliard .30
138 Hugh Douglas .15
139 Kurt Warner 1.50
140 Terry Glenn .50
141 Brian Urlacher 1.00
142 Charlie Garner .50
143 Jay Fiedler .50
144 Rob Johnson .30
145 Kordell Stewart .50
146 Mark Brunell .60
147 Travis Taylor .50
148 Laveranues Coles .50
149 Ed McCaffrey .50
150 Jacquez Green .15
151 Joe Horn .30
152 Darnay Scott .30
153 Torry Holt .50
154 Daunte Culpepper 1.00
155 Wesley Walls .30
156 Jeff Garcia .50
157 Derrick Alexander .30
158 Peerless Price .50
159 Bobby Shaw .15
160 Fred Taylor .60
161 Chris Redman .50
162 Tim Brown .50
163 Charlie Batch .50
164 Champ Bailey .30
165 Tiki Barber .50
166 Joey Galloway .50
167 Brad Johnson .50
168 Jeff Blake .30
169 Jon Kitna .50
170 Trent Green .50
171 Troy Brown .15
172 Eddie Kennison .30
173 J.J. Stokes .30
174 James McKnight .15
175 Jeremy McDaniel .15
176 Richard Huntley .15
177 Kyle Brady .15
178 Jamal Anderson .50
179 Chad Lewis .30
180 Ahman Green .50
181 *Michael Vick* 30.00
182 *Deuce McAllister* 15.00
183 *David Terrell* 8.00
184 *Koren Robinson* 8.00
185 *LaDainian Tomlinson* 15.00
186 *Michael Bennett* 10.00
187 *Chris Chambers* 10.00
188 *Chad Johnson* 10.00
189 *Santana Moss* 8.00
190 *Todd Heap* 6.00
191 *Freddie Mitchell* 6.00
192 *Quincy Morgan* 6.00
193 *Rod Gardner* 10.00
194 *Kevan Barlow* 10.00
195 *Drew Brees* 12.00
196 *Robert Ferguson* 4.00
197 *Ken-Yon Rambo* 4.00
198 *Travis Henry* 8.00
199 *LaMont Jordan* 3.00
200 *Chris Weinke* 8.00
201 *Sage Rosenfels* 4.00
202 *Josh Heupel* 3.00
203 *Quincy Carter* 8.00
204 *Jesse Palmer* 4.00
205 *Mike McMahon* 5.00
206 *Rudi Johnson* 10.00
207 *Anthony Thomas* 8.00
208 *James Jackson* 6.00
209 *Marvin "Snoop" Minnis* 4.00
210 *Derek Combs* 2.50
211 *Ronney Daniels* 2.50
212 *Alex Bannister* 4.00
213 *Cedrick Wilson* 3.00
214 *Travis Minor* 4.00
215 *Marques Tuiasosopo* 8.00
216 *Reggie Wayne* 10.00
217 *Josh Booty* 3.00
218 *Jamal Reynolds* 3.00
219 *Gerard Warren* 4.00
220 *Justin Smith* 3.00
221 *Andre Carter* 4.00
222 *Milton Wynn* 2.50
223 *Fred Smoot* 4.00
224 *Jamar Fletcher* 3.00
225 *Dan Morgan* 4.00
226 *Jon Carter* 2.50
227 *Correll Buckhalter* 6.00
228 *Kevin Kasper* 4.00
229 *Derrick Blaylock* 2.50
230 *Justin McCareins* 8.00

2001 Fleer Focus Certified Cuts

NM/M
Common Player: 15.00
Inserted 1:72
1CC Freddie Mitchell 15.00
2CC James Jackson 20.00
3CC Josh Heupel 25.00
4CC Kevan Barlow 20.00
5CC LaMont Jordan 15.00
6CC Chris Chambers 20.00
7CC Chris Weinke 50.00
8CC David Terrell 30.00
9CC Deuce McAllister 30.00
10CC Drew Brees 60.00
11CC Jesse Palmer 15.00
12CC Koren Robinson 20.00
13CC LaDainian Tomlinson 60.00
14CC Michael Vick 100.00
15CC Michael Bennett 50.00
16CC Quincy Morgan 15.00
17CC Reggie Wayne 20.00
18CC Rod Gardner 15.00
19CC Rudi Johnson 15.00
20CC Santana Moss 25.00
21CC Donovan McNabb 70.00

2001 Fleer Focus Numbers

NM/M
Common Player: 2.00
1 Marshall Faulk 253 6.00
2 Randy Moss 187 20.00
3 Cade McNown 154 5.00
4 Jeff Graham 165 2.00
5 Donovan McNabb 330 6.00
6 Shannon Sharpe 121 4.00
7 Todd Pinkston 181 3.00
8 Terrence Wilkins 132 8.00
9 Michael Strahan 51 6.00
10 Rich Gannon 284 2.50
11 Germane Crowell 126 5.00
12 Warren Sapp 43 10.00
13 La'Roi Glover 53 5.00
14 Peter Warrick 116 8.00
15 Shaun Alexander 64 15.00
16 Ray Lucas 21 20.00
17 Muhsin Muhammad 116 4.00
18 Curtis Conway 134 2.50
19 R. Jay Soward 110 3.00
20 Jamal Lewis 309 7.00
21 Tony Gonzalez 129 4.00
22 Bill Schroeder 154 2.00
23 Frank Sanders 139 4.00
24 Charles Woodson 16 25.00
25 Johnnie Morton 129 4.00
26 Frank Wycheck 91 4.00
27 Ron Dayne 228 7.00
28 Travis Prentice 16 20.00
29 Isaac Bruce 169 7.00
30 Drew Bledsoe 312 4.00
31 James Allen 290 2.50
32 Matt Hasselbeck 10 25.00
33 Zach Thomas 56 8.00
34 Shawn Bryson 161 2.00
35 Jerry Rice 107 20.00
36 Michael Cloud 30 6.00
37 Sammy Morris 93 5.00
38 Corey Simon 38 8.00
39 Peyton Manning 357 10.00
40 Thomas Jones 112 3.00
41 Tyrone Wheatley 232 2.50
42 Herman Moore 109 4.00
43 Jeff George 113 4.00
44 Kerry Collins 311 1.50
45 Raghib Ismail 140 3.00
46 Andre Rison 148 2.00
47 David Sloan 118 2.50
48 Michael Westbrook 114 4.00
49 Ron Dixon 153 2.50
50 Randall Cunningham 74 10.00
51 Keyshawn Johnson 123 7.00
52 Aaron Brooks 113 10.00
53 Corey Dillon 315 4.00
54 John Randle 25 15.00
55 Cris Carter 133 7.00
56 Donald Hayes 140 3.00
57 Hines Ward 140 2.00
58 Edgerrin James 387 10.00
59 Terance Mathis 119 2.50
60 Doug Johnson 93 6.00
61 Rod Smith 160 4.00
62 Kevin Dyson 173 3.00
63 Amani Toomer 140 3.00
64 Courtney Brown 62 5.00
65 Mike Alstott 131 7.00
66 Kevin Faulk 164 3.00
67 Shane Matthews 102 3.00
68 Ricky Watters 278 3.00
69 Peter Boulware 23 6.00
70 Tim Biakabutuka 173 3.00
71 Troy Aikman 156 10.00
72 Keenan McCardell 128 2.50
73 Priest Holmes 137 3.00
74 Duce Staley 79 10.00
75 AntonioFreeman 147 6.00
76 David Boston 163 6.00
77 Chad Pennington 2
78 Brian Griese 216 7.00
79 Stephen Davis 332 4.00
80 Curtis Martin 316 4.00
81 Tony Banks 150 3.00
82 Warrick Dunn 248 5.00
83 Willie McGinest 45 5.00
84 Marty Booker 104 4.00
85 James Williams 24 12.00
86 Oronde Gadsden 140 3.00
87 Patrick Jeffers 1
88 Junior Seau 102 4.00
89 Frank Moreau 67 4.00
90 Ray Lewis 108 8.00
91 Doug Flutie 132 10.00
92 Jimmy Smith 133 4.00
93 Qadry Ismail 134 2.50
94 Jeremiah Trotter 100 2.50
95 Dorsey Levens 77 5.00
96 Michael Pittman 184 2.00
97 Wayne Chrebet 136 4.00
98 Mike Anderson 297 10.00
99 Derrick Mason 142 3.00
100 Jason Sehorn 59 5.00
101 Kevin Johnson 117 8.00
102 Terrell Owens 150 7.00
103 Lamar Smith 309 3.00
104 Eric Moulds 141 4.00
105 Jerome Bettis 355 3.00
106 Marvin Harrison 139 8.00
107 Shawn Jefferson 137 2.50
108 Rickey Dudley 121 2.50
109 James Stewart 339 1.50
110 Bruce Smith 46 5.00
111 Matthew Hatchette 119 2.50
112 Emmitt Smith 294 12.00
113 Steve McNair 248 5.00
114 Ricky Williams 248 8.00
115 Tim Couch 137 10.00

116 Darrell Jackson 135 60.00
117 Doug Chapman 1
118 Jeff Lewis 16 15.00
119 Freddie Jones 108 3.00
120 Sylvester Morris 141 4.00
121 Elvis Grbac 326 2.00
122 Plaxico Burress 124 6.00
123 Marcus Pollard 146 2.00
124 Chris Chandler 192 3.00
125 James Thrash 131 2.50
126 Brett Favre 338 12.00
127 Jake Plummer 270 5.00
128 Vinny Testaverde 328 1.50
129 Terrell Davis 78 25.00
130 Jevon Kearse 36 20.00
131 Albert Connell 195 2.00
132 Dennis Northcutt 108 3.00
133 Az-Zahir Hakim 138 4.00
134 J.R. Redmond 125 3.00
135 Marcus Robinson 134 8.00
136 Eddie George 403 4.00
137 Ike Hilliard 143 3.00
138 Hugh Douglas 44 6.00
139 Kurt Warner 235 20.00
140 Terry Glenn 122 4.00
141 Brian Urlacher 98 20.00
142 Charlie Garner 258 3.00
143 Jay Fiedler 204 4.00
144 Rob Johnson 175 3.00
145 Kordell Stewart 151 6.00
146 Mark Brunell 311 4.00
147 Travis Taylor 99 5.00
148 Laveranues Coles 168 5.00
149 Ed McCaffrey 130 8.00
150 Jacquez Green 152 2.00
151 Joe Horn 143 3.00
152 Darnay Scott 1
153 Torry Holt 199 6.00
154 Daunte Culpepper 297 10.00
155 Wesley Walls 136 2.50
156 Jeff Garcia 355 4.00
157 Derrick Alexander 178 3.00
158 Peerless Price 147 3.00
159 Bobby Shaw 168 2.00
160 Fred Taylor 292 5.00
161 Chris Redman 2
162 Tim Brown 148 6.00
163 Charlie Batch 221 5.00
164 Champ Bailey 57 8.00
165 Tiki Barber 213 3.00
166 Joey Galloway 155 6.00
167 Brad Johnson 228 5.00
168 Jeff Blake 184 3.00
169 Jon Kitna 259 2.50
170 Trent Green 145 6.00
171 Troy Brown 114 2.50
172 Eddie Kennison 100 4.00
173 J.J. Stokes 175 3.00
174 James McKnight 178 3.00
175 Jeremy McDaniel 162 2.00
176 Richard Huntley 46 5.00
177 Kyle Brady 114 2.50
178 Jamal Anderson 282 5.00
179 Chad Lewis 107 2.50
180 Ahman Green 263 4.00
181 Michael Vick 87 100.00
182 Deuce McAllister 159 20.00
183 David Terrell 169 20.00
184 Koren Robinson 171 15.00
185 LaDainian Tomlinson 369 25.00
186 Michael Bennett 310 20.00
187 Chris Chambers 156 15.00
188 Chad Johnson 218 7.00
189 Santana Moss 166 12.00
190 Todd Heap 134 8.00
191 Freddie Mitchell 194 12.00
192 Quincy Morgan 182 10.00
193 Rod Gardner 181 15.00
194 Kevan Barlow 197 12.00
195 Drew Brees 309 20.00
196 Robert Ferguson 153 7.00
197 Ken-Yon Rambo 150 4.00
198 Travis Henry 253 12.00
199 LaMont Jordan 213 7.00
200 Chris Weinke 266 20.00
201 Sage Rosenfels 172 8.00
202 Josh Heupel 280 10.00
203 Quincy Carter 91 30.00
204 Jesse Palmer 116 10.00
205 Mike McMahon 169 8.00
206 Rudi Johnson 324 5.00
207 Anthony Thomas 319 8.00
208 James Jackson 201 8.00
209 Marvin "Snoop" Minnis 213 10.00
210 Derek Combs 175 6.00
211 Ronney Daniels 111 6.00
212 Alex Bannister 158 6.00
213 Cedrick Wilson 110 8.00
214 Travis Minor 181 6.00
215 Marques Tuiasosopo 176 12.00
216 Reggie Wayne 176 10.00
217 Josh Booty 145 6.00
218 Jamal Reynolds 58 15.00
219 Gerard Warren 76 15.00
220 Justin Smith 97 12.00
221 Andre Carter 59 15.00
222 Milton Wynn 185 5.00
223 Fred Smoot 55 15.00
224 Jamar Fletcher 34 15.00
225 Dan Morgan 138 8.00
226 Jon Carter 158 5.00
227 Correll Buckhalter 196 10.00
228 Kevin Kasper 123 10.00
229 Derrick Blaylock 202 4.00
230 Justin McCareins 177 5.00

2001 Fleer Focus Property Of

NM/M
Common Player: 15.00
Inserted 1:192
Shirts/Skins Cards: 4X
Production 50 Sets
1PO Brett Favre 45.00
2PO Dan Marino 50.00
3PO Jerry Rice 35.00
4PO Wayne Chrebet 15.00
5PO Marshall Faulk 20.00
6PO Kurt Warner 35.00
7PO Ray Lewis 15.00
8PO Rod Smith 15.00
9PO Corey Dillon 15.00
10PO Kordell Stewart 15.00

2001 Fleer Focus Rookie Premiere Jersey

NM/M
Common Player: 12.00
Inserted 1:65
Shirts/Skins Cards: 3X
Production 50 Sets
1RP Leonard Davis 12.00
2RP Michael Vick 60.00
3RP Todd Heap 12.00
4RP Travis Henry 15.00
5RP Dan Morgan 12.00
6RP Chris Weinke 20.00
7RP David Terrell 20.00
8RP Anthony Thomas 15.00
9RP Chad Johnson 15.00
10RP Justin Smith 12.00
11RP Rudi Johnson 15.00
12RP James Jackson 20.00
13RP Quincy Morgan 12.00
14RP Gerard Warren 12.00
15RP Quincy Carter 15.00
16RP Mike McMahon 15.00
17RP Robert Ferguson 12.00
18RP Reggie Wayne 15.00
19RP Marvin "Snoop" Minnis 12.00
20RP Chris Chambers 15.00
21RP Travis Minor 12.00
22RP Rod Gardner 15.00
23RP Michael Bennett 30.00
24RP Richard Seymour 12.00
25RP Deuce McAllister 20.00
26RP Jesse Palmer 12.00
27RP Santana Moss 15.00
28RP Marques Tuiasosopo 20.00
29RP Freddie Mitchell 12.00
30RP Drew Brees 35.00
31RP LaDainian Tomlinson 40.00
32RP Kevan Barlow 15.00
33RP Andre Carter 12.00
34RP Koren Robinson 15.00

2001 Fleer Focus Tag Team

NM/M
Common Player: 20.00
Inserted 1:140
1TGT Paul Hornung 30.00
2TGT Brett Favre 50.00
3TGT Troy Aikman 35.00
4TGT Roger Staubach 60.00
5TGT Bo Jackson 30.00
6TGT Marcus Allen 20.00
7TGT Daunte Culpepper 30.00
8TGT Warren Moon 20.00
9TGT John Elway 50.00
10TGT Terrell Davis 30.00
11TGT Marshall Faulk 25.00
12TGT Eric Dickerson 20.00
13TGT George Rogers 20.00
14TGT Deuce McAllister 25.00
15TGT Randy Moss 45.00
16TGT Dan Marino 50.00
17TGT Joe Montana 150.00
18TGT Steve Young 30.00
19TGT Steve McNair 20.00
20TGT Eddie George 25.00
21TGT Johnny Unitas 50.00
22TGT Edgerrin James 45.00
23TGT Emmitt Smith 45.00
24TGT Tony Dorsett 30.00
25TGT Walter Payton 125.00
26TGT Gale Sayers 20.00
27TGT Jerry Rice 40.00
28TGT William Perry 20.00
29TGT Brian Urlacher 30.00
30TGT Donovan McNabb 25.00
31TGT Randall Cunningham 25.00

2001 Fleer Focus Tag Team Tandems

NM/M
Common Player: 50.00
Production 50 Sets
1TGTT Paul Hornung, Brett Favre 150.00
2TGTT Troy Aikman, Roger Staubach 150.00
3TGTT Bo Jackson, Marcus Allen 85.00
4TGTT Daunte Culpepper, Warren Moon 100.00
5TGTT John Elway, Terrell Davis 150.00
6TGTT Marshall Faulk, Eric Dickerson 65.00
7TGTT Deuce McAllister, Ricky Williams 65.00
8TGTT Randy Moss, Daunte Culpepper 100.00
9TGTT Joe Montana, Steve Young 200.00
10TGTT Steve McNair, Eddie George 75.00
11TGTT Johnny Unitas, Edgerrin James 100.00
12TGTT Emmitt Smith, Tony Dorsett 150.00
14TGTT Jerry Rice, Steve Young 100.00
15TGTT William Perry, Brian Urlacher 50.00
16TGTT Donovan McNabb, Randall Cunningham 85.00

2001 Fleer Focus Toast of the Town

NM/M
Complete Set (20): 35.00
Common Player: .75
Minor Stars: 1.50
Inserted 1:6
1TT Donovan McNabb 2.50
2TT Brett Favre 6.00
3TT Jerome Bettis 1.50
4TT Stephen Davis 1.50
5TT Emmitt Smith 4.00
6TT Cris Carter 1.50
7TT Peyton Manning 5.00
8TT Eddie George 2.00
9TT Edgerrin James 4.00
10TT Daunte Culpepper 3.00
11TT Kurt Warner 4.00
12TT Mark Brunell 2.00
13TT Randy Moss 5.00
14TT Marvin Harrison 1.50
15TT Jamal Lewis 3.50
16TT Warren Sapp .75
17TT Jerry Rice 4.00
18TT Ricky Williams 2.50
19TT Ron Dayne 2.50
20TT Brian Griese 2.00

2001 Fleer Focus Ultra Rookie Update

1 Quincy Carter
2 Derrick Blaylock
3 Correll Buckhalter
4 Henry Burris
5 Cedric James
6 Kevin Kasper
7 Justin McCareins
8 Dave Dickenson
9 Steve Smith
10 Moran Norris

2001 Fleer Focus Vision Tunnel

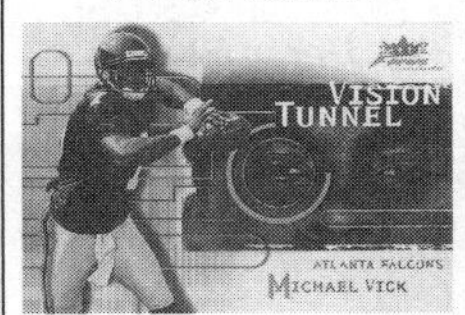

NM/M
Complete Set (15): 35.00
Common Player: 1.00
Minor Stars: 2.00
Inserted 1:12
1TV Peyton Manning 5.00
2TV Jamal Lewis 4.00
3TV Emmitt Smith 5.00
4TV Eddie George 2.50
5TV Michael Vick 12.00
6TV Brett Favre 6.00
7TV Ricky Williams 3.00
8TV Edgerrin James 3.00
9TV Ron Dayne 2.50
10TV Eric Moulds 2.00
11TV Tim Brown 2.00
12TV Terrell Davis 3.00
13TV Jevon Kearse 2.00
14TV Peter Warrick 2.00
15TV Ray Lewis 1.00

2001 Fleer Game Time

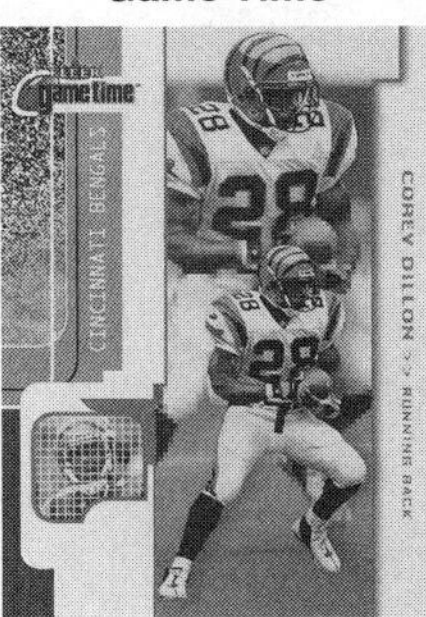

NM/M
Common Player: .15
Minor Stars: .30
Common Rookie: 1.00
Production 2001 Sets
Pack (5): 3.25
Wax Box (24): 65.00
1 Donovan McNabb .75
2 Travis Prentice .30
3 Keenan McCardell .15
4 Kurt Warner 1.50
5 Ray Lewis .30
6 Terrell Davis 1.00
7 Kevin Faulk .30
8 Terrell Owens .50
9 Jeff George .30
10 Dennis Northcutt .30
11 Fred Taylor .60
12 Cris Carter .50
13 Aaron Brooks .50
14 Marshall Faulk .60
15 David Boston .50
16 Raghib Ismail .15
17 Jerome Bettis .50
18 Warrick Dunn .50
19 Corey Dillon .50
20 Mark Brunell .60
21 Torry Holt .50
22 Michael McCrary .15
23 Rod Smith .30
24 Charlie Garner .30
25 Bruce Smith .15
26 Doug Johnson .30
27 Brian Griese .60
28 Jeff Garcia .50
29 Eddie George .60
30 Shawn Bryson .30
31 Marvin Harrison .50
32 Hugh Douglas .15
33 Terance Mathis .15
34 Emmitt Smith 1.25
35 Lamar Smith .50
36 Junior Seau .30
37 Steve McNair .50
38 Jake Plummer .50
39 Tim Couch .75
40 Jay Fiedler .50
41 Plaxico Burress .50
42 Keyshawn Johnson .50
43 Trent Dilfer .30
44 Charlie Batch .50
45 Terry Glenn .50
46 Laveranues Coles .50
47 Darrell Jackson .50
48 Jamal Lewis 1.50
49 Ed McCaffrey .30
50 Vinny Testaverde .50
51 Ricky Watters .50
52 Champ Bailey .50
53 Peter Warrick 1.00
54 Eric Moulds .50
55 Michael Strahan .15
56 Warren Sapp .30
57 Tony Gonzalez .50
58 Kerry Collins .50
59 Shaun King .50
60 Jason Sehorn .15
61 Marcus Robinson .50
62 James Stewart .50
63 Curtis Martin .50
64 Brian Urlacher 1.00
65 Germane Crowell .50
66 Wesley Walls .30
67 Antonio Freeman .50
68 Ron Dayne 1.00
69 Tyrone Wheatley .30
70 Zach Thomas .30
71 Shannon Sharpe .30
72 Mike Anderson 1.50
73 Wayne Chrebet .30
74 Shaun Alexander .50
75 Stephen Davis .50
76 Steve Beuerlein .30
77 Dorsey Levens .50
78 Jessie Armstead .15
79 Rich Gannon .30
80 Muhsin Muhammad .30
81 Brett Favre 2.00
82 Randy Moss 1.50
83 Joe Horn .50
84 Charles Woodson .30
85 Brad Hoover .50
86 Terrence Wilkins .30
87 Sylvester Morris .50
88 Tim Brown .30
89 Jamal Anderson .50
90 Joey Galloway .50
91 Drew Bledsoe .60
92 Rodney Harrison .15
93 Jevon Kearse .50
94 Rob Johnson .30
95 Edgerrin James 1.50
96 Thomas Jones .50
97 Courtney Brown .30
98 Jimmy Smith .50
99 Ricky Williams .75
100 Isaac Bruce .50
101 Akili Smith .50
102 Derrick Alexander .15
103 Daunte Culpepper 1.00
104 Amani Toomer .30
105 Mike Alstott .50
106 Sam Cowart .15
107 Peyton Manning 1.50
108 Robert Smith .30
109 Duce Staley .50
110 Cade McNown .50
111 *Michael Vick* 20.00
112 *David Terrell* 8.00
113 *Deuce McAllister* 15.00
114 *Koren Robinson* 10.00
115 *Rod Gardner* 10.00
116 *Chris Chambers* 10.00
117 *Santana Moss* 10.00
118 *Reggie Wayne* 10.00
119 *Quincy Morgan* 4.00
120 *Rudi Johnson* 10.00
121 *Robert Ferguson* 4.00
122 *Ja'Mar Toombs* 2.00
123 *Michael Bennett* 12.00
124 *Ronney Daniels* 2.00
125 *Drew Brees* 12.00
126 *Josh Heupel* 3.00
127 *Chris Weinke* 8.00
128 *LaDainian Tomlinson* 15.00
129 *Chad Johnson* 10.00
130 *LaMont Jordan* 2.00
131 *Freddie Mitchell* 5.00
132 *Anthony Thomas* 8.00
133 *Ben Leard* 2.00
134 *Sage Rosenfels* 4.00
135 *Marques Tuiasosopo* 6.00
136 *Gerard Warren* 3.00
137 *Jamar Fletcher* 3.00
138 *Justin Smith* 3.00
139 *Dan Morgan* 4.00
140 *Jamal Reynolds* 2.00
141 *Shaun Rogers* 1.00
142 *Todd Heap* 3.00
143 *Travis Minor* 2.00
144 *Mike McMahon* 4.00
145 *Travis Henry* 6.00
146 *Kevan Barlow* 10.00
147 *Javon Green* 2.00
148 *Ken-Yon Rambo* 3.00
149 *Tim Hasselbeck* 3.00
150 *Marvin "Snoop" Minnis* 3.00

2001 Fleer Game Time Extra

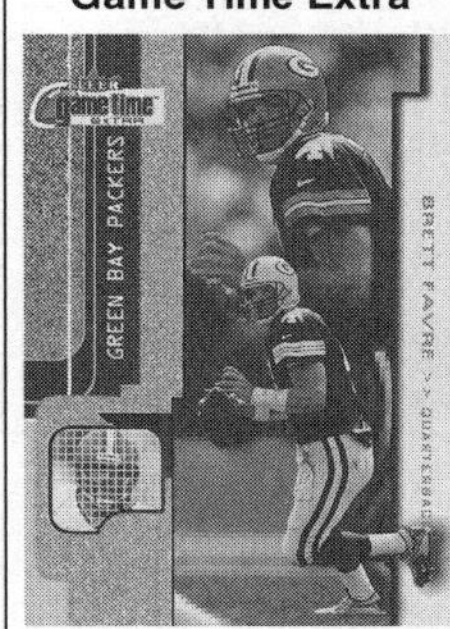

Extra Cards: 3X-6X
Inserted 1:8
Extra Rookies: 3X
Production 201 Sets

2001 Fleer Game Time CrunchTime

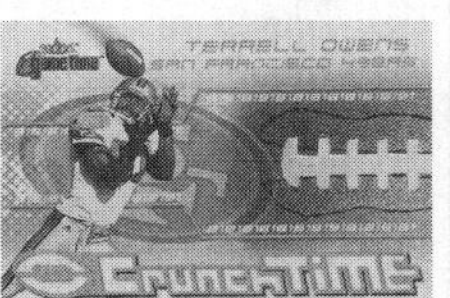

NM/M
Complete Set (20): 15.00
Common Player: .50
Minor Stars: 1.00
Inserted 1:4
1CT Emmitt Smith 3.50
2CT Isaac Bruce 1.00
3CT James Stewart .50
4CT Warrick Dunn 1.00
5CT Jake Plummer 1.00
6CT Shannon Sharpe .50
7CT Robert Smith 1.00
8CT Jamal Anderson 1.00
9CT Terrell Owens 1.00
10CT Marcus Robinson 1.00
11CT Ed McCaffrey .50
12CT Jamal Lewis .50
13CT Amani Toomer .50
14CT Jerome Bettis 1.00
15CT Cris Carter 1.00
16CT Stephen Davis 1.00
17CT Marvin Harrison 1.00
18CT Joe Horn 1.00
19CT Tim Couch 2.00
20CT Drew Bledsoe 1.75

2001 Fleer Game Time Double Trouble

NM/M
Complete Set (15): 35.00
Common Player: 1.00
Minor Stars: 2.00
Inserted 1:24
1DT Daunte Culpepper, Randy Moss 8.00
2DT Kurt Warner, Marshall Faulk 8.00
3DT Peyton Manning, Edgerrin James 8.00
4DT Warrick Dunn, Keyshawn Johnson 2.00
5DT Brett Favre, Antonio Freeman 8.00
6DT Tiki Barber, Ron Dayne 3.00
7DT Corey Dillon, Peter Warrick 4.00
8DT Donovan McNabb, Duce Staley 3.00
9DT Fred Taylor, Jimmy Smith 2.50
10DT Rich Gannon, Tim Brown 2.00
11DT Steve McNair, Eddie George 2.50
12DT Curtis Martin, Wayne Chrebet 2.00
13DT Ricky Williams, Aaron Brooks 3.50
14DT Derrick Alexander, Tony Gonzalez 1.00
15DT Brian Griese, Terrell Davis 4.00

2001 Fleer Game Time Eleven Up

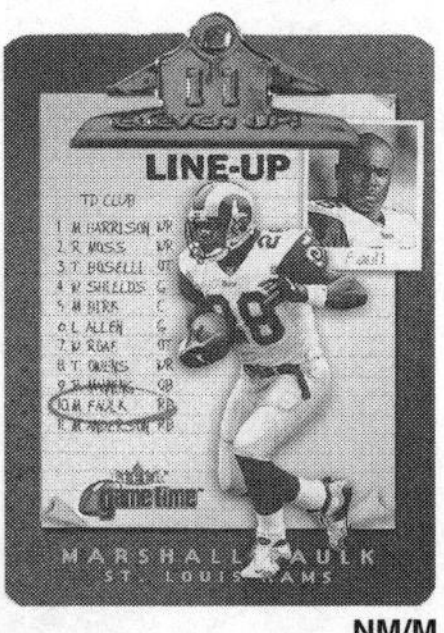

NM/M
Complete Set (15): 30.00
Common Player: 1.50
Inserted 1:12
1EU Jamal Lewis 4.00
2EU Randy Moss 5.00
3EU Ricky Williams 3.00
4EU Terrell Davis 3.00
5EU Donovan McNabb 3.00
6EU Curtis Martin 1.50
7EU Brett Favre 6.00
8EU Aaron Brooks 1.50
9EU Kurt Warner 3.00
10EU Eddie George 2.00
11EU Daunte Culpepper 4.00
12EU Jamal Anderson 1.50
13EU Marshall Faulk 2.00
14EU Ray Lewis 1.50
15EU Ron Dayne 1.00

2001 Fleer Game Time Fame Time

NM/M
Common Player: 35.00
Production 100 Sets
1 Terry Bradshaw 100.00
2 Eric Dickerson 35.00
3 Tony Dorsett 50.00
4 Paul Hornung 60.00
5 Howie Long 50.00
6 Joe Montana 150.00
7 Walter Payton 150.00
8 Roger Staubach 100.00
9 Fran Tarkenton 45.00
10 Lawrence Taylor 50.00
11 Johnny Unitas 60.00

2001 Fleer Game Time In the Zone

NM/M
Complete Set (14): 125.00
Common Player: 5.00
Inserted 1:73
Drew Bledsoe 15.00
Daunte Culpepper 30.00
Oronde Gadsden 5.00
Rich Gannon 5.00
Marvin Harrison 15.00
Edgerrin James 25.00
Peyton Manning 30.00
Curtis Martin 15.00
Randy Moss 30.00
Peerless Price 5.00
J.R. Redmond 5.00
Jimmy Smith 5.00
James Stewart 5.00
Tyrone Wheatley 5.00

2001 Fleer Game Time Uniformity

NM/M
Common Player: 10.00
Inserted 1:19
Jessie Armstead 10.00
Champ Bailey 15.00
David Boston 15.00
Kyle Brady Pants 10.00
Courtney Brown 12.00
Isaac Bruce 15.00
Mark Brunell 20.00
Plaxico Burress 15.00
Trung Canidate Pants 10.00
Wayne Chrebet 12.00
Tim Couch Pants 20.00
Marshall Faulk Pants 30.00
Marvin Harrison 15.00
Torry Holt 15.00
Kevin Johnson Pants 10.00
Jevon Kearse 15.00
Shaun King 15.00
Dorsey Levens 12.00
Dan Marino 50.00
Keenan McCardell 10.00
Donovan McNabb 25.00
Cade McNown 15.00
Jake Plummer 15.00
Travis Prentice 15.00
Peerless Price 12.00
Chris Redman 15.00
Jerry Rice 35.00
Marcus Robinson 15.00
Corey Simon 12.00
Jimmy Smith 12.00
Duce Staley 15.00

Kordell Stewart 15.00
Michael Strahan Pants 10.00
Fred Taylor 20.00
Kurt Warner 45.00

2001 Fleer Genuine

NM/M
Common Player: .20
Minor Stars: .40
Common Rookie: 10.00
Production 1000 Sets
Pack (5): 4.00
Wax Box (24): 75.00
1 Donovan McNabb 1.25
2 Daunte Culpepper 1.50
3 Derrick Alexander .20
4 Jessie Armstead .20
5 Hines Ward .40
6 Peter Warrick 1.50
7 Jay Fiedler .50

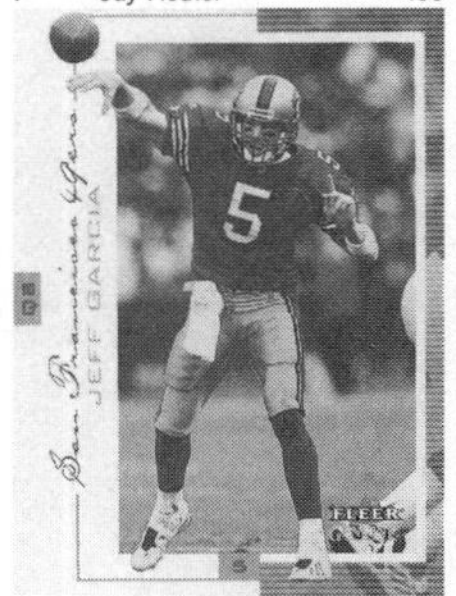

8 Cris Carter .75
9 Az-Zahir Hakim .40
10 Michael Westbrook .50
11 Akili Smith .75
12 Lamar Smith .75
13 Eric Moulds .75
14 Shaun Alexander 1.00
15 Jeff George .75
16 Brad Hoover .75
17 Brian Griese 1.00
18 Keenan McCardell .50
19 Freddie Jones .40
20 Brian Urlacher 1.50
21 Thomas Jones .75
22 Charlie Batch .75
23 Aaron Brooks .75
24 Hugh Douglas .20
25 Mike Alstott .75
26 Darrell Russell .20
27 Muhsin Muhammad .40
28 Raghib Ismail .20
29 Fred Taylor 1.00
30 Tyrone Wheatley .40
31 Rodney Harrison .20
32 Curtis Martin .75
33 Jason Sehorn .20
34 James McKnight .20
35 Jimmy Smith .50
36 Laveranues Coles .75
37 Jeff Garcia .75
38 Sam Cowart .20
39 Joey Galloway .75
40 Mark Brunell 1.00
41 Vinny Testaverde .50
42 Terrell Owens .75
43 Ray Lewis .50
44 Ahman Green .50
45 Ron Dayne 1.50
46 Samari Rolle .20
47 Shawn Bryson .20
48 Emmitt Smith 2.00
49 Terrence Wilkins .40
50 Charlie Garner .40
51 Rob Johnson .40
52 Courtney Brown .40
53 Edgerrin James 2.50
54 Kurt Warner 2.50
55 Michael McCrary .20
56 Dennis Northcutt .40
57 Marvin Harrison .75
58 Rich Gannon .50
59 Marshall Faulk 1.00
60 Travis Prentice .75
61 Terrell Davis 2.00
62 Charles Woodson .50
63 Isaac Bruce .75
64 Tim Couch 1.25
65 Oronde Gadsden .40
66 Randy Moss 2.50
67 Torry Holt .75
68 Shannon Sharpe .40
69 Antonio Freeman .75
70 Michael Strahan .20
71 Jevon Kearse .75
72 Jamal Lewis 2.00
73 Peyton Manning 2.50
74 Amani Toomer .40
75 Derrick Mason .75
76 Jake Plummer .75
77 Rod Smith .50
78 Terry Glenn .50
79 Plaxico Burress .75
80 Warren Sapp .40
81 Jamal Anderson .75
82 James Stewart .50
83 Ricky Williams 1.00
84 Chad Lewis .50
85 Shaun King .75
86 Wesley Walls .40
87 Mike Anderson 2.00
88 Corey Simon .40
89 Wayne Chrebet .50
90 Junior Seau .40
91 Terance Mathis .20
92 Germane Crowell .75
93 Joe Horn .50
94 Duce Staley .75
95 Keyshawn Johnson .75
96 Qadry Ismail .20
97 Dorsey Levens .75
98 Kerry Collins .50
99 Corey Dillon .75
100 Zach Thomas .40
101 Chad Pennington 1.50
102 Ricky Watters .50
103 Bruce Smith .20
104 David Boston .75
105 Ed McCaffrey .50
106 Kevin Faulk .50
107 Jerome Bettis .50
108 Warrick Dunn .50
109 Tim Brown .50
110 Marcus Robinson .75
111 Tony Gonzalez .50
112 Drew Bledsoe 1.00
113 Darrell Jackson .40
114 Stephen Davis .75
115 Doug Johnson .40
116 Brett Favre 3.00
117 Darren Howard .20
118 Cade McNown .75
119 Steve McNair .75
120 James Allen .50
121 Sylvester Morris .75
122 J.R. Redmond .50
123 Jacquez Green .20
124 Champ Bailey .40
125 Eddie George 1.00
126 *Michael Vick* 70.00
127 *David Terrell* 12.00
128 *Deuce McAllister* 35.00
129 *Koren Robinson* 12.00
130 *Rod Gardner* 20.00
131 *Chris Chambers* 15.00
132 *Santana Moss* 15.00
133 *Reggie Wayne* 20.00
134 *Quincy Morgan* 15.00
135 *Rudi Johnson* 15.00
136 *Robert Ferguson* 15.00
137 *Todd Heap* 10.00
138 *Michael Bennett* 30.00
139 *Jesse Palmer* 10.00
140 *Drew Brees* 25.00
141 *James Jackson* 15.00
142 *Chris Weinke* 15.00
143 *LaDainian Tomlinson* 40.00
144 *Chad Johnson* 25.00
145 *Quincy Carter* 20.00
146 *Freddie Mitchell* 15.00
147 *Anthony Thomas* 15.00
148 *Travis Henry* 20.00
149 *Marvin "Snoop" Minnis* 15.00
150 *Marques Tuiasosopo* 25.00
151 *Travis Minor* 10.00
152 *Mike McMahon* 15.00
153 *Josh Heupel* 10.00
154 *Sage Rosenfels* 15.00
155 *Kevan Barlow* 15.00

2001 Fleer Genuine Coverage Plus

NM/M
Common Player: 8.00
Inserted 1:24
1GC Isaac Bruce 12.00
2GC Mark Brunell 15.00
3GC Az-Zahir Hakim 8.00
4GC Marvin Harrison 12.00
5GC Edgerrin James 25.00
6GC Kevin Johnson 8.00
7GC Fred Taylor 15.00
8GC Kurt Warner 30.00
9GC Brian Urlacher 25.00
10GC Duce Staley 12.00
11GC Jimmy Smith 8.00
12GC Corey Simon 8.00
13GC Marcus Robinson 12.00
14GC Travis Prentice 12.00
15GC Jake Plummer 12.00
16GC Cade McNown 12.00
17GC Peyton Manning 35.00
18GC Thomas Jones 12.00
19GC Keenan McCardell 8.00
20GC Dez White 8.00
21GC Ed McCaffrey 8.00
22GC Eric Moulds 12.00
23GC Brad Johnson 12.00
24GC Rob Johnson 8.00
25GC Warren Sapp 8.00
26GC Courtney Brown 8.00
27GC Torry Holt 12.00

2001 Fleer Genuine Final Cut

NM/M
Complete Set (24): 275.00
Common Player: 8.00
Inserted 1:24
1FC Troy Aikman 35.00
2FC Jamal Anderson 12.00
3FC Charlie Batch 12.00
4FC David Boston 12.00
5FC Isaac Bruce 12.00
6FC Tim Couch 20.00
7FC Terrell Davis 25.00
8FC Kevin Dyson 8.00
9FC L.C. Greenwood 12.00
10FC Marvin Harrison 12.00
11FC Edgerrin James 25.00
12FC Rob Johnson 8.00
13FC Jevon Kearse 12.00
14FC Jim Kelly 25.00
15FC James Lofton 12.00
16FC Ed McCaffrey 12.00
17FC Rob Moore 8.00
18FC Johnnie Morton 8.00
19FC Jake Plummer 12.00
20FC Jerry Rice 35.00
21FC Mike Singletary 15.00
22FC Emmitt Smith 40.00
23FC Charles Woodson 12.00
24FC Steve Young 20.00

2001 Fleer Genuine Future Swatch Tandems

NM/M
Complete Set (5): 475.00
Common Player: 75.00
Production 50 Sets
1FST Michael Vick, Drew Brees 150.00
2FST David Terrell, Anthony Thomas 75.00
3FST Santana Moss, Reggie Wayne 75.00
4FST Deuce McAllister, LaDainian Tomlinson 150.00
5FST Koren Robinson, Rod Gardner 75.00

2001 Fleer Genuine Hawaii Live "O"

NM/M
Complete Set (15): 30.00
Common Player: 1.50
Minor Stars: 3.00
Inserted 1:23
1HL Daunte Culpepper 6.00
2HL Donovan McNabb 4.50
3HL Torry Holt 3.00
4HL Terrell Owens 3.00
5HL Jimmy Smith 1.50
6HL Jeff Garcia 3.00
7HL Rich Gannon 1.50
8HL Peyton Manning 8.00
9HL Joe Horn 3.00
10HL Tony Gonzalez 1.50
11HL Edgerrin James 4.00
12HL Eddie George 3.50
13HL Corey Dillon 3.00
14HL Warrick Dunn 3.00
15HL Marvin Harrison 3.00

2001 Fleer Genuine Names of the Game

NM/M
Common Player: 20.00
Production 100 Sets
1NG Daunte Culpepper 50.00
2NG Terrell Davis 40.00
3NG Ron Dayne 25.00
4NG Eric Dickerson 35.00
5NG Tony Dorsett 50.00
6NG Edgerrin James 65.00
7NG Jevon Kearse 25.00
8NG Curtis Martin 20.00
9NG Steve McNair 20.00
10NG Joe Montana 150.00
11NG Randy Moss 85.00
12NG Walter Payton 150.00
13NG William Perry 20.00
14NG Deion Sanders 50.00
15NG Roger Staubach 75.00
16NG Lawrence Taylor 45.00
17NG Johnny Unitas 75.00

2001 Fleer Genuine Pennant Aggression

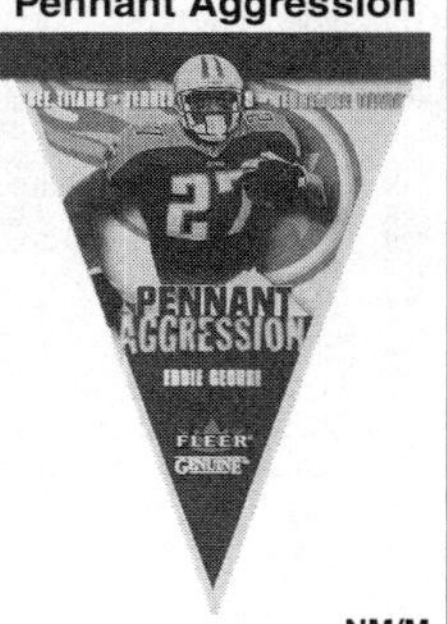

NM/M
Complete Set (10): 30.00
Common Player: 3.00
Inserted 1:23
1PA Kurt Warner 8.00
2PA Brett Favre 10.00
3PA Emmitt Smith 6.00
4PA Daunte Culpepper 4.50
5PA Terrell Davis 5.00
6PA Peyton Manning 8.00
7PA Eddie George 3.50
8PA Donovan McNabb 4.00
9PA Ricky Williams 4.00
10PA Tim Couch 3.50

2001 Fleer Genuine Seek and Deploy

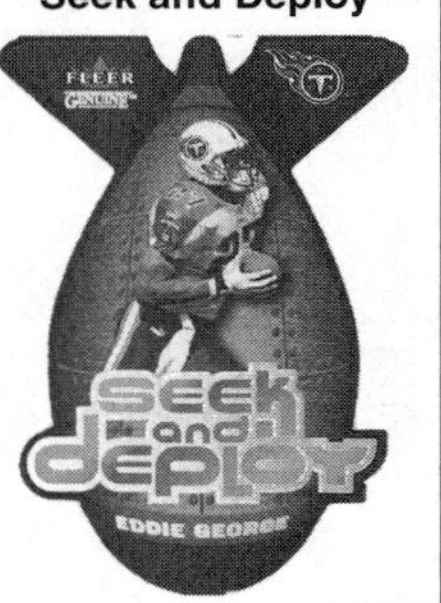

NM/M
Complete Set (15): 40.00
Common Player: 3.00
Inserted 1:23
1SD Jamal Lewis 4.00
2SD Randy Moss 8.00
3SD Ricky Williams 4.50
4SD Terrell Davis 4.00
5SD Donovan McNabb 4.50
6SD Curtis Martin 3.00
7SD Brett Favre 12.00
8SD Aaron Brooks 3.50
9SD Kurt Warner 4.00
10SD Eddie George 3.50
11SD Daunte Culpepper 6.00
12SD Jamal Anderson 3.00
13SD Marshall Faulk 3.50
14SD Ray Lewis 3.00
15SD Ron Dayne 2.00

2001 Fleer Genuine Donovan McNabb Uncut Sheet

1US Donovan McNabb

2001 Fleer Glossy

NM/M
Common Player: .20
Minor Stars: .40
Common Rookie (401-450): 2.50
Pack (10): 1.50
Box (24): 30.00
1 Thomas Jones .40
2 Bruce Smith .40
3 Marvin Harrison .60
4 Darrell Jackson .40
5 Trent Green .50
6 Wesley Walls .20
7 Jimmy Smith .50
8 Isaac Bruce .50
9 Jamal Anderson .50
10 Marty Booker .20
11 Elvis Grbac .60
12 Joe Jurevicius .20
13 Reidel Anthony .20
14 Darnay Scott .40
15 Oronde Gadsden .40
16 Shawn Bryson .20
17 Jonathan Ogden .20
18 Aaron Shea .20
19 Randy Moss 2.00
20 Eddie George .75
21 Stephen Davis .40
22 Emmitt Smith 1.50
23 Willie McGinest .20
24 Trent Dilfer .40
25 Peter Boulware .20
26 Rod Smith .50
27 Ricky Williams 1.00
28 Albert Connell .20
29 Robert Porcher .20
30 Jessie Armstead .20
31 Shane Matthews .20
32 Eric Moulds .50
33 Kurt Schulz .20
34 Richie Anderson .20
35 Ron Dugans .40
36 Steve Beuerlein .40
37 Darren Sharper .40
38 Andre Rison .40
39 Courtney Brown .40
40 Eddie Kennison .40
41 Ken Dilger .20
42 Charles Johnson .20
43 Dexter Coakley .20
44 Akili Smith .40
45 R. Jay Soward .20
46 Danny Farmer .40
47 Dez White .40
48 Olandis Gary .60
49 Wali Rainer .20
50 Derrick Alexander .40
51 Donnie Abraham .20
52 David Sloan .20
53 Larry Allen .20
54 Sam Madison .40
55 Troy Edwards .50
56 Ryan Longwell .20
57 Brian Griese .75
58 John Randle .20
59 Reggie Jones .20
60 Mike Peterson .20
61 Bill Romanowski .20
62 Kevin Faulk .40
63 Tai Streets .40
64 Tony Brackens .20
65 James Stewart .20
66 Joe Horn .40
67 Kurt Warner 2.00
68 Eric Hicks .20
69 Bryant Westbrook .20
70 Tiki Barber .50
71 Frank Sanders .40
72 Olindo Mare .20
73 Bill Schroeder .40
74 Anthony Becht .40
75 Rob Johnson .50
76 Troy Brown .40
77 Chad Bratzke .20
78 Rickey Dudley .20
79 Doug Johnson .20
80 Joe Johnson .20
81 Keenan McCardell .40
82 Tim Brown .60
83 Blaine Bishop .20
84 Ron Dixon .40
85 Mike Cloud .20
86 Todd Pinkston .50
87 Shannon Sharpe .50
88 Marvin Jones .20
89 Zach Thomas .50
90 Kordell Stewart .75
91 Champ Bailey .40
92 Jacquez Green .40
93 Daunte Culpepper 1.25
94 Freddie Jones .20
95 Donald Hayes .40
96 Rich Gannon .60
97 Ty Law .50
98 Grant Wilstrom .20
99 James Allen .20
100 Corey Simon .20
101 Jeff Blake .40
102 Bryant Young .40
103 Craig Yeast .20
104 Bobby Shaw .20
105 Kerry Collins .50
106 Brock Huard .50
107 JaJuan Dawson .40
108 Jeff Graham .20
109 Chad Pennington 1.25
110 Jake Plummer .50
111 James McKnight .20
112 Terrell Owens .60
113 Mo Lewis .20
114 Jeremy McDaniel .20
115 Ed McCaffrey .50
116 Ricky Watters .50
117 Jerry Porter .60
118 Shawn Jefferson .20
119 Charlie Batch .40
120 Justin Watson .20
121 Donovan McNabb 1.25
122 Shaun King .40
123 Brett Favre 2.50
124 Ronald McKinnon .20
125 Richard Huntley .20
126 Ray Lewis .60
127 Jerome Pathon .20
128 Sam Cowart .20
129 Ryan Leaf .40
130 Greg Clark .20
131 Tony Boselli .20
132 Frank Wycheck .20
133 Charlie Garner .40
134 Tony Siragusa .20
135 Sylvester Morris .50
136 Qadry Ismail .40
137 Jon Kitna .40
138 James Thrash .40
139 Lamar Smith .40
140 Brad Johnson .60
141 London Fletcher .20
142 Tim Biakabutuka .40
143 Ed McDaniel .20
144 Tony Parrish .20
145 David Boston .60
146 Brian Urlacher 1.25
147 Drew Bledsoe .75
148 David Patten .20
149 Marcellus Wiley .20
150 Peter Warrick .60
151 La'Roi Glover .20
152 Troy Aikman 1.25
153 Chris Chandler .20
154 Travis Prentice .40
155 Ike Hilliard .40
156 John Mobley .20
157 Warren Sapp .40
158 Joey Galloway .50
159 Laveranues Coles .50
160 Germane Crowell .40
161 Jamal Lewis 1.25
162 Mike Anderson 1.00
163 Charles Woodson .40
164 Antonio Freeman .50
165 Derrick Mason .50
166 Chris Claiborne .20
167 Brian Mitchell .20
168 Mike Vanderjagt .20
169 Rod Woodson .40
170 Doug Chapman .40
171 John Lynch .20
172 Kevin Hardy .20
173 Sam Shade .20
174 Edgerrin James 1.50
175 Brian Dawkins .20
176 Donnie Edwards .20
177 Patrick Jeffers .20
178 Mark Brunell .50
179 Junior Seau .40
180 Trace Armstrong .20
181 Marcus Robinson .50
182 Troy Edwards .60
183 J.J. Stokes .50
184 Jake Reed .20
185 Corey Dillon .40
186 Jay Fiedler .60
187 Christian Fauria .20
188 Sammy Knight .20
189 Kevin Johnson .50
190 Matthew Hatchette .20
191 Az-Zahir Hakim .40
192 Keith Hamilton .20
193 Darren Woodson .20
194 Terry Glenn .40
195 Simeon Rice .20
196 Keyshawn Johnson .60
197 Terrell Davis 1.25
198 Willie Roaf .20
199 Doug Flutie .75
200 Kevin Carter .20
201 Stephen Boyd .20
202 Michael Strahan .40
203 Ray Buchanan .20
204 Tyrone Wheatley .40
205 Jason Hanson .20
206 Wayne Chrebet .50
207 Samari Rolle .20
208 Duce Staley .50
209 Dorsey Levens .40
210 Sebastian Janikowski .40
211 Duane Starks .20
212 Jason Gildon .20
213 Terrence Wilkins .20
214 Eric Allen .20
215 Deion Sanders .50
216 Curtis Conway .20
217 Fred Taylor .75
218 Troy Vincent .20
219 Mike Minter .20
220 Jeff Garcia .75
221 Tony Richardson .20
222 Jerome Bettis .50
223 Chad Morton .20
224 Tony Horne .20
225 Dave Moore .20
226 Victor Green .20
227 Chris Sanders .20
228 Marshall Faulk .75
229 Cris Carter .60
230 Rodney Harrison .20
231 Tim Couch .75
232 Antowain Smith .60
233 Lawyer Milloy .20
234 Lance Schulters .20
235 Michael Wiley .20
236 Steve McNair .50
237 Aaron Brooks .75
238 Anthony Simmons .20
239 Dwayne Carswell .20
240 Priest Holmes .50
241 Amani Toomer .50
242 Aeneas Williams .40
243 MarTay Jenkins .20
244 Jeff George .40
245 Vinny Testaverde .50
246 Peerless Price .40
247 Bubba Franks .40
248 Randall Cunningham .40
249 Aaron Glenn .20
250 Terance Mathis .20
251 Peyton Manning 2.00
252 Terrell Buckley .20
253 Greg Biekert .20
254 Martin Gramatica .40
255 Kyle Brady .20
256 Johnnie Morton .40
257 Jeremiah Trotter .20
258 Travis Taylor .50
259 Frank Moreau .20
260 LeRoy Butler .40
261 Plaxico Burress .60
262 Randall Godfrey .20
263 Jason Taylor .20
264 Jeff Burris .20
265 Jim Harbaugh .40
266 Marco Coleman .20
267 Robert Smith .40
268 Mike Hollis .20
269 Jerry Rice 1.50
270 Muhsin Muhammad .40
271 J.R. Redmond .40
272 Brian Walker .20
273 Orlando Pace .20
274 Cade McNown .40
275 Darren Howard .20
276 Ron Dayne .50
277 Shaun Alexander 1.00
278 Brandon Bennett .20
279 Jason Sehorn .20
280 Matt Hasselbeck .40
281 Michael Pittman .20
282 Dennis Northcutt .20
283 Dedric Ward .20
284 Curtis Martin .50
285 Sammy Morris .20
286 Raghib Ismail .20
287 Jon Ritchie .20
288 Shaun Ellis .20
289 Tim Dwight .40
290 Trevor Pryce .20
291 Warrick Dunn .60
292 Napoleon Kaufman .20
293 Mike Alstott .50
294 Herman Moore .40
295 Chad Lewis .20
296 Hugh Douglas .20
297 Chris Redman .40
298 Ahman Green .50
299 Hines Ward .50
300 Mark Bruener .20
301 Jevon Kearse .20
302 Jermaine Fazande .20
303 Terrell Fletcher .20
304 Torry Holt .60
305 Chris McAlister .20
306 Jason Elam .20
307 Fred Beasley .20
308 Frank Wycheck .20
309 Michael McCrary .20
310 Mark Brunell .20
311 Tim Couch .40
312 Takeo Spikes .20
313 Jerome Bettis .20
314 Zach Thomas .20
315 Drew Bledsoe 1.00

316	Wayne Chrebet	.20
317	Jay Riemersma	.20
318	Marvin Harrison	.20
319	Ed McCaffrey	.20
320	Tony Gonzalez	.20
321	Tim Brown	.20
322	Junior Seau	.20
323	Shawn Springs	.20
324	Troy Aikman	.60
325	Pat Tilman	.20
326	David Akers	.20
327	Michael Strahan	.20
328	Darrell Green	.20
329	Kurt Warner	1.00
330	Jeff Garcia	.40
331	Aaron Brooks	.40
332	Jamal Anderson	.20
333	Brad Hoover	.20
334	Cris Carter	.20
335	Derrick Brooks	.20
336	Antonio Freeman	.20
337	Luther Elliss	.20
338	James Allen	.20
339	Cardinals	.20
340	Falcons	.20
341	Ravens	.20
342	Bills	.20
343	Panthers	.20
344	Bears	.20
345	Bengals	.20
346	Browns	.20
347	Cowboys	.60
348	Broncos	.20
349	Lions	.20
350	Packers	1.25
351	Colts	.60
352	Jaguars	.20
353	Chiefs	.20
354	Dolphins	.20
355	Vikings	.40
356	Patriots	.20
357	Saints	.20
358	Giants	.20
359	Jets	.20
360	Raiders	.20
361	Eagles	.40
362	Steelers	.40
363	Chargers	.20
364	49ers	.40
365	Seahawks	.20
366	Rams	1.00
367	Buccaneers	.20
368	Titans	.20
369	Redskins	.20
370	Bills	.20
371	Colts	.40
372	Dolphins	.20
373	Patriots	.20
374	Jets	.20
375	Ravens	.20
376	Bengals	.20
377	Browns	.20
378	Jaguars	.20
379	Steelers	.40
380	Titans	.40
381	Broncos	.20
382	Chiefs	.20
383	Raiders	.40
384	Chargers	.20
385	Seahawks	.20
386	Cardinals	.20
387	Cowboys	.60
388	Giants	.20
389	Eagles	.20
390	Redskins	.20
391	Bears	.20
392	Lions	.20
393	Packers	.60
394	Vikings	.40
395	Buccaneers	.20
396	Falcons	.20
397	Panthers	.20
398	Saints	.20
399	49ers	.40
400	Rams	.60
401	*Michael Vick*	30.00
402	*Drew Brees*	15.00
403	*Michael Bennett*	10.00
404	*David Terrell*	8.00
405	*Deuce McAllister*	15.00
406	*Santana Moss*	8.00
407	*Koren Robinson*	8.00
408	*Chris Weinke*	8.00
409	*Reggie Wayne*	8.00
410	*Rod Gardner*	8.00
411	*James Jackson*	5.00
412	*Travis Henry*	6.00
413	*Josh Heupel*	3.00
414	*LaDainian Tomlinson*	15.00
415	*Chad Johnson*	8.00
416	*Sage Rosenfels*	3.00
417	*Quincy Morgan*	5.00
418	*Ken-Yon Rambo*	3.00
419	*LaMont Jordan*	5.00
420	*Anthony Thomas*	8.00
421	*Dave Dickenson*	3.00
422	*Travis Minor*	3.00
423	*Kevan Barlow*	8.00
424	*Chris Chambers*	10.00
425	*Richard Seymour*	2.50
426	*Gerard Warren*	2.50
427	*Jamar Fletcher*	2.50
428	*Freddie Mitchell*	6.00
429	*Jamal Reynolds*	2.00
430	*Marques Tuiasosopo*	5.00
431	*Marvin "Snoop" Minnis*	6.00
432	*Mike McMahon*	8.00
433	*Robert Ferguson*	3.00
434	*Ronney Daniels*	2.00
435	*Rudi Johnson*	8.00
436	*Vinny Sutherland*	3.00
437	*Josh Booty*	4.00
438	*Reggie White*	2.50
439	*Todd Heap*	3.00
440	*Justin Smith*	2.50
441	*Andre Carter*	2.50
442	*Bobby Newcombe*	2.50
443	*Alex Bannister*	3.00
444	*Correll Buckhalter*	6.00
445	*Quincy Carter*	8.00
446	*Jesse Palmer*	5.00
447	*Heath Evans*	2.50
448	*Dan Morgan*	2.50
449	*Justin McCareins*	6.00
450	*Alge Crumpler*	3.00

2001 Fleer Glossy Nameplates

		NM/M
Common Player:		15.00
1NP	Ron Dayne	15.00
2NP	Kurt Warner	60.00
3NP	Curtis Martin	25.00
4NP	Jake Plummer	15.00
5NP	Mark Brunell	20.00
6NP	Drew Bledsoe	30.00
7NP	Kevin Johnson	15.00
8NP	Brian Griese	50.00
9NP	Terrell Owens	20.00
10NP	Brian Urlacher	65.00
11NP	Jamal Anderson	15.00
12NP	Isaac Bruce	20.00
13NP	Jerome Bettis	25.00
14NP	Fred Taylor	25.00
15NP	Tim Couch	40.00
16NP	Stephen Davis	15.00
17NP	Warrick Dunn	20.00
18NP	Rod Smith	20.00
19NP	Marshall Faulk	50.00
20NP	Thomas Jones	15.00
21NP	Emmitt Smith	80.00
22NP	Marcus Robinson	20.00
23NP	Daunte Culpepper	60.00
24NP	Antonio Freeman	25.00
25NP	Marvin Harrison	30.00
26NP	Dan Marino	100.00
27NP	Steve Young	60.00
28NP	Deion Sanders	60.00
29NP	Edgerrin James	60.00
30NP	Jerry Rice	80.00

2001 Fleer Glossy Rookie Mini

Mini Cards: 1X-1.5X
Production 350 Sets

2001 Fleer Glossy Rookie Sticker

Stickers: .5-1X
Production 699 Sets

2001 Fleer Glossy Throwbacks

		NM/M
Complete Set (20):		60.00
Common Player:		2.00
Inserted 1:12 Glossy		
Inserted 1:20 Tradition		
1TB	Jamal Lewis	3.00
2TB	Eddie George	3.00
3TB	Marvin Harrison	3.00
4TB	Brett Favre	8.00
5TB	Donovan McNabb	5.00
6TB	Troy Aikman	5.00
7TB	Edgerrin James	4.00
8TB	Brian Urlacher	5.00
9TB	Stephen Davis	2.00
10TB	Daunte Culpepper	5.00
11TB	Jerry Rice	6.00
12TB	Emmitt Smith	6.00
13TB	Kurt Warner	4.00
14TB	Ricky Williams	3.00
15TB	Cris Carter	2.00
16TB	Mark Brunell	3.00
17TB	Ron Dayne	2.00
18TB	Peyton Manning	6.00
19TB	Randy Moss	6.00
20TB	Brian Griese	3.00

2001 Fleer Glossy Traditional Threads

		NM/M
Common Player:		10.00
1TT	Troy Aikman	30.00
2TT	Jamal Anderson	10.00
3TT	Jerome Bettis	15.00
4TT	Drew Bledsoe	15.00
5TT	Isaac Bruce	12.00
6TT	Mark Brunell	12.00
7TT	Tim Couch	15.00
8TT	Daunte Culpepper	30.00
9TT	Stephen Davis	10.00
10TT	Ron Dayne	10.00
11TT	Warrick Dunn	12.00
12TT	Marshall Faulk	20.00
13TT	Brett Favre	50.00
14TT	Antonio Freeman	15.00
15TT	Eddie George	15.00
16TT	Brian Griese	15.00
17TT	Marvin Harrison	15.00
18TT	Edgerrin James	30.00
19TT	Kevin Johnson	10.00
20TT	Thomas Jones	10.00
21TT	Jevon Kearse	10.00
22TT	Ray Lewis	15.00
23TT	Dan Marino	60.00
24TT	Curtis Martin	15.00
25TT	Randy Moss	40.00
26TT	Terrell Owens	15.00
27TT	Jake Plummer	10.00
28TT	Jerry Rice	30.00
29TT	Rod Smith	12.00
30TT	Jimmy Smith	12.00
31TT	Kordell Stewart	15.00
32TT	Fred Taylor	12.00
33TT	Brian Urlacher	25.00
34TT	Kurt Warner	40.00
35TT	Steve Young	20.00

A player's name in *italic* type indicates a rookie card.

2001 Fleer Hot Prospects

		NM/M
Complete Set (150):		25.00
Common Player:		.20
Minor Stars:		.40
Pack (5):		6.25
Wax Box (15):		65.00
1	Aaron Brooks	.75
2	Tim Couch	1.00
3	Jeff George	.40
4	Brett Favre	3.00
5	Donovan McNabb	1.25
6	Ray Lucas	.20
7	Doug Flutie	1.00
8	Mark Brunell	1.00
9	Steve McNair	.75
10	Trent Green	.40
11	Daunte Culpepper	1.50
12	Rich Gannon	.40
13	Kurt Warner	2.50
14	Brian Griese	1.00
15	Kerry Collins	.40
16	Vinny Testaverde	.40
17	David Boston	.75
18	Peyton Manning	2.50
19	Keyshawn Johnson	.75
20	Tim Biakabutuka	.40
21	J.R. Redmond	.40
22	Emmitt Smith	2.00
23	Terry Glenn	.50
24	Tony Gonzalez	.50
25	Charlie Garner	.40
26	Lamar Smith	.50
27	Eddie George	1.00
28	Fred Taylor	1.00
29	Marvin Harrison	.75
30	Terrell Davis	1.50
31	Marcus Robinson	.75
32	Edgerrin James	2.50
33	Ed McCaffrey	.50
34	Ricky Williams	1.00
35	Todd Pinkston	.40
36	Jerome Bettis	.75
37	Shaun Alexander	.75
38	Mike Anderson	2.00
39	Keenan McCardell	.40
40	Mike Alstott	.75
41	Terrell Fletcher	.20
42	Kevin Johnson	.50
43	Wesley Walls	.20
44	Derrick Mason	.50
45	Sammy Morris	.40
46	Joey Galloway	.75
47	Sylvester Morris	.75
48	Stephen Davis	.75
49	Terrell Owens	.75
50	Troy Edwards	.20
51	Amani Toomer	.40
52	Ray Lewis	.50
53	Terance Mathis	.20
54	Brian Urlacher	1.50
55	Junior Seau	.50
56	Raghib Ismail	.40
57	Wayne Chrebet	.50
58	Peter Warrick	1.50
59	Andre Rison	.40
60	Desmond Howard	.20
61	Eric Moulds	.75
62	Jerry Rice	1.75
63	Stephen Alexander	.20
64	Isaac Bruce	.75
65	Travis Prentice	.50
66	James Stewart	.50
67	Jamal Anderson	.75
68	Ricky Watters	.50
69	Jamal Lewis	2.00
70	Priest Holmes	.40
71	Ahman Green	.50
72	Marshall Faulk	1.00
73	Warrick Dunn	.75
74	Curtis Martin	.75
75	Corey Dillon	.75
76	Ron Dayne	1.50
77	Thomas Jones	.50
78	Duce Staley	.75
79	Tiki Barber	.75
80	Cris Carter	.75
81	Tim Brown	.50
82	Jimmy Smith	.50
83	Elvis Grbac	.50
84	Randy Moss	2.50
85	Tim Dwight	.50
86	Antonio Freeman	.50
87	Muhsin Muhammad	.50
88	Torry Holt	.75
89	Frank Wycheck	.20
90	Jake Plummer	.75
91	Brad Johnson	.50
92	Chris Chandler	.40
93	Drew Bledsoe	1.00
94	Rob Johnson	.50
95	Matt Hasselbeck	.75
96	Jon Kitna	.50
97	Kordell Stewart	.75
98	Charlie Batch	.75
99	Cade McNown	.75
100	Jeff Garcia	.75
101	*Quincy Morgan*	1.00
102	*Jesse Palmer*	.50
103	*Reggie Wayne*	4.00
104	*Deuce McAllister*	8.00
105	*Chad Johnson*	5.00
106	*Chris Weinke*	1.00
107	*Michael Bennett*	6.00
108	*Rod Gardner*	4.00
109	*Michael Vick*	20.00
110	*Anthony Thomas*	4.00
111	*Santana Moss*	4.00
112	*Kevan Barlow*	5.00
113	*Koren Robinson*	4.00
114	*Rudi Johnson*	4.00
115	*Josh Heupel*	2.00
116	*James Jackson*	1.00
117	*Freddie Mitchell*	2.00
118	*LaDainian Tomlinson*	10.00
119	*Marques Tuiasosopo*	3.00
120	*Drew Brees*	8.00
121	*David Terrell*	3.00
122	*Chris Chambers*	5.00
123	*Mike McMahon*	2.00
124	*Robert Ferguson*	1.00
125	*Justin Smith*	1.00
126	*Leonard Davis*	.50
127	*Todd Heap*	2.00
128	*Dan Morgan*	.50
129	*Gerard Warren*	.50
130	*Travis Henry*	3.00
131	*Travis Minor*	.50
132	*Richard Seymour*	.50
133	*Quincy Carter*	2.00
134	*Marvin "Snoop" Minnis*	2.00
135	*Sage Rosenfels*	1.00

2001 Fleer Hot Prospects Draft Day Postmarks

	NM/M
Common Player:	12.00
Kevan Barlow	20.00
Michael Bennett	45.00
Drew Brees	50.00
Rod Gardner	20.00
Josh Heupel	20.00
James Jackson	20.00
Chad Johnson	15.00
Rudi Johnson	15.00
Deuce McAllister	25.00
Freddie Mitchell	20.00
Quincy Morgan	20.00
Santana Moss	25.00
Jesse Palmer	12.00
Koren Robinson	25.00
David Terrell	30.00
Anthony Thomas	20.00
LaDainian Tomlinson	50.00
Marques Tuiasosopo	20.00
Michael Vick	75.00
Reggie Wayne	20.00
Chris Weinke	45.00

2001 Fleer Hot Prospects Draft Day Postmarks Autographs

	NM/M
Common Player:	20.00
Kevan Barlow	25.00
Michael Bennett	75.00
Drew Brees	60.00
Rod Gardner	30.00
Josh Heupel	25.00
James Jackson	20.00
Chad Johnson	20.00
Rudi Johnson	20.00
Deuce McAllister	40.00
Freddie Mitchell	30.00
Quincy Morgan	30.00
Santana Moss	60.00
Jesse Palmer	20.00
Koren Robinson	30.00
David Terrell	40.00
Anthony Thomas	30.00
LaDainian Tomlinson	150.00
Marques Tuiasosopo	30.00
Michael Vick	250.00
Reggie Wayne	25.00
Chris Weinke	85.00

2001 Fleer Hot Prospects Honor Guard

		NM/M
Complete Set (49):		60.00
Common Player:		1.00
Minor Stars:		2.00
Inserted 1:5		
1HG	Troy Aikman	4.00
2HG	Marcus Allen	2.00
3HG	Mike Alstott	2.00
4HG	Jerome Bettis	2.00
5HG	Drew Bledsoe	2.25
6HG	Isaac Bruce	2.00
7HG	Mark Brunell	2.25
8HG	Wayne Chrebet	1.00
9HG	Daunte Culpepper	3.00
10HG	Randall Cunningham	1.00
11HG	Terrell Davis	3.00
12HG	Stephen Davis	2.00
13HG	Corey Dillon	2.00
14HG	Warrick Dunn	2.00
15HG	Marshall Faulk	2.25
16HG	Brett Favre	6.00
17HG	Doug Flutie	2.25
18HG	Jeff Garcia	2.00
19HG	Eddie George	2.25
20HG	Brian Griese	2.25
21HG	Bo Jackson	3.00
22HG	Jamal Lewis	4.50
23HG	Dan Marino	8.00
24HG	Donovan McNabb	2.50
25HG	Steve McNair	2.00
26HG	Joe Montana	10.00
27HG	Randy Moss	5.00
28HG	Jerry Rice	3.50
29HG	Jerry Rice	3.50
30HG	Deion Sanders	2.00
31HG	Emmitt Smith	4.50
32HG	Fred Taylor	2.25
33HG	John Elway	8.00
34HG	Kurt Warner	6.00
35HG	Ricky Williams	2.50
36HG	Marvin Harrison	2.00
37HG	Edgerrin James	5.00
38HG	Curtis Martin	2.00
39HG	Vinny Testaverde	1.00
40HG	Rod Smith	1.00
41HG	Warren Moon	2.00
42HG	Steve Young	2.50
43HG	Jamal Anderson	2.00
44HG	Tim Brown	2.00
45HG	Plaxico Burress	2.00
46HG	Tim Couch	2.25
47HG	Az-Zahir Hakim	1.00
48HG	Ed McCaffrey	2.00
49HG	Ron Dayne	2.50

2001 Fleer Hot Prospects Pigskin Prospects

		NM/M
Complete Set (15):		50.00
Common Player:		2.50
Inserted 1:15		
1PP	Drew Brees	10.00
2PP	Koren Robinson	4.00

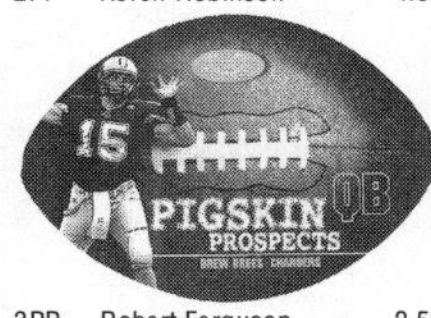

3PP	Robert Ferguson	2.50
4PP	Rod Gardner	4.00
5PP	Chad Johnson	2.50
6PP	Reggie Wayne	3.00
7PP	Chris Weinke	6.00
8PP	Deuce McAllister	5.00
9PP	Chris Chambers	2.50
10PP	Freddie Mitchell	3.50
11PP	Quincy Carter	5.00
12PP	LaDainian Tomlinson	8.00
13PP	Santana Moss	4.00
14PP	David Terrell	5.00
15PP	Michael Vick	15.00

2001 Fleer Hot Prospects Pigskin Prospects Jersey

		NM/M
Common Player:		15.00
Inserted 1:51		
1PPJ	Drew Brees	45.00
2PPJ	Robert Ferguson	20.00
3PPJ	Rod Gardner	25.00
4PPJ	Chad Johnson	15.00
5PPJ	Reggie Wayne	20.00
6PPJ	Chris Weinke	30.00

2001 Fleer Hot Prospects Rookie Premiere Postmarks

	NM/M
Complete Set (35):	450.00
Common Player:	8.00
Kevan Barlow	20.00
Michael Bennett	35.00
Drew Brees	50.00
Quincy Carter	25.00
Chris Chambers	25.00
Leonard Davis	8.00
Robert Ferguson	10.00
Rod Gardner	15.00
Todd Heap	10.00
Travis Henry	20.00
Josh Heupel	15.00
James Jackson	15.00
Chad Johnson	10.00
Rudi Johnson	10.00
Deuce McAllister	25.00
Mike McMahon	10.00
Marvin Minnis	20.00
Travis Minor	15.00
Freddie Mitchell	20.00
Dan Morgan	10.00
Quincy Morgan	15.00
Santana Moss	25.00
Jesse Palmer	10.00
Koren Robinson	20.00
Sage Rosenfels	10.00
Richard Seymour	8.00
Justin Smith	8.00
David Terrell	25.00
Anthony Thomas	15.00
LaDainian Tomlinson	50.00
Marques Tuiasosopo	20.00
Michael Vick	100.00
Gerard Warren	10.00
Reggie Wayne	20.00
Chris Weinke	40.00

2001 Fleer Hot Prospects TD Fever

		NM/M
Complete Set (15):		150.00
Common Player:		10.00
Inserted 1:21		
1TDF	Daunte Culpepper	25.00
2TDF	James Stewart	10.00
3TDF	Jimmy Smith	10.00
4TDF	Marvin Harrison	12.00
5TDF	Drew Bledsoe	15.00
6TDF	Randy Moss	35.00
7TDF	Oronde Gadsden	10.00
8TDF	Peyton Manning	35.00
9TDF	J.R. Redmond	10.00
10TDF	Rich Gannon	12.00
11TDF	Edgerrin James	30.00
12TDF	Peerless Price	10.00
13TDF	Tyrone Wheatley	10.00
14TDF	Curtis Martin	12.00

2001 Fleer Legacy

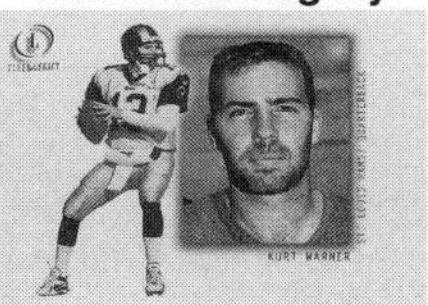

		NM/M
Common Player:		.25
Minor Stars:		.40
Common Rookie:		5.00
Production 999 Sets		
First 300 Are Rookie Postmarks		
Pack (5):		4.10
Box (24):		70.00
1	Donovan McNabb	1.50
2	Doug Flutie	1.00
3	Amani Toomer	.40
4	Jay Fiedler	.40
5	Antonio Freeman	.75
6	Jon Kitna	.40
7	Jake Plummer	.75
8	Ricky Watters	.40
9	Jerry Rice	2.00
10	Troy Brown	.40
11	Jimmy Smith	.40
12	Edgerrin James	2.00
13	Todd Pinkston	.25
14	Eric Moulds	.40
15	Stephen Davis	.75
16	Matt Hasselbeck	.40
17	Vinny Testaverde	.40
18	Priest Holmes	.75
19	Mike Anderson	1.25
20	Shane Matthews	.25
21	Qadry Ismail	.25
22	Torry Holt	.75
23	Duce Staley	.75
24	Ahman Green	.75
25	Corey Dillon	.75
26	Peerless Price	.40
27	Steve McNair	.75
28	Junior Seau	.40
29	Doug Chapman	.25
30	Mark Brunell	1.00
31	Joey Galloway	.40
32	James Allen	.25
33	David Boston	.75
34	Marshall Faulk	1.00
35	Shaun Alexander	1.00
36	Wayne Chrebet	.40
37	Randy Moss	2.50
38	Marvin Harrison	.75
39	Tim Couch	1.00
40	Jamal Anderson	.75
41	Warren Sapp	.40
42	Brad Johnson	.75
43	Kerry Collins	.40
44	Derrick Alexander	.25
45	Terrell Davis	1.50
46	Tiki Barber	.25
47	Trent Green	.40
48	James Stewart	.25
49	Kevin Johnson	.40
50	Ray Lewis	.75
51	Warrick Dunn	.75
52	Tim Brown	.75
53	Daunte Culpepper	1.50
54	Fred Taylor	1.00
55	Brian Griese	1.00
56	Wesley Walls	.25
57	Rob Johnson	.40
58	Jeff George	.25
59	Jeff Garcia	.75
60	Rich Gannon	.40
61	Cris Carter	.75
62	Peyton Manning	2.50
63	Peter Warrick	.75
64	Terance Mathis	.25
65	Kurt Warner	2.50
66	Kordell Stewart	.75
67	Aaron Brooks	.75
68	JaJuan Dawson	.25
69	Elvis Grbac	.40
70	Keyshawn Johnson	.75
71	Terrell Owens	.75
72	Curtis Martin	.75
73	Lamar Smith	.40
74	Rod Smith	.40
75	Tim Biakabutuka	.25
76	Thomas Jones	.40
77	Isaac Bruce	.75
78	Joe Horn	.40
79	Drew Bledsoe	1.00
80	Oronde Gadsden	.25
81	Brett Favre	3.00
82	Emmitt Smith	2.00

83 Muhsin Muhammad .40
84 Eddie George 1.00
85 Jerome Bettis .75
86 Ricky Williams 1.25
87 Tony Gonzalez .40
88 Germane Crowell .40
89 Brian Urlacher 1.50
90 Shawn Jefferson .25
91 *Michael Vick* 40.00
92 *David Terrell* 10.00
93 *Chris Chambers* 15.00
94 *Freddie Mitchell* 10.00
95 *Drew Brees* 15.00
96 *LaMont Jordan* 5.00
97 *Quincy Carter* 10.00
98 *Anthony Thomas* 12.00
99 *LaDainian Tomlinson* 30.00
100 *Santana Moss* 12.00
101 *Rod Gardner* 12.00
102 *Nick Goings* 2.00
103 *Sage Rosenfels* 3.00
104 *Mike McMahon* 10.00
105 *Marvin "Snoop" Minnis* 5.00
106 *Michael Bennett* 15.00
107 *Todd Heap* 5.00
108 *Kevan Barlow* 10.00
109 *Travis Henry* 10.00
110 *Jason Brookins* 6.00
111 *Rudi Johnson* 12.00
112 *Reggie Wayne* 10.00
113 *Koren Robinson* 8.00
114 *Chad Johnson* 12.00
115 *Quincy Morgan* 8.00
116 *Robert Ferguson* 6.00
117 *Chris Weinke* 8.00
118 *Jesse Palmer* 8.00
119 *James Jackson* 8.00
120 *Deuce McAllister* 20.00

2001 Fleer Legacy Hall of Fame Material

NM/M
Common Player: 20.00
Inserted 1:288
Troy Aikman 30.00
Marcus Allen 30.00
John Elway 60.00
Marshall Faulk 30.00
Brett Favre 60.00
Bo Jackson 40.00
Dan Marino 75.00
Jerry Rice 50.00
Junior Seau 20.00
Emmitt Smith 60.00

2001 Fleer Legacy Rookie Postmarks

NM/M
Common Player: 8.00
Production 300 Sets
First 100 Are Autographs
91 Michael Vick 50.00
92 David Terrell 25.00
93 Chris Chambers 20.00
94 Freddie Mitchell 15.00
95 Drew Brees 30.00
96 LaMont Jordan 8.00
97 Quincy Carter 20.00
98 Anthony Thomas 20.00
99 LaDainian Tomlinson 30.00
100 Santana Moss 15.00
101 Rod Gardner 15.00
102 Nick Goings 8.00
103 Sage Rosenfels 10.00
104 Mike McMahon 15.00
105 Marvin "Snoop" Minnis 12.00
106 Michael Bennett 20.00
107 Todd Heap 8.00
108 Kevan Barlow 12.00
109 Travis Henry 12.00
110 Jason Brookins 8.00
111 Rudi Johnson 8.00
112 Reggie Wayne 12.00
113 Koren Robinson 15.00
114 Chad Johnson 8.00
115 Quincy Morgan 10.00
116 Robert Ferguson 8.00
117 Chris Weinke 15.00
118 Jesse Palmer 10.00
119 James Jackson 10.00
120 Deuce McAllister 15.00

2001 Fleer Legacy NFL Game Issue

NM/M
Common Player: 6.00
2nd Quarter: 2X
Production 100 Sets
3rd Quarter: 2.5X
Production 50 Sets
4th Quarter: 3X-6X
Production 25 Sets
David Boston 10.00
Mark Brunell 12.00
Cris Carter 12.00
Germane Crowell 6.00
Daunte Culpepper 15.00
Ron Dayne 8.00
Brett Favre 20.00
Rich Gannon 10.00
Jeff Garcia 12.00
Brian Griese 15.00
Bo Jackson 20.00
Edgerrin James 15.00
Kevin Johnson 6.00
Rob Johnson 6.00
Ray Lewis 12.00
Donovan McNabb 15.00
Jake Plummer 6.00
Kordell Stewart 12.00
Vinny Testaverde 8.00
Kurt Warner 15.00

A player's name in *italic* type indicates a rookie card.

2001 Fleer Legacy Triple Threads

NM/M
1 Chris Weinke, Drew Brees, Quincy Carter 40.00
2 Michael Vick, Drew Brees, Quincy Carter 50.00
3 Jesse Palmer, Drew Brees, Sage Rosenfels 30.00
4 Josh Heupel, Quincy Carter, Michael Vick 40.00
5 LaDainian Tomlinson, Deuce McAllister, Michael Bennett 40.00
6 Anthony Thomas, James Jackson, Kevan Barlow 30.00
7 Reggie Wayne, Santana Moss, Koren Robinson 20.00
8 David Terrell, Freddie Mitchell, Rod Gardner 25.00
9 Rudi Johnson, James Jackson, Travis Minor 15.00
10 Chris Chambers, Marvin "Snoop" Minnis, Robert Ferguson 25.00
11 Chad Johnson, Todd Heap, Santana Moss 15.00
12 Mike McMahon, Chris Weinke, Marques Tuiasosopo 25.00
13 Travis Minor, Travis Henry, Michael Bennett 30.00
14 Michael Vick, LaDainian Tomlinson, David Terrell 60.00
15 Santana Moss, Freddie Mitchell, Chad Johnson 20.00
16 Kevan Barlow, Michael Bennett, Rudi Johnson 20.00
17 Koren Robinson, Freddie Mitchell, Quincy Morgan 20.00
18 Josh Heupel, Jesse Palmer, Marques Tuiasosopo 20.00
19 Mike McMahon, Jesse Palmer, Chris Weinke 25.00
20 Deuce McAllister, Travis Minor, Anthony Thomas 40.00
21 Robert Ferguson, Reggie Wayne, Marvin "Snoop" Minnis 20.00
22 Chris Chambers, Rod Gardner, Koren Robinson 30.00
23 Todd Heap, Quincy Morgan, Chris Chambers 20.00
24 LaDainian Tomlinson, Kevan Barlow, Travis Henry 20.00
25 Mike McMahon, Marques Tuiasosopo, Sage Rosenfels 25.00
26 David Terrell, Rod Gardner, Reggie Wayne 25.00
27 Josh Heupel, Sage Rosenfels, Todd Heap 15.00
28 Travis Henry, Anthony Thomas, James Jackson 30.00
29 Deuce McAllister, Rudi Johnson, Chad Johnson 15.00
30 Quincy Morgan, Robert Ferguson, Marvin "Snoop" Minnis 15.00

2001 Fleer Legacy 1,000 Yard Club

NM/M
Common Player: 12.00
Inserted 1:69
1YC Stephen Davis 12.00
2YC Warrick Dunn 12.00
3YC Barry Sanders 50.00
4YC Randy Moss 40.00
5YC Marvin Harrison 15.00
6YC Duce Staley 12.00
7YC Jamal Lewis 15.00
8YC Isaac Bruce 15.00
9YC Wayne Chrebet 15.00
10YC Terrell Owens 20.00
11YC Rod Smith 15.00
12YC Ed McCaffrey 12.00
13YC Jerome Bettis 15.00
14YC Fred Taylor 15.00
15YC Edgerrin James 25.00
16YC Curtis Martin 20.00
17YC Eric Moulds 15.00
18YC Corey Dillon 15.00
19YC Marcus Robinson 15.00
20YC Tiki Barber 15.00
21YC Jamal Anderson 15.00
22YC Torry Holt 20.00
23YC Frank Sanders 12.00

2001 Fleer Legacy 1,000 Yard Club Dual Swatch

NM/M
Common Player: 15.00
Production 400 Sets
1IB Stephen Davis, Warrick Dunn 15.00
2IB Stephen Davis, Duce Staley 15.00
3IB Stephen Davis, Terrell Davis 25.00
4IB Jamal Anderson, Barry Sanders 40.00
5IB Barry Sanders, Randy Moss 60.00
6IB Marvin Harrison, Isaac Bruce 25.00
7IB Marvin Harrison, Rod Smith 20.00
8IB Isaac Bruce, Terrell Owens 25.00
9IB Isaac Bruce, Marcus Robinson 20.00
10IB Wayne Chrebet, Curtis Martin 25.00
11IB Wayne Chrebet, Jimmy Smith 20.00
12IB Rod Smith, Ed McCaffrey 15.00
13IB Ed McCaffrey, Jimmy Smith 15.00
14IB Jerome Bettis, Fred Taylor 20.00
15IB Jerome Bettis, Edgerrin James 30.00
16IB Corey Dillon, Terrell Davis 25.00
17IB Marcus Robinson, Marvin Harrison 20.00
18IB Tiki Barber, Warrick Dunn 15.00
19IB Tiki Barber, Eddie George 20.00
20IB Eddie George, Warrick Dunn 20.00

2001 Fleer Legacy Ultimate Legacy

Veterans: 3X-6X
Rookies:
Production 250 Sets

2001 Fleer Premium

NM/M
Complete Set (250): 175.00
Common Player: .15
Minor Stars: .30
Common Rookies: 1.50
Production 2,001 Sets
Pack (8): 3.25
Wax Box (24): 55.00
1 Ricky Williams .75
2 Dez White .15
3 Jay Riemersma .15
4 Derrick Mason .30
5 Chad Lewis .15
6 Shaun King .50
7 Jevon Kearse .50
8 Bobby Engram .15
9 Warrick Dunn .50
10 Randall Cunningham .30
11 Stephen Alexander .15
12 Jimmy Smith .50
13 Az-Zahir Hakim .30
14 Antonio Freeman .50
15 Curtis Conway .30
16 Tim Biakabutuka .30
17 Peter Warrick 1.00
18 Kurt Warner 1.50
19 Brian Urlacher 1.00
20 Rod Smith .30
21 Frank Sanders .30
22 Trevor Pryce .15
23 Sammy Morris .15
24 Cade McNown .50
25 Keyshawn Johnson .50
26 Tim Couch .75
27 Dedric Ward .15
28 Bill Schroeder .15
29 John Randle .30
30 Donovan McNabb .75
31 Marvin Harrison .50
32 Trent Dilfer .30
33 David Boston .50
34 Donnell Bennett .15
35 Trace Armstrong .15
36 Sam Adams .15
37 Jeremiah Trotter .15
38 Zach Thomas .15
39 Shaun Jefferson .15
40 J.J. Stokes .30
41 Akili Smith .50
42 Tony Siragusa .15
43 William Roaf .15
44 Muhsin Muhammad .30
45 Terance Mathis .15
46 Tee Martin .30
47 Ray Lewis .50
48 Matt Hasselbeck .50
49 Todd Pinkston .50
50 Rob Johnson .30
51 Edgerrin James 1.25
52 Raghib Ismail .15
53 Trent Green .30
54 Tim Dwight .50
55 Anthony Becht .15
56 Jessie Armstead .15
57 Mike Anderson 1.25
58 Jamal Anderson .50
59 Anthony Wright .15
60 Regan Upshaw .15
61 John Holecek .15
62 Shaun Alexander .50
63 Troy Aikman 1.00
64 Peter Boulware .15
65 Hines Ward .15
66 Michael Strahan .15
67 Herman Moore .30
68 Rich Gannon .30
69 Ken Dilger .15
70 Terrell Davis 1.25
71 Terrence Wilkins .30
72 Fred Taylor .75
73 Napoleon Kaufman .15
74 Tony Horne .15
75 Ahman Green .30
76 Jay Fiedler .50
77 Albert Connell .15
78 Charlie Batch .50
79 James Allen .30
80 Sylvester Morris .30
81 Isaac Bruce .50
82 Charles Woodson .30
83 Lamar Smith .30
84 Peyton Manning 1.50
85 Sam Madison .15
86 Olandis Gary .50
87 Kevin Faulk .30
88 Jeff Garcia .50
89 JaJuan Dawson .15
90 Sam Cowart .15
91 David Sloan .15
92 Bobby Shaw .15
93 Travis Prentice .30
94 Terrell Owens .50
95 John Lynch .15
96 Jim Harbaugh .15
97 Brian Griese .60
98 Jeff Graham .15
99 La'Roi Glover .15
100 Joey Galloway .50
101 Wesley Walls .15
102 Vinny Testaverde .30
103 Jason Taylor .15
104 Darnay Scott .15
105 Samari Rolle .15
106 Adrian Murrell .15
107 Eric Moulds .30
108 Keenan McCardell .30
109 Donald Hayes .15
110 Brett Favre 2.00
111 Troy Edwards .30
112 Ron Dayne 1.00
113 Daunte Culpepper 1.00
114 Chris Chandler .30
115 Mark Brunell .60
116 Courtney Brown .30
117 Aaron Brooks .60
118 Fred Beasley .15
119 Mike Alstott .50
120 Tyrone Wheatley .30
121 R. Jay Soward .30
122 Deion Sanders .50
123 Jake Reed .15
124 Jamal Lewis 1.50
125 Tony Gonzalez .30
126 Terrell Fletcher .15
127 Wayne Chrebet .30
128 Cris Carter .50
129 Drew Bledsoe .60
130 Tiki Barber .30
131 Derrick Alexander .15
132 Frank Wycheck .15
133 Jerome Pathon .15
134 Warren Sapp .30
135 Joe Horn .30
136 Ricky Watters .30
137 Amani Toomer .30
138 Bruce Smith .30
139 Andre Rison .15
140 J.R. Redmond .15
141 Steve McNair .50
142 Michael McCrary .15
143 Ike Hillard .30
144 Charlie Garner .30
145 Mark Bruener .15
146 Emmitt Smith 1.25
147 Darren Sharper .15
148 Peerless Price .30
149 Johnnie Morton .30
150 Curtis Martin .50
151 Joe Johnson .15
152 MarTay Jenkins .15
153 Priest Holmes .50
154 Terry Glenn .30
155 Oronde Gadsden .30
156 Germane Crowell .50
157 Steve Beuerlein .15
158 Champ Bailey .50
159 Troy Vincent .15
160 James Stewart .30
161 Jerry Rice 1.25
162 Randy Moss 1.75
163 Dave Moore .15
164 Ed McCaffrey .30
165 Thomas Jones .30
166 Rickey Dudley .15
167 Hugh Douglas .15
168 Stephen Davis .50
169 Kerry Collins .30
170 Cam Cleeland .15
171 Stephen Boyd .15
172 Jerome Bettis .50
173 Aeneas Williams .15
174 Chad Pennington .75
175 Dorsey Levens .30
176 Desmond Howard .15
177 Torry Holt .50
178 Plaxico Burress .50
179 Kevin Johnson .30
180 Kyle Brady .15
181 Jake Plummer .50
182 Brad Johnson .50
183 Eddie George .60
184 Corey Dillon .50
185 Curtis Enis .15
186 Tim Brown .30
187 Tony Boselli .15
188 Duce Staley .50
189 Junior Seau .30
190 Marshall Faulk .60
191 Kordell Stewart .50
192 Corey Simon .30
193 Shannon Sharpe .30
194 Marcus Robinson .50
195 Carl Pickens .15
196 Doug Flutie .60
197 Freddie Jones .15
198 Patrick Jeffers .30
199 Shawn Bryson .15
200 Kevin Dyson .30
201 *David Terrell* 8.00
202 *Dan Morgan* 3.00
203 *Chris Weinke* 8.00
204 *Correll Buckhalter* 4.00
205 *Chad Johnson* 10.00
206 *LaDainian Tomlinson* 25.00
207 *Reggie Wayne* 10.00
208 *Tim Hasselbeck* 4.00
209 *Michael Vick* 35.00
210 *Heath Evans* 1.50
211 *Damione Lewis* 3.00
212 *Richard Seymour* 1.50
213 *Quincy Morgan* 6.00
214 *Drew Brees* 12.00
215 *Freddie Mitchell* 6.00
216 *Moran Norris* 3.00
217 *Mike McMahon* 4.00
218 *Derrick Gibson* 1.50
219 *Rudi Johnson* 8.00
220 *Todd Heap* 5.00
221 *Josh Booty* 3.00
222 *Justin Smith* 4.00
223 *Marcus Stroud* 3.00
224 *Rod Gardner* 10.00
225 *Vinny Sutherland* 3.00
226 *Marques Tuiasosopo* 8.00
227 *Anthony Thomas* 10.00
228 *Bobby Newcombe* 3.00
229 *Michael Bennett* 12.00
230 *Marvin "Snoop" Minnis* 3.00
231 *Travis Minor* 5.00
232 *Travis Henry* 10.00
233 *Kevan Barlow* 8.00
234 *Gerard Warren* 4.00
235 *Sage Rosenfels* 4.00
236 *Chris Chambers* 8.00
237 *James Jackson* 4.00
238 *Deuce McAllister* 15.00
239 *Koren Robinson* 10.00
240 *Andre Carter* 4.00
241 *Santana Moss* 10.00
242 *LaMont Jordan* 2.00
243 *Ken-Yon Rambo* 3.00
244 *Jamal Reynolds* 1.50
245 *Fred Smoot* 3.00
246 *Robert Ferguson* 4.00
247 *Ken Lucas* 3.00
248 *Dan Alexander* 3.00
249 *Nate Clements* 3.00
250 *Quincy Carter* 8.00

2001 Fleer Premium Star Ruby

Star Ruby Cards: 8X-16X
Star Ruby Rookies: 3X
Production 125 Sets

2001 Fleer Premium Clothes to the Game

NM/M
Common Player: 8.00
Inserted 1:59
1CG Jessie Armstead 8.00
2CG Todd Pinkston 8.00
3CG R. Jay Soward 8.00
4CG Travis Prentice 8.00
5CG Courtney Brown 8.00
6CG Ken Dilger 8.00
7CG Curtis Enis 8.00
8CG E.G. Green 8.00
9CG Torry Holt 12.00
10CG David Boston 12.00
11CG Michael Pittman 8.00
12CG Edgerrin James 25.00
13CG Marvin Harrison 12.00
14CG Johnnie Morton 8.00
15CG Cade McNown 12.00
16CG Isaac Bruce 12.00
17CG Jake Plummer 12.00
18CG Jerry Rice 25.00
19CG Champ Bailey 8.00
20CG Kordell Stewart 8.00
21CG Kurt Warner 20.00

2001 Fleer Premium Commanding Respect

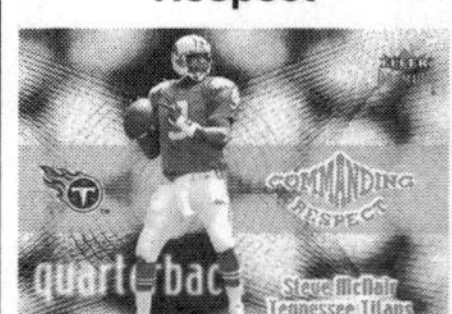

NM/M
Complete Set (15): 18.00
Common Player: 1.50
Inserted 1:20
Patch Cards: 8X-16X
Production 80 Sets
1CR Brian Griese 2.00
2CR Jamal Lewis 4.00
3CR Fred Taylor 2.00
4CR Stephen Davis 1.50
5CR Marcus Robinson 1.50
6CR Marvin Harrison 1.50
7CR Marshall Faulk 2.00
8CR Doug Flutie 2.00
9CR Jamal Anderson 1.50
10CR Donovan McNabb 3.00
11CR Steve McNair 1.50
12CR Jeff Garcia 1.50
13CR Daunte Culpepper 3.50
14CR Isaac Bruce 1.50
15CR Jimmy Smith 1.50

2001 Fleer Premium Greatest Plays

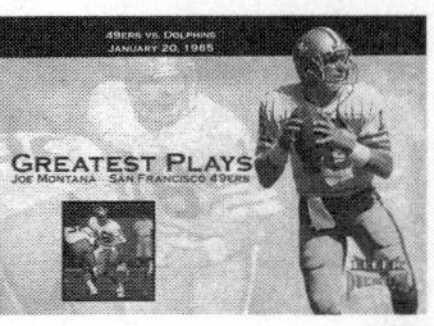

NM/M
Complete Set (21): 20.00
Common Player: .75
Inserted 1:10
#1 & #7 never released
2GP Emmitt Smith 3.00
3GP Roger Staubach 3.00
4GP Jerry Rice 3.00
5GP Doug Flutie 1.25
6GP Earl Campbell 1.50
8GP John Elway 5.00
9GP Joe Montana 5.00
10GP Dan Marino 5.00
11GP Dwight Clark .75
12GP Franco Harris 1.50
13GP Gale Sayers 1.50
14GP Ken Stabler 2.00
15GP Steve Young 2.00
16GP William Perry .75
17GP Michael Westbrook .75
18GP Kordell Stewart 1.50
19GP Terry Bradshaw 4.00
20GP Tony Dorsett 2.00
21GP Eric Dickerson 1.50

2001 Fleer Premium Home Field Advantage

NM/M
Complete Set (12): 50.00
Common Player: 3.00
Inserted 1:72
Turf Cards: 2X-4X
Production 314 Sets
1HA Eddie George 6.00
2HA Edgerrin James 8.00
3HA Ricky Williams 8.00
4HA Jeff Garcia 4.00
5HA Brett Favre 12.00
6HA Warrick Dunn 3.00
7HA Donovan McNabb 7.00
8HA Brian Urlacher 7.00
9HA Kurt Warner 8.00
10HA Emmitt Smith 10.00
11HA Rich Gannon 3.00
12HA Cris Carter 4.00

2001 Fleer Premium Premium Advantage

NM/M
Common Player: 8.00
Inserted 1:109
1SU Jessie Armstead 8.00
2SU Todd Pinkston 8.00
3SU R. Jay Soward 8.00
4SU Travis Prentice 12.00
5SU Courtney Brown 8.00
6SU Ken Dilger 8.00
7SU Curtis Enis 8.00
8SU E.G. Green 8.00
9SU Torry Holt 8.00
10SU David Boston 12.00
11SU Michael Pittman 8.00
12SU Edgerrin James 20.00
13SU Marvin Harrison 12.00
14SU Johnnie Morton 8.00
15SU Cade McNown 12.00
16SU Isaac Bruce 12.00
17SU Jake Plummer 12.00
18SU Jerry Rice 20.00
19SU Champ Bailey 8.00

2001 Fleer Premium Rookie Revolution

NM/M
Complete Set (10): 25.00
Common Player: 1.00

Inserted 1:10
Autographs: 20X
Production 50 Sets
1RR Deuce McAllister 3.00
2RR David Terrell 3.00
3RR Drew Brees 6.00
4RR Chad Johnson 1.00
5RR LaDainian Tomlinson 5.00
6RR Marques Tuiasosopo 2.00
7RR Michael Vick 10.00
8RR Michael Bennett 5.00
9RR Anthony Thomas 2.50
10RR Santana Moss 2.50

2001 Fleer Premium Solid Performers

NM/M
Complete Set (20): 30.00
Common Player: 1.00
Minor Stars: 2.00
Inserted 1:20
Jersey Cards: 5X
Production 900 Sets
1SP Jerome Bettis 2.00
2SP David Boston 2.00
3SP Cade McNown 2.00
4SP Keenan McCardell 1.00
5SP Thomas Jones 1.00
6SP Edgerrin James 4.00
7SP Torry Holt 2.00
8SP Az-Zahir Hakim 1.00
9SP Jake Plummer 2.00
10SP Travis Prentice 1.00
11SP Marcus Robinson 2.00
12SP Duce Staley 2.00
13SP Kurt Warner 4.00
14SP Kordell Stewart 2.00
15SP Rob Johnson 1.00
16SP Jamal Lewis 3.00
17SP Donovan McNabb 3.00
18SP Kevin Johnson 2.00
19SP Jim Kelly 2.00
20SP Jerry Rice 4.00

2001 Fleer Showcase

NM/M
Common Player: .20
Minor Stars: .40
Common Rookie: 5.00
Pack (5): 3.75
Wax Box (24): 65.00
1 Cris Carter .75
2 Sylvester Morris .75
3 Vinny Testaverde .50
4 Jevon Kearse .75
5 Terance Mathis .20
6 Mike Anderson 2.00
7 Aaron Brooks .75
8 Jerry Rice 2.00
9 Mike Alstott .75
10 Jon Kitna .40
11 Derrick Alexander .40
12 Shaun Alexander .75
13 Thomas Jones .75
14 James Stewart .50
15 Ron Dayne 1.25
16 Az-Zahir Hakim .40
17 Terrell Owens .75
18 Travis Prentice .50
19 Lamar Smith .75
20 James Thrash .40
21 Doug Flutie 1.00
22 Derrick Mason .75
23 Ray Lewis .75
24 Ed McCaffrey .75
25 Ricky Williams 1.00
26 Tyrone Wheatley .50
27 Chris Chandler .50
28 Rod Smith .75
29 Joe Horn .50
30 Jerome Bettis .75
31 Brian Urlacher 1.50
32 Dorsey Levens .50
33 Kordell Stewart .75
34 Michael Westbrook .50
35 Jamal Anderson .75
36 Charlie Batch .75
37 Kerry Collins .50
38 Jake Plummer .75
39 Robert Porcher .20
40 Jason Sehorn .40
41 Junior Seau .50
42 Warren Sapp .50
43 Champ Bailey .50
44 Jamal Lewis 2.00
45 Tony Banks .40
46 Doug Chapman .40
47 Stephen Davis .75
48 Elvis Grbac .50
49 Joey Galloway .75
50 Terry Glenn .50
51 Todd Pinkston .50
52 JaJuan Dawson .40
53 Zach Thomas .50
54 Tim Couch 1.00
55 Cade McNown .75
56 Charlie Garner .50
57 Jeff George .40
58 Peerless Price .50
59 Tony Gonzalez .50
60 Rob Johnson .50
61 Keenan McCardell .40
62 Eric Moulds .75
63 Jimmy Smith .75
64 Jeff Garcia .75
65 Rod Woodson .20
66 Brian Griese 1.00
67 Kevin Faulk .40
68 Plaxico Burress .75
69 Isaac Bruce .75
70 Keyshawn Johnson .75
71 Tim Biakabutuka .40
72 Mark Brunell 1.00
73 Wesley Walls .40
74 Jerome Pathon .20
75 Wayne Chrebet .75
76 Muhsin Muhammad .50
77 Marvin Harrison .75
78 David Boston .75
79 Germane Crowell .75
80 Tiki Barber .50
81 Laveranues Coles .50
82 Tim Brown .50
83 Matt Hasselbeck .75
84 Brad Johnson .50
85 Marcus Robinson .75
86 Ahman Green .75
87 Curtis Martin .75
88 Peter Warrick 1.00
89 Ray Lucas .40
90 Duce Staley .75
91 Darrell Jackson .50
92 Steve McNair .75
93 Rickey Dudley .40
94 Jason Taylor .40
95 Rich Gannon .50
96 Torry Holt .75
97 James Allen .75
98 Antonio Freeman .75
99 Trent Green .75
100 Ricky Watters .50
101 Corey Dillon 3.00
102 Emmitt Smith 8.00
103 Terrell Davis 7.00
104 Brett Favre 12.00
105 Peyton Manning 10.00
106 Edgerrin James 8.00
107 Fred Taylor 4.00
108 Daunte Culpepper 6.00
109 Randy Moss 10.00
110 Drew Bledsoe 4.00
111 Donovan McNabb 5.00
112 Kurt Warner 10.00
113 Marshall Faulk 4.00
114 Warrick Dunn 3.00
115 Eddie George 4.00
116 *Michael Vick* 100.00
117 *David Terrell* 15.00
118 *Deuce McAllister* 50.00
119 *Koren Robinson* 12.00
120 *Rod Gardner* 20.00
121 *Santana Moss* 25.00
122 *Drew Brees* 25.00
123 *Chris Weinke* 15.00
124 *LaDainian Tomlinson* 60.00
125 *Freddie Mitchell* 15.00
126 *Chris Chambers* 15.00
127 *Reggie Wayne* 15.00
128 *Quincy Morgan* 8.00
129 *Rudi Johnson* 15.00
130 *Robert Ferguson* 6.00
131 *Todd Heap* 6.00
132 *Michael Bennett* 20.00
133 *Jesse Palmer* 6.00
134 *James Jackson* 6.00
135 *Chad Johnson* 15.00
136 *LaMont Jordan* 3.00
137 *Anthony Thomas* 10.00
138 *Travis Henry* 15.00
139 *Marvin "Snoop" Minnis* 6.00
140 *Marques Tuiasosopo* 10.00
141 *Travis Minor* 3.00
142 *Mike McMahon* 6.00
143 *Josh Heupel* 6.00
144 *Sage Rosenfels* 3.00
145 *Quincy Carter* 6.00
146 *Alge Crumpler* 3.00
147 *Kevan Barlow* 10.00
148 *Heath Evans* 3.00
149 *Correll Buckhalter* 8.00
150 *Justin McCareins* 8.00
151 *Reggie Germany* 4.00
152 *Vinny Sutherland* 4.00
153 *Scotty Anderson* 3.00
154 *Tim Hasselbeck* 5.00
155 *Alex Bannister* 5.00
156 *Andre Carter* 5.00
157 *Adam Archuleta* 3.00
158 *Ken-Yon Rambo* 5.00
159 *Gerard Warren* 5.00
160 *Justin Smith* 5.00
NNO Donovan McNabb AU/300 75.00

2001 Fleer Showcase Awards Showcase

NM/M
Common Player: 35.00
1ASB Randy Moss 85.00
2ASB Marvin Harrison 35.00
3ASB Tony Gonzalez 35.00
4ASB Rich Gannon 35.00
5ASB Marshall Faulk 45.00
6ASB Edgerrin James 65.00
7ASB Warren Sapp 35.00
8ASB Ray Lewis 35.00
9ASB Brian Urlacher 60.00
10ASB Chris Weinke 65.00
11ASB Eric Moulds 35.00
12ASB Isaac Bruce 35.00
13ASB Daunte Culpepper 35.00
14ASB Curtis Martin 35.00
15ASB Kurt Warner 35.00
16ASB Mike Anderson 35.00
17ASB Robert Smith 35.00
18ASB Jamal Lewis 35.00
19ASB Rod Smith 35.00
20ASB Junior Seau 35.00

A card number in parenthese ( ) indicates the set is unnumbered.

2001 Fleer Showcase Awards Showcase Memorabilia

NM/M
Common Player: 45.00
Production 100 Sets
1AS Marcus Allen 45.00
2AS Terry Bradshaw 60.00
3AS Terrell Davis 60.00
4AS Eric Dickerson 45.00
5AS Tony Dorsett 65.00
6AS Marshall Faulk 50.00
7AS Brett Favre 85.00
8AS Eddie George 50.00
9AS Edgerrin James 70.00
10AS Joe Montana 125.00
11AS Randy Moss 85.00
12AS Walter Payton 125.00
13AS Jerry Rice 60.00
14AS Emmitt Smith 60.00
15AS Fran Tarkenton 60.00
16AS Lawrence Taylor 45.00
17AS Johnny Unitas 80.00
18AS Steve Young 45.00

2001 Fleer Showcase Patchwork

NM/M
Common Player: 10.00
Inserted 1:20:
1PW Bruce Smith 10.00
2PW Lawrence Taylor 20.00
3PW Brian Urlacher 25.00
4PW Warren Sapp 10.00
5PW Deion Sanders 20.00
6PW Dan Marino 60.00
7PW Junior Seau 10.00
8PW Jerry Rice 30.00
9PW Brian Griese 20.00
10PW Mark Brunell 15.00
11PW Ronnie Lott 15.00
12PW Marvin Harrison 15.00
13PW Edgerrin James 30.00
14PW Marshall Faulk 20.00
15PW Todd Pinkston 15.00
16PW Troy Aikman 25.00
17PW Charlie Batch 10.00
18PW Johnnie Morton 10.00
19PW Steve Young 20.00
20PW Terrell Davis 25.00
21PW Torry Holt 15.00
22PW Charles Woodson 15.00
23PW Steve McNair 15.00
24PW Rod Smith 15.00
25PW Jamal Anderson 15.00
26PW Drew Bledsoe 20.00
27PW Dorsey Levens 15.00
28PW Chris Chandler 10.00
29PW Kurt Warner 30.00
30PW Fred Taylor 15.00
31PW Chris Redman 15.00
32PW Travis Prentice 15.00
33PW Peerless Price 15.00

2001 Fleer Showcase Stitches

NM/M
Common Player: 15.00
Inserted 1:20
1SS Cris Carter 20.00
2SS Daunte Culpepper 25.00
3SS Corey Dillon 15.00
4SS John Elway 50.00
5SS Steve McNair 15.00
6SS Todd Pinkston 15.00
7SS Steve Young 20.00
8SS Marvin Harrison 15.00
9SS Fred Taylor 15.00
10SS Peter Warrick 15.00
11SS Ricky Williams 20.00
12SS Brett Favre 45.00
13SS Kurt Warner 30.00
14SS Marshall Faulk 20.00
15SS Robert Smith 15.00
16SS Dan Marino 50.00
17SS Joe Montana 75.00

2001 Fleer Showcase Signed Avant Card

1SAC Donovan McNabb

2001 Fleer Showcase Legacy

Legacy Cards (#1-100): 8X-16X
Legacy Cards (#101-115): 2X-4X
Legacy Rookies (#116-125): 2X
Legacy Rookies (#126-145): 4X
Legacy Rookies (#146-160): 6X

2001 Fleer Tradition

NM/M
Complete Set (450): 30.00
Common Player: .15
Minor Stars: .30
Common Rookie (401-450): .50
1 Thomas Jones .30
2 Bruce Smith .30
3 Marvin Harrison .50
4 Darrell Jackson .30
5 Trent Green .30
6 Wesley Walls .30
7 Jimmy Smith 1.50
8 Isaac Bruce .50
9 Jamal Anderson .40
10 Marty Booker .15
11 Elvis Grbac .50
12 Joe Jurevicius .15
13 Reidel Anthony .15
14 Darnay Scott .30
15 Oronde Gadsden .30
16 Shawn Bryson .15
17 Jonathan Ogden .15
18 Aaron Shea .15
19 Randy Moss 1.50
20 Eddie George .60
21 Stephen Davis .30
22 Emmitt Smith 1.25
23 Willie McGinest .15
24 Trent Dilfer .30
25 Peter Boulware .15
26 Rod Smith .40
27 Ricky Williams .75
28 Albert Connell .15
29 Robert Porcher .15
30 Jessie Armstead .15
31 Shane Matthews .15
32 Eric Moulds .40
33 Kurt Schulz .15
34 Richie Anderson .15
35 Ron Dugans .30
36 Steve Beuerlein .30
37 Darren Sharper .30
38 Andre Rison .30
39 Courtney Brown .30
40 Eddie Kennison .30
41 Ken Dilger .15
42 Charles Johnson .15
43 Dexter Coakley .15
44 Akili Smith .30
45 R. Jay Soward .15
46 Danny Farmer .30
47 Dez White .30
48 Olandis Gary .50
49 Wali Rainer .15
50 Derrick Alexander .30
51 Donnie Abraham .15
52 David Sloan .15
53 Larry Allen .15
54 Sam Madison .30
55 Troy Edwards .40
56 Ryan Longwell .15
57 Brian Griese .60
58 John Randle .15
59 Reggie Jones .15
60 Mike Peterson .15
61 Bill Romanowski .15
62 Kevin Faulk .30
63 Tai Streets .30
64 Tony Brackens .15
65 James Stewart .15
66 Joe Horn .15
67 Kurt Warner .15
68 Eric Hicks .15
69 Bryant Westbrook .15
70 Tiki Barber .40
71 Frank Sanders .30
72 Olindo Mare .15
73 Bill Schroeder .30
74 Anthony Becht .30
75 Rob Johnson .40
76 Troy Brown .30
77 Chad Bratzke .15
78 Rickey Dudley .15
79 Doug Johnson .15
80 Joe Johnson .15
81 Keenan McCardell .30
82 Tim Brown .50
83 Blaine Bishop .15
84 Ron Dixon .30
85 Mike Cloud .15
86 Todd Pinkston .40
87 Shannon Sharpe .40
88 Marvin Jones .15
89 Zach Thomas .40
90 Kordell Stewart .60
91 Champ Bailey .30
92 Jacquez Green .30
93 Daunte Culpepper 1.00
94 Freddie Jones .15
95 Donald Hayes .30
96 Rich Gannon .50
97 Ty Law .40
98 Grant Wilstrom .15
99 James Allen .15
100 Corey Simon .15
101 Jeff Blake .30
102 Bryant Young .30
103 Craig Yeast .15
104 Bobby Shaw .15
105 Kerry Collins .40
106 Brock Huard .40
107 JaJuan Dawson .30
108 Jeff Graham .15
109 Chad Pennington 1.00
110 Jake Plummer .40
111 James McKnight .15
112 Terrell Owens .50
113 Mo Lewis .15
114 Jeremy McDaniel .15
115 Ed McCaffrey .40
116 Ricky Watters .40
117 Jerry Porter .50
118 Shawn Jefferson .15
119 Charlie Batch .30
120 Justin Watson .15
121 Donovan McNabb 1.00
122 Shaun King .30
123 Brett Favre 2.00
124 Ronald McKinnon .15
125 Richard Huntley .15
126 Ray Lewis .50
127 Jerome Pathon .15
128 Sam Cowart .15
129 Ryan Leaf .30
130 Greg Clark .15
131 Tony Boselli .15
132 Frank Wycheck .15
133 Charlie Garner .30
134 Tony Siragusa .15
135 Sylvester Morris .40
136 Qadry Ismail .30
137 Jon Kitna .30
138 James Thrash .30
139 Lamar Smith .30
140 Brad Johnson .50
141 London Fletcher .15
142 Tim Biakabutuka .30
143 Ed McDaniel .15
144 Tony Parrish .15
145 David Boston .50
146 Brian Urlacher 1.00
147 Drew Bledsoe .60
148 David Patten .15
149 Marcellus Wiley .15
150 Peter Warrick .50
151 La'Roi Glover .15
152 Troy Aikman 1.00
153 Chris Chandler .15
154 Travis Prentice .30
155 Ike Hilliard .30
156 John Mobley .15
157 Warren Sapp .30
158 Joey Galloway .40
159 Laveranues Coles .40
160 Germane Crowell .30
161 Jamal Lewis 1.00
162 Mike Anderson .75
163 Charles Woodson .30
164 Antonio Freeman .40
165 Derrick Mason .40
166 Chris Claiborne .15
167 Brian Mitchell .15
168 Mike Vanderjagt .15
169 Rod Woodson .30
170 Doug Chapman .30
171 John Lynch .15
172 Kevin Hardy .15
173 Sam Shade .15
174 Edgerrin James 1.25
175 Brian Dawkins .15
176 Donnie Edwards .15
177 Patrick Jeffers .15
178 Mark Brunell .40
179 Junior Seau .30
180 Trace Armstrong .15
181 Marcus Robinson .40
182 Tony Gonzalez .50
183 J.J. Stokes .40
184 Jake Reed .15
185 Corey Dillon .30
186 Jay Fiedler .50
187 Christian Fauria .15
188 Sammy Knight .15
189 Kevin Johnson .40
190 Matthew Hatchette .15
191 Az-Zahir Hakim .30
192 Keith Hamilton .15
193 Darren Woodson .15
194 Terry Glenn .30
195 Simeon Rice .15
196 Keyshawn Johnson .50
197 Terrell Davis 1.00
198 Willie Roaf .15
199 Doug Flutie .60
200 Kevin Carter .15
201 Stephen Boyd .15
202 Michael Strahan .30
203 Ray Buchanan .15
204 Tyrone Wheatley .30
205 Jason Hanson .15
206 Wayne Chrebet .40
207 Samari Rolle .15
208 Duce Staley .40
209 Dorsey Levens .30
210 Sebastian Janikowski .30
211 Duane Starks .15
212 Jason Gildon .15
213 Terrence Wilkins .15
214 Eric Allen .15
215 Deion Sanders .40
216 Curtis Conway .15
217 Fred Taylor .60
218 Troy Vincent .15
219 Mike Minter .15
220 Jeff Garcia .60
221 Tony Richardson .15
222 Jerome Bettis .40
223 Chad Morton .15
224 Tony Horne .15
225 Dave Moore .15
226 Victor Green .15
227 Chris Sanders .15
228 Marshall Faulk .60
229 Cris Carter .50
230 Rodney Harrison .15
231 Tim Couch .60
232 Antowain Smith .50
233 Lawyer Milloy .15
234 Lance Schulters .15
235 Michael Wiley .15
236 Steve McNair .40
237 Aaron Brooks .60
238 Anthony Simmons .15
239 Dwayne Carswell .15
240 Priest Holmes .40
241 Amani Toomer .40
242 Aeneas Williams .30
243 MarTay Jenkins .15
244 Jeff George .30
245 Vinny Testaverde .40
246 Peerless Price .30
247 Bubba Franks .30
248 Randall Cunningham .30
249 Aaron Glenn .15
250 Terance Mathis .30
251 Peyton Manning 1.50
252 Terrell Buckley .15
253 Greg Biekert .15
254 Martin Gramatica .30
255 Kyle Brady .30
256 Johnnie Morton .30
257 Jeremiah Trotter .30
258 Travis Taylor .40
259 Frank Moreau .15
260 LeRoy Butler .30
261 Plaxico Burress .50
262 Randall Godfrey .15
263 Jason Taylor .15
264 Jeff Burris .15
265 Jim Harbaugh .30
266 Marco Coleman .15
267 Robert Smith .30
268 Mike Hollis .15
269 Jerry Rice 1.25
270 Muhsin Muhammad .30
271 J.R. Redmond .30
272 Brian Walker .15
273 Orlando Pace .15
274 Cade McNown .30
275 Darren Howard .15
276 Ron Dayne .40
277 Shaun Alexander .75
278 Brandon Bennett .15
279 Jason Sehorn .15
280 Matt Hasselbeck .30
281 Michael Pittman .15
282 Dennis Northcutt .15
283 Dedric Ward .30
284 Curtis Martin .40
285 Sammy Morris .15
286 Raghib Ismail .15
287 Jon Ritchie .15
288 Shaun Ellis .15
289 Tim Dwight .30
290 Trevor Pryce .15
291 Warrick Dunn .50
292 Napoleon Kaufman .15
293 Mike Alstott .40
294 Herman Moore .30
295 Chad Lewis .15
296 Hugh Douglas .15
297 Chris Redman .30
298 Ahman Green .40
299 Hines Ward .40
300 Mark Bruener .15
301 Jevon Kearse .15
302 Jermaine Fazande .15
303 Terrell Fletcher .15
304 Torry Holt .50
305 Chris McAlister .15
306 Jason Elam .15
307 Fred Beasley .15
308 Frank Wycheck .15
309 Michael McCrary .15
310 Mark Brunell .15
311 Tim Couch .30
312 Takeo Spikes .15
313 Jerome Bettis .15
314 Zach Thomas .15
315 Drew Bledsoe .30
316 Wayne Chrebet .15
317 Jay Riemersma .15
318 Marvin Harrison .15
319 Ed McCaffrey .15
320 Tony Gonzalez .15
321 Tim Brown .15
322 Junior Seau .15
323 Shawn Springs .15
324 Troy Aikman .50
325 Pat Tilman .15
326 David Akers .15
327 Michael Strahan .15
328 Darrell Green .15
329 Kurt Warner .75
330 Jeff Garcia .30
331 Aaron Brooks .30
332 Jamal Anderson .15
333 Brad Hoover .15
334 Cris Carter .15
335 Derrick Brooks .15
336 Antonio Freeman .15
337 Luther Elliss .15
338 James Allen .15
339 Cardinals .15
340 Falcons .15
341 Ravens .15
342 Bills .15
343 Panthers .15
344 Bears .15
345 Bengals .15
346 Browns .15
347 Cowboys .50
348 Broncos .15
349 Lions .15
350 Packers 1.00
351 Colts .50
352 Jaguars .15
353 Chiefs .15
354 Dolphins .15
355 Vikings .30
356 Patriots .15
357 Saints .15
358 Giants .15
359 Jets .15
360 Raiders .15
361 Eagles .30
362 Steelers .30
363 Chargers .15
364 49ers .30
365 Seahawks .15
366 Rams .75
367 Buccaneers .15
368 Titans .15
369 Redskins .15
370 Bills .15
371 Colts .30
372 Dolphins .15
373 Patriots .15
374 Jets .15
375 Ravens .15
376 Bengals .15
377 Browns .15
378 Jaguars .15
379 Steelers .30
380 Titans .30
381 Broncos .30
382 Chiefs .15
383 Raiders .30
384 Chargers .15
385 Seahawks .15
386 Cardinals .15
387 Cowboys .50
388 Giants .15
389 Eagles .15
390 Redskins .15
391 Bears .15
392 Lions .15
393 Packers .50
394 Vikings .30
395 Buccaneers .15
396 Falcons .15
397 Panthers .15
398 Saints .15
399 49ers .30
400 Rams .50
401 *Michael Vick* 5.00
402 *Drew Brees* 3.00
403 *Michael Bennett* 2.50

404	*David Terrell*	1.25
405	*Deuce McAllister*	3.00
406	*Santana Moss*	2.00
407	*Koren Robinson*	2.00
408	*Chris Weinke*	1.25
409	*Reggie Wayne*	2.00
410	*Rod Gardner*	2.00
411	*James Jackson*	1.25
412	*Travis Henry*	1.50
413	*Josh Heupel*	1.25
414	*LaDainian Tomlinson*	3.00
415	*Chad Johnson*	2.00
416	*Sage Rosenfels*	1.25
417	*Quincy Morgan*	1.25
418	*Ken-Yon Rambo*	.75
419	*LaMont Jordan*	1.00
420	*Anthony Thomas*	1.25
421	*Dave Dickenson*	.75
422	*Travis Minor*	1.25
423	*Kevan Barlow*	1.50
424	*Chris Chambers*	2.50
425	*Richard Seymour*	.50
426	*Gerard Warren*	.50
427	*Jamar Fletcher*	.50
428	*Freddie Mitchell*	2.00
429	*Jamal Reynolds*	.50
430	*Marques Tuiasosopo*	1.25
431	*Marvin "Snoop" Minnis*	1.25
432	*Mike McMahon*	1.50
433	*Robert Ferguson*	.75
434	*Ronney Daniels*	.50
435	*Rudi Johnson*	2.00
436	*Vinny Sutherland*	.75
437	*Josh Booty*	1.00
438	*Reggie White*	.50
439	*Todd Heap*	.75
440	*Justin Smith*	.50
441	*Andre Carter*	.50
442	*Bobby Newcombe*	.50
443	*Alex Bannister*	.75
444	*Correll Buckhalter*	1.50
445	*Quincy Carter*	1.25
446	*Jesse Palmer*	1.25
447	*Heath Evans*	.50
448	*Dan Morgan*	.50
449	*Justin McCareins*	2.00
450	*Alge Crumpler*	.75

2001 Fleer Autographics

		NM/M
Common Player:		10.00
Inserted 1:96		
1	Shaun Alexander	20.00
2	Mike Anderson	30.00
3	Drew Brees	70.00
4	Isaac Bruce	25.00
6	Chris Chambers	20.00
7	Wayne Chrebet	15.00
8	Daunte Culpepper	50.00
9	Stephen Davis	10.00
10	Ron Dayne	25.00
11	Corey Dillon	20.00
12	Marshall Faulk	35.00
13	Eddie George	30.00
14	Brian Griese	25.00
15	Travis Henry	15.00
16	Josh Heupel	15.00
17	Torry Holt	15.00
18	Edgerrin James	50.00
19	LaMont Jordan	15.00
20	Deuce McAllister	25.00
21	Donovan McNabb	50.00
22	Travis Minor	10.00
23	Randy Moss	60.00
24	Santana Moss	25.00
25	Ken-Yon Rambo	15.00
26	Koren Robinson	25.00
27	Marcus Robinson	20.00
28	Sage Rosenfels	15.00
29	Jimmy Smith	15.00
30	Duce Staley	15.00
31	David Terrell	25.00
32	Anthony Thomas	50.00
33	LaDainian Tomlinson	50.00
34	Marques Tuiasosopo	20.00
35	Michael Vick	100.00
36	Kurt Warner	50.00
37	Reggie Wayne	20.00
38	Chris Weinke	45.00

2001 Fleer Tradition Throwbacks

		NM/M
Complete Set (20):		40.00
Common Player:		2.00
Inserted 1:12 Glossy		
Inserted 1:20 Tradition		
1TB	Jamal Lewis	3.00
2TB	Eddie George	3.00
3TB	Marvin Harrison	2.00
4TB	Brett Favre	8.00
5TB	Donovan McNabb	5.00
6TB	Troy Aikman	5.00
7TB	Edgerrin James	4.00
8TB	Brian Urlacher	5.00
9TB	Stephen Davis	2.00
10TB	Daunte Culpepper	5.00
11TB	Jerry Rice	6.00
12TB	Emmitt Smith	6.00
13TB	Kurt Warner	4.00
14TB	Ricky Williams	4.00
15TB	Cris Carter	2.00
16TB	Mark Brunell	3.00
17TB	Ron Dayne	2.00
18TB	Peyton Manning	5.00
19TB	Randy Moss	5.00
20TB	Brian Griese	3.00

2001 Fleer Tradition Keeping Pace

		NM/M
Complete Set (15):		30.00
Common Player:		1.00
Inserted 1:12 Glossy		
Inserted 1:20 Tradition		
1KP	Michael Vick	6.00
2KP	Drew Brees	3.00
3KP	Michael Bennett	2.50
4KP	David Terrell	3.00
5KP	Deuce McAllister	2.50
6KP	Santana Moss	2.50
7KP	Koren Robinson	2.50
8KP	Chris Weinke	2.50
9KP	Reggie Wayne	2.50
10KP	Rod Gardner	2.50
11KP	James Jackson	1.50
12KP	Travis Henry	2.00
13KP	Josh Heupel	1.50
14KP	LaDainian Tomlinson	3.00
15KP	Chad Johnson	1.00

2001 Fleer Tradition Grass Roots

		NM/M
Complete Set (10):		30.00
Common Player:		3.00
Inserted 1:24 Glossy		
Inserted 1:40 Tradition		
1GR	Donovan McNabb	5.00
2GR	Edgerrin James	5.00
3GR	Ricky Williams	4.00
4GR	Fred Taylor	3.00
5GR	Terrell Davis	3.00
6GR	Eddie George	3.00
7GR	Jamal Lewis	3.00
8GR	Marshall Faulk	3.00
9GR	Daunte Culpepper	5.00
10GR	Emmitt Smith	6.00

2001 Fleer Tradition Grass Roots Turf

		NM/M
Common Player:		20.00
1GR	Donovan McNabb	30.00
2GR	Edgerrin James	50.00
3GR	Ricky Williams	25.00
4GR	Fred Taylor	20.00
5GR	Terrell Davis	30.00
6GR	Eddie George	20.00
7GR	Jamal Lewis	30.00
8GR	Marshall Faulk	25.00
9GR	Daunte Culpepper	30.00
10GR	Emmitt Smith	50.00

2001 Fleer Tradition Art of a Champion

		NM/M
Common Player:		6.00
Inserted 1:120 Glossy		
Inserted 1:240 Tradition		
1AC	Drew Brees	20.00
2AC	Daunte Culpepper	15.00
3AC	Ron Dayne	6.00
4AC	Marshall Faulk	10.00
5AC	Eddie George	10.00
6AC	Edgerrin James	20.00

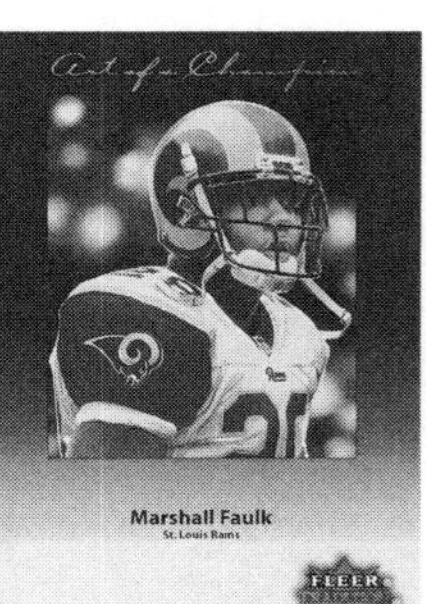

		NM/M
7AC	Jamal Lewis	15.00
8AC	Randy Moss	25.00
9AC	Fred Taylor	10.00
10AC	Michael Vick	30.00

2001 Fleer Tradition Art of a Champion Autographs

		NM/M
Common Player:		15.00
1AC	Drew Brees	75.00
2AC	Daunte Culpepper	50.00
3AC	Ron Dayne	25.00
4AC	Marshall Faulk	50.00
5AC	Eddie George	40.00
6AC	Edgerrin James	50.00
7AC	Jamal Lewis	40.00
8AC	Randy Moss	15.00
9AC	Fred Taylor	60.00
10AC	Michael Vick	150.00

2002 Fleer Authentix

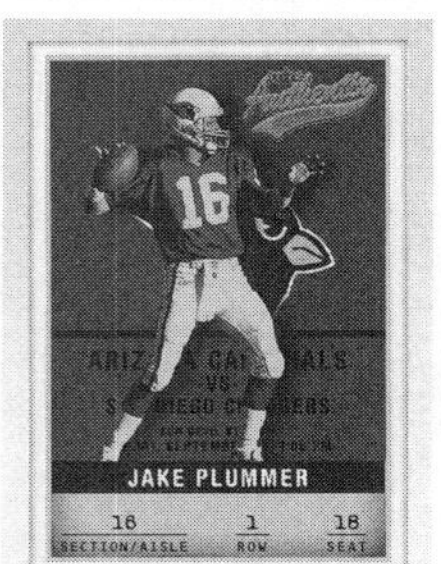

		NM/M
Common Player:		.20
Unlisted Stars:		.75
Minor Stars:		.50
Common Rookie (101-140):		
Minor Rookies:		
Production 1250 Sets		
Pack (5):		4.75
Wax Box (24):		80.00
1	Jake Plummer	.50
2	Chad Pennington	.50
3	Corey Bradford	.20
4	Mike Anderson	1.50
5	Donovan McNabb	2.00
6	Brian Griese	.75
7	Keyshawn Johnson	.50
8	Michael Strahan	.50
9	Rod Smith	.50
10	Warren Sapp	.50
11	Joe Horn	.20
12	Anthony Thomas	2.50
13	Jeff Garcia	.75
14	Michael Bennett	.75
15	Richard Huntley	.20
16	Doug Flutie	.75
17	Tony Gonzalez	.50
18	David Boston	.75
19	Freddie Mitchell	.50
20	Terrell Davis	1.50
21	Torry Holt	.59
22	Drew Bledsoe	2.00
23	Peter Warrick	.50
24	Darrell Jackson	.20
25	Chris Chambers	.75
26	Marvin Harrison	.50
27	Warrick Dunn	.50
28	Tim Brown	.75
29	Terry Glenn	.50
30	Rod Gardner	.50
31	Aaron Brooks	1.50
32	Johnnie Morton	.20
33	Steve McNair	.75
34	Deuce McAllister	1.50
35	Emmitt Smith	3.00
36	Isaac Bruce	.50
37	Cris Carter	.50
38	Marty Booker	.50
39	Garrison Hearst	.50
40	Jay Fiedler	.50
41	Eric Moulds	.50
42	Hines Ward	.50
43	Peyton Manning	3.00
44	Trent Dilfer	.50
45	Ricky Williams	2.00
46	Quincy Carter	2.00
47	Kurt Warner	3.00
48	Tom Brady	3.00
49	Chris Weinke	.75
50	LaDainian Tomlinson	2.50
51	Antowain Smith	.50
52	Corey Dillon	.75
53	Shaun Alexander	.75
54	Daunte Culpepper	2.00
55	Ray Lewis	.50
56	Kordell Stewart	.50
57	Trent Green	.50
58	Chris Redman	.50
59	Plaxico Burress	.75
60	Fred Taylor	.50
61	Marvin "Snoop" Minnis	.50
62	Jerry Rice	3.00
63	Charlie Rogers	.20
64	Peerless Price	.50
65	Curtis Martin	.50
66	Mike McMahon	.75
67	Brad Johnson	.50
68	Troy Brown	.75
69	Jamal Lewis	1.50
70	Jerome Bettis	.50
71	Dominic Rhodes	.20
72	Az-Zahir Hakim	.50
73	Rich Gannon	.50
74	Ahman Green	.75
75	Eddie George	.75
76	Tim Couch	1.50
77	Ricky Watters	.50
78	Randy Moss	3.00
79	Brian Urlacher	2.50
80	Terrell Owens	.75
81	Jimmy Smith	.20
82	Travis Henry	.75
83	Drew Brees	2.00
84	Priest Holmes	.20
85	Michael Vick	3.00
86	James Thrash	.20
87	Jamie Sharper	.20
88	Marcus Robinson	.20
89	Laveranues Coles	.50
90	Brett Favre	4.50
91	Stephen Davis	.50
92	Tiki Barber	.50
93	Kevin Johnson	.20
94	Marshall Faulk	2.00
95	Mark Brunell	.75
96	Jamal Anderson	.50
97	Duce Staley	.50
98	Edgerrin James	2.50
99	Kevan Barlow	.20
100	Kerry Collins	.50
101	*David Carr*	30.00
102	*Joey Harrington*	20.00
103	*William Green*	10.00
104	*Donte Stallworth*	15.00
105	*Ashley Lelie*	15.00
106	*Jabar Gaffney*	10.00
107	*Antonio Bryant*	10.00
108	*Josh Reed*	10.00
109	*Daniel Graham*	5.00
110	*Donald Reche Caldwell*	5.00
111	*Jeremy Shockey*	20.00
112	*T.J. Duckett*	12.00
113	*Marquise Walker*	4.00
114	*Lamar Gordon*	5.00
115	*DeShaun Foster*	6.00
116	*Patrick Ramsey*	12.00
117	*Andre Davis*	12.00
118	*Ron Johnson*	4.00
119	*Luke Staley*	5.00
120	*Clinton Portis*	30.00
121	*Kelly Campbell*	5.00
122	*Javon Walker*	15.00
123	*David Garrard*	5.00
124	*Kurt Kittner*	6.00
125	*Adrian Peterson*	6.00
126	*Roy Williams*	15.00
127	*Maurice Morris*	8.00
128	*Cliff Russell*	4.00
129	*Antwann Randle El*	15.00
130	*Verron Haynes*	4.00
131	*Eric Crouch*	8.00
132	*Kahlil Hill*	4.00
133	*Brian Westbrook*	10.00
134	*Travis Stephens*	4.00
135	*Julius Peppers*	12.00
136	*Quentin Jammer*	6.00
137	*Rohan Davey*	6.00
138	*Ladell Betts*	6.00
139	*Tim Carter*	4.00
140	*Josh McCown*	10.00

2002 Fleer Authentix Front Row

Stars:	4X-8X
Rookies:	1X-2X
Production 150 Sets	

2002 Fleer Authentix Second Row

Stars:	3X-6X
Rookies:	1.5X
Production 250 Sets	

2002 Fleer Authentix Jersey AuthenTIX (Ripped)

		NM/M
Common Player:		10.00
Inserted 1:11		
Unripped		2X to 3X
Production 50 sets		
1JA	Corey Dillon	10.00
2JA	Peter Warrick	10.00
3JA	Kurt Warner	20.00
4JA	Jeff Garcia	10.00
5JA	Marshall Faulk	25.00
6JA	Brett Favre	40.00
7JA	Kevin Johnson	10.00
8JA	Edgerrin James	25.00
9JA	Keenan McCardell	10.00
10JA	Drew Bledsoe	15.00
11JA	Ron Dayne	10.00
12JA	Chad Pennington	10.00
13JA	Tim Brown	10.00
14JA	Charles Woodson	10.00
15JA	Kordell Stewart	10.00
16JA	Warren Sapp	10.00
17JA	Isaac Bruce	10.00
18JA	Ed McCaffrey	10.00
19JA	Rod Smith	15.00
20JA	David Boston	10.00
21JA	Brian Urlacher	30.00
22JA	Dez White	10.00
23JA	Germane Crowell	10.00
24JA	Jimmy Smith	10.00
25JA	Stephen Davis	10.00
26JA	Thomas Jones	10.00
27JA	Jamal Anderson	10.00
28JA	Eric Moulds	10.00
29JA	Antonio Freeman	10.00
30JA	Todd Pinkston	10.00
31JA	Donovan McNabb	15.00
32JA	Torry Holt	10.00
33JA	Steve McNair	10.00

2002 Fleer Authentix Hometown Heroes

		NM/M
Complete Set (15):		35.00
Common Player:		2.00
Inserted 1:6		
1HH	Michael Vick	4.00
2HH	William Green	4.00
3HH	Donte Stallworth	3.00
4HH	Ashley Lelie	3.00
5HH	Anthony Thomas	3.00
6HH	Eddie George	2.00
7HH	Peyton Manning	3.00
8HH	Ricky Williams	2.00
9HH	Tom Brady	4.00
10HH	Kurt Warner	4.00
11HH	Daunte Culpepper	3.00
12HH	David Carr	6.00
13HH	Joey Harrington	4.00
14HH	Edgerrin James	3.00
15HH	Randy Moss	3.00

2002 Fleer Authentix Hometown Heroes Memorabilia

		NM/M
Common Player:		10.00
1HHM	Brett Favre	50.00
2HHM	Dorsey Levens	10.00
3HHM	Paul Hornung	50.00
4HHM	Bart Starr	60.00
5HHM	Ray Nitschke	40.00
6HHM	Todd Pinkston	10.00
7HHM	Corey Simon	10.00
8HHM	Duce Staley	10.00
9HHM	Donovan McNabb	25.00
10HHM	Brian Dawkins	10.00
11HHM	Troy Vincent	10.00
12HHM	Troy Aikman	40.00
13HHM	Emmitt Smith	50.00
14HHM	Tony Dorsett	30.00
15HHM	Roger Staubach	50.00
16HHM	Jeff Garcia	10.00
17HHM	Terrell Owens	10.00
18HHM	Jerry Rice	50.00
19HHM	Kordell Stewart	15.00
20HHM	Plaxico Burress	15.00
21HHM	Jerome Bettis	10.00
22HHM	Terry Bradshaw	50.00
23HHM	Zach Thomas	25.00
24HHM	Dan Marino	75.00

2002 Fleer Authentix Stadium Classics

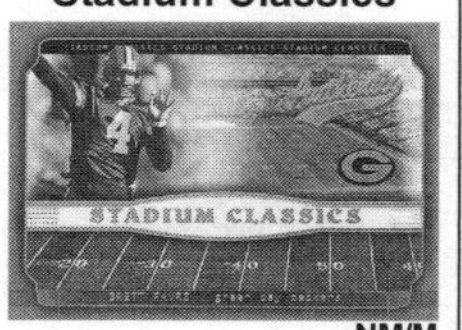

		NM/M
Complete Set (15):		35.00
Common Player:		2.00
Inserted 1:12		
1SC	Donovan McNabb	2.00
2SC	Marshall Faulk	3.00
3SC	Mark Brunell	2.00
4SC	Brett Favre	5.00
5SC	Emmitt Smith	3.00
6SC	Kurt Warner	3.00
7SC	Daunte Culpepper	2.00
8SC	Jerry Rice	2.00
9SC	Tim Couch	2.00
10SC	Edgerrin James	3.00
11SC	Randy Moss	3.00
12SC	Fred Taylor	2.00
13SC	Brian Urlacher	3.00
14SC	Jeff Garcia	2.00
15SC	Shaun Alexander	2.00

2002 Fleer Authentix Stadium Classics Memorabilia

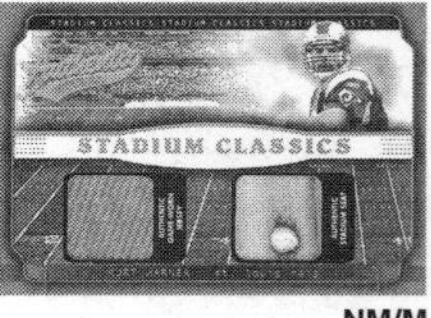

		NM/M
Common Player:		10.00
Gold:		1.5X
Production 100 sets		
1SC	Donovan McNabb	10.00
2SC	Marshall Faulk	20.00
3SC	Mark Brunell	10.00
4SC	Brett Favre	40.00
5SC	Emmitt Smith	40.00
6SC	Kurt Warner	35.00
7SC	Daunte Culpepper	15.00
8SC	Jerry Rice	35.00
9SC	Tim Couch	10.00
10SC	Edgerrin James	25.00
11SC	Randy Moss	30.00
12SC	Fred Taylor	20.00
13SC	Brian Urlacher	35.00
14SC	Jeff Garcia	10.00
15SC	Shaun Alexander	15.00

2002 Fleer Authentix Ticket For Four

		NM/M
Common Player:		75.00
Production 200 sets		
1TF	Brett Favre, Daunte Culpepper, Donovan McNabb, Peyton Manning	125.00
2TF	Bo Jackson, Ricky Williams, Marshall Faulk, Stephen Davis	75.00
3TF	Terrell Owens, David Boston, Rod Smith, Tim Brown	75.00
4TF	Junior Seau, Bruce Smith, Brian Urlacher, Warren Sapp	75.00
5TF	Kurt Warner, Marshall Faulk, Torry Holt, Isaac Bruce	100.00

2002 Fleer Box Score

		NM/M
Common Player:		.25
Unlisted Stars:		.75
Minor Stars:		.50
Common Rookie (116-150):		1.00
Unlisted Rookie Stars:		1.50
Minor Rookie Stars:		1.25
Rising Stars (151-180) Supplemental box		
QB Collection (181-210) Supplemental box		
All Pro (211-240) Supplemental box		
Box:		75.00
1	Brian Urlacher	1.50
2	Edgerrin James	1.50
3	Ricky Williams	1.25
4	Tim Brown	.75
5	Tim Couch	1.00
6	Kurt Warner	2.00
7	Kendrell Bell	.50
8	Daunte Culpepper	1.25
9	Anthony Thomas	1.25
10	Marvin Harrison	.75
11	Jerry Rice	2.00
12	Eddie George	.75
13	Donovan McNabb	1.25
14	Chris Chambers	.75
15	Emmitt Smith	2.00
16	David Boston	.75
17	Plaxico Burress	.75
18	Randy Moss	2.00
19	Peyton Manning	2.00
20	Michael Vick	2.00
21	Marshall Faulk	1.25
22	Tom Brady	2.00
23	LaDainian Tomlinson	1.50
24	Shaun Alexander	.75
25	Curtis Martin	.50
26	Brett Favre	2.50
27	Drew Bledsoe	1.25
28	Jeff Garcia	.75
29	Terrell Davis	1.00
30	Corey Dillon	.75
31	Troy Brown	.75
32	Drew Brees	1.50
33	Jamal Lewis	1.00
34	Derrick Alexander	.25
35	Az-Zahir Hakim	.50

36 Antowain Smith .50
37 Muhsin Muhammad .50
38 Warrick Dunn .50
39 Curtis Conway .25
40 Antonio Freeman .50
41 Bill Schroeder .25
42 Joe Horn .25
43 Peerless Price .50
44 Ahman Green .75
45 Marcus Robinson .50
46 Aaron Brooks 1.00
47 Cris Carter .50
48 Tiki Barber .25
49 Terry Glenn .50
50 Ed McCaffrey .50
51 Darrell Jackson .25
52 Garrison Hearst .50
53 Hines Ward .50
54 Deuce McAllister 1.00
55 Rod Gardner .50
56 Amani Toomer .50
57 Thomas Jones .25
58 Travis Henry .50
59 Koren Robinson .25
60 Travis Taylor .50
61 Ron Dayne .50
62 Robert Ferguson .25
63 Chad Pennington .50
64 James Allen .25
65 Chris Weinke .50
66 Torry Holt .75
67 Chris Chandler .25
68 Shane Matthews .25
69 Ike Hilliard .25
70 Charlie Garner .25
71 Laveranues Coles .25
72 Lamar Smith .25
73 Rob Johnson .50
74 Qadry Ismail .25
75 James Jackson .50
76 Wayne Chrebet .50
77 Priest Holmes 1.00
78 Michael Westbrook .25
79 Michael Pittman .25
80 Derrick Mason .50
81 Dominic Rhodes .25
82 Eric Moulds .25
83 Fred Taylor .50
84 Corey Bradford .25
85 Steve McNair .75
86 Tyrone Wheatley .25
87 Peter Warrick .50
88 Freddie Mitchell .50
89 Peter Boulware .25
90 Kevin Johnson .25
91 Jermaine Lewis .25
92 Joey Galloway .50
93 Stephen Davis .50
94 James Thrash .25
95 James Stewart .25
96 Quincy Morgan .25
97 Dorsey Levens .50
98 Johnnie Morton .25
99 Raghib Ismail .25
100 Rod Smith .50
101 David Terrell .25
102 Kordell Stewart .50
103 Marty Booker .25
104 Brian Griese .75
105 Marvin "Snoop" Minnis .50
106 Jake Plummer .50
107 Keenan McCardell .50
108 Duce Staley .50
109 Isaac Bruce .50
110 Bubba Franks .25
111 Keyshawn Johnson .50
112 Kevan Barlow .50
113 Reggie Wayne .50
114 Michael Bennett .75
115 Santana Moss .50
116 *David Carr* 15.00
117 *Joey Harrington* 10.00
118 *Antwann Randle El* 4.00
119 *Eric Crouch* 3.00
120 *Javon Walker* 8.00
121 *William Green* 4.00
122 *Patrick Ramsey* 8.00
123 *Clinton Portis* 15.00
124 *Andre Davis* 3.00
125 *T.J. Duckett* 5.00
126 *Ladell Betts* 2.50
127 *Marquise Walker* 2.50
128 *Maurice Morris* 3.00
129 *Brian Westbrook* 5.00
130 *Phillip Buchanon* 2.50
131 *Tim Carter* 1.50
132 *Zak Kustok* 1.00
133 *Chester Taylor* 1.00
134 *Josh Reed* 3.00
135 *Kurt Kittner* 2.50
136 *Cliff Russell* 1.50
137 *Travis Fisher* 1.00
138 *Jerramy Stevens* 1.50
139 *Vernon Hayes* 1.00
140 *Ricky Williams* 1.50
141 *Randy McMichael* 1.00
142 *Dwight Freeney* 1.00
143 *Lito Sheppard* 1.50
144 *Mike Williams* 1.00
145 *Jason McAddley* 1.00
146 *Deion Branch* 4.00
147 *Daniel Graham* 2.50
148 *J.T. O'Sullivan* 1.00
149 *Freddie Milons* 1.00
150 *Ron Johnson* 1.50
151 *Ashley Lelie* 5.00
152 *Roy Williams* 5.00
153 *Donte Stallworth* 3.00
154 *Randy Fasani* 1.00
155 *Antonio Bryant* 2.50
156 *Julius Peppers* 3.00
157 *Jabar Gaffney* 2.00
158 *Chad Hutchinson* 2.00
159 *DeShaun Foster* 2.00
160 *Micah Ross* 1.00
161 *Rocky Calmus* 1.50
162 *Travis Stephens* 1.00
163 *Quentin Jammer* 1.50
164 *Napoleon Harris* 1.00
165 *Jeremy Shockey* 6.00
166 *Rohan Davey* 2.00
167 *Najeh Davenport* 1.50
168 *Adrian Peterson* 1.50
169 *Edward Reed* 1.00
170 *Tavon Mason* 1.00
171 *Robert Thomas* 1.00
172 *Lamar Gordon* 1.50
173 *Donald Reche Caldwell* 1.50
174 *Michael Lewis* 1.00
175 *Ryan Sims* 1.50
176 *David Garrard* 1.50
177 *Jonathan Wells* 2.00
178 *Albert Haynesworth* 1.50
179 *Josh McCown* 1.50
180 *John Henderson* 1.50
181 Jake Plummer .25
182 Michael Vick 2.00
183 Chris Redman .25
184 Drew Bledsoe 1.00
185 Jim Miller .25
186 Jon Kitna .25
187 Tim Couch 1.00
188 Quincy Carter 1.00
189 Brian Griese .75
190 Mike McMahon .25
191 Brett Favre 3.00
192 David Carr 3.00
193 Peyton Manning 2.00
194 Mark Brunell .75
195 Trent Green .75
196 Jay Fiedler .25
197 Daunte Culpepper 1.50
198 Tom Brady 2.00
199 Aaron Brooks 1.00
200 Kerry Collins .25
201 Vinny Testaverde .25
202 Rich Gannon .50
203 Donovan McNabb 1.00
204 Kordell Stewart .50
205 Doug Flutie .75
206 Jeff Garcia .75
207 Trent Dilfer .25
208 Kurt Warner 2.00
209 Brad Johnson .25
210 Steve McNair 1.00
211 Sam Madison .25
212 Bruce Matthews .25
213 Brett Favre 3.00
214 Cris Carter .75
215 Michael Strahan .25
216 Ray Lewis .50
217 Randy Moss 2.00
218 Jerome Bettis .50
219 Warren Sapp .50
220 Junior Seau .50
221 Emmitt Smith 2.00
222 Jimmy Smith .25
223 Mike Alstott .25
224 Zach Thomas .25
225 Marshall Faulk 1.00
226 John Lynch .25
227 Larry Allen .25
228 Kurt Warner 2.00
229 Eddie George .75
230 Tony Gonzalez .25
231 Marvin Harrison .75
232 David Terrell .50
233 Peyton Manning 2.00
234 Terrell Owens .75
235 Jevon Kearse .25
236 Jerry Rice 2.00
237 Shannon Sharpe .50
238 Rod Woodson .25
239 Mark Brunell .75
240 Tim Brown .75

2002 Fleer Box Score All-Pro Roster Jerseys

NM/M

Common Player: 12.00
Supplemental box insert
1APR Michael Strahan, Jevon Kearse, Warren Sapp 12.00
2APR Junior Seau, Ray Lewis, Zach Thomas 12.00
3APR Sam Madison, John Lynch, Rod Woodson 12.00
4APR Tony Gonzalez, Shannon Sharpe, Mike Alstott 15.00
5APR Jimmy Smith, Marvin Harrison, Terrell Owens 15.00
6APR Brett Favre, Kurt Warner, Peyton Manning, Mark Brunell 50.00
7APR Emmitt Smith, Marshall Faulk, Eddie George, Terrell Davis 50.00
8APR Cris Carter, Randy Moss, Jerry Rice, Tim Brown 40.00
9APR Brett Favre, Emmitt Smith, Jerry Rice, Randy Moss 90.00
10APR Kurt Warner, Marshall Faulk, Peyton Manning, Eddie George 25.00

2002 Fleer Box Score Box Score Debuts

NM/M

Production 2002 sets
1BSD Antwann Randle El 5.00
2BSD T.J. Duckett 6.00
3BSD Donte Stallworth 5.00
4BSD Deion Branch 5.00
5BSD William Green 3.00
6BSD Brian Westbrook 2.50
7BSD Jabar Gaffney 2.50
8BSD Clinton Portis 6.00
9BSD Joey Harrington 8.00

NM/M

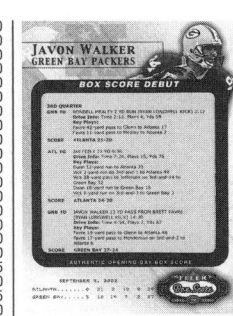

10BSD Andre Davis 3.00
11BSD Javon Walker 4.00
12BSD Antonio Bryant 4.00
13BSD Jeremy Shockey 4.00
14BSD Josh Reed 3.00
15BSD David Carr 8.00

2002 Fleer Box Score Classic Miniatures

NM/M

Common Player: .75
Supplemental box set
Gold 2X to 4X
Production 100 sets
1CM Brian Urlacher 1.50
2CM Edgerrin James 1.50
3CM Ricky Williams 1.25
4CM Tim Brown .75
5CM Tim Couch 1.00
6CM Kurt Warner 1.50
7CM Kendrell Bell .75
8CM Daunte Culpepper 1.25
9CM Anthony Thomas 1.50
10CM Marvin Harrison .75
11CM Jerry Rice 2.00
12CM Eddie George .75
13CM Donovan McNabb 1.25
14CM Chris Chambers .75
15CM Emmitt Smith 2.00
16CM David Boston .75
17CM Plaxico Burress .75
18CM Randy Moss 2.00
19CM Peyton Manning 2.00
20CM Michael Vick 2.00
21CM Marshall Faulk 1.25
22CM Tom Brady 2.00
23CM LaDainian Tomlinson 1.50
24CM Shaun Alexander .75
25CM Curtis Martin .75
26CM Brett Favre 2.50
27CM Drew Bledsoe 1.25
28CM Jeff Garcia .75
29CM Terrell Davis 1.00
30CM Corey Dillon .75

2002 Fleer Box Score Classic Miniatures Jerseys

NM/M

Common Player: 8.00
Supplemental box
1CMGU Brian Urlacher 20.00
2CMGU Ricky Williams 12.00
3CMGU Anthony Thomas 8.00
4CMGU Chris Chambers 8.00
5CMGU David Boston 8.00
6CMGU Plaxico Burress 12.00
7CMGU Tom Brady 15.00
8CMGU LaDainian Tomlinson 8.00
9CMGU Shaun Alexander
10CMGU Corey Dillon 8.00

2002 Fleer Box Score Jersey Rack Triples

NM/M

Common Player: 20.00
Production 300 sets
1JRT Kordell Stewart, Plaxico Burress, Jerome Bettis 20.00
2JRT Tom Brady, Brett Favre, Kurt Warner 40.00
3JRT Anthony Thomas, Ahman Green, Shawn Alexander 20.00
4JRT Randy Moss, Jerry Rice, Torry Holt 30.00
5JRT Michael Vick, Daunte Culpepper, Donovan McNabb 40.00

2002 Fleer Box Score Jersey Rack Quads

NM/M

Common Player: 30.00
Production 100 sets
1JRQ Eddie George, Steve McNair, Donovan McNabb, Freddie Mitchell 40.00
2JRQ Jeff Garcia, Terrell Owens, Marshall Faulk, Kurt Warner 40.00
3JRQ Randy Moss, Daunte Culpepper, Ahman Green, Brett Favre 50.00
4JRQ Jamal Lewis, Peyton Manning, Emmitt Smith, Fred Taylor 40.00
5JRQ David Boston, Marvin Harrison, LaDainian Tomlinson, Curtis Martin
6JRQ Ricky Williams, Chris Chambers, Edgerrin James, Marvin Harrison 30.00
7JRQ Tom Brady, Antowain Smith, Marshall Faulk, Kurt Warner 30.00

2002 Fleer Box Score Press Clippings

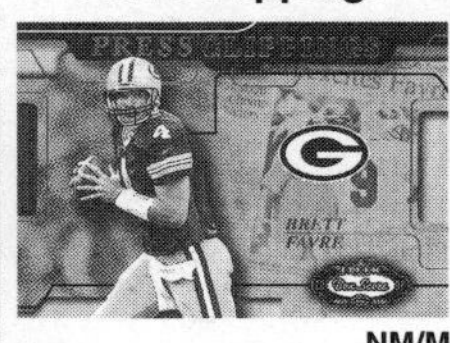

NM/M

Common Player: 2.00
Inserted 1:18
1PC David Carr 8.00
2PC Joey Harrington 8.00
3PC Drew Bledsoe 3.00
4PC Michael Vick 5.00
5PC Kordell Stewart 2.00
6PC Aaron Brooks 2.00
7PC Donovan McNabb 2.00
8PC Rich Gannon 2.00
9PC Drew Brees 2.00
10PC Peyton Manning 5.00
11PC Tom Brady 5.00
12PC Brett Favre 8.00
13PC Jeff Garcia 2.00
14PC Kurt Warner 4.00
15PC Daunte Culpepper 2.00

2002 Fleer Box Score Press Clippings Jerseys

NM/M

Common Player: 8.00
Inserted 1:14
1PCGU Marvin Harrison 8.00
2PCGU Shaun Alexander 8.00
3PCGU Curtis Martin 8.00
4PCGU David Boston 8.00
5PCGU Jamal Lewis 8.00
6PCGU Michael Vick 20.00
7PCGU Jerry Rice 20.00
8PCGU Anthony Thomas 8.00
9PCGU Jerome Bettis 8.00
10PCGU Fred Taylor 8.00
11PCGU Brian Urlacher 20.00
12PCGU LaDainian Tomlinson 15.00
13PCGU Tim Couch 8.00
14PCGU Torry Holt 8.00
15PCGU Emmitt Smith 20.00

2002 Fleer Box Score Press Clippings Patches

NM/M

Common Player: 15.00
Production 50 sets
1PCP Marvin Harrison 15.00
2PCP Shaun Alexander 15.00
3PCP Curtis Martin 15.00
4PCP David Boston 15.00
5PCP Jamal Lewis 15.00
6PCP Michael Vick 40.00
7PCP Jerry Rice 40.00
8PCP Anthony Thomas 25.00
9PCP Jerome Bettis 15.00
10PCP Fred Taylor 15.00
11PCP Brian Urlacher
12PCP LaDainian Tomlinson 25.00
13PCP Tim Couch 25.00
14PCP Torry Holt 15.00
15PCP Emmitt Smith 60.00

2002 Fleer Box Score QBXtra Jerseys

NM/M

Common Player: 8.00
Supplemental box
1QBX Michael Vick 18.00
2QBX Tim Couch 15.00
3QBX Brian Griese 12.00
4QBX Brett Favre 25.00
5QBX Peyton Manning 15.00
6QBX Daunte Culpepper 12.00
7QBX Tom Brady 15.00
8QBX Donovan McNabb 12.00
9QBX Jeff Garcia 8.00
10QBX Kurt Warner 15.00

2002 Fleer Box Score Red Shirt Freshman

NM/M

Supplemental box
1RSF Joey Harrington
2RSF DeShaun Foster 6.00
3RSF Javon Walker 8.00
4RSF Josh Reed 6.00
5RSF Antonio Bryant 8.00
6RSF Jeremy Shockey 8.00
7RSF Deion Branch 8.00
8RSF Clinton Portis
9RSF William Green 6.00
10RSF David Carr 20.00

2002 Fleer Box Score Yard Markers

NM/M

Common Player:
Inserted 1:9
1YM Tom Brady 4.00
2YM Antowain Smith 1.00
3YM Randy Moss 4.00
4YM Daunte Culpepper 2.00
5YM Edgerrin James 2.00
6YM Peyton Manning 4.00
7YM Eddie George 1.00
8YM Steve McNair 1.00
9YM Ricky Williams 2.00
10YM Chris Chambers 2.00
11YM Jeff Garcia 1.00
12YM Terrell Owens 1.00
13YM Marshall Faulk 1.00
14YM Kurt Warner 3.00
15YM Donovan McNabb 2.00
16YM Freddie Mitchell 1.00
17YM Ahman Green 1.00
18YM Brett Favre 6.00
19YM Plaxico Burress 2.00
20YM Kordell Stewart 1.00

2002 Fleer Box Score Yard Markers Dual

NM/M

Common Player: 2.00
Inserted 1:108
1YMD Tom Brady, Antowain Smith
2YMD Randy Moss, Daunte Culpepper
3YMD Edgerrin James, Peyton Manning 4.00
4YMD Eddie George, Steve McNair 2.00
5YMD Ricky Williams, Chris Chambers 3.00
6YMD Jeff Garcia, Terrell Owens 3.00
7YMD Marshall Faulk, Kurt Warner 5.00
8YMD Donovan McNabb, Freddie Mitchell 4.00
9YMD Ahman Green, Brett Favre
10YMD Plaxico Burress, Kordell Stewart 3.00

2002 Fleer Box Score Yard Markers Jerseys

NM/M

Common Player: 8.00
Inserted 1:14
1YMGU Tom Brady 15.00
2YMGU Antowain Smith 8.00
3YMGU Randy Moss 15.00
4YMGU Daunte Culpepper 10.00
5YMGU Edgerrin James 10.00
6YMGU Peyton Manning 15.00
7YMGU Eddie George 8.00
8YMGU Steve McNair 8.00
9YMGU Ricky Williams 10.00
10YMGU Chris Chambers 8.00
11YMGU Jeff Garcia 8.00
12YMGU Terrell Owens 8.00
13YMGU Marshall Faulk 10.00
14YMGU Kurt Warner 12.00
15YMGU Donovan McNabb 12.00
16YMGU Freddie Mitchell
17YMGU Ahman Green 8.00
18YMGU Brett Favre 20.00
19YMGU Plaxico Burress 8.00
20YMGU Kordell Stewart 8.00

2002 Fleer Box Score Yard Markers Dual Jerseys

NM/M

Common Player: 15.00
Production 100 sets
1YMDGU Tom Brady, Antowain Smith 20.00
2YMDGU Randy Moss, Daunte Culpepper 25.00
3YMDGU Edgerrin James, Peyton Manning 25.00
4YMDGU Eddie George, Steve McNair 15.00
5YMDGU Ricky Williams, Chris Chambers 20.00
6YMDGU Jeff Garcia, Terrell Owens 20.00
7YMDGU Marshall Faulk, Kurt Warner 20.00
8YMDGU Donovan McNabb, Freddie Mitchell
9YMDGU Ahman Green, Brett Favre 40.00
10YMDGU Plaxico Burress, Kordell Stewart 15.00

2002 Fleer Focus

NM/M

Common Player: .20
Unlisted Stars: .75
Minor Stars: .50
Common Rookie (101-160) 1.00
Minor Rookies: 1.50
Production 1850 sets
Pack (7): 3.00
Wax Box (24): 65.00
1 Tom Brady 3.00
2 Curtis Martin .60
3 Brett Favre 4.00
4 Michael Pittman .20
5 Donovan McNabb 2.00
6 Quincy Carter 2.00
7 Trent Dilfer .60
8 Troy Brown .75
9 Ed McCaffrey .60
10 Shaun Alexander .75
11 Daunte Culpepper 2.00
12 Marty Booker .50
13 Junior Seau .75
14 Zach Thomas .50
15 Muhsin Muhammad .50
16 Kordell Stewart .50
17 Jimmy Smith .50
18 David Boston .75
19 Laveranues Coles .50
20 Emmitt Smith 3.00
21 Darrell Jackson .20
22 Charlie Garner .50
23 Marcus Robinson .50
24 Drew Brees 2.50
25 Tony Gonzalez .50
26 James Allen .20
27 Steve McNair .75
28 Kerry Collins .50
29 Az-Zahir Hakim .50
30 Marshall Faulk 2.00
31 Derrick Mason .50
32 Rod Smith .50
33 Torry Holt .50
34 Jake Plummer .50
35 Kevin Johnson .20
36 Kevan Barlow .50
37 Priest Holmes .75
38 Anthony Thomas 2.50
39 Jerome Bettis .50
40 Johnnie Morton .20
41 Eric Moulds .50
42 James Thrash .20
43 Jamie Sharper .20
44 Eddie George .75
45 Randy Moss 3.00
46 Tim Couch 1.50
47 Terrell Owens .75
48 Jay Fiedler .50
49 Travis Henry .50
50 Hines Ward .50
51 Ricky Williams 2.00
52 Brian Urlacher 2.50
53 LaDainian Tomlinson 2.50
54 Trent Green .50
55 Chris Redman .50
56 Deuce McAllister 1.50
57 Mark Brunell .75
58 Jamal Lewis 1.50
59 Freddie Mitchell .50
60 Peyton Manning 3.00
61 Stephen Davis .50
62 Tiki Barber .50
63 Terry Glenn .50
64 Keyshawn Johnson .50
65 Aaron Brooks 1.50
66 Brian Griese .75
67 Koren Robinson .50
68 Michael Bennett .75
69 Ray Lewis .50
70 Rich Gannon .75
71 Marvin Harrison .50
72 Rod Gardner .50
73 Chad Pennington .50
74 Terrell Davis 1.50
75 Isaac Bruce .75
76 Peter Warrick .50
77 Jeff Garcia .75
78 Chris Chambers .75
79 Chris Weinke .75
80 Plaxico Burress .75
81 Edgerrin James 2.50
82 Drew Bledsoe 1.50
83 Duce Staley .50
84 Fred Taylor .50
85 Warrick Dunn .50
86 Jerry Rice 3.00
87 Ahman Green .75
88 Warren Sapp .50
89 Michael Strahan .50
90 Bill Schroeder .20
91 Kurt Warner 3.00
92 Antowain Smith .50
93 Corey Dillon .75
94 Garrison Hearst .50
95 Joey Galloway .50
96 Michael Vick 3.00
97 Tim Brown .75
98 Corey Bradford .20
99 Brad Johnson .50

100 Joe Horn .20
101 *Quentin Jammer* 2.50
102 *Rohan Davey* 3.00
103 *David Garrard* 1.50
104 *Ron Johnson* 1.50
105 *Jeremy Shockey* 6.00
106 *Marquise Walker* 2.50
107 *Luke Staley* 2.50
108 *Josh Scobey* 1.50
109 *Adrian Peterson* 1.50
110 *Lito Sheppard* 1.50
111 *Daniel Graham* 2.50
112 *Ryan Sims* 1.50
113 *William Green* 4.00
114 *Ashley Lelie* 5.00
115 *Deion Branch* 2.50
116 *Omar Easy* 1.50
117 *Jake Schifino* 1.50
118 *Donte Stallworth* 5.00
119 *Craig Nall* 1.50
120 *Clinton Portis* 15.00
121 *Brandon Doman* 1.00
122 *Eric Crouch* 3.00
123 *Josh McCown* 2.50
124 *Cliff Russell* 1.50
125 *T.J. Duckett* 5.00
126 *Jason McAddley* 1.00
127 *Chad Hutchinson* 1.50
128 *Jonathan Wells* 3.00
129 *Antwann Randle El* 4.00
130 *Terry Charles* 1.00
131 *Lamar Gordon* 2.50
132 *Antonio Bryant* 4.00
133 *Brian Westbrook* 1.50
134 *Javon Walker* 4.00
135 *J.T. O'Sullivan* 1.00
136 *Maurice Morris* 3.00
137 *Tim Carter* 1.50
138 *Antwoine Womack* 1.00
139 *Ladell Betts* 2.50
140 *Joey Harrington* 10.00
141 *Chester Taylor* 1.00
142 *David Carr* 15.00
143 *Roy Williams* 4.00
144 *Donald Reche Caldwell* 2.50
145 *Lamont Brightful* 1.00
146 *Patrick Ramsey* 3.00
147 *Travis Stephens* 2.50
148 *Andre Davis* 3.00
149 *Herb Haygood* 1.00
150 *Randy Fasani* 1.50
151 *Jabar Gaffney* 3.00
152 *Kahlil Hill* 1.00
153 *Julius Peppers* 4.00
154 *Kurt Kittner* 2.50
155 *DeShaun Foster* 3.00
156 *Verron Haynes* 1.00
157 *Josh Reed* 3.00
158 *Freddie Milons* 1.50
159 *Robert Thomas* 1.00
160 *Sam Simmons* 1.00

2002 Fleer Focus Franchise Focus

NM/M
Common Player: 1.00
Inserted 1:12
1FF David Boston 1.00
2FF Michael Vick 3.00
3FF Ray Lewis 1.00
4FF Drew Bledsoe 2.00
5FF Julius Peppers 3.00
6FF Brian Urlacher 3.00
7FF Corey Dillon 1.00
8FF Tim Couch 1.00
9FF Emmitt Smith 4.00
10FF Rod Smith 1.00
11FF Joey Harrington 8.00
12FF Brett Favre 5.00
13FF David Carr 10.00
14FF Peyton Manning 3.00
15FF Jimmy Smith 1.00
16FF Jimmy Gonzalez 1.00
17FF Ricky Williams 2.00
18FF Randy Moss 3.00
19FF Tom Brady 3.00
20FF Aaron Brooks 1.00
21FF Michael Strahan 1.00
22FF Curtis Martin 1.00
23FF Jerry Rice 2.00
24FF Donovan McNabb 1.50
25FF Jerome Bettis 1.00
26FF Junior Seau 1.00
27FF Jeff Garcia 1.00
28FF Shaun Alexander 1.50
29FF Kurt Warner 3.00
30FF Keyshawn Johnson 1.00
31FF Eddie George 1.00
32FF Stephen Davis 1.00

2002 Fleer Focus Franchise Focus Jersey

Inserted 1:82
1FFJ Jeff Garcia, Kurt Warner
2FFJ Donovan McNabb, Michael Strahan
3FFJ Curtis Martin, Tom Brady
4FFJ Aaron Brooks, Michael Vick
5FFJ Randy Moss, Brett Favre
6FFJ Tim Couch, Jerome Bettis
7FFJ Emmitt Smith, Stephen Davis
8FFJ Jerry Rice, Junior Seau
9FFJ Jimmy Smith, Eddie George
10FFJ David Boston, Shaun Alexander

2002 Fleer Focus Franchise Focus Rivals

NM/M
Production 100 sets
1FFJ Jeff Garcia, Kurt Warner 20.00
2FFJ Donovan McNabb, Michael Strahan 25.00
3FFJ Curtis Martin, Tom Brady 30.00
4FFJ Aaron Brooks, Michael Vick 35.00
5FFJ Randy Moss, Brett Favre 50.00
6FFJ Tim Couch, Jerome Bettis
7FFJ Emmitt Smith, Stephen Davis
8FFJ Jerry Rice, Junior Seau 35.00
9FFJ Jimmy Smith, Eddie George 15.00
10FFJ David Boston, Shaun Alexander 20.00

2002 Fleer Focus Freeze Frame

NM/M
Common Player: 5.00
Inserted 1:24
1FR Kurt Warner 8.00
2FR Eddie George 5.00
3FR Marshall Faulk 6.00
4FR Emmitt Smith 10.00
5FR Randy Moss 8.00
6FR Brett Favre 10.00
7FR Drew Bledsoe 5.00
8FR LaDainian Tomlinson 5.00
9FR Tom Brady 8.00
10FR Donovan McNabb 5.00
11FR Ricky Williams 5.00
12FR Jerry Rice 6.00
13FR Daunte Culpepper 5.00
14FR Peyton Manning 8.00
15FR Brian Urlacher 6.00

2002 Fleer Focus Freeze Frame Jersey

NM/M
Inserted 1:187
Patch versions: 1.5X-3X
Production 50 Sets
1FR Kurt Warner 20.00
2FR Eddie George 15.00
3FR Marshall Faulk 15.00
4FR Emmitt Smith 40.00
5FR Randy Moss 20.00
6FR Brett Favre 40.00
7FR Drew Bledsoe 15.00
12FR Jerry Rice 25.00
14FR Peyton Manning 25.00
15FR Brian Urlacher 25.00

2002 Fleer Focus Jersey Numbers

Stars/60-99: 5X-10X
Rookies/60-99: 1.5X
Stars/30-59: 10X-20X
Rookies/30-59: 1.5X-3X
Stars/15-29: 15X-30X
Rookies/15-29: 3X-6X

2002 Fleer Focus Jersey Numbers Century

Stars: 2X-4X
Rookies: 1X-2X
Production to jersey number plus 100

2002 Fleer Focus Lettermen

Production 1 set
1L Donovan McNabb
2L Troy Aikman
3L David Boston
4L Jerry Rice
5L Fred Taylor
6L Brian Griese
7L Jeff Garcia
8L Tim Couch
9L Brett Favre
10L Junior Seau
11L Kordell Stewart
12L Chad Pennington
13L Jimmy Smith
14L Daunte Culpepper
15L Tom Brady
16L LaDainian Tomlinson
17L Kurt Warner
18L Eddie George
19L Randy Moss
20L Jerome Bettis

2002 Fleer Focus Materialistic Home

NM/M
Common Player: 10.00
Inserted 1:24
Away versions: 1X-2X
Production 50 sets
1M Kurt Warner 10.00
2M Tom Brady 15.00
3M Daunte Culpepper 10.00
4M Drew Bledsoe 10.00
5M Emmitt Smith 15.00
6M Jerry Rice 12.00
7M Eddie George 10.00
8M Donovan McNabb 10.00
9M Brett Favre 15.00
10M Peyton Manning 10.00
11M Randy Moss 10.00
12M Marshall Faulk 10.00
13M Ricky Williams 10.00
14M Brian Urlacher 12.00
15M Edgerrin James 10.00

2002 Fleer Focus Materialistic Home Oversize

NM/M
Common Player: 6.00
Inserted 1:Box
Gold: 1X-2X
Gold Production 50 Sets
1MR Joey Harrington 12.00
2MR William Green 8.00
3MR Donte Stallworth 12.00
4MR Ashley Lelie 12.00
5MR Jabar Gaffney 8.00
6MR Antonio Bryant 8.00
7MR Josh Reed 8.00
8MR Antwann Randle El 10.00
9MR Donald Reche Caldwell 6.00
10MR Javon Walker 10.00
11MR T.J. Duckett 8.00
12MR Marquise Walker 6.00
13MR Clinton Portis 20.00
14MR DeShaun Foster 6.00
15MR Patrick Ramsey 10.00

2002 Fleer Focus Materialistic Plus

NM/M
Common Player: 15.00
Production 250 sets
1M Kurt Warner 20.00
5M Emmitt Smith 30.00
7M Eddie George 15.00
8M Donovan McNabb 25.00
9M Brett Favre 30.00
10M Peyton Manning 20.00
11M Randy Moss 20.00
12M Marshall Faulk 15.00
13M Ricky Williams 15.00
14M Brian Urlacher 20.00

2002 Fleer Focus ROY Collection

NM/M
Common Player: 3.00
Inserted 1:144
1ROY Emmitt Smith 8.00
2ROY Curtis Martin 4.00
3ROY Anthony Thomas 4.00
4ROY Brian Urlacher 5.00
5ROY Jerome Bettis 3.00
6ROY Edgerrin James 5.00
7ROY Jevon Kearse 3.00
8ROY Marshall Faulk 4.00
9ROY Eric Dickerson 3.00
10ROY Randy Moss 5.00
11ROY Tony Dorsett 3.00
12ROY Kendrell Bell 3.00
13ROY Eddie George 3.00
14ROY Charles Woodson 3.00
15ROY Warrick Dunn 3.00

2002 Fleer Focus ROY Collection Jerseys

NM/M
Common Player: 10.00
Inserted 1:187
2ROY Curtis Martin 15.00
3ROY Anthony Thomas 20.00
4ROY Brian Urlacher 30.00
7ROY Jevon Kearse 15.00
8ROY Marshall Faulk 30.00
10ROY Randy Moss 25.00
11ROY Tony Dorsett 25.00
12ROY Kendrell Bell 20.00
13ROY Eddie George 15.00
15ROY Warrick Dunn 10.00

2002 Fleer Focus ROY Collection Patches

NM/M
Common Player: 20.00
1 Warrick Dunn/97 20.00
2 Marshall Faulk/94 40.00
3 Eddie George/96 25.00
4 Jevon Kearse/99 20.00
5 Curtis Martin/95 25.00
6 Randy Moss/98 50.00
7 Anthony Thomas/101 20.00
8 Brian Urlacher/100 30.00

2002 Fleer Genuine

NM/M
Common Player: .30
Unlisted Stars: .75
Minor Stars: .50
Common Rookie (126-175): 2.00
Unlisted Rookie Star: 3.00
Minor Rookie Star: 2.50
Production 599 sets
Pack (5): 3.50
Wax Box (24): 60.00
1 Brian Urlacher 2.00
2 Keyshawn Johnson .50
3 Donovan McNabb 1.50
4 Tim Couch 1.25
5 Junior Seau .50
6 Eric Moulds .50
7 Randy Moss 2.50
8 Rod Smith .50
9 Torry Holt .75
10 Plaxico Burress .75
11 Kordell Stewart .50
12 Brett Favre 3.00
13 Stephen Davis .50
14 Santana Moss .50
15 Kurt Warner 2.00
16 Jake Plummer .50
17 Jimmy Smith .30
18 Quincy Carter 1.50
19 Marvin Harrison .75
20 Fred Taylor .50
21 Warren Sapp .50
22 Curtis Martin .50
23 Isaac Bruce .50
24 Drew Brees 2.00
25 Ray Lewis .50
26 Hines Ward .50
27 Koren Robinson .30
28 Jevon Kearse .50
29 Jerry Rice 2.50
30 Jeff Garcia .75
31 Edgerrin James 2.00
32 Warrick Dunn .50
33 Ricky Williams 1.50
34 Doug Flutie .75
35 Brian Griese .75
36 Chad Pennington .75
37 Duce Staley .50
38 Eddie George .75
39 Daunte Culpepper 1.50
40 Jerome Bettis .75
41 Michael Vick 2.50
42 Tim Brown .75
43 Tom Brady 2.50
44 Steve McNair .75
45 Terrell Owens .75
46 Corey Dillon .75
47 Peyton Manning 2.50
48 Rich Gannon .75
49 Emmitt Smith 2.50
50 David Boston .75
51 Mark Brunell .75
52 Ron Dayne .50
53 Wayne Chrebet .50
54 Terrell Davis 1.25
55 Zach Thomas .50
56 Kevin Johnson .30
57 Marshall Faulk 1.50
58 Anthony Thomas 1.50
59 Deuce McAllister 1.25
60 LaDainian Tomlinson 2.00
61 Thomas Jones .30
62 Ahman Green .75
63 Aaron Brooks 1.25
64 Courtney Brown .30
65 Chris Chambers .75
66 Jamal Lewis 1.00
67 David Terrell .75
68 Tony Gonzalez .50
69 Laveranues Coles .50
70 Shaun Alexander .75
71 Chris Weinke .50
72 Antowain Smith .50
73 Rod Gardner .50
74 Mike Anderson 1.00
75 Antonio Freeman .50
76 Kevan Barlow .50
77 Jim Miller .30
78 Bill Schroeder .30
79 Joe Horn .30
80 Travis Henry .50
81 Michael Bennett .75
82 Michael Pittman .30
83 Keenan McCardell .50
84 Amani Toomer .50
85 Peerless Price .50
86 Az-Zahir Hakim .50
87 James Thrash .30
88 Drew Bledsoe 1.50
89 Mike McMahon .50
90 Derrick Mason .50
91 Joey Galloway .50
92 Marvin "Snoop" Minnis .50
93 Ed McCaffrey .50
94 Johnnie Morton .30
95 Richard Huntley .30
96 Troy Brown .50
97 Shane Mathews .30
98 Muhsin Muhammad .50
99 David Patten .30
100 Jon Kitna .30
101 Terrence Wilkins .30
102 Kerry Collins .30
103 Tiki Barber .30
104 Fred Beasley .30
105 Trent Dilfer .30
106 Chris Redman .30
107 Jay Fiedler .30
108 Charlie Garner .50
109 Mike Alstott .50
110 Darnay Scott .50
111 Garrison Hearst .50
112 James Jackson .50
113 Darrell Jackson .30
114 Freddie Mitchell .50
115 Brad Johnson .30
116 Olandis Gary .30
117 Priest Holmes 1.25
118 Vinny Testaverde .50
119 Takeo Spikes .30
120 Marty Booker .50
121 Curtis Conway .50
122 Jacquez Green .30
123 Champ Bailey .30
124 Trent Green .50
125 Terry Glenn .50
126 *Ladell Betts* 3.00
127 *DeShaun Foster* 4.00
128 *Maurice Morris* 4.00
129 *Chester Taylor* 2.00
130 *Randy McMichael* 8.00
131 *Verron Haynes* 2.00
132 *Cliff Russell* 2.00
133 *Brandon Doman* 2.00
134 *Ashley Lelie* 10.00
135 *Roy Williams* 10.00
136 *Antonio Bryant* 6.00
137 *William Green* 6.00
138 *Clinton Portis* 15.00
139 *J.T. O'Sullivan* 2.00
140 *Javon Walker* 10.00
141 *Randy Fasani* 2.00
142 *Chad Hutchinson* 4.00
143 *Ben Leber* 4.00
144 *Tim Carter* 2.00
145 *Jason McAddley* 2.00
146 *Donte Stallworth* 6.00
147 *Andre Davis* 4.00
148 *Julius Peppers* 6.00
149 *Patrick Ramsey* 4.00
150 *Deion Branch* 6.00
151 *Jonathan Wells* 4.00
152 *Jabar Gaffney* 4.00
153 *Josh McCown* 8.00
154 *Jeremy Shockey* 8.00
155 *Eric Crouch* 4.00
156 *Joey Harrington* 15.00
157 *Jerramy Stevens* 2.00
158 *T.J. Duckett* 8.00
159 *Ron Johnson* 2.00
160 *Josh Reed* 4.00
161 *Donald Reche Caldwell* 3.00
162 *Lamar Gordon* 3.00
163 *David Garrard* 2.00
164 *Freddie Milons* 2.00
165 *Marquise Walker* 3.00
166 *Rohan Davey* 4.00
167 *Coy Wire* 6.00
168 *Quentin Jammer* 3.00
169 *Omar Easy* 2.00
170 *Kurt Kittner* 3.00
171 *Travis Stephens* 3.00
172 *David Carr* 20.00
173 *Daniel Graham* 2.00
174 *Antwann Randle El* 6.00
175 *Brian Westbrook* 8.00

2002 Fleer Genuine Reflection Ascending

Stars/100-125: 3X-6X
Stars/60-99: 5X-10X
Stars/30-59: 6X-12X
Stars/20-29: 10X-20X

2002 Fleer Genuine Reflection Descending

Stars/100-125: 4X-8X
Stars/60-99: 5X-10X
Stars/30-59: 6X-12X
Stars/20-29: 10X-20X

2002 Fleer Genuine Authen-Kicks

NM/M
Common Player: 10.00
Inserted 1:240
Jersey/Shoe Production 25 Sets
A-RG Rich Gannon 10.00
A-MH Marvin Harrison 15.00
A-TH Torry Holt 10.00
A-EJ Edgerrin James 15.00
A-PM Peyton Manning 25.00
A-DM Donovan McNabb 15.00

2002 Fleer Genuine Genuine Article

NM/M
Common Player: 8.00
Inserted 1:24
Insider versions: 1X
Insider Production 500 Sets
Tags Parallel is Unpriced
GA-JB Jerome Bettis 10.00
GA-TB Tom Brady 25.00
GA-DB Drew Brees 12.00
GA-IB Isaac Bruce 10.00
GA-QC Quincy Carter 15.00
GA-DC Daunte Culpepper 15.00
GA-SD Stephen Davis 8.00
GA-BF Brett Favre 35.00
GA-JG Jeff Garcia 12.00
GA-TH Torry Holt 8.00
GA-KJ Keyshawn Johnson 8.00
GA-RL Ray Lewis 12.00
GA-PM Peyton Manning 20.00
GA-RM Randy Moss 20.00
GA-SM Santana Moss 8.00
GA-JR Jerry Rice 20.00
GA-KR Koren Robinson 8.00
GA-WS Warren Sapp 8.00
GA-JS Junior Seau 12.00
GA-ES Emmitt Smith 35.00
GA-RS Rod Smith 8.00
GA-ZT Zach Thomas 12.00
GA-LT LaDainian Tomlinson 15.00
GA-BU Brian Urlacher 25.00

2002 Fleer Genuine Names of the Game

NM/M
Common Player: 1.00
Inserted 1:20
1NG Kurt Warner 3.00
2NG Brett Favre 5.00
3NG Brian Urlacher 3.00
4NG Jeff Garcia 1.00
5NG Donovan McNabb 2.00
6NG Tom Brady 4.00
7NG Tim Couch 1.50
8NG Daunte Culpepper 2.00
9NG Michael Vick 4.00
10NG Edgerrin James 2.00
11NG Marshall Faulk 2.00
12NG Emmitt Smith 4.00
13NG Eddie George 1.00
14NG Jerome Bettis 1.00
15NG Drew Brees 2.00
16NG Quincy Carter 2.00
17NG Randy Moss 4.00
18NG Isaac Bruce 1.00
19NG Jerry Rice 4.00
20NG Junior Seau 1.00

2002 Fleer Genuine Names of the Game Jerseys

NM/M
Common Player: 12.00
Production 500 sets
1NG Kurt Warner 15.00
2NG Brett Favre 30.00
3NG Brian Urlacher 20.00
4NG Jeff Garcia 12.00
5NG Donovan McNabb 15.00
6NG Tom Brady 20.00
7NG Tim Couch 12.00
8NG Daunte Culpepper 15.00
9NG Michael Vick 25.00
10NG Edgerrin James 12.00
11NG Marshall Faulk 12.00
12NG Emmitt Smith 30.00
13NG Eddie George 12.00
14NG Jerome Bettis 12.00
15NG Drew Brees 15.00
16NG Quincy Carter 12.00
17NG Randy Moss 20.00
18NG Isaac Bruce 12.00
19NG Jerry Rice 25.00
20NG Junior Seau 12.00

2002 Fleer Genuine Names of the Game Jerseys Dual

NM/M
Common Player: 20.00
Production 50 sets
KW-DM Kurt Warner, Donovan McNabb
BF-DC Brett Favre, Daunte Culpepper 60.00
MV-JG Michael Vick, Jeff Garcia
TB-TC Tom Brady, Tim Couch 35.00
BU-JS Brian Urlacher, Junior Seau 35.00
EJ-MF Edgerrin James, Marshall Faulk 25.00
EG-JB Eddie George, Jerome Bettis 20.00
DB-QC Drew Brees, Quincy Carter
RM-IB Randy Moss, Isaac Bruce 35.00
ES-JR Emmitt Smith, Jerry Rice 75.00

2002 Fleer Genuine TD Threats

NM/M
Common Player: 1.00
Inserted 1:8
1TD Edgerrin James, Eddie George 2.00
2TD Terrell Owens, Tim Brown 2.00
3TD Emmitt Smith, Marshall Faulk 3.00
4TD David Boston, Jimmy Smith 1.00
5TD Santana Moss, Randy Moss 3.00
6TD Daunte Culpepper, Tim Couch 2.00
7TD Donovan McNabb, Peyton Manning 3.00
8TD Jerry Rice, Chris Chambers 3.00
9TD Eric Moulds, Rod Smith 1.00
10TD Fred Taylor, LaDainian Tomlinson 2.00
11TD Duce Staley, Jerome Bettis 1.00
12TD Michael Vick, Brett Favre 4.00
13TD Tom Brady, Drew Brees 3.00
14TD Ahman Green, Curtis Martin 1.00
15TD Kurt Warner, Jeff Garcia 2.00
16TD Quincy Carter, Jake Plummer 1.00
17TD Terrell Davis, Corey Dillon 1.00
18TD Mark Brunell, Kordell Stewart 1.00
19TD Hines Ward, Plaxico Burress 1.00
20TD Joe Horn, Torry Holt 1.00
21TD Brian Griese, Drew Bledsoe 2.00
22TD Donte Stallworth, Darrell Jackson 2.00
23TD Rod Gardner, David Terrell 1.00
24TD Deuce McAllister, Anthony Thomas 2.00
25TD Aaron Brooks, David Carr 3.00

2002 Fleer Genuine TD Threats Jerseys

NM/M
Common Player: 8.00
Inserted 1:22
1TD Edgerrin James, Eddie George 12.00
2TD Terrell Owens, Tim Brown 15.00

3TD Emmitt Smith, Marshall Faulk 30.00
4TD David Boston, Jimmy Smith 8.00
5TD Santana Moss, Randy Moss 15.00
6TD Daunte Culpepper, Tim Couch 12.00
7TD Donovan McNabb, Peyton Manning 25.00
8TD Jerry Rice, Chris Chambers 20.00
9TD Eric Moulds, Rod Smith 8.00
10TD Fred Taylor, LaDainian Tomlinson 12.00
12TD Michael Vick, Brett Favre 50.00
13TD Tom Brady, Drew Brees 20.00
14TD Ahman Green, Curtis Martin 12.00
15TD Kurt Warner, Jeff Garcia 15.00
16TD Quincy Carter, Jake Plummer 10.00
17TD Terrell Davis, Corey Dillon 12.00
18TD Mark Brunell, Kordell Stewart 8.00
19TD Hines Ward, Plaxico Burress 15.00
20TD Joe Horn, Torry Holt 8.00

2002 Fleer Genuine TD Threats Patches

NM/M
Production to combined 2001 TD total
1TD Edgerrin James, Eddie George
2TD Terrell Owens, Tim Brown/26
3TD Emmitt Smith, Marshall Faulk
4TD David Boston, Jimmy Smith/16
5TD Santana Moss, Randy Moss
6TD Daunte Culpepper, Tim Couch/36 30.00
7TD Donovan McNabb, Peyton Manning/57
8TD Jerry Rice, Chris Chambers
9TD Eric Moulds, Rod Smith/16 35.00
10TD Fred Taylor, LaDainian Tomlinson
11TD Michael Vick, Brett Favre/36 125.00
12TD Tom Brady, Drew Brees
13TD Ahman Green, Curtis Martin
14TD Kurt Warner, Jeff Garcia/73
15TD Quincy Carter, Jake Plummer
16TD Terrell Davis, Corey Dillon
17TD Mark Brunell, Kordell Stewart/38
18TD Hines Ward, Plaxico Burress/10 70.00
20TD Joe Horn, Torry Holt

2002 Fleer Hot Prospects

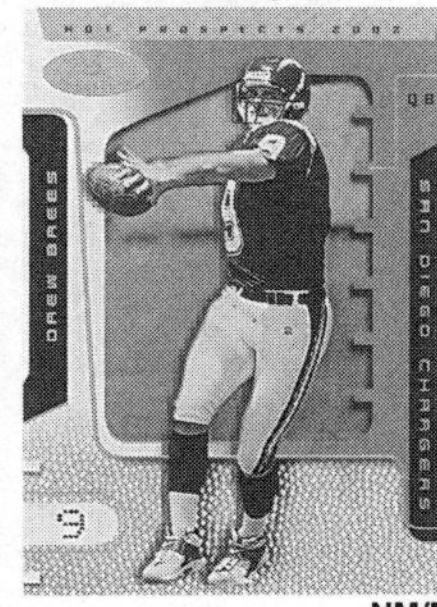

NM/M
Common Player: .20
Unlisted Stars: .75
Minor Stars: .50
Common Rookie JSY (82-112): 6.00
Minor Rookies: 8.00
Production 1000 sets
Pack (5): 13.00
Wax Box (15): 140.00
1 Donovan McNabb 2.00
2 Drew Brees 2.50
3 Curtis Martin .50
4 Priest Holmes .50
5 Quincy Carter 2.00
6 Chris Weinke .50
7 Marshall Faulk 2.00
8 Jake Plummer .50
9 Tom Brady 3.00
10 Ahman Green .75
11 Brian Urlacher 2.50
12 Keyshawn Johnson .50
13 Jerome Bettis .50
14 Tiki Barber .50
15 Edgerrin James 2.50
16 Jamal Lewis 1.50
17 Terrell Owens .75
18 Joe Horn .50
19 Daunte Culpepper 2.00
20 Terrell Davis 1.50
21 Fred Taylor .50
22 Emmitt Smith 3.00
23 Jamal Anderson .50
24 Garrison Hearst .50
25 Chad Pennington .50
26 Michael Bennett .75
27 James Allen .20
28 Marty Booker .50
29 Warren Sapp .50
30 Jerry Rice 3.00
31 Antowain Smith .50
32 Marvin Harrison .50
33 Tim Couch 1.50
34 Stephen Davis .50
35 Kordell Stewart .50
36 Tony Gonzalez .50
37 Mike McMahon .75
38 Eric Moulds .50
39 Kurt Warner 3.00
40 Ricky Williams 2.00
41 Michael Strahan .50
42 Trent Green .50
43 Brian Griese .75
44 David Boston .75
45 LaDainian Tomlinson 2.50
46 Tim Brown .75
47 Deuce McAllister 1.50
48 Jamie Sharper .20
49 Richard Huntley .20
50 Isaac Bruce .50
51 Freddie Mitchell .50
52 Kerry Collins .50
53 Mark Brunell .50
54 Corey Dillon .50
55 Steve McNair .75
56 Aaron Brooks 1.50
57 Chris Chambers .75
58 Bill Schroeder .20
59 Ray Lewis .50
60 Shaun Alexander .75
61 Kevin Johnson .20
62 Michael Vick 3.00
63 Jeff Garcia .75
64 Laveranues Coles .50
65 Jimmy Smith .20
66 Brett Favre 4.00
67 Anthony Thomas 2.00
68 Torry Holt .50
69 Duce Staley .50
70 Randy Moss 3.00
71 Peyton Manning 3.00
72 Peter Warrick .50
73 Eddie George .75
74 Plaxico Burress .75
75 Troy Brown .75
76 Rod Smith .50
77 Drew Bledsoe 2.00
78 Darrell Jackson .20
79 Rich Gannon .50
80 Jay Fiedler .50
81 *David Carr/250* 80.00
82 *Andre Davis JSY* 15.00
83 *Daniel Graham JSY* 8.00
84 *Ron Johnson JSY* 6.00
85 *Julius Peppers JSY* 15.00
86 *Josh Reed JSY* 15.00
87 *Travis Stephens JSY* 6.00
88 *Mike Williams JSY* 6.00
89 *Antonio Bryant JSY* 12.00
90 *Eric Crouch JSY* 12.00
91 *DeShaun Foster JSY* 10.00
92 *Joey Harrington JSY* 30.00
93 *Josh McCown JSY* 12.00
94 *Patrick Ramsey JSY* 15.00
95 *Jeremy Shockey JSY* 25.00
96 *Marquise Walker JSY* 6.00
97 *Donald Reche Caldwell JSY* 8.00
98 *Rohan Davey JSY* 8.00
99 *Jabar Gaffney JSY* 12.00
100 *Quentin Jammer JSY* 8.00
101 *Maurice Morris JSY* 10.00
102 *Antwann Randle El JSY* 20.00
103 *Donte Stallworth JSY* 20.00
104 *Roy Williams JSY* 20.00
105 *Ladell Betts JSY* 10.00
106 *Tim Carter JSY* 6.00
107 *T.J. Duckett JSY* 15.00
108 *William Green JSY* 15.00
109 *Ashley Lelie JSY* 20.00
110 *Clinton Portis JSY* 40.00
111 *Cliff Russell JSY* 6.00
112 *Javon Walker JSY* 20.00

2002 Fleer Hot Prospects Class Of

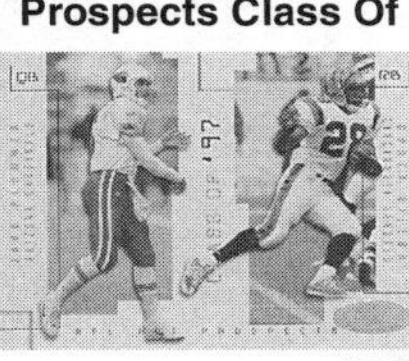

NM/M
Common Player: 3.00
Production 750 Sets
Jersey Cards: 1.5X-3X
Production 375 Sets
1CO Tim Couch, Donovan McNabb 3.00
2CO Torry Holt, David Boston 3.00
3CO Fred Taylor, Ahman Green 3.00
4CO Jake Plummer, Corey Dillon 3.00
5CO Keyshawn Johnson, Marvin Harrison 3.00
6CO Warren Sapp, Curtis Martin 3.00
7CO Aaron Brooks, Daunte Culpepper 4.00
8CO Marshall Faulk, Isaac Bruce 5.00
9CO Brian Griese, Peyton Manning 6.00
10CO Stephen Davis, Eddie George 3.00
11CO Edgerrin James, Ricky Williams 6.00
12CO Randy Moss, Hines Ward 6.00
13CO Michael Strahan, Jerome Bettis 3.00
14CO Terrell Owens, Mike Alstott 3.00
15CO Brett Favre, Ricky Watters 10.00
16CO Ron Dayne, Shaun Alexander 5.00
17CO Peter Warrick, Thomas Jones 3.00
18CO Tom Brady, Chad Pennington 8.00
19CO Michael Vick, Drew Brees 5.00
20CO LaDainian Tomlinson, Anthony Thomas 8.00

2002 Fleer Hot Prospects Hat Trick

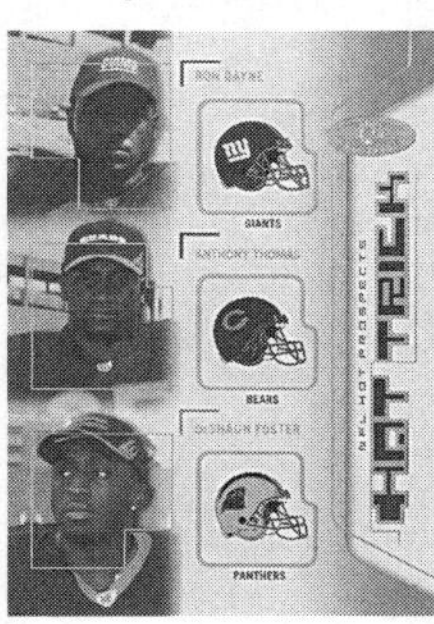

NM/M
Common Player: 2.00
Inserted 1:7
Jersey Cards: 5X-10X
Production 150 Sets
1HT Chad Pennington, Michael Vick, David Carr 8.00
2HT Chris Redman, Drew Brees, Joey Harrington 3.00
3HT Jamal Lewis, LaDainian Tomlinson, William Green 3.00
4HT Brian Urlacher, Dan Morgan, Julius Peppers 3.00
5HT Peter Warrick, Rod Gardner, Ashley Lelie 3.00
6HT Plaxico Burress, Freddie Mitchell, Donte Stallworth 4.00
7HT Shaun Alexander, Deuce McAllister, T.J. Duckett 5.00
8HT Bubba Franks, Todd Heap, Jeremy Shockey 4.00
9HT Travis Taylor, Koren Robinson, Jabar Gaffney 3.00
10HT Ron Dayne, Anthony Thomas, DeShaun Foster 7.00

2002 Fleer Hot Prospects Hot Materials

NM/M
Common Player: 15.00
Inserted 1:6
Red Hot Materials 1X-2X
Production 50 sets
1HM Donovan McNabb 15.00
2HM Daunte Culpepper 25.00
3HM Tom Brady 60.00
4HM Ricky Williams 15.00
5HM Drew Brees 20.00
6HM Emmitt Smith 50.00
7HM Randy Moss 40.00
8HM Torry Holt 15.00
9HM Marshall Faulk 25.00
10HM Kordell Stewart 15.00
11HM Anthony Thomas 30.00
12HM Brian Urlacher 30.00
13HM Jerry Rice 40.00
14HM Jeff Garcia 15.00
15HM Stephen Davis 15.00
16HM Eddie George 20.00
17HM Kurt Warner 40.00
18HM Terrell Owens 15.00
19HM Brett Favre 50.00
20HM Laveranues Coles 15.00
21HM Curtis Martin 15.00
22HM Tim Couch 25.00
23HM Trung Canidate 15.00
24HM Peter Warrick 20.00
25HM Aaron Brooks 15.00
26HM LaDainian Tomlinson 25.00
27HM Ahman Green 20.00
28HM Corey Dillon 15.00
29HM David Carr 75.00
30HM Joey Harrington 60.00
31HM William Green 50.00
32HM Donte Stallworth 40.00
33HM Ashley Lelie 40.00
34HM Jabar Gaffney 30.00
35HM Antonio Bryant 30.00
36HM Josh Reed 30.00
37HM Antwann Randle El 25.00
38HM Donald Reche Caldwell 20.00
39HM Javon Walker 30.00
40HM T.J. Duckett 40.00
41HM Marquise Walker 30.00
42HM Clinton Portis 40.00
43HM DeShaun Foster 40.00
44HM Patrick Ramsey 25.00

2002 Fleer Hot Prospects Hot Tandems

NM/M
Common Player: 15.00
Production 100 sets
Red Hot Production 10 Sets
1HTS Donovan McNabb, Daunte Culpepper 30.00
2HTS Kordell Stewart, Tim Couch 20.00
3HTS Ricky Williams, Anthony Thomas 30.00
4HTS Donovan McNabb, Aaron Brooks 15.00
5HTS Emmitt Smith, Marshall Faulk 25.00
6HTS Randy Moss, Terrell Owens 25.00
7HTS Torry Holt, Trung Canidate 15.00
8HTS Tom Brady, Kurt Warner 50.00
9HTS Jerry Rice, Brian Urlacher 40.00
10HTS Stephen Davis, Eddie George 15.00
11HTS Brett Favre, Curtis Martin 40.00
12HTS Jeff Garcia, LaDainian Tomlinson 30.00
13HTS Jeff Garcia, Ahman Green 25.00
14HTS Peter Warrick, Corey Dillon 20.00
15HTS David Carr, Joey Harrington 75.00
16HTS William Green, T.J. Duckett 50.00
17HTS Donte Stallworth, Marquise Walker 25.00
18HTS Ashley Lelie, Josh Reed 40.00
19HTS Antwann Randle El, Javon Walker 25.00
20HTS Jabar Gaffney, Antonio Bryant 25.00
21HTS Donald Reche Caldwell, Patrick Ramsey 20.00
22HTS Clinton Portis, DeShaun Foster 40.00
23HTS Kurt Warner, David Carr 50.00
24HTS Tom Brady, Joey Harrington 50.00
25HTS Emmitt Smith, William Green 50.00
26HTS Jerry Rice, Donte Stallworth 30.00
27HTS Terrell Owens, Brett Favre 40.00
28HTS Aaron Brooks, Ricky Williams 25.00
29HTS Daunte Culpepper, Randy Moss 40.00
30HTS Torry Holt, Marshall Faulk 25.00
31HTS Anthony Thomas, Brian Urlacher 40.00
32HTS Donovan McNabb, Tim Couch 25.00
33HTS Stephen Davis, Laveranues Coles 15.00
34HTS Tim Couch, Patrick Ramsey 15.00
35HTS DeShaun Foster, Curtis Martin 20.00
36HTS Ashley Lelie, Trung Canidate 20.00
37HTS Keyshawn Johnson, Marquise Walker 25.00
38HTS Eddie George, T.J. Duckett 20.00
39HTS LaDainian Tomlinson, Maurice Morris 20.00
40HTS Laveranues Coles, Jabar Gaffney 30.00
41HTS Ahman Green, Corey Dillon 20.00
42HTS Kordell Stewart, Antwann Randle El 30.00
43HTS Antonio Bryant, Josh Reed 30.00
44HTS Donald Reche Caldwell, Javon Walker 25.00

2002 Fleer Hot Prospects Sweet Selections

NM/M
Common Player: 3.00
Inserted 1:15
1SS David Carr 10.00
2SS Julius Peppers 5.00
3SS Joey Harrington 8.00
4SS Donte Stallworth 5.00
5SS William Green 6.00
6SS T.J. Duckett 5.00
7SS Ashley Lelie 5.00
8SS Javon Walker 4.00
9SS Patrick Ramsey 4.00
10SS Jabar Gaffney 4.00

2002 Fleer Hot Prospects Sweet Selections Autos

Production 50 sets
1SSA David Carr
2SSA Andre Davis
3SSA Daniel Graham
4SSA Ron Johnson
5SSA Julius Peppers
6SSA Josh Reed
7SSA Travis Stephens
8SSA Mike Williams
9SSA Antonio Bryant
10SSA Eric Crouch
11SSA DeShaun Foster
12SSA Joey Harrington
13SSA Josh McCown
14SSA Patrick Ramsey
15SSA Jeremy Shockey
16SSA Marquise Walker
17SSA Donald Reche Caldwell
18SSA Rohan Davey
19SSA Jabar Gaffney
20SSA Quentin Jammer
21SSA Maurice Morris
22SSA Antwann Randle El
23SSA Donte Stallworth
24SSA Roy Williams
25SSA Ladell Betts
26SSA Tim Carter
27SSA T.J. Duckett
28SSA William Green
29SSA Ashley Lelie
30SSA Clinton Portis
31SSA Cliff Russell
32SSA Javon Walker

2002 Fleer Maximum

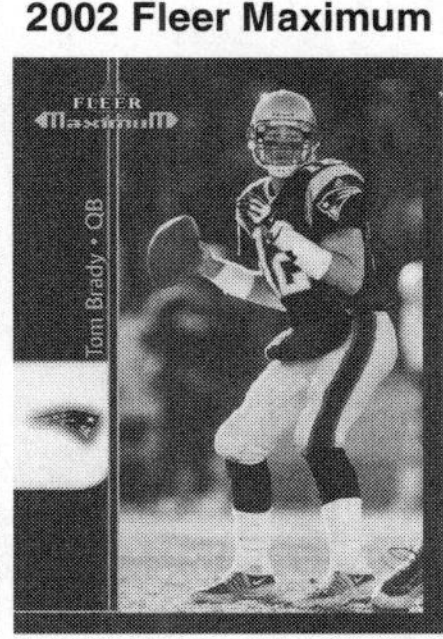

NM/M
Common Player: .20
Unlisted Stars: .60
Minor Stars: .40
Common Rookie (251-290): 1.00
Minor Rookies: 2.00
Pack (15): 2.75
Wax Box (16): 45.00
1 Tom Brady 2.00
2 Kurt Warner 2.00
3 Mike McMahon .60
4 Ronney Jenkins .20
5 Tyrone Wheatley .20
6 Germane Crowell .20
7 James Jackson .20
8 Eric Metcalf .20
9 Muhsin Muhammad .40
10 Tony Richardson .20
11 Wayne Chrebet .20
12 Daunte Culpepper 1.25
13 Trent Dilfer .40
14 Kevin Dyson .40
15 Chris Fuamatu-Ma'afala .20
16 Dominic Rhodes .20
17 David Terrell .60
18 Rod Woodson .40
19 Anthony Wright .20
20 Jerome Bettis .40
21 Kendrell Bell .40
22 Edgerrin James 1.50
23 Jamal Lewis 1.00
24 Jim Miller .50
25 Warren Sapp .40
26 Clint Stoerner .20
27 Michael Strahan .40
28 Vinny Sutherland .20
29 Mike Alstott .40
30 Jay Fiedler .40
31 Willie Jackson .20
32 Earl Little .20
33 Robert Porcher .20
34 Junior Seau .40
35 Darrick Vaughn .20
36 Wesley Walls .20
37 Michael Westbrook .40
38 Freddie Mitchell .50
39 Drew Bledsoe 1.25
40 Gus Frerotte .20
41 Travis Henry .40
42 MarTay Jenkins .20
43 Curtis Keaton .20
44 Keenan McCardell .40
45 Neil O'Donnell .20
46 Chad Pennington .40
47 Charlie Rogers .20
48 Hines Ward .40
49 Jason Gildon .20
50 Travis Taylor .20
51 Dre' Bly .20
52 Oronde Gadsden .20
53 Danny Wuerffel .20
54 Jamir Miller .20
55 Cory Schlesinger .20
56 LaDainian Tomlinson 1.50
57 Michael Vick 2.00
58 Chris Weinke .60
59 Brandon Stokley .20
60 James Allen .20
61 Correll Buckhalter .20
62 Jameel Cook .20
63 Deuce McAllister 1.00
64 Travis Minor .40
65 James Stewart .40
66 Kwamie Lassiter .20
67 Jamel White .20
68 Ronde Barber .20
69 Kevan Barlow .20
70 Marty Booker .40
71 Peter Boulware .20
72 Quincy Carter 1.25
73 Warrick Dunn .40
74 Brett Favre 2.50
75 Chad Lewis .20
76 Jeff Ogden .20
77 Todd Sauerbrun .20
78 Ricky Williams 1.25
79 Charlie Batch .20
80 Courtney Brown .20
81 Stephen Davis .50
82 Fred Smoot .20
83 Marshall Faulk 1.25
84 Doug Flutie .60
85 Rich Gannon .40
86 Dante Hall 2.00
87 Frank Sanders .20
88 Antowain Smith .40
89 Tiki Barber .40
90 Fred Beasley .20
91 Jason Brookins .20
92 Raghib Ismail .20
93 Bubba Franks .20
94 Joey Galloway .20
95 Keyshawn Johnson .40
96 Donovan McNabb 1.25
97 Lamar Smith .40
98 Corey Bradford .20
99 Kerry Collins .40
100 Autry Denson .20
101 Antonio Freeman .20
102 Fred Taylor .40
103 Troy Hambrick .20
104 Brad Johnson .40
105 Brian Mitchell .20
106 Zach Thomas .40
107 Michael Bennett .60
108 Ron Dayne .40
109 Jeff Garcia .60
110 Ahman Green .60
111 Scotty Anderson .20
112 Qadry Ismail .20
113 Ed McCaffrey .40
114 Shaun King .20
115 Duce Staley .40
116 Travis Brown .20
117 Mark Brunell .60
118 Chris Cole .20
119 Aaron Glenn .40
120 Darrell Jackson .20
121 Jevon Kearse .40
122 Randy Moss 2.00
123 Hank Poteat .20
124 Brian Urlacher 1.50
125 Mike Anderson .60
126 David Akers .20
127 Laveranues Coles .40
128 Eddie George .60
129 J.J. Stokes .20
130 Matt Hasselbeck .20
131 Nate Jacquet .20
132 Anthony Thomas 1.50
133 Terrence Wilkins .20
134 Tim Couch 1.00
135 Ty Detmer .20
136 Rod Gardner .50
137 Charlie Garner .20
138 Terry Glenn .40
139 Az-Zahir Hakim .40
140 Donald Hayes .20
141 Priest Holmes .60
142 Jermaine Wiggins .20
143 Aaron Brooks 1.00
144 Alge Crumpler .20
145 Benjamin Gay .20
146 Marcellus Wiley .20
147 Torry Holt .40
148 Desmond Howard .20
149 Richard Huntley .20
150 Bryan Johnson .20
151 Terry Kirby .20
152 Marvin "Snoop" Minnis .40
153 David Boston .60
154 Shawn Bryson .20
155 Scott Covington .20
156 Terrell Davis .20
157 Damon Gibson .20
158 Curtis Martin .40
159 Derrick Mason .40
160 Jacquez Green .20
161 Chad Scott .20
162 Tony Boselli .20
163 Derrick Alexander .20
164 Ian Gold .20
165 Rob Johnson .20
166 Thomas Jones .20
167 Steve Smith .20
168 Jonathan Quinn .20
169 Mack Strong .20
170 Vinny Testaverde .40
171 Frank Wycheck .20
172 Amos Zereoue .20
173 Chris Chambers .60
174 Joe Horn .20
175 Kevin Johnson .20
176 Ryan McNeil .20
177 Marcus Pollard .20

178 Jerry Rice 2.00
179 Jon Kitna .20
180 Maurice Smith .20
181 Jerome Pathon .20
182 Darrien Gordon .20
183 Champ Bailey .40
184 Drew Brees 1.50
185 Troy Brown .60
186 Brian Griese .60
187 Jamal Anderson .40
188 Eric Moulds .40
189 Darnay Scott .20
190 Jimmy Smith .20
191 Ricky Watters .40
192 Craig Yeast .20
193 Michael Bates .20
194 Trung Canidate .20
195 David Dunn .20
196 Tim Dwight .40
197 Trent Green .40
198 David Patten .20
199 Jake Plummer .40
200 Rod Smith .40
201 Alex Van Pelt .20
202 Peter Warrick .40
203 Shawn Alexander .60
204 Plaxico Burress .60
205 Byron Chamberlain .20
206 Peyton Manning 2.00
207 Marcus Robinson .40
208 Desmond Clark .20
209 Reggie Swinton .20
210 Amani Toomer .40
211 Karl Williams .20
212 Larry Centers .20
213 Corey Dillon .60
214 Jason Elam .20
215 Arnold Jackson .20
216 Stacey Mack .20
217 Steve McNair .60
218 Santana Moss .40
219 Koren Robinson .40
220 Kordell Stewart .40
221 Spergon Wynn .20
222 Todd Bouman .20
223 Marvin Harrison .40
224 Joe Jurevicius .40
225 Terry Allen .20
226 Jermaine Lewis .20
227 Terrell Owens .60
228 Shane Matthews .20
229 Emmitt Smith 2.00
230 Jeremiah Trotter .20
231 Tony Banks .20
232 Tim Brown .60
233 Isaac Bruce .40
234 Curtis Conway .20
235 Marc Edwards .20
236 Tony Gonzalez .40
237 Deltha O'Neal .20
238 Michael Pittman .20
239 Peerless Price .40
240 Takeo Spikes .20
241 Charlie Clemons .20
242 Garrison Hearst .40
243 Ike Hilliard .20
244 Leonard Johnson .20
245 Chris Redman .40
246 Ray Lewis .40
247 John Lynch .20
248 Bill Schroeder .20
249 James Thrash .20
250 Chad Johnson .20
251 *David Carr* 10.00
252 *Joey Harrington* 10.00
253 *DeShaun Foster* 3.00
254 *William Green* 4.00
255 *Travis Stephens* 2.50
256 *Javon Walker* 8.00
257 *Ashley Lelie* 6.00
258 *Adrian Peterson* 2.50
259 *Patrick Ramsey* 3.00
260 *Kurt Kittner* 2.50
261 *Josh Reed* 3.00
262 *David Garrard* 1.00
263 *Donald Reche Caldwell* 2.50
264 *Quentin Jammer* 2.50
265 *Roy Williams* 8.00
266 *Daniel Graham* 2.50
267 *Kahlil Hill* 1.00
268 *Antwaan Randle El* 4.00
269 *Josh McCown* 6.00
270 *Maurice Morris* 2.50
271 *Jeremy Shockey* 10.00
272 *Julius Peppers* 6.00
273 *Jonathan Wells* 3.00
274 *Rohan Davey* 3.00
275 *Brian Westbrook* 6.00
276 *Eric Crouch* 3.00
277 *Marquise Walker* 2.50
278 *Lamar Gordon* 2.50
279 *Jason McAddley* 1.00
280 *Jabar Gaffney* 5.00
281 *Luke Staley* 2.50
282 *Clinton Portis* 12.00
283 *Cliff Russell* 1.00
284 *Andre Davis* 3.00
285 *Ron Johnson* 1.00
286 *Ladell Betts* 1.00
287 *T.J. Duckett* 5.00
288 *Donte Stallworth* 5.00
289 *Antonio Bryant* 4.00
290 *Chad Hutchinson* 1.00

2002 Fleer Maximum To The Max

Stars: 3X-6X
Production 250 Sets
Rookies: 2X-4X
Production 100 Sets

2002 Fleer Maximum Dressed to Thrill

NM/M
Common Player: 10.00
Inserted 1:16
Jersey Number Swatches 1X-2X
Production 250 sets
1DTT Corey Dillon 10.00

NM/M
2DTT Trung Canidate 10.00
3DTT Brett Favre 50.00
4DTT Zach Thomas 25.00
5DTT Terrell Owens 20.00
6DTT LaDainian Tomlinson 30.00
7DTT Marvin Harrison 10.00
8DTT Rich Gannon 10.00
9DTT Plaxico Burress 15.00
10DTT Tim Brown 15.00
11DTT Courtney Brown 10.00
12DTT Peter Warrick 10.00
13DTT Ricky Williams 10.00
14DTT Mark Brunell 10.00
15DTT Jevon Kearse 10.00
16DTT Donovan McNabb 15.00
17DTT Warren Sapp 10.00
18DTT Eric Moulds 10.00
19DTT Jerry Rice 30.00
20DTT Marcus Robinson 10.00
21DTT Vinny Testaverde 10.00
22DTT Tony Gonzalez 12.00
23DTT Stephen Davis 12.00

2002 Fleer Maximum Dressed to Thrill Nameplates

NM/M
Common Player: 20.00
Production 100 sets
1DTTNA Corey Dillon 25.00
2DTTNA Trung Canidate 20.00
3DTTNA Brett Favre 150.00
4DTTNA Zach Thomas 40.00
5DTTNA Terrell Owens 30.00
6DTTNA LaDainian Tomlinson 75.00
7DTTNA Warren Sapp 20.00
8DTTNA Courtney Brown 20.00
9DTTNA Donovan McNabb 40.00
10DTTNA Tim Brown 40.00
11DTTNA Peter Warrick 25.00
12DTTNA Vinny Testaverde 20.00
13DTTNA Tony Gonzalez 25.00
14DTTNA Ricky Williams 30.00
15DTTNA Rich Gannon 30.00

2002 Fleer Maximum First and Ten

NM/M
Production 25 sets
Too uncommon to price at this time
1FAT Terrell Davis, Ricky Williams, Jerry Rice, Edgerrin James, Jamal Lewis, Kordell Stewart, Tim Couch, Brian Griese, Mark Brunell, Rich Gannon
2FAT Emmitt Smith, Brett Favre, Daunte Culpepper, Kurt Warner, Brian Urlacher, Donovan McNabb, Jeff Garcia, Jake Plummer, Randy Moss, Marshall Faulk

2002 Fleer Maximum K Corps

NM/M
Common Player: 1.00
Production to 2001 season yardage total
1KC Kurt Warner 4.00
2KC Peyton Manning 4.00
3KC Brett Favre 6.00
4KC Aaron Brooks 1.00
5KC Rich Gannon 1.00
6KC Trent Green 1.00
7KC Kerry Collins 1.00
8KC Jake Plummer 1.00
9KC Jeff Garcia 1.00
10KC Doug Flutie 1.00
11KC Brad Johnson 1.00
12KC Steve McNair 1.00
13KC Mark Brunell 1.00
14KC Jay Fiedler 1.00
15KC Donovan McNabb 2.00
16KC Jon Kitna 1.00
17KC Kordell Stewart 1.00
18KC Tim Couch 2.00
19KC David Boston 1.00
20KC Priest Holmes 1.00
21KC Marvin Harrison 1.00
22KC Curtis Martin 1.00
23KC Stephen Davis 1.00
24KC Terrell Owens 1.00
25KC Ahman Green 1.00
26KC Marshall Faulk 2.00
27KC Jimmy Smith 1.00
28KC Torry Holt 1.00
29KC Rod Smith 2.00
30KC Shaun Alexander 2.00
31KC Corey Dillon 1.00
32KC Keyshawn Johnson 1.00
33KC Joe Horn 1.00
34KC Ricky Williams 1.00
35KC LaDainian Tomlinson 3.00
36KC Randy Moss 4.00
37KC Garrison Hearst 1.00
38KC Troy Brown 1.00
39KC Anthony Thomas 4.00
40KC Tim Brown 2.00
41KC Antowain Smith 1.00
42KC Johnnie Morton 1.00
43KC Jerry Rice 3.00
44KC Derrick Mason 1.00
45KC Curtis Conway 1.00
46KC Keenan McCardell 1.00
47KC Isaac Bruce 1.00
48KC Dominic Rhodes 1.00
49KC Kevin Johnson 1.00
50KC Darrell Jackson 1.00
51KC Jerome Bettis 1.00
52KC Marty Booker 1.00
53KC Qadry Ismail 1.00
54KC Amani Toomer 1.00
55KC Willie Jackson 1.00
56KC Emmitt Smith 3.00
57KC Plaxico Burress 2.00
58KC Hines Ward 1.00

2002 Fleer Maximum Playbook X's & O's

NM/M
Common Player: 1.00
Inserted 1:6
1XO Tom Brady 6.00
2XO Tiki Barber 1.00
3XO Brian Griese 1.00
4XO Jake Plummer 1.00
5XO Chris Chambers 4.00
6XO Terrell Davis 2.00
7XO Daunte Culpepper 3.00
8XO Ron Dayne 1.00
9XO Cris Carter 1.00
10XO Jamal Lewis 1.00
11XO Duce Staley 1.00
12XO Brian Urlacher 4.00
13XO Edgerrin James 4.00
14XO Michael Vick 6.00
15XO Drew Brees 3.00
16XO Jerry Rice 4.00
17XO Marshall Faulk 3.00
18XO Brett Favre 8.00
19XO Jerome Bettis 1.00
20XO Kurt Warner 6.00

2002 Fleer Maximum Playbook X's & O's Jerseys

O's Jerseys: 1.5X-3X
O's Production 50 Sets

2002 Fleer Maximum Post Pattern

NM/M
Common Player: 10.00
Inserted 1:40
1PPN Edgerrin James 20.00
2PPN Marvin Harrison 10.00
3PPN Curtis Martin 10.00
4PPN Mark Brunell 10.00
5PPN Fred Taylor 10.00
6PPN Tim Brown 20.00
7PPN Randy Moss 25.00
8PPN Daunte Culpepper 20.00
9PPN Emmitt Smith 50.00
10PPN Steve McNair 12.00

2002 Fleer Platinum

NM/M
Common Player: .20
Unlisted Star: .60
Minor Star: .40
Common Rookie (231-290): 1.00
Minor Rookies: 1.50
Cards 291-300 Wax only #'d to 500
Cards 301-310 Jumbo only #'d to 350
Cards 311-320 Rack only #'d to 250
Pack (10): 5.00
Wax Box: 95.00
1 Donovan McNabb 1.25
2 Tom Brady 2.00
3 Kurt Warner 2.00
4 Jerry Porter .20
5 LaDainian Tomlinson 1.50
6 Rod Gardner .50
7 Dorsey Levens .20
8 Drew Bledsoe 1.25
9 David Terrell .50
10 Ahman Green .60
11 D'Wayne Bates .20
12 Wayne Chrebet .20
13 Doug Flutie .60
14 Steve McNair .60
15 Nate Clements .20
16 Gerard Warren .20
17 James Allen .20
18 David Patten .20
19 Jerry Rice 2.00
20 Garrison Hearst .60
21 Samari Rolle .20
22 Jay Riemersma .20
23 Quincy Carter 1.00
24 Lamar Smith .20
25 Jacquez Green .40
26 John Abraham .20
27 Kevin Dyson .40
28 James Thrash .20
29 Todd Heap .20
30 Gus Frerotte .20
31 Terry Glenn .40
32 Mark Brunell .60
33 Randy Moss 2.00
34 John Lynch .20
35 Curtis Conway .40
36 Bill Romanowski .20
37 Thomas Jones .20
38 Dez White .20
39 Greg Ellis .20
40 Trent Green .40
41 Deuce McAllister 1.00
42 Hines Ward .40
43 Isaac Bruce .40
44 Edgerrin James 1.50
45 Chad Lewis .20
46 Ray Lewis .40
47 Corey Dillon .60
48 Brett Favre 2.50
49 Daunte Culpepper 1.25
50 Vinny Testaverde .40
51 Warren Sapp .40
52 Corey Simon .40
53 Chris McAllister 1.00
54 Peter Warrick .40
55 Luther Elliss .20
56 Sam Madison .20
57 Will Allen .20
58 Michael Pittman .20
59 Jamal Lewis 1.00
60 Takeo Spikes .20
61 Robert Porcher .20
62 Peyton Manning 2.00
63 Robert Edwards .20
64 Rob Johnson .20
65 Willie Jackson .20
66 Dan Morgan .20
67 Ian Gold .20
68 Donald Driver .20
69 Fred Taylor .60
70 Dante Hall 2.00
71 Jerome Pathon .20
72 Amos Zereoue .20
73 Darrell Jackson .20
74 Chris Redman .40
75 Chad Johnson .40
76 Az-Zahir Hakim .40
77 Jermaine Lewis .20
78 Zach Thomas .40
79 Michael Strahan .40
80 Junior Seau .60
81 Brad Johnson .60
82 Keith Brooking .20
83 Shawn Springs .20
84 Tim Couch 1.00
85 Bill Schroeder .20
86 Jamie Sharper .20
87 Ricky Williams 1.25
88 Ron Dayne .40
89 Brian Finneran .20
90 Kevin Johnson .40
91 Scotty Anderson .20
92 Chris Chambers .60
93 Amani Toomer .60
94 Jeff Garcia .60
95 Chad Brown .20
96 Rodney Peete .20
97 Dennis Northcutt .20
98 Jamel White .20
99 Patrick Johnson .20
100 Ty Law .20
101 Charles Woodson .60
102 Stephen Davis .40
103 Charlie Garner .40
104 Courtney Brown .40
105 Aaron Glenn .20
106 Antowain Smith .40
107 Tim Brown .60
108 Shane Matthews .20
109 Warrick Dunn .40
110 Wesley Walls .40
111 Jason Elam .20
112 Jay Fiedler .40
113 Kerry Collins .40
114 Jerome Bettis .60
115 Koren Robinson .40
116 Patrick Kerney .20
117 Muhsin Muhammad .40
118 Mike McMahon .40
119 Qadry Ismail .20
120 Oronde Gadsden .20
121 Tiki Barber .40
122 Kordell Stewart .60
123 Shaun Alexander .60
124 Jake Plummer .40
125 Marty Booker .40
126 La'Roi Glover .20
127 Marvin Harrison .60
128 Bobby Shaw .20
129 Kevin Faulk .20
130 Drew Brees 1.50
131 Marshall Faulk 1.25
132 MarTay Jenkins .20
133 Anthony Thomas 1.00
134 Brian Griese .60
135 Johnnie Morton .40
136 Aaron Brooks 1.00
137 Ernie Conwell .20
138 Rod Smith .40
139 Antonio Freeman .20
140 Travis Taylor .40
141 Jon Kitna .20
142 Robert Ferguson .20
143 Derrick Alexander .20
144 Laveranues Coles .40
145 Keyshawn Johnson .60
146 Freddie Jones .20
147 Jim Miller .20
148 Mike Anderson .60
149 Marcus Pollard .20
150 Priest Holmes 1.00
151 Joe Horn .40
152 Plaxico Burress .60
153 Shannon Sharpe .40
154 Michael Vick 2.00
155 Steve Smith .20
156 Ed McCaffrey .40
157 Eddie Kennison .20
158 Darren Howard .20
159 Trent Dilfer .40
160 Peerless Price .40
161 Quincy Morgan .40
162 Corey Bradford .20
163 Jimmy Smith .40
164 Troy Brown .40
165 Rich Gannon .60
166 Kevan Barlow .40
167 Jevon Kearse .40
168 David Boston .60
169 Marcel Shipp .20
170 Joey Galloway .40
171 Kyle Brady .20
172 Donald Hayes .20
173 Chad Scott .20
174 Torry Holt .60
175 Champ Bailey .20
176 Travis Henry .40
177 Troy Hambrick .20
178 Hardy Nickerson .20
179 Michael Bennett .60
180 Chad Pennington 1.00
181 Eric Johnson .20
182 Derrick Mason .40
183 Kwamie Lassiter .20
184 Brian Urlacher 1.50
185 Olandis Gary .20
186 Tony Gonzalez .40
187 David Sloan .20
188 Kendrell Bell .40
189 Jamie Martin .20
190 Eric Moulds .40
191 Emmitt Smith 2.00
192 Bubba Franks .20
193 Byron Chamberlain .20
194 Santana Moss .40
195 Dana Stubblefield .20
196 Eddie George .60
197 Brian Dawkins .20
198 Stephen Alexander .20
199 Terrell Owens .60
200 Curtis Martin .60
201 Larry Izzo .20
202 Brian Simmons .20
203 Jason Fisk .20
204 Carlos Emmons .20
205 Justin McCareins .20
206 Adam Vinatieri .20
207 Cornelius Griffin .20
208 Trevor Pryce .20
209 Sam Shade .20
210 Rod Smart .50
211 Tony Richardson .20
212 Kevin Kasper .20
213 Rodney Harrison .20
214 Patrick Surtain .20
215 Fred Beasley .20
216 James Farrior .20
217 Rosevelt Colvin .50
218 Anthony McFarland .20
219 Dat Nguyen .20
220 Greg Comella .20
221 Rob Konrad .20
222 London Fletcher .20
223 Omar Stoutmire .20
224 Warrick Holdman .20
225 Bob Christian .20
226 David Akers .20
227 Tony Brackens .20
228 Deon Grant .20
229 Olin Kreutz .20
230 Gary Walker .20
231 *Lito Sheppard* 1.00
232 *Kalimba Edwards* 1.00
233 *Hayden Epstein* 4.00
234 *Napoleon Harris* 1.00
235 *Josh McCown* 4.00
236 *J.T. O'Sullivan* 1.00
237 *Omar Easy* 1.00
238 *Adrian Peterson* 1.00
239 *Jarrod Baxter* 1.00
240 *John Henderson* 1.00
241 *Jon McGraw* 2.00
242 *Terry Jones Jr.* 2.00
243 *Ron Johnson* 1.00
244 *Josh Reed* 2.00
245 *Jason McAddley* 1.00
246 *Sheldon Brown* 1.00
247 *Rocky Bernard* 4.00
248 *Nick Davis* 5.00
249 *Robert Thomas* 1.00
250 *Rohan Davey* 2.00
251 *Seth Burford* 1.00
252 *Najeh Davenport* 2.00
253 *Verron Haynes* 1.00
254 *Tellis Redmon* 1.00
255 *Vernon Fox* 2.00
256 *Willie Offord* 2.00
257 *Marquise Walker* 1.50
258 *Antonio Bryant* 4.00
259 *Andre Davis* 2.00
260 *Eddie Drummond* 1.00
261 *Marques Anderson* 2.00
262 *Charles Stackhouse* 2.00
263 *Rocky Calmus* 2.00
264 *Mike Williams* 2.00
265 *Brandon Doman* 2.00
266 *Maurice Morris* 2.00
267 *Ladell Betts* 2.00
268 *Ricky Williams* 1.00
269 *Tony Fisher* 3.00
270 *Michael Lewis* 1.00
271 *Jerramy Stevens* 1.00
272 *Donald Reche Caldwell* 2.00
273 *Antwann Randle El* 4.00
274 *Charles Grant* 1.00
275 *Lee Mays* 1.00
276 *Phillip Buchanon* 2.00
277 *Carlos Hall* 1.00
278 *Bill Cundiff* 2.00
279 *Saleem Rasheed* 1.00
280 *David Garrard* 1.00
281 *Preston Parsons* 1.00
282 *Travis Stephens* 1.00
283 *Clinton Portis* 10.00
284 *James Mungro* 3.00
285 *Tank Williams* 1.00
286 *Ed Reed* 1.00
287 *Javon Walker* 6.00
288 *Cliff Russell* 1.00
289 *Daryl Jones* 1.00
290 *Freddie Milons* 1.00
291 *Dwight Freeney* 2.00
292 *Lamar Gordon* 2.00
293 *Donte Stallworth* 6.00
294 *Craig Nall* 4.00
295 *Coy Wire* 4.00
296 *T.J. Duckett* 6.00
297 *Jeremy Shockey* 12.00
298 *Patrick Ramsey* 8.00
299 *Chester Taylor* 2.00
300 *Tim Carter* 2.00
301 *Joey Harrington* 20.00
302 *Roy Williams* 10.00
303 *Julius Peppers* 8.00
304 *William Green* 8.00
305 *Ashley Lelie* 12.00
306 *Rock Cartwright* 12.00
307 *DeShaun Foster* 6.00
308 *Marc Boerigter* 15.00
309 *Chad Hutchinson* 6.00
310 *Daniel Graham* 6.00
311 *Ryan Sims* 4.00
312 *Kurt Kittner* 6.00
313 *Jabar Gaffney* 10.00
314 *David Carr* 35.00
315 *Brian Westbrook* 10.00
316 *Randy Fasani* 4.00
317 *Randy McMichael* 12.00
318 *Ben Leber* 6.00
319 *Jonathan Wells* 8.00
320 *Deion Branch* 12.00

2002 Fleer Platinum Bad to the Bone

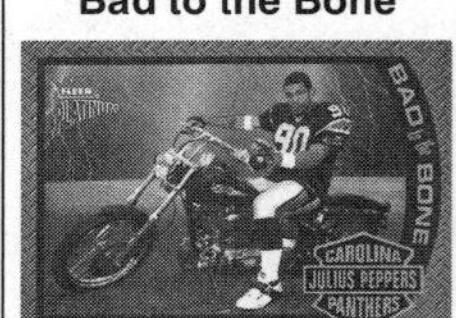

NM/M
Common Player: 2.00
Inserted 1:12
1BB Julius Peppers 4.00
2BB Josh Reed 2.00
3BB Antonio Bryant 4.00
4BB DeShaun Foster 3.00
5BB Joey Harrington 15.00
6BB Patrick Ramsey 6.00
7BB Jeremy Shockey 12.00
8BB Marquise Walker 4.00
9BB Reche Caldwell 3.00
10BB Jabar Gaffney 4.00
11BB Antwann Randle El 8.00
12BB Donte Stallworth 8.00
13BB Roy Williams 8.00
14BB Tim Carter 2.00
15BB T.J. Duckett 8.00
16BB William Green 8.00
17BB Ashley Lelie 8.00
18BB Clinton Portis 15.00
19BB Javon Walker 6.00
20BB Andre Davis 4.00

2002 Fleer Platinum Finish

NM/M
Stars: 3X-6X
Rookies/231-290: 2X-4X
Rookies/291-300: 1.5X-3X
Rookies/301-310: 1X-2X
Rookies/311-320: 1X-1.5X
Production 100 Sets

2002 Fleer Platinum Guts and Glory

NM/M
Common Player: 1.00
Inserted 1:4
1GG Zach Thomas 1.00
2GG Junior Seau 1.00
3GG Michael Strahan 1.00
4GG Mike Alstott 2.00

5GG Darren Woodson 1.00
6GG Garrison Hearst 1.00
7GG Jake Plummer 1.00
8GG Grant Wistrom 1.00
9GG Wayne Chrebet 1.00
10GG Rich Gannon 3.00
11GG Brian Griese 1.00
12GG Ed McCaffrey 1.00
13GG Jerome Bettis 1.00
14GG Ted Bruschi 1.00
15GG Keith Brooking 1.00
16GG Peter Boulware 1.00
17GG Brian Dawkins 1.00
18GG Vinny Testaverde 1.00
19GG Warren Sapp 2.00
20GG Antowain Smith 1.00

2002 Fleer Platinum Inside the Playbook

NM/M
Common Player: 2.00
Production 400 sets
1PB Jake Plummer 2.00
2PB Michael Vick 10.00
3PB Ray Lewis 2.00
4PB Drew Bledsoe 5.00
5PB Julius Peppers 5.00
6PB Brian Urlacher 5.00
7PB Corey Dillon 3.00
8PB Tim Couch 4.00
9PB Emmitt Smith 10.00
10PB Rod Smith 3.00
11PB Joey Harrington 12.00
12PB Brett Favre 12.00
13PB David Carr 12.00
14PB Peyton Manning 8.00
15PB Jimmy Smith 2.00
16PB Tony Gonzalez 2.00
17PB Ricky Williams 6.00
18PB Randy Moss 8.00
19PB Tom Brady 8.00
20PB Deuce McAllister 5.00
21PB Jeremy Shockey 10.00
22PB Curtis Martin 3.00
23PB Jerry Rice 8.00
24PB Donovan McNabb 5.00
25PB Hines Ward 2.00
26PB LaDainian Tomlinson 4.00
27PB Terrell Owens 2.00
28PB Shaun Alexander 2.00
29PB Marshall Faulk 4.00
30PB Keyshawn Johnson 2.00
31PB Steve McNair 3.00
32PB Stephen Davis 2.00

2002 Fleer Platinum Inside the Playbook Jerseys

NM/M
Common Player: 10.00
Production 250 sets
1PB Jake Plummer 10.00
2PB Michael Vick 40.00
3PB Ray Lewis 10.00
5PB Julius Peppers 15.00
6PB Brian Urlacher 25.00
7PB Corey Dillon 15.00
8PB Tim Couch 15.00
9PB Emmitt Smith 40.00
10PB Rod Smith 10.00
11PB Joey Harrington 40.00
12PB Brett Favre 40.00
14PB Peyton Manning 20.00
15PB Jimmy Smith 10.00
17PB Ricky Williams 20.00
18PB Randy Moss 20.00
22PB Curtis Martin 10.00
23PB Jerry Rice 20.00
24PB Donovan McNabb 15.00
25PB Hines Ward 15.00
26PB LaDainian Tomlinson 20.00
27PB Terrell Owens 15.00
29PB Marshall Faulk 15.00
30PB Keyshawn Johnson 10.00
31PB Steve McNair 15.00
32PB Stephen Davis 10.00

2002 Fleer Platinum Nameplates

NM/M
Common Player: 10.00
Jumbo Packs only
Production to varying quantities
1N Ahman Green/33 50.00
2N Az-Zahir Hakim/45 10.00
3N Antowain Smith/60 10.00
4N Brett Favre/33 100.00
5N Brian Griese/20 30.00
6N Bruce Smith
7N Chris Chambers/80 30.00
8N Corey Dillon/90 15.00
9N Clinton Portis/50 90.00
10N David Boston/48 15.00
11N Drew Brees
12N Daunte Culpepper/200 25.00
13N Doug Flutie/44 25.00
14N Ed McCaffrey/240 12.00
15N Eric Moulds/100 10.00
16N Emmitt Smith/150 50.00
17N Hines Ward/52 25.00
18N Isaac Bruce/95 15.00
19N Jerome Bettis/52 15.00
20N Jeff Garcia/70 15.00
21N Jevon Kearse/45 15.00
22N Johnnie Morton/90 10.00
23N Jake Plummer/125 10.00
24N Julius Peppers/54 35.00
25N Jerry Rice/35 65.00
26N Jimmy Smith/45 15.00
27N Kevin Dyson/80 12.00
28N Keyshawn Johnson
29N Kevin Johnson/75 10.00
30N Koren Robinson/60 12.00
31N Kordell Stewart/60 20.00
32N Kurt Warner/75 20.00
33N LaDainian Tomlinson/150 20.00
34N Mike Alstott/65 15.00
35N Mark Brunell/150 15.00
36N Marshall Faulk/40 25.00
37N Marvin Harrison/55 35.00
38N Plaxico Burress/130 25.00
39N Peyton Manning/55 35.00
40N Peter Warrick/70 10.00
41N Quincy Carter/95 10.00
42N Rich Gannon
43N Ray Lewis
44N Randy Moss/40 55.00
45N Rod Smith/110 12.00
46N Stephen Davis/75 10.00
47N Steve McNair/50 25.00
48N Santana Moss/20 25.00
49N Tim Brown/105 20.00
50N Tom Brady/61 20.00
51N Tim Couch/35 25.00
52N Terrell Davis/40 35.00
53N Torry Holt/60 12.00
54N Terrell Owens/45 30.00
55N Vinny Testaverde/75 12.00
56N Warren Sapp/110 15.00
57N Zach Thomas/60 15.00
58N Brian Urlacher/65 45.00

2002 Fleer Platinum Portraits

NM/M
Common Player: 2.00
Inserted 1:20
1PP Brett Favre 8.00
2PP Jerry Rice 6.00
3PP Emmitt Smith 6.00
4PP Michael Vick 6.00
5PP Marshall Faulk 3.00
6PP Peyton Manning 4.00
7PP Kurt Warner 3.00
8PP Donovan McNabb 3.00
9PP Tom Brady 4.00
10PP Ricky Williams 3.00
11PP LaDainian Tomlinson 3.00
12PP Drew Brees 3.00
13PP Daunte Culpepper 3.00
14PP Randy Moss 6.00
15PP Brian Urlacher 4.00
16PP Jeff Garcia 2.00
17PP Jerome Bettis 2.00
18PP Clinton Portis 10.00
19PP Fred Taylor 2.00
20PP Julius Peppers 3.00

2002 Fleer Platinum Portraits Memorabilia

NM/M
Common Player: 10.00
Inserted 1:66
Patch versions: 1X-2X
Production 100 Sets
1PP Brett Favre
2PP Jerry Rice 20.00
3PP Emmitt Smith 25.00
4PP Michael Vick 25.00
5PP Marshall Faulk 12.00
6PP Peyton Manning 20.00
7PP Kurt Warner 20.00
8PP Donovan McNabb 15.00
9PP Tom Brady
10PP Ricky Williams 15.00
11PP LaDainian Tomlinson 15.00
12PP Drew Brees 12.00
13PP Daunte Culpepper 15.00
14PP Randy Moss 20.00
15PP Brian Urlacher 20.00
16PP Jeff Garcia 15.00
17PP Jerome Bettis
18PP Clinton Portis 25.00
19PP Fred Taylor 10.00
20PP Julius Peppers 15.00

2002 Fleer Platinum Run with History Jerseys

NM/M
Common Player: 60.00
Duals numbered to 222
Autograph Production 20 Sets
1ES Emmitt Smith 40.00
2ES Emmitt Smith, Walter Payton 125.00
3ES Emmitt Smith, Troy Aikman Auto/20 300.00
4ES Emmitt Smith, Barry Sanders 60.00
5ES Emmitt Smith, Tony Dorsett 60.00
NNO Emmitt Smith, Deion Sanders, Troy Aikman, Tony Dorsett, Walter Payton/22

2002 Fleer Premium

NM/M
Common Player: .20
Unlisted Stars: .75
Minor Stars: .50
Common Rookie (131-170): 2.00
Minor Rookies: 3.00
Production 1250 sets
Pack (5): 3.00
Wax Box (24): 50.00
1 Kevin Dyson .50
2 Kerry Collins .50
3 Marty Booker .50
4 Curtis Conway .50
5 Drew Bledsoe 2.00
6 Kurt Warner 3.00
7 Hines Ward .50
8 Terrell Owens .75
9 Todd Pinkston .20
10 Eric Moulds .20
11 Quincy Morgan .20
12 Fred Taylor .50
13 Santana Moss .20
14 Peyton Manning 3.00
15 Qadry Ismail .20
16 Mike McMahon .75
17 David Patten .20
18 Wayne Chrebet .20
19 David Terrell .75
20 Corey Bradford .20
21 Derrick Mason .20
22 Anthony Thomas 2.50
23 James Allen .20
24 Vinny Testaverde .50
25 Trent Green .50
26 Thomas Jones .20
27 Raghib Ismail .20
28 Duce Staley .50
29 Drew Brees 2.50
30 Chris Chandler .40
31 Kordell Stewart .60
32 Koren Robinson .20
33 Jon Kitna .20
34 Jamie Sharper .20
35 Germane Crowell .20
36 Lamar Smith .20
37 LaDainian Tomlinson 2.50
38 Freddie Mitchell .50
39 Corey Dillon .75
40 Isaac Bruce .50
41 James Thrash .20
42 Brian Griese .75
43 Marvin Harrison .60
44 Aaron Brooks 1.50
45 Rich Gannon .75
46 Mike Alstott .50
47 Shannon Sharpe .50
48 Travis Henry .50
49 Keyshawn Johnson .50
50 Daunte Culpepper 2.00
51 James Jackson .50
52 Justin McCareins .20
53 Quincy Carter 2.00
54 Stephen Davis .50
55 Joey Galloway .50
56 Joe Horn .20
57 Plaxico Burress .75
58 Brett Favre 4.00
59 Brian Urlacher 2.50
60 David Boston .75
61 Darrell Jackson .75
62 Trung Canidate .20
63 Shaun Alexander .75
64 Steve McNair .75
65 Doug Flutie .75
66 LaMont Jordan .20
67 Rod Smith .50
68 Marshall Faulk 2.00
69 Tiki Barber .40
70 James Stewart .20
71 Frank Wycheck .20
72 Peerless Price .50
73 Derrick Alexander .20
74 Charlie Garner .50
75 Peter Warrick .50
76 Warren Sapp .40
77 Kevan Barlow .20
78 Edgerrin James 2.50
79 Willie Jackson .20
80 Keenan McCardell .20
81 Bill Schroeder .20
82 Curtis Martin .60
83 Torry Holt .50
84 Tony Gonzalez .40
85 Jeff Garcia .75
86 Travis Taylor .50
87 Johnnie Morton .20
88 Tim Couch 1.50
89 Troy Brown .75
90 Emmitt Smith 3.00
91 Aeneas Williams .20
92 Rod Gardner .50
93 Brandon Stokley .20
94 Warrick Dunn .40
95 Jay Riemersma .20
96 Kevin Johnson .20
97 Antowain Smith .40
98 James McKnight .20
99 Amani Toomer .40
100 Ricky Williams 2.00
101 Priest Holmes .75
102 Muhsin Muhammad .40
103 Jake Plummer .40
104 Marcus Robinson .40
105 Donovan McNabb 2.00
106 Tom Brady 3.00
107 Jimmy Smith .20
108 Jamal Lewis 1.50
109 Antonio Freeman .20
110 Ron Dayne .40
111 Tim Brown .75
112 Chris Chambers .75
113 Garrison Hearst .40
114 Michael Vick 3.00
115 Marvin "Snoop" Minnis .40
116 Terrell Davis 1.50
117 Ahman Green .75
118 Donald Hayes .20
119 Jermaine Lewis .20
120 Chad Johnson .20
121 Jay Fiedler .50
122 Randy Moss 3.00
123 Wesley Walls .20
124 Eddie George .75
125 Jerry Rice 3.00
126 Michael Bennett .75
127 Jerome Bettis .50
128 Mark Brunell .75
129 Adam Vinatieri .50
130 Ed McCaffrey .40
131 *Maurice Morris* 5.00
132 *Ron Johnson* 2.00
133 *Antwann Randle El* 10.00
134 *Brian Westbrook* 6.00
135 *Julius Peppers* 10.00
136 *Travis Stephens* 5.00
137 *David Carr* 25.00
138 *Clinton Portis* 25.00
139 *Donald Reche Caldwell* 5.00
140 *Tim Carter* 2.00
141 *Daniel Graham* 5.00
142 *Rohan Davey* 8.00
143 *T.J. Duckett* 10.00
144 *Luke Staley* 5.00
145 *Ashley Lelie* 10.00
146 *Josh Reed* 8.00
147 *Randy Fasani* 4.00
148 *Andre Davis* 5.00
149 *Joey Harrington* 20.00
150 *David Garrard* 3.00
151 *Ladell Betts* 5.00
152 *Donte Stallworth* 10.00
153 *Adrian Peterson* 5.00
154 *Lamar Gordon* 3.00
155 *Jonathan Wells* 5.00
156 *Jabar Gaffney* 8.00
157 *Patrick Ramsey* 8.00
158 *Roy Williams* 10.00
159 *Jeremy Shockey* 15.00
160 *Javon Walker* 10.00
161 *Marquise Walker* 5.00
162 *Antonio Bryant* 8.00
163 *Josh McCown* 6.00
164 *Najeh Davenport* 4.00
165 *William Green* 10.00
166 *Jerramy Stevens* 2.00
167 *DeShaun Foster* 8.00
168 *Cliff Russell* 3.00
169 *Kurt Kittner* 5.00
170 *Eric Crouch* 8.00
171 Michael Pittman .40
172 Darnay Scott .40
173 Charles Woodson .60
174 Ty Law .20
175 Tony Boselli .20
176 Zach Thomas .40
177 Trent Dilfer .20
178 Bubba Franks .20
179 Laveranues Coles .20
180 John Lynch .20
181 Kendrell Bell .20
182 Mike Anderson 1.00
183 Amos Zereoue .20
184 Michael Strahan .40
185 Chad Lewis .20
186 Travis Minor .20
187 Jevon Kearse .40
188 Darren Sharper .20
189 Az-Zahir Hakim .20
190 Ray Lewis .60
191 Deuce McAllister 1.00
192 Chris Weinke .40
193 Desmond Howard .20
194 Dominic Rhodes .40
195 Joe Jurevicius .20
196 Tim Dwight .60
197 Jeff Zgonina .20
198 Junior Seau .40
199 Rosevelt Colvin .20
200 Chad Pennington .75

2002 Fleer Premium Star Ruby

Stars: 2X-4X
Rookies: 1.5X-3X
Production 100 Sets

2002 Fleer Premium All-Rookie Team

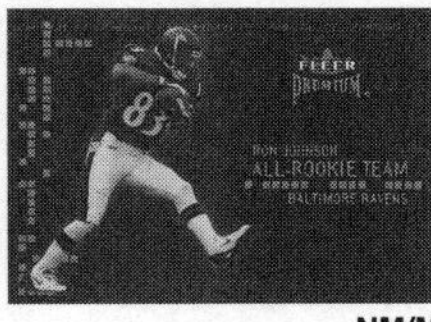

NM/M
Common Player: 2.00
Inserted 1:6
1ART David Carr 10.00
2ART William Green 4.00
3ART Ashley Lelie 4.00
4ART Clinton Portis 8.00
5ART Donald Reche Caldwell 2.00
6ART Donte Stallworth 4.00
7ART DeShaun Foster 4.00
8ART T.J. Duckett 4.00
9ART Antwann Randle El 5.00
10ART Julius Peppers 4.00
11ART Joey Harrington 5.00
12ART Jabar Gaffney 2.00
13ART Antonio Bryant 2.00
14ART Ladell Betts 2.00
15ART Ron Johnson 2.00

2002 Fleer Premium All-Rookie Team Jerseys

NM/M
Common Player: 12.00
Production 50 sets
1ART David Carr
2ART William Green 20.00
3ART Ashley Lelie 25.00
4ART Clinton Portis
5ART Donald Reche Caldwell
6ART Donte Stallworth 25.00
7ART DeShaun Foster 12.00
8ART T.J. Duckett 25.00
9ART Antwann Randle El
10ART Julius Peppers 15.00
11ART Joey Harrington 30.00
12ART Jabar Gaffney 15.00
13ART Antonio Bryant
14ART Ladell Betts
15ART Ron Johnson

2002 Fleer Premium All-Pro Team

NM/M
Common Player: 1.00
Production 1000 sets
1APT David Boston 1.00
2APT Jerome Bettis 1.00
3APT Brett Favre 4.00
4APT Brian Urlacher 2.00
5APT Marshall Faulk 2.00
6APT Rich Gannon 1.00
7APT Emmitt Smith 3.00
8APT Corey Dillon 1.00
9APT Jerry Rice 2.00
10APT Donovan McNabb 1.00
11APT Curtis Martin 1.00
12APT Isaac Bruce 1.00
13APT Junior Seau 1.00
14APT Jeff Garcia 1.00
15APT Mike Alstott 1.00
16APT Ray Lewis 1.00
17APT Daunte Culpepper 1.00
18APT Tony Gonzalez 1.00
19APT Terrell Owens 1.00
20APT Peyton Manning 2.00
21APT Randy Moss 3.00
22APT Kurt Warner 2.00
23APT Jimmy Smith 1.00
24APT Edgerrin James 1.00
25APT Tom Brady 4.00

2002 Fleer Premium All-Pro Team Jerseys

NM/M
Common Player: 5.00
Inserted 1:24
David Boston 5.00
Brett Favre 20.00
Brian Urlacher 20.00
Emmitt Smith 20.00
Corey Dillon 5.00
Jerry Rice 20.00
Curtis Martin 8.00
Junior Seau 10.00
Jeff Garcia 5.00
Ray Lewis 5.00
Daunte Culpepper 12.00
Terrell Owens 12.00
Randy Moss 15.00
Kurt Warner 15.00
Jimmy Smith 5.00
Tom Brady 20.00

2002 Fleer Premium All-Pro Team Patches

NM/M
Common Player: 5.00
Production 100 sets
David Boston 6.00
Jerome Bettis 8.00
Brett Favre 45.00
Brian Urlacher 45.00
Marshall Faulk 15.00
Rich Gannon 10.00
Emmitt Smith 45.00
Corey Dillon 8.00
Jerry Rice 40.00
Donovan McNabb 20.00
Curtis Martin 12.00
Isaac Bruce 12.00
Junior Seau 15.00
Jeff Garcia 12.00
Mike Alstott 10.00
Ray Lewis 10.00
Daunte Culpepper 20.00
Tony Gonzalez 10.00
Terrell Owens 12.00
Peyton Manning 35.00
Randy Moss 35.00
Kurt Warner 35.00
Jimmy Smith 12.00
Edgerrin James 20.00
Tom Brady 45.00

2002 Fleer Premium Fantasy Team

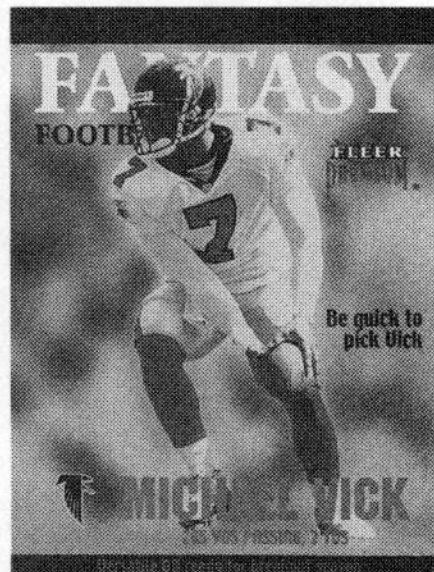

NM/M
Common Player: 2.00
Production 1200 sets
1FT Kurt Warner 3.00
2FT Peyton Manning 3.00
3FT Brett Favre 6.00
4FT Michael Vick 3.00
5FT Tom Brady 4.00
6FT Edgerrin James 3.00
7FT Marshall Faulk 2.00
8FT Ricky Williams 4.00
9FT Emmitt Smith 3.00
10FT Anthony Thomas 2.00
11FT Randy Moss 4.00
12FT Jerry Rice 3.00
13FT Marvin Harrison 2.00
14FT Chris Chambers 2.00
15FT Torry Holt 2.00
16FT David Carr 6.00
17FT Joey Harrington 4.00
18FT William Green 3.00
19FT Donte Stallworth 3.00
20FT Ashley Lelie 3.00

2002 Fleer Premium Fantasy Team Jerseys

NM/M
Inserted 1:35
Multi-patch versions: 2X-4X
Production 75 sets
Kurt Warner 15.00
Brett Favre 20.00
Michael Vick
Tom Brady 15.00
Edgerrin James 12.00
Marshall Faulk
Ricky Williams 10.00
Emmitt Smith
Anthony Thomas
Randy Moss 12.00
Jerry Rice 12.00
Marvin Harrison 5.00
Chris Chambers
Torry Holt 5.00
Joey Harrington 20.00
William Green 8.00
Ashley Lelie

2002 Fleer Premium Prem Team

NM/M
Common Player: 2.00
Inserted 1:12
Ruby versions: 1X-1.5X
Production 500 sets
1 Jeff Garcia 2.00
2 Garrison Hearst 2.00
3 Emmitt Smith 4.00
4 Brett Favre 5.00
5 Ahman Green 2.00
6 Plaxico Burress 2.00
7 Jerome Bettis 2.00
8 Kordell Stewart 2.00
9 Kendrell Bell 2.00
10 Randall Cunningham 2.00
11 Donovan McNabb 2.00
12 Duce Staley 2.00
13 Chad Lewis 2.00
14 Ricky Williams 2.00

15 Zach Thomas 2.00
16 Rich Gannon 2.00
17 Jerry Rice 3.00
18 Tim Brown 2.00
19 Brian Urlacher 3.00
20 Marcus Robinson 2.00
21 Anthony Thomas 2.00
22 Kurt Warner 3.00
23 Marshall Faulk 2.00
24 Isaac Bruce 2.00
25 Brian Griese 2.00
26 Terrell Davis 2.00
27 Ed McCaffrey 2.00

2002 Fleer Premium Prem Team Jerseys

NM/M

Inserted 1:13
Jeff Garcia 8.00
Emmitt Smith 25.00
Donovan McNabb 12.00
Duce Staley 8.00
Ricky Williams 12.00
Rich Gannon 8.00
Jerry Rice 20.00
Tim Brown 10.00
Brian Urlacher 20.00
Anthony Thomas 12.00
Kurt Warner 12.00
Brian Griese 12.00
Terrell Davis 8.00
Jerome Bettis 8.00

2002 Fleer Premium Prem Team Patch

NM/M

Common Player: 15.00
Production 100 sets
Jeff Garcia 15.00
Garrison Hearst
Emmitt Smith 50.00
Brett Favre 60.00
Ahman Green
Plaxico Burress
Jerome Bettis 15.00
Kordell Stewart 15.00
Kendrell Bell
Randall Cunningham
Donovan McNabb 30.00
Duce Staley 15.00
Chad Lewis
Ricky Williams 30.00
Zach Thomas
Rich Gannon 15.00
Jerry Rice 40.00
Tim Brown 20.00
Brian Urlacher 30.00
Marcus Robinson
Anthony Thomas 15.00
Kurt Warner 15.00
Marshall Faulk
Isaac Bruce
Brian Griese 15.00
Terrell Davis
Ed McCaffrey

2002 Fleer Showcase

NM/M

Common Player: .25
Unlisted Stars: .75
Minor Stars: .50
Common Avant (126-135): 2.00
136-141 Production 500 sets
Common Rookie (142-166): 5.00
Production 1500 sets
Pack (5): 3.25
Wax Box (24): 55.00
1 Kevin Johnson .25
2 Chris Walsh .25
3 Vinny Testaverde .50
4 Kordell Stewart .50
5 Chris Redman .50
6 Johnnie Morton .50
7 Tony Gonzalez .40
8 Torry Holt .40
9 Champ Bailey .25
10 Eric Moulds .25
11 Az-Zahir Hakim .40
12 Mark Brunell .75
13 Laveranues Coles .40
14 Kevan Barlow .40
15 Stephen Davis .50
16 Benjamin Gay .25
17 Randy Moss 3.00
18 Hines Ward .50
19 Brian Urlacher 2.50
20 Dominic Rhodes .25
21 David Patten .25
22 Tim Brown .75
23 Trent Dilfer .50
24 David Boston .75
25 Quincy Carter 2.00
26 Daunte Culpepper 2.00
27 Plaxico Burress .75
28 Michael Pittman .25
29 Joey Galloway .50
30 Jason Taylor .25
31 Drew Brees 2.50
32 Jamal Anderson .50
33 Dat Nguyen .25
34 Chris Chambers .75
35 Tiki Barber .50
36 LaDainian Tomlinson 2.50
37 Peter Warrick .50
38 Bubba Franks .25
39 Joey Horn .40
40 Correll Buckhalter .25
41 Mike Alstott .50
42 Brian Finneran .25
43 Troy Hambrick .25
44 Zach Thomas .40
45 Kerry Collins .40
46 Junior Seau .50
47 Alvis Whitted .25
48 Terrell Davis 1.50
49 Ricky Williams 2.00
50 Curtis Conway .40
51 Travis Taylor .40
52 Brian Griese .75
53 Sylvester Morris .25
54 Amani Toomer .40
55 Jeff Garcia .75
56 Michael McCrary .25
57 Ahman Green .75
58 Trent Green .50
59 Trung Canidate .25
60 Jamal Lewis 1.50
61 Larry Foster .25
62 Priest Holmes .75
63 Isaac Bruce .50
64 Bruce Smith .25
65 Darnay Scott .25
66 Terry Glenn .50
67 Darren Howard .25
68 Hugh Douglas .25
69 Milton Wynn .25
70 Tim Couch 1.50
71 Bill Schroeder .25
72 Michael Strahan .50
73 James Thrash .25
74 Steve McNair .75
75 Patrick Jeffers .25
76 Marcus Pollard .25
77 Willie McGinest .25
78 Santana Moss .50
79 Grant Wistrom .25
80 Jim Miller .25
81 Marvin Harrison .50
82 Troy Brown .25
83 Rich Gannon .50
84 Shaun Alexander .75
85 Jake Plummer .25
86 Quincy Morgan .50
87 Michael Bennett .75
88 Jerome Bettis .50
89 Marty Booker .25
90 Trevor Insley .25
91 Adam Vinatieri .40
92 Charles Woodon .25
93 Darrell Jackson .25
94 Corey Dillon .25
95 Corey Bradford .25
96 Deuce McAllister 1.50
97 Todd Pinkston .25
98 Warren Sapp .40
99 Alex Van Pelt .25
100 Mike McMahon .75
101 Fred Taylor .25
102 Ron Dayne .40
103 Ernie Conwell .25
104 Rod Gardner .75
105 Muhsin Muhammad .40
106 Reggie Wayne .25
107 Antowain Smith .25
108 Chad Pennington .50
109 Koren Robinson .50
110 Travis Henry .50
111 Ed McCaffrey .50
112 Keenan McCardell .25
113 Curtis Martin .50
114 Bryant Young .25
115 Derrick Mason .25
116 Anthony Thomas 2.50
117 Jermaine Lewis .25
118 Aaron Brooks 1.50
119 Charlie Garner .50
120 Keyshawn Johnson .40
121 Chris Weinke .75
122 Rod Smith .50
123 Jimmy Smith .50
124 Terrell Owens .75
125 Eddie George .75
126 Tom Brady Avant 3.00
127 Donovan McNabb Avant 2.00
128 Kurt Warner Avant 3.00
129 Peyton Manning Avant 3.00
130 Marshall Faulk Avant 2.00
131 Michael Vick Avant 3.00
132 Emmitt Smith Avant 3.00
133 Jerry Rice Avant 3.00
134 Edgerrin James Avant 2.50
135 Brett Favre Avant 4.00
136 *David Carr Avant* 50.00
137 *Joey Harrington Avant* 40.00
138 *Ashley Lelie Avant* 25.00
139 *William Green Avant* 20.00
140 *T.J. Duckett Avant* 20.00
141 *Donte Stallworth Avant* 25.00
142 *Ron Johnson* 5.00
143 *Jeremy Shockey* 25.00
144 *Daniel Graham* 6.00
145 *Donald Reche Caldwell* 6.00
146 *Antonio Bryant* 10.00
147 *DeShaun Foster* 8.00
148 *Clinton Portis* 40.00
149 *Patrick Ramsey* 12.00
150 *Lamar Gordon* 6.00
151 *Josh Reed* 10.00
152 *Ladell Betts* 6.00
153 *Kurt Kittner* 6.00
154 *Jabar Gaffney* 10.00
155 *Josh McCown* 10.00
156 *Marquise Walker* 6.00
157 *Brian Westbrook* 10.00
158 *Andre Davis* 10.00
159 *David Garrard* 4.00
160 *Cliff Russell* 5.00
161 *Julius Peppers* 12.00
162 *Adrian Peterson* 6.00
163 *Antwaan Randle El* 15.00
164 *Javon Walker* 15.00
165 *Rohan Davey* 10.00
166 *Luke Staley* 6.00

2002 Fleer Showcase Legacy

Stars: 5X-10X
Stars Avant: 2X-4X
Rookies Avant: 1.5X
Rookies: 1.5X-3X
Production 100 Sets

2002 Fleer Showcase Air to the Throne

NM/M

Common Player: 2.00
Inserted 1:8
Silver Jerseys: 2X-4X
Inserted 1:24
Gold Jerseys: 2X
Production 50 sets
1AT Mark Brunell 2.00
2AT Tim Couch 3.00
3AT Daunte Culpepper 3.00
4AT Brett Favre 6.00
5AT Rich Gannon 2.00
6AT Jeff Garcia 2.00
7AT Brian Griese 2.00
8AT Kurt Warner 4.00
9AT Donovan McNabb 3.00
10AT Steve McNair 2.00
11AT Jake Plummer 2.00
12AT Kordell Stewart 2.00
14AT Jim Kelly 2.00
15AT John Elway 8.00
18AT Dan Marino 8.00
20AT Roger Staubach 4.00

2002 Fleer Showcase Top 2 Bottom

NM/M

Common Player: 10.00
Production 250 sets
1TB David Boston 10.00
2TB Eddie George 12.00
3TB Marvin Harrison 12.00
4TB Edgerrin James 20.00
5TB Jake Plummer 10.00
6TB Marcus Robinson 10.00
7TB Duce Staley 12.00
8TB Brian Urlacher 40.00
9TB Kurt Warner 50.00
10TB Troy Aikman 40.00

2002 Fleer Showcase Football's Best

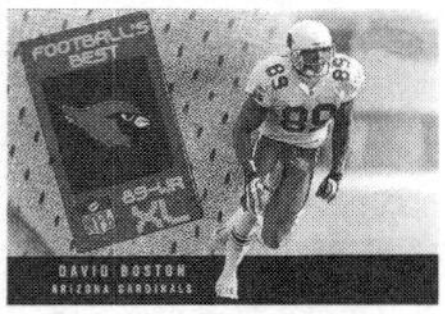

NM/M

Common Player: 2.00
Production 799 sets
Memorabilia cards: 1.5X-3X
Inserted 1:15
Silver Patches: 3X-6X
Production 100 sets
Gold Patches: 6X-12X
Production 25 sets
1FB Edgerrin James 4.00
2FB Shaun Alexander 3.00
3FB Mike Alstott 2.00
4FB Tiki Barber 2.00
5FB Jerome Bettis 2.00
6FB David Boston 3.00
7FB Tim Brown 3.00
8FB Isaac Bruce 3.00
9FB Plaxico Burress 3.00
10FB Tim Couch 4.00
11FB Wayne Chrebet 2.00
12FB Daunte Culpepper 5.00
13FB Stephen Davis 2.00
14FB Terrell Davis 2.00
15FB Ron Dayne 2.00
16FB Corey Dillon 2.00
17FB Marshall Faulk 4.00
18FB Brett Favre 8.00
19FB Rich Gannon 3.00
20FB Eddie George 4.00
21FB Randy Moss 5.00
22FB Junior Seau 3.00
23FB Jerry Rice 5.00
24FB Torry Holt 2.00
25FB Jamal Anderson 2.00
26FB Ray Lewis 2.00
27FB Antowain Smith 2.00
28FB Peter Warrick 2.00
29FB Ed McCaffrey 2.00
30FB Marvin Harrison 3.00
31FB Jimmy Smith 2.00
32FB Fred Taylor 2.00

2002 Fleer Throwbacks

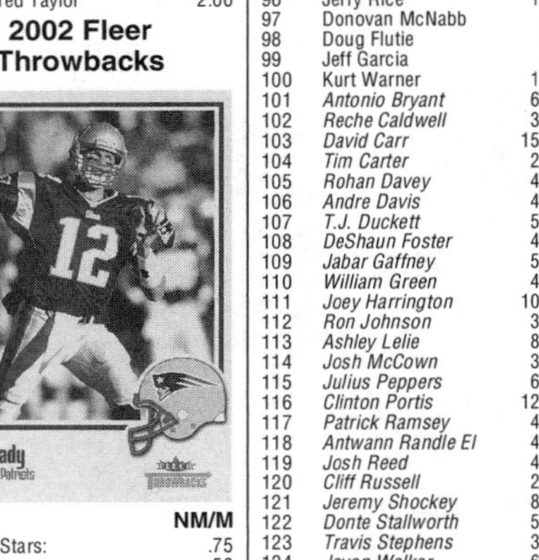

NM/M

Unlisted Stars: .75
Minor Stars: .50
Common Rookie (101-125): 2.00
Minor Rookies: 3.00
Pack (5): 8.00
Wax Box (24): 140.00
1 Terry Bradshaw 1.00
2 Franco Harris .40
3 Y.A. Tittle .25
4 Tony Dorsett .25
5 Paul Hornung 1.00
6 Rocky Bleier .25
7 Archie Griffin .25
8 Dwight Clark .25
9 Bo Jackson .75
10 Fran Tarkenton .75
11 Howie Long .75
12 Bob Griese .50
13 George Rogers .25
14 Roger Craig .25
15 Jim Plunkett .25
16 Eric Dickerson .50
17 Marcus Allen .50
18 Roger Staubach 1.00
19 Lawrence Taylor 1.00
20 Joe Greene .50
21 Earl Campbell .50
22 Dave Casper .25
23 Charles White .25
24 Fred Biletnikoff .25
25 Dan Pastorini .25
26 John Cappelletti .25
27 Paul Warfield .25
28 Ozzie Newsome .25
29 Johnny Rodgers .25
30 William Perry .50
31 Charley Taylor .25
32 Deacon Jones .25
33 Bubba Smith .25
34 James Lofton .25
35 Mike Rozier .25
36 Ray Nitschke 1.00
37 Dan Fouts .50
38 Bob Lilly .50
39 Ronnie Lott .50
40 Barry Sanders 1.00
41 Troy Aikman 1.00
42 John Elway 1.00
43 Irving Fryar .25
44 Jim Kelly .50
45 Jim McMahon .50
46 Joe Montana 1.00
47 Warren Moon .25
48 Jay Novacek .25
49 Mel Renfro .25
50 Mike Singletary .25
51 Johnny Unitas 1.00
52 Steve Young .50
53 Walter Payton 1.00
54 Dan Marino 1.00
55 Torry Holt .25
56 Rod Smith .25
57 Priest Holmes 1.00
58 Anthony Thomas 1.00
59 Curtis Martin .25
60 LaDainian Tomlinson 1.00
61 Antowain Smith .25
62 Terrell Owens .50
63 Tony Gonzalez .25
64 Steve McNair .25
65 Jerome Bettis .50
66 Rich Gannon .25
67 Jake Plummer .25
68 Jamal Lewis .50
69 Drew Brees .75
70 Jevon Kearse .25
71 Keyshawn Johnson .25
72 Kordell Stewart .50
73 Tim Brown .25
74 Vinny Testaverde .25
75 Tom Brady 2.00
76 Drew Bledsoe .50
77 Stephen Davis .25
78 Marvin Harrison .25
79 Brian Griese .25
80 Michael Vick 2.00
81 Emmitt Smith 2.00
82 Edgerrin James 1.00
83 Mark Brunell .25
84 Tim Couch .25
85 Randy Moss 2.00
86 Brian Urlacher 1.00
87 Marshall Faulk 1.00
88 Corey Dillon .25
89 Eddie George .25
90 Terrell Davis 1.00
91 Brett Favre 3.00
92 Peyton Manning 2.00
93 Fred Taylor .25
94 Daunte Culpepper .50
95 Ricky Williams .50
96 Jerry Rice 1.00
97 Donovan McNabb .50
98 Doug Flutie .50
99 Jeff Garcia .50
100 Kurt Warner 1.50
101 *Antonio Bryant* 6.00
102 *Reche Caldwell* 3.00
103 *David Carr* 15.00
104 *Tim Carter* 2.00
105 *Rohan Davey* 4.00
106 *Andre Davis* 4.00
107 *T.J. Duckett* 5.00
108 *DeShaun Foster* 4.00
109 *Jabar Gaffney* 5.00
110 *William Green* 4.00
111 *Joey Harrington* 10.00
112 *Ron Johnson* 3.00
113 *Ashley Lelie* 8.00
114 *Josh McCown* 3.00
115 *Julius Peppers* 6.00
116 *Clinton Portis* 12.00
117 *Patrick Ramsey* 4.00
118 *Antwann Randle El* 4.00
119 *Josh Reed* 4.00
120 *Cliff Russell* 2.00
121 *Jeremy Shockey* 8.00
122 *Donte Stallworth* 5.00
123 *Travis Stephens* 3.00
124 *Javon Walker* 6.00
125 *Marquise Walker* 3.00

2002 Fleer Throwbacks Classic Clippings

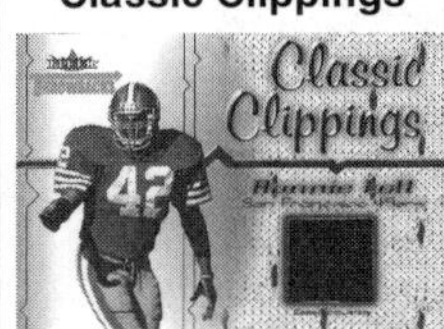

NM/M

Common Player: 8.00
Inserted 1:24
1CLIP Fred Biletnikoff 10.00
2CLIP Earl Campbell 15.00
3CLIP Dave Casper 10.00
4CLIP John Elway 25.00
5CLIP Irving Fryar 8.00
6CLIP Bob Lilly 15.00
7CLIP Ronnie Lott 10.00
8CLIP Joe Montana 45.00
9CLIP Dan Marino 40.00
10CLIP Jay Novacek 12.00
11CLIP Walter Payton 50.00
12CLIP Barry Sanders 25.00
13CLIP Steve Young 15.00

2002 Fleer Throwbacks Classic Numbers

NM/M

Production 100 sets
1CNUM Barry Sanders 50.00
2CNUM Marcus Allen 35.00
3CNUM Brett Favre 50.00
4CNUM Irving Fryar
5CNUM Steve Young 40.00
6CNUM Jim Plunkett

2002 Fleer Throwbacks Greats of the Game Autographs

NM/M

Common Player: 8.00
Inserted 1:24
1GOGA Marcus Allen 20.00
2GOGA Fred Biletnikoff 20.00
3GOGA Rocky Bleier 20.00
4GOGA Terry Bradshaw 85.00
5GOGA Earl Campbell 20.00
6GOGA John Cappelletti 15.00
7GOGA Dave Casper 15.00
8GOGA Dwight Clark 15.00
9GOGA Roger Craig 12.00
10GOGA Daunte Culpepper 25.00
11GOGA Eric Dickerson 20.00
12GOGA Joe Greene 25.00
13GOGA Bob Griese 20.00
14GOGA Archie Griffin 15.00
15GOGA Franco Harris 25.00
16GOGA Paul Hornung 35.00
17GOGA Bo Jackson 40.00
18GOGA Deacon Jones 15.00
19GOGA Ozzie Newsome 12.00
20GOGA Dan Pastorini 10.00
21GOGA William Perry 15.00
22GOGA Jim Plunkett 15.00
23GOGA George Rogers 8.00
24GOGA Johnny Rogers 8.00
25GOGA Mike Rozier 8.00
26GOGA Bubba Smith 12.00
27GOGA Roger Staubach 40.00
28GOGA Fran Tarkenton 25.00
29GOGA Charley Taylor 12.00
30GOGA Lawrence Taylor 15.00
31GOGA Y.A. Tittle 15.00
32GOGA Paul Warfield 15.00
33GOGA Charles White 12.00
34GOGA Emmitt Smith 200.00
35GOGA Johnny Unitas 140.00

2002 Fleer Throwbacks Lambeau Legends

NM/M

Common Player: 12.00
Inserted 1:48
1LL Paul Hornung 35.00
2LL Brett Favre 25.00
3LL Dorsey Levens 12.00
4LL Ray Nitschke 35.00
5LL Antonio Freeman 12.00
6LL Ahman Green 20.00

2002 Fleer Throwbacks On 2 Canton

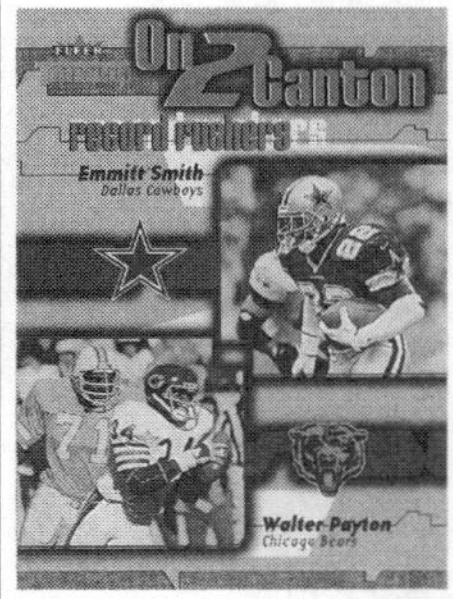

NM/M

Common Player: 2.00
Inserted 1:12
10TC Walter Payton, Emmitt Smith 5.00
20TC Brian Griese, Bob Griese 2.00
30TC Fran Tarkenton, Daunte Culpepper 2.00
40TC Randy Moss, Jerry Rice 4.00
50TC Earl Campbell, Ricky Williams 2.00

20302 Fleer Throwbacks On 2 Canton Memorabilia

NM/M

Production 50 sets
Walter Payton, Emmitt Smith 100.00
Brian Griese, Bob Griese
Fran Tarkenton, Daunte Culpepper 40.00
Randy Moss, Jerry Rice
Earl Campbell, Ricky Williams 40.00

2002 Fleer Throwbacks QB Collection

NM/M

Common Player: 2.00
Production 1500 sets
1QBC Donovan McNabb 2.00
2QBC Warren Moon 2.00
3QBC Jim Plunkett 2.00
4QBC Kurt Warner 3.00
5QBC Steve Young 3.00
6QBC Daunte Culpepper 2.00
7QBC Brett Favre 5.00
8QBC Peyton Manning 3.00
9QBC Jeff Garcia 2.00
10QBC Dan Fouts 2.00
11QBC John Elway 4.00
12QBC Jim McMahon 2.00
13QBC Jim Kelly 2.00
14QBC Troy Aikman 3.00
15QBC Y.A. Tittle 2.00
16QBC Fran Tarkenton 2.00
17QBC Bob Griese 2.00

2002 Fleer Throwbacks QB Collection Dream Backfield

NM/M

Common Player: 3.00
Inserted 1:24
1DB Brett Favre, Paul Hornung 8.00
2DB Warren Moon, Earl Campbell 5.00
3DB Kurt Warner, Eric Dickerson 5.00
4DB Dan Fouts, LaDainian Tomlinson 3.00

2002 Fleer Throwbacks QB Collection Dream Backfield JSY

	NM/M
Common Player:	12.00
Inserted 1:30	
Brett Favre, Paul Hornung	30.00
Warren Moon, Earl Campbell	15.00
Kurt Warner, Eric Dickerson	15.00
Dan Fouts, LaDainian Tomlinson	12.00

2002 Fleer Throwbacks QB Collection Dream Back JSY Dual

	NM/M
Common Player:	20.00
Inserted 1:1201	
Brett Favre, Paul Hornung	50.00
Warren Moon, Earl Campbell	25.00
Kurt Warner, Eric Dickerson	25.00
Dan Fouts, LaDainian Tomlinson	20.00

2002 Fleer Throwbacks QB Collection Memorabilia

	NM/M
Common Player:	12.00
Inserted 1:33	
Donovan McNabb	12.00
Warren Moon	12.00
Jim Plunkett	12.00
Kurt Warner	25.00
Steve Young	30.00
Daunte Culpepper	15.00
Brett Favre	25.00
Peyton Manning	
Jeff Garcia	15.00
Dan Fouts	15.00
John Elway	30.00
Jim McMahon	15.00
Jim Kelly	25.00
Troy Aikman	20.00
Y.A. Tittle	
Fran Tarkenton	
Bob Griese	

2002 Fleer Throwbacks Super Stars

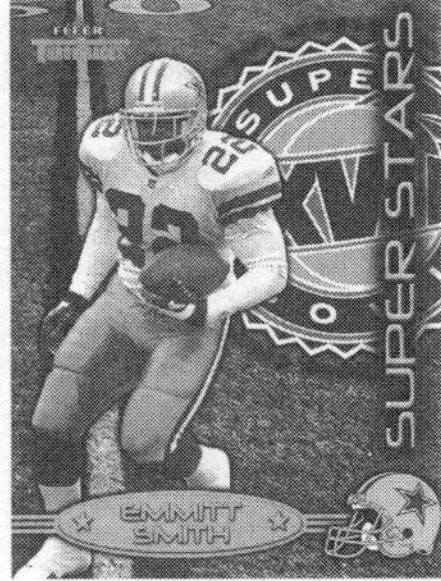

		NM/M
Common Player:		2.00
Inserted 1:6		
1STAR	Jerry Rice	3.00
2STAR	Terrell Davis	2.00
3STAR	Marcus Allen	2.00
4STAR	Jim Plunkett	2.00
5STAR	Fred Biletnikoff	2.00
6STAR	Emmitt Smith	6.00
7STAR	John Elway	4.00

2002 Fleer Throwbacks Super Stars Memorabilia

	NM/M
Common Player:	15.00
Inserted 1:48	
Jerry Rice	30.00
Terrell Davis	15.00
Marcus Allen	25.00
Jim Plunkett	20.00
Fred Biletnikoff	25.00
Emmitt Smith	40.00
John Elway	50.00

2002 Fleer

		NM/M
Complete Set (300):		100.00
Common Player:		.15
Unlisted Stars:		.60
Minor Stars:		.40
Common Rookie (261-300):		1.00
Minor Rookies:		2.00
Pack (10):		3.00
Wax Box (24):		65.00
1	Jeff Garcia	.60
2	Brian Simmons	.15
3	Kordell Stewart	.40
4	Chris Weinke	.60

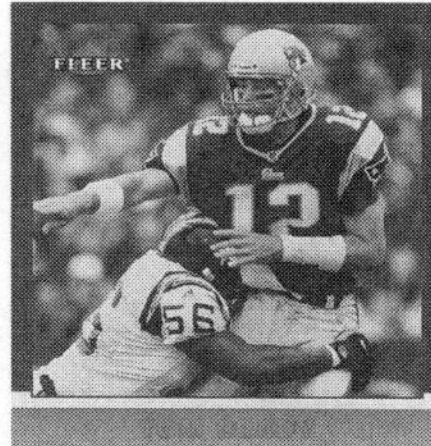

		NM/M
5	Donovan McNabb	1.25
6	Antoine Winfield	.15
7	Ray Lewis	.40
8	Drew Brees	1.50
9	Frank Sanders	.15
10	Rich Gannon	.40
11	Jamal Anderson	.15
12	Curtis Martin	.40
13	Darrell Jackson	.15
14	Micheal Barrow	.15
15	Jeff Wilkins	.15
16	Ricky Williams	1.25
17	Brad Johnson	.40
18	Tedy Bruschi	.15
19	Frank Wycheck	.15
20	Byron Chamberlain	.15
21	Terry Glenn	.40
22	James McKnight	.15
23	Thomas Jones	.15
24	Jamie Sharper	.15
25	Trent Green	.40
26	Mike Rucker	.15
27	Mark Brunell	.60
28	Takeo Spikes	.15
29	Dominic Rhodes	.15
30	Jim Miller	.40
31	Corey Bradford	.40
32	Jamir Miller	.15
33	Johnnie Morton	.40
34	Raghib Ismail	.15
35	Mike Anderson	1.00
36	James Allen	.40
37	Quincy Carter	1.25
38	Germane Crowell	.15
39	Quincy Morgan	.40
40	Kabeer Gbaja-Biamila	.40
41	Reggie Wayne	.40
42	Brian Urlacher	1.50
43	Stacey Mack	.15
44	Justin Smith	.15
45	Marvin "Snoop" Minnis	.40
46	Donald Hayes	.15
47	Jay Fiedler	.40
48	Nate Clements	.15
49	Drew Bledsoe	1.25
50	Peter Boulware	.15
51	Lawyer Malloy	.15
52	Michael Pittman	.15
53	Aaron Brooks	1.00
54	Maurice Smith	.15
55	Ike Hilliard	.40
56	Derrick Mason	.40
57	LaMont Jordan	.15
58	Charlie Garner	.40
59	Mike Alstott	.40
60	Freddie Mitchell	.40
61	Isaac Bruce	.40
62	Hines Ward	.40
63	John Randle	.15
64	Doug Flutie	.60
65	Terrell Owens	.60
66	Garrison Hearst	.40
67	Rodney Harrison	.15
68	Koren Robinson	.40
69	Amos Zereoue	.15
70	Aeneas Williams	.15
71	Hugh Douglas	.15
72	Jacquez Green	.40
73	Sebastian Janikowski	.15
74	Kevin Dyson	.40
75	Terance Mathis	.40
76	Vinny Testaverde	.40
77	Kwamie Lassiter	.15
78	Ron Dayne	.40
79	Jonathan Ogden	.15
80	Charlie Clemons	.15
81	Peter Warrick	.40
82	Adam Vinatieri	.15
83	Ted Washington	.15
84	Randy Moss	2.00
85	Rosevelt Colvin	.15
86	Oronde Gadsden	.15
87	Anthony Henry	.15
88	Priest Holmes	.60
89	Joey Galloway	.40
90	Jimmy Smith	.40
91	Bill Romanowski	.15
92	Chris Claiborne	.15
93	Marvin Harrison	.60
94	Vonnie Holliday	.15
95	Darren Sharper	.15
96	Chad Bratzke	.15
97	James Stewart	.40
98	Fred Taylor	.40
99	Jason Elam	.15
100	Keyshawn Johnson	.40
101	Dexter Coakley	.15
102	Zach Thomas	.40
103	Jamel White	.15
104	Antowain Smith	.40
105	Marty Booker	.40
106	Deuce McAllister	1.00
107	Adam Archuleta	.15
108	Rod Smith	.40
109	Tony Boselli	.15
110	Joe Johnson	.15
111	Simeon Rice	.15
112	Cory Schlesinger	.15
113	La'Roi Glover	.15
114	Tiki Barber	.40
115	Michael Westbrook	.40
116	Antonio Freeman	.40
117	Kerry Collins	.40
118	Laveranues Coles	.40
119	Jay Feeley	.15
120	Champ Bailey	.40
121	Peyton Manning	2.00
122	Chad Pennington	.60
123	Anthony Dorsett	.15
124	Jamal Lewis	1.00
125	Marcus Pollard	.15
126	Charles Woodson	.40
127	Duce Staley	.40
128	Travis Henry	.40
129	Tony Brackens	.15
130	Jeremiah Trotter	.15
131	Jerome Bettis	.40
132	Chad Johnson	.40
133	Lamar Smith	.40
134	Joey Porter	.15
135	Curtis Conway	.40
136	David Terrell	.60
137	Daunte Culpepper	1.25
138	Chris Fuamatu-Ma'afala	.15
139	J.J. Stokes	.15
140	Tim Couch	1.00
141	Ty Law	.15
142	Vinny Sutherland	.15
143	Trung Canidate	.15
144	Larry Allen	.15
145	Darren Howard	.15
146	Ricky Watters	.40
147	Grant Wistrom	.15
148	Brian Griese	.60
149	Jason Sehorn	.15
150	Marshall Faulk	1.25
151	Martin Gramatica	.15
152	Robert Porcher	.15
153	Richie Anderson	.15
154	Derrick Brooks	.15
155	Jevon Kearse	.40
156	Bill Schroeder	.40
157	Marvin Jones	.15
158	Eddie George	.60
159	Keith Brooking	.15
160	Ryan Longwell	.15
161	Brian Dawkins	.15
162	Chris Redman	.40
163	Az-Zahir Hakim	.40
164	James Thrash	.40
165	Rob Johnson	.40
166	Hardy Nickerson	.15
167	Chad Scott	.15
168	Jon Kitna	.15
169	Donnie Edwards	.15
170	Andre Carter	.15
171	Warrick Holdman	.15
172	Jason Taylor	.15
173	Levon Kirkland	.15
174	Mike Brown	.40
175	David Patten	.40
176	Kurt Warner	2.00
177	Fred Smoot	.15
178	Dat Nguyen	.15
179	Joe Horn	.40
180	John Lynch	.15
181	Troy Hambrick	.15
182	John Carney	.15
183	Wesley Walls	.15
184	Deltha O'Neal	.15
185	Joe Jurevicius	.15
186	Steve McNair	.60
187	Scotty Anderson	.15
188	John Abraham	.15
189	Stephen Davis	.60
190	Nate Wayne	.15
191	Corey Simon	.15
192	Joel Makovicka	.15
193	Rob Morris	.15
194	Correll Buckhalter	.40
195	Qadry Ismail	.15
196	Keenan McCardell	.40
197	Jason Gildon	.15
198	Peerless Price	.40
199	Tony Richardson	.15
200	Kevan Barlow	.15
201	Corey Dillon	.60
202	Sam Madison	.15
203	Chad Brown	.15
204	Dez White	.15
205	Troy Brown	.60
206	Orlando Pace	.15
207	Jermaine Lewis	.15
208	Willie Jackson	.40
209	Warrick Dunn	.40
210	James Jackson	.40
211	Sammy Knight	.15
212	Ronde Barber	.15
213	Ed McCaffrey	.40
214	Amani Toomer	.40
215	Rod Gardner	.40
216	Mike McMahon	.60
217	Wayne Chrebet	.40
218	Jake Plummer	.40
219	Bubba Franks	.40
220	Shane Lechler	.15
221	Travis Taylor	.40
222	Edgerrin James	1.50
223	David Akers	.15
224	Eric Moulds	.40
225	Mike Vanderjagt	.15
226	Kendrell Bell	.15
227	Darnay Scott	.40
228	Tony Gonzalez	.40
229	Marcellus Wiley	.15
230	Marcus Robinson	.40
231	Muhsin Muhammad	.40
232	Trent Dilfer	.40
233	Kevin Johnson	.40
234	Travis Minor	.40
235	London Fletcher	.15
236	Reggie Swinton	.15
237	Michael Bennett	.60
238	Brett Favre	2.50
239	Terrell Davis	1.00
240	Emmitt Smith	2.00
241	Shannon Sharpe	.40
242	Cris Carter	.40
243	Tim Brown	.60
244	Jerry Rice	2.00
245	Bruce Smith	.40
246	Warren Sapp	.40
247	Michael Strahan	.40
248	Junior Seau	.40
249	Darrell Green	.40
250	Rod Woodson	.40
251	David Boston	.60
252	Michael Vick	2.00
253	Anthony Thomas	1.50
254	Ahman Green	.60
255	Chris Chambers	.60
256	Tom Brady	2.00
257	Plaxico Burress	.60
258	LaDainian Tomlinson	1.50
259	Shaun Alexander	.60
260	Torry Holt	.40
261	*Julius Peppers*	4.00
262	*William Green*	4.00
263	*Joey Harrington*	10.00
264	*Jabar Gaffney*	3.00
265	*T.J. Duckett*	5.00
266	*Antwann Randle El*	4.00
267	*Javon Walker*	4.00
268	*David Carr*	10.00
269	*DeShaun Foster*	3.00
270	*Donte Stallworth*	5.00
271	*Antonio Bryant*	4.00
272	*Clinton Portis*	10.00
273	*Josh Reed*	3.00
274	*Ashley Lelie*	5.00
275	*Patrick Ramsey*	3.00
276	*Jonathan Wells, Adrian Peterson*	2.00
277	*Quentin Jammer, Roy Williams*	5.00
278	*Jeremy Shockey, Daniel Graham*	6.00
279	*Eric Crouch, Major Applewhite*	2.00
280	*Phillip Buchanon, Lito Sheppard*	2.00
281	*Kahlil Hill, Deion Branch*	3.00
282	*Ryan Sims, Wendell Bryant*	1.00
283	*Josh Scobey, Brian Westbrook*	3.00
284	*Ladell Betts, Omar Easy*	2.50
285	*Andre Davis, Daryl Jones*	3.00
286	*Cliff Russell, Chester Taylor*	1.00
287	*Jason McAddley, Josh McCown*	2.50
288	*David Garrard, Rohan Davey*	2.50
289	*Marquise Walker, Ron Johnson*	2.00
290	*Luke Staley, Lamar Gordon*	2.00
291	*Donald Reche Caldwell, Lee Mays*	2.00
292	*Robert Thomas, Napoleon Harris*	1.00
293	*Maurice Morris, Jerramy Stevens*	2.50
294	*Kurt Kittner, Randy Fasani*	2.50
295	*Rocky Calmus, Jake Schifino*	2.00
296	*Tim Carter, Freddie Milons*	1.00
297	*Tracey Wistrom, Travis Stephens*	2.00
298	*Mike Williams, Dwight Freeney*	2.50
299	*John Henderson, Albert Haynesworth*	1.00
300	*Najeh Davenport, Craig Nall*	2.00

2002 Fleer Tiffany

Stars:	4X-8X
Rookies:	2X-4X

Production 225 Sets

2002 Fleer Minis

Stars:	6X-12X
Rookies:	3X-6X

Production 125 Sets
Found In Retail Packs Only

2002 Fleer Classic Combinations Memorabilia Duals

		NM/M
Production 100 sets		
2CCDGU	Daunte Culpepper, Randy Moss	35.00
3CCDGU	Earl Campbell, Eddie George	15.00
4CCDGU	Paul Hornung, Brett Favre	60.00
6CCDGU	Donovan McNabb, Daunte Culpepper	25.00
7CCDGU	Brian Griese, Tom Brady	35.00
9CCDGU	Anthony Thomas, Walter Payton	75.00
11CCDGU	Jerry Rice, Cris Carter	40.00
13CCDGU	Michael Vick, Donovan McNabb	30.00
14CCDGU	Kurt Warner, Marshall Faulk	25.00
15CCDGU	Brett Favre, Daunte Culpepper	30.00
16CCDGU	Jeff Garcia, Kurt Warner	20.00
18CCDGU	Earl Campbell, Ricky Williams	15.00
20CCDGU	John Elway, Brian Griese	40.00
21CCDGU	Jeff Garcia, Terrell Owens	10.00
22CCDGU	Eric Dickerson, Marshall Faulk	20.00
23CCDGU	Emmitt Smith, Marcus Allen	30.00
24CCDGU	Roger Staubach, Emmitt Smith	50.00
25CCDGU	Terrell Davis, Curtis Martin	10.00
26CCDGU	Emmitt Smith, Walter Payton	100.00
27CCDGU	Joe Montana, Kurt Warner	50.00
30CCDGU	John Elway, Terrell Davis	40.00
34CCDGU	Randy Moss, Jerry Rice	40.00
35CCDGU	Emmitt Smith, Fred Taylor	30.00

2002 Fleer Classic Combinations Hobby

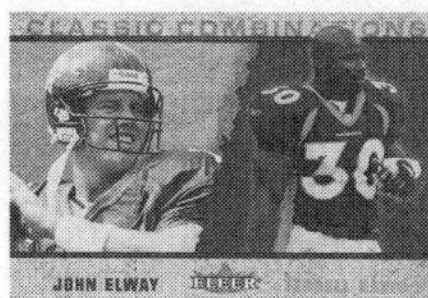

		NM/M
Common Player:		1.00
Production 2000, 1000, 500, or 250 sets		
1CCH	Kendrell Bell, Brian Urlacher/2000	2.00
2CCH	Daunte Culpepper, Randy Moss/2000	2.00
3CCH	Earl Campbell, Eddie George/2000	1.00
4CCH	Paul Hornung, Brett Favre/2000	5.00
5CCH	Peyton Manning, Edgerrin James/2000	1.00
6CCH	Donovan McNabb, Daunte Culpepper/2000	1.00
7CCH	Brian Griese, Tom Brady/2000	2.00
8CCH	Jerry Rice, Tim Brown/2000	2.00
9CCH	Anthony Thomas, Walter Payton/2000	4.00
10CCH	Torry Holt, Koren Robinson/2000	1.00
11CCH	Jerry Rice, Cris Carter/1000	2.00
12CCH	Chris Chambers, Plaxico Burress/1000	1.00
13CCH	Michael Vick, Donovan McNabb/1000	2.00
14CCH	Kurt Warner, Marshall Faulk/1000	2.00
15CCH	Brett Favre, Daunte Culpepper/1000	4.00
16CCH	Jeff Garcia, Kurt Warner/1000	2.00
17CCH	Peyton Manning, Jamal Lewis/1000	1.00
18CCH	Earl Campbell, Ricky Williams/1000	1.00
19CCH	David Carr, Peyton Manning/1000	3.00
20CCH	John Elway, Brian Griese/1000	3.00
21CCH	Jeff Garcia, Terrell Owens/500	2.00
22CCH	Eric Dickerson, Marshall Faulk/500	2.00
23CCH	Emmitt Smith, Marcus Allen/500	4.00
24CCH	Roger Staubach, Emmitt Smith/500	4.00
25CCH	Terrell Davis, Curtis Martin/500	2.00
26CCH	Emmitt Smith, Walter Payton/500	5.00
27CCH	Joe Montana, Kurt Warner/500	5.00
28CCH	Kordell Stewart, Jerome Bettis/500	2.00
29CCH	Eddie George, Archie Griffin/500	2.00
30CCH	John Elway, Terrell Davis/500	5.00
31CCH	Brian Griese, Bob Griese/250	5.00
32CCH	Joey Harrington, David Carr/250	8.00
33CCH	Bob Griese, Drew Brees/250	3.00
34CCH	Randy Moss, Jerry Rice/250	5.00
35CCH	Emmitt Smith, Fred Taylor/250	5.00

2002 Fleer Classic Combinations Memorabilia

		NM/M
1CCGU	Brian Urlacher	15.00
2CCGU	Daunte Culpepper	10.00
2CCGU	Randy Moss	15.00
3CCGU	Earl Campbell	12.00
3CCGU	Eddie George	10.00
4CCGU	Brett Favre	25.00
6CCGU	Donovan McNabb	10.00
6CCGU	Daunte Culpepper	10.00
7CCGU	Tom Brady	15.00
9CCGU	Anthony Thomas	12.00
9CCGU	Walter Payton	50.00
10CCGU	Torry Holt	10.00
11CCGU	Jerry Rice	30.00
11CCGU	Cris Carter	15.00
13CCGU	Michael Vick	15.00
13CCGU	Donovan McNabb	10.00
14CCGU	Kurt Warner	15.00
14CCGU	Marshall Faulk	15.00
15CCGU	Brett Favre	25.00
16CCGU	Jeff Garcia	10.00
17CCGU	Jamal Lewis	10.00
18CCGU	Earl Campbell	15.00
18CCGU	Ricky Williams	10.00
20CCGU	John Elway	25.00
21CCGU	Jeff Garcia	10.00
21CCGU	Terrell Owens	10.00
22CCGU	Eric Dickerson	15.00
22CCGU	Marshall Faulk	15.00
23CCGU	Emmitt Smith	25.00
23CCGU	Marcus Allen	15.00
24CCGU	Roger Staubach	20.00
26CCGU	Emmitt Smith	30.00
26CCGU	Walter Payton	60.00
27CCGU	Joe Montana	40.00
27CCGU	Kurt Warner	20.00
30CCGU	John Elway	25.00
33CCGU	Drew Brees	15.00
34CCGU	Randy Moss	20.00
34CCGU	Jerry Rice	35.00
35CCGU	Emmitt Smith	30.00

2002 Fleer Career Highlights

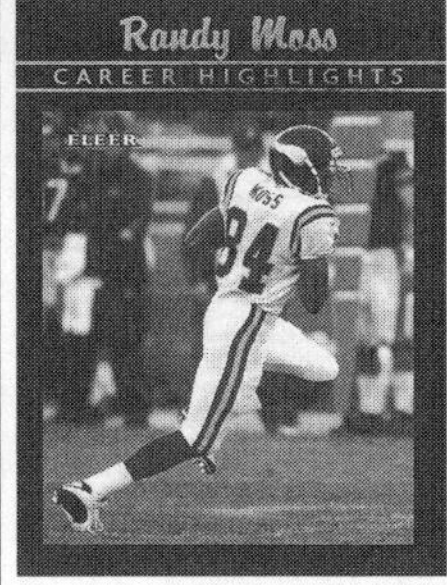

		NM/M
Common Player:		2.00
Inserted 1:24		
1CH	Peyton Manning	3.00
2CH	Brett Favre	5.00
3CH	Kurt Warner	4.00
4CH	Emmitt Smith	4.00
5CH	Marshall Faulk	3.00
6CH	Jerome Bettis	3.00
7CH	Jerry Rice	4.00
8CH	Cris Carter	2.00
9CH	Randy Moss	3.00
10CH	Michael Strahan	2.00

2002 Fleer Golden Memories

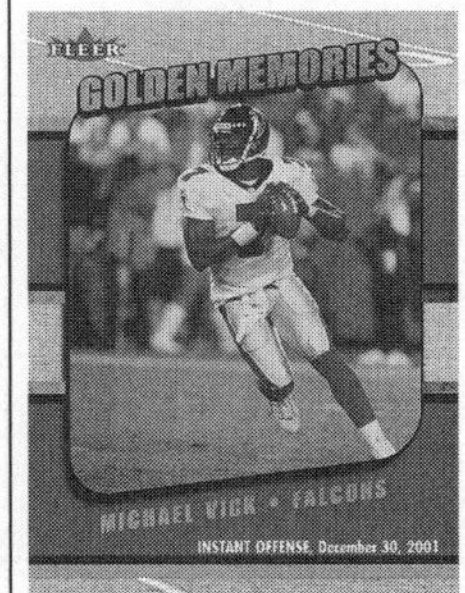

		NM/M
Common Player:		1.00
Inserted 1:8		
1GM	America Tribute	1.00
2GM	Kurt Warner	2.00
3GM	Tom Brady	3.00
4GM	David Carr	3.00
5GM	Shaun Alexander	1.00
6GM	Anthony Thomas	1.00
7GM	Kendrell Bell	1.00
8GM	Michael Vick	2.00
9GM	Donovan McNabb	1.00
10GM	LaDainian Tomlinson	1.00
11GM	Brian Urlacher	2.00
12GM	Marshall Faulk	1.00
13GM	Edgerrin James	1.00
14GM	Terrell Owens	1.00
15GM	Tim Brown	1.00

2002 Fleer Headliners

		NM/M
Common Player:		2.00
Inserted 1:24		
1HL	Donovan McNabb	2.00
2HL	Marshall Faulk	3.00
3HL	Randy Moss	4.00
4HL	Emmitt Smith	3.00
5HL	Jeff Garcia	2.00
6HL	Tim Brown	2.00
7HL	Brian Urlacher	3.00
8HL	Jerome Bettis	2.00
9HL	Edgerrin James	2.00
10HL	Kurt Warner	3.00
11HL	Terrell Davis	2.00

NM/M
12HL Tim Couch 2.00
13HL Ricky Williams 2.00
14HL Daunte Culpepper 2.00
15HL Jerry Rice 3.00
16HL Curtis Martin 2.00
17HL Peyton Manning 3.00
18HL Eddie George 2.00
19HL Tom Brady 4.00
20HL Brett Favre 5.00

2002 Fleer Rookie Sensations

NM/M
Common Player: 2.00
Production 1250 sets
1RS David Carr 10.00
2RS Joey Harrington 8.00
3RS William Green 6.00
4RS Ashley Lelie 4.00
5RS Donte Stallworth 4.00
6RS T.J. Duckett 4.00
7RS DeShaun Foster 3.00
8RS Josh Reed 4.00
9RS Jabar Gaffney 2.00
10RS Clinton Portis 6.00
11RS Antonio Bryant 4.00
12RS Donald Reche Caldwell 2.00
13RS Julius Peppers 3.00
14RS Ron Johnson 2.00
15RS Javon Walker 5.00
16RS Josh McCown 3.00
17RS Marquise Walker 2.00
18RS Patrick Ramsey 2.00
19RS Antwann Randle El 4.00
20RS Andre Davis 2.00

2002 Fleer School Colors

NM/M
Common Player: 3.00
Production 750 sets
1SC Santana Moss 3.00
2SC Edgerrin James 5.00
3SC David Terrell 4.00
4SC Anthony Thomas 4.00
5SC Dan Morgan 3.00
6SC Rod Gardner 3.00
7SC Archie Griffin 4.00
8SC Drew Brees 4.00
9SC Chad Johnson 3.00
10SC Chris Weinke 3.00
11SC Reggie Wayne 3.00
12SC DeShaun Foster 6.00
13SC Robert Ferguson 3.00
14SC Tom Brady 6.00
15SC David Carr 10.00

2002 Fleer School Colors Memorabilia

NM/M
Common Player: 8.00
Inserted 1:30
1SCGU Santana Moss 8.00
2SCGU Edgerrin James 15.00
3SCGU David Terrell 12.00
4SCGU Anthony Thomas 12.00
5SCGU Dan Morgan 8.00
6SCGU Rod Gardner 8.00
7SCGU Archie Griffin 15.00
8SCGU Drew Brees 12.00
9SCGU Chad Johnson 8.00
10SCGU Chris Weinke 8.00
11SCGU DeShaun Foster 15.00
12SCGU Robert Ferguson 8.00

A card number in parenthese ( ) indicates the set is unnumbered.

2002 Fleer School Colors Memorabilia Duals

NM/M
Common Player: 15.00
Inserted 1:211
1SCDGU Santana Moss 20.00
2SCDGU Edgerrin James 35.00
3SCDGU David Terrell 20.00
4SCDGU Anthony Thomas 20.00
5SCDGU Dan Morgan 15.00

2003 Fleer Authentix

NM/M
Common Player: .20
Unlisted Star: .60
Minor Star: .40

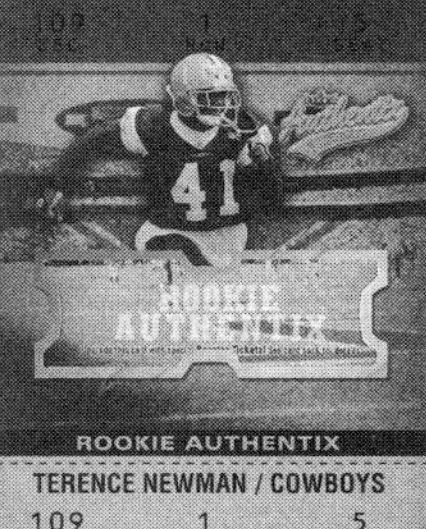

ROOKIE AUTHENTIX
ROOKIE AUTHENTIX
TERENCE NEWMAN / COWBOYS
109 SEC
1 ROW
5 SEAT

Common Rookie (101-130): 2.00
Pack (5): 4.00
Wax Box (24): 65.00
1 Donovan McNabb 1.25
2 Tim Brown .75
3 Donald Driver .60
4 Eddie George .75
5 Curtis Martin .60
6 Chad Hutchinson .20
7 Shaun Alexander .60
8 Kerry Collins .50
9 Trent Green .50
10 Marc Bulger .50
11 Donte Stallworth 1.00
12 Julius Peppers .50
13 Ronde Barber .20
14 Jason Taylor .20
15 Eric Moulds .50
16 Amos Zereoue .20
17 Fred Taylor .50
18 Jake Plummer .50
19 Jerry Rice 2.00
20 Quincy Morgan .20
21 Koren Robinson .20
22 Tom Brady 1.25
23 Brian Urlacher 1.50
24 Terrell Owens .60
25 Priest Holmes 1.00
26 Brett Favre 2.50
27 Derrick Mason .50
28 Charlie Garner .40
29 Clinton Portis 2.00
30 Warren Sapp .20
31 Joe Horn .20
32 Michael Lewis .20
33 Torry Holt .40
34 Aaron Brooks 1.00
35 William Green .60
36 Matt Hasselbeck .20
37 Ricky Williams 1.25
38 Travis Henry .50
39 Junior Seau .50
40 Duce Staley .50
41 Todd Heap .20
42 Hines Ward .50
43 David Carr 1.50
44 Rod Gardner .50
45 Deuce McAllister 1.00
46 Chad Johnson .20
47 Garrison Hearst .50
48 Daunte Culpepper 1.25
49 Ray Lewis .40
50 Plaxico Burress .60
51 Randy Moss 2.00
52 Drew Bledsoe 1.25
53 LaDainian Tomlinson 1.50
54 Chris Chambers .50
55 Chris Redman .50
56 Jerome Bettis .50
57 Tony Gonzalez .40
58 Michael Vick 2.50
59 Tommy Maddox .60
60 Marvin Harrison .60
61 Stephen Davis .40
62 Chad Pennington 1.00
63 James Stewart .20
64 Simeon Rice .20
65 Jeremy Shockey 1.50
66 Emmitt Smith 2.00
67 Marshall Faulk 1.25
68 Troy Brown .20
69 Warrick Dunn .20
70 David Boston .40
71 Edgerrin James 1.25
72 Patrick Ramsey .60
73 Rich Gannon .50
74 Ed McCaffrey .40
75 Kurt Warner 1.50
76 Marty Booker .20
77 Tai Streets .20
78 Michael Bennett .50
79 Peerless Price .60
80 Drew Brees 1.25
81 Mark Brunell .50
82 Jamal Lewis .20
83 Brad Johnson .20
84 Jimmy Smith .20
85 T.J. Duckett .60
86 Todd Pinkston .20
87 Joey Harrington 1.50
88 Derrick Brooks .20
89 Laveranues Coles .60
90 Shannon Sharpe .40
91 Keyshawn Johnson .60
92 Tiki Barber .60
93 Corey Dillon .40
94 Jeff Garcia .50
95 Peyton Manning 2.00
96 Marcel Shipp .20
97 Brian Dawkins .20
98 Ahman Green .60
99 Steve McNair .50
100 Amani Toomer .20
101 *Carson Palmer* 15.00
102 *Taylor Jacobs* 3.00
103 *Kyle Boller* 12.00
104 *Anquan Boldin* 12.00
105 *Willis McGahee* 15.00
106 *Kevin Curtis* 2.00
107 *Musa Smith* 4.00
108 *Dallas Clark* 6.00
109 *Larry Johnson* 10.00
110 *Billy McMullen* 2.00
111 *B.J. Askew* 4.00
112 *Bennie Joppru* 3.00
113 *Bryant Johnson* 5.00
114 *Byron Leftwich* 25.00
115 *Onterrio Smith* 8.00
116 *Justin Fargas* 6.00
117 *Terence Newman* 8.00
118 *Andre Johnson* 15.00
119 *Rex Grossman* 15.00
120 *Tyrone Calico* 8.00
121 *Chris Simms* 10.00
122 *Kelley Washington* 5.00
123 *Dave Ragone* 5.00
124 *Teyo Johnson* 3.00
125 *Seneca Wallace* 3.00
126 *Lee Suggs* 12.00
127 *Chris Brown* 10.00
128 *L.J. Smith* 2.00
129 *Charles Rogers* 10.00
130 *Terrell Suggs* 5.00
131 Antonio Bryant 3.00
132 Roy Williams 2.00
133 Joey Galloway 2.00
134 Dexter Coakley 1.00
135 Greg Ellis 1.00
136 Troy Hambrick 2.00
137 La'Roi Glover 1.00
138 Tony Fisher 2.00
139 Javon Walker 2.00
140 Robert Ferguson 2.00
141 Bubba Franks 2.00
142 Kabeer Gbaja-Biamila 1.00
143 Na'il Diggs 1.00
144 Darren Sharper 1.00
145 Jerry Porter 2.00
146 Doug Jolley 1.00
147 Sebastian Janikowski 1.00
148 Rod Woodson 1.50
149 Phillip Buchanon 2.00
150 Charles Woodson 2.00
151 Zack Crockett 1.00
152 Michael Strahan 1.50
153 Dontae' Jones 1.00
154 Will Allen 1.00
155 Will Peterson 1.00
156 Ron Dixon 1.00
157 Micheal Barrow 1.00
158 Ike Hilliard 1.50
159 Antwann Randle El 2.00
160 Joey Porter 1.00
161 Jason Gildon 1.00
162 Chris Fuamatu-Ma'afala 1.00
163 Kendrell Bell 1.50
164 Chad Scott 1.00
165 Dan Krieder 1.00

2003 Fleer Authentix Balcony

Stars: 2X-4X
Rookies: 1X-1.2X
Production 250 Sets

2003 Fleer Authentix Club Box

Stars: 3X-6X
Rookies: 1X-2X
Production 100 Sets

2003 Fleer Authentix Standing Room Only

Production 25 Sets

2003 Fleer Authentix Autographed Authentix

NM/M
Common Player: 15.00
1 Michael Vick 75.00
2 Chad Pennington 20.00
3 Willis McGahee 25.00
4 Clinton Portis 30.00
5 Michael Bennett 15.00
6 Antonio Bryant 15.00
7 Travis Henry 15.00
8 Brian Urlacher 40.00
9 Donovan McNabb 40.00
10 Plaxico Burress 15.00

2003 Fleer Authentix Hometown Heroes Memorabilia

NM/M
Common Player: 10.00
Available only in special team packs Packers,Cowboys,Giants,Steelers, Giants
1HHM Joey Galloway 10.00
2HHM Roy Williams 15.00
3HHM Antonio Bryant 10.00
4HHM Brett Favre 30.00
5HHM Ahman Green 15.00
6HHM Donald Driver 12.00
7HHM Rich Gannon 10.00
8HHM Jerry Rice 20.00
9HHM Tim Brown 12.00
10HHM Tiki Barber 10.00
11HHM Jeremy Shockey 15.00
12HHM Michael Strahan 10.00
13HHM Hines Ward 10.00
14HHM Plaxico Burress 10.00
15HHM Jerome Bettis 10.00
JG-AB Joey Galloway, Antonio Bryant 20.00
BF-AG Brett Favre, Ahman Green 40.00
JR-RG Jerry Rice, Rich Gannon 25.00
JS-TB Jeremy Shockey, Tiki Barber 25.00
HW-PB Hines Ward, Plaxico Burress 20.00

2003 Fleer Authentix Jersey Authentix Autos Reg Season

NM/M
Common Player: 50.00
1AJA Michael Vick/135 120.00
2AJA Chad Pennington/100 50.00
3AJA Willis McGahee/270 50.00

2003 Fleer Authentix Jersey Authentix Autos Pro Bowl

NM/M
Common Player: 60.00
Super Bowl Production 25 Sets
1AJA Michael Vick 150.00
2AJA Chad Pennington 80.00
3AJA Willis McGahee 60.00

2003 Fleer Authentix Jersey Authentix Game of the Week

NM/M
Common Player: 15.00
Production 250 sets
Unripped version: 1X-2X
Production 50 sets
1JAGW Joey Harrington, Michael Bennett 20.00
2JAGW Clinton Portis, LaDainian Tomlinson 30.00
3JAGW Chad Pennington, Donovan McNabb 25.00
4JAGW Travis Henry, Antonio Bryant 15.00
5JAGW Marshall Faulk, Jeff Garcia 20.00
6JAGW Randy Moss, Brian Urlacher 40.00
7JAGW Donovan McNabb, Ricky Williams 40.00
8JAGW Marshall Faulk, Plaxico Burress 25.00
9JAGW Antonio Bryant, Deuce McAllister 20.00
10JAGW Chad Pennington, Travis Henry 20.00

2003 Fleer Authentix Jersey Authentix Ripped

NM/M
Common Player: 6.00
Inserted 1:18
Unripped version 1X-2X
Production 50 sets
1JA Joey Harrington 12.00
2JA Clinton Portis 15.00
3JA Chad Pennington 10.00
4JA Michael Bennett 8.00
5JA Antonio Bryant 8.00
6JA Marshall Faulk 10.00
7JA Travis Henry 6.00
8JA Deuce McAllister 8.00
9JA Randy Moss 12.00
10JA Brian Urlacher 12.00
11JA LaDainian Tomlinson 8.00
12JA Ricky Williams 12.00
13JA Jeff Garcia 6.00
14JA Donovan McNabb 12.00
15JA Plaxico Burress 6.00

2003 Fleer Authentix Jersey Authentix Ripped Pro Bowl

NM/M
Common Player: 15.00
JAMB Michael Bennett/19 30.00
JAMF Marshall Faulk/80 25.00
JAJG Jeff Garcia/87 15.00
JATH Travis Henry/42 20.00
JADM Deuce McAllister/91 20.00
JADM Donovan McNabb/39 30.00
JARM Randy Moss/66 30.00
JALT LaDainian Tomlinson/103 20.00
JAJR Brian Urlacher/50 30.00
JARW Ricky Williams/74 30.00

2003 Fleer Authentix Stadium Classics

NM/M
Common Player: .75
Inserted 1:12
1SC Brian Urlacher 1.50
2SC Donovan McNabb 1.50
3SC Peyton Manning 2.00
4SC Deuce McAllister .75
5SC Brett Favre 2.50
6SC Chad Pennington 1.50
7SC Randy Moss 2.00
8SC Michael Vick 2.50
9SC Ricky Williams 1.50
10SC LaDainian Tomlinson .75

2003 Fleer Authentix Ticket Studs

NM/M
Common Player: 2.00
Inserted 1:26
1TS Michael Vick 6.00
2TS Tom Brady 4.00
3TS Brett Favre 6.00
4TS Emmitt Smith 6.00
5TS Randy Moss 4.00
6TS Jerry Rice 5.00
7TS Peyton Manning 4.00
8TS Chad Pennington 3.00
9TS Donovan McNabb 3.00
10TS LaDainian Tomlinson 3.00
11TS Jeremy Shockey 3.00
12TS Drew Brees 2.00
13TS Brian Urlacher 4.00
14TS Clinton Portis 5.00
15TS David Carr 4.00

2003 Fleer Authentix Ticket Studs Jersey

NM/M
Common Player: 10.00
Inserted 1:24
1TS Michael Vick 15.00
2TS Tom Brady 12.00
3TS Brett Favre 25.00
4TS Emmitt Smith 20.00
5TS Randy Moss 12.00
6TS Jerry Rice 15.00
7TS Peyton Manning 12.00
8TS Chad Pennington 12.00
9TS Donovan McNabb 12.00
10TS LaDainian Tomlinson 12.00
11TS Jeremy Shockey 12.00
12TS Drew Brees 10.00
13TS Brian Urlacher 12.00
14TS Clinton Portis 15.00
15TS David Carr 15.00

2003 Fleer Avant

NM/M
Common Player (1-60): .30
Minor Stars: .60
Unlisted Stars: .75
Common Rookie (61-90): 3.00
Minor Rookies: 4.00
Unlisted Rookies: 5.00
Production 699 Sets
Pack (4): 4.75
Box (18): 60.00
1 Priest Holmes .75
2 Hines Ward .75
3 Patrick Ramsey .75
4 Deuce McAllister .75
5 Tony Gonzalez .60
6 Daunte Culpepper .75
7 Edgerrin James 1.00
8 Jeremy Shockey 1.50
9 Donovan McNabb 1.00
10 Eddie George .75
11 Ray Lewis .60
12 LaDainian Tomlinson 1.00
13 Peyton Manning 3.00
14 Charlie Garner .60
15 Brad Johnson .60
16 David Carr 2.00
17 Jerry Rice 2.50
18 Keyshawn Johnson .60
19 Ahman Green .75
20 Rich Gannon .60
21 William Green .75
22 Torry Holt .75
23 Brett Favre 3.00
24 Curtis Martin .60
25 Derrick Brooks .30
26 Joey Harrington 1.50
27 Chad Pennington 1.00
28 Koren Robinson .60
29 Clinton Portis 2.00
30 Michael Strahan .30
31 Marvin Harrison .75
32 Travis Henry .60
33 Aaron Brooks .75
34 Antwann Randle El .60
35 Antonio Bryant .60
36 Shaun Alexander .75
37 Jake Plummer .60
38 Emmitt Smith 2.50
39 Plaxico Burress .60
40 Peerless Price .60
41 Drew Bledsoe 1.00
42 Jeff Garcia .75
43 Fred Taylor .75
44 Correll Buckhalter .30
45 Steve McNair .75
46 Stephen Davis .60
47 Terrell Owens .60
48 Corey Dillon .60
49 Marshall Faulk 1.00
50 Tom Brady 2.00
51 Tiki Barber .60
52 Michael Vick 3.00
53 Drew Brees 1.00
54 Chad Johnson .60
55 Randy Moss 1.50
56 Eric Moulds .60
57 Brian Urlacher 1.50
58 Kurt Warner .75
59 Ricky Williams 1.50
60 Laveranues Coles .60
61 *Carson Palmer* 15.00
62 *Charles Rogers* 8.00
63 *Andre Johnson* 10.00
64 *Dewayne Robertson* 3.00
65 *Terence Newman* 6.00
66 *Byron Leftwich* 20.00
67 *Terrell Suggs* 5.00
68 *Bryant Johnson* 4.00
69 *Kyle Boller* 8.00
70 *Rex Grossman* 10.00
71 *Willis McGahee* 10.00
72 *Dallas Clark* 5.00
73 *Larry Johnson* 8.00
74 *Bennie Joppru* 3.00
75 *Taylor Jacobs* 3.00
76 *Anquan Boldin* 10.00
77 *Tyrone Calico* 6.00
78 *L.J. Smith* 4.00
79 *Teyo Johnson* 4.00
80 *Kelley Washington* 5.00
81 *Jason Witten* 5.00
82 *Nate Burleson* 4.00
83 *Musa Smith* 3.00
84 *Tony Hollings* 3.00
85 *Chris Brown* 8.00
86 *Billy McMullen* 3.00
87 *Chris Simms* 6.00
88 *Artose Pinner* 3.00
89 *Quentin Griffin* 8.00
90 *Onterrio Smith* 8.00

2003 Fleer Avant Black

Stars: 2X-4X
Rookies: 1X-2X
Production 199 Sets

2003 Fleer Avant Candid Collection

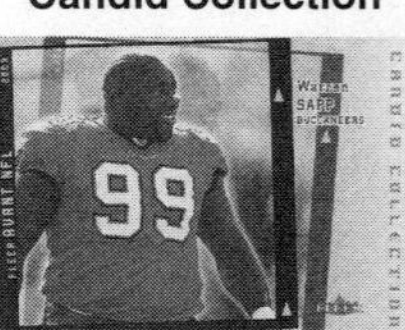

NM/M
Common Player: 4.00
Production 99 Sets
1CC Donovan McNabb 8.00
2CC Brett Favre 15.00
3CC Terrell Owens 6.00
4CC Michael Vick 15.00
5CC Kurt Warner 6.00
6CC Emmitt Smith 15.00
7CC Clinton Portis 10.00
8CC Rich Gannon 4.00
9CC Ricky Williams 8.00
10CC Daunte Culpepper 6.00
11CC Peyton Manning 10.00
12CC Chad Pennington 8.00
13CC Warren Sapp 4.00
14CC Shaun Alexander 6.00
15CC Priest Holmes 8.00
16CC LaDainian Tomlinson 6.00
17CC Jeremy Shockey 8.00
18CC Randy Moss 10.00

19CC Joey Harrington 8.00
20CC David Carr 10.00

2003 Fleer Avant Candid Collection Jerseys

NM/M
Common Player: 8.00
Production 100 Sets
1 Joey Harrington 12.00
2 Brett Favre 30.00
3 Clinton Portis 15.00
4 Peyton Manning 20.00
5 Daunte Culpepper 10.00
6 Warren Sapp 8.00
7 Priest Holmes 12.00
8 Donovan McNabb 12.00
9 Terrell Owens 10.00
10 Jeremy Shockey 12.00

2003 Fleer Avant Draw Play

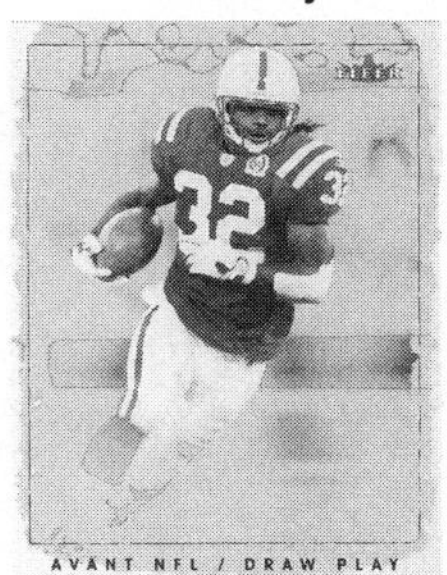

NM/M
Complete Set (15): 30.00
Common Player: 1.50
Production 535 Sets
1 Ricky Williams 3.00
2 Michael Vick 6.00
3 Travis Henry 1.50
4 Deuce McAllister 2.00
5 Clinton Portis 4.00
6 Ahman Green 2.00
7 Priest Holmes 3.00
8 Marshall Faulk 3.00
9 Emmitt Smith 6.00
10 LaDainian Tomlinson 3.00
11 Steve McNair 2.00
12 Daunte Culpepper 2.00
13 Tiki Barber 1.50
14 Donovan McNabb 3.00
15 Edgerrin James 3.00

2003 Fleer Avant Draw Play Jerseys

1 Deuce McAllister/26
2 Marshall Faulk/28
3 Edgerrin James/32
4 LaDainian Tomlinson/21
5 Donovan McNabb/5

2003 Fleer Avant Materials Blue

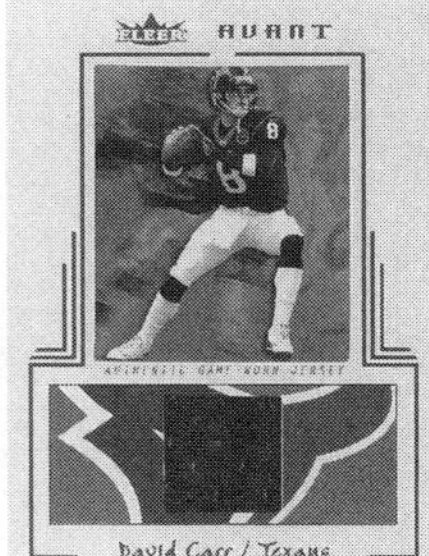

NM/M
Common Player: 6.00
Production 250 Sets
Red Materials: 1X-2X
Production 75 Sets
Patches: 3X-6X
Production 25 Sets
Drew Bledsoe 8.00
Tom Brady 12.00
Drew Brees 8.00
David Carr 12.00
Daunte Culpepper 8.00
Corey Dillon 6.00
Marshall Faulk 8.00
Brett Favre 20.00
Rich Gannon 6.00
Eddie George 6.00
Ahman Green 8.00
Rex Grossman 12.00
Joey Harrington 10.00
Torry Holt 8.00
Taylor Jacobs 6.00
Edgerrin James 8.00
Andre Johnson 12.00
Larry Johnson 10.00
Byron Leftwich 15.00
Peyton Manning 12.00
Deuce McAllister 8.00
Donovan McNabb 10.00
Steve McNair 8.00
Peerless Price 6.00
Antwann Randle El 6.00
Jeremy Shockey 8.00
Chris Simms 8.00
LaDainian Tomlinson 8.00
Brian Urlacher 10.00
Hines Ward 8.00

2003 Fleer Avant Work of Heart

NM/M
Complete Set (10): 40.00
Common Player: 3.00
Production 300 Sets
Jersey Cards: 2X
Production 300 Sets
1W Brett Favre 10.00
2W Marshall Faulk 5.00
3W Jerry Rice 8.00
4W Michael Vick 10.00
5W Jeff Garcia 3.00
6W Joey Harrington 5.00
7W Edgerrin James 5.00
8W Donovan McNabb 5.00
9W Jeremy Shockey 5.00
10W Randy Moss 6.00

2003 Fleer Focus

NM/M
Common Player: .20
Minor Stars: .50
Unlisted Stars: .60
Common Rookie (121-160): 2.50
Minor Rookies: 3.00
Unlisted Rookies: 4.00
Production 699 Sets
Pack (5): 3.00
Box (24): 60.00
1 Tony Gonzalez .50
2 Aaron Brooks .60
3 Joey Harrington 1.25
4 Brett Favre 2.00
5 Donovan McNabb .75
6 Jerome Bettis .50
7 Michael Vick 2.00
8 Travis Taylor .50
9 Jay Fiedler .50
10 David Boston .60
11 Peerless Price .50
12 Kevan Barlow .50
13 LaDainian Tomlinson .75
14 Jevon Kearse .50
15 Peyton Manning 1.00
16 T.J. Duckett .50
17 Drew Brees .60
18 Brian Dawkins .20
19 Charles Woodson .50
20 Emmitt Smith 1.50
21 Joe Jurevicius .20
22 Duce Staley .50
23 Rod Gardner .50
24 Jamal Lewis .60
25 Jeff Garcia .50
26 Clinton Portis 1.50
27 Priest Holmes .60
28 Mike Alstott .50
29 Shaun Alexander .60
30 Randy Moss 1.00
31 Eric Moulds .50
32 Troy Brown .50
33 Michael Bennett .60
34 Ricky Williams .75
35 Champ Bailey .50
36 Hugh Douglas .20
37 Travis Henry .50
38 Daunte Culpepper .60
39 Koren Robinson .50
40 Todd Heap .20
41 John Abraham .20
42 Drew Bledsoe .75
43 Tom Brady .75
44 Torry Holt .60
45 Jake Delhomme .50
46 Joe Horn .50
47 Julius Peppers .50
48 Ray Lewis .50
49 Deuce McAllister .60
50 Marshall Faulk .75
51 Takeo Spikes .20
52 Kordell Stewart .60
53 Brian Urlacher 1.00
54 Zach Thomas .20
55 Kurt Warner .75
56 Peter Warrick .50
57 Marty Booker .50
58 Warren Sapp .50
59 Jon Kitna .50
60 Chad Johnson .50
61 Jeremy Shockey 1.00
62 Keyshawn Johnson .50
63 Kelly Holcomb .20
64 Corey Dillon .60
65 Tiki Barber .60
66 Eddie George .60
67 Joey Galloway .50
68 Tim Couch .60
69 Amani Toomer .50
70 Steve McNair .60
71 Troy Hambrick .50
72 William Green .60
73 Chad Pennington .75
74 Laveranues Coles .50
75 Quincy Carter .60
76 Antonio Bryant .50
77 Curtis Martin .60
78 Terrell Owens .60
79 Patrick Ramsey .60
80 Ashley Lelie .50
81 Donte Stallworth .50
82 Roy Williams .50
83 Charlie Garner .50
84 Chris Chambers .60
85 Warrick Dunn .50
86 Shannon Sharpe .50
87 Rod Smith .50
88 Marvin Harrison .60
89 Rich Gannon .50
90 Stephen Davis .50
91 James Stewart .50
92 Tim Brown .50
93 Anthony Thomas .60
94 Stacey Mack .50
95 Jake Plummer .50
96 Jerry Rice 1.50
97 Quincy Morgan .50
98 Dwight Freeney .20
99 Jason Taylor .50
100 Ahman Green .60
101 Hines Ward .60
102 Kerry Collins .50
103 Plaxico Burress .60
104 Santana Moss .50
105 Michael Strahan .20
106 Donald Driver .50
107 Tommy Maddox .60
108 Jerry Porter .60
109 David Carr 1.25
110 Garrison Hearst .50
111 Edgerrin James .75
112 Isaac Bruce .50
113 Marc Bulger .60
114 Brad Johnson .50
115 Fred Taylor .60
116 Derrick Brooks .50
117 Jimmy Smith .50
118 Derrick Mason .50
119 Mark Brunell .50
120 Trent Green .50
121 *Mike Doss* 3.00
122 *Carson Palmer* 10.00
123 *Charles Rogers* 8.00
124 *Andre Johnson* 12.00
125 *Tony Hollings* 3.00
126 *Terence Newman* 5.00
127 *Byron Leftwich* 20.00
128 *Lee Suggs* 12.00
129 *Bryant Johnson* 4.00
130 *Kyle Boller* 8.00
131 *Rex Grossman* 12.00
132 *Willis McGahee* 8.00
133 *Dallas Clark* 4.00
134 *Bobby Wade* 3.00
135 *Tony Romo* 3.00
136 *Michael Haynes* 2.50
137 *Bethel Johnson* 3.00
138 *Anquan Boldin* 6.00
139 *Seneca Wallace* 3.00
140 *Nick Barnett* 4.00
141 *Teyo Johnson* 4.00
142 *Kelley Washington* 4.00
143 *Nate Burleson* 3.00
144 *Ken Dorsey* 5.00
145 *Dewayne White* 2.50
146 *Chris Kelsay* 2.50
147 *Dave Ragone* 3.00
148 *David Tyree* 2.50
149 *Billy McMullen* 2.50
150 *Chris Simms* 6.00
151 *Onterrio Smith* 6.00
152 *Marcus Trufant* 3.00
153 *Jason Witten* 3.00
154 *Jonathon Sullivan* 2.50
155 *Kevin Williams* 2.50
156 *Justin Fargas* 5.00
157 *Domanick Davis* 6.00
158 *LaBrandon Toefield* 3.00
159 *Shaun McDonald* 2.50
160 *Brandon Lloyd* 3.00

2003 Fleer Focus Anniversary Gold

Stars: 5X-10X
Rookies: 1X-2X
Production 50 Sets
Silver Production 25 Sets

2003 Fleer Focus Numbers Century

Stars: 3X-6X
Rookies: 1X-1.5X
Production 100 Sets
Decode Production 10 Sets

2003 Fleer Focus Diamond Focus

NM/M
Complete Set (15): 75.00
Common Player: 4.00
Production 350 Sets
1DF Ricky Williams 6.00
2DF Chad Pennington 5.00
3DF Michael Vick 10.00
4DF Brett Favre 10.00
5DF Peyton Manning 6.00
6DF Marshall Faulk 5.00
7DF Carson Palmer 8.00
8DF Charles Rogers 6.00
9DF Willis McGahee 6.00
10DF Andre Johnson 8.00
11DF Byron Leftwich 10.00
12DF Kyle Boller 6.00
13DF LaDainian Tomlinson 4.00
14DF Drew Bledsoe 5.00
15DF Jerry Rice 8.00

2003 Fleer Focus Diamond Focus Jerseys

NM/M
Common Player: 10.00
Production 200 Sets
Level 2: 1X-1.5X
Production 100 Sets
Level 3: 1X-2X
Production 50 Sets
Level 4 Production 5 Sets
Drew Bledsoe 10.00
Marshall Faulk 12.00
Brett Favre 25.00
Peyton Manning 15.00
Chad Pennington 12.00
Jerry Rice 20.00
Charles Rogers 12.00
LaDainian Tomlinson 10.00
Michael Vick 20.00
Ricky Williams 12.00

2003 Fleer Focus Emerald Focus

NM/M
Complete Set (10): 35.00
Common Player: 3.00
Production 500 Sets
1EF Donovan McNabb 5.00
2EF Kurt Warner 3.00
3EF David Carr 6.00
4EF Tom Brady 5.00
5EF Brian Urlacher 5.00
6EF Randy Moss 6.00
7EF Joey Harrington 5.00
8EF Edgerrin James 5.00
9EF Emmitt Smith 8.00
10EF Jeremy Shockey 5.00

2003 Fleer Focus Emerald Focus Jerseys

NM/M
Common Player: 8.00
Production 250 Sets
Level 2: 1X
Production 150 Sets
Level 3: 1X-1.5X
Production 75 Sets
Level 4 Production 10 Sets
Tom Brady 12.00
David Carr 12.00
Joey Harrington 10.00
Edgerrin James 12.00
Donovan McNabb 12.00
Randy Moss 15.00
Jeremy Shockey 10.00
Emmitt Smith 20.00
Brian Urlacher 12.00
Kurt Warner 8.00

2003 Fleer Focus Extra Effort

NM/M
Complete Set (10): 30.00
Common Player: 2.00
Production 500 Sets
1EE Emmitt Smith 8.00
2EE Brett Favre 10.00
3EE Hines Ward 3.00
4EE Jerry Rice 6.00
5EE Jeff Garcia 2.00
6EE Chad Pennington 4.00
7EE Eric Moulds 2.00
8EE Daunte Culpepper 3.00
9EE Fred Taylor 3.00
10EE Drew Brees 3.00

2003 Fleer Focus NFL Shirtified

NM/M
Complete Set (15): 30.00
Common Player: 2.00
Production 750 Sets
1NS Torry Holt 2.00
2NS Michael Vick 8.00
3NS Jeremy Shockey 3.00
4NS Terrell Owens 2.00
5NS Plaxico Burress 2.50
6NS Steve McNair 2.50
7NS Ricky Williams 5.00
8NS Tim Brown 2.00
9NS Brian Urlacher 4.00
10NS Priest Holmes 2.50
11NS Tommy Maddox 2.00
12NS Deuce McAllister 2.00
13NS Marvin Harrison 2.00
14NS Clinton Portis 6.00
15NS Tiki Barber 2.00

2003 Fleer Focus NFL Shirtified Jerseys

NM/M
Common Player: 6.00
Production 175 Sets
Level 2: 1.5X
Production 75 Sets
Nameplates: 1.5X-3X
Production 25 Sets
NFL Logo Production 1 Set
Shaun Alexander 10.00
Tiki Barber 8.00
Tim Brown 8.00
Plaxico Burress 8.00
Daunte Culpepper 10.00
Brett Favre 25.00
Eddie George 8.00
William Green 8.00
Marvin Harrison 10.00
Travis Henry 6.00
Priest Holmes 12.00
Torry Holt 8.00
Andre Johnson 12.00
Ray Lewis 10.00
Tommy Maddox 6.00
Deuce McAllister 8.00
Steve McNair 10.00
Terrell Owens 10.00
Julius Peppers 6.00
Clinton Portis 12.00
Jeremy Shockey 10.00
Emmitt Smith 20.00
Brian Urlacher 12.00
Michael Vick 20.00
Ricky Williams 12.00

2003 Fleer Genuine

NM/M
Common Player (1-100): .40
Minor Stars: 60.00
Unlisted Stars: 1.00
Common Rookie (101-130): 2.00
Minor Rookies: 3.00
Unlisted Rookies: 4.00
101-110 Production 499 Sets
111-130 Production 799 Sets
131-140 Production 350 Sets
Pack (5): 5.50
Box (24): 70.00
1 Donovan McNabb 1.50
2 Rich Gannon .60
3 Joey Harrington 2.00
4 Eddie George 1.00
5 Jeremy Shockey 2.00
6 Tim Couch 1.25
7 Shaun Alexander 1.00
8 Tiki Barber .60
9 Antonio Bryant 1.00
10 Marc Bulger 1.00
11 Tom Brady 2.00
12 Julius Peppers .60
13 Junior Seau .60
14 Trent Green .60
15 Eric Moulds .60
16 Santana Moss .60
17 Hugh Douglas .40
18 Emmitt Smith 2.50
19 Tim Brown 1.00
20 William Green 1.00
21 Koren Robinson .40
22 Randy Moss 2.50
23 Anthony Thomas .40
24 Terrell Owens 1.00
25 Fred Taylor 1.00
26 Ahman Green 1.00
27 Derrick Mason .60
28 Chad Pennington 1.25
29 Shannon Sharpe .60
30 Warren Sapp .60
31 Deuce McAllister 1.25
32 Rod Smith .60
33 Torry Holt 1.00
34 Joe Horn .40
35 Chad Johnson .60
36 Matt Hasselbeck .40
37 Chris Chambers 1.00
38 Travis Henry .60
39 David Boston 1.00
40 Tony Gonzalez .60
41 Todd Heap .40
42 Hines Ward .60
43 Brett Favre 3.00
44 Rod Gardner .60
45 Donte Stallworth .60
46 Corey Dillon 1.00
47 Garrison Hearst .60
48 Ricky Williams 1.50
49 Ray Lewis .60
50 Plaxico Burress 1.00
51 Michael Bennett 1.00
52 Stephen Davis .60
53 LaDainian Tomlinson 1.00
54 Priest Holmes .60
55 Jonathan Wells .40
56 Jerome Bettis .60
57 Jimmy Smith .60
58 Michael Vick 3.00
59 Tommy Maddox 1.00
60 Edgerrin James 1.50
61 Laveranues Coles 1.00
62 Curtis Conway .60
63 Clinton Portis 2.50
64 Derrick Brooks .60
65 Amani Toomer .60
66 Roy Williams 1.00
67 Marshall Faulk 1.50
68 Daunte Culpepper 1.00
69 Peerless Price .60
70 Marcel Shipp .60
71 David Carr 2.00
72 Patrick Ramsey 1.00
73 Charlie Garner .60
74 Jake Plummer .60
75 Kurt Warner 1.50
76 Brian Urlacher 1.00
77 Tai Streets .60
78 Jason Taylor .40
79 Drew Bledsoe 1.00
80 Drew Brees 1.00
81 Peyton Manning 2.50
82 Jamal Lewis 1.00
83 Antwann Randle El .60
84 Mark Brunell .60
85 Warrick Dunn .60
86 Brian Dawkins .40
87 James Stewart .60
88 Ronde Barber .40
89 Curtis Martin 1.00
90 Jon Kitna .40
91 Keyshawn Johnson .60
92 Aaron Brooks 1.00
93 Marty Booker .60
94 Jeff Garcia 1.00
95 Marvin Harrison 1.00
96 T.J. Duckett 1.00
97 Jerry Rice 2.50
98 Donald Driver 1.00
99 Steve McNair 1.00
100 Kerry Collins .60
101 *Carson Palmer* 20.00
102 *Kyle Boller* 12.00
103 *Willis McGahee* 15.00
104 *Larry Johnson* 10.00
105 *Bryant Johnson* 6.00
106 *Byron Leftwich* 25.00
107 *Andre Johnson* 15.00
108 *Rex Grossman* 15.00
109 *Kelley Washington* 6.00
110 *Charles Rogers* 15.00
111 *Taylor Jacobs* 4.00
112 *Sam Aiken* 2.00
113 *Dallas Clark* 6.00
114 *B.J. Askew* 3.00
115 *Quentin Griffin* 12.00
116 *Terence Newman* 6.00
117 *Chris Simms* 10.00
118 *Brandon Lloyd* 5.00
119 *Lee Suggs* 12.00
120 *L.J. Smith* 2.00
121 *Anquan Boldin* 12.00
122 *Musa Smith* 4.00
123 *Billy McMullen* 3.00
124 *Bennie Joppru* 2.00
125 *Justin Fargas* 4.00
126 *Tyrone Calico* 8.00
127 *Dave Ragone* 4.00
128 *Seneca Wallace* 4.00
129 *Chris Brown* 10.00
130 *Terrell Suggs* 5.00
131 Bethel Johnson 8.00
132 Nate Burleson 6.00
133 Teyo Johnson 8.00
134 Kevin Curtis 4.00
135 Jason Witten 6.00
136 Artose Pinner 8.00
137 Boss Bailey 6.00
138 Jerome McDougle 4.00
139 LaBrandon Toefield 6.00
140 *Domanick Davis* 12.00

2003 Fleer Genuine Minis

Stars: .5X
Production 149 Sets

2003 Fleer Genuine Reflection

Stars (1-100): 3X-6X
Rookies (101-130): 1X-2X
Production 99 Sets

2003 Fleer Genuine Autograph Insider

NM/M
Common Player: 15.00
Inserted 1:24
AI-MB Michael Bennett 15.00
AI-KB Kyle Boller 50.00
AI-DB Drew Brees 15.00
AI-DC David Carr 40.00
AI-LJ Larry Johnson 40.00
AI-TM Tommy Maddox 40.00
AI-CS Chris Simms 40.00
AI-KW Kelley Washington 15.00
AI-RW Roy Williams 20.00

2003 Fleer Genuine Genuine Article

NM/M
Common Player: 5.00
Inserted 1:24
GA-TB Tom Brady 8.00
GA-DB Drew Brees 6.00
GA-AB Aaron Brooks 5.00
GA-DC2 David Carr 8.00
GA-DC Daunte Culpepper 5.00
GA-MF Marshall Faulk 10.00
GA-BF Brett Favre 15.00
GA-JH Joey Harrington 8.00
GA-MH Marvin Harrison 5.00
GA-PM Peyton Manning SP 10.00
GA-DM2 Deuce McAllister 5.00
GA-DM Donovan McNabb 12.00
GA-RM Randy Moss 12.00
GA-TO Terrell Owens 5.00
GA-CP2 Chad Pennington 6.00
GA-CP Clinton Portis 12.00
GA-JR Jerry Rice 15.00
GA-JS Jeremy Shockey 10.00

GA-ES	Emmitt Smith	15.00
GA-LT	LaDainian Tomlinson	8.00
GA-BU	Brian Urlacher	10.00
GA-MV	Michael Vick SP	20.00
GA-KW	Kurt Warner	10.00
GA-RW	Ricky Williams	10.00

2003 Fleer Genuine Genuine Article Patch

		NM/M
	Common Player:	15.00
	Production 50 Sets	
GA-DB	Drew Brees	15.00
GA-DC2	David Carr	35.00
GA-DC	Daunte Culpepper	25.00
GA-MF	Marshall Faulk	30.00
GA-BF	Brett Favre	60.00
GA-JH	Joey Harrington	40.00
GA-MH	Marvin Harrison	15.00
GA-PM	Peyton Manning	40.00
GA-DM	Donovan McNabb	40.00
GA-RM	Randy Moss	40.00
GA-TO	Terrell Owens	15.00
GA-CP2	Chad Pennington	30.00
GA-JR	Jerry Rice	40.00
GA-JS	Jeremy Shockey	30.00
GA-ES	Emmitt Smith	50.00
GA-LT	LaDainian Tomlinson	30.00
GA-BU	Brian Urlacher	30.00
GA-MV	Michael Vick	60.00
GA-KW	Kurt Warner	30.00
GA-RW	Ricky Williams	40.00

2003 Fleer Genuine Tools of the Game

		NM/M
	Common Player:	1.00
	Inserted 1:8	
	Jersey Versions	3X-6X
	Production 199 Sets	
1TG	Brett Favre	4.00
2TG	Clinton Portis	3.00
3TG	Donovan McNabb	1.50
4TG	Daunte Culpepper	1.00
5TG	LaDainian Tomlinson	1.50
6TG	Tom Brady	1.50
7TG	Peyton Manning	2.00
8TG	Emmitt Smith	3.00
9TG	Brian Urlacher	2.00
10TG	Michael Vick	4.00
11TG	Randy Moss	2.00
12TG	Marshall Faulk	1.50
13TG	Kurt Warner	2.00
14TG	Marvin Harrison	1.00
15TG	Joey Harrington	2.50

2003 Fleer Genuine Tools of the Game Dual Jerseys

		NM/M
	Production 99 Sets	
TG-DC	Daunte Culpepper	15.00
TG-MF	Marshall Faulk	20.00
TG-BF	Brett Favre	50.00
TG-MH	Marvin Harrison	15.00
TG-PM	Peyton Manning	30.00
TG-DM	Donovan McNabb	30.00
TG-RM	Randy Moss	30.00
TG-BU	Brian Urlacher	30.00
TG-MV	Michael Vick	50.00
TG-KW	Kurt Warner	20.00

2003 Fleer Genuine Touchdown Threats

		NM/M
	Inserted 1:20	
	Jersey Versions	3X-6X
	Inserted 1:48	
1TD	Donovan McNabb, Michael Vick	5.00
2TD	Brett Favre, Peyton Manning	5.00
3TD	Jeremy Shockey, Todd Heap	2.00
4TD	Randy Moss, Terrell Owens	3.00
5TD	LaDainian Tomlinson, Clinton Portis	4.00
6TD	Emmitt Smith, Jerry Rice	4.00
7TD	Deuce McAllister, Travis Henry	1.50
8TD	Ricky Williams, Fred Taylor	2.50
9TD	Marshall Faulk, Edgerrin James	2.00
10TD	David Carr, Chad Pennington	4.00

2003 Fleer Genuine Touchdown Threats Dual Jerseys

		NM/M
	Common Player:	12.00
	Production 200 Sets	
DM-MV	Donovan McNabb, Michael Vick	30.00
BF-PM	Brett Favre, Peyton Manning	40.00
RM-TO	Randy Moss, Terrell Owens	20.00
LT-CP	LaDainian Tomlinson, Clinton Portis	20.00
ES-JR	Emmitt Smith, Jerry Rice	40.00
MF-EJ	Marshall Faulk, Edgerrin James	20.00
DC-CP	David Carr, Chad Pennington	20.00

2003 Fleer Hot Prospects

		NM/M
	Common Player (1-80):	.30
	Minor Stars:	.60
	Unlisted Stars:	.75
	Common Rookie (81-120):	2.00
	Minor Rookies:	3.00
	Unlisted Rookies:	4.00
	Cards 81-91 Production 400 Sets	
	Cards 92-103 Production 750 Sets	
	Cards 104-109 Production 300 Sets	
	Cards 110-120 Production 1,250 Sets	
	Pack (5):	7.50
	Box (15):	80.00
1	Emmitt Smith	2.50
2	Terrell Owens	.75
3	Tiki Barber	.75
4	Trent Green	.60
5	Quincy Morgan	.60
6	Eric Moulds	.60
7	Simeon Rice	.30
8	Hines Ward	.75
9	Michael Bennett	.75
10	Donald Driver	.60
11	Stephen Davis	.60
12	Steve McNair	.75
13	David Boston	.75
14	Deuce McAllister	.75
15	Marvin Harrison	.75
16	Peerless Price	.60
17	Matt Hasselbeck	.60
18	Jerry Rice	2.50
19	Junior Seau	.60
20	Clinton Portis	2.50
21	Fred Taylor	.75
22	William Green	.75
23	Warrick Dunn	.60
24	Koren Robinson	.60
25	Jeremy Shockey	1.50
26	Chris Chambers	.75
27	Brett Favre	3.00
28	Julius Peppers	.60
29	Eddie George	.75
30	Todd Pinkston	.30
31	Tom Brady	1.00
32	Edgerrin James	1.00
33	Chad Johnson	.60
34	Laveranues Coles	.60
35	LaDainian Tomlinson	1.00
36	Priest Holmes	.75
37	Shannon Sharpe	.75
38	Jamal Lewis	.75
39	Warren Sapp	.60
40	Tim Brown	.60
41	Kerry Collins	.60
42	Jimmy Smith	.60
43	Chad Hutchinson	.30
44	Marcel Shipp	.60
45	Jeff Garcia	.75
46	Donovan McNabb	1.00
47	Randy Moss	1.50
48	Ahman Green	.75
49	Travis Henry	.60
50	Brad Johnson	.60
51	Tommy Maddox	.60
52	Aaron Brooks	.75
53	Peyton Manning	1.50
54	Brian Urlacher	1.00
55	Rod Gardner	.60
56	Chad Pennington	1.00
57	Ricky Williams	1.50
58	James Stewart	.30
59	Todd Heap	.60
60	Marshall Faulk	1.00
61	Corey Dillon	.60
62	Michael Vick	3.00
63	Shaun Alexander	.75
64	Curtis Martin	.75
65	Mark Brunell	.60
66	Joey Harrington	2.00
67	Drew Bledsoe	1.00
68	Keyshawn Johnson	.60
69	Jerome Bettis	.60
70	Daunte Culpepper	.75
71	David Carr	2.00
72	Marty Booker	.60
73	Patrick Ramsey	.60
74	Drew Brees	.60
75	Donte Stallworth	.60
76	Jake Plummer	.60
77	Ray Lewis	.60
78	Kurt Warner	1.00
79	Rich Gannon	.60
80	Tony Gonzalez	.60
81	*Sam Aiken*	12.00
82	*Dave Ragone*	15.00
83	*Musa Smith*	15.00
84	*B.J. Askew*	15.00
85	*Kevin Curtis*	12.00
86	*Brandon Lloyd*	20.00
87	*E.J. Henderson*	10.00
88	*Justin Fargas*	20.00
89	*Lee Suggs*	30.00
90	*Chris Brown*	30.00
91	*Bennie Joppru*	12.00
92	*Dallas Clark*	10.00
93	*Terence Newman*	12.00
94	*Rex Grossman*	12.00
95	*Kelley Washington*	10.00
96	*Kyle Boller*	12.00
97	*Carson Palmer*	15.00
98	*Charles Rogers*	12.00
99	*Chris Simms*	12.00
100	*Larry Johnson*	10.00
101	*Andre Johnson*	15.00
102	*Taylor Jacobs*	8.00
103	*Byron Leftwich*	20.00
104	*Jason Witten*	35.00
105	*Teyo Johnson*	25.00
106	*Michael Haynes*	15.00
107	*Bryant Johnson*	30.00
108	*Terrell Suggs*	40.00
109	*L.J. Smith*	25.00
110	*Tyrone Calico*	4.00
111	*Billy McMullen*	2.00
112	*Jerome McDougle*	2.00
113	*Willis McGahee*	8.00
114	*Anquan Boldin*	6.00
115	*Artose Pinner*	3.00
116	*Kevin Williams*	2.00
117	*Bethel Johnson*	3.00
118	*Quentin Griffin*	12.00
119	*Nate Burleson*	3.00
120	*Dewayne Robertson*	2.00

2003 Fleer Hot Prospects Cream of the Crop

		NM/M
	Complete Set (15):	40.00
	Common Player:	2.00
	Inserted 1:5	
1COC	Byron Leftwich	6.00
2COC	Charles Rogers	5.00
3COC	Carson Palmer	6.00
4COC	Taylor Jacobs	2.00
5COC	Bryant Johnson	2.50
6COC	Kyle Boller	4.00
7COC	Rex Grossman	5.00
8COC	Andre Johnson	5.00
9COC	Kelley Washington	2.00
10COC	Larry Johnson	4.00
11COC	Willis McGahee	5.00
12COC	Chris Simms	3.00
13COC	Jason Witten	2.00
14COC	Anquan Boldin	4.00
15COC	Quentin Griffin	2.50

2003 Fleer Hot Prospects Hot Materials Game-Used

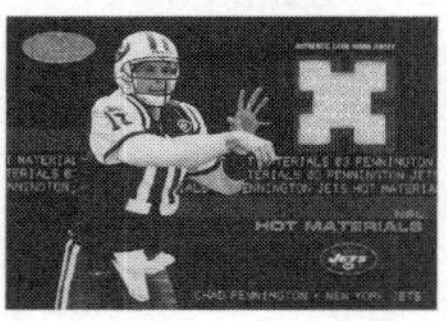

		NM/M
	Common Player:	6.00
	Production 150 Sets	
	Red Hots:	1X-1.5X
	Production 50 Sets	
HM-SA	Shaun Alexander	10.00
HM-DB	Drew Bledsoe	10.00
HM-TB	Tom Brady	15.00
HM-DB2	Drew Brees	6.00
HM-DC2	David Carr	12.00
HM-DC	Daunte Culpepper	10.00
HM-MF	Marshall Faulk	12.00
HM-BF	Brett Favre	25.00
HM-RG	Rich Gannon	6.00
HM-JG	Jeff Garcia	8.00
HM-RG	Rod Gardner	6.00
HM-EJ	Edgerrin James	12.00
HM-JH	Joey Harrington	10.00
HM-JL	Jamal Lewis	10.00
HM-PM	Peyton Manning	15.00
HM-DM	Deuce McAllister	8.00
HM-DM2	Donovan McNabb	12.00
HM-RM	Randy Moss	15.00
HM-TO	Terrell Owens	8.00
HM-CP2	Chad Pennington	12.00
HM-CP	Clinton Portis	20.00
HM-PR	Patrick Ramsey	8.00
HM-JR	Jerry Rice	20.00
HM-JS	Jeremy Shockey	10.00
HM-DS	Donte Stallworth	6.00
HM-LT	LaDainian Tomlinson	8.00
HM-BU	Brian Urlacher	10.00
HM-MV	Michael Vick	25.00
HM-KW	Kurt Warner	8.00
HM-RW	Ricky Williams	12.00

2003 Fleer Hot Prospects Hot Tandems Game-Used

		NM/M
	Common Player:	10.00
	Production 100 Sets	
	Red Hots Production 10 Sets	
TO-DS	Terrell Owens, Donte Stallworth	10.00
DM-SA	Deuce McAllister, Shaun Alexander	12.00
JR-RM	Jerry Rice, Randy Moss	25.00
CP-JL	Clinton Portis, Jamal Lewis	20.00
JS-RG	Jeremy Shockey, Rod Gardner	10.00
BF-TB	Brett Favre, Tom Brady	30.00
EJ-LT	Edgerrin James, LaDainianTomlinson	15.00
JG-DM	Jeff Garcia, Donovan McNabb	15.00
PM-BU	Peyton Manning, Brian Urlacher	20.00
CP-MV	Chad Pennington, Michael Vick	30.00
RW-MF	Ricky Williams, Marshall Faulk	20.00
JH-DC	Joey Harrington, Daunte Culpepper	15.00
DC-PR	David Carr, Patrick Ramsey	15.00
KW-RG	Kurt Warner, Rich Gannon	10.00
DB-DB	Drew Bledsoe, Drew Brees	10.00
DM-RM	Donovan McNabb, Randy Moss	25.00
DC-DC	Daunte Culpepper, David Carr	20.00
MF-MV	Marshall Faulk, Michael Vick	30.00
JS-BF	Jeremy Shockey, Brett Favre	30.00
TO-DM	Terrell Owens, Deuce McAllister	15.00
CP-RW	Chad Pennington, Ricky Williams	20.00
LT-JL	LaDainian Tomlinson, Jamal Lewis	15.00
JH-DB	Joey Harrington, Drew Bledsoe	15.00
BU-JR	Brian Urlacher, Jerry Rice	20.00
PM-KW	Peyton Manning, Kurt Warner	20.00

2003 Fleer Hot Prospects Hot Triple Patch

		NM/M
	Common Player:	25.00
	Production 50 Sets	
O-R-M	Terrell Owens, Jerry Rice, Randy Moss	80.00
F-M-M	Brett Favre, Peyton Manning, Donovan McNabb	100.00
M-P-T	Deuce McAllister, Clinton Portis, LaDainian Tomlinson	50.00
S-S-G	Jeremy Shockey, Donte Stallworth, Rod Gardner	25.00
B-G-P	Tom Brady, Jeff Garcia, Chad Pennington	50.00
J-L-A	Edgerrin James, Jamal Lewis, Shaun Alexander	40.00
C-R-B	David Carr, Patrick Ramsey, Drew Brees	30.00
W-G-B	Kurt Warner, Rich Gannon, Drew Bledsoe	25.00
V-H-C	Michael Vick, Joey Harrington, Daunte Culpepper	60.00
U-W-F	Brian Urlacher, Ricky Williams, Marshall Faulk	50.00
M-M-M	Donovan McNabb, Randy Moss, Peyton Manning	80.00
W-F-V	Ricky Williams, Marshall Faulk, Michael Vick	60.00
S-F-B	Jeremy Shockey, Brett Favre, Tom Brady	60.00
J-T-L	Edgerrin James, LaDainian Tomlinson, Jamal Lewis	40.00
H-B-C	Joey Harrington, Drew Bledsoe, Daunte Culpepper	40.00

Post-1980 cards in Near Mint condition will generally sell for about 75% of the quoted Mint value. Excellent-condition cards bring no more than 40%.

2003 Fleer Hot Prospects Sweet Selections

		NM/M
	Complete Set (10):	25.00
	Common Player:	2.00
	Inserted 1:15	
1SS	Carson Palmer, David Carr	5.00
2SS	LaDainian Tomlinson, Jamal Lewis	2.00
3SS	Joey Harrington, Steve McNair	3.00
4SS	Brian Urlacher, Fred Taylor	3.00
5SS	Michael Vick, Peyton Manning	10.00
6SS	Torry Holt, Tim Brown	2.00
7SS	Ricky Williams, Junior Seau	3.00
8SS	Donovan McNabb, Marshall Faulk	3.00
9SS	Plaxico Burress, David Boston	2.00
10SS	Keyshawn Johnson, Drew Bledsoe	3.00

2003 Fleer Hot Prospects Sweet Selections Game Used

		NM/M
	Common Player:	10.00
	Production 325 Sets	
PM-DC	Carson Palmer, David Carr	20.00
LT-JL	LaDainian Tomlinson, Jamal Lewis	10.00
JH-SM	Joey Harrington, Steve McNair	12.00
BU-FT	Brian Urlacher, Fred Taylor	12.00
MV-PM	Michael Vick, Peyton Manning	30.00
TH-TB	Torry Holt, Tim Brown	10.00
RW-JS	Ricky Williams, Junior Seau	12.00
DM-MF	Donovan McNabb, Marshall Faulk	15.00
PB-DB	Plaxico Burress, David Boston	10.00
KJ-DB	Keyshawn Johnson, Drew Bledsoe	10.00

2003 Fleer Mystique

		NM/M
	Common Player (1-80):	.40
	Minor Stars:	.75
	Unlisted Stars:	1.00
	Common Rookie (81-130):	3.00
	Minor Rookies:	4.00
	Unlisted Rookies:	5.00
	Production 699 Sets	
	Pack (4):	3.25
	Box (20):	45.00
1	Emmitt Smith	3.00
2	Marcel Shipp	.75
3	Michael Vick	4.00
4	Warrick Dunn	.75
5	T.J. Duckett	1.00
6	Peerless Price	.75
7	Ray Lewis	.75
8	Todd Heap	.40
9	Jamal Lewis	1.00
10	Eric Moulds	.75
11	Drew Bledsoe	1.50
12	Travis Henry	.75
13	Stephen Davis	.75
14	Julius Peppers	.75
15	Marty Booker	.75
16	Brian Urlacher	2.00
17	Chad Johnson	.75
18	Corey Dillon	1.00
19	William Green	1.00
20	Tim Couch	1.00
21	Joey Galloway	.75
22	Chad Hutchinson	.75
23	Jake Plummer	.75
24	Ed McCaffrey	.75
25	Clinton Portis	3.00
26	Joey Harrington	2.50
27	Ahman Green	1.00
28	Brett Favre	4.00
29	Jabar Gaffney	.75
30	David Carr	2.50
31	Peyton Manning	2.00
32	Marvin Harrison	1.00
33	Edgerrin James	1.50
34	Mark Brunell	.75
35	Fred Tayor	1.00
36	Trent Green	.75
37	Priest Holmes	1.00
38	Tony Gonzalez	.75
39	Chris Chambers	1.00
40	Zach Thomas	.40
41	Ricky Williams	2.00
42	Michael Bennett	1.00
43	Daunte Culpepper	1.00
44	Randy Moss	2.00
45	Deion Branch	.75
46	Tom Brady	1.50
47	Aaron Brooks	1.00
48	Deuce McAllister	1.00
49	Joe Horn	.75
50	Jeremy Shockey	2.50
51	Amani Toomer	.75
52	Tiki Barber	1.00
53	Chad Pennington	1.50
54	Curtis Martin	1.00
55	Rich Gannon	.75
56	Tim Brown	1.00
57	Jerry Rice	3.00
58	Donovan McNabb	1.50
59	Duce Staley	.75
60	Hines Ward	.75
61	Tommy Maddox	1.00
62	Plaxico Burress	1.00
63	Jerome Bettis	.75
64	David Boston	1.00
65	Drew Brees	1.50
66	LaDainian Tomlinson	1.50
67	Jeff Garcia	.75
68	Terrell Owens	1.00
69	Koren Robinson	.75
70	Shaun Alexander	1.00
71	Kurt Warner	2.00
72	Torry Holt	1.00
73	Marshall Faulk	1.50
74	Keyshawn Johnson	.75
75	Mike Alstott	.75
76	Warren Sapp	.75
77	Steve McNair	1.00
78	Eddie George	1.00
79	Patrick Ramsey	1.00
80	Rod Gardner	.75
81	*Bennie Joppru*	4.00
82	*Musa Smith*	5.00
83	*Ken Dorsey*	8.00
84	*Billy McMullen*	4.00
85	*Bethel Johnson*	6.00
86	*Terence Newman*	8.00
87	*Jason Witten*	6.00
88	*Jimmy Kennedy*	4.00
89	*Johnathan Sullivan*	3.00
90	*Chris Simms*	10.00
91	*Brian St. Pierre*	5.00
92	*Quentin Griffin*	12.00
93	*Tyrone Calico*	6.00
94	*Dewayne Robertson*	3.00
95	*Bryant Johnson*	6.00
96	*Charles Rogers*	12.00
97	*William Joseph*	5.00
98	*Dallas Clark*	8.00
99	*Michael Haynes*	4.00
100	*Larry Johnson*	10.00
101	*Terrell Suggs*	6.00
102	*Marcus Trufant*	4.00
103	*Dave Ragone*	6.00
104	*Seneca Wallace*	6.00
105	*Willis McGahee*	15.00
106	*Andre Woolfolk*	4.00
107	*LaBrandon Toefield*	4.00
108	*Andre Johnson*	15.00
109	*Lee Suggs*	6.00
110	*Brandon Lloyd*	6.00
111	*Kyle Boller*	15.00
112	*B.J. Askew*	4.00
113	*Anquan Boldin*	12.00
114	*Kelley Washington*	6.00
115	*Kevin Williams*	4.00
116	*Kliff Kingsbury*	5.00
117	*Jerome McDougle*	4.00
118	*L.J. Smith*	4.00
119	*J.R. Tolver*	4.00
120	*Carson Palmer*	20.00
121	*Kevin Curtis*	4.00
122	*Shaun McDonald*	3.00
123	*Byron Leftwich*	25.00
124	*Bobby Wade*	4.00
125	*Nate Burleson*	6.00
126	*Justin Fargas*	6.00
127	*Dewayne White*	3.00
128	*Taylor Jacobs*	5.00
129	*Rex Grossman*	15.00
130	*Boss Bailey*	5.00

2003 Fleer Mystique Blue Rookies

Rookies: 1X-5X
Production 350 Sets

2003 Fleer Mystique Gold

Stars: 5X-10X
Production 150 Sets
Rookies: 1X-2X
Production 75 Sets

2003 Fleer Mystique Awe Pairs

NM/M
Complete Set (20): 60.00
Common Player: 4.00
Production 250 Sets
1AP Drew Bledsoe, Travis Henry 5.00
2AP Peyton Manning, Marvin Harrison 6.00
3AP Tommy Maddox, Plaxico Burress 4.00
4AP Marshall Faulk, Torry Holt 6.00
5AP Ricky Williams, Chris Chambers 5.00
6AP Trent Green, Priest Holmes 4.00
7AP Steve McNair, Eddie George 4.00
8AP Donovan McNabb, Duce Staley 5.00
9AP Rich Gannon, Tim Brown 4.00
10AP Chad Pennington, Curtis Martin 4.00
11AP Drew Brees, LaDainian Tomlinson 4.00
12AP Kerry Collins, Jeremy Shockey 5.00
13AP Keyshawn Johnson, Mike Alstott 4.00
14AP Michael Bennett, Randy Moss 5.00
15AP Jeff Garcia, Terrell Owens 4.00
16AP Brett Favre, Donald Driver 10.00
17AP Jamal Lewis, Todd Heap 4.00
18AP Koren Robinson, Shaun Alexander 4.00
19AP Aaron Brooks, Deuce McAllister 4.00
20AP Michael Vick, Warrick Dunn 10.00

2003 Fleer Mystique Awe Pairs Gold

NM/M
Complete Set (20): 60.00
Common Player: 4.00
Production 250 Sets
1AP Drew Bledsoe/8, Travis Henry/8 5.00
2AP Peyton Manning/10, Marvin Harrison/10 6.00
3AP Tommy Maddox/10, Plaxico Burress/10 4.00
4AP Marshall Faulk/7, Torry Holt/7 6.00
5AP Ricky Williams/9, Chris Chambers/9 5.00
6AP Trent Green/8, Priest Holmes/8 4.00
7AP Steve McNair/11, Eddie George/11 4.00
8AP Donovan McNabb/12, Duce Staley/12 5.00
9AP Rich Gannon/11, Tim Brown/11 4.00
10AP Chad Pennington/9, Curtis Martin/9 4.00
11AP Drew Brees/8, LaDainian Tomlinson/8 4.00
12AP Kerry Collins/10, Jeremy Shockey/10 5.00
13AP Keyshawn Johnson/12, Mike Alstott/12 4.00
14AP Michael Bennett/6, Randy Moss/6 5.00
15AP Jeff Garcia/10, Terrell Owens/10 4.00
16AP Brett Favre/12, Donald Driver/12 10.00
17AP Jamal Lewis/7, Todd Heap/7 4.00
18AP Koren Robinson/7, Shaun Alexander/7 4.00
19AP Aaron Brooks/9, Deuce McAllister/9 4.00
20AP Michael Vick/9, Warrick Dunn/9 10.00

2003 Fleer Mystique Awe Pairs Jerseys

NM/M
Common Player: 10.00
Production 199 Sets
DB/TH Drew Bledsoe, Travis Henry 15.00
PM/MH Peyton Manning, Marvin Harrison 15.00
TM/PB Tommy Maddox, Plaxico Burress 10.00
MF/TH Marshall Faulk, Torry Holt 12.00
RW/CC Ricky Williams, Chris Chambers 15.00
SM/EG Steve McNair, Eddie George 12.00
DM/DS Donovan McNabb, Duce Staley 12.00
RG/TB Rich Gannon, Tim Brown 10.00
DB/LT Drew Brees, LaDainian Tomlinson 10.00
KC/JS Kerry Collins, Jeremy Shockey 10.00
KJ/MA Keyshawn Johnson, Mike Alstott 10.00
MB/RM Michael Bennett, Randy Moss 15.00
JG/TO Jeff Garcia, Terrell Owens 10.00
JL/TH Jamal Lewis, Todd Heap 10.00
KR/SA Koren Robinson, Shaun Alexander 10.00
AB/DM Aaron Brooks, Deuce McAllister 10.00

2003 Fleer Mystique End Zone Eminence

NM/M
Complete Set (10): 35.00
Common Player: 4.00
Production 100 Sets
1EZE Priest Holmes 4.00
2EZE Shaun Alexander 4.00
3EZE Ricky Williams 6.00
4EZE Clinton Portis 12.00
5EZE Deuce McAllister 4.00
6EZE LaDainian Tomlinson 6.00
7EZE Travis Henry 4.00
8EZE Eddie George 4.00
9EZE Terrell Owens 4.00
10EZE Hines Ward 4.00

2003 Fleer Mystique End Zone Eminence Gold

NM/M
Production 100 Sets
1EZE Priest Holmes/67 10.00
2EZE Shaun Alexander/88 6.00
3EZE Ricky Williams/63 10.00
4EZE Clinton Portis/66 12.00
5EZE Deuce McAllister/54 8.00
6EZE LaDainian Tomlinson/58 8.00
7EZE Travis Henry/26 10.00
8EZE Eddie George/54 6.00
9EZE Terrell Owens/79 8.00
10EZE Hines Ward/77 5.00

2003 Fleer Mystique End Zone Eminence Jerseys

NM/M
Common Player: 10.00
Production 150 Sets
EZE-SA Shaun Alexander 10.00
EZE-EG Eddie George 10.00
EZE-TH Travis Henry 10.00
EZE-PH Priest Holmes 12.00
EZE-DM Deuce McAllister 10.00
EZE-TO Terrell Owens 10.00
EZE-CP Clinton Portis 20.00
EZE-LT LaDainian Tomlinson 10.00
EZE-HW Hines Ward 10.00
EZE-RW Ricky Williams 15.00

2003 Fleer Mystique Ink Appeal

NM/M
IA-MB Michael Bennett
IA-TB Tom Brady 50.00
IA-PB Plaxico Burress
IA-JH Joey Harrington
IA-AJ Andre Johnson 75.00
IA-WM Willis McGahee 60.00
IA-DM Donovan McNabb
IA-CP Chad Pennington
IA-LT LaDainian Tomlinson 40.00

2003 Fleer Mystique Ink Appeal Gold

NM/M
IAG-MB Michael Bennett
IAG-TB Tom Brady
IAG-PB Plaxico Burress 25.00
IAG-JH Joey Harrington
IAG-AJ Andre Johnson 75.00
IAG-WM Willis McGahee
IAG-DM Donovan McNabb
IAG-CP Chad Pennington
IAG-LT LaDainian Tomlinson

2003 Fleer Mystique Rare Finds

NM/M
Complete Set (10): 30.00
Common Player: 3.00
Production 350 Sets
1RF Ricky Williams, Priest Holmes, LaDainian Tomlinson 5.00
2RF Marshall Faulk, Deuce McAllister, Shaun Alexander 5.00
3RF Rich Gannon, Drew Bledsoe, Peyton Manning 6.00
4RF Brett Favre, Aaron Brooks, Michael Vick 10.00
5RF Marvin Harrison, Hines Ward, Eric Moulds 3.00
6RF Randy Moss, Terrell Owens, Keyshawn Johnson 5.00
7RF Julius Peppers, Brian Urlacher, Ray Lewis 3.00
8RF David Carr, Joey Harrington, Patrick Ramsey 6.00
9RF Clinton Portis, Travis Henry, William Green 5.00
10RF Jerry Rice, Tim Brown, Jerry Porter 6.00

2003 Fleer Mystique Rare Finds Autograph

NM/M
Common Player: 30.00
Production 100 Sets
RFA-MB Michael Bennett 30.00
RFA-PB Plaxico Burress 30.00
RFA-JH Joey Harrington 50.00
RFA-DM Donovan McNabb 50.00
RFA-CP Chad Pennington 40.00

2003 Fleer Mystique Rare Finds Single Swatch

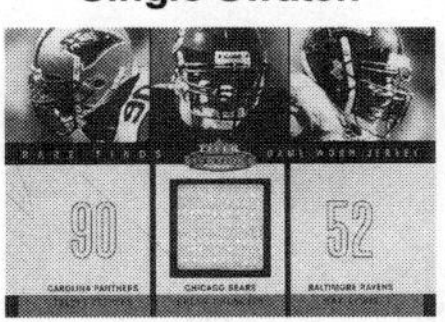

NM/M
RF-RW Ricky Williams Jsy, Priest Holmes, LaDainian Tomlinson 10.00
RF-MF Marshall Faulk Jsy, Deuce McAllister, Shaun Alexander 10.00
RF-DM Marshall Faulk, Deuce McAllister Jsy, Shaun Alexander 8.00
RF-DB Rich Gannon, Drew Bledsoe Jsy, Peyton Manning 12.00
RF-BF Brett Favre Jsy, Aaron Brooks, Michael Vick 20.00
RF-MH Marvin Harrison Jsy, Hines Ward, Eric Moulds 8.00
RF-HW Marvin Harrison, Hines Ward Jsy, Eric Moulds 8.00
RF-TO Randy Moss, Terrell Owens Jsy, Keyshawn Johnson 8.00
RF-JP Julius Peppers Jsy, Brian Urlacher, Ray Lewis 8.00
RF-BU Julius Peppers, Brian Urlacher Jsy, Ray Lewis 10.00
RF-DC David Carr Jsy, Joey Harrington, Patrick Ramsey 12.00
RF-JH David Carr, Joey Harrington Jsy, Patrick Ramsey 12.00
RF-CP Clinton Portis Jsy, Travis Henry, William Green 12.00
RF-WG Clinton Portis, Travis Henry, William Green Jsy 8.00

2003 Fleer Mystique Rare Finds Dual Swatch

NM/M
RW/PH Ricky Williams Jsy, Priest Holmes Jsy, LaDainian Tomlinson 15.00
RW/LT Ricky Williams Jsy, Priest Holmes, LaDainian Tomlinson Jsy 15.00
MF/DM Marshall Faulk Jsy, Deuce McAllister Jsy, Shaun Alexander 10.00
DM/SA Marshall Faulk, Deuce McAllister Jsy, Shaun Alexander Jsy 10.00
DB/PM Rich Gannon, Drew Bledsoe Jsy, Peyton Manning Jsy 15.00
MH/HW Marvin Harrison Jsy, Hines Ward Jsy, Eric Moulds 10.00
TO/KJ Randy Moss, Terrell Owens Jsy, Keyshawn Johnson Jsy 10.00
JP/BU Julius Peppers Jsy, Brian Urlacher Jsy, Ray Lewis 15.00
DC/JH David Carr Jsy, Joey Harrington Jsy, Patrick Ramsey 20.00
CP/TH Clinton Portis Jsy, Travis Henry Jsy, William Green 12.00

2003 Fleer Mystique Rare Finds Triple Swatch

NM/M
RWPHLT Ricky Williams, Priest Holmes, LaDainian Tomlinson 50.00
MFDMSA Marshall Faulk, Deuce McAllister, Shaun Alexander 25.00
RGDBPM Rich Gannon, Drew Bledsoe, Peyton Manning 25.00
MHHWEM Marvin Harrison, Hines Ward, Eric Moulds 20.00
JPBURL Julius Peppers, Brian Urlacher, Ray Lewis 40.00
DCJHPR David Carr, Joey Harrington, Patrick Ramsey 40.00
CPTHWG Clinton Portis, Travis Henry, William Green 25.00

2003 Fleer Mystique Rare Finds Jersey Autos

NM/M
Common Player: 50.00
Production 50 Sets
RFGA-MB Michael Bennett 50.00
RFGA-PB Plaxico Burress 50.00
RFGA-JH Joey Harrington 80.00
RFGA-DM Donovan McNabb 80.00
RFGA-CP Chad Pennington 60.00

2003 Fleer Mystique Secret Weapons

NM/M
Production 500 Sets
1SW Willis McGahee 5.00
2SW Carson Palmer 8.00
3SW Charles Rogers 6.00
4SW Byron Leftwich 8.00
5SW Andre Johnson 5.00
6SW Larry Johnson 5.00
7SW Quentin Griffin 3.00
8SW Dave Ragone 2.00
9SW Kyle Boller 6.00
10SW Chris Simms 4.00
11SW Terrell Suggs 2.00
12SW Rex Grossman 6.00
13SW Bryant Johnson 2.50
14SW Seneca Wallace 2.00
15SW Terence Newman 3.00

2003 Fleer Mystique Secret Weapons Gold

1SW Willis McGahee/21
2SW Carson Palmer/9
3SW Charles Rogers/80
4SW Byron Leftwich/7
5SW Andre Johnson/80
6SW Larry Johnson/34
7SW Quentin Griffin/22
8SW Dave Ragone/4
9SW Kyle Boller/8
10SW Chris Simms/2
11SW Terrell Suggs/55
12SW Rex Grossman/8
13SW Bryant Johnson/83
14SW Seneca Wallace/15
15SW Terence Newman/41

2003 Fleer Mystique Shining Stars

NM/M
Complete Set (15): 40.00
Common Player: 2.00
Production 500 Sets
1SS Emmitt Smith 6.00
2SS Michael Vick 8.00
3SS Brian Urlacher 4.00
4SS Joey Harrington 5.00
5SS Brett Favre 8.00
6SS Peyton Manning 4.00
7SS Tom Brady 3.00
8SS Kurt Warner 3.00
9SS Jeremy Shockey 4.00
10SS Jerry Rice 6.00
11SS Marshall Faulk 3.00
12SS Randy Moss 3.00
13SS Donovan McNabb 3.00
14SS Corey Dillon 2.00
15SS David Carr 5.00

2003 Fleer Mystique Shining Stars Gold

NM/M
Complete Set (15): 40.00
Common Player: 2.00
1SS Emmitt Smith/164 10.00
2SS Michael Vick/27 40.00
3SS Brian Urlacher/2
4SS Joey Harrington/12 30.00
5SS Brett Favre/326 8.00
6SS Peyton Manning/147 10.00
7SS Tom Brady/47 15.00
8SS Kurt Warner/102 6.00
9SS Jeremy Shockey/2
10SS Jerry Rice/192 10.00
11SS Marshall Faulk/120 8.00
12SS Randy Moss/60 15.00
13SS Donovan McNabb/85 12.00
14SS Corey Dillon/48 8.00
15SS David Carr/12 30.00

2003 Fleer Mystique Shining Stars Jerseys

NM/M
Common Player: 10.00
Production 250 Sets
SS-TB Tom Brady 10.00
SS-DC David Carr 15.00
SS-CD Corey Dillon 10.00
SS-MF Marshall Faulk 10.00
SS-BF Brett Favre 20.00
SS-JH Joey Harrington 12.00
SS-PM Peyton Manning 12.00
SS-DM Donovan McNabb 10.00
SS-JR Jerry Rice 15.00
SS-JS Jeremy Shockey 10.00
SS-ES Emmitt Smith 20.00
SS-BU Brian Urlacher 12.00
SS-KW Kurt Warner 10.00

2003 Fleer Mystique Shining Stars Patch

SSP-TB Tom Brady
SSP-DC David Carr
SSP-CD Corey Dillon
SSP-MF Marshall Faulk
SSP-BF Brett Favre
SSP-JH Joey Harrington
SSP-PM Peyton Manning
SSP-DM Donovan McNabb
SSP-JR Jerry Rice
SSP-JS Jeremy Shockey
SSP-ES Emmitt Smith
SSP-BU Brian Urlacher
SSP-KW Kurt Warner

2003 Fleer Platinum

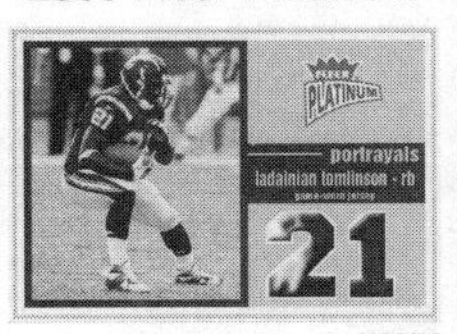

NM/M
Common Player (1-210): .15
Unlisted Star: .60
Minor Star: .40
Common Rookie (211-240): .50
Common Rookie (241-250): 2.00
Production 1500 Sets (Wax Only)
Common Rookie (251-260): 3.00
Production 750 Sets (Jumbo Only)
Common Rookie (261-270): 3.00
Production 500 Sets (Rack Only)
Wax Box (14+4+1): 35.00
1 Donovan McNabb 1.00
2 Jonathan Wells .50
3 Amos Zereoue .40
4 Ray Lewis .50
5 Trent Green .50
6 Jeff Garcia .40
7 Marty Booker .40
8 Antowain Smith .40
9 Brad Johnson .40
10 Joey Galloway .15
11 Chad Pennington .75
12 Patrick Ramsey .50
13 James Stewart .15
14 Charles Woodson .40
15 Warrick Dunn .15
16 Marvin Harrison .60
17 Jerome Bettis .40
18 Muhsin Muhammad .40
19 Zach Thomas .15
20 Darrell Jackson .15
21 Kelly Holcomb .40
22 Deuce McAllister .75
23 Mike Alstott .40
24 Kabeer Gbaja-Biamila .15
25 Todd Pinkston .15
26 Chris Redman .40
27 Jimmy Smith .40
28 Tim Dwight .15
29 Kordell Stewart .60
30 Daunte Culpepper 1.00
31 Isaac Bruce .50
32 William Green .60
33 Tiki Barber .40
34 Jevon Kearse .15
35 Ashley Lelie .75
36 Charlie Garner .40
37 Marcel Shipp .15
38 Corey Bradford .40
39 Hines Ward .50
40 Josh Reed .50
41 Jay Fiedler .40
42 Matt Hasselbeck .15
43 Corey Dillon .50
44 David Patten .15
45 Warren Sapp .30
46 Chad Johnson .40
47 Troy Brown .40
48 Keyshawn Johnson .50
49 Roy Williams .60
50 Curtis Martin .60
51 Rod Gardner .40
52 David Carr 1.25
53 Tommy Maddox .50
54 Todd Heap .40
55 Hugh Douglas .15
56 Julian Peterson .15
57 Julius Peppers .50
58 Sam Madison .15
59 Jerramy Stevens .15
60 Andre Davis .40
61 Joe Horn .40
62 Ronde Barber .15
63 Joey Harrington 1.25
64 Jerry Porter .40
65 T.J. Duckett .50
66 Edgerrin James 1.00
67 Joey Porter .40
68 Brian Urlacher 1.25
69 Randy Moss 1.50
70 Torry Holt .40
71 Quincy Morgan .40
72 Amani Toomer .40
73 Derrick Mason .40
74 Donald Driver .40
75 Duce Staley .30
76 Peerless Price .40
77 Mark Brunell .50
78 David Boston .50
79 Takeo Spikes .15
80 Ricky Williams 1.00
81 Shaun Alexander .60
82 Jon Kitna .30
83 Deion Branch .40
84 Derrick Brooks .15
85 Rod Smith .40
86 Rich Gannon .50
87 Jason McAddley .15
88 Jabar Gaffney .40
89 Plaxico Burress .50
90 Troy Hambrick .40
91 Santana Moss .40
92 Champ Bailey .15
93 Bubba Franks .15
94 Brian Westbrook .15
95 Ed Reed .15
96 Priest Holmes .75
97 Terrell Owens .60
98 Anthony Thomas .40
99 Michael Bennett .50
100 Marshall Faulk 1.00
101 Kevin Johnson .40
102 Kerry Collins .40
103 Eddie George .15
104 Shannon Sharpe .15
105 Tim Brown .60
106 Brian Finneran .15
107 Reggie Wayne .15
108 Drew Brees 1.00
109 Jake Delhomme .15
110 Chris Chambers .50
111 Maurice Morris .50
112 Antonio Bryant .60
113 Michael Strahan .15
114 Laveranues Coles .50
115 Ahman Green .60
116 Jeff Blake .15
117 Jamal Lewis .40
118 Fred Taylor .40
119 Marcellus Wiley .15
120 Stephen Davis .50
121 Randy McMichael .40
122 Kurt Warner 1.25
123 Tim Couch .75
124 Aaron Brooks .75
125 John Lynch .15
126 Clinton Portis 1.50
127 Wayne Chrebet .40
128 Emmitt Smith 1.50
129 Aaron Glenn .15

130 Antwann Randle El 1.00
131 Travis Henry .40
132 Tony Gonzalez .40
133 Garrison Hearst .40
134 Drew Bledsoe 1.00
135 Eddie Kennison .15
136 Kevan Barlow .40
137 David Terrell .40
138 Tom Brady 1.50
139 Joe Jurevicius .15
140 Terry Glenn .15
141 Curtis Conway .40
142 Trung Canidate .40
143 Javon Walker .50
144 Brian Dawkins .15
145 Keith Brooking .15
146 Dwight Freeney .15
147 LaDainian Tomlinson 1.25
148 Kevin Dyson .40
149 Jason Taylor .15
150 Koren Robinson .30
151 Dennis Northcutt .15
152 Donte Stallworth .75
153 Steve McNair .50
154 Ed McCaffrey .40
155 Jerry Rice 1.50
156 Travis Taylor .40
157 Kyle Brady .15
158 Quentin Jammer .15
159 DeShaun Foster .15
160 Derrius Thompson .15
161 Marc Bulger .50
162 Chad Hutchinson .40
163 Jeremy Shockey 1.25
164 Frank Wycheck .15
165 Brett Favre 2.00
166 Phillip Buchanon .40
167 Michael Vick 2.00
168 Peyton Manning 1.50
169 Kendrell Bell .40
170 Eric Moulds .40
171 Johnnie Morton .40
172 Tai Streets .15
173 Ron Dugans .15
174 Ty Law .15
175 Simeon Rice .15
176 Jake Plummer .50
177 John Abraham .15
178 Fred Smoot .15
179 Arizona Cardinals .15
180 Atlanta Falcons .75
181 Baltimore Ravens .15
182 Buffalo Bills .15
183 Carolina Panthers .15
184 Chicago Bears .15
185 Cincinnati Bengals .15
186 Cleveland Browns .15
187 Dallas Cowboys .40
188 Denver Broncos .40
189 Detroit Lions .15
190 Green Bay Packers .75
191 Houston Texans .50
192 Indianapolis Colts .15
193 Jacksonville Jaguars .15
194 Kansas City Chiefs .15
195 Miami Dolphins .50
196 Minnesota Vikings .50
197 New England Patriots .40
198 New Orleans Saints .15
199 New York Giants .15
200 New York Jets .40
201 Oakland Raiders .40
202 Philadelphia Eagles .15
203 Pittsburgh Steelers .40
204 San Diego Chargers .40
205 San Francisco 49ers .50
206 Seattle Seahawks .15
207 St. Louis Rams .40
208 Tampa Bay Buccaneers .75
209 Tennessee Titans .40
210 Washington Redskins .15
211 *L.J. Smith* .50
212 *Taylor Jacobs* 1.50
213 *J.R. Tolver* .50
214 *Musa Smith* 1.00
215 *Bennie Joppru* 1.50
216 *Ken Dorsey* 2.00
217 *Kareem Kelly* 1.00
218 *Andre Woolfolk* .75
219 *Brian St. Pierre* .75
220 *Jerome McDougle* .75
221 *Avon Cobourne* 1.00
222 *William Joseph* 1.50
223 *Dallas Clark* 3.00
224 *Anquan Boldin* 6.00
225 *Mike Doss* 1.00
226 *Cecil Sapp* .50
227 *Domanick Davis* 5.00
228 *Brad Banks* 1.50
229 *Justin Gage* 2.00
230 *Nate Burleson* 2.00
231 *Earnest Graham* .75
232 *Dewayne White* 1.00
233 *Kevin Williams* 1.00
234 *Billy McMullen* .75
235 *Talman Gardner* 1.00
236 *Marcus Trufant* 1.50
237 *Quentin Griffin* 8.00
238 *LaBrandon Toefield* 1.00
239 *Kliff Kingsbury* 1.00
240 *Doug Gabriel* .75
241 *Kyle Boller* 10.00
242 *Dave Ragone* 5.00
243 *Larry Johnson* 8.00
244 *Lee Suggs* 10.00
245 *Charles Rogers* 10.00
246 *Jimmy Kennedy* 2.00
247 *Onterrio Smith* 8.00
248 *Artose Pinner* 3.00
249 *Tyrone Calico* 6.00
250 *Terence Newman* 5.00
251 *Byron Leftwich* 25.00
252 *Kelley Washington* 4.00
253 *Justin Fargas* 5.00
254 *Dewayne Robertson* 5.00
255 *Boss Bailey* 4.00
256 *Sam Aiken* 3.00
257 *Bryant Johnson* 6.00
258 *Rex Grossman* 12.00
259 *Teyo Johnson* 4.00
260 *Willis McGahee* 15.00
261 *Carson Palmer* 20.00
262 *Chris Simms* 10.00
263 *Andre Johnson* 15.00
264 *Seneca Wallace* 5.00
265 *Terrell Suggs* 7.00
266 *Chris Brown* 10.00
267 *Kevin Curtis* 3.00
268 *Brandon Lloyd* 5.00
269 *Jason Witten* 5.00
270 *Bobby Wade* 4.00

2003 Fleer Platinum Finish

Stars: 5X-10X
Rookies (211-240): 2X-4X
Rookies (241-260): 1X-2X
Rookies (261-270): 1X-1.5X
Production 100 Sets

2003 Fleer Platinum Alma Materials

NM/M
Common Player: 6.00
Inserted 1:1 Rack Packs
1AM Carson Palmer 20.00
2AM Peyton Manning 15.00
3AM Michael Vick 25.00
4AM Ken Dorsey 8.00
5AM Edgerrin James 8.00
6AM Justin Fargas 6.00
7AM Quentin Griffin 6.00
8AM Seneca Wallace 8.00
9AM Julius Peppers 6.00

2003 Fleer Platinum Big Signs

NM/M
Common Player: 1.00
Platinum Finish: 1.5X-3X
Production 100 sets
1BS Donovan McNabb 2.00
2BS Brett Favre 4.00
3BS Ricky Williams 2.00
4BS Brian Urlacher 2.00
5BS Clinton Portis 3.00
6BS Jeremy Shockey 3.00
7BS Jerry Rice 2.00
8BS Randy Moss 2.00
9BS Chad Pennington 2.00
10BS Michael Vick 4.00

2003 Fleer Platinum Big Signs Autograph

NM/M
Common Player: 1.00
Production 200 sets
1BS Donovan McNabb 40.00
5BS Clinton Portis 40.00
9BS Chad Pennington 30.00

2003 Fleer Platinum Patch of Honor

NM/M
Common Player: 10.00
Inserted 1:8 Jumbo Packs
1PH Fred Taylor/220 15.00
2PH Jerry Rice/205 25.00
3PH Brian Urlacher/220 30.00
4PH Donovan McNabb/220 30.00
5PH Shaun Alexander/220 12.00
6PH Marshall Faulk/220 15.00
7PH Peyton Manning/220 15.00
8PH Ray Lewis/220 12.00
9PH Brett Favre/220 30.00
10PH Ricky Williams/220 15.00
11PH LaDainian Tomlinson/220 10.00
12PH Tom Brady/220 12.00
13PH Randy Moss/220 20.00
14PH Jeff Garcia/220 10.00
15PH Emmitt Smith/220 25.00
16PH Michael Vick/219 45.00
17PH Marvin Harrison/219 10.00
18PH Terrell Owens/220 10.00
19PH Daunte Culpepper/220 15.00
20PH Tim Brown/142 15.00
21PH Eddie George/220 12.00
22PH Curtis Martin/220 12.00
23PH Warren Sapp/220 10.00
24PH Clinton Portis/220 20.00
25PH Jeremy Shockey/220 20.00
26PH Chad Pennington/219 15.00
27PH Deuce McAllister/220 12.00
28PH Hines Ward/219 12.00
29PH Travis Henry/215 12.00
30PH Priest Holmes/220 15.00

2003 Fleer Platinum Platinum Portrayals

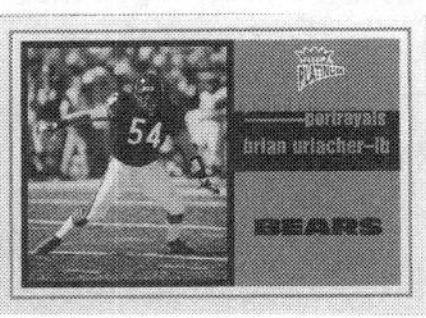

NM/M
Common Player: 1.00
Platinum Finish parallel 1X-2X
Production 100 sets
1PP LaDainian Tomlinson 1.50
2PP Shaun Alexander 1.00
3PP Ray Lewis 1.00
4PP Brett Favre 3.00
5PP Jerry Rice 2.00
6PP Joey Harrington 2.00
7PP Donovan McNabb 1.50
8PP Brian Urlacher 2.00
9PP Jeremy Shockey 2.00
10PP Emmitt Smith 2.00
11PP Chad Pennington 1.50
12PP Randy Moss 2.00
13PP Michael Vick 3.00
14PP Clinton Portis 2.00
15PP Ricky Williams 1.50

2003 Fleer Platinum Platinum Portrayals Jerseys

NM/M
Common Player: 10.00
Inserted 1:50 Wax Packs
Patch verions: 1X-2X
Production 100 sets
1PPGU Shaun Alexander 10.00
2PPGU Ray Lewis 10.00
3PPGU Randy Moss 25.00
4PPGU Brett Favre 35.00
5PPGU Donovan McNabb 20.00
6PPGU Brian Urlacher 25.00
7PPGU Jerry Rice 30.00
8PPGU Michael Vick
9PPGU Jeremy Shockey 15.00
10PPGU Joey Harrington 15.00

2003 Fleer Platinum Pro Bowl Scouting Report

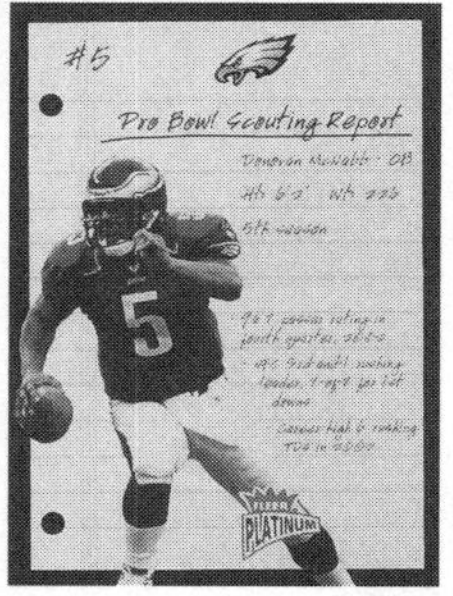

NM/M
Common Player: 1.00
Production 400 sets
Platinum Finish parallel 1X-1.5X
Production 100 sets
1PBSR Ricky Williams 2.00
2PBSR Rich Gannon 1.00
3PBSR Drew Bledsoe 1.50
4PBSR Brad Johnson 1.00
5PBSR Jeff Garcia 1.00
6PBSR Donovan McNabb 2.00
7PBSR Peyton Manning 3.00
8PBSR Todd Heap 1.00
9PBSR Terrell Owens 1.00
10PBSR Marshall Faulk 1.50
11PBSR Marvin Harrison 1.00
12PBSR Deuce McAllister 1.50
13PBSR LaDainian Tomlinson 2.00
14PBSR Eric Moulds 1.00
15PBSR Jerry Rice 3.00

A player's name in *italic* type indicates a rookie card.

2003 Fleer Platinum Pro Bowl Scouting Report Jerseys

NM/M
Common Player: 8.00
Production 250 Wax packs
1PBSGU Todd Heap 8.00
2PBSGU Peyton Manning 12.00
3PBSGU Deuce McAllister 10.00
4PBSGU LaDainian Tomlinson 10.00
5PBSGU Jerry Rice 15.00
6PBSGU Marvin Harrison 10.00
7PBSGU Rich Gannon 8.00
8PBSGU Jeff Garcia 8.00
8PBSGU Terrell Owens 8.00
10PBSGU Ricky Williams 12.00

2003 Fleer Showcase

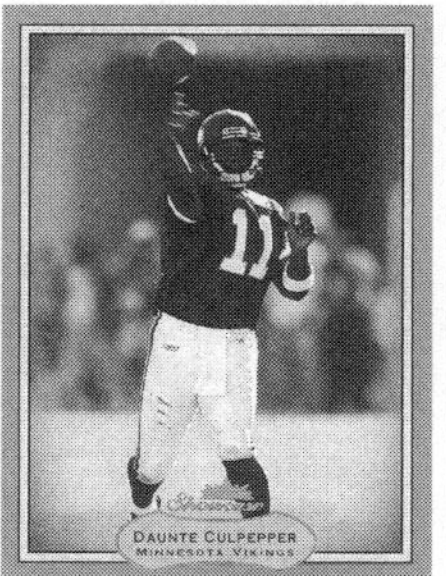

NM/M
Common Player: .20
Unlisted Star: .75
Minor Star: .50
Common Rookie (101-140): 4.00
Minor Rookies: 5.00
Cards 91-95 Production 650 sets
Cards 96-100 Production 350 sets
Cards 111-140 Production 750 sets
Pack (5): 3.00
Wax Box (24): 50.00
1 Edgerrin James 2.00
2 Donald Driver .50
3 Drew Brees 2.00
4 Corey Dillon .75
5 Jerome Bettis .50
6 Charlie Garner .40
7 Eddie George .75
8 Mark Brunell .75
9 David Boston .75
10 Todd Heap .20
11 Terrell Owens .75
12 Tommy Maddox .50
13 Keyshawn Johnson .75
14 Jamal Lewis .75
15 Zach Thomas .20
16 Isaac Bruce .50
17 Michael Bennett .75
18 Brian Griese .75
19 Eric Moulds .50
20 T.J. Duckett .75
21 Hines Ward .50
22 Tiki Barber .40
23 Julius Peppers .50
24 Rich Gannon .50
25 Rod Gardner .20
26 Curtis Martin .75
27 Donte Stallworth 1.00
28 Anthony Thomas .75
29 Warren Sapp .40
30 Jake Plummer .50
31 Patrick Ramsey .50
32 Tai Streets .20
33 Matt Hasselbeck .20
34 James Stewart .20
35 Chad Hutchinson .50
36 Hugh Douglas .20
37 Jimmy Smith .20
38 Kerry Collins .40
39 Junior Seau .50
40 Ed McCaffrey .40
41 Marshall Faulk 1.50
42 Deuce McAllister 1.00
43 Drew Bledsoe 1.50
44 Brian Urlacher 2.00
45 William Green .75
46 Chris Chambers .75
47 Daunte Culpepper 1.50
48 Warrick Dunn .40
49 Antwann Randle El 1.50
50 Joey Harrington 2.00
51 Tim Brown .75
52 Duce Staley .20
53 Laveranues Coles .50
54 Ray Lewis .40
55 Marvin Harrison .75
56 Tony Gonzalez .40
57 Torry Holt .40
58 Jeff Garcia .75
59 Peerless Price .75
60 Marcel Shipp .20
61 Brian Finneran .20
62 Fred Taylor .40
63 Koren Robinson .40
64 Shaun Alexander .75
65 Plaxico Burress .75
66 Ahman Green .75
67 Simeon Rice .20
68 Joe Horn .40
69 Steve McNair .75
70 Amani Toomer .20
71 Kendrell Bell .50
72 Marty Booker .40
73 Stephen Davis .40
74 David Carr 2.00
75 Garrison Hearst .40
76 Joey Galloway .40
77 Aaron Brooks 1.00
78 Mike Alstott .40
79 Shannon Sharpe .40
80 Derrick Mason .40
81 Tim Couch 1.00
82 Chad Johnson .20
83 Jason Taylor .20
84 Travis Henry .40
85 Curtis Conway .40
86 Peyton Manning 2.00
87 Kurt Warner 2.00
88 LaDainian Tomlinson 2.00
89 Emmitt Smith 2.50
90 Priest Holmes 1.00
91 Ricky Williams 4.00
92 Brett Favre 8.00
93 Clinton Portis 6.00
94 Randy Moss 6.00
95 Tom Brady 5.00
96 Chad Pennington 5.00
97 Michael Vick 9.00
98 Jeremy Shockey 8.00
99 Donovan McNabb 7.00
100 Jerry Rice 7.00
101 *Carson Palmer/350* 50.00
102 *Lee Suggs/350* 30.00
103 *Larry Johnson/350* 25.00
104 *Taylor Jacobs/650* 10.00
105 *Andre Johnson/350* 40.00
106 *Justin Fargas/650* 10.00
107 *Charles Rogers/350* 30.00
108 *Willis McGahee/650* 30.00
109 *Byron Leftwich/350* 50.00
110 *Kyle Boller/650* 20.00
111 *Bobby Wade* 2.00
112 *Brian St. Pierre* 4.00
113 *Doug Gabriel* 5.00
114 *Chris Brown* 10.00
115 *Dewayne Robertson* 4.00
116 *Anquan Boldin* 15.00
117 *Brandon Lloyd* 8.00
118 *Brad Banks* 4.00
119 *Dallas Clark* 8.00
120 *Artose Pinner* 5.00
121 *Dave Ragone* 8.00
122 *Arnaz Battle* 8.00
123 *Andrew Pinnock* 4.00
124 *Billy McMullen* 4.00
125 *Avon Cobourne* 8.00
126 *Terence Newman* 12.00
127 *Jimmy Kennedy* 5.00
128 *Terrell Suggs* 12.00
129 *Rex Grossman* 15.00
130 *Musa Smith* 5.00
131 *William Joseph* 5.00
132 *Tyrone Calico* 10.00
133 *Teyo Johnson* 5.00
134 *Onterrio Smith* 10.00
135 *Mike Doss* 4.00
136 *Kliff Kingsbury* 5.00
137 *Kelley Washington* 5.00
138 *Kareem Kelly* 4.00
139 *Jason Gesser* 4.00
140 *Chris Simms* 12.00

2003 Fleer Showcase Legacy

Stars (1-90): 3X-6X
Avant Stars (91-100): 1X-1.5X
Avant Rookies (101-110): 1X-1.5X
Rookies (111-140): 1X-2X
Production 125 Sets
Masterpiece Production 1 Set

2003 Fleer Showcase Avant Card Jerseys

NM/M
Common Player: 10.00
Production 999 sets
1AVGU Ricky Williams 14.00
2AVGU Brett Favre 18.00
3AVGU Clinton Portis 10.00
4AVGU Randy Moss 14.00
5AVGU Tom Brady 10.00
6AVGU Chad Pennington 10.00
7AVGU Michael Vick 20.00
8AVGU Jeremy Shockey 14.00
9AVGU Donovan McNabb 10.00
10AVGU Jerry Rice 14.00

2003 Fleer Showcase Football's Best

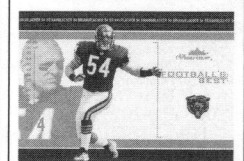

NM/M
Common Player: 1.00
Inserted 1:12
1FB Michael Vick 3.00
2FB Ricky Williams 2.00
3FB Brian Urlacher 2.00
4FB Jeff Garcia 1.00
5FB Chad Pennington 1.00
6FB William Green 1.00
7FB Kurt Warner 1.50
8FB Drew Bledsoe 1.50

A card number in parenthese ( ) indicates the set is unnumbered.

2003 Fleer Showcase Football's Best Memorabilia

NM/M
Common Player: 5.00
Inserted 1:38
Gold 1X-1.5X
Production 150 sets
1FBM Michael Vick 20.00
2FBM Ricky Williams 15.00
3FBM David Carr 10.00
4FBM Ahman Green 10.00
5FBM Keyshawn Johnson 8.00
6FBM William Green 8.00
7FBM Kurt Warner 8.00
8FBM Jeff Garcia 6.00
9FBM Michael Bennett 8.00
10FBM Jevon Kearse 5.00
11FBM Chad Pennington 8.00
12FBM Plaxico Burress 8.00
13FBM Koren Robinson 5.00
14FBM Eddie George 8.00
15FBM Tiki Barber 5.00
16FBM Warren Sapp 6.00
17FBM Eric Moulds 5.00
18FBM Brian Urlacher 15.00

2003 Fleer Showcase Hot Hands

NM/M
Common Player: 1.50
Inserted 1:144
1HH Jerry Rice 4.00
2HH Randy Moss 4.00
3HH Terrell Owens 2.00
4HH Marvin Harrison 2.00
5HH Jeremy Shockey 4.00
6HH Marshall Faulk 1.50
7HH Priest Holmes 2.00
8HH Deuce McAllister 1.50

2003 Fleer Showcase Hot Hands Jerseys

NM/M
Common Player: 6.00
Production 599 sets
1HHGU Jerry Rice 18.00
2HHGU Randy Moss 12.00
3HHGU Terrell Owens 6.00
4HHGU Marvin Harrison 6.00
5HHGU Jeremy Shockey 15.00
6HHGU Marshall Faulk 8.00
7HHGU Priest Holmes 12.00
8HHGU Deuce McAllister 6.00
9HHGU Peerless Price 6.00
10HHGU Todd Heap 10.00
11HHGU Daunte Culpepper 10.00
12HHGU Antonio Bryant 12.00
13HHGU Drew Brees 6.00
14HHGU Antwann Randle El 12.00
15HHGU Eric Moulds 6.00
16HHGU Koren Robinson 6.00
17HHGU Peyton Manning 12.00
18HHGU LaDainian Tomlinson 6.00
19HHGU David Boston 6.00
20HHGU Kurt Warner 10.00

2003 Fleer Showcase Sweet Stitch

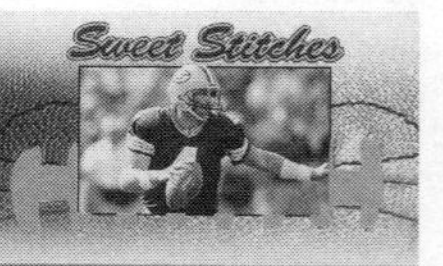

NM/M
Common Player: 2.00
Inserted 1:12
1SS Brett Favre 4.00
2SS Clinton Portis 3.00
3SS Donovan McNabb 2.00
4SS Daunte Culpepper 2.00
5SS LaDainian Tomlinson 2.00
6SS Tom Brady 2.00
7SS Peyton Manning 3.00
8SS Emmitt Smith 4.00

2003 Fleer Showcase Sweet Stitch Game-Used

NM/M
Common Player: 6.00
Production 899 sets
Patches: 1X-2X
Patch Production 201 Sets
1SSGU Brett Favre 18.00
2SSGU Clinton Portis 14.00
3SSGU Donovan McNabb 12.00
4SSGU Daunte Culpepper 10.00
5SSGU LaDainian Tomlinson 6.00
6SSGU Tom Brady
7SSGU Peyton Manning 8.00
8SSGU Emmitt Smith 16.00

		NM/M
9SSGU	Peerless Price	6.00
10SSGU	David Carr	12.00
11SSGU	Antonio Bryant	8.00
12SSGU	Antwann Randle El	10.00
13SSGU	Ahman Green	8.00
14SSGU	Drew Brees	8.00
15SSGU	Eddie George	6.00

2003 Fleer Snapshot

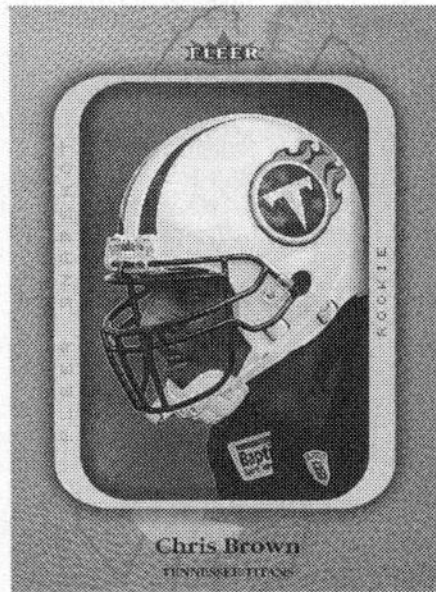

		NM/M
Common Player (1-90):		.20
Minor Stars:		.40
Unlisted Stars:		.60
Common Rookie (91-135):		3.00
Minor Rookie:		4.00
Unlisted Rookie:		5.00
Production 500 Sets		
Pack (5):		2.00
Box (24):		40.00
1	Trent Green	.40
2	Chad Johnson	.40
3	Randy Moss	1.00
4	Brett Favre	2.00
5	Terrell Owens	.60
6	LaDainian Tomlinson	.75
7	Michael Vick	2.00
8	Jerry Rice	1.50
9	David Carr	1.25
10	Chad Pennington	1.00
11	Torry Holt	.60
12	Edgerrin James	.75
13	Travis Henry	.40
14	Warrick Dunn	.40
15	Laveranues Coles	.40
16	Fred Taylor	.60
17	Todd Heap	.40
18	Tim Brown	.40
19	Donovan McNabb	.75
20	Marvin Harrison	.60
21	Patrick Ramsey	.60
22	Troy Brown	.40
23	Antonio Bryant	.40
24	Donte Stallworth	.40
25	Joe Horn	.40
26	Clinton Portis	1.50
27	Kurt Warner	.75
28	Quincy Morgan	.40
29	James Stewart	.40
30	Ashley Lelie	.40
31	Kerry Collins	.40
32	Julius Peppers	.40
33	Brad Johnson	.40
34	Ricky Williams	1.00
35	Ahman Green	.60
36	Plaxico Burress	.60
37	Amani Toomer	.40
38	Brian Urlacher	1.00
39	Eddie George	.60
40	Tony Gonzalez	.40
41	Chris Chambers	.60
42	Tommy Maddox	.40
43	Drew Brees	.75
44	Anthony Thomas	.40
45	Brian Griese	.40
46	Ray Lewis	.40
47	Peerless Price	.40
48	Charlie Garner	.40
49	Stacey Mack	.20
50	Rod Gardner	.40
51	Jevon Kearse	.40
52	Tim Couch	.60
53	Koren Robinson	.40
54	Daunte Culpepper	.60
55	Tom Brady	.75
56	Jeff Blake	.40
57	Jeff Garcia	.40
58	Mike Alstott	.40
59	Corey Dillon	.60
60	Antwann Randle El	.40
61	Deuce McAllister	.60
62	William Green	.60
63	Shaun Alexander	.60
64	Eric Moulds	.40
65	Jamal Lewis	.60
66	Rich Gannon	.40
67	Tiki Barber	.40
68	Peyton Manning	1.00
69	Marshall Faulk	.75
70	Hines Ward	.40
71	Drew Bledsoe	.75
72	Stephen Davis	.40
73	Mark Brunell	.40
74	Priest Holmes	.60
75	Duce Staley	.40
76	Jerome Bettis	.40
77	Rod Smith	.40
78	Marty Booker	.40
79	Aaron Brooks	.60
80	Jake Plummer	.40
81	Warren Sapp	.60
82	David Boston	.40
83	Joey Harrington	1.00
84	Emmitt Smith	1.50
85	Jimmy Smith	.40
86	Curtis Martin	.60
87	Keyshawn Johnson	.40
88	Steve McNair	.60
89	Donald Driver	.40
90	Jeremy Shockey	1.00
91	*Tyrone Calico*	8.00
92	*Sam Aiken*	3.00
93	*Jason Witten*	8.00
94	*Dave Ragone*	4.00
95	*Billy McMullen*	3.00
96	*Musa Smith*	4.00
97	*Kelley Washington*	5.00
98	*Larry Johnson*	8.00
99	*Dallas Clark*	8.00
100	*Andre Johnson*	12.00
101	*Artose Pinner*	4.00
102	*B.J. Askew*	4.00
103	*Rex Grossman*	12.00
104	*Kevin Williams*	3.00
105	*Terence Newman*	6.00
106	*Teyo Johnson*	4.00
107	*Kevin Curtis*	3.00
108	*Brandon Lloyd*	6.00
109	*Kyle Boller*	10.00
110	*Bethel Johnson*	6.00
111	*E.J. Henderson*	3.00
112	*Quentin Griffin*	10.00
113	*Jerome McDougle*	3.00
114	*Justin Fargas*	6.00
115	*Michael Haynes*	3.00
116	*Tony Hollings*	4.00
117	*Bryant Johnson*	4.00
118	*L.J. Smith*	4.00
119	*Nate Burleson*	6.00
120	*Taylor Jacobs*	4.00
121	*Byron Leftwich*	20.00
122	*Charles Rogers*	10.00
123	*Chris Brown*	10.00
124	*Dewayne Robertson*	3.00
125	*Terrell Suggs*	5.00
126	*Johnathan Sullivan*	3.00
127	*Willis McGahee*	15.00
128	*Anquan Boldin*	12.00
129	*Chris Simms*	8.00
130	*Carson Palmer*	15.00
131	*Marcus Trufant*	4.00
132	*Jimmy Kennedy*	3.00
133	*Onterrio Smith*	10.00
134	*Boss Bailey*	4.00
135	*William Joseph*	3.00

2003 Fleer Snapshot NFL Projections

		NM/M
Common Player:		2.50
Production 199 Sets		
1DP	Ricky Williams	5.00
2DP	Donovan McNabb	4.00
3DP	Brett Favre	10.00
4DP	Jerry Rice	8.00
5DP	Edgerrin James	4.00
6DP	Eddie George	3.00
7DP	Tom Brady	5.00
8DP	Marshall Faulk	4.00
9DP	Fred Taylor	3.00
10DP	Peyton Manning	5.00
11DP	Randy Moss	5.00
12DP	Chad Pennington	4.00
13DP	Kurt Warner	3.00
14DP	Tim Brown	2.50
15DP	Emmitt Smith	10.00

2003 Fleer Snapshot NFL Projections Jerseys Silver

		NM/M
Common Player:		6.00
Production 250 Sets		
Golds:		1X-2X
Production 50 Sets		
NPBF	Brett Favre	25.00
NPCP	Chad Pennington	10.00
NPDM	Donovan McNabb	10.00
NPEG	Eddie George	8.00
NPEJ	Edgerrin James	10.00
NPFT	Fred Taylor	8.00
NPJR	Jerry Rice	15.00
NPKW	Kurt Warner	8.00
NPMF	Marshall Faulk	10.00
NPPM	Peyton Manning	12.00
NPRM	Randy Moss	12.00
NPRW0	Ricky Williams	10.00
NPTB	Tim Brown	6.00
NPTB	Tom Brady	12.00

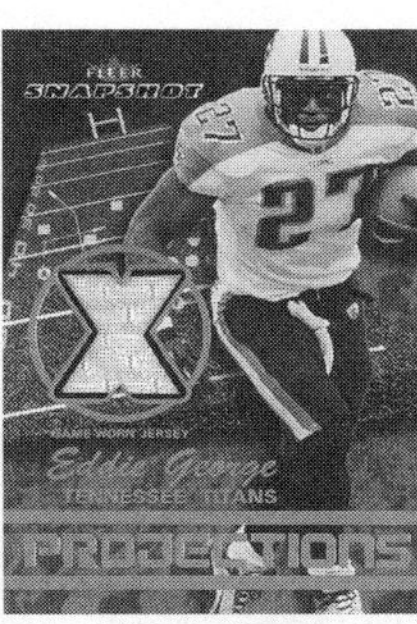

2003 Fleer Snapshot Rookie Slides

		NM/M
Common Player:		8.00
Production 50 Sets		
1	Tyrone Calico	15.00
2	Sam Aiken	8.00
3	Jason Witten	15.00
4	Dave Ragone	10.00
5	Billy McMullen	8.00
6	Musa Smith	8.00
7	Kelley Washington	12.00
8	Larry Johnson	20.00
9	Dallas Clark	12.00
10	Andre Johnson	30.00
11	Artose Pinner	10.00
12	B.J. Askew	10.00
13	Rex Grossman	30.00
14	Kevin Williams	8.00
15	Terence Newman	15.00
16	Teyo Johnson	12.00
17	Kevin Curtis	8.00
18	Brandon Lloyd	10.00
19	Kyle Boller	20.00
20	Bethel Johnson	15.00
21	E.J. Henderson	8.00
22	Quentin Griffin	20.00
23	Jerome McDougle	8.00
24	Justin Fargas	15.00
25	Michael Haynes	8.00
26	Tony Hollings	8.00
27	Bryant Johnson	12.00
28	L.J. Smith	8.00
29	Nate Burleson	8.00
30	Taylor Jacobs	40.00
31	Byron Leftwich	20.00
32	Charles Rogers	12.00
33	Chris Brown	12.00
34	Dewayne Robertson	8.00
35	Terrell Suggs	15.00
36	Johnathan Sullivan	8.00
37	Willis McGahee	25.00
38	Anquan Boldin	25.00
39	Chris Simms	20.00
40	Carson Palmer	30.00
41	Marcus Trufant	10.00
42	Jimmy Kennedy	8.00
43	Onterrio Smith	20.00
44	Boss Bailey	12.00
45	William Joseph	10.00

2003 Fleer Snapshot Seal of Approval

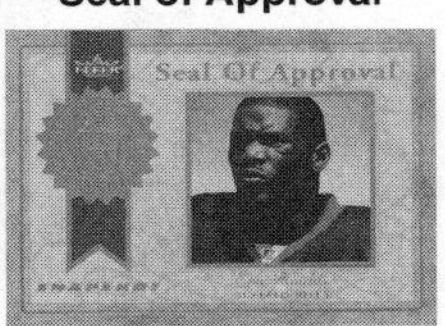

		NM/M
Common Player:		1.50
Inserted 1:12		
Golds:		1X-2X
Production 99 Sets		
1SA	Clinton Portis	4.00
2SA	David Carr	4.00
3SA	Joey Harrington	3.00
4SA	Antwann Randle El	2.00
5SA	Jeremy Shockey	3.00
6SA	Michael Vick	6.00
7SA	Drew Brees	2.50
8SA	Tommy Maddox	2.00
9SA	LaDainian Tomlinson	2.50
10SA	Deuce McAllister	2.00
11SA	Brett Favre	6.00
12SA	Jerry Rice	5.00
13SA	Eric Moulds	1.50
14SA	Ricky Williams	3.00
15SA	Terrell Owens	2.00
16SA	Taylor Jacobs	1.50
17SA	Larry Johnson	3.00
18SA	Rex Grossman	4.00
19SA	Bryant Johnson	2.00
20SA	Kyle Boller	3.00
21SA	Andre Johnson	4.00
22SA	Charles Rogers	3.00
23SA	Byron Leftwich	6.00
24SA	Willis McGahee	4.00
25SA	Carson Palmer	5.00

2003 Fleer Snapshot Seal of Approval Jerseys Bronze

		NM/M
Common Player:		6.00
Production 375 Sets		
Golds:		1.5X
Production 99 Sets		
SAAJ	Andre Johnson	12.00

		NM/M
SAAR	Antwann Randle El	8.00
SABF	Brett Favre	25.00
SABL	Byron Leftwich	15.00
SACP	Carson Palmer	15.00
SACP	Clinton Portis	12.00
SACR	Charles Rogers	10.00
SADB	Drew Brees	8.00
SADC	David Carr	12.00
SADM	Deuce McAllister	8.00
SAEM	Eric Moulds	6.00
SAJH	Joey Harrington	10.00
SAJR	Jerry Rice	15.00
SAKB	Kyle Boller	10.00
SALJ	Larry Johnson	10.00
SALT	LaDainian Tomlinson	8.00
SAMV	Michael Vick	20.00
SARG	Rex Grossman	12.00
SARW	Ricky Williams	10.00
SATJ	Taylor Jacobs	6.00
SATM	Tommy Maddox	6.00
SATO	Terrell Owens	8.00

2003 Fleer Snapshot Slides

		NM/M
Common Player:		6.00
Production 100 Sets		
1	Randy Moss	12.00
2	Brett Favre	25.00
3	LaDainian Tomlinson	8.00
4	Michael Vick	20.00
5	Jerry Rice	15.00
6	Chad Pennington	10.00
7	Donovan McNabb	10.00
8	Marvin Harrison	8.00
9	Clinton Portis	12.00
10	Ricky Williams	10.00
11	Daunte Culpepper	8.00
12	Tom Brady	15.00
13	Deuce McAllister	8.00
14	Shaun Alexander	8.00
15	Jamal Lewis	8.00
16	Peyton Manning	12.00
17	Marshall Faulk	10.00
18	Stephen Davis	6.00
19	Priest Holmes	10.00
20	Jeremy Shockey	10.00

2003 Fleer Snapshot Slides Autographs

		NM/M
Common Player:		12.00
Production 50 Sets		
1	T.J. Duckett	20.00
2	Joey Harrington	40.00
3	Josh Reed	15.00
4	Donte Stallworth	20.00
5	DeShaun Foster	25.00
6	Julius Peppers	20.00
7	Javon Walker	20.00
8	Daniel Graham	12.00
9	Ashley Lelie	20.00
10	Clinton Portis	50.00
11	Jabar Gaffney	15.00
12	Andre Davis	20.00
13	Antwann Randle El	25.00
14	William Green	20.00
15	Patrick Ramsey	30.00
16	Roy Williams	60.00
17	Antonio Bryant	20.00
18	Ladell Betts	12.00
19	Tim Carter	12.00
20	Josh McCown	15.00

2003 Fleer Snapshot We're Number One

		NM/M
1A	Carson Palmer/2003	5.00
1B	Carson Palmer/3	
2A	David Carr/2002	5.00
2B	David Carr/2	
3A	Michael Vick/2001	6.00
3B	Michael Vick/1	
4A	Tim Couch/1999	3.00
4B	Tim Couch/99	8.00
5A	Peyton Manning/1998	5.00
5B	Peyton Manning/98	15.00
6A	Keyshawn Johnson/1996	2.00
6B	Keyshawn Johnson/96	5.00
7A	Drew Bledsoe/1993	4.00
7B	Drew Bledsoe/93	10.00

2003 Fleer Snapshot We're Number One Jerseys

		NM/M
Common Player:		8.00
Production 11 Sets		
Gold Production 25 Sets		
1	Carson Palmer	20.00
2	David Carr	15.00
3	Michael Vick	25.00
4	Tim Couch	10.00
5	Peyton Manning	20.00
6	Keyshawn Johnson	8.00
7	Drew Bledsoe	10.00

2003 Fleer

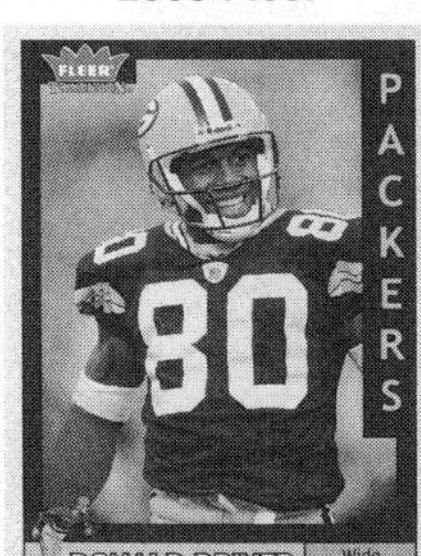

		NM/M
Complete Set (300):		50.00
Common Player (1-270):		.20
Minor Stars:		.40
Unlisted Stars:		.50
Common Rookie (271-300):		1.00
Minor Rookies:		1.25
Unlisted Rookies:		1.50
Pack (10):		1.25
Box (36):		35.00
1	Aaron Glenn	.20
2	Jerry Rice	1.50
3	Chad Hutchinson	.40
4	Kris Jenkins	.20
5	Ed Reed	.20
6	Ed McCaffrey	.40
7	Rod Gardner	.40
8	Aaron Brooks	.50
9	Chad Pennington	.60
10	Jevon Kearse	.40
11	Kurt Warner	.75
12	Eddie George	.50
13	Ron Dugans	.20
14	Adam Vinatieri	.20
15	Jimmy Smith	.40
16	Chad Johnson	.40
17	Kyle Brady	.20
18	Eddie Kennison	.40
19	Joe Jurevicius	.40
20	Ronde Barber	.20
21	Adam Archuleta	.20
22	Champ Bailey	.40
23	Joe Horn	.40
24	Ladell Betts	.40
25	Edgerrin James	.60
26	Rosevelt Colvin	.20
27	Ahman Green	.50
28	Joey Porter	.20
29	Charles Woodson	.40
30	Lance Schulters	.20
31	Edgerton Hartwell	.20
32	Joey Galloway	.40
33	Roy Williams	.50
34	Al Wilson	.20
35	Charlie Garner	.40
36	John Lynch	.40
37	La'Roi Glover	.20
38	Emmitt Smith	1.50
39	Ryan Longwell	.20
40	Alge Crumpler	.20
41	John Abraham	.20
42	Chris Hovan	.20
43	Laveranues Coles	.40
44	Eric Hicks	.20
45	Johnnie Morton	.40
46	Sam Madison	.20
47	Amani Toomer	.40
48	Chris Redman	.40
49	Jon Kitna	.40
50	Leonard Little	.20
51	Eric Moulds	.40
52	Santana Moss	.40
53	Amos Zereoue	.40
54	Jonathan Wells	.20
55	Chris Chambers	.50
56	London Fletcher	.20
57	Frank Wycheck	.20
58	Josh McCown	.40
59	Shannon Sharpe	.50
60	Andre Carter	.20
61	Corey Dillon	.50
62	Josh Reed	.40
63	Marc Boerigter	.40
64	Fred Smoot	.20
65	Shaun Alexander	.50
66	Andre Davis	.40
67	Julian Peterson	.20
68	Corey Bradford	.40
69	Marc Bulger	.50
70	Fred Taylor	.50
71	Junior Seau	.40
72	Simeon Rice	.40
73	Anthony Thomas	.50
74	Correll Buckhalter	.40
75	Justin Smith	.20
76	Marcel Shipp	.40
77	Garrison Hearst	.40
78	Stacey Mack	.40
79	Antowain Smith	.40
80	Kabeer Gbaja-Biamila	.20
81	Curtis Martin	.50
82	Marcellus Wiley	.20
83	Gary Walker	.20
84	Kalimba Edwards	.20
85	Stephen Davis	.40
86	Antwann Randle El	.50
87	Curtis Conway	.40
88	Keith Brooking	.20
89	Mark Word	.20
90	Greg Ellis	.20
91	Steve McNair	.50
92	Ashley Lelie	.50
93	Kelly Holcomb	.40
94	Darrell Jackson	.40
95	Mark Brunell	.40
96	Hugh Douglas	.20
97	Kendrell Bell	.40
98	Steve Smith	.40
99	Bill Schroeder	.20
100	Darren Howard	.20
101	Kevan Barlow	.40
102	Marshall Faulk	.60
103	Ike Hilliard	.40
104	T.J. Duckett	.50
105	Bobby Taylor	.20
106	Kevin Carter	.20
107	Darren Sharper	.20
108	Marty Booker	.40
109	Isaac Bruce	.50
110	Kevin Hardy	.20
111	Tai Streets	.40
112	Brad Johnson	.40
113	Daunte Culpepper	.50
114	Kevin Johnson	.40
115	Matt Hasselbeck	.40
116	Jabar Gaffney	.40
117	Takeo Spikes	.20
118	Brett Favre	2.00
119	Keyshawn Johnson	.40
120	David Akers	.20
121	Maurice Morris	.40
122	Jake Delhomme	.40
123	Kordell Stewart	.40
124	Terrell Davis	.50
125	Brian Kelly	.20
126	David Terrell	.40
127	Koren Robinson	.40
128	Michael Strahan	.40
129	Jake Plummer	.40
130	Terrell Owens	.50
131	Brian Urlacher	.75
132	David Patten	.40
133	Michael Vick	2.00
134	Jamal Lewis	.50
135	Terry Glenn	.40
136	Brian Simmons	.20
137	David Boston	.50
138	Michael Bennett	.50
139	James Stewart	.40
140	Tiki Barber	.50
141	Brian Griese	.50
142	Deion Branch	.40
143	Mike Peterson	.20
144	James Mungro	.40
145	Tim Couch	.50
146	Brian Dawkins	.20
147	Dennis Northcutt	.40
148	Mike Alstott	.40
149	James Thrash	.20
150	Tim Brown	.50
151	Brian Finneran	.40
152	Derrick Brooks	.40
153	Muhsin Muhammad	.40
154	Jason Elam	.20
155	Tim Dwight	.40
156	Bruce Smith	.40
157	Derrick Mason	.40
158	Napoleon Harris	.20
159	Jason Gildon	.20
160	Todd Heap	.40
161	Aaron Schobel	.20
162	Derrius Thompson	.40
163	Nate Clements	.20
164	Jason McAddley	.20
165	Todd Pinkston	.40
166	Bubba Franks	.40
167	Deuce McAllister	.50
168	Patrick Surtain	.20
169	Javon Walker	.40
170	Tom Brady	.60
171	Dexter Coakley	.20
172	Patrick Kerney	.20
173	Jay Fiedler	.40
174	Tommy Maddox	.50
175	Donald Driver	.40
176	Patrick Ramsey	.50
177	Olandis Gary	.40
178	Tony Gonzalez	.40
179	Donnie Edwards	.20
180	Peter Boulware	.20
181	Jeff Blake	.40
182	Torry Holt	.50
183	Donovan McNabb	.60
184	Peter Warrick	.40
185	Jeff Garcia	.50
186	Travis Henry	.40
187	Doug Jolley	.40
188	Peyton Manning	.75
189	Jerome Bettis	.40
190	Travis Taylor	.40
191	Drew Brees	.60
192	Phillip Buchanon	.20
193	Jerramy Stevens	.20
194	Trent Green	.40
195	Duce Staley	.40
196	Plaxico Burress	.50
197	Jerry Porter	.40
198	Trevor Pryce	.20
199	Dwight Freeney	.40
200	Quincy Morgan	.40
201	Troy Vincent	.20
202	Randy McMichael	.40
203	Troy Hambrick	.40
204	Randy Moss	.75
205	Troy Brown	.40
206	Ray Lewis	.40
207	Trung Canidate	.40

208 Raynoch Thompson .20
209 Ty Law .20
210 Reggie Wayne .40
211 Warren Sapp .40
212 Richard Seymour .20
213 Warrick Dunn .40
214 Robert Ferguson .40
215 Wayne Chrebet .40
216 Rod Coleman .20
217 Will Allen .20
218 Rod Woodson .40
219 Zach Thomas .40
220 Rod Smith .40
221 Ricky Williams .75
222 LaDainian Tomlinson .60
223 Priest Holmes .50
224 Rich Gannon .40
225 Drew Bledsoe .60
226 Kerry Collins .40
227 Marvin Harrison .50
228 Hines Ward .40
229 Peerless Price .40
230 Jason Taylor .40
231 Jeremy Shockey 1.00
232 Clinton Portis 1.50
233 Antonio Bryant .40
234 Donte Stallworth .50
235 David Carr 1.00
236 Joey Harrington 1.00
237 William Green .50
238 Julius Peppers .40
239 Marcel Shipp, Raynoch Thompson, Adrian Wilson .40
240 Michael Vick, Warrick Dunn, Brian Finneran, Keith Brooking 2.00
241 Jamal Lewis, Edgerton Hartwell, Travis Taylor, Ed Reed .50
242 Drew Bledsoe, Travis Henry, Eric Moulds, London Fletcher .60
243 Julius Peppers, Steve Smith, Muhsin Muhammad .40
244 Marty Booker, Brian Urlacher, Anthony Thomas .75
245 Corey Dillon, Justin Smith, Chad Johnson, Jon Kitna .50
246 Tim Couch, William Green, Quincy Morgan, Mark Word .50
247 Chad Hutchinson, Joey Galloway, Roy Williams, Greg Ellis .50
248 Clinton Portis, Rod Smith, Al Wilson 1.50
249 Joey Harrington, James Stewart, Bill Schroeder, Kalimba Edwards 1.00
250 Brett Favre, Ahman Green, Donald Driver, Kabeer Gbaja-Biamila 2.00
251 David Carr, Jonathan Wells, Corey Bradford, Aaron Glenn 1.00
252 Peyton Manning, Edgerrin James, Marvin Harrison, Dwight Freeney 1.00
253 Mark Brunell, Fred Taylor, Jimmy Smith, Marlon McCree .50
254 Trent Green, Priest Holmes, Eddie Kennison, Eric Hicks .50
255 Ricky Williams, Chris Chambers, Zach Thomas, Jason Taylor .60
256 Daunte Culpepper, Michael Bennett, Randy Moss, Moe Williams .75
257 Tom Brady, Antowain Smith, Troy Brown, Adam Vinatieri .60
258 Aaron Brooks, Deuce McAllister, Joe Horn, Darren Howard .50
259 Kerry Collins, Tiki Barber, Amani Toomer, Michael Strahan .50
260 Chad Pennington, Curtis Martin, Wayne Chrebet, John Abraham .60
261 Rich Gannon, Charlie Garner, Jerry Rice, Rod Woodson 1.50
262 Donovan McNabb, Duce Staley, Todd Pinkston, Bobby Taylor .60
263 Tommy Maddox, Amos Zereoue, Hines Ward, Jason Gildon, Joey Porter .50
264 Drew Brees, LaDainian Tomlinson, Donnie Edwards .75
265 Jeff Garcia, Garrison Hearst, Terrell Owens, Andre Carter .50
266 Matt Hasselbeck, Shaun Alexander, Koren Robinson, Reggie Tongue .50
267 Marc Bulger, Marshall Faulk, Torry Holt, Leonard Little .60
268 Brad Johnson, Keyshawn Johnson, Simeon Rice, Brian Kelly .50
269 Steve McNair, Eddie George, Derrick Mason, Lance Schulters .50
270 Patrick Ramsey, Rod Gardner, Fred Smoot .50
271 *Carson Palmer* 5.00
272 *Kyle Boller* 3.00
273 *Byron Leftwich* 6.00
274 *Willis McGahee* 5.00
275 *Larry Johnson* 3.00
276 *Charles Rogers* 3.00
277 *Andre Johnson* 3.00
278 *Bryant Johnson* 2.00
279 *Rex Grossman* 4.00
280 *Taylor Jacobs* 1.50
281 *Dewayne Robertson, Jonathon Sullivan, Kevin Williams* 1.00
282 *Bennie Joppru, Domanick Davis, Dave Ragone* 2.00
283 *Jason Witten, Dallas Clark, L.J. Smith* 1.25
284 *Terrence Edwards, Musa Smith, Boss Bailey* 1.50
285 *Lee Suggs, Chris Brown, Onterrio Smith* 2.00
286 *Quentin Griffin, Artose Pinner, B.J. Askew* 3.00
287 *Justin Fargas, Doug Gabriel, Teyo Johnson* 2.00
288 *Jimmy Kennedy, William Joseph, Ty Warren* 1.25
289 *Terrell Suggs, Michael Haynes, Jerome McDougle* 2.00
290 *Kelley Washington, Kevin Curtis, Nate Burleson* 1.50
291 *Seneca Wallace, Ken Dorsey, Chris Simms* 3.00
292 *Bobby Wade, Sam Aiken, Justin Gage* 1.00
293 *Sultan McCullough, Cecil Sapp, Earnest Graham* 1.25
294 *Kareem Kelly, Talman Gardner, J.R. Tolver* 1.00
295 *Bethel Johnson, Anquan Boldin, Tyrone Calico* 2.00
296 *Brandon Lloyd, Billy McMullen, Shaun McDonald* 1.25
297 *Chris Kelsay, Dewayne White, Mike Doss* 1.00
298 *Terence Newman, Marcus Trufant, Andre Woolfolk* 2.00
299 *Kliff Kingsbury, Tony Romo, Brian St. Pierre* 2.00
300 *Andrew Pinnock, LaBrandon Toefield, Avon Cobourne* 1.50

2003 Fleer Classic Combinations

NM/M
Complete Set (30): 110.00
Common Player: 2.00
1-10 Production 1500 Sets
11-20 Production 750 Sets
21-30 Production 375 Sets
1CC Earl Campbell, Priest Holmes 4.00
2CC Plaxico Burress, Charles Rogers 5.00
3CC Ed "Too Tall" Jones, Terrell Suggs 2.00
4CC Edgerrin James, Willis McGahee 5.00
5CC Marcus Allen, Carson Palmer 6.00
6CC Fran Tarkenton, Chad Pennington 2.00
7CC Michael Vick, Byron Leftwich 8.00
8CC Doug Flutie, Drew Bledsoe 2.00
9CC Peyton Manning, Travis Henry 3.00
10CC Ken Stabler, Rich Gannon 2.00
11CC Randy Moss, Terrell Owens 5.00
12CC Bob Griese, Ricky Williams 4.00
13CC Ronnie Lott, Roy Williams 2.00
14CC Jack Ham, Kendrell Bell 2.00
15CC David Carr, Andre Johnson 5.00
16CC Brett Favre, Kurt Warner 5.00
17CC Fred Biletnikoff, Jerry Rice 5.00
18CC Joey Harrington, Charles Rogers 5.00
19CC Chad Pennington, Byron Leftwich 6.00
20CC Ken Stabler, Michael Vick 6.00
21CC Fran Tarkenton, Brett Favre 10.00
22CC Donovan McNabb, Marvin Harrison 5.00
23CC Clinton Portis, Willis McGahee 10.00
24CC Emmitt Smith, Rex Grossman 10.00
25CC Jack Ham, Brian Urlacher 4.00
26CC Marcus Allen, Marshall Faulk 4.00
27CC Jeremy Shockey, Andre Johnson 6.00
28CC Fred Biletnikoff, Tim Brown 3.00
29CC Carson Palmer, Byron Leftwich 12.00
30CC Ed "Too Tall" Jones, Julius Peppers 3.00

2003 Fleer Classic Combinations Game-Used

NM/M
Common Player: 10.00
Inserted 1:72
1 Earl Campbell, Priest Holmes 12.00
2 Marcus Allen, Carson Palmer 12.00
3 Bob Griese, Ricky Williams 12.00
4 Ken Stabler, Michael Vick 20.00
5 Brett Favre, Kurt Warner 12.00
6 Fred Biletnikoff, Tim Brown 10.00
7 Fred Biletnikoff, Jerry Rice 12.00
8 Michael Vick, Byron Leftwich 25.00
9 Ed "Too Tall" Jones, Terrell Suggs 10.00
10 Ronnie Lott, Roy Williams 12.00
11 Doug Flutie, Drew Bledsoe 10.00
12 Fran Tarkenton, Chad Pennington 10.00
13 Clinton Portis, Willis McGahee 15.00
14 Marcus Allen, Marshall Faulk 12.00
15 Jeremy Shockey, Andre Johnson 12.00
16 Doug Flutie, Drew Bledsoe 10.00
17 Jack Ham, Brian Urlacher 12.00
18 Earl Campbell, Priest Holmes 12.00
19 Plaxico Burress, Charles Rogers 12.00
20 Peyton Manning, Travis Henry 12.00
21 Edgerrin James, Willis McGahee 12.00
22 Fred Biletnikoff, Tim Brown 10.00
23 Donovan McNabb, Marvin Harrison 10.00
24 Bob Griese, Ricky Williams 12.00
25 Randy Moss, Terrell Owens 12.00

2003 Fleer Classic Combinations Dual Swatch

NM/M
Common Player: 20.00
Production 100 Sets
1 Earl Campbell, Priest Holmes 25.00
2 Fred Biletnikoff, Tim Brown 20.00
3 Ed "Too Tall" Jones, Julius Peppers 20.00
4 Doug Flutie, Drew Bledsoe 20.00
5 Doug Flutie, Drew Bledsoe 25.00
6 Fred Biletnikoff, Jerry Rice 30.00
7 Donovan McNabb, Marvin Harrison 25.00
8 Peyton Manning, Travis Henry 20.00
9 Brett Favre, Kurt Warner 30.00
10 Randy Moss, Terrell Owens 25.00
11 Ronnie Lott, Roy Williams 25.00
12 Fran Tarkenton, Brett Favre 40.00
13 Brian Griese, Ricky Williams 25.00
14 Ken Stabler, Michael Vick 30.00
15 Fran Tarkenton, Chad Pennington 25.00

2003 Fleer Rookie Sensations

NM/M
Complete Set (20): 75.00
Common Player: 2.00

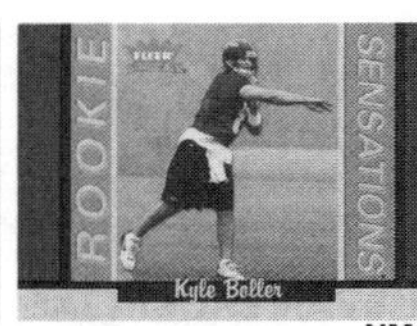

NM/M
Production 1250 Sets
1SS Kyle Boller 6.00
2SS Taylor Jacobs 2.50
3SS Terence Newman 4.00
4SS Kelley Washington 3.00
5SS Carson Palmer 10.00
6SS Byron Leftwich 10.00
7SS Willis McGahee 8.00
8SS Bethel Johnson 2.00
9SS Kevin Curtis 2.00
10SS Charles Rogers 8.00
11SS Rex Grossman 8.00
12SS Larry Johnson 6.00
13SS Anquan Boldin 5.00
14SS Andre Johnson 6.00
15SS Bryant Johnson 3.00
16SS Terrell Suggs 3.00
17SS Tyrone Calico 2.00
18SS Chris Simms 5.00
19SS Dewayne Robertson 2.00
20SS Nate Burleson 2.00

2003 Fleer Standouts

NM/M
Complete Set (10): 30.00
Common Player: 3.00
Inserted 1:36
1SO Ricky Williams 3.00
2SO Michael Vick 8.00
3SO Brett Favre 8.00
4SO Randy Moss 4.00
5SO Chad Pennington 3.00
6SO Jerry Rice 6.00
7SO Clinton Portis 6.00
8SO Brian Urlacher 4.00
9SO Donovan McNabb 3.00
10SO Tom Brady 3.00

2003 Fleer Throwbacks

NM/M
Complete Set (10): 50.00
Common Player: 5.00
Inserted 1:72
1TB Marcus Allen 10.00
2TB Bob Griese 6.00
3TB Jack Ham 5.00
4TB Ken Stabler 10.00
5TB Fran Tarkenton 10.00
6TB Earl Campbell 10.00
7TB Fred Biletnikoff 6.00
8TB Ed "Too Tall" Jones 5.00
9TB Ronnie Lott 5.00
10TB Doug Flutie 6.00

2003 Fleer Throwbacks Game-Used

NM/M
Common Player: 10.00
Inserted 1:288
Patches: 1X-2X
Production 100 Sets
TB-MA Marcus Allen 12.00
TB-EC Earl Campbell 12.00
TB-BG Bob Griese 10.00
TB-RL Ronnie Lott 10.00
TB-FT Fran Tarkenton 15.00

2004 Fleer Authentix

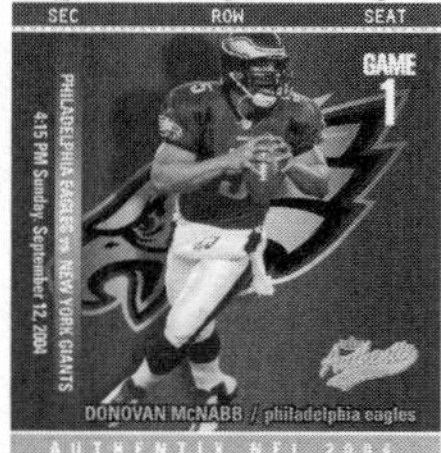

NM/M
Common Player (1-100): .25
Minor Stars (1-100): .50
Unlisted Stars (1-100): .75
Common Rookie (101-130): 1.50
Rookie Production 750 Sets
Common Executive Decision (131-140): 20.00
Production 250 Sets
Hometown Exclusive (141-150): .75
Pack (5): 5.50
Box (24): 95.00
1 Tom Brady 1.50
2 Amani Toomer .50
3 Terry Glenn .25
4 Eddie George .75
5 Bryant Johnson .25
6 Carson Palmer 1.00
7 Matt Hasselbeck .50
8 Randy Moss 1.50
9 Chad Johnson .50
10 Darrell Jackson .25
11 Chris Chambers .75
12 Jake Delhomme .75
13 Plaxico Burress .75
14 Marvin Harrison .75
15 Drew Bledsoe .75
16 Terrell Owens .75
17 Andre Johnson .75
18 Anquan Boldin .75
19 Jeremy Shockey .75
20 Champ Bailey .25
21 Shaun Alexander .75
22 Dante Hall .25
23 Julius Peppers .25
24 Duce Staley .25
25 Domanick Davis .75
26 Quentin Griffin .50
27 Clinton Portis 1.50
28 Aaron Brooks .75
29 Justin McCareins .25
30 Joey Galloway .25
31 David Boston .50
32 Lee Suggs .75
33 Torry Holt .75
34 Daunte Culpepper .75
35 Brian Urlacher .75
36 Kevan Barlow .25
37 Fred Taylor .75
38 Eric Moulds .25
39 Donovan McNabb 1.00
40 Edgerrin James 1.00
41 Ray Lewis .50
42 Rich Gannon .50
43 Joey Harrington .75
44 Laveranues Coles .50
45 Ricky Williams .75
46 Rex Grossman .75
47 Drew Brees .50
48 Priest Holmes 1.00
49 Travis Henry .25
50 Tim Rattay .25
51 Tony Gonzalez .50
52 Stephen Davis .50
53 Hines Ward .50
54 Peyton Manning 1.50
55 Peerless Price .50
56 Jerry Rice 2.00
57 David Carr 1.00
58 Jamal Lewis .75
59 Tim Brown .75
60 Warren Sapp .25
61 Tommy Maddox .50
62 Joe Horn .25
63 Roy Williams .50
64 Charlie Garner .25
65 Deion Branch .25
66 Corey Dillon .50
67 Marc Bulger .50
68 Trent Green .25
69 Michael Vick 2.00
70 Chad Pennington 1.00
71 Charles Rogers .75
72 Mark Brunell .50
73 Tiki Barber .25
74 Jeff Garcia .75
75 Marshall Faulk 1.00
76 DeShaun Foster .25
77 LaVar Arrington .50
78 Byron Leftwich 1.50
79 Willis McGahee .75
80 Brian Westbrook .25
81 Ahman Green .75
82 Kyle Boller .75
83 Jevon Kearse .25
84 Donald Driver .25
85 Warrick Dunn .25
86 Santana Moss .25
87 Keyshawn Johnson .50
88 Steve McNair .75
89 Deuce McAllister .75
90 A.J. Feeley .25
91 Keenan McCardell .25
92 Michael Bennett .75
93 Terrell Suggs .25
94 LaDainian Tomlinson 1.00
95 Brett Favre 2.50
96 Emmitt Smith 2.00
97 Curtis Martin .75
98 Jake Plummer .50
99 Derrick Mason .25
100 Ty Law .25
101 Ben Troupe 2.00
102 DeAngelo Hall 4.00
103 Eli Manning 20.00
104 Cody Pickett 2.50
105 Matt Schaub 2.50
106 J.P. Losman 6.00
107 Chris Perry 4.00
108 Steven Jackson 6.00
109 Kevin Jones 6.00
110 Michael Turner 1.50
111 Philip Rivers 10.00
112 Quincy Wilson 3.00
113 Luke McCown 2.50
114 Greg Jones 3.00
115 Julius Jones 6.00
116 Sean Taylor 5.00
117 Kellen Winslow Jr. 5.00
118 Rashaun Woods 5.00
119 Ben Watson 1.50
120 Devery Henderson 2.50
121 Ernest Wilford 1.50
122 Michael Jenkins 4.00
123 Roy Williams 8.00
124 Lee Evans 5.00
125 Bernard Berrian 1.50
126 Mewelde Moore 1.50
127 Jammal Lord 2.00
128 Darius Watts 2.50
129 Derrick Hamilton 1.50
130 Devard Darling 2.50
131 Andrew Hall w/Andy Reid Autograph 20.00
132 Tatum Bell w/Mike Shanahan Autograph 20.00
133 Drew Henson w/Bill Parcells Autograph 75.00
134 Ben Roethlisberger w/B. Cowher Autograph 75.00
135 Robert Gallery w/Norv Turner Autograph 40.00
136 Cedric Cobbs w/Bill Belichek Autograph 60.00
137 Reggie Williams w/Jack Del Rio Autograph 20.00
138 Larry Fitzgerald w/D. Green Autograph 40.00
139 Michael Clayton w/Jon Gruden Autograph 30.00
140 Keary Colbert w/John Fox Autograph 20.00
141 Najeh Davenport .75
142 Javon Walker .75
143 Robert Ferguson .75
144 Nick Barnett .75
145 Kabeer Gbaja-Biamila .75
146 Terence Newman .75
147 Dexter Coakley .75
148 Darren Woodson .75
149 Jason Witten .75
150 Antonio Bryant .75

2004 Fleer Authentix General Admission

Production 100 Sets
Stars (1-100): 4x-8x
Rookies (101-130): .5x-1.5x
Executive Decision (131-140): .5x-1x
Hometown Exclusive (141-150): 2x-4x

2004 Fleer Authentix Balcony

Production 75 Sets
Stars (1-100): 5x-10x
Rookies (101-130): .5x-1.5x
Executive Decision (131-140): .5x-1x
Hometown Exclusive (141-150): 2x-4x

2004 Fleer Authentix Mezzanine

Production 50 Sets
Stars (1-100): 6x-12x
Rookies (101-130): .75x-1.5x
Executive Decision (131-140): .5x-1.5x
Hometown Exclusive (141-150): 3x-5x

2004 Fleer Authentix Club Box

Production 25 Sets
No Pricing

2004 Fleer Authentix Standing Room Only

Production 10 Sets
No Pricing

2004 Fleer Authentix Autographed Authentix

Standing Room Only
No Pricing
Production 5 Sets
AA-TC Tyrone Calico
AA-DC David Carr
AA-JD Jake Delhomme
AA-DF DeShaun Foster
AA-DH Dante Hall
AA-MH Matt Hasselbeck
AA-MJ Michael Jenkins
AA-CJ Chad Johnson
AA-AL Ashley Lelie
AA-WM Willis McGahee
AA-DM Donovan McNabb
AA-DS Donte Stallworth
AA-JW Javon Walker
AA-BW Brian Westbrook
AA-JW2` Jason Witten

2004 Fleer Authentix Autographs General Admission

NM/M
Common Player: 15.00
Production 100 Sets
Balcony: .75X-1.5X
Production 75 Sets
Mezzanine: 1X-2X
Club Box: No Pricing
Production 25 Sets
There is a Club Box Donovan McNabb card.
AA-TC Tyrone Calico/100 20.00
AA-DF DeShaun Foster/100 15.00
AA-DH Dante Hall/100 30.00
AA-MJ Michael Jenkins/100 30.00
AA-CJ Chad Johnson/100 30.00

AA-AL Ashley Lelie/100 15.00
AA-WM Willis McGahee/100 25.00
AA-DS Donte Stallworth/100 15.00
AA-JW Javon Walker/100 15.00
AA-BW Brian Westbrook/100 15.00
AA-JW2 Jason Witten/100 15.00

2004 Fleer Authentix Autographed Jersey Authentix

NM/M
General Admission
Common Player: 20.00
Production 75 Sets
Balcony: 1X-2X
Production 50 Sets
There is a Balcony Donovan McNabb card.
AJA-TC Tyrone Calico/75 30.00
AJA-DC David Carr/75
AJA-JD Jake Delhomme/75 30.00
AJA-DF DeShaun Foster/75
AJA-DH Dante Hall/75 50.00
AJA-MH Matt Hasselbeck/75
AJA-CJ Chad Johnson/75
AJA-AL Ashley Lelie/75
AJA-WM Willis McGahee/75 30.00
AJA-DS Donte Stallworth/75
AJA-JW Javon Walker/75 20.00
AJA-BW Brian Westbrook/75
AJA-JW2 Jason Witten/75

2004 Fleer Authentix Autographed Jersey Mezzanine

No Pricing
Production 25 Sets
Club Box: No Pricing
Production 10 Sets
Standing Room Only: No Pricing
Production 1 Set
AJA-SA Shaun Alexander
AJA-PB Plaxico Burress
AJA-TC Tyrone Calico
AJA-DC David Carr
AJA-JD Jake Delhomme
AJA-DF DeShaun Foster
AJA-DH Dante Hall
AJA-MH Matt Hasselbeck
AJA-MJ Michael Jenkins
AJA-CJ Chad Johnson
AJA-AL Ashley Lelie
AJA-JL Jamal Lewis
AJA-DM Deuce McAllister
AJA-WM Willis McGahee
AJA-DM Donovan McNabb
AJA-CP Chad Pennington
AJA-DS Donte Stallworth
AJA-JW Javon Walker
AJA-BW Brian Westbrook
AJA-JW2 Jason Witten

2004 Fleer Authentix Hot Tickets

NM/M
Common Player: 1.50
Inserted 1:12
Jersey Version: 2X-4X
Production 500 Sets
Logo Version: No Pricing
Production 1 Set
1HT Donovan McNabb 2.00
2HT Tom Brady 3.00
3HT Brett Favre 5.00
4HT Clinton Portis 3.00
5HT Michael Vick 4.00
6HT Jeremy Shockey 1.50
7HT Peyton Manning 3.00
8HT Emmitt Smith 4.00
9HT Chad Pennington 2.00
10HT Randy Moss 3.00
11HT Ricky Williams 1.50
12HT Byron Leftwich 3.00
13HT Brian Urlacher 1.50
14HT Terrell Owens 1.50
15HT Jerry Rice 4.00

2004 Fleer Authentix Hot Tickets - Patch

NM/M
Numbered to player's jersey #
1HT Donovan McNabb/5
2HT Tom Brady/12
3HT Brett Favre/4
4HT Clinton Portis/26 20.00
5HT Michael Vick/7
6HT Jeremy Shockey/80 10.00
7HT Peyton Manning/18
8HT Emmitt Smith/22
9HT Chad Pennington/10
10HT Randy Moss/84 15.00
11HT Ricky Williams/34 25.00
12HT Byron Leftwich/7
13HT Brian Urlacher/54 25.00
14HT Terrell Owens/81 12.00
15HT Jerry Rice/80 20.00

2004 Fleer Authentix Jersey Authentix General Admission

NM/M
Common Player: 8.00
Numbered to indicated quantity
Balcony: 1X-2X
Production 150 Sets
Mezzanine: 2X-4X
Production 75 sets
Club Box: No Pricing
Production 25 Sets
Standing Room Only: No Pricing
Production 10 Sets
JA-SA Shaun Alexander/170 170.00
JA-LA LaVar Arrington/145 10.00
JA-AB Anquan Boldin/320 5.00
JA-TB Tom Brady/275 15.00
JA-QC Quincy Carter/315 5.00
JA-DC Daunte Culpepper/350 5.00
JA-KG Donald Driver/165 5.00
JA-MF Marshall Faulk/350 8.00
JA-BF Brett Favre/345 20.00
JA-AG Ahman Green/285 8.00
JA-JH Joey Harrington/225 5.00
JA-MH MarvinHarrison/350 5.00
JA-EJ Edgerrin James/145 8.00
JA-AJ Andre Johnson/350 5.00
JA-CJ Chad Johnson/350 5.00
JA-JL Jamal Lewis/350 5.00
JA-BL Byron Leftwich/350 8.00
JA-PM Peyton Manning/145 15.00
JA-DM2 Deuce McAllister/350 5.00
JA-DM Donovan McNabb/350 8.00
JA-SM Steve McNair/205 5.00
JA-RM Randy Moss/350 10.00
JA-SM Santana Moss/255 5.00
JA-TN Terence Newman/145 8.00
JA-TO Terrell Owens 8.00
JA-CP2 Chad Pennington/315 10.00
JA-CP Clinton Portis/210 8.00
JA-JR Jerry Rice/145 15.00
JA-JS Jeremy Shockey/350 5.00
JA-ES Emmitt Smith/145 20.00
JA-LT LaDainian Tomlinson/220 8.00
JA-MV Michael Vick/145 15.00
JA-BW Brian Westbrook/285 5.00
JA-RW Ricky Williams/212 5.00
JA-RW2 Roy Williams/350 8.00

2004 Fleer Authentix Monday Night Matchup Jerseys

NM/M
Numbered to indicated quantity
Patch Version: No Pricing
Production 10 Sets
JD-BF Jake Delhomme, Brett Favre/10
TO-RM Terrell Owens, Randy Moss/20
CP-RW Clinton Portis, Roy Williams/30
RL-PH Jamal Lewis, Priest Holmes/40
AG-EG Ahman Green, Eddie George/50
DB-MF Marshall Faulk, Derrick Brooks/60
CP-JP Carson Palmer, Jake Plummer/70
CP-RW Chad Pennington, Ricky Williams/80 12.00
DC-PM Peyton Manning, Daunte Culpepper/90
DM-KJ Keyshawn Johnson, Donovan McNabb/100
TG-TB Trent Green,Tom Brady/110
BF-MF Brett Favre, Marshall Faulk/120 30.00
SA-RW Shaun Alexander, Roy Williams/130
SM-TG Steve McNair, Tony Gonzalez/140
RW-TB Ricky Williams, Tom Brady/150
TH-TO Torry Holt, Terrell Owens/160

2004 Fleer Authentix NFL Draft Day Tickets

NM/M
Common Player: 12.00
Inserted 1:240
DDT-LE Lee Evans 12.00
DDT-LF Larry Fitzgerald 20.00
DDT-SJ Steven Jackson 15.00
DDT-EM Eli Manning 40.00
DDT-PR Philip Rivers 30.00
DDT-BR Ben Roethlisberger 40.00
DDT-RW2 Reggie Williams 12.00
DDT-RW Roy Williams 20.00
DDT-KW Kellen Winslow Jr. 10.00
DDT-RW3 Rashaun Woods 12.00

2004 Fleer Authentix Stadium Standouts

NM/M
Common Player: 1.00
Inserted 1:8
1SS Ricky Williams 1.00
2SS Anquan Boldin 1.00
3SS Tom Brady 2.00
4SS Brett Favre 4.00
5SS Peyton Manning 2.00
6SS Marshall Faulk 1.50
7SS Michael Vick 3.00
8SS David Carr 1.50
9SS Carson Palmer 1.50
10SS Randy Moss 2.00

2004 Fleer Authentix Tailgate Trios

NM/M
Common Card: 12.00
Production 75 Sets
Hometown Variation #1: No Pricing
Production 25 Sets
Hometown Variation #2: No Pricing
Production 5 Sets
O-M-W Donovan McNabb, Terrell Owens, Brian Westbrook 18.00
B-M-H Drew Bledsoe,Eric Moulds, Travis Henry 15.00
D-G-F Donald Driver,Ahman Green, Brett Favre 30.00
H-J-M Marvin Harrison, Edgerrin James, Peyton Manning 20.00
B-J-G Antonio Bryant, Keyshawn Johnson, Terry Glenn 12.00
M-C-B Randy Moss, Daunte Culpepper, Michael Bennett 20.00
B-H-M Aaron Brooks, Joe Horn, Deuce McAllister 15.00
P-M-M Chad Pennington, Santana Moss, Curtis Martin 15.00
G-R-B Rich Gannon, Jerry Rice, Tim Brown 18.00
B-W-M Plaxico Burress, Hines Ward, Tommy Maddox 12.00
H-J-A Matt Hasselbeck, Darrell Jackson, Shaun Alexander 12.00
H-B-F Torry Holt, Isaac Bruce, Marshall Faulk 15.00
M-M-G Steve McNair, Derrick Mason, Eddie George 18.00
P-C-B Clinton Portis, Laveranues Coles, Mark Brunell 20.00
T-S-B Amani Toomer, Jeremy Shockey, Tiki Barber 15.00

2004 Fleer Genuine

NM/M
Common Player (1-75): .40
Minor Stars (1-75): .60
Unlisted Stars (1-75): 1.00
Common Rookie (76-100): 3.00
Production 500 Sets
Pack (5): 10.00
Box (12): 90.00
1 Anquan Boldin 1.00
2 Rod Smith .40
3 Randy Moss 2.00
4 Drew Brees .60
5 Jamal Lewis 1.00
6 Ahman Green 1.00
7 Aaron Brooks 1.00
8 Torry Holt 1.00
9 Steve Smith .40
10 Marvin Harrison 1.00
11 Santana Moss .40
12 Eddie George 1.00
13 Lee Suggs .40
14 Randy McMichael .40
15 Hines Ward .60
16 Drew Bledsoe 1.00
17 Andre Johnson 1.00
18 Jeremy Shockey 1.00
19 Mike Alstott .40
20 Chad Johnson .60
21 Priest Holmes 1.50
22 Brian Westbrook .40
23 LaVar Arrington 1.00
24 Keyshawn Johnson .60
25 Chris Chambers 1.00
26 LaDainian Tomlinson 1.00
27 Ray Lewis .60
28 Brett Favre 3.00
29 Deuce McAllister 1.00
30 Marshall Faulk 1.50
31 Brian Urlacher 1.00
32 Byron Leftwich 2.00
33 Jerry Rice 2.50
34 Clinton Portis 2.00
35 Derrick Mason .40
36 David Boston .60
37 Plaxico Burress 1.00
38 Peerless Price .60
39 Joey Harrington 1.00
40 Corey Dillon .60
41 Matt Hasselbeck .60
42 Stephen Davis .60
43 Peyton Manning 2.00
44 Tiki Barber .40
45 Derrick Brooks .40
46 Jeff Garcia 1.00
47 Trent Green .40
48 Donovan McNabb 1.50
49 Michael Vick 2.50
50 Jake Plummer .60
51 Tom Brady 2.00
52 Brandon Lloyd .40
53 Eric Moulds .40
54 David Carr 1.50
55 Joe Horn .40
56 Isaac Bruce .60
57 Rex Grossman 1.00
58 Fred Taylor 1.00
59 Rich Gannon .60
60 Laveranues Coles .60
61 T.J. Duckett .60
62 Charles Rogers 1.00
63 Deion Branch .40
64 Shaun Alexander 1.00
65 Jake Delhomme 1.00
66 Edgerrin James 1.50
67 Chad Pennington 1.50
68 Steve McNair 1.00
69 Carson Palmer 1.50
70 Tony Gonzalez .60
71 Terrell Owens 1.00
72 Josh McCown .40
73 Ashley Lelie .60
74 Daunte Culpepper 1.00
75 Kevan Barlow .40
76 *Eli Manning* 20.00
77 *Larry Fitzgerald* 12.00
78 *Philip Rivers* 12.00
79 *Kellen Winslow Jr.* 5.00
80 *Roy Williams* 12.00
81 *Reggie Williams* 6.00
82 *Ben Roethlisberger* 60.00
83 *Lee Evans* 10.00
84 *Michael Clayton* 8.00
85 *J.P. Losman* 10.00
86 *Steven Jackson* 10.00
87 *Chris Perry* 6.00
88 *Michael Jenkins* 6.00
89 *Kevin Jones* 10.00
90 *Rashaun Woods* 6.00
91 *Ben Watson* 3.00
92 *Ben Troupe* 3.00
93 *Tatum Bell* 6.00
94 *Julius Jones* 10.00
95 *Devery Henderson* 3.00
96 *Darius Watts* 3.00
97 *Greg Jones* 5.00
98 *Keary Colbert* 5.00
99 *Derrick Hamilton* 3.00
100 *Drew Henson* 8.00

2004 Fleer Genuine Genuine Reflection

Veterans (1-75): 3X-5X
Rookies #'d to draft selection number
Rookies #'d to more than 100: .5X-1X
Rookies #'d 76-100: .75X-1X
Rookies #'d 51-75: .75X-1.25X
Rookies #'d 26-50: 1X-3X
Rookies #'d to 25 or less: No Pricing

2004 Fleer Genuine At Large

NM/M
Common Player: 3.00
Inserted 1:45
1 Anquan Boldin 4.00
2 LaDainian Tomlinson 5.00
3 Michael Vick 8.00
4 Daunte Culpepper 4.00
5 Brian Urlacher 4.00
6 Ahman Green 4.00
7 Peyton Manning 6.00
8 Byron Leftwich 6.00
9 Priest Holmes 5.00
10 Chad Pennington 5.00
11 Jeremy Shockey 4.00
12 Joe Horn 3.00
13 Santana Moss 3.00
14 Donovan McNabb 5.00
15 Randy Moss 6.00

2004 Fleer Genuine At Large Oversized Patch Autographs

No Pricing
Production 25 Sets
Anquan Boldin
Daunte Culpepper
Ahman Green
Priest Holmes
Joe Horn
Byron Leftwich
Peyton Manning
Donovan McNabb
Randy Moss
Santana Moss
Chad Pennington
Jeremy Shockey
LaDainian Tomlinson
Brian Urlacher
Michael Vick

2004 Fleer Genuine At Large Oversized Patch White

NM/M
Common Player: 10.00
Production 75 Sets
Black: .75X-1.5X
Production 35 Sets
Orange: No Pricing
Production 5 Sets
Mike Alstott 12.00
Anquan Boldin 10.00
Aaron Brooks 12.00
Derrick Brooks 10.00
Chris Chambers 12.00
Daunte Culpepper 12.00
Jake Delhomme 15.00
Justin Fargas 10.00
Marshall Faulk 15.00
Rich Gannon 10.00
Ahman Green 12.00
Rex Grossman 12.00
Joey Harrington 12.00
Matt Hasselbeck 12.00
Travis Henry 10.00
Priest Holmes 15.00
Joe Horn
Byron Leftwich
Jamal Lewis 12.00
Peyton Manning 30.00
Donovan McNabb 25.00
Randy Moss 30.00
Santana Moss
Chad Pennington
Jeremy Shockey
LaDainian Tomlinson 20.00
Brian Urlacher 12.00
Michael Vick 40.00
Hines Ward 15.00
Roy Williams 15.00

2004 Fleer Genuine Big Time

Common Player:
Inserted 1:500
1 Clinton Portis
2 Donovan McNabb
3 Jeff Garcia
4 Chad Johnson
5 Michael Vick
6 Tony Gonzalez
7 Deuce McAllister
8 Carson Palmer
9 Peyton Manning
10 LaDainian Tomlinson
11 Brett Favre
12 Marvin Harrison
13 Terrell Owens
14 Priest Holmes
15 Jamal Lewis

2004 Fleer Genuine Big Time Autographs Blue

NM/M
Common Player: 10.00
Production 150 Sets
Red: .75X-1.5X
Production 50 Sets
Orange: No Pricing
Production 25 Sets
Boss Bailey 10.00
Tiki Barber 15.00
Michael Bennett
Isaac Bruce 15.00
Plaxico Burress 15.00
David Carr 20.00
Brett Favre 125.00
Jeff Garcia 15.00
Tony Gonzalez 20.00
Marvin Harrison
Priest Holmes
Chad Johnson 20.00
Joe Jurevicius 12.00
Jamal Lewis 20.00
Curtis Martin 30.00
Deuce McAllister 20.00
Donovan McNabb
Freddie Mitchell 10.00
Terrell Owens
Carson Palmer
Julius Peppers
Chris Perry 10.00
Clinton Portis
Peerless Price 15.00
Donte Stallworth
Lee Suggs
Fred Taylor 15.00
Zach Thomas 15.00
LaDainian Tomlinson
Brian Urlacher
Peter Warrick
Reggie Williams 12.00

2004 Fleer Genuine Big Time Game-Used Autographs White

NM/M
Production 75 Sets
Black: No Pricing
Production 25 Sets
Jeff Garcia
Tony Gonzalez 20.00
Marvin Harrison
Chad Johnson 20.00
Jamal Lewis
Donovan McNabb
Terrell Owens
Carson Palmer
Clinton Portis
LaDainian Tomlinson

2004 Fleer Genuine Big Time Oversized Patch White

Numbered to player's jersey number
Black: No Pricing
Production 25 Sets
Orange: No Pricing
Production 5 Sets
Boss Bailey
Tiki Barber
Isaac Bruce
Plaxico Burress
David Carr
Brett Favre
Jeff Garcia
Tony Gonzalez
Marvin Harrison
Priest Holmes
Chad Johnson
Jamal Lewis
Peyton Manning
Curtis Martin
Deuce McAllister
Donovan McNabb
Freddie Mitchell
Terrell Owens
Carson Palmer
Julius Peppers
Clinton Portis
Peerless Price
Donte Stallworth
Lee Suggs
Fred Taylor
Zach Thomas
LaDainian Tomlinson
Brian Urlacher
Michael Vick
Peter Warrick

2004 Fleer Genuine Big Time Patch Autographs

No Pricing
Production 25 Sets
Brett Favre
Jeff Garcia
Tony Gonzalez
Marvin Harrison
Priest Holmes
Chad Johnson
Jamal Lewis
Peyton Manning
Deuce McAllister
Donovan McNabb
Terrell Owens
Carson Palmer
Clinton Portis
LaDainian Tomlinson
Michael Vick

2004 Fleer Genuine Genuine Article

NM/M
Common Player: 1.50
Inserted 1:7
1 Brett Favre 5.00
2 Marvin Harrison 1.50
3 Clinton Portis 3.00
4 Peyton Manning 3.00
5 Randy Moss 3.00
6 Donovan McNabb 2.00
7 Tom Brady 3.00
8 Terrell Owens 1.50
9 Torry Holt 1.50
10 Steve McNair 1.50
11 Ray Lewis 1.50
12 Michael Vick 4.00
13 Deuce McAllister 1.50
14 Shaun Alexander 1.50
15 Priest Holmes 2.00

2004 Fleer Gen. Genuine Article Oversized Patch White

NM/M
Common Player: 8.00
Production 150 Sets
Orange: No Pricing
Production 25 Sets
Shaun Alexander 10.00
Tom Brady 20.00
Brett Favre 40.00
Marvin Harrison 10.00
Priest Holmes 12.00
Torry Holt 10.00
Ray Lewis 8.00
Peyton Manning 15.00
Deuce McAllister
Donovan McNabb 12.00
Steve McNair 8.00
Randy Moss 15.00
Terrell Owens 10.00
Clinton Portis 15.00
Michael Vick 20.00

2004 Fleer Genuine Genuine Article Signature White

NM/M
Common Player: 25.00
Production 100 Sets
Black: .75X-1.5X
Production 50 Sets
Orange: No Pricing
Production 1 Set
Shaun Alexander 30.00
Marvin Harrison 25.00
Torry Holt 25.00
Ray Lewis
Deuce McAllister 25.00
Donovan McNabb 40.00
Steve McNair
Terrell Owens
Clinton Portis
Michael Vick

2004 Fleer Greats of the Game

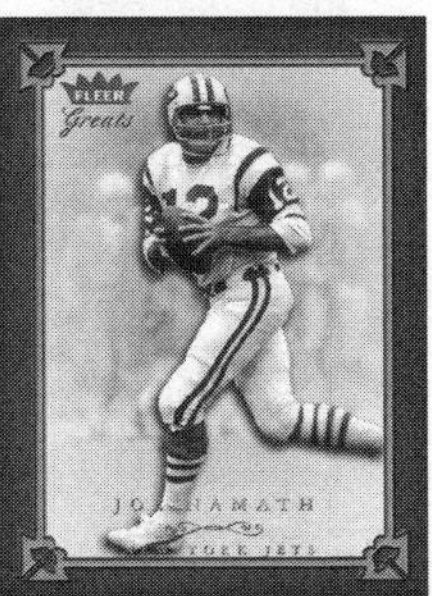

NM/M
Common Player (1-70): .50
Minor Stars (1-70): .75
Unlisted Stars (1-70): 1.50
Common Rookie (71-90): 4.00
Production 999 Sets
Pack (5): 8.00
Box (15): 90.00
1 Jim Brown 4.00
2 Jim Thorpe 4.00
3 Terry Bradshaw 4.00
4 Fran Tarkenton 3.00
5 Joe Namath 4.00
6 Joe Montana 5.00
7 George Rogers .50
8 Marcus Allen 3.00
9 Walter Payton 5.00
10 Dick Butkus 3.00

11 Dan Fouts 2.00
12 Kellen Winslow Sr. 2.00
13 Sammy Baugh 3.00
14 Bart Starr 4.00
15 Steve Young 3.00
16 Sid Luckman .75
17 Y.A. Tittle 3.00
18 Dan Marino 5.00
19 Paul Hornung 3.00
20 John Elway 5.00
21 Earl Campbell 2.00
22 Max McGee .50
23 Alan Ameche .50
24 Bronko Nagurski 2.00
25 Elroy Hirsch 2.00
26 Jack Lambert 3.00
27 Sam Huff 1.50
28 Jay Novacek .50
29 Roger Staubach 3.00
30 Bob Hayes 2.00
31 Ken Stabler 1.50
32 Chuck Bednarik .50
33 Ronnie Lott 1.50
34 Steve Van Buren .60
35 Art Monk .50
36 Gale Sayers 3.00
37 Jim Otto 2.00
38 Jim Plunkett 1.50
39 Mike Ditka 3.00
40 Don Maynard 2.00
41 John Riggins 2.00
42 Billy Sims 2.00
43 Franco Harris 2.00
44 Tony Dorsett 2.00
45 Wilbert Montgomery .50
46 Eric Dickerson 2.00
47 Jim Taylor 2.00
48 George Blanda 3.00
49 Cris Carter 1.50
50 Mike Quick .50
51 James Lofton 2.00
52 Lawrence Taylor 2.00
53 Roger Craig 2.00
54 Paul Warfield 2.00
55 Dan Pastorini .50
56 Ozzie Newsome 2.00
57 Charley Taylor 1.50
58 Deacon Jones 1.50
59 Bob Lilly 1.50
60 Mike Singletary 1.50
61 Warren Moon 2.00
62 Charles White .50
63 Bob Griese 2.00
64 Dwight Clark 2.00
65 Joe Greene 3.00
66 Dave Casper 2.00
67 Harold Carmichael .75
68 Drew Pearson .75
69 Tony Hill .50
70 Ray Nitschke 3.00
71 *Eli Manning* 20.00
72 *Philip Rivers* 10.00
73 *Ben Roethlisberger* 50.00
74 *Julius Jones* 10.00
75 *Larry Fitzgerald* 10.00
76 *Steven Jackson* 8.00
77 *Kevin Jones* 8.00
78 *Tatum Bell* 6.00
79 *Rashaun Woods* 5.00
80 *Roy Williams* 10.00
81 *Lee Evans* 8.00
82 *Michael Clayton* 8.00
83 *J.P. Losman* 8.00
84 *Drew Henson* 8.00
85 *Kellen Winslow Jr.* 6.00
86 *Chris Perry* 6.00
87 *Reggie Williams* 4.00
88 *Michael Jenkins* 5.00
89 *Darius Watts* 4.00
90 *Keary Colbert* 4.00

2004 Fleer Greats of the Game Green

Cards 1-70: 1X-3X
Production 500 Sets

2004 Fleer Greats of the Game Red

Cards 71-90: 1X-2X
Production 99 Sets

2004 Fleer Greats of the Game Classic Combos

NM/M

1CC Troy Aikman, Michael Irvin/1955 8.00
2CC John Elway, Shannon Sharpe
3CC Ken Stabler, Fred Biletnikoff/1975 3.00
4CC Roger Staubach, Drew Pearson/1974 6.00
5CC Joe Montana, Dwight Clark/1986 10.00
6CC Dan Marino, Mark Clayton/1984 10.00
7CC Steve Young, Jerry Rice/1995 6.00
8CC Joe Namath, Don Maynard/1965 8.00
9CC Bob Griese, Paul Warfield/1970 4.00
10CC Dan Fouts, Kellen Winslow Sr./1981 4.00

2004 Fleer Greats of the Game Classic Combos Autographs

NM/M

Sequentially Numbered
Dual: No Pricing
Production 10 Sets
1CC Troy Aikman, Michael Irvin
2CC Terry Bradshaw, Lynn Swann
3CC Ken Stabler, Fred Biletnikoff
4CC Roger Staubach,Drew Pearson
5CC Joe Montana, Dwight Clark
6CC Dan Marino, Mark Clayton
7CC Steve Young, Jerry Rice
8CC Joe Namath, Don Maynard
9CC Bob Griese, Paul Warfield
10CC Dan Fouts, Kellen Winslow Jr.

2004 Fleer Greats of the Game Comparison Cuts Autograph

No Pricing
Production 1 Set
AMEM Archie Manning, Eli Manning
DWBS Doak Walker, Barry Sanders
JBWP Jim Brown, Walter Payton
JEDM John Elway, Dan Marino
JMJN Joe Montana, Joe Namath
VLGH Vince Lombardi, George Halas

2004 Fleer Greats of the Game Etched in Time Autographs

No Pricing
Production 1 Set
ETSB Sammy Baugh
ETJB Jim Brown
ETOG Otto Graham
ETRG Harold "Red" Grange
ETDL Dick Lane
ETBL Bobby Layne
ETVL Vince Lombardi
ETBN Bronko Nagurski
ETRN Ray Nitschke
ETWP Walter Payton
ETJT Jim Thorpe

2004 Fleer Greats of the Game Glory of Their Time

NM/M

Common Player: 3.00
Sequentially #'d to indicated quantity
GOT1 Joe Namath/1967 8.00
GOT2 Troy Aikman/1992 8.00
GOT3 Walter Payton/1977 10.00
GOT4 Joe Montana/1987 10.00
GOT5 Bart Starr/1966 8.00
GOT6 Paul Hornung/1960 6.00
GOT7 Dan Marino/1984 10.00
GOT8 Roger Staubach/1979 6.00
GOT9 Warren Moon/1990 4.00
GOT10 Jack Lambert/1976 6.00
GOT11 Franco Harris/1979 4.00
GOT12 Steve Young/1994 6.00
GOT13 Eric Dickerson/1984
GOT14 Lawrence Taylor/1986 4.00
GOT15 Tony Dorsett/1981 4.00
GOT16 Ronnie Lott/1986 3.00
GOT17 Earl Campbell/1980 4.00
GOT18 Gale Sayers/1965 6.00
GOT19 Jim Kelly/1991 4.00
GOT20 Bob Griese/1977 4.00
GOT21 John Elway/1993 10.00
GOT22 Barry Sanders/1997 8.00
GOT23 Jim Plunkett/1985 3.00
GOT24 Bob Lilly/1963 3.00
GOT25 Fran Tarkenton/1975 6.00
GOT26 Mel Renfro/1969 4.00
GOT27 Fred Biletnikoff/1969 3.00
GOT28 Shannon Sharpe/1996
GOT29 Thurman Thomas/1992 3.00
GOT30 Michael Irvin/1995 4.00

2004 Fleer Greats of Game Glory of Their Time G-U Red

NM/M

Common Player: 8.00
Inserted 1:24
Silver: .75X-1.5X
Production 300 Sets
Patch: No Pricing
Production 25 Sets
TA Troy Aikman 15.00
FB Fred Biletnikoff 10.00
EC Earl Campbell 10.00
ED Eric Dickerson
TD Tony Dorsett 12.00
JE John Elway 25.00
BG Bob Griese 10.00
FH Franco Harris 15.00
PH Paul Hornung Pants 12.00
MI Michael Irvin 10.00
JK Jim Kelly 8.00
JL Jack Lambert 20.00
RL Ronnie Lott 8.00
BL Bob Lilly
DM Dan Marino 25.00
JM Joe Montana 40.00
WM Warren Moon 8.00
WP Walter Payton 40.00
JP Jim Plunkett 8.00
MF Mel Renfro 10.00
BS Barry Sanders 15.00
GS Gale Sayers 20.00
SS Shannon Sharpe
BS Bart Starr Pants 15.00
RS Roger Staubach 20.00
FT Fran Tarkenton
LT Lawrence Taylor 12.00
TT Thurman Thomas 8.00
SY Steve Young 12.00

2004 Fleer Greats of the Game Gold Border Autographs

NM/M

Common Player: 15.00
Inserted 1:15
MA Marcus Allen
SB Sammy Baugh
CB Chuck Bednarik 20.00
TBE Tatum Bell
GB George Blanda
TBR Terry Bradshaw
JB Jim Brown
DB Dick Butkus
EC Earl Campbell
HC Harold Carmichael 15.00
CC Cris Carter 30.00
DCA Dave Casper 20.00
DCL Dwight Clark 20.00
MC Michael Clayton
KC Keary Colbert 30.00
RC Roger Craig 15.00
ED Eric Dickerson
MD Mike Ditka
TD Tony Dorsett
JE John Elway 175.00
LE Lee Evans
LF Larry Fitzgerald
DF Dan Fouts 30.00
JG Joe Greene 50.00
BG Bob Griese 25.00
FH Franco Harris 40.00
DH Drew Henson
TH Tony Hill 30.00
PH Paul Hornung 30.00
SH Sam Huff 20.00
SJ Steven Jackson
MJ Michael Jenkins
DJ Deacon Jones 20.00
JJ Julius Jones
KJ Kevin Jones
JLA Jack Lambert
BL Bob Lilly 20.00
JLO James Lofton
JPL J.P. Losman
RL Ronnie Lott 30.00
EM Eli Manning
DM Dan Marino
DMY Don Maynard 20.00
MM Max McGee
AM Art Monk
JM Joe Montana 150.00
WMY Wilbert Montgomery 15.00
WMN Warren Moon 40.00
JNA Joe Namath 175.00
ON Ozzie Newsome 15.00
JN Jay Novacek 40.00
JO Jim Otto 30.00
DPA Dan Pastorini 20.00
WP Walter Payton
DPE Drew Pearson
CP Chris Perry
JP Jim Plunkett 20.00
MQ Mike Quick 20.00
JR John Riggins
PR Philip Rivers
BR Ben Roethlisberger 300.00
GR George Rogers
GS Gale Sayers 50.00
BSI Billy Sims 20.00
MS Mike Singletary 25.00
KS Ken Stabler 40.00
BST Bart Starr
RS Roger Staubach 80.00
FT Fran Tarkenton 30.00
CT Charley Taylor 20.00
JT Jim Taylor 60.00
LT Lawrence Taylor
YT Y.A. Tittle 30.00
SV Steve Van Buren
PW Paul Warfield 20.00
CW Charles White 15.00
REW Reggie Williams
RWI Roy Williams 100.00
KWJ Kellen Winslow Jr.
KWS Kellen Winslow Sr. 20.00
RWO Rashaun Woods
SY Steve Young 120.00

2004 Fleer Greats of the Game Legendary Nameplates

No Pricing
Numbered between 4 & 11
TA Troy Aikman/6
MA Marcus Allen Wht/5
MA2 Marcus Allen Red/5
FB Fred Biletnikoff/11
CC Cris Carter Purp/6
CC2 Cris Carter Wht/6
RC Randall Cunningham Grn/10
RC2 Randall Cunningham Wht/10
LG L.C. Greenwood/9
FH Franco Harris/6
MI Michael Irvin/5
BJ Bo Jackson/7
JK Jim Kelly/5
JL Jack Lambert/7
JL2 James Lofton/6
RL Ronnie Lott/4
DM Dan Marino/6
JM Joe Montana Wht/7
JM2 Joe Montana Red/7
JN Joe Namath/6
JN2 Jay Novacek/7
WP Walter Payton/6
JP Jim Plunkett/8
BS Barry Sanders/7
DS Deion Sanders Blue/7
DS2 Deion Sanders Wht/7
SS Shannon Sharpe Wht/6
SS2 Shannon Sharpe Blue/6
MS Mike Singletary/10
TT Thurman Thomas/6
SY Steve Young Red/5
SY2 Steve Young Wht/5

A player's name in *italic* type indicates a rookie card.

2004 Fleer Greats of Game Personality Cuts Autographs

No Pricing
Production 1 Set
PCPB Paul Brown
PCGH George Halas
PCCL Curly Lambeau
PCTL Tom Landry
PCVL Vince Lombardi
PCAR Art Rooney

2004 Fleer Hot Prospects

NM/M

Common Player: .40
Minor Stars (1-70): .60
Unlisted Stars (1-70): 1.00
Common Auto. Future Swatch (71-94): 40.00
Sequentially #'d to varying quantities
Common Future Swatch (95-102): 10.00
Production 350 Sets
Common Hot Prospects (103-112): 2.00
Production 1000 Sets
Pack (5): 20.00
Box (15): 220.00
1 Donovan McNabb 1.50
2 Charlie Garner .40
3 Tim Rattay .40
4 Drew Brees).60
5 Jerry Rice 2.50
6 Aaron Brooks 1.00
7 Chris Chambers 1.00
8 Byron Leftwich 2.00
9 Andre Johnson 1.00
10 Edgerrin James 1.50
11 Charles Rogers 1.00
12 Quentin Griffin .60
13 Carson Palmer 1.50
14 Ray Lewis .60
15 Clinton Portis 2.00
16 Marc Bulger .60
17 Matt Hasselbeck .60
18 Plaxico Burress 1.00
19 Priest Holmes 1.50
20 David Carr 1.50
21 Ahman Green 1.00
22 Roy Williams .60
23 Travis Henry .40
24 Michael Vick 2.50
25 Eddie George 1.00
26 Marshall Faulk 1.50
27 Kevan Barlow .40
28 Shaun Alexander 1.00
29 Hines Ward .60
30 Anquan Boldin 1.00
31 Chad Pennington 1.50
32 Randy Moss 2.00
33 Fred Taylor 1.00
34 Marvin Harrison 1.00
35 Joey Harrington 1.00
36 Rich Gannon .60
37 Deuce McAllister 1.00
38 Deion Branch .40
39 Tony Gonzalez .60
40 Brett Favre 3.00
41 Keyshawn Johnson .60
42 Lee Suggs .40
43 Jake Delhomme 1.00
44 Rex Grossman 1.00
45 Drew Bledsoe 1.00
46 Warrick Dunn .40
47 Steve McNair 1.00
48 Torry Holt 1.00
49 Brian Westbrook .40
50 Santana Moss .40
51 Jeremy Shockey 1.00
52 Daunte Culpepper 1.00
53 Jeff Garcia 1.00
54 Stephen Davis .60
55 Eric Moulds .40
56 Emmitt Smith 2.50
57 Keenan McCardell .40
58 LaDainian Tomlinson 1.50
59 Terrell Owens 1.00
60 Curtis Martin 1.00
61 Joe Horn .40
62 Tiki Barber .40
63 Tom Brady 2.00
64 Ricky Williams 1.00
65 Peyton Manning 2.00
66 Jake Plummer .60
67 Chad Johnson .60
68 Brian Urlacher 1.00
69 Jamal Lewis 1.00
70 Laveranues Coles .60
71 Tatum Bell/350 80.00
72 Bernard Berrian/344 40.00
73 Michael Clayton/350 80.00
74 Lee Evans/350 60.00
75 Larry Fitzgerald/140 175.00
76 Devery Henderson/350 60.00
77 Drew Henson/331 100.00
78 Steven Jackson/300 175.00
79 Michael Jenkins/350 50.00
80 Greg Jones/289 50.00
81 Kevin Jones/278 175.00
82 J.P. Losman/350 100.00
83 Eli Manning/350 200.00
84 Chris Perry/350 50.00
85 Philip Rivers/350 150.00
86 Ben Roethlisberger/150 500.00
87 Reggie Williams/350 80.00
88 Roy Williams/350 175.00
89 Kellen Winslow Jr./50 150.00
90 Rashaun Woods/350 100.00
91 Julius Jones/350 200.00
92 Luke McCown/350 50.00
93 Keary Colbert/349 40.00
94 Matt Schaub/120 60.00
95 Cedric Cobbs/350 12.00
96 Darius Watts/350 18.00
97 DeAngelo Hall/350 15.00
98 Derrick Hamilton/350 10.00
99 Devard Darling/350 10.00
100 Ben Troupe/350 10.00
101 Mewelde Moore/350 12.00
102 Ben Watson/350 10.00
103 Sean Taylor/1000 6.00
104 Ricky Ray/1000 3.00
105 Carlos Francis/1000 2.00
106 Samie Parker/1000 2.00
107 Jerricho Cotchery/1000 2.00
108 Ernest Wilford/1000 2.00
109 Craig Krenzel/1000 3.00
110 Robert Gallery/1000 4.00
111 Dunta Robinson/1000 2.00
112 Jonathan Vilma/1000 2.00

2004 Fleer Hot Prospects Red Hot

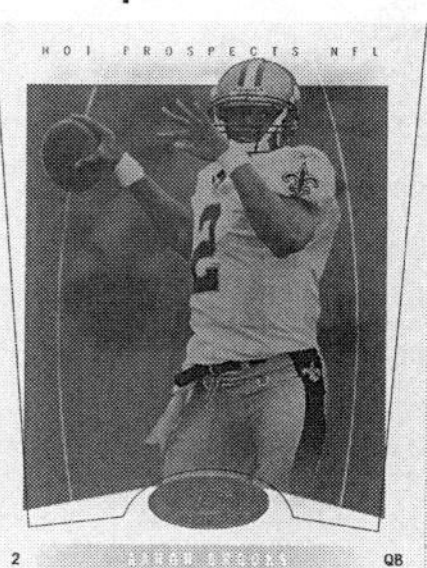

Stars (1-70): 1X-2X
Auto. Future Swatch (71-94): .75X-1.5X
Future Swatch (95-102): .75X-1.5X
Hot Prospects (103-112): 1X-2X
Production 50 Sets

2004 Fleer Hot Prospects White Hot

Cards 1-112: No Pricing
Production 1 Set

2004 Fleer Hot Prospects Alumni Ink

NM/M

Production 50 Sets
Red Hot: No Pricing
Production 10 Sets
White Hot: No Pricing
Production 1 Set
LE-CC Lee Evans, Chris Chambers 40.00
CP-BL Chad Pennington, Byron Leftwich 100.00
SJ-CJ Stephen Jackson, Chad Johnson 60.00
AB-LF Antonio Bryant, Larry Fitzgerald 75.00
MV-KJ Michael Vick, Kevin Jones 125.00
DH-TB Drew Henson, Tom Brady 150.00
DM-EM Deuce McAllister, Eli Manning 150.00
RW-RW Roy Williams, Ricky Williams 120.00
DH-MC Devery Henderson, Michael Clayton 50.00
TB-RW Tatum Bell, Rashaun Woods 75.00

2004 Fleer Hot Prospects Double Team Jerseys

NM/M

Common Player: 15.00
Production 100 Sets
Jersey Red Hot: 1X-2X
Production 25 Sets
Jersey White Hot: No Pricing
Production 1 Set
Patch: .75X-1.5X
Production 50 Sets
Patch Red Hot: No Pricing
Production 10 Sets
Patch White Hot: No Pricing
Production 1 Set
Auto Patch: 1.5X-3X
Production 25 Sets
Auto Patch Red Hot: No Pricing
Production 5 Sets
Auto Patch White Hot: No Pricing
Production 1 Set
DTLE Lee Evans 15.00
DTDF DeShaun Foster 15.00
GTQG Quentin Griffin 15.00
DTDH Drew Henson 25.00
DTSJ Steven Jackson 25.00
DTKJ Kevin Jones 25.00
DTEM Eli Manning 50.00
DTMS Matt Schaub 15.00
DTRW Roy Williams WR 30.00
DTKW Kellen Winslow Jr. 25.00

2004 Fleer Hot Prospects Draft Rewind

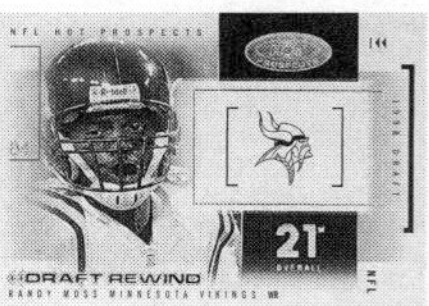

NM/M

Common Player: .75
Inserted 1:5
1DR Donovan McNabb 2.00
2DR Jerry Rice 4.00
3DR Andre Johnson 1.50
4DR Edgerrin James 2.00
5DR Charles Rogers 1.50
6DR Carson Palmer 2.00
7DR David Carr 2.00
8DR Roy Williams .75
9DR Michael Vick 4.00
10DR Eddie George 1.50
11DR Marshall Faulk 2.00
12DR Anquan Boldin 1.50
13DR Chad Pennington 2.00
14DR Randy Moss 3.00
15DR Marvin Harrison 1.50
16DR Joey Harrington 1.50
17DR Deuce McAllister 1.50
18DR Brett Favre 5.00
19DR Steve McNair 1.50
20DR Jeremy Shockey 1.50
21DR Daunte Culpepper 1.50
22DR Emmitt Smith 4.00
23DR LaDainian Tomlinson 2.00
24DR Terrell Owens 1.50
25DR Eli Manning 2.00
26DR Ricky Williams 1.50
27DR Peyton Manning 3.00
28DR Chad Johnson .75
29DR Brian Urlacher 1.50
30DR Jamal Lewis 1.50

2004 Fleer Hot Prospects Draft Rewind Jersey

NM/M

Seq. numbered to varying quantities
Red Hot: No Pricing
Production 10 Sets
White Hot: No Pricing
Production 1 Set
1DR Donovan McNabb/102 6.00
2DR Jerry Rice/116 15.00
3DR Andre Johnson/103 5.00
4DR Edgerrin James/104 6.00
5DR Charles Rogers/102 5.00
6DR Carson Palmer/101 6.00
7DR David Carr/101 6.00
8DR Roy Williams/108 4.00
9DR Michael Vick/101 15.00
10DR Eddie George/114 5.00
11DR Marshall Faulk/102 6.00
12DR Anquan Boldin/154 5.00
13DR Chad Pennington/118 6.00
14DR Randy Moss/121 10.00
15DR Marvin Harrison/119 5.00
16DR Joey Harrington/103 5.00
17DR Deuce McAllister/123 5.00
18DR Brett Favre/133 20.00
19DR Steve McNair/103 5.00
20DR Jeremy Shockey/114 5.00
21DR Daunte Culpepper/111 5.00
22DR Emmitt Smith/117 15.00
23DR LaDainian Tomlinson/105 6.00
24DR Terrell Owens/189 8.00
25DR Eli Manning/101 18.00
26DR Ricky Williams/105 5.00
27DR Peyton Manning/101 10.00
28DR Chad Johnson/136 4.00
29DR Brian Urlacher/109 5.00
30DR Jamal Lewis/105 5.00

2004 Fleer Hot Prospects Draft Rewind Patch

Seq. numbered to varying quantities
Cards #'d to less than 25 not priced
Red Hot: No Pricing
Production 5 Sets
White Hot: No Pricing
Production 1 Set
1DR Donovan McNabb/12
2DR Jerry Rice/26
3DR Andre Johnson/13
4DR Edgerrin James/14
5DR Charles Rogers/12
6DR Carson Palmer/11
7DR David Carr/11
8DR Roy Williams/18
9DR Michael Vick/11
10DR Eddie George/24
11DR Marshall Faulk/12
12DR Anquan Boldin/64
13DR Chad Pennington/28
14DR Randy Moss/31
15DR Marvin Harrison/29

16DR	Joey Harrington/13	
17DR	Deuce McAllister/33	
18DR	Brett Favre/43	
19DR	Steve McNair/13	
20DR	Jeremy Shockey/24	
21DR	Daunte Culpepper/21	
22DR	Emmitt Smith/27	
23DR	LaDainian Tomlinson/15	
24DR	Terrell Owens/99	
25DR	Eli Manning/11	
26DR	Ricky Williams/15	
27DR	Peyton Manning/11	
28DR	Chad Johnson/46	
29DR	Brian Urlacher/19	
30DR	Jamal Lewis/15	

2004 Fleer Hot Prospects NFL Hot Materials Game-Used

		NM/M
Common Player:		5.00
Production 500 Sets		
Red Hot:		1X-3X
Production 50 Sets		
White Hot:		No Pricing
Production 1 Set		
HM-AB	Anquan Boldin	5.00
HM-TB	Tom Brady	8.00
HM-DC	David Carr	6.00
HM-DC2	Daunte Culpepper	5.00
HM-LE	Lee Evans	4.00
HM-MF	Marshall Faulk	6.00
HM-BF	Brett Favre	12.00
HM-LF	Larry Fitzgerald	5.00
HM-JH	Joey Harrington	5.00
HM-MH	Marvin Harrison	5.00
HM-DH	Drew Henson	5.00
HM-EJ	Edgerrin James	6.00
HM-KJ	Kevin Jones	5.00
HM-JL	Jamal Lewis	5.00
HM-EM	Eli Manning	15.00
HM-PM	Peyton Manning	8.00
HM-DM2	Deuce McAllister	5.00
HM-DM	Donovan McNabb	6.00
HM-SM	Steve McNair	5.00
HM-RM	Randy Moss	8.00
HM-TO	Terrell Owens	6.00
HM-CP	Carson Palmer	6.00
HM-CP2	Chad Pennington	6.00
HM-JR	Jerry Rice	10.00
HM-PR	Philip Rivers	6.00
HM-BR	Ben Roethlisberger	20.00
HM-JS	Jeremy Shockey	5.00
HM-ES	Emmitt Smith	10.00
HM-LT	LaDainian Tomlinson	6.00
HM-BU	Brian Urlacher	5.00
HM-MV	Michael Vick	10.00
HM-RW3	Reggie Williams	5.00
HM-RW	Ricky Williams	5.00
HM-RW2	Roy Williams	6.00
HM-KW	Kellen Winslow Jr.	6.00

2004 Fleer Hot Prospects Notable Newcomers

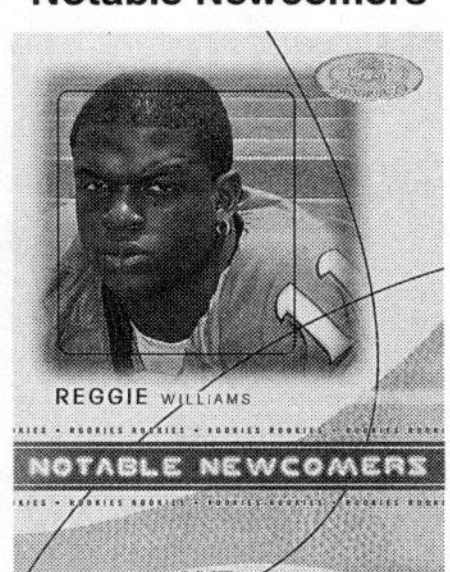

		NM/M
Common Player:		2.00
Inserted 1:15		
Autographs:		15X-25X
Production 50 Sets		
1NN	Eli Manning	6.00
2NN	Larry Fitzgerald	4.00
3NN	Ben Roethlisberger	6.00
4NN	Roy Williams	4.00
5NN	Kellen Winslow Jr.	3.00
6NN	Kevin Jones	3.00
7NN	Reggie Williams	2.50
8NN	Michael Clayton	2.50
9NN	Philip Rivers	5.00
10NN	Lee Evans	2.50
11NN	Drew Henson	3.00
12NN	Steven Jackson	3.00
13NN	Chris Perry	2.00
14NN	Greg Jones	2.00
15NN	J.P. Losman	2.50

2004 Fleer Inscribed

		NM/M
Common Player (1-75):		.40
Minor Stars (1-75):		.60
Unlisted Stars (1-75):		1.00
Common Rookie (76-100):		4.00
Minor Rookie (76-100):		5.00
Production 750 Sets		
Pack (5):		8.75
Box (12):		75.00
1	Terrell Owens	1.00
2	David Carr	1.50
3	Jerry Porter	.40
4	Charles Rogers	1.00
5	Torry Holt	1.00
6	Byron Leftwich	2.00
7	Laveranues Coles	.60

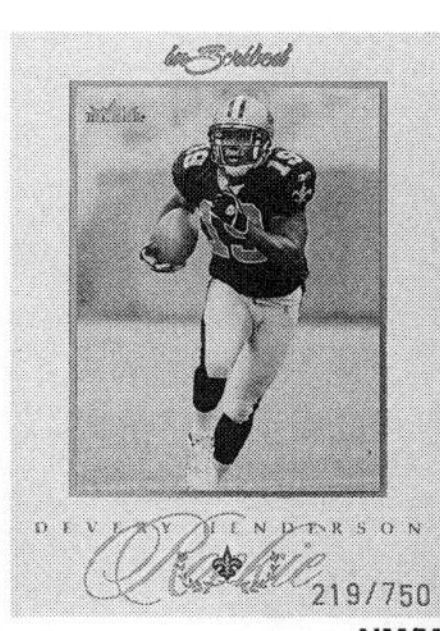

		NM/M
8	Edgerrin James	1.50
9	Brian Urlacher	1.00
10	Hines Ward	.60
11	LaDainian Tomlinson	1.50
12	Ahman Green	1.00
13	Kevan Barlow	.40
14	Trent Green	.40
15	Deuce McAllister	1.00
16	Lee Suggs	.40
17	Drew Brees	.60
18	Randy Moss	2.00
19	Brandon Lloyd	.40
20	Jeff Garcia	1.00
21	Roy Williams Cowboys	.60
22	Daunte Culpepper	1.00
23	Matt Hasselbeck	.60
24	Keyshawn Johnson	.60
25	Michael Vick	2.50
26	Shaun Alexander	1.00
27	Chad Pennington	1.50
28	Ashley Lelie	.60
29	Anquan Boldin	1.00
30	Carson Palmer	1.50
31	Jeremy Shockey	1.00
32	Peerless Price	.60
33	Chad Johnson	.60
34	Tiki Barber	.40
35	Warrick Dunn	.40
36	Jamal Lewis	1.00
37	Brian Westbrook	.40
38	Stephen Davis	.60
39	Steve McNair	1.00
40	Donovan McNabb	1.50
41	Fred Taylor	1.00
42	Clinton Portis	2.00
43	Santana Moss	.40
44	Rod Smith	.40
45	Josh McCown	.40
46	Ray Lewis	.60
47	Marshall Faulk	1.50
48	Eric Moulds	.40
49	Jerry Rice	2.50
50	Jake Delhomme	1.00
51	Tony Gonzalez	.60
52	Aaron Brooks	1.00
53	Randy McMichael	.40
54	David Boston	.60
55	Plaxico Burress	1.00
56	Rich Gannon	.60
57	Brett Favre	3.00
58	Isaac Bruce	.60
59	Tom Brady	2.00
60	Priest Holmes	1.50
61	Joe Horn	.40
62	Troy Brown	.40
63	Jake Plummer	.60
64	Derrick Brooks	.40
65	Marvin Harrison	1.00
66	LaVar Arrington	1.00
67	Drew Bledsoe	1.00
68	Steve Smith	.40
69	Peyton Manning	2.00
70	Rex Grossman	1.00
71	Corey Dillon	.60
72	Mike Alstott	.40
73	Andre Johnson	1.00
74	Joey Harrington	1.00
75	Tyrone Calico	.40
76	*Eli Manning*	25.00
77	*Larry Fitzgerald*	15.00
78	*Philip Rivers*	15.00
79	*Kellen Winslow Jr.*	8.00
80	*Roy Williams*	15.00
81	*Reggie Williams*	8.00
82	*Ben Roethlisberger*	50.00
83	*Lee Evans*	8.00
84	*Michael Clayton*	8.00
85	*J.P. Losman*	10.00
86	*Steven Jackson*	10.00
87	*Chris Perry*	6.00
88	*Michael Jenkins*	6.00
89	*Kevin Jones*	12.00
90	*Rashaun Woods*	8.00
91	*Ben Watson*	5.00
92	*Ben Troupe*	4.00
93	*Tatum Bell*	6.00
94	*Julius Jones*	15.00
95	*Devery Henderson*	4.00
96	*Darius Watts*	5.00
97	*Greg Jones*	5.00
98	*Keary Colbert*	5.00
99	*Derrick Hamilton*	4.00
100	*Bernard Berrian*	4.00

Post-1980 cards in Near Mint condition will generally sell for about 75% of the quoted Mint value. Excellent-condition cards bring no more than 40%.

2004 Fleer Inscribed Gold

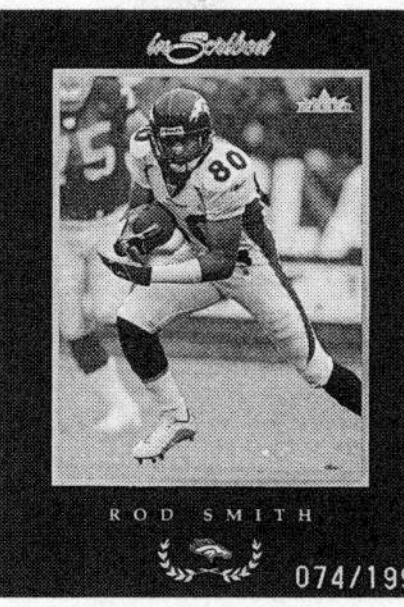

Veterans (1-75):		2X-5X
Rookies (76-100):		.75X-2X
Production 199 Sets		

2004 Fleer Inscribed Red

No Pricing
Production 5 Sets

2004 Fleer Inscribed Autographs

		NM/M
Common Player:		10.00
Sequentially Numbered		
CB	Champ Bailey/254	20.00
TB	Tatum Bell/100	20.00
BB	Bernard Berrian/100	20.00
AB	Antonio Bryant/300	15.00
TC	Tyrone Calico/238	10.00
CC	Chris Chambers/150	15.00
MC	Michael Clayton/100	20.00
KC	Keary Colbert/100	20.00
LE	Lee Evans/100	15.00
DF	DeShaun Foster/405	15.00
DH	Dante Hall/350	15.00
DH2	Derrick Hamilton/100	10.00
DH3	Devery Henderson/100	10.00
SJ	Steven Jackson/75	60.00
MJ	Michael Jenkins/100	10.00
CJ	Chad Johnson/340	15.00
GJ	Greg Jones	15.00
JJ	Julius Jones/75	60.00
AL	Ashley Lelie/340	15.00
JL	J.P. Losman/100	30.00
EM	Eli Manning/75	150.00
LM	Luke McCown/300	20.00
WM	Willis McGahee/350	25.00
SM	Santana Moss/10	
CP	Chris Perry/75	20.00
JP	Jerry Porter/191	15.00
PR	Philip Rivers/75	60.00
BR	Ben Roethlisberger/100	300.00
DS	Donte Stallworth/450	15.00
BT	Ben Troupe/100	10.00
AV	Adam Vinatieri/96	40.00
JW	Javon Walker/307	20.00
KW	Kelley Washington/124	15.00
BW	Ben Watson/100	10.00
DW	Darius Watts/100	15.00
BW	Brian Westbrook/289	15.00
RW	Reggie Williams/75	30.00
RW2	Roy Williams-Lions/75	60.00
KW2	Kellen Winslow Jr.	25.00
JW2	Jason Witten/243	15.00
RW3	Rashaun Woods/75	15.00

2004 Fleer Inscribed Autographs Purple

		NM/M
Common Purple:		20.00
Numbered to Jersey Number		
Red:		No Pricing
Production 25 Sets		
CB	Champ Bailey/21	
AB	Antonio Bryant/88	20.00
TC	Tyrone Calico/87	20.00
CC	Chris Chambers/84	20.00
DF	DeShaun Foster/26	
DH	Dante Hall/82	20.00
CJ	Chad Johnson/85	20.00
AL	Ashley Lelie/85	20.00
LM	Luke McCown/12	
WM	Willis McGahee/21	
SM	Santana Moss/83	20.00
JP	Jerry Porter/84	20.00
DS	Donte Stallworth/83	20.00
AV	Adam Vinatieri/4	
JW1	Javon Walker/84	30.00
KW	Kelley Washington/87	20.00
BW	Brian Westbrook/36	20.00
JW2	Jason Witten/82	25.00

2004 Fleer Inscribed Award Winners

		NM/M
Common Player:		2.00
Production 150 Sets		
1AW	Randy Moss	5.00
2AW	Ray Lewis	2.50
3AW	Warrick Dunn	2.00
4AW	Edgerrin James	4.00
5AW	Brian Urlacher	3.00
6AW	Derrick Brooks	2.00
7AW	Tommy Maddox	2.50
8AW	Marshall Faulk	4.00
9AW	Priest Holmes	4.00
10AW	Jevon Kearse	2.00
11AW	Warren Sapp	2.00
12AW	Michael Strahan	2.00
13AW	Eddie George	3.00
14AW	Clinton Portis	5.00
15AW	Anquan Boldin	4.00

2004 Fleer Inscribed Award Winners Autographs

		NM/M
Production 150 Sets		
Notated: No Pricing		
Numbered to final 2 digits of award year		
AWAAB	Anquan Boldin/100	
AWADB	Derrick Brooks	
AWAWD	Warrick Dunn	15.00
AWAMF	Marshall Faulk	
AWAEG	Eddie George	
AWAPH	Priest Holmes	
AWAEJ	Edgerrin James	
AWAJK	Jevon Kearse	
AWARL	Ray Lewis	
AWATM	Tommy Maddox	10.00
AWARM	Randy Moss	
AWACP	Clinton Portis	
AWAWS	Warren Sapp	
AWAMS	Michael Strahan	10.00
AWABU	Brian Urlacher	25.00

2004 Fleer Inscribed Award Winners Jersey Silver

		NM/M
Common Player:		5.00
Production 175 Sets		
Copper:		.75X-2X
Production 75 Sets		
Purple:		1X-3X
Production 49 Sets		
AWJAB	Anquan Boldin	8.00
AWJDB	Derrick Brooks	5.00
AWJWD	Warrick Dunn	5.00
AWJMF	Marshall Faulk	10.00
AWJEG	Eddie George	8.00
AWJPH	Priest Holmes	10.00
AWJEJ	Edgerrin James	10.00
AWJJK	Jevon Kearse	5.00
AWJRL	Ray Lewis	6.00
AWJTM	Tommy Maddox	6.00
AWJRM	Randy Moss	12.00
AWJCP	Clinton Portis	12.00
AWJWS	Warren Sapp	5.00
AWJMS	Michael Strahan	5.00
AWJBU	Brian Urlacher	8.00

2004 Fleer Inscribed Names of the Game

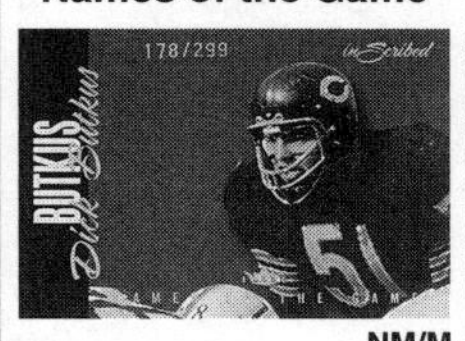

		NM/M
Common Player:		1.50
Production 299 Sets		
1NG	Priest Holmes	3.00
2NG	LaDainian Tomlinson	3.00
3NG	Donovan McNabb	3.00
4NG	Deuce McAllister	2.50
5NG	Edgerrin James	3.00
6NG	Plaxico Burress	2.50
7NG	Jake Plummer	2.00
8NG	Steve McNair	2.50
9NG	Eddie "Boo" Williams	1.50
10NG	Jevon Kearse	1.50
11NG	Tiki Barber	1.50
12NG	Peyton Manning	4.00
13NG	Peerless Price	1.50
14NG	Jerome Bettis	2.00
15NG	Tom Brady	4.00
16NG	Dante Hall	1.50
17NG	Randy Moss	4.00
18NG	Randy Moss	5.00
19NG	Ahman Green	2.50
20NG	Daunte Culpepper	2.50
21NG	Kellen Winslow Jr.	8.00
22NG	Terrell Owens	2.50
23NG	Larry Fitzgerald	8.00
24NG	Eli Manning	10.00
25NG	Dick Butkus	4.00
26NG	Ken Stabler	3.00
27NG	Paul Hornung	4.00
28NG	Earl Campbell	3.00
29NG	John Elway	10.00
30NG	Dan Marino	12.00

2004 Fleer Inscribed Names of the Game Autographs

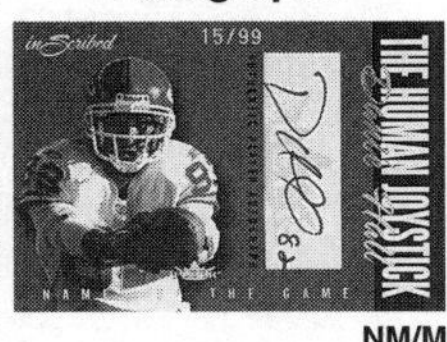

		NM/M
Common Player:		15.00
Production 99 Sets		
Notated:		No Pricing
Production 25 Sets		
NGATB	Tiki Barber	
NGAJB	Jerome Bettis	30.00
NGATB2	Tom Brady	
NGAPB	Plaxico Burress	30.00
NGADB	Dick Butkus	
NGAEC	Earl Campbell	30.00
NGADC	Daunte Culpepper	
NGAJE	John Elway	125.00
NGALF	Larry Fitzgerald	
NGAAG	Ahman Green	50.00
NGADH	Dante Hall	15.00
NGAPH2	Priest Holmes	
NGAPH	Paul Hornung	
NGAEJ	Edgerrin James	25.00
NGAJK	Jevon Kearse	
NGAEM	Eli Manning	
NGAPM	Peyton Manning	60.00
NGADM	Dan Marino	175.00
NGADM2	Deuce McAllister	25.00
NGADM3	Donovan McNabb	50.00
NGASM	Steve McNair	30.00
NGARM	Randy Moss	
NGATO	Terrell Owens	
NGAJP	Jake Plummer	
NGAPP	Peerless Price	
NGAES	Emmitt Smith	
NGAKS	Ken Stabler	
NGALT	LaDainian Tomlinson	40.00
NGABW	Eddie "Boo" Williams	
NGAKW	Kellen Winslow Jr.	

2004 Fleer Inscribed Names of the Game Jersey Silver

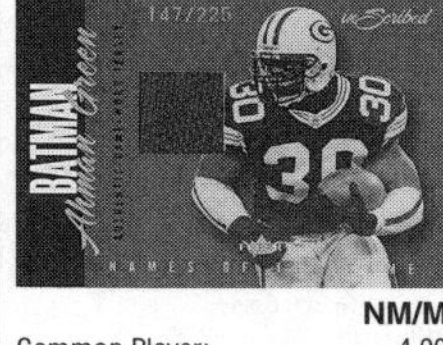

		NM/M
Common Player:		4.00
Copper:		.75X-1.5X
Production 225 Sets		
Gold:		1X-2X
Production 150 Sets		
Red:		2X-3X
Production 79 Sets		
Purple:		2X-4X
Production 33 Sets		
NGJTB	Tiki Barber	4.00
NGJJB	Jerome Bettis	5.00
NGJTB2	Tom Brady	10.00
NGJPB	Plaxico Burress	6.00
NGJEC	Earl Campbell	8.00
NGJDC	Daunte Culpepper	6.00
NGJJE	John Elway	20.00
NGJLF	Larry Fitzgerald	15.00
NGJAG	Ahman Green	6.00
NGJDH	Dante Hall	4.00
NGJPH2	Priest Holmes	8.00
NGJPH	Paul Hornung	15.00
NGJEJ	Edgerrin James	8.00
NGJJK	Jevon Kearse	4.00
NGJEM	Eli Manning	20.00
NGJPM	Peyton Manning	10.00
NGJDM	Dan Marino	25.00
NGJDM2	Deuce McAllister	6.00
NGJDM3	Donovan McNabb	8.00
NGJSM	Steve McNair	8.00
NGJRM	Randy Moss	10.00
NGJTO	Terrell Owens	8.00
NGJJP	Jake Plummer	5.00
NGJPP	Peerless Price	4.00
NGJES	Emmitt Smith	15.00
NGJKS	Ken Stabler	10.00
NGJLT	LaDainian Tomlinson	10.00
NGJBW	Eddie "Boo" Williams	4.00
NGJKW	Kellen Winslow Jr.	15.00

2004 Fleer Inscribed Valuable Players

		NM/M
Common Player:		4.00
Production 50 Sets		
1VP	Dan Marino/84	20.00
2VP	John Elway/87	15.00
3VP	Earl Campbell/79	6.00
4VP	Emmitt Smith/93	10.00
5VP	Ken Stabler/74	8.00
6VP	Brett Favre/95	12.00
7VP	Marshall Faulk/100	6.00
8VP	Rich Gannon/103	4.00
9VP	Steve McNair/104	5.00
10VP	Peyton Manning/104	8.00

2004 Fleer Inscribed Valuable Players Autographs

		NM/M
Production 199 Sets		
Notated:		No Pricing
Production 9 Sets		
VPAEC	Earl Campbell	25.00
VPAJE	John Elway	
VPAMF	Marshall Faulk	
VPABF	Brett Favre	
VPARG	Rich Gannon	
VPAPM	Peyton Manning	
VPADM	Dan Marino	
VPASM	Steve McNair	
VPAES	Emmitt Smith	
VPAKS	Ken Stabler	

2004 Fleer Inscribed Valuable Players Jersey

		NM/M
Common Player:		10.00
Numbered to MVP Year		
Masterpiece:		No Pricing
Production 1 Set		
EC	Earl Campbell/79	15.00
JE	John Elway/87	30.00
MF	Marshall Faulk/100	15.00
BF	Brett Favre/95	40.00
RG	Rich Gannon/103	10.00
PM	Peyton Manning/104	15.00
DM	Dan Marino/84	60.00
SM	Steve McNair/104	12.00
ES	Emmitt Smith/93	25.00
KS	Ken Stabler/74	20.00

2004 Fleer Platinum

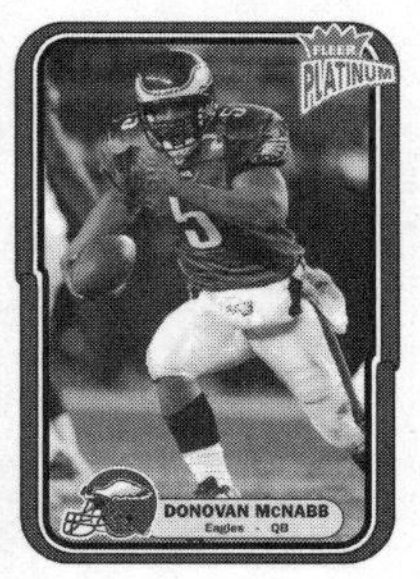

		NM/M
Common Player (1-135):		.25
Minor Stars (1-135):		.50
Unlisted Stars (1-135):		.75
Common Rookie (136-145):		5.00
Production 299 Sets		
Common Rookie (145-155):		1.50
Production 499 Sets		
Common Rookie (156-165):		1.00
Production 799 Sets		
Common Rookie (166-185):		1.00
Production 999 Sets		
Pack:		3.25
Box:		75.00
1	Joey Harrington	.75
2	Kyle Boller	.25
3	Randy McMichael	.25
4	David Tyree	.25
5	Darrell Jackson	.25
6	Brian Urlacher	.75
7	Ahman Green	.75
8	Onterrio Smith	.25
9	Jevon Kearse	.25
10	Eddie George	.75
11	Julius Peppers	.25
12	Donald Driver	.25
13	Randy Moss	1.50
14	Brian Westbrook	.25
15	Derrick Brooks	.25
16	Jamal Lewis	.75
17	Artose Pinner	.25
18	Ricky Williams	.75
19	Chad Pennington	1.00
20	Matt Hasselbeck	.50
21	Josh McCown	.25
22	Carson Palmer	1.00
23	Byron Leftwich	1.50
24	Tedy Bruschi	.25
25	Duce Staley	.25
26	Laveranues Coles	.50
27	Drew Bledsoe	.75
28	Shannon Sharpe	.50
29	A.J. Feeley	.25
30	Santana Moss	.25
31	Adam Archuleta	.25
32	Travis Henry	.50
33	Ashley Lelie	.50
34	Dante Hall	.25
35	Curtis Martin	.75
36	Isaac Bruce	.50
37	Eric Moulds	.25
38	Jake Plummer	.50
39	Trent Green	.25
40	Shaun Ellis	.25
41	Torry Holt	.75
42	T.J. Duckett	.50
43	Quincy Morgan	.25
44	Jabar Gaffney	.25
45	Tiki Barber	.25
46	Tim Rattay	.25
47	Champ Bailey	.25
48	Tony Gonzalez	.50
49	Rich Gannon	.50
50	Marshall Faulk	1.00
51	Jake Delhomme	.75
52	Antonio Bryant	.50
53	Priest Holmes	1.00
54	Jerry Rice	2.00
55	Marc Bulger	.50
56	Stephen Davis	.50
57	Roy Williams	.50
58	Kevin Johnson	.25
59	Julian Peterson	.25
60	Thomas Jones	.25
61	Dre' Bly	.25
62	Corey Dillon	.50
63	Tommy Maddox	.50
64	Derrick Mason	.25
65	Marty Booker	.25
66	Brett Favre	2.50
67	Tom Brady	1.50
68	Correll Buckhalter	.25
69	Steve McNair	.75
70	Alge Crumpler	.25
71	Quincy Carter	.75
72	Andre Johnson	.75
73	Jeremy Shockey	.75
74	Kevan Barlow	.25
75	Jerry Porter	.25
76	Ray Lewis	.50
77	Keyshawn Johnson	.50
78	Domanick Davis	.75

79	Michael Strahan	.25
80	Brandon Lloyd	.25
81	Anquan Boldin	.75
82	Chad Johnson	.50
83	Jimmy Smith	.25
84	Troy Brown	.50
85	Hines Ward	.50
86	Tyrone Calico	.25
87	Marcel Shipp	.25
88	Peter Warrick	.50
89	Reggie Wayne	.25
90	Aaron Brooks	.75
91	Antwann Randle El	.50
92	Mark Brunell	.50
93	Todd Heap	.50
94	Charles Rogers	.75
95	Chris Chambers	.75
96	Amani Toomer	.50
97	Shaun Alexander	.75
98	Michael Vick	2.00
99	Jeff Garcia	.75
100	Edgerrin James	1.00
101	Deuce McAllister	.75
102	LaDainian Tomlinson	1.00
103	Warrick Dunn	.25
104	Andre Davis	.25
105	Peyton Manning	1.50
106	Eddie "Boo" Williams	.25
107	Drew Brees	.50
108	Rex Grossman	.75
109	Javon Walker	.50
110	Michael Bennett	.75
111	Terrell Owens	.75
112	Michael Pittman	.25
113	Emmitt Smith	2.00
114	Rudi Johnson	.50
115	Fred Taylor	.75
116	Deion Branch	.25
117	Plaxico Burress	.75
118	Clinton Portis	1.50
119	DeShaun Foster	.25
120	Najeh Davenport	.25
121	Daunte Culpepper	.75
122	Donovan McNabb	1.00
123	Charles Lee	.25
124	Peerless Price	.50
125	Lee Suggs	.25
126	Marvin Harrison	.75
127	Joe Horn	.25
128	Antonio Gates	.25
129	Steve Smith	.25
130	David Carr	1.00
131	Jason Taylor	.25
132	Phillip Buchanon	.25
133	Brad Johnson	.25
134	Takeo Spikes	.25
135	Koren Robinson	.25
136	Eli Manning	20.00
137	Ben Roethlisberger	40.00
138	Drew Henson	6.00
139	Kellen Winslow Jr.	6.00
140	Kevin Jones	6.00
141	Larry Fitzgerald	8.00
142	Roy Williams	10.00
143	Philip Rivers	10.00
144	Lee Evans	5.00
145	Julius Jones	5.00
146	Chris Perry	2.50
147	Michael Clayton	3.00
148	Sean Taylor	3.00
149	Reggie Williams	3.00
150	Steven Jackson	6.00
151	Tatum Bell	2.50
152	Keary Colbert	2.00
153	J.P. Losman	6.00
154	Devery Henderson	1.50
155	Ben Troupe	1.50
156	Luke McCown	1.50
157	Greg Jones	2.00
158	Ben Watson	1.00
159	Bernard Berrian	1.50
160	Devard Darling	1.50
161	Cedric Cobbs	1.50
162	Darius Watts	1.50
163	Derrick Hamilton	1.00
164	Matt Schaub	1.50
165	Mewelde Moore	1.00
166	Michael Jenkins	2.00
167	Rashaun Woods	2.50
168	Quincy Wilson	1.50
169	Jonathan Vilma	1.50
170	Jerricho Cotchery	1.00
171	John Navarre	1.50
172	Josh Harris	1.00
173	Teddy Lehman	1.25
174	Ernest Wilford	1.00
175	P.K. Sam	1.50
176	Jeff Smoker	1.50
177	Chris Gamble	1.00
178	Johnnie Morant	1.00
179	DeAngelo Hall	2.00
180	Vince Wilfork	1.50
181	Michael Turner	1.50
182	Robert Gallery	1.50
183	Ricardo Colclough	1.00
184	Kenechi Udeze	1.00
185	Dunta Robinson	1.25

Post-1980 cards in Near Mint condition will generally sell for about 75% of the quoted Mint value. Excellent-condition cards bring no more than 40%.

2004 Fleer Platinum Platinum Finish

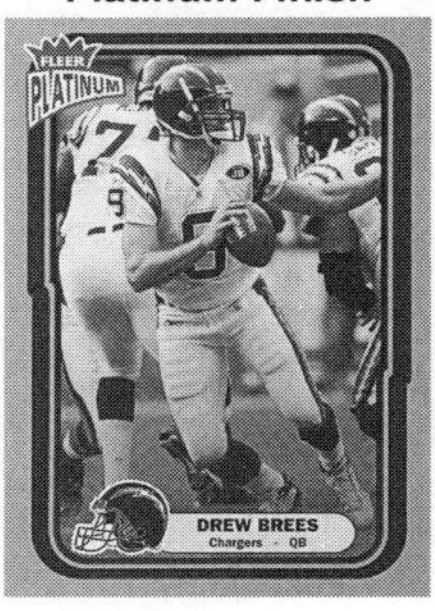

Cards 1-135:	.75X-3X
Cards 136-145:	1X-1.5X
Cards 146-155:	1X-2X
Cards 156-165:	1.25X-2.5X
Cards 166-185:	1.25X-3X

Production 100 Sets

2004 Fleer Platinum Deep Six

		NM/M
Common Player:		5.00
Inserted 1:108		
1CC	Joey Harrington, Roy Williams	5.00
2CC	Eli Manning, Jeremy Shockey	12.00
3CC	Donovan McNabb, Terrell Owens	8.00
4CC	Daunte Culpepper, Randy Moss	10.00
5CC	David Carr, Andre Johnson	8.00
6CC	Chad Pennington, Santana Moss	8.00
7CC	Michael Vick, Michael Jenkins	12.00
8CC	Peyton Manning, Marvin Harrison	8.00
9CC	Drew Bledsoe, Eric Moulds	5.00
10CC	Rich Gannon, Jerry Rice	10.00

2004 Fleer Platinum NFL Scouting Report

		NM/M
Common Player:		2.50
Production 250 Sets		
1SR	Tom Brady	5.00
2SR	Peyton Manning	5.00
3SR	Priest Holmes	4.00
4SR	Donovan McNabb	4.00
5SR	Torry Holt	3.00
6SR	Clinton Portis	5.00
7SR	LaDainian Tomlinson	4.00
8SR	Jeremy Shockey	3.00
9SR	Steve McNair	3.00
10SR	Chad Pennington	4.00
11SR	Michael Vick	6.00
12SR	Brett Favre	8.00
13SR	Randy Moss	5.00
14SR	Byron Leftwich	5.00
15SR	David Carr	4.00
16SR	Ricky Williams	3.00
17SR	Stephen Davis	2.50
18SR	Terrell Owens	3.00
19SR	Marvin Harrison	3.00
20SR	Jerry Rice	6.00

2004 Fleer Platinum Platinum Memorabilia

		NM/M
Common Player:		6.00
Inserted 1:24		
PM-SA	Shaun Alexander	8.00
PM-TB	Tom Brady	12.00
PM-DC	David Carr	10.00
PM-MF	Marshall Faulk	10.00
PM-BF	Brett Favre	20.00
PM-AG	Ahman Green	8.00
PM-JH	Joey Harrington	8.00
PM-MH	Marvin Harrison	8.00
PM-PH	Priest Holmes	10.00
PM-CJ	Chad Johnson	6.00
PM-BL	Byron Leftwich	12.00
PM-JL	Jamal Lewis	8.00
PM-PM	Peyton Manning	12.00
PM-DE	Deuce McAllister	8.00
PM-DM	Donovan McNabb	10.00
PM-SM	Steve McNair	8.00
PM-RM	Randy Moss	12.00
PM-CP	Chad Pennington	10.00
PM-CP2	Clinton Portis	12.00
PM-JR	Jerry Rice	15.00
PM-JS	Jeremy Shockey	8.00
PM-LT	LaDainian Tomlinson	10.00
PM-MV	Michael Vick	15.00
PM-RI	Ricky Williams	8.00
PM-RW	Roy Williams	6.00

2004 Fleer Platinum Platinum Memorabilia Dual

		NM/M
Common Player:		18.00
Production 50 Sets		
PMD-SA	Shaun Alexander	20.00
PMD-TB	Tom Brady	30.00
PMD-DC	David Carr	25.00
PMD-MF	Marshall Faulk	25.00
PMD-BF	Brett Favre	40.00
PMD-AG	Ahman Green	20.00
PMD-JH	Joey Harrington	20.00
PMD-MH	Marvin Harrison	20.00
PMD-PH	Priest Holmes	25.00
PMD-CJ	Chad Johnson	18.00
PMD-BL	Byron Leftwich	30.00
PMD-JL	Jamal Lewis	20.00
PMD-PM	Peyton Manning	30.00
PMD-DE	DeuceMcAllister	20.00
PMD-DM	Donovan McNabb	25.00
PMD-SM	Steve McNair	20.00
PMD-RM	Randy Moss	30.00
PMD-CP	Chad Pennington	25.00
PMD-CP2	Clinton Portis	30.00
PMD-JR	Jerry Rice	35.00
PMD-JS	Jeremy Shockey	20.00
PMD-LT	LaDainian Tomlinson	25.00
PMD-MV	Michael Vick	35.00
PMD-RI	Ricky Williams	20.00
PMD-RW	Roy Williams	18.00

2004 Fleer Platinum Platinum Portraits

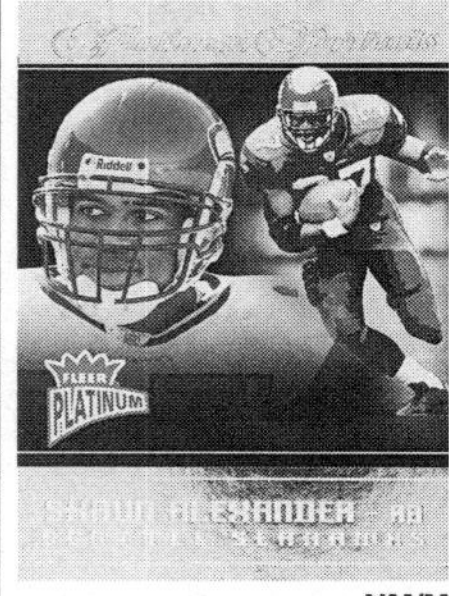

		NM/M
Common Player:		2.50
Inserted 1:18		
1PP	Deuce McAllister	4.00
2PP	Marshall Faulk	5.00
3PP	Brian Westbrook	2.50
4PP	Shaun Alexander	4.00
5PP	Andre Johnson	4.00
6PP	Charles Rogers	4.00
7PP	Brett Favre	10.00
8PP	Edgerrin James	5.00
9PP	Byron Leftwich	6.00
10PP	Hines Ward	3.00

2004 Fleer Platinum Platinum Portraits Jersey

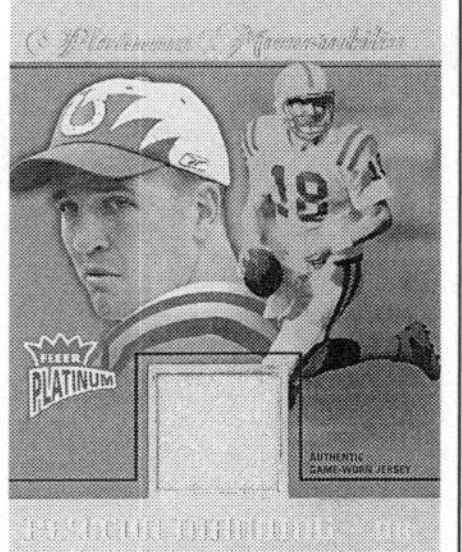

		NM/M
Common Player:		5.00
Inserted 1:48		
Patch:		1X-2X
Production 100 Sets		
PP-SA	Shaun Alexander	8.00
PP-MF	Marshall Faulk	10.00
PP-BF	Brett Favre	18.00
PP-EJ	Edgerrin James	10.00
PP-AJ	Andre Johnson	8.00
PP-BL	Byron Leftwich	12.00
PP-DM	Deuce McAllister	8.00
PP-CR	Charles Rogers	8.00
PP-HW	Hines Ward	8.00
PP-BW	Brian Westbrook	5.00

2004 Fleer Platinum Pro Material Jerseys

		NM/M
Common Player:		5.00
Production 250 Sets		
Die-Cut Jersey:		1X-3X
Production 99 Sets		
Die-Cut Patch:		No Pricing
Production 5 Sets		
PM-TB	Tatum Bell	10.00
PM-BB	Bernard Berrian	6.00
PM-MC	Michael Clayton	12.00
PM-CC	Cedric Cobbs	6.00
PM-KC	Keary Colbert	6.00
PM-DD	Devard Darling	6.00
PM-LE	Lee Evans	12.00
PM-LF	Larry Fitzgerald	20.00
PM-DH	DeAngelo Hall	10.00
PM-DH2	Derrick Hamilton	5.00
PM-DH3	Devery Henderson	6.00
PM-SJ	Steven Jackson	15.00
PM-MJ	Michael Jenkins	10.00
PM-GJ	Greg Jones	8.00
PM-JJ	Julius Jones	12.00
PM-KJ	Kevin Jones	15.00
PM-JL	J.P. Losman	12.00
PM-EM	Eli Manning	35.00
PM-LM	Luke McCown	6.00
PM-MM	Mewelde Moore	5.00
PM-CP	Chris Perry	10.00
PM-PR	Philip Rivers	20.00
PM-BR	Ben Roethlisberger	40.00
PM-MS	Matt Schaub	6.00
PM-BT	Ben Troupe	5.00
PM-BW	Ben Watson	5.00
PM-DW	Darius Watts	6.00
PM-RW	Reggie Williams	12.00
PM-RW2	Roy Williams WR	20.00
PM-KW	Kellen Winslow Jr.	15.00
PM-RW3	Rashaun Woods	12.00

2004 Fleer Platinum Scouting Report Jersey

		NM/M
Common Player:		5.00
Production 250 Sets		
SR-TB	Tom Brady	10.00
SR-DC	David Carr	8.00
SR-SD	Stephen Davis	5.00
SR-BF	Brett Favre	15.00
SR-MH	Marvin Harrison	6.00
SR-PH	Priest Holmes	8.00
SR-TH	Torry Holt	6.00
SR-BL	Byron Leftwich	10.00
SR-PM	Peyton Manning	10.00
SR-DM0	Donovan McNabb/35	
SR-SM	Steve McNair	6.00
SR-RM	Randy Moss	10.00
SR-TO	Terrell Owens	6.00
SR-CP	Chad Pennington	8.00
SR-CP2	Clinton Portis	10.00
SR-JR	Jerry Rice	12.00
SR-JS	Jeremy Shockey	6.00
SR-LT	LaDainian Tomlinson	8.00
SR-MV	Michael Vick	12.00
SR-RW	Ricky Williams	6.00

2004 Fleer Platinum Youth Movement

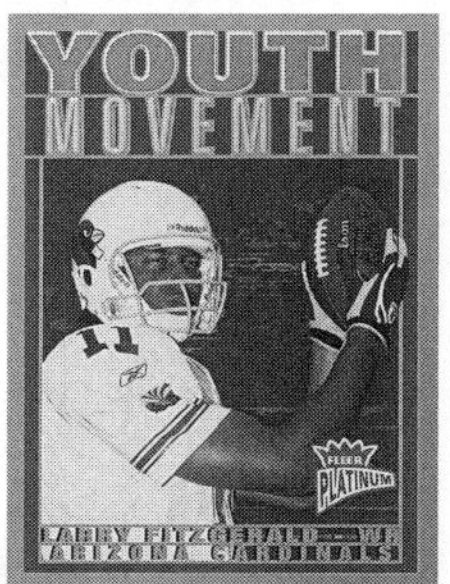

		NM/M
Common Player:		3.00
Inserted 1:9		
1BS	Eli Manning	8.00
2BS	Kevin Jones	4.00
3BS	Philip Rivers	6.00
4BS	Kellen Winslow Jr.	4.00
5BS	Ben Roethlisberger	8.00
6BS	Roy Williams	5.00
7BS	Drew Henson	4.00
8BS	Larry Fitzgerald	5.00
9BS	J.P. Losman	3.00
10BS	Steven Jackson	4.00
11BS	Chris Perry	3.00
12BS	Reggie Williams	3.00
13BS	Michael Clayton	3.00
14BS	Lee Evans	3.00
15BS	Tatum Bell	3.00

2004 Fleer Showcase

		NM/M
Common Player (1-100):		.40
Minor Stars:		.60
Unlisted Stars:		1.00
Common Rookie (101-149):		4.00
Production 599 Sets		
Pack (5):		8.75
Box (20):		125.00
1	Jamal Lewis	1.00
2	Kevan Barlow	.40
3	Travis Henry	.40
4	Jon Kitna	.40
5	David Boston	.60
6	Andre Davis	.60
7	Steve McNair	1.00
8	Freddie Mitchell	.40
9	Plaxico Burress	1.00
10	Jake Delhomme	1.00
11	Andre Johnson	1.00
12	T.J. Duckett	.60
13	Ray Lewis	.60
14	Shaun Alexander	1.00
15	Stephen Davis	.60
16	Priest Holmes	1.50
17	Edgerrin James	.50
18	Josh McCown	.40
19	Jerry Rice	2.50
20	Fred Taylor	1.00
21	Marty Booker	.40
22	Eddie George	1.00
23	Jake Plummer	.60
24	LaDainian Tomlinson	1.50
25	David Carr	1.50
26	Keenan McCardell	.40
27	Jerry Porter	.40
28	Drew Bledsoe	1.00
29	Brian Dawkins	.40
30	Curtis Martin	1.00
31	Troy Brown	.60
32	Peyton Manning	2.00
33	Clinton Portis	2.00
34	Brett Favre	3.00
35	Joey Harrington	1.00
36	Tiki Barber	.40
37	Hines Ward	.60
38	Laveranues Coles	.60
39	Deuce McAllister	1.00
40	Kyle Boller	1.00
41	Jeff Garcia	1.00
42	Julius Peppers	.40
43	Chris Chambers	1.00
44	Willis McGahee	1.00
45	Michael Vick	2.50
46	Carson Palmer	1.50
47	Ricky Williams	1.50
48	Matt Hasselbeck	.60
49	Anquan Boldin	1.00
50	Tony Gonzalez	.60
51	Marvin Harrison	1.00
52	Santana Moss	.40
53	Ahman Green	1.00
54	Eric Moulds	.40
55	Byron Leftwich	2.00
56	Daunte Culpepper	1.00
57	Terrell Owens	1.00
58	Kerry Collins	.40
59	Tommy Maddox	.60
60	Chad Johnson	.60
61	Rich Gannon	.60
62	Patrick Ramsey	.60
63	Quincy Morgan	.40
64	Koren Robinson	.40
65	Deion Branch	.40
66	Rex Grossman	1.00
67	Darnerian McCants	.40
68	Ashley Lelie	.60
69	Roy Williams	.60
70	Michael Bennett	1.00
71	Domanick Davis	1.00
72	Warren Sapp	.40
73	Randy Moss	2.00
74	Drew Brees	.60
75	Brian Westbrook	.40
76	Kelly Holcomb	.40
77	Jason Taylor	.40
78	Charles Rogers	1.00
79	Marc Bulger	.60
80	Donald Driver	.40
81	Trent Green	.40
82	Peerless Price	.60
83	Quincy Carter	1.00
84	Torry Holt	1.00
85	Derrick Mason	.40
86	Donte Stallworth	.60
87	Derrick Brooks	.40
88	Dre' Bly	.40
89	Antonio Bryant	.60
90	DeShaun Foster	.40
91	Emmitt Smith	2.50
92	Chad Pennington	1.50
93	Jeremy Shockey	1.00
94	Aaron Brooks	1.00
95	Marshall Faulk	1.50
96	Dante Hall	.40
97	Brian Urlacher	1.00
98	Corey Dillon	.60
99	Donovan McNabb	1.50
100	Tom Brady	2.00
101	Derrick Strait	4.00
102	Michael Clayton	8.00
103	Larry Fitzgerald	25.00
104	Chris Gamble	6.00
105	Devery Henderson	4.00
106	Steven Jackson	12.00
107	Michael Jenkins	8.00
108	Greg Jones	6.00
109	Kevin Jones	12.00
110	Eli Manning	40.00
111	Chris Perry	12.00
112	Philip Rivers	20.00
113	Ben Roethlisberger	50.00
114	Bernard Berrian	4.00
115	Sean Taylor	15.00
116	Reggie Williams	10.00
117	Roy Williams	25.00
118	Kellen Winslow Jr.	15.00
119	Rashaun Woods	10.00
120	J.P. Losman	12.00
121	Will Poole	4.00
122	Will Smith	4.00
123	Devard Darling	4.00
124	Jonathan Vilma	6.00
125	Drew Henson	12.00
126	Michael Turner	4.00
127	Lee Evans	12.00
128	Ernest Wilford	4.00
129	Cedric Cobbs	4.00
130	Ricardo Colclough	6.00
131	Ryan Dinwiddie	4.00
132	DeAngelo Hall	8.00
133	Cody Pickett	4.00
134	Quincy Wilson	6.00
135	Ahmad Carroll	8.00
136	Robert Gallery	10.00
137	John Navarre	6.00
138	P.K. Sam	6.00
139	Jeff Smoker	6.00
140	Ben Troupe	4.00
141	Marquise Hill	6.00
142	D.J. Williams	6.00
143	Tommie Harris	6.00
144	Ben Watson	4.00
145	Tatum Bell	12.00
146	B.J. Symons	4.00
147	Matt Schaub	6.00
148	Casey Clausen	6.00
149	Jason Fife	4.00

2004 Fleer Showcase Legacy

Stars:	1X-2X
Rookies (101-149):	.75X-2X

Production 125 Sets

2004 Fleer Showcase Masterpiece

No Pricing
Production 1 Set

2004 Fleer Showcase Feature Film

		NM/M
Common Player:		10.00
Production 50 Sets		
1FF	Brian Urlacher	15.00
2FF	Jerry Rice	25.00
3FF	Michael Vick	25.00
4FF	Jeremy Shockey	12.00
5FF	Emmitt Smith	25.00
6FF	Brett Favre	30.00
7FF	David Carr	25.00
8FF	Joey Harrington	10.00
9FF	Randy Moss	20.00
10FF	Peyton Manning	20.00

2004 Fleer Showcase Feature Film Game-Used

		NM/M
Common Player:		60.00
Production 25 Sets		
Hobby Only		
FF-DC	David Carr	75.00
FF-BF	Brett Favre	125.00
FF-JH	Joey Harrington	60.00
FF-PM	Peyton Manning	80.00
FF-RM	Randy Moss	75.00
FF-JR	Jerry Rice	80.00
FF-JS	Jeremy Shockey	60.00
FF-ES	Emmitt Smith	100.00
FF-BU	Brian Urlacher	75.00
FF-MV	Michael Vick	80.00

2004 Fleer Showcase Hothands

		NM/M
Common Player:		3.00
Inserted 1:240		
1HH	Anquan Boldin	5.00
2HH	Ahman Green	5.00
3HH	Chad Johnson	3.00
4HH	Jeremy Shockey	5.00
5HH	Priest Holmes	6.00
6HH	Torry Holt	3.00
7HH	Marvin Harrison	5.00
8HH	LaDainian Tomlinson	6.00
9HH	Deuce McAllister	5.00
10HH	Randy Moss	6.00

2004 Fleer Showcase Hothands Game-Used

		NM/M
Common Player:		12.00
Production 50 Sets		
HH-AB	Anquan Boldin	20.00
HH-AG	Ahman Green	40.00
HH-MH	Marvin Harrison	20.00
HH-PH	Priest Holmes	50.00
HH-TH	Torry Holt	20.00
HH-CJ	Chad Johnson	12.00
HH-DM	Deuce McCallister	30.00
HH-RM	Randy Moss	40.00
HH-JS	Jeremy Shockey	40.00
HH-LT	LaDainian Tomlinson	30.00

2004 Fleer Showcase Playmakers

		NM/M
Common Player:		2.50
Inserted 1:24		
1PM	Jamal Lewis	3.00
2PM	Michael Vick	5.00
3PM	Marvin Harrison	3.00
4PM	Ahman Green	3.00
5PM	Terrell Owens	3.00
6PM	Chad Johnson	2.00
7PM	Marshall Faulk	4.00
8PM	Priest Holmes	4.00
9PM	Hines Ward	2.50
10PM	Ricky Williams	4.00
11PM	Randy Moss	4.50
12PM	Charles Rogers	2.00

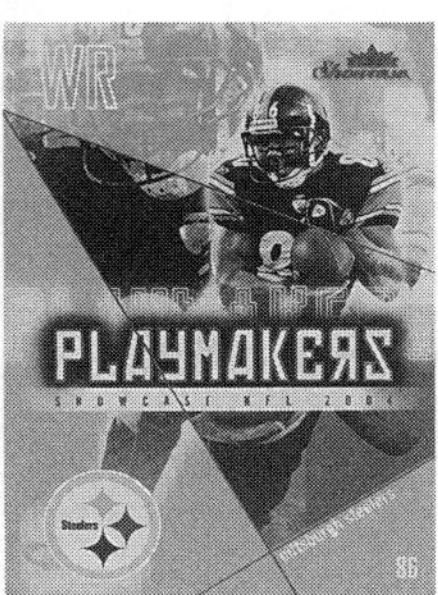

NM/M
13PM Donovan McNabb 4.00
14PM Anquan Boldin 3.00
15PM Chad Pennington 4.00

2004 Fleer Showcase Playmakers Game-Used Green

NM/M
Common Player: 5.00
Production 300 Sets
Silver Jersey: .75X-2X
Production 100
Gold: No Pricing
Numbered To Career TDs
Blue: No Pricing
Numbered To 2003 TD Total
Patch: No Pricing
Numbered To Jersey Number
Red Patch: No Pricing
Numbered To Games Started
Masterpiece: No Pricing
Production 1 Set
PM-AB Anquan Boldin 8.00
PM-MF Marshall Faulk 10.00
PM-AG Ahman Green 8.00
PM-MH Marvin Harrison 8.00
PM-PH Priest Holmes 10.00
PM-CJ Chad Johnson 6.00
PM-JL Jamal Lewis 8.00
PM-DM Donovan McNabb 10.00
PM-RM Randy Moss 12.00
PM-TO Terrell Owens 8.00
PM-CP Chad Pennington 10.00
PM-CR Charles Rogers 6.00
PM-MV Michael Vick 15.00
PM-HW Hines Ward 5.00
PM-RW Ricky Williams 10.00

2004 Fleer Showcase Showcase Grace

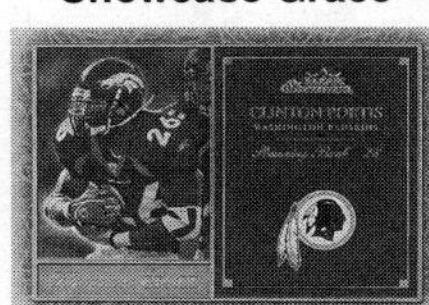

NM/M
Common Player: 1.00
Inserted 1:8
1SG Brian Urlacher 2.00
2SG Plaxico Burress 2.00
3SG Andre Johnson 2.00
4SG Shaun Alexander 2.00
5SG Stephen Davis 1.50
6SG Edgerrin James 3.00
7SG LaDainian Tomlinson 3.00
8SG Peyton Manning 3.50
9SG Clinton Portis 3.50
10SG Brett Favre 5.00
11SG Deuce McAllister 2.00
12SG Julius Peppers 1.00
13SG Jerry Rice 4.00
14SG Ricky Williams 3.00
15SG Daunte Culpepper 2.00
16SG Santana Moss 1.00
17SG Roy Williams 1.50
18SG Chad Pennington 3.00
19SG Donovan McNabb 3.00
20SG Tom Brady 3.50

2004 Fleer Showcase Showcase Grace Game-Used Blue

NM/M
Common Player: 5.00
Inserted 1:41
Green: 1X-1.5X
Production 300 Sets
Silver: 1X-2X
Production 100 Sets
Gold: No Pricing
Numbered To Career TDs
Patch: No Pricing
Numbered To Jersey Number
Red: No Pricing
Numbered To Team's 2003 Win Total

Masterpeice: No Pricing
Production 1 Set
SA Shaun Alexander 8.00
TB Tom Brady 12.00
PB Plaxico Burress 8.00
DC Daunte Culpepper 8.00
SD Stephen Davis 6.00
BF Brett Favre 18.00
EJ Edgerrin James 10.00
AJ Andre Johnson 8.00
PM Peyton Manning 12.00
DM Deuce McAllister 8.00
DM Donovan McNabb 10.00
SM Santana Moss 5.00
CHAD Chad Pennington 10.00
JP Julius Peppers 5.00
CP Clinton Portis 12.00
JR Jerry Rice 15.00
LT LaDainian Tomlinson 10.00
BU Brian Urlacher 8.00
RW Ricky Williams 10.00
ROY Roy Williams 6.00

2004 Fleer Sweet Sigs

NM/M
Common Player (1-75): .25
Minor Stars (1-75): .50
Unlisted Stars (1-75): .75
Common Rookie (76-100): 4.00
Production 999
Pack (6): 8.00
Box (12): 80.00
1 Brett Favre 2.50
2 Daunte Culpepper .75
3 Marshall Faulk 1.00
4 Ashley Lelie .50
5 Rex Grossman .75
6 Jeff Garcia .75
7 Jake Plummer .50
8 Tony Gonzalez .50
9 Terrell Owens .75
10 Plaxico Burress .75
11 Michael Vick 2.00
12 Carson Palmer 1.00
13 Charles Rogers .75
14 Corey Dillon .50
15 Aaron Brooks .75
16 Torry Holt .75
17 Joey Galloway .25
18 Mark Brunell .50
19 Anquan Boldin .75
20 Domanick Davis .75
21 Edgerrin James 1.00
22 Hines Ward .50
23 Kyle Boller .75
24 Kurt Warner .75
25 Matt Hasselbeck .50
26 Chris Chambers .75
27 Deuce McAllister .75
28 Chad Pennington 1.00
29 Eddie George .75
30 Ray Lewis .50
31 Ahman Green .75
32 Marvin Harrison .75
33 Tiki Barber .25
34 Jerry Rice 2.00
35 Emmitt Smith 2.00
36 Chad Johnson .50
37 Roy Williams Cowboys .50
38 Peyton Manning 1.50
39 Stephen Davis .50
40 Jamal Lewis .75
41 David Carr 1.00
42 A.J. Feeley .25
43 Jerry Porter .25
44 Willis McGahee .75
45 Quincy Morgan .25
46 Fred Taylor .75
47 Trent Green .25
48 Donovan McNabb 1.00
49 Marc Bulger .50
50 LaVar Arrington .75
51 Joey Harrington .75
52 Jake Delhomme .75
53 Jeremy Shockey .75
54 LaDainian Tomlinson 1.00
55 Brian Urlacher .75
56 Rudi Johnson .50
57 Shaun Alexander .75
58 Charlie Garner .25
59 Eric Moulds .25
60 Tom Brady 1.50
61 Curtis Martin .75
62 Koren Robinson .25
63 Steve McNair .75
64 Travis Henry .25
65 Julius Peppers .25
66 Keyshawn Johnson .50
67 Andre Johnson .75
68 Priest Holmes 1.00
69 Drew Brees .50
70 Rich Gannon .50
71 Randy Moss 1.50
72 Peerless Price .50
73 Drew Bledsoe .75
74 Byron Leftwich 1.50
75 Clinton Portis 1.50
76 *Roy Williams Lions* 12.00
77 *Eli Manning* 20.00
78 *Kevin Jones* 10.00
79 *Tatum Bell* 6.00
80 *DeAngelo Hall* 6.00
81 *Michael Clayton* 8.00
82 *Rashaun Woods* 5.00
83 *Darius Watts* 4.00
84 *J.P. Losman* 10.00
85 *Drew Henson* 10.00
86 *Philip Rivers* 12.00
87 *Ben Roethlisberger* 40.00
88 *Larry Fitzgerald* 12.00
89 *Chris Perry* 6.00
90 *Devery Henderson* 4.00
91 *Sean Taylor* 8.00
92 *Reggie Williams* 6.00
93 *Lee Evans* 8.00
94 *Julius Jones* 12.00
95 *Dunta Robinson* 4.00
96 *Michael Jenkins* 6.00
97 *Greg Jones* 5.00
98 *Kellen Winslow Jr.* 8.00
99 *Steven Jackson* 10.00
100 *Matt Schaub* 4.00

2004 Fleer Sweet Sigs Gold

Veterans (1-75): 3X-6X
Rookies (76-100): .75X-1.5X
Production 99 Sets

2004 Fleer Sweet Sigs Black

Veterans #'d 76-99: 3X-6X
Veterans #'d 51-75: 4X-8X
Veterans #'d 26-50: 5X-10X
Rookies #'d 51-99: .75X-1.5X
Rookies #'d 26-50: 1X-2X
Cards #'d 25 or less: No Pricing
Sequentially numbered to player's jersey number

2004 Fleer Sweet Sigs End Zone Kings

NM/M
Common Player: 1.50
Inserted 1:12
1 Ahman Green 2.00
2 Priest Holmes 3.00
3 LaDainian Tomlinson 3.00
4 Jamal Lewis 2.00
5 Clinton Portis 4.00
6 Marshall Faulk 3.00
7 Marvin Harrison 2.00
8 Tony Gonzalez 1.50
9 Hines Ward 1.50
10 Peyton Manning 4.00
11 Steve McNair 2.00
12 Daunte Culpepper 2.00
13 Terrell Owens 2.00
14 Chad Pennington 3.00
15 Randy Moss 4.00

2004 Fleer Sweet Sigs End Zone Kings Jersey Silver

NM/M
Common Player: 10.00
Sequentially #'d to indicated quantity
Gold Patch: 1X-2X
Production 50 Sets
Black Patch/Jersey: No Pricing
Sequentially #'d to highest TD total in a season
Masterpiece Logo: No Pricing
Production 1 Set
DC Daunte Culpepper/122 10.00
MF Marshall Faulk/208 12.00
TG Tony Gonzalez/225 10.00
AG Ahman Green/209 10.00
MH Marvin Harrison/221 10.00
PH Priest Holmes/175 12.00
JL Jamal Lewis/220 10.00
PM Peyton Manning/99 20.00
SM Steve McNair/136 10.00
RM Randy Moss/212 12.00
TO Terrell Owens/220 10.00
CP Chad Pennington/127 12.00
CP2 Clinton Portis/215 12.00
LT LaDainian Tomlinson/186 12.00
HW Hines Ward/223 10.00

2004 Fleer Sweet Sigs End Zone Kings Quads Patch

NM/M
Sequentially #'d between 12 & 35
PCMM Steve McNair, Chad Pennington, Daunte Culpepper, Peyton Manning/35 75.00
PTFH Clinton Portis, LaDainian Tomlinson, Marshall Faulk, Priest Holmes/26
WHMO Randy Moss, Terrell Owens, Hines Ward, Marvin Harrison/27
LHWH Hines Ward, Jamal Lewis, Priest Holmes, Marvin Harrison/12
GFMO Terrell Owens, Ahman Green, Marshall Faulk, Randy Moss/33

2004 Fleer Sweet Sigs Gridiron Heroes

NM/M
Common Player: 1.00
Inserted 1:6
1GH Brett Favre 5.00
2GH Michael Vick 4.00
3GH Jerry Rice 4.00
4GH Emmitt Smith 4.00
5GH Byron Leftwich 3.00
6GH Donovan McNabb 2.00
7GH Clinton Portis 3.00
8GH Shaun Alexander 1.50
9GH Tom Brady 3.00
10GH Eli Manning 5.00
11GH David Carr 2.00
12GH Chad Johnson 1.00
13GH Brian Urlacher 1.50
14GH Joey Harrington 1.50
15GH Andre Johnson 1.50
16GH Corey Dillon 1.00
17GH Drew Bledsoe 1.50
18GH Plaxico Burress 1.50
19GH Edgerrin James 2.00
20GH Larry Fitzgerald 4.00
21GH Carson Palmer 2.00
22GH Philip Rivers 4.00
23GH Kellen Winslow Jr. 3.00
24GH Charles Rogers 1.50
25GH Jeremy Shockey 1.50

2004 Fleer Sweet Sigs Gridiron Heroes Jersey Silver

NM/M
Common Player: 8.00
Sequentially #'d to indicated quantity
Gold Patch: 1X-2X
Production 50 Sets
Black Patch
Cards #'d 80-85: .75X-1.5X
Cards #'d 26-54: 1X-3X
Cards #'d 25 or less: No Pricing
Seq. #'d to player's jersey number
Masterpiece: No Pricing
Production 1 Set
DB Drew Bledsoe/203 10.00
TB Tom Brady/226 12.00
PB Plaxico Burress/209 10.00
DC David Carr/227 10.00
CD Corey Dillon/210 10.00
BF Brett Favre/230 20.00
JH Joey Harrington/230 8.00
EJ Edgerrin James/216 10.00
AJ Andre Johnson/198 8.00
CJ Chad Johnson/229 8.00
BL Byron Leftwich/100 12.00
DM Donovan McNabb/215 12.00
CAP Carson Palmer/223 10.00
CP2 Clinton Portis/189 12.00
JR Jerry Rice/200 15.00
CR Charles Rogers/228 8.00
JS Jeremy Shockey/224 10.00
ES Emmitt Smith/35 30.00
BU Brian Urlacher/155 10.00
MV Michael Vick/213 15.00

2004 Fleer Sweet Sigs Gridiron Heroes Duals Patch

NM/M
Sequentially numbered between 2 & 36
BD Tom Brady, Corey Dillon/36 50.00
CJ David Carr, Andre Johnson/34 30.00
FR Brett Favre, Jerry Rice
HR Joey Harrington, Charles Rogers/25
JP Edgerrin James, Clinton Portis/21
JP2 Chad Johnson, Carson Palmer/29
MR Eli Manning, Philip Rivers/9
MS Eli Manning, Jeremy Shockey
SF Emmitt Smith, Larry Fitzgerald/31
VL Michael Vick, Byron Leftwich/28

2004 Fleer Sweet Sigs Gridiron Heroes Quads Patch

NM/M
Sequentially numbered between 9 & 42
VCPM Eli Manning, Michael Vick, David Carr, Carson Palmer/9
BJJF Plaxico Burress, Chad Johnson, Andre Johnson, Larry Fitzgerald/29
JPDA Edgerrin James, Clinton Portis, Corey Dillon, Shaun Alexander/37 50.00
BFSR Emmitt Smith, Tom Brady, Brett Favre, Jerry Rice/32 150.00
VHLM Donovan McNabb, Byron Leftwich, Michael Vick, Joey Harrington/42 80.00

2004 Fleer Sweet Sigs Sweet Sigs Copper

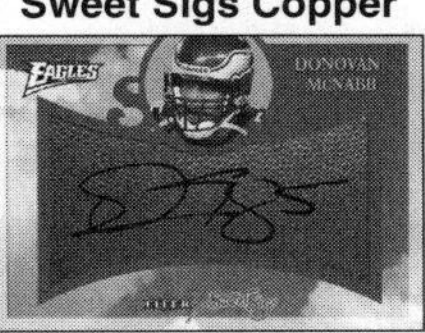

NM/M
Serially numbered
Silver
Cards #'d 101-153: .75X-1.5X
Cards #'d 51-100: 1X-2X
Cards #'d 26-50: 1X-3X
Cards #'d less than 25: No Pricing
Sequentially #'d to draft pick number
Gold: No Pricing
Sequentially #'d between 3 & 29
Masterpiece: No Pricing
Production 1 Set
TA Troy Aikman
SA Shaun Alexander
TB Tatum Bell 20.00
DB Drew Bennett 20.00
MIB Michael Bennett
BB Bernard Berrian 12.00
AB Anquan Boldin
KB Kyle Boller
MAB Marty Booker
TB Tom Brady
CB Chris Brown 15.00
AB2 Antonio Bryant 10.00
PB Plaxico Burress
TC Tyrone Calico 10.00
DC David Carr 40.00
CC Chris Chambers
MC Michael Clayton 15.00
KC Keary Colbert 15.00
DC2 Daunte Culpepper
DD Domanick Davis
JD Jake Delhomme
TD T.J. Duckett
JE John Elway
LE Lee Evans
MF Marshall Faulk
BF Brett Favre 225.00
AF A.J. Feeley
DF DeShaun Foster 10.00
EG Eddie George
AG Ahman Green 15.00
RG Rex Grossman 20.00
DAH Dante Hall
JH Joey Harrington
MH Matt Hasselbeck
DEH Devery Henderson 10.00
DRH Drew Henson 60.00
SJ Steven Jackson 40.00
EJ Edgerrin James
MJ Michael Jenkins 10.00
AJ Andre Johnson
CJ Chad Johnson
RJ Rudi Johnson 15.00
GJ Greg Jones 15.00
KJ Kevin Jones
JJ Joe Jurevicius
BYL Byron Leftwich
AL Ashley Lelie 10.00
JAL Jamal Lewis
BRL Brandon Lloyd
JPL J.P. Losman 20.00
EM Eli Manning
PM Peyton Manning
DAM Dan Marino
DEM Derrick Mason
DUM Deuce McAllister
WM Willis McGahee
DOM Donovan McNabb
JM Joe Montana
RM Randy Moss
SM Santana Moss
TO Terrell Owens
CAP Carson Palmer
CHP Chad Pennington
CRP Chris Perry 12.00
WP Will Poole
JP Jerry Porter 10.00
PR Philip Rivers 30.00
BR Ben Roethlisberger 250.00
BS Barry Sanders
JS Jeremy Shockey
OS Onterrio Smith 15.00
DS Donte Stallworth 15.00
LT LaDainian Tomlinson
BU Brian Urlacher
MV Michael Vick 125.00
AV Adam Vinatieri 30.00
JW Javon Walker 20.00
RW Reggie Wayne 15.00
BW Brian Westbrook 20.00
RW2 Reggie Williams 10.00
RW3 Ricky Williams
RW4 Roy Williams Lion
KW Kellen Winslow Jr.
RW5 Rashaun Woods 10.00
SY Steve Young

2004 Fleer Sweet Sigs Sweet Stitches Jersey Silver

NM/M
Common Player: 6.00
Sequentially #'d to indicated quantity
Gold Patch: 1X-2X
Production 50 Sets
Black Patch
Cards #'d 26-50: 1X-3X
Cards #'d less than 25: No Pricing
Masterpiece Logo: No Pricing
Production 1 Set
DB Drew Bledsoe/239 10.00
AB Anquan Boldin/244 8.00
KB Kyle Boller/226 8.00
DB2 Drew Brees/125 8.00
AB2 Aaron Brooks/250 8.00
CC Chris Chambers/236 8.00
DD Domanick Davis/198 8.00
SD Stephen Davis/238 6.00
JD Jake Delhomme/247 8.00
EGO Eddie George/236 8.00
TG Tony Gonzalez/201 6.00
RG Rex Grossman/246 10.00
DH Dante Hall/239 8.00
MH Matt Hasselbeck/190 8.00
DH2 Drew Henson/99 20.00
RJ Rudi Johnson/246 8.00
AL Ashley Lelie/230 6.00
RL Ray Lewis/247 8.00
CM Curtis Martin/248 8.00
SM Santana Moss/239 6.00
JP Julius Peppers/221 8.00
MP Marcus Pollard/210 6.00
PP Peerless Price/240 6.00
JS Jeremy Shockey/230 8.00
DS Donte Stallworth/223 6.00
LS Lee Suggs/231 6.00
ZT Zach Thomas/217 6.00
AT Amani Toomer/244 6.00
BU Brian Urlacher/189 8.00
HW Hines Ward/232 12.00

2004 Fleer Sweet Sigs Sweet Stitches Quads Patch

Sequentially numbered
DGBH Drew Henson, Jake Delhomme, Rex Grossman, Kyle Boller
BLSM Anquan Boldin, Ashley Lelie, Donte Stallworth, Santana Moss/33
PCTW Peerless Price, Chris Chambers, Amani Toomer, Hines Ward
JSDG Domanick Davis, Rudi Johnson, Lee Suggs, Quentin Griffin/27
LUTP Zach Thomas, Julius Peppers, Ray Lewis, Brian Urlacher
MGDG Curtis Martin, Eddie George, Stephen Davis, Charlie Garner/28 40.00
GSPF Marcus Pollard, Bubba Franks, Tony Gonzalez, Jeremy Shockey/27
BBGS Kyle Boller, Anquan Boldin, Rex Grossman, Lee Suggs/26
TTGD Amani Toomer, Zach Thomas, Eddie George, Stephen Davis
CTMM Curtis Martin, Santana Moss, Chris Chambers, Zach Thomas/33

2004 Fleer Tradition

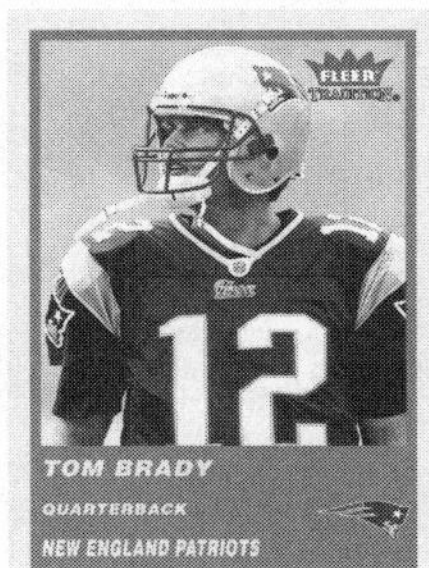

NM/M
Common Card (1-330): .15
Minor Stars (1-330): .25
Unlisted Stars (1-330): .50
Common Rookie (331-350): 2.50
Inserted 1:4
Common Trio Rookie (351-360): 3.00
Inserted 1:18
Pack (10): 3.25
Box (36): 80.00
1 Dolphins Team Leaders .40
2 Bills Team Leaders .15
3 Patriots Team Leaders .50
4 Jets Team Leaders .50
5 Colts Team Leaders .50
6 Jaguars Team Leaders .15
7 Titans Team Leaders .15
8 Texans Team Leaders .40
9 Raiders Team Leaders .75
10 Broncos Team Leaders .50
11 Chiefs Team Leaders .40
12 Chargers Team Leaders .40
13 Steelers Team Leaders .15
14 Browns Team Leaders .15
15 Bengals Team Leaders .15
16 Ravens Team Leaders .15
17 Eagles Team Leaders .40
18 Giants Team Leaders .15
19 Redskins Team Leaders .15
20 Cowboys Team Leaders .15
21 Vikings Team Leaders .50
22 Packers Team Leaders 1.00
23 Bears Team Leaders .25
24 Lions Team Leaders .15
25 49ers Team Leaders .25
26 Rams Team Leaders .40
27 Seahawks Team Leaders .15
28 Cardinals Team Leaders .15
29 Panthers Team Leaders .15
30 Buccaneers TeamLeaders .15
31 Falcons Team Leaders .15
32 Saints Team Leaders .25
33 Anquan Boldin .50
34 Michael Vick 1.50
35 Kyle Boller .50
36 Aeneas Williams .15
37 Jake Delhomme .50
38 Rex Grossman .50
39 Carson Palmer .75
40 Quincy Morgan .15
41 Terry Glenn .15
42 Jake Plummer .25
43 Joey Harrington .50
44 Brett Favre 2.00
45 Jeff Garcia .50
46 Peyton Manning 1.00
47 Byron Leftwich 1.00
48 Trent Green .15
49 A.J. Feeley .15
50 Daunte Culpepper .50
51 Tom Brady 1.00
52 Aaron Brooks .50
53 Kerry Collins .15
54 Chad Pennington .75
55 Rich Gannon .25
56 Donovan McNabb .75
57 Tommy Maddox .25
58 Drew Brees .25
59 Terrell Owens .50
60 Matt Hasselbeck .25
61 Kurt Warner .50
62 Brad Johnson .15
63 Jerome Bettis .25
64 Keith Bulluck .15
65 Rod Gardner .15
66 Eddie George .50
67 Warren Sapp .15
68 Marc Bulger .25

69	Shaun Alexander	.50
70	Tai Streets	.15
71	LaDainian Tomlinson	.75
72	Steve McNair	.50
73	Brian Westbrook	.15
74	Jerry Rice	1.50
75	Santana Moss	.15
76	Moe Williams	.15
77	Deuce McAllister	.50
78	Adam Vinatieri	.15
79	Randy Moss	1.00
80	Ricky Williams	.75
81	Priest Holmes	.75
82	Jimmy Smith	.15
83	Edgerrin James	.75
84	Andre Johnson	.50
85	Ahman Green	.50
86	Charles Rogers	.50
87	Champ Bailey	.15
88	Roy Williams	.25
89	Tim Couch	.25
90	Corey Dillon	.25
91	Thomas Jones	.15
92	Stephen Davis	.25
93	Travis Henry	.15
94	Jamal Lewis	.50
95	Warrick Dunn	.15
96	Emmitt Smith	1.50
97	Mark Brunell	.25
98	Willis McGahee	.50
99	Duce Staley	.15
100	Lee Suggs	.15
101	Rod Smith	.15
102	Marvin Harrison	.50
103	Larry Johnson	.15
104	Michael Bennett	.50
105	Donte Stallworth	.25
106	DeShaun Foster	.15
107	Hines Ward	.25
108	T.J. Duckett	.25
109	Brian Urlacher	.50
110	Boss Bailey	.15
111	Tim Brown	.50
112	David Boston	.25
113	Marshall Faulk	.75
114	Jason Witten	.15
115	Richard Seymour	.15
116	Domanick Davis	.50
117	Jon Kitna	.15
118	Ray Lewis	.25
119	Tedy Bruschi	.15
120	Chris Chambers	.50
121	Freddie Mitchell	.15
122	Amani Toomer	.25
123	Curtis Martin	.50
124	Eric Moulds	.15
125	Darrell Jackson	.15
126	Clinton Portis	1.00
127	Jay Fiedler	.15
128	Todd Heap	.25
129	Dexter Jackson	.15
130	James Jackson	.15
131	Shannon Sharpe	.25
132	Donald Driver	.15
133	Billy Miller	.15
134	Dante Hall	.15
135	Onterrio Smith	.15
136	Joe Horn	.15
137	Shaun Ellis	.15
138	L.J. Smith	.15
139	Jerry Porter	.15
140	Reggie Wayne	.15
141	Derrick Brooks	.15
142	Terrell Suggs	.15
143	Randy McMichael	.15
144	Mike Alstott	.15
145	Nathan Poole	.15
146	Chris Brown	.15
147	Torry Holt	.50
148	Adewale Ogunleye	.15
149	Peter Warrick	.25
150	Alge Crumpler	.15
151	Charlie Garner	.15
152	Jeremy Shockey	.50
153	Simeon Rice	.15
154	Julian Peterson	.15
155	Patrick Ramsey	.15
156	Shawn Springs	.15
157	Marcus Stroud	.15
158	Keyshawn Johnson	.25
159	Steve Smith	.15
160	Ty Law	.15
161	Derrick Mason	.15
162	Josh Reed	.15
163	Fred Smoot	.15
164	Muhsin Muhammad	.25
165	Justin Gage	.15
166	Chad Johnson	.25
167	Dennis Northcutt	.15
168	Joey Galloway	.15
169	Ashley Lelie	.15
170	Casey Fitzsimmons	.15
171	Dwight Freeney	.15
172	Nick Barnett	.15
173	LaBrandon Toefield	.15
174	Jabar Gaffney	.15
175	Tony Gonzalez	.25
176	Zach Thomas	.15
177	Nate Burleson	.15
178	Deion Branch	.15
179	Eddie "Boo" Williams	.15
180	Michael Strahan	.15
181	Anthony Becht	.15
182	Charles Woodson	.15
183	Sheldon Brown	.15
184	Kendrell Bell	.15
185	Kassim Osgood	.15
186	Tony Parrish	.15
187	Marcel Shipp	.15
188	Bobby Engram	.15
189	Keith Brooking	.15
190	Isaac Bruce	.25
191	Travis Taylor	.15
192	Charles Lee	.15
193	Takeo Spikes	.15
194	Justin McCareins	.15
195	Julius Peppers	.15
196	LaVar Arrington	.15
197	Dez White	.15
198	Rudi Johnson	.25
199	Andre Davis	.25
200	Quincy Carter	.50
201	Quentin Griffin	.15
202	Dallas Clark	.15
203	Artose Pinner	.15
204	Kevin Johnson	.15
205	Kabeer Gbaja-Biamila	.15
206	Marcus Coleman	.15
207	Johnnie Morton	.15
208	Jason Taylor	.15
209	Kevin Williams	.15
210	David Givens	.15
211	Charles Grant	.15
212	Ike Hilliard	.15
213	Wayne Chrebet	.15
214	Teyo Johnson	.15
215	Brian Dawkins	.15
216	Antwann Randle El	.25
217	Eric Parker	.25
218	Josh McCown	.15
219	Tim Rattay	.15
220	Brian Finneran	.15
221	Chad Brown	.15
222	Ed Reed	.15
223	Dane Looker	.15
224	Aaron Schobel	.15
225	Joe Jurevicius	.15
226	Ricky Manning	.15
227	Jevon Kearse	.15
228	Laveranues Coles	.25
229	Kelley Washington	.15
230	William Green	.25
231	Terence Newman	.15
232	Bryant Johnson	.15
233	Peerless Price	.15
234	Peter Boulware	.15
235	Drew Bledsoe	.50
236	Kris Jenkins	.15
237	Marty Booker	.15
238	Matt Schobel	.15
239	Earl Little	.15
240	Antonio Bryant	.25
241	Al Wilson	.15
242	Dre' Bly	.15
243	Javon Walker	.25
244	David Carr	.75
245	Mike Vanderjagt	.15
246	Fred Taylor	.50
247	Eddie Kennison	.15
248	Patrick Surtain	.15
249	Jim Kleinsasser	.15
250	Daniel Graham	.15
251	Jerome Pathon	.15
252	Tiki Barber	.15
253	John Abraham	.15
254	Justin Fargas	.15
255	Correll Buckhalter	.15
256	Plaxico Burress	.50
257	Quentin Jammer	.15
258	Kevan Barlow	.15
259	Koren Robinson	.15
260	Leonard Little	.15
261	John Lynch	.15
262	Tyrone Calico	.15
263	Taylor Jacobs	.15
264	Joey Porter	.15
265	Freddie Jones	.15
266	Marcus Pollard	.15
267	Mike Peterson	.15
268	Justin Griffith	.15
269	Shawn Bryson	.15
270	Will Allen	.15
271	Antonio Gates	.15
272	Chris McAllister	.15
273	Tony Hollings	.15
274	Cedrick Wilson	.15
275	Adam Archuleta	.15
276	London Fletcher	.15
277	Drew Bennett	.15
278	Rod Smart	.15
279	LaMont Jordan	.15
280	Jerry Azumah	.15
281	Bubba Franks	.15
282	Troy Edwards	.15
283	Willie McGinest	.15
284	Morten Anderson	.15
285	Dat Nguyen	.15
286	Samari Rolle	.15
287	Brian Simmons	.15
288	Chike Okeafor	.15
289	Rodney Harrison	.15
290	Jason Elam	.15
291	Tim Dwight	.15
292	Corey Bradford	.15
293	Charles Tillman	.15
294	Tim Carter	.15
295	Ahmed Plummer	.15
296	Troy Walters	.15
297	Michael Lewis	.15
298	Tony James	.15
299	Doug Flutie	.15
300	Az-Zahir Hakim	.15
301	Itula Mili	.15
302	Jamie Sharper	.15
303	Vonnie Holliday	.15
304	Brian Russell	.15
305	Bryan Gilmore	.15
306	Darren Sharper	.15
307	Kyle Brady	.15
308	David Tyree	.15
309	Andre Carter	.15
310	Lawyer Milloy	.15
311	David Terrell	.15
312	Richie Anderson	.15
313	Darren Howard	.15
314	Sebastian Janikowski	.15
315	Kimo Von Oelhoffen	.15
316	Donnie Edwards	.15
317	Brandon Lloyd	.15
318	Robert Ferguson	.15
319	Derek Smith	.15
320	Anthony Thomas	.25
321	Ken Hamlin	.15
322	Ronde Barber	.15
323	Erron Kinney	.15
324	Tom Brady	1.00
325	Peyton Manning	1.00
326	Steve McNair	.50
327	Jamal Lewis	.50
328	Ray Lewis	.25
329	Anquan Boldin	.50
330	Terrell Suggs	.15
331	Eli Manning	10.00
332	Larry Fitzgerald	6.00
333	Ben Roethlisberger	15.00
334	Tatum Bell	3.00
335	Roy Williams	6.00
336	Drew Henson	5.00
337	Philip Rivers	6.00
338	Rashaun Woods	4.00
339	Kevin Jones	6.00
340	Sean Taylor	4.00
341	Steven Jackson	5.00
342	Kellen Winslow Jr.	4.00
343	Chris Perry	3.00
344	J.P. Losman	4.00
345	Greg Jones	2.50
346	Reggie Williams	4.00
347	Michael Clayton	4.00
348	Jonathan Vilma	2.50
349	Julius Jones	6.00
350	Michael Jenkins	3.00
351	*Eli Manning, Philip Rivers, Ben Roethlisberger*	25.00
352	*Larry Fitzgerald, Reggie Williams, Roy Williams*	15.00
353	*Lee Evans, Bernard Berrian, Derrick Hamilton*	6.00
354	*Kenechi Udeze, Will Poole, Keary Colbert*	3.00
355	*Chris Gamble, Dunta Robinson, DeAngelo Hall*	5.00
356	*Ben Troupe, Ben Watson, Ben Hartsock*	3.00
357	*Devard Darling, Johnnie Morant, Ernest Wilford*	3.00
358	*Luke McCown, Cody Pickett, Matt Schaub*	3.00
359	*Tatum Bell, Michael Turner, Cedric Cobbs*	6.00
360	*Mewelde Moore, Quincy Wilson, Derrick Knight*	5.00

2004 Fleer Tradition Crystal

Stars (1-330):	2X-5X
Production 150 Sets	
Rookies (331-350):	2X-6X
Production 75 Sets	
Trio Rookies (351-360):	3X-6X
Production 25 Sets	

2004 Fleer Tradition Classic Combinations

		NM/M
Common Card:		3.00
Production 250 Sets		
1CC	Jerry Rice, Larry Fitzgerald	12.00
2CC	Philip Rivers, Eli Manning	12.00
3CC	Peyton Manning, Eli Manning	25.00
4CC	Carson Palmer, Chris Perry	4.00
5CC	Chad Pennington, Ben Roethlisberger	6.00
6CC	Clinton Portis, Tatum Bell	4.00
7CC	Tom Brady, Drew Henson	12.00
8CC	Jeremy Shockey, Kellen Winslow Jr.	6.00
9CC	Michael Vick, Kevin Jones	6.00
10CC	Roy Williams, Sean Taylor	4.00
11CC	Ricky Williams, Roy Williams	3.00
12CC	Anquan Boldin, Greg Jones	6.00
13CC	Chad Johnson, Steven Jackson	3.00
14CC	Byron Leftwich, Reggie Williams	5.00
15CC	Charles Rogers, Roy Williams	5.00
16CC	Brett Favre, Philip Rivers	10.00
17CC	Randy Moss, Rashaun Woods	6.00
18CC	Chris Chambers, Lee Evans	3.00
19CC	Drew Henson, Julius Jones	20.00
20CC	Patrick Ramsey, J.P. Losman	6.00

2004 Fleer Tradition Gridiron Tributes

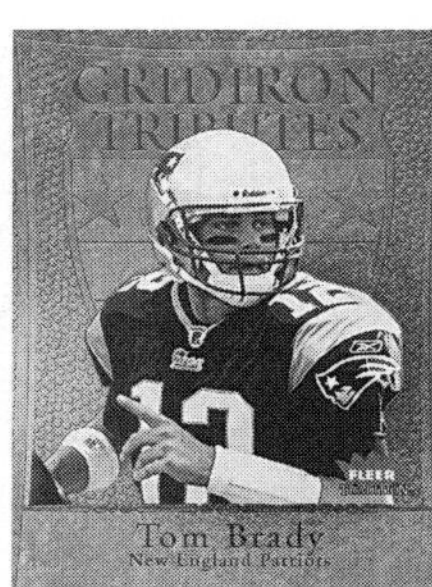

		NM/M
Common Player:		1.50
Inserted 1:6		
1GT	Steve McNair	1.50
2GT	Tom Brady	3.00
3GT	Peyton Manning	3.00
4GT	Chad Pennington	2.00
5GT	Donovan McNabb	2.00
6GT	Brett Favre	5.00
7GT	Jerry Rice	4.00
8GT	Emmitt Smith	4.00
9GT	Ricky Williams	2.00
10GT	Priest Holmes	2.00
11GT	LaDainian Tomlinson	2.00
12GT	Jeremy Shockey	1.50
13GT	Byron Leftwich	3.00
14GT	Marvin Harrison	1.50
15GT	Jamal Lewis	1.50
16GT	Ahman Green	1.50
17GT	Brian Urlacher	1.50
18GT	Michael Vick	4.00
19GT	Clinton Portis	3.00
20GT	Randy Moss	3.00

2004 Fleer Tradition Gridiron Tributes Game-Used Jersey

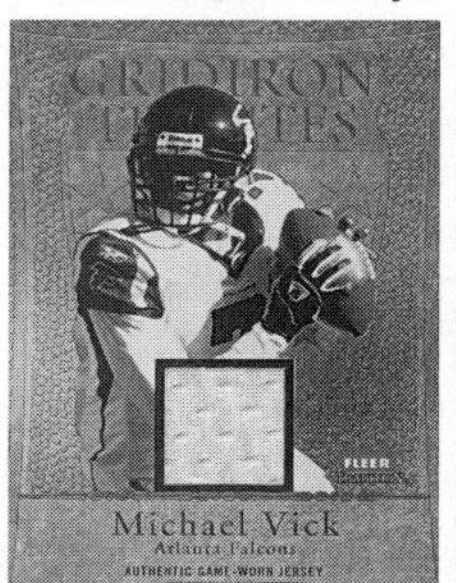

		NM/M
Common Player:		5.00
Inserted 1:51		
Patch:		1.5X-4X
Production 50 Sets		
GT-TB	Tom Brady	12.00
GT-BF	Brett Favre	20.00
GT-AG	Ahman Green	8.00
GT-MH	Marvin Harrison	8.00
GT-PH	Priest Holmes	10.00
GT-BL	Byron Leftwich	12.00
GT-JL	Jamal Lewis	8.00
GT-PM	Peyton Manning	12.00
GT-DM	Donovan McNabb	10.00
GT-SM	Steve McNair	5.00
GT-RM	Randy Moss	10.00
GT-CP	Chad Pennington	10.00
GT-CP2	Clinton Portis	10.00
GT-JR	Jerry Rice	15.00
GT-JS	Jeremy Shockey	8.00
GT-LT	LaDainian Tomlinson	10.00
GT-BU	Brian Urlacher	8.00
GT-MV	Michael Vick	15.00
GT-RW	Ricky Williams	8.00

2004 Fleer Tradition Rookie Hat's Off

		NM/M
Common Player:		15.00
Production 100 Sets		
HO-TB	Tatum Bell	20.00
HO-MC	Michael Clayton	20.00
HO-LF	Larry Fitzgerald	25.00
HO-LE	Lee Evans	20.00
HO-SJ	Steven Jackson	25.00
HO-MJ	Michael Jenkins	15.00
HO-GJ	Greg Jones	15.00
HO-JJ	Julius Jones	30.00
HO-KJ	Kevin Jones	20.00
HO-JL	J.P. Losman	15.00
HO-EM	Eli Manning	60.00
HO-CP	Chris Perry	15.00
HO-PR	Philip Rivers	30.00
HO-BR	Ben Roethlisberger	80.00
HO-RW3	Reggie Williams	15.00
HO-RW	Roy Williams	25.00
HO-KW	Kellen Winslow Jr.	30.00
HO-RW2	Rashaun Woods	15.00

2004 Fleer Tradition Rookie Throwback Threads Football

	NM/M
Common Player:	10.00
Inserted 1:108	
Helmet:	.75X-2X
Inserted 1:306	
Jersey:	.25X-1X
Inserted 1:58	

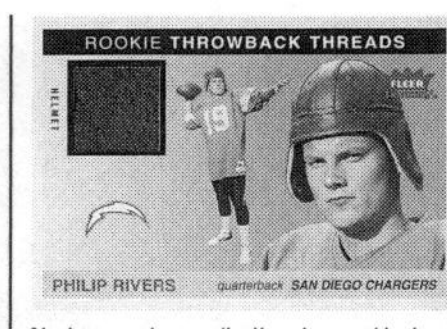

Rookie Throwback Threads
Philip Rivers
quarterback San Diego Chargers

No jersey, jersey/ball or jersey/ helmet cards for Larry Fitzgerald, Reggie Williams, Julius Jones, J.P. Losman, Matt Schaub

Jersey/Ball:		1X-3X
Production 50 Sets		
Jersey/Helmet:		3X-8X
Production 25 Sets		
TT-TB	Tatum Bell	12.00
TT-MC	Michael Clayton	15.00
TT-LE	Lee Evans	12.00
TT-LF	Larry Fitzgerald	20.00
TT-SJ	Steven Jackson	15.00
TT-MJ	Michael Jenkins	10.00
TT-GJ	Greg Jones	10.00
TT-JJ	Julius Jones	15.00
TT-KJ	Kevin Jones	15.00
TT-JL	J.P. Losman	15.00
TT-EM	Eli Manning	30.00
TT-EM2	Eli Manning	30.00
TT-LM	Luke McCown	10.00
TT-CP	Chris Perry	12.00
TT-PR	Philip Rivers	20.00
TT-BR	Ben Roethlisberger	30.00
TT-MS	Matt Schaub	10.00
TT-RW3	Reggie Williams	10.00
TT-RW	Roy Williams	15.00
TT-KW	Kellen Winslow Jr.	15.00
TT-KW2	Kellen Winslow Jr.	15.00
TT-RW2	Rashaun Woods	15.00

2004 Fleer Trad. Rookie Throwback Threads Dual Jersey

		NM/M
Common Card:		20.00
Production 100 Sets		
Dual Patch:		1X-2X
Production 75 Sets		
EM/PR	Eli Manning, Philip Rivers	
EM/KW	Eli Manning, Kellen Winslow Jr.	50.00
SJ/KJ	Steven Jackson, Kevin Jones	30.00
SJ/TB	Steven Jackson, Tatum Bell	25.00
RW/TB	Rashaun Woods, Tatum Bell	25.00
PR/BR	Philip Rivers, Ben Roethlisberger	40.00
KW/LM	Kellen Winslow Jr., Luke McCown	25.00
KJ/RW	Kevin Jones, Roy Williams	40.00
MJ/CP	Michael Jenkins, Chris Perry	20.00
EM/EM	Eli Manning	50.00
KW/KW	Kellen Winslow Jr.	40.00

2004 Fleer Tradition Signing Day

		NM/M
Common Player:		3.00
Inserted 1:12		
Parallel:		2X-5X
Production 50 Sets		
1SD	Eli Manning	10.00
2SD	Larry Fitzgerald	6.00
3SD	Ben Roethlisberger	10.00
4SD	J.P. Losman	4.00
5SD	Roy Williams	6.00
6SD	Steven Jackson	5.00
7SD	Rashaun Woods	4.00
8SD	Reggie Williams	4.00
9SD	Michael Jenkins	3.00
10SD	Philip Rivers	8.00
11SD	Drew Henson	5.00
12SD	Kevin Jones	5.00
13SD	Lee Evans	4.00
14SD	Michael Clayton	4.00
15SD	Chris Perry	3.00

1996 FlickBall Team Sets

These three team sets were regionally distributed. Each set consisted of five player cards and one team helmet card.

		NM/M
Complete Set (18):		17.00
Comp. Cowboys Set (6):		7.00
Comp. Vikings Set (6):		3.50
Comp. Packers Set (6):		7.00
Common Player:		.50
DC1	Troy Aikman	2.00
DC2	Deion Sanders	1.25
DC3	Emmitt Smith	4.00
DC4	Daryl Johnston	.75
DC5	Cowboys Helmet	.50
DC6	Darren Woodson	.50
MV1	Warren Moon	.75
MV2	Cris Carter	.75
MV3	Robert Smith	.75
MV4	Qadry Ismail	.50
MV5	Vikings Helmet	.50
MV6	David Palmer	.50
GBP1	Brett Favre	5.00
GBP2	Edgar Bennett	.75
GBP3	Reggie White	1.00
GBP4	Robert Brooks	1.00
GBP5	Packers Helmet	.50
GBP6	George Teague	.50

1995 Flickball NFL Helmets

Flickball debuted in 1995 and featured team helmets and Super Bowl logos. They arrived in six-card packs and featured two expansion team helmets, cards 61 and 62, that were found every 48 packs.

		NM/M
Complete Set (60):		12.00
Common Player:		.25
1	Dallas Cowboys	.50
2	New York Giants	.25
3	Arizona Cardinals	.25
4	Philadelphia Eagles	.25
5	Washington Redskins	.35
6	Minnesota Vikings	.25
7	Chicago Bears	.35
8	Green Bay Packers	.50
9	Detroit Lions	.25
10	Tampa Bay Buccaneers	.25
11	San Francisco 49ers	.50
12	New Orleans Saints	.25
13	Atlanta Falcons	.25
14	Carolina Panthers	.35
15	St. Louis Rams	.25
16	New England Patriots	.25
17	Miami Dolphins	.35
18	Buffalo Bills	.25
19	Indianapolis Colts	.25
20	New York Jets	.25
21	Pittsburgh Steelers	.35
22	Cleveland Browns	.25
23	Cincinnati Bengals	.25
24	Jacksonville Jaguars	.35
25	Houston Oilers	.25
26	San Diego Chargers	.25
27	Oakland Raiders	.35
28	Kansas City Chiefs	.25
29	Denver Broncos	.25
30	Seattle Seahawks	.25
31	Super Bowl I	.25
32	Super Bowl II	.25
33	Super Bowl III	.25
34	Super Bowl IV	.25
35	Super Bowl V	.25
36	Super Bowl VI	.25
37	Super Bowl VII	.25
38	Super Bowl VIII	.25
39	Super Bowl IX	.25
40	Super Bowl X	.25
41	Super Bowl XI	.25
42	Super Bowl XII	.25
43	Super Bowl XIII	.25
44	Super Bowl XIV	.25
45	Super Bowl XV	.25
46	Super Bowl XVI	.25
47	Super Bowl XVII	.25
48	Super Bowl XVIII	.25
49	Super Bowl XIX	.25
50	Super Bowl XX	.25
51	Super Bowl XXI	.25
52	Super Bowl XXII	.25
53	Super Bowl XXIII	.25
54	Super Bowl XXIV	.25
55	Super Bowl XXV	.25
56	Super Bowl XXVI	.25
57	Super Bowl XXVII	.25
58	Super Bowl XXVIII	.25
59	Super Bowl XXIX	.25
60	Super Bowl XXX Logo	.25
61	Carolina Panthers Inaugural Season	1.25
62	Jacksonville Jaguars Inaugural Season	1.25

1995 Flickball Prototypes

This unnumbered 10-card set was a prelude to the 1996 Flickball release. Each card arrived in the shape of a football and featured a finger-sized cut-out space used to flick the card as part of a game. Card No. 7 included a different player on each side and was called a "Double Flick". Each card in this prototype set contained the words "Pre-Production" on its back.

		NM/M
Complete Set (10):		5.00
Common Player:		.25
1	Bill Bates	.25
2	Jeff Blake	.50
3	Drew Bledsoe	1.00
4	Brett Favre	2.00
5	Kevin Greene	.25
6	Daryl Johnston	.25
7	Steve McNair, Kerry Collins	1.00
8	Jerry Rice	1.00
9	Tamarick Vanover	.50
10	Chris Warren	.25

1996 Flickball

The first Flickball set to feature players contained 100 top stars and arrived in seven-card packs. Inserts included in the release were: Commemoratives, DoubleFlicks, Hawaiian Flicks, PreviewFlick Cowboys and Rookies.

NM/M

Complete Set (100): 20.00
Common Player: .10
1 Troy Aikman 1.00
2 Emmitt Smith 2.00
3 Neil O'Donnell (UER, name spelled Niel) .10
4 Deion Sanders .50
5 Bill Bates .10
6 Rodney Peete .10
7 Ricky Watters .20
8 Fred Barnett .10
9 Dave Krieg .10
10 Larry Centers .10
11 Garrison Hearst .20
12 Dave Brown .10
13 Rodney Hampton .20
14 Mike Sherrard .10
15 Gus Frerotte .20
16 Henry Ellard .10
17 Darrell Green .10
18 Scott Mitchell .20
19 Barry Sanders 1.00
20 Herman Moore .30
21 Erik Kramer .10
22 Curtis Conway .25
23 Jeff Graham .10
24 Brett Favre 2.00
25 Edgar Bennett .20
26 Robert Brooks .30
27 Reggie White .25
28 Warren Moon .20
29 Robert Smith .20
30 Cris Carter .20
31 Trent Dilfer .30
32 Errict Rhett .75
33 Santana Dotson .10
34 Steve Young .75
35 Jerry Rice 1.00
36 Merton Hanks .10
37 Ken Norton .10
38 Jesse Sapolu .10
39 Jim Everett .10
40 Willie Roaf .10
41 Tyrone Hughes .10
42 Chris Miller .10
43 Isaac Bruce .75
44 Shane Conlan .10
45 Jeff George .20
46 Eric Metcalf .10
47 Craig Heyward .10
48 Sam Mills .10
49 Mark Carrier (WR) .10
50 Brett Maxie .10
51 Jim Kelly .20
52 Andre Reed .10
53 Bruce Smith .10
54 Bryce Paup .10
55 Jim Harbaugh .20
56 Marshall Faulk .75
57 Sean Dawkins .10
58 Dan Marino 2.00
59 Terry Kirby .10
60 O.J. McDuffie .20
61 Bernie Parmalee .10
62 Wayne Chrebet .20
63 Adrian Murrell .20
64 Ron Moore .10
65 Drew Bledsoe 1.00
66 Vincent Brisby .20
67 Vincent Brown .10
68 Neil O'Donnell .10
69 Erric Pegram .10
70 Rohn Stark .10
71 Kevin Greene .20
72 Greg Lloyd .20
73 Todd McNair .10
74 Mark Stepnoski .10
75 Bruce Matthews .10
76 Jeff Blake .75
77 Carl Pickens .20
78 John Copeland .10
79 Vinny Testaverde .10
80 Andre Rison .10
81 Leroy Hoard .10
82 Mark Brunell 1.00
83 Cedric Tillman .10
84 Desmond Howard .20
85 Stan Humphries .20
86 Natrone Means .30
87 Junior Seau .20
88 Steve Bono .20
89 Marcus Allen .20
90 Derrick Thomas .20
91 Neil Smith .20
92 Rick Mirer .30
93 Chris Warren .20
94 Cortez Kennedy .10
95 Jeff Hostetler .10
96 Tim Brown .20
97 Terry McDaniel .10
98 John Elway .75
99 Shannon Sharpe .20
100 Steve Atwater .10

1996 Flickball Commemoratives

This four-card Flickball insert was inserted every 357 packs, with each card being hand-numbered to 700.

NM/M

Complete Set (4): 75.00
Common Player: 15.00
C1 Emmitt Smith (25 Touchdowns) 20.00
C2 Dan Marino (Most passing yards) 20.00
C3 Brett Favre (MVP) 20.00
C4 Curtis Martin (Rookie of the Year) 15.00

1996 Flickball DoubleFlicks

This 12-card, double-sided insert set was inserted in every three packs. Cards feature a player on each side from the same position. The cards are numbered with the "DF" prefix.

NM/M

Complete Set (12): 18.00
Common Player: .75
1 Dan Marino, Drew Bledsoe 5.00
2 Troy Aikman, Steve Young 2.50
3 Kerry Collins, Steve McNair 2.50
4 Eric Zeier, Kordell Stewart 2.50
5 Emmitt Smith, Marshall Faulk 5.00
6 Barry Sanders, Errict Rhett 2.50
7 Curtis Martin, Terrell Davis 3.50
8 Rashaan Salaam, Napoleon Kaufman 1.50
9 Michael Irvin, Jerry Rice 2.50
10 Tim Brown, Cris Carter .75
11 Joey Galloway, J.J. Stokes 1.50
12 Frank Sanders, Michael Westbrook 1.25

1996 Flickball Hawaiian Flicks

Four different players that are native to Hawaii are featured in Hawaiian Flicks. These were found every eight packs.

NM/M

Complete Set (4): 4.00
Common Player: 1.00
H1 Mark Tuinei 1.00
H2 Jesse Sapolu 1.00
H3 Jason Elam 1.00
H4 Junior Seau 1.50

1996 Flickball PreviewFlick Cowboys

PreviewFlick Cowboys were included in every four packs. The set includes eight Cowboys, with cards carrying a "P" prefix on the card number.

NM/M

Complete Set (8): 6.00
Common Player: .50
1 Daryl Johnston 1.00
2 Jay Novacek 1.00
3 Kevin Williams (WR) 1.50
4 Charles Haley 1.00
5 Darren Woodson .50
6 Leon Lett .75
7 Chad Hennings .50
8 Mark Tuinei .50

1996 Flickball Rookies

This 20-card insert captured the top rookies from the 1995 season, and was inserted every two packs.

NM/M

Complete Set (20): 18.00
Common Player: .25
R1 Sherman Williams .25
R2 Mike Mamula .25
R3 Frank Sanders .50
R4 Steve Stentsrom .25
R5 Michael Westbrook 1.00
R6 Warren Sapp .50
R7 Rashaan Salaam 1.50
R8 J.J. Stokes 1.00
R9 Kevin Carter .25
R10 Kerry Collins 2.50
R11 Curtis Martin 3.00
R12 Kordell Stewart 2.50
R13 Steve McNair 2.00
R14 Rodney Thomas .25
R15 Eric Zeier .25
R16 Tony Boselli .25
R17 Tamarick Vanover 1.00
R18 Joey Galloway 1.75
R19 Napoleon Kaufman .75
R20 Terrell Davis 3.00

1988 Football Heroes Sticker Book

This 20-page booklet served as an introduction to American football, with a discussion of how the game is played and a glossary. The sticker book measures 9-1/4" x 12-1/2", while the stickers measure three inches in height. Stickers were issued on two sheets of 15 and were to be stuck in a glossy Football Heroes poster.

NM/M

Complete Set (30): 30.00
Common Player: .20
1 Marcus Allen .50
2 Gary Anderson .20
3 Brian Bosworth .20
4 Anthony Carter .20
5 Deron Cherry .20
6 Eric Dickerson .50
7 John Elway 2.00
8 Bo Jackson 1.00
9 Rich Karlis .20
10 Bernie Kosar .20
11 Steve Largent .50
12 Mick Luckhurst .20
13 Dexter Manley .20
14 Dan Marino 6.00
15 Jim McMahon .40
16 Joe Montana 3.00
17 Joe Morris .20
18 Anthony Munoz .20
19 Ozzie Newsome .20
20 Walter Payton 4.00
21 William Perry .40
22 Jerry Rice 3.00
23 Ricky Sanders .20
24 Phil Simms .40
25 Mike Singletary .40
26 Dwight Stephenson .20
27 Lawrence Taylor .50
28 Herschel Walker .40
29 Doug Williams .20
30 Kellen Winslow .40

1985-87 Football Immortals

FOOTBALL IMMORTALS
JOHN (Blood) McNALLY
Charter Enshrinee, 1963

Although this set was produced in both 1985 and 1987, they are similar enough to group together. The 1985 set had 135 cards, while the 1987 set featured 142 Hall of Famers, with their induction year on the front and back of each card. The first 45 cards feature a red border, while cards 46-90 feature a blue border, 91-135 have a green border and 136-142 have a yellow border.

NM/M

Complete Set (147): 75.00
Common Player: .35
1 Pete Rozelle .70
2 Joe Namath 1.50
3 Frank Gatski .35
4 O.J. Simpson 1.50
5 Roger Staubach 1.25
6 Herb Adderley .50
7 Lance Alworth .70
8 Doug Atkins .50
9 Morris "Red" Badgro .35
10 Cliff Battles .35
11 Sammy Baugh 1.00
12 Raymond Berry .70
13 Charles W. Bidwill .35
14 Chuck Bednarik .70
15 Bert Bell .35
16 Bobby Bell .50
17 George Blanda .70
18 Jim Brown 1.25
19 Paul Brown .75
20 Roosevelt Brown .50
21 Ray Flaherty .35
22 Len Ford .35
23 Dan Fortmann .35
24 Bill George .50
25 Art Donovan .75
26 John (Paddy) Driscoll .35
27 Jimmy Conzelman .35
28 Willie Davis .50
29 Earl "Dutch" Clark .50
30 George Connor .50
31 Guy Chamberlain .35
32 Jack Christiansen .50
33 Tony Canadeo .50
34 Joe Carr .35
35 Willie Brown .50
36 Dick Butkus 1.25
37 Bill Dudley .50
38 Glen Edwards .50
39 Weeb Ewbank .35
40 Tom Fears .50
41 Otto Graham 1.25
42 Harold "Red" Grange 1.25
43 Frank Gifford 1.25
44 Sid Gillman .35
45 Forrest Gregg .50
46 Lou Groza .75
47 Joe Guyon .35
48 George Halas 1.00
49 Ed Healy .35
50 Mel Hein .35
51 Fats Henry .50
52 Arnie Herber .35
53 Bill Hewitt .35
54 Clarke Hinkle .35
55 Elroy Hirsch .60
56 Robert "Cal" Hubbard .35
57 Sam Huff .50
58 Lamar Hunt .35
59 Don Hutson .50
60 Deacon Jones .75
61 Sonny Jurgensen .50
62 Walt Kiesling .35
63 Frank "Bruiser" Kinard .35
64 Earl (Curly) Lambeau .35
65 Dick "Night Train" Lane .50
66 Yale Lary .50
67 Dante Lavelli .50
68 Bobby Layne 1.00
69 Tuffy Leemans .35
70 Bob Lilly .50
71 Vince Lombardi 1.00
72 Sid Luckman 1.00
73 Link Lyman .35
74 Tim Mara .35
75 Gino Marchetti .50
76 Geo. Preston Marshall .35
77 Ollie Matson .60
78 George McAfee .50
79 Mike McCormack .50
80 Hugh McElhenny .60
81 Johnny "Blood" McNally .35
82 Mike Michalske .35
83 Wayne Millner .35
84 Bobby Mitchell .50
85 Ron Mix .50
86 Lenny Moore .60
87 Marion Motley .60
88 George Musso .35
89 Bronko Nagurski .75
90 Earl "Greasy" Neale .35
91 Ernie Nevers .50
92 Ray Nitschke .50
93 Leo Nomellini .50
94 Merlin Olsen .75
95 Jim Otto .50
96 Steve Owen .35
97 Clarence (Ace) Parker .35
98 Jim Parker .50
99 Joe Perry .60
100 Pete Pihos .50
101 Hugh (Shorty) Ray .35
102 Dan Reeves (OWN) .35
103 Jim Ringo .50
104 Andy Robustelli .50
105 Art Rooney .35
106 Gale Sayers 1.25
107 Joe Schmidt .50
108 Bart Starr 1.25
109 Ernie Stautner .50
110 Ken Strong .50
111 Joe Stydahar .35
112 Charley Taylor .50
113 Jim Taylor .60
114 Jim Thorpe 1.25
115 Y.A. Tittle 1.25
116 George Trafton .35
117 Charley Trippi .50
118 Emlen Tunnell .50
119 Clyde "Bulldog" Turner .50
120 Johnny Unitas 1.50
121 Norm Van Brocklin .75
122 Steve Van Buren .60
123 Paul Warfield .50
124 Bob Waterfield .75
125 Arnie Weinmeister .35
126 Bill Willis .35
127 Larry Wilson .50
128 Alex Wojciechowicz .35
129 Pro Football Hall of Fame (Entrance pictured) .35
130A Jim Thorpe Statue 1.00
130B Doak Walker 3.00
131A Enshrinement Galleries .75
131B Willie Lanier 1.75
132 Pro Football HOF on Enshrinement Day (Aerial shot of crowd) .35
133A Eric Dickerson (Display) 1.00
133B Paul Hornung 5.00
134A Walter Payton (Display) 1.50
134B Ken Houston 1.75
135A Super Bowl Display 1.00
135B Fran Tarkenton 5.00
136 Don Maynard 2.50
137 Larry Csonka 5.00
138 Joe Greene 5.00
139 Len Dawson 4.00
140 Gene Upshaw 2.00
141 Jim Langer 1.25
142 John Henry Johnson 1.50

1955 49ers White Border

This 38-card set was available direct from the team as part of a package to fans. Cards are unnumbered and very similar to other issues, except for the text on the back. The fronts feature a black and white posed photo, with the player's signature across the bottom.

NM/M

Complete Set (38): 185.00
Common Player: 3.00
1 Frankie Albert (CO One of Red) 3.00
2 Joe Arenas (The All-Time) 3.00
3 Harry Babcock 3.00
4 Ed Beatty (After searching) 3.00
5 Phil Bengtson (An All-America) 3.00
6 Rex Berry (One of the) 3.00
7 Hardy Brown 7.00
8 Marion Campbell 5.00
9 Al Carapella 3.00
10 Paul Carr (Drafted by) 3.00
11 Maury Duncan 3.00
12 Bob Hantla 3.00
13 Carroll Hardy 3.00
14 Matt Hazeltine (Won All-America) 4.00
15 Red Hickey (CO After 14 years) 4.00
16 Doug Hogland 3.00
17 Bill Johnson (Here's one..with ten lines of text) 3.00
18 John Henry Johnson 18.00
19 Eldred Kraemer 3.00
20 Bud Laughlin 3.00
21 Bobby Luna 3.00
22 George Maderos (The greatest..) 3.00
23 Clay Matthews 4.00
24 Hugh McElhenny (NFL Commissioner) 18.00
25 Dick Moegle (25 text lines) 4.00
26 Leo Nomellini (Leo was..) 14.00
27 Lou Palatella (Like Eldred) 3.00
28 Joe Perry (First man) 18.00
29 Charley Powell (Charley..) 4.00
30 Gordy Soltau (One of the..) 3.00
31 Bob St. Clair (In two years) 14.00
32 Tom Stolhandske 3.00
33 Roy Storey (ANN Bob Fouts ANN and Red Strader Co) 3.00
34 Red Strader (CO) 3.00
35 Y.A. Tittle (Jinxed by...) 20.00
36 Bob Toneff (Rated the..) 3.00
37 Billy Wilson (Named the..) 5.00
38 Sid Youngelman 3.00

1956 49ers White Border

This 29-card set was available direct from the team as part of a package for fans. Many of the cards are similar to other early issues, and are only distinguishable by the text on the back. Cards are black and white posed photos with the player's signature across the bottom.

NM/M

Complete Set (29): 125.00
Common Player: 3.00
1 Frankie Albert (Frank Culling Albert, who..) 3.00
2 Ed Beatty (Traded by..) 3.00
3 Phil Bengtson (Phil is known..) 3.00
4 Rex Berry (Unanimously..) 3.00
5 Bruce Bosley (Bosley was..) 4.00
6 Fred Bruney 3.00
7 Paul Carr (A redshirt..) 3.00
8 Clyde Conner (One of the..) 3.00
9 Paul Goad 3.00
10 Matt Hazeltine (Matt reported..) 3.00
11 Ed Henke (After attending) 3.00
12 Bill Herchman (Bill was..) 3.00
13 Red Hickey (Red Hickey..) 3.00
14 Bill Jessup (Bill is one..) 3.00
15 Bill Johnson (Here's one..with nine lines of text) 3.00
16 George Maderos (A 21st..) 3.00
17 Dick Moegle (San.. with 11 lines of text) 4.00
18 George Morris 3.00
19 Leo Nomellini (A 49er standby..) 14.00
20 Lou Palatella (Most.. same as 1957) 3.00
21 Joe Perry (Joe is..) 18.00
22 Charley Powell (Equipped..) 4.00
23 Leo Rucka 3.00
24 Ed Sharkey 3.00
25 Charles Smith 3.00
26 Gordy Soltau (No all-time) 3.00
27 Bob St. Clair (Tallest man) 10.00
28 Bob Toneff (Another..) 3.00
29 Billy Wilson (Billy is..) 4.00

1957 49ers White Border

As with many other early 49ers issues, this 43-card set is very similar to previous issues, except for the text on the card backs. For the players that were included in the 1956 set, the photos are the same. This issue features the first John Brodie card, which predates his Topps and Fleer rookies by four years.

NM/M

Complete Set (43): 180.00
Common Player: 3.00
1 Frankie Albert (CO Frank Culling Albert played.. same as 1958) 3.00
2 Joe Arenas (Again in 1956..) 3.00
3 Gene Babb (Drafted 19th..) 3.00
4 Larry Barnes 3.00
5 Phil Bengtson (CO Beginning his eighth..) 3.00
6 Bruce Bosley (After a same as 1958) 3.00
7 John Brodie (According to..) 30.00
8 Paul Carr (Versatile on..) 3.00
9 Clyde Conner (Football) 3.00
10 Ted Connolly (The 49er..) 3.00
11 Bob Cross 3.00
12 Mark Duncan (CO Mark.. same as 1958) 3.00
13 Bob Fouts (ANN Lon Simmons ANN and Frankie Albert CO same as 1958) 3.00
14 John Gonzaga (One of the) 3.00
15 Tom Harmon (Kids' ages are 11, 8 and 5) 5.00
16 Matt Hazeltine (An All-American) 3.00
17 Ed Henke (Studious-looking) 3.00
18 Bill Herchman (The 49ers) 3.00
19 Red Hickey (CO After 14 campaigns same as 1958) 3.00
20 Bobby Holladay 3.00
21 Bill Jessup (One of the) 3.00
22 Bill Johnson (CO No all-time same as 1958) 3.00
23 Marv Matuszak (Traded to) 4.00
24 Hugh McElhenny (Sidelined) 14.00
25 Dick Moegle (An with 11 lines of text) 3.00
26 Frank Morze (The 49ers, used) 3.00
27 Leo Nomellini (He was) 10.00
28 R.C. Owens (If the) 5.00
29 Lou Palatella (Most.. same as 1956) 3.00
30 Joe Perry (The greatest) 14.00
31 Charley Powell (Name almost) 3.00
32 Jim Ridlon (Teaming with) 3.00
33 Karl Rubke (The 16th) 3.00
34 J.D. Smith (J.D.'s football) 3.00
35 Gordy Soltau (Already listed) 3.00
36 Bob St. Clair (A born leader) 8.00
37 Bill Stits (An All-American) 3.00
38 Y.A. Tittle (For sheer) 18.00
39 Bob Toneff (After a) 3.00
40 Lynn Waldorf (Director of Personnel Vertical text, same as 1958) 3.00
41 Val Walker 3.00
42 Billy Wilson (Born on) 4.00
43 Bill Johnson, Phil Bengtson, Frankie Albert, Mark Duncan, Red Hickey 49ers Coaches (Blank back, same as 1958) 3.00

1958 49ers White Border

This 44-card set is very similar to other issues and is only distinguishable by the text on the card backs. The cards are in black and white, with posed photos and a signature across the bottom.

NM/M

Complete Set (44): 185.00
Common Player: 3.00
1 Frankie Albert (Frank Culling Albert played same as 1957) 3.00
2 Bill Atkins (Alabama) 3.00
3 Gene Babb (A great) 3.00
4 Phil Bengtson (CO Beginning his 9th) 3.00
5 Bruce Bosley (After a same as 1957) 3.00
6 John Brodie (With John) 18.00
7 Clyde Conner (In signing running pose) 3.00
8 Ted Connolly (When Santa Clara) 3.00

9 Fred Dugan (Butch Dugan) 3.00
10 Mark Duncan (CO Mark same as 1957) 3.00
11 Bob Fouts (Lon Simmons ANN and Frankie Albert CO same as 1957) 3.00
12 John Gonzaga (Recommended) 3.00
13 Tom Harmon (ANN Kids' ages are 12, 9 and 6) 4.00
14 Matt Hazeltine (Improved) 4.00
15 Ed Henke (The Frank Buck) 3.00
16 Bill Herchman (A lineman's) 3.00
17 Red Hickey (CO After 14 campaigns same as 1957) 3.00
18 Bill Jessup (Hard luck) 3.00
19 Bill Johnson (No all-time same as 1957) 3.00
20 Marv Matuszak (The best) 4.00
21 Hugh McElhenny (More people) 14.00
22 Jerry Mertens (A 20th draft selection, Jerry) 3.00
23 Dick Moegle (13 text lines) 3.00
24 Dennit Morris 3.00
25 Frank Morze (The 49ers drafted) 3.00
26 Leo Nomellini (Defensive) 10.00
27 R.C. Owens (There's always) 5.00
28 Jim Pace 3.00
29 Lou Palatella (When) 3.00
30 Joe Perry (The all-time) 12.00
31 Jim Ridlon (After a) 3.00
32 Karl Rubke (Desperately) 3.00
33 J.D. Smith (Used mainly) 3.00
34 Gordy Soltau (In the eight) 3.00
35 Bob St. Clair (The only) 8.00
36 Bill Stits (When the) 3.00
37 John Thomas (This is) 3.00
38 Y.A. Tittle (His real) 18.00
39 Bob Toneff (A chronic) 3.00
40 Lynn Waldorf (Director of Personnel Vertical text same as 1957) 3.00
41 Billy Wilson (Em Tunnell, great) 3.00
42 John Wittenborn (John) 3.00
43 Abe Woodson (The 49ers) 5.00
44 Bill Johnson, Phil Bengtson, Frankie Albert, Mark Duncan, Red Hickey 49ers Coachers (Blank back, same as 1957) 3.00

1959 49ers White Border

This 45-card set is very similar to other team issues around this time and can only be distinguished by the text on the back. Sets were available as part of a package available to fans. Fronts feature a black and white posed photo with a signature across the bottom.

NM/M
Complete Set (45): 185.00
Common Player: 3.00
1 Bill Atkins (Played defensive) 3.00
2 Dave Baker 3.00
3 Bruce Bosley (Starred as) 3.00
4 John Brodie (Led NFL) 18.00
5 Jack Christiansen (CO) 8.00
6 Monte Clark 4.00
7 Clyde Conner (Standing pose, uniform number 88) 3.00
8 Ted Connolly (Realized his) 3.00
9 Tommy Davis 4.00
10 Eddie Dove 3.00
11 Fred Dugan (Made) 3.00
12 Mark Duncan (CO A versatile) 3.00
13 Bob Fouts (ANN) 3.00
14 John Gonzaga (One of few) 3.00
15 Bob Harrison 3.00
16 Matt Hazeltine (One of the) 3.00
17 Ed Henke (Suffered a) 3.00
18 Bill Herchman (Starting) 3.00
19 Red Hickey (Baseball) 3.00
20 Russ Hodges (ANN) 4.00
21 Bill Johnson (CO Bill Johnson) 3.00
22 Charlie Krueger 3.00
23 Lenny Lyles 3.00
24 Hugh McElhenny (One of the) 14.00
25 Jerry Mertens (A 20th draft selection last) 3.00
26 Dick Moegle (7 text lines) 4.00
27 Frank Morze (Transferred) 3.00
28 Leo Nomellini (Has never) 10.00
29 Clancy Osborne 3.00
30 R.C. Owens (Have football) 5.00
31 Joe Perry (Football's) 14.00
32 Jim Ridlon (Showed) 3.00
33 Karl Rubke (Started his) 3.00
34 Bob St. Clair (Tallest player) 8.00
35 Henry Schmidt 3.00
36 Bob Shaw (CO) 3.00
37 Lon Simmons (ANN) 3.00
38 J.D. Smith (One of the) 3.00
39 John Thomas (Didn't make) 3.00
40 Y.A. Tittle (In 11 years) 18.00
41 Jerry Tubbs 4.00
42 Lynn Waldorf (Director of Personnel Horizontal text) 3.00
43 Billy Wilson (Emlen Tunnell, 12-year) 4.00
44 John Wittenborn (Handy) 3.00
45 Abe Woodson (Received) 4.00

1960 49ers White Border

This 44-card set was available through a package offered to fans and is similar to other issues in that time span, and can be distinguished by the text on the back. Players are featured in black and white posed photos, with a facsimile signature across the photo.

NM/M
Complete Set (44): 185.00
Common Player: 3.00
1 Dave Baker (David Lee Baker) 3.00
2 Bruce Bosley (Born in Fresno) 3.00
3 John Brodie (This could be) 14.00
4 Jack Christiansen (ACO) 8.00
5 Monte Clark (A special chapter) 5.00
6 Dan Colchico (Big Dan) 3.00
7 Clyde Conner (Clyde Raymond) 3.00
8 Ted Connolly (When Theodore) 3.00
9 Tommy Davis (San Francisco) 4.00
10 Eddie Dove (Edward Everett) 3.00
11 Mark Duncan (ACO A versatile) 3.00
12 Bob Fouts (ANN) 3.00
13 Bob Harrison (There is no more) 3.00
14 Matt Hazeltine (Matthew Hazeltine) 3.00
15 Ed Henke (Desire and) 3.00
16 Red Hickey (CO Baseball) 3.00
17 Russ Hodges (ANN) 3.00
18 Bill Johnson (CO Bill Johnson) 3.00
19 Gordon Kelley (This Southern) 3.00
20 Charlie Krueger (The 49ers) 4.00
21 Lenny Lyles (Leonard Lyles) 3.00
22 Hugh McElhenny (San Francisco's) 14.00
23 Mike Magac (Mike was) 3.00
24 Jerry Mertens (Jerome William) 3.00
25 Frank Morze (Anyone with) 3.00
26 Leo Nomellini (Leo Joseph) 10.00
27 Clancy Osborne (Desire) 4.00
28 R.C. Owens (Few players) 5.00
29 Jim Ridlon (James Ridlon) 3.00
30 C.R. Roberts (After trials) 3.00
31 Len Rohde (Len, a three) 3.00
32 Karl Rubke (Only 20 years) 3.00
33 Bob St. Clair (Robert Bruce) 8.00
34 Henry Schmidt (After two years) 3.00
35 Lon Simmons (ANN) 3.00
36 J.D. Smith (In J.D. Smith) 4.00
37 Gordy Soltau (ANN) 3.00
38 Monty Stickles (The football) 3.00
39 John Thomas (Noted more) 3.00
40 Y.A. Tittle (When Yelberton) 18.00
41 Lynn Waldorf (Director of Personnel) 3.00
42 Bobby Waters (A smart) 5.00
43 Billy Wilson (Only Don Hutson) 4.00
44 Abe Woodson (A Big 10) 4.00

1968 49ers White Border

This 35-card oversized set measures 8-1/2" x 11" and displays different 49ers players in posed, black and white photos. Card backs are blank, with no card numbers listed either. In addition, Steve Spurrier's card in this set predates his rookie by four years.

NM/M
Complete Set (35): 125.00
Common Player: 2.50
1 Kermit Alexander 2.50
2 Cas Banaszek 2.50
3 Ed Beard 2.50
4 Forrest Blue 4.00
5 Bruce Bosley 4.00
6 John Brodie 10.00
7 Elmer Collett 2.50
8 Doug Cunningham 2.50
9 Tommy Davis 4.00
10 Kevin Hardy 2.50
11 Matt Hazeltine 4.00
12 Stan Hindman 2.50
13 Tom Holzer 2.50
14 Jim Johnson 8.00
15 Charlie Krueger 4.00
16 Roland Lakes 2.50
17 Gary Lewis 2.50
18 Kay McFarland 2.50
19 Clifton McNeil 4.00
20 George Mira 5.00
21 Howard Mudd 2.50
22 Dick Nolan (CO) 4.00
23 Frank Nunley 2.50
24 Don Parker 2.50
25 Mel Phillips 4.00
26 Al Randolph 2.50
27 Len Rohde 2.50
28 Steve Spurrier 28.00
29 John Thomas 2.50
30 Bill Tucker 2.50
31 Dave Wilcox 4.00
32 Ken Willard 4.00
33 Bob Windsor 4.00
34 Dick Witcher 4.00
35 Team Photo 10.00

1972 49ers Redwood City Tribune

This six-card set measures 3" x 5-1/2" and contains a head shot of the featured player in black and white with white borders. There is a large white space below the photo that contains a facsimile autograph. Cards are unnumbered and listed below in alphabetical order.

NM/M
Complete Set (6): 50.00
Common Player: 8.00
1 Frank Edwards 8.00
2 Frank Nunley 8.00
3 Len Rohde 8.00
4 Larry Schrieber 8.00
5 Steve Spurrier 30.00
6 Gene Washington 12.00

1982 49ers Team Issue

This 5" x 8" set has 44 cards in black and white with white borders. The backs of the cards are blank and unnumbered.

NM/M
Complete Set (44): 55.00
Common Player: 1.00
1 Dan Audick 1.00
2 John Ayers 1.00
3 Guy Benjamin 1.00
4 Dwaine Board 1.00
5 Ken Bungarda 1.00
6 Dan Bunz 1.00
7 Dwight Clark 4.00
8 Ricky Churchman 1.00
9 Earl Cooper 1.00
10 Randy Cross 1.50
11 Johnny Davis 1.00
12 Fred Dean 1.00
13 Walt Downing 1.00
14 Walt Easley 1.00
15 Lenvil Elliott 1.00
16 Keith Fahnhorst 1.00
17 Rick Gervais 1.00
18 Willie Harper 1.00
19 John Harty 1.00
20 Pete Kugler 1.00
21 Amos Lawrence 1.00
22 Bobby Leopold 1.00
23 Saladin Martin 1.00
24 Milt McColl 1.00
25 Jim Miller 1.00
26 Joe Montana 22.00
27 Ricky Patton 1.00
28 Lawrence Pillers 1.00
29 Craig Puki 1.00
30 Fred Quillan 1.00
31 Eason Ramson 1.00
32 Archie Reese 1.00
33 Jack Reynolds 1.00
34 Mike Shumann 1.00
35 Freddie Solomon 1.50
36 Scott Stauch 1.00
37 Jim Stuckey 1.00
38 Lynn Thomas 1.00
39 Keena Turner 1.25
40 Ray Wersching 1.00
41 Carlton Williamson 1.00
42 Mike Wilson 1.00
43 Eric Wright 1.00
44 Charlie Young 1.00

1984 49ers Police

This 12-card set was issued in three panels of four cards each and measures 2-1/2" x 4". The set is unnumbered and sponsored by 7-Eleven, Dr. Pepper and KCB's.

NM/M
Complete Set (12): 25.00
Common Player: 1.00
1 Dwaine Board 1.00
2 Roger Craig 3.50
3 Riki Ellison 1.00
4 Keith Fahnhorst 1.00
5 Joe Montana, Dwight Clark 10.00
6 Jack Reynolds 1.00
7 Freddie Solomon 1.00
8 Keena Turner 1.00
9 Wendall Tyler 1.00
10 Bill Walsh (CO) 3.00
11 Ray Wersching 1.00
12 Eric Wright 1.00

1985 49ers Police

This 16-card set was issued in four panels of four cards each, and is very similar to the 1984 set except its sponsored only by Dr. Pepper and 7-Eleven. The cards are unnumbered and measure 2-1/2" x 4".

NM/M
Complete Set (16): 18.00
Common Player: .50
1 John Ayers .50
2 Roger Craig 2.00
3 Fred Dean .75
4 Riki Ellison .50
5 Keith Fahnhorst .50
6 Russ Francis .75
7 Dwight Hicks .50
8 Ronnie Lott 1.75
9 Dana McLemore .50
10 Joe Montana 10.00
11 Todd Shell .50
12 Freddie Solomon .75
13 Keena Turner .50
14 Bill Walsh (CO) 1.50
15 Ray Wersching .50
16 Eric Wright .50

1985 49ers Smokey

This seven-card oversized set measures approximately 3" x 4-3/8". It was issued by the 49ers and Smokey Bear, and features a cartoon fire safety tip and a facsimile signature of the player on the back.

NM/M
Complete Set (7): 30.00
Common Player: 2.00
1 Group Picture with (Smokey Player list on back of card) 6.00
2 Joe Montana 18.00
3 Jack Reynolds 3.00
4 Eric Wright 2.00
5 Dwight Hicks 2.00
6 Dwight Clark 4.00
7 Keena Turner 2.00

1988 49ers Police

This 20-card set included 19 players and one coach card and was sponsored by 7-Eleven and Oscar Mayer. The fronts are almost full-bleed photos with a thin white border. Backs have a football tip and a McGruff crime tip.

NM/M
Complete Set (20): 20.00
Common Player: .50
1 Harris Barton .75
2 Dwaine Board .50
3 Michael Carter .75
4 Roger Craig 1.50
5 Randy Cross .75
6 Riki Ellison .50
7 John Frank .50
8 Jeff Fuller .50
9 Pete Kugler .50
10 Ronnie Lott 2.00
11 Joe Montana 8.00
12 Tom Rathman 1.75
13 Jerry Rice 8.00
14 Jeff Stover .50
15 Keena Turner .75
16 Bill Walsh (CO) 1.50
17 Michael Walter .50
18 Mike Wilson .50
19 Eric Wright .75
20 Steve Young 8.00

1988 49ers Smokey

This 35-card set was printed on a 5" x 8" format and is unnumbered, except for the uniform number. Fronts feature a full-bleed shot with a thin white border around the inside of the card. Backs have a fire safety cartoon usually featuring Smokey the Bear.

NM/M
Complete Set (35): 100.00
Common Player: 1.00
1 Harris Barton 1.50
2 Dwaine Board (SP) 8.00
3 Michael Carter 1.50
4 Bruce Collie 1.00
5 Roger Craig 3.50
6 Randy Cross 1.75
7 Eddie DeBartolo (Jr Owner, President) 2.50
8 Riki Ellison 1.00
9 Kevin Fagan 1.00
10 Jim Fahnhorst 1.00
11 John Frank 1.00
12 Jeff Fuller 1.00
13 Don Griffin 1.50
14 Charles Haley 3.00
15 Ron Heller 1.00
16 Tom Holmoe 1.00
17 Pete Kugler 1.00
18 Ronnie Lott 4.00
19 Tim McKyer 1.50
20 Joe Montana 20.00
21 Tory Nixon 1.00
22 Bubba Paris 1.00
23 John Paye 1.00
24 Tom Rathman 3.00
25 Jerry Rice 20.00
26 Jeff Stover 1.00
27 Harry Sydney 1.00
28 John Taylor 4.00
29 Keena Turner 1.50
30 Steve Wallace 1.50
31 Bill Walsh (CO) 3.00
32 Michael Walter 1.00
33 Mike Wilson 1.00
34 Eric Wright 1.50
35 Steve Young 20.00

1990-91 49ers SF Examiner

This 16-card set was issued on two unperforated sheets measuring 14" x 11", and was issued by the San Francisco Examiner. Eight-card panels included a newspaper headline across the top reading "San Francisco Examiner Salutes the 49ers' Finest." Card fronts are in color with a thin orange border on the red-face card. Backs are horizontal and black and white with a head shot and stats.

NM/M
Complete Set (16): 10.00
Common Player: .50
1 Harris Barton .75
2 Michael Carter .50
3 Mike Cofer .50
4 Roger Craig 1.00
5 Kevin Fagan .50
6 Don Griffin .50
7 Charles Haley 1.25
8 Pierce Holt .50
9 Brent Jones 1.25
10 Ronnie Lott 1.25
11 Guy McIntyre .50
12 Matt Millen .75
13 Joe Montana 4.00
14 Tom Rathman 1.00
15 Jerry Rice 4.00
16 John Taylor 1.50

1992 49ers FBI

This 40-card set was available in different packs for free with 49ers' edition of GameDay Magazine at regular-season home games each week at Candlestick Park. The set was sponsored by the 49ers and the FBI and contains a public service message on the back in the form of a player quote.

NM/M
Complete Set (40): 45.00
Common Player: .50
1 Michael Carter .50
2 Kevin Fagan .50
3 Charles Haley 1.00
4 Guy McIntyre .50
5 George Seifert (CO) 1.00
6 Harry Sydney .50
7 John Taylor 1.00
8 Mike Walter .50
9 Steve Young 10.00
10 Mike Cofer .50
11 Keith DeLong .50
12 Don Griffin .50
13 Pierce Holt .50
14 Mike Sherrard .75
15 Larry Roberts .50
16 Bill Romanowski .50
17 Tom Rathman 1.00
18 Jesse Sapolu .75
19 Brent Jones 1.25
20 Brian Bollinger .50
21 Eric Davis .50
22 Antonio Goss .50
23 Alan Grant .50
24 Harris Barton .75
25 Ricky Watters 4.00
26 Darin Jordan .50
27 Odessa Turner .50
28 David Wilkins .50
29 Merton Hanks 1.00
30 David Whitmore .50
31 Joe Montana 10.00
32 Klaus Wilmsmeyer .50
33 Tim Harris .75
34 Roy Foster .50
35 Bill Musgrave .75
36 Dana Hall .75
37 Steve Wallace .75
38 Steve Bono 4.00
39 Jerry Rice 10.00
NNO Title Card 1.00

1994 49ers Pro Mags/Pro Tags

49ers Pro Mags and Pro Tags were each a six-card set issued in a black cardboard box and numbered out of 750. Each card is borderless and contains a gold-foil Super Bowl XXIX logo printed in the lower right corner. The tags feature Roman numerals XXIX in back of a superimposed shot of the player. Magnet backs are black and blank, Tags backs have a color close-up photo, an autograph strip and a player profile. The magnets are listed 1-6, while the tags are 7-12.

NM/M
Complete Set (12): 20.00
Common Player: 1.00
1 Ken Norton 1.00
2 Jerry Rice 4.00
3 Deion Sanders 2.50
4 John Taylor 1.00
5 Ricky Watters 1.50
6 Steve Young 3.00
7 Ken Norton 1.00
8 Jerry Rice 4.00
9 Deion Sanders 2.50
10 John Taylor 1.00
11 Ricky Watters 1.50
12 Steve Young 3.00

1996 49ers Save Mart

This nine-card set celebrates the 49ers' star Super Bowl players. Each full-bleed card front includes an action shot of the player, with his last name and San Francisco logo appearing along the right border. Each card back includes the 50-year anniversary and 49ers' logos along with the checklist. The Save Mart and UPI Marketing Inc. logos appear at the bottom, with the card number located in the lower right. One card and one coin were sold in each cello pack. The coins feature the player's likeness, name, team, years with the team and his jersey number on the front. The reverse side of the coin boasts the 49ers' 50-year logo. A coin holder was also given away.

NM/M
Complete Set (9): 12.00
Common Player: .50
1 Steve Young 3.00
2 Roger Craig 1.00
3 Jerry Rice 4.00
4 Ronnie Lott 1.00
5 Ken Norton Jr. .50
6 Dwight Clark .50
7 Brent Jones .50
8 Joe Montana 5.00
9 Super Bowl 1.00

1997 49ers Score

		NM/M
Complete Set (15):		10.00
Common Player:		.50
1	Jerry Rice	3.00
2	Steve Young	2.00
3	Garrison Hearst	1.00
4	Terry Kirby	.50
5	Brent Jones	.50
6	J.J. Stokes	.75
7	Terrell Owens	1.50
8	William Floyd	1.00
9	Ken Norton	.50
10	Bryant Young	.50
11	Dana Stubblefield	.50
12	Ted Popson	.50
13	Roy Barker	.50
14	Tyronne Drakeford	.50
15	Merton Hanks	.50

1989 Franchise Game

The 1989 Franchise Game is modeled after Monopoly, with players beginning with a sum of money and traveling around the board acquiring different players to fill out a 23-man roster. There are 304 players depicted and 28 different NFL teams. Fronts have the player's name, team, point value and salary. Backs contain the player's position written at the top, as well as a large acronym for the position in the middle of the player's city. Franchise was produced by Rohrwood Enterprises.

		NM/M
Complete Set (332):		200.00
Common Player:		.60
1	Neal Anderson	.60
2	Kevin Butler	.60
3	Jimbo Covert	.60
4	Dave Duerson	.60
5	Dan Hampton	1.00
6	Jay Hilgenberg	.60
7	Mike Richardson	.60
8	Ron Rivera	.60
9	Mike Singletary	1.00
10	Mike Tomczak	1.00
11	Keith Van Horne	.60
12	Lewis Billups	.60
13	Jim Breech	.60
14	James Brooks	.75
15	Eddie Brown	.60
16	Ross Browner	.60
17	Jason Buck	.60
18	Cris Collinsworth	.75
19	Eddie Edwards	.60
20	Boomer Esiason	.75
21	David Fulcher	.60
22	Ray Horton	.60
23	Tim Krumrie	.60
24	Max Montoya	.60
25	Anthony Munoz	1.50
26	Jim Skow	.60
27	Reggie Williams	.60
28	Ickey Woods	.60
29	Cornelius Bennett	1.00
30	Shane Conlan	1.00
31	Joe Devlin	.60
32	Nate Odomes	.60
33	Scott Norwood	.60
34	Andre Reed	1.50
35	Jim Ritcher	.60
36	Fred Smerlas	.60
37	Bruce Smith	1.50
38	Art Still	.60
39	Keith Bishop	.60
40	Bill Bryan	.60
41	Tony Dorsett	3.00
42	Simon Fletcher	.60
43	Mike Harden	.60
44	Mark Haynes	.60
45	Mike Horan	.60
46	Vance Johnson	.75
47	Rulon Jones	.60
48	Rich Karlis	.60
49	Karl Mecklenburg	1.00
50	Dennis Smith	.60
51	Dave Studdard	.60
52	Andre Townsend	.60
53	Steve Watson	.60
54	Sammy Winder	.60
55	Matt Bahr	.60
56	Rickey Bolden	.60
57	Earnest Byner	.75
58	Sam Clancy	.60
59	Hanford Dixon	.60
60	Bob Golic	.60
61	Carl Hairston	.60
62	Eddie Johnson	.60
63	Kevin Mack	.60
64	Clay Matthews	.75
65	Frank Minnifield	.60
66	Ozzie Newsome	1.00
67	Cody Risien	.60
68	John Cannon	.60
69	Ron Holmes	.60
70	Winston Moss	.60
71	Rob Taylor	.60
72	Joe Bostic	.60
73	Roy Green	.75
74	Ricky Hunley	.60
75	E.J. Junior	.60
76	Neil Lomax	.60
77	Tim McDonald	.60
78	Cedric Mack	.60
79	Freddie Joe Nunn	.60
80	Gary Anderson	.75
81	Keith Baldwin	.60
82	Gill Byrd	.60
83	Elvis Patterson	.60
84	Gary Plummer	.60
85	Billy Ray Smith	.60
86	Lee Williams	.60
87	Mike Bell	.60
88	Lloyd Burruss	.60
89	Carlos Carson	.60
90	Deron Cherry	.60
91	Jack Del Rio	.60
92	Irv Eatman	.60
93	Dino Hackett	.60
94	Bill Kenney	.60
95	Albert Lewis	.60
96	David Lutz	.60
97	Bill Maas	.60
98	Stephone Paige	.75
99	Neil Smith	1.50
100	Dean Biasucci	.60
101	Duane Bickett	.60
102	Chris Chandler	1.50
103	Eugene Daniel	.60
104	Ray Donaldson	.60
105	Jon Hand	.60
106	Chris Hinton	.60
107	Joe Klecko	.60
108	Cliff Odom	.60
109	Rohn Stark	.60
110	Donnell Thompson	.60
111	Willie Tullis	.60
112	Freddie Young	.60
113	Michael Downs	.60
114	Michael Irvin	3.00
115	Jim Jeffcoat	.60
116	Ed "Too Tall" Jones	1.00
117	Tom Rafferty	.60
118	Herschel Walker	1.25
119	Everson Walls	.60
120	Danny White	.75
121	Randy White	1.50
122	Bob Brudzinski	.60
123	Mark Clayton	.75
124	Mark Duper	1.00
125	Ron Jaworski	1.00
126	Paul Lankford	.60
127	Dan Marino	14.00
128	John Offerdahl	.60
129	Reggie Roby	.60
130	Dwight Stephenson	.60
131	Randall Cunningham	.75
132	Ron Heller	.60
133	Mike Quick	.75
134	Ken Reeves	.60
135	Dave Rimington	.60
136	Reggie Singletary	.60
137	Andre Waters	.60
138	Reggie White	2.00
139	Roynell Young	.60
140	Aundray Bruce	.60
141	Bobby Butler	.60
142	Bill Fralic	.60
143	Mike Kenn	.60
144	Chris Miller	.60
145	John Settle	.60
146	George Yarno	.60
147	Michael Carter	.60
148	Wes Chandler	1.00
149	Roger Craig	1.50
150	Randy Cross	.60
151	Riki Ellison	.60
152	Jim Fahnhorst	.60
153	Charles Haley	1.50
154	Barry Helton	.60
155	Guy McIntyre	.75
156	Tim McKyer	.60
157	Joe Montana	10.00
158	Jerry Rice	10.00
159	Keena Turner	.60
160	Eric Wright	.60
161	Steve Young	10.00
162	Raul Allegre	.60
163	Ottis Anderson	.75
164	Billy Ard	.60
165	Carl Banks	.60
166	Mark Bavaro	.75
167	Jim Burt	.60
168	Harry Carson	.75
169	John Elliott	.60
170	Terry Kinard	.60
171	Sean Landeta	.60
172	Lionel Manuel	.60
173	Joe Morris	.75
174	Bart Oates	.60
175	Phil Simms	1.00
176	Pat Leahy	.60
177	Marty Lyons	.60
178	Erik McMillan	.60
179	Freeman McNeil	1.00
180	Scott Mersereau	.60
181	Ken O'Brien	.60
182	Jim Sweeney	.60
183	Al Toon	.75
184	Wesley Walker	.75
185	Jim Arnold	.60
186	Bennie Blades	.60
187	Mike Cofer	.60
188	Keith Ferguson	.60
189	Steve Mott	.60
190	Eddie Murray	.75
191	Harvey Salem	.60
192	Bobby Watkins	.60
193	Keith Bostic	.60
194	Richard Byrd	.60
195	Ray Childress	.75
196	Ernest Givins	.75
197	Kenny Johnson	.75
198	Sean Jones	.75
199	Robert Lyles	.75
200	Bruce Matthews	.75
201	Johnny Meads	.60
202	Warren Moon	2.00
203	Mike Munchak	.75
204	Mike Rozier	.60
205	Dean Steinkuhler	.60
206	Tony Zendejas	.60
207	Mark Cannon	.60
208	Alphonso Carreker	.60
209	Phillip Epps	.60
210	Tim Harris	.75
211	Brian Noble	.60
212	Raymond Clayborn	.60
213	Steve Grogan	.75
214	Roland James	.60
215	Fred Marion	.60
216	Stanley Morgan	.75
217	Kenneth Sims	.60
218	Andre Tippett	.75
219	Marcus Allen	2.00
220	Chris Bahr	.60
221	Steve Beuerlein	.75
222	Tim Brown	4.00
223	Todd Christensen	.75
224	Ron Fellows	.60
225	Willie Gault	.75
226	Mike Haynes	.75
227	Bo Jackson	2.00
228	James Lofton	1.50
229	Howie Long	1.50
230	Vann McElroy	.60
231	Rod Martin	.60
232	Matt Millen	.75
233	Bill Pickel	.60
234	Jay Schroeder	.75
235	Stacey Toran	.60
236	Greg Townsend	.75
237	Greg Bell	.60
238	Henry Ellard	1.25
239	Jerry Gray	.60
240	Leroy Irvin	.60
241	Gary Jeter	.60
242	Johnnie Johnson	.60
243	Larry Kelm	.60
244	Mike Lansford	.60
245	Shawn Miller	.60
246	Mel Owens	.60
247	Jackie Slater	.60
248	Charles White	.60
249	Jeff Bostic	.60
250	Kelvin Bryant	.60
251	Dave Butz	.60
252	Gary Clark	1.50
253	Steve Cox	.60
254	Darryl Grant	.60
255	Darrell Green	.75
256	Joe Jacoby	.60
257	Mel Kaufman	.60
258	Jim Lachey	.60
259	Dexter Manley	.60
260	Charles Mann	.60
261	Mark May	.60
262	Art Monk	1.50
263	Ricky Sanders	.75
264	Alvin Walton	.60
265	Doug Williams	.75
266	Morten Andersen	.60
267	Bruce Clark	.60
268	Jim Dombrowski	.60
269	Mel Gray	.75
270	Bobby Hebert	.75
271	Rickey Jackson	.60
272	Van Jakes	.60
273	Steve Korte	.60
274	Rueben Mayes	.60
275	Sam Mills	.75
276	Dave Waymer	.60
277	Jeff Bryant	.60
278	Blair Bush	.60
279	Jacob Green	.60
280	Melvin Jenkins	.60
281	Norm Johnson	.60
282	Dave Krieg	.75
283	Bryan Millard	.60
284	Ruben Rodriquez	.60
285	Terry Taylor	.60
286	Curt Warner	1.00
287	Tony Woods	.60
288	Gary Anderson	.60
289	Tunch Ilkin	.60
290	Earnest Jackson	.60
291	Louis Lipps	.60
292	Mike Webster	.75
293	Rod Woodson	3.00
294	Joey Browner	.60
295	Anthony Carter	1.25
296	Chris Doleman	.75
297	Tim Irwin	.60
298	Tommy Kramer	.75
299	Carl Lee	.60
300	Kirk Lowdermilk	.60
301	Keith Millard	.60
302	Scott Studwell	.60
303	Wade Wilson	.75
304	Gary Zimmerman	.60
T1	Atlanta Falcons Team Helmet	.60
T2	Buffalo Bills	.60
T3	Chicago Bears	.60
T4	Cincinnati Bengals	.60
T5	Cleveland Browns	.60
T6	Dallas Cowboys	.75
T7	Denver Broncos	.60
T8	Detroit Lions	.60
T9	Green Bay Packers	.60
T10	Houston Oilers	.60
T11	Indianapolis Colts	.60
T12	Kansas City Chiefs	.60
T13	Los Angeles Raiders	.75
T14	Los Angeles Rams	.60
T15	Miami Dolphins	.75
T16	Minnesota Vikings	.60
T17	New England Patriots	.60
T18	New Orleans Saints	.60
T19	New York Giants	.60
T20	New York Jets	.60
T21	Philadelphia Eagles	.60
T22	Phoenix Cardinals	.60
T23	Pittsburgh Steelers	.60
T24	San Diego Chargers	.60
T25	San Francisco 49ers	.60
T26	Seattle Seahawks	.60
T27	Tampa Bay Buccaneers	.60
T28	Washington Redskins	.60

1993 Front Row Gold Collection

The 10-card, standard-size set features "Gold Collection" in gold foil on the card front over the color action photo. The card backs have another borderless color photo with a brief player summary (odd-numbered) and bio and stat information (even-numbered). Each of the 5,000 sets produced came with a certificate of authenticity.

		NM/M
Complete Set (10):		5.00
Common Player:		.50
1	Eric Curry	.75
2	Eric Curry	.75
3	Lincoln Kennedy	.50
4	Lincoln Kennedy	.50
5	O.J. McDuffie	1.00
6	O.J. McDuffie	1.00
7	Qadry Ismail	1.00
8	Qadry Ismail	1.00
9	Andre Hastings	1.00
10	Andre Hastings	1.00

1956 Giants Team Issue

This 36-card, black and white set contains posed player shots on the front surrounded by a white border and a facsimile signature. Backs are unnumbered, while each card measures approximately 5" x 7".

		NM/M
Complete Set (36):		200.00
Common Player:		4.00
1	Bill Austin	4.00
2	Ray Beck	4.00
3	Roosevelt Brown	10.00
4	Hank Burnine	4.00
5	Don Chandler	4.00
6	Bobby Clatterbuck	4.00
7	Charley Conerly	20.00
8	Frank Gifford	30.00
9	Rosevelt Grier	10.00
10	Don Heinrich	5.00
11	John Hermann	4.00
12	Jim Lee Howell (CO)	5.00
13	Sam Huff	16.00
14	Ed Hughes	4.00
15	Gerald Huth	4.00
16	Jim Katcavage	6.00
17	Gene Kirby (ANN)	4.00
18	Ken MacAfee	5.00
19	Dick Modzelewski (Misspelled Modelewski on the reverse)	5.00
20	Henry Moore	4.00
21	Dick Nolan	5.00
22	Jimmy Patton	5.00
23	Andy Robustelli	10.00
24	Kyle Rote	10.00
25	Chris Schenkel (ANN)	5.00
26	Bob Schnelker	4.00
27	Jack Stroud	4.00
28	Harland Svare	5.00
29	Bill Svoboda	4.00
30	Bob Topp	4.00
31	Mel Triplett	5.00
32	Emlen Tunnell	10.00
33	Alex Webster	5.00
34	Ray Wietecha	4.00
35	Dick Yelvington	4.00
36	Walt Yowarsky	4.00

1957 Giants Team Issue

This 1957 Giants team set measures approximately 5" x 7", with black and white photos and a glossy finish. The set contains 40 unnumbered cards that are listed below in alphabetical order.

		NM/M
Complete Set (40):		250.00
Common Player:		4.00
1	Ben Agajanian	4.00
2	Bill Austin	4.00
3	Ray Beck	4.00
4	John Bookman	4.00
5	Roosevelt Brown	8.00
6	Don Chandler	5.00
7	Bobby Clatterbuck	4.00
8	Charley Conerly	15.00
9	John Dell Isola (CO)	4.00
10	Gene Filipski	5.00
11	Frank Gifford	25.00
12	Don Heinrich	5.00
13	Jim Lee Howell (CO)	5.00
14	Sam Huff	10.00
15	Ed Hughes	4.00
16	Gerald Huth	4.00
17	Jim Katcavage	5.00
18	Ken Kavanaugh (CO)	5.00
19	Les Keiter (ANN)	4.00
20	Tom Landry (CO)	45.00
21	Cliff Livingston	4.00
22	Vince Lombardi (CO)	50.00
23	Ken MacAfee	5.00
24	Dennis Mendyk	4.00
25	Dick Modzelewski	5.00
26	Dick Nolan	5.00
27	Jim Patton	5.00
28	Andy Robustelli	10.00
29	Kyle Rote	10.00
30	Chris Schenkel (ANN)	5.00
31	Jack Spinks	4.00
32	Jack Stroud	4.00
33	Harland Svare	4.00
34	Bill Svoboda	4.00
35	Mel Triplett	5.00
36	Emlen Tunnell	8.00
37	Alex Webster	5.00
38	Ray Wietecha	5.00
39	Dick Yelvington	4.00
40	Walt Yowarsky	4.00

1960 Giants Jay Publishing

This 12-card set shows players in black and white on 5" x 7" cards. Cards were sold in 12-card packs and have blank, unnumbered backs.

		NM/M
Complete Set (12):		85.00
Common Player:		4.00
1	Roosevelt Brown	8.00
2	Don Chandler	4.00
3	Charley Conerly	8.00
4	Frank Gifford	20.00
5	Roosevelt Grier	8.00
6	Sam Huff	10.00
7	Phil King	4.00
8	Andy Robustelli	6.00
9	Kyle Rote	6.00
10	Bob Schnelker	4.00
11	Pat Summerall	6.00
12	Alex Webster	5.00

1960 Giants Shell/ Riger Posters

This set features 10 black and white posters by Robert Siger and distributed by Shell Oil in 1960. Each poster measures approximately 11-3/4" x 13-3/4".

		NM/M
Complete Set (10):		150.00
Common Player:		10.00
1	Charley Connerly	25.00
2	Frank Gifford	45.00
3	Sam Huff	20.00
4	Dick Modzelewski	10.00
5	Jim Patton	10.00
6	Andy Robustelli	16.00
7	Kyle Rote	16.00
8	Bob Schnelker	10.00
9	Pat Summerall	20.00
10	Alex Webster, Roosevelt Brown	16.00

1961 Giants Jay Publishing

Similar to the 1960 issue, this 12-card set is composed of black and white, 5" x 7" photos. It features traditional players and was available in 12-card packs.

		NM/M
Complete Set (12):		65.00
Common Player:		4.00
1	Roosevelt Brown	10.00
2	Don Chandler	4.00
3	Charley Conerly	10.00
4	Roosevelt Grier	8.00
5	Sam Huff	10.00
6	Dick Modzelewski	4.00
7	Jimmy Patton	5.00
8	Jim Podoley	4.00
9	Andy Robustelli	8.00
10	Allie Sherman (CO)	4.00
11	Del Shofner	5.00
12	Y.A. Tittle	15.00

1973 Giants Color Litho

Measuring 8-1/2" x 11", the eight-card set showcased color lithographs on the front. A facsimile player signature is printed at the bottom right inside a white triangle. The unnumbered cards are not bordered and have blank backs.

		NM/M
Complete Set (8):		50.00
Common Player:		5.00
1	Jim Files	5.00
2	Jack Gregory	5.00
3	Ron Johnson	7.50
4	Greg Larson	5.00
5	Spider Lockhart	7.50
6	Norm Snead	12.00
7	Bob Tucker	7.50
8	Brad Van Pelt	7.50

1987 Giants Police

Measuring 2-3/4" x 4-1/8", the 12-card set is anchored by a large photo on the front, with "New York Giants" printed at the top. Beneath the photo are the player's name and position printed between Giants' helmets. The card backs, which are unnumbered, have "Tips from the Giants" at the top, with two New Jersey law enforcement logos printed below. A safety tip and a McGruff the Crime Dog logo round out the backs. Overall, 10,000 sets were printed.

		NM/M
Complete Set (12):		75.00
Common Player:		3.00
1	Carl Banks	5.00
2	Mark Bavaro	5.00
3	Brad Benson	3.00
4	Jim Burt	3.00
5	Harry Carson	5.00
6	Maurice Carthon	3.00
7	Sean Landeta	3.00
8	Leonard Marshall	5.00
9	George Martin	3.00
10	Joe Morris	6.00
11	Bill Parcells (CO)	8.00
12	Phil Simms	25.00

1988 Giants Police

Measuring 2-3/4" x 4-1/8", the card fronts are anchored by a large photo. A Giants' helmet is printed in both corners at the top, with "New York Giants" located at the top center. Beneath the photo are the player's name, number, position and bio. The unnumbered backs have "Tips from the Giants" at the top, with two New Jersey law enforcement logos located underneath. A safety tip and a McGruff the Crime Dog logo round out the card backs.

		NM/M
Complete Set (12):		55.00
Common Player:		3.00
1	Billy Ard	3.00
2	Jim Burt	3.00
3	Harry Carson	5.00
4	Maurice Carthon	3.00
5	Leonard Marshall	5.00
6	George Martin	3.00
7	Phil McConkey	3.00
8	Joe Morris	6.00
9	Karl Nelson	3.00
10	Bart Oates	5.00
11	Bill Parcells (CO)	8.00
12	Phil Simms	16.00

1990 Giants Police

Measuring 2-3/4" x 4-1/8", the 12-card set is anchored by a large photo on the front, with a Giants' helmet in each of the top corners, with "New York Giants" printed at the top center. The player's name, position and bio are printed under the photo. The card backs, which are unnumbered, have "Tips from the Giants" at the top, with two New Jersey law enforcement logos beneath it. A safety tip and a McGruff the Crime Dog logo round out the card backs.

		NM/M
Complete Set (12):		45.00
Common Player:		2.50
1	Ottis Anderson	5.00
2	Matt Bahr	2.50
3	Eric Dorsey	2.50
4	John Elliott	2.50
5	Ray Handley (CO)	2.50
6	Jeff Hostetler	7.00
7	Erik Howard	2.50
8	Pepper Johnson	4.00
9	Leonard Marshall	4.00
10	Bart Oates	4.00
11	Gary Reasons	2.50
12	Phil Simms	8.00

1992 Giants Police

Measuring 2-3/4" x 4-1/8", the 12-card set is anchored on the front by a large photo and the player's name and bio beneath the photo. "New York Giants" is printed above the photo. The unnumbered card backs have "Tips from the Giants" at the top, a safety tip and a McGruff the Crime Dog logo at the bottom.

		NM/M
Complete Set (12):		20.00
Common Player:		1.00
1	Ottis Anderson	2.00
2	Matt Bahr	1.00
3	Eric Dorsey	1.00
4	John Elliott	1.00
5	Ray Handley (CO)	1.00
6	Jeff Hostetler	3.00
7	Erik Howard	1.00
8	Pepper Johnson	1.50
9	Leonard Marshall	1.50
10	Bart Oates	1.50
11	Gary Reasons	1.00
12	Phil Simms	5.00

1969 Glendale Stamps

These unnumbered stamps, which measure 1-13/16" x 3-15/16", feature a color player photo on the front; the back has his name, team and instructions on how to apply the stamp to the corresponding album which was produced. "Dampen strip and affix in ablum" is on the back. The album measures 9" x 12" and is arranged alphabetically by team city.

		NM/M
Complete Set (312):		200.00
Common Player:		.25

(1) Bob Berry .40
(2) Clark Miller .25
(3) Jim Butler .25
(4) Junior Coffey .25
(5) Paul Flatley .40
(6) Randy Johnson .45
(7) Charlie Bryant .25
(8) Billy Lothridge .25
(9) Tommy Nobis 2.00
(10) Claude Humphrey .40
(11) Ken Reaves .25
(12) Jerry Simmons .40
(13) Mike Curtis .75
(14) Dennis Gaubatz .25
(15) Jerry Logan .25
(16) Lenny Lyles .25
(17) John Mackey 2.00
(18) Tom Matte .50
(19) Lou Michaels .35
(20) Jimmy Orr .50
(21) Willie Richardson .35
(22) Don Shinnick .25
(23) Dan Sullivan .25
(24) Johnny Unitas 15.00
(25) Houston Antwine .25
(26) John Bramlett .25
(27) Aaron Marsh .25
(28) R.C. Gamble .25
(29) Gino Cappelletti .75
(30) John Charles .25
(31) Larry Eisenhauer .35
(32) Jon Morris .25
(33) Jim Nance .50
(34) Len St. Jean .25
(35) Mike Taliaferro .25
(36) Jim Whalen .25
(37) Stew Barber .35
(38) Al Bemiller .25
(39) George (Butch) Byrd .35
(40) Booker Edgerson .25
(41) Harry Jacobs .35
(42) Jack Kemp 18.00
(43) Ron McDole .35
(44) Joe O'Donnell .25
(45) John Pitts .25
(46) George Saimes .35
(47) Mike Stratton .35
(48) O.J. Simpson 35.00
(49) Ronnie Bull .35
(50) Dick Butkus 8.00
(51) Jim Cadile .25
(52) Jack Concannon .35
(53) Dick Evey .25
(54) Bennie McRae .25
(55) Ed O'Bradovich .25
(56) Brian Piccolo 10.00
(57) Mike Pyle .25
(58) Gale Sayers 10.00
(59) Dick Gordon .35
(60) Roosevelt Taylor .35
(61) Al Beauchamp .25
(62) Dave Middendorf .25
(63) Harry Gunner .25
(64) Bobby Hunt .25
(65) Bob Johnson .40
(66) Charley King .25
(67) Andy Rice .25
(68) Paul Robinson .35
(69) Bill Staley .25
(70) Pat Matson .25
(71) Bob Trumpy 2.00
(72) Sam Wyche 5.00
(73) Erich Barnes .35
(74) Gary Collins .35
(75) Ben Davis .25
(76) John Demarie .25
(77) Gene Hickerson .25
(78) Jim Houston .35
(79) Ernie Kellerman .25
(80) Leroy Kelly 3.00
(81) Dale Lindsey .25
(82) Bill Nelsen .75
(83) Jim Kanicki .25
(84) Dick Schafrath .35
(85) George Andrie .75
(86) Mike Clark .25
(87) Cornell Green .50
(88) Bob Hayes 1.50
(89) Chuck Howley .75
(90) Lee Roy Jordan 1.25
(91) Bob Lilly 3.00
(92) Craig Morton 1.00
(93) John Niland .25
(94) Dan Reeves 5.00
(95) Mel Renfro 1.00
(96) Lance Rentzel .50
(97) Tom Beer .25
(98) Billy Van Heusen .25
(99) Mike Current .25
(100) Al Denson .25
(101) Pete Duranko .25
(102) George Goeddeke .25
(103) John Huard .25
(104) Richard Jackson .25
(105) Pete Jaquess .35
(106) Fran Lynch .25
(107) Floyd Little 2.00
(108) Steve Tensi .50
(109) Lem Barney 3.00
(110) Nick Eddy .50
(111) Mel Farr .75
(112) Ed Flanagan .25
(113) Larry Hand .25
(114) Alex Karras 2.50
(115) Dick LeBeau .35
(116) Mike Lucci .35
(117) Earl McCullouch .35
(118) Bill Munson .40
(119) Jerry Rush .25
(120) Wayne Walker .35
(121) Herb Adderley 2.00
(122) Donny Anderson .50
(123) Lee Roy Caffey .25
(124) Carroll Dale .35
(125) Willie Davis 1.50
(126) Boyd Dowler .35
(127) Marv Fleming .50
(128) Bob Jeter .35
(129) Henry Jordan .35
(130) Dave Robinson .35
(131) Bart Starr 10.00
(132) Willie Wood 1.50
(133) Pete Beathard .75
(134) Jim Beirne .25
(135) Garland Boyette .25
(136) Woody Campbell .25
(137) Miller Farr .25
(138) Hoyle Granger .25
(139) Mac Haik .25
(140) Ken Houston 3.00
(141) Bobby Maples .35
(142) Alvin Reed .25
(143) Don Trull .35
(144) George Webster .50
(145) Bobby Bell 2.00
(146) Aaron Brown .25
(147) Buck Buchanan 2.00
(148) Len Dawson 5.00
(149) Mike Garrett .50
(150) Robert Holmes .35
(151) Willie Lanier 3.00
(152) Frank Pitts .25
(153) Johnny Robinson .75
(154) Jan Stenerud 3.00
(155) Otis Taylor .75
(156) Jim Tyrer .50
(157) Dick Bass .35
(158) Maxie Baughan .50
(159) Rich Petitbon .50
(160) Roger Brown .35
(161) Roman Gabriel 1.50
(162) Bruce Gossett .25
(163) David (Deacon) Jones 1.50
(164) Tom Mack 1.25
(165) Tommy Mason .50
(166) Ed Meador .35
(167) Merlin Olsen 3.00
(168) Pat Studstill .35
(169) Jack Clancy .25
(170) Maxie Williams .25
(171) Larry Csonka 10.00
(172) Jimmy Warren .25
(173) Norm Evans .35
(174) Rick Norton .25
(175) Bob Griese 7.50
(176) Howard Twilley .50
(177) Billy Neighbors .35
(178) Nick Buoniconti 1.25
(179) Tom Goode .25
(180) Dick Westmoreland .25
(181) Grady Alderman .25
(182) Bill Brown .75
(183) Fred Cox .35
(184) Clint Jones .35
(185) Joe Kapp 1.00
(186) Paul Krause 1.00
(187) Gary Larsen .25
(188) Jim Marshall 1.50
(189) Dave Osborn .25
(190) Alan Page 4.00
(191) Mike Tingelhoff .75
(192) Roy Winston .35
(193) Dan Abramowicz .50
(194) Doug Atkins 1.50
(195) Bo Burris .25
(196) John Douglas .25
(197) Don Shy .25
(198) Bill Kilmer .75
(199) Tony Lorick .25
(200) David Parks .50
(201) Dave Rowe .25
(202) Monty Stickles .25
(203) Steve Stonebreaker .35
(204) Del Williams .25
(205) Pete Case .25
(206) Tommy Crutcher .35
(207) Scott Eaton .25
(208) Tucker Frederickson .75
(209) Peter Gogolak .35
(210) Homer Jones .35
(211) Ernie Koy .35
(212) Carl (Spider) Lockhart .35
(213) Bruce Maher .25
(214) Aaron Thomas .35
(215) Fran Tarkenton 12.00
(216) Jim Katcavage .35
(217) Al Atkinson .25
(218) Emerson Boozer .35
(219) John Elliott .25
(220) Dave Herman .35
(221) Winston Hill .35
(222) Jim Hudson .25
(223) Pete Lammons .35
(224) Gerry Philbin .35
(225) George Sauer .50
(226) Joe Namath 20.00
(227) Matt Snell .50
(228) Jim Turner .35
(229) Fred Biletnikoff 3.00
(230) Willie Brown 1.50
(231) Billy Cannon .50
(232) Dan Conners .25
(233) Ben Davidson .75
(234) Hewritt Dixon .35
(235) Daryle Lamonica 1.00
(236) Ike Lassiter .25
(237) Ken McCloughan .25
(238) Jim Otto 1.50
(239) Harry Schuh .25
(240) Gene Upshaw 3.00
(241) Gary Ballman .35
(242) Joe Carollo .25
(243) Dave Lloyd .25
(244) Fred Hill .25
(245) Al Nelson .25
(246) Joe Scarpati .25
(247) Sam Baker .35
(248) Fred Brown .25
(249) Floyd Peters .50
(250) Nate Ramsey .25
(251) Norman Snead .50
(252) Tom Woodeshick .25
(253) John Hilton .25
(254) Kent Nix .25
(255) Paul Martha .50
(256) Ben McGee .25
(257) Andy Russell .50
(258) Dick Shiner .25
(259) J.R. Wilburn .25
(260) Marv Woodson .25
(261) Earl Gros .25
(262) Dick Hoak .50
(263) Roy Jefferson .50
(264) Larry Gagner .25
(265) Johnny Roland .75
(266) Jackie Smith 3.00
(267) Jim Bakken .50
(268) Don Brumm .25
(269) Bob DeMarco .35
(270) Irv Goode .25
(271) Ken Gray .35
(272) Charlie Johnson 1.00
(273) Ernie McMillan .35
(274) Larry Stallings .35
(275) Jerry Stovall .50
(276) Larry Wilson 1.50
(277) Chuck Allen .25
(278) Lance Alworth 3.00
(279) Kenny Graham .25
(280) Steve DeLong .35
(281) Willie Frazier .35
(282) Gary Garrison .35
(283) Sam Gruniesen .25
(284) John Hadl .75
(285) Brad Hubbert .25
(286) Ron Mix 2.00
(287) Dick Post .35
(288) Walt Sweeney .35
(289) Kermit Alexander .50
(290) Ed Beard .25
(291) Bruce Bosley .35
(292) John Brodie 3.00
(293) Stan Hindman .25
(294) Jim Johnson 1.50
(295) Charlie Krueger .35
(296) Clifton McNeil .35
(297) Gary Lewis .25
(298) Howard Mudd .35
(299) Dave Wilcox .50
(300) Ken Willard .50
(301) Charlie Gogolak .35
(302) Len Hauss .50
(303) Sonny Jurgensen 3.50
(304) Carl Kammerer .25
(305) Walt Rock .25
(306) Ray Schoenke .25
(307) Chris Hanburger .75
(308) Tom Brown .50
(309) Sam Huff 2.00
(310) Bob Long .25
(311) Vince Promuto .25
(312) Pat Richter .50

1989 Goal Line Hall of Fame

These postcard-size cards (4" x 6") feature full-color action paintings of inductees into the Pro Football Hall of Fame. The cards were part of an art series done by artist Gary Thomas and were offered by subscription. Each set was packaged in a custom box and was given a serial number (Set No. x of 5,000), which appears on each card, too. The back of the card is white and uses black ink. The player's name, college, position, biographical information, years he played, teams he played with and the year he was inducted are all listed, as well as a set and card number. A Football Hall of Fame logo is also given. Each of the first five series contains 30 cards; series 6 has 25. However, a card for Johnny Unitas (#174) was never issued. Series I was issued in 1989; a new series has followed each year since then. The cards are numbered alphabetically within each series.

NM/M
Complete Set (175): 400.00
Common Player: 2.00
1 Lance Alworth 6.00
2 Morris "Red" Badgro 2.50
3 Cliff Battles 2.50
4 Mel Blount 2.50
5 Terry Bradshaw 10.00
6 Jim Brown 12.00
7 George Connor 2.50
8 Turk Edwards 2.50
9 Tom Fears 2.50
10 Frank Gifford 10.00
11 Otto Graham 6.00
12 Harold "Red" Grange 5.00
13 George Halas 4.00
14 Clarke Hinkle 2.50
15 Robert "Cal" Hubbard 2.50
16 Sam Huff 2.50
17 Frank "Bruiser" Kinard 2.50
18 Dick "Night Train" Lane 2.50
19 Sid Luckman 6.00
20 Bobby Mitchell 2.50
21 Merlin Olsen 4.00
22 Jim Parker 2.50
23 Joe Perry 3.00
24 Pete Rozelle 3.00
25 Art Shell 3.00
26 Fran Tarkenton 9.00
27 Jim Thorpe 6.00
28 Paul Warfield 3.00
29 Larry Wilson 2.50
30 Willie Wood 2.50
31 Doug Atkins 2.00
32 Bobby Bell 2.00
33 Raymond Berry 3.00
34 Paul Brown 2.00
35 Guy Chamberlin 2.00
36 Earl "Dutch" Clark 2.00
37 Jimmy Conzelman 2.00
38 Len Dawson 3.00
39 Mike Ditka 8.00
40 Dan Fortmann 2.00
41 Frank Gatski 2.00
42 Bill George 2.00
43 Elroy Hirsch 3.00
44 Paul Hornung 4.00
45 John Henry Johnson 2.00
46 Walt Kiesling 2.00
47 Yale Lary 2.00
48 Bobby Layne 3.00
49 Tuffy Leemans 2.00
50 Geo. Preston Marshall 2.00
51 George McAfee 2.00
52 Wayne Millner 2.00
53 Bronko Nagurski 4.00
54 Joe Namath 12.00
55 Ray Nitschke 3.00
56 Jim Ringo 2.00
57 Art Rooney 2.00
58 Joe Stydahar 2.00
59 Charley Taylor 2.00
60 Charlie Trippi 2.00
61 Fred Biletnikoff 3.00
62 Buck Buchanan 2.00
63 Dick Butkus 6.00
64 Earl Campbell 8.00
65 Tony Canadeo 2.00
66 Art Donovan 3.00
67 Ray Flaherty 2.00
68 Forrest Gregg 2.50
69 Lou Groza 3.00
70 John Hannah 2.00
71 Don Hutson 2.50
72 David (Deacon) Jones 2.00
73 Stan Jones 2.00
74 Sonny Jurgensen 3.00
75 Vince Lombardi 3.00
76 Tim Mara 2.00
77 Ollie Matson 2.00
78 Mike McCormack 2.00
79 John "Blood" McNally 2.00
80 Marion Motley 2.00
81 George Musso 2.00
82 Earle "Greasy" Neale 2.00
83 Clarence (Ace) Parker 2.00
84 Pete Pihos 2.00
85 Tex Schramm 2.00
86 Roger Staubach 12.00
87 Jan Stenerud 2.00
88 Y.A. Tittle 3.00
89 Clyde "Bulldog" Turner 2.00
90 Steve Van Buren 2.00
91 Herb Adderley 2.00
92 Lem Barney 2.00
93 Sammy Baugh 5.00
94 Chuck Bednarik 3.00
95 Charles W. Bidwill 2.00
96 Willie Brown 2.00
97 Al Davis 4.00
98 Bill Dudley 2.00
99 Weeb Ewbank 2.00
100 Len Ford 2.00
101 Sid Gillman 2.00
102 Jack Ham 2.00
103 Mel Hein 2.00
104 Bill Hewitt 2.00
105 Dante Lavelli 2.00
106 Bob Lilly 3.00
107 John Mackey 2.00
108 Hugh McElhenny 3.00
109 Mike Michalske 2.00
110 Ron Mix 2.00
111 Leo Nomenllini 2.00
112 Steve Owen 2.00
113 Alan Page 2.50
114 Dan Reeves 2.00
115 John Riggins 3.00
116 Gale Sayers 6.00
117 Ken Strong 2.00
118 Gene Upshaw 3.00
119 Norm Van Brocklin 4.00
120 Alex Wojciechowicz 2.00
121 Bert Bell 2.00
122 George Blanda 4.00
123 Joe Carr 2.00
124 Larry Csonka 4.00
125 John (Paddy) Driscoll 2.00
126 Dan Fouts 3.00
127 Bob Griese 4.00
128 Ed Healy 2.00
129 Wilbur (Fats) Henry 2.00
130 Ken Houston 2.00
131 Lamar Hunt 2.00
132 Jack Lambert 2.50
133 Tom Landry 4.00
134 Willie Lanier 2.00
135 Larry Little 2.00
136 Don Maynard 3.00
137 Lenny Moore 3.00
138 Chuck Noll 3.00
139 Jim Otto 2.00
140 Walter Payton 10.00
141 Hugh (Shorty) Ray 2.00
142 Andy Robustelli 2.00
143 Bob St. Clair 2.00
144 Joe Schmidt 3.00
145 Jim Taylor 3.00
146 Doak Walker 3.00
147 Bill Walsh 3.00
148 Bob Waterfield 3.00
149 Arnie Weinmeister 2.00
150 Bill Willis 2.00
151 Roosevelt Brown 2.00
152 Jack Christiansen 2.00
153 Willie Davis 3.00
154 Tony Dorsett 6.00
155 Bud Grant 2.00
156 Joe Greene 5.00
157 Joe Guyon 2.00
158 Franco Harris 4.00
159 Ted Hendricks 2.00
160 Arnie Herber 2.00
161 Jimmy Johnson 2.00
162 Leroy Kelly 2.00
163 Curly Lambeau 2.00
164 Jim Langer 2.00
165 Link Lyman 2.00
166 Gino Marchetti 3.00
167 Ernie Nevers 3.00
168 O.J. Simpson 12.00
169 Jackie Smith 2.00
170 Bart Starr 6.00
171 Ernie Stautner 2.50
172 George Trafton 2.00
173 Emlen Tunnell 2.00
174 Johnny Unitas (not issued)
175 Randy White 2.00
176 Jim Finks 2.00
177 Henry Jordan 2.00
178 Steve Largent 4.00
179 Lee Roy Selmon 2.00
180 Kellen Winslow 2.00

1939 Gridiron Greats Blotters

The 12-card, 3-7/8" x 9" blotter set was sponsored by Louis F. Dow Company. The blotter card fronts feature a headshot on the left side, superimposed over a football, with the collegiate player's school letter appearing in a pennant below. The right side of the card blotters feature a player profile and a monthly calendar, as each of the 12 blotter cards have a different month. The backs are blank. The cards are numbered with the "B" prefix.

NM/M
Complete Set (12): 3,500
Common Player: 150.00
3941 Jim Thorpe 700.00
3942 Walter Eckersall 150.00
3943 Edward Mahan 150.00
3944 Sammy Baugh 550.00
3945 Thomas Shevlin 150.00
3946 Harold "Red" Grange 600.00
3947 Ernie Nevers 325.00
3948 George Gipp 525.00
3949 Pudge Heffelfinger 150.00
3950 Bronko Nagurski 600.00
3951 Willie Heston 150.00
3952 Jay Berwanger 150.00

1992 Gridiron Promos

The four-card, standard-size promo set was issued to show the design of the 1992 regular set. The cards are similar in design to the base set and each card has a "P" prefix.

NM/M
Complete Set (4): 5.00
Common Player: .50
1 Siran Stacy .50
2 Casey Weldon .75
3 Mike Saunders .50
4 Jeff Blake 5.00

1992 Gridiron

The 110-card, standard-size set, produced by Lafayette Sports-card Corporation, features the top players and coaches from the top 25 college teams. Three players and one coach represent each team. Production was limited to 50,000 sets. The card fronts feature a glossy color action shot while the back contains bio and stat information.

NM/M
Complete Set (110): 25.00
Common Player: .10
1 Robert Perez .20
2 Jason Jones .10
3 Jason Christ .10
4 Fisher DeBerry (CO) .20
5 Danny Woodson .10
6 Siran Stacy .20
7 Robert Stewart .10
8 Gene Stallings (CO) .75
9 Santana Dotson .50
10 Curtis Hafford .10
11 John Turnpaugh .10
12 Grant Teaff (CO) .30
13B Desmond Howard .50
14 Brian Treggs .10
15 Troy Auzenne .20
16 Bruce Snyder (CO) .10
17 DeChane Cameron .10
18 Levon Kirkland .35
19 *Ed McDaniel* .25
20 Ken Hatfield (CO) .25
21 Darian Hagan .20
22 Rico Smith .20
23 Joel Steed .20
24 Bill McCartney (CO) .75
25 Jeff Blake 4.00
26 David Daniels .10
27 Robert Jones .20
28 Bill Lewis (CO) .20
29 Tim Paulk .10
30 Arden Czyzewski .10
31 Cal Dixon .10
32 Steve Spurrier (CO) 2.00
33B Desmond Howard .50
34 Casey Weldon .35
35 Kirk Carruthers .10
36 Bobby Bowden (CO) 2.00
37 Mark Barsotti .10
38 Kelvin Means .10
39 Marquez Pope .20
40 Jim Sweeney (CO) .25
41 Kameno Bell .10
42 Elbert Turner .10
43 Marlin Primous .10
44 John Mackovic (CO) .50
45 Matt Rodgers .20
46 Mike Saunders .20
47 John Derby .10
48 Hayden Fry (CO) .75
49 Carlos Huerta .20
50 Leon Searcy .20
51 Claude Jones .10
52 Dennis Erickson (CO) .75
53 Erick Anderson .10
54 J.D. Carlson .10
55 Greg Skrepenak .35
56 Gary Moeller .20
57 Keithen McCant .20
58 Nate Turner .10
59 Pat Englebert .10
60 Tom Osborne (CO) 2.00
61 Charles Davenport .10
62 Mark Thomas .10
63 Clyde Hawley .10
64 Dick Sheridan (CO) .20
65 Derek Brown (TE) .20
66 Rodney Culver .20
67 Tony Smith .20
68 Lou Holtz (CO) 2.00
69 Kent Graham .35
70 Scottie Graham 1.25
71 John Kacherski .10
72 John Cooper (CO) .50
73 Mike Gaddis .20
74 Joe Bowden .20
75 Mike McKinley .10
76 Gary Gibbs (CO) .20
77 Sam Gash .20
78 Keith Goganious .20
79 Darren Perry .35
80 Joe Paterno (CO) 3.00
81 Steve Israel .20
82 Eric Seaman .10
83 Glen Deveaux .10
84 Paul Hackett (CO) .35
85 Tommy Vardell .35
86 Chris Walsh .10
87 Jason Palumbis .10
88 Dennis Green (CO) .75
89 Andy Kelly .10
90 Dale Carter .75
91 Shon Walker .10
92 Johnny Majors .50
93 Bucky Richardson .20
94 Quentin Coryatt 1.25
95 Kevin Smith .75
96 R.C. Slocum (CO) .75
97 Ed Cunningham .20
98 Mario Bailey .20
99 Donald Jones .10
100 Don James (CO) .75
101 Vaughn Dunbar .35
102 Reggie Yarbrough .10
103 Matt Blundin .35
104 Tony Sands .10
105B Desmond Howard .50
106 Ty Detmer .50
107B Desmond Howard .50
NNO Mario Bates CL, Jeff Blake 1.00
NNO Mike Gaddis CL, Tommy Vardell .20
NNO Title Card .10

1991 GTE Super Bowl Theme Art

The 25-card, 4-5/8" x 6" set was distributed by GTE in correlation with the 25th anniversary of the Super Bowl. The card fronts feature the Super Bowl program art while the backs contain game summaries and a GTE Telefact.

NM/M
Complete Set (25): 5.00
Common Player: .30
1 Super Bowl I .50
2 Super Bowl II .30
3 Super Bowl III .30

#	Player	NM/M
4	Super Bowl IV	.30
5	Super Bowl V	.30
6	Super Bowl VI	.30
7	Super Bowl VII	.30
8	Super Bowl VIII	.30
9	Super Bowl IX	.30
10	Super Bowl X	.30
11	Super Bowl XI	.30
12	Super Bowl XII	.30
13	Super Bowl XIII	.30
14	Super Bowl XIV	.30
15	Sueper Bowl XV	.30
16	Super Bowl XVI	.30
17	Super Bowl XVII	.30
18	Super Bowl XVIII	.30
19	Super Bowl XIX	.30
20	Super Bowl XX	.30
21	Super Bowl XXI	.30
22	Super Bowl XXII	.30
23	Super Bowl XXIII	.30
24	Super Bowl XXIV	.30
25	Super Bowl XXV	.30

H

1990 Hall of Fame Stickers

These 80 stickers feature members of the Pro Football Hall of Fame. Each sticker measures 1-7/8" x 2-1/8" and was created for inclusion in a book titled "The Official Pro Football Hall of Fame Fun and Fact Sticker Book." Artist Mark Rucker did the original artwork which appears on each sticker. The player's name, position and sticker number are given on the front.

		NM/M
Complete Set (80):		12.00
Common Player:		.15
1	Wilbur Henry	.20
2	George Trafton	.15
3	Mike Michalske	.15
4	Turk Edwards	.15
5	Bill Hewitt	.20
6	Mel Hein	.15
7	Joe Stydahar	.15
8	Dan Fortmann	.15
9	Alex Wojciechowicz	.15
10	George Connor	.20
11	Jim Thorpe	.75
12	Ernie Nevers	.35
13	John McNally	.25
14	Ken Strong	.15
15	Bronko Nagurski	.50
16	Clarke Hinkle	.15
17	Ace Parker	.15
18	Billy Dudley	.20
19	Don Hutson	.30
20	Dante Lavelli	.15
21	Elroy Hirsch	.25
22	Raymond Berry	.25
23	Bobby Mitchell	.15
24	Don Maynard	.25
25	Mike Ditka	.50
26	Lance Alworth	.25
27	Charley Taylor	.15
28	Paul Warfield	.30
29	Lou Groza	.35
30	Art Donovan	.25
31	Leo Nomellini	.15
32	Andy Robustelli	.20
33	Gino Marchetti	.15
34	Forrest Gregg	.15
35	Jim Otto	.20
36	Ron Mix	.15
37	Deacon Jones	.15
38	Bob Lilly	.25
39	Merlin Olsen	.25
40	Alan Page	.20
41	Joe Greene	.25
42	Art Shell	.25
43	Sammy Baugh	.35
44	Sid Luckman	.45
45	Bob Waterfield	.40
46	Bobby Layne	.25
47	Norm Van Brocklin	.25
48	Y.A. Tittle	.25
49	Johnny Unitas	.50
50	Bart Starr	.35
51	Sonny Jurgensen	.25
52	Joe Namath	.75
53	Roger Staubach	.75
54	Terry Bradshaw	.50
55	Steve Van Buren	.25
56	Marion Motley	.25
57	Joe Perry	.25
58	Hugh McElhenny	.25
59	Frank Gifford	.50
60	Jim Brown	1.00
61	Jim Taylor	.25
62	Gale Sayers	.35
63	Larry Csonka	.25
64	Emlen Tunnell	.15
65	Jack Christiansen	.15
66	Dick "Night Train" Lane	.15
67	Sam Huff	.25
68	Ray Nitschke	.15
69	Larry Wilson	.15
70	Willie Wood	.20
71	Bobby Bell	.15
72	Willie Brown	.20
73	Dick Butkus	.35
74	Jack Ham	.15
75	George Halas	.25
76	Steve Owen	.15
77	Art Rooney	.20
78	Bert Bell	.15
79	Paul Brown	.15
80	Pete Rozelle	.20

1993 Heads and Tails SB XXVII

The 25-card, regular-sized set, produced by Heads and Tails Inc., honored players from Super Bowl XXVII (Dallas vs. Buffalo), as well as past Super Bowl stars and current Pro Bowl players. The card fronts feature the player's name printed down one side with a silver foil "Rose Bowl" emblem along the bottom border. The card backs feature a filled Rose Bowl with Cowboys and Bills air-brushed end zones and player highlights. Gold-foil versions were randomly inserted (10,000) in the entire run (200,000).

		NM/M
Complete Set (25):		10.00
Common Player:		.25
1	Title Card CL	.25
2	Lawrence Taylor, Mike Singletary	.50
3	Dennis Byrd	.25
4	Junior Seau	.50
5	Steve Young	1.00
6	Sterling Sharpe	.50
7	Cortez Kennedy	.25
8	Terry Bradshaw	.75
9	Fred Biletnikoff	.25
10	John Riggins	.25
11	Phil Simms	.25
12	Cornelius Bennett	.50
13	Jim Kelly	.75
14	Bruce Smith	.50
15	Andre Reed	.50
16	Keith McKeller	.25
17	James Lofton	.25
18	Thurman Thomas	.75
19	Emmitt Smith	3.00
20	Kelvin Martin	.25
21	Troy Aikman	1.50
22	Charles Haley	.25
23	Alvin Harper	.25
24	Michael Irvin	.50
25	Jay Novacek	.25

1991 Heisman Collection I

The 20-card, regular-sized set, produced by College Classics in association with The Downtown Athletic Club of New York, features 20 Heisman winners in skip-numbered order (based on chronological order). The card fronts feature a color posed shot of the player with a Heisman trophy in the lower right corner. The card back informs collectors of the year the player won the award, player summary and a larger Heisman Trophy image. The production total was 100,000 sets and each case (1,000 sets) contained two player autograph cards. The set also had a serially numbered header card and a sample Bo Jackson card was also distributed.

		NM/M
Complete Set (21):		5.00
Common Player:		.15
1	Jay Berwanger	.15
6	Tom Harmon	.25
9	Angelo Bertelli	.15
11	Doc Blanchard	.25
13	John Lujack	.25
15	Leon Hart	.25
16	Vic Janowicz	.25
19	John Lattner	.25
23	John David Crow	.15
26	Joe Bellino	.15
30	John Huarte	.15
32	Steve Spurrier	1.00
36	Jim Plunkett	.40
40	Archie Griffin	.25
42	Tony Dorsett	1.00
43	Earl Campbell	1.00
45	Charles White	.15
48	Herschel Walker	.50
51	Bo Jackson	1.00
53	Tim Brown	.40
NNO	Title Card	.15
SAM	Bo Jackson (Sample Promo)	3.00

A player's name in *italic* type indicates a rookie card.

1992 Heisman Collection II

The 20-card, standard-size set is a continuation of the 1991 Hesiman Collection set, as the set is skip-numbered in chronological order. The card fronts and backs are identical in design with the 1991 set. As with the previous set, 100,000 sets were produced by College Classics and each set comes with a serially numbered header card. Sample cards of Barry Sanders and Roger Staubach were also available in 3-1/2" x 7-1/2" strips.

		NM/M
Complete Set (21):		10.00
Common Player:		.50
2	Larry Kelley	.50
3	Clint Frank	.50
5	Niles Kinnick	.75
7	Bruce Smith	.50
10	Les Horvath	.50
14	Doak Walker	.75
17	Dick Kazmaier	.50
20	Alan Ameche	.50
21	Howard Cassady	.50
25	Billy Cannon	.75
27	Ernie Davis	1.75
29	Roger Staubach	2.00
31	Mike Garrett	.50
35	Steve Owens	.50
38	Johnny Rodgers	.75
39	John Cappelletti	.50
44	Billy Sims	.75
50	Doug Flutie	1.50
52	Vinny Testaverde	.50
54	Barry Sanders	2.50
NNO	Title Card	.50
SAM	Barry Sanders (Sample Promo)	10.00
SAM	Roger Staubach (Sample Promo)	12.00

1970 Hi-C Posters

These posters were featured on the insides of Hi-C drink can labels. The featured players were statistical leaders at their positions during the 1969 season. Each poster measures 6-5/8" x 13-3/4" and is numbered below the player photo.

		NM/M
Complete Set (10):		700.00
Common Player:		75.00
(1)	Greg Cook	80.00
(2)	Fred Cox	75.00
(3)	Sonny Jurgensen	125.00
(4)	David Lee	75.00
(5)	Dennis Partee	75.00
(6)	Dick Post	75.00
(7)	Mel Renfro	90.00
(8)	Gale Sayers	175.00
(9)	Emmitt Thomas	80.00
(10)	Jim Turner	75.00

1991 Homers

In 1991, boxes of QB's Cookies contained one of six different cards featuring Hall of Fame football players. Each standard-size card has a sepia-toned photograph on the front, with a bronze frame. The player's name is in a bronze panel in the lower left. The numbered back has a checklist for the set, plus information about the player's accomplishments, biographical information and the year he was inducted into the Hall of Fame. The set was sponsored by Legend Food Products.

		NM/M
Complete Set (6):		10.00
Common Player:		1.00
1	Vince Lombardi	2.00
2	Hugh McElhenny	2.00
3	Elroy Hirsch	2.00
4	Jim Thorpe	4.00
5	Dick "Night Train" Lane	1.00
6	Bart Starr	3.00

I

1992-93 Intimidator Bio Sheets

The 36-card, 8-1/2" x 11" set features color action shots on the glossy card fronts with the player's name printed in gold foil down the right side, along wih his team name and uniform number. The card backs contain college and pro summaries, as well as biographical information.

		NM/M
Complete Set (36):		65.00
Common Player:		1.00
1	Troy Aikman	8.00
2	Jerry Ball	1.00
3	Cornelius Bennett	1.00
4	Earnest Byner	1.00
5	Randall Cunningham	1.00
6	Chris Doleman	1.00
7	John Elway	5.00
8	Jim Everett	1.00
9	Michael Irvin	2.50
10	Jim Kelly	2.50
11	James Lofton	1.00
12	Howie Long	1.50
13	Ronnie Lott	1.50
14	Nick Lowery	1.00
15	Charles Mann	1.00
16	Dan Marino	12.00
17	Art Monk	1.50
18	Joe Montana	8.00
19	Warren Moon	2.50
20	Christian Okoye	1.00
21	Leslie O'Neal	1.00
22	Andre Reed	2.50
23	Jerry Rice	8.00
24	Andre Rison	2.50
25	Deion Sanders	5.00
26	Junior Seau	2.50
27	Mike Singletary	1.50
28	Bruce Smith	2.50
29	Emmitt Smith	12.00
30	Neil Smith	2.50
31	Pat Swilling	1.00
32	Lawrence Taylor	2.50
33	Broderick Thomas	1.00
34	Derrick Thomas	2.50
35	Thurman Thomas	2.50
36	Lorenzo White	1.00

1984 Invaders Smokey

The five-card, 5" x 7" set featured four players and Smokey The Bear in a forestry promotion set. The card fronts feature a posed player shot with Smokey, as well as the player's signature. The card backs contain bio information. Notable in the set is future NFL linebacker Gary Plummer, who went on to play with San Diego and San Francisco.

		NM/M
Complete Set (5):		65.00
Common Player:		10.00
1	Dupre Marshall	10.00
2	Gary Plummer	20.00
3	David Shaw	10.00
4	Kevin Shea	10.00
5	Smokey Bear (With players above)	10.00

J

1986 Jeno's Pizza

Two players from each of the 28 NFL teams were selected for this 58-card set offered by Jeno's Pizza. Specially- marked Jeno's Pizza boxes each contained one card inside, sealed in plastic. Current and former stars are represented in the set. Each card back has a number which corresponds to the location in a Terry Bradshaw Action Play Book which was created to display the cards. The Play Book was available through a mail-in coupon. Each card back also has a summary of the player's career accomplishments.

		NM/M
Complete Set (56):		25.00
Common Player:		.40
1	Duane Thomas	.75
2	Butch Johnson	.40
3	Andy Headen	.40
4	Joe Morris	.60
5	Wilbert Montgomery	.50
6	Harold Carmichael	.75
7	Ottis Anderson	.60
8	Roy Green	.50
9	Mark Murphy	.40
10	Joe Theismann	1.50
11	Jim McMahon	1.00
12	Walter Payton	3.00
13	Billy Sims	.75
14	James Jones	.40
15	Willie Davis	.75
16	Eddie Lee Ivery	.40
17	Fran Tarkenton	2.00
18	Alan Page	.75
19	Ricky Bell	.60
20	Cecil Johnson	.40
21	Bubba Bean	.40
22	Gerald Riggs	.50
23	Eric Dickerson, Barry Redden	1.00
24	Jack Reynolds	.50
25	Archie Manning	1.00
26	Wayne Wilson	.60
27	Dan Bunz, Pete Johnson	.40
28	Roger Craig	1.00
29	O.J. Simpson	6.00
30	Joe Cribbs	.50
31	Rick Volk, Leroy Kelly	.60
32	Earl Morrall	.75
33	Jim Klick	.50
34	Dan Marino	5.00
35	Craig James	1.00
36	Julius Adams	.40
37	Joe Namath	4.00
38	Freeman McNeil	.60
39	Pete Johnson	.40
40	Larry Kinnebrew	.40
41	Brian Sipe	.50
42	Kevin Mack, Earnest Byner	.60
43	Dan Pastorini	.60
44	Elvin Bethea, Carter Hartwig	.40
45	Fran Tarkenton, Jack Lambert	1.00
46	Terry Bradshaw	3.00
47	Randy Gradishar, Steve Foley	.50
48	Sammy Winder	.40
49	Robert Holmes	.40
50	Buck Buchanan	.75
51	Willie Jones, Cedrick Hardman	.40
52	Marcus Allen	1.50
53	Dan Fouts, Don Macek	.75
54	Dan Fouts	1.50
55	Blair Bush	.40
56	Steve Largent	2.50
----	Terry Bradshaw Play Book	3.00

1966 Jets Team Issue

The nine-card, 5" x 7" set features black and white player photos on the fronts with blank backs.

		NM/M
Complete Set (9):		80.00
Common Player:		4.00
1	Ralph Baker	4.00
2	Larry Grantham	5.00
3	Bill Mathis	4.00
4	Don Maynard	15.00
5	Joe Namath	40.00
6	Gerry Philbin	5.00
7	Mark Smolinski	4.00
8	Matt Snell	8.00
9	Bake Turner	4.00

1969 Jets Tasco Prints

The six-card, 11" x 16" set, produced by Tasco Associates, features an artist's depiction of the players with blank backs.

		NM/M
Complete Set (6):		100.00
Common Player:		10.00
1	Winston Hill	10.00
2	Joe Namath	50.00
3	Gerry Philbin	15.00
4	Johnny Sample	10.00
5	Matt Snell	18.00
6	Jim Turner	10.00

1981 Jets Police

The 10-card, 2-5/8" x 4-1/8" set have green-bordered fronts and were sponsored by Frito-Lay, Kiwanis, local law enforcement and the Jets. The card backs contain a safety tip in red print. Apparently, four of the cards were short-printed and thus are more scarce.

		NM/M
Complete Set (10):		15.00
Common Player:		.70
14	Richard Todd (SP)	3.00
42	Bruce Harper	.70
51	Greg Buttle	.70
73	Joe Klecko	2.00
79	Marvin Powell	1.50
80	Johnny Lam Jones (SP)	2.75
85	Wesley Walker (SP)	3.75
93	Marty Lyons	2.00
99	Mark Gastineau	2.00
xx0	Team Effort (SP)	2.00

1997 John Elway Convenience Store News

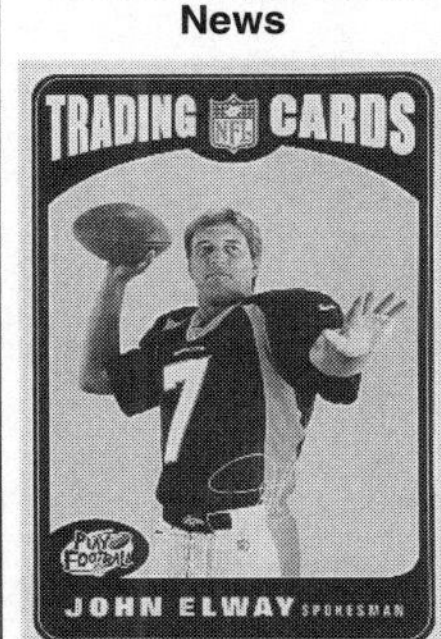

This 7" x 10" Elway card was rubber cemented inside the April 7, 1997 issue of Convenience Store News. The front features Elway in a posed shot of him passing the ball, with the words "Trading Cards" in bold white letters across the top, with the NFL logo in the middle. The back is split, with half containing facts and the other half featuring a comic.

	NM/M
Complete Set (1):	8.00
John Elway	8.00

A card number in parenthese ( ) indicates the set is unnumbered.

K

1959 Kahn's

Kahn's Wieners produced this set, which features members of the Cleveland Indians and Pittsburgh Steelers. The card front contains the Kahn's slogan (The Wiener the World Awaited), plus a black-and-white photograph and a facsimile autograph. Each back has biographical and statistical information. Each unnumbered card measures 3-1/4" x 3-15/16".

		NM/M
Complete Set (31):		1,250
Common Player:		30.00
(1)	Dick Alban	30.00
(2)	Jim Brown	375.00
(3)	Jack Butler	30.00
(4)	Lew Carpenter	35.00
(5)	Preston Carpenter	30.00
(6)	Vince Costello	30.00
(7)	Dale Dodrill	30.00
(8)	Bob Gain	30.00
(9)	Gary Glick	30.00
(10)	Lou Groza	75.00
(11)	Gene Hickerson	30.00
(12)	Billy Howton	35.00
(13)	Art Hunter	30.00
(14)	Joe Kruppa	30.00
(15)	Bobby Layne	65.00
(16)	Joe Lewis	30.00
(17)	Jack McClairen	30.00
(18)	Mike McCormack	45.00
(19)	Walt Michaels	40.00
(20)	Bobby Mitchell	75.00
(21)	Jim Ninowski	35.00
(22)	Chuck Noll	110.00
(23)	Jimmy Orr	35.00
(24)	Milt Plum	35.00
(25)	Ray Renfro	35.00
(26)	Mike Sandusky	30.00
(27)	Billy Ray Smith	30.00
(28)	Jim Ray Smith	30.00
(29)	Ernie Stautner	50.00
(30)	Tom Tracy	30.00
(31)	Frank Varrichione	30.00

1960 Kahn's

Kahn's once again featured members of the Pittsburgh Steelers and Cleveland Browns in this 38-card set. The 3-1/4" x 3-15/16" cards had black-and-white photos on the front, along with the Kahn's slogan. The back has statistical and biographical information, plus an offer for collectors to send in for a free album and instructional booklet. The cards are not numbered and are listed alphabetically.

		NM/M
Complete Set (38):		1,200
Common Player:		25.00
(1)	Sam Baker	25.00
(2)	Jim Brown	230.00
(3)	Ray Campbell	25.00
(4)	Preston Carpenter	25.00
(5)	Vince Costello	25.00
(6)	Willie Davis	65.00
(7)	Galen Fiss	25.00
(8)	Bob Gain	30.00
(9)	Lou Groza	50.00
(10)	Gene Hickerson	25.00
(11)	John Henry Johnson	55.00
(12)	Rich Kreitling	25.00
(13)	Joe Krupa	25.00
(14)	Bobby Layne	50.00
(15)	Jack McClairen	25.00
(16)	Mike McCormack	35.00
(17)	Walt Michaels	25.00
(18)	Bobby Mitchell	40.00
(19)	Dicky Moegle	25.00
(20)	John Morrow	25.00
(21)	Gern Nagler	25.00
(22)	John Nisby	25.00
(23)	Jimmy Orr	30.00
(24)	Bernie Parrish	25.00
(25)	Milt Plum	30.00
(26)	John Reger	25.00
(27)	Ray Renfro	30.00
(28)	Will Renfro	25.00
(29)	Mike Sandusky	30.00
(30)	Dick Schafrath	25.00
(31)	Jim Ray Smith	25.00
(32)	Billy Ray Smith	25.00
(33)	Ernie Stautner	40.00
(34)	George Tarasovic	25.00
(35)	Tom Tracy	30.00
(36)	Frank Varrichione	25.00
(37)	John Wooten	25.00
(38)	Lowe W. Wren	25.00

1961 Kahn's

In addition to featuring Cleveland Browns and Pittsburgh Steelers, as Kahn's sets from the two years before did, the 1961 set included players from the Baltimore Colts, Los Angeles Rams and Philadelphia Eagles. The cards are slightly larger than previous years' issues, measuring 3-1/4" x 4-1/16". The backs are similar to the 1961 backs, except the offer for the album and instructional booklet is slightly different. (The 1960 cards required two labels to be sent in for the album; the 1961 cards only required one.) The fronts are black-and-white and have a facsimile autograph and the Kahn's slogan. Once again, the cards are unnumbered.

		NM/M
Complete Set (36):		1,000
Common Player:		20.00
(1)	Sam Baker	20.00
(2)	Jim Brown	225.00
(3)	Preston Carpenter	20.00
(4)	Vince Costello	20.00
(5)	Buddy Dial	20.00
(6)	Dean Derby	25.00
(7)	Don Fleming	25.00
(8)	Bob Gain	20.00
(9)	Bobby Joe Green	20.00
(10)	Gene Hickerson	25.00
(11)	Jim Houston	25.00
(12)	Dan James	20.00
(13)	John Henry Johnson	40.00
(14)	Rich Kreitling	20.00
(15)	Joe Krupa	20.00
(16)	Larry Krutko (photo actually Tom Tracy)	20.00
(17)	Bobby Layne	60.00
(18)	Joe Lewis	20.00
(19)	Gene Lipscomb	40.00
(20)	Mike McCormack	30.00
(21)	Bobby Mitchell	45.00
(22)	John Morrow	20.00
(23)	John Nisby	20.00
(24)	Jimmy Orr	25.00
(25)	Milt Plum	25.00
(26)	John Reger	20.00
(27)	Ray Renfro	30.00
(28)	Will Renfro	20.00
(29)	Mike Sandusky	20.00
(30)	Dick Schafrath	20.00
(31)	Jim Ray Smith	20.00
(32)	Ernie Stautner	45.00
(33)	George Tarasovic	20.00
(34)	Tom Tracy (photo actually Larry Krutko)	20.00
(35)	Frank Varrichione	20.00
(36)	John Wooten	20.00

1962 Kahn's

This Kahn's set adds three new teams to the mix - the Chicago Bears, Detroit Lions and Minnesota Vikings. The unnumbered cards are 3-1/4" x 4-3/16" and can be identified from previous issues by the player's name on the back, which is in bold. The stats on the back are also double-spaced. Basically, the card design is similar to previous issues.

		NM/M
Complete Set (38):		1,000
Common Player:		20.00
(1)	Maxie Baughan	22.00
(2)	Charley Britt	20.00
(3)	Jim Brown	185.00
(4)	Preston Carpenter	20.00
(5)	Pete Case	22.00
(6)	Howard Cassady	25.00
(7)	Vince Costello	20.00
(8)	Buddy Dial	22.00
(9)	Gene Hickerson	20.00
(10)	Jim Houston	22.00
(11)	Dan James	20.00
(12)	Rich Kreitling	20.00
(13)	Joe Krupa	20.00
(14)	Bobby Layne	50.00
(15)	Ray Lemek	20.00
(16)	Gene Lipscomb	30.00
(17)	David Lloyd	20.00
(18)	Lou Michaels	22.00
(19)	Larry Morris	20.00
(20)	John Morrow	20.00
(21)	Jim Ninowski	20.00
(22)	Buzz Nutter	20.00
(23)	Jimmy Orr	25.00
(24)	Bernie Parrish	22.00
(25)	Milt Plum	22.00
(26)	Myron Pottios	22.00
(27)	John Reger	20.00
(28)	Ray Renfro	22.00
(29)	Frank Ryan	25.00
(30)	John Sample	22.00
(31)	Mike Sandusky	25.00
(32)	Dick Schafrath	20.00
(33)	Jim Shofner	22.00
(34)	Jim Ray Smith	20.00
(35)	Ernie Stautner	35.00
(36)	Fran Tarkenton	250.00
(37)	Paul Wiggin	22.00
(38)	John Wooten	20.00

1963 Kahn's

Kahn's included players from all 14 NFL teams this year, by adding players from the Dallas Cowboys, Green Bay Packers, New York Giants, St. Louis Cardinals, San Francisco 49ers and Washington Redskins to its 1963 lineup of eight teams. Although the backs are generally similar to those from previous sets, these cards can be distinguished from prior sets by the card front, which, for the first time, uses a white border around the black-and-white photo. Once again, the cards are unnumbered and measure 3-1/4" x 4-3/16".

		NM/M
Complete Set (92):		2,300
Common Player:		18.00
(1)	Bill Barnes	18.00
(2)	Erich Barnes	20.00
(3)	Dick Bass	20.00
(4)	Don Bosseler	18.00
(5)	Jim Brown	200.00
(6)	Roger Brown	20.00
(7)	Roosevelt Brown	25.00
(8)	Ron Bull	20.00
(9)	Preston Carpenter	18.00
(10)	Frank Clarke	18.00
(11)	Gail Cogdill	18.00
(12)	Bobby Joe Conrad	18.00
(13)	John David Crow	30.00
(14)	Dan Currie	18.00
(15)	Buddy Dial	20.00
(16)	Mike Ditka	70.00
(17)	Fred Dugan	18.00
(18)	Galen Fiss	18.00
(19)	Bill Forester	20.00
(20)	Bob Gain	18.00
(21)	Willie Gailmore	20.00
(22)	Bill George	25.00
(23)	Frank Gifford	125.00
(24)	Bill Glass	22.00
(25)	Forrest Gregg	25.00
(26)	Fred Hageman	18.00
(27)	Jimmy Hill	18.00
(28)	Sam Huff	30.00
(29)	Dan James	18.00
(30)	John Henry Johnson	25.00
(31)	Sonny Jurgensen	35.00
(32)	Jim Katcavage	20.00
(33)	Ron Kostelnik	18.00
(34)	Jerry Kramer	25.00
(35)	Ron Kramer	22.00
(36)	Dick "Night Train" Lane	25.00
(37)	Yale Lary	25.00
(38)	Eddie LeBaron	25.00
(39)	Dick Lynch	18.00
(40)	Tommy Mason	20.00
(41)	Tommy McDonald	20.00
(42)	Lou Michaels	18.00
(43)	Bobby Mithcell	30.00
(44)	Dick Modzelewski	18.00
(45)	Lenny Moore	30.00
(46)	John Morrow	18.00
(47)	John Nisby	18.00
(48)	Ray Nitschke	40.00
(49)	Leo Nomellini	25.00
(50)	Jimmy Orr	20.00
(51)	John Paluck	18.00
(52)	Jim Parker	25.00
(53)	Bernie Parrish	18.00
(54)	Jim Patton	18.00
(55)	Don Perkins	20.00
(56)	Richie Petitbon	18.00
(57)	Jim Phillips	18.00
(58)	Nick Pietrosante	18.00
(59)	Milt Plum	20.00
(60)	Myron Pottios	18.00
(61)	Sonny Randle	18.00
(62)	John Reger	18.00
(63)	Ray Renfro	22.00
(64)	Pete Retzlaff	20.00
(65)	Pat Richter	22.00
(66)	Jim Ringo	25.00
(67)	Andy Robustelli	25.00
(68)	Joe Rutgens	18.00
(69)	Bob St. Clair	25.00
(70)	John Sample	18.00
(71)	Lonnie Sanders	18.00
(72)	Dick Schafrath	18.00
(73)	Joe Schmidt	30.00
(74)	Del Shofner	20.00
(75)	J.D. Smith	18.00
(76)	Norm Snead	20.00
(77)	Billy Stacy	18.00
(78)	Bart Starr	60.00
(79)	Ernie Stautner	30.00
(80)	Jim Steffen	18.00
(81)	Andy Stynchula	18.00
(82)	Fran Tarkenton	110.00
(83)	Jim Taylor	40.00
(84)	Clendon Thomas	18.00
(85)	Fred (Fuzzy) Thurston	25.00
(86)	Y.A. Tittle	50.00
(87)	Bob Toneff	18.00
(88)	Jerry Tubbs	18.00
(89)	John Unitas	130.00
(90)	Billy Wade	18.00
(91)	Willie Wood	25.00
(92)	Abe Woodson	18.00

1964 Kahn's

Kahn's introduced color to its 1964 set, making it distinctively different from its prior black-and-white efforts. The Kahn's slogan has also been removed from the card fronts; it has been placed on the card back instead. The card backs are generally the same as those in previous issues. The unnumbered cards measure 3" x 3-5/8".

		NM/M
Complete Set (53):		1,400
Common Player:		15.00
(1)	Doug Atkins	25.00
(2)	Terry Barr	15.00
(3)	Dick Bass	20.00
(4)	Ordell Braase	15.00
(5)	Ed Brown	20.00
(6)	Jimmy Brown	160.00
(7)	Gary Collins	20.00
(8)	Bobby Joe Conrad	20.00
(9)	Mike Ditka	45.00
(10)	Galen Fiss	15.00
(11)	Paul Flatley	22.00
(12)	Joe Fortunato	18.00
(13)	Bill George	25.00
(14)	Bill Glass	18.00
(15)	Ernie Green	18.00
(16)	Dick Hoak	18.00
(17)	Paul Hornung	45.00
(18)	Sam Huff	35.00
(19)	Charlie Johnson	20.00
(20)	John Henry Johnson	30.00
(21)	Alex Karras	35.00
(22)	Jim Katcavage	18.00
(23)	Joe Krupa	15.00
(24)	Dick "Night Train" Lane	25.00
(25)	Tommy Mason	18.00
(26)	Don Meredith	60.00
(27)	Bobby Mitchell	30.00
(28)	Larry Morris	15.00
(29)	Jimmy Orr	18.00
(30)	Jim Parker	25.00
(31)	Bernie Parrish	20.00
(32)	Don Perkins	18.00
(33)	Jim Phillips	15.00
(34)	Sonny Randle	
(35)	Pete Retzlaff	18.00
(36)	Jim Ringo	25.00
(37)	Frank Ryan	20.00
(38)	Dick Schafrath	20.00
(39)	Joe Schmidt	25.00
(40)	Del Shofner	18.00
(41)	J.D. Smith	15.00
(42)	Norm Snead	18.00
(43)	Bart Starr	60.00
(44)	Fran Tarkenton	75.00
(45)	Jim Taylor	30.00
(46)	Clendon Thomas	15.00
(47)	Y.A. Tittle	50.00
(48)	Jerry Tubbs	18.00
(49)	John Unitas	80.00
(50)	Billy Wade	18.00
(51)	Paul Warfield	65.00
(52)	Alex Webster	18.00
(53)	Abe Woodson	15.00

1970 Kellogg's

Kellogg's cereal entered the football card market in 1970 with a set of 60 cards featuring the 3D effect utilized for many of its baseball card issues from the same period. The cards, which measure approximately 2-1/4" x 3-1/2", could be obtained inside cereal boxes or through a mail-in offer. Because of the process used to make the 3D effect, the cards are susceptible to cracking and curling, making perfect condition somewhat difficult.

		NM/M
Complete Set (60):		50.00
Common Player:		.40
1	Carl Eller	1.25
2	Jim Otto	1.25
3	Tom Matte	.60
4	Bill Nelson	.50
5	Travis Williams	.40
6	Len Dawson	2.00
7	Gene Washington	.60
8	Jim Nance	.50
9	Norm Snead	.60
10	Dick Butkus	4.00
11	George Sauer	.50
12	Billy Kilmer	.75
13	Alex Karras	3.00
14	Larry Wilson	1.25
15	Dave Robinson	.50
16	Bill Brown	.50
17	Bob Griese	4.00
18	Al Denson	.40
19	Dick Post	.40
20	Jan Stenerud	.60
21	Paul Warfield	1.50
22	Mel Farr	.50
23	Mel Renfro	.60
24	Roy Jefferson	.40
25	Mike Garrett	.50
26	Harry Jacobs	.40
27	Carl Garrett	.40
28	Dave Wilcox	.50
29	Matt Snell	.60
30	Tom Woodeshick	.40
31	Leroy Kelly	.75
32	Floyd Little	.75
33	Ken Willard	.60
34	John Mackey	1.25
35	Merlin Olsen	3.50
36	David Grayson	.40
37	Lem Barney	2.00
38	Deacon Jones	1.25
39	Bob Hayes	.75
40	Lance Alworth	2.00
41	Larry Csonka	3.00
42	Bobby Bell	1.25
43	George Webster	.50
44	John Roland	.50
45	Dick Shiner	.40
46	Charles (Bubba) Smith	2.00
47	Daryle Lamonica	.75
48	O.J. Simpson	20.00
49	Calvin Hill	1.00
50	Fred Biletnikoff	1.50
51	Gale Sayers	5.00
52	Homer Jones	.50
53	Sonny Jurgensen	2.50
54	Bob Lilly	2.00
55	Johnny Unitas	6.00
56	Tommy Nobis	.75
57	Ed Meador	.50
58	Carl Lockhart	.40
59	Don Maynard	1.25
60	Greg Cook	.50

1971 Kellogg's

The 1971 Kellogg's football set was again complete at 60 cards and featured the 3D effect. The cards measure approximately 2-1/4" x 3-1/2", and again, because of the process used to achieve the 3D effect, are susceptible to cracking and curling. Cards from the 1971 set were available only in boxes of cereal. Because sets were not available through a mail-in offer, the '71 Kellogg's set is considerably scarcer and more valuable than the '70 set.

		NM/M
Complete Set (60):		360.00
Common Player:		4.50
1	Tom Barrington	4.50
2	Chris Hanburger	5.00
3	Frank Nunley	4.50
4	Houston Antwine	4.50
5	Ron Johnson	5.00
6	Craig Morton	6.50
7	Jack Snow	5.00
8	Mel Renfro	5.00
9	Les Josephson	4.50
10	Gary Garrison	4.50
11	Dave Herman	4.50
12	Fred Dryer	6.50
13	Larry Brown	5.00
14	Gene Washington	4.50
15	Joe Greene	25.00
16	Marlin Briscoe	4.50
17	Bob Grant	4.50
18	Dan Conners	4.50
19	Mike Curtis	5.00
20	Harry Schuh	4.50
21	Rich Jackson	4.50
22	Clint Jones	4.50
23	Hewritt Dixon	4.50
24	Jess Phillips	4.50
25	Gary Cuozzo	4.50
26	Bo Scott	4.50
27	Glen Ray Hines	4.50
28	Johnny Unitas	27.00
29	John Gilliam	4.50
30	Harmon Wages	4.50
31	Walt Sweeney	4.50
32	Bruce Taylor	5.00
33	George Blanda	17.00
34	Ken Bowman	4.50
35	Johnny Robinson	5.00
36	Ed Podolak	4.50
37	Curley Culp	4.50
38	Jim Hart	6.50
39	Dick Butkus	20.00
40	Floyd Little	6.50
41	Nick Buoniconti	6.50
42	Larry Smith	4.50
43	Wayne Walker	4.50
44	MacArthur Lane	5.00
45	John Brodie	15.00
46	Dick LeBeau	4.50
47	Claude Humphrey	4.50
48	Jerry LeVias	4.50
49	Erich Barnes	4.50
50	Andy Russell	5.00
51	Donny Anderson	5.00
52	Mike Reid	7.50
53	Al Atkinson	4.50
54	Tom Dempsey	5.00
55	Bob Griese	18.00
56	Dick Gordon	4.50
57	Charlie Sanders	5.00
58	Doug Cunningham	4.50
59	Cyril Pinder	4.50
60	Dave Osborn	5.00

1978 Kellogg's Stickers

Measuring 2-1/2" x 2-5/8", the sticker fronts showcase the team's name beneath the team helmets. Spotlighted on the back are a brief history on each team and a referee's signals quiz. Each sticker is numbered on the back.

		NM/M
Complete Set (28):		30.00
Common Player:		1.00
1	Atlanta Falcons	1.00
2	Baltimore Colts	1.00
3	Buffalo Bills	1.00
4	Chicago Bears	1.00
5	Cincinnati Bengals	1.00
6	Cleveland Browns	1.00
7	Dallas Cowboys	2.00
8	Denver Broncos	1.00
9	Detroit Lions	1.00
10	Green Bay Packers	1.50
11	Houston Oilers	1.00
12	Kansas City Chiefs	1.00
13	Los Angeles Rams	1.00
14	Miami Dolphins	2.00
15	Minnesota Vikings	1.00
16	New England Patriots	1.00
17	New Orleans Saints	1.00
18	New York Giants	1.00
19	New York Jets	1.00
20	Oakland Raiders	2.00
21	Philadelphia Eagles	1.00
22	Pittsburgh Steelers	2.00
23	St. Louis Cardinals	1.00
24	San Diego Chargers	1.00
25	San Francisco 49ers	2.00
26	Seattle Seahawks	1.00
27	Tampa Bay Buccaneers	1.00
28	Washington Redskins	2.00

1982 Kellogg's

After a hiatus of more than a decade, Kellogg's returned in 1982 with a small (24-card) set that appeared in three-card panels on the backs of Raisin Bran boxes. The individual cards measure the standard 2-1/2" x 3-1/2", but the set is usually collected in panel-form, so it has little value if cut into individual cards. The prices below, therefore, are for complete panels. The cards are unnumbered and are checklisted here in alphabetical order based on the last name of the first player on each panel. Each panel measures approximately 4-1/8" x 7-1/2". Card fronts have the player's name, position and team on the bottom left, with the Kellogg's logo inside a football on the bottom right. Card backs feature the player's name and bio at the top, with his stats in the middle. His honors received are printed at the bottom, along with the team helmet and NFLPA and NFL logos. Billy Joe DuPree's photo is mistakenly labeled Harvey Martin, while Martin's is labeled DuPree.

		NM/M
Complete Set (8):		5.00
Common Panel:		.60
1	Ken Anderson, Frank Lewis, Gifford Nielsen	.75
2	Ottis Anderson, Chris Collinsworth, Franco Harris	1.75
3	William Andrews, Brian Sipe, Fred Smerlas	.60
4	Steve Bartkowski, Robert Brazile, Jack Rudnay	.60
5	Tony Dorsett, Eric Hipple, Pat McInally	1.25
6	Billy Joe DuPree, David Hill, John Stallworth	.75
7	Harvey Martin, Mike Pruitt, Joe Senser	.60
8	Art Still, Mel Gray, Tommy Kramer	.60

1982 Kellogg's Teams

Inserted into specially marked boxes of Kellogg's Raisin Bran cereal, this 28-poster set measures 8" x 10-1/2". Inside a black border, color artwork of generic players is featured, with a smaller color painting inset on one side. The team name, helmet and NFL shield are located inside an oval at the bottom. The backs include the official rules and an entry form for the "Raisin Bran Super Bowl Sweepstakes." If the team showcased on the front won the 1983 Super Bowl, the collector had to fill out the form and mail the poster to Kellogg's to win various prizes.

		NM/M
Complete Set (28):		100.00
Common Player:		5.00
1	Atlanta Falcons	5.00
2	Buffalo Bills	5.00
3	Chicago Bears	5.00
4	Cincinnati Bengals	5.00
5	Cleveland Browns	5.00
6	Dallas Cowboys	8.00
7	Denver Broncos	5.00
8	Detroit Lions	5.00
9	Green Bay Packers	8.00
10	Houston Oilers	5.00
11	Indianapolis Colts	5.00
12	Kansas City Chiefs	5.00
13	Los Angeles Raiders	8.00
14	Los Angeles Rams	5.00
15	Miami Dolphins	8.00
16	Minnesota Vikings	5.00
17	New England Patriots	5.00
18	New Orleans Saints	5.00
19	New York Giants	5.00
20	New York Jets	5.00
21	Philadelphia Eagles	5.00
22	Pittsburgh Steelers	5.00
23	St. Louis Cardinals	5.00
24	San Diego Chargers	5.00
25	San francisco 49ers	8.00
26	Seattle Seahawks	5.00
27	Tampa Bay Buccaneers	5.00
28	Washington Redskins	8.00

1989 King B Discs

These red-bordered discs, which feature 24 NFL stars, were included in specially-marked cans of King B beef jerky, one per can. The front has a color head shot of the player, along with the King B logo. "1st Annual Collectors Edition" is also written on the front. The back includes the King B and NFLPA logos, plus biographical information and 1988 and career statistics. A ring of stars runs along the border. The cards, produced by Michael Schechter Associates, are numbered on the back.

		NM/M
Complete Set (24):		50.00
Common Player:		1.00
1	Chris Miller	2.50
2	Shane Conlan	1.25
3	Richard Dent	1.75
4	Boomer Esiason	1.75
5	Frank Minnifield	1.00
6	Herschel Walker	2.00
7	Karl Mecklenburg	1.50
8	Mike Cofer	1.00
9	Warren Moon	3.00
10	Chris Chandler	1.50
11	Deron Cherry	1.00
12	Bo Jackson	2.00
13	Jim Everett	1.50
14	Dan Marino	12.00
15	Anthony Carter	1.25
16	Andre Tippett	1.50
17	Bobby Hebert	1.50
18	Phil Simms	1.75
19	Al Toon	1.50
20	Gary Anderson	1.50
21	Joe Montana	14.00
22	Dave Krieg	1.50
23	Randall Cunningham	2.50
24	Bubby Brister	1.00

1990 King B Discs

Once again, these discs were available in specially-marked cans of King B beef jerky, one per can. The front has a color mug shot of the player, surrounded by a red border with a yellow background. The year 1990 appears at the bottom of the card in green; the King B logo is underneath the year. Each card back is numbered and has a border of stars around it. Biographical information and a comment about the player's accomplishments are also given on the back, along with the King B and NFLPA logos.

		NM/M
Complete Set (24):		45.00
Common Player:		1.00
1	Jim Everett	2.00
2	Marcus Allen	2.00
3	Brian Blades	1.50
4	Bubby Brister	1.00
5	Mark Carrier	1.50
6	Steve Jordan	1.00
7	Barry Sanders	7.00
8	Ronnie Lott	2.00
9	Howie Long	2.00
10	Steve Atwater	1.50
11	Dan Marino	8.00
12	Boomer Esiason	2.00
13	Dalton Hilliard	1.00
14	Phil Simms	2.50
15	Jim Kelly	3.00
16	Mike Singletary	1.50
17	John Stephens	1.50
18	Christian Okoye	1.50
19	Art Monk	2.00
20	Chris Miller	2.50
21	Roger Craig	2.00
22	Duane Bickett	1.00
23	Don Majkowski	1.00
24	Eric Metcalf	2.50

1991 King B Discs

Specially-marked cans of King B beef jerky each contained a disc featuring one of 24 NFL stars. The front has a color mug shot of the player surrounded by a purple border. His name, team and position are printed in gold. The King B logo and 1991 are printed at the bottom of the disc. The back is numbered and includes 1990 and career statistics, plus brief biographical information, all in red ink. A ring of stars comprises the border. An NFLPA and King B logo are also included on the back. The discs were produced by Michael Schechter Associates.

		NM/M
Complete Set (24):		35.00
Common Player:		1.00
1	Mark Rypien	1.25
2	Art Monk	2.00
3	Sean Jones	1.00
4	Bubby Brister	1.00
5	Warren Moon	3.00
6	Andre Rison	2.00
7	Emmitt Smith	9.00
8	Mervyn Fernandez	1.00
9	Rickey Jackson	1.00
10	Bruce Armstrong	1.00
11	Neal Anderson	1.25
12	Christian Okoye	1.00
13	Thurman Thomas	3.00
14	Bruce Smith	1.25
15	Jeff Hostetler	1.50
16	Barry Sanders	6.00
17	Andre Reed	1.25
18	Derrick Thomas	2.50
19	Jim Everett	1.25
20	Boomer Esiason	1.50
21	Merril Hoge	1.00
22	Steve Atwater	1.25
23	Dan Marino	8.00
24	Mark Collins	1.00

1992 King B Discs

This fourth annual collectors' edition features 24 NFL stars on discs available in specially-marked cans of King B beef jerky. The front of each disc, which is black with a yellow border, has a color mug shot of the player. His name, team and position are written in white at the top of the card. A yellow King B logo and the year, 1992, are at the bottom. The back is numbered and includes 1991 and career statistics, plus brief biographical information. King B and NFLPA logos also appear. An alternating ring of white and black stars runs along the border of the back. Michael Schechter Associates again produced the set.

		NM/M
Complete Set (24):		30.00
Common Player:		1.00
1	Derrick Thomas	2.00
2	Wilber Marshall	1.50
3	Andre Rison	2.00
4	Thurman Thomas	2.50
5	Emmitt Smith	8.00
6	Charles Mann	1.00
7	Michael Irvin	3.00
8	Jim Everett	1.50
9	Gary Anderson	1.00
10	Trace Armstrong	1.00
11	John Elway	3.50
12	Chip Lohmiller	1.00
13	Bobby Hebert	1.00
14	Cornelius Bennett	1.25
15	Chris Miller	1.50
16	Warren Moon	2.00
17	Charles Haley	1.50
18	Mark Rypien	1.00
19	Darrell Green	1.25
20	Barry Sanders	5.00
21	Rodney Hampton	2.50
22	Shane Conlan	1.00
23	Jerry Ball	1.00
24	Morten Andersen	1.50

1993 King B Discs

These 2-3/8" discs were included one per specially-marked can of King B beef jerky. Twenty-four NFL stars are featured. The front of the card uses a green football field motif and features a color mug shot of the player. A black panel at the top includes the player's name, team and position, written in orange and white letters. A blue King B logo and the year appear at the bottom of the disc. The back is numbered and uses black ink to present brief biographical information, plus a brief career summary. King B and NFLPA logos are also included on the back, which has black and white stars along the rim. Each disc, produced by Michael Schechter Associates, measures 2-3/8". An uncut sheet, measuring 17-1/4" x 12-3/4", was also issued.

		NM/M
Complete Set (24):		30.00
Common Player:		1.00
1	Luis Sharpe	1.00
2	Erik McMillan	1.00
3	Chris Doleman	1.25
4	Cortez Kennedy	1.50
5	Howie Long	1.25
6	Bill Romanowski	1.00
7	Andre Tippett	1.00
8	Simon Fletcher	1.50
9	Derrick Thomas	2.00
10	Rodney Peete	1.00
11	Ronnie Lott	1.50
12	Duane Bickett	1.00
13	Steve Walsh	1.25
14	Stan Humphries	1.50
15	Jeff George	2.75
16	Jay Novacek	2.00
17	Andre Reed	2.00
18	Andre Rison	2.00
19	Emmitt Smith	8.00
20	Neal Anderson	1.00
21	Ricky Sanders	1.25
22	Thurman Thomas	2.50
23	Lorenzo White	1.00
24	Barry Foster	1.00

1994 King B Discs

The sixth edition of this set, issued by Michael Schechter Associates, was inserted one disc per specially marked can of King B beef jerky. Each disc measures 2-3/8" in diameter. Color headshots of the player are showcased over a green background. The player's name, position and team name are included in a yellow rectangle at the bottom of the photo. The white backs have the player's name with his team, position and bio listed at the top, along with the NFLPA logo. His stats are listed in the center. All print on the backs is in green. The back is bordered with stars.

		NM/M
Complete Set (24):		25.00
Common Player:		.75
1	Marcus Allen	1.50
2	Jerome Bettis	2.00
3	Terrell Buckley	.75
4	Craig Erickson	.75
5	Brett Favre	6.00
6	Barry Foster	.75
7	Irving Fryar	.75
8	Gary Brown	.75
9	Rodney Hampton	.75
10	Qadry Ismail	.75
11	Jim Jeffcoat	.75
12	Jim Lachey	.75
13	Natrone Means	2.00
14	Troy Meola	.75
15	Pete Metzelaars	.75
16	Scott Mitchell	1.00
17	Ronald Moore	.75
18	Andre Rison	.75
19	Jay Schroeder	.75
20	Junior Seau	1.25
21	Shannon Sharpe	1.00
22	Sterling Sharpe	1.00
23	Tim Brown	1.00
24	Chris Warren	1.00

1995 King B Discs

Labeled on the disc front as the "7th Annual Collectors Edition," these discs measure 2-5/8". A color headshot of the player is featured, with a background drawing of a running back chased by two defensive players. A brown and gold vertical striped background borders the left side of the disc. The King B logo also is printed at the left. The player's name and position are located at the bottom. The disc backs feature the player's name, team and bio at the top. His stats are in the middle, with the King B logo and the disc number at the bottom. Text is housed inside a circle of alternating stars and footballs. The discs were available either one disc per shredded beef jerky can or as a 17-1/4" x 12-1/2" collector sheet.

		NM/M
Complete Set (24):		18.00
Common Player:		.50
1	Errict Rhett	1.00
2	Andre Reed	.50
3	Rodney Hampton	.75
4	Kevin Greene	.50
5	Merton Hanks	.50
6	Jerome Bettis	1.50
7	Johnny Johnson	.50
8	Ricky Watters	1.00
9	Harvey Williams	.50
10	Mel Gray	.50
11	Craig Erickson	.50
12	Stan Humphries	.50
13	Natrone Means	1.50
14	Terance Mathis	.50
15	Ken Harvey	.50
16	Brian Mitchell	.50
17	Cris Carter	.50
18	Tim Brown	1.00
19	Marshall Faulk	2.00
20	Eric Turner	.50
21	Terry Allen	1.00
22	Chris Warren	1.00
23	Randy Baldwin	.50
24	Ben Coates	.50

1996 All King B Sack Attack Team

Measuring 2-3/8" in diameter, the 24-disc set focused on defensive players. The front of the disc includes a headshot of the player, his name at the top and a "Sack-It-To-'Em" logo at the bottom. A drawing of a defensive player is included along the left border. The disc backs feature the player's career sacks. One disc was included in each specially marked King B beef jerky canister.

		NM/M
Complete Set (24):		15.00
Common Player:		.50
1	Reggie White	2.00
2	Rickey Jackson	.50
3	Kevin Greene	1.00
4	Tony Bennett	.50
5	Bryce Paup	1.00
6	John Copeland	.50
7	Pat Swilling	.50
8	Willie McGinest	.50
9	Charles Haley	.50
10	Chris Doleman	.50
11	Clyde Simmons	.50
12	Hugh Douglas	.50
13	Henry Thomas	.50
14	John Randle	1.00
15	Phil Hansen	.50
16	Bruce Smith	1.00
17	Jim Flanigan	1.00
18	D'Marco Farr	.50
19	Ray Seals	.50
20	Neil Smith	1.00
21	Andy Harmon	.50
22	William Fuller	.50
23	Tracy Scoggins	.50
24	Leslie O'Neal	.50

1997 King B Discs

This 24-disc set includes only rookies from the 1997 season and were distributed one per specially marked package of the beef jerky snack. The discs contain the player's portrait over a purple background which features diagrammed plays. The King B logo is in the lower left portion of the photo, while "Rookies Collector Edition," the player's name and position are included inside a purple area at the bottom of the disc front.

		NM/M
Complete Set (24):		20.00
Common Player:		.50
1	Orlando Pace	1.00
2	Darrell Russell	.50
3	Shawn Springs	1.00
4	Peter Boulware	.50
5	Bryant Westbrook	.50
6	Walter Jones	.50
7	Ike Hilliard	1.50
8	James Farrior	.50
9	Tom Knight	.50
10	Chris Naeole	.50
11	Warrick Dunn	3.00
12	Tony Gonzalez	1.25
13	Reinard Wilson	.50
14	Yatil Green	.50
15	Reidel Anthony	1.50
16	Dwayne Rudd	1.50
17	Renaldo Wynn	.50
18	David LaFleur	1.00
19	Antowain Smith	2.00
20	Chad Scott	.50
21	Jim Druckenmiller	2.00
22	Rae Carruth	1.50
23	Jake Plummer	3.00
24	Ronnie McAda	.50

A card number in parenthese ( ) indicates the set is unnumbered.

1998 King B Discs

		NM/M
Complete Set (24):		15.00
Common Player:		.50
1	Grant Wistrom	.50
2	Jerome Pathon	.50
3	Skip Hicks	.50
4	Charles Woodson	.50
5	Joe Jurevicius	.50
6	Tra Thomas	.50
7	Andre Wadsworth	.50
8	Fred Taylor	2.00
9	Duane Starks	.50
10	Takeo Spikes	1.00
11	Anthony Simmons	.50
12	Brian Simmons	.50
13	Kevin Dyson	.50
14	Curtis Enis	.50
15	Robert Edwards	.50
16	Greg Ellis	.50
17	Marcus Nash	.50
18	Jason Peter	.50
19	Keith Brooking	.50
20	John Avery	.50
21	Ahman Green	3.00
22	Jacquez Green	.50
23	Brian Griese	1.00
24	Randy Moss	2.00

1999 King B Discs

		NM/M
Complete Set (24):		15.00
Common Player:		.50
1	Jevon Kearse	.50
2	Kevin Johnson	.50
3	Torry Holt	1.00
4	Jermaine Fazande	.50
5	Shaun King	.50
6	Edgerrin James	2.00
7	James Johnson	.50
8	Chris McAlister	.50
9	Antoine Winfield	.50
10	D'Wayne Bates	.50
11	Peerless Price	1.00
12	Troy Edwards	.50
13	Ebenezer Ekuban	.50
14	Andy Katzenmoyer	.50
15	Kevin Faulk	.50
16	David Boston	1.00
17	Brock Huard	.50
18	Daunte Culpepper	2.00
19	Akili Smith	.50
20	Mike Cloud	.50
21	Champ Bailey	.50
22	Rob Konrad	.50
23	Chris Claiborne	.50
24	Donovan McNabb	2.00

2000 King B Discs

		NM/M
Complete Set (24):		22.00
Common Player:		.50
1	Ron Dayne	.50
2	Trung Canidate	.50
3	Plaxico Burress	2.00
4	Courtney Brown	.50
5	Anthony Becht	.50
6	Shaun Alexander	2.00
7	Sylvester Morris	.50
8	Jamal Lewis	2.00
9	Thomas Jones	1.00
10	Bubba Franks	.50
11	Ron Dugans	.50
12	Reuben Droughns	.50
13	J.R. Redmond	.50
14	Travis Prentice	1.00
15	Jerry Porter	2.00
16	Todd Pinkston	.50
17	Chad Pennington	4.00
18	Dennis Northcutt	.50
19	Peter Warrick	.50
20	Brian Urlacher	2.00
21	Travis Taylor	1.00
22	R. Jay Soward	.50
23	Corey Simon	.50
24	Chris Samuels	.50

2002 King B Discs

		NM/M
Complete Set (24):		12.00
Common Player:		.25
	Shaun Alexander	.25
	Jerome Bettis	.25
	Tom Brady	1.00
	Tim Brown	.50
	Corey Dillon	.25
	Marshall Faulk	1.00
	Brett Favre	3.00
	Rich Gannon	.25
	Jeff Garcia	.25
	Eddie George	1.00
	Tony Gonzalez	.25
	Ahman Green	1.00
	Brian Griese	.25
	Marvin Harrison	1.00
	Edgerrin James	1.00
	Curtis Martin	1.00
	Terrell Owens	1.00
	Jerry Rice	2.00
	Warren Sapp	.25
	Rod Smith	.25
	Kordell Stewart	.25
	Michael Strahan	.25
	Adam Vinatieri	.25
	Kurt Warner	1.00

1989 Knudsen Raiders

Measuring 2" x 8", this bookmark set of 12 was introduced by Knudsen's Dairy of California. The bookmarks were available to children who checked out books from the Los Angeles Public Library during the 1989 season. The fronts featured a photo of a Raiders player, with "Knudsen presents Raiders Readers" at the top. The Raiders' logo, the player's name, position and bio, along with his highlights are listed below the photo. The unnumbered backs have reading tips, the player's name, L.A. Public Library, MCLS, Knudsen and Raiders' logos. The Mike Shanahan card is a tough one to locate, as it was not distributed or pulled after he left the Raiders for a position with another NFL team.

		NM/M
Complete Set (14):		30.00
Common Player:		1.50
6	Jeff Gossett	1.50
13	Jay Schroeder	2.00
26	Vann McElroy	1.50
35	Steve Smith	2.00
36	Terry McDaniel	2.00
70	Scott Davis	1.50
72	Don Mosebar	1.50
75	Howie Long	2.50
76	Steve Wisniewski	2.00
81	Tim Brown	6.00
83	Willie Gault	2.00
NNO	Mike Shanahan (SP) (CO)	16.00
NNO	Raiders/Super Bowl	1.50
NNO	Raiderettes (SP)	2.00

1990 Knudsen Chargers

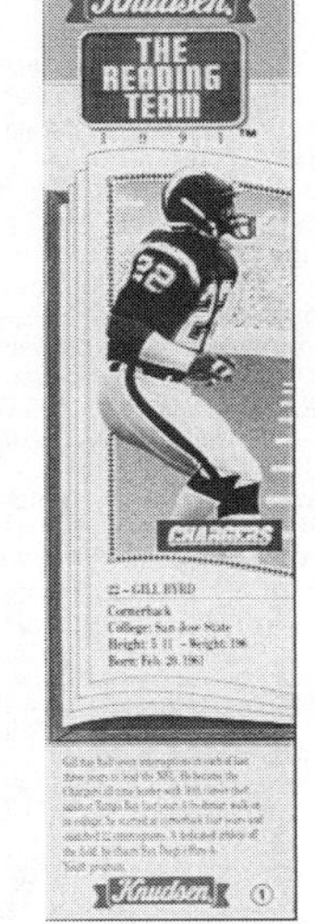

Measuring 2" x 8", the Chargers bookmarks were available at San Diego libraries. The fronts showcase the Knudsen logo at the top, with "The Reading Team" below it. The player photo is shown in the middle, with the Chargers' logo, player's name, uniform number and bio in a box under the photo. The unnumbered backs contain the Knudsen, American Library Association and San Diego libraries' logos.

		NM/M
Complete Set (6):		10.00
Common Player:		1.50
1	Marion Butts	2.50
2	Anthony Miller	3.50
3	Leslie O'Neal	2.50
4	Gary Plummer	1.50
5	Billy Ray Smith	1.50
6	Billy Joe Tolliver	2.00

1990 Knudsen 49ers

Measuring 2" x 8", this six-card bookmark set was given to children under 15 years of age at libraries in the San Francisco metro area. The design is basically the same as the Chargers set, with the Knudsen logo at the top and "The Reading Team" below it. The player's photo is in the center, above a box which contains the 49ers' logo and the player's name, uniform number and bio. The unnumbered backs have the Knudsen logo at the top and the San Francisco Public Library logo at the bottom. Two books are listed on the back of each bookmark.

		NM/M
Complete Set (6):		25.00
Common Player:		1.50
1	Roger Craig	2.50
2	Ronnie Lott	4.00
3	Joe Montana	12.00
4	Jerry Rice	12.00
5	George Siefert (CO)	3.00
6	Michael Walter	1.50

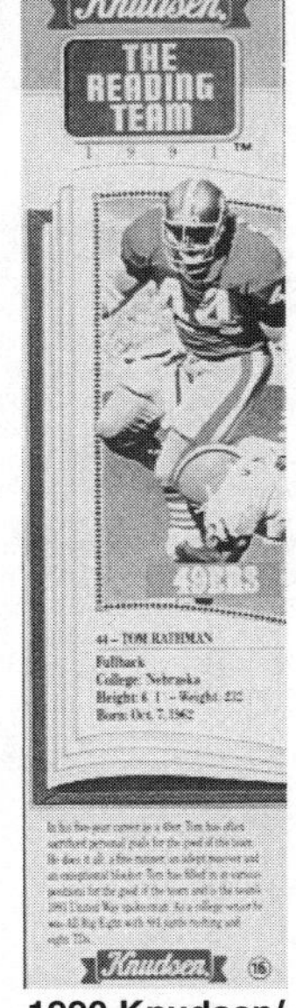

1990 Knudsen/ Sealtest Patriots

Measuring 2" x 8", this six-card bookmark set was sponsored by Knudsen's and Sealtest. Those children under 15 years of age in the New England area received the bookmarks at their local libraries. The Knudsen or Sealtest logos were located at the top of the front, with "The Reading Team" below it. The player's photo is showcased above a box which contains the Patriots' logo, player's name, uniform number and bio. The backs have the sponsor logos and information on two books.

		NM/M
Complete Set (6):		25.00
Common Player:		4.00
1	Steve Grogan	6.00
2	Ronnie Lippett	4.00
3	Eric Sievers	4.00
4	Mosi Tatupu	4.00
5	Andre Tippett	6.00
6	Garin Veris	4.00

1990 Knudsen Rams

Measuring 2" x 8", the six-bookmark set promoted reading to children under 15 years of age in the Los Angeles area. The front design is the same as the Chargers, 49ers and Patriots sets of 1990.

		NM/M
Complete Set (6):		25.00
Common Player:		4.00
1	Henry Ellard	8.00

2	Jim Everett	6.00
3	Jerry Gray	4.00
4	Pete Holohan	4.00
5	Mike Lansford	4.00
6	Irv Pankey	4.00

1991 Knudsen

Measuring 2" x 8", the 18-bookmark set was available to children who checked out books at San Diego, Los Angeles and San Francisco public libraries. The fronts have the Knudsen logo at the top, with "The Reading Team" printed below it. A photo of a player is included on a page of a book. The player's team name is superimposed over the photo. His name, position and bio are printed under the photo. The backs have the Knudsen and public library logos, along with information on two books. Each team's bookmarks were available only in its area. Nos. 1-6 are Chargers, Nos. 7-12 are Rams and Nos. 13-18 are 49ers.

		NM/M
Complete Set (18):		30.00
Common Player:		1.50
1	Gill Byrd	1.50
2	Courtney Hall	1.50
3	Ronnie Harmon	2.00
4	Anthony Miller	3.00
5	Joe Phillips	1.50
6	Junior Seau	5.00
7	Jim Everett	2.50
8	Kevin Greene	2.50
9	Damone Johnson	1.50
10	Tom Newberry	1.50
11	John Robinson (CO)	2.00
12	Michael Stewart	1.50
13	Michael Carter	1.50
14	Charles Haley	2.50
15	Joe Montana	10.00
16	Tom Rathman	2.00
17	Jerry Rice	10.00
18	George Seifert (CO)	3.00

L

1983 Latrobe Police

The black-and-white or sepia-toned standard sized cards were issued in Latrobe, Pa. Titled "Birthplace of Pro Football," the 30-card set featured a photo of the player in an oval, with his name and position in a box at the bottom of the card. The card backs, which came in two versions, have the 1895 "Birthplace of Pro Football" logo in the upper left, with the player's name and position at the right. A write-up of his career highlights also is included on the horizontal card backs. The cards were produced by Chess Promotions Inc. of Latrobe, Pa. The variation backs include safety tips.

		NM/M
Complete Set (30):		8.00
Common Player:		.30
1	John Brallier	1.00
2	John K. Brallier	.50
3	Latrobe YMCA Team 1895	.50
4	Brallier and Team at W and J 1895	.50
5	Latrobe A.A. Team 1896	.50
6	Latrobe A.A. 1897	.50
7	1st All Pro Team 1897	.50
8	David Berry (Mgr.)	.30
9	Harry Ryan (RT)	.30
10	Walter Okeson (LE)	.30
11	Edward Wood (RE)	.30
12	E. Hammer (C)	.30
13	Marcus Saxman (LH)	.30
14	Charles Shumaker (SUB)	.30
15	Charles McDyre (LE)	.30
16	Edward Abbatticchio (FB)	.30
17	George Flickinger (C/LT)	.30
18	Walter Howard (RH)	.30
19	Thomas Trenchard	.50
20	John Kinport Brallier (QB)	.75
21	Jack Gass (LH)	.30
22	Dave Campbell (LT)	.30
23	Edward Blair (RH)	.30
24	John Johnston (RG)	.30
25	Sam Johnston (LG)	.30
26	Alex Laird (SUB)	.30
27	Latrobe A.A. 1897 Team	.50
28	Pro Football Memorial Plaque	.30
29	Commemorative Medallion	.30
30	Birth of Pro Football Checklist Card	.50

1975 Laughlin Flaky Football

Artist R.G. Laughlin created this 26-card set in 1975 as a parody to the NFL. Measuring 2-1/2" x 3-3/8", the card fronts have the city name and a parody NFL nickname, such as the Green Bay Porkers, with artwork relating to the nickname. "Flaky Football" is printed at the top of the cards, with the card number in a white circle in one of the corners of the horizontal fronts. The backs of the cards are blank.

		NM/M
Complete Set (27):		125.00
Common Player:		4.50
1	Pittsburgh Stealers	8.00
2	Minnesota Spikings	6.00
3	Cincinnati Bungles	6.00
4	Chicago Bares	6.00
5	Miami Dullfins	8.00
6	Philadelphia Eggles	6.00
7	Cleveland Brawns	4.50
8	New York Gianuts	4.50
9	Buffalo Bulls	4.50
10	Dallas Plowboys	8.00
11	New England Pastry Nuts	4.50
12	Green Bay Porkers	8.00
13	Denver Bongos	4.50
14	St. Louis Cigardinals	4.50
15	New York Jests	4.50
16	Washington Redshins	8.00
17	Oakland Waders	8.00
18	Los Angeles Yams	4.50
19	Baltimore Kilts	4.50
20	New Orleans Scents	4.50
21	San Diego Charges	4.50
22	Detroit Loins	4.50
23	Kansas City Chefs	4.50
24	Atlanta Fakin's	4.50
25	Houston Owlers	4.50
26	San Francisco 40 Miners	8.00
NNO	Title Card Flaky Football	8.00

1948 Leaf

This 98-card set, the first of two Leaf sets to be issued in the late 1940s, features players posed in front of solid backgrounds (player hands and faces are in black and white). Cards measure 2-3/8" x 2-7/8", and the final 49 cards are more difficult to find than the first 49. Rookies in this set include Sid Luckman, Bulldog Turner, Doak Walker, Bobby Lane, Pete Pihos, George McAfee, Steve Van Buren, Bob Waterfield, Charlie Trippi, Sammy Baugh, Bill Dudley, George Connor, Frank Tripucka, Leo Nomellini, Charley Conerly, Leo Nomellini, Chuck Bednarik, and Jackie Jensen.

		NM/M
Complete Set (98):		5,800
Common Player (1-49):		20.00
Common Player (50-98):		100.00
1	*Sid Luckman*	300.00
2	Steve Suhey	20.00
3	*Bulldog Turner*	90.00
4	*Doak Walker*	125.00
5	Levi Jackson	20.00
6	*Bobby Layne*	350.00
7	Bill Fischer	20.00
8	Vice Banonis	20.00
9	*Tommy Thompson*	40.00
10	Perry Moss	20.00
11	*Terry Brennan*	20.00
12	*William Swiacki*	25.00
13	*Johnny Lujack*	125.00
14	Mal Kutner	20.00
15	*Charlie Justice*	60.00
16	*Pete Pihos*	95.00
17	*Kenny Washington*	55.00
18	*Harry Gilmer*	30.00
19	*George McAfee*	100.00
20	*George Taliaferro*	25.00
21	*Paul Christman*	40.00
22	*Steve Van Buren*	140.00
23	*Ken Kavanaugh*	25.00
24	*Jim Martin*	25.00
25	Bud Angsman	20.00
26	*Bob Waterfield*	200.00
27	Fred Davis	20.00
28	*Whitey Wistert*	20.00
29	*Charlie Trippi*	100.00
30	Paul Governali	20.00
31	Tom McWilliams	20.00
32	Larry Zimmerman	20.00
33	Pat Harder	40.00
34	*Sammy Baugh*	425.00
35	Ted Fritsch Sr.	20.00
36	*Bill Dudley*	85.00
37	*George Connor*	65.00
38	Frank Dancewicz	20.00
39	Billy Dewell	20.00
40	John Nolan	20.00
41	Harry Szulborski	20.00
42	Tex Coulter	20.00
43	Robert Nussbaumer	20.00
44	Bob Mann	20.00
45	Jim White	20.00
46	Jack Jacobs	20.00
47	John Clement	20.00
48	Frank Reagan	20.00
49	*Frank Tripucka*	30.00
50	*John Rauch*	100.00
51	Mike Dimitrio	100.00
52	*Leo Nomellini*	250.00
53	*Charlie Conerly*	250.00
54	*Chuck Bednarik*	400.00
55	Chick Jagade	100.00
56	*Bob Folsom*	100.00
57	*Eugene Rossides*	100.00
58	Art Weiner	100.00
59	Alex Sarkistian	100.00
60	Dick Harris	100.00
61	Len Younce	100.00
62	Gene Derricotte	100.00
63	Roy Steiner	100.00
64	Frank Seno	100.00
65	Bob Hendreen	100.00
66	Jack Cloud	100.00
67	Harrell Collins	100.00
68	Clyde LeForce	100.00
69	Larry Joe	100.00
70	Phil O'Reilly	100.00
71	Paul Campbell	100.00
72	Ray Evans	100.00
73	*Jackie Jensen*	300.00
74	Russ Steger	100.00
75	Tony Minisi	100.00
76	Clayton Tonnemaker	100.00
77	George Savitsky	100.00
78	Clarence Self	100.00
79	Rod Franz	100.00
80	Jim Youle	100.00
81	Billy Bye	100.00
82	Fred Enke	100.00
83	Fred Folger	100.00
84	Jug Girard	100.00
85	Joe Scott	100.00
86	Bob Demoss	100.00
87	Dave Templeton	100.00
88	Herb Siegert	100.00
89	Bucky O'Conner	100.00
90	Joe Whisler	100.00
91	*Leon Hart*	175.00
92	Earl Banks	100.00
93	Frank Aschenbrenner	100.00
94	John Golddsberry	100.00
95	Porter Payne	100.00
96	Pete Perini	100.00
97	Jay Rhodemyre	100.00
98	*Al DiMarco*	200.00

1949 Leaf

The 1949 Leaf issue is quite possibly the stupidest of what is considered the "major" football issues. There are but 49 cards in the set, but numerically the set jumps around until it reaches a 150 count. There are several gaps in the numbering sequence. Even less appealing is the fact that there is exactly one rookie card in the set - that of #1, Bob Hendren. Cards, which measure 2-3/8" x 2-7/8", bear close resemblance to the 1948 Leaf football set, as well as to the Leaf baseball sets of the era. The second-year cards in the set include those of Hall of Famers Sid Luckman, Charley Trippi, Bill Dudley, Sammy Baugh, Pete Pihos, George Connor, Ken McAfee (last card), Bobby Lane, Steve Van Buren, Bob Waterfield, Chuck Bednarik, and Bulldog Turner. Other sophomore cards include Charley Conerly, Johnny Lujack, and Frank Tripucka.

		NM/M
Complete Set (49):		2,000
Common Player:		25.00
1	Bob Hendren	75.00
2	Joe Scott	25.00
3	Frank Reagan	25.00
4	John Rauch	25.00
7	Bill Fischer	25.00
9	Bud Angsman	25.00
10	Billy Dewell	25.00
13	Tommy Thompson	25.00
15	Sid Luckman	100.00
16	Charlie Trippi	45.00
17	Bob Mann	25.00
19	Paul Christman	25.00
22	Bill Dudley	45.00
23	Clyde LeForce	25.00
26	Sammy Baugh	250.00
28	Pete Pihos	45.00
31	Tex Coulter	25.00
32	Mal Kutner	25.00
35	Whitey Wistert	25.00
37	Ted Fritsch Sr.	25.00
38	Vince Banonis	25.00
39	Jim White	25.00
40	George Connor	45.00
41	George McAfee	45.00
43	Frank Tripucka	25.00
47	Fred Enke	25.00
49	Charlie Conerly	80.00
51	Ken Kavanaugh	25.00
56	John Lujack	80.00
57	Jim Youle	25.00
62	Harry Gilmer	25.00
65	Robert Nussbaumer	25.00
67	Bobby Layne	140.00
70	Herb Siegert	25.00
74	Tony Minisi	25.00
79	Steve Van Buren	80.00
81	Perry Moss	25.00
89	Bob Waterfield	90.00
90	Jack Jacobs	25.00
95	Kenny Washington	30.00
101	Pat Harder	25.00
110	William Swiacki	25.00
118	Fred Davis	25.00
126	Jay Rhodemyre	25.00
134	Chuck Bednarik	100.00
144	George Savitsky	25.00
150	Bulldog Turner	125.00

1996 Leaf

Leaf Football contained 190 cards in the regular-issue set, plus 10 Gold Leaf Rookies that were numbered like inserts, but considered part of the regular-issue set. Leaf arrived for the first time since 1949, and was packaged in 10-card packs. The 190 players from the base set were also available in factory sets receiving special foil treatment and limited to 1,996 sets. The factory sets also included one of 25 different autographed future stars. Inserts found in Leaf Football included: 190-card Press Proof parallel set, Statistical Standouts, Grass Roots, Gold Leaf Stars, American All-Stars and Shirt Off My Back. Cards from regular packs had the bottom strip of the card in the player's team colors, with no foil, while pre- priced packs featured red foil and Collector's Edition cards had gold foil.

		NM/M
Complete Set (190):		20.00
Common Player:		.10
Minor Stars:		.20
Gold Press Proof Cards:		5X-10X
Hobby Pack (10):		1.50
Hobby Wax Box (18):		20.00
1	Troy Aikman	1.50
2	Ricky Watters	.20
3	Robert Brooks	.10
4	Ki-Jana Carter	.20
5	Drew Bledsoe	1.25
6	Eric Swann	.10
7	Hardy Nickerson	.10
8	Tony Martin	.10
9	Garrison Hearst	.10
10	Bernie Parmalee	.10
11	Neil Smith	.10
12	Aaron Craver	.10
13	Rashaan Salaam	.20
14	Greg Hill	.10
15	Charlie Garner	.10
16	Kimble Anders	.10
17	Steve McNair	1.00
18	Neil O'Donnell	.10
19	Greg Lloyd	.10
20	Warren Moon	.10
21	Bernie Kosar	.10
22	Derrick Thomas	.10
23	Andre Hastings	.10
24	Wayne Chrebet	.10
25	Mark Seay	.10
26	Eric Metcalf	.10
27	Shawn Jefferson	.10
28	Napoleon Kaufman	.10
29	Steve Walsh	.10
30	Derrick Alexander	.10
31	Rodney Peete	.10
32	Terance Mathis	.10
33	Michael Westbrook	.20
34	Kevin Carter	.10
35	Aaron Hayden	.10
36	J.J. Stokes	.20
37	Andre Reed	.10
38	Chris Warren	.20
39	Jerry Rice	1.50
40	Ben Coates	.10
41	Reggie White	.20
42	Joey Galloway	1.25
43	Sean Dawkins	.10
44	Brett Favre	3.00
45	Jeff George	.10
46	Robert Smith	.10
47	Ken Dilger	.10
48	Larry Centers	.10
49	Jackie Harris	.10
50	Hugh Douglas	.10
51	Herschel Walker	.10
52	Kerry Collins	.30
53	Michael Irvin	.20
54	Willie McGinest	.10
55	Herman Moore	.20
56	Leroy Hoard	.10
57	Scott Mitchell	.10
58	Terrell Davis	1.50
59	Kevin Greene	.10
60	Yancey Thigpen	.20
61	Kevin Smith	.10
62	Trent Dilfer	.10
63	Cortez Kennedy	.10
64	Carnell Lake	.10
65	Quinn Early	.10
66	Kyle Brady	.10
67	Marshall Faulk	.30
68	Fred Barnett	.10
69	Quentin Coryatt	.10
70	Dan Marino	3.00
71	Junior Seau	.10
72	Andre Coleman	.10
73	Terry Kirby	.10
74	Curtis Martin	2.00
75	Isaac Bruce	.75
76	Mark Chmura	.10
77	Edgar Bennett	.10
78	Mario Bates	.10
79	Eric Zeier	.10
80	Adrian Murrell	.10
81	Mark Brunell	1.00
82	Mark Rypien	.10
83	Erric Pegram	.10
84	Bryan Cox	.10
85	Heath Shuler	.10
86	Lake Dawson	.10
87	O.J. McDuffie	.10
88	Emmitt Smith	3.00
89	Jim Harbaugh	.10
90	Aaron Bailey	.10
91	Jim Kelly	.20
92	Rodney Hampton	.10
93	Cris Carter	.10
94	Henry Ellard	.10
95	Darnay Scott	.20
96	Daryl Johnston	.10
97	Tamarick Vanover	.20
98	Jeff Blake	.75
99	Anthony Miller	.10
100	Darren Woodson	.10
101	Irving Fryar	.10
102	Craig Heyward	.10
103	Derek Loville	.10
104	Ernie Mills	.10
105	Brian Blades	.10
106	Gus Frerotte	.10
107	Alvin Harper	.10
108	Tyrone Wheatley	.10
109	John Elway	1.00
110	Charles Haley	.10
111	Terrell Fletcher	.10
112	Vincent Brisby	.10
113	Jerome Bettis	.20
114	Barry Sanders	1.50
115	Ken Norton Jr.	.10
116	Sherman Williams	.10
117	Antonio Freeman	.10
118	Bert Emanuel	.10
119	Marcus Allen	.20
120	Stan Humphries	.10
121	Chris Sanders	.10
122	Jeff Graham	.10
123	Jay Novacek	.10
124	Aeneas Williams	.10
125	Kordell Stewart	1.25
126	Steve Young	1.00
127	Jake Reed	.10
128	Rick Mirer	.10
129	Jeff Hostetler	.10
130	Tim Brown	.10
131	Shannon Sharpe	.10
132	Dave Brown	.10
133	Harvey Williams	.10
134	Rodney Thomas	.10
135	Frank Sanders	.10
136	Brett Perriman	.10
137	Steve Bono	.10
138	Steve Atwater	.10
139	Andre Rison	.10
140	Orlando Thomas	.10
141	Terry Allen	.10
142	Carl Pickens	.20
143	William Floyd	.20
144	Bryce Paup	.10
145	James Stewart	.10
146	Eric Bjornson	.10
147	Errict Rhett	.20
148	Darick Holmes	.10
149	Bill Brooks	.10
150	Brent Jones	.10
151	Natrone Means	.10
152	Rod Woodson	.10
153	Bruce Smith	.10
154	Deion Sanders	.75
155	Kevin Williams	.10
156	Erik Kramer	.10
157	Jim Everett	.10
158	Vinny Testaverde	.10
159	Boomer Esiason	.10
160	Floyd Turner	.10
161	Curtis Conway	.20
162	Thurman Thomas	.20
163	Tony Brackens	.10
164	Stepfret Williams	.10
165	Alex Van Dyke	.75
166	Cedric Jones	.10
167	Stanley Pritchett	.10
168	Willie Anderson	.10
169	Regan Upshaw	.10
170	Daryl Gardener	.10
171	Alex Molden	.10
172	John Mobley	.10
173	*Danny Kanell*	.50
174	Marco Battaglia	.10
175	Simeon Rice	.10
176	*Tony Banks*	.75
177	*Stephen Davis*	2.00
178	Walt Harris	.30
179	Amani Toomer	.30
180	*Derrick Mayes*	1.00
181	*Jeff Lewis*	.50
182	Chris Darkins	.10
183	*Rickey Dudley*	.75
184	Jonathan Ogden	.10
185	*Mike Alstott*	1.75
186	*Eric Moulds*	2.00
187	*Karim Abdul-Jabbar*	.75
188	Checklist	.10
189	Checklist	.10
190	Checklist	.10

1996 Leaf Press Proofs

The first 190 cards in 1996 Leaf Football were die-cut and printed in gold foil to form this Press Proofs parallel set. Each Press Proof insert carried a 1 of 2,000 produced number.

	NM/M
Complete Set (190):	600.00
Press Proof Cards:	15X-30X

A player's name in *italic* type indicates a rookie card.

1996 Leaf Gold Leaf Rookies

Gold Leaf Rookies were numbered as an insert set, but are actually considered part of the base set. It features 10 rookies on a distinctly different design than base cards.

		NM/M
Complete Set (10):		40.00
Common Player:		3.00
1	Leeland McElroy	3.00
2	Marvin Harrison	6.00
3	Lawrence Phillips	2.00
4	Bobby Engram	3.00
5	Kevin Hardy	3.00
6	Keyshawn Johnson	5.00
7	Eddie Kennison	5.00
8	Tim Biakabutuka	4.00
9	Eddie George	8.00
10	Terry Glenn	4.00

1996 Leaf American All-Stars

American All-Stars showcased 20 NFL players who were All-America selections in college. The cards were printed on a simulated sailcloth card stock that attempts to have the look and feel of an American flag. American All-Stars arrived in regular and Gold Team versions, with 5,000 regular sets and 1,000 Gold Team sets.

		NM/M
Complete Set (20):		150.00
Common Player:		4.00
Gold Cards:		2X-3X
1	Emmitt Smith	20.00
2	Drew Bledsoe	10.00
3	Jerry Rice	20.00
4	Kerry Collins	10.00
5	Eddie George	10.00
6	Keyshawn Johnson	10.00
7	Lawrence Phillips	4.00
8	Rashaan Salaam	4.00
9	Deion Sanders	10.00
10	Marshall Faulk	15.00
11	Steve Young	15.00
12	Ki-Jana Carter	4.00
13	Curtis Martin	15.00
14	Joey Galloway	10.00
15	Troy Aikman	15.00
16	Barry Sanders	20.00
17	Dan Marino	20.00
18	John Elway	15.00
19	Steve McNair	4.00
20	Tim Biakabutuka	4.00

1996 Leaf American All-Stars Gold

American All-Stars Gold featured the same 20 cards found in the All-Stars Silver set, but with upgraded cloth stock and gold enhancements. Gold versions are sequentially numbered up to 1,000.

Gold Cards:	2X-3X

1996 Leaf Gold Leaf Stars

Fifteen of the top players in the NFL were included in Gold Leaf Stars. These were found in retail packs only and contain a 22kt. gold logo.

		NM/M
Common Player:		10.00
1	Drew Bledsoe	30.00
2	Jerry Rice	40.00
3	Emmitt Smith	80.00
4	Dan Marino	80.00
5	Isaac Bruce	20.00
6	Kerry Collins	30.00
7	Barry Sanders	40.00
8	Keyshawn Johnson	40.00
9	Errict Rhett	10.00
10	Joey Galloway	20.00
11	Brett Favre	80.00
12	Curtis Martin	60.00
13	Steve Young	30.00
14	Troy Aikman	40.00
15	John Elway	20.00

1996 Leaf Grass Roots

Printed on a card stock that simulates artificial turf, Grass Roots highlighted 20 running backs that perform the best on artificial turf. This insert was limited to 5,000 sets produced.

		NM/M
Complete Set (20):		125.00
Common Player:		4.00
Minor Stars:		8.00
1	Thurman Thomas	8.00
2	Eddie George	10.00
3	Rodney Hampton	4.00
4	Rashaan Salaam	4.00
5	Natrone Means	4.00
6	Errict Rhett	4.00
7	Leeland McElroy	4.00
8	Emmitt Smith	20.00
9	Marshall Faulk	8.00
10	Ricky Watters	4.00
11	Chris Warren	4.00
12	Tim Biakabutuka	4.00
13	Barry Sanders	20.00
14	Karim Abdul-Jabbar	4.00
15	Darick Holmes	4.00
16	Terrell Davis	10.00
17	Lawrence Phillips	4.00
18	Ki-Jana Carter	4.00
19	Curtis Martin	15.00
20	Kordell Stewart	6.00

1996 Leaf Shirt Off My Back

Shirt Off My Back inserts were found only in special pre-priced retail packs. The cards were printed on stock that simulates jersey material and includes 10 of the top quarterbacks. Shirt Off My Back was limited to 2,500 sets.

		NM/M
Complete Set (10):		80.00
Common Player:		3.00
1	Steve Young	6.00
2	Jeff Blake	3.00
3	Drew Bledsoe	8.00
4	Kordell Stewart	4.00
5	Troy Aikman	10.00
6	Steve McNair	6.00
7	John Elway	12.00
8	Dan Marino	15.00
9	Kerry Collins	3.00
10	Brett Favre	15.00

1996 Leaf Statisical Standouts

Printed on simulated leather and inserted only in hobby packs, Statistical Standouts includes 15 top players. These cards have the feel of leather and are individually numbered to 2,500.

		NM/M
Complete Set (15):		175.00
Common Player:		5.00
1	John Elway	20.00
2	Jerry Rice	25.00
3	Reggie White	5.00
4	Drew Bledsoe	15.00
5	Chris Warren	5.00
6	Bruce Smith	5.00
7	Barry Sanders	25.00
8	Greg Lloyd	5.00
9	Emmitt Smith	25.00
10	Dan Marino	25.00
11	Steve Young	15.00
12	Steve Atwater	5.00
13	Isaac Bruce	10.00
14	Deion Sanders	10.00
15	Brett Favre	30.00

1996 Leaf Collector's Edition Autographs

This 12-card autographed set was found one per Collector's Edition in factory sets from Leaf. The autographed cards all carry the words "Authentic Signature" on the front. Autographs of Leeland McElroy, Marvin Harrison, Lawrence Phillips, Bobby Engram and Eddie Kennison were printed on Gold Leaf Rookies inserts. Autographs of Tony Banks and Karim Abdul-Jabbar were on rookie subset cards, while the remaining autographs were found on regular-issue cards.

	NM/M
Common Player:	10.00
Karim Abdul-Jabbar	15.00
Tony Banks	15.00
Isaac Bruce	20.00
Terrell Davis	50.00
Bobby Engram	10.00
Joey Galloway	20.00
Marvin Harrison	35.00
Eddie Kennison	10.00
Leeland McElroy	10.00
Lawrence Phillips	15.00
Rashaan Salaam	10.00
Tamarick Vanover	10.00

1997 Leaf

Leaf Football is a 200-card set featuring a player action shot on the front and a close-up on the back. The backs also include the past season's statistics. The Fractal Matrix chase set makes its Leaf Football debut. This base set parallel features three different color schemes and three different die-cuts. The breakdown of die-cuts and colors is 100 X-Axis (5 gold/20 silver/75 bronze), 60 Y-Axis (10 gold/30 silver/20 bronze) and 40 Z-Axis (25 gold/10 silver/5 bronze). Inserts in this set include 1948 Leaf Reproductions, Lettermen, Run & Gun and Hardwear.

		NM/M
Complete Set (200):		20.00
Common Player:		.15
Minor Stars:		.30
Signature Proof Cards:		10X-20X
Signature Proof Rookies:		5X-10X
Production 200 Sets		
Pack (10):		2.75
Wax Box (24):		45.00
1	Steve Young	1.00
2	Brett Favre	3.00
3	Barry Sanders	3.00
4	Drew Bledsoe	1.50
5	Troy Aikman	1.50
6	Kerry Collins	.30
7	Dan Marino	2.00
8	Jerry Rice	1.50
9	John Elway	1.50
10	Emmitt Smith	2.00
11	Tony Banks	.30
12	Gus Frerotte	.15
13	Elvis Grbac	.15
14	Neil O'Donnell	.15
15	Michael Irvin	.30
16	Marshall Faulk	.50
17	Todd Collins	.15
18	Scott Mitchell	.15
19	Trent Dilfer	.30
20	Rick Mirer	.15
21	Frank Sanders	.15
22	Larry Centers	.15
23	Brad Johnson	.30
24	Garrison Hearst	.30
25	Steve McNair	.75
26	Dorsey Levens	.30
27	Eric Metcalf	.15
28	Jeff George	.30
29	Rodney Hampton	.15
30	Michael Westbrook	.15
31	Cris Carter	.50
32	Heath Shuler	.15
33	Warren Moon	.30
34	Rod Woodson	.15
35	Ken Dilger	.15
36	Ben Coates	.15
37	Andre Reed	.15
38	Terrell Owens	.75
39	Jeff Blake	.30
40	Vinny Testaverde	.30
41	Robert Brooks	.15
42	Shannon Sharpe	.30
43	Terry Allen	.30
44	Terance Mathis	.15
45	Bobby Engram	.15
46	Rickey Dudley	.15
47	Alex Molden	.15
48	Lawrence Phillips	.15
49	Curtis Martin	.75
50	Jim Harbaugh	.30
51	Wayne Chrebet	.30
52	Quentin Coryatt	.15
53	Eddie George	1.50
54	Michael Jackson	.15
55	Greg Lloyd	.15
56	Natrone Means	.30
57	Marcus Allen	.30
58	Desmond Howard	.15
59	Stan Humphries	.15
60	Reggie White	.30
61	Brett Perriman	.15
62	Warren Sapp	.15
63	Adrian Murrell	.30
64	Mark Brunell	1.50
65	Carl Pickens	.30
66	Kordell Stewart	1.50
67	Ricky Watters	.30
68	Tyrone Wheatley	.15
69	Stanley Pritchett	.15
70	Kevin Greene	.15
71	Karim Abdul-Jabbar	.30
72	Ki-Jana Carter	.15
73	Rashaan Salaam	.15
74	Simeon Rice	.15
75	Napoleon Kaufman	.75
76	Muhsin Muhammad	.15
77	Bruce Smith	.15
78	Eric Moulds	.50
79	O.J. McDuffie	.15
80	Danny Kanell	.15
81	Harvey Williams	.15
82	Greg Hill	.15
83	Terrell Davis	2.00
84	Dan Wilkinson	.15
85	Yancey Thigpen	.15
86	Darrell Green	.15
87	Tamarick Vanover	.15
88	Mike Alstott	.50
89	Johnnie Morton	.15
90	Dale Carter	.15
91	Jerome Bettis	.30
92	James Stewart	.15
93	Irving Fryar	.15
94	Junior Seau	.30
95	Sean Dawkins	.15
96	J.J. Stokes	.30
97	Tim Biakabutuka	.30
98	Bert Emanuel	.15
99	Eddie Kennison	.30
100	Ray Zellars	.15
101	Dave Brown	.15
102	Leeland McElroy	.15
103	Chris Warren	.15
104	Bam Morris	.15
105	Thurman Thomas	.30
106	Kyle Brady	.15
107	Anthony Miller	.15
108	Derrick Thomas	.15
109	Mark Chmura	.30
110	Deion Sanders	.50
111	Eric Swann	.15
112	Amani Toomer	.15
113	Raymont Harris	.15
114	Jake Reed	.15
115	Bryant Young	.15
116	Keenan McCardell	.30
117	Herman Moore	.30
118	Errict Rhett	.15
119	Henry Ellard	.15
120	Bobby Hoying	.15
121	Robert Smith	.30
122	Keyshawn Johnson	.50
123	Zach Thomas	.30
124	Charlie Garner	.15
125	Terry Kirby	.15
126	Darren Woodson	.15
127	Darnay Scott	.15
128	Chris Sanders	.15
129	Charles Johnson	.15
130	Joey Galloway	.50
131	Curtis Conway	.30
132	Isaac Bruce	.30
133	Bobby Taylor	.15
134	Jamal Anderson	.75
135	Ken Norton	.15
136	Darick Holmes	.30
137	Tony Brackens	.15
138	Tony Martin	.15
139	Antonio Freeman	.75
140	Neil Smith	.15
141	Terry Glenn	.30
142	Marvin Harrison	.30
143	Daryl Johnston	.15
144	Tim Brown	.30
145	Kimble Anders	.15
146	Derrick Alexander	.15
147	LeShon Johnson	.15
148	Anthony Johnson	.15
149	Leslie Shepherd	.15
150	Chris T. Jones	.15
151	Edgar Bennett	.15
152	Ty Detmer	.15
153	*Ike Hilliard*	1.00
154	*Jim Druckenmiller*	1.50
155	*Warrick Dunn*	1.50
156	*Yatil Green*	.30
157	*Reidel Anthony*	1.50
158	*Antowain Smith*	1.50
159	*Rae Carruth*	.75
160	*Tiki Barber*	1.00
161	*Byron Hanspard*	.50
162	*Jake Plummer*	3.00
163	*Joey Kent*	.30
164	*Corey Dillon*	3.00
165	*Kevin Lockett*	.15
166	*Will Blackwell*	.30
167	*Troy Davis*	.30
168	*James Farrior*	.15
169	*Danny Wuerffel*	.75
170	*Pat Barnes*	.50
171	*Darnell Autry*	.30
172	*Tom Knight*	.15
173	*David LaFleur*	.30
174	*Tony Gonzalez*	.75
175	*Kenny Holmes*	.15
176	*Reinard Wilson*	.15
177	*Renaldo Wynn*	.15
178	*Bryant Westbrook*	.30
179	*Darrell Russell*	.30
180	*Orlando Pace*	.30
181	*Shawn Springs*	.30
182	*Peter Boulware*	.30
183	Dan Marino (Legacy)	1.00
184	Brett Favre (Legacy)	1.50
185	Emmitt Smith (Legacy)	1.00
186	Eddie George (Legacy)	.75
187	Curtis Martin (Legacy)	.50
188	Tim Brown (Legacy)	.15
189	Mark Brunell (Legacy)	.75
190	Isaac Bruce (Legacy)	.15
191	Deion Sanders (Legacy)	.30
192	John Elway (Legacy)	.75
193	Jerry Rice (Legacy)	.75
194	Barry Sanders (Legacy)	1.50
195	Herman Moore (Legacy)	.15
196	Carl Pickens (Legacy)	.15
197	Karim Abdul-Jabbar (Legacy)	.15
198	Drew Bledsoe CL	.75
199	Troy Aikman CL	.75
200	Terrell Davis CL	.75

1997 Leaf Fractal Matrix

This 200-card parallel features multi-fractured technology. Each card is done in one of three colors: bronze (100 cards), silver (60 cards) or gold (40 cards).

		NM/M
Common Bronze X:		1.00
Common Bronze Y:		.75
Common Bronze Z:		.75
Common Silver X:		1.00
Common Silver Y:		1.00
Common Silver Z:		1.00
1	Steve Young GZ	10.00
2	Brett Favre GX	50.00
3	Barry Sanders GZ	35.00
4	Drew Bledsoe GZ	15.00
5	Troy Aikman GZ	15.00
6	Kerry Collins GZ	10.00
7	Dan Marino GX	50.00
8	Jerry Rice GZ	20.00
9	John Elway GZ	15.00
10	Emmitt Smith GX	40.00
11	Tony Banks GY	5.00
12	Gus Frerotte SX	1.00
13	Elvis Grbac SX	1.00
14	Neil O'Donnell BX	1.00
15	Michael Irvin SY	2.00
16	Marshall Faulk SY	2.00
17	Todd Collins SX	1.00
18	Scott Mitchell BX	1.00
19	Trent Dilfer SY	1.00
20	Rick Mirer SX	1.00
21	Frank Sanders SX	1.00
22	Larry Centers BX	1.00
23	Brad Johnson BX	1.00
24	Garrison Hearst SY	2.00
25	Steve McNair GZ	10.00
26	Dorsey Levens BX	1.00
27	Eric Metcalf BX	1.00
28	Jeff George SX	1.00
29	Rodney Hampton BX	1.00
30	Michael Westbrook SY	1.00
31	Cris Carter SY	1.00
32	Heath Shuler SX	1.00
33	Warren Moon BX	1.00
34	Rod Woodson SX	1.00
35	Ken Dilger BX	1.00
36	Ben Coates BX	1.00
37	Andre Reed BX	1.00
38	Terrell Owens SZ	2.00
39	Jeff Blake SY	1.00
40	Vinny Testaverde BX	1.00
41	Robert Brooks SY	1.00
42	Shannon Sharpe SX	1.00
43	Terry Allen SY	1.00
44	Terance Mathis BX	1.00
45	Bobby Engram BZ	1.00
46	Rickey Dudley BX	1.00
47	Alex Molden BX	1.00
48	Lawrence Phillips SY	1.00
49	Curtis Martin GZ	10.00
50	Jim Harbaugh BX	1.00
51	Wayne Chrebet BX	1.00
52	Quentin Coryatt BX	1.00
53	Eddie George GX	20.00
54	Michael Jackson BX	1.00
55	Greg Lloyd BX	1.00
56	Natrone Means SZ	1.00
57	Marcus Allen GY	5.00
58	Desmond Howard BX	1.00
59	Stan Humphries BX	1.00
60	Reggie White GY	4.00
61	Brett Perriman SY	1.00
62	Warren Sapp BX	2.00
63	Adrian Murrell SZ	1.00
64	Mark Brunell GZ	15.00
65	Carl Pickens GY	2.00
66	Kordell Stewart GZ	10.00
67	Ricky Watters GY	4.00
68	Tyrone Wheatley BX	1.00
69	Stanley Pritchett BX	1.00
70	Kevin Greene BX	1.00
71	Karim Abdul-Jabbar GZ	2.00
72	Ki-Jana Carter SY	1.00
73	Rashaan Salaam SY	1.00
74	Simeon Rice BX	2.00
75	Napoleon Kaufman SY	1.00
76	Muhsin Muhammad SZ	2.00
77	Bruce Smith GY	2.00
78	Eric Moulds SX	3.00
79	O.J. McDuffie BX	1.00
80	Danny Kanell BZ	1.50
81	Harvey Williams BX	1.00
82	Greg Hill SY	1.00
83	Terrell Davis GZ	20.00
84	Dan Wilkinson BX	1.00
85	Yancey Thigpen BX	1.00
86	Darrell Green SX	1.00
87	Tamarick Vanover SX	1.00
88	Mike Alstott BX	2.00
89	Johnnie Morton SX	2.00
90	Dale Carter BX	1.00
91	Jerome Bettis GY	4.00
92	James Stewart BX	2.00
93	Irving Fryar SX	2.00
94	Junior Seau SY	2.00
95	Sean Dawkins BX	1.00
96	J.J. Stokes BZ	1.50
97	Tim Biakabutuka SY	1.00
98	Bert Emanuel BX	1.00
99	Eddie Kennison GY	3.00
100	Ray Zellars BX	1.00
101	Dave Brown BX	1.00
102	Leeland McElroy SY	1.00
103	Chris Warren SY	1.00
104	Bam Morris BX	1.00
105	Thurman Thomas GY	5.00
106	Kyle Brady BX	1.00
107	Anthony Miller GY	1.00
108	Derrick Thomas SY	2.00
109	Mark Chmura BX	1.00
110	Deion Sanders GZ	3.00
111	Eric Swann BX	1.00
112	Amani Toomer SX	1.00
113	Raymont Harris BX	1.00
114	Jake Reed BX	2.00
115	Bryant Young BX	2.00
116	Keenan McCardell SX	2.00
117	Herman Moore GZ	3.00
118	Errict Rhett SZ	2.00
119	Henry Ellard BX	2.00
120	Bobby Hoying SX	1.00
121	Robert Smith BX	2.00
122	Keyshawn Johnson GZ	10.00
123	Zach Thomas BX	3.00
124	Charlie Garner BX	2.00
125	Terry Kirby BX	1.00
126	Darren Woodson BX	2.00
127	Darnay Scott SX	1.00
128	Chris Sanders SY	1.00
129	Charles Johnson SX	1.00
130	Joey Galloway SZ	2.00
131	Curtis Conway SY	2.00
132	Isaac Bruce GZ	4.00
133	Bobby Taylor BX	2.00
134	Jamal Anderson SY	3.00
135	Ken Norton BX	1.00
136	Darick Holmes BX	1.00
137	Tony Brackens BX	1.00
138	Tony Martin BX	1.00
139	Antonio Freeman SZ	2.00
140	Neil Smith BX	1.00
141	Terry Glenn GZ	5.00
142	Marvin Harrison SY	5.00
143	Daryl Johnston BX	2.00
144	Tim Brown GY	5.00
145	Kimble Anders BX	1.00
146	Derrick Alexander SX	1.00
147	LeShon Johnson BX	1.00
148	Anthony Johnson BX	1.00
149	Leslie Shepherd BX	1.00
150	Chris T. Jones BX	1.00
151	Edgar Bennett BX	1.00
152	Ty Detmer BX	2.00
153	*Ike Hilliard GX*	5.00
154	*Jim Druckenmiller SZ*	1.00
155	*Warrick Dunn GZ*	4.00
156	*Yatil Green GZ*	2.00
157	*Reidel Anthony GZ*	2.00
158	*Antowain Smith GZ*	2.00
159	*Rae Carruth SY*	1.00
160	*Tiki Barber GZ*	4.00
161	*Byron Hanspard SZ*	1.00
162	*Jake Plummer SY*	5.00
163	*Joey Kent SZ*	1.00
164	*Corey Dillon SY*	5.00
165	*Kevin Lockett BZ*	1.00
166	*Will Blackwell BY*	1.00
167	*Troy Davis GZ*	2.00
168	*James Farrior BX*	1.00
169	*Danny Wuerffel SY*	1.00
170	*Pat Barnes SY*	1.00
171	*Darnell Autry SY*	1.00
172	*Tom Knight BX*	1.00
173	*David LaFleur BY*	1.00
174	*Tony Gonzalez BY*	2.00
175	*Kenny Holmes BX*	1.00
176	*Reinard Wilson BX*	1.00
177	*Renaldo Wynn BX*	1.00
178	*Bryant Westbrook BX*	2.00
179	*Darrell Russell BX*	1.00
180	*Orlando Pace BX*	1.00
181	*Shawn Springs BX*	1.00
182	*Peter Boulware BX*	1.00
183	Dan Marino BY(Legacy)	10.00
184	Brett Favre BY (Legacy)	12.00
185	Emmitt Smith BY (Legacy)	10.00
186	Eddie George BY (Legacy)	4.00
187	Curtis Martin BY (Legacy)	4.00
188	Tim Brown BZ (Legacy)	4.00
189	Mark Brunell BY (Legacy)	4.00
190	Isaac Bruce BY (Legacy)	3.00
191	Deion Sanders BY (Legacy)	3.00
192	John Elway BY (Legacy)	4.00
193	Jerry Rice BY (Legacy)	5.00
194	Barry Sanders BY (Legacy)	10.00
195	Herman Moore BY (Legacy)	2.00
196	Carl Pickens BY (Legacy)	1.00
197	Karim Abdul-Jabbar BY (Legacy)	1.00
198	Drew Bledsoe BY Checklist	4.00
199	Troy Aikman BY Checklist	4.00
200	Terrell Davis BY Checklist	4.00

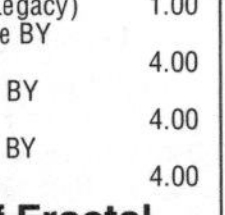

1997 Leaf Fractal Matrix Die-Cuts

This insert adds die-cutting to the Fractal Matrix parallel. The breakdown of cards is 100 X-Axis (5 gold/20 silver/75 bronze), 60 Y-Axis (10 gold/30 silver/20 bronze) and 40 Z-Axis (25 gold/10 silver/5 bronze).

		NM/M
Common X-Axis:		3.00
Common Y-Axis:		5.00
Common Z-Axis:		7.00
1	Steve Young GZ	25.00
2	Brett Favre GX	60.00
3	Barry Sanders GZ	70.00
4	Drew Bledsoe GZ	50.00
5	Troy Aikman GZ	50.00
6	Kerry Collins GZ	35.00
7	Dan Marino GX	50.00
8	Jerry Rice GZ	40.00
9	John Elway GZ	40.00
10	Emmitt Smith GX	40.00
11	Tony Banks GY	5.00
12	Gus Frerotte SX	3.00
13	Elvis Grbac SX	3.00
14	Neil O'Donnell BX	3.00
15	Michael Irvin SY	5.00
16	Marshall Faulk SY	7.00
17	Todd Collins SX	3.00
18	Scott Mitchell BX	3.00
19	Trent Dilfer SY	5.00
20	Rick Mirer SX	3.00
21	Frank Sanders SX	3.00
22	Larry Centers BX	3.00
23	Brad Johnson BX	5.00
24	Garrison Hearst SY	5.00
25	Steve McNair GZ	25.00
26	Dorsey Levens BX	3.00
27	Eric Metcalf BX	3.00
28	Jeff George SX	3.00
29	Rodney Hampton BX	3.00
30	Michael Westbrook SY	5.00
31	Cris Carter SY	5.00
32	Heath Shuler SX	3.00
33	Warren Moon BX	4.00
34	Rod Woodson SX	4.00
35	Ken Dilger BX	3.00
36	Ben Coates BX	3.00
37	Andre Reed BX	3.00
38	Terrell Owens SZ	15.00
39	Jeff Blake SY	5.00
40	Vinny Testaverde BX	3.00
41	Robert Brooks SY	5.00
42	Shannon Sharpe SX	3.00
43	Terry Allen SY	5.00
44	Terance Mathis BX	3.00
45	Bobby Engram BZ	7.00
46	Rickey Dudley BX	3.00
47	Alex Molden BX	3.00
48	Lawrence Phillips SY	5.00
49	Curtis Martin GZ	25.00
50	Jim Harbaugh BX	3.00
51	Wayne Chrebet BX	3.00
52	Quentin Coryatt BX	3.00
53	Eddie George GX	15.00
54	Michael Jackson BX	3.00
55	Greg Lloyd BX	3.00
56	Natrone Means SZ	7.00
57	Marcus Allen GY	7.00
58	Desmond Howard BX	3.00
59	Stan Humphries BX	3.00
60	Reggie White GY	7.00
61	Brett Perriman SY	5.00
62	Warren Sapp BX	4.00
63	Adrian Murrell SZ	7.00
64	Mark Brunell GZ	35.00
65	Carl Pickens GY	5.00
66	Kordell Stewart GZ	25.00
67	Ricky Watters GY	8.00
68	Tyrone Wheatley BX	3.00
69	Stanley Pritchett BX	3.00
70	Kevin Greene BX	3.00
71	Karim Abdul-Jabbar GZ	7.00
72	Ki-Jana Carter SY	5.00
73	Rashaan Salaam SY	5.00
74	Simeon Rice BX	3.00
75	Napoleon Kaufman SY	5.00
76	Muhsin Muhammad SZ	7.00
77	Bruce Smith GY	5.00
78	Eric Moulds SX	3.00
79	O.J. McDuffie BX	3.00
80	Danny Kanell BZ	7.00
81	Harvey Williams BX	3.00
82	Greg Hill SY	5.00
83	Terrell Davis GZ	60.00
84	Dan Wilkinson BX	3.00
85	Yancey Thigpen BX	3.00
86	Darrell Green SX	3.00
87	Tamarick Vanover SX	3.00
88	Mike Alstott BX	3.00
89	Johnnie Morton SX	3.00
90	Dale Carter BX	3.00
91	Jerome Bettis GY	5.00
92	James Stewart BX	3.00
93	Irving Fryar SX	3.00
94	Junior Seau SY	5.00
95	Sean Dawkins BX	3.00
96	J.J. Stokes BZ	7.00
97	Tim Biakabutuka SY	5.00
98	Bert Emanuel BX	3.00
99	Eddie Kennison GY	8.00
100	Ray Zellars BX	3.00
101	Dave Brown BX	3.00
102	Leeland McElroy SY	5.00
103	Chris Warren SY	5.00
104	Bam Morris BX	3.00
105	Thurman Thomas GY	8.00
106	Kyle Brady BX	3.00
107	Anthony Miller GY	5.00
108	Derrick Thomas SY	5.00
109	Mark Chmura BX	3.00
110	Deion Sanders GZ	12.00
111	Eric Swann BX	3.00
112	Amani Toomer SX	3.00

113 Raymont Harris BX 3.00
114 Jake Reed BX 3.00
115 Bryant Young BX 3.00
116 Keenan McCardell SX 3.00
117 Herman Moore GZ 10.00
118 Errict Rhett SZ 7.00
119 Henry Ellard BX 3.00
120 Bobby Hoying SX 3.00
121 Robert Smith BX 3.00
122 Keyshawn Johnson GZ 15.00
123 Zach Thomas BX 4.00
124 Charlie Garner BX 3.00
125 Terry Kirby BX 3.00
126 Darren Woodson BX 3.00
127 Darnay Scott SX 3.00
128 Chris Sanders SY 5.00
129 Charles Johnson SX 3.00
130 Joey Galloway SZ 8.00
131 Curtis Conway SY 5.00
132 Isaac Bruce GZ 8.00
133 Bobby Taylor BX 3.00
134 Jamal Anderson SY 5.00
135 Ken Norton BX 3.00
136 Darick Holmes BX 3.00
137 Tony Brackens BX 3.00
138 Tony Martin BX 3.00
139 Antonio Freeman SZ 10.00
140 Neil Smith BX 3.00
141 Terry Glenn GZ 10.00
142 Marvin Harrison SY 10.00
143 Daryl Johnston BX 3.00
144 Tim Brown GY 5.00
145 Kimble Anders BX 3.00
146 Derrick Alexander SX 3.00
147 LeShon Johnson BX 3.00
148 Anthony Johnson BX 3.00
149 Leslie Shepherd BX 3.00
150 Chris T. Jones BX 3.00
151 Edgar Bennett BX 3.00
152 Ty Detmer BX 3.00
153 *Ike Hilliard GX* 7.00
154 *Jim Druckenmiller SZ* 7.00
155 *Warrick Dunn GZ* 15.00
156 *Yatil Green GZ* 10.00
157 *Reidel Anthony GZ* 10.00
158 *Antowain Smith GZ* 15.00
159 *Rae Carruth SY* 5.00
160 *Tiki Barber GZ* 10.00
161 *Byron Hanspard SZ* 7.00
162 *Jake Plummer SY* 7.00
163 *Joey Kent SZ* 7.00
164 *Corey Dillon SY* 10.00
165 *Kevin Lockett BZ* 7.00
166 *Will Blackwell BY* 5.00
167 *Troy Davis GZ* 7.00
168 *James Farrior BX* 3.00
169 *Danny Wuerffel SY* 5.00
170 *Pat Barnes SY* 5.00
171 *Darnell Autry SY* 5.00
172 *Tom Knight BX* 3.00
173 *David LaFleur BY* 5.00
174 *Tony Gonzalez BY* 5.00
175 *Kenny Holmes BX* 3.00
176 *Reinard Wilson BX* 3.00
177 *Renaldo Wynn BX* 3.00
178 *Bryant Westbrook BX* 3.00
179 *Darrell Russell BX* 3.00
180 *Orlando Pace BX* 4.00
181 *Shawn Springs BX* 3.00
182 *Peter Boulware BX* 3.00
183 Dan Marino BY(Legacy) 40.00
184 Brett Favre BY(Legacy) 40.00
185 Emmitt Smith BY (Legacy) 30.00
186 Eddie George BY (Legacy) 20.00
187 Curtis Martin BY (Legacy) 20.00
188 Tim Brown BZ (Legacy) 12.00
189 Mark Brunell BY (Legacy) 15.00
190 Isaac Bruce BY (Legacy) 10.00
191 Deion Sanders BY (Legacy) 10.00
192 John Elway BY (Legacy) 25.00
193 Jerry Rice BY (Legacy) 35.00
194 Barry Sanders BY (Legacy) 35.00
195 Herman Moore BY (Legacy) 8.00
196 Carl Pickens BY (Legacy) 8.00
197 Karim Abdul-Jabbar BY (Legacy) 5.00
198 Drew Bledsoe BY Checklist 10.00
199 Troy Aikman BY Checklist 10.00
200 Terrell Davis BY Checklist 10.00

1997 Leaf Hardwear

Hardwear is a 20-card insert featuring top players on a plastic card. The cards are die-cut into a helmet-shaped design and sequentially numbered to 3,500.

NM/M

Complete Set (20): 125.00
Common Player: 2.00
Minor Stars: 4.00
Production 3,500 Sets
1 Dan Marino 15.00
2 Brett Favre 15.00
3 Emmitt Smith 15.00
4 Jerry Rice 12.00
5 Barry Sanders 15.00
6 Deion Sanders 4.00
7 Reggie White 4.00
8 Tim Brown 4.00
9 Steve McNair 6.00
10 Steve Young 10.00
11 Mark Brunell 6.00
12 Ricky Watters 2.00
13 Eddie Kennison 2.00
14 Kordell Stewart 4.00
15 Kerry Collins 2.00
16 Joey Galloway 4.00
17 Terrell Owens 6.00
18 Terry Glenn 4.00
19 Keyshawn Johnson 4.00
20 Eddie George 6.00

1997 Leaf Letterman

The cards in this 15-card insert look and feel like a college letter. The cards are also embossed and foil stamped. Each card is sequentially numbered to 1,000.

NM/M

Complete Set (15): 200.00
Common Player: 8.00
Production 1,000 Sets
1 Brett Favre 25.00
2 Emmitt Smith 25.00
3 Dan Marino 25.00
4 Jerry Rice 20.00
5 Mark Brunell 10.00
6 Barry Sanders 25.00
7 John Elway 20.00
8 Eddie George 15.00
9 Troy Aikman 20.00
10 Curtis Martin 12.00
11 Karim Abdul-Jabbar 8.00
12 Terrell Davis 15.00
13 Ike Hilliard 8.00
14 Yatil Green 8.00
15 Drew Bledsoe 15.00

1997 Leaf Run & Gun

This 18-card insert features a top quarterback/running back combo from the same team, one on each side of the card. One side features holographic foil stock and the other is foil stamped. The cards are numbered to 3,500.

NM/M

Complete Set (18): 100.00
Common Player: 3.00
Minor Stars: 5.00
Production 3,500 Sets
1 Dan Marino, Karim Abdul-Jabbar 15.00
2 Troy Aikman, Emmitt Smith 15.00
3 John Elway, Terrell Davis 15.00
4 Drew Bledsoe, Curtis Martin 12.00
5 Kordell Stewart, Jerome Bettis 8.00
6 Mark Brunell, Natrone Means 8.00
7 Kerry Collins, Tim Biakabutuka 6.00
8 Rick Mirer, Rashaan Salaam 3.00
9 Scott Mitchell, Barry Sanders 12.00
10 Steve McNair, Eddie George 8.00
11 Trent Dilfer, Warrick Dunn 6.00
12 Jeff Blake, Ki-Jana Carter 3.00
13 Tony Banks, Lawrence Phillips 3.00
14 Steve Young, Garrison Hearst 10.00
15 Jim Harbaugh, Marshall Faulk 8.00
16 Elvis Grbac, Marcus Allen 3.00
17 Neil O'Donnell, Adrian Murrell 3.00
18 Gus Frerotte, Terry Allen 3.00

1997 Leaf Reproductions

Twelve current and 12 former NFL stars are featured in this 24-card set. The cards are a reproduction of Leaf's 1948 set design. The first 500 cards of each former great are autographed. Each insert card is numbered to 1,948.

NM/M

Complete Set (24): 125.00
Common Player: 3.00
Minor Stars: 5.00
Production 1,948 Sets
Complete Autograph Set (11): 300.00
Common Autograph (13-24): 20.00
Minor Autograph Stars: 40.00
Production 500 Sets
1 Emmitt Smith 25.00
2 Brett Favre 25.00
3 Dan Marino 25.00
4 Barry Sanders 25.00
5 Jerry Rice 20.00
6 Terrell Davis 15.00
7 Curtis Martin 10.00
8 Troy Aikman 15.00
9 Drew Bledsoe 12.00
10 Herman Moore 3.00
11 Isaac Bruce 3.00
12 Carl Pickens 3.00
13 Len Dawson 6.00
14 Dan Fouts 6.00
15 Jim Plunkett 3.00
16 Ken Stabler 6.00
17 Joe Theismann 6.00
18 Billy Kilmer 6.00
19 Danny White 6.00
20 Archie Manning 3.00
21 Ron Jaworski 3.00
22 Y.A. Tittle 6.00
23 Sid Luckman 6.00
23a Sid Luckman AUTO 150.00
24 Sammy Baugh 14.00

1997 Leaf Signature

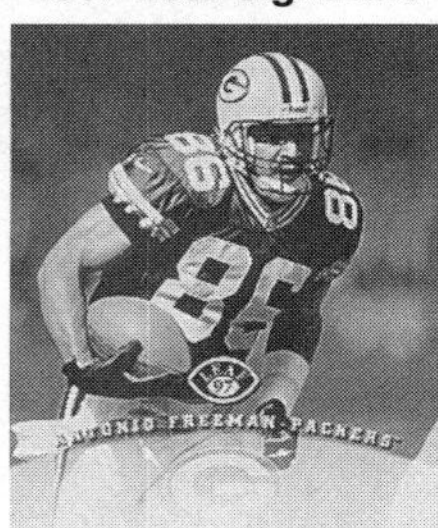

Leaf Signature Football consisted of 118 8" x 10" cards that featured top established players and rookies. The card fronts feature a large color shot of the player, with a large off-color oval taking up the bottom portion. The player's name is stamped in silver foil above this oval, with a Leaf '97 Football logo in silver and black above that. The backs are horizontal and unnumbered and contain a large close-up shot of the player on the left side with a brief biography on the right. Most of the players also arrive in an autographed version, which have the words "Authentic Signature" printed in black across the bottom. Also included in packs were Old School Draft Autographs, which featured 11 retired quarterbacks.

NM/M

Complete Set (118): 45.00
Common Player: .50
Minor Stars: 1.00
Pack (2): 17.50
Wax Box (8): 100.00
1 Karim Abdul-Jabbar 1.00
2 Troy Aikman 5.00
3 Derrick Alexander .50
4 Terry Allen 1.00
5 Mike Alstott 2.00
6 Jamal Anderson 3.00
7 Reidel Anthony 2.50
8 Darnell Autry 1.00
9 Tony Banks 1.00
10 Tiki Barber 1.00
11 Pat Barnes 1.00
12 Jerome Bettis 1.00
13 Tim Biakabutuka 1.00
14 Will Blackwell 1.00
15 Jeff Blake 1.00
16 Drew Bledsoe 3.00
17 Peter Boulware .50
18 Robert Brooks .50
19 Dave Brown .50
20 Tim Brown 1.00
21 Isaac Bruce 1.00
22 Mark Brunell 3.00
23 Rae Carruth 2.00
24 Cris Carter 2.00
25 Ki-Jana Carter .50
26 Larry Centers .50
27 Ben Coates 1.00
28 Kerry Collins 1.00
29 Todd Collins .50
30 Albert Connell .50
31 Curtis Conway 1.00
32 Terrell Davis 3.00
33 Troy Davis 1.00
34 Trent Dilfer 2.00
35 Corey Dillon 3.00
36 Jim Druckenmiller 1.00
37 Warrick Dunn 2.00
38 John Elway 5.00
39 Bert Emmanuel .50
40 Bobby Engram .50
41 Boomer Esiason .50
42 Jim Everett .50
43 Marshall Faulk 2.00
44 Brett Favre 6.00
45 Antonio Freeman 2.00
46 Gus Frerotte .50
47 Irving Fryar .50
48 Joey Galloway 2.00
49 Eddie George 2.00
50 Jeff George 1.00
51 Tony Gonzalez 2.00
52 Jay Graham 1.00
53 Elvis Grbac 1.00
54 Darrell Green .50
55 Yatil Green 1.00
56 Rodney Hampton .50
57 Byron Hanspard .50
58 Jim Harbaugh 1.00
59 Marvin Harrison 1.00
60 Garrison Hearst 2.00
61 Greg Hill .50
62 Ike Hilliard 2.00
63 Jeff Hostetler .50
64 Brad Johnson 2.00
65 Keyshawn Johnson 2.00
66 Darryl Johnston .50
67 Napoleon Kaufman 1.00
68 Jim Kelly 1.00
69 Eddie Kennison 1.00
70 Joey Kent 1.00
71 Bernie Kosar .50
72 Eric Kramer .50
73 Dorsey Levens 1.00
74 Kevin Lockett .50
75 Dan Marino 6.00
76 Curtis Martin 3.00
77 Tony Martin .50
78 Leeland McElroy .50
79 Steve McNair 3.00
80 Natrone Means 1.00
81 Eric Metcalf .50
82 Anthony Miller .50
83 Rick Mirer .50
84 Scott Mitchell .50
85 Warren Moon 1.00
86 Herman Moore 1.00
87 Muhsin Muhammad .50
88 Adrian Murrell 1.00
89 Neil O'Donnell .50
90 Terrell Owens 3.00
91 Brett Perriman .50
92 Lawrence Phillips .50
93 Jake Plummer 2.00
94 Andre Reed .50
95 Jerry Rice 5.00
96 Darrell Russell .50
97 Rashaan Salaam .50
98 Barry Sanders 6.00
99 Deion Sanders 2.00
100 Frank Sanders .50
101 Chris Sanders .50
102 Junior Seau .50
103 Darnay Scott .50
104 Shannon Sharpe 1.00
105 Sedrick Shaw .50
106 Heath Shuler .50
107 Antowain Smith 5.00
108 Bruce Smith .50
109 Emmitt Smith 6.00
110 Kordell Stewart 1.00
111 J.J. Stokes 1.00
112 Vinny Testaverde 1.00
113 Thurman Thomas 1.00
114 Tamarick Vanover .50
115 Herschel Walker .50
116 Michael Westbrook .50
117 Danny Wuerffel .50
118 Steve Young 3.00

1997 Leaf Signature Autographs

All but 11 of the players included in Leaf Signature Series Football signed cards for the product. Signature cards are identified by the player's autograph, usually found in the large, off-color oval part of the card and the words "Authentic Signature" in black letters across the bottom. Signature cards were inserted at a rate of one per pack. Included below with the player listing is the number of cards that was reported that each player signed.

NM/M

Common Player: 10.00
Minor Stars: 20.00
First Down Markers: 2X
Karim Abdul-Jabbar 2500 30.00
Derrick Alexander 4000 10.00
Terry Allen 3000 20.00
Mike Alstott 4000 30.00
Jamal Anderson 4000 20.00
Reidel Anthony 2000 30.00
Darnell Autry 4000 20.00
Tony Banks 500 45.00
Tiki Barber 4000 30.00
Pat Barnes 4000 20.00
Jerome Bettis 500 60.00
Tim Biakabutuka 3000 20.00
Will Blackwell 2500 20.00
Jeff Blake 500 45.00
Drew Bledsoe 500 75.00
Peter Boulware 4000 10.00
Robert Brooks 1000 30.00
Dave Brown 500 40.00
Tim Brown 2500 30.00
Isaac Bruce 2500 30.00
Mark Brunell 500 60.00
Rae Carruth 5000 20.00
Cris Carter 2500 20.00
Larry Centers 4000 10.00
Ben Coates 4000 10.00
Todd Collins 4000 10.00
Albert Connell 4000 10.00
Curtis Conway 3000 20.00
Terrell Davis 2500 75.00
Troy Davis 4000 20.00
Trent Dilfer 500 60.00
Corey Dillon 4000 60.00
Jim Druckenmiller 5000 50.00
Warrick Dunn 2000 35.00
John Elway 500 150.00
Bert Emmanuel 4000 10.00
Bobby Engram 3000 10.00
Boomer Esiason 500 50.00
Jim Everett 500 40.00
Marshall Faulk 3000 30.00
Antonio Freeman 2000 30.00
Gus Frerotte 500 40.00
Irving Fryar 3000 10.00
Joey Galloway 3000 30.00
Eddie George 300 75.00
Jeff George 500 40.00
Tony Gonzalez 3500 20.00
Jay Graham 1000 30.00
Elvis Grbac 500 40.00
Darrell Green 2500 10.00
Yatil Green 5000 30.00
Rodney Hampton 4000 10.00
Byron Hanspard 4000 20.00
Jim Harbaugh 500 40.00
Marvin Harrison 3000 30.00
Garrison Hearst 4000 10.00
Greg Hill 4000 10.00
Ike Hilliard 2000 20.00
Jeff Hostetler 500 40.00
Brad Johnson 2000 20.00
Keyshawn Johnson 900 35.00
Darryl Johnston 3000 10.00
Jim Kelly 500 75.00
Eddie Kennison 3000 20.00
Joey Kent 4000 10.00
Bernie Kosar 500 40.00
Eric Kramer 500 40.00
Dorsey Levens 3000 30.00
Kevin Lockett 4000 10.00
Tony Martin 4000 10.00
Leeland McElroy 4000 10.00
Natrone Means 3000 20.00
Eric Metcalf 4000 10.00
Anthony Miller 3000 10.00
Rick Mirer 500 40.00
Scott Mitchell 500 40.00
Warren Moon 500 50.00
Herman Moore 2500 20.00
Muhsin Muhammad 3000 10.00
Adrian Murrell 3000 20.00
Neil O'Donnell 500 40.00
Terrell Owens 3000 30.00
Brett Perriman 700 40.00
Lawrence Phillips 750 40.00
Jake Plummer 5000 60.00
Andre Reed 3000 10.00
Darrell Russell 2000 20.00
Rashaan Salaam 3000 10.00
Frank Sanders 3000 10.00
Chris Sanders 3000 10.00
Junior Seau 500 40.00
Darnay Scott 2000 20.00
Shannon Sharpe 1000 30.00
Sedrick Shaw 4000 20.00
Heath Shuler 500 40.00
Antowain Smith 5000 50.00
Kordell Stewart 500 40.00
J.J. Stokes 3000 10.00
Vinny Testaverde 250 40.00
Thurman Thomas 2500 20.00
TamarickVanover 4000 10.00
Herschel Walker 3000 10.00
Michael Westbrook 3000 10.00
Danny Wuerffel 3000 20.00
Steve Young 500 75.00

1997 Leaf Signature Old School Drafts Autographs

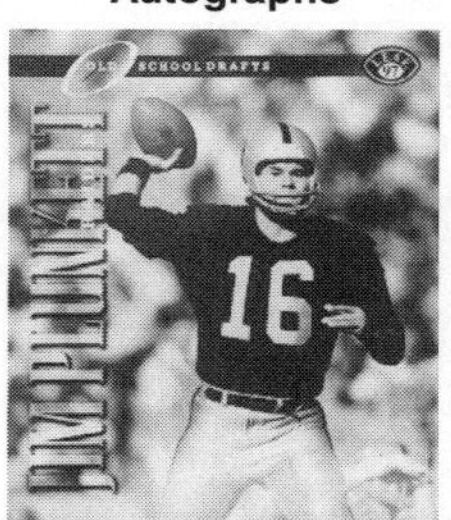

Old School Drafts Autographs included 11 former quarterbacks on 8" x 10" cards. The cards feature the insert name in large bold letters across the top and are individually numbered to 1,000. Card No. 10 is not available.

NM/M

Complete Set (11): 500.00
Common Player: 25.00
Card #10 not included
1 Joe Theismann 50.00
2 Archie Manning 50.00
3 Len Dawson 50.00
4 Sammy Baugh 120.00
5 Dan Fouts 75.00
6 Danny White 50.00
7 Ron Jaworski 25.00
8 Jim Plunkett 25.00
9 Y.A. Tittle 85.00
10 N/A
11 Ken Stabler 85.00
12 Billy Kilmer 25.00

1998 Leaf Rookies & Stars

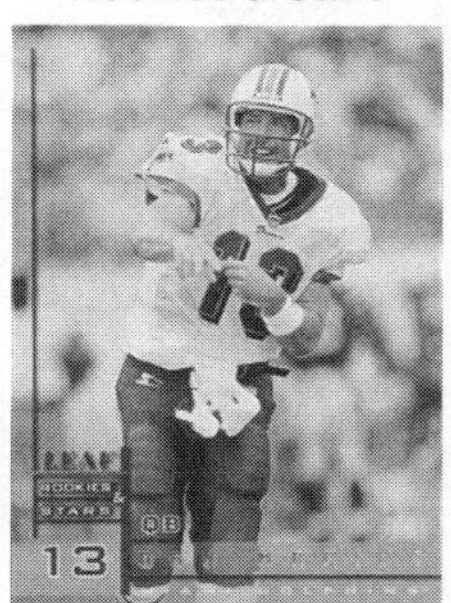

This is the first Leaf product released under Playoff. The 300-card set includes short-printed cards of 70 rookies and 30 Power Tools inserted 1:2 packs. Two parallel sets with the True Blue singles sequentially numbered to 500 and the Longevity parallel numbered to 50. The product also includes 13 other sequentially numbered inserts.

NM/M

Complete Set (300): 200.00
Common Player: .15
Minor Stars: .30
Common Rookie (171-240): 1.00
Common Power Tool (241-270): 1.00
Inserted 1:2
Longevity Cards: 25X-50X
Longevity Rookies: 2X
Longevity PT Cards: 6X-15X
Longevity PT Rookies: 2X-4X
Production 50 Sets
True Blue Cards: 5X-10X
True Blue Rookies: 1X
True Blue PT: 2X
Production 500 Sets
Pack (9): 4.00
Wax Box (24): 65.00
1 Keyshawn Johnson .50
2 Marvin Harrison .30
3 Eddie Kennison .15
4 Bryant Young .15
5 Darren Woodson .15
6 Tyrone Wheatley .15
7 Michael Westbrook .15
8 Charles Way .15
9 Ricky Watters .30
10 Chris Warren .15
11 Wesley Walls .15
12 Tamarick Vanover .15
13 Zach Thomas .30
14 Derrick Thomas .15
15 Yancey Thigpen .15
16 Vinny Testaverde .30
17 Dana Stubblefield .15
18 J.J. Stokes .30
19 James Stewart .15
20 Jeff George .30
21 John Randle .15
22 Gary Brown .15
23 Ed McCaffrey .30
24 James Jett .15
25 Rob Johnson .30
26 Daryl Johnston .15
27 Jermaine Lewis .15
28 Tony Martin .15
29 Derrick Mayes .15
30 Keenan McCardell .30
31 O.J. McDuffie .30
32 Chris Chandler .30
33 Doug Flutie .75
34 Scott Mitchell .30
35 Warren Moon .30
36 Rob Moore .30
37 Johnnie Morton .15
38 Neil O'Donnell .15
39 Rich Gannon .15
40 Andre Reed .15
41 Jake Reed .15
42 Errict Rhett .15
43 Simeon Rice .15
44 Andre Rison .30
45 Eric Moulds .30
46 Frank Sanders .15
47 Darnay Scott .15
48 Junior Seau .30
49 Shannon Sharpe .30
50 Bruce Smith .15
51 Jimmy Smith .30
52 Robert Smith .30
53 Derrick Alexander .15
54 Kimble Anders .15
55 Jamal Anderson .75
56 Mario Bates .15
57 Edgar Bennett .15
58 Tim Biakabutuka .15
59 Ki-Jana Carter .15
60 Larry Centers .15
61 Mark Chmura .30
62 Wayne Chrebet .30
63 Ben Coates .30
64 Curtis Conway .30
65 Randall Cunningham .75
66 Rickey Dudley .15

67 Bert Emanuel .15
68 Bobby Engram .15
69 William Floyd .15
70 Irving Fryar .15
71 Elvis Grbac .15
72 Kevin Greene .15
73 Jim Harbaugh .30
74 Raymont Harris .15
75 Garrison Hearst .50
76 Greg Hill .15
77 Desmond Howard .15
78 Bobby Hoying .30
79 Michael Jackson .15
80 Terry Allen .30
81 Jerome Bettis .50
82 Jeff Blake .30
83 Robert Brooks .15
84 Tim Brown .30
85 Isaac Bruce .30
86 Cris Carter .50
87 Ty Detmer .30
88 Trent Dilfer .30
89 Marshall Faulk .50
90 Antonio Freeman .75
91 Gus Frerotte .30
92 Joey Galloway .50
93 Michael Irvin .30
94 Brad Johnson .50
95 Danny Kanell .15
96 Napoleon Kaufman .50
97 Dorsey Levens .50
98 Natrone Means .50
99 Herman Moore .50
100 Adrian Murrell .30
101 Carl Pickens .30
102 Rod Smith .30
103 Thurman Thomas .30
104 Reggie White .50
105 Jim Druckenmiller .30
106 Antowain Smith .50
107 Reidel Anthony .30
108 Ike Hilliard .15
109 Rae Carruth .15
110 Troy Davis .15
111 Terrance Mathis .15
112 Brett Favre 3.00
113 Dan Marino 1.00
114 Emmitt Smith 1.00
115 Barry Sanders 3.00
116 Eddie George 1.25
117 Drew Bledsoe 1.25
118 Troy Aikman 1.50
119 Terrell Davis 2.50
120 John Elway 1.75
121 Mark Brunell 1.25
122 Jerry Rice 1.50
123 Kordell Stewart 1.25
124 Steve McNair .75
125 Curtis Martin .75
126 Steve Young 1.00
127 Kerry Collins .50
128 Terry Glenn .50
129 Deion Sanders .50
130 Mike Alstott .50
131 Tony Banks .30
132 Karim Abdul-Jabbar .50
133 Terrell Owens .75
134 Yatil Green .30
135 Tony Gonzalez .30
136 Byron Hanspard .30
137 David LaFleur .30
138 Danny Wuerffel .30
139 Tiki Barber .30
140 Peter Boulware .15
141 Will Blackwell .15
142 Warrick Dunn 1.00
143 Corey Dillon .75
144 Jake Plummer 1.25
145 Neil Smith .15
146 Charles Johnson .30
147 Fred Lane .30
148 Dan Wilkinson .15
149 Ken Norton Jr. .15
150 Stephen Davis .15
151 Gilbert Brown .15
152 Kenny Bynum .15
153 Derrick Cullors .15
154 Charlie Garner .30
155 Jeff Graham .15
156 Warren Sapp .15
157 Jerald Moore .15
158 Sean Dawkins .15
159 Charlie Jones .15
160 Kevin Lockett .15
161 James McKnight .15
162 Chris Penn .15
163 Leslie Shepherd .15
164 Karl Williams .15
165 Mark Bruener .15
166 Ernie Conwell .15
167 Ken Dilger .15
168 Troy Drayton .15
169 Freddie Jones .15
170 Dale Carter .15
171 *Charles Woodson* 8.00
172 *Alonzo Mayes* 1.00
173 *Andre Wadsworth* 3.00
174 *Grant Winstrom* 2.00
175 *Greg Ellis* 2.00
176 *Chris Howard* 1.00
177 *Keith Brooking* 2.00
178 *Takeo Spikes* 4.00
179 *Anthony Simmons* 2.00
180 *Brian Simmons* 2.00
181 *Sam Cowart* 1.00
182 *Ken Oxendine* 1.00
183 *Vonnie Holliday* 2.00
184 *Terry Fair* 1.00
185 *Shaun Williams* 1.00
186 *Tremayne Stephens* 1.00
187 *Duane Starks* 1.00
188 *Jason Peter* 1.00
189 *Tebucky Jones* 1.00
190 *Donovin Darius* 1.00
191 *R.W. McQuarters* 2.00
192 *Corey Chavous* 2.00
193 *Cameron Cleeland* 2.00
194 *Stephen Alexander* 4.00
195 *Rod Rutledge* 1.00
196 *Scott Frost* 1.00
197 *Fred Beasley* 1.00
198 *Dorian Boose* 1.00
199 *Randy Moss* 30.00
200 *Jacquez Green* 5.00
201 *Marcus Nash* 4.00
202 *Hines Ward* 12.00
203 *Kevin Dyson* 4.00
204 *E.G. Green* 4.00
205 *Germane Crowell* 4.00
206 *Joe Jurevicius* 6.00
207 *Tony Simmons* 4.00
208 *Tim Dwight* 5.00
209 *Az-Zahir Hakim* 5.00
210 *Jerome Pathon* 6.00
211 *Patrick Johnson* 2.00
212 *Mikhael Ricks* 2.00
213 *Donald Hayes* 4.00
214 *Jammi German* 1.00
215 *Larry Shannon* 1.00
216 *Brian Alford* 1.00
217 *Curtis Enis* 5.00
218 *Fred Taylor* 8.00
219 *Robert Edwards* 5.00
220 *Ahman Green* 30.00
221 *Tavian Banks* 4.00
222 *Skip Hicks* 5.00
223 *Robert Holcombe* 5.00
224 *John Avery* 4.00
225 *Chris Fuamatu-Ma'afala* 5.00
226 *Michael Pittman* 6.00
227 *Rashaan Shehee* 2.00
228 *Jonathon Linton* 4.00
229 *Jon Ritchie* 4.00
230 *Chris Floyd* 3.00
231 *Wilmont Perry* 1.00
232 *Raymond Priester* 1.00
233 *Peyton Manning* 40.00
234 *Ryan Leaf* 4.00
235 *Brian Griese* 15.00
236 *Jeff Ogden* 4.00
237 *Charlie Batch* 4.00
238 *Moses Moreno* 4.00
239 *Jonathan Quinn* 4.00
240 *Flozell Adams* 1.00
241 Brett Favre PT 12.00
242 Dan Marino PT 10.00
243 Emmitt Smith PT 10.00
244 Barry Sanders PT 10.00
245 Eddie George PT 6.00
246 Drew Bledsoe PT 6.00
247 Troy Aikman PT 7.00
248 Terrell Davis PT 6.00
249 John Elway PT 8.00
250 Carl Pickens PT 1.00
251 Jerry Rice PT 7.00
252 Kordell Stewart PT 6.00
253 Steve McNair PT 4.00
254 Curtis Martin PT 4.00
255 Steve Young PT 5.00
256 Herman Moore PT 1.00
257 Dorsey Levens PT 1.00
258 Deion Sanders PT 3.00
259 Napoleon Kaufman PT 1.00
260 Warrick Dunn PT 5.00
261 Corey Dillon PT 4.00
262 Jerome Bettis PT 1.00
263 Tim Brown PT 4.00
264 Cris Carter PT 3.00
265 Antonio Freeman PT 1.00
266 Randy Moss PT 12.00
267 Curtis Enis PT 1.00
268 Fred Taylor PT 6.00
269 Robert Edwards PT 8.00
270 Peyton Manning PT 15.00
271 Barry Sanders TL 1.50
272 Eddie George TL .50
273 Troy Aikman TL .75
274 Mark Brunell TL .50
275 Kordell Stewart TL .50
276 Kerry Collins TL .15
277 Terry Glenn TL .30
278 Mike Alstott TL .30
279 Tony Banks TL .15
280 Karim Abdul TL .30
281 Terrell Owens TL .40
282 Byron Hanspard TL .15
283 Jake Plummer TL .50
284 Terry Allen TL .15
285 Jeff Blake TL .15
286 Brad Johnson TL .30
287 Danny Kanell TL .15
288 Natrone Means TL .30
289 Rod Smith TL .15
290 Thurman Thomas TL .15
291 Reggie White TL .30
292 Troy Davis TL .15
293 Curtis Conway TL .15
294 Irving Fryar TL .15
295 Jim Harbaugh TL .15
296 Andre Rison TL .15
297 Ricky Watters TL .15
298 Keyshawn Johnson TL .30
299 Jeff George TL .15
300 Marshall Faulk TL .30

1998 Leaf Rookies & Stars Crosstraining

Each card in this 10-card set highlights the same player on front and back, demonstrating the different skills that make them great. All cards are printed on foil board and are sequentially numbered to 1,000.

NM/M
Complete Set (10): 40.00
Common Player: 3.00
Production 1,000 Sets
1 Brett Favre 15.00
2 Mark Brunell 6.00
3 Barry Sanders 15.00
4 John Elway 12.00
5 Jerry Rice 15.00
6 Kordell Stewart 5.00
7 Steve McNair 5.00
8 Deion Sanders 3.00
9 Jake Plummer 3.00
10 Steve Young 6.00

1998 Leaf Rookies & Stars Crusade

The 30-card set includes both stars and rookies from '98. Each of the Green singles are sequentially numbered to 250. A parallel Purple set is numbered to 100 and a parallel Red set is numbered to 25.

NM/M
Complete Set (30): 400.00
Common Player: 10.00
Production 250 Sets
Purple Cards: 2X
Production 100 Sets
Red Cards: 2X-4X
Production 25 Sets
1 Brett Favre 50.00
2 Dan Marino 45.00
3 Emmitt Smith 45.00
4 Barry Sanders 50.00
5 Eddie George 25.00
6 Drew Bledsoe 25.00
7 Troy Aikman 30.00
8 Terrell Davis 30.00
9 John Elway 40.00
10 Mark Brunell 25.00
11 Jerry Rice 30.00
12 Kordell Stewart 25.00
13 Steve McNair 10.00
14 Curtis Martin 10.00
16 Steve Young 20.00
18 Deion Sanders 10.00
22 Terrell Owens 10.00
23 Jamal Anderson 10.00
25 Jerome Bettis 10.00
30 Cris Carter 10.00
32 Marshall Faulk 10.00
33 Antonio Freeman 10.00
40 Dorsey Levens 10.00
49 Garrison Hearst 10.00
57 Warrick Dunn 20.00
59 Jake Plummer 25.00
66 Peyton Manning 50.00
69 Randy Moss 50.00
77 Fred Taylor 45.00
78 Robert Edwards 20.00

1998 Leaf Rookies & Stars Extreme Measures

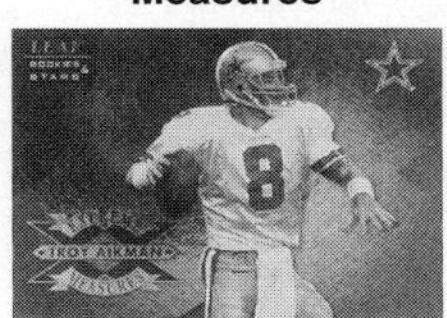

This 10-card set takes the top players in the game and highlights an outstanding but extreme statistic for each. These cards are each printed on foil board and sequentially numbered to 1,000.

NM/M
Complete Set (10): 60.00
Common Player: 5.00
1 Barry Sanders/918 15.00
2 Warrick Dunn/941 5.00
3 Curtis Martin/930 5.00
4 Terrell Davis/419 12.00
5 Troy Aikman/929 12.00
6 Drew Bledsoe/972 10.00
7 Eddie George/191 10.00
8 Emmitt Smith/888 15.00
9 Dan Marino/615 15.00
10 Brett Favre/965 15.00

1998 Leaf Rookies & Stars Extreme Measures Die Cuts

Each single in this set is sequentially numbered to a stat that was picked by the manufacturer. Each player in this set has a different amount of cards printed. Cards are identical to their Extreme Measures card except for being die cut in this set.

NM/M
Complete Set (10): 400.00
Common Player: 15.00
1 Barry Sanders/82 60.00
2 Warrick Dunn/59 20.00
3 Curtis Martin/70 35.00
4 Terrell Davis/581 15.00
5 Troy Aikman/71 40.00
6 Drew Bledsoe/28 60.00
7 Eddie George/809 15.00
8 Emmitt Smith/112 50.00
9 Dan Marino/385 40.00
10 Brett Favre/35 100.00

1998 Leaf Rookies & Stars Freshman Orientation

This 20-card set not only features the future stars of the game, but also highlights which round and overall number each player was selected in the NFL draft. Each card is sequentially numbered to 2,500 and printed on holographic foil.

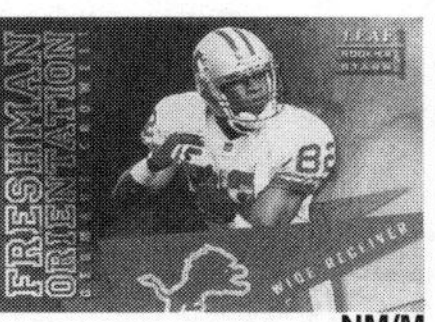

NM/M
Complete Set (20): 60.00
Common Player: 2.50
Minor Stars: 5.00
Production 2,500 Sets
1 Peyton Manning 15.00
2 Kevin Dyson 5.00
3 Joe Jurevicius 2.50
4 Tony Simmons 3.00
5 Marcus Nash 5.00
6 Ryan Leaf 3.00
7 Curtis Enis 3.00
8 Skip Hicks 5.00
9 Brian Griese 7.00
10 Jerome Pathon 2.50
11 John Avery 3.00
12 Fred Taylor 8.00
13 Robert Edwards 3.00
14 Robert Holcombe 3.00
15 Ahman Green 6.00
16 Hines Ward 2.50
17 Jacquez Green 3.00
18 Germane Crowell 3.00
19 Randy Moss 15.00
20 Charles Woodson 5.00

1998 Leaf Rookies & Stars Game Plan

Each card in this inside the game set is printed on foil board and sequentially numbered to 5,000. The first 500 of each card is treated with a "Master Game Plan" logo and unique color coating.

NM/M
Complete Set (20): 25.00
Common Player: .75
Minor Stars: 1.50
Production 5,000 Sets
Master Cards: 3X
Production First 500 Sets
1 Ryan Leaf .75
2 Peyton Manning 6.00
3 Brett Favre 4.00
4 Mark Brunell 2.00
5 Isaac Bruce 2.00
6 Dan Marino 3.00
7 Jerry Rice 2.00
8 Cris Carter 2.00
9 Emmitt Smith 4.00
10 Kordell Stewart 1.00
11 Corey Dillon 1.00
12 Barry Sanders 4.00
13 Curtis Martin 1.00
14 Carl Pickens .75
15 Eddie George 1.00
16 Warrick Dunn 1.00
17 Jake Plummer 1.00
18 Curtis Enis 1.75
19 Drew Bledsoe 2.00
20 Terrell Davis 2.00

1998 Leaf Rookies & Stars Great American Heroes

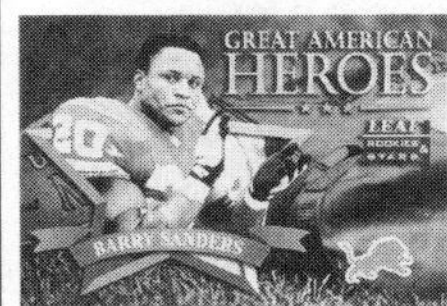

The theme to this insert is players that have helped make the great American game of football. Each card in this set is stamped with holographic foil and sequentially numbered to 2,500.

NM/M
Complete Set (20): 45.00
Common Player: 1.00
Minor Stars: 2.00
Production 2,500 Sets
1 Brett Favre 6.00
2 Dan Marino 6.00
3 Emmitt Smith 6.00
4 Barry Sanders 6.00
5 Eddie George 3.00
6 Drew Bledsoe 3.00
7 Troy Aikman 3.00
8 Terrell Davis 3.00
9 John Elway 4.00
10 Mark Brunell 2.00
11 Jerry Rice 4.00
12 Kordell Stewart 2.00
13 Steve McNair 2.00
14 Curtis Martin 2.00
15 Steve Young 3.00
16 Dorsey Levens 1.00
17 Herman Moore 1.00
18 Deion Sanders 1.00
19 Thurman Thomas 1.00
20 Peyton Manning 8.00

1998 Leaf Rookies & Stars Greatest Hits

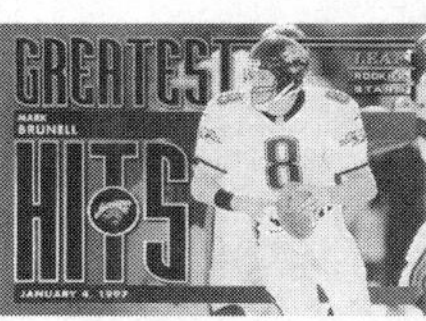

The top 20 players in the NFL are included in this insert and each card is sequentially numbered to 2,500.

NM/M
Complete Set (20): 45.00
Common Player: 1.00
Minor Stars: 2.00
Production 2,500 Sets
1 Brett Favre 6.00
2 Eddie George 3.00
3 John Elway 4.00
4 Steve Young 3.00
5 Napoleon Kaufman 1.00
6 Dan Marino 6.00
7 Drew Bledsoe 3.00
8 Mark Brunell 2.00
9 Warrick Dunn 2.00
10 Dorsey Levens 1.00
11 Emmitt Smith 6.00
12 Troy Aikman 4.00
13 Jerry Rice 5.00
14 Jake Plummer 1.00
15 Herman Moore 1.00
16 Barry Sanders 6.00
17 Terrell Davis 3.00
18 Kordell Stewart 1.00
19 Jerome Bettis 1.00
20 Isaac Bruce 1.00

1998 Leaf Rookies & Stars MVP Contenders

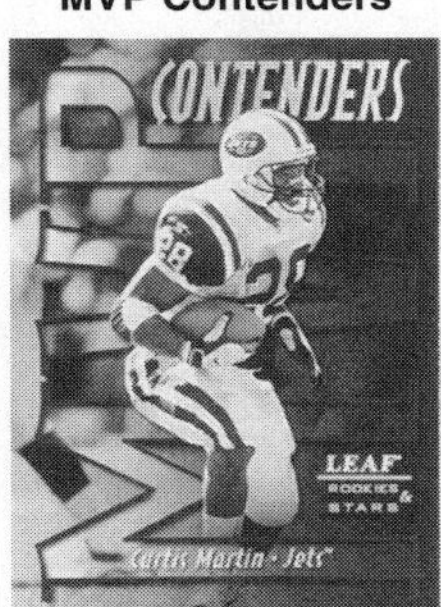

The set is made up of 20 of the league's top players who will contend for the MVP award. Each card is accented with holographic foil stamping and sequentially numbered to 2,500.

NM/M
Complete Set (20): 45.00
Common Player: 1.00
Minor Stars: 2.00
Production 2,500 Sets
1 Tim Brown 2.00
2 Herman Moore 1.00
3 Jake Plummer 1.00
4 Warrick Dunn 2.00
5 Dorsey Levens 1.00
6 Steve McNair 2.00
7 John Elway 3.00
8 Troy Aikman 3.00
9 Steve Young 3.00
10 Curtis Martin 3.00
11 Kordell Stewart 2.00
12 Jerry Rice 4.00
13 Mark Brunell 2.00
14 Terrell Davis 3.00
15 Drew Bledsoe 3.00
16 Eddie George 3.00
17 Barry Sanders 5.00
18 Emmitt Smith 5.00
19 Dan Marino 5.00
20 Brett Favre 5.00

1998 Leaf Rookies & Stars Standing Ovation

This 10-card set is printed with holographic foil stamping and sequentially numbered to 5,000. It features players who truly deserve a standing ovation for their accomplishments.

NM/M
Complete Set (10): 25.00
Common Player: 1.00
Minor Stars: 2.00
Production 5,000 Sets
1 Brett Favre 5.00
2 Dan Marino 5.00
3 Emmitt Smith 5.00
4 Barry Sanders 5.00
5 Terrell Davis 3.00
6 Jerry Rice 4.00
7 Steve Young 3.00
8 Reggie White 1.00
9 John Elway 3.00
10 Eddie George 1.00

1998 Leaf Rookies & Stars Ticket Masters

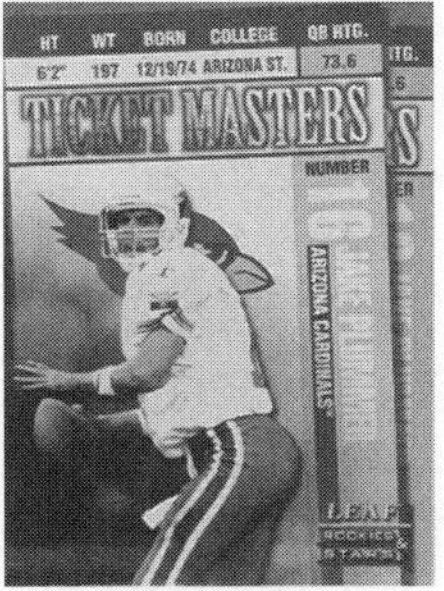

This double-sided 20-card set is printed on foil board and features players from the same team, like Terrell Davis and John Elway, that fill the seats for their franchise. Each card is sequentially numbered to 2,500 with the first 500 die-cut like a ticket.

NM/M
Complete Set (20): 60.00
Common Player: 1.00
Minor Stars: 2.00
Production 2,500 Sets
Die-Cut Cards: 3X
Production First 500 Sets
1 Brett Favre, Dorsey Levens 6.00
2 Dan Marino, Karim Abdul 6.00
3 Troy Aikman, Deion Sanders 4.00
4 Barry Sanders, Herman Moore 6.00
5 Steve McNair, Eddie George 3.00
6 Drew Bledsoe, Robert Edwards 3.00
7 Terrell Davis, John Elway 6.00
8 Jerry Rice, Steve Young 4.00
9 Kordell Stewart, Jerome Bettis 2.00
10 Curtis Martin, Keyshawn Johnson 3.00
11 Warrick Dunn, Trent Dilfer 2.00
12 Corey Dillon, Carl Pickens 2.00
13 Tim Brown, Napoleon Kaufman 2.00
14 Jake Plummer, Frank Sanders 2.00
15 Ryan Leaf, Natrone Means 1.00
16 Peyton Manning, Marshall Faulk 6.00
17 Mark Brunell, Fred Taylor 2.00
18 Curtis Enis, Curtis Conway 2.00
19 Cris Carter, Randy Moss 6.00
20 Isaac Bruce, Tony Banks 1.00

1998 Leaf Rookies & Stars Touchdown Club

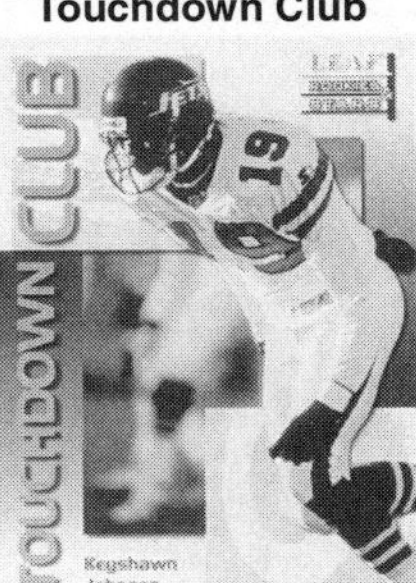

The 20 players showcased in this insert set are known for their ability to get into the end zone.

Whether it's through the air, on the ground or both, these NFL stars get the job done. Each card is printed on foil board and sequentially numbered to 5,000.

NM/M
Complete Set (20): 30.00
Common Player: 1.00
Minor Stars: 2.00
Production 5,000 Sets
1 Brett Favre 5.00
2 Dan Marino 5.00
3 Emmitt Smith 5.00
4 Barry Sanders 5.00
5 Eddie George 3.00
6 Drew Bledsoe 3.00
7 Terrell Davis 3.00
8 Mark Brunell 2.00
9 Jerry Rice 4.00
10 Kordell Stewart 2.00
11 Curtis Martin 2.00
12 Karim Abdul 1.00
13 Warrick Dunn 2.00
14 Corey Dillon 2.00
15 Jerome Bettis 1.00
16 Antonio Freeman 1.00
17 Keyshawn Johnson 1.00
18 John Elway 3.00
19 Steve Young 3.00
20 Jake Plummer 1.00

1999 Leaf Certified

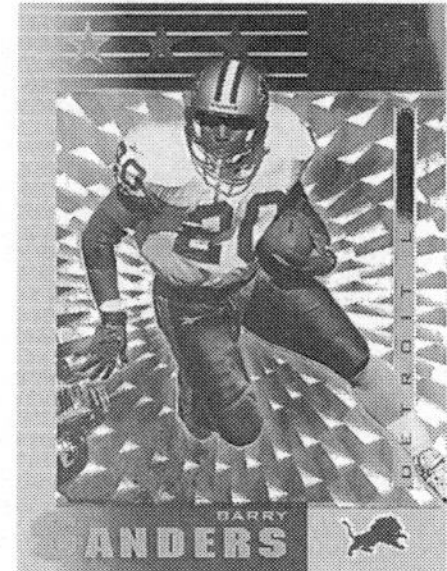

This was a 225-card set that was divided into four tiers. The first 100 cards contained one star and were found four to a pack. Two-star cards included #101-150 and they were inserted one-per-pack. Three-star cards included #151-175 and they were inserted 1:3 packs. The four-star singles were cards #176-225 and they were found 1:5 packs. Parallel sets included Mirror Red and Mirror Gold. Other inserts included: Certified Skills, Fabric of the Game, Gold Future, Gold Team and Gridiron Gear. SRP was $3.99 for five-card packs.

NM/M
Complete Set (225): 175.00
Common Player (1-100): .20
Minor Stars (1-100): .40
Inserted 4:1
Common Player (101-150): .50
Minor Stars (101-150): 1.00
Inserted 1:1
Common Player (151-175): 1.00
Minor Stars (151-175): 2.00
Inserted 1:3
Common Player (176-225): 5.00
Inserted 1:5
Pack (5): 5.00
Wax Box (18): 70.00
1 Simeon Rice .20
2 Frank Sanders .40
3 Andre Wadsworth .20
4 Larry Centers .20
5 Byron Hanspard .20
6 Terance Mathis .20
7 O.J. Santiago .20
8 Chris Calloway .20
9 Michael Jackson .20
10 Rod Woodson .20
11 Pat Johnson .20
12 Rob Johnson .40
13 Andre Reed .20
14 Tim Biakabutuka .20
15 Rae Carruth .20
16 Fred Lane .20
17 Muhsin Muhammad .40
18 Wesley Walls .20
19 Edgar Bennett .20
20 Curtis Conway .40
21 Bobby Engram .20
22 Jeff Blake .40
23 Darnay Scott .20
24 Ty Detmer .20
25 Sedrick Shaw .20
26 Leslie Shepherd .20
27 Keith Byars .20
28 Chris Warren .20
29 Raghib Ismail .20
30 Marcus Nash .20
31 Neil Smith .20
32 Bubby Brister .40
33 Brian Griese 1.50
34 Germane Crowell .40
35 Johnnie Morton .20
36 Gus Frerotte .20
37 Robert Brooks .20
38 Mark Chmura .40
39 Derrick Mayes .40
40 Jerome Pathon .20
41 Jimmy Smith .40
42 James Stewart .20
43 Tavian Banks .20
44 Derrick Alexander .20
45 Kimble Anders .20
46 Elvis Grbac .40
47 Derrick Thomas .20
48 Bam Morris .20
49 Tony Gonzalez .20
50 John Avery .20
51 Tyrone Wheatley .20
52 Zach Thomas .40
53 Lamar Thomas .20
54 Jeff George .40
55 John Randle .20
56 Jake Reed .20
57 Leroy Hoard .20
58 Robert Edwards .40
59 Ben Coates .40
60 Tony Simmons .40
61 Shawn Jefferson .20
62 Eddie Kennison .20
63 Lamar Smith .20
64 Tiki Barber .20
65 Kerry Collins .40
66 Ike Hilliard .20
67 Gary Brown .20
68 Joe Jurevicius .20
69 Kent Graham .20
70 Dedric Ward .20
71 Terry Allen .20
72 Neil O'Donnell .40
73 Desmond Howard .20
74 James Jett .20
75 Jon Ritchie .20
76 Rickey Dudley .20
77 Charles Johnson .20
78 Chris Fuamatu-Ma'afala .20
79 Hines Ward .40
80 Ryan Leaf .50
81 Jim Harbaugh .40
82 Junior Seau .40
83 Mikhael Ricks .20
84 J.J. Stokes .40
85 Ahman Green .40
86 Tony Banks .40
87 Robert Holcombe .20
88 Az-Zahir Hakim .40
89 Greg Hill .40
90 Trent Green .40
91 Eric Zeier .20
92 Reidel Anthony .40
93 Bert Emmanuel .20
94 Warren Sapp .20
95 Kevin Dyson .40
96 Yancey Thigpen .20
97 Frank Wycheck .20
98 Michael Westbrook .40
99 Albert Connell .20
100 Darrell Green .20
101 Rob Moore .50
102 Adrian Murrell .50
103 Jake Plummer .50
104 Chris Chandler .50
105 Jamal Anderson 1.00
106 Tim Dwight .75
107 Jermaine Lewis .50
108 Priest Holmes 1.50
109 Bruce Smith .50
110 Eric Moulds 1.00
111 Antowain Smith .75
112 Curtis Enis .50
113 Corey Dillon 1.00
114 Michael Irvin .50
115 Ed McCaffrey .50
116 Shannon Sharpe .50
117 Terrell Davis 2.00
118 Charlie Batch .50
119 Antonio Freeman .50
120 Dorsey Levens .50
121 Marvin Harrison 1.50
122 Peyton Manning 5.00
123 Keenan McCardell .50
124 Fred Taylor 2.00
125 Andre Rison .50
126 O.J. McDuffie .50
127 Karim Abdul .40
128 Randy Moss 5.00
129 Terry Glenn .50
130 Vinny Testaverde .50
131 Keyshawn Johnson 1.00
132 Curtis Martin 1.00
133 Wayne Chrebet .50
134 Napoleon Kaufman .40
135 Charles Woodson 1.00
136 Duce Staley .50
137 Kordell Stewart 1.00
138 Terrell Owens 1.00
139 Ricky Watters 1.00
140 Joey Galloway 1.00
141 Jon Kitna .50
142 Isaac Bruce 1.00
143 Jacquez Green .50
144 Warrick Dunn 1.00
145 Mike Alstott 1.00
146 Trent Dilfer 1.00
147 Steve McNair 1.50
148 Eddie George 1.50
149 Skip Hicks .50
150 Brad Johnson 1.00
151 Doug Flutie .50
152 Thurman Thomas 1.00
153 Carl Pickens 1.00
154 Emmitt Smith 8.00
155 Troy Aikman 5.00
156 Deion Sanders 2.00
157 John Elway 7.00
158 Rod Smith 1.00
159 Barry Sanders 8.00
160 Herman Moore 2.00
161 Brett Favre 10.00
162 Mark Brunell 1.00
163 Warren Moon 1.00
164 Dan Marino 8.00
165 Randall Cunningham 1.00
166 Robert Smith 1.00
167 Cris Carter 1.00
168 Drew Bledsoe 4.00
169 Tim Brown 2.00
170 Jerome Bettis 2.00
171 Natrone Means .50
172 Jerry Rice 5.00
173 Steve Young 3.00
174 Garrison Hearst 2.00
175 Marshall Faulk 2.00
176 *David Boston* 8.00
177 *Jeff Paulk* 4.00
178 *Reginald Kelly* 2.00
179 *Brandon Stokely* 3.00
180 *Chris McAlister* 4.00
181 *Shawn Bryson* 2.00
182 *Peerless Price* 6.00
183 *Cade McNown* 4.00
184 *Jerry Azumah* 2.00
185 *D'Wayne Bates* 3.00
186 *Marty Booker* 5.00
187 *Akili Smith* 4.00
188 *Craig Yeast* 2.00
189 *Tim Couch* 8.00
190 *Kevin Johnson* 4.00
191 *Wane McGarity* 2.00
192 *Olandis Gary* 8.00
193 *Travis McGriff* 3.00
194 *Sedrick Irvin* 3.00
195 *Chris Claiborne* 3.00
196 *De'Mond Parker* 3.00
197 *Dee Miller* 3.00
198 *Edgerrin James* 15.00
199 *Michael Cloud* 3.00
200 *Larry Parker* 3.00
201 *Cecil Collins* 4.00
202 *James Johnson* 4.00
203 *Rob Konrad* 3.00
204 *Daunte Culpepper* 15.00
205 *Jim Kleinsasser* 4.00
206 *Kevin Faulk* 4.00
207 *Andy Katzenmoyer* 4.00
208 *Ricky Williams* 10.00
209 *Joe Montgomery* 2.00
210 *Sean Bennett* 2.00
211 *Dameane Douglas* 2.00
212 *Donovan McNabb* 15.00
213 *Na Brown* 2.00
214 *Amos Zereoue* 5.00
215 *Troy Edwards* 4.00
216 *Jermaine Fazande* 2.00
217 *Tai Streets* 4.00
218 *Brock Huard* 3.00
219 *Charlie Rogers* 2.00
220 *Karsten Bailey* 3.00
221 *Joe Germaine* 3.00
222 *Torry Holt* 8.00
223 *Shaun King* 4.00
224 *Jevon Kearse* 5.00
225 *Champ Bailey* 5.00

1999 Leaf Certified Mirror Gold

This was a 225-card parallel to the base set found at four different tiers. Each single was printed on holographic stock with gold tint. The first 100 cards were sequentially numbered to 45. Cards 101-150 were numbered to 35. Cards 151-175 were numbered to 25 and cards 176-225 were numbered to 30.

NM/M
Common Player (1-100):
1-Star Cards: 20X-40X
Production 45 Sets
Common Player (101-150):
2-Star Cards: 10X-20X
Production 35 Sets
Common Player (151-175):
3-Star Cards: 10X-20X
Production 25 Sets
Common Player (176-225):
4-Star Cards: 2X-4X
Production 30 Sets

1999 Leaf Certified Mirror Red

This was a 225-card parallel to the base set found at four different tiers. Each single was printed on holographic stock with red tint. The first 100 cards were found 1:17 packs. Cards 101-150 were inserted 1:53 packs. Cards 151-175 were found 1:125 and cards 176-225 were inserted 1:89 packs.

NM/M
Common Player (1-100):
1-Star Cards: 5X-12X
Inserted 1:17
Common Player (101-150):
2-Star Cards: 4X-8X
Inserted 1:53
Common Player (151-175):
3-Star Cards: 4X-8X
Inserted 1:125
Common Player (176-225):
4-Star Cards: 1.5X
Inserted 1:89

1999 Leaf Certified Fabric of the Game

This was a 75-card insert set with the singles found at three levels. The three technologies used were nylon, leather and plastic. A total of 25 players were showcased according to Pro Bowl appearances, career TDs and career yards. Each level had five categories with different sequential numbering ranging from 100 to 1,000.

NM/M
Complete Set (75): 1,650
Common Player: 5.00
1 John Elway 100 100.00
2 Barry Sanders 100 100.00
3 Jerry Rice 100 60.00
4 Brett Favre 250 70.00
5 Steve Young 250 25.00
6 Troy Aikman 250 40.00
7 Deion Sanders 250 15.00
8 Terrell Davis 500 30.00
9 Mark Brunell 500 15.00
10 Drew Bledsoe 500 15.00
11 Randall Cunningham 500 10.00
12 Eddie George 500 12.00
13 Jamal Anderson 750 8.00
14 Doug Flutie 750 12.00
15 Robert Smith 750 8.00
16 Garrison Hearst 750 8.00
17 Keyshawn Johnson 750 8.00
18 Randy Moss 750 40.00
19 Eric Moulds 1000 8.00
20 Curtis Enis 1000 8.00
21 Ricky Williams 1000 30.00
22 Peyton Manning 1000 30.00
23 Tim Couch 1000 20.00
24 Cade McNown 1000 12.00
25 Akili Smith 1000 12.00
26 Dan Marino 100 100.00
27 Jerry Rice 100 60.00
28 Emmitt Smith 100 100.00
29 Cris Carter 250 15.00
30 Steve Young 250 25.00
31 Herman Moore 250 15.00
32 Tim Brown 250 15.00
33 Jerome Bettis 500 10.00
34 Natrone Means 500 5.00
35 Antonio Freeman 500 10.00
36 Terrell Davis 500 30.00
37 Carl Pickens 500 5.00
38 Karim Abdul 750 5.00
39 Mike Alstott 750 8.00
40 Jake Plummer 750 15.00
41 Steve McNair 750 8.00
42 Terrell Owens 750 8.00
43 Kordell Stewart 750 10.00
44 Randy Moss 1000 35.00
45 Fred Taylor 1000 20.00
46 Peyton Manning 1000 30.00
47 Tim Couch 1000 20.00
48 Akili Smith 1000 10.00
49 Torry Holt 1000 12.00
50 Donovan McNabb 1000 20.00
51 Barry Sanders 100 100.00
52 Dan Marino 100 100.00
53 Jerry Rice 100 60.00
54 John Elway 250 50.00
55 Brett Favre 250 70.00
56 Emmitt Smith 250 50.00
57 Mark Brunell 250 15.00
58 Jake Plummer 500 12.00
59 Ricky Watters 500 5.00
60 Dorsey Levens 500 10.00
61 Curtis Martin 500 10.00
62 Marshall Faulk 500 10.00
63 Eddie George 750 10.00
64 Corey Dillon 750 8.00
65 Warrick Dunn 750 10.00
66 Antowain Smith 750 8.00
67 Napoleon Kaufman 750 8.00
68 Joey Galloway 750 8.00
69 Fred Taylor 1000 20.00
70 Charlie Batch 1000 10.00
71 Ricky Williams 1000 20.00
72 Edgerrin James 1000 25.00
73 Jon Kitna 1000 10.00
74 Daunte Culpepper 1000 20.00
75 Skip Hicks 1000 5.00

1999 Leaf Certified Gold Future

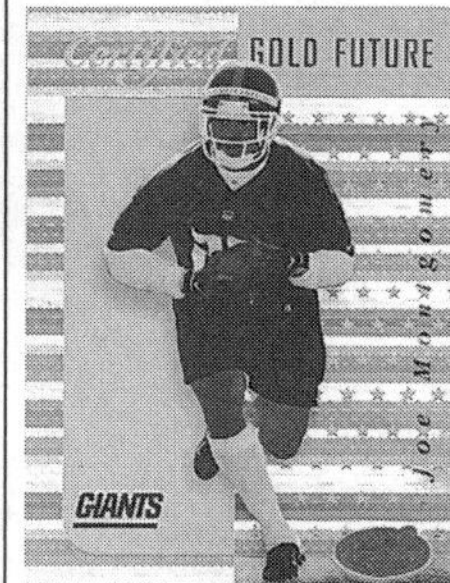

This 30-card insert set included the top rookies from the 1999 NFL Draft. Each single was printed on mirror Mylar with foil and micro-etching. Singles were found 1:17 packs. A parallel Mirror Black version was also made with each of those singles sequentially numbered to 25.

NM/M
Complete Set (30): 185.00
Common Player: 3.00
Inserted 1:17
Mirror Black Cards: 6X-12X
Production 25 Sets
1 Travis McGriff 1.00
2 Jermaine Fazande 1.00
3 Kevin Faulk 3.00
4 Edgerrin James 15.00
5 Ricky Williams 20.00
6 Tim Couch 15.00
7 Torry Holt 8.00
8 Kevin Johnson 8.00
9 Amos Zereoue 6.00
10 Joe Germaine 2.00
11 Shawn Bryson 1.00
12 D'Wayne Bates 3.00
13 Akili Smith 4.00
14 Shaun King 3.00
15 Joe Montgomery 1.00
16 Troy Edwards 4.00
17 Rob Konrad 2.00
18 David Boston 8.00
19 Reginald Kelly 3.00
20 Donovan McNabb 12.00
21 Champ Bailey 5.00
22 Craig Yeast 1.00
23 Daunte Culpepper 12.00
24 Peerless Price 8.00
25 Cecil Collins 4.00
26 Cade McNown 4.00
27 Karsten Bailey 3.00
28 James Johnson 3.00
29 Brock Huard 3.00
30 Michael Cloud 2.00

1999 Leaf Certified Gold Team

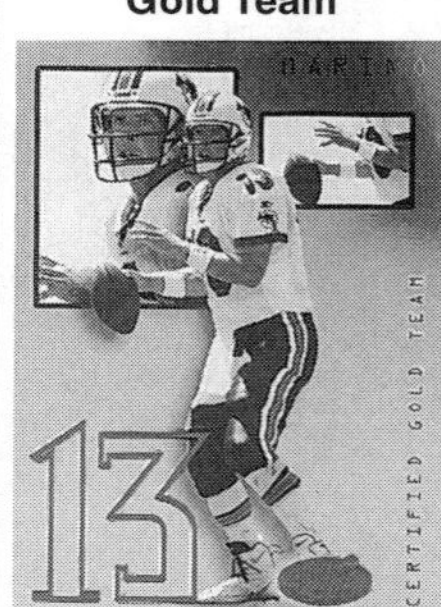

This 30-card insert set included the top veterans and pictured them on mirror Mylar board with foil. Singles were inserted 1:17 packs. A parallel Mirror Black version was also produced with each of those singles sequentially numbered to 25.

NM/M
Complete Set (30): 200.00
Common Player: 3.00
Inserted 1:17
Mirror Black Cards: 6X-12X
Production 25 Sets
1 Randy Moss 12.00
2 Terrell Davis 8.00
3 Peyton Manning 12.00
4 Fred Taylor 6.00
5 Jake Plummer 4.00
6 Drew Bledsoe 8.00
7 John Elway 12.00
8 Mark Brunell 4.00
9 Joey Galloway 3.00
10 Troy Aikman 12.00
11 Jerome Bettis 3.00
12 Tim Brown 3.00
13 Dan Marino 15.00
14 Antonio Freeman 3.00
15 Steve Young 7.00
16 Jamal Anderson 3.00
17 Brett Favre 15.00
18 Jerry Rice 12.00
19 Corey Dillon 3.00
20 Barry Sanders 15.00
21 Doug Flutie 3.00
22 Emmitt Smith 15.00
23 Curtis Martin 3.00
24 Dorsey Levens 3.00
25 Kordell Stewart 3.00
26 Eddie George 4.00
27 Terrell Owens 3.00
28 Keyshawn Johnson 3.00
29 Steve McNair 4.00
30 Cris Carter 3.00

1999 Leaf Certified Gridiron Gear

This 72-card insert set included pieces of game-used jerseys from the top veterans in the NFL. Each of the singles was sequentially numbered to 300.

NM/M
Common Player: 25.00
Multi-Colored Swatches: 1.5X
Production 300 Sets
KA33 Karim Abdul 25.00
TA8 Troy Aikman 75.00
JA32 Jamal Anderson 25.00
JB36 Jerome Bettis 40.00
DB11 Drew Bledsoe 75.00
TB71 Tony Boselli 25.00
RB87 Robert Brooks 25.00
TB81 Tim Brown 40.00
IB80 Isaac Bruce 40.00
MB8A Mark Brunell White 25.00
MB8H Mark Brunell Teal 25.00
MC89 Mark Chmura 25.00
BC87 Ben Coates 25.00
CC80 Curtis Conway 25.00
RC7 Randall Cunningham 40.00
TD30A Terrell Davis White 75.00
TD30H Terrell Davis Blue 75.00
TD12 Trent Dilfer 25.00
WD28 Warrick Dunn 40.00
JE7H John Elway Blue 75.00
JE7HC John Elway Orange 75.00
BF4A Brett Favre White 100.00
BF4H Brett Favre Green 100.00
DF7A Doug Flutie White 25.00
DF7H Doug Flutie Blue 25.00
AF86 Antonio Freeman 25.00
EG27 Eddie George 40.00
DG28 Darrell Green 25.00
MH88 Marvin Harrison 50.00
DH80 Desmond Howard 25.00
MI88 Michael Irvin 25.00
JJ82 James Jett 25.00
KJ19 Keyshawn Johnson 40.00
NK26A Napoleon Kaufman White 25.00
NK26H Napoleon Kaufman Black 25.00
JK12 Jim Kelly 40.00
RL16 Ryan Leaf 25.00
DL25A Dorsey Levens White 25.00
DL25H Dorsey Levens Green 25.00
PM18 Peyton Manning 75.00
DM13A Dan Marino White 100.00
DM13H Dan Marino Teal 100.00
CM28 Curtis Martin 40.00
KM87 Keenan McCardell 25.00
OM81 O.J. McDuffie 25.00
SM9 Steve McNair 40.00
NM20 Natrone Means 25.00
JM19 Joe Montana 100.00
WM1 Warren Moon 25.00
HMB4 Herman Moore 25.00
RM84A Randy Moss White 75.00
RM84H Randy Moss Purple 75.00
JP16 Jake Plummer 25.00
JR80A Jerry Rice White 75.00
JR80H Jerry Rice Red 75.00
BS20 Barry Sanders 100.00
CS81 Chris Sanders 25.00
DS21 Deion Sanders 40.00
WS99 Warren Sapp 25.00
JS55 Junior Seau 25.00
PH12 Phil Simms 25.00
ES22 Emmitt Smith 100.00
NS90 Neil Smith 25.00
JS82 Jimmy Smith 25.00
JS33 James Stewart 25.00
KS10 Kordell Stewart 40.00
VT12 Vinny Testaverde 25.00
DT58 Derrick Thomas 25.00
TT34 Thurman Thomas 25.00
ZT54 Zach Thomas 25.00
CW24 Charles Woodson 25.00
SY8 Steve Young 60.00

1999 Leaf Certified Skills

This 20-card insert set featured 20 pairs of NFL superstars

back-to-back on dual-sided mirror Mylar board. Singles were inserted 1:35 packs. A parallel Mirror Black version was also produced and each of those singles was sequentially numbered to 25.

		NM/M
Complete Set (20):		225.00
Common Player:		7.00
Inserted 1:35		
Mirror Black Cards:		5X-10X
Production 25 Sets		
1	Deion Sanders, Champ Bailey	5.00
2	John Elway, Cade McNown	12.00
3	Cris Carter, David Boston	7.00
4	Marshall Faulk, Edgerrin James	15.00
5	Jerry Rice, Randy Moss	20.00
6	Antonio Freeman, Terrell Owens	7.00
7	Terrell Davis, Ricky Williams	15.00
8	Drew Bledsoe, Doug Flutie	12.00
9	Eddie George, Jamal Anderson	10.00
10	Troy Aikman, Peyton Manning	20.00
11	Barry Sanders, Warrick Dunn	15.00
12	Randall Cunningham, Daunte Culpepper	10.00
13	Dan Marino, Tim Couch	20.00
14	Emmitt Smith, Fred Taylor	20.00
15	Keyshawn Johnson, Eric Moulds	7.00
16	Steve Young, Mark Brunell	12.00
17	Donovan McNabb, Akili Smith	10.00
18	Brett Favre, Jake Plummer	20.00
19	Kordell Stewart, Steve McNair	5.00
20	Torry Holt, Troy Edwards	5.00

1999 Leaf Rookies & Stars

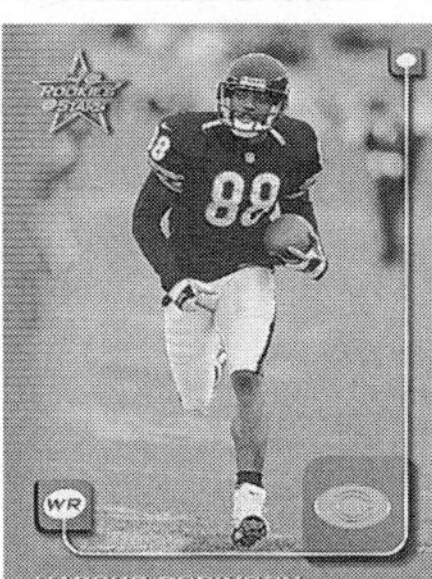

This was a 300-card base set that included 100 rookie cards found 1:2 packs. The Longevity insert was a parallel to the base with each card sequentially numbered. The first 200 cards were numbered to 50 and the 100 rookies were numbered to 30. Other inserts included: Cross Training, Dress for Success, John Elway Collection, Freshman Orientation, Game Plan, Great American Heroes, Greatest Hits, Prime Cuts, Signature Series, Slide Show, Statistical Standouts, Ticket Masters and Touchdown Club. SRP was $2.99 for 9-card packs.

		NM/M
Complete Set (300):		200.00
Common Player:		.15
Minor Stars:		.30
Common Rookie:		1.00
Inserted 1:2		
Pack (9):		4.00
Wax Box (24):		65.00
1	Frank Sanders	.15
2	Adrian Murrell	.15
3	Rob Moore	.30
4	Simeon Rice	.15
5	Michael Pittman	.30
6	Jake Plummer	.75
7	Chris Chandler	.30
8	Tim Dwight	.50
9	Chris Calloway	.15
10	Terance Mathis	.15
11	Jamal Anderson	.50
12	Byron Hanspard	.30
13	O.J. Santiago	.15
14	Ken Oxendine	.30
15	Priest Holmes	.50
16	Scott Mitchell	.15
17	Tony Banks	.30
18	Patrick Johnson	.15
19	Rod Woodson	.15
20	Jermaine Lewis	.15
21	Errict Rhett	.30
22	Stoney Case	.30
23	Andre Reed	.30
24	Eric Moulds	.50
25	Rob Johnson	.30
26	Doug Flutie	.75
27	Bruce Smith	.15
28	Jay Riemersma	.15
29	Antowain Smith	.50
30	Thurman Thomas	.30
31	Jonathon Linton	.30
32	Muhsin Muhammad	.30
33	Rae Carruth	.15
34	Wesley Walls	.30
35	Fred Lane	.30
36	Kevin Greene	.15
37	Tim Biakabutuka	.30
38	Curtis Enis	.50
39	Shane Matthews	.30
40	Bobby Engram	.15
41	Curtis Conway	.30
42	Marcus Robinson	1.00
43	Darnay Scott	.30
44	Carl Pickens	.30
45	Corey Dillon	.50
46	Jeff Blake	.30
47	Terry Kirby	.15
48	Ty Detmer	.15
49	Leslie Shepherd	.15
50	Karim Abdul	.30
51	Emmitt Smith	1.50
52	Deion Sanders	.50
53	Michael Irvin	.30
54	Raghib Ismail	.15
55	David LaFleur	.15
56	Troy Aikman	1.00
57	Ed McCaffrey	.50
58	Rod Smith	.50
59	Shannon Sharpe	.30
60	Brian Griese	1.00
61	John Elway	1.50
62	Bubby Brister	.30
63	Neil Smith	.15
64	Terrell Davis	1.00
65	John Avery	.30
66	Derek Loville	.15
67	Ron Rivers	.15
68	Herman Moore	.50
69	Johnnie Morton	.15
70	Charlie Batch	.75
71	Barry Sanders	2.00
72	Germane Crowell	.30
73	Greg Hill	.15
74	Gus Frerotte	.30
75	Corey Bradford	.30
76	Dorsey Levens	.50
77	Antonio Freeman	.50
78	Mark Chmura	.30
79	Brett Favre	2.00
80	Bill Schroeder	.30
81	Matt Hasselbeck	.50
82	E.G. Green	.30
83	Ken Dilger	.15
84	Jerome Pathon	.15
85	Marvin Harrison	.50
86	Peyton Manning	1.50
87	Tavian Banks	.30
88	Keenan McCardell	.30
89	Mark Brunell	.75
90	Fred Taylor	1.00
91	Jimmy Smith	.75
92	James Stewart	.50
93	Kyle Brady	.15
94	Derrick Thomas	.30
95	Rashaan Shehee	.15
96	Derrick Alexander	.15
97	Bam Morris	.15
98	Andre Rison	.30
99	Elvis Grbac	.30
100	Tony Gonzalez	.30
101	Donnell Bennett	.15
102	Warren Moon	.30
103	Zach Thomas	.30
104	Oronde Gadsden	.30
105	Dan Marino	1.50
106	O.J. McDuffie	.30
107	Tony Martin	.15
108	Randy Moss	2.00
109	Cris Carter	.50
110	Robert Smith	.50
111	Randall Cunningham	.50
112	Jake Reed	.30
113	John Randle	.30
114	Leroy Hoard	.15
115	Jeff George	.50
116	Ty Law	.15
117	Shawn Jefferson	.15
118	Troy Brown	.15
119	Robert Edwards	.30
120	Tony Simmons	.30
121	Terry Glenn	.50
122	Ben Coates	.30
123	Drew Bledsoe	.75
124	Terry Allen	.30
125	Cameron Cleeland	.30
126	Eddie Kennison	.15
127	Amani Toomer	.15
128	Kerry Collins	.30
129	Joe Jurevicius	.15
130	Tiki Barber	.15
131	Ike Hilliard	.30
132	Michael Strahan	.15
133	Gary Brown	.15
134	Jason Sehorn	.15
135	Curtis Martin	.50
136	Vinny Testaverde	.30
137	Dedric Ward	.30
138	Keyshawn Johnson	.50
139	Wayne Chrebet	.50
140	Tyrone Wheatley	.30
141	Napoleon Kaufman	.50
142	Tim Brown	.30
143	Rickey Dudley	.30
144	Jon Ritchie	.15
145	James Jett	.15
146	Rich Gannon	.30
147	Charles Woodson	.50
148	Charles Johnson	.15
149	Duce Staley	.50
150	Will Blackwell	.15
151	Kordell Stewart	.50
152	Jerome Bettis	.50
153	Hines Ward	.30
154	Richard Huntley	.30
155	Natrone Means	.30
156	Mikhael Ricks	.15
157	Junior Seau	.30
158	Jim Harbaugh	.30
159	Ryan Leaf	.50
160	Erik Kramer	.15
161	Terrell Owens	.50
162	J.J. Stokes	.30
163	Lawrence Phillips	.30
164	Charlie Garner	.30
165	Jerry Rice	1.00
166	Garrison Hearst	.50
167	Steve Young	.75
168	Derrick Mayes	.30
169	Ahman Green	.30
170	Joey Galloway	.50
171	Ricky Watters	.30
172	Jon Kitna	.50
173	Sean Dawkins	.15
174	Az-Zahir Hakim	.30
175	Robert Holcombe	.30
176	Isaac Bruce	.50
177	Amp Lee	.15
178	Marshall Faulk	.50
179	Trent Green	.30
180	Eric Zeier	.15
181	Bert Emanuel	.15
182	Jacquez Green	.30
183	Reidel Anthony	.30
184	Warren Sapp	.30
185	Mike Alstott	.50
186	Warrick Dunn	.50
187	Trent Dilfer	.30
188	Neil O'Donnell	.30
189	Eddie George	.60
190	Yancey Thigpen	.30
191	Steve McNair	.60
192	Kevin Dyson	.30
193	Frank Wycheck	.30
194	Stephen Davis	.50
195	Stephen Alexander	.15
196	Darrell Green	.15
197	Skip Hicks	.30
198	Brad Johnson	.50
199	Michael Westbrook	.30
200	Albert Connell	.15
201	*David Boston*	12.00
202	*Joel Makovicka*	1.00
203	*Chris Greisen*	1.00
204	*Jeff Paulk*	1.00
205	*Reginald Kelly*	1.00
206	*Chris McAlister*	2.00
207	*Brandon Stokley*	2.00
208	*Antoine Winfield*	1.00
209	*Bobby Collins*	1.00
210	*Peerless Price*	10.00
211	*Shawn Bryson*	1.00
212	*Sheldon Jackson*	1.00
213	*Kamil Loud*	1.00
214	*D'Wayne Bates*	2.00
215	*Jerry Azumah*	1.00
216	*Marty Booker*	3.00
217	*Cade McNown*	3.00
218	*James Allen*	1.00
219	*Nick Williams*	1.00
220	*Akili Smith*	4.00
221	*Craig Yeast*	1.00
222	*Damon Griffin*	1.00
223	*Scott Covington*	1.00
224	*Michael Basnight*	1.00
225	*Ronnie Powell*	1.00
226	*Rahim Abdullah*	1.00
227	*Tim Couch*	10.00
228	*Kevin Johnson*	4.00
229	*Darrin Chiaverini*	1.00
230	*Mark Campbell*	1.00
231	*Mike Lucky*	1.00
232	*Robert Thomas*	1.00
233	*Ebenezer Ekuban*	2.00
234	*Dat Nguyen*	3.00
235	*Wane McGarity*	3.00
236	*Jason Tucker*	2.00
237	*Olandis Gary*	8.00
238	*Al Wilson*	1.00
239	*Travis McGriff*	2.00
240	*Desmond Clark*	2.00
241	*Andre Cooper*	1.00
242	*Chris Watson*	1.00
243	*Sedrick Irvin*	5.00
244	*Chris Claiborne*	2.00
245	*Cory Sauter*	1.00
246	*Brock Olivo*	1.00
247	*De'Mond Parker*	4.00
248	*Aaron Brooks*	20.00
249	*Antwan Edwards*	3.00
250	*Basil Mitchell*	2.00
251	*Terrence Wilkins*	2.00
252	*Edgerrin James*	25.00
253	*Fernando Bryant*	1.00
254	*Michael Cloud*	2.00
255	*Larry Parker*	2.00
256	*Rob Konrad*	3.00
257	*Cecil Collins*	3.00
258	*James Johnson*	5.00
259	*Jim Kleinsasser*	3.00
260	*Daunte Culpepper*	25.00
261	*Michael Bishop*	4.00
262	*Andy Katzenmoyer*	4.00
263	*Kevin Faulk*	5.00
264	*Brett Bech*	1.00
265	*Ricky Williams*	20.00
266	*Sean Bennett*	3.00
267	*Joe Montgomery*	2.00
268	*Dan Campbell*	1.00
269	*Ray Lucas*	3.00
270	*Scott Dreisbach*	1.00
271	*Jed Weaver*	1.00
272	*Dameane Douglas*	1.00
273	*Cecil Martin*	3.00
274	*Donovan McNabb*	25.00
275	*Na Brown*	2.00
276	*Jerame Tuman*	1.00
277	*Amos Zereoue*	6.00
278	*Troy Edwards*	4.00
279	*Jermaine Fazande*	2.00
280	*Steve Heiden*	1.00
281	*Jeff Garcia*	25.00
282	*Terry Jackson*	3.00
283	*Charlie Rogers*	3.00
284	*Brock Huard*	4.00
285	*Karsten Bailey*	3.00
286	*Lamar King*	1.00
287	*Justin Watson*	1.00
288	*Kurt Warner*	20.00
289	*Torry Holt*	12.00
290	*Joe Germaine*	4.00
291	*Dre' Bly*	3.00
292	*Martin Gramatica*	3.00
293	*Rabih Abdullah*	2.00
294	*Shaun King*	4.00
295	*Anthony McFarland*	1.00
296	*Darnell McDonald*	1.00
297	*Kevin Daft*	1.00
298	*Jevon Kearse*	8.00
299	*Mike Sellers*	2.00
300	*Champ Bailey*	6.00

1999 Leaf Rookies & Stars Longevity

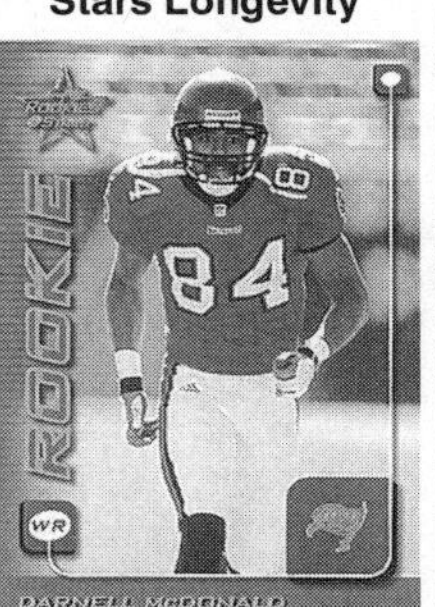

This was a 300-card parallel to the base set. Each single was printed on foil board with holographic foil stamping. The first 200 cards were sequentially numbered to 50 and the 100 rookies were numbered to 30.

	NM/M
Longevity Cards:	20X-40X
Production 50 Sets	
Longevity Rookies:	3X-6X
Production 30 Sets	

1999 Leaf Rookies & Stars Cross Training

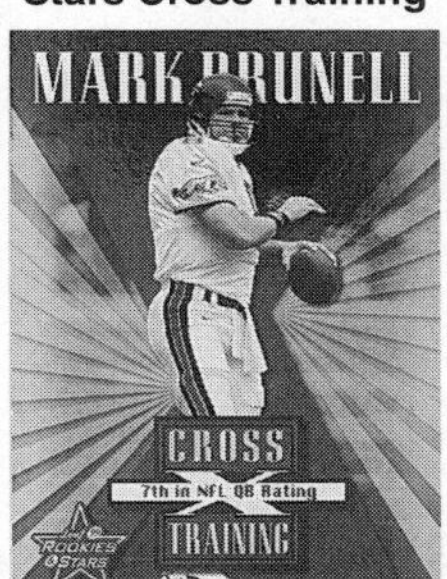

MARK BRUNELL
CROSS
7th in NFL QB Rating
TRAINING

This 25-card insert set included the most versatile players in the NFL. Each card highlighted the player's different skills, one on each side of the card. Each card in the set was sequentially numbered to 1,250.

		NM/M
Complete Set (25):		60.00
Common Player:		1.00
Production 1,250 Sets		
1	Champ Bailey	1.00
2	Mark Brunell	3.00
3	Daunte Culpepper	5.00
4	Randall Cunningham	1.00
5	Terrell Davis	5.00
6	Charlie Batch	1.00
7	Dorsey Levens	1.00
8	John Elway	6.00
9	Marshall Faulk	2.00
10	Brett Favre	10.00
11	Doug Flutie	6.00
12	Edgerrin James	12.00
13	Curtis Martin	1.00
14	Donovan McNabb	10.00
15	Steve McNair	4.00
16	Cade McNown	2.00
17	Randy Moss	8.00
18	Jake Plummer	3.00
19	Barry Sanders	10.00
20	Deion Sanders	1.00
21	Akili Smith	3.00
22	Kordell Stewart	1.00
23	Ricky Williams	15.00
24	Charles Woodson	1.00
25	Steve Young	6.00

1999 Leaf Rookies & Stars Dress for Success

This 30-card insert set included 20 of the top players in the NFL. Each single included a piece of a game-worn jersey by that player. Ten of the cards included two players on the front of the cards. Single-jersey cards were numbered to 200 and dual-jersey cards were numbered to 100.

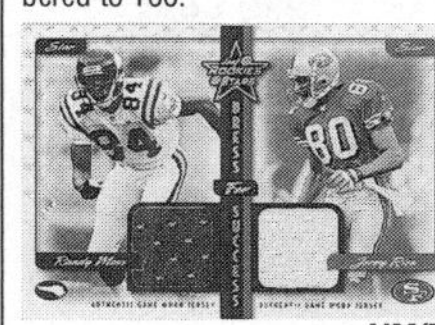

		NM/M
Common Player:		50.00
Single Jersey 200 Sets		
Dual Jersey 100 Sets		
1	Barry Sanders	100.00
2	Emmitt Smith	100.00
3	Barry Sanders, Emmitt Smith	200.00
4	Eddie George	50.00
5	Terrell Davis	50.00
6	Eddie George, Terrell Davis	100.00
7	Tim Couch	50.00
8	Dan Marino	100.00
9	Tim Couch, Dan Marino	200.00
10	Brett Favre	125.00
11	Troy Aikman	100.00
12	Brett Favre, Troy Aikman	225.00
13	Drew Bledsoe	50.00
14	Mark Brunell	40.00
15	Drew Bledsoe, Mark Brunell	75.00
16	Randy Moss	75.00
17	Jerry Rice	75.00
18	Randy Moss, Jerry Rice	200.00
19	Antonio Freeman	50.00
20	Terry Glenn	50.00
21	Antonio Freeman, Terry Glenn	75.00
22	Steve Young	50.00
23	Kordell Stewart	40.00
24	Steve Young, Kordell Stewart	75.00
25	Fred Taylor	50.00
26	Dorsey Levens	50.00
27	Fred Taylor, Dorsey Levens	75.00
28	Keyshawn Johnson	50.00
29	Herman Moore	50.00
30	Keyshawn Johnson, Herman Moore	75.00

1999 Leaf Rookies & Stars John Elway Collection

This 5-card insert set included pieces of authentic game-worn jerseys, shoes and helmets. The helmet and shoe singles were sequentially numbered to 125 and the jersey singles were numbered to 300.

		NM/M
Common Player:		100.00
Helmet/Shoes 125 Sets		
Jersey 300 Sets		
1	John Elway Home Jer.	100.00
2	John Elway Away Jer.	100.00
3	John Elway Shoe	150.00
4	John Elway Blue Hel.	200.00
5	John Elway Orange Hel.	200.00

1999 Leaf Rookies & Stars Freshman Orientation

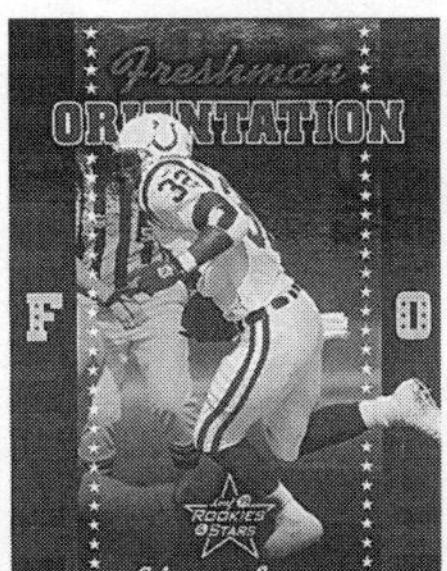

This 25-card insert set included the best rookies from the 1999 NFL Draft. Each card was printed on silver foil board and was sequentially numbered to 2,500.

		NM/M
Complete Set (25):		40.00
Common Player:		1.00
Production 2,500 Sets		
1	Champ Bailey	2.00
2	D'Wayne Bates	1.00
3	David Boston	4.00
4	Kurt Warner	5.00
5	Cecil Collins	4.00
6	Tim Couch	6.00
7	Daunte Culpepper	6.00
8	Troy Edwards	4.00
9	Kevin Faulk	3.00
10	Joe Germaine	3.00
11	Torry Holt	4.00
12	Brock Huard	3.00
13	Sedrick Irvin	3.00
14	Edgerrin James	8.00
15	Kevin Johnson	4.00
16	Shaun King	2.00
17	Rob Konrad	3.00
18	Sean Bennett	1.00
19	Donovan McNabb	6.00
20	Cade McNown	2.00
21	Peerless Price	3.00
22	Akili Smith	6.00
23	Ricky Williams	10.00
24	James Johnson	3.00
25	Olandis Gary	4.00

1999 Leaf Rookies & Stars Game Plan

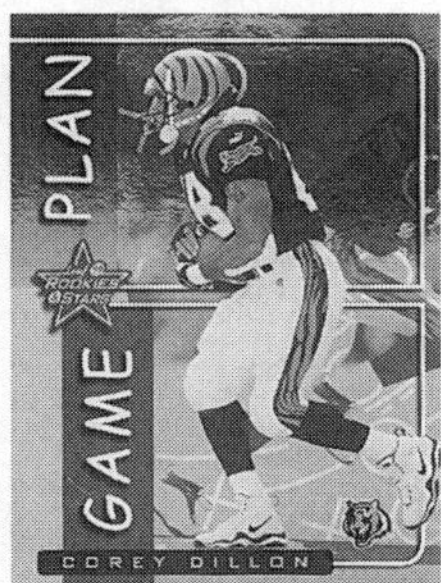

This 25-card insert set included a mix of veterans and rookies. Each card was printed on foil board and was sequentially numbered to 2,500. A Masters parallel was also produced on holographic foil board and each of those was numbered to 50.

		NM/M
Complete Set (25):		40.00
Common Player:		1.00
Production 2,500 Sets		
Masters Cards:		5X-10X
Production 50 Sets		
1	Jamal Anderson	1.00
2	Jerome Bettis	1.00
3	Drew Bledsoe	3.00
4	Tim Brown	1.00
5	Mark Brunell	2.00
6	Tim Couch	5.00
7	Terrell Davis	5.00
8	Corey Dillon	1.00
9	Warrick Dunn	1.00
10	Brad Johnson	1.00
11	Brett Favre	6.00
12	Doug Flutie	2.00
13	Joey Galloway	1.00
14	Eddie George	1.00
15	Keyshawn Johnson	1.00
16	Peyton Manning	5.00
17	Dan Marino	6.00
18	Donovan McNabb	4.00
19	Cade McNown	2.00
20	Randy Moss	5.00
21	Jake Plummer	2.00
22	Barry Sanders	6.00
23	Emmitt Smith	6.00
24	Ricky Williams	6.00
25	Steve Young	3.00

1999 Leaf Rookies & Stars Game Plan Masters

This was a 25-card parallel to the Game Plan insert. Each of these singles was printed on holographic foil board and was sequentially numbered to 50.

	NM/M
Masters Cards:	5X-10X
Production 50 Sets	

Values quoted in this guide reflect the retail price of a card—the price a collector can expect to pay when buying a card from a dealer. The wholesale price—that which a collector can expect to receive from a dealer when selling cards—will be significantly lower, depending on desirability and condition.

1999 Leaf Rookies & Stars Great American Heroes

This 25-card insert set included mostly veterans. Singles were sequentially numbered to 2,500.

NM/M
Complete Set (25): 40.00
Common Player: 1.00
Production 2,500 Sets
1 Troy Aikman 4.00
2 Jamal Anderson 1.00
3 Drew Bledsoe 3.00
4 Mark Brunell 21.00
5 Cris Carter 1.00
6 Randall Cunningham 1.00
7 Terrell Davis 4.00
8 John Elway 5.00
9 Brett Favre 6.00
10 Doug Flutie 2.00
11 Antonio Freeman 1.00
12 Eddie George 2.00
13 Peyton Manning 5.00
14 Dan Marino 6.00
15 Curtis Martin 1.00
16 Warren Moon 1.00
17 Randy Moss 5.00
18 Jake Plummer 2.00
19 Jerry Rice 5.00
20 Barry Sanders 6.00
21 Deion Sanders 1.00
22 Emmitt Smith 6.00
23 Fred Taylor 3.00
24 Ricky Williams 6.00
25 Steve Young 3.00

1999 Leaf Rookies & Stars Greatest Hits

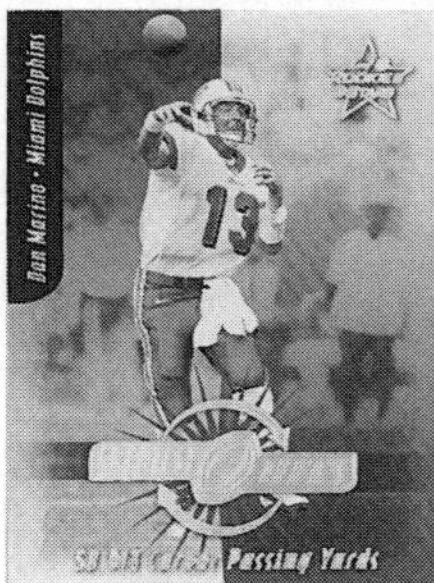

This 25-card insert set included the hottest superstars from the NFL. Singles were sequentially numbered to 2,500.

NM/M
Complete Set (25): 40.00
Common Player: 1.00
Production 2,500 Sets
1 Troy Aikman 4.00
2 Terry Glenn 1.00
3 Jamal Anderson 1.00
4 Drew Bledsoe 3.00
5 Cris Carter 1.00
6 Terrell Davis 4.00
7 John Elway 5.00
8 Brett Favre 6.00
9 Antonio Freeman 1.00
10 Eddie George 2.00
11 Priest Holmes 1.00
12 Keyshawn Johnson 1.00
13 Dorsey Levens 1.00
14 Dan Marino 6.00
15 Curtis Martin 1.00
16 Randy Moss 5.00
17 Eric Moulds 1.00
18 Terrell Owens 1.00
19 Carl Pickens 1.00
20 Jake Plummer 2.00
21 Jerry Rice 5.00
22 Barry Sanders 6.00
23 Marvin Harrison 1.00
24 Robert Smith 1.00
25 Fred Taylor 3.00

1999 Leaf Rookies & Stars Prime Cuts

This 15-card insert set included prime cuts from game-worn jerseys and incorporated them in this insert. Singles were randomly inserted.

NM/M
Common Player: 25.00
1 Tim Couch 75.00
2 Fred Taylor 50.00
3 Terry Glenn 25.00
4 Drew Bledsoe 75.00
5 Dan Marino 150.00
6 Jerry Rice 100.00
7 Barry Sanders 150.00
8 Mark Brunell 40.00
9 Brett Favre 150.00
10 Steve Young 75.00
11 Keyshawn Johnson 40.00
12 Antonio Freeman 25.00
13 Randy Moss 100.00
14 Troy Aikman 100.00
15 Emmitt Smith 150.00

1999 Leaf Rookies & Stars Signature Series

This 30-card insert set included signatures of the top veteran and rookies in the NFL. Single signed cards were sequentially numbered to 150 and dual signature cards were numbered to 50.

NM/M
Common Player: 20.00
Singles 150 Sets
Duals 50 Sets
1 Terrell Davis 50.00
2 Edgerrin James 100.00
3 Terrell Davis, Edgerrin James 200.00
4 Eddie George 50.00
5 Ricky Williams 100.00
6 Eddie George, Ricky Williams 150.00
7 Jake Plummer 40.00
8 Donovan McNabb 75.00
9 Jake Plummer, Donovan McNabb 100.00
10 Randall Cunningham 25.00
11 Daunte Culpepper 75.00
12 Randall Cunningham, Daunte Culpepper 100.00
13 Fred Taylor 60.00
14 Cecil Collins 25.00
15 Fred Taylor, Cecil Collins 75.00
16 Randy Moss 100.00
17 Torry Holt 50.00
18 Randy Moss, Torry Holt 150.00
19 Steve Young 75.00
20 Cade McNown 40.00
21 Steve Young, Cade McNown 125.00
22 Jerry Rice 100.00
23 David Boston 50.00
24 Jerry Rice, David Boston 150.00
25 Doug Flutie 40.00
26 Akili Smith 40.00
27 Doug Flutie, Akili Smith 75.00
28 Dan Marino 100.00
29 Tim Couch 75.00
30 Dan Marino, Tim Couch 150.00

1999 Leaf Rookies & Stars Slide Show

This 25-card insert set included mostly veterans and a few rookies. Each single was printed on red foil board and was sequentially numbered to 100. A parallel Green set was made with each of those singles numbered to 50. The parallel Blue set was numbered to 25 and the parallel Studios only had one card of each.

NM/M
Common Player: 5.00
Production 100 Sets
Green Cards: 2X
Production 50 Sets
Blue Cards: 3X
Production 25 Sets
Studio Cards: No Pricing
Production 1 Set
1 Troy Aikman 25.00
2 Drew Bledsoe 20.00
3 Mark Brunell 10.00
4 Tim Couch 20.00
5 Terrell Davis 20.00
6 John Elway 25.00
7 Brett Favre 30.00
8 Antonio Freeman 5.00
9 Eddie George 5.00
10 Torry Holt 20.00
11 Edgerrin James 25.00
12 Keyshawn Johnson 5.00
13 Jon Kitna 5.00
14 Dorsey Levens 5.00
15 Peyton Manning 20.00
16 Dan Marino 30.00
17 Randy Moss 25.00
18 Jake Plummer 10.00
19 Jerry Rice 25.00
20 Barry Sanders 30.00
21 Marvin Harrison 5.00
22 Emmitt Smith 30.00
23 Fred Taylor 12.00
24 Ricky Williams 30.00
25 Steve Young 15.00

1999 Leaf Rookies & Stars Statistical Standouts

This 25-card insert set included the top producers in receiving, rushing and passing, and highlighted them on simulated leather with white foil. Each single was sequentially numbered to 1,250. A parallel Die Cut version was also produced with each of those singles numbered to a 1998 stat.

NM/M
Complete Set (25): 50.00
Common Player: 1.00
Minor Stars: 4.00
Production 1,250 Sets
1 Jamal Anderson 2.00
2 Jerome Bettis 2.00
3 Drew Bledsoe 4.00
4 Cris Carter 2.00
5 Randall Cunningham 2.00
6 Terrell Davis 5.00
7 John Elway 6.00
8 Marshall Faulk 4.00
9 Brett Favre 8.00
10 Antonio Freeman 2.00
11 Joey Galloway 2.00
12 Eddie George 3.00
13 Garrison Hearst 1.00
14 Keyshawn Johnson 3.00
15 Peyton Manning 6.00
16 Steve McNair 4.00
17 Randy Moss 6.00
18 Eric Moulds 4.00
19 Terrell Owens 3.00
20 Jake Plummer 2.00
21 Barry Sanders 8.00
22 Emmitt Smith 8.00
23 Fred Taylor 3.00
24 Vinny Testaverde 1.00
25 Steve Young 3.00

1999 Leaf Rookies & Stars Ticket Masters

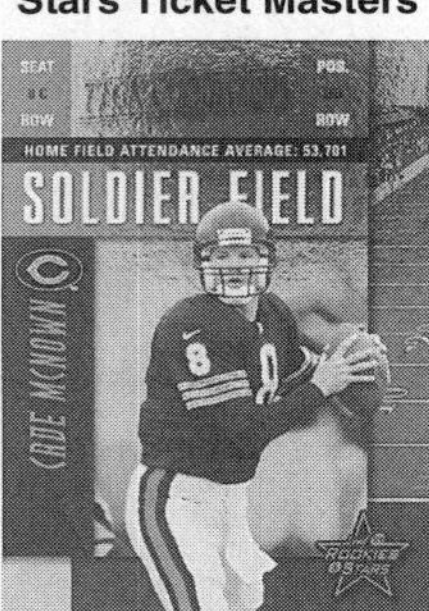

This 25-card insert set included the top NFL stars. Each single was sequentially numbered to 2,500. A parallel Executive Ticket Master set was also produced with each of those singles die cut and numbered to 50.

NM/M
Complete Set (25): 40.00
Common Player: 1.00
Production 2,500 Sets
Executive Cards: 5X-10X
Production 50 Sets
1 Randy Moss, Cris Carter 6.00
2 Brett Favre, Antonio Freeman 8.00
3 Cecil Collins, Dan Marino 8.00
4 Brian Griese, Terrell Davis 4.00
5 Edgerrin James, Peyton Manning 8.00
6 Emmitt Smith, Troy Aikman 8.00
7 Jerry Rice, Steve Young 6.00
8 Mark Brunell, Fred Taylor 4.00
9 David Boston, Jake Plummer 3.00
10 Terry Glenn, Drew Bledsoe 3.00
11 Charlie Batch, Herman Moore 2.00
12 Mike Alstott, Warrick Dunn 1.00
13 Eddie George, Steve McNair 3.00
14 Kordell Stewart, Jerome Bettis 1.00
15 Chris Chandler, Jamal Anderson 1.00
16 Akili Smith, Corey Dillon 3.00
17 Curtis Enis, Cade McNown 2.00
18 Isaac Bruce, Marshall Faulk 3.00
19 Eric Moulds, Doug Flutie 2.00
20 Joey Galloway, Ricky Watters 1.00
21 Michael Westbrook, Brad Johnson 1.00
22 Curtis Martin, Keyshawn Johnson 3.00
23 Napoleon Kaufman, Tim Brown 1.00
24 Kevin Johnson, Tim Couch 5.00
25 Duce Staley, Donovan McNabb 5.00

1999 Leaf Rookies & Stars Touchdown Club

This 20-card insert set included the players who see the end zone the most. Each of these singles was sequentially numbered to 1,000. A parallel Die Cut version was also produced with each of those singles numbered to 60.

NM/M
Complete Set (20): 75.00
Common Player: 2.00
Production 1,000 Sets
Die-Cut Cards: 3X-6X
Production 60 Sets
1 Randy Moss 10.00
2 Brett Favre 15.00
3 Dan Marino 15.00
4 Barry Sanders 15.00
5 John Elway 12.00
6 Terrell Davis 12.00
7 Peyton Manning 12.00
8 Emmitt Smith 15.00
9 Jerry Rice 12.00
10 Fred Taylor 6.00
11 Drew Bledsoe 6.00
12 Steve Young 6.00
13 Eddie George 3.00
14 Cris Carter 2.00
15 Antonio Freeman 2.00
16 Marvin Harrison 2.00
17 Kurt Warner 6.00
18 Stephen Davis 2.00
19 Terry Glenn 2.00
20 Brad Johnson 2.00

2000 Leaf Certified

NM/M
Complete Set (250): 650.00
Common Player (1-100): .20
Minor Stars: .40
Common Player (101-150): .30
Minor Stars: .60
Inserted 1:2
Common Rookie (151-190): 3.00
Production 2,000 Sets
Common Rookie (191-220): 4.00
Production 1,500 Sets
Common Rookie (221-250): 12.00
Production 1,000 Sets
Pack (5): 5.25
Wax Box (18): 65.00
1 Frank Sanders .40
2 Rob Moore .40
3 Simeon Rice .20
4 David Boston .75
5 Tim Dwight .75
6 Jamal Anderson .75
7 Chris Chandler .40
8 Terance Mathis .20
9 Priest Holmes .40
10 Rod Woodson .20
11 Tony Banks .40
12 Jermaine Lewis .20
13 Shannon Sharpe .40
14 Qadry Ismail .20
15 Doug Flutie .75
16 Antowain Smith .40
17 Peerless Price .40
18 Rob Johnson .40
19 Muhsin Muhammad .40
20 Wesley Walls .40
21 Tim Biakabutuka .40
22 Steve Beuerlein .40
23 Patrick Jeffers .75
24 Natrone Means .40
25 Curtis Enis .50
26 Bobby Engram .20
27 Marcus Robinson .75
28 Eddie Kennison .20
29 Marty Booker .20
30 Darnay Scott .40
31 Carl Pickens .40
32 Karim Abdul .20
33 Errict Rhett .40
34 Darrin Chiaverini .20
35 Randall Cunningham .40
36 Michael Irvin .40
37 Raghib Ismail .20
38 Ed McCaffrey .50
39 Rod Smith .50
40 Herman Moore .40
41 Johnnie Morton .40
42 James Stewart .40
43 Bill Schroeder .20
44 Ahman Green .40
45 Terrence Wilkins .40
46 Keenan McCardell .40
47 Derrick Alexander .20
48 Elvis Grbac .40
49 Tony Gonzalez .40
50 O.J. McDuffie .40
51 Tony Martin .20
52 James Johnson .20
53 Thurman Thomas .40
54 Jay Fiedler .20
55 Damon Huard .40
56 Leroy Hoard .20
57 Terry Glenn .75
58 Kevin Faulk .40
59 Jeff Blake .40
60 Jake Reed .20
61 Amani Toomer .20
62 Kerry Collins .40
63 Ike Hilliard .20
64 Joe Montgomery .20
65 Vinny Testaverde .40
66 Wayne Chrebet .40
67 Ray Lucas .50
68 Napoleon Kaufman .40
69 Charles Woodson .40
70 Tyrone Wheatley .40
71 Rich Gannon .40
72 Duce Staley .75
73 Kordell Stewart .75
74 Jerome Bettis .50
75 Troy Edwards .50
76 Junior Seau .40
77 Jim Harbaugh .40
78 Curtis Conway .20
79 Jermaine Fazande .40
80 Terrell Owens .75
81 Charlie Garner .40
82 Garrison Hearst .40
83 Jeff Garcia .75
84 Derrick Mayes .40
85 Az-Zahir Hakim .40
86 Mike Alstott .75
87 Warrick Dunn .75
88 Jacquez Green .20
89 Warren Sapp .20
90 Yancey Thigpen .20
91 Kevin Dyson .40
92 Frank Wycheck .20
93 Jevon Kearse .50
94 Adrian Murrell .40
95 Bruce Smith .20
96 Michael Westbrook .40
97 Albert Connell .40
98 Champ Bailey .40
99 Jeff George .50
100 Deion Sanders .75
101 Jake Plummer 1.25
102 Eric Moulds 1.25
103 Cade McNown 1.75
104 Corey Dillon 1.25
105 Akili Smith 1.50
106 Tim Couch 2.50
107 Kevin Johnson .60
108 Emmitt Smith 3.50
109 Troy Aikman 3.00
110 Joey Galloway 1.25
111 John Elway 4.00
112 Terrell Davis 2.00
113 Olandis Gary 1.25
114 Brian Griese 1.50
115 Charlie Batch 1.25
116 Barry Sanders 4.00
117 Germane Crowell 1.25
118 Brett Favre 5.00
119 Dorsey Levens 1.25
120 Antonio Freeman 1.25
121 Peyton Manning 4.00
122 Edgerrin James 5.00
123 Marvin Harrison 1.25
124 Mark Brunell 2.00
125 Fred Taylor 1.75
126 Jimmy Smith 1.25
127 Dan Marino 4.00
128 Randy Moss 5.00
129 Daunte Culpepper 2.50
130 Cris Carter 1.25
131 Robert Smith 1.25
132 Drew Bledsoe 2.00
133 Ricky Williams 2.00
134 Curtis Martin 1.25
135 Tim Brown 1.00
136 Donovan McNabb 3.00
137 Jerry Rice 3.00
138 Steve Young 1.75
139 Jon Kitna 1.00
140 Ricky Watters .75
141 Kurt Warner 3.00
142 Marshall Faulk 1.25
143 Torry Holt 1.25
144 Isaac Bruce 1.25
145 Shaun King 2.00
146 Keyshawn Johnson 1.25
147 Eddie George 1.50
148 Steve McNair 1.25
149 Stephen Davis 1.25
150 Brad Johnson 1.00
151 *Rogers Beckett* 3.00
152 *Erik Flowers* 3.00
153 *Demario Brown* 3.00
154 *Doug Johnson* 6.00
155 *Deon Grant* 3.00
156 *Ian Gold* 3.00
157 *Brian Urlacher* 20.00
158 *Frank Murphy* 3.00
159 *James Whalen* 3.00
160 *JaJuan Dawson* 8.00
161 *William Bartee* 3.00
162 *Aaron Shea* 3.00
163 *Deltha O'Neal* 6.00
164 *Jarious Jackson* 6.00
165 *Muneer Moore* 3.00
166 *Hank Poteat* 3.00
167 *Jacoby Shepherd* 3.00
168 *Ben Kelly* 3.00
169 *Orantes Grant* 3.00
170 *Chris Hovan* 3.00
171 *Leon Murray* 3.00
172 *Marc Bulger* 12.00
173 *Chad Morton* 8.00
174 *Na'il Diggs* 3.00
175 *Shaun Ellis* 3.00
176 *John Abraham* 3.00
177 *Fred Robbins* 3.00
178 *Marcus Knight* 3.00
179 *Thomas Hamner* 3.00
180 *Cornelius Griffin* 3.00
181 *Raynoch Thompson* 3.00
182 *Paul Smith* 3.00
183 *Ahmed Plummer* 4.00
184 *John Engelberger* 3.00
185 *Darren Howard* 3.00
186 *Corey Moore* 3.00
187 *Joe Hamilton* 4.00
188 *Rob Morris* 4.00
189 *Keith Bulluck* 3.00
190 *Todd Husak* 4.00
191 *Mareno Philyaw* 4.00
192 *Kwame Cavil* 4.00
193 *Sammy Morris* 12.00
194 *Avion Black* 4.00
195 *Bashir Yamini* 4.00
196 *Curtis Keaton* 6.00
197 *Mike Anderson* 10.00
198 *Bubba Franks* 10.00
199 *Anthony Lucas* 6.00
200 *Rondell Mealey* 6.00
201 *Terrelle Smith* 5.00
202 *Frank Moreau* 5.00
203 *Deon Dyer* 4.00
204 *Quinton Spotwood* 4.00
205 *Troy Walters* 5.00
206 *Doug Chapman* 4.00
207 *Tom Brady* 40.00
208 *Sherrod Gideon* 4.00
209 *Ron Dixon* 5.00
210 *Anthony Becht* 5.00
211 *James Williams* 4.00
212 *Sebastian Janikowski* 6.00
213 *Corey Simon* 5.00
214 *Gari Scott* 4.00
215 *Dante Hall* 15.00
216 *Tim Rattay* 10.00
217 *Chafie Fields* 4.00
218 *Trung Canidate* 6.00
219 *Chris Coleman* 4.00
220 *Erron Kinney* 4.00
221 *Thomas Jones* 12.00
222 *Travis Taylor* 8.00
223 *Chris Redman* 10.00
224 *Jamal Lewis* 20.00
225 *Dez White* 10.00
226 *Peter Warrick* 15.00
227 *Ron Dugans* 5.00
228 *Courtney Brown* 5.00
229 *Travis Prentice* 8.00
230 *Dennis Northcutt* 5.00
231 *Michael Wiley* 5.00
232 *Chris Cole* 5.00
233 *Reuben Droughns* 8.00
234 *R. Jay Soward* 5.00
235 *Shyrone Stith* 5.00
236 *Sylvester Morris* 5.00
237 *J.R. Redmond* 6.00
238 *Ron Dayne* 8.00
239 *Chad Pennington* 40.00
240 *Laveranues Coles* 15.00
241 *Jerry Porter* 15.00
242 *Todd Pinkston* 12.00
243 *Plaxico Burress* 25.00
244 *Danny Farmer* 8.00
245 *Tee Martin* 8.00
246 *Trevor Gaylor* 5.00
247 *Giovanni Carmazzi* 5.00
248 *Darrell Jackson* 15.00
249 *Shaun Alexander* 30.00
250 *Chris Samuels* 5.00

2000 Leaf Certified Mirror Gold

NM/M
One Star Cards: 20X-50X
Production 20 Sets
Two Star Cards: 20X-40X
Production 25 Sets
Three Star Cards: 4X-8X
Production 30 Sets
Four Star Cards: 2X-4X
Production 35 Sets
Five Star Cards: 2X
Production 40 Sets

2000 Leaf Certified Mirror Red

NM/M
One Star Cards: 3X-6X
Inserted 1:17
Two Star Cards: 3X-6X
Inserted 1:53
Three Star Cards: 2X
Inserted 1:89
Four Star Cards: 1.5X
Inserted 1:125
Five Star Cards: 1X
Inserted 1:161

Post-1980 cards in Near Mint condition will generally sell for about 75% of the quoted Mint value. Excellent-condition cards bring no more than 40%.

2000 Leaf Certified Rookie Die Cuts

Three Star Cards: 3X
Four Star Cards: 2X
Five Star Cards: 1.5X
Production 250 Sets

2000 Leaf Certified Fabric of the Game

NM/M
Complete Set (75): 700.00
Common Player: 5.00
Production 100 to 1,000 Sets
FG1 Barry Sanders 100 45.00
FG2 John Elway 100 45.00
FG3 Jerry Rice 100 30.00
FG4 Cris Carter 250 10.00
FG5 Emmitt Smith 250 25.00
FG6 Troy Aikman 250 20.00
FG7 Deion Sanders 250 5.00
FG8 Terrell Davis 500 20.00
FG9 Marshall Faulk 500 5.00
FG10 Mark Brunell 500 10.00
FG11 Randy Moss 500 25.00
FG12 Peyton Manning 500 20.00
FG13 Kurt Warner 750 20.00
FG14 Jamal Anderson 750 5.00
FG15 Edgerrin James 750 15.00
FG16 Isaac Bruce 750 5.00
FG17 Jimmy Smith 750 5.00
FG18 Keyshawn Johnson 750 5.00
FG19 Brian Griese 1000 5.00
FG20 Cade McNown 1000 5.00
FG21 Shaun King 1000 5.00
FG22 Chad Pennington 1000 12.00
FG23 Plaxico Burress 1000 10.00
FG24 Thomas Jones 1000 8.00
FG25 Peter Warrick 1000 15.00
FG26 Dan Marino 100 50.00
FG27 John Elway 100 50.00
FG28 Emmitt Smith 100 35.00
FG29 Brett Favre 250 30.00
FG30 Steve Young 250 10.00
FG31 Cris Carter 250 5.00
FG32 Michael Irvin 250 5.00
FG33 Eddie George 500 7.00
FG34 Drew Bledsoe 500 10.00
FG35 Antonio Freeman 500 5.00
FG36 Steve McNair 500 5.00
FG37 Randy Moss 500 20.00
FG38 Kurt Warner 750 15.00
FG39 Eric Moulds 750 5.00
FG40 Fred Taylor 750 5.00
FG41 Charlie Batch 750 5.00
FG42 Marvin Harrison 750 5.00
FG43 Joey Galloway 750 5.00
FG44 Tim Couch 1000 7.00
FG45 Ricky Williams 1000 8.00
FG46 Donovan McNabb 1000 5.00
FG47 Akili Smith 1000 5.00
FG48 Kevin Johnson 1000 5.00
FG49 Thomas Jones 1000 8.00
FG50 Ron Dayne 1000 20.00
FG51 Dan Marino 100 50.00
FG52 Barry Sanders 100 50.00
FG53 Jerry Rice 100 25.00
FG54 Brett Favre 250 30.00
FG55 Tim Brown 250 5.00
FG56 Steve Young 250 10.00
FG57 Thurman Thomas 250 5.00
FG58 Jeff George 500 5.00
FG59 Curtis Martin 500 5.00
FG60 Terrell Davis 500 20.00
FG61 Peyton Manning 500 20.00
FG62 Ricky Watters 500 5.00
FG63 Edgerrin James 750 15.00
FG64 Fred Taylor 750 5.00
FG65 Stephen Davis 750 5.00
FG66 Jake Plummer 750 5.00
FG67 Brad Johnson 750 5.00
FG68 Jon Kitna 750 5.00
FG69 Tim Couch 1000 7.00
FG70 Daunte Culpepper 1000 7.00
FG71 Olandis Gary 1000 5.00
FG72 Jamal Lewis 1000 12.00
FG73 Peter Warrick 1000 15.00
FG74 Shaun Alexander 1000 10.00
FG75 Travis Taylor 1000 8.00

2000 Leaf Certified Gold Future

NM/M
Complete Set (30): 60.00
Common Player: 2.00
Inserted 1:17
Mirror Black Cards: 10X-20X
Production 25 Sets
CGF1 Peter Warrick 3.00
CGF2 Chad Pennington 8.00
CGF3 Thomas Jones 4.00
CGF4 Plaxico Burress 5.00
CGF5 Jamal Lewis 4.00
CGF6 Travis Taylor 3.00
CGF7 Chris Redman 4.00

NM/M
CGF8 Dez White 2.00
CGF9 Shaun Alexander 5.00
CGF10 Sylvester Morris 4.00
CGF11 Ron Dayne 3.00
CGF12 R. Jay Soward 2.00
CGF13 Travis Prentice 3.00
CGF14 Giovanni Carmazzi 3.00
CGF15 Todd Pinkston 2.00
CGF16 J.R. Redmond 3.00
CGF17 Trevor Gaylor 2.00
CGF18 Trung Canidate 2.00
CGF19 Danny Farmer 2.00
CGF20 Tee Martin 2.00
CGF21 Darrell Jackson 2.00
CGF22 Gari Scott 2.00
CGF23 Dennis Northcutt 2.00
CGF24 Jerry Porter 2.00
CGF25 Reuben Droughns 2.00
CGF26 Laveranues Coles 3.00
CGF27 Bubba Franks 3.00
CGF28 Doug Chapman 2.00
CGF29 Chris Cole 2.00
CGF30 Ron Dugans 2.00

2000 Leaf Certified Gold Team

NM/M
Complete Set (40): 100.00
Common Player: 3.00
Inserted 1:17
Mirror Black Cards: 10X-20X
Production 25 Sets
CGT1 Randy Moss 8.00
CGT2 Brett Favre 8.00
CGT3 Dan Marino 8.00
CGT4 Barry Sanders 8.00
CGT5 John Elway 8.00
CGT6 Peyton Manning 6.00
CGT7 Terrell Davis 5.00
CGT8 Emmitt Smith 8.00
CGT9 Troy Aikman 5.00
CGT10 Jerry Rice 6.00
CGT11 Fred Taylor 3.50
CGT12 Jake Plummer 3.00
CGT13 Charlie Batch 3.00
CGT14 Drew Bledsoe 4.00
CGT15 Mark Brunell 4.00
CGT16 Steve Young 4.00
CGT17 Eddie George 3.50
CGT18 Tim Brown 3.00
CGT19 Cris Carter 3.00
CGT20 Stephen Davis 3.00
CGT21 Marshall Faulk 3.00
CGT22 Antonio Freeman 3.00
CGT23 Marvin Harrison 3.00
CGT24 Brad Johnson 3.00
CGT25 Keyshawn Johnson 3.00
CGT26 Jon Kitna 3.00
CGT27 Curtis Martin 3.00
CGT28 Steve McNair 3.00
CGT29 Isaac Bruce 3.00
CGT30 Kurt Warner 6.00
CGT31 Edgerrin James 6.00
CGT32 Tim Couch 5.00
CGT33 Ricky Williams 5.00
CGT34 Donovan McNabb 3.50
CGT35 Cade McNown 3.00
CGT36 Daunte Culpepper 4.50
CGT37 Torry Holt 3.00
CGT38 Robert Smith 3.00
CGT39 Mike Alstott 3.00
CGT40 Dorsey Levens 3.00

2000 Leaf Certified Gridiron Gear

NM/M
Common Jersey 300: 20.00
Common Jersey 100: 30.00
Century 300: 3X
Century 100: 2X
Production 21 Sets
Troy Aikman 100 75.00
Mike Alstott 300 30.00
Champ Bailey 300 20.00
Charlie Batch 300 20.00
Jerome Bettis 100 30.00
Drew Bledsoe 100 50.00
Tim Brown White 300 25.00
Tim Brown Black 300 25.00
Isaac Bruce White 100 40.00
Isaac Bruce Blue 300 30.00
Mark Brunell White 100 35.00
Mark Brunell Teal 300 25.00
Cris Carter 100 40.00
Wayne Chrebet 300 20.00
Tim Couch 100 25.00
Randall Cunningham 300 20.00
Terrell Davis 100 40.00
Corey Dillon 300 20.00
Warrick Dunn 300 20.00
John Elway 100 100.00
Curtis Enis White 300 20.00
Curtis Enis Blue 300 20.00
Marshall Faulk White 100 50.00
Marshall Faulk Blue 300 30.00
Brett Favre White 300 60.00
Brett Favre Green 100 100.00
Doug Flutie 300 30.00
Antonio Freeman 300 20.00
Olandis Gary 100 35.00
Eddie George 100 50.00
Brian Griese 100 25.00
Jim Harbaugh 300 20.00
Marvin Harrison 300 30.00
Damon Huard 300 20.00
Edgerrin James Blue 100 75.00
Edgerrin James PB 300 50.00
Napoleon Kaufman 100 25.00
Jevon Kearse 300 30.00
Shaun King 100 50.00
Dorsey Levens White 300 20.00
Dorsey Levens Green 300 20.00
Ray Lucas 100 30.00
Peyton Manning 100 100.00
Dan Marino White 300 100.00
Dan Marino Teal 100 125.00
Curtis Martin 100 40.00
Ed McCaffrey 300 20.00
Keenan McCardell 300 20.00
Donovan McNabb 300 30.00
Steve McNair 100 45.00
Cade McNown 300 20.00
Johnnie Morton 300 20.00
Randy Moss 100 80.00
Eric Moulds 300 30.00
Terrell Owens 300 30.00
Jake Plummer 300 30.00
Jerry Rice White 100 85.00
Jerry Rice Red 300 60.00
Barry Sanders 100 80.00
Deion Sanders 300 30.00
Emmitt Smith 100 80.00
Jimmy Smith White 100 40.00
Jimmy Smith Teal 300 25.00
Rod Smith 300 25.00
Kordell Stewart 300 30.00
Fred Taylor White 300 35.00
Fred Taylor Teal 100 50.00
Kurt Warner White 300 40.00
Kurt Warner Blue 100 75.00
Ricky Watters 300 20.00
Tyrone Wheatley 300 20.00
Ricky Williams White 100 50.00
Ricky Williams Black 100 50.00
Charles Woodson 300 20.00
Steve Young 100 60.00

2000 Leaf Certified Heritage Collection

NM/M
Production 100 Sets
Century Autographs: 3X
Century Non Auto: 2X
Marcus Allen White 50.00
Marcus Allen Red 50.00
Raymond Berry 35.00
Terry Bradshaw White 100.00
Terry Bradshaw PB 100.00
John Brodie 35.00
Jim Brown 80.00
Earl Campbell 50.00
Eric Dickerson White 50.00
Eric Dickerson Blue 50.00
Tony Dorsett 75.00
Boomer Esiason 35.00
Dan Fouts White 60.00
Dan Fouts Blue 60.00
Frank Gifford 85.00
Bob Griese 60.00
Ted Hendricks 35.00
Keith Jackson 35.00
Craig James 35.00
Bert Jones 35.00
Sonny Jurgensen 50.00
Jim Kelly 85.00
Bernie Kosar 35.00
Steve Largent 75.00
Howie Long 75.00
Ronnie Lott 35.00
Don Maynard 35.00
Joe Montana SF 200.00
Joe Montana KC 200.00
Warren Moon 35.00
Joe Namath 100.00
Ozzie Newsome 35.00
Ray Nitschke 100.00
Merlin Olsen 35.00
Walter Payton White 175.00
Walter Payton Blue 175.00
Jim Plunkett 50.00
Gale Sayers 75.00
Phil Simms 50.00
Ken Stabler 75.00
Bart Starr 125.00
Fran Tarkenton 75.00
Joe Theismann 50.00
Derrick Thomas 75.00
Johnny Unitas 150.00
Herschel Walker 35.00
Reggie White 35.00

2000 Leaf Certified Skills

NM/M
Complete Set (30): 75.00
Common Player: 2.00
Inserted 1:35:
Mirror Black Cards: 5X-10X
Production 25 Sets
CS1 Jamal Anderson, Thomas Jones 5.00
CS2 Randy Moss, Germane Crowell 6.00
CS3 Brett Favre, Donovan McNabb 8.00
CS4 Dan Marino, Tim Couch 8.00
CS5 Barry Sanders, James Stewart 8.00
CS6 John Elway, Brian Griese 6.00
CS7 Peyton Manning, Chad Pennington 8.00
CS8 Terrell Davis, Olandis Gary 4.00
CS9 Emmitt Smith, Duce Staley 7.00
CS10 Troy Aikman, Cade McNown 6.00
CS11 Jerry Rice, Isaac Bruce 6.00
CS12 Fred Taylor, Stephen Davis 3.50
CS13 Drew Bledsoe, Brad Johnson 4.00
CS14 Mark Brunell, Shaun King 4.00
CS15 Steve Young, Akili Smith 4.00
CS16 Eddie George, Ricky Williams 5.00
CS17 Kurt Warner, Jon Kitna 6.00
CS18 Edgerrin James, Corey Dillon 6.00
CS19 Cris Carter, Tim Brown 2.00
CS20 Keyshawn Johnson, Plaxico Burress 5.00
CS21 Marshall Faulk, Robert Smith 2.00
CS22 Antonio Freeman, Travis Taylor 3.00
CS23 Marvin Harrison, Kevin Johnson 2.00
CS24 Dorsey Levens, Jamal Lewis 4.00
CS25 Curtis Martin, Shaun Alexander 4.00
CS26 Steve McNair, Daunte Culpepper 3.50
CS27 Jimmy Smith, Peter Warrick 3.00
CS28 Jerome Bettis, Ron Dayne 3.00
CS29 Joey Galloway, Torry Holt 2.00
CS30 Eric Moulds, Terrell Owens 2.00

2000 Leaf Limited

NM/M
Complete Set (425): 3,000
Common Player (1-50): .50
Minor Stars (1-50): 1.00
Production 5,000 Sets
Common Player (51-100): .75
Minor Stars (51-100): 1.50
Production 4,000 Sets
Common Player (101-150): 1.00
Minor Stars (101-150): 2.00
Production 3,000 Sets
Common Player (151-200): 1.25
Minor Stars (151-200): 2.50
Production 2,000 Sets
Common Rookie (201-250): 3.50
Production 1,500 Sets
Common Rookie (251-300): 4.00
Production 1,000 Sets
Common Rookie (301-350): 7.50
Production 500 Sets
Common Rookie (351-400): 10.00
Production 350 Sets
Common Rookie (401-425): 20.00
Production 250,500,750 or 1,000 Sets
Pack (3): 6.00
Wax Box (18): 80.00
1 Ben Coates .50
2 Joe Horn .50
3 Jonathon Linton .50
4 Derrick Mason 1.00
5 Ray Lucas 1.00
6 Brock Huard 1.00
7 Frank Wycheck .50
8 Michael Strahan .50
9 Jessie Armstead .50
10 Stephen Alexander .50
11 Larry Centers .50
12 Michael Pittman .50
13 Priest Holmes 1.00
14 Jermaine Lewis .50
15 Jay Riemersma .50
16 Wesley Walls .50
17 Curtis Enis .50
18 Bobby Engram .50
19 Jim Miller .50
20 Eddie Kennison .50
21 Errict Rhett .50
22 Chris Warren .50
23 Byron Chamberlain .50
24 Desmond Howard .50
25 Lamar Smith .50
26 Robert Porcher .50
27 Corey Bradford .50
28 Donald Driver .50
29 Ahman Green 1.00
30 Ken Dilger .50
31 James McKnight .50
32 Kimble Anders .50
33 Zach Thomas .50
34 James Johnson .50
35 Lawyer Milloy .50
36 Ty Law .50
37 Willie McGinest .50
38 Jason Sehorn .50
39 Andre Rison .50
40 Rickey Dudley .50
41 Patrick Jeffers 1.00
42 Darrell Russell .50
43 Charles Johnson .50
44 Michael Westbrook .50
45 Levon Kirkland .50
46 Ryan Leahy .50
47 Sean Dawkins .50
48 Todd Lyght .50
49 Kevin Carter .50
50 Neil O'Donnell .50
51 Randall Cunningham 1.50
52 Oronde Gadsden .75
53 O.J. McDuffie .75
54 Jake Reed .75
55 Brian Mitchell .75
56 Kordell Stewart 1.75
57 Derrick Mayes .75
58 Az-Zahir Hakim 1.50
59 Jacquez Green .75
60 Andre Reed .75
61 Deion Sanders 1.75
62 Frank Sanders .75
63 Rob Moore .75
64 Shawn Jefferson .75
65 Patrick Johnson .75
66 Peter Boulware .75
67 Donald Hayes .75
68 Marty Booker .75
69 Leslie Shepherd .75
70 Jason Tucker .75
71 Johnnie Morton .75
72 Germane Crowell 1.50
73 Herman Moore 1.50
74 Bill Schroeder .75
75 E.G. Green .75
76 Jerome Pathon .75
77 Tony Brackens .75
78 Tony Richardson .75
79 Sam Madison .75
80 Jeff George 1.50
81 Matthew Hatchette .75
82 Kevin Faulk 1.50
83 Jeff Blake 1.50
84 Ike Hilliard 1.50
85 Napoleon Kaufman 1.50
86 Charles Woodson 1.50
87 Na Brown .75
88 Hines Ward 1.50
89 Troy Edwards 1.50
90 Curtis Conway .75
91 Junior Seau 1.50
92 Jim Harbaugh .75
93 J.J. Stokes .75
94 Jon Kitna 1.50
95 Reidel Anthony .75
96 Warrick Dunn 1.50
97 Carl Pickens 1.50
98 Yancey Thigpen .75
99 Albert Connell .75
100 Irving Fryar .75
101 Qadry Ismail 1.00
102 Shannon Sharpe 1.00
103 Joey Galloway 2.00
104 Ed McCaffrey 2.00
105 Rod Smith 2.00
106 Terrell Owens 2.00
107 Warren Sapp 1.00
108 Jevon Kearse 2.00
109 Bruce Smith 1.00
110 Champ Bailey 2.00
111 David Boston 2.00
112 Tim Dwight 2.00
113 Terance Mathis 1.00
114 Tony Banks 1.00
115 Shawn Bryson 1.00
116 Peerless Price 1.00
117 Muhsin Muhammad 1.00
118 Tim Biakabutuka 1.00
119 Steve Beuerlein 1.00
120 Corey Dillon 2.00
121 Kevin Johnson 2.00
122 Raghib Ismail 1.00
123 Charlie Batch 2.00
124 James Stewart 1.00
125 Terrence Wilkins 1.00
126 Keenan McCardell 1.00
127 Mark Brunell 3.00
128 Fred Taylor 3.00
129 Derrick Alexander 1.00
130 Tony Gonzalez 2.00
131 Warren Moon 1.00
132 Thurman Thomas 1.00
133 Tony Martin 1.00
134 Jay Fiedler 2.00
135 John Randle 1.00
136 Troy Brown 1.00
137 Amani Toomer 2.00
138 Kerry Collins 2.00
139 Tiki Barber 2.00
140 Wayne Chrebet 2.00
141 Tyrone Wheatley 1.00
142 Duce Staley 2.00
143 Jermaine Fazande 1.00
144 Charlie Garner 2.00
145 Torry Holt 2.00
146 Mike Alstott 2.00
147 Shaun King 2.50
148 Darrell Green 1.00
149 Brad Johnson 2.00
150 Olandis Gary 2.00
151 Jake Plummer 2.50
152 Chris Chandler 1.25
153 Jamal Anderson 2.50
154 Eric Moulds 2.50
155 Doug Flutie 3.00
156 Rob Johnson 1.25
157 Marcus Robinson 2.50
158 Cade McNown 2.50
159 Akili Smith 2.50
160 Tim Couch 4.00
161 Emmitt Smith 6.00
162 Troy Aikman 5.00
163 Brian Griese 3.00
164 John Elway 7.00
165 Terrell Davis 3.00
166 Dorsey Levens 2.50
167 Antonio Freeman 2.50
168 Brett Favre 10.00
169 Marvin Harrison 2.50
170 Peyton Manning 8.00
171 Edgerrin James 8.00
172 Jimmy Smith 2.50
173 Elvis Grbac 1.25
174 Dan Marino 7.00
175 Randy Moss 8.00
176 Cris Carter 2.50
177 Robert Smith 2.50
178 Daunte Culpepper 4.00
179 Terry Glenn 2.50
180 Drew Bledsoe 3.50
181 Ricky Williams 3.00
182 *Jake Delhomme* 4.00
183 Curtis Martin 2.50
184 Vinny Testaverde 1.25
185 Tim Brown 2.50
186 Rich Gannon 1.25
187 Donovan McNabb 4.00
188 Jerome Bettis 2.50
189 *Bobby Shaw* 5.00
190 Jerry Rice 5.00
191 Steve Young 3.50
192 Jeff Garcia 2.50
193 Ricky Watters 1.25
194 Isaac Bruce 2.50
195 Marshall Faulk 3.00
196 Kurt Warner 8.00
197 Keyshawn Johnson 2.50
198 Eddie George 3.00
199 Steve McNair 2.50
200 Stephen Davis 2.50
201 *Bobby Brooks* 3.50
202 *Cornelius Griffin* 3.50
203 *Danny Clark* 3.50
204 *Pat Dennis* 3.50
205 *Tommy Hendricks* 3.50
206 *Fred Jones* 3.50
207 *Isaiah Kacyvenski* 3.50
208 *Keith Miller* 3.50
209 *Andre O'Neal* 3.50
210 *Justin Snow* 3.50
211 *Armegis Spearman* 3.50
212 *Lester Towns* 3.50
213 *Antonio Wilson* 3.50
214 *Greg Wesley* 3.50
215 *Jabari Issa* 3.50
216 *Darwin Walker* 3.50
217 *Reggie Grimes* 3.50
218 *Rian Lindell* 3.50
219 *Chris Combs* 3.50
220 *Rashard Anderson* 5.00
221 *Erik Flowers* 5.00
222 *Corey Moore* 5.00
223 *Rob Meier* 3.50
224 *John Milem* 3.50
225 *Jeremiah Parker* 3.50
226 *Neil Rackers* 3.50
227 *Josh Taves* 5.00
228 *Mao Tosi* 3.50
229 *Gary Berry* 3.50
230 *Matt Bowen* 3.50
231 *Ralph Brown* 3.50
232 *Tony Darden* 3.50
233 *Arturo Freeman* 3.50
234 *David Gibson* 3.50
235 *Demario Brown* 5.00
236 *Deveron Harper* 3.50
237 *Johnnie Harris* 3.50
238 *Marcus Knight* 3.50
239 *Ronnie Heard* 3.50
240 *Eric Johnson* 3.50

241 John Keith 3.50
242 Anthony Malbrough 3.50
243 Anthony Mitchell 3.50
244 Aric Morris 3.50
245 Bobby Myers 3.50
246 Erik Olson 5.00
247 Lewis Sanders 3.50
248 Tony Scott 3.50
249 David Terrell 3.50
250 Travares Tillman 3.50
251 Dave Stachelski 4.00
252 Darren Howard 4.00
253 Frank Chamberlin 4.00
254 Na'il Diggs 8.00
255 Orantes Grant 6.00
256 Barrett Green 4.00
257 Kory Minor 4.00
258 Deon Grant 4.00
259 Mark Simoneau 8.00
260 Raynoch Thompson 4.00
261 Kenyatta Wright 4.00
262 Marcus Bell 4.00
263 Jack Golden 4.00
264 Thomas Hamner 4.00
265 Sekou Sanyika 4.00
266 Marcus Washington 4.00
267 Tim Seder 7.00
268 Paul Edinger 7.00
269 Micheal Boireau 4.00
270 Byron Frisch 4.00
271 Ketric Sanford 4.00
272 Frank Murphy 4.00
273 Robaire Smith 4.00
274 Adalius Thomas 4.00
275 William Bartee 4.00
276 Robert Bean 4.00
277 Tyrone Carter 4.00
278 Ike Charlton 4.00
279 Mario Edwards 4.00
280 Dwayne Goodrich 4.00
281 Michael Hawthorne 4.00
282 Kareem Larrimore 4.00
283 Mark Roman 4.00
284 Jacoby Shepherd 4.00
285 Jason Webster 4.00
286 Jimmy Wyrick 4.00
287 Rashidi Barnes 4.00
288 David Barrett 4.00
289 Ainsley Battles 4.00
290 Lamar Chapman 4.00
291 Todd Franz 4.00
292 Michael Green 4.00
293 Antwan Harris 4.00
294 Brandon Jennings 4.00
295 Darrick Vaughn 4.00
296 David Macklin 4.00
297 Bobby Brown 4.00
298 Reggie Stephens 4.00
299 Kenoy Kennedy 4.00
300 Raion Hill 4.00
301 Windrell Hayes 10.00
302 DaShon Polk 7.50
303 Tywan Mitchell 7.50
304 Casey Crawford 7.50
305 Hank Poteat 10.00
306 Mondriel Fulcher 7.50
307 Cory Geason 7.50
308 James Hill 7.50
309 Brian Jennings 7.50
310 John Jones 7.50
311 Anthony Lucas 7.50
312 Mike Leach 7.50
313 Dustin Lyman 7.50
314 Derek Rackley 7.50
315 Sebastian Janikowski 12.00
316 Brad St. Louis 7.50
317 Jay Tant 7.50
318 Austin Wheatley 7.50
319 Jermaine Wiggins 7.50
320 Todd Yoder 7.50
321 Deon Dyer 7.50
322 Jim Finn 7.50
323 Herbert Goodman 7.50
324 Mike Green 7.50
325 Dante Hall 25.00
326 Thabiti Davis 7.50
327 Kevin Houser 7.50
328 Jonas Lewis 7.50
329 Chad Morton 12.00
330 Patrick Pass 7.50
331 Maurice Smith 10.00
332 Paul Smith 7.50
333 Terrelle Smith 7.50
334 Craig Walendy 7.50
335 Jamel White 10.00
336 Jarious Jackson 12.00
337 Matt Lytle 7.50
338 Ron Powlus 7.50
339 Ian Gold 10.00
340 Brandon Short 7.50
341 T.J. Slaughter 10.00
342 Nate Webster 7.50
343 John Engelberger 7.50
344 Rogers Beckett 7.50
345 Mike Brown 7.50
346 Anthony Wright 12.00
347 Danny Farmer 10.00
348 Clint Stoerner 12.00
349 Julian Peterson 7.50
350 Ahmed Plummer 10.00
351 Avion Black 10.00
352 Kwame Cavil 10.00
353 Chris Cole 10.00
354 Chris Coleman 10.00
355 Trevor Gaylor 10.00
356 Damon Hodge 10.00
357 Darrell Jackson 30.00
358 Reggie Jones 10.00
359 Charles Lee 10.00
360 Jerry Porter 20.00
361 Bobby Shaw 15.00
362 Ron Dugans 12.00
363 James Williams 10.00
364 Bashir Yamini 10.00
365 Anthony Becht 12.00
366 Erron Kinney 10.00
367 Aaron Shea 12.00
368 Chris Samuels 12.00

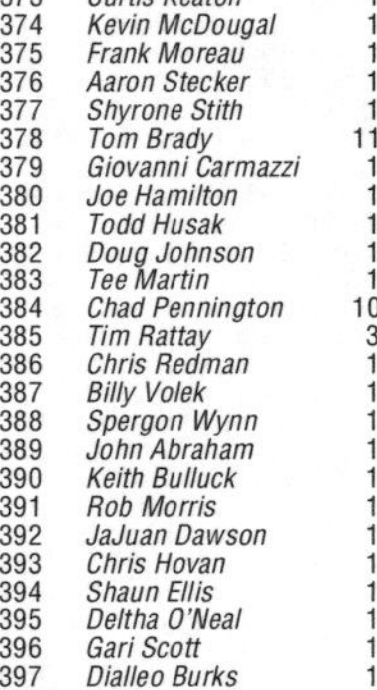

369 Trung Canidate 15.00
370 Obafemi Ayanbadejo 12.00
371 Doug Chapman 12.00
372 Ronney Jenkins 12.00
373 Curtis Keaton 12.00
374 Kevin McDougal 10.00
375 Frank Moreau 10.00
376 Aaron Stecker 12.00
377 Shyrone Stith 12.00
378 Tom Brady 110.00
379 Giovanni Carmazzi 15.00
380 Joe Hamilton 12.00
381 Todd Husak 10.00
382 Doug Johnson 15.00
383 Tee Martin 15.00
384 Chad Pennington 100.00
385 Tim Rattay 30.00
386 Chris Redman 15.00
387 Billy Volek 15.00
388 Spergon Wynn 12.00
389 John Abraham 12.00
390 Keith Bulluck 10.00
391 Rob Morris 12.00
392 JaJuan Dawson 15.00
393 Chris Hovan 12.00
394 Shaun Ellis 10.00
395 Deltha O'Neal 10.00
396 Gari Scott 10.00
397 Dialleo Burks 10.00
398 Shockmain Davis 12.00
399 Brad Hoover 15.00
400 Brian Finneran 10.00
401 Sylvester Morris 750 20.00
402 Dennis Northcutt 500 25.00
403 Todd Pinkston 1000 20.00
404 Larry Foster 500 20.00
405 R. Jay Soward 1000 20.00
406 Travis Taylor 250 40.00
407 Peter Warrick 1000 20.00
408 Dez White 1000 10.00
409 Ron Dayne 1000 15.00
410 Thomas Jones 500 25.00
411 Jamal Lewis 1000 20.00
412 Sammy Morris 500 20.00
413 Travis Prentice 500 20.00
414 J.R. Redmond 250 30.00
415 Michael Wiley 1000 10.00
416 Laveranues Coles 250 40.00
417 Bubba Franks 500 25.00
418 Mike Anderson 250 40.00
419 Plaxico Burress 250 100.00
420 Ron Dixon 1000 20.00
421 Troy Walters 1000 20.00
422 Shaun Alexander 1000 30.00
423 Brian Urlacher 1000 40.00
424 Corey Simon 1000 20.00
425 Courtney Brown 500 30.00

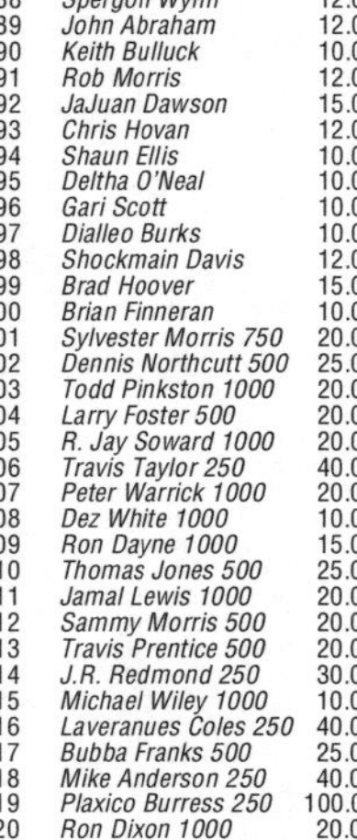

2000 Leaf Limited Limited Series

LS 1-50 Cards: 15X-30X
LS 51-100 Cards: 12X-24X
LS 101-150 Cards: 10X-20X
LS 151-200 Cards: 8X-16X
LS 151-200 Rookies: 4X
Production 35 Sets
LS 201-250 Rookies: 6X
LS 251-300 Rookies: 5X
LS 301-350 Rookies: 3X
LS 351-400 Rookies: 2X
Production 50 Sets
LS 401-425 Rookies: 2.5X
Production 25 Sets

2000 Leaf Limited Piece of the Game Previews

NM/M
Complete Set (25): 550.00
Common Player: 20.00
3rd Down Cards: 1.5X
Production 300 Sets
2nd Down Cards: 2X
Production 100 Sets
1st Down Cards: 4X
Production 25 Sets
JB36-B Jerome Bettis 20.00
IB80-W Isaac Bruce 20.00
MB8-W Mark Brunell 30.00
TC2-B Tim Couch 30.00
DC11-P Daunte Culpepper 30.00
SD48-W Stephen Davis 20.00
JE7-W John Elway 45.00
BF4-G Brett Favre 50.00
DF7-W Doug Flutie 25.00
BG14-N Brian Griese 25.00
EJ32-R Edgerrin James 45.00
JK12-W Jim Kelly 25.00
DM13-W Dan Marino 45.00
EM87-N Ed McCaffrey 20.00
DM5-W Donovan McNabb 25.00
RM84-P Randy Moss 40.00
JP16-W Jake Plummer 20.00
JR80-R Jerry Rice 40.00
BS20-B Barry Sanders 45.00
JS82-B Jimmy Smith 20.00
RS26-P Robert Smith 20.00
DS22-G Duce Staley 20.00
FT28-W Fred Taylor 25.00
KW13-W Kurt Warner 45.00
SY8-R Steve Young 30.00

2000 Leaf Rookies & Stars

NM/M
Common Player: .15
Minor Stars: .30
Common Rookie: 5.00
Production 1,000 Sets
Rookie Autographs: 2X
Production 200 Sets
Common Europe Prospect: 1.50
Production 3,000 Sets
Europe Autographs: 3X
Production 200 Sets
Pack (5): 5.00

NM/M
Wax Box (24): 85.00
1 Jake Plummer .50
2 David Boston .50
3 Tim Dwight .50
4 Jamal Anderson .50
5 Chris Chandler .30
6 Tony Banks .30
7 Qadry Ismail .15
8 Eric Moulds .50
9 Doug Flutie .75
10 Lamar Smith .30
11 Peerless Price .30
12 Rob Johnson .30
13 Reggie White .30
14 Muhsin Muhammad .30
15 Steve Beuerlein .30
16 Cade McNown .50
17 Derrick Alexander .15
18 Marcus Robinson .50
19 Corey Dillon .50
20 Akili Smith .50
21 Tim Couch 1.00
22 Kevin Johnson .30
23 Emmitt Smith 1.50
24 Troy Aikman 1.25
25 Joey Galloway .50
26 Raghib Ismail .15
27 John Elway 1.75
28 Terrell Davis 1.00
29 Brian Griese .75
30 Olandis Gary .50
31 Ed McCaffrey .30
32 Rod Smith .30
33 Barry Sanders 1.75
34 Charlie Batch .50
35 Germane Crowell .50
36 James Stewart .30
37 Brett Favre 2.00
38 Dorsey Levens .50
39 Antonio Freeman .50
40 Peyton Manning 1.75
41 Edgerrin James 2.00
42 Marvin Harrison .50
43 Fred Taylor .75
44 Mark Brunell .75
45 Jimmy Smith .50
46 Elvis Grbac .30
47 Tony Gonzalez .30
48 Dan Marino 1.75
49 Joe Horn .30
50 Jay Fiedler .30
51 James Allen .30
52 Randy Moss 1.75
53 Daunte Culpepper 1.00
54 Cris Carter .50
55 Robert Smith .50
56 Drew Bledsoe .75
57 Terry Glenn .50
58 Ricky Williams 1.25
59 Amani Toomer .30
60 Kerry Collins .50
61 Curtis Martin .50
62 Vinny Testaverde .30
63 Wayne Chrebet .30
64 Tim Brown .50
65 Tyrone Wheatley .30
66 Rich Gannon .30
67 Donovan McNabb .75
68 Duce Staley .50
69 Jerome Bettis .50
70 Donald Hayes .30
71 Junior Seau .30
72 Jermaine Fazande .30
73 Jerry Rice 1.25
74 Steve Young .75
75 Terrell Owens .50
76 Charlie Garner .30
77 Jeff Garcia .30
78 Tim Biakabutuka .30
79 Tiki Barber .50
80 Ricky Watters .30
81 Kurt Warner 1.50
82 Marshall Faulk .50
83 Isaac Bruce .50
84 Torry Holt .50
85 Mike Alstott .50
86 Warrick Dunn .50
87 Shaun King .75
88 Keyshawn Johnson .50
89 Warren Sapp .30
90 Eddie George .75
91 Jevon Kearse .50
92 Steve McNair .50
93 Carl Pickens .30
94 Deion Sanders .50
95 Stephen Davis .50
96 Brad Johnson .30
97 Bruce Smith .30
98 Michael Westbrook .30
99 Albert Connell .30
100 Jeff George .30
101 Thomas Jones 12.00
102 Bashir Yamini 5.00
103 Jamal Lewis 20.00
104 Travis Taylor 10.00

105 Chris Redman 10.00
106 Avion Black 5.00
107 Sammy Morris 10.00
108 Dez White 6.00
109 Peter Warrick 15.00
110 Ron Dugans 6.00
111 Curtis Keaton 6.00
112 Danny Farmer 7.00
113 Courtney Brown 8.00
114 Dennis Northcutt 8.00
115 Travis Prentice 10.00
116 JaJuan Dawson 8.00
117 Spergon Wynn 7.00
118 Michael Wiley 7.00
119 Chris Cole 5.00
120 Mike Anderson 7.00
121 Muneer Moore 5.00
122 Reuben Droughns 12.00
123 Bubba Franks 10.00
124 Anthony Lucas 5.00
125 Charles Lee 6.00
126 R. Jay Soward 8.00
127 Shyrone Stith 6.00
128 Sylvester Morris 5.00
129 Frank Moreau 8.00
130 Dante Hall 20.00
131 Doug Chapman 5.00
132 Troy Walters 6.00
133 J.R. Redmond 10.00
134 Tom Brady 60.00
135 Terrelle Smith 5.00
136 Chad Morton 7.00
137 Ron Dayne 10.00
138 Ron Dixon 6.00
139 Chad Pennington 40.00
140 Anthony Becht 6.00
141 Laveranues Coles 15.00
142 Windrell Hayes 5.00
143 Sebastian Janikowski 7.00
144 Jerry Porter 15.00
145 Corey Simon 8.00
146 Todd Pinkston 8.00
147 Gari Scott 5.00
148 Plaxico Burress 20.00
149 Tee Martin 8.00
150 Trevor Gaylor 7.00
151 Ronney Jenkins 5.00
152 Giovanni Carmazzi 8.00
153 Tim Rattay 15.00
154 Shaun Alexander 25.00
155 Darrell Jackson 15.00
156 James Williams 5.00
157 Trung Canidate 7.00
158 Joe Hamilton 8.00
159 Erron Kinney 5.00
160 Todd Husak 7.00
161 Raynoch Thompson 5.00
162 Darwin Walker 5.00
163 Jay Tant 5.00
164 Doug Johnson 12.00
165 Robert Bean 5.00
166 Mark Simoneau 5.00
167 John Jones 5.00
168 Obafemi Ayanbadejo 5.00
169 Mike Brown 5.00
170 Shockmain Davis 5.00
171 Erik Flowers 5.00
172 Corey Moore 5.00
173 Drew Haddad 5.00
174 Kwame Cavil 5.00
175 Pat Dennis 5.00
176 Rashard Anderson 6.00
177 Brian Finneran 5.00
178 Na'il Diggs 5.00
179 Marc Bulger 20.00
180 Mark Fulcher 5.00
181 Dwayne Carswell 5.00
182 Brian Urlacher 30.00
183 Paul Edinger 6.00
184 KaRon Coleman 5.00
185 Aaron Shea 5.00
186 Fabien Bownes 6.00
187 Damon Hodge 5.00
188 Dwayne Goodrich 5.00
189 Clint Stoerner 5.00
190 James Whalen 5.00
191 Deltha O'Neal 5.00
192 Ian Gold 6.00
193 Kenoy Kennedy 5.00
194 Jarious Jackson 7.00
195 Leroy Fields 5.00
196 Barrett Green 5.00
197 Joey Jamison 5.00
198 Rondell Mealey 7.00
199 Rob Morris 5.00
200 Marcus Washington 5.00
201 Trevor Insley 5.00
202 Jamel White 5.00
203 Kevin McDougal 5.00
204 Ibn Green 5.00
205 T.J. Slaughter 5.00
206 Emanuel Smith 5.00
207 Herbert Goodman 5.00
208 William Bartee 5.00
209 Rashidi Barnes 5.00
210 Brad Hoover 5.00
211 Deon Dyer 5.00
212 Jonas Lewis 5.00
213 Chris Hovan 5.00
214 Fred Robbins 5.00
215 Micheal Boireau 5.00
216 Giles Cole 5.00
217 Dave Stachelski 5.00
218 Patrick Pass 6.00
219 Darren Howard 5.00
220 Austin Wheatley 5.00
221 Kevin Houser 5.00
222 Rian Lindell 5.00
223 Jake Delhomme 25.00
224 Cornelius Griffin 5.00
225 Shaun Ellis 5.00
226 John Abraham 5.00
227 Travares Tillman 5.00
228 Julian Peterson 5.00
229 Marcus Knight 5.00
230 Thomas Hamner 5.00
231 Hank Poteat 5.00
232 Neil Rackers 5.00

233 Bobby Shaw 5.00
234 Rogers Beckett 5.00
235 Reggie Jones 8.00
236 Tim Seder 6.00
237 Durell Price 5.00
238 Ahmed Plummer 6.00
239 John Engelberger 5.00
240 Paul Smith 5.00
241 Chafie Fields 5.00
242 Kevin Feterik 5.00
243 Jacoby Shepherd 5.00
244 Nate Webster 5.00
245 Ketric Sanford 5.00
246 Tavarus Hogans 5.00
247 Keith Bulluck 5.00
248 Mike Green 5.00
249 Chris Coleman 5.00
250 Demario Brown 5.00
251 Billy Volek 8.00
252 Mareno Philyaw 5.00
253 Ethan Howell 5.00
254 Chris Samuels 7.00
255 Brandon Short 5.00
256 Maurice Smith 6.00
257 Frank Murphy 5.00
258 Darrick Vaughn 5.00
259 Payton Williams 5.00
260 JaJuan Seider 5.00
261 Antonio Banks 1.50
262 Jonathan Brown 1.50
263 Ontiwaun Carter 1.50
264 Jeremaine Copeland 1.50
265 Ralph Dawkins 1.50
266 Marques Douglas 1.50
267 Kevin Drake 1.50
268 Damon Dunn 1.50
269 Todd Floyd 1.50
270 Tony Graziani 2.00
271 Derrick Ham 1.50
272 Duane Hawthorne 1.50
273 Alonzo Johnson 1.50
274 Mark Kacmarynski 1.50
275 Eric Kresser 1.50
276 Jim Kubiak 1.50
277 Blaine McElmurry 1.50
278 Scott Milanovich 2.00
279 Norman Miller 1.50
280 Sean Morey 1.50
281 Jeff Ogden 2.50
282 Pepe Pearson 2.00
283 Ron Powlus 6.00
284 Jason Shelley 1.50
285 Ben Snell 1.50
286 Aaron Stecker 2.50
287 L.C. Stevens 1.50
288 Mike Sutton 1.50
289 Damian Vaughn 1.50
290 Ted White 1.50
291 Marcus Crandell 1.50
292 Darryl Daniel 1.50
293 Jesse Haynes 1.50
294 Matt Lytle 1.50
295 Deon Mitchell 1.50
296 Kendrick Nord 1.50
297 Ronnie Powell 1.50
298 Selucio Sanford 1.50
299 Corey Thomas 1.50
300 Vershan Jackson 1.50

2000 Leaf Rookies & Stars 2001 Draft Class

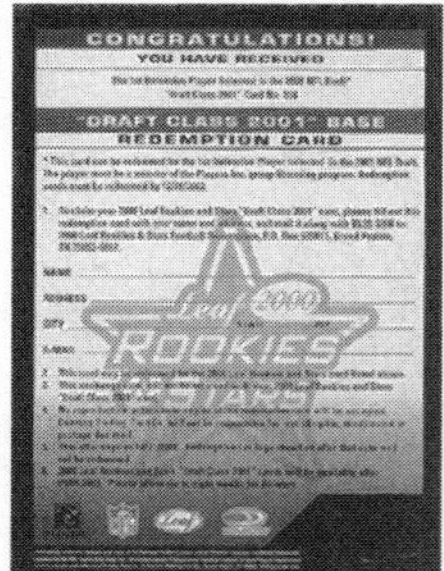

NM/M
Common Draft: 10.00
Inserted 1:2 Boxes
Redemptions expire 12/31/02
301 First QB 100.00
302 Second QB 50.00
303 Third QB 25.00
304 Fourth QB 25.00
305 Fifth QB 25.00
306 First RB 75.00
307 Second RB 50.00
308 Third RB 30.00
309 Fourth RB 25.00
310 Fifth RB 25.00
311 First WR 25.00
312 Second WR 25.00
313 Third WR 25.00
314 Fourth WR 20.00
315 Fifth WR 20.00
316 First Def 15.00
317 Second Def 15.00
318 Third Def 10.00
319 Fourth Def 10.00
320 Fifth Def 10.00

2000 Leaf Rookies & Stars Longevity

Longevity Cards: 15X-30X
Production 50 Sets
Longevity Rookies: 2X
Production 30 Sets
Longevity Europe: 3X-6X
Production 30 Sets

2000 Leaf Rookies & Stars Dress for Success

1 Jerry Rice
2 Eddie George
3 Troy Aikman
4 Mark Brunell
5 Barry Sanders
6 Marshall Faulk
7 Dan Marino
8 Stephen Davis
9 Terrell Davis
10 Brett Favre

2000 Leaf Rookies & Stars Freshman Orientation

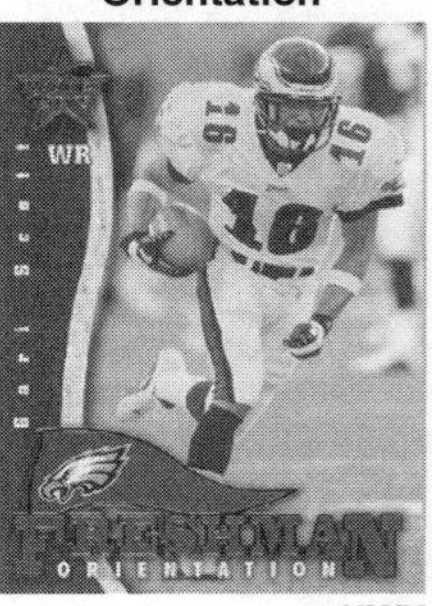

NM/M
Complete Set (30): 100.00
Common Player: 1.50
Minor Stars: 3.00
Production 2,000 Sets
FO1 Peter Warrick 3.00
FO2 Jamal Lewis 8.00
FO3 Thomas Jones 5.00
FO4 Plaxico Burress 6.00
FO5 Travis Taylor 4.00
FO6 Ron Dayne 4.00
FO7 Bubba Franks 3.00
FO8 Chad Pennington 8.00
FO9 Shaun Alexander 7.00
FO10 Sylvester Morris 6.00
FO11 R. Jay Soward 3.00
FO12 Trung Canidate 3.00
FO13 Dennis Northcutt 3.00
FO14 Todd Pinkston 3.00
FO15 Jerry Porter 3.00
FO16 Travis Prentice 4.00
FO17 Giovanni Carmazzi 3.50
FO18 Ron Dugans 3.00
FO19 Dez White 3.00
FO20 Mike Anderson 6.00
FO21 Ron Dixon 3.00
FO22 Chris Redman 5.00
FO23 J.R. Redmond 3.50
FO24 Laveranues Coles 3.50
FO25 JaJuan Dawson 3.00
FO26 Darrell Jackson 3.00
FO27 Sammy Morris 3.00
FO28 Doug Chapman 1.50
FO29 Tim Rattay 4.00
FO30 Gari Scott 1.50

2000 Leaf Rookies & Stars Game Plan

NM/M
Complete Set (30): 40.00
Common Player: 1.00
Production 2,000 Sets
Master Cards: 3X-6X
Production 50 Sets
GP1 Jerome Bettis 1.00
GP2 Charlie Garner 1.00
GP3 Jamal Lewis 6.00
GP4 Eric Moulds 1.00
GP5 Cade McNown 2.50
GP6 Peter Warrick 4.00
GP7 Tim Couch 3.50
GP8 Emmitt Smith 7.00
GP9 Troy Aikman 5.00
GP10 Terrell Davis 4.00
GP11 Brett Favre 8.00
GP12 Peyton Manning 5.00
GP13 Edgerrin James 5.00
GP14 Fred Taylor 3.00
GP15 Randy Moss 5.00
GP16 Daunte Culpepper 4.00
GP17 Drew Bledsoe 3.00
GP18 Ricky Williams 4.00
GP19 Ron Dayne 3.00
GP20 Curtis Martin 1.00
GP21 Donovan McNabb 2.50
GP22 Plaxico Burress 5.00
GP23 Jerry Rice 5.00
GP24 Shaun Alexander 4.00
GP25 Kurt Warner 4.00
GP26 Marshall Faulk 2.50
GP27 Keyshawn Johnson 1.00
GP28 Eddie George 2.50
GP29 Steve McNair 1.00
GP30 Stephen Davis 1.00

2000 Leaf Rookies & Stars Great American Heroes

		NM/M
Complete Set (10):		35.00
Common Player:		2.00
Production 1,000 Sets		
Signatures:		20X
Production 100 Sets		
Treasures:		20X
Production 100 Sets		
Treasures Autographs:		30X
Production 25 Sets		
GAH1	John Elway	6.00
GAH2	Terrell Davis	4.00
GAH3	Barry Sanders	7.00
GAH4	Edgerrin James	5.00
GAH5	Dan Marino	7.00
GAH6	Randy Moss	5.00
GAH7	Ricky Williams	4.00
GAH8	Jerry Rice	5.00
GAH9	Steve Young	2.00
GAH10	Kurt Warner	5.00

2000 Leaf Rookies & Stars Joe Montana Collection

		NM/M
Randomly Inserted		
Autographed:		2X
Production 25 Sets		
MC1	Joe Montana SF Jer/300	100.00
MC2	Joe Montana KC Jer/300	100.00
MC3	Joe Montana KC Helmet/125	225.00
MC4	Joe Montana Shoes/125	225.00
MC5	Joe Montana FB/125	225.00

2000 Leaf Rookies & Stars Prime Cuts

		NM/M
Common Player:		50.00
Production 25 Sets		
PC1	Eric Moulds	50.00
PC2	Cade McNown	60.00
PC3	Tim Couch	80.00
PC4	Emmitt Smith	150.00
PC5	John Elway	175.00
PC6	Terrell Davis	125.00
PC8	Barry Sanders	175.00
PC9	Brett Favre	200.00
PC10	Antonio Freeman	50.00
PC11	Peyton Manning	150.00
PC12	Edgerrin James	150.00
PC13	Marvin Harrison	50.00
PC14	Fred Taylor	60.00
PC15	Mark Brunell	60.00
PC16	Jimmy Smith	50.00
PC17	Dan Marino	175.00
PC18	Randy Moss	150.00
PC19	Cris Carter	50.00
PC20	Ricky Williams	100.00
PC21	Curtis Martin	50.00
PC22	Donovan McNabb	75.00
PC23	Jerry Rice	125.00
PC24	Steve Young	75.00
PC25	Kurt Warner	150.00
PC26	Marshall Faulk	60.00
PC27	Isaac Bruce	60.00
PC28	Shaun King	50.00
PC29	Eddie George	60.00
PC30	Steve McNair	50.00

2000 Leaf Rookies & Stars Slideshow

		NM/M
Complete Set (60):		75.00
Common Player:		1.00
Production 1,000 Sets		
Studio Cards:		6X-12X
Production 25 Sets		
S1	Jake Plummer	1.00
S2	Thomas Jones	2.00
S3	Jamal Anderson	2.00
S4	Jamal Lewis	5.00
S5	Travis Taylor	3.00
S6	Eric Moulds	2.00
S7	Cade McNown	1.00
S8	Marcus Robinson	1.00
S9	Corey Dillon	1.00
S10	Akili Smith	1.00
S11	Peter Warrick	2.00
S12	Tim Couch	3.00
S13	Travis Prentice	2.00
S14	Emmitt Smith	5.00
S15	Troy Aikman	4.00
S16	Mike Anderson	4.00
S17	John Elway	4.00
S18	Terrell Davis	4.00
S19	Brian Griese	3.00
S20	Terrell Owens	3.00
S21	Barry Sanders	5.00
S22	Charlie Batch	1.00
S23	Brett Favre	5.00
S24	Dorsey Levens	1.00
S25	Antonio Freeman	1.00
S26	Peyton Manning	4.00
S27	Edgerrin James	4.00
S28	Marvin Harrison	3.00
S29	Fred Taylor	3.00
S30	Mark Brunell	2.00
S31	Jimmy Smith	1.00
S32	Sylvester Morris	2.00
S33	Dan Marino	5.00
S34	Randy Moss	4.00
S35	Daunte Culpepper	2.00
S36	Cris Carter	2.00
S37	Robert Smith	1.00
S38	Drew Bledsoe	3.00
S39	Ricky Williams	4.00
S40	Ron Dayne	2.00
S41	Curtis Martin	3.00
S42	Chad Pennington	6.00
S43	Tim Brown	3.00
S44	Donovan McNabb	3.00
S45	Torry Holt	2.00
S46	Plaxico Burress	4.00
S47	Jerry Rice	4.00
S48	Steve Young	3.00
S49	Shaun Alexander	3.00
S50	Kurt Warner	4.00
S51	Marshall Faulk	3.00
S52	Isaac Bruce	2.00
S53	Shaun King	1.00
S54	Keyshawn Johnson	2.00
S55	Mike Alstott	2.00
S56	Eddie George	2.00
S57	Steve McNair	2.00
S58	Jevon Kearse	2.00
S59	Stephen Davis	2.00
S60	Brad Johnson	2.00

2000 Leaf Rookies & Stars Statistical Standouts

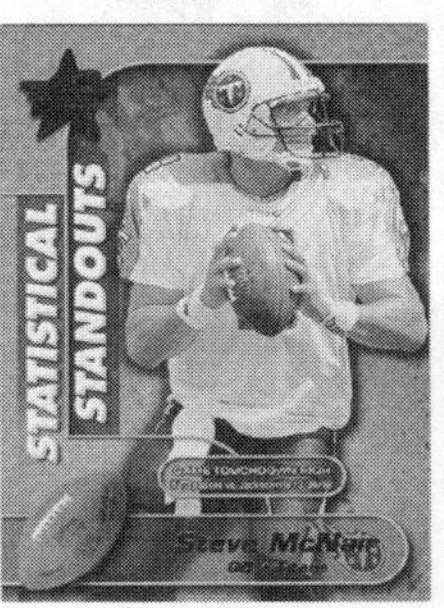

		NM/M
Complete Set (40):		100.00
Common Player:		2.00
Production 500 Sets		
SS1	Thomas Jones	3.00
SS2	Jamal Lewis	8.00
SS3	Travis Taylor	3.00
SS4	Cade McNown	2.00
SS5	Corey Dillon	2.00
SS6	Akili Smith	2.00
SS7	Peter Warrick	3.00
SS8	Tim Couch	4.00
SS9	Emmitt Smith	6.00
SS10	Troy Aikman	5.00
SS11	John Elway	5.00
SS12	Terrell Davis	4.00
SS13	Barry Sanders	6.00
SS14	Brett Favre	8.00
SS15	Dorsey Levens	2.00
SS16	Antonio Freeman	2.00
SS17	Peyton Manning	5.00
SS18	Edgerrin James	5.00
SS19	Marvin Harrison	2.00
SS20	Fred Taylor	3.00
SS21	Dan Marino	6.00
SS22	Randy Moss	5.00
SS23	Daunte Culpepper	4.00
SS24	Cris Carter	2.00
SS25	Drew Bledsoe	4.00
SS26	Ricky Williams	4.00
SS27	Ron Dayne	4.00
SS28	Curtis Martin	2.00
SS29	Chad Pennington	8.00
SS30	Plaxico Burress	5.00
SS31	Jerry Rice	6.00
SS32	Steve Young	5.00
SS33	Shaun Alexander	4.00
SS34	Kurt Warner	6.00
SS35	Marshall Faulk	2.00
SS36	Isaac Bruce	2.00
SS37	Eddie George	4.00
SS38	Steve McNair	2.00
SS39	Stephen Davis	2.00
SS40	Brad Johnson	2.00

2000 Leaf Rookies & Stars Ticket Masters

		NM/M
Complete Set (30):		40.00
Common Player:		1.00
Minor Stars:		2.00
Production 2,000 Sets		
TM1	Thomas Jones, Jake Plummer	2.00
TM2	Jamal Anderson, Chris Chandler	2.00
TM3	Travis Taylor, Jamal Lewis	4.00
TM4	Eric Moulds, Rob Johnson	2.00
TM5	Muhsin Muhammad, Steve Beuerlein	1.00
TM6	Cade McNown, Marcus Robinson	1.00
TM7	Peter Warrick, Akili Smith	2.00
TM8	Tim Couch, Kevin Johnson	2.50
TM9	Emmitt Smith, Troy Aikman	4.00
TM10	Terrell Davis, Brian Griese	3.00
TM11	Charlie Batch, James Stewart	2.00
TM12	Brett Favre, Antonio Freeman	5.00
TM13	Peyton Manning, Edgerrin James	5.00
TM14	Mark Brunell, Fred Taylor	3.00
TM15	Jay Fiedler, Lamar Smith	2.00
TM16	Randy Moss, Daunte Culpepper	5.00
TM17	Drew Bledsoe, Terry Glenn	3.00
TM18	Ricky Williams, Jeff Blake	3.00
TM19	Kerry Collins, Ron Dayne	3.00
TM20	Chad Pennington, Curtis Martin	6.00
TM21	Tim Brown, Rich Gannon	2.00
TM22	Donovan McNabb, Duce Staley	2.50
TM23	Plaxico Burress, Jerome Bettis	3.50
TM24	Ryan Leaf, Jermaine Fazande	1.00
TM25	Jerry Rice, Terrell Owens	4.00
TM26	Shaun Alexander, Ricky Watters	3.00
TM27	Kurt Warner, Marshall Faulk	5.00
TM28	Shaun King, Keyshawn Johnson	2.50
TM29	Eddie George, Steve McNair	2.50
TM30	Stephen Davis, Brad Johnson	2.00

2000 Quantum Leaf

		NM/M
Complete Set (350):		140.00
Common Player:		.20
Minor Stars:		.40
Common Rookie:		1.00
Inserted 1:2		
Pack (4):		4.25
Wax Box (24):		70.00
1	Frank Sanders	.40
2	Adrian Murrell	.40
3	Rob Moore	.40
4	Simeon Rice	.20
5	Michael Pittman	.20
6	Jake Plummer	1.00
7	David Boston	.75
8	Mario Bates	.20
9	Chris Chandler	.40
10	Tim Dwight	.75
11	Chris Calloway	.20
12	Terance Mathis	.20
13	Jamal Anderson	.75
14	Byron Hanspard	.40
15	Ken Oxendine	.20
16	Tony Graziani	.20
17	Bob Christian	.20
18	Priest Holmes	.40
19	Tony Banks	.40
20	Patrick Johnson	.40
21	Rod Woodson	.20
22	Jermaine Lewis	.40
23	Errict Rhett	.40
24	Stoney Case	.20
25	Peter Boulware	.20
26	Qadry Ismail	.20
27	Brandon Stokley	.20
28	Andre Reed	.40
29	Eric Moulds	.75
30	Doug Flutie	1.25
31	Bruce Smith	.20
32	Jay Riemersma	.20
33	Antowain Smith	.75
34	Thurman Thomas	.40
35	Jonathon Linton	.40
36	Peerless Price	.75
37	Rob Johnson	.40
38	Sam Gash	.20
39	Muhsin Muhammad	.40
40	Wesley Walls	.40
41	Fred Lane	.20
42	Kevin Greene	.20
43	Tim Biakabutuka	.40
44	Steve Beuerlein	.40
45	Donald Hayes	.20
46	Patrick Jeffers	1.00
47	Curtis Enis	.75
48	Bobby Engram	.20
49	Curtis Conway	.40
50	Marcus Robinson	1.00
51	Marty Booker	.20
52	Cade McNown	1.50
53	Shane Matthews	.40
54	Jim Miller	.40
55	Darnay Scott	.40
56	Carl Pickens	.40
57	Corey Dillon	.75
58	Jeff Blake	.40
59	Akili Smith	1.25
60	Michael Basnight	.20
61	Karim Abdul	.40
62	Tim Couch	2.00
63	Kevin Johnson	1.00
64	Terry Kirby	.20
65	Ty Detmer	.20
66	Leslie Shepherd	.20
67	Darrin Chiaverini	.20
68	Emmitt Smith	2.50
69	Deion Sanders	.75
70	Michael Irvin	.40
71	Raghib Ismail	.20
72	Troy Aikman	2.00
73	Daryl Johnston	.20
74	Chris Warren	.40
75	Jason Garrett	.20
76	Jason Tucker	1.00
77	Lawyer Milloy	.20
78	Dexter Coakley	.20
79	Greg Ellis	.20
80	David LaFleur	.20
81	Todd Lyght	.20
82	Ernie Mills	.20
83	Wane McGarity	.20
84	Chris Brazzell	.20
85	Ed McCaffrey	.40
86	Rod Smith	.40
87	Shannon Sharpe	.40
88	Brian Griese	1.00
89	John Elway	3.00
90	Neil Smith	.20
91	Terrell Davis	2.00
92	Olandis Gary	1.50
93	Derek Loville	.20
94	John Avery	.20
95	Bubby Brister	.40
96	Byron Chamberlain	.20
97	Dale Carter	.20
98	Johnnie Morton	.20
99	Charlie Batch	1.00
100	Barry Sanders	3.00
101	Germane Crowell	.40
102	Gus Frerotte	.20
103	Desmond Howard	.20
104	Terry Fair	.20
105	Ron Rivers	.20
106	Greg Hill	.20
107	Sedrick Irvin	.40
108	David Sloan	.20
109	Herman Moore	.75
110	Robert Porcher	.20
111	Corey Bradford	.40
112	Dorsey Levens	1.00
113	Antonio Freeman	1.00
114	Brett Favre	4.00
115	De'Mond Parker	.40
116	Bill Schroeder	.20
117	Matt Hasselbeck	.40
118	Donald Driver	.40
119	Basil Mitchell	.40
120	E.G. Green	.20
121	Ken Dilger	.20
122	Marvin Harrison	1.00
123	Peyton Manning	3.00
124	Terrence Wilkins	1.00
125	Edgerrin James	4.00
126	Jerome Pathon	.20
127	Marcus Pollard	.20
128	Keenan McCardell	.40
129	Mark Brunell	1.50
130	Fred Taylor	1.50
131	Jimmy Smith	.75
132	James Stewart	.75
133	Kyle Brady	.20
134	Tony Brackens	.20
135	Derrick Thomas	.40
136	Rashaan Shehee	.20
137	Derrick Alexander	.20
138	Bam Morris	.20
139	Andre Rison	.40
140	Elvis Grbac	.40
141	Tony Gonzalez	.40
142	Donnell Bennett	.20
143	Warren Moon	.75
144	Tamarick Vanover	.20
145	Kimble Anders	.20
146	Tony Richardson	.20
147	Zach Thomas	.40
148	Oronde Gadsden	.40
149	Dan Marino	3.00
150	O.J. McDuffie	.40
151	Tony Martin	.20
152	Cecil Collins	.40
153	James Johnson	.40
154	Rob Konrad	.20
155	Yatil Green	.20
156	Damon Huard	.75
157	Nate Jacquet	.20
158	Stanley Pritchett	.20
159	Sam Madison	.20
160	Randy Moss	3.00
161	Cris Carter	1.00
162	Robert Smith	1.00
163	Randall Cunningham	.75
164	Jake Reed	.40
165	John Randle	.40
166	Leroy Hoard	.20
167	Jeff George	.75
168	Daunte Culpepper	1.50
169	Matthew Hatchette	.20
170	Robert Tate	.20
171	Ty Law	.20
172	Troy Brown	.20
173	Tony Simmons	.40
174	Terry Glenn	.75
175	Ben Coates	.40
176	Drew Bledsoe	1.50
177	Terry Allen	.40
178	Kevin Faulk	.40
179	Shawn Jefferson	.20
180	Andy Katzenmoyer	.20
181	Willie McGinest	.20
182	Cameron Cleeland	.40
183	Eddie Kennison	.40
184	Ricky Williams	2.00
185	Danny Wuerffel	.20
186	Brett Bech	.20
187	Billy Joe Hobert	.20
188	*Jake Delhomme*	2.00
189	Wilmont Perry	.20
190	Keith Poole	.20
191	Ashley Ambrose	.20
192	Amani Toomer	.40
193	Kerry Collins	.40
194	Tiki Barber	.20
195	Ike Hilliard	.40
196	Jason Sehorn	.20
197	Joe Montgomery	.20
198	Joe Jurevicius	.20
199	Michael Strahan	.20
200	Sean Bennett	.20
201	Jessie Armstead	.20
202	Pete Mitchell	.20
203	Curtis Martin	.75
204	Vinny Testaverde	.40
205	Keyshawn Johnson	1.00
206	Wayne Chrebet	.75
207	Ray Lucas	1.00
208	Tyrone Wheatley	.40
209	Napoleon Kaufman	.75
210	Tim Brown	.75
211	Rickey Dudley	.20
212	James Jett	.20
213	Rich Gannon	.40
214	Charles Woodson	1.00
215	Zack Crockett	.20
216	Darrell Russell	.20
217	Duce Staley	1.00
218	Donovan McNabb	2.00
219	Charles Johnson	.20
220	Dameane Douglas	.20
221	Doug Pederson	.20
222	Torrance Small	.20
223	Troy Vincent	.20
224	Na Brown	.20
225	Kordell Stewart	1.00
226	Jerome Bettis	1.00
227	Hines Ward	.40
228	Troy Edwards	1.00
229	Richard Huntley	.40
230	Mark Bruener	.20
231	Pete Gonzalez	.40
232	Levon Kirkland	.20
233	*Bobby Shaw*	1.00
234	Amos Zereoue	.40
235	Natrone Means	.40
236	Junior Seau	.40
237	Jim Harbaugh	.40
238	Ryan Leaf	1.00
239	Mikhael Ricks	.20
240	Jermaine Fazande	.40
241	Jeff Graham	.20
242	Tremayne Stephens	.40
243	Terrell Owens	1.00
244	J.J. Stokes	.40
245	Charlie Garner	.40
246	Jerry Rice	2.00
247	Garrison Hearst	.40
248	Steve Young	1.50
249	Jeff Garcia	1.00
250	Fred Beasley	.20
251	Bryant Young	.20
252	Derrick Mayes	.40
253	Ahman Green	.40
254	Joey Galloway	1.00
255	Ricky Watters	.40
256	Jon Kitna	1.00
257	Sean Dawkins	.20
258	Sam Adams	.20
259	Christian Fauria	.20
260	Shawn Springs	.20
261	Az-Zahir Hakim	.40
262	Isaac Bruce	1.00
263	Marshall Faulk	1.00
264	Trent Green	.40
265	Kurt Warner	4.00
266	Torry Holt	1.00
267	Robert Holcombe	.20
268	Kevin Carter	.20
269	Amp Lee	.20
270	Roland Williams	.20
271	Jacquez Green	.40
272	Reidel Anthony	.40
273	Warren Sapp	.40
274	Mike Alstott	1.00
275	Warrick Dunn	1.00
276	Trent Dilfer	.40
277	Shaun King	1.50
278	Bert Emanuel	.20
279	Eric Zeier	.20
280	Neil O'Donnell	.40
281	Eddie George	1.00
282	Yancey Thigpen	.40
283	Steve McNair	1.00
284	Kevin Dyson	.40
285	Frank Wycheck	.20
286	Jevon Kearse	1.00
287	Bruce Matthews	.20
288	Lorenzo Neal	.20
289	Stephen Davis	.75
290	Stephen Alexander	.20
291	Darrell Green	.40
292	Skip Hicks	.40
293	Brad Johnson	.75
294	Michael Westbrook	.75
295	Albert Connell	.40
296	Irving Fryar	.20
297	Champ Bailey	1.00
298	Larry Centers	.20
299	Brian Mitchell	.20
300	James Thrash	.20
301	*LaVar Arrington*	10.00
302	*Peter Warrick*	4.00
303	*Courtney Brown*	3.00
304	*Plaxico Burress*	5.00
305	*Corey Simon*	2.00
306	*Thomas Jones*	3.00
307	*Travis Taylor*	3.00
308	*Shaun Alexander*	6.00
309	*Chris Redman*	3.00
310	*Chad Pennington*	10.00
311	*Jamal Lewis*	6.00
312	*Brian Urlacher*	5.00
313	*Keith Bullock*	1.50
314	*Daniel Franks*	3.00
315	*Dez White*	2.00
316	*Ahmed Plummer*	1.50
317	*Ron Dayne*	3.00
318	*Shaun Ellis*	1.50
319	*Sylvester Morris*	1.50
320	*Delthea O'Neal*	1.50
321	*R. Jay Soward*	2.50
322	*Sherrod Gideon*	1.50
323	*John Abraham*	1.50
324	*Travis Prentice*	3.00
325	*Darrell Jackson*	4.00
326	*Giovanni Carmazzi*	3.00
327	*Anthony Lucas*	1.50
328	*Danny Farmer*	2.50
329	*Dennis Northcutt*	3.00
330	*Troy Walters*	2.00
331	*Laveranues Coles*	4.00
332	*Tee Martin*	3.00
333	*J.R. Redmond*	3.00
334	*Jerry Porter*	4.00
335	*Sebastian Janikowski*	2.00
336	*Michael Wiley*	2.50
337	*Reuben Droughns*	4.00
338	*Trung Canidate*	2.00
339	*Shyrone Stith*	1.50
340	*Trevor Gaylor*	2.00
341	*Rob Morris*	1.50
342	*Marc Bulger*	5.00
343	*Tom Brady*	15.00
344	*Todd Husak*	1.50
345	*Gari Scott*	1.50
346	*Erron Kinney*	1.50
347	*Julian Peterson*	1.50
348	*Doug Chapman*	1.50
349	*Ron Dugans*	1.50
350	*Todd Pinkston*	2.50
351	*Deon Grant*	1.00
352	*Na'il Diggs*	1.00
353	*Raynoch Thompson*	1.00
354	*Mario Edwards*	1.00
355	*John Engelberger*	1.00
356	*Dwayne Goodrich*	1.00
357	*Ben Kelly*	1.00
358	*Sekou Sanyika*	1.00
359	*Brandon Short*	1.00
360	*Jabari Issa*	1.00
361	*Darwin Walker*	1.00
362	*Jerry Johnson*	1.00
363	*Robaire Smith*	1.00
364	*Mark Roman*	1.00
365	*Leonardo Carson*	1.00
366	*Mark Simoneau*	1.00
367	*Hank Poteat*	1.00
368	*Darren Howard*	1.00
369	*David Macklin*	1.00
370	*Adalius Thomas*	1.00
371	*Ralph Brown*	1.00
372	*Mondriel Fulcher*	1.00
373	*Sammy Morris*	2.50
374	*Rondell Mealey*	1.00
375	*Deon Dyer*	1.00
376	*Mareno Philyaw*	1.00
377	*Thomas Hamner*	1.00
378	*Jarious Jackson*	1.00
379	*Joe Hamilton*	2.50
380	*Tim Rattay*	3.00
381	*Chris Hovan*	2.00

2000 Quantum Leaf Infinity Green

	NM/M
Cards #1-100:	10X-20X
Production 100 Sets	
Cards #101-200:	20X-40X
Production 25 Sets	
Cards #201-300:	15X-30X
Production 50 Sets	
Cards #301-350:	4X-8X
Production 75 Sets	

2000 Quantum Leaf Infinity Purple

	NM/M
Cards #1-100:	20X-40X
Production 25 Sets	
Cards #101-200:	15X-30X
Production 50 Sets	
Cards #201-300:	10X-20X
Production 100 Sets	
Cards #301-350:	10X-20X
Production 15 Sets	

Post-1980 cards in Near Mint condition will generally sell for about 75% of the quoted Mint value. Excellent-condition cards bring no more than 40%.

2000 Quantum Leaf Infinity Red

		NM/M
Cards #1-100:		15X-30X
Production 50 Sets		
Cards #101-200:		10X-20X
Production 100 Sets		
Cards #201-300:		20X-40X
Production 25 Sets		
Cards #301-350:		5X-10X
Production 35 Sets		

2000 Quantum Leaf All-Millennium Team

		NM/M
Complete Set (28):		125.00
Common Player:		2.00
Minor Stars:		4.00
Production 1,000 Sets		
DM	Dan Marino	12.00
JE	John Elway	12.00
SB	Sammy Baugh	4.00
JU	Johnny Unitas	10.00
JM	Joe Montana	15.00
PH	Paul Hornung	4.00
JB	Jim Brown	12.00
TDO	Tony Dorsett	6.00
EC	Earl Campbell	6.00
BS	Barry Sanders	12.00
ES	Emmitt Smith	10.00
GS	Gale Sayers	8.00
TD	Terrell Davis	10.00
ED	Eric Dickerson	2.00
MA	Marcus Allen	4.00
JR	Jerry Rice	8.00
LA	Lance Alworth	2.00
KW	Kellen Winslow	2.00
FB	Fred Biletnikoff	6.00
RB	Raymond Berry	2.00
JL	James Lofton	2.00
RM	Randy Moss	12.00
PW	Paul Warfield	4.00
CC	Cris Carter	4.00
TB	Terry Bradshaw	10.00
RS	Roger Staubach	10.00
SL	Steve Largent	6.00
BST	Bart Starr	10.00

2000 Quantum Leaf All-Millennium Team Autographs

		NM/M
Complete Set (28):		2,800
Common Player:		35.00
Minor Stars:		70.00
Production 100 Sets		
DM	Dan Marino	200.00
JE	John Elway	200.00
SB	Sammy Baugh	70.00
JU	Johnny Unitas	175.00
JM	Joe Montana	250.00
PH	Paul Hornung	70.00
JB	Jim Brown	175.00
TDO	Tony Dorsett	100.00
EC	Earl Campbell	85.00
BS	Barry Sanders	200.00
ES	Emmitt Smith	175.00
GS	Gale Sayers	100.00
TD	Terrell Davis	125.00
ED	Eric Dickerson	35.00
MA	Marcus Allen	70.00
JR	Jerry Rice	150.00
LA	Lance Alworth	35.00
KW	Kellen Winslow	35.00
FB	Fred Biletnikoff	75.00
RB	Raymond Berry	35.00
JL	James Lofton	35.00
RM	Randy Moss	150.00
PW	Paul Warfield	70.00
CC	Cris Carter	70.00
TB	Terry Bradshaw	150.00
RS	Roger Staubach	150.00
SL	Steve Largent	75.00
BST	Bart Starr	175.00

2000 Quantum Leaf Banner Season

		NM/M
Complete Set (40):		85.00
Common Player:		1.50
Minor Stars:		3.00
Production #'d to 1999 Season Stat		
BS1	Brett Favre 4091	6.00
BS2	Marvin Harrison 1663	3.00
BS3	Tim Brown 1344	3.00
BS4	Randy Moss 1413	10.00
BS5	Edgerrin James 2139	8.00
BS6	Kurt Warner 4353	8.00
BS7	Marshall Faulk 2429	1.50
BS8	Dan Marino 2448	6.00
BS9	Tim Couch 2447	6.00
BS10	Ricky Williams 884	8.00
BS11	Eddie George 1304	4.00
BS12	Jerry Rice 830	8.00
BS13	Troy Aikman 2964	5.00
BS14	Emmitt Smith 1397	8.00
BS15	Antonio Freeman 1074	3.00
BS16	Jimmy Smith 1636	1.50
BS17	Charlie Batch 4857	1.50
BS18	Jake Plummer 2111	1.50
BS19	Drew Bledsoe 3985	3.00
BS20	Germane Crowell 1338	3.00
BS21	Cris Carter 1241	3.00
BS22	Deion Sanders 334	5.00
BS23	Donovan McNabb 948	5.00
BS24	Mark Brunell 3060	3.00
BS25	Fred Taylor 732	5.00
BS26	Stephen Davis 1405	3.00
BS27	Brad Johnson 4005	1.50
BS28	Jon Kitna 3346	1.50
BS29	Curtis Martin 1464	1.50
BS30	Keyshawn Johnson 1170	3.00
BS31	Shaun King 875	5.00
BS32	Isaac Bruce 1165	3.00
BS33	Kevin Johnson 986	3.00
BS34	Steve McNair 2179	1.50
BS35	Eric Moulds 994	3.00
BS36	Peyton Manning 4136	5.00
BS37	Dorsey Levens 1607	1.50
BS38	Olandis Gary 1159	3.00
BS39	James Stewart 931	1.50
BS40	Terry Glenn 1147	3.00

2000 Quantum Leaf Banner Season Century

		NM/M
Complete Set (40):		475.00
Common Player:		5.00
Minor Stars:		10.00
Production 99 Sets		
BS1	Brett Favre	40.00
BS2	Marvin Harrison	10.00
BS3	Tim Brown	10.00
BS4	Randy Moss	40.00
BS5	Edgerrin James	40.00
BS6	Kurt Warner	50.00
BS7	Marshall Faulk	12.00
BS8	Dan Marino	30.00
BS9	Tim Couch	25.00
BS10	Ricky Williams	25.00
BS11	Eddie George	12.00
BS12	Jerry Rice	25.00
BS13	Troy Aikman	25.00
BS14	Emmitt Smith	30.00
BS15	Antonio Freeman	10.00
BS16	Jimmy Smith	5.00
BS17	Charlie Batch	10.00
BS18	Jake Plummer	10.00
BS19	Drew Bledsoe	18.00
BS20	Germane Crowell	5.00
BS21	Cris Carter	10.00
BS22	Deion Sanders	10.00
BS23	Donovan McNabb	15.00
BS24	Mark Brunell	18.00
BS25	Fred Taylor	20.00
BS26	Stephen Davis	10.00
BS27	Brad Johnson	10.00
BS28	Jon Kitna	10.00
BS29	Curtis Martin	10.00
BS30	Keyshawn Johnson	10.00
BS31	Shaun King	10.00
BS32	Isaac Bruce	10.00
BS33	Kevin Johnson	10.00
BS34	Steve McNair	10.00
BS35	Eric Moulds	10.00
BS36	Peyton Manning	30.00
BS37	Dorsey Levens	10.00
BS38	Olandis Gary	10.00
BS39	James Stewart	5.00
BS40	Terry Glenn	10.00

2000 Quantum Leaf Double Team

		NM/M
Complete Set (30):		50.00
Common Player:		1.00
Minor Stars:		2.00
Production 1,500 Sets		
DT1	J.J. Johnson, Dan Marino	6.00
DT2	Edgerrin James, Peyton Manning	6.00
DT3	Kevin Faulk, Drew Bledsoe	3.00
DT4	Antowain Smith, Doug Flutie	2.00
DT5	Curtis Martin, Vinny Testaverde	2.00
DT6	Jerome Bettis, Kordell Stewart	2.00
DT7	Eddie George, Steve McNair	3.00
DT8	Fred Taylor, Mark Brunell	3.00
DT9	Errict Rhett, Tony Banks	1.00
DT10	Karim Abdul, Tim Couch	3.00
DT11	Corey Dillon, Akili Smith	2.00
DT12	Terrell Davis, Brian Griese	4.00
DT13	Donnell Bennett, Elvis Grbac	1.00
DT14	Ricky Watters, Jon Kitna	2.00
DT15	Tyrone Wheatley, Rich Gannon	1.00
DT16	Natrone Means, Jim Harbaugh	1.00
DT17	Emmitt Smith, Troy Aikman	6.00
DT18	Stephen Davis, Brad Johnson	2.00
DT19	Duce Staley, Donovan McNabb	3.00
DT20	Michael Pittman, Jake Plummer	2.00
DT21	Dorsey Levens, Brett Favre	6.00
DT22	Robert Smith, Jeff George	2.00
DT23	Mike Alstott, Shaun King	3.00
DT24	Curtis Enis, Cade McNown	3.00
DT25	Barry Sanders, Charlie Batch	6.00
DT26	Marshall Faulk, Kurt Warner	6.00
DT27	Ricky Williams, Jeff Blake	4.00
DT28	Charlie Garner, Steve Young	2.00
DT29	Tim Biakabutuka, Steve Beuerlein	1.00
DT30	Jamal Anderson, Chris Chandler	2.00

2000 Quantum Leaf Gamers

		NM/M
Common Player:		100.00
Production 25 Sets		
G1	Brett Favre	250.00
G2	Dan Marino	200.00
G3	Barry Sanders	200.00
G4	John Elway	150.00
G5	Peyton Manning	150.00
G6	Terrell Davis	100.00
G7	Fred Taylor	75.00
G8	Drew Bledsoe	100.00
G9	Mark Brunell	75.00
G10	Eddie George	75.00
G11	Isaac Bruce	75.00
G12	Jerry Rice	150.00
G13	Ray Lucas	50.00
G14	Olandis Gary	50.00
G15	Emmitt Smith	200.00
G16	Shaun King	50.00
G17	Edgerrin James	150.00
G18	Cris Carter	100.00
G19	Jimmy Smith	100.00
G20	Brian Griese	100.00

2000 Quantum Leaf Hardwear

		NM/M
Common Player:		30.00
Production 125 Sets		
HW1	Brett Favre	100.00
HW2	Dan Marino	100.00
HW3	Barry Sanders	100.00
HW4	John Elway	100.00
HW5	Terrell Davis	75.00
HW6	Troy Aikman	75.00
HW7	Steve Young	60.00
HW8	Eddie George	50.00
HW9	Brad Johnson	30.00
HW10	Herman Moore	30.00
HW11	Antowain Smith	30.00
HW12	Kordell Stewart	50.00
HW13	Dorsey Levens	30.00
HW14	Peyton Manning	100.00
HW15	Jerry Rice	75.00

2000 Quantum Leaf Millennium Moments

		NM/M
Complete Set (20):		75.00
Common Player:		2.00
Production 1,000 Sets		
MM1	Drew Bledsoe	4.00
MM2	Emmitt Smith	7.00
MM3	Mark Brunell	4.00
MM4	Brett Favre	10.00
MM5	Randy Moss	8.00
MM6	Kurt Warner	10.00
MM7	John Elway	8.00
MM8	Steve Young	4.00
MM9	Eddie George	3.00
MM10	Marshall Faulk	2.00
MM11	Edgerrin James	8.00
MM12	Antonio Freeman	2.00
MM13	Dan Marino	8.00
MM14	Terrell Davis	6.00
MM15	Doug Flutie	3.00
MM16	Jerry Rice	5.00
MM17	Fred Taylor	4.00
MM18	Peyton Manning	8.00
MM19	Troy Aikman	5.00
MM20	Barry Sanders	8.00

2000 Quantum Leaf Rookie Revolution

		NM/M
Complete Set (20):		30.00
Common Player:		1.00
Production 5,000 Sets		
First Strike Cards:		5X-10X
Production 50 Sets		
RR1	Peter Warrick	3.00
RR2	J.R. Redmond	3.00
RR3	Chris Redman	4.00
RR4	R. Jay Soward	3.00
RR5	Ron Dayne	2.00
RR6	Chad Pennington	7.00
RR7	Anthony Lucas	1.00
RR8	Tim Rattay	2.00
RR9	Shaun Alexander	4.00
RR10	Dez White	2.00
RR11	Tee Martin	3.00
RR12	Travis Taylor	4.00
RR13	Travis Prentice	3.00
RR14	Sylvester Morris	3.00
RR15	Jamal Lewis	5.00
RR16	Plaxico Burress	5.00
RR17	Sherrod Gideon	1.00
RR18	Shyrone Stith	1.00
RR19	Thomas Jones	4.00
RR20	Kwame Cavil	1.00

2000 Quantum Leaf Rookie Revolution First Strike

First Strike Cards:		5X-10X
Production 50 Cards		
1	Peter Warrick	
2	J.R. Redmond	
3	Chris Redman	
4	R. Jay Soward	
5	Ron Dayne	
6	Chad Pennington	
7	Anthony Lucas	
8	Tim Rattay	
9	Shaun Alexander	
10	Dez White	
11	Tee Martin	
12	Travis Taylor	
13	Travis Prentice	
14	Sylvester Morris	
15	Jamal Lewis	
16	Plaxico Burress	
17	Sherrod Gideon	
18	Shyrone Stith	
19	Thomas Jones	
20	Kwame Cavil	

2000 Quantum Leaf Shirt Off My Back

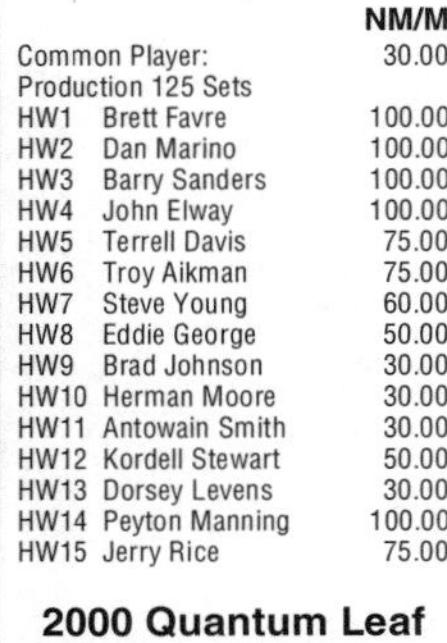

		NM/M
Common Player:		40.00
Production 100 Sets		
SB1	Brett Favre	150.00
SB2	Dan Marino	125.00
SB3	Barry Sanders	125.00
SB4	John Elway	125.00
SB5	Peyton Manning	100.00
SB6	Terrell Davis	75.00
SB7	Fred Taylor	50.00
SB8	Drew Bledsoe	75.00
SB9	Mark Brunell	75.00
SB10	Eddie George	60.00
SB11	Isaac Bruce	40.00
SB12	Jerry Rice	100.00
SB13	Ray Lucas	40.00
SB14	Olandis Gary	60.00
SB15	Emmitt Smith	125.00
SB16	Shaun King	85.00
SB17	Edgerrin James	100.00
SB18	Cris Carter	40.00
SB19	Jimmy Smith	40.00
SB20	Brian Griese	60.00

2000 Quantum Leaf Star Factor

		NM/M
Complete Set (40):		70.00
Common Player:		1.00
Minor Stars:		2.00
Production 2,500 Sets		
Quasar Cards:		8X-16X
Production 50 Sets		
SF1	Edgerrin James	3.00
SF2	Cris Carter	1.00
SF3	Terrell Owens	1.00
SF4	Brett Favre	5.00
SF5	Tim Couch	3.00
SF6	Terry Glenn	1.00
SF7	John Elway	4.00
SF8	Troy Aikman	4.00
SF9	Charlie Batch	1.00
SF10	Steve McNair	1.00
SF11	Drew Bledsoe	2.50
SF12	Joey Galloway	1.00
SF13	Dan Marino	5.00
SF14	Marshall Faulk	1.00
SF15	Jamal Anderson	1.00
SF16	Jake Plummer	2.00
SF17	Curtis Martin	1.00
SF18	Peyton Manning	4.00
SF19	Keyshawn Johnson	1.00
SF20	Barry Sanders	5.00
SF21	Jerry Rice	4.00
SF22	Emmitt Smith	4.00
SF23	Daunte Culpepper	2.00
SF24	Brad Johnson	1.00
SF25	Kurt Warner	4.00
SF26	Steve Young	2.50
SF27	Eddie George	2.00
SF28	Fred Taylor	3.00
SF29	Randy Moss	4.00
SF30	Terrell Davis	3.00
SF31	Eric Moulds	1.00
SF32	Antonio Freeman	1.00
SF33	Isaac Bruce	1.00
SF34	Ricky Williams	3.00
SF35	Donovan McNabb	2.00
SF36	Stephen Davis	1.00
SF37	Jon Kitna	1.00
SF38	Marvin Harrison	1.00
SF39	Doug Flutie	2.00
SF40	Mark Brunell	2.50

2000 Quantum Leaf Star Factor Quasar

Quasar Cards:		8X-16X
Production 50 Sets		

2000 Quantum Leaf Kurt Warner MVP

		NM/M
Complete Set (2):		20.00
Production 1,000 Sets		
Autographs:		10X
Production 100 Sets		
	Kurt Warner MVP	10.00
	Kurt Warner S.B. MVP	10.00

A card number in parenthese ( ) indicates the set is unnumbered.

2001 Leaf Certified Materials

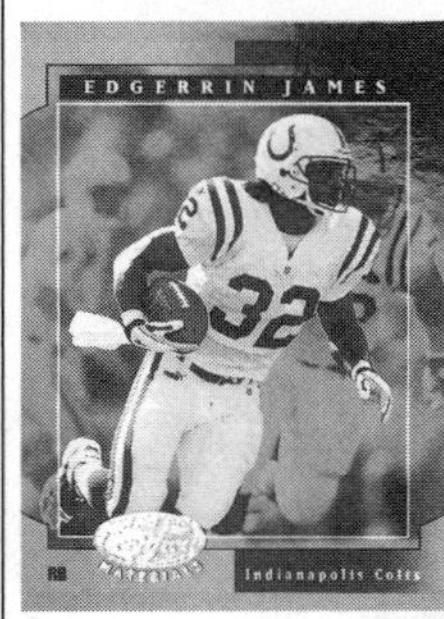

		NM/M
Complete Set (145):		600.00
Common Player:		.25
Minor Stars:		.50
Common Rookie (101-110):		6.00
Common Rookie Fabric (111-145):		10.00
Production 400 Sets		
Pack (5):		15.00
Box (12):		130.00
1	Aaron Brooks	1.00
2	Ahman Green	.75
3	Akili Smith	.25
4	Amani Toomer	.25
5	Antonio Freeman	.50
6	Barry Sanders	3.00
7	Brad Johnson	.50
8	Brett Favre	3.00
9	Brian Griese	1.00
10	Brian Urlacher	1.50
11	Bruce Smith	.50
12	Cade McNown	.25
13	Chad Pennington	2.00
14	Charlie Batch	.50
15	Charlie Garner	.50
16	Corey Dillon	.60
17	Cris Carter	.60
18	Curtis Martin	.60
19	Dan Marino	4.00
20	Darrell Jackson	.25
21	Daunte Culpepper	1.50
22	David Boston	.75
23	Derrick Alexander	.50
24	Donovan McNabb	1.50
25	Dorsey Levens	.50
26	Doug Flutie	1.00
27	Drew Bledsoe	1.00
28	Ed McCaffery	.50
29	Eddie George	1.00
30	Edgerrin James	2.00
31	Elvis Grbac	.50
32	Emmitt Smith	2.00
33	Eric Moulds	.60
34	Frank Wycheck	.25
35	Fred Taylor	1.00
36	Ike Hilliard	.50
37	Isaac Bruce	.75
38	Jacquez Green	.25
39	Jake Plummer	.50
40	Jamal Anderson	.50
41	Jamal Lewis	1.50
42	James Stewart	.25
43	Jay Fiedler	.60
44	Jeff Garcia	.75
45	Jeff George	.50
46	Jerome Bettis	.60
47	Jerry Rice	2.00
48	Jevon Kearse	.50
49	Jimmy Smith	.50
50	Joe Horn	.25
51	Joey Galloway	.50
52	John Elway	3.50
53	Junior Seau	.50
54	Keenan McCardell	.25
55	Kerry Collins	.75
56	Keyshawn Johnson	.75
57	Kurt Warner	2.50
58	Lamar Smith	.50
59	Laveranues Coles	.60
60	Marcus Robinson	.50
61	Mark Brunell	1.00
62	Marshall Faulk	1.00
63	Marvin Harrison	.75
64	Matt Hasselbeck	.50
65	Mike Alstott	.50
66	Mike Anderson	1.25
67	Muhsin Muhammad	.50
68	Peter Warrick	.60
69	Peyton Manning	3.00
70	Plaxico Burress	.60
71	Randy Moss	2.50
72	Ray Lewis	.50
73	Rich Gannon	.50
74	Ricky Watters	.50
75	Ricky Williams	1.25
76	Rob Johnson	.50
77	Rod Smith	.50
78	Ron Dayne	.50
79	Shannon Sharpe	.50
80	Shaun Alexander	1.25
81	Stephen Davis	.50
82	Steve McNair	.60
83	Steve Young	1.50
84	Sylvester Morris	.50
85	Terrell Davis	1.50
86	Terrell Owens	.75
87	Terry Glenn	.50
88	Thomas Jones	.25
89	Tiki Barber	.50
90	Tim Brown	.60
91	Tim Couch	1.00
92	Tony Gonzalez	.50
93	Torry Holt	.75

94 Travis Taylor .50
95 Troy Aikman 1.50
96 Tyrone Wheatley .25
97 Vinny Testaverde .50
98 Warren Sapp .50
99 Warrick Dunn .60
100 Wayne Chrebet .50
101 Chris Taylor 6.00
102 Ken-Yon Rambo 8.00
103 Correll Buckhalter 15.00
104 A.J. Feeley 10.00
105 Josh Booty 8.00
106 LaMont Jordan 8.00
107 Alge Crumpler 6.00
108 Jamal Reynolds 6.00
109 Nate Clements 6.00
110 Will Allen 6.00
111 Santana Moss 30.00
112 Chad Johnson 30.00
113 Chris Chambers 30.00
114 David Terrell 15.00
115 Freddie Mitchell 15.00
116 Koren Robinson 15.00
117 Quincy Morgan 20.00
118 Reggie Wayne 30.00
119 Robert Ferguson 15.00
120 Rod Gardner 30.00
121 Marvin "Snoop" Minnis 15.00
122 Josh Heupel 15.00
123 Anthony Thomas 20.00
124 Deuce McCallister 30.00
125 James Jackson 15.00
126 Travis Minor 15.00
127 Kevan Barlow 25.00
128 LaDainian Tomlinson 60.00
129 Todd Heap 12.00
130 Michael Bennett 40.00
131 Rudi Johnson 25.00
132 Travis Henry 25.00
133 Michael Vick 125.00
134 Drew Brees 30.00
135 Chris Weinke 15.00
136 Quincy Carter 20.00
137 Mike McMahon 15.00
138 Jesse Palmer 15.00
139 Marques Tuiasosopo 15.00
140 Dan Morgan 10.00
141 Gerard Warren 10.00
142 Leonard Davis 10.00
143 Andre Carter 10.00
144 Justin Smith 10.00
145 Sage Rosenfels 20.00

2001 Leaf Certified Materials Fabric of the Game

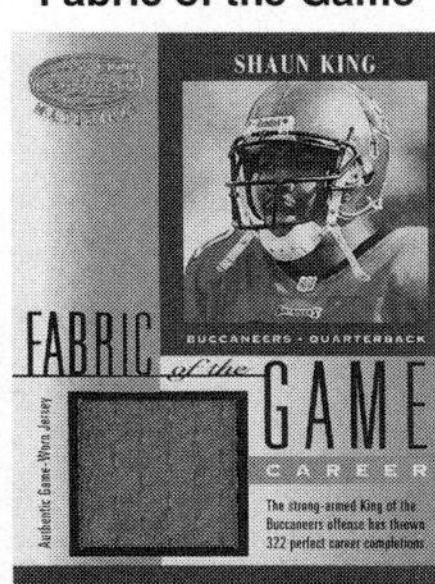

NM/M
Common Player: 15.00
1 Art Monk 30.00
2 Barry Sanders 60.00
3 Bart Starr 100.00
4 Bob Griese 60.00
5 Dan Fouts 25.00
6 Dan Fouts 25.00
7 Dan Marino 100.00
8 Dan Marino 100.00
9 Deacon Jones 20.00
10 Don Maynard 25.00
11 Earl Campbell 25.00
12 Eric Dickerson 25.00
13 Fran Tarkenton 35.00
14 Frank Gifford 45.00
15 Gale Sayers 50.00
16 George Blanda 25.00
17 Jim Brown 50.00
18 Joe Montana 125.00
19 Joe Montana 125.00
20 Joe Namath 100.00
21 John Elway 75.00
22 John Elway 75.00
23 Johnny Unitas 125.00
24 Larry Csonka 50.00
25 Lawrence Taylor 35.00
27 Marcus Allen 25.00
28 Marcus Allen 25.00
29 Ozzie Newsome 15.00
30 Raymond Berry 25.00
31 Roger Staubach 50.00
32 Sonny Jurgensen 40.00
33 Steve Largent 25.00
34 Steve Young 45.00
35 Steve Young 45.00
36 Terry Bradshaw 60.00
37 Terry Bradshaw 50.00
38 Tony Dorsett 40.00
39 Walter Payton 150.00
40 Walter Payton 150.00
41 Brett Favre 100.00
42 Brett Favre 100.00
43 Brian Griese 25.00
44 Charley Taylor 25.00
45 Daunte Culpepper 35.00
46 Daunte Culpepper 35.00
47 Donovan McNabb 35.00
48 Donovan McNabb 35.00
49 Drew Bledsoe 35.00
50 Eddie George 75.00
51 Edgerrin James 35.00
52 Edgerrin James 35.00
53 Emmitt Smith 50.00
54 Emmitt Smith 50.00
55 Jamal Lewis 15.00
56 Jerry Rice 40.00
57 Jerry Rice 40.00
58 Kurt Warner 35.00
59 Kurt Warner 35.00
60 Marshall Faulk 35.00
61 Marshall Faulk 35.00
62 Mike Anderson 25.00
63 Peyton Manning 40.00
64 Peyton Manning 40.00
65 Randy Moss 40.00
66 Randy Moss 40.00
67 Ricky Williams 35.00
68 Terrell Davis 35.00
69 Troy Aikman 45.00
70 Warren Moon 15.00
71 Antonio Freeman 15.00
72 Antonio Freeman 15.00
73 Bernie Kosar 15.00
74 Boomer Esiason 15.00
75 Cade McNown 15.00
76 Charlie Batch 15.00
77 Corey Dillon 15.00
78 Cris Carter 15.00
79 Curtis Martin 25.00
80 Deion Sanders 25.00
81 Duce Staley 15.00
82 Ed McCaffrey 15.00
83 Eric Moulds 15.00
84 Fred Taylor 15.00
85 Isaac Bruce 15.00
86 Isaac Bruce 20.00
87 Jake Plummer 15.00
88 Jamal Anderson 15.00
89 Jerome Bettis 20.00
90 Jerome Bettis 15.00
91 Jevon Kearse 15.00
92 Jim Kelly 15.00
93 Keyshawn Johnson 20.00
94 Mark Brunell 15.00
95 Mark Brunell 15.00
96 Marvin Harrison 25.00
97 Michael Irvin 30.00
98 Mike Alstott 15.00
99 Olandis Gary 15.00
100 Peter Warrick 15.00
101 Ron Dayne 15.00
102 Shaun Alexander 25.00
103 Stephen Davis 15.00
104 Steve McNair 35.00
105 Steve McNair 35.00
106 Terrell Owens 25.00
107 Tim Brown 35.00
108 Tim Couch 35.00
109 Torry Holt 15.00
110 Warrick Dunn 15.00
111 Akili Smith 15.00
112 Amani Toomer 15.00
113 Az-Zahir Hakim 15.00
114 Champ Bailey 15.00
115 Charles Woodson 15.00
116 Chris Redman 15.00
117 Courtney Brown 15.00
118 Darrell Green 15.00
119 Dorsey Levens 15.00
120 Frank Sanders 15.00
121 Herman Moore 15.00
122 J.J. Stokes 15.00
123 James Allen 15.00
124 Jason Sehorn 15.00
125 Jay Fiedler 15.00
126 Jimmy Smith 15.00
127 Johnnie Morton 15.00
128 Junior Seau 35.00
129 Keenan McCardell 15.00
130 Kevin Johnson 15.00
131 Kordell Stewart 15.00
132 Lamar Smith 15.00
133 Laveranues Coles 25.00
134 Michael Strahan 15.00
135 Rich Gannon 15.00
136 Ricky Watters 15.00
137 Rob Johnson 15.00
138 Rod Smith 25.00
139 Sebastian Janikowski 15.00
140 Shaun King 15.00
141 Terry Glenn 15.00
142 Thurman Thomas 15.00
143 Tony Gonzalez 15.00
144 Travis Prentice 15.00
145 Tyrone Wheatley 15.00
146 Vinny Testaverde 15.00
147 Warren Sapp 15.00
148 Wayne Chrebet 15.00
149 Wesley Walls 15.00
150 JaJuan Dawson 15.00

2001 Leaf Certified Materials Mirror Gold

Veterans: 15X-30X
Rookies: 3X
Production 25 Sets

2001 Leaf Certified Materials Mirror Red

Veterans: 5X-10X
Rookies: 1.5X
1-110 Production 75 Sets
111-145 Production 150 Sets
111-145 Are Autos
Inserted 1:4

2001 Leaf Rookies & Stars

NM/M
Complete Set (100): 25.00
Common Player: .15
Mirror Stars: .30
Common Rookie (101-200): 2.00
Inserted 1:4
Common Rookie (201-300): 4.00

NM/M
Inserted 1:24
Pack (5): 3.00
Box (24): 55.00
1 Aaron Brooks .60
2 Ahman Green .50
3 Antonio Freeman .40
4 Brad Johnson .30
5 Brett Favre 2.00
6 Brian Griese .60
7 Brian Urlacher 1.00
8 Bruce Smith .30
9 Cade McNown .15
10 Chad Pennington .40
11 Champ Bailey .30
12 Charles Woodson .30
13 Charlie Batch .30
14 Charlie Garner .30
15 Corey Dillon .50
16 Cris Carter .50
17 Curtis Martin .40
18 Dan Marino 3.00
19 Daunte Culpepper 1.00
20 David Boston .60
21 Deion Sanders .40
22 Donovan McNabb 1.00
23 Doug Flutie .60
24 Drew Bledsoe .60
25 Duce Staley .30
26 Ed McCaffrey .30
27 Eddie George .60
28 Edgerrin James 1.25
29 Elvis Grbac .30
30 Emmitt Smith 1.25
31 Eric Moulds .50
32 Fred Taylor .50
33 Germane Crowell .30
34 Ike Hilliard .15
35 Isaac Bruce .50
36 Jake Plummer .40
37 Jamal Anderson .40
38 Jamal Lewis 1.00
39 James Allen .15
40 James Stewart .30
41 Jay Fiedler .30
42 Jeff Garcia .50
43 Jeff George .30
44 Jeff Lewis .30
45 Jerome Bettis .50
46 Jerry Rice 1.25
47 Jevon Kearse .30
48 Jimmy Smith .30
49 Joey Galloway .40
50 John Elway 2.50
51 Junior Seau .30
52 Keenan McCardell .30
53 Kerry Collins .40
54 Kevin Johnson .30
55 Keyshawn Johnson .50
56 Kordell Stewart .50
57 Kurt Warner 1.50
58 Lamar Smith .30
59 Marcus Robinson .30
60 Mark Brunell .60
61 Marshall Faulk .60
62 Marvin Harrison .50
63 Matt Hasselbeck .15
64 Mike Alstott .30
65 Mike Anderson .75
66 Muhsin Muhammad .30
67 Peter Warrick .40
68 Peyton Manning 1.50
69 Priest Holmes .50
70 Randy Moss 1.50
71 Ray Lewis .40
72 Rich Gannon .40
73 Ricky Watters .40
74 Ricky Williams .75
75 Rob Johnson .30
76 Rod Smith .40
77 Ron Dayne .30
78 Shannon Sharpe .30
79 Shaun Alexander .75
80 Stephen Davis .30
81 Steve McNair .60
82 Steve Young 1.00
83 Sylvester Morris .30
84 Terrell Davis 1.00
85 Terrell Owens .50
86 Thomas Jones .30
87 Tim Brown .40
88 Tim Couch .60
89 Tony Banks .30
90 Tony Gonzalez .30
91 Torry Holt .40
92 Travis Taylor .30
93 Trent Green .30
94 Troy Aikman 1.00
95 Tyrone Wheatley .30
96 Vinny Testaverde .30
97 Warren Sapp .30
98 Warrick Dunn .40
99 Wayne Chrebet .30
100 Zach Thomas .15
101 *A.J. Feeley* 6.00
102 *Josh Booty* 4.00
103 *Roderick Robinson* 2.00
104 *Renaldo Hill* 2.00
105 *Harold Blackmon* 2.00
106 *Rudi Johnson* 8.00
107 *Curtis Fuller* 2.00
108 *Dan Alexander* 4.00
109 *Anthony Thomas* 8.00
110 *Travis Minor* 4.00
111 *Heath Evans* 2.00
112 *Joe Walker* 2.00
113 *Moran Norris* 2.00
114 *Quincy Carter* 6.00
115 *Michael Vick* 20.00
116 *Vinny Sutherland* 4.00
117 *Scotty Anderson* 2.00
118 *Eddie Berlin* 2.00
119 *Jonathan Carter* 2.00
120 *Monty Beisel* 2.00
121 *T.J. Houshmandzadeh* 2.00
122 *Rodney Bailey* 2.00
123 *Reggie Germany* 4.00
124 *Ellis Wyms* 2.00
125 *Koren Robinson* 6.00
126 *Antonio Pierce* 2.00
127 *Arnold Jackson* 2.00
128 *Andre Rone* 2.00
129 *Richard Newsome* 2.00
130 *Ifeanyi Ohalete* 2.00
131 *Dan O'Leary* 2.00
132 *Shad Meier* 2.00
133 *Jay Feeley* 2.00
134 *Brandon Manumaleuna* 2.00
135 *Riall Johnson* 2.00
136 *Marvin "Snoop" Minnis* 4.00
137 *Jermaine Hampton* 2.00
138 *Johnny Huggins* 2.00
139 *Marcellus Rivers* 2.00
140 *Andre Carter* 2.00
141 *Michael Stone* 2.00
142 *Tony Dixon* 2.00
143 *Bhawoh Jue* 2.00
144 *Will Peterson* 2.00
145 *Anthony Henry* 6.00
146 *Marques Tuiasosopo* 4.00
147 *Reggie Swinton* 4.00
148 *Robert Carswell* 2.00
149 *Freddie Mitchell* 4.00
150 *Idrees Bashir* 2.00
151 *James Boyd* 2.00
152 *Chris Chambers* 8.00
153 *Aaron Schobel* 2.00
154 *Dominic Rajola* 2.00
155 *Derrick Burgess* 2.00
156 *DeLawrence Grant* 2.00
157 *Karon Riley* 2.00
158 *Cedric Scott* 2.00
159 *David Warren* 2.00
160 *Eric Johnson* 5.00
161 *Tevita Ofahengaue* 2.00
162 *Chris Cooper* 2.00
163 *Fred Wakefield* 2.00
164 *Kenny Smith* 2.00
165 *Marcus Bell* 2.00
166 *Mario Fatafehi* 2.00
167 *Anthony Herron* 2.00
168 *Joe Tafoya* 2.00
169 *Morlon Greenwood* 2.00
170 *Orlando Huff* 2.00
171 *Carlos Polk* 2.00
172 *Edgerton Hartwell* 2.00
173 *Zeke Moreno* 2.00
174 *Alex Lincoln* 2.00
175 *Quinton Caver* 2.00
176 *Matt Stewart* 2.00
177 *Markus Steele* 2.00
178 *Dwight Smith* 2.00
179 *Reggie Wayne* 6.00
180 *Jerametrius Butler* 2.00
181 *Jason Doering* 2.00
182 *John Howell* 2.00
183 *Alvin Porter* 2.00
184 *Eric Downing* 2.00
185 *John Nix* 2.00
186 *Tim Baker* 2.00
187 *Robert Garza* 2.00
188 *Randy Chevrier* 2.00
189 *Drew Brees* 8.00
190 *Shawn Worthen* 2.00
191 *Drew Bennett* 5.00
192 *Marlon McCree* 2.00
193 *David Terrell* 5.00
194 *Jeff Backus* 2.00
195 *Otis Leverette* 2.00
196 *Jason Glenn* 2.00
197 *Rashad Holman* 2.00
198 *T.J. Turner* 2.00
199 *Lynn Scott* 2.00
200 *Bill Gramatica* 4.00
201 *Michael Vick* 45.00
202 *Drew Brees* 15.00
203 *Quincy Carter* 8.00
204 *Jesse Palmer* 10.00
205 *Mike McMahon* 8.00
206 *Dave Dickerson* 8.00
207 *Jameel Cook* 6.00
208 *Marques Tuiasosopo* 8.00
209 *Chris Weinke* 8.00
210 *Sage Rosenfels* 8.00
211 *Josh Heupel* 8.00
212 *LaDainian Tomlinson* 35.00
213 *Michael Bennett* 20.00
214 *Anthony Thomas* 12.00
215 *Travis Henry* 12.00
216 *James Jackson* 8.00
217 *Correll Buckhalter* 12.00
218 *Derrick Blaylock* 6.00
219 *Dadrian Brown* 6.00
220 *LaVar Woods* 4.00
221 *Deuce McAllister* 15.00
222 *LaMont Jordan* 10.00
223 *Kevan Barlow* 12.00
224 *Travis Minor* 10.00
225 *David Terrell* 10.00
226 *Koren Robinson* 15.00
227 *Rod Gardner* 15.00
228 *Santana Moss* 15.00
229 *Freddie Mitchell* 8.00
230 *Reggie Wayne* 15.00
231 *Quincy Morgan* 10.00
232 *Chris Chambers* 15.00
233 *Steve Smith* 8.00
234 *Marvin "Snoop" Minnis* 8.00
235 *Justin McCareins* 10.00
236 *Onome Ojo* 6.00
237 *Darnerian McCants* 6.00
238 *Bobby Newcombe* 10.00
239 *Cedrick Wilson* 6.00
240 *Kevin Kasper* 8.00
241 *Chris Taylor* 6.00
242 *Ken-Yon Rambo* 6.00
243 *Richmond Flowers* 6.00
244 *Andre King* 6.00
245 *Eddie "Boo" Williams* 6.00
246 *Adrian Wilson* 4.00
247 *Cory Bird* 4.00
248 *Alex Bannister* 6.00
249 *Elvis Joseph* 6.00
250 *Chad Johnson* 20.00
251 *Robert Ferguson* 10.00
252 *David Martin* 8.00
253 *Quentin McCord* 6.00
254 *Todd Heap* 6.00
255 *Alge Crumpler* 6.00
256 *Nate Clements* 6.00
257 *Will Allen* 6.00
258 *Willie Middlebrooks* 6.00
259 *Fred Smoot* 6.00
260 *Andre Dyson* 6.00
261 *Gary Baxter* 4.00
262 *Jamar Fletcher* 6.00
263 *Ken Lucas* 4.00
264 *Tay Cody* 4.00
265 *Eric Kelly* 4.00
266 *Adam Archuleta* 8.00
267 *Derrick Gibson* 6.00
268 *Jarrod Cooper* 4.00
269 *Hakim Akbar* 4.00
270 *Tony Driver* 4.00
271 *Justin Smith* 6.00
272 *Andre Carter* 6.00
273 *Jamal Reynolds* 4.00
274 *Gerard Warren* 8.00
275 *Richard Seymour* 8.00
276 *Damione Lewis* 6.00
277 *Casey Hampton* 4.00
278 *Marcus Stroud* 4.00
279 *Benjamin Gay* 8.00
280 *Shaun Rogers* 4.00
281 *Dan Morgan* 4.00
282 *Kendrell Bell* 20.00
283 *Tommy Polley* 10.00
284 *Jamie Winborn* 4.00
285 *Sedrick Hodge* 4.00
286 *Torrance Marshall* 4.00
287 *Eric Westmoreland* 4.00
288 *Brian Allen* 4.00
289 *Brandon Spoon* 4.00
290 *Henry Burris* 4.00
291 *Leonard Davis* 4.00
292 *Kenyatta Walker* 4.00
293 *Cedric James* 6.00
294 *Sean Brewer* 4.00
295 *Jason Brookins* 8.00
296 *Kyle Vanden Bosch* 8.00
297 *Nick Goings* 6.00
298 *Kris Jenkins* 4.00
299 *Dominic Rhodes* 8.00
300 *Leonard Myers* 4.00

2001 Leaf Rookies & Stars Crosstraining

NM/M
Common Player: 20.00
Production 100 Sets
1 Terrell Davis, Michael Bennett 30.00
2 Troy Aikman, Quincy Carter 50.00
3 Donovan McNabb, Michael Vick 100.00
4 Randy Moss, Rod Gardner 50.00
5 Corey Dillon, Kevan Barlow 20.00
6 Warren Sapp, Gerard Warren 20.00
7 Marshall Faulk, Deuce McAllister 40.00
8 Edgerrin James, James Jackson 30.00
9 Cris Carter, Reggie Wayne 30.00
10 Barry Sanders, LaDainian Tomlinson 100.00
11 Tim Couch, Drew Brees 50.00
12 Peter Warrick, Marvin "Snoop" Minnis 25.00
13 Torry Holt, Koren Robinson 25.00
14 Isaac Bruce, Santana Moss 25.00
15 Jerry Rice, David Terrell 50.00
16 Tim Brown, Chris Chambers 30.00
17 Emmitt Smith, Travis Henry 60.00
18 Eddie George, Anthony Thomas 50.00
19 Drew Bledsoe, Chris Weinke 25.00
20 Dan Marino, Josh Heupel 100.00
21 Jerome Bettis, Rudi Johnson 20.00
22 Keyshawn Johnson, Chad Johnson 20.00
23 Mark Brunell, Marques Tuiasosopo 25.00
24 Jevon Kearse, Andre Carter 20.00
25 Steve Young, Mike McMahon 50.00

A player's name in *italic* type indicates a rookie card.

2001 Leaf Rookies & Stars Dress For Success

NM/M
Common Player: 12.00
Inserted 1:96
Prime Cuts: 1X-2X
Production 50 Sets
1 Tim Brown 25.00
2 Lamar Smith 12.00
3 Boomer Esiason 12.00
4 Dan Marino 100.00
5 Lawrence Taylor 25.00
6 Marshall Faulk 40.00
7 Isaac Bruce 25.00
8 Stephen Davis 20.00
9 Marvin Harrison 20.00
10 Michael Strahan 12.00
11 Jerome Bettis 25.00
12 Cris Carter 25.00
13 Emmitt Smith 75.00
14 Jevon Kearse 12.00
15 Eric Moulds 20.00
16 Curtis Martin 25.00
17 Randy Moss 75.00
18 Peyton Manning 75.00
19 John Elway 100.00
20 Warrick Dunn 25.00
21 Steve Young 50.00
22 Donovan McNabb 40.00
23 Keyshawn Johnson 30.00
24 Ron Dayne 20.00
25 Rich Gannon 12.00

2001 Leaf Rookies & Stars Dress for Success Auto.

Production 25 Sets
Too uncommon to price
1 Tim Brown
3 Boomer Esiason
4 Dan Marino
6 Marshall Faulk
7 Isaac Bruce
8 Stephen Davis
9 Marvin Harrison
12 Cris Carter
13 Emmitt Smith
15 Eric Moulds
19 John Elway
21 Steve Young
24 Ron Dayne

2001 Leaf Rookies & Stars Freshman Orientation

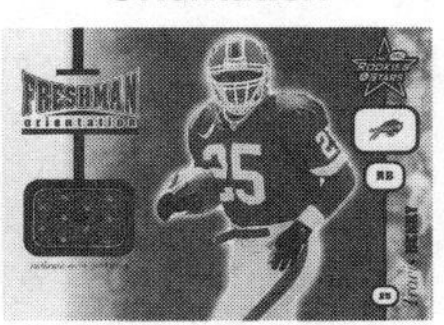

NM/M
Common Player: 12.00
Inserted 1:96
Class Officers: 2X-4X
Production 50 Sets
1 Michael Vick 75.00
2 Drew Brees 40.00
3 Quincy Carter 25.00
4 Chris Weinke 20.00
5 Santana Moss 20.00
6 Mike McMahon 20.00
7 Jesse Palmer 15.00
8 Deuce McAllister 20.00
9 LaDainian Tomlinson 40.00
10 Anthony Thomas 25.00
11 Michael Bennett 25.00
12 Travis Henry 15.00
13 James Jackson 15.00
14 Kevan Barlow 15.00
15 Rudi Johnson 12.00
16 Travis Minor 15.00
17 David Terrell 25.00
18 Rod Gardner 20.00
19 Quincy Morgan 12.00
20 Freddie Mitchell 20.00
21 Reggie Wayne 20.00
22 Koren Robinson 20.00
23 Chris Chambers 25.00
24 Marvin "Snoop" Minnis 15.00
25 Chad Johnson 15.00

2001 Leaf Rookies & Stars Freshman Orientation Auto.

Production 25 Sets
Too uncommon to price
4 Chris Weinke
9 LaDainian Tomlinson
19 Quincy Morgan
24 Marvin "Snoop" Minnis
25 Chad Johnson

2001 Leaf Rookies & Stars Player's Collection

NM/M
Common Player: 25.00
Production 100 Sets
Combo Production 25 Sets
1 Eddie George gloves 25.00
2 Eddie George jersey 25.00
3 Eddie George helmet 25.00
4 Eddie George shoes 25.00
5 Eddie George combo

6 Troy Aikman ball 30.00
7 Troy Aikman jersey 50.00
8 Troy Aikman helmet 50.00
9 Troy Aikman shoes 50.00
10 Troy Aikman combo
11 Kurt Warner pants 50.00
12 Kurt Warner jersey 50.00
13 Kurt Warner helmet 50.00
14 Kurt Warner shoes 50.00
15 Kurt Warner combo

2001 Leaf Rookies & Stars Rookie Autographs

NM/M
Common Player: 10.00
Production 230 Sets
106 Rudi Johnson 15.00
111 Heath Evans 10.00
113 Moran Norris 10.00
118 Eddie Berlin 10.00
119 Jonathan Carter 10.00
121 T.J. Houshmandzadeh 10.00
123 Reggie Germany 12.00
201 Michael Vick 225.00
202 Drew Brees 80.00
204 Jesse Palmer 20.00
205 Mike McMahon 40.00
206 Dave Dickenson 20.00
209 Chris Weinke 40.00
212 LaDainian Tomlinson 80.00
213 Michael Bennett 40.00
214 Anthony Thomas 60.00
215 Travis Henry 20.00
216 James Jackson 20.00
217 Correll Buckhalter 25.00
218 Derrick Blaylock 12.00
219 Dadrian Brown 10.00
221 Deuce McAllister 40.00
222 LaMont Jordan 15.00
223 Kevan Barlow 15.00
224 Travis Minor 20.00
225 David Terrell 50.00
226 Koren Robinson 30.00
228 Santana Moss 30.00
229 Freddie Mitchell 30.00
231 Quincy Morgan 20.00
233 Steve Smith 15.00
234 Marvin "Snoop" Minnis 25.00
235 Justin McCareins 10.00
236 Onome Ojo 10.00
239 Cedrick Wilson 10.00
240 Kevin Kasper 15.00
242 Ken-Yon Rambo 20.00
248 Alex Bannister 15.00
250 Chad Johnson 20.00
251 Robert Ferguson 20.00
254 Todd Heap 15.00
255 Alge Crumpler 15.00
256 Nate Clements 12.00
257 Will Allen 12.00
271 Justin Smith 12.00
273 Jamal Reynolds 10.00
275 Richard Seymour 12.00
276 Damione Lewis 10.00
277 Casey Hampton 10.00
280 Shaun Rogers 10.00

2001 Leaf Rookies & Stars Slideshow

NM/M
Common Player: 15.00
Production 100 Sets
View Masters: 4X-8X
Production 25 Sets
1 Barry Sanders 60.00
2 Brett Favre 75.00
3 Brian Griese 20.00
4 Cris Carter 20.00
5 Dan Marino 100.00
6 Daunte Culpepper 30.00
7 Donovan McNabb 30.00
8 Drew Bledsoe 20.00
9 Eddie George 25.00
10 Edgerrin James 40.00
11 Emmitt Smith 60.00
12 Fred Taylor 15.00
13 John Elway 100.00
14 Kurt Warner 60.00
15 Marshall Faulk 30.00
16 Peyton Manning 60.00
17 Randy Moss 60.00
18 Ricky Williams 30.00
19 Ron Dayne 15.00
20 Steve McNair 15.00
21 Steve Young 40.00
22 Terrell Davis 30.00
23 Tim Brown 25.00
24 Tim Couch 25.00
25 Troy Aikman 40.00

2001 Leaf Rookies & Stars Slideshow Auto.

Production 25 Sets
Too uncommon to price
3 Brian Griese
4 Cris Carter
18 Ricky Williams
21 Steve Young
23 Tim Brown

2001 Leaf Rookies & Stars Statistical Standouts

NM/M
Common Player: 10.00
Inserted 1:96
Supers: 1X-2X
Production 50 Sets
1 Peyton Manning 25.00
2 Jeff Garcia 15.00
3 Donovan McNabb 20.00
4 Daunte Culpepper 20.00
5 Kurt Warner 25.00
6 Vinny Testaverde 12.00
7 Mark Brunell 12.00
8 Edgerrin James 20.00
9 Eddie George 15.00
10 Mike Anderson 15.00
11 Corey Dillon 12.00
12 Fred Taylor 15.00
13 Marshall Faulk 20.00
14 Stephen Davis 10.00
15 Torry Holt 15.00
16 Rod Smith 12.00
17 Isaac Bruce 15.00
18 Terrell Owens 15.00
19 Randy Moss 30.00
20 Marvin Harrison 15.00
21 Kerry Collins 12.00
22 Junior Seau 10.00
23 Warren Sapp 10.00
24 Donnie Abraham 10.00
25 Dexter McCleon 10.00

2001 Leaf Rookies & Stars Statistical Standouts Auto.

Production 25 Sets
Too uncommon to price
4 Daunte Culpepper
5 Kurt Warner
6 Vinny Testaverde
7 Mark Brunell
8 Edgerrin James
10 Mike Anderson
11 Corey Dillon
13 Marshall Faulk
14 Stephen Davis
15 Torry Holt
17 Isaac Bruce
18 Terrell Owens
20 Marvin Harrison

2001 Leaf Rookies & Stars Triple Threads

NM/M
Common Player: 30.00
Production 100 Sets
1 Cris Carter, Daunte Culpepper, Randy Moss 75.00
2 Fred Taylor, Jimmy Smith, Mark Brunell 30.00
3 Edgerrin James, Marvin Harrison, Peyton Manning 100.00
4 Antonio Freeman, Brett Favre, Dorsey Levens 100.00
5 Brian Griese, Ed McCaffrey, Terrell Davis 50.00
6 Isaac Bruce, Kurt Warner, Marshall Faulk 100.00
7 Troy Aikman, Emmitt Smith, Michael Irvin 100.00
8 Keyshawn Johnson, Warren Sapp, Warrick Dunn 30.00
9 Jim Kelly, Thurman Thomas, Andre Reed 50.00
10 Eddie George, Jevon Kearse, Steve McNair 50.00

2001 Leaf Rookies & Stars View Masters Auto.

Production 5 Sets
Too uncommon to price
1 Barry Sanders
2 Brett Favre
5 Dan Marino
6 Daunte Culpepper
11 Emmitt Smith

2001 Quantum Leaf

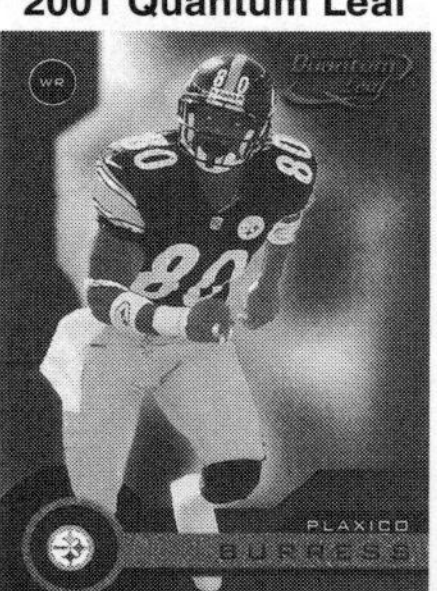

NM/M
Common Player: .25
Minor Stars: .50
Common Rookie: 2.00
Inserted 1:2
Common Rookie SP: 70.00
Inserted 1:720
Pack (5): 4.00
Wax Box (24): 65.00
1 David Boston .75
2 Frank Sanders .50
3 Jake Plummer .75
4 Michael Pittman .25
5 Rob Moore .25
6 Thomas Jones .75
7 Chris Chandler .50
8 Doug Johnson .50
9 Jamal Anderson .50
10 Tim Dwight .50
11 Chris Redman .75
12 Jamal Lewis 1.50
13 Qadry Ismail .25
14 Ray Lewis .50
15 Rod Woodson .25
16 Shannon Sharpe .50
17 Travis Taylor .75
18 Trent Dilfer .50
19 Doug Flutie 1.00
20 Eric Moulds .75
21 Jay Riemersma .25
22 Peerless Price .50
23 Rob Johnson .50
24 Sammy Morris .50
25 Shawn Bryson .25
26 Donald Hayes .25
27 Muhsin Muhammad .50
28 Patrick Jeffers .50
29 Reggie White .50
30 Steve Beuerlein .50
31 Tim Biakabutuka .25
32 Wesley Walls .25
33 Brian Urlacher 1.00
34 Cade McNown .75
35 Dez White .25
36 James Allen .50
37 Marcus Robinson .75
38 Marty Booker .25
39 Akili Smith .75
40 Corey Dillon .75
41 Danny Farmer .50
42 Peter Warrick 1.25
43 Ron Dugans .25
44 Courtney Brown .50
45 Dennis Northcutt .50
46 JaJuan Dawson .50
47 Kevin Johnson .50
48 Tim Couch 1.00
49 Travis Prentice .75
50 Anthony Wright .50
51 Emmitt Smith 1.25
52 James McKnight .25
53 Joey Galloway .75
54 Raghib Ismail .25
55 Randall Cunningham .50
56 Troy Aikman 1.25
57 Brian Griese .75
58 Ed McCaffrey .50
59 Gus Frerotte .25
60 John Elway 1.50
61 Mike Anderson 1.50
62 Olandis Gary .75
63 Rod Smith .50
64 Terrell Davis 1.50
65 Barry Sanders 2.00
66 Charlie Batch .75
67 Germane Crowell .75
68 Herman Moore .50
69 James Stewart .50
70 Johnnie Morton .50
71 Ahman Green .50
72 Antonio Freeman .50
73 Bill Schroeder .25
74 Brett Favre 2.50
75 Dorsey Levens .50
76 Matt Hasselbeck .75
77 Edgerrin James 1.75
78 Jerome Pathon .25
79 Ken Dilger .25
80 Marvin Harrison .75
81 Peyton Manning 1.75
82 Fred Taylor 1.00
83 Hardy Nickerson .25
84 Jimmy Smith .50
85 Keenan McCardell .50
86 Mark Brunell 1.00
87 Tony Brackens .25
88 Derrick Alexander .25
89 Elvis Grbac .50
90 Sylvester Morris .75
91 Tony Gonzalez .50
92 Tony Richardson .25
93 Warren Moon .50
94 Dan Marino 1.50
95 Jay Fiedler .50
96 Lamar Smith .50
97 Oronde Gadsden .25
98 Sam Madison .25
99 Thurman Thomas .50
100 Tony Martin .25
101 Zach Thomas .25
102 Cris Carter .75
103 Daunte Culpepper 1.00
104 John Randle .25
105 Randy Moss 1.75
106 Robert Smith .50
107 Drew Bledsoe 1.00
108 J.R. Redmond .50
109 Kevin Faulk .50
110 Michael Bishop .75
111 Terry Glenn .75
112 Troy Brown .25
113 Aaron Brooks .75
114 Jake Reed .50
115 Jeff Blake .50
116 Joe Horn .50
117 La'Roi Glover .25
118 Ricky Williams 1.25
119 Willie Jackson .25
120 Amani Toomer .25
121 Ike Hilliard .25
122 Jason Sehorn .25
123 Kerry Collins .50
124 Michael Strahan .25
125 Ron Dayne 1.25
126 Ron Dixon .50
127 Tiki Barber .50
128 Chad Pennington 1.00
129 Curtis Martin .75
130 Dedric Ward .25
131 Laveranues Coles .75
132 Vinny Testaverde .50
133 Wayne Chrebet .50
134 Charles Woodson .50
135 Napoleon Kaufman .50
136 Rich Gannon .50
137 Tim Brown .50
138 Tyrone Wheatley .50
139 Charles Johnson .25
140 Donovan McNabb 1.00
141 Duce Staley .75
142 Hugh Douglas .25
143 Na Brown .25
144 Todd Pinkston .50
145 Bobby Shaw .25
146 Hines Ward .50
147 Jerome Bettis .50
148 Kordell Stewart .75
149 Levon Kirkland .25
150 Plaxico Burress 1.00
151 Richard Huntley .50
152 Troy Edwards .50
153 Jim Harbaugh .25
154 Junior Seau .50
155 Ryan Leaf .50
156 Charlie Garner .50
157 Jeff Garcia .75
158 Jerry Rice 1.25
159 Steve Young 1.00
160 Terrell Owens .75
161 Brock Huard .75
162 Darrell Jackson .50
163 Derrick Mayes .25
164 Ricky Watters .50
165 Shaun Alexander 1.00
166 Az-Zahir Hakim .50
167 Isaac Bruce .75
168 Kurt Warner 1.50
169 Marshall Faulk .75
170 Torry Holt .50
171 Trent Green .50
172 Derrick Brooks .25
173 Jacquez Green .25
174 John Lynch .25
175 Keyshawn Johnson .75
176 Mike Alstott .50
177 Reidel Anthony .25
178 Shaun King .75
179 Warren Sapp .25
180 Warrick Dunn .50
181 Carl Pickens .50
182 Derrick Mason .50
183 Eddie George .75
184 Frank Wycheck .25
185 Jevon Kearse .50
186 Neil O'Donnell .25
187 Steve McNair .75
188 Yancey Thigpen .25
189 Albert Connell .25
190 Andre Reed .25
191 Brad Johnson .50
192 Bruce Smith .25
193 Champ Bailey .50
194 Darrell Green .25
195 Deion Sanders .75
196 Irving Fryar .25
197 James Thrash .50
198 Jeff George .50
199 Michael Westbrook .50
200 Stephen Davis .50
201 *Michael Vick* 15.00
202 *Drew Brees* 8.00
203 *Chris Weinke* 3.00
204 *Sage Rosenfels* 3.00
205 *Josh Heupel* 3.00
206 *Marques Tuiasosopo* 3.00
207 *Mike McMahon SP* 50.00
208 *Deuce McAllister SP* 80.00
209 *LaMont Jordan* 3.00
210 *LaDainian Tomlinson* 12.00
211 *James Jackson* 2.00
212 *Anthony Thomas* 3.00
213 *Travis Henry* 3.00
214 *Travis Minor* 2.00
215 *Rudi Johnson* 3.00
216 *Michael Bennett* 3.00
217 *Kevan Barlow* 2.00
218 *Dan Alexander* 2.00
219 *Correll Buckhalter SP* 50.00
220 *Moran Norris* 2.00
221 *Jesse Palmer* 3.00
222 *Heath Evans* 2.00
223 *David Terrell SP* 25.00
224 *Santana Moss* 5.00
225 *Rod Gardner* 5.00
226 *Quincy Morgan SP* 50.00
227 *Freddie Mitchell* 3.00
228 *Reggie Wayne* 4.00
229 *Bobby Newcombe* 3.00
230 *Reggie Germany* 2.00
231 *Robert Ferguson* 3.00
232 *Ken-Yon Rambo* 3.00
233 *Alex Bannister* 3.00
234 *Koren Robinson* 4.00
235 *Chad Johnson* 4.00
236 *Chris Chambers* 3.00
237 *Marvin "Snoop" Minnis* 2.00
238 *Vinny Sutherland* 2.00
239 *Cedrick Wilson* 2.00
240 *T.J. Houshmandzadeh* 2.00
241 *Todd Heap* 3.00
242 *Alge Crumpler* 3.00
243 *Jabari Holloway* 3.00
244 *Tony Stewart* 2.00
245 *Jamal Reynolds* 2.00
246 *Andre Carter SP* 50.00
247 *Justin Smith SP* 40.00
248 *Richard Seymour* 2.00
249 *Marcus Stroud* 2.00
250 *Damione Lewis* 2.00
251 *Gerard Warren SP* 60.00
252 *Tommy Polley SP* 50.00
253 *Dan Morgan* 2.00
254 *Jamar Fletcher* 3.00
255 *Ken Lucas* 2.00
256 *Fred Smoot SP* 50.00
257 *Nate Clements* 3.00
258 *Will Allen* 2.00
259 *Derrick Gibson* 3.00
260 *Adam Archuleta* 3.00

2001 Quantum Leaf All-Millennium Marks

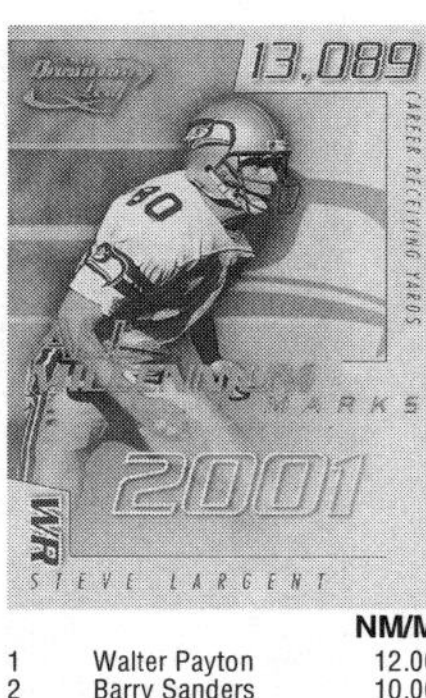

NM/M
Complete Set (30): 100.00
Common Player: 2.50
Production 1,000 Sets
Autograph Cards: 6X-12X
Production 100 Sets
1 Walter Payton 12.00
2 Barry Sanders 10.00
3 Emmitt Smith 10.00
4 Eric Dickerson 2.50
5 Ricky Watters 2.50
6 Jim Brown 10.00
7 Marcus Allen 4.00
8 Jerome Bettis 2.50
9 Thurman Thomas 2.50
10 Earl Campbell 4.00
11 Jerry Rice 8.00
12 Ozzie Newsome 2.50
13 Henry Ellard 2.50
14 Charlie Taylor 2.50
15 Steve Largent 4.00
16 Cris Carter 4.00
17 Art Monk 2.50
18 Irving Fryar 2.50
19 Michael Irvin 4.00
20 Tim Brown 4.00
21 Dan Marino 10.00
22 John Elway 10.00
23 Warren Moon 2.50
24 Fran Tarkenton 4.00
25 Dan Fouts 4.00
26 Joe Montana 12.00
27 Johnny Unitas 12.00
28 Boomer Esiason 2.50
29 Jim Kelly 5.00
30 Vinny Testaverde 2.50

2001 Quantum Leaf All-Millennium Materials

NM/M
Common Player: 25.00
Production 100 Sets
Autograph Cards: 2X-3X
Production 25 Sets
1 Walter Payton 150.00
2 Barry Sanders 100.00
3 Emmitt Smith 85.00
4 Eric Dickerson 25.00
5 Ricky Watters 25.00
6 Jim Brown 75.00
7 Marcus Allen 35.00
8 Jerome Bettis 25.00
9 Thurman Thomas 25.00
10 Earl Campbell 40.00
11 Jerry Rice 75.00
12 Ozzie Newsome 25.00
13 Henry Ellard 25.00
14 Charlie Taylor 25.00
15 Steve Largent 35.00
16 Cris Carter 35.00
17 Art Monk 25.00
18 Irving Fryar 25.00
19 Michael Irvin 35.00
20 Tim Brown 35.00
21 Dan Marino 85.00
22 John Elway 85.00
23 Warren Moon 25.00
24 Fran Tarkenton 35.00
25 Dan Fouts 35.00
26 Joe Montana 150.00
27 Johnny Unitas 100.00
28 Boomer Esiason 25.00
29 Jim Kelly 40.00
30 Vinny Testaverde 25.00

2001 Quantum Leaf All-Millennium Milestones

NM/M
Complete Set (4): 50.00
Common Player: 10.00
Production 1,000 Sets
Autograph Cards: 10X
Production 25 Sets
1 Dan Marino, John Elway 20.00
2 Jerry Rice, Cris Carter 15.00
3 Emmitt Smith, Barry Sanders, Walter Payton 20.00
5 Jerry Rice, Dan Marino, Emmitt Smith 20.00

2001 Quantum Leaf Century Season

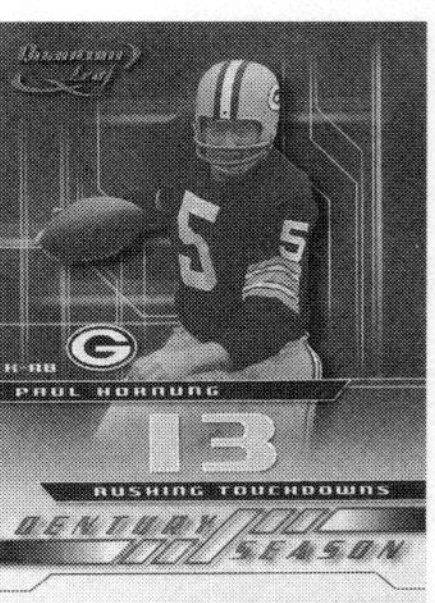

NM/M
Complete Set (65): 200.00
Common Player: 1.50
Minor Stars: 3.00
Production 1,000 Sets
Autograph Cards: 10X-20X
Production 21 Sets
1 Eric Dickerson 1.50
2 Barry Sanders 12.00
3 John Elway 10.00
4 Jim Brown 10.00
5 Sammy Baugh 1.50
6 Marcus Allen 3.00
7 Tony Gonzalez 1.50
8 Franco Harris 4.00
9 Dan Marino 10.00
10 Mike Singletary 1.50
11 Fred Biletnikoff 1.50
12 Warren Moon 1.50
13 Steve Largent 5.00
14 Fran Tarkenton 3.00
15 Lawrence Taylor 3.00
16 Roger Staubach 8.00
17 Roger Craig 1.50
18 Bart Starr 10.00
19 Gale Sayers 6.00
20 Steve Young 6.00
21 Don Maynard 1.50
22 Joe Montana 12.00
23 Tony Dorsett 4.00
24 Joe Namath 10.00
25 Johnny Unitas 10.00
26 Paul Hornung 5.00
27 Bob Griese 4.00
28 Isaac Bruce 3.00
29 Dan Fouts 3.00
30 Earl Campbell 4.00
31 Terry Bradshaw 8.00
32 Larry Csonka 3.00
33 Jim Kelly 4.00
34 Lance Alworth 1.50
35 Dick Butkus 4.00
36 Sonny Jurgensen 3.00
37 Ozzie Newsome 1.50
38 Kellen Winslow 1.50
39 Stephen Davis 3.00
40 Frank Gifford 5.00
41 Terrell Davis 7.00
42 Reggie White 3.00
43 Edgerrin James 10.00
44 Jerry Rice 8.00
45 Marshall Faulk 4.00
46 Kurt Warner 10.00
47 Cris Carter 3.00
48 Bruce Smith 1.50
49 Emmitt Smith 10.00
50 Ray Lewis 1.50
51 Jamal Lewis 8.00
52 Marvin Harrison 3.00
53 Eric Moulds 3.00
54 Eddie George 4.00
55 Ricky Williams 5.00
56 Mark Brunell 5.00
57 Brian Griese 3.00
58 Brett Favre 12.00
59 Daunte Culpepper 6.00
60 Mike Anderson 7.00
61 Donovan McNabb 5.00
62 Randall Cunningham 1.50
63 Drew Bledsoe 5.00
64 Troy Aikman 8.00
65 Randy Moss 10.00

2001 Quantum Leaf Gamers

NM/M
Common Player: 100.00
Production 25 Sets
1 Akili Smith 100.00
2 Corey Dillon 130.00
3 Donovan McNabb 175.00
4 Edgerrin James 250.00
5 Fred Taylor 150.00
6 Isaac Bruce 140.00
7 Shaun King 100.00
8 Tim Couch 150.00
9 Dan Marino, John Elway, Jim Kelly 400.00
10a Tim Couch, Daunte Culpepper, Donovan McNabb, Akili Smith, Cade McNown, Shaun King 400.00

2001 Quantum Leaf Hardwear

NM/M
Common Player: 25.00
Production 100 Sets
1 Akili Smith 35.00
2 Charlie Garner 25.00
3 Corey Dillon 35.00
4 Dan Marino 125.00
5 Donovan McNabb 70.00
6 Duce Staley 35.00
7 Edgerrin James 100.00
8 Fred Taylor 40.00
9 Isaac Bruce 40.00
10 Jamal Anderson 35.00
11 Jason Sehorn 25.00
12 Jay Fiedler 35.00
13 Jerome Bettis 35.00
14 Jerry Rice 85.00
15 John Elway 125.00
16 Junior Seau 25.00
17 Ray Lewis 35.00
18 Reggie White 35.00

19	Ricky Watters	25.00
20	Ryan Leaf	35.00
21	Shaun King	35.00
22	Steve Young	70.00
23	Terrell Davis	85.00
24	Terry Glenn	35.00
25	Tim Couch	75.00
26	Torry Holt	35.00
27	Vinny Testaverde	35.00
28	Warren Sapp	35.00
29	Wayne Chrebet	35.00
30	Zach Thomas	35.00

2001 Quantum Leaf Rookie Revolution

		NM/M
	Complete Set (20):	45.00
	Common Player:	1.50
	Minor Stars:	3.00
	Production 4,000 Sets	
	Autograph Cards:	10X-20X
1	Michael Vick	12.00
2	David Terrell	4.00
3	Deuce McAllister	6.00
4	Drew Brees	6.00
5	Santana Moss	4.00
6	Anthony Thomas	4.00
7	Chris Weinke	2.00
8	Rod Gardner	4.00
9	LaDainian Tomlinson	8.00
10	Quincy Carter	1.50
11	Koren Robinson	3.00
12	Travis Henry	3.50
13	Quincy Morgan	3.00
14	LaMont Jordan	3.50
15	Rudi Johnson	3.50
16	Reggie Wayne	4.00
17	Michael Bennett	6.00
18	Freddie Mitchell	3.50
19	Chris Chambers	3.00
20	Chad Johnson	1.50

2001 Quantum Leaf Shirt Off My Back

		NM/M
	Common Player:	30.00
	Production 100 Sets	
1	Jamal Lewis	50.00
2	Mike Anderson	50.00
3	Ron Dayne	40.00
4	Peter Warrick	40.00
5	Shaun Alexander	40.00
6	Warrick Dunn	30.00
7	Shaun King	30.00
8	Tim Couch	50.00
9	Cade McNown	35.00
10	Akili Smith	35.00
11	Rich Gannon	30.00
12	Daunte Culpepper	75.00
13	Randy Moss	100.00
14	Cris Carter	35.00
15	Robert Smith	30.00
16	Kurt Warner	75.00
17	Marshall Faulk	60.00
18	Ricky Williams	50.00
19	Terrell Owens	30.00
20	Corey Dillon	35.00
21	Fred Taylor	40.00
22	Edgerrin James	75.00
23	Curtis Martin	35.00
24	Donovan McNabb	50.00
25	Steve McNair	40.00
26	Peyton Manning	100.00
27	Eric Moulds	35.00
28	Stephen Davis	35.00
29	Brian Griese	40.00
30	Isaac Bruce	35.00

2001 Quantum Leaf Star Factor

		NM/M
	Complete Set (40):	50.00
	Common Player:	1.50
	Production 2,000 Sets	
	X-Factor Cards:	5X-10X
	Production 25 Sets	
1	Peyton Manning	6.00
2	Edgerrin James	5.00
3	Marvin Harrison	1.50
4	Curtis Martin	1.50
5	Eric Moulds	1.50
6	Dan Marino	6.00
7	Jake Plummer	1.50
8	Troy Aikman	5.00
9	Jamal Lewis	4.00
10	Eddie George	2.50
11	Steve McNair	1.50
12	Steve Young	3.00
13	Jerome Bettis	1.50
14	Tim Couch	4.00
15	Mark Brunell	3.00
16	Fred Taylor	3.00
17	Corey Dillon	1.50
18	Chad Pennington	6.00
19	Brian Griese	2.50
20	Mike Anderson	3.00
21	John Elway	5.00
22	Terrell Owens	1.50
23	Rich Gannon	1.50
24	Jerry Rice	5.00
25	Ricky Williams	4.00
26	Aaron Brooks	3.00
27	Kurt Warner	5.00
28	Marshall Faulk	3.00
29	Isaac Bruce	2.50
30	Brett Favre	6.00
31	Antonio Freeman	1.50
32	Daunte Culpepper	4.00
33	Randy Moss	5.00
34	Cris Carter	1.50
35	Barry Sanders	6.00
36	Emmitt Smith	6.00
37	Stephen Davis	1.50
38	Ron Dayne	2.00
39	Donovan McNabb	3.00
40	Peter Warrick	2.00

2001 Quantum Leaf Touchdown Club

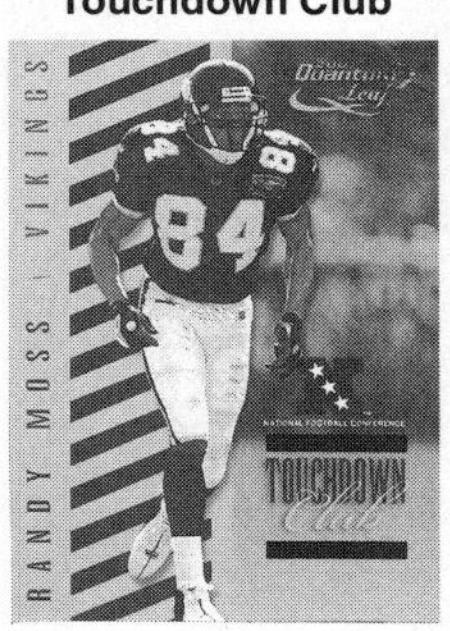

		NM/M
	Common Player:	1.50
	Production 2,000 Sets	
1	Marshall Faulk	3.00
2	Edgerrin James	4.00
3	Randy Moss	5.00
4	Eddie George	2.50
5	Terrell Owens	2.00
6	Mike Anderson	3.00
7	Stephen Davis	2.00
8	Marvin Harrison	2.00
9	Robert Smith	1.50
10	Fred Taylor	2.50
11	Daunte Culpepper	3.50
12	Curtis Martin	1.50
13	Emmitt Smith	6.00
14	Jamal Lewis	3.00
15	Ricky Williams	3.50
16	John Elway	5.00
17	Jerry Rice	5.00
18	Peyton Manning	6.00
19	Kurt Warner	4.00
20	Tim Brown	1.50
21	Brett Favre	6.00
22	Jimmy Smith	1.50
23	Cris Carter	2.00
24	Terrell Davis	3.00
25	Jeff Garcia	2.00
26	Peter Warrick	3.00
27	Ron Dayne	3.00
28	Tony Gonzalez	1.50
29	Isaac Bruce	2.00
30	Drew Bledsoe	2.50
31	Marcus Robinson	2.00
32	Ricky Watters	1.50
33	Ahman Green	1.50
34	Dan Marino	6.00
35	Donovan McNabb	2.50
36	Eric Moulds	1.50
37	Aaron Brooks	2.00
38	Steve McNair	1.50
39	Barry Sanders	6.00
40	Brian Griese	2.50

2001 Quantum Leaf X-Ponential Power

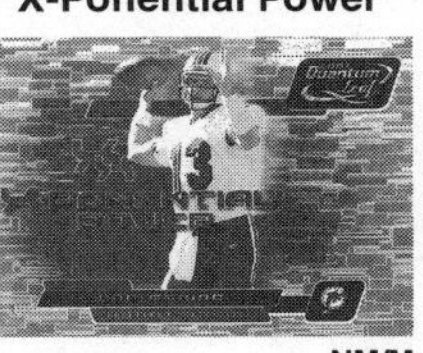

		NM/M
	Common Player:	6.00
1	Kurt Warner	6.00
2	Peyton Manning	6.00
3	Steve Young	6.00
4	Dan Marino	10.00
5	Jerry Rice	6.00
6	John Elway	10.00
7	Barry Sanders	10.00
8	Steve McNair	6.00
9	Brett Favre	10.00
10	Terrell Davis	6.00

2002 Leaf Certified

		NM/M
	Common Player:	.25
	Unlisted Stars:	.75
	Minor Stars:	.50
	Common Rookie JSY (101-132):	5.00
	Minor Rookies:	6.00
	Production 800 Sets	
	Pack (5):	7.00
	Wax Box (16):	75.00
1	David Boston	.60
2	Jake Plummer	.40
3	Michael Vick	2.50
4	Jamal Anderson	.25
5	Chris Redman	.40
6	Ray Lewis	.40
7	Eric Moulds	.40
8	Travis Henry	.40
9	Nate Clements	.25
10	Chris Weinke	.60
11	Muhsin Muhammad	.40
12	Wesley Walls	.25
13	Anthony Thomas	2.00
14	Brian Urlacher	2.00
15	Dez White	.40
16	Corey Dillon	.60
17	Peter Warrick	.40
18	Tim Couch	1.25
19	Kevin Johnson	.40
20	James Jackson	.50
21	Emmitt Smith	2.50
22	Quincy Carter	1.50
23	Brian Griese	.60
24	Ed McCaffrey	.40
25	Rod Smith	.40
26	Terrell Davis	1.25
27	Mike Anderson	1.25
28	Germane Crowell	.25
29	James Stewart	.25
30	Charlie Batch	.25
31	Antonio Freeman	.25
32	Brett Favre	3.00
33	Ahman Green	.60
34	LeRoy Butler	.25
35	Edgerrin James	2.00
36	Marvin Harrison	.60
37	Peyton Manning	2.50
38	Fred Taylor	.50
39	Jimmy Smith	.40
40	Mark Brunell	.60
41	Keenan McCardell	.25
42	Tony Gonzalez	.40
43	Priest Holmes	.60
44	Jay Fiedler	.25
45	Chris Chambers	.60
46	Zach Thomas	.40
47	Travis Minor	.25
48	Cris Carter	.40
49	Daunte Culpepper	1.50
50	Randy Moss	2.50
51	Drew Bledsoe	1.50
52	Tom Brady	2.50
53	Antowain Smith	.40
54	Troy Brown	.40
55	Aaron Brooks	1.25
56	Ricky Williams	1.50
57	Ron Dayne	.40
58	Kerry Collins	.40
59	Michael Strahan	.40
60	Amani Toomer	.25
61	Chad Pennington	.50
62	Curtis Martin	.50
63	Vinny Testaverde	.40
64	Wayne Chrebet	.25
65	Charles Woodson	.25
66	Rich Gannon	.50
67	Tim Brown	.60
68	Jerry Rice	2.50
69	Tyrone Wheatley	.25
70	Donovan McNabb	1.50
71	Duce Staley	.40
72	Todd Pinkston	.25
73	Correll Buckhalter	.25
74	Jerome Bettis	.50
75	Kordell Stewart	.50
76	Plaxico Burress	.60
77	Hines Ward	.25
78	Junior Seau	.75
79	LaDainian Tomlinson	2.00
80	Doug Flutie	.60
81	Terrell Owens	.75
82	Jeff Garcia	.75
83	Ricky Watters	.40
84	Shawn Alexander	.75
85	Koren Robinson	.25
86	Isaac Bruce	.60
87	Kurt Warner	2.50
88	Marshall Faulk	1.50
89	Torry Holt	.40
90	Keyshawn Johnson	.40
91	Mike Alstott	.40
92	Warren Sapp	.40
93	Brad Johnson	.40
94	Eddie George	.75
95	Jevon Kearse	.40
96	Steve McNair	.75
97	Derrick Mason	.25
98	Frank Wycheck	.25
99	Champ Bailey	.25
100	Stephen Davis	.75
101	*Ladell Betts*	8.00
102	*Antonio Bryant*	12.00
103	*Donald Reche Caldwell*	6.00
104	*David Carr*	30.00
105	*Tim Carter*	6.00
106	*Eric Crouch*	10.00
107	*Rohan Davey*	8.00
108	*Andre Davis*	12.00
109	*T.J. Duckett*	12.00
110	*DeShaun Foster*	8.00
111	*Jabar Gaffney*	10.00
112	*Daniel Graham*	8.00
113	*William Green*	10.00
114	*Joey Harrington*	25.00
115	*David Garrard*	8.00
116	*Ron Johnson*	5.00
117	*Ashley Lelie*	20.00
118	*Josh McCown*	10.00
119	*Maurice Morris*	6.00
120	*Julius Peppers*	15.00
121	*Clinton Portis*	30.00
122	*Patrick Ramsey*	12.00
123	*Antwann Randle El*	15.00
124	*Josh Reed*	10.00
125	*Cliff Russell*	5.00
126	*Jeremy Shockey*	25.00
127	*Donte Stallworth*	12.00
128	*Travis Stephens*	5.00
129	*Javon Walker*	15.00
130	*Marquise Walker*	5.00
131	*Roy Williams*	15.00
132	*Mike Williams*	5.00

2002 Leaf Certified Mirror Red

Red Stars:	10X-20X
1-100 Red Production 100 Sets	
Red Rookies:	1X-2X
101-132 Red Production 250 Sets	
Blue Stars:	20X-40X
1-100 Blue Production 50 Sets	
Blue Rookies:	2X-4X
101-132 Blue Production 100 Sets	
Gold Stars:	30X-60X
Gold Rookies:	3X-6X
Gold Production 25 Sets	

2002 Leaf Certified Mirror Signatures

		NM/M
	Mirror Red Production 50 Sets	
	Mirror Blue versions:	1X to2X
	Mirror Blue Production 25 Sets	
	Mirror Gold versions:	2X to4X
	Mirror Gold Production 10 Sets	
1	Joe Montana	200.00
2	Joe Namath	150.00
3	Ronnie Lott	40.00
4	Thurman Thomas	25.00
5	John Riggins	80.00
6	Barry Sanders	100.00
7	Phil Simms	30.00
8	Steve Young	40.00
9	Troy Aikman	80.00
10	Deuce McAllister	40.00
11	Justin Smith	15.00
12	Eric Moulds	20.00
13	Chris Weinke	15.00
14	Aaron Brooks	25.00
15	Kurt Warner	60.00
16	Drew Brees	30.00
17	Edgerrin James	50.00
18	Correll Buckhalter	12.00
19	Jimmy Smith	12.00
20	Elvis Grbac	12.00
21	Tim Brown	30.00
22	Stephen Davis	20.00
23	Dan Morgan	12.00
24	Robert Ferguson	20.00
25	Peter Warrick	30.00
26	Kerry Collins	25.00
27	Isaac Bruce	40.00
28	David Terrell	15.00
29	Jamal Lewis	30.00
30	Jeff Blake	15.00
31	Santana Moss	20.00
32	Mark Brunell	20.00
33	Gerard Warren	12.00
34	Marcus Robinson	12.00
35	Randall Cunningham	15.00
36	Quincy Carter	30.00
37	Marshall Faulk	60.00
38	LaMont Jordan	15.00

2002 Leaf Certified Certified Future

		NM/M
	Common Player:	1.00
	Inserted 1:15	
1	David Carr	10.00
2	Joey Harrington	8.00
3	Kurt Kittner	2.50
4	Patrick Ramsey	3.00
5	William Green	4.00
6	T.J. Duckett	5.00
7	Clinton Portis	8.00
8	DeShaun Foster	3.00
9	Brian Westbrook	2.50
10	Javon Walker	4.00
11	Donte Stallworth	5.00
12	Antonio Bryant	4.00
13	Ashley Lelie	5.00
14	Jabar Gaffney	3.00
15	Donald Reche Caldwell	2.50
16	Josh Reed	3.00
17	Julius Peppers	4.00
18	Albert Haynesworth	1.50
19	Quentin Jammer	2.50
20	Roy Williams	4.00

2002 Leaf Certified Certified Skills

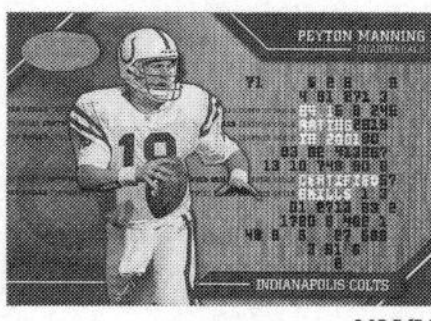

		NM/M
	Common Player:	1.00
	Inserted 1:15	
1	Donovan McNabb	1.50
2	Kordell Stewart	1.00
3	Mark Brunell	1.00
4	Peyton Manning	3.00
5	Daunte Culpepper	1.50
6	Brian Griese	1.00
7	Eddie George	1.00
8	Ahman Green	1.00
9	Shaun Alexander	1.50
10	LaDainian Tomlinson	1.50
11	Anthony Thomas	2.00
12	Priest Holmes	1.00
13	Torry Holt	1.00
14	Rod Smith	1.00
15	Terrell Owens	1.00
16	Troy Brown	1.00
17	Derrick Mason	1.00
18	Jimmy Smith	1.00
19	Jevon Kearse	1.00
20	Zach Thomas	1.00

2002 Leaf Certified Fabric of the Game

		NM/M
	Common Player:	12.00
	Production 100 Sets	
	Team Logo	1.5X
	Production 50 Sets	
1	Andre Reed	20.00
2	Art Monk	30.00
3	Barry Sanders	50.00
4	Bert Jones	12.00
5	Bob Griese	30.00
6	Craig Morton	15.00
7	Deacon Jones	12.00
8	Dick Butkus	60.00
9	Don Maynard	15.00
10	Earl Campbell	20.00
11	Eric Dickerson	20.00
12	Fran Tarkenton	25.00
13	Franco Harris	50.00
14	Gale Sayers	40.00
15	Henry Ellard	12.00
16	Herschel Walker	15.00
17	Howie Long	30.00
18	Jim McMahon	20.00
19	Joe Theismann	20.00
20	John Riggins	30.00
21	Ken Stabler	30.00
22	L.C. Greenwood	12.00
23	Marcus Allen	20.00
24	Ozzie Newsome	12.00
25	Raymond Berry	20.00
26	Roger Staubach	50.00
27	Sterling Sharpe	25.00
28	Steve Bartkowski	12.00
29	Steve Largent	25.00
30	Terry Bradshaw	50.00
31	Tony Dorsett	20.00
32	Joe Montana	100.00
33	Joe Namath	50.00
34	Ronnie Lott	20.00
35	Thurman Thomas	15.00
36	Boomer Esiason	12.00
37	Dan Marino	60.00
38	Jim Kelly	30.00
39	John Elway	60.00
40	Phil Simms	12.00
41	Steve Young	25.00
42	Troy Aikman	30.00
43	Warren Moon	20.00
44	Daunte Culpepper	15.00
45	Edgerrin James	20.00
46	Emmitt Smith	50.00
47	Kurt Warner	20.00
48	Marshall Faulk	20.00
49	Tim Brown	15.00
50	Terrell Owens	12.00

2002 Leaf Certified Fabric of the Game Autos

		NM/M
	Common Player:	30.00
1	Andre Reed/83	40.00
2	Art Monk/81	60.00
3	Barry Sanders/20	
4	Bert Jones/7	
5	Bob Griese/12	
6	Craig Morton/14	
7	Deacon Jones/75	50.00
8	Dick Butkus/51	100.00
9	Don Maynard/13	
10	Earl Campbell/34	100.00
11	Eric Dickerson/29	100.00
12	Fran Tarkenton/10	
13	Franco Harris/32	100.00
14	Gale Sayers/40	150.00
15	Henry Ellard/80	50.00
16	Herschel Walker/34	60.00
17	Howie Long/75	80.00
18	Jim McMahon/9	
19	Joe Theismann/7	
20	John Riggins/44	100.00
21	Ken Stabler/12	
22	L.C. Greenwood/68	50.00
23	Marcus Allen/32	100.00
24	Ozzie Newsome/82	30.00
25	Raymond Berry/82	40.00
26	Roger Staubach/12	
27	Sterling Sharpe/84	50.00
28	Steve Bartkowski/10	
29	Steve Largent/80	100.00
30	Terry Bradshaw/12	
31	Tony Dorsett/33	125.00
32	Joe Montana/16	
33	Joe Namath/12	
34	Ronnie Lott/42	60.00
35	Thurman Thomas/34	50.00
36	Boomer Esiason/7	
37	Dan Marino/13	
38	Jim Kelly/12	
39	John Elway/7	
40	Phil Simms/11	
41	Steve Young/8	
42	Troy Aikman/8	
43	Warren Moon/1	
44	Daunte Culpepper/11	
45	Edgerrin James/32	60.00
46	Emmitt Smith/22	
47	Kurt Warner/13	
48	Marshall Faulk/28	100.00
49	Tim Brown/81	40.00
50	Terrell Owens/81	40.00

2002 Leaf Certified Gold Team

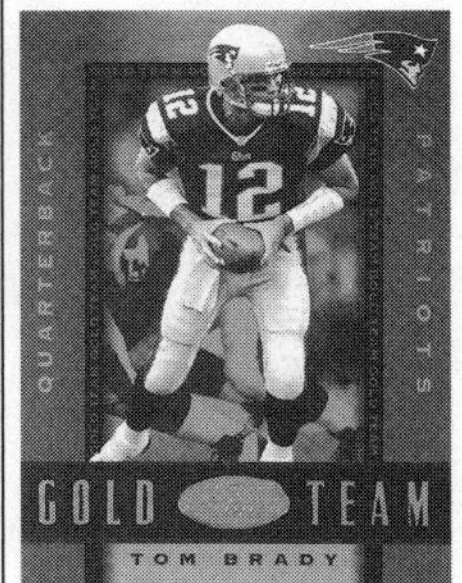

		NM/M
	Common Player:	1.00
	Inserted 1:15	
1	Kurt Warner	3.00
2	Brett Favre	5.00
3	Jeff Garcia	1.00
4	Rich Gannon	1.00
5	Steve McNair	1.00
6	Tom Brady	4.00
7	Edgerrin James	2.00
8	Curtis Martin	1.00
9	Marshall Faulk	2.00
10	Emmitt Smith	3.00
11	Ricky Williams	1.50
12	Garrison Hearst	1.00
13	David Boston	1.00
14	Jerry Rice	2.00
15	Randy Moss	3.00
16	Keyshawn Johnson	1.00
17	Tim Brown	1.00
18	Marvin Harrison	1.00
19	Michael Strahan	1.00
20	Brian Urlacher	2.00

2002 Leaf Rookies & Stars

		NM/M
	Complete Set (300):	250.00
	Common Player:	.20
	Unlisted Star:	.60
	Minor Star:	.40
	Common Rookie (101-300):	1.50
	Minor Rookie Star:	2.00
	Pack (6):	2.00
	Wax Box (24):	35.00
1	Jake Plummer	.40
2	David Boston	.60
3	Thomas Jones	.20
4	Michael Vick	2.00
5	Warrick Dunn	.40
6	Jamal Lewis	1.00
7	Chris Redman	.40
8	Ray Lewis	.40

9 Drew Bledsoe 1.25
10 Travis Henry .40
11 Eric Moulds .40
12 Steve Smith .20
13 Chris Weinke .20
14 Lamar Smith .20
15 Anthony Thomas 1.00
16 David Terrell .40
17 Brian Urlacher 1.50
18 Corey Dillon .60
19 Michael Westbrook .40
20 Peter Warrick .20
21 Tim Couch 1.00
22 James Jackson .40
23 Kevin Johnson .20
24 Quincy Carter 1.00
25 Joey Galloway .40
26 Emmitt Smith 2.00
27 Terrell Davis 1.00
28 Brian Griese .60
29 Ed McCaffrey .40
30 Rod Smith .40
31 Mike McMahon .20
32 Germane Crowell .20
33 Az-Zahir Hakim .40
34 Terry Glenn .40
35 Brett Favre 3.00
36 Ahman Green .60
37 James Allen .20
38 Corey Bradford .20
39 Peyton Manning 2.00
40 Edgerrin James 1.50
41 Marvin Harrison .60
42 Qadry Ismail .20
43 Fred Taylor .40
44 Mark Brunell .60
45 Jimmy Smith .20
46 Priest Holmes 1.00
47 Tony Gonzalez .40
48 Trent Green .40
49 Johnnie Morton .40
50 Chris Chambers .60
51 Ricky Williams 1.25
52 Zach Thomas .40
53 Randy Moss 2.00
54 Michael Bennett .60
55 Derrick Alexander .20
56 Daunte Culpepper 1.25
57 Tom Brady 2.00
58 Troy Brown .40
59 Antowain Smith .20
60 Joe Horn .40
61 Aaron Brooks 1.00
62 Deuce McAllister 1.00
63 Kerry Collins .40
64 Amani Toomer .40
65 Michael Strahan .20
66 Laveranues Coles .40
67 Vinny Testaverde .20
68 Curtis Martin .60
69 Rich Gannon .60
70 Tim Brown .60
71 Jerry Rice 2.00
72 Donovan McNabb 1.25
73 Freddie Mitchell .40
74 Duce Staley .40
75 Kordell Stewart .40
76 Jerome Bettis .40
77 Plaxico Burress .60
78 Drew Brees 1.50
79 LaDainian Tomlinson 1.50
80 Junior Seau .40
81 Jeff Garcia .60
82 Garrison Hearst .40
83 Terrell Owens .60
84 Shaun Alexander .60
85 Koren Robinson .20
86 Kurt Warner 2.00
87 Marshall Faulk 1.50
88 Isaac Bruce .40
89 Torry Holt .40
90 Rob Johnson .40
91 Brad Johnson .40
92 Keyshawn Johnson .20
93 Mike Alstott .40
94 Eddie George .60
95 Steve McNair .60
96 Derrick Mason .40
97 Jevon Kearse .40
98 Stephen Davis .40
99 Sage Rosenfels .20
100 Rod Gardner .40
101 Adrian Peterson 2.00
102 Nick Rolovich 8.00
103 Lew Thomas 2.00
104 David Carr 20.00
105 Daryl Jones 1.00
106 Brandon Doman 1.00
107 Ed Reed 1.50
108 Tellis Redmon 1.50
109 Andra Davis 1.00
110 Kendall Newson 1.00
111 Joe Burns 1.00
112 Maurice Morris 2.00
113 Craig Nall 1.50
114 Phillip Buchanon 2.00
115 Mike Echols 1.00
116 Terry Jones Jr. 2.00
117 Anthony Weaver 1.00
118 Jeb Putzier 6.00
119 Tony Fisher 4.00
120 Joey Harrington 10.00
121 Lamar Gordon 2.00
122 Tracey Wistrom 1.00
123 Ashley Lelie 10.00
124 Will Witherspoon 5.00
125 Travis Stephens 2.00
126 J.T. O'Sullivan 1.00
127 Brian Westbrook 6.00
128 James Mungro 2.00
129 Lamont Thompson 1.00
130 Jarrod Baxter 1.00
131 Andre Lott 1.00
132 Steve Bellisari 1.00
133 David Garrard 1.50
134 Michael Lewis 5.00
135 James Allen 1.00
136 Bryant McKinnie 2.00
137 Marques Anderson 2.00
138 Rohan Davey 4.00
139 Kyle Johnson 1.00
140 Dusty Bonner 1.00
141 DeShaun Foster 4.00
142 Chad Hutchinson 4.00
143 Jack Brewer 1.00
144 Eddie Freeman 1.00
145 Seth Burford 1.00
146 Roosevelt Williams 1.50
147 Jamin Elliott 1.00
148 Charles Grant 1.00
149 Jeff Kelly 1.00
150 Cliff Russell 1.50
151 Josh Scobey 1.00
152 Tank Williams 1.00
153 Larry Tripplett 1.50
154 Clinton Portis 20.00
155 Javin Hunter 1.00
156 DeVeren Johnson 3.00
157 Donald Reche Caldwell 2.00
158 Ronald Curry 2.00
159 Chris Hope 1.00
160 Damien Anderson 1.00
161 Saleem Rasheed 2.00
162 Albert Haynesworth 1.50
163 Bryan Gilmore 1.00
164 Wes Pate 1.00
165 Deion Branch 6.00
166 Ben Leber 3.00
167 Andre Davis 4.00
168 Darrell Hill 1.00
169 Rodney Wright 5.00
170 Demontray Carter 1.00
171 Zak Kustok 4.00
172 James Wofford 1.00
173 David Priestly 1.00
174 Donte Stallworth 8.00
175 Marc Boerigter 3.00
176 Freddie Milons 1.50
177 John Simon 3.00
178 Josh Norman 8.00
179 Jabar Gaffney 6.00
180 Doug Jolley 2.00
181 Preston Parsons 2.00
182 Chris Baker 2.00
183 Javon Walker 10.00
184 Justin Peelle 1.00
185 Josh Reed 4.00
186 Omar Easy 1.00
187 Jerramy Stevens 2.00
188 Shaun Hill 1.00
189 David Thornton 1.00
190 John Henderson 1.50
191 Verron Haynes 1.00
192 Dennis Johnson 1.00
193 Napoleon Harris 1.50
194 Jonathan Wells 4.00
195 Howard Green 1.00
196 Travis Fisher 1.00
197 Anton Palepoi 3.00
198 Ed Ieremia-Stansbury 1.00
199 Josh McCown 8.00
200 Alex Brown 2.00
201 Joseph Jefferson 1.00
202 Julius Peppers 6.00
203 Larry Ned 1.00
204 Rock Cartwright 5.00
205 Kalimba Edwards 1.00
206 Matt Schobel 1.00
207 Maurice Jackson 1.00
208 Kelly Campbell 2.00
209 Mel Mitchell 3.00
210 Ken Simonton 1.00
211 Brian Allen 1.00
212 Darnell Sanders 1.00
213 Jesse Chatman 1.00
214 Keyuo Craver 1.00
215 Chester Taylor 1.00
216 Kurt Kittner 4.00
217 Derek Ross 2.00
218 Charles Hill 1.00
219 Jarvis Green 1.00
220 Mike Jenkins 1.00
221 Robert Royal 1.00
222 Ladell Betts 2.00
223 Antwoine Womack 1.00
224 Raonall Smith 1.00
225 Charles Stackhouse 5.00
226 Quinn Gray 1.00
227 Lito Sheppard 1.50
228 Ryan Van Dyke 1.00
229 Will Overstreet 2.00
230 Leonard Henry 1.00
231 Dorsett Davis 4.00
232 Marquand Manuel 1.00
233 Luke Staley 2.00
234 Carlos Hall 4.00
235 Marcus Brady 1.00
236 Ryan Denney 1.00
237 Eric McCoo 1.00
238 Major Applewhite 3.00
239 Adam Tate 1.00
240 Marquise Walker 2.00
241 Little John Flowers 2.00
242 Levar Fisher 1.00
243 Ricky Williams 1.50
244 Mike Rumph 1.50
245 Delvin Joyce 5.00
246 Bryan Thomas 1.00
247 Mike Williams 2.00
248 Sam Brandon 1.00
249 Eddie Drummond 1.00
250 Najeh Davenport 2.00
251 Brian Williams 2.00
252 Scott Fujita 4.00
253 Dwight Freeney 6.00
254 Herb Haygood 1.00
255 Patrick Ramsey 10.00
256 Atnaf Harris .20
257 Jason McAddley 1.00
258 Peter Rebstock 1.00
259 Quentin Jammer 2.00
260 Luke Butkus 5.00
261 Jeremy Allen 1.00
262 Jake Schifino 1.00
263 Randy Fasani 1.50
264 Bryan Fletcher 1.00
265 Jeremy Shockey 8.00
266 Kevin Bentley 1.00
267 Jon McGraw 4.00
268 Robert Thomas 2.00
269 Coy Wire 4.00
270 Brian Poli-Dixon 1.00
271 Willie Offord 3.00
272 Rocky Calmus 2.00
273 Sheldon Brown 1.00
274 Terry Charles 1.00
275 Ron Johnson 1.50
276 Roy Williams 6.00
277 Sam Simmons 1.00
278 Andre Goodman 1.00
279 Ryan Sims 1.50
280 Antwann Randle El 6.00
281 Allan Harper 1.00
282 Tavon Mason 1.00
283 Kahlil Hill 1.00
284 Antonio Bryant 6.00
285 Akin Ayodele 1.00
286 T.J. Duckett 8.00
287 Kenyon Coleman 1.00
288 Tim Carter 1.50
289 Lamont Brightful 1.00
290 Trev Faulk 1.00
291 Randy McMichael 2.00
292 Daniel Graham 2.00
293 Wendell Bryant 1.50
294 Jamar Martin 1.00
295 Chris Luzar 2.00
296 William Green 6.00
297 Lee Mays 1.00
298 Eric Crouch 4.00
299 Steve Smith 6.00
300 Woodrow Dantzler III 2.00

2002 Leaf Rookies & Stars Longevity

Stars: 10X-20X
Rookies: 2X-4X
Production 50 Sets

2002 Leaf Rookies & Stars Rookie Autographs

NM/M
Common Player 10.00
Production 150 Sets
101 Adrian Peterson 25.00
109 Andra Davis 10.00
117 Anthony Weaver 10.00
123 Ashley Lelie 50.00
127 Brian Westbrook 25.00
131 Andre Lott 10.00
136 Bryant McKinnie 12.00
142 Chad Hutchinson 25.00
148 Charles Grant 10.00
150 Cliff Russell 12.00
154 Clinton Portis 125.00
160 Damien Anderson 10.00
165 Deion Branch 30.00
170 Demontray Carter 10.00
174 Donte Stallworth 50.00
176 Freddie Milons 12.00
179 Jabar Gaffney 20.00
183 Javon Walker 40.00
190 John Henderson 12.00
194 Jonathan Wells 15.00
199 Josh McCown 40.00
202 Julius Peppers 60.00
205 Kalimba Edwards 10.00
208 Kelly Campbell 15.00
210 Ken Simonton 10.00
214 Keyuo Craver 10.00
216 Kurt Kittner 30.00
222 Ladell Betts 25.00
227 Lito Sheppard 12.00
233 Luke Staley 12.00
240 Marquise Walker 12.00
244 Mike Rumph 12.00
247 Mike Williams 10.00
250 Najeh Davenport 15.00
255 Patrick Ramsey 50.00
259 Quentin Jammer 15.00
263 Randy Fasani 10.00
268 Robert Thomas 10.00
272 Rocky Calmus 12.00
275 Ron Johnson 12.00
276 Roy Williams 50.00
279 Ryan Sims 10.00
282 Tavon Mason 10.00
284 Antonio Bryant 30.00
286 T.J. Duckett 30.00
288 Tim Carter 12.00
290 Trev Faulk 10.00
293 Wendell Bryant 12.00
296 William Green 30.00
300 Woodrow Dantzler III 15.00

2002 Leaf Rookies & Stars Action Packed Bronze

NM/M
Common Player: 2.00
Production 1850 sets
Silver: 1X-2X
Silver Production 500 Sets
Gold: 1.5X-3X
Gold Production 150 Sets
1 Brian Urlacher 3.00
2 Randy Moss 3.00
3 T.J. Duckett 3.00
4 Peyton Manning 3.00
5 Edgerrin James 2.50
6 Donte Stallworth 3.00
7 Joey Harrington 6.00
8 Drew Brees 2.50
9 Anthony Thomas 2.50
10 William Green 3.00
11 LaDainian Tomlinson 2.50
12 Donovan McNabb 2.50
13 Patrick Ramsey 2.00
14 Shaun Alexander 2.00
15 Kurt Warner 3.00
16 Michael Vick 5.00
17 Antonio Bryant 3.00
18 Jeff Garcia 2.00
19 David Carr 6.00
20 Chris Chambers 2.00

2002 Leaf Rookies & Stars Dress For Success

NM/M
Common Player: 5.00
Production 400 sets
1 LaDainian Tomlinson 15.00
2 Quincy Carter 10.00
3 Freddie Mitchell
4 Anthony Thomas
5 Quincy Morgan 5.00
6 Chris Weinke

2002 Leaf Rookies & Stars Freshman Orientation

NM/M
Common Player: 8.00
Production 650 Sets
Auto Production 25 Sets
1 Ashley Lelie 20.00
2 David Garrard 8.00
3 Javon Walker 12.00
4 Jeremy Shockey 20.00
5 Josh McCown 8.00
6 Josh Reed 12.00
7 Ladell Betts 10.00
8 Patrick Ramsey 10.00
9 Tim Carter 8.00
10 Joey Harrington 30.00
11 Roy Williams 12.00
12 David Carr 30.00
13 Antonio Bryant 12.00
14 T.J. Duckett 12.00
15 Donald Reche Caldwell 8.00
16 Julius Peppers 12.00
17 Maurice Morris 8.00
18 Clinton Portis 20.00
19 DeShaun Foster 12.00
20 Donte Stallworth 15.00
21 Eric Crouch 12.00
22 Andre Davis 10.00
23 Marquise Walker 8.00
24 Rohan Davey 8.00
25 Antwann Randle El 20.00
26 Jabar Gaffney 8.00
27 Travis Stephens 12.00
28 Ron Johnson 8.00
29 Daniel Graham 8.00
30 Cliff Russell 8.00
31 Mike Williams 8.00
32 William Green 15.00

2002 Leaf Rookies & Stars Great American Heroes

NM/M
Common Player: 1.00
Production 2000 sets
1 Steve Young 4.00
2 Troy Aikman 5.00
3 Daunte Culpepper 2.00
4 Correll Buckhalter 1.00
5 Marshall Faulk 2.00
6 Kevan Barlow 1.00
7 Marvin Harrison 1.00
8 Peter Warrick 1.00
9 LaMont Jordan 1.00
10 Rod Gardner 1.00
11 Charlie Batch 1.00
12 Reggie Wayne 1.00
13 Ricky Watters 1.00
14 Ken-Yon Rambo 1.00
15 Kurt Warner 2.00
16 Ahman Green 1.00
17 Dan Morgan 1.00
18 Isaac Bruce 1.00
19 Chad Pennington 2.00
20 Josh Heupel 1.00
21 Tony Stewart 1.00
22 Rudi Johnson 1.00
23 Michael Bennett 1.50
24 Quincy Carter 1.50
25 Aaron Brooks 1.50
26 Jesse Palmer 1.00
27 Cade McNown 1.00
28 Jeff Garcia 1.50
29 Jevon Kearse 1.00
30 Justin Smith 1.00
31 Kerry Collins 1.00
32 Kordell Stewart 1.00
33 Michael Vick 5.00
34 Ricky Williams 3.00
35 Vinny Testaverde 1.00
36 Terrell Davis 1.50
37 Jake Plummer 1.00
38 Drew Bledsoe 2.00
39 Santana Moss 1.00
40 Elvis Grbac 1.00

2002 Leaf Rookies & Stars Great American Heroes Autos

NM/M
Common Player: 10.00
1 Steve Young/15
2 Troy Aikman/15
3 Daunte Culpepper/33
4 Correll Buckhalter/90 15.00
5 Marshall Faulk/67
6 Kevan Barlow/30
7 Marvin Harrison/25
8 Peter Warrick/110 15.00
9 LaMont Jordan/40 20.00
10 Rod Gardner/25
11 Charlie Batch/20
12 Reggie Wayne/35
13 Ricky Watters/100 15.00
14 Ken-Yon Rambo/20
15 Kurt Warner/15 175.00
16 Ahman Green/10
17 Dan Morgan/15
18 Isaac Bruce/25
19 Chad Pennington/50
20 Josh Heupel/120 15.00
21 Tony Stewart/199 10.00
22 Rudi Johnson/59 25.00
23 Michael Bennett/242 20.00
24 Quincy Carter/106 30.00
25 Aaron Brooks/25
26 Jesse Palmer/25
27 Cade McNown/25
28 Jeff Garcia/25 40.00
29 Jevon Kearse/25
30 Justin Smith/40
31 Kerry Collins/25
32 Kordell Stewart/25
33 Michael Vick/57 150.00
34 Ricky Williams/25
35 Vinny Testaverde/15
36 Terrell Davis/10
37 Jake Plummer/25 40.00
38 Drew Bledsoe/25
39 Santana Moss/200 20.00
40 Elvis Grbac/40 15.00

2002 Leaf Rookies & Stars Initial Steps

NM/M
Common Player: 10.00
Production 125 sets
1 Jabar Gaffney 10.00
2 Cliff Russell 10.00
3 T.J. Duckett
4 Josh Reed 10.00
5 Daniel Graham 12.00
6 Antonio Bryant
7 Ashley Lelie 25.00
8 Mike Williams 10.00
9 Ladell Betts 15.00
10 Jeremy Shockey 35.00
11 Josh McCown 10.00
12 Andre Davis
13 Travis Stephens 12.00
14 Roy Williams 25.00
15 Rohan Davey 10.00
16 Julius Peppers 15.00
17 Javon Walker
18 Donald Reche Caldwell 10.00
19 Clinton Portis 60.00
20 Antwann Randle El 35.00
21 Eric Crouch 15.00
22 Patrick Ramsey
23 Marquise Walker
24 David Garrard 10.00
25 David Carr 60.00

2002 Leaf Rookies & Stars Rookie Masks

NM/M
Common Player: 10.00
Production 250 sets
1 Ladell Betts 12.00
2 Antonio Bryant 25.00
3 Donald Reche Caldwell 10.00
4 David Carr 50.00
5 Tim Carter 10.00
6 Eric Crouch 15.00
7 Rohan Davey 10.00
8 Andre Davis 12.00
9 T.J. Duckett 25.00
10 DeShaun Foster 12.00
11 Jabar Gaffney 10.00
12 Daniel Graham 10.00
13 William Green 25.00
14 Joey Harrington 50.00
15 Ron Johnson 10.00
16 Ashley Lelie 25.00
17 Josh McCown 10.00
18 Maurice Morris 10.00
19 Julius Peppers
20 Clinton Portis 40.00
21 Patrick Ramsey 15.00
22 Antwaan Randle El 30.00
23 Josh Reed 15.00
24 Cliff Russell
25 Jeremy Shockey 30.00
26 Donte Stallworth 25.00
27 Travis Stephens 15.00
28 Javon Walker 20.00
29 Marquise Walker 10.00
30 Roy Williams 30.00
31 Mike Williams 10.00
32 David Garrard

2002 Leaf Rookies & Stars Run With History

NM/M
Common Player: 25.00
Production to rushing total for year
Autographs: 250.00
Auto Production 22 Sets
Cards 1, 3, 4, 6 Have Auto versions
1 Emmitt Smith/937 35.00
2 Emmitt Smith/1563 25.00
3 Emmitt Smith/1713 25.00
4 Emmitt Smith/1486 25.00
5 Emmitt Smith/1484 25.00
6 Emmitt Smith/1773 25.00
7 Emmitt Smith/1204 25.00
8 Emmitt Smith/1074 25.00
9 Emmitt Smith/1332 25.00
10 Emmitt Smith/1397 25.00
11 Emmitt Smith/1203 25.00
12 Emmitt Smith/1021 25.00

2002 Leaf Rookies & Stars Slideshow

NM/M
Common Player: 2.00
Production 1500 sets
1 Anthony Thomas 2.00
2 Eddie George 2.00
3 Kurt Warner 3.00
4 Ricky Williams 2.50
5 Donovan McNabb 2.50
6 Jeff Garcia 2.00
7 Randy Moss 3.00
8 Shaun Alexander 2.00
9 Brett Favre 5.00
10 Jerry Rice 4.00
11 Emmitt Smith 4.00
12 Marshall Faulk 2.00
13 Michael Vick 4.00
14 Zach Thomas 2.00
15 Peyton Manning 4.00

2002 Leaf Rookies & Stars Standing Ovation

NM/M
Common Player: 2.00
Production 2500 sets
1 Tom Brady 4.00
2 Kordell Stewart 2.00
3 Kurt Warner 3.00
4 Jeff Garcia 2.00
5 Priest Holmes 3.00
6 Shaun Alexander 2.00
7 Marshall Faulk 3.00
8 Anthony Thomas 2.00
9 Jerry Rice 4.00
10 David Boston 2.00
11 Terrell Owens 2.50
12 Michael Strahan 2.00
13 New England Patriots 3.00

2002 Leaf Rookies & Stars Ticket Masters

NM/M
Common Player: 1.00
Production 2500 sets
1 Michael Vick, T.J. Duckett 5.00
2 Jamal Lewis, Ray Lewis 1.00
3 Drew Bledsoe, Travis Henry 3.00
4 Chris Weinke, DeShaun Foster 1.00
5 Anthony Thomas, Brian Urlacher 3.00
6 Tim Couch, William Green 3.00
7 Quincy Carter, Emmitt Smith 5.00
8 Brian Griese, Ashley Lelie 3.00
9 Joey Harrington, Germane Crowell 5.00
10 Brett Favre, Ahman Green 5.00
11 David Carr, Jabar Gaffney 5.00
12 Peyton Manning, Edgerrin James 3.00
13 Ricky Williams, Chris Chambers 2.00
14 Randy Moss, Daunte Culpepper 3.00
15 Aaron Brooks, Donte Stallworth 1.00
16 Jerry Rice, Tim Brown 4.00
17 Drew Brees, LaDainian Tomlinson 3.00
18 Jeff Garcia, Garrison Hearst 1.00
19 Kurt Warner, Marshall Faulk 3.00
20 Steve McNair, Eddie George 2.00

2002 Leaf Rookies & Stars Triple Threads

NM/M
Common Player: 40.00
Production 50 sets
1 Kordell Stewart, Jerome Bettis, Plaxico Burress 40.00
2 Jeff Garcia, Terrell Owens, Garrison Hearst 40.00
3 Tim Brown, Jerry Rice, Rich Gannon 90.00
4 Anthony Thomas, Brian Urlacher, David Terrell 40.00
5 Brett Favre, Ahman Green, Terry Glenn

2003 Leaf Certified

NM/M
Common Player (1-150): .50
Minor Stars: 1.00
Unlisted Stars: 1.50
Common Rookie (151-180): 4.00
Minor Rookies: 5.00
Unlisted Rookies: 6.00
Production 1250 Sets
Pack (5): 20.00
Box (10): 140.00
1 Jake Plummer 1.00
2 David Boston 1.50
3 MarTay Jenkins .50
4 Marcel Shipp .50
5 Michael Vick 5.00
6 T.J. Duckett 1.50
7 Chris Redman 1.00
8 Ray Lewis 1.00

NM/M
9 Jamal Lewis 1.50
10 Eric Moulds 1.00
11 Nate Clements .50
12 Travis Henry 1.00
13 Drew Bledsoe 2.00
14 Peerless Price 1.00
15 Josh Reed 1.00
16 Wesley Walls .50
17 Muhsin Muhammad 1.00
18 Julius Peppers 1.00
19 Dez White 1.00
20 Mike Brown .50
21 Brian Urlacher 2.50
22 Anthony Thomas 1.50
23 David Terrell 1.00
24 Corey Dillon 1.50
25 Peter Warrick 1.00
26 Josh McCown 1.00
27 Dennis Northcutt 1.00
28 Kevin Johnson 1.00
29 Tim Couch 1.50
30 Gerard Warren .50
31 William Green 1.50
32 Antonio Bryant 1.00
33 Darren Woodson 1.00
34 Emmitt Smith 4.00
35 Quincy Carter 1.50
36 Roy Williams 1.50
37 Brian Griese 1.50
38 Ed McCaffrey 1.00
39 Mike Anderson 1.00
40 Rod Smith 1.00
41 Clinton Portis 4.00
42 Ashley Lelie 1.50
43 Cory Schlesinger .50
44 Germane Crowell .50
45 James Stewart 1.00
46 Scotty Anderson .50
47 Joey Harrington 3.00
48 Brett Favre 5.00
49 Terry Glenn 1.00
50 Ahman Green 1.50
51 Donald Driver 1.00
52 Javon Walker 1.00
53 David Carr 3.00
54 Ron Dayne 1.00
55 Terrell Davis 1.50
56 Edgerrin James 2.00
57 Marvin Harrison 1.50
58 Peyton Manning 4.00
59 Fred Taylor 1.50
60 Jimmy Smith 1.00
61 Kyle Brady 1.00
62 Mark Brunell 1.00
63 Tony Gonzalez 1.00
64 Priest Holmes 1.50
65 Trent Green 1.00
66 Jason Taylor 1.00
67 Jay Fiedler 1.00
68 Zach Thomas 1.00
69 Chris Chambers 1.50
70 Ricky Williams 2.50
71 Randy McMichael 1.00
72 Daunte Culpepper 1.50
73 Randy Moss 2.50
74 Michael Bennett 1.50
75 Ty Law 1.00
76 Tom Brady 2.00
77 Troy Brown 1.00
78 Antowain Smith 1.00
79 Aaron Brooks 1.50
80 Donte Stallworth 1.50
81 Joe Horn 1.00
82 Deuce McAllister 1.50
83 Amani Toomer 1.00
84 Kerry Collins 1.00
85 Michael Strahan 1.00
86 Tiki Barber 1.50
87 Jeremy Shockey 3.00
88 Chad Pennington 2.00
89 Curtis Martin 1.50
90 Laveranues Coles 1.00
91 Vinny Testaverde 1.00
92 Santana Moss 1.00
93 Charles Woodson 1.00
94 Sebastian Janikowski .50
95 Tim Brown 1.50
96 Rich Gannon 1.00
97 Jerry Rice 4.00
98 Donovan McNabb 2.00
99 Duce Staley 1.00
100 Todd Pinkston 1.00
101 Chad Lewis .50
102 A.J. Feeley 1.00
103 Jerome Bettis 1.00
104 Plaxico Burress 1.50
105 Hines Ward 1.50
106 Antwann Randle El 1.50
107 Kendrell Bell 1.00
108 Junior Seau 1.00
109 LaDainian Tomlinson 2.00
110 Doug Flutie 1.50
111 Drew Brees 2.00
112 Terrell Owens 1.50
113 Jeff Garcia 1.50
114 Garrison Hearst 1.00
115 Koren Robinson 1.00
116 Shaun Alexander 1.50
117 Isaac Bruce 1.00
118 Kurt Warner 2.50
119 Marshall Faulk 2.00
120 Torry Holt 1.50
121 Keyshawn Johnson 1.00
122 Warren Sapp 1.00
123 Mike Alstott 1.00
124 Brad Johnson 1.00
125 Eddie George 1.50
126 Jevon Kearse 1.00
127 Steve McNair 1.50
128 Derrick Mason 1.00
129 Keith Bulluck .50
130 Champ Bailey 1.00
131 Darrell Green 1.00
132 Stephen Davis 1.00
133 Rod Gardner 1.00
134 Barry Sanders .50
135 Cris Carter 1.00
136 Dan Marino .50
137 Deion Sanders .50
138 Jim Kelly .50
139 Joe Montana .50
140 John Elway .50
141 Marcus Allen .50
142 Reggie White .50
143 Sterling Sharpe .50
144 Steve Young .50
145 Thurman Thomas .50
146 Troy Aikman .50
147 Warren Moon .50
148 Drew Bledsoe .50
149 Jerry Rice .50
150 Ricky Williams .50
151 *Carson Palmer* 20.00
152 *Byron Leftwich* 30.00
153 *Kyle Boller* 15.00
154 *Rex Grossman* 15.00
155 *Dave Ragone* 5.00
156 *Kliff Kingsbury* 5.00
157 *Seneca Wallace* 5.00
158 *Larry Johnson* 10.00
159 *Willis McGahee* 15.00
160 *Justin Fargas* 8.00
161 *Onterrio Smith* 8.00
162 *Chris Brown* 10.00
163 *Musa Smith* 5.00
164 *Artose Pinner* 4.00
165 *Andre Johnson* 12.00
166 *Kelley Washington* 6.00
167 *Taylor Jacobs* 5.00
168 *Bryant Johnson* 6.00
169 *Tyrone Calico* 8.00
170 *Anquan Boldin* 12.00
171 *Bethel Johnson* 6.00
172 *Nate Burleson* 6.00
173 *Kevin Curtis* 5.00
174 *Dallas Clark* 8.00
175 *Teyo Johnson* 6.00
176 *Terrell Suggs* 6.00
177 *Dewayne Robertson* 4.00
178 *Brian St. Pierre* 5.00
179 *Terence Newman* 8.00
180 *Marcus Trufant* 4.00

2003 Leaf Certified Mirror Blue

Stars: 1X-2X
Rookies: 2X Red
Production 50 Sets

2003 Leaf Certified Mirror Gold

Stars: 2X-4X Red
Rookies: 1.5X-3X Red
Production 25 Sets

2003 Leaf Certified Mirror Red

Stars: 5X-10X
Rookies (151-180): 2X-3X
Production 150 Sets

2003 Leaf Certified Mirror Signatures

NM/M
Common Player: 20.00
1 Jim Brown/100 80.00
2 Joe Montana/100 150.00
3 John Riggins/100 40.00
4 Randy White/100 40.00
5 Terry Bradshaw/100 100.00
6 Deion Branch/50 25.00
7 Jeff Garcia/25 50.00
8 Joe Horn/50 25.00
9 Joey Harrington/25
10 Kurt Warner/100 40.00
11 Randy Moss/25
12 Tim Brown/25
13 Torry Holt/25
14 TBD
15 Byron Leftwich/25
16 Carson Palmer/25
18 Larry Johnson/25
19 Bryant Johnson/50 30.00
20 Kelley Washington/50 30.00
21 Terrell Suggs/50 30.00
22 Terence Newman/100 50.00
23 Musa Smith/100 20.00
24 Dave Ragone/100 20.00
25 Chris Brown/100 20.00

2003 Leaf Certified Potential

NM/M
Common Player: 12.00
Production 125 Sets
1 Antonio Bryant 8.00
2 Antwann Randle El 10.00
3 Ashley Lelie 10.00
4 Chris Chambers 10.00
5 Clinton Portis 15.00
6 David Carr 12.00
7 Drew Brees 10.00
8 Javon Walker 8.00
9 Jeremy Shockey 12.00
10 Joey Harrington 12.00
11 Josh Reed 8.00
12 Julius Peppers 10.00
13 Koren Robinson 8.00
14 LaDainian Tomlinson 10.00
15 Marcel Shipp 6.00
16 Roy Williams 10.00
17 T.J. Duckett 8.00
18 Travis Henry 8.00

2003 Leaf Certified Skills

NM/M
Common Player: 5.00
Production 100 Sets
1 Rich Gannon 10.00
2 Drew Bledsoe 12.00
3 Peyton Manning 15.00
4 Kerry Collins 8.00
5 Daunte Culpepper 10.00
6 Tom Brady 10.00
7 Trent Green 8.00
8 Brett Favre 25.00
9 Aaron Brooks 10.00
10 Steve McNair 10.00
11 Jeff Garcia 8.00
12 Drew Brees 10.00
13 Brian Griese 8.00
14 Chad Pennington 12.00
15 Brad Johnson 8.00
16 Ricky Williams 15.00
17 LaDainian Tomlinson 10.00
18 Priest Holmes 12.00
19 Clinton Portis 12.00
20 Travis Henry 8.00
21 Deuce McAllister 10.00
22 Tiki Barber 8.00
23 Jamal Lewis 10.00
24 Fred Taylor 10.00
25 Corey Dillon 8.00
26 Michael Bennett 8.00
27 Ahman Green 10.00
28 Shaun Alexander 10.00
29 Eddie George 8.00
30 Curtis Martin 8.00
31 Duce Staley 8.00
32 James Stewart 5.00
33 Marvin Harrison 12.00
34 Randy Moss 15.00
35 Amani Toomer 8.00
36 Hines Ward 10.00
37 Plaxico Burress 10.00
38 Torry Holt 10.00
39 Terrell Owens 12.00
40 Eric Moulds 10.00
41 Laveranues Coles 10.00
42 Peerless Price 10.00
43 Koren Robinson 10.00
44 Jerry Rice 20.00
45 Emmitt Smith 25.00
46 Keyshawn Johnson 10.00
47 Isaac Bruce 10.00
48 Donald Driver 10.00
49 Jimmy Smith 5.00
50 Rod Smith 8.00

2003 Leaf Limited

NM/M
Common Player (1-100): 1.00
Minor Stars: 1.50
Unlisted Stars: 2.00
1-100 Production 999 Sets
Common Rookie (101-125): 3.00
Minor Rookie: 4.00
Unlisted Rookie: 5.00
101-125 Production 750 Sets
Common Rookie Auto (126-150): 20.00
126-150 Auto Production 150 Sets
Pack (4): 70.00
Box (4): 200.00
1 Emmitt Smith 6.00
2 Michael Vick 6.00

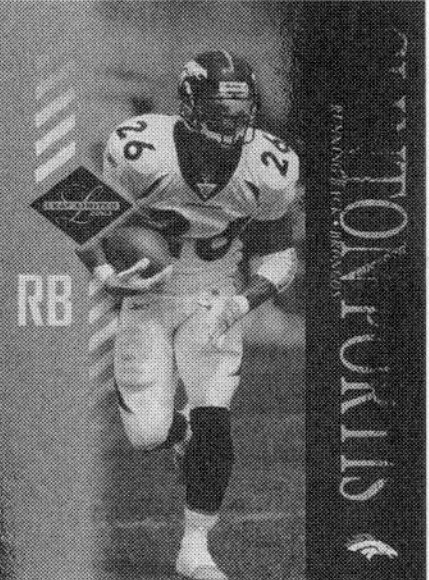
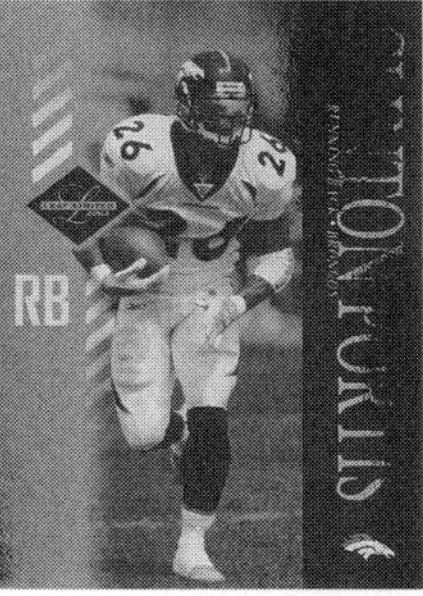

NM/M
3 Peerless Price 1.00
4 T.J. Duckett 1.50
5 Jamal Lewis 2.00
6 Drew Bledsoe 2.00
7 Eric Moulds 1.00
8 Travis Henry 1.00
9 Jim Kelly 4.00
10 Julius Peppers 1.50
11 Dick Butkus 3.00
12 Mike Singletary 2.00
13 Walter Payton 8.00
14 Anthony Thomas 2.00
15 Brian Urlacher 3.00
16 Marty Booker 1.00
17 Corey Dillon 1.00
18 Jim Thorpe 3.00
19 Jim Brown 6.00
20 Tim Couch 1.00
21 William Green 1.50
22 Deion Sanders 2.00
23 Michael Irvin 2.00
24 Roger Staubach 4.00
25 Troy Aikman 4.00
26 Tony Dorsett 3.00
27 Antonio Bryant 1.00
28 Clinton Portis 3.00
29 Jake Plummer 1.00
30 Rod Smith 1.00
31 Barry Sanders 6.00
32 Doak Walker 2.00
33 Joey Harrington 3.00
34 Bart Starr 4.00
35 Ahman Green 2.00
36 Brett Favre 6.00
37 Donald Driver 1.50
38 David Carr 4.00
39 Don Shula 2.00
40 Johnny Unitas 5.00
41 Edgerrin James 2.00
42 Marvin Harrison 2.00
43 Peyton Manning 3.00
44 Fred Taylor 2.00
45 Jimmy Smith 1.00
46 Mark Brunell 1.00
47 Marcus Allen 2.00
48 Priest Holmes 3.00
49 Tony Gonzalez 1.50
50 Trent Green 1.00
51 Dan Marino 6.00
52 Bob Griese 2.00
53 Chris Chambers 2.00
54 Ricky Williams 3.00
55 Fran Tarkenton 3.00
56 Daunte Culpepper 2.00
57 Michael Bennett 2.00
58 Randy Moss 3.00
59 Tom Brady 3.00
60 Aaron Brooks 2.00
61 Deuce McAllister 2.00
62 Donte Stallworth 1.50
63 Mark Bavaro 1.00
64 Jeremy Shockey 3.00
65 Kerry Collins 1.00
66 Tiki Barber 1.50
67 Joe Namath 5.00
68 Chad Pennington 3.00
69 Curtis Martin 2.00
70 Jerry Porter 1.50
71 Jerry Rice 5.00
72 Rich Gannon 1.50
73 Tim Brown 2.00
74 Donovan McNabb 2.00
75 Terry Bradshaw 4.00
76 Antwann Randle El 2.00
77 Plaxico Burress 2.00
78 Tommy Maddox 2.00
79 David Boston 2.00
80 Drew Brees 2.00
81 LaDainian Tomlinson 2.00
82 Joe Montana 10.00
83 Steve Young 3.00
84 Jeff Garcia 2.00
85 Terrell Owens 2.00
86 Koren Robinson 1.50
87 Matt Hasselbeck 1.50
88 Shaun Alexander 2.00
89 Isaac Bruce 2.00
90 Kurt Warner 2.00
91 Marshall Faulk 3.00
92 Torry Holt 2.00
93 Brad Johnson 1.00
94 Keyshawn Johnson 1.00
95 Earl Campbell 3.00
96 Eddie George 2.00
97 Steve McNair 2.00
98 John Riggins 3.00
99 Laveranues Coles 1.50
100 Patrick Ramsey 2.00
101 *LaTarence Dunbar* 3.00
102 *Sam Aiken* 3.00
103 *Bobby Wade* 4.00
104 *Justin Gage* 6.00
105 *Lee Suggs* 15.00
106 *Jason Witten* 8.00
107 *Quentin Griffin* 15.00
108 *Domanick Davis* 10.00
109 *LaBrandon Toefield* 5.00
110 *J.R. Tolver* 3.00
111 *Kliff Kingsbury* 4.00
112 *Talman Gardner* 4.00
113 *Teyo Johnson* 4.00
114 *Billy McMullen* 3.00
115 *L.J. Smith* 4.00
116 *Brian St. Pierre* 4.00
117 *Brandon Lloyd* 6.00
118 *Seneca Wallace* 4.00
119 *Kevin Curtis* 3.00
120 *Shaun McDonald* 3.00
121 *Terrell Suggs* 5.00
122 *Terence Newman* 6.00
123 *Tony Romo* 3.00
124 *Dewayne Robertson* 3.00
125 *Marcus Trufant* 3.00
126 *Artose Pinner Auto* 20.00
127 *Bryant Johnson Auto* 25.00
128 *Kelley Washington Auto* 25.00
129 *Dallas Clark Auto* 25.00
130 *Onterrio Smith Auto* 40.00
131 *Tony Hollings Auto* 20.00
132 *Tyrone Calico Auto* 30.00
133 *Carson Palmer Auto* 120.00
134 *Byron Leftwich Auto* 140.00
135 *Rex Grossman Auto* 100.00
136 *Kyle Boller Auto* 60.00
137 *Chris Simms Auto* 60.00
138 *Dave Ragone Auto* 25.00
139 *Ken Dorsey Auto* 40.00
140 *Willis McGahee Auto* 80.00
141 *Larry Johnson Auto* 40.00
142 *Musa Smith Auto* 25.00
143 *Chris Brown Auto* 50.00
144 *Charles Rogers Auto* 80.00
145 *Andre Johnson Auto* 100.00
146 *Taylor Jacobs Auto* 20.00
147 *Anquan Boldin Auto* 80.00
148 *Bethel Johnson Auto* 40.00
149 *Justin Fargas Auto* 30.00
150 *Nate Burleson Auto* 30.00

2003 Leaf Limited Bronze Spotlight

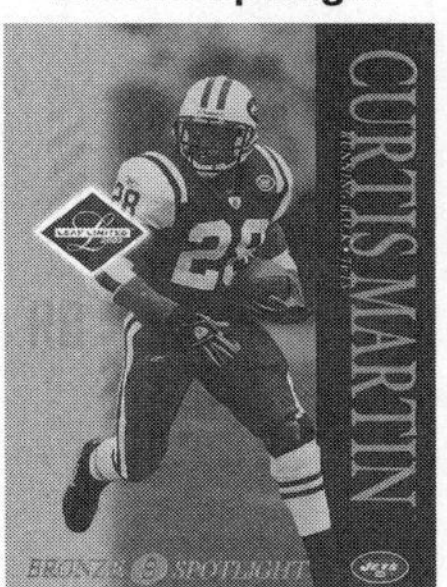

Stars: 1X-2X
Rookies: 1X-1.5X
1-125 Production 150 Sets
126-150 Production 25 Sets

2003 Leaf Limited Gold Spotlight

Stars: 3X-6X
Rookies: 2X-4X
1-125 Production 25 Sets
126-150 AU Production 10 Sets

2003 Leaf Limited Silver Spotlight

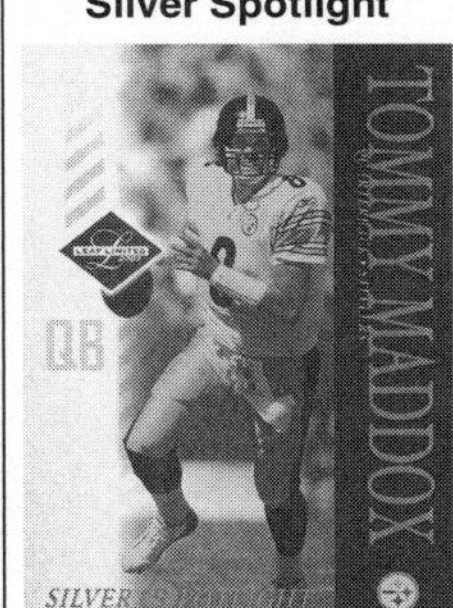

Stars: 1.5X-3X
Rookies: 1X-2X
1-125 Production 75 Sets
126-150 AU Production 15 Sets

2003 Leaf Limited Contenders Previews

103 Brandon Lloyd/10
107 Jerome McDougle/10
108 Jimmy Kennedy/10
109 William Joseph/10
111 Mike Doss/25
112 Chris Simms/25
114 Justin Gage/25
115 Sam Aiken/10
116 Doug Gabriel/10
117 Jason Witten/25
119 Chris Kelsay/10
121 Kevin Williams/10
124 Boss Bailey/10
126 Carson Palmer/25
127 Byron Leftwich/25
128 Kyle Boller/25
129 Rex Grossman/25
130 Dave Ragone/10
131 Brian St. Pierre/10
132 Kliff Kingsbury/10
133 Seneca Wallace/25
134 Larry Johnson/25
136 Justin Fargas/25
138 Chris Brown/25
139 Musa Smith/25
140 Artose Pinner/25
141 Andre Johnson/25
142 Kelley Washington/25
143 Taylor Jacobs/25
144 Bryant Johnson/25
145 Tyrone Calico/25
146 Anquan Boldin/25
147 Bethel Johnson/25
149 Kevin Curtis/25
150 Dallas Clark/25
151 Teyo Johnson/25
152 Terrell Suggs/25
154 Terence Newman/25
155 Marcus Trufant/25
157 Brooks Bollinger/25
158 Ken Dorsey/25
163 Avon Cobourne/25
165 Tony Hollings/25
167 Arlen Harris/25
168 Sultan McCullough/10
170 L.J. Smith/25
172 Walter Young/10
173 Bobby Wade/10
174 Zuriel Smith/10
176 Ken Hamlin/10
178 Cortez Hankton/10
179 J.R. Tolver/10
182 Arnaz Battle/10
184 Andre Woolfolk/10
190 Troy Polamalu/10
191 Eric Parker/10
192 Justin Griffith/10
195 Rashean Mathis/10
196 Mike Sherman/25
197 Dave Wannstedt/25
198 Dick Vermeil/25
199 Tony Dungy/25
200 Mike Martz/25

2003 Leaf Limited Double Threads

NM/M
Common Player: 20.00
Production 100 Sets
Prime Production 10 Sets
DT-1 Johnny Unitas, Peyton Manning/25 100.00
DT-2 Don Shula, Edgerrin James 40.00
DT-3 Jim Kelly, Drew Bledsoe 25.00
DT-4 Jim Kelly, Bruce Smith 30.00
DT-5 Dick Butkus, Brian Urlacher 60.00
DT-6 Walter Payton, Mike Singletary 80.00
DT-7 Dick Butkus, Mike Singletary 40.00
DT-8 Jim Brown, Bernie Kosar 50.00
DT-9 Roger Staubach, Troy Aikman 40.00
DT-10 Tony Dorsett, Emmitt Smith 60.00
DT-11 Michael Irvin, Antonio Bryant 20.00
DT-12 Deion Sanders, Roy Williams 25.00
DT-13 Terrell Davis, Clinton Portis 30.00
DT-14 John Elway, Terrell Davis 50.00
DT-15 Tony Dorsett, Clinton Portis 30.00
DT-16 Doak Walker, Barry Sanders 50.00
DT-17 Bart Starr, Brett Favre 80.00
DT-18 Earl Campbell, Eddie George 20.00
DT-19 Joe Montana, Rich Gannon 60.00
DT-20 Marcus Allen, Priest Holmes 30.00
DT-21 Bob Griese, Dan Marino 60.00
DT-22 Fran Tarkenton, Daunte Culpepper 20.00
DT-23 Drew Bledsoe, Tom Brady 25.00
DT-24 Ricky Williams, Deuce McAllister 25.00
DT-25 Mark Bavaro, Jeremy Shockey 20.00
DT-26 Joe Namath, Chad Pennington 50.00
DT-27 Joe Namath, John Riggins 50.00
DT-28 Marcus Allen, Jerry Rice 30.00
DT-29 Terry Bradshaw, Antwann Randle El 30.00
DT-30 Drew Brees, LaDainian Tomlinson 20.00
DT-31 Joe Montana, Jeff Garcia 60.00
DT-32 Steve Young, Jerry Rice 40.00
DT-33 Joe Montana, Jerry Rice 80.00
DT-34 Jerry Rice, Terrell Owens 30.00
DT-35 Kurt Warner, Marshall Faulk 20.00
DT-36 John Riggins, Deion Sanders 30.00

DT-37 Michael Vick, Donovan McNabb 30.00
DT-38 Joey Harrington, David Carr 20.00
DT-39 John Elway, Brett Favre 80.00
DT-40 Jim Kelly, Dan Marino 50.00
DT-41 Joe Montana, Donovan McNabb 60.00
DT-42 Steve Young, Michael Vick 40.00
DT-43 Walter Payton, Emmitt Smith 100.00
DT-44 Jim Brown, Barry Sanders 60.00
DT-45 Ricky Williams, Priest Holmes 30.00
DT-46 Emmitt Smith, LaDainian Tomlinson 30.00
DT-47 Marshall Faulk, Edgerrin James 25.00
DT-48 Earl Campbell, Ricky Williams 30.00
DT-49 Edgerrin James, Clinton Portis 30.00
DT-50 Jeremy Shockey, Andre Johnson 20.00

2003 Leaf Limited Hardwear

NM/M
Common Player: 15.00
Production 100 Sets
Limited: 1X-2X
Production 25 Sets
H-1 Jeremy Shockey 20.00
H-2 Dan Marino 80.00
H-3 Joe Montana 80.00
H-4 Emmitt Smith 60.00
H-5 Brian Urlacher 25.00
H-6 Brett Favre 80.00
H-7 Ricky Williams 30.00
H-8 Earl Campbell 25.00
H-9 Jerry Rice 50.00
H-10 John Elway 80.00
H-11 Marcus Allen 25.00
H-12 Randy Moss 30.00
H-13 Steve Young 40.00
H-14 Troy Aikman 40.00
H-15 Tony Dorsett 25.00
H-16 Jim Kelly 40.00
H-17 Marshall Faulk 20.00
H-18 Jeff Garcia 15.00
H-19 Tom Brady 30.00
H-20 Chad Pennington 25.00
H-21 Deuce McAllister 20.00
H-22 Marcus Allen 25.00
H-23 Travis Henry 15.00
H-24 Roger Staubach 40.00
H-25 Terrell Owens 20.00

2003 Leaf Limited Limited Cuts

NM/M
LC-1 John Elway/75 200.00
LC-2 Michael Vick/94 250.00
LC-3 Warren Moon/100 50.00
LC-4 Aaron Brooks/100 40.00

2003 Leaf Limited Limited Legends

NM/M
Common Player: 20.00
Production 50 Sets
Prime Production 5 Sets
LL-1 Barry Sanders 40.00
LL-2 Bart Starr 40.00
LL-3 Brett Favre 60.00
LL-4 Dan Marino 80.00
LL-5 Doak Walker 50.00
LL-6 Don Shula Auto 60.00
LL-7 Earl Campbell 20.00
LL-8 Emmitt Smith 50.00
LL-9 Fran Tarkenton Auto 60.00
LL-10 Jerry Rice 50.00
LL-11 Jim Brown Auto 100.00
LL-12 Jim Kelly 25.00
LL-13 Jim Thorpe 125.00
LL-14 Joe Montana 80.00
LL-15 Joe Namath 60.00
LL-16 John Elway 60.00
LL-17 John Riggins 20.00
LL-18 Roger Staubach 40.00
LL-19 Terry Bradshaw 40.00
LL-20 Walter Payton 80.00

2003 Leaf Limited Limited Legends Seasons

LL-1 Barry Sanders Auto/10
LL-2 Bart Starr/16
LL-3 Brett Favre/13
LL-4 Dan Marino Auto/17
LL-5 Doak Walker/6
LL-6 Don Shula Auto/7
LL-7 Earl Campbell Auto/8
LL-8 Emmitt Smith/14
LL-9 Fran Tarkenton Auto/18
LL-10 Jerry Rice/19
LL-11 Jim Brown/9
LL-12 Jim Kelly Auto/11
LL-13 Jim Thorpe/13
LL-14 Joe Montana/16
LL-15 Joe Namath Auto/13
LL-16 John Elway/16
LL-17 John Riggins/14
LL-18 Roger Staubach/11
LL-19 Terry Bradshaw Auto/14
LL-20 Walter Payton/13

2003 Leaf Limited Limited Threads

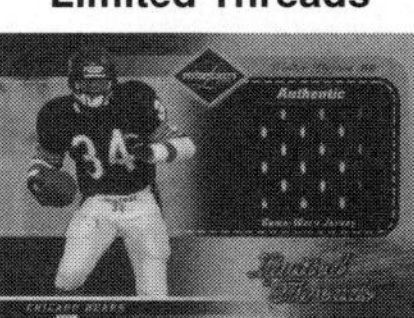

NM/M
Common Player: 10.00
Production 100 Sets
Prime Production 25 Sets
LT-1 Aaron Brooks 8.00
LT-2 Aaron Brooks 8.00
LT-3 Ahman Green 20.00
LT-4 Ahman Green Nebraska 25.00
LT-5 Barry Sanders 30.00
LT-6 Barry Sanders 30.00
LT-7 Bart Starr 40.00
LT-8 Bob Griese 15.00
LT-9 Brett Favre 40.00
LT-10 Brett Favre 40.00
LT-11 Brian Urlacher 20.00
LT-12 Chad Pennington 20.00
LT-13 Clinton Portis 20.00
LT-14 Clinton Portis 20.00
LT-15 Clinton Portis Miami 25.00
LT-16 Dan Marino 50.00
LT-17 Dan Marino 50.00
LT-18 Daunte Culpepper 12.00
LT-19 Daunte Culpepper 12.00
LT-20 Daunte Culpepper Pro Bowl 12.00
LT-21 David Carr 15.00
LT-22 Deion Sanders Cowboys 20.00
LT-23 Deion Sanders Redskins 15.00
LT-24 Deuce McAllister 12.00
LT-25 Dick Butkus 30.00
LT-26 Doak Walker 25.00
LT-27 Don Shula Auto 60.00
LT-28 Donovan McNabb 15.00
LT-29 Donovan McNabb 15.00
LT-30 Drew Bledsoe Bills 12.00
LT-31 Drew Bledsoe Patriots 12.00
LT-32 Drew Bledsoe Patriots 12.00
LT-33 Drew Bledsoe Wash. St. 15.00
LT-34 Drew Brees 10.00
LT-35 Earl Campbell/66 Oilers 20.00
LT-35A Earl Campbell Auto/34 50.00
LT-36 Earl Campbell Texas 20.00
LT-37 Edgerrin James 15.00
LT-38 Edgerrin James Pro Bowl 15.00
LT-39 Edgerrin James Miami 20.00
LT-40 Emmitt Smith 30.00
LT-41 Fran Tarkenton 60.00
LT-42 Jeff Garcia 10.00
LT-43 Jeff Garcia Pro Bowl 10.00
LT-44 Jeremy Shockey 12.00
LT-45 Jeremy Shockey Miami 12.00
LT-46 Jerry Rice Raiders 25.00
LT-47 Jerry Rice 49ers 25.00
LT-48 Jerry Rice 49ers 25.00
LT-49 Jim Brown 40.00
LT-50 Jim Kelly 20.00
LT-51 Jim Thorpe 100.00
LT-52 Joe Montana 49ers 50.00
LT-53 Joe Montana 49ers 50.00
LT-54 Joe Montana Chiefs 50.00
LT-55 Joe Namath 50.00
LT-56 Joey Harrington 12.00
LT-57 John Elway 40.00
LT-58 John Elway 40.00
LT-59 John Elway 40.00
LT-60 John Elway Stanford 50.00
LT-61 John Riggins Redskins 25.00
LT-62 John Riggins Jets 25.00
LT-63 Johnny Unitas 40.00
LT-64 Kurt Warner Auto 40.00
LT-65 LaDainian Tomlinson 12.00
LT-66 Shaun Alexander 12.00
LT-67 Marcus Allen Raiders 20.00
LT-68 Marcus Allen Chiefs 20.00
LT-69 Mark Bavaro 10.00
LT-70 Marshall Faulk Rams 12.00
LT-71 Marshall Faulk Rams 12.00
LT-72 Marshall Faulk SD State 15.00
LT-73 Marvin Harrison 12.00
LT-74 Marvin Harrison 12.00
LT-75 Michael Vick 40.00
LT-76 Mike Singletary Bears 20.00
LT-77 Mike Singletary Baylor 25.00
LT-78 Peyton Manning 20.00
LT-79 Peyton Manning 20.00
LT-80 Peyton Manning Pro Bowl 20.00
LT-81 Priest Holmes Chiefs 15.00
LT-82 Priest Holmes Ravens 15.00
LT-83 Randy Moss 20.00
LT-84 Randy Moss 20.00
LT-85 Ricky Williams Saints 15.00
LT-86 Ricky Williams Saints 15.00
LT-87 Ricky Williams Dolphins 15.00
LT-88 Ricky Williams Texas 20.00
LT-89 Roger Staubach 30.00
LT-90 Steve Young 20.00
LT-91 Terrell Owens 12.00
LT-92 Terry Bradshaw 30.00
LT-93 Tom Brady 20.00
LT-94 Tom Brady Pro Bowl 20.00
LT-95 Tony Dorsett Cowboys 15.00
LT-96 Tony Dorsett Broncos 15.00
LT-97 Troy Aikman 25.00
LT-98 Troy Aikman 25.00
LT-99 Walter Payton 60.00
LT-100 Walter Payton 60.00

2003 Leaf Limited Limited Threads At the Half

NM/M
Stars: 1X-1.5X
Production 50 Sets
LT-1 Aaron Brooks Auto 30.00
LT-2 Aaron Brooks Auto 30.00
LT-24 Deuce McAllister Auto 50.00
LT-27 Don Shula 30.00
LT-41 Fran Tarkenton 25.00
LT-56 Joey Harrington Auto 60.00
LT-64 Kurt Warner Auto 50.00
LT-67 Marcus Allen Auto 60.00
LT-68 Marcus Allen Auto 60.00
LT-69 Mark Bavaro Auto 40.00
LT-76 Mike Singletary Auto 80.00
LT-81 Priest Holmes Auto 80.00
LT-82 Priest Holmes Auto 80.00
LT-96 Tony Dorsett Auto 80.00

2003 Leaf Limited Limited Threads Jersey

LT-1 Aaron Brooks Auto/2
LT-2 Aaron Brooks Auto/2
LT-3 Ahman Green Auto/30
LT-4 Ahman Green Auto/30
LT-5 Barry Sanders Auto/20
LT-6 Barry Sanders Auto/20
LT-7 Bart Starr/15
LT-8 Bob Griese Auto/21
LT-9 Brett Favre Auto/4
LT-10 Brett Favre Auto/4
LT-11 Brian Urlacher Auto/54
LT-12 Chad Pennington Auto/10
LT-13 Clinton Portis Auto/26
LT-14 Clinton Portis Auto/26
LT-15 Clinton Portis Auto/28
LT-16 Dan Marino Auto/13
LT-17 Dan Marino Auto/13
LT-18 Daunte CulpepperAuto/11
LT-19 Daunte Culpepper Auto/11
LT-20 Daunte Culpepper Auto/11
LT-21 David Carr/8
LT-22 Deion Sanders Auto/21
LT-23 Deion Sanders Auto/21
LT-24 Deuce McAllister Auto/26
LT-25 Dick Butkus Auto/51
LT-26 Doak Walker/37
LT-27 Don Shula Auto/25
LT-28 Donovan McNabb/5
LT-29 Donovan McNabb/5
LT-30 Drew Bledsoe/11
LT-31 Drew Bledsoe/11
LT-32 Drew Bledsoe/11
LT-33 Drew Bledsoe/11
LT-34 Drew Brees/9
LT-35 Earl Campbell Auto/34
LT-36 Earl Campbell Auto/20
LT-37 Edgerrin James/32
LT-38 Edgerrin James/32
LT-39 Edgerrin James/32
LT-40 Emmitt Smith/22
LT-41 Fran Tarkenton Auto/10
LT-42 Jeff Garcia/5
LT-43 Jeff Garcia/5
LT-44 Jeremy Shockey/80
LT-45 Jeremy Shockey/80
LT-46 Jerry Rice/80
LT-47 Jerry Rice/80
LT-48 Jerry Rice/80
LT-49 Jim Brown/32
LT-50 Jim Kelly Auto/12
LT-51 Jim Thorpe/1
LT-52 Joe Montana/16
LT-53 Joe Montana/16
LT-54 Joe Montana/19
LT-55 Joe Namath Auto/12
LT-56 Joey Harrington Auto/3
LT-57 John Elway/7
LT-58 John Elway/7
LT-59 John Elway/7
LT-60 John Elway/7
LT-61 John Riggins/44
LT-62 John Riggins/44
LT-63 Johnny Unitas/19
LT-64 Kurt Warner Auto/13
LT-65 LaDainian Tomlinson/21
LT-66 Shaun Alexander Auto/37
LT-67 Marcus Allen/32
LT-68 Marcus Allen/32
LT-69 Mark Bavaro Auto/89
LT-70 Marshall Faulk/28
LT-71 Marshall Faulk/28
LT-72 Marshall Faulk/28
LT-73 Marvin Harrison/88
LT-74 Marvin Harrison/88
LT-75 Michael Vick Auto/7
LT-76 Mike Singletary/50
LT-77 Michael Singletary/63
LT-78 Peyton Manning/18
LT-79 Peyton Manning/18
LT-80 Peyton Manning/18
LT-81 Priest Holmes Auto/31
LT-82 Priest Holmes Auto/33
LT-83 Randy Moss/84
LT-84 Randy Moss/84
LT-85 Ricky Williams/34
LT-86 Ricky Williams/34
LT-87 Ricky Williams/34
LT-88 Ricky Williams/34
LT-89 Roger Staubach/12
LT-90 Steve Young/8
LT-91 Terrell Owens/81
LT-92 Terry Bradshaw Auto/12
LT-93 Tom Brady Auto/12
LT-94 Tom Brady Auto/12
LT-95 Tony Dorsett Auto/33
LT-96 Tony Dorsett Auto/33
LT-97 Troy Aikman Auto/8
LT-98 Troy Aikman Auto/8
LT-99 Walter Payton/34
LT-100 Walter Payton/34

2003 Leaf Limited Limited Threads Positions

NM/M
Stars: 1X-1.2X
Production 75 Sets
LT-27 Don Shula 25.00
LT-41 Fran Tarkenton 20.00
LT-64 Kurt Warner 15.00

2003 Leaf Limited Player Threads

NM/M
Common Player: 20.00
Production 50 Sets
Prime Production 10 Sets
PT-1 Barry Sanders 60.00
PT-2 Brett Favre 80.00
PT-3 Dan Marino 100.00
PT-4 Donovan McNabb 20.00
PT-5 Earl Campbell/34 30.00
PT-6 Emmitt Smith 60.00
PT-7 Fran Tarkenton 30.00
PT-8 Jeremy Shockey 20.00
PT-9 Jim Kelly 40.00
PT-10 John Riggins 30.00
PT-11 LaDainian Tomlinson 20.00
PT-12 Mike Singletary 30.00
PT-13 Peyton Manning 30.00
PT-14 Priest Holmes 25.00
PT-15 Randy Moss 30.00
PT-16 Roger Staubach 50.00
PT-17 Steve Young 30.00
PT-18 Terry Bradshaw 50.00
PT-19 Tom Brady 30.00
PT-20 Tony Dorsett 20.00
PT-21 Troy Aikman 30.00
PT-22 Walter Payton 100.00
PT-23 Clinton Portis 40.00
PT-24 Drew Bledsoe 25.00
PT-25 Edgerrin James 25.00
PT-26 Jerry Rice 60.00
PT-27 Joe Montana 100.00
PT-28 John Elway 80.00
PT-29 Marshall Faulk 30.00
PT-30 Ricky Williams 30.00

2003 Leaf Limited Monikers

M-1 Dan Marino/15
M-2 Dan Marino/10
M-3 Jim Brown/25
M-4 Jim Kelly/25
M-5 Joe Montana/25
M-6 Joe Montana/15
M-7 Joe Montana/10
M-8 John Riggins/25
M-9 John Riggins/25
M-10 Mark Bavaro/25
M-11 Walter Payton/5
M-12 Joe Namath/10
M-13 Daunte Culpepper/25
M-14 Troy Aikman/15
M-15 Troy Aikman/10
M-16 Michael Vick/25
M-17 Roger Staubach/25
M-18 Drew Bledsoe/25
M-19 Brian Urlacher/25
M-20 Clinton Portis/10
M-21 Clinton Portis/10
M-22 Joey Harrington/20
M-23 Ahman Green/10
M-24 Brett Favre/10
M-25 David Carr/20
M-26 Marvin Harrison/15
M-27 Marvin Harrison/10
M-28 Priest Holmes/15
M-29 Priest Holmes/10
M-30 Ricky Williams/20
M-31 Earl Campbell/25
M-32 Randy Moss/9
M-33 Tom Brady/20
M-34 Deuce McAllister/10
M-35 Chad Pennington/10
M-36 Jerry Rice/20
M-37 Dick Butkus/25
M-38 Jeff Garcia/20
M-39 Joe Namath/15
M-40 Kurt Warner/25
M-41 Jim Brown, Jamal Lewis/20
M-42 Kurt Warner, Torry Holt/20
M-43 Kurt Warner, Isaac Bruce/25
M-44 Joe Montana, Marcus Allen/25
M-45 Joe Montana, Jeff Garcia/25
M-46 Jerry Rice, Tim Brown/10
M-47 Joe Namath, Chad Pennington/10
M-48 Steve McNair, Eddie George/25
M-49 Brett Favre, Ahman Green/10
M-50 Deuce McAllister, Aaron Brooks/10

2003 Leaf Limited Team Trademark Autos

NM/M
Common Player: 25.00
Production 50 Sets
Limited: 1X-2X
Production 25 Sets
LT-1 Aaron Brooks 30.00
LT-2 Ahman Green 75.00
LT-3 Bart Starr/10
LT-4 Bob Griese 60.00
LT-5 Brian Urlacher 60.00
LT-6 Chad Pennington 60.00
LT-7 Chris Chambers 50.00
LT-8 Clinton Portis 80.00
LT-9 Dan Marino 200.00
LT-10 David Carr 50.00
LT-11 Deion Sanders 100.00
LT-12 Deuce McAllister 50.00
LT-13 Dick Butkus 80.00
LT-14 Don Shula 50.00
LT-15 Drew Bledsoe 50.00
LT-16 Earl Campbell 60.00
LT-17 Ashley Lelie 25.00
LT-18 Eric Moulds 30.00
LT-19 Fran Tarkenton 60.00
LT-20 Isaac Bruce 30.00
LT-21 Jamal Lewis 80.00
LT-22 Jim Kelly 80.00
LT-23 Joe Namath 175.00
LT-24 Joey Harrington 60.00
LT-25 Johnny Unitas/5
LT-26 Kendrell Bell 30.00
LT-27 Kurt Warner 50.00
LT-28 Antwann Randle El 40.00
LT-29 Marcus Allen 60.00
LT-30 Marvin Harrison 50.00
LT-31 Michael Irvin 60.00
LT-32 Michael Vick 200.00
LT-33 Mike Alstott 40.00
LT-34 Mike Singletary 50.00
LT-35 Priest Holmes 80.00
LT-36 Ricky Williams 60.00
LT-37 Roger Staubach 100.00
LT-38 Roy Williams 50.00
LT-39 Santana Moss 40.00
LT-40 Shaun Alexander 40.00
LT-41 Steve Largent 80.00
LT-42 Steve McNair 80.00
LT-43 Steve Young 80.00
LT-44 Terrell Owens 40.00
LT-45 Tim Brown 60.00
LT-46 Tom Brady 100.00
LT-47 Tony Dorsett 60.00
LT-48 Quincy Carter 50.00
LT-49 Troy Aikman 100.00
LT-50 Warren Moon 40.00

2003 Leaf Rookies & Stars

NM/M
Common Player (1-100): .20
Minor Stars: .40
Unlisted Stars: .60
Common Rookie (101-200): 2.00
Minor Rookie: 3.00
Unlisted Rookie: 4.00
Common Rookie (201-250):
201-250 Production 750 Sets
Common Rookie (251-280):
251-280 Production 550 Sets
201-250 First 150 Signed
Cards 251-280 First 50 Signed
Pack (6): 3.00
Box (24): 50.00
1 Emmitt Smith 1.50
2 Michael Vick 2.00
3 Peerless Price .40
4 T.J. Duckett .60
5 Warrick Dunn .40
6 Jamal Lewis .60
7 Ray Lewis .40
8 Drew Bledsoe .75
9 Eric Moulds .40
10 Josh Reed .40
11 Travis Henry .40
12 Julius Peppers .40
13 Anthony Thomas .40
14 Brian Urlacher .75
15 Marty Booker .40
16 Kordell Stewart .40
17 Corey Dillon .40
18 Chad Johnson .40
19 Tim Couch .40
20 William Green .60
21 Antonio Bryant .40
22 Roy Williams .40
23 Ashley Lelie .40
24 Clinton Portis 1.50
25 Ed McCaffrey .20
26 Jake Plummer .40
27 Rod Smith .40
28 Joey Harrington 1.25
29 Ahman Green .60
30 Brett Favre 2.00
31 Donald Driver .40
32 Javon Walker .40
33 David Carr 1.25
34 Edgerrin James 1.00
35 Marvin Harrison .60
36 Peyton Manning 1.00
37 Fred Taylor .60
38 Jimmy Smith .40
39 Mark Brunell .40
40 Priest Holmes .60
41 Tony Gonzalez .40
42 Trent Green .40
43 Chris Chambers .60
44 Jay Fiedler .40
45 Junior Seau .40
46 Ricky Williams 1.00
47 Zach Thomas .40
48 Daunte Culpepper .60
49 Michael Bennett .60
50 Randy Moss 1.00
51 Tom Brady .75
52 Troy Brown .40
53 Aaron Brooks .60
54 Deuce McAllister .60
55 Donte Stallworth .40
56 Joe Horn .40
57 Jeremy Shockey 1.00
58 Kerry Collins .40
59 Michael Strahan .40
60 Tiki Barber .60
61 Chad Pennington .75
62 Curtis Martin .60
63 Santana Moss .40
64 Charles Woodson .40
65 Jerry Rice 1.50
66 Rich Gannon .40
67 Tim Brown .40
68 Donovan McNabb .75
69 Antwann Randle El .40
70 Tommy Maddox .60
71 Jerome Bettis .40
72 Kendrell Bell .40
73 Plaxico Burress .60
74 David Boston .60
75 Drew Brees .75
76 LaDainian Tomlinson .75
77 Kevan Barlow .40
78 Jeff Garcia .40
79 Terrell Owens .60
80 Matt Hasselbeck .40
81 Koren Robinson .40
82 Shaun Alexander .60
83 Isaac Bruce .60
84 Kurt Warner .60
85 Marshall Faulk .60
86 Torry Holt .40
87 Brad Johnson .40
88 Keyshawn Johnson .40
89 Mike Alstott .40
90 Warren Sapp .40
91 Eddie George .60
92 Jevon Kearse .60
93 Steve McNair .60
94 Laveranues Coles .40
95 Rod Gardner .40
96 Patrick Ramsey .40
97 Kyle Boller, Terrell Suggs, Musa Smith .60
98 Rex Grossman, Taylor Jacobs .60
99 Anquan Boldin, Bryant Johnson .60
100 Tyrone Calico, Chris Brown .40
101 *Charles Tillman* 5.00
102 *Justin Griffith* 2.00
103 *Ovie Mughelli* 2.00
104 *Chris Edmonds* 2.00
105 *Jeremi Johnson* 3.00
106 *Malaefou MacKenzie* 2.00
107 *James Lynch* 2.00
108 *B.J. Askew* 4.00
109 *Andrew Pinnock* 5.00
110 *Chris Davis* 2.00
111 *Dan Curley* 2.00
112 *Lenny Walls* 2.00
113 *Travis Fisher* 2.00
114 *Ahmaad Galloway* 3.00
115 *Joe Smith* 2.00
116 *Reno Mahe* 3.00
117 *Torrie Cox* 2.00
118 *Kerry Carter* 2.00
119 *Dwone Hicks* 3.00
120 *Cato June* 2.00
121 *Terry Pierce* 2.00
122 *Eddie Moore* 2.00
123 *Mike Seidman* 2.00
124 *Michael Nattiel* 3.00
125 *Casey Fitzsimmons* 3.00
126 *George Wrighster* 2.00
127 *Mike Pinkard* 3.00
128 *Donald Lee* 2.00
129 *Sean Berton* 3.00
130 *Solomon Bates* 2.00
131 *Zach Hilton* 2.00
132 *Antonio Gates* 8.00
133 *Aaron Walker* 2.00
134 *Richard Angulo* 2.00
135 *Will Heller* 2.00
136 *Theo Sanders* 2.00

137 *Jimmy Farris* 3.00
138 *Ryan Nece* 3.00
139 *Antonio Brown* 3.00
140 *Clarence Coleman* 3.00
141 *Lawrence Hamilton* 3.00
142 *C.J. Jones* 3.00
143 *Frisman Jackson* 2.00
144 *Antonio Chatman* 4.00
145 *Rocky Boiman* 3.00
146 *Tron LaFavor* 2.00
147 *Derick Armstrong* 2.00
148 *J.J. Moses* 3.00
149 *Aaron Moorehead* 3.00
150 *Brad Pyatt* 3.00
151 *Arland Bruce* 3.00
152 *Chris Horn* 3.00
153 *Kareem Kelly* 3.00
154 *Talman Gardner* 3.00
155 *David Tyree* 3.00
156 *Willie Ponder* 2.00
157 *Greg Lewis* 2.00
158 *Eric Parker* 3.00
159 *Kassim Osgood* 3.00
160 *Jason Willis* 3.00
161 *Akbar Gbaja-Biamila* 3.00
162 *Mike Furrey* 3.00
163 *Chris Kelsay* 3.00
164 *Cory Redding* 2.00
165 *Kenny Peterson* 3.00
166 *Osi Umenyiora* 2.00
167 *Tyler Brayton* 3.00
168 *Dewayne White* 2.00
169 *Kevin Williams* 3.00
170 *Dan Klecko* 4.00
171 *Johnathan Sullivan* 3.00
172 *William Joseph* 3.00
173 *Rien Long* 2.00
174 *Angelo Crowell* 2.00
175 *Chaun Thompson* 2.00
176 *Bradie James* 3.00
177 *Antwan Peek* 3.00
178 *Kawicka Mitchell* 2.00
179 *Cie Grant* 3.00
180 *E.J. Henderson* 3.00
181 *Victor Hobson* 3.00
182 *Alonzo Jackson* 3.00
183 *Matt Wilhelm* 2.00
184 *Pisa Tinoisamoa* 4.00
185 *Ricky Manning Jr.* 4.00
186 *Dennis Weathersby* 2.00
187 *Donald Strickland* 2.00
188 *Asante Samuel* 3.00
189 *Eugene Wilson* 3.00
190 *Nnamdi Asomugha* 2.00
191 *Ike Taylor* 3.00
192 *Drayton Florence* 2.00
193 *DeJuan Groce* 3.00
194 *Shane Walton* 2.00
195 *Terrence Holt* 2.00
196 *Rashean Mathis* 2.00
197 *Julian Battle* 2.00
198 *Hanik Milligan* 3.00
199 *Terrence Kiel* 2.00
200 *David Kircus* 3.00
201 *Lee Suggs* 10.00
202 *Charles Rogers* 10.00
203 *Brandon Lloyd* 6.00
204 *Terrence Edwards* 5.00
205 *Tony Romo* 5.00
206 *Brooks Bollinger* 5.00
207 *Jerome McDougle* 4.00
208 *Jimmy Kennedy* 3.00
209 *Ken Dorsey* 8.00
210 *Kirk Farmer* 3.00
211 *Mike Doss* 4.00
212 *Chris Simms* 10.00
213 *Cecil Sapp* 4.00
214 *Justin Gage* 6.00
215 *Sam Aiken* 3.00
216 *Doug Gabriel* 4.00
217 *Jason Witten* 6.00
218 *Bennie Joppru* 4.00
219 *Jason Gesser* 4.00
220 *Brock Forsey* 10.00
221 *Quentin Griffin* 8.00
222 *Avon Cobourne* 5.00
223 *Domanick Davis* 10.00
224 *Boss Bailey* 5.00
225 *Tony Hollings* 4.00
226 *LaBrandon Toefield* 5.00
227 *Arlen Harris* 8.00
228 *Sultan McCullough* 4.00
229 *Visanthe Shiancoe* 3.00
230 *L.J. Smith* 5.00
231 *LaTarence Dunbar* 4.00
232 *Walter Young* 4.00
233 *Bobby Wade* 5.00
234 *Zuriel Smith* 5.00
235 *Adrian Madise* 3.00
236 *Ken Hamlin* 5.00
237 *Carl Ford* 3.00
238 *Cortez Hankton* 3.00
239 *J.R. Tolver* 4.00
240 *Keenan Howry* 5.00
241 *Billy McMullen* 4.00
242 *Arnaz Battle* 4.00
243 *Shaun McDonald* 4.00
244 *Andre Woolfolk* 4.00
245 *Sammy Davis* 4.00
246 *Calvin Pace* 3.00
247 *Michael Haynes* 4.00
248 *Ty Warren* 4.00
249 *Nick Barnett* 8.00
250 *Troy Polamalu* 6.00
251 *Carson Palmer Jsy* 20.00
252 *Byron Leftwich Jsy* 25.00
253 *Kyle Boller Jsy* 12.00
254 *Rex Grossman Jsy* 15.00
255 *Dave Ragone Jsy* 6.00
256 *Brian St. Pierre Jsy* 6.00
257 *Kliff Kingsbury Jsy* 6.00
258 *Seneca Wallace Jsy* 6.00
259 *Larry Johnson Jsy* 12.00
260 *Willis McGahee Jsy* 15.00
261 *Justin Fargas Jsy* 10.00
262 *Onterrio Smith Jsy* 10.00
263 *Chris Brown Jsy* 12.00
264 *Musa Smith Jsy* 6.00
265 *Artose Pinner Jsy* 6.00
266 *Andre Johnson Jsy* 20.00
267 *Kelley Washington Jsy* 8.00
268 *Taylor Jacobs Jsy* 6.00
269 *Bryant Johnson Jsy* 8.00
270 *Tyrone Calico Jsy* 10.00
271 *Anquan Boldin Jsy* 15.00
272 *Bethel Johnson Jsy* 8.00
273 *Nate Burleson Jsy* 8.00
274 *Kevin Curtis Jsy* 6.00
275 *Dallas Clark Jsy* 10.00
276 *Teyo Johnson Jsy* 8.00
277 *Terrell Suggs Jsy* 8.00
278 *Dewayne Robertson Jsy* 6.00
279 *Terence Newman Jsy* 10.00
280 *Marcus Trufant Jsy* 6.00
281 Carson Palmer, Byron Leftwich 30.00
282 Kyle Boller, Dave Ragone 12.00
283 Rex Grossman, Brian St. Pierre 15.00
284 Kliff Kingsbury, Seneca Wallace 10.00
285 Larry Johnson, Willis McGahee 15.00
286 Justin Fargas, Onterrio Smith 12.00
287 Chris Brown, Musa Smith 8.00
288 Artose Pinner, Andre Johnson 15.00
289 Kelley Washington, Taylor Jacobs 10.00
290 Bryant Johnson, Tyrone Calico 10.00
291 Anquan Boldin, Bethel Johnson 15.00
292 Nate Burleson, Kevin Curtis 10.00
293 Dallas Clark, Teyo Johnson 10.00
294 Terrell Suggs, Dewayne Robertson 8.00
295 Terence Newman, Marcus Trufant 10.00

2003 Leaf Rookies & Stars Longevity

Stars: 5X-10X
1-100 Production 100 Sets
Rookies (101-200): 3X-6X
101-200 Production 50 Sets
201-250, 281-295 Production 25 Sets
251-280 Production 10 Sets

2003 Leaf Rookies & Stars Rookie Autographs

NM/M
201 Lee Suggs EXCH 40.00
202 Charles Rogers EXCH 50.00
203 Brandon Lloyd 25.00
204 Terrence Edwards 12.00
205 Tony Romo EXCH 15.00
206 Brooks Bollinger 15.00
207 Jerome McDougle 10.00
208 Jimmy Kennedy 10.00
209 Ken Dorsey 30.00
210 Kirk Farmer 10.00
211 Mike Doss 20.00
212 Chris Simms 30.00
213 Cecil Sapp 12.00
214 Justin Gage 30.00
215 Sam Aiken 10.00
216 Doug Gabriel 12.00
217 Jason Witten 20.00
218 Bennie Joppru 10.00
219 Jason Gesser 20.00
220 Brock Forsey 30.00
221 Quentin Griffin EXCH 50.00
222 Avon Cobourne 20.00
223 Domanick Davis EXCH 60.00
224 Boss Bailey 25.00
225 Tony Hollings 20.00
226 LaBrandon Toefield EXCH 15.00
227 Arlen Harris 25.00
228 Sultan McCullough 15.00
229 Visanthe Shiancoe 20.00
230 L.J. Smith 15.00
231 LaTarence Dunbar 10.00
232 Walter Young 12.00
233 Bobby Wade EXCH 20.00
234 Zuriel Smith 15.00
235 Adrian Madise 12.00
236 Ken Hamlin 15.00
237 Carl Ford 20.00
238 Cortez Hankton 10.00
239 J.R. Tolver 10.00
240 Keenan Howry EXCH 20.00
241 Billy McMullen EXCH 20.00
242 Arnaz Battle 15.00
243 Shaun McDonald 15.00
244 Andre Woolfolk 20.00
245 Sammy Davis 10.00
246 Calvin Pace 10.00
247 Michael Haynes 10.00
248 Ty Warren EXCH 15.00
249 Nick Barnett EXCH 40.00
250 Troy Polamalu 25.00
251 Carson Palmer JSY 100.00
252 Byron Leftwich JSY 120.00
253 Kyle Boller JSY 60.00
254 Rex Grossman JSY 80.00
255 Dave Ragone JSY 25.00
256 Brian St. Pierre JSY 25.00
257 Kliff Kingsbury JSY 25.00
258 Seneca Wallace JSY 25.00
259 Larry Johnson JSY 30.00
260 Willis McGahee JSY EXCH 80.00
261 Justin Fargas JSY 40.00
262 Onterrio Smith JSY EXCH 50.00
263 Chris Brown JSY 50.00
264 Musa Smith JSY 25.00
265 Artose Pinner JSY 30.00
266 Andre Johnson JSY 80.00
267 Kelley Washington JSY 30.00
268 Taylor Jacobs JSY 25.00
269 Bryant Johnson JSY 30.00
270 Tyrone Calico JSY 50.00
271 Anquan Boldin JSY 80.00
272 Bethel Johnson JSY 40.00
273 Nate Burleson JSY EXCH 30.00
274 Kevin Curtis JSY 20.00
275 Dallas Clark JSY 30.00
276 Teyo Johnson JSY 30.00
277 Terrell Suggs JSY 30.00
278 Dewayne Robertson JSY EXCH 20.00
279 Terence Newman JSY 50.00
280 Marcus Trufant JSY 30.00

2003 Leaf Rookies & Stars Freshman Orientation

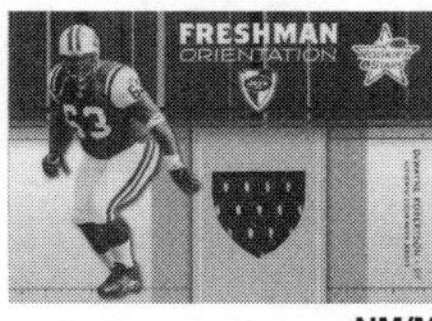

NM/M
Common Player: 5.00
Production 600 Sets
Class Officers: 2X-4X
Production 25 Sets
1 Carson Palmer 15.00
2 Byron Leftwich 20.00
3 Kyle Boller 10.00
4 Rex Grossman 15.00
5 Dave Ragone 5.00
6 Brian St. Pierre 5.00
7 Kliff Kingsbury 5.00
8 Seneca Wallace 6.00
9 Larry Johnson 10.00
10 Willis McGahee 12.00
11 Justin Fargas 8.00
12 Onterrio Smith 10.00
13 Chris Brown 6.00
14 Musa Smith 5.00
15 Artose Pinner 5.00
16 Andre Johnson 15.00
17 Kelley Washington 8.00
18 Taylor Jacobs 5.00
19 Bryant Johnson 8.00
20 Tyrone Calico 10.00
21 Anquan Boldin 12.00
22 Bethel Johnson 8.00
23 Nate Burleson 6.00
24 Kevin Curtis 5.00
25 Dallas Clark 6.00
26 Teyo Johnson 5.00
27 Terrell Suggs 6.00
28 Dewayne Robertson 5.00
29 Terence Newman 10.00
30 Marcus Trufant 5.00

2003 Leaf Rookies & Stars Great American Heroes

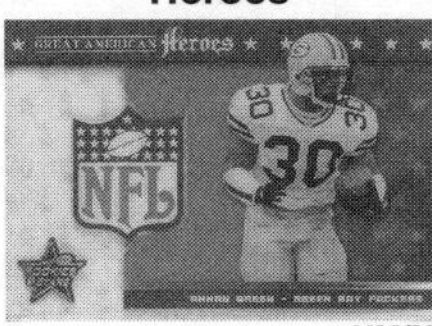

NM/M
Common Player: 1.50
Production 1,325 Sets
1 Brian Urlacher 3.00
2 Bob Griese 2.00
3 Mel Blount 1.50
4 Ahman Green 2.00
5 Aaron Brooks 2.00
6 Chad Pennington 3.00
7 Clinton Portis 4.00
8 Isaac Bruce 2.00
9 Jamal Lewis 2.00
10 Jeff Garcia 2.00
11 Jerry Rice 5.00
12 Joey Harrington 3.00
13 Kurt Warner 2.00
14 LaDainian Tomlinson 2.00
15 Rod Smith 1.50
16 Tommy Maddox 1.50
17 Rex Grossman 4.00
18 Cecil Sapp 1.50
19 Byron Leftwich 5.00
20 Kenny Peterson 1.50

2003 Leaf Rookies & Stars Great American Heroes Autos

NM/M
1 Brian Urlacher/25
2 Bob Griese/17
3 Mel Blount/53 25.00
4 Ahman Green/25
5 Aaron Brooks/75 20.00
6 Chad Pennington/10
7 Clinton Portis/30 100.00
8 Isaac Bruce/75 25.00
9 Jamal Lewis/25
10 Jeff Garcia/25
11 Jerry Rice/25
12 Joey Harrington/30 50.00
13 Kurt Warner/25
14 LaDainian Tomlinson/25
15 Rod Smith/150 12.00
16 Tommy Maddox/50 20.00
17 Rex Grossman/50 50.00
18 Cecil Sapp/100 10.00
19 Byron Leftwich/25
20 Kenny Peterson/100 10.00

2003 Leaf Rookies & Stars Initial Steps

NM/M
Common Player: 6.00
Production 100 Sets
1 Carson Palmer 20.00
2 Byron Leftwich 30.00
3 Kyle Boller 12.00
4 Rex Grossman 20.00
5 Dave Ragone 6.00
6 Brian St. Pierre 6.00
7 Kliff Kingsbury 6.00
8 Seneca Wallace 6.00
9 Larry Johnson 12.00
10 Willis McGahee 15.00
11 Justin Fargas 10.00
12 Onterrio Smith 12.00
13 Chris Brown 8.00
14 Musa Smith 6.00
15 Artose Pinner 6.00
16 Andre Johnson 20.00
17 Kelley Washington 8.00
18 Taylor Jacobs 6.00
19 Bryant Johnson 8.00
20 Tyrone Calico 10.00
21 Anquan Boldin 15.00
22 Bethel Johnson 8.00
23 Nate Burleson 8.00
24 Kevin Curtis 6.00
25 Dallas Clark 6.00
26 Teyo Johnson 6.00
27 Terrell Suggs 8.00
28 Dewayne Robertson 6.00
29 Terence Newman 8.00
30 Marcus Trufant 6.00

2003 Leaf Rookies & Stars Masks

NM/M
Common Player: 5.00
Production 350 Sets
Dual Masks:
Production: First 100 Sets
1 Carson Palmer 15.00
2 Byron Leftwich 20.00
3 Kyle Boller 12.00
4 Rex Grossman 15.00
5 Dave Ragone 5.00
6 Brian St. Pierre 5.00
7 Kliff Kingsbury 5.00
8 Seneca Wallace 6.00
9 Larry Johnson 10.00
10 Willis McGahee 15.00
11 Justin Fargas 10.00
12 Onterrio Smith 12.00
13 Chris Brown 8.00
14 Musa Smith 6.00
15 Artose Pinner 5.00
16 Andre Johnson 15.00
17 Kelley Washington 8.00
18 Taylor Jacobs 6.00
19 Bryant Johnson 6.00
20 Tyrone Calico 12.00
21 Anquan Boldin 15.00
22 Bethel Johnson 8.00
23 Nate Burleson 6.00
24 Kevin Curtis 5.00
25 Dallas Clark 6.00
26 Teyo Johnson 6.00
27 Terrell Suggs 8.00
28 Dewayne Robertson 5.00
29 Terence Newman 10.00
30 Marcus Trufant 5.00

2003 Leaf Rookies & Stars Prime Cuts

Production 25 Sets
1 Aaron Brooks
2 Ahman Green
3 Antonio Bryant
4 Antwann Randle El
5 Ashley Lelie
6 Brett Favre
7 Brian Urlacher
8 Chad Pennington
9 Chris Chambers
10 Clinton Portis
11 Daunte Culpepper
12 David Carr
13 Deuce McAllister
14 Donovan McNabb
15 Donte Stallworth
16 Drew Bledsoe
17 Drew Brees
18 Edgerrin James
19 Jeff Garcia
20 Jeremy Shockey
21 Jerry Rice
22 Joey Harrington
23 Julius Peppers
24 Kurt Warner
25 LaDainian Tomlinson
26 Marshall Faulk
27 Marvin Harrison
28 Michael Vick
29 Peyton Manning
30 Priest Holmes
31 Randy Moss
32 Ricky Williams
33 Shaun Alexander
34 Steve McNair
35 Tom Brady
36 William Green

2003 Leaf Rookies & Stars Slideshow

NM/M
Common Player: 1.50
Production 1,500 Sets
1 Clinton Portis 5.00
2 Drew Bledsoe 2.50
3 Michael Vick 8.00
4 Donovan McNabb 3.00
5 Brett Favre 8.00
6 Deuce McAllister 2.50
7 Ricky Williams 4.00
8 Jeremy Shockey 4.00
9 Brian Urlacher 3.00
10 Chad Pennington 3.00

2003 Leaf Rookies & Stars Ticket Masters

NM/M
Common Player: 2.00
Production 1,325 Sets
1 Brett Favre, Ahman Green 6.00
2 Joey Harrington, Charles Rogers 4.00
3 Brian Urlacher, Anthony Thomas 3.00
4 Randy Moss, Daunte Culpepper 4.00
5 Kurt Warner, Marshall Faulk 3.00
6 Jeff Garcia, Terrell Owens 2.00
7 Ricky Williams, Zach Thomas 3.00
8 LaDainian Tomlinson, Drew Brees 3.00
9 Jerry Rice, Rich Gannon 4.00
10 Priest Holmes, Tony Gonzalez 3.00
11 Clinton Portis, Rod Smith 3.00
12 Drew Bledsoe, Travis Henry 2.00
13 Chad Johnson, Carson Palmer 5.00
14 Chad Pennington, Curtis Martin 3.00
15 Steve McNair, Eddie George 3.00
16 Peyton Manning, Marvin Harrison 4.00
17 Deuce McAllister, Aaron Brooks 2.00
18 Donovan McNabb, Duce Staley 3.00
19 Michael Vick, Peerless Price 5.00
20 Jeremy Shockey, Tiki Barber 2.00

2003 Leaf Rookies & Stars Triple Threads

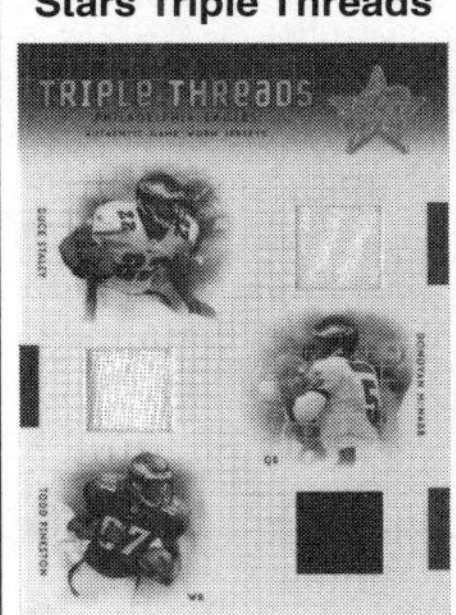

NM/M
Common Player: 12.00
Production 100 Sets
1 Michael Vick, T.J. Duckett, Warrick Dunn 25.00
2 Kurt Warner, Marshall Faulk, Torry Holt 20.00
3 Drew Bledsoe, Eric Moulds, Travis Henry 15.00
4 Brian Urlacher, Anthony Thomas, Mike Brown 20.00
5 Clinton Portis, Ed McCaffrey, Rod Smith 20.00
6 Brett Favre, Ahman Green, Donald Driver 40.00
7 Peyton Manning, Edgerrin James, Marvin Harrison 40.00
8 Mark Brunell, Fred Taylor, Jimmy Smith 12.00
9 Trent Green, Priest Holmes, Tony Gonzalez 20.00
10 Ricky Williams, Chris Chambers, Zach Thomas 20.00
11 Daunte Culpepper, Michael Bennett, Randy Moss 25.00
12 Tom Brady, Antowain Smith, Troy Brown 25.00
13 Aaron Brooks, Deuce McAllister, Donte Stallworth 15.00
14 Kerry Collins, Jeremy Shockey, Michael Strahan 20.00
15 Chad Pennington, Curtis Martin, Santana Moss 20.00
16 Rich Gannon, Jerry Rice, Tim Brown 20.00
17 Donovan McNabb, Duce Staley, Todd Pinkston 20.00
18 Jerome Bettis, Kendrell Bell, Plaxico Burress 12.00
19 Drew Brees, Doug Flutie, LaDainian Tomlinson 15.00
20 Jeff Garcia, Garrison Hearst, Terrell Owens 15.00

2004 Leaf Certified Materials

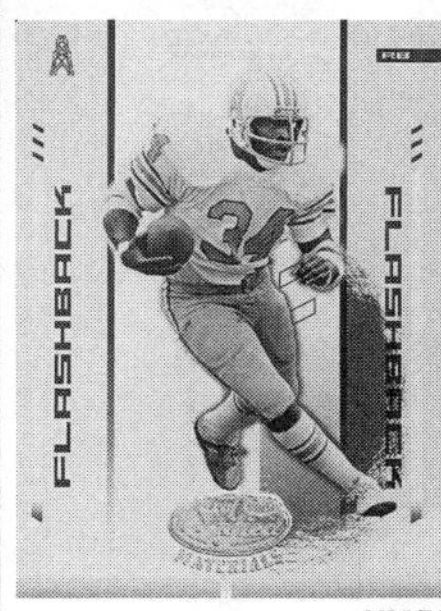

NM/M
Common Card (1-150): .25
Minor Stars (1-150): .50
Unlisted Stars (1-150): .75
Unsigned Rookies (150-200): 4.00
Common Signed Rookie (150-200): 6.00
Production 1,000 Sets
Common Rookie (201-233): 5.00
Production 1,250 Sets
Pack (5): 12.75
Box (10): 110.00
1 Anquan Boldin .75
2 Emmitt Smith 2.00
3 Josh McCown .25
4 Marcel Shipp .25
5 Michael Vick 2.00
6 Peerless Price .50
7 T.J. Duckett .50
8 Warrick Dunn .25
9 Jamal Lewis .75
10 Kyle Boller .75
11 Ray Lewis .50
12 Terrell Suggs .25
13 Todd Heap .50
14 Drew Bledsoe .50
15 Eric Moulds .25
16 Travis Henry .25
17 Julius Peppers .25
18 Muhsin Muhammad .50
19 Stephen Davis .50
20 Anthony Thomas .50
21 Brian Urlacher .75
22 Rex Grossman .75
23 Chad Johnson .50
24 Corey Dillon .50
25 Peter Warrick .50
26 Jeff Garcia .75
27 Tim Couch .50
28 Willie Green .50
29 Antonio Bryant .50
30 Keyshawn Johnson .50
31 Quincy Carter .75
32 Roy Williams-Cowboys .50
33 Terence Newman .25
34 Ashley Lelie .50
35 Ed McCaffrey .25
36 Jake Plummer .50
37 Mike Anderson .25
38 Rod Smith .25
39 Charles Rogers .75
40 Joey Harrington .75
41 Ahman Green .75
42 Brett Favre 2.50
43 Donald Driver .25
44 Javon Walker .50
45 Robert Ferguson .25
46 Andre Johnson .75

47 David Carr 1.00
48 Edgerrin James 1.00
49 Marvin Harrison .75
50 Peyton Manning 1.50
51 Reggie Wayne .25
52 Byron Leftwich 1.50
53 Fred Taylor .75
54 Jimmy Smith .25
55 Dante Hall .25
56 Priest Holmes 1.00
57 Tony Gonzalez .50
58 Trent Green .25
59 A.J. Feeley .25
60 Chris Chambers .75
61 David Boston .50
62 Jason Taylor .25
63 Jay Fiedler .25
64 Junior Seau .25
65 Randy McMichael .25
66 Ricky Williams .75
67 Zach Thomas .25
68 Daunte Culpepper .75
69 Michael Bennett .75
70 Randy Moss 1.50
71 Tom Brady 1.50
72 Troy Brown .25
73 Ty Law .25
74 Aaron Brooks .75
75 Deuce McAllister .75
76 Donte Stallworth .50
77 Amani Toomer .50
78 Jeremy Shockey .75
79 Kerry Collins .25
80 Michael Strahan .25
81 Tiki Barber .25
82 Chad Pennington 1.00
83 Curtis Martin .75
84 Justin McCareins .25
85 Santana Moss .25
86 Charles Woodson .25
87 Jerry Rice 2.00
88 Rich Gannon .25
89 Tim Brown .75
90 Warren Sapp .25
91 Correll Buckhalter .25
92 Donovan McNabb 1.00
93 Freddie Mitchell .25
94 Jevon Kearse .25
95 Terrell Owens .75
96 Antwann Randle El .50
97 Duce Staley .25
98 Hines Ward .50
99 Jerome Bettis .50
100 Plaxico Burress .75
101 Doug Flutie .50
102 LaDainian Tomlinson 1.00
103 Koren Robinson .25
104 Matt Hasselbeck .50
105 Shaun Alexander .75
106 Isaac Bruce .50
107 Kurt Warner .75
108 Marc Bulger .50
109 Marshall Faulk 1.00
110 Torry Holt .75
111 Brad Johnson .25
112 Mike Alstott .25
113 Derrick Mason .25
114 Drew Bennett .25
115 Eddie George .75
116 Frank Wycheck .25
117 Keith Bulluck .25
118 Steve McNair .75
119 Tyrone Calico .25
120 Clinton Portis 1.50
121 LaVar Arrington .75
122 Laveranues Coles .50
123 Mark Brunell .50
124 Patrick Ramsey .50
125 Rod Gardner .25
126 Jake Plummer .50
127 Thomas Jones .50
128 Priest Holmes 1.00
129 Jim Kelly 1.00
130 Doug Flutie .50
131 Walter Payton 2.50
132 Troy Aikman 1.50
133 John Elway 2.00
134 Barry Sanders 2.00
135 Mark Brunell .50
136 Earl Campbell .75
137 Joe Montana 2.50
138 Dan Marino 2.00
139 Curtis Martin .75
140 Drew Bledsoe .75
141 Ricky Williams .75
142 Junior Seau .25
143 Charlie Garner .25
144 Jerry Rice 2.00
145 Ahman Green .75
146 Jerome Bettis .50
147 Trent Green .25
148 Warrick Dunn .25
149 Deion Sanders .75
150 Stephen Davis .75
151 *Adimchinobe Echemandu Auto* 6.00
152 *Ahmad Carroll* 4.00
153 *Andy Hall Auto* 6.00
154 *B.J. Johnson Auto* 10.00
155 *B.J. Symons Auto* 6.00
156 *Bradlee Van Pelt Auto* 10.00
157 *Brandon Miree Auto* 6.00
158 *Bruce Perry Auto* 10.00
159 *Carlos Francis Auto* 10.00
160 *Casey Bramlet Auto* 10.00
161 *Chris Gamble* 4.00
162 *Clarence Moore Auto* 15.00
163 *Cody Pickett Auto* 8.00
164 *Craig Krenzel Auto* 10.00
165 *D.J. Hackett* 4.00
166 *D.J. Williams* 4.00
167 *Derrick Ward Auto* 6.00
168 *Drew Carter Auto* 8.00
169 *Ernest Wilford* 6.00
170 *Drew Henson* 10.00
171 *Jamaar Taylor Auto* 8.00
172 *Jared Lorenzen Auto* 10.00
173 *Jarrett Payton Auto* 10.00
174 *Jason Babin Auto* 10.00
175 *Jeff Smoker Auto* 15.00
176 *Jeris McIntyre Auto* 8.00
177 *Jerricho Cotchery* 4.00
178 *Jim Sorgi Auto* 8.00
179 *John Navarre Auto* 10.00
180 *Patrick Crayton Auto* 8.00
181 *Johnnie Morant* 4.00
182 *Sean Taylor* 8.00
183 *Jonathan Vilma* 4.00
184 *Josh Harris* 6.00
185 *Kenechi Udeze* 4.00
186 *Mark Jones Auto* 6.00
187 *Matt Mauck Auto* 10.00
188 *Maurice Mann Auto* 8.00
189 *Michael Turner* 4.00
190 *P.K. Sam* 4.00
191 *Quincy Wilson* 4.00
192 *Ran Carthon Auto* 6.00
193 *Ryan Krause Auto* 6.00
194 *Samie Parker* 4.00
195 *Sloan Thomas Auto* 8.00
196 *Tommie Harris* 4.00
197 *Triandos Luke Auto* 10.00
198 *Troy Fleming Auto* 6.00
199 *Vince Wilfork* 4.00
200 *Will Smith* 4.00
201 *Larry Fitzgerald Jsy* 12.00
202 *DeAngelo Hall Jsy* 6.00
203 *Matt Schaub Jsy* 5.00
204 *Michael Jenkins Jsy* 6.00
205 *Devard Darling Jsy* 5.00
206 *J.P. Losman Jsy* 10.00
207 *Lee Evans Jsy* 10.00
208 *Keary Colbert Jsy* 6.00
209 *Bernard Berrian Jsy* 5.00
210 *Chris Perry Jsy* 6.00
211 *Kellen Winslow Jr. Jsy* 8.00
212 *Luke McCown Jsy* 5.00
213 *Julius Jones Jsy* 12.00
214 *Darius Watts Jsy* 5.00
215 *Tatum Bell Jsy* 6.00
216 *Kevin Jones Jsy* 10.00
217 *Roy Williams Jsy* 12.00
218 *Dunta Robinson Jsy* 5.00
219 *Greg Jones Jsy* 5.00
220 *Reggie Williams Jsy* 8.00
221 *Mewelde Moore Jsy* 5.00
222 *Ben Watson Jsy* 5.00
223 *Cedric Cobbs Jsy* 5.00
224 *Devery Henderson Jsy* 5.00
225 *Eli Manning Jsy* 30.00
226 *Robert Gallery Jsy* 5.00
227 *Ben Roethlisberger Jsy* 50.00
228 *Philip Rivers Jsy* 12.00
229 *Derrick Hamilton Jsy* 5.00
230 *Rashaun Woods Jsy* 8.00
231 *Steven Jackson Jsy* 10.00
232 *Michael Clayton Jsy* 8.00
233 *Ben Troupe Jsy* 5.00

2004 Leaf Certified Materials Mirror White

Current (1-150): 2X-4X
Rookies (151-200): 1X-3X
Production 150 Sets

2004 Leaf Certified Materials Mirror Red

Current (1-150): 2X-4.5X
Rookies (151-200): 1X-3.5X
Production 100 Sets

2004 Leaf Certified Materials Mirror Blue

Current (1-150): 2.5X-5X
Rookies (151-200): 1.5X-4X
Production 50 Sets

2004 Leaf Certified Materials Mirror Gold

No Pricing
Production 25 Sets

2004 Leaf Certified Materials Mirror Emerald

No Pricing
Production 5 Sets

2004 Leaf Certified Materials Mirror Black

No Pricing
Production 1 Set

2004 Leaf Certified Materials Certified Skills Jersey

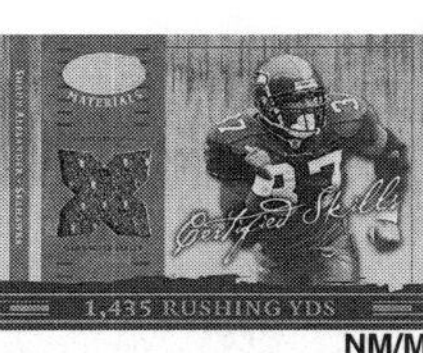

NM/M
Common Player: 8.00
Production 175 Sets
Positions: .75X-1.5X
Production 75 Sets
Positions Prime: No Pricing
Production 25 Sets
Black: No Pricing
Production 1 Set
CS1 Peyton Manning 15.00
CS2 Trent Green 8.00
CS3 Marc Bulger 8.00
CS4 Matt Hasselbeck 8.00
CS5 Brad Johnson 8.00
CS6 Tom Brady 15.00
CS7 Aaron Brooks 10.00
CS8 Daunte Culpepper 10.00
CS9 Brett Favre 25.00
CS10 Quincy Carter 10.00
CS11 Donovan McNabb 12.00
CS12 Steve McNair 10.00
CS13 Kerry Collins 8.00
CS14 Dan Marino 40.00
CS15 John Elway 30.00
CS16 Warren Moon 12.00
CS17 Fran Tarkenton 15.00
CS18 Brett Favre 25.00
CS19 Joe Montana 40.00
CS20 Jamal Lewis 10.00
CS21 Ahman Green 10.00
CS22 LaDainian Tomlinson 12.00
CS23 Deuce McAllister 10.00
CS24 Clinton Portis 15.00
CS25 Fred Taylor 10.00
CS26 Stephen Davis 8.00
CS27 Shaun Alexander 10.00
CS28 Priest Holmes 12.00
CS29 Ricky Williams 10.00
CS30 Travis Henry 8.00
CS31 Curtis Martin 10.00
CS32 Edgerrin James 12.00
CS33 Tiki Barber 8.00
CS34 Eddie George 10.00
CS35 Anthony Thomas 8.00
CS36 Emmitt Smith 20.00
CS37 Walter Payton 50.00
CS38 Barry Sanders 40.00
CS39 Torry Holt 10.00
CS40 Randy Moss 15.00
CS41 Anquan Boldin 10.00
CS42 Chad Johnson 8.00
CS43 Derrick Mason 8.00
CS44 Marvin Harrison 10.00
CS45 Laveranues Coles 8.00
CS46 Hines Ward 8.00
CS47 Santana Moss 8.00
CS48 Terrell Owens 10.00
CS49 Jerry Rice 20.00
CS50 Tim Brown 10.00

2004 Leaf Certified Materials Cert. Potential Jersey

NM/M
Common Player: 6.00
Production 150 Sets
Infinite: .75X-1.5X
Production 75 Sets
Infinite Prime: No Pricing
Production 25 Sets
Black: No Pricing
Production 1 Set
CP1 A.J. Feeley 6.00
CP2 Andre Johnson 8.00
CP3 Anquan Boldin 8.00
CP4 Antonio Bryant 6.00
CP5 Antwann Randle El 6.00
CP6 Ashley Lelie 6.00
CP7 Bryant Johnson 6.00
CP8 Byron Leftwich 10.00
CP9 Charles Rogers 8.00
CP10 Correll Buckhalter 6.00
CP11 Dallas Clark 6.00
CP12 David Carr 10.00
CP13 Donte Stallworth 6.00
CP14 Drew Bennett 6.00
CP15 Javon Walker 8.00
CP16 Joey Harrington 8.00
CP17 Josh McCown 6.00
CP18 Justin McCareins 6.00
CP19 Kyle Boller 8.00
CP20 Marcel Shipp 6.00
CP21 Nick Barnett 6.00
CP22 Rex Grossman 8.00
CP23 Terence Newman 6.00
CP24 Terrell Suggs 6.00
CP25 Tyrone Calico 6.00

2004 Leaf Certified Materials Fabric of the Game

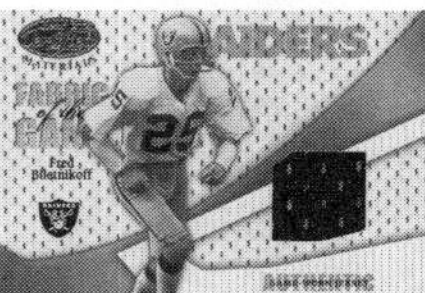

NM/M
Common Player: 10.00
Production 100 Sets
Debut Year
Cards #74-103: .5X-1.5X
Cards #50-73: .75X-2X
21st Century: No Pricing
Production 21 Sets
Team Logo: No Pricing
Production 5 Sets
FG1 Aaron Brooks 12.00
FG2 Ahman Green 12.00
FG3 Andre Johnson 12.00
FG4 Anquan Boldin 12.00
FG5 Antwann Randle El 10.00
FG6 Barry Sanders 30.00
FG7 Bart Starr 30.00
FG8 Bob Griese 15.00
FG9 Brett Favre 40.00
FG10 Brian Urlacher 12.00
FG11 Bruce Smith 12.00
FG12 Byron Leftwich 20.00
FG13 Chad Johnson 10.00
FG14 Chad Pennington 15.00
FG15 Charles Rogers 12.00
FG16 Charles Woodson 10.00
FG17 Chris Chambers 12.00
FG18 Clinton Portis 20.00
FG19 Dan Marino 40.00
FG20 Daryl Johnston 12.00
FG21 Daunte Culpepper 12.00
FG22 David Carr 15.00
FG23 Deacon Jones 12.00
FG24 Deion Sanders 15.00
FG25 Derrick Mason 10.00
FG26 Deuce McAllister 12.00
FG27 Doak Walker 30.00
FG28 Don Maynard 10.00
FG29 Don Shula 15.00
FG30 Donovan McNabb 15.00
FG31 Drew Bledsoe 12.00
FG32 Earl Campbell 15.00
FG33 Eddie George 12.00
FG34 Edgerrin James 15.00
FG35 Emmitt Smith 30.00
FG36 Fran Tarkenton 12.00
FG37 Franco Harris 20.00
FG38 Fred Biletnikoff 15.00
FG39 George Blanda 15.00
FG40 Harvey Martin 12.00
FG41 Herman Edwards 12.00
FG42 Hines Ward 10.00
FG43 Jake Plummer 10.00
FG44 Jamal Lewis 12.00
FG45 James Lofton 15.00
FG46 Javon Walker 12.00
FG47 Jeremy Shockey 12.00
FG48 Jerry Rice 30.00
FG49 Jim Brown 25.00
FG50 Jim Kelly 20.00
FG51 Jim Plunkett 12.00
FG52 Jim Thorpe 100.00
FG53 Joe Greene 15.00
FG54 Joe Montana 40.00
FG55 Joe Namath 25.00
FG56 Joey Harrington 12.00
FG57 John Elway 25.00
FG58 John Riggins 15.00
FG59 Kendrell Bell 10.00
FG60 L.C. Greenwood 15.00
FG61 LaDainian Tomlinson 15.00
FG62 Lawrence Taylor 20.00
FG63 Leroy Kelly 10.00
FG64 Lynn Swann 40.00
FG65 Marc Bulger 10.00
FG66 Mark Bavaro 10.00
FG67 Marshall Faulk 15.00
FG68 Matt Hasselbeck 10.00
FG69 Mel Blount 15.00
FG70 Michael Irvin 12.00
FG71 Michael Vick 30.00
FG72 Mike Singletary 12.00
FG73 Ozzie Newsome 12.00
FG74 Paul Warfield 15.00
FG75 Peyton Manning 20.00
FG76 Priest Holmes 15.00
FG77 Quincy Carter 12.00
FG78 Randy Moss 20.00
FG79 Ray Nitschke 25.00
FG80 Reggie White 15.00
FG81 Rex Grossman 12.00
FG82 Richard Dent 12.00
FG83 Ricky Williams 12.00
FG84 Roger Staubach 30.00
FG85 Roy Williams-Cowboys 10.00
FG86 Santana Moss 10.00
FG87 Shaun Alexander 12.00
FG88 Sterling Sharpe 15.00
FG89 Steve McNair 12.00
FG90 Terrell Davis 15.00
FG91 Terry Bradshaw 30.00
FG92 Thurman Thomas 12.00
FG93 Tiki Barber 10.00
FG94 Todd Heap 10.00
FG95 Tom Brady 20.00
FG96 Tony Dorsett 15.00
FG97 Trent Green 10.00
FG98 Troy Aikman 30.00
FG99 Walter Payton 50.00
FG100 Warren Moon 15.00

2004 Leaf Certified Materials Gold Team Jersey

NM/M
Common Player: 12.00
Production 150 Sets
24K: .75X-1.5X
Production 75 Sets
24K Prime: No Pricing
Production 25 Sets
Black: No Pricing
Production 1 Set
GT1 Barry Sanders 25.00
GT2 Brett Favre 40.00
GT3 Brian Urlacher 12.00
GT4 Byron Leftwich 20.00
GT5 Chad Pennington 15.00
GT6 Dan Marino 40.00
GT7 Daunte Culpepper 12.00
GT8 David Carr 15.00
GT9 Deuce McAllister 12.00
GT10 Donovan McNabb 15.00
GT11 Emmitt Smith 30.00
GT12 Jerry Rice 30.00
GT13 Joe Montana 40.00
GT14 Joey Harrington 12.00
GT15 John Elway 30.00
GT16 LaDainian Tomlinson 15.00
GT17 Michael Vick 30.00
GT18 Peyton Manning 20.00
GT19 Priest Holmes 15.00
GT20 Randy Moss 20.00
GT21 Ricky Williams 12.00
GT22 Steve McNair 12.00
GT23 Tom Brady 20.00
GT24 Troy Aikman 30.00
GT25 Walter Payton 50.00

2004 Leaf Certified Materials Mirror Red Signatures

NM/M
Common Player: 15.00
Sequentially Numbered
Numbered 25 or less: No Pricing
1 Anquan Boldin/89 25.00
3 Josh McCown/135 15.00
5 Michael Vick/120 80.00
14 Drew Bledsoe/20
21 Brian Urlacher/50 50.00
22 Rex Grossman/237 25.00
30 Keyshawn Johnson/40 25.00
32 Roy Williams-Cowboys/125 25.00
40 Joey Harrington/32 50.00
41 Ahman Green/60 40.00
44 Javon Walker/31 25.00
49 Marvin Harrison/20
50 Peyton Manning/20
56 Priest Holmes/63 75.00
60 Chris Chambers/31 25.00
69 Michael Bennett/125 15.00
71 Tom Brady/20
75 Deuce McAllister/85 30.00
80 Michael Strahan/60 30.00
82 Chad Pennington/30 50.00
85 Santana Moss/250 15.00
96 Antwann Randle El/50 25.00
98 Hines Ward/49 30.00
102 LaDainian Tomlinson/60 50.00
104 Matt Hasselbeck/150 20.00
105 Shaun Alexander/60 25.00
115 Eddie George/20
120 Clinton Portis/20
129 Jim Kelly/48 40.00
132 Troy Aikman/20
136 Earl Campbell/20
137 Joe Montana/60 150.00
145 Ahman Green/100 40.00
152 Ahmad Carroll/90 30.00
161 Chris Gamble/100 15.00
165 D.J. Hackett/90 15.00
166 D.J. Williams/250 20.00
169 Ernest Wilford/55 15.00
177 Jerricho Cotchery/90 15.00
181 Johnnie Morant/90
182 Sean Taylor/25 15.00
183 Jonathan Vilma/225 15.00
185 Kenechi Udeze/165 15.00
189 Michael Turner/130 15.00
190 P.K. Sam/215 15.00
191 Quincy Wilson/90 15.00
194 Samie Parker/140 15.00
196 Tommie Harris/75 20.00
199 Vince Wilfork/225 15.00
200 Will Smith/100 15.00

2004 Leaf Certified Materials Mirror Blue Signatures

NM/M
Common Player: 20.00
Sequentially Numbered
Numbered 25 or less: No Pricing
Mirror Gold Signatures: No Pricing
Production between 10 & 25 Sets
Mirror Emerald Signatures: No Pricing
Production 5 Sets
Mirror Black Signatures: No Pricing
Production 1 Set
1 Anquan Boldin/50 30.00
3 Josh McCown/100 20.00
5 Michael Vick/100 80.00
14 Drew Bledsoe/15
21 Brian Urlacher/40 50.00
22 Rex Grossman/100 30.00
30 Keyshawn Johnson/20
32 Roy Williams-Cowboys/89 30.00
40 Joey Harrington/20
41 Ahman Green/60 40.00
44 Javon Walker/20
49 Marvin Harrison/15
50 Peyton Manning/15
56 Priest Holmes/25
60 Chris Chambers/20
69 Michael Bennett/84 20.00
71 Tom Brady/15
74 Aaron Brooks/28 25.00
75 Deuce McAllister/50 30.00
80 Michael Strahan/25
82 Chad Pennington/20
85 Santana Moss/100 25.00
96 Antwann Randle El/38 30.00
98 Hines Ward/25
102 LaDainian Tomlinson/25
104 Matt Hasselbeck/87 20.00
105 Shaun Alexander/25
115 Eddie George/15
120 Clinton Portis/15
129 Jim Kelly/25
132 Troy Aikman/15
136 Earl Campbell/15
137 Joe Montana/25
152 Ahmad Carroll/25
161 Chris Gamble/75 20.00
165 D.J. Hackett/75 20.00
166 D.J. Williams/100 20.00
169 Ernest Wilford/25
170 Drew Henson/15
177 Jerricho Cotchery/75 20.00
181 Johnnie Morant/50
182 Sean Taylor/15
183 Jonathan Vilma/75 20.00
184 Josh Harris/25
185 Kenechi Udeze/100 20.00
189 Michael Turner/100 20.00
190 P.K. Sam/100 20.00
191 Quincy Wilson/50 20.00
194 Samie Parker/75 20.00
196 Tommie Harris/50 25.00
199 Vince Wilfork/100 20.00
200 Will Smith/75 20.00

2004 Leaf Certified Materials Mirror White Materials

NM/M
Common Player: 5.00
Production 250 Sets
Mirror Red Materials: .75X-1.5X
Production 150 Sets
Mirror Blue Materials: 1X-3X
Production 50 Sets
Mirror Gold Materials: No Pricing
Production 25 Sets
Mirror Emerald Materials: No Pricing
Production 5 Sets
Mirror Black Materials: No Pricing
Production 1 Set
1 Anquan Boldin 8.00
2 Emmitt Smith 15.00
3 Josh McCown 5.00
4 Marcel Shipp 5.00
5 Michael Vick 15.00
6 Peerless Price 6.00
7 T.J. Duckett 6.00
8 Warrick Dunn 5.00
9 Jamal Lewis 8.00
10 Kyle Boller 8.00
11 Ray Lewis 8.00
12 Terrell Suggs 5.00
13 Todd Heap 6.00
14 Drew Bledsoe 8.00
15 Eric Moulds 5.00
16 Travis Henry 5.00
17 Julius Peppers 5.00
18 Muhsin Muhammad 6.00
19 Stephen Davis 6.00
20 Anthony Thomas 6.00
21 Brian Urlacher 8.00
22 Rex Grossman 8.00
23 Chad Johnson 6.00
24 Corey Dillon 6.00
25 Peter Warrick 6.00
26 Jeff Garcia 8.00
27 Tim Couch 6.00
28 Willie Green 6.00
29 Antonio Bryant 6.00
30 Keyshawn Johnson 6.00
31 Quincy Carter 8.00
32 Roy Williams-Cowboys 6.00
33 Terence Newman 5.00
34 Ashley Lelie 6.00
35 Ed McCaffrey 5.00
36 Jake Plummer 6.00
37 Mike Anderson 5.00
38 Rod Smith 5.00
39 Charles Rogers 8.00
40 Joey Harrington 8.00
41 Ahman Green 8.00
42 Brett Favre 20.00
43 Donald Driver 5.00
44 Javon Walker 6.00
45 Robert Ferguson 5.00
46 Andre Johnson 8.00
47 David Carr 10.00
48 Edgerrin James 10.00
49 Marvin Harrison 8.00
50 Peyton Manning 12.00
51 Reggie Wayne 5.00
52 Byron Leftwich 12.00
53 Fred Taylor 8.00
54 Jimmy Smith 5.00
55 Dante Hall 5.00
56 Priest Holmes 10.00
57 Tony Gonzalez 6.00
58 Trent Green 5.00
59 A.J. Feeley 5.00
60 Chris Chambers 8.00
61 David Boston 6.00
62 Jason Taylor 5.00
63 Jay Fiedler 5.00
64 Junior Seau 6.00
65 Randy McMichael 5.00
66 Ricky Williams 8.00
67 Zach Thomas 5.00
68 Daunte Culpepper 8.00
69 Michael Bennett 8.00

70 Randy Moss 12.00
71 Tom Brady 12.00
72 Troy Brown 5.00
73 Ty Law 5.00
74 Aaron Brooks 8.00
75 Deuce McAllister 8.00
76 Donte Stallworth 6.00
77 Amani Toomer 6.00
78 Jeremy Shockey 8.00
79 Kerry Collins 5.00
80 Michael Strahan 5.00
81 Tiki Barber 5.00
82 Chad Pennington 10.00
83 Curtis Martin 8.00
84 Justin McCareins 5.00
85 Santana Moss 5.00
86 Charles Woodson 5.00
87 Jerry Rice 15.00
88 Rich Gannon 6.00
89 Tim Brown 8.00
90 Warren Sapp 5.00
91 Correll Buckhalter 5.00
92 Donovan McNabb 10.00
93 Freddie Mitchell 5.00
94 Jevon Kearse 5.00
95 Terrell Owens 8.00
96 Antwann Randle El 6.00
97 Duce Staley 5.00
98 Hines Ward 6.00
99 Jerome Bettis 6.00
100 Plaxico Burress 8.00
101 Doug Flutie 6.00
102 LaDainian Tomlinson 10.00
103 Koren Robinson 5.00
104 Matt Hasselbeck 6.00
105 Shaun Alexander 8.00
106 Isaac Bruce 6.00
107 Kurt Warner 8.00
108 Marc Bulger 6.00
109 Marshall Faulk 10.00
110 Torry Holt 8.00
111 Brad Johnson 5.00
112 Mike Alstott 5.00
113 Derrick Mason 5.00
114 Drew Bennett 5.00
115 Eddie George 8.00
116 Frank Wycheck 5.00
117 Keith Bulluck 5.00
118 Steve McNair 8.00
119 Tyrone Calico 5.00
120 Clinton Portis 12.00
121 LaVar Arrington 8.00
122 Laveranues Coles 6.00
123 Mark Brunell 6.00
124 Patrick Ramsey 6.00
125 Rod Gardner 5.00
126 Jake Plummer 6.00
127 Thomas Jones 6.00
128 Priest Holmes 10.00
129 Jim Kelly 10.00
130 Doug Flutie 6.00
131 Walter Payton 40.00
132 Troy Aikman 15.00
133 John Elway 20.00
134 Barry Sanders 30.00
135 Mark Brunell 6.00
136 Earl Campbell 10.00
137 Joe Montana 40.00
138 Dan Marino 40.00
139 Curtis Martin 8.00
140 Drew Bledsoe 8.00
141 Ricky Williams 8.00
142 Junior Seau 6.00
143 Charlie Garner 5.00
144 Jerry Rice 15.00
145 Ahman Green 8.00
146 Jerome Bettis 6.00
147 Trent Green 5.00
148 Warrick Dunn 5.00
149 Deion Sanders 8.00
150 Stephen Davis 6.00
201 Larry Fitzgerald 20.00
202 DeAngelo Hall 10.00
203 Matt Schaub 6.00
204 Michael Jenkins 10.00
205 Devard Darling 6.00
206 J.P. Losman 12.00
207 Lee Evans 12.00
208 Keary Colbert 6.00
209 Bernard Berrian 6.00
210 Chris Perry 10.00
211 Kellen Winslow Jr. 15.00
212 Luke McCown 6.00
213 Julius Jones 20.00
214 Darius Watts 6.00
215 Tatum Bell 10.00
216 Kevin Jones 15.00
217 Roy Williams-Lions 20.00
218 Dunta Robinson 6.00
219 Greg Jones 8.00
220 Reggie Williams 12.00
221 Mewelde Moore 6.00
222 Ben Watson 6.00
223 Cedric Cobbs 6.00
224 Devery Henderson 6.00
225 Eli Manning 50.00
226 Robert Gallery 8.00
227 Ben Roethlisberger 80.00
228 Philip Rivers 30.00
229 Derrick Hamilton 6.00
230 Rashaun Woods 12.00
231 Steven Jackson 15.00
232 Michael Clayton 12.00
233 Ben Troupe 6.00

2004 Leaf Limited

NM/M

Common Player (1-150): 1.00
Minor Stars (1-150): 2.00
Unlisted Stars (1-150): 3.00
Production 799 Sets
Common Rookie (151-200): 6.00
Production 350 Sets
Common Rookie (201-233): 25.00
Production 150 Sets
Pack (4): 75.00
Box (4): 215.00

1 A.J. Feeley 1.00
2 Aaron Brooks 3.00
3 Ahman Green 8.00
4 Andre Johnson 3.00
5 Anquan Boldin 3.00
6 Antwann Randle El 2.00
7 Ashley Lelie 2.00
8 Brad Johnson 1.00
9 Brett Favre 8.00
10 Brian Urlacher 3.00
11 Brian Westbrook 1.00
12 Byron Leftwich 5.00
13 Carson Palmer 4.00
14 Chad Johnson 3.00
15 Chad Pennington 4.00
16 Charlie Garner 1.00
17 Charles Rogers 3.00
18 Chris Brown 2.00
19 Chris Chambers 3.00
20 Clinton Portis 3.00
21 Corey Dillon 2.00
22 Deion Sanders 3.00
23 Curtis Martin 3.00
24 Daunte Culpepper 3.00
25 David Terrell 1.00
26 David Carr 4.00
27 Deion Branch 1.00
28 Derrick Mason 1.00
29 DeShaun Foster 1.00
30 Deuce McAllister 3.00
31 Domanick Davis 3.00
32 Donovan McNabb 4.00
33 Donte Stallworth 2.00
34 Drew Bledsoe 3.00
35 Duce Staley 1.00
36 Eddie George 3.00
37 Edgerrin James 4.00
38 Emmitt Smith 6.00
39 Eric Moulds 1.00
40 Fred Taylor 3.00
41 Hines Ward 2.00
42 Isaac Bruce 2.00
43 Jake Delhomme 3.00
44 Jake Plummer 2.00
45 Javon Walker 2.00
46 Jeff Garcia 3.00
47 Jeremy Shockey 3.00
48 Jerome Bettis 2.00
49 Jerry Porter 1.00
50 Jerry Rice 6.00
51 Jevon Kearse 1.00
52 Jimmy Smith 1.00
53 Joe Horn 1.00
54 Joey Harrington 3.00
55 Josh McCown 1.00
56 Kevan Barlow 1.00
57 Koren Robinson 1.00
58 Kyle Boller 3.00
59 LaDainian Tomlinson 4.00
60 LaVar Arrington 3.00
61 Laveranues Coles 2.00
62 Lee Suggs 1.00
63 Marc Bulger 2.00
64 Mark Brunell 2.00
65 Marshall Faulk 4.00
66 Marvin Harrison 3.00
67 Matt Hasselbeck 2.00
68 Michael Bennett 3.00
69 Michael Strahan 1.00
70 Michael Vick 6.00
71 Peerless Price 2.00
72 Peter Warrick 2.00
73 Peyton Manning 5.00
74 Priest Holmes 4.00
75 Quentin Griffin 1.00
76 Randy Moss 5.00
77 Ray Lewis 2.00
78 Rex Grossman 3.00
79 Lamar Gordon 1.00
80 Rod Smith 1.00
81 Roy Williams 2.00
82 Rudi Johnson 2.00
83 Santana Moss 1.00
84 Shaun Alexander 3.00
85 Stephen Davis 2.00
86 Steve McNair 3.00
87 Steve Smith 1.00
88 T.J. Duckett 2.00
89 Terrell Owens 3.00
90 Thomas Jones 2.00
91 Tiki Barber 2.00
92 Tim Brown 3.00
93 Tom Brady 5.00
94 Tony Gonzalez 2.00
95 Torry Holt 3.00
96 Travis Henry 1.00
97 Trent Green 1.00
98 Warren Sapp 1.00
99 William Green 2.00
100 Willis McGahee 3.00
101 Barry Sanders 6.00
102 Bart Starr 5.00
103 Bo Jackson 5.00
104 Bob Griese 4.00
105 Bronko Nagurski 3.00
106 Dan Marino 8.00
107 Deion Sanders 3.00
108 Dick Butkus 4.00
109 Doak Walker 4.00
110 Don Maynard 3.00
111 Don Shula 3.00
112 Earl Campbell 3.00
113 Fran Tarkenton 4.00
114 Franco Harris 4.00
115 Fred Biletnikoff 3.00
116 Gale Sayers 5.00
117 Herman Edwards 3.00
118 Jim Brown 6.00
119 Jim Kelly 3.00
120 Jim Thorpe 6.00
121 Jimmie Johnson 3.00
122 Joe Greene 3.00
123 Joe Montana 8.00
124 Joe Namath 6.00
125 John Elway 6.00
126 John Riggins 4.00
127 Johnny Unitas 8.00
128 Larry Csonka 3.00
129 Lawrence Taylor 4.00
130 Marcus Allen 4.00
131 Mark Bavaro 3.00
132 Michael Irvin 3.00
133 Mike Ditka 4.00
134 Mike Singletary 4.00
135 Ozzie Newsome 3.00
136 Paul Warfield 4.00
137 Randall Cunningham 3.00
138 Ray Nitschke 5.00
139 Harold "Red" Grange 5.00
140 Reggie White 4.00
141 Roger Staubach 6.00
142 Sterling Sharpe 3.00
143 Steve Largent 3.00
144 Terrell Davis 3.00
145 Terry Bradshaw 8.00
146 Thurman Thomas 3.00
147 Tony Dorsett 4.00
148 Troy Aikman 5.00
149 Walter Payton 10.00
150 Warren Moon 3.00
151 *Ahmad Carroll* 8.00
152 *Andy Hall* 6.00
153 *Antwan Odom* 6.00
154 *B.J. Symons* 6.00
155 *Carlos Francis* 6.00
156 *Casey Bramlet* 8.00
157 *Chris Cooley* 6.00
158 *Chris Gamble* 8.00
159 *Clarence Moore* 8.00
160 *Cody Pickett* 6.00
161 *Courtney Watson* 6.00
162 *Craig Krenzel* 8.00
163 *D.J. Hackett* 6.00
164 *D.J. Williams* 8.00
165 *Derrick Strait* 8.00
166 *Dontarrious Thomas* 6.00
167 *Drew Henson* 15.00
168 *Ernest Wilford* 6.00
169 *Jamaar Taylor* 10.00
170 *Jason Babin* 6.00
171 *Jeff Smoker* 12.00
172 *Jerricho Cotchery* 6.00
173 *Jim Sorgi* 8.00
174 *Joey Thomas* 6.00
175 *John Navarre* 8.00
176 *Johnnie Morant* 6.00
177 *Jonathan Vilma* 10.00
178 *Josh Harris* 10.00
179 *Keiwan Ratliff* 6.00
180 *Kenechi Udeze* 8.00
181 *Kris Wilson* 6.00
182 *Marcus Tubbs* 6.00
183 *Marquise Hill* 6.00
184 *Matt Mauck* 8.00
185 *Maurice Mann* 6.00
186 *Michael Boulware* 8.00
187 *Michael Turner* 6.00
188 *P.K. Sam* 8.00
189 *Patrick Crayton* 6.00
190 *Ricardo Colclough* 6.00
191 *Richard Smith* 6.00
192 *Samie Parker* 8.00
193 *Sean Taylor* 12.00
194 *Teddy Lehman* 8.00
195 *Thomas Tapeh* 6.00
196 *Tommie Harris* 8.00
197 *Triandos Luke* 6.00
198 *Troy Fleming* 6.00
199 *Vince Wilfork* 8.00
200 *Will Smith* 6.00
201 *Larry Fitzgerald Jsy/Auto* 100.00
202 *DeAngelo Hall Jsy/Auto* 40.00
203 *Matt Schaub Jsy/Auto* 40.00
204 *Michael Jenkins Jsy/Auto* 40.00
205 *Devard Darling Jsy/Auto* 25.00
206 *J.P. Losman Jsy/Auto* 100.00
207 *Lee Evans Jsy/Auto* 75.00
208 *Keary Colbert Jsy/Auto* 30.00
209 *Bernard Berrian Jsy/Auto* 25.00
210 *Chris Perry Jsy/Auto* 50.00
211 *Kellen Winslow Jr. Jsy/Auto* 40.00
212 *Luke McCown Jsy/Auto* 25.00
213 *Julius Jones Jsy/Auto* 150.00
214 *Darius Watts Jsy/Auto* 25.00
215 *Tatum Bell Jsy/Auto* 40.00
216 *Kevin Jones Jsy/Auto* 80.00
217 *Roy Williams Jsy/Auto* 100.00
218 *Dunta Robinson Jsy/Auto* 30.00
219 *Greg Jones Jsy/Auto* 30.00
220 *Reggie Williams Jsy/Auto* 30.00
221 *Mewelde Moore Jsy/Auto* 30.00
222 *Ben Watson Jsy/Auto* 25.00
223 *Cedric Cobbs Jsy/Auto* 30.00
224 *Devery Henderson Jsy/Auto* 30.00
225 *Eli Manning Jsy/Auto* 200.00
226 *Robert Gallery Jsy/Auto* 30.00
227 *Ben Roethlisberger Jsy/Auto* 400.00
228 *Philip Rivers Jsy/Auto* 125.00
229 *Derrick Hamilton Jsy/Auto* 30.00
230 *Rashaun Woods Jsy/Auto* 25.00
231 *Steven Jackson Jsy/Auto* 80.00
232 *Michael Clayton Jsy/Auto* 60.00
233 *Ben Troupe Jsy/Auto* 25.00

2004 Leaf Limited Bronze Spotlight

Cards 1-150: 1X-2X
Production 100 Sets
Rookies (151-200): .75X-1.5X
Production 100 Sets
Rookies (201-233): No Pricing
Production 25 Sets

2004 Leaf Limited Silver Spotlight

Cards 1-150: 1X-3X
Production 50 Sets
Rookies (151-200): .75X-2X
Production 50 Sets
Rookies (201-233): No Pricing
Production 15 Sets

2004 Leaf Limited Gold Spotlight

Cards 1-150: No Pricing
Production 25 Sets
Rookies (151-200): No Pricing
Production 25 Sets
Rookies (201-233): No Pricing
Production 10 Sets

2004 Leaf Limited Platinum Spotlight

Cards 1-233: No Pricing
Production 1 Set

2004 Leaf Limited Bound by Round

NM/M

Common Card: 20.00
Production 50 Sets
Prime: No Pricing
Production 25 Sets

BR-1 Brett Favre, Anquan Boldin 40.00
BR-2 Dan Marino, Barry Sanders 75.00
BR-3 John Elway, Emmitt Smith 60.00
BR-4 Walter Payton, Jerry Rice 80.00
BR-5 Bo Jackson, Michael Vick 60.00
BR-6 Marcus Allen, Tim Brown 30.00
BR-7 Joe Montana, Terrell Owens 75.00
BR-8 Tom Brady, Matt Hasselbeck 40.00
BR-9 Donovan McNabb, Marvin Harrison 20.00
BR-10 Ricky Williams, Deuce McAllister 25.00
BR-11 Clinton Portis, Antwann Randle El 20.00
BR-12 Hines Ward, Ahman Green 20.00
BR-13 Marshall Faulk, Edgerrin James 25.00
BR-14 Terrell Davis, Marc Bulger 20.00
BR-15 Mark Bavaro, Stephen Davis 20.00
BR-16 Aaron Brooks, Rudi Johnson 20.00
BR-17 Ed McCaffrey, Steve Largent 20.00
BR-18 Chad Johnson, Travis Henry 20.00
BR-19 Chris Chambers, Fred Biletnikoff 25.00
BR-20 Mike Singletary, Randall Cunningham 20.00
BR-21 Fran Tarkenton, Ray Nitschke 30.00
BR-22 Trent Green, Leroy Kelly 20.00
BR-23 Michael Irvin, Sterling Sharpe 25.00
BR-24 Jamal Lewis, Ray Lewis 20.00
BR-25 Brian Urlacher, Daunte Culpepper 25.00
BR-26 Joe Namath, Chad Pennington 40.00
BR-27 Byron Leftwich, Randy Moss 25.00
BR-28 Jim Kelly, Drew Bledsoe 30.00
BR-29 Tony Dorsett, LaDainian Tomlinson 25.00
BR-30 Dick Butkus, Lawrence Taylor 60.00
BR-31 Gale Sayers, Shaun Alexander 30.00
BR-32 Earl Campbell, David Carr 25.00
BR-33 Deion Sanders, Roy Williams 30.00
BR-34 Ozzie Newsome, Jeremy Shockey 20.00
BR-35 Joey Harrington, Bob Griese 25.00
BR-36 Reggie White, Peyton Manning 50.00
BR-37 John Riggins, Larry Csonka 25.00
BR-38 James Lofton, Torry Holt 20.00
BR-39 Joe Greene, Julius Peppers 20.00
BR-40 Paul Warfield, Santana Moss 20.00
BR-41 Troy Aikman, Steve McNair 20.00
BR-42 Walter Payton, Michael Vick 60.00
BR-43 Clinton Portis, Brett Favre 30.00
BR-44 Dan Marino, Emmitt Smith 75.00
BR-45 Bo Jackson, Jerry Rice 100.00
BR-46 Joe Namath, Troy Aikman 40.00
BR-47 John Elway, Barry Sanders 50.00
BR-48 Peyton Manning, David Carr 25.00
BR-49 Brian Urlacher, Randy Moss 30.00
BR-50 Ricky Williams, Donovan McNabb 20.00

2004 Leaf Limited Common Threads

NM/M

Common Card: 20.00
Production 50 Sets
Prime: No Pricing
Production 10 Sets

CT-1 Daunte Culpepper, Steve McNair 20.00
CT-2 Randall Cunningham, Donovan McNabb 20.00
CT-3 Byron Leftwich, Aaron Brooks 25.00
CT-4 John Elway, David Carr 40.00
CT-5 Joe Montana, Tom Brady 150.00
CT-6 Joe Montana, Trent Green 40.00
CT-7 Troy Aikman, Joey Harrington 25.00
CT-8 Joe Namath, Chad Pennington 40.00
CT-9 Fran Tarkenton, Michael Vick 30.00
CT-10 Marc Bulger, Matt Hasselbeck 20.00
CT-11 Dan Marino, Peyton Manning 100.00
CT-12 Bart Starr, Brett Favre 75.00
CT-13 Jim Kelly, Drew Bledsoe 25.00
CT-14 Earl Campbell, Ricky Williams 20.00
CT-15 Marcus Allen, Priest Holmes 25.00
CT-16 Walter Payton, LaDainian Tomlinson 60.00
CT-17 Barry Sanders, Clinton Portis 50.00
CT-18 Bo Jackson, Jamal Lewis 30.00
CT-19 Terrell Davis, Edgerrin James 25.00
CT-20 Larry Csonka, Deuce McAllister 20.00
CT-21 Gale Sayers, Shaun Alexander 30.00
CT-22 Tony Dorsett, Ahman Green 25.00
CT-23 Leroy Kelly, John Riggins 25.00
CT-24 Emmitt Smith, Travis Henry 30.00
CT-25 Bo Jackson, Rudi Johnson 30.00
CT-26 Jerry Rice, Anquan Boldin 25.00
CT-27 Jerry Rice, Marvin Harrison 30.00
CT-28 Randy Moss, Chris Chambers 25.00
CT-29 Michael Irvin, Terrell Owens 20.00
CT-30 Fred Biletnikoff, Tim Brown 20.00
CT-31 Torry Holt, Chad Johnson 20.00
CT-32 James Lofton, Sterling Sharpe 20.00
CT-33 Steve Largent, Laveranues Coles 20.00
CT-34 Paul Warfield, Santana Moss 20.00
CT-35 Reggie White, Julius Peppers 30.00
CT-36 Mike Singletary, Ray Lewis 30.00
CT-37 Dick Butkus, Brian Urlacher 50.00
CT-38 Lawrence Taylor, LaVar Arrington 40.00
CT-39 Deion Sanders, Terence Newman 25.00
CT-40 Mark Bavaro, Jeremy Shockey 20.00
CT-41 Michael Vick, Donovan McNabb 40.00
CT-42 John Elway, Brett Favre 75.00
CT-43 Joe Montana, Dan Marino 100.00
CT-44 Troy Aikman, Tom Brady 40.00
CT-45 Joe Montana, Chad Pennington 60.00
CT-46 Jim Kelly, Peyton Manning 25.00
CT-47 Dan Marino, John Elway 100.00
CT-48 Walter Payton, Barry Sanders 80.00
CT-49 Walter Payton, Emmitt Smith 80.00
CT-50 Jerry Rice, Randy Moss 40.00

2004 Leaf Limited Contenders Rookie Ticket Preview Auto

NM/M

Common Player: 30.00
Sequentially #'d to 15, 20 or 25
Cards #'d 20 or less: No Pricing

102 Ahmad Carroll/25 50.00
106 Ben Roethlisberger/15
107 Ben Troupe/25 40.00
108 Ben Watson/25 40.00
109 Bernard Berrian/25 30.00
114 Cedric Cobbs/25 30.00
116 Chris Perry/25 60.00
117 Clarence Moore/25 30.00
119 Craig Krenzel/25 30.00
121 D.J. Williams/25 40.00
123 DeAngelo Hall/20
124 Derrick Hamilton/25 30.00
126 Devard Darling/25 30.00
127 Devery Henderson/25 30.00
129 Drew Henson/15
131 Eli Manning/15
132 Ernest Wilford/25 30.00
133 Greg Jones/25 40.00
134 J.P. Losman/25 75.00
135 Jamaar Taylor/25 30.00
138 Jason Babin/25 40.00
144 Jonathan Vilma/25 60.00
146 Julius Jones/25 275.00
147 Keary Colbert/25 50.00
149 Kenechi Udeze/25 30.00
150 Kevin Jones/20
152 Lee Evans/25 60.00
153 Luke McCown/25 40.00
154 Matt Mauck/25 50.00
155 Matt Schaub/25 60.00
157 Mewelde Moore/25 50.00
158 Michael Clayton/25 80.00
159 Michael Jenkins/25 40.00
162 Philip Rivers/25 100.00
165 Rashaun Woods/25 30.00
166 Reggie Williams/20
167 Ricardo Colclough/25 40.00
169 Roy Williams/25 150.00
174 Steven Jackson/25 150.00
175 Tatum Bell/25 80.00
178 Troy Fleming/25 30.00
182 Michael Boulware/25 30.00
186 Chris Cooley/20
188 Willie Parker/25 50.00
194 Erik Coleman/25 30.00
196 Andy Reid/15
197 Brian Billick/15
198 Jeff Fisher/15
199 John Gruden/15
200 Marvin Lewis/15

2004 Leaf Limited Hardwear

NM/M

Common Player: 12.00
Production 100 Sets
Limited: No Pricing
Production 25 Sets
Limited Shield: No Pricing
Production 1 Set

H-1 Anquan Boldin 15.00
H-2 Ahman Green 15.00
H-3 Brian Urlacher 15.00
H-4 Chad Johnson 12.00
H-5 Chad Pennington 20.00
H-6 Chris Chambers 12.00
H-7 Eddie George 15.00
H-8 Jake Plummer 12.00
H-9 Jerry Rice 30.00
H-10 Larry Csonka 20.00
H-11 LaDainian Tomlinson 20.00
H-12 Lawrence Taylor 20.00
H-13 Marc Bulger 12.00
H-14 Marcus Allen 25.00
H-15 Matt Hasselbeck 12.00
H-16 Michael Bennett 12.00
H-17 Marvin Harrison 15.00
H-18 Michael Irvin 20.00
H-19 Peyton Manning 25.00
H-20 Randy Moss 25.00
H-21 Ray Lewis 15.00
H-22 Ricky Williams 15.00
H-23 Shaun Alexander 15.00
H-24 Steve McNair 15.00
H-25 Torry Holt 15.00

2004 Leaf Limited Lettermen

No Pricing
Sequentially #'d between 4 & 10

LM-1 Barry Sanders/8
LM-2 Brett Favre/5
LM-3 Brian Urlacher/8
LM-4 Chad Pennington/10
LM-5 Dan Marino/6
LM-6 David Carr/4
LM-7 Donovan McNabb/6
LM-8 Drew Bledsoe/7
LM-9 Edgerrin James/5
LM-10 Emmitt Smith/6
LM-11 Jeremy Shockey/7
LM-12 Jerry Rice/4
LM-13 Joe Montana/7
LM-14 Joe Montana/7
LM-15 Joey Harrington/10
LM-16 John Elway/5
LM-17 Marshall Faulk/5
LM-18 Michael Vick/4
LM-19 Peyton Manning/7
LM-20 Priest Holmes/6
LM-21 Randy Moss/4
LM-22 Ricky Williams/9
LM-23 Shaun Alexander/9
LM-24 Tom Brady/5
LM-25 Walter Payton/6

2004 Leaf Limited Limited Cuts Autographs

NM/M

Common Player: 30.00
Sequentially #'d to indicated quantity

LC-1 Tom Brady/50 200.00
LC-2 Priest Holmes/50 100.00
LC-3 Dan Marino/50 200.00
LC-4 LaDainian Tomlinson/50 100.00
LC-5 Jake Plummer/100 30.00
LC-6 Bronko Nagurski/30 350.00
LC-7 Vince Lombardi/25 400.00
LC-8 Aaron Brooks/55 40.00
LC-9 Warren Moon/55 60.00

2004 Leaf Limited Limited Legends

NM/M

Common Player: 15.00
Production 50 Sets
Seasons: No Pricing
Sequentially #'d between 6 & 18
Prime: No Pricing
Production 5 Sets

LL-1 Barry Sanders 40.00
LL-2 Bart Starr 80.00
LL-3 Brett Favre 40.00
LL-4 Dick Butkus 40.00
LL-5 Doak Walker 20.00
LL-6 Fran Tarkenton 25.00
LL-7 Franco Harris 25.00
LL-8 Fred Biletnikoff 15.00
LL-9 Gale Sayers 30.00
LL-10 Jim Brown/Auto. 100.00
LL-11 Jim Kelly 25.00
LL-12 Jim Thorpe 125.00
LL-13 Joe Montana 80.00
LL-14 Joe Namath/Auto. 120.00
LL-15 John Elway 40.00
LL-16 John Riggins 25.00
LL-17 Johnny Unitas 40.00
LL-18 Steve Largent 25.00
LL-19 Terry Bradshaw 40.00
LL-20 Walter Payton 50.00

2004 Leaf Limited Limited Threads

NM/M

Common Player: 10.00
Production 75 or 100 Sets
Positions: .5X-1.5X
Production 50 or 75 Sets
Prime: No Pricing
Production 25 Sets

LT-1 Aaron Brooks/75 10.00
LT-2 Ahman Green Seattle Seahawks/75 12.00
LT-3 Ahman Green Green Bay Packers/75 12.00
LT-4 Andre Johnson Miami/75 12.00
LT-5 Andre Johnson Houston Texans/75 10.00
LT-6 Anquan Boldin Florida State/75 12.00
LT-7 Anquan Boldin Arizona Cardinals/75 15.00
LT-8 Barry Sanders Oklahoma State/100 50.00
LT-9 Barry Sanders Detroit Lions/100 40.00
LT-10 Bart Starr/100 30.00
LT-11 Bo Jackson/100 20.00
LT-12 Bob Griese/75 15.00
LT-13 Brett Favre/100 30.00
LT-14 Brian Urlacher/75 15.00
LT-15 Byron Leftwich/75 15.00
LT-16 Carson Palmer USC/75 20.00
LT-17 Carson Palmer Cincinnati Bengals/75 15.00
LT-18 Chad Pennington/75 12.00
LT-19 Clinton Portis Miami/75 15.00
LT-20 Clinton Portis Washington Redskins/75 15.00
LT-21 David Carr/75 12.00
LT-22 Dan Marino Miami Dolphins/100 40.00
LT-23 Dan Marino Pro Bowl/100 40.00
LT-24 Daunte Culpepper Minnesota Vikings/75 12.00
LT-25 Daunte Culpepper Pro Bowl/75 10.00
LT-26 Deion Sanders Dallas Cowboys/75 20.00
LT-27 Deion Sanders Washington Redskins/75 15.00
LT-28 Deuce McAllister Auto/100 25.00
LT-29 Dick Butkus/75 30.00
LT-30 Domanick Davis Auto/100 20.00
LT-31 Don Maynard/75 15.00
LT-32 Donovan McNabb/75 15.00
LT-33 Drew Bledsoe Washinton State/75 20.00
LT-34 Drew Bledsoe Buffalo Bills/75 15.00
LT-35 Earl Campbell/75 15.00
LT-36 Edgerrin James Miami/75 20.00
LT-37 Edgerrin James Indianapolis Colts/75 15.00
LT-38 Emmitt Smith/100 25.00
LT-39 Fran Tarkenton Minnesota Vikings/75 15.00
LT-40 Fran Tarkenton New York Giants/75 15.00
LT-41 George Blanda/75 20.00
LT-42 Jake Delhomme Auto/100 30.00
LT-43 Jamal Lewis/75 15.00
LT-44 Jeremy Shockey Miami/75 20.00
LT-45 Jeremy Shockey New York Giants/75 20.00
LT-46 Jerry Rice/100 25.00
LT-47 Jevon Kearse/75 15.00
LT-48 Jim Kelly/75 15.00
LT-49 Joe Greene/75 20.00
LT-50 Joe Greene/75 20.00
LT-51 Joe Montana San Francisco 49ers/100 40.00
LT-52 Joe Montana Kansas City Chiefs/100 30.00
LT-53 Joe Namath/100 30.00
LT-54 Joey Harrington/75 12.00
LT-55 John Elway Stanford/100 30.00
LT-56 John Elway Denver Broncos/100 30.00
LT-57 John Riggins New York Jets/75 15.00
LT-58 John Riggins Washington Redskins/75 15.00
LT-59 Josh McCown/75 10.00
LT-60 Kellen Winslow Jr./75 15.00
LT-61 Kyle Boller/75 12.00
LT-62 Michael Vick/100 30.00
LT-63 LaDainian Tomlinson/75 15.00
LT-64 Larry Fitzgerald/75 12.00
LT-65 Lawrence Taylor/75 20.00
LT-66 Marc Bulger/75 12.00
LT-67 Marcus Allen Los Angeles Raiders/75 20.00
LT-68 Marcus Allen Kansas City Chiefs/75 15.00
LT-69 Marshall Faulk San Diego State Univ./75 20.00
LT-70 Marshall Faulk St. Louis Rams/75 15.00
LT-71 Matt Hasselbeck Auto/100 20.00
LT-72 Michael Clayton/75 15.00
LT-73 Michael Irvin Dallas Cowboys/75 15.00
LT-74 Michael Irvin Pro Bowl/75 12.00
LT-75 Michael Vick/100 20.00
LT-76 Michael Singletary/75 15.00
LT-77 Ozzie Newsome/75 15.00
LT-78 Peyton Manning Indianapolis Colts/75 30.00
LT-79 Peyton Manning Pro Bowl/75 25.00
LT-80 Priest Holmes Kansas City Chiefs/75 15.00
LT-81 Priest Holmes Baltimore Ravens/75 15.00
LT-82 Randy Moss/75 20.00
LT-83 Reggie White/75 25.00
LT-84 Reggie Williams/75 12.00
LT-85 Rex Grossman/75 12.00
LT-86 Ricky Williams/75 15.00
LT-87 Roger Staubach/75 25.00
LT-88 Shaun Alexander/75 15.00
LT-89 Steve Largent/75 20.00
LT-90 Steve McNair/75 12.00
LT-91 Sonny Jurgensen/75 15.00
LT-92 Steve Smith Auto/100 20.00
LT-93 Terrell Davis/75 15.00
LT-94 Terry Bradshaw 20.00
LT-95 Tom Brady New England Patriots/100 30.00
LT-96 Tom Brady Pro Bowl/100 25.00
LT-97 Tony Dorsett/75 20.00
LT-98 Trent Green/75 12.00
LT-99 Troy Aikman/75 20.00
LT-100 Walter Payton/100 40.00

2004 Leaf Limited Limited Threads at the Half

NM/M

Unsigned Cards: .75X-1.5X Limited Threads
Production 35 or 50 Sets

LT-3 Ahman Green 30.00
LT-7 Anquan Boldin 30.00
LT-28 Deuce McAllister 30.00
LT-30 Domanick Davis 30.00
LT-35 Earl Campbell 40.00
LT-42 Jake Delhomme 30.00
LT-49 Joe Greene 75.00
LT-53 Joe Namath 100.00
LT-63 LaDainian Tomlinson 50.00
LT-71 Matt Hasselbeck 30.00
LT-83 Reggie White 80.00
LT-85 Rex Grossman 30.00
LT-91 Sonny Jurgensen 80.00
LT-92 Steve Smith 20.00
LT-98 Trent Green 30.00

2004 Leaf Limited Limited Threads Jersey Numbers

NM/M

Unsigned Cards #'d 51-92: .75X-1.5X
Unsigned Cards #'d 26-50: 1X-2X
Unsigned Cards #d 25 or less: No Pricing
Auto Cards #'d 25 or less: No Pricing
Sequentially #'d to player's jersey #

LT-2 Ahman Green Auto/30 40.00
LT-14 Brian Urlacher Auto/54 80.00
LT-19 Clinton Portis Auto/28 60.00
LT-20 Clinton Portis Auto/26 60.00
LT-28 Deuce McAllister Auto/26 50.00
LT-30 Domanick Davis Auto/37 40.00
LT-35 Earl Campbell Auto/34 50.00
LT-57 John Riggins Auto/44 60.00
LT-58 John Riggins Auto/44 100.00
LT-80 Priest HolmesAuto/31 80.00
LT-92 Steve Smith Auto/89 20.00
LT-97 Tony Dorsett Auto/33 75.00

2004 Leaf Limited Material Monikers

NM/M

Common Player: 40.00
Sequentially #'d to indicated quantity
Cards #'d less than 25: No Pricing
Limited Material Monikers: No Pricing
Production 1 Set

MM-1 Ahman Green/25 50.00
MM-2 Barry Sanders/25 200.00
MM-3 Bart Starr/31 125.00
MM-4 Brett Favre/6
MM-5 Bob Griese/15
MM-6 Dan Marino/15
MM-7 Chad Pennington/15
MM-8 Joe Namath/50 80.00
MM-9 Byron Leftwich/25 60.00
MM-10 Donovan McNabb/25 80.00
MM-11 Daunte Culpepper/40 40.00
MM-12 Fran Tarkenton/50 50.00
MM-13 Jamal Lewis/25 50.00
MM-14 Jim Brown/25 150.00
MM-15 Jerry Rice/15
MM-16 Anquan Boldin/25 40.00
MM-17 Joe Montana/5
MM-18 Jerry Rice/10
MM-19 Joe Montana/10
MM-20 Tom Brady/25 200.00
MM-21 John Elway/15
MM-22 Jim Kelly/25 60.00
MM-23 Clinton Portis/25 50.00
MM-24 John Riggins/25 60.00
MM-25 Roy Williams/25 40.00
MM-26 Deion Sanders/25 75.00
MM-27 Earl Campbell/20
MM-28 Priest Holmes/50 60.00
MM-29 Larry Csonka/25 50.00
MM-30 Gale Sayers/15
MM-31 LaDainian Tomlinson/25 75.00
MM-32 Michael Vick/15
MM-33 Steve McNair/50 40.00
MM-34 Peyton Manning/45 100.00
MM-35 Johnny Unitas/5
MM-36 Terry Bradshaw/50 150.00
MM-37 Bo Jackson/25 100.00
MM-38 Jim Thorpe/2
MM-39 Bart Starr, Brett Favre/15
MM-40 Bob Griese, Dan Marino/10
MM-41 Joe Namath, Chad Pennington/10
MM-42 Jim Brown, Jamal Lewis/25 150.00
MM-43 Joe Montana, Tom Brady/10
MM-44 John Elway, Jim Kelly/10
MM-45 John Riggins, Clinton Portis/25 75.00
MM-46 Deion Sanders, Roy Williams/25 100.00
MM-47 Gale Sayers, LaDainian Tomlinson/10
MM-48 Johnny Unitas, Peyton Manning/5
MM-49 Michael Vick, Donovan McNabb/10
MM-50 Bart Starr, Ray Nitschke/9

2004 Leaf Limited Player Threads

NM/M

Common Card: 25.00
Production 50 Sets
Prime: No Pricing
Production 25 Sets
Limited: No Pricing
Production 1 Set

PT-1 Ahman Green 40.00
PT-2 Barry Sanders 75.00
PT-3 Brett Favre 50.00
PT-4 Brian Urlacher 30.00
PT-5 Carson Palmer 25.00
PT-6 Clinton Portis 30.00
PT-7 Dan Marino 75.00
PT-8 Daunte Culpepper 25.00
PT-9 Donovan McNabb 25.00
PT-10 Drew Bledsoe 25.00
PT-11 Edgerrin James 30.00
PT-12 Emmitt Smith 75.00
PT-13 Fran Tarkenton 25.00
PT-14 Jeremy Shockey 25.00
PT-15 Jerry Rice 75.00
PT-16 Joe Montana 175.00
PT-17 John Elway 75.00
PT-18 Marcus Allen 40.00
PT-19 Marshall Faulk 25.00
PT-20 Michael Vick 40.00
PT-21 Mike Singletary 25.00
PT-22 Peyton Manning 30.00
PT-23 Priest Holmes 25.00
PT-24 Randy Moss 25.00
PT-25 Ricky Williams 25.00
PT-26 Roger Staubach 40.00
PT-27 Terry Bradshaw 50.00
PT-28 Tom Brady 30.00
PT-29 Troy Aikman 30.00
PT-30 Walter Payton 75.00

2004 Leaf Limited Team Trademarks

NM/M

Common Player: 30.00
Production 50 Sets
Limited Team Trademarks: No Pricing
Production 25 Sets

TT-1 Ahman Green 40.00
TT-2 Anquan Boldin 30.00
TT-3 Bo Jackson 100.00
TT-4 Bob Griese 40.00
TT-5 Brian Urlacher 75.00
TT-6 Chad Johnson 30.00
TT-7 Chad Pennington 60.00
TT-8 Clinton Portis 40.00
TT-9 Dan Marino 200.00
TT-10 Deuce McAllister 30.00
TT-11 Domanick Davis 30.00
TT-12 Don Shula 40.00
TT-13 Drew Bledsoe 50.00
TT-14 Fran Tarkenton 50.00
TT-15 Franco Harris 60.00
TT-16 Fred Biletnikoff 40.00
TT-17 Gale Sayers 75.00
TT-18 Herman Edwards 30.00
TT-19 Jake Delhomme 30.00
TT-20 Jim Brown 100.00
TT-21 Jimmie Johnson 30.00
TT-22 Joe Montana 175.00
TT-23 Joe Namath 100.00
TT-24 Joey Harrington 40.00
TT-25 John Riggins 75.00
TT-26 LaDainian Tomlinson 50.00
TT-27 Lawrence Taylor 50.00
TT-28 Marvin Harrison 50.00
TT-29 Matt Hasselbeck 40.00
TT-30 Michael Irvin 50.00
TT-31 Michael Strahan 30.00
TT-32 Michael Vick 125.00
TT-33 Mike Singletary 40.00
TT-34 Ozzie Newsome 30.00
TT-35 Priest Holmes 50.00
TT-36 Steve Smith 30.00
TT-37 Rex Grossman 30.00
TT-38 Earl Campbell 40.00
TT-39 Roger Staubach 75.00
TT-40 Roy Williams 40.00
TT-41 Santana Moss 30.00
TT-42 Shaun Alexander 40.00
TT-43 Stephen Davis 30.00
TT-44 Steve Largent 50.00
TT-45 Thurman Thomas 30.00
TT-46 Tom Brady 200.00
TT-47 Tony Dorsett 60.00
TT-48 Torry Holt 40.00
TT-49 Trent Green 40.00
TT-50 Troy Aikman 80.00

2004 Leaf Limited Team Threads Dual

NM/M

Common Card: 20.00
Production 50 Sets
Prime: No Pricing
Production 10 Sets

TT-1 Anquan Boldin, Larry Fitzgerald 20.00
TT-2 Michael Vick, Peerless Price 30.00
TT-3 Jamal Lewis, Ray Lewis 20.00
TT-4 Drew Bledsoe, Jim Kelly 30.00
TT-5 Brian Urlacher, Walter Payton 75.00
TT-6 Carson Palmer, Chad Johnson 20.00
TT-7 Emmitt Smith, Troy Aikman 30.00
TT-8 John Elway, Terrell Davis 30.00
TT-9 Barry Sanders, Joey Harrington 30.00
TT-10 Brett Favre, Sterling Sharpe 30.00
TT-11 Andre Johnson, David Carr 20.00
TT-12 Edgerrin James, Peyton Manning 40.00
TT-13 Byron Leftwich, Fred Taylor 20.00
TT-14 Priest Holmes, Joe Montana 60.00
TT-15 Dan Marino, Ricky Williams 50.00
TT-16 Daunte Culpepper, Randy Moss 30.00
TT-17 Tom Brady, Drew Bledsoe 40.00
TT-18 Lawrence Taylor, Jeremy Shockey 20.00
TT-19 Chad Pennington, Joe Namath 40.00
TT-20 Jerry Rice, Bo Jackson 80.00
TT-21 Donovan McNabb, Randall Cunningham 20.00
TT-22 Jerry Rice, Joe Montana 80.00
TT-23 Matt Hasselbeck, Steve Largent 20.00
TT-24 Steve McNair, Earl Campbell 20.00
TT-25 Clinton Portis, Laveranues Coles 20.00

2004 Leaf Limited Team Thread Triples

No Pricing
Production 25 Sets
Prime: No Pricing
Production 5 Sets

TT-1 Michael Vick, Peerless Price, Warrick Dunn
TT-2 Drew Bledsoe, Jim Kelly, Bruce Smith
TT-3 Brian Urlacher, Dick Butkus, Walter Payton
TT-4 Emmitt Smith, Michael Irvin, Troy Aikman
TT-5 Jake Plummer, John Elway, Terrell Davis
TT-6 Barry Sanders, Joey Harrington, Doak Walker
TT-7 Ahman Green, Brett Favre, Sterling Sharpe
TT-8 Edgerrin James, Marvin Harrison, Peyton Manning
TT-9 Joe Montana, Priest Holmes, Marcus Allen
TT-10 Bob Griese, Dan Marino, Ricky Williams
TT-11 Daunte Culpepper, Fran Tarkenton, Randy Moss
TT-12 Jeremy Shockey, Lawrence Taylor, Mark Bavaro
TT-13 Joe Namath, Chad Pennington, Curtis Martin
TT-14 Bo Jackson, Marcus Allen, Jerry Rice
TT-15 Clinton Portis, Laveranues Coles, John Riggins

A player's name in *italic* type indicates a rookie card.

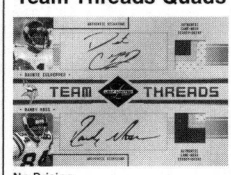

2004 Leaf Limited Team Threads Quads

No Pricing
Production 10 Sets
Prime Signatures: No Pricing
Production 1 Set

TT-1 Walter Payton, Mike Singletary, Brian Urlacher, Dick Butkus
TT-2 Deion Sanders, Emmitt Smith, Michael Irvin, Troy Aikman
TT-3 John Elway, Terrell Davis, Tony Dorsett, Jake Plummer
TT-4 Ahman Green, Bart Starr, Brett Favre, Sterling Sharpe
TT-5 Marvin Harrison, Peyton Manning, Johnny Unitas, Don Shula
TT-6 Joe Montana, Marcus Allen, Priest Holmes, Trent Green
TT-7 Bo Jackson, Marcus Allen, Jerry Rice, Fred Biletnikoff
TT-8 Antwann Randle El, Franco Harris, Joe Greene, Terry Bradshaw
TT-9 Ahman Green, Matt Hasselbeck, Shaun Alexander, Steve Largent
TT-10 Earl Campbell, Warren Moon, Eddie George, Steve McNair

2004 Leaf Rookies & Stars

NM/M

Common Card (1-100): .25
Minor Stars (1-100): .50
Unlisted Stars (1-100): .75
Common Rookie (101-200): 2.00
Common Rookie (201-250): 4.00
Production 750 Sets
Common Rookie (251-283): 6.00
Production 750 Sets
Common Card (284-299): 8.00
Production 500 Sets
Pack: (6): 5.25
Box: (24): 90.00

1 Anquan Boldin .75
2 Emmitt Smith 2.00
3 Josh McCown .25
4 Michael Vick 2.00
5 Peerless Price .50
6 T.J. Duckett .50
7 Warrick Dunn .75
8 Jamal Lewis .75
9 Kyle Boller .75
10 Ray Lewis .50
11 Drew Bledsoe .75
12 Eric Moulds .25
13 Travis Henry .75
14 Jake Delhomme .75
15 Stephen Davis .50
16 Steve Smith .75
17 Brian Urlacher .75
18 Rex Grossman .75
19 Thomas Jones .50
20 Carson Palmer 1.00
21 Chad Johnson .50
22 Rudi Johnson .50
23 Jeff Garcia .75
24 Willie Green .50
25 Keyshawn Johnson .50
26 Terence Newman .25
27 Roy Williams .50
28 Jake Plummer .50
29 Quentin Griffin .25
30 Rod Smith .25
31 Charles Rogers .75
32 Joey Harrington .75
33 Ahman Green .75
34 Brett Favre 2.50
35 Javon Walker .50
36 Andre Johnson .75
37 David Carr 1.00
38 Domanick Davis .75
39 Edgerrin James 1.00
40 Marvin Harrison .75
41 Peyton Manning 1.50
42 Byron Leftwich 1.50
43 Fred Taylor .75
44 Jimmy Smith .25
45 Priest Holmes 1.00
46 Tony Gonzalez .50
47 Trent Green .25
48 A.J. Feeley .25
49 Chris Chambers .75
50 Deion Sanders .75
51 Daunte Culpepper .75
52 Michael Bennett .75
53 Randy Moss 1.50
54 Corey Dillon .50
55 Deion Branch .25
56 Tom Brady 1.50
57 Aaron Brooks .75
58 Deuce McAllister .75
59 Joe Horn .25
60 Jeremy Shockey .75
61 Michael Strahan .25
62 Tiki Barber .25
63 Chad Pennington 1.00
64 Curtis Martin .75
65 Santana Moss .25
66 Jerry Porter .25
67 Jerry Rice 2.00
68 Warren Sapp .25
69 Donovan McNabb 1.00
70 Jevon Kearse .25
71 Terrell Owens .75
72 Duce Staley .25
73 Hines Ward .50
74 Jerome Bettis .50
75 LaDainian Tomlinson 1.00
76 Kevan Barlow .25
77 Tim Rattay .25
78 Koren Robinson .25
79 Matt Hasselbeck .50
80 Shaun Alexander .75
81 Isaac Bruce .50
82 Marc Bulger .50
83 Marshall Faulk 1.00
84 Torry Holt .75
85 Brad Johnson .25
86 Derrick Brooks .25
87 Chris Brown .50
88 Derrick Mason .50
89 Eddie George .75
90 Steve McNair .75
91 Clinton Portis 1.50
92 LaVar Arrington .75
93 Laveranues Coles .50
94 Mark Brunell .50
95 DeAngelo Hall, Matt Schaub, Michael Jenkins .50
96 J.P. Losman, Lee Evans .75
97 Kellen Winslow Jr., Luke McCown .75
98 Darius Watts, Tatum Bell .75
99 Kevin Jones, Roy Williams .75
100 Greg Jones, Reggie Williams .50
101 *Darnell Dockett* 2.00
102 *Karlos Dansby* 3.00
103 *Larry Croom* 3.00
104 *Chad Lavalais* 2.00
105 *Demorrio Williams* 3.00
106 *B.J. Sams* 2.00
107 *Dwan Edwards* 2.00
108 *Jason Peters* 3.00
109 *Shaud Williams* 5.00
110 *Tim Anderson* 2.00
111 *Tim Euhus* 3.00
112 *Michael Gaines* 2.00
113 *Rod Rutherford* 2.00
114 *Leon Joe* 2.00
115 *Nathan Vasher* 2.00
116 *Caleb Miller* 3.00
117 *Jamall Broussard* 2.00
118 *Keiwan Ratliff* 2.00
119 *Landon Johnson* 2.00
120 *Madieu Williams* 3.00
121 *Matthias Askew* 2.00
122 *Robert Geathers* 3.00
123 *Richard Alston* 2.00
124 *Bruce Thornton* 2.00
125 *Patrick Crayton* 3.00
126 *Bradlee Van Pelt* 3.00
127 *Charlie Adams* 3.00
128 *Nate Jackson* 3.00
129 *Roc Alexander* 3.00
130 *Romar Crenshaw* 2.00
131 *Keith Smith* 2.00
132 *Joey Thomas* 3.00
133 *Kelvin Kight* 2.00
134 *Scott McBrien* 3.00
135 *Andrae Thurman* 2.00
136 *Derrick Armstrong* 2.00
137 *Glenn Earl* 3.00
138 *Kendrick Starling* 2.00
139 *Ben Hartsock* 2.00
140 *Gilbert Gardner* 3.00
141 *Jason David* 4.00
142 *Daryl Smith* 2.00
143 *Jared Allen* 4.00
144 *Jeris McIntyre* 2.00
145 *John Booth* 5.00
146 *Jonathan Smith* 3.00
147 *Junior Siavii* 2.00
148 *Keyaron Fox* 2.00
149 *Kris Wilson* 3.00
150 *Doug Easlick* 3.00
151 *Fred Russell* 4.00
152 *Tony Bua* 3.00
153 *Will Poole* 3.00
154 *Ben Nelson* 2.00
155 *Brock Lesnar* 5.00
156 *Butchie Wallace* 2.00
157 *Darrion Scott* 3.00
158 *Dontarrious Thomas* 2.00
159 *Richard Owens* 2.00
160 *Rod Davis* 3.00
161 *Dexter Reid* 2.00
162 *Kory Chapman* 2.00
163 *Marquise Hill* 2.00
164 *Courtney Watson* 2.00
165 *Mike Karney* 2.00
166 *Gibril Wilson* 2.00
167 *Reggie Torbor* 2.00
168 *Darrell McClover* 2.00
169 *Derrick Strait* 2.00
170 *Erik Coleman* 2.00
171 *Jonathan Reese* 2.00
172 *Rashad Washington* 5.00
173 *Courtney Anderson* 2.00
174 *Stuart Schweigert* 3.00
175 *J.R. Reed* 2.00
176 *Justin Jenkins* 2.00
177 *Matt Ware* 3.00
178 *Nate Lawrie* 2.00
179 *Thomas Tapeh* 2.00
180 *Matt Kranchick* 3.00
181 *Willie Parker* 5.00
182 *Igor Olshansky* 4.00
183 *Ryan Krause* 3.00
184 *Shaun Philips* 2.00
185 *Wes Welker* 2.00
186 *Richard Seigler* 2.00
187 *Shawntae Spencer* 3.00
188 *Marcus Tubbs* 2.00
189 *Niko Koutouvides* 2.00
190 *Brandon Chillar* 2.00
191 *Tony Hargrove* 2.00
192 *Mark Jones* 3.00

193 *Marquis Cooper* 2.00
194 *Antwan Odom* 3.00
195 *Michael Waddell* 2.00
196 *Randy Starks* 2.00
197 *Rich Gardner* 2.00
198 *Travis LaBoy* 2.00
199 *Vick King* 2.00
200 *Chris Cooley* 3.00
201 *Adimchinobe Echemandu* 4.00
202 *Ahmad Carroll* 5.00
203 *Andy Hall* 4.00
204 *B.J. Johnson* 5.00
205 *B.J. Symons* 4.00
206 *Brandon Miree* 4.00
207 *Bruce Perry* 5.00
208 *Carlos Francis* 4.00
209 *Casey Bramlet* 6.00
210 *Chris Gamble* 6.00
211 *Clarence Moore* 4.00
212 *Cody Pickett* 4.00
213 *Craig Krenzel* 5.00
214 *D.J. Hackett* 4.00
215 *D.J. Williams* 5.00
216 *Derrick Ward* 5.00
217 *Drew Carter* 4.00
218 *Drew Henson* 8.00
219 *Ernest Wilford* 5.00
220 *Jamaar Taylor* 5.00
221 *Jared Lorenzen* 4.00
222 *Jarrett Payton* 5.00
223 *Jason Babin* 4.00
224 *Jeff Smoker* 6.00
225 *Jerricho Cotchery* 5.00
226 *Jim Sorgi* 4.00
227 *John Navarre* 5.00
228 *Johnnie Morant* 4.00
229 *Jonathan Vilma* 6.00
230 *Josh Harris* 4.00
231 *Kenechi Udeze* 5.00
232 *Matt Mauck* 4.00
233 *Maurice Mann* 4.00
234 *Michael Turner* 4.00
235 *P.K. Sam* 5.00
236 *Quincy Wilson* 5.00
237 *Ran Carthon* 4.00
238 *Ricardo Colclough* 5.00
239 *Samie Parker* 5.00
240 *Sean Jones* 4.00
241 *Sean Taylor* 6.00
242 *Sloan Thomas* 4.00
243 *Tommie Harris* 5.00
244 *Triandos Luke* 4.00
245 *Troy Fleming* 4.00
246 *Vince Wilfork* 6.00
247 *Will Smith* 5.00
248 *Michael Boulware* 5.00
249 *Richard Smith* 4.00
250 *Teddy Lehman* 5.00
251 *Larry Fitzgerald Jersey* 15.00
252 *DeAngelo Hall Jersey* 8.00
253 *Matt Schaub Jersey* 6.00
254 *Michael Jenkins Jenkins* 8.00
255 *Devard Darling Jersey* 6.00
256 *J.P. Losman Jersey* 15.00
257 *Lee Evans Jersey* 10.00
258 *Keary Colbert Jersey* 8.00
259 *Bernard Berrian Jersey* 6.00
260 *Chris Perry Jersey* 8.00
261 *Kellen Winslow Jr. Jersey* 10.00
262 *Luke McCown Jersey* 6.00
263 *Julius Jones Jersey* 15.00
264 *Darius Watts Jersey* 6.00
265 *Tatum Bell Jersey* 8.00
266 *Kevin Jones Jersey* 15.00
267 *Roy Williams Jersey* 15.00
268 *Dunta Robinson Jersey* 6.00
269 *Greg Jones Jersey* 6.00
270 *Reggie Williams Jersey* 8.00
271 *Mewelde Moore Jersey* 6.00
272 *Ben Watson Jersey* 6.00
273 *Cedric Cobbs Jersey* 6.00
274 *Devery Henderson Jersey* 6.00
275 *Eli Manning Jersey* 30.00
276 *Robert Gallery Jersey* 6.00
277 *Ben Roethlisberger Jersey* 75.00
278 *Philip Rivers Jersey* 15.00
279 *Derrick Hamilton Jersey* 6.00
280 *Rashaun Woods Jersey* 8.00
281 *Steven Jackson Jersey* 12.00
282 *Michael Clayton Jersey* 10.00
283 *Ben Troupe Jersey* 6.00
284 *Eli Manning Jersey, Philip Rivers Jersey* 30.00
285 *Larry Fitzgerald Jersey, Roy Williams Jersey* 20.00
286 *Kellen Winslow Jr. Jersey, Greg Jones Jersey* 15.00
287 *DeAngelo Hall Jersey, Dunta Robinson Jersey* 8.00
288 *Reggie Williams Jersey, Devard Darling Jersey* 10.00
289 *Ben Roethlisberger Jersey, J.P. Losman Jersey* 75.00
290 *Michael Clayton Jersey, Devery Henderson Jersey* 12.00
291 *Steven Jackson Jersey, Chris Perry Jersey* 15.00
292 *Lee Evans Jersey, Michael Jenkins Jersey* 12.00
293 *Rashaun Woods Jersey, Tatum Bell Jersey* 15.00
294 *Kevin Jones Jersey, Bernard Berrian Jersey* 15.00
295 *Ben Watson Jersey, Ben Troupe Jersey* 8.00
296 *Julius Jones Jersey, Mewelde Moore Jersey* 20.00
297 *Matt Schaub Jersey, Derrick Hamilton Jersey* 8.00
298 *Luke McCown Jersey, Darius Watts Jersey* 8.00
299 *Keary Colbert Jersey, Cedric Cobbs Jersey* 8.00

2004 Leaf Rookies & Stars Longevity

Cards 1-100: 3X-5X
Production 125 Sets
Rookies (101-200): 3X-6X
Production 75 Sets
Autographed Rookies (201-250): .5X-8X
Production 50 Sets
Auto./Mat.Rookies (251-283): No Pricing
Production 10 Sets
Rookies (284-299): No Pricing
Production 25 Sets

2004 Leaf Rookies & Stars Longevity Holofoil

Cards 1-100: 4X-8X
Production 75 Sets
Rookies (101-200): No Pricing
Production 25 Sets
Auto. Rookies (201-250): No Pricing
Production 10 Sets
Auto./Mat. Rookies (251-283): No Pricing
Production 5 Sets
Rookies (284-299): No Pricing
Production 10 Sets

2004 Leaf Rookies & Stars True Blue Longevity

Cards 1-100: 1X-3X
Production 249 Sets
Rookies (101-200): 3X-6X
Production 75 Sets
Rookies (201-250): No Pricing
Production 25 Sets

2004 Leaf Rookies & Stars Crusade Red

NM/M
Common Player: 3.00
Production 1,250 Sets
Red Die-Cut: No Pricing
Production 10 Sets
Green: .75X-1.5X
Production 750 Sets
Green Die-Cut: No Pricing
Production 25 Sets
Purple: 1X-2X
Production 250 Sets
Purple Die-Cut: 1X-3X
Production 50 Sets
C-1 Brett Favre 8.00
C-2 Brian Urlacher 3.00
C-3 Byron Leftwich 5.00
C-4 Carson Palmer 4.00
C-5 Chad Pennington 4.00
C-6 Clinton Portis 5.00
C-7 Daunte Culpepper 3.00
C-8 David Carr 4.00
C-9 Deuce McAllister 3.00
C-10 Donovan McNabb 4.00
C-11 Emmitt Smith 6.00
C-12 Jamal Lewis 3.00
C-13 Jeremy Shockey 3.00
C-14 Jerry Rice 6.00
C-15 Joe Namath 6.00
C-16 Joey Harrington 3.00
C-17 LaDainian Tomlinson 4.00
C-18 LaVar Arrington 3.00
C-19 Michael Vick 6.00
C-20 Peyton Manning 5.00
C-21 Priest Holmes 4.00
C-22 Randy Moss 5.00
C-23 Ricky Williams 3.00
C-24 Steve McNair 3.00
C-25 Tom Brady 5.00

2004 Leaf Rookies & Stars Face Mask

NM/M
Common Player: 5.00
Production 325 Sets
M-1 Eli Manning 25.00
M-2 Robert Gallery 6.00
M-3 Larry Fitzgerald 15.00
M-4 Philip Rivers 15.00
M-5 Kellen Winslow Jr. 12.00
M-6 Roy Williams 15.00
M-7 DeAngelo Hall 8.00
M-8 Reggie Williams 8.00
M-9 Dunta Robinson 5.00
M-10 Ben Roethlisberger 50.00
M-11 Lee Evans 10.00
M-12 Michael Clayton 10.00
M-13 J.P. Losman 10.00
M-14 Steven Jackson 12.00
M-15 Chris Perry 8.00
M-16 Michael Jenkins 8.00
M-17 Kevin Jones 12.00
M-18 Rashaun Woods 8.00
M-19 Ben Watson 5.00
M-20 Ben Troupe 5.00
M-21 Tatum Bell 8.00
M-22 Julius Jones 15.00
M-23 Devery Henderson 5.00
M-24 Darius Watts 5.00
M-25 Greg Jones 6.00
M-26 Keary Colbert 6.00
M-27 Derrick Hamilton 5.00
M-28 Bernard Berrian 5.00
M-29 Devard Darling 5.00
M-30 Matt Schaub 6.00
M-31 Luke McCown 6.00
M-32 Mewelde Moore 6.00
M-33 Cedric Cobbs 5.00

2004 Leaf Rookies & Stars Fans of the Game

NM/M
Common Card: 2.00
300 Tony Hawk 3.00
301 Michael Phelps 3.00
302 Damien Fahey 2.00
303 Jackie Mason 2.00
304 Bob Saget 2.00
305 Linda Cohn 2.00

2004 Leaf Rookies & Stars Fans of the Game Auto

NM/M
Common Card: 20.00
300 Tony Hawk 125.00
301 Michael Phelps 75.00
302 Damien Fahey 20.00
303 Jackie Mason 30.00
304 Bob Saget 30.00
305 Linda Cohn 30.00

2004 Leaf Rookies & Stars Freshman Orientation

NM/M
Common Player: 5.00
Production 500 Sets
Class Officers: .75X-1.5X
Production 100 Sets
FO-1 Eli Manning 20.00
FO-2 Robert Gallery 6.00
FO-3 Larry Fitzgerald 15.00
FO-4 Philip Rivers 15.00
FO-5 Kellen Winslow Jr. 10.00
FO-6 Roy Williams 15.00
FO-7 DeAngelo Hall 8.00
FO-8 Reggie Williams 8.00
FO-9 Dunta Robinson 5.00
FO-10 Ben Roethlisberger 60.00
FO-11 Lee Evans 10.00
FO-12 Michael Clayton 10.00
FO-13 J.P. Losman 10.00
FO-14 Steven Jackson 12.00
FO-15 Chris Perry 8.00
FO-16 Michael Jenkins 8.00
FO-17 Kevin Jones 12.00
FO-18 Rashaun Woods 8.00
FO-19 Ben Watson 5.00
FO-20 Ben Troupe 5.00
FO-21 Tatum Bell 8.00
FO-22 Julius Jones 15.00
FO-23 Devery Henderson 5.00
FO-24 Darius Watts 5.00
FO-25 Greg Jones 6.00
FO-26 Keary Colbert 6.00
FO-27 Derrick Hamilton 5.00
FO-28 Bernard Berrian 5.00
FO-29 Devard Darling 5.00
FO-30 Matt Schaub 6.00
FO-31 Luke McCown 6.00
FO-32 Mewelde Moore 6.00
FO-33 Cedric Cobbs 5.00

2004 Leaf R & S Great American Heroes Red

NM/M
Common Player: 2.00
Production 1,250 Sets
White: .75X-1.5X
Production 750 Sets
Blue: 1X-2X
Production 250 Sets
GAH-1 Anquan Boldin 3.00
GAH-2 Chad Pennington 4.00
GAH-3 Christian Okoye 2.00
GAH-4 Dante Hall 2.00
GAH-5 Derrick Mason 2.00
GAH-6 Domanick Davis 3.00
GAH-7 Hines Ward 2.00
GAH-8 Joe Horn 2.00
GAH-9 Joe Namath 6.00
GAH-10 Laveranues Coles 2.00
GAH-11 Matt Hasselbeck 2.00
GAH-12 Patrick Ramsey 2.00
GAH-13 Rex Grossman 3.00
GAH-14 Rudi Johnson 3.00
GAH-15 Sammy Baugh 4.00
GAH-16 Steve Smith 2.00
GAH-17 Terrell Suggs 2.00
GAH-18 Todd Heap 2.00
GAH-19 Tom Brady 5.00
GAH-20 Adam Vinatieri 2.00
GAH-21 Craig Krenzel 3.00
GAH-22 DeAngelo Hall 3.00
GAH-23 Matt Mauck 2.00
GAH-24 Philip Rivers 5.00
GAH-25 Tatum Bell 4.00

2004 Leaf R&S Great American Heroes Signatures

NM/M
Common Player: 15.00
Sequentially #'d to indicated quantity
GAH-1 Anquan Boldin/50 15.00
GAH-2 Chad Pennington/25
GAH-3 Christian Okoye/100 20.00
GAH-4 Dante Hall/50
GAH-5 Derrick Mason/50 15.00
GAH-6 Domanick Davis/75 15.00
GAH-7 Hines Ward/50 50.00
GAH-8 Joe Horn/100 15.00
GAH-9 Joe Namath/100 75.00
GAH-10 Laveranues Coles/25
GAH-11 Matt Hasselbeck/25
GAH-12 Patrick Ramsey/25
GAH-13 Rex Grossman/25
GAH-14 Rudi Johnson/50 15.00
GAH-15 Sammy Baugh/100 75.00
GAH-16 Steve Smith/75 15.00
GAH-18 Todd Heap/25
GAH-19 Tom Brady/25
GAH-20 Adam Vinatieri/75 30.00
GAH-21 Craig Krenzel/25
GAH-22 DeAngelo Hall/25
GAH-23 Matt Mauck/25
GAH-24 Philip Rivers/25
GAH-25 Tatum Bell/25

2004 Leaf Rookies & Stars Initial Steps Shoes

NM/M
Common Player: 6.00
Production 100 Sets
IS-1 Eli Manning 30.00
IS-2 Robert Gallery 8.00
IS-3 Larry Fitzgerald 20.00
IS-4 Philip Rivers 20.00
IS-5 Kellen Winslow Jr. 12.00
IS-6 Roy Williams 20.00
IS-7 DeAngelo Hall 10.00
IS-8 Reggie Williams 10.00
IS-9 Dunta Robinson 6.00
IS-10 Ben Roethlisberger 60.00
IS-11 Lee Evans 12.00
IS-12 Michael Clayton 12.00
IS-13 J.P. Losman 12.00
IS-14 Steven Jackson 15.00
IS-15 Chris Perry 10.00
IS-16 Michael Jenkins 10.00
IS-17 Kevin Jones 15.00
IS-18 Rashaun Woods 10.00
IS-19 Ben Watson 6.00
IS-20 Ben Troupe 6.00
IS-21 Tatum Bell 10.00
IS-22 Julius Jones 20.00
IS-23 Devery Henderson 6.00
IS-24 Darius Watts 6.00
IS-25 Greg Jones 8.00
IS-26 Keary Colbert 8.00
IS-27 Derrick Hamilton 6.00
IS-28 Bernard Berrian 6.00
IS-29 Devard Darling 6.00
IS-30 Matt Schaub 8.00
IS-31 Luke McCown 8.00
IS-32 Mewelde Moore 8.00
IS-33 Cedric Cobbs 6.00

2004 Leaf Rookies & Stars Prime Cuts

No Pricing
Production 25 Sets
PC-1 Brett Favre
PC-2 Brian Urlacher
PC-3 Byron Leftwich
PC-4 Chad Pennington
PC-5 Daunte Culpepper
PC-6 David Carr
PC-7 Deuce McAllister
PC-8 Donovan McNabb
PC-9 Emmitt Smith
PC-10 Jamal Lewis
PC-11 Jeremy Shockey
PC-12 Jerry Rice
PC-13 Joe Namath
PC-14 Joey Harrington
PC-15 LaDainian Tomlinson
PC-16 LaVar Arrington
PC-17 Marc Bulger
PC-18 Matt Hasselbeck
PC-19 Michael Vick
PC-20 Peyton Manning
PC-21 Priest Holmes
PC-22 Randy Moss
PC-23 Ricky Williams
PC-24 Steve McNair
PC-25 Tom Brady

2004 Leaf Rookies & Stars Rookie Autographs

NM/M
Common Player (201-250): 12.00
Production 150 Sets
Common Player (251-283): 25.00
Production 50 Sets
201 Adimchinobe Echemandu 15.00
202 Ahmad Carroll 25.00
203 Andy Hall 12.00
204 B.J. Johnson 15.00
205 B.J. Symons 12.00
206 Brandon Miree 12.00
207 Bruce Perry 15.00
208 Carlos Francis 20.00
209 Casey Bramlet 20.00
210 Chris Gamble 25.00
211 Clarence Moore 20.00
212 Cody Pickett 12.00
213 Craig Krenzel 20.00
214 D.J. Hackett 12.00
215 D.J. Williams 15.00
216 Derrick Ward 15.00
217 Drew Carter 12.00
218 Drew Henson 60.00
219 Ernest Wilford 15.00
220 Jamaar Taylor 15.00
221 Jared Lorenzen 12.00
222 Jarrett Payton 15.00
223 Jason Babin 30.00
224 Jeff Smoker 20.00
225 Jerricho Cotchery 15.00
226 Jim Sorgi 12.00
227 John Navarre 20.00
228 Johnnie Morant 12.00
229 Jonathan Vilma 30.00
230 Josh Harris 20.00
231 Kenechi Udeze 30.00
232 Matt Mauck 12.00
233 Maurice Mann 12.00
234 Michael Turner 12.00
235 P.K. Sam 15.00
236 Quincy Wilson 20.00
237 Ran Carthon 12.00
238 Ricardo Colclough 15.00
239 Samie Parker 15.00
240 Sean Jones 15.00
241 Sean Taylor 40.00
242 Sloan Thomas 12.00
243 Tommie Harris 30.00
244 Triandos Luke 12.00
245 Troy Fleming 12.00
246 Vince Wilfork 20.00
247 Will Smith 15.00
248 Michael Boulware 15.00
249 Richard Smith 20.00
250 Teddy Lehman 15.00
251 Larry Fitzgerald/10 Jersey
252 DeAngelo Hall Jersey 40.00
253 Matt Schaub Jersey 30.00
254 Michael Jenkins Jersey 30.00
255 Devard Darling Jersey 25.00
256 J.P. Losman Jersey 50.00
257 Lee Evans Jersey 50.00
258 Keary Colbert Jersey 40.00
259 Bernard Berrian Jersey 25.00
260 Chris Perry Jersey 40.00
261 Kellen Winslow Jr. Jersey 40.00
262 Luke McCown Jersey 25.00
263 Julius Jones Jersey 120.00
264 Darius Watts Jersey 30.00
265 Tatum Bell Jersey 60.00
266 Kevin Jones Jersey 80.00
267 Roy Williams Jersey 120.00
268 Dunta Robinson Jersey 25.00
269 Greg Jones Jersey 30.00
270 Reggie Williams Jersey 40.00
271 Mewelde Moore Jersey 40.00
272 Ben Watson Jersey 25.00
273 Cedric Cobbs Jersey 25.00
274 Devery Henderson Jersey 25.00
275 Eli Manning Jersey 200.00
276 Robert Gallery Jersey 30.00
277 Ben Roethlisberger Jersey 500.00
278 Philip Rivers Jersey 80.00
279 Derrick Hamilton Jersey 25.00
280 Rashaun Woods Jersey 30.00
281 Steven Jackson Jersey 75.00
282 Michael Clayton Jersey 75.00
283 Ben Troupe Jersey 30.00

2004 Leaf Rookies & Stars Slideshow

NM/M
Common Player: 2.00
Production 1,250 Sets
Slideshow Studio: .75X-1.5X
Production 750 Sets
Slideshow View Masters: 1X-2X
Production 250 Sets
SS-1 Aaron Brooks 3.00
SS-2 Ahman Green 3.00
SS-3 Anquan Boldin 3.00
SS-4 Chad Johnson 2.00
SS-5 Chris Chambers 3.00
SS-6 Drew Bledsoe 3.00
SS-7 Edgerrin James 4.00
SS-8 Jake Delhomme 3.00
SS-9 Jake Plummer 2.00
SS-10 Joe Namath 6.00
SS-11 Kevan Barlow 2.00
SS-12 Kyle Boller 3.00
SS-13 LaVar Arrington 3.00
SS-14 Marc Bulger 2.00
SS-15 Marshall Faulk 4.00
SS-16 Marvin Harrison 3.00
SS-17 Matt Hasselbeck 2.00
SS-18 Roy Williams 2.00
SS-19 Rudi Johnson 2.00
SS-20 Shaun Alexander 3.00
SS-21 Stephen Davis 2.00
SS-22 Tom Brady 5.00
SS-23 Travis Henry 2.00
SS-24 Trent Green 2.00
SS-25 Donovan McNabb 4.00

2004 Leaf Rookies & Stars Ticket Masters

NM/M
Common Card: 2.00
Production 1,250 Sets
Season Ticket Masters: .75X-1.5X
Production 750 Sets
Championship Ticket Masters: 1X-2X
Production 250 Sets
TM-1 Emmitt Smith, Anquan Boldin 5.00
TM-2 Michael Vick, Michael Jenkins 5.00
TM-3 Jamal Lewis, Ray Lewis 2.00
TM-4 Drew Bledsoe, Travis Henry 2.00
TM-5 Jake Delhomme, Julius Peppers 2.00
TM-6 Brian Urlacher, Rex Grossman 2.00
TM-7 Carson Palmer, Chad Johnson 3.00
TM-8 Kellen Winslow Jr., Jeff Garcia 3.00
TM-9 Joey Harrington, Roy Williams 3.00
TM-10 Brett Favre, Ahman Green 6.00
TM-11 David Carr, Andre Johnson 3.00
TM-12 Peyton Manning, Edgerrin James 4.00
TM-13 Byron Leftwich, Fred Taylor 4.00
TM-14 Priest Holmes, Trent Green 3.00
TM-15 Ricky Williams, Chris Chambers 2.00
TM-16 Daunte Culpepper, Randy Moss 4.00
TM-17 Tom Brady, Corey Dillon 4.00
TM-18 Eli Manning, Jeremy Shockey 6.00
TM-19 Chad Pennington, Curtis Martin 3.00
TM-20 Jerry Rice, Tim Brown 5.00
TM-21 Donovan McNabb, Terrell Owens 3.00
TM-22 Ben Roethlisberger, Hines Ward 8.00
TM-23 Philip Rivers, LaDainian Tomlinson 4.00
TM-24 Marc Bulger, Marshall Faulk 3.00
TM-25 Clinton Portis, LaVar Arrington 4.00

2004 Leaf Rookies & Stars Triple Threads

NM/M
Common Card: 15.00
Production 100 Sets
1 Anquan Boldin, Josh McCown, Larry Fitzgerald 15.00
2 Michael Vick, Warrick Dunn, Peerless Price 30.00
3 Jamal Lewis, Kyle Boller, Ray Lewis 15.00
4 Drew Bledsoe, Eric Moulds, Travis Henry 15.00
5 Jake Delhomme, Stephen Davis, Steve Smith 15.00
6 Brian Urlacher, Rex Grossman, Anthony Thomas 20.00
7 Chad Johnson, Rudi Johnson, Peter Warrick 15.00
8 Darren Woodson, Roy Williams, Terence Newman 20.00
9 Jake Plummer, Rod Smith, Shannon Sharpe 15.00
10 Brett Favre, Ahman Green, Javon Walker 40.00
11 Patrick Ramsey, Laveranues Coles, LaVar Arrington 25.00
12 Peyton Manning, Edgerrin James, Marvin Harrison 25.00
13 Byron Leftwich, Fred Taylor, Jimmy Smith 25.00
14 Trent Green, Priest Holmes, Dante Hall 20.00
15 Ricky Williams, Chris Chambers, Zach Thomas 20.00
16 Daunte Culpepper, Michael Bennett, Randy Moss 25.00
17 Tom Brady, Bethel Johnson, Ty Law 25.00
18 Aaron Brooks, Deuce McAllister, Donte Stallworth 15.00
19 Tiki Barber, Jeremy Shockey, Amani Toomer 20.00
20 Chad Pennington, Curtis Martin, Santana Moss 25.00
21 Jerry Rice, Rich Gannon, Tim Brown 30.00
22 Jerome Bettis, Hines Ward, Plaxico Burress 25.00
23 Matt Hasselbeck, Shaun Alexander, Koren Robinson 15.00
24 Marc Bulger, Marshall Faulk, Isaac Bruce 20.00
25 Steve McNair, Chris Brown, Derrick Mason 15.00
26 David Carr, Domanick Davis, Andre Johnson 20.00

2004 Leaf Rookies and Stars Longevity

NM/M
Common Player (1-94): .40
Minor Player (1-100): .60
Unlisted Player (1-94): 1.00
Common Card (95-100): 3.00
Common Rookie (101-200): 3.00
Unlisted Rookie (101-200): 4.00
Production 999 Sets
Common Rookie (201-250): 4.00
Unlisted Rookie (201-250): 5.00
Production 499 Sets
Common Rookie (251-283): 6.00
Unlisted Rookie (251-283): 8.00
Production 299 Sets
Pack (5): 6.00
Box (24): 140.00
1 Anquan Boldin 1.00
2 Emmitt Smith 2.50
3 Josh McCown .40
4 Michael Vick 2.50
5 Peerless Price .60
6 T.J. Duckett .60
7 Warrick Dunn .40
8 Jamal Lewis 1.00
9 Kyle Boller 1.00
10 Ray Lewis .60
11 Drew Bledsoe 1.00
12 Eric Moulds .40
13 Travis Henry .40
14 Jake Delhomme 1.00
15 Stephen Davis .60
16 Steve Smith .40
17 Brian Urlacher 1.00
18 Rex Grossman 1.00

19 Thomas Jones .60
20 Carson Palmer 1.50
21 Chad Johnson .60
22 Rudi Johnson .60
23 Jeff Garcia 1.00
24 William Green .60
25 Keyshawn Johnson .60
26 Terence Newman .40
27 Roy Williams .60
28 Jake Plummer .60
29 Quentin Griffin .40
30 Rod Smith .40
31 Charles Rogers 1.00
32 Joey Harrington 1.00
33 Ahman Green 1.00
34 Brett Favre 3.00
35 Javon Walker .60
36 Andre Johnson 1.00
37 David Carr 1.50
38 Domanick Davis 1.00
39 Edgerrin James 1.50
40 Marvin Harrison 1.00
41 Peyton Manning 2.00
42 Byron Leftwich 2.00
43 Fred Taylor 1.00
44 Jimmy Smith .40
45 Priest Holmes 1.50
46 Tony Gonzalez .60
47 Trent Green .40
48 A.J. Feeley .40
49 Chris Chambers 1.00
50 Deion Sanders 1.00
51 Daunte Culpepper 1.00
52 Michael Bennett 1.00
53 Randy Moss 2.00
54 Corey Dillon .60
55 Deion Branch .40
56 Tom Brady 2.00
57 Aaron Brooks 1.00
58 Deuce McAllister 1.00
59 Joe Horn .60
60 Jeremy Shockey 1.00
61 Michael Strahan .40
62 Tiki Barber .40
63 Chad Pennington 1.50
64 Curtis Martin 1.00
65 Santana Moss .40
66 Jerry Porter .40
67 Jerry Rice 2.50
68 Warren Sapp .40
69 Donovan McNabb 1.50
70 Jevon Kearse .40
71 Terrell Owens 1.00
72 Duce Staley .40
73 Hines Ward .60
74 Jerome Bettis .60
75 LaDainian Tomlinson 1.50
76 Kevan Barlow .40
77 Tim Rattay .40
78 Koren Robinson .40
79 Matt Hasselbeck .60
80 Shaun Alexander 1.00
81 Isaac Bruce .60
82 Marc Bulger .60
83 Marshall Faulk 1.50
84 Torry Holt 1.00
85 Brad Johnson .40
86 Derrick Brooks .40
87 Chris Brown .60
88 Derrick Mason .40
89 Eddie George 1.00
90 Steve McNair 1.00
91 Clinton Portis 2.00
92 LaVar Arrington 1.00
93 Laveranues Coles .60
94 Mark Brunell .60
95 DeAngelo Hall, Matt Schaub, Michael Jenkins 3.00
96 J.P. Losman, Lee Evans 3.00
97 Kellen Winslow Jr., Luke McCown 3.00
98 Darius Watts, Tatum Bell 3.00
99 Kevin Jones, Roy Williams 4.00
100 Greg Jones, Reggie Williams 3.00
101 *Darnell Dockett* 3.00
102 *Karlos Dansby* 3.00
103 *Larry Croom* 3.00
104 *Chad Lavalais* 4.00
105 *Demorrio Williams* 3.00
106 *B.J. Sams* 3.00
107 *Dwan Edwards* 4.00
108 *Jason Peters* 3.00
109 *Shaud Williams* 4.00
110 *Tim Anderson* 4.00
111 *Tim Euhus* 3.00
112 *Michael Gaines* 3.00
113 *Rod Rutherford* 3.00
114 *Leon Joe* 3.00
115 *Nathan Vasher* 4.00
116 *Caleb Miller* 3.00
117 *Jamall Broussard* 4.00
118 *Keiwan Ratliff* 3.00
119 *Landon Johnson* 3.00
120 *Madieu Williams* 4.00
121 *Matthias Askew* 3.00
122 *Robert Geathers* 3.00
123 *Richard Alston* 4.00
124 *Bruce Thornton* 3.00
125 *Patrick Crayton* 4.00
126 *Bradlee Van Pelt* 4.00
127 *Charlie Adams* 3.00
128 *Nate Jackson* 3.00
129 *Roc Alexander* 3.00
130 *Romar Crenshaw* 3.00
131 *Keith Smith* 3.00
132 *Joey Thomas* 5.00
133 *Kelvin Kight* 3.00
134 *Scott McBrien* 4.00
135 *Andrae Thurman* 4.00
136 *Derick Armstrong* 3.00
137 *Glenn Earl* 4.00
138 *Kendrick Starling* 4.00
139 *Ben Hartsock* 4.00
140 *Gilbert Gardner* 5.00
141 *Jason David* 3.00
142 *Daryl Smith* 3.00
143 *Jared Allen* 4.00
144 *Jeris McIntyre* 4.00
145 *John Booth* 6.00
146 *Jonathan Smith* 3.00
147 *Junior Siavii* 4.00
148 *Keyaron Fox* 3.00
149 *Kris Wilson* 3.00
150 *Doug Easlick* 4.00
151 *Fred Russell* 3.00
152 *Tony Bua* 5.00
153 *Will Poole* 4.00
154 *Ben Nelson* 3.00
155 *Brock Lesnar* 6.00
156 *Butchie Wallace* 4.00
157 *Darrion Scott* 3.00
158 *Dontarrious Thomas* 3.00
159 *Richard Owens* 4.00
160 *Rod Davis* 3.00
161 *Dexter Reid* 3.00
162 *Kory Chapman* 3.00
163 *Marquise Hill* 5.00
164 *Courtney Watson* 3.00
165 *Mike Karney* 4.00
166 *Gibril Wilson* 4.00
167 *Reggie Torbor* 4.00
168 *Darrell McClover* 3.00
169 *Derrick Strait* 3.00
170 *Erik Coleman* 3.00
171 *Jonathan Reese* 3.00
172 *Rashad Washington* 3.00
173 *Courtney Anderson* 3.00
174 *Stuart Schweigert* 3.00
175 *J.R. Reed* 3.00
176 *Justin Jenkins* 4.00
177 *Matt Ware* 4.00
178 *Nate Lawrie* 3.00
179 *Thomas Tapeh* 3.00
180 *Matt Kranchick* 3.00
181 *Willie Parker* 4.00
182 *Igor Olshansky* 3.00
183 *Ryan Krause* 3.00
184 *Shaun Phillips* 3.00
185 *Wes Welker* 4.00
186 *Richard Seigler* 3.00
187 *Shawntae Spencer* 3.00
188 *Marcus Tubbs* 3.00
189 *Niko Koutouvides* 3.00
190 *Brandon Chillar* 3.00
191 *Anthony Hargrove* 3.00
192 *Mark Jones* 4.00
193 *Marquis Cooper* 3.00
194 *Antwan Odom* 3.00
195 *Michael Waddell* 3.00
196 *Randy Starks* 4.00
197 *Rich Gardner* 4.00
198 *Travis LaBoy* 3.00
199 *Vick King* 3.00
200 *Chris Cooley* 3.00
201 *Adimchinobe Echemandu* 5.00
202 *Ahmad Carroll* 6.00
203 *Andy Hall* 4.00
204 *B.J. Johnson* 3.00
205 *B.J. Symons* 4.00
206 *Brandon Miree* 4.00
207 *Bruce Perry* 4.00
208 *Carlos Francis* 4.00
209 *Casey Bramlet* 6.00
210 *Chris Gamble* 5.00
211 *Clarence Moore* 6.00
212 *Cody Pickett* 4.00
213 *Craig Krenzel* 5.00
214 *D.J. Hackett* 5.00
215 *D.J. Williams* 5.00
216 *Derrick Ward* 5.00
217 *Drew Carter* 4.00
218 *Drew Henson* 8.00
219 *Ernest Wilford* 4.00
220 *Jamaar Taylor* 5.00
221 *Jared Lorenzen* 4.00
222 *Jarrett Payton* 5.00
223 *Jason Babin* 5.00
224 *Jeff Smoker* 6.00
225 *Jericho Cotchery* 6.00
226 *Jim Sorgi* 4.00
227 *John Navarre* 5.00
228 *Johnnie Morant* 5.00
229 *Jonathan Vilma* 5.00
230 *Josh Harris* 5.00
231 *Kenechi Udeze* 4.00
232 *Matt Mauck* 4.00
233 *Maurice Mann* 4.00
234 *Michael Turner* 4.00
235 *P.K. Sam* 5.00
236 *Quincy Wilson* 5.00
237 *Ran Carthon* 5.00
238 *Ricardo Colclough* 5.00
239 *Samie Parker* 6.00
240 *Sean Jones* 4.00
241 *Sean Taylor* 8.00
242 *Sloan Thomas* 5.00
243 *Tommie Harris* 5.00
244 *Triandos Luke* 4.00
245 *Troy Fleming* 4.00
246 *Vince Wilfork* 4.00
247 *Will Smith* 4.00
248 *Michael Boulware* 4.00
249 *Richard Smith* 4.00
250 *Teddy Lehman* 4.00
251 *Larry Fitzgerald* 20.00
252 *DeAngelo Hall* 10.00
253 *Matt Schaub* 8.00
254 *Michael Jenkins* 10.00
255 *Devard Darling* 6.00
256 *J.P. Losman* 20.00
257 *Lee Evans* 12.00
258 *Keary Colbert* 6.00
259 *Bernard Berrian* 6.00
260 *Chris Perry* 8.00
261 *Kellen Winslow Jr.* 12.00
262 *Luke McCown* 6.00
263 *Julius Jones* 30.00
264 *Darius Watts* 6.00
265 *Tatum Bell* 10.00
266 *Kevin Jones* 25.00
267 *Roy Williams* 20.00
268 *Dunta Robinson* 6.00
269 *Greg Jones* 8.00
270 *Reggie Williams* 8.00
271 *Mewelde Moore* 8.00
272 *Ben Watson* 6.00
273 *Cedric Cobbs* 6.00
274 *Devery Henderson* 6.00
275 *Eli Manning* 40.00
276 *Robert Gallery* 8.00
277 *Ben Roethlisberger* 60.00
278 *Philip Rivers* 25.00
279 *Derrick Hamilton* 6.00
280 *Rashaun Woods* 12.00
281 *Steven Jackson* 20.00
282 *Michael Clayton* 15.00
283 *Ben Troupe* 6.00

2004 Leaf Rookies and Stars Longevity Ruby

Common Player (1-100): 1X-1.5X
Production 250 Sets
Common Rookie (101-200): .75X-1.5X
Production 199 Sets
Common Rookie (201-250): .5X-1.25X
Production 150 Sets
Com. Rookie RPS Mat. (251-283): .5X-1.25X
Production 99 Sets

2004 Leaf Rookies and Stars Longevity Sapphire

Common Player (1-100): 1X-2X
Production 199 Sets
Common Rookie (101-200): .75X-1.75X
Production 150 Sets
Common Rookie (201-250): .5X-1.5X
Production 99 Sets
Com. Rookie RPS Mat. (251-283): .5X-1.25X
Production 75 Sets

2004 Leaf Rookies and Stars Longevity Gold

Common Player (1-100): 1.25X-2X
Production 150 Sets
Common Rookie (101-200): 1X-2X
Production 99 Sets
Common Rookie (201-250): .75X-1.5X
Production 75 Sets
Com. Rookie RPS Mat. (251-283): 1X-2X
Production 50 Sets

2004 Leaf Rookies and Stars Longevity Emerald

NM/M
Common Player (1-100): 1.5X-2X
Production 99 Sets
Common Rookie (101-200): 1X-2X
Production 75 Sets
Common Rookie (201-250): .75X-2X
Production 50 Sets
Com. Rookie RPS Mat (251-283): No Pricing
Production 25 Sets

2004 Leaf Rookies and Stars Longevity Black

Common Player (1-100): 1.5X-3X
Production 75 Sets
Common Rookie (101-200): 1X-3X
Production 50 Sets
Common Rookie (201-250): No Pricing
Production 25 Sets
Com. Rookie RPS Materials: No Pricing
Production 10 Sets

2004 Leaf R/S Longevity Draft Class 2001 Autos

NM/M
301 Michael Vick 200.00
302 Drew Brees
304 Marques Tuiasosopo
305 Chris Weinke 10.00
307 Deuce McAllister
309 Anthony Thomas
311 David Terrell
312 Koren Robinson
313 Rod Gardner
314 Santana Moss
315 Freddie Mitchell 15.00
316 Gerard Warren
317 Justin Smith
318 Jamal Reynolds

2004 Leaf R and S Longevity Materials Ruby

NM/M
Common Card: 5.00
Sequentially #'d to indicated quantity
4 Michael Vick/150 20.00
6 T.J. Duckett/125 6.00
11 Drew Bledsoe/150 8.00
14 Jake Delhomme/150 8.00
15 Stephen Davis/99 6.00
16 Steve Smith/150 5.00
18 Rex Grossman/150 8.00
19 Thomas Jones/150 6.00
20 Carson Palmer/99 10.00
23 Jeff Garcia/99 8.00
24 William Green/125 6.00
26 Terence Newman/125 5.00
29 Quentin Griffin/99 6.00
32 Joey Harrington/99 8.00
36 Andre Johnson/99 8.00
37 David Carr/150 10.00
38 Domanick Davis/150 8.00
40 Marvin Harrison/150 8.00
42 Byron Leftwich/150 15.00
43 Fred Taylor/135 8.00
44 Jimmy Smith/99 6.00
46 Tony Gonzalez/150 6.00
48 A.J. Feeley/99 5.00
50 Deion Sanders/150 10.00
52 Michael Bennett/99 8.00
53 Randy Moss/125 15.00
54 Corey Dillon/99 6.00
57 Aaron Brooks/150 8.00
58 Deuce McAllister/99 8.00
60 Jeremy Shockey/125 8.00
61 Michael Strahan/125 5.00
62 Tiki Barber/125 8.00
63 Chad Pennington/150 10.00
64 Curtis Martin/125 8.00
66 Jerry Porter/150 5.00
67 Jerry Rice/150 20.00
68 Warren Sapp/125 5.00
69 Donovan McNabb/150 10.00
70 Jevon Kearse/150 6.00
72 Duce Staley/99 8.00
73 Hines Ward/150 8.00
74 Jerome Bettis/50 10.00
75 LaDainian Tomlinson/50 10.00
78 Koren Robinson/150 5.00
79 Matt Hasselbeck/150 6.00
80 Shaun Alexander/50 12.00
81 Isaac Bruce/75 6.00
82 Marc Bulger/150 6.00
85 Brad Johnson/99 5.00
87 Chris Brown/80 6.00
88 Derrick Mason/99 5.00
90 Steve McNair/150 8.00
92 LaVar Arrington/99 20.00
93 Laveranues Coles/125 6.00
94 Mark Brunell/125 6.00

2004 Leaf R and S Longevity Materials Sapphire

NM/M
Common Player: 5.00
Sequentially #'d to indicated quantity
1 Anquan Boldin/99 8.00
3 Josh McCown/84 5.00
4 Michael Vick/99 25.00
6 T.J. Duckett/99 6.00
8 Jamal Lewis/75 8.00
9 Kyle Boller/99 8.00
11 Drew Bledsoe/99 8.00
13 Travis Henry/99 5.00
14 Jake Delhomme/75 8.00
16 Steve Smith/99 5.00
17 Brian Urlacher/99 8.00
18 Rex Grossman/99 8.00
19 Thomas Jones/99 6.00
24 William Green/99 6.00
25 Keyshawn Johnson/50 10.00
26 Terence Newman/99 6.00
27 Roy Williams/50 10.00
28 Jake Plummer/50 6.00
29 Quentin Griffin/75 6.00
36 Andre Johnson/75 8.00
37 David Carr/99 10.00
38 Domanick Davis/99 8.00
40 Marvin Harrison/99 8.00
41 Peyton Manning/50 20.00
42 Byron Leftwich/99 15.00
44 Jimmy Smith/50 8.00
46 Tony Gonzalez/99 6.00
48 A.J. Feeley/75 5.00
50 Deion Sanders/99 12.00
51 Daunte Culpepper/50 15.00
52 Michael Bennett/50 8.00
53 Randy Moss/75 15.00
54 Corey Dillon/99 6.00
56 Tom Brady/75 20.00
57 Aaron Brooks/99 8.00
58 Deuce McAllister/75 8.00
60 Jeremy Shockey/99 8.00
61 Michael Strahan/99 5.00
62 Tiki Barber/99 10.00
63 Chad Pennington/99 10.00
64 Curtis Martin/99 8.00
65 Santana Moss/25 15.00
66 Jerry Porter/99 6.00
67 Jerry Rice/99 20.00
68 Warren Sapp/99 8.00
69 Donovan McNabb/99 12.00
70 Jevon Kearse/99 8.00
72 Duce Staley/75 8.00
73 Hines Ward/99 8.00
78 Koren Robinson/99 6.00
79 Matt Hasselbeck/99 6.00
81 Isaac Bruce/50 8.00
82 Marc Bulger/99 8.00
85 Brad Johnson/75 6.00
89 Eddie George/75 6.00
91 Clinton Portis/50 15.00
92 LaVar Arrington/50 25.00
93 Laveranues Coles/75 5.00
94 Mark Brunell/75 8.00

2004 Leaf R and S Longevity Materials Emerald

NM/M
Common Player: 10.00
Sequentially #'d to indicated quantity
No pricing for cards #'d to 25 or less
1 Anquan Boldin/35 20.00
2 Emmitt Smith/50
3 Josh McCown/35 10.00
4 Michael Vick/50 40.00
5 Peerless Price/25
6 T.J. Duckett/35
7 Warrick Dunn/35
8 Jamal Lewis/25
9 Kyle Boller/25
10 Ray Lewis/25
11 Drew Bledsoe/25
12 Eric Moulds/35 10.00
13 Travis Henry/35 10.00
14 Jake Delhomme/35
15 Stephen Davis/35 12.00
16 Steve Smith/35
17 Brian Urlacher/35 15.00
18 Rex Grossman/35
19 Thomas Jones/35
20 Carson Palmer/25
21 Chad Johnson/35
22 Rudi Johnson/35
23 Jeff Garcia/35
24 William Green/25
25 Keyshawn Johnson/35 15.00
26 Terence Newman/25
27 Roy Williams/35 25.00
28 Jake Plummer/35 15.00
29 Quentin Griffin/25
30 Rod Smith/25
31 Charles Rogers/35 15.00
32 Joey Harrington/35 15.00
33 Ahman Green/35
34 Brett Favre/50
35 Javon Walker/35 15.00
36 Andre Johnson/35
37 David Carr/25
38 Domanick Davis/35 15.00
39 Edgerrin James/35 20.00
40 Marvin Harrison/35
41 Peyton Manning/50 25.00
42 Byron Leftwich/10
43 Fred Taylor/35
44 Jimmy Smith/25
45 Priest Holmes/40
46 Tony Gonzalez/35 20.00
47 Trent Green/35 20.00
49 Chris Chambers/35 20.00
51 Daunte Culpepper/40
52 Michael Bennett/35
53 Randy Moss/40 30.00
54 Corey Dillon/40 12.00
56 Tom Brady/50 30.00
57 Aaron Brooks/35
58 Deuce McAllister/35 12.00
60 Jeremy Shockey/35
61 Michael Strahan/35 10.00
62 Tiki Barber/35 12.00
63 Chad Pennington/35 20.00
64 Curtis Martin/35
65 Santana Moss/35 10.00
66 Jerry Porter/35
67 Jerry Rice/50
69 Donovan McNabb/50
70 Jevon Kearse/25
71 Terrell Owens/35 15.00
72 Duce Staley/25
73 Hines Ward/25
74 Jerome Bettis/35 15.00
75 LaDainian Tomlinson/40
78 Koren Robinson/35
79 Matt Hasselbeck/35 12.00
80 Shaun Alexander/35
81 Isaac Bruce/25
82 Marc Bulger/35 15.00
83 Marshall Faulk/35 15.00
84 Torry Holt/35 20.00
85 Brad Johnson/25
87 Chris Brown/35 20.00
88 Derrick Mason/25
89 Eddie George/35 12.00
90 Steve McNair/35
91 Clinton Portis/35
92 LaVar Arrington/35 25.00
93 Laveranues Coles/25

2004 Leaf R and S Longevity Materials Gold

NM/M
Common Player: 10.00
Sequentially #'d to indicated quantity
No pricing for cards #'d to 25 or less
1 Anquan Boldin/75 10.00
4 Michael Vick/75 25.00
6 T.J. Duckett/75 10.00
8 Jamal Lewis/50 12.00
9 Kyle Boller/65 12.00
10 Ray Lewis/50 15.00
11 Drew Bledsoe/75 12.00
13 Travis Henry/75 8.00
14 Jake Delhomme/50 15.00
16 Steve Smith/75 8.00
17 Brian Urlacher/75 12.00
18 Rex Grossman/75 12.00
19 Thomas Jones/75 12.00
21 Chad Johnson/50 10.00
23 Jeff Garcia/50 12.00
24 William Green/75 10.00
25 Keyshawn Johnson/50 15.00
26 Terence Newman/75 12.00
28 Jake Plummer/50 10.00
29 Quentin Griffin/50 15.00
32 Joey Harrington/50 12.00
36 Andre Johnson/50 12.00
37 David Carr/75 15.00
38 Domanick Davis/75 12.00
40 Marvin Harrison/75 12.00
42 Byron Leftwich/75 20.00
43 Fred Taylor/25
46 Tony Gonzalez/75 12.00
48 A.J. Feeley/50 10.00
50 Deion Sanders/75 20.00
53 Randy Moss/50 20.00
54 Corey Dillon/75 12.00
57 Aaron Brooks/75 12.00
58 Deuce McAllister/50 15.00
59 Joe Horn/25 10.00
60 Jeremy Shockey/75 12.00
61 Michael Strahan/75 10.00
62 Tiki Barber/75 12.00
63 Chad Pennington/75 15.00
64 Curtis Martin/75 12.00
65 Santana Moss/50 10.00
66 Jerry Porter/75 10.00
67 Jerry Rice/75 25.00
68 Warren Sapp/75 12.00
69 Donovan McNabb/75 15.00
70 Jevon Kearse/75 12.00
72 Duce Staley/60 12.00
73 Hines Ward/75 12.00
78 Koren Robinson/75 10.00
79 Matt Hasselbeck/75 12.00
81 Isaac Bruce/50 12.00
82 Marc Bulger/75 12.00
83 Marshall Faulk/75 15.00
84 Torry Holt/50 12.00
85 Brad Johnson/50 10.00
88 Derrick Mason/50 10.00
89 Eddie George/50 12.00
93 Laveranues Coles/50 10.00
94 Mark Brunell/50 12.00

2004 Leaf R and S Longevity Materials Black

No Pricing
Sequentially numbered to 25 or less
1 Anquan Boldin/25
2 Emmitt Smith/25
3 Josh McCown/25
4 Michael Vick/25
5 Peerless Price/10
6 T.J. Duckett/25
7 Warrick Dunn/25
8 Jamal Lewis/10
9 Kyle Boller/25
10 Ray Lewis/10
11 Drew Bledsoe/10
12 Eric Moulds/25
13 Travis Henry/25
14 Jake Delhomme/25
15 Stephen Davis/25
16 Steve Smith/25
17 Brian Urlacher/25
18 Rex Grossman/25
19 Thomas Jones/25
20 Carson Palmer/25
21 Chad Johnson/25
22 Rudi Johnson/25
23 Jeff Garcia/20
24 William Green/10
25 Keyshawn Johnson/25
26 Terence Newman/10
27 Roy Williams/25
28 Jake Plummer/25
29 Quentin Griffin/10
30 Rod Smith/10
31 Charles Rogers/25
32 Joey Harrington/25
33 Ahman Green/25
34 Brett Favre/25
35 Javon Walker/25
36 Andre Johnson/25
37 David Carr/25
38 Domanick Davis/25
39 Edgerrin James/25
40 Marvin Harrison/25
41 Peyton Manning/25
42 Byron Leftwich/5
43 Fred Taylor/25
44 Jimmy Smith/10
45 Priest Holmes/25
46 Tony Gonzalez/25
47 Trent Green/25
49 Chris Chambers/25
51 Daunte Culpepper/25
52 Michael Bennett/25
53 Randy Moss/25
54 Corey Dillon/25
56 Tom Brady/25
57 Aaron Brooks/25
58 Deuce McAllister/25
60 Jeremy Shockey/25
61 Michael Strahan/25
62 Tiki Barber/25
63 Chad Pennington/25
64 Curtis Martin/25
65 Santana Moss/25
66 Jerry Porter/25
67 Jerry Rice/25
69 Donovan McNabb/25
70 Jevon Kearse/10
71 Terrell Owens/25
72 Duce Staley/10
73 Hines Ward/25
74 Jerome Bettis/25
75 LaDainian Tomlinson/25
78 Koren Robinson/25
79 Matt Hasselbeck/25
80 Shaun Alexander/25
81 Isaac Bruce/10
82 Marc Bulger/25
83 Marshall Faulk/25
84 Torry Holt/25
85 Brad Johnson/10
87 Chris Brown/25
88 Derrick Mason/10
89 Eddie George/25
90 Steve McNair/25
91 Clinton Portis/25
92 LaVar Arrington/25
93 Laveranues Coles/10

1961 Lions Jay Publishing

Measuring approximately 5" x 7", the 12-card set showcases black-and-white photos of players in the vintage football card poses. The blank-backed cards were sold in 12-

card packs for 25 cents. The cards were unnumbered.

		NM/M
Complete Set (12):		65.00
Common Player:		5.00
1	Carl Brettschneider	5.00
2	Howard Cassady	6.00
3	Gail Cogdill	5.00
4	Jim Gibbons	6.00
5	Alex Karras	12.00
6	Yale Lary	10.00
7	Jim Martin	5.00
8	Earl Morrall	8.00
9	Jim Ninowski	6.00
10	Nick Pietrosante	6.00
11	Joe Schmidt	10.00
12	George Wilson	5.00

1964 Lions White Border

Measuring 7-3/8" x 9-3/8", the 24-card set includes black-and-white photos that are bordered in white. The player's name and position, along with the Detroit Lions, are printed under the photo. The unnumbered cards could have been released in many series, as later cards have a date stamped on the otherwise blank backs.

		NM/M
Complete Set (24):		90.00
Common Player:		4.00
1	Dick Compton	4.00
2	Larry Ferguson	4.00
3	Dennis Gaubatz	4.00
4	Jim Gibbons	5.00
5	John Gonzaga	4.00
6	John Gordy	5.00
7	Tom Hall	4.00
8	Roger LaLonde	4.00
9	Dan LaRose	4.00
10	Yale Lary	10.00
11	Dan Lewis	5.00
12	Gary Lowe	4.00
13	Bruce Maher	5.00
14	Hugh McInnis	4.00
15	Max Messner	4.00
16	Floyd Peters	6.00
17	Daryl Sanders	4.00
18	Joe Schmidt	12.00
19	Bob Scholtz	4.00
20	James Simon	4.00
21	J.D. Smith	5.00
22	Bill Quinlan	4.00
23	Bob Whitlow	4.00
24	Sam Williams	4.00

1966 Lions Marathon Oil

The 5" x 7" photos showcase black-and-white photos on the front, surrounded by white borders. The player's name, position and Detroit Lions are printed under the photo. The backs are unnumbered and blank.

		NM/M
Complete Set (7):		42.00
Common Player:		5.00
1	Gail Cogdill	5.00
2	John Gordy	5.00
3	Alex Karras	15.00
4	Ron Kramer	6.00
5	Milt Plum	8.00
6	Wayne Rasmussen	5.00
7	Daryl Sanders	5.00

1986 Lions Police

Measuring 2-5/8" x 4-1/8", this 14-card police set is sponsored by Oscar Mayer, WJR/WHYT, Detroit Lions, Claussen, Pontiac Police Athletic League and the Detroit Crime Prevention Section. Card fronts have the player's name, uniform number and position in a box at the bottom center, while the Lions' logo is at the top center. A white border surrounds the photo. The card backs have the player's name, bio and highlights in a box on the left of the horizontal backed cards. A safety tip is located on the right.

		NM/M
Complete Set (14):		5.00
Common Player:		.50
1	William Gay	.50
2	Pontiac Silverdome	.60
3	Leonard Thompson	.60
4	Eddie Murray	1.00
5	Eric Hipple	1.00
6	James Jones	.75
7	Darryl Rogers (CO)	.50
8	Chuck Long	.75
9	Garry James	.60
10	Michael Cofer	.60
11	Jeff Chadwick	.60
12	Jimmy Williams	.50
13	Keith Dorney	.50
14	Bobby Watkins	.50

1987 Lions Police

Measuring 2-5/8" x 4-1/8", the 14-card set is sponsored by Oscar Mayer, WJR/WHYT, Claussen, Detroit Lions, Pontiac Police Athletic League and the Detroit Crime Prevention Section. The card fronts have the Lions and NFL logos at the top, with the photo in the center. The player's name, uniform number and position are printed inside a box at the bottom center. The Oscar Mayer and Claussen logos are in the lower corners of the card front. The card backs include a cartoon in the upper left, with the player's highlights. The upper left has a safety tip.

		NM/M
Complete Set (14):		5.00
Common Player:		.40
1	Michael Cofer, Vernon Maxwell, William Gay	.50
2	Rich Strenger	.40
3	Keith Ferguson	.40
4	James Jones	.50
5	Jeff Chadwick	.50
6	Devon Mitchell	.40
7	Eddie Murray	.75
8	Reggie Rogers	.50
9	Chuck Long	.50
10	Jimmie Giles	.60
11	Eric Williams	.40
12	Lomas Brown	.50
13	Jimmy Williams	.40
14	Garry James	.50

1988 Lions Police

Measuring 2-5/8" x 4-1/8", the 14-card set boasts 13 single-player cards which feature veterans. The remaining card has three of the Lions' top three 1988 draft picks. The card fronts have the Lions logo under the photo, which is opposite the 1987 Lions Police set. The card backs have the standard career highlights and safety tips.

		NM/M
Complete Set (14):		5.00
Common Player:		.50
1	Rob Rubick	.50
2	Paul Butcher	.50
3	Pete Mandley	.60
4	Jimmy Williams	.50
5	Harvey Salem	.50
6	Chuck Long	.60
7	Pat Carter, Bennie Blades, Chris Spielman	1.00
8	Jerry Ball	.75
9	Lomas Brown	.60
10	Dennis Gibson	.50
11	Jim Arnold	.50
12	Michael Cofer	.50
13	James Jones	.60
14	Steve Mott	.50

1989 Lions Police

Measuring 2-5/8" x 4-1/8", the 12-card set has the Lions logo and NFL shields at the top. The player's name, uniform number and position are printed in a box at the bottom, sandwiched between Oscar Mayer and Claussen logos. The backs feature a cartoon in the upper left, with a highlight directly under it. The horizontal backs also include a safety tip in the upper right. A WWJ logo is printed at the bottom left, with the card number located at bottom center. The cards are printed on thin paper stock. These cards were distributed in Michigan and Ontario.

		NM/M
Complete Set (12):		14.00
Common Player:		.35
1	George Jamison	.35
2	Wayne Fontes (CO)	.75
3	Kevin Glover	.35
4	Chris Spielman	1.00
5	Eddie Murray	.75
6	Bennie Blades	.75
7	Joe Milinichik	.35
8	Michael Cofer	.35
9	Jerry Ball	.50
10	Dennis Gibson	.35
11	Barry Sanders	10.00
12	Jim Arnold	.35

A player's name in *italic* type indicates a rookie card.

1990 Lions Police

Measuring 2-5/8" x 4-1/8", the 12-card set includes the player's name and position at the bottom center, with his uniform number printed in much larger type. The Oscar Mayer and Claussen logos are in the lower left and right corners, respectively. The card backs have the player's name at the top, with a drawing of him and highlight directly under. A "Little Oscar" safety tip is included in the lower left. The card number is in the lower right, along with the WWJ Radio logo.

		NM/M
Complete Set (12):		5.00
Common Player:		.35
1	William White	.35
2	Chris Spielman	.75
3	Rodney Peete	.75
4	Jimmy Williams	.35
5	Bennie Blades	.50
6	Barry Sanders	3.00
7	Jerry Ball	.50
8	Richard Johnson	.50
9	Michael Cofer	.35
10	Lomas Brown	.50
11	Joe Schmidt, Andre Ware, Wayne Fontes	.50
12	Eddie Murray	.50

1991 Lions Police

Measuring 2-5/8" x 4-1/8", the 12-card set was available through Michigan police officers. The yellow-bordered cards feature a color action photo, with the Oscar Mayer logo in the lower left, the player's name in the lower center and Lions helmet in the lower right. Above and below the player's name are blue horizontal lines. Card backs include a player photo at the top, with his position and name below it. A Little Oscar safety tip is in the lower left. The cards are numbered and are located in the lower right. The WWJ Radio logo is in the lower right.

		NM/M
Complete Set (12):		5.00
Common Player:		.35
1	Mel Gray	.50
2	Ken Dallafior	.35
3	Chris Spielman	.50
4	Bennie Blades	.50
5	Robert Clark	.50
6	Eric Andolsek	.50
7	Rodney Peete	.75
8	William White	.35
9	Lomas Brown	.50
10	Jerry Ball	.50
11	Michael Cofer	.35
12	Barry Sanders	3.00

1993 Lions 60th Season Commemorative

After years of odd-sized cards, the Lions finally introduced a standard-sized set. The 16-card set features full-bleed photos on the front, with the Lions' 60th anniversary logo in one of the upper corners. The player's name or, in some cases, the card's caption are printed in a rectangle at the bottom. The horizontal card backs feature the player's name and the years he played with the team in the upper left. His career highlights are printed along the left side, with a black-and-white headshot of the player in the upper right. The Lions' 60th anniversary logo is in the lower right, along with the card number. The cards were housed in a 6" x 8" black binder.

		NM/M
Complete Set (16):		10.00
Common Player:		.50
1	Barry Sanders	5.00
2	Joe Schmidt	1.00
3	Sam Williams, Roger Brown, Alex Karras, Darris McCord The Fearsome Foursome	.75
4	Chris Spielman	.75
5	Billy Sims	.75
6	Alex Wojciechowicz, Byron White '40s Phenoms	.75
7	Bennie Blades, Mel Gray Thunder and Lightning	.50
8	Bobby Layne	1.50
9	Dutch Clark	.75
10	Great Games, Thanksgiving 1962	.50
11	Charlie Sanders	.75
12	Lomas Brown	.50
13	Doug English	.75
14	Doak Walker	1.50
15	Lem Barney, Billy Sims, Barry Sanders Roaring 20's	2.00
16	Anniversary Card	.50

1990 Little Big Leaguers

Boyhood photos and the highlights of the player's early athletic career are included in this 45-card set. The book, published by Simon and Schuster, included five 8-1/2" x 11" sheets, which included nine perforated cards. The card fronts included a black-and-white photo of the athlete as a child. A white border surrounds the card, with the player's name printed in a blue band at the top and "Little Football Big Leaguers" printed in a blue band at the bottom. The backs include the player's name, position, team, bio and write-up. The cards are unnumbered.

		NM/M
Complete Set (45):		40.00
Common Player:		.50
1	Troy Aikman	10.00
2	Morten Andersen	.50
3	Jerry Ball	.50
4	Carl Banks	.75
5	Bennie Blades	.50
6	Brian Blades	.75
7	Joey Browner	.50
8	Keith Byars	.75
9	Anthony Carter	.75
10	Deron Cherry	.50
11	Roger Craig	.75
12	John Elway	7.00
13	Doug Flutie	1.00
14	Tim Goad	.50
15	Bob Golic	.50
16	Dino Hackett	.50
17	Dan Hampton	.75
18	Bobby Hebert	.75
19	Darryl Henley	.50
20	Wes Hopkins	.50
21	Hank Ilesic	.50
22	Tunch Ilkin	.50
23	Perry Kemp	.50
24	Bernie Kosar	.75
25	Mike Lansford	.50
26	Shawn Lee	.50
27	Charles Mann	.75
28	Dan Marino	14.00
29	Bruce Matthews	.75
30	Clay Matthews	.75
31	Freeman McNeil	.75
32	Warren Moon	2.00
33	Anthony Munoz	.75
34	Andre Reed	1.00
35	Andre Rison	.75
36	Phil Simms	.75
37	Mike Singletary	.75
38	Rohn Stark	.50
39	Kelly Stouffer	.50
40	Vinny Testaverde	.75
41	Doug Williams	.50
42	Marc Wilson	.50
43	Craig Wolfley	.50
44	Ron Wolfley	.50
45	Steve Young	7.00

M

1977 Marketcom Test

With posters measuring approximately 5-1/2" x 8-1/2", the set boasts only two confirmed mini-posters. The unnumbered posters each have folds in them. They are blank-backed, except for a Marketcom 1977 copyright tag line at the bottom.

		NM/M
Complete Set (2):		100.00
1	Greg Pruitt	50.00
2	Jack Youngblood	50.00

1978 Marketcom Test

These unnumbered posters, featuring 32 NFL stars, measure 5-1/2" x 8-1/2". The fronts feature full-color photos, along with the player's name in the upper left corner. Marketcom, which produced the set, is listed in the lower right corner. The backs are blank.

		NM/M
Complete Set (32):		225.00
Common Player:		4.00
(1)	Otis Armstrong	6.00
(2)	Steve Bartkowski	9.00
(3)	Terry Bradshaw	25.00
(4)	Earl Campbell	25.00
(5)	Dave Casper	5.00
(6)	Dan Dierdorf	10.00
(7)	Dan Fouts	15.00
(8)	Tony Galbreath	4.00
(9)	Randy Gradishar	7.00
(10)	Bob Griese	12.00
(11)	Steve Grogan	5.00
(12)	Ray Guy	6.00
(13)	Pat Haden	8.00
(14)	Jack Ham	7.00
(15)	Cliff Harris	7.00
(16)	Franco Harris	8.00
(17)	Jim Hart	5.00
(18)	Ron Jaworski	5.00
(19)	Bert Jones	10.00
(20)	Jack Lambert	10.00
(21)	Reggie McKenzie	4.00
(22)	Karl Mecklenberg	7.00
(23)	Craig Morton	5.00
(24)	Dan Pastorini	4.00
(25)	Walter Payton	25.00
(26)	Lee Roy Selmon	5.00
(27)	Roger Staubach	25.00
(28)	Joe Theismann (misspelled Theisman)	9.00
(29)	Wesley Walker	7.00
(30)	Randy White	7.00
(31)	Jack Youngblood	12.00
(32)	Jim Zorn	5.00

1980 Marketcom

These white-bordered posters, measuring 5-1/2" x 8-1/2", feature 50 NFL stars. The player's name appears at the top of the card; Marketcom, the set's producer, is credited in the bottom lower right corner. A white facsimile autograph also appears on the card front. The back has the player's name at the top, and a card number on the bottom (Mini-Poster 1 of 50, etc.). Marketcom, of St. Louis, sold the posters in packs of five.

		NM/M
Complete Set (50):		25.00
Common Player:		.50
1	Ottis Anderson	1.00
2	Brian Sipe	.60
3	Lawrence McCutcheon	.60
4	Ken Anderson	1.25
5	Roland Harper	.50
6	Chuck Foreman	.75
7	Gary Danielson	.50
8	Wallace Francis	.50
9	John Jefferson	.75
10	Charlie Waters	.75
11	Jack Ham	1.00
12	Jack Lambert	1.25
13	Walter Payton	5.00
14	Bert Jones	1.00
15	Harvey Martin	.75
16	Jim Hart	.60
17	Craig Morton	.75
18	Reggie McKenzie	.50
19	Keith Wortman	.50
20	Otis Armstrong	.75
21	Steve Grogan	.75
22	Jim Zorn	.75
23	Bob Griese	2.00
24	Tony Dorsett	2.00
25	Wesley Walker	.75
26	Dan Fouts	2.00
27	Dan Dierdorf	1.00
28	Steve Bartkowski	.75
29	Archie Manning	1.00
30	Randy Gradishar	.75
31	Randy White	1.25
32	Joe Theismann	2.00
33	Tony Galbreath	.50
34	Cliff Harris	.75
35	Ray Guy	1.00
36	Dave Casper	.75
37	Ron Jaworski	.75
38	Greg Pruitt	.75
39	Ken Burrough	.60
40	Robert Brazile	.60
41	Pat Haden	1.00
42	Dan Pastorini	.60
43	Lee Roy Selmon	.75
44	Franco Harris	2.00
45	Jack Youngblood	1.25
46	Terry Bradshaw	5.00
47	Roger Staubach	6.00
48	Earl Campbell	5.00
49	Phil Simms	3.00
50	Delvin Williams	.50

1981 Marketcom

The 1981 Marketcom posters are the first set to include detailed information on the back of the poster. Along with biographical and statistical information for 1980 and for the player's career, a comprehensive summary of the player's accomplishments is provided. A poster number is also given. Each poster, measuring 5-1/2" x 8-1/2", has a full-color action photo of the player on the front, along with his facsimile signature. His name is listed in the upper left corner.

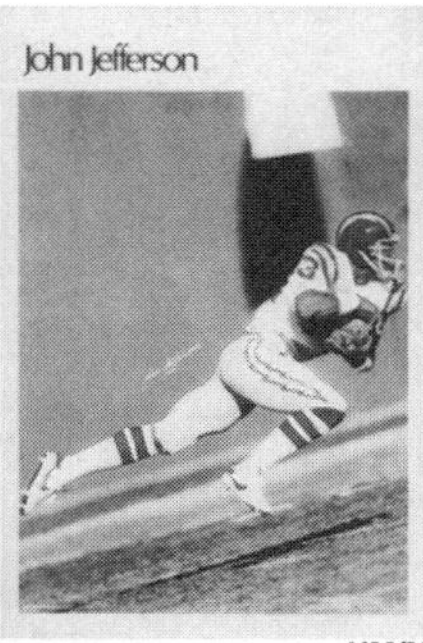

		NM/M
Complete Set (50):		24.00
Common Player:		.40
1	Ottis Anderson	.60
2	Brian Sipe	.45
3	Rocky Bleier	.60
4	Ken Anderson	.70
5	Roland Harper	.40
6	Steve Furness	.40
7	Gary Danielson	.40
8	Wallace Francis	.45
9	John Jefferson	.45
10	Charlie Waters	.60
11	Jack Ham	.60
12	Jack Lambert	.90
13	Walter Payton	3.75
14	Bert Jones	.70
15	Harvey Martin	.60
16	Jim Hart	.60
17	Craig Morton	.60
18	Reggie McKenzie	.40
19	Keith Wortman	.40
20	Joe Greene	1.25
21	Steve Grogan	.60
22	Jim Zorn	.60
23	Bob Griese	1.50
24	Tony Dorsett	2.00
25	Wesley Walker	.60
26	Dan Fouts	1.50
27	Dan Dierdorf	.70
28	Steve Bartkowski	.60
29	Archie Manning	.70
30	Randy Gradishar	.60
31	Randy White	.90
32	Joe Theismann	1.50
33	Tony Galbreath	.40
34	Cliff Harris	.60
35	Ray Guy	.70
36	Joe Ferguson	.60
37	Ron Jaworski	.60
38	Greg Pruitt	.60
39	Ken Burrough	.45
40	Robert Brazile	.40
41	Pat Haden	.70
42	Ken Stabler	1.50
43	Lee Roy Selmon	.60
44	Franco Harris	1.50
45	Jack Youngblood	.90
46	Terry Bradshaw	4.50
47	Roger Staubach	4.50
48	Earl Campbell	3.00
49	Phil Simms	1.25
50	Delvin Williams	.40

1982 Marketcom

These 50 mini-posters from Marketcom are similar in design to the previous year's issue. Each poster is 5-1/2" x 8-1/2" and has a full-color action photo on the front, along with a facsimile signature in white letters. The backs are similar to the backs of the 1981 posters - they have a detailed career summary and biographical information, plus statistics for the player's career and 1981 season. In addition to a number, the back also says "St. Louis - Marketcom - Series C".

		NM/M
Complete Set (48):		175.00
Common Player:		2.00
1	Joe Ferguson	2.50
2	Kellen Winslow	3.00
3	Jim Hart	2.50
4	Archie Manning	4.00
5	Earl Campbell	15.00
6	Wallace Francis	2.00
7	Randy Gradishar	2.50
8	Ken Stabler	5.00
9	Danny White	3.00
10	Jack Ham	4.00
11	Lawrence Taylor	20.00
12	Eric Hipple	2.00
13	Ron Jaworski	2.50
14	George Rogers	2.00
15	Jack Lambert	5.00
16	Randy White	5.00
17	Terry Bradshaw	20.00
18	Ray Guy	3.00
19	Rob Carpenter	2.00
20	Reggie McKenzie	2.00
21	Tony Dorsett	7.50
22	Wesley Walker	2.50
23	Tommy Kramer	2.50
24	Dwight Clark	3.00
25	Franco Harris	5.00
26	Craig Morton	2.50
27	Harvey Martin	2.50
28	Jim Zorn	2.50
29	Steve Bartkowski	2.50
30	Joe Theismann	5.00

31	Dan Dierdorf	3.00
32	Walter Payton	25.00
33	John Jefferson	2.50
34	Phil Simms	5.00
35	Lee Roy Selmon	2.50
36	Joe Montana	40.00
37	Robert Brazile	2.00
38	Steve Grogan	2.50
39	Dave Logan	2.00
40	Ken Anderson	4.00
41	Richard Todd	2.50
42	Jack Youngblood	3.00
43	Ottis Anderson	3.00
44	Brian Sipe	2.50
45	Mark Gastineau	2.50
46	Mike Pruitt	2.00
47	Cris Collinsworth	2.50
48	Dan Fouts	5.00

1982 Marketcom Cowboys

Measuring 5-1/2" x 8-1/2", these nine NFL mini-posters feature the player's name at the top left, with a color photo dominating the white-bordered fronts. The player's facsimile autograph also appears on the photo. The unnumbered card backs showcase the player's name at the top, with his bio directly underneath. His career highlights are also included. "St. Louis Marketcom" is printed in the lower right of the back. Some experts say a 10th card may exist.

		NM/M
Complete Set (9):		50.00
Common Player:		5.00
1	Bob Breunig	5.00
2	Pat Donovan	5.00
3	Michael Downs	5.00
4	Butch Johnson	6.00
5	Harvey Martin	6.00
6	Timmy Newsome	5.00
7	Drew Pearson	6.00
8	Danny White	8.00
9	Randy White	10.00

1971 Mattel Mini-Records

Measuring approximately 2-1/2" in diameter, each of the 17 discs in the set were to be played on a specially made Mattel mini-record player. Some discs were packaged four to a pack, like Olsen, Hayes, Sayers and Brodie or Mackey, Lamonica, Simpson and Butkus. Other packs showcased eight discs and a Joe Namath or Bart Starr booklet. The discs have color artwork on one side and the recording on the reverse. The recording side has the player's name and "Instant Replay."

		NM/M
Complete Set (17):		200.00
Common Player:		4.00
1	Donny Anderson	4.00
2	Lem Barney	6.00
3	John Brodie (DP)	6.00
4	Dick Butkus (DP)	15.00
5	Bob Hayes (DP)	6.00
6	Sonny Jurgensen	10.00
7	Alex Karras	10.00
8	Leroy Kelly	9.00
9	Daryle Lamonica (DP)	4.00
10	John Mackey (DP)	6.00
11	Earl Morrall	4.00
12	Joe Namath	50.00
13	Merlin Olsen (DP)	6.00
14	Alan Page	9.00
15	Gale Sayers (DP)	20.00
16	O.J. Simpson (DP)	25.00
17	Bart Starr	30.00
NNO	Record Player	100.00

1894 Mayo

Thirty-five Ivy League college football players are included in this 35-card set. The card fronts include a sepia-toned photo and a black border. The player's name, college and Mayo Cut Plug advertisement are listed at the bottom. The unnumbered cards measure 1-5/8" x 2-7/8".

		NM/M
Complete Set (35):		32,500
Common Player:		750.00
1	R Acton (Harvard)	1,000
2	George Adee (Yale AA94)	1,500
3	R. Armstrong (Yale)	1,000
4	H.W. Barnett (Princeton)	1,200
5	A.M. Beale (Harvard)	825.00
6	Anson Beard (Yale)	1,600
7	Charles Brewer (Harvard AA92/93/95)	750.00
8	Brown (Princeton)	1,200
9	Burt (Princeton)	1,000
10	Frank Butterworth (Yale AA93/94)	750.00
11	Eddie Crowdis (Princeton)	900.00
12	Robert Emmons (Harvard)	1,000
13	M.G. Gonterman (UER Harvard) (Misspelled Gouterman)	1,000
14	G.A. Grey (Harvard)	750.00
15	John Greenway (Yale)	900.00
16	William Hickok (Yale AA93/94)	1,000
17	Frank Hinkey (Yale AA91/92/93/94)	4,500
18	Augustus Holly (Princeton)	1,000
19	Langdon Lea (Princeton AA93/94/95)	900.00
20	W.C. Mackie (Harvard)	1,000
21	T.J. Manahan (Harvard)	1,000
22	Jim McCrea (Yale)	1,000
23	Frank Morse (Princeton AA93)	750.00
24	Fred Murphy (Yale AA95/96)	1,000
25	Poe (Princeton thought to be Neilson or Arthur)	3,500
26	Dudley Riggs (Princeton AA95)	1,200
27	Phillip Stillman (Yale AA94)	1,200
28	Knox Taylor (Princeton)	1,500
29	Brinck Thorne (Yale AA95)	800.00
30	Thomas Trenchard (Princeton AA93)	750.00
31	William Ward (Princeton)	800.00
32	Bert Waters (Harvard AA92/94)	1,000
33	Arthur Wheeler (Princeton AA92/93/94)	1,000
34	Edgar Wrightington (Harvard AA96)	1,000
35	Anonymous (reportedly John Dunlop-Harvard)	3,000

1975 McDonald's Quarterbacks

Measuring 2-1/2" x 3-7/16", this four-card set was a McDonald's promotion. The yellow-bordered card fronts showcase the player's name and team at the top, with a photo in the center. Printed below the photo is "Get a quarter back..." The McDonald's logo is in the lower right. The backs of each card have different colors. The unnumbered card backs have the player's name, position and team at the top, with his stats below. The perforated coupon below explains the promotion. Each card was good for one week. Prices are for cards which have the coupons intact.

		NM/M
Complete Set (4):		10.00
Common Player:		.50
1	Terry Bradshaw	6.00
2	Joe Ferguson	1.00
3	Ken Stabler	4.00
4	Al Woodall	.50

1985 McDonald's Bears

This 32-card set picturing only Chicago Bears was issued by McDonald's in the Chicago area, apparently to test the concept of using football cards as a promotion. The full-color cards have three different tab colors (blue, orange, yellow), each referring to a specific week in the playoffs or Super Bowl. The cards measure approximately 4-1/2" x 5-7/8" with the tab intact. The prices below are for cards with the tab intact. Cards without the tabs have little collector value and are worth considerably less. Because of space limitations, only players with a significant value over common price are listed individually. Players not listed are worth approximately the common price (or perhaps slightly above for minor stars). The individual values listed are for the least expensive color tabs (yellow or orange). Cards with blue tabs are worth about twice as much as values listed. Card numbers refer to a player's uniform number.

		NM/M
Complete Set (Blue):		45.00
Complete Set (Orange):		25.00
Complete Set (Yellow):		20.00
Common Player:		.50
4	Steve Fuller	.75
6	Kevin Butler	1.00
8	Maury Buford	.50
9	Jim McMahon	2.50
21	Leslie Frazier	.50
22	Dave Duerson	.50
26	Matt Suhey	.75
27	Mike Richardson	.50
29	Dennis Gentry	.50
33	Calvin Thomas	.50
34	Walter Payton	7.00
45	Gary Fencik	.75
50	Mike Singletary	2.50
55	Otis Wilson	.50
58	Wilber Marshall	1.00
62	Mark Bortz	.50
63	Jay Hilgenberg	.75
72	William Perry	1.25
73	Mike Hartenstine	.50
74	Jim Covert	.75
75	Stefan Humphries	.50
76	Steve McMichael	1.00
78	Keith Van Horne	.50
80	Tim Wrightman	.50
82	Ken Margerum	.50
83	Willie Gault	1.00
85	Dennis McKinnon	.75
87	Emery Moorehead	.50
95	Richard Dent	2.00
99	Dan Hampton	2.00
	Mike Ditka (CO)	2.50
	Buddy Ryan (ACO)	1.50

1986 McDonald's All-Stars

Measuring 3-1/16" x 4-11/16" with the tab intact or 3-1/16" x 3-5/8" without, this 30-card set was for participating McDonald's outside of an NFL market. Released over four weeks, the set featured different colored tabs -- with blue (first week), black or gray (second week), gold or orange (third week) and green (fourth week). The backs feature McDonald's All-Star Team printed at the top. Also included on the backs are the player's name, jersey number, career and 1985 highlights and a 1986 copyright date.

		NM/M
Complete Set (Blue):		6.00
Complete Set (Black):		6.00
Complete Set (Gold):		6.00
Complete Set (Green):		6.00
Common Player:		.15
9	Jim McMahon	.35
11	Phil Simms	.35
13	Dan Marino	2.50
14	Dan Fouts	.35
16	Joe Montana	2.00
20A	Deron Cherry	.15
20B	Joe Morris	.15
32	Marcus Allen	.35
33	Roger Craig	.25
34A	Kevin Mack	.15
35B	Walter Payton	1.75
42	Gerald Riggs	.15
45	Kenny Easley	.15
47A	Joey Browner	.15
47B	LeRoy Irvin	.15
52	Mike Webster	.25
54A	E.J. Junior	.15
54B	Randy White	.25
56	Lawrence Taylor	.35
63	Mike Munchak	.15
66	Joe Jacoby	.15
73	John Hannah	.25
75A	Chris Hinton	.15
75B	Rulon Jones	.15
75C	Howie Long	.25
78	Anthony Munoz	.25
81	Art Monk	.35
82A	Ozzie Newsome	.35
82B	Mike Quick	.15
99	Mark Gastineau	.15

1986 McDonald's Chicago Bears

Released in the Chicago area, the 24-card set was released over four weeks at participating McDonald's. The tab colors were as follows: blue (first week), black or gray (second), gold or orange (third) and green (fourth). With the tab intact, the cards measure 3-1/16" x 4-11/16" and 3-1/16" x 3-5/8" without. The card fronts have the McDonald's logo in the upper left, Bears helmet in the upper right, NFL shield in the lower left and the NFLPA logo in the lower right. The card backs have "Super Bowl Collectors Edition" at the top. The player's name, uniform number, bio and 1986 and career highlights are also listed on the backs.

		NM/M
Complete Set (Blue):		15.00
Complete Set (Black):		7.50
Complete Set (Gold):		7.50
Complete Set (Green):		7.50
Common Player:		.30
6	Kevin Butler (DP)	.40
8	Maury Buford	.30
9	Jim McMahon (DP)	1.25
22	Dave Duerson	.30
26	Matt Suhey	.40
27	Mike Richardson	.30
34	Walter Payton (DP)	1.75
45	Gary Fencik	.40
50	Mike Singletary (DP)	1.25
55	Otis Wilson	.30
57	Tom Thayer	.30
58	Wilber Marshall	.50
62	Mark Bortz (DP)	.30
63	Jay Hilgenberg	.40
72	William Perry (DP)	.50
74	Jim Covert	.40
76	Steve McMichael	.50
78	Keith Van Horne	.30
80	Tim Wrightman	.30
82	Ken Margerum	.30
83	Willie Gault	.50
87	Emery Moorehead	.30
95	Richard Dent	1.00
99	Dan Hampton	1.00

1986 McDonald's Cincinnati Bengals

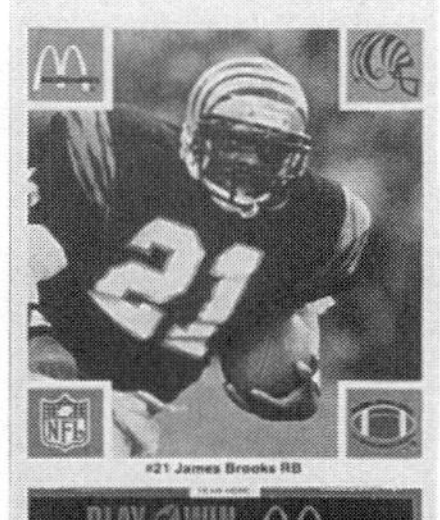

The Cincinnati area received the benefits of this 24-card set, which was part of the McDonald's promotion of 1986. The card fronts showcase the McDonald's logo in the upper left, with the Cincinnati helmet in the upper right. The NFL shield and NFLPA logos appear in the bottom left and right, respectively, of the color action photo. Card backs feature the player's number, name, bio, stats and highlights. The cards measure 3-1/16" x 4-11/16" with the tab and 3-1/16" x 3-5/8" without. Released over four weeks, the first week's cards had blue tabs, second had black or gray, third had gold or orange and the fourth week tabs were green.

		NM/M
Complete Set (Blue):		25.00
Complete Set (Black):		12.50
Complete Set (Gold):		12.50
Complete Set (Green):		12.50
Common Player:		.50
7	Boomer Esiason	2.50
14	Ken Anderson (DP)	1.00
20	Ray Horton	.60
21	James Brooks (DP)	1.00
22	James Griffin	.50
28	Larry Kinnebrew	.60
34	Louis Breeden (DP)	.50
37	Robert Jackson	.50
40	Charles Alexander (DP)	.50
52	Dave Rimington	.60
57	Reggie Williams	.75
65	Max Montoya	.60
69	Tim Krumrie	.75
73	Eddie Edwards	.60
74	Brian Blados (DP)	.50
77	Mike Wilson	.50
78	Anthony Munoz	1.25
79	Ross Browner	.60
80	Cris Collinsworth	1.00
81	Eddie Brown (DP)	.75
82	Rodney Holman	.60
83	M.L. Harris	.50
90	Emanuel King	.50
91	Carl Zander	.50

1986 McDonald's Buffalo Bills

Measuring 3-1/16" x 4-11/16" with the tab and 3-1/16" x 3-5/8" without, the 24-card set was distributed over four weeks of the 1986 season in the Buffalo area. In the top corners of the color action photo on the card front were the McDonald's logo and Bills helmet. At the bottom corners of the photo were the NFL shield and NFLPA logo. The player's name, number and position appear under the photo. The card backs have the player's name, jersey number and highlights. Each week featured a different colored tab: blue (first), black or gray (second), gold or orange (third) and green (fourth).

		NM/M
Complete Set (Blue):		150.00
Complete Set (Black):		30.00
Complete Set (Gold):		15.00
Complete Set (Green):		15.00
Common Player:		.75
4	John Kidd	.75
7	Bruce Mathison	.75
11	Scott Norwood	1.00
22	Steve Freeman	.75
26	Charles Romes	.75
28	Greg Bell (DP)	1.00
29	Derrick Burroughs (DP)	.75
43	Martin Bayless (DP)	.75
51	Jim Ritcher	1.00
54	Eugene Marve	.75
55	Jim Haslett	.75
57	Lucius Sanford	.75
63	Justin Cross	.75
65	Tim Vogler	.75
70	Joe Devlin	.75
72	Ken Jones	.75
76	Fred Smerlas	1.00
77	Ben Williams	1.00
78	Bruce Smith	5.00
80	Jerry Butler (DP)	1.00
83	Andre Reed	5.00
85	Chris Burkett (DP)	1.00
87	Eason Ramson	.75
95	Sean McNanie	.75

1986 McDonald's Denver Broncos

Released over four weeks in the Denver area during the 1986 season, this 24-card set measured 3-1/16" x 4-11/16" with the tab and 3-1/16" x 3-5/8" without. The card fronts and backs followed the same format as the other McDonald's sets of that season. Each week's cards featured a different colored tab: blue (first), black or gray (second), gold or orange (third) and green (fourth).

		NM/M
Complete Set (Blue):		25.00
Complete Set (Black):		8.00
Complete Set (Gold):		8.00
Complete Set (Green):		8.00
Common Player:		.30
3	Rich Karlis	.30
7	John Elway	3.50
20	Louis Wright	.40
22	Tony Lily	.30
23	Sammy Winder	.40
30	Steve Sewell	.40
31	Mike Harden	.40
43	Steve Foley	.40
47	Gerald Wilhite	.40
49	Dennis Smith	.50
50	Jim Ryan	.30
54	Keith Bishop (DP)	.30
55	Rick Dennison (DP)	.30
57	Tom Jackson	1.25
60	Paul Howard	.30
64	Bill Bryan (DP)	.30
68	Rubin Carter (DP)	.30
70	Dave Studdard	.30
75	Rulon Jones	.40
77	Karl Mecklenburg	.60
79	Barney Chavous (DP)	.30
81	Steve Watson	.40
82	Vance Johnson	.60
84	Clint Sampson	.30

1986 McDonald's Cleveland Browns

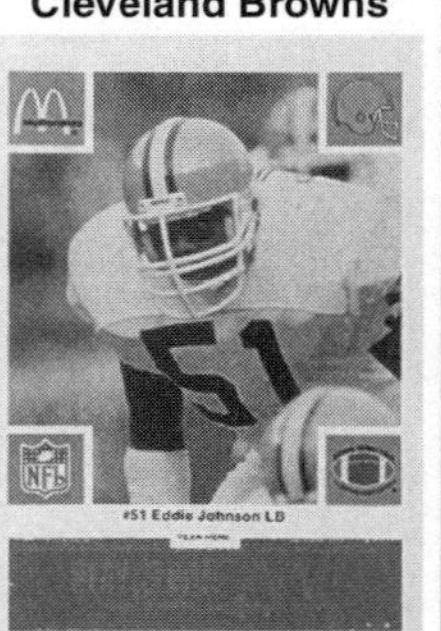

Issued over four weeks of the 1986 season in the Cleveland area, the 24-card set measure 3-1/16" x 4-11/16" with the tab and 3-1/16" x 3-5/8" without. The card fronts feature a color photo, with the McDonald's logo in the upper left and Browns helmet in the upper right. The NFL shields and NFLPA logo are on the bottom corners, left and right respectively. The card backs have the player's name, jersey number, bio and highlights. Each week's cards featured different colored tabs: blue (first), black or gray (second), gold or orange (third) and green (fourth).

		NM/M
Complete Set (Blue):		10.00
Complete Set (Black):		6.00
Complete Set (Gold):		6.00
Complete Set (Green):		6.00
Common Player:		.25
9	Matt Bahr (DP)	.25
18	Gary Danielson	.25
19	Bernie Kosar (DP)	1.75
27	Al Gross	.25
29	Hanford Dixon	.35
31	Frank Minnifield	.35
34	Kevin Mack	.50
37	Chris Rockins	.25
44	Earnest Byner	.75
51	Eddie Johnson	.25
55	Curtis Weathers	.25
56	Chip Banks (DP)	.25
57	Clay Matthews	.50
60	Tom Cousineau	.25
61	Mike Baab (DP)	.25
63	Cody Risien	.35
77	Rickey Bolden (DP)	.25
78	Carl Hairston	.25
79	Bob Golic	.35
82	Ozzie Newsome	1.00
84	Glen Young	.25
85	Clarence Weathers	.25
86	Brian Brennan (DP)	.35
96	Reggie Camp	.25

1986 McDonald's Tampa Bay Buccaneers

Issued over four weeks in the Tampa area during the 1986 season, the 24-card set measures 3-1/16" x 4-11/16" with the tab and 3-1/16" x 3-5/8" without. The card fronts have a color photo, with the McDonald's logo in the upper left and Tampa Bay helmet in the upper right. The NFL shield and NFLPA logo are in the bottom corners, left and right respectively. The card backs have the player's name, jersey number, bio and highlights. Each week's cards had different colored tabs: blue (first), black or gray (second), gold or orange (third) and green (fourth).

		NM/M
Complete Set (Blue):		15.00
Complete Set (Black):		15.00
Complete Set (Gold):		15.00
Complete Set (Green):		15.00
Common Player:		.30
1	Donald Igwebuike	.30
8	Steve Young	8.00
17	Steve DeBerg	.75
21	John Holt	.30
23	Jeremiah Castille (DP)	.30
30	David Greenwood	.30
32	James Wilder	.50
44	Ivory Sully	.30
51	Chris Washington	.30
52	Scot Brantley (DP)	.30
54	Ervin Randle	.30
58	Jeff Davis (DP)	.30
60	Randy Grimes	.30
62	Sean Farrell	.40
66	George Yarno	.30
73	Ron Heller	.30
76	David Logan	.30
78	John Cannon (DP)	.30
82	Jerry Bell (DP)	.30
86	Calvin Magee	.30
87	Gerald Carter	.30
88	Jimmie Giles	.50
89	Kevin House	.50
90	Ron Holmes	.40

1986 McDonald's St. Louis Cardinals

Released over four weeks in the St. Louis area during the 1986 season, the 24-card set measures 3-1/16" x 4-11/16" with the tabs and 3-1/16" x 3-5/8" without. The card fronts showcase a color photo, with the McDonald's logo in the upper left and the Cardinals' helmet in the upper right. The NFL shield and NFLPA logo appear at the bottom, left and right respectively. The player's name, jersey number and position are printed under the photo. The card backs showcase the player's name, jersey number, bio and highlights. Each week's card had a different colored tab: blue (first), black or gray (second), gold or orange (third) and green (fourth).

		NM/M
Complete Set (Blue):		10.00
Complete Set (Black):		6.00
Complete Set (Gold):		6.00
Complete Set (Green):		6.00
Common Player:		.25
15	Neil Lomax	.50
18	Carl Birdsong (DP)	.25
30	Stump Mitchell	.35
32	Ottis Anderson (DP)	.75
43	Lonnie Young	.25
45	Leonard Smith	.25
47	Cedric Mack	.25
48	Lionel Washington	.25
53	Freddie Joe Nunn	.35
54	E.J. Junior	.35
57	Niko Noga	.25
60	Al "Bubba" Baker (DP)	.35
63	Tootie Robbins	.25
65	David Galloway	.25
66	Doug Dawson (DP)	.25
67	Luis Sharpe	.25
71	Joe Bostic (DP)	.25
73	Mark Duda (DP)	.25
75	Curtis Greer	.25
80	Doug Marsh	.25
81	Roy Green	.50
83	Pat Tilley	.25
84	J.T. Smith	.35
89	Greg Lafleur	.25

1986 McDonald's San Diego Chargers

Released over four weeks in the San Diego area, the 24-card set measures 3-1/16" x 4-11/16" with the tab and 3-1/16" x 3-5/8" without. The card fronts showcase a color photo, with the McDonald's logo in the upper left, Chargers' helmet in the upper right, NFL shield in the bottom left and NFLPA logo in the lower right. The player's name, jersey number and position are printed under the photo. The card backs include the player's name, number, position, bio and highlights. Each week's cards had a different colored tab: blue (first), black or gray (second), gold or orange (third) and green (fourth).

		NM/M
Complete Set (Blue):		20.00
Complete Set (Black):		15.00
Complete Set (Gold):		10.00
Complete Set (Green):		10.00
Common Player:		.40
9	Mark Herrmann	.40
14	Dan Fouts	1.50
18	Charlie Joiner	1.25
21	Buford McGee	.40
22	Gill Byrd (DP)	.50
26	Lionel James	.50
29	John Hendy	.40
37	Jeff Dale (DP)	.40
40	Gary Anderson (RB) (DP)	.75
43	Tim Spencer	.40
51	Woodrow Lowe	.40
54	Bill Ray Smith	.50
60	Dennis McKnight	.40
62	Don Macek	.40
67	Ed White	.40
74	Jim Lachey	.50
78	Chuck Ehin (DP)	.40
80	Kellen Winslow	1.50
83	Trumaine Johnson	.40
85	Eric Sievers	.40
88	Pete Holohan	.50
89	Wes Chandler (DP)	.50
93	Earl Wilson	.40
99	Lee Williams	.50

1986 McDonald's Kansas City Chiefs

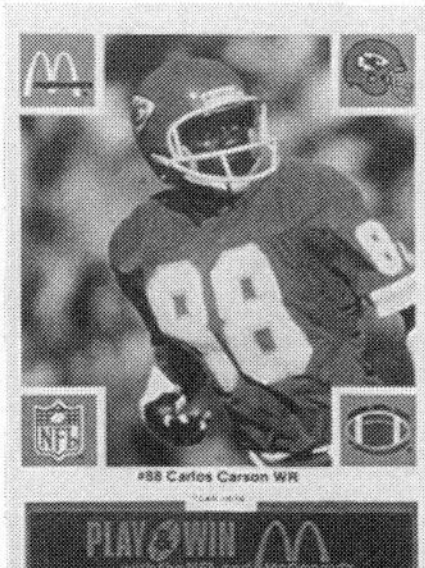

Released over a four-week time span at Kansas City area McDonald's, the 24-card set measures 3-1/16" x 4-11/16" with the tab and 3-1/16" x 3-5/8" without. Anchored with a color photo on the card front, the McDonald's logo is in the upper left and Chiefs' helmet in the upper right. The NFL shield and NFLPA logo are in the bottom corners, left and right respectively. The player's name, jersey number and position are located under the photo. The card backs have the player's name, jersey number, position, bio and career highlights. Each week's cards had different colored tabs: blue (first), black or gray (second), gold or orange (third) and green (fourth).

		NM/M
Complete Set (Blue):		20.00
Complete Set (Black):		40.00
Complete Set (Gold):		20.00
Complete Set (Green):		20.00
Common Player:		.75
6	Jim Arnold (DP)	.75
8	Nick Lowery	1.00
9	Bill Kenney	.75
14	Todd Blackledge (DP)	1.00
20	Deron Cherry (DP)	1.25
29	Albert Lewis	1.50
31	Kevin Ross	1.25
34	Lloyd Burruss (DP)	.75
41	Garcia Lane	.75
42	Jeff Smith	.75
43	Mike Pruitt	1.00
44	Herman Heard	.75
50	Calvin Daniels	.75
59	Gary Spani	.75
63	Bill Maas	.75
64	Bob Olderman	.75
66	Brad Budde (DP)	.75
67	Art Still	.75
72	David Lutz	.75
83	Stephone Paige	1.25
85	Jonathan Hayes	1.00
88	Carlos Carson (DP)	1.00
89	Henry Marshall	.75
97	Scott Radecic	.75

1986 McDonald's Indianapolis Colts

Released during a four-week time span at Indianapolis McDonald's, the 24-card set measures 3-1/16" x 4-11/16" with the tab and 3-1/16" x 3-5/8" without. Anchored with a color photo, the card fronts have a McDonald's logo in the upper left and a Colts' helmet in the upper right. The NFL shield and NFLPA logo are in the bottom corners, left and right respectively. The player's name, number and position are printed below the photo. The card backs showcase the player's name, number, bio and highlights. Each week's cards featured different colored tabs: blue (first), black or gray (second), gold or orange (third) and green (fourth).

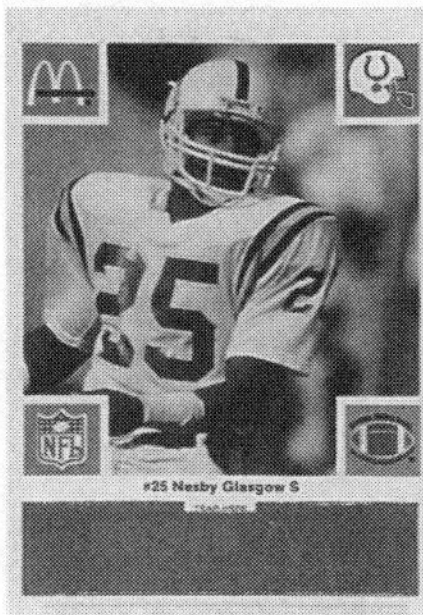

		NM/M
Complete Set (Blue):		100.00
Complete Set (Black):		20.00
Complete Set (Gold):		15.00
Complete Set (Green):		20.00
Common Player:		.60
2	Raul Allegre (DP)	.60
3	Rohn Stark	.75
25	Nesby Glasgow	.60
27	Preston Davis	.60
32	Randy McMillian	.75
34	George Wonsley	.60
38	Eugene Daniel	.75
44	Owen Gill	.60
47	Leonard Coleman	.60
50	Duane Bickett (DP)	1.00
53	Ray Donaldson	.75
55	Barry Krauss	.60
64	Ben Utt	.60
66	Ron Solt	.60
72	Karl Baldischwiler (DP)	.60
75	Chris Hinton	.75
81	Pat Beach (DP)	.60
85	Matt Bouza (DP)	.60
87	Wayne Capers (DP)	.60
88	Robbie Martin	.60
92	Brad White	.60
93	Cliff Odom	.60
96	Blaise Winter	.60
98	Johnie Cooks	.60

1986 McDonald's Dallas Cowboys

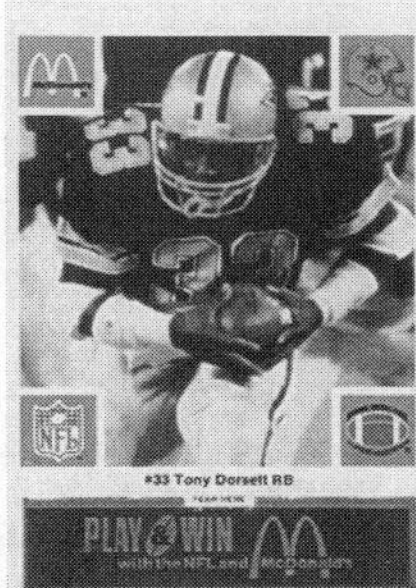

Issued over four weeks at Dallas-area McDonald's, the 25-card set measures 3-1/16" x 4-11/16" with the tab and 3-1/16" x 3-5/8" without. The card fronts boast a color photo, with the McDonald's logo in the upper left and Dallas helmet in the upper right. The NFL shield and NFLPA logo are located in the lower corners, left and right respectively. The player's name, number and position are printed under the photo. The card backs feature the player's name, number, bio and highlights. Each week's cards featured a different colored tab: blue (first), black or gray (second), gold or orange (third) and green (fourth).

		NM/M
Complete Set (Blue):		10.00
Complete Set (Black):		10.00
Complete Set (Gold):		10.00
Complete Set (Green):		10.00
Common Player:		.25
1	Rafael Septien	.25
11	Danny White	.50
24	Everson Walls	.35
26	Michael Downs (DP)	.25
27	Ron Fellows	.25
30	Timmy Newsome	.25
33	Tony Dorsett (DP)	1.50
34	Herschel Walker	2.00
40	Bill Bates (DP)	.50
47	Dexter Clinkscale (DP)	.25
50	Jeff Rohrer	.25
54	Randy White	.75
56	Eugene Lockhart	.35
58	Mike Hegman	.25
61	Jim Cooper (DP)	.25
63	Glen Titensor	.25
64	Tom Rafferty	.25
65	Kurt Peterson	.25
72	Ed "Too Tall" Jones	.75
75	Phil Pozderac	.25
77	Jim Jeffcoat	.50
78	John Dutton	.35
80	Tony Hill	.35
82	Mike Renfro	.25
84	Doug Cosbie (DP)	.25

1986 McDonald's Miami Dolphins

Issued over four weeks at Miami-area McDonald's, the 25-card set measure 3-1/16" x 4-11/16" with the tab and 3-1/16" x 3-5/8" without. Each card front is anchored with a color photo, with the McDonald's logo in the upper left and Miami helmet in the upper right. The NFL shield and NFLPA logo are in the bottom corners, left and right respectively. Below the photo are the player's name, number and position. The card backs showcase the player's name, number, position and highlights. Each week's cards featured a different colored tab: blue (first), black or gray (second), gold or orange (third) and green (fourth).

		NM/M
Complete Set (Blue):		40.00
Complete Set (Black):		20.00
Complete Set (Gold):		20.00
Complete Set (Green):		20.00
Common Player:		.50
4	Reggie Roby	.75
7	Fuad Reveiz	.75
10	Don Strock	.75
13	Dan Marino	10.00
22	Tony Nathan	.75
23A	Joe Carter (ERR) (Photo actually Tony Nathan 22)	.75
23B	Joe Carter (COR)	.50
27	Lorenzo Hampton	.50
30	Ron Davenport	.50
43	Bud Brown (DP)	.50
47	Glenn Blackwood (DP)	.50
49	William Judson	.50
55	Hugh Green	.75
57	Dwight Stephenson	.75
58	Kim Bokamper (DP)	.50
59	Bob Brudzinski (DP)	.50
61	Roy Foster	.50
71	Mike Charles	.50
75	Doug Betters (DP)	.50
79	Jon Giesler	.50
83	Mark Clayton	2.00
84	Bruce Hardy	.50
85	Mark Duper	1.00
89	Nat Moore	.75
91	Mack Moore	.50

1986 McDonald's Philadelphia Eagles

Issued over a four-week time span at Philadelphia-area McDonald's, the 24-card set measures 3-1/16" x 4-11/16" with the tab and 3-1/16" x 3-5/8" without. A color photo anchors the card front, with the McDonald's logo in the upper left and the Eagles' helmet in the upper right. The NFL shield and NFLPA logos are in the bottom corners, left and right respectively. The player's name, number and position are printed under the photo. The card backs have the player's name, number, bio and highlights. Each week's cards featured a different colored tab: blue (first), black or gray (second), gold or orange (third) and green (fourth).

		NM/M
Complete Set (Blue):		60.00
Complete Set (Black):		20.00
Complete Set (Gold):		10.00
Complete Set (Green):		10.00
Common Player:		.25
7	Ron Jaworski	.50
8	Paul McFadden	.25
12	Randall Cunningham (DP)	2.00
22	Brenard Wilson	.25
24	Ray Ellis	.25
29	Elbert Foules	.25
36	Herman Hunter	.35
41	Earnest Jackson	.35
43	Roynell Young	.35
48	Wes Hopkins	.25
50	Garry Cobb (DP)	.25
63	Ron Baker (DP)	.25
66	Ken Reeves	.25
71	Ken Clarke (DP)	.25
73	Steve Kenney	.25
74	Leonard Mitchell	.25
81	Kenny Jackson	.35
82	Mike Quick	.35
85	Ron Johnson	.25
88	John Spagnola	.25
91	Reggie White	4.00
93	Thomas Strauthers	.25
94	Byron Darby (DP)	.25
98	Greg Brown (DP)	.25

1986 McDonald's Atlanta Falcons

Released over a four-week time span at Atlanta-area McDonald's, the 24-card set measures 3-1/16" x 4-11/16" with the tab and 3-1/16" x 3-5/8" without. The card fronts are anchored with a color photo, with the McDonald's logo in the upper left and Falcons' helmet in the upper right. The NFL shield and NFLPA logo are located at the bottom, left and right respectively. The player's name, number and position are printed below the photo. The card backs include the player's name, number, position, bio and highlights. Each week featured a different colored tab: blue (first), black or gray (second), gold or orange (third) and green (fourth). The values listed are for cards with the tabs intact.

		NM/M
Complete Set (Blue):		60.00
Complete Set (Black):		200.00
Complete Set (Gold):		40.00
Complete Set (Green):		15.00
Common Player:		.60
3	Rick Donnelly	.60
16	Dave Archer (DP)	1.00
18	Mick Luckhurst	.60
23	Bobby Butler	.60
26	James Britt (DP)	.60
37	Kenny Johnson	.60
39	Cliff Austin	.60
42	Gerald Riggs	.75
50	Buddy Curry	.60
56	Al Richardson	.60
57	Jeff Van Note	.75
58	David Frye	.60
61	John Scully	.60
62	Brett Miller	.60
74	Mike Pitts	.60
76	Mike Gann	.60
77	Rick Bryan	.60
78	Mike Kenn	.75
79	Bill Fralic	1.00
81	Billy Johnson	.75
82	Stacey Bailey (DP)	.60
87	Cliff Benson (DP)	.60
88	Arthur Cox	.60
89	Charlie Brown (DP)	.75

1986 McDonald's San Francisco 49ers

Released over a four-week time span at San Francisco-area McDonald's, the 24-card set measures 3-1/16" x 4-11/16" with the tab and 3-1/16" x 3-5/8" without. The card fronts are anchored with a color photo, with the McDonald's logo in the upper left and 49ers' helmet in the upper right. The NFL shield and NFLPA logo are located at the bottom, left and right respectively. The player's name, number and position are printed below the photo. The card backs include the player's name, number, position, bio and highlights. Each week featured a different colored tab: blue (first), black or gray (second), gold or orange (third) and green (fourth). The values listed are for cards with the tabs intact.

		NM/M
Complete Set (Blue):		50.00
Complete Set (Black):		25.00
Complete Set (Gold):		25.00
Complete Set (Green):		25.00
Common Player:		.75
16	Joe Montana	12.00
21	Eric Wright	1.00
26	Wendell Tyler	1.00
27	Carlton Williamson	.75
33	Roger Craig (DP)	1.25
42	Ronnie Lott	2.00
49	Jeff Fuller	.75
50	Riki Ellison	.75
51	Randy Cross (DP)	1.00
56	Fred Quillan	.75
58	Keena Turner	.75
62	Guy McIntyre	.75
68	John Ayers (DP)	.75
71	Keith Fahnhorst	.75
72	Jeff Stover	.75
76	Dwaine Board (DP)	.75
77	Bubba Paris	.75
78	Manu Tuiasosopo	.75
80	Jerry Rice	12.00
81	Russ Francis	1.00
86	John Frank	.75
87	Dwight Clark (DP)	1.00
90	Todd Shell	.75
95	Michael Carter (DP)	1.00

1986 McDonald's New York Giants

Released over a four-week time span at New York-area McDonald's, the 24-card set measures 3-1/16" x 4-11/16" with the tab and 3-1/16" x 3-5/8" without. The card fronts are anchored with a color photo, with the McDonald's logo in the upper left and Giants' helmet in the upper right. The NFL shield and NFLPA logo are located at the bottom, left and right respectively. The player's name, number and position are printed below the photo. The card backs include the player's name, number, position, bio and highlights. Each week featured a different colored tab: blue (first), black or gray (second), gold or orange (third) and green (fourth). The values listed are for cards with the tabs intact.

		NM/M
Complete Set (Blue):		12.00
Complete Set (Black):		10.00
Complete Set (Gold):		6.00
Complete Set (Green):		6.00
Common Player:		.25
5	Sean Landeta	.35
11	Phil Simms	1.00
20	Joe Morris	.50
23	Perry Williams	.25
26	Rob Carpenter (DP)	.25
33	George Adams (DP)	.25
34	Elvis Patterson	.35
43	Terry Kinard	.25
44	Maurice Carthon	.25
48	Kenny Hill	.25
53	Harry Carson	.35
54	Andy Headen	.25
56	Lawrence Taylor	1.50
60	Brad Benson (DP)	.25
63	Karl Nelson	.25
64	Jim Burt (DP)	.35
67	Billy Ard (DP)	.25
70	Leonard Marshall	.35
75	George Martin	.35
80	Phil McConkey	.35
84	Zeke Mowatt	.25
85	Don Hasselbeck	.25
86	Lionel Manuel	.35
89	Mark Bavaro (DP)	.35

1986 McDonald's New York Jets

Released over a four-week time span at New York-area McDonald's, the 24-card set measures 3-1/16" x 4-11/16" with the tab and 3-1/16" x 3-5/8" without. The card fronts are anchored with a color photo, with the McDonald's logo in the upper left and Jets' helmet in the upper right. The NFL shield and NFLPA logo are located at the bottom, left and right respectively. The player's name, number and position are printed below the photo. The card backs include the player's name, number, position, bio and highlights. Each week featured a different colored tab: blue (first), black or gray (second), gold or orange (third) and green (fourth). The values listed are for cards with the tabs intact.

		NM/M
Complete Set (Blue):		150.00
Complete Set (Black):		150.00
Complete Set (Gold):		25.00
Complete Set (Green):		25.00
Common Player:		1.00
5	Pat Leahy	1.00
7	Ken O'Brien	1.50
21	Kirk Springs	1.00
24	Freeman McNeil	2.00
27	Russell Carter (DP)	1.00
29	Johnny Lynn	1.00
34	Johnny Hector	1.00

39	Harry Hamilton	1.00
49	Tony Paige	1.00
53	Jim Sweeney	1.00
56	Lance Mehl	1.00
59	Kyle Clifton (DP)	1.00
60	Dan Alexander (DP)	1.00
65	Joe Fields (DP)	1.00
73	Joe Klecko	1.25
78	Barry Bennett (DP)	1.00
80	Johnny Lam Jones	1.00
82	Mickey Shuler	1.00
85	Wesley Walker	1.25
87	Kurt Sohn	1.00
88	Al Toon	2.00
89	Rocky Klever	1.00
93	Marty Lyons	1.00
99	Mark Gastineau (DP)	1.50

1986 McDonald's Detroit Lions

Released over a four-week time span at Detroit-area McDonald's, the 24-card set measures 3-1/16" x 4-11/16" with the tab and 3-1/16" x 3-5/8" without. The card fronts are anchored with a color photo, with the McDonald's logo in the upper left and Lions' helmet in the upper right. The NFL shield and NFLPA logo are located at the bottom, left and right respectively. The player's name, number and position are printed below the photo. The card backs include the player's name, number, position, bio and highlights. Each week featured a different colored tab: blue (first), black or gray (second), gold or orange (third) and green (fourth). The values listed are for cards which have the tabs intact.

		NM/M
Complete Set (Blue):		6.00
Complete Set (Black):		6.00
Complete Set (Gold):		6.00
Complete Set (Green):		6.00
Common Player:		.25
3	Eddie Murray	.35
11	Michael Black (DP)	.25
17	Eric Hipple	.35
20	Billy Sims	.50
21	Demetrious Johnson	.25
27	Bobby Watkins	.25
29	Bruce McNorton	.25
30	James Jones	.35
33	William Graham	.25
35	Alvin Hall	.25
39	Leonard Thompson	.35
50	August Curley (DP)	.25
52	Steve Mott	.25
55	Mike Cofer (DP)	.35
59	Jimmy Williams	.25
70	Keith Dorney (DP)	.25
71	Rich Strenger	.25
75	Lomas Brown (DP)	.35
76	Eric Williams	.25
79	William Gay	.25
82	Pete Mandley	.25
86	Mark Nichols	.25
87	David Lewis	.25
89	Jeff Chadwick (DP)	.25

1986 McDonald's Houston Oilers

Released over a four-week time span at Houston-area McDonald's, the 24-card set measures 3-1/16" x 4-11/16" with the tab and 3-1/16" x 3-5/8" without. The card fronts are anchored with a color photo, with the McDonald's logo in the upper left and Oilers' helmet in the upper right. The NFL shield and NFLPA logo are located at the bottom, left and right respectively. The player's name, number and position are printed below the photo. The card backs include the player's name, number, position, bio and highlights. Each week featured a different colored tab: blue (first), black or gray (second), gold or orange (third) and green (fourth). The values listed are for cards which have the tabs intact.

		NM/M
Complete Set (Blue):		12.00
Complete Set (Black):		8.00
Complete Set (Gold):		8.00
Complete Set (Green):		8.00
Common Player:		.30
1	Warren Moon	4.00
7	Tony Zendejas	.30
10	Oliver Luck	.40
21	Bo Eason	.30
23	Richard Johnson	.30
24	Steve Brown (DP)	.30
25	Keith Bostic (DP)	.30
29	Patrick Allen (DP)	.30
33	Mike Rozier	.50
40	Butch Woolfolk	.30
53	Avon Riley	.30
56	Robert Abraham (DP)	.30
63	Mike Munchak	.40
67	Mike Stensrud	.30
70	Dean Steinkuhler	.40
71	Richard Byrd (DP)	.30
73	Harvey Salem	.30
74	Bruce Matthews	.75
79	Ray Childress	.75
83	Tim Smith	.30
85	Drew Hill	.75
87	Jamie Williams	.30
91	Johnny Meads	.30
94	Frank Bush (DP)	.30

1986 McDonald's Green Bay Packers

Released over a four-week time span at Green Bay-area McDonald's, the 24-card set measures 3-1/16" x 4-11/16" with the tab and 3-1/16" x 3-5/8" without. The card fronts are anchored with a color photo, with the McDonald's logo in the upper left and Packers' helmet in the upper right. The NFL shield and NFLPA logo are located at the bottom, left and right respectively. The player's name, number and position are printed below the photo. The card backs include the player's name, number, position, bio and highlights. Each week featured a different colored tab: blue (first), black or gray (second), gold or orange (third) and green (fourth). The values listed are for cards which have the tabs intact.

		NM/M
Complete Set (Blue):		6.00
Complete Set (Black):		6.00
Complete Set (Gold):		6.00
Complete Set (Green):		6.00
Common Player:		.25
10	Al Del Greco (DP)	.25
12	Lynn Dickey	.35
16	Randy Wright	.35
18	Jim Zorn	.35
22	Mark Lee	.25
26	Tim Lewis	.25
31	Gerry Ellis	.25
33	Jessie Clark (DP)	.25
37	Mark Murphy	.35
41	Tom Flynn	.25
42	Gary Ellerson	.25
53	Mike Douglass	.25
55	Randy Scott	.25
59	John Anderson (DP)	.25
67	Karl Swanke	.25
75	Ken Ruettgers	.25
76	Alphonso Carreker (DP)	.25
77	Mike Butler (DP)	.25
79	Donnie Humphrey	.25
82	Paul Coffman (DP)	.25
85	Phillip Epps	.35
90	Ezra Johnson	.25
91	Brian Noble	.35
94	Charles Martin	.25

1986 McDonald's New England Patriots

Released over a four-week time span at New England-area McDonald's, the 24-card set measures 3-1/16" x 4-11/16" with the tab and 3-1/16" x 3-5/8" without. The card fronts are anchored with a color photo, with the McDonald's logo in the upper left and Patriots' helmet in the upper right. The NFL shield and NFLPA logo are located at the bottom, left and right respectively. The player's name, number and position are printed below the photo. The card backs include the player's name, number, position, bio and highlights. Each week featured a different colored tab: blue (first), black or gray (second), gold or orange (third) and green (fourth). The values listed are for cards which have the tabs intact.

		NM/M
Complete Set (Blue):		6.00
Complete Set (Black):		6.00
Complete Set (Gold):		6.00
Complete Set (Green):		6.00
Common Player:		.25
3	Rich Camarillo (DP)	.25
11	Tony Eason (DP)	.35
14	Steve Grogan	.50
24	Robert Weathers	.25
26	Raymond Clayborn (DP)	.25
30	Mosi Tatupu	.25
31	Fred Marion	.25
32	Craig James	.50
33	Tony Collins (DP)	.35
38	Roland James	.25
42	Ronnie Lippett	.25
50	Larry McGrew	.25
55	Don Blackmon (DP)	.25
56	Andre Tippett	.50
57	Steve Nelson	.25
58	Pete Brock (DP)	.25
60	Garin Veris	.25
61	Ron Wooten	.25
73	John Hannah	.50
77	Kenneth Sims	.25
80	Irving Fryar	1.00
81	Stephen Starring	.25
83	Cedric Jones	.25
86	Stanley Morgan	.50

1986 McDonald's Los Angeles Raiders

Released over a four-week time span at Los Angeles-area McDonald's, the 24-card set measures 3-1/16" x 4-11/16" with the tab and 3-1/16" x 3-5/8" without. The card fronts are anchored with a color photo, with the McDonald's logo in the upper left and Raiders' helmet in the upper right. The NFL shield and NFLPA logo are located at the bottom, left and right respectively. The player's name, number and position are printed below the photo. The card backs include the player's name, number, position, bio and highlights. Each week featured a different colored tab: blue (first), black or gray (second), gold or orange (third) and green (fourth). The values listed are for cards which have the tabs intact.

		NM/M
Complete Set (Blue):		20.00
Complete Set (Black):		10.00
Complete Set (Gold):		6.00
Complete Set (Green):		6.00
Common Player:		.25
1	Marc Wilson	.35
8	Ray Guy (DP)	.50
10	Chris Bahr (DP)	.25
16	Jim Plunkett	.50
22	Mike Haynes	.35
26	Vann McElroy	.25
27	Frank Hawkins	.25
32	Marcus Allen (DP)	1.50
36	Mike Davis (DP)	.25
37	Lester Hayes	.35
46	Todd Christensen (DP)	.50
53	Rod Martin	.35
54	Reggie McKenzie	.25
55	Matt Millen	.35
70	Henry Lawrence	.25
71	Bill Pickel	.25
72	Don Mosebar	.35
73	Charley Hannah	.25
75	Howie Long	1.00
79	Bruce Davis (DP)	.25
84	Jessie Hester	.50
85	Dokie Williams	.25
91	Brad Van Pelt	.25
99	Sean Jones	.50

A player's name in *italic* type indicates a rookie card.

1986 McDonald's Los Angeles Rams

Released over a four-week time span at Los Angeles-area McDonald's, the 24-card set measures 3-1/16" x 4-11/16" with the tab and 3-1/16" x 3-5/8" without. The card fronts are anchored with a color photo, with the McDonald's logo in the upper left and Rams' helmet in the upper right. The NFL shield and NFLPA logo are located at the bottom, respectively. The player's name, number and position are printed below the photo. The card backs include the player's name, number, position, bio and highlights. Each week featured a different colored tab: first week (blue), second (black or gray), third (gold or orange) and fourth (green). The values listed are for cards which have the tabs intact.

		NM/M
Complete Set (Blue):		9.00
Complete Set (Black):		6.00
Complete Set (Gold):		6.00
Complete Set (Green):		6.00
Common Player:		.25
1	Mike Lansford	.25
3	Dale Hatcher	.25
5	Dieter Brock (DP)	.25
20	Johnnie Johnson	.25
21	Nolan Cromwell (DP)	.35
22	Vince Newsome	.25
27	Gary Green	.25
29	Eric Dickerson (DP)	1.00
44	Mike Guman	.25
47	LeRoy Irvin	.35
50	Jim Collins (DP)	.25
54	Mike Wilcher	.25
55	Carl Ekern	.25
56	Doug Smith	.25
58	Mel Owens	.25
60	Dennis Harrah	.25
71	Reggie Doss (DP)	.25
72	Kent Hill	.25
75	Irv Pankey	.25
78	Jackie Slater	.50
80	Henry Ellard	.75
81	David Hill	.25
87	Tony Hunter	.25
89	Ron Brown (DP)	.35

1986 McDonald's Washington Redskins

Released over a four-week time span at Washington, D.C.- area McDonald's, the 24-card set measures 3-1/16" x 4-11/16" with the tab and 3-1/16" x 3-5/8" without. The card fronts are anchored with a color photo, with the McDonald's logo in the upper left and Redskins' helmet in the upper right. The NFL shield and NFLPA logo are located at the bottom, left and right respectively. The player's name, number and position are printed below the photo. The card backs include the player's name, number, position, bio and highlights. Each week featured a different colored tab: blue (first), black or gray (second), gold or orange (third) and green (fourth). The values listed are for cards which have the tabs intact.

		NM/M
Complete Set (Blue):		6.00
Complete Set (Black):		6.00
Complete Set (Gold):		6.00
Complete Set (Green):		6.00
Common Player:		.25
3	Mark Moseley	.25
10	Jay Schroeder	.50
22	Curtis Jordan	.25
28	Darrell Green	.50
32	Vernon Dean (DP)	.25
35	Keith Griffin	.25
37	Raphel Cherry (DP)	.25
38	George Rogers	.35
51	Monte Coleman (DP)	.35
52	Neal Olkewicz	.25
53	Jeff Bostic (DP)	.25
55	Mel Kaufman	.25
57	Rich Milot	.25
65	Dave Butz (DP)	.35
66	Joe Jacoby	.35
68	Russ Grimm	.35
71	Charles Mann	.50
72	Dexter Manley	.35
73	Mark May	.35
77	Darryl Grant	.25
81	Art Monk	1.00
84	Gary Clark (DP)	1.00
85	Don Warren	.35
86	Clint Didier	.25

1986 McDonald's New Orleans Saints

Released over a four-week time span at New Orleans-area McDonald's, the 24-card set measures 3-1/16" x 4-11/16" with the tab and 3-1/16" x 3-5/8" without. The card fronts are anchored with a color photo, with the McDonald's logo in the upper left and Saints' helmet in the upper right. The NFL shield and NFLPA logo are located at the bottom, left and right respectively. The player's name, number and position are printed below the photo. The card backs include the player's name, number, position, bio and highlights. Each week featured a different colored tab: blue (first), black or gray (second), gold or orange (third) and green (fourth). The values listed are for cards which have the tabs intact.

		NM/M
Complete Set (Blue):		150.00
Complete Set (Black):		30.00
Complete Set (Gold):		20.00
Complete Set (Green):		25.00
Common Player:		.75
3	Bobby Hebert	2.00
7	Morten Andersen (DP)	1.00
10	Brian Hansen	.75
18	Dave Wilson	.75
20	Russell Gary	.75
25	Johnnie Poe	.75
30	Wayne Wilson	.75
44	Dave Waymer	.75
46	Hokie Gajan	.75
49	Frank Wattelett	.75
50	Jack Del Rio (DP)	1.00
57	Rickey Jackson	1.00
60	Steve Korte	.75
61	Joel Hilgenberg	.75
63	Brad Edelman (DP)	.75
64	Dave Lafary	.75
67	Stan Brock (DP)	.75
73	Frank Warren	.75
75	Bruce Clark (DP)	.75
84	Eric Martin	1.50
85	Hoby Brenner (DP)	.75
88	Eugene Goodlow	.75
89	Tyrone Young	.75
99	Tony Elliott	.75

1986 McDonald's Seattle Seahawks

Released over a four-week time span at Seattle-area McDonald's, the 24-card set measures 3-1/16" x 4-11/16" with the tab and 3-1/16" x 3-5/8" without. The card fronts are anchored with a color photo, with the McDonald's logo in the upper left and Seahawks' helmet in the upper right. The NFL shield and NFLPA logo are located at the bottom, left and right respectively. The player's name, number and position are printed below the photo. The card backs include the player's name, number, position, bio and highlights. Each week featured a different colored tab: blue (first), black or gray (second), gold or orange (third) and green (fourth). The values listed are for cards which have the tabs intact.

		NM/M
Complete Set (Blue):		10.00
Complete Set (Black):		7.00
Complete Set (Gold):		7.00
Complete Set (Green):		7.00
Common Player:		.25
9	Norm Johnson	.35
17	Dave Krieg	.50
20	Terry Taylor	.25
22	Dave Brown (DP)	.25
28	Curt Warner (DP)	.50
33	Dan Doornink	.25
44	John Harris	.25
45	Kenny Easley	.35
46	David Hughes	.25
50	Fredd Young	.25
53	Keith Butler (DP)	.25
55	Michael Jackson	.25
58	Bruce Scholtz	.25
59	Blair Bush (DP)	.25
61	Robert Pratt	.25
64	Ron Essink	.25
65	Edwin Bailey (DP)	.25
72	Joe Nash	.25
77	Jeff Bryant (DP)	.25
78	Bob Cryder (DP)	.25
79	Jacob Green	.35
80	Steve Largent	2.00
81	Daryl Turner	.25
82	Paul Skansi	.25

1986 McDonald's Pittsburgh Steelers

Released over a four-week time span at Pittsburgh-area McDonald's, the 24-card set measures 3-1/16" x 4-11/16" with the tab and 3-1/16" x 3-5/8" without. The card fronts are anchored with a color photo, with the McDonald's logo in the upper left and Steelers' helmet in the upper right. The NFL shield and NFLPA logo are located at the bottom, left and right respectively. The player's name, number and position are printed below the photo. The card backs include the player's name, number, position, bio and highlights. Each week featured a different colored tab: blue (first), black or gray (second), gold or orange (third) and green (fourth). The values listed are for cards which have the tabs intact.

		NM/M
Complete Set (Blue):		50.00
Complete Set (Black):		25.00
Complete Set (Gold):		10.00
Complete Set (Green):		10.00

Common Player: .40
1 Gary Anderson (K) (DP) .50
16 Mark Malone .50
21 Eric Williams .40
24 Rich Erenberg (DP) .40
30 Frank Pollard .40
31 Donnie Shell .50
34 Walter Abercrombie (DP) .40
49 Dwayne Woodruff .40
50 David Little .40
52 Mike Webster .50
53 Bryan Hinkle .50
56 Robin Cole (DP) .40
57 Mike Merriweather .50
62 Tunch Ilkin .40
65 Ray Pinney .40
67 Gary Dunn (DP) .40
73 Craig Wolfley .40
74 Terry Long .40
82 John Stallworth .75
83 Louis Lipps .75
87 Weegie Thompson .40
92 Keith Gary (DP) .40
93 Keith Willis .40
99 Darryl Sims .40

1986 McDonald's Minnesota Vikings

Released over a four-week time span at Minneapolis-area McDonald's, the 24-card set measures 3-1/16" x 4-11/16" with the tab and 3-1/16" x 3-5/8" without. The card fronts are anchored with a color photo, with the McDonald's logo in the upper left and Vikings' helmet in the upper right. The NFL shield and NFLPA logo are located at the bottom, left and right respectively. The player's name, number and position are printed below the photo. The card backs include the player's name, number, position, bio and highlights. Each week featured a different colored tab: blue (first), black or gray (second), gold or orange (third) and green (fourth). The values listed are for cards which have the tabs intact.

NM/M
Complete Set (Blue): 45.00
Complete Set (Black): 30.00
Complete Set (Gold): 15.00
Complete Set (Green): 15.00
Common Player: .60
8 Greg Coleman (DP) .60
9 Tommy Kramer .75
11 Wade Wilson .75
20 Darrin Nelson .75
23 Ted Brown (DP) .60
37 Willie Teal .60
39 Carl Lee .75
46 Alfred Anderson (DP) .60
47 Joey Browner (DP) .75
55 Scott Studwell .60
56 Chris Doleman .75
59 Matt Blair (DP) .75
67 Dennis Swilley .60
68 Curtis Rouse .60
75 Keith Millard .75
76 Tim Irwin .60
77 Mark Mullaney .60
79 Doug Martin .60
81 Anthony Carter (DP) 1.25
83 Steve Jordan .75
87 Leo Lewis .75
89 Mike Jones .60
96 Tim Newton .60
99 David Howard .60

1993 McDonald's GameDay

These cards were issued as part of the McDonald's/NFL Kickoff Playoff promotion. With a certain food combination purchase, customers received a game piece which offered prizes ranging from a trip to the Super Bowl to food. Or, the game piece had a point value on it - 6 (touchdown), 3 (field goal) or 1 (extra point). For 10 points, a collector could obtain a six-card panel featuring players from the NFL team in that participating McDonald's market. A different six-player sheet was given away in each of three weeks, making a complete set three panels, or 18 cards. The cards are identical in size to the regular issues (2-1/2" x 4-3/4"), but have a McDonald's logo on each side. Cards are also numbered using a McD prefix. Some restaurants also offered three sheets featuring 18 different All-Stars.

NM/M
Complete Set: 35.00
Common Player: 1.50
1 Deion Sanders, Thurman Thomas, Troy Aikman, John Elway, Barry Sanders, Sterling Sharpe All-Stars A 1.50
2 Derrick Thomas, Howie Long, Dan Marino, Chris Doleman, Vaughan Johnson, Phil Simms All-Stars B 1.50
3 Randall Cunningham, Barry Foster, Jerry Rice, Junior Seau, Cortez Kennedy, Mark Rypien All-Stars C 1.00
4 Deion Sanders, Moe Gardner, Tim Green, Michael Haynes, Chris Hinton, Tim McKyer Atlanta Falcons A 1.50
5 Chris Miller, Bruce Pickens, Mike Pritchard, Andre Rison, Chris Miller, Bruce Pickens, Mike Pritchard, Andre Rison, Darion Conner, Jessie Tuggle Atlanta Falcons B 1.00
6 Drew Hill, Pierce Holt, Elbert Shelley, Jesse Solomon, Bobby Hebert, Lincoln Kennedy Atlanta Falcons C .75
7 Howard Ballard, Don Beebe, Cornelius Bennett, Phil Hansen, Henry Jones, Jim Kelly Buffalo Bills A 1.00
8 Nate Odomes, Andre Reed, Frank Reich, Bruce Smith, Darryl Talley, Steve Tasker Buffalo Bills B .75
9 Bill Brooks, Jim Ritcher, Thurman Thomas, Kenneth Davis, Jeff Wright, Thomas Smith Buffalo Bills C 1.25
10 Neal Anderson, Trace Armstrong, Mark Carrier DB, Wendell Davis, Richard Dent, Shaun Gayle Chicago Bears A .75
11 Jim Harbaugh, Darren Lewis, Jim Morrissey, William Perry, Alonzo Spellman, Tom Waddle Chicago Bears B .75
12 Steve McMichael, Craig Heyward, Lemuel Stinson, Keith Van Horne, Donnell Woolford, Curtis Conway Chicago Bears C 1.00
13 Derrick Fenner, James Francis, David Fulcher, Harold Green, Rod Jones CB, David Klingler Cincinnati Bengals A .75
14 Bruce Kozerski, Tim Krumrie, Ricardo McDonald, Carl Pickens, Reggie Rembert, Daniel Stubbs Cincinnati Bengals B .75
15 Eddie Brown, Gary Reasons, Lamar Rogers, Alfred Williams, Darryl Williams, John Copeland Cincinnati Bengals C .75
16 Rob Burnett, Jay Hilgenberg, Leroy Hoard, Michael Jackson, Mike Johnson, Bernie Kosar Cleveland Browns A 1.00
17 Eric Metcalf, Michael Dean Perry, Clay Matthews, Lawyer Tillman, Eric Turner, Tommy Vardell Cleveland Browns B 1.00
18 David Brandon, Tony Jones T, Scott Galbraith, James Jones DT, Vinny Testaverde, Steve Everitt Cleveland Browns C .75
19 Troy Aikman, Tony Casillas, Thomas Everett, Charles Haley, Alvin Harper, Michael Irvin Dallas Cowboys A 1.75
20 Jim Jeffcoat, Daryl Johnston, Robert Jones, Nate Newton, Ken Norton Jr., Jay Novacek Dallas Cowboys B 1.00
21 Russell Maryland, Emmitt Smith, Kevin Smith, Mark Stepnoski, Tony Tolbert, Larry Brown DB Dallas Cowboys C 2.00
22 Steve Atwater, Mike Croel, Shane Dronett, John Elway, Simon Fletcher, Reggie Rivers Denver Broncos A 1.50
23 Vance Johnson, Greg Lewis, Tommy Maddox, Arthur Marshall, Shannon Sharpe, Dennis Smith Denver Broncos B .75
24 Rod Bernstine, Michael Brooks, Wymon Henderson, Greg Kragen, Karl Mecklenburg, Dan Williams Denver Broncos C .75
25 Bennie Blades, Michael Cofer, Ray Crockett, Mel Gray, Willie Green, Jason Hanson Detroit Lions A .75
26 Herman Moore, Rodney Peete, Brett Perriman, Kelvin Pritchett, Barry Sanders, Tracy Scroggins Detroit Lions B 1.50
27 Pat Swilling, Lomas Brown, Erik Kramer, Chris Spielman, Andre Ware, William White Detroit Lions C 1.00
28 Tony Bennett, Matt Brock, Terrell Buckley, LeRoy Butler, Chris Jacke, Brett Favre Green Bay Packers A 2.00
29 Jackie Harris, Brian Noble, Bryce Paup, Sterling Sharpe, Ed West, Johnny Holland Green Bay Packers B 1.00
30 Tunch Ilkin, George Teague, Reggie White, Ken O'Brien, John Stephens, Wayne Simmons Green Bay Packers C 1.50
31 Cody Carlson, Ray Childress, Curtis Duncan, William Fuller, Haywood Jeffires, Lamar Lathon Houston Oilers A .75
32 Bruce Matthews, Bubba McDowell, Warren Moon, Mike Munchak, Eddie Robinson, Webster Slaughter Houston Oilers B 1.00
33 Ernest Givins, Cris Dishman, Al Smith, Lorenzo White, Lee Williams, Brad Hopkins Houston Oilers C .75
34 Chip Banks, Kerry Cash, Quentin Coryatt, Rodney Culver, Steve Emtman, Reggie Langhorne Indianapolis Colts A .75
35 Jeff Herrod, Anthony Johnson, Jeff George, Rohn Stark, Jack Trudeau, Clarence Verdin Indianapolis Colts B 1.00
36 Duane Bickett, Eugene Daniel, Jessie Hester, Chris Goode, Kirk Lowdermilk, Sean Dawkins Indianapolis Colts C .75
37 Dale Carter, Willie Davis, Dave Krieg, Albert Lewis, Nick Lowery, J.J. Birden Kansas City Chiefs A .75
38 Charles Mincy, Christian Okoye, Kevin Ross, Dan Saleaumua, Tracy Simien, Harvey Williams Kansas City Chiefs B .75
39 Todd McNair, Neil Smith, Derrick Thomas, Leonard Griffin, Barry Word, Joe Montana Kansas City Chiefs C 1.50
40 Eddie Anderson, Jeff Gossett, Ethan Horton, Jeff Jaeger, Howie Long, Todd Marinovich Los Angeles Raiders A .75
41 Terry McDaniel, Don Mosebar, Anthony Smith, Greg Townsend, Aaron Wallace, Steve Wisniewski Los Angeles Raiders B .75
42 Nick Bell, Tim Brown, Eric Dickerson, James Lofton, Jeff Hostetler, Patrick Bates Los Angeles Raiders C 1.00
43 Flipper Anderson, Marc Boutte, Henry Ellard, Bill Hawkins, Cleveland Gary, David Lang Los Angeles Rams A .75
44 Jim Everett, Darryl Henley, Todd Lyght, Anthony Newman, Roman Phifer, Jim Price Los Angeles Rams B 1.00
45 Shane Conlan, Henry Rolling, Larry Kelm, Jackie Slater, Fred Stokes, Jerome Bettis Los Angeles Rams C 1.25
46 Marco Coleman, Bryan Cox, Jeff Cross, Mark Duper, Keith Sims, Mark Higgs Miami Dolphins A .75
47 Keith Jackson, Dan Marino, John Offerdahl, Louis Oliver, Tony Paige, Pete Stoyanovich Miami Dolphins B 2.00
48 Tony Martin, Irving Fryar, Troy Vincent, Richmond Webb, Jarvis Williams, O.J. McDuffie Miami Dolphins C 1.00
49 Terry Allen, Anthony Carter, Cris Carter, Jack Del Rio, Chris Doleman, Rich Gannon Minnesota Vikings A 1.00
50 Steve Jordan, Carl Lee, Randall McDaniel, John Randle, Sean Salisbury, Todd Scott Minnesota Vikings B .75
51 Jim McMahon, Audray McMillian, Mike Merriweather, Henry Thomas, Gary Zimmerman, Robert Smith Minnesota Vikings C .75
52 Ray Agnew, Bruce Armstrong, Vincent Brown, Eugene Chung, Marv Cook, Maurice Hurst New England Patriots A .75
53 Pat Harlow, Eugene Lockhart, Greg McMurtry, Scott Zolak, Leonard Russell, Andre Tippett New England Patriots B 1.00
54 David Howard, Johnny Rembert, Jon Vaughn, Brent Williams, Scott Secules, Drew Bledsoe New England Patriots C 1.50
55 Morten Andersen, Gene Atkins, Toi Cook, Richard Cooper, Jim Dombrowski, Vaughn Dunbar New Orleans Saints A .75
56 Joel Hilgenberg, Rickey Jackson, Vaughan Johnson, Wayne Martin, Renaldo Turnbull, Frank Warren New Orleans Saints B .75
57 Irv Smith, Brad Muster, Dalton Hilliard, Eric Martin, Sam Mills, Willie Roaf New Orleans Saints C .75
58 Jarrod Bunch, Mark Collins, Howard Cross, Rodney Hampton, Erik Howard, Greg Jackson New York Giants A 1.00
59 Pepper Johnson, Sean Landeta, Ed McCaffrey, Dave Meggett, Bart Oates, Phil Simms New York Giants B 1.00
60 Carlton Bailey, Carl Banks, John Elliott, Eric Dorsey, Lawrence Taylor, Mike Sherrard New York Giants C 1.00
61 Brad Baxter, Scott Mersereau, Chris Burkett, Kyle Clifton, Jeff Lageman, Mo Lewis New York Jets A .75
62 Johnny Mitchell, Rob Moore, Browning Nagle, Blair Thomas, Brian Washington, Marvin Washington New York Jets B .75
63 Boomer Esiason, James Hasty, Ronnie Lott, Leonard Marshall, Terance Mathis, Marvin Jones New York Jets C 1.00
64 Eric Allen, Fred Barnett, Randall Cunningham, Byron Evans, Andy Harmon, Seth Joyner Philadelphia Eagles A 1.00
65 Heath Sherman, Vai Sikahema, Clyde Simmons, Herschel Walker, Andre Waters, Calvin Williams Philadelphia Eagles B 1.00
66 Keith Byars, Mike Golic, Leonard Renfro, William Thomas, Antone Davis, Lester Holmes Philadelphia Eagles C .75
67 Johnny Bailey, Rich Camarillo, Larry Centers, Chris Chandler, Ken Harvey, Randal Hill Phoenix Cardinals A .75
68 Mark May, Robert Massey, Freddie Joe Nunn, Ricky Proehl, Eric Hill, Eric Swann Phoenix Cardinals B 1.00
69 Gary Clark, John Booty, Chuck Cecil, Steve Beuerlein, Ernest Dye, Garrison Hearst Phoenix Cardinals C 1.00
70 Dermontti Dawson, Barry Foster, Jeff Graham, Eric Green, Carlton Haselrig, Bryan Hinkle Pittsburgh Steelers A 1.00
71 Merril Hoge, D.J. Johnson, Carnell Lake, David Little, Neil O'Donnell, Darren Perry Pittsburgh Steelers B 1.00
72 Bubby Brister, Kevin Greene, Greg Lloyd, Leon Searcy, Rod Woodson, Deon Figures Pittsburgh Steelers C 1.00
73 Eric Bieniemy, Marion Butts, Burt Grossman, Ronnie Harmon, Stan Humphries, Nate Lewis San Diego Chargers A 1.00
74 Chris Mims, Leslie O'Neal, Stanley Richard, Junior Seau, Harry Swayne, Derrick Walker San Diego Chargers B 1.00
75 Jerrol Williams, Gill Byrd, John Friesz, Anthony Miller, Gary Plummer, Darrien Gordon San Diego Chargers C 1.00
76 Ricky Watters, Michael Carter, Don Griffin, Dana Hall, Brent Jones, Harris Barton San Francisco 49ers A 1.00
77 Tom Rathman, Jerry Rice, Bill Romanowski, John Taylor, Steve Wallace, Mike Walter San Francisco 49ers B 1.50
78 Kevin Fagan, Todd Kelly, Guy McIntyre, Tim McDonald, Steve Young, Dana Stubblefield San Francisco 49ers C 1.50
79 Robert Blackmon, Brian Blades, Jeff Bryant, Dwayne Harper, Andy Heck, Tommy Kane Seattle Seahawks A .75
80 Cortez Kennedy, Dan McGwire, Rufus Porter, Ray Roberts, Eugene Robinson, Chris Warren Seattle Seahawks B 1.00
81 Ferrell Edmunds, Kelvin Martin, John L. Williams, Tony Woods, David Wyman, Rick Mirer Seattle Seahawks C 1.25
82 Gary Anderson RB, Tyji Armstrong, Reggie Cobb, Lawrence Dawsey, Steve DeBerg, Santana Dotson Tampa Bay Buccaneers A .75
83 Ron Hall, Courtney Hawkins, Keith McCants, Charles McRae, Ricky Reynolds, Broderick Thomas Tampa Bay Buccaneers B .75
84 Vince Workman, Paul Gruber, Hardy Nickerson, Marty Carter, Mark Wheeler, Eric Curry Tampa Bay Buccaneers C .75
85 Earnest Byner, Andre Collins, Brad Edwards, Ricky Ervins, Darrell Green, Desmond Howard Washington Redskins A 1.00
86 Tim Johnson, Jim Lachey, Chip Lohmiller, Mark Rypien, Ricky Sanders, Mark Schlereth Washington Redskins B 1.00
87 Al Noga, Kurt Gouveia, Charles Mann, Wilber Marshall, Art Monk, Tom Carter Washington Redskins C 1.00

1996 McDonald's Looney Tunes Cups

These four cups were available at McDonalds during the 1996 NFL season. Each cup featured a player and a Looney Tunes character.

NM/M
Complete Set (4): 6.00
Common Cup: 1.00
1 Drew Bledsoe, Wile E. Coyote 1.00
2 Dan Marino, Daffy Duck 2.00
3 Barry Sanders, Tazmanian Devil 1.50
4 Emmitt Smith, Bugs Bunny 2.00

1995 Metal

Fleer's 1995 Metal features the set's computer-generated metallic, hand foil-etched fronts with a color action photo. The player's name is written in a foil panel at the bottom of the card, next to the brand logo. The cards have a triangle in the lower left which has the card number; cards are numbered as subsets by team, alphabetically by city name and then by player name. An action photo comprises the top part of the card, with a bar graph depicting 1994 and career totals. Biographical information is also included. The team name is written along the right side of the card. Three insert sets were created: Silver Flashers, Gold Blasters and Platinum Portraits. As an added bonus, a Super Bowl XXX instant win card was randomly included in a pack; the finder was entitled to a trip to Super Bowl XXX in Phoenix.

NM/M
Complete Set (200): 25.00
Common Player: .10
Minor Stars: .20
Pack (8): 1.00
Wax Box (36): 20.00
1 Garrison Hearst .25
2 Seth Joyner .10
3 Dave Krieg .10
4 Lorenzo Lynch .10
5 Rob Moore .10
6 Eric Swann .10
7 Aeneas Williams .10
8 Chris Doleman .10
9 Bert Emanuel .50
10 Jeff George .25
11 Craig Heyward .10
12 Terance Mathis .10
13 Eric Metcalf .10
14 Cornelius Bennett .10
15 Bucky Brooks .10
16 Jeff Burris .10
17 Jim Kelly .20
18 Andre Reed .20
19 Bruce Smith .10
20 Don Beebe .10
21 *Kerry Collins* 1.50
22 Barry Foster .20
23 Lamar Lathon .10
24 Sam Mills .10
25 *Tyrone Poole* .20
26 Frank Reich .10
27 Joe Cain .10
28 Curtis Conway .10
29 Jeff Graham .10
30 Erik Kramer .10
31 *Rashaan Salaam* .50
32 Lewis Tillman .10
33 Chris Zorich .10
34 *Jeff Blake* .75
35 *Ki-Jana Carter* .50
36 Carl Pickens .50
37 Corey Sawyer .10
38 Darnay Scott .75
39 Dan Wilkinson .10
40 Darryl Williams .10
41 Derrick Alexander .30
42 Leroy Hoard .10
43 Michael Jackson .10
44 Antonio Langham .10
45 Andre Rison .20
46 Vinny Testaverde .10
47 Eric Turner .10
48 Troy Aikman 1.50
49 Charles Haley .10
50 Michael Irvin .50
51 Daryl Johnston .10
52 Jay Novacek .10
53 Emmitt Smith 3.00
54 Kevin Williams .10
55 Steve Atwater .10
56 Rod Bernstine .10
57 John Elway .75
58 Glyn Milburn .10
59 Anthony Miller .10
60 Mike Pritchard .10
61 Shannon Sharpe .10
62 Mike Johnson .10
63 Scott Mitchell .10
64 Herman Moore .50
65 Brett Perriman .10
66 Barry Sanders 2.50
67 Chris Spielman .10
68 Edgar Bennett .10
69 Robert Brooks .10
70 Brett Favre 3.00
71 LeShon Johnson .10
72 George Koonce .10
73 Reggie White .20
74 Gary Brown .10
75 Cris Dishman .10
76 Mel Gray .10
77 *Steve McNair* 4.50
78 Webster Slaughter .10
79 *Rodney Thomas* .20
80 Trev Alberts .10
81 Quentin Coryatt .10
82 Sean Dawkins .10
83 Craig Erickson .10
84 Marshall Faulk 2.00
85 Stephen Grant .20
86 Steve Beuerlein .10
87 *Tony Boselli* .50
88 Desmond Howard .10
89 *James Stewart* 1.50
90 Marcus Allen .20
91 Kimble Anders .10
92 Steve Bono .30
93 Lake Dawson .40
94 Greg Hill .40
95 Neil Smith .10

96	Derrick Thomas	.20
97	Tim Bowens	.10
98	Brian Cox	.10
99	Irving Fryar	.10
100	Eric Green	.10
101	Dan Marino	3.00
102	O.J. McDuffie	.10
103	Bernie Parmalee	.40
104	Cris Carter	.20
105	Jack Del Rio	.10
106	Qadry Ismail	.10
107	Warren Moon	.20
108	Jake Reed	.10
109	DeWayne Washington	.10
110	Bruce Armstrong	.10
111	Drew Bledsoe	2.00
112	Vincent Brisby	.10
113	Ben Coates	.10
114	Willie McGinnest	.10
115	David Meggett	.10
116	Chris Slade	.10
117	Mario Bates	.50
118	Quinn Early	.10
119	Jim Everett	.20
120	Michael Haynes	.10
121	Tyrone Hughes	.20
122	Renaldo Turnbull	.10
123	*Ray Zellers*	.50
124	Dave Brown	.10
125	Chris Calloway	.10
126	Rodney Hampton	.20
127	Thomas Lewis	.10
128	Phillippi Sparks	.10
129	*Tyrone Wheatley*	.50
130	*Kyle Brady*	.75
131	Boomer Esiason	.10
132	Aaron Glenn	.10
133	Bobby Houston	.10
134	Mo Lewis	.10
135	Johnny Mitchell	.10
136	Ron Moore	.10
137	Greg Biekert	.10
138	Tim Brown	.20
139	Jeff Hostetler	.20
140	Raghib Ismail	.10
141	*Napoleon Kaufman*	1.00
142	Chester McGlockton	.10
143	Harvey Williams	.10
144	Fred Barnett	.10
145	Randall Cunningham	.10
146	William Fuller	.10
147	Charlie Garner	.10
148	Andy Harmon	.10
149	Ricky Watters	.20
150	Calvin Williams	.10
151	Kevin Greene	.10
152	Charles Johnson	.40
153	Greg Lloyd	.10
154	Bam Morris	.75
155	Neil O'Donnell	.10
156	Darren Perry	.10
157	Rod Woodson	.10
158	Jerome Bettis	.50
159	Isaac Bruce	.50
160	Troy Drayton	.10
161	Sean Gilbert	.10
162	Todd Lyght	.10
163	Chris Miller	.10
164	Andre Coleman	.10
165	Stan Humphries	.20
166	Shawn Jefferson	.10
167	Natrone Means	1.25
168	Leslie O'Neal	.10
169	Junior Seau	.30
170	Mark Seay	.10
171	William Floyd	.60
172	Merton Hanks	.10
173	Brent Jones	.10
174	Jerry Rice	2.00
175	Deion Sanders	1.25
176	*J.J. Stokes*	2.00
177	Lee Woodall	.10
178	Bryant Young	.10
179	Steve Young	1.50
180	Brian Blades	.10
181	*Joey Galloway*	2.00
182	Cortez Kennedy	.10
183	Kevin Mawae	.10
184	Rick Mirer	.50
185	Chris Warren	.20
186	Lawrence Dawsey	.10
187	Trent Dilfer	.75
188	Paul Gruber	.10
189	Hardy Nickerson	.10
190	Errict Rhett	.20
191	*Warren Sapp*	.75
192	Tom Carter	.10
193	Henry Ellard	.10
194	Darrell Green	.10
195	Brian Mitchell	.10
196	Heath Shuler	.30
197	*Michael Westbrook*	1.50
198	Checklist	.10
199	Checklist	.10
200	Checklist	.10

1995 Metal Gold Blasters

This 1995 Fleer Metal set highlights 18 of the players who have had a major impact on the NFL. Cards were randomly inserted into every fifth pack of 1995 Fleer Metal football. The card front has color action photo against a swirled, gold metallic background. The player's name is in a bar at the bottom of the card, next to the brand logo. The card back, numbered 1 of 18, etc., at the bottom, has the insert set icon in the lower left corner. A player profile is in the upper right corner.

		NM/M
Complete Set (18):		35.00
Common Player:		1.00
1	Troy Aikman	3.00
2	Jerome Bettis	2.00
3	Tim Brown	1.00
4	Ben Coates	1.00
5	John Elway	3.00
6	Brett Favre	5.00
7	William Floyd	1.00
8	Joey Galloway	2.00
9	Rodney Hampton	1.00
10	Dan Marino	5.00
11	Steve McNair	3.00
12	Herman Moore	1.00
13	Errict Rhett	1.00
14	Rashaan Salaam	1.00
15	Chris Warren	1.00
16	Michael Westbrook	2.00
17	Rod Woodson	1.00
18	Steve Young	4.00

1995 Metal Platinum Portraits

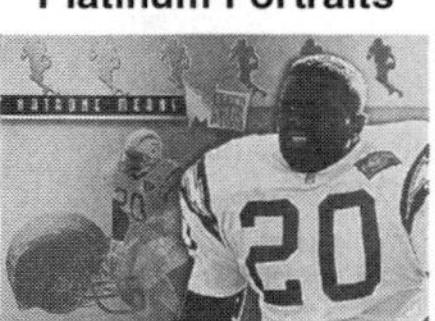

Twelve of the NFL's elite players are featured on these 1995 Fleer Metal insert football cards. Cards, numbered on the back "number x of 12!", were random inserts, one in every ninth pack. The horizontal card front has a color closeup of the player on the left, with ghosted images of his team logo and him in action on the right. The metallic background features his team's primary uniform color. Along the upper top of the card are several player icons, with the player's name and brand logo just below in the right corner. The back has a player profile written towards the top, with small and large icons from the front incorporated into the design.

		NM/M
Complete Set (12):		30.00
Common Player:		1.00
1	Drew Bledsoe	3.00
2	Ki-Jana Carter	1.00
3	Marshall Faulk	3.00
4	Natrone Means	1.00
5	Bam Morris	1.00
6	Jerry Rice	4.00
7	Andre Rison	1.00
8	Barry Sanders	5.00
9	Deion Sanders	3.00
10	Emmitt Smith	5.00
11	J.J. Stokes	2.00
12	Ricky Watters	1.00

1995 Metal Silver Flashers

This 50-card set features some of the NFL's flashiest performers. Cards were random inserts, one every two packs of 1995 Fleer Metal football. The card front has a silver metallic background, with a color action photo superimposed in the foreground. The player's name is in a silver foil panel at the bottom, next to the brand logo in the lower right corner. The back's design has the brand logo incorporated into its design at the top, with a written player profile also included. A card number is in a triangle in the lower left corner.

		NM/M
Complete Set (50):		40.00
Common Player:		.20
Minor Stars:		1.00
1	Troy Aikman	2.00
2	Marcus Allen	.20
3	Jerome Bettis	1.00
4	Drew Bledsoe	2.00
5	Tim Brown	.20
6	Cris Carter	.20
7	Ki-Jana Carter	.40
8	Ben Coates	.20
9	Kerry Collins	1.00
10	Randall Cunningham	1.00
11	Lake Dawson	.20
12	Trent Dilfer	1.00
13	John Elway	2.00
14	Jim Everett	.20
15	Marshall Faulk	2.00
16	Brett Favre	4.00
17	William Floyd	.40
18	Jeff George	.20
19	Rodney Hampton	.20
20	Jeff Hostetler	.20
21	Stan Humphries	.20
22	Michael Irvin	1.00
23	Cortez Kennedy	.20
24	Dan Marino	4.00
25	Terance Mathis	.20
26	Willie McGinnest	.20
27	Natrone Means	.50
28	Rick Mirer	.40
29	Warren Moon	.20
30	Herman Moore	.20
31	Bam Morris	.40
32	Carl Pickens	1.00
33	Errict Rhett	.40
34	Jerry Rice	3.00
35	Andre Rison	.20
36	Rashaan Salaam	.40
37	Barry Sanders	4.00
38	Deion Sanders	1.00
39	Junior Seau	.20
40	Shannon Sharpe	.20
41	Heath Shuler	.40
42	Emmitt Smith	4.00
43	J.J. Stokes	1.00
44	Chris Warren	.20
45	Ricky Watters	.20
46	Michael Westbrook	.40
47	Tyrone Wheatley	.40
48	Reggie White	.20
49	Rod Woodson	.20
50	Steve Young	2.00

1996 Metal

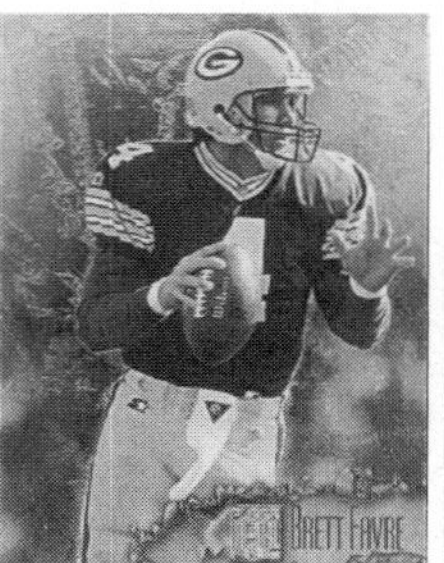

Fleer's 1996 Metal set has an all-new look for 1996 - metalized foil engraved by hand on each card front, meaning no two player cards are alike. The basic set includes 123 regular cards, 25 rookies and two checklists. The card front has a full-bleed color photograph, with the player's name "tearing through" the lower right-hand corner of the card. The back has another photo, a close-cropped headshot bursting through the card, 1995 and career statistics, and biographical information. An extra-rare parallel set - Precious Metal - was also produced. These cards, seeded one per box, feature an all-silver front and were limited to less than 550 each. They are numbered on the back using a PM prefix. There were five other insert sets included in packs - Goldfingers, Goldflingers, Platinum Portraits, Molten Metal and Freshly Forged.

		NM/M
Complete Set (150):		30.00
Common Player:		.10
Minor Stars:		.20
Comp. Precious Metal (148):		800.00
Precious Metal Cards:		10X-20X
Pack (8):		1.25
Wax Box (24):		20.00
1	Garrison Hearst	.10
2	Rob Moore	.10
3	Frank Sanders	.10
4	Eric Swann	.10
5	Jeff George	.20
6	Craig Heyward	.10
7	Terance Mathis	.10
8	Eric Metcalf	.10
9	Derrick Alexander	.10
10	Andre Rison	.10
11	Vinny Testaverde	.10
12	Eric Turner	.10
13	Jim Kelly	.10
14	Bryce Paup	.10
15	Bruce Smith	.10
16	Thurman Thomas	.20
17	Bob Christian	.10
18	Kerry Collins	.40
19	Lamar Lathon	.10
20	Tyrone Poole	.10
21	Curtis Conway	.10
22	Bryan Cox	.10
23	Erik Kramer	.10
24	Rashaan Salaam	.50
25	Jeff Blake	.20
26	Ki-Jana Carter	.50
27	Carl Pickens	.20
28	Darnay Scott	.30
29	Troy Aikman	1.50
30	Michael Irvin	.20
31	Daryl Johnston	.10
32	Deion Sanders	.75
33	Emmitt Smith	3.00
34	Terrell Davis	1.25
35	John Elway	.75
36	Anthony Miller	.10
37	Shannon Sharpe	.10
38	Scott Mitchell	.10
39	Herman Moore	.75
40	Brett Perriman	.10
41	Barry Sanders	2.00
42	Edgar Bennett	.10
43	Robert Brooks	.20
44	Mark Chmura	.30
45	Brett Favre	3.00
46	Reggie White	.20
47	Mel Gray	.10
48	Steve McNair	1.00
49	Chris Sanders	.30
50	Rodney Thomas	.20
51	Quentin Coryatt	.10
52	Sean Dawkins	.10
53	Ken Dilger	.10
54	Marshall Faulk	.75
55	Jim Harbaugh	.20
56	Tony Boselli	.10
57	Mark Brunell	1.00
58	Natrone Means	.20
59	James Stewart	.10
60	Marcus Allen	.20
61	Steve Bono	.20
62	Neil Smith	.10
63	Tamarick Vanover	.20
64	Eric Green	.10
65	Terry Kirby	.10
66	Dan Marino	3.00
67	O.J. McDuffie	.10
68	Cris Carter	.10
69	Qadry Ismail	.10
70	Warren Moon	.10
71	Jake Reed	.10
72	Drew Bledsoe	1.25
73	Ben Coates	.10
74	Curtis Martin	2.50
75	David Meggett	.10
76	Mario Bates	.10
77	Jim Everett	.10
78	Michael Haynes	.10
79	Tyrone Hughes	.10
80	Dave Brown	.10
81	Rodney Hampton	.10
82	Thomas Lewis	.10
83	Tyrone Wheatley	.10
84	Kyle Brady	.10
85	Hugh Douglas	.10
86	Adrian Murrell	.10
87	Neil O'Donnell	.10
88	Tim Brown	.10
89	Jeff Hostetler	.10
90	Napoleon Kaufman	.30
91	Harvey Williams	.10
92	Charlie Garner	.10
93	Rodney Peete	.10
94	Ricky Watters	.10
95	Calvin Williams	.10
96	Jerome Bettis	.20
97	Greg Lloyd	.10
98	Kordell Stewart	1.00
99	Yancey Thigpen	.30
100	Rod Woodson	.10
101	Isaac Bruce	.30
102	Kevin Carter	.10
103	Steve Walsh	.10
104	Aaron Hayden	.10
105	Stan Humphries	.10
106	Junior Seau	.10
107	William Floyd	.10
108	Brent Jones	.10
109	Jerry Rice	1.50
110	J.J. Stokes	.20
111	Steve Young	1.00
112	Brian Blades	.10
113	Joey Galloway	1.00
114	Rick Mirer	.10
115	Chris Warren	.20
116	Trent Dilfer	.10
117	Alvin Harper	.10
118	Hardy Nickerson	.10
119	Errict Rhett	.30
120	Terry Allen	.10
121	Brian Mitchell	.10
122	Heath Shuler	.10
123	Michael Westbrook	.20
124	*Karim Abdul-Jabbar*	.75
125	*Tim Biakabutuka*	.50
126	*Duane Clemons*	.10
127	*Stephen Davis*	4.00
128	*Rickey Dudley*	.75
129	*Bobby Engram*	.50
130	*Daryl Gardener*	.10
131	*Eddie George*	4.00
132	*Terry Glenn*	2.00
133	*Kevin Hardy*	.20
134	*Walt Harris*	.20
135	*Marvin Harrison*	4.00
136	*Keyshawn Johnson*	2.00
137	*Cedric Jones*	.10
138	*Eddie Kennison*	.30
139	*Sam Manuel, Sean Manuel*	.10
140	*Leeland McElroy*	.30
141	*Ray Mickens*	.10
142	*Jonathan Ogden*	.10
143	*Lawrence Phillips*	.75
144	*Kavika Pittman*	.10
145	*Simeon Rice*	.20
146	*Regan Upshaw*	.10
147	*Alex Van Dyke*	.20
148	*Stepfret Williams*	.10
149	Checklist	.10
150	Checklist	.10

1996 Metal Precious Metal

One Precious Metals parallel card was found in each box of Metal Football in 1996. The set included each card in the regular-issue set (minus the two checklists), but featured all-silver fronts and the letters "PM" preceding the card number on the back.

	NM/M
Complete Set (148):	800.00
Precious Metal Cards:	10X-20X

1996 Metal Goldfingers

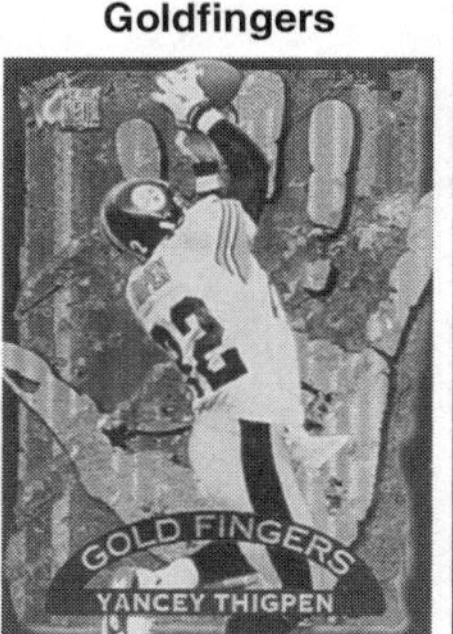

These 24-karat etched gold foil-stamped inserts feature some of the NFL's top-flight receivers. Each card front has a color action photo against a metallic background with an image of a gold hand. The Fleer logo is in the upper left corner. The player's name and "Goldfingers" are in gold foil in an arch at the bottom. The card back, numbered 1 of 10, etc., has a color photo on one side, with the player's name in the upper left corner. A brief player profile is below. Cards were seeded one per every eight packs.

		NM/M
Complete Set (12):		25.00
Common Player:		1.00
1	Isaac Bruce	2.00
2	Joey Galloway	3.00
3	Michael Irvin	2.00
4	Herman Moore	1.00
5	Carl Pickens	1.00
6	Jerry Rice	4.00
7	Chris Sanders	1.00
8	Frank Sanders	1.00
9	J.J. Stokes	2.00
10	Yancey Thigpen	2.00
11	Tamarick Vanover	1.00
12	Michael Westbrook	2.00

1996 Metal Goldflingers

Twelve of the top quarterbacks in football were included in the Goldflingers insert, not to be confused with Goldfingers, which were both out of Metal. Goldflingers was a retail exclusive insert found every 12 packs.

		NM/M
Complete Set (12):		30.00
Common Player:		1.00
1	Troy Aikman	4.00
2	Steve Bono	1.00
3	Kerry Collins	2.00
4	Trent Dilfer	1.00
5	Brett Favre	6.00
6	Gus Frerotte	1.00
7	Stan Humphries	1.00
8	Dan Marino	6.00
9	Steve McNair	4.00
10	Scott Mitchell	1.00
11	Steve Young	5.00
12	Eric Zeier	1.00

1996 Metal Platinum Portraits

This 1996 Fleer Metal set uses the serillusion process to profile 10 NFL stars. The front shows a close-up head shot of the player, using a silvery embossed effect to create depth. The Fleer Metal logo is in the upper left corner; "Platinum Portraits" is written along the right side of the card. The player's name is along the bottom. The horizontal card back shows an image of the photo from the front as a background, with a brief writeup over it. One side of the card has a color action photo on it. The card number, 1 of 12, etc., is in the upper left corner, with the player's name next to it.

		NM/M
Complete Set (10):		60.00
Common Player:		2.00
1	Isaac Bruce	4.00
2	Terrell Davis	6.00
3	John Elway	8.00
4	Joey Galloway	6.00
5	Steve McNair	6.00
6	Errict Rhett	4.00
7	Rashaan Salaam	2.00
8	Barry Sanders	10.00
9	Chris Warren	2.00
10	Steve Young	8.00

1996 Metal Molten Metal

Featuring 10 red-hot superstars, these 1996 Fleer inserts use foil embossing on the front. The Fleer Metal logo is in an upper corner; Molten Metal, in gold foil, is in the lower left corner. The player's name is in gold foil, too, along the right side of the card. The card back, numbered 1 of 10, etc., has a photo on one side. The other side has a white rectangle which includes a brief player profile. The player's name is above the box. These cards were the scarcest of the Fleer Metal inserts; they were seeded one per every 120 packs.

		NM/M
Complete Set (10):		150.00
Common Player:		5.00
1	Troy Aikman	15.00
2	Ki-Jana Carter	5.00
3	Kerry Collins	10.00
4	Terrell Davis	15.00
5	Marshall Faulk	15.00
6	Brett Favre	25.00
7	Keyshawn Johnson	10.00
8	Curtis Martin	15.00
9	Deion Sanders	15.00
10	Emmitt Smith	25.00

1996 Metal Freshly Forged

These 1996 Fleer Metal inserts highlight second-year NFL standouts and flashy rookies. The cards, seeded one per every 30 hobby packs only, are acrylic. The card front has a color action photo on it, with an NFL logo and line drawing of the photo as the background. The Fleer Metal logo is in an upper corner. The player's name and "Freshly Forged" are stamped in gold foil along the bottom. The card back shows the entire NFL logo, with a description of the player's skills inside. A card number, 1 of 10, etc., is also on the back.

		NM/M
Complete Set (10):		60.00
Common Player:		1.00
1	Tim Biakabutuka	1.00
2	Jeff Blake	2.00
3	Ki-Jana Carter	1.00
4	Eddie George	6.00
5	Terry Glenn	3.00
6	Keyshawn Johnson	5.00
7	Curtis Martin	8.00
8	Leeland McElroy	1.00
9	Lawrence Phillips	1.00
10	Kordell Stewart	6.00

1997 Metal

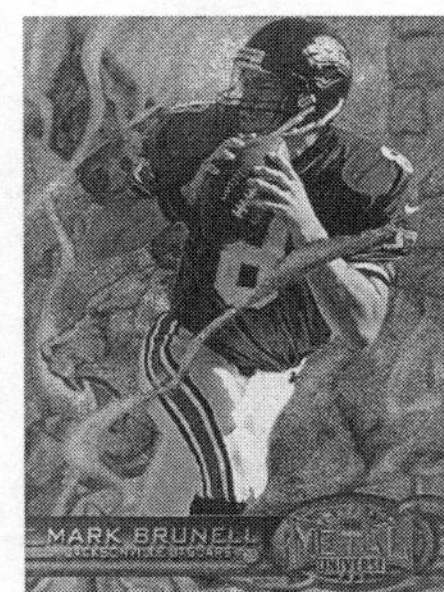

The 200-card set contains 173 player cards, two checklists and 25 rookies. Each card featured all etched foil. The players are presented in original Marvel comic illustrations on full-bleed backgrounds, with the player's name, team, position and Metal Universe logo located near the bottom of the card. Card backs contain another player photo and stats.

		NM/M
Complete Set (200):		30.00
Common Player:		.10
Minor Stars:		.20
Precious Metal Stars:		15X-30X
Precious Metal Rookies:		10X-20X
Pack (8):		2.50
Wax Box (24):		50.00
1	Terry Glenn	.30
2	Terry Kirby	.10
3	Thomas Lewis	.10
4	Tim Biakabutuka	.20
5	Tim Brown	.10
6	Todd Collins	.10
7	Tony Banks	.40
8	Tony Brackens	.10
9	Tony Martin	.10
10	Trent Dilfer	.20
11	Troy Aikman	1.00
12	Ty Detmer	.10
13	Tyrone Wheatley	.10
14	Vinny Testaverde	.10
15	Wayne Chrebet	.10
16	Wesley Walls	.10
17	William Floyd	.10
18	Willie McGinest	.10
19	Yancey Thigpen	.10
20	Zach Thomas	.30
21	Terry Allen	.10
22	Terrell Owens	.50
23	Terrell Davis	1.25
24	Terance Mathis	.10
25	Ted Johnson	.10
26	Tamarick Vanover	.20
27	Steve Young	.75
28	Steve McNair	.75
29	Stan Humphries	.10
30	Simeon Rice	.10
31	Shannon Sharpe	.10
32	Sean Jones	.10
33	Scott Mitchell	.10
34	Sam Mills	.10
35	Rodney Hampton	.10
36	Rod Woodson	.10
37	Robert Smith	.10
38	Rob Moore	.10
39	Ricky Watters	.20
40	Rickey Dudley	.10
41	Rick Mirer	.10
42	Reggie White	.20
43	Ray Zellars	.10
44	Ray Lewis	.10
45	Rashaan Salaam	.20
46	Quentin Coryatt	.10
47	Qadry Ismail	.10
48	O.J. McDuffie	.10
49	Nilo Silvan	.10
50	Neil Smith	.10
51	Neil O'Donnell	.10
52	Natrone Means	.20
53	Napoleon Kaufman	.10
54	Mike Tomczak	.10
55	Mike Alstott	.20
56	Michael Westbrook	.10
57	Michael Jackson	.10
58	Michael Irvin	.20
59	Michael Haynes	.10
60	Michael Bates	.10
61	Mel Gray	.10
62	Marvin Harrison	.50
63	Marshall Faulk	.30
64	Mark Brunell	1.00
65	Mario Bates	.10
66	Marcus Allen	.20
67	Lorenzo Neal	.10
68	Levon Kirkland	.10
69	Leonard Russell	.10
70	Leeland McElroy	.10
71	Lawyer Milloy	.10
72	Lawrence Phillips	.20
73	Larry Centers	.10
74	Lamar Lathon	.10
75	Kordell Stewart	.75
76	Kimble Anders	.10
77	Ki-Jana Carter	.10
78	Keyshawn Johnson	.50
79	Kevin Turner	.10
80	Jermaine Lewis	.10
81	Jerome Bettis	.20
82	Jerris McPhail	.10
83	Joey Galloway	.40
84	Jerry Rice	1.00
85	Jim Everett	.10
86	Jimmy Smith	.10
87	Jim Harbaugh	.10
88	John Elway	.75
89	John Friez	.10
90	John Mobley	.10
91	Johnnie Morton	.10
92	Junior Seau	.10
93	Karim Abdul-Jabbar	.30
94	Keenan McCardell	.10
95	Ken Dilger	.10
96	Ken Norton	.10
97	Kent Graham	.10
98	Kerry Collins	.30
99	Kevin Greene	.10
100	Kevin Hardy	.10
101	Jeff Lewis	.10
102	Jeff George	.10
103	Jeff Graham	.10
104	Jeff Blake	.30
105	Jason Sehorn	.10
106	Jason Dunn	.10
107	Jamie Asher	.10
108	Jamal Anderson	.30
109	Jake Reed	.10
110	Isaac Bruce	.30
111	Irving Fryar	.10
112	Iheanyi Uwaezuoke	.10
113	Hugh Douglas	.10
114	Herman Moore	.20
115	Harvey Williams	.10
116	Hardy Nickerson	.10
117	Gus Frerotte	.10
118	Greg Hill	.10
119	Glyn Milburn	.10
120	Frank Wycheck	.10
121	Frank Sanders	.10
122	Errict Rhett	.20
123	Erik Kramer	.10
124	Eric Moulds	.10
125	Eric Metcalf	.10
126	Emmitt Smith	2.00
127	Edgar Bennett	.10
128	Eddie Kennison	.50
129	Eddie George	1.50
130	Drew Bledsoe	1.00
131	Dorsey Levens	.20
132	Desmond Howard	.10
133	Derrick Thomas	.10
134	Derrick Alexander	.10
135	Deion Sanders	.50
136	Dave Brown	.10
137	Daryl Johnston	.10
138	Darnay Scott	.10
139	Darick Holmes	.10
140	Dan Marino	2.00
141	Curtis Martin	1.25
142	Curtis Conway	.10
143	Cris Carter	.10
144	Chris Warren	.10
145	Chris T. Jones	.10
146	Chris Slade	.10
147	Chris Sanders	.10
148	Chester McGlockton	.10
149	Charlie Jones	.10
150	Charles Way	.10
151	Carl Pickens	.10
152	Bryan Still	.10
153	Bruce Smith	.10
154	Brian Mitchell	.10
155	Brett Perriman	.10
156	Brett Favre	2.50
157	Brad Johnson	.10
158	Thurman Thomas	.20
159	Bobby Engram	.10
160	Bert Emanuel	.10
161	Ben Coates	.10
162	Barry Sanders	1.50
163	Bam Morris	.10
164	Ashley Ambrose	.10
165	Antonio Freeman	.30
166	Anthony Miller	.10
167	Anthony Johnson	.10
168	Andre Rison	.10
169	Andre Reed	.10
170	Alex Molden	.10
171	Aeneas Williams	.10
172	Adrian Murrell	.10
173	Aaron Hayden	.10
174	*Darnell Autry*	.20
175	*Orlando Pace*	.30
176	*Darrell Russell*	.10
177	*Peter Boulware*	.10
178	*Shawn Springs*	.30
179	*Bryant Westbrook*	.10
180	*Dwayne Rudd*	.10
181	*Rae Carruth*	.25
182	*Troy Davis*	.50
183	*Antowain Smith*	2.50
184	*James Farrior*	.10
185	*Walter Jones*	.10
186	*Sam Madison*	.10
187	*Tom Knight*	.10
188	*Reidel Anthony*	1.00
189	*Warrick Dunn*	2.00
190	*Reinard Wilson*	.10
191	*Tyrus McCloud*	.10
192	*Michael Booker*	.10
193	*Tony Gonzalez*	1.25
194	*Pat Barnes*	.30
195	*Tiki Barber*	1.00
196	*Sedrick Shaw*	.50
197	*Corey Dillon*	4.00
198	*Danny Wuerffel*	.40
199	Checklist	.10
200	Checklist	.10

1997 Metal Precious Metal Gems

The 198-card parallel of the base set, not including the two checklists, was randomly seeded in packs. SkyBox produced 150 serial numbered sets. The first 15 cards of the print run were printed with green foil.

Precious Metal Stars:	15X-30X
Precious Metal Rookies:	10X-20X

1997 Metal Autographics Previews

Inserted 1:500 packs, autographed cards of 10 of the 75 NFL players appearing in the debut of the Autographics program are found here.

	NM/M
Common Player:	15.00
Karim Abdul-Jabbar	20.00
Mike Alstott	50.00
Darnell Autry	20.00
Rae Carruth	15.00
Ty Detmer	25.00
Eddie Kennison	20.00
Brian Manning	15.00
Ed McCaffrey	35.00
Jerry Rice	200.00
Shannon Sharpe	40.00
Mike Vrabel	15.00
Chris Warren	15.00

1997 Metal Body Shop

Inserted 1:96 packs, the 15-card set mixes photography and technology. Drew Bledsoe's arm and Jamal Anderson's legs turn bionic on these cards. The cards are numbered with a "BS" prefix.

		NM/M
Complete Set (15):		100.00
Common Player:		3.00
Minor Stars:		20.00
1	Zach Thomas	8.00
2	Steve Young	12.00
3	Steve McNair	12.00
4	Simeon Rice	3.00
5	Shannon Sharpe	4.00
6	Napoleon Kaufman	3.00
7	Mike Alstott	5.00
8	Michael Westbrook	3.00
9	Kordell Stewart	10.00
10	Kevin Hardy	3.00
11	Kerry Collins	6.00
12	Junior Seau	3.00
13	Jamal Anderson	3.00
14	Drew Bledsoe	12.00
15	Deion Sanders	8.00

1997 Metal Gold Universe

The 10-card set was inserted 1:120 retail packs. The players are illustrated in space on the card fronts. The cards are numbered with a "GU" prefix.

		NM/M
Complete Set (10):		100.00
Common Player:		3.00
1	Dan Marino	30.00
2	Deion Sanders	15.00
3	Drew Bledsoe	20.00
4	Isaac Bruce	15.00
5	Joey Galloway	10.00
6	Karim Abdul-Jabbar	5.00
7	Lawrence Phillips	3.00
8	Marshall Faulk	15.00
9	Marvin Harrison	15.00
10	Steve Young	20.00

1997 Metal Iron Rookies

Inserted 1:24 packs, the 15-card set features the top players who were chosen in the 1997 NFL Draft. The cards are numbered with an "IC" prefix.

		NM/M
Complete Set (15):		40.00
Common Player:		1.00
Minor Stars:		5.00
1	Darnell Autry	2.00
2	Orlando Pace	2.00
3	Peter Boulware	1.00
4	Shawn Springs	1.00
5	Bryant Westbrook	2.00
6	Rae Carruth	1.00
7	Troy Davis	1.00
8	Antowain Smith	6.00
9	James Farrior	1.00
10	Dwayne Rudd	2.00
11	Darrell Russell	1.00
12	Warrick Dunn	10.00
13	Sedrick Shaw	1.00
14	Danny Wuerffel	2.00
15	Sam Madison	2.00

1997 Metal Marvel Metal

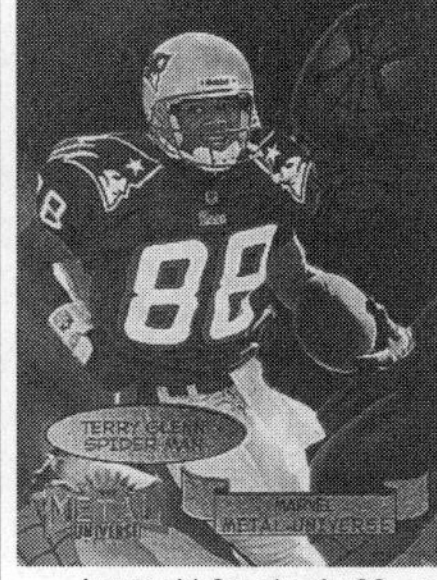

Inserted 1:6 packs, the 20-card set compares the players with Marvel Superheroes. For example, Isaac Bruce is pictured with Spider-Man. The cards are numbered with the "MM" prefix.

		NM/M
Complete Set (20):		20.00
Common Player:		.25
Minor Stars:		2.00
1	Barry Sanders	4.00
2	Bruce Smith	.25
3	Desmond Howard	.25
4	Eddie George	3.00
5	Eddie Kennison	2.50
6	Jerry Rice	3.00
7	Joey Galloway	2.00
8	John Elway	3.00
9	Karim Abdul-Jabbar	.50
10	Kerry Collins	2.00
11	Kevin Hardy	.25
12	Kordell Stewart	2.00
13	Mark Brunell	2.00
14	Marshall Faulk	2.00
15	Michael Westbrook	.25
16	Simeon Rice	.25
17	Steve McNair	3.00
18	Terry Glenn	2.00
19	Tony Brackens	.25
20	Tony Martin	.25

1997 Metal Platinum Portraits

Inserted 1:288 packs, the 10-card set features the players on the card fronts with an etched-foil look. This was the third year for the chase set. The cards are numbered with a "PP" prefix.

		NM/M
Complete Set (10):		200.00
Common Player:		5.00
1	Troy Aikman	20.00
2	Terrell Davis	20.00
3	Marvin Harrison	10.00
4	Keyshawn Johnson	8.00
5	Jerry Rice	25.00
6	Emmitt Smith	30.00
7	Dan Marino	30.00
8	Curtis Martin	15.00
9	Brett Favre	30.00
10	Barry Sanders	30.00

1997 Metal Titanium

Inserted 1:72 hobby packs, the 20-card set featured a titanium background on die-cut cards. The cards are numbered with a "TT" prefix.

		NM/M
Complete Set (20):		200.00
Common Player:		3.00
Minor Stars:		5.00
1	Barry Sanders	20.00
2	Brett Favre	20.00
3	Curtis Martin	10.00
4	Eddie George	10.00
5	Eddie Kennison	3.00
6	Emmitt Smith	20.00
7	Herman Moore	3.00
8	Isaac Bruce	5.00
9	Jerry Rice	15.00
10	John Elway	15.00
11	Keyshawn Johnson	5.00
12	Lawrence Phillips	3.00
13	Mark Brunell	10.00
14	Mike Alstott	5.00
15	Steve McNair	10.00
16	Steve Young	15.00
17	Terrell Davis	15.00
18	Terry Glenn	5.00
19	Tony Banks	5.00
20	Troy Aikman	20.00

1998 Metal Universe

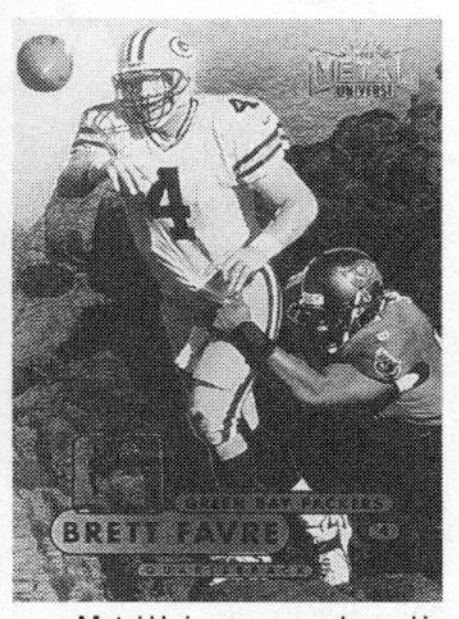

Metal Universe was released in a single series, 200-card set for 1998. The cards featured foil-etched designs in the background pertaining to the player or the city they play in. The set was paralleled in a Precious Metal Gems set. Inserts in Metal Universe include: Decided Edge, E-X2001 Previews, Planet Football, Quasars and Titanium.

		NM/M
Complete Set (200):		35.00
Common Player:		.10
Minor Stars:		.20
Precious Metal Gem Cards:		30X-75X
Precious Metal Gem Rookies:		10X-20X
Pack (8):		3.00
Wax Box (24):		50.00
1	Jerry Rice	1.00
2	Muhsin Muhammad	.10
3	Ed McCaffrey	.10
4	Brett Favre	2.50
5	Troy Brown	.10
6	Brad Johnson	.20
7	John Elway	1.00
8	Herman Moore	.20
9	O.J. McDuffie	.10
10	Tim Brown	.20
11	Byron Hanspard	.10
12	Rae Carruth	.10
13	Rod Smith	.10
14	John Randle	.10
15	Karim Abdul-Jabbar	.20
16	Bobby Hoying	.10
17	Steve Young	.50
18	Andre Hastings	.10
19	Chidi Ahanotu	.10
20	Barry Sanders	2.00
21	Bruce Smith	.10
22	Kimble Anders	.10
23	Troy Davis	.10
24	Jamal Anderson	.10
25	Curtis Conway	.20
26	Mark Chmura	.20
27	Reggie White	.20
28	Jake Reed	.10
29	Willie McGinest	.10
30	Terrell Davis	1.00
31	Joey Galloway	.20
32	Leslie Shepherd	.10
33	Peter Boulware	.10
34	Chad Lewis	.10
35	Marcus Allen	.20
36	Randal Hill	.10
37	Jerome Bettis	.20
38	William Floyd	.10
39	Warren Moon	.20
40	Mike Alstott	.40
41	Jay Graham	.10
42	Emmitt Smith	2.00
43	James Stewart	.10
44	Charlie Garner	.10
45	Merton Hanks	.10
46	Shawn Springs	.10
47	Chris Calloway	.10
48	Larry Centers	.10
49	Michael Jackson	.10
50	Deion Sanders	.50
51	Jimmy Smith	.10
52	Jason Sehorn	.10
53	Charles Johnson	.10
54	Garrison Hearst	.10
55	Chris Warren	.10
56	Warren Sapp	.10
57	Corey Dillon	.75
58	Marvin Harrison	.20
59	Chris Sanders	.10
60	Jamie Asher	.10
61	Yancey Thigpen	.10
62	Freddie Jones	.10
63	Rob Moore	.10
64	Jermaine Lewis	.10
65	Michael Irvin	.20
66	Natrone Means	.20
67	Charles Way	.10
68	Terry Kirby	.10
69	Tony Banks	.20
70	Steve McNair	.50
71	Vinny Testaverde	.10
72	Dexter Coakley	.10
73	Keenan McCardell	.10
74	Glenn Foley	.10
75	Isaac Bruce	.20
76	Terry Allen	.10

77	Todd Collins	.10
78	Troy Aikman	1.00
79	Damon Jones	.10
80	Leon Johnson	.10
81	James Jett	.10
82	Frank Wycheck	.10
83	Andre Reed	.10
84	Derrick Alexander	.10
85	Jason Taylor	.10
86	Wayne Chrebet	.10
87	Napoleon Kaufman	.50
88	Eddie George	1.00
89	Ernie Conwell	.10
90	Antowain Smith	.50
91	Johnnie Morton	.10
92	Jerris McPhail	.10
93	Cris Carter	.10
94	Danny Kanell	.10
95	Stan Humphries	.10
96	Terrell Owens	.10
97	Willie Davis	.10
98	David Dunn	.10
99	Tony Brackens	.10
100	Kordell Stewart	1.00
101	Rodney Thomas	.10
102	Keyshawn Johnson	.20
103	Carl Pickens	.10
104	Mark Brunell	.75
105	Jeff George	.20
106	Bert Emanuel	.10
107	Wesley Walls	.10
108	Bryant Westbrook	.10
109	Dorsey Levens	.20
110	Drew Bledsoe	1.00
111	Adrian Murrell	.20
112	Aeneas Williams	.10
113	Raymont Harris	.10
114	Tony Gonzalez	.20
115	Sean Dawkins	.10
116	Billy Joe Hobert	.10
117	James McKnight	.10
118	Reidel Anthony	.10
119	Terance Mathis	.10
120	Darrien Gordon	.10
121	Dale Carter	.10
122	Duce Staley	.10
123	Jerald Moore	.10
124	Eric Swann	.10
125	Antonio Freeman	.20
126	Chris Penn	.10
127	Ken Dilger	.10
128	Robert Smith	.20
129	Tiki Barber	.30
130	Mark Bruener	.10
131	Junior Seau	.20
132	Trent Dilfer	.20
133	Gus Frerotte	.10
134	Jake Plummer	1.00
135	Jeff Blake	.20
136	Jim Harbaugh	.20
137	Michael Strahan	.10
138	Gary Brown	.10
139	Tony Martin	.10
140	Stephen Davis	.10
141	Thurman Thomas	.20
142	Scott Mitchell	.10
143	Dan Marino	2.00
144	David Palmer	.10
145	J.J. Stokes	.10
146	Chris Chandler	.10
147	Darnell Autry	.20
148	Robert Brooks	.10
149	Derrick Mayes	.10
150	Curtis Martin	.75
151	Steve Broussard	.10
152	Eddie Kennison	.20
153	Kerry Collins	.30
154	Shannon Sharpe	.20
155	Andre Rison	.20
156	Dwayne Rudd	.10
157	Orlando Pace	.10
158	Terry Glenn	.20
159	Frank Sanders	.10
160	Ricky Proehl	.10
161	Marshall Faulk	.20
162	Irving Fryar	.10
163	Courtney Hawkins	.10
164	Eric Metcalf	.10
165	Warrick Dunn	1.00
166	Cris Dishman	.10
167	Fred Lane	.10
168	John Mobley	.10
169	Elvis Grbac	.10
170	Ben Coates	.10
171	Rickey Dudley	.10
172	Ricky Watters	.20
173	*Alonzo Mayes*	.30
174	*Andre Wadsworth*	.50
175	*Brian Simmons*	1.00
176	*Charles Woodson*	3.00
177	*Curtis Enis*	1.00
178	*Fred Taylor*	3.00
179	*Germane Crowell*	1.00
180	*Greg Ellis*	.30
181	*Jacquez Green*	2.00
182	*Jason Peter*	.30
183	*John Dutton*	.30
184	*Kevin Dyson*	2.00
185	*Kivuusama Mays*	.10
186	*Marcus Nash*	.75
187	*Michael Myers*	.10
188	*Ahman Green*	6.00
189	*Peyton Manning*	8.00
190	*Randy Moss*	6.00
191	*Robert Edwards*	1.00
192	*Robert Holcombe*	1.00
193	*Ryan Leaf*	1.00
194	*Takeo Spikes*	.50
195	*Tavian Banks*	1.00
196	*Tim Dwight*	2.00
197	*Vonnie Holliday*	.50
198	Dorsey Levens	.10
199	Jerry Rice	.50
200	Dan Marino	1.00

A player's name in *italic* type indicates a rookie card.

1998 Metal Universe Precious Metal Gems

Precious Metal Gems was a 200-card parallel set found only in hobby packs. Cards were sequentially numbered to 50 sets on the back.

Metal Gem Cards:	30X-75X
Metal Gem Rookies:	10X-20X

1998 Metal Universe Decided Edge

Decided Edge was a 10-card insert that was seeded one per 288 packs. The outside of these cards was silver foil with the player's image etched into it, while the inside could be pulled out to reveal another card of the player. Three circles were cut into the outside of the front, and one circle was on the back - each allowed you to see the inner card. When lined up, the player's face could be seen through each of the circles. Decided Edge inserts were numbered with a "CE" prefix on the inside card.

		NM/M
Complete Set (10):		250.00
Common Player:		10.00
1	Terrell Davis	20.00
2	Brett Favre	35.00
3	John Elway	30.00
4	Barry Sanders	35.00
5	Eddie George	20.00
6	Jerry Rice	30.00
7	Emmitt Smith	35.00
8	Dan Marino	35.00
9	Troy Aikman	30.00
10	Marcus Allen	10.00

1998 Metal Universe E-X2001 Previews

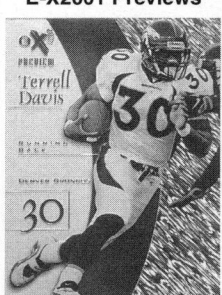

This 15-card insert previewed the upcoming E-X2001 set. Cards featured the two layered, plastic design, but added the word "Preview" in gold foil under the E-X2001 logo. The Metal Universe logo does not appear anywhere on the card. Preview inserts were seeded one per 144 packs. Cards are numbered with a "EX" prefix.

		NM/M
Complete Set (15):		200.00
Common Player:		3.00
Minor Stars:		6.00
1	Barry Sanders	25.00
2	Brett Favre	25.00
3	Corey Dillon	10.00
4	John Elway	20.00
5	Drew Bledsoe	15.00
6	Eddie George	12.00
7	Emmitt Smith	25.00
8	Joey Galloway	3.00
9	Karim Abdul-Jabbar	3.00
10	Kordell Stewart	6.00
11	Mark Brunell	6.00
12	Mike Alstott	6.00
13	Warrick Dunn	6.00
14	Antonio Freeman	3.00
15	Terrell Davis	15.00

1998 Metal Universe Planet Football

Planet Football was a 15-card insert that was seeded one per eight packs. The player's color image was shown over a foil etched background that contained a large football in space. Cards are numbered with a "PF" prefix.

		NM/M
Complete Set (15):		30.00
Common Player:		.50
1	Barry Sanders	4.00
2	Corey Dillon	2.00
3	Warrick Dunn	1.00
4	Jake Plummer	1.00
5	John Elway	3.00
6	Kordell Stewart	2.00
7	Curtis Martin	2.00
8	Mark Brunell	2.00
9	Dorsey Levens	.50
10	Troy Aikman	3.00
11	Terry Glenn	.50
12	Eddie George	2.00
13	Keyshawn Johnson	.50
14	Steve McNair	2.00
15	Jerry Rice	4.00

1998 Metal Universe Quasars

This 15-card set showcased the top rookies from the 1998 NFL Draft. Cards had a color shot of the player in his college uniform over a etched foil background. These were inserted one per 20 packs. Cards are numbered with a "QS" prefix.

		NM/M
Complete Set (15):		60.00
Common Player:		1.00
1	Peyton Manning	12.00
2	Ryan Leaf	2.00
3	Charles Woodson	5.00
4	Randy Moss	12.00
5	Curtis Enis	2.00
6	Tavian Banks	2.00
7	Germane Crowell	1.00
8	Kevin Dyson	4.00
9	Robert Edwards	3.00
10	Jacquez Green	4.00
11	Alonzo Mayes	1.00
12	Brian Simmons	1.00
13	Takeo Spikes	3.00
14	Andre Wadsworth	1.00
15	Ahman Green	8.00

1998 Metal Universe Titanium

Titanium was a 10-card insert printed on a silver holofoil background. The insert name runs up the left side with the letters in circles. These were inserted one per 96 packs. Cards are numbered with a "TM" prefix.

		NM/M
Complete Set (10):		75.00
Common Player:		4.00
1	Corey Dillon	8.00
2	Emmitt Smith	15.00
3	Terrell Davis	10.00
4	Brett Favre	15.00
5	Mark Brunell	6.00
6	Dan Marino	15.00
7	Curtis Martin	8.00
8	Kordell Stewart	5.00
9	Warrick Dunn	5.00
10	Steve McNair	6.00

1999 Metal Universe

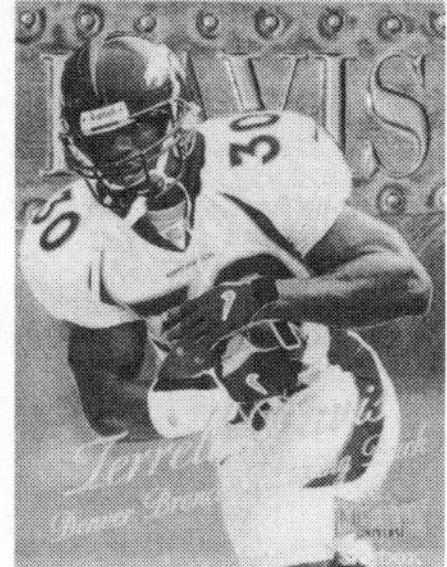

The 250-card base set features each player's name stamped in a steel-look foil across the top and stats laid into another steel motif on the card backs. The 182 player cards are joined by the 25 all-foil "N.F.L.P.D." subset. The base set also includes forty non-seeded rookies and three checklists. Top inserts include: Precious Metal, Gem Masters, Autographics, Linchpins, Planet Metal, Quasars and Starchild.

		NM/M
Complete Set (250):		50.00
Common Player:		.10
Minor Stars:		.20
Common Rookie:		.50
Hobby Pack (8):		2.50
Hobby Wax Box (24):		50.00
1	Eric Moulds	.50
2	David Palmer	.10
3	Ricky Watters	.20
4	Antonio Freeman	.50
5	Hugh Douglas	.10
6	Johnnie Morton	.10
7	Corey Fuller	.10
8	J.J. Stokes	.20
9	Keith Poole	.10
10	Steve Beuerlein	.10
11	Keenan McCardell	.10
12	Carl Pickens	.20
13	Mark Bruener	.10
14	Warren Sapp	.10
15	Rich Gannon	.10
16	Bruce Smith	.10
17	Mark Chmura	.20
18	Drew Bledsoe	.75
19	Charles Woodson	.50
20	Ahman Green	.20
21	Ricky Proehl	.10
22	Corey Dillon	.50
23	Terry Fair	.10
24	Mark Brunell	.75
25	Leroy Hoard	.10
26	La'Roi Glover	.10
27	Tim Brown	.20
28	Kevin Turner	.10
29	Terrell Owens	.50
30	Mike Alstott	.50
31	Rob Moore	.20
32	Troy Aikman	1.00
33	Derrick Alexander	.10
34	Chris Calloway	.10
35	Kordell Stewart	.75
36	Reidel Anthony	.20
37	Michael Westbrook	.20
38	Ray Lewis	.10
39	Alonzo Mayes	.10
40	Rod Smith	.20
41	Reggie Barlow	.10
42	Sean Dawkins	.10
43	Duce Staley	.10
44	R.W. McQuarters	.10
45	Robert Holcombe	.10
46	Priest Holmes	.50
47	Erik Kramer	.10
48	Shannon Sharpe	.20
49	Mike Vanderjagt	.10
50	Cris Carter	.50
51	Billy Joe Tolliver	.10
52	Vinny Testaverde	.20
53	Antonio Langham	.10
54	Damon Gibson	.10
55	Garrison Hearst	.30
56	Brad Johnson	.50
57	Randall Cunningham	.50
58	Jim Harbaugh	.20
59	Curtis Enis	.50
60	Bill Romanowski	.10
61	Marcus Pollard	.10
62	Zach Thomas	.20
63	Cameron Cleeland	.20
64	Curtis Martin	.50
65	Charlie Garner	.10
66	Jerris McPhail	.10
67	Jon Kitna	.75
68	Chris Chandler	.20
69	Emmitt Smith	1.50
70	Andre Rison	.20
71	Wayne Chrebet	.50
72	Mikhael Ricks	.10
73	Yancey Thigpen	.20
74	Peter Boulware	.10
75	Bobby Engram	.10
76	John Mobley	.10
77	Peyton Manning	1.50
78	O.J. McDuffie	.20
79	Tony Simmons	.20
80	Mo Lewis	.10
81	Bryan Still	.10
82	Eugene Robinson	.10
83	Curtis Conway	.20
84	Ed McCaffrey	.30
85	Marvin Harrison	.30
86	Dan Marino	1.50
87	Ty Law	.10
88	Leon Johnson	.10
89	Junior Seau	.20
90	Terance Mathis	.10
91	Wesley Walls	.10
92	John Elway	1.50
93	Marshall Faulk	.50
94	Oronde Gadsden	.20
95	Keyshawn Johnson	.50
96	Muhsin Muhammad	.10
97	Dorsey Levens	.50
98	Shawn Jefferson	.10
99	Rocket Ismail	.10
100	Vonnie Holliday	.20
101	Terry Glenn	.30
102	Shawn Springs	.10
103	Tim Dwight	.50
104	Terrell Davis	1.00
105	Karim Abdul	.30
106	Bryan Cox	.10
107	Steve McNair	.75
108	Tony Martin	.10
109	Jason Elam	.10
110	John Avery	.20
111	Aaron Glenn	.10
112	Eddie George	.75
113	Larry Centers	.10
114	Darnay Scott	.10
115	Jimmy Smith	.20
116	Tiki Barber	.10
117	Charles Johnson	.10
118	Mike Archie	.10
119	Adrian Murrell	.10
120	Dexter Coakley	.10
121	Dale Carter	.10
122	Kent Graham	.10
123	Hines Ward	.20
124	Greg Hill	.10
125	Skip Hicks	.50
126	Doug Flutie	.75
127	Leslie Shepherd	.10
128	Neil O'Donnell	.20
129	Herman Moore	.50
130	Kevin Hardy	.10
131	Randy Moss	2.00
132	Andre Hastings	.10
133	Rickey Dudley	.10
134	Jerome Bettis	.50
135	Jerry Rice	1.00
136	Jake Plummer	.50
137	Billy Davis	.10
138	Tony Gonzalez	.20
139	Ike Hilliard	.20
140	Freddie Jones	.10
141	Isaac Bruce	.30
142	Darrell Green	.10
143	Trent Green	.50
144	Jamal Anderson	.50
145	Deion Sanders	.50
146	Bam Morris	.20
147	Charles Way	.10
148	Natrone Means	.30
149	Frank Wycheck	.10
150	Brett Favre	2.00
151	Michael Bates	.10
152	Ben Coates	.20
153	Koy Detmer	.10
154	Eddie Kennison	.10
155	Eric Metcalf	.10
156	Takeo Spikes	.10
157	Fred Taylor	.50
158	Gary Brown	.10
159	Levon Kirkland	.10
160	Trent Dilfer	.30
161	Antowain Smith	.50
162	Robert Brooks	.10
163	Robert Smith	.50
164	Napoleon Kaufman	.50
165	Chad Brown	.10
166	Warrick Dunn	.75
167	Joey Galloway	.50
168	Frank Sanders	.20
169	Michael Irvin	.20
170	Elvis Grbac	.20
171	Michael Strahan	.10
172	Ryan Leaf	.50
173	Stephen Alexander	.10
174	Andre Reed	.10
175	Barry Sanders	2.00
176	Jake Reed	.10
177	James Jett	.10
178	Steve Young	.75
179	Jermaine Lewis	.20
180	Charlie Batch	.75
181	Jacquez Green	.20
182	Kevin Dyson	.20
183	Roell Preston	.10
184	Randall Cunningham	.20
185	Charlie Batch	.20
186	Kordell Stewart	.20
187	Bennie Thompson	.10
188	Deion Sanders	.20
189	Jake Plummer	.50
190	Eric Moulds	.20
191	Derrick Brooks	.10
192	Steve McNair	.20
193	Ryan Leaf	.20
194	Keyshawn Johnson	.20
195	Eddie George	.20
196	Warrick Dunn	.20
197	Jessie Tuggle	.10
198	Rodney Harrison	.10
199	Vinny Testaverde	.10
200	Marshall Faulk	.20
201	Ray Buchanon	.10
202	Garrison Hearst	.10
203	John Randle	.10
204	Drew Bledsoe	.50
205	Sam Gash	.10
206	Troy Aikman	.50
207	Michael McCrary	.10
208	*Chris Claiborne*	1.00
209	*Ricky Williams*	10.00
210	*Tim Couch*	5.00
211	*Champ Bailey*	1.50
212	*Torry Holt*	3.00
213	*Donovan McNabb*	6.00
214	*David Boston*	3.00
215	*Chris McAlister*	.75
216	*Aaron Gibson*	.50
217	*Daunte Culpepper*	6.00
218	*Matt Stinchcomb*	.50
219	*Edgerrin James*	8.00
220	*Jevon Kearse*	4.00
221	*Ebenezer Ekuban*	.50
222	*Kris Farris*	.50
223	*Chris Terry*	.50
224	*Cecil Collins*	1.00
225	*Akili Smith*	3.00
226	*Shaun King*	2.00
227	*Rahim Abdullah*	.50
228	*Peerless Price*	3.00
229	*Antoine Winfield*	.50
230	*Antwan Edwards*	.50
231	*Rob Konrad*	.75
232	*Troy Edwards*	2.00
233	*John Thornton*	.50
234	*Fred Vinson*	.50
235	*Gary Stills*	.50
236	*Desmond Clark*	.50
237	*Lamar King*	.50
238	*Jared DeVries*	.50
239	*Martin Gramatica*	.50
240	*Montae Reagor*	.50
241	*Andy Katzenmoyer*	1.00
242	*Rufus French*	.50
243	*D'Wayne Bates*	.75
244	*Amos Zereoue*	1.00
245	*Dre' Bly*	.75
246	*Kevin Johnson*	3.00
247	*Cade McNown*	2.00
248	Kordell Stewart	.20
249	Deion Sanders	.20
250	Vinny Testaverde	.10

1999 Metal Universe Precious Metal Gem

This is a 250-card parallel to the base that is sequentially numbered to 50.

	NM/M
Precious Metal Cards:	25X-60X
Precious Metal Rookies:	10X-20X
Production 50 Sets	

1999 Metal Universe Linchpins

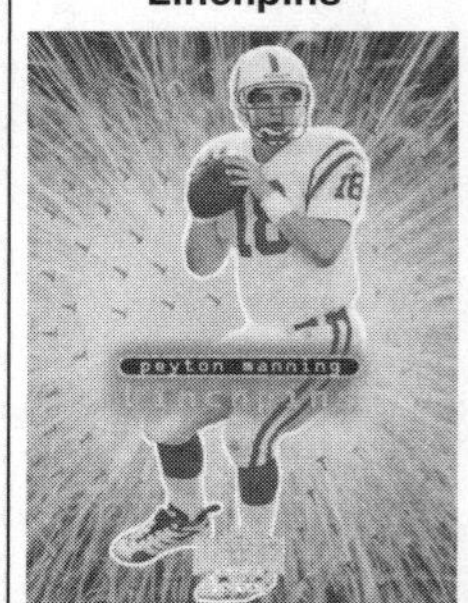

This 10-card set spotlights a laser die-cut design and highlights key players who hold their teams together on the field and in the clubhouse. Singles were found 1:360 packs.

		NM/M
Complete Set (10):		200.00
Common Player:		10.00
Inserted 1:360		
1	Emmitt Smith	30.00
2	Charlie Batch	10.00
3	Fred Taylor	15.00
4	Jake Plummer	15.00
5	Brett Favre	30.00
6	Barry Sanders	30.00
7	Mark Brunell	15.00
8	Peyton Manning	25.00
9	Randy Moss	25.00
10	Terrell Davis	20.00

1999 Metal Universe Planet Metal

Each player in this 15-card set is printed on a die-cut card that features a metallic view of the planet. Singles were inserted 1:36 packs.

		NM/M
Complete Set (15):		75.00
Common Player:		2.00
Inserted 1:36		
1	Terrell Davis	8.00
2	Troy Aikman	10.00
3	Peyton Manning	10.00
4	Mark Brunell	5.00
5	John Elway	10.00
6	Doug Flutie	3.00
7	Dan Marino	12.00
8	Brett Favre	12.00
9	Barry Sanders	12.00
10	Emmitt Smith	12.00
11	Fred Taylor	6.00
12	Jerry Rice	10.00
13	Jamal Anderson	2.00
14	Randall Cunningham	2.00
15	Randy Moss	10.00

1999 Metal Universe Quasars

This 15-card set features the top rookies from 1999 and puts them on a silver rainbow holofoil card. They were inserted 1:18 packs.

		NM/M
Complete Set (15):		50.00
Common Player:		1.00
Inserted 1:18		
1	Ricky Williams	15.00
2	Tim Couch	10.00
3	Shaun King	3.00
4	Champ Bailey	3.00
5	Torry Holt	5.00
6	Donovan McNabb	8.00
7	David Boston	6.00
8	Andy Katzenmoyer	1.00
9	Daunte Culpepper	8.00
10	Edgerrin James	10.00
11	Cade McNown	3.00
12	Troy Edwards	4.00
13	Akili Smith	3.00
14	Peerless Price	6.00
15	Amos Zereoue	4.00

1999 Metal Universe Starchild

This 20-card insert has a young star theme to it and prints each player on a silver rainbow holofoil background. Singles were found 1:6 packs.

		NM/M
Complete Set (20):		15.00
Common Player:		.50
Minor Stars:		1.00
Inserted 1:6		
1	Skip Hicks	1.00
2	Mike Alstott	1.00
3	Joey Galloway	1.00
4	Tony Simmons	.50
5	Jamal Anderson	1.00
6	John Avery	.50
7	Charles Woodson	1.00
8	Jon Kitna	1.00
9	Marshall Faulk	2.00
10	Eric Moulds	1.00
11	Keyshawn Johnson	1.00
12	Ryan Leaf	.50
13	Curtis Enis	.50
14	Steve McNair	1.00
15	Corey Dillon	1.00
16	Tim Dwight	1.00
17	Brian Griese	2.00
18	Drew Bledsoe	3.00
19	Eddie George	2.00
20	Terrell Owens	2.00

2000 Metal

		NM/M
Complete Set (300):		75.00
Common Player:		.15
Minor Stars:		.30
Common Rookie (#201-250):		.50
Common Rookie (#251-300):		1.00
Inserted 1:2		
Pack (10):		2.00
Wax Box (24):		35.00
1	Tim Couch	.75
2	Olandis Gary	.50
3	Andre Hastings	.15
4	Donovan McNabb	.75
5	Bobby Engram	.15
6	Bert Emanuel	.15
7	Levon Kirkland	.15
8	Chris Chandler	.30
9	Herman Moore	.30
10	Jeff Blake	.30
11	Cortez Kennedy	.15
12	Antowain Smith	.30
13	Marvin Harrison	.50
14	Bryant Young	.15
15	Peerless Price	.30
16	Peyton Manning	1.75
17	Darrell Russell	.15
18	Darrell Green	.15
19	James Allen	.30
20	Tedy Bruschi	.15
21	Jon Kitna	.50
22	Doug Flutie	.75
23	Bill Schroeder	.15
24	Curtis Martin	.50
25	Kevin Lockett	.15
26	Errict Rhett	.30
27	Kevin Faulk	.30
28	J.J. Stokes	.30
29	Jonathon Linton	.30
30	Jimmy Smith	.50
31	Brian Dawkins	.15
32	Michael Westbrook	.30
33	Randall Cunningham	.30
34	Oronde Gadsden	.30
35	Shawn Springs	.15
36	Shannon Sharpe	.30
37	Terrence Wilkins	.30
38	Aaron Glenn	.15
39	Torrance Small	.15
40	Sean Dawkins	.15
41	Terrell Davis	1.25
42	Ike Hilliard	.30
43	Warrick Dunn	.50
44	Jeremiah Trotter	.15
45	O.J. McDuffie	.30
46	Richard Huntley	.30
47	Aeneas Williams	.15
48	Raghib Ismail	.30
49	Terry Glenn	.50
50	Derrick Mayes	.30
51	Wayne Chrebet	.50
52	Kevin Dyson	.30
53	Takeo Spikes	.15
54	Matthew Hatchette	.30
55	Shawn Bryson	.15
56	Qadry Ismail	.15
57	Jerome Pathon	.15
58	Rich Gannon	.30
59	Stephen Davis	.50
60	Marcus Robinson	.50
61	Damon Huard	.30
62	Junior Seau	.30
63	Curtis Enis	.30
64	Tony Richardson	.15
65	Troy Edwards	.30
66	Robert Brooks	.15
67	Antonio Freeman	.50
68	Kerry Collins	.30
69	Jacquez Green	.15
70	Akili Smith	.50
71	Zach Thomas	.30
72	Kordell Stewart	.60
73	Deion Sanders	.50
74	David Patten	.15
75	Drew Bledsoe	.75
76	Shaun King	.50
77	Eddie Kennison	.15
78	Stacey Mack	.15
79	Jim Harbaugh	.30
80	Shawn Jefferson	.15
81	James Stewart	.50
82	Pete Mitchell	.15
83	Mike Alstott	.50
84	Marty Booker	.15
85	Hardy Nickerson	.15
86	Charles Johnson	.15
87	Jeff George	.30
88	Jermaine Lewis	.15
89	Edgerrin James	1.00
90	Rickey Dudley	.15
91	Eddie George	.60
92	Darren Woodson	.15
93	Willie McGinest	.15
94	Jeff Garcia	.50
95	Eric Moulds	.50
96	Tony Brackens	.15
97	Charles Woodson	.50
98	Warren Sapp	.30
99	Corey Dillon	.50
100	Tony Martin	.15
101	Bruce Smith	.15
102	Troy Aikman	1.00
103	Daunte Culpepper	1.00
104	Christian Fauria	.15
105	Steve Beuerlein	.30
106	Fred Taylor	.75
107	Ricky Watters	.30
108	Brian Mitchell	.15
109	Emmitt Smith	1.25
110	Robert Smith	.50
111	Jerry Rice	1.00
112	Priest Holmes	1.00
113	Jay Fiedler	.30
114	Curtis Conway	.30
115	Jamal Anderson	.50
116	E.G. Green	.15
117	Kent Graham	.15
118	Frank Wycheck	.15
119	Jake Plummer	.50
120	Randy Moss	1.25
121	Charlie Garner	.30
122	Frank Sanders	.30
123	Germane Crowell	.50
124	Jason Sehorn	.15
125	Marshall Faulk	.50
126	David Sloan	.15
127	Cris Carter	.50
128	Robert Chancey	.15
129	Tony Banks	.30
130	Ken Dilger	.15
131	Dedric Ward	.30
132	Yancey Thigpen	.30
133	Jeremy McDaniel	.15
134	John Randle	.30
135	Jerome Bettis	.50
136	Tim Dwight	.50
137	Charlie Batch	.50
138	Mark Brunell	.75
139	Tyrone Wheatley	.30
140	Champ Bailey	.30
141	Brian Griese	.60
142	Keith Poole	.15
143	Kurt Warner	1.75
144	Tim Biakabutuka	.30
145	Elvis Grbac	.30
146	Cade McNown	.50
147	Albert Connell	.30
148	Donald Driver	.30
149	Donald Hayes	.30
150	Terrell Owens	.50
151	Johnnie Morton	.30
152	Tiki Barber	.50
153	Keyshawn Johnson	.50
154	Carl Pickens	.30
155	Thurman Thomas	.30
156	Jeff Graham	.15
157	Peter Boulware	.15
158	Brett Favre	2.00
159	Vinny Testaverde	.30
160	Derrick Brooks	.15
161	Wesley Walls	.30
162	Derrick Alexander	.15
163	Duce Staley	.50
164	Troy Brown	.15
165	Keenan McCardell	.30
166	James Jett	.15
167	Simeon Rice	.15
168	Rod Smith	.50
169	Ricky Williams	1.25
170	Az-Zahir Hakim	.30
171	Muhsin Muhammad	.30
172	Andre Rison	.30
173	Tim Brown	.50
174	Brad Johnson	.30
175	Darrin Chiaverini	.15
176	Jake Reed	.30
177	Kevin Carter	.15
178	Jay Riemersma	.15
179	Tony Gonzalez	.30
180	Hines Ward	.30
181	David Boston	.50
182	Ed McCaffrey	.30
183	Amani Toomer	.30
184	Torry Holt	.50
185	Rob Johnson	.30
186	Kevin Hardy	.15
187	Napoleon Kaufman	.50
188	Jevon Kearse	.50
189	Terance Mathis	.15
190	Dorsey Levens	.50
191	Kyle Brady	.15
192	Steve McNair	.50
193	Kevin Johnson	.30
194	Lamar Smith	.15
195	Ryan Leaf	.50
196	Rod Woodson	.15
197	Corey Bradford	.15
198	Joe Horn	.30
199	Isaac Bruce	.50
200	Steve Young, Dan Marino	1.50
201	*Demario Brown*	.50
202	*Chad Morton*	1.50
203	*Quinton Spotwood*	.50
204	*Mike Anderson*	3.00
205	*Jarious Jackson*	1.25
206	*Hank Poteat*	.75
207	*Rogers Beckett*	.50
208	*Deon Dyer*	.50
209	*Charles Lee*	.75
210	*Barrett Green*	.50
211	*T.J. Slaughter*	.75
212	*Chris Hovan*	.75
213	*Mark Simoneau*	.50
214	*Rashard Anderson*	1.25
215	*Trevor Insley*	.50
216	*Paul Smith*	.75
217	*Doug Johnson*	1.50
218	*Dwayne Goodrich*	.50
219	*Julian Peterson*	.75
220	*Keith Bulluck*	.50
221	*Chris Samuels*	1.00
222	*Shaun Ellis*	.75
223	*Na'il Diggs*	1.00
224	*William Bartee*	.50
225	*John Abraham*	.50
226	*Trevor Gaylor*	1.25
227	*Dante Hall*	4.00
228	*Marcus Knight*	.50
229	*Patrick Pass*	.75
230	*Bashir Yamini*	.50
231	*Deltha O'Neal*	.75
232	*Vaughn Sanders*	.50
233	*Todd Husak*	1.50
234	*Thomas Hamner*	.50
235	*Chafie Fields*	1.00
236	*Orantes Grant*	.50
237	*Muneer Moore*	.50
238	*Kwame Cavil*	.75
239	*Spergon Wynn*	1.25
240	*Leon Murray*	.50
241	*Rob Morris*	1.00
242	*Ben Kelly*	.50
243	*Darren Howard*	.75
244	*Raynoch Thompson*	1.00
245	*Mike Green*	.50
246	*Sammy Morris*	1.75
247	*Ahmed Plummer*	1.00
248	*Ian Gold*	.75
249	*Chris Coleman*	.50
250	*Ron Dixon*	1.75
251	*Peter Warrick*	4.00
252	*Joe Hamilton*	1.50
253	*Dennis Northcutt*	1.50
254	*Laveranues Coles*	4.00
255	*Michael Wiley*	1.50
256	*Plaxico Burress*	5.00
257	*Danny Farmer*	1.50
258	*Aaron Shea*	1.00
259	*Sebastian Janikowski*	1.50
260	*Corey Simon*	1.50
261	*Frank Murphy*	1.00
262	*JaJuan Dawson*	1.50
263	*Ron Dayne*	2.00
264	*Tim Rattay*	3.00
265	*Troy Walters*	1.25
266	*J.R. Redmond*	2.00
267	*Tom Brady*	12.00
268	*Jamal Lewis*	6.00
269	*Anthony Lucas*	1.00
270	*Reuben Droughns*	2.00
271	*James Williams*	1.00
272	*Shyrone Stith*	1.00
273	*Jerry Porter*	4.00
274	*Brian Urlacher*	5.00
275	*Avion Black*	1.00
276	*Thomas Jones*	2.00
277	*Chad Pennington*	10.00
278	*Travis Prentice*	2.00
279	*Chris Redman*	3.00
280	*Travis Taylor*	2.00
281	*Giovanni Carmazzi*	1.50
282	*Sherrod Gideon*	1.00
283	*Bubba Franks*	1.50
284	*Sylvester Morris*	2.00
285	*Curtis Keaton*	1.00
286	*Frank Moreau*	1.25
287	*Terrelle Smith*	1.00
288	*Shaun Alexander*	6.00
289	*Tee Martin*	1.50
290	*R. Jay Soward*	1.50
291	*Dez White*	1.25
292	*Trung Canidate*	1.25
293	*Darrell Jackson*	1.50
294	*Marc Bulger*	1.00
295	*Courtney Brown*	1.50
296	*Todd Pinkston*	1.50
297	*Anthony Becht*	1.25
298	*Doug Chapman*	1.00
299	*Gari Scott*	1.00
300	*Chris Cole*	1.00

2000 Metal Emerald

	NM/M
Emerald Cards:	2X-4X
Inserted 1:4	
Emerald Rookies (#201-250):	2X
Emerald Rookies (#251-300):	1X
Inserted 1:7	

2000 Metal Heavy Metal

		NM/M
Complete Set (10):		30.00
Common Player:		1.50
Inserted 1:20		
1	Emmitt Smith	5.00
2	Randy Moss	6.00
3	Kurt Warner	7.00
4	Keyshawn Johnson	1.50
5	Ricky Williams	3.00
6	Peyton Manning	6.00
7	Edgerrin James	6.00
8	Peter Warrick	6.00
9	Brett Favre	7.00
10	Tim Couch	2.50

2000 Metal Hot Commodities

		NM/M
Complete Set (10):		20.00
Common Player:		1.25
Inserted 1:14		
1	Kurt Warner	3.00
2	Jerry Rice	4.00
3	Terrell Davis	3.00
4	Peyton Manning	3.00
5	Stephen Davis	1.25
6	Brett Favre	4.00
7	Ron Dayne	1.00
8	Troy Aikman	3.00
9	Edgerrin James	2.50
10	Eddie George	1.75

2000 Metal Steel of the Draft

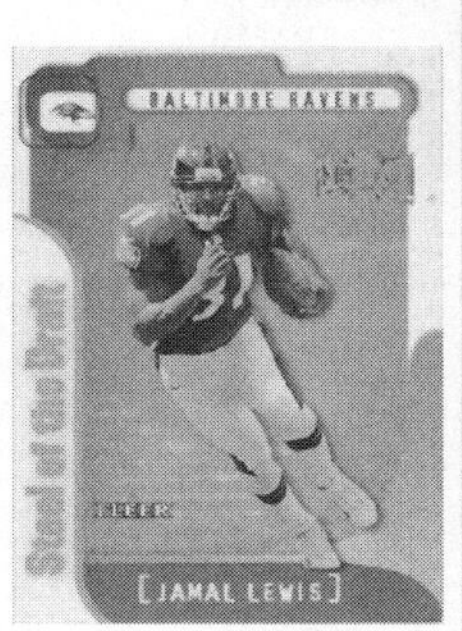

		NM/M
Complete Set (10):		25.00
Common Player:		1.00
Inserted 1:28		
1	Peter Warrick	2.00
2	Ron Dayne	2.00
3	Plaxico Burress	3.50
4	Thomas Jones	3.00
5	Jamal Lewis	5.00
6	Shaun Alexander	5.00
7	Chad Pennington	6.00
8	Travis Taylor	1.00
9	Chris Redman	3.00
10	J.R. Redmond	1.00

2000 Metal Sunday Showdown

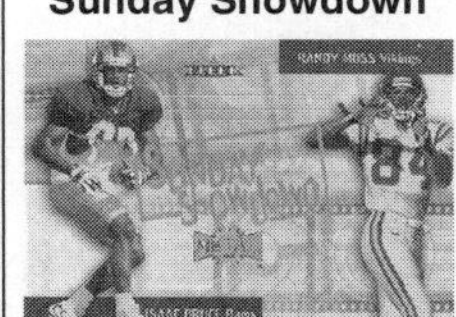

		NM/M
Complete Set (15):		18.00
Common Player:		1.00
Inserted 1:4		
1	Emmitt Smith, Stephen Davis	2.25
2	Mark Brunell, Tim Couch	1.50
3	Randy Moss, Isaac Bruce	2.00
4	Shaun King, Akili Smith	1.00
5	Peter Warrick, Plaxico Burress	2.00
6	Chad Pennington, Peyton Manning	2.50
7	Ricky Williams, Edgerrin James	2.00
8	Marshall Faulk, Jamal Anderson	1.00
9	Troy Aikman, Donovan McNabb	2.00
10	Daunte Culpepper, Cade McNown	1.75
11	Terrell Davis, Shaun Alexander	1.50
12	Brett Favre, Brad Johnson	3.00
13	Jevon Kearse, Fred Taylor	1.25
14	Thomas Jones, Ron Dayne	1.50
15	Jerry Rice, Keyshawn Johnson	2.00

1992 Metallic Images Tins

These collector's tins were used to package two decks of playing cards. Two active quarterbacks and two Hall of Famers were selected for the tins. The Marino and Moon tins have playing cards which incorporate the Quarterback Club logo into the design; the other two use a Quarterback Legends emblem on the card front. The unnumbered tins were produced by Metallic Images Inc. and were sold in 7-Eleven stores to benefit the Children's Miracle Network.

		NM/M
Complete Set (4):		15.00
Common Player:		3.00
1	Dan Marino	10.00
2	Warren Moon	4.00
3	Y.A. Tittle	3.00
4	Johnny Unitas	5.00

1993 Metallic Images QB Legends

These metal cards, honoring 20 star NFL quarterbacks, each measures 2-9/16" x 3-9/16" and was included inside a special collectors tin. Metallic Images produced the cards; each has a color action shot against a team color-coded background with gold stripes running through it. The player's team logo, uniform number and mug shot are also featured on the front. The back is numbered and gives a career summary of the player, framed by a team color-coded border. There were 49,000 numbered sets produced; each includes a certificate of authenticity.

		NM/M
Complete Set (20):		35.00
Common Player:		1.50
1	Steve Bartkowski	1.50
2	John Brodie	2.50
3	Charley Conerly	2.50
4	Lynn Dickey	1.50
5	Tom Flores	2.00
6	Roman Gabriel	2.00
7	Bob Griese	5.00
8	Steve Grogan	1.50
9	James Harris	1.50
10	Jim Hart	1.50
11	Sonny Jurgensen	3.00
12	Billy Kilmer	2.00
13	Daryle Lamonica	2.50
14	Archie Manning	3.00
15	Craig Morton	1.50
16	Dan Pastorini	1.50
17	Jim Plunkett	2.50
18	Y.A. Tittle	5.00
19	Johnny Unitas	7.50
20	Danny White	2.00

1985 Miller Lite Beer

Measuring 4-3/4" x 7", the eight-card set is anchored on the front with a large player photo. The player's name, position, team helmet, player bio and NFL/Lite logo are beneath the photo. The card backs, which are unnumbered, have the Lite logo in the upper left, with the player's name and position on the upper right. The player's highlights on the field and off the field are printed at the bottom of the card.

		NM/M
Complete Set (6):		150.00
Common Player:		15.00
1	Larry Csonka	35.00
2	John Hadl (CO)	15.00
3	Freeman McNeil (NFL Man of the Year)	15.00
4	Jack Reynolds (Lite Beer All-Stars)	15.00
5	Steve Young (USFL Man of the Year)	80.00
6	1985 LA Express (Cheerleaders)	15.00

1988 Monte Gum

Monte Gum, in Europe, produced these 100 cards along with an album to hold them. The cards, 1-15/16" x 2-3/4", feature a generic team action photo and caption describing the play on the front. A card number is also included on the front, which has a yellow border around the photo. The backs are blank.

	NM/M
Complete Set (100):	85.00

Common Player:		1.00
1	Atlanta Falcons	1.75
2	Atlanta Falcons	1.00
3	Atlanta Falcons	1.00
4	Buffalo Bills	1.00
5	Chicago Bears	1.25
6	Chicago Bears	1.00
7	Cincinnati Bengals	1.00
8	Cincinnati Bengals	1.00
9	Cincinnato Bengals	5.00
10	Cincinnati Bengals	1.00
11	Cincinnati Bengals	1.50
12	Cleveland Browns	1.00
13	Cleveland Browns	2.50
14	Cleveland Browns	1.00
15	Cleveland Browns	1.00
16	Dallas Cowboys	1.00
17	Dallas Cowboys	1.25
18	Dallas Cowboys	1.25
19	Denver Broncos	1.00
20	Denver Broncos	1.00
21	Denver Broncos	2.00
22	Detroit Lions	1.00
23	Green Bay Packers	1.00
24	Green Bay Packers	1.00
25	Houston Oilers	1.00
26	Houston Oilers	1.00
27	Indianapolis Colts	1.00
28	Kansas City Chiefs	1.00
29	Kansas City Chiefs	1.00
30	Kansas City Chiefs	1.25
31	Los Angeles Raiders	1.00
32	Los Angeles Raiders	1.00
33	Los Angeles Raiders	1.00
34	Los Angeles Raiders	2.00
35	Los Angeles Rams	1.00
36	Los Angeles Rams	2.00
37	Los Angeles Rams	1.00
38	Miami Dolphins	1.25
39	Miami Dolphins	1.25
40	Minnesota Vikings	1.00
41	Minnesota Vikings	1.00
42	New England Patriots	1.00
43	New England Patriots	1.25
44	New England Patriots	3.00
45	New Orleans Saints	1.50
46	New Orleans Saints (photo actually shows Washington and Michigan in '81 Rose Bowl game)	1.25
47	New York Giants	1.25
48	New York Giants	1.00
49	New York Jets	1.00
50	New York Jets	1.00
51	Philadelphia Eagles	1.00
52	Philadelphia Eagles	1.00
53	Philadelphia Eagles	1.00
54	Philadelphia Eagles	1.00
55	Pittsburgh Steelers	1.00
56	Pittsburgh Steelers	1.50
57	Pittsburgh Steelers	1.00
58	St. Louis Cardinals	1.00
59	St. Louis Cardinals	1.00
60	St. Louis Cardinals	1.00
61	St. Louis Cardinals	1.00
62	San Diego Chargers	1.00
63	San Diego Chargers	1.00
64	San Diego Chargers	1.25
65	San Diego Chargers	1.00
66	San Francisco 49ers	1.00
67	San Francisco 49ers	1.25
68	San Francisco 49ers	10.00
69	San Francisco 49ers	1.25
70	Seattle Seahawks	1.00
71	Seattle Seahawks	1.00
72	Tampa Bay Buccaneers	1.00
73	Tampa Bay Buccaneers	1.00
74	Tampa Bay Buccaneers	1.00
75	Tampa Bay Buccaneers	1.00
76	Washington Redskins	1.00
77	Washington Redskins	1.00
78	Washington Redskins	1.00
79	Washington Redskins	1.00
80	Official NFL Football	1.00
81	Helmets: Falcons/Bills	1.00
82	Helmets: Bears/Bengals	1.00
83	Helmets: Browns/ Cowboys	1.00
84	Helmets: Broncos/Lions	1.00
85	Helmets: Packers/Oilers	1.00
86	Helmets: Colts/Chiefs	1.00
87	Helmets: Raiders/Rams	1.00
88	Helmets: Dolphins/Vikings	1.00
89	Helmets: Patriots/Saints	1.00
90	Helmets: Giants/Jets	1.00
91	Philadelphia Eagles Helmet	1.00
92	Pittsburgh Steelers Helmet	1.00
93	St. Louis Cardinals Helmet	1.00
94	San Diego Chargers Helmet	1.00
95	San Francisco 49ers Helmet	1.00
96	Seattle Seahawks Helmet	1.00
97	Tampa Bay Buccaneers Helmet	1.00
98	Washington Redskins Helmet	1.00
99	National Football League Logo	1.00
100	American Football Fans	1.50

1996 Motion Vision

Motion Vision debuted in 1996 with two, 12-card series. The first was called Motion Vision, the second carried a 2.0 suffix. This product arrived in one card "packs" that actually resembled a compact disk case, with the cards inside a polysleeve. Motion Vision used Kodak technology to simulate actual game footage with tremendous clarity. The cards carried a Movi Motion Vision logo in the upper left-hand corner and the card number in the upper right- hand corner. The bottom of the card has the player's name, with nothing on the back. The card is best viewed by holding the plastic card up to light and rotating it to see game action. Motion Vision also had a 10-card Limited Digital Replay insert that was differentiated by having 25,000 produced.

		NM/M
Complete Set (24):		50.00
Comp. Series 1 (12):		25.00
Comp. Series 2 (12):		25.00
Common Player:		1.00
Series 1 Pack (1):		2.00
Series 1 Wax Box (25):		50.00
Series 2 Pack (1):		2.00
Series 2 Wax Box (25):		50.00
1	Troy Aikman	4.00
2	Dan Marino	5.00
3	Steve Young	3.00
4	Emmitt Smith	5.00
5	Drew Bledsoe	3.00
6	Kordell Stewart	2.00
7	Jerry Rice	4.00
8	Warren Moon	1.00
9	Junior Seau	1.00
10	Barry Sanders	5.00
11	Jim Harbaugh	1.00
12	John Elway	4.00
13	Brett Favre	5.00
14	Brett Favre	5.00
15	Troy Aikman	4.00
16	Emmitt Smith	5.00
17	Dan Marino	5.00
18	Kordell Stewart	2.00
19	John Elway	4.00
20	Kerry Collins	2.00
21	Jim Kelly	2.00
22	Drew Bledsoe	3.00
23	Mark Brunell	2.00
24	Jerry Rice	4.00

1996 Motion Vision Limited Digital Replays

Limited Digital Replays were the only insert set in 1996 Motion Vision. The first six cards were inserted every 25 packs of Series I, with only 2,500 sets produced, while the last four were found in Series 2.0 at a rate of one per 22 packs, with 3,500 sets produced. LDRs are distinguished by having a card back that features another shot of the player and statistics (regular-issue cards have no backs). LDR fronts also carry no logos on the front and instead of a phrase at the bottom describing the play, LDRs have only the player's name. Cards are numbered LDR1-LDR10.

		NM/M
Complete Set (10):		60.00
Comp. Series 1 (6):		30.00
Comp. Series 2 (4):		30.00
Autographs of Aikman, Bledsoe, Stewart and Young:		10X
1	Troy Aikman	10.00
2	Dan Marino	15.00
3	Steve Young	10.00
4	Emmitt Smith	15.00
5	Drew Bledsoe	10.00
6	Kordell Stewart	6.00
7	Brett Favre	15.00
8	Brett Favre	15.00
9	Emmitt Smith	15.00
10	Kerry Collins	10.00

1996 Motion Vision LDR Autographs

Limted Digital Replays Autographs consisted of four players who signed their LDR insert in 1996 Motion Vision. Drew Bledsoe, Kordell Stewart and Steve Young were inserted in Series I, while Troy Aikman and the remaining Steve Young cards were in Series 2.0. Fronts of these were the same, with the autograph on the back along with a seal to prove its autheticity.

		NM/M
Complete Set (4):		1,000
Common Player:		250.00
1	Troy Aikman AUTO	125.00
3	Steve Young AUTO	100.00
5	Drew Bledsoe AUTO	125.00
6	Kordell Stewart AUTO	75.00

1997 Motion Vision

Motion Vision second year in football cards produced 28 cards, with 20 cards in Series I and eight in Series II. Packs consisted of compact disc-like cases that could be opened to expose the card, which is more like a video shown on thick plastic. The card is best viewed when held up to light and moved slightly with the hand. Each series had four insert cards, which were inserted one per 25, with Series I containing LDR1-4 and a Terrell Davis autograph version, while Series II had LDR5-6 and two redemption cards.

		NM/M
Complete Set (28):		50.00
Complete Series 1 (20):		30.00
Complete Series 2 (8):		25.00
Common Player:		1.00
Pack (1):		2.00
Wax Box (25):		50.00
1	Terrell Davis	3.00
2	Curtis Martin	3.00
3	Joey Galloway	2.00
4	Eddie George	3.00
5	Isaac Bruce	1.00
6	Antonio Freeman	1.00
7	Terry Glenn	1.00
8	Deion Sanders	2.00
9	Jerome Bettis	2.00
10	Reggie White	1.00
11	Brett Favre	5.00
12	Dan Marino	5.00
13	Emmitt Smith	5.00
14	Mark Brunell	2.00
15	John Elway	4.00
16	Drew Bledsoe	3.00
17	Barry Sanders	5.00
18	Jeff Blake	1.00
19	Kerry Collins	1.00
20	Jerry Rice	4.00
21	Dan Marino	5.00
22	Troy Aikman	4.00
23	Brett Favre	5.00
24	Emmitt Smith	5.00
25	Kordell Stewart	2.00
26	Terrell Davis	3.00
27	Eddie George	2.00
28	Drew Bledsoe	3.00

1997 Motion Vision Box Toppers

Five different box toppers were offered with boxes of Motion Vision Series II Football. The cards measure 4" x 6" and were included at a rate of one per box.

	NM/M
Complete Set (4):	30.00
Common Player:	5.00
John Elway	6.00
Brett Favre	8.00
Dan Marino	8.00
Steve Young	5.00

1997 Motion Vision Limited Digital Replays

Each series of Motion Vision included four inserts at a rate of one per 25 packs. The Limited Digital Replays are numbered LDR1-6, with numbers 5 and 6 being trade cards for Warrick Dunn and Antoine Smith. Also included are Dunn and Smith XVRR cards. In addition, a autographed version of Terrell Davis' LDR was available.

		NM/M
Complete Set (8):		50.00
Complete Series 1 (4):		30.00
Complete Series 2 (4):		25.00
Common Player:		2.00
1	Terrell Davis	6.00
1A	Terrell Davis AUTO	100.00
2	Curtis Martin	5.00
3	Brett Favre	10.00
4	Barry Sanders	10.00
5	Warrick Dunn	3.00
6	Antowain Smith	3.00
XVRR	Warrick Dunn	3.00
XVRR	Antowain Smith	5.00

1997 Motion Vision Super Bowl XXXI

This four-card set was available through a redemption offer in 1996 MotionVision Series Two packs. The cards commemorate the Conference Championships and Super Bowl XXXI. The fourth card is jumbo format (5-5/8" x 3-3/4"). Each card is numbered one of 5,000.

		NM/M
Complete Set (4):		75.00
Common Player:		15.00
1	Drew Bledsoe AFC Championship Game	15.00
2	Brett Favre NFC Championship Game	20.00
3	Brett Favre Super Bowl XXXI	20.00
4	Brett Favre Jumbo Super Bowl XXXI	20.00

1981 Michael Schechter Associates Test Discs

These discs, produced by Michael Schecter Associates, were included in specially-marked packages of bread. The front shows a head shot of the player, but team logos have been airbrushed off the helmets. An NFLPA logo appears on the card front, along with the player's name, team, position and biographical information. Four stars appear at the top of the card. The unnumbered cards have blank backs. Holsum and Gardner's are among the brands of bread which included the cards inside packages. These two companies also made different posters which were intended to be used to display the discs.

		NM/M
Complete Set (32):		131.00
Common Player:		2.00
(1)	Ken Anderson	3.00
(2)	Ottis Anderson	4.50
(3)	Steve Bartkowski	2.25
(4)	Ricky Bell	2.25
(5)	Terry Bradshaw	13.00
(6)	Harold Carmichael	2.25
(7)	Joe Cribbs	2.00
(8)	Gary Danielson	2.00
(9)	Lynn Dickey	2.00
(10)	Dan Doornink	2.00
(11)	Vince Evans	2.25
(12)	Joe Ferguson	2.25
(13)	Vagas Ferguson	2.00
(14)	Dan Fouts	6.00
(15)	Steve Fuller	2.00
(16)	Archie Griffin	2.25
(17)	Steve Grogan	2.25
(18)	Bruce Harper	2.00
(19)	Jim Hart	2.25
(20)	Jim Jensen	2.00
(21)	Bert Jones	2.25
(22)	Archie Manning	3.00
(23)	Ted McKnight	2.00
(24)	Joe Montana	64.00
(25)	Craig Morton	2.25
(26)	Robert Newhouse	2.25
(27)	Phil Simms	6.75
(28)	Billy Taylor	2.00
(29)	Joe Theismann	3.75
(30)	Mark Van Eeghen	2.00
(31)	Delvin Williams	2.00
(32)	Tim Wilson	2.00

1990 Michael Schechter Associates Superstars

These unnumbered cards, produced by Michael Schechter Associates, were included two per box of Ralston Purina's Staff and Food Club Frosted Flakes cereal. Each card front has a color closeup shot of the player, with "Superstars" written at the top, and the player's name and team at the bottom. Three footballs are in different corners; an NFLPA logo is in the fourth corner. The card back also has the NFLPA logo, plus biographical information and statistics.

		NM/M
Complete Set (12):		15.00
Common Player:		.75
(1)	Carl Banks	.75
(2)	Cornelius Bennett	.75
(3)	Roger Craig	1.50
(4)	Jim Everett	1.00
(5)	Bo Jackson	2.00
(6)	Ronnie Lott	1.50
(7)	Don Majkowski	.75
(8)	Dan Marino	8.00
(9)	Karl Mecklenburg	.75
(10)	Christian Okoye	.75
(11)	Mike Singletary	1.00
(12)	Herschel Walker	1.00

N

1994 Nabisco A.1. "Masters of the Grill"

A.1. Masters of the Grill features 28 of the larger NFL stars, one from each team, equipped with all the necessary grill utensils and A.1. clothing, from chef hats to aprons. All the cards present grill recipes on the back; each recipe has A.1. as a key ingredient. The cards are surrounded by a black border and have an A.1. Masters of the Grill logo.

		NM/M
Complete Set (28):		7.00
Common Player:		.25
(1)	Harris Barton	.25
(2)	Jerome Bettis	1.50
(3)	Ray Childress	.25
(4)	Eugene Chung	.25
(5)	Jamie Dukes	.25
(6)	Steve Emtman	.25
(7)	Burt Grossman	.25
(8)	Courney Hall	.25
(9)	Ken Harvey	.35
(10)	Chris Hinton	.35
(11)	Jeff Hull	.25
(12)	Keith Jackson	.50
(13)	Rickey Jackson	.30
(14)	Cortez Kennedy	.35
(15)	Tim Krumrie	.25
(16)	Jeff Lageman	.25
(17)	Greg Lloyd	.35
(18)	Howie Long	.35
(19)	Hardy Nickerson	.30
(20)	Bart Oates	.25
(21)	Ken Ruettgers	.25
(22)	Dan Saleaumua	.25
(23)	Alonzo Spellman	.30
(24)	Eric Swann	.25
(25)	Pat Swilling	.25
(26)	Tommy Vardell	.25
(27)	Eric Williams	.25
(28)	Gary Zimmerman	.25

1935 National Chicle

The granddaddy of all football card sets, the 36-card National Chicle set was the first to be circulated nationally and the first set to feature only football players (all were pro football players except for Notre Dame coach Knute Rockne). Cards measure 2-3/8" x 2-7/8". The first 24 cards are easier to obtain than the final 12. Rookie cards in this set include Hall of Famers Earl "Dutch" Clark, Cliff Battles, Ken Strong, Turk Edwards, Clarke Hinkle and Bronko Nagurski. Nagurski's card is the most valuable football card in existence.

		NM/M
Complete Set (36):		18,000
Common Player (1-24):		110.00
Common Player (25-36):		375.00
1	*Earl "Dutch" Clark*	1,000
2	Bo Molenda	110.00
3	George Kenneally	110.00
4	Ed Matesic	110.00
5	Glenn Presnell	110.00
6	Pug Rentner	110.00
7	Ken Strong	225.00
8	Jim Zyntell	110.00
9	Knute Rockne	3,000
10	*Cliff Battles*	220.00
11	*Turk Edwards*	220.00
12	Tom Hupke	110.00
13	Homer Griffiths	110.00
14	Phil Sorboe	110.00
15	Ben Ciccone	110.00
16	Ben Smith	110.00
17	Tom Jones	110.00
18	Mike Mikulak	110.00
19	Ralph Kercheval	110.00
20	Warren Heller	110.00
21	Cliff Montgomery	110.00
22	Shipwreck Kelley	110.00
23	Beattie Feathers	220.00
24	Clarke Hinkle	200.00
25	Dale Burnett	375.00
26	John Isola	375.00
27	Bill Tosi	375.00
28	Stan Kosta	375.00
29	Jim MacMurdo	375.00
30	Ernie Caddel	375.00
31	Nic Niccola	375.00
32	Swede Johnston	375.00
33	Ernie Smith	375.00
34	*Bronko Nagurski*	7,000
35	Luke Johnson	375.00
36	Bernie Masterson	1,600

1992 NewSport

NewSport was issued exclusively in France, with four cards being distributed each month from November 1991 to June 1992. The 32-card glossy set was either issued in individual cards or in four-card strips. Each card measures 4" x 6", with card backs written in French.

		NM/M
Complete Set (32):		200.00
Common Player:		6.00
1	Bubby Brister	6.00
2	James Brooks	6.00
3	Joey Browner	6.00
4	Gill Byrd	6.00
5	Eric Dickerson	8.00
6	Henry Ellard	6.00
7	John Elway	20.00
8	Mervyn Fernandez	6.00
9	David Fulcher	6.00
10	Ernest Givins	6.00
11	Jay Hilgenberg	6.00
12	Michael Irvin	10.00
13	Dave Krieg	6.00
14	Albert Lewis	6.00
15	James Lofton	6.00
16	Dan Marino	45.00
17	Wilber Marshall	6.00
18	Freeman McNeil	6.00
19	Karl Mecklenberg	6.00
20	Joe Montana	35.00
21	Christian Okoye	6.00
22	Michael Dean Perry	6.00
23	Tom Rathman	6.00
24	Mark Rypien	6.00
25	Barry Sanders	30.00
26	Deion Sanders	20.00
27	Sterling Sharpe	8.00
28	Pat Swilling	6.00
29	Lawrence Taylor	10.00
30	Vinny Testaverde	6.00
31	Andre Tippett	6.00
32	Reggie White	10.00

1991 NFL Experience

These oversized cards feature artwork highlights from the first 25 Super Bowls. The black-bordered cards, which measure 2-1/2" x 4-3/4", were produced by the NFL, so each has an NFL Experience logo on the front. The back is in a horizontal format, with a pink bar at the top which has "The NFL Experience" written in it, plus the card number. A pink bar at the bottom carries a description of the action on the front. Sandwiched between the two bars is a brief comment about life in the NFL, plus a sponsor logo.

		NM/M
Complete Set (28):		4.00
Common Player:		.20
1	NFL Experience Theme Art	.20
2	Max McGee Super Bowl I	.20
3	Vince Lombardi, Bart Starr Super Bowl II	.50
4	Don Shula, Joe Namath Super Bowl III	.75
5	Super Bowl IV	.20
6	Super Bowl V - Colts vs. Cowboys	.20
7	Duane Thomas, Bob Lily, Roger Staubach, Tom Landry, Tex Schramm Super Bowl VI	.60
8	Super Bowl VII	.20
9	Larry Csonka Super Bowl VIII	.30
10	Super Bowl IX	.20
11	Lynn Swann, Jack Lambert Super Bowl X	.30
12	John Madden Super Bowl XI - Raiders vs. Vikings	.30
13	Randy White, Harvey Martin, Craig Morton Super Bowl XII	.30
14	Super Bowl XIII - Steelers vs. Cowboys	.20
15	Terry Bradshaw Super Bowl XIV	.60
16	Super Bowl XV - Raiders vs. Eagles	.20
17	Super Bowl XVI - 49ers vs. Bengals	.20
18	John Riggins Super Bowl XVII	.30

19	Marcus Allen Super Bowl XVIII	.30
20	Super Bowl XIX - 49ers vs. Dolphins	.20
21	Richard Dent Super Bowl XX	.30
22	Super Bowl XXI	.20
23	John Elway, Doug Williams Super Bowl XXII	.30
24	Super Bowl XXIII - 49ers vs. Bengals	.20
25	Joe Montana Super Bowl XXIV	1.00
26	Collage of 25 Super Bowls	.20
27	Super Bowl XXVI - Lombardi Trophy	.20
28	Joe Theismann	.30

1993 NFL Properties Santa Claus

This 12-card set was available through a mail-in offer of any 30 1993 NFL trading card wrappers and $1.50 for postage and handling. In addition, sets were sent out to dealers with a season's greeting card. All 12 NFL trading card licensees produced a Santa Claus card, and there was a checklist card issued by NFL Properties included.

		NM/M
Complete Set (13):		15.00
Common Player:		1.50
1	Santa Claus Action Packed (Action Packed)	1.50
2	Santa Claus Classic	1.50
3	Santa Claus Collector's Edge	1.50
4	Santa Claus Fleer	1.50
5	Santa Claus Pacific	1.50
6	Santa Claus Pinnacle	1.50
7	Santa Claus Playoff	1.50
8	Santa Claus Pro Set	1.50
9	Santa Claus SkyBox	1.50
10	Santa Claus Topps	1.50
11	Santa Claus Upper Deck	1.50
12	Santa Claus Wild Card	1.50
13	Checklist Card NFL Properties	1.50

1993-95 NFL Properties Show Redemption Cards

This NFL Properties product was handed out to attendees at card shows over a three-year span, with a banner at the top of each card showing the city and dates that the show was held. The first card was issued at Chicago and is the only unnumbered card (others have roman numerals on the back). Card No. 2 was given out at a Labor Day Weekend Show in San Francisco and is the only card in the set to show the team's schedule on the back (others have text about players on the front). Card No. 4B was limited to 3,000 total cards, and replaced card No. 4A, which was done to commemorate the St. Louis Stallions NFL franchise that never materialized so it was not issued. Card No. 6A was issued at the Cocktail Reception sponsored by NFL Properties at the 15th National Sports Collectors Convention, with the three players autographing the card in blue ink. Card No. 6B was issued as part of the Back-to- School promotion, with collectors redeeming two proof of purchases for the oversized Elway NFL FACT card.

		NM/M
Complete Set (9):		750.00
Common Player:		10.00
1	Dick Butkus, Mike Ditka, Gale Sayers Chicago Bears Saluting Hall of Famers (7/24/93) (200) (Signed in silver ink)	100.00
2	NFL Kickoff '93, Ricky Watters, Steve Young, Keith DeLong, Jerry Rice, John Taylor, Tim McDonald San Francisco 49ers Labor Day Weekend (9/93) (1,000) (1993 49er schedule on card back)	20.00
3	Y.A. Tittle, Ken Stabler San Francisco 49ers Labor Day Weekend (9/93)(1,000) Saluting Bay Area Legends, (Career summaries on back)	15.00
3AU	Y.A. Tittle, Ken Stabler Weekend (9/93) (1,000) Saluting Bay Area Legends Signed by both players)	180.00
4B	Jim Hart, Charlie Johnson, Neil Lomax Decades of Gateway City QBs (10/29-31/93) (3000)	10.00
5	Michael Irvin, Troy Aikman, Emmitt Smith, Jay Novacek, Russell Maryland, Ken Norton Champions (11/19-21/93) 3000)	15.00
6A	Earl Campbell, Dan Pastorini, Ken Stabler Legends (Autographed) 8/4-7/94) (200)	180.00
6B	John Elway 1995 Spokesman NFL Trading Cards (Autographed) (300)	100.00
7	Joe Namath, John Elway (Autographed) (300)	180.00

1994 NFL Back-to-School

This 11-card set had one card by each of the 11 NFL licensees and was available to collectors who sent in 20 wrappers from NFL licensed products by the deadline of Nov. 30, 1994. Cards are unnumbered on the backs, except Action Packed (BS1) and Upper Deck (19) and are standard sized. At one point Pro Set had planned to do a Brett Favre card, however it went out of business before the card could be issued.

		NM/M
Complete Set (11):		15.00
Common Player:		.50
1	NFL Quarterback Club (Action Packed)	1.50
2	Emmitt Smith (Classic)	4.00
3	John Elway (Collector's Edge)	1.25
4	Jerome Bettis (Fleer)	1.00
5	Sterling Sharpe(Pacific)	.75
6	Drew Bledsoe (Pinnacle)	2.00
7	Dana Stubblefield (Playoff)	.75
8	Jim Kelly (SkyBox)	.75
9	Jerry Rice (Topps)	2.00
10	Joe Montana (Upper Deck)	2.50
11	Checklist NFL Properties	.50

1994 NFL Properties Santa Claus

Each of the NFL's 10 card licensees printed a Santa card for the set, which was available through a mail in exchange for 20 NFL-licensed card wrappers and $1.50 postage. There is no consistent design throughout the set, as each company was allowed to create their own design. Some cards are numbered and others are not. The fronts each include Santa artwork, while the backs have holiday greetings.

		NM/M
Complete Set (10):		10.00
Common Player:		1.25
1	Santa Claus Action Packed	1.25
2	Santa Claus Classic	1.25
3	Santa Claus Collector's Edge	1.25
4	Santa Claus Fleer	1.25
5	Santa Claus Pacific	1.25
6	Santa Claus Pinnacle	1.25
7	Santa Claus Playoff	1.25
8	Santa Claus SkyBox	1.25
9	Santa Claus Upper Deck	1.25
10	Checklist Card, NFL Properties	1.25

1995 NFL Properties Santa Claus

Eight of the NFL's card licensees produced cards for this nine-card set. The fronts and backs do not have a consistent design. The set was available for 20 wrappers and $1.50 shipping.

		NM/M
Complete Set (9):		10.00
Common Player:		1.00
1	Title Card (Santa and friend)	1.00
2	Emmitt Smith, Drew Bledsoe Santa Claus Classic ProLine	2.00
3	Santa Claus Collector's Edge	1.00
4	Santa Claus Pacific	1.00
5	Dan Marino, Emmitt Smith, Steve Young Santa Claus Pinnacle	4.00
6	Santa Claus Playoff	1.00
7	Santa Claus SkyBox	1.00
8	Santa Claus Topps	1.00
9	Santa Claus Upper Deck	1.00

1996 NFL Properties 7-11

Fleer/SkyBox, Pinnacle, Topps and Upper Deck, along with NFL Properties, combined to produce this nine-card set. Each card front and back is designed identically to the companies' sets from 1996. The cards are numbered 1-9 on the backs. To receive the cards, collectors needed to send in two wrappers from any 1996 NFL trading card product, a 7-11 store receipt with the trading card purchase circled, completed entry form or 3 x 5 card and $1 for shipping had to be sent to a redemption house in Minnesota.

		NM/M
Complete Set (9):		20.00
Common Player:		1.00
1	John Elway	3.00
2	Jerry Rice	3.00
3	Dan Marino	4.00
4	Barry Sanders	5.00
5	Kordell Stewart	3.00
6	Steve Young	2.00
7	Joe Namath	3.00
8	Brett Favre	6.00
9	Trent Dilfer	1.00

1996 NFL Properties Back-to-School

One of each of the NFL's card licensees, along with NFL Properties, joined forces to produce this nine-card set. To receive the set, collectors needed to send in 20 wrappers from any 1996 NFL-licensed trading cards and $1.50 for shipping to a redemption house in Minnesota. The offer expired Nov. 30, 1996.

	NM/M
Complete Set (9):	10.00
Common Player:	.50
Chris Warren Pacific	.50
Dan Marino, Steve Young Pinnacle	2.00
John Elway NFLP	1.50
Steve Young Topps	1.00
Brett Favre Fleer	3.00
Steve Bono Collector's Edge	.50
Dan Marino Upper Deck	2.00
Emmitt Smith Classic	2.00
Deion Sanders Playoff	1.00

1996 NFL Properties Santa Claus

This nine-card set consists of cards produced by the eight NFL trading card licensees. All the cards feature Santa Claus and some have NFL players as well. The cards could be obtained via redemption of 20 wrappers of any participating manufacturers football products.

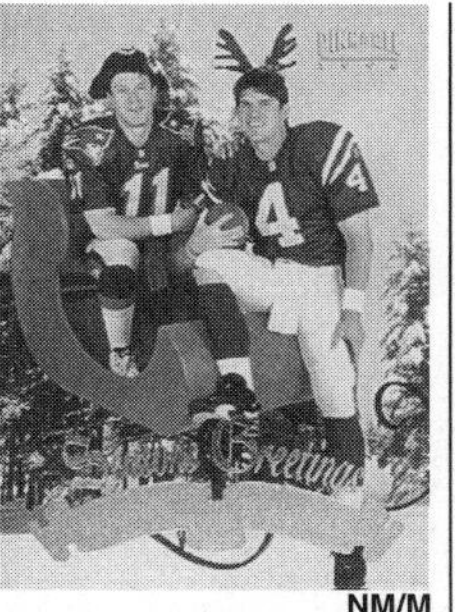

		NM/M
Complete Set (9):		8.00
Common Player:		1.00
1	Title Card - Santa Claus	1.00
2	Santa Claus (Collector's Edge with Jeff Blake and Steve Bono)	1.00
3	Santa Claus (Fleer/Skybox with Brett Favre on back)	1.00
4	Santa Claus (Pacific)	1.00
5	Santa Claus (Pinnacle with Drew Bledsoe and Jim Harbaugh)	1.00
6	Santa Claus (Playoff)	1.00
7	Santa Claus (Score Board with Troy Aikman)	1.00
8	Santa Claus (Topps)	1.00
9	Santa Claus (Upper Deck)	1.00

1972 NFLPA Wonderful World Stamps

These numbered stamps, which each measure 1-15/16" x 2-7/8", feature stars from each team in the NFL. The front of each stamp has a color photo of the player; the back has player's name, a stamp number and a place for it to be glued so it can be put into an accompanying album. The 30-page 9-1/2" x 13-1/4" album traces the history of pro football in the United States and provides short biographies of the players who are featured on the stamps. The NFLPA sponsored the album, which is titled "The Wonderful World of Pro Football USA." Stamps which are listed in the checklist with an A were issued in 1971.

		NM/M
Complete Set (390):		275.00
Common Player:		.35
1	Bob Berry	.50
2	Greg Brezina	.35
3	Ken Burrow	.35
4	Jim Butler	.40
5	Wes Chesson	.35
6	Claude Humphrey	.50
7	George Kunz	1.00
8	Tom McCauley	.35
9	Jim Mitchell	.50
10	Tommy Nobis	3.00
11	Ken Reaves	.35
12	Bill Sandeman	.35
13	John Small	.35
14	Harmon Wages	.35
15	John Zook	.50
16	Norm Bulaich	.60
17	Bill Curry	.75
18	Mike Curtis	.75
19	Ted Hendricks	3.00
20	Roy Hilton	.35
21	Eddie Hinton	.35
22	David Lee	.35
23	Jerry Logan	.35
24	John Mackey	2.00
25	Tom Matte	.75
26	Jim O'Brien	.50
27	Glenn Ressler	.35
28	Johnny Unitas	15.00
29	Bob Vogel	.50
30	Rick Volk	.50
31	Paul Costa	.35
32	Jim Dunaway	.50
33	Paul Guidry	.35
34	Jim Harris	.35
35	Robert James	.35
36	Mike McBath	.35
37	Haven Moses	1.00
38	Wayne Patrick	.35
39	John Pitts	.35
40	Jim Reilly	.35
41	Pete Richardson	.35
42	Dennis Shaw	.50
43	O.J. Simpson	25.00
44	Mike Stratton	.50
45	Bob Tatarek	.35
46	Dick Butkus	8.00
47	Jim Cadile	.35
48	Jack Concannon	.50
49	Bobby Douglass	.75
50	George Farmer	.50
51	Dick Gordon	.50
52	Bobby Joe Green	.35
53	Ed O'Bradovich	.35
54A	Bob Hyland	.35
54B	Mac Percival	.35
55A	Ed O'Bradovich	.50
55B	Gale Sayers	9.00
56A	Mac Percival	.35
56B	George Seals	.35
57	Jim Seymour	.35
58A	George Seals	.35
58B	Ron Smith	.50
59	Bill Staley	.35
60	Cecil Turner	.40
61	Al Beauchamp	.45
62	Virgil Carter	.50
63	Vernon Holland	.35
64	Bob Johnson	.50
65	Ron Lamb	.35
66	Dave Lewis	.35
67	Rufus Mayes	.50
68	Horst Muhlmann	.35
69	Lemar Parrish	.75
70	Jess Phillips	.35
71	Mike Reid	2.00
72	Ken Riley	1.00
73	Paul Robinson	.50
74	Bob Trumpy	2.25
75	Fred Willis	.35
76	Don Cockroft	.50
77	Gary Collins	.50
78	Gene Hickerson	.50
79	Fair Hooker	.75
80	Jim Houston	.50
81	Walter Johnson	.50
82	Joe Jones	.35
83	Leroy Kelly	3.00
84	Milt Morin	.50
85	Reece Morrison	.35
86	Bill Nelsen	.50
87	Mike Phipps	.75
88	Bo Scott	.50
89	Jerry Sherk	.50
90	Ron Snidow	.35
91	Herb Adderley	3.00
92	George Andrie	.75
93	Mike Clark	.35
94	Dave Edwards	.50
95	Walt Garrison	1.50
96	Cornell Green	.75
97	Bob Hayes	2.00
98	Calvin Hill	2.00
99	Chuck Howley	.75
100	Lee Roy Jordan	2.50
101	Dave Manders	.50
102	Craig Morton	1.25
103	Ralph Neely	.50
104	Mel Renfro	1.00
105	Roger Staubach	30.00
106	Bobby Anderson	.75
107	Sam Brunelli	.35
108	Dave Costa	.35
109	Mike Current	.35
110	Pete Duranko	.35
111	George Goeddeke	.35
112	Cornell Gordon	.35
113	Don Horn	.50
114	Rich Jackson	.35
115	Larry Kaminski	.35
116	Floyd Little	1.50
117	Marv Montgomery	.35
118	Steve Ramsey	.50
119	Paul Smith	.50
120	Billy Thompson	.75
121	Lem Barney	3.00
122	Nick Eddy	.50
123	Mel Farr	.75
124	Ed Flanagan	.35
125	Larry Hand	.35
126	Greg Landry	.75
127	Dick LeBeau	.50
128	Mike Lucci	.50
129	Earl McCullouch	.50
130	Bill Munson	.75
131	Wayne Rasmussen	.35
132	Joe Robb	.35
133	Jerry Rush	.35
134	Altie Taylor	.50
135	Wayne Walker	.50
136	Ken Bowman	.35
137	John Brockington	.75
138	Fred Carr	.50
139	Carroll Dale	.50
140	Ken Ellis	.35
141	Gale Gillingham	.50
142	Dave Hampton	.50
143	Doug Hart	.35
144A	John Hilton	.35
144B	MacArthur Lane	.35
145	Mike McCoy	.50
146	Ray Nitschke	2.50
147	Frank Patrick	.35
148	Francis Peay	.35
149	Dave Robinson	.75
150	Bart Starr	9.00
151	Bob Atkins	.35
152	Elvin Bethea	.75
153	Garland Boyette	.35
154	ken Burrough	.75
155	Woody Campbell	.35
156	John Charles	.35
157	Lynn Dickey	.75
158	Elbert Drungo	.35
159	Gene Ferguson	.35
160	Charlie Johnson	.75
161	Charlie Joyner	3.00
162	Dan Patorini	.75
163	Ron Pritchard	.35
164	Walt Suggs	.35
165	Mike Tilleman	.35
166	Bobby Bell	3.00
167	Aaron Brown	.50
168	Buck Buchanan	2.00
169	Ed Buddle	.75
170	Curley Culp	1.00
171	Len Dawson	6.00
172	Willie Lanier	2.50
173	Jim Lynch	.50
174	Jim Marsalis	.50
175	Mo Moorman	.35
176	Ed Podolak	.50
177	Johnny Robinson	.75
178	Jan Stenerud	2.00
179	Otis Taylor	1.50
180	Jim Tyrer	.75
181	Kermit Alexander	.50
182	Coy Bacon	.35
183	Dick Buzin	.35
184	Roman Gabriel	1.00
185	Gene Howard	.35
186	Ken Iman	.35
187	Les Josephson	.50
188	Marlin McKeever	.50
189	Merlin Olsen	4.00
190A	Richie Petitbon	.75
190B	Phil Olsen	.35
191	David Ray	.35
192	Lance Rentzel	.75
193	Isiah Robertson	.50
194	Larry Smith	.35
195	Jack Snow	.75
196	Nick Buoniconti	2.00
197	Doug Crusan	.35
198	Larry Csonka	8.00
199	Bob DeMarco	.50
200	Marv Fleming	.50
201	Bob Griese	10.00
202	Jim Klick	1.00
203	Bob Kuechenberg	1.00
204	Mercury Morris	1.25
205A	Jim Riley	.35
205B	John Richardson	.35
206	Jim Riley	.35
207	Jake Scott	.75
208	Howard Twilley	.75
209	Paul Warfield	5.00
210	Garo Yepremian	.75
211	Grady Alderman	.50
212	John Beasley	.35
213	John Henderson	.35
214	Wally Hilgenberg	.50
215	Clinton Jones	.50
216	Karl Kassulke	.35
217	Paul Krause	1.25
218	Dave Osborn	.50
219	Alan Page	2.00
220	Ed Sharockman	.35
221	Fran Tarkenton	10.00
222	Mick Tingelhoff	.75
223	Charlie West	.35
224	Lonnie Warwick	.35
225	Gene Washington	.75
226	Hank Barton	.35
227A	Larry Carwell	.35
227B	Ron Berger	.35
228	Larry Carwell	.35
229A	Carl Garrett	.50
229B	Jim Cheyunski	.50
230A	Jim Hunt	.35
230B	Carl Garrett	.50
231	Rickie Harris	.35
232	Daryl Johnson	.35
233	Steve Kiner	.35
234	Jon Morris	.35
235	Jim Nance	.75
236	Tom Neville	.35
237	Jim Plunkett	4.00
238	Ron Sellers	.50
239	Len St. Jean	.35
240A	Gerald Warren	.35
240B	Don Webb	.35
241	Dan Abramowicz	.75
242A	Tony Baker	.35
242B	Dick Absher	.35
243	Leo Carroll	.35
244	Jim Duncan	.35
245	Al Dodd	.35
246	Jim Flanigan	.35
247	Hoyle Granger	.35
248	Edd Hargett	.75
249	Glen Ray Hines	.35
250	Hugo Hollas	.35
251	Jake Kupp	.35
252	Dave Long	.35
253	Mike Morgan	.35
254	Tom Roussel	.35
255	Del Williams	.35
256	Otto Brown	.35
257	Bobby Duhon	.50
258	Scott Eaton	.35
259	Jim Flies	.35
260	Tucker Fredrickson	.75
261A	Don Herrmann	.35
261B	Pete Gogolak	.50
262	Bob Grim	.50
263	Don Herrmann	.35
264A	Ernie Koy	.75
264B	Ron Johnson	1.00
265A	Spider Lockhart	.50
265B	Jim Kanicki	.35
266	Spider Lockhart	.50
267	Joe Morrison	.75
268	Bob Tucker	2.00
269	Willie Williams	.35
270	Willie Young	.35
271	Al Atkinson	.35
272	Ralph Baker	.35
273	Emerson Boozer	.75
274	John Elliott	.35
275	Dave Herman	.35
276A	Dave Herman	.35
276B	Winston Hill	.50
277	Gus Hollomon	.35
278	Bob Howfield	.35
279	Pete Lammons	.50
280	Joe Namath (numbered 281)	22.00
281	Gerry Philbin	.50
282	Matt Snell	.75
283	Steve Tannen	.35
284	Earlie Thomas	.35
285	Al Woodall	.50
286	Fred Biletnikoff	4.00
287	George Blanda	6.00
288	Willie Brown	3.00
289	Ray Chester	1.00
290	Tony Cline	.35
291	Dan Conners	.35
292	Ben Davidson	1.50
293	Hewritt Dixon	.50
294	Tom Keating	.50
295	Daryle Lamonica	1.50
296	Gus Otto	.35
297	Jim Otto	3.00
298	Rod Sherman	.35
299	Bubba Smith	.35
300A	Warren Wells	.50
300B	Gene Upshaw	3.00
301	Rick Arrington	.35
302	Gary Ballman	.50
303	Lee Bouggess	.35
304	Bill Bradley	.75
305A	Richard Harris	.35

305B	Happy Feller	.75
306A	Ben Hawkins	.35
306B	Richard Harris	.35
307	Ben Hawkins	.35
308	Harold Jackson	1.50
309	Pete Liske	.75
310	Al Nelson	.35
311	Gary Pettigrew	.35
312	Tim Rossovich	.75
313	Tom Woodeshick	.50
314	Adrian Young	.50
315	Steve Zabel	.50
316	Chuck Allen	.35
317	Warren Bankston	.50
318	Chuck Beatty	.35
319	Terry Bradshaw	20.00
320	John Fuqua	.50
321	Terry Hanratty	1.00
322	Ray Mansfield	.35
323	Ben McGee	.35
324	John Rowser	.35
325	Andy Russell	1.00
326	Ron Shanklin	.50
327	Dave Smith	.35
328	Bruce Van Dyke	.35
329	Lloyd Voss	.35
330	Bobby Walden	.35
331	Donny Anderson	.75
332	Jim Bakken	.75
333	Pete Beathard	.75
334A	Mel Gray	2.00
334B	Miller Farr	.50
335A	Jim Hart	1.00
335B	Mel Gray	1.00
336	Jim Hart	1.00
337A	Chuck Latourette	.35
337B	Rol Krueger	.35
338	Chuck Latourette	.35
339A	Bob Reynolds	.35
339B	Ernie McMillan	.50
340	Bob Reynolds	.35
341	Jackie Smith	3.50
342	Larry Stallings	.50
343	Chuck Walker	.35
344	Roger Wehrli	.75
345	Larry Wilson	2.00
346	Bob Babich	.35
347	Pete Barnes	.35
348A	Marty Domres	.50
348B	Steve DeLong	.50
349	Marty Domres	.50
350	Gary Garrison	.50
351A	Walker Gillette	.35
351B	John Hadl	1.25
352	Kevin Hardy	.35
353	Bob Howard	.35
354A	Jim Hill	.35
354B	Deacon Jones	1.75
355	Terry Owens	.75
356	Dennis Partee	.35
357A	Dennis Partee	.35
357B	Jeff Queen	.35
358	Jim Tolbert	.35
359	Russ Washington	.35
360	Doug Wilkerson	.35
361	John Brodie	3.50
362	Doug Cunningham	.35
363	Bruce Gossett	.35
364	Stan Hindman	.35
365	John Isenbarger	.50
366	Charlie Krueger	.50
367	Frank Nunley	.35
368	Woody Peoples	.35
369	Len Rohde	.35
370	Steve Spurrier	6.50
371	Gene Washington	1.00
372	Dave Wilcox	.75
373	Ken Willard	1.00
374	Bob Windsor	.50
375	Dick Witcher	.50
376	Verlon Biggs	.75
377	Larry Brown	3.00
378	Speedy Duncan	.50
379	Chris Hanburger	1.00
380	Charlie Harraway	.50
381	Sonny Jurgensen	5.00
382	Bill Kilmer	1.50
383	Tommy Mason	.50
384	Ron McDole	.50
385	Brig Owens	.35
386	Jack Pardee	2.00
387	Myron Pottios	1.00
388	Jerry Smith	.50
389	Diron Talbert	.50
390	Charley Taylor	4.00
---	Album	25.00

1972 NFLPA Iron Ons

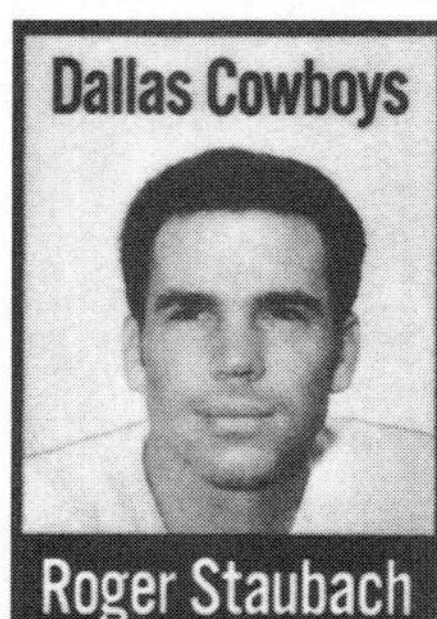

These 35 cards were created as cloth patches to be ironed onto clothes. Hence, the backs are blank. The front of the card has a full color head shot of the player, with his name and 1972 NFLPA copyright at the bottom. The player's name is above the photo, which is framed by a black border. The cards, which were sold through vending machines, measure 2-1/4" x 3-1/2" and are unnumbered.

		NM/M
	Complete Set (35):	175.00
	Common Player:	2.00
(1)	Donny Anderson	2.00
(2)	George Blanda	7.50
(3)	Terry Bradshaw	20.00
(4)	John Brockington	2.00
(5)	John Brodie	5.00
(6)	Dick Butkus	10.00
(7)	Larry Csonka	10.00
(8)	Mike Curtis	2.00
(9)	Len Dawson	6.00
(10)	Carl Eller	3.00
(11)	Mike Garrett	2.00
(12)	Joe Greene	8.00
(13)	Bob Griese	9.00
(14)	Dick Gordon	2.00
(15)	John Hadl	3.00
(16)	Bob Hayes	3.00
(17)	Ron Johnson	2.00
(18)	Deacon Jones	3.00
(19)	Sonny Jurgensen	6.00
(20)	Leroy Kelly	3.00
(21)	Jim Kiick	2.50
(22)	Greg Landry	2.00
(23)	Floyd Little	3.00
(24)	Mike Lucci	2.00
(25)	Archie Manning	5.00
(26)	Joe Namath	35.00
(27)	Tommy Nobis	3.00
(28)	Alan Page	3.00
(29)	Jim Plunkett	4.00
(30)	Gale Sayers	10.00
(31)	O.J. Simpson	35.00
(32)	Roger Staubach	30.00
(33)	Duane Thomas	2.00
(34)	Johnny Unitas	25.00
(35)	Paul Warfield	5.00

1972 NFLPA Vinyl Stickers

These stickers feature 20 of the NFL's stars and were sold through vending machines. Each sticker is 2-3/4" x 4-3/4" and is copyrighted on the front by the NFLPA. Each player's head appears on a caricature drawing of him in a football uniform; the outline of his body is what can actually be used as a sticker. Consequently, the backs are blank. The stickers are unnumbered.

		NM/M
	Complete Set (20):	95.00
	Common Player:	2.00
(1)	Donny Anderson	2.00
(2)	George Blanda	5.00
(3)	Terry Bradshaw	17.00
(4)	John Brockington	2.00
(5)	John Brodie	4.00
(6)	Dick Butkus	8.00
(7)	Dick Gordon	2.00
(8)	Joe Greene	5.00
(9)	John Hadl	2.00
(10)	Bob Hayes	3.00
(11)	Ron Johnson	9.00
(12)	Floyd Little	3.00
(13)	Joe Namath	25.00
(14)	Tommy Nobis	3.00
(15)	Alan Page	15.00
(16)	Jim Plunkett	5.00
(17)	Gale Sayers	10.00
(18)	Roger Staubach	22.00
(19)	Johnny Unitas	18.00
(20)	Paul Warfield	4.00

1979 NFLPA Pennant Stickers

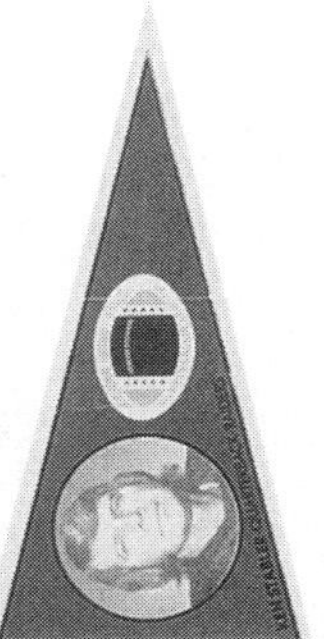

Each of these 50 stickers, sponsored by the NFLPA, is shaped like a pennant and features a black-and-white head shot of a player inside a circle. The NFLPA football logo is also on the front of the sticker. Different colors are used for the backgrounds of the stickers; some stickers can be found with various colors for a background, too. The stickers measure 2-1/2" x 5" and have the player's name, position and team on the front.

		NM/M
	Complete Set (50):	425.00
	Common Player:	2.50
(1)	Lyle Alzado	5.00
(2)	Ken Anderson	7.50
(3)	Steve Bartkowski	10.00
(4)	Ricky Bell	4.00
(5)	Elvin Bethea	2.50
(6)	Tom Blanchard	2.50
(7)	Terry Bradshaw	25.00
(8)	Bob Breunig	4.00
(9)	Greg Brezina	5.00
(10)	Doug Buffone	9.00
(11)	Earl Campbell	50.00
(12)	John Cappelletti	3.00
(13)	Harold Carmichael	4.00
(14)	Chuck Crist	15.00
(15)	Sam Cunningham	4.00
(16)	Joe DeLamielleure	2.50
(17)	Tom Dempsey	4.00
(18)	Tony Dorsett	15.00
(19)	Dan Fouts	20.00
(20)	Roy Gerela	4.00
(21)	Bob Griese (misspelled Greise)	12.00
(22)	Franco Harris	15.00
(23)	Jim Hart	12.00
(24)	Charlie Joiner	6.00
(25)	Paul Krause	4.00
(26)	Bob Kuechenberg	4.00
(27)	Greg Landry	2.50
(28)	Archie Manning	6.00
(29)	Chester Marcol	2.50
(30)	Harvey Martin	4.00
(31)	Lawrence McCutcheon	12.00
(32)	Craig Morton	4.00
(33)	Haven Moses	2.50
(34)	Steve Odom	3.00
(35)	Morris Owens	2.50
(36)	Dan Pastorini	9.00
(37)	Walter Payton	35.00
(38)	Greg Pruitt	14.00
(39)	John Riggins	9.00
(40)	Jake Scott	3.00
(41)	Ken Stabler	20.00
(42)	Roger Staubach	30.00
(43)	Jan Stenerud	6.00
(44)	Art Still	9.00
(45)	Mick Tingelhoff	4.00
(46)	Richard Todd	2.50
(47)	Phil Villapiano	9.00
(48)	Wesley Walker	5.00
(49)	Roger Werhli	9.00
(50)	Jim Zorn	12.00

1995 NFLPA Super Bowl Party Giveaways

Produced as a premium for the NFLPA Super Bowl XXIX party, each NFL card licensee designed one card for the 10-card set. Overall, 500 of each card were printed. The cards are unnumbered. The NFL Players logo is included on the front of each card.

		NM/M
	Complete Set (10):	200.00
	Common Player:	10.00
1	Marcus Allen (Pinnacle)	12.00
2	Jerome Bettis (Fleer)	12.00
3	Tim Brown (Collector's Edge)	10.00
4	Trent Dilfer (SkyBox)	12.00
5	Marshall Faulk (Pacific)	30.00
6	Ronnie Lott (Classic)	10.00
7	Dan Marino (Upper Deck)	80.00
8	Junior Seau (Stadium Club)	12.00
9	Sterling Sharpe (Action Packed)	10.00
10	Heath Shuler (Playoff)	20.00

1996 NFLPA Super Bowl Party Giveaways

Produced as a premium for the NFLPA Sega Sports Super Bowl XXX party, each NFL card licensee created one card for the 12-card set. The NFL Players' logo appears on the front and backs of the unnumbered cards.

		NM/M
	Complete Set (12):	15.00
	Common Player:	.75
1	Marcus Allen, Ronnie Lott (Collector's Edge)	1.00
2	Steve Beuerlein (Topps)	.75
3	Jeff Blake (Pacific)	1.50
4	Tim Brown (Action Packed)	1.00
5	Kerry Collins (Classic)	3.00
6	Kevin Greene (Playoff)	.75
7	Garrison Hearst (Fleer Metal)	1.00
8	Daryl Johnston (SkyBox Impact)	.75
9	Joe Montana (Upper Deck)	3.00
10	Deion Sanders (Donruss Red Zone)	1.50
11	Herschel Walker (Pinnacle)	.75
12	Logo Card (Checklist back)	.75

1997 NFLPA Super Bowl Player's Party

This 11-card set was distributed at the NFLPA Super Bowl XXXI player's party. Cards were contributed by each NFL trading card licensee. The cards are unnumbered.

		NM/M
	Complete Set (11):	12.00
	Common Player:	.75
1	Morten Andersen SkyBox	.75
2	Steve Bono Collector's Edge	.75
3	Robert Brooks Pacific	.75
4	Tony Dorsett Topps	1.50
5	Gus Frerotte Donruss	.75
6	Kevin Hardy Pinnacle	.75
7	Tyrone Hughes Score Board	.75
8	Dan Marino Upper Deck	3.00
9	Curtis Martin SkyBox	2.00
10	Deion Sanders Playoff	1.50
11	Checklist Card - Upper Deck	.75

2002 NFL Properties Punt, Pass, and Kick

		NM/M
	Common Player:	2.00
1	Troy Aikman Fleer	5.00
2	Drew Bledsoe Pacific	4.00
3	Randall Cunningham Donruss	3.00
4	Brett Favre Donruss	8.00
5	Bert Jones Fleer	2.00
6	Jim Kelly Topps	4.00
7	Bernie Kosar Upper Deck	3.00
8	Dan Marino Upper Deck	8.00
9	Vinny Testaverde Topps	2.00
10	Danny White Pacific	2.00

O

1961 Oilers Jay Publishing

Measuring 5" x 7", the 24-card set is anchored by a black-and-white player photo on the front. The player's name and team appear in the white border beneath the photo. The player's facsimile signature is printed on the photo. The cards are unnumbered and have blank backs. Originally, the cards were sold in 12-card packs for 25 cents.

		NM/M
	Complete Set (24):	125.00
	Common Player:	5.00
1	Dalva Allen	5.00
2	Tony Banfield	5.00
3	George Blanda	12.00
4	Billy Cannon	6.00
5	Doug Cline	5.00
6	Willard Dewveall	5.00
7	Mike Dukes	5.00
8	Don Floyd	6.00
9	Freddy Glick	6.00
10	Bill Groman	6.00
11	Charlie Hennigan	6.00
12	Ed Husmann	5.00
13	Al Jamison	5.00
14	Mark Johnston	5.00
15	Jacky Lee	6.00
16	Bob McLeod	5.00
17	Rich Michael	5.00
18	Dennit Morris	5.00
19	Jim Norton	6.00
20	Bob Schmidt	5.00
21	Dave Smith	5.00
22	Bob Talamini	6.00
23	Charles Tolar	6.00
24	Hogan Wharton	5.00

1964-65 Oilers Color Team Issue

Measuring 7-3/4" x 9-3/4", the 16-photo set is anchored by a color photo on the front, bordered in white. A facsimile signature is printed over the photo. The photos are unnumbered and have blank backs. The photos were sold in eight-photo packs for 50 cents.

		NM/M
	Complete Set (16):	80.00
	Common Player:	5.00
1	Scott Appleton	6.00
2	Tony Banfield	6.00
3	Sonny Bishop	6.00
4	George Blanda	12.00
5	Sid Blanks	6.00
6	Danny Brabham	5.00
7	Ode Burrell	6.00
8	Doug Cline	5.00
9	Don Floyd	6.00
10	Freddy Glick	6.00
11	Charlie Hennigan	6.00
12	Ed Husmann	5.00
13	Walt Suggs	6.00
14	Bob Talamini	5.00
15	Charley Tolar	6.00
16	Don Trull	6.00

1967 Oilers Team Issue

Measuring 5-1/8" x 7", the 14-card set is anchored on the front with a black-and-white photo. The cards, which are unnumbered, have blank backs.

		NM/M
	Complete Set (14):	45.00
	Common Player:	4.00
1	Pete Barnes	4.00
2	Sonny Bishop	5.00
3	Ode Burrell	5.00
4	Ronnie Caveness	4.00
5	Joe Childress (CO)	4.00
6	Glen Ray Hines	5.00
7	Pat Holmes	4.00
8	Bobby Jancik	5.00
9	Pete Johns	4.00
10	Jim Norton	5.00
11	Willie Parker	4.00
12	Bob Poole	4.00
13	Alvin Reed	4.00
14	Olen Underwood	4.00

1969 Oilers Team Issue

Measuring 8" x 10", the 39-photo set is anchored by a large black-and-white photo on the front, bordered in white. The player's name, team and position are located beneath the photo. The unnumbered photos have blank backs.

		NM/M
	Complete Set (39):	125.00
	Common Player:	3.00
1	Jim Beirne (Wide receiver)	4.00
2	Jim Beirne (Split end)	4.00
3	Elvin Bethea	5.00
4	Sonny Bishop	4.00
5	Garland Boyette	4.00
6	Ode Burrell	4.00
7	Ed Carrington	3.00
8	Joe Childress (CO)	3.00
9	Bob Davis	3.00
10	Hugh Devore (CO)	3.00
11	Tom Domres	3.00
12	F.A. Dry	3.00
13	Miller Farr	4.00
14	Mac Haik (Action shot)	3.00
15	Mac Haik (Portrait)	3.00
16	W.K. Hicks	3.00
17	Glen Ray Hines	4.00
18	Pat Holmes	3.00
19	Roy Hopkins	3.00
20	Charlie Joiner	18.00
21	Jim LeMoine	3.00
22	Bobby Maples	4.00
23	Richard Marshall	3.00
24	Zeke Moore	4.00
25	Willie Parker	3.00
26	Johnny Peacock	3.00
27	Ron Pritchard (Back peddling)	3.00
28	Ron Pritchard (Cutting left)	3.00
29	Ron Pritchard (Preparing to fend off blocker)	3.00
30	Tom Regner	3.00
31	George Rice	3.00
32	George Rice	3.00
33	Bob Robertson	3.00
34	Walt Suggs	3.00
35	Don Trull	4.00
36	Olen Underwood	3.00
37	Loyd Wainscott	3.00
38	Wayne Walker	4.00
39	Glenn Woods	3.00

1971 Oilers Team Issue

Measuring 4" x 5-1/2", the 23-card set showcases a black-and-white photo on the front, with an Oilers' helmet in the upper left, "Houston Oilers" at the top center and the NFL shield in the upper right. The player's name and position are printed beneath the photo. The blank-backed cards are unnumbered.

		NM/M
	Complete Set (23):	50.00
	Common Player:	2.00
1	Willie Alexander	2.50
2	Jim Beirne	2.50
3	Elvin Bethea	3.00
4	Ron Billingsley	2.00
5	Garland Boyette	2.50
6	Leo Brooks	2.00
7	Ken Burrough	4.00
8	Woody Campbell	2.00
9	Lynn Dickey	4.00
10	Elbert Drungo	2.00
11	Pat Holmes	2.00
12	Robert Holmes	2.50
13	Ken Houston	10.00
14	Charlie Johnson	4.00
15	Charlie Joiner	12.00
16	Zeke Moore	2.50
17	Mark Moseley	4.00
18	Dan Pastorini	5.00
19	Alvin Reed	2.00
20	Tom Regner	2.00
21	Floyd Rice	2.00
22	Mike Tilleman	2.00
23	George Webster	3.00

1972 Oilers Team Issue

Measuring 5" x 7", the 11-card set showcases full-bleed black-and-white photos on the front. The unnumbered backs are blank.

		NM/M
	Complete Set (11):	25.00
	Common Player:	2.00
1	Ron Billingsley	2.00
2	Garland Boyette	2.00
3	Levert Carr	2.00
4	Walter Highsmith	2.00
5	Albert Johnson	2.00
6	Benny Johnson	2.00
7	Guy Murdock	2.00
8	Ron Saul	3.00
9	Mike Tilleman	2.00
10	Ward Walsh	2.00
11	George Webster	4.00

1973 Oilers McDonald's

Measuring 8" x 10", the three-photo card set is anchored by a color photo on the front, with the player's name and team beneath it. The fronts are bordered in white. The backs, which are unnumbered, have the player's name, bio, highlights and stats, along with the 1973 Oilers' schedule. The McDonald's logo is printed in the lower right.

		NM/M
	Complete Set (3):	25.00
	Common Player:	6.00
1	John Matuszak	12.00
2	Zeke Moore	6.00
3	Dan Pastorini	12.00

1973 Oilers Team Issue

Measuring 5" x 8", the 17-card set is anchored by a large black-and-white photo on the front of the white-bordered cards. The blank-backed cards are unnumbered.

		NM/M
	Complete Set (17):	35.00
	Common Player:	2.00
1	Mack Alston	2.00
2	Bob Atkins	2.00
3	Skip Butler	2.00
4	Al Cowlings	3.00
5	Lynn Dickey	3.00
6	Mike Fanucci	2.00
7	Edd Hargett	2.50
8	Lewis Jolley	2.00
9	Clifton McNeil	2.50
10	Ralph Miller	2.00
11	Zeke Moore	2.50
12	Dave Parks	2.50
13	Willie Rodgers	2.00
14	Greg Sampson	2.00
15	Finn Seemann	2.00
16	Jeff Severson	2.00
17	Fred Willis	2.50

1980 Oilers Police

The 14-card, 2-5/8" x 4-1/8" set, sponsored by Kiwanis, local law enforcement and the Oilers, features front color action photos with "Oilers Tips" appearing on the backs.

		NM/M
	Complete Set (14):	12.00
	Common Player:	.75
1	Gregg Bingham	1.00
2	Robert Brazile	.75
3	Ken Burrough	1.50
4	Rob Carpenter	1.00
5	Ronnie Coleman	1.00
6	Curley Culp	1.00
7	Carter Hartwig	.75
8	Billy Johnson	1.50
9	Carl Mauck	.75
10	Gifford Nielsen	1.00
11	Cliff Parsley	.75
12	Bum Phillips (CO)	1.00
13	Mike Renfro	1.00
14	Ken Stabler	4.00

P

1984 Pacific Legends

The 30-card, regular-size set features well-known athletes from the Pac 10 football conference, including John Wayne, Pop Warner, Jackie Robinson, Frank Gifford and Lynn Swann.

		NM/M
Complete Set (30):		20.00
Common Player:		.30
1	O.J. Simpson	5.00
2	Mike Garrett	.50
3	Pop Warner	.50
4	Bob Schloredt	.30
5	Pat Haden	.60
6	Ernie Nevers	.50
7	Jackie Robinson	2.50
8	Arnie Weinmeister	.50
9	Gary Beban	.50
10	Jim Plunkett	.60
11	Bobby Grayson	.30
12	Craig Morton	.50
13	Ben Davidson	.60
14	Jim Hardy	.30
15	Vern Burke	.30
16	Hugh McElhenny	.75
17	John Wayne	4.00
18	Ricky Bell (UER) (Name spelled Rickey on both sides)	.50
19	George Wildcat Wilson	.30
20	Bob Waterfield	.75
21	Charlie Mitchell	.30
22	Donn Moomaw	.30
23	Don Heinrich	.30
24	Terry Baker	.50
25	Jack Thompson	.50
26	Charles White	.50
27	Frank Gifford	1.50
28	Lynn Swann	1.75
29	Brick Muller	.30
30	Ron Yary	.50

1989 Pacific Steve Largent

This 110-card set is devoted to Hall of Fame wide receiver Steve Largent and commemorates his career with the Seattle Seahawks. Each card front, with a silver border, captures an event in Largent's career. The horizontally-designed backs describe the action on the front and have light blue borders. There were 85 cards in the set which were numbered; the remaining 25 cards form a 12-1/2" x 17-1/2" poster of Largent. The entire set was available as a factory set or wax packs of 10 cards each. Pacific Trading Cards produced them.

		NM/M
Complete Set (110):		25.00
Common Player (1-85):		.25
1	Steve Largent Title Card (Checklist 1-42 On Back)	1.00
2	Steve Largent Santa, Can You Please	.25
3	Steve Largent Age 9	.25
4	Steve Largent Junior High 1968	.25
5	Steve Largent High School 1971	.25
6	Steve Largent Baseball or Football	.25
7	Steve Largent Tulsa, Senior Bowl	.25
8	Steve Largent Led Nation in TD's	.25
9	Coach Patera, Coach Jerry Rhome	.40
10	Steve Largent Rookie 1976	.50
11	Steve Largent First NFL TD	.25
12	Steve Largent Seahawk's First Win	.25
13	Steve Largent First Team All-Rookie	.40
14	Steve Largent Beats Buffalo 56-7	.25
15	Steve Largent The Huddle	.25
16	Steve Largent, Norm Evans Captains	.40
17	Steve Largent First Win Against Raiders	.25
18	Steve Largent 3000 Yards Receiving	.25
19	Jerry Rhome, Steve Largent	.50
20	Steve Largent Great Hands	.25
21	Steve Largent Climbs Mt. Rainier	.25
22	Steve Largent Zorn Connection	.40
23	Steve Largent, Jim Zorn	.40
24	Steve Largent First Team All-AFC	.25
25	Steve Largent Seahawks MVP 1981	.40
26	Steve Largent Strike Season 1982	.25
27	Steve Largent Training Camp 1983	.25
28	Chuck Knox Head Coach	.40
29	Steve Largent 50 Career TD's	.25
30	Steve Largent 7000 Yards Receiving	.25
31	Tilley and Largent	.50
32	Steve Largent Cold Day in Cincy	.25
33	Steve Largent Catches 3 TD Passes	.25
34	Steve Largent Seahawks 12-4 in 1984	.25
35	Steve Largent Defeated in AFC Championships	.25
36	Steve Largent Preparing for 1985	.25
37	Steve Largent Career High 79 Catches	.25
38	Steve Largent Career High 1287 Yards	.25
39	Steve Largent 10000 Yards Receiving	.25
40	Steve Largent Throws a Pass	.25
41	Steve Largent Game Day 1985	.25
42	Steve Largent Seattle Sports Star of the Year	.40
43	Steve Largent A Very Sore Elbow	.25
44	Steve Largent The Concentration	.25
45	Steve Largent, Eugene Robinson	.40
46	Steve Largent Breaks Carmichael's Record	.35
47	Steve Largent Seahawks 37, Raiders 0	.25
48	Steve Largent 11000 Yards Receiving	.25
49	Steve Largent Rough Game	.25
50	Steve Largent Streak Continues	.25
51	Captains Lane, Brown and Largent	.40
52	Steve Largent Steve & Kyle Catch a Big One	.25
53	Steve Largent Krieg Connection	.40
54	Steve Largent Seahawk Camp	.25
55	Steve Largent NFL All-Time Leading Receiver	.40
56	Steve Largent Hall of Fame Bowl	.25
57	Steve Largent, Coach Knox	.40
58	Steve Largent 1987 Seahawks MVP	.40
59	Steve Largent Largent at Quarterback	.50
60	Steve Largent NFL All-Time Great	.40
61	Steve Largent Travelers' NFL Man of the Year 1988	.40
62	Steve Largent, Terry Largent	.25
63	Steve Largent Holding for Norm Johnson	.40
64	Steve Largent Great Moves	.25
65	Steve Largent Great Hands	.25
66	Steve Largent Seven-Time Pro Bowl Selection	.25
67	Agee, Steve Largent, Paul Skansi	.40
68	Steve Largent Signing for Fans	.25
69	Miller, Joe Nash, Steve Largent, Bryan Millard	.25
70	Steve Largent, John Elway Pro Bowl Greats	1.50
71	Steve Largent Hanging onto the Ball	.25
72	Steve Largent 1618 Career Yards vs. Denver	.25
73	Steve Largent 17 Pro Bowl Receptions	.25
74	Jim Zorn, Steve Largent	.40
75	Steve Largent Mr. Seahawk	.40
76	Steve Largent Sets NFL Career Yardage Record	.40
77	Steve Largent Two of the Greatest	.50
78	Steve Largent, Jerry Rhome, Charlie Joiner	.50
79	Steve Largent NFL All-Time Leader in Receptions	.40
80	Steve Largent Leader in Consecutive Game Receptions	.40
81	Steve Largent All-Time Leader 12686 Receiving Yards	.25
82	Steve Largent NFL All-Time Leader 1000 Yard Seasons	.40
83	Steve Largent First Recipient of the Bart Starr Trophy	.50
84	Steve Largent	.40
85	Steve Largent Future Hall of Famer	.75

A player's name in *italic* type indicates a rookie card.

1991 Pacific Prototypes

These cards were produced by Pacific Trading Cards to promote its 1991 set, its debut set. The cards, which are numbered on the back, use different numbers than their counterparts in the regular set, and can also be identified from the regular by the statistics line on the card back. The prototype cards use zeroes to fill in the stats on the back. Approximately 5,000 sets were made and distributed to dealers.

		NM/M
Complete Set (5):		100.00
Common Player:		6.00
1	Joe Montana	25.00
2	Barry Sanders	25.00
3	Bo Jackson	10.00
4	Eric Metcalf	6.00
5	Troy Aikman	20.00

1991 Pacific

Pacific's inaugural issue features full-color fronts with ultra-violet coating and full-color backs. Cards began shipping in late June and were numbered alphabetically by city name and player name. Pacific's border colors echo the player's team colors.

		NM/M
Complete Set (660):		20.00
Complete Series 1 (550):		10.00
Complete Series 2 (110):		10.00
Common Player:		.04
Series 1 Pack (14):		.50
Series 1 Wax Box (36):		10.00
Series 2 Pack (14):		.75
Series 2 Wax Box (36):		15.00
1	Deion Sanders	.25
2	Steve Broussard	.04
3	Aundray Bruce	.04
4	Rick Bryant	.04
5	John Rade	.04
6	Scott Case	.04
7	Tony Casillas	.04
8	Shawn Collins	.04
9	Darion Conner	.04
10	Tory Epps	.04
11	Bill Fralic	.04
12	Mike Gann	.04
13	Tim Green	.04
14	Chris Hinton	.04
15	Houston Hoover	.04
16	Chris Miller	.04
17	Andre Rison	.25
18	Mike Rozier	.04
19	Jessie Tuggle	.04
20	Don Beebe	.04
21	Ray Bentley	.04
22	Shane Conlan	.04
23	Kent Hull	.04
24	Mark Kelso	.04
25	James Lofton	.04
26	Scott Norwood	.04
27	Andre Reed	.20
28	Leonard Smith	.04
29	Bruce Smith	.04
30	Leon Seals	.04
31	Darryl Talley	.04
32	Steve Tasker	.04
33	Thurman Thomas	.50
34	James Williams	.04
35	Will Wolford	.04
36	Frank Reich	.04
37	*Jeff Wright*	.12
38	Neal Anderson	.10
39	Trace Armstrong	.04
40	Johnny Bailey	.04
41	Mark Bortz	.04
42	Cap Boso	.04
43	Kevin Butler	.04
44	Mark Carrier	.04
45	Jim Covert	.04
46	Wendell Davis	.10
47	Richard Dent	.04
48	Shaun Gayle	.04
49	Jim Harbaugh	.10
50	Jay Hilgenberg	.04
51	Brad Muster	.04
52	William Perry	.04
53	Mike Singletary	.04
54	Peter Tom Willis	.04
55	Donnell Woolford	.04
56	Steve McMichael	.04
57	Eric Ball	.04
58	Lewis Billups	.04
59	Jim Breech	.04
60	James Brooks	.04
61	Eddie Brown	.04
62	Rickey Dixon	.04
63	Boomer Esiason	.15
64	James Francis	.04
65	David Fulcher	.04
66	David Grant	.04
67	Harold Green	.15
68	Rodney Holman	.04
69	Stanford Jennings	.04
70	Tim Krumrie	.04
71	Tim McGee	.04
72	Anthony Munoz	.04
73	Mitchell Price	.04
74	Eric Thomas	.04
75	Ickey Woods	.04
76	Mike Baab	.04
77	Thane Gash	.04
78	David Grayson	.04
79	Mike Johnson	.04
80	Reggie Langhorne	.04
81	Kevin Mack	.04
82	Clay Matthews	.04
83	Eric Metcalf	.04
84	Frank Minnifield	.04
85	Mike Oliphant	.04
86	Mike Pagel	.04
87	John Talley	.04
88	Lawyer Tillman	.04
89	Felix Wright	.04
90	Bryan Wagner	.04
91	*Bob Burnett*	.10
92	Tommie Agee	.04
93	Troy Aikman	1.00
94	Bill Bates	.04
95	Jack Del Rio	.04
96	Issiac Holt	.04
97	Michael Irvin	.50
98	Jim Jeffcoat	.04
99	Jimmy Jones	.04
100	Kelvin Martin	.04
101	Nate Newton	.04
102	Danny Noonan	.04
103	Ken Norton	.04
104	Jay Novacek	.15
105	Mike Saxon	.04
106	Derrick Sheppard	.04
107	Emmitt Smith	2.00
108	Daniel Stubbs	.04
109	Tony Tolbert	.04
110	Alexander Wright	.09
111	Steve Atwater	.04
112	Melvin Bratton	.04
113	Tyrone Braxton	.04
114	Alphonso Carreker	.04
115	John Elway	.35
116	Simon Fletcher	.04
117	Bobby Humphrey	.04
118	Mark Jackson	.04
119	Vance Johnson	.04
120	Greg Kragen	.04
121	Karl Mecklenburg	.04
122	Orson Mobley	.04
123	Alton Montgomery	.04
124	Rickey Nattiel	.04
125	Steve Sewell	.04
126	Shannon Sharpe	.50
127	Dennis Smith	.04
128	Andre Townsend	.50
129	Mike Horan	.04
130	Jerry Ball	.04
131	Bennie Blades	.04
132	Lomas Brown	.04
133	Jeff Campbell	.04
134	Robert Clark	.04
135	Michael Cofer	.04
136	Dennis Gibson	.04
137	Mel Gray	.04
138	LeRoy Irvin	.04
139	*George Jamison*	.12
140	Richard Johnson	.04
141	Eddie Murray	.04
142	Dan Owens	.04
143	Rodney Peete	.04
144	Barry Sanders	1.25
145	Chris Spielman	.04
146	Mark Spindler	.04
147	Andre Ware	.12
148	William White	.04
149	Tony Bennett	.04
150	Robert Brown	.04
151	LeRoy Butler	.04
152	Anthony Dilweg	.04
153	Michael Haddix	.04
154	Ron Hallstrom	.04
155	Tim Harris	.04
156	Johnny Holland	.04
157	Chris Jacke	.04
158	Perry Kemp	.04
159	Mark Lee	.04
160	Don Majkowski	.04
161	Tony Mandarich	.04
162	Mark Murphy	.04
163	Brian Noble	.04
164	Shawn Patterson	.04
165	Jeff Query	.04
166	Sterling Sharpe	.60
167	Darrell Thompson	.12
168	Ed West	.04
169	Ray Childress	.04
170	*Chris Dishman*	.35
171	Curtis Duncan	.04
172	William Fuller	.04
173	Ernest Givins	.04
174	Drew Hill	.04
175	Haywood Jeffires	.20
176	Sean Jones	.04
177	Lamar Lathon	.04
178	Bruce Matthews	.04
179	Bubba McDowell	.04
180	Johnny Meads	.04
181	Warren Moon	.15
182	Mike Munchak	.04
183	Allen Pinkett	.04
184	Dean Steinkuhler	.04
185	Lorenzo White	.25
186	John Grimsby	.04
187	Pat Beach	.04
188	Albert Bentley	.04
189	Dean Biasucci	.04
190	Duane Bickett	.04
191	Bill Brooks	.04
192	Eugene Daniel	.04
193	Jeff George	.30
194	Jon Hand	.04
195	Jeff Herrod	.04
196	Jesse Hester	.04
197	Mike Prior	.04
198	Stacey Simmons	.04
199	Rohn Stark	.04
200	Pat Tomberlin	.04
201	Clarence Verdin	.04
202	Keith Taylor	.04
203	Jack Trudeau	.04
204	Chip Banks	.04
205	John Alt	.04
206	Deron Cherry	.04
207	Steve DeBerg	.04
208	Tim Grunhard	.04
209	Albert Lewis	.04
210	Nick Lowery	.04
211	Bill Maas	.04
212	Chris Martin	.04
213	Todd McNair	.04
214	Christian Okoye	.04
215	Stephone Paige	.04
216	Steve Pelluer	.04
217	Kevin Porter	.04
218	Kevin Ross	.04
219	Dan Sealeaumua	.04
220	Neil Smith	.04
221	David Szott	.04
222	Derrick Thomas	.25
223	Barry Word	.12
224	Percy Snow	.04
225	Marcus Allen	.04
226	Eddie Anderson	.04
227	Steve Beuerlein	.25
228	Tim Brown	.20
229	Scott Davis	.04
230	Mike Dyal	.04
231	Mervyn Fernandez	.04
232	Willie Gault	.04
233	Ethan Horton	.04
234	Bo Jackson	.50
235	Howie Long	.04
236	Terry McDaniel	.04
237	Max Montoya	.04
238	Don Mosebar	.04
239	Jay Schroeder	.04
240	Steve Smith	.04
241	Greg Townsend	.04
242	Aaron Wallace	.04
243	Lionel Washington	.04
244	Steve Wisniewski	1.00
245	Willie Anderson	.04
246	Latin Berry	.04
247	Robert Delpino	.04
248	Marcus Dupree	.04
249	Henry Ellard	.04
250	Jim Everett	.04
251	Cleveland Gary	.04
252	Jerry Gray	.04
253	Kevin Greene	.04
254	Pete Holohan	.04
255	Buford McGee	.04
256	Tom Newberry	.04
257	Irv Pankey	.04
258	Jackie Slater	.04
259	Doug Smith	.04
260	Frank Stams	.04
261	Michael Stewart	.04
262	Fred Strickland	.04
263	J.D. Brown	.04
264	Mark Clayton	.04
265	Jeff Cross	.04
266	Mark Dennis	.08
267	Mark Duper	.04
268	Ferrell Edmunds	.04
269	Dan Marino	2.00
270	John Offerdahl	.04
271	Louis Oliver	.04
272	Tony Paige	.04
273	Reggie Roby	.04
274	Sammie Smith	.04
275	Keith Sims	.04
276	Brian Sochia	.04
277	Pete Stoyanovich	.04
278	Richmond Webb	.04
279	Jarvis Williams	.04
280	Tim McKyer	.04
281	Jim Jensen	.04
282	*Scott Secules*	.12
283	Ray Berry	.04
284	Joey Browner	.04
285	Anthony Carter	.04
286	Cris Carter	.25
287	Chris Doleman	.04
288	Mark Dusbabek	.04
289	Hassan Jones	.04
290	Steve Jordan	.04
291	Carl Lee	.04
292	Kirk Lowdermilk	.04
293	Randall McDaniel	.04
294	Mike Merriweather	.04
295	Keith Millard	.04
296	Al Noga	.04
297	Scott Studwell	.04
298	Henry Thomas	.04
299	Herschel Walker	.04
300	Gary Zimmerman	.04
301	Rich Gannon	.10
302	Wade Wilson	.04
303	Vincent Brown	.04
304	Marv Cook	.04
305	Hart Lee Dykes	.04
306	Irving Fryar	.04
307	Tom Hodson	.04
308	Maurice Hurst	.04
309	Ronnie Lippett	.04
310	Fred Marion	.04
311	Greg McMurty	.04
312	Johnny Rembert	.04
313	Chris Singleton	.04
314	Ed Reynolds	.04
315	Andre Tippett	.04
316	Garin Veris	.04
317	Brent Williams	.04
318	John Stephens	.75
319	Sammy Martin	.04
320	Bruce Armstrong	.04
321	Morten Andersen	.10
322	Gene Atkins	.04
323	Vince Buck	.04
324	John Fourcade	.04
325	Kevin Haverdink	.04
326	Bobby Hebert	.04
327	Craig Heyward	.04
328	Dalton Hilliard	.04
329	Rickey Jackson	.04
330	Vaughan Johnson	.04
331	Eric Martin	.04
332	Wayne Martin	.04
333	Rueben Mayes	.04
334	Sam Mills	.04
335	Brett Perriman	.04
336	Pat Swilling	.04
337	Renaldo Turnbull	.04
338	Lonzell Hill	.04
339	Steve Walsh	.04
340	Carl Banks	.04
341	Mark Bavaro	.04
342	Maurice Carthon	.04
343	*Pat Harlow*	.08
344	Eric Dorsey	.04
345	John Elliott	.04
346	Rodney Hampton	.50
347	Jeff Hostetler	.20
348	Erik Howard	.04
349	Pepper Johnson	.04
350	Sean Landeta	.50
351	Leonard Marshall	.04
352	David Meggett	.04
353	Bart Oates	.04
354	Gary Reasons	.04
355	Phil Simms	.10
356	Lawrence Taylor	.10
357	Reyna Thompson	.04
358	Brian Williams	.04
359	Matt Boyer	.04
360	Mark Ingram	.04
361	Brad Baxter	.15
362	Mark Boyer	.04
363	Dennis Byrd	.04
364	Dave Cadigan	.04
365	Kyle Clifton	.04
366	James Hasty	.04
367	Joe Kelly	.04
368	Jeff Lageman	.04
369	Pat Leahy	.04
370	Terance Mathis	.10
371	Erik McMillan	.04
372	Rob Moore	.25
373	Ken O'Brien	.04
374	Tony Stargell	.04
375	Jim Sweeney	.04
376	Al Toon	.04
377	Johnny Hector	.04
378	Jeff Criswell	.04
379	Mike Haight	.04
380	Troy Benson	.04
381	Eric Allen	.04
382	Fred Barnett	.15
383	Jerome Brown	.04
384	Keith Byars	.04
385	Randall Cunningham	.20
386	Byron Evans	.04
387	Wes Hopkins	.04
388	Keith Jackson	.20
389	Seth Joyner	.04
390	*Bobby Wilson*	.10
391	Heath Sherman	.10
392	Clyde Simmons	.04
393	Ben Smith	.04
394	Andre Waters	.04
395	Reggie White	.20
396	Calvin Williams	.15
397	Al Harris	.04
398	Anthony Toney	.04
399	Mike Quick	.04
400	Anthony Bell	.04
401	Rich Camarillo	.04
402	Roy Green	.04
403	Ken Harvey	.04
404	Eric Hill	.04
405	*Garth Jax*	.07
406	Ernie Jones	.04
407	Cedric Mack	.04
408	Dexter Manley	.04
409	Tim McDonald	.04
410	Freddie Joe Nunn	.04
411	Ricky Proehl	.10
412	*Moe Gardner*	.12
413	Timm Rosenbach	.04
414	Luis Sharpe	.04
415	Vai Sikahema	.04
416	Anthony Thompson	.04
417	Ron Wolfley	.04
418	Lonnie Young	.04
419	Gary Anderson	.04
420	Bubby Brister	.04
421	Thomas Everett	.04
422	Eric Green	.10
423	Delton Hall	.04
424	Bryan Hinkle	.04
425	Merril Hoge	.04
426	Carnell Lake	.04
427	Louis Lipps	.04
428	David Little	.04
429	Greg Lloyd	.04
430	Mike Mularkey	.04
431	Keith Willis	.04
432	Dwayne Woodruff	.04
433	Rod Woodson	.04
434	Tim Worley	.04
435	Warren Williams	.04
436	Terry Long	.04
437	Martin Bayless	.04
438	*Jarrod Bunch*	.15
439	Marion Butts	.04
440	Gill Byrd	.04
441	Arthur Cox	.04
442	John Friesz	.15
443	Leo Goeas	.04
444	Burt Grossman	.04

445 Courtney Hall .04
446 Ronnie Harmon .04
447 *Nate Lewis* .25
448 Anthony Miller .04
449 Leslie O'Neal .04
450 Gary Plummer .04
451 Junior Seau .30
452 Billy Ray Smith .04
453 Billy Joe Tolliver .04
454 Broderick Thompson .04
455 Lee Williams .04
456 Michael Carter .04
457 Mike Cofer .04
458 Kevin Fagan .04
459 Charles Haley .04
460 Pierce Holt .04
461 Johnny Jackson .04
462 Brent Jones .04
463 Guy McIntyre .04
464 Joe Montana 1.00
465 Bubba Paris .04
466 Tom Rathman .04
467 Jerry Rice 1.00
468 Mike Sherrard .04
469 John Taylor .15
470 Steve Young .75
471 Dennis Brown .04
472 Dexter Carter .04
473 Bill Romanowski .04
474 Dave Waymer .04
475 Robert Blackmon .04
476 Derrick Fenner .10
477 Nesby Glasgow .04
478 Jacob Green .04
479 Andy Heck .04
480 Norm Johnson .04
481 Tommy Kane .04
482 Cortez Kennedy .30
483 Dave Krieg .04
484 Bryan Millard .04
485 Joe Nash .04
486 Rufus Porter .04
487 Eugene Robinson .04
488 *Mike Tice* .10
489 Chris Warren .50
490 John L. Williams .04
491 Terry Wooden .04
492 Tony Woods .04
493 Brian Blades .04
494 Paul Skansi .04
495 Gary Anderson .04
496 Mark Carrier .04
497 Chris Chandler .04
498 Steve Christie .04
499 Reggie Cobb .25
500 Reuben Davis .04
501 Willie Drewery .04
502 Randy Grimes .04
503 Paul Gruber .04
504 Wayne Haddix .04
505 Ron Hall .04
506 Harry Hamilton .04
507 Bruce Hill .04
508 Eugene Marve .04
509 Keith McCants .04
510 Winston Moss .04
511 Kevin Murphy .04
512 Mark Robinson .04
513 Vinny Testaverde .08
514 Broderick Thomas .04
515 Jeff Bostic .04
516 Todd Bowles .04
517 Earnest Byner .04
518 Gary Clark .20
519 *Craig Erickson* .50
520 Darryl Grant .04
521 Darrell Green .04
522 Russ Grimm .04
523 Stan Humphries .30
524 Joe Jacoby .04
525 Jim Lachey .04
526 Chip Lohmiller .04
527 Charles Mann .04
528 Wilber Marshall .04
529 Art Monk .04
530 Tracy Rocker .04
531 Mark Rypien .12
532 Ricky Sanders .04
533 Alvin Walton .04
534 *Todd Marinovich* .15
535 Mike Dumas .04
536 Russell Maryland .50
537 *Eric Turner* .20
538 *Ernie Mills* .20
539 *Ed King* .10
540 Michael Stonebreaker .04
541 *Chris Zorich* .25
542 Mike Croel .35
543 *Eric Moten* .10
544 *Dan McGwire* .15
545 *Keith Cash* .10
546 *Kenny Walker* .12
547 Leroy Hoard .08
548 Luis Chrisobol .04
549 Stacy Danley .04
550 *Todd Lyght* .10
551 *Brett Favre* 6.00
552 *Mike Pritchard* .50
553 Moe Gardner .05
554 Tim McKyer .05
555 *Erric Pegram* .50
556 Norm Johnson .05
557 *Bruce Pickens* .10
558 *Henry Jones* .35
559 *Phil Hansen* .20
560 Cornelius Bennett .05
561 Stan Thomas .05
562 Chris Zorich .10
563 *Anthony Morgan* .15
564 *Darren Lewis* .30
565 Mike Stonebreaker .05
566 *Alfred Williams* .15
567 Lamar Rogers .05
568 *Erik Wilhelm* .30
569 Ed King .05
570 *Michael Jackson* .75
571 *James Jones* .15
572 Russell Maryland .15
573 *Dixon Edwards* .10
574 Derrick Brownlow .05
575 *Larry Brown* .50
576 Mike Croel .20
577 *Keith Traylor* .08
578 Kenny Walker .05
579 *Reggie Johnson* .12
580 *Herman Moore* 2.50
581 *Kelvin Pritchett* .10
582 *Kevin Scott* .10
583 *Vinnie Clark* .10
584 *Esera Tuaolo* .10
585 Don Davey .05
586 *Blair Kiel* .12
587 Mike Dumas .05
588 *Darryll Lewis* .10
589 *John Flannery* .10
590 Kevin Donnally .05
591 Shane Curry .05
592 *Mark Vander Poel* .08
593 Dave McCloughan .05
594 *Mel Agee* .10
595 *Kerry Cash* .12
596 *Harvey Williams* .50
597 Joe Valerio .05
598 *Tim Barnett* .30
599 Todd Marinovich .05
600 *Nick Bell* .20
601 Roger Craig .05
602 Ronnie Lott .10
603 *Mike Jones* .10
604 Todd Lyght .10
605 *Roman Phifer* .10
606 *David Lang* .15
607 *Aaron Craver* .10
608 *Mark Higgs* .75
609 Chris Green .05
610 *Randy Baldwin* .10
611 Pat Harlow .05
612 *Leonard Russell* .20
613 *Jerome Henderson* .10
614 *Scott Zolak* .20
615 *Jon Vaughn* .15
616 *Harry Colon* .12
617 *Wesley Carroll* .15
618 Quinn Early .05
619 *Reggie Jones* .15
620 Jarrod Bunch .10
621 *Kanavis McGhee* .15
622 *Ed McCaffrey* 3.00
623 *Browning Nagle* .35
624 *Mo Lewis* .10
625 Blair Thomas .10
626 Antone Davis .10
627 Jim McMahon .05
628 *Scott Kowalkowski* .10
629 *Brad Goebel* .15
630 *William Thomas* .10
631 *Eric Swann* .20
632 *Mike Jones* .10
633 *Aeneas Williams* .12
634 Dexter Davis .05
635 Tom Tupa .05
636 Johnny Johnson .20
637 Randal Hill .30
638 *Jeff Graham* .75
639 Ernie Mills .10
640 *Adrian Cooper* .15
641 *Stanley Richard* .35
642 *Eric Bieniemy* .15
643 Eric Moten .05
644 *Shawn Jefferson* .35
645 *Ted Washington* .10
646 *John Johnson* .10
647 Dan McGwire .10
648 *Doug Thomas* .05
649 David Daniels .05
650 *John Kasay* .12
651 Jeff Kemp .05
652 *Charles McRae* .08
653 *Lawrence Dawsey* .20
654 Robert Wilson .05
655 Dexter Manley .05
656 Chuck Weatherspoon .05
657 Tim Ryan .05
658 Bobby Wilson .05
659 *Ricky Ervins* .35
660 Matt Millen .05

1991 Pacific Checklists

These checklists were issued for Pacific's first series of 1991 football cards and were randomly included in late-issue foil and wax packs. Pacific stated it only produced 10,000 checklist sets. Cards were numbered on the back.

NM/M

Complete Set (5): 2.00
Common Player: .50
1 Checklist 1 .50
2 Checklist 2 .50
3 Checklist 3 .50
4 Checklist 4 .50
5 Checklist 5 .50

1991 Pacific Picks The Pros

Pacific produced a 25-card insert set, including its choice as the best player at each position offensively and defensively plus a card of 1991 #1 draft choice Russell Maryland. Cards were either bordered in silver or gold, with 10,000 of each type produced and randomly inserted (gold in foil packs, silver in cello).

NM/M

Complete Set (25): 35.00
Common Player: .30
1 Russell Maryland 1.00
2 Andre Reed 3.00
3 Jerry Rice 8.00
4 Keith Jackson 1.00
5 Jim Lachey .30
6 Anthony Munoz .50
7 Randall McDaniel .30
8 Bruce Matthews .30
9 Kent Hull .30
10 Joe Montana 10.00
11 Barry Sanders 10.00
12 Thurman Thomas 5.00
13 Morten Anderson 3.00
14 Jerry Ball .50
15 Jerome Brown .50
16 Reggie White 2.00
17 Bruce Smith 2.00
18 Derrick Thomas 2.00
19 Lawrence Taylor 3.00
20 Charles Haley 1.00
21 Albert Lewis 1.00
22 Rod Woodson 3.00
23 David Fulcher 1.00
24 Joey Browner 1.00
25 Sean Landeta 1.00

1991 Pacific Flash Cards

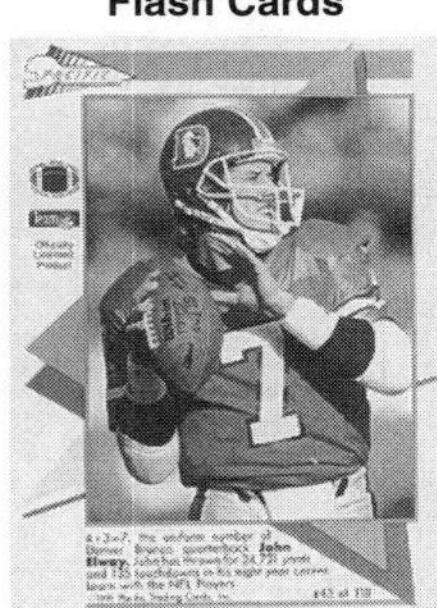

These mathematical flash cards contain a problem on the front which, when worked out correctly, equals the uniform number of the player pictured on the card back. The back of the card has a glossy picture of the player and either a career summary or highlights from the previous season. A card number also appears on the back. The cards are standard size.

NM/M

Complete Set (110): 8.00
Common Player: .05
1 Steve Young .40
2 Hart Lee Dykes .05
3 Timm Rosenbach .05
4 Andre Collins .05
5 Johnny Johnson .20
6 Nick Lowery .05
7 John Stephens .05
8 Jim Arnold .05
9 Steve DeBerg .15
10 Christian Okoye .05
11 Eric Swann .10
12 Jerry Robinson .05
13 Steve Wisniewski .05
14 Jim Harbaugh .10
15 Steve Broussard .05
16 Mike Singletary .15
17 Tim Green .05
18 Roger Craig .15
19 Maury Buford .05
20 Marcus Allen .25
21 Deion Sanders .40
22 Chris Miller .20
23 Joey Browner .10
24 Bubby Brister .10
25 Buford McGee .05
26 Ed West .05
27 Mark Murphy .05
28 Tim Worley .10
29 Keith Willis .05
30 Rich Gannon .05
31 Jim Everett .15
32 Duval Love .05
33 Bob Nelson .05
34 Anthony Munoz .15
35 Boomer Esiason .20
36 Kenny Walker .05
37 Mike Horan .05
38 Gary Kubiak .05
39 David Treadwell .05
40 Robert Wilson .05
41 Lewis Billups .05
42 Kevin Mack .05
43 John Elway .50
44 Lee Johnson .05
45 Ken Willis .05
46 Herman Moore .40
47 Eddie Murray .05
48 Mike Saxon .05
49 John L. Williams .10
50 Barry Sanders 1.00
51 Andre Ware .15
52 Dave Krieg .10
53 Cortez Kennedy .25
54 Bo Jackson .50
55 Derrick Fenner .05
56 Steve Walsh .10
57 Brett Maxie .05
58 Stan Brock .05
59 DeMond Winston .05
60 Sam Mills .10
61 Eric Martin .10
62 Michael Carter .10
63 Steve Wallace .05
64 Jesse Sapolu .05
65 Bill Romanowski .05
66 Joe Montana 2.00
67 Sean Landeta .05
68 Doug Riesenberg .05
69 Myron Guyton .05
70 Andre Reed .15
71 John Elliott .05
72 Jeff Hostetler .15
73 Rohn Stark .05
74 Jeff George .20
75 Duane Bickett .05
76 Emmitt Smith 2.00
77 Michael Irvin .50
78 Tony Stargell .05
79 Kyle Clifton .05
80 John Booty .05
81 Fred Barnett .20
82 Blair Thomas .10
83 Erik McMillan .05
84 Broderick Thomas .10
85 Jim Skow .05
86 Gary Anderson .10
87 Mark Robinson .05
88 Steve Christie .05
89 Cody Carlson .15
90 Warren Moon .35
91 Lorenzo White .10
92 Reggie Roby .05
93 Jim C. Jensen .05
94 Mark Clayton .10
95 Willie Gault .10
96 Don Mosebar .05
97 Gary Plummer .05
98 Leslie O'Neal .10
99 Neal Anderson .15
100 Derrick Thomas .25
101 Luis Sharpe .05
102 D.J. Dozier .05
103 Jarrod Bunch .05
104 Mark Ingram .05
105 James Lofton .15
106 Jay Schroeder .10
107 Ronnie Lott .15
108 Todd Marinovich .10
109 Chris Zorich .15
110 Charles McRae .05

1992 Pacific Prototypes

These 1992 prototypes feature Pacific's new design for 1992. A full-color glossy photo is on the card front, framed by a white border. A color stripe, containing the player's name and team helmet, runs along the left side of the card. The back is numbered and includes a mug shot and career summary. Approximately 5,000 sets were produced; most were given away at the Super Bowl Card Show in Minneapolis.

NM/M

Complete Set (6): 15.00
Common Player: 2.00
1 Warren Moon 3.00
2 Pat Swilling 2.00
3 Michael Irvin 3.00
4 Haywood Jeffires 3.00
5 Thurman Thomas 5.00
6 Leonard Russell 2.00

1992 Pacific

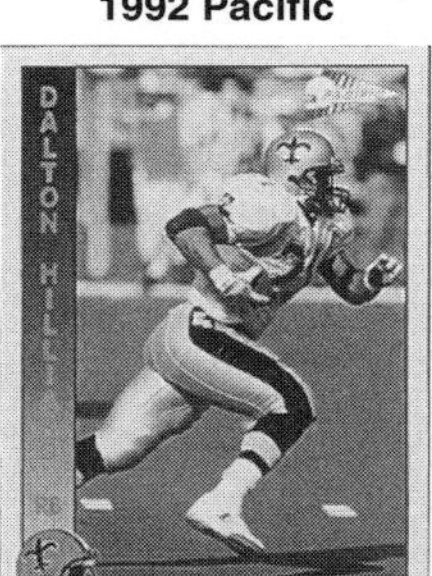

Pacific issued this set of 660 standard-sized cards in two series of 330 cards each. The glossy fronts feature color action shots framed by white borders. The player's name and team helmet run in a stripe down the left side. The backs are done in a horizontal format and also feature a color photo, plus statistics and a player profile. Cards are numbered alphabetically by player, by team, beginning with Atlanta and ending with Washington. Draft Picks are featured in a subset. Insert sets include Checklists (8 cards randomly inserted in packs); Bob Griese and Steve Largent (9 Legends of the Game cards for each, plus 1,000 autographed cards each; all are random inserts); Prisms (10 cards featuring top running backs, randomly inserted); Statistical Leaders (30 cards featuring the 28 statistical leaders from the 28 NFL teams, plus two cards devoted to the AFC and NFC rushing leaders; all were randomly inserted); and Pacific Picks the Pros (25 cards, Pacific's selection of the top players at each position). The Picks the Pros cards come in two versions - with gold foil or silver foil borders, and corresponding lettering.

NM/M

Complete Set (660): 20.00
Complete Series 1 (330): 10.00
Complete Series 2 (330): 10.00
Complete Factory Set (690): 25.00
Common Player: .05
Pack (17): .25
Wax Box (36): 7.00
1 Steve Broussard .05
2 Darion Connor .05
3 Tory Epps .05
4 Michael Haynes .30
5 Chris Hinton .05
6 Mike Kenn .05
7 Tim McKyer .05
8 Chris Miller .05
9 Erric Pegram .20
10 Mike Pritchard .20
11 Moe Gardner .05
12 Tim Green .05
13 Norm Johnson .05
14 Don Beebe .05
15 Cornelius Bennett .05
16 Al Edwards .05
17 Mark Kelso .05
18 James Lofton .05
19 Frank Reich .05
20 Leon Seals .05
21 Darryl Talley .05
22 Thurman Thomas .40
23 Kent Hall .05
24 Jeff Wright .05
25 Nate Odomes .05
26 Carwell Gardner .05
27 Neal Anderson .10
28 Mark Carrier .05
29 Johnny Bailey .05
30 Jim Harbaugh .05
31 Jay Hilgenberg .05
32 William Perry .05
33 Wendell Davis .05
34 Donnell Woolford .05
35 Keith Van Horne .05
36 Shaun Gayle .05
37 Tom Waddle .12
38 Chris Zorich .05
39 Tom Thayer .05
40 Rickey Dixon .05
41 James Francis .05
42 David Fulcher .05
43 Reggie Rembert .05
44 Anthony Munoz .05
45 Harold Green .05
46 Mitchell Price .05
47 Rodney Holman .05
48 Bruce Kozerski .05
49 Bruce Reimers .05
50 Erik Wilhelm .05
51 Harlon Barnett .05
52 Mike Johnson .05
53 Brian Brennan .05
54 Ed King .05
55 Reggie Langhorne .05
56 James Jones .05
57 Mike Baab .05
58 Dan Fike .05
59 Frank Minnifield .05
60 Clay Matthews .05
61 Kevin Mack .05
62 Tony Casillas .05
63 Jay Novacek .15
64 Larry Brown .05
65 Michael Irvin .25
66 Jack Del Rio .05
67 Ken Willis .05
68 Emmitt Smith 2.25
69 Alan Veingrad .05
70 John Gesek .05
71 Steve Beuerlein .20
72 *Vinson Smith* .08
73 Steve Atwater .05
74 Mike Croel .05
75 John Elway .35
76 Gaston Green .05
77 Mike Horan .05
78 Vance Johnson .05
79 Karl Mecklenburg .05
80 Shannon Sharpe .05
81 David Treadwell .05
82 Kenny Walker .05
83 Greg Lewis .05
84 Shawn Moore .05
85 Alton Montgomery .05
86 Michael Young .05
87 Jerry Ball .05
88 Bennie Blades .05
89 Mel Gray .05
90 Herman Moore .50
91 Erik Kramer .05
92 Willie Green .12
93 George Jamison .05
94 Chris Spielman .05
95 Kelvin Pritchett .05
96 William White .05
97 Mike Utley .12
98 Tony Bennett .05
99 LeRoy Butler .05
100 Vinnie Clark .05
101 Ron Hallstrom .05
102 Chris Jacke .05
103 Tony Mandarich .05
104 Sterling Sharpe .45
105 Don Majkowski .05
106 Johnny Holland .05
107 Esera Tuaolo .05
108 Darrell Thompson .05
109 Bubba McDowell .05
110 Curtis Duncan .05
111 Lamar Lathon .05
112 Drew Hill .05
113 Bruce Matthews .05
114 *Bo Orlando* .15
115 Don Maggs .05
116 Lorenzo White .05
117 Ernest Givins .05
118 Tony Jones .05
119 Dean Steinkuhler .05
120 Dean Biasucci .05
121 Duane Bickett .05
122 Bill Brooks .05
123 Ken Clark .05
124 Jessie Hester .05
125 Anthony Johnson .05
126 Chip Banks .05
127 Mike Prior .05
128 Rohn Stark .05
129 Jeff Herrod .05
130 Clarence Verdin .05
131 Tim Manoa .05
132 *Brian Baldinger* .05
133 Tim Barnett .05
134 J.J. Birden .05
135 Deron Cherry .05
136 Steve DeBerg .05
137 Nick Lowery .05
138 Todd McNair .05
139 Christian Okoye .05
140 Mark Vlasic .05
141 Dan Saleaumua .05
142 Neil Smith .05
143 Robb Thomas .05
144 Eddie Anderson .05
145 Nick Bell .12
146 Tim Brown .30
147 Roger Craig .05
148 Jeff Gossett .05
149 Ethan Horton .05
150 Jamie Holland .05
151 Jeff Jaeger .05
152 Todd Marinovich .05
153 Marcus Allen .05
154 Steve Smith .05
155 Flipper Anderson .05
156 Robert Delpino .05
157 Cleveland Gary .05
158 Kevin Greene .05
159 Dale Hatcher .05
160 Duval Love .05
161 Ron Brown .05
162 Jackie Slater .05
163 Doug Smith .05
164 Aaron Cox .05
165 Larry Kelm .05
166 Mark Clayton .05
167 Louis Oliver .05
168 Mark Higgs .15
169 Aaron Craver .05
170 Sammie Smith .05
171 Tony Paige .05
172 Jeff Cross .05
173 David Griggs .05
174 Richmond Webb .05
175 Vestee Jackson .05
176 Jim C. Jensen .05
177 Anthony Carter .05
178 Cris Carter .05
179 Chris Doleman .05
180 Rich Gannon .10
181 Al Noga .05
182 Randall McDaniel .05
183 Todd Scott .05
184 Henry Thomas .05
185 Felix Wright .05
186 Gary Zimmerman .05
187 Herschel Walker .05
188 Vincent Brown .05
189 Harry Colon .05
190 Irving Fryar .05
191 Marv Cook .05
192 Leonard Russell .25
193 Hugh Millen .05
194 Pat Harlow .05
195 Jon Vaughn .12
196 *Ben Coates* 2.00
197 Johnny Rembert .05
198 Greg McMurtry .05
199 Morten Andersen .05
200 Tommy Barnhardt .05
201 Bobby Hebert .05
202 Dalton Hilliard .05
203 Sam Mills .05
204 Pat Swilling .05
205 Rickey Jackson .05
206 Stan Brock .05
207 Reggie Jones .05
208 Gill Fenerty .05
209 Eric Martin .05
210 Matt Bahr .05
211 Rodney Hampton .40
212 Jeff Hostetler .15
213 Pepper Johnson .05
214 Leonard Marshall .05
215 Doug Riesenberg .05
216 Stephen Baker .05
217 Mike Fox .05
218 Bart Oates .05
219 Everson Walls .05
220 Gary Reasons .05
221 Jeff Lageman .05
222 Joe Kelly .05
223 Mo Lewis .05
224 Tony Stargell .05
225 Jim Sweeney .05
226 Freeman McNeil .05
227 Brian Washington .05
228 Johnny Hector .05
229 Terance Mathis .05
230 Rob Moore .20
231 Brad Baxter .05
232 Eric Allen .05
233 Fred Barnett .20
234 Jerome Brown .05
235 Keith Byars .05
236 William Thomas .05
237 Jessie Small .05
238 Robert Drummond .05

No.	Player	Price
239	Reggie White	.15
240	James Joseph	.05
241	Brad Goebel	.08
242	Clyde Simmons	.05
243	Rich Camarillo	.05
244	Ken Harvey	.05
245	Garth Jax	.05
246	Johnny Johnson	.15
247	Mike Jones	.05
248	Ernie Jones	.05
249	Tom Tupa	.05
250	Ron Wolfley	.05
251	Luis Sharpe	.05
252	Eric Swann	.05
253	Anthony Thompson	.05
254	Gary Anderson	.05
255	Dermontti Dawson	.05
256	Jeff Graham	.12
257	Eric Green	.05
258	Louis Lipps	.05
259	Neil O'Donnell	.25
260	Rod Woodson	.05
261	Dwight Stone	.05
262	Aaron Jones	.05
263	Keith Willis	.05
264	Ernie Mills	.05
265	Martin Bayless	.05
266	Rod Bernstine	.05
267	John Carney	.05
268	John Friesz	.05
269	Nate Lewis	.05
270	Shawn Jefferson	.05
271	Burt Grossman	.05
272	Eric Moten	.05
273	Gary Plummer	.05
274	Henry Rolling	.05
275	*Steve Hendrickson*	.10
276	Michael Carter	.05
277	*Steve Bono*	1.00
278	Dexter Carter	.05
279	Mike Cofer	.05
280	Charles Haley	.05
281	Tom Rathman	.05
282	Guy McIntyre	.05
283	John Taylor	.05
284	Dave Waymer	.05
285	Steve Wallace	.05
286	Jamie Williams	.05
287	Brian Blades	.05
288	Jeff Bryant	.05
289	Grant Feasel	.05
290	Jacob Green	.05
291	Andy Heck	.05
292	Kelly Stouffer	.05
293	John Kasay	.05
294	Cortez Kennedy	.15
295	Bryan Millard	.05
296	Eugene Robinson	.05
297	Tony Woods	.05
298	Jesse Anderson	.05
299	Gary Anderson	.05
300	Mark Carrier	.05
301	Reggie Cobb	.12
302	Robert Wilson	.05
303	Jesse Solomon	.05
304	Broderick Thomas	.05
305	Lawrence Dawsey	.05
306	Charles McRae	.05
307	Paul Gruber	.05
308	Vinny Testaverde	.05
309	Brian Mitchell	.05
310	Darrell Green	.05
311	Art Monk	.05
312	Russ Grimm	.05
313	Mark Rypien	.20
314	Bobby Wilson	.05
315	Wilber Marshall	.05
316	Gerald Riggs	.05
317	Chip Lohmiller	.05
318	Joe Jacoby	.05
319	Martin Mayhew	.05
320	*Amp Lee*	.35
321	*Terrell Buckley*	.30
322	*Tommy Vardell*	.25
323	*Ricardo McDonald*	.10
324	*Joe Bowden*	.08
325	*Darryl Williams*	.20
326	Carlos Huerta	.05
327	*Patrick Rowe*	.10
328	*Siran Stacy*	.15
329	*Dexter McNabb*	.08
330	*Willie Clay*	.10
331	Oliver Barnett	.05
332	Aundray Bruce	.05
333	*Ken Tippins*	.10
334	Jessie Tuggle	.05
335	Brian Jordan	.06
336	Andre Rison	.30
337	Houston Hoover	.05
338	Bill Fralic	.05
339	*Pat Chaffey*	.15
340	Keith Jones	.05
341	*Jamie Dukes*	.08
342	Chris Mohr	.05
343	John Davis	.05
344	Ray Bentley	.05
345	Scott Norwood	.05
346	Shane Conlan	.06
347	Steve Tasker	.06
348	Will Wolford	.05
349	*Gary Baldinger*	.10
350	Kirby Jackson	.05
351	Jamie Mueller	.05
352	Pete Metzelaars	.05
353	Richard Dent	.05
354	Ron Rivera	.05
355	Jim Morrissey	.05
356	John Roper	.05
357	Steve McMichael	.05
358	Ron Morris	.05
359	Darren Lewis	.15
360	Anthony Morgan	.10
361	Stan Thomas	.05
362	James Thornton	.05
363	Brad Muster	.05
364	Tim Krumrie	.05
365	Lee Johnson	.05
366	Eric Ball	.05
367	Alonzo Mitz	.10
368	David Grant	.05
369	Lynn James	.05
370	Lewis Billups	.05
371	Jim Breech	.05
372	Alfred Williams	.05
373	Wayne Haddix	.05
374	Tim McGee	.05
375	Michael Jackson	.10
376	Leroy Hoard	.05
377	Tony Jones	.05
378	Vince Newsome	.05
379	*Todd Philcox*	.15
380	Eric Metcalf	.05
381	John Rienstra	.05
382	Matt Stover	.05
383	Brian Hansen	.05
384	Joe Morris	.05
385	Anthony Pleasant	.05
386	Mark Stepnoski	.05
387	Eric Williams	.05
388	Jimmie Jones	.05
389	Kevin Gogan	.05
390	Manny Hendrix	.10
391	Issiac Holt	.05
392	Ken Norton	.05
393	Tommie Agee	.05
394	Alvin Harper	.10
395	Alexander Wright	.05
396	Mike Saxon	.05
397	Michael Brooks	.05
398	Bobby Humphrey	.05
399	Ken Lanier	.05
400	Steve Sewell	.05
401	Robert Perryman	.05
402	Wymon Henderson	.05
403	Keith Kartz	.05
404	Clarence Kay	.05
405	Keith Traylor	.05
406	Doug Widell	.05
407	Dennis Smith	.05
408	Marc Spindler	.05
409	Lomas Brown	.05
410	Robert Clark	.05
411	Eric Andolsek	.05
412	Mike Farr	.05
413	Ray Crockett	.05
414	Jeff Campbell	.05
415	Dan Owens	.05
416	Jim Arnold	.05
417	Barry Sanders	1.25
418	Eddie Murray	.05
419	Vince Workman	.10
420	Ed West	.05
421	Charles Wilson	.05
422	Perry Kemp	.05
423	Chuck Cecil	.05
424	James Campen	.05
425	Robert Brown	.05
426	Brian Noble	.05
427	Rich Moran	.05
428	Vai Sikahema	.05
429	Allen Rice	.05
430	Haywood Jeffires	.15
431	Warren Moon	.20
432	Greg Montgomery	.05
433	Sean Jones	.05
434	Richard Johnson	.05
435	Al Smith	.05
436	Johnny Meads	.05
437	William Fuller	.05
438	Mike Munchak	.05
439	Ray Childress	.05
440	Cody Carlson	.05
441	Scott Radecic	.05
442	*Quintus McDonald*	.10
443	Eugene Daniel	.05
444	Mark Herrmann	.15
445	*John Baylor*	.12
446	Dave McCloughan	.05
447	Mark Vander Poel	.05
448	Randy Dixon	.05
449	Keith Taylor	.05
450	Alan Grant	.05
451	Tony Siragusa	.05
452	Rich Baldinger	.05
453	Derrick Thomas	.20
454	Bill Jones	.05
455	Troy Stradford	.05
456	Barry Word	.15
457	Tim Grunhard	.05
458	Tim Martin	.05
459	*Jayice Pearson*	.10
460	Dino Hackett	.05
461	David Lutz	.05
462	Albert Lewis	.06
463	*Fred Jones*	.12
464	Winston Moss	.05
465	*Sam Graddy*	.20
466	Steve Wisniewski	.05
467	Jay Schroeder	.05
468	Ronnie Loft	.05
469	Willie Gault	.05
470	Greg Townsend	.05
471	Max Montoya	.05
472	Howie Long	.05
473	Lionel Washington	.05
474	Riki Ellison	.05
475	Tom Newberry	.05
476	Damone Johnson	.05
477	Pat Terrell	.05
478	Marcus Dupree	.05
479	Todd Lyght	.10
480	Buford McGee	.05
481	Bern Brostek	.05
482	Jim Price	.05
483	Robert Young	.05
484	Tony Zendejas	.05
485	*Robert Bailey*	.10
486	Alvin Wright	.05
487	Pat Carter	.05
488	Pete Stoyanovich	.05
489	Reggie Roby	.05
490	Harry Galbreath	.05
491	*Michael McGruder*	.10
492	J.B. Brown	.05
493	E.J. Junior	.05
494	Ferrell Edmunds	.05
495	Scott Secules	.05
496	*Greg Baty*	.15
497	Mike Iaquaniello	.05
498	Keith Sims	.05
499	John Randle	.05
500	Joey Browner	.05
501	Steve Jordan	.08
502	Darrin Nelson	.05
503	Audray McMillian	.05
504	Harry Newsome	.05
505	Hassan Jones	.05
506	Ray Berry	.05
507	Mike Merriweather	.05
508	Leo Lewis	.05
509	Tim Irwin	.05
510	Kirk Lowdermilk	.05
511	Alfred Anderson	.05
512	*Michael Timpson*	.75
513	Jerome Henderson	.05
514	Andre Tippett	.05
515	Chris Singleton	.05
516	John Stephens	.05
517	Ronnie Lippett	.05
518	Bruce Armstrong	.05
519	*Marion Hobby*	.10
520	Tim Goad	.05
521	*Mickey Washington*	.08
522	Fred Smerlas	.05
523	Wayne Martin	.05
524	Frank Warren	.05
525	Floyd Turner	.05
526	Wesley Carroll	.05
527	Gene Atkins	.05
528	Vaughan Johnson	.05
529	Hoby Brenner	.05
530	Renaldo Turnbull	.05
531	Joel Hilgenberg	.05
532	Craig Heyward	.05
533	Vince Buck	.05
534	Jim Dombrowski	.05
535	*Fred McAfee*	.12
536	Phil Simms	.10
537	Lewis Tillman	.05
538	John Elliott	.05
539	Dave Meggett	.05
540	Mark Collins	.05
541	Ottis Anderson	.05
542	*Bobby Abrams*	.10
543	Sean Landeta	.05
544	Brian Williams	.05
545	Erik Howard	.05
546	Mark Ingram	.05
547	Kanavis McGhee	.05
548	Kyle Clifton	.05
549	Marvin Washington	.05
550	Jeff Criswell	.05
551	Dave Cadigan	.05
552	Chris Burkett	.05
553	Erik McMillan	.05
554	James Hasty	.05
555	*Louie Aguiar*	.10
556	*Troy Johnson*	.10
557	*Troy Taylor*	.10
558	*Pat Kelly*	.08
559	Heath Sherman	.05
560	Roger Ruzek	.05
561	Andre Waters	.05
562	Izel Jenkins	.05
563	Keith Jackson	.15
564	Byron Evans	.05
565	Wes Hopkins	.05
566	Rich Miano	.05
567	Seth Joyner	.05
568	Thomas Sanders	.05
569	David Alexander	.05
570	Jeff Kemp	.05
571	*Jock Jones*	.10
572	*Craig Patterson*	.10
573	Robert Massey	.05
574	Bill Lewis	.05
575	Freddie Joe Nunn	.05
576	Aeneas Williams	.05
577	John Jackson	.05
578	Tim McDonald	.05
579	*Michael Zordich*	.10
580	Eric Hill	.05
581	Lorenzo Lynch	.05
582	*Vernice Smith*	.10
583	Greg Lloyd	.05
584	Carnell Lake	.05
585	Hardy Nickerson	.05
586	Delton Hall	.05
587	Gerald Williams	.05
588	Bryan Hinkle	.05
589	Barry Foster	.45
590	Bubby Brister	.05
591	*Rick Strom*	.15
592	David Little	.05
593	*Leroy Thompson*	.40
594	Eric Bieniemy	.05
595	Courtney Hall	.05
596	George Thornton	.05
597	Donnie Elder	.05
598	Billy Ray Smith	.05
599	Gill Byrd	.05
600	Marion Butts	.10
601	Ronnie Harmon	.05
602	Anthony Shelton	.05
603	Mark May	.05
604	*Craig McEwen*	.10
605	Steve Young	1.00
606	Keith Henderson	.05
607	Pierce Holt	.05
608	Roy Foster	.05
609	Don Griffin	.05
610	Harry Sydney	.05
611	Todd Bowles	.05
612	Ted Washington	.05
613	Johnny Jackson	.05
614	Jesse Sapolu	.05
615	Brent Jones	.05
616	Travis McNeal	.05
617	*Darrick Brilz*	.10
618	Terry Wooden	.05
619	Tommy Kane	.05
620	Nesby Glasgow	.05
621	Dwayne Harper	.05
622	Rick Tuten	.05
623	Chris Warren	.30
624	John L. Williams	.05
625	Rufus Porter	.05
626	David Daniels	.05
627	Keith McCants	.05
628	Reuben Davis	.05
629	Mark Royals	.05
630	*Marty Carter*	.15
631	Ian Beckles	.05
632	Ron Hall	.05
633	Eugene Marve	.05
634	Willie Drewrey	.05
635	*Tom McHale*	.10
636	Kevin Murphy	.05
637	Robert Hardy	.10
638	Ricky Sanders	.05
639	Gary Clark	.10
640	Andre Collins	.05
641	Brad Edwards	.05
642	Monte Coleman	.05
643	*Clarence Vaughn*	.10
644	Fred Stokes	.05
645	Charles Mann	.05
646	Earnest Byner	.05
647	Jim Lachey	.05
648	Jeff Bostic	.05
649	*Chris Mims*	.30
650	*George Williams*	.10
651	Ed Cunningham	.08
652	*Tony Smith*	.10
653	*Will Furrer*	.15
655	*Mike Mooney*	.08
656	*Eddie Blake*	.10
657	*Leon Searcy*	.12
658	*Kevin Turner*	.20
659	*Keith Hamilton*	.15
660	*Alan Haller*	.10

1992 Pacific Checklists

These inserts were released in 1992 Pacific foil, jumbo and 25-cent packs. Each card is numbered on the back 1 of 8, etc. Cards 1-4 were in Series I packs; cards 5-8 were in Series II packs.

		NM/M
Complete Set (8):		3.00
Common Player:		.50
1	Checklist 1 - (1-110)	.50
2	Checklist 2 - (111-220)	.50
3	Checklist 3 - (221-330)	.50
4	Checklist 4 (Highlight Cards)	.50
5	Checklist 5 - (1-110)	.50
6	Checklist 6 - (111-220)	.50
7	Checklist 7 - (221-330)	.50
8	Checklist 8 (Highlight Cards)	.50

1992 Pacific Legends of the Game Bob Griese

Miami Dolphins Hall of Fame quarterback Bob Griese is featured on this nine-card insert set. The cards, subtitled "Legends of the Game," were random inserts in 1992 Pacific Series II foil and jumbo packs. Each white-bordered card front has a color action shot, along with a caption and Griese's name in a colorful stripe at the bottom next to the Pacific logo. The back is in a horizontal format and features another photo of the player, plus a career summary. The cards are a continuation of the "Legends of the Game" series, so they start at 10, where the 1992 Steve Largent set ended. The Griese cards were also randomly inserted in triple folder card packs and five-card changemaker packs. Griese also autographed 1,000 cards.

		NM/M
Complete Set (9):		5.00
Common Griese:		.50
10	Bob Griese Purdue Star	.50
11	Bob Griese AFL Star	.50
12	Bob Griese Super Bowl Star	.50
13	Bob Griese Thinking Man's QB	.50
14	Bob Griese 349 Yards	.50
15	Bob Griese All Star	.50
16	Bob Griese The 25,000 Yard Club	.50
17	Bob Griese Number 12 Retired	.50
18	Bob Griese Hall of Fame	.50

1992 Pacific Legends of the Game Steve Largent

Seattle Seahawks Hall of Fame wide receiver Steve Largent is featured in this nine-card insert set. Cards were randomly inserted in Series I and jumbo packs. Fronts feature color action photos with white borders. The card title and Largent's name are in a colored panel at the bottom. The backs have a photo, career summary and card number, 1 of 9, etc. They are in a horizontal format. Largent autographed 1,000 cards.

		NM/M
Complete Set (9):		5.00
Common Player:		.50
1	Great Rookie Start	.50
2	Largent Leads NFL	.50
3	Hi-Steppin'	.50
4	NFL Leader	.50
5	Team Captain	.50
6	Pro Bowl	.50
7	Man of the Year	.50
8	The Final Season	.50
9	Retirement Celebration	.50

1992 Pacific Picks The Pros

Pacific selected the best player at each position for this 25-card insert set. Gold foil versions of the cards, which say "Pacific Picks The Pros" in gold foil down the left side, were randomly inserted in Series I foil packs. Silver versions were also made and were random inserts in Series I jumbo packs. The backs present a career summary in a diagonal format with a red and yellow background. A card number is also included. The cards have the same value for both versions.

		NM/M
Complete Set (25):		15.00
Common Player:		.50
1	Mark Rypien	.50
2	Marv Cook	.50
3	Jim Lachey	.50
4	Darrell Green	.50
5	Derrick Thomas	1.00
6	Thurman Thomas	3.00
7	Kent Hull	.50
8	Tim McDonald	.50
9	Mike Croel	.50
10	Anthony Munoz	.50
11	Jerome Brown	.50
12	Reggie White	2.00
13	Gill Byrd	.50
14	Jessie Tuggle	.50
15	Randall McDaniel	.50
16	Sam Mills	.50
17	Pat Swilling	.50
18	Eugene Robinson	.50
19	Michael Irvin	3.00
20	Emmitt Smith	6.00
21	Jeff Gossett	.50
22	Jeff Jaeger	.50
23	William Fuller	.50
24	Mike Munchak	.50
25	Andre Rison	1.00

1992 Pacific Prism Inserts

The top 10 running backs in the NFL are featured in this set. Pacific stated it produced only 10,000 of each card and randomly inserted them in 1992 Pacific Series II foil packs and triple folder card packs. The front of each card features a player photo superimposed against a prism-patterned background. A color streak at the bottom contains the player's name. Each back has a green football field for a background and uses team-color bar graphics to give the back's rushing totals for each game in 1991. Backs are numbered 1 of 10, etc.

		NM/M
Complete Set (10):		12.00
Common Player:		1.00
1	Thurman Thomas	1.00
2	Gaston Green	1.00
3	Christian Okoye	1.00
4	Leonard Russell	1.00
5	Mark Higgs	1.00
6	Emmitt Smith	4.00
7	Barry Sanders	4.00
8	Rodney Hampton	1.00
9	Earnest Byner	1.00
10	Herschel Walker	2.00

1992 Pacific Statistical Leaders

These cards, which feature statistical leaders from each NFL team, were random inserts in Series I foil packs. The front of the card has a glossy action photo bordered by a white frame. The player's name and category he lead are at the bottom in a multi-colored stripe. Three other team leaders are featured on each back, plus small photos of the player in action. The cards are also numbered on the back. Additional cards were made for the AFC and NFC rushing leaders.

		NM/M
Complete Set (30):		9.00
Common Player:		.25
1	Chris Miller	.25
2	Thurman Thomas	1.25
3	Jim Harbaugh	.25
4	Jim Breech	.25
5	Kevin Mack	.25
6	Emmitt Smith	4.00
7	Gaston Green	.25
8	Barry Sanders	2.50
9	Tony Bennett	.25
10	Warren Moon	.50
11	Bill Brooks	.25
12	Christian Okoye	.25
13	Jay Schroeder	.30
14	Robert Delpino	.25
15	Mark Higgs	.25
16	John Randle	.25
17	Leonard Russell	.25
18	Pat Swilling	.30
19	Rodney Hampton	.50
20	Terance Mathis	.40
21	Fred Barnett	.25
22	Aeneas Williams	.25
23	Neil O'Donnell	.35
24	Marion Butts	.25
25	Steve Young	1.25
26	John L. Williams	.25
27	Reggie Cobb	.25
28	Mark Rypien	.35
29	Thurman Thomas	.50
30	Emmitt Smith	1.50

1992 Pacific Triple Folders

One player from each NFL team was selected for this 28-card Pacific Trading Cards set. Each card front has two panels which, when closed, form a 3-1/2" x 5" glossy color action photo. The player's name and team helmet are on one side, while his position is on the other side. When opened up, the inside of the card reveals three smaller photos of the featured player. The cards use team color-coding for the background and have statistics and a player profile on the back, along with a card number. Each Triple Folder pack also included one card as an insert from the following sets: Steve Largent, Bob Griese, Statistical Leaders, Gold/Foil Prisms, Rushing Leaders Prisms, or checklists.

		NM/M
Complete Set (28):		17.00
Common Player:		.50
1	Chris Miller	.50
2	Thurman Thomas	1.50
3	Neal Anderson	.50
4	Tim McGee	.50
5	Kevin Mack	.50
6	Emmitt Smith	4.00
7	John Elway	2.00
8	Barry Sanders	4.00
9	Sterling Sharpe	1.00
10	Warren Moon	.75
11	Bill Brooks	.50
12	Christian Okoye	.50
13	Nick Bell	.50
14	Robert Delpino	.50
15	Mark Higgs	.75
16	Rich Gannon	.50
17	Leonard Russell	.50
18	Pat Swilling	.75
19	Rodney Hampton	.75
20	Rob Moore	.75
21	Reggie White	1.00
22	Johnny Johnson	.50
23	Neil O'Donnell	1.00
24	Marion Butts	.50
25	Steve Young	2.00
26	John L. Williams	.50
27	Reggie Cobb	.50
28	Mark Rypien	1.00

1993 Pacific Protypes

The five-card, standard-size set was issued at the 1993 National Convention in Chicago as samples, with a production total of 5,000 sets.

		NM/M
Complete Set (5):		12.00
Common Player:		1.00
1	Emmitt Smith	5.00
2	Barry Sanders	5.00
3	Derrick Thomas	1.00
4	Jim Everett	1.00
5	Steve Young	3.00

1993 Pacific

Pacific's 1993 set features glossy cards with team color-coded marble backgrounds. The 440-card set has two subsets - "NFL Stars" (#s 393-417) and "Rookies" (#s 418-440). Random inserts include Prism (20 cards) and Pacific Picks the Pros (25) cards. The five prototype cards are similar to the regular set, except they say "1993 Prototypes" on the back. Approximately 5,000 sets were made; many were given away at the 1993 National Sports Collectors Convention in Chicago in July.

		NM/M
Complete Set (440):		18.00
Common Player:		.05
Minor Stars:		.10
Checklist Set (4):		4.00
Pack (12):		.60
Wax Box (36):		20.00
1	Emmitt Smith	1.50
2	Troy Aikman	.75
3	Larry Brown	.05
4	Tony Castillas	.05
5	Thomas Everett	.05
6	Alvin Harper	.10
7	Michael Irvin	.30
8	Charles Haley	.05
9	*Leon Lett*	.30
10	Kevin Smith	.05
11	Robert Jones	.05
12	Jimmy Smith	.25
13	*Derrick Gainer*	.05
14	*Lin Elliott*	.05
15	William Thomas	.05
16	Clyde Simmons	.05
17	Seth Joyner	.05
18	Randall Cunningham	.10
19	Byron Evans	.05
20	Fred Barnett	.05
21	Calvin Williams	.05
22	James Joseph	.05
23	Heath Sherman	.05
24	Siran Stacy	.05
25	*Andy Harmon*	.05
26	Eric Allen	.05
27	Herschel Walker	.05
28	Vai Sikahema	.05
29	Ernest Byner	.05
30	Jeff Bostic	.05
31	Monte Coleman	.05
32	Ricky Ervins	.05
33	Darrell Green	.05
34	Mark Schlereth	.05
35	Mark Rypien	.05
36	Art Monk	.10
37	Brian Mitchell	.05
38	Chip Lohmiller	.05
39	Charles Mann	.05
40	Shane Collins	.05
41	Jim Lachey	.05
42	Joe Jacoby	.05
43	Rodney Hampton	.10
44	*Dave Brown*	.60
45	Mark Collins	.05
46	Jerrod Bunch	.05
47	William Roberts	.05
48	Sean Landetta	.05
49	Lawrence Taylor	.10
50	Ed McCaffrey	.05
51	Bart Oates	.05
52	Pepper Johnson	.05
53	Eric Dorsey	.05
54	Erik Howard	.05
55	Phil Simms	.10
56	Derek Brown	.05
57	Johnny Bailey	.05
58	Rich Camarillo	.05
59	*Larry Centers*	.50
60	Chris Chandler	.05
61	Randal Hill	.05
62	Ricky Proehl	.05
63	Freddie Joe Nunn	.05
64	Robert Massey	.05
65	Aeneas Williams	.05
66	Luis Sharpe	.05
67	Eric Swann	.05
68	Timm Rosenbach	.05
69	*Anthony Edwards*	.10
70	Greg Davis	.05
71	Terry Allen	.10
72	Anthony Carter	.05
73	Cris Carter	.10
74	Roger Craig	.05
75	Jack Del Rio	.05
76	Chris Doleman	.05
77	Rich Gannon	.05
78	Hassan Jones	.05
79	Steve Jordan	.05
80	Randall McDaniel	.05
81	Sean Salisbury	.05
82	Harry Newsome	.05
83	Carlos Jenkins	.05
84	Jake Reed	.05
85	Edgar Bennett	.10
86	Tony Bennett	.05
87	Terrell Buckley	.05
88	Ty Detmer	.05
89	Brett Favre	1.50
90	Chris Jackie (Jacke)	.05
91	Sterling Sharpe	.10
92	James Campen	.05
93	Brian Noble	.05
94	*Lester Archambeau*	.05
95	Harry Sydney	.05
96	Corey Harris	.05
97	Don Majkowski	.05
98	Ken Ruettgers	.05
99	Lomas Brown	.05
100	Jason Hanson	.05
101	Robert Porcher	.05
102	Chris Spielman	.05
103	Erik Kramer	.05
104	Tracy Scroggins	.05
105	Rodney Peete	.05
106	Barry Sanders	1.25
107	Herman Moore	.30
108	Brett Perriman	.05
109	Mel Gray	.05
110	Dennis Gibson	.05
111	Bennie Blades	.05
112	Andre Ware	.05
113	Gary Anderson	.05
114	Tyji Armstrong	.05
115	Reggie Cobb	.05
116	Marty Carter	.05
117	Lawrence Dawsey	.05
118	Steve DeBerg	.05
119	Ron Hall	.05
120	Courtney Hawkins	.05
121	Broderick Thomas	.05
122	Keith McCants	.05
123	Bruce Reimers	.05
124	Darrick Brownlow	.05
125	Mark Wheeler	.05
126	Ricky Reynolds	.05
127	Neal Anderson	.05
128	Trace Armstrong	.05
129	Mark Carrier	.05
130	Richard Dent	.05
131	Wendall Davis	.05
132	Darren Lewis	.05
133	Tom Waddle	.05
134	Jim Harbaugh	.05
135	Steve McMichael	.05
136	William Perry	.05
137	Alonzo Spellman	.05
138	John Roper	.05
139	Peter Tom Willis	.05
140	Dante Jones	.05
141	Harris Barton	.05
142	Michael Carter	.05
143	Eric Davis	.05
144	Dana Hall	.05
145	Amp Lee	.05
146	Don Griffin	.05
147	Jerry Rice	.75
148	Ricky Watters	.20
149	Steve Young	.75
150	Bill Romanowski	.05
151	Klaus Wilmsmeyer	.05
152	Steve Bono	.30
153	Tom Rathman	.05
154	Odessa Turner	.05
155	Morten Andersen	.05
156	Richard Cooper	.05
157	Toi Cook	.05
158	Quinn Early	.05
159	Vaughn Dunbar	.05
160	Rickey Jackson	.05
161	Wayne Mottin	.05
162	Hoby Brenner	.05
163	Joel Hilgenberg	.05
164	Mike Buck	.05
165	Torrance Small	.05
166	Eric Martin	.05
167	Vaughan Johnson	.05
168	Sam Mills	.05
169	Steve Broussard	.05
170	Darion Connel	.05
171	Drew Hill	.05
172	Chris Hinton	.05
173	Chris Miller	.05
174	Tim McKyer	.05
175	Norm Johnson	.05
176	Mike Pritchard	.05
177	Andre Rison	.10
178	Deion Sanders	.40
179	Tony Smith	.05
180	Bruce Pickens	.05
181	Michael Haynes	.05
182	Jessie Tuggle	.05
183	Makr Boutte	.05
184	Don Bracken	.05
185	Bern Brostek	.05
186	Henry Ellard	.05
187	Jim Everett	.10
188	Sean Gilbert	.05
189	Cleveland Gary	.05
190	Todd Kinchen	.10
191	Pat Terrell	.05
192	Jackie Slater	.05
193	David Lang	.05
194	Willie Anderson	.05
195	Tony Zendejas	.05
196	Roman Phifer	.05
197	Steve Christie	.05
198	Cornelius Bennett	.05
199	Phil Hansen	.05
200	Don Beebe	.05
201	Mark Kelso	.05
202	Bruce Smith	.05
203	Darryl Talley	.05
204	Andre Reed	.05
205	Mike Lodish	.05
206	Jim Kelly	.20
207	Thurman Thomas	.20
208	Kenneth Davis	.05
209	Frank Reich	.05
210	Kent Hall	.05
211	Marco Coleman	.05
212	Bryan Cox	.05
213	Jeff Cross	.05
214	Mark Higgs	.05
215	Keith Jackson	.05
216	Scott Miller	.05
217	John Offerdahl	.05
218	Dan Marino	1.50
219	Keith Sims	.05
220	Chuck Klingbell	.05
221	Troy Vincent	.05
222	*Mike Williams*	.05
223	Pete Stoyanovich	.05
224	J.B. Brown	.05
225	Ashley Ambrose	.05
226	*Jason Belser*	.05
227	Jeff George	.10
228	Quentin Coryatt	.05
229	Duane Bickett	.05
230	Steve Emtmann	.05
231	Anthony Johnson	.05
232	Rohn Stark	.05
233	Jessie Hester	.05
234	Reggie Langhorne	.05
235	Clarence Verdin	.05
236	Dean Biasucci	.05
237	Jack Trudeau	.05
238	Tony Siragusa	.05
239	Chris Burkett	.05
240	Brad Baxter	.05
241	Rob Moore	.05
242	Browning Nagle	.05
243	Jim Sweeney	.05
244	Kent Barber	.05
245	*Siupeli Malamala*	.05
246	Mike Brim	.05
247	Mo Lewis	.05
248	Johnny Mitchell	.05
249	*Ken Whisenhunt*	.05
250	James Hasty	.05
251	Kyle Clifton	.05
252	Terance Mathis	.05
253	Ray Agnew	.05
254	Eugene Chung	.05
255	Marv Cook	.05
256	Johnny Rembert	.05
257	Maurice Hurst	.05
258	John Vaughn	.05
259	Leonard Russell	.05
260	Pat Harlow	.05
261	Andre Tippet	.05
262	Michael Timpson	.05
263	Greg McCarthy	.05
264	Chris Singleton	.05
265	*Reggie Redding*	.05
266	Walter Stanley	.05
267	Gary Anderson	.05
268	Merril Hoge	.05
269	Barry Foster	.10
270	Charles Davenport	.05
271	Jeff Graham	.05
272	Adrian Cooper	.05
273	David Little	.05
274	Neil O'Donnell	.10
275	Rod Woodson	.10
276	Ernie Mills	.05
277	Dwight Stone	.05
278	Darren Perry	.05
279	Dermontti Dawson	.05
280	Carlton Haselrig	.05
281	Pat Coleman	.05
282	Ernest Givins	.05
283	Warren Moon	.10
284	Haywood Jeffires	.05
285	Cody Carlson	.05
286	Ray Childress	.05
287	Bruce Matthews	.05
288	Webster Slaughter	.05
289	Bo Orlando	.05
290	Lorenzo White	.05
291	Eddie Robinson	.05
292	Bubba McDowell	.05
293	Bucky Richardson	.10
294	Sean Jones	.05
295	David Brandon	.05
296	Shawn Collins	.05
297	Lawyer Tillman	.05
298	Bob Dahl	.05
299	Kevin Mack	.05
300	Bernie Kosar	.05
301	Tommy Vardell	.05
302	Jay Hilgenberg	.05
303	Michael Dean Perry	.05
304	Michael Jackson	.05
305	Eric Metcalf	.05
306	*Rico Smith*	.05
307	*Stevon Moore*	.05
308	Leroy Hoard	.05
309	Eric Ball	.05
310	Derrick Fenner	.05
311	James Francis	.05
312	Ricardo McDonald	.05
313	Tim Krumrie	.05
314	Carl Pickens	.50
315	David Klingler	.10
316	Donald Hollas	.05
317	Harold Green	.05
318	Daniel Stubbs	.05
319	Alfred Williams	.05
320	Darryl Williams	.05
321	*Mike Arthur*	.05
322	Leonard Wheeler	.05
323	Gil Byrd	.05
324	Eric Bieniemy	.05
325	Marion Butts	.05
326	John Carney	.05
327	Stan Humphries	.10
328	Ronnie Harmon	.05
329	Junior Seau	.10
330	Nate Lewis	.05
331	Harry Swayne	.05
332	Leslie O'Neal	.05
333	Eric Moten	.05
334	*Blaise Winter*	.05
335	Anthony Miller	.05
336	Gary Plummer	.05
337	Willie Davis	.05
338	J.T. Birden	.05
339	Tim Barnett	.05
340	Dave Krieg	.05
341	Barry Word	.05
342	Tracy Simien	.05
343	Christian Okoye	.05
344	Todd McNair	.05
345	Dan Salesaumua	.05
346	Derrick Thomas	.10
347	Harvey Williams	.05
348	*Kimble Anders*	.10
349	Tim Grunhard	.05
350	*Tony Hargain*	.05
351	Simon Fletcher	.05
352	John Elway	.30
353	Mike Croel	.05
354	Steve Atwater	.05
355	Tommy Maddox	.05
356	Karl Mecklenberg	.05
357	Shane Dronett	.05
358	Kenny Walker	.05
359	*Reggie Rivers*	.05
360	*Cedric Tillman*	.05
361	*Arthur Marshall*	.10
362	Greg Lewis	.05
363	Shannon Sharpe	.10
364	Doug Widell	.05
365	Todd Marinovich	.05
366	Nick Bell	.05
367	Eric Dickerson	.05
368	Max Montoya	.05
369	Winston Moss	.05
370	Howie Long	.05
371	Willie Gault	.05
372	Tim Brown	.10
373	Steve Smith	.05
374	Steve Wisniewski	.05
375	Alexander Wright	.05
376	Ethan Horton	.05
377	Napoleon McCallum	.05
378	Terry McDaniel	.05
379	Patrick Hunter	.05
380	Robert Blackmon	.05
381	John Kasay	.05
382	Cortez Kennedy	.10
383	Andy Heck	.05
384	*Bill Hitchcock*	.05
385	*Rick Mirer*	.30
386	Jeff Bryant	.05
387	Eugene Robinson	.05
388	John L. Williams	.05
389	Chris Warren	.20
390	Rufus Porter	.05
391	*Joe Tofflemire*	.05
392	Dan McGwire	.05
393	Boomer Esiason	.10
394	Brad Muster	.05
395	James Lofton	.05
396	Tim McGee	.05
397	Steve Beurlein	.10
398	Gaston Green	.05
399	Bill Brooks	.05
400	Ronnie Lott	.05
401	Jay Schroeder	.05
402	Marcus Allen	.10
403	Kevin Green	.05
404	Kirk Lowdermilk	.05
405	Hugh Millen	.05
406	Pat Swilling	.05
407	Bobby Herbert	.05
408	Carl Banks	.05
409	Jeff Hostetler	.10
410	Leonard Marshall	.05
411	Ken O'Brien	.05
412	Joe Montana	1.00
413	Reggie White	.10
414	Gary Clark	.05
415	Johnny Johnson	.05
416	Tim McDonald	.05
417	Pierce Holt	.05
418	*Gino Torretta*	.10
419	*Glyn Milburn*	.30
420	*O.J. McDuffie*	.60
421	*Coleman Rudolph*	.10
422	*Reggie Brooks*	.10
423	*Garrison Hearst*	1.50
424	*Leonard Renfro*	.10
425	*Kevin Williams*	.30
426	*Demetrius DuBose*	.10
427	*Elvis Grbac*	1.50
428	*Lincoln Kennedy*	.10
429	*Carlton Gray*	.10
430	*Micheal Barrow*	.10
431	*George Teague*	.25
432	*Curtis Conway*	1.00
433	*Natrone Means*	1.00
434	*Jerome Bettis*	1.00
435	*Drew Bledsoe*	3.00
436	*Robert Smith*	1.00
437	*Deon Figures*	.20
438	*Qadry Ismail*	.50
439	*Chris Slade*	.30
440	*Dana Stubblefield*	.50

1993 Pacific Picks the Pros Gold

Pacific's top picks at each position are featured in this 25-card insert set. Cards were randomly included in packs and have a color action photo on the front with a gold-foil border. The player's name and position are at the bottom in a gold-foil panel. The back is in a horizontal format and includes the player's name, position, team name and season recap in black letters on a blue and gray background. A card number is also given. A silver version was also made for these cards; these cards were randomly included in 1993 Pacific Triple Folders.

		NM/M
Complete Set (25):		30.00
Common Player:		1.00
Minor Stars:		2.00
1	Jerry Rice	5.00
2	Sterling Sharpe	2.00
3	Richmond Webb	1.00
4	Harris Barton	1.00
5	Randall McDaniel	1.00
6	Steve Wisniewski	1.00
7	Mark Stepnoski	1.00
8	Steve Young	4.00
9	Emmitt Smith	6.00
10	Barry Foster	2.00
11	Nick Lowery	1.00
12	Reggie White	2.00
13	Leslie O'Neal	1.00
14	Cortez Kennedy	2.00
15	Ray Childress	1.00
16	Vaughan Johnson	1.00
17	Wilber Marshall	1.00
18	Junior Seau	3.00
19	Sam Mills	1.00
20	Rod Woodson	2.00
21	Ricky Reynolds	1.00
22	Steve Atwater	1.00
23	Chuck Cecil	1.00
24	Rich Camarillo	1.00
25	Dale Carter	1.00

1993 Pacific Silver Prism Inserts

Pacific produced three versions of its 1993 Prism inserts. The first version, the regular prism inserts, have triangular prisms for a background. There were 8,000 of each of these cards made; they were randomly included in 1993 Pacific packs and 1993 Pacific Triple Folder packs. A circular version background was also made; these cards were randomly included in retail packs and were easier to find than the triangular versions. The third type of prism insert was limited to 1,000 per card and features a gold triangular prism background. They were randomly included in 1993 Pacific Triple Folder packs. Each card design is basically the same for all three versions. The front has a color action photo against the prism background; the player's name is at the bottom in block letters in team colors. The back has the same photo used for the front, except the entire background of the photo is also used. The player's name and position are given in scripted white letters. A card number is also given (1 of 20, etc.).

		NM/M
Complete Set (20):		60.00
Common Player:		1.00
Minor Stars:		2.00
Comp. Gold Set (20):		150.00
Gold Cards:		1.5X-3X
1	Troy Aikman	5.00
2	Jerome Bettis	2.00
3	Drew Bledsoe	5.00
4	Reggie Brooks	2.00
5	Brett Favre	8.00
6	Barry Foster	2.00
7	Garrison Hearst	2.00
8	Michael Irvin	2.00
9	Cortez Kennedy	1.00
10	David Klingler	1.00
11	Dan Marino	8.00
12	Rick Mirer	2.00
13	Joe Montana	8.00
14	Jay Novacek	1.00
15	Jerry Rice	6.00
16	Barry Sanders	8.00
17	Sterling Sharpe	2.00
18	Emmitt Smith	8.00
19	Thurman Thomas	2.00
20	Steve Young	5.00

1993 Pacific Prisms

Approximately 17,000 of each card in this 108-card set were produced. Each card front has a player action photo against a prism-like foil background. The player's name is in team colors and appears at the bottom of the card. The back is numbered and includes a player profile, two photos, a team helmet and the

Pacific logo. The card back is in a horizontal format and uses a gray background. There were also two promotional cards made for the set - (22) Emmitt Smith and (61) Drew Bledsoe. The cards, which were given away at the 1993 National Card Collectors Convention in Chicago, are similar in design to the regular set.

NM/M

Complete Set (108): 35.00
Common Player: .10
Minor Stars: .50
Checklist (NNO): .25
Pack (1): 1.00
Wax Box (36): 35.00
1 Chris Miller .10
2 Mike Pritchard .10
3 Andre Rison .50
4 Deion Sanders 1.00
5 Tony Smith .10
6 Jim Kelly 2.00
7 Andre Reed .50
8 Thurman Thomas 2.00
9 Neal Anderson .10
10 Jim Harbaugh .10
11 Donnell Woolford .10
12 David Klingler .10
13 Carl Pickens 1.00
14 Alfred Williams .10
15 Michael Jackson .10
16 Bernie Kosar .50
17 Tommy Vardell .10
18 Troy Aikman 4.00
19 Alvin Harper .50
20 Michael Irvin 1.00
21 Russell Maryland .10
22 Emmitt Smith 5.00
23 John Elway 4.00
24 Tommy Maddox .10
25 Shannon Sharpe .50
26 Herman Moore 1.00
27 Rodney Peete .10
28 Barry Sanders 5.00
29 Pat Swilling .10
30 Terrell Buckley .10
31 Brett Favre 5.00
32 Sterling Sharpe 1.00
33 Reggie White .50
34 Ernest Givins .10
35 Haywood Jeffires .10
36 Warren Moon 1.00
37 Lorenzo White .10
38 Steve Emtman .10
39 Jeff George .50
40 Reggie Langhorne .10
41 Dale Carter .10
42 Joe Montana 5.00
43 Derrick Thomas .50
44 Barry Word .10
45 Nick Bell .10
46 Eric Dickerson .50
47 Jeff Jaeger .10
48 Jerome Bettis 1.00
49 Henry Ellard .10
50 Jim Everett .50
51 Cleveland Gary .10
52 Marco Coleman .10
53 Mark Higgs .10
54 Keith Jackson .10
55 Dan Marino 5.00
56 Troy Vincent .10
57 Terry Allen .10
58 Jack Del Rio .10
59 Sean Salisbury .10
60 Robert Smith 1.00
61 Drew Bledsoe 10.00
62 Marv Cook .10
63 Irving Fryar .10
64 Leonard Russell .10
65 Andre Tippett .10
66 Morten Andersen .10
67 Vaughn Dunbar .10
68 Eric Martin .10
69 David Brown .40
70 Rodney Hampton 1.00
71 Phil Simms .10
72 Lawrence Taylor .50
73 Ronnie Lott .10
74 Johnny Mitchell .10
75 Rob Moore .10
76 Browning Nagle .10
77 Fred Barnett .10
78 Randall Cunningham .50
79 Herschel Walker .10
80 Gary Clark .10
81 Ken Harvey .10
82 Garrison Hearst 3.00
83 Ricky Proehl .10
84 Barry Foster .50
85 Ernie Mills .10
86 Neil O'Donnell 1.50
87 Stan Humpheries 1.50
88 Leslie O'Neil .10
89 Junior Seau 2.00
90 Amp Lee .10
91 Jerry Rice 4.00
92 Ricky Watters 1.00
93 Steve Young 3.00
94 Cortez Kennedy .10
95 Rick Mirer .50
96 Eugene Robinson .10
97 Chris Warren .50
98 John L. Williams .10
99 Reggie Cobb .10
100 Lawrence Dawsey .10
101 Santana Dotson .10
102 Courtney Hawkins .10
103 Reggie Brooks .50
104 Ricky Ervins .10
105 Desmond Howard .50
106 Art Monk .50
107 Mark Rypien .10
108 Ricky Sanders .10

1993 Pacific Triple Folders

These cards feature two panels on the front which, when closed, form a color action photo of an NFL star player. The player's name and team helmet are on one panel; his position is printed on the other side. When opened up, the inside of the card panels reveal additional player photos. The card back is numbered and has 1992 statistics, a career summary, the player's name and team helmet, and position, all against a team color-coded marble-like background. Approximately 2,500 cases were produced.

NM/M

Complete Set (30): 18.00
Common Player: .45
1 Thurman Thomas 1.25
2 Carl Pickens .75
3 Glyn Milburn .75
4 Lorenzo White .45
5 Anthony Johnson .45
6 Joe Montana 3.50
7 Nick Bell .45
8 Dan Marino 2.50
9 Anthony Carter .45
10 Drew Bledsoe 2.00
11 Rob Moore .75
12 Barry Foster 1.00
13 Stan Humphries .75
14 Cortez Kennedy .75
15 Rick Mirer .50
16 Deion Sanders 1.50
17 Curtis Conway 1.00
18 Tommy Vardell .75
19 Emmitt Smith 3.00
20 Barry Sanders 3.00
21 Brett Favre 3.00
22 Cleveland Gary .45
23 Morten Andersen .45
24 Marcus Buckley .45
25 Rodney Hampton .75
26 Herschel Walker .75
27 Garrison Hearst 1.00
28 Jerry Rice 2.00
29 Lawrence Dawsey .45
30 Desmond Howard 1.00

1993 Pacific Triple Folder Superstars

These 20 cards were randomly inserted into 1993 Pacific Triple Folder packs. Each card front has a borderless, full-color action photo, with the player's name in white letters at the bottom of the card. His position is also given. The back is numbered and has a player profile, along with the player's name, position and team helmet. The background uses the player's team colors. Some of the players featured in the set were rookies.

NM/M

Complete Set (20): 15.00
Common Player: .35
1 Troy Aikman 2.00
2 *Victor Bailey* .50
3 *Jerome Bettis* 2.00
4 *Drew Bledsoe* 3.50
5 *Reggie Brooks* 1.00
6 *Derek Brown* .50
7 *Marcus Buckley* .35
8 *Curtis Conway* .75
9 Brett Favre 3.00
10 Barry Foster .75
11 *Garrison Hearst* .75
12 Cortez Kennedy .50
13 *Rick Mirer* .50
14 Joe Montana 2.00
15 Jerry Rice 2.00
16 Barry Sanders 2.50
17 Sterling Sharpe 1.50
18 Emmitt Smith 3.00
19 *Robert Smith* .50
20 Thurman Thomas 1.00

1994 Pacific

Crown Collection 1994 Football from Pacific Trading Cards contained 450 cards in the primary set, with three insert sets called Gems of the Crown, Crown Collection Crystalline and Knights of the Gridiron. There were only 7,000 of each insert set produced and a card from one of the three was inserted into each 12-card pack.

NM/M

Complete Set (450): 28.00
Common Player: .05
Pack (12): 1.25
Wax Box (36): 30.00
1 Troy Aikman 1.00
2 Charles Haley .05
3 Alvin Harper .05
4 Michael Irvin .10
5 Jim Jeffcoat .05
6 Daryl Johnston .05
7 Robert Jones .05
8 *Brock Marion* .05
9 Russell Maryland .05
10 Ken Norton .05
11 Jay Novacek .05
12 Emmitt Smith 2.00
13 Kevin Smith .05
14 Tony Tolbert .05
15 Kevin Williams .40
16 Don Beebe .05
17 Cornelius Bennett .05
18 Bill Brooks .05
19 Steve Christie .05
20 Russell Copeland .05
21 Kenneth Davis .05
22 Kent Hull .05
23 Jim Kelly .10
24 Pete Metzelaars .05
25 Andre Reed .05
26 Frank Reich .05
27 Bruce Smith .05
28 Darryl Talley .05
29 Steve Tasker .05
30 Thurman Thomas .10
31 Steve Bono .20
32 Dexter Carter .05
33 Kevin Fagan .05
34 Dana Hall .05
35 Brent Jones .05
36 Amp Lee .05
37 Marc Logan .05
38 Tim McDonald .05
39 Guy McIntyre .05
40 Tom Rathman .05
41 Jerry Rice 1.00
42 Dana Stubblefield .05
43 Steve Wallace .05
44 Ricky Watters .10
45 Steve Young 1.00
46 Marcus Allen .10
47 Kimble Anders .05
48 Tim Barnett .05
49 J.J. Birden .05
50 Dale Carter .05
51 Jonathan Hayes .05
52 Dave Krieg .05
53 Albert Lewis .05
54 Nick Lowery .05
55 Joe Montana 1.00
56 Neil Smith .05
57 John Stephens .05
58 Derrick Thomas .10
59 Harvey Williams .05
60 Micheal Barrow .05
61 Gary Brown .05
62 Cody Carlson .05
63 Ray Childress .05
64 Curtis Duncan .05
65 Ernest Givins .05
66 Haywood Jeffires .05
67 Wilber Marshall .05
68 Bubba McDowell .05
69 Warren Moon .10
70 Mike Munchak .05
71 Marcus Robertson .05
72 Webster Slaughter .05
73 *Gary Wellman* .05
74 Lorenzo White .05
75 Ray Crockett .05
76 Jason Hanson .05
77 Rodney Holman .05
78 George Jamison .05
79 Erik Kramer .05
80 Ryan McNeil .05
81 Derrick Moore .05
82 Herman Moore .50
83 Rodney Peete .05
84 Brett Perriman .05
85 Barry Sanders 1.25
86 Chris Spielman .05
87 Pat Swilling .05
88 Vernon Turner .05
89 Andre Ware .05
90 Michael Brooks .05
91 Dave Brown .05
92 Derek Brown .05
93 Jarrod Bunch .05
94 Chris Calloway .05
95 Kent Graham .05
96 Rodney Hampton .10
97 Mark Jackson .05
98 Ed McCaffrey .05
99 Dave Meggett .05
100 Aaron Pierce .05
101 Mike Sherrard .05
102 Phil Simms .05
103 Lewis Tillman .05
104 Eddie Anderson .05
105 Patrick Bates .05
106 Nick Bell .05
107 Tim Brown .10
108 Willie Gault .05
109 Jeff Gossett .05
110 Ethan Horton .05
111 Jeff Hostetler .05
112 Rocket Ismail .05
113 Chester McGlockton .05
114 Anthony Smith .05
115 Steve Smith .05
116 Greg Townsend .05
117 Steve Wisniewski .05
118 Alexander Wright .05
119 Steve Atwater .05
120 Rod Bernstine .05
121 Mike Croel .05
122 Shane Dronett .05
123 Jason Elam .05
124 John Elway .30
125 Brian Habib .05
126 Rondell Jones .05
127 Tommy Maddox .05
128 Karl Mecklenburg .05
129 Glyn Milburn .05
130 Derek Russell .05
131 Shannon Sharpe .05
132 Dennis Smith .05
133 Edgar Bennett .05
134 Tony Bennett .05
135 Robert Brooks .20
136 Terrell Buckley .05
137 LeRoy Butler .05
138 Mark Clayton .05
139 Ty Detmer .05
140 Brett Favre 2.00
141 *John Jurkovic* .10
142 Bryce Paup .05
143 Sterling Sharpe .10
144 George Teague .05
145 Darrell Thompson .05
146 Ed West .05
147 Reggie White .10
148 Terry Allen .05
149 Anthony Carter .05
150 Cris Carter .10
151 Roger Craig .05
152 Jack Del Rio .05
153 Chris Doleman .05
154 *Scottie Graham* .10
155 Eric Guliford .05
156 Qadry Ismail .10
157 Steve Jordan .05
158 Randall McDaniel .05
159 Jim McMahon .05
160 Audray McMillian .05
161 Sean Salisbury .05
162 Robert Smith .25
163 Henry Thomas .05
164 Gary Anderson .05
165 Deon Figures .05
166 Barry Foster .10
167 Jeff Graham .05
168 Kevin Greene .05
169 *Dave Hoffman* .05
170 Merril Hoge .05
171 Gary Jones .05
172 Greg Lloyd .05
173 Ernie Mills .05
174 Neil O'Donnell .10
175 Darren Perry .05
176 Leon Searcy .05
177 Leroy Thompson .05
178 *Willie Williams* .05
179 Rod Woodson .05
180 Keith Byars .05
181 Marco Coleman .05
182 Bryan Cox .05
183 Irving Fryar .05
184 John Grimsley .05
185 Mark Higgs .05
186 Mark Ingram .05
187 Keith Jackson .05
188 Terry Kirby .10
189 Dan Marino 2.00
190 O.J. McDuffie .25
191 Scott Mitchell .10
192 Pete Stoyanovich .05
193 Troy Vincent .05
194 Richmond Webb .05
195 Brad Baxter .05
196 Chris Burkett .05
197 Rob Carpenter .05
198 Boomer Esiason .05
199 Johnny Johnson .05
200 Jeff Lageman .05
201 Mo Lewis .05
202 Ronnie Lott .05
203 Leonard Marshall .05
204 Terance Mathis .05
205 Johnny Mitchell .05
206 Rob Moore .05
207 Anthony Prior .05
208 Blair Thomas .05
209 Brian Washington .05
210 Eric Bieniemy .05
211 Marion Butts .05
212 Gill Byrd .05
213 John Carney .05
214 Darren Carrington .05
215 John Friesz .05
216 Ronnie Harmon .05
217 Stan Humphries .05
218 Nate Lewis .05
219 Natrone Means .25
220 Anthony Miller .05
221 Chris Mims .05
222 Eric Moten .05
223 Leslie O'Neal .05
224 Junior Seau .10
225 Morten Andersen .05
226 Gene Atkins .05
227 Derek Brown .05
228 Toi Cook .05
229 Vaughn Dunbar .05
230 Quinn Early .05
231 Reggie Freeman .05
232 Tyrone Hughes .05
233 Rickey Jackson .05
234 Eric Martin .05
235 Sam Mills .05
236 Brad Muster .05
237 Torrance Small .05
238 Irv Smith .05
239 Wade Wilson .05
240 Eric Allen .05
241 Victor Bailey .05
242 Fred Barnett .05
243 Mark Bavaro .05
244 Bubby Brister .05
245 Randall Cunningham .05
246 Antone Davis .05
247 *Britt Hager* .05
248 Vaughn Hebron .05
249 James Joseph .05
250 Seth Joyner .05
251 Rich Maino .05
252 Heath Sherman .05
253 Clyde Simmons .05
254 Herschel Walker .05
255 Calvin Williams .05
256 Jerry Ball .05
257 Mark Carrier .05
258 Michael Jackson .05
259 Mike Johnson .05
260 James Jones .05
261 Brian Kinchen .05
262 Clay Matthews .05
263 Eric Metcalf .05
264 Stevon Moore .05
265 Michael Dean Perry .05
266 Todd Philcox .05
267 Anthony Pleasant .05
268 Vinny Testaverde .05
269 Eric Turner .05
270 Tommy Vardell .05
271 Neal Anderson .05
272 Trace Armstrong .05
273 Mark Carrier .05
274 Bob Christian .05
275 Curtis Conway .30
276 Richard Dent .05
277 Robert Green .05
278 Jim Harbaugh .05
279 Craig Heyward .05
280 Terry Obee .05
281 Alonzo Spellman .05
282 Tom Waddle .05
283 Peter Tom Willis .05
284 Donnell Woolford .05
285 Tim Worley .05
286 Chris Zorich .05
287 Steve Broussard .05
288 Darion Conner .05
289 James Geathers .05
290 Michael Haynes .05
291 Bobby Hebert .05
292 Lincoln Kennedy .05
293 Chris Miller .05
294 *David Mims* .05
295 Erric Pegram .05
296 Mike Pritchard .05
297 Andre Rison .10
298 Deion Sanders .50
299 Chuck Smith .05
300 Tony Smith .05
301 Johnny Bailey .05
302 Steve Beuerlein .05
303 Chuck Cecil .05
304 Chris Chandler .05
305 Gary Clark .05
306 *Rick Cunningham* .05
307 Ken Harvey .05
308 Garrison Hearst .50
309 Randal Hill .05
310 Robert Massey .05
311 Ron Moore .05
312 Ricky Proehl .05
313 Eric Swann .05
314 Aeneas Williams .05
315 Michael Bates .05
316 Brian Blades .05
317 Carlton Gray .05
318 *Paul Green* .05
319 Patrick Hunter .05
320 John Kasay .05
321 Cortez Kennedy .05
322 Kelvin Martin .05
323 Dan McGwire .05
324 Rick Mirer .30
325 Eugene Robinson .05
326 Rick Tuten .05
327 Chris Warren .15
328 John L. Williams .05
329 Reggie Cobb .05
330 Horace Copeland .05
331 Lawrence Dawsey .05
332 Santana Dotson .05
333 Craig Erickson .05
334 Ron Hall .05
335 Courtney Hawkins .05
336 Keith McCants .05
337 Hardy Nickerson .05
338 *Mazio Royster* .05
339 Broderick Thomas .05
340 *Casey Weldon* .10
341 Mark Wheeler .05
342 Vince Workman .05
343 Willie Anderson .05
344 Jerome Bettis .30
345 *Richard Buchanan* .05
346 Shane Conlan .05
347 Troy Drayton .05
348 Henry Ellard .05
349 Jim Everett .05
350 Cleveland Gary .05
351 Sean Gilbert .05
352 David Lang .05
353 Todd Lyght .05
354 *T.J. Rubley* .10
355 Jackie Slater .05
356 Russell White .05
357 Bruce Armstrong .05
358 Drew Bledsoe 1.00
359 Vincent Brisby .05
360 Vincent Brown .05
361 Ben Coates .10
362 Marv Cook .05
363 *Ray Crittenden* .10
364 *Corey Croom* .05
365 Pat Harlow .05
366 Dion Lambert .05
367 Greg McMurtry .05
368 Leonard Russell .05
369 Scott Secules .05
370 Chris Slade .05
371 Michael Timpson .05
372 Kevin Turner .05
373 Ashley Ambrose .05
374 Dean Biasucci .05
375 Duane Bickett .05
376 Quentin Coryatt .05
377 Rodney Culver .05
378 *Sean Dawkins* .25
379 Jeff George .10
380 Jeff Herrod .05
381 Jessie Hester .05
382 Anthony Johnson .05
383 Reggie Langhorne .05
384 Roosevelt Potts .05
385 *William Schultz* .05
386 Rohn Stark .05
387 Clarence Verdin .05
388 Carl Banks .05
389 Reggie Brooks .10
390 Earnest Byner .05
391 Tom Carter .05
392 Cary Conklin .05
393 *Pat Ellers* .05
394 Ricky Ervins .05
395 Rich Gannon .05
396 Darrell Green .05
397 Desmond Howard .05
398 Chip Lohmiller .05
399 *Sterling Palmer* .05
400 Mark Rypien .05
401 Ricky Sanders .05
402 *Johnny Thomas* .05
403 John Copeland .05
404 Derrick Fenner .05
405 Alex Gordon .05
406 Harold Green .05
407 Lance Gunn .05
408 David Klingler .05
409 Ricardo McDonald .05
410 Tim McGee .05
411 Reggie Rembert .05
412 Patrick Robinson .05
413 Jay Schroeder .05
414 Erik Wilhelm .05
415 Alfred Williams .05
416 Darryl Williams .05
417 *Sam Adams* .10
418 *Mario Bates* .10
419 *James Bostic* .10
420 *Bucky Brooks* .10
421 *Jeff Burris* .10
422 *Shante Carver* .10
423 *Jeff Cothran* .05
424 *Lake Dawson* .10
425 *Trent Dilfer* 2.00
426 *Marshall Faulk* 4.00
427 *Cory Fleming* .10
428 *William Floyd* .50
429 *Glenn Foley* .75
430 *Rob Fredrickson* .10
431 *Charles Garner* 2.00
432 *Greg Hill* .50
433 *Charles Johnson* .50
434 *Calvin Jones* .10
435 *Jimmy Klingler* .05
436 *Antonio Langham* .10
437 *Kevin Lee* .10
438 *Chuck Levy* .10
439 *Willie McGinest* .25
440 *Jamir Miller* .10
441 *Johnnie Morton* .30
442 *David Palmer* .25
443 *Errict Rhett* .75
444 *Cory Sawyer* .10
445 *Darnay Scott* .50
446 *Heath Shuler* .25
447 *Lamar Smith* 1.00
448 *Dan Wilkinson* .10
449 *Bernard Williams* .10
450 *Bryant Young* .30

1994 Pacific Crystalline

Crown Collection Crystalline features an action shot of one of the top 20 running backs in the NFL. These cards are made of plastic and have a multi-color pattern on the left half of the card and clear plastic on the right half. The player's name is in the top-left corner, with his position under it and the Pacific Crown Collection logo under it. The player is postioned mostly on the clear side with a small portion of his body located over the pattern. The back features a close-up and stats on the pattern side and the reverse-angle player on the clear.

		NM/M
Complete Set (20):		40.00
Common Player:		1.00
1	Emmitt Smith	15.00
2	Jerome Bettis	4.00
3	Thurman Thomas	5.00
4	Erric Pegram	1.00
5	Barry Sanders	15.00
6	Leonard Russell	1.00
7	Rodney Hampton	2.00
8	Chris Warren	1.00
9	Reggie Brooks	1.00
10	Ron Moore	1.00
11	Gary Brown	1.00
12	Ricky Watters	2.00
13	Johnny Johnson	1.00
14	Rod Bernstine	1.00
15	Marcus Allen	1.00
16	Leroy Thompson	1.00
17	Marion Butts	1.00
18	Herschel Walker	1.00
19	Barry Foster	1.00
20	Roosevelt Potts	1.00

1994 Pacific Gems of the Crown

Gems of the Crown present a top offensive player on a card with an etched gold foil border. The Pacific logo appears in the bottom-left corner of this 20-card set, with the player name at the bottom in etched gold foil. The back contains a player close-up and a brief statistics, along with "Gems of the Crown" written across the top-right corner and card numbers in the opposite corner.

		NM/M
Complete Set (36):		75.00
Common Player:		1.00
Minor Stars:		2.00
1	Troy Aikman	4.00
2	Marcus Allen	2.00
3	Jerome Bettis	2.00
4	Drew Bledsoe	3.00
5	Reggie Brooks	1.00
6	Gary Brown	1.00
7	Tim Brown	2.00
8	Cody Carlson	1.00
9	John Elway	4.00
10	Boomer Esiason	1.00
11	Brett Favre	6.00
12	Rodney Hampton	2.00
13	Alvin Harper	1.00
14	Jeff Hostetler	1.00
15	Jim Kelly	2.00
16	Dan Marino	6.00
17	Eric Martin	1.00
18	O.J. McDuffie	1.00
19	Natrone Means	1.00
20	Rick Mirer	1.00
21	Joe Montana	6.00
22	Herman Moore	1.00
23	Ron Moore	1.00
24	Neil O'Donnell	2.00
25	Erric Pegram	1.00
26	Roosevelt Potts	1.00
27	Jerry Rice	5.00
28	Barry Sanders	6.00
29	Shannon Sharpe	1.00
30	Sterling Sharpe	2.00
31	Emmitt Smith	6.00
32	Thurman Thomas	2.00
33	Herschel Walker	1.00
34	Chris Warren	2.00
35	Ricky Watters	2.00
36	Steve Young	4.00

A card number in parenthese ( ) indicates the set is unnumbered.

1994 Pacific Knights of the Gridiron

Knights of the Gridiron is a 20-card prism insert that showcases the top rookies and draft picks. Cards show an action-shot of the player with his name at the bottom. His first name is in a color box, depending on his team colors, and his last name is in gold prism and shadowed in a team color. The Pacific logo appears in the top left corner of this shiny gold prism card. The backs show a picture of the player with a large Pacific Crown Collection logo and Knight of the Gridiron, player name and team above the logo.

		NM/M
Complete Set (20):		45.00
Common Player:		1.00
Minor Stars:		2.00
1	Mario Bates	1.00
2	Jerome Bettis	2.00
3	Drew Bledsoe	5.00
4	Vincent Brisby	1.00
5	Reggie Brooks	1.00
6	Derek Brown	1.00
7	Jeff Burris	1.00
8	Trent Dilfer	2.00
9	Troy Drayton	1.00
10	Marshall Faulk	8.00
11	William Floyd	2.00
12	Rocket Ismail	1.00
13	Terry Kirby	1.00
14	Thomas Lewis	1.00
15	Natrone Means	2.00
16	Rick Mirer	1.00
17	David Palmer	1.00
18	Errict Rhett	2.00
19	Darnay Scott	2.00
20	Heath Shuler	1.00

1994 Pacific Marquee Prisms

These 36 cards, produced in both silver and gold versions, feature several veteran and younger stars of the NFL. Each card front has a player photo superimposed over either a gold or silver foil background. The Crown Collection logo is in the upper left corner; the player's name and position are at the bottom in a marquee banner. The card back has a player photo on the left and a marquee billboard on the right which says "Now Appearing," followed by the player's name, position and team, plus a card number. A gold or silver card was issued in every pack of 1994 Pacific marquee prism, but gold cards were found at a ratio of only two per every box.

		NM/M
Complete Set (36):		20.00
Common Player:		.25
Minor Stars:		.50
Gold Cards:		4X-8X
1	Troy Aikman	2.00
2	Marcus Allen	.50
3	Jerome Bettis	.50
4	Drew Bledsoe	3.00
5	Reggie Brooks	.25
6	Dave Brown	.25
7	Ben Coates	.25
8	Reggie Cobb	.25
9	Curtis Conway	.50
10	John Elway	2.00
11	Marshall Faulk	3.00
12	Brett Favre	5.00
13	Barry Foster	.25
14	Rodney Hampton	.50
15	Michael Irvin	.50
16	Terry Kirby	.25
17	Dan Marino	5.00
18	Natrone Means	.50
19	Rick Mirer	.50
20	Joe Montana	3.00
21	Warren Moon	.50
22	Ron Moore	.25
23	David Palmer	.25
24	Errict Rhett	.50
25	Jerry Rice	3.00
26	Bucky Richardson	.25
27	Barry Sanders	3.00
28	Shannon Sharpe	.25
29	Sterling Sharpe	.50
30	Heath Shuler	.50
31	Emmitt Smith	5.00
32	Irving Spikes	.25
33	Thurman Thomas	.50
34	Chris Warren	.50
35	Ricky Watters	.50
36	Steve Young	2.00

1994 Pacific Prisms

This set offers Pacific's splashy design and technology. The cards have full-color fronts and backs and are printed on a heavier card stock. Production is limited to a maximum of 2,999 individually-numbered 20-box cases. Four or five players from each team are represented in the set, which also includes top draft picks. The cards were done in silver versions (only 16,000 of each card were made) and gold versions (1,138 of each card). The borderless card front has an action photo superimposed on a prism-like background. The card back has the same cutout photo as the front, but the background is blurred. Gold versions are generally worth 4 to 7 times the value of the listed prices.

		NM/M
Complete Set (126):		50.00
Common Player:		.20
Unlisted Gold Stars:		2X-4X
Comp. Helmet Set (30):		2.50
Pack (1):		1.00
Wax Box (36):		35.00
1	Troy Aikman	4.00
2	Marcus Allen	1.00
3	Morten Andersen	.20
4	Fred Barnett	.20
5	*Mario Bates*	.40
6	Edgar Bennett	.20
7	Rod Bernstine	.20
8	Jerome Bettis	1.00
9	Steve Beuerlein	.20
10	Brian Blades	.20
11	Drew Bledsoe	4.00
12	Vincent Brisby	1.00
13	Reggie Brooks	.20
14	Derek Brown	.20
15	Gary Brown	.20
16	Tim Brown	1.00
17	Marion Butts	.20
18	Keith Byars	.20
19	Cody Carlson	.20
20	Anthony Carter	.20
21	Tom Carter	.20
22	Gary Clark	.20
23	Ben Coates	1.00
24	Reggie Cobb	.20
25	Curtis Conway	1.50
26	John Copeland	.20
27	Randall Cunningham	.20
28	Willie Davis	.20
29	*Sean Dawkins*	.50
30	Lawrence Dawsey	.20
31	Richard Dent	.20
32	*Trent Dilfer*	2.00
33	Troy Drayton	.20
34	Vaughn Dunbar	.20
35	Henry Ellard	.20
36	John Elway	4.00
37	Craig Erickson	.20
38	Boomer Esiason	.20
39	*Marshall Faulk*	15.00
40	Brett Favre	6.00
41	*William Floyd*	1.50
42	*Glenn Foley*	1.00
43	Barry Foster	.20
44	Irving Fryar	.20
45	Jeff George	1.00
46	*Scottie Graham*	1.50
47	Rodney Hampton	1.00
48	Jim Harbaugh	.20
49	Alvin Harper	.20
50	Courtney Hawkins	.20
51	Garrison Hearst	1.00
52	Vaughn Hebron	.20
53	*Greg Hill*	.75
54	Jeff Hostetler	.50
55	Michael Irvin	1.00
56	Qadry Ismail	.20
57	Rocket Ismail	.20
58	Anthony Johnson	.20
59	*Charles Johnson*	.50
60	Johnny Johnson	.20
61	Brent Jones	.20
62	Kyle Clifton	.20
63	Jim Kelly	1.00
64	Cortez Kennedy	.20
65	Terry Kirby	.50
66	David Klingler	.20
67	Erik Kramer	.20
68	Reggie Langhorne	.20
69	*Chuck Levy*	.50
70	Dan Marino	6.00
71	O.J. McDuffie	1.00
72	Natrone Means	.50
73	Eric Metcalf	.20
74	Glyn Milburn	.20
75	Anthony Miller	.20
76	Rick Mirer	.50
77	Johnny Mitchell	.20
78	Scott Mitchell	.50
79	Joe Montana	6.00
80	Warren Moon	1.00
81	Derrick Moore	.20
82	Herman Moore	1.00
83	Rob Moore	.20
84	Ron Moore	.20
85	*Johnnie Morton*	2.00
86	Neil O'Donnell	.20
87	*David Palmer*	1.00
88	Erric Pegram	.20
89	Carl Pickens	.75
90	Anthony Pleasant	.20
91	Roosevelt Potts	.20
92	Mike Pritchard	.20
93	Andre Reed	1.00
94	*Errict Rhett*	2.00
95	Jerry Rice	5.00
96	Andre Rison	1.00
97	Greg Robinson	.20
98	T.J. Rubley	.20
99	Leonard Russell	.20
100	Barry Sanders	6.00
101	Deion Sanders	2.00
102	Ricky Sanders	.20
103	Junior Seau	1.00
104	Shannon Sharpe	1.00
105	Sterling Sharpe	1.00
106	*Heath Shuler*	.50
107	Phil Simms	.20
108	Webster Slaughter	.20
109	Bruce Smith	.20
110	Emmitt Smith	6.00
111	Irv Smith	.20
112	Robert Smith	.50
113	Vinny Testaverde	.50
114	Derrick Thomas	.50
115	Thurman Thomas	1.00
116	Leroy Thompson	.20
117	Lewis Tillman	.20
118	Michael Timpson	.20
119	Herschel Walker	.20
120	Chris Warren	.50
121	Ricky Watters	1.00
122	Lorenzo White	.20
123	Reggie White	1.00
124	*Dan Wilkinson*	.50
125	Kevin Williams	.50
126	Steve Young	3.00

1994 Pacific Prisms Team Helmets

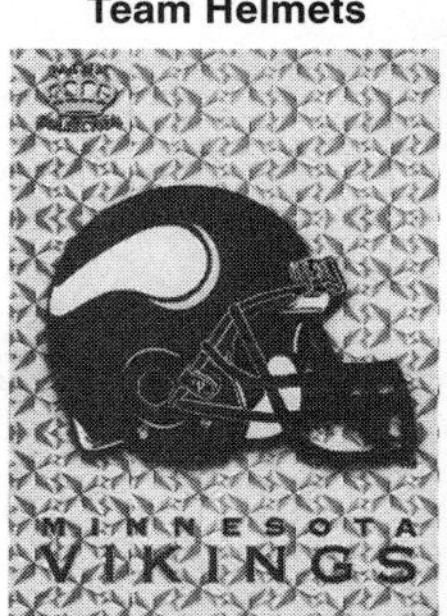

Each of these prism cards features the helmet of an NFL team on the card front, along with a team history and ghosted helmet on the back. The cards, which are numbered on the back (1 of 30, etc.) were random inserts in 1994 Pacific Prisms foil packs. The card front has a borderless prism-like background.

		NM/M
Complete Set (30):		2.50
Common Player:		.10
1	Arizona Cardinals	.10
2	Atlanta Falcons	.10
3	Buffalo Bills	.10
4	Carolina Panthers	.10
5	Chicago Bears	.10
6	Cincinnati Bengals	.10
7	Cleveland Browns	.10
8	Dallas Cowboys	.10
9	Denver Broncos	.10
10	Detroit Lions	.10
11	Green Bay Packers	.10
12	Houston Oilers	.10
13	Indianapolis Colts	.10
14	Jacksonville Jaguars	.10
15	Kansas City Chiefs	.10
16	Los Angeles Raiders	.10
17	Los Angeles Rams	.10
18	Miami Dolphins	.10
19	Minnesota Vikings	.10
20	New England Patriots	.10
21	New Orleans Saints	.10
22	New York Giants	.10
23	New York Jets	.10
24	Philadelphia Steelers	.10
25	Pittsburgh Steelers	.10
26	San Diego Chargers	.10
27	San Francisco 49ers	.10
28	Seattle Seahawks	.10
29	Tampa Bay Buccaneers	.10
30	Washington Redskins	.10

1994 Pacific Prisms Gold

The 126-card, regular-sized cards are a parallel to the base prism issue. Only 10 percent of the total print run were produced in gold foil.

Complete Set (126):		
Common Player:		
Veteran Stars:		2.5X-5X
Young Stars/RCs:		1.5X-3X

1994 Pacific Triple Folders

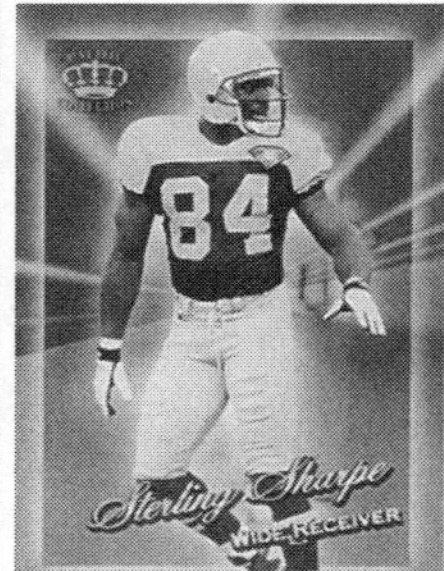

Each card in the 33-card set measures 3-1/2" x 5" when folded, features color photos on all panels. The front panels can be closed and merged into a single action photo. The set, arranged into alphabetical order by teams, was limited to a production run of less than 3,000.

		NM/M
Complete Set (33):		15.00
Common Player:		.30
1	Ron Moore	.30
2	Erric Pegram	.30
3	Jim Kelly	.75
4	Thurman Thomas	.75
5	Curtis Conway	1.00
6	Vinny Testaverde	.30
7	Troy Aikman	1.75
8	Emmitt Smith	3.00
9	John Elway	1.00
10	Shannon Sharpe	.30
11	Barry Sanders	1.75
12	Brett Favre	3.00
13	Sterling Sharpe	.75
14	Gary Brown	.30
15	Marshall Faulk	1.50
16	Joe Montana	2.00
17	Rocket Ismail	.75
18	Jerome Bettis	.50
19	Dan Marino	3.00
20	David Palmer	.30
21	Drew Bledsoe	2.00
22	Ben Coates	.75
23	Derrick Ned	.30
24	Rodney Hampton	.75
25	Boomer Esiason	.30
26	Barry Foster	.30
27	Charles Johnson	.30
28	Natrone Means	.50
29	Steve Young	1.50
30	Rick Mirer	.75
31	Chris Warren	.50
32	Trent Dilfer	1.00
33	Heath Shuler	.50

1994 Pacific Triple Folders Rookies/Stars

The 40-card, regular-sized set was randomly inserted in Triple Folder packs. The fronts feature color action shots with the player's name and position in gold-foil on the card bottom.

		NM/M
Complete Set (40):		20.00
Common Player:		.20
1	Ronald Moore	.20
2	Jeff George	.50
3	Jim Kelly	.50
4	Thurman Thomas	.50
5	Curtis Conway	.75
6	Darnay Scott	.60
7	Vinny Testaverde	.20
8	Troy Aikman	1.50
9	Emmitt Smith	3.00
10	John Elway	1.00
11	Shannon Sharpe	.20
12	Barry Sanders	1.50
13	LeShon Johnson	.20
14	Sterling Sharpe	.50
15	Gary Brown	.20
16	Marshall Faulk	1.00
17	Lake Dawson	.20
18	Greg Hill	.60
19	Joe Montana	2.00
20	Tim Brown	.50
21	Jerome Bettis	.60
22	Dan Marino	3.00
23	Terry Allen	.50
24	David Palmer	.20
25	Drew Bledsoe	1.75
26	Ben Coates	.50
27	Michael Haynes	.20
28	Rodney Hampton	.50
29	Thomas Lewis	.20
30	Aaron Glenn	.20
31	Charlie Garner	.20
32	Charles Johnson	.20
33	Byron "Bam" Morris	.50
34	Natrone Means	.75
35	Ricky Watters	.50
36	Steve Young	1.25
37	Rick Mirer	.60
38	Trent Dilfer	1.00
39	Errict Rhett	2.00
40	Heath Shuler	.50

1995 Pacific

Pacific's 1995 Crown Collection set includes 450 cards, each using double-etched foil technology and etched gold foil. A 40-card subset features the season's top rookie draft picks. Two parallel sets were also created - a hobby only Royal Platinum Pt and a retail only Techn-Chrome Cr (both sets' cards were randomly included nine per every 37 packs). The regular card design has a gold-foiled panel which includes the player's name and position outlined in his team's colors. A full-bleed color photo is on the right, with the Pacific Crown Collection in the upper right. The card back has the player's name at the top, along with a mug shot, position, biographical information and a brief profile. Complete yearly statistics are also included on the back, which incorporates a team logo and the team's colors into the background. Seven insert sets were produced: Gems of the Crown; Gold Die-Cut Crown; Rookies 95; Young Warriors; G-Force; Hometown Heroes; and Cramer's Choice Awards.

		NM/M
Complete Set (450):		25.00
Common Player:		.05
Minor Stars:		.10
Comp. Platinum Set (450):		100.00
Platinum Cards:		3X-6X
Pack (12):		1.50
Wax Box (36):		50.00
1	Randy Baldwin	.05
2	Tommy Barnhardt	.05
3	Tim McKyer	.05
4	Sam Mills	.05
5	Brian O'Neal	.05
6	Frank Reich	.05
7	Jack Trudeau	.05
8	Vernon Turner	.05
9	*Kerry Collins*	1.00
10	Shawn King	.10
11	Steve Beuerlein	.05
12	Derek Brown	.05
13	Reggie Clark	.10
14	Reggie Cobb	.05
15	Desmond Howard	.05
16	Jeff Lageman	.05
17	Kelvin Pritchett	.05
18	Cedric Tillman	.05
19	*Tony Boselli*	.20

No.	Player	Price
20	*James Stewart*	1.50
21	Eric Davis	.05
22	William Floyd	.30
23	Elvis Grbac	.05
24	Brent Jones	.05
25	Ken Norton Jr.	.05
26	Bart Oates	.05
27	Jerry Rice	.75
28	Deion Sanders	.40
29	John Taylor	.05
30	*Adam Walker*	.10
31	Steve Wallace	.05
32	Ricky Watters	.15
33	Lee Woodall	.05
34	Bryant Young	.05
35	Steve Young	.75
36	*J.J. Stokes*	1.00
37	Troy Aikman	.50
38	Larry Allen	.05
39	Chris Boniol	.05
40	Lincoln Coleman	.05
41	Charles Haley	.05
42	Alvin Harper	.10
43	Chad Hennings	.05
44	Michael Irvin	.20
45	Daryl Johnston	.05
46	Leon Lett	.05
47	Nate Newton	.05
48	Jay Novacek	.05
49	Emmitt Smith	2.00
50	James Washington	.05
51	Kevin Williams	.05
52	*Sherman Williams*	.30
53	Barry Foster	.05
54	Eric Green	.05
55	Kevin Greene	.05
56	Andre Hastings	.05
57	Charles Johnson	.20
58	Greg Lloyd	.05
59	Ernie Mills	.05
60	Byron "Bam" Morris	.10
61	Neil O'Donnell	.10
62	Darren Perry	.05
63	*Yancey Thigpen*	.50
64	Mike Tomczak	.05
65	John L. Williams	.05
66	Rod Woodson	.05
67	*Mark Bruener*	.50
68	*Kordell Stewart*	2.00
69	Jeff Brohm	.10
70	Andre Coleman	.05
71	Rueben Davis	.05
72	Dennis Gibson	.05
73	Darrien Gordon	.05
74	Stan Humphries	.15
75	Shawn Jefferson	.05
76	Tony Martin	.05
77	Natrone Means	.40
78	Shannon Mitchell	.10
79	Leslie O'Neal	.05
80	Alfred Pupunu	.05
81	Stanley Richard	.05
82	Junior Seau	.10
83	Mark Seay	.05
84	Derrick Alexander	.20
85	Carl Banks	.05
86	Issac Booth	.10
87	Rob Burnett	.05
88	Earnest Byner	.05
89	Steve Everitt	.05
90	Leroy Hoard	.05
91	Pepper Johnson	.05
92	Antonio Langham	.05
93	Eric Metcalf	.05
94	Anthony Pleasant	.05
95	Frank Stams	.05
96	Vinny Testaverde	.05
97	Eric Turner	.05
98	Mike Miller	.10
99	Craig Powell	.05
100	Gene Atkins	.05
101	Aubrey Beavers	.05
102	Tim Bowens	.05
103	Keith Byars	.05
104	Bryan Cox	.05
105	Aaron Craver	.05
106	Jeff Cross	.05
107	Irving Fryar	.05
108	Dan Marino	2.00
109	O.J. McDuffie	.05
110	Bernie Parmalee	.20
111	James Saxon	.05
112	Keith Sims	.05
113	Irving Spikes	.05
114	Pete Mitchell	.10
115	Terry Allen	.05
116	Cris Carter	.10
117	Adrian Cooper	.05
118	Bernard Dafney	.05
119	Jack Del Rio	.05
120	Vencie Glenn	.05
121	Qadry Ismail	.05
122	Carlos Jenkins	.05
123	Andrew Jordan	.05
124	Ed McDaniel	.05
125	Warren Moon	.10
126	David Palmer	.05
127	John Randle	.05
128	Jake Reed	.05
129	Derrick Alexander	.15
130	*Chad May*	.30
131	Korey Stringer	.10
132	Bruce Armstrong	.05
133	Drew Bledsoe	1.00
134	Vincent Brisby	.05
135	Troy Brown	.10
136	Vincent Brown	.05
137	Marion Butts	.05
138	Ben Coates	.05
139	Ray Crittenden	.05
140	Maurice Hurst	.05
141	Aaron Jones	.05
142	Willie McGinest	.05
143	Marty Moore	.10
144	Mike Pitts	.05
145	Leroy Thompson	.05
146	Michael Timpson	.05
147	Bennie Blades	.05
148	Jocelyn Borgella	.05
149	Anthony Carter	.05
150	Willie Clay	.05
151	Mel Gray	.05
152	Mike Johnson	.05
153	Dave Kreig	.05
154	Robert Massey	.05
155	Scott Mitchell	.10
156	Herman Moore	.10
157	Johnnie Morton	.05
158	Barry Sanders	1.25
159	Chris Spielman	.05
160	Broderick Thomas	.05
161	Cory Schlesinger	.10
162	Marcus Allen	.10
163	Donnell Bennett	.05
164	J.J. Birden	.05
165	Matt Blundin	.05
166	Steve Bono	.15
167	Dale Carter	.05
168	Lake Dawson	.20
169	Ron Dickerson	.05
170	Lin Elliott	.05
171	Jaime Fields	.05
172	Greg Hill	.20
173	Danan Hughes	.05
174	Neil Smith	.05
175	*Steve Stenstrom*	.20
176	Edgar Bennett	.05
177	Robert Brooks	.05
178	Mark Brunell	.75
179	Doug Evans	.05
180	Brett Favre	2.00
181	Corey Harris	.05
182	LeShon Johnson	.05
183	Sean Jones	.05
184	Lenny McGill	.10
185	Terry Mickens	.05
186	Sterling Sharpe	.10
187	Joe Sims	.05
188	Darrell Thompson	.05
189	Reggie White	.10
190	Craig Newsome	.15
191	Tim Brown	.10
192	Vince Evans	.05
193	Rob Fredrickson	.05
194	*Andrew Glover*	.10
195	Jeff Hostetler	.10
196	Raghib Ismail	.05
197	Jeff Jaeger	.05
198	James Jett	.05
199	Chester McGlockton	.05
200	Don Mosebar	.05
201	Tom Rathman	.05
202	Harvey Williams	.05
203	Steve Wisniewski	.05
204	Alexander Wright	.05
205	*Napoleon Kaufman*	1.00
206	Trace Armstrong	.05
207	Curtis Conway	.10
208	Raymont Harris	.05
209	Erik Kramer	.05
210	Nate Lewis	.05
211	*Shane Matthews*	2.00
212	John Thierry	.05
213	Lewis Tillman	.05
214	Tom Waddle	.05
215	Steve Walsh	.05
216	James Williams	.05
217	Donnell Woolford	.05
218	Chris Zorich	.05
219	*Rashaan Salaam*	.50
220	John Booty	.05
221	Michael Brooks	.05
222	Dave Brown	.05
223	Chris Calloway	.05
224	Gary Downs	.10
225	Kent Graham	.05
226	Keith Hamilton	.05
227	Rodney Hampton	.05
228	Brian Kozlowski	.15
229	Thomas Lewis	.05
230	Dave Meggett	.05
231	Aaron Pierce	.05
232	Mike Sherrard	.05
233	Phillippi Sparks	.05
234	*Tyrone Wheatley*	.40
235	Trev Alberts	.05
236	Aaron Bailey	.05
237	Jason Belser	.05
238	Tony Bennett	.05
239	Kerry Cash	.05
240	Marshall Faulk	1.00
241	Stephen Grant	.10
242	Jeff Herrod	.05
243	Ronald Humphrey	.10
244	Kirk Lowdermilk	.05
245	Don Majkowski	.05
246	Tony McCoy	.05
247	Floyd Turner	.05
248	Lamont Warren	.05
249	Zack Crockett	.10
250	Michael Bankston	.05
251	Larry Centers	.05
252	Gary Clark	.05
253	Ed Cunningham	.05
254	Garrison Hearst	.10
255	Eric Hill	.05
256	Terry Irving	.05
257	Lorenzo Lynch	.05
258	Jamir Miller	.05
259	Ron Moore	.05
260	Terry Samuels	.10
261	Jay Schroeder	.05
262	Eric Swann	.05
263	Aeneas Williams	.05
264	*Frank Sanders*	.75
265	Morten Andersen	.05
266	Mario Bates	.20
267	Derek Brown	.05
268	Darion Conner	.05
269	Quinn Early	.05
270	Jim Everett	.10
271	Michael Haynes	.05
272	Wayne Martin	.05
273	Derrell Mitchell	.10
274	Lorenzo Neal	.05
275	Jimmy Spencer	.05
276	Winfred Tubbs	.05
277	Renaldo Turnbull	.05
278	Jeff Uhlenhake	.05
279	Steve Atwater	.05
280	Keith Burns	.10
281	Butler By'not'e	.15
282	Jeff Campbell	.05
283	Derrick Clark	.10
284	Shane Dronett	.05
285	Jason Elam	.05
286	John Elway	.30
287	Jerry Evans	.10
288	Karl Mecklenburg	.05
289	Glyn Milburn	.05
290	Anthony Miller	.05
291	Tom Rouen	.05
292	Leonard Russell	.05
293	Shannon Sharpe	.05
294	Steve Russ	.10
295	Mel Agee	.05
296	Lester Archambeau	.05
297	Bert Emanuel	.20
298	Jeff George	.10
299	Craig Heyward	.05
300	Bobby Hebert	.05
301	D.J. Johnson	.05
302	Mike Kenn	.05
303	Terance Mathis	.05
304	Clay Matthews	.05
305	Erric Pegram	.05
306	Andre Rison	.10
307	Chuck Smith	.05
308	Jessie Tuggle	.05
309	Lorenzo Styles	.10
310	Cornelius Bennett	.05
311	Bill Brooks	.05
312	Jeff Burris	.05
313	Carwell Gardner	.05
314	Kent Hull	.05
315	Yonel Jourdain	.15
316	Jim Kelly	.10
317	Vince Marrow	.05
318	Pete Metzelaars	.05
319	Andre Reed	.05
320	Kurt Schulz	.05
321	Bruce Smith	.05
322	Darryl Talley	.05
323	Matt Darby	.05
324	Justin Armour	.10
325	*Todd Collins*	.30
326	David Alexander	.05
327	Eric Allen	.05
328	Fred Barnett	.05
329	Randall Cunningham	.05
330	William Fuller	.05
331	Charlie Garner	.05
332	Vaughn Hebron	.05
333	James Joseph	.05
334	Bill Romanowski	.05
335	Ken Rose	.05
336	Jeff Snyder	.05
337	William Thomas	.05
338	Herschel Walker	.05
339	Calvin Williams	.05
340	*Dave Barr*	.25
341	Chidi Ahanotu	.05
342	Barney Bussey	.05
343	Horace Copeland	.05
344	Trent Dilfer	.40
345	Craig Erickson	.05
346	Paul Gruber	.05
347	Courtney Hawkins	.05
348	Lonnie Marts	.05
349	Martin Mayhew	.05
350	Hardy Nickerson	.05
351	Errict Rhett	.50
352	Lamar Thomas	.05
353	Charles Wilson	.05
354	Vince Workman	.05
355	Derrick Brooks	1.00
356	*Warren Sapp*	1.00
357	Sam Adams	.05
358	Michael Bates	.05
359	Brian Blades	.05
360	Carlton Gray	.05
361	Bill Hitchcock	.05
362	Cortez Kennedy	.05
363	Rick Mirer	.30
364	Eugene Robinson	.05
365	Michael Sinclair	.05
366	Steve Smith	.05
367	Bob Spitulski	.05
368	Rick Tuten	.05
369	Chris Warren	.10
370	Terrence Warren	.10
371	*Christian Fauria*	.10
372	*Joey Galloway*	2.00
373	Boomer Esiason	.05
374	Aaron Glenn	.05
375	Victor Green	.10
376	Johnny Johnson	.05
377	Mo Lewis	.05
378	Ronnie Lott	.05
379	Nick Lowery	.05
380	Johnny Mitchell	.05
381	Rob Moore	.05
382	Adrian Murrell	.05
383	Anthony Prior	.05
384	Brian Washington	.05
385	Matt Willig	.05
386	*Kyle Brady*	.25
387	Willie Anderson	.05
388	Johnny Bailey	.05
389	Jerome Bettis	.25
390	Isaac Bruce	.30
391	Shane Conlan	.05
392	Troy Drayton	.05
393	D'Marco Farr	.05
394	Jessie Hester	.05
395	Todd Kinchen	.05
396	Ron Middleton	.05
397	Chris Miller	.05
398	Marquez Pope	.05
399	Robert Young	.05
400	Tony Zendejas	.05
401	*Kevin Carter*	.20
402	Reggie Brooks	.05
403	Tom Carter	.05
404	Andre Collins	.05
405	Pat Eilers	.05
406	Henry Ellard	.05
407	Ricky Ervins	.05
408	Gus Frerotte	.25
409	Ken Harvey	.05
410	Jim Lachey	.05
411	Brian Mitchell	.05
412	Reggie Roby	.05
413	Heath Shuler	.50
414	Tyronne Stowe	.05
415	Tydus Winans	.05
416	Cory Raymer	.05
417	*Michael Westbrook*	1.00
418	*Jeff Blake*	.50
419	Steve Broussard	.05
420	Dave Cadigan	.05
421	Jeff Cothran	.05
422	Derrick Fenner	.05
423	James Francis	.05
424	Lee Johnson	.05
425	Louis Oliver	.05
426	Carl Pickens	.20
427	Jeff Query	.05
428	Corey Sawyer	.05
429	Darnay Scott	.30
430	Dan Wilkinson	.05
431	Alfred Williams	.05
432	*Ki-Jana Carter*	.50
433	David Dunn	.15
434	*John Walsh*	.25
435	Gary Brown	.05
436	Pat Carter	.05
437	Ray Childress	.05
438	Ernest Givins	.05
439	Haywood Jeffires	.05
440	Lamar Lathon	.05
441	Bruce Matthews	.05
442	Marcus Robertson	.05
443	Eddie Robinson	.05
444	*Malcolm Seabron*	.10
445	Webster Slaughter	.05
446	Al Smith	.05
447	Billy Joe Tolliver	.05
448	Lorenzo White	.05
449	*Steve McNair*	3.00
450	*Rodney Thomas*	.20

1995 Pacific Blue/ Platinum

The two, 450-card card parallel sets were inserted every 37 packs (blue in retail, platinum in hobby).

	NM/M
Complete Set (45):	225.00
Common Player:	.30
Veteran Stars:	3X-6X
Young Stars:	2X-4X
RCs:	1.5X-3X

1995 Pacific Cramer's Choice

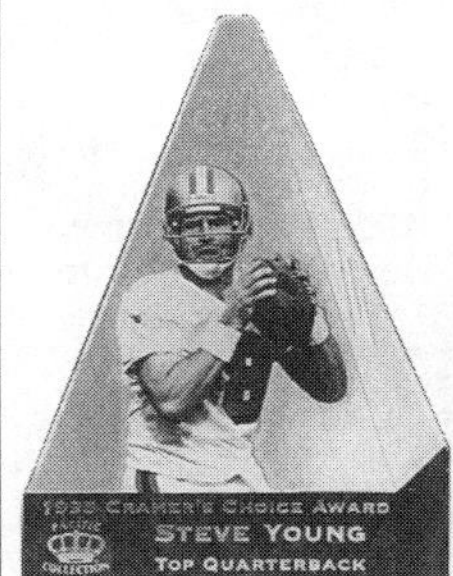

These 1995 Pacific Crown Collection inserts feature six top NFL players in six different categories, as selected by Pacific President and CEO Michael Cramer. The die-cut cards, done in a trophy design, were seeded one per every 720 packs. The front has a marble-like base which includes the Crown logo and designation of the award, plus who won it. The player photo appears in the middle of the metallic silver pyramid design, with another Crown Collection logo at the top of the point. The card back is marble-like, with an extensive quote from Cramer about the player. A small closeup shot is also provided, as is a card number, which uses a "CC" prefix.

		NM/M
Complete Set (6):		175.00
Common Player:		20.00
1	Ki-Jana Carter	20.00
2	Emmitt Smith	75.00
3	Marshall Faulk	50.00
4	Jerry Rice	60.00
5	Deion Sanders	35.00
6	Steve Young	60.00

1995 Pacific Gems of the Crown

These 36 insert cards feature a color photo on the front, etched by a gold frame. The Pacific Crown Collection logo is in the upper right corner; the player's name is in the bottom right corner, with gold foil outlining the letters. The horizontal back has a closeup shot of the player on the left, with his name, position and team name underneath. On the right is a paragraph summarizing the player's career, plus an insert set logo and a card number (using a GC prefix). Cards were random inserts, two per every 37 packs of 1995 Pacific Crown Collection football.

		NM/M
Complete Set (36):		60.00
Common Player:		1.00
1	Jim Kelly	3.00
2	Kerry Collins	2.00
3	Darnay Scott	1.00
4	Jeff Blake	1.00
5	Terry Allen	1.00
6	Emmitt Smith	6.00
7	Michael Irvin	2.00
8	Troy Aikman	5.00
9	John Elway	5.00
10	Dave Krieg	1.00
11	Barry Sanders	6.00
12	Brett Favre	6.00
13	Marshall Faulk	4.00
14	Marcus Allen	2.00
15	Tim Brown	1.00
16	Bernie Parmalee	1.00
17	Dan Marino	6.00
18	Cris Carter	1.00
19	Drew Bledsoe	4.00
20	Mario Bates	1.00
21	Rodney Hampton	1.00
22	Ben Coates	1.00
23	Charles Johnson	1.00
24	Byron "Bam" Morris	1.00
25	Stan Humphries	1.00
26	Deion Sanders	2.00
27	Jerry Rice	5.00
28	Ricky Watters	2.00
29	Steve Young	4.00
30	Natrone Means	1.00
31	William Floyd	1.00
32	Chris Warren	1.00
33	Rick Mirer	1.00
34	Jerome Bettis	2.00
35	Errict Rhett	1.00
36	Heath Shuler	1.00

1995 Pacific G-Force

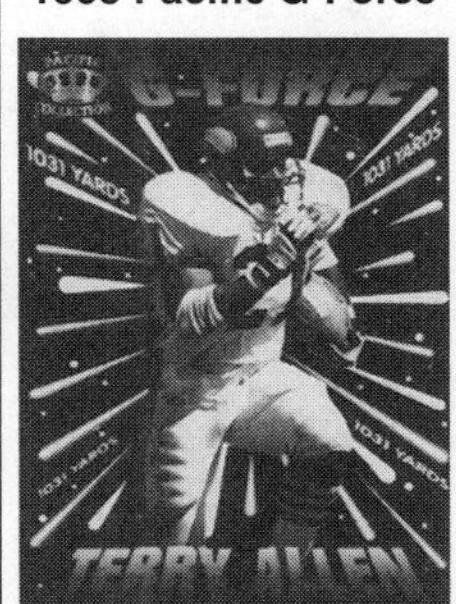

Ten of the NFL's top running backs are featured on these insert cards, randomly included one per every 37 packs of Pacific's 1995 Crown Collection football. The card front has a color photo of the player against a black background which includes several starbursts, plus the number of yards he gained rushing in 1994. "G-Force" is written at the top of the card; the player's name is at the bottom. The card back has a similar design for the background, with a closeup shot of the player in the upper right corner. His name, team name and card number, using a "GF" prefix, are to the left of the photo. A paragraph recapping the player's 1994 accomplishments is featured in the middle of the card.

		NM/M
Complete Set (10):		25.00
Common Player:		1.00
1	Marcus Allen	2.00
2	Terry Allen	1.00
3	Emmitt Smith	6.00
4	Barry Sanders	6.00
5	Marshall Faulk	3.00
6	Rodney Hampton	1.00
7	Natrone Means	1.00
8	Chris Warren	1.00
9	Jerome Bettis	2.00
10	Errict Rhett	1.00

1995 Pacific Gold Crown Die-Cuts

These 36 insert cards could be randomly found two per every 37 packs of 1995 Pacific Crown Collection football. The cards, numbered on the back using a "DC" prefix, feature a full-bleed color action photo on the front, with a die-cut foiled crown at the top. The player's name is at the bottom in foil.

		NM/M
Complete Set (20):		75.00
Common Player:		2.00
Flat Gold Cards:		1X-2X
1	Ki-Jana Carter	2.00
2	Michael Irvin	2.00
3	Emmitt Smith	20.00
4	Troy Aikman	15.00
5	John Elway	15.00
6	Barry Sanders	20.00
7	Marshall Faulk	12.00
8	Dan Marino	20.00
9	Ben Coates	2.00
10	Drew Bledsoe	15.00
11	Byron "Bam" Morris	2.00
12	Jerry Rice	15.00
13	William Floyd	2.00
14	Steve Young	15.00
15	Natrone Means	2.00
16	Deion Sanders	4.00
17	Rick Mirer	2.00
18	Chris Warren	2.00
19	Jerome Bettis	3.00
20	Errict Rhett	2.00

1995 Pacific Hometown Heroes

These insert cards feature 10 top NFL stars and pay tribute to the players' hometown. Each card front has a color photo of the player, with his hometown's state flag flying on the left side. His name and "Hometown Hereos" are written in foil at the bottom of the card. The horizontal card back has two photos - one a close-up, the other an action photo of the player framed by the borders of his state. A star is used to pinpoint his city's location on the map. A banner at the top of the card includes the insert set's name, with a recap of where the player started his football career. Cards, randomly included one per every 37 packs of Pacific Crown Collection football, are numbered with an "HH" prefix.

		NM/M
Complete Set (10):		35.00
Common Player:		1.00
1	Emmitt Smith	6.00
2	Troy Aikman	5.00
3	Barry Sanders	6.00
4	Marshall Faulk	3.00
5	Dan Marino	6.00
6	Drew Bledsoe	4.00
7	Natrone Means	1.00
8	Steve Young	4.00
9	Jerry Rice	5.00
10	Errict Rhett	1.00

1995 Pacific Rookies

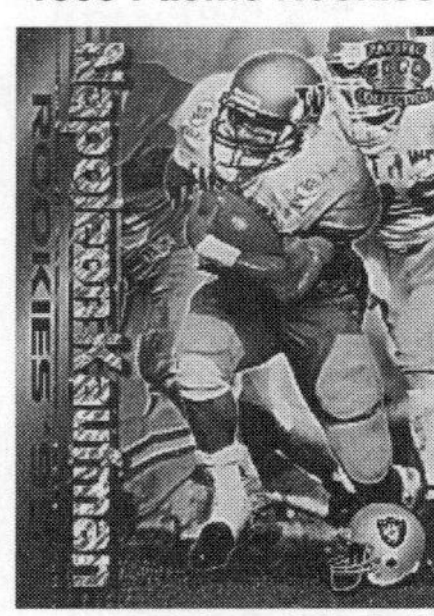

Inserted into 1995 Pacific Crown Collection football packs at a rate of two per every 37 packs, these 20 cards feature top rookies of 1995. The card front has a color photo of the player in his college uniform, with his name in silver foil running down the left side. "Rookies '95" is also written along the side. A football helmet of the team which drafted the player is in the lower right corner. The card back has another photo of the player in the upper left, with his pro team's helmet on the right. The player's name runs across the center of the card, just above a paragraph which summarizes his skills.

		NM/M
Complete Set (20):		25.00
Common Player:		.25
1	Dave Barr	.25
2	Kyle Brady	.50
3	Mark Bruener	.25
4	Ki-Jana Carter	.50
5	Kerry Collins	5.00
6	Todd Collins	.25
7	Christian Fauria	.25
8	Joey Galloway	3.00
9	Chris Jones	.25
10	Napoleon Kaufman	.50
11	Chad May	.25
12	Steve McNair	6.00
13	Rashaan Salaam	.25
14	Warren Sapp	3.00
15	James Stewart	2.00
16	Kordell Stewart	4.00
17	J.J. Stokes	1.00
18	Michael Westbrook	1.00
19	Tyrone Wheatley	.25
20	Sherman Williams	.25

1995 Pacific Young Warriors

Twenty of the NFL's top second-year stars are featured on these 1995 Pacific Crown Collection inserts. The card front is full gold foil, with "Young Warrior" written down the right side of the card. The Pacific logo is in the upper left corner; the player's name is at the bottom in his team's colors. The back has two pillars, with the insert set name and the player's team name inside at the top. His name is at the very top of the card. Between the two pillars is an image of the player in action. A brief 1994 recap is also given, below the image.

		NM/M
Complete Set (20):		25.00
Common Player:		1.00
Minor Stars:		2.00
1	Bert Emanuel	2.00
2	Darnay Scott	2.00
3	Dan Wilkinson	1.00
4	Derrick Alexander	1.00
5	Willie McGinest	1.00
6	Marshall Faulk	6.00
7	Lake Dawson	1.00
8	Greg Hill	2.00
9	Tim Bowens	1.00
10	David Palmer	1.00
11	Aaron Glenn	1.00
12	Mario Bates	2.00
13	Charles Johnson	2.00
14	Byron "Bam" Morris	2.00
15	William Floyd	2.00
16	Adam Walker	1.00
17	Bryant Young	2.00
18	Trent Dilfer	2.00
19	Errict Rhett	2.00
20	Heath Shuler	2.00

1995 Pacific Crown Royale

Pacific's 1995 Crown Collection II Crown Royale football set features a hobby first - all cards are die-cut. The horizontal card front has a die-cut crown at the top in gold foil, which is also used for the player's name and position at the bottom. A team helmet also appears at the bottom in the lower right corner. The card back has another color photo of the player, along with a recap of his 1994 season. Hobby and retail versions of Crown Royale were produced. Two distinct parallel sets exist, with distinguishing foils for both hobby and retail versions, and are seeded four per every 25 packs. Three insert sets were created - Pro Bowl Die-Cut, Pride of the NFL and Cramer's Choice Awards.

		NM/M
Complete Set (144):		45.00
Common Player:		.25
Minor Stars:		.50
Copper Cards:		2X-4X
Blue Cards:		3X-6X
Pack (4):		4.00
Wax Box (24):		80.00
1	Lake Dawson	.25
2	Steve Beuerlein	.25
3	Jake Reed	.25
4	Jim Everett	.25
5	Sean Dawkins	.25
6	Jeff Hostetler	.25
7	Marshall Faulk	4.00
8	*Jeff Blake*	1.00
9	Dave Brown	.25
10	Frank Reich	.25
11	Raghib Ismail	.25
12	Jerry Jones	1.00
13	Dan Marino	5.00
14	Ricky Watters	1.00
15	Herman Moore	1.50
16	Daryl Johnston	.25
17	Craig Erickson	.25
18	Alexander Wright	.25
19	Reggie White	1.00
20	Andre Rison	.25
21	Fred Barnett	.25
22	*Tyrone Wheatley*	1.00
23	Charles Johnson	.50
24	*Rashaan Salaam*	.50
25	Mark Brunell	3.00
26	Derek Loville	.25
27	Garrison Hearst	1.00
28	Ken Norton Jr.	.25
29	*Kerry Collins*	5.00
30	Isaac Bruce	2.00
31	Andre Reed	.25
32	Leon Lett	.25
33	Deion Sanders	2.00
34	Terance Mathis	.25
35	Tim Bowens	.25
36	Shannon Sharpe	.25
37	Quinn Early	.25
38	Jerry Rice	4.00
39	Bruce Smith	.25
40	Drew Bledsoe	4.00
41	Alvin Harper	.25
42	Jim Kelly	1.00
43	*Napoleon Kaufman*	1.00
44	Errict Rhett	1.00
45	Henry Ellard	.25
46	Barry Sanders	5.00
47	Vincent Brisby	.25
48	Chris Zorich	.25
49	Zack Crockett	.25
50	Haywood Jeffires	.25
51	Byron "Bam" Morris	1.00
52	John Kasay	.25
53	Scott Mitchell	.25
54	Boomer Esiason	.25
55	Eric Metcalf	.25
56	Kevin Greene	.25
57	Courtney Hawkins	.25
58	Adrian Murrell	.25
59	Larry Centers	.25
60	Leroy Hoard	.25
61	Lorenzo White	.25
62	Chris Spielman	.25
63	Carl Pickens	1.50
64	Steve Young	4.00
65	Trent Dilfer	1.00
66	Eric Kramer	.25
67	Cortez Kennedy	.25
68	Ray Childress	.25
69	Rick Mirer	1.00
70	Kevin Williams	.25
71	*Joey Galloway*	5.00
72	Dan Wilkinson	.25
73	*Antonio Freeman*	3.00
74	Curtis Conway	1.00
75	Troy Aikman	4.00
76	Natrone Means	1.00
77	Jeff George	1.00
78	*Curtis Martin*	8.00
79	William Floyd	1.00
80	Anthony Miller	.25
81	Greg Hill	1.00
82	Craig Heyward	.25
83	Brian Mitchell	.25
84	Anthony Carter	.25
85	Jerome Bettis	1.00
86	Jim Harbaugh	.25
87	Harvey Williams	.25
88	Tony Martin	.25
89	Rob Moore	.25
90	Neil O'Donnell	.25
91	Cris Carter	.25
92	*Warren Sapp*	3.00
93	Terry Allen	.25
94	Michael Irvin	1.00
95	Heath Shuler	2.00
96	Cornelius Bennett	.25
97	Randy Baldwin	.25
98	Vince Workman	.25
99	Irving Fryar	.25
100	Randall Cunningham	.25
101	*James Stewart*	4.00
102	Stan Humphries	.25
103	Mario Bates	.25
104	Ben Coates	.25
105	Charlie Garner	.25
106	*Todd Collins*	1.00
107	Tim Brown	1.00
108	Edgar Bennett	.25
109	*J.J. Stokes*	3.00
110	Michael Timpson	.25
111	Junior Seau	1.00
112	Bernie Parmalee	1.00
113	Willie McGinest	.25
114	David Dunn	.25
115	*Kyle Brady*	1.50
116	Vinny Testaverde	.25
117	Ernest Givins	.25
118	*Eric Zeier*	1.00
119	Michael Jackson	.25
120	*Chad May*	1.00
121	Dave Krieg	.25
122	Rodney Hampton	.25
123	Darnay Scott	2.00
124	Chris Miller	.25
125	Emmitt Smith	5.00
126	*Steve McNair*	8.00
127	Warren Moon	.25
128	Robert Brooks	1.00
129	Bert Emanuel	1.50
130	John Elway	4.00
131	Chris Warren	1.00
132	Herschel Walker	.25
133	Terry Kirby	.25
134	*Michael Westbrook*	3.00
135	*Kordell Stewart*	3.00
136	*Terrell Davis*	6.00
137	Desmond Howard	.25
138	*Rodney Thomas*	1.00
139	Brett Favre	5.00
140	*Ray Zellars*	1.00
141	Marcus Allen	1.00
142	Gus Frerotte	.50
143	Steve Bono	1.00
144	Aaron Craver	.25

1995 Pacific Crown Royale Blue Holofoil

The 144-card, regular-size set was inserted into retail packs with the fronts having blue holographic background rather than gold-foil backgrounds.

Veteran Stars:	3.5X-7X
Young Stars:	2.5X-5X
RCs:	2X-4X

1995 Pacific Crown Royale Copper

The 144-card, regular-sized parallel set was randomly inserted in hobby packs and features copper foil instead of gold foil on the die-cut crown.

Veteran Stars:	2.5X-5X
Young Stars:	2X-4X
RCs:	1.5X-3X

1995 Pacific Crown Royale Cramer's Choice Jumbos

These six cards are similar to their 1995 Pacific counterparts, except they are oversized, in a new foil format. One player is also different; Rashaan Salaam replaces Ki-Jana Carter in the set. The cards are included one per every 16 boxes of Crown Royale football product and represent Mike Cramer's top picks in offensive and defensive categories. Cramer is Pacific's CEO and president. The cards are numbered and have a "CC" prefix.

		NM/M
Complete Set (6):		200.00
Common Player:		15.00
1	Rashaan Salaam	15.00
2	Emmitt Smith	75.00
3	Marshall Faulk	40.00
4	Jerry Rice	65.00
5	Deion Sanders	25.00
6	Steve Young	60.00

1995 Pacific Crown Royale Pride of the NFL

This set represents 36 of the NFL's top players, using a new foil wave design on the card front. The card back is numbered using a "PN" prefix. Cards were random inserts in three of every 25 packs.

		NM/M
Complete Set (36):		125.00
Common Player:		2.00
1	Jim Kelly	4.00
2	Kerry Collins	5.00
3	Darnay Scott	2.00
4	Jeff Blake	2.00
5	Terry Allen	2.00
6	Emmitt Smith	10.00
7	Michael Irvin	3.00
8	Troy Aikman	8.00
9	John Elway	8.00
10	Napoleon Kaufman	2.00
11	Barry Sanders	10.00
12	Brett Favre	12.00
13	Michael Westbrook	2.00
14	Marcus Allen	2.00
15	Tim Brown	4.00
16	Bernie Parmalee	2.00
17	Dan Marino	12.00
18	Cris Carter	2.00
19	Drew Bledsoe	8.00
20	Mario Bates	2.00
21	Rodney Hampton	2.00
22	Ben Coates	2.00
23	Charles Johnson	2.00
24	Bam Morris	2.00
25	Stan Humphries	2.00
26	Rashaan Salaam	2.00
27	Jerry Rice	8.00
28	Ricky Watters	2.00
29	Steve Young	8.00
30	Natrone Means	2.00
31	William Floyd	2.00
32	Chris Warren	2.00
33	Rick Mirer	2.00
34	Jerome Bettis	4.00
35	Errict Rhett	2.00
36	Heath Shuler	2.00

1995 Pacific Crown Royale Pro Bowl Die Cuts

These 1995 Pacific Crown Royale die-cut cards feature 20 players who participated in the 1995 Pro Bowl game, played in Honolulu, Hawaii. Thus, a palm tree foiled die-cut design is used, and the Pro Bowl logo is displayed on each card. Cards were random inserts, one per every 25 packs. The cards are numbered with the "PB" prefix.

		NM/M
Complete Set (20):		300.00
Common Player:		6.00
1	Drew Bledsoe	25.00
2	Ben Coates	6.00
3	John Elway	30.00
4	Marshall Faulk	25.00
5	Dan Marino	40.00
6	Natrone Means	6.00
7	Junior Seau	10.00
8	Chris Warren	6.00
9	Rod Woodson	6.00
10	Tim Brown	12.00
11	Troy Aikman	30.00
12	Jerome Bettis	8.00
13	Michael Irvin	8.00
14	Jerry Rice	30.00
15	Barry Sanders	40.00
16	Deion Sanders	15.00
17	Emmitt Smith	40.00
18	Steve Young	25.00
19	Reggie White	8.00
20	Cris Carter	6.00

1995 Pacific Gridiron

These 3-1/2" x 5" oversized cards capture the NFL's toughest players in their most aggressive and powerful moments on the field. The card front features a full-bleed color photo. The card back details the play on the front in a newspaper-style article and includes a closeup shot of the player. Only 1,500 cases of Pacific's Gridiron were produced. There were 750 hobby cases produced, with each card stamped with blue foil for the player's name on the front. There were also 750 retail cases produced; these cards are stamped with red foil. Each of these sets will also have a "Presidential Series" parallel set, too. The hobby parallel set will be stamped in platinum foil and represent 10 percent of the sets produced. The retail parallel set is stamped in copper foil and represents 10 percent of the sets produced.

		NM/M
Complete Set (100):		35.00
Common Player:		.20
Copper-Platinum Stars:		3X-6X
Pack (1):		1.00
Wax Box (36):		30.00
1	Natrone Means	.50
2	Dave Meggett	.20
3	Curtis Conway	.20
4	Sam Adams	.20
5	Qadry Ismail	.20
6	Steve Young	2.00
7	Errict Rhett	1.00
8	Nate Lewis	.20
9	Barry Sanders	3.00
10	Sterling Sharpe	.20
11	Steve Beuerlein	.20
12	Irving Spikes	.20
13	Byron "Bam" Morris	.20
14	Eric Metcalf	.20
15	Michael Irvin	1.00
16	Dan Marino	4.00
17	Stan Humphries	.20
18	Leroy Hoard	.20
19	Marcus Allen	.20
20	Barry Foster	.20
21	Rob Moore	.20
22	Rodney Hampton	.20
23	Ben Coates	.20
24	Vernon Turner	.20
25	Shannon Sharpe	.20
26	Larry Centers	.20
27	*Mack Strong*	.20
28	Reggie White	.20
29	Harvey Williams	.20
30	Darnay Scott	.50
31	Drew Bledsoe	2.00
32	Marshall Faulk	2.00
33	Troy Aikman	2.00
34	Boomer Esiason	.20
35	Bobby Hebert	.20
36	Brian Mitchell	.20
37	Andre Rison	.20
38	Brett Favre	5.00
39	Don Majkowski	.20
40	Johnny Johnson	.20
41	Mark Carrier	.20
42	James Joseph	.20
43	Mario Bates	.50
44	Craig Heyward	.20
45	Henry Ellard	.20
46	Thurman Thomas	1.00
47	Jerome Bettis	1.00
48	Dave Brown	.20
49	Lorenzo White	.20
50	Joe Montana	5.00
51	Vinny Testaverde	.20
52	Lake Dawson	.50
53	Michael Timpson	.20
54	Ricky Ervins	.20
55	Cris Carter	.20
56	Raymont Harris	.50
57	Andre Coleman	.20
58	Craig Erickson	.20
59	Jeff Hostetler	.20
60	Deion Sanders	1.00
61	Eric Turner	.20
62	Darryl Johnston	.20
63	Bernie Parmalee	.20
64	Ricky Watters	.20
65	David Palmer	.20
66	Aaron Glenn	.20
67	Todd Kinchen	.20
68	Edgar Bennett	.20
69	Mel Gray	.20
70	Randall Cunningham	.20
71	Michael Haynes	.20
72	Chris Miller	.20
73	Glyn Milburn	.20
74	*Steve McNair*	7.00
75	Lewis Tillman	.20
76	Chuck Levy	.20
77	Carl Pickens	.20
78	Michael Bates	.20
79	*Jeff Blake*	2.00
80	O.J. McDuffie	.20
81	Tim Brown	.20
82	Haywood Jeffires	.20
83	Jeff Burris	.20
84	John Elway	3.00
85	Charles Johnson	.50
86	Emmitt Smith	4.00
87	William Floyd	.50
88	Herschel Walker	.20
89	Rick Mirer	.50
90	Roosevelt Potts	.20
91	Rod Woodson	.20
92	Greg Hill	.50
93	Junior Seau	.20
94	Dave Krieg	.20
95	Jim Kelly	.20
96	Warren Moon	.20
97	Leroy Thompson	.20
98	*Ki-Jana Carter*	2.00
99	Herman Moore	.75
100	Jerry Rice	4.00

1995 Pacific Gridiron Copper/Platinum

The 100-card, regular-size parallel set featured copper/ platinum foil rather than the blue foil. Only 10 percent of the sets produced were copper/platinum.

Veteran Stars:	4X-8X
Young Stars:	3X-6X
RCs:	2X-4X

1995 Pacific Gridiron Gold

The 100-card, regular-sized parallel set features gold foil on the card front instead of red foil. Of the sets produced, only 10 percent were in gold foil.

Veteran Stars:	20X-40X
Young Stars/RCs:	10X-20X

1995 Pacific Prisms

Pacific released its 1995 set in two 108-card series, with each of the 216 cards reprinted in a parallel Gold Prism set (one every 30 Series I packs, two every 37 Series II packs). Each card front has an action photo on the left, along with the player's name in silver foil. A closeup shot appears on the right side of the horizontally-designed card. The back has another action photo of the player against a backdrop with a photo of his team's helmet. A few career accomplishment tidbits are also included on the back. The player's name runs down the right side. Production was limted to 1,500 hobby and 1,500 retail cases for each series. Series I inserts include Red Hot Super Stars, Red Hot Rookies and two Expansion Extra inserts, a Barry Foster card for Carolina and a Steve Beuerlein card for Jacksonville. Series II inserts include Royal Connections, and Kings of the NFL.

	NM/M
Complete Set (216):	100.00
Complete Series 1 Set (108):	50.00
Complete Series 2 Set (108):	50.00
Common Player:	.50
Minor Stars:	1.00
Series 1 or 2 Pack (1):	1.00
Series 1 or 2 Wax Box (36):	35.00

1	Chuck Levy	.50
2	Ron Moore	.50
3	Jay Schroeder	.50
4	Bert Emanuel	.50
5	Terance Mathis	.50
6	Andre Rison	.50
7	Bucky Brooks	.50
8	Jeff Burris	.50
9	Jim Kelly	2.00
10	Lewis Tillman	.50
11	Steve Walsh	.50
12	Chris Zorich	.50
13	*Jeff Blake*	2.00
14	Steve Broussard	.50
15	Jeff Cothran	.50
16	Ernest Byner	.50
17	Leroy Hoard	.50
18	Vinny Testaverde	1.00
19	Troy Aikman	4.00
20	Alvin Harper	.50
21	Leon Lett	.50
22	Jay Novacek	.50
23	John Elway	4.00
24	Karl Mecklenburg	.50
25	Leonard Russell	.50
26	Mel Gray	.50
27	Barry Sanders	5.00
28	Dave Krieg	.50
29	Chris Spielman	.50
30	Robert Brooks	1.00
31	LeShon Johnson	.50
32	Sterling Sharpe	1.00
33	Ernest Givins	.50
34	Billy Joe Tolliver	.50
35	Lorenzo White	.50
36	Charles Arbuckle	.50
37	Sean Dawkins	.75
38	Marshall Faulk	4.00
39	Marcus Allen	2.00
40	Donnell Bennett	.50
41	*Matt Blundin*	.50
42	Greg Hill	.75
43	Tim Brown	2.00
44	Billy Joe Hobert	.75
45	Raghib Ismail	.50
46	James Jett	.50
47	Tim Bowens	.50
48	Irving Fryar	.50
49	O.J. McDuffie	.75
50	Irving Spikes	.50
51	Terry Allen	.75
52	Cris Carter	1.00
53	Amp Lee	.50
54	Drew Bledsoe	4.00
55	Willie McGinest	.50
56	Leroy Thompson	.50
57	Michael Timpson	.50
58	Michael Haynes	.50
59	Derrell Mitchell	.50
60	Dave Brown	.50
61	Thomas Lewis	.50
62	Dave Meggett	.50
63	Boomer Esiason	.50
64	Aaron Glenn	.50
65	Ronnie Lott	.50
66	Randall Cunningham	1.00
67	Charlie Garner	.50
68	Herschel Walker	.50
69	Barry Foster	.50
70	Charles Johnson	.75
71	*Jim Miller*	1.00
72	Rod Woodson	1.00
73	Andre Coleman	.50
74	Natrone Means	1.00
75	Shannon Mitchell	.50
76	Junior Seau	1.00
77	Elvis Grbac	.75
78	Deion Sanders	2.00
79	*Adam Walker*	.50
80	Ricky Watters	1.00
81	Michael Bates	.50
82	Brian Blades	.50
83	Eugene Robinson	.50
84	Chris Warren	.75
85	Jerome Bettis	1.00
86	Troy Drayton	.50
87	Chris Miller	.50
88	Trent Dilfer	1.00
89	Hardy Nickerson	.50
90	Errict Rhett	1.00
91	Henry Ellard	.50
92	Gus Frerotte	.75
93	Ricky Irvins	.50
94	*Dave Barr*	.50
95	*Kyle Brady*	.50
96	*Mark Bruener*	.75
97	*Ki-Jana Carter*	2.00
98	*Kerry Collins*	5.00
99	*Joey Galloway*	5.00
100	*Napoleon Kaufman*	2.00
101	*Steve McNair*	12.00
102	*Craig Newsome*	.50
103	*Rashaan Salaam*	1.00
104	*Kordell Stewart*	3.00
105	*J.J. Stokes*	2.00
106	*Rodney Thomas*	1.00
107	*Michael Westbrook*	2.00
108	*Tyrone Wheatley*	1.00
109	Larry Centers	.50
110	Garrison Hearst	1.00
111	Jamir Miller	.50
112	Jeff George	.75
113	Craig Heyward	.50
114	Cornelius Bennett	.50
115	Andre Reed	.50
116	Randy Baldwin	.50
117	Tommy Barnhardt	.50
118	Sam Mills	.50
119	Brian O'Neal	.50
120	Frank Reich	.50
121	Tony Smith	.50
122	Lawyer Tillman	.50
123	Jack Trudeau	.50
124	Vernon Turner	.50
125	Curtis Conway	1.00
126	Erik Kramer	.50
127	Nate Lewis	.50
128	Carl Pickens	1.00
129	Darnay Scott	1.00
130	Dan Wilkinson	.50
131	Derrick Alexander	.50
132	Carl Banks	.50
133	Michael Irvin	1.00
134	Emmitt Smith	5.00
135	Kevin Williams	.50
136	Glyn Milburn	.50
137	Anthony Miller	.50
138	Shannon Sharpe	.50
139	Scott Mitchell	.50
140	Herman Moore	1.00
141	Edgar Bennett	.50
142	Brett Favre	5.00
143	Reggie White	1.00
144	Gary Brown	.50
145	Haywood Jeffires	.50
146	Webster Slaughter	.50
147	Craig Erickson	.50
148	Paul Justin	.50
149	Lamont Warren	.50
150	Steve Beuerlein	.50
151	Derek Brown	.50
152	Mark Brunell	2.00
153	Reggie Cobb	.50
154	Desmond Howard	.50
155	Kelvin Pritchett	.50
156	*James Stewart*	4.00
157	Cedric Tillman	.50
158	Kimble Anders	.50
159	Lake Dawson	.50
160	Keith Byars	.50
161	Dan Marino	5.00
162	Bernie Parmalee	.50
163	Qadry Ismail	.50
164	Warren Moon	1.00
165	Jake Reed	.50
166	Marion Butts	.50
167	Ben Coates	.50
168	Mario Bates	.50
169	Quinn Early	.50
170	Jim Everett	.50
171	Rodney Hampton	.50
172	Mike Horan	.50
173	Mike Sherrard	.50
174	Johnny Johnson	.50
175	Adrian Murrell	.75
176	*Andrew Glover*	.50
177	Jeff Hostetler	.50
178	Harvey Williams	.50
179	Fred Barnett	.50
180	Vaughn Hebron	.50
181	Jeff Sydner	.50
182	Kevin Greene	.50
183	Byron "Bam" Morris	.50
184	Neil O'Donnell	.50
185	Stan Humphries	1.00
186	Tony Martin	.75
187	Mark Seay	.50
188	William Floyd	.75
189	Rickey Jackson	.50
190	Jerry Rice	4.00
191	Steve Young	4.00
192	Cortez Kennedy	.50
193	Rick Mirer	3.00
194	Jessie Hester	.50
195	*Curtis Martin*	10.00
196	Horace Copeland	.50
197	Charles Wilson	.50
198	Reggie Brooks	.50
199	Brian Mitchell	.50
200	Heath Shuler	.75
201	*Justin Armour*	.50
202	*Jay Barker*	.50
203	*Zack Crockett*	.50
204	*Christian Fauria*	.50
205	*Antonio Freeman*	3.00
206	*Chad May*	.50
207	*Frank Sanders*	1.00
208	*Steve Stenstrom*	.50
209	*Lorenzo Styles*	.50
210	*Sherman Williams*	.50
211	*Ray Zellars*	.50
212	*Eric Zeier*	.50
213	Joey Galloway	4.00
214	Napoleon Kaufman	.50
215	Rashaan Salaam	.75
216	J.J. Stokes	2.00
NNO	Barry Foster (Carolina)	1.00
NNO	Steve Beuerlein (Jacksonville)	1.00

1995 Pacific Prisms Gold

The 216-card, standard-sized parallel set was inserted every 37 packs. The cards feature gold backgrounds instead of silver.

Veteran Stars:	2.5X-5X
Young Stars:	2X-4X
RCs:	1.75X-3.5X

1995 Pacific Prisms Connections

These 1995 Pacific Prism Series II inserts feature 10 top quarterback/receiver combinations; there are 20 cards in the set. Hobby cases feature the receiver halves; retail packs have the 10 quarterback cards. Both appear in one per every 73 of their respective packs. The cards are fitted together to form a particular team's qb/receiver tandem. The quarterback cards, numbered 1-10 using an (A) suffix, have the city name along the top; receiver cards (B) have the team nickname. The players' names run along the bottom of the cards. The foiled background includes team logos, plus half of the Royal Connections logo, which fits with its counterpart to form a circle. The quarterback cards have a throwing quarterback symbol as part of its design; receiver cards have a symbol of a player making a catch. Card backs also have the Royal Connections symbol, a player mug shot and a career summary. In addition to (A) and (B) suffixes, cards are numbered using an "RC" prefix.

		NM/M
Complete Green Set (20):		100.00
Common Green Player:		2.00
Complete Blue Set (20):		1,000
Common Blue Player:		20.00
Blue Cards:		2X-4X
1A	Steve Young	10.00
1B	Jerry Rice	10.00
2A	Dan Marino	12.00
2B	Irving Fryar	2.00
3A	Drew Bledsoe	8.00
3B	Ben Coates	2.00
4A	John Elway	8.00
4B	Shannon Sharpe	2.00
5A	Jeff Hostetler	2.00
5B	Tim Brown	4.00
6A	Warren Moon	2.00
6B	Cris Carter	2.00
7A	Neil O'Donnell	2.00
7B	Charles Johnson	2.00
8A	Troy Aikman	10.00
8B	Michael Irvin	3.00
9A	Stan Humphries	2.00
9B	Shawn Jefferson	2.00
10A	Jim Kelly	4.00
10B	Andre Reed	2.00

1995 Pacific Prisms Kings of the NFL

These 10 1995 Pacific Prism Series II football inserts feature statistical leaders from the 1994 season. Cards were inserted one per every 361 packs. The card front has a color action photo of the player, forming the body of a gold foil hourglass which has the category he led the league in listed at the top, along with the statistical number he reached. The bottom of the hourglass has the Pacific Collection Crown icon and the player's name. The card back has a square with a color mug shot inside, with the number he reached adjacent to it, at the top, but below the category heading he led in. His name runs across the middle of the card, followed by a player profile and a few specific examples of when he had productive weeks in his particular category.

		NM/M
Complete Set (10):		275.00
Common Player:		20.00
1	Emmitt Smith	50.00
2	Steve Young	40.00
3	Jerry Rice	40.00
4	Deion Sanders	25.00
5	Emmitt Smith	50.00
6	Dan Marino	50.00
7	Drew Bledsoe	40.00
8	Barry Sanders	50.00
9	Marshall Faulk	30.00
10	Marshall Faulk, Natrone Means	30.00

1995 Pacific Prisms Red Hot Rookies

These nine insert cards could be found in 1995 Pacific Prism Series I packs, one per every 73 hobby packs. The cards have a color action photo of the player in his collegiate uniform against a red foil background which has his pro team's nickname printed several times within it. His name runs along the left side of the card. The back, numbered using 1, 2, 3, etc., is horizontal and includes a closeup shot of the player on the left side. A photo of his new pro team appears on the right side. His name, position and pro team are superimposed over the helmet, as is a summary of when the player was selected in the 1995 draft.

		NM/M
Complete Set (9):		90.00
Common Player:		3.00
Inserted 1:73		
1	Ki-Jana Carter	3.00
2	Joey Galloway	8.00
3	Steve McNair	20.00
4	Tyrone Wheatley	3.00
5	Kerry Collins	8.00
6	Rashaan Salaam	3.00
7	Michael Westbrook	8.00
8	J.J. Stokes	8.00
9	Napoleon Kaufman	6.00

1995 Pacific Prisms Red Hot Stars

These 1995 Pacific Prism Series I inserts feature nine of the NFL's top stars. The cards were included one per every 73 retail packs. The card front has a color action photo of the player against a red foil spiderweb pattern. The player's name appears at the bottom of the card. The card back, numbered 1, 2, 3, etc., is horizontal and has a closeup shot of the player on the left side. The other side has his name, position, team name and 1994 season recap all superimposed against a football background.

		NM/M
Complete Set (9):		150.00
Common Player:		10.00
1	Barry Sanders	50.00
2	Steve Young	40.00
3	Emmitt Smith	50.00
4	Drew Bledsoe	35.00
5	Natrone Means	10.00
6	Dan Marino	50.00
7	Marshall Faulk	20.00
8	Jerry Rice	35.00
9	Errict Rhett	10.00

1995 Pacific Prisms Super Bowl Logos

This 30-card insert features the game-specific Super Bowl logo on the front and details of the game on the back. The cards are unnumbered.

		NM/M
Complete Set (30):		4.00
Common Player:		.15
1	Super Bowl I	.15
2	Super Bowl II	.15
3	Super Bowl III	.15
4	Super Bowl IV	.15
5	Super Bowl V	.15
6	Super Bowl VI	.15
7	Super Bowl VII	.15
8	Super Bowl VIII	.15
9	Super Bowl IX	.15
10	Super Bowl X	.15
11	Super Bowl XI	.15
12	Super Bowl XII	.15
13	Super Bowl XIII	.15
14	Super Bowl XIV	.15
15	Super Bowl XV	.15
16	Super Bowl XVI	.15
17	Super Bowl XVII	.15
18	Super Bowl XVIII	.15
19	Super Bowl XIX	.15
20	Super Bowl XX	.15
21	Super Bowl XXI	.15
22	Super Bowl XXII	.15
23	Super Bowl XXIII	.15
24	Super Bowl XXIV	.15
25	Super Bowl XXV	.15
26	Super Bowl XXVI	.15
27	Super Bowl XXVII	.15
28	Super Bowl XXVIII	.15
29	Super Bowl XXIX	.15
30	Super Bowl XXX	.15

1995 Pacific Prisms Team Helmets

This 30-card insert includes one card for each NFL team. The fronts feature the team helmet and the backs have team history.

		NM/M
Complete Set (30):		4.00
Common Player:		.15
1	Arizona Cardinals	.15
2	Atlanta Falcons	.15
3	Buffalo Bills	.15
4	Carolina Panthers	.15
5	Chicago Bears	.15
6	Cincinnati Bengals	.15
7	Cleveland Browns	.15
8	Dallas Cowboys	.25
9	Denver Broncos	.15
10	Detroit Lions	.15
11	Green Bay Packers	.25
12	Detroit Lions	.15
13	Indianapolis Colts	.15
14	Jacksonville Jaguars	.15
15	Kansas City Chiefs	.15
16	Los Angeles Raiders	.25
17	Miami Dolphins	.25
18	Minnesota Vikings	.15
19	New England Patriots	.15
20	New Orleans Saints	.15
21	New York Giants	.15
22	New York Jets	.15
23	Philadelphia Eagles	.15
24	Pittsburgh Steelers	.25
25	San Diego Chargers	.15
26	San Francisco 49ers	.25
27	Seattle Seahawks	.15
28	St. Louis Rams	.15
29	Tampa Bay Buccaneers	.15
30	Washington Redskins	.25

1995 Pacific Prisms Team Uniforms

This 30-card insert includes one card per NFL team. The cards feature a horizontal layout with the team uniform on the front and team history on the back.

		NM/M
Complete Set (30):		4.00
Common Player:		.15
1	Arizona Cardinals	.15
2	Atlanta Falcons	.15
3	Buffalo Bills	.15
4	Carolina Panthers	.15
5	Chicago Bears	.15
6	Cincinnati Bengals	.15
7	Cleveland Browns	.15
8	Dallas Cowboys	.25
9	Denver Broncos	.15
10	Detroit Lions	.15
11	Green Bay Packers	.25
12	Detroit Lions	.15
13	Indianapolis Colts	.15
14	Jacksonville Jaguars	.15
15	Kansas City Chiefs	.15
16	Los Angeles Raiders	.25
17	Miami Dolphins	.25
18	Minnesota Vikings	.15
19	New England Patriots	.15
20	New Orleans Saints	.15
21	New York Giants	.15
22	New York Jets	.15
23	Philadelphia Eagles	.15
24	Pittsburgh Steelers	.25
25	San Diego Chargers	.15
26	San Francisco 49ers	.25
27	Seattle Seahawks	.15
28	St. Louis Rams	.15
29	Tampa Bay Buccaneers	.15
30	Washington Redskins	.25

1995 Pacific Triple Folders

These cards feature two panels on the front which, when closed, form a color action photo of an NFL star player. The format is the same as previous editions, but the 1995 cards have been reduced in size to standard-sized cards. The player's name and the Pacific Crown Collection are on one panel on the front; a team helmet is on the other. When opened up, the inside of the card panels reveal three more photos, with the player's team name in the center. The card back, a green football field, contains a closeup photo of the player, a card number and a brief recap of the 1994 season. Insert sets include: Rookies and Stars (which have different color foil versions for hobby and retail versions, plus another parallel set, with yet another different color foil for each); Team Triple Folders; Crystalline; Big Guns; and Careers.

		NM/M
Complete Set (48):		25.00
Common Player:		.25
Minor Stars:		.50
Wax Box:		30.00
1	Garrison Hearst	.50
2	*Kerry Collins*	1.00
3	Jeff George	.50
4	Herschel Walker	.25
5	Lake Dawson	.25
6	Cris Carter	.50
7	Byron "Bam" Morris	.25
8	Jim Kelly	.50
9	*Rashaan Salaam*	.50
10	*Eric Zeier*	.50
11	*Curtis Martin*	3.00
12	Jerry Rice	2.00
13	Chris Warren	.50
14	Trent Dilfer	1.00
15	Terry Allen	.50
16	*Jeff Blake*	1.25
17	Drew Bledsoe	2.00
18	Tim Brown	.50
19	*Wayne Chrebet*	2.00
20	Bernie Parmalee	.25
21	Stan Humphries	.25
22	Jerome Bettis	.50
23	*Michael Westbrook*	1.00
24	Charlie Garner	.50
25	Mario Bates	.25
26	Marcus Allen	.50
27	*James Stewart*	2.00
28	Ben Coates	.50
29	*Tyrone Wheatley*	1.00
30	Steve Young	1.50
31	Natrone Means	.50
32	*Terrell Davis*	5.00
33	*Napoleon Kaufman*	.75
34	Charles Johnson	.50
35	Barry Sanders	4.00
36	John Elway	3.00
37	*Joey Galloway*	2.50
38	Brett Favre	4.00
39	Errict Rhett	.50
40	Gary Brown	.25
41	Reggie White	.50
42	Steve Bono	.50
43	Marshall Faulk	2.00
44	Dan Marino	4.00
45	Emmitt Smith	4.00
46	Troy Aikman	2.00
47	Ricky Watters	.25
48	Michael Irvin	.50
P1	Natrone Means Promo	.50

1995 Pacific Triple Folders Big Guns

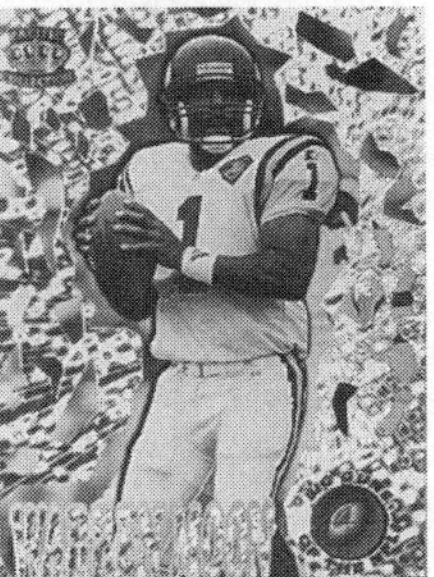

Twelve of the NFL's top quarterbacks are featured on these 1995 Pacific Triple Folder inserts, seeded two per every 37 packs. The card front has a color photo of the player against a prism background which has several geometric shapes cut into it. The player's name is in gold foil in the lower left corner; the insert set logo is in the bottom right corner. The horizontal card back has a football as the background, with a mug shot, brief career summary and cannon firing a football superimposed over it. Three opponents' helmets, representing games in which the quarterback had big numbers, are also shown on the back, along with the statistics from those games.

		NM/M
Complete Set (12):		40.00
Common Player:		1.00
Minor Stars:		2.00
Inserted 2:37		
1	Drew Bledsoe	4.00
2	Dan Marino	6.00
3	Warren Moon	2.00
4	John Elway	5.00
5	Jeff Blake	2.00
6	Brett Favre	6.00
7	Steve Young	4.00
8	Boomer Esiason	2.00
9	Jim Everett	1.00
10	Jim Kelly	2.00
11	Jeff George	2.00
12	Dave Kreig	1.00

1995 Pacific Triple Folders Careers

Eight of the NFL's top stars are featured on these 1995 Pacific Triple Folder inserts, seeded one every 181 packs. The metallic card front has a color photo of the player, with his name in the upper left corner, adjacent to the Pacific logo. "Careers" runs down the right side of the card front, which includes several of the player's career numbers scattered throughout the card background. The back, numbered using a "C" prefix, has a closeup shot of the player, plus a recap of some of the key numbers from his career statistics.

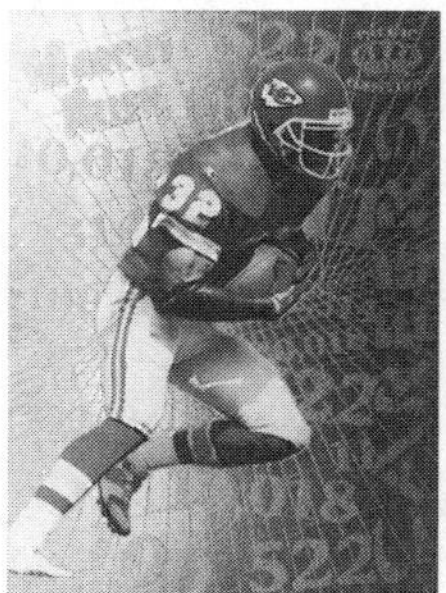

		NM/M
Complete Set (8):		100.00
Common Player:		8.00
Inserted 1:181		
1	Troy Aikman	20.00
2	Marcus Allen	8.00
3	John Elway	25.00
4	Dan Marino	30.00
5	Jerry Rice	20.00
6	Barry Sanders	30.00
7	Emmitt Smith	30.00
8	Steve Young	15.00

1995 Pacific Triple Folders Crystalline

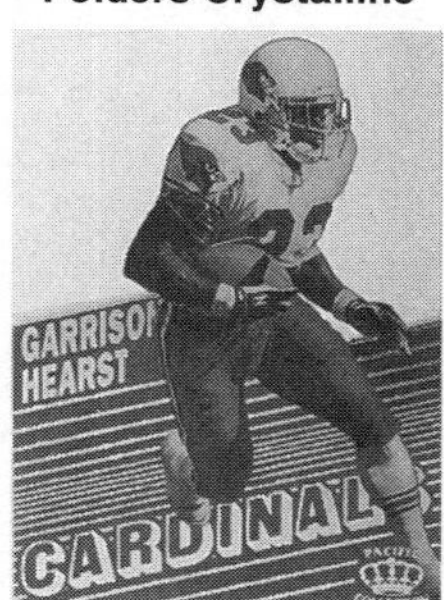

These 1995 Pacific Triple Folder inserts were seeded four per every 37 packs. Each is a plastic card with clear area above the player photo and his team's primary color and gold foil at the bottom for his name, team nickname and Pacific logo. The card back, numbered using a "Cr" prefix, contains the player's name, position, team and biographical information against the shadow of the card front photo. A team helmet, mug shot and brief career summary are also included on the back.

		NM/M
Complete Set (20):		40.00
Common Player:		.75
Minor Stars:		2.00
Inserted 4:37		
1	Troy Aikman	4.00
2	Jeff Blake	1.00
3	Drew Bledsoe	4.00
4	Kerry Collins	2.00
5	John Elway	4.00
6	Marshall Faulk	2.00
7	Gus Frerotte	.75
8	Joey Galloway	2.00
9	Garrison Hearst	.75
10	Jeff Hostetler	.75
11	Dan Marino	5.00
12	Natrone Means	1.00
13	Errict Rhett	1.00
14	Rashaan Salaam	.75
15	Barry Sanders	5.00
16	Deion Sanders	1.00
17	Emmitt Smith	5.00
18	J.J. Stokes	2.00
19	Steve Young	3.00
20	Eric Zeier	.75

1995 Pacific Triple Folders Rookies and Stars

This set features a mix of 36 stars and rookies, featured on different color foiled cards for the retail and hobby versions, plus a third parallel set which uses yet another color for the foil. The hobby and retail inserts were each seeded three per every four of their respective packs, while the parallel cards are seeded three per every 37 packs. The card front features a full-bleed color photo, with foil for the insert set logo and at the bottom for the player's name. The card back, numbered using an "RS" prefix, has a mug shot of the player, plus a brief recap of the player's previous season.

		NM/M
Complete Set (36):		30.00
Common Gold Player:		.50
Inserted 3:4		
Blue Cards:		1X
Inserted 3:4		
Raspberry Cards:		2X-4X
Inserted 3:37		
Silver Cards:		2X-4X
Inserted 3:37		
1	Garrison Hearst	.50
2	Darrick Holmes	.50
3	Kerry Collins	1.50
4	Rashaan Salaam	.75
5	Jeff Blake	1.00
6	Eric Zeier	1.00
7	Troy Aikman	1.50
8	Eric Bjorson	.50
9	Deion Sanders	1.00
10	Emmitt Smith	2.50
11	Sherman Williams	.50
12	Terrell Davis	4.00
13	John Elway	2.50
14	Barry Sanders	3.00
15	Steve McNair	3.00
16	Marshall Faulk	1.00
17	James Stewart	1.50
18	Steve Bono	.50
19	Tamarick Vanover	.50
20	Dan Marino	2.50
21	Drew Bledsoe	1.50
22	Curtis Martin	3.00
23	Tyrone Wheatley	1.00
24	Tim Brown	.75
25	Napoleon Kaufman	1.00
26	Ricky Watters	.50
27	Natrone Means	.50
28	Jerry Rice	2.00
29	J.J. Stokes	1.00
30	Steve Young	1.25
31	Joey Galloway	1.00
32	Chris Warren	.50
33	Jerome Bettis	.75
34	Errict Rhett	.50
35	Terry Allen	.50
36	Michael Westbrook	1.50

1995 Pacific Triple Folders Teams

These 1995 Pacific Triple Folders feature three players from a team. The two flaps feature one player; the inside features another player, while the back features a third teammate and a card number. The inside of the card uses gold foil stamping for that player's name and the Pacific Crown Collection logo, plus a circle which surrounds the players' team helmet, which is at the bottom of the card. These inserts were randomly included one per every 37 packs.

		NM/M
Complete Set (30):		40.00
Common Player:		.50
Minor Stars:		1.00
Inserted 9:37		
1	Garrison Hearst, Dave Kreig, Rob Moore	1.00
2	Jeff George, Terance Mathis, Eric Metcalf	1.00
3	Darick Holmes, Jim Kelly, Andre Reed	1.00
4	Edgar Bennett, Brett Favre, Reggie White	5.00
5	Haywood Jeffires, Chris Chandler, Steve McNair	2.00
6	Marshall Faulk, Jim Harbaugh, Sean Dawkins	2.00
7	Bob Christian, Tim McKyer, Kerry Collins	2.00
8	Rashaan Salaam, Erik Kramer, Michael Timpson	1.00
9	Carl Pickens, Jeff Blake, Darnay Scott	1.00
10	Leroy Hoard, Andre Rison, Vinny Testaverde	1.00
11	Troy Aikman, Michael Irvin, Emmitt Smith	5.00
12	John Elway, Terrell Davis, Shannon Sharpe	6.00
13	Scott Mitchell, Herman Moore, Barry Sanders	4.00
14	James Stewart, Mark Brunell, Desmond Howard	2.00
15	Marcus Allen, Steve Bono, Greg Hill	1.00
16	Bernie Parmalee, Dan Marino, Irving Fryar	5.00
17	Robert Smith, Warren Moon, Cris Carter	1.50
18	Curtis Martin, Drew Bledsoe, Ben Coates	4.00
19	Mario Bates, Jim Everett, Michael Haynes	.50
20	Rodney Hampton, Dave Brown, Herschel Walker	.50
21	Wayne Chrebet, Kyle Brady, Adrian Murrell	2.50
22	Napoleon Kaufman, Jeff Hostetler, Tim Brown	2.00
23	Ricky Watters, Charlie Garner, Mike Malmua	.75
24	Bam Morris, Mike Tomczak, Charles Johnson	.50
25	Natrone Means, Stan Humphries, Tony Martin	1.00
26	Jerry Rice, Steve Young, J.J. Stokes	3.00
27	Chris Warren, Rick Mirer, Joey Galloway	2.00
28	Jerome Bettis, Kelvin Carter, Isaac Bruce	1.50
29	Errict Rhett, Trent Dilfer, Alvin Harper	1.50
30	Terry Allen, Gus Frerotte, Michael Westbrook	1.00

1996 Pacific Super Bowl Bronze/Gold

The six-card, standard-size set was produced with both bronze and gold. The bronze set was available to collectors through a special wrapper redemption program at the 1996 Super Bowl Card Show in Phoenix. The gold set was available through a wrapper redemption program with 1995 Triple Folders. The gold cards are parallel to the bronze set, except with a Super Bowl XXX logo on the card fronts.

		NM/M
Complete Set (6):		14.00
Common Player:		1.00
1	Chris Warren	1.00
2	Kordell Stewart	2.00
3	Curtis Martin	5.00
4	Errict Rhett	1.00
5	Neil O'Donnell	1.00
6	Barry Sanders	4.00

1996 Pacific

Pacific's 1996 Crown Collection set includes 450 cards (no subsets), each of which has gold-foiled etching along the bottom for the player's name, team helmet and a gridiron. The Pacific logo is also stamped in gold on the front, which features a full-bleed color action photo. The horizontal back has a color closeup shot on one side, with the player's name and position in team colors on the opposite side in the top corner. Underneath is biographical information and a career recap. The card number and a Pacific logo are in the lower right corner. Two parallel versions of the regular set were also made - Scorching Red Foil (nine in every 37 retail packs) and Electric Blue Foil (nine in every 37 hobby packs). There are six insert sets - Card-Supials, Cramer's Choice Awards, Bomb Squad, Gold Crown Die-Cuts, Gems of the Crown and The Zone.

		NM/M
Complete Set (450):		40.00
Common Player:		.05
Minor Stars:		.10
Comp. Blue or Red (450):		300.00
Blue or Red Cards:		4X-8X
Pack (12):		1.00
Wax Box (36):		35.00
1	Jeff Feagles	.05
2	Rob Moore	.05
3	Clyde Simmons	.05
4	Mike Buck	.05
5	Aeneas Williams	.05
6	*Simeon Rice*	.25
7	Garrison Hearst	.10
8	Eric Swann	.05
9	Dave Krieg	.05
10	*Leeland McElroy*	.75
11	Oscar McBride	.05
12	Frank Sanders	.05
13	Larry Centers	.05
14	Seth Joyner	.05
15	Stevie Anderson	.05
16	Craig Heyward	.05
17	Devin Bush	.05
18	Eric Metcalf	.05
19	Jeff George	.10
20	*Richard Huntley*	1.00
21	*Jamal Anderson*	2.00
22	Bert Emanuel	.05
23	Terance Mathis	.05
24	Roman Fortin	.05
25	Jessie Tuggle	.05
26	Morten Andersen	.05
27	Chris Doleman	.05
28	D.J. Johnson	.05
29	Kevin Ross	.05
30	Michael Jackson	.05
31	Eric Zeier	.05
32	Jonathan Ogden	.05
33	Eric Turner	.05
34	Andre Rison	.05
35	Lorenzo White	.05
36	Earnest Byner	.05
37	Derrick Alexander	.05
38	Brian Kinchen	.05
39	Anthony Pleasant	.05
40	Vinny Testaverde	.05
41	Pepper Johnson	.05
42	Frank Hartley	.05
43	Craig Powell	.05
44	Leroy Hoard	.05
45	Kent Hull	.05
46	Bryce Paup	.05
47	Andre Reed	.05
48	Darick Holmes	.05
49	Russell Copeland	.05
50	Jerry Ostroski	.05
51	Chris Green	.05
52	*Eric Moulds*	2.00
53	Justin Armour	.05
54	Jim Kelly	.10
55	Cornelius Bennett	.05
56	Steve Tasker	.05
57	Thurman Thomas	.10
58	Bruce Smith	.05
59	Todd Collins	.05
60	Shawn King	.05
61	Don Beebe	.05
62	John Kasay	.05
63	Tim McKyer	.05
64	Darion Conner	.05
65	Pete Metzelaars	.05
66	Derrick Moore	.05
67	Blake Brockermeyer	.05
68	*Tim Biakabutuka*	.50
69	Sam Mills	.05
70	Vince Workman	.05
71	Kerry Collins	.75
72	Carlton Bailey	.05
73	Mark Carrier	.05
74	Donnell Woolford	.05
75	*Walt Harris*	.25
76	John Thierry	.05
77	Al Fontenot	.05
78	Lewis Tillman	.05
79	Curtis Conway	.10
80	Chris Zorich	.05
81	Mark Carrier	.05
82	*Bobby Engram*	.75
83	Alonzo Spellman	.05
84	Rashaan Salaam	.50
85	Michael Timpson	.05
86	Nate Lewis	.05
87	James Williams	.05
88	Jeff Graham	.05
89	Erik Kramer	.05
90	Willie Anderson	.05
91	Tony McGee	.05
92	Marco Battaglia	.05
93	Dan Wilkinson	.05
94	John Walsh	.05
95	Eric Bieniemy	.05
96	Ricardo McDonald	.05
97	Carl Pickens	.10
98	Kevin Sargent	.05
99	David Dunn	.05
100	Jeff Blake	.50
101	Harold Green	.05
102	James Francis	.05
103	John Copeland	.05
104	Darnay Scott	.05
105	Darren Woodson	.05
106	Jay Novacek	.05
107	Charles Haley	.05
108	Mark Tuinei	.05
109	Michael Irvin	.10
110	Troy Aikman	.75
111	Chris Boniol	.05
112	Sherman Williams	.05
113	Deion Sanders	.50
114	Emmitt Smith	2.00
115	Eric Bjornson	.05
116	Nate Newton	.05
117	Larry Allen	.05
118	Kevin Williams	.05
119	Leon Lett	.05
120	John Mobley	.05
121	Anthony Miller	.05
122	Brian Habib	.05
123	Aaron Craver	.05
124	Glyn Milburn	.05
125	Shannon Sharpe	.05
126	Steve Atwater	.05
127	Jason Elam	.05
128	John Elway	.35
129	Reggie Rivers	.05
130	Mike Pritchard	.05
131	Vance Johnson	.05
132	Terrell Davis	1.25
133	Tyrone Braxton	.05
134	Ed McCaffrey	.05
135	Brett Perriman	.05
136	Chris Spielman	.05
137	Luther Elliss	.05
138	Johnnie Morton	.05
139	Zefross Moss	.05
140	Barry Sanders	1.25
141	Lomas Brown	.05
142	Cory Schlesinger	.05
143	Jason Hanson	.05
144	Kevin Glover	.05
145	*Ron Rivers*	.50
146	Aubrey Matthews	.05
147	Reggie Brown	.05
148	Herman Moore	.30
149	Scott Mitchell	.05
150	Brett Favre	2.00
151	Sean Jones	.05
152	Leroy Butler	.05
153	Mark Chmura	.20
154	*Derrick Mayes*	.50
155	Mark Ingram	.05
156	Antonio Freeman	.05
157	*Chris Darkins*	.25
158	Robert Brooks	.10
159	William Henderson	.05
160	George Koonce	.05
161	Craig Newsome	.05
162	Darius Holland	.05
163	George Teague	.05
164	Edgar Bennett	.05
165	Reggie White	.10
166	Micheal Barrow	.05
167	Mel Gray	.05
168	Anthony Dorsett Jr.	.05
169	Roderick Lewis	.05
170	Henry Ford	.05
171	Mark Stepnoski	.05
172	Chris Sanders	.05
173	Anthony Cook	.05
174	Eddie Robinson	.05
175	Steve McNair	.50
176	Haywood Jeffires	.05
177	*Eddie George*	3.50
178	Marion Butts	.05
179	Malcolm Seabron	.05
180	Rodney Thomas	.05
181	Ken Dilger	.05
182	Zack Crockett	.05
183	Tony Bennett	.05
184	Quentin Coryatt	.05
185	Marshall Faulk	.50
186	Sean Dawkins	.05
187	Jim Harbaugh	.05
188	Eugene Daniel	.05
189	Roosevelt Potts	.05
190	Lamont Warren	.05
191	Will Wolford	.05
192	Tony Siragusa	.05
193	Aaron Bailey	.05
194	Trev Alberts	.05
195	*Kevin Hardy*	.10
196	Greg Spann	.05
197	Steve Beuerlein	.05
198	Steve Taneyhill	.05
199	Vaughn Dunbar	.05
200	Mark Brunell	.75
201	Bernard Carter	.05
202	James Stewart	.05
203	Tony Boselli	.05
204	Chris Doering	.05
205	Willie Jackson	.05
206	*Tony Brackens*	.30
207	Ernest Givins	.05
208	Le'Shai Maston	.05
209	Pete Mitchell	.05
210	Desmond Howard	.05
211	Vinnie Clark	.05
212	Jeff Lageman	.05
213	Derrick Walker	.05
214	Dan Saleaumua	.05
215	Derrick Thomas	.05
216	Neil Smith	.05
217	Willie Davis	.05
218	Mark Collins	.05
219	Lake Dawson	.05
220	Greg Hill	.05
221	Anthony Davis	.05
222	Kimble Anders	.05
223	Webster Slaughter	.05
224	Tamarick Vanover	.50
225	Marcus Allen	.10
226	Steve Bono	.10
227	Will Shields	.05
228	*Karim Abdul-Jabbar*	.75
229	Tim Bowens	.05
230	Keith Sims	.05
231	Terry Kirby	.05
232	Gene Atkins	.05
233	Dan Marino	2.00
234	Richmond Webb	.05
235	Gary Clark	.05
236	O.J. McDuffie	.05
237	Marco Coleman	.05
238	Bernie Parmalee	.05
239	Randal Hill	.05
240	Bryan Cox	.05
241	Irving Fryar	.05
242	Derrick Alexander	.05
243	Qadry Ismail	.05
244	Warren Moon	.05
245	Cris Carter	.05
246	Chad May	.05
247	Robert Smith	.05
248	Fuad Reveiz	.05
249	Orlando Thomas	.05
250	Chris Hinton	.05
251	Jack Del Rio	.05
252	Moe Williams	.05
253	Roy Barker	.05
254	Jake Reed	.05
255	Adrian Cooper	.05
256	Curtis Martin	1.50
257	Ben Coates	.05
258	Drew Bledsoe	.75
259	Maurice Hurst	.05
260	Troy Brown	.05
261	Bruce Armstrong	.05
262	Myron Guyton	.05
263	Dave Meggett	.05
264	*Terry Glenn*	1.75
265	Chris Slade	.05
266	Vincent Brisby	.05
267	Willie McGinest	.05
268	Vincent Brown	.05
269	Will Moore	.05
270	Jay Barker	.05
271	Ray Zellars	.05
272	Derek Brown	.05
273	William Roaf	.05
274	Quinn Early	.05
275	Michael Haynes	.05
276	Rufus Porter	.05
277	Renaldo Turnbull	.05
278	Wayne Martin	.05
279	Tyrone Hughes	.05
280	Irv Smith	.05
281	Eric Allen	.05
282	Mark Fields	.05
283	Mario Bates	.05
284	Jim Everett	.05
285	Vince Buck	.05
286	Alex Molden	.05
287	Tyrone Wheatley	.05
288	Chris Calloway	.05
289	Jessie Armstead	.05
290	Arthur Marshall	.05
291	Aaron Pierce	.05
292	Dave Brown	.05
293	Rodney Hampton	.05

294 John Elliott .05
295 Mike Sherrard .05
296 Howard Cross .05
297 Michael Brooks .05
298 Herschel Walker .05
299 *Danny Kanell* .75
300 Keith Elias .05
301 Bobby Houston .05
302 Dexter Carter .05
303 Tony Casillas .05
304 Kyle Brady .05
305 Glenn Foley .05
306 Ron Moore .05
307 Ryan Yarborough .05
308 Aaron Glenn .05
309 Adrian Murrell .05
310 Boomer Esiason .05
311 Kyle Clifton .05
312 Wayne Chrebet .05
313 Erik Howard .05
314 *Keyshawn Johnson* 2.50
315 Marvin Washington .05
316 Johnny Mitchell .05
317 *Alex Van Dyke* .50
318 Billy Joe Hobert .05
319 Andrew Glover .05
320 Vince Evans .05
321 Chester McGlockton .05
322 Pat Swilling .05
323 Raghib Ismail .05
324 Eddie Anderson .05
325 *Rickey Dudley* .75
326 Steve Wisniewski .05
327 Harvey Williams .05
328 Napoleon Kaufman .05
329 Tim Brown .10
330 Jeff Hostetler .05
331 Anthony Smith .05
332 Terry McDaniel .05
333 Charlie Garner .05
334 Ricky Watters .05
335 Brian Dawkins .05
336 Randall Cunningham .05
337 Gary Anderson .05
338 Calvin Williams .05
339 Chris T. Jones .05
340 *Bobby Hoying* .75
341 William Fuller .05
342 William Thomas .05
343 Mike Mamula .05
344 Fred Barnett .05
345 Rodney Peete .05
346 Mark McMillian .05
347 Bobby Taylor .05
348 Yancey Thigpen .35
349 Neil O'Donnell .05
350 Rod Woodson .05
351 Kordell Stewart .75
352 Dermontti Dawson .05
353 Norm Johnson .05
354 Ernie Mills .05
355 Bam Morris .05
356 Mark Bruener .05
357 Kevin Greene .05
358 Greg Lloyd .05
359 Andre Hastings .05
360 Erric Pegram .05
361 Carnell Lake .05
362 Dwayne Harper .05
363 Ronnie Harmon .05
364 Leslie O'Neal .05
365 John Carney .05
366 Stan Humphries .05
367 Brian Roche .05
368 Terrell Fletcher .05
369 Shaun Gayle .05
370 Alfred Pupunu .05
371 Shawn Jefferson .05
372 Junior Seau .05
373 Mark Seay .05
374 Aaron Hayden .05
375 Tony Martin .05
376 Steve Young .75
377 J.J. Stokes .50
378 Jerry Rice .75
379 Derek Loville .05
380 Lee Woodall .05
381 *Terrell Owens* 4.00
382 Elvis Grbac .05
383 Ricky Ervins .05
384 Eric Davis .05
385 Dana Stubblefield .05
386 Gary Plummer .05
387 Tim McDonald .05
388 William Floyd .05
389 Ken Norton Jr. .05
390 Merton Hanks .05
391 Bart Oates .05
392 Brent Jones .05
393 Steve Broussard .05
394 Robert Blackmon .05
395 Rick Tuten .05
396 Pete Kendall .05
397 John Friesz .05
398 Terry Wooden .05
399 Rick Mirer .05
400 Chris Warren .10
401 Joey Galloway .50
402 Howard Ballard .05
403 Jason Kyle .05
404 Kevin Mawae .05
405 Mack Strong .05
406 Reggie Brown .05
407 Cortez Kennedy .05
408 Sean Gilbert .05
409 J.T. Thomas .05
410 Shane Conlan .05
411 Johnny Bailey .05
412 Mark Rypien .05
413 Leonard Russell .05
414 Troy Drayton .05
415 Jerome Bettis .05
416 Jessie Hester .05
417 Isaac Bruce .50
418 Roman Phifer .05
419 Todd Kinchen .05
420 Alexander Wright .05
421 Marcus Jones .05
422 Horace Copeland .05
423 Eric Curry .05
424 Courtney Hawkins .05
425 Alvin Harper .05
426 Derrick Brooks .05
427 Errict Rhett .25
428 Trent Dilfer .05
429 Hardy Nickerson .05
430 Brad Culpepper .05
431 Warren Sapp .05
432 Reggie Roby .05
433 Santana Dotson .05
434 Jerry Ellison .05
435 Lawrence Dawsey .05
436 Heath Shuler .05
437 Stanley Richard .05
438 Rod Stephens .05
439 *Stephen Davis* 3.00
440 Terry Allen .05
441 Michael Westbrook .40
442 Ken Harvey .05
443 Coleman Bell .05
444 Marvcus Patton .05
445 Gus Frerotte .05
446 Leslie Shepherd .05
447 Tom Carter .05
448 Brian Mitchell .05
449 Darrell Green .05
450 Tony Woods .05

1996 Pacific Blue/Red/Silver

Pacific Crown Collection Football was offered in three different parallel versions - blue, red and silver. Electric Blue versions of the 450-card set were available in hobby packs, with Scorching Red versions in retail, both seeded nine per 37 packs. There was also a Silver version available in special retail packs, with roughly the same production as the Red and Blue set. The only differences in these cards from the base cards is the color of the foil stamping.

	NM/M
Complete Blue Set (450):	300.00
Blue Cards:	4X-8X
Complete Red Set (450):	300.00
Red Cards:	4X-8X
Complete Silver Set (450):	300.00
Silver Cards:	4X-8X

1996 Pacific Bomb Squad

The NFL's finest quarterback/receiver combinations are spotlighted on these 1996 Pacific inserts. The cards, seeded one per every 73 packs, feature a player on each side against a background of team-colored swirls. The Pacific logo is in the upper left corner; the player's name and position run down the right side of the card. One side has a card number, which uses a "BS" prefix.

		NM/M
Complete Set (10):		125.00
Common Player:		5.00
1	Jeff Blake, Carl Pickens	5.00
2	John Elway, Anthony Miller	10.00
3	Scott Mitchell, Herman Moore	5.00
4	Troy Aikman, Jay Novacek	15.00
5	Brett Favre, Robert Brooks	25.00
6	Steve McNair, Chris Sanders	10.00
7	Dan Marino, Irving Fryar	25.00
8	Drew Bledsoe, Terry Glenn	20.00
9	Kordell Stewart, Kordell Stewart	10.00
10	Steve Young, Jerry Rice	25.00

1996 Pacific Card-Supials

This 36-card Pacific insert set features cards with flashy gold embossing on the front for the Pacific logo, player's name and outline of the letters in the player's position and team name. The back has a little cut in the card, creating a pouch for another mini (1-1/4" x 1-3/4") card of the player - a marsupial. Hence, the name Card-Supials. The card back of the regular card is black-and-white; the mini card, when placed in the pouch, fills in the area with color. The bottom of the card has a brief paragraph about the player, plus a card number (1 of 36, etc.). The mini card's back has the player's name and position along the side. A closeup shot and player profile complete the back. The card is numbered 1a of 36, etc. Cards were seeded one per every 37 packs, but the minis were not always matched up with the larger card.

		NM/M
Complete Set (72):		350.00
Comp. Large Set (36):		225.00
Comp. Small Set (36):		125.00
Common Large:		2.00
Small Cards: Half Price		
1	Garrison Hearst	2.00
2	Jeff George	2.00
3	Eric Zeier	2.00
4	Jim Kelly	2.00
5	Kerry Collins	5.00
6	Rashaan Salaam	2.00
7	Jeff Blake	2.00
8	Troy Aikman	15.00
9	Emmitt Smith	20.00
10	Terrell Davis	12.00
11	John Elway	15.00
12	Deion Sanders	6.00
13	Barry Sanders	20.00
14	Brett Favre	25.00
15	Steve McNair	10.00
16	Marshall Faulk	10.00
17	Mark Brunell	6.00
18	Tamarick Vanover	6.00
19	Dan Marino	25.00
20	Cris Carter	2.00
21	Keyshawn Johnson	6.00
22	Rodney Hampton	2.00
23	Curtis Martin	12.00
24	Drew Bledsoe	15.00
25	Mario Bates	2.00
26	Napoleon Kaufman	2.00
27	Ricky Watters	2.00
28	Kordell Stewart	8.00
29	Junior Seau	5.00
30	Steve Young	15.00
31	Jerry Rice	20.00
32	Isaac Bruce	8.00
33	Joey Galloway	8.00
34	Chris Warren	2.00
35	Errict Rhett	4.00
36	Michael Westbrook	4.00

1996 Pacific Cramer's Choice Awards

Cramer's Choice Awards return as an insert for Pacific's 1996 football line. The die-cut cards, which showcase some of the NFL's most amazing athletes, have a silver background for the card, which is shaped like a trophy. The cards are the rarest in this product line; they are seeded one per every 721 packs. The back has comments about the player by Michael Cramer, CEO and president of Pacific, who made the selections.

		NM/M
Complete Set (10):		400.00
Common Player:		10.00
1	Emmitt Smith	50.00
2	John Elway	40.00
3	Barry Sanders	50.00
4	Brett Favre	55.00
5	Reggie White	15.00
6	Dan Marino	55.00
7	Curtis Martin	20.00
8	Keyshawn Johnson	10.00
9	Kordell Stewart	10.00
10	Jerry Rice	40.00

1996 Pacific The Zone

Only the NFL's most productive players who found the end zone on a regular basis in 1995 are featured on these die-cut inserts. The cards were seeded one per every 145 packs. Each card front has a die-cut goal post, with the player photo between the posts. The player's name is in gold foil on the cross bar. His team's name is on the post. Pacific and the logo are in gold foil on the bottom of the card, which has a grassy background. The card back has a closeup shot of the player, his name and a team logo between the posts. His position and city name are on the cross bar. The bottom of the card has a grassy background with a recap of some of the player's accomplishments. The card number is also at the bottom, using a "Z" prefix.

		NM/M
Complete Set (20):		300.00
Common Player:		4.00
1	Jim Kelly	15.00
2	Rashaan Salaam	4.00
3	Carl Pickens	4.00
4	Jeff Blake	4.00
5	Kerry Collins	12.00
6	Emmitt Smith	45.00
7	Troy Aikman	35.00
8	John Elway	35.00
9	Barry Sanders	45.00
10	Herman Moore	4.00
11	Scott Mitchell	4.00
12	Brett Favre	50.00
13	Robert Brooks	4.00
14	Marshall Faulk	15.00
15	Dan Marino	50.00
16	Drew Bledsoe	30.00
17	Curtis Martin	25.00
18	Steve Young	30.00
19	Jerry Rice	40.00
20	Chris Warren	4.00

1996 Pacific Gold Crown Die-Cuts

These 1996 Pacific inserts were seeded one per every 37 packs. Each card features a full-bleed color action photo on the front, with a die-cut gold foiled crown at the top. The player's name is at the bottom in foil, too, next to a team helmet. The card back has the crown image at the top. The player's name runs across the middle, with a closeup shot of the player in a diamond on one side and brief player profile on the other. A card number, using a "GC" prefix, is in the lower left corner.

		NM/M
Complete Set (20):		175.00
Common Player:		2.00
1	Emmitt Smith	25.00
2	Troy Aikman	20.00
3	Barry Sanders	25.00
4	Kerry Collins	4.00
5	Jeff Blake	2.00
6	John Elway	20.00
7	Terrell Davis	20.00
8	Deion Sanders	12.00
9	Brett Favre	25.00
10	Dan Marino	25.00
11	Eddie George	12.00
12	Curtis Martin	15.00
13	Drew Bledsoe	15.00
14	Keyshawn Johnson	10.00
15	Napoleon Kaufman	2.00
16	Kordell Stewart	8.00
17	Steve Young	15.00
18	Jerry Rice	20.00
19	Joey Galloway	4.00
20	Chris Warren	2.00

1996 Pacific Gems of the Crown

These 1996 Pacific inserts, numbered 19-36, were seeded one per every 37 packs. (Cards 1-18 were inserts in 1996 Dynagon Prism packs.) The horizontal card front has a color photo in the middle, with an outline around it. The team name is stamped in gold along the left side; the player's last name is stamped in gold along the right. A gold-foiled panel along the top has the Pacific logo and the player's first name in the upper right corner.

		NM/M
Complete Set (18):		130.00
Common Player:		2.00
19	Garrison Hearst	3.00
20	Jeff Blake	2.00
21	Troy Aikman	12.00
22	Deion Sanders	6.00
23	Brett Favre	20.00
24	Robert Smith	2.00
25	Mario Bates	2.00
26	Napoleon Kaufman	2.00
27	Kordell Stewart	6.00
28	Jim Kelly	6.00
29	Jim Harbaugh	2.00
30	Tamarick Vanover	2.00
31	Dan Marino	20.00
32	Warren Moon	2.00
33	Curtis Martin	12.00
34	Rodney Hampton	2.00
35	Ricky Watters	2.00
36	Joey Galloway	5.00

1996 Pacific Power Corps

Power Corps was a 20-card insert that was only available in special retail packs on Pacific Crown Collection in 1996. The cards contained the words "Power Corps" running down the left side, with the player's name running down the right side. The cards were numbered PC1-PC20. There were also foil parallel versions of card numbers 1, 11, 14, 17 and 19.

		NM/M
Complete Set (20):		60.00
Common Player:		1.00
1	Troy Aikman	6.00
2	Jeff Blake	1.00
3	Drew Bledsoe	6.00
4	Kerry Collins	3.00
5	Terrell Davis	6.00
6	John Elway	8.00
7	Marshall Faulk	3.00
8	Brett Favre	10.00
9	Joey Galloway	1.00
10	Garrison Hearst	1.00
11	Dan Marino	8.00
12	Curtis Martin	5.00
13	Steve McNair	4.00
14	Jerry Rice	6.00
15	Rashaan Salaam	1.00
16	Barry Sanders	8.00
17	Emmitt Smith	8.00
18	Kordell Stewart	2.00
19	Chris Warren	1.00
20	Steve Young	4.00

1996 Pacific Crown Royale

Pacific's 1996 Crown Royale release features 144 regular-size cards that are highlighted by etched, die-cut cards. Each horizontal card is topped with a die-cut gold crown and the front has the player's name, position and team logo. Two parallel versions are available: Royale Blue (hobby) and Royale Silver (retail). Also, five insert sets were inserted: Cramer's Choice Awards, Field Force Etch-Tech, Pro Bowl Die-Cut, Triple Crown Die-Cut and NFL Regime. The 144-card base set was sold in five-card packs and each regular card back was listed by the "CR" prefix.

		NM/M
Complete Set (144):		50.00
Common Player:		.25
Minor Stars:		1.00
Blue Cards:		2X-4X
Silver Cards:		3X-6X
Pack (5):		3.00
Wax Box (24):		50.00
1	Dan Marino	5.00
2	Frank Sanders	.25
3	*Bobby Engram*	.50
4	Cornelius Bennett	.25
5	Steve Bono	.25
6	Aaron Hayden	.25
7	Leroy Hoard	.25
8	Brett Perriman	.25
9	Irv Smith	.25
10	Jim Kelly	1.00
11	Rodney Thomas	.25
12	Eric Bieniemy	.25
13	Darnay Scott	.50
14	Ki-Jana Carter	.50
15	Kerry Collins	1.00
16	Shannon Sharpe	.25
17	Michael Westbrook	1.00
18	Steve McNair	3.00
19	*Tony Banks*	2.00
20	Rashaan Salaam	.50
21	Terrell Fletcher	.25
22	Michael Timpson	.25
23	*Bobby Hoying*	1.00
24	Quinn Early	.25
25	Warren Moon	1.00
26	Tommy Vardell	.25
27	*Marvin Harrison*	12.00
28	Lake Dawson	.25
29	*Karim Abdul-Jabbar*	1.00
30	Chris Warren	.50
31	Heath Shuler	.50
32	Bert Emanuel	.25
33	Howard Griffith	.25
34	*Alex Van Dyke*	.50
35	Isaac Bruce	1.00
36	Mark Brunell	2.00
37	Winslow Oliver	.25
38	O.J. McDuffie	.25
39	*Terrell Owens*	12.00
40	Jerry Rice	4.00
41	Henry Ellard	.25
42	Chris Sanders	.25
43	Craig Heyward	.25
44	*Eddie Kennison*	2.00
45	Terrell Davis	4.00
46	Rodney Hampton	.25
47	Bryan Still	.25
48	Tim Brown	.25
49	*Keyshawn Johnson*	10.00
50	Barry Sanders	5.00
51	Terry Allen	.50
52	Sean Dawkins	.25
53	Bryce Paup	.25
54	Brett Favre	6.00
55	Deion Sanders	1.00
56	*Kevin Hardy*	.50
57	Kevin Williams	.25
58	Jeff George	.25
59	*Tim Biakabutuka*	1.00
60	Drew Bledsoe	3.00
61	Michael Jackson	.25
62	James Stewart	.25
63	Mario Bates	.25
64	Daryl Johnston	.25
65	Herman Moore	1.00
66	Ben Coates	.25
67	*Terry Glenn*	4.00
68	Robert Smith	.25
69	Irving Fryar	.25
70	Napoleon Kaufman	.25
71	*Rickey Dudley*	2.00
72	Bernie Parmalee	.25
73	Kyle Brady	.25
74	Neil O'Donnell	.25
75	*Lawrence Phillips*	.50
76	Hardy Nickerson	.25
77	John Elway	4.00
78	Pete Mitchell	.25
79	Jason Dunn	.25
80	Reggie White	1.00
81	J.J. Stokes	1.00
82	Jake Reed	.25
83	Yancey Thigpen	.25
84	Jonathan Ogden	.25
85	Larry Centers	.25
86	Scott Mitchell	.25
87	Eric Zeier	.25
88	Anthony Miller	.25
89	Brian Blades	.25
90	Cris Carter	.25
91	Kordell Stewart	2.00
92	Charles Way	.25
93	Jeff Hostetler	.25
94	Brad Johnson	2.00
95	Marcus Allen	1.00
96	Errict Rhett	1.00
97	Stan Humphries	.25
98	Michael Haynes	.25
99	Curtis Martin	3.00

100 Troy Aikman 4.00
101 Earnest Byner .25
102 Vincent Brisby .25
103 Zack Crockett .25
104 Haywood Jeffires .25
105 Joey Galloway 1.00
106 Carl Pickens 1.00
107 *Leeland McElroy* .40
108 Adrian Murrell .25
109 *Joe Horn* 10.00
110 Steve Young 4.00
111 Andre Rison .25
112 Jim Everett .25
113 *Jamie Asher* .40
114 Steve Walsh .25
115 Robert Brooks .50
116 *Eric Moulds* 8.00
117 Edgar Bennett .25
118 Greg Lloyd .25
119 Jerris McPhail .25
120 Marshall Faulk 3.00
121 Dave Brown .25
122 Harvey Williams .25
123 Trent Dilfer 1.00
124 *Eddie George* 12.00
125 Jeff Blake .50
126 Mark Chmura .25
127 Boomer Esiason .25
128 Jim Harbaugh .25
129 Bryan Cox .25
130 Ricky Watters 1.00
131 *Amani Toomer* 2.00
132 Jim Miller .25
133 Cortez Kennedy .25
134 Courtney Hawkins .25
135 Junior Seau .25
136 Tamarick Vanover 1.00
137 Jerome Bettis 1.00
138 Chris Calloway .25
139 Rick Mirer .25
140 Thurman Thomas 1.00
141 Sheddrick Wilson .25
142 Charlie Garner .25
143 Erik Kramer .25
144 Emmitt Smith 5.00

1996 Pacific Crown Royale Blue/Silver

Each card in the 144-card 1996 Crown Royale set were reprinted in two different versions. Hobby packs had Royale Blue parallels, while retail packs had Royale Silver parallels, with both seeded four per 25 packs. These parallel sets are distinguished only by the color of the foil stamping.

Blue Cards: 2X-4X
Silver Cards: 3X-6X

1996 Pacific Crown Royale Cramer's Choice Awards

The large-sized set (5-1/2" x 4") was offered as part of a redemption offer in the Crown Royale set. Redemption cards, inserted every 385 packs, enabled collectors to obtain the 10-card, die-cut set. The cards are cut into the shape of a pyramid and the players honored were chosen by Pacific President and CEO Michael Cramer. The card backs are each listed with the "CC" prefix.

		NM/M
Complete Set (10):		500.00
Common Player:		40.00
1	John Elway	80.00
2	Brett Favre	100.00
3	Keyshawn Johnson	40.00
4	Dan Marino	100.00
5	Curtis Martin	75.00
6	Jerry Rice	85.00
7	Barry Sanders	100.00
8	Emmitt Smith	100.00
9	Kordell Stewart	40.00
10	Reggie White	40.00

1996 Pacific Crown Royale Triple Crown Die-Cut

The 10-card, regular-sized, die-cut set honors 10 players who led the league in at least three different categories. Inserted every 73 packs in 1996 Crown Royale, the cards feature a similar die-cut crown design with gold foil as the base cards in Crown Royale. The card backs are labeled with the "TC" prefix and are individually numbered.

		NM/M
Complete Set (10):		225.00
Common Player:		8.00
1	Troy Aikman	35.00
2	John Elway	40.00
3	Brett Favre	50.00
4	Keyshawn Johnson	8.00
5	Dan Marino	50.00
6	Curtis Martin	35.00
7	Jerry Rice	40.00
8	Barry Sanders	50.00
9	Emmitt Smith	50.00
10	Steve Young	35.00

1996 Pacific Crown Royale Field Force

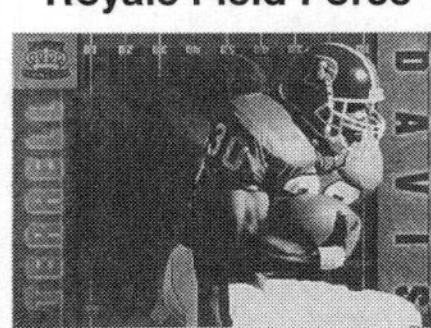

The 20-card, regular-sized set was inserted in 1996 packs of Crown Royale. Inserted every 49 packs, the horizontal cards employ etch-tech design and feature the player's name written on the side margins in foil etching of the player's team colors. The card backs contain a headshot of the player and are numbered with the "FF" prefix.

		NM/M
Complete Set (20):		375.00
Common Player:		5.00
1	Troy Aikman	35.00
2	Karim Abdul-Jabbar	10.00
3	Jeff Blake	10.00
4	Drew Bledsoe	35.00
5	Lawrence Phillips	10.00
6	Kerry Collins	25.00
7	Terrell Davis	35.00
8	John Elway	40.00
9	Brett Favre	50.00
10	Eddie George	35.00
11	Dan Marino	50.00
12	Curtis Martin	35.00
13	Jerry Rice	45.00
14	Rashaan Salaam	5.00
15	Barry Sanders	50.00
16	Deion Sanders	25.00
17	Emmitt Smith	50.00
18	Kordell Stewart	20.00
19	Chris Warren	5.00
20	Steve Young	40.00

1996 Pacific Crown Royale Pro Bowl Die-Cut

The 20-card, regular-sized, die-cut cards were inserted every 25 packs of Crown Royale. Each player is pictured in his Pro Bowl jersey and is backdropped with a die-cut palm tree and pineapple. The card backs feature an exploding volcano and a headshot of the player and are numbered with the "PB" prefix.

		NM/M
Complete Set (20):		275.00
Common Player:		5.00
1	Jeff Blake	5.00
2	Mark Chmura	5.00
3	Marshall Faulk	12.00
4	Brett Favre	55.00
5	Charles Haley	5.00
6	Merton Hanks	5.00
7	Greg Lloyd	5.00
8	Dan Marino	55.00
9	Curtis Martin	35.00
10	Anthony Miller	5.00
11	Herman Moore	12.00
12	Bryce Paup	5.00
13	Jerry Rice	45.00
14	Barry Sanders	50.00
15	Junior Seau	15.00
16	Emmitt Smith	50.00
17	Yancey Thigpen	5.00
18	Chris Warren	5.00
19	Ricky Watters	5.00
20	Steve Young	35.00

1996 Pacific Crown Royale NFL Regime

The 110-card, regular-sized set was included in each of the 1996 Crown Royale five-card packs. The card fronts feature a gray border with the player's name on top in red lettering and a white globe centered on a red ribbon which reads "NFL Regime." The card backs contain a headshot of the player and the prefix "NR."

		NM/M
Complete Set (110):		25.00
Common Player:		.10
Minor Stars:		.40
1	Steve Young	1.00
2	Jamir Miller	.10
3	Tyrone Brown	.10
4	Chris Shelling	.10
5	Warren Moon	.10
6	Shane Bonham	.10
7	Gary Brown	.10
8	Chris Chandler	.10
9	Bradford Banta	.10
10	John Elway	.75
11	Tom McManus	.10
12	Alfred Jackson	.10
13	Jay Barker	.10
14	Kirk Botkin	.10
15	Jim Kelly	.10
16	Lou Benfatti	.10
17	Billy Joe Hobert	.10
18	John Jackson	.10
19	Torin Dorn	.10
20	Drew Bledsoe	1.00
21	Gale Gilbert	.10
22	James Atkins	.10
23	John Lynch	.10
24	James Jenkins	.10
25	Kerry Collins	.50
26	Eric Swann	.10
27	Dan Stryzinski	.10
28	Mike Groh	.10
29	Tim Tindale	.10
30	Kordell Stewart	.75
31	Frank Garcia	.10
32	Mill Coleman	.10
33	Bracey Walker	.10
34	Ryan McNeil	.10
35	Rodney Hampton	.10
36	John Mobley	.10
37	Derek Russell	.10
38	Jeff George	.10
39	Steve Morrison	.10
40	Rashaan Salaam	.40
41	Ryan Christopherson	.10
42	Darren Anderson	.10
43	Ronnie Williams	.10
44	Scottie Graham	.10
45	Thurman Thomas	.40
46	Corwin Brown	.10
47	Lee DeRamus	.10
48	Ray Agnew	.10
49	Erik Howard	.10
50	Emmitt Smith	2.50
51	Dan Land	.10
52	Vinny Testaverde	.10
53	Myron Bell	.10
54	Keith Lyle	.10
55	Aaron Hayden	.10
56	Jeff Brohm	.10
57	Ronnie Harris	.10
58	Trent Dilfer	.10
59	Browning Nagle	.10
60	Jeff Blake	.75
61	Rich Owens	.10
62	Anthony Edwards	.10
63	Orlando Brown	.10
64	Matthew Campbell	.10
65	Ricky Watters	.40
66	Travis Hannah	.10
67	Melvin Tuten	.10
68	Aaron Taylor	.10
69	Dale Hellestrae	.10
70	Marshall Faulk	1.00
71	Gary Anderson	.10
72	David Williams	.10
73	Jim Harbaugh	.10
74	Ray Hall	.10
75	Dan Marino	2.50
76	Chris Mims	.10
77	Matt Blundin	.10
78	Roy Barker	.10
79	John Burke	.10
80	Troy Aikman	1.25
81	Ed King	.10
82	Stan White	.10
83	Vance Joseph	.10
84	David Klingler	.10
85	Terrell Davis	1.00
86	Bobby Hoying	.10
87	Lethon Flowers	.10
88	Dwayne White	.10
89	Vaughn Parker	.10
90	Jerry Rice	1.25
91	Casey Weldon	.10
92	Rick Mirer	.10
93	Jim Pyne	.10
94	Matt Turk	.10
95	Marcus Allen	.10
96	Rob Moore	.10
97	Ruben Brown	.10
98	Zach Thomas	.10
99	Carwell Gardner	.10
100	Barry Sanders	1.75
101	Ben Coleman	.10
102	Steve Rhem	.10
103	Everett McIver	.10
104	Cole Ford	.10
105	Dave Krieg	.10
106	Anthony Parker	.10
107	Michael Brandon	.10
108	Michael McCrary	.10
109	Chad Fann	.10
110	Brett Favre	2.50

1996 Pacific Dynagon

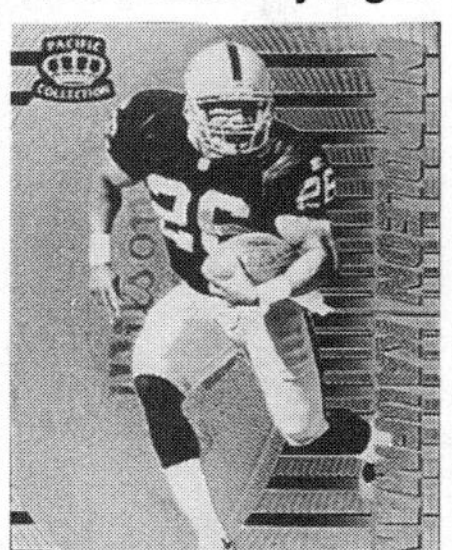

Pacific's 1996 Dynagon Prism set has 144 regular-issue cards and five insert sets. It is sold as a retail and hobby product, with inserts exclusive to both. The regular card front has a gold-foiled football stamped on the left, with a player photo in the middle. The player's name is written along the right side. The card uses the team's primary colors in the design. The horizontal back has a player profile shot on one side, flanked by his name, position and team name, card number and brief career summary. The five insert sets are Dynamic Duos, Gems of the Crown, Kings of the NFL, Tandems and Best Kept Secrets.

		NM/M
Complete Set (144):		50.00
Common Player:		.25
Minor Stars:		1.00
Comp. Best Kept Secrets (100):		15.00
Common Best Kept Sec.:		.25
Pack (2):		1.00
Wax Box (36):		30.00
1	Larry Centers	.25
2	Garrison Hearst	1.00
3	Dave Krieg	.25
4	Frank Sanders	.75
5	Jeff George	.75
6	Craig Heyward	.25
7	Terance Mathis	.25
8	Eric Metcalf	.25
9	Todd Collins	.25
10	Darick Holmes	.25
11	Jim Kelly	1.50
12	*Eric Moulds*	5.00
13	Bryce Paup	.25
14	Thurman Thomas	1.50
15	*Tim Biakabutuka*	1.50
16	Blake Brockermeyer	.25
17	Mark Carrier	.25
18	Kerry Collins	2.00
19	Derrick Moore	.25
20	*Bobby Engram*	1.00
21	Jeff Graham	.25
22	Erik Kramer	.25
23	Rashaan Salaam	.50
24	Steve Stenstrom	.25
25	Chris Zorich	.25
26	Jeff Blake	.75
27	David Dunn	.25
28	Carl Pickens	1.00
29	Darnay Scott	.25
30	Earnest Byner	.25
31	Leroy Hoard	.25
32	Keenan McCardell	.25
33	Eric Zeier	.25
34	Troy Aikman	4.00
35	Chris Boniol	.25
36	Michael Irvin	1.50
37	Daryl Johnston	.25
38	Deion Sanders	2.00
39	Emmitt Smith	5.00
40	*Stepfret Williams*	.75
41	John Elway	4.00
42	Terrell Davis	4.00
43	Anthony Miller	.25
44	Shannon Sharpe	.25
45	Scott Mitchell	.25
46	Herman Moore	1.50
47	Brett Perriman	.25
48	Barry Sanders	5.00
49	Cory Schlesinger	.25
50	Edgar Bennett	.25
51	Robert Brooks	.25
52	Mark Chmura	.75
53	Brett Favre	5.00
54	Reggie White	1.50
55	*Eddie George*	6.00
56	Steve McNair	2.00
57	Chris Sanders	.75
58	Rodney Thomas	.50
59	Ben Bronsen	.25
60	Zack Crockett	.25
61	Marshall Faulk	2.50
62	Jim Harbaugh	.25
63	Mark Brunell	2.00
64	*Kevin Hardy*	.75
65	Willie Jackson	.25
66	Pete Mitchell	.25
67	James Stewart	.25
68	Marcus Allen	1.50
69	Steve Bono	.75
70	Lake Dawson	.25
71	Neil Smith	.25
72	Tamarick Vanover	.75
73	Irving Fryar	.25
74	Terry Kirby	.25
75	Dan Marino	5.00
76	O.J. McDuffie	.25
77	Bernie Parmalee	.25
78	*Stanley Pritchett*	.25
79	Cris Carter	.25
80	Qadry Ismail	.25
81	Chad May	.25
82	Warren Moon	.25
83	Robert Smith	.25
84	Drew Bledsoe	4.00
85	Ben Coates	.25
86	*Terry Glenn*	4.00
87	Curtis Martin	3.00
88	Willie McGinest	.25
89	Mario Bates	.25
90	Jim Everett	.25
91	Wayne Martin	.25
92	Shane Pahukoa	.25
93	Ray Zellars	.25
94	Dave Brown	.25
95	Chris Calloway	.25
96	Rodney Hampton	.25
97	Tyrone Wheatley	.25
98	Wayne Chrebet	.25
99	Glenn Foley	.25
100	*Keyshawn Johnson*	6.00
101	Adrian Murrell	.25
102	*Alex Van Dyke*	.50
103	Tim Brown	.25
104	Harvey Williams	.25
105	Billy Joe Hobert	.25
106	Raghib Ismail	.25
107	Napoleon Kaufman	.50
108	Charlie Garner	.25
109	Rodney Peete	.25
110	Ricky Watters	.25
111	Calvin Williams	.25
112	Mark Bruener	.25
113	Kevin Greene	.25
114	Ernie Mills	.25
115	Kordell Stewart	2.00
116	Yancey Thigpen	.50
117	Dave Barr	.25
118	Jerome Bettis	.25
119	Isaac Bruce	1.50
120	*Lawrence Phillips*	.50
121	J.T. Thomas	.25
122	Ronnie Harmon	.25
123	Aaron Hayden	.50
124	Stan Humphries	.25
125	Junior Seau	1.50
126	William Floyd	.25
127	Elvis Grbac	.25
128	Jerry Rice	4.00
129	J.J. Stokes	1.50
130	Steve Young	4.00
131	Joey Galloway	2.00
132	Cortez Kennedy	.25
133	Kevin Mawae	.25
134	Rick Mirer	.25
135	Chris Warren	.25
136	Trent Dilfer	.25
137	Jerry Ellison	.25
138	Alvin Harper	.25
139	Errict Rhett	.50
140	Terry Allen	.25
141	Brian Mitchell	.25
142	Gus Frerotte	.25
143	Michael Westbrook	1.00
144	Heath Shuler	.50

1996 Pacific Dynagon Dynamic Duos

This 24-card 1996 Pacific Dynagon insert set showcases football's best one-two combinations on 12 teams. Cards 1-12 are found in hobby cases, while 13-24 can be found in retail cases; they are seeded in every 37th pack. Each card front has a color action photo against a metallic background which has one half of the team's helmet on it; the two cards can be placed next to each other to complete the helmet and showcase the duo. The back has a closeup shot of the player, with his name, team name and card number (using a "DD" prefix) at the top. His career accomplishments are also summarized.

		NM/M
Complete Set (24):		140.00
Common Player:		1.00
Minor Stars:		3.00
1	Troy Aikman	12.00
2	Jerry Rice	15.00
3	Brett Favre	20.00
4	Marshall Faulk	8.00
5	Carl Pickens	1.00
6	Terrell Davis	12.00
7	Curtis Martin	12.00
8	Dan Marino	20.00
9	Herman Moore	1.00
10	Kordell Stewart	6.00
11	Emmitt Smith	20.00
12	Trent Dilfer	3.00
13	Deion Sanders	6.00
14	Steve Young	12.00
15	Robert Brooks	1.00
16	Jim Harbaugh	1.00
17	Jeff Blake	1.00
18	John Elway	15.00
19	Drew Bledsoe	15.00
20	Bernie Parmalee	1.00
21	Barry Sanders	20.00
22	Kevin Greene	1.00
23	Sherman Williams	1.00
24	Errict Rhett	3.00

1996 Pacific Dynagon Gems of the Crown

These 36 Pacific insert cards are distributed in two base brands; cards 1-18 are seeded two per every 37 packs of Dynamic Prism, while 19-36 are seeded in Crown Collection Football packs. The horizontal card front has a color action photo in the center. The top has a gold-foiled panel which has the Pacific logo in the upper left corner; the player's last name is in the upper right corner, with his last name stamped in gold down the side. The player's team logo is in gold along the left side, on a panel using team colors. The horizontal back has a color closeup shot on one side, with the player's position and team name below. The opposite side has the player's name in the upper corner, with a brief career summary underneath. The card is numbered using a "GC" prefix.

		NM/M
Complete Set (18):		45.00
Common Player:		1.00
1	Kerry Collins	2.00
2	Rashaan Salaam	1.00
3	Steve Young	6.00
4	Rodney Thomas	1.00
5	Michael Westbrook	4.00
6	Cris Carter	2.00
7	Jerry Rice	8.00
8	Drew Bledsoe	6.00
9	Steve McNair	6.00
10	Terrell Davis	8.00
11	Barry Sanders	10.00
12	Robert Brooks	1.00
13	Chris Warren	1.00
14	Marshall Faulk	6.00
15	John Elway	6.00
16	Isaac Bruce	4.00

17	Emmitt Smith	10.00
18	Thurman Thomas	3.00

1996 Pacific Dynagon Kings of the NFL

Ten of the NFL's biggest stars are featured on these 1996 Pacific Dynagon inserts. The cards, numbered using a "K" prefix, were seeded one per every 361 packs. The card front is covered with etched foil at the top around the player's name, and at the bottom is a crown with a significant achievement inside it. A color action photo dominates the center of the card. The back has the player's name and team name at the top, with a career summary along the left side. A color action photo is on the right side. The accomplishment highlighted on the front is indicated at the bottom of the card.

		NM/M
Complete Set (10):		175.00
Common Player:		8.00
1	Emmitt Smith	40.00
2	Dan Marino	40.00
3	Barry Sanders	40.00
4	Curtis Martin	8.00
5	Brett Favre	40.00
6	Kordell Stewart	8.00
7	Emmitt Smith	40.00
8	Jerry Rice	30.00
9	John Elway	30.00
10	Dan Marino	40.00

1996 Pacific Dynagon Gold Tandems

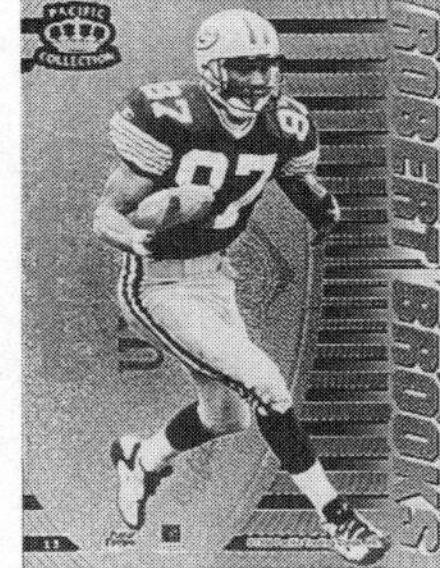

This 72-card parallel set pairs the fronts of two cards from Pacific's main 1996 Dynagon set. The cards were seeded one per every 37 packs.

		NM/M
Complete Set (72):		375.00
Common Player:		2.00
1	Dan Marino, Troy Aikman	45.00
2	Emmitt Smith, Rashaan Salaam	40.00
3	Jim Kelly, John Elway	45.00
4	Steve Young, Brett Favre	60.00
5	Curtis Martin, Terrell Davis	35.00
6	Kordell Stewart, Napoleon Kaufman	15.00
7	Barry Sanders, Jerry Rice	50.00
8	Joey Galloway, J.J. Stokes	20.00
9	Kerry Collins, Jeff Blake	15.00
10	Deion Sanders, Reggie White	15.00
11	Herman Moore, Mark Chmura	10.00
12	Eric Zeier, Tyrone Wheatley	5.00
13	Errict Rhett, Robert Brooks	10.00
14	Trent Dilfer, Steve McNair	20.00
15	Marshall Faulk, Drew Bledsoe	35.00
16	Tamarick Vanover, Michael Westbrook	5.00
17	Heath Shuler, Jerome Bettis	10.00
18	Isaac Bruce, Tim Brown	15.00
19	Terry Allen, Chris Warren	6.00
20	Brian Mitchell, Alex Van Dyke	2.00
21	Jerry Ellison, Kevin Mawae	2.00
22	Alvin Harper, Stanley Pritchett	2.00
23	Rick Mirer, Elvis Grbac	2.00
24	Cortez Kennedy, Junior Seau	5.00
25	William Floyd, Aaron Hayden	2.00
26	Stan Humphries, Dave Barr	2.00
27	J.T. Thomas, Stepfret Williams	2.00
28	Ronnie Harmon, Yancey Thigpen	2.00
29	Ernie Mills, Calvin Williams	2.00
30	Mark Bruener, Eddie George	15.00
31	Kevin Greene, Eric Moulds	12.00
32	Ricky Watters, Harvey Williams	6.00
33	Rodney Peete, Keyshawn Johnson	12.00
34	Charlie Garner, Adrian Murrell	2.00
35	Raghib Ismail, Wayne Chrebet	6.00
36	Billy Jo Hobert, Glenn Foley	2.00
37	Rodney Hampton, Ben Coates	6.00
38	Chris Calloway, Qadry Ismail	4.00
39	Dave Brown, Warren Moon	4.00
40	Ray Zellars, Robert Smith	2.00
41	Shane Pahukoa, Bernie Parmalee	2.00
42	Wayne Martin, Neil Smith	2.00
43	Jim Everett, Steve Bono	5.00
44	Mario Bates, Terry Kirby	2.00
45	Willie McGinest, Lawrence Phillips	2.00
46	Chad May, Mark Brunell	12.00
47	Cris Carter, O.J. McDuffie	6.00
48	Irving Fryar, Lake Dawson	6.00
49	Marcus Allen, James Stewart	12.00
50	Willie Jackson, Terry Glenn	15.00
51	Pete Mitchell, Kevin Hardy	4.00
52	Jim Harbaugh, Scott Mitchell	5.00
53	Zack Crockett, Rodney Thomas	10.00
54	Ben Bronson, Chris Sanders	2.00
55	Edgar Bennett, Tim Biakabutuka	4.00
56	Brett Perriman, Anthony Miller	2.00
57	Cory Schlesinger, Daryl Johnston	2.00
58	Shannon Sharpe, Michael Irvin	12.00
59	Chris Boniol, Thurman Thomas	10.00
60	Keenan McCardell, Darnay Scott	6.00
61	Leroy Hoard, Chris Zorich	2.00
62	Earnest Byner, Jeff Graham	2.00
63	Carl Pickens, Darick Holmes	5.00
64	David Dunn, Mark Carrier	2.00
65	Steve Stenstrom, Todd Collins	2.00
66	Eric Kramer, Derrick Moore	2.00
67	Larry Centers, Bobby Engram	5.00
68	Garrison Hearst, Jeff George	10.00
69	Dave Krieg, Craig Heyward	2.00
70	Frank Sanders, Terance Mathis	5.00
71	Gus Frerotte, Eric Metcalf	2.00
72	Bryce Paup, Blake Brockermeyer	2.00

1996 Pacific Gridiron

The only oversized football card set on the market returned for a second year in 1996 under the Pacific Pure Gridiron brand. A total of 1,500 cases of the product were produced, meaning the various inserts are rather limited in availability. Each card front uses gold foil stamping for the player's name and Crown Collection logo at the bottom. The photo on the front is a full-bleed color action shot. The back recaps the game from which the photo was taken, and another photo. Five parallel sets were made - Electric Blue (hobby), Scorching Red (retail), Presidential Copper (hobby, four per 37 packs), Presidential Platinum (retail, four per 37) and Presidential Gold (two per 721 packs of both retail and hobby; only 30 of these sets exist). Insert sets include Gold Crown die-cuts, Driving Force, Gridiron Performers and Gridiron Gems.

		NM/M
Complete Set (125):		40.00
Common Player:		.10
Pack (2):		1.00
Wax Box (36):		35.00
1	Larry Centers	.10
2	Garrison Hearst	.10
3	Dave Krieg	.10
4	Frank Sanders	.10
5	*Jamal Anderson*	3.00
6	J.J. Birden	.10
7	Eric Metcalf	.10
8	Jeff George	.50
9	Cornelius Bennett	.10
10	Todd Collins	.10
11	Darick Holmes	.40
12	Jim Kelly	1.00
13	Bryce Paup	.10
14	Bob Christian	.10
15	Kerry Collins	2.00
16	Pete Metzelaars	.10
17	Derrick Moore	.10
18	Curtis Conway	.10
19	Jim Flanigan	.10
20	Erik Kramer	.10
21	Rashaan Salaam	.40
22	Eric Bieniemy	.10
23	Jeff Blake	.50
24	Tony McGee	.10
25	Darnay Scott	.10
26	Vashone Adams	.10
27	Leroy Hoard	.10
28	Andre Rison	.10
29	Tommy Vardell	.10
30	Troy Aikman	3.00
31	Michael Irvin	1.00
32	Daryl Johnston	.10
33	Deion Sanders	1.00
34	Emmitt Smith	4.00
35	Terrell Davis	3.00
36	John Elway	3.00
37	Ed McCaffrey	.10
38	Anthony Miller	.10
39	Scott Mitchell	.10
40	Brett Perriman	.10
41	Barry Sanders	4.00
42	Chris Spielman	.10
43	Edgar Bennett	.10
44	Robert Brooks	.10
45	Brett Favre	4.00
46	Antonio Freeman	.10
47	Reggie White	.10
48	Haywood Jeffires	.10
49	Steve McNair	2.00
50	Rodney Thomas	.50
51	Frank Wycheck	.10
52	Ashley Ambrose	.10
53	Mark Brunell	2.00
54	Ken Dilger	.10
55	Marshall Faulk	2.00
56	Jim Harbaugh	.10
57	Tony Boselli	.10
58	Pete Mitchell	.10
59	James Stewart	.10
60	Marcus Allen	.10
61	Steve Bono	.10
62	Lake Dawson	.10
63	Tamarick Vanover	.50
64	Bryan Cox	.10
65	Dan Marino	4.00
66	O.J. McDuffie	.10
67	Bernie Parmalee	.10
68	Cris Carter	.10
69	Qadry Ismail	.10
70	Warren Moon	.10
71	Robert Smith	.10
72	Drew Bledsoe	3.00
73	Vincent Brisby	.10
74	Ben Coates	.10
75	Curtis Martin	3.00
76	Mario Bates	.10
77	Derek Brown	.10
78	Jim Everett	.10
79	Dave Brown	.10
80	Chris Calloway	.10
81	Rodney Hampton	.10
82	Tyrone Wheatley	.10
83	Kyle Brady	.10
84	Wayne Chrebet	.10
85	Adrian Murrell	.10
86	Tim Brown	1.00
87	Rob Carpenter	.10
88	Charlie Garner	.10
89	Daryl Hobbs	.10
90	Napoleon Kaufman	.50
91	Rodney Peete	.10
92	Ricky Watters	.10
93	Calvin Williams	.10
94	Kevin Greene	.10
95	Greg Lloyd	.10
96	Neil O'Donnell	.10
97	Erric Pegram	.10
98	Kordell Stewart	1.00
99	Yancey Thigpen	.50
100	Rod Woodson	.10
101	Isaac Bruce	2.00
102	Jerome Bettis	.10
103	J.T. Thomas	.10
104	Ronnie Harmon	.10
105	*Aaron Hayden*	.30
106	Stan Humphries	.10
107	Alfred Pupunu	.10
108	William Floyd	.10
109	Brent Jones	.10
110	Jerry Rice	3.00
111	J.J. Stokes	1.00
112	John Taylor	.10
113	Steve Young	3.00
114	Harvey Williams	.10
115	John Friesz	.10
116	Joey Galloway	1.00
117	Cortez Kennedy	.10
118	Rick Mirer	.10
119	Chris Warren	.40
120	Trent Dilfer	.10
121	Alvin Harper	.10
122	Errict Rhett	.50
123	Terry Allen	.10
124	Gus Frerotte	.10
125	Michael Westbrook	1.00

1996 Pacific Gridiron Copper/Platinum

The 125-card, regular-size parallel set to the Gridiron issue, these sets can be distinguished by the foil on the card fronts. Both Copper and platinum were inserted four times every 37 packs.

	NM/M
Common Player:	.25
Semistars:	.50
Cop./Plat.:	3X-6X

1996 Pacific Gridiron Gold

The 125-card, regular-sized set paralleled the Gridiron issue. The cards were inserted twice every 721 packs, with just 30 sets produced.

Common Player (1-125):

1996 Pacific Gridiron Driving Force

The top 10 running backs in the NFL are highlighted in this 1996 Pacific Pure Gridiron insert set. Cards were seeded one per every 73 packs. The card front has a color action photo, with a team color-coordinated hourglass with gold foil highlights behind the player. Gold foil is also used for the card's background, set name and player's name, which is highlighted in his team's color. The Crown logo is in the upper left corner. The back also uses the player's primary team color for the background, and has a color action photo in the center, with the set name above the photo and the player's name below. A brief recap of the player's 1995 season accomplishments is below the photo. A card number, using a "DF" prefix, is in the lower right corner.

		NM/M
Complete Set (10):		40.00
Common Player:		2.00
1	Chris Warren	2.00
2	Emmitt Smith	12.00
3	Barry Sanders	12.00
4	Rashaan Salaam	2.00
5	Errict Rhett	3.00
6	Curtis Martin	8.00
7	Garrison Hearst	4.00
8	Marshall Faulk	8.00
9	Terrell Davis	10.00
10	Edgar Bennett	2.00

A player's name in *italic* type indicates a rookie card.

1996 Pacific Gridiron Gems

These 1996 Pacific Pure Gridiron inserts feature 50 top NFL stars. Cards, numbered on the back using a GG prefix, were randomly inserted three per every four packs. The front has a color action photo in the center, with the Crown logo in the upper left corner. A puzzle-like border is used to frame three sides; a gridiron, with the player's name and brand logo, is stamped along the bottom of the card in green foil. The horizontal back repeats the puzzle pattern and has a color photo on one side and a recap of the player's 1995 achievements on the other.

		NM/M
Complete Set (50):		25.00
Common Player:		.25
1	J.J. Birden	.25
2	Garrison Hearst	1.00
3	Bryce Paup	.25
4	Kerry Collins	1.00
5	Alonzo Spellman	.25
6	Chris Zorich	.25
7	Harold Green	.25
8	Lee Johnson	.25
9	Eric Zeier	.25
10	Troy Aikman	3.00
11	Deion Sanders	1.50
12	Emmitt Smith	4.00
13	John Elway	3.00
14	Mike Pritchard	.25
15	Shane Bonham	.25
16	Barry Sanders	4.00
17	Edgar Bennett	.25
18	Brett Favre	4.00
19	Reggie White	.25
20	Eddie Robinson	.25
21	Marshall Faulk	3.00
22	Brian Stablein	.25
23	Don Davey	.25
24	Neil Smith	.25
25	Derrick Thomas	.25
26	Eric Green	.25
27	Jake Reed	.25
28	Troy Brown	.25
29	Will Moore	.25
30	Wesley Walls	.25
31	Herschel Walker	.25
32	Keyshawn Johnson	1.00
33	Billy Joe Hobert	.25
34	Ricky Watters	.25
35	Ernie Mills	.25
36	Kordell Stewart	1.00
37	Terrell Fletcher	.25
38	Junior Seau	.50
39	Elvis Grbac	.25
40	Gary Plummer	.25
41	Jerry Rice	3.00
42	Steve Young	3.00
43	Carlester Crumpler	.25
44	Joey Galloway	1.00
45	Cortez Kennedy	.25
46	Chris Warren	.25
47	Greg Robinson	.25
48	Errict Rhett	1.00
49	Terry Allen	.25
50	Stanley Richard	.25

1996 Pacific Gridiron Gold Crown Die-Cut

These cards could be obtained by sending in a redemption card bearing the player's name and card number. The cards were seeded one per every 37 packs of 1996 Pacific Pure Gridiron product. The front is a die-cut crown, with gold foil used to complete the crown. Gold foil is also used for the player's name, which is at the bottom adjacent to a team helmet. A full-bleed color action photo is in the center of the card. The back, numbered using a "GC" prefix, has a crown at the top, with a player photo in the center and his name below. Career, 1995 and most prolific games are recapped in brief summaries below.

		NM/M
Complete Set (20):		110.00
Common Player:		2.00
1	Barry Sanders	12.00
2	Ricky Watters	2.00
3	Troy Aikman	10.00
4	Deion Sanders	6.00
5	Kerry Collins	6.00
6	Dan Marino	15.00
7	Steve Young	10.00
8	Drew Bledsoe	10.00
9	Jerry Rice	12.00
10	Steve McNair	10.00
11	Joey Galloway	6.00
12	John Elway	12.00
13	Terrell Davis	12.00
14	Rashaan Salaam	4.00
15	Kordell Stewart	8.00
16	Emmitt Smith	15.00
17	Curtis Martin	12.00
18	Marshall Faulk	10.00
19	Brett Favre	15.00
20	Chris Warren	2.00

1996 Pacific Gridiron Rock Solid Rookies

Six of the NFL's top rookies from the 1995 season are featured on these 1996 Pacific Pure Gridiron inserts. The cards, seeded one per every 121 packs, are numbered on the back using an "RP" prefix. The front has a color action photo in the center, with a granite rock background and gold-foil borders. The player's team helmet is at the bottom in gold, too. "Rock Solid Rookie" is written in rock-like letters at the bottom. The Pacific Crown logo is in the upper left corner. The back has the player's name and set name running along opposite sides. A color photo is in a square at the top of the card, while a recap of the player's rookie season is underneath. The background is a gray marble.

		NM/M
Complete Set (6):		75.00
Common Player:		5.00
1	Joey Galloway	10.00
2	Napoleon Kaufman	5.00
3	Michael Westbrook	10.00
4	Kerry Collins	15.00
5	Aaron Hayden	5.00
6	Kordell Stewart	15.00

1996 Pacific Invincible

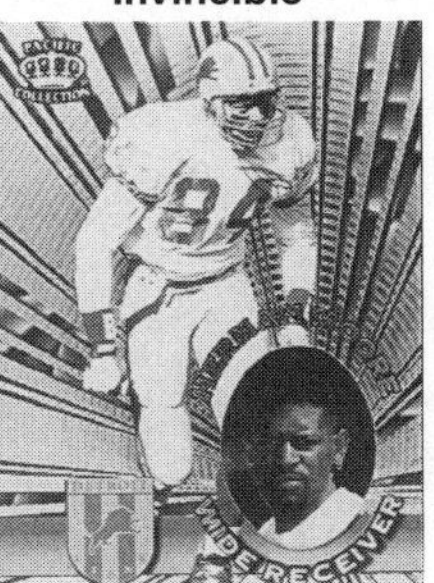

Pacific's 1996 Invincible Football (Prism II) has 150 cards in the set. Each is paralleled in four different versions. The regular card front has a color action photo in the middle, with a gold-foiled sunburst design as a background pattern. The Pacific logo is in the upper left corner; the player's team logo is in a team color-coordinated banner at the bottom. The lower left corner has a small oval with a plastic piece inside featuring the player's mug shot. His name is in gold foil above the photo; his position is below. The back side has a rectangle at the top, with a color photo inside it. The Pacific logo is in the upper left corner. The player's name is below the photo, with a recap of his career comprising most of the back side. The plastic mug shot is reversed on the front and is in the lower left corner. The card number (using an "I" prefix) is at the bottom of the card. The regular cards have four parallel versions. Hobby packs have a bronze parallel (four per 25 packs), while retail packs have a silver parallel (four per 25 packs). Then a platinum (one per 25) and a gold parallel set are found in both hobby and retail packs. There are also four insert sets - Kick-Starters Die-Cuts, Pro Bowl Stars, Smash Mouth, and a 10-card Chris Warren set.

	NM/M
Complete Set (150):	50.00
Common Player:	.25
Minor Stars:	1.00
Bronze/Silver Cards:	3X
Platinum Cards:	6X
Comp. C.Warren Set (10):	2.00
Common Warren:	.25
Pack (3):	2.00
Wax Box (24):	45.00

#	Player	NM/M
1	Larry Centers	.25
2	Garrison Hearst	.25
3	Seth Joyner	.25
4	*Simeon Rice*	1.00
5	Eric Swann	.25
6	Bert Emanuel	.25
7	Jeff George	.25
8	Craig Heyward	.25
9	Terance Mathis	.25
10	Eric Metcalf	.25
11	Derrick Alexander	.25
12	Leroy Hoard	.25
13	Andre Rison	.25
14	Tommy Vardell	.25
15	Eric Zeier	.25
16	Jim Kelly	1.00
17	*Eric Moulds*	5.00
18	Bryce Paup	.25
19	Bruce Smith	.25
20	Thurman Thomas	1.00
21	*Tim Biakabutuka*	1.00
22	Blake Brockermeyer	.25
23	Kerry Collins	3.00
24	Howard Griffith	.25
25	Lamar Lathon	.25
26	Mark Carrier	.25
27	Curtis Conway	.25
28	Erik Kramer	.25
29	Rashaan Salaam	.50
30	Alonzo Spellman	.25
31	Jeff Blake BR	1.00
32	Harold Green	.25
33	Carl Pickens	1.00
34	Darnay Scott	.50
35	Dan Wilkinson	.25
36	Troy Aikman	4.00
37	Jay Novacek	.25
38	Deion Sanders	3.00
39	Emmitt Smith	5.00
40	Kevin Williams	.25
41	Terrell Davis	4.00
42	John Elway	4.00
43	Anthony Miller	.25
44	Michael Dean Perry	.25
45	Shannon Sharpe	.25
46	Scott Mitchell	.25
47	Herman Moore	1.00
48	Brett Perriman	.25
49	Barry Sanders	5.00
50	Chris Spielman	.25
51	Edgar Bennett	.25
52	Robert Brooks	.25
53	Brett Favre	6.00
54	*Derrick Mayes*	1.00
55	Reggie White	1.00
56	*Eddie George*	8.00
57	Haywood Jeffires	.25
58	Steve McNair	3.00
59	Chris Sanders	.50
60	Rodney Thomas	.40
61	Tony Bennett	.25
62	Quentin Coryatt	.25
63	Ken Dilger	.25
64	Marshall Faulk	3.00
65	Jim Harbaugh	.25
66	Tony Boselli	.25
67	Mark Brunell	2.00
68	Kevin Hardy	.25
69	Desmond Howard	.25
70	James Stewart	.25
71	Marcus Allen	1.00
72	Steve Bono	.25
73	Neil Smith	.25
74	Derrick Thomas	.25
75	Tamarick Vanover	.50
76	*Karim Abdul-Jabbar*	.50
77	Irving Fryar	.25
78	Eric Green	.25
79	Dan Marino	6.00
80	Bernie Parmalee	.25
81	Cris Carter	.25
82	Warren Moon	.25
83	Jake Reed	.25
84	Robert Smith	.25
85	Moe Williams	.25
86	Drew Bledsoe	4.00
87	Ben Coates	.25
88	*Terry Glenn*	4.00
89	Curtis Martin	4.00
90	Dave Meggett	.25
91	Mario Bates	.25
92	Jim Everett	.25
93	Michael Haynes	.25
94	Torrance Small	.25
95	Ray Zellars	.25
96	Kyle Brady	.25
97	Wayne Chrebet	.25
98	*Keyshawn Johnson*	6.00
99	Adrian Murrell	.25
100	*Alex Van Dyke*	.50
101	Michael Brooks	.25
102	Dave Brown	.25
103	Chris Calloway	.25
104	Rodney Hampton	.25
105	*Amani Toomer*	1.00
106	Tyrone Wheatley	.25
107	Tim Brown	.25
108	*Rickey Dudley*	1.00
109	Billy Joe Hobert	.25
110	Raghib Ismail	.25
111	Napoleon Kaufman	.25
112	Harvey Williams	.25
113	Charlie Garner	.25
114	*Bobby Hoying*	1.00
115	Rodney Peete	.25
116	Ricky Watters	1.00
117	Greg Lloyd	.25
118	Erric Pegram	.25
119	Kordell Stewart	3.00
120	Yancey Thigpen	1.00
121	Jon Witman	.25
122	Aaron Hayden	.25
123	Stan Humphries	.25
124	Tony Martin	.25
125	Leslie O'Neal	.25
126	Junior Seau	.25
127	Jerome Bettis	1.00
128	Isaac Bruce	1.00
129	Ernie Conwell	.25
130	*Lawrence Phillips*	.50
131	William Floyd	.25
132	*Terrell Owens*	6.00
133	Jerry Rice	4.00
134	J.J. Stokes	1.00
135	Steve Young	4.00
136	Brian Blades	.25
137	Christian Fauria	.25
138	Joey Galloway	3.00
139	Rick Mirer	.25
140	Chris Warren	.50
141	Horace Copeland	.25
142	Trent Dilfer	.50
143	Alvin Harper	.25
144	Dave Moore	.25
145	Errict Rhett	1.00
146	Terry Allen	.25
147	Gus Frerotte	.25
148	Brian Mitchell	.25
149	Heath Shuler	.25
150	Michael Westbrook	1.00

1996 Pacific Invincible Bronze/ Silver/ Platinum

Pacific's 150-card Invincible set was paralleled in a total of four different versions. Hobby packs contained Bronze parallels, while retail packs had Silver versions of the base set, with both seeded four per 25 packs. In addition, Invincible Platinums (1:25) and Golds were available in both types of packs at a reduced rate. Each version is distinguished by the color foil used.

Bronze Cards:	3X
Silver Cards:	3X
Platinum Cards:	6X

1996 Pacific Invincible Chris Warren

This 10-card set is entirely devoted to Seattle Seahawks running back Chris Warren. Each card features a different action shot of Warren, with cards found every 10 packs.

	NM/M
Complete Set (10):	2.00
Common Warren:	.25

#	Player	NM/M
1	Chris Warren	.25
2	Chris Warren	.25
3	Chris Warren	.25
4	Chris Warren	.25
5	Chris Warren	.25
6	Chris Warren	.25
7	Chris Warren	.25
8	Chris Warren	.25
9	Chris Warren	.25
10	Chris Warren	.25

1996 Pacific Invincible Kick-Starters

These 1996 Pacific Invincible inserts are the most limited; they are seeded one per every 49 packs. The cards are die-cut into a gold-foiled football with a color action photo on it. The player's name is written along the left side of the card against a grassy background. The Pacific logo is in the upper left corner. The card back has a color action photo on the football part of the card; the right side has the player's name and a recap of a time when the player jump-started his team. The card is numbered using a "KS" prefix.

	NM/M
Complete Set (20):	225.00
Common Player:	5.00

#	Player	NM/M
1	Jeff Blake	5.00
2	Tim Brown	10.00
3	Kerry Collins	10.00
4	John Elway	15.00
5	Marshall Faulk	12.00
6	Brett Favre	25.00
7	Keyshawn Johnson	12.00
8	Dan Marino	25.00
9	Curtis Martin	15.00
10	Steve McNair	15.00
11	Errict Rhett	5.00
12	Jerry Rice	20.00
13	Rashaan Salaam	5.00
14	Barry Sanders	20.00
15	Deion Sanders	12.00
16	Emmitt Smith	25.00
17	Kordell Stewart	10.00
18	Tamarick Vanover	5.00
19	Chris Warren	5.00
20	Ricky Watters	10.00

1996 Pacific Invincible Pro Bowl

Every 25th pack of 1996 Pacific Invincible has one of these insert cards devoted to participants in the previous Pro Bowl game. Each card front shows the player in his Pro Bowl uniform against a colorful metallic background which incorporates the Pacific logo into the pattern. The player's name is written along the bottom. The horizontal back, numbered using a "PB" prefix, has a close-up shot of the player in his uniform, along with a Pro Bowl logo and a recap of some of his accomplishments as a Pro Bowler.

	NM/M
Complete Set (20):	110.00
Common Player:	2.00

#	Player	NM/M
1	Jeff Blake	2.00
2	Steve Bono	2.00
3	Tim Brown	5.00
4	Cris Carter	4.00
5	Ben Coates	2.00
6	Brett Favre	20.00
7	Jim Harbaugh	2.00
8	Curtis Martin	15.00
9	Warren Moon	4.00
10	Herman Moore	4.00
11	Carl Pickens	2.00
12	Jerry Rice	15.00
13	Barry Sanders	20.00
14	Shannon Sharpe	4.00
15	Emmitt Smith	20.00
16	Yancey Thigpen	4.00
17	Chris Warren	2.00
18	Ricky Watters	4.00
19	Reggie White	4.00
20	Steve Young	10.00

1996 Pacific Invincible Smash-Mouth

Some of the NFL's most intense players and hardest hitters are featured on these 1996 Pacific Invincible inserts. The cards, numbered on the back using an "SM" prefix, were seeded two per pack. Each card front shows a player busting through a hole against a football field background. The Pacific logo is in the upper right corner; the player's name is along the bottom. The back has a square in the upper right corner which has a mug shot inside. A summary of some of his accomplishments is given below the photo. The player's name, team name and position are written along the left side of the card, below the Pacific logo.

	NM/M
Complete Set (180):	20.00
Common Player:	.10
Minor Stars:	.40

#	Player	NM/M
1	Marcus Dowdell	.10
2	Karl Dunbar	.10
3	Eric England	.10
4	Garrison Hearst	.10
5	Bryan Reeves	.10
6	Simeon Rice	.40
7	Jeff George	.10
8	Bobby Hebert	.10
9	Craig Heyward	.10
10	Dave Richard	.10
11	Elbert Shelley	.10
12	Lonnie Johnson	.10
13	Jim Kelly	1.00
14	Corbin Lacina	.10
15	Bryce Paup	.10
16	Sam Rogers	.10
17	Bruce Smith	.10
18	Thurman Thomas	1.00
19	Carl Banks	.10
20	Dan Footman	.10
21	Louis Riddick	.10
22	Matt Stover	.10
23	Tommy Barnhardt	.10
24	Kerry Collins	.75
25	Mark Dennis	.10
26	Matt Elliott	.10
27	Eric Guliford	.10
28	Lamar Lathon	.10
29	Joe Cain	.10
30	Marty Carter	.10
31	Robert Green	.10
32	Erik Kramer	.10
33	Todd Perry	.10
34	Rashaan Salaam	.10
35	Alonzo Spellman	.10
36	Jeff Blake	.75
37	Andre Collins	.10
38	Todd Kelly	.10
39	Carl Pickens	.10
40	Kevin Sargent	.10
41	Troy Aikman	1.25
42	Charles Haley	.10
43	Daryl Johnston	.10
44	Nate Newton	.10
45	Deion Sanders	.75
46	Emmitt Smith	3.00
47	Steve Atwater	.10
48	Terrell Davis	1.00
49	John Elway	.75
50	Michael Dean Perry	.10
51	Shannon Sharpe	.10
52	Dave Wyman	.10
53	Bennie Blades	.10
54	Kevin Glover	.10
55	Herman Moore	.50
56	Robert Porcher	.10
57	Barry Sanders	1.25
58	Henry Thomas	.10
59	Edgar Bennett	.10
60	Robert Brooks	.10
61	Brett Favre	3.00
62	Harry Galbreath	.10
63	Sean Jones	.10
64	Reggie White	.40
65	Blaine Bishop	.10
66	Chuck Cecil	.10
67	Cris Dishman	.10
68	Steve McNair	.75
69	Rodney Thomas	.10
70	Jason Belser	.10
71	Ray Buchanan	.10
72	Quentin Coryatt	.10
73	Marshall Faulk	1.00
74	Jim Harbaugh	.10
75	Devon McDonald	.10
76	Tony Boselli	.10
77	Tony Brackens	.10
78	Mark Brunell	.75
79	Don Davey	.10
80	Rich Griffith	.10
81	Kevin Hardy	.10
82	Mickey Washington	.10
83	Louis Aguiar	.10
84	Dan Saleaumua	.10
85	Will Shields	.10
86	Neil Smith	.10
87	Derrick Thomas	.10
88	Tamarick Vanover	.75
89	Gene Atkins	.10
90	Bryan Cox	.10
91	Steve Emtman	.10
92	Chris Gray	.10
93	Dan Marino	3.00
94	Derrick Alexander	.10
95	Cris Carter	.10
96	Jeff Christy	.10
97	Robert Smith	.10
98	Korey Stringer	.10
99	Orlando Thomas	.10
100	Esera Tuaolo	.10
101	Drew Bledsoe	1.00
102	Eddie Cade	.10
103	Mike Jones	.10
104	Curtis Martin	2.00
105	Willie McGinest	.10
106	Chris Slade	.10
107	Eric Allen	.10
108	Mario Bates	.10
109	Jim Dombrowski	.10
110	Wayne Martin	.10
111	William Roaf	.10
112	Irv Smith	.10
113	Michael Brooks	.10
114	Stacey Dillard	.10
115	Rodney Hampton	.10
116	Doug Riesenberg	.10
117	Coleman Rudolph	.10
118	Tyrone Wheatley	.10
119	Kyle Brady	.10
120	Roger Duffy	.10
121	Keyshawn Johnson	1.00
122	Gary Jones	.10
123	Eddie Anderson	.10
124	Rickey Dudley	.40
125	Napoleon Kaufman	.10
126	Greg Skrepenak	.10
127	Pat Swilling	.10
128	Steve Wisniewski	.10
129	William Fuller	.10
130	Kurt Gouvela	.10
131	Andy Harmon	.10
132	Mike Mamula	.10
133	Guy McIntyre	.10
134	Ricky Watters	.10
135	Kevin Greene	.10
136	Bill Johnson	.10
137	Carnell Lake	.10
138	Greg Lloyd	.10
139	Erric Pegram	.10
140	Leon Searcy	.10
141	Shane Conlan	.10
142	Troy Drayton	.10
143	Wayne Gandy	.10
144	Sean Gilbert	.10
145	Carlos Jenkins	.10
146	Lawrence Phillips	.10
147	Aaron Hayden	.10
148	Stan Humphries	.40
149	Leslie O'Neal	.10
150	Bo Orlando	.10
151	Junior Seau	.10
152	Harry Swayne	.10
153	Harris Barton	.10
154	Merton Hanks	.10
155	Rod Milstead	.10
156	Ken Norton Jr.	.10
157	Gary Plummer	.10
158	Jerry Rice	1.50
159	Steve Wallace	.10
160	Steve Young	1.00
161	James Atkins	.10
162	Brian Blades	.10
163	Matt Joyce	.10
164	Cortez Kennedy	.10
165	Kevin Mawae	.10
166	Winston Moss	.10
167	Chris Warren	.40
168	Derrick Brooks	.10
169	Trent Dilfer	1.00
170	Santana Dotson	.10
171	Alvin Harper	.10
172	Hardy Nickerson	.10
173	Errict Rhett	.40
174	Warren Sapp	.40
175	Terry Allen	.10
176	John Gesek	.10
177	Ken Harvey	.10
178	Tre Johnson	.10
179	Rod Stephens	.10
180	Michael Westbrook	.40

1996 Pacific Litho-Cel

The 100-card, regular-sized set actually is two 100-card sets, with Cel and Litho versions. The Cel cards feature a clear oval center with a blue color image. The Litho cards are the same card fronts, but with a red color, non-clear oval center image. When the Cel card is placed over the Litho card, a 3-D effect makes the center oval image appear in full color. The card backs of the Cel cards are numbered with the "Cel" prefix while the Litho cards feature the same corresponding number with a "Litho" prefix. Litho-Cel came in three-card packs and included Moments In Time, Feature Performers, Game Time, Litho-Proof and Certified Litho-Proof inserts, as well as parallel silver foil (3:25) and Blue-Platinum (retail 3:25) versions. Pacific Litho-Cel was available in three-card packs which contained one Cel card, one Litho card and one Game Time card or other insert card.

	NM/M
Complete Set (100):	55.00
Common Player:	.20
Minor Stars:	.50
Bronze/Silver:	2X-4X
Prices are for both Litho and Cel cards together.	
Pack (3):	2.00
Wax Box (24):	45.00

#	Player	NM/M
1	Kent Graham	.20
2	LeShon Johnson	.20
3	*Leeland McElroy*	.75
4	Frank Sanders	.20
5	*Jamal Anderson*	10.00
6	Cornelius Bennett	.20
7	Bobby Hebert	.20
8	Earnest Byner	.20
9	Michael Jackson	.20
10	Vinny Testaverde	.50
11	Jim Kelly	1.00
12	Andre Reed	.50
13	Bruce Smith	.20
14	Thurman Thomas	1.00
15	Kerry Collins	1.00
16	Lamar Lathon	.20
17	Kevin Greene	.20
18	*Bobby Engram*	.75
19	Erik Kramer	.20
20	Rashaan Salaam	.50
21	Jeff Blake	.50
22	Garrison Hearst	1.00
23	Carl Pickens	.50
24	Darnay Scott	.50
25	Troy Aikman	3.00
26	Eric Bjornson	.20
27	Deion Sanders	1.00
28	Emmitt Smith	5.00
29	Terrell Davis	5.00
30	John Elway	5.00
31	Anthony Miller	.20
32	John Mobley	.20
33	Scott Mitchell	.20
34	Herman Moore	1.00
35	Brett Perriman	.20
36	Barry Sanders	6.00
37	Edgar Bennett	.20
38	Robert Brooks	.20
39	Brett Favre	6.00
40	Reggie White	1.00
41	Chris Chandler	.75
42	*Eddie George*	10.00
43	Steve McNair	3.00
44	Chris Sanders	.20
45	Ken Dilger	.20
46	Marshall Faulk	1.00
47	Jim Harbaugh	.50
48	Mark Brunell	2.00
49	Keenan McCardell	.50
50	James Stewart	.50
51	Marcus Allen	1.00
52	Steve Bono	.50
53	Greg Hill	.50
54	Tamarick Vanover	.50
55	*Karim Abdul-Jabbar*	2.00
56	Dan Marino	5.00
57	*Zach Thomas*	1.50
58	Cris Carter	1.00
59	Warren Moon	.50
60	Robert Smith	1.00
61	Drew Bledsoe	3.00
62	*Terry Glenn*	4.00
63	Curtis Martin	2.00
64	Mario Bates	.20
65	Jim Everett	.50
66	Haywood Jeffires	.20
67	Dave Brown	.20
68	Rodney Hampton	.20
69	*Amani Toomer*	1.00
70	Adrian Murrell	.50
71	Neil O'Donnell	.50
72	*Alex Van Dyke*	.50

73 Tim Brown .50
74 Jeff Hostetler .20
75 Napoleon Kaufman .75
76 Irving Fryar .20
77 Chris T. Jones .20
78 Ricky Watters 1.00
79 Jerome Bettis 1.00
80 Kordell Stewart 1.00
81 *Tony Banks* 1.00
82 *Eddie Kennison* .75
83 *Lawrence Phillips* .50
84 Stan Humphries .20
85 Tony Martin .20
86 Leonard Russell .20
87 Junior Seau .50
88 Jerry Rice 3.00
89 J.J. Stokes .50
90 Tommy Vardell .20
91 Steve Young 2.00
92 Joey Galloway 1.00
93 Rick Mirer .50
94 Chris Warren .20
95 *Mike Alstott* 3.00
96 Trent Dilfer .75
97 Nilo Silvan .20
98 Terry Allen .50
99 Gus Frerotte .50
100 Michael Westbrook .75

1996 Pacific Litho-Cel Bronze/Silver

Each card in the 100-card Litho-Cel set was reprinted in two different foil versions. Silver foil parallels were found in three per 25 hobby packs, while bronze versions were found in three per 25 retail packs. The only difference between these parallels and the regular-issue cards is the color of the foil stamping.

Bronze Cards: 2X-4X
Silver Cards: 2X-4X

1996 Pacific Litho-Cel Feature Performers

The 20-card, regular-sized inserts were included in every 25 packs of Litho-Cel cards. The card fronts feature the player over gold foil with his respective team helmet outline on the bottom half of the card. The player's name is written in the player's team color down the right side while the backs are numbered with the "FP" prefix.

NM/M
Complete Set (20): 175.00
Common Player: 4.00
1 Jim Kelly 4.00
2 Troy Aikman 10.00
3 Deion Sanders 8.00
4 Emmitt Smith 15.00
5 Terrell Davis 12.00
6 John Elway 12.00
7 Herman Moore 6.00
8 Barry Sanders 12.00
9 Robert Brooks 4.00
10 Brett Favre 15.00
11 Eddie George 12.00
12 Jim Harbaugh 4.00
13 Marcus Allen 4.00
14 Karim Abdul-Jabbar 4.00
15 Dan Marino 15.00
16 Joey Galloway 6.00
17 Curtis Martin 12.00
18 Jerome Bettis 6.00
19 Jerry Rice 12.00
20 Steve Young 12.00

1996 Pacific Litho-Cel Litho-Proof

The 36-card, regular-sized set was inserted in every 97 packs of 1996 Litho-Cel cards. The card fronts feature the same color photo and design as the basic Litho-Cel set, without the clear blue cel imaging. Also differentiating between the two sets is a gray seal in the lower left section of the card front which reads, "1996 Pacific Litho Cards - Litho-Proof." The cards are sequentially numbered as "x of 360" and are listed with a "Litho-Proof" prefix. A parallel version, Certified Litho-Proof, features a second seal "Pacific Collection" and is inserted every 481 packs.

NM/M
Complete Set (36): 1,000
Common Player: 5.00
Certified Cards: 2X-4X
1 Jim Kelly 15.00
2 Kerry Collins 15.00
3 Rashaan Salaam 5.00
4 Jeff Blake 10.00
5 Carl Pickens 10.00
6 Troy Aikman 50.00
7 Deion Sanders 35.00
8 Emmitt Smith 65.00
9 Terrell Davis 45.00
10 John Elway 45.00
11 Herman Moore 15.00
12 Barry Sanders 60.00
13 Robert Brooks 5.00
14 Brett Favre 70.00
15 Reggie White 5.00
16 Eddie George 35.00
17 Marshall Faulk 35.00
18 Jim Harbaugh 5.00
19 Mark Brunell 25.00
20 Marcus Allen 12.00
21 Steve Bono 5.00
22 Karim Abdul-Jabbar 10.00
23 Dan Marino 65.00
24 Warren Moon 12.00
25 Drew Bledsoe 35.00
26 Curtis Martin 35.00
27 Amani Toomer 5.00
28 Tim Brown 15.00
29 Napoleon Kaufman 5.00
30 Ricky Watters 12.00
31 Jerome Bettis 12.00
32 Kordell Stewart 15.00
33 Jerry Rice 45.00
34 Steve Young 45.00
35 Joey Galloway 25.00
36 Terry Allen 5.00

1996 Pacific Litho-Cel Certified Litho-Proofs

Certified Litho-Proofs are similar to the regular Litho-Proof inserts, but contain a large Pacific Crown Collection logo over top of the Litho-Proof logo in the bottom left corner. Certified Litho-Proofs were inserted at a rate of one per 481 packs.

Complete Set (36):
Certified Litho-Proofs: 2X-4X

1996 Pacific Litho-Cel Game Time

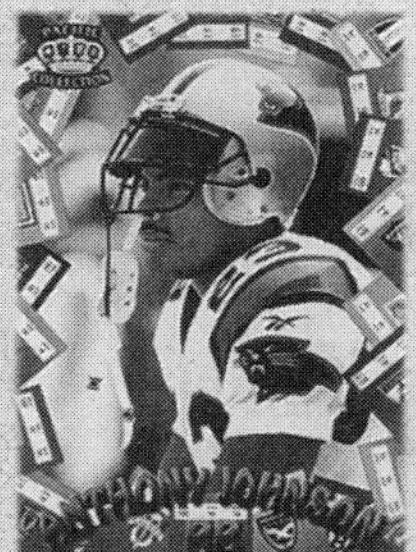

The 96-card, regular-sized set was inserted in each pack of Litho-Cel cards. The card fronts feature the player centered in an array of statistical cut-out boxes and the player's name is written in a curved pattern over the position on the bottom. The card backs feature headshots of the players in the lower lefthand corner, framed in a stop watch. The cards are numbered with the "GT" prefix.

NM/M
Complete Set (96): 25.00
Common Player: .10
Minor Stars: .40
1 Eddie George 2.00
2 Larry Bowie .10
3 Jarius Hayes .10
4 Jamal Anderson 2.00
5 Earnest Hunter .10
6 Darick Holmes .10
7 Kerry Collins .50
8 Raymont Harris .10
9 Jeff Blake .50
10 Troy Aikman 1.50
11 Terrell Davis 2.00
12 Kevin Glover .10
13 Brett Favre 3.00
14 Al Del Greco .10
15 Marshall Faulk .75
16 Bryan Barker .10
17 Rich Gannon .10
18 Dwight Hollier .10
19 Dixon Edwards .10
20 Drew Bledsoe 1.00
21 Paul Green .10
22 Lawrence Dawsey .10
23 Ron Carpenter .10
24 Joe Aska .10
25 Joe Panos .10
26 Norm Johnson .10
27 Tony Banks .50
28 Darren Bennett .10
29 Steve Israel .10
30 Mike Barber .10
31 Dexter Nottage .10
32 Kwamie Lassiter .10
33 Travis Hall .10
34 Greg Montgomery .10
35 Jim Kelly 1.00
36 Matt Elliott .10
37 Jack Jackson .10
38 Ki-Jana Carter .40
39 Deion Sanders .50
40 Jason Elam .10
41 Johnnie Morton .10
42 Darius Holland .10
43 Sheddrick Wilson .10
44 Derrick Frazier .10
45 Travis Davis .10
46 Pellom McDaniels .10
47 Dan Marino 3.00
48 Ben Hanks .10
49 Tedy Bruschi .10
50 Tom Hodson .10
51 Amani Toomer .50
52 Brian Hansen .10
53 Paul Butcher .10
54 Kevin Turner .10
55 Darren Perry .10
56 Mike Gruttadauria .10
57 Charlie Jones .10
58 Iheanyi Uwaezuoke .10
59 Glenn Montgomery .10
60 Mike Alstott .75
61 Joe Patton .10
62 Leeland McElroy .75
63 Robbie Tobeck .10
64 Vinny Testaverde .50
65 Chris Spielman .10
66 Anthony Johnson .10
67 Todd Sauerbrun .10
68 Jeff Hill .10
69 Emmitt Smith 3.00
70 John Elway 2.00
71 Barry Sanders 3.00
72 Brian Williams .10
73 Chris Gardocki .10
74 Jimmy Smith .10
75 Ricky Siglar .10
76 Tim Ruddy .10
77 Moe Williams .10
78 Willie Clay .10
79 Henry Lusk .10
80 Brian Williams .10
81 Ronald Moore .10
82 Trey Junkin .10
83 James Willis .10
84 Joel Steed .10
85 Jamie Martin .10
86 Shawn Lee .10
87 Steve Young 1.00
88 Barrett Robbins .10
89 Charles Dimry .10
90 Darryl Pounds .10
91 Herschel Walker .10
92 Bill Romanowski .10
93 David Tate .10
94 Marrio Grier .10
95 Rodney Young .10
96 Lamar Smith .10

1996 Pacific Litho-Cel Moments in Time

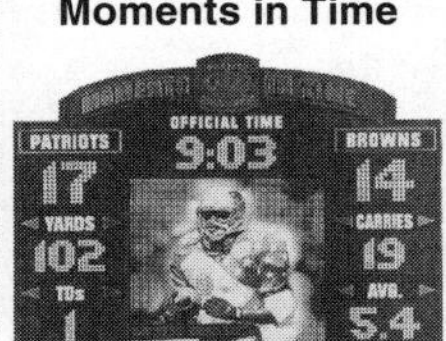

The 20-card, regular-sized, die-cut set was inserted every 49 packs of Litho-Cel cards. The horizontal cards are die-cut in the shape of a scoreboard and feature red-foil printing. The score of a particular game, along with the player's statistics for that game are included on the card front in scoreboard script, while the card back describes the player's performance with a highlight. The cards are numbered with the "MT" prefix.

NM/M
Complete Set (20): 325.00
Common Player: 4.00
1 Jim Kelly 12.00
2 Kerry Collins 12.00
3 Rashann Salaam 4.00
4 Troy Aikman 25.00
5 Deion Sanders 15.00
6 Emmitt Smith 35.00
7 Terrell Davis 25.00
8 John Elway 30.00
9 Barry Sanders 35.00
10 Robert Brooks 4.00
11 Brett Favre 40.00
12 Marshall Faulk 20.00
13 Jim Harbaugh 4.00
14 Steve Bono 4.00
15 Dan Marino 40.00
16 Drew Bledsoe 25.00
17 Curtis Martin 20.00
18 Jerry Rice 30.00
19 Steve Young 30.00
20 Terry Allen 4.00

1997 Pacific

The 450-card set showcases a full-bleed photo on the front, with the Pacific Crown Collection logo in the upper left. The team's helmet is in color in the lower left and reproduced in gold foil towards the bottom center. The player's name is printed in capital gold-foil letters in the lower right of the front. A Copper parallel was inserted 1:1 hobby packs, while a Silver parallel was seeded 1:1 retail packs. A Platinum Blue hobby and retail parallel was included in 1:73 packs. Red-foil parallels were found one per Treat Entertainment U.S. retail pack.

NM/M
Complete Set (450): 25.00
Common Player: .05
Minor Stars: .10
Copper/Silver Cards: 3X-6X
Blue Cards: 20X-30X
Pack (12): 1.00
Wax Box (36): 35.00
1 Lomas Brown .05
2 Pat Carter .05
3 Larry Centers .05
4 Matt Darby .05
5 Marcus Dowdell .05
6 Aaron Graham .05
7 Kent Graham .10
8 LeShon Johnson .05
9 Seth Joyner .05
10 Leeland McElroy .10
11 Rob Moore .05
12 Simeon Rice .05
13 Eric Swann .05
14 Aeneas Williams .05
15 Morten Andersen .05
16 Jamal Anderson .20
17 Lester Archambeau .05
18 Cornelius Bennett .05
19 J.J. Birden .05
20 Antone Davis .05
21 Bert Emanuel .05
22 Travis Hall .05
23 Bobby Hebert .05
24 Craig Heyward .05
25 Terance Mathis .05
26 Tim McKyer .05
27 Eric Metcalf .05
28 Jessie Tuggle .05
29 Derrick Alexander .05
30 Orlando Brown .05
31 Rob Burnett .05
32 Earnest Byner .05
33 Ray Ethridge .05
34 Steve Everett .05
35 Carwell Gardner .05
36 Michael Jackson .05
37 Jamal Lewis .05
38 Stevon Moore .05
39 Bam Morris .05
40 Jonathan Ogden .05
41 Vinny Testaverde .10
42 Todd Collins .10
43 Russell Copeland .05
44 Quinn Early .05
45 John Fina .05
46 Phil Hansen .05
47 Eric Moulds .15
48 Bryce Paup .05
49 Andre Reed .05
50 Kurt Schulz .05
51 Bruce Smith .05
52 Chris Spielman .05
53 Steve Tasker .05
54 Thurman Thomas .10
55 Carlton Bailey .05
56 Michael Bates .05
57 Blake Brockermeyer .05
58 Mark Carrier .05
59 Kerry Collins .25
60 Eric Davis .05
61 Kevin Greene .05
62 Raghib Ismail .05
63 Anthony Johnson .05
64 Shawn King .05
65 Greg Kragen .05
66 Sam Mills .05
67 Tyrone Poole .05
68 Wesley Walls .05
69 Mark Carrier .05
70 Curtis Conway .10
71 Bobby Engram .10
72 Jim Flanigan .05
73 Al Fontenot .05
74 Raymont Harris .05
75 Walt Harris .05
76 Andy Heck .05
77 Dave Krieg .05
78 Rashaan Salaam .10
79 Vinson Smith .05
80 Alonzo Spellman .05
81 Michael Timpson .05
82 James Williams .05
83 Ashley Ambrose .05
84 Eric Bieniemy .05
85 Jeff Blake .15
86 Ki-Jana Carter .10
87 John Copeland .05
88 David Dunn .05
89 Jeff Hill .05
90 Ricardo McDonald .05
91 Tony McGee .05
92 Greg Myers .05
93 Carl Pickens .10
94 Corey Sawyer .05
95 Darnay Scott .05
96 Dan Wilkinson .05
97 Troy Aikman 1.00
98 Larry Allen .05
99 Eric Bjornson .05
100 Ray Donaldson .05
101 Michael Irvin .10
102 Daryl Johnson .05
103 Nate Newton .05
104 Deion Sanders .40
105 Jim Schwantz .05
106 Emmitt Smith 1.75
107 Broderick Thomas .05
108 Tony Tolbert .05
109 Eric Williams .05
110 Sherman Williams .05
111 Darren Woodson .05
112 Steve Atwater .05
113 Aaron Craver .05
114 Ray Crockett .05
115 Terrell Davis 1.25
116 Jason Elam .05
117 John Elway .60
118 Todd Kinchen .05
119 Ed McCaffrey .05
120 Anthony Miller .05
121 John Mobley .05
122 Michael Dean Perry .05
123 Reggie Rivers .05
124 Shannon Sharpe .05
125 Alfred Williams .05
126 Reggie Brown .05
127 Luther Elliss .05
128 Kevin Glover .05
129 Jason Hanson .05
130 Pepper Johnson .05
131 Glyn Milburn .05
132 Scott Mitchell .05
133 Herman Moore .15
134 Johnnie Morton .05
135 Brett Perriman .05
136 Robert Porcher .05
137 Ron Rivers .05
138 Barry Sanders 1.25
139 Henry Thomas .05
140 Don Beebe .05
141 Edgar Bennett .05
142 Robert Brooks .05
143 LeRoy Butler .05
144 Mark Chmura .05
145 Brett Favre 2.00
146 Antonio Freeman .25
147 Chris Jacke .05
148 Travis Jervey .05
149 Sean Jones .05
150 Dorsey Levens .10
151 John Michels .05
152 Craig Newsome .05
153 Eugene Robinson .05
154 Reggie White .10
155 Micheal Barrow .05
156 Blaine Bishop .05
157 Chris Chandler .05
158 Anthony Cook .05
159 Malcolm Floyd .05
160 Eddie George 1.25
161 Roderick Lewis .05
162 Steve McNair .75
163 John Henry Mills .05
164 Derek Russell .05
165 Chris Sanders .05
166 Mark Stepnoski .05
167 Frank Wycheck .05
168 Robert Young .05
169 Trev Alberts .05
170 Aaron Bailey .05
171 Tony Bennett .05
172 Ray Buchanan .05
173 Quentin Coryatt .05
174 Eugene Daniel .05
175 Sean Dawkins .05
176 Ken Dilger .05
177 Marshall Faulk .10
178 Jim Harbaugh .05
179 Marvin Harrison .40
180 Paul Justin .05
181 Lamont Warren .05
182 Bernard Whittingham .05
183 Tony Bosselli .05
184 Tony Brackens .05
185 Mark Brunell .75
186 Brian DeMarco .05
187 Rich Griffith .05
188 Kevin Hardy .05
189 Willie Jackson .05
190 Jeff Lageman .05
191 Keenan McCardell .10
192 Natrone Means .10
193 Pete Mitchell .05
194 Joel Smeenge .05
195 Jimmy Smith .10
196 James Stewart .10
197 Marcus Allen .10
198 John Art .05
199 Kimble Anders .05
200 Steve Bono .10
201 Vaughn Booker .05
202 Dale Carter .05
203 Mark Collins .05
204 Greg Hill .05
205 Joe Horn .05
206 Dan Saleaumua .05
207 Will Shields .05
208 Neil Smith .05
209 Derrick Thomas .10
210 Tamarick Vanover .10
211 Karim Abdul-Jabbar .25
212 Fred Barnett .05
213 Tim Bowens .05
214 Kirby Dar Dar .05
215 Troy Drayton .05
216 Craig Erickson .05
217 Daryl Gardener .05
218 Randal Hill .05
219 Dan Marino 1.75
220 O.J. McDuffie .05
221 Bernie Parmalee .05
222 Stanley Pritchett .05
223 Daniel Stubbs .05
224 Zach Thomas .20
225 Derrick Alexander .05
226 Cris Carter .10
227 Jeff Christy .05
228 Qadry Ismail .05
229 Brad Johnson .05
230 Andrew Jordan .05
231 Randall McDaniel .05
232 David Palmer .05
233 John Randle .05
234 Jake Reed .05
235 Scott Sisson .05
236 Korey Stringer .05
237 Darryl Talley .05
238 Orlando Thomas .05
239 Bruce Armstrong .05
240 Drew Bledsoe 1.00
241 Willie Clay .05
242 Ben Coates .05
243 Frank Collins .05
244 Terry Glenn .25
245 Jerome Henderson .05
246 Shawn Jefferson .05
247 Dietrich Jells .05
248 Ty Law .05
249 Curtis Martin 1.25
250 Willie McGinest .05
251 David Meggett .05
252 Lawyer Milloy .05
253 Chris Slade .05
254 Je'Rod Cherry .05
255 Jim Everett .05
256 Mark Fields .05
257 Michael Haynes .05
258 Tyrone Hughes .05
259 Haywood Jeffires .05
260 Wayne Martin .05
261 Mark McMillian .05
262 Rufus Porter .05
263 William Roaf .05
264 Torrance Small .05
265 Renaldo Turnbull .05
266 Ray Zellars .05
267 Jessie Armstead .05
268 Chad Bratzke .05
269 Dave Brown .05
270 Chris Calloway .05
271 Howard Cross .05
272 Lawrence Dawsey .05
273 Rodney Hampton .05
274 Danny Kanell .05
275 Arthur Marshall .05
276 Aaron Pierce .05
277 Phillippi Sparks .05
278 Amani Toomer .05
279 Charles Way .05
280 Richie Anderson .05
281 Fred Baxter .05
282 Wayne Chrebet .05
283 Kyle Clifton .05
284 John Elliott .05
285 Aaron Glenn .05
286 Jeff Graham .05
287 Bobby Hamilton .05
288 Keyshawn Johnson .40
289 Adrian Murrell .05
290 Neil O'Donnell .05
291 Webster Slaughter .05
292 Alex Van Dyke .05
293 Marvin Washington .05
294 Joe Aska .05
295 Jerry Ball .05
296 Tim Brown .10
297 Rickey Dudley .10
298 Pat Harlow .05
299 Nolan Harrison .05
300 Billy Joe Hobert .05
301 James Jett .05
302 Napoleon Kaufman .10
303 Lincoln Kennedy .05
304 Albert Lewis .05
305 Chester McGlockton .05
306 Pat Swilling .05
307 Steve Wisniewski .05
308 Darion Conner .05
309 Ty Detmer .05
310 Jason Dunn .05
311 Irving Fryar .05
312 Jeff Fuller .05
313 William Fuller .05
314 Charlie Garner .05
315 Bobby Hoying .05
316 Tom Hutton .05
317 Chris T. Jones .05
318 Mike Mamula .05
319 Mark Seay .05

320	Bobby Taylor	.05
321	Ricky Watters	.10
322	Jahine Arnold	.05
323	Jerome Bettis	.10
324	Chad Brown	.05
325	Mark Bruener	.05
326	Andre Hastings	.05
327	Norm Johnson	.05
328	Levon Kirkland	.05
329	Carnell Lake	.05
330	Greg Lloyd	.05
331	Ernie Mills	.05
332	Orpheus Roye	.05
333	Kordell Stewart	.75
334	Yancey Thigpen	.05
335	Mike Tomczak	.05
336	Rod Woodson	.05
337	Tony Banks	.25
338	Bern Brostek	.05
339	Isaac Bruce	.15
340	Ernie Conwell	.05
341	Keith Crawford	.05
342	Wayne Gandy	.05
343	Harold Green	.05
344	Carlos Jenkins	.05
345	Jimmie Jones	.05
346	Eddie Kennison	.40
347	Todd Lyght	.05
348	Leslie O'Neal	.05
349	Lawrence Phillips	.10
350	Greg Robinson	.05
351	Darren Bennett	.05
352	Lewis Bush	.05
353	Eric Castle	.05
354	Terrell Fletcher	.05
355	Darrien Gordon	.05
356	Kurt Gouveia	.05
357	Aaron Hayden	.05
358	Stan Humphries	.05
359	Tony Martin	.05
360	Vaughn Parker	.05
361	Brian Roche	.05
362	Leonard Russell	.05
363	Junior Seau	.10
364	Roy Barker	.05
365	Harris Barton	.05
366	Dexter Carter	.05
367	Chris Doleman	.05
368	Tyronne Drakeford	.05
369	Elvis Grbac	.05
370	Derek Loville	.05
371	Tim McDonald	.05
372	Ken Norton	.05
373	Terrell Owens	.50
374	Gary Plummer	.05
375	Jerry Rice	1.00
376	Dana Stubblefield	.05
377	Lee Woodall	.05
378	Steve Young	.60
379	Robert Blackman	.05
380	Brian Blades	.05
381	Carlester Crumpler	.05
382	Christian Fauria	.05
383	John Friesz	.05
384	Joey Galloway	.25
385	Derrick Graham	.05
386	Cortez Kennedy	.05
387	Warren Moon	.10
388	Winston Moss	.05
389	Mike Pritchard	.05
390	Michael Sinclair	.05
391	Lamar Smith	.05
392	Chris Warren	.05
393	Chidi Ahanotu	.05
394	Mike Alstott	.15
395	Reggie Brooks	.05
396	Trent Dilfer	.10
397	Jerry Ellison	.05
398	Paul Gruber	.05
399	Alvin Harper	.05
400	Courtney Hawkins	.05
401	Dave Moore	.05
402	Errict Rhett	.10
403	Warren Sapp	.05
404	Nilo Silvan	.05
405	Regan Upshaw	.05
406	Casey Weldon	.05
407	Terry Allen	.05
408	Jamie Asher	.05
409	Bill Brooks	.05
410	Tom Carter	.05
411	Henry Ellard	.05
412	Gus Frerotte	.05
413	Darrell Green	.05
414	Ken Harvey	.05
415	Tre' Johnson	.05
416	Brian Mitchell	.05
417	Rich Owens	.05
418	Heath Shuler	.10
419	Michael Westbrook	.05
420	*Tony Woods*	.10
421	*Reidel Anthony*	1.50
422	*Darnell Autry*	.50
423	*Tiki Barber*	2.00
424	*Pat Barnes*	.30
425	*Terry Battle*	.10
426	*Will Blackwell*	.30
427	*Peter Boulware*	.10
428	*Rae Carruth*	.10
429	*Troy Davis*	.50
430	*Jim Druckenmiller*	.50
431	*Warrick Dunn*	1.25
432	*Marc Edwards*	.10
433	*James Farrior*	.10
434	*Yatil Green*	.50
435	*Byron Hanspard*	.50
436	*Ike Hilliard*	1.50
437	*David LaFleur*	.50
438	*Kevin Lockett*	.25
439	*Sam Madison*	.10
440	*Brian Manning*	.10
441	*Orlando Pace*	.50
442	*Jake Plummer*	1.00
443	*Chad Scott*	.10
444	*Sedrick Shaw*	.30
445	*Antowain Smith*	1.25
446	*Shawn Springs*	.30
447	*Ross Verba*	.20
448	*Bryant Webster*	.10
449	*Renaldo Wynn*	.10
450	Jimmy Johnson	.30

1997 Pacific Big Number Die-Cuts

Inserted 1:37 packs, the 20-card die-cut set features the player's last name and jersey number on the front of the card. The backs have the player's name at the top, with the Pacific Crown logo in the upper right. A player photo is in the center, with his highlights located inside a box near the bottom.

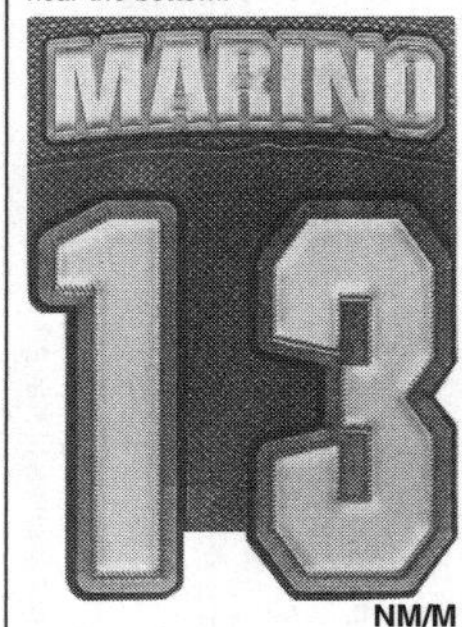

		NM/M
Complete Set (20):		75.00
Common Player:		1.00
Minor Stars:		2.00
Inserted 1:37		
1	Jamal Anderson	5.00
2	Kerry Collins	5.00
3	Troy Aikman	10.00
4	Emmitt Smith	12.00
5	Terrell Davis	10.00
6	John Elway	10.00
7	Barry Sanders	12.00
8	Brett Favre	15.00
9	Eddie George	8.00
10	Mark Brunell	6.00
11	Marcus Allen	6.00
12	Karim Abdul-Jabbar	2.00
13	Dan Marino	15.00
14	Drew Bledsoe	10.00
15	Curtis Martin	10.00
16	Napoleon Kaufman	2.00
17	Jerome Bettis	4.00
18	Eddie Kennison	1.00
19	Jerry Rice	10.00
20	Steve Young	10.00

1997 Pacific Card Supials

Inserted 1:37 packs, the 36-card set features a player photo superimposed on the front, with a gold-foil version of the same photo printed along the right side of the front. The Crown logo is in the upper left, while the player's first name is in the upper right. His last name is printed vertically along the left edge of the front. The backs include a slot where a miniature die-cut card of the player can be inserted. The mini card includes a photo inside a die-cut football, which is sitting on a tee. The team's logo is in the lower right of the mini-card front.

		NM/M
Complete Set (72):		175.00
Complete Large Set (36):		100.00
Complete Small Set (36):		75.00
Common Large Player:		.50
Minor Large Stars:		2.00
Small Cards:		.7X
Inserted 1:37		
1	Todd Collins	.50
2	Kerry Collins	2.00
3	Wesley Walls	.50
4	Jeff Blake	2.00
5	Troy Aikman	8.00
6	Emmitt Smith	10.00
7	Terrell Davis	8.00
8	John Elway	8.00
9	Herman Moore	2.00
10	Barry Sanders	10.00
11	Brett Favre	12.00
12	Dorsey Levens	2.00
13	Eddie George	6.00
14	Steve McNair	6.00
15	Marshall Faulk	6.00
16	Mark Brunell	4.00
17	Natrone Means	2.00
18	Marcus Allen	2.00
19	Karim Abdul-Jabbar	2.00
20	Dan Marino	12.00
21	Brad Johnson	4.00
22	Drew Bledsoe	10.00
23	Terry Glenn	6.00
24	Curtis Martin	10.00
25	Napoleon Kaufman	2.00
26	Ricky Watters	2.00
27	Jerome Bettis	2.00
28	Kordell Stewart	6.00
29	Tony Banks	2.00
30	Isaac Bruce	2.00
31	Eddie Kennison	2.00
32	Jerry Rice	8.00
33	Steve Young	8.00
34	Joey Galloway	4.00
35	Chris Warren	.50
36	Gus Frerotte	.50

1997 Pacific Cramer's Choice Awards

Inserted 1:721 packs, the 10-card set showcases a player photo superimposed over a pyramid die-cut background. "1997 Cramer's Choice Awards" and the Crown logo are printed at the top of the award, while the gold base of the award includes the Crown logo, player's name and position.

		NM/M
Complete Set (10):		425.00
Common Player:		10.00
Inserted 1:721		
1	Kevin Greene	10.00
2	Emmitt Smith	100.00
3	Terrell Davis	75.00
4	John Elway	75.00
5	Barry Sanders	100.00
6	Brett Favre	110.00
7	Eddie George	50.00
8	Mark Brunell	40.00
9	Terry Glenn	25.00
10	Jerry Rice	75.00

1997 Pacific Gold Crown Die-Cuts

The 36-card set was inserted 1:37 packs. The top of the cards feature a die-cut gold crown at the top. The player's photo is superimposed over the crown. The bottom of the card front has three gold-foil stripes, with the player's name printed in the center of the middle stripe. A circle at the bottom center features the team logo inside a shield. Eight sun rays are printed diagonally at the bottom of the front.

		NM/M
Complete Set (36):		150.00
Common Player:		2.00
Minor Stars:		4.00
Inserted 1:37		
1	Larry Centers	2.00
2	Vinny Testaverde	4.00
3	Kerry Collins	4.00
4	Kevin Green	2.00
5	Anthony Johnson	2.00
6	Jeff Blake	4.00
7	Troy Aikman	12.00
8	Emmitt Smith	15.00
9	Terrell Davis	12.00
10	John Elway	12.00
11	Barry Sanders	15.00
12	Brett Favre	18.00
13	Antonio Freeman	4.00
14	Eddie George	6.00
15	Marshall Faulk	8.00
16	Mark Brunell	6.00
17	Jimmy Smith	4.00
18	Marcus Allen	6.00
19	Karim Abdul-Jabbar	4.00
20	Dan Marino	18.00
21	Brad Johnson	6.00
22	Drew Bledsoe	10.00
23	Terry Glenn	6.00
24	Curtis Martin	10.00
25	Adrian Murrell	2.00
26	Tim Brown	6.00
27	Jerome Bettis	6.00
28	Kordell Stewart	6.00
29	Tony Banks	4.00
30	Terrell Owens	10.00
31	Jerry Rice	12.00
32	Steve Young	12.00
33	Chris Warren	2.00
34	Terry Allen	4.00
35	Gus Frerotte	2.00
36	Jim Druckenmiller	2.00

1997 Pacific Mark Brunell

The four-card set was split between Crown Collection and Invincible. Card Nos. 1-2 were seeded 1:72 packs of Crown, while Nos. 3-4 were inserted 1:72 in Invincible packs.

	NM/M
Complete Set (4):	20.00
Common Player:	5.00

1997 Pacific Team Checklists

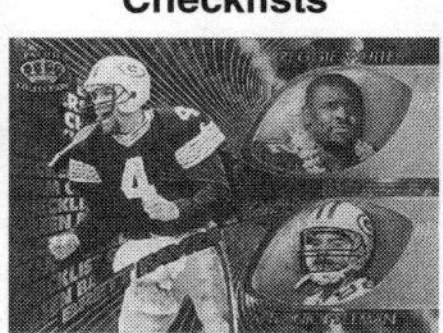

The 30-card set is inserted 1:37 packs. The fronts feature an action shot of a player on the left side, with his name printed in gold across his body, while the team's two other stars have each of their head shot printed on football-shaped acetate pieces on the right. Their names appear above the top football and below the bottom football. The team's name and the word "checklist" are repeated many times beginning on the left border and continuing to a thin area on the right side.

		NM/M
Complete Set (30):		150.00
Common Player:		2.00
Minor Stars:		12.00
Inserted 1:37		
1	Arizona Cardinals	2.00
2	Atlanta Falcons	2.00
3	Baltimore Ravens	2.00
4	Buffalo Bills	6.00
5	Carolina Panthers	6.00
6	Chicago Bears	2.00
7	Cincinnati Bengals	6.00
8	Dallas Cowboys	10.00
9	Denver Broncos	10.00
10	Detroit Lions	12.00
11	Green Bay Packers	12.00
12	Houston Oilers	6.00
13	Indianapolis Colts	2.00
14	Jacksonville Jaguars	6.00
15	Kansas City Chiefs	2.00
16	Miami Dolphins	12.00
17	Minnesota Vikings	8.00
18	New England Patriots	8.00
19	New Orleans Saints	2.00
20	New York Giants	4.00
21	New York Jets	2.00
22	Oakland Raiders	2.00
23	Philadelphia Eagles	2.00
24	Pittsburgh Steelers	10.00
25	St. Louis Rams	6.00
26	San Diego Chargers	2.00
27	San Francisco 49ers	10.00
28	Seattle Seahawks	2.00
29	Tampa Bay Buccaneers	2.00
30	Washington Redskins	2.00

1997 Pacific The Zone

Inserted 1:73 packs, the 20-card set is die-cut in the shape of a goal post. The front has a photo of the player inside the uprights, while his name and position are printed at the base of the goal post.

		NM/M
Complete Set (20):		175.00
Common Player:		2.00
Minor Stars:		12.00
Inserted 1:73		
1	Kerry Collins	4.00
2	Jeff Blake	2.00
3	Emmitt Smith	25.00
4	Terrell Davis	15.00
5	John Elway	15.00
6	Barry Sanders	20.00
7	Brett Favre	25.00
8	Mark Brunell	12.00
9	Karim Abdul-Jabbar	2.00
10	Dan Marino	25.00
11	Drew Bledsoe	15.00
12	Terry Glenn	6.00
13	Curtis Martin	12.00
14	Napoleon Kaufman	2.00
15	Jerome Bettis	6.00
16	Eddie Kennison	2.00
17	Tony Martin	2.00
18	Jerry Rice	15.00
19	Steve Young	15.00
20	Terry Allen	4.00

1997 Pacific Crown Royale

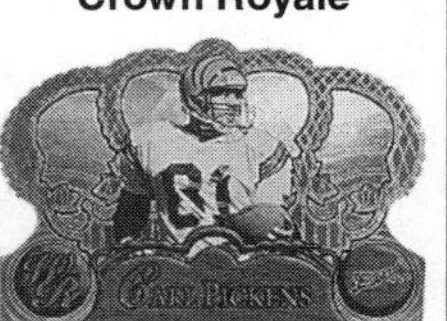

Crown Royale is a 144-card, all die-cut set. The base cards feature a player shot on a crown-shaped die-cut card. The two parallel sets are silver and holographic gold foil (4:25) and silver and holographic blue foil (1:25). Insert sets include NFL Cel-Fusions, Chalk Talk Laser Cuts, Pro Bowl Die-Cuts, Firestone on Football and Premium-sized Cramer's Choice Awards.

		NM/M
Complete Set (144):		150.00
Common Player:		.50
Minor Stars:		1.00
Gold/Silver Cards:		2X-4X
Gold/Silver Rookies:		2X
Blue Cards:		6X-12X
Blue Rookies:		3X-6X
Pack (4):		4.00
Wax Box (24):		80.00
1	Larry Centers	.50
2	Kent Graham	1.00
3	LeShon Johnson	.50
4	Leeland McElroy	.50
5	*Jake Plummer*	4.00
6	Jamal Anderson	1.00
7	Chris Chandler	.50
8	*Byron Hanspard*	.50
9	Michael Haynes	.50
10	Derrick Alexander	.50
11	*Jay Graham*	.50
12	Michael Jackson	.50
13	Vinny Testaverde	.50
14	Todd Collins	.50
15	Jay Riemersma	.50
16	*Antowain Smith*	6.00
17	Steve Tasker	.50
18	Thurman Thomas	1.00
19	*Rae Carruth*	.50
20	Kerry Collins	1.00
21	Anthony Johnson	.50
22	*Fred Lane*	.50
23	Muhsin Muhammad	.50
24	Wesley Walls	.50
25	*Darnell Autry*	1.00
26	Raymont Harris	.50
27	Erik Kramer	.50
28	Rick Mirer	.50
29	Rashaan Salaam	.50
30	Jeff Blake	1.00
31	Ki-Jana Carter	.50
32	*Corey Dillon*	10.00
33	Carl Pickens	.50
34	Troy Aikman	4.00
35	Michael Irvin	1.00
36	Daryl Johnston	.50
37	*David LaFleur*	.50
38	Deion Sanders	2.00
39	Emmitt Smith	5.00
40	Terrell Davis	4.00
41	John Elway	4.00
42	Ed McCaffrey	.50
43	Shannon Sharpe	.50
44	Neil Smith	.50
45	Scott Mitchell	.50
46	Herman Moore	1.00
47	Johnnie Morton	.50
48	Barry Sanders	5.00
49	Robert Brooks	.50
50	Mark Chmura	.50
51	Brett Favre	6.00
52	Antonio Freeman	.50
53	Dorsey Levens	.50
54	Reggie White	1.00
55	Ken Dilger	.50
56	Marshall Faulk	1.00
57	Jim Harbaugh	.50
58	Marvin Harrison	2.00
59	Mark Brunell	3.00
60	Rob Johnson	.50
61	Keenan McCardell	.50
62	Natrone Means	.50
63	Jimmy Smith	.50
64	Marcus Allen	1.00
65	*Tony Gonzalez*	6.00
66	Elvis Grbac	.50
67	Greg Hill	.50
68	Tamarick Vanover	.50
69	Karim Abdul-Jabbar	.50
70	Fred Barnett	.50
71	Dan Marino	6.00
72	O.J. McDuffie	.50
73	Jerris McPhail	.50
74	Cris Carter	.50
75	Randall Cunningham	.50
76	Brad Johnson	1.00
77	Jake Reed	.50
78	Robert Smith	1.00
79	Drew Bledsoe	4.00
80	Ben Coates	.50
81	Terry Glenn	1.50
82	Curtis Martin	4.00
83	*Troy Davis*	.50
84	Heath Shuler	.50
85	Irv Smith	.50
86	*Danny Wuerffel*	1.00
87	*Tiki Barber*	8.00
88	Dave Brown	.50
89	Rodney Hampton	.50
90	*Ike Hilliard*	1.50
91	Amani Toomer	.50
92	Wayne Chrebet	.50
93	Keyshawn Johnson	2.00
94	Adrian Murrell	.50
95	Neil O'Donnell	.50
96	Dedric Ward	.50
97	Tim Brown	1.00
98	Jeff George	.50
99	Desmond Howard	.50
100	Napoleon Kaufman	.50
101	Ty Detmer	.50
102	Irving Fryar	.50
103	Bobby Hoying	.50
104	Ricky Watters	1.00
105	Jerome Bettis	1.00
106	*Will Blackwell*	.50
107	Charles Johnson	.50
108	*George Jones*	.50
109	Kordell Stewart	3.00
110	Tony Banks	2.00
111	Isaac Bruce	1.00
112	Eddie Kennison	1.00
113	Lawrence Phillips	.50
114	Jim Everett	.50
115	Stan Humphries	.50
116	*Freddie Jones*	.50
117	Tony Martin	.50
118	Junior Seau	1.00
119	*Jim Druckenmiller*	1.00
120	Garrison Hearst	.50
121	Brent Jones	.50
122	Terrell Owens	3.00
123	Jerry Rice	4.00
124	Steve Young	4.00
125	Chad Brown	.50
126	Joey Galloway	1.00
127	*Jon Kitna*	2.00
128	Warren Moon	.50
129	Chris Warren	.50
130	Mike Alstott	3.00
131	*Reidel Anthony*	2.00
132	Trent Dilfer	1.00
133	*Warrick Dunn*	6.00
134	Karl Williams	.50
135	Willie Davis	.50
136	Eddie George	3.00
137	*Joey Kent*	.50
138	Steve McNair	3.00
139	Chris Sanders	.50
140	Terry Allen	.50
141	Jamie Asher	.50
142	Stephen Davis	.50
143	Henry Ellard	.50
144	Gus Frerotte	.50

1997 Pacific Crown Royale Cel-Fusions

This 20-card insert consists of a die-cut cel football fused to a trading card. The cards were inserted 1:49.

		NM/M
Complete Set (20):		300.00
Common Player:		5.00
1	Antowain Smith	10.00
2	Troy Aikman	35.00

3 Emmitt Smith 45.00
4 Terrell Davis 35.00
5 John Elway 35.00
6 Barry Sanders 45.00
7 Brett Favre 50.00
8 Mark Brunell 20.00
9 Elvis Grbac 5.00
10 Karim Abdul-Jabbar 5.00
11 Dan Marino 50.00
12 Drew Bledsoe 35.00
13 Curtis Martin 35.00
14 Danny Wuerffel 5.00
15 Tiki Barber 12.00
16 Jeff George 5.00
17 Kordell Stewart 12.00
18 Tony Banks 5.00
19 Jerry Rice 35.00
20 Steve Young 35.00

1997 Pacific Crown Royale Chalk Talk

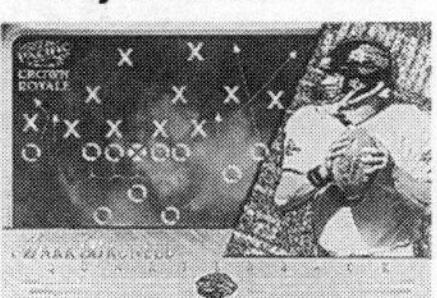

This 20-card insert features a player action shot with a laser cut diagram of one of their signature plays. This set was inserted 1:73.

NM/M
Complete Set (20): 350.00
Common Player: 10.00
1 Kerry Collins 12.00
2 Troy Aikman 35.00
3 Emmitt Smith 45.00
4 Terrell Davis 35.00
5 John Elway 35.00
6 Barry Sanders 45.00
7 Brett Favre 50.00
8 Mark Brunell 25.00
9 Marcus Allen 10.00
10 Dan Marino 50.00
11 Drew Bledsoe 35.00
12 Curtis Martin 35.00
13 Troy Davis 10.00
14 Napoleon Kaufman 10.00
15 Jerome Bettis 12.00
16 Jim Druckenmiller 10.00
17 Jerry Rice 40.00
18 Steve Young 40.00
19 Warrick Dunn 20.00
20 Eddie George 20.00

1997 Pacific Crown Royale Cramer's Choice Jumbos

Cramer's Choice is a jumbo-sized insert featuring 10 players on cards die-cut to look like trophies. This insert was found one card per box.

NM/M
Complete Set (10): 55.00
Common Player: 2.00
1 Deion Sanders 5.00
2 Emmitt Smith 12.00
3 Terrell Davis 8.00
4 John Elway 8.00
5 Barry Sanders 12.00
6 Brett Favre 15.00
7 Mark Brunell 6.00
8 Drew Bledsoe 10.00
9 Jim Druckenmiller 2.00
10 Eddie George 6.00

1997 Pacific Crown Royale Firestone on Football

These 20 cards feature players on an etched-foil design. The backs have comments from Roy Firestone. A #21 card was made featuring Firestone with comments from a future Hall of Fame QB on the back. This set was inserted 1:25.

NM/M
Complete Set (21): 150.00
Common Player: 2.00
1 Kerry Collins 4.00
2 Troy Aikman 12.00
3 Deion Sanders 8.00
4 Emmitt Smith 15.00
5 Terrell Davis 12.00
6 John Elway 12.00
7 Barry Sanders 15.00
8 Brett Favre 20.00
9 Reggie White 2.00
10 Mark Brunell 8.00
11 Marcus Allen 4.00
12 Dan Marino 20.00
13 Drew Bledsoe 15.00
14 Terry Glenn 6.00
15 Curtis Martin 12.00
16 Jerome Bettis 4.00
17 Jerry Rice 15.00
18 Steve Young 15.00
19 Eddie George 12.00
20 Gus Frerotte 2.00
21 Roy Firestone 2.00

1997 Pacific Crown Royale Pro Bowl Die-Cuts

These die-cut cards feature Pro Bowl players against an ocean background. The 20 cards were inserted 1:25.

NM/M
Complete Set (20): 225.00
Common Player: 5.00
1 Kerry Collins 8.00
2 Troy Aikman 25.00
3 Deion Sanders 15.00
4 Terrell Davis 25.00
5 John Elway 25.00
6 Shannon Sharpe 5.00
7 Barry Sanders 30.00
8 Brett Favre 35.00
9 Reggie White 5.00
10 Mark Brunell 12.00
11 Derrick Thomas 5.00
12 Drew Bledsoe 20.00
13 Ben Coates 5.00
14 Curtis Martin 20.00
15 Jerome Bettis 5.00
16 Isaac Bruce 5.00
17 Jerry Rice 25.00
18 Steve Young 25.00
19 Terry Allen 5.00
20 Gus Frerotte 5.00

1997 Pacific Dynagon

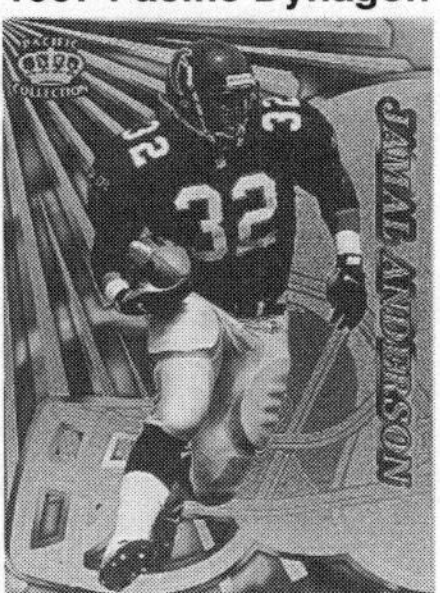

The 1997 Pacific Dynagon prism set consists of 144 regular-sized cards. The card fronts feature a gold-foil helmet background with the player's image outlined on top. The background also has the player's team colors with the player's name printed down the right side. The card backs include a head shot in the upper right-hand corner and a brief career highlight. Included with Dynagon Prism football are Tandems, Careers, Player Of The Week, Royal Connections and Best Kept Secrets insert sets. Each pack of Dynagon Prism contains three cards: one base card, one Best Kept Secrets card and one other insert card. A Silver parallel was available in retail packs (2:37), while a Copper parallel was included in 2:37 hobby packs. Red-foil parallels were found in 4:21 Treat Entertainment U.S. retail packs.

NM/M
Complete Set (144): 50.00
Common Player: .20
Minor Stars: 1.00
Copper/Red/Silver 3X to6X
Pack (3): 2.00
Wax Box (36): 45.00
1 Larry Centers .20
2 Kent Graham .20
3 Leeland McElroy .20
4 Frank Sanders .20
5 Jamal Anderson 1.00
6 Bert Emanuel .20
7 Bobby Hebert .20
8 Terance Mathis .20
9 Eric Metcalf .20
10 Derrick Alexander .20
11 Earnest Byner .20
12 Michael Jackson .20
13 Vinny Testaverde .20
14 Quinn Early .20
15 Jim Kelly .20
16 Eric Moulds 2.00
17 Andre Reed .20
18 Bruce Smith .20
19 Thurman Thomas 1.00
20 Tshimanga Biakabutuka .40
21 Mark Carrier .20
22 Kerry Collins 1.00
23 Kevin Greene .20
24 Anthony Johnson .20
25 Wesley Walls .20
26 Curtis Conway .20
27 Bobby Engram .40
28 Raymont Harris .20
29 Dave Krieg .20
30 Rashaan Salaam .40
31 Jeff Blake .40
32 Ki-Jana Carter .20
33 Garrison Hearst .20
34 Carl Pickens .20
35 Darnay Scott .20
36 Troy Aikman 3.00
37 Chris Boniol .20
38 Michael Irvin 1.00
39 Deion Sanders 2.00
40 Emmitt Smith 5.00
41 Herschel Walker .20
42 Terrell Davis 4.00
43 John Elway 4.00
44 Ed McCaffrey .20
45 Shannon Sharpe .20
46 Alfred Williams .20
47 Scott Mitchell .20
48 Herman Moore 1.00
49 Brett Perriman .20
50 Barry Sanders 5.00
51 Edgar Bennett .20
52 Robert Brooks .20
53 Mark Chmura .20
54 Brett Favre 5.00
55 Antonio Freeman .75
56 Desmond Howard .20
57 Reggie White .75
58 Chris Chandler .20
59 Eddie George 3.00
60 James McKeehan .20
61 Steve McNair 3.00
62 Chris Sanders .20
63 Sean Dawkins .20
64 Ken Dilger .20
65 Marshall Faulk 2.00
66 Jim Harbaugh .20
67 Marvin Harrison 2.50
68 Tony Boselli .20
69 Mark Brunell 2.00
70 Keenan McCardell .20
71 Natrone Means .50
72 Jimmy Smith .20
73 Marcus Allen 1.00
74 Kimble Anders .20
75 Dale Carter .20
76 Greg Hill .20
77 Derrick Thomas .20
78 Tamarick Vanover .50
79 Karim Abdul-Jabbar .50
80 Dan Marino 5.00
81 O.J. McDuffie .20
82 Jerris McPhail .20
83 Zach Thomas 1.00
84 Cris Carter .20
85 Brad Johnson .20
86 Jake Reed .20
87 Robert Smith .20
88 Drew Bledsoe 3.00
89 Ben Coates .20
90 Terry Glenn 1.00
91 Curtis Martin 3.00
92 Willie McGinest .20
93 Jim Everett .20
94 Michael Haynes .20
95 Haywood Jeffires .20
96 Ray Zellars .20
97 Dave Brown .20
98 Rodney Hampton .20
99 Danny Kanell .20
100 Thomas Lewis .20
101 Wayne Chrebet .20
102 Keyshawn Johnson 2.00
103 Adrian Murrell .20
104 Neil O'Donnell .20
105 Tim Brown 1.00
106 Rickey Dudley .50
107 Jeff Hostetler .20
108 Napoleon Kaufman .20
109 Ty Detmer .20
110 Jason Dunn .20
111 Irving Fryar .20
112 Chris T. Jones .20
113 Ricky Watters .20
114 Jerome Bettis 1.00
115 Chad Brown .20
116 Kordell Stewart 2.00
117 Mike Tomczak .20
118 Rod Woodson .20
119 Tony Banks 1.00
120 Isaac Bruce 1.50
121 Eddie Kennison .50
122 Lawrence Phillips .20
123 Terrell Fletcher .20
124 Stan Humphries .20
125 Tony Martin .20
126 Junior Seau .20
127 Elvis Grbac .20
128 Terrell Owens 2.00
129 Ted Popson .20
130 Jerry Rice 4.00
131 Steve Young 4.00
132 John Friesz .20
133 Joey Galloway 2.00
134 Michael McCrary .20
135 Lamar Smith .20
136 Chris Warren .20
137 Mike Alstott 1.00
138 Trent Dilfer .20
139 Courtney Hawkins .20
140 Errict Rhett 1.00
141 Terry Allen .20
142 Henry Ellard .20
143 Gus Frerotte .20
144 Leslie Shepherd .20

1997 Pacific Dynagon Careers

The 10-card, regular-sized cards were inserted every 360 packs in Dynagon Prism. The card fronts feature gold foil in an outline of a football. The player's name is printed down the right side in blue and the player's image is outlined over a crescent-shaped swirl of the player's statistics. The card backs feature a circular photo of the player with several career highlights and are numbered 1-10.

NM/M
Complete Set (10): 225.00
Common Player: 10.00
1 Jim Kelly 15.00
2 Emmitt Smith 45.00
3 John Elway 35.00
4 Barry Sanders 45.00
5 Brett Favre 50.00
6 Reggie White 10.00
7 Dan Marino 50.00
8 Drew Bledsoe 25.00
9 Jerry Rice 35.00
10 Steve Young 35.00

1997 Pacific Dynagon Player of the Week

The 20-card, regular-sized set was inserted every 37 packs of Dynagon Prism. The card fronts feature an action shot centered in a diamond. The player's first name is printed on the upper right section of the diamond while the last name appears on the lower left section. The player's team helmet is located in the upper right part of the horizontal card front, centered in a diamond. The card backs feature another shot of the player, again centered in a diamond. The card number corresponds with the week the player excelled during the 1996 season and was voted by visitors to Pacific's website as the Player Of The Week.

NM/M
Complete Set (20): 125.00
Common Player: 2.00
1 Karim Abdul-Jabbar 2.00
2 Eddie George 5.00
3 Curtis Martin 8.00
4 Mark Brunell 6.00
5 John Elway 10.00
6 Drew Bledsoe 8.00
7 Emmitt Smith 12.00
8 Terrell Davis 8.00
9 Troy Aikman 8.00
10 Jerry Rice 10.00
11 Dan Marino 15.00
12 Barry Sanders 12.00
13 Brett Favre 15.00
14 Steve Young 10.00
15 Kerry Collins 2.00
16 Eddie Kennison 2.00
17 Terry Allen 2.00
18 Brett Favre 15.00
19 Desmond Howard 2.00
20 Mark Brunell 6.00

1997 Pacific Dynagon Royal Connections

Royal Connections, inserted every 73 packs of 1997 Dynagon Prism, is actually a 30-card, regular-sized, die-cut set that can be fitted with its counterpart to form 15 3-1/2" x 4-1/4" cards. The cards are numbered to 15 with "A" and "B" versions. The A versions feature quarterbacks and the right edge of the card is die-cut in the shape of a football with laces. The "B" versions highlight a wide receiver from a corresponding team and the left side is die-cut to allow the "A" version to fit with it to form a single card.

NM/M
Complete Set (30): 225.00
Common Player: 4.00
Minor Stars: 8.00
Inserted 1:73
1A Kent Graham 4.00
1B Larry Centers 4.00
2A Jim Kelly 8.00
2B Andre Reed 4.00
3A Kerry Collins 8.00
3B Wesley Walls 4.00
4A Jeff Blake 4.00
4B Carl Pickens 4.00
5A Troy Aikman 15.00
5B Michael Irvin 8.00
6A John Elway 15.00
6B Shannon Sharpe 8.00
7A Brett Favre 25.00
7B Antonio Freeman 8.00
8A Mark Brunell 10.00
8B Keenan McCardell 4.00
9A Dan Marino 25.00
9B O.J. McDuffie 4.00
10A Brad Johnson 8.00
10B Jake Reed 4.00
11A Drew Bledsoe 15.00
11B Terry Glenn 8.00
12A Ty Detmer 4.00
12B Irving Fryar 4.00
13A Kordell Stewart 8.00
13B Charles Johnson 4.00
14A Tony Banks 4.00
14B Isaac Bruce 8.00
15A Steve Young 15.00
15B Jerry Rice 15.00

1997 Pacific Dynagon Tandems

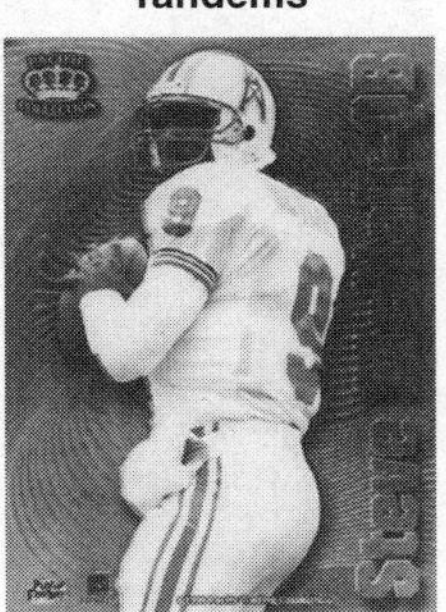

Inserted 1:37 packs, the 72 double-fronted cards feature the same 144 players from the base set, with one player on each side. Foiled in emerald, the cards have the numbers printed in the upper right.

NM/M
Complete Set (72): 600.00
Common Player: 4.00
Minor Stars: 8.00
Inserted 1:37
1 Jerome Bettis, Eddie George 15.00
2 Jamal Anderson, Eric Moulds 15.00
3 Kerry Collins, Kordell Stewart 15.00
4 Jeff Blake, Ty Detmer 4.00
5 Michael Irvin, Tim Brown 8.00
6 Deion Sanders, Ray Zellars 8.00
7 Emmitt Smith, Steve Young 25.00
8 Terrell Davis, Barry Sanders 25.00
9 John Elway, Dan Marino 25.00
10 Robert Brooks, Eddie Kennison 4.00
11 Mark Chmura, Shannon Sharpe 8.00
12 Brett Favre, Mark Brunell 25.00
13 Antonio Freeman, Isaac Bruce 10.00
14 Desmond Howard, Natrone Means 8.00
15 Reggie White, Keyshawn Johnson 8.00
16 Edgar Bennett, Chris Sanders 4.00
17 Terry Glenn, Jerry Rice 20.00
18 Steve McNair, Karim Abdul-Jabbar 15.00
19 Marshall Faulk, Tamarick Vanover 8.00
20 Gus Frerotte, Brad Johnson 4.00
21 Jim Kelly, Tim Biakabutuka 8.00
22 Lawrence Phillips, Ben Coates 4.00
23 Napoleon Kaufman, Terrell Owens 12.00
24 Elvis Grbac, Junior Seau 8.00
25 Drew Bledsoe, Tony Banks 15.00
26 Curtis Martin, Troy Aikman 20.00
27 Curtis Conway, Brett Perriman 4.00
28 Bobby Engram, Larry Centers 4.00
29 Raymont Harris, Eric Metcalf 4.00
30 Dave Krieg, Derrick Alexander 4.00
31 Rashaan Salaam, Leeland McElroy 4.00
32 Ki-Jana Carter, Herman Moore 8.00
33 Garrison Hearst, Earnest Byner 4.00
34 Carl Pickens, Frank Sanders 4.00
35 Darnay Scott, Michael Jackson 4.00
36 Chris Boniol, Kent Graham 4.00
37 Herschel Walker, Thurman Thomas 8.00
38 Ed McCaffrey, Quinn Early 8.00
39 Alfred Williams, Mike Alstott 4.00
40 Scott Mitchell, Mark Carrier 4.00
41 Bert Emanuel, Henry Ellard 4.00
42 Bobby Hebert, Trent Dilfer 8.00
43 Terance Mathis, Andre Reed 4.00
44 Vinny Testaverde, Chris Warren 4.00
45 Bruce Smith, Kevin Greene 4.00
46 Anthony Johnson, Terry Allen 4.00
47 Wesley Walls, Errict Rhett 4.00
48 John Friesz, Jeff Hostetler 4.00
49 Joey Galloway, Leslie Shepherd 8.00
50 Michael McCrary, Chris T. Jones 4.00
51 Lamar Smith, Courtney Hawkins 4.00
52 Rickey Dudley, Jason Dunn 4.00
53 Irving Fryar, Tony Martin 4.00
54 Ted Popson, Ricky Watters 4.00
55 Chad Brown, Zach Thomas 8.00
56 Mike Tomczak, Stan Humphries 4.00
57 Rod Woodson, Willie McGinnest 4.00
58 Terrell Fletcher, Jerris McPhail 4.00
59 O.J. McDuffie, Cris Carter 8.00
60 Jake Reed, Marcus Allen 8.00
61 Robert Smith, Greg Hill 4.00
62 Jim Everett, Dave Brown 4.00
63 Michael Haynes, James McKeehan 4.00
64 Haywood Jeffires, Sean Dawkins 4.00
65 Rodney Hampton, Adrian Murrell 4.00
66 Danny Kanell, Marvin Harrison 8.00
67 Thomas Lewis, Dale Carter 4.00
68 Wayne Chrebet, Ken Dilger 8.00
69 Neil O'Donnell, Chris Chandler 4.00
70 Jim Harbaugh, Jimmy Smith 4.00
71 Derrick Thomas, Tony Boselli 4.00
72 Keenan McCardell, Kimble Anders 4.00

1997 Pacific Invincible

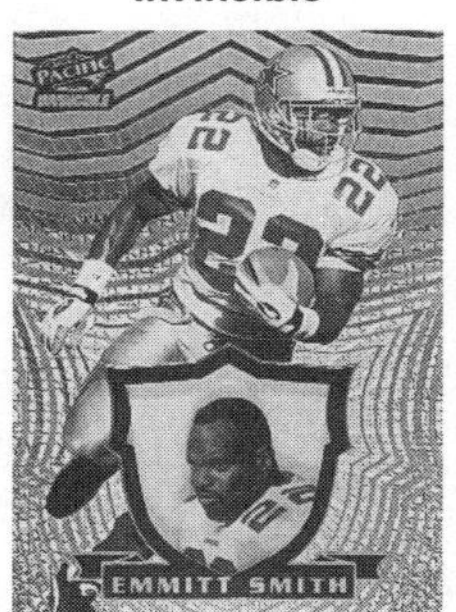

The 150-card set features a player action photo superimposed over a multicolored and gold-foiled background. At the bottom center of the card front is a player head shot printed on acetate. The player's name is printed in gold foil inside a black banner beneath the shield. The Pacific Invincible logo is located in the upper left. The base set is paralleled in Copper foil in hobby packs (2:37), Silver parallel in retail (2:37) and Platinum Blue (1:73). Red-foil parallel was seeded 4:37 in Treat Entertainment U.S. retail packs.

		NM/M
Complete Set (150):		75.00
Common Player:		.25
Minor Stars:		1.00
Copper Cards:		3X-6X
Silver Cards:		3X-6X
Blue Cards:		5X-10X
Pack (3):		2.00
Wax Box (36):		55.00
1	Larry Centers	.25
2	Kent Graham	.25
3	LeShon Johnson	.25
4	Leeland McElroy	1.00
5	*Jake Plummer*	7.00
6	Frank Sanders	.25
7	Morten Andersen	.25
8	Jamal Anderson	1.00
9	Bert Emanuel	.25
10	Bobby Hebert	.25
11	Roell Preston	.25
12	Derrick Alexander	.25
13	Michael Jackson	.25
14	Bam Morris	.25
15	Vinny Testaverde	.25
16	Todd Collins	.50
17	Andre Reed	.25
18	*Antowain Smith*	3.00
19	Steve Tasker	.25
20	Thurman Thomas	1.00
21	Tim Biakabutuka	.50
22	*Rae Carruth*	.50
23	Kerry Collins	2.00
24	Kevin Greene	.25
25	Anthony Johnson	.25
26	Wesley Walls	.25
27	*Darnell Autry*	1.00
28	Curtis Conway	.25
29	Raymont Harris	.25
30	Rashaan Salaam	1.00
31	Jeff Blake	.50
32	Ki-Jana Carter	1.00
33	David Dunn	.25
34	Carl Pickens	.25
35	Darnay Scott	.25
36	Troy Aikman	4.00
37	Michael Irvin	1.00
38	Deion Sanders	3.00
39	Emmitt Smith	5.00
40	Herschel Walker	.25
41	Kevin Williams	.25
42	Steve Atwater	.25
43	Terrell Davis	4.00
44	John Elway	4.00
45	Ed McCaffrey	.25
46	Shannon Sharpe	.25
47	Scott Mitchell	.25
48	Herman Moore	1.00
49	Brett Perriman	.25
50	Barry Sanders	5.00
51	Edgar Bennett	.25
52	Robert Brooks	.25
53	Brett Favre	6.00
54	Antonio Freeman	.50
55	Dorsey Levens	.25
56	Reggie White	1.00
57	Eddie George	3.00
58	Steve McNair	3.00
59	Chris Sanders	.25
60	Sean Dawkins	.25
61	Marshall Faulk	1.00
62	Jim Harbaugh	.25
63	Marvin Harrison	2.50
64	Brian Stablein	.25
65	Mark Brunell	2.00
66	Keenan McCardell	.25
67	Natrone Means	.50
68	Pete Mitchell	.25
69	Jimmy Smith	.25
70	Marcus Allen	1.00
71	Kimble Anders	.25
72	Greg Hill	.25
73	Kevin Lockett	.25
74	Derrick Thomas	.25
75	Tamarick Vanover	.25
76	Karim Abdul-Jabbar	.50
77	*Yatil Green*	.50
78	Randal Hill	.25
79	Dan Marino	6.00
80	Stanley Pritchett	.25
81	Irving Spikes	.25
82	Cris Carter	.25
83	Brad Johnson	.25
84	Robert Smith	.25
85	Darryl Talley	.25
86	Drew Bledsoe	3.00
87	Ben Coates	.25
88	Terry Glenn	.75
89	Curtis Martin	3.00
90	*Sedrick Shaw*	.50
91	Mario Bates	.25
92	*Troy Davis*	.50
93	Jim Everett	.25
94	Michael Haynes	.25
95	*Tiki Barber*	4.00
96	Dave Brown	.25
97	Rodney Hampton	.25
98	*Ike Hilliard*	4.00
99	Danny Kanell	.25
100	Wayne Chrebet	.25
101	Keyshawn Johnson	1.00
102	Adrian Murrell	.25
103	Neil O'Donnell	.25
104	Alex Van Dyke	.25
105	Joe Aska	.25
106	Tim Brown	1.00
107	Rickey Dudley	.25
108	Napoleon Kaufman	.50
109	Carl Kidd	.25
110	Ty Detmer	.25
111	Jason Dunn	.25
112	Irving Fryar	.25
113	Bobby Hoying	.25
114	Ricky Watters	1.00
115	Jerome Bettis	1.00
116	Charles Johnson	.25
117	Greg Lloyd	.25
118	Kordell Stewart	2.00
119	Rod Woodson	.25
120	Tony Banks	1.00
121	Isaac Bruce	1.00
122	Eddie Kennison	.50
123	Lawrence Phillips	.50
124	Stan Humphries	.25
125	Tony Martin	.25
126	*Corey Dillon*	6.00
127	Leonard Russell	.25
128	Junior Seau	1.00
129	*Jim Druckenmiller*	1.00
130	Marc Edwards	.25
131	Ken Norton Jr.	.25
132	Terrell Owens	2.00
133	Jerry Rice	5.00
134	Iheanyi Uwaezuoke	.25
135	Steve Young	4.00
136	John Friesz	.25
137	Joey Galloway	2.00
138	Warren Moon	.25
139	Todd Peterson	.25
140	Chris Warren	.25
141	Mike Alstott	.25
142	*Reidel Anthony*	1.00
143	Trent Dilfer	1.00
144	*Warrick Dunn*	2.00
145	Errict Rhett	1.00
146	Terry Allen	.25
147	Henry Ellard	.25
148	Gus Frerotte	.25
149	Brian Mitchell	.25
150	Leslie Shepherd	.25

1997 Pacific Invincible Canton, Ohio

The 10-card Canton, Ohio, chase set was inserted 1:361 packs. The player's photo is superimposed over a crown and multicolored background. The player is standing on an oval, while his name is printed directly beneath it. The chase set's name is printed at the top, with the Invincible logo at the top center.

		NM/M
Complete Set (10):		250.00
Common Player:		10.00
1	Troy Aikman	25.00
2	Emmitt Smith	35.00
3	John Elway	25.00
4	Barry Sanders	35.00
5	Brett Favre	40.00
6	Reggie White	10.00
7	Marcus Allen	10.00
8	Dan Marino	40.00
9	Jerry Rice	30.00
10	Steve Young	30.00

A player's name in *italic* type indicates a rookie card.

1997 Pacific Invincible Moments in Time

The 20-card Moments in Time was inserted 1:73 packs. The die-cut cards have a scoreboard-like front, with a player photo on the left. His name is printed beneath his team's and opponent's helmets. The date of the game, his yards and stats, along with the score of the game are printed on the front.

		NM/M
Complete Set (20):		225.00
Common Player:		5.00
1	Kerry Collins	8.00
2	Troy Aikman	15.00
3	Emmitt Smith	20.00
4	Terrell Davis	15.00
5	John Elway	20.00
6	Barry Sanders	25.00
7	Brett Favre	30.00
8	Reggie White	5.00
9	Eddie George	12.00
10	Mark Brunell	12.00
11	Marcus Allen	10.00
12	Karim Abdul-Jabbar	5.00
13	Dan Marino	30.00
14	Drew Bledsoe	20.00
15	Terry Glenn	12.00
16	Curtis Martin	15.00
17	Jerome Bettis	10.00
18	Eddie Kennison	5.00
19	Jerry Rice	25.00
20	Steve Young	25.00

1997 Pacific Invincible Pop Cards

The 10-card set was inserted 2:37 packs. The front of the card included a player photo, which was surrounded by gold-foil squares. The player's name and position are printed at the bottom center. The Pop Card redemption program worked like this: Remove the Pop Card piece from the card back to reveal a player photo and create a new card. If a collector collected all four pieces of a given player's card, the pieces could be sent to Pacific to receive a limited edition gold-foil card of that same player. Details are provided on the backs of each card.

		NM/M
Complete Set (10):		35.00
Common Player:		2.00
1	Kerry Collins	2.00
2	Troy Aikman	6.00
3	Emmitt Smith	10.00
4	John Elway	6.00
5	Barry Sanders	10.00
6	Brett Favre	12.00
7	Mark Brunell	4.00
8	Dan Marino	12.00
9	Drew Bledsoe	6.00
10	Jerry Rice	8.00

1997 Pacific Invincible Smash Mouth

This 220-card bonus set was inserted one or two per pack. The cards feature a player photo on the front inside an oval, surrounded by a metal-diamond-type border. The team's logo is in the lower left, while the player's position is in the lower right. The player's name runs along the bottom of the front. In addition, a Smash Mouth X-tra 59-card set was also inserted one or two cards per pack. The card fronts include a large photo on the left, with the player's name printed in a stencil font vertically along the right border. The backs include a photo in the upper right corner.

		NM/M
Complete Set (220):		15.00
Common Player:		.10
Minor Stars:		.20
1	Don Majkowski	.10
2	Leo Araguz	.10
3	John Carney	.10
4	Brett Favre	2.25
5	Cole Ford	.10
6	Marty Carter	.10
7	John Elway	.75
8	Mark Brunell	1.00
9	Rodney Peete	.10
10	Jeff Feagles	.10
11	Drew Bledsoe	1.00
12	Kerry Collins	.75
13	Dan Marino	2.00
14	Torrian Gray	.10
15	Reidel Anthony	.75
16	Jim Druckenmiller	1.00
17	Jim Everett	.10
18	Pat Barnes	.20
19	Ike Hilliard	.50
20	Barry Sanders	1.25
21	Terry Allen	.20
22	Emmitt Smith	2.00
23	Antowain Smith	.75
24	Robert Griffith	.10
25	Mickey Washington	.10
26	Napoleon Kaufman	.30
27	Eddie George	1.50
28	Curtis Martin	1.00
29	Anthony Lynn	.10
30	Terrell Davis	1.00
31	Steve Broussard	.10
32	Ricky Watters	.20
33	Karim Abdul-Jabbar	.50
34	Thurman Thomas	.20
35	Ross Verba	.10
36	Jerome Bettis	.20
37	Chad Cota	.10
38	Antonio Langham	.10
39	Brett Maxie	.10
40	James Hasty	.10
41	Conrad Hamilton	.10
42	Chris Warren	.10
43	George Jones	.10
44	Byron Hanspard	.50
45	Henri Crockett	.10
46	Brent Alexander	.10
47	John Lynch	.10
48	Renaldo Wynn	.10
49	Jared Tomich	.10
50	James Francis	.10
51	Brian Williams	.10
52	Kevin Mawae	.10
53	Marvcus Patton	.10
54	Mike Barber	.10
55	Robert Jones	.10
56	Ernest Dixon	.10
57	Mo Lewis	.10
58	Peter Boulware	.10
59	Wayne Simmons	.10
60	Anthony Redmon	.10
61	Tim Ruddy	.10
62	Victor Green	.10
63	Kirk Lowdermilk	.10
64	John Jurkovic	.10
65	John Jackson	.10
66	Kevin Gogan	.10
67	Adam Schrieber	.10
68	Mike Morris	.10
69	Albert Connell	.10
70	Tony Mayberry	.10
71	Mark Tuinei	.10
72	Harry Swayne	.10
73	Todd Steussie	.10
74	Glenn Parker	.10
75	D'Marco Farr	.10
76	Ed Simmons	.10
77	Tarik Glenn	.10
78	Rick Hamilton	.10
79	Dave Szott	.10
80	Jerry Rice	1.00
81	Tim Brown	.20
82	Charlie Jones	.10
83	Jerry Wunsch	.10
84	Lonnie Johnson	.10
85	Reggie Johnson	.10
86	Willie Davis	.10
87	Greg Clark	.10
88	Deems May	.10
89	J.J. Birden	.10
90	Chuck Smith	.10
91	Coleman Rudolph	.10
92	Leon Johnson	.10
93	Trace Armstrong	.10
94	John Thierry	.10
95	Dean Wells	.10
96	Mike Jones	.10
97	Mike Lodish	.10
98	Tony Siragusa	.10
99	Daved Benefield	.10
100	Michael Bankston	.10
101	Jamal Anderson	.50
102	Greg Montgomery	.10
103	Mark Maddox	.10
104	Matt Elliott	.10
105	Joe Cain	.10
106	Jeff Blake	.20
107	Troy Aikman	1.00
108	Brian Habib	.10
109	Pete Chryplewicz	.10
110	Earl Dotson	.10
111	Joe Bowden	.10
112	Marshall Faulk	1.00
113	Reggie Barlow	.10
114	Marcus Allen	.50
115	Jeff Buckey	.10
116	Mitch Berger	.10
117	Corwin Brown	.10
118	Troy Davis	.10
119	Rodney Hampton	.10
120	Tom Knight	.10
121	Michael Booker	.10
122	Matt Stover	.10
123	Mark Pike	.10
124	Rohn Stark	.10
125	Todd Sauerbrun	.10
126	Corey Dillon	.50
127	Tyji Armstrong	.10
128	Vaughn Hebron	.10
129	Antonio London	.10
130	Santana Dotson	.10
131	Cris Dishman	.10
132	Stephen Grant	.10
133	Mike Hollis	.10
134	Martin Bayless	.10
135	Sam Madison	.10
136	Esera Tuaolo	.10
137	Hason Graham	.10
138	Jim Dombrowski	.10
139	Bernard Holsey	.10
140	Kyle Brady	.10
141	David Klingler	.10
142	Don Griffin	.10
143	Bernard Dafney	.10
144	Derrick Harris	.10
145	Charles Johnson	.10
146	Dedrick Dodge	.10
147	Antonio Edwards	.10
148	Jorge Diaz	.10
149	Marc Logan	.10
150	Lou D'Agostino	.10
151	Lance Johnstone	.10
152	Ray Farmer	.10
153	Brentson Buckner	.10
154	Tony Banks	.50
155	'OMar Ellison	.10
156	Derrick Deese	.10
157	Howard Ballard	.10
158	Ronde Barber	.10
159	Gus Frerotte	.10
160	Leeland McElroy	.10
161	Devin Bush	.10
162	Eddie Sutter	.10
163	Sam Rogers	.10
164	Carl Simpson	.10
165	Lee Johnson	.10
166	Tony Casillas	.10
167	Randy Hilliard	.10
168	Ryan McNeil	.10
169	William Henderson	.10
170	Irv Eatman	.10
171	Derwin Gray	.10
172	Rob Johnson	.10
173	Derrick Walker	.10
174	Chris Singleton	.10
175	Chris Walsh	.10
176	Marty Moore	.10
177	Paul Green	.10
178	Brian Williams	.10
179	Robert Farmer	.10
180	Derrick Witherspoon	.10
181	Jim Miller	.10
182	James Harris	.10
183	Shannon Mitchell	.10
184	Steve Young	.75
185	Ronnie Harris	.10
186	Trent Dilfer	.25
187	Joe Patton	.10
188	Jake Plummer	.30
189	Ron George	.10
190	Vinny Testaverde	.10
191	Ryan Wetnight	.10
192	Steve Tovar	.10
193	Godfrey Myles	.10
194	Rod Smith	.30
195	Zefross Moss	.10
196	Jerald Sowell	.10
197	Jason Layman	.10
198	Ray McElroy	.10
199	Tom McManus	.10
200	Shawn Wooden	.10
201	Tony Johnson	.10
202	James Farrior	.10
203	Marc Woodard	.10
204	Chad Scott	.10
205	Dwayne White	.10
206	Warrick Dunn	1.00
207	Joe Wolf	.10
208	Dedric Ward	.10
209	Bennie Thompson	.10
210	Bracey Walker	.10
211	Tracy Scroggins	.10
212	Derrick Mason	.30
213	Ed King	.10
214	Harry Galbreath	.10
215	Joel Steed	.10
216	Jackie Harris	.10
217	Craig Sauer	.10
218	Reinard Wilson	.10
219	Barron Wortham	.10
220	Errict Rhett	.10

1997 Pacific Invincible Smash Mouth X-tra

This 59-card set was randomly inserted into packs of Invincible. The card features the player's name running up the right side in team colors, and is numbered in the bottom right corner on the back where the insert name is also indicated.

		NM/M
Complete Set (59):		15.00
Common Player:		.10
Minor Stars:		.20
1	Steve Young	.75
2	Jeff Blake	.20
3	Troy Aikman	1.00
4	Brett Favre	2.25
5	Gus Frerotte	.10
6	Tony Banks	.50
7	John Elway	.75
8	Mark Brunell	1.00
9	Rodney Peete	.10
10	Trent Dilfer	.30
11	Drew Bledsoe	1.00
12	Kerry Collins	.75
13	Dan Marino	2.00
14	Vinny Testaverde	.10
15	Reidel Anthony	.75
16	Jim Druckenmiller	.30
17	Jim Everett	.10
18	Pat Barnes	.30
19	Ike Hilliard	.50
20	Barry Sanders	1.25
21	Terry Allen	.20
22	Emmitt Smith	2.00
23	Antowain Smith	.75
24	Jake Plummer	.30
25	Vaughn Hebron	.10
26	Napoleon Kaufman	.25
27	Eddie George	1.50
28	Curtis Martin	1.00
29	Rodney Hampton	.10
30	Terrell Davis	1.00
31	Marshall Faulk	.20
32	Ricky Watters	.20
33	Karim Abdul-Jabbar	.50
34	Thurman Thomas	.20
35	Troy Davis	.50
36	Jerome Bettis	.20
37	Warrick Dunn	1.00
38	Leeland McElroy	.10
39	William Henderson	.10
40	Jamal Anderson	.20
41	Errict Rhett	.10
42	Chris Warren	.10
43	George Jones	.10
44	Byron Hanspard	.50
45	Jerald Sowell	.10
46	Marcus Allen	.20
47	Kirk Lowdermilk	.10
48	Brian Habib	.10
49	Derrick Mason	.30
50	Jerry Rice	1.00
51	Albert Connell	.10
52	Kyle Brady	.10
53	Tim Brown	.20
54	Charles Johnson	.10
55	Jackie Harris	.10
56	Lonnie Johnson	.10
57	Deems May	.10
58	Peter Boulware	.10
59	Wayne Simmons	.10

1997 Pacific Philadelphia

The 330-card set features a white border on the front of the cards, surrounding the player photo. The Philadelphia logo is in the upper left. The bottom left of the photo includes the player's name, team and position. The team's logo is printed in the lower right. The backs included the player's name inside a stripe at the top left, with the card number inside a circle in the upper right. The player's bio, highlights and stats round out the back. Two football player images are printed in the background of the highlights and stats. Red-foil parallels were included one per Treat Entertainment U.S. retail pack.

		NM/M
Complete Set (330):		25.00
Common Player:		.05
Minor Stars:		.10
Pack (8):		1.00
Wax Box (36):		35.00
1	Kevin Butler	.05
2	Larry Centers	.05
3	Kent Graham	.05
4	Leeland McElroy	.10
5	Ronald McKinnon	.05
6	Johnny McWilliams	.05
7	Brad Ottis	.05
8	Frank Sanders	.05
9	Rob Selby	.05
10	Cedric Smith	.05
11	Joe Staysniak	.05
12	Cornelius Bennett	.05
13	David Brandon	.05
14	Tyrone Brown	.05
15	John Burrough	.05
16	Browning Nagle	.05
17	Dan Owens	.05
18	Anthony Phillips	.05
19	Roell Preston	.05
20	Darnell Walker	.05
21	Bob Whitfield	.05
22	Mike Zandofsky	.05
23	Vashone Adams	.05
24	Derrick Alexander	.05
25	Harold Bishop	.05
26	Jeff Blackshear	.05
27	Donny Brady	.05
28	Mike Frederick	.05
29	Tim Goad	.05
30	DeRon Jenkins	.05
31	Ray Lewis	.05
32	Rick Lyle	.05
33	Bam Morris	.05
34	Chris Brantley	.05
35	Jeff Burris	.05
36	Todd Collins	.10
37	Rob Coons	.05
38	Corbin Lacina	.05
39	Emanuel Martin	.05
40	Marlo Perry	.05
41	Sahwn Price	.05
42	Thomas Smith	.05
43	Matt Stevens	.05
44	Thurman Thomas	.15
45	Jay Barker	.05
46	Tshimanga Biakabutuka	.10
47	Kerry Collins	1.50
48	Matt Elliott	.05
49	Howard Griffith	.05
50	Anthony Johnson	.05
51	John Kasay	.05
52	Muhsin Muhammad	.40
53	Winslow Oliver	.05
54	Walter Rasby	.05
55	Gerald Williams	.05
56	Mark Butterfield	.05
57	Bryan Cox	.05
58	Mike Faulkerson	.05
59	Paul Grasmanis	.05
60	Robert Green	.05
61	Jack Jackson	.05
62	Bob Neely	.05
63	Todd Perry	.05
64	Evan Pilgrim	.05
65	Octus Polk	.05
66	Rashaan Salaam	.10
67	Willie Anderson	.05
68	Jeff Blake	.20
69	Scott Brumfield	.05
70	Jeff Cothran	.05
71	Gerald Dixon	.05
72	Garrison Hearst	.05
73	James Hundon	.05
74	Brian Milne	.05
75	Troy Sadowski	.05
76	Tom Tumulty	.05
77	Kimo Von Oelhoffen	.05
78	Troy Aikman	1.50
79	Dale Hellestrae	.05
80	Roger Harper	.05
81	Michael Irvin	.10
82	John Jett	.05
83	Kelvin Martin	.05
84	Deion Sanders	.75
85	Darrin Smith	.05
86	Emmitt Smith	3.00
87	Herschel Walker	.05
88	Charlie Williams	.05
89	Glenn Cadrez	.05
90	Dwayne Carswell	.05
91	Terrell Davis	1.75
92	David Diaz-Infante	.05
93	John Elway	1.00
94	Harold Hasselbach	.05
95	Tory James	.05
96	Bill Musgrave	.05
97	Ralph Tamm	.05
98	Maa Tunavasa	.05
99	Gary Zimmerman	.05
100	Shane Bonham	.05
101	Stephen Boyd	.05
102	Jeff Hartings	.05
103	Hessley Hempstead	.05
104	Scott Kowalkowski	.05
105	Herman Moore	.20
106	Barry Sanders	1.50
107	Tony Semple	.05
108	Ryan Stewart	.05
109	Mike Wells	.05
110	Richard Woodley	.05
111	Brett Favre	3.00
112	Bernardo Harris	.05
113	Keith McKenzie	.05
114	Terry Mickens	.05
115	Doug Pederson	.05
116	Jeff Thomason	.05
117	Adam Timmerman	.05
118	Reggie White	.20
119	Bruce Wilkerson	.05
120	Gabe Wilkens	.05
121	Tyrone Williams	.05
122	Al Del Greco	.05
123	Anthony Dorsett	.05
124	Josh Evans	.05
125	Eddie George	2.00
126	Lemanski Hall	.05
127	Ronnie Harmon	.05
128	Steve McNair	1.00
129	Michael Roan	.05
130	Marcus Robertson	.05
131	Jon Runyan	.05
132	Chris Sanders	.05
133	Kerwin Bell	.05
134	Marshall Faulk	.30
135	Clif Groce	.05
136	Jim Harbaugh	.05
137	Marvin Harrison	1.00
138	Eric Mahlum	.05
139	Tony Mandarich	.05
140	Dedric Mathis	.05
141	Marcus Pollard	.05
142	Scott Slutzker	.05
143	Mark Stock	.05
144	Bucky Brooks	.05
145	Mark Brunell	1.50
146	Kendricke Bullard	.05
147	Randy Jordan	.05
148	Jeff Kopp	.05
149	Le'Shai Maston	.05
150	Keenan McCardell	.05
151	Clyde Simmons	.05
152	Jimmy Smith	.05
153	Rich Tylski	.05
154	Dave Widell	.05
155	Marcus Allen	.10
156	Keith Cash	.05
157	Donnie Edwards	.05
158	Trezelle Jenkins	.05
159	Sean LaChapelle	.05
160	Greg Manusky	.05
161	Steve Matthews	.05
162	Pellom McDaniels	.05
163	Chris Penn	.05
164	Danny Villa	.05
165	Jerome Woods	.05
166	Karim Abdul-Jabbar	.50
167	John Bock	.05
168	O.J. Brigance	.05
169	Norman Hand	.05
170	Anthony Harris	.05
171	Larry Izzo	.05
172	Charles Jordan	.05
173	Dan Marino	3.00
174	Everett McIver	.05
175	Joe Nedney	.05
176	Robert Wilson	.05
177	David Dixon	.05
178	Charlie Evans	.05
179	Hunter Goodwin	.05
180	Ben Hanks	.05
181	Warren Moon	.10
182	Harold Morrow	.05
183	Fernando Smith	.05
184	Robert Smith	.10
185	Sean Vanhorse	.05
186	Jay Walker	.05
187	DeWayne Washington	.05
188	Moe Williams	.05
189	Mike Bartrum	.05
190	Drew Bledsoe	1.50
191	Troy Brown	.05
192	Chad Eaton	.05
193	Sam Gash	.05
194	Mike Gisler	.05
195	Curtis Martin	1.75
196	Dave Richards	.05
197	Todd Rucci	.05
198	Chris Sullivan	.05
199	Adam Vinatieri	8.00
200	Doug Brien	.05
201	Derek Brown	.05
202	Lee DeRamus	.05
203	Jim Everett	.05
204	Mercury Hayes	.05
205	Joe Johnson	.05
206	Henry Lusk	.05
207	Andy McCollum	.05
208	Alex Molden	.05
209	Ray Zellars	.05
210	Marcus Buckley	.05
211	Doug Coleman	.05
212	Percy Ellsworth	.05
213	Rodney Hampton	.05
214	Brian Saxton	.05
215	Jason Sehorn	.05
216	Stan White	.05
217	Corey Widmer	.05
218	Rodney Young	.05
219	Rob Zatechka	.05
220	Henry Bailey	.05
221	Chad Cascadden	.05
222	Wayne Chrebet	.05
223	Tyrone Davis	.05
224	Kwame Ellis	.05
225	Glenn Foley	.05
226	Erik Howard	.05
227	Gary Jones	.05
228	Adrian Murrell	.05
229	Marc Spindler	.05
230	Lonnie Young	.05
231	Eric Zomalt	.05
232	Tim Brown	.10
233	Aundray Bruce	.05
234	Darren Carrington	.05
235	Rick Cunningham	.05
236	Rob Homberg	.05
237	Jeff Hostetler	.05
238	Lorenzo Lynch	.05
239	Barrett Robbins	.05
240	Dan Turk	.05
241	Harvey Williams	.05
242	Brian Dawkins	.05
243	Ty Detmer	.05
244	Troy Drake	.05
245	Rhett Hall	.05
246	Joe Panos	.05
247	Johnny Thomas	.05
248	Kevin Turner	.05
249	Ricky Watters	.10
250	Derrick Whiterspoon	.05
251	Sylvester Wright	.05
252	Jerome Bettis	.20
253	Carlos Emmons	.05
254	Jason Gildon	.05
255	Jonathan Hayes	.05
256	Kevin Henry	.05
257	Jerry Olsavsky	.05
258	Erric Pegram	.05
259	Brenden Stai	.05
260	Justin Strzelczyk	.05
261	Mike Tomczak	.05
262	Tony Banks	.50
263	Hayward Clay	.05
264	Percell Gaskins	.05
265	Eddie Kennison	.05
266	Aaron Laing	.05
267	Keith Lyle	.05
268	Jamie Martin	.05
269	Lawrence Phillips	.10
270	Zach Wiegert	.05
271	Toby Wright	.05
272	Darren Bennett	.05
273	Tony Berti	.05
274	Freddie Bradley	.05
275	Joe Cocozzo	.05
276	Andre Coleman	.05
277	Marco Coleman	.05
278	Rodney Harrison	.05
279	David Hendrix	.05
280	Leonard Russell	.05
281	Sean Salisbury	.05
282	Dennis Brown	.05
283	Chris Dalman	.05
284	Brent Jones	.05
285	Sean Manuel	.05
286	Marquez Pope	.05
287	Jerry Rice	1.50
288	Kirk Scrafford	.05
289	Iheanyi Uwaezuoke	.05
290	Tommy Vardell	.05
291	Steve Young	1.00
292	James Atkins	.05
293	T.J. Cunningham	.05
294	Stan Gelbaugh	.05
295	James Logan	.05
296	James McKnight	.05
297	Rick Mirer	.10
298	Todd Peterson	.05
299	Fred Thomas	.05
300	Rick Tuten	.05
301	Chris Warren	.05
302	Donnie Abraham	.05
303	Trent Dilfer	.10
304	Kenneth Gant	.05
305	Jeff Gooch	.05
306	Courtney Hawkins	.05
307	Tyoka Jackson	.05
308	Melvin Johnson	.05
309	Lonnie Marts	.05
310	Hardy Nickerson	.05
311	Errict Rhett	.20
312	Terry Allen	.10
313	Flipper Anderson	.05
314	William Bell	.05
315	Scott Blanton	.05
316	Leomont Evans	.05
317	Gus Frerotte	.05
318	Darryl Morrison	.05
319	Matt Turk	.05
320	Jeff Uhlenhake	.05
321	Bryan Walker	.05
322	Mark Brunell (1996 Statistical Leaders)	.75
323	Barry Sanders (1996 Statistical Leaders)	.75
324	Isaac Bruce (1996 Statistical Leaders)	.05
325	Terry Allen (1996 Statistical Leaders)	.05
326	Steve Young (1996 Statistical Leaders)	.50
327	Jerry Rice (1996 Statistical Leaders)	.75
328	Ricky Watters (1996 Statistical Leaders)	.05
329	Kevin Greene (1996 Statistical Leaders)	.05
330	Brett Favre (1996 Statistical Leaders)	1.50

1997 Pacific Philadelphia Gold

The 200-card set was a bonus in packs of the product. Each pack contained two Philadelphia Gold cards and either one insert card or an additional Philadelphia Gold card per pack. The card fronts showcased a full-bleed photo, with the Philadelphia logo in the upper left. The player's name is printed in gold foil over a gold-foil "spiral background" at the bottom left of the card. The team's logo is printed inside a banner over a football in the lower right. The backs have the player's name, position and highlights along the left, with a photo on the right. The card number is printed inside a circle in the lower right. A Hobby parallel version was printed with copper foil and inserted 2:37 packs. A Retail parallel version was produced with silver foil and inserted 2:37 packs.

		NM/M
Complete Set (200):		30.00
Common Player:		.15
Minor Stars:		.30
Copper Cards:		2X-4X
Silver Cards:		3X-6X
1	Ryan Christopherson	.15
2	James Dexter	.15
3	Boomer Esiason	.15
4	Jarius Hayes	.15
5	Eric Hill	.15
6	Trey Junkin	.15
7	Kwamie Lassiter	.15
8	Patrick Bates	.15
9	Brad Edwards	.15
10	Roman Fortin	.15
11	Harper LeBel	.15
12	Lorenzo Styles	.15
13	Robbie Tobeck	.15
14	Mike Caldwell	.15
15	Eric Green	.15
16	Brian Kinchen	.15
17	Eric Turner	.15
18	Jerrol Williams	.15
19	Eric Zeier	.15
20	Darick Holmes	.30
21	Ken Irvin	.15
22	Jerry Ostroski	.15
23	Andre Reed	.15
24	Steve Tasker	.15
25	Thurman Thomas	.30
26	Steve Beuerlein	.15
27	Kerry Collins	2.00
28	Eric Davis	.15
29	Norberto Garrido	.15
30	Lamar Lathon	.15
31	Andre Royal	.15
32	Tony Carter	.15
33	Jerry Fontenot	.15
34	Raymont Harris	.30
35	Anthony Marshall	.15
36	Barry Minter	.15
37	Steve Stenstrom	.15
38	Donnell Woolford	.15
39	Ken Blackman	.15
40	Jeff Blake	.50
41	Carl Pickens	.30
42	Artie Smith	.15
43	Ramondo Stallings	.15
44	Melvin Tuten	.15
45	Joe Walter	.15
46	Troy Aikman	2.00
47	Billy Davis	.15
48	Chad Hennings	.15
49	Emmitt Smith	4.00
50	George Teague	.15
51	Kevin Williams	.15
52	Terrell Davis	2.50
53	John Elway	2.00
54	Tom Nalen	.15
55	Bill Romanowski	.15
56	Rod Smith	.15
57	Dan Williams	.15
58	Mike Compton	.15
59	Eric Lynch	.15
60	Aubrey Matthews	.15
61	Pete Metzelaars	.15
62	Herman Moore	.30
63	Barry Sanders	4.00
64	Keith Washington	.15
65	Edgar Bennett	.15
66	Brett Favre	4.00
67	Lamont Hollinquest	.15
68	Keith Jackson	.15
69	Derrick Mayes	.15
60	Andre Rison	.15
71	Eddie George	2.50
72	Mel Gray	.15
73	Darryll Lewis	.15
74	John Henry Mills	.15
75	Rodney Thomas	.15
76	Gary Walker	.15
77	Troy Auzenne	.15
78	Sammie Burroughs	.15
79	Jim Harbaugh	.15
80	Tony McCoy	.15
81	Brian Stablein	.15
82	Kipp Vickers	.15
83	Aaron Beasley	.15
84	Mark Brunell	2.00
85	Don Davey	.15
86	Chris Hudson	.15
87	Greg Huntington	.15
88	Ernie Logan	.15
89	Donnell Bennett	.15
90	Anthony Davis	.15
91	Tim Grunhard	.15
92	Danan Hughes	.15
93	Tony Richardson	.15
94	Tracy Simien	.15
95	Karim Abdul-Jabbar	1.50
96	Dwight Hollier	.15
97	John Kidd	.15
98	Dan Marino	4.00
99	Jerris McPhail	.15
100	Irving Spikes	.15
101	Richmond Webb	.15
102	Jeff Brady	.15
103	Richard Brown	.15
104	Corey Fuller	.15
105	John Gerak	.15
106	Scottie Graham	.15
107	Amp Lee	.15
108	Drew Bledsoe	2.00
109	Tedy Bruschi	.15
110	Todd Collins	.15
111	Bob Kratch	.15
112	Curtis Martin	2.50
113	David Meggett	.15
114	Tom Tupa	.15
115	Eric Allen	.15
116	Mario Bates	.15
117	Clarence Jones	.15
118	Sean Lumpkin	.15
119	Doug Nussmeier	.15
120	Irv Smith	.15
121	Winfred Tubbs	.15
122	Willie Beamon	.15
123	Greg Bishop	.15
124	Dave Brown	.15
125	Gary Downs	.15
126	Thomas Lewis	.15
127	Michael Strahan	.15
128	Tyrone Wheatley	.15
129	Matt Brock	.15
130	Mike Chalenski	.15
131	Roger Duffy	.15
132	John Hudson	.15
133	Frank Reich	.15
134	David Williams	.15
135	Greg Biekert	.15
136	Mike Jones	.15
137	Napoleon Kaufman	.15
138	Carl Kidd	.15
139	Terry McDaniel	.15
140	Mike Morton	.15
141	Orlanda Truitt	.15
142	Gary Anderson	.15
143	Richard Cooper	.15
144	Jimmie Johnson	.15
145	Joe Kelly	.15
146	William Thomas	.15
147	Ricky Watters	.30
148	Ed West	.15
149	Michael Zordich	.15
150	Jerome Bettis	.50
151	Dermontti Dawson	.15
152	Lethon Flowers	.15
153	Charles Johnson	.15
154	Darren Perry	.15
155	Kordell Stewart	1.00
156	Will Wolford	.15
157	Isaac Bruce	.75
158	Kevin Carter	.15
159	Torin Dorn	.15
160	Leo Goeas	.15
161	Gerald McBurrows	.15
162	Chuck Osborne	.15
163	J.T. Thomas	.15
164	Dwayne Gordon	.15
165	Stan Humphries	.15
166	Shawn Lee	.15
167	Chris Mims	.15
168	John Parrella	.15
169	Junior Seau	.15
170	Bryan Still	.15
171	Curtis Buckley	.15
172	William Floyd	.15
173	Merton Hanks	.15
174	Terry Kirby	.15
175	Jerry Rice	2.00
176	J.J. Stokes	.15
177	Jeff Wilkins	.15
178	Bryant Young	.15
179	Sam Adams	.15
180	John Friesz	.15
181	Joey Galloway	.75
182	Pete Kendall	.15
183	Jason Kyle	.15
184	Darryl Williams	.15
185	Ronnie Williams	.15
186	Mike Alstott	.30
187	Trent Dilfer	.30
188	Tyrone Legette	.15
189	Martin Mayhew	.15
190	Jason Odom	.15
191	Warren Sapp	.15
192	Karl Williams	.15
193	Terry Allen	.15
194	Romeo Bandison	.15
195	Alcides Catanho	.15
196	Gus Frerotte	.15
197	William Gaines	.15
198	Ken Harvey	.15
199	Trevor Matich	.15
200	Scott Turner	.15

1997 Pacific Philadelphia Heart of the Game

The 20-card set was inserted 1:73 packs. The fronts showcased a full-bleed photo, with the Philadelphia logo in the upper left corner. The player's name is printed in large gold-foil letters at the bottom of the front. In the bottom center of the name is an oval globe. A red heartbeat runs from the lower left to the lower right, with the date of a key game printed in red in the center.

		NM/M
Complete Set (20):		160.00
Common Player:		2.00
Minor Stars:		4.00
1	Thurman Thomas	4.00
2	Kerry Collins	6.00
3	Troy Aikman	10.00
4	Emmitt Smith	15.00
5	Terrell Davis	12.00
6	John Elway	12.00
7	Barry Sanders	15.00
8	Brett Favre	18.00
9	Antonio Freeman	4.00
10	Marshall Faulk	8.00
11	Mark Brunell	6.00
12	Marcus Allen	4.00
13	Dan Marino	18.00
14	Drew Bledsoe	12.00
15	Curtis Martin	12.00
16	Napoleon Kaufman	2.00
17	Jerome Bettis	4.00
18	Isaac Bruce	4.00
19	Jerry Rice	15.00
20	Steve Young	15.00

1997 Pacific Philadelphia Milestones

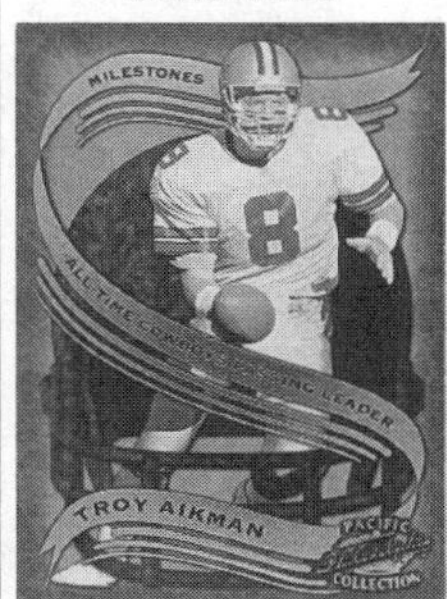

The 20-card set was inserted 1:37 packs. The fronts feature a red-orange border, with a player photo superimposed over a helmet and gold-foil Milestones banner that runs from the upper right to the lower left. The player's milestone is printed in the center of the banner, with his name in the lower left of the banner. The Philadelphia logo is located in the lower right.

		NM/M
Complete Set (20):		110.00
Common Player:		2.00
Minor Stars:		4.00
1	Simeon Rice	3.00
2	Thurman Thomas	4.00
3	Troy Aikman	8.00
4	Emmitt Smith	12.00
5	Terrell Davis	10.00
6	John Elway	10.00
7	Brett Favre	15.00
8	Desmond Howard	2.00
9	Reggie White	4.00
10	Mark Brunell	6.00
11	Marcus Allen	4.00
12	Karim Abdul-Jabbar	2.00
13	Dan Marino	15.00
14	Drew Bledsoe	10.00
15	Terry Glenn	6.00
16	Curtis Martin	10.00
17	Tony Banks	4.00
18	Jerry Rice	10.00
19	Steve Young	10.00
20	Terry Allen	2.00

1997 Pacific Philadelphia Photoengravings

Inserted 2:37 packs, the 36-card set has the look and feel of playing cards. The rounded-bordered cards have a player photo in the center of the card surrounded by a brown border and background. The player's name is printed in black at the bottom center. The Philadelphia logo is located in the upper left of the card front.

		NM/M
Complete Set (36):		110.00
Common Player:		2.00
Minor Stars:		3.00
1	Thurman Thomas	3.00
2	Kerry Collins	4.00
3	Jeff Blake	3.00
4	Troy Aikman	8.00
5	Deion Sanders	4.00
6	Emmitt Smith	10.00
7	Terrell Davis	8.00
8	John Elway	8.00
9	Herman Moore	3.00
10	Barry Sanders	10.00
11	Brett Favre	12.00
12	Desmond Howard	2.00
13	Dorsey Levens	2.00
14	Eddie George	6.00
15	Marshall Faulk	3.00
16	Jim Harbaugh	2.00
17	Marvin Harrison	3.00
18	Mark Brunell	4.00
19	Keenan McCardell	2.00
20	Karim Abdul-Jabbar	2.00
21	Dan Marino	12.00
22	Brad Johnson	2.00
23	Drew Bledsoe	8.00
24	Terry Glenn	4.00
25	Curtis Martin	8.00
26	Keyshawn Johnson	3.00
27	Tim Brown	4.00
28	Napoleon Kaufman	2.00
29	Ricky Watters	2.00
30	Jerome Bettis	3.00
31	Kordell Stewart	3.00
32	Eddie Kennison	3.00
33	Jerry Rice	8.00
34	Steve Young	8.00
35	Chris Warren	2.00
36	Terry Allen	2.00

1997 Pacific Revolution

Revolution is a 150-card set. The base cards all feature holographic foil, etching and embossing. Three parallel sets were created: Silver & Holographic Gold (retail, 2:25), Copper & Holographic Silver (hobby, 2:25) and Platinum Blue & Holographic Gold (1:49). The inserts included Proteges, Air Mail Die-Cuts, Silks and Ring Bearer Laser-Cuts.

		NM/M
Complete Set (150):		45.00
Common Player:		.20
Minor Stars:		.50
Copper/Red Cards:		3X-5X
Copper/Red Rookies:		2X-4X
Silver Cards:		4X-8X
Silver Rookies:		2X-4X
Blue Cards:		5X-8X
Blue Rookies:		2X-5X
Pack (3):		2.00
Wax Box (24):		45.00
1	Larry Centers	.20
2	Kent Graham	.20
3	Leeland McElroy	.20
4	Rob Moore	.20
5	*Jake Plummer*	5.00
6	Jamal Anderson	.50
7	Bert Emanuel	.20
8	*Byron Hanspard*	.40
9	Terance Mathis	.20
10	O.J. Santiago	.20
11	Derrick Alexander	.20
12	Peter Boulware	.20
13	*Jay Graham*	.50
14	Michael Jackson	.20
15	Vinny Testaverde	.20
16	Todd Collins	.50
17	Andre Reed	.20
18	Jay Riemersma	.20
19	*Antowain Smith*	3.00
20	Bruce Smith	.20
21	Thurman Thomas	.50
22	*Rae Carruth*	.75
23	Kerry Collins	.50
24	Anthony Johnson	.20
25	Muhsin Muhammad	.20
26	Wesley Walls	.20
27	Curtis Conway	.50
28	Bobby Engram	.20
29	Raymont Harris	.20
30	Rick Mirer	.20
31	Rashaan Salaam	.20
32	Jeff Blake	.50
33	*Corey Dillon*	6.00
34	Carl Pickens	.20
35	Darnay Scott	.20
36	Troy Aikman	3.00
37	Michael Irvin	.50
38	Daryl Johnston	.20
39	Deion Sanders	1.00
40	Emmitt Smith	4.00
41	Terrell Davis	3.00
42	John Elway	3.00
43	Ed McCaffrey	.20
44	Shannon Sharpe	.20
45	Neil Smith	.20
46	Scott Mitchell	.20
47	Herman Moore	.50
48	Johnnie Morton	.20
49	Barry Sanders	4.00
50	Robert Brooks	.20
51	LeRoy Butler	.20
52	Brett Favre	5.00
53	Antonio Freeman	.50
54	Dorsey Levens	.50
55	Reggie White	.50
56	Sean Dawkins	.20
57	Ken Dilger	.20
58	Marshall Faulk	.50
59	Jim Harbaugh	.20
60	Marvin Harrison	2.00
61	Mark Brunell	2.00
62	Keenan McCardell	.20
63	Natrone Means	.50
64	Jimmy Smith	.20
65	James Stewart	.20
66	Marcus Allen	.50
67	*Tony Gonzalez*	3.00
68	Elvis Grbac	.20
69	Greg Hill	.20
70	Andre Rison	.20
71	Karim Abdul-Jabbar	.40
72	Fred Barnett	.20
73	Dan Marino	5.00
74	O.J. McDuffie	.20
75	Irving Spikes	.20
76	Cris Carter	.20
77	*Matthew Hatchette*	1.00
78	Brad Johnson	.50
79	Jake Reed	.20
80	Robert Smith	.50
81	Drew Bledsoe	2.00
82	Ben Coates	.20
83	Terry Glenn	1.50
84	Curtis Martin	2.00
85	Dave Meggett	.20
86	*Troy Davis*	.50
87	Andre Hastings	.20
88	Heath Shuler	.20
89	Irv Smith	.20
90	*Danny Wuerffel*	.50
91	Ray Zellars	.20
92	*Tiki Barber*	3.00
93	Dave Brown	.20
94	Chris Calloway	.20
95	Rodney Hampton	.20
96	Amani Toomer	.20
97	Wayne Chrebet	.20
98	Keyshawn Johnson	2.00
99	Adrian Murrell	.50
100	Neil O'Donnell	.20
101	Dedric Ward	.20
102	Tim Brown	.50
103	Rickey Dudley	.20
104	Jeff George	.20
105	Desmond Howard	.20
106	Napoleon Kaufman	.50
107	Ty Detmer	.20
108	Jason Dunn	.20
109	Irving Fryar	.20
110	Rodney Peete	.20
111	Ricky Watters	.50
112	Jerome Bettis	.50
113	*Will Blackwell*	.50
114	Charles Johnson	.20
115	Kordell Stewart	2.00
116	Tony Banks	.50
117	Isaac Bruce	.50
118	Ernie Conwell	.20
119	Eddie Kennison	.50
120	Lawrence Phillips	.20
121	Stan Humphries	.20
122	Tony Martin	.20
123	Eric Metcalf	.20
124	Junior Seau	.50
125	*Jim Druckenmiller*	.50
126	Kevin Greene	.20
127	Garrison Hearst	.20
128	Terrell Owens	2.00
129	Jerry Rice	3.00
130	J.J. Stokes	.20
131	Rod Woodson	.20
132	Steve Young	3.00
133	Joey Galloway	.50
134	Cortez Kennedy	.20
135	*Jon Kitna*	2.00
136	Warren Moon	.20
137	Chris Warren	.20
138	Mike Alstott	1.00
139	*Reidel Anthony*	2.00
140	Trent Dilfer	.50
141	*Warrick Dunn*	3.00
142	Willie Davis	.20
143	Eddie George	2.00
144	Steve McNair	2.00
145	Chris Sanders	.20
146	Terry Allen	.20
147	Jamie Asher	.20
148	Henry Ellard	.20
149	Gus Frerotte	.20
150	Leslie Shepherd	.20

1997 Pacific Revolution Air Mail

The cards in this 36-card insert are die-cut to look like stamps. They were inserted once in every 25 packs.

		NM/M
Complete Set (36):		125.00
Common Player:		1.00
Minor Stars:		2.00
1	Vinny Testaverde	1.00
2	Andre Reed	1.00
3	Kerry Collins	2.00
4	Jeff Blake	2.00
5	Troy Aikman	6.00
6	Deion Sanders	4.00
7	Emmitt Smith	10.00
8	Michael Irvin	2.00
9	Terrell Davis	8.00
10	John Elway	8.00
11	Barry Sanders	10.00
12	Brett Favre	12.00
13	Antonio Freeman	2.00
14	Mark Brunell	6.00
15	Marcus Allen	2.00
16	Elvis Grbac	1.00
17	Dan Marino	12.00
18	Brad Johnson	2.00
19	Drew Bledsoe	8.00
20	Terry Glenn	2.00
21	Curtis Martin	8.00
22	Danny Wuerffel	2.00
23	Jeff George	1.00
24	Napoleon Kaufman	2.00
25	Kordell Stewart	5.00
26	Tony Banks	2.00
27	Isaac Bruce	2.00
28	Jim Druckenmiller	2.00
29	Jerry Rice	8.00
30	Steve Young	8.00
31	Warren Moon	1.00
32	Trent Dilfer	2.00
33	Warrick Dunn	6.00
34	Eddie George	6.00
35	Steve McNair	6.00
36	Gus Frerotte	1.00

1997 Pacific Revolution Proteges

These 20 insert cards feature a proven veteran alongside their young understudy. The foiled cards were inserted 2:25.

		NM/M
Complete Set (20):		65.00
Common Player:		1.00
1	Kent Graham, Jake Plummer	2.00
2	Jamal Anderson, Byron Hanspard	1.00
3	Thurman Thomas, Antowain Smith	3.00
4	Troy Aikman, Jason Garrett	5.00
5	Emmitt Smith, Sherman Williams	8.00
6	John Elway, Jeff Lewis	6.00
7	Barry Sanders, Ron Rivers	8.00
8	Brett Favre, Doug Pederson	10.00
9	Mark Brunell, Rob Johnson	5.00
10	Marcus Allen, Greg Hill	1.00
11	Dan Marino, Damon Huard	10.00
12	Curtis Martin, Marrio Grier	6.00
13	Heath Shuler, Danny Wuerffel	2.00
14	Rodney Hampton, Tiki Barber	2.00
15	Jerome Bettis, George Jones	2.00
16	Jerry Rice, Terrell Owens	8.00
17	Steve Young, Jim Druckenmiller	6.00
18	Warren Moon, Jon Kitna	2.00
19	Errict Rhett, Warrick Dunn	4.00
20	Terry Allen, Stephen Davis	1.00

A card number in parenthese ( ) indicates the set is unnumbered.

1997 Pacific Revolution Ring Bearers

These 10 fully foiled and embossed cards are die-cut and laser-cut to look like a championship ring. The cards feature 10 of the NFL's best and were inserted 1:121.

		NM/M
Complete Set (12):		110.00
Common Player:		5.00
Inserted 1:121		
1	Emmitt Smith	25.00
2	John Elway	15.00
3	Barry Sanders	25.00
4	Brett Favre	30.00
5	Mark Brunell	10.00
6	Dan Marino	30.00
7	Drew Bledsoe	10.00
8	Steve Young	12.00
9	Warrick Dunn	5.00
10	Eddie George	50.00
11	Troy Aikman	50.00
12	Jerry Rice	50.00

1997 Pacific Revolution Silks

This 18-card, oversized insert features top NFL players on a silk-like material. The cards were inserted 1:49.

		NM/M
Complete Set (18):		75.00
Common Player:		2.00
1	Kerry Collins	4.00
2	Troy Aikman	8.00
3	Deion Sanders	6.00
4	Emmitt Smith	10.00
5	Terrell Davis	8.00
6	John Elway	8.00
7	Barry Sanders	10.00
8	Brett Favre	12.00
9	Mark Brunell	6.00
10	Marcus Allen	2.00
11	Dan Marino	12.00
12	Drew Bledsoe	6.00
13	Curtis Martin	6.00
14	Jerome Bettis	2.00
15	Jim Druckenmiller	2.00
16	Jerry Rice	8.00
17	Warrick Dunn	5.00
18	Eddie George	5.00

1998 Pacific

The 450-card silver-foiled main set captures the NFL's pinpoint passes, touchdown runs and goal-line stands with the sharpest action photography. The set is designed with the die-hard football fan in mind, this set delivers outstanding player selection, including the strong crop of rookies from 1998. Each card back includes full year-by-year career stats. A parallel Red version can be found one per special retail pack and the Platinum Blue parallel singles can be found 1:73 packs.

		NM/M
Complete Set (450):		70.00
Common Player:		.10
Minor Stars:		.20
Common Rookie:		1.00
Platinum Blue Cards:		15X-30X
Platinum Blue Rookies:		5X-10X
Inserted 1:73		
Pack (10):		2.00
Wax Box (36):		50.00
1	Mario Bates	.10
2	Lomas Brown	.10
3	Larry Centers	.10
4	Chris Gedney	.10
5	Terry Irving	.10
6	Tom Knight	.10
7	Eric Metcalf	.10
8	Jamir Miller	.10
9	Rob Moore	.20
10	Joe Nedney	.10
11	Jake Plummer	1.00
12	Simeon Rice	.10
13	Frank Sanders	.10
14	Eric Swann	.10
15	Aeneas Williams	.10
16	Morten Andersen	.10
17	Jamal Anderson	.50
18	Michael Booker	.10
19	Keith Brooking	.10
20	Ray Buchanan	.10
21	Devin Bush	.10
22	Chris Chandler	.20
23	Tony Graziani	.10
24	Harold Green	.10
25	Byron Hanspard	.10
26	Todd Kinchen	.10
27	Tony Martin	.10
28	Terance Mathis	.10
29	Eugene Robinson	.10
30	O.J. Santiago	.10
31	Chuck Smith	.10
32	Jessie Tuggle	.10
33	Bob Whitfield	.10
34	Peter Boulware	.10
35	Jay Graham	.10
36	Eric Green	.10
37	Jim Harbaugh	.20
38	Michael Jackson	.10
39	Jermaine Lewis	.10
40	Ray Lewis	.10
41	Michael McCrary	.10
42	Stevon Moore	.10
43	Jonathan Ogden	.10
44	Errict Rhett	.10
45	Matt Stover	.10
46	Rod Woodson	.10
47	Eric Zeier	.10
48	Ruben Brown	.10
49	Steve Christie	.10
50	Quinn Early	.10
51	John Fina	.10
52	Doug Flutie	.75
53	Phil Hansen	.10
54	Lonnie Johnson	.10
55	Rob Johnson	.20
56	Henry Jones	.10
57	Eric Moulds	.20
58	Andre Reed	.10
59	Antowain Smith	.50
60	Bruce Smith	.10
61	Thurman Thomas	.20
62	Ted Washington	.10
63	Michael Bates	.10
64	Tim Biakabutuka	.10
65	Blake Brockermeyer	.10
66	Mark Carrier	.10
67	Rae Carruth	.10
68	Kerry Collins	.20
69	Doug Evans	.10
70	William Floyd	.10
71	Sean Gilbert	.10
72	Raghib Ismail	.10
73	John Kasay	.10
74	Fred Lane	.20
75	Lamar Lathon	.10
76	Muhsin Muhammad	.10
77	Wesley Walls	.10
78	Edgar Bennett	.10
79	Tom Carter	.10
80	Curtis Conway	.20
81	Bobby Engram	.10
82	*Curtis Enis*	.75
83	Jim Flanigan	.10
84	Walt Harris	.10
85	Jeff Jaeger	.10
86	Erik Kramer	.10
87	John Mangum	.10
88	Glyn Milburn	.10
89	Barry Minter	.10
90	Chris Penn	.10
91	Todd Sauerbrun	.10
92	James Williams	.10
93	Ashley Ambrose	.10
94	Willie Anderson	.10
95	Eric Bieniemy	.10
96	Jeff Blake	.20
97	Ki-Jana Carter	.10
98	John Copeland	.10
99	Corey Dillon	.75
100	Tony McGee	.10
101	Neil O'Donnell	.20
102	Carl Pickens	.20
103	Kevin Sargent	.10
104	Darnay Scott	.20
105	*Takeo Spikes*	1.00
106	Troy Aikman	1.50
107	Larry Allen	.10
108	Eric Bjornson	.10
109	Billy Davis	.10
110	Jason Garrett	.10
111	Michael Irvin	.20
112	Daryl Johnston	.10
113	David LaFleur	.10
114	Everett McIver	.10
115	Ernie Mills	.10
116	Nate Newton	.10
117	Deion Sanders	.50
118	Emmitt Smith	2.00
119	Kevin Smith	.10
120	Eric Williams	.10
121	Steve Atwater	.10
122	Tyrone Braxton	.10
123	Ray Crockett	.10
124	Terrell Davis	2.00
125	Jason Elam	.10
126	John Elway	1.50
127	Willie Green	.10
128	*Brian Griese*	5.00
129	Tony Jones	.10
130	Ed McCaffrey	.20
131	John Mobley	.10
132	Tom Nalen	.10
133	*Marcus Nash*	2.00
134	Bill Romanowski	.10
135	Shannon Sharpe	.20
136	Neil Smith	.10
137	Rod Smith	.20
138	Keith Traylor	.10
139	Stephen Boyd	.10
140	Mark Carrier	.10
141	*Charlie Batch*	1.00
142	Jason Hanson	.10
143	Scott Mitchell	.20
144	Herman Moore	.50
145	Johnnie Morton	.10
146	Robert Porcher	.10
147	Ron Rivers	.10
148	Barry Sanders	3.00
149	Tracy Scroggins	.10
150	David Sloan	.10
151	Tommy Vardell	.10
152	Kerwin Waldroup	.10
153	Bryant Westbrook	.10
154	Robert Brooks	.10
155	Gilbert Brown	.10
156	LeRoy Butler	.10
157	Mark Chmura	.20
158	Earl Dotson	.10
159	Santana Dotson	.10
160	Brett Favre	3.00
161	Antonio Freeman	.50
162	Raymont Harris	.10
163	William Henderson	.10
164	*Vonnie Holliday*	.50
165	George Koonce	.10
166	Dorsey Levens	.20
167	Derrick Mayes	.10
168	Craig Newsome	.10
169	Ross Verba	.10
170	Reggie White	.50
171	Elijah Alexander	.10
172	Aaron Bailey	.10
173	Jason Belser	.10
174	Robert Blackmon	.10
175	Zack Crockett	.10
176	Ken Dilger	.10
177	Marshall Faulk	.50
178	Tarik Glenn	.10
179	Marvin Harrison	.20
180	Tony Mandarich	.10
181	*Peyton Manning*	10.00
182	Marcus Pollard	.10
183	Lamont Warren	.10
184	*Tavian Banks*	2.00
185	Reggie Barlow	.10
186	Tony Boselli	.10
187	Tony Brackens	.10
188	Mark Brunell	1.00
189	Kevin Hardy	.10
190	Mike Hollis	.10
191	Jeff Lageman	.10
192	Keenan McCardell	.20
193	Pete Mitchell	.10
194	Bryce Paup	.10
195	Leon Searcy	.10
196	Jimmy Smith	.20
197	James Stewart	.10
198	*Fred Taylor*	3.00
199	Renaldo Wynn	.10
200	Derrick Alexander	.10
201	Kimble Anders	.10
202	Donnell Bennett	.10
203	Dale Carter	.10
204	Anthony Davis	.10
205	Rich Gannon	.10
206	Tony Gonzalez	.20
207	Elvis Grbac	.20
208	James Hasty	.10
209	Leslie O'Neal	.10
210	Andre Rison	.10
211	*Rashaan Shehee*	.40
212	Will Shields	.10
213	Pete Stoyanovich	.10
214	Derrick Thomas	.20
215	Tamarick Vanover	.10
216	Karim Abdul-Jabbar	.20
217	Trace Armstrong	.10
218	*John Avery*	.50
219	Tim Bowens	.10
220	Terrell Buckley	.10
221	Troy Brayton	.10
222	Daryl Gardener	.10
223	*Damon Huard*	1.00
224	Charles Jordan	.10
225	Dan Marino	2.00
226	O.J. McDuffie	.10
227	Bernie Parmalee	.10
228	Stanley Pritchett	.10
229	Derrick Rodgers	.10
230	Lamar Thomas	.10
231	Zach Thomas	.20
232	Richmond Webb	.10
233	Derrick Alexander	.10
234	Jerry Ball	.10
235	Cris Carter	.50
236	Randall Cunningham	.50
237	Charles Evans	.10
238	Corey Fuller	.10
239	Andrew Glover	.10
240	Leroy Hoard	.10
241	Brad Johnson	.50
242	Ed McDaniel	.10
243	Randall McDaniel	.10

244	*Randy Moss*	8.00
245	John Randle	.10
246	Jake Reed	.10
247	Dwayne Rudd	.10
248	Robert Smith	.20
249	Bruce Armstrong	.10
250	Drew Bledsoe	1.00
251	Vincent Brisby	.10
252	Tedy Bruschi	.10
253	Ben Coates	.20
254	Derrick Cullors	.10
255	Terry Glenn	.20
256	Shawn Jefferson	.10
257	Ted Johnson	.10
258	Ty Law	.10
259	Willie McGinest	.10
260	Lawyer Milloy	.10
261	Sedrick Shaw	.10
262	Chris Slade	.10
263	Troy Davis	.10
264	Mark Fields	.10
265	Andre Hastings	.10
266	Billy Joe Hobert	.10
267	Qadry Ismail	.10
268	Tony Johnson	.10
269	Sammy Knight	.10
270	Wayne Martin	.10
271	Chris Naeole	.10
272	Keith Poole	.10
273	William Roaf	.10
274	Pio Sagapolutele	.10
275	Danny Wuerffel	.20
276	Ray Zellars	.10
277	Jessie Armstead	.10
278	Tiki Barber	.20
279	Chris Calloway	.10
280	Percy Ellsworth	.10
281	Sam Garnes	.10
282	Kent Graham	.10
283	Ike Hilliard	.10
284	Danny Kanell	.10
285	Corey Miller	.10
286	Phillippi Sparks	.10
287	Michael Strahan	.10
288	Amani Toomer	.10
289	Charles Way	.10
290	Tyrone Wheatley	.10
291	Tito Wooten	.10
292	Kyle Brady	.10
293	Keith Byars	.10
294	Wayne Chrebet	.20
295	John Elliott	.10
296	Glenn Foley	.20
297	Aaron Glenn	.10
298	Keyshawn Johnson	.50
299	Curtis Martin	.50
300	Otis Smith	.10
301	Vinny Testaverde	.20
302	Alex Van Dyke	.10
303	Dedric Ward	.10
304	Greg Biekert	.10
305	Tim Brown	.20
306	Rickey Dudley	.10
307	Jeff George	.20
308	Pat Harlow	.10
309	Desmond Howard	.10
310	James Jett	.10
311	Napoleon Kaufman	.50
312	Lincoln Kennedy	.10
313	Russell Maryland	.10
314	Darrell Russell	.10
315	Eric Turner	.10
316	Steve Wisniewski	.10
317	*Charles Woodson*	2.00
318	James Darling	.10
319	Jason Dunn	.10
320	Irving Fryar	.10
321	Charlie Garner	.20
322	Jeff Graham	.10
323	Bobby Hoying	.20
324	Chad Lewis	.10
325	Rodney Peete	.10
326	Freddie Solomon	.10
327	Duce Staley	.10
328	Bobby Taylor	.10
329	William Thomas	.10
330	Kevin Turner	.10
331	Troy Vincent	.10
332	Jerome Bettis	.50
333	Will Blackwell	.10
334	Mark Bruener	.10
335	Andre Coleman	.10
336	Dermontti Dawson	.10
337	Jason Gildon	.10
338	Courtney Hawkins	.10
339	Charles Johnson	.10
340	Levon Kirkland	.10
341	Carnell Lake	.10
342	Tim Lester	.10
343	Joel Steed	.10
344	Kordell Stewart	1.00
345	Will Wolford	.10
346	Tony Banks	.20
347	Isaac Bruce	.20
348	Ernie Conwell	.10
349	D'Marco Farr	.10
350	Wayne Gandy	.10
351	*Robert Holcombe*	.50
352	Eddie Kennison	.20
353	Amp Lee	.10
354	Keith Lyle	.10
355	Ryan McNeil	.10
356	Jerald Moore	.20
357	Orlando Pace	.10
358	Roman Phifer	.10
359	David Thompson	.10
360	Darren Bennett	.10
361	John Carney	.10
362	Marco Coleman	.10
363	Terrell Fletcher	.10
364	William Fuller	.10
365	Charlie Jones	.10
366	Freddie Jones	.10
367	*Ryan Leaf*	.50
368	Natrone Means	.50
369	Junior Seau	.20
370	Terrance Shaw	.10
371	Tremayne Stephens	.10
372	Bryan Still	.10
373	Aaron Taylor	.10
374	Greg Clark	.10
375	Ty Detmer	.10
376	Jim Druckenmiller	.20
377	Marc Edwards	.10
378	Merton Hanks	.10
379	Garrison Hearst	.20
380	Chuck Levy	.10
381	Ken Norton	.10
382	Terrell Owens	.75
383	Marquez Pope	.10
384	Jerry Rice	1.50
385	Irv Smith	.10
386	J.J. Stokes	.20
387	Iheanyi Uwaezuoke	.10
388	Bryant Young	.10
389	Steve Young	.75
390	Sam Adams	.10
391	Chad Brown	.10
392	Christian Fauria	.10
393	Joey Galloway	.50
394	*Ahman Green*	8.00
395	Walter Jones	.10
396	Cortez Kennedy	.10
397	Jon Kitna	.50
398	James McKnight	.10
399	Warren Moon	.20
400	Mike Pritchard	.10
401	Michael Sinclair	.10
402	Shawn Springs	.10
403	Ricky Watters	.20
404	Darryl Williams	.10
405	Mike Alstott	.50
406	Reidel Anthony	.20
407	Derrick Brooks	.10
408	Brad Culpepper	.10
409	Trent Dilfer	.50
410	Warrick Dunn	1.00
411	Bert Emanuel	.10
412	*Jacquez Green*	2.50
413	Paul Gruber	.10
414	Patrick Hape	.10
415	Dave Moore	.10
416	Hardy Nickerson	.10
417	Warren Sapp	.10
418	Robb Thomas	.10
419	Regan Upshaw	.10
420	Karl Williams	.10
421	Blaine Bishop	.10
422	Anthony Cook	.10
423	Willie Davis	.10
424	Al Del Greco	.10
425	*Kevin Dyson*	2.00
426	Henry Ford	.10
427	Eddie George	1.00
428	Jackie Harris	.10
429	Steve McNair	.75
430	Chris Sanders	.10
431	Mark Stepnoski	.10
432	Yancey Thigpen	.20
433	Barron Wortham	.10
434	Frank Wycheck	.10
435	Stephen Alexander	.10
436	Terry Allen	.20
437	Jamie Asher	.10
438	Bob Dahl	.10
439	Stephen Davis	.10
440	Cris Dishman	.10
441	Gus Frerotte	.10
442	Darrell Green	.10
443	Trent Green	.20
444	Ken Harvey	.10
445	*Skip Hicks*	1.00
446	Jeff Hostetler	.10
447	Brian Mitchell	.10
448	Leslie Shepherd	.10
449	Michael Westbrook	.20
450	Dan Wilkinson	.10

1998 Pacific Cramer's Choice Awards

Pacific President/CEO Michael Cramer selected and wrote about the 10 players that are on these die-cut awards. Each card is in the shape of a triangle and were inserted 1:721 packs.

		NM/M
Complete Set (10):		400.00
Common Player:		30.00
Inserted 1:721		
1	Terrell Davis	50.00
2	John Elway	50.00
3	Barry Sanders	70.00
4	Brett Favre	70.00
5	Peyton Manning	50.00
6	Mark Brunell	25.00
7	Dan Marino	70.00
8	Ryan Leaf	30.00
9	Jerry Rice	50.00
10	Warrick Dunn	30.00

1998 Pacific Dynagon Turf

This sparkling insert features action photography and a mirror-patterned full-foil background. Singles from this 20-card set were inserted 4:37 packs. A parallel Titanium Turf set was added for hobby-only packs. Each single is sequentially numbered to 99.

		NM/M
Complete Set (20):		60.00
Common Player:		1.00
Inserted 4:37		
Titanium Cards:		4X-10X
Production 99 Sets		
1	Corey Dillon	2.00
2	Troy Aikman	3.00
3	Emmitt Smith	5.00
4	Terrell Davis	4.00
5	John Elway	4.00
6	Barry Sanders	5.00
7	Brett Favre	5.00
8	Peyton Manning	4.00
9	Mark Brunell	3.00
10	Dan Marino	5.00
11	Drew Bledsoe	3.00
12	Curtis Martin	3.00
13	Napoleon Kaufman	1.00
14	Jerome Bettis	1.00
15	Kordell Stewart	2.00
16	Ryan Leaf	1.00
17	Jerry Rice	4.00
18	Steve Young	4.00
19	Warrick Dunn	2.00
20	Eddie George	2.00

1998 Pacific Gold Crown Die-Cuts

This die-cut dual-foiled insert honors 36 of football's elite players. These singles were created with Pacific's cutting-edge technology and feature super-thick 24-point stock. Singles were inserted 1:37 packs.

		NM/M
Complete Set (36):		175.00
Common Player:		2.00
Minor Stars:		5.00
Inserted 1:37		
1	Jake Plummer	5.00
2	Antowain Smith	5.00
3	Curtis Enis	2.00
4	Corey Dillon	5.00
5	Troy Aikman	8.00
6	Deion Sanders	5.00
7	Emmitt Smith	12.00
8	Terrell Davis	10.00
9	John Elway	10.00
10	Barry Sanders	12.00
11	Brett Favre	15.00
12	Dorsey Levens	2.00
13	Marshall Faulk	5.00
14	Peyton Manning	10.00
15	Mark Brunell	6.00
16	Fred Taylor	6.00
17	Derrick Thomas	2.00
18	Dan Marino	15.00
19	Brad Johnson	5.00
20	Robert Smith	5.00
21	Drew Bledsoe	8.00
22	Glenn Foley	2.00
23	Curtis Martin	8.00
24	Napoleon Kaufman	2.00
25	Charles Woodson	5.00
26	Jerome Bettis	5.00
27	Kordell Stewart	5.00
28	Ryan Leaf	2.00
29	Garrison Hearst	2.00
30	Jerry Rice	10.00
31	J.J. Stokes	2.00
32	Steve Young	10.00
33	Joey Galloway	5.00
34	Ricky Watters	2.00
35	Warrick Dunn	5.00
36	Eddie George	5.00

1998 Pacific Team Checklists

This uniquely-designed insert highlights a team leader side-by-side with the holographic silver-foiled NFL logo of his respective team. On the back you'll find another photo of that player and a complete team checklist. Singles were inserted 2:37 packs.

		NM/M
Complete Set (30):		110.00
Common Player:		1.00
Minor Stars:		2.00
Inserted 2:37		
1	Jake Plummer	2.00
2	Jamal Anderson	2.00
3	Eric Zeier	1.00
4	Rob Johnson	1.00
5	Fred Lane	1.00
6	Curtis Enis	1.00
7	Corey Dillon	2.00
8	Troy Aikman	6.00
9	John Elway	6.00
10	Barry Sanders	8.00
11	Brett Favre	10.00
12	Peyton Manning	8.00
13	Mark Brunell	5.00
14	Elvis Grbac	1.00
15	Dan Marino	10.00
16	Robert Smith	2.00
17	Drew Bledsoe	6.00
18	Danny Wuerffel	1.00
19	Tiki Barber	1.00
20	Curtis Martin	6.00
21	Napoleon Kaufman	1.00
22	Duce Staley	1.00
23	Kordell Stewart	4.00
24	Tony Banks	2.00
25	Ryan Leaf	2.00
26	Jerry Rice	8.00
27	Warren Moon	2.00
28	Warrick Dunn	4.00
29	Eddie George	3.00
30	Terry Allen	1.00

1998 Pacific Timelines

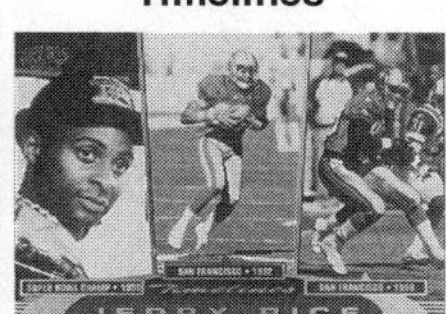

Timelines features 20 superstars, giving a chronological history of each player complete with photos from early in their careers. These singles could be found in hobby-only packs at a ratio of 1:181.

		NM/M
Complete Set (20):		350.00
Common Player:		5.00
Minor Stars:		10.00
Inserted 1:181 Hobby		
1	Troy Aikman	25.00
2	Deion Sanders	10.00
3	Emmitt Smith	35.00
4	Terrell Davis	25.00
5	John Elway	25.00
6	Barry Sanders	35.00
7	Brett Favre	40.00
8	Peyton Manning	35.00
9	Mark Brunell	25.00
10	Dan Marino	40.00
11	Drew Bledsoe	25.00
12	Curtis Martin	10.00
13	Jerome Bettis	5.00
14	Kordell Stewart	10.00
15	Ryan Leaf	5.00
16	Jerry Rice	25.00
17	Steve Young	25.00
18	Ricky Watters	5.00
19	Warrick Dunn	10.00
20	Eddie George	10.00

1998 Pacific Aurora

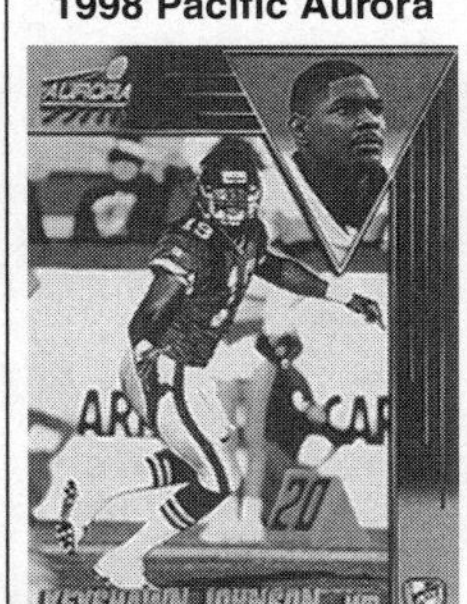

The Aurora main set shines its light on 200 of football's most exciting players, each featured on their own 24-point stock card. Each card back gives you the latest in-depth player information and statistics along with a trivia question.

		NM/M
Complete Set (200):		75.00
Common Player:		.20
Minor Stars:		.40
Pack (6):		3.00
Wax Box (36):		100.00
1	Rob Moore	.20
2	Jake Plummer	1.00
3	Frank Sanders	.20
4	Eric Swann	.20
5	Jamal Anderson	.75
6	Chris Chandler	.20
7	Byron Hanspard	.20
8	Terance Mathis	.20
9	O.J. Santiago	.20
10	Chuck Smith	.20
11	Jessie Tuggle	.20
12	Jay Graham	.20
13	Jim Harbaugh	.20
14	Michael Jackson	.20
15	*Patrick Johnson*	.40
16	Jermaine Lewis	.20
17	Errict Rhett	.20
18	Rod Woodson	.20
19	Quinn Early	.20
20	Andre Reed	.20
21	Antowain Smith	1.00
22	Bruce Smith	.20
23	Thurman Thomas	.40
24	Ted Washington	.20
25	Michael Bates	.20
26	Rae Carruth	.20
27	Kerry Collins	.40
28	Fred Lane	.40
29	Wesley Walls	.20
30	Edgar Bennett	.20
31	Curtis Conway	.40
32	*Curtis Enis*	.50
33	Walt Harris	.20
34	Erik Kramer	.20
35	Barry Minter	.20
36	Jeff Blake	.40
37	Corey Dillon	1.25
38	Carl Pickens	.20
39	Darnay Scott	.20
40	Troy Aikman	2.00
41	Michael Irvin	.40
42	Deion Sanders	.75
43	Emmitt Smith	3.00
44	Chris Warren	.20
45	Terrell Davis	3.00
46	John Elway	2.00
47	*Brian Griese*	5.00
48	Ed McCaffrey	.20
49	John Mobley	.20
50	Shannon Sharpe	.40
51	Neil Smith	.20
52	Rod Smith	.20
53	Stephen Boyd	.20
54	Scott Mitchell	.20
55	Herman Moore	.75
56	Johnnie Morton	.20
57	Robert Porcher	.20
58	Barry Sanders	4.00
59	Robert Brooks	.20
60	Mark Chmura	.40
61	Brett Favre	4.00
62	Antonio Freeman	.75
63	*Vonnie Holliday*	1.00
64	Dorsey Levens	.40
65	Ross Verba	.20
66	Reggie White	.40
67	Elijah Alexander	.20
68	Ken Dilger	.20
69	Marshall Faulk	.75
70	Marvin Harrison	.40
71	*Peyton Manning*	10.00
72	Bryan Barker	.20
73	Mark Brunell	1.50
74	Keenan McCardell	.20
75	Jimmy Smith	.20
76	James Stewart	.20
77	Derrick Alexander	.20
78	Kimble Anders	.20
79	Donnell Bennett	.20
80	Elvis Grbac	.20
81	Andre Rison	.20
82	*Rashaan Shehee*	.75
83	Derrick Thomas	.20
84	Karim Abdul-Jabbar	.40
85	Trace Armstrong	.20
86	Charles Jordan	.20
87	Dan Marino	3.00
88	O.J. McDuffie	.20
89	Zach Thomas	.40
90	Cris Carter	.40
91	Charles Evans	.20
92	Andrew Glover	.20
93	Brad Johnson	.40
94	*Randy Moss*	8.00
95	John Randle	.20
96	Jake Reed	.20
97	Robert Smith	.40
98	Bruce Armstrong	.20
99	Drew Bledsoe	1.50
100	Ben Coates	.20
101	*Robert Edwards*	1.00
102	Terry Glenn	.40
103	Willie McGinest	.20
104	Sedrick Shaw	.20
105	*Tony Simmons*	.50
106	Chris Slade	.20
107	Billy Joe Hobert	.20
108	Qadry Ismail	.20
109	Heath Shuler	.20
110	Lamar Smith	.20
111	Ray Zellars	.20
112	Tiki Barber	.20
113	Chris Calloway	.20
114	Ike Hilliard	.20
115	*Joe Jurevicius*	1.00
116	Danny Kanell	.20
117	Amani Toomer	.20
118	Charles Way	.20
119	Tyrone Wheatley	.20
120	Wayne Chrebet	.20
121	John Elliott	.20
122	Glenn Foley	.20
123	*Scott Frost*	.40
124	Aaron Glenn	.20
125	Keyshawn Johnson	.40
126	Curtis Martin	1.00
127	Vinny Testaverde	.20
128	Tim Brown	.40
129	Rickey Dudley	.20
130	Jeff George	.40
131	James Jett	.20
132	Napoleon Kaufman	.75
133	Darrell Russell	.20
134	*Charles Woodson*	3.00
135	James Darling	.20
136	Koy Detmer	.20
137	Irving Fryar	.20
138	Charlie Garner	.20
139	Bobby Hoying	.20
140	Chad Lewis	.20
141	Duce Staley	.20
142	Kevin Turner	.20
143	Jerome Bettis	.40
144	Will Blackwell	.20
145	Mark Bruener	.20
146	Dermontti Dawson	.20
147	Charles Johnson	.20
148	Levon Kirkland	.20
149	Tim Lester	.20
150	Kordell Stewart	1.50
151	Tony Banks	.75
152	Isaac Bruce	.40
153	*Robert Holcombe*	2.00
154	Eddie Kennison	.40
155	Amp Lee	.20
156	Jerald Moore	.20
157	Charlie Jones	.20
158	Freddie Jones	.20
159	*Ryan Leaf*	.50
160	Natrone Means	.40
161	Junior Seau	.40
162	Bryan Still	.20
163	Marc Edwards	.20
164	Merton Hanks	.20
165	Garrison Hearst	.40
166	Terrell Owens	.40
167	Jerry Rice	2.00
168	J.J. Stokes	.20
169	Bryant Young	.20
170	Steve Young	1.00
171	Chad Brown	.20
172	Joey Galloway	.75
173	Walter Jones	.20
174	Cortez Kennedy	.20
175	Jon Kitna	.20
176	James McKnight	.20
177	Warren Moon	.40
178	Michael Sinclair	.20
179	Mike Alstott	.40
180	Reidel Anthony	.20
181	Derrick Brooks	.20
182	Trent Dilfer	.40
183	Warrick Dunn	1.50
184	Hardy Nickerson	.20
185	Warren Sapp	.20
186	Willie Davis	.20
187	Eddie George	1.25
188	Steve McNair	.75
189	Jon Runyan	.20
190	Chris Sanders	.20
191	Frank Wycheck	.20
192	Stephen Alexander	.20
193	Terry Allen	.20
194	Stephen Davis	.20
195	Cris Dishman	.20
196	Gus Frerotte	.20
197	Darrell Green	.20
198	*Skip Hicks*	1.50
199	Dana Stubblefield	.20
200	Michael Westbrook	.20

1998 Pacific Aurora Championship Fever

Each of the singles in this 50-card set are printed on gold foil and etched. Singles were inserted one-per-pack. This insert also has three parallel sets. The easiest being the Silvers that are found in retail packs and are sequentially numbered to 250. The Platinum Blues are numbered to 100 and can be found in both hobby and retail packs. The Copper cards are limited to 20 and are found in hobby packs.

		NM/M
Complete Set (50):		40.00
Common Player:		.30
Minor Stars:		.60
Inserted 1:1		
Silver Cards:		5X-10X
Production 250 Sets		
Platinum Blue Cards:		10X-20X
Production 100 Sets		
Copper Cards:		20X-40X
Production 20 Sets		
1	Jake Plummer	1.00
2	Antowain Smith	1.00
3	Bruce Smith	.30
4	Kerry Collins	.60
5	Kevin Greene	.30
6	Jeff Blake	.30
7	Corey Dillon	1.50
8	Carl Pickens	.30
9	Troy Aikman	3.00
10	Michael Irvin	.60
11	Deion Sanders	.75
12	Emmitt Smith	4.00

13	Terrell Davis	4.00
14	John Elway	3.00
15	Shannon Sharpe	.30
16	Herman Moore	.60
17	Barry Sanders	6.00
18	Brett Favre	6.00
19	Antonio Freeman	.75
20	Dorsey Levens	.60
21	Marshall Faulk	.75
22	Peyton Manning	5.00
23	Mark Brunell	2.00
24	Elvis Grbac	.30
25	Andre Rison	.30
26	Rashaan Shehee	.60
27	Derrick Thomas	.30
28	Dan Marino	4.00
29	Cris Carter	.30
30	Robert Smith	.60
31	Drew Bledsoe	2.00
32	Robert Edwards	3.00
33	Terry Glenn	.60
34	Danny Kanell	.30
35	Keyshawn Johnson	.60
36	Tim Brown	.30
37	Napoleon Kaufman	.75
38	Bobby Hoying	.30
39	Jerome Bettis	.60
40	Kordell Stewart	2.00
41	Ryan Leaf	.50
42	Jerry Rice	3.00
43	Steve Young	1.50
44	Joey Galloway	.75
45	Mike Alstott	.60
46	Trent Dilfer	.60
47	Warrick Dunn	2.00
48	Eddie George	2.00
49	Steve McNair	.75
50	Gus Frerotte	.30

1998 Pacific Aurora Cubes

The Cubes insert could only be found in hobby boxes and were inserted one per box. Only 20 of the top players from the NFL were included in this insert.

		NM/M
Complete Set (20):		60.00
Common Player:		1.00
One Per Box		
1	Corey Dillon	3.00
2	Troy Aikman	5.00
3	Emmitt Smith	7.00
4	Terrell Davis	5.00
5	John Elway	5.00
6	Barry Sanders	7.00
7	Brett Favre	8.00
8	Dorsey Levens	1.00
9	Peyton Manning	7.00
10	Mark Brunell	3.00
11	Dan Marino	8.00
12	Drew Bledsoe	4.00
13	Napoleon Kaufman	1.00
14	Jerome Bettis	1.00
15	Kordell Stewart	2.00
16	Ryan Leaf	1.00
17	Jerry Rice	6.00
18	Steve Young	6.00
19	Warrick Dunn	3.00
20	Eddie George	3.00

1998 Pacific Aurora Face Mask Cel-Fusions

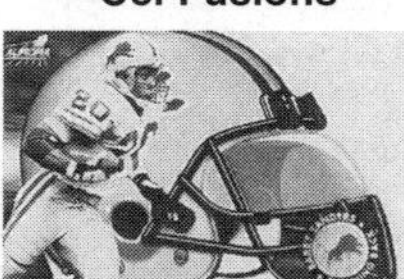

Each player in this 20-card foiled and etched set is profiled against a die-cut helmet that is fused to a cel-portion face mask. Singles were inserted 1:73 packs.

		NM/M
Complete Set (20):		110.00
Common Player:		3.00
Inserted 1:73		
1	Corey Dillon	5.00
2	Troy Aikman	10.00
3	Emmitt Smith	15.00
4	Terrell Davis	10.00
5	John Elway	10.00
6	Barry Sanders	15.00
7	Brett Favre	18.00
8	Antonio Freeman	3.00
9	Peyton Manning	15.00
10	Mark Brunell	5.00
11	Dan Marino	18.00
12	Drew Bledsoe	10.00
13	Napoleon Kaufman	3.00
14	Jerome Bettis	3.00
15	Kordell Stewart	6.00
16	Ryan Leaf	3.00
17	Jerry Rice	12.00
18	Steve Young	12.00
19	Warrick Dunn	6.00
20	Eddie George	6.00

1998 Pacific Aurora Gridiron Laser-Cuts

Each single in this 20-card set is laser cut and was inserted 4:37 packs. They could only be found in hobby packs.

		NM/M
Complete Set (20):		70.00
Common Player:		2.00
Inserted 4:37 Hobby		
1	Jake Plummer	3.00
2	Corey Dillon	5.00
3	Troy Aikman	6.00
4	Emmitt Smith	8.00
5	Terrell Davis	6.00
6	John Elway	6.00
7	Barry Sanders	8.00
8	Brett Favre	10.00
9	Peyton Manning	8.00
10	Mark Brunell	4.00
11	Dan Marino	10.00
12	Drew Bledsoe	4.00
13	Jerome Bettis	2.00
14	Kordell Stewart	2.00
15	Ryan Leaf	2.00
16	Jerry Rice	6.00
17	Steve Young	6.00
18	Warrick Dunn	3.00
19	Eddie George	3.00
20	Steve McNair	3.00

1998 Pacific Aurora NFL Command

This insert salutes 10 NFL stars with this coveted fully-foiled and etched insert. Singles were inserted 1:361 packs.

		NM/M
Complete Set (10):		325.00
Common Player:		5.00
Inserted 1:361		
1	Terrell Davis	25.00
2	John Elway	25.00
3	Barry Sanders	35.00
4	Brett Favre	40.00
5	Peyton Manning	35.00
6	Mark Brunell	15.00
7	Dan Marino	100.00
8	Drew Bledsoe	20.00
9	Ryan Leaf	5.00
10	Warrick Dunn	15.00

1998 Pacific Crown Royale

This 144-card base set features football's brightest stars and top rookies on the Crown Royale double-foiled, double-etched, all-die-cut format. The parallel Limited Series cards are printed on 24-point stock and are sequentially numbered to 99.

		NM/M
Complete Set (144):		75.00
Common Player:		.50
Minor Stars:		1.00
Common Rookie:		1.00
Limited Series Cards:		5X-10X
Limited Series Rookies:		2X-4X
Production 99 Sets		
Pack (6):		5.00
Wax Box (24):		115.00
1	Larry Centers	.50
2	Rob Moore	.50
3	Adrian Murrell	.50
4	Jake Plummer	1.00
5	Jamal Anderson	1.50
6	Chris Chandler	.50
7	*Tim Dwight*	3.00
8	Tony Martin	.50
9	Jay Graham	.50
10	*Patrick Johnson*	.50
11	Jermaine Lewis	.50
12	Eric Zeier	.50
13	Rob Johnson	.50
14	Eric Moulds	1.00
15	Antowain Smith	1.50
16	Bruce Smith	.50
17	Steve Beuerlein	.50
18	Anthony Johnson	.50
19	Fred Lane	.40
20	Muhsin Muhammad	.50
21	Curtis Conway	1.00
22	*Curtis Enis*	1.00
23	Erik Kramer	.50
24	*Tony Parrish*	.40
25	Corey Dillon	2.00
26	Neil O'Donnell	.50
27	Carl Pickens	1.00
28	*Takeo Spikes*	2.00
29	Troy Aikman	4.00
30	Michael Irvin	1.00
31	Deion Sanders	1.50
32	Emmitt Smith	6.00
33	Chris Warren	.50
34	Terrell Davis	3.00
35	John Elway	4.00
36	*Brian Griese*	6.00
37	Ed McCaffrey	1.00
38	Shannon Sharpe	1.00
39	Rod Smith	1.00
40	*Charlie Batch*	1.00
41	Herman Moore	1.00
42	Johnnie Morton	.50
43	Barry Sanders	6.00
44	Bryant Westbrook	.50
45	Robert Brooks	.50
46	Brett Favre	8.00
47	Antonio Freeman	1.50
48	Raymont Harris	.50
49	*Vonnie Holliday*	1.00
50	Reggie White	1.00
51	Marshall Faulk	1.50
52	*E.G. Green*	.50
53	Marvin Harrison	1.00
54	*Peyton Manning*	20.00
55	*Jerome Pathon*	2.00
56	*Tavian Banks*	1.00
57	Mark Brunell	2.00
58	Keenan McCardell	.50
59	Jimmy Smith	1.00
60	*Fred Taylor*	6.00
61	Derrick Alexander	.50
62	Tony Gonzalez	.50
63	Elvis Grbac	.50
64	Andre Rison	.50
65	*Rashaan Shehee*	2.00
66	Derrick Thomas	1.00
67	Karim Abdul-Jabbar	.50
68	*John Avery*	1.00
69	*Oronde Gadsden*	1.00
70	Dan Marino	6.00
71	O.J. McDuffie	.50
72	Cris Carter	1.50
73	Randall Cunningham	1.00
74	Brad Johnson	1.00
75	*Randy Moss*	15.00
76	John Randle	.50
77	Jake Reed	.50
78	Robert Smith	1.00
79	Drew Bledsoe	3.00
80	*Robert Edwards*	3.00
81	Terry Glenn	1.00
82	*Tebucky Jones*	1.00
83	*Tony Simmons*	1.00
84	Mark Fields	.50
85	Andre Hastings	.50
86	Danny Wuerffel	.50
87	Ray Zellars	.50
88	Tiki Barber	1.00
89	Ike Hilliard	.50
90	*Joe Jurevicius*	2.00
91	Danny Kanell	.50
92	Wayne Chrebet	1.00
93	Glenn Foley	.50
94	Keyshawn Johnson	1.50
95	Leon Johnson	.50
96	Curtis Martin	1.50
97	Tim Brown	1.00
98	Jeff George	.50
99	Napoleon Kaufman	.50
100	*Jon Ritchie*	1.00
101	*Charles Woodson*	4.00
102	Irving Fryar	.50
103	Bobby Hoying	1.00
104	*Allen Rossum*	.50
105	Duce Staley	.50
106	Jerome Bettis	1.00
107	*Chris Fuamatu-Ma'afala*	3.00
108	Charles Johnson	1.00
109	Levon Kirkland	.50
110	Kordell Stewart	2.00
111	*Hines Ward*	6.00
112	Tony Banks	1.00
113	*Tony Horne*	1.00
114	Eddie Kennison	1.00
115	Amp Lee	.50
116	Freddie Jones	.50
117	*Ryan Leaf*	.75
118	Natrone Means	.50
119	*Mikhael Ricks*	.50
120	Bryan Still	.50
121	Marc Edwards	.50
122	Garrison Hearst	1.50
123	Terrell Owens	1.50
124	Jerry Rice	4.00
125	J.J. Stokes	1.00
126	Steve Young	2.50
127	Joey Galloway	1.50
128	*Ahman Green*	15.00
129	Warren Moon	1.00
130	Ricky Watters	1.00
131	Mike Alstott	1.50
132	Trent Dilfer	1.00
133	Warrick Dunn	1.00
134	*Jacquez Green*	3.00
135	Warren Sapp	.50
136	*Kevin Dyson*	3.00
137	Eddie George	2.00
138	Steve McNair	2.00
139	Yancey Thigpen	1.00
140	*Stephen Alexander*	1.00
141	Terry Allen	1.00
142	Trent Green	1.00
143	*Skip Hicks*	3.00
144	Michael Westbrook	1.00

1998 Pacific Crown Royale Cramer's Choice Awards Jumbos

These singles are identical to the Cramer's Choice awards found in Pacific except for the size. Singles from this set are larger and found on top of boxes at one per. The twist to this insert is the six different parallels with varying foil colors and number of sets produced. The Dark Blues are numbered to 35, Greens are numbered to 30, Reds to 25, Light Blues to 20, Golds to 10 and only one Purple set.

		NM/M
Complete Set (10):		110.00
Common Player:		10.00
One Per Box		
Dark Blue Cards:		10X-20X
Production 35 Sets		
Green Cards:		10X-20X
Production 30 Sets		
Red Cards:		10X-20X
Production 25 Sets		
Light Blue Cards:		10X-20X
Production 20 Sets		
Gold Cards:		15X-30X
Production 10 Sets		
1	Terrell Davis	12.00
2	John Elway	12.00
3	Barry Sanders	20.00
4	Brett Favre	20.00
5	Peyton Manning	20.00
6	Mark Brunell	10.00
7	Dan Marino	15.00
8	Randy Moss	20.00
9	Jerry Rice	12.00
10	Warrick Dunn	10.00

1998 Pacific Crown Royale Living Legends

The players selected for this insert were based on the dozens of records, awards and championships that each player has earned. Each card in this insert is sequentially numbered to 375.

		NM/M
Complete Set (10):		125.00
Common Player:		8.00
Production 375 Sets		
1	Troy Aikman	15.00
2	Emmitt Smith	25.00
3	Terrell Davis	15.00
4	John Elway	15.00
5	Barry Sanders	25.00
6	Brett Favre	30.00
7	Mark Brunell	8.00
8	Dan Marino	30.00
9	Drew Bledsoe	15.00
10	Jerry Rice	20.00

1998 Pacific Crown Royale Master Performers

Master Performers includes the top 20 players from the NFL and was inserted 2:25 hobby packs.

		NM/M
Complete Set (20):		45.00
Common Player:		1.00
Minor Stars:		4.00
Inserted 2:25 Hobby		
1	Corey Dillon	2.00
2	Troy Aikman	5.00
3	Emmitt Smith	7.00
4	Terrell Davis	5.00
5	John Elway	5.00
6	Charlie Batch	2.00
7	Barry Sanders	7.00
8	Brett Favre	8.00
9	Peyton Manning	8.00
10	Mark Brunell	3.00
11	Fred Taylor	3.00
12	Dan Marino	8.00
13	Randy Moss	8.00
14	Drew Bledsoe	4.00
15	Curtis Martin	4.00
16	Kordell Stewart	2.00
17	Ryan Leaf	1.00
18	Jerry Rice	5.00
19	Steve Young	5.00
20	Warrick Dunn	2.00

1998 Pacific Crown Royale Pillars of the Game

These holographic gold foil cards served as the bottom card in every pack and featured a strong mix of NFL mainstays and rising stars. These could only be found in hobby packs.

		NM/M
Complete Set (25):		15.00
Common Player:		.20
Minor Stars:		.50
Inserted 1:1 Hobby		
1	Antowain Smith	.20
2	Corey Dillon	.50
3	Troy Aikman	1.50
4	Emmitt Smith	2.00
5	Terrell Davis	2.00
6	John Elway	1.50
7	Charlie Batch	.50
8	Barry Sanders	3.00
9	Brett Favre	3.00
10	Antonio Freeman	.50
11	Peyton Manning	4.00
12	Mark Brunell	1.25
13	Dan Marino	2.00
14	Randy Moss	4.00
15	Drew Bledsoe	1.25
16	Curtis Martin	.50
17	Napoleon Kaufman	.50
18	Jerome Bettis	.50
19	Kordell Stewart	1.25
20	Ryan Leaf	.50
21	Jerry Rice	1.50
22	Steve Young	.50
23	Ricky Watters	.20
24	Eddie George	1.25
25	Warrick Dunn	1.25

1998 Pacific Crown Royale Pivotal Players

This 25-card holographic silver foil insert featured some of football's most dynamic superstars along with several top rookies from 1998. Singles were found one-per-pack in hobby packs only.

		NM/M
Complete Set (25):		15.00
Common Player:		.25
Inserted 1:1 Hobby		
1	Jake Plummer	.50
2	Antowain Smith	.25
3	Corey Dillon	.75
4	Troy Aikman	1.50
5	Deion Sanders	.25
6	Emmitt Smith	2.00
7	Terrell Davis	2.00
8	John Elway	1.50
9	Charlie Batch	.50
10	Barry Sanders	3.00
11	Brett Favre	3.00
12	Peyton Manning	4.00
13	Mark Brunell	1.00
14	Fred Taylor	2.00
15	Dan Marino	2.00
16	Randy Moss	5.00
17	Drew Bledsoe	1.25
18	Curtis Martin	.75
19	Napoleon Kaufman	.25
20	Jerome Bettis	.25
21	Kordell Stewart	1.25
22	Ryan Leaf	.50
23	Jerry Rice	1.50
24	Eddie George	1.25
25	Warrick Dunn	1.00

1998 Pacific Crown Royale Rookie Paydirt

The fully foiled and etched Rookie Paydirt set gave collectors an early look at the top 20 rookies from 1998. Singles were inserted into hobby packs at a ratio of 1:25.

		NM/M
Complete Set (20):		90.00
Common Player:		1.00
Inserted 1:25 Hobby		
1	Curtis Enis	1.00
2	Marcus Nash	2.00
3	Charlie Batch	2.00
4	Vonnie Holliday	2.00
5	E.G. Green	1.00
6	Peyton Manning	25.00
7	Jerome Pathon	1.00
8	Tavian Banks	6.00
9	Fred Taylor	15.00
10	Rashaan Shehee	1.00
11	John Avery	3.00
12	Randy Moss	25.00
13	Robert Edwards	5.00
14	Charles Woodson	8.00
15	Hines Ward	5.00
16	Ryan Leaf	3.00
17	Mikhael Ricks	2.00
18	Ahman Green	10.00
19	Jacquez Green	4.00
20	Kevin Dyson	5.00

1998 Pacific Omega

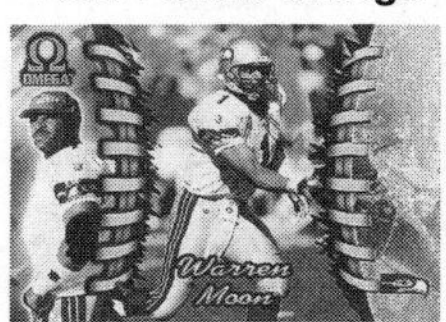

Omega football consists of a 250-card base set and five inserts. The base cards have a horizontal layout. The fronts feature three photos separated by a football stitching pattern. The color center photo is duplicated in silver foil on the right. Another color photo is on the left.

		NM/M
Complete Set (250):		50.00
Common Player:		.10
Minor Stars:		.20
Pack (8):		2.00
Wax Box (36):		60.00
1	Larry Centers	.10
2	Rob Moore	.10
3	Michael Pittman	.10
4	Jake Plummer	1.00
5	Simeon Rice	.10
6	Frank Sanders	.10
7	Eric Swann	.10
8	Morten Anderson	.10
9	Jamal Anderson	.20
10	Chris Chandler	.10
11	Harold Green	.10
12	Byron Hanspard	.10
13	Terance Mathis	.10
14	O.J. Santiago	.10
15	Peter Boulware	.10
16	Jay Graham	.10
17	Eric Green	.10
18	Michael Jackson	.10
19	Jermaine Lewis	.10
20	Ray Lewis	.10
21	Jonathan Ogden	.10
22	Eric Zeier	.10
23	Steve Christie	.10
24	Todd Collins	.10
25	Quinn Early	.10
26	Eric Moulds	.20
27	Andre Reed	.10
28	Antowain Smith	1.00
29	Bruce Smith	.10
30	Thurman Thomas	.20
31	Ted Washington	.10
32	Michael Bates	.10
33	Tim Biakabutuka	.10
34	Mark Carrier	.10
35	Rae Carruth	.20
36	Kerry Collins	.30
37	Kevin Greene	.10
38	Fred Lane	.20
39	Muhsin Muhammad	.10
40	Wesley Walls	.10
41	Curtis Conway	.20
42	Bobby Engram	.10
43	*Curtis Enis*	.75
44	Raymont Harris	.10
45	Erik Kramer	.10
46	Chris Penn	.10
47	Ryan Wetnight	.10
48	Jeff Blake	.20
49	Ki-Jana Carter	.10
50	John Copeland	.10
51	Corey Dillon	1.00
52	Tony McGee	.10
53	Carl Pickens	.20
54	Darnay Scott	.10
55	Takeo Spikes	.10
56	Troy Aikman	1.50
57	Eric Bjornson	.10
58	*Greg Ellis*	.20
59	Michael Irvin	.20
60	Daryl Johnston	.10
61	David LaFleur	.10
62	Deion Sanders	.50
63	Emmitt Smith	2.50
64	Jason Garrett	.10
65	Nicky Sualua	.10
66	Steve Atwater	.10
67	Terrell Davis	1.50
68	John Elway	1.50
69	*Brian Griese*	3.00
70	Ed McCaffrey	.10
71	John Mobley	.10
72	*Marcus Nash*	2.00
73	Shannon Sharpe	.20
74	Neil Smith	.10
75	Rod Smith	.20
76	*Charlie Batch*	1.00
77	*Germane Crowell*	1.00
78	Jason Hanson	.10
79	Scott Mitchell	.10
80	Herman Moore	.20
81	Johnnie Morton	.10
82	Barry Sanders	3.00
83	Tommy Vardell	.10
84	Robert Brooks	.10
85	Gilbert Brown	.10
86	Leroy Butler	.10
87	Mark Chmura	.20
88	Brett Favre	3.00
89	Antonio Freeman	.20
90	William Henderson	.10
91	*Vonnie Holliday*	.20
92	Dorsey Levens	.20
93	Reggie White	.20
94	Aaron Bailey	.10
95	Quentin Coryatt	.10
96	Zack Crockett	.10
97	Ken Dilger	.10
98	Marshall Faulk	.20
99	*E.G. Green*	.20
100	Marvin Harrison	.20
101	*Peyton Manning*	8.00
102	Jerome Pathon	.10
103	*Tavian Banks*	2.00
104	Tony Boselli	.10
105	Tony Brackens	.10
106	Mark Brunell	1.25
107	Kevin Hardy	.10
108	Keenan McCardell	.10
109	Pete Mitchell	.10
110	Jimmy Smith	.20
111	James Stewart	.20
112	*Fred Taylor*	3.00
113	Kimble Anders	.10
114	Dale Carter	.10
115	Tony Gonzalez	.10
116	Elvis Grbac	.10
117	Donnell Bennett	.10
118	Andre Rison	.10
119	*Rashaan Shehee*	.50
120	Derrick Thomas	.20
121	Tamarick Vanover	.10
122	Karim Abdul-Jabbar	.30
123	*John Avery*	1.00
124	Troy Drayton	.10
125	John Dutton	.10
126	Craig Erickson	.10
127	Dan Marino	2.50
128	O.J. McDuffie	.10
129	Jerris McPhail	.10
130	Stanley Pritchett	.10
131	Larry Shannon	.10
132	Zach Thomas	.20
133	Cris Carter	.20
134	Randall Cunningham	.20
135	Andrew Glover	.10
136	Brad Johnson	.20
137	Randall McDaniel	.10
138	David Palmer	.10
139	John Randle	.10
140	Jake Reed	.10
141	Robert Smith	.20
142	Drew Bledsoe	1.25
143	Ben Coates	.10
144	*Robert Edwards*	2.00
145	Terry Glenn	.30
146	Shawn Jefferson	.10
147	Willie McGinest	.10
148	Tony Simmons	.10
149	Chris Slade	.10
150	Troy Davis	.10

151 Mark Fields .10
152 Andre Hastings .10
153 Billy Joe Hobert .10
154 William Roaf .10
155 Heath Shuler .10
156 Danny Wuerffel .10
157 Ray Zellars .10
158 Jessie Armstead .10
159 Tiki Barber .20
160 Chris Calloway .10
161 Mike Cherry .10
162 Danny Kanell .10
163 Amani Toomer .10
164 Charles Way .10
165 Tyrone Wheatley .10
166 Kyle Brady .10
167 Wayne Chrebet .10
168 Glenn Foley .20
169 *Scott Frost* .20
170 Keyshawn Johnson .20
171 Leon Johnson .10
172 Alex Van Dyke .10
173 Dedric Ward .10
174 Tim Brown .20
175 Rickey Dudley .10
176 Jeff George .20
177 Desmond Howard .10
178 James Jett .10
179 Napoleon Kaufman .50
180 Darrell Russell .10
181 *Charles Woodson* 2.00
182 Jason Dunn .10
183 Irving Fryar .10
184 Charlie Garner .20
185 Bobby Hoying .10
186 Chris T. Jones .10
187 Michael Timpson .10
188 Kevin Turner .10
189 Jerome Bettis .20
190 Will Blackwell .10
191 Mark Bruener .10
192 Charles Johnson .10
193 George Jones .10
194 Levon Kirkland .10
195 Kordell Stewart 1.25
196 *Hines Ward* 3.00
197 Tony Banks .20
198 Isaac Bruce .20
199 Ernie Conwell .10
200 *Robert Holcombe* 2.00
201 Eddie Kennison .20
202 Amp Lee .10
203 Orlando Pace .10
204 Charlie Jones .10
205 Freddie Jones .10
206 *Ryan Leaf* .75
207 Natrone Means .20
208 Junior Seau .20
209 Bryan Still .10
210 Greg Clark .10
211 Jim Druckenmiller .20
212 Marc Edwards .10
213 Garrison Hearst .20
214 Terrell Owens .20
215 Jerry Rice 1.50
216 J.J. Stokes .10
217 Bryant Young .10
218 Steve Young 1.00
219 Chad Brown .10
220 Joey Galloway .30
221 Cortez Kennedy .10
222 Jon Kitna .10
223 James McKnight .10
224 Warren Moon .20
225 Michael Sinclair .10
226 Ricky Watters .20
227 Mike Alstott .30
228 Reidel Anthony .20
229 Derrick Brooks .10
230 Trent Dilfer .20
231 Warrick Dunn 2.00
232 Dave Moore .10
233 Hardy Nickerson .10
234 Warren Sapp .10
235 Karl Williams .10
236 Willie Davis .10
237 *Kevin Dyson* 2.00
238 Eddie George 1.25
239 Derrick Mason .10
240 Steve McNair .75
241 Chris Sanders .10
242 Frank Wycheck .10
243 Terry Allen .10
244 Jamie Asher .10
245 Gus Frerotte .10
246 Darrell Green .10
247 *Skip Hicks* 1.50
248 Brian Mitchell .10
249 Leslie Shepherd .10
250 Michael Westbrook .10

1998 Pacific Omega EO Portraits

EO Portraits is a 20-card insert seeded 1:73. The cards feature a color player photo with a closeup photo of the player's face laser-cut into the card. A hoobby-only parallel version is numbered to one.

NM/M
Complete Set (20): 150.00
Common Player: 5.00
Inserted 1:73
1 Jake Plummer 10.00
2 Corey Dillon 15.00
3 Troy Aikman 25.00
4 Emmitt Smith 35.00
5 Terrell Davis 25.00
6 John Elway 25.00
7 Barry Sanders 35.00
8 Brett Favre 40.00
9 Dorsey Levens 5.00
10 Peyton Manning 40.00
11 Mark Brunell 15.00
12 Dan Marino 40.00
13 Drew Bledsoe 20.00
14 Jerome Bettis 5.00
15 Kordell Stewart 5.00
16 Ryan Leaf 5.00
17 Jerry Rice 25.00
18 Steve Young 15.00
19 Warrick Dunn 12.00
20 Eddie George 12.00

1998 Pacific Omega Face To Face

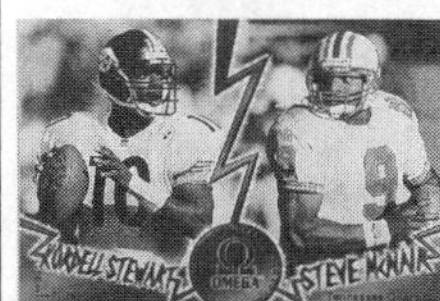

Face To Face is a 10-card insert seeded 1:145. The cards have a horizontal layout and feature two NFL stars on the front.

NM/M
Complete Set (10): 110.00
Common Player: 8.00
Inserted 1:145
1 Peyton Manning, Ryan Leaf 15.00
2 Barry Sanders, Warrick Dunn 15.00
3 Dan Marino, John Elway 20.00
4 Jerry Rice, Antonio Freeman 15.00
5 Jake Plummer, Drew Bledsoe 10.00
6 Corey Dillon, Eddie George 8.00
7 Emmitt Smith, Terrell Davis 15.00
8 Steve Young, Mark Brunell 10.00
9 Kordell Stewart, Steve McNair 10.00
10 Troy Aikman, Brett Favre 25.00

1998 Pacific Omega Online

Online is a 36-card insert seeded 4:37. The card is designed to resemble a computer, with the color player photo on the monitor. The player's name, position, team logo and team web page appear on the keyboard at the bottom.

NM/M
Complete Set (36): 50.00
Common Player: 1.00
Inserted 4:37
1 Jake Plummer 2.00
2 Antowain Smith 2.00
3 Curtis Enis 1.00
4 Corey Dillon 3.00
5 Troy Aikman 5.00
6 Emmitt Smith 7.00
7 Terrell Davis 5.00
8 John Elway 5.00
9 Shannon Sharpe 1.00
10 Herman Moore 1.00
11 Barry Sanders 7.00
12 Brett Favre 8.00
13 Antonio Freeman 1.00
14 Dorsey Levens 1.00
15 Peyton Manning 8.00
16 Marshall Faulk 3.00
17 Mark Brunell 3.00
18 Fred Taylor 3.00
19 Dan Marino 8.00
20 Robert Smith 1.00
21 Drew Bledsoe 4.00
22 Tiki Barber 1.00
23 Danny Kanell 1.00
24 Tim Brown 2.00
25 Napoleon Kaufman 1.00
26 Charles Woodson 3.00
27 Jerome Bettis 1.00
28 Kordell Stewart 2.00
29 Ryan Leaf 1.00
30 Jerry Rice 6.00
31 Steve Young 6.00
32 Joey Galloway 1.00
33 Trent Dilfer 1.00
34 Warrick Dunn 2.00
35 Eddie George 2.00
36 Steve McNair 2.00

1998 Pacific Omega Prisms

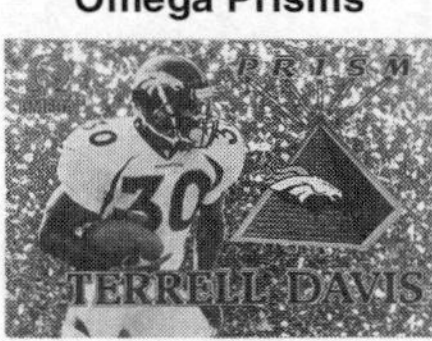

Prism is a 20-card insert seeded one per 37 packs. The cards have a horizontal layout on prismatic foil. A color player photo is on the left with a pyramid and team logo on the right.

NM/M
Complete Set (20): 70.00
Common Player: 1.00
Inserted 1:37
1 Jake Plummer 3.00
2 Corey Dillon 3.00
3 Troy Aikman 5.00
4 Emmitt Smith 7.00
5 Terrell Davis 5.00
6 John Elway 5.00
7 Barry Sanders 7.00
8 Brett Favre 8.00
9 Peyton Manning 8.00
10 Mark Brunell 3.00
11 Dan Marino 8.00
12 Drew Bledsoe 5.00
13 Napoleon Kaufman 1.00
14 Jerome Bettis 1.00
15 Kordell Stewart 2.00
16 Ryan Leaf 1.00
17 Jerry Rice 6.00
18 Steve Young 6.00
19 Warrick Dunn 3.00
20 Eddie George 3.00

1998 Pacific Omega Rising Stars

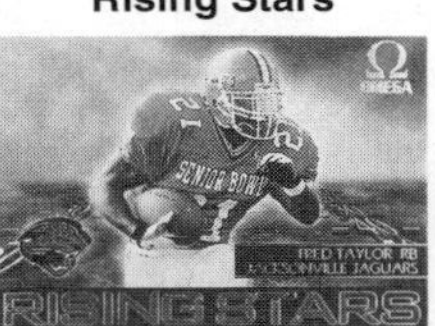

Rising Stars is a 30-card insert seeded 4:37. The set features NFL rookies from 1998. The insert is paralleled five times, each with a different foil color. The blue foil parallel is numbered to 100, red to 75, green to 50, purple to 25 and gold to one.

NM/M
Complete Set (30): 55.00
Common Player: 1.00
Inserted 4:37 Hobby
1 Michael Pittman 1.00
2 Keith Brooking 1.00
3 Duane Starks 1.00
4 Curtis Enis 1.00
5 Marcus Nash 2.00
6 Brian Griese 6.00
7 Terry Fair 1.00
8 Germane Crowell 5.00
9 Charlie Batch 2.00
10 E.G. Green 1.00
11 Peyton Manning 12.00
12 Jerome Pathon 1.00
13 Fred Taylor 8.00
14 Tavian Banks 2.00
15 Rashaan Shehee 1.00
16 John Avery 2.00
17 John Dutton 1.00
18 Robert Edwards 2.00
19 Tony Simmons 2.00
20 Joe Jurevicius 4.00
21 Scott Frost 1.00
22 Charles Woodson 6.00
23 Hines Ward 6.00
24 Robert Holcombe 4.00
25 Az-Zahir Hakim 3.00
26 Ryan Leaf 1.00
27 Ahman Green 8.00
28 Kevin Dyson 5.00
29 Stephen Alexander 3.00
30 Skip Hicks 3.00

1998 Pacific Paramount

Paramount Football consists of a 250-card base set with three parallels and four inserts. The base cards feature full-bleed photos with the player's name, position and team logo at the bottom. The regular cards have Copper, Silver and Platinum Blue parallels. Inserts include Pro Bowl Die-Cuts, Super Bowl XXXII Highlights, Personal Bests and Kings of the NFL.

NM/M
Complete Set (250): 40.00
Common Player: .10
Minor Stars: .20
Copper/Silver Cards: 2X-4X
Platinum Blue Cards: 10X-20X
Pack (6): 1.50
Wax Box (36): 50.00
1 Larry Centers .10
2 Chris Gedney .10
3 Rob Moore .10
4 Jake Plummer 1.00
5 Simeon Rice .10
6 Frank Sanders .10
7 Mark Smith .10
8 Eric Swann .10
9 Jamal Anderson .20
10 Chris Chandler .10
11 Bert Emanuel .10
12 Tony Graziani .10
13 Byron Hanspard .20
14 Terance Mathis .10
15 O.J. Santiago .10
16 Chuck Smith .10
17 Derrick Alexander .10
18 Peter Boulware .10
19 Jay Graham .10
20 *Priest Holmes* 20.00
21 Michael Jackson .10
22 Bam Morris .10
23 Vinny Testaverde .20
24 Eric Zeier .10
25 Todd Collins .10
26 Quinn Early .10
27 Bryce Paup .10
28 Andre Reed .10
29 Jay Riemersma .10
30 Antowain Smith .50
31 Bruce Smith .10
32 Thurman Thomas .20
33 Michael Bates .10
34 Mark Carrier .10
35 Rae Carruth .20
36 Kerry Collins .30
37 Fred Lane .10
38 Lamar Lathon .10
39 Muhsin Muhammad .10
40 Wesley Walls .10
41 Darnell Autry .20
42 Curtis Conway .20
43 Raymont Harris .20
44 Tyrone Hughes .10
45 Chris Penn .10
46 Ricky Proehl .10
47 Steve Stenstrom .10
48 Ryan Wetnight .10
49 Jeff Blake .20
50 Ki-Jana Carter .10
51 Corey Dillon .75
52 David Dunn .10
53 Boomer Esiason .10
54 Brian Milne .10
55 Carl Pickens .20
56 Darnay Scott .10
57 Troy Aikman 1.00
58 Eric Bjornson .10
59 Michael Irvin .20
60 Daryl Johnston .10
61 Anthony Miller .10
62 Deion Sanders .40
63 Emmitt Smith 1.50
64 Omar Stoutmire .10
65 Sherman Williams .10
66 Terrell Davis 1.25
67 John Elway 1.00
68 Darrien Gordon .10
69 Ed McCaffrey .10
70 Bill Romanowski .10
71 Shannon Sharpe .20
72 Neil Smith .10
73 Rod Smith .20
74 Maa Tanuvasa .10
75 Tommie Boyd .10
76 Glyn Milburn .10
77 Scott Mitchell .10
78 Herman Moore .20
79 Johnnie Morton .10
80 Robert Porcher .10
81 Barry Sanders 1.50
82 Bryant Westbrook .10
83 Robert Brooks .10
84 LeRoy Butler .10
85 Mark Chmura .20
86 Brett Favre 2.00
87 Antonio Freeman .20
88 Dorsey Levens .20
89 Eugene Robinson .10
90 *Bill Schroeder* 2.00
91 Reggie White .20
92 Aaron Bailey .10
93 Quentin Coryatt .10
94 Zack Crockett .10
95 Sean Dawkins .10
96 Ken Dilger .10
97 Marshall Faulk .20
98 Jim Harbaugh .20
99 Marvin Harrison .20
100 Bryan Barker .10
101 Tony Boselli .10
102 Tony Brackens .10
103 Mark Brunell 1.00
104 Mike Hollis .10
105 Keenan McCardell .10
106 Natrone Means .20
107 Jimmy Smith .10
108 James Stewart .10
109 Marcus Allen .20
110 Kimble Anders .10
111 Dale Carter .10
112 Tony Gonzalez .20
113 Elvis Grbac .20
114 Greg Hill .10
115 Andre Rison .10
116 Will Shields .10
117 Derrick Thomas .10
118 Karim Abdul-Jabbar .30
119 Trace Armstrong .10
120 *Damon Huard* 2.00
121 Charles Jordan .10
122 Dan Marino 1.50
123 O.J. McDuffie .10
124 Irving Spikes .10
125 Zach Thomas .10
126 Cris Carter .10
127 *Charles Woodson* 2.00
128 Brad Johnson .20
129 Randall McDaniel .10
130 John Randle .10
131 Jake Reed .10
132 Robert Smith .10
133 Todd Steussie .10
134 Bruce Armstrong .10
135 Drew Bledsoe 1.00
136 Ben Coates .10
137 Derrick Cullors .10
138 Terry Glenn .30
139 Shawn Jefferson .10
140 Curtis Martin .75
141 Chris Slade .10
142 Larry Whigham .10
143 Troy Davis .20
144 Andre Hastings .10
145 Randal Hill .10
146 Sammy Knight .10
147 William Roaf .10
148 Heath Shuler .10
149 Danny Wuerffel .20
150 Ray Zellars .10
151 Jessie Armstead .10
152 Tiki Barber .40
153 Chris Calloway .10
154 Danny Kanell .10
155 David Patten .10
156 Michael Strahan .10
157 Charles Way .10
158 Tyrone Wheatley .10
159 Kyle Brady .10
160 Wayne Chrebet .10
161 Glenn Foley .10
162 Aaron Glenn .10
163 Leon Johnson .10
164 Adrian Murrell .20
165 Neil O'Donnell .10
166 Dedric Ward .10
167 Tim Brown .20
168 Rickey Dudley .10
169 Jeff George .20
170 Desmond Howard .10
171 James Jett .10
172 Napoleon Kaufman .20
173 Chester McGlockton .10
174 Darrell Russell .10
175 Ty Detmer .10
176 Irving Fryar .10
177 Charlie Garner .10
178 Bobby Hoying .10
179 Chad Lewis .10
180 Duce Staley .10
181 Kevin Turner .10
182 Ricky Watters .20
183 Jerome Bettis .20
184 Will Blackwell .10
185 Charles Johnson .10
186 George Jones .10
187 Levon Kirkland .10
188 Carnell Lake .10
189 Kordell Stewart 1.00
190 Yancey Thigpen .10
191 Tony Banks .30
192 Isaac Bruce .20
193 Ernie Conwell .10
194 Craig Heyward .10
195 Eddie Kennison .20
196 Amp Lee .10
197 Orlando Pace .10
198 Torrance Small .10
199 Gary Brown .10
200 Kenny Bynum .10
201 Freddie Jones .10
202 Tony Martin .10
203 Eric Metcalf .10
204 Junior Seau .20
205 Craig Whelihan .10
206 William Floyd .20
207 Merton Hanks .10
208 Garrison Hearst .10
209 Brent Jones .10
210 Terrell Owens .20
211 Jerry Rice 1.00
212 J.J. Stokes .10
213 Rod Woodson .10
214 Steve Young .50
215 Steve Broussard .10
216 Joey Galloway .20
217 Cortez Kennedy .10
218 Jon Kitna .10
219 James McKnight .10
220 Warren Moon .20
221 Michael Sinclair .10
222 *Ryan Leaf* 1.00
223 Darryl Williams .10
224 Mike Alstott .30
225 Reidel Anthony .20
226 Derrick Brooks .10
227 Horace Copeland .10
228 Trent Dilfer .20
229 Warrick Dunn 1.00
230 Hardy Nickerson .10
231 Warren Sapp .10
232 Karl Williams .10
233 Blaine Bishop .10
234 Willie Davis .10
235 Eddie George 1.25
236 Derrick Mason .10
237 Bruce Matthews .10
238 Steve McNair .75
239 Chris Sanders .10
240 Rodney Thomas .10
241 Frank Wycheck .10
242 Terry Allen .10
243 Jamie Asher .10
244 Larry Bowie .10
245 Albert Connell .10
246 Stephen Davis .10
247 Gus Frerotte .10
248 Ken Harvey .10
249 Leslie Shepherd .10
250 Michael Westbrook .10

1998 Pacific Paramount Copper/Silver

The 250-card base set is paralleled in the Copper hobby-only and Silver retail-only sets (1:1).

Copper/Silver Cards: 2X-4X

1998 Pacific Paramount Platinum Blue

Platinum Blue is a full parallel of the Paramount base set, seeded one per 73 packs.

Platinum Blue Cards: 10X-20X

1998 Pacific Paramount Kings of the NFL

Kings of the NFL is a fully-foiled 20-card insert seeded one per 73 packs. The cards have a color photo with the player's name, position and team logo at the bottom.

NM/M
Complete Set (20): 110.00
Common Player: 3.00
1 Antowain Smith 5.00
2 Corey Dillon 5.00
3 Troy Aikman 10.00
4 Emmitt Smith 15.00
5 Terrell Davis 10.00
6 John Elway 10.00
7 Barry Sanders 15.00
8 Brett Favre 18.00
9 Dorsey Levens 3.00
10 Reggie White 3.00
11 Mark Brunell 5.00
12 Dan Marino 18.00
13 Curtis Martin 8.00
14 Drew Bledsoe 10.00
15 Jerome Bettis 3.00
16 Kordell Stewart 4.00
17 Jerry Rice 12.00
18 Steve Young 12.00

19	Warrick Dunn	6.00
20	Eddie George	6.00

1998 Pacific Paramount Personal Bests

Personal Bests is a 36-card insert seeded 4:37. The cards have a color player photo on holographic silver foil. The player's name is printed vertically on the left.

		NM/M
Complete Set (36):		60.00
Common Player:		1.00
1	Jake Plummer	2.00
2	Antowain Smith	2.00
3	Kerry Collins	2.00
4	Raymont Harris	1.00
5	Corey Dillon	3.00
6	Troy Aikman	5.00
7	Deion Sanders	3.00
8	Emmitt Smith	8.00
9	Terrell Davis	6.00
10	John Elway	6.00
11	Shannon Sharpe	1.00
12	Herman Moore	1.00
13	Barry Sanders	8.00
14	Brett Favre	10.00
15	Antonio Freeman	1.00
16	Dorsey Levens	1.00
17	Marshall Faulk	3.00
18	Mark Brunell	3.00
19	Dan Marino	10.00
20	Robert Smith	1.00
21	Curtis Martin	4.00
22	Drew Bledsoe	6.00
23	Danny Kanell	1.00
24	Adrian Murrell	1.00
25	Napoleon Kaufman	1.00
26	Jerome Bettis	1.00
27	Kordell Stewart	3.00
28	Terrell Owens	1.00
29	Jerry Rice	6.00
30	Steve Young	5.00
31	Warren Moon	1.00
32	Mike Alstott	3.00
33	Trent Dilfer	1.00
34	Warrick Dunn	3.00
35	Eddie George	3.00
36	Steve McNair	3.00

1998 Pacific Paramount Pro Bowl Die-Cuts

Pro Bowl Die-Cuts is a 20-card insert featuring players in their uniforms from the 1998 Pro Bowl. The background has a Hawaiian theme and the left side of the card features a die-cut outrigger. This set was inserted 1:37.

		NM/M
Complete Set (20):		80.00
Common Player:		2.00
1	Terrell Davis	8.00
2	John Elway	8.00
3	Shannon Sharpe	2.00
4	Herman Moore	2.00
5	Barry Sanders	10.00
6	Mark Chmura	2.00
7	Brett Favre	12.00
8	Dorsey Levens	2.00
9	Mark Brunell	5.00
10	Andre Rison	2.00
11	Cris Carter	2.00
12	Drew Bledsoe	6.00
13	Ben Coates	2.00
14	Jerome Bettis	2.00
15	Steve Young	8.00
16	Warren Moon	2.00
17	Mike Alstott	4.00
18	Trent Dilfer	2.00
19	Warrick Dunn	4.00
20	Eddie George	4.00

1998 Pacific Paramount Super Bowl XXXII Highlights

Super Bowl XXXII Highlights is a 10-card insert seeded two per 37 packs. The cards feature photography from the Super Bowl.

		NM/M
Complete Set (10):		25.00
Common Player:		1.00
1	Terrell Davis	4.00
2	John Elway	4.00
3	John Elway	4.00
4	Brett Favre	8.00
5	Antonio Freeman	2.00
6	Dorsey Levens	2.00
7	Ed McCaffrey	1.00
8	Eugene Robinson	1.00
9	Bill Romanowski	1.00
10	Darren Sharper	1.00

1998 Pacific Revolution

Pacific Revolution Football consists of a 150-card base set with one parallel and five inserts. The base cards feature a color player photo with a swirled foil background. The cards are etched and embossed. The player's name and his team helmet are featured on a black bar on the bottom. The base set is paralleled by Shadow Series. The inserts include Icons, Prime Time Performers, Rookies & Stars, Showstoppers and Touchdown Laser-Cuts.

		NM/M
Complete Set (150):		65.00
Common Player:		.10
Minor Stars:		.50
Shadow Cards:		5X-10X
Shadow Rookies:		3X-5X
Production 99 Sets		
Pack (3):		4.00
Wax Box (24):		80.00
1	Larry Centers	.10
2	Leeland McElroy	.10
3	Rob Moore	.10
4	Jake Plummer	2.00
5	Frank Sanders	.10
6	Jamal Anderson	.10
7	Chris Chandler	.10
8	Byron Hanspard	.10
9	Jay Graham	.10
10	Michael Jackson	.10
11	Vinny Testaverde	.10
12	Eric Zeier	.10
13	Todd Collins	.10
14	Quinn Early	.10
15	Andre Reed	.10
16	Antowain Smith	2.00
17	Bruce Smith	.10
18	Thurman Thomas	.50
19	Rae Carruth	.50
20	Kerry Collins	.50
21	Wesley Walls	.10
22	Darnell Autry	.50
23	Curtis Conway	.50
24	Bobby Engram	.10
25	*Curtis Enis*	1.00
26	Raymont Harris	.10
27	Jeff Blake	.50
28	Corey Dillon	3.00
29	Carl Pickens	.10
30	Darnay Scott	.10
31	Troy Aikman	4.00
32	Michael Irvin	.50
33	Deion Sanders	2.00
34	Emmitt Smith	5.00
35	Steve Atwater	.10
36	Terrell Davis	4.00
37	John Elway	4.00
38	*Brian Griese*	6.00
39	Ed McCaffrey	.10
40	*Marcus Nash*	1.00
41	Shannon Sharpe	.10
42	Neil Smith	.10
43	Rod Smith	.10
44	*Charlie Batch*	1.00
45	*Germane Crowell*	1.00
46	Scott Mitchell	.10
47	Herman Moore	.50
48	Barry Sanders	5.00
49	Robert Brooks	.10
50	Mark Chmura	.10
51	Brett Favre	6.00
52	Antonio Freeman	.50
53	Dorsey Levens	.50
54	Sean Dawkins	.10
55	Ken Dilger	.10
56	Marshall Faulk	.50
57	Marvin Harrison	.50
58	*Peyton Manning*	12.00
59	*Tavian Banks*	1.00
60	Tony Brackens	.10
61	Mark Brunell	2.00
62	Keenan McCardell	.10
63	Natrone Means	.50
64	Jimmy Smith	.10
65	James Stewart	.10
66	*Fred Taylor*	5.00
67	Tony Gonzalez	.50
68	Elvis Grbac	.10
69	Greg Hill	.10
70	Andre Rison	.10
71	Derrick Thomas	.10
72	Karim Abdul-Jabbar	.50
73	*John Avery*	1.00
74	Troy Drayton	.10
75	Dan Marino	6.00
76	O.J. McDuffie	.10
77	Cris Carter	.10
78	Brad Johnson	.50
79	John Randle	.10
80	Jake Reed	.10
81	Robert Smith	.50
82	Drew Bledsoe	3.00
83	Ben Coates	.10
84	*Robert Edwards*	2.00
85	Terry Glenn	.50
86	*Tony Simmons*	.10
87	Troy Davis	.50
88	Heath Shuler	.10
89	Danny Wuerffel	.10
90	Ray Zellars	.10
91	Tiki Barber	1.00
92	*Joe Jurevicius*	1.50
93	Danny Kanell	.10
94	Charles Way	.10
95	Tyrone Wheatley	.10
96	Wayne Chrebet	.10
97	Glenn Foley	.10
98	Keyshawn Johnson	.50
99	Curtis Martin	3.00
100	Tim Brown	.50
101	Rickey Dudley	.10
102	Jeff George	.50
103	Desmond Howard	.10
104	Napoleon Kaufman	.50
105	*Charles Woodson*	4.00
106	Jason Dunn	.10
107	Irving Fryar	.10
108	Charlie Garner	.10
109	Bobby Hoying	.50
110	Jerome Bettis	.50
111	Mark Bruener	.10
112	Charles Johnson	.10
113	Levon Kirkland	.10
114	Kordell Stewart	2.00
115	*Hines Ward*	5.00
116	Tony Banks	.50
117	Isaac Bruce	.50
118	*Robert Holcombe*	3.00
119	Eddie Kennison	.50
120	Freddie Jones	.10
121	*Ryan Leaf*	1.00
122	Tony Martin	.10
123	Junior Seau	.50
124	Jim Druckenmiller	.50
125	Garrison Hearst	.10
126	Terrell Owens	.50
127	Jerry Rice	4.00
128	J.J. Stokes	.10
129	Steve Young	2.00
130	Joey Galloway	.50
131	*Ahman Green*	10.00
132	Cortez Kennedy	.10
133	Jon Kitna	.50
134	James McKnight	.10
135	Warren Moon	.50
136	Mike Alstott	2.00
137	Reidel Anthony	.50
138	Trent Dilfer	.50
139	Warrick Dunn	2.00
140	Warren Sapp	.10
141	*Kevin Dyson*	3.00
142	Eddie George	2.00
143	Steve McNair	2.00
144	Chris Sanders	.10
145	Frank Wycheck	.10
146	Stephen Alexander	.10
147	Terry Allen	.10
148	Gus Frerotte	.10
149	*Skip Hicks*	1.00
150	Michael Westbrook	.10

1998 Pacific Revolution Icons

Icons is a 10-card insert seeded one per 121 packs. The cards have a die-cut design resembling the NFL's shield logo.

		NM/M
Complete Set (10):		110.00
Common Player:		10.00
1	Emmitt Smith	20.00
2	Terrell Davis	15.00
3	John Elway	15.00
4	Barry Sanders	20.00
5	Brett Favre	25.00
6	Mark Brunell	10.00
7	Dan Marino	25.00
8	Jerry Rice	20.00
9	Warrick Dunn	10.00
10	Eddie George	10.00

1998 Pacific Revolution Prime Time Performers

Prime Time Performers is a 20-card insert seeded 1:25. The cards feature a small player photo on the left and a football with the team's logo laser-cut on the right. The cards have a horizontal layout.

		NM/M
Complete Set (20):		75.00
Common Player:		2.00
1	Jake Plummer	3.00
2	Corey Dillon	3.00
3	Troy Aikman	5.00
4	Deion Sanders	3.00
5	Emmitt Smith	7.00
6	Terrell Davis	5.00
7	John Elway	5.00
8	Barry Sanders	7.00
9	Brett Favre	8.00
10	Peyton Manning	8.00
11	Mark Brunell	3.00
12	Dan Marino	8.00
13	Drew Bledsoe	5.00
14	Jerome Bettis	2.00
15	Kordell Stewart	3.00
16	Jerry Rice	6.00
17	Steve Young	6.00
18	Warrick Dunn	3.00
19	Eddie George	3.00
20	Steve McNair	3.00

1998 Pacific Revolution Rookies and Stars

Rookies & Stars is a 30-card hobby-only insert. Seeded 4:25, the set features 20 rookies and 10 established stars. A gold parallel version was also produced. The parallel cards are numbered to 50.

		NM/M
Complete Set (30):		60.00
Common Player:		1.00
Minor Stars:		3.00
Inserted 4:25 Hobby		
Gold Cards:		4X-8X
Production 50 Sets		
1	Michael Pittman	1.00
2	Curtis Enis	1.00
3	Takeo Spikes	1.00
4	Greg Ellis	1.00
5	Emmitt Smith	6.00
6	Terrell Davis	5.00
7	John Elway	5.00
8	Brian Griese	4.00
9	Marcus Nash	1.00
10	Charlie Batch	1.00
11	Barry Sanders	6.00
12	Brett Favre	8.00
13	Vonnie Holliday	1.00
14	E.G. Green	1.00
15	Peyton Manning	8.00
16	Fred Taylor	4.00
17	John Avery	1.00
18	Dan Marino	8.00
19	Drew Bledsoe	3.00
20	Robert Edwards	2.00
21	Joe Jurevicius	1.00
22	Charles Woodson	2.00
23	Kordell Stewart	2.00
24	Robert Holcombe	2.00
25	Ryan Leaf	1.00
26	Warrick Dunn	2.00
27	Jacquez Green	2.00
28	Kevin Dyson	2.00
29	Eddie George	3.00
30	Stephen Alexander	2.00

1998 Pacific Revolution Shadows

Shadows are a full parallel of the Revolution base set. The parallel cards are numbered to 99.

Shadow Cards:	5X-10X
Shadow Rookies:	3X-5X

1998 Pacific Revolution Showstoppers

Showstoppers is a 36-card insert seeded two per 25 packs. The background features the player's name and team name printed in holographic silver foil.

		NM/M
Complete Set (36):		80.00
Common Player:		1.00
Minor Stars:		2.00
1	Jake Plummer	2.00
2	Antowain Smith	2.00
3	Kerry Collins	2.00
4	Corey Dillon	3.00
5	Troy Aikman	5.00
6	Deion Sanders	3.00
7	Emmitt Smith	7.00
8	Terrell Davis	15.00
9	John Elway	5.00
10	Shannon Sharpe	1.00
11	Herman Moore	2.00
12	Barry Sanders	7.00
13	Brett Favre	8.00
14	Antonio Freeman	2.00
15	Dorsey Levens	2.00
16	Peyton Manning	8.00
17	Mark Brunell	4.00
18	Dan Marino	8.00
19	Robert Smith	1.00
20	Drew Bledsoe	5.00
21	Danny Kanell	1.00
22	Curtis Martin	5.00
23	Tim Brown	1.00
24	Napoleon Kaufman	1.00
25	Jerome Bettis	2.00
26	Kordell Stewart	3.00
27	Ryan Leaf	1.00
28	Terrell Owens	1.00
29	Jerry Rice	6.00
30	Steve Young	6.00
31	Ricky Watters	1.00
32	Mike Alstott	3.00
33	Trent Dilfer	1.00
34	Warrick Dunn	3.00
35	Eddie George	3.00
36	Steve McNair	3.00

1998 Pacific Revolution Touchdown

Touchdown Laser-Cuts is a 20-card insert seeded one per 49 packs. The cards have a color player photo in the foreground with a set of goal posts in the background. The netting behind the goal posts is laser-cut.

		NM/M
Complete Set (20):		110.00
Common Player:		2.00
1	Jake Plummer	3.00
2	Corey Dillon	3.00
3	Troy Aikman	5.00
4	Emmitt Smith	8.00
5	Terrell Davis	5.00
6	John Elway	7.00
7	Barry Sanders	8.00
8	Brett Favre	10.00
9	Dorsey Levens	2.00
10	Peyton Manning	25.00
11	Mark Brunell	4.00
12	Marcus Allen	2.00
13	Dan Marino	10.00
14	Drew Bledsoe	6.00
15	Jerome Bettis	2.00
16	Kordell Stewart	3.00
17	Jerry Rice	6.00
18	Steve Young	6.00
19	Warrick Dunn	4.00
20	Eddie George	4.00

1999 Pacific

Pacific Football is a 450-card set that includes more than 30 unseeded rookie cards. Copper, Gold, Opening Day and Platinum Blue are the four different parallel sets. Other inserts include: Cramer's Choice, Dynagon Turf, Gold Crown Die Cuts, Pro Bowl Die Cuts, Record Breakers and Team Checklists.

		NM/M
Complete Set (450):		100.00
Common Player:		.15
Minor Stars:		.30
Common Rookie:		.50
Pack (12):		4.00
Wax Box (24):		80.00
1	Mario Bates	.15
2	Larry Centers	.15
3	Chris Gedney	.15
4	Kwamie Lassiter	.15
5	Johnny McWilliams	.15
6	Eric Metcalf	.15
7	Rob Moore	.30
8	Adrian Murrell	.15
9	Jake Plummer	.50
10	Simeon Rice	.15
11	Frank Sanders	.30
12	Andre Wadsworth	.30
13	Aeneas Williams	.15
14	Michael Pittman, Ronnie Anderson	.15
15	Morten Andersen	.15
16	Jamal Anderson	.50
17	Lester Archambeau	.15
18	Chris Chandler	.15
19	Bob Christian	.15
20	Steve DeBerg	.15
21	Tim Dwight	.50
22	Tony Martin	.15
23	Terance Mathis	.15
24	Eugene Robinson	.15
25	O.J. Santiago	.15
26	Chuck Smith	.15
27	Jessie Tuggle	.15
28	Jammi German, Ken Oxendine	.15
29	Peter Boulware	.15
30	Jay Graham	.15
31	Jim Harbaugh	.30
32	Priest Holmes	.75
33	Michael Jackson	.15
34	Jermaine Lewis	.15
35	Ray Lewis	.15
36	Michael McCrary	.15
37	Jonathan Ogden	.15
38	Errict Rhett	.15
39	James Roe	.15
40	Floyd Turner	.15
41	Rod Woodson	.15
42	Eric Zeier	.15
43	Wally Richardson, Patrick Johnson	.15
44	Ruben Brown	.15
45	Quinn Early	.15
46	Doug Flutie	.50
47	Sam Gash	.15
48	Phil Hansen	.15
49	Lonnie Johnson	.15
50	Rob Johnson	.30
51	Eric Moulds	.50
52	Andre Reed	.15
53	Jay Riemersma	.15
54	Antowain Smith	.30
55	Bruce Smith	.15

56	Thurman Thomas	.30
57	Ted Washington	.15
58	Jonathon Linton, Kamil Loud	.15
59	Michael Bates	.15
60	Steve Beuerlein	.15
61	Tshimanga Biakabutuka	.15
62	Mark Carrier	.15
63	Eric Davis	.15
64	William Floyd	.15
65	Sean Gilbert	.15
66	Kevin Greene	.15
67	Raghib Ismail	.15
68	Anthony Johnson	.15
69	Fred Lane	.15
70	Muhsin Muhammad	.15
71	Winslow Oliver	.15
72	Wesley Walls	.15
73	Dameyune Craig, Shane Matthews	.15
74	Edgar Bennett	.15
75	Curtis Conway	.30
76	Bobby Engram	.15
77	Curtis Enis	.50
78	Ty Hallock	.15
79	Walt Harris	.15
80	Jeff Jaeger	.15
81	Erik Kramer	.15
82	Glyn Milburn	.15
83	Chris Penn	.15
84	Steve Stenstrom	.15
85	Ryan Wetnight	.15
86	Moses Moreno, James Allen	.15
87	Ashley Ambrose	.15
88	Brandon Bennett	.15
89	Eric Bieniemy	.15
90	Jeff Blake	.30
91	Corey Dillon	.50
92	Paul Justin	.15
93	Eric Kresser	.15
94	Tremain Mack	.15
95	Tony McGee	.15
96	Neil O'Donnell	.15
97	Carl Pickens	.30
98	Darnay Scott	.15
99	Takeo Spikes	.15
100	Ty Detmer	.15
101	Chris Gardocki	.15
102	Damon Gibson	.15
103	Antonio Langham	.15
104	Jerris McPhail	.15
105	Irv Smith	.15
106	Freddie Solomon	.15
107	Scott Milanovich, Fred Brock	.15
108	Troy Aikman	1.25
109	Larry Allen	.15
110	Eric Bjornson	.15
111	Billy Davis	.15
112	Michael Irvin	.30
113	David LaFleur	.15
114	Ernie Mills	.15
115	Nate Newton	.15
116	Deion Sanders	.50
117	Emmitt Smith	1.75
118	Chris Warren	.15
119	Bubby Brister	.15
120	Terrell Davis	1.00
121	Jason Elam	.15
122	John Elway	2.00
123	Willie Green	.15
124	Howard Griffith	.15
125	Vaughn Hebron	.15
126	Ed McCaffrey	.30
127	John Mobley	.15
128	Bill Romanowski	.15
129	Shannon Sharpe	.30
130	Neil Smith	.15
131	Rod Smith	.30
132	Brian Griese, Marcus Nash	.50
133	Charlie Batch	1.00
134	Stephen Boyd	.15
135	Mark Carrier	.15
136	Germane Crowell	.30
137	Terry Fair	.15
138	Jason Hanson	.15
139	Greg Jeffries	.15
140	Herman Moore	.30
141	Johnnie Morton	.15
142	Robert Porcher	.15
143	Ron Rivers	.15
144	Barry Sanders	2.00
145	Tommy Vardell	.15
146	Bryant Westbrook	.15
147	Robert Brooks	.15
148	LeRoy Butler	.15
149	Mark Chmura	.15
150	Tyrone Davis	.15
151	Brett Favre	2.50
152	Antonio Freeman	.50
153	Raymont Harris	.15
154	Vonnie Holliday	.30
155	Darick Holmes	.15
156	Dorsey Levens	.30
157	Brian Manning	.15
158	Derrick Mayes	.15
159	Roell Preston	.15
160	Jeff Thomason	.15
161	Tyrone Williams	.15
162	Corey Bradford, Michael Blair	.15
163	Aaron Bailey	.15
164	Ken Dilger	.15
165	Marshall Faulk	.50
166	E.G. Green	.30
167	Marvin Harrison	.30
168	Craig Heyward	.15
169	Peyton Manning	2.00
170	Jerome Pathon	.30
171	Marcus Pollard	.15
172	Torrance Small	.15
173	Mike Vanderjagt	.15
174	Lamont Warren	.15
175	Tavian Banks	.30
176	Reggie Barlow	.15
177	Tony Boselli	.15
178	Tony Brackens	.15
179	Mark Brunell	1.00
180	Kevin Hardy	.15
181	Damon Jones	.15
182	Jamie Martin	.15
183	Keenan McCardell	.15
184	Pete Mitchell	.15
185	Bryce Paup	.15
186	Jimmy Smith	.30
187	Fred Taylor	1.00
188	Alvis Whitted, Chris Howard	.15
189	Derrick Alexander	.15
190	Kimble Anders	.15
191	Donnell Bennett	.15
192	Dale Carter	.15
193	Rich Gannon	.15
194	Tony Gonzalez	.15
195	Elvis Grbac	.15
196	Joe Horn	.15
197	Kevin Lockett	.15
198	Bam Morris	.15
199	Andre Rison	.30
200	Derrick Thomas	.15
201	Tamarick Vanover	.15
202	Gregory Favors, Rashaan Shehee	.15
203	Karim Abdul	.30
204	Trace Armstrong	.15
205	John Avery	.30
206	Lorenzo Bromell	.15
207	Terrell Buckley	.15
208	Oronde Gadsden	.30
209	Sam Madison	.15
210	Dan Marino	1.75
211	O.J. McDuffie	.15
212	Ed Perry	.15
213	Jason Taylor	.15
214	Lamar Thomas	.15
215	Zach Thomas	.30
216	Henry Lusk, Nate Jacquet	.15
217	Damon Huard, Todd Doxzon	.15
218	Gary Anderson	.15
219	Cris Carter	.50
220	Randall Cunningham	.50
221	Andrew Glover	.15
222	Matthew Hatchette	.15
223	Brad Johnson	.50
224	Ed McDaniel	.15
225	Randall McDaniel	.15
226	Randy Moss	2.00
227	David Palmer	.15
228	John Randle	.15
229	Jake Reed	.15
230	Robert Smith	.30
231	Todd Steussie	.15
232	Stalin Colinet, Kivuusama Mays	.15
233	*Jay Fiedler, Todd Bouman*	10.00
234	Drew Bledsoe	1.00
235	Troy Brown	.15
236	Ben Coates	.30
237	Derrick Cullors	.15
238	Robert Edwards	.30
239	Terry Glenn	.30
240	Shawn Jefferson	.15
241	Ty Law	.15
242	Lawyer Milloy	.15
243	Lovett Purnell	.15
244	Sedrick Shaw	.15
245	Tony Simmons	.30
246	Chris Slade	.15
247	Rod Rutledge, Anthony Ladd	.15
248	Chris Floyd, Harold Shaw	.15
249	Ink Aleaga	.15
250	Cameron Cleeland	.30
251	Kerry Collins	.30
252	Troy Davis	.15
253	Sean Dawkins	.15
254	Mark Fields	.15
255	Andre Hastings	.15
256	Sammy Knight	.15
257	Keith Poole	.15
258	William Roaf	.15
259	Lamar Smith	.15
260	Danny Wuerffel	.15
261	Josh Wilcox, Brett Bech	.15
262	Chris Bordeleau, Wilmont Perry	.15
263	Jessie Armstead	.15
264	Tiki Barber	.15
265	Chad Bratzke	.15
266	Gary Brown	.15
267	Chris Calloway	.15
268	Howard Cross	.15
269	Kent Graham	.15
270	Ike Hilliard	.15
271	Danny Kanell	.15
272	Michael Strahan	.15
273	Amani Toomer	.15
274	Charles Way	.15
275	Mike Cherry, Greg Comella	.15
276	Kyle Brady	.15
277	Keith Byars	.15
278	Chad Cascadden	.15
279	Wayne Chrebet	.30
280	Bryan Cox	.15
281	Glenn Foley	.30
282	Aaron Glenn	.15
283	Keyshawn Johnson	.50
284	Leon Johnson	.15
285	Mo Lewis	.15
286	Curtis Martin	.50
287	Otis Smith	.15
288	Vinny Testaverde	.30
289	Dedric Ward	.15
290	Tim Brown	.30
291	Rickey Dudley	.15
292	Jeff George	.30
293	Desmond Howard	.15
294	James Jett	.15
295	Lance Johnstone	.15
296	Randy Jordan	.15
297	Napoleon Kaufman	.50
298	Lincoln Kennedy	.15
299	Terry Mickens	.15
300	Darrell Russell	.15
301	Harvey Williams	.15
302	Jon Ritchie, Charles Woodson	.30
303	Rodney Williams, Jermaine Williams	.15
304	Koy Detmer	.15
305	Hugh Douglas	.15
306	Jason Dunn	.15
307	Irving Fryar	.15
308	Charlie Garner	.15
309	Jeff Graham	.15
310	Bobby Hoying	.15
311	Rodney Peete	.15
312	Allen Rossum	.15
313	Duce Staley	.15
314	William Thomas	.15
315	Kevin Turner	.15
316	Kaseem Sinceno, Corey Walker	.15
317	Jahine Arnold	.15
318	Jerome Bettis	.30
319	Will Blackwell	.15
320	Mark Bruener	.15
321	Dermontti Dawson	.15
322	Chris Fuamatu-Ma'afala	.15
323	Courtney Hawkins	.15
324	Richard Huntley	.15
325	Charles Johnson	.15
326	Levon Kirkland	.15
327	Kordell Stewart	.75
328	Hines Ward	.30
329	DeWayne Washington	.15
330	Tony Banks	.30
331	Steve Bono	.15
332	Isaac Bruce	.30
333	June Henley	.15
334	Robert Holcombe	.30
335	Mike Jones	.15
336	Eddie Kennison	.15
337	Amp Lee	.15
338	Jerald Moore	.15
339	Ricky Proehl	.15
340	J.T. Thomas	.15
341	Derrick Harris, Az-Zahir Hakim	.15
342	Roland Williams, Grant Wistrom	.15
343	*Kurt Warner, Tony Horne*	15.00
344	Terrell Fletcher	.15
345	Greg Jackson	.15
346	Charlie Jones	.15
347	Freddie Jones	.15
348	Ryan Leaf	1.00
349	Natrone Means	.30
350	Mikhael Ricks	.15
351	Junior Seau	.30
352	Bryan Still	.15
353	Tremayne Stephens, Ryan Thelwell	.15
354	Greg Clark	.15
355	Marc Edwards	.15
356	Merton Hanks	.15
357	Garrison Hearst	.30
358	R.W. McQuarters	.15
359	Ken Norton Jr.	.15
360	Terrell Owens	.50
361	Jerry Rice	1.25
362	J.J. Stokes	.30
363	Bryant Young	.15
364	Steve Young	1.00
365	Chad Brown	.15
366	Christian Fauria	.15
367	Joey Galloway	.50
368	Ahman Green	.30
369	Cortez Kennedy	.15
370	Jon Kitna	.75
371	James McKnight	.15
372	Mike Pritchard	.15
373	Michael Sinclair	.15
374	Shawn Springs	.15
375	Ricky Watters	.30
376	Darryl Williams	.15
377	Robert Wilson, Kerry Joseph	.15
378	Mike Alstott	.30
379	Reidel Anthony	.15
380	Derrick Brooks	.15
381	Trent Dilfer	.30
382	Warrick Dunn	.75
383	Bert Emanuel	.15
384	Jacquez Green	.30
385	Patrick Hape	.15
386	John Lynch	.15
387	Dave Moore	.15
388	Hardy Nickerson	.15
389	Warren Sapp	.15
390	Karl Williams	.15
391	Blaine Bishop	.15
392	Joe Bowden	.15
393	Isaac Byrd	.15
394	Willie Davis	.15
395	Al Del Greco	.15
396	Kevin Dyson	.30
397	Eddie George	.75
398	Jackie Harris	.15
399	Dave Krieg	.15
400	Steve McNair	.50
401	Michael Roan	.15
402	Yancey Thigpen	.15
403	Frank Wycheck	.15
404	Derrick Mason, Steve Matthews	.15
405	Stephen Alexander	.15
406	Terry Allen	.30
407	Jamie Asher	.15
408	Stephen Davis	.15
409	Darrell Green	.15
410	Trent Green	.30
411	Skip Hicks	.30
412	Brian Mitchell	.15
413	Leslie Shepherd	.15
414	Michael Westbrook	.15
415	Terry Hardy, Rabih Abdullah	.15
416	Corey Thomas, Mike Quinn	.15
417	Jonathan Quinn, Kelly Holcomb	.15
418	Brian Alford, Blake Spence	.15
419	Andy Haase, Carlos King	.15
420	Karl Hankton, James Thrash	.15
421	Fred Beasley, Itula Mili	.15
422	*Champ Bailey*	2.00
423	*D'Wayne Bates*	1.00
424	*Michael Bishop*	2.00
425	*David Boston*	3.00
426	*Shawn Bryson*	.50
427	*Tim Couch*	3.00
428	*Scott Covington*	1.00
429	*Daunte Culpepper*	6.00
430	*Autry Denson*	1.00
431	*Troy Edwards*	1.50
432	*Kevin Faulk*	2.00
433	*Joe Germaine*	2.00
434	*Torry Holt*	3.00
435	*Brock Huard*	2.00
436	*Sedrick Irvin*	1.50
437	*Edgerrin James*	6.00
438	*Andy Katzenmoyer*	1.00
439	*Shaun King*	2.00
440	*Rob Konrad*	.50
441	*Donovan McNabb*	6.00
442	*Cade McNown*	1.50
443	*Billy Miller*	1.00
444	*Dee Miller*	1.00
445	*Sirr Parker*	1.00
446	*Peerless Price*	2.50
447	*Akili Smith*	1.50
448	*Tai Streets*	1.00
449	*Ricky Williams*	3.00
450	*Amos Zereoue*	2.00

1999 Pacific Copper

This 450-card parallel was a hobby-only release and was sequentially numbered to 99.

	NM/M
Copper Cards:	10X-20X
Copper Rookies:	3X-5X
Production 99 Sets	

1999 Pacific Gold

This 450-card set is a parallel to the base and was hobby only and is sequentially numbered to 199.

	NM/M
Gold Cards:	5X-10X
Gold Rookies:	2X-4X
Production 199 Sets	

1999 Pacific Opening Day

This 450-card set is a parallel to the base and each card is sequentially numbered to 45.

	NM/M
Opening Day Cards:	15X-30X
Opening Day Rookies:	5X-10X
Production 45 Sets	

1999 Pacific Platinum Blue

This is a 450-card set that is a parallel to the base with each single sequentially numbered to 75.

	NM/M
Platinum Blue Cards:	10X-25X
Platinum Blue Rookies:	4X-8X
Production 75 Sets	

1999 Pacific Cramer's Choice Awards

This insert includes the top ten players in the NFL and captures them on a dual-foiled trophy card. Each is die cut in the shape of a pyramid and is sequentially numbered to 299.

		NM/M
Complete Set (10):		300.00
Common Player:		15.00
Production 299 Sets		
1	Jamal Anderson	15.00
2	Terrell Davis	35.00
3	John Elway	35.00
4	Barry Sanders	45.00
5	Brett Favre	50.00
6	Peyton Manning	50.00
7	Fred Taylor	25.00
8	Dan Marino	50.00
9	Randall Cunningham	15.00
10	Randy Moss	50.00

1999 Pacific Dynagon Turf

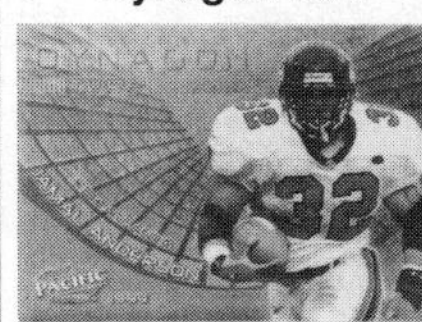

Each card in this 20-card set is printed on a silver-foil card and is horizontal. Singles were inserted 2:25 packs. A parallel Titanium Turf was made and is sequentially numbered to 99.

		NM/M
Complete Set (20):		45.00
Common Player:		.75
Minor Stars:		1.50
Inserted 2:25		
Titanium Turf Singles:		3X-6X
Production 99 Sets		
1	Jake Plummer	2.00
2	Jamal Anderson	1.50
3	Doug Flutie	1.50
4	Emmitt Smith	5.00
5	Terrell Davis	4.00
6	John Elway	4.00
7	Barry Sanders	5.00
8	Brett Favre	6.00
9	Peyton Manning	5.00
10	Mark Brunell	3.00
11	Fred Taylor	3.00
12	Dan Marino	6.00
13	Randall Cunningham	1.50
14	Randy Moss	5.00
15	Drew Bledsoe	3.00
16	Curtis Martin	1.50
17	Jerome Bettis	.75
18	Jerry Rice	4.00
19	Jon Kitna	1.50
20	Eddie George	2.00

1999 Pacific Gold Crown Die-Cuts

Each card in this 36-card set is printed on dual-foil board and is die cut in the shape of a gold crown. Singles were inserted 1:25 packs.

		NM/M
Complete Set (36):		100.00
Common Player:		1.00
Minor Stars:		2.00
Inserted 1:25		
1	Jake Plummer	2.00
2	Jamal Anderson	2.00
3	Priest Holmes	4.00
4	Doug Flutie	2.00
5	Antowain Smith	1.00
6	Corey Dillon	2.00
7	Troy Aikman	6.00
8	Emmitt Smith	8.00
9	Terrell Davis	6.00
10	John Elway	6.00
11	Brian Griese	4.00
12	Charlie Batch	2.00
13	Barry Sanders	8.00
14	Brett Favre	10.00
15	Antonio Freeman	2.00
16	Marshall Faulk	2.00
17	Peyton Manning	10.00
18	Mark Brunell	4.00
19	Fred Taylor	4.00
20	Dan Marino	10.00
21	Randall Cunningham	2.00
22	Randy Moss	10.00
23	Drew Bledsoe	6.00
24	Keyshawn Johnson	2.00
25	Curtis Martin	2.00
26	Napoleon Kaufman	1.00
27	Jerome Bettis	2.00
28	Kordell Stewart	4.00
29	Terrell Owens	4.00
30	Jerry Rice	6.00
31	Steve Young	6.00
32	Joey Galloway	2.00
33	Jon Kitna	2.00
34	Trent Dilfer	2.00
35	Warrick Dunn	3.00
36	Eddie George	3.00

1999 Pacific Pro Bowl Die-Cuts

The 20 players in this set are printed on a die-cut card with an erupting volcano in the background. Singles were inserted 1:49 packs.

		NM/M
Complete Set (20):		70.00
Common Player:		2.00
Inserted 1:49		
1	Jamal Anderson	3.00
2	Chris Chandler	2.00
3	Doug Flutie	2.00
4	Deion Sanders	3.00
5	Emmitt Smith	10.00
6	Terrell Davis	6.00
7	John Elway	6.00
8	Barry Sanders	10.00
9	Antonio Freeman	3.00
10	Marshall Faulk	6.00
11	Randall Cunningham	2.00
12	Randy Moss	12.00
13	Robert Smith	2.00
14	Ty Law	2.00
15	Keyshawn Johnson	2.00
16	Curtis Martin	3.00
17	Jerry Rice	6.00
18	Steve Young	6.00
19	Mike Alstott	3.00
20	Eddie George	3.00

1999 Pacific Record Breakers

This was a hobby only insert that included record-breaking achievements from 1998. Singles from this 20-card insert were sequentially numbered to 199.

		NM/M
Complete Set (20):		140.00
Common Player:		5.00
Production 199 Sets		
1	Jake Plummer	5.00
2	Jamal Anderson	5.00
3	Doug Flutie	5.00
4	Troy Aikman	15.00
5	Emmitt Smith	20.00
6	Terrell Davis	15.00
7	John Elway	15.00
8	Barry Sanders	20.00
9	Brett Favre	25.00
10	Marshall Faulk	12.00
11	Peyton Manning	20.00
12	Mark Brunell	10.00
13	Fred Taylor	10.00
14	Dan Marino	25.00
15	Randall Cunningham	5.00
16	Randy Moss	20.00
17	Drew Bledsoe	12.00
18	Curtis Martin	10.00
19	Jerry Rice	15.00
20	Steve Young	15.00

1999 Pacific Team Checklists

Each card in this 31-card set includes each team with a star player from that team on the fronts of the horizontal card. The backs include the team checklist for each player in the base set. Singles were inserted 2:25 packs.

		NM/M
Complete Set (31):		40.00
Common Player:		1.00
Minor Stars:		2.00
Inserted 2:25		
1	Jake Plummer	1.00
2	Jamal Anderson	1.00
3	Priest Holmes	2.00
4	Doug Flutie	1.00
5	Muhsin Muhammad	1.00
6	Curtis Enis	1.00
7	Corey Dillon	2.00
8	Ty Detmer	1.00
9	Emmitt Smith	5.00
10	John Elway	4.00
11	Barry Sanders	5.00

12	Brett Favre	6.00
13	Peyton Manning	5.00
14	Fred Taylor	3.00
15	Andre Rison	1.00
16	Dan Marino	5.00
17	Randy Moss	5.00
18	Drew Bledsoe	3.00
19	Cameron Cleeland	1.00
20	Ike Hilliard	1.00
21	Curtis Martin	2.00
22	Napoleon Kaufman	1.00
23	Duce Staley	1.00
24	Jerome Bettis	2.00
25	Isaac Bruce	1.00
26	Ryan Leaf	1.00
27	Steve Young	3.00
28	Joey Galloway	1.00
29	Warrick Dunn	1.00
30	Eddie George	2.00
31	Michael Westbrook	1.00

1999 Pacific Aurora

Each card in this 200-card set has a large posed photo and a smaller action photo in a vintage looking sepia color. A total of 150 players were used with 50 star players and rookies duplicated with a pinstripe background and posed photo on front. Inserts include: Premiere Date, Canvas Creations, Championship Fever, Complete Players, Leather Bound and Styrotechs.

		NM/M
Complete Set (200):		45.00
Common Player:		.15
Minor Stars:		.30
Pack (6):		3.00
Wax Box (24):		65.00
1	*David Boston*	3.00
2	Larry Centers	.15
3	Rob Moore	.30
4	Adrian Murrell	.15
5C	Jake Plummer	1.00
5D	Jake Plummer	1.00
6C	Jamal Anderson	.50
6D	Jamal Anderson	.50
7	Chris Chandler	.30
8	Tim Dwight	.50
9	Terance Mathis	.15
10	O.J. Santiago	.15
11C	Priest Holmes	.50
11D	Priest Holmes	.50
12	Michael Jackson	.15
13	Jermaine Lewis	.30
14	Ray Lewis	.15
15	Michael McCrary	.15
16C	Doug Flutie	.75
16D	Doug Flutie	.75
17C	Eric Moulds	.50
17D	Eric Moulds	.50
18	*Peerless Price*	2.50
19	Antowain Smith	.50
20	Bruce Smith	.15
21	Steve Beuerlein	.15
22	Tshimanga Biakabutuka	.15
23	Kevin Greene	.15
24	Muhsin Muhammad	.15
25	Wesley Walls	.15
26	Curtis Conway	.30
27	Bobby Engram	.15
28	Curtis Enis	.30
29	Erik Kramer	.15
30C	*Cade McNown*	1.00
30D	*Cade McNown*	1.00
31	Jeff Blake	.30
32C	Corey Dillon	.50
32D	Corey Dillon	.50
33	Carl Pickens	.30
34	Darnay Scott	.15
35C	*Akili Smith*	1.00
35D	*Akili Smith*	1.00
36C	*Tim Couch*	3.00
36D	*Tim Couch*	3.00
37	Ty Detmer	.15
38	*Kevin Johnson*	2.00
39	Terry Kirby	.15
40C	Troy Aikman	1.00
40D	Troy Aikman	1.00
41	Michael Irvin	.30
42	Raghib Ismail	.15
43C	Deion Sanders	.50
43D	Deion Sanders	.50
44C	Emmitt Smith	1.50
44D	Emmitt Smith	1.50
45	Bubby Brister	.30
46C	Terrell Davis	1.50
46D	Terrell Davis	1.50
47	Brian Griese	1.00
48	Ed McCaffrey	.30
49C	Shannon Sharpe	.30
49D	Shannon Sharpe	.30
50	Rod Smith	.30
51C	Charlie Batch	.75
51D	Charlie Batch	.75
52	*Sedrick Irvin*	.50
53C	Herman Moore	.50
53D	Herman Moore	.50
54	Johnnie Morton	.15
55C	Barry Sanders	2.00
55D	Barry Sanders	2.00
56	Robert Brooks	.15
57C	Brett Favre	2.00
57D	Brett Favre	2.00
58C	Antonio Freeman	.50
58D	Antonio Freeman	.50
59	Dorsey Levens	.50
60	Derrick Mayes	.30
61	Marvin Harrison	.50
62C	*Edgerrin James*	6.00
62D	*Edgerrin James*	6.00
63C	Peyton Manning	1.50
63D	Peyton Manning	1.50
64	Jerome Pathon	.15
65	Tavian Banks	.30
66C	Mark Brunell	.75
66D	Mark Brunell	.75
67	Keenan McCardell	.15
68	Jimmy Smith	.30
69C	Fred Taylor	1.00
69D	Fred Taylor	1.00
70	Derrick Alexander	.15
71	Kimble Anders	.15
72	*Michael Cloud*	1.50
73	Elvis Grbac	.30
74	Andre Rison	.30
75	Karim Abdul	.30
76	*James Johnson*	2.00
77C	Dan Marino	1.50
77D	Dan Marino	1.50
78	O.J. McDuffie	.30
79	Lamar Thomas	.15
80C	Cris Carter	.50
80D	Cris Carter	.50
81	*Daunte Culpepper*	6.00
82C	Randall Cunningham	.50
82D	Randall Cunningham	.50
83C	Randy Moss	2.50
83D	Randy Moss	2.50
84	John Randle	.15
85C	Robert Smith	.50
85D	Robert Smith	.50
86C	Drew Bledsoe	.75
86D	Drew Bledsoe	.75
87	Ben Coates	.30
88	*Kevin Faulk*	2.00
89C	Terry Glenn	.50
89D	Terry Glenn	.50
90	Ty Law	.15
91	Cameron Cleeland	.30
92	Andre Hastings	.15
93	Billy Joe Hobert	.15
94C	*Ricky Williams*	6.00
94D	*Ricky Williams*	6.00
95	Tiki Barber	.15
96	Kent Graham	.15
97	Ike Hilliard	.15
98	Charles Way	.15
99	Wayne Chrebet	.50
100C	Keyshawn Johnson	.50
100D	Keyshawn Johnson	.50
101C	Curtis Martin	.50
101D	Curtis Martin	.50
102C	Vinny Testaverde	.30
102D	Vinny Testaverde	.30
103	Dedric Ward	.15
104C	Tim Brown	.30
104D	Tim Brown	.30
105	Rickey Dudley	.15
106	James Jett	.15
107	Napoleon Kaufman	.50
108	Charles Woodson	.50
109	Jeff Graham	.15
110	Charles Johnson	.15
111C	*Donovan McNabb*	6.00
111D	*Donovan McNabb*	6.00
112	Duce Staley	.30
113C	Jerome Bettis	.50
113D	Jerome Bettis	.50
114	*Troy Edwards*	2.00
115	Courtney Hawkins	.15
116C	Kordell Stewart	.50
116D	Kordell Stewart	.50
117	*Amos Zereoue*	2.00
118	Isaac Bruce	.30
119C	Marshall Faulk	.50
119D	Marshall Faulk	.50
120	*Joe Germaine*	2.00
121C	*Torry Holt*	3.00
121D	*Torry Holt*	3.00
122	Amp Lee	.15
123	Charlie Jones	.15
124	Ryan Leaf	.50
125	Natrone Means	.30
126	Junior Seau	.30
127	Garrison Hearst	.50
128C	Terrell Owens	.50
128D	Terrell Owens	.50
129C	Jerry Rice	1.00
129D	Jerry Rice	1.00
130	J.J. Stokes	.30
131C	Steve Young	.75
131D	Steve Young	.75
132	Chad Brown	.15
133C	Joey Galloway	.50
133D	Joey Galloway	.50
134	*Brock Huard*	2.00
135C	Jon Kitna	.50
135D	Jon Kitna	.50
136C	Ricky Watters	.30
136D	Ricky Watters	.30
137C	Mike Alstott	.50
137D	Mike Alstott	.50
138	Reidel Anthony	.30
139	Trent Dilfer	.30
140C	Warrick Dunn	.50
140D	Warrick Dunn	.50
141	Jacquez Green	.30
142	*Shaun King*	1.00
143C	Eddie George	.50
143D	Eddie George	.50
144C	Steve McNair	.50
144D	Steve McNair	.50
145	Yancey Thigpen	.30
146	Frank Wycheck	.15
147	*Champ Bailey*	2.00
148	Skip Hicks	.50
149	Brad Johnson	.50
150	Michael Westbrook	.30

1999 Pacific Aurora Premiere Date

This 200-card set is a parallel to the base and is sequentially numbered to 77. Singles were only found in hobby product and were inserted 1:25 packs.

		NM/M
Premiere Date Cards:		10X-30X
Premiere Date Rookies:		5X-10X
Production 77 Sets		
1	*David Boston*	3.00
2	Larry Centers	.15
3	Rob Moore	.30
4	Adrian Murrell	.15
5C	Jake Plummer	1.00
5D	Jake Plummer	1.00
6C	Jamal Anderson	.50
6D	Jamal Anderson	.50
7	Chris Chandler	.30
8	Tim Dwight	.50
9	Terance Mathis	.15
10	O.J. Santiago	.15
11C	Priest Holmes	10.00
11D	Priest Holmes	10.00
12	Michael Jackson	.15
13	Jermaine Lewis	.30
14	Ray Lewis	.15
15	Michael McCrary	.15
16C	Doug Flutie	.75
16D	Doug Flutie	.75
17C	Eric Moulds	.50
17D	Eric Moulds	.50
18	*Peerless Price*	2.50
19	Antowain Smith	.50
20	Bruce Smith	.15
21	Steve Beuerlein	.15
22	Tshimanga Biakabutuka	.15
23	Kevin Greene	.15
24	Muhsin Muhammad	.15
25	Wesley Walls	.15
26	Curtis Conway	.30
27	Bobby Engram	.15
28	Curtis Enis	.30
29	Erik Kramer	.15
30C	*Cade McNown*	5.00
30D	*Cade McNown*	5.00
31	Jeff Blake	.30
32C	Corey Dillon	.50
32D	Corey Dillon	.50
33	Carl Pickens	.30
34	Darnay Scott	.15
35C	*Akili Smith*	4.00
35D	*Akili Smith*	4.00
36C	*Tim Couch*	12.00
36D	*Tim Couch*	12.00
37	Ty Detmer	.15
38	*Kevin Johnson*	3.00
39	Terry Kirby	.15
40C	Troy Aikman	1.00
40D	Troy Aikman	1.00
41	Michael Irvin	.30
42	Raghib Ismail	.15
43C	Deion Sanders	.50
43D	Deion Sanders	.50
44C	Emmitt Smith	1.50
44D	Emmitt Smith	1.50
45	Bubby Brister	.30
46C	Terrell Davis	1.50
46D	Terrell Davis	1.50
47	Brian Griese	1.00
48	Ed McCaffrey	.30
49C	Shannon Sharpe	.30
49D	Shannon Sharpe	.30
50	Rod Smith	.30
51C	Charlie Batch	.75
51D	Charlie Batch	.75
52	*Sedrick Irvin*	2.00
53C	Herman Moore	.50
53D	Herman Moore	.50
54	Johnnie Morton	.15
55C	Barry Sanders	2.00
55D	Barry Sanders	2.00
56	Robert Brooks	.15
57C	Brett Favre	2.00
57D	Brett Favre	2.00
58C	Antonio Freeman	.50
58D	Antonio Freeman	.50
59	Dorsey Levens	.50
60	Derrick Mayes	.30
61	Marvin Harrison	.50
62C	*Edgerrin James*	7.00
62D	*Edgerrin James*	7.00
63C	Peyton Manning	75.00
63D	Peyton Manning	75.00
64	Jerome Pathon	.15
65	Tavian Banks	.30
66C	Mark Brunell	.75
66D	Mark Brunell	.75
67	Keenan McCardell	.15
68	Jimmy Smith	.30
69C	Fred Taylor	1.00
69D	Fred Taylor	1.00
70	Derrick Alexander	.15
71	Kimble Anders	.15
72	*Michael Cloud*	1.50
73	Elvis Grbac	.30
74	Andre Rison	.30
75	Karim Abdul	.30
76	*James Johnson*	2.00
77C	Dan Marino	1.50
77D	Dan Marino	1.50
78	O.J. McDuffie	.30
79	Lamar Thomas	.15
80C	Cris Carter	.50
80D	Cris Carter	.50
81	*Daunte Culpepper*	5.00
82C	Randall Cunningham	.50
82D	Randall Cunningham	.50
83C	Randy Moss	2.50
83D	Randy Moss	2.50
84	John Randle	.15
85C	Robert Smith	.50
85D	Robert Smith	.50
86C	Drew Bledsoe	.75
86D	Drew Bledsoe	.75
87	Ben Coates	.30
88	*Kevin Faulk*	3.00
89C	Terry Glenn	.50
89D	Terry Glenn	.50
90	Ty Law	.15
91	Cameron Cleeland	.30
92	Andre Hastings	.15
93	Billy Joe Hobert	.15
94C	*Ricky Williams*	12.00
94D	*Ricky Williams*	12.00
95	Tiki Barber	.15
96	Kent Graham	.15
97	Ike Hilliard	.15
98	Charles Way	.15
99	Wayne Chrebet	.50
100C	Keyshawn Johnson	.50
100D	Keyshawn Johnson	.50
101C	Curtis Martin	.50
101D	Curtis Martin	.50
102C	Vinny Testaverde	.30
102D	Vinny Testaverde	.30
103	Dedric Ward	.15
104C	Tim Brown	.30
104D	Tim Brown	.30
105	Rickey Dudley	.15
106	James Jett	.15
107	Napoleon Kaufman	.50
108	Charles Woodson	.50
109	Jeff Graham	.15
110	Charles Johnson	.15
111C	*Donovan McNabb*	5.00
111D	*Donovan McNabb*	5.00
112	Duce Staley	.30
113C	Jerome Bettis	.50
113D	Jerome Bettis	.50
114	*Troy Edwards*	3.00
115	Courtney Hawkins	.15
116C	Kordell Stewart	.50
116D	Kordell Stewart	.50
117	*Amos Zereoue*	2.50
118	Isaac Bruce	.30
119C	Marshall Faulk	.50
119D	Marshall Faulk	.50
120	*Joe Germaine*	2.00
121C	*Torry Holt*	3.00
121D	*Torry Holt*	3.00
122	Amp Lee	.15
123	Charlie Jones	.15
124	Ryan Leaf	.50
125	Natrone Means	.30
126	Junior Seau	.30
127	Garrison Hearst	.50
128C	Terrell Owens	.50
128D	Terrell Owens	.50
129C	Jerry Rice	1.00
129D	Jerry Rice	1.00
130	J.J. Stokes	.30
131C	Steve Young	.75
131D	Steve Young	.75
132	Chad Brown	.15
133C	Joey Galloway	.50
133D	Joey Galloway	.50
134	*Brock Huard*	2.00
135C	Jon Kitna	.50
135D	Jon Kitna	.50
136C	Ricky Watters	.30
136D	Ricky Watters	.30
137C	Mike Alstott	.50
137D	Mike Alstott	.50
138	Reidel Anthony	.30
139	Trent Dilfer	.30
140C	Warrick Dunn	.50
140D	Warrick Dunn	.50
141	Jacquez Green	.30
142	*Shaun King*	2.00
143C	Eddie George	.50
143D	Eddie George	.50
144C	Steve McNair	.50
144D	Steve McNair	.50
145	Yancey Thigpen	.30
146	Frank Wycheck	.15
147	*Champ Bailey*	2.00
148	Skip Hicks	.50
149	Brad Johnson	.50
150	Michael Westbrook	.30

1999 Pacific Aurora Canvas Creations

Each player in this 10-card set was printed on real canvas. Singles were inserted 1:193 packs.

		NM/M
Complete Set (10):		75.00
Common Player:		5.00
Inserted 1:193		
1	Troy Aikman	10.00
2	Terrell Davis	10.00
3	Barry Sanders	15.00
4	Brett Favre	18.00
5	Peyton Manning	15.00
6	Dan Marino	18.00
7	Randy Moss	15.00
8	Drew Bledsoe	10.00
9	Steve Young	10.00
10	Jon Kitna	5.00

1999 Pacific Aurora Championship Fever

This 20-card set was issued at 4:25 packs. Each card has a parallel Copper issue that was only found in hobby product and are sequentially numbered to 20. A Platinum Blue parallel was also made and are numbered to 100. The retail only Silver parallel are numbered to 250.

		NM/M
Complete Set (20):		25.00
Common Player:		.50
Inserted 4:25		
Copper Cards:		5X-10X
Production 20 Sets		
Platinum Blue Cards:		3X-5X
Production 100 Sets		
1	Jake Plummer	1.00
2	Jamal Anderson	.50
3	Tim Couch	3.00
4	Troy Aikman	2.50
5	Emmitt Smith	3.50
6	Terrell Davis	2.00
7	Barry Sanders	3.00
8	Brett Favre	4.00
9	Peyton Manning	3.50
10	Fred Taylor	2.00
11	Dan Marino	3.50
12	Randy Moss	4.00
13	Drew Bledsoe	2.00
14	Ricky Williams	4.00
15	Keyshawn Johnson	.50
16	Terrell Owens	.50
17	Jerry Rice	2.50
18	Steve Young	1.50
19	Jon Kitna	.50
20	Eddie George	1.00

1999 Pacific Aurora Complete Players

Ten players were used in this insert with two different cards. One in hobby product and the other in retail. Each product has a 10-card set with each single sequentially numbered to 299. Each card is printed on 10-point double laminated stock with full foil on both sides. A parallel Hologold set was made and inserted into both products and are sequentially numbered to 25.

		NM/M
Complete Set (10):		60.00
Common Player:		3.00
Production 299 Sets		
Hologold Cards:		3X-5X
Production 25 Sets		
1	Troy Aikman	5.00
2	Terrell Davis	5.00
3	Barry Sanders	7.00
4	Brett Favre	8.00
5	Peyton Manning	7.00
6	Dan Marino	8.00
7	Randy Moss	7.00
8	Drew Bledsoe	3.00
9	Jerry Rice	5.00
10	Steve Young	3.00

1999 Pacific Aurora Leather Bound

This hobby-only insert features 20 players on a laminated leather football card with white foil embossed laces. They were found 2:25 packs.

		NM/M
Complete Set (20):		45.00
Common Player:		1.00
Inserted 2:25		
1	Jake Plummer	2.00
2	Jamal Anderson	1.00
3	Tim Couch	3.00
4	Troy Aikman	3.00
5	Emmitt Smith	5.00
6	Terrell Davis	4.00
7	Barry Sanders	5.00
8	Brett Favre	6.00
9	Peyton Manning	4.00
10	Fred Taylor	3.00
11	Dan Marino	6.00
12	Randy Moss	4.00
13	Drew Bledsoe	3.00
14	Ricky Williams	5.00
15	Curtis Martin	1.00
16	Jerome Bettis	1.00
17	Jerry Rice	4.00
18	Steve Young	4.00
19	Jon Kitna	1.00
20	Eddie George	2.00

1999 Pacific Aurora Terrell Owens Autograph

Owens signed a total of 197 cards for Aurora Football. Each card is full foil and hand sequentially numbered.

		NM/M
Production 197 Sets		
AU1	Terrell Owens Auto	50.00

1999 Pacific Aurora Styrotechs

Each card in this 20-card set is horizontal with two photos of the player. One in color and the other a smaller photo of the player in black and white. Singles are printed on styrene and were inserted 1:25.

		NM/M
Complete Set (20):		45.00
Common Player:		1.00
Inserted 1:25		
1	Jake Plummer	1.00
2	Jamal Anderson	1.00
3	Tim Couch	3.00
4	Troy Aikman	3.00
5	Emmitt Smith	4.00
6	Terrell Davis	3.00
7	Barry Sanders	4.00
8	Brett Favre	5.00
9	Peyton Manning	4.00
10	Fred Taylor	2.00
11	Dan Marino	5.00
12	Randy Moss	4.00
13	Drew Bledsoe	2.00
14	Ricky Williams	5.00
15	Curtis Martin	1.00
16	Jerry Rice	3.00
17	Steve Young	3.00
18	Joey Galloway	1.00
19	Jon Kitna	1.00
20	Eddie George	2.00

1999 Pacific Crown Royale

This was a 144-card base set that featured each single die-cut, double-etched and on a double-foiled format. Each veteran card had a gold foil crown while the rookies were printed on a silver foil crown. Parallel sets included Limited Series and Premier Date. Other inserts included: Card Supials, Century 21, Cramer's Choice Jumbos, Franchise Glory, Gold Crown Die Cuts, Rookie Gold and Test of Time. SRP was $5.99 for six-card packs.

	NM/M
Complete Set (144):	140.00
Common Player:	.30
Minor Stars:	.60
Common Rookie:	2.00
Pack (6):	6.00
Wax Box (24):	120.00

1 *David Boston* 6.00
2 *Chris Greisen* 1.00
3 Rob Moore .60
4 Jake Plummer 2.00
5 Frank Sanders .60
6 Jamal Anderson 1.50
7 Chris Chandler .60
8 Tim Dwight 1.50
9 Byron Hanspard .60
10 Stoney Case .30
11 Priest Holmes 2.00
12 Jermaine Lewis .60
13 *Chris McCalister* 2.00
14 *Brandon Stokley* 2.00
15 Doug Flutie 2.00
16 Eric Moulds 1.50
17 *Peerless Price* 4.00
18 Antowain Smith 1.50
19 Steve Beuerlein .60
20 Tshimanga Biakabutuka .60
21 Muhsin Muhammad 1.00
22 Curtis Conway .60
23 Curtis Enis .50
24 Shane Matthews .50
25 *Cade McNown* 3.00
26 Marcus Robinson 1.00
27 Jeff Blake 1.00
28 *Scott Covington* 1.00
29 Corey Dillon 1.50
30 *Damon Griffin* 1.00
31 Carl Pickens 1.00
32 *Akili Smith* 3.00
33 *Tim Couch* 6.00
34 *Kevin Johnson* 3.00
35 Terry Kirby .30
36 Leslie Shepherd .30
37 Troy Aikman 3.00
38 Raghib Ismail .30
39 *Wane McGarity* 1.00
40 Deion Sanders 1.50
41 Emmitt Smith 4.00
42 Terrell Davis 2.00
43 Brian Griese 3.00
44 Ed McCaffrey 1.50
45 Shannon Sharpe .75
46 Rod Smith 1.50
47 Charlie Batch .50
48 Germane Crowell .75
49 *Sedrick Irvin* 1.00
50 Herman Moore 1.50
51 Barry Sanders 4.00
52 Brett Favre 6.00
53 Antonio Freeman 1.50
54 Matt Hasselbeck 1.50
55 Dorsey Levens 1.50
56 *Basil Mitchell* 1.00
57 E.G. Green .60
58 Marvin Harrison 1.50
59 *Edgerrin James* 12.00
60 Peyton Manning 4.00
61 *Terrence Wilkins* 3.00
62 Mark Brunell 2.00
63 Keenan McCardell .60
64 Jimmy Smith 1.50
65 Fred Taylor 1.00
66 Derrick Alexander .30
67 Elvis Grbac .60
68 Warren Moon .60
69 *Larry Parker* 1.00
70 Andre Rison .60
71 *Cecil Collins* 3.00
72 Damon Huard .50
73 *James Johnson* 2.00
74 *Rob Konrad* 3.00
75 Dan Marino 4.00
76 O.J. McDuffie .60
77 Cris Carter 1.50
78 *Daunte Culpepper* 12.00
79 Randall Cunningham 1.50
80 Randy Moss 4.00
81 Robert Smith 1.50
82 *Michael Bishop* 1.00
83 Drew Bledsoe 2.00
84 Ben Coates .60
85 *Kevin Faulk* 1.00
86 Terry Glenn 1.50
87 Billy Joe Hobert .30
88 Eddie Kennison .60
89 Keith Poole .30
90 *Ricky Williams* 6.00
91 *Sean Bennett* 1.00
92 Kerry Collins .60
93 Pete Mitchell .30
94 Amani Toomer .60
95 Wayne Chrebet 1.50
96 Keyshawn Johnson 1.50
97 Curtis Martin 1.50
98 Tim Brown 1.00
99 *Scott Dreisbach* 1.00
100 Rich Gannon .60
101 Napoleon Kaufman .50
102 Tyrone Wheatley .60
103 Charles Johnson .30
104 *Donovan McNabb* 12.00
105 Torrance Small .30
106 Duce Staley 1.50
107 *Jed Weaver* 1.00
108 Jerome Bettis 1.50
109 *Troy Edwards* 3.00
110 Kordell Stewart 1.50
111 *Amos Zereoue* 4.00
112 Isaac Bruce 1.50
113 Marshall Faulk 1.50
114 *Joe Germaine* 1.50
115 *Torry Holt* 6.00
116 *Kurt Warner* 15.00
117 Jim Harbaugh .60
118 Erik Kramer .30
119 Natrone Means .75
120 Junior Seau .75
121 *Jeff Garcia* 12.00
122 Terrell Owens 1.50
123 Jerry Rice 3.00
124 J.J. Stokes .60
125 Steve Young 2.00
126 Sean Dawkins .30
127 *Brock Huard* 1.00
128 Jon Kitna 2.00
129 Derrick Mayes .75
130 *Charlie Rogers* 2.00
131 Ricky Watters 1.00
132 Mike Alstott 1.50
133 Trent Dilfer 1.00
134 Warrick Dunn 1.50
135 Eric Zeier .30
136 *Kevin Daft* 1.00
137 Kevin Dyson .60
138 Eddie George 1.75
139 Steve McNair 1.75
140 Neil O'Donnell .60
141 *Champ Bailey* 3.00
142 Albert Connell .30
143 Stephen Davis 1.50
144 Brad Johnson 1.50

1999 Pacific Crown Royale Limited Series

This was a 144-card parallel to the base set. Each single was sequentially numbered to 99.

	NM/M
Limited Ser. Cards:	5X-10X
Limited Ser. Rookies:	2X-4X
Production 99 Sets	

1999 Pacific Crown Royale Premiere Date

This was a 144-card parallel to the base set. Singles were sequentially numbered to 68 and found 1:25 packs.

Premiere Date Cards:	5X-10X
Premiere Date Rookies:	3X-6X
Inserted 1:25	
Production 68 Sets	

1999 Pacific Crown Royale Card Supials

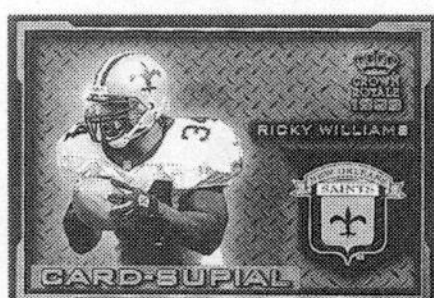

This 20-card insert set included a full-size card with a "Card-Supial" inserted into a special die-cut pouch on the back of the full-size card. The mini (1/4 the full card size) card is inserted into a different player's full-size card. Singles were inserted 2:25 packs.

	NM/M
Complete Set (20):	45.00
Common Player:	1.00
Small Cards:	.7X
Inserted 2:25	

1 Cade McNown 1.00
2 Tim Couch 3.00
3 Troy Aikman 3.00
4 Emmitt Smith 6.00
5 Barry Sanders 6.00
6 Brett Favre 6.00
7 Edgerrin James 6.00
8 Peyton Manning 4.00
9 Mark Brunell 2.00
10 Fred Taylor 2.00
11 Damon Huard 1.00
12 Dan Marino 5.00
13 Randy Moss 5.00
14 Drew Bledsoe 4.00
15 Ricky Williams 6.00
16 Jerome Bettis 1.00
17 Kurt Warner 6.00
18 Terrell Owens 1.00
19 Jerry Rice 4.00
20 Jon Kitna 1.00

1999 Pacific Crown Royale Century 21

This 10-card insert set included football's most dominating players. Each of the singles were sequentially numbered to 375.

	NM/M
Complete Set (10):	45.00
Common Player:	3.00
Production 375 Sets	

1 Jake Plummer 3.00
2 Tim Couch 6.00
3 Terrell Davis 6.00
4 Peyton Manning 8.00
5 Mark Brunell 3.00
6 Fred Taylor 5.00
7 Randy Moss 8.00
8 Drew Bledsoe 3.00
9 Ricky Williams 8.00
10 Kurt Warner 15.00

1999 Pacific Crown Royale Cramer's Choice Jumbos

This 10-card insert set included both veterans and a few of the hot rookies from 1999. Singles were inserted one per box. Six different parallel sets were also issued and they include: Dark Blue (#'d to 35), Green (#'d to 30), Red (#'d to 25), Light Blue (#'d to 20), Gold (#'d to 10) and Purple (#'d to 1).

	NM/M
Complete Set (10):	60.00
Common Player:	3.00
1:Box	
Dark Blue Cards:	6X-12X
Production 35 Sets	
Gold Cards:	10X-20X
Production 10 Sets	
Green Cards:	6X-12X
Production 30 Sets	
Light Blue Cards:	8X-15X
Production 20 Sets	
Purple Cards:	No Pricing
Production 1 Set	
Red Cards:	8X-15X
Production 25 Sets	

1 Cade McNown 2.00
2 Tim Couch 4.00
3 Emmitt Smith 6.00
4 Edgerrin James 8.00
5 Mark Brunell 4.00
6 Fred Taylor 4.00
7 Randy Moss 6.00
8 Kurt Warner 8.00
9 Jon Kitna 2.00
10 Eddie George 3.00

1999 Pacific Crown Royale Franchise Glory

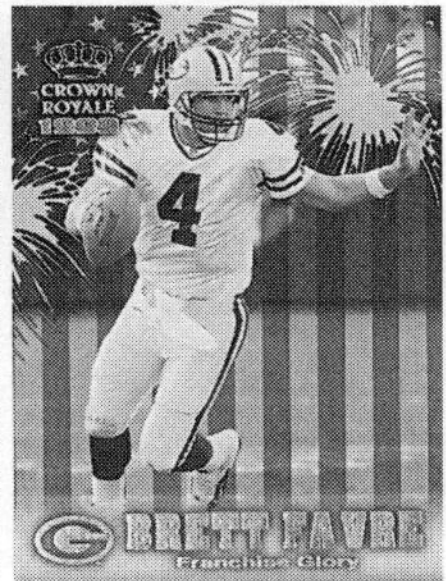

This 25-card insert set included NFL team leaders, veterans and rising stars. Each is printed with the American flag and fireworks in the background. They were found one-per-pack.

	NM/M
Complete Set (25):	30.00
Common Player:	.50
Inserted 1:1	

1 Doug Flutie 1.00
2 Corey Dillon 1.00
3 Troy Aikman 3.00
4 Emmitt Smith 4.00
5 Terrell Davis 3.00
6 Herman Moore .50
7 Barry Sanders 4.00
8 Brett Favre 4.00
9 Antonio Freeman .50
10 Peyton Manning 3.00
11 Mark Brunell 2.00
12 Fred Taylor 2.00
13 Dan Marino 4.00
14 Randy Moss 4.00
15 Drew Bledsoe 2.00
16 Keyshawn Johnson .50
17 Jerome Bettis .50
18 Marshall Faulk 1.00
19 Kurt Warner 8.00
20 Terrell Owens .50
21 Jerry Rice 3.00
22 Steve Young 2.00
23 Warrick Dunn .50
24 Eddie George .50
25 Brad Johnson .50

1999 Pacific Crown Royale Gold Crown Die Cuts

Singles from this six-card insert set were over-sized and sequentially numbered to 976.

	NM/M
Complete Set (6):	35.00
Common Player:	2.00
Production 976 Sets	

1 Tim Couch 6.00
2 Troy Aikman 6.00
3 Emmitt Smith 8.00
4 Damond Huard 2.00
5 Randy Moss 8.00
6 Kurt Warner 10.00

A player's name in *italic* type indicates a rookie card.

1999 Pacific Crown Royale Rookie Gold

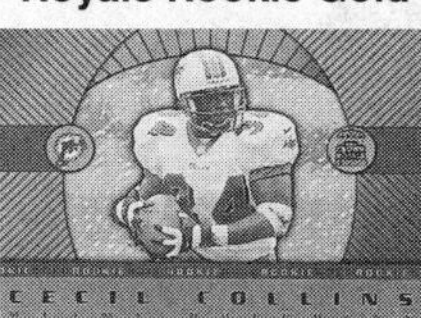

This 25-card insert set included the top rookies from 1999. Singles were found one-per-pack. A parallel die-cut version was also made and each of those singles was sequentially numbered to 10.

	NM/M
Complete Set (25):	30.00
Common Player:	.50
Inserted 1:1	

1 David Boston 2.00
2 Brandon Stokley .50
3 Cade McNown 1.00
4 Akili Smith 1.00
5 Tim Couch 3.00
6 Kevin Johnson 2.00
7 Wane McGarity .50
8 Edgerrin James 5.00
9 Terrence Wilkins 2.00
10 Cecil Collins 1.00
11 Rob Konrad .50
12 James Johnson .50
13 Daunte Culpepper 4.00
14 Michael Bishop 1.50
15 Kevin Faulk 1.50
16 Ricky Williams 6.00
17 Scott Dreisbach .50
18 Donovan McNabb 4.00
19 Troy Edwards 3.00
20 Amos Zereoue .50
21 Joe Germaine .50
22 Torry Holt 3.00
23 Brock Huard 1.50
24 Charlie Rogers .50
25 Champ Bailey 1.50

1999 Pacific Crown Royale Test of Time

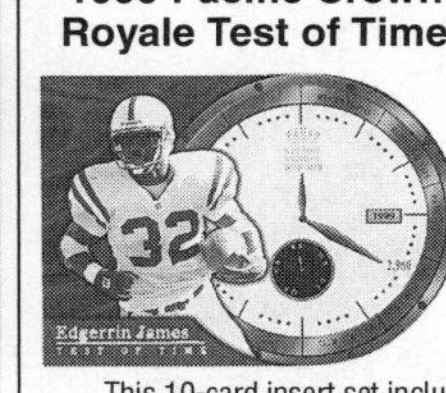

This 10-card insert set included seasoned veterans along with a few rookies. Each player was pictured on a die-cut single with a clock-shaped design. Singles were inserted 1:25 packs.

	NM/M
Complete Set (10):	45.00
Common Player:	2.00
Inserted 1:25	

1 Tim Couch 6.00
2 Emmitt Smith 6.00
3 Terrell Davis 4.00
4 Barry Sanders 6.00
5 Brett Favre 6.00
6 Antonio Freeman 2.00
7 Edgerrin James 6.00
8 Mark Brunell 3.00
9 Dan Marino 6.00
10 Jerry Rice 4.00

1999 Pacific Omega

This was a 250-card set that included 48 unseeded rookie cards. Each single was horizontal and used silver foil. Four parallel sets were issued and they include: Copper, Gold, Platinum Blue and Premiere Date. Other inserts include: 5-Star Attack, Draft Class, EO Portraits, Gridiron Masters and TD 99. SRP was $1.99 for six-card packs.

	NM/M
Complete Set (250):	30.00
Common Player:	.10
Minor Stars:	.30
Common Rookie:	.50
Pack (6):	1.00
Wax Box (36):	35.00

1 Mario Bates .10
2 *David Boston* 2.50
3 Rob Moore .30
4 Adrian Murrell .10
5 Jake Plummer 1.00
6 Frank Sanders .10
7 Aeneas Williams .10
8 *Joel Makovicka, L.J. Shelton* 1.00
9 Jamal Anderson .50
10 Ray Buchanan .10
11 Chris Chandler .30
12 Tim Dwight .50
13 Byron Hanspard .10
14 Terance Mathis .10
15 O.J. Santiago .10
16 Danny Kanell, Chris Calloway .10
17 Peter Boulware .10
18 Priest Holmes .50
19 Patrick Johnson .10
20 Jermaine Lewis .10
21 Ray Lewis .10
22 Michael McCrary .10
23 Jonathan Ogden .10
24 Tony Banks, Scott Mitchell .10
25 Doug Flutie .75
26 Rob Johnson .10
27 Eric Moulds .50
28 Andre Reed .10
29 Antowain Smith .30
30 Bruce Smith .10
31 Kevin Williams .10
32 *Shawn Bryson, Peerless Price* 2.00
33 Steve Beuerlein .10
34 Tshimanga Biakabutuka .30
35 Rae Carruth .10
36 *Dameyune Craig* 1.50
37 William Floyd .10
38 Kevin Greene .10
39 Muhsin Muhammad .30
40 Wesley Walls .10
41 Edgar Bennett .10
42 *Robert Chancey* 1.00
43 Curtis Conway .30
44 Bobby Engram .10
45 Curtis Enis .50
46 *Cade McNown* 1.00
47 Ryan Wetnight .10
48 *D'Wayne Bates, Marty Booker* 1.50
49 Jeff Blake .30
50 *Scott Covington* 1.00
51 Corey Dillon .50
52 James Hundon .10
53 Carl Pickens .30
54 Darnay Scott .30
55 *Akili Smith* 1.50
56 *Craig Yeast* 1.00
57 *Tim Couch* 2.50
58 Ty Detmer .10
59 Marc Edwards .10
60 *Kevin Johnson* 1.50
61 Terry Kirby .10
62 Sedrick Shaw .10
63 Leslie Shepherd .10
64 *Rahim Abdullah, Daylon McCutcheon* .50
65 Troy Aikman 1.00
66 Michael Irvin .30
67 David LaFleur .10
68 *Wane McGarity* 1.00
69 Ernie Mills .10
70 Deion Sanders .50
71 Emmitt Smith 1.50
72 Raghib Ismail, James McKnight .10
73 Bubby Brister .30
74 *Byron Chamberlain* 1.25
75 Terrell Davis 1.50
76 *Olandis Gary* 2.00
77 Brian Griese 1.00
78 Ed McCaffrey .50
79 Shannon Sharpe .30
80 Rod Smith .30
81 *Travis McGriff, Al Wilson* 1.00
82 Charlie Batch .75
83 *Chris Claiborne* 1.00
84 Germane Crowell .30
85 Terry Fair .10
86 *Sedrick Irvin* 1.50
87 Herman Moore .50
88 Johnnie Morton .10
89 Barry Sanders 2.00
90 Mark Chmura .30
91 Brett Favre 2.00
92 Antonio Freeman .50
93 Desmond Howard .10
94 Dorsey Levens .50
95 Derrick Mayes .50
96 Bill Schroeder .30
97 *Aaron Brooks, Dee Miller* 5.00
98 Ken Dilger .10
99 E.G. Green .10
100 Marvin Harrison .50
101 *Edgerrin James* 5.00
102 Peyton Manning 1.50
103 Jerome Pathon .10
104 Marcus Pollard .10
105 Derrick Alexander .10
106 Reggie Barlow .10
107 Tony Boselli .10
108 Mark Brunell .75
109 George Jones .10
110 Keenan McCardell .30
111 Jimmy Smith .30
112 James Stewart .30
113 Fred Taylor 1.00
114 Kimble Anders .10
115 *Michael Cloud* 1.00
116 Tony Gonzalez .30
117 Elvis Grbac .30
118 Bam Morris .10
119 Andre Rison .30
120 Derrick Thomas .30
121 Karim Abdul .30
122 Oronde Gadsden .30
123 *James Johnson* 1.75
124 *Rob Konrad* 1.00
125 Dan Marino 1.50
126 O.J. McDuffie .30
127 Lamar Thomas .10
128 Zach Thomas .30
129 Cris Carter .50
130 *Daunte Culpepper* 5.00
131 Randall Cunningham .50
132 Matthew Hatchette .10
133 Leroy Hoard .30
134 David Palmer .10
135 John Randle .10
136 Randy Moss 2.00
137 Robert Smith .50
138 Drew Bledsoe .75
139 Ben Coates .30
140 *Kevin Faulk* 2.00
141 Terry Glenn .50
142 Shawn Jefferson .10
143 Ty Law .10
144 Tony Simmons .30
145 *Michael Bishop, Andy Katzenmoyer* 1.75
146 Cameron Cleeland .30
147 Andre Hastings .10
148 Billy Joe Hobert .10
149 Joe Johnson .10
150 Keith Poole .10
151 William Roaf .10
152 Billy Joe Tolliver .10
153 *Ricky Williams* 5.00
154 Tiki Barber .30
155 Gary Brown .10
156 Kent Graham .10
157 Ike Hilliard .10
158 David Patten .10
159 Jason Sehorn .10
160 Amani Toomer .10
161 *Joe Montgomery, Luke Petitgout* 1.25
162 Wayne Chrebet .30
163 Bryan Cox .10
164 Aaron Glenn .10
165 Keyshawn Johnson .50
166 Leon Johnson .10
167 Curtis Martin .50
168 Vinny Testaverde .30
169 Dedric Ward .10
170 Tim Brown .30
171 Rickey Dudley .30
172 James Jett .10
173 Napoleon Kaufman .50
174 Jon Ritchie .10
175 Darrell Russell .10
176 Charles Woodson .50
177 Rich Gannon, Heath Shuler .10
178 Hugh Douglas .10
179 *Donovan McNabb* 5.00
180 Allen Rossum .10
181 Duce Staley .30
182 Kevin Turner .10
183 Charles Johnson, Doug Pederson .10
184 *Barry Gardner, Cecil Martin* .50
185 Jerome Bettis .50
186 Mark Bruener .10
187 *Troy Edwards* 1.50
188 Courtney Hawkins .10
189 Levon Kirkland .10
190 Kordell Stewart .50
191 Hines Ward .30
192 *Malcolm Johnson, Amos Zereoue* 1.75
193 Greg Clark .10
194 Terrell Fletcher .10
195 Charlie Jones .10
196 *Cecil Collins* 1.00
197 Natrone Means .30
198 Mikhael Ricks .10
199 Junior Seau .30
200 Bryan Still .10
201 Ryan Thelwell .10
202 Garrison Hearst .30
203 *Terry Jackson* .50
204 R.W. McQuarters .10
205 Terrell Owens .50
206 Jerry Rice 1.00
207 J.J. Stokes .30
208 Tommy Vardell .10
209 Steve Young .75
210 *Karsten Bailey* 1.00
211 Chad Brown .10
212 Christian Fauria .10
213 Joey Galloway .50
214 Ahman Green .30
215 *Brock Huard* 1.50
216 Cortez Kennedy .10
217 Jon Kitna .75
218 Ricky Watters .50
219 Isaac Bruce .50
220 Az-Zahir Hakim .30
221 June Henley .10
222 Greg Hill .10
223 *Torry Holt* 2.50
224 Amp Lee .10
225 Ricky Proehl .10
226 Marshall Faulk, Trent Green .50
227 Mike Alstott .50
228 Reidel Anthony .30
229 Trent Dilfer .30
230 Warrick Dunn .50
231 Bert Emanuel .10
232 Jacquez Green .30
233 Warren Sapp .10
234 *Shaun King, Anthony McFarland* 1.00
235 *Mike Archie* .50
236 Kevin Dyson .30
237 Eddie George .75
238 Derrick Mason .10
239 Steve McNair .75
240 Yancey Thigpen .30
241 Frank Wycheck .10
242 *Darran Hall, Jevon Kearse* 2.00
243 Stephen Alexander .10
244 *Champ Bailey* 1.50

245	Stephen Davis	.50
246	Skip Hicks	.30
247	James Thrash	.10
248	Michael Westbrook	.30
249	Dan Wilkinson	.10
250	Brad Johnson, Larry Centers	.50

1999 Pacific Omega Copper

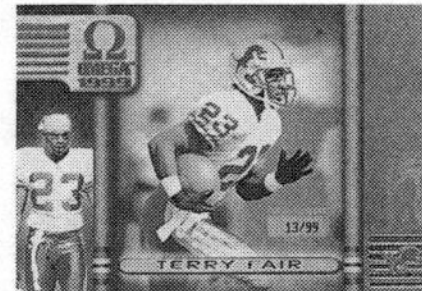

This was a 250-card parallel to the base set. Each of these singles used copper foil rather than silver foil on the base cards. These were only found in hobby packs and each was sequentially numbered to 99.

Copper Cards:	3X-8X
Copper Rookies:	2X-5X
Production 99 Sets	

1999 Pacific Omega Gold

This was a 250-card parallel to the base set. Each of these singles used gold foil rather than silver foil on the base cards. These were only found in retail packs and each was sequentially numbered to 299.

Gold Cards:	2X-5X
Gold Rookies:	1X-3X
Production 299 Sets	

1999 Pacific Omega Platinum Blue

This was a 250-card parallel to the base set. Each of these singles used blue foil rather than silver foil on the base cards. These were found in both hobby and retail packs and each was sequentially numbered to 75.

Platinum Blue Cards:	3X-8X
Platinum Blue Rookies:	2X-5X
Production 75 Sets	

1999 Pacific Omega Premiere Date

This was a 250-card parallel to the base set. Each of these singles used red foil rather than silver foil on the base cards. Each of these singles was sequentially numbered to 60.

Premiere Date Cards:	3X-8X
Premiere Date Rookies:	2X-5X
Production 60 Sets	

1999 Pacific Omega 5-Star Attack

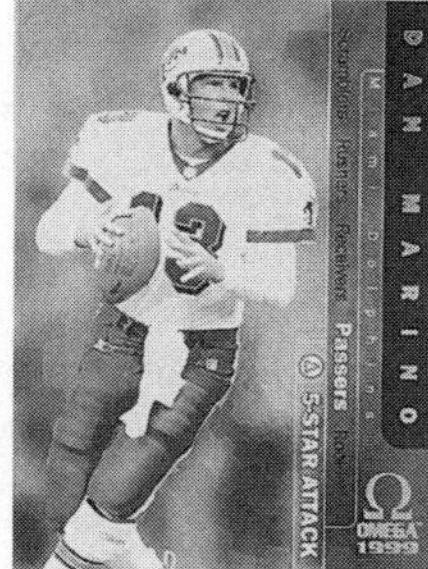

This was a 30-card insert that included the NFL's top stars and premier rookies. Singles were inserted 4:37 packs and could only be found in hobby packs. Five parallel sets were issued and include: Blue (#'d to 100), Red (#'d to 75), Green (#'d to 50), Purple (#'d to 25) and Gold (#'d to 1).

		NM/M
Complete Set (30):		35.00
Common Player:		.50
Minor Stars:		1.00
Inserted 4:37		
Blue Cards:		2X-3X
Production 100 Sets		
Gold Cards:		No Pricing
Production 1 Set		
Green Cards:		2X-5X
Production 50 Sets		
Purple Cards:		3X-6X
Production 25 Sets		
Red Cards:		2X-5X
Production 75 Sets		
1	Chris Chandler	.50
2	Tim Couch	4.00
3	Peyton Manning	4.00
4	Dan Marino	4.00
5	Drew Bledsoe	2.00
6	Vinny Testaverde	.50
7	Randall Cunningham	1.00
8	Doug Flutie	1.00
9	Charlie Batch	1.00
10	Mark Brunell	2.00
11	Steve Young	1.75
12	Jon Kitna	.50
13	Jamal Anderson	1.00
14	Priest Holmes	2.00
15	Emmitt Smith	4.00
16	Fred Taylor	2.00
17	Curtis Martin	1.00
18	Eddie George	1.50
19	Ed McCaffrey	.50
20	Antonio Freeman	1.00
21	Randy Moss	4.00
22	Keyshawn Johnson	1.00
23	Terrell Owens	1.00
24	Joey Galloway	1.00
25	Cade McNown	1.00
26	Akili Smith	1.00
27	Edgerrin James	3.00
28	Daunte Culpepper	3.00
29	Ricky Williams	4.00
30	Donovan McNabb	3.00

1999 Pacific Omega Draft Class

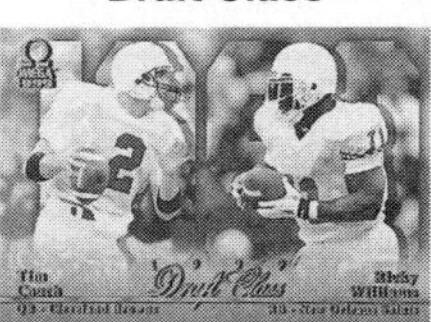

This 10-card insert included two players from the same draft year and pictured them on the front of each card. Singles were inserted 1:145 packs.

		NM/M
Complete Set (10):		65.00
Common Player:		5.00
Inserted 1:145		
1	Darrell Green, Dan Marino 1983	12.00
2	Jerry Rice, Bruce Smith 1985	10.00
3	Troy Aikman, Barry Sanders 1989	15.00
4	Shannon Sharpe, Emmitt Smith 1990	12.00
5	Brett Favre, Herman Moore 1991	15.00
6	Drew Bledsoe, Mark Brunell 1993	8.00
7	Terrell Davis, Curtis Martin 1995	10.00
8	Warrick Dunn, Jake Plummer 1997	5.00
9	Peyton Manning, Randy Moss 1998	15.00
10	Tim Couch, Ricky Williams 1999	15.00

1999 Pacific Omega EO Portraits

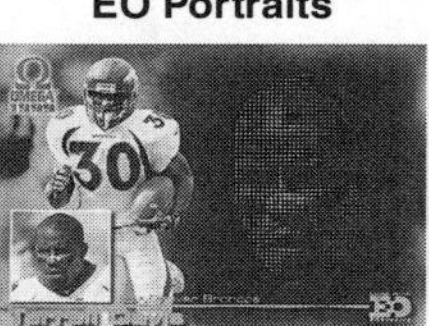

This 20-card insert included mostly veterans and a few rookies. Each single used electro-optical technology and each had the player's portrait laser cut into the card. Singles were inserted 1:73 packs.

		NM/M
Complete Set (20):		85.00
Common Player:		2.00
Inserted 1:73		
1	Jake Plummer	4.00
2	Jamal Anderson	4.00
3	Akili Smith	4.00
4	Tim Couch	8.00
5	Troy Aikman	10.00
6	Emmitt Smith	12.00
7	Terrell Davis	8.00
8	Barry Sanders	10.00
9	Brett Favre	12.00
10	Peyton Manning	8.00
11	Mark Brunell	4.00
12	Fred Taylor	4.00
13	Dan Marino	12.00
14	Randy Moss	8.00
15	Ricky Williams	10.00
16	Curtis Martin	2.00
17	Jerry Rice	8.00
18	Jon Kitna	2.00
19	Warrick Dunn	2.00
20	Eddie George	4.00

1999 Pacific Omega Gridiron Masters

This 36-card insert included both veterans and rookies. Singles were inserted 4:37 packs.

		NM/M
Complete Set (36):		30.00
Common Player:		.25
Minor Stars:		.50
Inserted 4:37		
1	David Boston	1.00
2	Jake Plummer	1.00
3	Jamal Anderson	.50
4	Chris Chandler	.25
5	Priest Holmes	1.00
6	Doug Flutie	1.00
7	Akili Smith	1.00
8	Cade McNown	.50
9	Tim Couch	3.00
10	Deion Sanders	1.00
11	Emmitt Smith	3.50
12	Rod Smith	.50
13	Charlie Batch	.50
14	Herman Moore	.50
15	Barry Sanders	4.00
16	Antonio Freeman	.50
17	Edgerrin James	4.00
18	Mark Brunell	.50
19	Fred Taylor	1.00
20	Randall Cunningham	.50
21	Randy Moss	4.00
22	Terry Glenn	.50
23	Keyshawn Johnson	.50
24	Curtis Martin	.50
25	Vinny Testaverde	.25
26	Donovan McNabb	3.00
27	Jerome Bettis	.50
28	Terrell Owens	.50
29	Jerry Rice	2.50
30	Steve Young	1.75
31	Joey Galloway	.50
32	Jon Kitna	.25
33	Warrick Dunn	.50
34	Shaun King	.50
35	Eddie George	1.00
36	Steve McNair	1.00

1999 Pacific Omega TD '99

This 20-card insert included the NFL's most renown TD leaders. Each was printed on a prism-style holographic foil board. Singles were inserted 1:37 packs.

		NM/M
Complete Set (20):		35.00
Common Player:		1.00
Inserted 1:37		
1	Jamal Anderson	1.00
2	Priest Holmes	2.00
3	Doug Flutie	1.00
4	Tim Couch	5.00
5	Troy Aikman	4.00
6	Emmitt Smith	5.00
7	Terrell Davis	4.00
8	Herman Moore	1.00
9	Brett Favre	5.00
10	Antonio Freeman	1.00
11	Mark Brunell	2.00
12	Fred Taylor	3.00
13	Randall Cunningham	1.00
14	Randy Moss	5.00
15	Drew Bledsoe	3.00
16	Terrell Owens	2.00
17	Steve Young	3.00
18	Jon Kitna	1.00
19	Warrick Dunn	1.00
20	Eddie George	2.00

1999 Pacific Paramount

Pacific Paramount Football is a 250-card set that includes all of the top rookies from 1999. The base has six different parallel sets with Copper, Gold, Premiere Date, HoloGold, HoloSilver and Platinum Blue. Other inserts include: Canton Bound, End Zone Net-Fusions, Personal Bests and Team Checklists.

		NM/M
Complete Set (250):		40.00
Common Player:		.10
Minor Stars:		.20
Common Rookie:		.50
Pack (6):		1.00
Wax Box (36):		35.00
1	*David Boston*	2.50
2	Larry Centers	.10
3	*Joel Makovicka*	1.00
4	Eric Metcalf	.10
5	Rob Moore	.20
6	Adrian Murrell	.20
7	Jake Plummer	1.00
8	Frank Sanders	.20
9	Aeneas Williams	.10
10	Morten Anderson	.10
11	Jamal Anderson	.50
12	Chris Chandler	.20
13	Tim Dwight	.50
14	Terance Mathis	.10
15	*Jeff Paulk*	.40
16	O.J. Santiago	.10
17	Chuck Smith	.10
18	Peter Boulware	.10
19	Priest Holmes	.50
20	Michael Jackson	.10
21	Jermaine Lewis	.20
22	Ray Lewis	.10
23	Michael McCrary	.10
24	Bennie Thompson	.10
25	Rod Woodson	.10
26	*Shawn Bryson*	.50
27	Doug Flutie	.75
28	Eric Moulds	.50
29	*Peerless Price*	2.00
30	Andre Reed	.10
31	Jay Riemersma	.10
32	Antowain Smith	.50
33	Bruce Smith	.10
34	Michael Bates	.10
35	Steve Beuerlein	.10
36	Tshimanga Biakabutuka	.10
37	Kevin Greene	.10
38	Anthony Johnson	.10
39	Fred Lane	.10
40	Muhsin Muhammad	.10
41	Wesley Walls	.10
42	*D'Wayne Bates*	.75
43	Edgar Bennett	.10
44	*Marty Booker*	.50
45	Curtis Conway	.20
46	Bobby Engram	.10
47	Curtis Enis	.50
48	Erik Kramer	.10
49	*Cade McNown*	1.00
50	Jeff Blake	.20
51	*Scott Covington*	.50
52	Corey Dillon	.50
53	*Quincy Jackson*	.50
54	Carl Pickens	.20
55	Darnay Scott	.10
56	*Akili Smith*	2.00
57	*Craig Yeast*	.50
58	Jerry Ball	.10
59	*Darrin Chiaverini*	.50
60	*Tim Couch*	2.50
61	Ty Detmer	.10
62	*Kevin Johnson*	1.25
63	Terry Kirby	.10
64	*Daylon McCutcheon*	.50
65	Irv Smith	.10
66	Troy Aikman	1.00
67	*Ebenezer Ekuban*	.50
68	Michael Irvin	.20
69	Daryl Johnston	.10
70	*Wayne McGarity*	.75
71	*Dat Nguyen*	1.00
72	Deion Sanders	.50
73	Emmitt Smith	1.50
74	Bubby Brister	.30
75	Terrell Davis	1.50
76	Jason Elam	.10
77	*Olandis Gary*	2.00
78	Brian Griese	.75
79	Ed McCaffrey	.30
80	*Travis McGriff*	1.00
81	Shannon Sharpe	.20
82	Rod Smith	.20
83	Charlie Batch	.75
84	*Chris Claiborne*	1.00
85	Germane Crowell	.20
86	*Sedrick Irvin*	1.50
87	Herman Moore	.50
88	Johnnie Morton	.10
89	Barry Sanders	2.00
90	Robert Brooks	.10
91	*Aaron Brooks*	5.00
92	Mark Chmura	.20
93	Brett Favre	2.00
94	Antonio Freeman	.50
95	Vonnie Holliday	.20
96	Dorsey Levens	.50
97	*De'Mond Parker*	.75
98	Ken Dilger	.10
99	Marvin Harrison	.30
100	*Edgerrin James*	5.00
101	Peyton Manning	1.50
102	Jerome Pathon	.10
103	*Mike Peterson*	.50
104	Marcus Pollard	.10
105	Tavian Banks	.20
106	Reggie Barlow	.10
107	Tony Boselli	.10
108	Mark Brunell	.75
109	Keenan McCardell	.10
110	Bryce Paup	.10
111	Jimmy Smith	.20
112	Fred Taylor	1.00
113	Dave Thomas	.10
114	Kimble Anders	.10
115	Donnell Bennett	.10
116	*Mike Cloud*	1.00
117	Tony Gonzalez	.20
118	Elvis Grbac	.20
119	*Larry Parker*	.50
120	Andre Rison	.20
121	*Brian Shay*	.50
122	Karim Abdul	.30
123	Oronde Gadsden	.20
124	*James Johnson*	1.50
125	*Rob Konrad*	1.00
126	Dan Marino	1.50
127	O.J. McDuffie	.20
128	Zach Thomas	.20
129	Cris Carter	.50
130	*Daunte Culpepper*	5.00
131	Randall Cunningham	.50
132	Matthew Hatchette	.10
133	Leroy Hoard	.10
134	Randy Moss	2.00
135	John Randle	.10
136	Jake Reed	.10
137	Robert Smith	.50
138	*Michael Bishop*	2.00
139	Drew Bledsoe	.75
140	Ben Coates	.20
141	*Kevin Faulk*	2.50
142	Terry Glenn	.30
143	Shawn Jefferson	.10
144	*Andy Katzenmoyer*	1.00
145	Tony Simmons	.20
146	*Cuncho Brown*	.50
147	Cameron Cleeland	.20
148	Mark Fields	.10
149	La'Roi Glover	.10
150	Andre Hastings	.10
151	Billy Joe Hobert	.10
152	William Roaf	.10
153	Billy Joe Tolliver	.10
154	*Ricky Williams*	3.00
155	Jessie Armstead	.10
156	Tiki Barber	.20
157	Gary Brown	.10
158	Kent Graham	.10
159	Ike Hilliard	.20
160	*Joe Montgomery*	1.25
161	Amani Toomer	.10
162	Charles Way	.10
163	Wayne Chrebet	.50
164	Bryan Cox	.10
165	Aaron Glenn	.10
166	Keyshawn Johnson	.50
167	Leon Johnson	.10
168	Curtis Martin	.50
169	Vinny Testaverde	.20
170	Dedric Ward	.10
171	Tim Brown	.20
172	*Dameane Douglas*	.75
173	Rickey Dudley	.20
174	James Jett	.10
175	Napoleon Kaufman	.50
176	Darrell Russell	.10
177	Harvey Williams	.10
178	Charles Woodson	.50
179	*Na Brown*	.50
180	Hugh Douglas	.10
181	*Cecil Martin*	.50
182	*Donovan McNabb*	5.00
183	Duce Staley	.10
184	Kevin Turner	.10
185	Jerome Bettis	.50
186	*Troy Edwards*	2.00
187	Jason Gildon	.10
188	Courtney Hawkins	.10
189	*Malcolm Johnson*	.50
190	Kordell Stewart	.75
191	*Jerame Tuman*	.50
192	*Amos Zereoue*	2.00
193	Isaac Bruce	.30
194	Kevin Carter	.10
195	*Jeremaine Copeland*	.50
196	*Joe Germaine*	1.75
197	Az-Zahir Hakim	.20
198	*Torry Holt*	2.50
199	Amp Lee	.10
200	Ricky Proehl	.10
201	Charlie Jones	.10
202	Freddie Jones	.10
203	Ryan Leaf	.50
204	Natrone Means	.30
205	Mikhael Ricks	.10
206	Junior Seau	.20
207	Bryan Still	.10
208	Garrison Hearst	.30
209	*Terry Jackson*	.50
210	R.W. McQuarters	.10
211	Ken Norton Jr.	.10
212	Terrell Owens	.50
213	Jerry Rice	1.00
214	J.J. Stokes	.20
215	*Tai Streets*	1.00
216	Steve Young	.75
217	*Karsten Bailey*	1.00
218	Chad Brown	.10
219	Joey Galloway	.50
220	Ahman Green	.20
221	*Brock Huard*	1.50
222	Cortez Kennedy	.10
223	Jon Kitna	.75
224	Shawn Springs	.10
225	Ricky Watters	.20
226	Mike Alstott	.50
227	Reidel Anthony	.20
228	Trent Dilfer	.30
229	Warrick Dunn	.75
230	Bert Emanuel	.10
231	*Martin Gramatica*	.50
232	Jacquez Green	.20
233	*Shaun King*	2.00
234	*Anthony McFarland*	1.00
235	Warren Sapp	.10
236	Willie Davis	.10
237	Kevin Dyson	.20
238	Eddie George	.75
239	*Darran Hall*	.50
240	Jackie Harris	.10
241	Steve McNair	.50
242	Yancey Thigpen	.20
243	Frank Wycheck	.10
244	Stephen Alexander	.10
245	*Champ Bailey*	1.50
246	Stephen Davis	.10
247	Darrell Green	.10
248	Skip Hicks	.50
249	Brian Mitchell	.10
250	Michael Westbrook	.20

1999 Pacific Paramount Copper

This is a parallel to the base and could only be found in hobby product at one-per-pack.

	NM/M
Complete Set (250):	135.00
Copper Cards:	2X
Copper Rookies:	1.5X
Inserted 1:1	

1999 Pacific Paramount HoloGold

This is a parallel to the base set and was only found in retail product. Each card was sequentially numbered to 199.

HoloGold Cards:	3X-5X
HoloGold Rookies:	2X-4X
Production 199 Sets	

1999 Pacific Paramount Holographic Silver

This is a parallel to the base and was inserted into hobby product. Each card was sequentially numbered to 99.

Silver Cards:	3X-8X
Silver Rookies:	2X-5X
Production 99 Sets	

1999 Pacific Paramount Platinum Blue

This is a parallel to the base and was inserted in both hobby and retail product. Cards were found 1:73 packs.

Blue Cards:	3X-6X
Blue Rookies:	2X-4X
Inserted 1:73	

1999 Pacific Paramount Premiere Date

This is a parallel to the base that was found 1:37 hobby packs and each is sequentially numbered to 62.

Premiere Date Cards:	3X-10X
Premiere Date Rookies:	2X-8X
Inserted 1:37	

1999 Pacific Paramount Canton Bound

Each card is fully foiled and etched with just ten of the top players heading to Canton. Each card is horizontal and were inserted 1:361 packs. A parallel Proof set was also issued with each card sequentially numbered to 20.

		NM/M
Complete Set (10):		125.00
Common Player:		10.00
Inserted 1:361		
Proofs:		4X
Production 20 Sets		
1	Troy Aikman	15.00
2	Emmitt Smith	20.00
3	Terrell Davis	15.00
4	Barry Sanders	20.00
5	Brett Favre	25.00
6	Dan Marino	25.00
7	Randy Moss	20.00
8	Drew Bledsoe	15.00
9	Jerry Rice	15.00
10	Steve Young	15.00

1999 Pacific Paramount End Zone Net-Fusions

Each card in this 20-card set has a die-cut design that includes actual netting from behind the goal posts. Singles were inserted 1:73 packs.

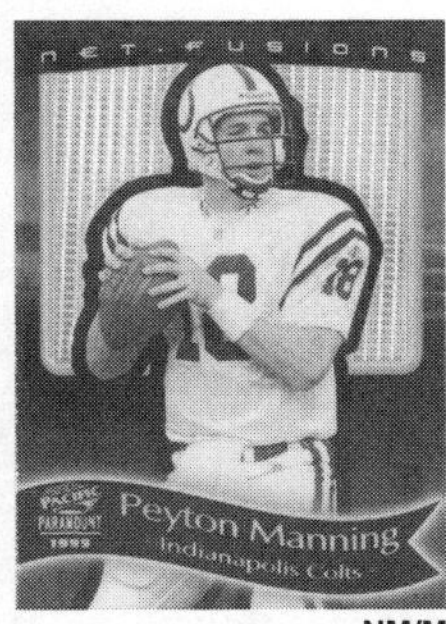

#	Player	NM/M
	Complete Set (20):	325.00
	Common Player:	10.00
	Inserted 1:73	
1	Jake Plummer	20.00
2	Jamal Anderson	10.00
3	Doug Flutie	15.00
4	Tim Couch	40.00
5	Troy Aikman	20.00
6	Emmitt Smith	30.00
7	Terrell Davis	30.00
8	Barry Sanders	40.00
9	Brett Favre	40.00
10	Peyton Manning	30.00
11	Mark Brunell	15.00
12	Fred Taylor	15.00
13	Dan Marino	30.00
14	Randy Moss	40.00
15	Drew Bledsoe	15.00
16	Ricky Williams	40.00
17	Jerry Rice	20.00
18	Steve Young	15.00
19	Jon Kitna	10.00
20	Eddie George	12.00

1999 Pacific Paramount Personal Bests

Thirty-six of the NFL's top players are featured on these holographic patterned foil cards. Singles were inserted 1:37 packs.

#	Player	NM/M
	Complete Set (36):	85.00
	Common Player:	1.00
	Inserted 1:37	
1	Jake Plummer	2.00
2	Jamal Anderson	1.00
3	Priest Holmes	4.00
4	Doug Flutie	2.00
5	Antowain Smith	1.00
6	Corey Dillon	2.00
7	Akili Smith	2.00
8	Tim Couch	5.00
9	Troy Aikman	4.00
10	Emmitt Smith	5.00
11	Terrell Davis	4.00
12	Barry Sanders	5.00
13	Brett Favre	6.00
14	Antonio Freeman	1.00
15	Edgerrin James	4.00
16	Peyton Manning	4.00
17	Mark Brunell	2.00
18	Fred Taylor	3.00
19	Dan Marino	5.00
20	Randall Cunningham	1.00
21	Randy Moss	4.00
22	Drew Bledsoe	3.00
23	Kevin Faulk	2.00
24	Ricky Williams	6.00
25	Curtis Martin	2.00
26	Napoleon Kaufman	1.00
27	Donovan McNabb	4.00
28	Jerome Bettis	1.00
29	Kordell Stewart	2.00
30	Terrell Owens	4.00
31	Jerry Rice	5.00
32	Steve Young	3.00
33	Jon Kitna	1.00
34	Warrick Dunn	2.00
35	Eddie George	3.00
36	Steve McNair	3.00

1999 Pacific Paramount Team Checklists

Each card in this 31-card set highlights one player from each team and uses his photo on the front with his name in gold foil. The back has a smaller photo with a checklist of players from that team. Singles were inserted 2:37 packs.

#	Player	NM/M
	Complete Set (31):	65.00
	Common Player:	1.00
	Minor Stars:	2.00
	Inserted 2:37	
1	Jake Plummer	2.00
2	Jamal Anderson	2.00
3	Priest Holmes	3.00
4	Doug Flutie	2.00
5	Muhsin Muhammad	1.00
6	Cade McNown	1.00
7	Corey Dillon	2.00
8	Tim Couch	5.00
9	Troy Aikman	4.00
10	Terrell Davis	4.00
11	Barry Sanders	5.00
12	Brett Favre	6.00
13	Peyton Manning	4.00
14	Fred Taylor	3.00
15	Elvis Grbac	1.00
16	Dan Marino	6.00
17	Randy Moss	4.00
18	Drew Bledsoe	3.00
19	Ricky Williams	5.00
20	Ike Hilliard	1.00
21	Curtis Martin	3.00
22	Napoleon Kaufman	1.00
23	Donovan McNabb	5.00
24	Jerome Bettis	2.00
25	Torry Holt	3.00
26	Natrone Means	1.00
27	Jerry Rice	4.00
28	Jon Kitna	1.00
29	Warrick Dunn	2.00
30	Eddie George	3.00
31	Skip Hicks	1.00

1999 Pacific Prisms

This 150-card base set pictured players on a holographic prismatic background. A total of five parallel sets were issued and they include: Holographic Blue, Holographic Gold, Holographic Mirror, Holographic Purple and Premiere Date. Other inserts include: Dial-a-Stats, Ornaments, Prospects and Sunday's Best. SRP was $4.99 for five-card packs.

#	Player	NM/M
	Complete Set (150):	60.00
	Common Player:	.10
	Minor Stars:	.40
	Common Rookie:	.50
	Pack (5):	3.00
	Wax Box (24):	65.00
1	*David Boston*	4.00
2	Rob Moore	.40
3	Adrian Murrell	.10
4	Jake Plummer	1.50
5	Frank Sanders	.40
6	Jamal Anderson	.75
7	Chris Chandler	.40
8	Tim Dwight	.75
9	Terance Mathis	.10
10	Peter Boulware	.10
11	Priest Holmes	.75
12	Patrick Johnson	.40
13	Jermaine Lewis	.10
14	Doug Flutie	1.25
15	Eric Moulds	.75
16	*Peerless Price*	3.00
17	Antowain Smith	.75
18	Bruce Smith	.10
19	Steve Beuerlein	.40
20	Tim Biakabutuka	.40
21	Muhsin Muhammad	.75
22	Wesley Walls	.10
23	Edgar Bennett	.10
24	Curtis Conway	.40
25	Bobby Engram	.10
26	Curtis Enis	.75
27	*Cade McNown*	2.00
28	Jeff Blake	.40
29	*Scott Covington*	1.00
30	Corey Dillon	.75
31	Carl Pickens	.40
32	*Akili Smith*	2.00
33	*Craig Yeast*	1.00
34	*Tim Couch*	4.00
35	Ty Detmer	.10
36	*Kevin Johnson*	2.00
37	Terry Kirby	.10
38	Leslie Shepherd	.10
39	Troy Aikman	1.50
40	Michael Irvin	.40
41	Deion Sanders	.75
42	Emmitt Smith	2.00
43	Bubby Brister	.40
44	Terrell Davis	1.00
45	Brian Griese	1.50
46	Ed McCaffrey	.75
47	Shannon Sharpe	.40
48	Rod Smith	.75
49	Charlie Batch	1.25
50	Germane Crowell	.75
51	*Sedrick Irvin*	2.00
52	Herman Moore	.75
53	Johnnie Morton	.40
54	Barry Sanders	2.00
55	Mark Chmura	.40
56	Brett Favre	3.00
57	Antonio Freeman	.75
58	Dorsey Levens	.75
59	Ken Dilger	.10
60	Marvin Harrison	.75
61	*Edgerrin James*	8.00
62	Peyton Manning	2.00
63	Jerome Pathon	.10
64	Mark Brunell	1.25
65	Keenan McCardell	.40
66	Jimmy Smith	.75
67	Fred Taylor	1.50
68	Derrick Alexander	.10
69	*Michael Cloud*	1.00
70	Tony Gonzalez	.40
71	Elvis Grbac	.40
72	Andre Rison	.40
73	*Cecil Collins*	2.00
74	Oronde Gadsden	.40
75	*James Johnson*	2.00
76	Dan Marino	2.00
77	O.J. McDuffie	.40
78	Lamar Thomas	.10
79	Cris Carter	.75
80	*Daunte Culpepper*	8.00
81	Randall Cunningham	.75
82	Matthew Hatchette	.40
83	Randy Moss	2.00
84	John Randle	.10
85	Robert Smith	.75
86	Drew Bledsoe	1.25
87	Ben Coates	.40
88	*Kevin Faulk*	2.00
89	Terry Glenn	.75
90	Shawn Jefferson	.10
91	Cameron Cleeland	.40
92	Billy Joe Hobert	.10
93	Keith Poole	.10
94	*Ricky Williams*	4.00
95	Gary Brown	.10
96	Kent Graham	.10
97	Ike Hilliard	.40
98	Amani Toomer	.40
99	Wayne Chrebet	.75
100	Keyshawn Johnson	.75
101	Curtis Martin	.75
102	Vinny Testaverde	.40
103	Tim Brown	.40
104	James Jett	.10
105	Napoleon Kaufman	.75
106	Charles Woodson	.75
107	Koy Detmer	.10
108	*Donovan McNabb*	8.00
109	Duce Staley	.75
110	Kevin Turner	.10
111	Jerome Bettis	.75
112	Mark Bruener	.10
113	*Troy Edwards*	2.00
114	Levon Kirkland	.10
115	Kordell Stewart	.75
116	*Amos Zereoue*	1.50
117	Ryan Leaf	.75
118	Natrone Means	.40
119	Mikhael Ricks	.40
120	Junior Seau	.40
121	Garrison Hearst	.40
122	Terrell Owens	.75
123	Jerry Rice	1.50
124	J.J. Stokes	.40
125	Steve Young	1.25
126	Chad Brown	.10
127	Joey Galloway	.75
128	*Brock Huard*	.75
129	Jon Kitna	1.00
130	Ricky Watters	.40
131	Isaac Bruce	.75
132	*Joe Germaine*	1.50
133	Marshall Faulk	.75
134	*Torry Holt*	4.00
135	Trent Green	.40
136	Mike Alstott	.75
137	Reidel Anthony	.40
138	Trent Dilfer	.40
139	Warrick Dunn	.75
140	Jacquez Green	.40
141	*Shaun King*	1.00
142	*Darnell McDonald*	1.50
143	Eddie George	1.00
144	Steve McNair	1.00
145	Yancey Thigpen	.40
146	Frank Wycheck	.10
147	*Champ Bailey*	2.00
148	Albert Connell	.40
149	Skip Hicks	.40
150	Michael Westbrook	.40

1999 Pacific Prisms Holographic Blue

This was a 150-card parallel to the base set. Each of these singles was printed with blue foil on the background. Singles were found in both hobby and retail packs. Each was sequentially numbered on the front to 80.

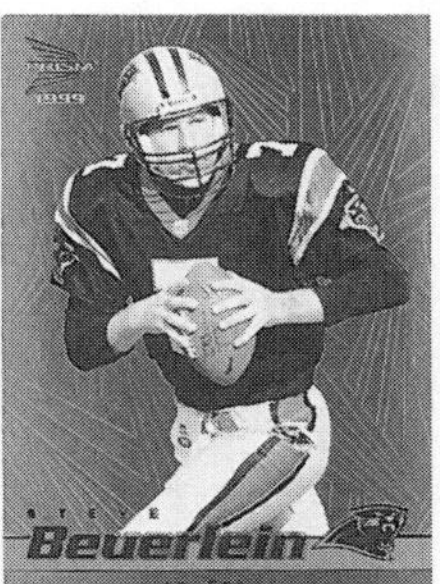

Blue Cards:	5X-10X
Blue Rookies:	3X-6X
Production 80 Sets	

1999 Pacific Prisms Holographic Gold

This was a 150-card parallel to the base set. Each of these singles was printed with gold foil on the background. Singles were found in both hobby and retail packs. Each was sequentially numbered on the front to 480.

Gold Cards:	2X-4X
Gold Rookies:	2X
Production 480 Sets	

1999 Pacific Prisms Holographic Mirror

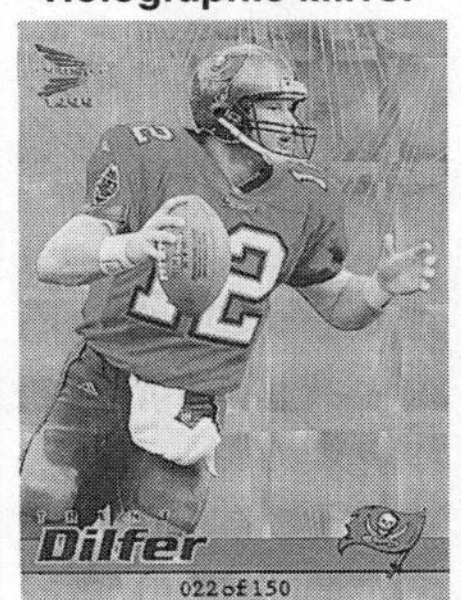

This was a 150-card parallel to the base set. Each of these singles was printed with a mirror foil background. Singles were found in both hobby and retail packs. Each was sequentially numbered on the front to 160.

Mirror Cards:	4X-8X
Mirror Rookies:	2X-4X
Production 160 Sets	

1999 Pacific Prisms Holographic Purple

This was a 150-card parallel to the base set. Each of these singles was printed with purple foil on the background. Singles were found only in hobby packs. Each was sequentially numbered on the front to 320.

Purple Cards:	3X-5X
Purple Rookies:	2X
Production 320 Sets	

1999 Pacific Prisms Premiere Date

This was a 150-card parallel to the base set. Each of these singles was printed with red foil on the background. Singles were found only in hobby packs. Cards were found one-per-box and each was sequentially numbered to 61.

Premiere Date Cards:	5X-10X
Premiere Date Rookies:	3X-5X
Production 61 Sets	

1999 Pacific Prisms Dial-a-Stats

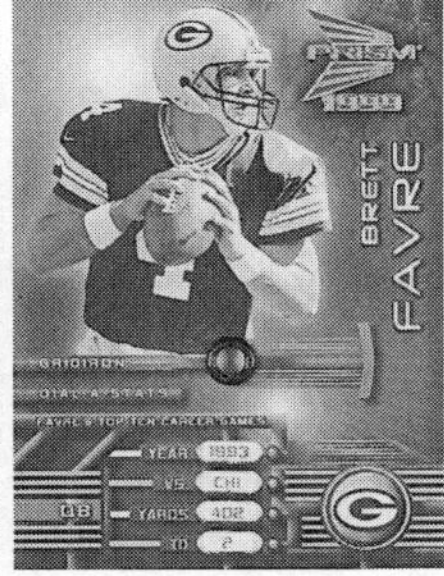

This 10-card insert included a spinning wheel on the card that allowed collectors to dial up a player's top performances. Singles were inserted 1:193 packs.

#	Player	NM/M
	Complete Set (10):	75.00
	Common Player:	5.00
	Inserted 1:193	
1	Tim Couch	12.00
2	Emmitt Smith	15.00
3	Terrell Davis	10.00
4	Barry Sanders	12.00
5	Brett Favre	15.00
6	Mark Brunell	6.00
7	Dan Marino	15.00
8	Ricky Williams	12.00
9	Curtis Martin	5.00
10	Terrell Owens	5.00

1999 Pacific Prisms Ornaments

This 20-card insert had a Christmas theme to each single. Five different die cuts could be found in the shapes of Christmas trees, stockings, balls, etc. Each came with a string attached so collectors could hang these on their Christmas trees. Cards were found 1:25 packs.

#	Player	NM/M
	Complete Set (20):	75.00
	Common Player:	2.00
	Inserted 1:25	
1	Jake Plummer	3.00
2	Jamal Anderson	3.00
3	Cade McNown	2.00
4	Tim Couch	8.00
5	Troy Aikman	8.00
6	Deion Sanders	3.00
7	Emmitt Smith	10.00
8	Terrell Davis	8.00
9	Barry Sanders	10.00
10	Brett Favre	12.00
11	Peyton Manning	8.00
12	Mark Brunell	3.00
13	Fred Taylor	3.00
14	Dan Marino	12.00
15	Randy Moss	8.00
16	Drew Bledsoe	5.00
17	Terrell Owens	3.00
18	Jerry Rice	8.00
19	Steve Young	8.00
20	Jon Kitna	2.00

A card number in parenthese ( ) indicates the set is unnumbered.

1999 Pacific Prisms Prospects

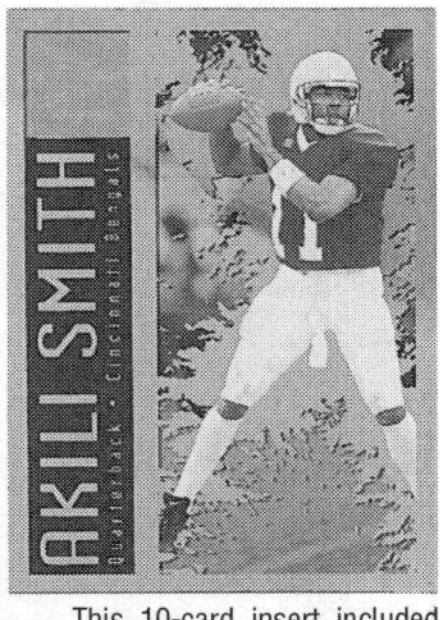

This 10-card insert included rookies from the 1999 NFL Draft. Singles were only found in hobby product and inserted 1:97 packs.

#	Player	NM/M
	Complete Set (10):	45.00
	Common Player:	2.00
	Inserted 1:97	
1	David Boston	4.00
2	Cade McNown	2.00
3	Akili Smith	2.00
4	Tim Couch	6.00
5	Edgerrin James	10.00
6	Cecil Collins	2.00
7	Daunte Culpepper	8.00
8	Ricky Williams	12.00
9	Donovan McNabb	8.00
10	Torry Holt	3.00

1999 Pacific Prisms Sunday's Best

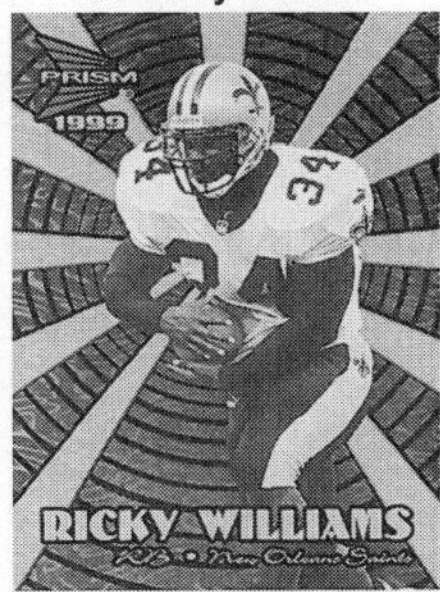

This 20-card insert included a mix of veterans and rookies. Singles were inserted 2:25 packs.

#	Player	NM/M
	Complete Set (20):	45.00
	Common Player:	1.00
	Inserted 2:25	
1	Jake Plummer	2.00
2	Akili Smith	2.00
3	Tim Couch	5.00
4	Emmitt Smith	5.00
5	Terrell Davis	4.00
6	Barry Sanders	5.00
7	Brett Favre	6.00
8	Peyton Manning	4.00
9	Mark Brunell	2.00
10	Fred Taylor	2.00
11	Dan Marino	6.00
12	Randy Moss	4.00
13	Drew Bledsoe	3.00
14	Ricky Williams	5.00
15	Curtis Martin	2.00
16	Terrell Owens	2.00
17	Jerry Rice	4.00
18	Steve Young	3.00
19	Jon Kitna	1.00
20	Eddie George	2.00

1999 Pacific Revolution

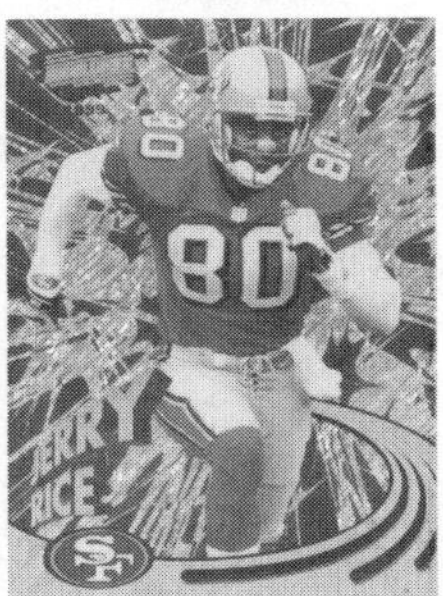

Pacific Revolution is a 175-card set that includes 50 seeded rookies at 1:4 packs. Each card includes dual foiling, etching and embossing. Opening Day, Shadow and Red are three parallel sets. Other inserts include: Chalk Talk, Icons, Showstoppers and Thorn in the Side.

		NM/M
Complete Set (175):		75.00
Common Player:		.15
Minor Stars:		.50
Common Rookie:		1.00
Inserted 1:4		
Pack (3):		2.50
Wax Box (24):		50.00
1	*David Boston*	4.00
2	*Joel Makovicka*	2.00
3	Rob Moore	.50
4	Adrian Murrell	.15
5	Jake Plummer	2.00
6	Frank Sanders	.15
7	Jamal Anderson	1.00
8	Chris Chandler	.50
9	Tim Dwight	.75
10	Terance Mathis	.15
11	*Jeff Paulk*	2.00
12	O.J. Santiago	.15
13	Peter Boulware	.15
14	Priest Holmes	2.00
15	Michael Jackson	.15
16	Jermaine Lewis	.15
17	Doug Flutie	1.50
18	Eric Moulds	1.00
19	*Peerless Price*	3.00
20	Andre Reed	.50
21	Antowain Smith	1.00
22	Bruce Smith	.15
23	Steve Beuerlein	.15
24	Kevin Greene	.15
25	Fred Lane	.15
26	Muhsin Muhammad	.15
27	Wesley Walls	.15
28	*Marty Booker*	1.00
29	Curtis Conway	.50
30	Bobby Engram	.15
31	Curtis Enis	1.00
32	Erik Kramer	.15
33	*Cade McNown*	2.00
34	*Scott Covington*	2.00
35	Corey Dillon	1.25
36	Carl Pickens	.50
37	Darnay Scott	.15
38	*Akili Smith*	2.00
39	*Craig Yeast*	2.00
40	*Darrin Chiaverini*	1.00
41	*Tim Couch*	4.00
42	Ty Detmer	.15
43	*Kevin Johnson*	2.00
44	Terry Kirby	.15
45	*Daylon McCutcheon*	1.00
46	Irv Smith	.15
47	Troy Aikman	2.00
48	Michael Irvin	.75
49	*Wayne McGarity*	1.00
50	*Dat Nguyen*	2.00
51	Deion Sanders	1.00
52	Emmitt Smith	3.00
53	Terrell Davis	1.00
54	John Elway	3.00
55	Brian Griese	1.50
56	Ed McCaffrey	.75
57	*Travis McGriff*	1.00
58	Shannon Sharpe	.50
59	Rod Smith	.50
60	Charlie Batch	.75
61	*Chris Claiborne*	1.00
62	*Sedrick Irvin*	1.00
63	Herman Moore	1.00
64	Johnnie Morton	.15
65	Barry Sanders	2.00
66	*Aaron Brooks*	10.00
67	Mark Chmura	.50
68	Brett Favre	4.00
69	Antonio Freeman	1.00
70	Dorsey Levens	.75
71	*De'Mond Parker*	1.00
72	Marvin Harrison	.50
73	*Edgerrin James*	8.00
74	Peyton Manning	3.00
75	Jerome Pathon	.15
76	*Mike Peterson*	2.00
77	Reggie Barlow	.15
78	Mark Brunell	1.50
79	Keenan McCardell	.50
80	Jimmy Smith	.75
81	Fred Taylor	1.00
82	*Mike Cloud*	1.00
83	Tony Gonzalez	.50
84	Elvis Grbac	.15
85	*Larry Parker*	1.00
86	Andre Rison	.50
87	*Brian Shay*	1.00
88	Karim Abdul	.75
89	Oronde Gadsden	.50
90	*James Johnson*	3.00
91	*Rob Konrad*	2.00
92	Dan Marino	3.00
93	O.J. McDuffie	.50
94	Cris Carter	1.00
95	*Daunte Culpepper*	8.00
96	Randall Cunningham	1.00
97	*Jim Kleinsasser*	2.00
98	Randy Moss	3.00
99	Jake Reed	.15
100	Robert Smith	.75
101	Drew Bledsoe	1.50
102	Ben Coates	.50
103	*Kevin Faulk*	2.00
104	Terry Glenn	.75
105	Shawn Jefferson	.15
106	*Andy Katzenmoyer*	2.00
107	Cameron Cleeland	.50
108	Andre Hastings	.15
109	Billy Joe Tolliver	.15
110	*Ricky Williams*	8.00
111	Gary Brown	.15
112	Kent Graham	.15
113	Ike Hilliard	.15
114	*Joe Montgomery*	2.00
115	Amani Toomer	.15
116	Wayne Chrebet	.75
117	Keyshawn Johnson	1.00
118	Leon Johnson	.15
119	Curtis Martin	1.00
120	Vinny Testaverde	.50
121	Dedric Ward	.15
122	Tim Brown	.75
123	*Dameane Douglas*	2.00
124	Rickey Dudley	.50
125	James Jett	.15
126	Napoleon Kaufman	1.00
127	Charles Woodson	1.00
128	*Na Brown*	2.00
129	*Cecil Martin*	2.00
130	*Donovan McNabb*	8.00
131	Duce Staley	.15
132	Kevin Turner	.15
133	Jerome Bettis	1.00
134	*Troy Edwards*	2.00
135	Courtney Hawkins	.15
136	*Malcolm Johnson*	2.00
137	Kordell Stewart	1.25
138	*Jerame Tuman*	1.00
139	*Amos Zereoue*	3.00
140	Isaac Bruce	1.00
141	*Joe Germaine*	2.00
142	*Torry Holt*	4.00
143	Amp Lee	.15
144	Ricky Proehl	.15
145	Freddie Jones	.15
146	Ryan Leaf	.50
147	Natrone Means	1.00
148	Mikhael Ricks	.15
149	Garrison Hearst	.75
150	*Terry Jackson*	2.00
151	Terrell Owens	1.00
152	Jerry Rice	2.00
153	J.J. Stokes	.50
154	Steve Young	1.50
155	*Karsten Bailey*	2.00
156	Joey Galloway	1.00
157	Ahman Green	.50
158	*Brock Huard*	2.00
159	Jon Kitna	1.00
160	Ricky Watters	.75
161	Mike Alstott	1.00
162	Reidel Anthony	.50
163	Trent Dilfer	.75
164	Warrick Dunn	1.25
165	*Shaun King*	2.00
166	*Anthony McFarland*	1.00
167	Kevin Dyson	.50
168	Eddie George	1.25
169	*Darran Hall*	1.00
170	Steve McNair	1.00
171	Frank Wycheck	.15
172	Stephen Alexander	.15
173	*Champ Bailey*	2.50
174	Skip Hicks	.50
175	Michael Westbrook	.15

1999 Pacific Revolution Opening Day

This is a parallel to the base set and each single is sequentially numbered to 68.

Opening Day Cards:	6X-15X
Opening Day Rookies:	3X-5X
Production 68 Sets	

1999 Pacific Revolution Red

This is a parallel to the base set and each single is sequentially numbered to 299.

Red Cards	3X-6X
Red Rookies:	2X
Production 299 Sets	

1999 Pacific Revolution Shadow

This is a parallel to the base set and each single is sequentially numbered to 99.

Shadow Cards:	5X-12X
Shadow Rookies:	3X-5X
Production 99 Sets	

1999 Pacific Revolution Chalk Talk

Each card in this 20-card set has the player pictured on a chalk board with a diagram of an offensive play. Singles were inserted 1:49 packs.

		NM/M
Complete Set (20):		75.00
Common Player:		2.00
Inserted 1:49		
1	Jake Plummer	3.00
2	Jamal Anderson	3.00
3	Doug Flutie	2.00
4	Tim Couch	8.00
5	Troy Aikman	6.00
6	Emmitt Smith	8.00
7	Terrell Davis	6.00
8	John Elway	6.00
9	Barry Sanders	8.00
10	Brett Favre	10.00
11	Peyton Manning	6.00
12	Mark Brunell	3.00
13	Fred Taylor	3.00
14	Dan Marino	10.00
15	Randy Moss	6.00
16	Drew Bledsoe	5.00
17	Ricky Williams	12.00
18	Jerry Rice	6.00
19	Jon Kitna	2.00
20	Eddie George	3.00

1999 Pacific Revolution Icons

Each card is silver foiled, etched and die-cut. The 10 players in the set were found 1:121 packs.

		NM/M
Complete Set (10):		75.00
Common Player:		3.00
Inserted 1:121		
1	Emmitt Smith	15.00
2	Terrell Davis	10.00
3	John Elway	10.00
4	Barry Sanders	15.00
5	Brett Favre	18.00
6	Peyton Manning	12.00
7	Dan Marino	18.00
8	Randy Moss	12.00
9	Jerry Rice	10.00
10	Jon Kitna	3.00

1999 Pacific Revolution Showstoppers

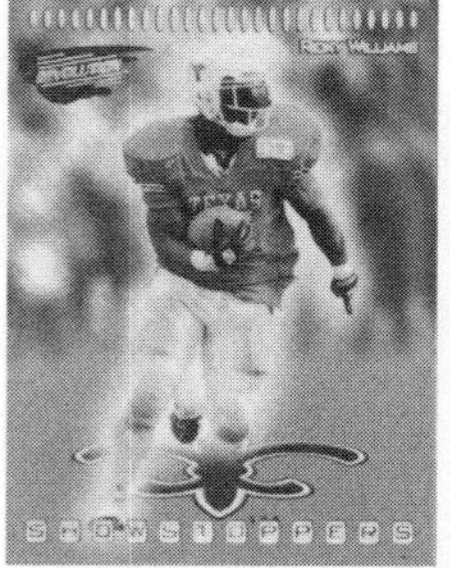

The top 36 players in the NFL are in this insert that is etched and includes silver foil on the fronts. Singles were inserted 2:25 packs.

		NM/M
Complete Set (36):		75.00
Common Player:		1.00
Minor Stars:		2.00
Inserted 2:25		
1	Jake Plummer	2.00
2	Jamal Anderson	2.00
3	Priest Holmes	3.00
4	Doug Flutie	2.00
5	Antowain Smith	2.00
6	Cade McNown	2.00
7	Tim Couch	6.00
8	Corey Dillon	2.00
9	Akili Smith	2.00
10	Troy Aikman	5.00
11	Emmitt Smith	6.00
12	Terrell Davis	5.00
13	John Elway	5.00
14	Charlie Batch	2.00
15	Barry Sanders	6.00
16	Brett Favre	7.00
17	Antonio Freeman	1.00
18	Edgerrin James	6.00
19	Peyton Manning	5.00
20	Mark Brunell	3.00
21	Fred Taylor	3.00
22	Dan Marino	7.00
23	Randall Cunningham	2.00
24	Randy Moss	5.00
25	Drew Bledsoe	4.00
26	Ricky Williams	7.00
27	Curtis Martin	2.00
28	Napoleon Kaufman	1.00
29	Donovan McNabb	5.00
30	Kordell Stewart	3.00
31	Terrell Owens	2.00
32	Jerry Rice	5.00
33	Steve Young	4.00
34	Jon Kitna	2.00
35	Warrick Dunn	2.00
36	Eddie George	3.00

A player's name in *italic* type indicates a rookie card.

1999 Pacific Revolution Thorn in the Side

Each card is die cut and on the back includes an analysis of how that player has hurt an opposing team. A total of 20 players were used for this insert and were found 1:25 packs.

		NM/M
Complete Set (20):		65.00
Common Player:		1.00
Minor Stars:		2.00
Inserted 1:25		
1	Jake Plummer	2.00
2	Jamal Anderson	2.00
3	Doug Flutie	2.00
4	Tim Couch	5.00
5	Troy Aikman	5.00
6	Emmitt Smith	6.00
7	Terrell Davis	5.00
8	John Elway	5.00
9	Barry Sanders	6.00
10	Brett Favre	7.00
11	Peyton Manning	5.00
12	Fred Taylor	3.00
13	Dan Marino	7.00
14	Randy Moss	5.00
15	Drew Bledsoe	3.00
16	Ricky Williams	7.00
17	Curtis Martin	2.00
18	Jerome Bettis	1.00
19	Jerry Rice	5.00
20	Jon Kitna	1.00

2000 Pacific

		NM/M
Complete Set (450):		50.00
Common Player:		.10
Minor Stars:		.20
Common Rookie:		.50
Pack (12):		1.50
Wax Box (36):		45.00
1	Mario Bates	.10
2	David Boston	.50
3	Rob Fredrickson	.10
4	Terry Hardy	.10
5	Rob Moore	.20
6	Adrian Murrell	.20
7	Michael Pittman	.10
8	Jake Plummer	.50
9	Simeon Rice	.10
10	Frank Sanders	.10
11	Aeneas Williams	.10
12	Mac Cody, Andy McCullough	.10
13	Dennis McKinley, Joel Makovicka	.50
14	Jamal Anderson	.50
15	Chris Calloway	.10
16	Chris Chandler	.20
17	Bob Christian	.10
18	Tim Dwight	.50
19	Jammi German	.10
20	Ronnie Harris	.10
21	Terance Mathis	.10
22	Ken Oxendine	.10
23	O.J. Santiago	.10
24	Bob Whitfield	.10
25	Eugene Baker, Reggie Kelly	.10
26	Justin Armour	.10
27	Tony Banks	.20
28	Peter Boulware	.10
29	Stoney Case	.10
30	Priest Holmes	1.00
31	Qadry Ismail	.10
32	Patrick Johnson	.10
33	Michael McCrary	.10
34	Jonathan Ogden	.10
35	Errict Rhett	.20
36	Duane Starks	.10
37	Doug Flutie	.75
38	Rob Johnson	.20
39	Jonathon Linton	.20
40	Eric Moulds	.50
41	Peerless Price	.30
42	Andre Reed	.20
43	Jay Riemersma	.10
44	Antowain Smith	.30
45	Bruce Smith	.10
46	Thurman Thomas	.20
47	Kevin Williams	.10
48	Bobby Collins, Sheldon Jackson	.10
49	Michael Bates	.10
50	Steve Beuerlein	.20
51	Tshimanga Biakabutuka	.20
52	Antonio Edwards	.10
53	Donald Hayes	.10
54	Patrick Jeffers	.30
55	Anthony Johnson	.10
56	Jeff Lewis	.10
57	Eric Metcalf	.10
58	Muhsin Muhammad	.20
59	Jason Peter	.10
60	Wesley Walls	.20
61	John Allred	.10
62	Marty Booker	.10
63	Curtis Conway	.20
64	Bobby Engram	.10
65	Curtis Enis	.30
66	Shane Matthews	.10
67	Cade McNown	.75
68	Glyn Milburn	.10
69	Jim Miller	.10
70	Marcus Robinson	.50
71	Ryan Wetnight	.10
72	James Allen, Macey Brooks	.10
73	Jeff Blake	.20
74	Corey Dillon	.30
75	Rodney Heath	.10
76	Willie Jackson	.10
77	Tremain Mack	.10
78	Tony McGee	.10
79	Carl Pickens	.20
80	Darnay Scott	.20
81	Akili Smith	.60
82	Takeo Spikes	.10
83	Craig Yeast	.10
84	Michael Basnight, Nick Williams	.10
85	Karim Abdul	.20
86	Darren Chiaverini	.10
87	Tim Couch	1.25
88	Marc Edwards	.10
89	Kevin Johnson	.50
90	Terry Kirby	.10
91	Daylon McCutcheon	.10
92	Jamir Miller	.10
93	Leslie Shepherd	.10
94	Irv Smith	.10
95	Mark Campbell, James Dearth	.10
96	Zola Davis, Damon Dunn	.10
97	Madre Hill, Tarek Selah	.10
98	Troy Aikman	1.25
99	Eric Bjornson	.10
100	Dexter Coakley	.10
101	Greg Ellis	.10
102	Raghib Ismail	.10
103	David LaFleur	.10
104	Ernie Mills	.10
105	Jeff Ogden	.10
106	Ryan Neufeld, Robert Thomas	.10
107	Deion Sanders	.50
108	Emmitt Smith	2.00
109	Chris Warren	.20
110	Mike Lucky, Jason Tucker	.30
111	Byron Chamberlain	.10
112	Terrell Davis	1.00
113	Jason Elam	.10
114	Olandis Gary	.60
115	Brian Griese	.60
116	Ed McCaffrey	.50
117	Trevor Pryce	.10
118	Bill Romanowski	.10
119	Shannon Sharpe	.30
120	Rod Smith	.50
121	Al Wilson	.10
122	Andre Cooper, Chris Watson	.10
123	Charlie Batch	.50
124	Stephen Boyd	.10
125	Chris Claiborne	.10
126	Germane Crowell	.20
127	Terry Fair	.10
128	Gus Frerotte	.10
129	Jason Hanson	.10
130	Greg Hill	.10
131	Herman Moore	.30
132	Johnnie Morton	.10
133	Barry Sanders	2.00
134	David Sloan	.10
135	Brock Olivo, Cory Sauter	.10
136	Corey Bradford	.20
137	Tyrone Davis	.10
138	Brett Favre	2.50
139	Antonio Freeman	.50
140	Vonnie Holliday	.10
141	Dorsey Levens	.50
142	Keith McKenzie	.10
143	Mike McKenzie	.10
144	Bill Schroeder	.10
145	Jeff Thomason	.10
146	Frank Winters	.10
147	Cornelius Bennett	.10
148	Tony Blevins	.10
149	Chad Bratzke	.10
150	Ken Dilger	.10
151	Tarik Glenn	.10
152	E.G. Green	.10
153	Marvin Harrison	.50
154	Edgerrin James	2.50
155	Peyton Manning	2.00
156	Jerome Pathon	.10
157	Marcus Pollard	.10
158	Terrence Wilkins	.10
159	*Issac Jones, Paul Shields*	.50
160	Reggie Barlow	.10
161	Aaron Beasley	.10
162	Tony Boselli	.10
163	Tony Brackens	.10
164	Kyle Brady	.10
165	Mark Brunell	.75
166	Jay Fiedler	.20
167	Kevin Hardy	.10
168	Carnell Lake	.10
169	Keenan McCardell	.20
170	Jonathan Quinn	.10
171	Jimmy Smith	.30
172	James Stewart	.30
173	Fred Taylor	.75
174	Lenzie Jackson, Stacey Mack	.50
175	Derrick Alexander	.10
176	Donnell Bennett	.10
177	Donnie Edwards	.10
178	Tony Gonzalez	.30
179	Elvis Grbac	.20
180	James Hasty	.10
181	Joe Horn	.10
182	Lonnie Johnson	.10
183	Kevin Lockett	.10
184	Larry Parker	.10
185	Tony Richardson	.10
186	Rashaan Shehee	.10
187	Tamarick Vanover	.10
188	Trace Armstrong	.10
189	Oronde Gadsden	.10
190	Damon Huard	.20
191	Nate Jacquet	.10
192	J.J. Johnson	.20
193	Rob Konrad	.10
194	Sam Madison	.10
195	Dan Marino	2.00
196	Tony Martin	.10
197	O.J. McDuffie	.20
198	Stanley Pritchett	.10
199	Tim Ruddy	.10
200	Patrick Surtain	.10
201	Zach Thomas	.20
202	Cris Carter	.50
203	Duane Clemons	.10
204	Carlester Crumpler	.10
205	Daunte Culpepper	.75
206	Jeff George	.30
207	Matthew Hatchette	.10
208	Leroy Hoard	.10
209	Randy Moss	2.00
210	John Randle	.10
211	Jake Reed	.10
212	Robert Smith	.50
213	Robert Tate	.10
214	Terry Allen	.20
215	Bruce Armstrong	.10
216	Drew Bledsoe	.75
217	Ben Coates	.20
218	Kevin Faulk	.20
219	Terry Glenn	.30
220	Shawn Jefferson	.10
221	Andy Katzenmoyer	.10
222	Ty Law	.10
223	Willie McGinest	.10
224	Lawyer Milloy	.10
225	Tony Simmons	.10
226	Michael Bishop, Sean Morey	.10
227	Cameron Cleeland	.20
228	Troy Davis	.10
229	*Jake Delhomme*	.50
230	Andre Hastings	.10
231	Eddie Kennison	.20
232	Wilmont Perry	.10
233	Dino Philyaw	.10
234	Keith Poole	.10
235	William Roaf	.10
236	Billy Joe Tolliver	.10
237	Fred Weary	.10
238	Ricky Williams	1.50
239	*P.J. Franklin, Marvin Powell*	.50
240	Jessie Armstead	.10
241	Tiki Barber	.20
242	Daniel Campbell	.10
243	Kerry Collins	.20
244	Percy Ellsworth	.10
245	Kent Graham	.10
246	Ike Hilliard	.20
247	Cedric Jones	.10
248	Bashir Livingston	.10
249	Pete Mitchell	.10
250	Michael Strahan	.10
251	Amani Toomer	.20
252	Charles Way	.10
253	Andre Weathers	.10
254	Richie Anderson	.10
255	Wayne Chrebet	.50
256	Marcus Coleman	.10
257	Bryan Cox	.10
258	Jason Fabini	.10
259	*Robert Farmer*	.50
260	Keyshawn Johnson	.50
261	Ray Lucas	.30
262	Curtis Martin	.50
263	Kevin Mawae	.10
264	Eric Ogbogu	.10
265	Bernie Parmalee	.10
266	Vinny Testaverde	.30
267	Dedric Ward	.10
268	Eric Barton	.10
269	Tim Brown	.30
270	Tony Bryant	.10
271	Rickey Dudley	.20
272	Rich Gannon	.20
273	Bobby Hoying	.30
274	James Jett	.10
275	Napoleon Kaufman	.30
276	Jon Ritchie	.10
277	Darrell Russell	.10
278	Kenny Shedd	.10
279	Marquis Walker	.10
280	Tyrone Wheatley	.20
281	Charles Woodson	.50
282	Luther Broughton	.10

283 Al Harris .10
284 Greg Jefferson .10
285 Dietrich Jells .10
286 Charles Johnson .10
287 Chad Lewis .10
288 Mike Mamula .10
289 Donovan McNabb 1.50
290 Doug Pederson .10
291 Allen Rossum .10
292 Torrance Small .10
293 Duce Staley .30
294 Jerome Bettis .50
295 Kris Brown .10
296 Mark Bruener .10
297 Troy Edwards .50
298 Jason Gildon .10
299 Richard Huntley .10
300 Bobby Shaw .10
301 Scott Shields .10
302 Kordell Stewart .50
303 Hines Ward .20
304 Amos Zereoue .20
305 Matt Cushing, Jerame Tuman .10
306 *Pete Gonzalez, Anthony Wright* 1.00
307 Isaac Bruce .50
308 Kevin Carter .10
309 Marshall Faulk .50
310 London Fletcher .10
311 Joe Germaine .20
312 Az-Zahir Hakim .20
313 Torry Holt .50
314 Tony Horne .20
315 Mike Jones .10
316 Dexter McCleon .10
317 Orlando Pace .10
318 Ricky Proehl .10
319 Kurt Warner 3.00
320 Roland Williams .10
321 Grant Winstrom .10
322 James Hodgins, Justin Watson .10
323 Jermaine Fazande .20
324 Jeff Graham .10
325 Jim Harbaugh .10
326 Raylee Johnson .10
327 Charlie Jones .10
328 Freddie Jones .10
329 Natrone Means .20
330 Chris Penn .10
331 Mikhael Ricks .10
332 Junior Seau .20
333 Reginald Davis, Robert Reed .10
334 Fred Beasley .10
335 Brentson Buckner .10
336 Greg Clark .10
337 Dave Fiore .10
338 Charlie Garner .20
339 *Mark Harris* .50
340 Ramos McDonald .10
341 Terrell Owens .50
342 Jerry Rice 1.25
343 Lance Schulters .10
344 J.J. Stokes .20
345 Bryant Young .10
346 Steve Young .75
347 Jeff Garcia .50
348 Fabien Bownes .10
349 Chad Brown .10
350 Reggie Brown .10
351 Sean Dawkins .10
352 Christian Fauria .10
353 Ahman Green .20
354 Walter Jones .10
355 Cortez Kennedy .10
356 Jon Kitna .50
357 Derrick Mayes .20
358 Charlie Rogers .10
359 Shawn Springs .10
360 Ricky Watters .20
361 Donnie Abraham .10
362 Mike Alstott .50
363 Reidel Anthony .20
364 Ronde Barber .10
365 Derrick Brooks .10
366 Warrick Dunn .50
367 Jacquez Green .20
368 Marcus Jones .10
369 Shaun King .75
370 John Lynch .10
371 Warren Sapp .10
372 Steve White .10
373 Martin Gramatica, Kevin McCloud .10
374 Blaine Bishop .10
375 Al Del Greco .10
376 Kevin Dyson .20
377 Eddie George .60
378 Jevon Kearse .60
379 Derrick Mason .10
380 Bruce Matthews .10
381 Steve McNair .60
382 Neil O'Donnell .20
383 Yancey Thigpen .20
384 Frank Wycheck .10
385 Kevin Daft, Larry Brown .10
386 Stephen Alexander .10
387 Champ Bailey .30
388 Larry Centers .10
389 Marco Coleman .10
390 Albert Connell .30
391 Stephen Davis .50
392 Irving Fryar .10
393 Skip Hicks .20
394 Brad Johnson .50
395 Michael Westbrook .30
396 Obafemi Ayanbadejo, Lennox Gordon .10
397 Donald Driver, Ronnie Powell .10
398 *Todd Bouman, Jeremy Brigham* .50
399 Brock Huard, Sherdrick Bonner .30
400 Mike Sellers, Spencer George .10
401 *Shaun Alexander* 3.00
402 *Lavar Arrington* 6.00
403 *Tom Brady* 8.00
404 *Demario Brown* .50
405 *Plaxico Burress* 2.00
406 *Trung Canidate* 1.00
407 *Giovanni Carmazzi* .50
408 *Kwame Cavil* 1.00
409 *Chrys Chukwuma* .50
410 *Ron Dayne* 1.00
411 *Reuben Droughns* 1.50
412 *Ron Dugans* 1.00
413 *Deon Dyer* 1.00
414 *Danny Farmer* 1.00
415 *Chafie Fields* 1.00
416 *Trevor Gaylor* 1.00
417 *Sherrod Gideon* 1.00
418 *Joey Goodspeed* 1.00
419 *Joe Hamilton* .50
420 *Tony Hartley* 1.00
421 *Todd Husak* 1.00
422 *Trevor Insley* .50
423 *Thomas Jones* 1.50
424 *Marcus Knight* .50
425 *Jamal Lewis* 3.00
426 *Anthony Lucas* .50
427 *Tee Martin* 1.50
428 *Rondell Mealey* 1.00
429 *Sylvester Morris* .75
430 *Chad Morton* 1.00
431 *Dennis Northcutt* .75
432 *Chad Pennington* 5.00
433 *Rodnick Phillips* .50
434 *Mareno Philyaw* .50
435 *Jerry Porter* 1.00
436 *Travis Prentice* .75
437 *Tim Rattay* 1.50
438 *Chris Redman* 1.50
439 *J.R. Redmond* .75
440 *Gari Scott* 1.00
441 *Keith Smith* 1.00
442 *Terrelle Smith* 1.00
443 *R. Jay Soward* .75
444 *Quinton Spotwood* 1.00
445 *Shyrone Stith* 1.00
446 *Travis Taylor* .75
447 *Troy Walters* 1.00
448 *Peter Warrick* 2.00
449 *Dez White* 1.00
450 *Michael Wiley* 1.00

2000 Pacific Copper

Copper Cards: 10X-20X
Copper Rookies: 5X-10X
Production 75 Sets

2000 Pacific Gold

Gold Cards: 5X-12X
Gold Rookies: 3X-6X
Production 199 Sets

2000 Pacific Platinum Blue Draft Picks

Plat. Blue Cards: 2X-4X
Production 399 Sets

2000 Pacific Premiere Date

Premiere Date Cards: 10X-20X
Premiere Date Rookies: 5X-10X
Production 78 Sets

2000 Pacific Draft Picks 999

999 Cards: 3X
Production 999 Sets

2000 Pacific AFC Leaders

NM/M
Complete Set (10): 25.00
Common Player: 1.00
Minor Stars: 2.00
Inserted 1:37
1 Tim Couch 5.00
2 Olandis Gary 2.50
3 Marvin Harrison 2.50
4 Edgerrin James 6.00
5 Peyton Manning 5.00
6 Mark Brunell 3.00
7 Jimmy Smith 1.00
8 Drew Bledsoe 3.00
9 Keyshawn Johnson 2.00
10 Eddie George 2.50

2000 Pacific Autographs

NM/M
Common Player: 7.50
Minor Stars: 15.00
Random Inserts
51 Tim Biakabutuka 7.50
70 Marcus Robinson 25.00
87 Tim Couch 60.00
229 Jake Delhomme 25.00
307 Isaac Bruce 20.00
319 Kurt Warner 75.00
362 Mike Alstott 20.00
391 Stephen Davis 20.00
401 Shaun Alexander 40.00
403 Tom Brady 50.00
404 Demario Brown 15.00
405 Plaxico Burress 50.00
406 Trung Canidate 15.00
407 Giovanni Carmazzi 25.00
408 Kwame Cavil 7.50
410 Ron Dayne 25.00
411 Reuben Droughns 15.00
412 Ron Dugans 15.00
414 Danny Farmer 15.00
415 Chafie Fields 7.50
417 Sherrod Gideon 7.50
420 Tony Hartley 7.50
421 Todd Husak 7.50
423 Thomas Jones 50.00
424 Marcus Knight 7.50
426 Anthony Lucas 15.00
427 Tee Martin 25.00
428 Rondell Mealey 7.50
429 Sylvester Morris 25.00
431 Dennis Northcutt 25.00
432 Chad Pennington 60.00
434 Mareno Philyaw 7.50
435 Jerry Porter 25.00
436 Travis Prentice 20.00
437 Tim Rattay 20.00
438 Chris Redman 25.00
439 J.R. Redmond 25.00
443 R. Jay Soward 20.00
445 Shyrone Stith 15.00
446 Travis Taylor 25.00
447 Troy Walters 15.00
448 Peter Warrick 35.00
449 Dez White 20.00
450 Michael Wiley 20.00

2000 Pacific Cramer's Choice Awards

NM/M
Complete Set (10): 145.00
Common Player: 10.00
Inserted 1:721
1 Tim Couch 15.00
2 Emmitt Smith 20.00
3 Brett Favre 25.00
4 Edgerrin James 20.00
5 Peyton Manning 20.00
6 Randy Moss 20.00
7 Marshall Faulk 10.00
8 Kurt Warner 20.00
9 Eddie George 10.00
10 Peter Warrick 10.00

2000 Pacific Finest Hour

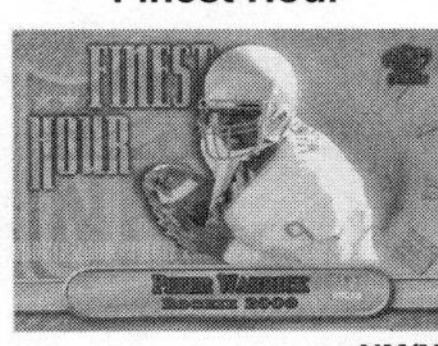

NM/M
Complete Set (20): 75.00
Common Player: 3.00
Inserted 1:73
1 Terrell Davis 4.00
2 Barry Sanders 5.00
3 Brett Favre 6.00
4 Edgerrin James 4.00
5 Drew Bledsoe 3.00
6 Damon Huard 2.00
7 Randy Moss 4.00
8 Kurt Warner 5.00
9 Jerry Rice 4.00
10 Stephen Davis 3.00
11 Shaun Alexander 3.00
12 Peter Warrick 3.00
13 Chris Redman 4.00
14 Chad Pennington 10.00
15 Tom Brady 10.00
16 Plaxico Burress 8.00
17 Todd Husak 3.00
18 Jamal Lewis 6.00
19 Thomas Jones 5.00
20 Ron Dayne 3.00

2000 Pacific Game-Worn Jerseys

NM/M
Common Player: 15.00
Inserted 1:5 Boxes
1 Kurt Warner 40.00
2 Fred Taylor 25.00
3 Ricky Williams 45.00
4 Ike Hilliard 15.00
5 Tim Brown 15.00
6 Brett Favre 60.00
7 Jon Kitna 15.00
8 Kordell Stewart 20.00
9 Natrone Means 15.00

2000 Pacific Gold Crown Die-Cuts

NM/M
Complete Set (36): 100.00
Common Player: 2.50
Inserted 1:37
1 Jake Plummer 2.50
2 Cade McNown 3.00
3 Corey Dillon 2.50
4 Akili Smith 2.50
5 Tim Couch 5.00
6 Kevin Johnson 2.50
7 Olandis Gary 4.00

NM/M
8 Brian Griese 4.00
9 Marvin Harrison 2.50
10 Edgerrin James 6.00
11 Mark Brunell 3.00
12 Fred Taylor 3.00
13 Damon Huard 2.50
14 Dan Marino 6.00
15 Randy Moss 4.00
16 Drew Bledsoe 3.00
17 Ricky Williams 5.00
18 Keyshawn Johnson 2.50
19 Donovan McNabb 4.00
20 Marshall Faulk 2.50
21 Kurt Warner 5.00
22 Jon Kitna 2.50
23 Jerry Rice 4.00
24 Shaun King 2.50
25 Eddie George 3.00
26 Steve McNair 3.00
27 Stephen Davis 2.50
28 Brad Johnson 2.50
29 Shaun Alexander 4.00
30 Plaxico Burress 6.00
31 Ron Dayne 3.00
32 Joe Hamilton 3.00
33 Thomas Jones 5.00
34 Chad Pennington 12.00
35 Chris Redman 5.00
36 Peter Warrick 4.00

2000 Pacific NFC Leaders

NM/M
Complete Set (10): 15.00
Common Player: 1.00
Minor Stars: 2.00
Inserted 1:37
1 Marcus Robinson 1.00
2 Troy Aikman 3.00
3 Emmitt Smith 4.00
4 Cris Carter 2.00
5 Randy Moss 4.00
6 Isaac Bruce 2.00
7 Marshall Faulk 2.00
8 Kurt Warner 5.00
9 Stephen Davis 1.00
10 Brad Johnson 1.00

2000 Pacific Pro Bowl Die Cuts

NM/M
Complete Set (20): 40.00
Common Player: 1.50
Minor Stars: 3.00
Inserted 1:37
1 Steve Beuerlein 1.50
2 Corey Dillon 3.00
3 Emmitt Smith 5.00
4 Marvin Harrison 3.00
5 Edgerrin James 5.00
6 Peyton Manning 4.00
7 Mark Brunell 3.00
8 Jimmy Smith 1.50
9 Tony Gonzalez 1.50
10 Cris Carter 2.00
11 Randy Moss 4.00
12 Rich Gannon 1.50
13 Keyshawn Johnson 2.00
14 Terry Glenn 2.00
15 Marshall Faulk 3.00
16 Kurt Warner 5.00
17 Mike Alstott 3.00
18 Eddie George 3.00
19 Stephen Davis 1.50
20 Brad Johnson 1.50

2000 Pacific Reflections

NM/M
Complete Set (20): 75.00
Common Player: 3.00
Inserted 1:145
1 Cade McNown 3.00
2 Tim Couch 6.00
3 Troy Aikman 5.00
4 Emmitt Smith 6.00
5 Terrell Davis 4.00
6 Barry Sanders 6.00
7 Brett Favre 7.00
8 Marvin Harrison 3.00
9 Edgerrin James 5.00
10 Mark Brunell 3.00
11 Fred Taylor 3.00
12 Dan Marino 7.00
13 Randy Moss 5.00
14 Ricky Williams 6.00
15 Marshall Faulk 3.00
16 Kurt Warner 6.00
17 Jon Kitna 3.00
18 Shaun King 3.00
19 Eddie George 3.00
20 Stephen Davis 3.00

2000 Pacific Aurora

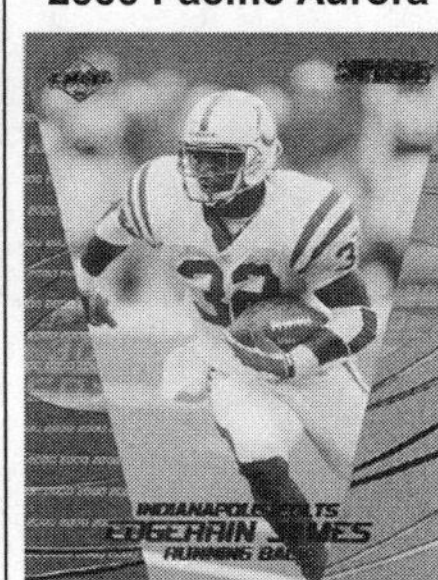

NM/M
Complete Set (150): 25.00
Common Player: .10
Minor Stars: .30
Common Rookie: .50
Pack (6): 1.00
Wax Box (36): 35.00
1 David Boston .50
2 *Thomas Jones* 1.00
3 Rob Moore .30
4 Jake Plummer .50
5 Frank Sanders .10
6 Jamal Anderson .50
7 Chris Chandler .30
8 Tim Dwight .50
9 *Doug Johnson* .50
10 Tony Banks .30
11 Qadry Ismail .10
12 *Jamal Lewis* 3.00
13 *Chris Redman* 1.50
14 *Travis Taylor* 1.50
15 Doug Flutie .50
16 Rob Johnson .30
17 Eric Moulds .50
18 Peerless Price .50
19 Antowain Smith .50
20 Steve Beuerlein .30
21 Tim Biakabutuka .10
22 Patrick Jeffers .50
23 Muhsin Muhammad .30
24 Curtis Enis .50
25 Cade McNown .75
26 Marcus Robinson .50
27 *Dez White* .50
28 Corey Dillon .50
29 *Ron Dugans* .50
30 Darnay Scott .30
31 Akili Smith .60
32 *Peter Warrick* 1.50
33 Tim Couch 1.00
34 *JaJuan Dawson* .50
35 Kevin Johnson .50
36 *Dennis Northcutt* .50
37 *Travis Prentice* 1.50
38 Troy Aikman 1.00
39 Raghib Ismail .10
40 Emmitt Smith 1.25
41 Jason Tucker .30
42 Terrell Davis 1.25
43 Olandis Gary .60
44 Brian Griese .60
45 Ed McCaffrey .30
46 Rod Smith .30
47 Charlie Batch .50
48 Germane Crowell .30
49 *Reuben Droughns* .50
50 Herman Moore .30
51 Barry Sanders 1.75
52 Brett Favre 2.00
53 *Bubba Franks* 1.50
54 Antonio Freeman .50
55 Dorsey Levens .50
56 Bill Schroeder .10
57 Marvin Harrison .50
58 Edgerrin James 1.50
59 Peyton Manning 1.50
60 Terrence Wilkins .30
61 Mark Brunell .75
62 Keenan McCardell .30
63 Jimmy Smith .50
64 *R. Jay Soward* .50
65 *Shyrone Stith* .50
66 Fred Taylor .75
67 Derrick Alexander .10
68 Donnell Bennett .10
69 Tony Gonzalez .30
70 Elvis Grbac .30
71 *Sylvester Morris* 1.00
72 Damon Huard .30
73 J.J. Johnson .30
74 Dan Marino 1.75
75 Tony Martin .10
76 O.J. McDuffie .30
77 *Quinton Spotwood* .50
78 Cris Carter .50
79 Daunte Culpepper .75
80 Randy Moss 1.50
81 Robert Smith .50
82 *Troy Walters* .50
83 Drew Bledsoe .75
84 *Tom Brady* 5.00
85 Kevin Faulk .50
86 Terry Glenn .50
87 *J.R. Redmond* 1.50
88 *Marc Bulger* 2.00
89 *Sherrod Gideon* .50
90 Keith Poole .10
91 Ricky Williams 1.25
92 Kerry Collins .30
93 *Ron Dayne* 1.50
94 Ike Hilliard .30
95 Amani Toomer .30
96 Wayne Chrebet .30
97 *Laveranues Coles* 1.50
98 Curtis Martin .50
99 *Chad Pennington* 4.00
100 Vinny Testaverde .30
101 Tim Brown .30
102 Rich Gannon .30
103 Napoleon Kaufman .50
104 *Jerry Porter* 2.00
105 Tyrone Wheatley .30
106 Charles Johnson .10
107 Donovan McNabb .75
108 *Todd Pinkston* 1.00
109 Duce Staley .50
110 Jerome Bettis .50
111 *Plaxico Burress* 2.00
112 Troy Edwards .50
113 Richard Huntley .30
114 *Tee Martin* 1.25
115 Kordell Stewart .50
116 Isaac Bruce .50
117 *Trung Canidate* 1.00
118 Marshall Faulk .50
119 Torry Holt .50
120 Kurt Warner 2.50
121 Jermaine Fazande .50
122 *Trevor Gaylor* .50
123 Jim Harbaugh .10
124 Junior Seau .30
125 *Giovanni Carmazzi* .50
126 Charlie Garner .30
127 Terrell Owens .50
128 Jerry Rice 1.00
129 J.J. Stokes .30
130 Steve Young .75
131 *Shaun Alexander* 3.00
132 Sean Dawkins .10
133 Jon Kitna .50
134 Derrick Mayes .30
135 Ricky Watters .30
136 Mike Alstott .50
137 Warrick Dunn .50
138 Jacquez Green .30
139 *Joe Hamilton* .50
140 Shaun King .75
141 Eddie George .60
142 Jevon Kearse .50
143 Steve McNair .50
144 Yancy Thigpen .10
145 Frank Wycheck .10
146 Albert Connell .30
147 Stephen Davis .50
148 *Todd Husak* .50
149 Brad Johnson .50
150 Michael Westbrook .30

2000 Pacific Aurora Premiere Date

NM/M
Prem. Date Cards: 10X-20X
Prem. Date Rookies: 5X-10X
Production 85 Sets
1 David Boston 1.00
2 *Thomas Jones* 3.00
3 Rob Moore .30
4 Jake Plummer .50
5 Frank Sanders .15
6 Jamal Anderson .50

NM/M
7 Chris Chandler .30
8 Tim Dwight .50
9 *Doug Johnson* 1.00
10 Tony Banks .30
11 Qadry Ismail .15
12 *Jamal Lewis* 3.00
13 *Chris Redman* 2.00
14 *Travis Taylor* 2.00
15 Doug Flutie .50
16 Rob Johnson .30
17 Eric Moulds .50
18 Peerless Price .50
19 Antowain Smith .50
20 Steve Beuerlein .30
21 Tim Biakabutuka .15
22 Patrick Jeffers .50
23 Muhsin Muhammad .30
24 Curtis Enis .50
25 Cade McNown .75
26 Marcus Robinson .50
27 *Dez White* 1.00
28 Corey Dillon .50
29 *Ron Dugans* 1.00
30 Darnay Scott .30
31 Akili Smith .60
32 *Peter Warrick* 5.00
33 Tim Couch 1.25
34 *JaJuan Dawson* 1.50
35 Kevin Johnson .50
36 *Dennis Northcutt* 1.25
37 *Travis Prentice* 1.50
38 Troy Aikman 1.00
39 Raghib Ismail .15
40 Emmitt Smith 1.25
41 Jason Tucker .30
42 Terrell Davis 1.25
43 Olandis Gary .60
44 Brian Griese .60
45 Ed McCaffrey .30
46 Rod Smith .30
47 Charlie Batch .50
48 Germane Crowell .30
49 *Reuben Droughns* 1.00
50 Herman Moore .30
51 Barry Sanders 1.75
52 Brett Favre 2.00
53 *Bubba Franks* 1.50
54 Antonio Freeman .50
55 Dorsey Levens .50
56 Bill Schroeder .15
57 Marvin Harrison .50
58 Edgerrin James 2.00
59 Peyton Manning 1.50
60 Terrence Wilkins .30
61 Mark Brunell .75
62 Keenan McCardell .30
63 Jimmy Smith .50
64 *R. Jay Soward* 1.25
65 *Shyrone Stith* 1.00
66 Fred Taylor .75
67 Derrick Alexander .15
68 Donnell Bennett .15
69 Tony Gonzalez .30
70 Elvis Grbac .30
71 *Sylvester Morris* 1.50
72 Damon Huard .30
73 J.J. Johnson .30
74 Dan Marino 1.75
75 Tony Martin .15
76 O.J. McDuffie .30
77 *Quinton Spotwood* .50
78 Cris Carter .50
79 Daunte Culpepper .75
80 Randy Moss 1.50
81 Robert Smith .50
82 *Troy Walters* .50
83 Drew Bledsoe .75
84 *Tom Brady* 10.00
85 Kevin Faulk .50
86 Terry Glenn .50
87 *J.R. Redmond* 1.50
88 *Marc Bulger* 1.00
89 *Sherrod Gideon* .50
90 Keith Poole .15
91 Ricky Williams 1.25
92 Kerry Collins .30
93 *Ron Dayne* 5.00
94 Ike Hilliard .30
95 Amani Toomer .30
96 Wayne Chrebet .30
97 *Laveranues Coles* 1.00
98 Curtis Martin .50
99 *Chad Pennington* 4.00
100 Vinny Testaverde .30
101 Tim Brown .30
102 Rich Gannon .30
103 Napoleon Kaufman .50
104 *Jerry Porter* 1.25
105 Tyrone Wheatley .30
106 Charles Johnson .15
107 Donovan McNabb .75
108 *Todd Pinkston* 1.00
109 Duce Staley .50
110 Jerome Bettis .50
111 *Plaxico Burress* 4.00
112 Troy Edwards .50
113 Richard Huntley .30
114 *Tee Martin* 1.25
115 Kordell Stewart .50
116 Isaac Bruce .50
117 *Trung Canidate* 1.00
118 Marshall Faulk .50
119 Torry Holt .50
120 Kurt Warner 2.50
121 Jermaine Fazande .50
122 *Trevor Gaylor* .50
123 Jim Harbaugh .15
124 Junior Seau .30
125 *Giovanni Carmazzi* 1.50
126 Charlie Garner .30
127 Terrell Owens .50
128 Jerry Rice 1.00
129 J.J. Stokes .30
130 Steve Young .75
131 *Shaun Alexander* 3.00
132 Sean Dawkins .15
133 Jon Kitna .50
134 Derrick Mayes .30
135 Ricky Watters .30
136 Mike Alstott .50
137 Warrick Dunn .50
138 Jacquez Green .30
139 *Joe Hamilton* 1.25
140 Shaun King .75
141 Eddie George .60
142 Jevon Kearse .50
143 Steve McNair .50
144 Yancy Thigpen .15
145 Frank Wycheck .15
146 Albert Connell .30
147 Stephen Davis .50
148 *Todd Husak* .50
149 Brad Johnson .50
150 Michael Westbrook .30

2000 Pacific Aurora Autographs

NM/M
Common Player: 8.00
Randomly Inserted
2 Thomas Jones 350 30.00
26 Marcus Robinson 350 25.00
27 Dez White 350 8.00
32 Peter Warrick Exch 30.00
34 JaJuan Dawson 350 12.00
43 Olandis Gary 350 20.00
61 Mark Brunell 100 30.00
63 Jimmy Smith 350 20.00
71 Sylvester Morris 350 20.00
77 Quinton Spotwood 350 8.00
88 Marc Bulger 350 8.00
93 Ron Dayne 150 35.00
131 Shaun Alexander 350 30.00
147 Stephen Davis 350 20.00

2000 Pacific Aurora Championship Fever

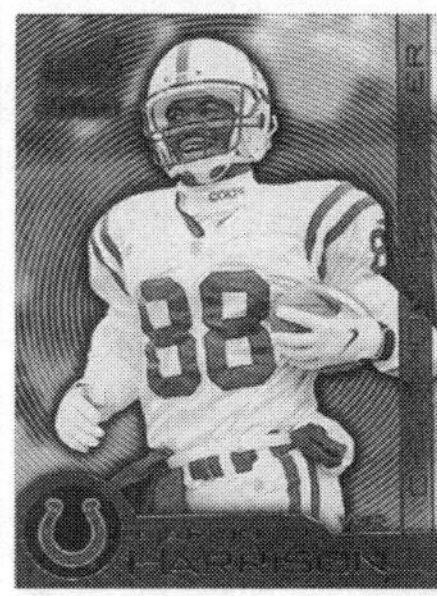

NM/M
Complete Set (20): 25.00
Common Player: .50
Inserted 4:37
Copper Cards: 4X-8X
Production 160 Sets
Platinum Blue Cards: 4X-8X
Production 145 Sets
1 Thomas Jones 2.00
2 Jamal Lewis 2.00
3 Peter Warrick 1.00
4 Tim Couch 2.00
5 Emmitt Smith 2.50
6 Olandis Gary 1.50
7 Marvin Harrison 1.00
8 Edgerrin James 2.00
9 Mark Brunell 1.50
10 Fred Taylor 1.50
11 Randy Moss 2.00
12 Chad Pennington 4.00
13 Plaxico Burress 3.00
14 Marshall Faulk .50
15 Kurt Warner 2.00
16 Shaun Alexander 3.00
17 Jon Kitna .50
18 Eddie George 1.50
19 Shaun King .50
20 Stephen Davis .50

2000 Pacific Aurora Game-Worn Jerseys

NM/M
Common Player: 20.00
Randomly Inserted
Patch Cards: No Pricing
Production 10 Sets
1 Olandis Gary 20.00
2 Brett Favre 45.00
3 Mark Brunell 20.00
4 Cris Carter 25.00
5 Randy Moss 35.00
6 Ricky Williams 35.00
7 Donovan McNabb 30.00
8 Duce Staley 20.00
9 Junior Seau 20.00
10 Steve McNair 25.00

2000 Pacific Aurora Helmet Styrotechs

NM/M
Complete Set (20): 40.00
Common Player: 1.00
Inserted 1:37
1 Jake Plummer 1.00
2 Cade McNown 1.00
3 Tim Couch 3.00
4 Troy Aikman 3.00
5 Emmitt Smith 4.00
6 Barry Sanders 4.00
7 Terrell Davis 3.00
8 Brett Favre 5.00
9 Edgerrin James 3.00
10 Peyton Manning 4.00
11 Mark Brunell 2.00
12 Fred Taylor 2.00
13 Drew Bledsoe 3.00
14 Ricky Williams 4.00
15 Randy Moss 4.00
16 Kurt Warner 4.00
17 Jerry Rice 4.00
18 Jon Kitna 1.00
19 Shaun King 1.00
20 Eddie George 2.00

2000 Pacific Aurora Rookie Draft Board

NM/M
Complete Set (20): 35.00
Common Player: 1.00
Inserted 2:37
1 Thomas Jones 2.00
2 Jamal Lewis 3.00
3 Chris Redman 2.00
4 Travis Taylor 2.00
5 Peter Warrick 2.00
6 Dez White 2.00
7 Dennis Northcutt 2.00
8 Travis Prentice 2.50
9 Reuben Droughns 1.00
10 R. Jay Soward 2.00
11 Sylvester Morris 2.50
12 J.R. Redmond 2.50
13 Ron Dayne 2.00
14 Laveranues Coles 3.00
15 Chad Pennington 6.00
16 Plaxico Burress 4.00
17 Tee Martin 2.00
18 Trung Canidate 2.00
19 Giovanni Carmazzi 1.00
20 Shaun Alexander 4.00

2000 Pacific Aurora Team Players

NM/M
Complete Set (10): 15.00
Common Player: 1.00
Inserted 1:37
1 Troy Aikman 3.00
2 Terrell Davis 3.00
3 Antonio Freeman 1.00
4 Peyton Manning 4.00
5 Fred Taylor 2.00
6 Randy Moss 4.00
7 Marshall Faulk 2.00
8 Jerry Rice 3.50
9 Steve McNair 1.00
10 Stephen Davis 1.00

2000 Pacific Crown Royale

NM/M
Complete Set (144): 125.00
Common Player: .15
Minor Stars: .30
Common Rookie: .50
Pack (6): 3.00
Wax Box (24): 55.00
1 Rob Moore .30
2 Jake Plummer .50
3 Frank Sanders .30
4 Jamal Anderson .75
5 Chris Chandler .30
6 Tim Dwight .75
7 Tony Banks .30
8 Priest Holmes .50
9 Qadry Ismail .15
10 Doug Flutie .50
11 Rob Johnson .30
12 Eric Moulds .75
13 Peerless Price .50
14 Steve Beuerlein .30
15 Patrick Jeffers .75
16 Muhsin Muhammad .30
17 Curtis Enis .50
18 Cade McNown .50
19 Marcus Robinson .75
20 Corey Dillon .75
21 Darnay Scott .30
22 Akili Smith .50
23 Karim Abdul .30
24 Tim Couch 2.00
25 Kevin Johnson .75
26 Troy Aikman 1.50
27 Joey Galloway .75
28 Emmitt Smith 2.00
29 Terrell Davis 1.00
30 Olandis Gary 1.00
31 Brian Griese 1.00
32 Ed McCaffrey .30
33 Charlie Batch .75
34 Herman Moore .75
35 Barry Sanders 3.00
36 James Stewart .50
37 Brett Favre 3.00
38 Antonio Freeman .75
39 Dorsey Levens .75
40 Marvin Harrison .75
41 Edgerrin James 2.00
42 Peyton Manning 2.00
43 Mark Brunell 1.25
44 Keenan McCardell .30
45 Jimmy Smith .50
46 Fred Taylor 1.25
47 Derrick Alexander .15
48 Tony Gonzalez .30
49 Elvis Grbac .30
50 Damon Huard .50
51 J.J. Johnson .30
52 Dan Marino 2.00
53 O.J. McDuffie .30
54 Cris Carter .75
55 Daunte Culpepper 1.25
56 Jeff George .50
57 Randy Moss 2.50
58 Robert Smith .75
59 Drew Bledsoe 1.25
60 Terry Glenn .75
61 Lawyer Milloy .15
62 Jeff Blake .30
63 Keith Poole .15
64 Ricky Williams 2.00
65 Kerry Collins .30
66 Ike Hilliard .30
67 Amani Toomer .30
68 Wayne Chrebet .50
69 Keyshawn Johnson .75
70 Ray Lucas .75
71 Curtis Martin .75
72 Vinny Testaverde .50
73 Tim Brown .50
74 Rich Gannon .30
75 Napoleon Kaufman .50
76 Tyrone Wheatley .30
77 Donovan McNabb 2.00
78 Torrance Small .15
79 Duce Staley .75
80 Jerome Bettis .75
81 Troy Edwards .75
82 Kordell Stewart .75
83 Isaac Bruce .75
84 Marshall Faulk .75
85 Torry Holt .75
86 Kurt Warner 2.50
87 Jim Harbaugh .30
88 Jermaine Fazande .30
89 Junior Seau .30
90 Charlie Garner .30
91 Terrell Owens .75
92 Jerry Rice 1.50
93 Steve Young 1.00
94 Sean Dawkins .15
95 Jon Kitna .50
96 Derrick Mayes .30
97 Ricky Watters .50
98 Mike Alstott .75
99 Warrick Dunn .75
100 Jacquez Green .30
101 Shaun King .50
102 Kevin Dyson .30
103 Eddie George 1.00
104 Jevon Kearse .75
105 Steve McNair 1.00
106 Stephen Davis .75
107 Brad Johnson .75
108 Michael Westbrook .50
109 *Shaun Alexander* 6.00
110 *Tom Brady* 15.00
111 *Marc Bulger* 5.00
112 *Plaxico Burress* 4.00
113 *Giovanni Carmazzi* 1.00
114 *Kwame Cavil* .50
115 *Chris Cole* .50
116 *Chris Coleman* 1.00
117 *Laveranues Coles* 3.00
118 *Ron Dayne* 2.00
119 *Reuben Droughns* .50
120 *Ron Dugans* .50
121 *Danny Farmer* 2.00
122 *Chafie Fields* .50
123 *Joe Hamilton* 2.00
124 *Todd Husak* 2.00
125 *Darrell Jackson* 1.00
126 *Thomas Jones* 3.00
127 *Jamal Lewis* 6.00
128 *Tee Martin* 2.00
129 *Rondell Mealey* 2.00
130 *Sylvester Morris* 2.00
131 *Chad Morton* 2.00
132 *Dennis Northcutt* 1.00
133 *Chad Pennington* 10.00
134 *Travis Prentice* 2.00
135 *Tim Rattay* 1.00
136 *Chris Redman* 2.00
137 *J.R. Redmond* 2.00
138 *R. Jay Soward* 2.00
139 *Shyrone Stith* 1.00
140 *Travis Taylor* 2.00
141 *Troy Walters* 1.00
142 *Peter Warrick* 4.00
143 *Dez White* 2.00
144 *Michael Wiley* 2.00

2000 Pacific Crown Royale Draft Picks 499

NM/M
Complete Set (35): 250.00
#'d to 499 Cards: 2.5X
Production 499 Sets
109 *Shaun Alexander* 7.00
110 *Tom Brady* 20.00
111 *Marc Bulger* 1.00
112 *Plaxico Burress* 10.00
113 *Giovanni Carmazzi* 5.00
114 *Kwame Cavil* 1.00
115 *Chris Cole* 1.00
116 *Chris Coleman* 1.00
117 *Laveranues Coles* 2.00
118 *Ron Dayne* 12.00
119 *Reuben Droughns* 3.00
120 *Ron Dugans* 3.00
121 *Danny Farmer* 2.00
122 *Chafie Fields* 1.00
123 *Joe Hamilton* 2.00
124 *Todd Husak* 2.00
125 *Darrell Jackson* 2.00
126 *Thomas Jones* 7.00
127 *Jamal Lewis* 7.00
128 *Tee Martin* 4.00
129 *Rondell Mealey* 2.00
130 *Sylvester Morris* 4.00
131 *Chad Morton* 2.00
132 *Dennis Northcutt* 3.00
133 *Chad Pennington* 10.00
134 *Travis Prentice* 3.00
135 *Tim Rattay* 3.00
136 *Chris Redman* 5.00
137 *J.R. Redmond* 4.00
138 *R. Jay Soward* 4.00
139 *Shyrone Stith* 2.00
140 *Travis Taylor* 5.00
141 *Troy Walters* 2.00
142 *Peter Warrick* 12.00
143 *Dez White* 3.00
144 *Michael Wiley* 2.00

2000 Pacific Crown Royale Limited Series

Limited Cards: 3X-8X
Limited Rookies: 2X-4X
Production 144 Cards

2000 Pacific Crown Royale Premiere Date

Premiere Cards: 3X-8X
Premiere Rookies: 2X-4X
Production 145 Sets

2000 Pacific Crown Royale Autographs

NM/M
Common Player: 10.00
Minor Stars: 20.00
Randomly Inserted
109 Shaun Alexander 30.00
110 Tom Brady 50.00
111 Marc Bulger 50.00
112 Plaxico Burress 40.00
113 Giovanni Carmazzi 30.00
114 Kwame Cavil 10.00
115 Chris Cole 10.00
116 Chris Coleman 10.00
117 Laveranues Coles 20.00
118 Ron Dayne 45.00
119 Reuben Droughns 20.00
120 Ron Dugans 20.00
121 Danny Farmer 20.00
122 Chafie Fields 10.00
123 Joe Hamilton 20.00
124 Todd Husak 10.00
125 Darrell Jackson 10.00
126 Thomas Jones 40.00
127 Jamal Lewis 40.00
128 Tee Martin 25.00
129 Rondell Mealey 10.00
130 Sylvester Morris 25.00
131 Chad Morton 10.00
132 Dennis Northcutt 20.00
133 Chad Pennington 75.00
134 Travis Prentice 25.00
135 Tim Rattay 20.00
136 Chris Redman 30.00
137 J.R. Redmond 25.00
138 R. Jay Soward 25.00
139 Shyrone Stith 10.00
140 Travis Taylor 30.00
141 Troy Walters 10.00
142 Peter Warrick 30.00
143 Dez White 20.00
144 Michael Wiley 20.00

2000 Pacific Crown Royale Cramer's Choice Jumbos

NM/M
Complete Set (10): 45.00
Common Player: 2.00
One Per Hobby Box
Dark Blue Cards: 5X-10X
Production 35 Sets
Gold Cards: 15X-30X
Production 10 Sets
Green Cards: 5X-10X
Production 30 Sets
Light Blue Cards: 7X-14X
Production 20 Sets
Purple Cards: No Pricing
Production 1 Set
Red Cards: 7X-14X
Production 25 Sets
1 Tim Couch 5.00
2 Emmitt Smith 6.00
3 Edgerrin James 6.00
4 Damon Huard 2.00
5 Randy Moss 6.00
6 Kurt Warner 5.00
7 Jon Kitna 2.00
8 Eddie George 3.00
9 Chad Pennington 8.00
10 Peter Warrick 3.00

2000 Pacific Crown Royale Fifth Anniversary Jumbos

NM/M
Complete Set (6): 25.00
Common Player: 2.50
Inserted 6:10 Boxes
1 Terrell Davis 4.00
2 Eddie George 3.00
3 Jon Kitna 2.50
4 Randy Moss 6.00
5 Kurt Warner 5.00
6 Peter Warrick 3.00

2000 Pacific Crown Royale First and Ten

NM/M
Complete Set (10): 45.00
Common Player: 4.00
Production 375 Sets
1 Tim Couch 4.00
2 Troy Aikman 5.00
3 Emmitt Smith 6.00
4 Terrell Davis 5.00
5 Brett Favre 7.00
6 Edgerrin James 5.00
7 Peyton Manning 5.00
8 Randy Moss 5.00
9 Kurt Warner 5.00
10 Jerry Rice 5.00

2000 Pacific Crown Royale Jersey Cards

NM/M
Common Player: 25.00
Randomly Inserted
1 Eric Moulds 30.00
2 Brett Favre 75.00
3 Antonio Freeman 25.00
4 Ricky Williams 60.00
5 Tiki Barber 25.00
6 Charles Woodson 30.00
7 Isaac Bruce 30.00
8 Kurt Warner 40.00
9 Tim Couch 35.00

2000 Pacific Crown Royale In the Pocket

NM/M
Complete Set (20): 45.00
Common Player: 2.00
Mini Cards: .5X
Inserted 2:25
1 Tim Couch 3.00
2 Troy Aikman 4.00
3 Emmitt Smith 5.00
4 Charlie Batch 2.00
5 Edgerrin James 4.00
6 Peyton Manning 4.00
7 Mark Brunell 2.00
8 Randy Moss 4.00
9 Drew Bledsoe 3.00
10 Donovan McNabb 3.00
11 Kurt Warner 4.00
12 Jon Kitna 2.00
13 Eddie George 3.00
14 Steve McNair 3.00
15 Brad Johnson 2.00
16 Plaxico Burress 6.00
17 Ron Dayne 4.00
18 Thomas Jones 5.00
19 Chad Pennington 10.00
20 Peter Warrick 3.00

2000 Pacific Crown Royale In Your Face

NM/M
Complete Set (25): 15.00
Common Player: .50
Inserted 1:1
Rainbow Cards: 10X-25X

Production 20 Sets
1 Jake Plummer .75
2 Cade McNown .75
3 Marcus Robinson .50
4 Corey Dillon .50
5 Tim Couch 1.25
6 Emmitt Smith 1.50
7 Terrell Davis 1.50
8 Barry Sanders 2.00
9 Marvin Harrison .50
10 Edgerrin James 1.50
11 Mark Brunell 1.00
12 Fred Taylor 1.00
13 Dan Marino 1.50
14 Randy Moss 2.00
15 Drew Bledsoe 1.00
16 Ricky Williams 1.25
17 Curtis Martin .50
18 Isaac Bruce .50
19 Marshall Faulk .50
20 Kurt Warner 1.75
21 Jerry Rice 1.50
22 Jon Kitna .75
23 Shaun King .75
24 Eddie George .75
25 Stephen Davis .50

2000 Pacific Crown Royale Productions

NM/M
Complete Set (20): 45.00
Common Player: 1.00
Inserted 1:25
1 Cade McNown 2.00
2 Tim Couch 3.00
3 Emmitt Smith 5.00
4 Olandis Gary 1.00
5 Barry Sanders 5.00
6 Brett Favre 6.00
7 Edgerrin James 4.00
8 Peyton Manning 4.00
9 Fred Taylor 3.00
10 Damon Huard 1.00
11 Dan Marino 6.00
12 Randy Moss 5.00
13 Drew Bledsoe 4.00
14 Ricky Williams 4.00
15 Marshall Faulk 1.00
16 Kurt Warner 4.00
17 Jerry Rice 4.00
18 Shaun King 1.00
19 Eddie George 3.00
20 Stephen Davis 1.00

2000 Pacific Crown Royale Rookie Royalty

NM/M
Complete Set (25): 25.00
Common Player: .50
Inserted 1:1
Die-Cut Cards: 10X-30X
Production 10 Sets
1 Shaun Alexander 2.50
2 Tom Brady 10.00
3 Plaxico Burress 4.00
4 Ron Dayne 2.00
5 Reuben Droughns 1.00
6 Danny Farmer 1.00
7 Chafie Fields .50
8 Joe Hamilton 1.00
9 Todd Husak 1.00
10 Thomas Jones 3.00
11 Jamal Lewis 3.00
12 Tee Martin 1.50
13 Sylvester Morris 2.00
14 Dennis Northcutt 1.25
15 Chad Pennington 12.00
16 Travis Prentice 1.50
17 Tim Rattay 1.50
18 Chris Redman 1.75
19 J.R. Redmond 1.50
20 R. Jay Soward 1.50
21 Shyrone Stith .50
22 Travis Taylor 2.00
23 Troy Walters .50
24 Peter Warrick 2.00
25 Dez White 1.25

2000 Pacific Omega

NM/M
Common Player: .10
Minor Stars: .30
Common Rookie: 1.00
Production 500 Sets
Pack (6): 1.50
Wax Box (36): 40.00
1 David Boston .50
2 Dave Brown .10
3 Rob Moore .30
4 Jake Plummer .30
5 Simeon Rice .10
6 Frank Sanders .30
7 Jamal Anderson .50
8 Chris Chandler .30
9 Tim Dwight .50
10 Terance Mathis .10
11 Tony Banks .30
12 Peter Boulware .30
13 Priest Holmes .50
14 Qadry Ismail .10
15 Doug Flutie .75
16 Rob Johnson .30
17 Jonathon Linton .10
18 Eric Moulds .50
19 Peerless Price .30
20 Antowain Smith .30
21 Steve Beuerlein .30
22 Tshimanga Biakabutuka .30
23 Patrick Jeffers .50
24 Muhsin Muhammad .30
25 Wesley Walls .30
26 Bobby Engram .10
27 Curtis Enis .50
28 Cade McNown .50
29 Marcus Robinson .50
30 Willie Anderson .10
31 Michael Basnight .10
32 Corey Dillon .50
33 Akili Smith .50
34 Tim Couch 1.00
35 Kevin Johnson .50
36 Wali Rainer .10
37 Troy Aikman 1.25
38 Dexter Coakley .10
39 Raghib Ismail .10
40 Emmitt Smith 2.00
41 Chris Warren .30
42 Terrell Davis 1.50
43 Olandis Gary .50
44 Brian Griese .75
45 Ed McCaffrey .30
46 Rod Smith .30
47 Charlie Batch .50
48 Germane Crowell .50
49 Herman Moore .50
50 Johnnie Morton .30
51 Barry Sanders 1.75
52 Corey Bradford .30
53 Brett Favre 2.50
54 Antonio Freeman .50
55 Dorsey Levens .30
56 Bill Schroeder .10
57 Ken Dilger .10
58 Marvin Harrison .50
59 Edgerrin James 2.00
60 Peyton Manning 1.75
61 Jerome Pathon .10
62 Terrence Wilkins .10
63 Mark Brunell .75
64 Keenan McCardell .30
65 Jimmy Smith .50
66 Fred Taylor .75
67 Derrick Alexander .10
68 Donnell Bennett .10
69 Tony Gonzalez .10
70 Elvis Grbac .30
71 Tony Richardson .10
72 Oronde Gadsden .10
73 Damon Huard .50
74 J.J. Johnson .30
75 Dan Marino 2.00
76 Tony Martin .10
77 O.J. McDuffie .30
78 Cris Carter .50
79 Daunte Culpepper 1.00
80 Randy Moss 1.75
81 Robert Smith .50
82 Drew Bledsoe .75
83 Kevin Faulk .30
84 Terry Glenn .50
85 P.J. Franklin .10
86 Keith Poole .10
87 Ricky Williams 1.25
88 Tiki Barber .50
89 Kerry Collins .30
90 Ike Hilliard .30
91 Amani Toomer .30
92 Wayne Chrebet .50
93 Ray Lucas .50
94 Curtis Martin .50
95 Vinny Testaverde .30
96 Tim Brown .50
97 Rich Gannon .30
98 James Jett .10
99 Napoleon Kaufman .50
100 Tyrone Wheatley .30
101 Charles Woodson .50
102 Brian Dawkins .10
103 Charles Johnson .10
104 Donovan McNabb .75
105 Torrance Small .10
106 Duce Staley .50
107 Jerome Bettis .50
108 Troy Edwards .30
109 Richard Huntley .30
110 Kordell Stewart .60
111 Hines Ward .30
112 Isaac Bruce .50
113 Marshall Faulk .50
114 Az-Zahir Hakim .30
115 Torry Holt .50
116 Tony Horne .10
117 Kurt Warner 2.50
118 Jermaine Fazande .30
119 Jeff Graham .10
120 Jim Harbaugh .30
121 Mikhael Ricks .10
122 Junior Seau .30
123 Jeff Garcia .50
124 Charlie Garner .30
125 Terrell Owens .50
126 Jerry Rice 1.25
127 J.J. Stokes .30
128 Jon Kitna .50
129 Derrick Mayes .30
130 Charlie Rogers .10
131 Shawn Springs .10
132 Ricky Watters .30
133 Mike Alstott .50
134 Reidel Anthony .10
135 Warrick Dunn .50
136 Jacquez Green .10
137 Shaun King .75
138 Warren Sapp .30
139 Kevin Dyson .30
140 Eddie George .60
141 Jevon Kearse .50
142 Steve McNair .50
143 Yancy Thigpen .30
144 Frank Wycheck .10
145 Champ Bailey .30
146 Larry Centers .10
147 Albert Connell .30
148 Stephen Davis .50
149 Brad Johnson .30
150 Michael Westbrook .30
151 *Thomas Jones* 10.00
152 *Jay Tant* 1.00
153 *Doug Johnson* 7.50
154 *Mareno Philyaw* 1.00
155 *Jamal Lewis* 25.00
156 *Chris Redman* 10.00
157 *Travis Taylor* 10.00
158 *Kwame Cavil* 1.00
159 *Corey Moore* 1.00
160 *Deon Grant* 1.00
161 *Frank Murphy* 1.00
162 *Dez White* 1.00
163 *Ron Dugans* 2.00
164 *Tony Hartley* 1.00
165 *Curtis Keaton* 1.00
166 *Peter Warrick* 15.00
167 *Courtney Brown* 7.50
168 *JaJuan Dawson* 7.50
169 *Dennis Northcutt* 7.50
170 *Travis Prentice* 8.00
171 *Aaron Shea* 1.00
172 *Michael Wiley* 6.00
173 *Chris Cole* 1.00
174 *Jarious Jackson* 6.00
175 *Deltha O'Neal* 1.00
176 *Reuben Droughns* 1.00
177 *Bubba Franks* 7.50
178 *Anthony Lucas* 1.00
179 *Rondell Mealey* 6.00
180 *Ibn Green* 1.00
181 *Kevin McDougal* 1.00
182 *R. Jay Soward* 7.50
183 *Shyrone Stith* 2.00
184 *Dante Hall* 20.00
185 *Frank Moreau* 2.00
186 *Sylvester Morris* 6.00
187 *Deon Dyer* 1.00
188 *Ben Kelly* 1.00
189 *Quinton Spotwood* 1.00
190 *Troy Walters* 6.00
191 *Tom Brady* 40.00
192 *J.R. Redmond* 10.00
193 *David Stachelski* 1.00
194 *Marc Bulger* 20.00
195 *Sherrod Gideon* 1.00
196 *Chad Morton* 6.00
197 *Ron Dayne* 10.00
198 *Anthony Becht* 2.00
199 *Laveranues Coles* 12.00
200 *Chad Pennington* 40.00
201 *Sebastian Janikowski* 6.00
202 *Marcus Knight* 1.00
203 *Jerry Porter* 15.00
204 *Todd Pinkston* 7.50
205 *Gari Scott* 1.00
206 *Plaxico Burress* 15.00
207 *Danny Farmer* 6.00
208 *Tee Martin* 6.00
209 *Hank Poteat* 1.00
210 *Trung Canidate* 6.00
211 *Patrick Batteaux* 1.00
212 *Trevor Gaylor* 2.00
213 *Ronney Jenkins* 1.00
214 *Terrence McCaskey* 1.00
215 *JaJuan Seider* 1.00
216 *Giovanni Carmazzi* 3.00
217 *Chafie Fields* 1.00
218 *Jonas Lewis* 1.00
219 *Tim Rattay* 10.00
220 *Shaun Alexander* 25.00
221 *Darrell Jackson* 7.50
222 *James Williams* 1.00
223 *Joe Hamilton* 7.50
224 *Erron Kinney* 1.00
225 *Todd Husak* 6.00
226 Plaxico Burress, Danny Farmer 10.00
227 Ron Dayne, Joe Hamilton 8.00
228 Peter Warrick, Ron Dugans 8.00
229 Thomas Jones, Curtis Keaton 10.00
230 Shaun Alexander, Reuben Droughns 8.00
231 Travis Taylor, Darrell Jackson 8.00
232 Giovanni Carmazzi, Tim Rattay 4.00
233 Trung Canidate, J.R. Redmond 6.00
234 Sylvester Morris, R. Jay Soward 6.00
235 Travis Prentice, Trevor Gaylor 8.00
236 Todd Pinkston, Sherrod Gideon 1.00
237 Frank Murphy, Dez White 1.00
238 Chris Redman, Tom Brady 15.00
239 Jamal Lewis, Tee Martin 10.00
240 Rondell Mealey, Shyrone Stith 1.00
241 Michael Wiley, Chad Morton 4.00
242 Laveranues Coles, Sebastian Janikowski 6.00
243 Troy Walters, Todd Husak 1.00
244 Marc Bulger, Jerry Porter 12.00
245 Mareno Philyaw, Doug Johnson 1.00
246 Dennis Northcutt, Courtney Dyson 6.00
247 Jarious Jackson, Chris Cole 1.00
248 JaJuan Dawson, Gari Scott 6.00
249 Quinton Spotwood, Chafie Fields 1.00
250 Chad Pennington, James Williams 12.00

2000 Pacific Omega Copper

Copper Cards: 8X-20X
Production 51 Sets
Inserted 1:73
No Rookies

2000 Pacific Omega Gold

Gold Cards: 5X-15X
Production 95 Sets
Inserted 1:37
No Rookies

2000 Pacific Omega Platinum Blue

NM/M
Platinum Blue Cards: 10X-25X
Production 51 Sets
Inserted 1:145
No Rookies

2000 Pacific Omega Premiere Date

Premiere Date Cards: 5X-15X
Production 92 Sets
Inserted 1:37
No Rookies

2000 Pacific Omega AFC Conference Contenders

NM/M
Complete Set (18): 25.00
Common Player: 1.00
Minor Stars: 2.00
Inserted 2:37
1 Jamal Lewis 4.00
2 Akili Smith 2.00
3 Peter Warrick 2.00
4 Tim Couch 2.50
5 Terrell Davis 4.00
6 Brian Griese 2.00
7 Marvin Harrison 2.00
8 Edgerrin James 6.00
9 Mark Brunell 2.50
10 Fred Taylor 2.50
11 Jimmy Smith 1.00
12 Curtis Martin 2.00
13 Tim Brown 2.00
14 Jerome Bettis 2.00
15 Plaxico Burress 4.00
16 Jon Kitna 1.00
17 Eddie George 2.50
18 Steve McNair 2.00

2000 Pacific Omega Autographs

NM/M
Common Player: 12.00
Inserted 1:4 Boxes
1 Brett Favre 100.00
2 Edgerrin James 55.00
3 Peyton Manning 85.00
4 Mark Brunell 40.00
5 Fred Taylor 40.00
6 Drew Bledsoe 40.00
7 Tyrone Wheatley 12.00
8 Torry Holt 20.00
9 Kurt Warner 55.00
10 Stephen Davis 12.00

2000 Pacific Omega EO Portraits

NM/M
Complete Set (20): 45.00
Common Player: 1.00
Inserted 1:73
1 Jake Plummer 1.00
2 Peter Warrick 2.00
3 Tim Couch 3.00
4 Troy Aikman 4.00
5 Emmitt Smith 5.00
6 Terrell Davis 4.00
7 Brett Favre 6.00
8 Edgerrin James 4.00
9 Peyton Manning 4.00
10 Mark Brunell 2.00
11 Fred Taylor 2.00
12 Randy Moss 4.00
13 Drew Bledsoe 3.00
14 Ricky Williams 4.00
15 Ron Dayne 2.00
16 Chad Pennington 8.00
17 Marshall Faulk 1.00
18 Kurt Warner 4.00
19 Jerry Rice 4.00
20 Eddie George 3.00

2000 Pacific Omega Fourth & Goal

NM/M
Complete Set (36): 35.00
Common Player: .50
Minor Stars: 1.00
Inserted 4:37
#1-9 Parallel: 2X-4X
Production 100 Sets
#10-18 Parallel: 3X-8X
Production 50 Sets
#19-27 Parallel: 5X-20X
Production 25 Sets
#28-36 Parallel: 10X-25X
Production 10 Sets
1 Eric Moulds 1.00
2 Marcus Robinson 1.00
3 Antonio Freeman 1.00
4 Marvin Harrison 1.00
5 Jimmy Smith 1.00
6 Cris Carter 1.00
7 Randy Moss 3.00
8 Tim Brown 1.00
9 Isaac Bruce 1.00
10 Emmitt Smith 3.50
11 Edgerrin James 3.00
12 Fred Taylor 2.00
13 Robert Smith 1.00
14 Curtis Martin 1.00
15 Marshall Faulk 1.50
16 Warrick Dunn 1.00
17 Eddie George 1.50
18 Stephen Davis 1.00
19 Steve Beuerlein .50
20 Akili Smith 1.00
21 Tim Couch 2.50
22 Brian Griese 1.50
23 Mark Brunell 2.00
24 Daunte Culpepper 2.50
25 Kurt Warner 3.00
26 Jon Kitna 1.00
27 Shaun King 1.50
28 Thomas Jones 2.50
29 Jamal Lewis 4.00
30 Travis Taylor 1.50
31 Peter Warrick 2.00
32 Ron Dayne 2.00
33 Chad Pennington 6.00
34 Plaxico Burress 3.00
35 Giovanni Carmazzi 1.50
36 Shaun Alexander 2.50

2000 Pacific Omega Game Worn Jerseys

NM/M
Complete Set (10): 15.00
Common Player: 15.00
1 Keenan McCardell 15.00
2 Fred Taylor 30.00
3 Dan Marino 75.00
4 Wayne Chrebet 25.00
5 Jerome Bettis 25.00
6 Charles Johnson 15.00
7 Donovan McNabb 35.00
8 Kevin Turner 15.00
9 Brock Huard 20.00
10 Cortez Kennedy 15.00

2000 Pacific Omega Generations

NM/M
Complete Set (20): 70.00
Common Player: 2.00
Inserted 1:145
1 Cade McNown, Dez White 2.00
2 Tim Couch, Dennis Northcutt 5.00
3 Troy Aikman, Chad Pennington 12.00
4 Emmitt Smith, Thomas Jones 10.00
5 Terrell Davis, Jamal Lewis 8.00
6 Brett Favre, Giovanni Carmazzi 10.00
7 Marvin Harrison, Travis Taylor 6.00
8 Edgerrin James, Shaun Alexander 8.00
9 Peyton Manning, Tee Martin 8.00
10 Mark Brunell, R. Jay Soward 3.00
11 Cris Carter, Sylvester Morris 3.00
12 Randy Moss, Peter Warrick 8.00
13 Drew Bledsoe, Tom Brady 12.00
14 Jerome Bettis, Ron Dayne 3.00
15 Marshall Faulk, Trung Canidate 4.00
16 Kurt Warner, Chris Redman 6.00
17 Jerry Rice, Plaxico Burress 8.00
18 Warrick Dunn, J.R. Redmond 3.00
19 Eddie George, Reuben Droughns 3.00
20 Stephen Davis, Travis Prentice 3.00

2000 Pacific Omega NFC Conference Contenders

NM/M
Complete Set (18): 25.00
Common Player: .50
Minor Stars: 1.00
Inserted 2:37
1 Thomas Jones 2.00
2 Cade McNown 1.00
3 Ron Dayne 2.00
4 Donovan McNabb 2.50
5 Emmitt Smith 4.00
6 Jake Plummer 2.00
7 Randy Moss 4.00
8 Marshall Faulk 2.00
9 Kurt Warner 3.00
10 Ricky Williams 3.00
11 Marcus Robinson 2.00
12 Warrick Dunn 2.00
13 Jerry Rice 4.00
14 Jamal Anderson 2.00
15 Cris Carter 2.00
16 Brad Johnson .50
17 Stephen Davis 1.00
18 Shaun King .50

2000 Pacific Omega Stellar Performers

NM/M
Complete Set (20): 40.00
Common Player: 1.00
Inserted 1:37
1 Tim Couch 3.00
2 Troy Aikman 4.00
3 Emmitt Smith 5.00
4 Brian Griese 3.00
5 Brett Favre 6.00
6 Edgerrin James 4.00
7 Peyton Manning 4.00
8 Mark Brunell 2.00
9 Fred Taylor 2.00
10 Randy Moss 4.00
11 Drew Bledsoe 3.50
12 Isaac Bruce 1.00
13 Marshall Faulk 1.00
14 Kurt Warner 4.00
15 Jerry Rice 4.00
16 Jon Kitna 1.00
17 Shaun King 1.00
18 Eddie George 2.00
19 Steve McNair 1.00
20 Stephen Davis 1.00

2000 Pacific Paramount

NM/M
Complete Set (249): 35.00
Common Player: .10
Minor Stars: .20
Common Rookie: .50
Pack (6): 1.00
Wax Box (36): 30.00
Card #242 Never Released
1 David Boston .30
2 *Thomas Jones* 1.00
3 Rob Moore .20
4 Jake Plummer .50
5 Simeon Rice .10
6 Frank Sanders .20
7 *Raynoch Thompson* .50
8 Jamal Anderson .40
9 Chris Chandler .20
10 Bob Christian .10
11 Tim Dwight .30
12 Byron Hanspard .10
13 Terance Mathis .10
14 *Mareno Philyaw* .50
15 Tony Banks .20
16 Priest Holmes .30
17 Qadry Ismail .10
18 Patrick Johnson .10
19 *Jamal Lewis* 2.00
20 *Chris Redman* 1.25
21 Shannon Sharpe .20
22 *Travis Taylor* 1.25
23 *Erik Flowers* .75
24 Doug Flutie .50
25 Rob Johnson .20
26 Jonathon Linton .10
27 *Corey Moore* .50
28 Eric Moulds .40
29 Peerless Price .30
30 Jay Riemersma .20
31 Antowain Smith .30
32 *Rashard Anderson* .75
33 Steve Beuerlein .20
34 Tshimanga Biakabutuka .20
35 Donald Hayes .10
36 Patrick Jeffers .30
37 Jeff Lewis .20
38 Muhsin Muhammad .30
39 Wesley Walls .20
40 Bobby Engram .10
41 Curtis Enis .30
42 Cade McNown .75
43 Jim Miller .10
44 Marcus Robinson .40
45 *Brian Urlacher* 2.00
46 *Dez White* 1.00
47 Michael Basnight .10
48 Corey Dillon .30
49 *Ron Dugans* .75
50 Willie Jackson .10
51 Darnay Scott .20
52 Akili Smith .50
53 *Peter Warrick* 1.50
54 *Courtney Brown* 1.00
55 Darrin Chiaverini .20
56 Tim Couch 1.00
57 Kevin Johnson .40
58 Terry Kirby .10

59 *Dennis Northcutt* 1.00
60 *Travis Prentice* 1.00
61 Leslie Shepherd .10
62 Troy Aikman 1.00
63 Joey Galloway .30
64 Raghib Ismail .10
65 David LaFleur .10
66 Emmitt Smith 1.25
67 Jason Tucker .20
68 Chris Warren .10
69 *Michael Wiley* 1.00
70 Desmond Clark .10
71 *Chris Cole* .50
72 Terrell Davis 1.00
73 Olandis Gary .50
74 Brian Griese .50
75 *Jarious Jackson* .75
76 Ed McCaffrey .30
77 *Delthea O'Neal* .50
78 Rod Smith .30
79 Charlie Batch .40
80 Germane Crowell .30
81 *Reuben Droughns* 1.00
82 Terry Fair .10
83 Herman Moore .30
84 Johnnie Morton .20
85 Barry Sanders 1.50
86 James Stewart .20
87 Corey Bradford .20
88 Tyrone Davis .10
89 Brett Favre 1.50
90 *Bubba Franks* 1.25
91 Antonio Freeman .30
92 Matt Hasselbeck .20
93 Dorsey Levens .30
94 *Anthony Lucas* .75
95 Bill Schroeder .20
96 Ken Dilger .10
97 E.G. Green .10
98 Marvin Harrison .40
99 Edgerrin James 1.50
100 Peyton Manning 1.25
101 Jerome Pathon .10
102 *Marcus Washington* .50
103 Terrence Wilkins .30
104 Kyle Brady .10
105 Mark Brunell .60
106 Kevin Hardy .10
107 Keenan McCardell .20
108 Jimmy Smith .30
109 *R. Jay Soward* 1.25
110 *Shyrone Stith* .50
111 Fred Taylor .60
112 Alvis Whitted .10
113 Derrick Alexander .10
114 Kimble Anders .10
115 Donnell Bennett .10
116 Tony Gonzalez .20
117 Elvis Grbac .20
118 Kevin Lockett .10
119 *Sylvester Morris* 1.25
120 Tony Richardson .10
121 *Deon Dyer* .50
122 Oronde Gadsden .20
123 Damon Huard .30
124 J.J. Johnson .20
125 Dan Marino 1.25
126 Tony Martin .10
127 O.J. McDuffie .20
128 Zach Thomas .20
129 Cris Carter .30
130 Daunte Culpepper .75
131 Leroy Hoard .10
132 *Chris Hovan* .50
133 Randy Moss 1.50
134 John Randle .20
135 Robert Smith .30
136 *Troy Walters* .75
137 Drew Bledsoe .60
138 *Tom Brady* 4.00
139 Troy Brown .10
140 Kevin Faulk .20
141 Terry Glenn .30
142 *J.R. Redmond* 1.25
143 Tony Simmons .20
144 *David Stachelski* .75
145 Jeff Blake .20
146 *Marc Bulger* 2.00
147 Cameron Cleeland .20
148 *Sherrod Gideon* .50
149 *Darren Howard* .50
150 *Chad Morton* .50
151 Keith Poole .10
152 Ricky Williams 1.00
153 Tiki Barber .20
154 Kerry Collins .20
155 *Ron Dayne* 1.00
156 Ike Hilliard .20
157 Joe Jurevicius .10
158 Pete Mitchell .10
159 Joe Montgomery .10
160 Amani Toomer .20
161 *John Abraham* .50
162 *Anthony Becht* .75
163 Wayne Chrebet .30
164 *Laveranues Coles* 1.50
165 Ray Lucas .30
166 Curtis Martin .30
167 *Chad Pennington* 4.00
168 Vinny Testaverde .30
169 Dedric Ward .20
170 Tim Brown .30
171 Rich Gannon .20
172 Bobby Hoying .20
173 James Jett .10
174 Napoleon Kaufman .30
175 *Jerry Porter* 1.50
176 Tyrone Wheatley .20
177 Charles Woodson .30
178 Dameane Douglas .10
179 Charles Johnson .20
180 Donovan McNabb .75
181 *Todd Pinkston* .75
182 *Gari Scott* .50
183 Torrance Small .10
184 Duce Staley .30
185 Jerome Bettis .30
186 *Plaxico Burress* 1.50
187 Troy Edwards .30
188 *Danny Farmer* .75
189 Richard Huntley .20
190 *Tee Martin* 1.25
191 Kordell Stewart .40
192 Hines Ward .20
193 Isaac Bruce .30
194 *Trung Canidate* .75
195 Marshall Faulk .40
196 Az-Zahir Hakim .20
197 Torry Holt .40
198 Tony Horne .10
199 Ricky Proehl .10
200 Kurt Warner 1.75
201 Jermaine Fazande .20
202 *Trevor Gaylor* .75
203 Jeff Graham .10
204 Jim Harbaugh .20
205 Freddie Jones .20
206 Mikhael Ricks .10
207 Junior Seau .20
208 Fred Beasley .10
209 *Giovanni Carmazzi* 1.00
210 Jeff Garcia .30
211 Charlie Garner .20
212 Terrell Owens .40
213 *Tim Rattay* 1.25
214 Jerry Rice 1.00
215 J.J. Stokes .20
216 Steve Young .60
217 *Shaun Alexander* 2.00
218 Sean Dawkins .10
219 *Darrell Jackson* 1.00
220 Jon Kitna .40
221 Derrick Mayes .20
222 Charlie Rogers .10
223 Shawn Springs .10
224 Ricky Watters .30
225 Mike Alstott .40
226 Reidel Anthony .20
227 Warrick Dunn .40
228 Jacquez Green .20
229 *Joe Hamilton* 1.00
230 Keyshawn Johnson .40
231 Shaun King .75
232 Warren Sapp .20
233 *Keith Bulluck* .50
234 Kevin Dyson .20
235 Eddie George .50
236 Jevon Kearse .50
237 *Erron Kinney* .50
238 Steve McNair .50
239 Neil O'Donnell .20
240 Yancy Thigpen .20
241 Frank Wycheck .10
243 Champ Bailey .20
244 Larry Centers .10
245 Albert Connell .20
246 Stephen Davis .30
247 *Todd Husak* .75
248 Brad Johnson .30
249 *Chris Samuels* .75
250 Michael Westbrook .20

2000 Pacific Paramount Draft Picks 325

Draft Pick Cards: 5X-10X
Production 325 Sets

2000 Pacific Paramount HoloGold

HoloGold Cards: 10X-20X
HoloGold Rookies: 6X-12X
Production 199 Sets
Retail Only

2000 Pacific Paramount HoloSilver

HoloSilver Cards: 15X-30X
HoloSilver Rookies: 8X-16X
Production 99 Sets
Hobby Only

2000 Pacific Paramount Platinum Blue

Platinum Blue Cards: 15X-30X
Platinum Blue Rookies: 8X-16X
Production 67 Sets

2000 Pacific Paramount Premiere Date

Premiere Date Cards: 15X-30X
Premiere Date Rookies: 8X-16X
Production 79 Sets
Hobby Only

2000 Pacific Paramount Draft Report

NM/M
Complete Set (31): 40.00
Common Player: .50
Minor Stars: 1.00
Inserted 2:37
1 Thomas Jones 2.00
2 Mareno Philyaw .50
3 Jamal Lewis 4.00
4 Erik Flowers .50
5 Rashard Anderson .50
6 Dez White 1.00
7 Peter Warrick 1.00
8 Dennis Northcutt 1.00
9 Michael Wiley 1.00
10 Delthea O'Neal .50
11 Reuben Droughns 1.00
12 Anthony Lucas .50
13 Marcus Washington .50
14 R. Jay Soward 2.00
15 Sylvester Morris 2.50
16 Deon Dyer .50
17 Troy Walters 1.00
18 J.R. Redmond 3.00
19 Marc Bulger .50
20 Ron Dayne 2.00
21 Chad Pennington 8.00
22 Jerry Porter 1.00
23 Todd Pinkston .50
24 Plaxico Burress 6.00
25 Trung Canidate 1.00
26 Trevor Gaylor .50
27 Giovanni Carmazzi 2.00
28 Shaun Alexander 4.00
29 Joe Hamilton 1.00
30 Erron Kinney .50
31 Todd Husak 1.50

2000 Pacific Paramount End Zone Net-Fusions

NM/M
Complete Set (20): 85.00
Common Player: 2.00
Inserted 1:73
1 Jake Plummer 2.00
2 Cade McNown 2.00
3 Tim Couch 4.00
4 Troy Aikman 5.00
5 Emmitt Smith 6.00
6 Terrell Davis 4.00
7 Brett Favre 7.00
8 Edgerrin James 5.00
9 Peyton Manning 5.00
10 Mark Brunell 3.00
11 Fred Taylor 3.00
12 Drew Bledsoe 6.00
13 Ricky Williams 5.00
14 Randy Moss 5.00
15 Marshall Faulk 2.00
16 Kurt Warner 5.00
17 Jerry Rice 4.00
18 Jon Kitna 2.00
19 Eddie George 3.00
20 Stephen Davis 2.00

2000 Pacific Paramount Game Used Footballs

NM/M
Common Player: 15.00
Randomly Inserted
1 Troy Aikman 25.00
2 Emmitt Smith 30.00
3 Olandis Gary 15.00
4 Brett Favre 35.00
5 Edgerrin James 25.00
6 Peyton Manning 25.00
7 Randy Moss 25.00
8 Drew Bledsoe 25.00
9 Kurt Warner 25.00
10 Jerry Rice 30.00

2000 Pacific Paramount Sculptures

NM/M
Complete Set (10): 100.00
Common Player: 6.00
Inserted 1:361
Proof Cards: 4X-8X
Production 20 Sets
Canvas Proof Cards:
Production 1 Set
1 Peter Warrick 12.00
2 Tim Couch 20.00
3 Emmitt Smith 25.00
4 Edgerrin James 20.00
5 Mark Brunell 12.00
6 Fred Taylor 12.00
7 Randy Moss 20.00
8 Kurt Warner 20.00
9 Eddie George 12.00
10 Stephen Davis 6.00

2000 Pacific Paramount Zoned In

NM/M
Complete Set (36): 80.00
Common Player: 1.00
Inserted 1:37
1 Thomas Jones 3.00
2 Jake Plummer 1.00
3 Jamal Lewis 4.00
4 Cade McNown 1.00
5 Marcus Robinson 1.00
6 Peter Warrick 2.00
7 Tim Couch 4.00
8 Troy Aikman 5.00
9 Emmitt Smith 6.00
10 Barry Sanders 6.00
11 Terrell Davis 4.00
12 Brian Griese 3.00
13 Brett Favre 7.00
14 Marvin Harrison 2.00
15 Edgerrin James 5.00
16 Peyton Manning 5.00
17 Mark Brunell 3.00
18 Fred Taylor 3.00
19 Drew Bledsoe 3.00
20 Ricky Williams 5.00
21 Ron Dayne 3.00
22 Chad Pennington 10.00
23 Randy Moss 5.00
24 Donovan McNabb 3.00
25 Plaxico Burress 8.00
26 Isaac Bruce 1.00
27 Marshall Faulk 2.00
28 Kurt Warner 5.00
29 Jerry Rice 5.00
30 Shaun Alexander 4.00
31 Jon Kitna 1.00
32 Shaun King 1.00
33 Eddie George 2.00
34 Steve McNair 2.00
35 Stephen Davis 1.00
36 Brad Johnson 1.00

2000 Pacific Prism

NM/M
Common Player: .15
Minor Stars: .30
Common Rookie: 1.00
Production 1,000 Sets
Pack (5): 2.00
Wax Box (24): 40.00
1 David Boston .50
2 Jake Plummer .50
3 Jamal Anderson .50
4 Chris Chandler .30
5 Tim Dwight .50
6 Terance Mathis .15
7 Tony Banks .30
8 Priest Holmes .30
9 Doug Flutie .75
10 Rob Johnson .30
11 Eric Moulds .50
12 Antowain Smith .30
13 Steve Beuerlein .30
14 Tim Biakabutuka .30
15 Muhsin Muhammad .30
16 Bobby Engram .15
17 Curtis Enis .50
18 Cade McNown .75
19 Marcus Robinson .50
20 Corey Dillon .50
21 Akili Smith .50
22 Tim Couch 1.25
23 Kevin Johnson .50
24 Troy Aikman 1.50
25 Joey Galloway .50
26 Raghib Ismail .15
27 Emmitt Smith 1.75
28 Terrell Davis 1.00
29 Olandis Gary .75
30 Brian Griese .75
31 Charlie Batch .50
32 Herman Moore .30
33 Johnnie Morton .15
34 Brett Favre 2.50
35 Antonio Freeman .50
36 Dorsey Levens .50
37 Marvin Harrison .50
38 Edgerrin James 2.00
39 Peyton Manning 2.00
40 Mark Brunell 1.00
41 Keenan McCardell .30
42 Jimmy Smith .50
43 Fred Taylor 1.00
44 Donnell Bennett .15
45 Tony Gonzalez .30
46 Elvis Grbac .30
47 Damon Huard .50
48 J.J. Johnson .15
49 Cris Carter .50
50 Daunte Culpepper 1.25
51 Randy Moss 2.00
52 Robert Smith .50
53 Drew Bledsoe 1.00
54 Kevin Faulk .30
55 Terry Glenn .50
56 Jeff Blake .30
57 Ricky Williams 2.00
58 Kerry Collins .30
59 Ike Hilliard .30
60 Amani Toomer .30
61 Wayne Chrebet .50
62 Curtis Martin .50
63 Vinny Testaverde .50
64 Tim Brown .50
65 Rich Gannon .30
66 Napoleon Kaufman .50
67 Tyrone Wheatley .30
68 Donovan McNabb 1.50
69 Duce Staley .50
70 Jerome Bettis .50
71 Troy Edwards .50
72 Kordell Stewart .60
73 Isaac Bruce .50
74 Torry Holt .50
75 Marshall Faulk .50
76 Kurt Warner 2.00
77 Jermaine Fazande .30
78 Jim Harbaugh .30
79 Ryan Leaf .30
80 Junior Seau .30
81 Jeff Garcia .50
82 J.J. Stokes .30
83 Terrell Owens .50
84 Jerry Rice 1.50
85 Jon Kitna .50
86 Derrick Mayes .30
87 Ricky Watters .30
88 Mike Alstott .50
89 Warrick Dunn .50
90 Jacquez Green .15
91 Shaun King .75
92 Eddie George .75
93 Jevon Kearse .50
94 Steve McNair .60
95 Carl Pickens .30
96 Stephen Davis .50
97 Jeff George .50
98 Brad Johnson .50
99 Deion Sanders .50
100 Michael Westbrook .30
101 *Jabari Issa* 1.00
102 *Thomas Jones* 8.00
103 *Sekou Sanyika* 1.00
104 *Jay Tant* 1.00
105 *Raynoch Thompson* 1.00
106 *Doug Johnson* 2.00
107 *Mark Simoneau* 1.00
108 *Jamal Lewis* 20.00
109 *Chris Redman* 8.00
110 *Travis Taylor* 4.00
111 *Kwame Cavil* 2.00
112 *Corey Moore* 1.00
113 *Rashard Anderson* 2.00
114 *Lester Towns* 1.00
115 *Paul Edinger* 2.00
116 *Brian Urlacher* 20.00
117 *Dez White* 6.00
118 *Ron Dugans* 2.00
119 *Danny Farmer* 6.00
120 *Curtis Keaton* 2.00
121 *Peter Warrick* 15.00
122 *Courtney Brown* 8.00
123 *Lamar Chapman* 2.00
124 *JaJuan Dawson* 2.00
125 *Dennis Northcutt* 2.00
126 *Travis Prentice* 4.00
127 *Aaron Shea* 2.00
128 *Spergon Wynn* 3.00
129 *Dwayne Goodrich* 2.00
130 *Orantes Grant* 1.00
131 *Kareem Larrimore* 1.00
132 *Michael Wiley* 2.00
133 *Mike Anderson* 10.00
134 *Chris Cole* 2.00
135 *Jarious Jackson* 8.00
136 *Jerry Johnson* 1.00
137 *Kenoy Kennedy* 1.00
138 *Deltha O'Neal* 6.00
139 *Reuben Droughns* 2.00
140 *Barret Green* 2.00
141 *Bubba Franks* 8.00
142 *Kevin McDougal* 2.00
143 *Marcus Washington* 2.00
144 *T.J. Slaughter* 2.00
145 *R. Jay Soward* 2.00
146 *Shyrone Stith* 2.00
147 *William Bartee* 1.00
148 *Dante Hall* 20.00
149 *Frank Moreau* 2.00
150 *Sylvester Morris* 4.00
151 *Deon Dyer* 1.00
152 *Ben Kelly* 1.00
153 *Tyrone Carter* 2.00
154 *Doug Chapman* 2.00
155 *Troy Walters* 2.00
156 *Tom Brady* 40.00
157 *Patrick Pass* 2.00
158 *J.R. Redmond* 10.00
159 *Marc Bulger* 20.00
160 *Darren Howard* 2.00
161 *Chad Morton* 8.00
162 *Mareno Philyaw* 1.00
163 *Terrelle Smith* 1.00
164 *Ralph Brown* 1.00
165 *Ron Dayne* 6.00
166 *Brandon Short* 2.00
167 *John Abraham* 2.00
168 *Anthony Becht* 2.00
169 *Laveranues Coles* 12.00
170 *Shaun Ellis* 2.00
171 *Chad Pennington* 30.00
172 *Sebastian Janikowski* 6.00
173 *Jerry Porter* 15.00
174 *Todd Pinkston* 8.00
175 *Gari Scott* 2.00
176 *Corey Simon* 8.00
177 *Plaxico Burress* 15.00
178 *Tee Martin* 8.00
179 *Hank Poteat* 2.00
180 *Rogers Beckett* 2.00
181 *Trevor Gaylor* 2.00
182 *Ronney Jenkins* 6.00
183 *Giovanni Carmazzi* 4.00
184 *Chafie Fields* 2.00
185 *Ahmed Plummer* 2.00
186 *Tim Rattay* 10.00
187 *Jeff Ulenhake* 2.00
188 *Shaun Alexander* 20.00
189 *Darrell Jackson* 4.00
190 *Rodnick Phillips* 2.00
191 *James Williams* 2.00
192 *Trung Canidate* 10.00
193 *Joe Hamilton* 8.00
194 *Demario Brown* 2.00
195 *Keith Bulluck* 2.00
196 *Chris Coleman* 4.00
197 *Erron Kinney* 2.00
198 *Billy Volek* 1.00
199 *Todd Husak* 6.00
200 *Chris Samuels* 2.00

2000 Pacific Prism Graded Series

7.5 .5X Reg. Set
8.0 .75X Reg. Set
8.5 1X Reg. Set
9.0 1.5X Reg.Set
101 Jabari Issa 8.0 (133)
102 Thomas Jones 8.0 (91)
102 Thomas Jones 8.5 (42)
103 Sekou Sanyika 8.0 (129)
103 Sekou Sanyika 8.5 (4)
104 Jay Tant 8.0 (2)
104 Jay Tant 8.5 (105)
104 Jay Tant 9.0 (26)
105 Raynoch Thompson 8.0 (128)
105 Raynoch Thompson 8.5 (5)
106 Doug Johnson 8.0 (133)
107 Mark Simoneau 8.0 (127)
107 Mark Simoneau 8.5 (6)
108 Jamal Lewis 8.0 (133)
109 Chris Redman 8.0 (68)
109 Chris Redman 8.5 (63)
109 Chris Redman 9.0 (2)
110 Travis Taylor 7.5 (1)
110 Travis Taylor 8.0 (132)
111 Kwame Cavil 8.0 (133)
112 Corey Moore 8.0 (125)
112 Corey Moore 8.5 (8)
113 Rashard Anderson 8.0 (128)
113 Rashard Anderson 8.5 (5)
114 Lester Towns 8.0 (126)
114 Lester Towns 8.5 (7)
115 Paul Edinger 8.0 (99)
115 Paul Edinger 8.5 (33)
115 Paul Edinger 9.0 (1)
116 Brian Urlacher 8.0 (132)
116 Brian Urlacher 8.5 (1)
117 Dez White 8.0 (133)
118 Ron Dugans 8.0 (133)
119 Danny Farmer 8.0 (96)
119 Danny Farmer 8.5 (37)
121 Peter Warrick 8.0 (131)
121 Peter Warrick 8.5 (2)
122 Courtney Brown 8.0 (64)
122 Courtney Brown 8.5 (68)
122 Courtney Brown 9.0 (1)
123 Lamar Chapman 8.0 (132)
123 Lamar Chapman 8.5 (1)
124 JaJuan Dawson 8.0 (116)
124 JaJuan Dawson 8.5 (16)
124 JaJuan Dawson 9.0 (1)
125 Dennis Northcutt 8.0 (130)
125 Dennis Northcutt 8.5 (3)
126 Travis Prentice 8.0 (133)
127 Aaron Shea 8.0 (133)
128 Spergon Wynn 8.0 (132)
128 Spergon Wynn 8.5 (1)
129 Dwayne Goodrich 8.0 (133)
130 Orantes Grant 8.0 (129)
130 Orantes Grant 8.5 (4)
131 Kareem Larrimore 8.0 (116)
131 Kareem Larrimore 8.5 (17)
132 Michael Wiley 8.0 (128)
132 Michael Wiley 8.5 (5)
133 Mike Anderson 8.0 (132)
133 Mike Anderson 8.5 (1)
134 Chris Cole 8.0 (132)
134 Chris Cole 8.5 (1)
135 Jarious Jackson 8.0 (132)
135 Jarious Jackson 8.5 (1)
136 Jerry Johnson 8.0 (124)
136 Jerry Johnson 8.5 (9)
137 Kenoy Kennedy 8.0 (72)
137 Kenoy Kennedy 8.5 (59)
137 Kenoy Kennedy 9.0 (2)
138 Deltha O'Neal 8.0 (131)
138 Deltha O'Neal 8.5 (2)
139 Reuben Droughns 8.0 (3)
139 Reuben Droughns 8.5 (129)
139 Reuben Droughns 9.0 (1)
140 Barrett Green 8.0 (121)
140 Barrett Green 8.5 (12)
141 Bubba Franks 8.5 (103)
141 Bubba Franks 9.0 (30)
142 Kevin McDougal 8.0 (123)
142 Kevin McDougal 8.5 (10)
144 T.J. Slaughter 8.0 (133)
145 R. Jay Soward 8.5 (27)
145 R. Jay Soward 9.0 (106)
146 Shyrone Stith 8.0 (18)
146 Shyrone Stith 8.5 (109)
146 Shyrone Stith 9.0 (6)
147 William Bartee 8.0 (133)
148 Dante Hall 8.0 (121)
148 Dante Hall 8.5 (12)
149 Frank Moreau 8.0 (133)
150 Sylvester Morris 8.0 (90)
150 Sylvester Morris 8.5 (43)
151 Deon Dyer 8.0 (131)
151 Deon Dyer 8.5 (2)
155 Troy Walters 8.5 (21)
155 Troy Walters 9.0 (102)
155 Troy Walters 9.5 (10)
157 Patrick Pass 8.0 (133)
158 J.R. Redmond 8.0 (133)
159 Marc Bulger 8.0 (2)

159 Marc Bulger 8.5 (60)
159 Marc Bulger 9.0 (70)
159 Marc Bulger 9.5 (1)
161 Chad Morton 8.0 (130)
161 Chad Morton 8.5 (3)
162 Mareno Philyaw 8.0 (16)
162 Mareno Philyaw 8.5 (115)
162 Mareno Philyaw 9.0 (2)
164 Ralph Brown 8.0 (126)
164 Ralph Brown 8.5 (7)
165 Ron Dayne 8.0 (42)
165 Ron Dayne 8.5 (83)
165 Ron Dayne 9.0 (8)
166 Brandon Short 8.0 (122)
166 Brandon Short 8.5 (11)
167 John Abraham 8.0 (4)
167 John Abraham 8.5 (26)
167 John Abraham 9.0 (95)
167 John Abraham 9.5 (8)
168 Anthony Becht 8.0 (133)
169 Laveranues Coles 8.0 (133)
170 Shaun Ellis 8.0 (132)
170 Shaun Ellis 8.5 (1)
171 Chad Pennington 8.0 (133)
172 Sebastian Janikowski 8.0 (123)
172 Sebastian Janikowski 8.5 (10)
173 Jerry Porter 8.0 (133)
174 Todd Pinkston 8.0 (129)
174 Todd Pinkston 8.5 (4)
175 Gari Scott 8.0 (133)
176 Corey Simon 8.0 (130)
176 Corey Simon 8.5 (3)
177 Plaxico Burress 8.0 (132)
177 Plaxico Burress 8.5 (1)
178 Tee Martin 8.0 (133)
179 Hank Poteat 8.0 (133)
180 Rogers Beckett 8.0 (133)
181 Trevor Gaylor 8.0 (133)
182 Ronney Jenkins 8.0 (133)
183 Giovanni Carmazzi 8.0 (110)
183 Giovanni Carmazzi 8.5 (23)
184 Chafie Fields 8.0 (130)
184 Chafie Fields 8.5 (3)
185 Ahmed Plummer 8.0 (133)
186 Tim Rattay 8.0 (129)
186 Tim Rattay 8.5 (4)
187 Jeff Ulbrich 8.0 (85)
187 Jeff Ulbrich 8.5 (48)
188 Shaun Alexander 7.5 (1)
188 Shaun Alexander 8.0 (130)
188 Shaun Alexander 8.5 (2)
189 Darrell Jackson 8.0 (22)
189 Darrell Jackson 8.5 (84)
189 Darrell Jackson 9.0 (27)
190 Rodnick Phillips 8.0 (133)
191 James Williams 8.0 (133)
192 Trung Canidate 8.0 (133)
193 Joe Hamilton 8.0 (132)
193 Joe Hamilton 8.5 (1)
194 Demario Brown 8.0 (133)
195 Keith Bulluck 8.0 (133)
196 Chris Coleman 8.0 (132)
196 Chris Coleman 8.5 (1)
197 Erron Kinney 8.5 (133)
198 Billy Volek 8.0 (77)
198 Billy Volek 8.5 (55)
198 Billy Volek 9.0 (1)
199 Todd Husak 8.0 (133)
200 Chris Samuels 8.0 (131)
200 Chris Samuels 8.5 (2)

2000 Pacific Prism Holographic Blue

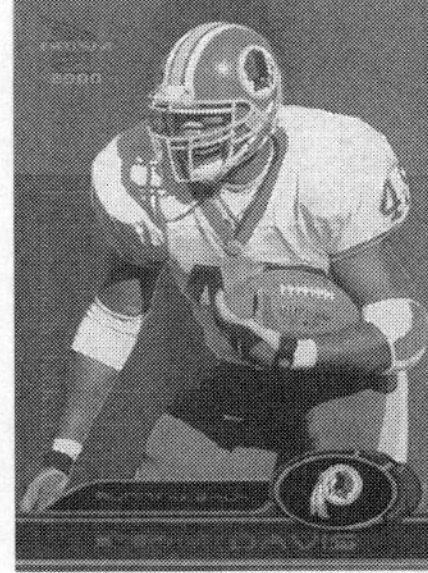

Blue Cards: 5X-10X
Production 100 Sets

2000 Pacific Prism Holographic Gold

Gold Cards: 10X-20X
Production 50 Sets

2000 Pacific Prism Holographic Mirror

Mirror Cards: 8X-15X
Production 75 Sets

2000 Pacific Prism Premiere Date

Premiere Date Cards: 4X-8X
Production 138 Sets

2000 Pacific Prism Fortified with Stars

NM/M
Complete Set (10): 60.00
Common Player: 4.00
Inserted 1:97
1 Jake Plummer Apple Jakes 4.00
2 Drew Bledsoe BledsOe's 5.00
3 Tim Couch Cap'n Couch 5.00
4 Plaxico Burress Frosted PlaxicO's 12.00
5 Brett Favre Frosted Favre's 15.00
6 Jerome Bettis Alpha-Bettis 5.00
7 Peerless Price Peerless Price Krispies 6.00
8 Jon Kitna Special K itna 4.00
9 Jerry Rice Jerry Rice Chex 12.00
10 Tyrone Wheatley Tyrone Wheatley's 4.00

2000 Pacific Prism Game Worn Jerseys

NM/M
Common Player: 15.00
Randomly Inserted
1 Mark Brunell 20.00
2 Wayne Chrebet 15.00
3 Randall Cunningham 15.00
4 Drew Bledsoe 20.00
5 Kordell Stewart 20.00
6 Dan Marino 60.00
7 Steve Young 30.00
8 Jerry Rice 35.00
9 Fred Taylor 25.00
10 Jon Kitna 15.00

2000 Pacific Prism MVP Candidates

NM/M
Complete Set (10): 30.00
Common Player: 1.00
Inserted 1:25
1 Peter Warrick 2.00
2 Emmitt Smith 5.00
3 Brett Favre 6.00
4 Edgerrin James 4.00
5 Peyton Manning 4.00
6 Randy Moss 4.00
7 Ricky Williams 5.00
8 Marshall Faulk 1.00
9 Kurt Warner 4.00
10 Eddie George 3.00

2000 Pacific Prism Rookie Dial-A-Stats

NM/M
Complete Set (10): 75.00
Common Player: 3.00
Inserted 1:193
1 Thomas Jones 12.00
2 Jamal Lewis 25.00
3 Peter Warrick 8.00
4 Plaxico Burress 15.00
5 Ron Dayne 8.00
6 Chad Pennington 35.00
7 Shaun Alexander 20.00
8 Chris Redman 12.00
9 R. Jay Soward 3.00
10 Laveranues Coles 8.00

2000 Pacific Prism ROY Candidates

NM/M
Complete Set (10): 30.00
Common Player: 1.50
Inserted 1:25
1 Thomas Jones 3.00
2 Jamal Lewis 5.00
3 Travis Taylor 2.00
4 Peter Warrick 2.00
5 Sylvester Morris 3.50
6 Doug Chapman 1.50
7 Ron Dayne 2.00
8 Chad Pennington 8.00
9 Plaxico Burress 3.50
10 Shaun Alexander 5.00

2000 Pacific Prism Sno-Globe Die Cuts

NM/M
Complete Set (20): 75.00
Common Player: 2.00
Inserted 1:25

NM/M
1 Jamal Anderson 2.00
2 Cade McNown 2.00
3 Tim Couch 4.00
4 Troy Aikman 6.00
5 Emmitt Smith 7.00
6 Terrell Davis 6.00
7 Brian Griese 5.00
8 Brett Favre 8.00
9 Peyton Manning 6.00
10 Edgerrin James 6.00
11 Mark Brunell 3.00
12 Damon Huard 2.00
13 Randy Moss 6.00
14 Drew Bledsoe 4.00
15 Jon Kitna 2.00
16 Marshall Faulk 3.00
17 Kurt Warner 6.00
18 Eddie George 3.00
19 Steve McNair 2.00
20 Stephen Davis 2.00

2000 Pacific Private Stock

NM/M
Common Player: .20
Minor Stars: .40
Common Rookie: 5.00
Production 278 Sets
Pack (7): 4.00
Wax Box (22): 70.00
1 Rob Moore .40
2 Jake Plummer .75
3 Frank Sanders .40
4 Jamal Anderson .75
5 Chris Chandler .40
6 Tim Dwight .75
7 Tony Banks .40
8 Priest Holmes .75
9 Doug Flutie 1.00
10 Rob Johnson .40
11 Eric Moulds .75
12 Antowain Smith .40
13 Steve Beuerlein .40
14 Tshimanga Biakabutuka .40
15 Patrick Jeffers .75
16 Muhsin Muhammad .40
17 Curtis Enis .40
18 Cade McNown .50
19 Marcus Robinson .75
20 Corey Dillon .75
21 Akili Smith .75
22 Tim Couch 1.25
23 Kevin Johnson .40
24 Troy Aikman 1.75
25 Raghib Ismail .20
26 Emmitt Smith 2.25
27 Terrell Davis 1.50
28 Olandis Gary .75
29 Brian Griese 1.00
30 Ed McCaffrey .75
31 Charlie Batch .75
32 Germane Crowell .75
33 Herman Moore .75
34 Barry Sanders 2.50
35 Brett Favre 3.00
36 Antonio Freeman .75
37 Dorsey Levens .75
38 Marvin Harrison .75
39 Edgerrin James 2.00
40 Peyton Manning 2.50
41 Terrence Wilkins .75
42 Mark Brunell 1.25
43 Keenan McCardell .40
44 Jimmy Smith .75
45 Fred Taylor 1.25
46 Derrick Alexander .20
47 Donnell Bennett .20
48 Tony Gonzalez .40
49 Elvis Grbac .40
50 Damon Huard .75
51 J.J. Johnson .20
52 Dan Marino 2.50
53 O.J. McDuffie .20
54 Cris Carter .75
55 Daunte Culpepper 1.50
56 Randy Moss 2.50
57 Robert Smith .75
58 Drew Bledsoe 1.25
59 Kevin Faulk .40
60 Terry Glenn .75
61 Keith Poole .20
62 Ricky Williams 2.50
63 Kerry Collins .40
64 Ike Hilliard .20
65 Amani Toomer .20
66 Wayne Chrebet .75
67 Ray Lucas .75
68 Curtis Martin .75
69 Tim Brown .75
70 Rich Gannon .40
71 Napoleon Kaufman .75
72 Donovan McNabb 2.00
73 Duce Staley .75
74 Jerome Bettis .75
75 Troy Edwards .75
76 Kordell Stewart .75
77 Isaac Bruce .75
78 Marshall Faulk .75
79 Torry Holt .75
80 Kurt Warner 2.00
81 Jermaine Fazande .20
82 Jim Harbaugh .20
83 Junior Seau .40
84 Charlie Garner .40
85 Terrell Owens .75
86 Jerry Rice 1.75
87 Jon Kitna .75
88 Derrick Mayes .40
89 Ricky Watters .40
90 Mike Alstott .75
91 Warrick Dunn .75
92 Jacquez Green .20
93 Shaun King 1.25
94 Eddie George 1.00
95 Jevon Kearse .75
96 Steve McNair .75
97 Yancey Thigpen .20
98 Stephen Davis .75
99 Brad Johnson .75
100 Michael Westbrook .40
101 *Thomas Jones* 25.00
102 *Doug Johnson* 10.00
103 *Mareno Philyaw* 5.00
104 *Jamal Lewis* 20.00
105 *Chris Redman* 15.00
106 *Travis Taylor* 20.00
107 *Frank Murphy* 5.00
108 *Dez White* 20.00
109 *Ron Dugans* 10.00
110 *Curtis Keaton* 5.00
111 *Peter Warrick* 30.00
112 *Courtney Brown* 15.00
113 *JaJuan Dawson* 10.00
114 *Dennis Northcutt* 15.00
115 *Travis Prentice* 20.00
116 *Michael Wiley* 10.00
117 *Chris Cole* 5.00
118 *Jarious Jackson* 10.00
119 *Reuben Droughns* 10.00
120 *Bubba Franks* 20.00
121 *Anthony Lucas* 5.00
122 *Rondell Mealey* 5.00
123 *R. Jay Soward* 15.00
124 *Shyrone Stith* 10.00
125 *Sylvester Morris* 15.00
126 *Quinton Spotwood* 10.00
127 *Troy Walters* 15.00
128 *Tom Brady* 125.00
129 *J.R. Redmond* 15.00
130 *Marc Bulger* 40.00
131 *Sherrod Gideon* 5.00
132 *Ron Dayne* 15.00
133 *Anthony Becht* 5.00
134 *Laveranues Coles* 30.00
135 *Chad Pennington* 100.00
136 *Sebastian Janikowski* 20.00
137 *Jerry Porter* 30.00
138 *Todd Pinkston* 15.00
139 *Gari Scott* 5.00
140 *Plaxico Burress* 40.00
141 *Danny Farmer* 20.00
142 *Tee Martin* 20.00
143 *Trung Canidate* 25.00
144 *Trevor Gaylor* 10.00
145 *Giovanni Carmazzi* 10.00
146 *Tim Rattay* 15.00
147 *Shaun Alexander* 50.00
148 *Darrell Jackson* 25.00
149 *Joe Hamilton* 10.00
150 *Todd Husak* 15.00

2000 Pacific Private Stock Retail Version

Retail Cards: 1x
Retail Rookies: 1x
Production 650 Sets

2000 Pacific Private Stock Gold

Gold Cards: 2X-5X
Gold Rookies: 2X
Production 181 Sets

2000 Pacific Private Stock Premiere Date

Premiere Date Cards: 5X-10X
Premiere Date Rookies: 1X
Production 95 Sets

2000 Pacific Private Stock Silver

Silver Cards: 2x-4x
Silver Rookies: 1x
Production 330 Sets

2000 Pacific Private Stock Artist's Canvas

NM/M
Complete Set (20): 125.00
Common Player: 4.00
Inserted 1:45
1 Jamal Lewis 6.00
2 Peter Warrick 5.00
3 Tim Couch 6.00
4 Emmitt Smith 12.00
5 Olandis Gary 4.00
6 Marvin Harrison 4.00
7 Edgerrin James 10.00
8 Mark Brunell 6.00
9 Fred Taylor 6.00
10 Randy Moss 10.00
11 Ron Dayne 5.00
12 Chad Pennington 20.00

NM/M
13 Jerome Bettis 4.00
14 Plaxico Burress 10.00
15 Marshall Faulk 4.00
16 Kurt Warner 10.00
17 Jon Kitna 4.00
18 Eddie George 6.00
19 Shaun King 4.00
20 Stephen Davis 4.00

2000 Pacific Private Stock Extreme Action

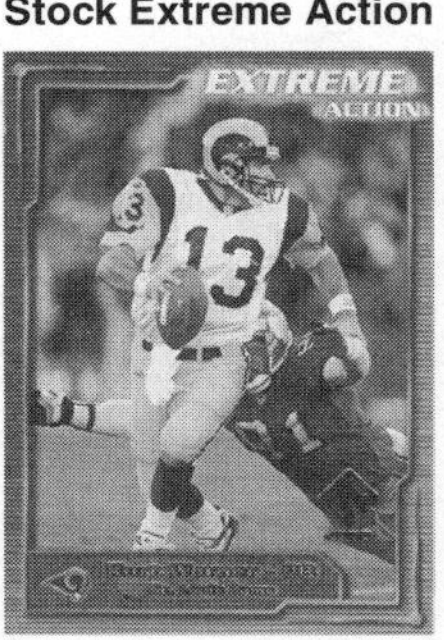

NM/M
Complete Set (20): 40.00
Common Player: 1.00
Inserted 2:23
1 Jake Plummer 1.00
2 Tim Couch 3.00
3 Emmitt Smith 4.00
4 Olandis Gary 1.00
5 Marvin Harrison 2.00
6 Edgerrin James 4.00
7 Mark Brunell 2.00
8 Fred Taylor 2.00
9 Randy Moss 4.00
10 Drew Bledsoe 3.00
11 Ricky Williams 4.00
12 Ron Dayne 3.00
13 Donovan McNabb 3.00
14 Isaac Bruce 1.00
15 Marshall Faulk 2.00
16 Kurt Warner 4.00
17 Jon Kitna 1.00
18 Shaun King 1.00
19 Steve McNair 2.00
20 Stephen Davis 1.00

2000 Pacific Private Stock Private Signings

NM/M
Common Player: 10.00
1 Thomas Jones 20.00
2 Jamal Lewis 30.00
3 Chris Redman 25.00
4 Travis Taylor 20.00
5 Dez White 15.00
6 Peter Warrick 25.00
7 Courtney Brown 25.00
8 JaJuan Dawson 10.00
9 Dennis Northcutt 10.00
10 Travis Prentice 10.00
11 Michael Wiley 10.00
12 Chris Cole 10.00
13 Reuben Droughns 10.00
14 Anthony Lucas 10.00
15 Rondell Mealey 10.00
16 R. Jay Soward 10.00
17 Shyrone Stith 10.00
18 Sylvester Morris 20.00
19 Quinton Spotwood 10.00
20 Troy Walters 10.00
21 J.R. Redmond 20.00
22 Marc Bulger 25.00
23 Ron Dayne 25.00
24 Laveranues Coles 10.00
25 Chad Pennington 60.00
26 Jerry Porter 10.00
27 Todd Pinkston 10.00
28 Plaxico Burress 40.00
29 Danny Farmer 15.00
30 Tee Martin 15.00
31 Chafie Fields 10.00
32 Tim Rattay 10.00
33 Shaun Alexander 50.00
34 Darrell Jackson 10.00
35 Joe Hamilton 15.00
36 Todd Husak 15.00

2000 Pacific Private Stock PS 2000 Action

NM/M
Complete Set (60): 25.00

NM/M
Common Player: .30
Minor Stars: .60
Inserted 2:1
1 Thomas Jones .75
2 Jake Plummer .60
3 Jamal Lewis 1.00
4 Chris Redman .75
5 Travis Taylor .60
6 Doug Flutie .60
7 Cade McNown .60
8 Marcus Robinson .60
9 Dez White .30
10 Akili Smith .60
11 Peter Warrick .60
12 Tim Couch .75
13 Dennis Northcutt .60
14 Travis Prentice .60
15 Troy Aikman 1.00
16 Emmitt Smith 1.25
17 Terrell Davis 1.25
18 Olandis Gary .60
19 Brian Griese .60
20 Reuben Droughns .30
21 Barry Sanders 1.50
22 Brett Favre 1.75
23 Antonio Freeman .30
24 Marvin Harrison .60
25 Edgerrin James 1.50
26 Peyton Manning 1.50
27 Mark Brunell .60
28 R. Jay Soward .30
29 Fred Taylor .75
30 Sylvester Morris .75
31 Dan Marino 1.50
32 Cris Carter .60
33 Randy Moss 1.50
34 Drew Bledsoe .75
35 J.R. Redmond .60
36 Ricky Williams .75
37 Ron Dayne .75
38 Laveranues Coles .60
39 Curtis Martin .60
40 Chad Pennington 2.00
41 Napoleon Kaufman .30
42 Donovan McNabb .60
43 Jerome Bettis .30
44 Plaxico Burress .75
45 Tee Martin .60
46 Isaac Bruce .60
47 Marshall Faulk .60
48 Kurt Warner 1.50
49 Giovanni Carmazzi .60
50 Terrell Owens .60
51 Jerry Rice 1.00
52 Shaun Alexander 1.00
53 Jon Kitna .60
54 Warrick Dunn .60
55 Joe Hamilton .60
56 Shaun King .60
57 Eddie George .60
58 Steve McNair .60
59 Stephen Davis .60
60 Brad Johnson .30

2000 Pacific Private Stock PS 2000 New Wave

NM/M
Complete Set (25): 85.00
Common Player: 2.00
Minor Stars: 4.00
Production 202 Sets
1 Jake Plummer 3.00
2 Eric Moulds 3.00
3 Cade McNown 2.00
4 Marcus Robinson 4.00
5 Akili Smith 2.00
6 Tim Couch 4.00
7 Kevin Johnson 2.00
8 Olandis Gary 4.00
9 Brian Griese 5.00
10 Marvin Harrison 5.00
11 Edgerrin James 8.00
12 Peyton Manning 8.00
13 Fred Taylor 4.00
14 Tony Gonzalez 2.00
15 Damon Huard 2.00
16 Randy Moss 8.00
17 Ricky Williams 6.00
18 Donovan McNabb 5.00
19 Duce Staley 4.00
20 Kurt Warner 6.00
21 Terrell Owens 4.00
22 Jon Kitna 2.00
23 Shaun King 2.00
24 Steve McNair 4.00
25 Stephen Davis 4.00

2000 Pacific Private Stock PS 2000 Rookies

NM/M
Complete Set (25): 125.00
Common Player: 2.00
Production 106 Sets

1 Thomas Jones 5.00
2 Jamal Lewis 12.00
3 Chris Redman 10.00
4 Travis Taylor 6.00
5 Dez White 2.00
6 Ron Dugans 2.00
7 Peter Warrick 4.00
8 Dennis Northcutt 5.00
9 Travis Prentice 8.00
10 Reuben Droughns 2.00
11 R. Jay Soward 2.00
12 Sylvester Morris 5.00
13 Troy Walters 2.00
14 J.R. Redmond 6.00
15 Ron Dayne 4.00
16 Laveranues Coles 8.00
17 Chad Pennington 18.00
18 Jerry Porter 8.00
19 Todd Pinkston 2.00
20 Plaxico Burress 12.00
21 Tee Martin 5.00
22 Giovanni Carmazzi 5.00
23 Shaun Alexander 12.00
24 Joe Hamilton 5.00
25 Todd Husak 2.00

2000 Pacific Private Stock PS 2000 Stars

NM/M
Complete Set (25): 65.00
Common Player: 2.00
Minor Stars: 4.00
Production 298 Sets

1 Jamal Anderson 3.00
2 Doug Flutie 3.00
3 Troy Aikman 5.00
4 Emmitt Smith 6.00
5 Terrell Davis 5.00
6 Herman Moore 2.00
7 Barry Sanders 6.00
8 Brett Favre 7.00
9 Antonio Freeman 3.00
10 Dorsey Levens 3.00
11 Mark Brunell 4.00
12 Dan Marino 7.00
13 Cris Carter 3.00
14 Robert Smith 3.00
15 Drew Bledsoe 5.00
16 Curtis Martin 4.00
17 Tim Brown 4.00
18 Napoleon Kaufman 2.00
19 Jerome Bettis 3.00
20 Isaac Bruce 3.00
21 Marshall Faulk 4.00
22 Jerry Rice 5.00
23 Warrick Dunn 3.00
24 Eddie George 3.00
25 Brad Johnson 2.00

2000 Pacific Private Stock Reserve

NM/M
Complete Set (20): 80.00
Common Player: 2.00
Inserted 1:23

1 Cade McNown 2.00
2 Peter Warrick 3.00
3 Tim Couch 4.00
4 Troy Aikman 5.00
5 Emmitt Smith 6.00
6 Terrell Davis 5.00
7 Barry Sanders 6.00
8 Brett Favre 7.00
9 Edgerrin James 5.00
10 Peyton Manning 5.00
11 Mark Brunell 3.00
12 Fred Taylor 3.00
13 Randy Moss 5.00
14 Ron Dayne 3.00
15 Chad Pennington 12.00
16 Marshall Faulk 3.00
17 Kurt Warner 5.00
18 Jerry Rice 5.00
19 Shaun Alexander 8.00
20 Eddie George 3.00

2000 Pacific Revolution

NM/M
Common Player: .20
Minor Stars: .40
Common Rookie: 2.00
Production 300 Sets
Pack (3plus Graded): 15.00
Wax Box (6): 70.00

1 David Boston 1.00

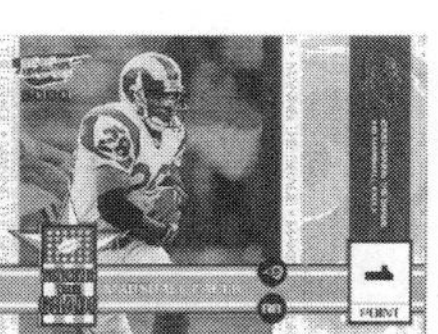

NM/M
2 Jake Plummer 1.00
3 Frank Sanders .40
4 Jamal Anderson 1.00
5 Chris Chandler .40
6 Tim Dwight .75
7 Terance Mathis .20
8 Tony Banks .40
9 Qadry Ismail .20
10 Shannon Sharpe .40
11 Rob Johnson .75
12 Eric Moulds 1.00
13 Peerless Price .75
14 Antowain Smith .40
15 Steve Beuerlein .40
16 Tshimanga Biakabutuka .40
17 Muhsin Muhammad .40
18 Curtis Enis .40
19 Cade McNown .75
20 Marcus Robinson 1.00
21 Corey Dillon 1.00
22 Akili Smith 1.00
23 Tim Couch 2.00
24 Kevin Johnson .75
25 Troy Aikman 2.50
26 Raghib Ismail .20
27 Emmitt Smith 3.00
28 Terrell Davis 1.50
29 Brian Griese 1.25
30 Ed McCaffrey .75
31 Charlie Batch 1.00
32 Herman Moore .75
33 James Stewart .40
34 Brett Favre 4.00
35 Antonio Freeman .75
36 Dorsey Levens .75
37 Marvin Harrison 1.00
38 Edgerrin James 2.50
39 Peyton Manning 3.00
40 Terrence Wilkins .40
41 Mark Brunell 1.50
42 Keenan McCardell .40
43 Jimmy Smith .75
44 Fred Taylor 1.50
45 Derrick Alexander .20
46 Tony Gonzalez .50
47 Elvis Grbac .50
48 Damon Huard .75
49 J.J. Johnson .40
50 O.J. McDuffie .40
51 Cris Carter 1.00
52 Daunte Culpepper 2.00
53 Randy Moss 3.00
54 Robert Smith 1.00
55 Drew Bledsoe 1.50
56 Terry Glenn 1.00
57 Jeff Blake .75
58 Ricky Williams 2.50
59 Tiki Barber .75
60 Kerry Collins .50
61 Ike Hilliard .40
62 Amani Toomer .40
63 Wayne Chrebet .75
64 Curtis Martin 1.00
65 Vinny Testaverde .75
66 Dedric Ward .40
67 Tim Brown .75
68 Napoleon Kaufman .50
69 Tyrone Wheatley .50
70 Charles Johnson .40
71 Donovan McNabb 2.00
72 Duce Staley 1.00
73 Jerome Bettis 1.00
74 Troy Edwards .50
75 Kordell Stewart .75
76 Isaac Bruce 1.00
77 Marshall Faulk 1.25
78 Az-Zahir Hakim .50
79 Torry Holt .75
80 Kurt Warner 3.00
81 Curtis Conway .40
82 Jermaine Fazande .50
83 Ryan Leaf .50
84 Junior Seau .40
85 Jeff Garcia 1.00
86 Charlie Garner .50
87 Terrell Owens 1.00
88 Jerry Rice 2.50
89 Jon Kitna .75
90 Derrick Mayes .40
91 Ricky Watters .75
92 Mike Alstott 1.00
93 Warrick Dunn 1.00
94 Keyshawn Johnson 1.00
95 Shaun King 1.00
96 Eddie George 1.25
97 Jevon Kearse 1.00
98 Steve McNair 1.00
99 Stephen Davis 1.00
100 Brad Johnson .75
101 *Thomas Jones* 15.00
102 *Doug Johnson* 10.00
103 *Jamal Lewis* 30.00
104 *Chris Redman* 12.00
105 *Travis Taylor* 15.00
106 *Avion Black* 2.00
107 *Kwame Cavil* 2.00
108 *Sammy Morris* 15.00
109 *Dez White* 10.00
110 *Ron Dugans* 4.00
111 *Danny Farmer* 10.00
112 *Curtis Keaton* 2.00
113 *Peter Warrick* 15.00
114 *Dennis Northcutt* 10.00
115 *Travis Prentice* 12.00
116 *Kevin Thompson* 2.00
117 *Spergon Wynn* 4.00
118 *Michael Wiley* 4.00
119 *Mike Anderson* 15.00
120 *Chris Cole* 2.00
121 *Jarious Jackson* 8.00
122 *Charles Lee* 2.00
123 *Anthony Lucas* 2.00
124 *R. Jay Soward* 10.00
125 *Shyrone Stith* 8.00
126 *Sylvester Morris* 10.00
127 *Doug Chapman* 6.00
128 *Tom Brady* 100.00
129 *Shockmain Davis* 3.00
130 *J.R. Redmond* 12.00
131 *Ron Dayne* 10.00
132 *Ron Dixon* 4.00
133 *Laveranues Coles* 15.00
134 *Windrell Hayes* 2.00
135 *Chad Pennington* 60.00
136 *Jerry Porter* 15.00
137 *Todd Pinkston* 10.00
138 *Plaxico Burress* 20.00
139 *Trung Canidate* 10.00
140 *Trevor Gaylor* 4.00
141 *Giovanni Carmazzi* 4.00
142 *Tim Rattay* 12.00
143 *Shaun Alexander* 30.00
144 *Darrell Jackson* 12.00
145 *James Williams* 2.00
146 *Joe Hamilton* 6.00
147 *Aaron Stecker* 4.00
148 *Billy Volek* 2.00
149 *Bashir Yamini* 2.00
150 *Todd Husak* 10.00

2000 Pacific Revolution Premiere Date

Premiere Date Cards: 5X-10X
Inserted 1:7
Production 85 Sets

2000 Pacific Revolution Red

Red Cards: 5X-10X
Production 99 Sets

2000 Pacific Revolution Silver

Silver Cards: 5X-10X
Production 80 Sets

2000 Pacific Revolution First Look

NM/M
Complete Set (36): 50.00
Common Player: .50
Minor Stars: 1.00
Inserted 4:25

1 Thomas Jones 2.00
2 Doug Johnson .50
3 Jamal Lewis 5.00
4 Chris Redman 3.00
5 Travis Taylor 2.50
6 Sammy Morris 2.50
7 Dez White 1.00
8 Ron Dugans .50
9 Curtis Keaton .50
10 Peter Warrick 2.00
11 Courtney Brown 1.00
12 Dennis Northcutt 1.00
13 Travis Prentice 3.00
14 Mike Anderson 5.00
15 Bubba Franks 1.00
16 R. Jay Soward 1.00
17 Frank Moreau 1.00
18 Sylvester Morris 4.00
19 Deon Dyer .50
20 Doug Chapman 3.00
21 Tom Brady 10.00
22 Aaron Brooks 1.00
23 Ron Dayne 3.00
24 Laveranues Coles 2.50
25 Chad Pennington 12.00
26 Jerry Porter 1.00
27 Todd Pinkston 1.00
28 Plaxico Burress 6.00
29 Tee Martin 2.50
30 Trung Canidate 1.00
31 JaJuan Seider .50
32 Giovanni Carmazzi 2.00
33 Paul Smith .50
34 Darrell Jackson 2.50
35 Shaun Alexander 5.00
36 Joe Hamilton 2.50

2000 Pacific Revolution Game Worn Jerseys

NM/M
Common Player: 15.00

1 Rod Woodson 1145 15.00
2 Jamir Miller 1295 15.00
3 Olandis Gary 75 35.00
4 Brett Favre 15 175.00
5 Mark Brunell 735 30.00
6 Keenan McCardell 679 15.00
7 Fred Taylor 380 35.00
8 Dan Marino 777 50.00
9 Cris Carter 235 35.00
10 Randy Moss 85 85.00
11 Drew Bledsoe 645 30.00
12 Ricky Williams 35 100.00
13 Koy Detmer 726 15.00
14 Torrance Small 481 15.00
15 Duce Staley 35 75.00
16 Jerome Bettis 65 30.00
17 Junior Seau 60 25.00
18 Jerry Rice 828 50.00
19 Brock Huard 20.00
20 Steve McNair 52 50.00

A player's name in *italic* type indicates a rookie card.

2000 Pacific Revolution Making The Grade Black

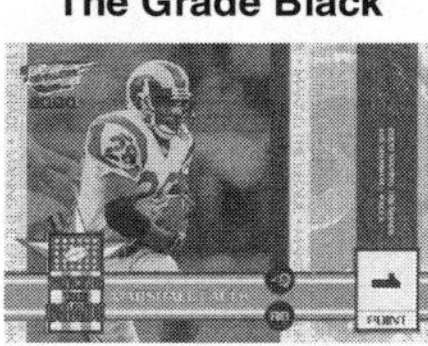

NM/M
Complete Set (20): 30.00
Common Player: .50
Inserted 4:13
Red Cards: 2X
Inserted 1:49
Gold Cards: 3X
Inserted 1:97

1 Peter Warrick 1.00
2 Tim Couch 2.00
3 Troy Aikman 3.00
4 Emmitt Smith 4.00
5 Terrell Davis 2.50
6 Brian Griese 1.50
7 Brett Favre 6.00
8 Peyton Manning 4.00
9 Edgerrin James 3.00
10 Mark Brunell 2.00
11 Fred Taylor 2.00
12 Randy Moss 4.00
13 Ricky Williams 2.50
14 Ron Dayne 2.00
15 Chad Pennington 4.00
16 Marshall Faulk 1.50
17 Kurt Warner 3.00
18 Jerry Rice 3.00
19 Eddie George 1.50
20 Steve McNair .50

2000 Pacific Revolution Ornaments

NM/M
Complete Set (20): 75.00
Common Player: 2.00
Inserted 1:25

1 Thomas Jones 4.00
2 Jake Plummer 2.00
3 Jamal Anderson 2.00
4 Jamal Lewis 10.00
5 Cade McNown 2.00
6 Corey Dillon 2.00
7 Peter Warrick 4.00
8 Troy Aikman 6.00
9 Emmitt Smith 7.00
10 Mike Anderson 6.00
11 Marvin Harrison 3.00
12 Edgerrin James 5.00
13 Peyton Manning 6.00
14 Mark Brunell 4.00
15 Daunte Culpepper 4.00
16 Ron Dayne 3.00
17 Plaxico Burress 8.00
18 Marshall Faulk 6.00
19 Kurt Warner 6.00
20 Jerry Rice 6.00

2000 Pacific Revolution Shields

NM/M
Complete Set (20): 90.00
Common Player: 3.00
Inserted 1:97

1 Peter Warrick 5.00
2 Tim Couch 6.00
3 Troy Aikman 6.00
4 Emmitt Smith 8.00
5 Terrell Davis 6.00
6 Brett Favre 10.00
7 Edgerrin James 6.00
8 Peyton Manning 6.00
9 Mark Brunell 4.00
10 Daunte Culpepper 5.00
11 Randy Moss 6.00
12 Drew Bledsoe 5.00
13 Ricky Williams 6.00
14 Chad Pennington 15.00
15 Marshall Faulk 5.00
16 Kurt Warner 7.00
17 Eddie George 4.00
18 Steve McNair 3.00
19 Stephen Davis 3.00
20 Brad Johnson 3.00

2000 Pacific Vanguard

NM/M
Common Player: .15
Minor Stars: .50
Common Rookie: 5.00
Production 762 Sets
Pack (4): 3.00
Wax Box (24): 50.00

1 Tony Banks .50
2 Priest Holmes .50
3 Qadry Ismail .15
4 Doug Flutie 1.00
5 Rob Johnson .50
6 Eric Moulds .75
7 Peerless Price .75
8 Antowain Smith .75
9 Corey Dillon .75
10 Darnay Scott .50
11 Akili Smith 1.00
12 Tim Couch 2.00
13 Kevin Johnson .75
14 Terry Kirby .15
15 Terrell Davis 1.50
16 Olandis Gary 1.00
17 Brian Griese 1.00
18 Ed McCaffrey .50
19 Rod Smith .75
20 Marvin Harrison .75
21 Edgerrin James 2.00
22 Peyton Manning 2.50
23 Terrence Wilkins .75
24 Mark Brunell 1.25
25 Keenan McCardell .50
26 Jimmy Smith .75
27 Fred Taylor 1.50
28 Derrick Alexander .15
29 Donnell Bennett .15
30 Tony Gonzalez .50
31 Elvis Grbac .50
32 Damon Huard .50
33 J.J. Johnson .50
34 Dan Marino 2.50
35 Tony Martin .15
36 O.J. McDuffie .15
37 Drew Bledsoe 1.25
38 Kevin Faulk .50
39 Terry Glenn .75
40 Wayne Chrebet .50
41 Ray Lucas .75
42 Curtis Martin .75
43 Vinny Testaverde .75
44 Tim Brown .50
45 Rich Gannon .50
46 Napoleon Kaufman .75
47 Tyrone Wheatley .50
48 Jerome Bettis .75
49 Troy Edwards .50
50 Richard Huntley .50
51 Kordell Stewart .75
52 Jermaine Fazande .50
53 Jim Harbaugh .50
54 Mikhael Ricks .15
55 Junior Seau .50
56 Brock Huard .50
57 Jon Kitna .75
58 Derrick Mayes .50
59 Ricky Watters .50
60 Eddie George 1.00
61 Jevon Kearse 1.00
62 Steve McNair 1.00
63 Yancy Thigpen .15
64 David Boston .75
65 Rob Moore .50
66 Jake Plummer .75
67 Frank Sanders .15
68 Jamal Anderson .75
69 Chris Chandler .50
70 Tim Dwight .75
71 Terance Mathis .15
72 Steve Beuerlein .50
73 Tshimanga Biakabutuka .50
74 Patrick Jeffers .15
75 Muhsin Muhammad .50
76 Bobby Engram .15
77 Curtis Enis .75
78 Cade McNown 1.25
79 Marcus Robinson .75
80 Troy Aikman 1.75
81 Raghib Ismail .15
82 Emmitt Smith 2.25
83 Jason Tucker .15
84 Chris Warren .15
85 Charlie Batch .75
86 Germane Crowell .75
87 Herman Moore .50
88 Johnnie Morton .15
89 Barry Sanders 2.50
90 Brett Favre 3.00
91 Antonio Freeman .75
92 Dorsey Levens .75
93 Bill Schroeder .15
94 Cris Carter .75
95 Daunte Culpepper 1.25
96 Randy Moss 2.00
97 Robert Smith .75
98 Cameron Cleeland .50
99 Keith Poole .15
100 Ricky Williams 2.00
101 Tiki Barber .75
102 Kerry Collins .50
103 Ike Hilliard .50
104 Amani Toomer .50
105 Charles Johnson .15
106 Donovan McNabb 1.25
107 Torrance Small .15
108 Duce Staley .75
109 Isaac Bruce .75
110 Marshall Faulk .75
111 Torry Holt .75
112 Kurt Warner 2.00
113 Charlie Garner .50
114 Terrell Owens .75
115 Jerry Rice 1.75
116 J.J. Stokes .50
117 Steve Young 1.25
118 Mike Alstott .75
119 Reidel Anthony .50
120 Warrick Dunn .75
121 Jacquez Green .50
122 Shaun King 1.25
123 Stephen Davis .75
124 Brad Johnson .50
125 Michael Westbrook .50
126 *Thomas Jones* 15.00
127 *Jamal Lewis* 30.00
128 *Chris Redman* 15.00
129 *Travis Taylor* 15.00
130 *Dez White* 15.00
131 *Ron Dugans* 10.00
132 *Peter Warrick* 20.00
133 *Dennis Northcutt* 10.00
134 *Travis Prentice* 10.00
135 *Reuben Droughns* 10.00
136 *R. Jay Soward* 10.00
137 *Sylvester Morris* 10.00
138 *Troy Walters* 10.00
139 *Tom Brady* 50.00
140 *J.R. Redmond* 15.00
141 *Marc Bulger* 25.00
142 *Ron Dayne* 15.00
143 *Laveranues Coles* 20.00
144 *Chad Pennington* 50.00
145 *Jerry Porter* 20.00
146 *Plaxico Burress* 25.00
147 *Trung Canidate* 15.00
148 *Giovanni Carmazzi* 10.00
149 *Shaun Alexander* 30.00
150 *Todd Husak* 10.00

2000 Pacific Vanguard Premiere Date

Premiere Date Cards: 5X-10X
Production 138 Sets

2000 Pacific Vanguard Purple

Purple Cards: 5X-10X

2000 Pacific Vanguard Cosmic Force

NM/M
Complete Set (10): 40.00
Common Player: 3.00
Inserted 1:73

1 Tim Couch 3.00
2 Troy Aikman 4.00
3 Emmitt Smith 5.00
4 Terrell Davis 4.00
5 Barry Sanders 5.00
6 Brett Favre 6.00
7 Edgerrin James 4.00
8 Peyton Manning 4.00
9 Randy Moss 4.00
10 Kurt Warner 4.00

2000 Pacific Vanguard Game-Worn Jerseys

NM/M
Common Player: 10.00
Randomly Inserted

1 Cris Carter 25.00
2 Randall Cunningham 25.00
3 Randy Moss 35.00
4 Ricky Williams 35.00
5 Wayne Chrebet 20.00
6 Koy Detmer 10.00
7 Donovan McNabb 25.00
8 Torrance Small 10.00
9 Duce Staley 20.00
10 Jerome Bettis 20.00
11 Kordell Stewart 20.00
12 Jerry Rice 35.00
13 Steve Young 30.00
14 Steve McNair 25.00

2000 Pacific Vanguard Game-Worn Jerseys Duals

NM/M
Common Player: 45.00
Production 200 Sets

1 Cris Carter, Randy Moss 100.00
2 Ricky Williams, Jerome Bettis 100.00
3 Duce Staley, Donovan McNabb 85.00
4 Jerome Bettis, Kordell Stewart 45.00
5 Jerry Rice, Randy Moss 125.00
6 Steve Young, Steve McNair 60.00

2000 Pacific Vanguard Game-Worn Jerseys Dual Patches

NM/M
Inserted 1:5,000

1 Olandis Gary, Ricky Williams 12 100.00
2 Mark Brunell, Steve Young 15 150.00
3 Cris Carter, Randy Moss 25 200.00
4 Jerome Bettis, Kordell Stewart 35 125.00

5 Jerry Rice, Randy Moss 19 250.00
6 Steve McNair, Donovan McNabb 25 125.00

2000 Pacific Vanguard Gridiron Architects

NM/M
Complete Set (20): 40.00
Common Player: 1.00
Inserted 1:25
1 Jake Plummer 1.00
2 Cade McNown 1.00
3 Tim Couch 3.00
4 Troy Aikman 4.00
5 Emmitt Smith 5.00
6 Terrell Davis 4.00
7 Brett Favre 6.00
8 Edgerrin James 4.00
9 Peyton Manning 4.00
10 Fred Taylor 2.00
11 Dan Marino 6.00
12 Randy Moss 4.00
13 Drew Bledsoe 3.00
14 Curtis Martin 1.00
15 Terrell Owens 1.00
16 Marshall Faulk 2.00
17 Kurt Warner 4.00
18 Shaun King 1.00
19 Eddie George 2.00
20 Stephen Davis 1.00

2000 Pacific Vanguard High Voltage

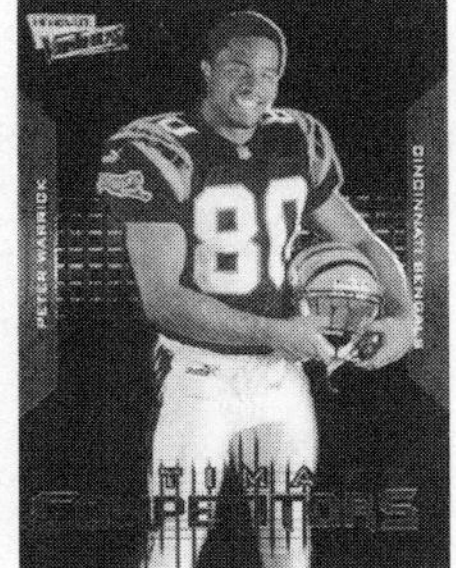

NM/M
Complete Set (36): 18.00
Common Player: .50
Inserted 1:1
Gold Cards: 3X-8X
Production 199 Sets
Green Cards: 5X-10X
Production 99 Sets
Red Cards: 2X-4X
Production 299 Sets
1 Thomas Jones 1.00
2 Jamal Lewis 1.50
3 Eric Moulds .50
4 Marcus Robinson .50
5 Corey Dillon .50
6 Peter Warrick 1.00
7 Tim Couch 1.00
8 Kevin Johnson .50
9 Emmitt Smith 1.25
10 Olandis Gary .75
11 Brian Griese .75
12 Charlie Batch .50
13 Antonio Freeman .50
14 Marvin Harrison .50
15 Edgerrin James 1.50
16 Mark Brunell .75
17 Fred Taylor .75
18 Damon Huard .50
19 Cris Carter .50
20 Daunte Culpepper .75
21 Randy Moss 1.50
22 Ron Dayne 1.00
23 Curtis Martin .50
24 Chad Pennington 4.00
25 Jerome Bettis .50
26 Plaxico Burress 2.00
27 Isaac Bruce .50
28 Marshall Faulk .50
29 Kurt Warner 1.75
30 Giovanni Carmazzi 1.00
31 Shaun Alexander 1.50
32 Jon Kitna .50
33 Eddie George .50
34 Warrick Dunn .50
35 Shaun King .75
36 Stephen Davis .50

2000 Pacific Vanguard Press Hobby

NM/M
Complete Set (10): 15.00
Common Player: 1.00
Inserted 2:25 Hobby
1 Peter Warrick 1.00
2 Tim Couch 1.50
3 Terrell Davis 2.00
4 Edgerrin James 3.00
5 Peyton Manning 3.00
6 Fred Taylor 1.25
7 Drew Bledsoe 1.25
8 Chad Pennington 5.00
9 Jon Kitna 1.00
10 Eddie George 1.00

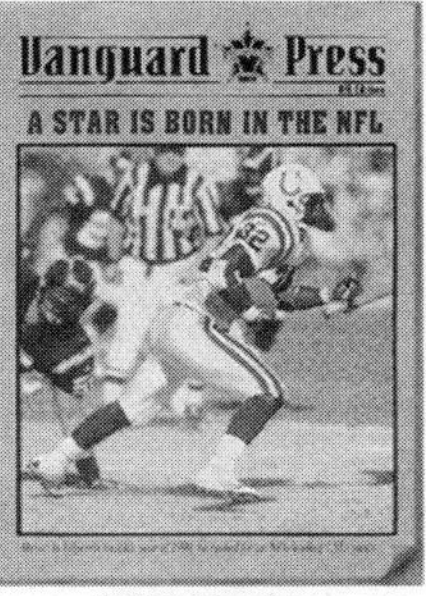

Vanguard Press
A STAR IS BORN IN THE NFL

2000 Pacific Vanguard Press Retail

NM/M
Complete Set (10): 15.00
Common Player: 1.00
Inserted 2:25 Retail
1 Thomas Jones 1.00
2 Cade McNown 1.00
3 Troy Aikman 1.75
4 Emmitt Smith 2.00
5 Brett Favre 3.00
6 Randy Moss 2.00
7 Ron Dayne 1.00
8 Marshall Faulk 1.00
9 Kurt Warner 2.00
10 Stephen Davis 1.00

2001 Pacific National Convention (Brown Royale)

NM/M
Complete Set (9): 10.00
Common Player: 1.00
1 Spergon Wynn, Drew Brees 2.00
2 Tim Couch, Marques Tuiasosopo 2.00
3 Errict Rhett, Anthony Thomas 1.00
4 Jamel White, James Jackson 1.00
5 Travis Prentice, LaDainian Tomlinson 3.00
6 Dennis Northcutt, Koren Robinson 1.00
7 JaJuan Dawson, Rod Gardner 1.00
8 Kevin Johnson, David Terrell 1.00
9 Quincy Morgan, Santana Moss 2.00

2001 Pacific

NM/M
Common Player: .15
Minor Stars: .30
Common Rookie: 2.00
Rookie QB Numbered to 1,000
Rookie RB Numbered to 1,500
Rookie WR Numbered to 1,750
Rookie Other Numbered to 2,500
Pack (10): 2.00
Wax Box (36): 50.00
1 David Boston .50
2 Mac Cody .15
3 Chris Gedney .15
4 Chris Griesen .15
5 Terry Hardy .15
6 Mar Tay Jenkins .15
7 Thomas Jones .50
8 Joel Makovicka .15
9 Tywan Mitchell .15
10 Rob Moore .15
11 Michael Pittman .15
12 Jake Plummer .50
13 Frank Sanders .15
14 Aeneas Williams .15
15 Jamal Anderson .50
16 Eugene Baker .15
17 Chris Chandler .30
18 Tim Dwight .30
19 Brian Finneran .15
20 Jammi German .15
21 Shawn Jefferson .15
22 Doug Johnson .30
23 Danny Kanell .15
24 Reggie Kelly .15
25 Terance Mathis .15
26 Derek Rackley .15
27 Ron Rivers .15
28 Maurice Smith .15
29 Sam Adams .15
30 Obafemi Ayanbadejo .15
31 Tony Banks .30
32 Trent Dilfer .30
33 Sam Gash .15
34 Priest Holmes .30
35 Qadry Ismail .15
36 Pat Johnson .15
37 Jamal Lewis 1.50
38 Jermaine Lewis .15
39 Ray Lewis .30
40 Chris Redman .75
41 Shannon Sharpe .30
42 Brandon Stokley .15
43 Travis Taylor .50
44 Shawn Bryson .15
45 Kwame Cavil .15
46 Sam Cowart .15
47 Doug Flutie .75
48 Rob Johnson .30
49 Jonathon Linton .15
50 Jeremy McDaniel .15
51 Sammy Morris .50
52 Eric Moulds .50
53 Peerless Price .30
54 Jay Riemersma .15
55 Antowain Smith .30
56 Chris Watson .15
57 Marcellus Wiley .15
58 Michael Bates .15
59 Steve Beuerlein .30
60 Tshimanga Biakabutuka .30
61 Isaac Byrd .15
62 Dameyune Craig .30
63 William Floyd .15
64 Karl Hankton .15
65 Donald Hayes .15
66 Chris Hetherington .15
67 Brad Hoover .50
68 Patrick Jeffers .30
69 Muhsin Muhammad .30
70 Iheanyi Uwaezuoke .15
71 Wesley Walls .15
72 James Allen .30
73 Marlon Barnes .15
74 D'Wayne Bates .15
75 Marty Booker .15
76 Macey Brooks .15
77 Bobby Engram .15
78 Curtis Enis .30
79 Mark Hartsell .15
80 Eddie Kennison .15
81 Shane Matthews .15
82 Cade McNown .50
83 Jim Miller .15
84 Marcus Robinson .50
85 Brian Urlacher 1.00
86 Dez White .15
87 Brandon Bennett .15
88 Steve Bush .15
89 Corey Dillon .50
90 Ron Dugans .15
91 Danny Farmer .15
92 Damon Griffin .15
93 Clif Groce .15
94 Curtis Keaton .15
95 Scott Mitchell .15
96 Darnay Scott .15
97 Akili Smith .50
98 Peter Warrick 1.00
99 Nick Williams .15
100 Craig Yeast .15
101 Bobby Brown .15
102 Darrin Chiaverini .15
103 Tim Couch .75
104 JaJuan Dawson .15
105 Marc Edwards .15
106 Kevin Johnson .30
107 Dennis Northcutt .30
108 David Patten .15
109 Doug Pederson .15
110 Travis Prentice .50
111 Errict Rhett .15
112 Aaron Shea .15
113 Kevin Thompson .15
114 Jamel White .15
115 Spergon Wynn .15
116 Troy Aikman 1.00
117 Chris Brazzell .15
118 Randall Cunningham .30
119 Jackie Harris .15
120 Damon Hodge .15
121 Raghib Ismail .15
122 David LaFleur .15
123 Wane McGarity .15
124 James McKnight .15
125 Emmitt Smith 1.25
126 Clint Stoerner .50
127 Jason Tucker .15
128 Michael Wiley .30
129 Anthony Wright .30
130 Mike Anderson 1.25
131 Dwayne Carswell .15
132 Byron Chamberlain .15
133 Desmond Clark .15
134 Chris Cole .15
135 KaRon Coleman .15
136 Terrell Davis 1.25
137 Gus Frerotte .15
138 Olandis Gary .50
139 Brian Griese .50
140 Howard Griffith .15
141 Jarious Jackson .15
142 Ed McCaffrey .30
143 Scottie Montgomery .15
144 Rod Smith .30
145 Charlie Batch .30
146 Stoney Case .15
147 Germane Crowell .30
148 Larry Foster .15
149 Desmond Howard .15
150 Sedrick Irvin .15
151 Herman Moore .30
152 Johnnie Morton .15
153 Robert Porcher .15
154 Cory Sauter .15
155 Cory Schlesinger .15
156 David Sloan .15
157 Brian Stablein .15
158 James Stewart .30
159 Corey Bradford .15
160 Tyrone Davis .15
161 Donald Driver .15
162 Brett Favre 2.00
163 Bubba Franks .30
164 Antonio Freeman .30
165 Herbert Goodman .15
166 Ahman Green .30
167 Matt Hasselbeck .50
168 William Henderson .15
169 Charles Lee .15
170 Dorsey Levens .30
171 Bill Schroeder .30
172 Darren Sharper .15
173 Matt Snider .15
174 Danny Wuerffel .15
175 Ken Dilger .15
176 Jim Finn .15
177 Lennox Gordon .15
178 E.G. Green .15
179 Marvin Harrison .50
180 Kelly Holcomb .15
181 Trevor Insley .15
182 Edgerrin James 1.50
183 Peyton Manning 1.50
184 Kevin McDougal .15
185 Jerome Pathon .15
186 Marcus Pollard .15
187 Justin Snow .15
188 Terrence Wilkins .15
189 Reggie Barlow .15
190 Kyle Brady .15
191 Mark Brunell .75
192 Kevin Hardy .15
193 Anthony Johnson .15
194 Stacey Mack .15
195 Jamie Martin .15
196 Keenan McCardell .30
197 Daimon Shelton .15
198 Jimmy Smith .50
199 R. Jay Soward .15
200 Shyrone Stith .15
201 Fred Taylor .60
202 Alvis Whitted .15
203 Jermaine Williams .15
204 Derrick Alexander .15
205 Kimble Anders .15
206 Donnell Bennett .15
207 Mike Cloud .15
208 Todd Collins .15
209 Tony Gonzalez .30
210 Elvis Grbac .30
211 Dante Hall .15
212 Kevin Lockett .15
213 Warren Moon .30
214 Frank Moreau .15
215 Sylvester Morris .50
216 Larry Parker .15
217 Tony Richardson .15
218 Trace Armstrong .15
219 Autry Denson .15
220 Bert Emanuel .15
221 Jay Fiedler .30
222 Oronde Gadsden .15
223 Damon Huard .30
224 J.J. Johnson .15
225 Rob Konrad .15
226 Tony Martin .15
227 O.J. McDuffie .30
228 Mike Quinn .15
229 Lamar Smith .50
230 Jason Taylor .15
231 Thurman Thomas .30
232 Zach Thomas .15
233 Todd Bouman .15
234 Bubby Brister .30
235 Cris Carter .50
236 Daunte Culpepper 1.00
237 John Davis .15
238 Robert Griffith .15
239 Matthew Hatchette .15
240 Jim Kleinsasser .15
241 Randy Moss 1.50
242 John Randle .30
243 Robert Smith .30
244 Chris Walsh .15
245 Troy Walters .15
246 Moe Williams .15
247 Michael Bishop .50
248 Drew Bledsoe .75
249 Troy Brown .15
250 Tedy Bruschi .15
251 Tony Carter .15
252 Shockmain Davis .15
253 Kevin Faulk .30
254 Terry Glenn .50
255 Ty Law .15
256 Lawyer Milloy .15
257 J.R. Redmond .30
258 Harold Shaw .15
259 Tony Simmons .30
260 Jermaine Wiggins .15
261 Jeff Blake .30
262 Aaron Brooks .50
263 Cameron Cleeland .30
264 Andrew Glover .15
265 La'Roi Glover .15
266 Joe Horn .30
267 Kevin Houser .15
268 Willie Jackson .15
269 Jerald Moore .15
270 Chad Morton .30
271 Keith Poole .15
272 Terrelle Smith .30
273 Ricky Williams .75
274 Robert Wilson .15
275 Jessie Armstead .15
276 Tiki Barber .50
277 Mike Cherry .15
278 Kerry Collins .30
279 Greg Comella .15
280 Thabiti Davis .15
281 Ron Dayne 1.00
282 Ron Dixon .30
283 Ike Hilliard .30
284 Joe Jurevicius .30
285 Jason Sehorn .15
286 Michael Strahan .15
287 Amani Toomer .30
288 Craig Walendy .15
289 Damon Washington .15
290 Richie Anderson .15
291 Anthony Becht .15
292 Wayne Chrebet .30
293 Laveranues Coles .50
294 Bryan Cox .15
295 Marvin Jones .15
296 Mo Lewis .15
297 Ray Lucas .30
298 Curtis Martin .50
299 Bernie Parmalee .15
300 Chad Pennington 1.00
301 Jerald Sowell .15
302 Dwight Stone .15
303 Vinny Testaverde .30
304 Dedric Ward .15
305 Tim Brown .30
306 Zack Crockett .15
307 Scott Dreisbach .15
308 Rickey Dudley .15
309 David Dunn .15
310 Mondriel Fulcher .15
311 Rich Gannon .30
312 James Jett .15
313 Randy Jordan .15
314 Napoleon Kaufman .30
315 Rodney Peete .15
316 Jerry Porter .30
317 Andre Rison .30
318 Tyrone Wheatley .30
319 Charles Woodson .30
320 Darnell Autry .30
321 Na Brown .15
322 Hugh Douglas .15
323 Charles Johnson .15
324 Chad Lewis .15
325 Cecil Martin .15
326 Donovan McNabb .75
327 Brian Mitchell .15
328 Todd Pinkston .30
329 Ron Powlus .30
330 Stanley Pritchett .15
331 Torrance Small .15
332 Duce Staley .50
333 Troy Vincent .15
334 Chris Warren .30
335 Jerome Bettis .50
336 Plaxico Burress .50
337 Troy Edwards .30
338 Chris Fuamatu-Ma'afala .15
339 Cory Geason .15
340 Kent Graham .15
341 Courtney Hawkins .15
342 Richard Huntley .15
343 Tee Martin .30
344 Bobby Shaw .30
345 Kordell Stewart .50
346 Hines Ward .30
347 Destry Wright .15
348 Amos Zereoue .15
349 Isaac Bruce .50
350 Trung Canidate .30
351 Marshall Faulk .60
352 London Fletcher .15
353 Joe Germaine .30
354 Trent Green .50
355 Az-Zahir Hakim .30
356 James Hodgins .15
357 Robert Holcombe .15
358 Torry Holt .30
359 Tony Horne .15
360 Ricky Proehl .15
361 Chris Thomas .15
362 Kurt Warner 1.75
363 Justin Watson .15
364 Kenny Bynum .15
365 Robert Chancey .15
366 Curtis Conway .15
367 Jermaine Fazande .30
368 Terrell Fletcher .15
369 Trevor Gaylor .15
370 Jeff Graham .15
371 Jim Harbaugh .30
372 Rodney Harrison .15
373 Ronney Jenkins .15
374 Freddie Jones .15
375 Reggie Jones .30
376 Ryan Leaf .30
377 Junior Seau .30
378 Fred Beasley .15
379 Greg Clark .15
380 Jeff Garcia .50
381 Charlie Garner .30
382 Terry Jackson .15
383 Brian Jennings .15
384 Travis Jervey .15
385 Jonas Lewis .15
386 Terrell Owens .50
387 Jerry Rice 1.00
388 Paul Smith .15
389 J.J. Stokes .30
390 Tai Streets .30
391 Justin Swift .15
392 Shaun Alexander .50
393 Karsten Bailey .15
394 Chad Brown .15
395 Sean Dawkins .15
396 Christian Fauria .15
397 Brock Huard .30
398 Darrell Jackson .30
399 Jon Kitna .30
400 Derrick Mayes .30
401 Itula Mili .15
402 Charlie Rogers .15
403 Mack Strong .15
404 Ricky Watters .30
405 James Williams .15
406 Rabih Abdullah .15
407 Mike Alstott .50
408 Reidel Anthony .15
409 Derrick Brooks .15
410 Warrick Dunn .50
411 Jacquez Green .30
412 Joe Hamilton .30
413 Keyshawn Johnson .50
414 Shaun King .50
415 *Charles Kirby* 1.00
416 Warren Sapp .30
417 Aaron Stecker .15
418 Todd Yoder .15
419 Eric Zeier .15
420 Chris Coleman .15
421 Kevin Dyson .30
422 Eddie George .60
423 Jevon Kearse .50
424 Erron Kinney .15
425 Mike Leach .15
426 Derrick Mason .30
427 Steve McNair .50
428 Lorenzo Neal .15
429 Carl Pickens .30
430 Chris Sanders .15
431 Yancey Thigpen .15
432 Rodney Thomas .15
433 Frank Wycheck .15
434 Stephen Alexander .15
435 Champ Bailey .30
436 Larry Centers .15
437 Albert Connell .15
438 Stephen Davis .50
439 Zeron Flemister .15
440 Irving Fryar .15
441 Jeff George .30
442 Skip Hicks .15
443 Todd Husak .30
444 Brad Johnson .30
445 Adrian Murrell .15
446 Deion Sanders .50
447 Mike Sellers .15
448 Derrius Thompson .15
449 James Thrash .30
450 Michael Westbrook .30
451 *Alex Bannister AUTO* 10.00
452 *Kevan Barlow AUTO* 10.00
453 *Drew Brees AUTO* 75.00
454 *Travis Henry AUTO* 20.00
455 *Chad Johnson AUTO* 15.00
456 *Mike McMahon AUTO* 15.00
457 *Bobby Newcombe AUTO* 15.00
458 *Sage Rosenfels AUTO* 20.00
459 *LaDainian Tomlinson AUTO* 60.00
460 *Chris Weinke AUTO* 35.00
461 *Tay Cody* 4.00
462 *Adam Archuleta* 4.00
463 *Will Allen* 4.00
464 *Moran Norris* 4.00
465 *Tommy Polley* 4.00
466 *Ennis Davis* 4.00
467 *Jamar Fletcher* 5.00
468 *Derrick Gibson* 4.00
469 *Sedrick Hodge* 4.00
470 *Willie Howard* 4.00
471 *Steve Hutchinson* 4.00
472 *Michael Stone* 2.00
473 *Vinny Sutherland* 6.00
474 *Joe Tafoya* 2.00
475 *Maurice Williams* 4.00
476 *Pork Chop Womack* 4.00
477 *Chad Ward* 4.00
478 *Scotty Anderson* 4.00
479 *Gary Baxter* 4.00
480 *Marques Tuiasosopo* 15.00
481 *Tim Hasselbeck* 8.00
482 *Clevan Thomas* 4.00
483 *Marcus Stroud* 4.00
484 *John Schlecht* 2.00
485 *Brandon Spoon* 4.00
486 *Alex Lincoln* 4.00
487 *Anthony Thomas* 30.00
488 *Freddie Mitchell* 10.00
489 *Brian Allen* 4.00
490 *Zeke Moreno* 4.00
491 *Tony Driver* 4.00
492 *Kynan Forney* 2.00
493 *Reggie Wayne* 12.00
494 *Larry Casher* 4.00
495 *Fred Wakefield* 4.00
496 *Jeff Backus* 4.00
497 *Jarrod Cooper* 2.00
498 *Heath Evans* 4.00
499 *James Jackson* 8.00
500 *Jabari Holloway* 4.00
501 *Quincy Morgan* 10.00
502 *Josh Booty* 8.00
503 *Ja'Mar Toombs* 4.00
504 *Jason McKinley* 6.00
505 *Reggie White* 5.00
506 *Todd Heap* 5.00
507 *Rudi Johnson* 6.00
508 *Marvin "Snoop" Minnis* 5.00
509 *David Terrell* 20.00
510 *Torrance Marshall* 4.00
511 *Michael Bennett* 25.00
512 *Chris Chambers* 15.00
513 *Ben Leard* 6.00
514 *Rod Gardner* 12.00
515 *Michael Vick* 75.00
516 *Josh Heupel 1000 RED* 20.00
517 *Jesse Palmer 1000 RED* 12.00
518 *Quincy Carter 1000 RED* 12.00
519 *A.J. Freely 1000 RED* 8.00
520 *David Rivers 1000 RED* 8.00
521 *Deuce McAllister 1500 RED* 25.00
522 *LaMont Jordan 1500 RED* 15.00
523 *David Allen 1500 RED* 10.00
524 *Correll Buckhelter 1500 RED* 10.00
525 *Travis Minor 1500 RED* 10.00
526 *Koren Robinson 1750 RED* 20.00
527 *Santana Moss 1750 RED* 20.00
528 *Robert Ferguson 1750 RED* 15.00
529 *T.J. Houshmandzadeh 1750 RED* 10.00
530 *Cedrick Wilson 1750 RED* 10.00

2001 Pacific Hobby LTD

LTD Cards: 12X-24X
Production 99 Sets

2001 Pacific Retail LTD

Retail LTD Cards: 6X-12X
Production 299 Sets

2001 Pacific Premier Date

Premiere Date Cards: 15X-30X
Production 45 Sets

2001 Pacific All-Rookie Team

NM/M
Complete Set (10): 35.00
Common Player: 4.00
Inserted 1:37
1 Kevan Barlow 5.00
2 Travis Henry 5.00
3 Chad Johnson 4.00
4 LaDainian Tomlinson 10.00
5 Chris Weinke 6.00
6 Drew Brees 12.00
7 Anthony Thomas 5.00
8 Freddie Mitchell 5.00
9 Reggie Wayne 5.00
10 Marques Tuiasosopo 6.00

2001 Pacific Cramer's Choice Awards

NM/M
Complete Set (10): 200.00
Common Player: 12.00
Production 99 Sets
1 Trent Dilfer 12.00
2 Jamal Lewis 25.00
3 Emmitt Smith 40.00
4 Brett Favre 60.00
5 Edgerrin James 40.00
6 Peyton Manning 40.00
7 Randy Moss 40.00
8 Marshall Faulk 25.00
9 Kurt Warner 35.00
10 Eddie George 20.00

2001 Pacific Game-Worn Jerseys

NM/M
Common Player: 20.00
Production 99 Sets
1 Thomas Jones 25.00
2 Jake Plummer 15.00
3 Rod Woodson 20.00
4 Rob Johnson 20.00
5 Corey Dillon 25.00
6 Akili Smith 25.00
7 Peter Warrick 15.00
8 Mark Brunell 25.00
9 Keenan McCardell 20 35.00
10 Fred Taylor 30.00
11 Dan Marino 120.00
12 Trent Green 25.00
13 Kurt Warner 80.00
14 Jerry Rice 20 100.00
15 Brock Huard 20 40.00

2001 Pacific Game-Used Footballs

NM/M
Common Player: 20.00
Production 99 Sets
1 Jamal Lewis 40.00
2 Peter Warrick 25.00
3 Mike Anderson 40.00
4 Edgerrin James 45.00
5 Daunte Culpepper 40.00
6 Randy Moss 45.00
7 Ron Dayne 25.00
8 Marshall Faulk 35.00
9 Kurt Warner 35.00
10 Eddie George 20.00

2001 Pacific Gold Crown Die-Cuts

NM/M
Complete Set (30): 80.00
Common Player: 1.00
Minor Stars: 2.00
Inserted 1:73
1 Jamal Lewis 5.00
2 Corey Dillon 2.00
3 Peter Warrick 3.00
4 Troy Aikman 6.00
5 Emmitt Smith 8.00
6 Mike Anderson 6.00
7 Terrell Davis 5.00
8 Brian Griese 4.00
9 Brett Favre 10.00
10 Marvin Harrison 4.00
11 Edgerrin James 6.00
12 Peyton Manning 6.00
13 Mark Brunell 4.00
14 Fred Taylor 4.00
15 Cris Carter 2.00
16 Daunte Culpepper 5.00
17 Randy Moss 7.00
18 Drew Bledsoe 5.00
19 Ricky Williams 6.00
20 Kerry Collins 1.00
21 Ron Dayne 3.00
22 Curtis Martin 2.00
23 Donovan McNabb 5.00
24 Jerome Bettis 2.00
25 Isaac Bruce 2.00
26 Marshall Faulk 5.00
27 Kurt Warner 5.00
28 Jeff Garcia 2.00
29 Jerry Rice 7.00
30 Steve McNair 2.00

2001 Pacific Impact Zone

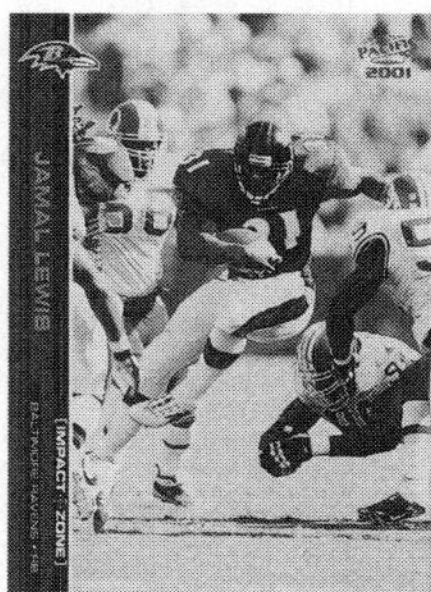

NM/M
Complete Set (20): 40.00
Common Player: 1.00
Minor Stars: 2.00
Inserted 1:37
1 Jamal Lewis 4.00
2 Corey Dillon 2.00
3 Peter Warrick 2.00
4 Emmitt Smith 5.00
5 Mike Anderson 3.00
6 Brian Griese 2.00
7 Edgerrin James 4.00
8 Mark Brunell 2.50
9 Fred Taylor 2.50
10 Randy Moss 4.00
11 Ricky Williams 2.50
12 Ron Dayne 3.00
13 Curtis Martin 2.00
14 Rich Gannon 1.00
15 Donovan McNabb 3.00
16 Marshall Faulk 2.50
17 Jerry Rice 5.00
18 Mike Alstott 2.00
19 Warrick Dunn 2.00
20 Eddie George 2.50

2001 Pacific Pro Bowl Die-Cuts

NM/M
Complete Set (20): 40.00
Common Player: 1.50
Minor Stars: 3.00
Inserted 1:37
1 Eric Moulds 3.00
2 Corey Dillon 3.00
3 Marvin Harrison 3.00
4 Edgerrin James 5.00
5 Peyton Manning 5.00
6 Jimmy Smith 1.50
7 Tony Gonzalez 1.50
8 Elvis Grbac 1.50
9 Cris Carter 3.00
10 Daunte Culpepper 5.00
11 Joe Horn 1.50
12 Rich Gannon 1.50
13 Donovan McNabb 4.00
14 Torry Holt 3.00
15 Jeff Garcia 3.00
16 Terrell Owens 3.00
17 Warrick Dunn 3.00
18 Eddie George 4.00
19 Derrick Mason 1.50
20 Stephen Davis 3.00

2001 Pacific War Room

NM/M
Complete Set (20): 35.00
Common Player: 1.00
Inserted 2:37
1 Alex Bannister 1.00
2 Kevan Barlow 3.00
3 Travis Henry 3.00
4 Chad Johnson 3.00
5 Mike McMahon 3.00
6 Sage Rosenfels 3.00
7 LaDainian Tomlinson 10.00
8 Chris Weinke 4.00
9 Drew Brees 12.00
10 Anthony Thomas 5.00
11 Freddie Mitchell 4.00
12 Reggie Wayne 4.00
13 Marques Tuiasosopo 5.00
14 Quincy Morgan 4.00
15 Josh Booty 1.00
16 Tim Hasselbeck 4.00
17 James Jackson 1.00
18 Rudi Johnson 1.00
19 Marvin Minnis 1.00
20 Bobby Newcombe 3.00

2001 Pacific Canvas Impressions

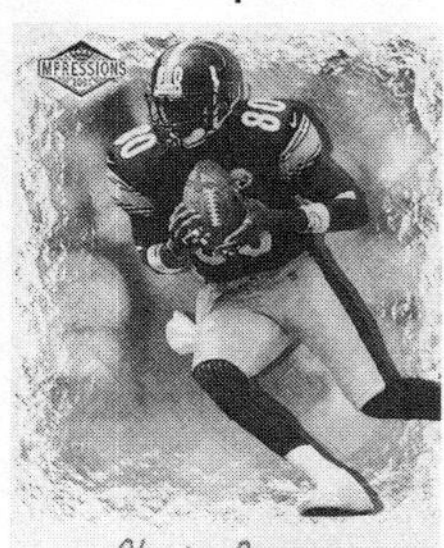

NM/M
Complete Set (144): 75.00
Common Player: .30
Minor Stars: .60
Common Rookie: 5.00
Inserted 1:17
Production 117 Sets
Pack (3): 6.00
Wax Box (16): 75.00
1 David Boston 1.00
2 Thomas Jones .60
3 Rob Moore .30
4 Michael Pittman .60
5 Jake Plummer 1.00
6 Jamal Anderson 1.00
7 Chris Chandler .60
8 Shawn Jefferson .30
9 Terance Mathis .30
10 Elvis Grbac .75
11 Qadry Ismail .60
12 Jamal Lewis 2.75
13 Ray Lewis .75
14 Shannon Sharpe .60
15 Shawn Bryson .30
16 Rob Johnson .75
17 Sammy Morris .60
18 Eric Moulds 1.00
19 Peerless Price 1.00
20 Tim Biakabutuka .60
21 Richard Huntley .30
22 Patrick Jeffers .75
23 Jeff Lewis .30
24 Muhsin Muhammad .75
25 James Allen .75
26 Marcus Robinson 1.00
27 Brian Urlacher 2.50
28 Corey Dillon 1.25
29 Jon Kitna .75
30 Akili Smith .75
31 Peter Warrick 1.25
32 Tim Couch 1.50
33 Kevin Johnson .75
34 Dennis Northcutt .60
35 Travis Prentice .75
36 Joey Galloway 1.00
37 Raghib Ismail .60
38 Emmitt Smith 3.00
39 Mike Anderson 2.25
40 Terrell Davis 2.75
41 Brian Griese 1.25
42 Ed McCaffrey 1.00
43 Rod Smith 1.00
44 Charlie Batch 1.00
45 Germane Crowell .75
46 Herman Moore .60
47 Johnnie Morton .30
48 James Stewart .60
49 Brett Favre 5.00
50 Antonio Freeman 1.25
51 Ahman Green 1.25
52 Dorsey Levens .60
53 Bill Schroeder .60
54 Marvin Harrison 1.25
55 Edgerrin James 3.50
56 Peyton Manning 4.00
57 Jerome Pathon .30
58 Terrence Wilkins .60
59 Mark Brunell 1.25
60 Keenan McCardell .60
61 Jimmy Smith 1.00
62 Fred Taylor 1.25
63 Derrick Alexander .60
64 Tony Gonzalez .75
65 Trent Green .75
66 Priest Holmes 1.00
67 Jay Fiedler 1.00
68 Oronde Gadsden .60
69 O.J. McDuffie .60
70 Cade McNown .75
71 Lamar Smith 1.00
72 Zach Thomas .75
73 Cris Carter 1.25
74 Daunte Culpepper 2.50
75 Randy Moss 4.00
76 Moe Williams .30
77 Drew Bledsoe 1.50
78 Kevin Faulk .60
79 Charles Johnson .30
80 J.R. Redmond .60
81 Jeff Blake .75
82 Aaron Brooks 1.25
83 Albert Connell .60
84 Joe Horn 1.00
85 Ricky Williams 2.00
86 Tiki Barber .75
87 Kerry Collins 1.00
88 Ron Dayne 2.50
89 Ike Hilliard .60
90 Amani Toomer .60
91 Richie Anderson .30
92 Wayne Chrebet 1.00
93 Laveranues Coles 1.00
94 Curtis Martin 1.25
95 Chad Pennington 2.00
96 Vinny Testaverde 1.00
97 Tim Brown 1.25
98 Rich Gannon 1.00
99 Charlie Garner .75
100 Jerry Rice 2.75
101 Tyrone Wheatley .60
102 Charles Woodson .75
103 Darnell Autry .30
104 Donovan McNabb 2.00
105 Duce Staley .60
106 James Thrash .60
107 Jerome Bettis 1.25
108 Plaxico Burress 1.25
109 Bobby Shaw .60
110 Kordell Stewart 1.25
111 Hines Ward .75
112 Isaac Bruce 1.25
113 Marshall Faulk 1.50
114 Az-Zahir Hakim 1.00
115 Torry Holt 1.25
116 Kurt Warner 5.00
117 Curtis Conway .60
118 Tim Dwight .75
119 Doug Flutie 1.25
120 Jeff Graham .30
121 Jeff Garcia 1.25
122 Garrison Hearst 1.25
123 Terrell Owens 1.25
124 J.J. Stokes 1.00
125 Tai Streets 1.00
126 Shaun Alexander 1.50
127 Matt Hasselbeck 1.00
128 Darrell Jackson 1.00
129 Ricky Watters 1.25
130 Mike Alstott 1.25
131 Warrick Dunn 1.25
132 Jacquez Green .75
133 Brad Johnson 1.00
134 Keyshawn Johnson 1.25
135 Warren Sapp .75
136 Kevin Dyson .60
137 Eddie George 1.50
138 Jevon Kearse 1.00
139 Derrick Mason 1.00
140 Steve McNair 1.00
141 Champ Bailey 1.00
142 Stephen Davis 1.25
143 Jeff George 1.00
144 Michael Westbrook 1.00
145 *Bobby Newcombe* 10.00
146 *Corey Brown* 10.00
147 *Quentin McCord* 5.00
148 *Vinny Sutherland* 12.00
149 *Michael Vick* 80.00
150 *Chris Barnes* 12.00
151 *Tim Hasselbeck* 10.00
152 *Todd Heap* 12.00
153 *Nate Clements* 10.00
154 *Reggie Germany* 10.00
155 *Travis Henry* 25.00
156 *Dee Brown* 5.00
157 *Dan Morgan* 12.00
158 *Steve Smith* 10.00
159 *Chris Weinke* 30.00
160 *David Terrell* 40.00
161 *Anthony Thomas* 40.00
162 *T.J. Houshmandzadeh* 10.00
163 *Chad Johnson* 12.00
164 *Rudi Johnson* 12.00
165 *James Jackson* 15.00
166 *Andre King* 8.00
167 *Quincy Morgan* 15.00
168 *Quincy Carter* 30.00
169 *Kevin Kasper* 12.00
170 *Scotty Anderson* 10.00
171 *Mike McMahon* 25.00
172 *Robert Ferguson* 12.00
173 *Jamal Reynolds* 10.00
174 *Reggie Wayne* 20.00
175 *Marcus Stroud* 10.00
176 *Derrick Blaylock* 10.00
177 *Ryan Helming* 10.00
178 *Marvin "Snoop" Minnis* 20.00
179 *Chris Chambers* 30.00
180 *Josh Heupel* 15.00
181 *Travis Minor* 12.00
182 *Michael Bennett* 35.00
183 *Deuce McAllister* 40.00
184 *Onomo Ojo* 5.00
185 *Will Allen* 10.00
186 *Jonathan Carter* 10.00
187 *Jesse Palmer* 12.00
188 *Corey Alston* 5.00
189 *LaMont Jordan* 15.00
190 *Santana Moss* 25.00
191 *Derek Combs* 10.00
192 *Derrick Gibson* 10.00
193 *Ken-Yon Rambo* 10.00
194 *Marques Tuiasosopo* 25.00
195 *Correll Buckhalter* 20.00
196 *Freddie Mitchell* 20.00
197 *Chris Taylor* 10.00
198 *Adam Archuleta* 12.00
199 *Damione Lewis* 10.00
200 *Francis St.Paul* 10.00
201 *Milton Wynn* 10.00
202 *Drew Brees* 50.00
203 *LaDainian Tomlinson* 50.00
204 *Kevan Barlow* 20.00
205 *Andre Carter* 12.00
206 *Cedrick Wilson* 8.00
207 *Alex Bannister* 12.00
208 *Josh Booty* 12.00
209 *Heath Evans* 8.00
210 *Ken Lucas* 8.00
211 *Koren Robinson* 25.00
212 *Dan Alexander* 12.00
213 *Eddie Berlin* 10.00
214 *Rod Gardner* 25.00
215 *Darnerian McCants* 8.00
216 *Sage Rosenfels* 15.00

2001 Pacific Canvas Impressions Premiere Date

Premiere Date Cards: 9X-18X
Premiere Date Rookies: 2X
Inserted 1:17
Production 50 Sets

2001 Pacific Canvas Impressions Red Backs

Red Back Stars: 2X-4X
Red Back Rookies: 80%
Inserted 2:4
Production 280 Sets

2001 Pacific Canvas Impressions Classic Images

NM/M
Complete Set (10): 40.00
Common Player: 4.00
Inserted 1:65
1 Emmitt Smith 5.00
2 Terrell Davis 4.00
3 Brett Favre 8.00
4 Edgerrin James 6.00
5 Peyton Manning 6.00
6 Daunte Culpepper 5.00
7 Randy Moss 6.00
8 Jerry Rice 8.00
9 Donovan McNabb 6.00
10 Kurt Warner 6.00

2001 Pacific Canvas Impressions First Impressions

NM/M
Complete Set (20): 85.00
Common Player: 3.00
Inserted 1:33
1 Michael Vick 15.00
2 Travis Henry 5.00
3 Chris Weinke 6.00
4 David Terrell 7.00
5 Anthony Thomas 10.00
6 Chad Johnson 3.00
7 Quincy Carter 6.00
8 Reggie Wayne 4.00
9 Chris Chambers 6.00
10 Michael Bennett 8.00
11 Deuce McAllister 5.00
12 Jesse Palmer 3.00
13 LaMont Jordan 3.00
14 Santana Moss 5.00
15 Marques Tuiasosopo 5.00
16 Freddie Mitchell 5.00
17 Drew Brees 12.00
18 LaDainian Tomlinson 12.00
19 Rod Gardner 5.00
20 Sage Rosenfels 3.00

2001 Pacific Canvas Impressions Future Foundations

NM/M
Common Player: 25.00
Inserted 1:257
Production 50 Sets
1 Michael Vick 70.00
2 Chris Weinke 35.00
3 David Terrell 40.00
4 Michael Bennett 40.00
5 Deuce McAllister 30.00
6 Santana Moss 25.00
7 Freddie Mitchell 25.00
8 Drew Brees 50.00
9 LaDainian Tomlinson 60.00
10 Koren Robinson 25.00

2001 Pacific Canvas Impressions Lasting Impressions

NM/M
Complete Set (20): 45.00
Common Player: 1.00
Inserted 1:17
1 Jamal Lewis 3.00
2 Peter Warrick 1.00
3 Emmitt Smith 5.00
4 Mike Anderson 3.00
5 Terrell Davis 4.00
6 Brian Griese 2.00
7 Brett Favre 6.00
8 Edgerrin James 4.00
9 Peyton Manning 4.00
10 Mark Brunell 2.00
11 Daunte Culpepper 4.00
12 Randy Moss 4.00
13 Drew Bledsoe 2.00
14 Ricky Williams 3.00
15 Ron Dayne 2.00
16 Jerry Rice 4.00
17 Donovan McNabb 3.00
18 Marshall Faulk 2.00
19 Kurt Warner 4.00
20 Eddie George 2.00

2001 Pacific Canvas Impressions Renderings

NM/M
Complete Set (20): 35.00
Common Player: 1.00
Inserted 2:17
1 Michael Vick 6.00
2 Travis Henry 2.00
3 Chris Weinke 3.00
4 David Terrell 3.50
5 Anthony Thomas 3.00
6 Chad Johnson 1.00
7 James Jackson 1.25
8 Quincy Carter 2.75
9 Reggie Wayne 1.50
10 Chris Chambers 2.50
11 Michael Bennett 3.00
12 Deuce McAllister 2.00
13 LaMont Jordan 1.00
14 Santana Moss 2.00
15 Marques Tuiasosopo 2.00
16 Freddie Mitchell 2.00
17 Drew Brees 3.00
18 LaDainian Tomlinson 4.00
19 Kevan Barlow 1.50
20 Rod Gardner 2.00

2001 Pacific Canvas Impressions Triple Threads

NM/M
Common Player: 12.00
Inserted 3:17
1 David Boston, Thomas Jones, Jake Plummer 20.00
2 Joel Makovicka, Dennis McKinley, Stephen Davis 12.00
3 Jamal Anderson, Mike Alstott, Stephen Davis 20.00
4 Qadry Ismail, Pat Johnson, Brandon Stokley 12.00
5 Tim Biakabutuka, Brad Hoover, Muhsin Muhammad 12.00
6 Chris Weinke, Marques Tuiasosopo, Drew Brees 40.00

7 Richard Huntley, Dan Kreider, Amos Zereoue 15.00
8 Shane Matthews, Cade McNown, Jim Miller 18.00
9 Bobby Engram, Marcus Robinson, Dez White 20.00
10 Ron Dugans, Danny Farmer, Craig Yeast 12.00
11 Steve Bush, Tony McGee, Brad St. Louis 12.00
12 Corey Dillon, Ricky Watters, Eddie George 25.00
13 JaJuan Dawson, Travis Prentice, Errict Rhett 12.00
14 Tim Couch, Troy Aikman, Kurt Warner 45.00
15 Desmond Clark, KaRon Coleman, Howard Griffith 12.00
16 Gus Frerotte, Ed McCaffrey, Rod Smith 20.00
17 Brian Griese, Brett Favre, Drew Bledsoe 60.00
18 Terrell Davis, Curtis Martin, LaDainian Tomlinson 50.00
19 Charlie Batch, Johnnie Morton, James Stewart 18.00
20 Herbert Goodman, Ahman Green, Dorsey Levens 18.00
21 Marvin Harrison, Edgerrin James, Peyton Manning 55.00
22 Ken Dilger, Lennox Gordon, Terrence Wilkins 12.00
23 Mark Brunell, Jimmy Smith, Fred Taylor 20.00
24 Jay Fiedler, Oronde Gadsden, Lamar Smith 20.00
25 Cris Carter, Daunte Culpepper, Randy Moss 60.00
26 Shockmain Davis, Kevin Faulk, Terry Glenn 15.00
27 Jeff Blake, Aaron Brooks, Joe Horn 20.00
28 Tiki Barber, Kerry Collins, Ron Dayne 25.00
29 Wayne Chrebet, Dwight Stone, Vinny Testaverde 15.00
30 Tim Brown, Rich Gannon, Tyrone Wheatley 25.00
31 Plaxico Burress, Troy Edwards, Courtney Hawkins 25.00
32 Giovanni Carmazzi, Rick Mirer, Tim Rattay 18.00
33 Shaun Alexander, Darrell Jackson, James Williams 20.00
34 Reggie Brown, Charlie Rogers, Mack Strong 12.00
35 Reidel Anthony, Jacquez Green, Keyshawn Johnson 18.00

2001 Pacific Canvas Impressions Shadow

NM/M
Shadow Cards: 15X-30X
Shadow Rookies: 3X
Inserted 1:65
Production 25 Sets

2001 Pacific Crown Royale

NM/M
Common Player: .25
Minor Stars: .50
Common Rookie: 4.00
Production 1,750 Sets
Pack (6): 5.00
Wax Box (20): 90.00
1 David Boston .75
2 Thomas Jones .75
3 Rob Moore .50
4 Michael Pittman .50
5 Jake Plummer .75
6 Jamal Anderson .75
7 Chris Chandler .50
8 Tim Dwight .50
9 Shawn Jefferson .25
10 Doug Johnson .75
11 Terance Mathis .25
12 Tony Banks .50
13 Trent Dilfer .50
14 Priest Holmes .50
15 Qadry Ismail .25
16 Jamal Lewis 2.50
17 Ray Lewis .50
18 Shannon Sharpe .50
19 Shawn Bryson .25
20 Doug Flutie .75
21 Rob Johnson .50
22 Eric Moulds .75
23 Peerless Price .50
24 Antowain Smith .50
25 Steve Beuerlein .50
26 Tim Biakabutuka .50
27 Patrick Jeffers .50
28 Muhsin Muhammad .50
29 James Allen .75
30 Bobby Engram .25
31 Cade McNown .75
32 Marcus Robinson .75
33 Brian Urlacher 1.50
34 Corey Dillon .75
35 Akili Smith .75
36 Peter Warrick 1.50
37 Tim Couch 1.00
38 Kevin Johnson .50
39 Travis Prentice .75
40 Troy Aikman 1.25
41 Raghib Ismail .25
42 James McKnight .25
43 Emmitt Smith 2.00
44 Mike Anderson 1.00
45 Terrell Davis 2.00
46 Olandis Gary .75
47 Brian Griese .75
48 Ed McCaffrey .50
49 Rod Smith .50
50 Charlie Batch .75
51 Herman Moore .50
52 Johnnie Morton .50
53 James Stewart .50
54 Brett Favre 3.00
55 Antonio Freeman .50
56 Ahman Green .50
57 Dorsey Levens .50
58 Bill Schroeder .50
59 Marvin Harrison .75
60 Edgerrin James 2.50
61 Peyton Manning 2.50
62 Jerome Pathon .25
63 Mark Brunell 1.00
64 Keenan McCardell .50
65 Jimmy Smith .75
66 Fred Taylor 1.00
67 Derrick Alexander .25
68 Tony Gonzalez .50
69 Elvis Grbac .50
70 Sylvester Morris .75
71 Tony Richardson .25
72 Jay Fiedler .75
73 Oronde Gadsden .50
74 Tony Martin .25
75 Lamar Smith .75
76 Cris Carter .75
77 Daunte Culpepper 1.50
78 Randy Moss 2.50
79 Robert Smith .50
80 Drew Bledsoe 1.00
81 Troy Brown .25
82 Kevin Faulk .50
83 Terry Glenn .75
84 J.R. Redmond .75
85 Jeff Blake .50
86 Aaron Brooks .75
87 Joe Horn .50
88 Ricky Williams 1.25
89 Tiki Barber .50
90 Kerry Collins .75
91 Ron Dayne 1.50
92 Ike Hilliard .50
93 Amani Toomer .50
94 Wayne Chrebet .75
95 Curtis Martin .75
96 Chad Pennington 1.50
97 Vinny Testaverde .50
98 Dedric Ward .50
99 Tim Brown .50
100 Rich Gannon .50
101 Napoleon Kaufman .50
102 Andre Rison .50
103 Tyrone Wheatley .75
104 Charles Johnson .50
105 Donovan McNabb 1.25
106 Torrance Small .25
107 Duce Staley .75
108 Jerome Bettis .75
109 Plaxico Burress .75
110 Kordell Stewart .75
111 Hines Ward .50
112 Isaac Bruce .75
113 Marshall Faulk 1.00
114 Trent Green .75
115 Az-Zahir Hakim .50
116 Torry Holt .75
117 Kurt Warner 3.00
118 Curtis Conway .25
119 Jeff Graham .25
120 Ryan Leaf .50
121 Junior Seau .50
122 Jeff Garcia .75
123 Charlie Garner .50
124 Terrell Owens .75
125 Jerry Rice 1.75
126 Shaun Alexander 1.00
127 Darrell Jackson .50
128 Jon Kitna .50
129 Ricky Watters .75
130 Mike Alstott .75
131 Warrick Dunn .75
132 Keyshawn Johnson .75
133 Shaun King .50
134 Warren Sapp .50
135 Kevin Dyson .25
136 Eddie George 1.00
137 Jevon Kearse .75
138 Derrick Mason .25
139 Steve McNair .75
140 Stephen Davis .75
141 Jeff George .50
142 Brad Johnson .50
143 Deion Sanders .75
144 Michael Westbrook .50
145 *Michael Bennett 250* 100.00
146 *Drew Brees 250* 125.00
147 *Chris Chambers 250* 75.00
148 *Rod Gardner 250* 50.00
149 *David Terrell 250* 90.00
150 *Anthony Thomas 250* 125.00
151 *LaDainian Tomlinson 250* 160.00
152 *Marques Tuiasosopo 250* 45.00
153 *Michael Vick 250* 200.00
154 *Chris Weinke 250* 75.00
155 *Dan Alexander 1750* 8.00
156 *Brian Allen 1750* 4.00
157 *David Allen 1750* 4.00
158 *Will Allen 1750* 4.00
159 *Scotty Anderson 1000* 8.00
160 *Adam Archuleta 1750* 6.00
161 *Jeff Backus 1750* 4.00
162 *Alex Bannister 1000* 6.00
163 *Kevan Barlow 750* 18.00
164 *Gary Baxter 1750* 4.00
165 *Josh Booty 500* 15.00
166 *Larry Casher 1750* 4.00
167 *Tay Cody 1750* 4.00
168 *Jarrod Cooper 1750* 4.00
169 *Ennis Davis 1750* 4.00
170 *Leonard Davis 1750* 4.00
171 *Tony Dixon 1750* 4.00
172 *Tony Driver 1750* 6.00
173 *Heath Evans 1750* 4.00
174 *Jamar Fletcher 1750* 6.00
175 *Derrick Gibson 1750* 4.00
176 *Morlon Greenwood 1750* 4.00
177 *Edgerton Hartwell 1750* 4.00
178 *Tim Hasselbeck 500* 16.00
179 *Todd Heap 1750* 6.00
180 *Travis Henry 750* 30.00
181 *Josh Heupel 500* 30.00
182 *Sedrick Hodge 1750* 4.00
183 *Jabari Holloway 1750* 5.00
184 *Willie Howard 1750* 4.00
185 *Steve Hutchinson 1750* 4.00
186 *James Jackson 750* 15.00
187 *Chad Johnson 1000* 7.00
188 *Rudi Johnson 750* 15.00
189 *LaMont Jordan 750* 18.00
190 *Ben Leard 500* 12.00
191 *Alex Lincoln 1750* 4.00
192 *Torrance Marshall 1750* 6.00
193 *Deuce McAllister 750* 45.00
194 *Jason McKinley 500* 12.00
195 *Mike McMahon 500* 18.00
196 *Marvin "Snoop" Minnis 1000* 16.00
197 *Travis Minor 750* 18.00
198 *Freddie Mitchell 1000* 20.00
199 *Zeke Moreno 1750* 4.00
200 *Santana Moss 1000* 25.00
201 *Quincy Morgan 1000* 12.00
202 *Bobby Newcombe 1000* 4.00
203 *Moran Norris 1750* 4.00
204 *Tommy Polley 1750* 4.00
205 *Ken-Yon Rambo 1000* 10.00
206 *Koren Robinson 1000* 25.00
207 *Sage Rosenfels 500* 6.00
208 *John Schlecht 1750* 4.00
209 *Brandon Spoon 1750* 4.00
210 *Michael Stone 1750* 4.00
211 *Marcus Stroud 1750* 6.00
212 *Vinny Sutherland 1000* 8.00
213 *Joe Tafoya 1750* 4.00
214 *Clevan Thomas 1750* 4.00
215 *Ja'Mar Toombs 1750* 4.00
216 *Fred Wakefield 1750* 4.00
217 *Reggie Wayne 1000* 25.00
218 *Reggie White 750* 10.00

2001 Pacific Crown Royale Coming Soon

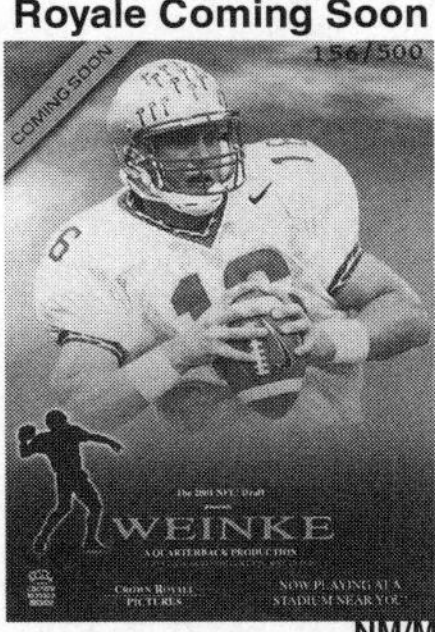

NM/M
Complete Set (10): 100.00
Common Player: 6.00
Production 500 Sets
1 Drew Brees 25.00
2 Chris Chambers 6.00
3 Rod Gardner 12.00
4 Travis Henry 10.00
5 Deuce McAllister 15.00
6 David Terrell 18.00
7 Anthony Thomas 12.00
8 LaDainian Tomlinson 20.00
9 Michael Vick 35.00
10 Chris Weinke 12.00

2001 Pacific Crown Royale Cramer's Choice Jumbos

NM/M
Complete Set (10): 100.00
Common Player: 10.00
Inserted 1:Box
1 Jamal Lewis 25.00
2 Corey Dillon 10.00
3 Peter Warrick 20.00
4 Brett Favre 35.00
5 Fred Taylor 15.00
6 Daunte Culpepper 25.00
7 Randy Moss 30.00
8 Ricky Williams 15.00
9 Marshall Faulk 20.00
10 Kurt Warner 30.00

A player's name in *italic* type indicates a rookie card.

2001 Pacific Crown Royale Game-Worn Jerseys

NM/M
Complete Set (15): 350.00
Common Player: 15.00
1 Thomas Jones 277 20.00
2 Rob Johnson 277 20.00
3 Thurman Thomas 276 25.00
4 Corey Dillon 277 25.00
5 Peter Warrick 277 35.00
6 Brett Favre 277 100.00
7 Jay Fiedler 521 15.00
8 Lamar Smith 506 20.00
9 Aaron Brooks 523 25.00
10 Joe Horn 522 15.00
11 Ricky Williams 519 25.00
12 Marshall Faulk 277 30.00
13 Az-Zahir Hakim 519 15.00
14 Torry Holt 523 20.00
15 Kurt Warner 277 100.00

2001 Pacific Crown Royale Jewels of the Crown

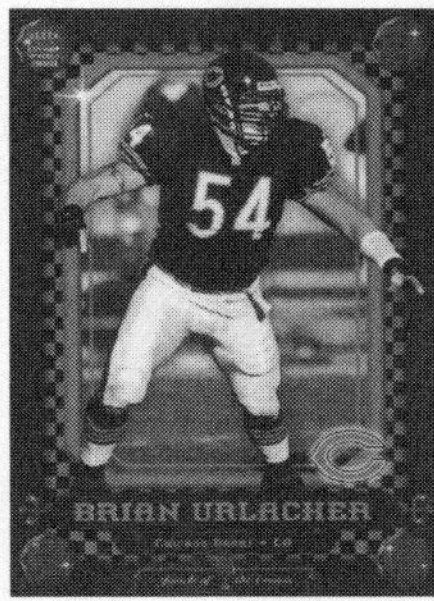

NM/M
Complete Set (25): 15.00
Common Player: .50
Inserted 1:1
1 Trent Dilfer .50
2 Brian Urlacher 1.50
3 Corey Dillon .75
4 Peter Warrick 1.25
5 Tim Couch 1.00
6 Emmitt Smith 2.00
7 Mike Anderson 2.00
8 Brian Griese .75
9 Marvin Harrison .75
10 Edgerrin James 2.00
11 Mark Brunell 1.00
12 Fred Taylor .75
13 Daunte Culpepper 1.50
14 Randy Moss 2.50
15 Drew Bledsoe 1.00
16 Ron Dayne 1.25
17 Curtis Martin .75
18 Rich Gannon .50
19 Jerome Bettis .75
20 Marshall Faulk 1.00
21 Kurt Warner 2.50
22 Jeff Garcia .75
23 Eddie George 1.00
24 Steve McNair .75
25 Stephen Davis .75

2001 Pacific Crown Royale Landmarks

NM/M
Complete Set (10): 200.00
Common Player: 15.00
Production 99 Sets
1 Emmitt Smith 35.00
2 Brian Griese 15.00
3 Brett Favre 45.00
4 Edgerrin James 40.00
5 Peyton Manning 40.00
6 Ricky Williams 20.00
7 Marshall Faulk 20.00
8 Kurt Warner 40.00
9 Jerry Rice 30.00
10 Eddie George 20.00

2001 Pacific Crown Royale Living Legends

NM/M
Complete Set (20): 100.00
Common Player: 1.75
Production 950 Sets
1 Tim Couch 5.00
2 Troy Aikman 7.00
3 Emmitt Smith 10.00
4 Terrell Davis 8.00
5 Brian Griese 4.00
6 Brett Favre 15.00
7 Edgerrin James 12.00
8 Mark Brunell 5.00
9 Daunte Culpepper 8.00
10 Cris Carter 3.00
11 Randy Moss 12.00
12 Drew Bledsoe 5.00
13 Ricky Williams 6.00
14 Marshall Faulk 4.00
15 Kurt Warner 12.00
16 Junior Seau 1.75
17 Jerry Rice 8.00
18 Eddie George 5.00
19 Steve McNair 1.75
20 Stephen Davis 1.75

2001 Pacific Crown Royale Now Playing

NM/M
Complete Set (20): 100.00
Common Player: 1.75
Production 1,000 Sets
1 Peter Warrick 6.00
2 Tim Couch 4.00
3 Troy Aikman 8.00
4 Emmitt Smith 10.00
5 Terrell Davis 8.00
6 Brian Griese 3.00
7 Brett Favre 15.00
8 Edgerrin James 12.00
9 Mark Brunell 3.00
10 Daunte Culpepper 8.00
11 Randy Moss 12.00
12 Drew Bledsoe 3.00
13 Ricky Williams 5.00
14 Ron Dayne 5.00
15 Marshall Faulk 3.00
16 Kurt Warner 12.00
17 Jeff Garcia 3.00
18 Jerry Rice 8.00
19 Eddie George 3.00
20 Steve McNair 1.75

2001 Pacific Crown Royale Pro Bowl Honors

NM/M
Complete Set (20): 70.00
Common Player: 1.75
Production 850 Sets
1 Eric Moulds 3.00
2 Corey Dillon 3.00
3 Brian Griese 3.00
4 Marvin Harrison 3.00
5 Peyton Manning 12.00
6 Edgerrin James 12.00
7 Jimmy Smith 1.75
8 Tony Gonzalez 1.75
9 Elvis Grbac 1.75
10 Cris Carter 3.00
11 Daunte Culpepper 8.00
12 Randy Moss 12.00
13 Rich Gannon 1.75
14 Marshall Faulk 3.50
15 Torry Holt 3.00
16 Kurt Warner 15.00
17 Jeff Garcia 3.00
18 Terrell Owens 3.00
19 Warrick Dunn 3.00
20 Eddie George 3.50

2001 Pacific Crown Royale Rookie Jumbos

NM/M
Complete Set (25): 250.00
Common Player: 6.00
Production 499 Sets
1 Dan Alexander 6.00
2 Alex Bannister 6.00
3 Kevan Barlow 6.00
4 Michael Bennett 25.00
5 Drew Brees 35.00
6 Chris Chambers 8.00
7 Rod Gardner 15.00
8 Travis Henry 12.00
9 Chad Johnson 8.00
10 Rudi Johnson 8.00
11 LaMont Jordan 8.00
12 Ben Leard 6.00
13 Deuce McAllister 20.00
14 Mike McMahon 8.00
15 Freddie Mitchell 8.00
16 Quincy Morgan 8.00
17 Koren Robinson 15.00
18 Sage Rosenfels 8.00
19 David Terrell 25.00
20 Anthony Thomas 15.00
21 LaDainian Tomlinson 30.00
22 Marques Tuiasosopo 12.00
23 Michael Vick 45.00
24 Reggie Wayne 12.00
25 Chris Weinke 20.00

2001 Pacific Crown Royale Rookie Signatures

NM/M
Common Player: 10.00
Production 500 Sets
1 Scotty Anderson 10.00
2 Alex Bannister 10.00
3 Kevan Barlow 10.00
4 Michael Bennett 100 85.00
5 Josh Booty 10.00
6 Drew Brees 100 120.00
7 Chris Chambers 250 25.00
8 Heath Evans 10.00
9 Jamar Fletcher 10.00
10 Rod Gardner 20.00
11 Tim Hasselbeck 12.00
12 Todd Heap 10.00
13 Travis Henry 18.00
14 Jabari Holloway 10.00
15 James Jackson 12.00
16 Chad Johnson 12.00
17 Rudi Johnson 12.00
18 Ben Leard 10.00
19 Jason McKinley 10.00
20 Mike McMahon 12.00
21 Marvin "Snoop" Minnis 15.00
22 Freddie Mitchell 18.00
23 Quincy Morgan 10.00
24 Bobby Newcombe 10.00
25 Moran Norris 10.00
26 Sage Rosenfels 10.00
27 Vinny Sutherland 10.00
28 David Terrell 250 50.00
29 Anthony Thomas 250 30.00
30 LaDainian Tomlinson 100 120.00
31 Ja'Mar Toombs 10.00
32 Marques Tuiasosopo 250 25.00
33 Michael Vick 100 200.00
34 Reggie Wayne 20.00
35 Chris Weinke 100 45.00
36 Reggie White 10.00

2001 Pacific Crown Royale Rookie Royalty

MARQUES TUIASOSOPO
0699/1250
ROOKIE CROWN ROYALE 2001 ROYALTY

NM/M
Complete Set (20): 70.00
Common Player: 2.00
Production 1,250 Sets
1 Alex Bannister 2.00
2 Kevan Barlow 2.00
3 Michael Bennett 10.00
4 Drew Brees 15.00
5 Rod Gardner 6.00
6 Travis Henry 4.00
7 Chad Johnson 3.00
8 Rudi Johnson 2.50
9 Mike McMahon 2.00
10 Freddie Mitchell 4.00
11 Quincy Morgan 3.00
12 Koren Robinson 6.00
13 Sage Rosenfels 2.00
14 David Terrell 6.00
15 Anthony Thomas 6.00
16 LaDainian Tomlinson 12.00
17 Marques Tuiasosopo 5.00
18 Michael Vick 20.00
19 Reggie Wayne 5.00
20 Chris Weinke 8.00

Post-1980 cards in Near Mint condition will generally sell for about 75% of the quoted Mint value. Excellent-condition cards bring no more than 40%.

2001 Pacific Crown Royale 21st Century Rookies

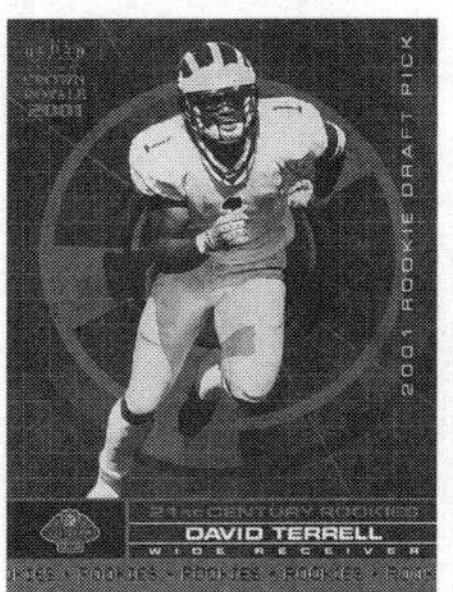

NM/M
Complete Set (25): 25.00
Common Player: 1.00
Inserted 1:1
1 Kevan Barlow 1.00
2 Michael Bennett 5.00
3 Josh Booty 1.00
4 Drew Brees 7.00
5 Chris Chambers 2.00
6 Rod Gardner 3.00
7 Tim Hasselbeck 1.50
8 Todd Heap 1.00
9 Travis Henry 2.50
10 Chad Johnson 1.50
11 Rudi Johnson 1.50
12 LaMont Jordan 1.50
13 Ben Leard 1.00
14 Deuce McAllister 4.00
15 Mike McMahon 1.50
16 Freddie Mitchell 2.00
17 Quincy Morgan 1.50
18 Sage Rosenfels 1.50
19 David Terrell 5.00
20 Anthony Thomas 3.00
21 LaDainian Tomlinson 6.00
22 Marques Tuiasosopo 2.50
23 Michael Vick 10.00
24 Reggie Wayne 2.50
25 Chris Weinke 3.50

2001 Pacific Dynagon DMX

NM/M
Common Player: .15
Minor Stars: .50
Cards #132, 136, 148 never released
Pack (5): 3.50
Wax Box (22): 60.00
1 David Boston 1.00
2 Thomas Jones 1.00
3 Jake Plummer .75
4 Jamal Anderson 1.00
5 Tim Dwight 1.00
6 Elvis Grbac .50
7 Jamal Lewis 2.00
8 Ray Lewis .50
9 Shannon Sharpe .50
10 Rob Johnson .50
11 Eric Moulds 1.00
12 Peerless Price .75
13 Tim Biakabutuka .50
14 Patrick Jeffers .75
15 Muhsin Muhammad .75
16 James Allen .50
17 Cade McNown 1.00
18 Marcus Robinson 1.00
19 Brian Urlacher 2.00
20 Corey Dillon 1.00
21 Akili Smith 1.00
22 Peter Warrick 2.00
23 Tim Couch 1.50
24 Kevin Johnson 1.00
25 Randall Cunningham 1.00
26 Emmitt Smith 2.50
27 Mike Anderson 3.00
28 Terrell Davis 2.50
29 Brian Griese 1.25
30 Ed McCaffrey 1.00
31 Rod Smith 1.00
32 Charlie Batch 1.00
33 Johnnie Morton .50
34 James Stewart .75
35 Brett Favre 4.00
36 Antonio Freeman 1.00
37 Ahman Green 1.00
38 Marvin Harrison 1.00
39 Edgerrin James 3.00
40 Peyton Manning 3.00
41 Mark Brunell 1.25
42 Keenan McCardell .50
43 Jimmy Smith 1.00
44 Fred Taylor 1.25
45 Derrick Alexander .50
46 Tony Gonzalez .50
47 Sylvester Morris 1.00
48 Jay Fiedler 1.00
49 Oronde Gadsden .15
50 Lamar Smith 1.00
51 Cris Carter 1.00
52 Daunte Culpepper 2.00
53 Randy Moss 3.00
54 Drew Bledsoe 1.25
55 Terry Glenn 1.00
56 J.R. Redmond 1.00
57 Aaron Brooks 1.00
58 Joe Horn 1.00
59 Ricky Williams 1.50
60 Tiki Barber 1.00
61 Kerry Collins 1.00
62 Ron Dayne 2.00
63 Amani Toomer .15
64 Wayne Chrebet .75
65 Curtis Martin 1.00
66 Vinny Testaverde .75
67 Tim Brown 1.00
68 Rich Gannon 1.00
69 Tyrone Wheatley 1.00
70 Charles Johnson .50
71 Donovan McNabb 1.50
72 Duce Staley 1.00
73 Jerome Bettis 1.00
74 Plaxico Burress 1.00
75 Kordell Stewart 1.00
76 Isaac Bruce 1.50
77 Marshall Faulk 1.25
78 Torry Holt 1.00
79 Kurt Warner 3.50
80 Curtis Conway .50
81 Doug Flutie 1.25
82 Jeff Garcia 1.00
83 Charlie Garner .75
84 Terrell Owens 1.00
85 Jerry Rice 2.50
86 Shaun Alexander 1.00
87 Matt Hasselbeck 1.00
88 Darrell Jackson 1.00
89 Mike Alstott 1.00
90 Warrick Dunn 1.00
91 Brad Johnson 1.00
92 Keyshawn Johnson 1.00
93 Shaun King 1.00
94 Eddie George 1.25
95 Jevon Kearse 1.00
96 Derrick Mason 1.00
97 Steve McNair 1.00
98 Stephen Davis 1.00
99 Jeff George 1.00
100 Deion Sanders 1.00
101 *Michael Bennett 199* 60.00
102 *Drew Brees 199* 110.00
103 *Chris Chambers 199* 60.00
104 *LaMont Jordan 199* 30.00
105 *Deuce McAllister 199* 80.00
106 *Koren Robinson 199* 50.00
107 *David Terrell 199* 75.00
108 *LaDainian Tomlinson 199* 160.00
109 *Marques Tuiasosopo 199* 45.00
110 *Michael Vick 199* 200.00
111 *Chris Weinke 199* 60.00
112 *Kevan Barlow 499* 20.00
113 *Josh Booty 499* 15.00
114 *Rod Gardner 499* 30.00
115 *Todd Heap 499* 15.00
116 *Travis Henry 499* 30.00
117 *James Jackson 499* 20.00
118 *Chad Johnson 499* 20.00
119 *Rudi Johnson 499* 20.00
120 *Ben Leard 499* 12.00
121 *Quincy Morgan 499* 20.00
122 *Marvin "Snoop" Minnis 499* 25.00
123 *Freddie Mitchell 499* 25.00
124 *Sage Rosenfels 499* 20.00
125 *Anthony Thomas 499* 75.00
126 *Reggie Wayne 499* 30.00
127 *Dan Alexander 699* 12.00
128 *Will Allen 699* 10.00
129 *Scotty Anderson 699* 10.00
130 *Adam Archuleta 699* 12.00
131 *Alex Bannister 699* 12.00
133 *Tay Cody 699* 8.00
134 *Tony Dixon 699* 8.00
135 *Heath Evans 699* 8.00
137 *Derrick Gibson 699* 8.00
138 *Edgerton Hartwell 699* 8.00
139 *Tim Hasselbeck 699* 12.00
140 *Jabari Holloway 699* 10.00
141 *Torrance Marshall 699* 10.00
142 *Jason McKinley 699* 10.00
143 *Mike McMahon 699* 15.00
144 *Bobby Newcombe 699* 12.00
145 *Moran Norris 699* 8.00
146 *Tommy Polley 699* 8.00
147 *Vinny Sutherland 699* 12.00
149 *Reggie White 699* 12.00
150 *Cedrick Wilson 699* 10.00

2001 Pacific Dynagon DMX Premiere Date

Premiere Date Cards: 4X-8X
Production 135 Sets

2001 Pacific Dynagon DMX Red

Red Cards: 5X-10X
Production 99 Sets

2001 Pacific Dynagon DMX Retail

NM/M
Complete Set (150): 150.00
Common Rookie: 1.00
Inserted 1:4
101 Michael Bennett 7.00
102 Drew Brees 12.00
103 Chris Chambers 2.00
104 LaMont Jordan 2.00
105 Deuce McAllister 5.00
106 Koren Robinson 4.00
107 David Terrell 6.00
108 LaDainian Tomlinson 8.00
109 Marques Tuiasosopo 3.00
110 Michael Vick 18.00
111 Chris Weinke 5.00
112 Kevan Barlow 2.00
113 Josh Booty 2.00
114 Rod Gardner 4.00
115 Todd Heap 1.50
116 Travis Henry 3.00
117 James Jackson 2.00
118 Chad Johnson 2.00
119 Rudi Johnson 1.50
120 Ben Leard 1.00
121 Quincy Morgan 2.50
122 Marvin "Snoop" Minnis 2.50
123 Freddie Mitchell 2.50
124 Sage Rosenfels 2.00
125 Anthony Thomas 8.00
126 Reggie Wayne 3.00
127 Dan Alexander 2.00
128 Will Allen 1.00
129 Scotty Anderson 1.00
130 Adam Archuleta 1.50
131 Alex Bannister 2.00
132 Gary Baxter 1.00
133 Tay Cody 1.00
134 Tony Dixon 1.00
135 Heath Evans 1.00
136 Jamar Fletcher 1.50
137 Derrick Gibson 1.00
138 Edgerton Hartwell 1.00
139 Tim Hasselbeck 1.50
140 Jabari Holloway 1.50
141 Torrance Marshall 1.00
142 Jason McKinley 1.00
143 Mike McMahon 2.00
144 Bobby Newcombe 1.50
145 Moran Norris 1.00
146 Tommy Polley 1.00
147 Vinny Sutherland 1.50
148 Ja'Mar Toombs 1.00
149 Reggie White 1.50
150 Cedrick Wilson 1.00

2001 Pacific Dynagon DMX Big Numbers

NM/M
Complete Set (20): 50.00
Common Player: 3.00
Production 799 Sets
1 Cade McNown 3.00
2 Peter Warrick 3.00
3 Tim Couch 5.00
4 Mike Anderson 5.00
5 Brian Griese 5.00
6 Cris Carter 3.00
7 Mark Brunell 5.00
8 Drew Bledsoe 5.00
9 Ricky Williams 6.00
10 Ron Dayne 3.00
11 Curtis Martin 3.00
12 Rich Gannon 3.00
13 Jerome Bettis 3.00
14 Torry Holt 3.00
15 Jeff Garcia 3.00
16 Jerry Rice 8.00
17 Warrick Dunn 3.00
18 Eddie George 3.50
19 Steve McNair 3.00
20 Stephen Davis 3.00

2001 Pacific Dynagon DMX Canton Bound

NM/M
Complete Set (10): 225.00
Common Player: 15.00
Production 99 Sets
1 Emmitt Smith 40.00
2 Brett Favre 50.00
3 Edgerrin James 35.00
4 Peyton Manning 35.00
5 Dan Marino 50.00
6 Cris Carter 15.00
7 Randy Moss 35.00
8 Marshall Faulk 20.00
9 Kurt Warner 30.00
10 Jerry Rice 30.00

2001 Pacific Dynagon DMX Dynamic Duos

NM/M
Complete Set (20): 45.00
Common Player: 2.00
Production 1,499 Sets
1 Jake Plummer, David Boston 2.00
2 Jamal Lewis, Priest Holmes 6.00
3 Rob Johnson, Eric Moulds 2.00
4 Cade McNown, Marcus Robinson 2.00
5 Corey Dillon, Peter Warrick 3.00
6 Tim Couch, Kevin Johnson 3.00
7 Mike Anderson, Terrell Davis 4.00
8 Brian Griese, Rod Smith 3.00
9 Brett Favre, Antonio Freeman 8.00
10 Peyton Manning, Marvin Harrison 8.00
11 Mark Brunell, Fred Taylor 3.00
12 Daunte Culpepper, Randy Moss 8.00
13 Drew Bledsoe, Terry Glenn 3.00
14 Tiki Barber, Ron Dayne 4.00
15 Rich Gannon, Tim Brown 2.00
16 Donovan McNabb, Duce Staley 3.00
17 Kurt Warner, Torry Holt 5.00
18 Jeff Garcia, Terrell Owens 2.00
19 Mike Alstott, Warrick Dunn 2.00
20 Steve McNair, Derrick Mason 2.00

2001 Pacific Dynagon DMX Freshman Phenoms

NM/M
Complete Set (10): 130.00
Common Player: 7.00
Production 599 Sets
1 Michael Bennett 18.00
2 Drew Brees 30.00
3 Josh Heupel 12.00
4 Deuce McAllister 15.00
5 Santana Moss 15.00
6 Ken-Yon Rambo 7.00
7 Koren Robinson 12.00
8 David Terrell 12.00
9 LaDainian Tomlinson 25.00
10 Michael Vick 50.00

2001 Pacific Dynagon DMX Game-Used Footballs

NM/M
Common Player: 15.00
Inserted 1:82
Production 214 Sets
1 Jamal Lewis 25.00
2 Peter Warrick 25.00
3 Tim Couch 20.00
4 Emmitt Smith 40.00
5 Mike Anderson 30.00
6 Terrell Davis 30.00
7 Brett Favre 50.00
8 Edgerrin James 40.00
9 Peyton Manning 40.00
10 Mark Brunell 20.00
11 Fred Taylor 15.00
12 Daunte Culpepper 30.00
13 Randy Moss 40.00
14 Drew Bledsoe 20.00
15 Ricky Williams 25.00
16 Donovan McNabb 25.00
17 Marshall Faulk 20.00
18 Kurt Warner 40.00
19 Jerry Rice 35.00
20 Eddie George 20.00

2001 Pacific Dynagon DMX Logo Optics

NM/M
Complete Set (20): 40.00
Common Player: 1.50
Production 499 Sets
1 Jamal Lewis 3.00
2 Eric Moulds 2.00
3 Corey Dillon 2.00
4 Emmitt Smith 5.00
5 Terrell Davis 4.00
6 Brian Griese 2.50
7 Edgerrin James 4.00
8 Fred Taylor 2.50
9 Lamar Smith 1.50
10 Daunte Culpepper 4.00
11 Ricky Williams 4.00
12 Curtis Martin 2.00
13 Tyrone Wheatley 1.50
14 Donovan McNabb 4.00
15 Jerome Bettis 2.00
16 Marshall Faulk 2.00
17 Jeff Garcia 2.00
18 Warrick Dunn 2.00
19 Eddie George 2.00
20 Stephen Davis 2.00

A card number in parenthese ( ) indicates the set is unnumbered.

2001 Pacific Dynagon DMX Premiere Players

NM/M
Complete Set (20): 100.00
Common Player: 2.00
Production 999 Sets
1 David Allen 2.00
2 Kevan Barlow 3.00
3 Michael Bennett 10.00
4 Drew Brees 15.00
5 Chris Chambers 3.00
6 Josh Heupel 7.00
7 James Jackson 3.00
8 LaMont Jordan 3.00
9 Deuce McAllister 8.00
10 Freddie Mitchell 4.00
11 Santana Moss 8.00
12 Ken-Yon Rambo 2.00
13 Koren Robinson 7.00
14 David Terrell 10.00
15 Anthony Thomas 7.00
16 LaDainian Tomlinson 12.00
17 Marques Tuiasosopo 5.00
18 Michael Vick 25.00
19 Reggie Wayne 6.00
20 Chris Weinke 7.00

2001 Pacific Dynagon DMX Top of the Class

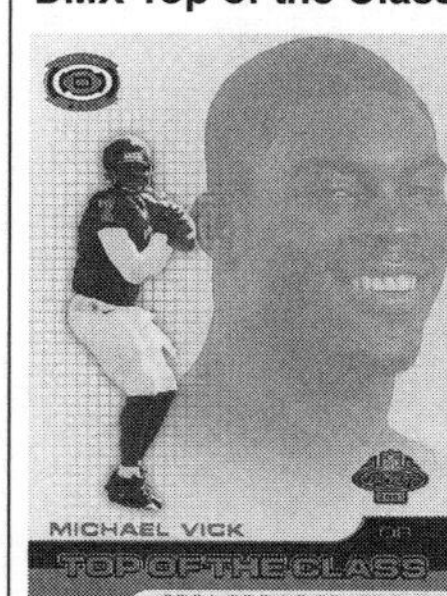

NM/M
Complete Set (25): 40.00
Common Player: 1.00
Inserted 1:1
1 Kevan Barlow 1.50
2 Michael Bennett 2.00
3 Drew Brees 7.00
4 Chris Chambers 1.50
5 Rod Gardner 2.50
6 Travis Henry 2.00
7 Josh Heupel 3.00
8 James Jackson 1.00
9 Chad Johnson 1.00
10 LaMont Jordan 1.00
11 Deuce McAllister 3.00
12 Mike McMahon 1.00
13 Marvin "Snoop" Minnis 1.50
14 Travis Minor 1.50
15 Freddie Mitchell 2.00
16 Santana Moss 3.00
17 Ken-Yon Rambo 1.00
18 Koren Robinson 2.50
19 David Terrell 4.00
20 Anthony Thomas 2.50
21 LaDainian Tomlinson 5.00
22 Marques Tuiasosopo 2.00
23 Michael Vick 10.00
24 Reggie Wayne 2.50
25 Chris Weinke 3.00

2001 Pacific Invincible

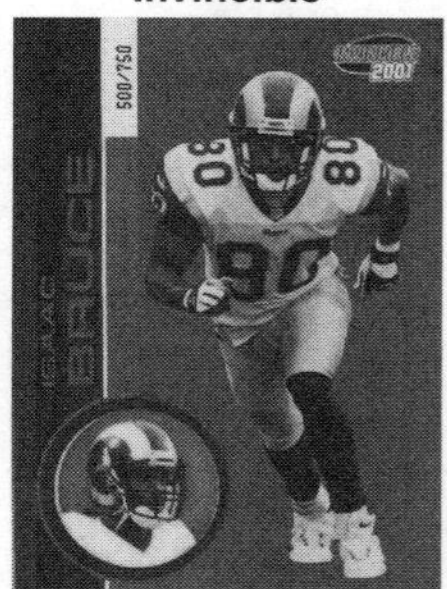

NM/M
Common Player: .40
Minor Stars: 1.00
Common Rookie: 4.00
Production 299 Sets
Common RK Jersey: 40.00
Production 250 Sets
Pack (3): 3.00
Wax Box (20): 55.00
1 David Boston 2.50
2 Mar Tay Jenkins .40
3 Thomas Jones .40
4 Rob Moore .40
5 Michael Pittman .40
6 Jake Plummer 2.50
7 Frank Sanders .40
8 Jamal Anderson 2.50
9 Chris Chandler .40
10 Jammi German .40
11 Shawn Jefferson .40
12 Doug Johnson .40
13 Terance Mathis .40
14 Elvis Grbac .40
15 Qadry Ismail .40
16 Jamal Lewis 6.00
17 Jermaine Lewis .40
18 Ray Lewis .40
19 Chris Redman 2.50
20 Shannon Sharpe .40
21 Travis Taylor .40
22 Shawn Bryson .40
23 Rob Johnson .40
24 Jeremy McDaniel .40
25 Sammy Morris .40
26 Eric Moulds .40
27 Peerless Price .40
28 Antowain Smith .40
29 Michael Bates .40
30 Tim Biakabutuka .40
31 Isaac Byrd .40
32 Brad Hoover 2.50
33 Patrick Jeffers .40
34 Jeff Lewis .40
35 Muhsin Muhammad .40
36 Wesley Walls .40
37 James Allen .40
38 Marty Booker .40
39 Macey Brooks .40
40 Bobby Engram .40
41 Cade McNown 2.50
42 Marcus Robinson 2.50
43 Brian Urlacher 5.00
44 Dez White .40
45 Brandon Bennett .40
46 Corey Dillon 2.50
47 Danny Farmer .40
48 Jon Kitna 2.50
49 Darnay Scott .40
50 Akili Smith 2.50
51 Peter Warrick 5.00
52 Craig Yeast .40
53 Tim Couch 3.00
54 JaJuan Dawson .40
55 Curtis Enis .40
56 Kevin Johnson 2.50
57 Dennis Northcutt .40
58 Travis Prentice .40
59 Errict Rhett .40
60 Tony Banks .40
61 Randall Cunningham 1.30
62 Raghib Ismail .40
63 Wane McGarity .40
64 Carl Pickens .40
65 Emmitt Smith 4.00
66 Jason Tucker .40
67 Michael Wiley .40
68 Mike Anderson 6.00
69 Terrell Davis 6.00
70 Gus Frerotte .40
71 Olandis Gary .40
72 Brian Griese 3.00
73 Eddie Kennison .40
74 Ed McCaffrey 2.50
75 Rod Smith .40
76 Charlie Batch 2.50
77 Germane Crowell .40
78 Larry Foster .40
79 Desmond Howard .40
80 Herman Moore .40
81 Johnnie Morton .40
82 Robert Porcher .40
83 James Stewart .40
84 Donald Driver .40
85 Brett Favre 10.00
86 Bubba Franks .40
87 Antonio Freeman 2.50
88 Ahman Green .40
89 William Henderson .40
90 Dorsey Levens .40
91 Bill Schroeder .40
92 Ken Dilger .40
93 E.G. Green .40
94 Marvin Harrison 2.50
95 Edgerrin James 4.00
96 Peyton Manning 8.00
97 Jerome Pathon .40
98 Marcus Pollard .40
99 Terrence Wilkins .40
100 Kyle Brady .40
101 Mark Brunell 3.00
102 Stacey Mack .40
103 Keenan McCardell .40
104 Jimmy Smith .40
105 R. Jay Soward .40
106 Shyrone Stith .40
107 Fred Taylor 3.00
108 Derrick Alexander .40
109 Kimble Anders .40
110 Todd Collins .40
111 Tony Gonzalez .40
112 Trent Green .40
113 Priest Holmes .40
114 Frank Moreau .40
115 Sylvester Morris .40
116 Tony Richardson .40
117 Jay Fiedler 2.50
118 Oronde Gadsden .40
119 J.J. Johnson .40
120 Ray Lucas .40
121 Tony Martin .40
122 O.J. McDuffie .40

123 James McKnight .40
124 Lamar Smith .40
125 Jason Taylor .40
126 Zach Thomas .40
127 Cris Carter 2.50
128 Daunte Culpepper 5.00
129 Randy Moss 8.00
130 Chris Walsh .40
131 Troy Walters .40
132 Moe Williams .40
133 Drew Bledsoe 3.00
134 Troy Brown .40
135 Kevin Faulk .40
136 Terry Glenn .40
137 Ty Law .40
138 Lawyer Milloy .40
139 David Patten .40
140 J.R. Redmond .40
141 Tony Simmons .40
142 Jeff Blake .40
143 Aaron Brooks 2.50
144 Albert Connell .40
145 Joe Horn .40
146 Willie Jackson .40
147 Chad Morton .40
148 Keith Poole .40
149 Ricky Williams 4.00
150 Robert Wilson .40
151 Jessie Armstead .40
152 Tiki Barber .40
153 Kerry Collins .40
154 Ron Dayne 5.00
155 Ron Dixon .40
156 Ike Hilliard .40
157 Jason Sehorn .40
158 Michael Strahan .40
159 Amani Toomer .40
160 Richie Anderson .40
161 Wayne Chrebet .40
162 Laveranues Coles 2.50
163 Matthew Hatchette .40
164 Marvin Jones .40
165 Curtis Martin 2.50
166 Chad Pennington 5.00
167 Vinny Testaverde .40
168 Dedric Ward .40
169 Tim Brown 2.50
170 Zack Crockett .40
171 Rich Gannon .40
172 James Jett .40
173 Randy Jordan .40
174 Andre Rison .40
175 Tyrone Wheatley .40
176 Charles Woodson .40
177 Darrell Autry .40
178 Charles Johnson .40
179 Chad Lewis .40
180 Donovan McNabb 4.00
181 Todd Pinkston .40
182 Stanley Pritchett .40
183 Torrance Small .40
184 Duce Staley 2.50
185 Jerome Bettis 2.50
186 Plaxico Burress 2.50
187 Troy Edwards .40
188 Courtney Hawkins .40
189 Richard Huntley .40
190 Bobby Shaw .40
191 Kordell Stewart 2.50
192 Hines Ward .40
193 Isaac Bruce 2.50
194 Trung Canidate .40
195 Marshall Faulk 3.00
196 Az-Zahir Hakim .40
197 Torry Holt 2.50
198 Tony Horne .40
199 Ricky Proehl .40
200 Kurt Warner 8.00
201 Aeneas Williams .40
202 Curtis Conway .40
203 Tim Dwight 2.50
204 Jermaine Fazande .40
205 Terrell Fletcher .40
206 Doug Flutie 3.00
207 Jeff Graham .40
208 Freddie Jones .40
209 Reggie Jones .40
210 Junior Seau .40
211 Fred Beasley .40
212 Jeff Garcia 2.50
213 Charlie Garner .40
214 Terrell Owens 2.50
215 Jerry Rice 6.00
216 Paul Smith .40
217 J.J. Stokes .40
218 Tai Streets .40
219 Shaun Alexander 3.00
220 Karsten Bailey .40
221 Matt Hasselbeck .40
222 Brock Huard .40
223 Darrell Jackson 2.50
224 Shawn Springs .40
225 Ricky Watters .40
226 James Williams .40
227 Mike Alstott 2.50
228 Reidel Anthony .40
229 Warrick Dunn 2.50
230 Jacquez Green .40
231 Keyshawn Johnson 2.50
232 Brad Johnson 2.50
233 Shaun King 2.50
234 Warren Sapp .40
235 Kevin Dyson .40
236 Eddie George 3.00
237 Jevon Kearse 2.50
238 Derrick Mason .40
239 Steve McNair 2.50
240 Chris Sanders .40
241 Rodney Thomas .40
242 Frank Wycheck .40
243 Stephen Alexander .40
244 Larry Centers .40
245 Stephen Davis 2.50
246 Irving Fryar .40
247 Jeff George .40
248 Kevin Lockett .40
249 James Thrash .40
250 Michael Westbrook .40
251 *Bobby Newcombe* 10.00
252 *Alge Crumpler* 10.00
253 *Vinny Sutherland* 10.00
254 *Michael Vick* 125.00
255 *Travis Henry* 20.00
256 *Dan Morgan* 15.00
257 *Chris Weinke* 30.00
258 *David Terrell* 40.00
259 *Anthony Thomas* 50.00
260 *T.J. Houshmandzadeh* 4.00
261 *Chad Johnson* 12.00
262 *Rudi Johnson* 12.00
263 *James Jackson* 12.00
264 *Quincy Morgan* 15.00
265 *Scotty Anderson* 4.00
266 *Mike McMahon* 10.00
267 *Robert Ferguson* 15.00
268 *Reggie Wayne* 15.00
269 *Marvin "Snoop" Minnis* 15.00
270 *Chris Chambers* 12.00
271 *Josh Heupel* 15.00
272 *Travis Minor* 15.00
273 *Michael Bennett* 30.00
274 *Ben Leard* 4.00
275 *Deuce McAllister* 50.00
276 *Moran Norris* 4.00
277 *Jesse Palmer* 12.00
278 *LaMont Jordan* 12.00
279 *Santana Moss* 25.00
280 *Ken-Yon Rambo* 10.00
281 *Marques Tuiasosopo* 40.00
282 *Correll Buckhalter* 15.00
283 *A.J. Feely* 4.00
284 *Freddie Mitchell* 40.00
285 *Joey Getherall* 12.00
286 *Chris Taylor* 10.00
287 *Adam Archuleta* 10.00
288 *David Rivers* 4.00
289 *Drew Brees* 60.00
290 *LaDainian Tomlinson* 70.00
291 *Kevan Barlow* 12.00
292 *Cedrick Wilson* 10.00
293 *Alex Bannister* 12.00
294 *Josh Booty* 10.00
295 *Heath Evans* 4.00
296 *Koren Robinson* 30.00
297 *Dan Alexander* 12.00
298 *Rod Gardner* 30.00
299 *Sage Rosenfels* 12.00
300 *David Allen* 10.00

2001 Pacific Invincible Blue

Stars: 2X
Production 250 Sets
Rookies: 2X
Production 99 Sets

2001 Pacific Invincible Premiere Date

Stars: 3X-6X
Rookies: 2X
Production 55 Sets

2001 Pacific Invincible Red

Stars: 1X
Production 750 Sets
Rookies: 1X
Production 199 Sets

2001 Pacific Invincible Retail

NM/M
Complete Set (300): 150.00
Retail Cards: 30%
Retail Rookies: 15%

2001 Pacific Invincible Afterburners

NM/M
Complete Set (20): 30.00
Common Player: 1.00
Production 2,000 Sets
1 Jamal Lewis 2.00
2 Eric Moulds 1.00
3 David Terrell 2.00
4 Corey Dillon 2.00
5 Peter Warrick 2.00
6 Marvin Harrison 2.00
7 Edgerrin James 4.00
8 Jimmy Smith 1.00
9 Fred Taylor 2.00
10 Sylvester Morris 1.00
11 Chris Chambers 3.00
12 Michael Bennett 5.00
13 Randy Moss 6.00
14 Santana Moss 3.00
15 Tim Brown 2.00
16 Isaac Bruce 2.00
17 Marshall Faulk 2.00
18 Torry Holt 2.00
19 LaDainian Tomlinson 8.00
20 Warrick Dunn 2.00

Post-1980 cards in Near Mint condition will generally sell for about 75% of the quoted Mint value. Excellent-condition cards bring no more than 40%.

2001 Pacific Invincible Fast Forward

NM/M
Complete Set (20): 85.00
Common Player: 2.00
Production 1,000 Sets
1 Jamal Lewis 4.00
2 Eric Moulds 2.00
3 Emmitt Smith 12.00
4 Mike Anderson 6.00
5 Marvin Harrison 4.00
6 Jimmy Smith 2.00
7 Cris Carter 4.00
8 Daunte Culpepper 8.00
9 Randy Moss 10.00
10 Ricky Williams 6.00
11 Ron Dayne 2.00
12 Curtis Martin 4.00
13 Rich Gannon 2.00
14 Jerome Bettis 4.00
15 Isaac Bruce 4.00
16 Marshall Faulk 5.00
17 Torry Holt 4.00
18 Kurt Warner 8.00
19 Jeff Garcia 4.00
20 Jerry Rice 10.00

2001 Pacific Invincible Heat-Seekers

NM/M
Complete Set (20): 100.00
Common Player: 2.50
Production 750 Sets
1 Jake Plummer 5.00
2 Michael Vick 25.00
3 Rob Johnson 2.50
4 Cade McNown 5.00
5 Akili Smith 5.00
6 Tim Couch 7.00
7 Brian Griese 6.00
8 Charlie Batch 5.00
9 Brett Favre 15.00
10 Peyton Manning 12.00
11 Mark Brunell 6.00
12 Daunte Culpepper 10.00
13 Drew Bledsoe 6.00
14 Aaron Brooks 6.00
15 Rich Gannon 2.50
16 Marques Tuiasosopo 5.00
17 Kurt Warner 10.00
18 Jeff Garcia 5.00
19 Steve McNair 5.00
20 Jeff George 2.50

2001 Pacific Invincible Main Set Jersey Variations-Blue

NM/M
Complete Set (50):
Common Player: 10.00
1 David Boston 15.00
4 Rob Moore 10.00
8 Jamal Anderson 10.00
9 Chris Chandler 10.00
23 Rob Johnson 10.00
26 Eric Moulds 10.00
30 Tim Biakabutuka 10.00
37 James Allen 10.00
40 Bobby Engram 10.00
53 Tim Couch 20.00
56 Kevin Johnson 10.00
65 Emmitt Smith 30.00
68 Mike Anderson 15.00
69 Terrell Davis 20.00
72 Brian Griese 15.00
76 Charlie Batch 10.00
83 James Stewart 10.00
85 Brett Favre 40.00
101 Mark Brunell 20.00
103 Keenan McCardell 10.00
104 Jimmy Smith 10.00
108 Derrick Alexander 10.00
115 Sylvester Morris 10.00
117 Jay Fiedler 10.00
127 Cris Carter 10.00
128 Daunte Culpepper 20.00
129 Randy Moss 20.00
142 Jeff Blake 10.00
145 Joe Horn 10.00
149 Ricky Williams 15.00
152 Tiki Barber 10.00
153 Kerry Collins 10.00
159 Amani Toomer 10.00
165 Curtis Martin 15.00
166 Chad Pennington 15.00
167 Vinny Testaverde 10.00
169 Tim Brown 15.00
171 Rich Gannon 10.00
175 Tyrone Wheatley 10.00
196 Az-Zahir Hakim 10.00
200 Kurt Warner 30.00
206 Doug Flutie 20.00
210 Junior Seau 15.00
215 Jerry Rice 25.00
219 Shaun Alexander 15.00
223 Darrell Jackson 10.00
225 Ricky Watters 10.00
235 Kevin Dyson 10.00
236 Eddie George 15.00
239 Steve McNair 15.00

2001 Pacific Invincible Main Set Jersey Variations-Red

NM/M
Common Player: 5.00
2 Mar Tay Jenkins 5.00
5 Michael Pittman 5.00
10 Jammi German 5.00
11 Shawn Jefferson 5.00
14 Elvis Grbac 5.00
22 Shawn Bryson 5.00
27 Peerless Price 5.00
31 Isaac Byrd 5.00
33 Patrick Jeffers 5.00
35 Muhsin Muhammad 5.00
39 Macey Brooks 5.00
42 Marcus Robinson 10.00
49 Darnay Scott 5.00
50 Akili Smith 10.00
52 Craig Yeast 5.00
55 Curtis Enis 5.00
57 Dennis Northcutt 5.00
62 Raghib Ismail 5.00
67 Michael Wiley 5.00
73 Eddie Kennison 5.00
74 Ed McCaffrey 5.00
75 Rod Smith 5.00
77 Germane Crowell 5.00
80 Herman Moore 5.00
87 Antonio Freeman 5.00
91 Bill Schroeder 5.00
100 Kyle Brady 5.00
105 R. Jay Soward 5.00
106 Shyrone Stith 5.00
109 Kimble Anders 5.00
118 Oronde Gadsden 5.00
122 O.J. McDuffie 5.00
126 James McKnight 5.00
147 Chad Morton 5.00
155 Ron Dixon 5.00
160 Richie Anderson 5.00
161 Wayne Chrebet 5.00
163 Matthew Hatchette 5.00
174 Andre Rison 5.00
176 Charles Woodson 10.00
194 Trung Canidate 5.00
199 Ricky Proehl 5.00
202 Curtis Conway 5.00
203 Tim Dwight 5.00
204 Jermaine Fazande 5.00
217 J.J. Stokes 10.00
218 Tai Streets 5.00
220 Karsten Bailey 5.00
238 Derrick Mason 5.00
248 Kevin Lockett 5.00

2001 Pacific Invincible New Sensations

NM/M
Complete Set (30): 60.00
Common Player: 1.25
Production 1,250 Sets
1 Vinny Sutherland 1.00
2 Michael Vick 15.00
3 Travis Henry 2.50
4 Chris Weinke 2.00
5 David Terrell 4.00
6 Anthony Thomas 4.00
7 Chad Johnson 1.50
8 James Jackson 1.50
9 Quincy Morgan 2.00
10 Mike McMahon 1.50
11 Reggie Wayne 2.50
12 Marvin "Snoop" Minnis 2.00
13 Chris Chambers 1.50
14 Josh Heupel 4.00
15 Travis Minor 2.00
16 Michael Bennett 7.00
17 Deuce McAllister 5.00
18 LaMont Jordan 1.50
19 Santana Moss 4.00
20 Ken-Yon Rambo 1.25
21 Marques Tuiasosopo 2.50
22 Correll Buckhalter 2.00
23 Freddie Mitchell 3.00
24 Drew Brees 8.00
25 LaDainian Tomlinson 8.00
26 Kevan Barlow 2.00
27 Josh Booty 1.25
28 Koren Robinson 4.00
29 Rod Gardner 4.00
30 Sage Rosenfels 1.50

2001 Pacific Invincible Rookie Die-Cuts

NM/M
Complete Set (10): 175.00
Common Player: 15.00
Production 100 Sets
1 Michael Vick 70.00
2 Chris Weinke 20.00
3 David Terrell 20.00
4 Michael Bennett 30.00
5 Deuce McAllister 25.00
6 Freddie Mitchell 15.00
7 Drew Brees 40.00
8 LaDainian Tomlinson 40.00
9 Koren Robinson 15.00
10 Rod Gardner 15.00

2001 Pacific Invincible School Colors

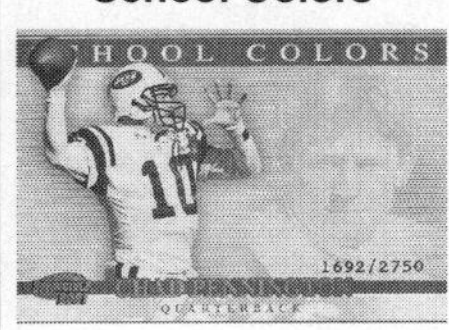

NM/M
Complete Set (60): 75.00
Common Player: .50
Minor Stars: 1.00
Production 2,750 Sets
1 Doug Flutie 1.00
2 Tim Hasselbeck 1.00
3 Darrell Jackson 1.00
4 Jesse Palmer .50
5 Emmitt Smith 4.00
6 Fred Taylor 1.00
7 Warrick Dunn 1.00
8 Marvin "Snoop" Minnis 1.00
9 Travis Minor 1.00
10 Peter Warrick 2.00
11 Chris Weinke 1.00
12 Terrell Davis 3.00
13 Olandis Gary 2.00
14 Randy Moss 3.00
15 Chad Pennington 5.00
16 James Jackson 1.00
17 Edgerrin James 4.00
18 Santana Moss 3.00
19 Reggie Wayne 3.00
20 Brian Griese 3.00
21 David Terrell 2.00
22 Anthony Thomas 3.00
23 Tyrone Wheatley .50
24 Ahman Green .50
25 Dan Alexander 1.00
26 Correll Buckhalter 1.00
27 Bobby Newcombe .50
28 Torry Holt 1.00
29 Koren Robinson 2.00
30 Jerome Bettis 1.00
31 Tim Brown 1.00
32 Joey Getherall .50
33 Jabari Holloway .50
34 David Boston 1.00
35 Cris Carter 1.00
36 Eddie George 3.00
37 Ken-Yon Rambo .50
38 Kevan Barlow 1.00
39 Curtis Martin 1.00
40 Mike Alstott 1.00
41 Drew Brees 8.00
42 Vinny Sutherland .50
43 Marvin Harrison 1.00
44 Kevin Johnson 1.00
45 Donovan McNabb 4.00
46 Travis Henry 3.00
47 Jamal Lewis 5.00
48 Peyton Manning 8.00
49 Troy Aikman 3.00
50 Cade McNown 1.00
51 Freddie Mitchell 3.00
52 Keyshawn Johnson 1.00
53 Junior Seau .50
54 Rob Johnson .50
55 Mark Brunell 2.00
56 Corey Dillon 1.00
57 Marques Tuiasosopo 2.00
58 Ron Dayne 2.00
59 Michael Bennett 4.00
60 Chris Chambers 1.00

2001 Pacific Invincible Widescreen

NM/M
Complete Set (20): 35.00
Common Player: 1.00
Production 2,500 Sets
1 Corey Dillon 2.00
2 Peter Warrick 2.00
3 Tim Couch 3.00
4 Kevin Johnson 2.00
5 Brian Griese 3.00
6 Brett Favre 6.00
7 Peyton Manning 4.00
8 Fred Taylor 3.00
9 Sylvester Morris 1.00
10 Drew Bledsoe 3.00
11 Tyrone Wheatley 1.00
12 Donovan McNabb 3.00
13 Jerome Bettis 2.00
14 Plaxico Burress 2.00
15 Jeff Garcia 2.00
16 Terrell Owens 2.00
17 Shaun Alexander 3.00
18 Eddie George 3.00
19 Derrick Mason 2.00
20 Steve McNair 2.00

2001 Pacific Invincible XXXVI

NM/M
Complete Set (20): 75.00
Common Player: 2.50
Production 499 Sets
1 Jamal Lewis 5.00
2 Rob Johnson 2.50
3 Mike Anderson 5.00
4 Terrell Davis 8.00
5 Brett Favre 15.00
6 Marvin Harrison 5.00
7 Edgerrin James 10.00
8 Mark Brunell 6.00
9 Cris Carter 5.00
10 Daunte Culpepper 8.00
11 Ricky Williams 8.00
12 Ron Dayne 8.00
13 Curtis Martin 5.00
14 Rich Gannon 2.50
15 Donovan McNabb 8.00
16 Marshall Faulk 6.00
17 Kurt Warner 8.00
18 Warrick Dunn 5.00
19 Eddie George 6.00
20 Steve McNair 5.00

2001 Pacific Prism Atomic

NM/M
Common Player: .15
Pack(5): 4.00
Wax Box(24): 75.00
1 David Boston .60
2 Thomas Jones .15
3 Rob Moore .15
4 Michael Pittman .15
5 Jake Plummer .15
6 Jamal Anderson .15
7 Chris Chandler .15
8 Shawn Jefferson .15
9 Terance Mathis .15
10 Elvis Grbac .15
11 Qadry Ismail .15
12 Jamal Lewis 1.50
13 Ray Lewis .15
14 Shannon Sharpe .15
15 Shawn Bryson .15
16 Rob Johnson .15
17 Sammy Morris .15
18 Eric Moulds .15
19 Peerless Price .15
20 Tim Biakabutuka .15
21 Richard Huntley .15
22 Patrick Jeffers .15
23 Jeff Lewis .15
24 Muhsin Muhammad .15
25 James Allen .15
26 Cade McNown .15
27 Marcus Robinson .15
28 Brian Urlacher 1.50
29 Corey Dillon .60
30 Jon Kitna .15
31 Akili Smith .60
32 Peter Warrick .60
33 Tim Couch 1.00
34 Kevin Johnson .15
35 Dennis Northcutt .15
36 Travis Prentice .15
37 Tony Banks .15
38 Joey Galloway .15
39 Raghib Ismail .15
40 Emmitt Smith 2.00
41 Anthony Wright .15
42 Mike Anderson 1.00
43 Terrell Davis 1.00
44 Olandis Gary .15
45 Brian Griese .75
46 Ed McCaffrey .15
47 Rod Smith .15
48 Charlie Batch .15
49 Germane Crowell .15
50 Herman Moore .15
51 Johnnie Morton .15
52 James Stewart .15
53 Brett Favre 4.00
54 Antonio Freeman .15
55 Ahman Green .75
56 Dorsey Levens .15
57 Bill Schroeder .15
58 Marvin Harrison .60
59 Edgerrin James 3.00
60 Peyton Manning 3.00
61 Jerome Pathon .15
62 Terrence Wilkins .15
63 Mark Brunell .75
64 Keenan McCardell .15
65 Jimmy Smith .15
66 Fred Taylor .60
67 Derrick Alexander .15
68 Tony Gonzalez .15
69 Trent Green .50
70 Priest Holmes .50

71	Sylvester Morris	.15
72	Jay Fiedler	.15
73	Oronde Gadsden	.15
74	O.J. McDuffie	.15
75	Lamar Smith	.15
76	Zach Thomas	.50
77	Daunte Culpepper	2.00
78	Cris Carter	.15
79	Randy Moss	3.00
80	Chris Walsh	.15
81	Moe Williams	.15
82	Drew Bledsoe	1.00
83	Kevin Faulk	.15
84	Terry Glenn	.50
85	Charles Johnson	.15
86	J.R. Redmond	.15
87	Jeff Blake	.15
88	Aaron Brooks	1.00
89	Albert Connell	.15
90	Joe Horn	.15
91	Ricky Williams	1.00
92	Tiki Barber	.15
93	Kerry Collins	.15
94	Ron Dayne	.75
95	Ike Hilliard	.15
96	Amani Toomer	.15
97	Richie Anderson	.15
98	Wayne Chrebet	.15
99	Curtis Martin	.50
100	Chad Pennington	.15
101	Vinny Testaverde	.15
102	Tim Brown	.50
103	Rich Gannon	.15
104	Charlie Garner	.15
105	Jerry Rice	2.00
106	Tyrone Wheatley	.15
107	Charles Woodson	.75
108	Darnell Autry	.15
109	Donovan McNabb	1.00
110	Duce Staley	.15
111	James Thrash	.15
112	Jerome Bettis	.60
113	Plaxico Burress	1.00
114	Bobby Shaw	.15
115	Kordell Stewart	.75
116	Hines Ward	.15
117	Isaac Bruce	.75
118	Marshall Faulk	2.00
119	Az-Zahir Hakim	.15
120	Torry Holt	.15
121	Kurt Warner	3.00
122	Curtis Conway	.15
123	Tim Dwight	.15
124	Doug Flutie	.75
125	Dave Dickerson	.15
126	Jeff Garcia	.50
127	Terrell Owens	.75
128	J.J. Stokes	.15
129	Tai Streets	.15
130	Shaun Alexander	.50
131	Matt Hasselbeck	.15
132	Darrell Jackson	.15
133	Ricky Watters	.15
134	Mike Alstott	.50
135	Warrick Dunn	.50
136	Jacquez Green	.15
137	Brad Johnson	.15
138	Keyshawn Johnson	.50
139	Warren Sapp	.15
140	Kevin Dyson	.15
141	Eddie George	1.00
142	Jevon Kearse	.15
143	Derrick Mason	.15
144	Steve McNair	1.00
145	Champ Bailey	.75
146	Stephen Davis	.50
147	Jeff George	.15
148	Michael Westbrook	.15
149	*Quentin McCord*	3.00
150	*Vinny Sutherland*	3.00
151	*Michael Vick*	60.00
152	*Chris Barnes*	3.00
153	*Reggie Germany*	3.00
154	*Travis Henry*	5.00
155	*Dee Brown*	3.00
156	*Dan Morgan*	5.00
157	*Steve Smith*	.15
158	*Chris Weinke*	15.00
159	*David Terrell*	15.00
160	*Anthony Thomas*	30.00
161	*Chad Johnson*	5.00
162	*Rudi Johnson*	5.00
163	*James Jackson*	3.00
164	*Andre King*	3.00
165	*Quincy Morgan*	5.00
166	*Quincy Carter*	10.00
167	*Kevin Kasper*	5.00
168	*Scotty Anderson*	5.00
169	*Mike McMahon*	15.00
170	*Robert Ferguson*	5.00
171	*Reggie Wayne*	10.00
172	*Derrick Blaylock*	5.00
173	*Marvin "Snoop" Minnis*	10.00
174	*Chris Chambers*	25.00
175	*Josh Heupel*	10.00
176	*Travis Minor*	10.00
177	*Michael Bennett*	25.00
178	*Deuce McAllister*	25.00
179	*Jonathan Carter*	5.00
180	*Jesse Palmer*	5.00
181	*LaMont Jordan*	5.00
182	*Santana Moss*	10.00
183	*Ken-Yon Rambo*	3.00
184	*Marques Tuiasosopo*	10.00
185	*Correll Buckhalter*	5.00
186	*Freddie Mitchell*	10.00
187	*Milton Wynn*	3.00
188	*Drew Brees*	25.00
189	*LaDainian Tomlinson*	40.00
190	*Kevan Barlow*	5.00
191	*Cedrick Wilson*	3.00
192	*Alex Bannister*	3.00
193	*Josh Booty*	3.00
194	*Koren Robinson*	5.00
195	*Eddie Berlin*	3.00
196	*Rod Gardner*	10.00
197	*Darnerian McCants*	5.00
198	*Sage Rosenfels*	5.00

2001 Pacific Prism Atomic Atomic Energy

		NM/M
Complete Set (20):		35.00
Common Player:		1.00
1	Michael Vick	8.00
2	Travis Henry	2.00
3	Chris Weinke	2.00
4	David Terrell	2.00
5	Anthony Thomas	3.00
6	Quincy Carter	2.00
7	Reggie Wayne	2.00
8	Josh Heupel	2.00
9	Michael Bennett	4.00
10	Deuce McAllister	4.00
11	Jesse Palmer	2.00
12	LaMont Jordan	1.00
13	Santana Moss	3.00
14	Marques Tuiasosopo	2.00
15	Freddie Mitchell	3.00
16	Drew Brees	4.00
17	LaDainian Tomlinson	4.00
18	Koren Robinson	2.00
19	Rod Gardner	2.00
20	Sage Rosenfels	1.00

2001 Pacific Prism Atomic Core Players

		NM/M
Complete Set (20):		30.00
Common Player:		1.00
1	Jamal Lewis	2.00
2	Peter Warrick	1.00
3	Tim Couch	2.00
4	Emmitt Smith	3.00
5	Mike Anderson	2.00
6	Terrell Davis	1.00
7	Brett Favre	5.00
8	Edgerrin James	3.00
9	Peyton Manning	3.00
10	Fred Taylor	1.00
11	Randy Moss	4.00
12	Ricky Williams	1.00
13	Ron Dayne	1.00
14	Jerry Rice	3.00
15	Donovan McNabb	2.00
16	Marshall Faulk	2.00
17	Kurt Warner	3.00
18	Jeff Garcia	1.00
19	Eddie George	2.00
20	Steve McNair	1.00

2001 Pacific Prism Atomic Game-Worn Jerseys

		NM/M
Common Player:		10.00
1	Mac Cody	10.00
2	MarTay Jenkins	10.00
3	Thomas Jones	10.00
4	Rob Moore	10.00
5	Chris Chandler	10.00
6	Bob Christian	10.00
7	Jamal Lewis	15.00
8	Larry Centers	10.00
9	Rob Johnson	10.00
10	Peerless Price	10.00
11	Brad Hoover	10.00
12	Muhsin Muhammad	10.00
13	Chris Weinke	12.00
14	James Allen	10.00
15	Macey Brooks	10.00
16	Bobby Engram	10.00
17	Anthony Thomas	25.00
18	Brian Urlacher	30.00
19	Corey Dillon	10.00
20	Bobby Brown	10.00
21	Tim Couch	15.00
22	Curtis Enis	10.00
23	Emmitt Smith	50.00
24	Anthony Wright	10.00
25	Mike Anderson	25.00
26	Eddie Kennison	10.00
27	James Stewart	10.00
28	Brett Favre	50.00
29	Bubba Franks	10.00
30	William Henderson	10.00
31	Marvin Harrison	15.00
32	Edgerrin James	30.00
33	Peyton Manning	30.00
34	Mark Brunell	10.00
35	Keenan McCardell	10.00
36	Jimmy Smith	10.00
37	R. Jay Soward	10.00
38	Fred Taylor	15.00
39	Sylvester Morris	10.00
40	Autrey Denson	10.00
41	Jay Fiedler	10.00
42	J.J. Johnson	10.00
43	Zach Thomas	10.00
44	Cris Carter	10.00
45	Daunte Culpepper	25.00
46	Randy Moss	35.00
47	Drew Bledsoe	15.00
48	Aaron Brooks	15.00
49	Joe Horn	10.00
50	Terrelle Smith	10.00
51	Tiki Barber	10.00
52	Kerry Collins	10.00
53	Greg Comella	10.00
54	Ron Dixon	10.00
55	Ike Hilliard	10.00
56	Joe Jurevicius	10.00
57	Richie Anderson	10.00
58	Laveranues Coles	15.00
59	Matthew Hatchette	10.00
60	Curtis Martin	10.00
61	Dwight Stone	10.00
62	Vinny Testaverde	10.00
63	David Dunn	10.00
64	Napoleon Kaufman	10.00
65	Jerry Porter	30.00
66	Jerry Rice	10.00
67	Andre Rison	10.00
68	Marques Tuiasosopo	25.00
69	Tyrone Wheatley	10.00
70	Charles Woodson	10.00
71	Donovan McNabb	25.00
72	Freddie Mitchell	25.00
73	Duce Staley	10.00
74	Ernie Conwell	10.00
75	Marshall Faulk	25.00
76	Az-Zahir Hakim	10.00
77	Torry Holt	10.00
78	Ricky Proehl	10.00
79	Drew Brees	30.00
80	Curtis Conway	10.00
81	Freddie Jones	10.00
82	Junior Seau	10.00
83	LaDainian Tomlinson	30.00
84	Jeff Garcia	10.00
85	Terrell Owens	15.00
86	J.J. Stokes	10.00
87	Tai Streets	10.00
88	Karsten Bailey	10.00
89	Brock Huard	10.00
90	James Williams	10.00
91	Reidel Anthony	10.00
92	Jacquez Green	10.00
93	Joe Hamilton	10.00
94	Keyshawn Johnson	15.00
95	Warren Sapp	10.00
96	Kevin Dyson	10.00
97	Jevon Kearse	10.00
98	Derrick Mason	10.00
99	Stephen Alexander	10.00
100	Kevin Lockett	10.00
101	Michael Pittman	10.00
102	Jake Plummer	10.00
103	Jamal Anderson	10.00
104	Qadry Ismail	10.00
105	Pat Johnson	10.00
106	Chris Redman	10.00
107	Brandon Stokley	10.00
108	Travis Taylor	10.00
109	Tim Biakabutuka	10.00
110	Richard Huntley	10.00
111	Marcus Robinson	10.00
112	Ron Dugans	10.00
113	Scott Mitchell	10.00
114	Darnay Scott	10.00
115	Akili Smith	10.00
116	Craig Yeast	10.00
117	JaJuan Dawson	10.00
118	Travis Prentice	10.00
119	Errict Rhett	10.00
120	Spergon Wynn	10.00
121	Brian Griese	15.00
122	Germane Crowell	10.00
123	Herman Moore	10.00
124	Antonio Freeman	10.00
125	Tom Brady	35.00
126	Shockmain Davis	10.00
127	Kevin Faulk	10.00
128	Curtis Jackson	10.00
129	Jeff Blake	10.00
130	Amani Toomer	10.00
131	Wayne Chrebet	10.00
132	Chad Pennington	15.00
133	Tim Brown	15.00
134	Rich Gannon	10.00
135	Darnell Autry	10.00
136	Brian Mitchell	10.00
137	Plaxico Burress	20.00
138	Troy Edwards	10.00
139	Courtney Hawkins	10.00
140	Dan Kreider	10.00
141	Bobby Shaw	10.00
142	Hines Ward	10.00
143	Amos Zereoue	10.00
144	Giovanni Carmazzi	10.00
145	Greg Clark	10.00
146	Rick Mirer	10.00
147	Tim Rattay	10.00
148	Darrell Jackson	10.00
149	Ricky Watters	15.00
150	Chris Sanders	10.00

Post-1980 cards in Near Mint condition will generally sell for about 75% of the quoted Mint value. Excellent-condition cards bring no more than 40%.

2001 Pacific Prism Atomic Rookie Reaction

		NM/M
Complete Set (20):		50.00
Common Player:		1.00
1	Michael Vick	8.00
2	Travis Henry	2.00
3	Chris Weinke	2.00
4	David Terrell	3.00
5	Anthony Thomas	3.00
6	James Jackson	2.00
7	Quincy Carter	3.00
8	Reggie Wayne	2.00
9	Josh Heupel	1.00
10	Michael Bennett	4.00
11	Deuce McAllister	4.00
12	LaMont Jordan	1.00
13	Santana Moss	3.00
14	Marques Tuiasosopo	3.00
15	Freddie Mitchell	4.00
16	Drew Brees	5.00
17	LaDainian Tomlinson	6.00
18	Kevan Barlow	2.00
19	Koren Robinson	2.00
20	Rod Gardner	3.00

2001 Pacific Prism Atomic Strategic Arms

		NM/M
Complete Set (10):		150.00
Common Player:		10.00
1	Michael Vick	40.00
2	Tim Couch	10.00
3	Brian Griese	10.00
4	Brett Favre	35.00
5	Peyton Manning	25.00
6	Mark Brunell	10.00
7	Daunte Culpepper	15.00
8	Drew Bledsoe	15.00
9	Donovan McNabb	15.00
10	Kurt Warner	20.00

2001 Pacific Prism Atomic Statosphere

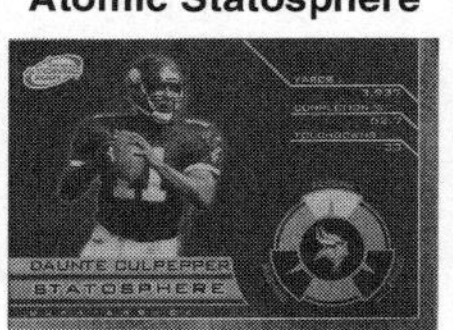

		NM/M
Complete Set (20):		30.00
Common Player:		1.00
1	Chris Weinke	1.00
2	Tim Couch	1.00
3	Brian Griese	1.00
4	Peyton Manning	3.00
5	Mark Brunell	1.00
6	Daunte Culpepper	2.50
7	Drew Bledsoe	1.50
8	Kurt Warner	3.00
9	Jeff Garcia	1.00
10	Steve McNair	1.00
11	Jamal Lewis	2.50
12	Peter Warrick	1.00
13	Emmitt Smith	3.00
14	Terrell Davis	1.00
15	Edgerrin James	3.00
16	Fred Taylor	1.00
17	Randy Moss	4.00
18	Ricky Williams	1.00
19	Jerry Rice	3.00
20	Marshall Faulk	2.00

2001 Pacific Prism Atomic Team Nucleus

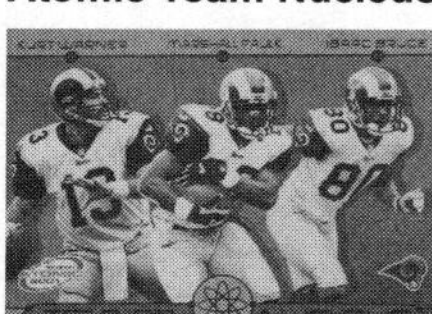

		NM/M
Complete Set (10):		30.00
Common Player:		2.00
1	Brian Urlacher, Anthony Thomas, David Terrell	3.00
2	Chad Johnson, Corey Dillon, Peter Warrick	2.00
3	Brian Griese, Terrell Davis, Mike Anderson	2.00
4	Reggie Wayne, Edgerrin James, Marvin Harrison	4.00
5	Mark Brunell, Fred Taylor, Jimmy Smith	2.00
6	Daunte Culpepper, Michael Bennett, Randy Moss	5.00
7	Chad Pennington, LaMont Jordan, Santana Moss	3.00
8	Kurt Warner, Marshall Faulk, Isaac Bruce	4.00
9	Doug Flutie, Drew Brees, LaDainian Tomlinson	5.00
10	Steve McNair, Eddie George, Derrick Mason	2.00

2001 Pacific Private Stock

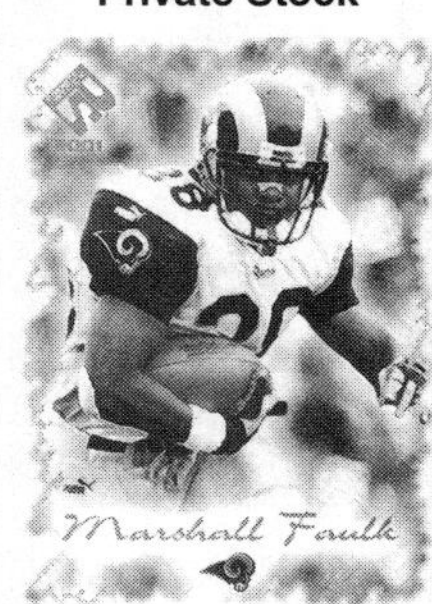

		NM/M
Common Player:		.15
Minor Stars:		.50
Common Rookie:		5.00
Production 200 Sets		
Pack (7):		10.00
Wax Box (10):		85.00
1	David Boston	1.00
2	Thomas Jones	.50
3	Jake Plummer	1.00
4	Jamal Anderson	1.00
5	Chris Chandler	.50
6	Eric Zeier	.15
7	Elvis Grbac	.75
8	Jamal Lewis	2.50
9	Shannon Sharpe	.50
10	Rob Johnson	.75
11	Eric Moulds	1.00
12	Peerless Price	.75
13	Tim Biakabutuka	.50
14	Jeff Lewis	.50
15	Muhsin Muhammad	.75
16	James Allen	.75
17	Cade McNown	1.00
18	Marcus Robinson	1.00
19	Brian Urlacher	2.00
20	Corey Dillon	1.00
21	Jon Kitna	.75
22	Akili Smith	1.00
23	Peter Warrick	2.00
24	Tim Couch	1.25
25	Kevin Johnson	.75
26	Travis Prentice	.75
27	Raghib Ismail	.50
28	Emmitt Smith	2.50
29	Mike Anderson	2.50
30	Terrell Davis	2.00
31	Brian Griese	1.25
32	Ed McCaffrey	1.00
33	Charlie Batch	1.00
34	Germane Crowell	.75
35	James Stewart	.75
36	Brett Favre	4.00
37	Antonio Freeman	.75
38	Ahman Green	.75
39	Marvin Harrison	1.00
40	Edgerrin James	2.75
41	Peyton Manning	3.00
42	Mark Brunell	1.25
43	Jimmy Smith	.75
44	Fred Taylor	1.25
45	Derrick Alexander	.50
46	Tony Gonzalez	.75
47	Trent Green	.75
48	Priest Holmes	.50
49	Jay Fiedler	1.00
50	Oronde Gadsden	.50
51	Lamar Smith	.75
52	Cris Carter	1.00
53	Daunte Culpepper	2.00
54	Randy Moss	3.00
55	Drew Bledsoe	1.25
56	Kevin Faulk	.50
57	Terry Glenn	.75
58	Jeff Blake	.50
59	Aaron Brooks	1.00
60	Joe Horn	.75
61	Ricky Williams	1.50
62	Tiki Barber	1.00
63	Kerry Collins	.75
64	Ron Dayne	1.75
65	Amani Toomer	.50
66	Wayne Chrebet	.75
67	Curtis Martin	1.00
68	Vinny Testaverde	.75
69	Tim Brown	.75
70	Rich Gannon	.50
71	Charlie Garner	.50
72	Jerry Rice	2.00
73	Tyrone Wheatley	.50
74	Donovan McNabb	1.50
75	Duce Staley	1.00
76	Jerome Bettis	1.00
77	Kordell Stewart	1.00
78	Hines Ward	.50
79	Isaac Bruce	1.00
80	Marshall Faulk	1.25
81	Torry Holt	1.00
82	Kurt Warner	3.00
83	Curtis Conway	.50
84	Doug Flutie	1.25
85	Jeff Garcia	1.00
86	Terrell Owens	1.00
87	Shaun Alexander	1.25
88	Matt Hasselbeck	1.00
89	Darrell Jackson	.50
90	Ricky Watters	.75
91	Mike Alstott	1.00
92	Warrick Dunn	1.00
93	Keyshawn Johnson	1.00
94	Brad Johnson	.75
95	Eddie George	1.25
96	Derrick Mason	.75
97	Steve McNair	1.00
98	Stephen Davis	1.00
99	Jeff George	.75
100	Michael Westbrook	.75
101	*Bobby Newcombe*	12.00
102	*Corey Brown*	10.00
103	*Alge Crumpler*	12.00
104	*Vinny Sutherland*	12.00
105	*Michael Vick*	125.00
106	*Chris Barnes*	12.00
107	*Todd Heap*	12.00
108	*Nate Clements*	10.00
109	*Tim Hasselbeck*	12.00
110	*Travis Henry*	40.00
111	*Dee Brown*	10.00
112	*Dan Morgan*	12.00
113	*Steve Smith*	10.00
114	*Chris Weinke*	20.00
115	*John Capel*	12.00
116	*David Terrell*	40.00
117	*Anthony Thomas*	50.00
118	*T.J. Houshmandzadeh*	10.00
119	*Chad Johnson*	20.00
120	*Rudi Johnson*	20.00
121	*James Jackson*	25.00
122	*Quincy Morgan*	25.00
123	*Quincy Carter*	40.00
124	*Kevin Kasper*	12.00
125	*Scotty Anderson*	5.00
126	*Mike McMahon*	15.00
127	*Robert Ferguson*	20.00
128	*David Martin*	5.00
129	*Jamal Reynolds*	12.00
130	*Reggie Wayne*	30.00
131	*Richmond Flowers*	10.00
132	*Marcus Stroud*	10.00
133	*Derrick Blaylock*	5.00
134	*Marvin "Snoop" Minnis*	25.00
135	*Chris Chambers*	40.00
136	*Jamar Fletcher*	12.00
137	*Josh Heupel*	35.00
138	*Travis Minor*	20.00
139	*Michael Bennett*	40.00
140	*Deuce McAllister*	65.00
141	*Moran Norris*	5.00
142	*Onomo Ojo*	10.00
143	*Will Allen*	10.00
144	*Jonathan Carter*	5.00
145	*Jesse Palmer*	15.00
146	*LaMont Jordan*	20.00
147	*Santana Moss*	35.00
148	*Derek Combs*	10.00
149	*Derrick Gibson*	5.00
150	*Javon Green*	5.00
151	*Ken-Yon Rambo*	15.00
152	*Marques Tuiasosopo*	35.00
153	*Correll Buckhalter*	20.00
154	*Freddie Mitchell*	35.00
155	*Joey Getherall*	5.00
156	*Chris Taylor*	5.00
157	*Adam Archuleta*	15.00
158	*David Rivers*	10.00
159	*Francis St. Paul*	5.00
160	*Drew Brees*	70.00
161	*LaDainian Tomlinson*	90.00
162	*David Allen*	12.00
163	*Kevan Barlow*	25.00
164	*Andre Carter*	10.00
165	*Cedrick Wilson*	12.00
166	*Alex Bannister*	15.00
167	*Josh Booty*	12.00
168	*Heath Evans*	5.00
169	*Koren Robinson*	35.00
170	*Margin Hooks*	5.00
171	*Dan Alexander*	15.00
172	*Eddie Berlin*	5.00
173	*Rod Gardner*	35.00
174	*Darnerian McCants*	10.00
175	*Sage Rosenfels*	20.00

2001 Pacific Private Stock Blue

Blue Cards:	8X-16X
Blue Rookies:	1.5X
Production 75 Sets	

2001 Pacific Private Stock Gold

Gold Cards:	10X-20X
Gold Rookies:	2X
Production 49 Sets	

2001 Pacific Private Stock Premiere Date

Premiere Date Cards:	6X-12X
Premiere Date Rookies:	1.2X
Production 95 Sets	

2001 Pacific Private Stock Artist's Reserve

		NM/M
Common Player:		20.00
Production 99 Sets		
1	Michael Vick	75.00
2	Chris Weinke	15.00

3 David Terrell 25.00
4 Quincy Carter 20.00
5 Michael Bennett 40.00
6 Deuce McAllister 25.00
7 Marques Tuiasosopo 20.00
8 Drew Brees 50.00
9 LaDainian Tomlinson 50.00
10 Koren Robinson 20.00

2001 Pacific Private Stock Game-Worn Jersey

NM/M
Common Player: 5.00
1 Thomas Jones 5.00
2 Rob Moore 5.00
3 Jake Plummer 5.00
4 Frank Sanders 5.00
5 Chris Chandler 5.00
6 Doug Johnson 5.00
7 Terance Mathis 5.00
8 Randall Cunningham 5.00
9 Elvis Grbac 5.00
10 Jamal Lewis 15.00
11 Ray Lewis 10.00
12 Shawn Bryson 5.00
13 Kwame Cavil 5.00
14 Jonathon Linton 5.00
15 Jeremy McDaniel 5.00
16 Eric Moulds 5.00
17 Thurman Thomas 10.00
18 Michael Bates 5.00
19 Dameyune Craig 5.00
20 William Floyd 5.00
21 Patrick Jeffers 5.00
22 Wesley Walls 5.00
23 Chris Weinke (college) 18.00
24 Marlon Barnes 5.00
25 D'Wayne Bates 5.00
26 Marty Booker 5.00
27 Cade McNown 10.00
28 Anthony Thomas (college) 25.00
29 Brian Urlacher 15.00
30 Brandon Bennett 5.00
31 Curtis Keaton 5.00
32 Jon Kitna 5.00
33 Peter Warrick 10.00
34 Darrin Chiaverini 5.00
35 Tim Couch 10.00
36 Rickey Dudley 5.00
37 Curtis Enis 5.00
38 Kevin Johnson 5.00
39 Dennis Northcutt 5.00
40 Troy Aikman 15.00
41 Wane McGarity 5.00
42 Carl Pickens 5.00
43 Emmitt Smith 20.00
44 Michael Wiley 5.00
45 Anthony Wright 5.00
46 Mike Anderson 5.00
47 Steve Beuerlein 5.00
48 Terrell Davis 10.00
49 Olandis Gary 5.00
50 Brian Griese 10.00
51 Eddie Kennison 5.00
52 Deltha O'Neal 5.00
53 Keith Poole 5.00
54 Bill Romanowski 5.00
55 Charlie Batch 5.00
56 Desmond Howard 5.00
57 Sedrick Irvin 5.00
58 Tyrone Davis 5.00
59 Donald Driver 5.00
60 Brett Favre 30.00
61 Ahman Green 10.00
62 Charles Lee 5.00
63 Bill Schroeder 5.00
64 E.G. Green 5.00
65 Edgerrin James 20.00
66 Peyton Manning 25.00
67 Jerome Pathon 5.00
68 Marcus Pollard 5.00
69 Kyle Brady 5.00
70 Mark Brunell 10.00
71 Jamie Martin 5.00
72 Keenan McCardell 5.00
73 Shyrone Stith 5.00
74 Fred Taylor 10.00
75 Alvis Whitted 5.00
76 Derrick Alexander 5.00
77 Kimble Anders 5.00
78 Mike Cloud 5.00
79 Trent Green 5.00
80 Tony Horne 5.00
81 Warren Moon 10.00
82 Rob Konrad 5.00
83 Ray Lucas 5.00
84 Tony Martin 5.00
85 O.J. McDuffie 5.00
86 James McKnight 5.00
87 Leslie Shepherd 5.00
88 Dedric Ward 5.00
89 Cris Carter 10.00
90 Daunte Culpepper 15.00
91 Randy Moss 25.00
92 Jake Reed 5.00
93 Robert Smith 5.00
94 Moe Williams 5.00
95 Michael Bishop 5.00
96 Drew Bledsoe 10.00
97 Troy Brown 5.00
98 Bert Emanuel 5.00
99 David Patten 5.00
100 J.R. Redmond 10.00
101 Albert Connell 5.00
102 Willie Jackson 5.00
103 Chad Morton 5.00
104 Ricky Williams 10.00
105 Ron Dayne 10.00
106 Ron Dixon 5.00
107 Joe Jurevicius 5.00
108 Richie Anderson 5.00
109 Matthew Hatchette 5.00
110 Chad Pennington 10.00
111 Reggie Barlow 5.00
112 Napoleon Kaufman 5.00
113 Jerry Rice 20.00
114 Andre Rison 5.00
115 Marques Tuiasosopo (college) 15.00
116 Charles Woodson 10.00
117 Donovan McNabb 10.00
118 Freddie Mitchell (college) 10.00
119 Trung Canidate 5.00
120 Marshall Faulk 15.00
121 Kurt Warner 20.00
122 Drew Brees (college) 25.00
123 Tim Dwight 5.00
124 Jermaine Fazande 5.00
125 Doug Flutie 15.00
126 LaDainian Tomlinson (college) 25.00
127 Jeff Garcia 10.00
128 Tai Streets 5.00
129 Shaun Alexander 10.00
130 Matt Hasselbeck 5.00
131 Warrick Dunn 5.00
132 Shaun King 5.00
133 Ryan Leaf 5.00
134 Eddie George 10.00
135 Jevon Kearse 5.00
136 Steve McNair 10.00
137 Chris Sanders 5.00
138 Donnell Bennett 5.00
139 Kevin Lockett 5.00
140 David Boston 10.00
141 Thomas Jones 5.00
142 Jake Plummer 5.00
143 Corey Dillon 10.00
144 Akili Smith 10.00
145 Peter Warrick 10.00
146 Isaac Bruce 10.00
147 Marshall Faulk 15.00
148 Az-Zahir Hakim 5.00
149 Torry Holt 10.00
150 Kurt Warner 20.00

2001 Pacific Private Stock Game Worn Gear

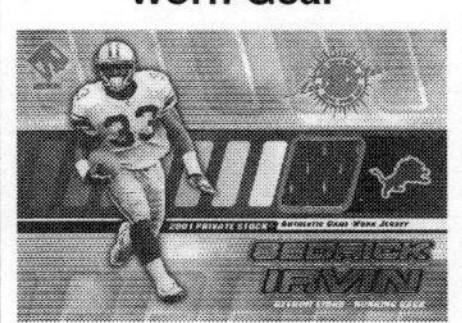

NM/M
Common Player: 7.00
Inserted 1:1
1 Thomas Jones 600 10.00
2 Rob Moore 500 10.00
3 Jake Plummer 1148 10.00
4 Frank Sanders 250 10.00
5 Chris Chandler 600 10.00
6 Doug Johnson 2000 7.00
7 Terance Mathis 750 10.00
8 Randall Cunningham 1000 7.00
9 Elvis Grbac 1250 10.00
10 Jamal Lewis 500 30.00
11 Ray Lewis 1250 7.00
12 Shawn Bryson 500 7.00
13 Kwame Cavil 2000 7.00
14 Jonathon Linton 2000 7.00
15 Jeremy McDaniel 1500 7.00
16 Eric Moulds 1250 10.00
17 Thurman Thomas 1224 12.00
18 Michael Bates 200 10.00
19 Dameyune Craig 2000 7.00
20 William Floyd 2000 7.00
21 Patrick Jeffers 500 12.00
22 Wesley Walls 500 7.00
23 Chris Weinke 1000 10.00
24 Marlon Barnes 2000 7.00
25 D'Wayne Bates 2000 7.00
26 Marty Booker 2000 7.00
27 Cade McNown 1000 12.00
28 Anthony Thomas 1000 20.00
29 Brian Urlacher 625 25.00
30 Brandon Bennett 2000 7.00
31 Curtis Keaton 500 10.00
32 Jon Kitna 2000 12.00
33 Peter Warrick 400 20.00
34 Darrin Chiaverini 2000 7.00
35 Tim Couch 500 20.00
36 Rickey Dudley 2000 7.00
37 Curtis Enis 750 7.00
38 Kevin Johnson 1250 10.00
39 Dennis Northcutt 750 12.00
40 Troy Aikman 1250 30.00
41 Wane McGarity 500 7.00
42 Carl Pickens 1000 7.00
43 Emmitt Smith 400 45.00
44 Michael Wiley 1250 7.00
45 Anthony Wright 750 12.00
46 Mike Anderson 400 30.00
47 Steve Beuerlein 750 10.00
48 Terrell Davis 400 30.00
49 Olandis Gary 1250 12.00
50 Brian Griese 400 25.00
51 Eddie Kennison 750 10.00
52 Deltha O'Neal 2000 7.00
53 Bill Romanowski 2000 7.00
54 Charlie Batch 1250 10.00
55 Desmond Howard 500 12.00
56 Sedrick Irvin 2000 7.00
57 Tyrone Davis 500 7.00
58 Donald Driver 2000 7.00
59 Brett Favre 723 45.00
60 Ahman Green 400 12.00
61 Charles Lee 2000 7.00
62 Bill Schroeder 500 10.00
63 E.G. Green 1500 7.00
64 Edgerrin James 500 40.00
65 Peyton Manning 500 50.00
66 Jerome Pathon 1500 7.00
67 Marcus Pollard 2000 7.00
68 Kyle Brady 1250 7.00
69 Mark Brunell 500 25.00
70 Jamie Martin 2000 7.00
71 Keenan McCardell 750 10.00
72 Shyrone Stith 1250 7.00
73 Fred Taylor 1500 20.00
74 Alvis Whitted 2000 7.00
75 Derrick Alexander 1000 7.00
76 Kimble Anders 1250 7.00
77 Mike Cloud 2000 7.00
78 Trent Green 1398 10.00
79 Tony Horne 1500 7.00
80 Warren Moon 2000 15.00
81 Rob Konrad 2000 7.00
82 Ray Lucas 2000 7.00
83 Tony Martin 500 10.00
84 O.J. McDuffie 750 10.00
85 James McKnight 500 10.00
86 Leslie Shepherd 2000 7.00
87 Dedric Ward 2000 7.00
88 Cris Carter 1000 15.00
89 Daunte Culpepper 400 30.00
90 Randy Moss 400 45.00
91 Jake Reed 2000 7.00
92 Robert Smith 1500 7.00
93 Moe Williams 500 10.00
94 Michael Bishop 2000 10.00
95 Drew Bledsoe 500 20.00
96 Troy Brown 2000 7.00
97 Bert Emanuel 500 10.00
98 David Patten 2000 7.00
99 J.R. Redmond 2000 7.00
100 Albert Connell 2000 7.00
101 Willie Jackson 250 15.00
102 Chad Morton 250 12.00
103 Keith Poole 2000 7.00
104 Ricky Williams 731 20.00
105 Ron Dayne 625 15.00
106 Ron Dixon 750 10.00
107 Joe Jurevicius 1000 7.00
108 Richie Anderson 750 7.00
109 Matthew Hatchette 750 10.00
110 Chad Pennington 625 20.00
111 Reggie Barlow 1500 7.00
112 Napoleon Kaufman 1000 7.00
113 Jerry Rice 750 30.00
114 Andre Rison 750 10.00
115 Marques Tuiasosopo 1000 15.00
116 Charles Woodson 750 10.00
117 Donovan McNabb 500 25.00
118 Freddie Mitchell 1000 20.00
119 Trung Canidate 750 10.00
120 Marshall Faulk 400 20.00
121 Kurt Warner 200 40.00
122 Drew Brees 1000 45.00
123 Tim Dwight 500 12.00
124 Jermaine Fazande 1250 7.00
125 Doug Flutie 1250 15.00
126 LaDainian Tomlinson 1000 45.00
127 Jeff Garcia 1400 15.00
128 Tai Streets 750 12.00
129 Shaun Alexander 500 20.00
130 Matt Hasselbeck 750 12.00
131 Warrick Dunn 1500 12.00
132 Shaun King 2000 10.00
133 Ryan Leaf 2000 7.00
134 Eddie George 400 25.00
135 Jevon Kearse 750 15.00
136 Steve McNair 900 12.00
137 Chris Sanders 750 7.00
138 Donnell Bennett 2000 7.00
139 Kevin Lockett 750 7.00
140 David Boston 200 25.00
141 Thomas Jones 200 12.00
142 Jake Plummer 200 15.00
143 Corey Dillon 200 25.00
144 Akili Smith 200 20.00
145 Peter Warrick 200 25.00
146 Isaac Bruce 200 25.00
147 Marshall Faulk 200 30.00
148 Az-Zahir Hakim 200 15.00
149 Torry Holt 200 20.00
150 Kurt Warner 200 50.00

2001 Pacific Private Stock Game Worn Gear Patch

NM/M
Common Player: 12.00
1 Thomas Jones 100 20.00
2 Rob Moore 200 15.00
3 Jake Plummer 225 20.00
4 Frank Sanders 250 15.00
5 Chris Chandler 150 20.00
6 Doug Johnson 300 15.00
7 Terance Mathis 250 12.00
8 Randall Cunningham 200 18.00
9 Elvis Grbac 300 20.00
10 Jamal Lewis 100 40.00
11 Ray Lewis 300 20.00
12 Shawn Bryson 300 15.00
13 Kwame Cavil 300 12.00
14 Jonathon Linton 300 12.00
15 Jeremy McDaniel 300 12.00
16 Eric Moulds 250 20.00
17 Thurman Thomas 250 25.00
18 Michael Bates 300 12.00
19 Dameyune Craig 300 12.00
20 William Floyd 300 12.00
21 Patrick Jeffers 250 15.00
22 Wesley Walls 250 12.00
24 Marlon Barnes 300 12.00
25 D'Wayne Bates 300 12.00
26 Marty Booker 300 12.00
27 Cade McNown 200 20.00
29 Brian Urlacher 100 50.00
30 Brandon Bennett 300 12.00
31 Curtis Keaton 50 20.00
32 Jon Kitna 300 20.00
33 Peter Warrick 25 30.00
34 Darrin Chiaverini 300 12.00
35 Tim Couch 100 35.00
36 Rickey Dudley 300 12.00
37 Curtis Enis 250 12.00
38 Kevin Johnson 250 15.00
39 Dennis Northcutt 300 12.00
40 Troy Aikman 225 50.00
41 Wane McGarity 250 12.00
42 Carl Pickens 200 12.00
43 Emmitt Smith 100 70.00
44 Michael Wiley 300 12.00
45 Anthony Wright 150 30.00
46 Mike Anderson 100 50.00
47 Steve Beuerlein 200 15.00
48 Terrell Davis 100 50.00
49 Olandis Gary 225 15.00
50 Brian Griese 100 40.00
51 Eddie Kennison 250 12.00
52 Deltha O'Neal 300 12.00
53 Bill Romanowski 300 12.00
54 Charlie Batch 250 20.00
55 Desmond Howard 250 12.00
56 Sedrick Irvin 300 12.00
57 Tyrone Davis 250 12.00
58 Donald Driver 300 12.00
59 Brett Favre 125 85.00
60 Ahman Green 75 25.00
61 Charles Lee 300 12.00
62 Bill Schroeder 300 12.00
63 E.G. Green 250 12.00
64 Edgerrin James 100 60.00
65 Peyton Manning 100 75.00
66 Jerome Pathon 300 12.00
67 Marcus Pollard 300 12.00
68 Kyle Brady 300 12.00
69 Mark Brunell 100 40.00
70 Jamie Martin 300 12.00
71 Keenan McCardell 100 20.00
72 Shyrone Stith 300 12.00
73 Fred Taylor 250 30.00
74 Alvis Whitted 300 12.00
75 Derrick Alexander 300 12.00
76 Kimble Anders 300 12.00
77 Mike Cloud 300 12.00
78 Trent Green 250 12.00
79 Tony Horne 250 15.00
80 Warren Moon 250 25.00
81 Rob Konrad 300 12.00
82 Ray Lucas 300 12.00
83 Tony Martin 250 12.00
84 O.J. McDuffie 250 15.00
85 James McKnight 250 12.00
86 Leslie Shepherd 300 12.00
87 Dedric Ward 300 12.00
88 Cris Carter 225 25.00
89 Daunte Culpepper 25 100.00
90 Randy Moss 25 150.00
91 Jake Reed 300 12.00
92 Robert Smith 275 12.00
93 Moe Williams 250 12.00
94 Michael Bishop 300 18.00
95 Drew Bledsoe 100 40.00
96 Troy Brown 300 12.00
97 Bert Emanuel 250 12.00
98 David Patten 300 12.00
99 J.R. Redmond 300 12.00
100 Albert Connell 300 12.00
101 Willie Jackson 250 12.00
102 Chad Morton 300 12.00
103 Keith Poole 300 12.00
104 Ricky Williams 100 45.00
105 Ron Dayne 100 45.00
106 Ron Dixon 250 20.00
107 Joe Jurevicius 200 12.00
108 Richie Anderson 250 12.00
109 Matthew Hatchette 250 12.00
110 Chad Pennington 100 45.00
111 Reggie Barlow 250 12.00
112 Napoleon Kaufman 200 20.00
113 Jerry Rice 100 80.00
114 Andre Rison 250 15.00
116 Charles Woodson 250 20.00
117 Donovan McNabb 100 40.00
119 Trung Canidate 250 15.00
120 Marshall Faulk 25 75.00
121 Kurt Warner 25 75.00
123 Tim Dwight 250 25.00
124 Jermaine Fazande 300 12.00
125 Doug Flutie 250 35.00
127 Jeff Garcia 250 30.00
128 Tai Streets 250 15.00
129 Shaun Alexander 100 30.00
130 Matt Hasselbeck 200 25.00
131 Warrick Dunn 250 25.00
132 Shaun King 300 18.00
133 Ryan Leaf 300 12.00
134 Eddie George 100 40.00
135 Jevon Kearse 150 30.00
136 Steve McNair 225 25.00
137 Chris Sanders 150 15.00
138 Donnell Bennett 300 12.00
139 Kevin Lockett 250 12.00

2001 Pacific Private Stock Moments In Time

NM/M
Complete Set (15): 130.00
Common Player: 8.00
Production 499 Sets
1 Michael Vick 45.00
2 Travis Henry 10.00
3 Chris Weinke 15.00
4 David Terrell 12.00
5 Anthony Thomas 10.00
6 Quincy Carter 12.00
7 Michael Bennett 20.00
8 Deuce McAllister 12.00
9 Santana Moss 10.00
10 Marques Tuiasosopo 8.00
11 Freddie Mitchell 10.00
12 Drew Brees 30.00
13 LaDainian Tomlinson 30.00
14 Koren Robinson 10.00
15 Rod Gardner 10.00

2001 Pacific Private Stock PS-2001

NM/M
Common Player: .20
1 David Boston .50
2 Thomas Jones .20
3 Jake Plummer .20
4 Jamal Anderson .20
5 Terance Mathis .20
6 Elvis Grbac .20
7 Jamal Lewis 1.00
8 Chris Redman .20
9 Shannon Sharpe .40
10 Travis Taylor .20
11 Rob Johnson .40
12 Eric Moulds .20
13 Peerless Price .40
14 Tim Biakabutuka .20
15 Patrick Jeffers .20
16 Muhsin Muhammad .20
17 James Allen .20
18 Cade McNown .40
19 Marcus Robinson .20
20 Brian Urlacher 1.50
21 Corey Dillon .40
22 Peter Warrick .40
23 Tim Couch 1.00
24 Kevin Johnson .20
25 Dennis Northcutt .20
26 Travis Prentice .20
27 Raghib Ismail .20
28 Emmitt Smith 2.00
29 Mike Anderson .50
30 Terrell Davis .50
31 Brian Griese .50
32 Ed McCaffrey .20
33 Charlie Batch .20
34 Johnnie Morton .20
35 James Stewart .20
36 Brett Favre 3.00
37 Antonio Freeman .20
38 Ahman Green .75
39 Marvin Harrison .50
40 Jerome Pathon .20
41 Terrence Wilkins .20
42 Mark Brunell .50
43 Keenan McCardell .20
44 Jimmy Smith .20
45 Fred Taylor .50
46 Derrick Alexander .20
47 Tony Gonzalez .20
48 Trent Green .20
49 Sylvester Morris .20
50 Jay Fiedler .20
51 Oronde Gadsden .20
52 Lamar Smith .20
53 Cris Carter .50
54 Doug Chapman .20
55 Daunte Culpepper 2.00
56 Drew Bledsoe 1.00
57 Kevin Faulk .20
58 Terry Glenn .20
59 J.R. Redmond .50
60 Jeff Blake .20
61 Aaron Brooks 1.00
62 Joe Horn .20
63 Ricky Williams 1.00
64 Tiki Barber .20
65 Kerry Collins .20
66 Ron Dayne 1.00
67 Amani Toomer .20
68 Curtis Martin .50
69 Chad Pennington 1.00
70 Vinny Testaverde .20
71 Tim Brown .50
72 Rich Gannon .20
73 Jerry Rice 1.00
74 Tyrone Wheatley .20
75 Donovan McNabb .50
76 Duce Staley .20
77 Jerome Bettis .50
78 Kordell Stewart .50
79 Isaac Bruce .50
80 Marshall Faulk 1.00
81 Az-Zahir Hakim .20
82 Torry Holt .50
83 Tim Dwight .20
84 Doug Flutie 1.00
85 Jeff Garcia .50
86 Terrell Owens .50
87 Shaun Alexander 1.00
88 Matt Hasselbeck .20
89 Darrell Jackson .20
90 Ricky Watters .40
91 Mike Alstott .40
92 Warrick Dunn .40
93 Brad Johnson .20
94 Keyshawn Johnson .40
95 Eddie George 1.00
96 Derrick Mason .20
97 Steve McNair .50
98 Stephen Davis .50
99 Jeff George .20
100 Michael Westbrook .20
101 Bobby Newcombe 1.00
102 Alge Crumpler 1.00
103 Vinny Sutherland 1.00
104 Todd Heap 1.00
105 Tim Hasselbeck 1.00
106 Travis Henry 1.00
107 Dee Brown 1.00
108 Dan Morgan 1.00
109 Steve Smith 1.00
110 Chris Weinke 2.00
111 Anthony Thomas 2.50
112 T.J. Houshmandzadeh 1.00
113 Chad Johnson 1.00
114 Rudi Johnson 1.00
115 James Jackson 1.00
116 Quincy Morgan 1.50
117 Quincy Carter 1.50
118 Kevin Kasper 1.00
119 Scotty Anderson 1.00
120 Mike McMahon 2.00
121 Robert Ferguson 1.00
122 Reggie Wayne 1.00
123 Derrick Blaylock 1.00
124 Marvin "Snoop" Minnis 1.50
125 Chris Chambers 2.00
126 Jamar Fletcher 1.00
127 Josh Heupel 1.50
128 Travis Minor 1.00
129 Michael Bennett 2.50
130 Deuce McAllister 2.50
131 Moran Norris 1.00
132 Will Allen 1.00
133 Jonathan Carter 1.00
134 Jesse Palmer 1.00
135 LaMont Jordan 1.00
136 Ken-Yon Rambo 1.00
137 Marques Tuiasosopo 2.00
138 Correll Buckhelter 1.00
139 Freddie Mitchell 2.00
140 Chris Taylor 1.00
141 Adam Archuleta 1.00
142 Francis St. Paul 1.00
143 Kevan Barlow 1.00
144 Cedrick Wilson 1.00
145 Alex Bannister 1.00
146 Josh Booty 1.00
147 Heath Evans 1.00
148 Dan Alexander 1.00
149 Eddie Berlin 1.00
150 Rod Gardner 1.50
151 Darnerian McCants 1.00
152 Sage Rosenfels 1.00

2001 Pacific Private Stock PS-2001 Blue Back

Not priced due to limited production
153 Michael Vick
154 David Terrell
155 Edgerrin James
156 Peyton Manning
157 Randy Moss
158 Santana Moss
159 Kurt Warner
160 Drew Brees
161 LaDainian Tomlinson
162 Koren Robinson

2001 Pacific Private Stock Reserve

NM/M
Complete Set (20): 65.00
Common Player: 3.00
Inserted 1:21
1 Jamal Lewis 3.00
2 Peter Warrick 3.00
3 Emmitt Smith 6.00
4 Mike Anderson 4.00
5 Terrell Davis 5.00
6 Brian Griese 4.00
7 Brett Favre 8.00
8 Edgerrin James 5.00
9 Peyton Manning 5.00
10 Mark Brunell 4.00
11 Daunte Culpepper 4.00
12 Randy Moss 5.00
13 Drew Bledsoe 4.00
14 Ricky Williams 5.00
15 Ron Dayne 2.00
16 Donovan McNabb 4.00
17 Marshall Faulk 4.00
18 Kurt Warner 5.00
19 Eddie George 4.00
20 Steve McNair 3.00

2001 Pacific Titanium Hobby

NM/M
Commons .25
Rookie commons 5.00
Wax Box(24): 80.00

No.	Player	NM/M
1	David Boston	1.00
2	Thomas Jones	.25
3	Rob Moore	.25
4	Michael Pittman	.25
5	Jake Plummer	.25
6	Jamal Anderson	.50
7	Chris Chandler	.25
8	Shawn Jefferson	.25
9	Terance Mathis	.25
10	Terry Allen	.25
11	Jason Brookins	1.50
12	Elvis Grbac	.25
13	Qadry Ismail	.25
14	Jamal Lewis	2.00
15	Ray Lewis	.50
16	Shannon Sharpe	.50
17	Shawn Bryson	.25
18	Rob Johnson	.25
19	Sammy Morris	.40
20	Eric Moulds	.25
21	Peerless Price	.25
22	Tim Biakabutuka	.25
23	Patrick Jeffers	.25
24	Muhsin Muhammad	.25
25	James Allen	.25
26	Shane Mathews	.25
27	Marcus Robinson	.50
28	Brian Urlacher	2.50
29	Corey Dillon	.50
30	Jon Kitna	.25
31	Akili Smith	.50
32	Peter Warrick	.50
33	Tim Couch	1.25
34	Kevin Johnson	.25
35	Dennis Northcutt	.25
36	Joey Galloway	.25
37	Raghib Ismail	.25
38	Emmitt Smith	2.50
39	Mike Anderson	1.50
40	Terrell Davis	1.50
41	Brian Griese	1.25
42	Ed McCaffrey	.25
43	Rod Smith	.25
44	Charlie Batch	.25
45	Germane Crowell	.25
46	Herman Moore	.25
47	Johnnie Morton	.25
48	James Stewart	.25
49	Brett Favre	4.00
50	Antonio Freeman	.25
51	Ahman Green	.60
52	Bill Schroeder	.25
53	Marvin Harrison	.60
54	Edgerrin James	2.50
55	Peyton Manning	3.00
56	Jerome Pathon	.25
57	Terrence Wilkins	.25
58	Mark Brunell	1.00
59	Keenan McCardell	.25
60	Jimmy Smith	.25
61	Fred Taylor	1.00
62	Derrick Alexander	.25
63	Tony Gonzalez	.25
64	Trent Green	.25
65	Priest Holmes	.60
66	Jay Fiedler	.25
67	Oronde Gadsden	.25
68	James McKnight	.25
69	Lamar Smith	.25
70	Zach Thomas	.60
71	Cris Carter	.60
72	Daunte Culpepper	2.00
73	Randy Moss	3.00
74	Drew Bledsoe	1.00
75	Troy Brown	.25
76	Charles Johnson	.25
77	J.R. Redmond	1.00
78	Antowain Smith	.25
79	Jeff Blake	.25
80	Aaron Brooks	1.00
81	Albert Connell	.25
82	Joe Horn	.25
83	Ricky Williams	1.50
84	Tiki Barber	.25
85	Kerry Collins	.25
86	Ron Dayne	.60
87	Ike Hilliard	.25
88	Amani Toomer	.25
89	Richie Anderson	.25
90	Wayne Chrebet	.25
91	Laveranues Coles	.25
92	Curtis Martin	.60
93	Chad Pennington	.75
94	Vinny Testaverde	.25
95	Tim Brown	.60
96	Rich Gannon	.25
97	Charlie Garner	.25
98	Jerry Rice	2.50
99	Tyrone Wheatley	.25
100	Charles Woodson	.75
101	Donovan McNabb	2.00
102	Todd Pinkston	.25
103	Duce Staley	.25
104	James Thrash	.25
105	Jerome Bettis	.60
106	Plaxico Burress	1.00
107	Tommy Maddox	.25
108	Bobby Shaw	.25
109	Kordell Stewart	.60
110	Hines Ward	.25
111	Isaac Bruce	.60
112	Marshall Faulk	1.50
113	Az-Zahir Hakim	.25
114	Torry Holt	.25
115	Kurt Warner	2.50
116	Curtis Conway	.25
117	Tim Dwight	.25
118	Doug Flutie	1.00
119	Jeff Graham	.25
120	Jeff Garcia	.60
121	Garrison Hearst	.25
122	Terrell Owens	.60
123	J.J. Stokes	.25
124	Tai Streets	.25
125	Shaun Alexander	1.50
126	Matt Hasselbeck	.25
127	Darrell Jackson	.25
128	Ricky Watters	.60
129	Mike Alstott	.60
130	Warrick Dunn	.60
131	Jacquez Green	.25
132	Brad Johnson	.25
133	Keyshawn Johnson	.60
134	Warren Sapp	.50
135	Kevin Dyson	.25
136	Eddie George	1.25
137	Mike Green	.25
138	Jevon Kearse	.25
139	Derrick Mason	.25
140	Steve McNair	.60
141	Champ Bailey	.50
142	Stephen Davis	.75
143	Jeff George	.25
144	Michael Westbrook	.25
145	*Bill Gramatica*	5.00
146	*Arnold Jackson*	5.00
147	*Bobby Newcombe*	5.00
148	*Marcel Shipp*	25.00
149	*Quentin McCord*	10.00
150	*Michael Vick*	175.00
151	*Chris Barnes*	5.00
152	*Todd Heap*	35.00
153	*Reggie Germany*	10.00
154	*Travis Henry*	40.00
155	*Chris Taylor*	10.00
156	*Dee Brown*	10.00
157	*Dan Morgan*	10.00
158	*Steve Smith*	10.00
159	*Chris Weinke*	25.00
160	*David Terrell*	75.00
161	*Anthony Thomas*	80.00
162	*T.J. Houshmandzadeh*	10.00
163	*Chad Johnson*	10.00
164	*Rudi Johnson*	10.00
165	*James Jackson*	40.00
166	*Andre King*	10.00
167	*Quincy Morgan*	40.00
168	*Quincy Carter*	75.00
169	*Ken-Yon Rambo*	10.00
170	*Kevin Kasper*	10.00
171	*Scotty Anderson*	15.00
172	*Mike McMahon*	75.00
173	*Robert Ferguson*	15.00
174	*David Martin*	15.00
175	*Reggie Wayne*	50.00
176	*Richmond Flowers*	10.00
177	*Derrick Blaylock*	10.00
178	*Marvin "Snoop" Minnis*	40.00
179	*Chris Chambers*	75.00
180	*Josh Heupel*	40.00
181	*Travis Minor*	15.00
182	*Michael Bennett*	75.00
183	*Cedric James*	10.00
184	*Deuce McAllister*	100.00
185	*Onomo Ojo*	10.00
186	*Jonathan Carter*	10.00
187	*Jesse Palmer*	25.00
188	*LaMont Jordan*	15.00
189	*Derek Combs*	10.00
190	*Marques Tuiasosopo*	75.00
191	*Correll Buckhalter*	40.00
192	*Freddie Mitchell*	40.00
193	*Adam Archuleta*	10.00
194	*Francis St. Paul*	10.00
195	*Drew Brees*	100.00
196	*LaDainian Tomlinson*	125.00
197	*Kevan Barlow*	40.00
198	*Vinny Sutherland*	10.00
199	*Cedrick Wilson*	10.00
200	*Alex Bannister*	10.00
201	*Koren Robinson*	20.00
202	*Milton Wynn*	10.00
203	*Dan Alexander*	10.00
204	*Eddie Berlin*	10.00
205	*Justin McCareins*	10.00
206	*Rod Gardner*	40.00
207	*Darnerian McCants*	10.00
208	*Sage Rosenfels*	25.00

2001 Pacific Titanium Hobby Double-Sided Jerseys

		NM/M
Common Player:		10.00
1	Bobby Newcombe, Arnold Jackson	10.00
2	Marcel Shipp, Bill Gramatica	10.00
3	LaMont Jordan, Rod Gardner	20.00
4	Quentin McCord, Vinny Sutherland	10.00
5	Michael Vick, Quincy Carter	60.00
6	Chris Barnes, Todd Heap	10.00
7	Reggie Germany, Travis Henry	15.00
8	Dee Brown, Steve Smith	10.00
9	Chris Weinke, Josh Heupel	25.00
10	Dan Morgan, Adam Archuleta	10.00
11	David Terrell, Anthony Thomas	30.00
12	T.J. Houshmandzadeh, Chad Johnson	10.00
13	Rudi Johnson, James Jackson	20.00
14	Andre King, Quincy Morgan	15.00
15	Kevin Kasper, Richmond Flowers	10.00
16	Scotty Anderson, Mike McMahon	20.00
17	Robert Ferguson, David Martin	20.00
18	Reggie Wayne, Freddie Mitchell	25.00
19	Derrick Blaylock, Marvin "Snoop" Minnis	20.00
20	Chris Chambers, Travis Minor	40.00
21	Michael Bennett, Cedric James	40.00
22	Deuce McAllister, Onomo Ojo	40.00
23	Jonathan Carter, Jesse Palmer	15.00
24	Derek Combs, Ken-Yon Rambo	10.00
25	Marques Tuiasosopo, Sage Rosenfels	25.00
26	Correll Buckhalter, Dan Alexander	10.00
27	Chris Taylor, Darnerian McCants	10.00
28	Francis St. Paul, Milton Wynn	10.00
29	Drew Brees, LaDainian Tomlinson	50.00
30	Kevan Barlow, Cedrick Wilson	10.00
31	Alex Bannister, Koren Robinson	10.00
32	Eddie Berlin, Justin McCareins	10.00
33	Na Brown, Chad Lewis	10.00
34	Terry Hardy, David Sloan	10.00
35	Tywan Mitchell, Dennis McKinley	10.00
36	Bryan Gilmore, Jermaine Lewis	10.00
37	David Boston, Jimmy Smith	20.00
38	MarTay Jenkins, R. Jay Soward	10.00
39	Thomas Jones, Fred Taylor	20.00
40	Frank Sanders, Terrell Owens	15.00
41	Chris Gedney, Frank Wycheck	10.00
42	Chris Griesen, Neil O'Donnell	10.00
43	Jammi German, Shawn Jefferson	10.00
44	Reggie Kelly, Maurice Smith	10.00
45	Tony Martin, Derrick Alexander	10.00
46	Jamal Anderson, Curtis Martin	15.00
47	Jamal Lewis, Mike Anderson	25.00
48	Shannon Sharpe, Tony Gonzalez	15.00
49	Ray Lewis, Bryan Cox	15.00
50	Elvis Grbac, Kerry Collins	10.00
51	Obafemi Ayanbadejo, Chris Fuamatu-Ma'afala	10.00
52	Antowain Smith, Sammy Morris	10.00
53	Thurman Thomas, J.J. Johnson	15.00
54	Donald Hayes, Chris Hetherington	10.00
55	Isaac Byrd, Reggie White	10.00
56	Brad Hoover, Steve Beuerlein	10.00
57	Tim Biakabutuka, William Floyd	10.00
58	Shane Matthews, Jim Miller	10.00
59	Marcus Robinson, Johnnie Morton	10.00
60	Dez White, Sylvester Morris	10.00
61	Brian Urlacher, Zach Thomas	45.00
62	Clif Groce, Nick Williams	10.00
63	Corey Dillon, Peter Warrick	15.00
64	Damon Griffin, Tremain Mack	10.00
65	Danny Farmer, Craig Yeast	10.00
66	Marco Battaglia, Takeo Spikes	10.00
67	Damay Scott, Bill Schroeder	10.00
68	Kevin Thompson, Jamel White	10.00
69	Tim Couch, Jake Plummer	20.00
70	Kevin Johnson, Antonio Freeman	10.00
71	Dennis Northcutt, Keenan McCardell	10.00
72	Aaron Shea, Marc Edwards	10.00
73	Raghib Ismail, Jason Tucker	10.00
74	Troy Hambrick, Darren Woodson	10.00
75	Jeff Garcia, Warren Moon	20.00
76	Wane McGarity, James McKnight	10.00
77	Emmitt Smith, Eddie George	50.00
78	Dwayne Carswell, Byron Chamberlain	10.00
79	Terrell Davis, Brian Griese	25.00
80	Rod Smith, Oronde Gadsden	10.00
81	Ed McCaffrey, Torry Holt	10.00
82	Germane Crowell, Herman Moore	10.00
83	Larry Foster, Allen Rossum	10.00
84	James Stewart, Robert Smith	10.00
85	Charlie Batch, Steve McNair	15.00
86	Herbert Goodman, De'Mond Parker	10.00
87	Dorsey Levens, Lamar Smith	10.00
88	Brett Favre, Kurt Warner	75.00
89	E.G. Green, Jerome Pathon	10.00
90	Edgerrin James, Peyton Manning	50.00
91	Marvin Harrison, Amani Toomer	15.00
92	Anthony Johnson, Stacey Mack	10.00
93	Mark Brunell, Chris Chandler	20.00
94	Sean Dawkins, Derrick Mayes	10.00
95	Priest Holmes, Charlie Garner	15.00
96	Kimble Anders, Mike Alstott	10.00
97	Leslie Shepherd, Bert Emanuel	10.00
98	O.J. McDuffie, J.J. Stokes	10.00
99	Chris Walsh, Troy Walters	10.00
100	Daunte Culpepper, Randy Moss	50.00
101	Cris Carter, Wayne Chrebet	10.00
102	Charles Johnson, Torrance Small	10.00
103	Drew Bledsoe, Rich Gannon	15.00
104	Damon Huard, Brock Huard	10.00
105	Jeff Blake, Chad Morton	10.00
106	Willie Jackson, Kevin Dyson	10.00
107	Ron Dayne, Tiki Barber	15.00
108	Jason Sehorn, Charles Woodson	15.00
109	Ron Dixon, Az-Zahir Hakim	10.00
110	Chad Pennington, Vinny Testaverde	15.00
111	Tim Brown, Jerry Rice	50.00
112	Andre Rison, Tai Streets	10.00
113	Tyrone Wheatley, Shaun Alexander	20.00
114	Donovan McNabb, Duce Staley	20.00
115	Jerome Bettis, Kordell Stewart	25.00
116	Orlando Pace, Justin Watson	10.00
117	Curtis Conway, Doug Flutie	20.00
118	Fred Beasley, Paul Smith	10.00
119	Christian Fauria, Itula Mili	10.00
120	Darrell Jackson, Ricky Watters	10.00
121	Trent Dilfer, Tony Banks	10.00
122	Rabih Abdullah, Aaron Stecker	10.00
123	Dave Moore, Erron Kinney	10.00
124	Yancey Thigpen, Rodney Thomas	10.00
125	Deion Sanders, Champ Bailey	20.00

2001 Pacific Titanium Hobby Fantasy Football

		NM/M
Complete Set (25):		60.00
Common Player:		2.00
1	Michael Vick	10.00
2	Travis Henry	3.00
3	Chris Weinke	2.00
4	David Terrell	3.00
5	Anthony Thomas	4.00
6	Chad Johnson	2.00
7	James Jackson	3.00
8	Quincy Morgan	3.00
9	Quincy Carter	3.00
10	Kevin Kasper	2.00
11	Reggie Wayne	4.00
12	Marvin "Snoop" Minnis	3.00
13	Chris Chambers	5.00
14	Travis Minor	3.00
15	Michael Bennett	5.00
16	Deuce McAllister	5.00
17	Santana Moss	4.00
18	Marques Tuiasosopo	5.00
19	Correll Buckhalter	2.00
20	Freddie Mitchell	5.00
21	Drew Brees	5.00
22	LaDainian Tomlinson	6.00
23	Kevan Barlow	3.00
24	Koren Robinson	3.00
25	Rod Gardner	5.00

2001 Pacific Titanium Hobby Monday Knights

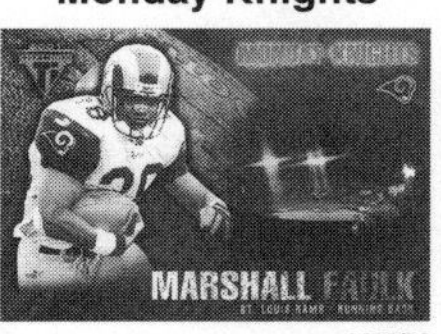

		NM/M
Complete Set (25):		40.00
Common Player:		1.00
1	Emmitt Smith	4.00
2	Mike Anderson	2.00
3	Terrell Davis	2.00
4	Brian Griese	2.00
5	Rod Smith	1.00
6	Brett Favre	5.00
7	Antonio Freeman	1.00
8	Ahman Green	1.50
9	Edgerrin James	4.00
10	Peyton Manning	4.00
11	Mark Brunell	2.00
12	Jimmy Smith	1.00
13	Fred Taylor	1.00
14	Cris Carter	1.00
15	Daunte Culpepper	3.00
16	Randy Moss	4.00
17	Rich Gannon	1.00
18	Jerry Rice	4.00
19	Donovan McNabb	3.00
20	Duce Staley	2.00
21	Isaac Bruce	1.50
22	Marshall Faulk	3.00
23	Kurt Warner	4.00
24	Eddie George	2.50
25	Steve McNair	1.50

2001 Pacific Titanium Hobby Titanium Team

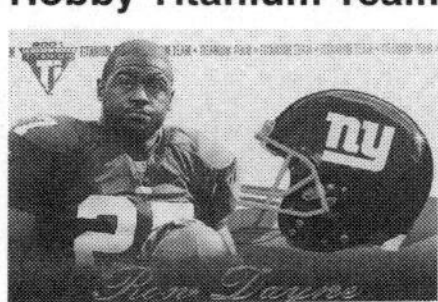

		NM/M
Complete Set (25):		70.00
Common Player:		1.00
1	Corey Dillon	1.00
2	Peter Warrick	1.00
3	Tim Couch	3.00
4	Emmitt Smith	5.00
5	Mike Anderson	3.00
6	Olandis Gary	1.00
7	Brian Griese	3.00
8	Brett Favre	6.00
9	Edgerrin James	3.00
10	Peyton Manning	4.00
11	Mark Brunell	2.00
12	Fred Taylor	2.00
13	Daunte Culpepper	3.00
14	Randy Moss	4.00
15	Drew Bledsoe	4.00
16	Aaron Brooks	3.00
17	Ricky Williams	4.00
18	Ron Dayne	2.00
19	Jerry Rice	4.00
20	Donovan McNabb	4.00
21	Marshall Faulk	4.00
22	Kurt Warner	4.00
23	Jeff Garcia	1.00
24	Eddie George	3.00
25	Steve McNair	1.00

2001 Pacific Titanium Retail

Common Player:
#'s 1-144 .5X of hobby
#'s 145-216 .1X of hobby

2001 Pacific Vanguard

		NM/M
Common Player:		.20
Minor Stars:		.50
Common Rookie:		2.00
Production 450 Sets		
Pack (4):		3.00
Wax Box (24):		55.00

No.	Player	NM/M
1	David Boston	.75
2	Thomas Jones	.75
3	Jake Plummer	.75
4	Jamal Anderson	.75
5	Chris Chandler	.50
6	Elvis Grbac	.75
7	Jamal Lewis	2.00
8	Shannon Sharpe	.50
9	Rob Johnson	.50
10	Eric Moulds	.75
11	Peerless Price	.50
12	Tim Biakabutuka	.50
13	Muhsin Muhammad	.50
14	James Allen	.75
15	Cade McNown	.75
16	Marcus Robinson	.75
17	Corey Dillon	.75
18	Akili Smith	.75
19	Peter Warrick	.75
20	Tim Couch	1.00
21	Kevin Johnson	.75
22	Travis Prentice	.50
23	Raghib Ismail	.50
24	Emmitt Smith	2.00
25	Mike Anderson	2.00
26	Terrell Davis	1.75
27	Brian Griese	1.00
28	Ed McCaffrey	.75
29	Rod Smith	.75
30	Charlie Batch	.75
31	Johnnie Morton	.50
32	James Stewart	.75
33	Brett Favre	3.00
34	Antonio Freeman	.75
35	Ahman Green	.75
36	Bill Schroeder	.50
37	Marvin Harrison	.75
38	Edgerrin James	2.00
39	Peyton Manning	2.50
40	Terrence Wilkins	.50
41	Mark Brunell	.75
42	Keenan McCardell	.50
43	Jimmy Smith	.75
44	Fred Taylor	1.00
45	Derrick Alexander	.50
46	Tony Gonzalez	.75
47	Sylvester Morris	.75
48	Jay Fiedler	.75
49	Oronde Gadsden	.50
50	Lamar Smith	.75
51	Cris Carter	.75
52	Daunte Culpepper	1.50
53	Randy Moss	2.50
54	Drew Bledsoe	1.00
55	Terry Glenn	.75
56	J.R. Redmond	.50
57	Jeff Blake	.50
58	Joe Horn	.50
59	Ricky Williams	1.25
60	Tiki Barber	.75
61	Kerry Collins	.50
62	Ron Dayne	1.25
63	Amani Toomer	.50
64	Wayne Chrebet	.50
65	Curtis Martin	.75
66	Vinny Testaverde	.50
67	Tim Brown	.50
68	Rich Gannon	.50
69	Tyrone Wheatley	.50
70	Charles Johnson	.20
71	Donovan McNabb	1.25
72	Duce Staley	.75
73	Jerome Bettis	.75
74	Kordell Stewart	.50
75	Hines Ward	.50
76	Isaac Bruce	.75
77	Marshall Faulk	1.00
78	Torry Holt	.75
79	Kurt Warner	2.50
80	Curtis Conway	.50
81	Tim Dwight	.75
82	Doug Flutie	1.00
83	Junior Seau	.50
84	Jeff Garcia	.75
85	Terrell Owens	.75
86	Jerry Rice	2.00
87	Shaun Alexander	1.00
88	Matt Hasselbeck	.75
89	Darrell Jackson	.50
90	Mike Alstott	.75
91	Warrick Dunn	.75
92	Keyshawn Johnson	.75
93	Brad Johnson	.50
94	Kevin Dyson	.20
95	Eddie George	1.00
96	Derrick Mason	.75
97	Steve McNair	.75
98	Stephen Davis	.75
99	Jeff George	.50
100	Michael Westbrook	.50
101	*Bobby Newcombe*	10.00
102	*Alge Crumpler*	10.00
103	*Vinny Sutherland*	10.00
104	*Michael Vick*	85.00
105	*Todd Heap*	10.00
106	*Nate Clements*	2.00

107 *Travis Henry* 25.00
108 *Dan Morgan* 10.00
109 *Chris Weinke* 30.00
110 *David Terrell* 25.00
111 *Anthony Thomas* 50.00
112 *T.J. Houshmandzadeh* 2.00
113 *Chad Johnson* 12.00
114 *Rudi Johnson* 12.00
115 *James Jackson* 15.00
116 *Quincy Morgan* 15.00
117 *Quincy Carter* 25.00
118 *Scotty Anderson* 2.00
119 *Mike McMahon* 10.00
120 *Robert Ferguson* 10.00
121 *Reggie Wayne* 15.00
122 *Marvin "Snoop" Minnis* 15.00
123 *Chris Chambers* 15.00
124 *Jamar Fletcher* 8.00
125 *Josh Heupel* 18.00
126 *Travis Minor* 10.00
127 *Michael Bennett* 30.00
128 *Deuce McAllister* 35.00
129 *Will Allen* 2.00
130 *Jesse Palmer* 10.00
131 *LaMont Jordan* 12.00
132 *Santana Moss* 18.00
133 *Ken-Yon Rambo* 10.00
134 *Marques Tuiasosopo* 25.00
135 *Correll Buckhalter* 15.00
136 *A.J. Feeley* 2.00
137 *Freddie Mitchell* 20.00
138 *Chris Taylor* 2.00
139 *Adam Archuleta* 10.00
140 *Drew Brees* 50.00
141 *LaDainian Tomlinson* 60.00
142 *Kevan Barlow* 15.00
143 *Cedrick Wilson* 8.00
144 *Alex Bannister* 8.00
145 *Josh Booty* 8.00
146 *Heath Evans* 2.00
147 *Koren Robinson* 20.00
148 *Dan Alexander* 8.00
149 *Rod Gardner* 25.00
150 *Sage Rosenfels* 10.00

2001 Pacific Vanguard Blue

Blue Cards: 2X-4X
Blue Rookies: 1X
Production 299 Sets

2001 Pacific Vanguard Gold

Gold Cards: 5X-8X
Gold Rookies: 1.5X
Production 99 Sets

2001 Pacific Vanguard Premiere Date

Premiere Date Cards: 3X-6X
Premiere Date Rookies: 1.5X
Production 115 Sets

2001 Pacific Vanguard Bombs Away

NM/M
Complete Set (30): 75.00
Common Player: 1.00
1 Michael Vick 12.00
2 Chris Weinke 3.00
3 Tim Couch 4.00
4 Brian Griese 3.00
5 Brett Favre 6.00
6 Peyton Manning 4.00
7 Mark Brunell 3.00
8 Daunte Culpepper 4.00
9 Drew Bledsoe 4.00
10 Rich Gannon 1.00
11 Donovan McNabb 4.00
12 Kurt Warner 4.00
13 Drew Brees 5.00
14 Jeff Garcia 3.00
15 Steve McNair 3.00
16 Eric Moulds 1.00
17 David Terrell 3.00
18 Peter Warrick 2.00
19 Marvin Harrison 3.00
20 Jimmy Smith 1.00
21 Cris Carter 1.00
22 Santana Moss 4.00
23 Tim Brown 3.00
24 Freddie Mitchell 4.00
25 Isaac Bruce 3.00
26 Torry Holt 1.00
27 Terrell Owens 3.00
28 Jerry Rice 4.00
29 Koren Robinson 3.00
30 Rod Gardner 3.00

A player's name in *italic* type indicates a rookie card.

2001 Pacific Vanguard Double Sided Jerseys

NM/M
Common Player: 12.00
Inserted 2:25
1 Jake Plummer, David Boston 20.00
2 Rob Moore, Frank Sanders 12.00
3 Thomas Jones, Michael Pittman 12.00
4 Chris Gedney, Ernie Conwell 12.00
5 Chris Griesen, Neil O'Donnell 12.00
6 Chris Chandler, Terance Mathis 12.00
7 Tim Biakabutuka, Steve Beuerlein 15.00
8 Brad Hoover, Moe Williams 12.00
9 Chris Weinke, Freddie Mitchell 45.00
10 Patrick Jeffers, Tim Dwight 20.00
11 Reggie White, Jevon Kearse 20.00
12 Wesley Walls, Frank Wycheck 15.00
13 Bobby Engram, Dez White 12.00
14 Cade McNown, James Allen 20.00
15 Shane Matthews, Jim Miller 15.00
16 Brian Urlacher, Zach Thomas 60.00
17 Anthony Thomas, LaDainian Tomlinson 40.00
18 Corey Dillon, Peter Warrick 25.00
19 Ron Dugans, Danny Farmer 15.00
20 Randall Cunningham, Anthony Wright 12.00
21 Troy Aikman, Emmitt Smith 60.00
22 Wane McGarity, James McKnight 15.00
23 Jason Tucker, Ricky Proehl 12.00
24 Carl Pickens, Kevin Dyson 15.00
25 Brian Griese, Olandis Gary 30.00
26 Dwayne Carswell, Byron Chamberlain 12.00
27 Mike Anderson, Terrell Davis 40.00
28 Gus Frerotte, Matt Hasselbeck 18.00
29 Herman Moore, Johnnie Morton 15.00
30 James Stewart, Larry Foster 15.00
31 Desmond Howard, Tony Martin 12.00
32 Ahman Green, Herbert Goodman 20.00
33 Brett Favre, Antonio Freeman 50.00
34 Dorsey Levens, De'Mond Parker 15.00
35 Tyrone Davis, Bubba Franks 15.00
36 William Henderson, Greg Comella 12.00
37 Autry Denson, J.J. Johnson 12.00
38 Chris Walsh, Troy Walters 12.00
39 Cris Carter, Robert Smith 25.00
40 Daunte Culpepper, Randy Moss 70.00
41 Damon Huard, Bert Emanuel 15.00
42 Jeff Blake, Willie Jackson 15.00
43 Kerry Collins, Joe Jurevicius 15.00
44 Tiki Barber, Ron Dayne 25.00
45 Jason Sehorn, Aeneas Williams 15.00
46 Amani Toomer, Chris Sanders 15.00
47 Tyrone Wheatley, Napoleon Kaufman 15.00
48 Marques Tuiasosopo, Drew Brees 45.00
49 Kurt Warner, Marshall Faulk 50.00
50 Eddie George, Steve McNair 25.00

2001 Pacific Vanguard In Focus

NM/M
Common Player: 10.00
Production 99 Sets
1 Jamal Lewis 15.00
2 Emmitt Smith 25.00
3 Mike Anderson 20.00
4 Terrell Davis 25.00
5 Brett Favre 30.00
6 Edgerrin James 20.00
7 Peyton Manning 20.00
8 Mark Brunell 15.00
9 Daunte Culpepper 20.00
10 Randy Moss 25.00
11 Ricky Williams 20.00
12 Donovan McNabb 20.00
13 Marshall Faulk 20.00
14 Kurt Warner 20.00
15 Jerry Rice 25.00

2001 Pacific Vanguard Prime Prospects

NM/M
Complete Set (36): 45.00
Common Player: .75
Inserted 1:1
1 Michael Vick 10.00
2 Travis Henry 2.50
3 Dan Morgan .75
4 Chris Weinke 2.00
5 David Terrell 2.50
6 Anthony Thomas 2.00
7 Chad Johnson 1.00
8 James Jackson 1.25
9 Quincy Morgan 1.50
10 Quincy Carter 2.50
11 Mike McMahon 1.25
12 Robert Ferguson .75
13 Reggie Wayne 1.50
14 Marvin "Snoop" Minnis 1.50
15 Chris Chambers 1.50
16 Josh Heupel 1.75
17 Travis Minor .75
18 Michael Bennett 5.00
19 Deuce McAllister 2.50
20 Jesse Palmer .75
21 LaMont Jordan 1.25
22 Santana Moss 1.75
23 Ken-Yon Rambo .75
24 Marques Tuiasosopo 2.00
25 Correll Buckhalter 1.50
26 Freddie Mitchell 1.75
27 Adam Archuleta 1.00
28 Drew Brees 4.50
29 LaDainian Tomlinson 6.00
30 Kevan Barlow 1.50
31 Cedrick Wilson .75
32 Alex Bannister .75
33 Koren Robinson 2.00
34 Dan Alexander 1.00
35 Rod Gardner 2.50
36 Sage Rosenfels 1.00

2001 Pacific Vanguard V-Team

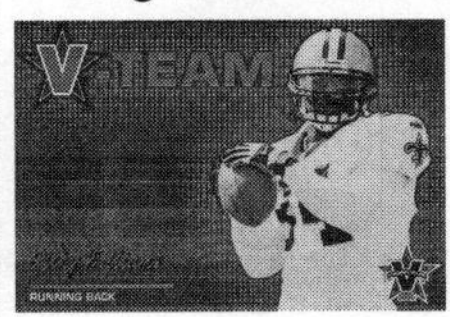

NM/M
Complete Set (25): 45.00
Common Player: 1.00
Production 1,499 Sets
1 Jamal Lewis 3.00
2 Corey Dillon 1.00
3 Peter Warrick 2.00
4 Tim Couch 4.00
5 Emmitt Smith 5.00
6 Mike Anderson 3.00
7 Terrell Davis 4.00
8 Brian Griese 3.50
9 Marvin Harrison 1.00
10 Edgerrin James 43.00
11 Peyton Manning 4.00
12 Mark Brunell 3.50
13 Fred Taylor 3.00
14 Cris Carter 1.00
15 Randy Moss 4.00
16 Drew Bledsoe 3.50
17 Ricky Williams 4.00
18 Ron Dayne 2.00
19 Donovan McNabb 4.00
20 Marshall Faulk 4.00
21 Kurt Warner 4.00
22 Jeff Garcia 1.00
23 Jerry Rice 5.00
24 Eddie George 3.00
25 Steve McNair 1.00

2001 Pacific Vanguard V-Team Rookies

NM/M
Complete Set (30): 100.00
Common Player: 2.00
Production 999 Sets
1 Michael Vick 18.00
2 Travis Henry 6.00
3 Chris Weinke 4.00
4 David Terrell 5.00
5 Anthony Thomas 5.00
6 Chad Johnson 3.00
7 James Jackson 4.00
8 Quincy Morgan 4.00
9 Quincy Carter 6.00
10 Mike McMahon 3.00
11 Robert Ferguson 2.00
12 Reggie Wayne 4.00
13 Marvin "Snoop" Minnis 4.00
14 Chris Chambers 4.00
15 Josh Heupel 5.00
16 Travis Minor 2.50
17 Michael Bennett 12.00
18 Deuce McAllister 6.00
19 Jesse Palmer 2.00
20 LaMont Jordan 3.00
21 Santana Moss 5.00
22 Marques Tuiasosopo 5.00
23 Correll Buckhalter 4.00
24 A.J. Feeley 2.00
25 Freddie Mitchell 5.00
26 Drew Brees 10.00
27 LaDainian Tomlinson 12.00
28 Koren Robinson 5.00
29 Rod Gardner 6.00
30 Sage Rosenfels 3.00

2002 Pacific

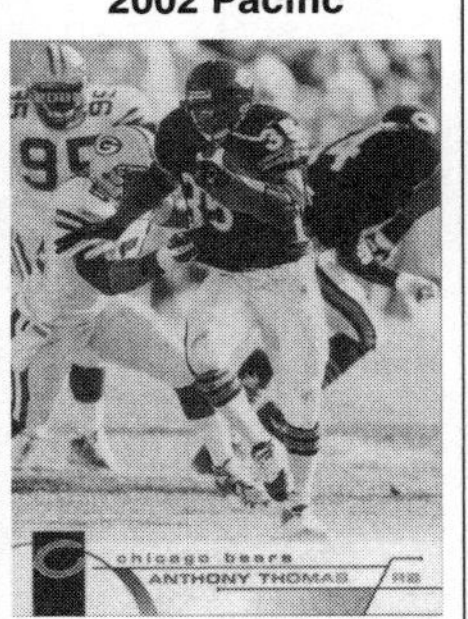

NM/M
Complete Set (500): 130.00
Common Player: .15
Unlisted Stars: .60
Minor Stars: .40
Pack (10): 2.00
Wax Box (36): 60.00
1 David Boston .60
2 Arnold Jackson .15
3 MarTay Jenkins .15
4 Thomas Jones .15
5 Kwamie Lassiter .15
6 Joel Makovicka .15
7 Ronald McKinnon .15
8 Tywan Mitchell .15
9 Michael Pittman .15
10 Jake Plummer .40
11 Frank Sanders .15
12 Kyle Vanden Bosch .15
13 Jamal Anderson .15
14 Keith Brooking .15
15 Chris Chandler .15
16 Bob Christian .15
17 Alge Crumpler .15
18 Brian Finneran .15
19 Shawn Jefferson .15
20 Patrick Kerney .15
21 Terance Mathis .15
22 Maurice Smith .15
23 Rodney Thomas .15
24 Darrick Vaughn .15
25 Michael Vick 2.00
26 Sam Adams .15
27 Terry Allen .15
28 Obafemi Ayanbadejo .15
29 Peter Boulware .15
30 Jason Brookins .15
31 Randall Cunningham .15
32 Elvis Grbac .15
33 Todd Heap .15
34 Qadry Ismail .15
35 Jamal Lewis 1.00
36 Ray Lewis .40
37 Chris Redman .40
38 Shannon Sharpe .40
39 Brandon Stokley .15
40 Travis Taylor .15
41 Moe Williams .15
42 Rod Woodson .40
43 Shawn Bryson .15
44 Larry Centers .15
45 Nate Clements .15
46 London Fletcher .15
47 Reggie Germany .15
48 Travis Henry .40
49 Jeremy McDaniel .15
50 Sammy Morris .15
51 Eric Moulds .40
52 Peerless Price .40
53 Jay Riemersma .15
54 Alex Van Pelt .15
55 Tim Biakabutuka .15
56 Isaac Byrd .15
57 Doug Evans .15
58 Donald Hayes .15
59 Chris Hetherington .15
60 Brad Hoover .15
61 Richard Huntley .15
62 Patrick Jeffers .15
63 Matt Lytle .15
64 Dan Morgan .15
65 Muhsin Muhammad .40
66 Mike Rucker .15
67 Steve Smith .15
68 Wesley Walls .15
69 Chris Weinke .60
70 James Allen .15
71 Fred Baxter .15
72 Marty Booker .40
73 Mike Brown .40
74 Rosevelt Colvin .15
75 Phillip Daniels .15
76 Leon Johnson .15
77 Shane Matthews .15
78 Jim Miller .40
79 Tony Parrish .15
80 Marcus Robinson .15
81 David Terrell .60
82 Anthony Thomas 1.50
83 Brian Urlacher 1.50
84 Ted Washington .15
85 Dez White .15
86 Brandon Bennett .15
87 Corey Dillon .60
88 Ron Dugans .15
89 Danny Farmer .15
90 T.J. Houshmandzadeh .15
91 Chad Johnson .15
92 Curtis Keaton .15
93 Jon Kitna .15
94 Tony McGee .15
95 Lorenzo Neal .15
96 Darnay Scott .15
97 Akili Smith .15
98 Justin Smith .15
99 Takeo Spikes .15
100 Peter Warrick .40
101 Tim Couch 1.00
102 JaJuan Dawson .15
103 Benjamin Gay .15
104 Anthony Henry .15
105 James Jackson .40
106 Kevin Johnson .15
107 Andre King .15
108 Jamir Miller .15
109 Quincy Morgan .40
110 Dennis Northcutt .15
111 O.J. Santiago .15
112 Jamel White .15
113 Quincy Carter 1.25
114 Darrin Chiaverini .15
115 Dexter Coakley .15
116 Joey Galloway .15
117 Troy Hambrick .15
118 Raghib Ismail .15
119 Dat Nguyen .15
120 Ken-Yon Rambo .15
121 Emmitt Smith 2.00
122 Reggie Swinton .15
123 Robert Thomas .15
124 Michael Wiley .15
125 Anthony Wright .15
126 Mike Anderson 1.00
127 Dwayne Carswell .15
128 Desmond Clark .15
129 Chris Cole .15
130 Terrell Davis 1.00
131 Gus Frerotte .15
132 Olandis Gary .15
133 Brian Griese .60
134 Kevin Kasper .15
135 Ed McCaffrey .40
136 Phil McGeoghan .15
137 John Mobley .15
138 Scottie Montgomery .15
139 Deltha O'Neal .15
140 Trevor Pryce .15
141 Rod Smith .40
142 Al Wilson .15
143 Scotty Anderson .15
144 Charlie Batch .15
145 Aveion Cason .15
146 Germane Crowell .15
147 Reuben Droughns .15
148 Bert Emanuel .15
149 Larry Foster .15
150 Az-Zahir Hakim .40
151 Desmond Howard .15
152 Mike McMahon .60
153 Herman Moore .15
154 Johnnie Morton .15
155 Robert Porcher .15
156 Cory Schlesinger .15
157 David Sloan .15
158 James Stewart .15
159 Lamont Warren .15
160 Donald Driver .15
161 Brett Favre 2.50
162 Bubba Franks .40
163 Antonio Freeman .40
164 Kabeer Gbaja-Biamila .15
165 Terry Glenn .40
166 Ahman Green .60
167 William Henderson .15
168 Dorsey Levens .15
169 David Martin .15
170 Rondell Mealey .15
171 Bill Schroeder .15
172 Darren Sharper .15
173 Avion Black .15
174 Tony Boselli .15
175 Corey Bradford .15
176 Marcus Coleman .15
177 Leomont Evans .15
178 Aaron Glenn .15
179 Trevor Insley .15
180 Jermaine Lewis .15
181 Anthony Malbrough .15
182 Frank Moreau .15
183 Mike Quinn .15
184 Charlie Rogers .15
185 Jamie Sharper .15
186 Matt Snider .15
187 Gary Walker .15
188 Kevin Williams .15
189 Kailee Wong .15
190 Chad Bratzke .15
191 Ken Dilger .50
192 Marvin Harrison .60
193 Edgerrin James 1.50
194 Kevin McDougal .15
195 Rob Morris .15
196 Jerome Pathon .15
197 Marcus Pollard .15
198 Dominic Rhodes .15
199 Marcus Washington .15
200 Reggie Wayne 1.25
201 Terrence Wilkins .15
202 Tony Brackens .15
203 Kyle Brady .15
204 Mark Brunell .75
205 Donovin Darius .15
206 Sean Dawkins .40
207 Damon Gibson .15
208 Elvis Joseph .15
209 Stacey Mack .15
210 Keenan McCardell .15
211 Hardy Nickerson .15
212 Jonathan Quinn .15
213 Micah Ross .15
214 Jimmy Smith .15
215 Fred Taylor .60
216 Patrick Washington .15
217 Derrick Alexander .15
218 Mike Cloud .15
219 Donnie Edwards .15
220 Tony Gonzalez .40
221 Trent Green .40
222 Dante Hall .15
223 Priest Holmes .60
224 Eddie Kennison .15
225 Marvin "Snoop" Minnis .40
226 Larry Parker .15
227 Marvcus Patton .15
228 Tony Richardson .15
229 Mikhael Ricks .15
230 Chris Chambers .75
231 Jay Fiedler .40
232 Oronde Gadsden .15
233 Rob Konrad .15
234 Sam Madison .15
235 Brock Marion .15
236 James McKnight .15
237 Travis Minor .15
238 Jeff Ogden .15
239 Lamar Smith .15
240 Jason Taylor .15
241 Zach Thomas .40
242 Dedric Ward .15
243 Ricky Williams 1.25
244 Michael Bennett .75
245 Todd Bouman .15
246 Cris Carter .40
247 Byron Chamberlain .15
248 Doug Chapman .15
249 Kenny Clark .15
250 Daunte Culpepper 1.25
251 Nate Jacquet .15
252 Jim Kleinsasser .15
253 Harold Morrow .15
254 Randy Moss 2.00
255 Jake Reed .15
256 Spergon Wynn .15
257 Drew Bledsoe 1.25
258 Tom Brady 2.00
259 Troy Brown .60
260 Fred Coleman .15
261 Marc Edwards .15
262 Kevin Faulk .15
263 Bobby Hamilton .15
264 Ty Law .15
265 Lawyer Milloy .15
266 David Patten .15
267 J.R. Redmond .15
268 Antowain Smith .40
269 Adam Vinatieri .15
270 Jermaine Wiggins .15
271 Aaron Brooks 1.00
272 Cam Cleeland .15
273 Charlie Clemons .15
274 James Fenderson .15
275 La'Roi Glover .15
276 Joe Horn .15
277 Willie Jackson .15
278 Sammy Knight .15
279 Michael Lewis .15
280 Deuce McAllister 1.00
281 Terrelle Smith .15
282 Eddie Williams .15
283 Robert Wilson .15
284 Tiki Barber .40
285 Micheal Barrow .15
286 Kerry Collins .40
287 Greg Comella .15
288 Thabiti Davis .15
289 Ron Dayne .40
290 Ron Dixon .15
291 Ike Hilliard .15
292 Joe Jurevicius .15
293 Michael Strahan .40
294 Amani Toomer .40
295 Damon Washington .15
296 John Abraham .15
297 Richie Anderson .15
298 Anthony Becht .15

299 Wayne Chrebet .40
300 Laveranues Coles .40
301 James Farrior .15
302 Marvin Jones .15
303 LaMont Jordan .15
304 Curtis Martin .40
305 Santana Moss .40
306 Chad Pennington .60
307 Kevin Swayne .15
308 Vinny Testaverde .40
309 Craig Yeast .15
310 Greg Biekert .15
311 Tim Brown .75
312 Zack Crockett .15
313 Rich Gannon .50
314 Charlie Garner .15
315 Sebastian Janikowski .15
316 Randy Jordan .15
317 Terry Kirby .15
318 Jerry Porter .15
319 Jerry Rice 2.00
320 Jon Ritchie .15
321 Tyrone Wheatley .15
322 Roland Williams .15
323 Charles Woodson .40
324 Correll Buckhalter .15
325 Brian Dawkins .15
326 Hugh Douglas .15
327 A.J. Feeley .15
328 Chad Lewis .15
329 Cecil Martin .15
330 Brian Mitchell .15
331 Freddie Mitchell .50
332 Todd Pinkston .15
333 Rod Smart .15
334 Duce Staley .15
335 James Thrash .15
336 Jeremiah Trotter .15
337 Troy Vincent .15
338 Kendrell Bell .40
339 Jerome Bettis .60
340 Demetrius Brown .15
341 Plaxico Burress .75
342 Troy Edwards .15
343 Chris Fuamatu-Ma'afala .15
344 Jason Gildon .15
345 Earl Holmes .15
346 Joey Porter .15
347 Chad Scott .15
348 Bobby Shaw .15
349 Kordell Stewart .60
350 Hines Ward .40
351 Amos Zereoue .15
352 Adam Archuleta .15
353 Dre' Bly .15
354 Isaac Bruce .60
355 Trung Canidate .15
356 Ernie Conwell .15
357 Marshall Faulk 1.25
358 Torry Holt .15
359 Leonard Little .15
360 Yo Murphy .15
361 Ricky Proehl .15
362 Kurt Warner 2.00
363 Aeneas Williams .15
364 Drew Brees 1.50
365 Curtis Conway .40
366 Tim Dwight .15
367 Terrell Fletcher .15
368 Doug Flutie .75
369 Jeff Graham .15
370 Rodney Harrison .15
371 Ronney Jenkins .15
372 Raylee Johnson .15
373 Freddie Jones .15
374 Ryan McNeil .15
375 Junior Seau .60
376 LaDainian Tomlinson 1.50
377 Marcellus Wiley .15
378 Kevan Barlow .50
379 Fred Beasley .15
380 Zack Bronson .15
381 Andre Carter .15
382 Jeff Garcia .60
383 Garrison Hearst .40
384 Terry Jackson .15
385 Eric Johnson .15
386 Saladin McCullough .15
387 Terrell Owens .60
388 Ahmed Plummer .15
389 J.J. Stokes .15
390 Tai Streets .15
391 Vinny Sutherland .15
392 Bryant Young .15
393 Shaun Alexander .60
394 Chad Brown .15
395 Kerwin Cook .15
396 Trent Dilfer .40
397 Bobby Engram .15
398 Christian Fauria .15
399 Matt Hasselbeck .15
400 Darrell Jackson .15
401 John Randle .15
402 Koren Robinson .50
403 Anthony Simmons .15
404 Mack Strong .15
405 Ricky Watters .40
406 James Williams .15
407 Mike Alstott .40
408 Ronde Barber .15
409 Derrick Brooks .15
410 Jameel Cook .15
411 Warrick Dunn .40
412 Jacquez Green .15
413 Brad Johnson .50
414 Keyshawn Johnson .50
415 Rob Johnson .40
416 John Lynch .15
417 Dave Moore .15
418 Warren Sapp .40
419 Aaron Stecker .15
420 Karl Williams .15
421 Drew Bennett .15
422 Eddie Berlin .15
423 Rafael Cooper .15
424 Kevin Dyson .40
425 Eddie George .75
426 Mike Green .15
427 Skip Hicks .15
428 Jevon Kearse .40
429 Erron Kinney .15
430 Derrick Mason .40
431 Justin McCareins .15
432 Steve McNair .60
433 Neil O'Donnell .15
434 Frank Wycheck .15
435 Reidel Anthony .15
436 Jessie Armstead .15
437 Champ Bailey .15
438 Tony Banks .15
439 Michael Bates .15
440 Donnell Bennett .15
441 Ki-Jana Carter .15
442 Stephen Davis .50
443 Zeron Flemister .15
444 Rod Gardner .50
445 Kevin Lockett .15
446 Eric Metcalf .15
447 Sage Rosenfels .50
448 Fred Smoot .15
449 Michael Westbrook .15
450 Danny Wuerffel .15
451 *Jason McAddley* .15
452 *Freddie Milons* .15
453 *Bryan Thomas* .15
454 *Levi Jones* .15
455 *William Green* 2.00
456 *Luke Staley* 1.00
457 *Daniel Graham* 1.00
458 *David Garrard* 1.00
459 *Donald Reche Caldwell* 1.25
460 *Andra Davis* .50
461 *Lito Sheppard* 1.00
462 *Chris Hope* .50
463 *Javon Walker* 2.00
464 *David Carr* 5.00
465 *Alan Harper* .50
466 *Adrian Peterson* 1.00
467 *Kelly Campbell* 1.00
468 *Ashley Lelie* 3.00
469 *Kurt Kittner* 1.25
470 *Antwann Randle El* 2.00
471 *Ladell Betts* 1.25
472 *Josh Reed* 1.50
473 *Clinton Portis* 5.00
474 *Ron Johnson* 1.00
475 *Eric Crouch* 1.50
476 *Tracey Wistrom* .50
477 *David Neill* .50
478 *Ronald Curry* 1.00
479 *Lamar Gordon* 1.25
480 *Damien Anderson* .50
481 *Napoleon Harris* 1.00
482 *Zak Kustok* 1.00
483 *Rocky Calmus* 1.25
484 *Roy Williams* 2.00
485 *Joey Harrington* 5.00
486 *Maurice Morris* 1.25
487 *Antonio Bryant* 2.00
488 *Josh McCown* 1.25
489 *John Henderson* 1.00
490 *Quentin Jammer* 1.25
491 *Mike Williams* 1.00
492 *Patrick Ramsey* 1.50
493 *Kenyon Coleman* .50
494 *DeShaun Foster* 1.50
495 *Brian Poli-Dixon* 1.00
496 *Cliff Russell* 1.00
497 *Brian Westbrook* 1.25
498 *Andre Davis* 1.50
499 *Larry Triplett* .50
500 *Lamont Thompson* .50

2002 Pacific Authentic Game-Used Jersey Cards

NM/M

Common Player: 3.00
Common SP Player: 6.00
1 David Boston 433 6.00
2 MarTay Jenkins 3.00
3 Jake Plummer 3.00
4 Michael Vick 30.00
5 Jamal Lewis 496 10.00
6 Travis Henry 3.00
7 Steve Smith 393 6.00
8 Anthony Thomas 30.00
9 Peter Warrick 285 6.00
10 Quincy Carter 10.00
11 Terrell Davis 3.00
12 Mike McMahon 3.00
13 Brett Favre 40.00
14 Antonio Freeman 497 6.00
15 Ahman Green 404 10.00
16 Marvin Harrison 492 6.00
17 Reggie Wayne 3.00
18 Mark Brunell 315 10.00
19 Priest Holmes (Balt jsy) 3.00
20 Marvin "Snoop" Minnis 8.00
21 Chris Chambers 371 30.00
22 Ricky Williams 457 6.00
23 Daunte Culpepper 580 20.00
24 Randy Moss 30.00
25 Spergon Wynn (Clev jsy) 3.00
26 Drew Bledsoe 639 6.00
27 Tom Brady 30.00
28 Aaron Brooks 707 10.00
29 Jesse Palmer 3.00
30 Curtis Martin 3.00
31 Santana Moss 3.00
32 Tim Brown 3.00
33 Jerry Rice 574 (SF jsy) 25.00
34 Marques Tuiasosopo 15.00
35 Correll Buckhalter 3.00
36 Jerome Bettis 3.00
37 Marshall Faulk 10.00
38 Kurt Warner 775 30.00
39 Aeneas Williams 240 (Ari jsy) 6.00
40 LaDainian Tomlinson 858 20.00
41 Kevan Barlow 3.00
42 Terrell Owens 707 10.00
43 Shaun Alexander 8.00
44 Trent Dilfer (Balt jsy) 3.00
45 Matt Hasselbeck 242 (GB jsy) 6.00
46 Warrick Dunn 3.00
47 Justin McCareins 3.00
48 Steve McNair 569 6.00
49 Tony Banks (Bal jsy) 3.00
50 Sage Rosenfels 3.00

2002 Pacific Cramer's Choice

NM/M

Complete Set (10): 200.00
Common Player: 15.00
1 David Boston 15.00
2 Anthony Thomas 40.00
3 Emmitt Smith 40.00
4 Brett Favre 60.00
5 Priest Holmes 15.00
6 Tom Brady 40.00
7 Marshall Faulk 15.00
8 Kurt Warner 40.00
9 Terrell Owens 15.00
10 Shaun Alexander 15.00

2002 Pacific Draft Force

NM/M

Complete Set (20): 140.00
Common Player: 5.00
1 William Green 15.00
2 Luke Staley 5.00
3 Donald Reche Caldwell 5.00
4 David Carr 30.00
5 Ashley Lelie 15.00
6 Kurt Kittner 5.00
7 Antwann Randle El 12.00
8 Ladell Betts 5.00
9 Josh Reed 12.00
10 Clinton Portis 5.00
11 Eric Crouch 15.00
12 Lamar Gordon 5.00
13 Joey Harrington 30.00
14 Maurice Morris 5.00
15 Antonio Bryant 5.00
16 Josh McCown 5.00
17 Patrick Ramsey 10.00
18 DeShaun Foster 10.00
19 Brian Westbrook 5.00
20 Andre Davis 5.00

2002 Pacific Feature Attractions

NM/M

Complete Set (20): 60.00
Common Player: 2.00
1 Michael Vick 10.00
2 Anthony Thomas 10.00
3 Emmitt Smith 8.00
4 Brian Griese 2.00
5 Brett Favre 20.00
6 Ahman Green 2.00
7 Edgerrin James 10.00
8 Priest Holmes 2.00
9 Ricky Williams 2.00
10 Daunte Culpepper 6.00
11 Tom Brady 6.00
12 Ron Dayne 2.00
13 Curtis Martin 2.00
14 Jerry Rice 6.00
15 Marshall Faulk 2.00
16 Torry Holt 2.00
17 Kurt Warner 6.00
18 LaDainian Tomlinson 2.00
19 Warrick Dunn 2.00
20 Eddie George 2.00

2002 Pacific Pro Bowl

NM/M

Complete Set (20): 50.00
Common Player: 2.00
1 David Boston 5.00
2 Brian Urlacher 10.00
3 Corey Dillon 5.00
4 Ahman Green 5.00
5 Marvin Harrison 2.00
6 Priest Holmes 2.00
7 Troy Brown 2.00
8 Curtis Martin 2.00
9 Tim Brown 5.00
10 Rich Gannon 2.00
11 Kordell Stewart 2.00
12 Hines Ward 6.00
13 Marshall Faulk 4.00
14 Torry Holt 2.00
15 Kurt Warner 6.00
16 Jeff Garcia 2.00
17 Garrison Hearst 2.00
18 Terrell Owens 2.00
19 Mike Alstott 2.00
20 Keyshawn Johnson 2.00

2002 Pacific Rocket Launchers

NM/M

Complete Set (20): 40.00
Common Player: 1.00
1 Jake Plummer 1.00
2 Michael Vick 3.00
3 Chris Weinke 1.00
4 Tim Couch 1.00
5 Quincy Carter 1.00
6 Brian Griese 1.00
7 Mark Brunell 1.00
8 Daunte Culpepper 2.00
9 Drew Bledsoe 1.00
10 Tom Brady 3.00
11 Aaron Brooks 2.00
12 Kerry Collins 1.00
13 Kordell Stewart 1.00
14 Drew Brees 2.00
15 Jeff Garcia 1.00
16 Brad Johnson 1.00
17 Steve McNair 1.00
18 David Carr 10.00
19 Joey Harrington 10.00
20 Patrick Ramsey 5.00

2002 Pacific War Room

NM/M

Complete Set (10): 35.00
Common Player: 2.00
1 William Green 5.00
2 David Carr 8.00
3 Ashley Lelie 5.00
4 Kurt Kittner 2.00
5 Josh Reed 4.00
6 Clinton Portis 3.00
7 Joey Harrington 8.00
8 Josh McCown 2.00
9 Patrick Ramsey 3.00
10 DeShaun Foster 3.00

2002 Pacific Adrenaline

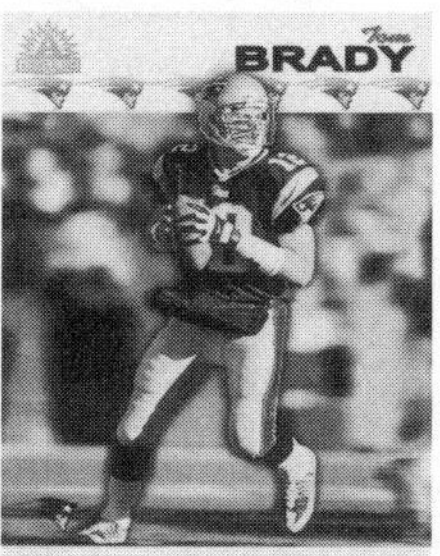

NM/M

Complete Set (288): 50.00
Common Player: .20
Unlisted Stars: .60
Minor Stars: .40
Red Variation (1-288) 1X to2X
Inserted 1:1
Blue Variation (Rookies only) 2X to 3X
Production 165 sets
Wax Box (36): 60.00
1 Damien Anderson (RK) .75
2 David Boston .75
3 *Wendell Bryant* .75
4 Thomas Jones .20
5 *Jason McAddley (RK)* .75
6 *Josh McCown* 1.00
7 Jake Plummer .40
8 Frank Sanders .20
9 Josh Scobey (RK) .75
10 Keith Brooking .20
11 *T.J. Duckett* 3.00
12 Warrick Dunn .40
13 Brian Finneran .20
14 *Kahlil Hill (RK)* .75
15 Shawn Jefferson .20
16 *Kurt Kittner* 1.00
17 *Will Overstreet (RK)* .75
18 Michael Vick 2.00
19 *Ron Johnson (RK)* .75
20 Jamal Lewis 1.00
21 Ray Lewis .40
22 Chris Redman .40
23 *Tellis Redmon (RK)* .75
24 Brandon Stokley .20
25 *Chester Taylor* .75
26 Travis Taylor .20
27 *Anthony Weaver* .75
28 Drew Bledsoe 1.25
29 Shawn Bryson .20
30 Larry Centers .20
31 *Ryan Denney* .75
32 Travis Henry .50
33 Richard Huntley .20
34 Eric Moulds .20
35 Peerless Price .40
36 *Josh Reed* 1.50
37 Isaac Byrd .20
38 *Randy Fasani* 1.00
39 *DeShaun Foster* 1.50
40 *Kyle Johnson* .75
41 Muhsin Muhammad .40
42 *Julius Peppers* 2.00
43 Lamar Smith .20
44 Steve Smith .20
45 Chris Weinke .50
46 Marty Booker .20
47 Chris Chandler .20
48 *Eric McCoo* .75
49 Jim Miller .20
50 *Adrian Peterson* 1.00
51 Marcus Robinson .20
52 David Terrell .75
53 Anthony Thomas 1.50
54 Brian Urlacher 1.50
55 Corey Dillon .75
56 Gus Frerotte .20
57 Chad Johnson .20
58 Jon Kitna .20
59 Justin Smith .20
60 Takeo Spikes .20
61 *Lamont Thompson* .75
62 Peter Warrick .40
63 Michael Westbrook .20
64 Tim Couch 1.00
65 *Andre Davis* 1.50
66 JaJuan Dawson .20
67 *William Green* 2.00
68 James Jackson .50
69 Kevin Johnson .20
70 Jamir Miller .20
71 Quincy Morgan .40
72 Jamel White .20
73 *Antonio Bryant* 2.00
74 Quincy Carter 1.25
75 *Woodrow Dantzler III* .75
76 Joey Galloway .20
77 *Ennis Haywood* .75
78 *Chad Hutchinson* .75
79 Raghib Ismail .20
80 Emmitt Smith 2.00
81 *Roy Williams* 2.00
82 Mike Anderson 1.00
83 Terrell Davis 1.00
84 Brian Griese .75
85 *Herb Haygood* .75
86 *Ashley Lelie* 3.00
87 Ed McCaffrey .40
88 Deltha O'Neal .20
89 *Clinton Portis* 5.00
90 Rob Smith .20
91 Scotty Anderson .20
92 *Eddie Drummond* .75
93 Az-Zahir Hakim .50
94 *Joey Harrington* 5.00
95 Mike McMahon .75
96 *James Mungro* .75
97 Bill Schroeder .20
98 *Luke Staley* 1.00
99 James Stewart .20
100 *Marques Anderson* 1.00
101 *Najeh Davenport* 1.00
102 Brett Favre 2.50
103 Robert Ferguson .40
104 Bubba Franks .20
105 Terry Glenn .40
106 Ahman Green .75
107 *Craig Nall* .75
108 *Javon Walker* 2.00
109 James Allen .20
110 *Jarrod Baxter* .75
111 Corey Bradford .20
112 *David Carr* 5.00
113 *Delvon Flowers* .75
114 *Jabar Gaffney* 1.50
115 Jermaine Lewis .20
116 Travis Prentice .20
117 *Jonathan Wells* 1.00
118 *Brian Allen* .75
119 Chad Bratzke .20
120 Marvin Harrison .50
121 Qadry Ismail .20
122 Edgerrin James 1.50
123 Peyton Manning 2.00
124 Rob Morris .20
125 Dominic Rhodes .20
126 Reggie Wayne .20
127 Tony Brackens .20
128 Mark Brunell .75
129 Donovin Darius .20
130 *David Garrard* 1.00
131 *John Henderson* 1.00
132 Stacey Mack .20
133 Bobby Shaw .20
134 Jimmy Smith .20
135 Fred Taylor .40
136 *Omar Easy* .75
137 *Eddie Freeman* .75
138 Tony Gonzalez .40
139 Trent Green .50
140 Priest Holmes .75
141 Eddie Kennison .20
142 Marvin "Snoop" Minnis .50
143 Johnnie Morton .20
144 *Ryan Sims* 1.00
145 Chris Chambers .75
146 Jay Fiedler .40
147 Oronde Gadsden .20
148 *Leonard Henry* 1.00
149 James McKnight .20
150 Travis Minor .20
151 *Sam Simmons* .75
152 Zach Thomas .40
153 Ricky Williams 1.25
154 Derrick Alexander .20
155 *Jeremy Allen* .75
156 *Atrews Bell* .75
157 Michael Bennett .75
158 *Kelly Campbell* 1.00
159 Byron Chamberlain .20
160 Doug Chapman .20
161 Daunte Culpepper 1.25
162 Randy Moss 2.00
163 Tom Brady 2.00
164 *Deion Branch* 1.25
165 Troy Brown .50
166 *Rohan Davey* 1.50
167 Kevin Faulk .20
168 *Daniel Graham* 1.00
169 David Patten .20
170 Antowain Smith .40
171 *Antwoine Womack* .75
172 Aaron Brooks 1.00
173 Charlie Clemons .20
174 Joe Horn .20
175 Sammy Knight .20
176 Deuce McAllister 1.00
177 *J.T. O'Sullivan* .75
178 Jerome Pathon .20
179 *Donte Stallworth* 3.00
180 *Ricky Williams* 1.00
181 Tiki Barber .20
182 *Tim Carter* 1.00
183 Kerry Collins .50
184 Ron Dayne .50
185 Ike Hilliard .20
186 *Daryl Jones* .75
187 *Jeremy Shockey* 3.00
188 Michael Strahan .40
189 Amani Toomer .20
190 Wayne Chrebet .20
191 Laveranues Coles .20
192 *Alan Harper* .75
193 *LaMont Jordan* 1.00
194 Curtis Martin .50
195 Chad Morton .20
196 Santana Moss .40
197 Vinny Testaverde .20
198 *Bryan Thomas* .75
199 Tim Brown .75
200 *Ronald Curry* 1.00
201 Rich Gannon .50
202 Charlie Garner .40
203 *Napoleon Harris* .75
204 *Larry Ned* .75
205 Jerry Rice 2.00
206 Tyrone Wheatley .20
207 Charles Woodson .40
208 *Michael Lewis* .75
209 Donovan McNabb 1.25
210 *Freddie Milions* 1.00
211 Freddie Mitchell .75
212 Todd Pinkston .20
213 *Lito Sheppard* 1.00
214 Duce Staley .40
215 James Thrash .20
216 *Brian Westbrook* 1.00
217 Kendrell Bell .50
218 Jerome Bettis .50
219 Plaxico Burress .75
220 *Verron Haynes* .75
221 *Chris Hope* .75
222 *Lee Mays* .75
223 *Antwann Randle El* 2.00
224 Kordell Stewart .50
225 Hines Ward .20
226 Isaac Bruce .50
227 *Eric Crouch* 1.50
228 Marshall Faulk 1.25
229 Lamar Gordon .20
230 Torry Holt .20
231 Leonard Little .20
232 *Robert Thomas* .75
233 Kurt Warner 2.00
234 Terrence Wilkins .20
235 Drew Brees 1.50
236 *Seth Burford* .75
237 *Donald Reche Caldwell* 1.00
238 Curtis Conway .40
239 Doug Flutie .75
240 *Quentin Jammer* 1.00
241 *Brian Poli-Dixon* 1.00
242 Junior Seau .50
243 LaDainian Tomlinson 1.50
244 Kevan Barlow .20
245 Andre Carter .20
246 *Brandon Doman* .75
247 Jeff Garcia .20
248 Garrison Hearst .40
249 Terrell Owens .50
250 Derek Smith .20
251 J.J. Stokes .20
252 Vinny Sutherland .20
253 Shaun Alexander .75
254 Chad Brown .20
255 Trent Dilfer .40
256 Bobby Engram .20
257 Darrell Jackson .20
258 *Nakoa McElrath* .75
259 *Maurice Morris* 1.50
260 Koren Robinson .20
261 *Jerramy Stevens* 1.00
262 Mike Alstott .40
263 Derrick Brooks .20
264 Brad Johnson .40
265 Keyshawn Johnson .50
266 Keenan McCardell .20
267 Michael Pittman .20
268 Warren Sapp .40
269 *Travis Stephens* 1.00
270 *Marquise Walker* 1.00
271 *Rocky Calmus* 1.00
272 Kevin Dyson .20
273 Eddie George .75
274 *Albert Haynesworth* 1.00
275 Derrick Mason .50
276 Steve McNair .50
277 *Dicenzo Miller* .75
278 *Jake Schifino* .75
279 *Clevan Williams* .75
280 Champ Bailey .20
281 *Ladell Betts* 1.00
282 Stephen Davis .50
283 Rod Gardner .50
284 Jacquez Green .20
285 Shane Matthews .20
286 *Patrick Ramsey* 1.50
287 *Cliff Russell* 1.00
288 Jeremiah Trotter .20

2002 Pacific Adrenaline Adrenaline Rush

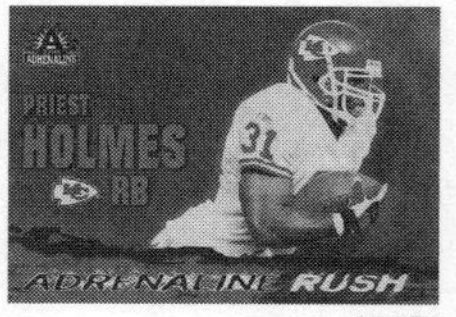

NM/M

Common Player: 1.00
Inserted 1:5
1 T.J. Duckett 3.00
2 DeShaun Foster 2.00
3 Anthony Thomas 2.00
4 Corey Dillon 1.00
5 William Green 2.00
6 Emmitt Smith 4.00
7 Terrell Davis 1.00
8 Clinton Portis 3.00
9 Ahman Green 1.00
10 Edgerrin James 1.00
11 Priest Holmes 1.00
12 Ricky Williams 1.00
13 Curtis Martin 1.00
14 Jerome Bettis 1.00
15 Marshall Faulk 1.00
16 LaDainian Tomlinson 1.00
17 Shaun Alexander 1.00
18 Eddie George 1.00

A card number in parenthese ( ) indicates the set is unnumbered.

2002 Pacific Adrenaline Driven

		NM/M
Common Player:		1.00
Inserted 1:5		
1	T.J. Duckett	3.00
2	Michael Vick	2.00
3	Drew Bledsoe	1.00
4	DeShaun Foster	1.50
5	Anthony Thomas	1.00
6	William Green	2.00
7	Emmitt Smith	2.00
8	Ashley Lelie	3.00
9	Clinton Portis	3.00
10	Joey Harrington	4.00
11	Brett Favre	4.00
12	Javon Walker	2.00
13	David Carr	5.00
14	Edgerrin James	2.00
15	Ricky Williams	1.00
16	Daunte Culpepper	1.00
17	Randy Moss	2.00
18	Tom Brady	2.00
19	Donte Stallworth	3.00
20	Jerry Rice	1.50
21	Antwann Randle El	2.00
22	Eric Crouch	1.50
23	Marshall Faulk	1.00
24	Kurt Warner	2.00
25	Drew Brees	1.50
26	LaDainian Tomlinson	1.50
27	Patrick Ramsey	1.50

2002 Pacific Adrenaline Game-Used Jersey Cards

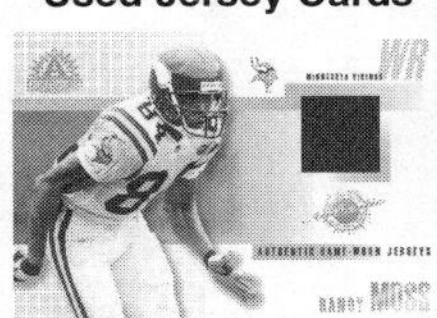

		NM/M
Common Player:		5.00
Inserted 2:37		
Gold version		2X to5X
Production 25 sets		
1	Thomas Jones	8.00
2	Jake Plummer	5.00
3	Michael Vick	20.00
4	Chris Redman	10.00
5	Drew Bledsoe (NE)	8.00
6	Peerless Price	10.00
7	Brian Urlacher	20.00
8	Corey Dillon	5.00
9	Takeo Spikes	5.00
10	Tim Couch	10.00
11	Ken-Yon Rambo (Oak)	5.00
12	Emmitt Smith	20.00
13	Mike Anderson	10.00
14	Brett Favre	25.00
15	Terry Glenn (NE)	5.00
16	Edgerrin James	12.00
17	Peyton Manning	15.00
18	Mark Brunell	5.00
19	Stacey Mack	5.00
20	Fred Taylor	5.00
21	Tony Richardson	8.00
22	Ricky Williams (NO)	10.00
23	Daunte Culpepper	12.00
24	Jim Kleinsasser	10.00
25	Randy Moss	20.00
26	Christian Fauria (Sea)	5.00
27	Patrick Pass	5.00
28	Ron Dayne	5.00
29	Anthony Becht	5.00
30	LaMont Jordan	5.00
31	Curtis Martin	5.00
32	Jerry Rice	20.00
33	Jon Ritchie	5.00
34	Donovan McNabb	10.00
35	Brian Mitchell	8.00
36	Jerome Bettis	8.00
37	Mark Bruener	5.00
38	Kordell Stewart	10.00
39	Marshall Faulk	10.00
40	Kurt Warner	10.00
41	Terrence Wilkins (Ind)	5.00
42	Drew Brees	5.00
43	Trevor Gaylor	5.00
44	LaDainian Tomlinson	15.00
45	Jeff Garcia	10.00
46	Terrell Owens	10.00
47	Shaun Alexander	10.00
48	Eddie George	12.00
49	Steve McNair	10.00
50	Shane Matthews (Chi)	8.00

2002 Pacific Adrenaline Playmakers

		NM/M
Common Player:		1.00
Inserted 1:5		
1	T.J. Duckett	2.00
2	Michael Vick	2.00
3	Anthony Thomas	1.00
4	William Green	1.00
5	Emmitt Smith	3.00
6	Ashley Lelie	2.00
7	Joey Harrington	4.00
8	Brett Favre	4.00
9	David Carr	5.00
10	Randy Moss	2.00
11	Tom Brady	3.00
12	Donte Stallworth	2.00
13	Jerry Rice	2.00
14	Donovan McNabb	1.00
15	Eric Crouch	1.00
16	Marshall Faulk	1.00
17	Kurt Warner	2.00
18	LaDainian Tomlinson	1.00

2002 Pacific Adrenaline Power Surge

		NM/M
Common Player:		4.00
Inserted 2:37		
1	Michael Vick	4.00
2	Emmitt Smith	4.00
3	Joey Harrington	6.00
4	Brett Favre	6.00
5	David Carr	8.00
6	Tom Brady	4.00

2002 Pacific Adrenaline Rookie Report

		NM/M
Common Player:		1.50
Inserted 1:7		
1	T.J. Duckett	3.00
2	DeShaun Foster	1.50
3	William Green	2.00
4	Ashley Lelie	3.00
5	Clinton Portis	3.00
6	Joey Harrington	4.00
7	Javon Walker	2.00
8	David Carr	5.00
9	Jabar Gaffney	1.50
10	Donte Stallworth	3.00
11	Antwann Randle El	2.00
12	Patrick Ramsey	1.50

2002 Pacific Atomic

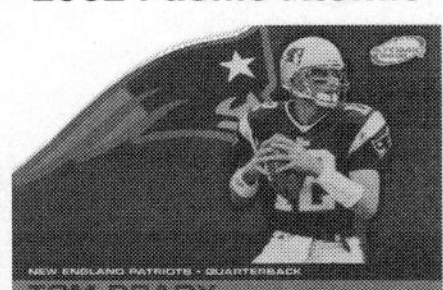

		NM/M
Common Player:		.20
Unlisted Stars:		.75
Minor Stars:		.50
Red		1X to2X
Gold		2X to10X
Production to player's jersey #		
Pack (5):		5.00
Wax Box (20):		85.00
1	David Boston	.75
2	Thomas Jones	.20
3	Jake Plummer	.20
4	Jamal Anderson	.20
5	Warrick Dunn	.40
6	Michael Vick	3.00
7	Jamal Lewis	1.50
8	Chris Redman	.40
9	Travis Taylor	.40
10	Travis Henry	.50
11	Eric Moulds	.20
12	Peerless Price	.20
13	Muhsin Muhammad	.50
14	Lamar Smith	.50
15	Chris Weinke	.60
16	Marty Booker	.40
17	Jim Miller	.20
18	Anthony Thomas	2.50
19	Corey Dillon	.75
20	Jon Kitna	.20
21	Peter Warrick	.40
22	Tim Couch	1.50
23	Kevin Johnson	.20
24	Quincy Morgan	.50
25	Quincy Carter	2.00
26	Joey Galloway	.50
27	Emmitt Smith	3.00
28	Terrell Davis	1.50
29	Brian Griese	.75
30	Ed McCaffrey	.20
31	Rod Smith	.20
32	Scotty Anderson	.20
33	Az-Zahir Hakim	.40
34	Mike McMahon	.75
35	Brett Favre	4.00
36	Terry Glenn	.40
37	Ahman Green	.75
38	James Allen	.20
39	Corey Bradford	.20
40	Jermaine Lewis	.20
41	Marvin Harrison	.60
42	Edgerrin James	2.50
43	Peyton Manning	3.00
44	Mark Brunell	.75
45	Jimmy Smith	.20
46	Fred Taylor	.75
47	Tony Gonzalez	.40
48	Trent Green	.40
49	Priest Holmes	.60
50	Chris Chambers	.75
51	Jay Fiedler	.20
52	Ricky Williams	2.00
53	Michael Bennett	.75
54	Daunte Culpepper	2.00
55	Randy Moss	3.00
56	Tom Brady	3.00
57	Troy Brown	.20
58	Antowain Smith	.20
59	Aaron Brooks	1.50
60	Joe Horn	.20
61	Deuce McAllister	1.50
62	Tiki Barber	.20
63	Kerry Collins	.40
64	Ron Dayne	.40
65	Wayne Chrebet	.40
66	Curtis Martin	.50
67	Vinny Testaverde	.20
68	Tim Brown	.75
69	Rich Gannon	.40
70	Charlie Garner	.20
71	Jerry Rice	3.00
72	Correll Buckhalter	.20
73	Donovan McNabb	2.00
74	Duce Staley	.40
75	Jerome Bettis	.40
76	Kordell Stewart	.40
77	Hines Ward	.20
78	Isaac Bruce	.75
79	Marshall Faulk	2.00
80	Torry Holt	.20
81	Kurt Warner	3.00
82	Drew Brees	2.50
83	Tim Dwight	.20
84	Doug Flutie	.75
85	LaDainian Tomlinson	2.50
86	Jeff Garcia	.75
87	Garrison Hearst	.20
88	Terrell Owens	.75
89	Shaun Alexander	.75
90	Trent Dilfer	.20
91	Darrell Jackson	.20
92	Mike Alstott	.40
93	Brad Johnson	.20
94	Keyshawn Johnson	.40
95	Eddie George	.75
96	Derrick Mason	.20
97	Steve McNair	.75
98	Stephen Davis	.75
99	Rod Gardner	.20
100	Jacquez Green	.20
101	*Damien Anderson*	2.00
102	*Ladell Betts*	4.00
103	*Antonio Bryant*	8.00
104	*Donald Reche Caldwell*	4.00
105	*Kelly Campbell*	2.00
106	*David Carr*	20.00
107	*Rohan Davey*	5.00
108	*Andre Davis*	5.00
109	*T.J. Duckett*	10.00
110	*DeShaun Foster*	5.00
111	*David Garrard*	2.00
112	*Lamar Gordon*	3.00
113	*William Green*	8.00
114	*Joey Harrington*	15.00
115	*Kurt Kittner*	4.00
116	*Ashley Lelie*	10.00
117	*Josh McCown*	4.00
118	*Clinton Portis*	20.00
119	*Patrick Ramsey*	5.00
120	*Antwann Randle El*	8.00
121	*Josh Reed*	5.00
122	*Luke Staley*	4.00
123	*Donte Stallworth*	10.00
124	*Marquise Walker*	4.00
125	*Michael Westbrook*	4.00
126	*Jason McAddley*	2.00
127	*Josh Scobey*	2.00
128	*Kahlil Hill*	2.00
129	*Ron Johnson*	2.00
130	*Julius Peppers*	8.00
131	*Adrian Peterson*	4.00
132	*Woodrow Dantzler III*	2.00
133	*Roy Williams*	8.00
134	*Najeh Davenport*	3.00
135	*Javon Walker*	8.00
136	*Jabar Gaffney*	5.00
137	*John Henderson*	2.00
138	*Leonard Henry*	3.00
139	*Daniel Graham*	4.00
140	*Jeremy Shockey*	12.00
141	*Ronald Curry*	4.00
142	*Napoleon Harris*	2.00
143	*Freddie Milons*	2.00
144	*Lito Sheppard*	3.00
145	*Eric Crouch*	5.00
146	*Robert Thomas*	2.00
147	*Quentin Jammer*	4.00
148	*Maurice Morris*	5.00
149	*Travis Stephens*	4.00
150	*Cliff Russell*	2.00

2002 Pacific Atomic Arms Race

		NM/M
Complete Set (18):		45.00
Common Player:		3.00
Inserted 1:21		
1	Michael Vick	6.00
2	Tim Couch	3.00
3	Brian Griese	3.00
4	Joey Harrington	6.00
5	Brett Favre	8.00
6	David Carr	10.00
7	Peyton Manning	4.00
8	Mark Brunell	3.00
9	Daunte Culpepper	3.00
10	Tom Brady	6.00
11	Aaron Brooks	3.00
12	Donovan McNabb	3.00
13	Kurt Warner	4.00
14	Drew Brees	4.00
15	Doug Flutie	4.00
16	Jeff Garcia	3.00
17	Steve McNair	3.00
18	Patrick Ramsey	6.00

2002 Pacific Atomic Authentic Game-Worn Jerseys

		NM/M
Common Player:		10.00
Inserted 3:21		
Patch Variation		2X to4X
Production 100 sets		
Gold		2X to6X
Production 25 sets		
1	David Boston	10.00
2	Freddie Jones	10.00
3	Joel Makovicka	10.00
4	Jake Plummer	10.00
5	Jamal Anderson	10.00
6	Warrick Dunn	10.00
7	Shawn Jefferson	10.00
8	Maurice Smith	10.00
9	Dave Moore	10.00
10	Peerless Price	15.00
11	Jay Riemersma	10.00
12	Lamar Smith	10.00
13	Rabih Abdullah	10.00
14	Chris Chandler	10.00
15	Brian Urlacher	30.00
16	Dez White	10.00
17	Corey Dillon	10.00
18	Scott Mitchell	10.00
19	Akili Smith	10.00
20	Takeo Spikes	10.00
21	Tim Couch	20.00
22	Jammi German	10.00
23	Jamel White	10.00
24	La'Roi Glover	10.00
25	Emmitt Smith	30.00
26	Darren Woodson	10.00
27	Mike Anderson	10.00
28	Terrell Davis	15.00
29	Gus Frerotte	10.00
30	Brian Griese	12.00
31	Howard Griffith	10.00
32	Deltha O'Neal	10.00
33	Shannon Sharpe	10.00
34	Charlie Batch	10.00
35	Az-Zahir Hakim	10.00
36	Brett Favre	40.00
37	Antonio Freeman	10.00
38	Terry Glenn	10.00
39	Ahman Green	15.00
40	Dorsey Levens	10.00
41	James Allen	10.00
42	Avion Black	10.00
43	Jermaine Lewis	10.00
44	Charlie Rogers	10.00
45	Qadry Ismail	10.00
46	Trent Green	10.00
47	Tony Richardson	10.00
48	Ricky Williams	15.00
49	Cris Carter	10.00
50	Corey Chavous	10.00
51	Daunte Culpepper	20.00
52	Jim Kleinsasser	10.00
53	Randy Moss	30.00
54	Tom Brady	40.00
55	Donald Hayes	10.00
56	Curtis Jackson	10.00
57	Patrick Pass	10.00
58	Aaron Brooks	10.00
59	Bryan Cox	10.00
60	Jerome Pathon	10.00
61	Robert Wilson	10.00
62	Tiki Barber	10.00
63	Kerry Collins	10.00
64	Ron Dayne	10.00
65	Laveranues Coles	10.00
66	James Jett	10.00
67	Randy Jordan	10.00
68	Jerry Rice	40.00
69	Cecil Martin	10.00
70	Donovan McNabb	15.00
71	Brian Mitchell	10.00
72	Jerome Bettis	12.00
73	Mark Bruener	10.00
74	Troy Edwards	10.00
75	Kordell Stewart	12.00
76	Isaac Bruce	10.00
77	Trung Canidate	10.00
78	Ernie Conwell	10.00
79	Marshall Faulk	25.00
80	Torry Holt	10.00
81	Kurt Warner	40.00
82	Aeneas Williams	10.00
83	Stephen Alexander	10.00
84	Drew Brees	25.00
85	Tim Dwight	10.00
86	Terrell Fletcher	10.00
87	Doug Flutie	15.00
88	Ronney Jenkins	10.00
89	Fred Beasley	10.00
90	Shaun Alexander	20.00
91	Itula Mili	10.00
92	Ken Dilger	10.00
93	Michael Pittman	10.00
94	Eddie George	15.00
95	Jevon Kearse	10.00
96	Erron Kinney	10.00
97	Steve McNair	12.00
98	Dameyune Craig	10.00
99	Stephen Davis	15.00

2002 Pacific Atomic Countdown to Stardom

		NM/M
Complete Set (18):		50.00
Common Player:		2.00
Inserted 2:21		
1	Josh McCown	3.00
2	T.J. Duckett	5.00
3	Brian Griese	2.00
4	Joey Harrington	8.00
5	Brett Favre	6.00
6	David Carr	10.00
7	Ashley Lelie	5.00
8	Clinton Portis	3.00
9	Joey Harrington	8.00
10	Javon Walker	4.00
11	David Carr	10.00
12	Jabar Gaffney	3.00
13	Donte Stallworth	5.00
14	Brian Westbrook	3.00
15	Lamar Gordon	3.00
16	Donald Reche Caldwell	3.00
17	Maurice Morris	3.00
18	Patrick Ramsey	4.00

2002 Pacific Atomic Fusion Force

		NM/M
Complete Set (18):		70.00
Common Player:		5.00
Inserted 1:41		
1	T.J. Duckett	10.00
2	Michael Vick	8.00
3	DeShaun Foster	8.00
4	Anthony Thomas	8.00
5	William Green	10.00
6	Emmitt Smith	5.00
7	Terrell Davis	5.00
8	Ashley Lelie	6.00
9	Joey Harrington	8.00
10	Brett Favre	6.00
11	David Carr	10.00
12	Randy Moss	6.00
13	Donte Stallworth	6.00
14	Jerry Rice	5.00
15	Marshall Faulk	5.00
16	Kurt Warner	6.00
17	LaDainian Tomlinson	6.00
18	Patrick Ramsey	6.00

2002 Pacific Atomic Super Colliders

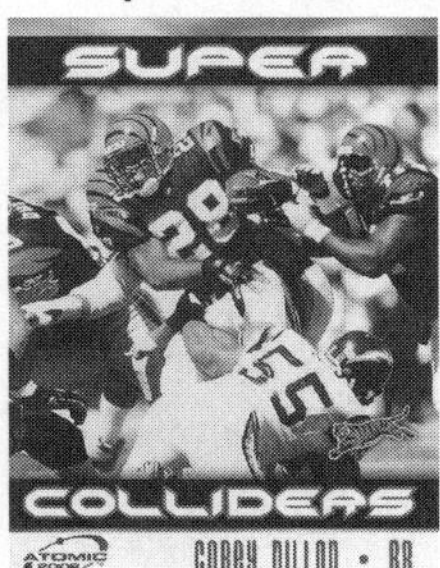

		NM/M
Complete Set (9):		25.00
Common Player:		2.00
Inserted 1:21		
1	Anthony Thomas	6.00
2	Corey Dillon	2.00
3	Emmitt Smith	6.00
4	Edgerrin James	4.00
5	Ricky Williams	2.00
6	Jerome Bettis	2.00
7	Marshall Faulk	3.00
8	LaDainian Tomlinson	5.00
9	Shaun Alexander	4.00

2002 Pacific Crown Royale

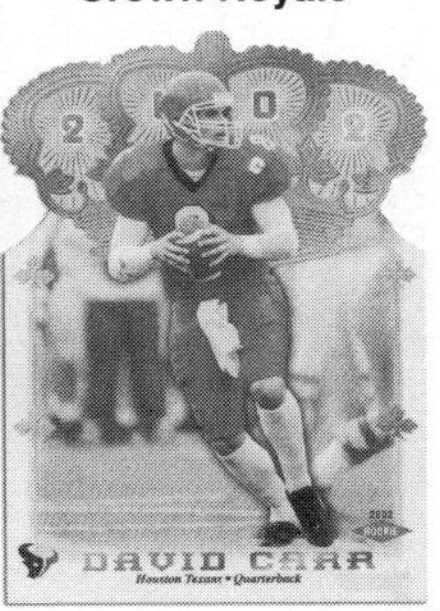

		NM/M
Common Player:		.25
Unlisted Stars:		.75
Minor Stars:		.50
Common Rookie:		
Minor Rookie Stars:		
Red Version Inserted 10:box		1X to 3X
Blue Version Inserted 2:box		2X to 5X
Rookies short-printed 1:pack		
Pack (5):		4.00
Wax Box (24):		80.00
1	David Boston	.75
2	Thomas Jones	.25
3	Jake Plummer	.50
4	Frank Sanders	.25
5	Jamal Anderson	.50
6	Warrick Dunn	.50
7	Brian Finneran	.25
8	Shawn Jefferson	.25
9	Michael Vick	3.00
10	Jeff Blake	.25
11	Jamal Lewis	1.50
12	Ray Lewis	.25
13	Chris Redman	.50
14	Travis Taylor	.50
15	Drew Bledsoe	2.00
16	Travis Henry	.50
17	Eric Moulds	.25
18	Peerless Price	.25
19	Isaac Byrd	.25
20	Muhsin Muhammad	.50
21	Lamar Smith	.25

22 Chris Weinke .75
23 Marty Booker .50
24 Jim Miller .25
25 Marcus Robinson .25
26 Anthony Thomas 2.50
27 Brian Urlacher 2.50
28 Corey Dillon .75
29 Gus Frerotte .25
30 Jon Kitna .25
31 Darnay Scott .25
32 Peter Warrick .50
33 Tim Couch 1.50
34 James Jackson .50
35 Kevin Johnson .25
36 Quincy Morgan .50
37 Quincy Carter 2.00
38 Joey Galloway .50
39 Raghib Ismail .25
40 Emmitt Smith 3.00
41 Mike Anderson 1.50
42 Terrell Davis .50
43 Brian Griese .75
44 Ed McCaffrey .50
45 Rod Smith .50
46 Germane Crowell .25
47 Az-Zahir Hakim .50
48 Mike McMahon .75
49 Bill Schroeder .50
50 Brett Favre 4.00
51 Bubba Franks .25
52 Antonio Freeman .40
53 Terry Glenn .50
54 Ahman Green .75
55 James Allen .25
56 Corey Bradford .25
57 Kent Graham .25
58 Jermaine Lewis .25
59 Marvin Harrison .75
60 Edgerrin James 2.50
61 Peyton Manning 3.00
62 Dominic Rhodes .25
63 Reggie Wayne .25
64 Mark Brunell .75
65 Patrick Johnson .25
66 Jimmy Smith .50
67 Fred Taylor .50
68 Tony Gonzalez .50
69 Trent Green .50
70 Priest Holmes .75
71 Johnnie Morton .25
72 Chris Chambers .75
73 Jay Fiedler .50
74 James McKnight .25
75 Ricky Williams 2.00
76 Derrick Alexander .25
77 Michael Bennett .75
78 Daunte Culpepper 2.00
79 Randy Moss 3.00
80 Tom Brady 3.00
81 Troy Brown .75
82 Kevin Faulk .25
83 David Patten .25
84 Antowain Smith .40
85 Aaron Brooks 1.50
86 Joe Horn .40
87 Deuce McAllister 1.50
88 Jerome Pathon .25
89 Tiki Barber .50
90 Kerry Collins .50
91 Ron Dayne .50
92 Ike Hilliard .25
93 Michael Strahan .50
94 Amani Toomer .40
95 Wayne Chrebet .40
96 Laveranues Coles .50
97 Curtis Martin .50
98 Vinny Testaverde .40
99 Tim Brown .75
100 Rich Gannon .50
101 Charlie Garner .40
102 Jerry Rice 3.00
103 Tyrone Wheatley .25
104 Charles Woodson .50
105 Donovan McNabb 2.00
106 Todd Pinkston .25
107 Duce Staley .75
108 James Thrash .25
109 Jerome Bettis .50
110 Plaxico Burress .50
111 Kordell Stewart .50
112 Hines Ward .50
113 Isaac Bruce .75
114 Marshall Faulk 2.00
115 Torry Holt .25
116 Kurt Warner 3.00
117 Drew Brees 2.50
118 Curtis Conway .25
119 Tim Dwight .50
120 Doug Flutie .75
121 Junior Seau .50
122 LaDainian Tomlinson 2.50
123 Jeff Garcia .75
124 Garrison Hearst .50
125 Terrell Owens .75
126 J.J. Stokes .25
127 Shaun Alexander .75
128 Trent Dilfer .25
129 Darrell Jackson .25
130 Koren Robinson .25
131 Mike Alstott .50
132 Brad Johnson .50
133 Keyshawn Johnson .50
134 Keenan McCardell .25
135 Michael Pittman .25
136 Warren Sapp .50
137 Kevin Dyson .25
138 Eddie George .75
139 Derrick Mason .25
140 Steve McNair .75
141 Stephen Davis .60
142 Rod Gardner .25
143 Jacquez Green .25
144 Shane Matthews .25
145 *Jason McAddley* 1.00
146 *Josh McCown* 4.00
147 *Josh Scobey* 1.00
148 *T.J. Duckett* 10.00
149 *Kahlil Hill* .50
150 *Kurt Kittner* 4.00
151 *Ron Johnson* 1.00
152 *Tellis Redmon* 1.00
153 *Chester Taylor* 1.00
154 *Josh Reed* 5.00
155 *Randy Fasani* 1.00
156 *DeShaun Foster* 5.00
157 *Julius Peppers* 8.00
158 *Adrian Peterson* 4.00
159 *Andre Davis* 5.00
160 *William Green* 8.00
161 *Antonio Bryant* 8.00
162 *Woody Dantzler* 1.00
163 *Ennis Haywood* 1.00
164 *Chad Hutchinson* 3.00
165 *Jamar Martin* 1.00
166 *Roy Williams* 8.00
167 *Herb Haygood* 1.00
168 *Ashley Lelie* 10.00
169 *Clinton Portis* 15.00
170 *Eddie Drummond* 1.00
171 *Joey Harrington* 20.00
172 *Luke Staley* 4.00
173 *Craig Nall* 3.00
174 *Javon Walker* 10.00
175 *Jarrod Baxter* 1.00
176 *David Carr* 20.00
177 *Delvon Flowers* 1.00
178 *Jabar Gaffney* 5.00
179 *Jonathan Wells* 5.00
180 *David Garrard* 4.00
181 *John Henderson* 3.00
182 *Omar Easy* 1.00
183 *Leonard Henry* 2.00
184 *Atrews Bell* 1.00
185 *Deion Branch* 1.00
186 *Rohan Davey* 5.00
187 *Daniel Graham* 4.00
188 *Antwoine Womack* 1.00
189 *J.T. O'Sullivan* 1.00
190 *Donte Stallworth* 15.00
191 *Tim Carter* 2.00
192 *Daryl Jones* 2.00
193 *Jeremy Shockey* 12.00
194 *Ronald Curry* 4.00
195 *Napoleon Harris* 1.00
196 *Larry Ned* 1.00
197 *Freddie Milons* 3.00
198 *Lito Sheppard* 3.00
199 *Brian Westbrook* 4.00
200 *Lee Mays* 1.00
201 *Antwaan Randle El* 8.00
202 *Eric Crouch* 5.00
203 *Lamar Gordon* 4.00
204 *Robert Thomas* 1.00
205 *Seth Burford* 1.00
206 *Donald Reche Caldwell* 4.00
207 *Quentin Jammer* 4.00
208 *Brandon Doman* 1.00
209 *Maurice Morris* 5.00
210 *Jerramy Stevens* 1.00
211 *Travis Stephens* 4.00
212 *Marquise Walker* 4.00
213 *Jake Schifino* 1.00
214 *Ladell Betts* 4.00
215 *Patrick Ramsey* 5.00
216 *Cliff Russell* 2.00

2002 Pacific Crown Royale Crowning Glory

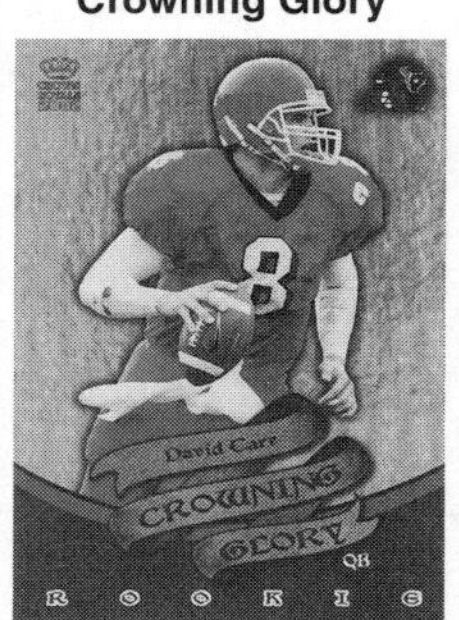

NM/M
Complete Set (20): 50.00
Common Player: 2.00
Inserted 1:25
Card #'s 1-10, rookies, hobby only
Card #'s 11-20, veterans, retail only
1 T.J. Duckett 3.00
2 DeShaun Foster 2.00
3 William Green 3.00
4 Ashley Lelie 3.00
5 Clinton Portis 3.00
6 Joey Harrington 4.00
7 David Carr 5.00
8 Jabar Gaffney 2.00
9 Donte Stallworth 3.00
10 Patrick Ramsey 3.00
11 Michael Vick 2.00
12 Anthony Thomas 2.00
13 Emmitt Smith 5.00
14 Brett Favre 5.00
15 Peyton Manning 4.00
16 Randy Moss 4.00
17 Tom Brady 5.00
18 Jerry Rice 3.00
19 Kurt Warner 4.00
20 LaDainian Tomlinson 2.00

2002 Pacific Crown Royale Legendary Heroes

NM/M
Common Player: 8.00
Inserted 1:392
1 Emmitt Smith/80 12.00
2 Terrell Davis/80 8.00
3 Brett Favre/80 30.00
4 Peyton Manning 20.00
5 Ricky Williams 15.00
6 Randy Moss 20.00
7 Jerry Rice/80 15.00
8 Donovan McNabb 15.00
9 Marshall Faulk 15.00
10 Kurt Warner 20.00

2002 Pacific Crown Royale Majestic Motion

NM/M
Complete Set (10): 60.00
Common Player: 5.00
Inserted 1:24
1 Michael Vick 5.00
2 Anthony Thomas 5.00
3 Emmitt Smith 15.00
4 Brett Favre 15.00
5 Peyton Manning 10.00
6 Randy Moss 10.00
7 Jerry Rice 8.00
8 Marshall Faulk 5.00
9 Kurt Warner 8.00
10 LaDainian Tomlinson 5.00

2002 Pacific Crown Royale Pro Bowl Honors

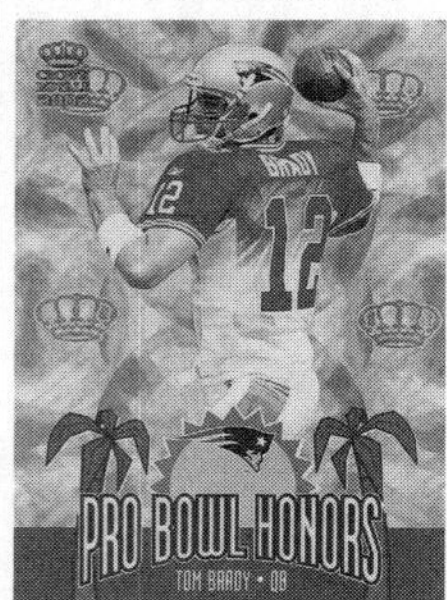

NM/M
Complete Set (20): 50.00
Common Player: 2.00
Inserted 1:6
1 Brian Urlacher 6.00
2 Corey Dillon 2.00
3 Emmitt Smith 8.00
4 Terrell Davis 2.00
5 Ahman Green 3.00
6 Marvin Harrison 2.00
7 Edgerrin James 4.00
8 Peyton Manning 5.00
9 Daunte Culpepper 4.00
10 Randy Moss 4.00
11 Tom Brady 6.00
12 Curtis Martin 2.00
13 Rich Gannon 2.00
14 Jerry Rice 4.00
15 Donovan McNabb 2.00
16 Kordell Stewart 2.00
17 Marshall Faulk 2.00
18 Kurt Warner 6.00
19 Junior Seau 2.00
20 Eddie George 2.00

2002 Pacific Crown Royale Triple Threads

NM/M
Common Player: 8.00
Inserted 1:12
Gold 2X to 5X
Production 25 sets
1 David Boston, Thomas Jones, Jake Plummer 15.00
2 MarTay Jenkins, Tywan Mitchell, Frank Sanders 8.00
3 Ray Lewis, Chris Redman, Travis Taylor 12.00
4 Reggie Germany, Eric Moulds, Peerless Price 8.00
5 Shawn Bryson, Sammy Morris, Jay Riemersma 8.00
6 Jim Miller, David Terrell, Brian Urlacher 15.00
7 T.J. Houshmandzadeh, Chad Johnson, Peter Warrick 8.00
8 JaJuan Dawson, Dennis Northcutt, Jamel White 8.00
9 Mike Anderson, Ed McCaffrey, Rod Smith 20.00
10 Scotty Anderson, Germane Crowell, Desmond Howard 8.00
11 Mark Brunell, Jimmy Smith, Fred Taylor 15.00
12 Derrick Blaylock, Trent Green, Tony Richardson 8.00
13 Richie Anderson, Chad Pennington, Vinny Testaverde 12.00
14 Tim Brown, James Jett, Randy Jordan 12.00
15 Chad Lewis, Cecil Martin, Todd Pinkston 8.00
16 Mark Bruener, Hines Ward, Amos Zereoue 8.00
17 Chris Fuamatu-Ma'afala, Dan Kreider, Tee Martin 8.00
18 Doug Flutie, Ronney Jenkins, Junior Seau 12.00
19 Champ Bailey, Stephen Davis, Darnerian McCants 8.00
20 Terrell Davis, Edgerrin James, Ricky Williams 30.00
21 Daunte Culpepper, Tom Brady, Donovan McNabb 50.00
22 Corey Dillon, Shaun Alexander, Eddie George 20.00
23 Emmitt Smith, Marshall Faulk, LaDainian Tomlinson 50.00
24 Michael Vick, Chris Weinke, Drew Brees 50.00
25 Brett Favre, Peyton Manning, Kurt Warner 100.00
26 Ahman Green, Curtis Martin, Jerome Bettis 25.00
27 Drew Bledsoe, Tim Couch, Brian Griese 25.00
28 Aaron Brooks, Kordell Stewart, Steve McNair 12.00
29 Randy Moss, Jerry Rice, Isaac Bruce 50.00
30 Marvin Harrison, Cris Carter, Terrell Owens 20.00
31 Jamal Anderson, Bob Christian, Reggie Kelly 8.00
32 Joey Galloway, Troy Hambrick, Darren Woodson 8.00
33 Matt Hasselbeck, Itula Mili, Mack Strong 10.00
34 Bryan Gilmore, Chris Greisen, Arnold Jackson 8.00
35 Todd Heap, Chris Redman, Brandon Stokley 12.00
36 Donald Hayes, Patrick Pass, Antowain Smith 8.00
37 Derrick Alexander, D'Wayne Bates, Chris Walsh 8.00
38 Emmitt Smith, Ahman Green, Ricky Williams 50.00
39 Brett Favre, Mark Brunell, Donovan McNabb 75.00
40 Drew Brees, Anthony Thomas, Chris Weinke 40.00

2002 Pacific Crown Royale Sunday Soldiers

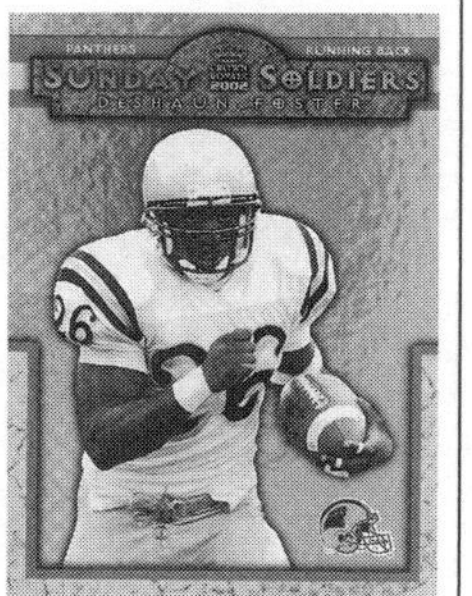

NM/M
Complete Set (20): 50.00
Common Player: 2.00
Inserted 1:15
1 T.J. Duckett 3.00
2 Michael Vick 3.00
3 Drew Bledsoe 2.00
4 DeShaun Foster 3.00
5 William Green 3.00
6 Emmitt Smith 10.00
7 Ashley Lelie 4.00
8 Joey Harrington 5.00
9 Brett Favre 10.00
10 David Carr 5.00
11 Peyton Manning 4.00
12 Randy Moss 6.00
13 Tom Brady 8.00
14 Donte Stallworth 3.00
15 Donovan McNabb 2.00
16 Marshall Faulk 3.00
17 Kurt Warner 5.00
18 LaDainian Tomlinson 2.00
19 Shaun Alexander 2.00
20 Patrick Ramsey 3.00

2002 Pacific Exclusive

NM/M
Common Player: .20
Unlisted Stars: .50
Minor Stars: .40

NM/M
Common Rookie: .75
Minor Rookie Stars: 1.00
Gold 1X to 3X
Inserted 1:1
Blue Rookie 2X to 5X
Inserted 1:21
Rookie Autographs
Inserted 1:21
Pack (6): 4.00
Wax Box (20): 75.00
1 David Boston .50
2 Thomas Jones .20
3 Jake Plummer .40
4 Frank Sanders .20
5 *Josh Scobey* .75
6 Warrick Dunn .40
7 *Brian Finneran* .75
8 *Kahlil Hill* .75
9 Shawn Jefferson .20
10 *Kurt Kittner* 1.25
11 Michael Vick 2.00
12 *Ron Johnson* 1.00
13 Jamal Lewis .75
14 Ray Lewis .40
15 Chris Redman .40
16 Brandon Stokley .20
17 Chester Taylor .20
18 Travis Taylor .40
19 Drew Bledsoe 1.00
20 Travis Henry .40
21 Eric Moulds .40
22 Peerless Price .20
23 *Randy Fasani* 1.00
24 Muhsin Muhammad .40
25 Lamar Smith .20
26 Steve Smith .20
27 Chris Weinke .50
28 Marty Booker .40
29 Jim Miller .40
30 *Adrian Peterson* 1.00
31 Marcus Robinson .40
32 David Terrell .50
33 Anthony Thomas 1.25
34 Brian Urlacher 1.25
35 Corey Dillon .50
36 Chad Johnson .20
37 Jon Kitna .20
38 Peter Warrick .40
39 Michael Westbrook .20
40 Tim Couch .75
41 *JaJuan Dawson* .75
42 James Jackson .40
43 Kevin Johnson .20
44 Quincy Morgan .20
45 Quincy Carter 1.00
46 Joey Galloway .40
47 *Troy Hambrick* .75
48 *Chad Hutchinson* 1.00
49 Raghib Ismail .20
50 Emmitt Smith 2.00
51 Mike Anderson .75
52 Terrell Davis .75
53 Brian Griese .50
54 *Herb Haygood* .75
55 Ed McCaffrey .40
56 Rod Smith .40
57 Germane Crowell .20
58 Az-Zahir Hakim .40
59 Mike McMahon .50
60 Bill Schroeder .20
61 *Luke Staley* 1.50
62 James Stewart .40
63 Brett Favre 2.50
64 Robert Ferguson .20
65 Bubba Franks .20
66 Terry Glenn .40
67 Ahman Green .50
68 *Craig Nall* .75
69 James Allen .20
70 Corey Bradford .20
71 Jermaine Lewis .20
72 Travis Prentice .20
73 *Brian Allen* .75
74 Marvin Harrison .40
75 Edgerrin James 1.25
76 Peyton Manning 2.00
77 Reggie Wayne .20
78 Mark Brunell .50
79 Patrick Johnson .20
80 Jimmy Smith .20
81 Fred Taylor .40
82 Tony Gonzalez .40
83 Trent Green .40
84 Priest Holmes .50
85 Johnnie Morton .20
86 Chris Chambers .50
87 Jay Fiedler .40
88 Oronde Gadsden .20
89 Leonard Henry .40
90 Travis Minor .20
91 Sam Simmons .20
92 Ricky Williams 1.00
93 Derrick Alexander .20
94 Michael Bennett .50
95 Daunte Culpepper 1.00
96 Randy Moss 2.00
97 Tom Brady 2.00
98 *Deion Branch* 1.50
99 Troy Brown .50
100 *Rohan Davey* 1.50
101 Donald Hayes .20
102 David Patten .20
103 Antowain Smith .40
104 *Antwoine Womack* .75
105 Aaron Brooks .75
106 Joe Horn .20
107 Deuce McAllister .75
108 *J.T. O'Sullivan* .75
109 Jerome Pathon .20
110 Tiki Barber .40
111 *Tim Carter* 1.25
112 Kerry Collins .40
113 Ron Dayne .40
114 Ike Hilliard .40
115 Amani Toomer .40
116 Wayne Chrebet .40
117 Laveranues Coles .40
118 Curtis Martin .40
119 Santana Moss .40
120 Vinny Testaverde .40
121 Tim Brown .50
122 *Ronald Curry* 1.25
123 Rich Gannon .50
124 Charlie Garner .40
125 *Larry Ned* .75
126 Jerry Rice 2.00
127 Tyrone Wheatley .20
128 Donovan McNabb 1.00
129 Freddie Mitchell .40
130 Todd Pinkston .20
131 Duce Staley .40
132 James Thrash .20
133 Jerome Bettis .40
134 Plaxico Burress .50
135 Kordell Stewart .40
136 Hines Ward .40
137 Amos Zereoue .20
138 Isaac Bruce .50
139 Trung Canidate .20
140 *Eric Crouch* 1.50
141 Marshall Faulk 1.00
142 Lamar Gordon .20
143 Torry Holt .40
144 Kurt Warner 2.00
145 Terrence Wilkins .20
146 Drew Brees 1.25
147 *Seth Burford* .75
148 *Donald Reche Caldwell* 1.25
149 Curtis Conway .40
150 Tim Dwight .40
151 Doug Flutie .50
152 LaDainian Tomlinson 1.25
153 Kevan Barlow .20
154 *Brandon Doman* .75
155 Jeff Garcia .50
156 Garrison Hearst .40
157 Terrell Owens .50
158 J.J. Stokes .20
159 Shaun Alexander .50
160 Trent Dilfer .40
161 Darrell Jackson .20
162 Koren Robinson .40
163 Mike Alstott .40
164 Brad Johnson .40
165 Keyshawn Johnson .40
166 Keenan McCardell .20
167 Michael Pittman .20
168 *Travis Stephens* 1.25
169 Marquise Walker 1.25
170 Kevin Dyson .40
171 Eddie George .50
172 Derrick Mason .40
173 Steve McNair .50
174 Reidel Anthony .20
175 *Ladell Betts* 1.25
176 Stephen Davis .50
177 Rod Gardner .40
178 Jacquez Green .20
179 Shane Matthews .20
180 *Cliff Russell* 1.00
181 *Josh McCown* 1.25
182 *T.J. Duckett* 4.00
183 *Josh Reed* 1.50
184 *DeShaun Foster* 1.50
185 *Andre Davis* 1.50
186 *William Green* 3.00
187 *Antonio Bryant* 3.00
188 *Ashley Lelie* 4.00
189 *Clinton Portis* 6.00
190 *Joey Harrington* 5.00
191 *Javon Walker* 3.00
192 *David Carr* 5.00
193 *Jabar Gaffney* 1.50
194 *Jonathan Wells* 1.50
195 *David Garrard* 1.25
196 *Donte Stallworth* 4.00
197 *Brian Westbrook* 1.25
198 *Antwaan Randle El* 3.00
199 *Maurice Morris* 1.50
200 *Patrick Ramsey* 1.50

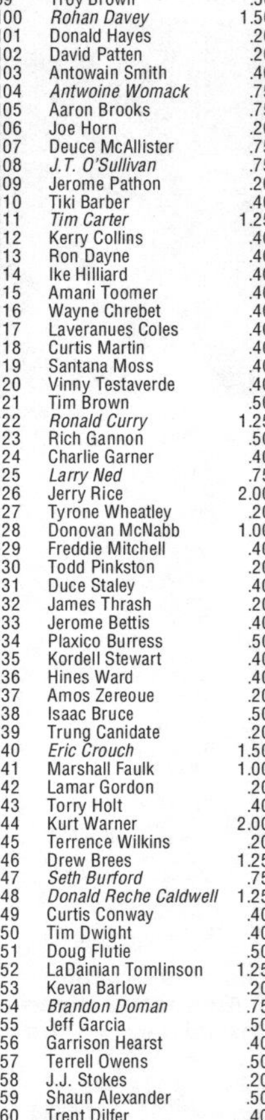

2002 Pacific Exclusive Authentic Game-Worn Jerseys

NM/M
Common Player: 6.00
Inserted 2:21
Gold 2X to5X
Production 25 sets
1 Frank Sanders/610 6.00
2 Jamal Anderson/610 6.00
3 Quentin McCord/610 6.00
4 Michael Vick/150 15.00
5 Jeremy McDaniel/610 6.00
6 Jay Riemersma/610 6.00
7 Charlie Rogers/610 6.00
8 Marcus Robinson/610 6.00
9 Brian Urlacher/250 20.00
10 Corey Dillon/250 8.00
11 Michael Westbrook/610 6.00
12 Tim Couch/250 10.00
13 Aaron Shea/610 6.00
14 Emmitt Smith/250 20.00

NM/M
15 Kevin Kasper/575 6.00
16 Rob Moore/610 6.00
17 Brett Favre/250 30.00
18 Robert Ferguson/350 6.00
19 Ahman Green/250 12.00
20 Avion Black/610 6.00
21 Clif Groce/610 6.00
22 Brock Huard/610 6.00
23 Peyton Manning/250 15.00
24 Troy Walters/610 6.00
25 Mark Brunell/610 6.00
26 Bobby Shaw/610 6.00
27 Jimmy Smith/610 6.00
28 Ricky Williams/610 12.00
29 Daunte Culpepper/500 12.00
30 Randy Moss/250 20.00
31 Aaron Brooks/450 8.00
32 Terrelle Smith/610 6.00
33 Laveranues Coles/500 6.00
34 Curtis Martin/250 6.00
35 Rich Gannon/210 6.00
36 Jerry Rice/300 25.00
37 Donovan McNabb/610 12.00
38 James Thrash/610 6.00
39 Jerome Bettis/250
40 Plaxico Burress/200 10.00
41 Chris Fuamatu-Ma'afala/610 10.00
42 Marshall Faulk/295 12.00
43 Kurt Warner/500 15.00
44 Drew Brees/295 10.00
45 Terrell Fletcher/610 6.00
46 Shaun Alexander/175 10.00
47 Brad Johnson/610 6.00
48 Michael Pittman 610 6.00
49 Aaron Stecker/610 6.00
50 Erron Kinney/610 6.00

2002 Pacific Exclusive Destined For Greatness

NM/M
Common Player: 3.00
Inserted 1:11
1 T.J. Duckett 4.00
2 DeShaun Foster 3.00
3 William Green 3.00
4 Ashley Lelie 4.00
5 Clinton Portis 4.00
6 Joey Harrington 6.00
7 David Carr 6.00
8 Donte Stallworth 4.00
9 Antwann Randle El 3.00
10 Patrick Ramsey 3.00

2002 Pacific Exclusive Diamond Rookie Autograph

NM/M
Common Player: 10.00
Production to varying quantities
Antonio Bryant/62 50.00
David Carr/73 100.00
Andre Davis/467 15.00
DeShaun Foster/78 35.00
Jabar Gaffney/77 25.00
David Garrard/466 15.00
Ashley Lelie/73 40.00
Josh McCown/470 15.00
Maurice Morris/695 10.00
Clinton Portis/361 70.00
Antwann Randle El/476 50.00
Jonathan Wells/536 25.00
Brian Westbrook/645 20.00
Javon Walker 30.00

2002 Pacific Exclusive Etched in Stone

NM/M
Common Player: 4.00
Inserted 1:21
1 Michael Vick 5.00
2 Anthony Thomas 4.00
3 Emmitt Smith 6.00
4 Brett Favre 8.00
5 Peyton Manning 5.00
6 Randy Moss 5.00
7 Tom Brady 5.00
8 Jerry Rice 5.00
9 Marshall Faulk 4.00
10 Kurt Warner 5.00

2002 Pacific Exclusive Exclusive Advantage

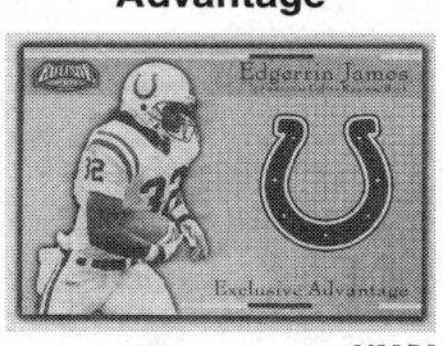

NM/M
Common Player: 2.00
Inserted 1:6
1 Michael Vick 4.00
2 Drew Bledsoe 2.00
3 Anthony Thomas 2.00
4 Corey Dillon 2.00
5 Tim Couch 2.00
6 Emmitt Smith 4.00
7 Brett Favre 5.00
8 Edgerrin James 2.00
9 Peyton Manning 3.00
10 Ricky Williams 2.00
11 Daunte Culpepper 2.00
12 Randy Moss 3.00
13 Tom Brady 4.00
14 Jerry Rice 4.00
15 Donovan McNabb 2.00
16 Marshall Faulk 2.00
17 Kurt Warner 3.00
18 Drew Brees 2.00
19 LaDainian Tomlinson 2.00
20 Shaun Alexander 2.00

2002 Pacific Exclusive Great Expectations

NM/M
Common Player: 2.00
Inserted 1:6
1 Josh McCown 2.00
2 T.J. Duckett 4.00
3 Josh Reed 2.00
4 DeShaun Foster 2.00
5 Andre Davis 2.00
6 William Green 3.00
7 Antonio Bryant 3.00
8 Ashley Lelie 4.00
9 Clinton Portis 4.00
10 Joey Harrington 5.00
11 Javon Walker 3.00
12 David Carr 5.00
13 Jabar Gaffney 2.00
14 Jonathan Wells 2.00
15 David Garrard 2.00
16 Donte Stallworth 4.00
17 Brian Westbrook 2.00
18 Antwann Randle El 3.00
19 Maurice Morris 2.00
20 Patrick Ramsey 2.00

2002 Pacific Exclusive Maximum Overdrive

NM/M
Common Player: 2.00
Inserted 1:6
1 T.J. Duckett 4.00
2 Michael Vick 4.00
3 DeShaun Foster 2.00
4 Anthony Thomas 2.00
5 Tim Couch 2.00
6 Andre Davis 2.00
7 William Green 3.00
8 Antonio Bryant 3.00
9 Emmitt Smith 4.00
10 Ashley Lelie 4.00
11 Clinton Portis 4.00
12 Joey Harrington 5.00
13 Brett Favre 6.00
14 Javon Walker 3.00
15 David Carr 5.00
16 Jabar Gaffney 2.00
17 Peyton Manning 4.00
18 Ricky Williams 2.00
19 Daunte Culpepper 2.00
20 Randy Moss 4.00
21 Tom Brady 4.00
22 Donte Stallworth 4.00
23 Jerry Rice 4.00
24 Donovan McNabb 2.00
25 Antwann Randle El 3.00
26 Marshall Faulk 2.00
27 Kurt Warner 4.00
28 Drew Brees 4.00
29 LaDainian Tomlinson 3.00
30 Patrick Ramsey 2.00

2002 Pacific Exclusive Pinwheel Rookie Autograph

NM/M
Common Player: 10.00
Production to varying quantities
Antonio Bryant/513 45.00
David Carr/27 125.00
Andre Davis/311 15.00
DeShaun Foster/27 45.00
Jabar Gaffney/26 35.00
David Garrard/321 20.00
Ashley Lelie/27 55.00
Josh McCown/309 15.00
Maurice Morris/350 10.00
Clinton Portis/162 70.00
Antwann Randle El/312 50.00
Jonathan Wells/82 35.00
Brian Westbrook/285 20.00
Javon Walker 30.00

2002 Pacific Heads Up

NM/M
Common Player: .25
Unlisted Stars: .75
Minor Stars: .50
Blue Variation 1X to3X
Inserted 2:19
Red Variation 1X to4X
Inserted 1:19
Purple Variation 2X to8X
Production 25 sets
Pack (5): 4.00
Wax Box (18): 75.00
1 David Boston .75
2 Thomas Jones .25
3 Jake Plummer .40
4 Jamal Anderson .25
5 Warrick Dunn .40
6 Shawn Jefferson .25
7 Michael Vick 3.00
8 Jamal Lewis .25
9 Chris Redman .40
10 Brandon Stokley .25
11 Travis Taylor .50
12 Drew Bledsoe 2.00
13 Travis Henry .50
14 Eric Moulds .25
15 Peerless Price .50
16 Alex Van Pelt .25
17 Muhsin Muhammad .50
18 Lamar Smith .50
19 Steve Smith .25
20 Chris Weinke .75
21 Marty Booker .40
22 Jim Miller .40
23 David Terrell .75
24 Anthony Thomas 2.50
25 Corey Dillon .75
26 Chad Johnson .25
27 Jon Kitna .25
28 Peter Warrick .50
29 Tim Couch 1.50
30 James Jackson .75
31 Kevin Johnson .25
32 Quincy Morgan .50
33 Quincy Carter 2.00
34 Joey Galloway .25
35 Raghib Ismail .25
36 Emmitt Smith 3.00
37 Terrell Davis 1.50
38 Brian Griese .75
39 Ed McCaffrey .25
40 Rod Smith .50
41 Scotty Anderson .25
42 Az-Zahir Hakim .50
43 Mike McMahon .75
44 Bill Schroeder .25
45 Brett Favre 4.00
46 Robert Ferguson .25
47 Terry Glenn .50
48 Ahman Green .25
49 James Allen .25
50 Corey Bradford .25
51 Jermaine Lewis .25
52 Marvin Harrison .60
53 Edgerrin James 2.50
54 Peyton Manning 3.00
55 Reggie Wayne .25
56 Mark Brunell .75
57 Keenan McCardell .25
58 Jimmy Smith .25
59 Fred Taylor .50
60 Derrick Alexander .25
61 Tony Gonzalez .40
62 Trent Green .40
63 Priest Holmes .75
64 Chris Chambers .75
65 Jay Fiedler .25
66 James McKnight .25
67 Ricky Williams 2.00
68 Michael Bennett .75
69 Daunte Culpepper 2.00
70 Randy Moss 3.00
71 Tom Brady 3.00
72 Troy Brown .75
73 Antowain Smith .50
74 Aaron Brooks 1.50
75 Joe Horn .50
76 Willie Jackson .25
77 Deuce McAllister 1.50
78 Tiki Barber .40
79 Kerry Collins .40
80 Ron Dayne .40
81 Ike Hilliard .40
82 Wayne Chrebet .40
83 Laveranues Coles .40
84 Curtis Martin .40
85 Vinny Testaverde .40
86 Tim Brown .75
87 Rich Gannon .50
88 Charlie Garner .40
89 Jerry Rice 3.00
90 Correll Buckhalter .25
91 Donovan McNabb 2.00
92 Duce Staley .40
93 James Thrash .25
94 Jerome Bettis .50
95 Plaxico Burress .75
96 Kordell Stewart .50
97 Hines Ward .25
98 Isaac Bruce .50
99 Marshall Faulk 2.00
100 Torry Holt .50
101 Kurt Warner 3.00
102 Drew Brees 2.00
103 Tim Dwight .25
104 Doug Flutie .75
105 LaDainian Tomlinson 2.50
106 Jeff Garcia .75
107 Garrison Hearst .25
108 Terrell Owens .75
109 J.J. Stokes .25
110 Shaun Alexander .75
111 Trent Dilfer .40
112 Darrell Jackson .25
113 Koren Robinson .40
114 Mike Alstott .40
115 Brad Johnson .40
116 Keyshawn Johnson .40
117 Michael Pittman .25
118 Kevin Dyson .40
119 Eddie George .75
120 Derrick Mason .25
121 Steve McNair .75
122 Reidel Anthony .25
123 Stephen Davis .50
124 Rod Gardner .40
125 Jacquez Green .25
126 *Jason McAddley* 2.00
127 *Josh McCown* 4.00
128 *T.J. Duckett* 10.00
129 *Kahlil Hill* 2.00
130 *Kurt Kittner* 4.00
131 *Ron Johnson* 2.00
132 *Josh Reed* 5.00
133 *DeShaun Foster* 5.00
134 *Julius Peppers* 8.00
135 *Adrian Peterson* 4.00
136 *Andre Davis* 5.00
137 *William Green* 8.00
138 *Antonio Bryant* 8.00
139 *Roy Williams* 8.00
140 *Ashley Lelie* 10.00
141 *Clinton Portis* 15.00
142 *Joey Harrington* 15.00
143 *Luke Staley* 4.00
144 *Javon Walker* 8.00
145 *David Carr* 20.00
146 *Jabar Gaffney* 5.00
147 *David Garrard* 3.00
148 *Leonard Henry* 2.00
149 *Rohan Davey* 5.00
150 *Daniel Graham* 5.00
151 *Donte Stallworth* 10.00
152 *Jeremy Shockey* 10.00
153 *Ronald Curry* 4.00
154 *Freddie Milons* 3.00
155 *Brian Westbrook* 4.00
156 *Antwann Randle El* 8.00
157 *Eric Crouch* 5.00
158 *Lamar Gordon* 4.00
159 *Donald Reche Caldwell* 4.00
160 *Maurice Morris* 5.00
161 *Marquise Walker* 4.00
162 *Ladell Betts* 4.00
163 *Patrick Ramsey* 5.00
164 *Cliff Russell* 3.00
165 *Travis Stephens* 4.00
166 *Deion Branch* 4.00
167 *Eric McCoo* 3.00
168 *Antwoine Womack* 3.00

2002 Pacific Heads Up Authentic Game-Worn Jersey Quads

NM/M
Common Player: 25.00
Inserted 2:21
Gold 3X to5X
Inserted 1:145
1 David Boston, Thomas Jones, Jake Plummer, Frank Sanders 25.00
2 Martin Gramatica, MarTay Jenkins, Joel Makovicka, Tywan Mitchell 25.00
3 Obafemi Ayanbadejo, Todd Heap, Chris Redman, Travis Taylor 25.00
4 Shawn Bryson, Reggie Germany, Sammy Morris, Jay Riemersma 25.00

A player's name in *italic* type indicates a rookie card.

5 Isaac Byrd, Muhsin Muhammad, Wesley Walls, Chris Weinke 30.00
6 Marty Booker, Jim Miller, David Terrell, Brian Urlacher 60.00
7 Corey Dillon, Chad Johnson, Darnay Scott, Peter Warrick 25.00
8 Curtis Keaton, Scott Mitchell, Brad St. Louis, Nick Williams 25.00
9 Tim Couch, JaJuan Dawson, Kevin Johnson, Jamel White 35.00
10 Quincy Carter, Joey Galloway, Raghib Ismail, Emmitt Smith 75.00
11 Troy Hambrick, Michael Wiley, Darren Woodson, Anthony Wright 25.00
12 Mike Anderson, Olandis Gary, Brian Griese, Rod Smith 35.00
13 Brett Favre, Antonio Freeman, Ahman Green, David Martin 60.00
14 Tyrone Davis, Robert Ferguson, Bubba Franks, William Henderson 35.00
15 Marvin Harrison, Edgerrin James, Peyton Manning, Marcus Pollard 40.00
16 Mark Brunell, Keenan McCardell, Jimmy Smith, Fred Taylor 25.00
17 Tony Gonzalez, Trent Green, Sylvester Morris, Tony Richardson 25.00
18 Jay Fiedler, Oronde Gadsden, Travis Minor, Zach Thomas 30.00
19 Michael Bennett, Cris Carter, Daunte Culpepper, Randy Moss 60.00
20 Drew Bledsoe, Tom Brady, Troy Brown, Patrick Pass 75.00
21 Aaron Brooks, Joe Horn, Deuce McAllister, Robert Wilson 25.00
22 Tiki Barber, Kerry Collins, Ron Dayne, Amani Toomer 25.00
23 Jonathan Carter, Ron Dixon, Ike Hilliard, Jason Sehorn 25.00
24 Anthony Becht, Laveranues Coles, Curtis Martin, Chad Pennington 25.00
25 Tim Brown, Zack Crockett, Jerry Rice, Charles Woodson 50.00
26 David Dunn, James Jett, Randy Jordan, Jerry Porter 25.00
27 Chad Lewis, Donovan McNabb, Brian Mitchell, Todd Pinkston 25.00
28 Jerome Bettis, Plaxico Burress, Kordell Stewart, Hines Ward 35.00
29 Isaac Bruce, Marshall Faulk, Torry Holt, Kurt Warner 60.00
30 Drew Brees, Doug Flutie, Junior Seau, LaDainian Tomlinson 60.00
31 Terrell Fletcher, Trevor Gaylor, Ronney Jenkins, Fred McCrary 25.00
32 Jeff Garcia, Terrell Owens, Tim Rattay, J.J. Stokes 25.00
33 Fred Beasley, Greg Clark, Paul Smith, Cedrick Wilson 25.00
34 Shaun Alexander, Alex Bannister, Matt Hasselbeck, Darrell Jackson 25.00
35 Brock Huard, Itula Mili, Mack Strong, James Williams 25.00
36 Joe Hamilton, Brad Johnson, Rob Johnson, Shaun King 25.00
37 Mike Alstott, Keyshawn Johnson, Warren Sapp, Aaron Stecker 25.00
38 Kevin Dyson, Eddie George, Derrick Mason, Steve McNair 35.00
39 David Boston, Jake Plummer, Corey Dillon, Peter Warrick 35.00
40 Isaac Bruce, Marshall Faulk, Torry Holt, Kurt Warner 60.00

2002 Pacific Heads Up Bobble Head Dolls

NM/M
Inserted one per hobby box
1 Michael Vick 35.00
2 Anthony Thomas 35.00
3 Emmitt Smith 50.00
4 Brett Favre 50.00
5 David Carr 65.00
0 Ricky Williams 40.00

NM/M
7 Daunte Culpepper 35.00
8 Randy Moss 40.00
9 Tom Brady 50.00
10 Jerry Rice 50.00
11 Jerome Bettis 30.00
12 Marshall Faulk 35.00
13 Kurt Warner 40.00
14 LaDainian Tomlinson 40.00

2002 Pacific Heads Up Head First

NM/M
Common Player: 2.00
Inserted 1:19
1 Michael Vick 3.00
2 Brian Urlacher 3.00
3 Tim Couch 2.00
4 William Green 4.00
5 Emmitt Smith 4.00
6 Joey Harrington 5.00
7 David Carr 8.00
8 Edgerrin James 3.00
9 Peyton Manning 3.00
10 Ricky Williams 2.00
11 Randy Moss 2.00
12 Jerry Rice 4.00
13 Donovan McNabb 2.00
14 Marshall Faulk 3.00
15 LaDainian Tomlinson 3.00
16 Shaun Alexander 2.00

2002 Pacific Heads Up Inside The Numbers

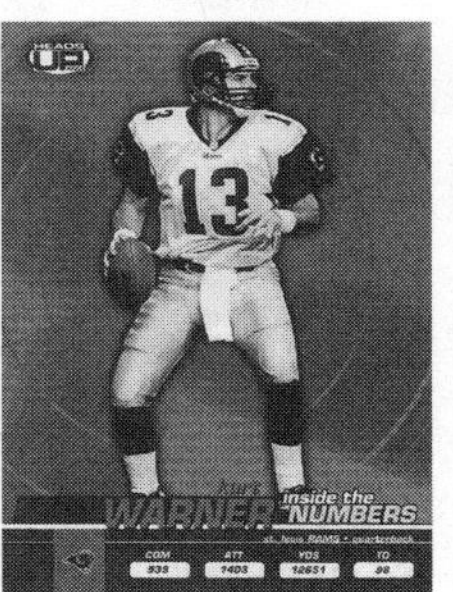

NM/M
Common Player: 2.00
Inserted 2:19
1 T.J. Duckett 3.00
2 Michael Vick 3.00
3 DeShaun Foster 3.00
4 Anthony Thomas 3.00
5 William Green 4.00
6 Emmitt Smith 3.00
7 Terrell Davis 2.00
8 Joey Harrington 5.00
9 Brett Favre 5.00
10 David Carr 8.00
11 Jabar Gaffney 2.00
12 Edgerrin James 3.00
13 Peyton Manning 3.00
14 Ricky Williams 2.00
15 Daunte Culpepper 3.00
16 Randy Moss 3.00
17 Tom Brady 5.00
18 Donte Stallworth 4.00
19 Jerry Rice 4.00
20 Donovan McNabb 2.00
21 Marshall Faulk 3.00
22 Kurt Warner 4.00
23 LaDainian Tomlinson 3.00
24 Patrick Ramsey 3.00

2002 Pacific Heads Up Prime Picks

NM/M
Common Player: 4.00
Inserted 1:37
1 T.J. Duckett 5.00
2 DeShaun Foster 5.00
3 William Green 6.00

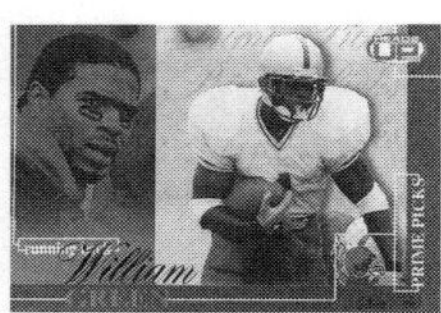

		NM/M
4	Ashley Lelie	4.00
5	Joey Harrington	8.00
6	Jevon Walker	6.00
7	David Carr	12.00
8	Jabar Gaffney	4.00
9	Donte Stallworth	5.00
10	Patrick Ramsey	4.00

2002 Pacific Heads Update

		NM/M
Complete Set (175):		75.00
Common Player:		.20
Unlisted Star:		.40
Minor Star:		.50
Blue Hobby only- Red Retail only		
Pack (6):		4.00
Wax Box (18):		80.00
1	David Boston	.75
2	*Wendell Bryant*	1.00
3	Thomas Jones	.20
4	*Jason McAddley*	1.00
5	*Josh McCown*	1.25
6	Jake Plummer	.50
7	*T.J. Duckett*	3.00
8	Warrick Dunn	.50
9	Shawn Jefferson	.20
10	*Kurt Kittner*	1.25
11	Michael Vick	2.00
12	*Dameon Hunter*	1.00
13	*Javin Hunter*	2.00
14	*Ron Johnson*	1.00
15	Jamal Lewis	1.00
16	Ray Lewis	.50
17	Chris Redman	.50
18	*Tellis Redmon*	1.00
19	*Ed Reed*	1.00
20	*Chester Taylor*	1.00
21	Drew Bledsoe	1.25
22	Travis Henry	.50
23	Eric Moulds	.50
24	*Josh Reed*	1.50
25	*Randy Fasani*	1.25
26	*DeShaun Foster*	1.50
27	Muhsin Muhammad	.50
28	*Julius Peppers*	2.00
29	Lamar Smith	.20
30	Chris Weinke	.20
31	Marty Booker	.50
32	*Jamin Elliott*	1.00
33	Jim Miller	.40
34	*Adrian Peterson*	1.25
35	Anthony Thomas	1.25
36	Brian Urlacher	1.50
37	Corey Dillon	.75
38	Gus Frerotte	.20
39	Peter Warrick	.50
40	Michael Westbrook	.20
41	Tim Couch	1.00
42	*Andre Davis*	1.50
43	*William Green*	2.00
44	Kevin Johnson	.40
45	Quincy Morgan	.40
46	*Antonio Bryant*	2.00
47	Quincy Carter	1.25
48	Joey Galloway	.50
49	*Chad Hutchinson*	1.25
50	Emmitt Smith	2.00
51	*Roy Williams*	2.00
52	Terrell Davis	1.00
53	Brian Griese	.75
54	*Ashley Lelie*	3.00
55	*Clinton Portis*	5.00
56	Rod Smith	.50
57	*Eddie Drummond*	1.00
58	*Joey Harrington*	5.00
59	Mike McMahon	.50
60	Bill Schroeder	.20
61	James Stewart	.20
62	*Najeh Davenport*	1.00
63	Brett Favre	2.50
64	*Tony Fisher*	1.00
65	Terry Glenn	.50
66	Ahman Green	.75
67	*Craig Nall*	1.00
68	*Javon Walker*	2.00
69	James Allen	.20
70	*Jarrod Baxter*	1.00
71	Corey Bradford	.20
72	*David Carr*	5.00
73	*Jabar Gaffney*	1.50
74	Jermaine Lewis	.20
75	*Edmond Stansbury*	1.00
76	*Jonathan Wells*	1.50
77	*Dwight Freeney*	1.00
78	Marvin Harrison	.75
79	Edgerrin James	1.50
80	Peyton Manning	2.00
81	*Ricky Williams*	1.00
82	Mark Brunell	.75
83	*David Garrard*	1.25
84	*John Henderson*	1.00
85	Jimmy Smith	.20
86	Fred Taylor	.50
87	*Marc Boerigter*	2.00
88	*Omar Easy*	1.00
89	Tony Gonzalez	.50
90	Trent Green	.50
91	Priest Holmes	1.00
92	Chris Chambers	.75
93	Jay Fiedler	.50
94	Ricky Williams	1.25
95	Michael Bennett	.75
96	*Kelly Campbell*	1.00
97	Daunte Culpepper	1.25
98	Shaun Hill	.20
99	Randy Moss	2.00
100	Tom Brady	2.00
101	*Deion Branch*	2.00
102	Troy Brown	.50
103	*Rohan Davey*	1.50
104	*Daniel Graham*	1.25
105	Antowain Smith	.50
106	Aaron Brooks	1.00
107	Joe Horn	.20
108	Deuce McAllister	1.00
109	*J.T. O'Sullivan*	1.00
110	*Donte Stallworth*	3.00
111	Tiki Barber	.20
112	*Tim Carter*	1.00
113	Kerry Collins	.40
114	*Daryl Jones*	1.00
115	*Jeremy Shockey*	3.00
116	Amani Toomer	.40
117	Laveranues Coles	.40
118	Curtis Martin	.50
119	Vinny Testaverde	.40
120	*Bryan Thomas*	1.00
121	Tim Brown	.75
122	*Phillip Buchanon*	1.25
123	Rich Gannon	.50
124	*Napoleon Harris*	1.25
125	Jerry Rice	2.00
126	Donovan McNabb	1.25
127	*Freddie Milons*	1.00
128	*Lito Sheppard*	1.00
129	Duce Staley	.50
130	James Thrash	.20
131	*Brian Westbrook*	1.00
132	Jerome Bettis	.50
133	*Verron Haynes*	1.50
134	*Lee Mays*	1.00
135	*Antwaan Randle El*	2.00
136	Kordell Stewart	.50
137	Hines Ward	.50
138	Isaac Bruce	.50
139	Marshall Faulk	1.25
140	*Lamar Gordon*	1.25
141	Torry Holt	.75
142	*Robert Thomas*	2.00
143	Kurt Warner	2.00
144	Drew Brees	1.50
145	*Seth Burford*	2.00
146	*Donald Reche Caldwell*	1.25
147	Doug Flutie	.75
148	*Quentin Jammer*	1.25
149	LaDainian Tomlinson	1.50
150	*Brandon Doman*	1.00
151	Jeff Garcia	.75
152	Garrison Hearst	.50
153	Terrell Owens	.75
154	*Mike Rumph*	1.00
155	Shaun Alexander	.75
156	Trent Dilfer	.50
157	*Darrell Jackson*	.75
158	*Maurice Morris*	1.50
159	Koren Robinson	.50
160	*Jerramy Stevens*	1.00
161	Brad Johnson	.50
162	Keyshawn Johnson	.50
163	Keenan McCardell	.40
164	*Travis Stephens*	1.25
165	*Marquise Walker*	1.25
166	Eddie George	.75
167	*Albert Haynesworth*	1.00
168	Derrick Mason	.50
169	Steve McNair	.75
170	*Ladell Betts*	1.25
171	Stephen Davis	.50
172	Rod Gardner	.50
173	Shane Matthews	.20
174	*Patrick Ramsey*	1.50
175	*Cliff Russell*	1.00

2002 Pacific Heads Update Atomic Updated Rookies

		NM/M
Common Player:		1.00
Inserted 1:10		
151	Dameon Hunter	1.00
152	Javin Hunter	1.00
153	Tellis Redmon	1.00
154	Chester Taylor	1.00
155	Randy Fasani	1.00
156	Jamin Elliott	1.00
157	Chad Hutchinson	2.00
158	Eddie Drummond	1.00
159	Craig Nall	1.00
160	Jarrod Baxter	1.00
161	Jonathan Wells	1.50
162	Shaun Hill	1.00
163	Deion Branch	2.50
164	J.T. O'Sullivan	1.00
165	Tim Carter	1.00
166	Darryl Jones	1.50
167	Lee Mays	1.00
168	Seth Burford	1.00
169	Brandon Doman	1.00
170	Jerramy Stevens	1.00

2002 Pacific Heads Update Authentic Game-Worn Patches

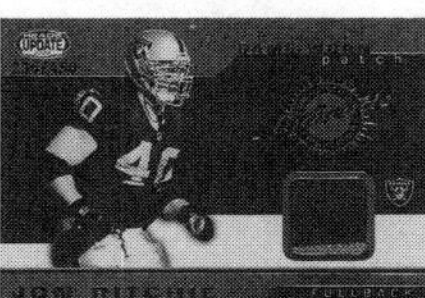

		NM/M
Common Player:		8.00
Production to varying quantities		
Gold version		2X to4X
Production 25 sets		
1	David Boston/215	12.00
2	Bryan Gilmore/250	8.00
3	Thomas Jones/350	8.00
4	Jake Plummer/215	8.00
5	Frank Sanders/335	8.00
6	Warrick Dunn/315	10.00
7	Michael Vick/250	25.00
8	Drew Bledsoe/160	15.00
9	Corey Dillon/350	12.00
10	Peter Warrick/410	8.00
11	Tim Couch/50	15.00
12	Jamel White/105	8.00
13	Emmitt Smith/270	35.00
14	Mike Anderson/215	15.00
15	Terrell Davis/250	15.00
16	Brian Griese/115	12.00
17	Ed McCaffrey/225	12.00
18	Brett Favre/50	35.00
19	Ahman Green/95	15.00
20	Marvin Harrison/150	15.00
21	Qadry Ismail/95	8.00
22	Peyton Manning/180	25.00
23	Mark Brunell/390	8.00
24	Jimmy Smith/200	8.00
25	Fred Taylor/425	8.00
26	Tony Gonzalez/305	8.00
27	Desmond Clark/275	8.00
28	Zach Thomas/195	10.00
29	Ricky Williams/125	20.00
30	Derrick Alexander/225	8.00
31	Cris Carter/305	15.00
32	Randy Moss/350	25.00
33	Tom Brady/85	25.00
34	Christian Fauria/255	8.00
35	Deuce McAllister/95	20.00
36	Curtis Martin/175	12.00
37	Tim Brown/375	15.00
38	Rich Gannon/165	12.00
39	Jerry Rice/255	25.00
40	Jon Ritchie/450	8.00
41	Correll Buckhalter/305	8.00
42	Donovan McNabb/315	15.00
43	Marshall Faulk/225	15.00
44	Kurt Warner/185	20.00
45	Terrence Wilkins/225	8.00
46	Shaun Alexander/400	12.00
47	Trent Dilfer/115	8.00
48	Itula Mili/185	8.00
49	Joe Jurevicius/100	10.00
50	Michael Pittman/145	8.00

2002 Pacific Heads Update Big Numbers Die-Cuts

		NM/M
Common Player:		2.00
Inserted 1:5		
1	Michael Vick	5.00
2	Anthony Thomas	2.00
3	Tim Couch	2.00
4	William Green	2.00
5	Antonio Bryant	3.00
6	Emmitt Smith	5.00
7	Ashley Lelie	3.00
8	Joey Harrington	10.00
9	Brett Favre	10.00
10	David Carr	10.00
11	Peyton Manning	5.00
12	Ricky Williams	2.00
13	Daunte Culpepper	2.00
14	Randy Moss	5.00
15	Tom Brady	5.00
16	Donte Stallworth	3.00
17	Jerry Rice	5.00
18	Marshall Faulk	2.00
19	Kurt Warner	4.00
20	LaDainian Tomlinson	3.00

A card number in parenthese ( ) indicates the set is unnumbered.

2002 Pacific Heads Update Bobble Head Dolls

		NM/M
Common Player:		25.00
Inserted 1:Box		
1	T.J. Duckett	30.00
2	Drew Bledsoe	30.00
3	William Green	25.00
4	Joey Harrington	40.00
5	Ahman Green	30.00
6	Peyton Manning	30.00
7	Eddie George	25.00

2002 Pacific Heads Update Command Performance

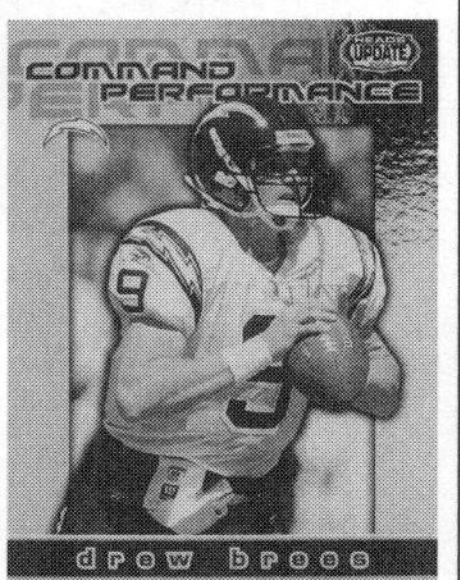

		NM/M
Common Player:		2.00
Inserted 1:5		
1	David Boston	2.00
2	Anthony Thomas	2.00
3	Corey Dillon	2.00
4	Tim Couch	2.00
5	Emmitt Smith	4.00
6	Brett Favre	6.00
7	Ahman Green	2.00
8	Ricky Williams	2.00
9	Daunte Culpepper	2.00
10	Randy Moss	4.00
11	Tom Brady	4.00
12	Curtis Martin	2.00
13	Jerry Rice	4.00
14	Donovan McNabb	2.00
15	Marshall Faulk	2.00
16	Kurt Warner	3.00
17	Drew Brees	2.00
18	LaDainian Tomlinson	3.00
19	Shaun Alexander	2.00
20	Steve McNair	2.00

2002 Pacific Heads Update Generations

		NM/M
Common Player:		2.00
Inserted 1:5		
1	Brett Favre, David Carr	8.00
2	Peyton Manning, Joey Harrington	5.00
3	Kurt Warner, Patrick Ramsey	3.00
4	Emmitt Smith, William Green	3.00
5	Jerome Bettis, T.J. Duckett	2.00
6	Randy Moss, Ashley Lelie	3.00
7	Jerry Rice, Donte Stallworth	3.00
8	Tom Brady, Josh McCown	3.00
9	Anthony Thomas, DeShaun Foster	2.00
10	Michael Vick, David Garrard	3.00
11	Marshall Faulk, Maurice Morris	2.00
12	Daunte Culpepper, Rohan Davey	2.00
13	Tim Couch, Randy Fasani	2.00
14	LaDainian Tomlinson, Clinton Portis	3.00
15	Isaac Bruce, Jabar Gaffney	2.00
16	Marvin Harrison, Javon Walker	2.00
17	Kordell Stewart, Antwaan Randle El	3.00
18	David Boston, Antonio Bryant	2.00
19	Terrell Owens, Andre Davis	2.00
20	Ricky Williams, Jonathan Wells	2.00

2002 Pacific Heads Update Heads Up Updated Rookies

		NM/M
Common Player:		1.00
Inserted 1:10		
176	Dameon Hunter	1.00
177	Javin Hunter	1.00
178	Tellis Redmon	1.00
179	Ed Reed	1.00
180	Jamin Elliott	1.00
181	Chad Hutchinson	2.00
182	Eddie Drummond	1.00
183	Najeh Davenport	1.00
184	Craig Nall	1.00
185	Jarrod Baxter	1.00
186	Marc Boerigter	1.00
187	Kelly Campbell	1.00
188	Shaun Hill	1.00
189	Tim Carter	1.00
190	Daryl Jones	1.50
191	Phillip Buchanon	1.50
192	Napoleon Harris	1.50
193	Seth Burford	1.00
194	Brandon Doman	1.00
195	Jerramy Stevens	1.00

2002 Pacific Heads Update Pacific Updated Rookies

		NM/M
Common Player:		1.00
501	T.J. Duckett	3.00
502	Dameon Hunter	1.00
503	Javin Hunter	1.00
504	Tellis Redmon	1.00
505	Chester Taylor	1.00
506	Randy Fasani	1.00
507	Julius Peppers	2.00
508	Jamin Elliott	1.00
509	Chad Hutchinson	2.00
510	Eddie Drummond	1.00
511	Craig Nall	1.00
512	Jabar Gaffney	1.00
513	Jonathan Wells	1.50
514	Shaun Hill	1.00
515	Deion Branch	2.00
516	Rohan Davey	1.50
517	J.T. O'Sullivan	1.00
518	Tim Carter	1.00
519	Daryl Jones	1.00
520	Jeremy Shockey	2.00
521	Seth Burford	1.00
522	Brandon Doman	1.00
523	Jerramy Stevens	1.00
524	Travis Stephens	1.50
525	Marquise Walker	1.50

2002 Pacific Private Stock Reserve

		NM/M
Common Player:		.40
Unlisted Stars:		1.00
Minor Stars:		.60
Hobby rookies		
Production to jersey #		
Pack (8):		12.00
Wax Box (8):		80.00
1	David Boston	1.00
2	Thomas Jones	.40
3	Jake Plummer	.60
4	Jamal Anderson	.60
5	Warrick Dunn	.60
6	Shawn Jefferson	.40
7	Michael Vick	5.00
8	Jamal Lewis	.40
9	Chris Redman	.40
10	Travis Taylor	.40
11	Travis Henry	.60
12	Eric Moulds	.40
13	Peerless Price	.40
14	Muhsin Muhammad	.40
15	Lamar Smith	.40
16	Chris Weinke	1.00
17	Marty Booker	.40
18	Jim Miller	.40
19	Anthony Thomas	3.00
20	Corey Dillon	1.00
21	Darnay Scott	.40
22	Peter Warrick	.60
23	Tim Couch	1.50
24	James Jackson	.40
25	Kevin Johnson	.40
26	Quincy Carter	2.50
27	Raghib Ismail	.40
28	Emmitt Smith	5.00
29	Mike Anderson	1.50
30	Terrell Davis	1.50
31	Brian Griese	1.00
32	Rod Smith	.60
33	Mike McMahon	1.00
34	Johnnie Morton	.40
35	Brett Favre	6.00
36	Antonio Freeman	.40
37	Ahman Green	1.00
38	Corey Bradford	.40
39	Jermaine Lewis	.40
40	Jamie Sharper	.40
41	Marvin Harrison	.75
42	Edgerrin James	3.00
43	Mark Brunell	1.00
44	Jimmy Smith	.40
45	Fred Taylor	.40
46	Tony Gonzalez	.40
47	Trent Green	.40
48	Priest Holmes	1.00
49	Chris Chambers	1.00
50	Jay Fiedler	.40
51	James McKnight	.40
52	Ricky Williams	2.50
53	Michael Bennett	1.00
54	Cris Carter	.40
55	Daunte Culpepper	2.50
56	Randy Moss	5.00
57	Drew Bledsoe	2.50
58	Tom Brady	5.00
59	Troy Brown	1.00
60	Antowain Smith	.40
61	Aaron Brooks	1.50
62	Joe Horn	.40
63	Deuce McAllister	1.50
64	Tiki Barber	.40
65	Kerry Collins	.40
66	Ron Dayne	.40
67	Laveranues Coles	.40
68	Curtis Martin	.75
69	Vinny Testaverde	.40
70	Tim Brown	1.00
71	Rich Gannon	.75
72	Jerry Rice	5.00
73	Correll Buckhalter	.40
74	Duce Staley	.75
75	James Thrash	.40
76	Jerome Bettis	.75
77	Plaxico Burress	1.00
78	Kordell Stewart	.75
79	Hines Ward	.40
80	Isaac Bruce	.75
81	Marshall Faulk	2.50
82	Torry Holt	.40
83	Kurt Warner	5.00
84	Drew Brees	3.00
85	Doug Flutie	1.00
86	LaDainian Tomlinson	3.00
87	Jeff Garcia	1.00
88	Garrison Hearst	.40
89	Terrell Owens	1.00
90	Shaun Alexander	1.00
91	Trent Dilfer	.40
92	Darrell Jackson	.40
93	Ricky Watters	.40
94	Brad Johnson	.40
95	Keyshawn Johnson	.75
96	Eddie George	1.00
97	Derrick Mason	.40
98	Steve McNair	1.00
99	Stephen Davis	.75
100	Rod Gardner	.40
101	*Damien Anderson*	1.00
102	*Ladell Betts*	2.00
103	*Antonio Bryant*	50.00
104	*Wendell Bryant*	1.00
105	*Donald Reche Caldwell*	1.00
106	*Kelly Campbell*	1.00
107	*David Carr*	18.00
108	*Eric Crouch*	15.00
109	*Ronald Curry*	1.00
110	*Rohan Davey*	2.00
111	*Andre Davis*	2.00
112	*T.J. Duckett*	8.00
113	*DeShaun Foster*	6.00
114	*Jabar Gaffney*	2.00
115	*David Garrard*	2.00
116	*Lamar Gordon*	2.00
117	*Daniel Graham*	2.00
118	*William Green*	10.00
119	*Joey Harrington*	15.00
120	*Napoleon Harris*	1.00
121	*Verron Haynes*	1.00
122	*John Henderson*	1.00
123	*Kahlil Hill*	1.00
124	*Quentin Jammer*	2.00
125	*Ron Johnson*	1.00
126	*Kurt Kittner*	2.00
127	*Zak Kustok*	2.00
128	*Ashley Lelie*	8.00
129	*Josh McCown*	2.00
130	*Freddie Milons*	2.00
131	*Maurice Morris*	2.00
132	*James Mungro*	2.00
133	*David Neill*	1.00
134	*Adrian Peterson*	1.00
135	*Brian Poli-Dixon*	1.00
136	*Clinton Portis*	6.00
137	*Patrick Ramsey*	2.00
138	*Antwaan Randle El*	4.00
139	*Josh Reed*	8.00
140	*Cliff Russell*	1.00
141	*Josh Scobey*	1.00
142	*Lito Sheppard*	2.00
143	*Jeremy Shockey*	100.00
144	*Luke Staley*	2.00
145	*Donte Stallworth*	8.00
146	*Lamont Thompson*	1.00
147	*Javon Walker*	75.00
148	*Marquise Walker*	3.00

149 *Brian Westbrook* 2.00
150 *Roy Williams* 18.00

2002 Pacific Private Stock Res. Auth. Game-Worn Jerseys

NM/M
Common Player: 5.00
Patch version 1X to2X
Team Logo 1X to3X
Production 2X jersey #
Number version
Production to jersey #

1 David Boston 10.00
2 Steve Bush 5.00
3 Arnold Jackson 5.00
4 Thomas Jones 5.00
5 Rob Moore 5.00
6 Jake Plummer 5.00
7 Jamal Anderson 8.00
8 Maurice Smith 5.00
9 Michael Vick 30.00
10 Todd Heap 5.00
11 Travis Taylor 5.00
12 Randall Cunningham 10.00
13 Elvis Grbac 5.00
14 Jamal Lewis 25.00
15 Ray Lewis 10.00
16 Shannon Sharpe 5.00
17 Moe Williams 5.00
18 Larry Centers 5.00
19 Travis Henry 15.00
20 Isaac Byrd 5.00
21 Jim Harbaugh 5.00
22 Richard Huntley 5.00
23 Chris Weinke 15.00
24 Autry Denson 5.00
25 David Terrell 25.00
26 Anthony Thomas 25.00
27 Brian Urlacher 30.00
28 Corey Dillon 10.00
29 T.J. Houshmandzadeh 5.00
30 Chad Johnson 5.00
31 Rudi Johnson 5.00
32 Jon Kitna 5.00
33 Peter Warrick 10.00
34 Tim Couch 15.00
35 Darrin Chiaverini 5.00
36 Richmond Flowers 5.00
37 Joey Galloway 5.00
38 La'Roi Glover 5.00
39 Troy Hambrick 5.00
40 Emmitt Smith 40.00
41 Mike Anderson 20.00
42 Tony Carter 5.00
43 Terrell Davis 10.00
44 Brian Griese 5.00
45 Todd Husak 5.00
46 Kevin Kasper 5.00
47 Scotty Anderson 5.00
48 Karsten Bailey 5.00
49 Reggie Brown 5.00
50 Brett Favre 40.00
51 Robert Ferguson 5.00
52 Antonio Freeman 5.00
53 Ahman Green 15.00
54 David Martin 5.00
55 Jermaine Lewis 5.00
56 Frank Moreau 5.00
57 Marvin Harrison 10.00
58 Edgerrin James 25.00
59 Tony Simmons 5.00
60 Mark Brunell 10.00
61 Sean Dawkins 5.00
62 Jimmy Smith 10.00
63 Fred Taylor 10.00
64 Tony Gonzalez 10.00
65 Trent Green 10.00
66 Mikhael Ricks 5.00
67 Cade McNown 5.00
68 Ricky Williams 10.00
69 Michael Bennett 20.00
70 Cris Carter 10.00
71 Corey Chavous 5.00
72 Daunte Culpepper 25.00
73 Randy Moss 40.00
74 Travis Prentice 5.00
75 Drew Bledsoe 15.00
76 Tom Brady 40.00
77 Marc Edwards 5.00
78 Kevin Faulk 5.00
79 Antowain Smith 5.00
80 Aaron Brooks 10.00
81 Albert Connell 5.00
82 Deuce McAllister 20.00
83 Wane McGarity 5.00
84 Jake Reed 5.00
85 Ron Dayne 5.00
86 Curtis Martin 10.00
87 Chad Morton 5.00
88 Craig Yeast 5.00
89 Tim Brown 10.00
90 Rich Gannon 5.00
91 Charlie Garner 10.00
92 Jerry Rice 30.00
93 Freddie Mitchell 15.00
94 Todd Pinkston 5.00
95 James Thrash 5.00
96 Jerome Bettis 10.00
97 Kordell Stewart 10.00
98 Hines Ward 5.00
99 Isaac Bruce 10.00
100 Marshall Faulk 25.00
101 Damon Griffin 5.00
102 Kurt Warner 35.00
103 Drew Brees 15.00
104 Doug Flutie 10.00
105 LaDainian Tomlinson 20.00
106 Jeff Garcia 10.00
107 Terrell Owens 10.00
108 Tim Rattay 5.00
109 Shockmain Davis 5.00
110 Bobby Engram 5.00
111 Matt Hasselbeck 5.00
112 Koren Robinson 5.00
113 Ricky Watters 5.00
114 Mike Alstott 5.00
115 Marco Battaglia 5.00
116 Rob Johnson 5.00
117 Brad Johnson 5.00
118 Michael Pittman 5.00
119 Dan Alexander 5.00
120 Eddie Berlin 5.00
121 Eddie George 15.00
122 Skip Hicks 5.00
123 Derrick Mason 5.00
124 Steve McNair 10.00
125 Rod Gardner 10.00

2002 Pacific Private Stock Reserve Banner Year

NM/M
Common Player: 2.00
Inserted 1:17

1 Michael Vick 4.00
2 Anthony Thomas 4.00
3 Emmitt Smith 3.00
4 Brett Favre 8.00
5 Randy Moss 4.00
6 Tom Brady 8.00
7 Jerry Rice 4.00
8 Marshall Faulk 3.00
9 Kurt Warner 5.00
10 LaDainian Tomlinson 4.00

2002 Pacific Private Stock Reserve Class Acts

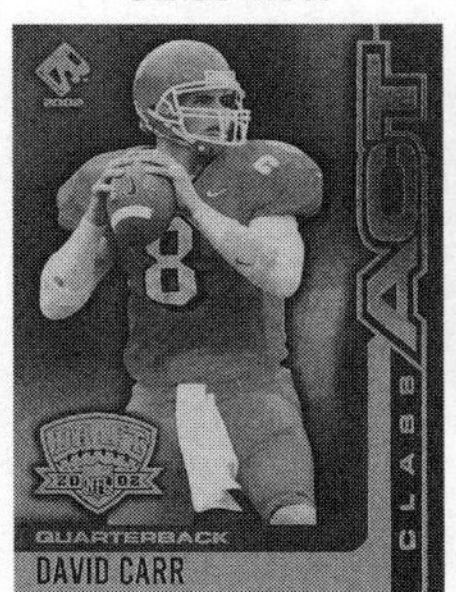

NM/M
Complete Set (20): 70.00
Common Player: 2.00
Inserted 2:9

1 Antonio Bryant 5.00
2 Donald Reche Caldwell 2.00
3 David Carr 10.00
4 Eric Crouch 8.00
5 Rohan Davey 3.00
6 Andre Davis 2.00
7 T.J. Duckett 5.00
8 DeShaun Foster 5.00
9 Lamar Gordon 2.00
10 William Green 8.00
11 Joey Harrington 8.00
12 Kurt Kittner 3.00
13 Ashley Lelie 5.00
14 Josh McCown 3.00
15 Clinton Portis 3.00
16 Patrick Ramsey 4.00
17 Antwann Randle El 4.00
18 Josh Reed 5.00
19 Luke Staley 2.00
20 Donte Stallworth 5.00

2002 Pacific Private Stock Res. Divisional Realignment

NM/M
Complete Set (32): 50.00
Common Player: 2.00
Inserted 1:9

1 David Boston 2.00
2 Michael Vick 4.00
3 Jamal Lewis 2.00
4 Travis Henry 2.00
5 Chris Weinke 3.00
6 Anthony Thomas 4.00
7 Corey Dillon 2.00
8 Tim Couch 2.00
9 Emmitt Smith 4.00
10 Terrell Davis 2.00
11 Mike McMahon 2.00
12 Brett Favre 6.00
13 Jermaine Lewis 2.00
14 Edgerrin James 4.00
15 Mark Brunell 2.00
16 Priest Holmes 2.00
17 Chris Chambers 3.00
18 Randy Moss 4.00
19 Tom Brady 5.00
20 Aaron Brooks 2.00
21 Ron Dayne 2.00
22 Curtis Martin 2.00
23 Jerry Rice 4.00
24 Duce Staley 2.00
25 Jerome Bettis 2.00
26 Kurt Warner 4.00
27 LaDainian Tomlinson 3.00
28 Jeff Garcia 2.00
29 Shaun Alexander 2.00
30 Mike Alstott 2.00
31 Eddie George 2.00
32 Rod Gardner 2.00

2002 Pacific Private Stock Reserve Moments In Time

NM/M
Common Player: 10.00
Inserted 1:193

1 Antonio Bryant 25.00
2 David Carr 50.00
3 T.J. Duckett 30.00
4 DeShaun Foster 25.00
5 William Green 40.00
6 Joey Harrington 40.00
7 Kurt Kittner 15.00
8 Clinton Portis 15.00
9 Patrick Ramsey 20.00
10 Donte Stallworth 30.00

2002 Pacific Private Stock Titanium

NM/M
Common Player: .25
101-175 Star Jersey/Rookie Combinations
Production to varying quantities
Unlisted Star (1-100): .75
Minor Star (1-100): .50
Unlisted Rookie (101-175): 5.00
Minor Rookie (101-175): 4.00
Pack (10): 20.00
Wax Box (6): 100.00

1 David Boston .60
2 Thomas Jones .25
3 Jake Plummer .40
4 Warrick Dunn .40
5 Shawn Jefferson .25
6 Michael Vick 2.50
7 Jamal Lewis 1.25
8 Chris Redman .40
9 Travis Taylor .40
10 Drew Bledsoe 2.50
11 Travis Henry .40
12 Eric Moulds .40
13 Peerless Price .40
14 Muhsin Muhammad .40
15 Rodney Peete .25
16 Lamar Smith .25
17 Chris Weinke .25
18 Marty Booker .40
19 Jim Miller .25
20 Anthony Thomas 1.25
21 Corey Dillon .75
22 Gus Frerotte .25
23 Peter Warrick .25
24 Tim Couch 1.25
25 Kevin Johnson .25
26 Jamel White .25
27 Quincy Carter 1.25
28 Joey Galloway .40
29 Emmitt Smith 2.50
30 Olandis Gary .25
31 Brian Griese .75
32 Ed McCaffrey .50
33 Rod Smith .50
34 Mike McMahon .25
35 Bill Schroeder .25
36 James Stewart .25
37 Brett Favre 3.00
38 Terry Glenn .40
39 Ahman Green .75
40 James Allen .25
41 Corey Bradford .25
42 Jermaine Lewis .25
43 Marvin Harrison .75
44 Edgerrin James 2.00
45 Peyton Manning 2.50
46 Mark Brunell .75
47 Jimmy Smith .25
48 Fred Taylor .50
49 Tony Gonzalez .40
50 Trent Green .40
51 Priest Holmes 1.25
52 Chris Chambers .75
53 Jay Fiedler .40
54 Ricky Williams 1.50
55 Michael Bennett .75
56 Daunte Culpepper 1.50
57 Randy Moss 2.50
58 Tom Brady 2.50
59 Troy Brown .40
60 Antowain Smith .40
61 Aaron Brooks 1.25
62 Joe Horn .40
63 Deuce McAllister 1.25
64 Tiki Barber .50
65 Kerry Collins .40
66 Amani Toomer .40
67 Laveranues Coles .50
68 Curtis Martin .75
69 Vinny Testaverde .25
70 Tim Brown .75
71 Rich Gannon .75
72 Jerry Rice 2.50
73 Donovan McNabb 1.50
74 Duce Staley .40
75 James Thrash .25
76 Jerome Bettis .50
77 Kordell Stewart .50
78 Hines Ward .50
79 Isaac Bruce .50
80 Marshall Faulk 1.50
81 Torry Holt .75
82 Kurt Warner 2.50
83 Drew Brees 2.00
84 LaDainian Tomlinson 2.00
85 Jeff Garcia .75
86 Garrison Hearst .40
87 Terrell Owens .75
88 Shaun Alexander .75
89 Trent Dilfer .25
90 Koren Robinson .25
91 Brad Johnson .40
92 Keyshawn Johnson .75
93 Keenan McCardell .40
94 Eddie George .75
95 Derrick Mason .50
96 Steve McNair .75
97 Stephen Davis .50
98 Rod Gardner .50
99 Shane Matthews .25
100 Derrius Thompson .25
101 *Freddie Jones, Jason McAddley/1000* 5.00
102 *Jake Plummer, Josh McCown/250* 5.00
103 *Kyle Vanden Bosch, Wendell Bryant/200* 15.00
104 *Thomas Jones, Chester Taylor/1100* 5.00
105 *Bryan Gilmore, Tim Carter/1100* 8.00
106 *Michael Vick, Kurt Kittner/300* 25.00
107 *Brandon Stokley, Ron Johnson/150* 8.00
108 *Chris Redman, Javin Hunter* 8.00
109 *Peerless Price, Josh Reed/275* 8.00
110 *Isaac Byrd, Julius Peppers/250* 10.00
111 *Dez White, Jamin Elliott/110* 8.00
112 *Rabih Abdullah, Adrian Peterson/1000* 5.00
113 *Brian Urlacher, Napoleon Harris/500* 15.00
114 *Michael Westbrook, Lamont hompson/1100* 5.00
115 *Corey Dillon, T.J. Duckett/750* 10.00
116 *Takeo Spikes, Roy Williams/500* 8.00
117 *Akili Smith, Craig Nall/1000* 5.00
118 *Tim Couch, Andre Davis/200* 8.00
119 *Jamel White, Tellis Redmon/500* 5.00
120 *Quincy Carter, Chad Hutchinson* 8.00
121 *Troy Hambrick, Antonio Bryant/50* 10.00
122 *Emmitt Smith, William Green/500* 25.00
123 *La'Roi Glover, John Henderson/1100* 5.00
124 *Deltha O'Neal, Mike Rumph/200* 5.00
125 *Larry Foster, Eddie Drummond/1100* 5.00
126 *Ahman Green, Najeh Davenport/200* 8.00
127 *Donald Driver, Javon Walker* .25
128 *Brett Favre, David Carr/500* 40.00
129 *James Allen, Jonathan Wells/300* .25
130 *Jermaine Lewis, Jabar Gaffney/200* .25
131 *Edgerrin James, Ricky Williams* 8.00
132 *Peyton Manning, Dwight Freeney* 10.00
133 *Mark Brunell, David Garrard* 5.00
134 *Jimmy Smith, Marquise Walker* 5.00
135 *Curtis Jackson, Marc Boerigter* 5.00
136 *Tony Richardson, Omar Easy* 5.00
137 *Desmond Clark, Randy McMichael* 5.00
138 *Zach Thomas, Robert Thomas/200* 12.00
139 *Chris Walsh, Shaun Hill* 5.00
140 *Daunte Culpepper, Randy Fasani/1000* 10.00
141 *Jim Kleinsasser, Jarrod Baxter/1100* 8.00
142 *Randy Moss, Donte Stallworth/500* 15.00
143 *Corey Chavous, Phillip Buchanon/1100* 5.00
144 *Christian Fauria, Daniel Graham/750* 5.00
145 *Damon Huard, Rohan Davey/300* 5.00
146 *Donald Hayes, Deion Branch/500* 5.00
147 *Terrelle Smith, J.T. O'Sullivan/200* 5.00
148 *Jonathan Carter, Daryl Jones* 5.00
149 *Ron Dayne, Jeremy Shockey/165* 15.00
150 *Anthony Becht, Bryan Thomas/1100* 5.00
151 *Curtis Martin, Dameon Hunter/75* 10.00
152 *Jerry Rice, Ashley Lelie/750* 15.00
153 *Jon Ritchie, Ed Stansbury/1100* 5.00
154 *Cecil Martin, Freddie Milons/1100* 5.00
155 *Donovan McNabb, Lito Sheppard/1100* 10.00
156 *James Thrash, Brian Westbrook/1000* 5.00
157 *Jerome Bettis, Verron Haynes/1000* 8.00
158 *Kordell Stewart, Antwann Randle El/500* 12.00
159 *Marshall Faulk, Lamar Gordon/200* 8.00
160 *Kurt Warner, Joey Harrington/500* 15.00
161 *Drew Brees, Quentin Jammer/1100* 10.00
162 *Fred McCrary, Seth Burford/1100* 5.00
163 *Stephen Alexander, Donald Reche Caldwell/1100* 5.00
164 *LaDainian Tomlinson, Clinton Portis/500* 12.00
165 *Jeff Garcia, Brandon Doman/200* 8.00
166 *Paul Smith, Lee Mays/250* 5.00
167 *Shaun Alexander, Maurice Morris/130* 8.00
168 *Michael Pittman, Travis Stephens/500* 8.00
169 *Ken Dilger, Jerramy Stevens/750* 5.00
170 *Eddie Berlin, Darrell Hill* 5.00
171 *Steve McNair, Albert Haynesworth/500* 8.00
172 *Eddie George, DeShaun Foster/200* 8.00
173 *Jacquez Green, Ladell Betts* 5.00
174 *Rod Gardner, Cliff Russell* 5.00
175 *Shane Matthews, Patrick Ramsey* 5.00

2002 Pacific Private Stock Titanium High Capacity

NM/M
Common Player: 2.00
Inserted 1:7

1 Michael Vick 4.00
2 Anthony Thomas 2.00
3 Emmitt Smith 4.00
4 Brett Favre 5.00
5 Peyton Manning 4.00
6 Randy Moss 4.00
7 Tom Brady 4.00
8 Jerry Rice 4.00
9 Marshall Faulk 3.00
10 Kurt Warner 3.00

2002 Pacific Private Stock Titanium Monday Knights

NM/M
Common Player: 1.00
Inserted 1:3

1 Jamal Lewis 1.00
2 Anthony Thomas 1.00
3 Brian Griese 1.00
4 Ashley Lelie 3.00
5 Clinton Portis 5.00

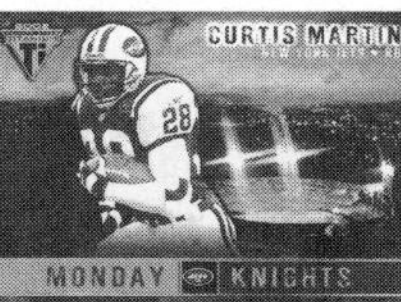

NM/M
6 Brett Favre 5.00
7 Edgerrin James 2.00
8 Peyton Manning 3.00
9 Tom Brady 3.00
10 Curtis Martin 1.00
11 Jerry Rice 3.00
12 Donovan McNabb 2.00
13 Jerome Bettis 1.00
14 Antwann Randle El 3.00
15 Marshall Faulk 1.00
16 Kurt Warner 2.00
17 Jeff Garcia 1.00
18 Terrell Owens 1.00
19 Shaun Alexander 1.00
20 Eddie George 1.00
21 Steve McNair 1.00

2002 Pacific Private Stock Titanium Shadows

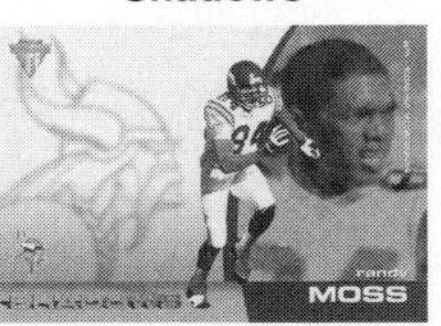

NM/M
Common Player: 3.00
Inserted 1:5

1 Michael Vick 4.00
2 Emmitt Smith 4.00
3 Joey Harrington 5.00
4 Brett Favre 5.00
5 David Carr 5.00
6 Randy Moss 4.00
7 Tom Brady 4.00
8 Jerry Rice 4.00
9 Kurt Warner 3.00

2002 Pacific Priv. Stock Titanium Titanium Rookie Team

NM/M
Common Player: 2.00
Inserted 1:13

1 Josh Reed 3.00
2 DeShaun Foster 2.00
3 William Green 3.00
4 Antonio Bryant 3.00
5 Ashley Lelie 3.00
6 Clinton Portis 4.00
7 Joey Harrington 5.00
8 David Carr 5.00
9 Donte Stallworth 3.00
10 Antwann Randle El 3.00

2002 Pacific Private Stock Titanium Postseason Edition

NM/M
Common Player: 2.00
Unlisted Star: 3.00
Minor Star: 5.00
Cards 1-50 numbered to 699
Cards 51-125 numbered to 435/ Jersey

1 *Damien Anderson* 2.00
2 *Preston Parsons* 2.00
3 *T.J. Duckett* 5.00
4 *Kurt Kittner* 2.50
5 *Javin Hunter* 3.00
6 *Ed Reed* 3.00
7 *Anthony Weaver* 2.00
8 *Coy Wire* 8.00
9 *Randy Fasani* 2.00
10 *Matt Schobel* 2.00
11 *Derek Ross* 4.00
12 *Chris Cash* 2.00
13 *Najeh Davenport* 4.00
14 *Tony Fisher* 4.00
15 *Craig Nall* 2.00
16 *Dwight Freeney* 2.00
17 *Larry Tripplett* 2.00
18 *Ricky Williams* 2.00
19 *Akin Ayodele* 2.00
20 *John Henderson* 2.00
21 *Randy McMichael* 4.00
22 *Shaun Hill* 10.00
23 *Deion Branch* 4.00
24 *Rohan Davey* 3.00
25 *David Givens* 5.00
26 *Daniel Graham* 2.00
27 *Charles Grant* 4.00
28 *J.T. O'Sullivan* 2.00
29 *Daryl Jones* 2.00
30 *Jeremy Shockey* 15.00
31 *Charles Stackhouse* 2.00
32 *Phillip Buchanon* 2.00
33 *Napoleon Harris* 2.00
34 *Larry Foote* 6.00
35 *Lee Mays* 4.00
36 *Travis Fisher* 2.00
37 *Robert Thomas* 2.00
38 *Seth Burford* 5.00
39 *Quentin Jammer* 3.00
40 *Ben Leber* 2.00
41 *Josh Norman* 2.00
42 *Brandon Doman* 4.00
43 *Jeff Kelly* 4.00
44 *Jerramy Stevens* 2.00
45 *Travis Stephens* 2.00
46 *Carlos Hall* 2.00
47 *Darrell Hill* 2.00
48 *John Simon* 2.00
49 *Tank Williams* 3.00
50 *Rock Cartwright* 10.00
51 *Josh McCown* 8.00
52 *Ron Johnson* 8.00
53 *Josh Reed* 12.00
54 *DeShaun Foster* 12.00
55 *Julius Peppers* 15.00
56 *Andre Davis* 12.00
57 *William Green* 20.00
58 *Antonio Bryant* 20.00
59 *Chad Hutchinson* 15.00
60 *Roy Williams* 20.00
61 *Ashley Lelie* 20.00
62 *Clinton Portis* 25.00
63 *Joey Harrington* 25.00
64 *Javon Walker* 15.00
65 *David Carr* 25.00
66 *Jabar Gaffney* 8.00
67 *Jonathan Wells* 8.00
68 *David Garrard* 8.00
69 *Donte Stallworth* 15.00
70 *Tim Carter* 8.00
71 *Brian Westbrook* 8.00
72 *Antwann Randle El* 15.00
73 *Lamar Gordon* 8.00
74 *Donald Reche Caldwell* 8.00
75 *Maurice Morris* 8.00
76 *Ladell Betts* 12.00
77 *Patrick Ramsey* 12.00
78 *Cliff Russell* 8.00
79 David Boston 8.00
80 Jamal Lewis 8.00
81 Drew Bledsoe 15.00
82 Eric Moulds 12.00
83 Anthony Thomas 10.00
84 Brian Urlacher 20.00
85 Corey Dillon 10.00
86 Tim Couch 15.00
87 Quincy Carter 8.00
88 Emmitt Smith 25.00
89 Terrell Davis 10.00
90 Brian Griese 10.00
91 Ed McCaffrey 10.00
92 Brett Favre 30.00
93 Terry Glenn 8.00
94 Ahman Green 15.00
95 Corey Bradford 8.00
96 Marvin Harrison 15.00
97 Edgerrin James 15.00
98 Peyton Manning 20.00
99 Fred Taylor 8.00
100 Trent Green 8.00
101 Priest Holmes 15.00
102 Chris Chambers 12.00
103 Ricky Williams 15.00
104 Derrick Alexander 8.00
105 Michael Bennett 15.00
106 Randy Moss 15.00
107 Aaron Brooks 12.00
108 Deuce McAllister 8.00
109 Tiki Barber 8.00
110 Curtis Martin 8.00
111 Tim Brown 12.00
112 Duce Staley 8.00
113 Jerome Bettis 10.00
114 Kordell Stewart 10.00
115 Isaac Bruce 10.00
116 Marshall Faulk 15.00
117 Torry Holt 12.00
118 Kurt Warner 12.00
119 Drew Brees 12.00
120 LaDainianTomlinson 15.00
121 Jeff Garcia 8.00
122 Terrell Owens 12.00
123 Shaun Alexander 8.00
124 Eddie George 8.00
125 Steve McNair 12.00

A player's name in *italic* type indicates a rookie card.

2002 Pacific National Promo

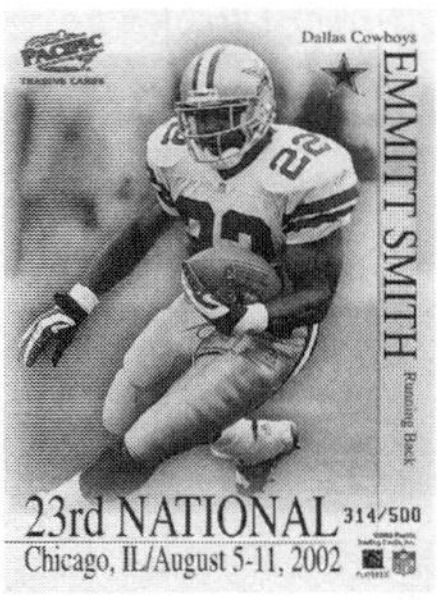

NM/M
Complete Set (8): 12.00
Common Player: 1.00
1 Ilya Kovalchuk, Michael Vick 3.00
2 Joe Thornton, Tom Brady 1.00
3 Eric Daze, Anthony Thomas 1.00
4 Peter Forsberg, Brian Griese 2.00
5 Mike Modano, Emmitt Smith 4.00
6 Steve Yzerman, Joey Harrington 5.00
7 Eric Lindros, Ron Dayne 1.00
8 Chris Pronger, Kurt Warner 1.00

2003 Pacific CFL

NM/M
Complete Set (110): 42.00
Common Player: .20
Unlisted Star: .75
Red version 1X-2X
Inserted 1:1
Pack (5): 2.79
Wax Box (30): 75.00
1 Damon Allen 1.00
2 Bret Anderson .20
3 Chris Brazzell .20
4 Eric Carter .20
5 Jason Clermont .20
6 Dave Dickenson 1.00
7 Willie Hurst .20
8 Carl Kidd .20
9 Bo Lewis .20
10 Geroy Simon 1.50
11 Barrin Simpson .20
12 Ryan Thelwell .20
13 Spergon Wynn .20
14 Kelvin Anderson 1.50
15 Don Blair .20
16 Albert Connell .20
17 Marcus Crandell 1.00
18 Kevin Feterik .20
19 Joe Fleming .20
20 Alondra Johnson .20
21 Demetrious Maxie .20
22 Wane McGarity 1.00
23 Mark McLoughlin .20
24 Lawrence Phillips .40
25 Reidel Anthony .50
26 Mike Bradley .20
27 Sean Fleming .20
28 Edward Hervey 1.50
29 Jason Maas .20
30 Singor Mobley .20
31 Winston October .20
32 Elfrid Payton .20
33 Mike Pringle 1.00
34 Ricky Ray 1.50
35 Jason Tucker .20
36 Terry Vaughn 1.00
37 Ricky Walters .20
38 Tony Akins .20
39 Archie Amerson .20
40 Troy Davis 1.00
41 Tyree Davis .20
42 Pete Gonzalez .20
43 Rob Hitchcock .20
44 Danny McManus 1.00
45 Joe Montford .20
46 Paul Osbaldiston .20
47 Chris Shelling .20
48 Jarrett Smith .20
49 Jason Brookins .20
50 Ben Cahoon 1.00
51 Anthony Calvillo 4.00
52 Chris Coleman .20
53 Jermaine Copeland 2.00
54 Sylvain Girard .20
55 Bruno Heppell .20
56 Kevin Johnson .20
57 Eric Lapointe .20
58 Marc Megna .20
59 Barron Miles .20
60 Quinton Spotwood .20
61 Demetris Bendross .20
62 Donovan Carter .20
63 Dameyune Craig .20
64 Dan Crowley .20
65 Aubrey Cummings .20
66 Darren Davis .20
67 John Grace 1.00
68 Denis Montana .20
69 Mark Nohra .20
70 Josh Ranek .20
71 Gerald Vaughn 1.00
72 Kelly Wiltshire .20
73 Jason French .20
74 Kevin Glenn .20
75 Nealon Greene 1.00
76 Rocky Henry .20
77 Corey Holmes .20
78 Quincy Jackson .20
79 Paul McCallum .20
80 Travis Moore .20
81 Omarr Morgan .20
82 Shonte Peoples .20
83 Sedrick Shaw .20
84 Michael Bishop .50
85 Marcus Brady .20
86 Ben Gay .40
87 Clifford Ivory .20
88 Alfred Jackson .20
89 Michael Jenkins 1.00
90 Tony Miles .20
91 Derrell Mitchell .20
92 Mike Morreale .20
93 Jimmy Oliver .20
94 Michael O'Shea .20
95 Johnny Scott .20
96 Reggie Slack .20
97 Adrion Smith .20
98 Doug Brown .20
99 Tom Europe .20
100 Denny Fortney .20
101 Robert Gordon .20
102 Markus Howell .20
103 Khari Jones 1.50
104 Lamar McGriggs .20
105 Harold Nash Jr. .20
106 Chad Plummer .20
107 Charles Roberts 2.00
108 Mike Sellers .20
109 Milt Stegall 1.00
110 Troy Westwood .20

2003 Pacific CFL Authentic Game-Worn Jerseys

NM/M
Common Player: 10.00
Inserted 1:16
1 Marcus Crandell 10.00
2 Edward Hervey 10.00
3 Terry Vaughn 10.00
4 Danny McManus 10.00
5 Anthony Calvillo 20.00
6 John Grace 14.00
7 Khari Jones 12.00
8 Charles Roberts 10.00

2003 Pacific CFL Division Collision

NM/M
Common Player: 1.50
Inserted 1:11
1 Damon Allen 1.50
2 Marcus Crandell 1.50
3 Ricky Ray 3.00
4 Danny McManus 2.00
5 Anthony Calvillo 5.00
6 John Grace 4.00
7 Nealon Greene 1.50
8 Derrell Mitchell 1.50
9 Khari Jones 1.50

2003 Pacific CFL Grey Cup Heroes

NM/M
Common Player: 15.00

NM/M
Randomly inserted
1 Doug Flutie 15.00
2 Jeff Garcia 15.00

2003 Pacific CFL Grey Expectations

NM/M
Common Player: 1.50
Inserted 1:16
1 Damon Allen 1.50
2 Mike Pringle 4.00
3 Ricky Ray 3.00
4 Danny McManus 2.00
5 Anthony Calvillo 5.00
6 Khari Jones 1.50
7 Milt Stegall 4.50

2003 Pacific CFL Maximum Overdrive

NM/M
Common Player: 2.00
Inserted 1:16
1 Mike Pringle 4.00
2 Terry Vaughn 2.50
3 Troy Davis 3.00
4 Ben Cahoon 4.00
5 Corey Holmes 4.00
6 Michael Jenkins 2.00
7 Charles Roberts 5.00
8 Milt Stegall 4.00

1961 Packers Lake to Lake

The 36-card, 2-1/2" x 3-1/4" set was issued by Lake to Lake out of Sheboygan, Wis. The card fronts feature a player shot with the card number and the player's number, height, weight and college attended. The card backs give offers for premium upgrades, such as a football or a ceramic figurine. Cards 1-8 and 17-24 are much more difficult to obtain.

NM/M
Complete Set (36): 625.00
Common Player (1-8/17-24): 25.00
Common Player (9-16/25-32): 2.50
Common Player (33-36): 5.00
Common SP: 25.00
1 Jerry Kramer (SP) 45.00
2 Norm Masters (SP) 25.00
3 Willie Davis (SP) 50.00
4 Bill Quinlan (SP) 25.00
5 Jim Temp (SP) 25.00
6 Emlen Tunnell (SP) 45.00
7 Gary Knafelc (SP) 25.00
8 Hank Jordan (SP) 45.00
9 Bill Forester 25.00
10 Paul Hornung 15.00
11 Jesse Whittenton 2.50
12 Andy Cverko 2.50
13 Jim Taylor 15.00
14 Hank Gremminger 2.50
15 Tom Moore 3.00
16 John Symank 2.50
17 Max McGee (SP) 40.00
18 Bart Starr (SP) 85.00
19 Ray Nitschke (SP) 65.00
20 Dave Hanner (SP) 30.00
21 Tom Bettis (SP) 25.00
22 Fuzzy Thurston (SP) 30.00
23 Lew Carpenter (SP) 25.00
24 Boyd Dowler (SP) 30.00
25 Ken Iman 2.50
26 Bob Skoronski 2.50
27 Forrest Gregg 7.50
28 Jim Ringo 7.50
29 Ron Kramer 3.00
30 Herb Adderley 12.00
31 Dan Currie 2.50
32 John Roach 2.50
33 Dale Hackbart 5.00
34 Larry Hickman 5.00
35 Nelson Toburen 5.00
36 Willie Wood 12.00

1966 Packers Mobil Posters

The eight-poster, 11" x 14" set features color action art with blank backs. The posters were available with envelopes which gave the art's title and number.

NM/M
Complete Set (8): 80.00
Common Player: 10.00
1 The Pass (Bart Star back to pass) 25.00
2 The Block (Jerry Kramer blocking for Elijah Pitts) 12.00
3 The Punt (Don Chandler punting) 10.00
4 The Sweep (Jim Taylor following blocking) 15.00
5 Boyd Dowler The Catch 12.00
6 The Tackle 10.00
7 The Touchdown (Tom Moore scoring) 12.00
8 The Extra Point (Don Chandler with Bart Starr holding) 12.00

1969 Packers Drenks Potato Chip Pins

The 20-pin, 1-1/8" in diameter set were issued by Drenks Potato Chips. The pins have a black and white headshot with green and white backgrounds. "Green Bay Packers" appears on the top edge while the bottom edge has the player's name and position.

NM/M
Complete Set (20): 80.00
Common Player: 2.00
1 Herb Adderley 8.00
2 Lionel Aldridge 2.00
3 Donny Anderson 3.00
4 Ken Bowman 2.00
5 Carroll Dale 2.00
6 Willie Davis 8.00
7 Boyd Dowler 3.00
8 Marv Fleming 3.00
9 Gale Gillingham 2.00
10 Jim Grabowski 3.00
11 Forrest Gregg 8.00
12 Don Horn 2.00
13 Bob Jeter 2.00
14 Hank Jordan 8.00
15 Ray Nitschke 10.00
16 Elijah Pitts 3.00
17 Dave Robinson 3.00
18 Bart Starr 16.00
19 Travis Williams 3.00
20 Willie Wood 8.00

1969 Packers Tasco Prints

The seven-piece, 11" x 16" print set features artwork of the player with his name and position, with the backs blank.

NM/M
Complete Set (7): 50.00
Common Player: 10.00
1 Donny Anderson 10.00
2 Boyd Dowler 10.00
3 Jim Grabowski 10.00
4 Hank Jordan 15.00
5 Ray Nitschke 25.00
6 Bart Starr 30.00
7 Willie Wood 15.00

1972 Packers Team Issue

The 45-card, 8" x 10" set was printed on glossy paper and featured posed player shots. The card front bottoms have the player's name and position while the backs are blank.

NM/M
Complete Set (45): 50.00
Common Player: 2.00
1 Ken Bowman 2.00
2 John Brockington 4.00
3 Bob Brown (DT) 2.00
4 Willie Buchanon 3.00
5 Fred Carr 3.00
6 Jim Carter 2.00
7 Carroll Dale 3.00
8 Carroll Dale (Action pose)) 3.00
9 Dan Devine (CO/GM) 3.00
10 Ken Ellis 2.00
11 Len Garrett 2.00
12 Gale Gillingham 2.00
13 Leland Glass 2.00
14 Charlie Hall 2.00
15 Jim Hill 2.00
16 Dick Himes 2.00
17 Bob Hudson (Head shot)) 2.00
18 Bob Hudson (Kneeling pose)) 2.00
19 Kevin Hunt 2.00
20 Scott Hunter 3.00
21 Dave Kopay 2.00
22 Bob Kroll 2.00
23 Pete Lammons 2.00
24 MacArthur Lane 4.00
25 Bill Lueck 2.00
26 Al Matthews 2.00
27 Mike McCoy 2.00
28 Rich McGeorge 2.00
29 Charlie Napper 2.00
30 Ray Nitschke 10.00
31 Charles Pittman 3.00
32 Malcolm Snider (action pose, Falcons Uniform) 2.00
33 Malcolm Snider (Kneeling pose) 2.00
34 Jon Staggers 3.00
35 Bart Starr 12.00
36 Jerry Tagge 3.00
37 Isaac Thomas (Action pose) 2.00
38 Isaac Thomas (Kneeling pose) 2.00
39 Vern Vanoy 2.00
40 Ron Widby (Action pose, Cowboys uniform) 2.00
41 Ron Widby (Kneeling pose) 2.00
42 Clarence Williams 2.00
43 Perry Williams 2.00
44 Keith Wortman 2.00
45 Bart Starr, Hank Kuhlmann, Dave Hanner, Burt Gustafson, John Polonchek, Don Doll, Red Cochran, Dan Devine, Rollie Dotsch Coaching Staff 12.00

1974 Packers Team Issue

The 14-card, 6" x 9" set featured the players in posed shots with facsimile autographs and blank backs.

NM/M
Complete Set (14): 25.00
Common Player: 3.00
1 John Brockington 5.00
2 Willie Buchanon 4.00
3 Fred Carr 4.00
4 Jim Carter 4.00
5 Jack Concannon 4.00
6 Bill Curry 5.00
7 John Hadl 5.00
8 Bill Lueck 3.00
9 Chester Marcol 4.00
10 Rich McGeorge 4.00
11 Alden Roche 3.00
12 Barry Smith 3.00
13 Barty Smith 3.00
14 Clarence Williams 3.00

1983 Packers Police

The 19-card, 2-5/8" x 4-1/8" set featured action shots on white card stock with three different card backs: First Wisconsin Bank, Waukesha Police and without First Wisconsin Bank, with the latter one being the most rare set. "Packer Tips" are given on the back.

NM/M
Complete Set (19): 20.00
Common Player: 1.00
10 Jan Stenerud 2.00
12 Lynn Dickey 1.50
24 Johnnie Gray 1.00
29 Mike McCoy 1.25
31 Gerry Ellis 1.00
40 Eddie Lee Ivery 1.50
52 George Cumby 1.00
53 Mike Douglass 1.25
54 Larry McCarren 1.00
59 John Anderson 1.25
63 Terry Jones 1.00
64 Sid Kitson 1.00
68 Greg Koch 1.00
80 James Lofton 4.00
82 Paul Coffman 1.50
83 John Jefferson 2.00
85 Phillip Epps 1.50
90 Ezra Johnson 1.00
Bart Starr (CO) 4.00

1984 Packers Police

The 25-card, 2-5/8" x 4" set was sponsored by First Wisconsin Bank, local law enforcement and the Packers. The card backs contain "Packer Tips."

NM/M
Complete Set (25): 10.00
Common Player: .40
1 John Jefferson .60
2 Forrest Gregg (CO) 2.00
3 John Anderson .50
4 Eddie Garcia .40

5	Tim Lewis	.40
6	Jessie Clark	.40
7	Karl Swanke	.40
8	Lynn Dickey	1.00
		NM/M
9	Eddie Lee Ivery	.60
10	Dick Modzelewski (CO) (Defensive Coord.)	.40
11	Mark Murphy	.40
12	Dave Drechsler	.40
13	Mike Douglass	.40
14	James Lofton	2.50
15	Bucky Scribner	.40
16	Randy Scott	.40
17	Mark Lee	.50
18	Gerry Ellis	.40
19	Terry Jones	.40
20	Bob Schnelker (CO) (Offensive Coord.)	.40
21	George Cumby	.40
22	George Cumby	.40
23	Larry McCarren	.40
24	Sid Kitson	.40
25	Paul Coffman	.50

1985 Packers Police

The 25-card, 2-3/4" x 4" set, as with the previous year's, was issued by First Wisconsin Bank, local law enforcement and Green Bay and contains "Packer Tips" on the card backs.

		NM/M
Complete Set (25):		8.00
Common Player:		.40
1	Forrest Gregg (CO)	1.75
2	Paul Coffman	.60
3	Terry Jones	.40
4	Ron Hallstrom	.40
5	Eddie Lee Ivery	.60
6	John Anderson	.40
7	Tim Lewis	.40
8	Bob Schnelker (CO) (Offensive Coord.)	.40
9	Al Del Greco	.40
10	Mark Murphy	.40
11	Tim Huffman	.40
12	Del Rodgers	.40
13	Mark Lee	.40
14	Tom Flynn	.40
15	Dick Modzelewski (CO) (Defensive Corrd.)	.40
16	Randy Scott	.40
17	Bucky Scribner	.40
18	George Cumby	.40
19	James Lofton	2.50
20	Mike Douglass	.50
21	Alphonso Carreker	.40
22	Greg Koch	.40
23	Gerry Ellis	.40
24	Ezra Johnson	.40
25	Lynn Dickey	.75

1986 Packers Police

The 25-card, 2-3/4" x 4" set was sponsored by local law enforcement, First Wisconsin Bank and the Packers. The card backs feature player bios and stats, as well as a safety tip.

		NM/M
Complete Set (25):		8.00
Common Player:		.35
10	Al Del Greco	.35
12	Lynn Dickey	.60
16	Randy Wright	.60
26	Tim Lewis	.35
31	Gerry Ellis	.35
33	Jessie Clark	.35
37	Mark Murphy	.50
40	Eddie Lee Ivery	.50
41	Tom Flynn	.35
42	Gary Ellerson	.35
55	Randy Scott	.35
58	Mark Cannon	.35
59	John Anderson	.50
65	Ron Hallstrom	.35
67	Karl Swanke	.35
76	Alphonso Carreker	.35
80	James Lofton	1.50
82	Paul Coffman	.50
85	Phillip Epps	.50
90	Ezra Johnson	.35
91	Brian Noble	.50
93	Robert Brown	.35
94	Charles Martin	.35
99	John Dorsey	.35
	Forrest Gregg (CO)	1.25

1987 Packers Police

Measuring 2-3/4" x 4", the 22-card set showcased "1987 Packers" at the top, with a photo in the center and the Packers' helmet, player's jersey number and name under the photo. The card backs, printed in green on white paper stock, has the player's name and jersey number at the top, his bio and highlights follow. A safety tip is also included on the back. The cards were sponsored by local law enforcement agencies, the Packers, Employers Health Insurance Co. and Arson Task Force. Approximately 35,000 sets were handed out. Card Nos. 5, 6 and 20 were never distributed as they featured players who were waived or traded before the set was released.

		NM/M
Complete Set (22):		8.00
Common Player:		.35
1	Forrest Gregg (CO)	1.00
2	George Greene	.35
3	Ron Hallstrom	.35
4	Ezra Johnson	.35
7	Robert Brown	.35
8	Tom Neville	.35
9	Rich Moran	.35
10	Ken Ruettgers	.50
11	Alan Veingrad	.35
12	Mark Lee	.50
13	John Dorsey	.35
14	Paul Ott Carruth	.35
15	Randy Wright	.50
16	Phillip Epps	.50
17	Al Del Greco	.35
18	Tim Harris	1.00
19	Kenneth Davis	1.00
21	John Anderson	.50
22	Mark Murphy	.50
23	Ken Stills	.35
24	Brian Noble	.50
25	Mark Cannon	.35

1988 Packers Police

Measuring 2-3/4" x 4", the 25-card set was anchored by a large photo on the front, with the player's name, number, height, weight and position listed at the bottom. The Packers' helmet appears in the lower right. The card backs included a Packers' helmet at the top, with a "Packers Tips" boxed in section underneath. The set was sponsored by Copps, Brown County Arson Task Force, local law enforcement agencies and the Packers.

		NM/M
Complete Set (25):		10.00
Common Player:		.40
1	John Anderson	.50
2	Jerry Boyarsky	.40
3	Don Bracken	.40
4	Dave Brown	.40
5	Mark Cannon	.40
6	Alphonso Carreker	.40
7	Paul Ott Carruth	.40
8	Kenneth Davis	.75
9	John Dorsey	.40
10	Brent Fullwood	.40
11	Tiger Greene	.40
12	Ron Hallstrom	.40
13	Tim Harris	.75
14	Johnny Holland	.50
15	Lindy Infante (CO)	.75
16	Mark Lee	.50
17	Don Majkowski	.75
18	Rich Moran	.40
19	Mark Murphy	.40
20	Ken Ruettgers	.50
21	Walter Stanley	.60
22	Keith Uecker	.40
23	Ed West	.50
24	Randy Wright	.40
25	Max Zendejas	.40

1989 Packers Police

Measuring 2-3/4" x 4", the 15-card set showcases a photo on the card front, with the player's name, jersey number, position and year in the league listed below. The Packers' helmet is at the bottom center. The backs have a Packers Tip boxed in the center, with the Packers' logo at the top. The card number is listed at the bottom center of the text box. The front photo is bordered in yellow, with the card printed on white stock.

		NM/M
Complete Set (15):		5.00
Common Player:		.35
1	Lindy Infante (CO)	.50
2	Don Majkowski	.60
3	Brent Fullwood	.35
4	Mark Lee	.50
5	Dave Brown	.35
6	Mark Murphy	.50
7	Johnny Holland	.50
8	John Anderson	.50
9	Ken Ruettgers	.50
10	Sterling Sharpe	2.00
11	Ed West	.35
12	Walter Stanley	.50
13	Brian Noble	.50
14	Shawn Patterson	.35
15	Tim Harris	.50

1990 Packers Police

Measuring 2-3/4" x 4", the 20-card set is anchored by a large photo on the front. "Packers '90" is printed at the top, with the player's name, number, position and year in the league listed under the photo. The Packers' helmet is located in the lower left.

		NM/M
Complete Set (20):		5.00
Common Player:		.25
1	Lindy Infante (CO)	.35
2	Keith Woodside	.25
3	Chris Jacke	.35
4	Chuck Cecil	.35
5	Tony Mandarich	.25
6	Brent Fullwood	.25
7	Robert Brown	.25
8	Scott Stephen	.25
9	Anthony Dilweg	.25
10	Mark Murphy	.25
11	Johnny Holland	.35
12	Sterling Sharpe	1.00
13	Tim Harris	.35
14	Ed West	.25
15	Jeff Query	.25
16	Mark Lee	.25
17	Rich Moran	.25
18	Perry Kemp	.35
19	Brian Noble	.35
20	Don Majkowski	.50

1990 Packers 25th Anniversary

Pacific Trading Cards produced this 45-card standard sized set, while Champion Cards released it. The card fronts feature a 25th Anniversary pennant in the upper left, either a color or sepia-toned photo and the player's name and position. The Packers' helmet is pictured in the lower right corner. The backs feature the player's name, position and number at the top. His bio and career highlights are also listed. The card's number is printed in the lower right.

		NM/M
Complete Set (45):		10.00
Common Player:		.25
1	Introduction Card	.50
2	Bart Starr	2.00
3	Herb Adderley	.75
4	Bob Skoronski	.25
5	Tom Brown	.35
6	Lee Roy Caffey	.35
7	Ray Nitschke	1.00
8	Carroll Dale	.35
9	Jim Taylor	1.25
10	Ken Bowman	.25
11	Gale Gillingham	.35
12	Jim Grabowski	.50
13	Dave Robinson	.50
14	Donny Anderson	.50
15	Willie Wood	.75
16	Zeke Bratkowski	.50
17	Doug Hart	.25
18	Jerry Kramer	.75
19	Marv Fleming	.35
20	Lionel Aldridge	.35
21	Red Mack (UER) (Text reads returned to football before the following season should be retired)	.25
22	Ron Kostelnik	.25
23	Boyd Dowler	.50
24	Vince Lombardi (CO)	1.25
25	Forrest Gregg	.75
26	Max McGee (Superstar)	.35
27	Fuzzy Thurston	.50
28	Bob Brown (DT)	.35
29	Willie Davis	.75
30	Elijah Pitts	.50
31	Hank Jordan	.50
32	Bart Starr	2.00
33	Jim Taylor Super Bowl I	.75
34	1996 Packers	.50
35	Max McGee	.50
36	Jim Weatherwax	.25
37	Bob Long	.25
38	Don Chandler	.35
39	Bill Anderson	.25
40	Tommy Crutcher	.35
41	Dave Hathcock	.25
42	Steve Wright	.25
43	Phil Vandersea	.25
44	Bill Curry	.50
45	Bob Jeter	.35

1991 Packers Police

The green-bordered, 20-card set features a yellow banner in the upper left corner of the card front which includes "1991 Packers." The photo is surrounded by a green and yellow border. The player's name and position are printed in the upper right, while his year in the league and his college are printed inside a yellow band at the bottom of the card. The Packers' logo is printed in the lower right of the photo. Numbered "of 20," the card backs feature "1991 Packer Tips." The sponsors' logos appear at the bottom of the standard-sized card backs. Each card back is vertical, except for the Lambeau Field card which is horizontal.

		NM/M
Complete Set (20):		5.00
Common Player:		.30
1	Lambeau Field	.30
2	Sterling Sharpe	1.00
3	James Campen	.30
4	Chuck Cecil	.40
5	Lindy Infante (CO)	.40
6	Keith Woodside	.30
7	Perry Kemp	.30
8	Johnny Holland	.40
9	Don Majkowski	.40
10	Tony Bennett	.50
11	Leroy Butler	.40
12	Tony Mandarich	.30
13	Darrell Thompson	.40
14	Matt Brock	.30
15	Charles Wilson	.50
16	Brian Noble	.40
17	Ed West	.30
18	Chris Jacke	.30
19	Blair Kiel	.40
20	Mark Murphy	.30

1991 Packers Super Bowl II

The 25th anniversary of the Packers' Super Bowl II victory is honored on this standard-sized 50-card set. The card fronts include a photo which is surrounded by a dark green border. The player's name, Packers' logo and Super Bowl II are located inside a yellow band at the bottom of the card. The card backs feature the player's name, bio and highlights, along with his stats. A photo credit and "Copyright Champion Cards" appear at the bottom left. The card number is printed at the bottom center inside a football.

		NM/M
Complete Set (50):		10.00
Common Player:		.25
1	Intro Card Super Bowl Trophy	.50
2	Steve Wright	.25
3	Jim Flanigan	.25
4	Tom Brown	.35
5	Tommy Joe Crutcher	.35
6	Doug Hart	.35
7	Bob Hyland	.25
8	John Rowser	.25
9	Bob Skoronski	.25
10	Jim Weatherwax	.25
11	Ben Wilson	.25
12	Don Horn	.35
13	Allen Brown	.25
14	Dick Capp	.25
15	Donny Anderson Super Bowl II Action	.50
16	Bart Starr Ice Bowl: The Play	1.00
17	Chuck Mercein	.35
18	Herb Adderley	.75
19	Ken Bowman	.25
20	Lee Roy Caffey	.35
21	Carroll Dale	.35
22	Marv Fleming	.35
23	Jim Grabowski	.50
24	Bob Jeter	.35
25	Jerry Kramer	.75
26	Max McGee	.50
27	Elijah Pitts	.50
28	Bart Starr	1.50
29	Fuzzy Thurston	.50
30	Willie Wood	.75
31	Lionel Aldridge	.35
32	Donny Anderson	.50
33	Zeke Bratkowski	.50
34	Bob Brown (DT)	.35
35	Don Chandler	.35
36	Willie Davis	.75
37	Boyd Dowler	.50
38	Gale Gillingham	.35
39	Hank Jordan	.75
40	Ron Kostelnik	.25
41	Vince Lombardi (CO)	1.25
42	Bob Long	.25
43	Ray Nitschke	1.00
44	Dave Robinson	.50
45	Bart Starr (MVP)	1.25
46	Travis Williams	.35
47	1967 Packers Team	.50
48	Ice Bowl Game Summary	.25
49	Ice Bowl	.25
50	NNO Packer Pro Shop	.25

1992 Packers Hall of Fame

This 110-card set, available only at the Packer Hall of Fame Gift Shop, honors 106 members of the Packer Hall of Fame. The card fronts are anchored by a photo inside an oval. The Packers Hall of Fame logo appears in the upper left, with an old Packers' logo in the upper right. The player's name, position and jersey number are included inside a gold rectangle at the bottom of the card, which is bordered in green. Card backs have the player's name in green inside a gold banner at the top. His bio and highlights appear at the center of the horizontal card back. The card number is printed at the bottom center inside a helmet. Card No. 1 does not exist, but two No. 45 cards were printed.

		NM/M
Complete Set (110):		20.00
Common Player:		.10
2	Red Dunn	.20
3	Mike Michalske	.50
4	Cal Hubbard	.50
5	Johnny "Blood" McNally	.50
6	Verne Lewellen	.10
7	Cub Buck	.10
8	Whitey Woodin	.10
9	Jug Earp	.10
10	Charlie Mathys	.10
11	Andrew Turnbull (PRES)	.10
12	Curly Lambeau (Founder/Coach)	.50
13	George Calhoun (PUB)	.10
14	Boob Darling	.10
15	Eddie Jankowski	.10
16	Swede Johnston	.10
17	George Svendsen	.10
18	Bob Monnett	.10
19	Joe Laws	.10
20	Tiny Engebretsen	.10
21	Milt Gantenbein	.10
22	Hank Bruder	.10
23	Clarke Hinkle	.50
24	Lon Evans	.10
25	Buckets Goldenberg	.10
26	Nate Barrager	.10
27	Arnie Herber	.30
28	Lee Joannes (PRES)	.10
29	Jerry Clifford (VP)	.10
30	Pete Tinsley	.10
31	Buford Ray	.10
32	Andy Uram	.10
33	Larry Craig	.10
34	Charlie Brock	.10
35	Ted Fritsch	.20
36	Lou Brock	.10
37	Carl Mulleneaux	.10
38	Harry Jacunski	.10
39	Cecil Isbell	.30
40	Bud Svendsen	.10
41	Russ Letlow	.10
42	Don Hutson	.75
43	Irv Comp	.10
44	John Martinkovic	.10
45A	Bobby Dillon	.20
45B	Lavern Dilweg (UER) (Back is that of card 45 card, Bobby Dillon)	.50
46	Wilner Burke (Band Director)	.10
47	Dick Wildung	.10
48	Billy Howton	.30
49	Tobin Rote	.30
50	Jim Ringo	.50
51	Deral Teteak	.10
52	Bob Forte	.10
53	Tony Canadeo	.50
54	Al Carmichael	.10
55	Bob Mann	.10
56	Jack Vainisi (Scout)	.10
57	Ken Bowman	.10
58	Bob Skoronski	.10
59	Dave Hanner	.20
60	Bill Forester	.20
61	Fred Cone	.10
62	Lionel Aldridge	.20
63	Carroll Dale	.20
64	Howard Ferguson	.10
65	Gary Knafelc	.10
66	Ron Kramer	.20
67	Forrest Gregg	.50
68	Phil Bengtson (CO)	.10
69	Dan Currie	.10
70	Al Schneider (Contributor)	.10
71	Bob Jeter	.20
72	Jesse Whittenton	.20
73	Hank Gremminger	.10
74	Ron Kostelnik	.10
75	Gale Gillingham	.20
76	Lee Roy Caffey	.20
77	Hank Jordan	.50
78	Boyd Dowler	.30
79	Fred Carr	.20
80	Bud Jorgensen (TR)	.10
81	Eugene Brusky (Team Physician)	.10
82	Fred Trowbridge (Executive Committee)	.10
83	Jan Stenerud	.50
84	Jerry Atkinson (Contributor)	.10
85	Larry McCarren	.10
86	Fred Leicht (Executive Committee)	.10
87	Max McGee	.30
88	Zeke Bratkowski	.30
89	Dave Robinson	.30
90	Herb Adderley	.50
91	Dominic Olejniczak (President)	.20
92	Jerry Kramer	.50
93	Super Bowl I	.20
94	Don Chandler	.10
95	John Brockington	.30
96	Lynn Dickey	.20
97	Bart Starr	1.00
98	Willie Wood	.50
99	Packer Hall of Fame	.20
100	Donny Anderson	.20
101	Chester Marcol	.20
102	Fuzzy Thurston	.20
103	Paul Hornung	.75
14	Jim Taylor	.75
105	Vince Lombardi (CO)	.75
106	Willie Davis	.50
107	Ray Nitschke	.50
108	Elijah Pitts	.20
109	NNO Honor Roll (Checklist Card)	.20
110	NNO Packer Hall of Fame (Catalog Order Form)	.20

1992 Packers Police

This unnumbered 20-card set is anchored by a color photo on the front. The backs of the cards have text printed in green on a white background. The logos of the various sponsors also appear. This set has one of the first cards to feature Brett Favre as a Packer.

		NM/M
Complete Set (20):		10.00
Common Player:		.25
1	Tony Bennett	.50
2	Matt Brock	.25
3	Leroy Butler	.25
4	Vinnie Clark	.35
5	Brett Favre	6.00
6	Jackie Harris	.50
7	Johnny Holland	.25
8	Mike Holmgren (CO)	1.50
9	Chris Jacke	.25
10	Sherman Lewis (CO)	.25
11	Don Majkowski	.35
12	Tony Mandrich	.25
13	Paul McJulien	.25
14	Brian Noble	.35
14	Bryce Paup	2.00
16	Ray Rhodes (CO)	1.00
17	Tootie Robbins	.25
18	Sterling Sharpe	.75
19	Darrell Thompson	.25
20	Ron Wolf (GM)	.35

1993 Packers Archives Postcards

Measuring 3-1/2" x 5-1/2", this 40-postcard set features Packer players from the team's 75-year history. A photo dominates the card fronts, which are bordered in white. Card fronts also include the Packers' 75th anniversary logo and the player's name and year the photo was taken. The horizontal card backs are divided in half, with the player's name, bio and highlights printed on the left side. The right side of the card back includes the Champion Cards' logo printed over the Vince Lombardi Trophy. The card number is printed inside a football at the bottom center.

		NM/M
Complete Set (40):		10.00
Common Player:		.50
1	The First Team 1919	.75
2	The 1920s	.50
3	The 1930s	.50
4	The 1940s	.50
5	The 1950s	.50
6	The 1960s	.50
7	The 1970s	.50
8	The 1980s	.50
9	The 1990s	.50
10	Curly Lambeau (1919)	.75
11	Jim Ringo (1953)	.75
12	Ice Bowl 1967	.75
13	Jerry Kramer (1958)	.75

14	Ray Nitschke (1958)	1.00
15	Fuzzy Thurston (1959)	.75
16	James Lofton (1978-86)	.75
17	Super Bowl I Action	.75
18	Don Hutson (1935-45)	1.00
19	Tony Canadeo (1941-43, 46-52)	.75
20	Bobby Dillon (1952-59)	.50
21	The Quarterback	.75
22	Willie Wood (1960-71)	.75
23	Dave Beverly (1975-80)	.50
24	James Lofton (1978)	.75
25	Tim Harris (1986-90)	.75
26	1929 Championship Team	.50
27	1930 Championship Team	.50
28	1931 ChampionshipTeam	.50
29	1936 Championship Team	.50
30	1939 Championship Team	.50
31	1944 Championship Team	.50
32	1961 ChampionshipTeam	.75
33	1962 ChampionshipTeam	.75
34	1965 ChampionshipTeam	.75
35	1966 ChampionshipTeam	.75
36	1967 ChampionshipTeam	.75
37	Old City Stadium	.50
38	New City Stadium	.50
39	Lambeau Field-1992	.50
40	NNO Title Card (3-3/4" x 5-3/4")	.75

1993 Packers Police

The 20-card set is bordered in white on the front, with a color photo anchoring it. The Packers' 75th anniversary logo appears inside the photo in the upper left. "Celebrating 75 seasons of Pro Football 1919-1993" is printed under the photo. The vertical card backs have the Packers' helmet in the upper left, with the player's name, position, year in the league and college listed to the right. Elementary students' saftey tips are printed in the center of the card. The card number "of 20" is located under the tip. Various sponsor logos appear at the bottom of the card backs.

		NM/M
Complete Set (20):		8.00
Common Player:		.25
1	Ron Wolf (GM)	.25
2	Wayne Simmons	.35
3	James Campen	.25
4	Matt Brock	.25
5	Mike Holmgren (CO)	1.00
6	Brian Noble	.35
7	Ken O'Brien	.35
8	George Teague	.35
9	Brett Favre	4.00
10	LeRoy Butler	.35
11	Harry Galbreath	.25
12	Chris Jacke	.35
13	Sterling Sharpe	.75
14	Terrell Buckley	.35
15	Ken Ruettgers	.35
16	Johnny Holland	.35
17	Edgar Bennett	1.50
18	Jackie Harris	.50
19	Tony Bennett	.50
20	Reggie White	1.50

1994 Packers Police

The 20-card set includes a color photo on the front, with "1994 Green Bay Packers" printed at the top. The player's name and jersey number are printed inside a green band under the photo. Numbered "of 20," the card backs include the Packers' logo in the upper left, with the player's number, name, position, year in the league and college listed to the right. A student tip is printed in the center of the card back. Logos from the various sponsors are printed at the bottom.

		NM/M
Complete Set (20):		8.00
Common Player:		.30
1	Sherman Lewis	.30
2	Sterling Sharpe	.75
3	Ken Ruettgers	.40
4	Reggie White	1.00
5	Edgar Bennett	1.00
6	Fritz Shurmur (CO)	.40
7	Brett Favre	3.00
8	John Jurkovic	.50
9	Robert Brooks	2.00
10	Reggie Cobb	.30
11	Bryce Paup	.75
12	Harry Galbreath	.30
13	Mike Holmgren (CO)	.50
14	Ed West	.30
15	Sean Jones	.50
16	Ron Wolf (GM)	.30
17	Chris Jacke	.40
18	Wayne Simmons	.40
19	LeRoy Butler	.30
20	George Teague	.40

1995 Packers Safety Fritsch

Produced by Larry Fritsch Cards, the 20-card set showcases a color photo on the front, with "Packers" printed vertically along the left side inside a ghosted area. A 1995 diamond logo is located at the upper left. The player's name and number are printed inside a yellow stripe at the bottom. The cards are bordered in green on the front. Card backs feature the player's name, number, position, year in the league and college at the top, with a student tip printed below it. The card number "of 20" is printed in the lower center, above the various sponsors' names.

		NM/M
Complete Set (20):		8.00
Common Player:		.30
1	Mike Holmgren (CO)	.40
2	Ron Wolf (VP/GM)	.30
3	Brett Favre	3.00
4	Ty Detmer	1.00
5	Chris Jacke	.50
6	Craig Hentrich	.30
7	Craig Newsome	.30
8	George Teague	.50
9	Edgar Bennett	1.00
10	LeRoy Butler	.30
11	George Koonce	.30
12	John Jurkovic	.50
13	Aaron Taylor	.30
14	Ken Ruettgers	.30
15	Robert Brooks	1.50
16	Mark Chmura	1.50
17	Reggie White	1.00
18	Doug Evans	.30
19	Sean Jones	.50
20	Wayne Simmons	.50

1996 Packers Police

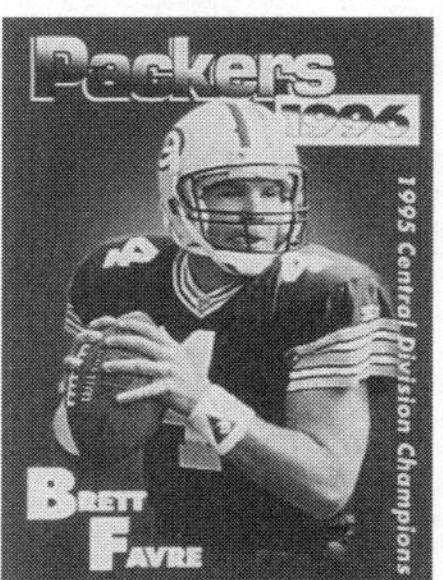

The 20-card standard-sized set features a photo of the player placed over a two-toned green background. "Packers 1996" is featured at the top, while "1995 Central Division Champions" is printed in yellow along the right side of the card. The player's name is printed in yellow in the lower left. The card backs, numbered "of 20," has the player's name position, jersey number and university at the top. A student tip is located in the center, with the card number underneath it. The various sponsors are listed at the bottom.

		NM/M
Complete Set (20):		8.00
Common Player:		.30
1	Edgar Bennett	.30
2	Robert Brooks	.50
3	Gilbert Brown	.75
4	LeRoy Butler	.30
5	Mark Chmura	.50
6	Santana Dotson	.30
7	Doug Evans	.30
8	Brett Favre	3.00
9	Antonio Freeman	.75
10	Craig Hendricks	.30
11	Chris Jacke	.30
12	Wayne Simmons	.30
13	George Koonce	.30
14	Craig Newsome	.30
15	Ron Wolf	.50
16	Ken Ruettgers	.20
17	Keith Jackson	.30
18	Aaron Taylor	.30
19	Reggie White	1.00
20	Mike Holmgren	.50

1997 Packers Playoff

This 50-card set commemorates the Packers' Super Bowl XXXI victory. The card fronts contain a color action shot and the Super Bowl logo. The backs have player information and the final score of the Super Bowl with the Superdome as the background.

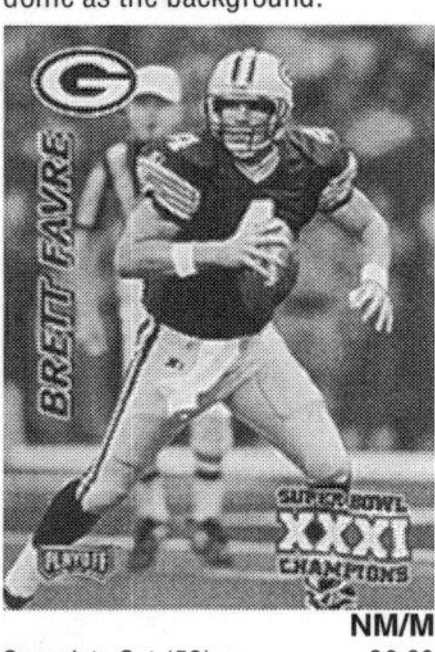

		NM/M
Complete Set (50):		30.00
Common Player:		.40
1	Super Bowl XXXI Champions (Scoreboard Photo)	.50
2	Brett Favre MVP	3.00
3	Reggie White Minister of Defense	1.50
4	Desmond Howard MVP	.50
5	NFC Championship Trophy Presentation	.40
6	Mike Holmgren CO	.50
7	Brett Favre	5.00
8	Chris Jacke	.40
9	Craig Hentrich	.40
10	Craig Newsome	.50
11	Dorsey Levens	2.00
12	Doug Evans	.40
13	Edgar Bennett	.50
14	Leroy Butler	.50
15	Eugene Robinson	.40
16	Brian Williams	.50
17	Frank Winters	.40
18	Ron Cox	.40
19	Wayne Simmons	.50
20	Adam Timmerman	.40
21	Bruce Wilkerson	.40
22	Santana Dotson	.40
23	Earl Dotson	.50
24	Aaron Taylor	.40
25	Desmond Howard	.50
26	Don Beebe	.50
27	Andre Rison	.50
28	Antonio Freeman	2.00
29	Terry Mickens	.40
30	Keith Jackson	.50
31	Mark Chmura	1.00
32	Reggie White	1.50
33	Gilbert Brown	.50
34	Sean Jones	.50
35	Robert Brooks, George Koonce	.75
36	Derrick Mayes, Gary Brown	.50
37	Jim McMahon	.50
38	William Henderson	.40
39	Travis Jervey, Roderick Mullen	.50
40	Tyrone Williams	.40
41	John Michels	.50
42	Mike Prior	.40
43	Calvin Jones, Jeff Thomason	.40
44	Brett Favre	3.00
45	Jeff Dellenbach	.40
46	Bernardo Harris	.40
47	Darius Holland	.40
48	Lamont Hollinquest	.40
49	Lindsay Knapp	.40
50	Gabe Wilkins	.40

1997 Packers Police

This 20-card Packers set boasts the Vince Lombardi Trophy in the lower right and the words "96 Super Bowl Champs" down the right side. Fronts capture a color photo of the player cut out over a purple background, with the player's name down the left side in a vertical gold strip. Card backs are numbered "of 20" and have the player's name, number, position, college and various sponsors. Included in the background is a photo of the Packers' three Super Bowl trophies.

		NM/M
Complete Set (20):		8.00
Common Player:		.30
1	Super Bowl XXXI Trophy	.50
2	Mike Holmgren	.50
3	Ron Wolf	.50
4	Brett Favre	3.00
5	Reggie White	1.00
6	LeRoy Butler	.30
7	Frank Winters	.30
8	Aaron Taylor	.30
9	Robert Brooks	.50
10	Gilbert Brown	.75
11	Mark Chmura	.50
12	Earl Dotson	.30
13	Santana Dotson	.30
14	Doug Evans	.30
15	Antonio Freeman	.75
16	William Henderson	.30
17	Craig Hentrich	.30
18	Dorsey Levens	1.00
19	Craig Newsome	.30
20	Edgar Bennett	.30

1997 Packers Score

		NM/M
Complete Set (15):		6.00
Common Player:		.30
Platinum Club		1X to 2X
Premiere Club		2X to 5X
1	Brett Favre	2.00
2	Andre Rison	.30
3	Robert Brooks	.30
4	Keith Jackson	.30
5	Edgar Bennett	.50
6	Reggie White	.75
7	Dorsey Levens	.50
8	Antonio Freeman	.30
9	Mark Chmura	.30
10	Wayne Simmons	.30
11	Eugene Robinson	.30
12	Brian Williams	.30
13	Doug Evans	.30
14	LeRoy Butler	.75
15	Gilbert Brown	.30

1998 Packers Police

		NM/M
Complete Set (20):		6.00
Common Player:		.25
	Robert Brooks	.25
	Gilbert Brown	.25
	LeRoy Butler	.50
	Mark Chmura	.25
	Earl Dotson	.25
	Santana Dotson	.25
	Brett Favre	2.00
	Antonio Freeman	.25
	Bernardo Harris	.25
	William Henderson	.25
	Mike Holmgren	.50
	Dorsey Levens	.50
	Craig Newsome	.25
	Adam Timmerman	.25
	Ross Verba	.25
	Reggie White	1.00
	Brian Williams	.25
	Tyrone Williams	.25
	Frank Winters	.25
	Ron Wolf	.25

1999 Packers Police

		NM/M
Complete Set (20):		6.00
Common Player:		.25
1	Gilbert Brown	.25
2	LeRoy Butler	.50
3	Mark Chmura	.25
4	Earl Dotson	.25
5	Santana Dotson	.25
6	Brett Favre	2.00
7	Antonio Freeman	.25
8	Bernardo Harris	.25
9	William Henderson	.25
10	Vonnie Holliday	.25
11	George Koonce	.25
12	Dorsey Levens	.50
13	Ryan Longwell	.25
14	Marco Rivera	.25
15	Darren Sharper	.50
16	Ross Verba	.25
17	Brian Williams	.25
18	Tyrone Williams	.25
19	Ron Wolf	.25
20	Coach Ray Rhodes	.25

2000 Packers Police

		NM/M
Complete Set (20):		6.00
Common Player:		.25
	LeRoy Butler	.50
	Earl Dotson	.25
	Santana Dotson	.25
	Brett Favre	2.00
	Antonio Freeman	.25
	Bernardo Harris	.25
	William Henderson	.25
	Vonnie Holliday	.25
	Dorsey Levens	.50
	Russell Maryland	.25
	Mike McKenzie	.25
	Bill Schroeder	.25
	Darren Sharper	.50
	Mike Sherman	.25
	Ross Verba	.25
	Mike Wahle	.25
	Brian Williams	.25
	Tyrone Williams	.25
	Frank Winters	.25
	Ron Wolf	.25

Values quoted in this guide reflect the retail price of a card—the price a collector can expect to pay when buying a card from a dealer. The wholesale price—that which a collector can expect to receive from a dealer when selling cards—will be significantly lower, depending on desirability and condition.

2001 Packers Police

		NM/M
Complete Set (20):		6.00
Common Player:		.25
	LeRoy Butler	.50
	Na'il Diggs	.25
	Santana Dotson	.25
	Brett Favre	2.00
	Mike Flanagan	.25
	Antonio Freeman	.25
	Ahman Green	.75
	Bernardo Harris	.25
	William Henderson	.25
	Vonnie Holliday	.25
	Ryan Longwell	.25
	Russell Maryland	.25
	Marco Rivera	.25
	Allen Rossum	.25
	Bill Schroeder	.25
	Darren Sharper	.50
	Mike Sherman	.25
	John Thierry	.25
	Nate Wayne	.25
	Tyrone Williams	.25

2002 Packers Police

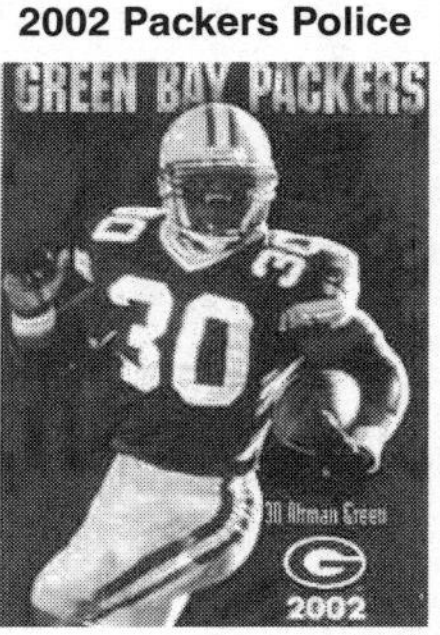

		NM/M
Complete Set (20):		6.00
Common Player:		.25
	Gilbert Brown	.25
	Chad Clifton	.25
	Na'il Diggs	.25
	Brett Favre	2.00
	Robert Ferguson	.25
	Bubba Franks	.50
	Kabeer Gbaja-Biamila	.25
	Terry Glenn	.50
	Ahman Green	.75
	William Henderson	.25
	Vonnie Holliday	.25
	Joe Johnson	.25
	Ryan Longwell	.25
	Mike McKenzie	.25
	Darren Sharper	.50
	Mike Sherman	.25
	Mark Tauscher	.25
	Mike Wahle	.25
	Nate Wayne	.25
	Tyrone Williams	.25

2003 Packers Police

		NM/M
Common Player:		.25
1	Mike Sherman	.25
2	Brett Favre	2.00
3	Ryan Longwell	.25
4	Ahman Green	.75
5	William Henderson	.25
6	Mike McKenzie	.25
7	Darren Sharper	.50
8	Mike Flanagan	.25
9	Na'il Diggs	.25
10	Marco Rivera	.25
11	Mark Tauscher	.25
12	Chad Clifton	.50
13	Donald Driver	.50
14	Javon Walker	.75
15	Bubba Franks	.50
16	Robert Ferguson	.50
17	Joe Johnson	.25
18	Kabeer Gbaja-Biamila	.50
19	Rod Walker	.25
20	Cletidus Hunt	.25

1988 Panini Stickers

These stickers, which each measure 2-1/8" x 2-3/4", were made to be stored in a special collector's album which was produced. John Elway is featured on the cover of the album, which has the stickers arranged on pages according to the way they are numbered. The sticker number appears on both sides of the sticker. The front of the sticker has a close-up shot of the player, between two team color-coded bars. His team's name is above the photo; his name is below the photo. The stickers were sold in packs which also included one of three types of foil stickers - team name stickers, team helmet stickers, and team uniform stickers. Each team name sticker was produced with a player sticker, listed in parenthesis. Backs for the team name stickers had a referee signal, while helmet foils had a stadium shot and uniform foils had a mascot cartoon on the back.

		NM/M
Complete Set (447):		35.00
Common Player:		.05
1	Super Bowl XXII Program Cover	.15
2	Bills Helmet	.05
3	Bills Action	.05
4	Cornelius Bennett	.50
5	Chris Burkett	.05
6	Derrick Burroughs	.05
7	Shane Conlan	.25
8	Ronnie Harmon	.25
9	Jim Kelly	.80
10	Buffalo Bills	.05
11	Mark Kelso	.05
12	Nate Odomes	.05
13	Andre Reed	.25
14	Fred Smerlas	.05
15	Bruce Smith	.25
16	Uniform	.05
17	Bengals Helmet	.05
18	Bengals Action	.05
19	Jim Breech	.05
20	James Brooks	.10
21	Eddie Brown	.10
22	Cris Collinsworth	.10
23	Boomer Esiason	.20
24	Rodney Holman	.10
25	Bengals	.05
26	Larry Kinnebrew	.05
27	Tim Krumrie	.05
28	Anthony Munoz	.15
29	Reggie Williams	.10
30	Carl Zander	.05
31	Uniform	.05
32	Browns Helmet	.05
33	Browns Action	.15
34	Earnest Byner	.10
35	Hanford Dixon	.05
36	Bob Golic	.10
37	Mike Johnson	.05
38	Bernie Kosar	.30
39	Kevin Mack	.10
40	Browns	.05
41	Clay Matthews	.15
42	Gerald McNeil	.05
43	Frank Minnifield	.05
44	Ozzie Newsome	.15
45	Cody Risien	.05
46	Uniform	.05
47	Broncos Helmet	.05
48	Broncos Action	.05
49	Keith Bishop	.05
50	Tony Dorsett	.35
51	John Elway	1.25
52	Simon Fletcher	.25
53	Mark Jackson	.10
54	Vance Johnson	.10
55	Broncos	.05
56	Rulon Jones	.05
57	Rick Karlis	.05
58	Karl Mecklenburg	.10
59	Ricky Nattiel	.10
60	Sammy Winder	.05
61	Uniform	.05
62	Oilers Helmet	.05
63	Oilers Action	.25
64	Keith Bostic	.05
65	Steve Brown	.05
66	Ray Childress	.15
67	Jeff Donaldson	.05
68	John Grimsley	.05
69	Robert Lyles	.05
70	Oilers	.05
71	Drew Hill	.10
72	Warren Moon	.85
73	Mike Munchak	.15
74	Mike Rozier	.10
75	Johnny Meads	.05
76	Uniform	.05
77	Colts Helmet	.05
78	Colts Action	.15
79	Albert Bentley	.10
80	Dean Biasucci	.05
81	Duane Bickett	.15
82	Bill Brooks	.15
83	Johnny Cooks	.05
84	Eric Dickerson	.40
85	Colts	.05
86	Ray Donaldson	.05
87	Chris Hinton	.10
88	Cliff Odom	.05
89	Barry Krauss	.10
90	Jack Trudeau	.15
91	Uniform	.05
92	Chiefs Helmet	.05
93	Chiefs Action	.05
94	Carlos Carson	.05
95	Deron Cherry	.10
96	Dino Hackett	.05
97	Bill Kenney	.05
98	Albert Lewis	.10
99	Nick Lowery	.10
100	Chiefs	.05
101	Bill Maas	.05
102	Christian Okoye	.15
103	Stephone Paige	.10
104	Paul Palmer	.05
105	Kevin Ross	.05
106	Uniform	.05
107	Raiders Helmet	.05

No.	Sticker	Price
108	Raiders Action	.25
109	Marcus Allen	.35
110	Todd Christensen	.15
111	Mike Haynes	.15
112	Bo Jackson	.60
113	James Lofton	.20
114	Howie Long	.15
115	Raiders	.05
116	Rod Martin	.05
117	Vann McElroy	.05
118	Bill Pickel	.05
119	Don Mosebar	.05
120	Stacey Toran	.05
121	Uniform	.05
122	Dolphins Helmet	.05
123	Dolphins Action	.05
124	John Bosa	.05
125	Mark Clayton	.15
126	Mark Duper	.10
127	Lorenzo Hampton	.05
128	William Judson	.05
129	Dan Marino	2.50
130	Dolphins	.05
131	John Offerdahl	.10
132	Reggie Roby	.05
133	Jackie Shipp	.05
134	Dwight Stephenson	.10
135	Troy Stradford	.10
136	Uniform	.05
137	Patriots Helmet	.05
138	Patriots Action	.05
139	Bruce Armstrong	.05
140	Raymond Clayborn	.05
141	Reggie Dupard	.05
142	Steve Grogan	.10
143	Craig James	.25
144	Ronnie Lippett	.05
145	Patriots	.05
146	Fred Marion	.05
147	Stanley Morgan	.15
148	Mosi Tatupu	.05
149	Andre Tippett	.10
150	Garin Veris	.05
151	Uniform	.05
152	Jets Helmet	.05
153	Jets Action	.05
154	Bob Crable	.05
155	Mark Gastineau	.10
156	Pat Leahy	.05
157	Johnny Hector	.10
158	Marty Lyons	.10
159	Freeman McNeil	.15
160	Jets	.05
161	Ken O'Brien	.10
162	Mickey Shuler	.05
163	Al Toon	.10
164	Roger Vick	.05
165	Wesley Walker	.10
166	Uniform	.05
167	Steelers Helmet	.05
168	Steelers Action	.05
169	Walter Abercrombie	.05
170	Gary Anderson	.05
171	Todd Blackledge	.05
172	Thomas Everett	.15
173	Delton Hall	.05
174	Bryan Hinkle	.05
175	Steelers	.05
176	Earnest Jackson	.10
177	Louis Lipps	.10
178	David Little	.05
179	Mike Merriweather	.10
180	Mike Webster	.15
181	Uniform	.05
182	Chargers Helmet	.05
183	Chargers Action	.05
184	Gary Anderson	.15
185	Chip Banks	.10
186	Martin Bayless	.05
187	Chuck Ehin	.05
188	Venice Glenn	.05
189	Lionel James	.05
190	Chargers	.05
191	Mark Malone	.05
192	Ralf Mojsiejenko	.05
193	Billy Ray Smith	.10
194	Lee Williams	.15
195	Kellen Winslow	.15
196	Uniform	.05
197	Seahawks Helmet	.05
198	Seahawks Action	.10
199	Eugene Robinson	.05
200	Jeff Bryant	.05
201	Ray Butler	.05
202	Jacob Green	.10
203	Norm Johnson	.10
204	Dave Krieg	.10
205	Seahawks	.05
206	Steve Largent	.75
207	Joe Nash	.05
208	Curt Warner	.10
209	Bobby Joe Edmonds	.10
210	Daryl Turner	.05
211	Uniform	.05
212	AFC Logo	.05
213	Bernie Kosar	.35
214	Curt Warner	.10
215	Jerry Rice, Steve Largent	1.25
216	Mark Bavaro, Anthony Munoz	.15
217	Gary Zimmerman, Bill Fralic	.10
218	Dwight Stephenson, Mike Munchak	.10
219	Joe Montana	3.00
220	Charles White, Eric Dickerson	.40
221	Morten Andersen, Vai Sikahema	.10
222	Bruce Smith, Reggie White	.30
223	Michael Carter, Steve McMichael	.10
224	Jim Arnold	.05
225	Carl Banks, Andre Tippett	.10
226	Barry Wilburn, Mike Singletary	.10
227	Hanford Dixon, Frank Minnifield	.05
228	Ronnie Lott, Joey Browner	.15
229	NFC Logo	.05
230	Gary Clark	.15
231	Richard Dent	.15
232	Falcons Helmet	.05
233	Falcons Action	.05
234	Rick Bryan	.10
235	Bobby Butler	.05
236	Tony Casillas	.15
237	Floyd Dixon	.05
238	Rick Donnelly	.05
239	Bill Fralic	.10
240	Falcons	.05
241	Mike Gann	.05
242	Chris Miller	.40
243	Robert Moore	.05
244	John Rade	.05
245	Gerald Riggs	.10
246	Uniform	.05
247	Bears Helmet	.05
248	Bears Action	.15
249	Neal Anderson	.30
250	Jim Covert	.10
251	Richard Dent	.15
252	Dave Duerson	.05
253	Dennis Gentry	.05
254	Jay Hilgenberg	.10
255	Bears	.05
256	Jim McMahon	.20
257	Steve McMichael	.10
258	Matt Suhey	.05
259	Mike Singletary	.20
260	Otis Wilson	.10
261	Uniform	.05
262	Cowboys Helmet	.05
263	Cowboys Action	.15
264	Bill Bates	.10
265	Doug Crosbie	.05
266	Ron Francis	.05
267	Jim Jeffcoat	.15
268	Ed "Too Tall" Jones	.20
269	Eugene Lockhart	.05
270	Cowboys	.05
271	Danny Noonan	.05
272	Steve Pelleur	.10
273	Herschel Walker	.10
274	Everson Walls	.20
275	Randy White	.05
276	Uniform	.05
277	Lions Helmet	.05
278	Lions Action	.05
279	Jim Arnold	.10
280	Jerry Ball	.05
281	Michael Cofer	.05
282	Keith Ferguson	.05
283	Dennis Gibson	.05
284	James Griffin	.05
285	Lions	.05
286	James Jones	.10
287	Chuck Long	.10
288	Pete Mandley	.05
289	Eddie Murray	.05
290	Garry James	.05
291	Uniform	.05
292	Packers Helmet	.05
293	Packers Action	.05
294	John Anderson	.05
295	Dave Brown	.10
296	Alphonso Carreker	.05
297	Kenneth Davis	.20
298	Phillip Epps	.05
299	Brent Fullwood	.05
300	Packers	.05
301	Tim Harris	.15
302	Johnny Holland	.10
303	Mark Murphy	.05
304	Brian Noble	.05
305	Walter Stanley	.10
306	Uniform	.05
307	Rams Helmet	.05
308	Rams Action	.10
309	Jim Collins	.05
310	Henry Ellard	.15
311	Jim Everett	.30
312	Jerry Gray	.05
313	LeRoy Irvin	.05
314	Mike Lansford	.05
315	Los Angeles Rams	.05
316	Mel Owens	.05
317	Jackie Slater	.10
318	Doug Smith	.05
319	Charles White	.10
320	Mike Wilcher	.05
321	Uniform	.05
322	Vikings Helmet	.05
323	Vikings Action	.05
324	Joey Browner	.10
325	Anthony Carter	.15
326	Chris Doleman	.15
327	D.J. Dozier	.10
328	Steve Jordan	.10
329	Tommy Kramer	.10
330	Vikings	.05
331	Darrin Nelson	.10
332	Jesse Solomon	.10
333	Scott Studwell	.10
334	Wade Wilson	.35
335	Gary Zimmerman	.05
336	Uniform	.05
337	Saints Helmet	.05
338	Saints Action	.15
339	Morten Andersen	.10
340	Bruce Clark	.05
341	Brad Edelman	.05
342	Bobby Hebert	.15
343	Dalton Hilliard	.10
344	Rickey Jackson	.15
345	Saints	.05
346	Vaughan Johnson	.10
347	Rueben Mayes	.10
348	Sam Mills	.10
349	Lionel Manuel	.35
350	Dave Waymer	.05
351	Uniform	.05
352	Giants Helmet	.05
353	Giants Action	.05
354	Carl Banks	.15
355	Mark Bavaro	.15
356	Jim Burt	.05
357	Harry Carson	.10
358	Terry Kinard	.05
359	Lionel Manuel	.05
360	Giants	.05
361	Leonard Marshall	.10
362	George Martin	.05
363	Joe Morris	.10
364	Phil Simms	.50
365	George Adams	.05
366	Uniform	.05
367	Eagles Helmet	.05
368	Eagles Action	.25
369	Jerome Brown	.30
370	Keith Byars	.15
371	Randall Cunningham	.40
372	Terry Hoage	.05
373	Seth Joyner	.20
374	Mike Quick	.15
375	Eagles	.05
376	Clyde Simmons	.20
377	Anthony Toney	.05
378	Andre Waters	.10
379	Reggie White	.35
380	Roynell Young	.05
381	Uniform	.05
382	Cardinals Helmet	.05
383	Cardinals Action	.05
384	Robert Awalt	.05
385	Roy Green	.15
386	Neil Lomax	.10
387	Stump Mitchell	.10
388	Niko Noga	.06
389	Freddie Joe Nunn	.05
390	Cardinals	.05
391	Luis Sharpe	.10
392	Vai Sikahema	.10
393	J.T. Smith	.10
394	Leonard Smith	.05
395	Lonnie Young	.05
396	Uniform	.05
397	49ers Helmet	.05
398	49ers Action	1.50
399	Dwaine Board	.05
400	Michael Carter	.10
401	Roger Craig	.25
402	Jeff Fuller	.05
403	Don Griffin	.05
404	Ronnie Lott	.20
405	49ers	.05
406	Joe Montana	3.00
407	Tom Rathman	.25
408	Jerry Rice	1.50
409	Keena Turner	.05
410	Michael Walter	.05
411	Uniform	.05
412	Bucs Helmet	.05
413	Bucs Action	.05
414	Mark Carrier	.25
415	Gerald Carter	.05
416	Ron Holmes	.10
417	Rod Jones	.05
418	Calvin Magee	.05
419	Ervin Randle	.05
420	Buccaneers	.05
421	Donald Igwebuike	.05
422	Vinny Testaverde	.25
423	Jackie Walker	.05
424	Chris Washington	.05
425	James Wilder	.10
426	Uniform	.05
427	Redskins Helmet	.05
428	Redskins Action	.10
429	Gary Clark	.15
430	Monte Coleman	.05
431	Darrell Green	.10
432	Charles Mann	.10
433	Kelvin Bryant	.10
434	Art Monk	.25
435	Redskins	.05
436	Ricky Sanders	.15
437	Jay Schroeder	.15
438	Alvin Walton	.05
439	Barry Wilburn	.10
440	Doug Williams	.10
441	Uniform	.05
442	Super Bowl Action	.05
443	Super Bowl Action	.05
444	Doug Williams (Super Bowl MVP)	.15
445	Super Bowl Action	.05
446	Super Bowl Action	.05
447	Super Bowl Action	.05
----	Panini Album (John Elway on cover)	2.00

1989 Panini Stickers

These 1989 stickers from Panini are slightly larger than those issued in 1988, measuring 1-15/16" x 3."

		NM/M
Complete Set (416):		30.00
Common Player:		.05
1	SB XXIII Program	.10
2	SB XXIII Program	.05
3	Floyd Dixon	.05
4	Tony Casillas	.10
5	Bill Fralic	.10
6	Aundray Bruce	.05
7	Scott Case	.05
8	Rick Donnelly	.05
9	Atlanta logo	.05
10	Helmet	.05
11	Marcus Cotton	.05
12	Chris Miller	.25
13	Robert Moore	.05
14	Bobby Butler	.05
15	Rick Bryan	.05
16	John Settle	.10
17	Jim McMahon	.15
18	Neal Anderson	.15
19	Dave Duerson	.05
20	Steve McMichael	.05
21	Jay Hilgenberg	.05
22	Dennis McKinnon	.05
23	Chicago logo	.05
24	Helmet	.05
25	Richard Dent	.15
26	Dennis Gentry	.05
27	Mike Singletary	.15
28	Vestee Jackson	.05
29	Mike Tomczak	.15
30	Dan Hampton	.15
31	Michael Irvin	1.75
32	Eugene Lockhart	.10
33	Herschel Walker	.30
34	Kelvin Martin	.15
35	Jim Jeffcoat	.10
36	Everson Walls	.10
37	Dallas logo	.05
38	Helmet	.05
39	Danny Noonan	.05
40	Ray Alexander	.05
41	Garry Cobb	.05
42	Ed "Too Tall" Jones	.15
43	Kevin Brooks	.05
44	Bill Bates	.10
45	Detroit logo	.05
46	Chuck Long	.10
47	Jim Arnold	.05
48	Michael Cofer	.05
49	Eddie Murray	.05
50	Keith Ferguson	.05
51	Pete Mandley	.05
52	Helmet	.05
53	Jerry Ball	.05
54	Bennie Blades	.15
55	Dennis Gibson	.05
56	Chris Spielman	.15
57	Eric Williams	.05
58	Lomas Brown	.05
59	Johnny Holland	.10
60	Tim Harris	.15
61	Mark Murphy	.05
62	Walter Stanley	.10
63	Brent Fullwood	.05
64	Ken Ruettgers	.10
65	Green Bay logo	.05
66	Helmet	.05
67	John Anderson	.05
68	Brian Noble	.05
69	Sterling Sharpe	1.50
70	Keith Woodside	.10
71	Mark Lee	.05
72	Don Majkowski	.15
73	Aaron Cox	.10
74	LeRoy Irvin	.05
75	Jim Everett	.15
76	Mike Lansford	.05
77	Mike Wilcher	.05
78	Henry Ellard	.10
79	Rams helmet	.05
80	Jerry Gray	.05
81	Doug Smith	.05
82	Tom Newberry	.10
83	Jackie Slater	.10
84	Greg Bell	.10
85	Kevin Greene	.10
86	Chris Doleman	.10
87	Steve Jordan	.10
88	Jesse Solomon	.05
89	Randall McDaniel	.05
90	Hassan Jones	.10
91	Joey Browner	.10
92	Vikings logo	.05
93	Helmet	.05
94	Anthony Carter	.10
95	Gary Zimmerman	.05
96	Wade Wilson	.15
97	Scott Studwell	.10
98	Keith Millard	.10
99	Carl Lee	.10
100	Morten Andersen	.10
101	Bobby Hebert	.15
102	Rueben Mayes	.10
103	Sam Mills	.10
104	Vaughan Johnson	.10
105	Pat Swilling	.15
106	Saints logo	.05
107	Helmet	.05
108	Brad Edelman	.05
109	Craig Heyward	.15
110	Eric Martin	.10
111	Dalton Hilliard	.10
112	Lonzell Hill	.05
113	Rickey Jackson	.10
114	Erik Howard	.05
115	Phil Simms	.35
116	Leonard Marshall	.10
117	Joe Morris	.10
118	Bart Oates	.10
119	Mark Bavaro	.10
120	Giants logo	.05
121	Helmet	.05
122	Terry Kinard	.05
123	Carl Banks	.10
124	Lionel Manuel	.05
125	Stephen Baker	.15
126	Pepper Johnson	.10
127	Jim Burt	.05
128	Cris Carter	.35
129	Mike Quick	.10
130	Terry Hoage	.05
131	Keith Jackson	.80
132	Clyde Simmons	.15
133	Eric Allen	.05
134	Eagles logo	.05
135	Helmet	.05
136	Randall Cunningham	.40
137	Mike Pitts	.05
138	Keith Byars	.10
139	Seth Joyner	.15
140	Jerome Brown	.15
141	Reggie White	.30
142	Jay Novacek	.30
143	Neil Lomax	.10
144	Ken Harvey	.10
145	Freddie Joe Nunn	.05
146	Robert Awalt	.05
147	Niko Noga	.05
148	Phoenix logo	.05
149	Helmet	.05
150	Tim McDonald	.25
151	Roy Green	.10
152	Stump Mitchell	.10
153	J.T. Smith	.10
154	Luis Sharpe	.05
155	Vai Sikhema	.10
156	Jeff Fuller	.05
157	Joe Montana	3.00
158	Harris Barton	.05
159	Michael Carter	.10
160	Jeff Fuller	.05
161	Jerry Rice	2.00
162	49ers logo	.05
163	Helmet	.05
164	Tom Rathman	.15
165	Roger Craig	.20
166	Ronnie Lott	.30
167	Charles Haley	.15
168	John Taylor	.50
169	Michael Walter	.05
170	Ron Hall	.05
171	Ervin Randle	.05
172	James Wilder	.10
173	Ron Holmes	.05
174	Mark Carrier	.15
175	William Howard	.05
176	Tampa Bay logo	.05
177	Helmet	.05
178	Lars Tate	.05
179	Vinny Testaverde	.20
180	Paul Gruber	.15
181	Bruce Hill	.10
182	Reuben Davis	.05
183	Ricky Reynolds	.05
184	Ricky Sanders	.15
185	Gary Clark	.15
186	Mark May	.05
187	Darrell Green	.10
188	Jim Lachey	.10
189	Doug Williams	.10
190	Helmet	.05
191	Redskins logo	.05
192	Kelvin Bryant	.05
193	Charles Mann	.05
194	Alvin Walton	.05
195	Art Monk	.20
196	Barry Wilburn	.05
197	Mark Rypien	.25
198	NFC logo	.05
199	Scott Case	.05
200	Herschel Walker	.30
201	Herschel Walker, Roger Craig	.25
202	Henry Ellard, Jerry Rice	.65
203	Bruce Matthews, Tom Newberry	.05
204	Gary Zimmerman, Anthony Munoz	.10
205	Boomer Esiason	.15
206	Jay Hilgenberg	.10
207	Keith Jackson	.25
208	Reggie White, Bruce Smith	.25
209	Keith Millard, Tim Krumrie	.10
210	Carl Lee, Frank Minnifield	.05
211	Joey Browner, Deron Cherry	.10
212	Shane Conlan	.10
213	Mike Singletary	.15
214	Cornelius Bennett	.10
215	AFC logo	.05
216	Boomer Esiason	.25
217	Erik McMillan	.10
218	Jim Kelly	.60
219	Cornelius Bennett	.15
220	Fred Smerlas	.10
221	Shane Conlan	.10
222	Scott Norwood	.05
223	Mark Kelso	.05
224	Bills logo	.05
225	Helmet	.05
226	Thurman Thomas	1.50
227	Pete Metzelaars	.05
228	Bruce Smith	.25
229	Art Still	.10
230	Kent Hull	.10
231	Andre Reed	.25
232	Tim Krumrie	.05
233	Boomer Esiason	.25
234	Ickey Woods	.10
235	Eric Thomas	.10
236	Rodney Holman	.10
237	Jim Skow	.05
238	Bengals helmet	.05
239	James Brooks	.10
240	David Fulcher	.10
241	Carl Zander	.05
242	Eddie Brown	.10
243	Max Montoya	.05
244	Anthony Munoz	.15
245	Felix Wright	.05
246	Clay Matthews	.15
247	Hanford Dixon	.05
248	Ozzie Newsome	.15
249	Bernie Kosar	.25
250	Kevin Mack	.10
251	Bengals Helmet	.05
252	Brian Brennan	.05
253	Reggie Langhorne	.05
254	Cody Risien	.05
255	Webster Slaughter	.15
256	Mike Johnson	.05
257	Frank Minnifield	.05
258	Mike Horan	.05
259	Dennis Smith	.10
260	Ricky Nattiel	.05
261	Karl Mecklenburg	.10
262	Keith Bishop	.05
263	John Elway	1.50
264	Broncos helmet	.05
265	Broncos logo	.05
266	Simon Fletcher	.15
267	Vance Johnson	.10
268	Tony Dorsett	.35
269	Greg Kragen	.10
270	Mike Harden	.05
271	Mark Jackson	.05
272	Warren Moon	.75
273	Mike Rozier	.10
274	Houston logo	.05
275	Allen Pinkett	.10
276	Tony Zendejas	.05
277	Alonzo Highsmith	.10
278	Johnny Meads	.05
279	Helmet	.05
280	Mike Munchak	.10
281	John Grimsley	.05
282	Ernest Givins	.15
283	Drew Hill	.10
284	Bruce Matthews	.10
285	Ray Childress	.10
286	Colts logo	.05
287	Chris Hinton	.10
288	Clarence Verdin	.10
289	Jon Hand	.15
290	Chris Chandler	.15
291	Eugene Daniel	.05
292	Dean Biasucci	.05
293	Helmet	.05
294	Duane Bickett	.10
295	Rohn Stark	.05
296	Albert Bentley	.10
297	Bill Brooks	.10
298	O'Brien Alston	.05
299	Ray Donaldson	.05
300	Carlos Carson	.05
301	Lloyd Burruss	.05
302	Steve DeBerg	.15
303	Irv Eatman	.05
304	Dino Hackett	.05
305	Albert Lewis	.10
306	Chiefs helmet	.05
307	Chiefs logo	.05
308	Deron Cherry	.10
309	Paul Palmer	.05
310	Neil Smith	.40
311	Christian Okoye	.10
312	Stephone Paige	.10
313	Bill Maas	.05
314	Marcus Allen	.40
315	Vann McElroy	.05
316	Mervyn Fernandez	.10
317	Bill Pickel	.05
318	Greg Townsend	.10
319	Tim Brown	1.25
320	Raiders logo	.05
321	Helmet	.05
322	James Lofton	.15
323	Willie Gault	.10
324	Jay Schroeder	.10
325	Matt Millen	.05
326	Howie Long	.10
327	Bo Jackson	.50
328	Lorenzo Hampton	.05
329	Jarvis Williams	.05
330	Jim C. Jensen	.05
331	Dan Marino	2.50
332	John Offerdahl	.10
333	Brian Sochia	.05
334	Miami logo	.05
335	Helmet	.05
336	Ferrell Edmunds	.05
337	Mark Brown	.05
338	Mark Duper	.05
339	Troy Stradford	.05
340	T.J. Turner	.05
341	Mark Clayton	.15
342	Patriots logo	.05
343	Johnny Rembert	.05
344	Garin Veris	.05
345	Stanley Morgan	.10
346	John Stephens	.15
347	Fred Marion	.05
348	Irving Fryar	.15
349	Helmet	.05
350	Andre Tippett	.10
351	Roland James	.05
352	Brent Williams	.05
353	Raymond Clayborn	.05
354	Tony Eason	.10
355	Bruce Armstrong	.05
356	Jets logo	.05
357	Marty Lyons	.10
358	Bobby Humphrey	.05
359	Pat Leahy	.05
360	Mickey Shuler	.05
361	James Hasty	.05
362	Ken O'Brien	.10
363	Helmet	.05
364	Alex Gordon	.05
365	Al Toon	.10
366	Erik McMillan	.10
367	Johnny Hector	.10
368	Wesley Walker	.10
369	Freeman McNeil	.10
370	Steelers logo	.05

371 Gary Anderson .05
372 Rodney Carter .05
373 Merril Hoge .10
374 David Little .05
375 Bubby Brister .15
376 Thomas Everett .10
377 Helmet .05
378 Rod Woodson .40
379 Bryan Hinkle .05
380 Tunch Ilkin .05
381 Aaron Jones .05
382 Louis Lipps .10
383 Warren Williams .05
384 Anthony Miller .75
385 Gary Anderson .15
386 Lee Williams .10
387 Lionel James .10
388 Gary Plummer .05
389 Gill Byrd .10
390 Chargers helmet .05
391 Ralf Mojsiejenko .05
392 Rod Bernstine .25
393 Keith Browner .05
394 Billy Ray Smith .10
395 Leslie O'Neal .15
396 Jamie Holland .05
397 Tony Woods .10
398 Bruce Scholtz .05
399 Joe Nash .05
400 Curt Warner .10
401 John L. Williams .10
402 Bryan Millard .05
403 Seahawks logo .05
404 Helmet .05
405 Steve Largent .30
406 Norm Johnson .10
407 Jacob Green .10
408 Dave Krieg .10
409 Paul Moyer .05
410 Brian Blades .50
411 SB XXIII .05
412 Jerry Rice 1.50
413 SB XXIII .10
414 SB XXIII .10
415 SB XXIII .10
416 SB XXIII .10
---- Panini Album (Joe Montana on conver) 4.00

1990 Panini Stickers

These stickers were intended to be stored in an album titled "The Hitters." Ronnie Lott, Mike Singletary and Lawrence Taylor are featured on the album cover. The stickers measure 1-7/8" x 2-15/16" and have a color action photo on the front, using a design distinctly different from those used the two years before.

NM/M
Complete Set (396): 20.00
Common Player: .05
1 Super Bowl XXIV Program Cover (top) .15
2 Super Bowl XXIV Program Cover (bottom) .10
3 Bills Crest .05
4 Thurman Thomas .50
5 Nate Odomes .05
6 Jim Kelly .45
7 Cornelius Bennett .20
8 Scott Norwood .05
9 Mark Kelso .05
10 Kent Hull .05
11 Jim Ritcher .05
12 Darryl Talley .10
13 Bruce Smith .15
14 Shane Conlan .10
15 Andre Reed .15
16 Jason Buck .05
17 David Fulcher .10
18 Jim Skow .05
19 Anthony Munoz .15
20 Eric Thomas .05
21 Eric Ball .05
22 Tim Krumrie .05
23 James Brooks .10
24 Bengals Crest .05
25 Rodney Holman .05
26 Boomer Esiason .25
27 Eddie Brown .10
28 Tim McGee .10
29 Browns Crest .05
30 Mike Johnson .05
31 David Grayson .05
32 Thane Gash .05
33 Robert Banks .05
34 Eric Metcalf .20
35 Kevin Mack .10
36 Reggie Langhorne .05
37 Webster Slaughter .10
38 Felix Wright .05
39 Bernie Kosar .25
40 Frank Minnifield .05
41 Clay Matthews .15
42 Vance Johnson .10
43 Ron Holmes .05
44 Melvin Bratton .10
45 Greg Kragen .05
46 Karl Mecklenburg .10
47 Dennis Smith .10
48 Bobby Humphrey .10
49 Simon Fletcher .10
50 Broncos Crest .05
51 Michael Brooks .05
52 Steve Atwater .10
53 John Elway .80
54 David Treadwell .05
55 Oilers Crest .05
56 Bubba McDowell .05
57 Ray Childress .10
58 Bruce Matthews .05
59 Allen Pinkett .10
60 Warren Moon .55
61 John Grimsley .05
62 Alonzo Highsmith .10
63 Mike Munchak .10
64 Ernest Givins .10
65 Johnny Meads .05
66 Drew Hill .10
67 William Fuller .05
68 Duane Bickett .10
69 Jack Trudeau .10
70 Jon Hand .10
71 Chris Hinton .10
72 Bill Brooks .10
73 Donnell Thompson .05
74 Jeff Herrod .05
75 Andre Rison .25
76 Colts Crest .05
77 Chris Chandler .10
78 Ray Donaldson .05
79 Albert Bentley .10
80 Keith Taylor .05
81 Chiefs Crest .05
82 Leonard Griffin .05
83 Dino Hackett .05
84 Christian Okoye .10
85 Chris Martin .10
86 John Alt .05
87 Kevin Ross .05
88 Steve DeBerg .05
89 Albert Lewis .10
90 Stephone Paige .05
91 Derrick Thomas .40
92 Neil Smith .15
93 Pete Mandley .05
94 Howie Long .10
95 Greg Townsend .05
96 Mervyn Fernandez .10
97 Scott Davis .05
98 Steve Beuerlein .40
99 Mike Dyal .05
100 Willie Gault .10
101 Eddie Anderson .05
102 Raiders Crest .05
103 Trey McDaniel .05
104 Bo Jackson .30
105 Steve Wisniewski .05
106 Steve Smith .10
107 Dolphins Crest .05
108 Mark Clayton .15
109 Louis Oliver .10
110 Jarvis Williams .05
111 Ferrell Edmunds .05
112 Jeff Cross .05
113 John Offerdahl .10
114 Brian Sochia .05
115 Dan Marino 2.00
116 Jim C. Jensen .05
117 Sammie Smith .05
118 Reggie Roby .05
119 Roy Foster .05
120 Bruce Armstrong .05
121 Steve Grogan .10
122 Hart Lee Dykes .05
123 Andre Tippett .10
124 Johnny Rembert .05
125 Ed Reynolds .05
126 Cedric Jones .05
127 Vincent Brown .05
128 Patriots Crest .05
129 Brent Williams .05
130 John Stephens .10
131 Eric Sievers .05
132 Maurice Hurst .05
133 Jets Crest .05
134 Johnny Hector .10
135 Eric McMillan .05
136 Jeff Lageman .05
137 Al Toon .10
138 James Hasty .05
139 Kyle Clifton .05
140 Ken O'Brien .10
141 Jim Sweeney .05
142 JoJo Townsell .10
143 Dennis Byrd .20
144 Mickey Shuler .10
145 Alex Gordon .05
146 Keith Willis .05
147 Louis Lipps .10
148 David Little .05
149 Greg Lloyd .05
150 Carnell Lake .05
151 Tim Worley .10
152 Dwayne Woodruff .05
153 Gerald Williams .05
154 Steelers Crest .05
155 Merril Hoge .10
156 Bubby Brister .10
157 Tunch Ilkin .05
158 Rod Woodson .15
159 Charger Crest .05
160 Leslie O'Neal .10
161 Billy Ray Smith .05
162 Marion Butts .15
163 Lee Williams .10
164 Gill Byrd .10
165 Jim McMahon .15
166 Courtney Hall .05
167 Burt Grossman .15
168 Gary Plummer .05
169 Anthony Miller .40
170 Billy Joe Tolliver .15
171 Venice Glenn .05
172 Andy Heck .05
173 Brian Blades .15
174 Bryan Millard .05
175 Tony Woods .05
176 Rufus Porter .05
177 Dave Wyman .05
178 John L. Williams .10
179 Jacob Green .05
180 Seahawks Crest .05
181 Eugene Robinson .05
182 Jeff Bryant .05
183 Dave Krieg .10
184 Joe Nash .05
185 Christian Okoye .05
186 Felix Wright .05
187 Rod Woodson .10
188 Barry Sanders, Christian Okoye .75
189 Jerry Rice, Sterling Sharpe 1.00
190 Bruce Matthews .05
191 Jay Hilgenberg .05
192 Tom Newbury .05
193 Anthony Munoz .10
194 Jim Lachey .05
195 Keith Jackson .15
196 Joe Montana 1.50
197 David Fulcher, Ronnie Lott .10
198 Albert Lewis, Eric Allen .05
199 Reggie White .20
200 Keith Millard .05
201 Chris Doleman .05
202 Mike Singletary .15
203 Tim Harris .05
204 Lawrence Taylor .20
205 Rich Camarrilo .05
206 Sterling Sharpe .25
207 Chris Doleman .05
208 Barry Sanders .55
209 Falcons Crest .05
210 Michael Haynes .30
211 Scott Case .05
212 Marcus Cotton .05
213 Chris Miller .15
214 Keith Jones .05
215 Tim Green .05
216 Deion Sanders .50
217 Shawn Collins .10
218 John Settle .05
219 Bill Fralic .05
220 Aundray Bruce .05
221 Jessie Tuggle .05
222 James Thornton .05
223 Dennis Gentry .05
224 Richard Dent .15
225 Jay Hilgenberg .05
226 Steve McMichael .05
227 Brad Muster .10
228 Donnell Woodford .05
229 Mike Singletary .15
230 Bears Crest .05
231 Mark Bortz .05
232 Kevin Butler .05
233 Neal Anderson .10
234 Trace Armstrong .05
235 Cowboys Crest .05
236 Mark Tuinei .10
237 Tony Tolbert .05
238 Eugene Lockhart .10
239 Daryl Johnston .25
240 Troy Aikman 3.00
241 Jim Jeffcoat .10
242 James Dixon .05
243 Jesse Solomon .05
244 Ken Norton .25
245 Kelvin Martin .05
246 Danny Noonan .05
247 Michael Irvin .50
248 Eric Williams .05
249 Richard Johnson .05
250 Michael Cofer .05
251 Chris Spielman .10
252 Rodney Peete .20
253 Bennie Blades .10
254 Jerry Ball .10
255 Eddie Murray .08
256 Lions Crest .05
257 Barry Sanders 1.75
258 Jerry Holmes .05
259 Dennis Gibson .05
260 Lomas Brown .05
261 Packers Crest .05
262 Dave Brown .05
263 Mark Murphy .05
264 Perry Kemp .05
265 Don Majkowski .10
266 Chris Jacke .05
267 Keith Woodside .10
268 Tony Mandarich .10
269 Robert Brown .05
270 Sterling Sharpe .75
271 Tim Harris .10
272 Brent Fullwood .05
273 Brian Noble .05
274 Alvin Wright .05
275 Flipper Anderson .10
276 Jackie Slater .10
277 Kevin Greene .10
278 Pete Holohan .05
279 Tom Newberry .05
280 Jerry Gray .05
281 Henry Ellard .10
282 Rams Crest .05
283 LeRoy Irvin .05
284 Jim Everett .15
285 Greg Bell .10
286 Doug Smith .05
287 Vikings Crest .05
288 Joey Browner .10
289 Wade Wilson .15
290 Chris Doleman .10
291 Al Noga .05
292 Herschel Walker .20
293 Henry Thomas .10
294 Steve Jordan .10
295 Anthony Carter .10
296 Keith Millard .10
297 Carl Lee .05
298 Randall McDaniel .05
299 Gary Zimmerman .05
300 Morten Andersen .05
301 Rickey Jackson .10
302 Sam Mills .05
303 Hoby Brenner .05
304 Dalton Hilliard .05
305 Robert Massey .05
306 John Fourcade .10
307 Lonzell Hill .05
308 Saints Crest .05
309 Jim Dombrowski .05
310 Pat Swilling .15
311 Vaughan Johnson .05
312 Eric Martin .10
313 Giants Crest .05
314 Ottis Anderson .10
315 Myron Guyton .05
316 Terry Kinard .05
317 Mark Bavaro .10
318 Phil Simms .25
319 Lawrence Taylor .30
320 Odessa Turner .05
321 Erik Howard .05
322 Mark Collins .05
323 Dave Meggett .15
324 Leonard Marshall .05
325 Carl Banks .10
326 Anthony Toney .05
327 Seth Joyner .15
328 Cris Carter .20
329 Eric Allen .05
330 Keith Jackson .20
331 Clyde Simmons .10
332 Byron Evans .05
333 Keith Byars .10
334 Eagles Crest .05
335 Reggie White .25
336 Izel Jenkins .05
337 Jerome Brown .15
338 David Alexander .05
339 Cardinals Crest .05
340 Rich Camarillo .05
341 Ken Harvey .05
342 Luis Sharpe .05
343 Timm Rosenbach .10
344 Tim McDonald .15
345 Vai Sikahema .05
346 Freddie Joe Nunn .05
347 Ernie Jones .05
348 J.T. Smith .10
349 Eric Hill .05
350 Roy Green .10
351 Anthony Bell .05
352 Kevin Fagan .05
353 Roger Craig .15
354 Ronnie Lott .20
355 Mike Cofer .05
356 John Taylor .20
357 Joe Montana 3.00
358 Charles Haley .10
359 Guy McIntyre .05
360 49ers Crest .05
361 Pierce Holt .15
362 Tom Rathman .15
363 Jerry Rice 1.50
364 Michael Carter .10
365 Buccaneers Crest .05
366 Lars Tate .05
367 Paul Gruber .10
368 Winston Moss .05
369 Reuben Davis .05
370 Mark Robinson .05
371 Bruce Hill .05
372 Kevin Murphy .05
373 Ricky Reynolds .05
374 Harry Hamilton .05
375 Vinny Testaverde .15
376 Mark Carrier .15
377 Ervin Randle .05
378 Ricky Sanders .10
379 Charles Mann .10
380 Jim Lachey .10
381 Wilber Marshall .10
382 A.J. Johnson .10
383 Darrell Green .10
384 Mark Rypien .15
385 Gerald Riggs .10
386 Redskins Crest .05
387 Alvin Walton .05
388 Art Monk .15
389 Gary Clark .15
390 Earnest Byner .10
391 SB XXIV Action (Jerry Rice) .75
392 SB XXIV Action (49er Offensive Line) .15
393 SB XXIV Action (Tom Rathman) .25
394 SB XXIV Action (Chet Brooks) .10
395 SB XXIV Action (John Elway) 1.00
396 SB XXIV Action (Joe Montana) 3.00
---- Panini Album 2.00

1995 Panthers SkyBox

The Panthers' inaugural season is commemorated on this 21-card set. The card fronts feature a full-bleed photo, with the player's name and position listed on a team-colored band near the bottom. The Panther logo is featured next to the name. The backs include a photo on the right, with the player's name, bio and highlights inside a box on the left. The card number is printed inside a circle in the upper right. Stats are located in the lower right.

NM/M
Complete Set (21): 15.00
Common Player: .75
1 John Kasay .75
2 Kerry Collins 4.00
3 Frank Reich 1.25
4 Rod Smith .75
5 Tim McKyer .75
6 Randy Baldwin .75
7 Bubba McDowell .75
8 Tyrone Poole 1.00
9 Sam Mills 1.00
10 Carlton Bailey .75
11 Darion Conner .75
12 Lamar Lathon .75
13 Blake Brockermeyer 1.00
14 Mike Fox .75
15 Don Beebe 1.00
16 Mark Carrier 1.00
17 Pete Metzelaars .75
18 Shawn King .75
19 Howard Griffith .75
20 Bob Christian 1.00
NNO Cover Card (checklist back) .75

1996 Panthers Fleer/SkyBox Impact Promo Sheet

This six-card promo sheet was distributed by Fleer/SkyBox at the NFL Experience Card Show in Charlotte in 1996. It features six players from the Carolina Panthers.

NM/M
1 Tim Biakabutuka, Lamar Lathon, Muhsin Muhammad, Kerry Collins, Tyrone Poole, Mark Carrier WR Promo Sheet 5.00

1974 Parker Brothers Pro Draft

These 50 cards were included inside a Parker Brothers board game called Pro Draft. The cards, featuring only offensive players, were produced by Topps and use the identical design as the 1974 Topps set. However, some differences can be noted on certain cards. Some of the game cards have 1972 statistics on the card backs, and others have different player poses on the front (#s 23, 49, 116, 124, 126 and 127). Players with an * have 1972 statistics. Card numbers in this set are identical to the card numbers the players have in the regular 1974 Topps set.

NM/M
Complete Set (50): 75.00
Common Player: 1.25
4 Ken Bowman 1.25
6 Jerry Smith 3.00
7 Ed Podolak 2.50
9 Pat Matson 1.25
11 Frank Pitts 2.00
15 Winston Hill 1.25
18 Rich Coady 2.00
19 Ken Willard 3.75
21 Ben Hawkins 2.00
23 Norm Snead (vertical pose) 10.00
24 Jim Yarborough 2.00
28 Bob Hayes 5.00
32 Dan Dierdorf 8.00
35 Essex Johnson 2.00
39 Mike Siani 1.25
42 Del Williams 1.25
43 Don McCauley 2.00
44 Randy Jackson 2.00
46 Gene Washington 3.50
49 Bob Windsor (vertical pose) 6.00
50 John Hadl 4.00
52 Steve Owens 4.00
54 Rayfield Wright 2.00
57 Milt Sunde 2.00
58 Bill Kilmer 5.50
61 Rufus Mayes 2.00
63 Gene Washington 2.50
65 Eugene Upshaw 4.50
75 Fred Willis 2.00
77 Tom Neville 1.25
78 Ted Kwalick 3.00
80 John Niland 2.00
81 Ted Fritsch Jr. 1.25
83 Jack Snow 3.00
87 Mike Phipps 3.00
90 MacArthur Lane 3.00
95 Calvin Hill 3.50
98 Len Rohde 1.25
101 Gary Garrison 2.50
103 Len St. Jean 1.25
107 Jim Mitchell 2.00
109 Harry Schuh 1.25
110 Greg Pruitt 5.00
111 Ed Flanagan 1.25
113 Chuck Foreman 6.00
116 Charlie Johnson (vertical pose) 8.00
119 Roy Jefferson 4.00
124 Forrest Blue (not All-Pro on card) 6.00
126 Tom Mack (not All-Pro on card) 8.00
127 Bob Tucker (not All-Pro on card) 6.00

1989 Parker Brothers Talking Football

Licensed by the NFL Players Association, the 34-card set features a "Superstar Lineup Talking Football" logo in the upper left. Up to three player photos can appear on the front of the card. The NFLPA logo also appears on the front of the card. The backs of the cards, which are unnumbered, include the name of player(s), bio and highlights. The bottom right of the card back carries a Parker Brothers copyright.

NM/M
Complete Set (34): 90.00
Common Player: 2.00
1 AFC Team Roster 2.00
2 Marcus Allen 5.00
3 Cornelius Bennett, John Offerdahl 3.00
4 Keith Bishop, Mike Munchak 2.00
5 Keith Bostic, Deron Cherry, Hanford Dixon 2.00
6 Carlos Carson, Stanley Morgan 2.00
7 Todd Christensen, Mickey Shuler 2.50
8 Eric Dickerson 4.00
9 Ray Donaldson, Irving Fryar 2.00
10 Jacob Green, Bruce Smith 2.00
11 Mark Haynes, Frank Minnifield, Dennis Smith 2.00
12 Chris Hinton, Anthony Munoz 2.50
13 Steve Largent, Al Toon 5.00
14 Howie Long, Bill Maas 3.00
15 Nick Lowery, Reggie Roby 2.00
16 Dan Marino 25.00
17 Karl Mecklenburg, Andre Tippett 2.50
18 NFC Team Roster 2.00
19 Morten Andersen, Jim Arnold 2.00
20 Carl Banks, Mike Singletary 3.00
21 Mark Bavaro, Doug Cosbie 2.50
22 Joey Browner, Darrell Green, Leonard Smith 2.00
23 Anthony Carter, Jerry Rice 12.00
24 Gary Clark, Mike Quick 4.00
25 Richard Dent, Chris Doleman 3.00
26 Brad Edelman, Bill Fralic 2.00
27 Carl Ekern, Rickey Jackson 2.00
28 Jerry Gray, LeRoy Irvin, Ronnie Lott 2.50
29 Mel Gray, Jay Hilgenberg 3.00
30 Dexter Manley, Reggie White 2.50
31 Rueben Mayes 2.00
32 Joe Montana 20.00
33 Jackie Slater, Gary Zimmerman 2.00
34 Herschel Walker 3.00

1988 Patriots Holsum

Available only in specially marked packages of Holsum Bread, the 12 standard-sized cards feature the Holsum logo in the upper left, with "1988 Annual Collectors' Edition" printed in the upper right. The player photo dominates the front, while the player's name and team are located inside a box beneath the photo. The card backs include the player's facsimile autograph, jersey number, bio and card number "of 12" printed at the top. The remainder of the card back is filled with stats and various logos.

NM/M
Complete Set (12): 40.00
Common Player: 4.00
1 Andre Tippett 4.00
2 Stanley Morgan 6.00
3 Steve Grogan 6.00
4 Ronnie Lippett 4.00
5 Kenneth Sims 4.00
6 Pete Brock 4.00
7 Sean Farrell 4.00
8 Garin Veris 4.00
9 Mosi Tatupu 4.00
10 Raymond Clayborn 5.00
11 Tony Franklin 4.00
12 Reggie Dupard 4.00

A player's name in *italic* type indicates a rookie card.

1988 Walter Payton Commemorative

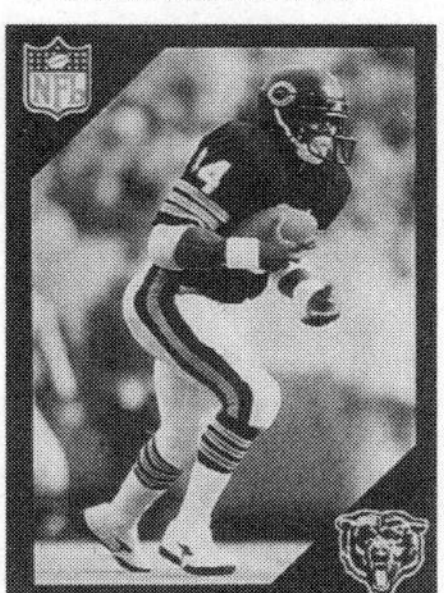

Chicagoland Processing Corp. produced 16,726 of these sets to commemorate the total rushing yards Hall of Fame running back Walter Payton gained during his career with the Chicago Bears. The 132-card set chronicles his illustrious career; each card recaptures a significant moment. The standard-size cards were packaged in a blue plastic box and were issued in conjunction with a softcover book titled "Sweetness." Each card front has a dark blue border around an action photo. The Bears' logo and NFL logo are also on the front. The cards are numbered on the back and have a title and text which ties to the photo on the front. The cards are listed by the title used on the back.

		NM/M
Complete Set (132):		50.00
Common Player:		.50
1	Leading Scorer in NCAA History	2.00
2	1975 Game-by-Game	.50
3	Vs. New York Jets	.50
4	Vs. Miami Dolphins	.50
5	Vs. Baltimore/ Indianapolis Colts	.50
6	Vs. Buffalo Bills	.50
7	Vs. New England Patriots	.50
8	Vs. Houston Oilers	.50
9	Vs. Pittsburgh Steelers	.50
10	Vs. Cincinnati Bengals	.50
11	Vs. Cleveland Browns	.50
12	Vs. Kansas City Chiefs	.50
13	Vs. Oakland/ Los Angeles Raiders	.50
14	Vs. San Diego Chargers	.50
15	Vs. Denver Broncos	.50
16	Vs. Seattle Seahawks	.50
17	Vs. Washington Redskins	.50
18	Vs. New York Giants	.50
19	Vs. Dallas Cowboys	.50
20	Vs. St. Louis Cardinals	.50
21	Vs. Philadelphia Eagles	.50
22	Vs. New Orleans Saints	.50
23	Vs. Atlanta Falcons	.50
24	Vs. Los Angeles Rams	.50
25	Vs. San Francisco 49ers	.50
26	Vs. Detroit Lions	.50
27	Vs. Minnesota Vikings	.50
28	Vs. Tampa Bay Buccaneers	.50
29	Vs. Green Bay Packers	.50
30	1976 Game-by-Game	.50
31	Appears in Nine Pro Bowls	.50
32	Post-Season Stats	.50
33	Owns 23 Bear Records	.50
34	Season-by-Season Statistics	.50
35	1977 Game-by-Game	.50
36	Most Yards Gained, Rushing	.50
37	Most Combined Yards, Career	.50
38	Most Rushing Touchdowns	.50
39	Most Games, 100 Yards Rushing, Career	.50
40	Consecutive Combined 2000-Yard Seasons	.50
41	Most Yards Gained, Rushing, Game	.50
42	Most Rushing Attempts, Career	.50
43	Most Combined Attempts, Career	.50
44	Most Seasons, 1000 Yards Rushing	.50
45	1978 Game-by-Game	.50
46	Top 10 Average Per Carry Days 1	.50
47	Top 10 Average Per Carry Days 2	.50
48	Top 10 Average Per Carry Days 3	.50
49	Top 10 Average Per Carry Days 4	.50
50	Top 10 Average Per Carry Days 5	.50
51	Top 10 Average Per Carry Days 6	.50
52	Top 10 Average Per Carry Days 7	.50
53	Top 10 Average Per Carry Days 8	.50
54	Top 10 Average Per Carry Days 9	.50
55	Top 10 Average Per Carry Days 10	.50
56	1979 Game-by-Game	.50
57	In Training Didn't Play Until 11th Grad	.50
58	In Training Running the Hill	.50
59	In Training Jumping Rope	.50
60	In Training	.50
61	Personal Life Interests Include...	.50
62	Personal Life Corporate Spokesman	.50
63	Personal Life Family Man	.50
64	Personal Life Realtives in NFL	.50
65	"Sweetness" autobiography written, 1978	.50
66	National Committee, Child Abuse Preven.	.50
67	Chicago 1986 Sports Father of the Year	.50
68	Active in Many Charities	.50
69	Personal Life Parade Grand Marshall	.50
70	1980 Game-by-Game	.50
71	1976 TSN MFC Player of the Year	.50
72	1976 Chicago Red Cloud Athlete of the Y	.50
73	1977 UPI Atlete of the Year	.50
74	1977 PFWA NFL MVP	.50
75	1977 UPI and TSN NFC Player of the Year	.50
76	1977 All Pro Pick AP, UPI, and NEA	.50
77	1977 PFWA,NEA,Mut.Radio, AP,FB Dig., POT	.50
78	TSN NFC All-Star 1976-79	.50
79	TSN NFL All-Star 1980,1984, and 1985	.50
80	1981 Game-by-Game	.50
81	As Quarterback	.50
82	Kickoff Return	.50
83	Complete Player	.50
84	Toouchdown	.50
85	1982 Game-by-Game	.50
86	Most Consecutive Games, Career	.50
87	Five Longest Runs	.50
88	Pass Receiving	.50
89	Ditka on Payton	.50
90	1983 Game-by-Game	.50
91	Breaks Career Rushing Record	.50
92	Breaks Career Rushing	.50
93	Breaks Career Rushing	.50
94	Breaks Career Rushing	.50
95	1984 Game-by-Game	.50
96	Bears Win 1985 NFC Champ. over Rams	.50
97	Super Bowl XX	.50
98	Super Bowl XX	.50
99	Super Bowl XX	.50
100	Super Bowl XX	.50
101	1985 Game-by-Game	.50
102	Sweetness	.50
103	Sweetness Choice to Pro Bowl Squad 1977	.50
104	Sweetness	.50
105	Sweetness 1979 Pro Bowl Starter,AP NFC	.50
106	Sweetness	.50
107	Sweetness	.50
108	Sweetness	.50
109	Sweetness	.50
110	1986 Game-by-Game	.50
111	Final Season Goodbye to Green Bay	.50
112	Final Season	.50
113	Last Regular Season Home Game	.50
114	Last Reg.Season Home Game,Number Retire	.50
115	Last Home Game,Presented with Portrait	.50
116	Last Regular Season Home Game	.50
117	Soldier Field,Known As Payton's Place	.50
118	Last Regular Season Home Game	.50
119	Last Regular Season Game vs. Raiders	.50
120	Last Regular Season Game	.50
121	Last Reg. Season Game, Catches 2 Passes	.50
122	Last Regular Season Game	.50
123	Last Regular Season Game	.50
124	Plays 190th Game, Bears All-Time Record	.50
125	Last Regular Season Game	.50
126	Ends Career with 21,803 Combined Yards	.50
127	Finishes w/4542 Career Receiving Yards	.50
128	16,726 Career Rushing Yards	.50
129	1987 Game-by-Game	.50
130	The End of an Era	.50
131	Thanks for the Memories	.50
132	Last Few Moments	2.00

1976 Pepsi Discs

This set was regionally produced in the Cincinnati area; hence the majority of the discs feature members of the Cincinnati Bengals (#s 21-40). The remaining discs feature top NFL stars. The cards are valued with the tab intact; this is how they are commonly found. The tab was used to hang the disc from a bottle included in six packs of Pepsi products. Each disc is 3-1/2" in diameter and features a player photo, biographical information and 1975 statistics on the front. Discs 1, 5, 7, 8 and 14 are reportedly scarcer than the others because they were short-printed. A free, personalized T-shirt was also offered to those who sent in 200 capliners which read "Pepsi Players." The shirt would picture either Ken Anderson or Archie Griffin, with the collector's first name. It would say "To my buddy xxxx, Best Wishes, Ken Anderson."

		NM/M
Complete Set (40):		90.00
Common Player:		.50
1	Steve Bartkowski	22.00
2	Lydell Mitchell	1.50
3	Wally Chambers	.50
4	Doug Buffone	.50
5	Jerry Sherk	22.00
6	Drew Pearson	1.00
7	Otis Armstrong	22.00
8	Charlie Sanders	20.00
9	John Brockington	.75
10	Curley Culp	.75
11	Jan Stenerud	1.50
12	Lawrence McCutcheon	.75
13	Chuck Foreman	1.00
14	Bob Pollard	20.00
15	Ed Marinaro	12.00
16	Jack Lambert	5.00
17	Terry Metcalf	.75
18	Mel Gray	.75
19	Russ Washington	.50
20	Charley Taylor	2.50
21	Ken Anderson	2.50
22	Bob Brown	.50
23	Ron Carpenter	.50
24	Tom Casanova	1.25
25	Boobie Clark	1.00
26	Isaac Curtis	1.00
27	Lenvil Elliott	.50
28	Stan Fritts	.50
29	Vernon Holland	.50
30	Bob Johnson	1.00
31	Ken Johnson	.50
32	Bill Kollar	.50
33	Jim LeClair	.75
34	Chip Myers	.50
35	Lemar Parrish	.75
36	Rob Pritchard	.50
37	Bob Trumpy	1.50
38	Sherman White	.50
39	Archie Griffin	1.50
40	John Shinners	.50

1964 Philadelphia

This was Philly's first of four straight 198-card sets, and Philly covered the NFL players while Topps, possibly unable to reach an agreement with the NFL, showcased only American Football League players. For the first time, a card with a team play and a black-and-white photo of the coach was included in a football card set. As would be the case throughout the Philly run, cards are numbered alphabetically by player's last name and by city name. Two checklists appear at the end of each of the four Philly sets. Rookies in this set include John Mackey, Tom Matte, Jack Pardee, Mick Tingelhoff, Irv Cross, and Hall of Famers Herb Adderly, Willie Davis and Merlin Olsen. Making their debut on cards on coaches' issues were Don Shula, Vince Lombardi and Allie Sherman. Second-year cards in the set include Bob Lilly and Jim Marshall. This set held the final regular-issue cards of Gino Marchetti, Night Train Lane, Joe Schmidt, Jerry Kramer, Frank Gifford, Y.A. Tittle, and Bob St. Clair. One error does exist in the set -- card #169 does not picture Garland Boyette as advertised, it's unclear who the player actually is.

		NM/M
Complete Set (198):		875.00
Common Player:		1.75
Wax Pack (5):		190.00
1	Raymond Berry	20.00
2	Tom Gilburg	1.75
3	*John Mackey*	25.00
4	Gino Marchetti	4.00
5	Jim Martin	1.75
6	*Tom Matte*	6.00
7	Jimmy Orr	1.75
8	Jim Parker	3.00
9	Bill Pellington	1.75
10	Alex Sandusky	1.75
11	Dick Szymanski	1.75
12	Johnny Unitas	40.00
13	Baltimore Colts Team	1.75
14	Don Shula	25.00
15	Doug Atkins	2.50
16	Ron Bull	1.75
17	Mike Ditka	32.00
18	Joe Fortunato	1.75
19	Willie Galimore	1.75
20	Joe Marconi	1.75
21	*Bennie McRae*	2.00
22	Johnny Morris	1.75
23	*Richie Petitbon*	2.50
24	Mike Pyle	1.75
25	*Roosevelt Taylor*	4.00
26	Bill Wade	1.75
27	Chicago Bears Team	1.75
28	George Halas	10.00
29	Johnny Brewer	1.75
30	Jim Brown	65.00
31	*Gary Collins*	6.00
32	Vince Costello	1.75
33	Galen Fiss	1.75
34	Bill Glass	1.75
35	*Ernie Green*	4.00
36	Rich Kreitling	1.75
37	John Morrow	1.75
38	Frank Ryan	3.00
39	*Charlie Scales*	3.00
40	*Dick Schafrath*	2.00
41	Cleveland Browns Team	1.75
42	Blanton Collier Cleveland Browns Play of the Year	1.75
43	Don Bishop	1.75
44	*Frank Clarke*	3.00
45	Mike Connelly	1.75
46	Lee Folkins	1.75
47	*Cornell Green*	5.00
48	Bob Lilly	40.00
49	Amos Marsh	1.75
50	Tommy McDonald	1.75
51	Don Meredith	35.00
52	*Pettis Norman*	2.00
53	Don Perkins	2.00
54	Guy Resse	1.75
55	Dallas Cowboys Team	1.75
56	Tom Landry	12.00
57	Terry Barr	1.75
58	Roger Brown	1.75
59	Gail Cogdill	1.75
60	John Gordy	1.75
61	Dick "Night Train" Lane	4.00
62	Yale Lary	4.00
63	Dan Lewis	1.75
64	Darris McCord	1.75
65	Earl Morrall	5.00
66	Joe Schmidt	4.00
67	*Pat Studstill*	4.00
68	*Wayne Walker*	4.00
69	Detroit Lions Team	1.75
70	George Wilson Detroit Lions Player of the Year	1.75
71	*Herb Adderley*	30.00
72	*Willie Davis*	30.00
73	Forrest Gregg	4.00
74	Paul Hornung	25.00
75	Henry Jordan	1.75
76	Jerry Kramer	5.00
77	Tom Moore	1.75
78	Jim Ringo	4.00
79	Bart Starr	40.00
80	Jim Taylor	15.00
81	*Jess Whittenton*	2.50
82	Willie Wood	8.00
83	Green Bay Packers Team	1.75
84	Vince Lombardi	24.00
85	Jon Arnett	1.75
86	*Pervis Atkins*	2.00
87	Dick Bass	1.75
88	Carroll Dale	1.75
89	Roman Gabriel	6.00
90	Ed Meador	1.75
91	*Merlin Olsen*	50.00
92	*Jack Pardee*	7.00
93	Jim Phillips	1.75
94	Carver Shannon	1.75
95	Frank Varrichione	1.75
96	Danny Villanueva	1.75
97	Los Angeles Rams Team	1.75
98	Harland Svare Los Angeles Rams Play of the Year	1.75
99	*Grady Alderman*	2.00
100	Larry Bowie	1.75
101	*Bill Brown*	5.00
102	*Paul Flatley*	2.00
103	Rip Hawkins	1.75
104	Jim Marshall	8.00
105	Tommy Mason	1.75
106	Jim Prestel	1.75
107	Jerry Reichow	1.75
108	Ed Sharockman	1.75
109	Fran Tarkenton	30.00
110	*Mick Tingelhoff*	8.00
111	Minnesota Vikings Team	1.75
112	Norm Van Brocklin	4.00
113	Erich Barnes	1.75
114	Roosevelt Brown	3.00
115	Don Chandler	1.75
116	Darrell Dess	1.75
117	Frank Gifford	45.00
118	Dick James	1.75
119	Jim Katcavage	1.75
120	John Lovetere	1.75
121	*Dick Lynch*	2.00
122	Jim Patton	1.75
123	Del Shofner	1.75
124	Y.A. Tittle	20.00
125	New York Giants Team	1.75
126	Allie Sherman Player of the year	1.75
127	Sam Baker	1.75
128	Maxie Baughan	1.75
129	Timmy Brown	1.75
130	Mike Clark	1.75
131	*Irv Cross*	6.00
132	Ted Dean	1.75
133	Ron Goodwin	1.75
134	King Hill	1.75
135	Clarence Peaks	1.75
136	Pete Retzlaff	1.75
137	Jim Schrader	1.75
138	Norm Snead	3.00
139	Philadelphia Eagles Team	1.75
140	Joe Kuharich Philadelphia Eagles Play of the Year	1.75
141	*Gary Ballman*	3.00
142	Charley Bradshaw	1.75
143	Ed Brown	1.75
144	John Henry Johnson	5.00
145	Joe Krupa	1.75
146	Bill Mack	1.75
147	Lou Michaels	1.75
148	Buzz Nutter	1.75
149	Myron Pottios	1.75
150	John Reger	1.75
151	Mike Sandusky	1.75
152	Clendon Thomas	1.75
153	Pittsburgh Steelers Team	1.75
154	Buddy Parker Pittsburgh Steelers Play of the Year	1.75
155	*Kermit Alexander*	3.00
156	Bernie Casey	1.75
157	Dan Colchico	1.75
158	Clyde Conner	1.75
159	Tommy Davis	1.75
160	Matt Hazeltine	1.75
161	*Jim Johnson*	15.00
162	*Don Lisbon*	2.00
163	Lamar McHan	1.75
164	Bob St. Clair	4.00
165	J.D. Smith	1.75
166	Abe Woodson	1.75
167	San Francisco 49ers Team	1.75
168	Red Hickey San Francisco 49ers Play of the Year	1.75
169	Garland Boyette	1.75
170	Bobby Joe Conrad	1.75
171	*Bob DeMarco*	3.00
172	*Ken Gray*	3.00
173	Jimmy Hill	1.75
174	Charlie Johnson	3.00
175	Ernie McMillan	1.75
176	Dale Meinert	1.75
177	Luke Owens	1.75
178	Sonny Randle	1.75
179	Joe Robb	1.75
180	Bill Stacy	1.75
181	St. Louis Cardinals Team	1.75
182	Wally Lem St. Louis Cardinals Play of the Year	1.75
183	Bill Barnes	1.75
184	Don Bosseler	1.75
185	Sam Huff	6.00
186	Sonny Jurgensen	18.00
187	Ed Khayat	1.75
188	Riley Mattson	1.75
189	Bobby Mitchell	6.00
190	John Nisby	1.75
191	Vince Promuto	1.75
192	Joe Rutgens	1.75
193	Lonnie Sanders	1.75
194	Jim Steffen	1.75
195	Washington Redskins Team	1.75
196	Bill McPeak Washington Redskins Play of the Year	1.75
197	Checklist 1	20.00
198	Checklist 2	40.00

1965 Philadelphia

This Philly set was the second one of NFLers issued in its four-year run during the mid-60s. The standard-size 198-card set lists players alphabetically by last name, and alphabetically by city name. Card fronts show the player name in a black box below the photo, with the NFL logo to the right. Card backs had a rub-off game below the statistics. Play of the year cards displayed a diagrammed play the team had used; accompanying it on the front of the card is a small black-and-white picture of the coach. Team cards were once again issued, as were set checklists. One error in the set has Merlin Olsen spelled "Olson" on the checklist card. Rookies in this set include Hall of Famers Paul Warfield and Charley Taylor; all-time interception leader Paul Krause; future NFL head coach Floyd Peters; Carl Eller; Fred Cox; Jack Concannon; Jim Bakken and Pat Fischer. Second-year cards in the set depict Hall of Famers Herb Adderly, Willie Davis, Ray Nitschke (his first Philly card), Vince Lombardi, Deacon Jones, and Merlin Olsen. Others include Mick Tinglehoff, Allie Sherman and Irv Cross. The final regular-issue cards of these players are also in the set: Hall of Famers Yale Lary, Norm Van Brocklin (on a play of the year card), John Henry Johnson, and Sam Huff. This set also had the last regular-issue card of Roosevelt Grier.

		NM/M
Complete Set (198):		775.00
Common Player:		1.50
Wax Pack (5):		190.00
1	Baltimore Colts Team	11.00
2	Raymond Berry	6.00
3	Bob Boyd	1.50
4	Wendell Harris	1.50
5	Jerry Logan	1.50
6	Tony Lorick	1.50
7	Lou Michaels	1.50
8	Lenny Moore	6.00
9	Jimmy Orr	1.50
10	Jim Parker	3.00
11	Dick Szymanski	1.50
12	Johnny Unitas	35.00
13	*Bob Vogel*	1.50
14	Don Shula	14.00
15	Chicago Bears Team	1.50
16	Jon Arnett	1.50
17	Doug Atkins	3.00
18	*Rudy Bukich*	3.00
19	Mike Ditka	25.00
20	Dick Evey	1.50
21	Joe Fortunato	1.50
22	*Bobby Joe Green*	1.50
23	Johnny Morris	1.50
24	Mike Pyle	1.50
25	Roosevelt Taylor	1.50
26	Bill Wade	1.50
27	Bob Wetoska	1.50
28	George Halas	6.00
29	Cleveland Browns Team	1.50
30	Walter Beach	1.50
31	Jim Brown	60.00
32	Gary Collins	1.50
33	Bill Glass	1.50
34	Ernie Green	1.50
35	*Jim Houston*	3.00
36	Dick Modzelewski	1.50
37	Bernie Parrish	1.50
38	Walter Roberts	1.50
39	Frank Ryan	1.50
40	Dick Schafrath	1.50
41	*Paul Warfield*	75.00
42	Blanton Collier Cleveland Browns Play of the Year	1.50
43	Dallas Cowboys Team	1.50
44	Frank Clarke	1.50
45	Mike Connelly	1.50
46	Buddy Dial	1.50
47	Bob Lilly	20.00
48	*Tony Liscio*	1.75
49	Tommy McDonald	1.50
50	Don Meredith	25.00
51	Pettis Norman	1.50
52	Don Perkins	2.00
53	*Mel Renfro*	30.00
54	Jim Ridlon	1.50
55	Jerry Tubbs	1.50
56	Tom Landry	7.00
57	Detroit Lions Team	1.50
58	Terry Barr	1.50
59	Roger Brown	1.50
60	Gail Cogdill	1.50
61	Jim Gibbons	1.50
62	John Gordy	1.50
63	Yale Lary	3.00
64	*Dick LeBeau*	4.00
65	Earl Morrall	4.00
66	Nick Pietrosante	1.50
67	Pat Studstill	1.50
68	Wayne Walker	1.50
69	Tom Watkins	1.50
70	George Wilson Detroit Lions Play of the Year	1.50
71	Green Bay Packers Team	1.50
72	Herb Adderley	8.00
73	Willie Davis	8.00
74	Boyd Dowler	1.50
75	Forrest Gregg	4.00
76	Paul Hornung	25.00
77	Henry Jordan	1.50
78	Tom Moore	1.50
79	Ray Nitschke	15.00
80	*Elijah Pitts*	5.00
81	Bart Starr	25.00
82	Jim Taylor	14.00
83	Willie Wood	8.00
84	Vince Lombardi	12.00
85	Los Angeles Rams Team	1.50
86	Dick Bass	1.50
87	Roman Gabriel	5.00
88	Roosevelt Grier	3.00
89	Deacon Jones	8.00
90	*Lamar Lundy*	3.00
91	Marlin McKeever	1.50
92	Ed Meador	1.50
93	*Bill Munson*	3.00
94	Merlin Olsen	17.00
95	Bobby Smith	1.50
96	Frank Varrichione	1.50
97	Ben Wilson	1.50
98	Harland Svare Los Angeles Rams Play of the Year	1.50

99 Minnesota Vikings Team 1.50
100 Grady Alderman 1.50
101 *Hal Bedsole* 1.50
102 Bill Brown 1.50
103 Bill Butler 1.50
104 *Fred Cox* 4.00
105 *Carl Eller* 26.00
106 Paul Flatley 1.50
107 Jim Marshall 6.00
108 Tommy Mason 1.50
109 George Rose 1.50
110 Fran Tarkenton 30.00
111 Mick Tingelhoff 2.00
112 Norm Van Brocklin 3.00
113 New York Giants Team 1.50
114 Erich Barnes 1.50
115 Roosevelt Brown 4.00
116 Clarence Childs 1.50
117 Jerry Hillebrand 1.50
118 Greg Larson 1.50
119 Dick Lynch 1.50
120 *Joe Morrison* 4.00
121 Lou Slaby 1.50
122 *Aaron Thomas* 2.50
123 Steve Thurlow 1.50
124 Ernie Wheelwright 1.50
125 *Gary Wood* 1.50
126 Allie Sherman New York Giants Play of the Year 1.50
127 Philadelphia Eagles Team 1.50
128 Sam Baker 1.50
129 Maxie Baughan 1.50
130 Timmy Brown 1.50
131 *Jack Concannon* 1.50
132 Irv Cross 2.50
133 Earl Gros 1.50
134 Dave Lloyd 1.50
135 Floyd Peters 4.00
136 Nate Ramsey 1.50
137 Pete Retzlaff 1.50
138 Jim Ringo 4.00
139 Norm Snead 2.00
140 Joe Kuharich Philadelphia Eagles Play of the Year 1.50
141 Pittsburgh Steelers Team 1.50
142 John Baker 1.50
143 Gary Ballman 1.50
144 Charley Bradshaw 1.50
145 Ed Brown 1.50
146 Dick Haley 1.50
147 John Henry Johnson 4.50
148 Brady Keys 1.50
149 Ray Lemek 1.50
150 Ben McGee 1.50
151 Clarence Peaks 1.50
152 Myron Pottios 1.50
153 Clendon Thomas 1.50
154 Buddy Parker Pittsburgh Steelers Play of the Year 1.50
155 St. Louis Cardinals Team 1.50
156 *Jim Bakken* 4.50
157 Joe Childress 1.50
158 Bobby Joe Conrad 1.50
159 Bob DeMarco 1.50
160 *Pat Fischer* 4.50
161 Irv Goode 1.50
162 Ken Gray 1.50
163 Charlie Johnson 1.50
164 Bill Koman 1.50
165 Dale Meinert 1.50
166 *Jerry Stovall* 2.50
167 Abe Woodson 1.50
168 Wally Lemon St. Louis Cardinals Play of the Year 1.50
169 San Francisco 49ers Team 1.50
170 Kermit Alexander 1.50
171 John Brodie 12.00
172 Bernie Casey 1.50
173 John David Crow 1.50
174 Tommy Davis 1.50
175 Matt Hazeltine 1.50
176 Jim Johnson 1.50
177 Charlie Krueger 1.50
178 Roland Lakes 1.50
179 *George Mira* 5.00
180 *Dave Parks* 4.00
181 John Thomas 1.50
182 Jack Christiansen 2.00
183 Washington Redskins Team 1.50
184 Pervis Atkins 1.50
185 Preston Carpenter 1.50
186 Angelo Coia 1.50
187 Sam Huff 6.00
188 Sonny Jurgensen 15.00
189 *Paul Krause* 16.00
190 Jim Martin 1.50
191 Bobby Mitchell 6.00
192 John Nisby 1.50
193 John Paluck 1.50
194 Vince Promuto 1.50
195 *Charley Taylor* 60.00
196 Bill McPeak 1.50
197 Checklist 1 20.00
198 Checklist 2 40.00

Values quoted in this guide reflect the retail price of a card—the price a collector can expect to pay when buying a card from a dealer. The wholesale price—that which a collector can expect to receive from a dealer when selling cards—will be significantly lower, depending on desirability and condition.

1966 Philadelphia

This 198-card set of NFL players is best known for the inclusion of rookie cards of Gale Sayers and Dick Butkus (the other significant rookie card is that of Bob Hayes). This was the final year regular-issue cards were produced of players including Hall of Famers Lenny Moore, Jim Parker, Jim Brown, Roosevelt Brown, and Jim Ringo. The 198-card set lists players in alphabetical order according to city. The play card for each team features a color action photo on the front, with a description of the play on the back.

NM/M

Complete Set (198): 875.00
Common Player: 1.50
Wax Pack (5): 225.00
1 Falcons Logo 8.00
2 Larry Benz 1.50
3 Dennis Claridge 1.50
4 Perry Lee Dunn 1.50
5 Dan Grimm 1.50
6 Alex Hawkins 1.50
7 Ralph Heck 1.50
8 Frank Lasky 1.50
9 Guy Reese 1.50
10 Bob Richards 1.50
11 Ron Smith 1.50
12 Ernie Wheelwright 1.50
13 Atlanta Falcons Roster 1.50
14 Baltimore Colts Team Card 1.50
15 Raymond Berry 7.00
16 Bob Boyd 1.50
17 Jerry Logan 1.50
18 John Mackey 6.00
19 Tom Matte 1.50
20 Lou Michaels 1.50
21 Lenny Moore 6.00
22 Jimmy Orr 1.50
23 Jim Parker 1.50
24 Johnny Unitas 30.00
25 Bob Vogel 1.50
26 Baltimore Colts Play Card 1.50
27 Chicago Bears Team Card 1.50
28 Doug Atkins 1.50
29 Rudy Bukich 1.50
30 Ron Bull 1.50
31 *Dick Butkus* 185.00
32 Mike Ditka 25.00
33 Joe Fortuanto 1.50
34 Bobby Joe Green 1.50
35 Roger LeClerc 1.50
36 Johnny Morris 1.50
37 Mike Pyle 1.50
38 *Gale Sayers* 210.00
39 Gale Sayers (Bears) 25.00
40 Cleveland Browns Team Card 1.50
41 Jim Brown 55.00
42 Gary Collins 1.50
43 Ross Fichtner 1.50
44 Ernie Green 1.50
45 *Gene Hickerson* 2.00
46 Jim Houston 1.50
47 John Morrow 1.50
48 Walter Roberts 1.50
49 Frank Ryan 1.50
50 Dick Schafrath 1.50
51 *Paul Wiggin* 2.00
52 Cleveland Browns Play Card 1.50
53 Dallas Cowboys Team Card 1.50
54 *George Andrie* 2.00
55 Frank Ryan 1.50
56 Mike Connelly 1.50
57 Cornell Green 1.50
58 *Bob Hayes* 25.00
59 *Chuck Howley* 10.00
60 Bob Lilly 15.00
61 Don Meredith 25.00
62 Don Perkins 1.50
63 Mel Renfro 8.00
64 Danny Villanueva 1.50
65 Dallas Cowboys Play Card 1.50
66 Detroit Lions Team Card 1.50
67 Roger Brown 1.50
68 John Gordy 1.50
69 Alex Karras 10.00
70 Dick LeBeau 1.50
71 Amos Marsh 1.50
72 Milt Plum 1.50
73 Bobby Smith 1.50
74 Wayne Rasmussen 1.50
75 Pat Studstill 1.50
76 Wayne Walker 1.50
77 Tom Watkins 1.50
78 Detroit Lions Play Card 1.50
79 Green Bay Packers Team Card 1.50
80 Herb Adderley 5.00
81 *Lee Roy Caffey* 2.00
82 Don Chandler 1.50
83 Willie Davis 5.00
84 Boyd Dowler 1.50
85 Forrest Gregg 4.00
86 Tom Moore 1.50
87 Ray Nitschke 10.00
88 Bart Starr 25.00
89 Jim Taylor 13.00
90 Willie Wood 4.50
91 Green Bay Packers Play Card 1.50
92 Los Angeles Rams Team Card 1.50
93 Willie Brown 1.50
94 Dick Bass, Roman Gabriel 2.50
95 Bruce Gossett 2.50
96 Deacon Jones 6.00
97 Tommy McDonald 1.50
98 Marlin McKeever 1.50
99 Aaron Martin 1.50
100 Ed Meador 1.50
101 Bill Munson 2.00
102 Merlin Olsen 9.00
103 Jim Stiger 1.50
104 Los Angeles Rams Play Card 1.50
105 Minnesota Vikings Team Card 1.50
106 Grady Alderman 1.50
107 Bill Brown 1.50
108 Fred Cox 1.50
109 Paul Flatley 1.50
110 Rip Hawkins 1.50
111 Tommy Mason 1.50
112 Ed Sharockman 1.50
113 Gordon Smith 1.50
114 Fran Tarkenton 20.00
115 Mick Tinglehoff 2.00
116 *Bobby Walden* 2.00
117 Minnesota Vikings Play Card 1.50
118 New York Giants Team Card 1.50
119 Roosevelt Brown 4.00
120 *Henry Carr* 2.00
121 Clarence Childs 1.50
122 *Tucker Frederickson* 2.00
123 Jerry Hillebrand 1.50
124 Greg Larson 1.50
125 *Spider Lockhart* 3.00
126 Dick Lynch 1.50
127 Earl Morrall, Bob Scholtz 1.50
128 Joe Morrison 1.50
129 Steve Thurlow 1.50
130 New York Giants Play Card 1.50
131 Philadelphia Ealges Team Card 1.50
132 Sam Baker 1.50
133 Maxie Baughan 1.50
134 *Bob Brown* 6.00
135 Timmy Brown 1.50
136 Irv Cross 2.00
137 Earl Gros 1.50
138 Ray Poage 1.50
139 Nate Ramsey 1.50
140 Pete Retzlaff 1.50
141 Jim Ringo 3.50
142 Norm Snead 2.00
143 Philadelphia Eagles Play Card 1.50
144 Pittsburgh Steelers Team Card 1.50
145 Gary Ballman 1.50
146 Charley Bradshaw 1.50
147 Jim Butler 1.50
148 Mike Clark 1.50
149 *Dick Hoak* 2.00
150 *Roy Jefferson* 2.00
151 Frank Lambert 1.50
152 Mike Lind 1.50
153 *Bill Nelsen* 4.00
154 Clarence Peaks 1.50
155 Clendon Thomas 1.50
156 Pittsburgh Steelers Play Card 1.50
157 St. Louis Cardinals Team Card 1.50
158 Jim Bakken 1.50
159 Bobby Joe Conrad 1.50
160 *Willis Crenshaw* 2.00
161 Bob DeMarco 1.50
162 Pat Fischer 2.00
163 Charlie Johnson 2.00
164 Dale Meinert 1.50
165 Sonny Randle 1.50
166 *Sam Silas* 2.00
167 Bill Triplett 1.50
168 Larry Wilson 4.00
169 St. Louis Cardinals Play Card 1.50
170 San Francisco 49ers Team Card 1.50
171 Kermit Alexander 1.50
172 Bruce Bosley 1.50
173 John Brodie 9.00
174 Bernie Casey 1.50
175 John David Crow 1.50
176 Tommy Davis 1.50
177 Jim Johnson 1.50
178 Gary Lewis 1.50
179 Dave Parks 1.50
180 Walter Rock 1.50
181 *Ken Willard* 4.00
182 San Francisco 49ers Play Card 1.50
183 Washington Redskins Team Card 1.50
184 Rickie Harris 1.50
185 Sonny Jurgensen 9.00
186 Paul Krause 5.00
187 Bobby Mitchell 5.00
188 Vince Promuto 1.50
189 *Pat Richter* 3.00
190 Joe Rutgens 1.50
191 John Sample 1.50
192 Lonnie Sanders 1.50
193 Jim Steffen 1.50
194 Charley Taylor 18.00
195 Washington Redskins Play Card 1.50
196 Referee signals 5.00
197 Checklist 1 20.00
198 Checklist 2 40.00

1967 Philadelphia

This was the last time until 1989 that Topps would face a direct challenge in the football card market, as the Philadelphia Chewing Gum Corp. ceased production of football cards after this issue. (The company returned with sets of NFL Hall of Famers in 1988 and 1989). The 198-card set has yellow borders on the front, and backs were printed on white or brown card stock. As usual, teams were grouped alphabetically by city name, players were grouped alphabetically by last name. Team logo cards rounded out the grouping of each team. There is an error in the set: on card #14, Raymond Berry, the picture actually shows Bob Boyd. Also, the roster for the New Orleans Saints team card (#121) was included on the back of the logo card (#132); the set includes team picture cards and team logo cards for all other teams except the expansion Saints (The front of the card reads, "On the back of this card are names of New Orleans players and the teams from which they were picked" while the back simply has a capsule on the Saints' New Orleans impact). Another error, on card #26 reads "Bukich" on the front and "Buckich" on the back. Rookies in this set include Tommy Nobis, Leroy Kelly, Lee Roy Jordan, and Chris Hanburger. Second-year cards include Dick Butkus, Gale Sayers, Bob Brown, Roy Jefferson, Jim Bakken and Ken Willard. This was the last year for regular-issue cards of Hall of Famers Forrest Gregg and Paul Hornung. The first members of the New Orleans Saints made their debut in the '67 Philly set.

NM/M

Complete Set (198): 650.00
Common Player: 1.50
Wax Pack (5): 180.00
1 Falcons Team 5.00
2 *Junior Coffey* 1.50
3 Alex Hawkins 1.50
4 *Randy Johnson* 3.00
5 Lou Kirouac 1.50
6 Billy Martin 1.50
7 *Tommy Nobis* 16.00
8 *Jerry Richardson* 6.00
9 Marion Rushing 1.50
10 Ron Smith 1.50
11 Ernie Wheelwright 1.50
12 Atlanta Falcons Insignia 1.50
13 Baltimore Colts Team 1.50
14 Raymond Berry 5.00
15 Bob Boyd 1.50
16 Ordell Braase 1.50
17 Alvin Haymond 1.50
18 Tony Lorick 1.50
19 Lenny Lyles 1.50
20 John Mackey 5.00
21 Tom Matte 1.50
22 Lou Michaels 1.50
23 Johnny Unitas 30.00
24 Baltimore Colts Insignia 1.50
25 Chicago Bears Team 1.50
26 Rudy Bukich 1.50
27 Ron Bull 1.50
28 Dick Butkus 60.00
29 Mike Ditka 25.00
30 *Dick Gordon* 1.50
31 Roger LeClerc 1.50
32 Bennie McRae 1.50
33 Richie Petibon 2.50
34 Mike Pyle 1.50
35 Gale Sayers 75.00
36 Chicago Bears Insignia 1.50
37 Cleveland Browns Team 1.50
38 Johnny Brewer 1.50
39 Gary Collins 1.50
40 Ross Fichtner 1.50
41 Ernie Green 1.50
42 Gene Hickerson 1.50
43 *Leroy Kelly* 30.00
44 Frank Ryan 1.50
45 Dick Schafrath 1.50
46 Paul Warfield 20.00
47 John Wooten 1.50
48 Cleveland Browns Insignia 1.50
49 Dallas Cowboys Team 1.50
50 George Andrie 1.50
51 Cornell Green 1.50
52 Bob Hayes 10.00
53 Chuck Howley 1.50
54 *Lee Roy Jordan* 22.00
55 Bob Lilly 12.00
56 *Dave Manders* 2.00
57 Don Meredith 20.00
58 *Dan Reeves* 33.00
59 Mel Renfro 2.50
60 Dallas Cowboys Insignia 1.50
61 Detroit Lions Team 1.50
62 Roger Brown 1.50
63 Gail Cogdill 1.50
64 John Gordy 1.50
65 Ron Kramer 1.50
66 Dick LeBeau 1.50
67 *Mike Lucci* 6.00
68 Amos Marsh 1.50
69 Tom Nowatzke 1.50
70 Pat Studstill 1.50
71 Karl Sweetan 1.50
72 Detroit Lions Insignia 1.50
73 Green Bay Packers Team 1.50
74 Herb Adderley 4.50
75 Lee Roy Caffey 1.50
76 Willie Davis 4.50
77 Forrest Gregg 4.00
78 Henry Jordan 1.50
79 Ray Nitschke 6.00
80 *Dave Robinson* 5.00
81 Bob Skoronski 1.50
82 Bart Starr 20.00
83 Willie Wood 5.00
84 Green Bay Packers Insignia 1.50
85 Los Angeles Rams Team 1.50
86 Dick Bass 1.50
87 Maxie Baughan 1.50
88 Roman Gabriel 4.00
89 Bruce Gossett 1.50
90 Deacon Jones 5.00
91 Tommy McDonald 1.50
92 Marlin McKeever 1.50
93 Tom Moore 1.50
94 Merlin Olsen 7.00
95 Clancy Williams 1.50
96 Los Angeles Rams Insignia 1.50
97 Minnesota Vikings Team 1.50
98 Grady Alderman 1.50
99 Bill Brown 1.50
100 Fred Cox 1.50
101 Paul Flatley 1.50
102 Dale Hackbart 1.50
103 Jim Marshall 3.00
104 Tommy Mason 1.50
105 Milt Sunde 1.50
106 Fran Tarkenton 20.00
107 Mick Tingelhoff 2.00
108 Minnesota Vikings Insignia 1.50
109 New York Giants Team 1.50
110 Henry Carr 1.50
111 Clarence Childs 1.50
112 Allen Jacobs 1.50
113 *Homer Jones* 2.00
114 Tom Kennedy 1.50
115 Spider Lockhart 1.50
116 Joe Morrison 1.50
117 Francis Peay 1.50
118 Jeff Smith 1.50
119 Aaron Thomas 1.50
120 New York Giants Team 1.50
121 New Orleans Saints Team 2.00
122 Charley Bradshaw 1.50
123 Paul Hornung 18.00
124 Elbert Kimbrough 1.50
125 Earl Leggett 1.50
126 Obert Logan 1.50
127 Riley Mattson 1.50
128 John Morrow 1.50
129 Bob Scholtz 1.50
130 *Dave Whitsell* 2.00
131 Gary Wood 1.50
132 New Orleans Saints Insignia 1.50
133 Philadelphia Eagles Team 1.50
134 Sam Baker 1.50
135 Bob Brown 2.00
136 Jim Brown 1.50
137 Earl Gros 1.50
138 Dave Lloyd 1.50
139 Floyd Peters 1.50
140 Pete Retzlaff 1.50
141 Joe Scarpati 1.50
142 Norm Snead 2.00
143 Jim Skaggs 1.50
144 Philadelphia Eagles Insignia 1.50
145 Pittsburgh Steelers Team 1.50
146 Bill Asbury 1.50
147 John Baker 1.50
148 Gary Ballman 1.50
149 Mike Clark 1.50
150 Riley Gunnels 1.50
151 John Hilton 1.50
152 Roy Jefferson 1.50
153 Brady Keys 1.50
154 Ben McGee 1.50
155 Bill Nelsen 2.00
156 Pittsburgh Steelers Insignia 1.50
157 St. Louis Cardinals Team 1.50
158 Jim Bakken 1.50
159 Bobby Joe Conrad 1.50
160 Ken Gray 1.50
161 Charlie Johnson 2.00
162 Joe Robb 1.50
163 *Johnny Roland* 4.00
164 Roy Shivers 1.50
165 *Jackie Smith* 15.00
166 Jerry Stovall 1.50
167 Larry Wilson 4.00
168 St. Louis Cardinals Insignia 1.50
169 San Francisco 49ers Team 1.50
170 Kermit Alexander 1.50
171 Bruce Bosley 1.50
172 John Brodie 7.50
173 Bernie Casey 1.50
174 Tommy Davis 1.50
175 Howard Mudd 1.50
176 Dave Parks 1.50
177 John Thomas 1.50
178 *Dave Wilcox* 5.00
179 Ken Willard 1.50
180 San Francisco 49ers Insignia 1.50
181 Washington Redskins Team 1.50
182 *Charlie Gogolak* 2.00
183 *Chris Hanburger* 8.00
184 *Len Hauss* 3.00
185 Sonny Jurgensen 8.00
186 Bobby Mitchell 5.00
187 Bris Owens 1.50
188 Jim Shorter 1.50
189 *Jerry Smith* 2.00
190 Charley Taylor 7.50
191 A.D. Whitfield 1.50
192 Washington Redskins Insignia 1.50
193 Cleveland Browns 5.00
194 Joe Morrison New York Giants Play Card 1.50
195 Ernie Wheelwright Atlanta Falcons Play Card 1.50
196 Referee Signals 2.00
197 Checklist 1 18.00
198 Checklist 2 35.00

1991 Pinnacle Promo Panels

The 18-card, 5" x 7" panel set each features four preview cards from Pinnacle's 1991 football debut and were issued at the Super Bowl XXVI Card Show. The four-card panels have the same design as the regular-issue set.

NM/M

Complete Set (18): 100.00
Common Player: 3.00
1 John Alt, Eric Green, Don Mosebar, Greg Townsend 3.00
2 Bruce Armstrong, Joe Montana, Jim Lachey, Bruce Matthews 8.00
3 Don Beebe, Irving Fryar, Ricky Proehl, Vinny Testaverde 4.00
4 Duane Bickett, Tony Bennett, John Friesz, Rob Burnett 3.00
5 Mark Bortz, Warren Moon, Jim Breech, Eric Metcalf 4.00
6 Roger Craig, Issiac Holt, Kevin Mack, Shane Conlan 4.00
7 Wendell Davis, Gaston Green, Tony Mandarich, Merril Hoge 3.00
8 Dermontti Dawson, Jerry Gray, Nick Lowery, Scott Case 3.00
9 Chris Doleman, Troy Aikman, Sterling Sharpe, Sean Landeta 8.00
10 Darryl Henley, Karl Mecklenberg, Sam Mills, Rod Woodson 4.00
11 Mark Higgs, Jay Schroeder, Mark Carrier, Jim Everett 4.00
12 Jay Hilgenberg, Dan Marino, Anthony Carter, Howie Long 15.00
13 Louis Lipps, John Offerdahl, Herschel Walker, Jeff George 4.00
14 Greg McMurtry, Henry Ellard, Brian Mitchell, Mark Clayton 4.00
15 Nate Odomes, Allen Pinkett, Don Majkowski, Dave Meggett 3.00
16 Andre Rison, Jeff Hostetler, Hugh Millen, Jack Del Rio 4.00
17 Emmitt Smith, Dennis Smith, Bill Brooks, Bobby Hebert 18.00
18 Reyna Thompson, Louis Oliver, Steve Broussard, Andre Reed 4.00

1991 Pinnacle

Score's first effort at a premium edition is its 415-card 1991 Pinnacle set. Each card front features an action shot and a mug shot against a black background with white borders. The back has an action photo superimposed against a black background, plus statistics, a profile and a biography. An anti-counterfeit band appears on the back of each card. Subsets include Head-to-Head, Technicians, Game Winners, Idols and Sidelines. There are also 58 rookies featured in the set; their cards have green backgrounds on the front, and a mug shot on the back. A standard-size Emmitt Smith promotional card was also created. It is identical in design to its regular set's counterpart, except the text on the back of the promo card mentions Smith's holdout before the season. Twelve four-card panels (5" x 7" each) were also made and use the same design as the regular 1991 cards. Each card in the panel has the same number as its counterpart in the regular set, but the panel is unnumbered.

		NM/M
Complete Set (415):		35.00
Common Player:		.10
Minor Stars:		.20
Foil Pack (12):		1.00
Foil Wax Box (36):		25.00
1	Warren Moon	.30
2	Morten Andersen	.10
3	Rohn Stark	.10
4	Mark Bortz	.10
5	*Mark Higgs*	.10
6	Troy Aikman	4.00
7	John Elway	1.50
8	Neal Anderson	.10
9	Chris Doleman	.10
10	Jay Schroeder	.10
11	Sterling Sharpe	.40
12	Steve DeBerg	.10
13	Ronnie Lott	.10
14	Sea Landeta	.10
15	Jim Everett	.10
16	Jim Breech	.10
17	Barry Foster	.10
18	Mike Merriweather	.10
19	Eric Metcalf	.40
20	Mark Carrier	.10
21	James Brooks	.10
22	Nate Odomes	.10
23	Rodney Hampton	.50
24	Chris Miller	.10
25	Roger Craig	.10
26	Louis Oliver	.10
27	Allen Pinkett	.10
28	Bubby Brister	.10
29	Reyna Thompson	.10
30	Issiac Holt	.10
31	Steve Broussard	.10
32	Christian Okoye	.10
33	Dave Meggett	.10
34	Andre Reed	.20
35	Shane Conlan	.10
36	Eric Ball	.10
37	Johnny Bailey	.10
38	Don Majkowski	.10
39	Gerald Williams	.10
40	Kevin Mack	.10
41	Jeff Herrod	.10
42	Emmitt Smith	6.00
43	Wendell Davis	.10
44	Lorenzo White	.10
45	Andre Rison	.20
46	Jerry Gray	.10
47	Dennis Smith	.10
48	Gaston Green	.10
49	Dermontti Dawson	.10
50	Jeff Hostetler	.30
51	Nick Lowery	.10
52	Merril Hoge	.10
53	Bobby Hebert	.10
54	Scott Case	.10
55	Jack Del Rio	.10
56	Cornelius Bennett	.10
57	Tony Mandarich	.10
58	Bill Brooks	.10
59	Jessie Tuggle	.10
60	*Hugh Millen*	.10
61	Tony Bennett	.10
62	*Chris Dishman*	.10
63	*Darryl Henley*	.10
64	Duane Bickett	.10
65	Jay Hilgenberg	.10
66	Joe Montana	3.50
67	Bill Fralic	.10
68	Sam Mills	.10
69	Bruce Armstrong	.10
70	Dan Marino	5.00
71	Jim Lachey	.10
72	Rod Woodson	.10
73	Simon Fletcher	.10
74	Bruce Matthews	.10
75	Howie Long	.10
76	John Friesz	.10
77	Karl Mecklenburg	.10
78	John L. Williams	.10
79	*Rob Burnett*	.10
80	Anthony Carter	.10
81	Henry Ellard	.10
82	Don Beebe	.10
83	Louis Lipps	.10
84	Greg McMurty	.10
85	Will Wolford	.10
86	Eric Green	.20
87	Irving Fryar	.10
88	John Offerdahl	.10
89	John Alt	.10
90	Tom Tupa	.10
91	Don Mosebar	.10
92	Jeff George	.50
93	Vinny Testaverde	.20
94	Greg Townsend	.10
95	Derrick Fenner	.10
96	Brian Mitchell	.20
97	Herschel Walker	.10
98	Ricky Proehl	.10
99	Mark Clayton	.10
100	Derrick Thomas	.20
101	Jim Harbaugh	.50
102	Barry Word	.10
103	Jerry Rice	4.00
104	Keith Byars	.10
105	Marion Butts	.10
106	Rich Moran	.10
107	Thurman Thomas	.75
108	Stephone Paige	.10
109	David Johnson	.10
110	William Perry	.10
111	Haywood Jeffires	.10
112	Rodney Peete	.10
113	Andy Heck	.10
114	Kevin Ross	.10
115	Michael Carter	.10
116	Tim McKyer	.10
117	Kenneth Davis	.10
118	Richmond Webb	.10
119	Rich Camarillo	.10
120	James Francis	.10
121	Craig Heyward	.10
122	Hardy Nickerson	.10
123	Michael Brooks	.10
124	Fred Barnett	.30
125	Cris Carter	.40
126	Brian Jordan	.10
127	Pat Leahy	.10
128	Kevin Greene	.10
129	Trace Armstrong	.10
130	Eugene Lockhart	.10
131	Albert Lewis	.10
132	Ernie Jones	.10
133	Eric Martin	.10
134	Anthony Thompson	.10
135	Tim Krumrie	.10
136	James Lofton	.10
137	John Taylor	.10
138	Jeff Cross	.10
139	Tommy Kane	.10
140	Robb Thomas	.10
141	Gary Anderson	.10
142	Mark Murphy	.10
143	Rickey Jackson	.10
144	Ken O'Brien	.10
145	Ernest Givins	.10
146	Jessie Hester	.10
147	Deion Sanders	1.75
148	*Keith Henderson*	.10
149	Chris Singleton	.10
150	Rod Bernstine	.10
151	Quinn Early	.10
152	Boomer Esiason	.10
153	Mike Gann	.10
154	Dino Hackett	.10
155	Perry Kemp	.10
156	Mark Ingram	.10
157	Daryl Johnston	.75
158	Eugene Daniel	.10
159	Dalton Hilliard	.10
160	Rufus Porter	.10
161	Tunch Ilkin	.10
162	James Hasty	.10
163	Keith McKeller	.10
164	Heath Sherman	.10
165	Vai Sikahema	.10
166	Pat Terrell	.10
167	Anthony Munoz	.10
168	*Brad Edwards*	.10
169	Tom Rathman	.10
170	Steve McMichael	.10
171	Vaughan Johnson	.10
172	*Nate Lewis*	.10
173	Mark Rypien	.10
174	Rob Moore	.10
175	Tim Green	.10
176	Tony Casillas	.10
177	Jon Hand	.10
178	Todd McNair	.10
179	*Toi Cook*	.10
180	Eddie Brown	.10
181	Mark Jackson	.10
182	Pete Stoyanovich	.10
183	*Bryce Paup*	2.00
184	Anthony Miller	.20
185	Dan Saleaumua	.10
186	Guy McIntyre	.10
187	Broderick Thomas	.10
188	Frank Warren	.10
189	Drew Hill	.10
190	Reggie White	.40
191	Chris Hinton	.10
192	David Little	.10
193	David Fulcher	.10
194	Clarence Verdin	.10
195	Junior Seau	1.00
196	Blair Thomas	.10
197	Stan Brock	.10
198	Gary Clark	.10
199	Michael Irvin	.75
200	Ronnie Harmon	.10
201	Steve Young	3.00
202	Brian Noble	.10
203	Dan Stryzinski	.10
204	Darryl Talley	.10
205	David Alexander	.10
206	Pat Swilling	.10
207	Gary Plummer	.10
208	Robert Delpino	.10
209	Norm Johnson	.10
210	Mike Singletary	.10
211	Anthony Johnson	.10
212	Eric Allen	.10
213	Gill Fenerty	.10
214	Neil Smith	.10
215	Joe Phillips	.10
216	Ottis Anderson	.10
217	LeRoy Butler	.10
218	Ray Childress	.10
219	Rodney Holman	.10
220	Kevin Fagan	.10
221	Bruce Smith	.10
222	Brad Muster	.10
223	Mike Horan	.10
224	Steve Atwater	.10
225	Rich Gannon	.10
226	Anthony Pleasant	.10
227	Steve Jordan	.10
228	Lomas Brown	.10
229	Jackie Slater	.10
230	Brad Baxter	.10
231	Joe Morris	.10
232	Marcus Allen	.20
233	Chris Warren	1.00
234	Johnny Johnson	.10
235	Phil Simms	.10
236	Dave Krieg	.10
237	Jim McMahon	.10
238	Richard Dent	.10
239	*John Washington*	.10
240	Sammie Smith	.10
241	Brian Brennan	.10
242	Cortez Kennedy	.20
243	Tim McDonald	.10
244	Charles Haley	.10
245	Joey Browner	.10
246	Eddie Murray	.10
247	Bob Golic	.10
248	Myron Guyton	.10
249	Dennis Byrd	.10
250	Barry Sanders	4.00
251	Clay Matthews	.10
252	Pepper Johnson	.10
253	*Eric Swann*	1.00
254	Lamar Lathon	.10
255	Andre Tippett	.10
256	Tom Newberry	.10
257	Kyle Clifton	.10
258	Leslie O'Neal	.10
259	Bubba McDowell	.10
260	Scott Davis	.10
261	Wilber Marshall	.10
262	Marv Cook	.10
263	Jeff Lageman	.10
264	Mike Young	.10
265	Gary Zimmerman	.10
266	Mike Munchak	.10
267	David Treadwell	.10
268	Steve Wisniewski	.10
269	Mark Duper	.10
270	Chris Spielman	.10
271	Brett Perriman	.50
272	Lionel Washington	.10
273	Lawrence Taylor	.20
274	Mark Collins	.10
275	Mark Carrier	.10
276	Paul Gruber	.10
277	Earnest Byner	.10
278	Andre Collins	.10
279	Reggie Cobb	.10
280	Art Monk	.20
281	*Henry Jones*	.20
282	*Mike Pritchard*	.75
283	*Moe Gardner*	.20
284	*Chris Zorich*	.50
285	*Keith Traylor*	.20
286	*Mike Dumas*	.20
287	*Ed King*	.20
288	*Russell Maryland*	.20
289	*Alfred Williams*	.20
290	*Derek Russell*	.20
291	*Vinnie Clark*	.20
292	*Mike Croel*	.20
293	*Todd Marinovich*	.20
294	*Phil Hansen*	.20
295	*Aaron Craver*	.20
296	*Nick Bell*	.20
297	*Kenny Walker*	.20
298	*Roman Phifer*	.20
299	*Kanavis McGhee*	.20
300	*Ricky Ervins*	.20
301	*Jim Price*	.20
302	*John Johnson*	.20
303	George Thornton	.20
304	Huey Richardson	.10
305	*Harry Colon*	.20
306	*Antone Davis*	.20
307	*Todd Lyght*	.30
308	*Bryan Cox*	1.00
309	*Brad Goebel*	.20
310	*Eric Moten*	.20
311	*John Kasay*	.30
312	*Esera Tuaolo*	.20
313	*Bobby Wilson*	.20
314	*Mo Lewis*	.20
315	*Harvey Williams*	1.00
316	Mike Stonebreaker	.10
317	*Charles McRae*	.20
318	*John Flannery*	.20
319	*Ted Washington*	.20
320	*Stanley Richard*	.20
321	*Browning Nagle*	.20
322	*Ed McCaffery*	3.50
323	*Jeff Graham*	.50
324	Stan Thomas	.10
325	*Lawrence Dawsey*	.20
326	*Eric Bieniemy*	.30
327	*Tim Barnett*	.20
328	*Eric Pegram*	1.50
329	Lamar Rogers	.10
330	*Ernie Mills*	.20
331	*Pat Harlow*	.20
332	*Greg Lewis*	.20
333	*Jarrod Bunch*	.20
334	*Dan McGwire*	.20
335	*Randal Hill*	.50
336	*Leonard Russell*	.50
337	Carnell Lake	.10
338	Brian Blades	.10
339	Darrell Green	.10
340	Bobby Humphrey	.10
341	Mervyn Fernandez	.10
342	Ricky Sanders	.10
343	Keith Jackson	.20
344	Carl Banks	.10
345	Gill Byrd	.10
346	Al Toon	.10
347	Stephen Baker	.10
348	Randall Cunningham	.10
349	Flipper Anderson	.10
350	Jay Novacek	.10
351	Young/Smith (HH)	.40
352	Sanders/Browner (HH)	.75
353	Montana/Carrier (HH)	.50
354	Thomas/Taylor (HH)	.20
355	Rice/Green (HH)	.50
356	Warren Moon (TECH)	.20
357	Anthony Munoz (TECH)	.10
358	Barry Sanders (TECH)	1.50
359	Jerry Rice (TECH)	1.00
360	Joey Browner (TECH)	.10
361	Morten Andersen (TECH)	.10
362	Sean Landeta (TECH)	.10
363	Thurman Thomas (GW)	.20
364	Emmitt Smith (GW)	3.00
365	Gaston Green (GW)	.10
366	Barry Sanders (GW)	2.00
367	Christian Okoye (GW)	.10
368	Earnest Byner (GW)	.10
369	Neal Anderson (GW)	.10
370	Herschel Walker (GW)	.10
371	Rodney Hampton (GW)	.20
372	Darryl Talley (IDOL)	.10
373	Mark Carrier (IDOL)	.10
374	Jim Breech (IDOL)	.10
375	Rodney Hampton (IDOL)	.20
376	Kevin Mack (IDOL)	.10
377	Steve Jordan (IDOL)	.10
378	Boomer Esiason (IDOL)	.10
379	Steve DeBerg (IDOL)	.10
380	Al Toon (IDOL)	.10
381	Ronnie Lott (IDOL)	.10
382	Henry Ellard (IDOL)	.10
383	Troy Aikman (IDOL)	1.25
384	Thurman Thomas	.50
385	Dan Marino (IDOL)	1.75
386	Howie Long (IDOL)	.10
387	Franco Harris Immaculate Reception	.10
388	Esera Tuaolo	.10
389	Super Bowl XXVI (Super Bowl Records)	.10
390	Charles Mann	.10
391	Kenny Walker	.10
392	Reggie Roby	.10
393	*Bruce Pickens*	.20
394	Ray Childress (SL)	.10
395	Karl Mecklenburg (SL)	.10
396	Dean Biasucci (SL)	.10
397	John Alt (SL)	.10
398	Marcus Allen (SL)	.10
399	John Offerdahl (SL)	.10
400	Richard Tardits (SL)	.10
401	Al Toon (SL)	.10
402	Joey Browner (SL)	.10
403	Spencer Tillman (SL)	.10
404	Jay Novacek (SL)	.10
405	Stephen Braggs (SL)	.10
406	Mike Tice (SL)	.10
407	Kevin Greene (SL)	.10
408	Reggie White (SL)	.20
409	Brian Noble (SL)	.10
410	Bart Oates (SL)	.10
411	Art Monk (SL)	.10
412	Ron Wolfley (SL)	.10
413	Louis Lipps (SL)	.10
414	*Dante Jones* (SL)	.20
415	Kenneth Davis (SL)	.10

1992 Pinnacle Samples

The six-card, standard-size set features six cards from the 1992 Pinnacle football set with the same design, as well as the same card numbers on the backs as their regular-issue counterparts.

		NM/M
Complete Set (6):		5.00
Common Player:		1.00
1	Reggie White	2.00
5	Pepper Johnson	1.00
19	Chris Spielman	1.00
59	Mike Croel	1.00
100	Bobby Hebert	1.00
102	Rodney Hampton	1.50

Values quoted in this guide reflect the retail price of a card—the price a collector can expect to pay when buying a card from a dealer. The wholesale price—that which a collector can expect to receive from a dealer when selling cards—will be significantly lower, depending on desirability and condition.

1992 Pinnacle

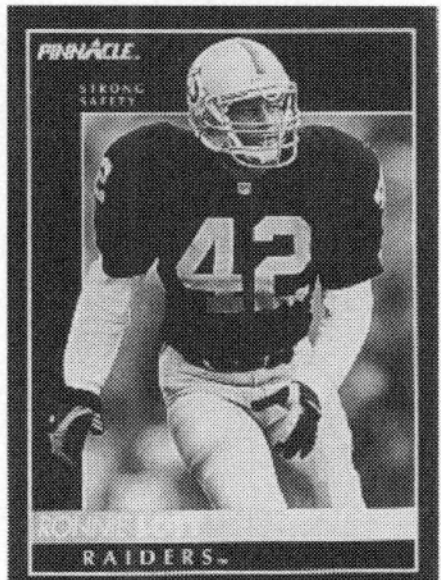

Score decreased its second Pinnacle set to 360 cards. The fronts have action shots with a white frame and black border. Parts of the photos extend over the background, giving them a cut-out look. The player's name is at the bottom of the card in a team color-coded bar. The horizontal backs have black backgrounds with white borders and a purple band that contains the player's name. Also included on the backs are a profile, biography, statistics and a mug shot. Subsets include Rookies, Sidelines, Game Winners, Hall of Famers and Idols. Insert sets include Team Pinnacle cards (13) and Team 2000 (30 cards). A six-card promotional set was also produced to preview the regular set. The cards have a similar design to the regular set, but each card back is marked as a "SAMPLE."

		NM/M
Complete Set (360):		20.00
Common Player:		.05
Minor Stars:		.10
Pack (16):		.75
Wax Box (36):		25.00
1	Reggie White	.10
2	Eric Green	.05
3	Craig Heyward	.05
4	Phil Simms	.05
5	Pepper Johnson	.05
6	Sean Landeta	.05
7	Dino Hackett	.05
8	Andre Ware	.05
9	Ricky Nattiel	.05
10	Jim Price	.05
11	Jim Ritcher	.05
12	Kelly Stouffer	.05
13	Ray Crockett	.05
14	Steve Tasker	.05
15	Barry Sanders	3.50
16	Pat Swilling	.05
17	Moe Gardner	.05
18	Steve Young	2.50
19	Chris Spielman	.05
20	Richard Dent	.05
21	Anthony Munoz	.05
22	Thurman Thomas	.50
23	Ricky Sanders	.05
24	Steve Atwater	.05
25	Tony Tolbert	.05
26	Haywood Jeffires	.05
27	Duane Bickett	.05
28	Tim McDonald	.05
29	Cris Carter	.10
30	Derrick Thomas	.10
31	Hugh Millen	.05
32	Bart Oates	.05
33	Darryl Talley	.05
34	Marion Butts	.05
35	Pete Stoyanovich	.05
36	Ronnie Lott	.05
37	Simon Fletcher	.05
38	Morten Andersen	.05
39	Clyde Simmons	.05
40	Mark Rypien	.05
41	Henry Ellard	.05
42	Michael Irvin	.50
43	Louis Lipps	.05
44	John L. Williams	.05
45	Broderick Thomas	.05
46	Don Majkowski	.05
47	William Perry	.05
48	David Fulcher	.05
49	Tony Bennett	.05
50	Clay Matthews	.05
51	Warren Moon	.10
52	Bruce Armstrong	.05
53	Bill Brooks	.05
54	Greg Townsend	.05
55	Steve Broussard	.05
56	Mel Gray	.05
57	Kevin Mack	.05
58	Emmitt Smith	5.00
59	Mike Croel	.05
60	Brian Mitchell	.05
61	Bennie Blades	.05
62	Carnell Lake	.05
63	Cornelius Bennett	.05
64	Darrell Thompson	.05
65	Jessie Hester	.05
66	Marv Cook	.05
67	Tim Brown	.10
68	Mark Duper	.05
69	Robert Delpino	.05
70	Eric Martin	.05
71	Wendell Davis	.05
72	Vaughan Johnson	.05
73	Brian Blades	.05
74	Ed King	.05
75	Gaston Green	.05
76	Christian Okoye	.05
77	Rohn Stark	.05
78	Kevin Greene	.05
79	Jay Novacek	.10
80	Chip Lohmiller	.05
81	Cris Dishman	.05
82	Ethan Horton	.05
83	Pat Harlow	.05
84	Mark Ingram	.05
85	Mark Carrier	.05
86	Sam Mills	.05
87	Mark Higgs	.05
88	Keith Jackson	.10
89	Gary Anderson	.05
90	Ken Harvey	.05
91	Anthony Carter	.05
92	Randall McDaniel	.05
93	Johnny Johnson	.10
94	Shane Conlan	.05
95	Sterling Sharpe	.10
96	Guy McIntyre	.05
97	Albert Lewis	.05
98	Chris Doleman	.05
99	Andre Rison	.10
100	Bobby Hebert	.05
101	Dan Owens	.05
102	Rodney Hampton	.10
103	Ernie Jones	.05
104	Reggie Cobb	.05
105	Wilber Marshall	.05
106	Mike Munchak	.05
107	Cortez Kennedy	.05
108	Todd Lyght	.05
109	Burt Grossman	.05
110	Ferrell Edmunds	.05
111	Jim Everett	.05
112	Hardy Nickerson	.05
113	Andre Tippett	.05
114	Ronnie Harmon	.05
115	Andre Waters	.05
116	Ernest Givins	.05
117	Eric Hill	.05
118	Erric Pegram	.10
119	Jarrod Bunch	.05
120	Marcus Allen	.10
121	Barry Foster	.05
122	Kent Hull	.05
123	Neal Anderson	.05
124	Stephen Braggs	.05
125	Nick Lowery	.05
126	Jeff Hostetler	.10
127	Michael Carter	.05
128	Don Warren	.05
129	Brad Baxter	.05
130	John Taylor	.05
131	Harold Green	.05
132	Mike Merriweather	.05
133	Gary Clark	.05
134	Vince Buck	.05
135	Dan Saleaumua	.05
136	Gary Zimmerman	.05
137	Richmond Webb	.05
138	Art Monk	.10
139	Mervyn Fernandez	.05
140	Mark Jackson	.05
141	Freddie Joe Nunn	.05
142	Jeff Lageman	.05
143	Kenny Walker	.05
144	Mark Carrier	.05
145	Jon Vaughn	.05
146	Greg Davis	.05
147	Bubby Brister	.05
148	Mo Lewis	.05
149	Howie Long	.05
150	Rod Bernstine	.05
151	Nick Bell	.05
152	Terry Allen	.50
153	William Fuller	.05
154	Dexter Carter	.05
155	Gene Atkins	.05
156	Don Beebe	.05
157	Mark Collins	.05
158	Jerry Ball	.05
159	Fred Barnett	.05
160	Rodney Holman	.05
161	Stephen Baker	.05
162	Jeff Graham	.10
163	Leonard Russell	.10
164	Jeff Gossett	.05
165	Vinny Testaverde	.05
166	Maurice Hurst	.05
167	Louis Oliver	.05
168	Jim Morrissey	.05
169	Greg Kragen	.05
170	Andre Collins	.05
171	Dave Meggett	.05
172	Keith Henderson	.05
173	Vince Newsome	.05
174	Chris Hinton	.05
175	James Hasty, Steve Sewell	.05
176	John Offerdahl	.05
177	Lomas Brown	.05
178	Neil O'Donnell	.10
179	Leonard Marshall	.05
180	Bubba McDowell	.05
181	Herman Moore	2.00
182	Rob Moore	.05
183	Earnest Byner	.05
184	Keith McCants	.05
185	Floyd Turner	.05
186	Steve Jordan	.05
187	Nate Odomes	.05
188	Jeff Herrod	.05
189	Jim Harbaugh	.10
190	Jessie Tuggle	.05
191	Al Smith	.05
192	Lawrence Dawsey	.05
193	*Steve Bono*	1.00
194	Greg Lloyd	.10
195	Steve Wisniewski	.05
196	Larry Kelm	.05
197	Tommy Kane	.05
198	*Mark Schlereth*	.05

199	Ray Childress	.05
200	Vincent Brown	.05
201	Rodney Peete	.10
202	Dennis Smith	.05
203	Bruce Matthews	.05
204	Rickey Jackson	.05
205	Eric Allen	.05
206	Rich Camarillo	.05
207	Jim Lachey	.05
208	Kevin Ross	.05
209	Irving Fryar	.05
210	Mark Clayton	.05
211	Keith Byars	.05
212	John Elway	.75
213	Harris Barton	.05
214	Aeneas Williams	.05
215	Rich Gannon	.05
216	Toi Cook	.05
217	Rod Woodson	.10
218	Gary Anderson	.05
219	Reggie Roby	.05
220	Karl Mecklenburg	.05
221	Rufus Porter	.05
222	Jon Hand	.05
223	Tim Barnett	.05
224	Eric Swann	.10
225	Eugene Robinson	.05
226	Mike Young	.05
227	Frank Warren	.05
228	Mike Kenn	.05
229	Tim Green	.05
230	Barry Word	.05
231	Mike Pritchard	.05
232	John Kasay	.05
233	Derek Russell	.05
234	Jim Breech	.05
235	Pierce Holt	.05
236	Tim Krumrie	.05
237	William Roberts	.05
238	Erik Kramer	.10
239	Brett Perriman	.10
240	Reyna Thompson	.05
241	Chris Miller	.05
242	Drew Hill	.05
243	Curtis Duncan	.05
244	Seth Joyner	.05
245	Ken Norton	.05
246	Calvin Williams	.05
247	James Joseph	.05
248	*Bennie Thompson*	.05
249	Tunch Ilkin	.05
250	Brad Edward	.05
251	Jeff Jaeger	.05
252	Gill Byrd	.05
253	Jeff Feagles	.05
254	*Jamie Dukes*	.05
255	Greg McMurtry	.05
256	Anthony Johnson	.05
257	Lamar Lathon	.05
258	John Roper	.05
259	Lorenzo White	.05
260	Brian Noble	.05
261	Chris Singleton	.05
262	Todd Marinovich	.05
263	Jay Hilgenberg	.05
264	Kyle Clifton	.05
265	Tony Casillas	.05
266	James Francis	.05
267	Eddie Anderson	.05
268	Tim Harris	.05
269	James Lofton	.05
270	Jay Schroeder	.05
271	Ed West	.05
272	Don Mosebar	.05
273	Jackie Slater	.05
274	*Fred McAfee*	.05
276	Charles Mann	.05
277	Ron Hall	.05
278	Darrell Green	.05
279	Jeff Cross	.05
280	Jeff Wright	.05
281	Issiac Holt	.05
282	Dermontti Dawson	.05
283	Michael Haynes	.05
284	Tony Mandarich	.05
285	Leroy Hoard	.05
286	Darryl Henley	.05
287	Tim McGee	.05
288	Willie Gault	.05
289	Dalton Hilliard	.05
290	Tim McKyer	.05
291	Tom Waddle	.05
292	Eric Thomas	.05
293	Herschel Walker	.05
294	Donnell Woolford	.05
295	James Brooks	.05
296	Brad Muster	.05
297	Brent Jones	.05
298	Erik Howard	.05
299	Alvin Harper	.10
300	Joey Browner	.05
301	Jack Del Rio	.05
302	Cleveland Gary	.05
303	Brett Favre	5.00
304	Freeman McNeil	.05
305	Willie Green	.05
306	Percy Snow	.05
307	Neil Smith	.05
308	Eric Bieniemy	.05
309	Keith Traylor	.05
310	Ernie Mills	.05
311	Will Wolford	.05
312	Robert Young	.05
313	Anthony Smith	.05
314	*Robert Porcher*	.50
315	*Leon Searcy*	.05
316	*Amp Lee*	.20
317	*Siran Stacy*	.05
318	*Patrick Rowe*	.05
319	*Chris Mims*	.05
320	*Matt Elliott*	.05
321	*Ricardo McDonald*	.05
322	*Keith Hamilton*	.05
323	*Edgar Bennett*	1.00
324	*Chris Hakel*	.05
325	*Dexter McNabb*	.05
326	*Roderick Milstead*	.05
327	*Joe Bowden*	.05
328	*Brian Bollinger*	.05
329	*Darryl Williams*	.05
330	*Tommy Vardell*	.15
331	Glenn Parker	.05
332	Herschel Walker	.05
333	Mike Cofer	.05
334	Mark Rypien	.05
335	Andre Rison	.10
336	Henry Ellard	.05
337	Rob Moore	.05
338	Fred Barnett	.05
339	Mark Clayton	.05
340	Eric Martin	.05
341	Irving Fryar	.05
342	Tim Brown	.10
343	Sterling Sharpe	.10
344	Gary Clark	.05
345	John Mackey	.05
346	Lem Barney	.05
347	John Riggins	.05
348	Marion Butts	.05
349	Jeff Lageman	.05
350	Eric Green	.05
351	Reggie White	.10
352	Marv Cook	.05
353	John Elway, Roger Staubach	.50
354	Steve Tasker	.05
355	Nick Lowery	.05
356	Mark Clayton	.05
357	Warren Moon	.10
358	Eric Metcalf	.05
359	Charles Haley	.05
360	*Terrell Buckley*	.05

1992 Pinnacle Team Pinnacle

Each of these 13 insert cards features two players on it, one on each side. Score randomly included the cards in 1992 Score Pinnacle packs at a rate of one per every 36 packs. The cards have a gold foil stripe at the bottom with the player's name and position. A black stripe beneath this gold stripe has a card number (1 of 13, etc.), but this number only appears on one side of the card. An offensive player is featured on one side, while a standout defensive counterpart is on the other. The cards feature the artwork of Christopher Greco.

		NM/M
Complete Set (13):		20.00
Common Player:		1.00
Minor Stars:		2.00
1	Mark Rypien, Ronnie Lott	1.00
2	Barry Sanders, Derrick Thomas	5.00
3	Thurman Thomas, Pat Swilling	2.00
4	Eric Green, Steve Atwater	1.00
5	Haywood Jeffires, Darrell Green	1.00
6	Michael Irvin, Eric Allen	2.00
7	Bruce Matthews, Jerry Ball	1.00
8	Steve Wisniewski, Pepper Johnson	1.00
9	William Roberts, Karl Mecklenburg	1.00
10	Jim Lachey, William Fuller	1.00
11	Anthony Munoz, Reggie White	2.00
12	Mel Gray, Steve Tasker	1.00
13	Jeff Jaeger, Jeff Gossett	1.00

1992 Pinnacle Team 2000

The NFL's projected stars of the year 2000 are featured on these inserts, available randomly two per 27-card jumbo pack of 1992 Score Pinnacle football. The card is framed on the left and bottom by a black border. "Team 2000" is written in gold foil along the left side of the card; the player's name is in gold foil at the bottom. A team helmet logo intersects the two borders. The card back has a career summary and player photo against a black background. The horizontally-designed back also has a card number (1 of 30, etc.).

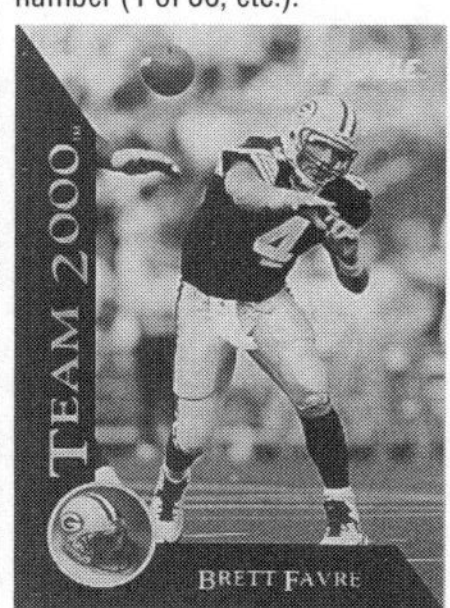

		NM/M
Complete Set (30):		15.00
Common Player:		.25
Minor Stars:		.50
1	Todd Marinovich	.25
2	Rodney Hampton	.50
3	Mike Croel	.25
4	Leonard Russell	.50
5	Herman Moore	.75
6	Rob Moore	.50
7	Jon Vaughn	.25
8	Lamar Lathon	.25
9	Ed King	.25
10	Moe Gardner	.25
11	Barry Foster	.25
12	Eric Green	.25
13	Kenny Walker	.25
14	Tim Barnett	.25
15	Derrick Thomas	.50
16	Steve Atwater	.25
17	Nick Bell	.25
18	John Friesz	.50
19	Emmitt Smith	3.00
20	Eric Swann	.25
21	Barry Sanders	4.00
22	Mark Carrier	.25
23	Brett Favre	4.00
24	James Francis	.25
25	Lawrence Dawsey	.25
26	Keith McCants	.25
27	Broderick Thomas	.25
28	Mike Pritchard	.25
29	Bruce Pickens	.25
30	Todd Lyght	.25

1993 Pinnacle Samples

The six-card, standard size set gave collectors a preview of the 1993 base set by issuing the first six cards of the regular-issue set. The cards were distributed in 7-1/2" x 7" panels with two rows of three cards.

		NM/M
Complete Set (6):		8.00
Common Player:		1.00
1	Brett Favre	6.00
2	Tommy Vardell	1.00
3	Jarrod Bunch	1.00
4	Mike Croel	1.00
5	Morten Andersen	1.00
6	Barry Foster	1.00

1993 Pinnacle

Score's 1993 Pinnacle set has 360 cards and includes two subsets - Hall of Famers and Hometown Heroes. The cards have black backgrounds, with the player's team name at the top and his name at the bottom of the card. Backs have a mug shot, one-year and career statistics, a profile and biographical information. Insert sets include Men of Autumn (55 cards), Rookies (25), Super Bowl XXVII (10), Team 2001 (30) and Team Pinnacle (13 cards). Six sample cards on a 7-1/2" x 7" panel was also produced as previews of the regular set. The cards are similar in design to the regular set, including numbers, but the sample cards are labeled as such on the backs under the anti-counterfeit band.

		NM/M
Complete Set (360):		25.00
Common Player:		.10
Minor Stars:		.20
Autograph F. Harris:		25.00
Wax Box:		25.00
1	Brett Favre	4.00
2	Tommy Vardell	.10
3	Jarrod Bunch	.10
4	Mike Croel	.10
5	Morten Andersen	.10
6	Barry Foster	.30
7	Chris Spielman	.10
8	Jim Jeffcoat	.10
9	Ken Ruettgers	.10
10	Cris Dishman	.10
11	Ricky Watters	.30
12	Alfred Williams	.10
13	Mark Kelso	.10
14	Moe Gardner	.10
15	Terry Allen	.10
16	Willie Gault	.10
17	Bubba McDowell	.10
18	Brian Mitchell	.10
19	Karl Mecklenburg	.10
20	Jim Everett	.20
21	Bobby Humphrey	.10
22	Tim Krumrie	.10
23	Ken Norton	.10
24	Wendell Davis	.10
25	Brad Baxter	.10
26	Mel Gray	.10
27	Jon Vaughn	.10
28	James Hasty	.10
29	Chris Warren	.50
30	Tim Harris	.10
31	Eric Metcalf	.10
32	Rob Moore	.10
33	Charles Haley	.10
34	Leonard Marshall	.10
35	Jeff Graham	.10
36	Eugene Robinson	.10
37	Darryl Talley	.10
38	Brent Jones	.10
39	Reggie Roby	.10
40	Bruce Armstrong	.10
41	Audray McMillian	.10
42	Bern Brostek	.10
43	Tony Bennett	.10
44	Albert Lewis	.10
45	Derrick Thomas	.25
46	Cris Carter	.20
47	Richmond Webb	.10
48	Sean Landeta	.10
49	Cleveland Gary	.10
50	Mark Carrier	.10
51	Lawrence Dawsey	.10
52	Lamar Lathon	.10
53	Nick Bell	.10
54	Curtis Duncan	.10
55	Irving Fryar	.10
56	Seth Joyner	.10
57	Jay Novacek	.10
58	John L. Williams	.10
59	Amp Lee	.10
60	Marion Butts	.10
61	Clyde Simmons	.10
62	Rich Gannon	.10
63	Anthony Johnson	.10
64	Dave Meggett	.10
65	James Francis	.10
66	Trace Armstrong	.10
67	Mo Lewis	.10
68	Cornelius Bennett	.10
69	Mark Duper	.10
70	Frank Reich	.10
71	Eric Green	.10
72	Bruce Matthews	.10
73	Steve Broussard	.10
74	Anthony Carter	.10
75	Sterling Sharpe	.30
76	Mike Kenn	.10
77	Andre Rison	.30
78	Todd Marinovich	.10
79	Vincent Brown	.10
80	Harold Green	.10
81	Art Monk	.10
82	Reggie Cobb	.10
83	Johnny Johnson	.10
84	Tommy Kane	.10
85	Rohn Stark	.10
86	Steve Tasker	.10
87	Ronnie Harmon	.10
88	Pepper Johnson	.10
89	Hardy Nickerson	.10
90	Alvin Harper	.20
91	Louis Oliver	.10
92	Rod Woodson	.25
93	Sam Mills	.10
94	Randall McDaniel	.10
95	Johnny Holland	.10
96	Jackie Slater	.10
97	Don Mosebar	.10
98	Andre Ware	.10
99	Kelvin Martin	.10
100	Emmitt Smith	4.00
101	Michael Brooks	.10
102	Dan Saleaumua	.10
103	John Elway	1.00
104	Henry Jones	.10
105	William Perry	.10
106	James Lofton	.10
107	Carnell Lake	.10
108	Chip Lohmiller	.10
109	Andre Tippett	.10
110	Barry Word	.10
111	Haywood Jeffires	.10
112	Kenny Walker	.10
113	John Randle	.10
114	Donnell Woolford	.10
115	Johnny Bailey	.10
116	Marcus Allen	.25
117	Mark Jackson	.10
118	Ray Agnew	.10
119	Gill Byrd	.10
120	Kyle Clifton	.10
121	Marv Cook	.10
122	Jerry Ball	.10
123	Steve Jordan	.10
124	Shannon Sharpe	.25
125	Brian Blades	.10
126	Rodney Hampton	.30
127	Bobby Hebert	.10
128	Jessie Tuggle	.10
129	Tom Newberry	.10
130	Keith McCants	.10
131	Richard Dent	.10
132	Herman Moore	1.00
133	Michael Irvin	.50
134	Ernest Givins	.10
135	Mark Rypien	.10
136	Leonard Russell	.10
137	Reggie White	.25
138	Thurman Thomas	.50
139	Nick Lowery	.10
140	Al Smith	.10
141	Jackie Harris	.10
142	Duane Bickett	.10
143	Lawyer Tillman	.10
144	Steve Wisniewski	.10
145	Derrick Fenner	.10
146	Harris Barton	.10
147	Rich Camarillo	.10
148	John Offerdahl	.10
149	Mike Johnson	.10
150	Ricky Reynolds	.10
151	Fred Barnett	.10
152	Nate Newton	.10
153	Chris Doleman	.10
154	Todd Scott	.10
155	Tim McKyer	.10
156	Ken Harvey	.10
157	Jeff Feagles	.10
158	Vince Workman	.10
159	Bart Oates	.10
160	Chris Miller	.10
161	Pete Stoyanovich	.10
162	Steve Wallace	.10
163	Dermontti Dawson	.10
164	Kenneth Davis	.10
165	Mike Munchak	.10
166	George Jamison	.10
167	Christian Okoye	.10
168	Chris Hinton	.10
169	Vaughan Johnson	.10
170	Gaston Green	.10
171	Kevin Greene	.10
172	Rob Burnett	.10
173	Norm Johnson	.10
174	Eric Hill	.10
175	Lomas Brown	.10
176	Chip Banks	.10
177	Greg Townsend	.10
178	David Fulcher	.10
179	Gary Anderson	.10
180	Brian Washington	.10
181	Brett Perriman	.10
182	Chris Chandler	.10
183	Phil Hansen	.10
184	Mark Clayton	.10
185	Frank Warren	.10
186	Tim Brown	.30
187	Mark Stepnoski	.10
188	Bryan Cox	.10
189	Gary Zimmerman	.10
190	Neil O'Donnell	.30
191	Anthony Smith	.10
192	Craig Heyward	.10
193	Keith Byars	.10
194	Sean Salisbury	.10
195	Todd Lyght	.10
196	Jessie Hester	.10
197	Rufus Porter	.10
198	Steve Christie	.10
199	Nate Lewis	.10
200	Barry Sanders	3.00
201	Michael Haynes	.10
202	John Taylor	.10
203	John Friesz	.10
204	William Fuller	.10
205	Dennis Smith	.10
206	Adrian Cooper	.10
207	Henry Thomas	.10
208	Gerald Williams	.10
209	Chris Burkett	.10
210	Broderick Thomas	.10
211	Marvin Washington	.10
212	Bennie Blades	.10
213	Tony Casillas	.10
214	Bubby Brister	.10
215	Don Griffin	.10
216	Jeff Cross	.10
217	Derrick Walker	.10
218	Lorenzo White	.10
219	Ricky Sanders	.10
220	Rickey Jackson	.10
221	Simon Fletcher	.10
222	Troy Vincent	.10
223	Gary Clark	.10
224	Stanley Richard	.10
225	Dave Krieg	.10
226	Warren Moon	.25
227	Reggie Langhorne	.10
228	Kent Hull	.10
229	Ferrell Edmunds	.10
230	Cortez Kennedy	.20
231	Hugh Millen	.10
232	Eugene Chung	.10
233	Rodney Peete	.10
234	Tom Waddle	.10
235	David Klingler	.10
236	Mark Carrier	.10
237	Jay Schroeder	.10
238	James Jones	.10
239	Phil Simms	.10
240	Steve Atwater	.10
241	Jeff Herrod	.10
242	Dale Carter	.10
243	*Glenn Cadrez*	.10
244	Wayne Martin	.10
245	Willie Davis	.10
246	Lawrence Taylor	.20
247	Stan Humphries	.50
248	Byron Evans	.10
249	Wilber Marshall	.10
250	*Michael Bankston*	.10
251	Steve McMichael	.10
252	Brad Edwards	.10
253	Will Wolford	.10
254	Paul Gruber	.10
255	Steve Young	2.00
256	Chuck Cecil	.10
257	Pierce Holt	.10
258	Anthony Miller	.20
259	Carl Banks	.10
260	Brad Muster	.10
261	Clay Matthews	.10
262	Rod Bernstine	.10
263	Tim Barnett	.10
264	Greg Lloyd	.10
265	Sean Jones	.10
266	J.J. Birden	.10
267	Tim McDonald	.10
268	Charles Mann	.10
269	Bruce Smith	.10
270	Sean Gilbert	.10
271	Ricardo McDonald	.10
272	Jeff Hostetler	.20
273	Russell Maryland	.10
274	*Dave Brown*	1.00
275	Ronnie Lott	.10
276	Jim Kelly	.25
277	Joe Montana	3.00
278	Eric Allen	.10
279	Browning Nagle	.10
280	Neal Anderson	.10
281	Troy Aikman	2.00
282	Ed McCaffrey	.10
283	Robert Jones	.10
284	Dalton Hilliard	.10
285	Johnny Mitchell	.10
286	Jay Hilgenberg	.10
287	Eric Martin	.10
288	Steve Emtman	.10
289	Vaughn Dunbar	.10
290	Mark Wheeler	.10
291	Leslie O'Neal	.10
292	Jerry Rice	2.00
293	Neil Smith	.10
294	Kerry Cash	.10
295	Dan McGwire	.10
296	Carl Pickens	1.00
297	Terrell Buckley	.10
298	Randall Cunningham	.25
299	Santana Dotson	.10
300	Keith Jackson	.10
301	Jim Lachey	.10
302	Dan Marino	3.50
303	Lee Williams	.10
304	Burt Grossman	.10
305	Kevin Mack	.10
306	Pat Swilling	.10
307	*Arthur Marshall*	.20
308	Jim Harbaugh	.10
309	Kurt Barber	.10
310	Harvey Williams	.10
311	Ricky Ervins	.10
312	Willie Anderson	.10
313	Bernie Kosar	.20
314	Boomer Esiason	.20
315	Deion Sanders	1.00
316	Ray Childress	.10
317	Howie Long	.10
318	Henry Ellard	.10
319	Marco Coleman	.10
320	Chris Mims	.10
321	Quentin Coryatt	.10
322	Jason Hanson	.10
323	Ricky Proehl	.10
324	Randal Hill	.10
325	Vinny Testaverde	.20
326	Jeff George	.20
327	Junior Seau	.40
328	Earnest Byner	.10
329	Andre Reed	.20
330	Phillippi Sparks	.10
331	Kevin Ross	.10
332	Clarence Verdin	.10
333	Darryl Henley	.10
334	Dana Hall	.10
335	Greg McMurtry	.10
336	Ron Hall	.10
337	Darrell Green	.10
338	Carlton Bailey	.10
339	Irv Eatman	.10
340	Greg Kragen	.10
341	Wade Wilson	.10
342	Klaus Wilmsmeyer	.10
343	Derek Brown	.10
344	Eric Williams	.10
345	Jim McMahon	.10
346	Mike Sherrard	.10
347	Mark Bavaro	.10
348	Anthony Munoz	.10
349	Eric Dickerson	.10
350	Steve Beuerlein	.10
351	Tim McGee	.10
352	Terry McDaniel	.10
353	Dan Fouts (Hall of Fame)	.20
354	Chuck Noll (Hall of Fame)	.10
355	Bill Walsh (Hall of Fame)	.10
356	Larry Little (Hall of Fame)	.10
357	Todd Marinovich (Hometown Hero)	.10
358	Jeff George (Hometown Hero)	.20
359	Bernie Kosar (Hometown Hero)	.10
360	Rob Moore (Hometown Hero)	.10

1993 Pinnacle Men of Autumn

These 55 cards were randomly inserted into 1993 Score football 16-card foil packs. The cards feature a glossy black laminate with a color action photo with a red frame. The set's logo is at the bottom, along with the player's name and position, which are in gold foil. Each back is horizontal and numbered and has a closeup shot of the player, plus a brief career summary.

		NM/M
Complete Set (55):		15.00
Common Player:		.25
Minor Stars:		.50
1	Andre Rison	.50
2	Thurman Thomas	.50
3	Wendell Davis	.25
4	Harold Green	.25
5	Eric Metcalf	.25
6	Michael Irvin	.50
7	John Elway	1.50
8	Barry Sanders	3.00
9	Sterling Sharpe	.50
10	Warren Moon	.50
11	Rohn Stark	.25
12	Derrick Thomas	.50
13	Terry McDaniel	.25
14	Cleveland Gary	.25
15	Dan Marino	3.00

16	Terry Allen	.25
17	Marv Cook	.25
18	Bobby Hebert	.25
19	Rodney Hampton	.50
20	Brad Baxter	.25
21	Reggie White	.50
22	Ricky Proehl	.25
23	Barry Foster	.50
24	Junior Seau	.50
25	Steve Young	2.00
26	Cortez Kennedy	.25
27	Reggie Cobb	.25
28	Mark Rypien	.25
29	Deion Sanders	1.00
30	Bruce Smith	.25
31	Richard Dent	.25
32	Alfred Williams	.25
33	Clay Matthews	.25
34	Emmitt Smith	4.00
35	Simon Fletcher	.25
36	Chris Spielman	.25
37	Brett Favre	4.00
38	Bruce Matthews	.25
39	Jeff Herrod	.25
40	Nick Lowery	.25
41	Steve Wisniewski	.25
42	Jim Everett	.25
43	Keith Jackson	.25
44	Chris Doleman	.25
45	Irving Fryar	.25
46	Rickey Jackson	.25
47	Pepper Johnson	.25
48	Randall Cunningham	.50
49	Rich Camarillo	.25
50	Rod Woodson	.50
51	Ronnie Harmon	.25
52	Ricky Watters	.50
53	Chris Warren	.50
54	Lawrence Dawsey	.25
55	Wilber Marshall	.25

1993 Pinnacle Rookies

These inserts cards have a black front with a color action photo emerging from a diamond-shaped metallic design in the middle. The set's name and Pinnacle logo are foil stamped in copper on the card, too. A metallic bar in team colors contains the player's name and team. The back is black and has a copper panel which includes career information. The player's name is in copper at the top of the card, which is also numbered 1 of 25, etc. Cards were reportedly randomly inserted one per every 36 1993 Pinnacle foil packs and feature several of the NFL's top rookies in 1993.

		NM/M
Complete Set (25):		400.00
Common Player:		7.00
1	Drew Bledsoe	150.00
2	Garrison Hearst	30.00
3	John Copeland	7.00
4	Eric Curry	7.00
5	Curtis Conway	25.00
6	Lincoln Kennedy	7.00
7	Jerome Bettis	50.00
8	Dan Williams	7.00
9	Patrick Bates	7.00
10	Brad Hopkins	7.00
11	Wayne Simmons	7.00
12	Rick Mirer	10.00
13	Tom Carter	7.00
14	Irv Smith	7.00
15	Marvin Jones	7.00
16	Deon Figures	7.00
17	Leonard Renfro	7.00
18	O.J. McDuffie	20.00
19	Dana Stubblefield	14.00
20	Carlton Gray	7.00
21	Demetrius DuBose	7.00
22	Troy Drayton	7.00
23	Natrone Means	30.00
24	Reggie Brooks	7.00
25	Glyn Milburn	14.00

1993 Pinnacle Super Bowl XXVII

The 1993 Super Bowl Champion Dallas Cowboys are featured on this 10-card insert set. Cards were randomly inserted in foil packs, one per hobby box of 1993 Pinnacle. Horizontal fronts feature a borderless color photo, plus a blue stripe that has the set name in blue foil. The backs are horizontal, too, and has the player's name, game highlights, Buffalo Bills and Cowboys helmets and the Super Bowl logo. Each card is numbered 1 of 10, etc.

		NM/M
Complete Set (10):		40.00
Common Player:		3.00
1	Rose Bowl	3.00
2	Dominant "D"	3.00
3	Emmitt Smith	25.00
4	Ken Norton Jr.	3.00
5	Michael Irvin	5.00
6	Jay Novacek	3.00
7	Charles Haley	3.00
8	Leon Lett	3.00
9	Alvin Harper	3.00
10	Sweet Victory	3.00

1993 Pinnacle Team Pinnacle

Each of these cards features two player paintings on it - one per side. An AFC player is featured with his NFC counterpart at that position. The paintings are framed by a thin white border and a larger black one. The player's name, position and conference are given in a stripe at the bottom. Both sides are numbered 1 of 13, etc. Cards were random inserts in 1993 Pinnacle foil packs, at least one per every 90 packs.

		NM/M
Complete Set (13):		90.00
Common Player:		3.00
1	Troy Aikman, Joe Montana	40.00
2	Thurman Thomas, Emmitt Smith	30.00
3	Rodney Hampton, Barry Foster	3.00
4	Sterling Sharpe, Anthony Miller	5.00
5	Haywood Jeffires, Michael Irvin	8.00
6	Jay Novacek, Keith Jackson	3.00
7	Richmond Webb, Steve Wallace	3.00
8	Reggie White, Leslie O'Neal	3.00
9	Cortez Kennedy, Sean Gilbert	3.00
10	Derrick Thomas, Wilber Marshall	3.00
11	Sam Mills, Junior Seau	8.00
12	Rod Woodson, Deion Sanders	10.00
13	Steve Atwater, Tim McDonald	3.00

1993 Pinnacle Team 2001

Promising young NFL players who might become stars by the year 2001 are featured in this 30-card insert set. A wide black stripe along the left and bottom of the card front borders a color action photo of the player. The set's and player's name are stamped in gold foil at the bottom, too, near a team logo. The back is done in a horizontal format and has a player mug shot and a black panel with a 1992 recap, team name and position, plus the player's name in gold foil. Cards, numbered 1 of 27, etc., were randomly inserted in 1993 Pinnacle 27-card super packs, one per pack.

		NM/M
Complete Set (30):		15.00
Common Player:		.50
Minor Stars:		1.00
1	Junior Seau	1.00
2	Cortez Kennedy	.50
3	Carl Pickens	3.00
4	David Klingler	.50
5	Santana Dotson	.50
6	Sean Gilbert	.50
7	Brett Favre	8.00
8	Steve Emtman	.50
9	Rodney Hampton	1.00
10	Browning Nagle	.50
11	Amp Lee	.50
12	Vaughn Dunbar	.50
13	Quentin Coryatt	.50
14	Marco Coleman	.50
15	Johnny Mitchell	.50
16	Arthur Marshall	.50
17	Dale Carter	.50
18	Henry Jones	.50
19	Terrell Buckley	.50
20	Tommy Vardell	.50
21	Tommy Maddox	.50
22	Barry Foster	1.00
23	Herman Moore	3.00
24	Ricky Watters	1.00
25	Mike Croel	.50
26	Russell Maryland	.50
27	Terry Allen	.50
28	Jon Vaughn	.50
29	Todd Marinovich	.50
30	Jeff Graham	.50

1994 Pinnacle Samples

The 10-card, regular-size set was issued as a preview for the 1994 regular-issue set. The cards have the same design as the cards in the base set, complete with same card-back numbers, but with a hole punched in a corner.

		NM/M
Complete Set (10):		10.00
Common Player:		.75
1	Deion Sanders (last line of text reads "es for a 17.7-yard...")	1.50
3	Barry Sanders Trophy Collection (name in brown ink on back)	2.50
24	Sean Gilbert (last line on text reads "mage to earn...")	.75
30	Alvin Harper (last line of text reads "tions and scored...")	.75
32	Derrick Thomas (last line of text reads "bles last season")	.75
85	James Jett (hometown/drafted line 1-3/16" long instead of 1-5/16")	.75
214	Chuck Levy (card number in white letters)	.75
DP8	William Floyd (last line of text reads "over would-be tacklers.")	1.25
NNO	Ad Card	.75
NNO	Pick Pinnacle Redemp. Card. (no player name on front)	.75

1994 Pinnacle

Pinnacle football 1994 contained full-bleed action shots with a gold foil football appearing on top of a large, textured, gold foil pyramid. Each player's name also appears in gold foil. The backs contain a close-up of the player and statistics on a football background. There were six insert sets in Pinnacle football: Trophy Collection, Team Pinnacle, Pick Pinnacle, Draft Pinnacle, Pinnacle Passer and Performers. Trophy is a 270-card parallel set that utilizes the Dufex printing process on regular-issue cards. Cards from the set are inserted at a rate of one-per-four packs. These cards feature the same shot as in the regular set, but have a Dufex background (shiny with silver highlights). Card backs are the same, except for a Trophy Collection logo in the bottom-right corner. Three insert sets were also made: Draft Picks, Performers and Team Pinnacle.

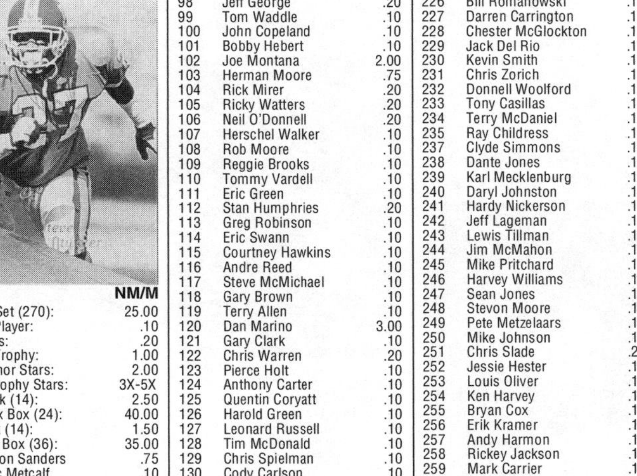

		NM/M
Complete Set (270):		25.00
Common Player:		.10
Minor Stars:		.20
Common Trophy:		1.00
Trophy Minor Stars:		2.00
Unlisted Trophy Stars:		3X-5X
Hobby Pack (14):		2.50
Hobby Wax Box (24):		40.00
Retail Pack (14):		1.50
Retail Wax Box (36):		35.00
1	Deion Sanders	.75
2	Eric Metcalf	.10
3	Barry Sanders	2.50
4	Ernest Givins	.10
5	Phil Simms	.10
6	Rod Woodson	.20
7	Michael Irvin	.20
8	Cortez Kennedy	.20
9	Eric Martin	.10
10	Jeff Hostetler	.20
11	Sterling Sharpe	.30
12	John Elway	1.00
13	Neal Anderson	.10
14	Terry Kirby	.20
15	Jim Everett	.10
16	Lawrence Dawsey	.10
17	Kelvin Martin	.10
18	Tim McGee	.10
19	Cris Carter	.20
20	Ronnie Harmon	.10
21	Jim Kelly	.30
22	Steve Young	1.50
23	Johnny Johnson	.10
24	Sean Gilbert	.10
25	Brian Mitchell	.10
26	Carl Pickens	.10
27	Tim Brown	.20
28	Reggie Langhorne	.10
29	Webster Slaughter	.10
30	Alvin Harper	.20
31	Andre Rison	.20
32	Derrick Thomas	.20
33	Irving Fryar	.10
34	Vinny Testaverde	.10
35	Steve Beuerlein	.10
36	Brett Favre	4.00
37	Barry Foster	.20
38	Vaughan Johnson	.10
39	Carlton Bailey	.10
40	Steve Emtman	.10
41	Anthony Miller	.10
42	Jeff Cross	.10
43	Trace Armstrong	.10
44	Derek Russell	.10
45	Vincent Brisby	.30
46	Mark Jackson	.10
47	Eugene Robinson	.10
48	John Friesz	.10
49	Scott Mitchell	.20
50	Steve Atwater	.10
51	Ken Norton	.10
52	Vincent Brown	.10
53	Morten Andersen	.10
54	Gary Anderson	.10
55	Eric Curry	.10
56	Henry Jones	.10
57	Willie Anderson	.10
58	Pat Swilling	.10
59	Erric Pegram	.10
60	Bruce Matthews	.10
61	Willie Davis	.10
62	O.J. McDuffie	.20
63	Qadry Ismail	.20
64	Anthony Smith	.10
65	Eric Allen	.10
66	Marion Butts	.10
67	Chris Miller	.10
68	Terrell Buckley	.10
69	Thurman Thomas	.30
70	Roosevelt Potts	.10
71	Tony McGee	.10
72	Jason Hanson	.10
73	Victor Bailey	.10
74	Albert Lewis	.10
75	Nate Odomes	.10
76	Ben Coates	.20
77	Warren Moon	.20
78	Derek Brown	.10
79	David Klingler	.10
80	Cleveland Gary	.10
81	Emmitt Smith	3.00
82	Jay Novacek	.10
83	Dana Stubblefield	.20
84	Michael Brooks	.10
85	James Jett	.10
86	J.J. Birden	.10
87	William Fuller	.10
88	Glyn Milburn	.10
89	Tim Worley	.10
90	Brett Perriman	.10
91	Randall Cunningham	.20
92	Drew Bledsoe	2.00
93	Jerome Bettis	1.00
94	Boomer Esiason	.10
95	Garrison Hearst	.20
96	Bruce Smith	.10
97	Jackie Harris	.10
98	Jeff George	.20
99	Tom Waddle	.10
100	John Copeland	.10
101	Bobby Hebert	.10
102	Joe Montana	2.00
103	Herman Moore	.75
104	Rick Mirer	.20
105	Ricky Watters	.20
106	Neil O'Donnell	.20
107	Herschel Walker	.10
108	Rob Moore	.10
109	Reggie Brooks	.10
110	Tommy Vardell	.10
111	Eric Green	.10
112	Stan Humphries	.20
113	Greg Robinson	.10
114	Eric Swann	.10
115	Courtney Hawkins	.10
116	Andre Reed	.10
117	Steve McMichael	.10
118	Gary Brown	.10
119	Terry Allen	.10
120	Dan Marino	3.00
121	Gary Clark	.10
122	Chris Warren	.20
123	Pierce Holt	.10
124	Anthony Carter	.10
125	Quentin Coryatt	.10
126	Harold Green	.10
127	Leonard Russell	.10
128	Tim McDonald	.10
129	Chris Spielman	.10
130	Cody Carlson	.10
131	Ron Moore	.10
132	Renaldo Turnbull	.10
133	Ronnie Lott	.10
134	Natrone Means	.75
135	Keith Byars	.10
136	Henry Ellard	.10
137	Steve Jordan	.10
138	Calvin Williams	.10
139	Brian Blades	.10
140	Michael Jackson	.10
141	Charles Haley	.10
142	Curtis Conway	.10
143	Nick Lowery	.10
144	Bill Brooks	.10
145	Michael Haynes	.10
146	Willie Green	.10
147	Duane Bickett	.10
148	Shannon Sharpe	.20
149	Ricky Proehl	.10
150	Troy Aikman	1.50
151	Mike Sherrard	.10
152	Reggie Cobb	.10
153	Norm Johnson	.10
154	Neil Smith	.10
155	James Francis	.10
156	Greg McMurtry	.10
157	Greg Townsend	.10
158	Mel Gray	.10
159	Rocket Ismail	.10
160	Leslie O'Neal	.10
161	Johnny Mitchell	.10
162	Brent Jones	.10
163	Chris Doleman	.10
164	Seth Joyner	.10
165	Marco Coleman	.10
166	Mark Higgs	.10
167	John L. Williams	.10
168	Darrell Green	.10
169	Mark Carrier	.10
170	Reggie White	.20
171	Darryl Talley	.10
172	Russell Maryland	.10
173	Mark Collins	.10
174	Chris Jacke	.10
175	Richard Dent	.10
176	John Taylor	.10
177	Rodney Hampton	.20
178	Dwight Stone	.10
179	Cornelius Bennett	.10
180	Cris Dishman	.10
181	Jerry Rice	1.50
182	Rod Bernstine	.10
183	Keith Hamilton	.10
184	Keith Jackson	.10
185	Craig Erickson	.10
186	Marcus Allen	.20
187	Marcus Robertson	.10
188	Junior Seau	.20
189	*LeShon Johnson*	.40
190	*Perry Klein*	.30
191	*Bryant Young*	.50
192	*Byron Morris*	.50
193	*Jeff Cothran*	.20
194	*Lamar Smith*	1.00
195	*Calvin Jones*	.40
196	*James Bostic*	.20
197	*Dan Wilkinson*	.40
198	*Marshall Faulk*	6.00
199	*Heath Shuler*	.50
200	*Willie McGinest*	.40
201	*Trev Alberts*	.30
202	*Trent Dilfer*	3.00
203	*Sam Adams*	.30
204	*Charles Johnson*	.50
205	*Johnnie Morton*	.75
206	*Thomas Lewis*	.20
207	*Greg Hill*	.50
208	*William Floyd*	1.00
209	*Derrick Alexander*	.50
210	*Darnay Scott*	.75
211	*Lake Dawson*	.30
212	*Errict Rhett*	.75
213	*Kevin Lee*	.30
214	*Chuck Levy*	.30
215	*David Palmer*	.50
216	*Ryan Yarborough*	.30
217	*Charlie Garner*	3.00
218	*Mario Bates*	.30
219	*Jamir Miller*	.30
220	*Bucky Brooks*	.30
221	*Donnell Bennett*	.30
222	Kevin Greene	.10
223	LeRoy Butler	.10
224	Anthony Pleasant	.10
225	Steve Christie	.10
226	Bill Romanowski	.10
227	Darren Carrington	.10
228	Chester McGlockton	.10
229	Jack Del Rio	.10
230	Kevin Smith	.10
231	Chris Zorich	.10
232	Donnell Woolford	.10
233	Tony Casillas	.10
234	Terry McDaniel	.10
235	Ray Childress	.10
237	Clyde Simmons	.10
238	Dante Jones	.10
239	Karl Mecklenburg	.10
240	Daryl Johnston	.10
241	Hardy Nickerson	.10
242	Jeff Lageman	.10
243	Lewis Tillman	.10
244	Jim McMahon	.10
245	Mike Pritchard	.10
246	Harvey Williams	.10
247	Sean Jones	.10
248	Stevon Moore	.10
249	Pete Metzelaars	.10
250	Mike Johnson	.10
251	Chris Slade	.20
252	Jessie Hester	.10
253	Louis Oliver	.10
254	Ken Harvey	.10
255	Bryan Cox	.10
256	Erik Kramer	.10
257	Andy Harmon	.10
258	Rickey Jackson	.10
259	Mark Carrier	.10
260	Greg Lloyd	.10
261	Robert Brooks	.10
262	Dave Brown	.20
263	Dennis Smith	.10
264	Michael Dean Perry	.10
265	Dan Saleaumua	.10
266	Mo Lewis	.10
267	Checklist	.10
268	Checklist	.10
269	Checklist	.10
270	Checklist	.10
271SP	Jerry Rice TD King	7.00
NNO	Drew Bledsoe Pin. Pass.	70.00

1994 Pinnacle Trophy Collection

The 270-card, regular-size set was a parallel Dufex version of the base card set, inserted every four packs.

	NM/M
Complete Set (270):	600.00
Common Player:	1.50
Veteran Stars:	3X-5X
Young Stars:	3X-5X
RCs:	2X-4X

1994 Pinnacle Draft Pinnacle

Draft Pinnacle displays the NFL's top 10 picks in their NFL uniforms. The bottom of the card shows a football texture background with "Draft" printed in gold, along with the Pinnacle logo, while "Pinnacle '94" is printed in white. The rest of the front pictures the draft pick. The back is made of half football texture with a brief biography and the other half contains a picture of the player. Cards are numbered DP 1 through DP 10.

	NM/M
Complete Set (10):	25.00
Common Player:	.50
Minor Stars:	1.00

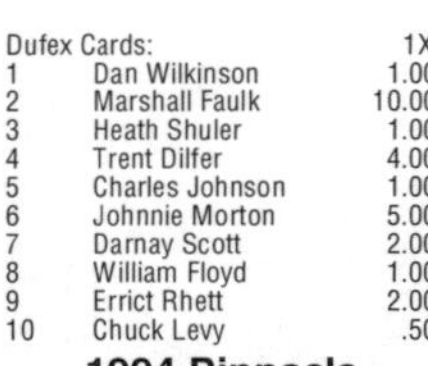

Dufex Cards: 1X
1 Dan Wilkinson 1.00
2 Marshall Faulk 10.00
3 Heath Shuler 1.00
4 Trent Dilfer 4.00
5 Charles Johnson 1.00
6 Johnnie Morton 5.00
7 Darnay Scott 2.00
8 William Floyd 1.00
9 Errict Rhett 2.00
10 Chuck Levy .50

1994 Pinnacle Performers

Pinnacle Performers was an 18-card insert set featuring some of the top talent in the NFL. These were inserted exclusively into jumbo packs at a rate of one every four packs.

NM/M
Complete Set (18): 35.00
Common Player: .50
Minor Stars: 1.00
Inserted 1:4 Jumbo
1 Troy Aikman 4.00
2 Emmitt Smith 5.00
3 Sterling Sharpe 1.00
4 Barry Sanders 5.00
5 Jerry Rice 4.00
6 Steve Young 3.00
7 John Elway 4.00
8 Michael Irvin 1.00
9 Jerome Bettis 1.00
10 Tim Brown 1.00
11 Joe Montana 5.00
12 Reggie Brooks .50
13 Brett Favre 6.00
14 Drew Bledsoe 4.00
15 Ricky Watters 1.00
16 Garrison Hearst 1.00
17 Rodney Hampton .50
18 Dan Marino 5.00

1994 Pinnacle Team Pinnacle

Team Pinnacle is a double-fronted, 10-card insert set that was found one in every 90 packs. Cards feature two top performers at a variety of different positions.

NM/M
Complete Set (10): 110.00
Common Player: 3.00
1 Troy Aikman, Joe Montana 30.00
2 Brett Favre, Rick Mirer 25.00
3 Thurman Thomas, Emmitt Smith 20.00
4 Barry Sanders, Barry Foster 20.00
5 Jerome Bettis, Natrone Means 5.00
6 Tim Brown, Sterling Sharpe 5.00
7 Anthony Miller, Jerry Rice 20.00
8 Michael Irvin, James Jett 3.00
9 Reggie White, Bruce Smith 5.00
10 Cortez Kennedy, Sean Gilbert 3.00

1994 Pinnacle Canton Bound

The Canton Bound NFL boxed set was released by Pinnacle containing 25 cards. It featured the game's most accomplished veterans and the brightest young stars. Pinnacle produced 100,000 numbered sets, each came with a factory seal and serial number. The cards showcase a full-bleed design with the player's name and Pinnacle logo in gold-foil. At the bottom of the card is the "Canton Bound" neon logo. The back of the card includes two photos, the player's bio, highlights, 1993 and career stats.

NM/M
Complete Set (25): 10.00
Common Player: .25
1 Troy Aikman 1.50
2 Emmitt Smith 3.00
3 Barry Sanders 1.50
4 Jerry Rice 1.50
5 Sterling Sharpe .35
6 Ronnie Lott .35
7 John Elway 1.00
8 Joe Montana 1.50
9 Reggie White .35
10 Thurman Thomas .50
11 Bruce Smith .35
12 Cortez Kennedy .35
13 Dan Marino 3.00
14 James Lofton .35
15 Art Monk .35
16 Warren Moon .35
17 Barry Foster .25
18 Steve Young 1.00
19 Phil Simms .35
20 Richard Dent .25
21 Marcus Allen .35
22 Junior Seau .50
23 Michael Irvin .50
24 Deion Sanders .75
25 Jerome Bettis .50
26 Ronnie Lott Sample 1.50

1994 Pinnacle/ Sportflics Super Bowl

This seven-card set was distributed at the 1994 Super Bowl Show in Atlanta, and was available by exchanging three Pinnacle Brands wrappers for one card. These Magic Motion cards were produced in the following quantities: Gary Brown and Emmitt Smith (3,000); Sterling Sharpe and Jerome Bettis/Reggie Brooks and Drew Bledsoe/Rick Mirer (2,000); and Jerry Rice and Deion Sanders (1,000).

NM/M
Complete Set (7): 35.00
Common Player: 2.00
1 Gary Brown 2.00
2 Emmitt Smith 10.00
3 Sterling Sharpe 5.00
4 Jerome Bettis, Reggie Brooks 5.00
5 Drew Bledsoe, Rick Mirer 8.00
6 Jerry Rice 10.00
7 Deion Sanders 10.00

1995 Pinnacle Promos

This four-card set was used to promote the 1995 Pinnacle set. It included two regular-issue cards, one Showcase insert and a header card.

NM/M
Complete Set (4): 7.00
Common Player: .50
1 Dan Marino Showcase Card 4.00
39 Barry Sanders 2.00
62 Steve Young 1.25
NNO Ad Card .50

1995 Pinnacle

Pinnacle's 1995 football set has 250 cards plus two Dufex parallel sets. Each regular card front has a full-bleed color action photo on the front, with a Pinnacle logo in an upper corner. The player's name and position are stamped in gold foil at the bottom of the card, along with the seams of a football. The card back has a color photo, player profile, biographical information and 1994 and career statistics. There are four subsets within the main set - Draft Picks, Pinnacle Passers, Checklists and a "Judge" card, which pays tribute to Steve Young for passing the bar exam. Parallel sets are Trophy Collection, which reprints all 250 cards on a dufex design, and Artist's Proofs, which parallels the Trophy Collection, but has an Artist's Proof stamp on each card. Five insert sets were made: Showcase, Black 'n Blue, Team Pinnacle, Clear Shots and Gamebreakers.

NM/M
Complete Set (250): 15.00
Common Player: .10
Minor Stars: .20
Comp. Trophy Coll. Set (250):
Trophy Collection Cards: 3X-5X
Comp. Art. Proof Set (250):
Artist Proof Cards: 10X-20X
Card #193 Montana AP was never made.
Hobby Pack (12): 1.00
Hobby Wax Box (24): 20.00
Retail Pack (12): 1.00
Retail Wax Box (24): 20.00
1 Reggie White .20
2 Troy Aikman 1.00
3 Willie Davis .10
4 Jerry Rice 1.00
5 Bruce Smith .10
6 Keith Byars .10
7 Chris Warren .20
8 Erik Kramer .10
9 Leon Lett .10
10 Greg Lloyd .10
11 Jackie Harris .10
12 Irving Fryar .10
13 Rodney Hampton .10
14 Michael Irvin .30
15 Michael Haynes .10
16 Irving Spikes .10
17 Calvin Williams .10
18 Ken Norton Jr. .10
19 Herman Moore .20
20 Lewis Tillman .10
21 Cortez Kennedy .10
22 Dan Marino 2.50
23 Erric Pegram .10
24 Tim Brown .20
25 *Jeff Blake* .50
26 Brett Favre 2.50
27 Garrison Hearst .20
28 Ronnie Harmon .10
29 Qadry Ismail .10
30 Ben Coates .10
31 Deion Sanders .60
32 John Elway .50
33 Natrone Means .60
34 Derrick Alexander .30
35 Craig Heyward .10
36 Jake Reed .10
37 Steve Walsh .10
38 John Randle .10
39 Barry Sanders 2.00
40 Tydus Winans .10
41 Thomas Lewis .10
42 Jim Kelly .30
43 Gus Frerotte .40
44 Cris Carter .20
45 Kevin Williams .10
46 Dave Meggett .10
47 Pat Swilling .10
48 Neil O'Donnell .20
49 Terance Mathis .10
50 Desmond Howard .10
51 Bryant Young .10
52 Stan Humphries .20
53 Alvin Harper .10
54 Henry Ellard .10
55 Jessie Hester .10
56 Lorenzo White .10
57 John Friesz .10
58 Anthony Smith .10
59 Bert Emanuel .40
60 Gary Clark .10
61 Bill Brooks .10
62 Steve Young 1.00
63 Jerome Bettis .30
64 John Taylor .10
65 Ricky Proehl .10
66 Junior Seau .20
67 Bubby Brister .10
68 Neil Smith .10
69 Dan McGwire .10
70 Brett Perriman .10
71 Chris Spielman .10
72 Jeff George .20
73 Emmitt Smith 2.50
74 Chris Penn .10
75 Derrick Fenner .10
76 Reggie Brooks .10
77 Chris Chandler .10
78 Rod Woodson .10
79 Isaac Bruce .30
80 Reggie Cobb .10
81 Bryce Paup .10
82 Warren Moon .20
83 Bryan Reeves .10
84 Lake Dawson .30
85 Larry Centers .10
86 Marshall Faulk 1.00
87 Jim Harbaugh .10
88 Ray Childress .10
89 Eric Metcalf .10
90 Ernie Mills .10
91 Lamar Lathon .10
92 Errict Rhett .20
93 David Klingler .10
94 Vincent Brown .10
95 Andre Rison .10
96 Brian Mitchell .10
97 Mark Rypien .10
98 Eugene Robinson .10
99 Eric Green .10
100 Rocket Ismail .10
101 Flipper Anderson .10
102 Randall Cunningham .10
103 Ricky Watters .20
104 Amp Lee .10
105 Ernest Givins .10
106 Daryl Johnston .10
107 Dave Krieg .10
108 Dana Stubblefield .10
109 Torrance Small .10
110 *Yancey Thigpen* .50
111 Chester McGlockton .10
112 Craig Erickson .10
113 Herschel Walker .10
114 Mike Sherrard .10
115 Tony McGee .10
116 Adrian Murrell .10
117 Frank Reich .10
118 Hardy Nickerson .10
119 Andre Reed .10
120 Leonard Russell .10
121 Eric Allen .10
122 Jeff Hostetler .10
123 Barry Foster .10
124 Anthony Miller .10
125 Shawn Jefferson .10
126 Richie Anderson .10
127 Steve Bono .20
128 Seth Joyner .10
129 Darnay Scott .60
130 Johnny Mitchell .10
131 Eric Swann .10
132 Drew Bledsoe 1.50
133 Marcus Allen .20
134 Carl Pickens .20
135 Michael Brooks .10
136 John L. Williams .10
137 Steve Beuerlein .10
138 Robert Smith .10
139 O.J. McDuffie .10
140 Haywood Jeffires .10
141 Aeneas Williams .10
142 Rick Mirer .40
143 William Floyd .50
144 Fred Barnett .10
145 Leroy Hoard .10
146 Terry Kirby .10
147 Boomer Esiason .10
148 Ken Harvey .10
149 Cleveland Gary .10
150 Brian Blades .10
151 Eric Turner .10
152 Vinny Testaverde .10
153 Ron Moore .10
154 Curtis Conway .10
155 Johnnie Morton .10
156 Kenneth Davis .10
157 Scott Mitchell .10
158 Sean Gilbert .10
159 Shannon Sharpe .10
160 Mark Seay .10
161 Cornelius Bennett .10
162 Heath Shuler .75
163 Bam Morris .50
164 Robert Brooks .10
165 Glyn Milburn .10
166 Gary Brown .10
167 Jim Everett .10
168 Steve Atwater .10
169 Darren Woodson .10
170 Mark Ingram .10
171 Donnell Woolford .10
172 Trent Dilfer .50
173 Charlie Garner .10
174 Charles Johnson .40
175 Mike Pritchard .10
176 Derek Brown .10
177 Chris Miller .10
178 Charles Haley .10
179 J.J. Birden .10
180 Jeff Graham .10
181 Bernie Parmalee .30
182 Mark Brunell 1.00
183 Greg Hill .40
184 Michael Timpson .10
185 Terry Allen .10
186 Ricky Ervins .10
187 Dave Brown .10
188 Dan Wilkinson .10
189 Jay Novacek .10
190 Harvey Williams .10
191 Mario Bates .30
192 Steve Young .50
193 Joe Montana 2.00
194 Steve Young .50
195 Troy Aikman .40
196 Drew Bledsoe .75
197 Dan Marino 1.00
198 John Elway .20
199 Brett Favre .75
200 Heath Shuler .40
201 Warren Moon .20
202 Jim Kelly .20
203 Jeff Hostetler .20
204 Rick Mirer .20
205 Dave Brown .10
206 Randall Cunningham .10
207 Neil O'Donnell .10
208 Jim Everett .10
209 *Ki-Jana Carter* .30
210 *Steve McNair* 4.00
211 *Michael Westbrook* 1.50
212 *Kerry Collins* 2.00
213 *Joey Galloway* 3.00
214 *Kyle Brady* .20
215 *J.J. Stokes* 1.50
216 *Tyrone Wheatley* .50
217 *Rashaan Salaam* .30
218 *Napoleon Kaufman* 1.50
219 *Frank Sanders* .30
220 *Stoney Case* .20
221 *Todd Collins* .30
222 *Warren Sapp* .75
223 *Sherman Williams* .20
224 *Rob Johnson* 1.50
225 *Mark Bruener* .20
226 *Derrick Brooks* .20
227 *Chad May* .20
228 *James Stewart* .20
229 *Ray Zellars* .20
230 *Dave Barr* .20
231 *Kordell Stewart* 3.00
232 *Jimmy Oliver* .20
233 *Tony Boselli* .30
234 *James Stewart* 1.75
235 *Derrick Alexander* .20
236 *Lovell Pinkney* .20
237 *John Walsh* .20
238 *Tyrone Davis* .20
239 *Joe Aska* .20
240 *Korey Stringer* .20
241 *Hugh Douglas* .20
242 *Christian Fauria* .20
243 *Terrell Fletcher* .20
244 Dan Marino CL .40
245 Drew Bledsoe CL .40
246 John Elway CL .20
247 Emmitt Smith CL .40
248 Steve Young CL .25
249 Barry Sanders CL .50
250 Jerry Rice CL .25

1995 Pinnacle Artist's Proof

Artist's Proofs were a parallel set of the 1995 Pinnacle set, minus Joe Montana, who didn't have an Artist's Proof card. This 249-card set features the same all-foil dufex printing as the Trophy Collection parallel, but is identified by a round seal that includes the Artist's Proof logo. This parallel set was seeded every 48 packs.

193 Montana AP Not Issued
AP Veteran Stars: 10X-20X
AP Young Stars: 10X-20X
AP RCs: 5X-10X

1995 Pinnacle Trophy Collection

This 250-card parallel set was included in every four packs of Pinnacle Football and is printed in all-foil dufex. The cards have the same photo on the front as regular-issue cards, but have the words Trophy Collection written in large letters on the back.

NM/M
Complete Set (250): 600.00
Common Player: 1.25
Veteran Stars: 3X-5X
Young Stars: 2X-4X
RCs: 1.5X-3X

A card number in parenthese ( ) indicates the set is unnumbered.

1995 Pinnacle Black 'N Blue

These 1995 Pinnacle football cards picture some of the NFL's toughest players. The cards, featuring a micro-etched foil design for the front, were seeded one per every 18 jumbo packs.

NM/M
Complete Set (30): 90.00
Common Player: 1.00
1 Junior Seau 3.00
2 Bam Morris 1.00
3 Craig Heyward 1.00
4 Drew Bledsoe 10.00
5 Barry Sanders 12.00
6 Jerome Bettis 1.00
7 William Floyd 1.00
8 Greg Lloyd 1.00
9 John Elway 10.00
10 Jerry Rice 10.00
11 Kevin Greene 1.00
12 Errict Rhett 1.00
13 Steve Young 10.00
14 Bruce Smith 1.00
15 Steve Atwater 1.00
16 Natrone Means 1.00
17 Ben Coates 1.00
18 Reggie White 1.00
19 Ken Harvey 1.00
20 Dan Marino 12.00
21 Marshall Faulk 1.00
22 Seth Joyner 1.00
23 Rod Woodson 1.00
24 Hardy Nickerson 1.00
25 Brett Favre 14.00
26 Bryan Cox 1.00
27 Rodney Hampton 1.00
28 Jeff Hostetler 1.00
29 Brent Jones 1.00
30 Emmitt Smith 12.00

1995 Pinnacle Clear Shots

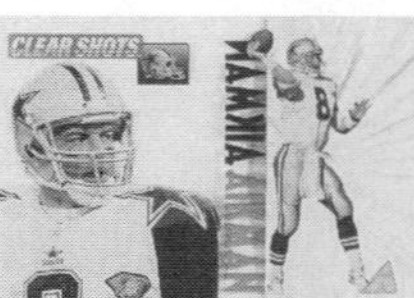

These 1995 Pinnacle football inserts are one of the most exclusive ones in the base brand; they are seeded one per every 60 packs. The cards display 10 of the league's best veterans on a clear plastic card stock overprinted with rainbow holographic foil. The process is called Spectroview.

NM/M
Complete Set (10): 50.00
Common Player: 2.00
1 Jerry Rice 6.00
2 Dan Marino 8.00
3 Steve Young 6.00
4 Drew Bledsoe 6.00
5 Emmitt Smith 8.00
6 Barry Sanders 8.00
7 Marshall Faulk 4.00
8 Troy Aikman 6.00
9 Ki-Jana Carter 2.00
10 Steve McNair 4.00

1995 Pinnacle Gamebreakers

These 15 insert cards were exclusive to 1995 Pinnacle hobby packs, one per every 24 hobby packs. The card front has a metallic shine to it, with the insert set name featured at the top of the card. The player's name and team name are in the lower left corner, opposite the Pinnacle base brand logo.

		NM/M
Complete Set (15):		60.00
Common Player:		1.00
1	Marshall Faulk	3.00
2	Emmitt Smith	6.00
3	Steve Young	4.00
4	Ki-Jana Carter	1.00
5	Drew Bledsoe	4.00
6	Troy Aikman	4.00
7	Rashaan Salaam	1.00
8	Tyrone Wheatley	1.00
9	Dan Marino	6.00
10	Natrone Means	1.00
11	Barry Sanders	6.00
12	Jerry Rice	4.00
13	Bam Morris	1.00
14	Steve McNair	3.00
15	Kerry Collins	2.00

1995 Pinnacle Showcase

This 1995 Pinnacle insert set features 21 top NFL stars, using black-and-white portraits for the card fronts. The front design also uses silver foil stamping for the player's name and brand name. A silver bar outlines the letters in the word "Showcase." The card back, numbered 1 of 21, etc., has another black-and-white photo, but this one is an action shot, unlike the front one, which shows the player without his helmet on. The insert set icon and a facsimile autograph are also included on the card back. Cards were seeded one per every 18 packs.

		NM/M
Complete Set (21):		35.00
Common Player:		1.00
1	Drew Bledsoe	2.00
2	Joey Galloway	2.00
3	Steve Young	3.00
4	Joe Aska	1.00
5	Barry Sanders	4.00
6	Troy Aikman	3.00
7	Dan Marino	5.00
8	Randall Cunningham	1.00
9	John Elway	3.00
10	Brett Favre	5.00
11	Jim Kelly	1.00
12	Warren Moon	1.00
13	Dave Brown	1.00
14	Jeff Hostetler	1.00
15	Rick Mirer	1.00
16	Ki-Jana Carter	1.00
17	Kerry Collins	1.00
18	J.J. Stokes	1.00
19	Kordell Stewart	2.00
20	Michael Westbrook	1.00
21	Todd Collins	1.00

1995 Pinnacle Team Pinnacle

These cards are the rarest of all 1995 Pinnacle football inserts, seeded one per every 90 packs. The 10 cards feature some of the hottest AFC and NFC players at their positions, back-to-back. The set has 20 variations, because each card exists with just one side printed with Pinnacle's exclusive textured-foil process. The player is pictured against a background which shows his team's logo.

		NM/M
Complete Set (10):		80.00
Common Player:		2.00
1	Steve Young, Drew Bledsoe	8.00
2	Emmitt Smith, Marshall Faulk	12.00
3	Barry Sanders, Natrone Means	10.00
4	Troy Aikman, Dan Marino	12.00
5	Jerry Rice, Tim Brown	10.00
6	Errict Rhett, Bam Morris	2.00
7	Brett Favre, John Elway	12.00
8	Ki-Jana Carter, Rashaan Salaam	2.00
9	Steve McNair, Kerry Collins	5.00
10	Michael Westbrook, Joey Galloway	2.00

1995 Pinnacle Super Bowl Card Show

The four-card, standard-size set was available at the 1995 NFL Experience in exchange for five Pinnacle-brand wrappers. Gold Zone (2,000) and Platinum (1,000) cards were also randomly issued.

		NM/M
Complete Set (4):		6.00
Common Player:		1.00
1	Jeff Blake	1.00
2	Drew Bledsoe	3.00
3	Marshall Faulk	3.00
4	Natrone Means	1.00

1995 Pinnacle Club Collection Promos

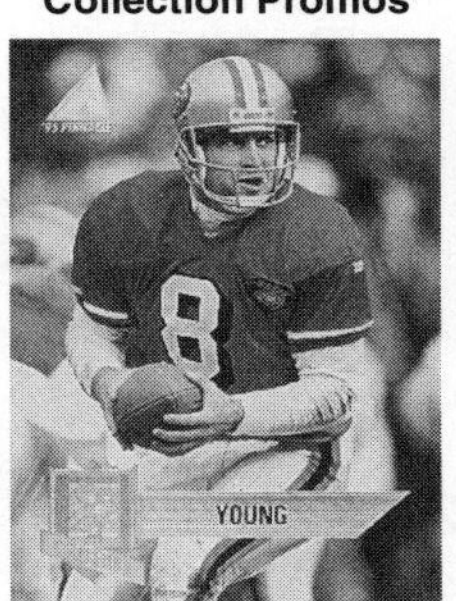

The four-card, standard-size set, issued in a cello pack, previewed the 1995 Pinnacle Club Collection series. The set contained two base cards, one Arms Race card and an advertisement card. The card backs are identified with a "Promo" stamp.

		NM/M
Complete Set (4):		8.00
Common Player:		.50
1	Steve Young	2.00
11	Dan Marino	4.00
AR11	Drew Bledsoe Arm's Race	2.00
NNO	Pinnacle Ad Card	.50

1995 Pinnacle Club Collection

This set, in conjunction with Pinnacle's sponsorship of the NFL Quarterback Club, features 20 members of the NFL's Quarterback Club. Each player in the 261-card set has at least four cards - a regular one and three subset cards. The subset cards are: Xs and Os, which feature the players with an Xs and Os graphic design of their favorite plays; Rookie Replay, which shows the players from their rookie season; and Defining Moment, which highlights top performances for each player. A pin redemption card was also produced; it was seeded one per every 24 packs and entitles the finder to one of 20 Quarterback Club pins if the card is mailed in. There were three insert sets made: Arms Race and Aerial Assault, both of which are dedicated to the quarterbacks, and Spotlight, which focuses on non-quarterbacks. An interactive game that goes along with the Arms Race insert was also designed; as each featured quarterback accumulates statistics, collectors earned chances at winning prizes.

		NM/M
Complete Set (261):		25.00
Common Player:		.05
Minor Stars:		.10
Each player has nine cards.		
Pack (12):		1.50
Wax Box (24):		25.00
1	Steve Young (R)	.50
2	Steve Young	.50
3	Steve Young	.50
4	Steve Young	.50
5	Steve Young	.50
6	Steve Young	.50
7	Steve Young (XO)	.50
8	Steve Young (RR)	.50
9	Steve Young (DM)	.50
10	Dan Marino (R)	1.00
11	Dan Marino	1.00
12	Dan Marino	1.00
13	Dan Marino	1.00
14	Dan Marino	1.00
15	Dan Marino	1.00
16	Dan Marino (XO)	1.00
17	Dan Marino (RR)	1.00
18	Dan Marino (DM)	1.00
19	Troy Aikman (R)	.40
20	Troy Aikman	.40
21	Troy Aikman	.40
22	Troy Aikman	.40
23	Troy Aikman	.40
24	Troy Aikman	.40
25	Troy Aikman (XO)	.40
26	Troy Aikman (RR)	.40
27	Troy Aikman (DM)	.40
28	Drew Bledsoe (R)	.50
29	Drew Bledsoe	.50
30	Drew Bledsoe	.50
31	Drew Bledsoe	.50
32	Drew Bledsoe	.50
33	Drew Bledsoe	.50
34	Drew Bledsoe (XO)	.50
35	Drew Bledsoe (RR)	.50
36	Drew Bledsoe (DM)	.50
37	Bubby Brister (R)	.05
38	Bubby Brister	.05
39	Bubby Brister	.05
40	Bubby Brister	.05
41	Bubby Brister	.05
42	Bubby Brister	.05
43	Bubby Brister (XO)	.05
44	Bubby Brister (RR)	.05
45	Bubby Brister (DM)	.05
46	Dave Brown (R)	.05
47	Dave Brown	.05
48	Dave Brown	.05
49	Dave Brown	.05
50	Dave Brown	.05
51	Dave Brown	.05
52	Dave Brown (XO)	.05
53	Dave Brown (RR)	.05
54	Dave Brown (DM)	.05
55	Randall Cunningham (R)	.10
56	Randall Cunningham	.10
57	Randall Cunningham	.10
58	Randall Cunningham	.10
59	Randall Cunningham	.10
60	Randall Cunningham	.10
61	Randall Cunningham (XO)	.10
62	Randall Cunningham (RR)	.10
63	Randall Cunningham (DM)	.10
64	John Elway (R)	.30
65	John Elway	.30
66	John Elway	.30
67	John Elway	.30
68	John Elway	.30
69	John Elway	.30
70	John Elway (XO)	.30
71	John Elway (RR)	.30
72	John Elway (DM)	.30
73	Boomer Esiason (R)	.05
74	Boomer Esiason	.05
75	Boomer Esiason	.05
76	Boomer Esiason	.05
77	Boomer Esiason	.05
78	Boomer Esiason	.05
79	Boomer Esiason (XO)	.05
80	Boomer Esiason (RR)	.05
81	Boomer Esiason (DM)	.05
82	Jim Everett (R)	.05
83	Jim Everett	.05
84	Jim Everett	.05
85	Jim Everett	.05
86	Jim Everett	.05
87	Jim Everett	.05
88	Jim Everett (XO)	.05
89	Jim Everett (RR)	.05
90	Jim Everett (DM)	.05
91	Brett Favre (R)	.50
92	Brett Favre	.50
93	Brett Favre	.50
94	Brett Favre	.50
95	Brett Favre	.50
96	Brett Favre	.50
97	Brett Favre (XO)	.50
98	Brett Favre (RR)	.50
99	Brett Favre (DM)	.50
100	Jim Harbaugh (R)	.05
101	Jim Harbaugh	.05
102	Jim Harbaugh	.05
103	Jim Harbaugh	.05
104	Jim Harbaugh	.05
105	Jim Harbaugh	.05
106	Jim Harbaugh (XO)	.05
107	Jim Harbaugh (RR)	.05
108	Jim Harbaugh (DM)	.05
109	Jeff Hostetler (R)	.05
110	Jeff Hostetler	.05
111	Jeff Hostetler	.05
112	Jeff Hostetler	.05
113	Jeff Hostetler	.05
114	Jeff Hostetler	.05
115	Jeff Hostetler (XO)	.05
116	Jeff Hostetler (RR)	.05
117	Jeff Hostetler (DM)	.05
118	Michael Irvin (R)	.25
119	Michael Irvin	.25
120	Michael Irvin	.25
121	Michael Irvin	.25
122	Michael Irvin	.25
123	Michael Irvin	.25
124	Michael Irvin (XO)	.25
125	Michael Irvin (RR)	.25
126	Michael Irvin (DM)	.25
127	Jim Kelly (R)	.20
128	Jim Kelly	.20
129	Jim Kelly	.20
130	Jim Kelly	.20
131	Jim Kelly	.20
132	Jim Kelly	.20
133	Jim Kelly (XO)	.20
134	Jim Kelly (RR)	.20
135	Jim Kelly (DM)	.20
136	David Klingler (R)	.05
137	David Klingler	.05
138	David Klingler	.05
139	David Klingler	.05
140	David Klingler	.05
141	David Klingler	.05
142	David Klingler (XO)	.05
143	David Klingler (RR)	.05
144	David Klingler (DM)	.05
145	Bernie Kosar (R)	.05
146	Bernie Kosar	.05
147	Bernie Kosar	.05
148	Bernie Kosar	.05
149	Bernie Kosar	.05
150	Bernie Kosar	.05
151	Bernie Kosar (XO)	.05
152	Bernie Kosar (RR)	.05
153	Bernie Kosar (DM)	.05
154	Chris Miller (R)	.05
155	Chris Miller	.05
156	Chris Miller	.05
157	Chris Miller	.05
158	Chris Miller	.05
159	Chris Miller	.05
160	Chris Miller (XO)	.05
161	Chris Miller (RR)	.05
162	Chris Miller (DM)	.05
163	Rick Mirer (R)	.25
164	Rick Mirer	.25
165	Rick Mirer	.25
166	Rick Mirer	.25
167	Rick Mirer	.25
168	Rick Mirer	.25
169	Rick Mirer (XO)	.25
170	Rick Mirer (RR)	.25
171	Rick Mirer (DM)	.25
172	Warren Moon (R)	.10
173	Warren Moon	.10
174	Warren Moon	.10
175	Warren Moon	.10
176	Warren Moon	.10
177	Warren Moon	.10
178	Warren Moon (XO)	.10
179	Warren Moon (RR)	.10
180	Warren Moon (DM)	.10
181	Neil O'Donnell (R)	.05
182	Neil O'Donnell	.05
183	Neil O'Donnell	.05
184	Neil O'Donnell	.05
185	Neil O'Donnell	.05
186	Neil O'Donnell	.05
187	Neil O'Donnell (XO)	.05
188	Neil O'Donnell (RR)	.05
189	Neil O'Donnell (DM)	.05
190	Jerry Rice (R)	.50
191	Jerry Rice	.50
192	Jerry Rice	.50
193	Jerry Rice	.50
194	Jerry Rice	.50
195	Jerry Rice	.50
196	Jerry Rice (XO)	.50
197	Jerry Rice (RR)	.50
198	Jerry Rice (DM)	.50
199	Mark Rypien (R)	.05
200	Mark Rypien	.05
201	Mark Rypien	.05
202	Mark Rypien	.05
203	Mark Rypien	.05
204	Mark Rypien	.05
205	Mark Rypien (XO)	.05
206	Mark Rypien (RR)	.05
207	Mark Rypien (DM)	.05
208	Barry Sanders (R)	.50
209	Barry Sanders	.50
210	Barry Sanders	.50
211	Barry Sanders	.50
212	Barry Sanders	.50
213	Barry Sanders	.50
213	Barry Sanders (XO)	.50
215	Barry Sanders (RR)	.50
216	Barry Sanders (DM)	.50
217	Junior Seau (R)	.10
218	Junior Seau	.10
219	Junior Seau	.10
220	Junior Seau	.10
221	Junior Seau	.10
222	Junior Seau	.10
223	Junior Seau (XO)	.10
224	Junior Seau (RR)	.10
225	Junior Seau (DM)	.10
226	Emmitt Smith (R)	1.00
227	Emmitt Smith	1.00
228	Emmitt Smith	1.00
229	Emmitt Smith	1.00
230	Emmitt Smith	1.00
231	Emmitt Smith	1.00
232	Emmitt Smith (XO)	1.00
233	Emmitt Smith (RR)	1.00
234	Emmitt Smith (DM)	1.00
235	Phil Simms (R)	.05
236	Phil Simms	.05
237	Phil Simms	.05
238	Phil Simms	.05
239	Phil Simms	.05
240	Phil Simms	.05
241	Phil Simms (XO)	.05
242	Phil Simms (RR)	.05
243	Phil Simms (DM)	.05
244	Heath Shuler (R)	.30
245	Heath Shuler	.30
246	Heath Shuler	.30
247	Heath Shuler	.30
248	Heath Shuler	.30
249	Heath Shuler	.30
250	Heath Shuler (XO)	.30
251	Heath Shuler (RR)	.30
252	Heath Shuler (DM)	.30
253	Frank Reich (R)	.05
254	Frank Reich	.05
255	Frank Reich	.05
256	Frank Reich	.05
257	Frank Reich	.05
258	Frank Reich (XO)	.05
259	Frank Reich (RR)	.05
260	Frank Reich (DM)	.05
261	Frank Reich	.05

1995 Pinnacle Club Collection Aerial Assault

These 18 cards have all-foil printing on one side, and Pinnacle's exclusive Dufex textured-foil printing on the other. Both sides say "Aerial Assault," but only the all-foil side has a card number, which uses an "AA" prefix. This side also has a brief recap of the player's accomplishments. Cards were random inserts, one per every 36 packs of 1995 Pinnacle Club Collection football.

		NM/M
Complete Set (18):		45.00
Common Player:		1.00
1	Troy Aikman	4.00
2	Dave Brown	1.00
3	Drew Bledsoe	4.00
4	Randall Cunningham	1.00
5	Jim Everett	1.00
6	Jeff Hostetler	1.00
7	David Klingler	1.00
8	Dan Marino	6.00
9	Rick Mirer	1.00
10	Neil O'Donnell	1.00
11	Brett Favre	6.00
12	Boomer Esiason	1.00
13	Jim Harbaugh	1.00
14	John Elway	4.00
15	Steve Young	4.00
16	Warren Moon	1.00
17	Jim Kelly	1.00
18	Heath Shuler	1.00

1995 Pinnacle Club Collection Arms Race

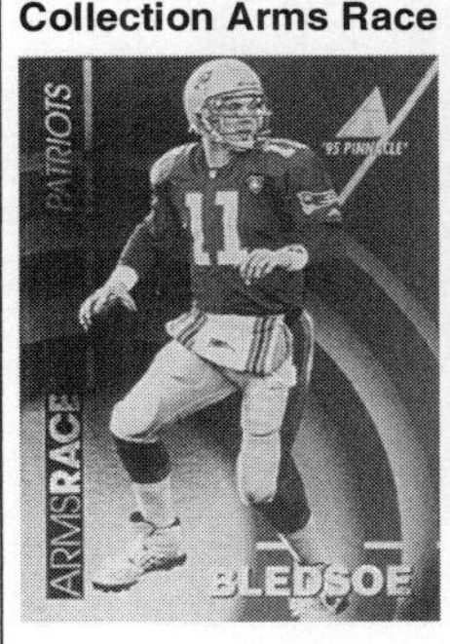

These cards, featuring double-sided Gold Rush technology that puts all-foil printing on both sides of the card, were from an interactive game-card insert set comprised of 18 members of the Quarterback Club. As each quarterback gained points for TD passes, victories and in six statistical categories, the card holder would move closer toward winning prizes. Collectors who had the card of the highest point total finisher at the end of the season had chances at the prizes. Cards were seeded one per every 18 packs. The front of the card had a gold-foiled scope as a background, with the color action photo in the foreground. Arms Race and the player's team name are along the left side of the card. The player's last name is in the lower left corner. The card back, numbered 1 of 18, etc., has a closeup shot of the player on the top half, with a scope as a background. The bottom half has contest rules for the game sweepstakes, plus the set logo.

		NM/M
Complete Set (18):		30.00
Common Player:		1.00
1	Steve Young	3.00
2	Troy Aikman	3.00
3	John Elway	3.00
4	Dan Marino	5.00
5	Brett Favre	5.00
6	Heath Shuler	1.00
7	Jim Kelly	2.00
8	Randall Cunningham	1.00
9	Dave Brown	1.00
10	Jim Everett	1.00
11	Drew Bledsoe	3.00
12	Rick Mirer	1.00
13	Jeff Hostetler	1.00
14	Neil O'Donnell	1.00
15	Warren Moon	2.00
16	Boomer Esiason	1.00
17	Chris Miller	1.00
18	David Klingler	1.00

1995 Pinnacle Club Collection Spotlight

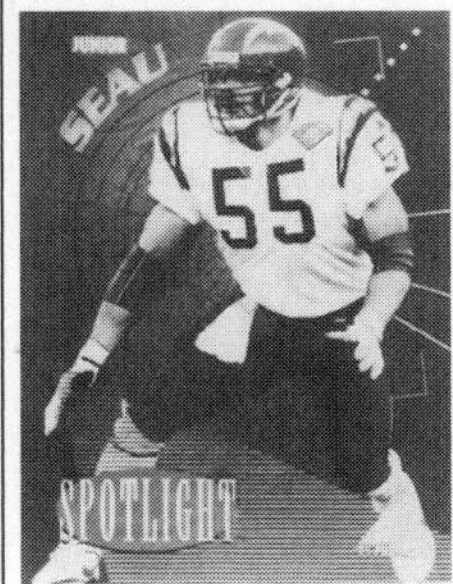

These five cards pay a special tribute to superstars who are not quarterbacks. The cards use a micro-etching process that puts fine textured lines into a holographic foil, creating a flashy effect for the front. Cards were random inserts, one per every 90 packs of 1995 Pinnacle Club Collection.

		NM/M
Complete Set (5):		30.00
Common Player:		2.00
1	Emmitt Smith	10.00
2	Barry Sanders	8.00
3	Jerry Rice	8.00
4	Michael Irvin	2.00
5	Junior Seau	2.00

1995 Pinnacle Dial Corporation

The 30-card, regular-sized cards were issued as part of a promotion sponsored by Dial soap and Purex laundry products. UPC labels from these products could be sent in, with $2.50, for the set. As part of the promotion, 90-card sheets were awarded with Bruce Smith signatures. The cards are numbered with the "DC" prefix.

		NM/M
Complete Set (30):		15.00
Common Player:		.30
1	Troy Aikman	1.50
2	Frank Reich	.30
3	Drew Bledsoe	1.50
4	Bubby Brister	.30
5	Dave Brown	.30
6	Randall Cunningham	.30
7	John Elway	1.00
8	Boomer Esiason	.30
9	Jim Everett	.30
10	Bruce Smith	.40
11	Brett Favre	3.00
12	Jim Harbaugh	.40
13	Jeff Hostetler	.30
14	Michael Irvin	.60
15	Jim Kelly	.40
16	David Klingler	.30
17	Bernie Kosar	.30
18	Dan Marino	3.00
19	Chris Miller	.30
20	Rick Mirer	.60
21	Warren Moon	.40
22	Neil O'Donnell	.40
23	Jerry Rice	1.50
24	Mark Rypien	.30
25	Barry Sanders	1.50
26	Junior Seau	.60
27	Heath Shuler	.40
28	Phil Simms	.30
29	Emmitt Smith	3.00
30	Steve Young	1.00
P1	Uncut Sheet Prize	45.00

1996 Pinnacle Super Bowl Card Show

The 15-card, standard-size set features color action shots over a metallic Dufex background. The card fronts feature a Super Bowl XXX Card Show logo while the horizontal backs have a player shot with a highlight. Pinnacle distributed the set in three-card packs in exchange for two Pinnacle wrappers.

		NM/M
Complete Set (15):		15.00
Common Player:		.40
1	Steve Young	1.25
2	Dan Marino	3.00
3	Troy Aikman	1.50
4	Drew Bledsoe	1.50
5	John Elway	3.00
6	Brett Favre	3.00
7	Jim Harbaugh	.40
8	Jeff Hostetler	.40
9	Michael Irvin	.75
10	Jim Kelly	.75
11	Warren Moon	.75
12	Jerry Rice	1.50
13	Barry Sanders	3.00
14	Junior Seau	.75
15	Emmitt Smith	2.50

1996 Pinnacle

Pinnacle's 1996 football set includes 200 cards in the regular set, including 30 Rookies, six Bid For Six subset cards, five checklists and a Brett Favre Cheesehead card. The set is paralleled twice in normal packs - Trophy Collection (one in five packs, these cards use all-foil Dufex) and Artist's Proof (one in 47 packs, these have a holographic gold foil stamp). These parallel cards are labeled accordingly on them. Each regular card has a full-bleed color action photo on the front, with a Pinnacle logo in an upper corner. The player's name is in a gold-foiled triangle at the bottom. The card back has logo in an upper corner, with the card number in white in a black square. The upper half of the card has a photo; the lower half has a brief profile, stats, biographical information, the player's name and team logo, and his position. Insert sets include Black 'N Blue, Double Disguise, On the Line, Team Pinnacle and 321 Die-Cut Jersey cards. Pinnacle also offers hobby-exclusive packs called premium stock, which contain 25 cards and carry a suggested retail price of $6.99. In these packs each common card in the set is printed on a super-premium, 24-point card stock featuring silver foil stamping. Premium stock packs also have five inserts - Trophy Collection, Artist's Proofs, Team Pinnacle, Double Disguise and an exclusive rainbow holographic foil version of 321.

		NM/M
Complete Set (200):		15.00
Common Player:		.05
Minor Stars:		.20
Trophy Coll. Cards:		3X-5X
Artist's Proof Cards:		5X-10X
Premium Cards:		2X
Hobby Pack (10):		1.00
Hobby Wax Box (24):		20.00
Prem. Stock Pack (25):		3.00
Prem. Stock Wax Box (8):		20.00
1	Emmitt Smith	2.50
2	Robert Brooks	.20
3	Joey Galloway	.75
4	Dan Marino	2.50
5	Frank Sanders	.20
6	Cris Carter	.05
7	Jeff Blake	.75
8	Steve McNair	.75
9	Tamarick Vanover	.75
10	Andre Reed	.05
11	Junior Seau	.05
12	Alvin Harper	.05
13	Trent Dilfer	.05
14	Kordell Stewart	1.00
15	Kyle Brady	.05
16	Charles Haley	.05
17	Greg Lloyd	.05
18	Mario Bates	.05
19	Shannon Sharpe	.05
20	Scott Mitchell	.05
21	Craig Heyward	.05
22	Marcus Allen	.05
23	Curtis Martin	1.75
24	Drew Bledsoe	1.00
25	Jerry Rice	1.00
26	Charlie Garner	.05
27	Michael Irvin	.05
28	Curtis Conway	.05
29	Terrell Davis	1.25
30	Jeff Hostetler	.05
31	Neil O'Donnell	.05
32	Errict Rhett	.50
33	Stan Humphries	.05
34	Jeff Graham	.05
35	Floyd Turner	.05
36	Vincent Brisby	.05
37	Steve Young	1.00
38	Carl Pickens	.05
39	Terance Mathis	.05
40	Brett Favre	2.50
41	Ki-Jana Carter	.40
42	Jim Everett	.05
43	Marshall Faulk	.75
44	William Floyd	.05
45	Deion Sanders	.50
46	Garrison Hearst	.05
47	Chris Sanders	.05
48	Isaac Bruce	.75
49	Natrone Means	.05
50	Troy Aikman	1.25
51	Ben Coates	.05
52	Tony Martin	.05
53	Rod Woodson	.05
54	Edgar Bennett	.05
55	Eric Zeier	.05
56	Steve Bono	.05
57	Tim Brown	.05
58	Kevin Williams	.05
59	Erik Kramer	.05
60	Jim Kelly	.05
61	Larry Centers	.05
62	Terrell Fletcher	.05
63	Michael Westbrook	.20
64	Kerry Collins	.50
65	Jay Novacek	.05
66	J.J. Stokes	.20
67	John Elway	.50
68	Jim Harbaugh	.05
69	Aeneas Williams	.05
70	Tyrone Wheatley	.05
71	Chris Warren	.20
72	Rodney Thomas	.05
73	Jeff George	.05
74	Rick Mirer	.05
75	Yancey Thigpen	.50
76	Herman Moore	.50
77	Gus Frerotte	.05
78	Anthony Miller	.05
79	Ricky Watters	.05
80	Sherman Williams	.05
81	Hardy Nickerson	.05
82	Henry Ellard	.05
83	Aaron Craver	.05
84	Rodney Peete	.05
85	Eric Metcalf	.05
86	Brian Blades	.05
87	Rob Moore	.05
88	Kimble Anders	.05
89	Harvey Williams	.05
90	Thurman Thomas	.20
91	Dave Brown	.05
92	Terry Allen	.05
93	Ken Norton	.05
94	Reggie White	.20
95	Mark Chmura	.20
96	Bert Emanuel	.05
97	Brett Perriman	.05
98	Antonio Freeman	.05
99	Brian Mitchell	.05
100	Orlando Thomas	.05
101	Aaron Hayden	.05
102	Quinn Early	.05
103	Lovell Pinkney	.05
104	Napoleon Kaufman	.20
105	Daryl Johnston	.05
106	Steve Tasker	.05
107	Brent Jones	.05
108	Mark Brunell	.75
109	Leslie O'Neal	.05
110	Irving Fryar	.05
111	Jim Miller	.05
112	Sean Dawkins	.05
113	Boomer Esiason	.05
114	Heath Shuler	.05
115	Bruce Smith	.05
116	Russell Maryland	.05
117	Jake Reed	.05
118	O.J. McDuffie	.05
119	Eric Williams	.05
120	Willie McGinest	.05
121	Terry Kirby	.05
122	Fred Barnett	.05
123	Andre Hastings	.05
124	Dale Hellestrae	.05
125	Darren Woodson	.05
126	Steve Atwater	.05
127	Quentin Coryatt	.05
128	Derrick Thomas	.05
129	Nate Newton	.05
130	Kevin Greene	.05
131	Barry Sanders	1.25
132	Warren Moon	.05
133	Rashaan Salaam	.50
134	Rodney Hampton	.05
135	James Stewart	.05
136	Erric Pegram	.05
137	Bryan Cox	.05
138	Adrian Murrell	.05
139	Robert Smith	.05
140	Bernie Parmalee	.05
141	Bryce Paup	.05
142	Darick Holmes	.05
143	Hugh Douglas	.05
144	Ken Dilger	.05
145	Derek Loville	.05
146	Horace Copeland	.05
147	Wayne Chrebet	.05
148	Andre Coleman	.05
149	Greg Hill	.05
150	Eric Swann	.05
151	Tyrone Hughes	.05
152	Ernie Mills	.05
153	*Terry Glenn*	2.00
154	*Cedric Jones*	.05
155	*Leeland McElroy*	.30
156	*Bobby Engram*	.50
157	*Willie Anderson*	.05
158	*Mike Alstott*	1.75
159	*Alex Van Dyke*	.20
160	*Jeff Lewis*	.50
161	*Keyshawn Johnson*	3.00
162	*Regan Upshaw*	.05
163	*Eric Moulds*	2.50
164	*Tim Biakabutuka*	1.00
165	*Kevin Hardy*	.20
166	*Marvin Harrison*	3.00
167	*Karim Abdul-Jabbar*	1.00
168	*Tony Brackens*	.30
169	*Stepfret Williams*	.05
170	*Eddie George*	4.00
171	*Lawrence Phillips*	.75
172	*Danny Kanell*	.50
173	*Derrick Mayes*	1.00
174	*Daryl Gardener*	.05
175	*Jonathan Ogden*	.05
176	*Alex Molden*	.05
177	*Chris Darkins*	.20
178	*Stephen Davis*	4.00
179	*Rickey Dudley*	.30
180	*Eddie Kennison*	.50
181	*Simeon Rice*	.40
182	*Bobby Hoying*	.75
183	Troy Aikman	.50
184	Emmitt Smith	1.00
185	Michael Irvin	.05
186	Deion Sanders	.25
187	Daryl Johnston	.05
188	Jay Novacek	.05
189	Steve Young	.40
190	Jerry Rice	.50
191	J.J. Stokes	.05
192	Ken Norton	.05
193	William Floyd	.05
194	Brent Jones	.05
195	Dan Marino CL	.40
196	Brett Favre CL	.30
197	Emmitt Smith CL	.40
198	Barry Sanders CL	.30
199	Emmitt Smith, Dan Marino, Brett Favre, Barry Sanders CL Checklist	.30
200	Brett Favre Cheese	2.50

1996 Pinnacle Trophy Collection

Trophy Collection features all 200 cards from 1996 Pinnacle, reprinted in Dufex foil fronts and a stamp on the back that reads "Trophy Collection." Regular packs had Trophy Collection cards every five packs, while Premium Stock packs contained them every two packs. There is no difference between regular and Premium Stock cards in Trophy Collection.

	NM/M
Complete Trophy Set (200):	500.00
Trophy Cards:	3X-5X

1996 Pinnacle Foils

Pinnacle Foils were available only in All-Foil packs, which were available in retail locations. These Foils were the "regular-issue" cards of All-Foil packs that also included Black and Blue inserts.

	NM/M
Complete Set (200):	35.00
Foil Cards:	1.5X

1996 Pinnacle Artist's Proofs

This 200-card parallel set features each card in 1996 Pinnacle Football, but includes a holographic Artist's Proof logo on the front, as well as a logo on the back. Artist's Proofs were included in every 48 hobby and retail packs. Regular Artist's Proofs contained gold foil at the bottom of the card in contrast to Premium Stock Artist's Proofs that included silver foil and are included in a separate entry.

	NM/M
Artist's Proof Cards:	5X-10X

1996 Pinnacle Premium Stock

Pinnacle Premium Stock was issued as a hobby exclusive product that was offered in addition to regular Pinnacle Football. The base cards were different in that they had silver foil at the bottom instead of gold foil. Packs of Premium Stock contained 25 cards, and included Artist's Proofs, Trophy Collection, Team Pinnacle, Die-Cut Jerseys and Double Disguise inserts. Only the Artist's Proofs and Die-Cut Jerseys are different than regular-issue inserts.

	NM/M
Premium Stock Cards:	2X

1996 Pinnacle Premium Stock Artist's Proofs

Each card in the 200-card Premium Stock set was featured in the parallel Artist's Proof insert. This means that the Premium Stock Artist's Proofs feature silver foil on the fronts instead of gold foil on the regular-issue Artist's Proofs. Premium Stock Artist's Proofs were inserted every 12 packs.

	NM/M
Complete Set (200):	1,500
PS Artist's Proofs:	25X-50X

1996 Pinnacle Die-Cut Jerseys

The best and youngest players in the NFL - those with three or less years of experience - are featured on these die-cut Pinnacle insert cards. The cards are hobby-exclusive; they were seeded one per every 23 hobby packs. The card front has a color action shot against a die-cut version of his jersey. "3-2-1" is included as a tag in the jersey's collar. The Pinnacle logo and player's name are stamped in gold foil along the bottom of the card. The back of the card uses the back of the player's jersey as a background. A second photo appears, along with a team logo, a brief summary of one of his accomplishments, and a card number (1 of 20, etc.).

		NM/M
Complete Set (20):		45.00
Common Player:		1.00
Holofoil Cards:		2X
1	Errict Rhett	1.00
2	Marshall Faulk	3.00
3	Isaac Bruce	2.00
4	William Floyd	1.00
5	Heath Shuler	1.00
6	Kerry Collins	2.00
7	Kordell Stewart	3.00
8	Rashaan Salaam	1.00
9	Terrell Davis	4.00
10	Rodney Thomas	1.00
11	Curtis Martin	4.00
12	Steve McNair	3.00
13	J.J. Stokes	2.00
14	Joey Galloway	2.00
15	Michael Westbrook	2.00
16	Keyshawn Johnson	3.00
17	Lawrence Phillips	1.00
18	Terry Glenn	3.00
19	Tim Biakabutuka	1.00
20	Eddie George	4.00

1996 Pinnacle Premium Stock Die-Cut Jerseys

Premium Stock packs included a unique version of the Die-cut Jerseys that featured the fronts in prismatic foil. These versions of Die-Cut Jerseys were inserted every six packs and only included in Premium Stock.

	NM/M
Complete Set (20):	320.00
PS Die-Cut Jerseys:	2X

Post-1980 cards in Near Mint condition will generally sell for about 75% of the quoted Mint value. Excellent-condition cards bring no more than 40%.

1996 Pinnacle Double Disguise

These 1996 Pinnacle inserts showcase five players in 20 different combinations. The cards are printed on plastic and are covered with an opaque plastic protector which is meant to be peeled off. Each side features combinations of Emmitt Smith, Dan Marino, Brett Favre, Kerry Collins and Steve Young matched up. The card's background shows the length of a football field as seen through a fish-eye lens. The front side uses gold-foil stamping for the Pinnacle logo, player's name and set name. These are not in foil on the opposite side, which has a card number (1 of 20, etc.). The cards were seeded one per every 18 packs.

		NM/M
Complete Set (20):		45.00
Common Player:		1.00
1	Emmitt Smith, Emmitt Smith	4.00
2	Emmitt Smith, Dan Marino	4.00
3	Emmitt Smith, Brett Favre	4.00
4	Emmitt Smith, Steve Young	3.00
5	Dan Marino, Dan Marino	4.00
6	Dan Marino, Emmitt Smith	4.00
7	Dan Marino, Kerry Collins	3.00
8	Dan Marino, Steve Young	3.00
9	Kerry Collins, Kerry Collins	1.00
10	Kerry Collins, Dan Marino	3.00
11	Kerry Collins, Brett Favre	3.00
12	Kerry Collins, Steve Young	1.00
13	Brett Favre, Brett Favre	4.00
14	Brett Favre, Kerry Collins	3.00
15	Brett Favre, Dan Marino	5.00
16	Brett Favre, Emmitt Smith	5.00
17	Steve Young, Steve Young	1.00
18	Steve Young, Brett Favre	3.00
19	Steve Young, Emmitt Smith	4.00
20	Steve Young, Kerry Collins	1.00

1996 Pinnacle Black 'N Blue

Twenty-five of the NFL's most rugged players show the hard-nosed, aggressive play which has earned them a spot in this set. The cards were seeded one per every 33 magazine packs. Each card front has two photos on it.

		NM/M
Complete Set (25):		65.00
Common Player:		1.00
1	Steve Young	4.00
2	Troy Aikman	4.00

3	Dan Marino	6.00
4	Michael Irvin	1.00
5	Jerry Rice	4.00
6	Emmitt Smith	5.00
7	Brett Favre	6.00
8	Drew Bledsoe	3.00
9	John Elway	4.00
10	Barry Sanders	5.00
11	Cris Carter	1.00
12	Jeff Blake	1.00
13	Chris Warren	1.00
14	Kerry Collins	2.00
15	Natrone Means	1.00
16	Herman Moore	1.00
17	Steve McNair	3.00
18	Ricky Watters	1.00
19	Tamarick Vanover	2.00
20	Deion Sanders	3.00
21	Terrell Davis	4.00
22	Rodney Thomas	1.00
23	Rashaan Salaam	1.00
24	Darick Holmes	1.00
25	Eric Zeier	1.00

1996 Pinnacle Team Pinnacle

These 1996 Pinnacle inserts feature the best AFC player at each position on a card that is complemented by the top NFC position player on the flip side. The cards were seeded one per every 90 packs for both hobby and retail packs. The design shows a pinstripe-framed color action photo against a football background. The player's name, position and Team Pinnacle are written in a rectangle at the bottom. The card is numbered 1 of 20, etc.

		NM/M
Complete Set (10):		70.00
Common Player:		2.00
Inserted 1:90		
1	Troy Aikman, Drew Bledsoe	6.00
2	Steve Young, Jeff Blake	5.00
3	Brett Favre, John Elway	14.00
4	Kerry Collins, Dan Marino	12.00
5	Emmitt Smith, Curtis Martin	12.00
6	Barry Sanders, Chris Warren	10.00
7	Errict Rhett, Marshall Faulk	4.00
8	Jerry Rice, Carl Pickens	10.00
9	Michael Irvin, Joey Galloway	2.00
10	Isaac Bruce, Kordell Stewart	4.00

1996 Pinnacle On the Line

The NFL's top pass catchers are featured on these 1996 Pinnacle inserts. The cards, seeded one per every 23 retail packs, use Dufex for the design. The card front has a full-bleed color action photo on it, with the player's name at the bottom near a grid which says "On the Line." The Pinnacle logo is in an upper corner.

		NM/M
Complete Set (15):		45.00
Common Player:		1.00
1	Michael Irvin	1.00
2	Robert Brooks	1.00
3	Herman Moore	2.00
4	Cris Carter	1.00
5	Chris Sanders	1.00
6	Jerry Rice	5.00
7	Michael Westbrook	1.00
8	Carl Pickens	1.00
9	Bobby Engram	2.00
10	Alex Van Dyke	1.00
11	Keyshawn Johnson	4.00
12	Terry Glenn	4.00
13	Eric Moulds	4.00
14	Marvin Harrison	6.00
15	Eddie Kennison	4.00

1996 Laser View

Each of these 1996 Pinnacle Laserview cards features nearly four seconds of taped replay action from NFL Films in the form of a hologram. Each regular card has the hologram on one side, with a small action photo, the player's name and the LaserView logo on the opposite. The background of the horizontal card front is black. The card back has a ghosted image for the background, with a small action photo, biographical information, a card number, team logo and brief write-up toward the top of the card. Two team-colored stripes separate this information from the player's name, position and 1995 and career statistics at the bottom. Laser-view Gold parallel gold-foiled cards were seeded every 12th pack. Other inserts include Eye on the Prize and Inscriptions. Every box also comes with a Pinnacle authenticator lens that allows collectors to prove the authenticity of the printing. A small box on the back of each card has a multi-colored pattern of lines that can only be read by the lens; the message "PBI 96" appears when this is done. If the lens is turned another way, a rainbow pattern appears. Pinnacle claims no counterfeit techniques would be able to duplicate this printing because the pattern of lines is so thin.

		NM/M
Complete Set (40):		35.00
Common Player:		.50
Minor Stars:		1.00
Gold Cards:		2X-3X
Pack (1):		4.00
Wax Box (24):		75.00
1	Jim Kelly	1.00
2	Troy Aikman	5.00
3	Michael Irvin	1.00
4	Emmitt Smith	6.00
5	John Elway	4.00
6	Barry Sanders	5.00
7	Brett Favre	6.00
8	Jim Harbaugh	.50
9	Dan Marino	6.00
10	Warren Moon	.50
11	Drew Bledsoe	5.00
12	Jim Everett	.50
13	Jeff Hostetler	.50
14	Neil O'Donnell	.50
15	Junior Seau	.50
16	Jerry Rice	5.00
17	Steve Young	4.00
18	Rick Mirer	1.00
19	Boomer Esiason	.50
20	Bernie Kosar	.50
21	Heath Shuler	1.00
22	Dave Brown	.50
23	Jeff Blake	1.00
24	Kerry Collins	1.50
25	Kordell Stewart	5.00
26	Scott Mitchell	.50
27	Kerry Collins PE	3.00
28	Troy Aikman PE	3.00
29	Kordell Stewart PE	3.00
30	Michael Irvin PE	.50
31	Emmitt Smith PE	5.00
32	John Elway PE	1.00
33	Barry Sanders PE	3.00
34	Brett Favre PE	5.00
35	Dan Marino PE	5.00
36	Drew Bledsoe PE	3.00
37	Neil O'Donnell PE	.50
38	Jerry Rice PE	3.00
39	Steve Young PE	2.00
40	Jeff Blake PE	2.00

A card number in parenthese ( ) indicates the set is unnumbered.

1996 Laser View Golds

This 40-card parallel set used all 40 cards in the regular-issue LaserView set in a gold version. Gold parallels were found every 12 packs.

Golds: 2X-3X

1996 Laser View Eye on the Prize

This 1996 Pinnacle Laserview insert spotlights 12 of the NFL's elite superstars as they compete for the coveted Lombardi Trophy as winners of the Super Bowl. The cards put a different holographic angle on the players by picturing the player with a holographic background. The cards were seeded one per every 24 packs.

		NM/M
Complete Set (12):		40.00
Common Player:		1.00
1	Troy Aikman	5.00
2	Emmitt Smith	7.00
3	Michael Irvin	1.00
4	Steve Young	8.00
5	Jerry Rice	5.00
6	Dan Marino	7.00
7	John Elway	4.00
8	Junior Seau	1.00
9	Neil O'Donnell	1.00
10	Jeff Hostetler	1.00
11	Jim Kelly	1.00
12	Kordell Stewart	3.00

1996 Laser View Inscriptions

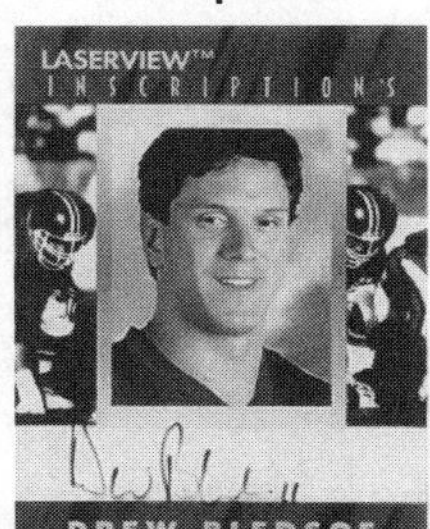

This 1996 Pinnacle Laserview insert set features 25 of the top members of the NFL Quarterback Club who each signed a serial-numbered card. The cards, seeded one per every 24 packs, are printed on clear plastic stock which gives collectors a backwards-forwards look at the signature. The front has a color panel at the top which includes the brand and set names, with a color mug shot underneath framed in yellow. The closeup shot is flanked by a black-and-white action scene. The player's signature is below his photo, followed by another colored band at the bottom which has the player's name and team name inside. The back, which shows reverse images of the front, includes the serial number in a white rectangle at the top.

	NM/M
Complete Set (25):	
Jeff Blake 3125	40.00
Drew Bledsoe 2775	75.00
Dave Brown 3100	20.00
Mark Brunell 3200	50.00
Kerry Collins 3000	50.00
John Elway 3100	100.00
Boomer Esiason 1500	100.00
Jim Everett 3100	20.00
Brett Favre 4850	100.00
Jeff George 2900	30.00
Jim Harbaugh 3500	25.00
Jeff Hostetler 3750	20.00
Michael Irvin 3050	25.00
Jim Kelly 3100	40.00
Bernie Kosar 3200	20.00
Erik Kramer 3150	20.00
Rick Mirer 3150	30.00
Scott Mitchell 4900	20.00
Warren Moon 2800	25.00
Neil O'Donnell 1600	50.00
Jerry Rice 900	125.00
Barry Sanders 2900	100.00
Junior Seau 3000	25.00
Heath Shuler 3100	25.00
Steve Young 1950	75.00

1996 Pinnacle Mint Cards

The 30-card, regular-sized set comes in three-card packs and contains two coin cards and one regular-issue card. The die-cut coin cards feature a closeup player shot and an action shot on the front with the same action shot in black and white on the back. The cards have a circular cutout in the upper right quadrant where the included brass, nickel- silver or gold coins fit. The regular-issue cards feature a foil team emblem (where the hole is on the coin cards) in brass (common), silver (1:20) or gold (1:48). Each of the 30 players represented in the set are members of the Quarterback Club.

		NM/M
Complete Die-Cut (30):		18.00
Common Player:		.20
Minor Stars:		.40
Bronze Cards:		2X
Silver Cards:		3X-5X
Gold Cards:		4X-8X
Wax Box:		30.00
1	Troy Aikman	1.50
2	John Elway	.75
3	Jim Kelly	.40
4	Dan Marino	3.00
5	Warren Moon	.20
6	Steve Young	1.50
7	Jerry Rice	1.50
8	Boomer Esiason	.20
9	Jim Everett	.20
10	Brett Favre	3.00
11	Jim Harbaugh	.40
12	Jeff Hostetler	.20
13	Neil O'Donnell	.20
14	Drew Bledsoe	1.50
15	Rick Mirer	.20
16	Emmitt Smith	3.00
17	Barry Sanders	1.50
18	Junior Seau	.20
19	Dave Brown	.20
20	Heath Shuler	.20
21	Jeff Blake	.40
22	Kerry Collins	.75
23	Scott Mitchell	.20
24	Kordell Stewart	1.50
25	Jeff George	.20
26	Mark Brunell	1.00
27	Erik Kramer	.20
28	Bernie Kosar	.20
29	Frank Reich	.20
30	Randall Cunningham	.20

1996 Pinnacle Mint Coins

The 30-piece set was included twice in every three-pack of Pinnacle Mint Collection football. Two variations of the common brass coin were available: nickel-silver (1:20) and 24 kt. gold (1:48). Solid silver coins were also inserted every 2,300 packs and one redemption card was available for an all-gold coin with the odds being one in 47,200. The coin face has the image of the player's face with his name, team and uniform number. The coin backs feature the Quarterback Club logo, as each of the 30 players represented in the set are members.

		NM/M
Complete Brass (30):		50.00
Common Brass Coin:		.75
Minor Brass Stars:		1.50
Nickel Coins:		1X-2X
Gold Plated Coins:		2X-4X
1	Troy Aikman	4.00
2	John Elway	3.00
3	Jim Kelly	1.50
4	Dan Marino	8.00
5	Warren Moon	.75
6	Steve Young	3.00
7	Jerry Rice	4.00
8	Boomer Esiason	.75
9	Jim Everett	.75
10	Brett Favre	8.00
11	Jim Harbaugh	.75
12	Jeff Hostetler	.75
13	Neil O'Donnell	.75
14	Drew Bledsoe	4.00
15	Rick Mirer	.75
16	Emmitt Smith	8.00
17	Barry Sanders	4.00
18	Junior Seau	1.50
19	Dave Brown	.75
20	Heath Shuler	.75
21	Jeff Blake	1.50
22	Kerry Collins	1.50
23	Scott Mitchell	.75
24	Kordell Stewart	4.00
25	Jeff George	.75
26	Mark Brunell	3.00
27	Erik Kramer	.75
28	Bernie Kosar	.75
29	Frank Reich	.75
30	Randall Cunningham	.75

1996 Pinnacle Bimbo Bread

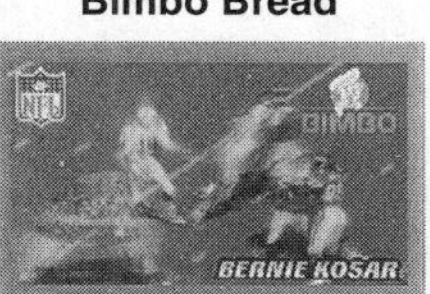

These magic motion cards were distributed in Mexico through Bimbo Bakery products. The 30 cards measure 1-1/2" x 2-1/2" and feature a magic motion photo and the Bimbo logo on the front. The backs have another player photo and biographical information.

		NM/M
Complete Set (30):		75.00
Common Player:		1.00
1	Troy Aikman	6.00
2	Michael Irvin	3.00
3	Emmitt Smith	8.00
4	Jim Kelly	4.00
5	John Elway	6.00
6	Barry Sanders	8.00
7	Brett Favre	10.00
8	Jim Harbaugh	1.00
9	Dan Marino	10.00
10	Warren Moon	1.00
11	Drew Bledsoe	6.00
12	Jim Everett	1.00
13	Jeff Hostetler	1.00
14	Neil O'Donnell	1.00
15	Junior Seau	3.00
16	Jerry Rice	8.00
17	Steve Young	6.00
18	Rick Mirer	1.00
19	Jeff Blake	1.00
20	David Klingler	1.00
21	Boomer Esiason	1.00
22	Heath Shuler	1.00
23	Dave Brown	1.00
24	Bernie Kosar	1.00
25	Kordell Stewart	3.00
26	Mark Brunell	4.00
27	Kerry Collins	3.00
28	Scott Mitchell	1.00
29	Erik Kramer	1.00
30	Jeff George	1.00

1997 Pinnacle

Pinnacle Football has a 200-card base set. Both sides feature a player action photo. Pinnacle Football also has two partial base set parallels (Artist's Proof and Trophy Collection) and three inserts. Trophy Collection utilizes Dufex technology. Artist's Proof parallels Trophy Collection by adding the Artist's Proof stamp. The parallel sets are re-numbered. The inserts include Epix (24 cards, 1:19), Scoring Core (24 cards, 1:89) and Team Pinnacle (10 cards, 1:240).

		NM/M
Complete Set (200):		25.00
Common Player:		.10
Minor Stars:		.20
Trophy Cards:		3X-5X
Trophy Rookies:		2X-4X
Inserted 1:9		
Artist Proof Cards:		5X-10X
Artist Proof Rookies:		3X-6X
Inserted 1:39		
Pack (10):		3.00
Wax Box (18):		48.00
1	Brett Favre	2.50
2	Dan Marino	2.00
3	Emmitt Smith	2.00
4	Steve Young	.75
5	Drew Bledsoe	1.00
6	Eddie George	1.50
7	Barry Sanders	1.25
8	Jerry Rice	1.00
9	John Elway	.75
10	Troy Aikman	1.00
11	Kerry Collins	.25
12	Rick Mirer	.10
13	Jim Harbaugh	.10
14	Elvis Grbac	.10
15	Gus Frerotte	.10
16	Neil O'Donnell	.10
17	Jeff George	.10
18	Kordell Stewart	1.00
19	Junior Seau	.20
20	Vinny Testaverde	.10
21	Terry Glenn	.30
22	Anthony Johnson	.10
23	Boomer Esiason	.10
24	Terrell Owens	.50
25	Natrone Means	.20
26	Marcus Allen	.20
27	James Jett	.10
28	Chris T. Jones	.10
29	Stan Humphries	.10
30	Keith Byars	.10
31	John Friesz	.10
32	Mike Alstott	.20
33	Eddie Kennison	.40
34	Eric Moulds	.10
35	Frank Sanders	.10
36	Daryl Johnston	.10
37	Cris Carter	.10
38	Errict Rhett	.20
39	Ben Coates	.10
40	Shannon Sharpe	.10
41	Jamal Anderson	.20
42	Tim Biakabutuka	.10
43	Jeff Blake	.20
44	Michael Irvin	.20
45	Terrell Davis	1.00
46	Bam Morris	.10
47	Rashaan Salaam	.10
48	Adrian Murrell	.20
49	Ty Detmer	.10
50	Terry Allen	.10
51	Mark Brunell	1.00
52	O.J. McDuffie	.10
53	Willie McGinest	.10
54	Chris Warren	.10
55	Trent Dilfer	.20
56	Jerome Bettis	.20
57	Tamarick Vanover	.10
58	Ki-Jana Carter	.10
59	Ray Zellars	.10
60	J.J. Stokes	.10
61	Cornelius Bennett	.10
62	Scott Mitchell	.10
63	Tyrone Wheatley	.10
64	Steve McNair	.75
65	Tony Banks	.40
66	James Stewart	.10
67	Robert Smith	.10
68	Thurman Thomas	.20
69	Mark Chmura	.10
70	Napoleon Kaufman	.20
71	Ken Norton	.10
72	Herschel Walker	.10
73	Joey Galloway	.20
74	Neil Smith	.10
75	Simeon Rice	.10
76	Michael Jackson	.10
77	Muhsin Muhammad	.10
78	Kevin Hardy	.10
79	Irving Fryar	.10
80	Eric Swann	.10
81	Yancey Thigpen	.10
82	Jim Everett	.10
83	Karim Abdul-Jabbar	.30
84	Garrison Hearst	.10
85	Lawrence Phillips	.20
86	Bryan Cox	.10
87	Larry Centers	.10
88	Wesley Walls	.10
89	Curtis Conway	.10
90	Darnay Scott	.10
91	Anthony Miller	.10
92	Edgar Bennett	.10
93	Willie Green	.10
94	Kent Graham	.10
95	Dave Brown	.10
96	Wayne Chrebet	.10
97	Ricky Watters	.20
98	Tony Martin	.10
99	Warren Moon	.10
100	Curtis Martin	1.00
101	Dorsey Levens	.30
102	Jim Pyne	.10
103	Antonio Freeman	.30
104	Leeland McElroy	.10
105	Isaac Bruce	.20
106	Chris Sanders	.10
107	Tim Brown	.10
108	Greg Lloyd	.10
109	Terrell Buckley	.10
110	Deion Sanders	.40
111	Carl Pickens	.10
112	Bobby Engram	.10
113	Andre Reed	.10
114	Terance Mathis	.10
115	Herman Moore	.20
116	Robert Brooks	.10
117	Ken Dilger	.10
118	Keenan McCardell	.10
119	Andre Hastings	.10
120	Willie Davis	.10
121	Bruce Smith	.10
122	Rob Moore	.10
123	Johnnie Morton	.10
124	Sean Dawkins	.10
125	Mario Bates	.10
126	Henry Ellard	.10
127	Derrick Alexander	.10
128	Kevin Green	.10
129	Derrick Thomas	.10

130	Rod Woodson	.10
131	Rodney Hampton	.10
132	Marshall Faulk	.20
133	Michael Westbrook	.10
134	Erik Kramer	.10
135	Todd Collins	.10
136	Bill Romanowski	.10
137	Jake Reed	.10
138	Heath Shuler	.10
139	Keyshawn Johnson	.40
140	Marvin Harrison	.40
141	Andre Rison	.10
142	Zach Thomas	.20
143	Eric Metcalf	.10
144	Amani Toomer	.10
145	Desmond Howard	.10
146	Jimmy Smith	.10
147	Brad Johnson	.10
148	Troy Vincent	.10
149	Bryce Paup	.10
150	Reggie White	.20
151	*Jake Plummer*	2.50
152	*Darnell Autry*	.25
153	*Tiki Barber*	.75
154	*Pat Barnes*	.30
155	*Orlando Pace*	.20
156	*Peter Boulware*	.10
157	*Shawn Springs*	.20
158	*Troy Davis*	.30
159	*Ike Hilliard*	.75
160	*Jim Druckenmiller*	1.50
161	*Warrick Dunn*	1.25
162	*James Farrior*	.10
163	*Tony Gonzalez*	.75
164	*Darrell Russell*	.10
165	*Byron Hanspard*	.50
166	*Corey Dillon*	2.00
167	*Kenny Holmes*	.10
168	*Walter Jones*	.10
169	*Danny Wuerffel*	.75
170	*Tom Knight*	.10
171	*David LaFleur*	.40
172	*Kevin Lockett*	.10
173	*Will Blackwell*	.20
174	*Reidel Anthony*	1.00
175	*Dwayne Rudd*	.10
176	*Yatil Green*	.30
177	*Antowain Smith*	1.25
178	*Rae Carruth*	.75
179	*Bryant Westbrook*	.10
180	*Reinard Wilson*	.10
181	*Joey Kent*	.30
182	*Renaldo Wynn*	.10
183	Brett Favre	1.25
184	Emmitt Smith	1.00
185	Dan Marino	1.00
186	Troy Aikman	.50
187	Jerry Rice	.50
188	Drew Bledsoe	.50
189	Eddie George	.75
190	Terry Glenn	.10
191	John Elway	.30
192	Steve Young	.30
193	Mark Brunell	.30
194	Barry Sanders	.50
195	Kerry Collins	.30
196	Curtis Martin	.50
197	Terrell Davis	.50
198	Checklist	.10
199	Checklist	.10
200	Checklist	.10

1997 Pinnacle Trophy Collection

Trophy Collection is a 100-card partial parallel of the base set. The cards were re-numbered and feature Dufex technology. They were inserted one per nine packs.

		NM/M
Complete Set (100):		250.00
Common Player:		1.00
Minor Stars:		3X to 5X
P1	Brett Favre	25.00
P2	Dan Marino	20.00
P3	Emmitt Smith	20.00
P4	Steve Young	8.00
P5	Drew Bledsoe	12.00
P6	Eddie George	16.00
P7	Barry Sanders	12.00
P8	Jerry Rice	12.00
P9	John Elway	10.00
P10	Troy Aikman	12.00
P11	Kerry Collins	3.00
P12	Rick Mirer	1.00
P13	Jim Harbaugh	1.00
P14	Elvis Grbac	1.00
P15	Gus Frerotte	1.00
P16	Neil O'Donnell	1.00
P17	Jeff George	1.00
P18	Kordell Stewart	12.00
P19	Junior Seau	1.00
P20	Vinny Testaverde	1.00
P21	Terry Glenn	10.00
P22	Natrone Means	2.00
P23	Marcus Allen	2.00
P24	Stan Humphries	1.00
P25	John Friesz	1.00
P26	Cris Carter	1.00
P27	Shannon Sharpe	1.00
P28	Tim Biakabutuka	1.00
P29	Jeff Blake	2.00
P30	Michael Irvin	2.00
P31	Terrell Davis	12.00
P32	Rashaan Salaam	1.00
P33	Adrian Murrell	2.00
P34	Ty Detmer	1.00
P35	Mark Brunell	12.00
P36	Chris Warren	1.00
P37	Trent Dilfer	2.00
P38	Jerome Bettis	2.00
P39	Scott Mitchell	1.00
P40	Steve McNair	10.00
P41	Tony Banks	3.00
P42	Joey Galloway	2.00
P43	Karim Abdul-Jabbar	8.00
P44	Lawrence Phillips	2.00
P45	Dave Brown	1.00
P46	Warren Moon	1.00
P47	Curtis Martin	12.00
P48	Dorsey Levens	2.00
P49	Deion Sanders	5.00
P50	Herman Moore	2.00
P51	Bruce Smith	1.00
P52	Keyshawn Johnson	2.00
P53	Reggie White	2.00
P54	Jake Plummer	10.00
P55	Darnell Autry	4.00
P56	Tiki Barber	8.00
P57	Pat Barnes	4.00
P58	Orlando Pace	2.00
P59	Peter Boulware	1.00
P60	Shawn Springs	2.00
P61	Troy Davis	3.00
P62	Ike Hilliard	6.00
P63	Jim Druckenmiller	12.00
P64	Warrick Dunn	20.00
P65	James Farrior	1.00
P66	Tony Gonzalez	5.00
P67	Darrell Russell	1.00
P68	Byron Hanspard	3.00
P69	Corey Dillon	12.00
P70	Kenny Holmes	1.00
P71	Walter Jones	1.00
P72	Danny Wuerffel	10.00
P73	Tom Knight	1.00
P74	David LaFleur	5.00
P75	Kevin Lockett	1.00
P76	Will Blackwell	2.00
P77	Reidel Anthony	8.00
P78	Dwayne Rudd	1.00
P79	Yatil Green	6.00
P80	Antowain Smith	12.00
P81	Rae Carruth	6.00
P82	Bryant Westbrook	2.00
P83	Reinard Wilson	2.00
P84	Joey Kent	2.00
P85	Renaldo Wynn	1.00
P86	Brett Favre	12.00
P87	Emmitt Smith	10.00
P88	Dan Marino	10.00
P89	Troy Aikman	6.00
P90	Jerry Rice	6.00
P91	Drew Bledsoe	6.00
P92	Eddie George	8.00
P93	Terry Glenn	4.00
P94	John Elway	4.00
P95	Steve Young	4.00
P96	Mark Brunell	6.00
P97	Barry Sanders	6.00
P98	Kerry Collins	2.00
P99	Curtis Martin	6.00
P100	Terrell Davis	6.00

1997 Pinnacle Artist's Proof

Artist's Proof is a 100-card partial parallel of Pinnacle Football. The cards feature Dufex technology and the Artist's Proof stamp. The cards are re-numbered from one to 100.

		NM/M
Complete Set (100):		850.00
Common Player:		3.00
Minor Stars:		3X-10X
P1	Brett Favre	75.00
P2	Dan Marino	60.00
P3	Emmitt Smith	60.00
P4	Steve Young	20.00
P5	Drew Bledsoe	40.00
P6	Eddie George	50.00
P7	Barry Sanders	40.00
P8	Jerry Rice	40.00
P9	John Elway	30.00
P10	Troy Aikman	40.00
P11	Kerry Collins	8.00
P12	Rick Mirer	3.00
P13	Jim Harbaugh	3.00
P14	Elvis Grbac	3.00
P15	Gus Frerotte	3.00
P16	Neil O'Donnell	3.00
P17	Jeff George	3.00
P18	Kordell Stewart	40.00
P19	Junior Seau	3.00
P20	Vinny Testaverde	3.00
P21	Terry Glenn	30.00
P22	Natrone Means	6.00
P23	Marcus Allen	6.00
P24	Stan Humphries	3.00
P25	John Friesz	3.00
P26	Cris Carter	3.00
P27	Shannon Sharpe	3.00
P28	Tim Biakabutuka	3.00
P29	Jeff Blake	6.00
P30	Michael Irvin	6.00
P31	Terrell Davis	40.00
P32	Rashaan Salaam	3.00
P33	Adrian Murrell	6.00
P34	Ty Detmer	3.00
P35	Mark Brunell	40.00
P36	Chris Warren	3.00
P37	Trent Dilfer	6.00
P38	Jerome Bettis	6.00
P39	Scott Mitchell	3.00
P40	Steve McNair	30.00
P41	Tony Banks	8.00
P42	Joey Galloway	6.00
P43	Karim Abdul-Jabbar	20.00
P44	Lawrence Phillips	6.00
P45	Dave Brown	3.00
P46	Warren Moon	3.00
P47	Curtis Martin	40.00
P48	Dorsey Levens	6.00
P49	Deion Sanders	20.00
P50	Herman Moore	6.00
P51	Bruce Smith	3.00
P52	Keyshawn Johnson	6.00
P53	Reggie White	6.00
P54	Jake Plummer	25.00
P55	Darnell Autry	12.00
P56	Tiki Barber	20.00
P57	Pat Barnes	10.00
P58	Orlando Pace	6.00
P59	Peter Boulware	3.00
P60	Shawn Springs	6.00
P61	Troy Davis	8.00
P62	Ike Hilliard	15.00
P63	Jim Druckenmiller	30.00
P64	Warrick Dunn	50.00
P65	James Farrior	3.00
P66	Tony Gonzalez	12.00
P67	Darrell Russell	3.00
P68	Byron Hanspard	8.00
P69	Corey Dillon	30.00
P70	Kenny Holmes	3.00
P71	Walter Jones	3.00
P72	Danny Wuerffel	25.00
P73	Tom Knight	3.00
P74	David LaFleur	12.00
P75	Kevin Lockett	3.00
P76	Will Blackwell	6.00
P77	Reidel Anthony	20.00
P78	Dwayne Rudd	3.00
P79	Yatil Green	15.00
P80	Antowain Smith	25.00
P81	Rae Carruth	15.00
P82	Bryant Westbrook	6.00
P83	Reinard Wilson	3.00
P84	Joey Kent	6.00
P85	Renaldo Wynn	3.00
P86	Brett Favre	40.00
P87	Emmitt Smith	30.00
P88	Dan Marino	30.00
P89	Troy Aikman	20.00
P90	Jerry Rice	20.00
P91	Drew Bledsoe	20.00
P92	Eddie George	25.00
P93	Terry Glenn	15.00
P94	John Elway	15.00
P95	Steve Young	15.00
P96	Mark Brunell	20.00
P97	Barry Sanders	20.00
P98	Kerry Collins	8.00
P99	Curtis Martin	20.00
P100	Terrell Davis	20.00

1997 Pinnacle Epix

Epix is a 24-card insert which features holographic effects. The set consists of Game, Moment and Season cards which highlight each player's top performances. Orange, Purple and Emerald versions of each card were produced. The overall insertion rate for Epix was 1:19.

		NM/M
Complete Set (24):		65.00
Common Game (E1-E8):		1.00
Common Moment (E9-E16):		3.00
Common Season (E17-E24):		2.00
Purple Cards:		2X
Emerald Cards:		3X
1	Emmitt Smith	6.00
2	Troy Aikman	5.00
3	Terrell Davis	5.00
4	Drew Bledsoe	4.00
5	Jeff George	1.00
6	Kerry Collins	2.00
7	Antonio Freeman	1.00
8	Herman Moore	1.00
9	Barry Sanders	6.00
10	Brett Favre	12.00
11	Michael Irvin	3.00
12	Steve Young	6.00
13	Mark Brunell	5.00
14	Jerome Bettis	3.00
15	Deion Sanders	4.00
16	Jeff Blake	3.00
17	Dan Marino	12.00
18	Eddie George	5.00
19	Jerry Rice	6.00
20	John Elway	6.00
21	Curtis Martin	5.00
22	Kordell Stewart	3.00
23	Junior Seau	2.00
24	Reggie White	2.00

1997 Pinnacle Scoring Core

Scoring Core is a 24-card insert seeded 1:89 packs. Each card is specially die-cut and features foil-etching.

		NM/M
Complete Set (24):		160.00
Common Player:		1.00
Minor Stars:		2.00
1	Emmitt Smith	10.00
2	Troy Aikman	8.00
3	Michael Irvin	2.00
4	Robert Brooks	1.00
5	Brett Favre	12.00
6	Antonio Freeman	2.00
7	Curtis Martin	6.00
8	Drew Bledsoe	6.00
9	Terry Glenn	2.00
10	Tim Biakabutuka	1.00
11	Kerry Collins	2.00
12	Muhsin Muhammad	1.00
13	Karim Abdul-Jabbar	2.00
14	Dan Marino	12.00
15	O.J. McDuffie	1.00
16	Terrell Davis	6.00
17	John Elway	8.00
18	Shannon Sharpe	1.00
19	Garrison Hearst	1.00
20	Steve Young	6.00
21	Jerry Rice	8.00
22	Natrone Means	2.00
23	Mark Brunell	4.00
24	Keenan McCardell	1.00

1997 Pinnacle Team Pinnacle

Team Pinnacle is a 10-card insert consisting of double-sided foil cards. The cards feature two players from the same position, one from each conference. Team Pinnacle cards were inserted 1:240.

		NM/M
Complete Set (10):		110.00
Common Player:		5.00
1	Dan Marino, Troy Aikman	25.00
2	Drew Bledsoe, Brett Favre	30.00
3	Mark Brunell, Kerry Collins	10.00
4	John Elway, Steve Young	20.00
5	Terrell Davis, Emmitt Smith	30.00
6	Curtis Martin, Barry Sanders	25.00
7	Eddie George, Tim Biakabutuka	10.00
8	Karim Abdul-Jabbar, Lawrence Phillips	5.00
9	Terry Glenn, Jerry Rice	15.00
10	Joey Galloway, Michael Irvin	5.00

1997 Pinnacle Certified

Pinnacle Certified consists of a 150-card base set, four parallels and two inserts. The base cards were printed on silver mirror board. The parallel sets include Certified Red (1:5), Mirror Red (1:99), Mirror Blue (1:199) and Mirror Blue (1:299). The inserts are Certified Team (20 cards, 1:19) and Epix (24 cards, 1:15). All cards in the set have a clear-coat protector.

		NM/M
Complete Set (150):		40.00
Common Player:		.10
Minor Stars:		.50
Certified Red Cards:		2X-4X
Certified Red Rookies:		2X-3X
Mirror Red Stars:		3X-8X
Mirror Red Rookies:		2X-5X
Mirror Blue Stars:		5X-12X
Mirror Blue Rookies:		2X-10X
Mirror Gold Stars:		10X-25X
Mirror Gold Rookies:		5X-15X
Pack (6):		1.75
Wax Box (20):		25.00
1	Emmitt Smith	5.00
2	Dan Marino	5.00
3	Brett Favre	6.00
4	Steve Young	2.00
5	Kerry Collins	.75
6	Troy Aikman	2.50
7	Drew Bledsoe	2.50
8	Eddie George	4.00
9	Jerry Rice	3.00
10	John Elway	2.00
11	Barry Sanders	4.00
12	Mark Brunell	2.50
13	Elvis Grbac	.10
14	Tony Banks	1.50
15	Vinny Testaverde	.10
16	Rick Mirer	.10
17	Carl Pickens	.10
18	Deion Sanders	1.50
19	Terry Glenn	2.50
20	Heath Shuler	.10
21	Dave Brown	.10
22	Keyshawn Johnson	1.00
23	Jeff George	.50
24	Ricky Watters	.50
25	Kordell Stewart	2.50
26	Junior Seau	.10
27	Terrell Owens	2.00
28	Warren Moon	.50
29	Isaac Bruce	.50
30	Steve McNair	2.00
31	Gus Frerotte	.10
32	Trent Dilfer	.50
33	Shannon Sharpe	.10
34	Scott Mitchell	.10
35	Antonio Freeman	.50
36	Jim Harbaugh	.10
37	Natrone Means	.50
38	Marcus Allen	.50
39	Karim Abdul-Jabbar	1.75
40	Tim Biakabutuka	.10
41	Jeff Blake	.50
42	Michael Irvin	.50
43	Herschel Walker	.10
44	Curtis Martin	2.50
45	Eddie Kennison	.50
46	Napoleon Kaufman	.75
47	Larry Centers	.10
48	Jamal Anderson	.50
49	Derrick Alexander	.10
50	Bruce Smith	.10
51	Wesley Walls	.10
52	Rod Smith	.10
53	Keenan McCardell	.10
54	Robert Brooks	.10
55	Willie Green	.10
56	Jake Reed	.10
57	Joey Galloway	.50
58	Eric Metcalf	.10
59	Chris Sanders	.10
60	Jeff Hostetler	.10
61	Kevin Greene	.10
62	Frank Sanders	.10
63	Dorsey Levens	.50
64	Sean Dawkins	.10
65	Cris Carter	.10
66	Andre Hastings	.10
67	Amani Toomer	.10
68	Adrian Murrell	.50
69	Ty Detmer	.10
70	Yancey Thigpen	.10
71	Jim Everett	.10
72	Todd Collins	.10
73	Curtis Conway	.50
74	Herman Moore	.50
75	Neil O'Donnell	.10
76	Rod Woodson	.10
77	Tony Martin	.10
78	Kent Graham	.10
79	Andre Reed	.10
80	Reggie White	.50
81	Thurman Thomas	.50
82	Garrison Hearst	.10
83	Chris Warren	.10
84	Wayne Chrebet	.10
85	Chris T. Jones	.10
86	Anthony Miller	.10
87	Chris Chandler	.10
88	Terrell Davis	3.00
89	Mike Alstott	1.50
90	Terry Allen	.10
91	Jerome Bettis	.50
92	Stan Humphries	.10
93	Andre Rison	.10
94	Marshall Faulk	.50
95	Erik Kramer	.10
96	O.J. McDuffie	.10
97	Robert Smith	.10
98	Keith Byars	.10
99	Rodney Hampton	.10
100	Desmond Howard	.10
101	Lawrence Phillips	.50
102	Michael Westbrook	.10
103	Johnnie Morton	.10
104	Ben Coates	.10
105	J.J. Stokes	.50
106	Terance Mathis	.10
107	Errict Rhett	.10
108	Tim Brown	.10
109	Marvin Harrison	1.00
110	Muhsin Muhammad	.10
111	Bam Morris	.10
112	Mario Bates	.10
113	Jimmy Smith	.10
114	Irving Fryar	.10
115	Tamarick Vanover	.10
116	Brad Johnson	.50
117	Rashaan Salaam	.10
118	Ki-Jana Carter	.10
119	Tyrone Wheatley	.10
120	John Friesz	.10
121	*Orlando Pace*	.50
122	*Jim Druckenmiller*	6.00
123	*Byron Hanspard*	.75
124	*David LaFleur*	1.50
125	*Reidel Anthony*	3.00
126	*Antowain Smith*	4.00
127	*Bryant Westbrook*	.50
128	*Fred Lane*	2.00
129	*Tiki Barber*	4.00
130	*Shawn Springs*	.50
131	*Ike Hilliard*	3.00
132	*James Farrior*	.10
133	*Darrell Russell*	.10
134	*Walter Jones*	.10
135	*Tom Knight*	.10
136	*Yatil Green*	1.00
137	*Joey Kent*	.50
138	*Kevin Lockett*	.10
139	*Troy Davis*	1.00
140	*Darnell Autry*	.50
141	*Pat Barnes*	.75
142	*Rae Carruth*	3.00
143	*Will Blackwell*	.50
144	*Warrick Dunn*	4.00
145	*Corey Dillon*	8.00
146	*Dwayne Rudd*	.10
147	*Reinard Wilson*	.10
148	*Peter Boulware*	.10
149	*Tony Gonzalez*	1.50
150	*Danny Wuerffel*	4.00

1997 Pinnacle Certified Red

Certified Red was a parallel to the Certified set. Inserted in one per five packs, the cards were printed on a red surface, with the words "Certified Red" printed down the side.

Certified Red Cards:	3X-6X
Certified Red Rookies:	2X-3X

1997 Pinnacle Certified Mirror Blue

Mirror Blue is a parallel of the Certified base set. Inserted 1:199, the cards feature a holographic blue finish.

1997 Pinnacle Certified Mirror Gold

Mirror Gold is a parallel of the Certified base set. The cards have a holographic gold finish. They were inserted one per 299 packs.

1997 Pinnacle Certified Mirror Red

Mirror Red is a parallel of the Certified base set. Seeded one per 99 packs, the cards feature a holographic red finish.

1997 Pinnacle Certified Epix

Epix is a 24-card insert which features holographic effects. The set consists of Game, Moment and Season cards that highlight each player's top performances. Orange, Purple and Emerald versions of each card were produced. Epix was inserted 1:15.

		NM/M
Complete Set (24):		400.00
Common Moment (E1-E8):		12.00
Common Season (E9-E16):		8.00
Common Game (E17-E24):		4.00
1	Emmitt Smith	70.00
2	Troy Aikman	40.00
3	Terrell Davis	40.00
4	Drew Bledsoe	40.00
5	Jeff George	12.00
6	Kerry Collins	12.00
7	Antonio Freeman	12.00

8 Herman Moore 12.00
9 Barry Sanders 35.00
10 Brett Favre 50.00
11 Michael Irvin 8.00
12 Steve Young 20.00
13 Mark Brunell 25.00
14 Jerome Bettis 8.00
15 Deion Sanders 15.00
16 Jeff Blake 8.00
17 Dan Marino 30.00
18 Eddie George 20.00
19 Jerry Rice 15.00
20 John Elway 12.00
21 Curtis Martin 12.00
22 Kordell Stewart 20.00
23 Junior Seau 4.00
24 Reggie White 4.00

1997 Pinnacle Certified Gold Team

Certified Gold Teams were a parallel set to the Certified Team inserts, but added a gold foil pattern to the card front. Gold Team included 20 cards and were inserted one per 19 packs. In addition, 25 of each card was also done in a Mirror Gold version.

Gold Cards: 2X-4X
Mirror Gold Cards: 20X-40X

1997 Pinnacle Certified Team

Certified Team is a 20-card insert that was seeded 1:19 in packs of Certified Football. The cards were printed on silver mirror board. Gold (inserted 1:119) and Mirror Gold (25 numbered sets) parallels were also issued.

NM/M
Complete Set (20): 60.00
Common Player: 1.00
Inserted 1:19
Gold Cards: 2X-4X
Inserted 1:119
Mirror Golds: 3X-8X
Production 25 Sets
1 Brett Favre 12.00
2 Dan Marino 12.00
3 Emmitt Smith 10.00
4 Eddie George 6.00
5 Jerry Rice 8.00
6 Troy Aikman 6.00
7 Barry Sanders 10.00
8 Terrell Davis 6.00
9 Drew Bledsoe 6.00
10 Curtis Martin 6.00
11 Terry Glenn 2.00
12 Kerry Collins 3.00
13 John Elway 6.00
14 Kordell Stewart 2.00
15 Karim Abdul-Jabbar 1.00
16 Steve Young 6.00
17 Steve McNair 4.00
18 Terrell Owens 2.00
19 Keyshawn Johnson 3.00
20 Mark Brunell 3.00

1997 Pinnacle Inscriptions

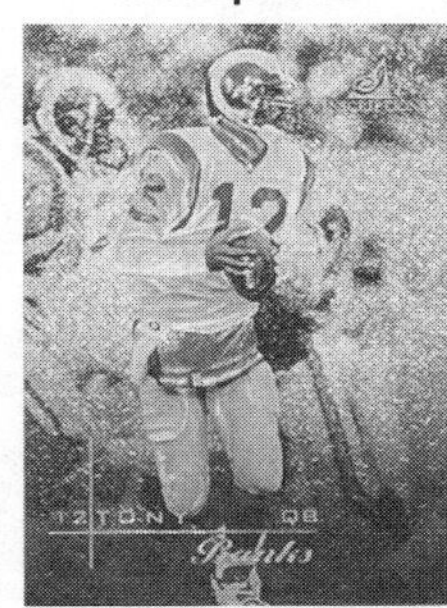

Inscriptions consists of a 50-card base set, two parallel sets and two inserts. The base set features a color player photo with a black and white background. The parallel sets are Challenge Collection (1:7) and Artist's Proof (1:35). Artist's Proof features Dufex technology and the Artist's Proof seal. The inserts are Autographs (30 cards, 1:23) and V2 (18 cards, 1:11). Each pack contained three cards and was packaged in a collectable box.

NM/M
Complete Set (50): 20.00
Common Player: .25
Minor Stars: .50
Artist Proof Cards: 3X-6X
Chall. Collection Cards: 1X-2X
Pack (3): 3.00
Wax Box (24): 55.00
1 Mark Brunell 1.00
2 Steve Young 2.00
3 Rick Mirer .25
4 Brett Favre 4.00
5 Tony Banks .50
6 Elvis Grbac .25
7 John Elway 3.00
8 Troy Aikman 3.00
9 Neil O'Donnell .25
10 Kordell Stewart 1.00
11 Drew Bledsoe 2.00
12 Kerry Collins .50
13 Dan Marino 4.00
14 Jeff George .50
15 Scott Mitchell .25
16 Jim Harbaugh .25
17 Dave Brown .25
18 Jeff Blake .50
19 Trent Dilfer .50
20 Barry Sanders 4.00
21 Jerry Rice 3.00
22 Emmitt Smith 4.00
23 Vinny Testaverde .25
24 Warren Moon .25
25 Junior Seau .25
26 Gus Frerotte .25
27 Heath Shuler .25
28 Erik Kramer .25
29 Boomer Esiason .25
30 Jim Kelly .50
31 Mark Brunell 1.00
32 Steve Young 1.50
33 Brett Favre 4.00
34 Tony Banks .50
35 John Elway 1.50
36 Troy Aikman 2.00
37 Kordell Stewart 1.00
38 Drew Bledsoe 2.00
39 Kerry Collins .50
40 Dan Marino 4.00
41 Jim Harbaugh .25
42 Jeff Blake .25
43 Barry Sanders 2.50
44 Jerry Rice 2.00
45 Emmitt Smith 4.00
46 Rick Mirer .25
47 Jeff George .25
48 Neil O'Donnell .25
49 Elvis Grbac .25
50 Scott Mitchell .25

1997 Pinnacle Inscriptions Autographs

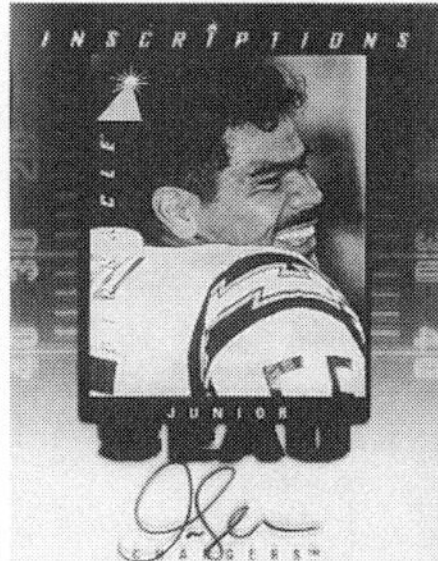

Autographs is a 30-card insert which was seeded one per 23 packs. The cards are plastic, signed by the player and hand-numbered. Each player signed a different number of cards.

NM/M
Common Player: 10.00
Minor Stars: 25.00
Tony Banks 1925 12.00
Jeff Blake 1470 12.00
Drew Bledsoe 1970 50.00
Dave Brown 1970 10.00
Mark Brunell 2000 50.00
Kerry Collins 1300 40.00
Trent Dilfer 1950 25.00
John Elway 1975 100.00
Jim Everett 2000 10.00
Brett Favre 215 250.00
Gus Frerotte 1975 10.00
Jeff George 1935 10.00
Elvis Grbac 1985 10.00
Jim Harbaugh 1975 10.00
Jeff Hostetler 2000 10.00
Jim Kelly 1925 25.00
Bernie Kosar 1975 10.00
Eric Kramer 2000 10.00
Dan Marino 440 250.00
Rick Mirer 2000 10.00
Scott Mitchell 1995 10.00
Warren Moon 1975 10.00
Neil O'Donnell 1990 10.00
Jerry Rice 950 200.00
Junior Seau 1900 10.00
Heath Shuler 1965 10.00
Emmitt Smith 220 225.00
Kordell Stewart 1495 25.00
Vinny Testaverde 1975 10.00
Steve Young 1900 60.00

1997 Pinnacle Inscriptions Artist Proofs

This 50-card parallel set utilized a Dufex background to parallel the entire base set. Card fronts also added an Artist's Proof logo in the bottom right corner. These parallels were inserted into one per 35 packs of Inscriptions.

Artist Proof Cards: 8X-16X

1997 Pinnacle Inscriptions Challenge Collection

Challenge Collection was a 50-card parallel that featured each base card with printed on a red foil background with the player's signature appearing repeatedly in black. There is also a Challenge Collection logo in the lower right corner. These were inserted one per seven packs.

Challenge Collection Cards: 2X-4X

1997 Pinnacle Inscriptions V2

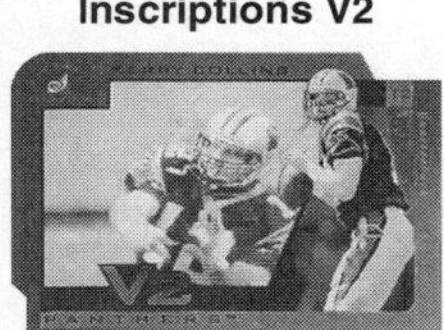

V2 is a 18-card insert consisting of plastic motion cards. Inserted 1:11, the cards came with a clear-coat protector.

NM/M
Complete Set (18): 30.00
Common Player: 1.00
Minor Stars: 2.00
1 Mark Brunell 2.00
2 Steve Young 3.00
3 Brett Favre 6.00
4 Tony Banks 1.00
5 John Elway 3.00
6 Troy Aikman 3.00
7 Kordell Stewart 2.00
8 Drew Bledsoe 3.00
9 Isaac Bruce 2.00
10 Dan Marino 6.00
11 Barry Sanders 5.00
12 Jerry Rice 4.00
13 Emmitt Smith 5.00
14 Neil O'Donnell 1.00
15 Scott Mitchell 1.00
16 Jim Harbaugh 1.00
17 Jeff Blake 1.00
18 Trent Dilfer 2.00

1997 Pinnacle Inside

Pinnacle Inside featured a 150-card base set and 28 collectible cans. The base cards include three different player shots. Silver Lining (1:7) and Gridiron Gold (1:63) were the parallel sets. The inserts are Fourth & Goal and Autographed Cards.

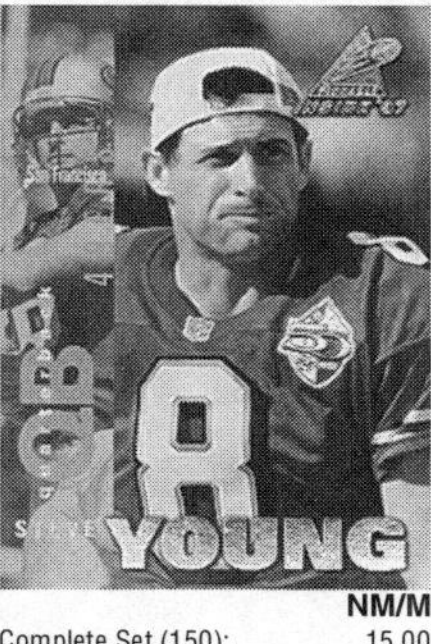

NM/M
Complete Set (150): 15.00
Common Player: .05
Minor Stars: .40
Silver Cards: 2X-4X
Silver Rookies: 1X-2X
Inserted 1:7
Gridiron Gold Cards: 3X-8X
Gridiron Gold Rookies: 2X-4X
Inserted 1:63
Wax Box (48): 50.00
1 Troy Aikman 1.50
2 Dan Marino 3.00
3 Barry Sanders 1.50
4 Drew Bledsoe 1.50
5 Kerry Collins .50
6 Emmitt Smith 3.00
7 Brett Favre 3.00
8 John Elway 1.00
9 Jerry Rice 1.50
10 Mark Brunell 1.50
11 Elvis Grbac .05
12 Junior Seau .05
13 Eddie George 1.75
14 Steve Young 1.00
15 Terrell Davis 1.50
16 Thurman Thomas .40
17 Deion Sanders .75
18 Terrell Owens .75
19 Neil O'Donnell .05
20 Carl Pickens .05
21 Marcus Allen .40
22 Ricky Watters .40
23 Vinny Testaverde .05
24 Kordell Stewart 1.25
25 Tony Banks .75
26 Terry Glenn .50
27 Todd Collins .05
28 Robert Brooks .40
29 Heath Shuler .05
30 Shannon Sharpe .05
31 Michael Westbrook .05
32 Reggie White .40
33 Brad Johnson .05
34 Tamarick Vanover .05
35 Larry Centers .05
36 Terance Mathis .05
37 Hardy Nickerson .05
38 Jamal Anderson .40
39 Kevin Hardy .05
40 Stan Humphries .05
41 Chris Warren .05
42 Tim Brown .05
43 Joey Galloway .60
44 Boomer Esiason .05
45 Jake Reed .05
46 Kent Graham .05
47 Marshall Faulk .40
48 Sean Dawkins .05
49 Dave Brown .05
50 Willie Green .05
51 Andre Hastings .05
52 Erik Kramer .05
53 Michael Irvin .40
54 Gus Frerotte .05
55 Winslow Oliver .05
56 Jimmy Smith .05
57 Derrick Alexander .05
58 Adrian Murrell .05
59 Ki-Jana Carter .05
60 Garrison Hearst .05
61 Chris Sanders .05
62 Johnnie Morton .05
63 Lawrence Phillips .40
64 Bobby Engram .05
65 Tim Biakabutuka .40
66 Anthony Johnson .05
67 Keyshawn Johnson .60
68 Jeff George .05
69 Errict Rhett .05
70 Cris Carter .05
71 Chris T. Jones .05
72 Eric Moulds .05
73 Rick Mirer .05
74 Keenan McCardell .05
75 Simeon Rice .05
76 Eddie Kennison .75
77 Herman Moore .40
78 Jim Harbaugh .05
79 Robert Smith .05
80 Bruce Smith .05
81 John Friesz .05
82 Irving Fryar .05
83 Edgar Bennett .05
84 Ty Detmer .05
85 Curtis Conway .05
86 Napoleon Kaufman .05
87 Tony Martin .05
88 Amani Toomer .05
89 Willie McGinest .05
90 Daryl Johnston .05
91 Stanley Pritchett .05
92 Chris Chandler .05
93 Natrone Means .05
94 Kimble Anders .05
95 Steve McNair 1.00
96 Curtis Martin 1.50
97 O.J. McDuffie .05
98 Ben Coates .05
99 Jerome Bettis .40
100 Andre Reed .05
101 Jeff Blake .40
102 Wesley Walls .05
103 Warren Moon .05
104 Isaac Bruce .40
105 Terry Allen .05
106 Rodney Hampton .05
107 Karim Abdul-Jabbar .50
108 Marvin Harrison .75
109 Dorsey Levens .05
110 Rashaan Salaam .40
111 Scott Mitchell .05
112 Darnay Scott .05
113 Aeneas Williams .05
114 Trent Dilfer .05
115 Antonio Freeman .40
116 Jim Everett .05
117 Muhsin Muhammad .05
118 Rickey Dudley .05
119 Mike Alstott .05
120 *Jim Druckenmiller* .60
121 *Tiki Barber* 1.50
122 *Ike Hilliard* 1.25
123 *Orlando Pace* .50
124 *Jake Plummer* 2.00
125 *Yatil Green* .75
126 *Byron Hanspard* .75
127 *James Farrior* .05
128 *Corey Dillon* 2.50
129 *Pat Barnes* .50
130 *Kenny Holmes* .05
131 *Rae Carruth* 1.25
132 *Danny Wuerffel* 1.50
133 *Darnell Autry* .75
134 *Reidel Anthony* 1.00
135 *Darrell Russell* .05
136 *Will Blackwell* .50
137 *Peter Boulware* .05
138 *Shawn Springs* .50
139 *Joey Kent* .75
140 *Troy Davis* .75
141 *Antowain Smith* 1.50
142 *Walter Jones* .05
143 *Tony Gonzalez* .75
144 *David LaFleur* .75
145 *Warrick Dunn* 1.25
146 *Bryant Westbrook* .05
147 *Dwayne Rudd* .05
148 *Tom Knight* .05
149 *Kevin Lockett* .05
150 Checklist .05

1997 Pinnacle Inside Silver

This 150-card parallel set features each base card printed with silver foil highlights. The lettering and words "Silver Lining" are printed in bronze foil. These parallels are inserted one per seven packs.

Silver Cards: 6X-12X
Silver Rookies: 3X-6X
Inserted 1:7

1997 Pinnacle Inside Gridiron Gold

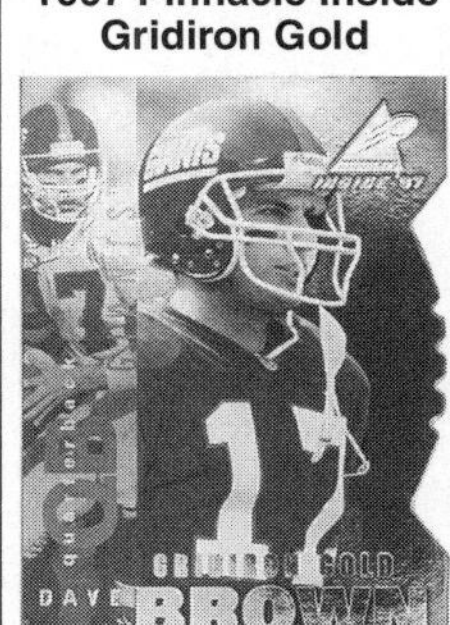

This 150-card parallel set featured each base card printed on a gold foil format that is die-cut on the right side. The logo, player's name and words "Gridiron Gold" are one per 63 hobby/retail packs.

Gridiron Gold Cards: 20X-40X
Gridiron Gold Rookies: 10X-20X
Inserted 1:63

1997 Pinnacle Inside Autographed Cards

These 34 cards highlight members of the NFL Quarterback Club. The cards are autographed by the player featured on them. They were inserted 1:251.

1 Brett Favre
2 Emmitt Smith
3 Dan Marino
4 Troy Aikman
5 Barry Sanders
6 John Elway
7 Steve Young
8 Drew Bledsoe
9 Jerry Rice
10 Jeff Blake
11 Kerry Collins
12 Scott Mitchell
13 Kordell Stewart
14 Jeff George
15 Mark Brunell
16 Neil O'Donnell
17 Jim Everett
18 Jim Harbaugh
19 Junior Seau
20 Dave Brown
21 Jeff Hostetler
22 Erik Kramer
23 Rick Mirer
24 Tony Banks
25 Elvis Grbac
26 Vinny Testaverde
27 Jim Kelly
28 Warren Moon
29 Bernie Kosar
30 Boomer Esiason
31 Heath Shuler
32 Steve McNair
33 Trent Dilfer
34 Gus Frerotte

1997 Pinnacle Inside Cans

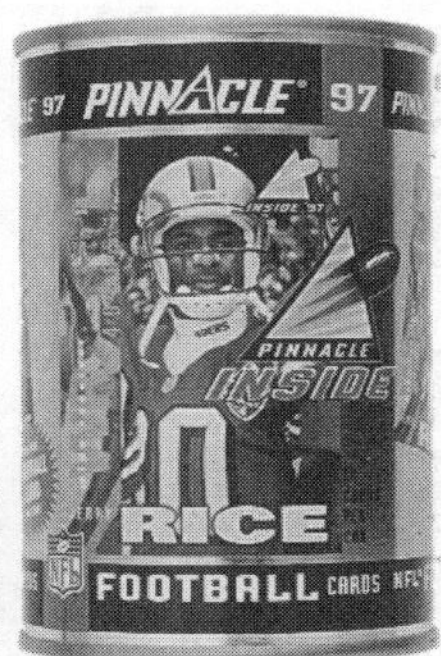

Inside cards were available in 28 different cans. The first 25 cans featured a single player with the image of their Inside card on the outside of the can. Three special cans - Brett Favre MVP, Dan Marino passing record and Ice Bowl commemorative - were also issued. A Gold Can parallel set was also created. Gold Cans were found once per 47 cans.

NM/M
Complete Set (28): 15.00
Common Can: .25
Common Sealed Can: 1.00
Sealed Cans: 1X-2X
Gold Cans: 2X-4X
Gold Sealed Cans: 3X-6X
1 Brett Favre 3.00
2 Dan Marino 2.50
3 Emmitt Smith 2.50
4 Troy Aikman 1.50
5 Barry Sanders 1.50
6 Kerry Collins 1.00
7 Mark Brunell 1.50
8 John Elway 1.00
9 Steve Young 1.00
10 Jerry Rice 1.50
11 Terrell Davis 1.50
12 Curtis Martin 1.50
13 Terry Glenn 1.00
14 Eddie George 2.00
15 Jeff Blake .25
16 Kordell Stewart 1.50
17 Rick Mirer .25
18 Karim Abdul-Jabbar 1.00
19 Jeff George .25
20 Keyshawn Johnson .25
21 Jim Harbaugh .25
22 Drew Bledsoe 1.50
23 Deion Sanders 1.00
24 Tony Banks 1.00
25 Jerome Bettis .25
26 Brett Favre (MVP) 4.00
27 Dan Marino (Passing) 2.50
28 Ice Bowl 2.50

1997 Pinnacle Inside Fourth & Goal

This 20-card insert features clutch players on a foil card. These cards were inserted 1:23.

NM/M
Complete Set (20): 80.00

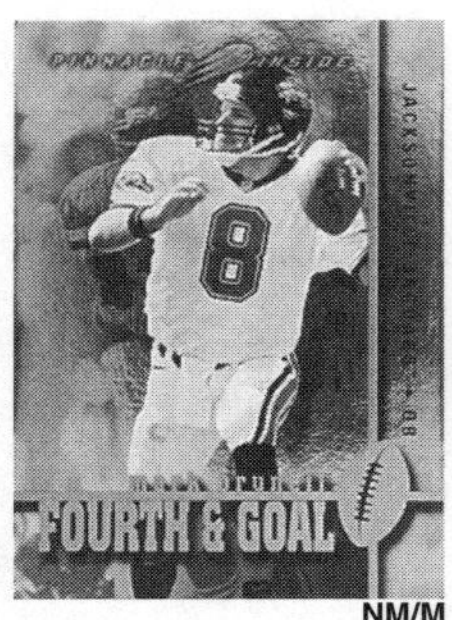

		NM/M
Common Player:		2.00
1	Brett Favre	10.00
2	Drew Bledsoe	6.00
3	Troy Aikman	6.00
4	Mark Brunell	4.00
5	Steve Young	6.00
6	Vinny Testaverde	2.00
7	Dan Marino	10.00
8	Kerry Collins	3.00
9	John Elway	6.00
10	Emmitt Smith	8.00
11	Barry Sanders	8.00
12	Eddie George	4.00
13	Terrell Davis	5.00
14	Curtis Martin	4.00
15	Terry Glenn	3.00
16	Jerry Rice	5.00
17	Herman Moore	2.00
18	Jeff Blake	2.00
19	Warrick Dunn	3.00
20	Antowain Smith	3.00

1997 Pinnacle Mint Cards

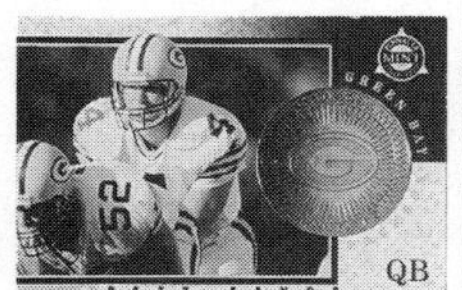

This 30-card base set features a player photo and a foil stamped bronze medallion on the front. A die-cut parallel was created to hold the set's coins. The other parallels are Silver Team Pinnacle (silver foil printing, 1:15) and Gold Team Pinnacle (gold Dufex etched foil, 1:47). Inserts include Commemorative Collection, a six-card set capturing the top moments of 1996 with silver foil and inserted 1:31. Pinnacle Mint also includes Solid Gold Redemption Cards. The solid gold cards are a parallel of the regular set. One redemption card per player was issued and they were inserted 1:47,000.

		NM/M
Complete Die-Cut (30):		20.00
Common Player:		.20
Minor Stars:		.40
Bronze Cards:		1X-2X
Silver Cards:		2X-4X
Gold Cards:		3X-6X
Wax Box:		60.00
1	Brett Favre	2.50
2	Drew Bledsoe	1.25
3	Mark Brunell	1.25
4	Kerry Collins	.50
5	Troy Aikman	1.25
6	Steve Young	1.00
7	Dan Marino	2.00
8	Barry Sanders	1.25
9	John Elway	1.00
10	Emmitt Smith	2.00
11	Rick Mirer	.20
12	Kordell Stewart	1.25
13	Tony Banks	.75
14	Jeff George	.20
15	Jerry Rice	1.25
16	Jeff Blake	.40
17	Jim Harbaugh	.20
18	Heath Shuler	.20
19	Scott Mitchell	.20
20	Neil O'Donnell	.20
21	Brett Favre (Minted Highlights)	1.25
22	Drew Bledsoe (Minted Highlights)	.75
23	Mark Brunell (Minted Highlights)	.75
24	Kerry Collins (Minted Highlights)	.40
25	Troy Aikman (Minted Highlights)	.50
26	Dan Marino (Minted Highlights)	1.00
27	Barry Sanders (Minted Highlights)	.75
28	Emmitt Smith (Minted Highlights)	1.00
29	Tony Banks (Minted Highlights)	.20
30	John Elway (Minted Highlights)	.50

1997 Pinnacle Mint Coins

The 30-base coins feature each players face and match up with one of the base cards. Six parallels of the base coins were made. Nickel-Silver (1:20), Gold Plated (1:47), Brass Proof (numbered to 500), Silver Proof (numbered to 250), Gold Proof (numbered to 100) and Solid Silver (1:288) versions were all added to Pinnacle Mint. The only insert is Commemorative Collection.

		NM/M
Complete Brass (30):		30.00
Common Brass Coin:		.40
Minor Brass Stars:		1.00
Nickel Coins:		1X-2X
Gold Plated Coins:		2X-4X
1	Brett Favre	5.00
2	Drew Bledsoe	3.00
3	Mark Brunell	2.00
4	Kerry Collins	2.00
5	Troy Aikman	3.00
6	Steve Young	3.00
7	Dan Marino	5.00
8	Barry Sanders	4.00
9	John Elway	3.00
10	Emmitt Smith	4.00
11	Rick Mirer	.40
12	Kordell Stewart	2.00
13	Tony Banks	1.00
14	Jeff George	.40
15	Jerry Rice	4.00
16	Jeff Blake	1.00
17	Jim Harbaugh	.40
18	Heath Shuler	.40
19	Scott Mitchell	.40
20	Neil O'Donnell	.40
21	Brett Favre (Minted Highlights)	4.00
22	Drew Bledsoe (Minted Highlights)	2.50
23	Mark Brunell (Minted Highlights)	2.50
24	Kerry Collins (Minted Highlights)	1.00
25	Troy Aikman (Minted Highlights)	1.75
26	Dan Marino (Minted Highlights)	3.00
27	Barry Sanders (Minted Highlights)	2.50
28	Emmitt Smith (Minted Highlights)	3.00
29	Tony Banks (Minted Highlights)	.40
30	John Elway (Minted Highlights)	1.75

1997 Pinnacle Mint Commemorative Cards

This six-card insert highlights six top moments of 1996. The cards feature silver foil and were inserted 1:31.

		NM/M
Complete Set (6):		30.00
Common Player:		3.00
1	Barry Sanders	10.00
2	Brett Favre	12.00
3	Mark Brunell	3.00
4	Emmitt Smith	10.00
5	Dan Marino	12.00
6	Jerry Rice	5.00

1997 Pinnacle Mint Commemorative Coins

These six coins are double-sized brass and match up with the Commemorative Collection cards. They also highlight top events of 1996 and were inserted 1:31.

		NM/M
Complete Set (6):		40.00
Common Player:		4.00
1	Barry Sanders	12.00
2	Brett Favre	14.00
3	Mark Brunell	4.00
4	Emmitt Smith	12.00
5	Dan Marino	14.00
6	Jerry Rice	8.00

1997 Pinnacle Totally Certified Platinum Red

Platinum Red is considered the "base set" for Totally Certified. Each card in the 150-card set is sequentially-numbered to 4,999. The cards feature a micro-etched holographic mylar finish. Platinum Blue (one per pack) and Platinum Gold (1:79) parallels were also included in this series.

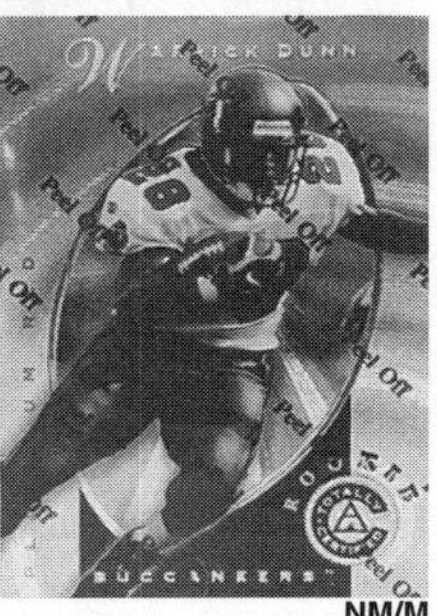

		NM/M
Complete Set (150):		100.00
Common Player:		3X
Minor Stars:		1.00
Common Rookie:		.50
Reds Sequentially #'d to 4,999		
Pack (3):		7.00
Wax Box (18):		100.00
1	Emmitt Smith	5.00
2	Dan Marino	6.00
3	Brett Favre	6.00
4	Steve Young	4.00
5	Kerry Collins	1.50
6	Troy Aikman	4.00
7	Drew Bledsoe	4.00
8	Eddie George	3.00
9	Jerry Rice	4.00
10	John Elway	4.00
11	Barry Sanders	5.00
12	Mark Brunell	3.00
13	Elvis Grbac	1.50
14	Tony Banks	1.50
15	Vinny Testaverde	1.50
16	Rick Mirer	.25
17	Carl Pickens	1.50
18	Deion Sanders	2.00
19	Terry Glenn	3.00
20	Heath Shuler	.25
21	Dave Brown	.25
22	Keyshawn Johnson	3.00
23	Jeff George	1.00
24	Ricky Watters	1.50
25	Kordell Stewart	1.00
26	Junior Seau	1.50
27	Terrell Owens	2.00
28	Warren Moon	1.50
29	Isaac Bruce	3.00
30	Steve McNair	3.00
31	Gus Frerotte	.25
32	Trent Dilfer	1.50
33	Shannon Sharpe	1.50
34	Scott Mitchell	.25
35	Antonio Freeman	1.00
36	Jim Harbaugh	1.50
37	Natrone Means	1.50
38	Marcus Allen	2.00
39	Karim Abdul-Jabbar	1.50
40	Tim Biakabutuka	1.50
41	Jeff Blake	1.00
42	Michael Irvin	3.00
43	Herschel Walker	.25
44	Curtis Martin	3.00
45	Eddie Kennison	1.50
46	Napoleon Kaufman	.50
47	Larry Centers	.25
48	Jamal Anderson	2.00
49	Derrick Alexander	.25
50	Bruce Smith	1.50
51	Wesley Walls	.25
52	Rod Smith	1.50
53	Keenan McCardell	1.50
54	Robert Brooks	1.50
55	Willie Green	.25
56	Jake Reed	.25
57	Joey Galloway	2.00
58	Eric Metcalf	.25
59	Chris Sanders	.25
60	Jeff Hostetler	.25
61	Kevin Greene	.25
62	Frank Sanders	1.50
63	Dorsey Levens	1.00
64	Sean Dawkins	.25
65	Cris Carter	1.00
66	Andre Hastings	.25
67	Amani Toomer	1.50
68	Adrian Murrell	1.00
69	Ty Detmer	1.00
70	Yancey Thigpen	1.50
71	Jim Everett	1.50
72	Todd Collins	.25
73	Curtis Conway	1.50
74	Herman Moore	2.00
75	Neil O'Donnell	1.50
76	Rod Woodson	1.50
77	Tony Martin	.25
78	Kent Graham	.25
79	Andre Reed	1.50
80	Reggie White	2.00
81	Thurman Thomas	2.00
82	Garrison Hearst	1.50
83	Chris Warren	1.50
84	Wayne Chrebet	2.00
85	Chris T. Jones	.25
86	Anthony Miller	.25
87	Chris Chandler	1.50
88	Terrell Davis	4.00
89	Mike Alstott	3.00
90	Terry Allen	1.50
91	Jerome Bettis	3.00
92	Stan Humphries	.25
93	Andre Rison	1.50
94	Marshall Faulk	4.00
95	Erik Kramer	.25
96	O.J. McDuffie	1.50
97	Robert Smith	3.00
98	Keith Byars	.25
99	Rodney Hampton	.25
100	Desmond Howard	.25
101	Lawrence Phillips	1.50
102	Michael Westbrook	1.50
103	Johnnie Morton	1.50
104	Ben Coates	1.50
105	J.J. Stokes	1.50
106	Terance Mathis	1.50
107	Errict Rhett	1.50
108	Tim Brown	3.00
109	Marvin Harrison	3.00
110	Muhsin Muhammad	1.50
111	Bam Morris	.25
112	Mario Bates	.25
113	Jimmy Smith	2.00
114	Irving Fryar	1.50
115	Tamarick Vanover	.25
116	Brad Johnson	3.00
117	Rashaan Salaam	.25
118	Ki-Jana Carter	.25
119	Tyrone Wheatley	1.50
120	John Friesz	1.50
121	*Orlando Pace*	2.00
122	*Jim Druckenmiller*	1.00
123	*Byron Hanspard*	1.00
124	*David LaFleur*	1.00
125	*Reidel Anthony*	2.00
126	*Antowain Smith*	3.00
127	*Bryant Westbrook*	2.00
128	*Fred Lane*	1.00
129	*Tiki Barber*	8.00
130	*Shawn Springs*	2.00
131	*Ike Hilliard*	6.00
132	*James Farrior*	1.00
133	*Darrell Russell*	1.00
134	*Walter Jones*	1.00
135	*Tom Knight*	1.00
136	*Yatil Green*	1.00
137	*Joey Kent*	1.00
138	*Kevin Lockett*	1.00
139	*Troy Davis*	2.00
140	*Darnell Autry*	2.00
141	*Pat Barnes*	1.00
142	*Rae Carruth*	.50
143	*Will Blackwell*	1.00
144	*Warrick Dunn*	6.00
145	*Corey Dillon*	10.00
146	*Dwayne Rudd*	2.00
147	*Reinard Wilson*	1.00
148	*Peter Boulware*	2.00
149	*Tony Gonzalez*	6.00
150	*Danny Wuerffel*	1.00

1997 Pinnacle Totally Certified Platinum Blue

Platinum Blue cards are sequentially-numbered to 2,499. They feature a micro-etched holographic mylar finish and were seeded one per pack.

Platinum Blue Cards:	2X
Production 2,499 Sets	
Inserted 1:1	

1997 Pinnacle Totally Certified Platinum Gold

Platinum Gold cards feature a micro-etched holographic mylar finish. Each card is sequentially-numbered to 30 and they were inserted 1:79.

	NM/M
Platinum Gold Cards:	3X-8X
Platinum Gold Rookies:	2X-4X
Production 30 Sets	
Inserted 1:79	

1997 Pinnacle X-Press

This 150-base card set features a 22-card Rookie subset, a 10-card Peak Performers subset and three checklist cards. The base cards are laid-out horizontally with two player photos on the front. The inserts included the Pursuit of Paydirt interactive game, Metal Works, Bombs Away and Divide & Conquer. Autumn Warriors is a base set parallel. The silver foil cards were inserted 1:7.

		NM/M
Complete Set (150):		20.00
Common Player:		.05
Minor Stars:		.10
Aut. Warrior Cards:		3X-6X
Aut. Warrior Rookies:		1X-3X
Hobby Pack (8):		2.00
Hobby Wax Box (24):		42.00
Retail Pack (8):		2.00
Retail Wax Box (36):		65.00
Metal Works Wax Box:		15.00
1	Drew Bledsoe	1.00
2	Steve Young	.75
3	Brett Favre	2.25
4	John Elway	.75
5	Dan Marino	2.00
6	Jerry Rice	1.00
7	Tony Banks	.40
8	Kerry Collins	.25
9	Mark Brunell	1.00
10	Troy Aikman	1.00
11	Barry Sanders	1.25
12	Elvis Grbac	.05
13	Eddie George	1.50
14	Terry Glenn	.25
15	Kordell Stewart	1.00
16	Junior Seau	.10
17	Herman Moore	.10
18	Gus Frerotte	.05
19	Warren Moon	.05
20	Emmitt Smith	2.00
21	Chris Chandler	.05
22	Rashaan Salaam	.05
23	Sean Dawkins	.05
24	Tyrone Wheatley	.05
25	Lawrence Phillips	.05
26	Ty Detmer	.05
27	Vinny Testaverde	.05
28	Dorsey Levens	.10
29	Ricky Watters	.10
30	Natrone Means	.10
31	Curtis Conway	.05
32	Larry Centers	.05
33	Johnnie Morton	.05
34	Desmond Howard	.05
35	Marcus Allen	.10
36	Cris Carter	.05
37	James Stewart	.05
38	Frank Sanders	.05
39	Bruce Smith	.05
40	Carl Pickens	.05
41	Neil O'Donnell	.05
42	Trent Dilfer	.10
43	Rodney Peete	.05
44	Terance Mathis	.05
45	Muhsin Muhammad	.05
46	Jake Reed	.05
47	Jim Harbaugh	.05
48	Todd Collins	.05
49	Ki-Jana Carter	.05
50	Scott Mitchell	.05
51	Kevin Hardy	.05
52	Stanley Pritchett	.05
53	Dave Brown	.05
54	Jeff George	.05
55	Stan Humphries	.05
56	Isaac Bruce	.10
57	Eric Moulds	.05
58	Robert Brooks	.05
59	Steve McNair	.75
60	Adrian Murrell	.10
61	Mike Alstott	.10
62	Michael Jackson	.05
63	Tamarick Vanover	.05
64	Edgar Bennett	.05
65	Andre Hastings	.05
66	Robert Smith	.05
67	Thurman Thomas	.10
68	Tim Biakabutuka	.05
69	Rick Mirer	.05
70	Deion Sanders	.50
71	Curtis Martin	1.00
72	Garrison Hearst	.05
73	Kent Graham	.05
74	Anthony Johnson	.05
75	Antonio Freeman	.10
76	Marshall Faulk	.10
77	O.J. McDuffie	.05
78	Heath Shuler	.05
79	Napoleon Kaufman	.10
80	Aeneas Williams	.05
81	Hardy Nickerson	.05
82	Keenan McCardell	.05
83	Erik Kramer	.05
84	Ben Coates	.05
85	Shannon Sharpe	.05
86	Tony Martin	.05
87	Chris Sanders	.05
88	Jamal Anderson	.05
89	Karim Abdul-Jabbar	.50
90	Keyshawn Johnson	.40
91	Terrell Owens	.50
92	Michael Irvin	.10
93	John Friesz	.05
94	Chris Warren	.05
95	Errict Rhett	.05
96	Terry Allen	.10
97	Michael Westbrook	.05
98	Simeon Rice	.05
99	Willie Green	.05
100	Jerome Bettis	.10
101	Reggie White	.10
102	Bert Emanuel	.05
103	Zach Thomas	.10
104	Tim Brown	.05
105	Darnay Scott	.05
106	Terrell Davis	1.00
107	Andre Reed	.05
108	Amani Toomer	.05
109	Irving Fryar	.05
110	Joey Galloway	.10
111	Marvin Harrison	.40
112	Derrick Alexander	.05
113	Jeff Blake	.20
114	Brad Johnson	.05
115	Eddie Kennison	.40
116	*Rae Carruth*	.75
117	*Tony Gonzalez*	.50
118	*Joey Kent*	.10
119	*Peter Boulware*	.10
120	*Orlando Pace*	.20
121	*David LaFleur*	.50
122	*Darnell Autry*	.50
123	*Tiki Barber*	1.00
124	*Troy Davis*	.50
125	*Jim Druckenmiller*	1.50
126	*Corey Dillon*	2.00
127	*Ike Hilliard*	.75
128	*Reidel Anthony*	1.00
129	*Byron Hanspard*	.50
130	*Antowain Smith*	1.00
131	*Jake Plummer*	1.25
132	*Warrick Dunn*	1.00
133	*Bryant Westbrook*	.10
134	*Darrell Russell*	.10
135	*Yatil Green*	.50
136	*Shawn Springs*	.10
137	*Danny Wuerffel*	.75
138	Brett Favre (Peak Performer)	1.00
139	Emmitt Smith (Peak Performer)	1.00
140	Barry Sanders (Peak Performer)	.50
141	Troy Aikman (Peak Performer)	.50
142	Drew Bledsoe (Peak Performer)	.50
143	Jerry Rice (Peak Performer)	.50
144	Dan Marino (Peak Performer)	1.00
145	John Elway (Peak Performer)	.30
146	Kerry Collins (Peak Performer)	.30
147	Mark Brunell (Peak Performer)	.30
148	Brett Favre Checklist	.50
149	Dan Marino Checklist	.50
150	Troy Aikman Checklist	.25

1997 Pinnacle X-Press Metal Works

Each card in this 20-card set features an image of the player printed on Bronze card stock. Redemption cards for Silver (400 made) and Gold (200 made) were randomly inserted. The redemption program ended on 7/1/98.

		NM/M
Complete Set (20):		150.00
Common Player:		2.50
Minor Stars:		5.00
Inserted 1:1 Special		
Silver Cards:		3X-6X
Inserted 1:470		
Production 400 Sets		
Gold Cards:		5X-10X
Inserted 1:950		
Production 200 Sets		
1	Troy Aikman	10.00
2	Emmitt Smith	15.00
3	Dan Marino	15.00
4	Brett Favre	20.00
5	Barry Sanders	20.00
6	Drew Bledsoe	10.00
7	Kerry Collins	5.00
8	Mark Brunell	10.00
9	John Elway	15.00
10	Steve Young	8.00
11	Jerry Rice	10.00
12	Terrell Davis	15.00
13	Curtis Martin	7.00
14	Terry Glenn	5.00
15	Eddie George	10.00
16	Jerome Bettis	5.00
17	Jeff Blake	5.00
18	Kordell Stewart	10.00
19	Jeff George	2.50
20	Deion Sanders	5.00

1997 Pinnacle X-Press Autumn Warrior

This 150-card set paralleled each card in X-Press. They were found in one per seven packs.

Autumn Warrior Cards:	6X-12X

Autumn Warrior Rookies: 3X-6X
Inserted 1:7

1997 Pinnacle X-Press Bombs Away

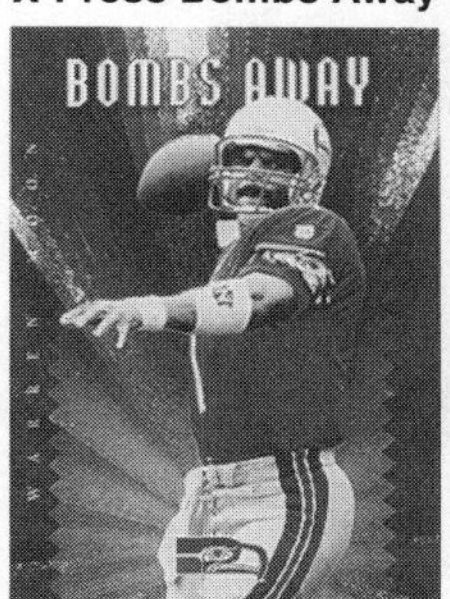

This 18-card insert features top quarterbacks on a full foil, micro-etched card. Bombs Away was inserted 1:19.

		NM/M
Complete Set (18):		60.00
Common Player:		1.00
Minor Stars:		2.00
1	Brett Favre	6.00
2	Dan Marino	6.00
3	Troy Aikman	4.00
4	Drew Bledsoe	4.00
5	Kerry Collins	3.00
6	Mark Brunell	3.00
7	John Elway	4.00
8	Steve Young	4.00
9	Jeff Blake	2.00
10	Kordell Stewart	2.00
11	Jeff George	1.00
12	Rick Mirer	1.00
13	Neil O'Donnell	1.00
14	Scott Mitchell	1.00
15	Jim Harbaugh	1.00
16	Warren Moon	1.00
17	Trent Dilfer	2.00
18	Jim Druckenmiller	1.00

1997 Pinnacle X-Press Divide & Conquer

Divide & Conquer is a 20-card insert on full foil, micro-etched card stock. The cards feature a player action shot and heliogram print technology. They are numbered to 500.

		NM/M
Complete Set (20):		110.00
Common Player:		7.00
1	Tim Biakabutuka	2.00
2	Karim Abdul-Jabbar	2.00
3	Jerome Bettis	5.00
4	Eddie George	8.00
5	Terrell Davis	8.00
6	Barry Sanders	10.00
7	Emmitt Smith	10.00
8	Brett Favre	12.00
9	Dan Marino	12.00
10	Troy Aikman	8.00
11	Jerry Rice	8.00
12	Drew Bledsoe	6.00
13	Kerry Collins	4.00
14	Mark Brunell	4.00
15	John Elway	8.00
16	Steve Young	6.00
17	Warrick Dunn	5.00
18	Byron Hanspard	2.00
19	Troy Davis	2.00
20	Jeff Blake	2.00

1997 Pinnacle X-Press Pursuit of Paydirt-Quarterbacks

The Pursuit of Paydirt insert was an interactive game which ran during the 1997 season. This 30-card insert (found 1:2) featured quarterbacks and gave collectors the chance to win if they found the QB who led the league in touchdowns during the season.

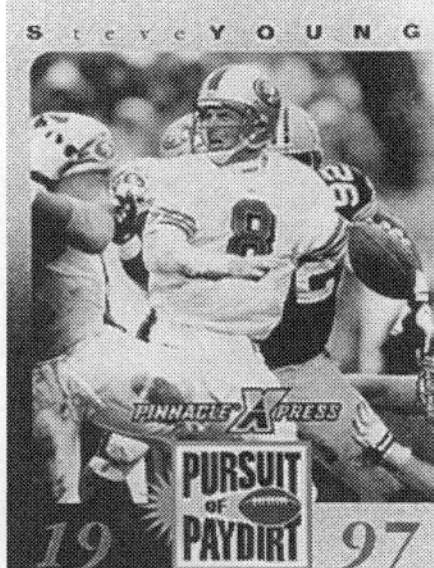

		NM/M
Complete Set (30):		22.00
Common Player:		.25
Minor Stars:		.50
1	Drew Bledsoe	2.00
2	Steve Young	1.50
3	Brett Favre	4.50
4	John Elway	1.50
5	Dan Marino	4.00
6	Tony Banks	1.00
7	Kerry Collins	.75
8	Mark Brunell	1.00
9	Troy Aikman	2.00
10	Elvis Grbac	.25
11	Kordell Stewart	1.00
12	Gus Frerotte	.25
13	Warren Moon	.25
14	Chris Chandler	.25
15	Rick Mirer	.25
16	Vinny Testaverde	.25
17	Neil O'Donnell	.25
18	Trent Dilfer	.50
19	Rodney Peete	.25
20	Jim Harbaugh	.25
21	Todd Collins	.25
22	Scott Mitchell	.25
23	Dave Brown	.25
24	Jeff George	.25
25	Stan Humphries	.25
26	Steve McNair	1.50
27	Heath Shuler	.25
28	Jeff Blake	.50
29	Brad Johnson	.25
30	Jim Druckenmiller	.50

1997 Pinnacle X-Press Pursuit of Paydirt-Running Backs

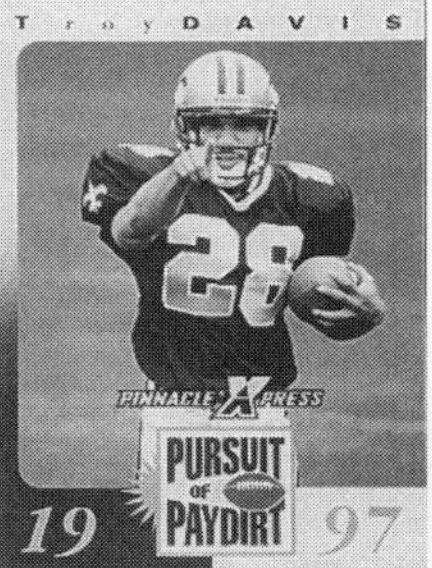

This 30-card insert featured running backs and gave collectors the chance to win prizes if they could match the leading TD scorer with the number of TDs he made. This insert was found 1:2.

		NM/M
Complete Set (30):		25.00
Common Player:		.25
Minor Stars:		.50
1	Errict Rhett	.25
2	Terry Allen	.50
3	Jerome Bettis	.50
4	Terrell Davis	2.00
5	Tiki Barber	1.50
6	Troy Davis	1.25
7	Byron Hanspard	1.25
8	Greg Hill	.25
9	Barry Sanders	4.00
10	Eddie George	3.00
11	Emmitt Smith	4.00
12	Rashaan Salaam	.25
13	Tyrone Wheatley	.25
14	Lawrence Phillips	.25
15	Ricky Watters	.50
16	Natrone Means	.50
17	Marcus Allen	1.00
18	James Stewart	.25
19	Ki-Jana Carter	.25
20	Dorsey Levens	.50
21	Robert Smith	.25
22	Thurman Thomas	1.00
23	Tim Biakabutuka	.25
24	Curtis Martin	2.00
25	Garrison Hearst	.25
26	Marshall Faulk	2.00
27	Napoleon Kaufman	.50
28	Jamal Anderson	.25
29	Karim Abdul-Jabbar	.50
30	Chris Warren	.25

1997 Pinnacle Rembrandt

This nine-card set was inserted one per box of Rembrandt's Ultra-PRO plastic sheets. The cards feature an action shot and a bronze-colored foil section. Silver and gold foil parallel sets were also created. Collectors who assembled an entire bronze, silver or gold set could redeem them for prizes from Rembrandt.

		NM/M
Complete Set (9):		20.00
Common Player:		1.50
*Gold Cards:		3X-5X
*Silver Cards:		2X-4X
1	Brett Favre	5.00
2	Troy Aikman	2.00
3	John Elway	1.50
4	Dan Marino	4.00
5	Drew Bledsoe	2.00
6	Emmitt Smith	4.00
7	Jerry Rice	2.00
8	Barry Sanders	2.50
9	Mark Brunell	2.00

1992 Playoff Promos

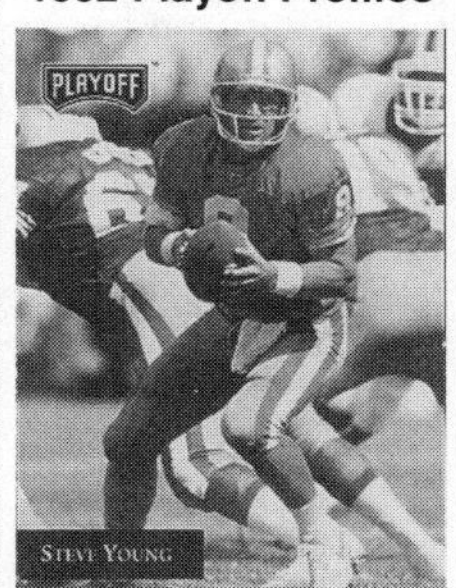

This seven-card promotional set gave collectors a glimpse of what Playoff's 1992 set would look like. These cards were printed on 22-point stock. The player's names were printed in silver inside a black box at the bottom of the card. The card backs, numbered "of 6 promo," feature a full-bleed photo, with the player's name located along the left margin of the card. A write-up about the player was included in the lower left of the card back.

		NM/M
Complete Set (7):		15.00
Common Player:		1.00
1	Calvin Williams	1.25
2	John Elway	4.00
3	Dalton Hilliard	1.00
4	Steve Young	4.00
5	Emmitt Smith	8.00
6	Mike Golic	1.00
NNO	Header/Intro Card	1.00

1992 Playoff

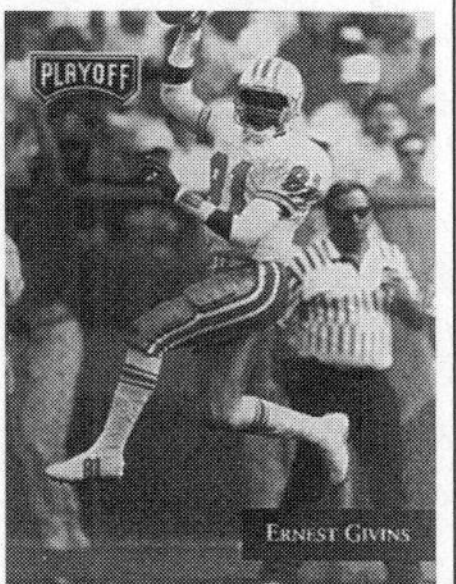

This 150-card set features standard-size cards printed on stock which is thicker than usual. The card front has a full-bleed color photo, plus the player's name in a black bar at the bottom. Most of the backgrounds are black-and-white and, using a metallic-like process, give the cards depth. The card back has a close-up shot of the player, plus his team's name in a team color-coded bar. Information contained in a black box details the player's performance from a key game during the previous season. There were also seven promotional cards made as previews of the regular 1992 set.

		NM/M
Complete Set (150):		25.00
Common Player:		.05
Minor Stars:		.50
Pack (8):		1.25
Wax Box (36):		30.00
1	Emmitt Smith	6.00
2	Steve Young	3.00
3	Jack Del Rio	.05
4	Bobby Hebert	.05
5	Shannon Sharpe	.05
6	Gary Clark	.05
7	Christian Okoye	.05
8	Ernest Givins	.05
9	Mike Horan	.05
10	Dennis Gentry	.05
11	Michael Irvin	1.00
12	Eric Floyd	.05
13	Brent Jones	.05
14	Anthony Carter	.05
15	Tony Martin	.75
16	Greg Lewis ("Returning" should be "returned" on back)	.05
17	Todd McNair	.05
18	Earnest Byner	.05
19	Steve Beuerlein	.05
20	Roger Craig	.05
21	Mark Higgs	.05
22	Guy McIntyre	.05
23	Don Warren	.05
24	Alvin Harper	.50
25	Mark Jackson	.05
26	Chris Doleman	.05
27	Jesse Sapolu	.05
28	Tony Talbert	.05
29	Wendell Davis	.05
30	Dan Saleaumua	.05
31	Jeff Bostic	.05
32	Jay Novacek	.05
33	Cris Carter	.50
34	Tony Paige	.05
35	Greg Kragen	.05
36	Jeff Dellenbach	.05
37	Keith DeLong	.05
38	Todd Scott	.05
39	Jeff Feagles	.05
40	Mike Saxon	.05
41	Martin Mayhew	.05
42	*Steve Bono*	1.00
43	*Willie Davis*	.50
44	Mark Stepnoski	.05
45	Harry Newsome	.05
46	Thane Gash	.05
47	Gaston Green	.05
48	James Washington	.05
49	Kenny Walker	.05
50	*Jeff Davidson*	.05
51	Shane Conlan	.05
52	Richard Dent	.05
53	Haywood Jeffires	.05
54	Harry Galbreath	.05
55	Terry Allen	.40
56	Tommy Barnhardt	.05
57	Mike Golic	.05
58	Dalton Hilliard	.05
59	Danny Copeland	.05
60	*Jerry Fontenot*	.05
61	Kelvin Martin	.05
62	Mark Kelso	.05
63	Wymon Henderson	.05
64	Mark Rypien	.05
65	Bobby Humphrey	.05
66	Rich Gannon (Tarkington misspelled, Minneapolis instead of Minnesota on back)	.05
67	Darren Lewis	.05
68	Barry Foster	.05
69	Ken Norton	.05
70	James Lofton	.05
71	Trace Armstrong	.05
72	Vestee Jackson	.05
73	Clyde Simmons	.05
74	Brad Muster	.05
75	Cornelius Bennett	.05
76	Mike Merriweather	.05
77	John Elway	4.00
78	Herschel Walker	.05
79	Hassan Jones (Minneapolis instead of Minnesota on back)	.05
80	Jim Harbaugh	.50
81	Issiac Holt	.05
82	David Alexander	.05
83	Brian Mitchell	.05
84	Mark Tuinei	.05
85	Tom Rathman	.05
86	Reggie White	.50
87	William Perry	.05
88	Jeff Wright	.05
89	Keith Kartz	.05
90	Andre Waters	.05
91	Darryl Talley	.05
92	Morten Andersen	.05
93	Tom Waddle	.05
94	Felix Wright (Minneapolis instead of Minnesota on back)	.05
95	Keith Jackson	.05
96	Art Monk	.50
97	Seth Joyner	.05
98	Steve McMichael	.05
99	Thurman Thomas	1.00
100	Warren Moon	.75
101	Tony Casillas	.05
102	Vance Johnson	.05
103	*Doug Dawson*	.05
104	Bill Maas	.05
105	Mark Clayton	.05
106	Hoby Brenner	.05
107	Gary Anderson	.05
108	Marc Logan	.05
109	Ricky Sanders	.05
110	Vai Sikahema	.05
111	Neil Smith	.05
112	Cody Carlson	.05
113	Jimmie Jones	.05
114	Pat Swilling	.05
115	Neil O'Donnell	1.00
116	Chip Lohmiller	.05
117	Mike Croel	.05
118	Pete Metzelaars	.05
119	Ray Childress	.05
120	Fred Banks	.05
121	Derek Kennard	.05
122	Daryl Johnston	.05
123	Lorenzo White (Minneapolis instead of Minnesota on back)	.05
124	Hardy Nickerson	.05
125	Derrick Thomas	.50
126	Steve Walsh	.05
127	Doug Widell	.05
128	Calvin Williams	.05
129	Tim Harris	.05
130	Rod Woodson	.50
131	Craig Heyward	.05
132	Barry Word	.05
133	Mark Duper	.05
134	Tim Johnson	.05
135	John Gesek	.05
136	Steve Jackson	.05
137	Dave Krieg	.05
138	Barry Sanders	6.00
139	Michael Haynes	.05
140	Eric Metcalf	.05
141	Stan Humphries	.50
142	Sterling Sharpe	.50
143	Todd Marinovich	.05
144	Rodney Hampton	.50
145	Rodney Peete	.50
146	*Darryl Williams*	.05
147	*Darren Perry*	.05
148	*Terrell Buckley*	.05
149	*Amp Lee*	.75
150	Ricky Watters	1.50

1993 Playoff Promos

This six-card promotional set gave collectors a glimpse of what the 1993 Playoff set would look like. The card fronts feature the Playoff logo at the top and the player's name, printed in silver inside a black box, near the bottom of the card. The card backs have a full-bleed photo, with the player's name inside a box on the upper left corner. A write-up about the player is included in the lower right. The cards, printed on 22-point stock, are numbered "of 6 promo."

		NM/M
Complete Set (6):		12.00
Common Player:		1.00
1	Emmitt Smith	6.00
2	Barry Foster	1.00
3	Quinn Early	1.00
4	Tim Brown	1.50
5	Steve Young	3.00
6	Sterling Sharpe	1.50

1993 Playoff

Playoff increased its 1993 set to 315 cards. Subsets within the regular set include "The Backs" (#s 277-282, featuring top running backs), "Connections" (#s 283-292, featuring top quarterback/wide receiver combinations), and "Rookies" (#s 293-315). Redemption cards were randomly inserted in packs for "Headliner" (six cards) and "Rookie Roundup" (10 cards) sets. Other insert sets included Checklists (eight cards), Playoff Club (seven cards), and Brett Favre and Ricky Watters (five cards each). Six promotional cards, which have the same design as the regular cards, were also made.

		NM/M
Complete Set (315):		30.00
Common Player:		.15
Minor Stars:		.25
Comp. Promo Set (6):		10.00
Hobby Pack (8):		1.75
Hobby Wax Box (24):		30.00
Retail Pack (8):		1.50
Retail Wax Box (24):		25.00
1	Troy Aikman	3.00
2	Jerry Rice	3.00
3	Keith Jackson	.15
4	Sean Gilbert	.15
5	Jim Kelly	.25
6	Junior Seau	.25
7	Deion Sanders	2.00
8	Joe Montana	4.00
9	Terrell Buckley	.15
10	Emmitt Smith	5.00
11	Pete Stoyanovich	.15
12	Randall Cunningham	.25
13	Boomer Esiason	.25
14	Mike Saxon	.15
15	Chuck Cecil	.15
16	Vinny Testaverde	.25
17	Jeff Hostetler	.25
18	Mark Clayton	.15
19	Nick Bell	.15
20	Frank Reich	.15
21	Henry Ellard	.15
22	Andre Reed	.25
23	Mark Ingram	.15
24	Mike Brim	.15
25	Bernie Kosar	.25
26	Jeff George	.25
27	Tommy Maddox	.15
28	*Kent Graham*	.75
29	David Klingler	.15
30	Robert Delpino	.15
31	Kevin Fagan	.15
32	Mark Bavaro	.15
33	Harold Green	.15
34	Shawn McCarthy	.15
35	Ricky Proehl	.15
36	Eugene Robinson	.15
37	Phil Simms	.15
38	David Lang	.15
39	Santana Dotson	.15
40	Brett Perriman	.15
41	Jim Harbaugh	.15
42	Keith Byars	.15
43	Quentin Coryatt	.15
44	Louis Oliver	.15
45	Howie Long	.15
46	Mike Sherrard	.15
47	Earnest Byner	.15
48	Neil Smith	.15
49	Audray McMillan	.15
50	Vaughn Dunbar	.15
51	Ronnie Lott	.15
52	Clyde Simmons	.15
53	Kevin Scott	.15
54	Bubby Brister	.15
55	Randal Hill	.15
56	Pat Swilling	.15
57	Steve Beuerlein	.15
58	Gary Clark	.15
59	Brian Noble	.15
60	Leslie O'Neal	.15
61	Vincent Brown	.15
62	Edgar Bennett	.25
63	Anthony Carter	.15
64	Glenn Cadez	.15
65	Dalton Hilliard	.15
66	James Lofton	.15
67	Walter Stanley	.15
68	Tim Harris	.15
69	Carl Banks	.15
70	Andre Ware	.15
71	Karl Mecklenburg	.15
72	Russell Maryland	.15
73	LeRoy Thompson	.15
74	Tommy Kane	.15
75	Dan Marino	5.00
76	Darrell Fullington	.15
77	Jessie Tuggle	.15
78	Bruce Smith	.15
79	Neal Anderson	.15
80	Kevin Mack	.15
81	Shane Dronett	.15
82	Nick Lowery	.15
83	Sheldon White	.15
84	Willie (Flipper) Anderson	.15
85	Jeff Herrod	.15
86	Dwight Stone	.15
87	Dave Krieg	.15
88	Bryan Cox	.15
89	Greg McMurty	.15
90	Rickey Jackson	.15
91	Ernie Mills	.15
92	Browning Nagle	.15
93	John Taylor	.15
94	Eric Dickerson	.15
95	Johnny Holland	.15
96	Anthony Miller	.15
97	Fred Barnett	.15
98	Ricky Ervins	.15
99	Leonard Russell	.15
100	Lawrence Taylor	.25
101	Tony Casillas	.15
102	John Elway	1.50
103	Bennie Blades	.15
104	Harry Sydney	.15
105	Bubba McDowell	.15
106	Todd McNair	.15
107	Steve Smith	.15
108	Jim Everett	.25
109	Bobby Humphrey	.15
110	Rich Gannon	.15
111	Marv Cook	.15
112	Wayne Martin	.15
113	Sean Landeta	.15
114	Brad Baxter	.15
115	Reggie White	.25
116	Johnny Johnson	.15
117	Jeff Graham	.15
118	*Darren Carrington*	.25
119	Ricky Watters	.25
120	Art Monk	.25
121	Cornelius Bennett	.15
122	Wade Wilson	.15

123 Daniel Stubbs .15
124 Brad Muster .15
125 Mike Tomczak .15
126 Jay Novacek .15
127 Shannon Sharpe .25
128 Rodney Peete .15
129 Daryl Johnston .15
130 Warren Moon .25
131 Willie Gault .15
132 Tony Martin .15
133 Terry Allen .15
134 Hugh Millen .15
135 Rob Moore .15
136 *Andy Harmon* .15
137 Kelvin Martin .15
138 Rod Woodson .25
139 Nate Lewis .15
140 Darryl Talley .15
141 Guy McIntyre .15
142 John L. Williams .15
143 Brad Edwards .15
144 Trace Armstrong .15
145 Kenneth Davis .15
146 Clay Matthews .15
147 Gaston Green .15
148 Chris Spielman .15
149 Cody Carlson .15
150 Derrick Thomas .25
151 Terry McDaniel .15
152 Kevin Greene .15
153 Roger Craig .15
154 Craig Heyward .15
155 Rodney Hampton .25
156 Heath Sherman .15
157 Mark Stepnoski .15
158 Chris Chandler .15
159 Rob Berstine .15
160 Pierce Holt .15
161 Wilber Marshall .15
162 Reggie Cobb .15
163 Tom Rathman .15
164 Michael Haynes .15
165 Nate Odomes .15
166 Tom Waddle .15
167 Eric Ball .15
168 Brett Favre 5.00
169 Michael Jackson .15
170 Lorenzo White .15
171 Cleveland Gary .15
172 Jay Schroeder .15
173 Tony Paige .15
174 Jack Del Rio .15
175 Jon Vaughn .15
176 Morten Andersen .15
177 Chris Burkett .15
178 Vai Sikahema .15
179 Ronnie Harmon .15
180 Amp Lee .15
181 Chip Lohmiller .15
182 Steve Broussard .15
183 Don Beebe .15
184 Tommy Vardell .15
185 Keith Jennings .15
186 Simon Fletcher .15
187 Mel Gray .15
188 Vince Workman .15
189 Haywood Jeffires .15
190 Barry Word .15
191 Ethan Horton .15
192 Mark Higgs .15
193 Irving Fryar .15
194 Charles Haley .15
195 Steve Bono .50
196 Mike Golic .15
197 Gary Anderson .15
198 Sterling Sharpe .25
199 Andre Tippett .15
200 Thurman Thomas 1.00
201 Chris Miller .15
202 Henry Jones .15
203 Mo Lewis .15
204 Marion Butts .15
205 Mike Johnson .15
206 Alvin Harper .25
207 Ray Childress .15
208 Anthony Newman .15
209 Tony Bennett .15
210 *Antony Newman* .15
211 Christian Okoye .15
212 Marcus Allen .25
213 Jackie Harris .15
214 Mark Duper .15
215 Cris Carter .25
216 John Stephens .15
217 Barry Sanders 3.50
218 Herman Moore 1.00
219 Marvin Washington .15
220 Calvin Williams .15
221 John Randle .15
222 Marco Coleman .15
223 Eric Martin .15
224 David Meggett .15
225 Brian Washington .15
226 Barry Foster .25
227 Michael Zordich .15
228 Stan Humphries .25
229 Mike Cofer .15
230 Chris Warren .50
231 Keith McCants .15
232 Mark Rypien .15
233 James Francis .15
234 Andre Rison .25
235 William Perry .15
236 Chip Banks .15
237 Willie Davis .15
238 Chris Doleman .15
239 Tim Brown .25
240 Darren Perry .15
241 Johnny Bailey .15
242 Ernest Givins .15
243 John Carney .15
244 Cortez Kennedy .25
245 Lawrence Dawsey .15
246 Martin Mayhew .15
247 Shane Conlan .15
248 J.J. Birden .15
249 Quinn Early .15
250 Michael Irvin .25
251 Neil O'Donnell .25
252 Stan Gelbaugh .15
253 Drew Hill .15
254 Wendell Davis .15
255 Tim Johnson .15
256 Seth Joyner .15
257 Derrick Fenner .15
258 Steve Young 3.00
259 Jackie Slater .15
260 Eric Metcalf .15
261 Rufus Porter .15
262 Ken Norton .15
263 Tim McDonald .15
264 Mark Jackson .15
265 Hardy Nickerson .15
266 Anthony Munoz .15
267 Mark Carrier .15
268 Mike Pritchard .15
269 Steve Emtman .15
270 Ricky Sanders .15
271 Robert Massey .15
272 Pete Metzelaars .15
273 Reggie Langhorne .15
274 Tim McGee .15
275 *Reggie Rivers* .15
276 Jimmie Jones .15
277 Lorenzo White .15
278 Emmitt Smith 3.00
279 Thurman Thomas .25
280 Barry Sanders 2.00
281 Rodney Hampton .25
282 Barry Foster .25
283 Troy Aikman 1.50
284 Michael Irvin .25
285 Brett Favre 2.00
286 Sterling Sharpe .25
287 Steve Young 2.00
288 Jerry Rice 2.00
289 Stan Humphries .25
290 Anthony Miller .25
291 Dan Marino 3.00
292 Keith Jackson .15
293 *Patrick Bates* .25
294 *Jerome Bettis* 3.00
295 *Drew Bledsoe* 8.00
296 *Tom Carter* .25
297 *Curtis Conway* 2.00
298 *John Copeland* .25
299 *Eric Curry* .25
300 *Reggie Brooks* .25
301 *Steve Everitt* .25
302 *Deon Figures* .25
303 *Garrison Hearst* 3.00
304 *Qadry Ismail* 1.00
305 *Marvin Jones* .25
306 *Lincoln Kennedy* .25
307 *O.J. McDuffie* 2.00
308 *Rick Mirer* .50
309 *Wayne Simmons* .25
310 *Irv Smith* .25
311 *Robert Smith* 2.00
312 *Dana Stubblefield* 1.00
313 *George Teague* .25
314 *Dan Williams* .25
315 *Kevin Williams* .50

1993 Playoff Checklists

Randomly seeded in packs, this eight-card set showcases an action shot of a player. A silver box, featuring highlights about the player, is included at the bottom of the card. The box is bordered on the left side by a black box which has "Check It Out" inside it. The card back features a portion of the checklist printed inside a white area in the center of the card. The top of the card has a red stripe, while the bottom of the card has a black stripe.

		NM/M
Complete Set (8):		7.00
Common Player:		.75
1A	Warren Moon (UER) (Kosar misspelled Kozar)	1.00
1B	Warren Moon (COR)	1.00
2	Barry Sanders	1.00
3	Deion Sanders	1.00
4	Ron Woodson	1.00
5	Junior Seau	1.00
6	Mark Rypien	.75
7	Derrick Thomas	1.00
8	Daryl Johnston, Alvin Harper, Michael Irvin Dallas Players (UER) (Stan Humphries listed as 299; should be 289)	.75

1993 Playoff Club

These insert cards feature a gold Playoff Club logo on the card front which distinguishes it as an insert card from the regular Playoff cards. A color player closeup shot, surrounded by a black-and-white background, is also included on the card front. The player has also signed his signature in gold ink. The back, numbered using a "PC" prefix, gives a summary of the player's career against a grey Playoff Club logo which is ghosted in the background. These were inserted into retail and hobby boxes.

		NM/M
Complete Set (7):		25.00
Common Player:		2.00
1	Joe Montana	15.00
2	Art Monk	2.00
3	Lawrence Taylor	4.00
4	Ronnie Lott	2.00
5	Reggie White	4.00
6	Anthony Munoz	2.00
7	Jackie Slater	2.00

1993 Playoff Brett Favre

Green Bay Packer quarterback Brett Favre is featured in this five-card insert set. The fronts have a metallic shine to them and feature a full-bleed color photo. A black box at the bottom contains Favre's name. The card back has a ghosted image of Favre throwing a pass, plus season highlights against a green background. Cards, numbered 1 of 5, etc., were randomly inserted in hobby display boxes.

		NM/M
Complete Set (5):		100.00
Common Favre:		20.00
1	Brett Favre The Early Years	20.00
2	Brett Favre The College Years	20.00
3	Brett Favre Turning Pro	20.00
4	Brett Favre Green Bay Star	20.00
5	Brett Favre 1992: The Storybook Season	20.00

1993 Playoff Headliners Redemption

Randomly seeded in retail foil packs, the redemption card could be redeemed for this six-card set. Overall, 48,475 redemption cards were inserted into packs. The card front features a gray background with silver type. A color photo of the player is featured, with the player's name located inside a black box at the top of the card front. The Headliners' logo is printed to the right of the player's name. The card backs showcase the player's name and highlights printed inside a black box at the top, with the card number in the upper right. A headshot of the player is located in the center of the card back. The cards are numbered with an "H" prefix.

		NM/M
Complete Set (6):		25.00
Common Player:		1.00
1	Brett Favre	14.00
2	Sterling Sharpe	2.00
3	Emmitt Smith	14.00
4	Jerry Rice	7.00
5	Thurman Thomas	2.00
6	David Klingler	1.00
NNO	Headliner Redemption	1.00

1993 Playoff Promo Inserts

Each 1993 Playoff special retail pack included one promo insert (or Playoff Ricky Watters card). The full-bleed photo on the card front includes the Playoff logo at the top and the player's name in silver inside a black rectangle, located at the bottom left. The player is highlighted in color, with the background in black-and-white. Showcased on the card back are highlights from the player's career. With the card number in the upper right (labeled "Promo X of 6"), the player's name appears in white inside a black band in the upper left corner.

		NM/M
Complete Set (6):		10.00
Common Player:		1.50
1	Michael Irvin	1.50
2	Barry Foster	1.50
3	Quinn Early	1.50
4	Tim Brown	1.50
5	Reggie White	2.00
6	Sterling Sharpe	2.00

1993 Playoff Rookie Roundup Redemption

A 10-card set would be given to collectors in exchange for a 1993 Playoff Rookie Roundup Redemption card, which was found in hobby foil packs. The mail-in offer expired on July 3, 1994. Silver type over a gray background served as the backdrop to the color photo of the player. The Rookie Roundup and the Playoff logos also appear on the card front. The player's name is printed in the lower right corner. The card back has a color photo of the player in the center, over a white background with gray team logos in the background. A black box at the bottom of the card back houses the player's name and 1993 highlights. Overall, 15,683 exchange cards were printed. Cards are prefixed with "R."

		NM/M
Complete Set (10):		40.00
Common Player:		2.00
1	Jerome Bettis	10.00
2	Drew Bledsoe	15.00
3	Reggie Brooks	3.00
4	Derek Brown (RB)	3.00
5	Garrison Hearst	6.00
6	Terry Kirby	3.00
7	Glyn Milburn	3.00
8	Rick Mirer	6.00
9	Roosevelt Potts	2.00
10	Dana Stubblefield	3.00
NNO	Rookie Roundup Redemption Card	.50

1993 Playoff Ricky Watters

This five-card set features San Francisco 49er running back Ricky Watters. The front has a full-bleed color photo against a metallic background. Watters' name is at the bottom of the card in a black box. The Playoff logo is also on the front. The back has a ghosted image of Watters running the ball, plus career highlights against a tan background. Cards, which are numbered 1 of 5, etc., were randomly inserted in retail display boxes.

		NM/M
Complete Set (5):		20.00
Common Watters:		4.00
1	Ricky Watters The Early Years	4.00
2	Ricky Watters Irish Eyes Were Smiling	4.00
3	Ricky Watters The Bay Watters	4.00
4	Ricky Watters A Second-Year Rookie	4.00
5	Ricky Watters Rookie of the Year	4.00

1993 Playoff Contenders Promos

This six-card promotional set gave collectors a glimpse of what the 1993 Contenders set would look like. The borderless fronts showcase the Playoff logo and player's name inside of a silver box at the bottom of the card. A color photo of the player is located on the left of the horizontal card back. The right side is a team-colored area which includes the player's team helmet, his name and his season highlight. In the upper right is the card number, which is indicated with a Roman numeral.

		NM/M
Complete Set (6):		12.00
Common Player:		.75
1	Drew Bledsoe	3.00
2	Neil Smith	.75
3	Rick Mirer	1.00
4	Rodney Hampton	.75
5	Barry Sanders	2.50
6	Emmitt Smith	4.00

1993 Playoff Contenders

This 150-card Playoff Contenders set uses a unique ink-on-foil printing process called Tekchrome. The cards are printed on a heavy card stock, making them among the thickest and sturdiest in the hobby. Cards include photos and game information from the 1993 season; the set is primarily composed of players from teams that were most likely to make the NFL playoffs, plus 49 top rookies and free agents from the season. The set also includes two insert sets - "Rookie Contenders" (10 of the top first-year players) and a five-card set tracing the collegiate and professional career of Seattle Seahawk rookie quarterback Rick Mirer. The regular cards have the player's name and Playoff logo in a silver box on the card front.

		NM/M
Complete Set (150):		20.00
Common Player:		.15
Minor Stars:		.25
Pack (7):		1.50
Wax Box (24):		25.00
1	Brett Favre	5.00
2	Thurman Thomas	.25
3	Barry Word	.15
4	Herman Moore	1.00
5	Reggie Langhorne	.15
6	Wilber Marshall	.15
7	Ricky Watters	.25
8	Marcus Allen	.25
9	Jeff Hostetler	.25
10	Steve Young	2.00
11	Bobby Hebert	.15
12	David Klingler	.15
13	Craig Heyward	.15
14	Andre Reed	.25
15	Tommy Vardell	.15
16	Anthony Carter	.15
17	Mel Gray	.15
18	Dan Marino	4.00
19	Haywood Jeffires	.15
20	Joe Montana	3.00
21	Tim Brown	.25
22	Jim McMahon	.15
23	Scott Mitchell	.25
24	Rickey Jackson	.15
25	Troy Aikman	2.00
26	Rodney Hampton	.25
27	Fred Barnett	.15
28	Gary Clark	.15
29	Barry Foster	.25
30	Brian Blades	.15
31	Tim McDonald	.15
32	Kelvin Martin	.15
33	Henry Jones	.15
34	Erric Pegram	.15
35	Don Beebe	.15
36	Eric Metcalf	.15
37	Charles Haley	.15
38	Robert Delpino	.15
39	Leonard Russell	.15
40	Jackie Harris	.15
41	Ernest Givins	.15
42	Willie Davis	.15
43	Alexander Wright	.15
44	Keith Byars	.15
45	David Meggett	.15
46	Johnny Johnson	.15
47	Mark Bavaro	.15
48	Seth Joyner	.15
49	Junior Seau	.25
50	Emmitt Smith	4.00
51	Shannon Sharpe	.25
52	Rodney Peete	.15
53	Andre Rison	.25
54	Cornelius Bennett	.15
55	Mark Carrier	.15
56	Mark Clayton	.15
57	Warren Moon	.25
58	J.J. Birden	.15
59	Howie Long	.15
60	Irving Fryar	.15
61	Mark Jackson	.15
62	Eric Martin	.15
63	Herschel Walker	.15
64	Cortez Kennedy	.25
65	Steve Beuerlein	.15
66	Jim Kelly	.25
67	Bernie Kosar	.25
68	Pat Swilling	.15
69	Michael Irvin	.25
70	Harvey Williams	.15
71	Steve Smith	.15
72	Wade Wilson	.15
73	Phil Simms	.15
74	Vinny Testaverde	.25
75	Barry Sanders	2.50
76	Ken Norton	.15
77	Rod Woodson	.25
78	Webster Slaughter	.15
79	Derrick Thomas	.25
80	Mike Sherrard	.15
81	Calvin Williams	.15
82	Jay Novacek	.15
83	Michael Brooks	.15
84	Randall Cunningham	.25
85	Chris Warren	.50
86	Johnny Mitchell	.15
87	Jim Harbaugh	.15
88	Rod Bernstine	.15
89	John Elway	1.00
90	Jerry Rice	2.00
91	Brent Jones	.15
92	Cris Carter	.25
93	Alvin Harper	.25
94	*Horace Copeland*	.50
95	Raghib Ismail	.25
96	*Darrin Smith*	.25
97	*Reggie Brooks*	.25
98	*Demetrius DuBose*	.25
99	*Eric Curry*	.25
100	*Rick Mirer*	.75
101	*Carlton Gray*	.15
102	*Dana Stubblefield*	1.00
103	*Todd Kelly*	.15
104	*Natrone Means*	1.00
105	*Darrien Gordon*	.50
106	*Deon Figures*	.30
107	*Garrison Hearst*	3.00
108	*Ron Moore*	.50
109	*Leonard Renfro*	.15
110	*Lester Holmes*	.15
111	*Vaughn Hebron*	.25
112	*Marvin Jones*	.25
113	*Irv Smith*	.25
114	*Willie Roaf*	.25
115	*Derek Brown*	.25
116	*Vincent Brisby*	1.00
117	*Drew Bledsoe*	8.00
118	*Gino Torretta*	.25
119	*Robert Smith*	3.00
120	*Qadry Ismail*	1.00
121	*O.J. McDuffie*	1.75
122	*Terry Kirby*	.75
123	*Troy Drayton*	1.00
124	*Jerome Bettis*	3.00
125	*Patrick Bates*	.25
126	*Rossevelt Potts*	.25
127	*Tom Carter*	.40
128	*Patrick Robinson*	.25
129	*Brad Hopkins*	.15
130	*George Teague*	.40
131	Wayne Simmons	.15
132	*Mark Brunell*	7.00
133	*Ryan McNeil*	.15
134	*Dan Williams*	.15
135	*Glyn Milburn*	.50
136	*Kevin Williams*	1.50
137	*Derrick Lassic*	.25
138	Steve Everitt	.25
139	*Lance Gunn*	.25
140	*John Copeland*	.25
141	*Curtis Conway*	2.00
142	*Thomas Smith*	.25
143	*Russell Copeland*	1.00
144	*Lincoln Kennedy*	.25
145	Boomer Esiason	.15
146	Neil Smith	.15
147	Jack Del Rio	.15
148	Morten Andersen	.15
149	Sterling Sharpe (CL)	.15
150	Reggie White	.25

A player's name in *italic* type indicates a rookie card.

1993 Playoff Contenders Rick Mirer

These five cards, devoted to Seattle Seahawks first-round draft pick Rick Mirer, were randomly inserted in 1993 Playoff Contenders packs. The fronts have a borderless color action shot with a metallic shine. Mirer's name is at the bottom in a black box. Mirer's photo from the front of card 3 is used as a ghosted image for all five card backs. Career highlights and a card number, 1 of 5, etc., are also given on the backs.

		NM/M
Complete Set (5):		5.00
Common Mirer:		1.00
1	Rick Mirer This Kid Can Play	1.00
2	Rick Mirer Notre Dame All-American	1.00
3	Rick Mirer First-Round Draft Pick	1.00
4	Rick Mirer Seattle in the Hunt	1.00
5	Rick Mirer A Tough Guy	1.00

1993 Playoff Contenders Rookie Contenders

These 10 inserts cards, randomly included in 1993 Playoff Contenders packs, feature 10 of the top rookies in 1993. Each card front has a borderless color action photo, with a metallic shine and blurred background. The player's name and set logo appear in the lower left corner in a gold box. Each card is white and has the player's name at the top; the set name is given in white in two black bands, one on top and the other on the bottom. The backs are numbered and include a summary of the player's collegiate accomplishments.

		NM/M
Complete Set (10):		65.00
Common Player:		1.00
1	Jerome Bettis	12.00
2	Drew Bledsoe	20.00
3	Reggie Brooks	1.00
4	Derek Brown	1.00
5	Garrison Hearst	8.00
6	Vaughn Hebron	1.00
7	Qadry Ismail	5.00
8	Derrick Lassic	1.00
9	Glyn Milburn	1.00
10	Dana Stubblefield	4.00

1994 Playoff Prototypes

This six-card set gave collectors a glimpse of what the 1994 Playoff set would look like. A full-bleed color photo dominates the front, with the Playoff logo near the bottom, located inside an oval that also housed the player's name. The card back also had a full-bleed shot of the player, with his name in a black box next to his helmet. Below the name on the unnumbered card back is the player's career highlights.

		NM/M
Complete Set (6):		8.00
Common Player:		1.00
1	Marcus Allen	1.00
2	Rick Mirer	1.25
3	Barry Sanders	2.00
4	Junior Seau	1.25
5	Sterling Sharpe	1.00
6	Emmitt Smith	3.00

1994 Playoff

These Playoff cards use the company's Tekchrome II ink-on-foil process for the full-color card fronts. The photo is full-bleed and has the set's logo in the upper right corner. The card back has another photo of the player, along with his name and team helmet. A brief player profile is also included. Subsets within the main set include Sack Pack, Ground Attack, Summerall's Best and Rookies. Insert sets include the Silver Playoff Club, which features Gale Sayers (some of them are autographed); the Jerome Bettis Collection; the Jerry Rice Collection; the Playoff Club; the Barry Sanders Collection; and the Headliners. Six prototype cards were also produced, previewing the regular cards.

		NM/M
Complete Set (336):		30.00
Common Player:		.05
Pack (8):		1.25
Wax Box (24):		20.00
1	Joe Montana	2.00
2	Derrick Thomas	.35
3	Dan Marino	4.00
4	Cris Carter	.25
5	Boomer Esiason	.30
6	Bruce Smith	.25
7	Andre Rison	.40
8	Curtis Conway	.40
9	Michael Irvin	.50
10	Shannon Sharpe	.35
11	Pat Swilling	.25
12	John Parrella	.05
13	Mel Gray	.05
14	Ray Childress	.05
15	Willie Davis	.05
16	Raghib Ismail	.45
17	Jim Everett	.20
18	Mark Higgs	.05
19	Trace Armstrong	.05
20	Jim Kelly	.60
21	Rob Burnett	.05
22	Jay Novacek	.35
23	Robert Delpino	.05
24	Brett Perriman	.05
25	Troy Aikman	2.00
26	Reggie White	.30
27	Lorenzo White	.05
28	Bubba McDowell	.05
29	Steve Emtman	.05
30	Brett Favre	4.00
31	Derek Russell	.05
32	Jeff Hostetler	.20
33	Henry Ellard	.05
34	Jack Del Rio	.05
35	Mike Saxon	.05
36	Rickey Jackson	.05
37	Phil Simms	.25
38	Quinn Early	.05
39	Russell Copeland	.05
40	Carl Pickens	.25
41	Lance Gunn	.05
42	Bernie Kosar	.05
43	John Elway	1.00
44	George Teague	.30
45	Nick Lowery	.25
46	Haywood Jeffires	.25
47	Will Shields	.05
48	Daryl Johnson	.20
49	Pete Metzelaars	.05
50	Warren Moon	.25
51	Cornelius Bennett	.20
52	Vinny Testaverde	.20
53	*John Mangun*	.05
54	Tommy Vardell	.25
55	*Lincoln Coleman*	.60
56	Karl Mecklenburg	.05
57	Jackie Harris	.20
58	Curtis Duncan	.05
59	Quentin Coryatt	.25
60	Tim Brown	.35
61	Irving Fryar	.30
62	Sean Gilbert	.25
63	Qadry Ismail	.25
64	Irv Smith	.25
65	Mark Jackson	.05
66	Ronnie Lott	.20
67	Henry Jones	.05
68	Horace Copeland	.25
69	John Copeland	.05
70	Mark Carrier	.05
71	Michael Jackson	.25
72	Jason Elam	.20
73	Rod Bernstine	.20
74	Wayne Simmons	.25
75	Cody Carlson	.05
76	Alexander Wright	.05
77	Shane Conlan	.05
78	Keith Jackson	.25
79	Sean Salisbury	.05
80	Vaughan Johnson	.05
81	Rob Moore	.05
82	Andre Reed	.30
83	David Klingler	.35
84	Jim Harbaugh	.05
85	*John Jett*	.30
86	Sterling Sharpe	.25
87	Webster Slaughter	.20
88	J.J. Birden	.05
89	O.J. McDuffie	.60
90	Andre Tippett	.05
91	Don Beebe	.05
92	Mark Stepnoski	.05
93	Neil Smith	.20
94	Terry Kirby	.85
95	Wade Wilson	.05
96	Darryl Talley	.05
97	Anthony Smith	.05
98	Willie Roaf	.25
99	Mo Lewis	.05
100	James Washington	.05
101	Nate Odomes	.05
102	Chris Gedney	.05
103	Joe Walter	.05
104	Alvin Harper	.20
105	Simon Fletcher	.25
106	Rodney Peete	.05
107	Terrell Buckley	.05
108	Jeff George	.30
109	James Jett	.50
110	Tony Casillas	.05
111	Marco Coleman	.05
112	Anthony Carter	.05
113	Lincoln Kennedy	.20
114	Chris Calloway	.05
115	Randall Cunningham	.20
116	Steve Beuerlein	.25
117	Neil O'Donnell	.30
118	Stan Humphries	.05
119	John Taylor	.20
120	Cortez Kennedy	.20
121	Santana Dotson	.05
122	Thomas Smith	.05
123	Kevin Williams	.30
124	Andre Ware	.05
125	Ethan Horton	.05
126	Mike Sherrard	.05
127	Fred Barnett	.05
128	Ricky Proehl	.05
129	Kevin Greene	.05
130	John Carney	.05
131	Tim McDonald	.25
132	Rick Mirer	.75
133	Blair Thomas	.05
134	Hardy Nickerson	.05
135	Heath Sherman	.05
136	Andre Hastings	.05
137	Randal Hill	.05
138	Mike Cofer	.05
139	Brian Blades	.05
140	Earnest Byner	.05
141	Bill Bates	.05
142	Junior Seau	.20
143	Johnny Bailey	.05
144	Dwight Stone	.05
145	Todd Kelly	.05
146	Tyrone Montgomery	.05
147	Herschel Walker	.05
148	Gary Clark	.05
149	Eric Green	.20
150	Steve Young	2.00
151	Anthony Miller	.25
152	Dana Stubblefield	.50
153	*Dean Wells*	.50
154	Vincent Brisby	.60
155	Chris Chandler	.05
156	Clyde Simmons	.05
157	Rod Woodson	.20
158	Nate Lewis	.05
159	Martin Harrison	.05
160	Kelvin Martin	.05
161	Craig Erickson	.25
162	Johnny Mitchell	.20
163	Calvin Williams	.20
164	Deon Figures	.30
165	Tom Rathman	.05
166	Rick Hamilton	.05
167	John L. Williams	.05
168	Demetrius Dubose	.05
169	Michael Brooks	.05
170	Marion Butts	.30
171	Brent Jones	.20
172	Bobby Hebert	.20
173	Brad Edwards	.05
174	Dave Wyman	.05
175	Herman Moore	1.00
176	Leroy Butler	.20
177	Reggie Langhorne	.05
178	Dave Krieg	.05
179	Patrick Bates	.05
180	Erik Kramer	.05
181	Troy Drayton	.30
182	David Meggett	.05
183	Eric Allen	.30
184	Mark Bavaro	.05
185	Leslie O'Neal	.25
186	Jerry Rice	2.00
187	Desmond Howard	.25
188	Deion Sanders	1.00
189	Bill Maas	.05
190	Frank Wycheck	.05
191	Ernest Givins	.25
192	Terry McDaniel	.05
193	Bryan Cox	.20
194	Guy McIntyre	.05
195	Pierce Holt	.05
196	Fred Stokes	.05
197	Mike Pritchard	.25
198	Terry Obee	.05
199	Mark Collins	.05
200	Drew Bledsoe	3.00
201	Barry Wood	.05
202	Derrick Lassic	.35
203	Chris Spielman	.05
204	*John Jurkovic*	.25
205	Ken Norton Jr.	.05
206	Dale Carter	.20
207	Chris Doleman	.25
208	Keith Hamilton	.05
209	Andy Harmon	.05
210	John Friesz	.05
211	Steve Bono	.20
212	Mark Rypien	.05
213	Ricky Sanders	.05
214	Michael Haynes	.35
215	Todd McNair	.05
216	Leon Lett	.05
217	Scott Mitchell	.50
218	*Mike Morris*	.05
219	Darrin Smith	.05
220	Jim McMahon	.05
221	Garrison Hearst	1.50
222	Leroy Thompson	.05
223	Darren Carrington	.05
224	Pete Stoyanovich	.05
225	Chris Miller	.20
226	Bruce Smith	.30
227	Simon Fletcher	.30
228	Reggie White	.20
229	Neil Smith	.20
230	Chris Doleman	.20
231	Keith Hamilton	.05
232	Dana Stubblefield	.20
233	Erric Pegram	.40
234	Thurman Thomas	.50
235	Lewis Tillman	.05
236	Harold Green	.05
237	Eric Metcalf	.20
238	Emmitt Smith	4.00
239	Glyn Milburn	.20
240	Barry Sanders	3.00
241	Edgar Bennett	.20
242	Gary Brown	.20
243	Rossevelt Potts	.05
244	Marcus Allen	.25
245	Greg Robinson	.05
246	Jerome Bettis	.75
247	Keith Byars	.05
248	Robert Smith	.50
249	Leonard Russell	.20
250	Derek Brown	.55
251	Rodney Hampton	.55
252	Johnny Johnson	.05
253	Vaughn Hebron	.05
254	Ron Moore	.40
255	Barry Foster	.50
256	Natrone Means	.75
257	Ricky Watters	.30
258	Chris Warren	.05
259	Vince Workman	.05
260	Reggie Brooks	.30
261	Carolina Panthers	.20
262	Jacksonville Jaguars	.20
263	Troy Aikman	1.75
264	Barry Sanders	1.50
265	Emmitt Smith	2.00
266	Michael Irvin	.40
267	Jerry Rice	1.00
268	Shannon Sharpe	.25
269	Bob Kratch	.05
270	Howard Ballard	.05
271	Eric Williams	.05
272	Guy McIntyre	.05
273	Kelvin Williams	.25
274	Mel Gray	.05
275	Eddie Murray	.05
276	Mark Stepnoski	.05
277	Tommy Barnhardt	.05
278	Derrick Thomas	.30
279	Ken Norton Jr.	.20
280	Chris Spielman	.05
281	Deion Sanders	.75
282	Mark Collins	.05
283	Bruce Smith	.20
284	Reggie White	.20
285	Sean Gilbert	.25
286	Cortez Kennedy	.20
287	Steve Atwater	.05
288	Tim McDonald	.05
289	Jerome Bettis	.75
290	Dana Stubblefield	.20
291	*Bert Emanuel*	.75
292	*Jeff Burris*	.30
293	*Bucky Brooks*	.65
294	*Dan Wilkinson*	.85
295	*Darnay Scott*	.75
296	*Derrick Alexander*	.75
297	*Antonio Langham*	.50
298	*Shante Carver*	.40
299	*Shelby Hill*	.25
300	*Larry Allen*	.30
301	*Johnnie Morton*	.75
302	*Van Malone*	.25
303	*Aaron Taylor*	.35
304	*Marshall Faulk*	8.00
305	*Eric Mahlum*	.25
306	*Trev Alberts*	.90
307	*Greg Hill*	.50
308	*Donnell Bennett*	.30
309	*Rob Fredrickson*	.25
310	*James Folston*	.25
311	*Isaac Bruce*	5.00
312	*Tim Ruddy*	.25
313	*Aubrey Beavers*	.25
314	*David Palmer*	.50
315	*DeWayne Washington*	.45
316	*Willie McGinest*	.50
317	*Mario Bates*	.30
318	*Kevin Lee*	.50
319	*Jason Sehorn*	.05
320	*Thomas Randolph*	.35
321	*Ryan Yarborough*	.40
322	*Bernard Williams*	.25
323	*Chuck Levy*	.75
324	*Jamir Miller*	.50
325	*Charles Johnson*	.50
326	*Bryant Young*	.35
327	*William Floyd*	.50
328	*Kevin Mitchell*	.25
329	*Sam Adams*	.50
330	*Kevin Mawae*	.05
331	*Errict Rhett*	.75
332	*Trent Dilfer*	1.00
333	*Heath Shuler*	.50
334	*Aaron Glenn*	.40
335	*Todd Steussie*	.30
336	*Toby Wright*	.05

1994 Playoff Jerome Bettis

1993 NFL Rookie of the Year Jerome Bettis is featured in this five-card insert set. Cards devoted to the Los Angeles Rams running back were random inserts in 1994 Playoff hobby packs. Each card front has a color action photo against a silver foil background which has Bettis' name written on it in several different typefaces. The "1994 Playoff Collection" logo is also on the front, in the lower right corner. The yellow backs have biographical information about Bettis, and the card title, plus a card number.

		NM/M
Complete Set (5):		20.00
Common Bettis:		4.00
1	Jerome Bettis	4.00
2	Jerome Bettis	4.00
3	Jerome Bettis	4.00
4	Jerome Bettis	4.00
5	Jerome Bettis	4.00

1994 Playoff Checklists

Full-bleed metallic color photos dominate the front, with the featured player's highlights printed inside a silver box at the bottom center. The card backs, numbered "of 10," highlight a portion of the set's checklists. The cards were randomly seeded.

		NM/M
Complete Set (10):		5.00
Common Player:		.50
1	Keith Cash	.50
2	Kerry Cash	.50
3	Qadry Ismail	.75
4	Rocket Ismail	.75
5	Bruce Matthews	.50
6	Clay Matthews	.50
7	Shannon Sharpe	1.00
8	Sterling Sharpe	1.00
9	John Taylor	.50
10	Keith Taylor	.50

1994 Playoff Club

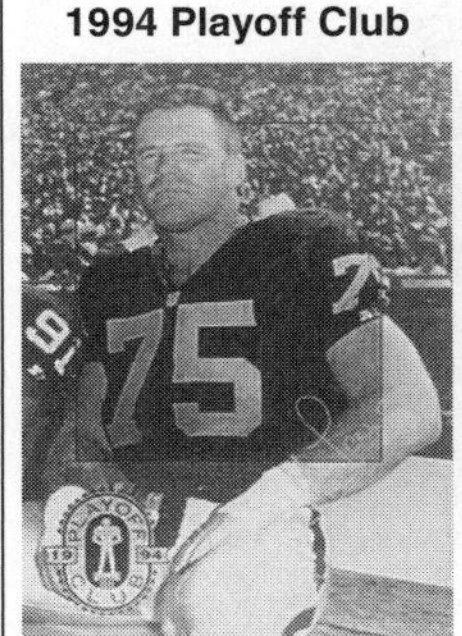

These inserts, randomly included in 1994 Playoff packs, feature six future Hall of Famers. Each card has a borderless front with a metallic action photo. The set logo appears at the bottom of the card, along with a facsimile autograph. The card back is white and has the player's name and a career summary. Backs are numbered with a "PC" prefix.

		NM/M
Complete Set (6):		35.00
Commom Player:		2.75
8	Jerry Rice	20.00
9	Marcus Allen	5.00
10	Howie Long	5.00
11	Clay Matthews	2.75
12	Richard Dent	2.75
13	Morten Andersen	2.75

1994 Playoff Headliners Redemption

In exchange for a redemption card, a collector would receive this six-card set. Card fronts have a prism effect, with the player's name and Headliners' logo printed at the bottom. Showcased on the horizontal card back is a headshot of the player, his name and an explanation of his 1994 milestone.

		NM/M
Complete Set (6):		12.00
Common Player:		1.00
1	Tim Brown	3.00
2	Bernie Parmalee	1.00
3	Sterling Sharpe	3.00
4	Natrone Means	2.00
5	Alvin Harper	1.00
6	Deion Sanders	4.00
NNO	Headliners Redemption	.50

1994 Playoff Jerry Rice

San Francisco 49er wide receiver Jerry Rice is featured in this five-card insert set. Cards were randomly included in 1994 Playoff retail display packs. The card front has a color action photo against a foil background, plus a "1994 Playoff Collection" logo. The card back has another photo and career summary, plus a card number.

		NM/M
Complete Set (5):		50.00
Common Rice:		10.00
1	Jerry Rice Born to Run	10.00
2	Jerry Rice All American	10.00
3	Jerry Rice The 49ers Start the Dynasty	10.00
4	Jerry Rice The Offensive Player of the Year (Again)	10.00
5	Jerry Rice Breaking Jim Brown's Record	10.00

1994 Playoff Rookie Roundup Redemption

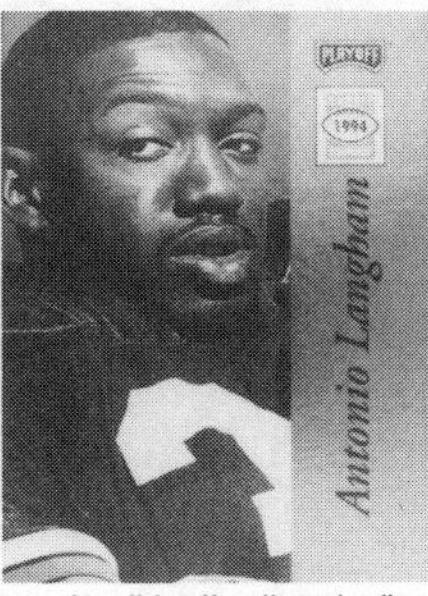

A mail-in offer allowed collectors to exchange the redemption card for this nine-card set. The exchange card was randomly seeded in packs. Card fronts have a photo of the player, with a team-colored border on either side of the card.

Located on the horizontal backs are a full-bleed photo, with his name and biographical information printed inside boxes. This offer expired Dec. 31, 1995.

		NM/M
Complete Set (9):		20.00
Common Player:		1.00
1	Heath Shuler	1.00
2	David Palmer	1.00
3	Dan Wilkinson	1.00
4	Marshall Faulk	10.00
5	Charlie Garner	4.00
6	Errict Rhett	4.00
7	Trent Dilfer	5.00
8	Antonio Langham	1.00
9	Gus Frerotte	1.00
NNO	Redemption Card	.50

1994 Playoff Barry Sanders

Detroit Lions running back Barry Sanders is highlighted in this five-card insert set. Cards were randomly included in Playoff's Four Star Edition of the set. These sets were distributed to selected hobby stores, Wal-Mart, Books-A-Million, Walden Books and other retail stores.

		NM/M
Complete Set (5):		50.00
Common Sanders:		10.00
1	Barry Sanders	10.00
2	Barry Sanders	10.00
3	Barry Sanders	10.00
4	Barry Sanders	10.00
5	Barry Sanders	10.00

1994 Playoff Super Bowl Redemption

This six-card set, which featured Dallas players, was traded to collectors in exchange for a redemption card through a mail-in offer. The redemption card was randomly seeded in packs. A Super Bowl Playoff logo, along with the player's name, are printed at the top of the full-bleed card fronts. The horizontal card backs have the Super Bowl Playoff logo, Cowboys and Bills helmets and the player's Super Bowl accomplishments.

		NM/M
Complete Set (6):		15.00
Common Player:		1.00
1	Troy Aikman	5.00
2	Emmitt Smith	8.00
3	Leon Lett	1.00
4	Michael Irvin	3.00
5	James Washington	1.00
6	Darrin Smith	1.00
NNO	Super Bowl Redemption	1.00

1994 Playoff Julie Bell Art Redemption

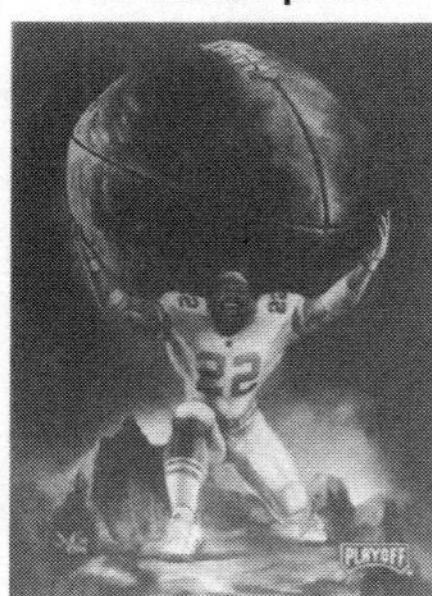

Fantasy artist Julie Bell used her talents to create this six-card set,featuring players in superhuman poses. The fronts are borderless, with a Playoff logo. The backs have a repeat of a portion of the artwork, along with a quote from Bell. "Julie Bell's Fantasy Football" is printed at the top. The set was available as a mail-in offer with a redemption found randomly inserted in packs.

		NM/M
Complete Set (6):		20.00
Common Player:		2.00
1	Emmitt Smith	10.00
2	Marcus Allen	2.00
3	Junior Seau	3.00
4	Barry Sanders	5.00
5	Rick Mirer	2.00
6	Sterling Sharpe	2.00

1994 Playoff Super Bowl Promos

To commemorate Super Bowl XXVIII, Playoff produced this six-card set. The full-bleed fronts have the player's name and the Playoff logo printed in an oval at the bottom of the card. The white card backs, numbered "of 6 promo," showcase the Super Bowl XXVIII logo in the center.

		NM/M
Complete Set (6):		16.00
Common Player:		1.50
1	Jerry Rice	6.00
2	Daryl Johnston	1.50
3	Herschel Walker	1.50
4	Reggie White	2.50
5	Scott Mitchell	2.00
6	Thurman Thomas	2.50

1994 Playoff Contenders Promos

This seven-card set gave collectors a glimpse of what the 1994 Playoff Contenders set would look like. The city name of the player's team was printed at the top of the card fronts, with the player's name in silver foil on a green border at the bottom. The Playoff Contenders' logo is also included at the bottom. The unnumbered card backs have a headshot of the player, with his highlights printed below. The NFL's 75th anniversary logo is located above the write-up.

		NM/M
Complete Set (7):		10.00
Common Player:		1.00
1	Qadry Ismail	2.50
2	Daryl Johnston	1.50
3	John Jurkovic	1.00
4	Eric Metcalf	2.00
5	Andre Reed	1.50
6	Calvin Williams	1.00
7	Title Card	1.00

1994 Playoff Contenders

This 120-card set uses Playoff's patented, ink-on-foil Tekchrome printing process. Fronts capture the player in an intense game action photo. A grass strip at the bottom contains the player's name; his team's name is at the top of the card. A set logo appears in the lower right corner. The card back has a close-up shot of the player, which takes up two-thirds of the card. A blue strip at the bottom of the card contains some biographical information. The entire background is grey marble. A 27-card Draft Pick subset is contained within the main set. There were also four insert sets produced - 75th Anniversary Throwbacks, Rookie Contenders, Sophomore Contenders and Back-To-Backs.

		NM/M
Complete Set (120):		20.00
Common Player:		.10
Minor Stars:		.30
Pack (7):		3.25
Wax Box (24):		55.00
1	Drew Bledsoe	3.00
2	Barry Sanders	3.00
3	Jerry Rice	3.00
4	Rod Woodson	.30
5	Irving Fryar	.10
6	Charles Haley	.10
7	Chris Warren	.30
8	Craig Erickson	.10
9	Eric Metcalf	.10
10	Marcus Allen	.30
11	Chris Miller, Charles Johnson	.10
12	Andre Rison	.30
13	Art Monk	.30
14	Calvin Williams	.10
15	Shannon Sharpe, Bryant Young	.10
16	Rodney Hampton	.30
17	Marion Butts	.10
18	John Jurkovic	.50
19	Jim Kelly	.30
20	Emmitt Smith	5.00
21	Jeff Hostetler	.30
22	Barry Foster	.30
23	Boomer Esiason	.30
24	Jim Harbaugh	.10
25	Joe Montana	3.00
26	Jeff George	.50
27	Warren Moon	.30
28	Steve Young	3.00
29	Randall Cunningham	.30
30	Shawn Jefferson	.10
31	Cortez Kennedy	.30
32	Reggie Brooks	.10
33	Alvin Harper	.30
34	Brent Jones	.10
35	O.J. McDuffie	.40
36	Jerome Bettis	1.00
37	Daryl Johnston	.10
38	Herman Moore	1.00
39	Dave Meggett	.10
40	Reggie White	.30
41	Junior Seau	.50
42	Dan Marino	5.00
43	Scott Mitchell	.10
44	John Elway	4.00
45	Troy Aikman	3.00
46	Terry Allen	.10
47	David Klingler	.10
48	Stan Humphries	.40
49	Rick Mirer	.30
50	Neil O'Donnell	.30
51	Keith Jackson	.10
52	Ricky Watters	.30
53	Dave Brown	.30
54	Neil Smith	.10
55	Johnny Mitchell	.10
56	Jackie Harris	.10
57	Terry Kirby	.10
58	Willie Davis	.10
59	Rob Moore	.10
60	Nate Newton	.10
61	Deion Sanders	2.00
62	John Taylor	.10
63	Sterling Sharpe	.30
64	Natrone Means	.50
65	Steve Beuerlein	.10
66	Erik Kramer	.10
67	Qadry Ismail	.10
68	Johnny Johnson	.10
69	Herschel Walker	.10
70	Mark Stepnoski	.10
71	Brett Favre	5.00
72	Dana Stubblefield	.10
73	Bruce Smith	.10
74	Leroy Hoard	.10
75	Steve Walsh	.10
76	Jay Novacek	.10
77	Derrick Thomas	.30
78	Keith Byars	.10
79	Ben Coates	.40
80	Lorenzo Neal	.10
81	Ronnie Lott	.10
82	Tim Brown	.30
83	Michael Irvin	.50
84	Ron Moore	.10
85	Andre Reed	.30
86	James Jett	.10
87	Curtis Conway	.10
88	*Bernie Parmalee*	.30
89	Keith Cash	.10
90	Russell Copeland	.10
91	Kevin Williams	.50
92	Gary Brown	.10
93	Thurman Thomas	.50
94	*Jamir Miller*	.30
95	*Bert Emanuel*	1.00
96	*Buck Brooks*	.50
97	*Jeff Burris*	.50
98	*Antonio Langham*	.50
99	*Derrick Alexander*	.50
100	*Dan Wilkinson*	.50
101	*Shante Carver*	.40
102	*Johnnie Morton*	.75
103	*LeShon Johnson*	.50
104	*Marshall Faulk*	6.00
105	*Greg Hill*	.50
106	*Lake Dawson*	.30
107	*Irving Spikes*	.50
108	*David Palmer*	.50
109	*Willie McGinest*	.50
110	*Joe Johnson*	.30
111	*Aaron Glenn*	.30
112	*Charlie Garner*	3.00
113	*Charles Johnson*	.50
114	*Byron Bam Morris*	.50
115	*Bryant Young*	.75
116	*William Floyd*	.50
117	*Trent Dilfer*	3.00
118	*Errict Rhett*	1.00
119	*Heath Shuler*	.50
120	*Gus Frerotte*	.50

1994 Playoff Contenders Back-to-Back

Each card in this 60-card insert set shows two card fronts from the 120 regular cards. The card fronts are matched up so that two key players from the same position appear on the card. Team names and Playoff Contenders logos are foil stamped on the cards, and the photos are embossed, meaning they are raised up off the card.

		NM/M
Common Player:		4.00
Minor Stars:		10.00
Inserted 1:24		
1	Joe Montana, Dan Marino	50.00
2	Drew Bledsoe, John Elway	40.00
3	Jerry Rice, Sterling Sharpe	40.00
4	Barry Sanders, Emmitt Smith	50.00
5	Troy Aikman, Steve Young	40.00
6	Erik Kramer, Steve Walsh	4.00
7	Nate Newton, Bruce Smith	4.00
8	Johnny Mitchell, Aaron Glenn	4.00
9	Neil O'Donnell, Charles Johnson	4.00
10	Herman Moore, Calvin Williams	6.00
11	Alvin Harper, Michael Irvin	10.00
12	Jim Harbaugh, Curtis Conway	10.00
13	Brett Favre, LeShon Johnson	45.00
14	Marshall Faulk, Eric Metcalf	25.00
15	Qadry Ismail, David Palmer	4.00
16	Deion Sanders, Andre Rison	10.00
17	Jackie Harris, Errict Rhett	4.00
18	Keith Jackson, Keith Byars	4.00
19	Dave Meggett, Jeff Burris	4.00
20	Dana Stubblefield, William Floyd	4.00
21	Randall Cunningham, Reggie White	15.00
22	Shannon Sharpe, Keith Cash	15.00
23	Marcus Allen, Greg Hill	10.00
24	Irving Fryar, Russell Copeland	4.00
25	Johnny Johnson, Willie McGinest	4.00
26	John Taylor, Brent Jones	4.00
27	Terry Kirby, Bernie Parmalee	4.00
28	Ricky Watters, Ronnie Lott	15.00
29	Scott Mitchell, Johnnie Morton	4.00
30	O.J. McDuffie, Irving Spikes	4.00
31	Shawn Jefferson, Andre Reed	4.00
32	Rodney Hampton, Lorenzo Neal	4.00
33	Chris Miller, Joe Johnson	4.00
34	Charles Haley, Thurman Thomas	12.00
35	Herschel Walker, Charlie Garner	4.00
36	Natrone Means, Stan Humphries	6.00
37	Willie Davis, Lake Dawson	4.00
38	Dave Brown, Gary Brown	4.00
39	Jerome Bettis, Terry Allen	15.00
40	Cortez Kennedy, Junior Seau	8.00
41	David Klingler, Derrick Alexander	4.00
42	Chris Warren, Bucky Brooks	4.00
43	Mark Stepnoski, Kevin Williams	4.00
44	Steve Beuerlein, Ron Moore	4.00
45	Rob Moore, James Jett	4.00
46	Neil Smith, Derrick Thomas	4.00
47	Rick Mirer, Bryant Young	4.00
48	Daryl Johnston, Jay Novacek	4.00
49	Reggie Brooks, Gus Frerotte	4.00
50	Barry Foster, Byron "Bam" Morris	4.00
51	Art Monk, Heath Shuler	4.00
52	Craig Erickson, Trent Dilfer	10.00
53	Jeff George, Bert Emanuel	4.00
54	Rod Woodson, Antonio Langham	4.00
55	Marion Butts, Ben Coates	4.00
56	John Jurkovic, Dan Wilkinson	4.00
57	Jim Kelly, Shante Carver	15.00
58	Jeff Hostetler, Tim Brown	8.00
59	Boomer Esiason, Jamir Miller	8.00
60	Warren Moon, Terry Allen	12.00

1994 Playoff Contenders Rookie Contenders

Six first-year standouts are showcased in this 1994 Playoff Contenders insert set, which combines three different foil effects. Each card has a split background, with the left side having a glittery silver foil and the right side having a purple foil. The player's name is written in silver foil within the purple foil. Above his name is a Rookie Contender logo stamped in foil. Below his name is a Playoff logo. These cards are inserted one per 48 packs.

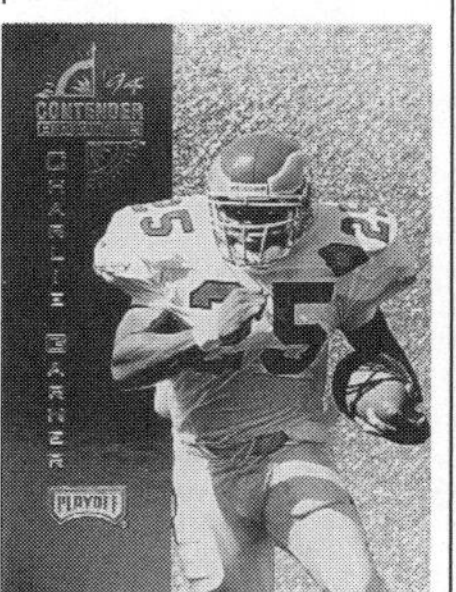

		NM/M
Complete Set (6):		40.00
Common Player:		1.00
Minor Stars:		5.00
1	Marshall Faulk	25.00
2	Charles Garner	5.00
3	Trent Dilfer	5.00
4	Heath Shuler	1.00
5	Dan Wilkinson	1.00
6	David Palmer	1.00

1994 Playoff Contenders Sophomore Contenders

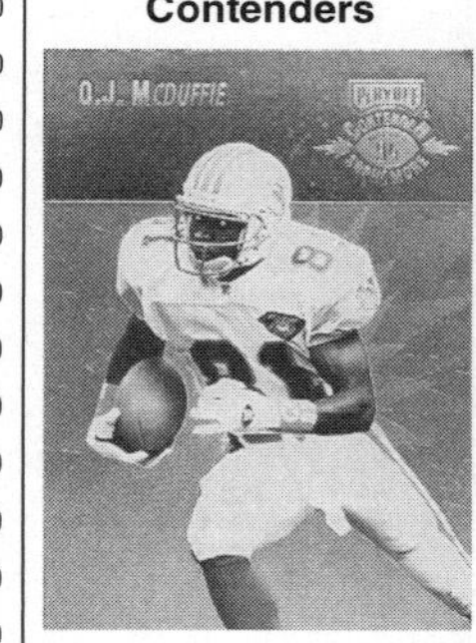

Six of the top second-year NFL players are featured on these insert cards, available at a rate of one per 48 packs. These cards feature a foil-etched burst-pattern design. The top one third of the card has a purple prism design. It has the player's name on the left and a Sophomore Contenders logo on the right, both in silver foil. The bottom two-thirds has the player on a silver burst-patterned background.

		NM/M
Complete Set (6):		20.00
Common Player:		1.00
1	Drew Bledsoe	10.00
2	Jerome Bettis	5.00
3	Natrone Means	2.00
4	Rick Mirer	1.00
5	Reggie Brooks	1.00
6	O.J. McDuffie	2.00

1994 Playoff Contenders Throwbacks

This 30-card insert set shows at least one star from each NFL team in his "Throwback" uniform. The front shows the player in a foil-enhanced background. A strip across the bottom contains the player's name in silver foil, with an NFL Throwback Week logo centered on this strip. These cards were randomly included in Playoff Contender packs at a ratio of one per 12 packs.

		NM/M
Complete Set (30):		75.00
Common Player:		.50
1	Larry Centers	.50
2	Andre Rison	.50
3	Jim Kelly	4.00
4	Curtis Conway	.50
5	David Klingler	.50
6	Vinny Testaverde	.50
7	Troy Aikman	8.00
8	Emmitt Smith	10.00
9	John Elway	8.00
10	Barry Sanders	10.00
11	Sterling Sharpe	4.00
12	Gary Brown	.50
13	Jim Harbaugh	.50
14	Joe Montana	10.00
15	Tim Brown	4.00
16	Chris Miller	.50
17	Dan Marino	12.00
18	Terry Allen	.50
19	Marion Butts	.50
20	Jim Everett	.50
21	Dave Brown	.50
22	Johnny Johnson	.50
23	Randall Cunningham	.50
24	Barry Foster	.50
25	Stan Humphries	1.00
26	Jerry Rice	8.00
27	Steve Young	8.00
28	Chris Warren	1.00
29	Errict Rhett	.50
30	John Freisz	.50

1995 Playoff Absolute-Prime

Playoff's 1995 200-card football set was released in two different designs - a hobby version (Absolute) and a totally different retail version (Prime). The hobby-only Absolute features a Pigskins Preview insert set devoted to six NFC players, a Quad Series parallel set (four players per card), and Die-Cut Helmets. Common to both Absolute and Prime packs are Unsung Heroes and First Draft Picks for the two new expansion teams - Jacksonville and Carolina. Playoff Prime has the remaining six Pigskin Preview cards, which are devoted to AFC players. Draft Picks cards are a subset of the regular set.

		NM/M
Complete Absolute Set (200):		20.00
Common Absolute Player:		.05
Minor Absolute Stars:		.30
Prime Cards:		.5X
Absolute Pack (8):		1.00
Absolute Box (24):		20.00
Prime Pack (8):		.75
Prime Wax Box (24):		15.00
1	John Elway	.50
2	Reggie White	.30
3	Errict Rhett	.30
4	Deion Sanders	.75
5	Raghib Ismail	.05
6	Jerome Bettis	.30
7	Randall Cunningham	.05
8	Mario Bates	.50
9	Dave Brown	.05
10	Stan Humphries	.30
11	Drew Bledsoe	1.50
12	Neil O'Donnell	.30
13	Dan Marino	3.00
14	Larry Centers	.05
15	Craig Heyward	.05
16	Bruce Smith	.05
17	Erik Kramer	.05
18	*Jeff Blake*	.50
19	Vinny Testaverde	.05
20	Barry Sanders	2.00
21	Boomer Esiason	.05
22	Emmitt Smith	3.00
23	Warren Moon	.30
24	Junior Seau	.30
25	Heath Shuler	.50
26	Jackie Harris	.05
27	Terance Mathis	.05
28	Raymont Harris	.05
29	Jim Kelly	.30
30	Dan Wilkinson	.05
31	Herman Moore	.50
32	Shannon Sharpe	.05
33	Antonio Langham	.05
34	Charles Haley	.05
35	Brett Favre	3.00
36	Marshall Faulk	.30
37	Neil Smith	.05
38	Harvey Williams	.05
39	Johnny Bailey	.05
40	O.J. McDuffie	.05
41	David Palmer	.05
42	Willie McGinest	.05
43	Quinn Early	.05
44	Johnny Johnson	.05
45	Derek Brown	.05
46	Charlie Garner	.05
47	Bam Morris	.30
48	Natrone Means	.30
49	Ken Norton	.05
50	Troy Aikman	1.25
51	Reggie Brooks	.05
52	Trent Dilfer	.50
53	Cortez Kennedy	.05
54	Chuck Levy	.05
55	Jeff George	.30
56	Steve Young	1.25
57	Lewis Tillman	.05
58	Carl Pickens	.30
59	Brett Perriman	.05
60	Jay Novacek	.05
61	Greg Hill	.30
62	James Jett	.05
63	Terry Kirby	.05
64	Qadry Ismail	.05
65	Ben Coates	.05
66	Kevin Greene	.05
67	Bryant Young	.05
68	Brian Mitchell	.05
69	Steve Walsh	.05
70	Darnay Scott	.75
71	Daryl Johnston	.05
72	Glyn Milburn	.05
73	Tim Brown	.30
74	Isaac Bruce	.50
75	Bernie Parmalee	.30
76	Terry Allen	.05
77	Jim Everett	.05
78	Thomas Lewis	.05
79	Vaughn Hebron	.05
80	Rod Woodson	.05
81	Rick Mirer	.40
82	Dana Stubblefield	.05
83	Bert Emanuel	.50
84	Andre Reed	.05
85	Jeff Graham	.05
86	Johnnie Morton	.05
87	LeShon Johnson	.05
88	Michael Irvin	.40
89	Derrick Alexander	.05
90	Lake Dawson	.50
91	Cody Carlson	.05
92	Chris Warren	.30
93	William Floyd	.50
94	Charles Johnson	.30
95	Roosevelt Potts	.05
96	Cris Carter	.30
97	Aaron Glenn	.05
98	Curtis Conway	.30
99	Kevin Williams	.05
100	Jerry Rice	1.25
101	Frank Reich	.05
102	Harold Green	.05
103	Russell Copeland	.05
104	Rob Moore	.05
105	Edgar Bennett	.05
106	Darren Carrington	.05
107	Tommy Maddox	.05
108	Dave Meggett	.05
109	Fred Barnett	.05
110	Mark Seay	.05
111	Gus Frerotte	.50
112	Brent Jones	.05
113	Chris Miller	.05
114	Cedric Tillman	.05
115	Mark Ingram	.05
116	Eric Turner	.05
117	Mark Carrier	.05
118	Garrison Hearst	.30
119	Craig Erickson	.05
120	Derek Russell	.05
121	Mike Sherrard	.05
122	Horace Copeland	.05
123	Jack Trudeau	.05
124	Leroy Hoard	.05
125	Gary Brown	.05
126	Mel Gray	.05
127	Steve Beuerlein	.05
128	Marcus Allen	.30
129	Irving Fryar	.05
130	Marion Butts	.05
131	Ricky Watters	.30
132	Tony Martin	.05
133	Lawrence Dawsey	.05
134	Ronnie Harmon	.05
135	Herschel Walker	.05
136	Michael Haynes	.05
137	Eric Green	.05
138	Steve Bono	.40
139	Jamir Miller	.05
140	Rod Smith	.05
141	Andre Rison	.30
142	Eric Metcalf	.05
143	Michael Timpson	.05
144	Cornelius Bennett	.05
145	Sean Dawkins	.30
146	Scott Mitchell	.05
147	Ray Childress	.05
148	Jim Harbaugh	.30
149	Reggie Cobb	.05
150	Willie Roaf	.05
151	Stevie Anderson	.05
152	Barry Foster	.05
153	Joe Montana	2.00
154	David Klingler	.05
155	Chris Chandler	.05
156	Carnell Lake	.05
157	Calvin Williams	.05
158	Kenneth Davis	.05
159	Tydus Winans	.05
160	Sam Adams	.05
161	Ron Moore	.05
162	Vincent Brisby	.05
163	Alvin Harper	.05
164	Jake Reed	.05
165	Jeff Hostetler	.05
166	Mark Brunell	1.50
167	Leonard Russell	.05
168	Greg Truitt	.05
169	Pete Metzelaars	.05
170	Dave Krieg	.05
171	Lorenzo White	.05
172	Robert Brooks	.30
173	Willie Davis	.05
174	Irving Spikes	.05
175	Rodney Hampton	.05
176	Eric Pegram	.05
177	Brian Blades	.05
178	Shawn Jefferson	.05
179	Tyrone Poole	.05
180	*Rob Johnson*	3.00
181	*Ki-Jana Carter*	1.00
182	*Steve McNair*	5.00
183	*Michael Westbrook*	1.00
184	*Kerry Collins*	2.00
185	*Kevin Carter*	.30
186	*Tony Boselli*	.30
187	*Joey Galloway*	3.00
188	*Kyle Brady*	.50
189	*J.J. Stokes*	1.00
190	*Warren Sapp*	.75
191	*Tyrone Wheatley*	.75
192	*Napoleon Kaufman*	.50
193	*James Stewart*	2.00
194	*Rashaan Salaam*	.50
195	*Ray Zellars*	.75
196	*Todd Collins*	.75
197	*Sherman Williams*	.50
198	*Frank Sanders*	1.00
199	*Terrell Fletcher*	.50
200	*Chad May*	.50
DP1	Tony Boselli Draft	1.00
DP2	Kerry Collins Draft	5.00

1995 Playoff Unsung Heroes

These 28 cards were inserted in both 1995 Playoff Absolute and Prime packs, one per 13 packs. The card front has a color photo of the player against a football field pattern. "Unsung Heroes" and the Playoff logo are stamped in gold in the upper corners. The player's name is in the lower left corner. The card back has goal posts which have a brief recap of the player's 1994 season between them.

		NM/M
Complete Set (28):		15.00
Common Player:		.25
Minor Stars:		1.00
1	Garth Jax	.25
2	Craig Heyward	.25
3	Steve Tasker	.25
4	Raymont Harris	.25
5	Jeff Blake	1.00
6	Bob Dahl	.25
7	Jason Garrett	.25
8	Gary Zimmerman	.25
9	Tom Beer	.25
10	John Jurkovic	.25
11	Spencer Tillman	.25
12	Devon McDonald	.25
13	John Alt	.25
14	Steve Wisniewski	.25
15	Tim Bowens	.25
16	Amp Lee	.25
17	Todd Rucci	.25
18	Tyrone Hughes	.25
19	Michael Strahan	.25
20	Brad Baxter	.25
21	Mark Bavaro	.25
22	Yancy Thigpen	.50
23	Courtney Hall	.25
24	Eric Davis	.25
25	Rufus Porter	.25
26	Jackie Slater	.25
27	Courtney Hawkins	.25
28	Gus Frerotte	.40

1995 Playoff Absolute Die Cut Helmets

These die-cut cards feature all 30 teams with a star player from each club on a clear plastic card. The front has a color photo of the player against a background of his team's helmet. His name appears in the lower right corner. The back of the card, numbered using an "HDC" prefix, has a white outline of the helmet and photo depicted on the front. These inserts were randomly included in hobby-only 1995 Playoff Absolute Packs, one per 25.

		NM/M
Complete Set (30):		100.00
Common Player:		1.00
Minor Stars:		3.00
1	Garrison Hearst	3.00
2	Jim Kelly	3.00
3	Jeff Blake	1.00
4	Emmitt Smith	10.00
5	John Elway	8.00
6	Brett Favre	12.00
7	Marshall Faulk	6.00
8	Marcus Allen	3.00
9	Jerome Bettis	3.00
10	Dan Marino	12.00
11	Cris Carter	3.00
12	Drew Bledsoe	8.00
13	Jim Everett	1.00
14	Rodney Hampton	1.00
15	Natrone Means	1.00
16	Steve Young	8.00
17	Rick Mirer	3.00
18	Errict Rhett	3.00
19	Heath Shuler	3.00
20	Lewis Tillman	1.00
21	Barry Sanders	10.00
22	Leroy Hoard	1.00
23	Rod Woodson	3.00
24	Gary Brown	1.00
25	Terance Mathis	1.00
26	Frank Reich	1.00
27	Steve Beuerlein	1.00
28	Raghib Ismail	1.00
29	Johnny Johnson	1.00
30	Charlie Garner	1.00

1995 Playoff Absolute Pigskin Previews

These hobby-only 1995 Playoff Absolute inserts feature six NFC stars. Cards were randomly included one per 145 packs. The front has a color photo superimposed over a leather football. Gold foil stamping is used at the bottom for the player's name and insert set logo. The card back has a color photo of the player against his team's city skyline. A brief recap of the player's 1994 accomplishments is given at the top of the card; his 1994 and career stats are listed in a panel at the bottom.

		NM/M
Complete Set (6):		100.00
Common Player:		5.00
1	Emmitt Smith	40.00
2	Steve Young	30.00
3	Barry Sanders	40.00
4	Deion Sanders	10.00
5	Cris Carter	5.00
6	Errict Rhett	5.00

1995 Playoff Absolute Quad Series

These 50 cards are a creative variation as a parallel set to Playoff's 1995 Absolute set. Each card features four players on it, two per side. Their names and the set and insert set logos are stamped in gold foil down the middle of the card. The backgrounds for each player are a pattern of metallic swirls. One side has a card number, using a "Q" prefix.

		NM/M
Complete Set (50):		300.00
Common Player:		3.00
Minor Stars:		5.00
1	Joe Montana, Steve Young, Dan Marino, John Elway	40.00
2	Troy Aikman, Drew Bledsoe, Brett Favre, Rick Mirer	40.00
3	Trent Dilfer, Heath Shuler, Mark Brunell, Jeff Blake	10.00
4	Randall Cunningham, Warren Moon, Jim Kelly, Boomer Esiason	5.00
5	Dave Brown, Jeff George, Stan Humphries, Jim Everett	5.00
6	Barry Sanders, Emmitt Smith, Marshall Faulk, Errict Rhett	40.00
7	Marcus Allen, Ricky Watters, William Floyd, Natrone Means	8.00
8	Garrison Hearst, Jerome Bettis, Lewis Tillman, Gary Brown	8.00
9	Michael Irvin, Jerry Rice, Tim Brown, Cris Carter	25.00
10	Pete Metzelaars, Bam Morris, Ben Coates, Andre Rison	5.00
11	Reggie White, Bruce Smith, Junior Seau, Deion Sanders	8.00
12	Rob Moore, Larry Centers, Jamir Miller, Chuck Levy	3.00
13	Craig Haywood, Terance Mathis, Bert Emanuel, Eric Metcalf	3.00
14	Kenneth Davis, Andre Reed, Russell Copeland, Cornelius Bennett	3.00
15	Frank Reich, Jack Trudeau, Mark Carrier, Tyrone Poole	3.00
16	Jeff Graham, Curtis Conway, Erik Kramer, Steve Walsh	3.00
17	Carl Pickens, Darnay Scott, Harold Green, David Klinger	3.00
18	Vinny Testaverde, Derrick Alexander, Leroy Hoard, Lorenzo White	3.00
19	Charles Haley, Kevin Williams, Daryl Johnston, Jay Novacek	3.00
20	Glyn Milburn, Leonard Russell, Derek Russell, Shannon Sharpe	3.00
21	Scott Mitchell, Brett Perriman, Herman Moore, Johnnie Morton	5.00
22	Edgar Bennett, LeShon Johnson, Robert Brooks, Mark Ingram	3.00
23	Cody Carlson, Mel Gray, Chris Chandler, Ray Childress	3.00
24	Jim Harbaugh, Craig Erickson, Roosevelt Potts, Sean Dawkins	3.00
25	Steve Beuerlein, Rob Johnson, Cedric Tillman, Reggie Cobb	3.00
26	Greg Hill, Willie Davis, Lake Dawson, Steve Bono	3.00
27	Jeff Hostetler, Harvey Williams, James Jett, Raghib Ismail	3.00
28	Bernie Parmalee, Irving Spikes, Terry Kirby, Irving Fryar	3.00
29	Terry Allen, David Palmer, Qadry Ismail, Jake Reed	3.00
30	Marion Butts, Vincent Brisby, Dave Meggett, Willie McGinest	3.00
31	Willie Roaf, Mario Bates, Quinn Early, Michael Haynes	3.00
32	Herschel Walker, Mike Sherrard, Derek Brown, Thomas Lewis	3.00
33	Stevie Anderson, Aaron Glenn, Johnny Johnson, Ron Moore	3.00
34	Calvin Williams, Fred Barnett, Vaughn Hebron, Charlie Garner	3.00
35	Neil O'Donnell, Charles Johnson, Rod Woodson, Eric Pegram	5.00
36	Ronnie Harmon, Shawn Jefferson, Tony Martin, Mark Seay	3.00
37	Brent Jones, Dana Stubblefield, Bryant Young, Ken Norton	3.00
38	Chris Warren, Cortez Kennedy, Sam Adams, Brian Blades	3.00
39	Tommy Maddox, Chris Miller, Johnny Bailey, Isaac Bruce	8.00
40	Lawrence Dawsey, Alvin Harper, Jackie Harris, Horace Copeland	3.00
41	Gus Frerotte, Brian Mitchell, Reggie Brooks, Tydus Winans	4.00
42	Steve McNair, Kerry Collins, Todd Collins, Chad May	20.00
43	Ki-Jana Carter, Tyrone Wheatley, Napoleon Kaufman, Rashaan Salaam	5.00
44	Terrell Fletcher, Sherman Williams, Ray Zellars, James Stewart	5.00
45	Michael Westbrook, Joseph Galloway, J.J. Stokes, Frank Sanders	5.00
46	Kevin Carter, Tony Boselli, Warren Sapp, Kyle Brady	5.00
47	Greg Truitt, Dan Wilkinson, Eric Turner, Antonio Langham	3.00
48	Carnell Lake, Neil Smith, Rod Smith, Kevin Greene	3.00
49	O.J. McDuffie, Darren Carrington, Michael Timpson, Raymont Harris	3.00
50	Rodney Hampton, Dave Krieg, Barry Foster, Kevin Greene	3.00

1995 Playoff Prime Fantasy Team

These inserts, available in 1995 Playoff Prime retail packs, were seeded at a ratio of one per 25 packs. Each clear plastic card features a star player against an exciting multi-color holographic foil background. If the card is moved to change the angle of the light, the phrase "Playoff Fantasy Team" flashes in three different dimensions.

		NM/M
Complete Set (20):		65.00
Common Player:		1.00
Minor Stars:		2.00
1	Jerome Bettis	2.00
2	Shannon Sharpe	1.00
3	Fuad Reveiz	1.00
4	John Carney	1.00
5	Steve Young	6.00
6	Brett Favre	12.00
7	Tim Brown	2.00
8	Ben Coates	1.00
9	Marshall Faulk	6.00
10	Stan Humphries	1.00
11	Dan Marino	12.00
12	Jerry Rice	10.00
13	Errict Rhett	2.00
14	Chris Warren	2.00
15	Barry Sanders	10.00
16	Cris Carter	2.00
17	Michael Irvin	2.00
18	Emmitt Smith	10.00
19	Terance Mathis	1.00
20	Herman Moore	2.00

1995 Playoff Prime Minis

These 1995 Playoff Prime Mini insert cards were seeded one per every seven retail packs. The cards are a miniature version of the 200-card base set; each measures 2-1/4" x 3-1/8" and isolates the corresponding base set player photo against a holographic foil background. Blue foil is used for the player's name along the right side of the card, and the set icon, printed in the lower left corner. The card back has a closeup shot of the player toward the top, along with the card number. Below the photo is a brief player profile.

		NM/M
Complete Set (200):		100.00
Common Player:		.25
Minor Stars:		1.00
1	John Elway	4.00
2	Reggie White	1.00
3	Errict Rhett	1.00
4	Deion Sanders	3.00
5	Raghib Ismail	.25
6	Jerome Bettis	3.00
7	Randall Cunningham	1.00
8	Mario Bates	1.00
9	Dave Brown	.25
10	Stan Humphries	1.00
11	Drew Bledsoe	4.00
12	Neil O'Donnell	1.00
13	Dan Marino	10.00
14	Larry Centers	.25
15	Craig Heyward	.25
16	Bruce Smith	.25
17	Erik Kramer	1.00
18	Jeff Blake	1.00
19	Vinny Testaverde	1.00
20	Barry Sanders	8.00
21	Boomer Esiason	.25
22	Emmitt Smith	8.00
23	Warren Moon	1.00
24	Junior Seau	1.00
25	Heath Shuler	.50
26	Jackie Harris	.25
27	Terance Mathis	.25
28	Raymont Harris	1.00
29	Jim Kelly	4.00
30	Dan Wilkinson	.25
31	Herman Moore	2.00
32	Shannon Sharpe	1.00
33	Antonio Langham	.25
34	Charles Haley	.25
35	Brett Favre	10.00
36	Marshall Faulk	6.00
37	Neil Smith	.25
38	Harvey Williams	.25
39	Johnny Bailey	.25
40	O.J. McDuffie	.25
41	David Palmer	.25
42	Willie McGinest	.25
43	Quinn Early	.25
44	Johnny Johnson	.25
45	Derek Brown	.25
46	Charlie Garner	.25
47	Bam Morris	1.00
48	Natrone Means	1.00
49	Ken Norton	.25
50	Troy Aikman	6.00
51	Reggie Brooks	.25
52	Trent Dilfer	3.00
53	Cortez Kennedy	.25
54	Chuck Levy	.25
55	Jeff George	1.00
56	Steve Young	7.00
57	Lewis Tillman	.25
58	Carl Pickens	1.00
59	Brett Perriman	1.00
60	Jay Novacek	.25
61	Greg Hill	1.00
62	James Jett	.25

63	Terry Kirby	.25
64	Qadry Ismail	.25
65	Ben Coates	.25
66	Kevin Greene	.25
67	Bryant Young	.25
68	Brian Mitchell	.25
69	Steve Walsh	.25
70	Darnay Scott	1.00
71	Daryl Johnston	.25
72	Glyn Milburn	.25
73	Tim Brown	3.00
74	Isaac Bruce	5.00
75	Bernie Parmalee	.25
76	Terry Allen	.25
77	Jim Everett	.25
78	Thomas Lewis	.25
79	Vaughn Hebron	.25
80	Rod Woodson	1.00
81	Rick Mirer	1.00
82	Dana Stubblefield	1.00
83	Bert Emanuel	1.00
84	Andre Reed	1.00
85	Jeff Graham	.25
86	Johnnie Morton	.25
87	LeShon Johnson	.25
88	Michael Irvin	2.00
89	Derrick Alexander	.25
90	Lake Dawson	.50
91	Cody Carlson	.25
92	Chris Warren	1.00
93	William Floyd	1.00
94	Charles Johnson	1.00
95	Roosevelt Potts	.25
96	Cris Carter	1.00
97	Aaron Glenn	.25
98	Curtis Conway	1.00
99	Kevin Williams	1.00
100	Jerry Rice	8.00
101	Frank Reich	.25
102	Harold Green	.25
103	Russell Copeland	.25
104	Rob Moore	.25
105	Edgar Bennett	.25
106	Darren Carrington	.25
107	Tommy Maddox	2.00
108	Dave Meggett	.25
109	Fred Barnett	.25
110	Mark Seay	.25
111	Gus Frerotte	.50
112	Brent Jones	.25
113	Chris Miller	.25
114	Cedric Tillman	.25
115	Mark Ingram	.25
116	Eric Turner	.25
117	Mark Carrier	.25
118	Garrison Hearst	2.00
119	Craig Erickson	.25
120	Derek Russell	.25
121	Mike Sherrard	.25
122	Horace Copeland	.25
123	Jack Trudeau	.25
124	Leroy Hoard	.25
125	Gary Brown	.25
126	Mel Gray	.25
127	Steve Beuerlein	.25
128	Marcus Allen	2.00
129	Irving Fryar	.25
130	Marion Butts	.25
131	Ricky Watters	2.00
132	Tony Martin	.25
133	Lawrence Dawsey	.25
134	Ronnie Harmon	.25
135	Herschel Walker	.25
136	Michael Haynes	.25
137	Eric Green	.25
138	Steve Bono	1.00
139	Jamir Miller	.25
140	Rod Smith	.25
141	Andre Rison	1.00
142	Eric Metcalf	.25
143	Michael Timpson	.25
144	Cornelius Bennett	.25
145	Sean Dawkins	1.00
146	Scott Mitchell	1.00
147	Ray Childress	.25
148	Jim Harbaugh	1.00
149	Reggie Cobb	.25
150	Willie Roaf	.25
151	Stevie Anderson	.25
152	Barry Foster	.25
153	Joe Montana	10.00
154	David Klingler	.25
155	Chris Chandler	.25
156	Carnell Lake	.25
157	Calvin Williams	.25
158	Kenneth Davis	.25
159	Tydus Winans	.25
160	Sam Adams	.25
161	Ron Moore	.25
162	Vincent Brisby	.25
163	Alvin Harper	1.00
164	Jake Reed	.25
165	Jeff Hostetler	1.00
166	Mark Brunell	4.00
167	Leonard Russell	.25
168	Greg Truitt	.25
169	Pete Metzelaars	.25
170	Dave Krieg	.25
171	Lorenzo White	.25
172	Robert Brooks	1.00
173	Willie Davis	.25
174	Irving Spikes	.25
175	Rodney Hampton	.25
176	Erric Pegram	.25
177	Brian Blades	.25
178	Shawn Jefferson	.25
179	Tyrone Poole	.25
180	Rob Johnson	1.00
181	Ki-Jana Carter	1.00
182	Steve McNair	5.00
183	Michael Westbrook	1.00
184	Kerry Collins	5.00
185	Kevin Carter	1.00
186	Tony Boselli	1.00
187	Joseph Galloway	2.00
188	Kyle Brady	1.00
189	J.J. Stokes	2.00
190	Warren Sapp	2.00
191	Tyrone Wheatley	1.00
192	Napoleon Kaufman	1.00
193	James Stewart	1.00
194	Rashaan Salaam	1.00
195	Ray Zellars	.50
196	Todd Collins	.50
197	Sherman Williams	.50
198	Frank Sanders	1.00
199	Terrell Fletcher	.50
200	Chad May	.50

1995 Playoff Prime Pigskin Previews

These retail-only 1995 Playoff Prime inserts feature six AFC stars. Cards were randomly included one per 145 packs. The front has a color photo superimposed over a leather football. Gold foil stamping is used for the player's name and insert set logo. The card back has a color photo of the player against his team's city skyline. A brief recap of the player's 1994 accomplishments is given at the top of the card; his 1994 and career stats are listed in a panel at the bottom.

		NM/M
Complete Set (6):		75.00
Common Player:		5.00
7	Dan Marino	20.00
8	Marshall Faulk	15.00
9	Natrone Means	5.00
10	Tim Brown	10.00
11	Drew Bledsoe	15.00
12	Marcus Allen	10.00

1995 Playoff Night of the Stars

Playoff produced this six-card set to hand out to those attending the 1995 National Sports Collectors Convention Trade Show in St. Louis. The set was also available at the Playoff booth during the National by exchanging 10 wrappers for one of the six cards. The borderless fronts featured the "Night of the Stars," the player's name, Playoff logo and team helmet at the bottom. The backs include the player's name and an endorsement for the 1995 National.

		NM/M
Complete Set (6):		20.00
Common Player:		2.00
1	Jerome Bettis	4.00
2	Ben Coates	2.00
3	Deion Sanders	5.00
4	Ki-Jana Carter	2.00
5	Steve McNair	8.00
6	Errict Rhett	2.00

1995 Playoff Super Bowl Card Show

To commemorate the Super Bowl XXIX Card Show, Playoff produced this eight-card set. Overall, 3,000 of each card was issued. A color photo of the player is printed over a red, silver and gold-foil background. In the upper left is the player's name in silver foil. The card backs have the player's name, highlights and the Super Bowl XXIX logo. The card number is printed in the upper right of the card back, which sports a black background.

		NM/M
Complete Set (8):		25.00
Common Player:		2.00
1	Marshall Faulk	8.00
2	Heath Shuler	3.00
3	David Palmer	2.00
4	Errict Rhett	3.00
5	Charlie Garner	3.00
6	Irving Spikes	2.00
7	Shante Carver	2.00
8	Greg Hill	3.00

1995 Playoff Contenders

As with previous editions, Playoff's 1995 Contenders set emphasizes players whose teams are in contention for post-season play. The 150-card set includes a 30-card Rookies subset and three insert sets. The regular card uses a metallic process which gives the card a depth to it. The band at the top and the player's name use a team-related color, as does the back, which includes a closeup shot of the player and a brief recap of a game in which he had a key role. Insert sets include Hog Heaven Pigskins, Rookie Kickoff and Back-to-Backs, a 75-card parallel set which includes two players per card.

		NM/M
Complete Set (150):		20.00
Common Player:		.05
Minor Stars:		.40
Pack (6):		1.75
Wax Box (24):		30.00
1	Steve Young	1.50
2	*Jeff Blake*	1.00
3	Rick Mirer	.40
4	Brett Favre	4.00
5	Heath Shuler	.40
6	Steve Bono	.40
7	John Elway	.50
8	Troy Aikman	2.00
9	Rodney Peete	.05
10	Gus Frerotte	.50
11	Drew Bledsoe	1.50
12	Jim Kelly	.40
13	Dan Marino	3.00
14	Errict Rhett	1.00
15	Jeff Hostetler	.05
16	Erik Kramer	.05
17	Jim Everett	.05
18	Elvis Grbac	.05
19	Scott Mitchell	.05
20	Barry Sanders	1.50
21	Deion Sanders	1.00
22	Emmitt Smith	4.00
23	Garrison Hearst	.40
24	Mario Bates	.40
25	Mark Brunell	1.00
26	Robert Smith	.05
27	Rodney Hampton	.05
28	Marshall Faulk	.40
29	Greg Hill	.40
30	Bernie Parmalee	.05
31	Natrone Means	.40
32	Marcus Allen	.40
33	Bam Morris	.40
34	Edgar Bennett	.05
35	Vincent Brisby	.05
36	Jerome Bettis	.40
37	Craig Heyward	.05
38	Anthony Miller	.05
39	Curtis Conway	.05
40	William Floyd	.40
41	Chris Warren	.40
42	Terry Kirby	.05
43	Herschel Walker	.05
44	Eric Metcalf	.05
45	Darnay Scott	.40
46	Jackie Harris	.05
47	Dana Stubblefield	.05
48	Daryl Johnston	.05
49	Dave Meggett	.05
50	Ricky Watters	.40
51	Ken Norton	.05
52	Boomer Esiason	.05
53	Lake Dawson	.40
54	Eric Green	.05
55	Junior Seau	.40
56	*Yancey Thigpen*	1.00
57	James Jett	.05
58	Leonard Russell	.05
59	Brent Jones	.05
60	Trent Dilfer	.40
61	Terance Mathis	.05
62	Jeff George	.05
63	Alvin Harper	.05
64	Terry Allen	.05
65	Stan Humphries	.05
66	Robert Green	.05
67	Bryce Paup	.40
68	*Tamarick Vanover*	.75
69	Desmond Howard	.05
70	Derek Loville	.05
71	Dave Brown	.05
72	Carl Pickens	.40
73	Gary Clark	.05
74	Gary Brown	.05
75	Brett Perriman	.05
76	Charlie Garner	.05
77	Ben Coates	.05
78	Bruce Smith	.05
79	Erric Pegram	.05
80	Jerry Rice	1.50
81	Tim Brown	.05
82	John Taylor	.05
83	Will Moore	.05
84	Jay Novacek	.05
85	Kevin Williams	.05
86	Raghib Ismail	.05
87	Robert Brooks	.40
88	Michael Irvin	.40
89	Mark Chmura	.75
90	Shannon Sharpe	.05
91	Henry Ellard	.05
92	Reggie White	.40
93	Isaac Bruce	.50
94	Charles Haley	.05
95	Jake Reed	.05
96	Pete Metzelaars	.05
97	Dave Krieg	.05
98	Tony Martin	.05
99	Charles Jordan	.05
100	Bert Emanuel	.50
101	Andre Rison	.05
102	Jeff Graham	.05
103	O.J. McDuffie	.05
104	Randall Cunningham	.05
105	Harvey Williams	.05
106	Cris Carter	.05
107	Irving Fryar	.05
108	Jim Harbaugh	.05
109	Bernie Kosar	.05
110	Charles Johnson	.40
111	Warren Moon	.40
112	Neil O'Donnell	.40
113	Fred Barnett	.05
114	Herman Moore	.75
115	Chris Miller	.05
116	Vinny Testaverde	.05
117	Craig Erickson	.05
118	Qadry Ismail	.05
119	Willie Davis	.05
120	Michael Jackson	.05
121	*Stoney Case*	.40
122	*Frank Sanders*	.50
123	*Todd Collins*	.40
124	*Kerry Collins*	2.00
125	*Sherman Williams*	.40
126	*Terrell Davis*	3.00
127	*Luther Elliss*	.40
128	*Steve McNair*	4.00
129	*Chris Sanders*	1.00
130	*Ki-Jana Carter*	1.00
131	*Rodney Thomas*	.50
132	*Tony Boselli*	.40
133	*Rob Johnson*	2.00
134	*James Stewart*	1.50
135	*Chad May*	.40
136	*Eric Bjorson*	.40
137	*Tyrone Wheatley*	.50
138	*Kyle Brady*	.40
139	*Curtis Martin*	4.00
140	*Eric Zeier*	.50
141	*Ray Zellars*	.40
142	*Napoleon Kaufman*	1.50
143	*Mike Mamula*	.40
144	*Mark Bruener*	.50
145	*Kordell Stewart*	1.00
146	*J.J. Stokes*	1.00
147	*Joey Galloway*	2.50
148	*Warren Sapp*	.75
149	*Michael Westbrook*	1.00
150	*Rashaan Salaam*	1.00

1995 Playoff Contenders Back-to-Back

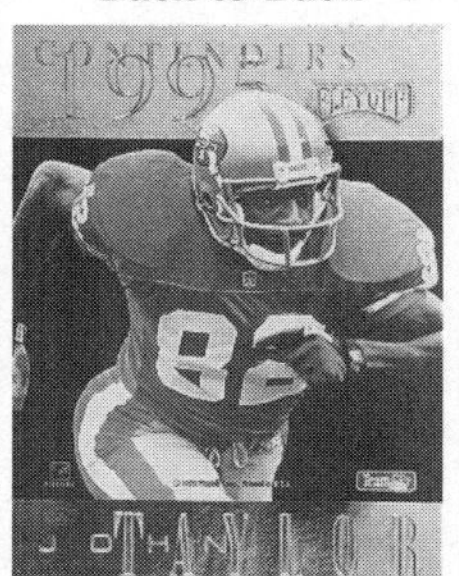

This 1995 Playoff Contenders insert set is a 75-card parallel set which features two players per card, one on each side. The cards use foil stamping for the player's name and set logo, which appear at the bottom and top, respectively. The cards have a glossier finish than their regular counterparts. These inserts are seeded one per 19 packs.

		NM/M
Complete Set (75):		400.00
Common Player:		1.00
Minor Stars:		3.00
Inserted 1:19		
1	Troy Aikman, Dan Marino	18.00
2	Emmitt Smith, Marshall Faulk	18.00
3	Brett Favre, John Elway	18.00
4	Steve Young, Drew Bledsoe	12.00
5	Barry Sanders, Errict Rhett	12.00
6	Deion Sanders, Jerry Rice	12.00
7	Jeff Blake, Rick Mirer	1.00
8	Michael Irvin, Tim Brown	3.00
9	Chris Warren, Ricky Watters	3.00
10	Herman Moore, Vincent Brisby	3.00
11	James Jett, Eric Metcalf	1.00
12	Henry Ellard, Terance Mathis	1.00
13	Curtis Conway, Isaac Bruce	3.00
14	Steve Bono, Jeff Hostetler	1.00
15	Greg Hill, Harvey Williams	1.00
16	Garrison Hearst, Jerome Bettis	3.00
17	Jay Novacek, Brent Jones	1.00
18	Reggie White, Bruce Smith	3.00
19	Eric Green, Shannon Sharpe	3.00
20	Gus Frerotte, Jeff George	3.00
21	Erik Kramer, Brian Mitchell	1.00
22	Warren Moon, Jim Kelly	3.00
23	Mark Chmura, Ben Coates	1.00
24	Trent Dilfer, Heath Shuler	3.00
25	Craig Heyward, Edgar Bennett	1.00
26	Jim Everett, Dave Brown	1.00
27	Bert Emanuel, Andre Rison	1.00
28	Robert Brooks, Alvin Harper	1.00
29	Desmond Howard, Tony Martin	1.00
30	Rodney Peete, Fred Barnett	1.00
31	Natrone Means, William Floyd	3.00
32	Brett Perriman, Raghib Ismail	1.00
33	Cris Carter, Irving Fryar	3.00
34	Tamarick Vanover, Darnay Scott	1.00
35	Charles Haley, Dana Stubblefield	1.00
36	Bryce Paup, Ken Norton	1.00
37	Marcus Allen, Herschel Walker	3.00
38	Leonard Russell, Terry Allen	1.00
39	Junior Seau, Derrick Loville	3.00
40	Lake Dawson, Charles Johnson	1.00
41	Kevin Williams, Charles Jordan	1.00
42	Jeff Graham, Carl Pickens	1.00
43	Anthony Miller, O.J. McDuffie	1.00
44	Elvis Grbac, Jim Harbaugh	1.00
45	Dave Meggett, Terry Kirby	1.00
46	Dave Krieg, Stan Humphries	1.00
47	Mark Brunell, Boomer Esiason	10.00
48	Craig Erickson, Vinny Testaverde	1.00
49	Randall Cunningham, Bernie Kosar	3.00
50	Erric Pegram, Charlie Garner	1.00
51	Will Moore, Gary Clark	1.00
52	Qadry Ismail, Willie Davis	1.00
53	Neil O'Donnell, Chris Miller	1.00
54	Mario Bates, Robert Smith	1.00
55	Rodney Hampton, Bernie Parmalee	1.00
56	Bam Morris, Daryl Johnston	1.00
57	Jackie Harris, Jake Reed	1.00
58	John Taylor, Pete Metzelaars	1.00
59	Yancey Thigpen, Michael Jackson	1.00
60	Gary Brown, Robert Green	1.00
61	Rashaan Salaam, Napoleon Kaufman	3.00
62	Mark Bruener, Kyle Brady	1.00
63	Ki-Jana Carter, Rodney Thomas	1.00
64	Chad May, Steve McNair	8.00
65	Frank Sanders, J.J. Stokes	3.00
66	Mike Mamula, Warren Sapp	3.00
67	Stoney Case, Kordell Stewart	8.00
68	Terrell Davis, Curtis Martin	12.00
69	Sherman Williams, Chris Sanders	1.00
70	James Stewart, Eric Bjornson	1.00
71	Tyrone Wheatley, Ray Zellars	1.00
72	Tony Boselli, Luther Elliss	1.00
73	Rob Johnson, Todd Collins	15.00
74	Kerry Collins, Eric Zeier	3.00
75	Joey Galloway, Michael Westbrook	4.00

1995 Playoff Contenders Hog Heaven

Hog Heaven Pigskins cards were randomly inserted one per 48 packs of 1995 Playoff Contenders football packs. The thick cards, which showcase 30 players, feature a photo among cloud formations, next to a leather football. The set logo is in the upper left corner; the player's name is in gold foil in the lower right hand corner of the horizontally-designed card. The card back is all leather and features a caricature of the player, plus his name, position and team name. The card number uses an "HH" prefix.

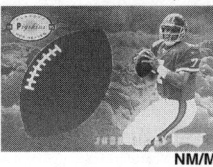

		NM/M
Complete Set (30):		100.00
Common Player:		1.00
Minor Stars:		2.00
Inserted 1:48		
1	Troy Aikman	8.00
2	Marcus Allen	2.00
3	Jeff Blake	2.00
4	Drew Bledsoe	8.00
5	Steve Bono	1.00
6	Isaac Bruce	2.00
7	Trent Dilfer	2.00
8	John Elway	8.00
9	Marshall Faulk	6.00
10	Brett Favre	12.00
11	Gus Frerotte	1.00
12	Irving Fryar	1.00
13	Jeff George	2.00
14	Rodney Hampton	1.00
15	Garrison Hearst	2.00
16	Michael Irvin	2.00
17	Erik Kramer	1.00
18	Dan Marino	12.00
19	Natrone Means	2.00
20	Errict Rhett	1.00
21	Jerry Rice	8.00
22	Barry Sanders	10.00
23	Deion Sanders	4.00
24	Shannon Sharpe	1.00
25	Emmitt Smith	10.00
26	Robert Smith	2.00
27	Chris Warren	1.00
28	Reggie White	2.00
29	Harvey Williams	1.00
30	Steve Young	8.00

1995 Playoff Contenders Rookie Kick Off

These 1995 Playoff Absolute inserts were seeded one per 24 packs. Thirty rookies appear on a plastic die-cut card shaped like a football waiting to be kicked off. The player's name and set logo are in gold foil at the bottom. The card back is blank.

		NM/M
Complete Set (30):		100.00
Common Player:		1.00
1	Eric Bjornson	1.00
2	Tony Boselli	2.00
3	Kyle Brady	2.00
4	Mark Bruener	1.00
5	Ki-Jana Carter	2.00
6	Stoney Case	1.00
7	Kerry Collins	8.00
8	Todd Collins	1.00
9	Terrell Davis	25.00
10	Luther Elliss	1.00
11	Joey Galloway	5.00
12	Rob Johnson	3.00
13	Napoleon Kaufman	2.00
14	Mike Mamula	1.00
15	Curtis Martin	10.00
16	Chad May	1.00
17	Steve McNair	18.00
18	Rashaan Salaam	1.00
19	Chris Sanders	1.00
20	Frank Sanders	3.00
21	Warren Sapp	3.00
22	James Stewart	4.00
23	Kordell Stewart	5.00
24	J.J. Stokes	4.00
25	Rodney Thomas	1.00
26	Michael Westbrook	4.00
27	Tyrone Wheatley	1.00
28	Sherman Williams	1.00
29	Eric Zeier	1.00
30	Ray Zellars	1.00

A player's name in *italic* type indicates a rookie card.

1996 Playoff National Promos

Handed out at the 1996 National Sports Collectors Convention in Anaheim, this seven-card set was available through a wrapper redemption program at the show. Three wrappers from a Playoff product could be exchanged for one card. A foil box of wrappers was good for the complete set. The card fronts featured a photo of the player over a background of a California scene. The "17th National Sports Collectors Convention" is printed along one side of the acetate card. The card backs are the reverse of the fronts, with the player's bio written in the shadow of the player. The cards are numbered "x/7." Kordell Stewart's card was only available through the foil box complete set redemption offer.

		NM/M
Complete Set (7):		35.00
Common Player:		3.00
1	Kordell Stewart	8.00
2	Curtis Martin	10.00
3	Tyrone Wheatley	3.00
4	Joey Galloway	5.00
5	Steve McNair	6.00
6	Kerry Collins	8.00
7	Napoleon Kaufman	4.00

1996 Playoff Super Bowl Card Show

As a redemption offer at the Super Bowl XXX Card Show, Playoff issued this six-card set. Player photos are showcased over Arizona desert scenery. The player's name is printed along one side of the card, with the Playoff logo in one of the lower corners. The Super Bowl Card Show logo is located in one of the upper corners. The card back features the Super Bowl Card Show logo at the top, with the player's highlights printed in a box at the bottom. The cards are numbered "X/6." A collector could exchange a Playoff wrapper for a different card each day of the show, which was held in Tempe, Ariz. A collector could receive the entire set in exchange for 10 wrappers. The cards have a 1995 copyright date on the card back.

		NM/M
Complete Set (6):		17.00
Common Player:		2.00
1	Deion Sanders	4.00
2	Rashaan Salaam	3.00
3	Garrison Hearst	2.00
4	Robert Brooks	2.00
5	Barry Sanders	5.00
6	Errict Rhett	3.00

1996 Playoff Absolute Promos

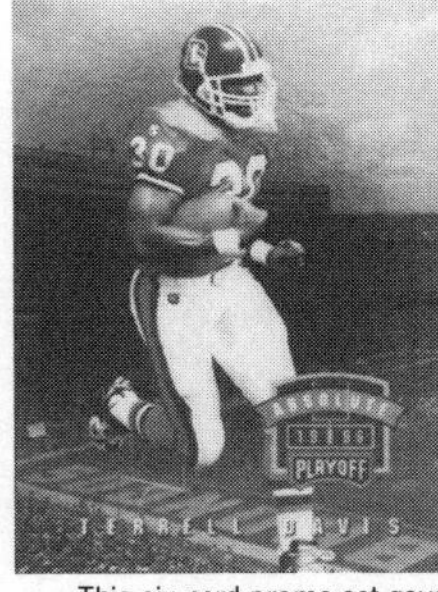

This six-card promo set gave collectors and dealers a sneak peak at the designs for 1996 Playoff Absolute. The same six players are featured in Prime Promos, but the photos and logos are different.

	NM/M
Complete Set (6):	20.00
Common Player:	1.50
Terrell Davis	7.00
Tamarick Vanover	3.00
Rashaan Salaam	3.00
J.J. Stokes	3.00
Antonio Freeman	3.00
Zack Crockett	1.50

1996 Playoff Absolute

Playoff's 1996 Absolute football cards feature a full-color player action photo on the front, set against a colorful snapshot of the player's stadium with a game in progress. Each card back has a head-and-shoulder shot of the player, complete career and 1995 NFL statistics and an intriguing or unusual fact about the player. A 20-card subset of the top 1996 draft choices is included within the main set. Four insert sets were also produced: Metal X (also in Prime), Xtreme Team, Quad Series and Unsung Heroes (also in Prime). In an innovative pack-within-a-pack concept, three types of color-coded packs are available within 1996 Playoff Absolute boxes. Each box of 1996 Playoff Absolute contains 24 Red packs, each containing five cards, and either a White or Blue inner pack. Each Red pack contains five base cards from the #1-100 low level series, plus one White or Blue inner pack, and a potential random insert card. Each White inner pack contains one base card from the #101-150 mid level series, or a random insert card. Each box includes approximately 18 White inner packs. Each Blue inner pack has one base card from the #150-200 high level series, or a random insert card. Each box includes approximately six Blue inner packs.

		NM/M
Complete Set (200):		75.00
Common Red (1-100):		.10
Common White (101-150):		.20
Common Blue (151-200):		.40
Pack (6):		2.25
Wax Box (24):		35.00
1	Jim Kelly	.50
2	Michael Irvin	.20
3	Jim Harbaugh	.10
4	Warren Moon	.40
5	Rick Mirer	.10
6	Drew Bledsoe	1.25
7	Steve Young	1.50
8	Junior Seau	.20
9	Sherman Williams	.10
10	Jay Novacek	.10
11	Bill Brooks	.10
12	Steve Bono	.20
13	Leroy Hoard	.10
14	Willie Jackson	.10
15	Irving Fryer	.10
16	Tony McGee	.10
17	Neil O'Donnell	.20
18	Fred Barnett	.10
19	Erric Pegram	.10
20	Derrick Moore	.10
21	Johnnie Morton	.10
22	James Jett	.10
23	Tim Brown	.20
24	Kevin Miniefield	.10
25	Jim McMahon	.10
26	Brian Blades	.10
27	Henry Ellard	.10
28	Calvin Williams	.10
29	Chris Chandler	.10
30	Rod Woodson	.10
31	Ronnie Harmon	.10
32	Brent Jones	.10
33	Qadry Ismail	.10
34	Steve Tasker	.10
35	Eric Green	.10
36	Brian Mitchell	.10
37	Herschel Walker	.10
38	Sean Dawkins	.10
39	Bryce Paup	.10
40	Dorsey Levens	.25
41	Andre Rison	.10
42	Lamont Warren	.10
43	Earnest Byner	.10
44	*Bobby Engram*	1.00
45	*Simeon Rice*	.25
46	Michael Jackson	.10
47	*Marvin Harrison*	5.00
48	Thurman Thomas	.20
49	Charles Haley	.10
50	Rob Moore	.10
51	Bryan Cox	.10
52	Horace Copeland	.10
53	Rodney Peete	.10
54	Jeff Graham	.10
55	Charles Johnson	.10
56	Natrone Means	.20
57	Terrell Fletcher	.10
58	Eric Bieniemy	.10
59	*Karim Abdul-Jabbar*	1.00
60	Quinn Early	.10
61	Mark Bruener	.10
62	Shawn Jefferson	.10
63	Vinny Testaverde	.10
64	*Derrick Mayes*	1.25
65	Mario Bates	.10
66	J.J. Birden	.10
67	*Eddie Kennison*	.75
68	Steve Walsh	.10
69	Mark Chmura	.30
70	Mike Sherrard	.10
71	Boomer Esiason	.10
72	*Alex Van Dyke*	.75
73	Jake Reed	.10
74	Jackie Harris	.10
75	Mark Rypien	.10
76	Chris Calloway	.10
77	*Amani Toomer*	.50
78	Terrell Davis	4.00
79	Raghib Ismail	.10
80	Derek Loville	.10
81	Ben Coates	.10
82	Kyle Brady	.10
83	Willie Green	.10
84	Randall Cunningham	.10
85	Amp Lee	.10
86	Bert Emanual	.10
87	*Jason Dunn*	.25
88	Michael Haynes	.10
89	Robert Green	.10
90	Willie Davis	.10
91	O.J. McDuffie	.10
92	Harold Green	.10
93	Ken Dilger	.10
94	Brett Perriman	.10
95	Eric Zeier	.10
96	Jerome Bettis	.10
97	*Rickey Dudley*	.75
98	Darnay Scott	.10
99	Mark Brunell	1.00
100	Christian Fauria	.10
101	Jeff Blake	.75
102	Troy Aikman	5.00
103	John Elway	3.00
104	Barry Sanders	6.00
105	Curtis Conway	.75
106	Wayne Chrebet	.20
107	Lake Dawson	.20
108	Jerry Rice	5.00
109	Kevin Williams	.20
110	Zack Crockett	.20
111	Vincent Brisby	.20
112	Rodney Thomas	.75
113	Rodney Hampton	.20
114	Adrian Murrell	.20
115	Bruce Smith	.20
116	Napoleon Kaufman	.75
117	Bam Morris	.20
118	Anthony Miller	.20
119	*Aaron Hayden*	1.00
120	Joey Galloway	2.00
121	Trent Dilfer	.75
122	Stoney Case	.20
123	Tamarick Vanover	.75
124	Eric Metcalf	.20
125	Marcus Allen	.20
126	James Stewart	.20
127	Charlie Garner	.20
128	Yancey Thigpen	1.25
129	William Floyd	.20
130	Terry Allen	.20
131	Robert Smith	.20
132	Todd Kinchen	.20
133	Gus Frerotte	.20
134	Frank Sanders	.75
135	Scott Mitchell	.20
136	Greg Hill	.20
137	Edgar Bennett	.20
138	Alvin Harper	.20
139	Reggie White	.50
140	Craig Heyward	.20
141	Todd Collins	.20
142	Ernie Mills	.20
143	*Keyshawn Johnson*	6.00
144	Mark Carrier	.20
145	Robert Brooks	.20
146	Bernie Parmalee	.20
147	Carl Pickens	.75
148	*Kevin Hardy*	.75
149	*Jonathan Ogden*	.75
150	*Lawrence Phillips*	.50
151	Emmitt Smith	10.00
152	Brett Favre	12.00
153	Dan Marino	12.00
154	Jim Everett	1.00
155	Dave Brown	1.00
156	Jeff Hostetler	1.00
157	Heath Shuler	1.00
158	Daryl Johnston	1.00
159	Terance Mathis	1.00
160	Curtis Martin	8.00
161	Ray Zellars	1.00
162	Ricky Watters	1.00
163	Chris Warren	1.00
164	Larry Centers	1.00
165	Steve McNair	8.00
166	Terry Kirby	1.00
167	Rob Johnson	1.00
168	Dave Meggett	1.00
169	Antonio Freeman	1.00
170	Marshall Faulk	5.00
171	Andre Hastings	1.00
172	Stan Humphries	1.00
173	Errict Rhett	1.00
174	Michael Westbrook	1.50
175	Deion Sanders	4.00
176	Jeff George	2.00
177	Cris Carter	1.50
178	Chris Sanders	1.50
179	Ki-Jana Carter	1.50
180	Kordell Stewart	4.00
181	Isaac Bruce	2.00
182	*Terry Glenn*	4.00
183	Garrison Hearst	1.00
184	Erik Kramer	1.00
185	*Leeland McElroy*	2.00
186	Rashaan Salaam	2.00
187	Kimble Anders	1.00
188	Chad May	1.00
189	Tony Martin	1.00
190	J.J. Stokes	7.00
191	Darick Holmes	1.00
192	*Eric Moulds*	10.00
193	Shannon Sharpe	1.00
194	*Tim Biakabutuka*	2.00
195	*Eddie George*	15.00
196	*Mike Alstott*	7.00
197	Kerry Collins	3.00
198	Harvey Williams	1.00
199	Herman Moore	2.00
200	Tyrone Wheatley	1.00

1996 Playoff Absolute/ Prime Metal XL

These cards were available in both 1996 Playoff Absolute (#s 1-18) and 1996 Playoff Prime (#s 19-36). The cards introduce the first-ever concept of a collector coin and card in one. A metal coin commemorating each player's team is imbedded in each card. Cards were available only in Blue inner packs, one in 96 packs.

		NM/M
Complete Set (36):		200.00
Comp. Absolute Set (18):		125.00
Comp. Prime Set (18):		75.00
Common Player:		1.00
1	Troy Aikman	10.00
2	Emmitt Smith	12.00
3	Barry Sanders	12.00
4	Brett Favre	15.00
5	Dan Marino	15.00
6	Jerry Rice	10.00
7	Marshall Faulk	8.00
8	Curtis Martin	8.00
9	Rashaan Salaam	2.00
10	Harvey Williams	1.00
11	Ricky Watters	3.00
12	Yancey Thigpen	1.00
13	Chris Warren	1.00
14	Errict Rhett	3.00
15	Terry Allen	1.00
16	Robert Brooks	1.00
17	Anthony Miller	1.00
18	Erik Kramer	1.00
19	Michael Irvin	1.00
20	John Elway	10.00
21	Jim Harbaugh	1.00
22	Steve Young	10.00
23	Deion Sanders	6.00
24	Terrell Davis	15.00
25	Reggie White	1.00
26	Herman Moore	4.00
27	Rodney Hampton	1.00
28	Cris Carter	1.00
29	Isaac Bruce	4.00
30	Kordell Stewart	4.00
31	Brett Perriman	1.00
32	Joey Galloway	3.00
33	Drew Bledsoe	8.00
34	J.J. Stokes	4.00
35	Napoleon Kaufman	1.00
36	Tim Brown	5.00

1996 Playoff Absolute Quad Series

These 35 insert cards were avaiable only in Playoff's 1996 Absolute Red packs, one in 24. Each card features four players on it. There were also five rookies-only Quad cards produced. The background is foiled, with a silver-stamped insert set logo with the player's team name around it. The player's names are stamped in copper foil on each side of the card. Copper is also used for a card number, which appears on one side only.

		NM/M
Complete Set (35):		250.00
Common Player:		2.00
Minor Stars:		5.00
1	Stoney Case, Garrison Hearst, Rob Moore, Frank Sanders	2.00
2	J.J. Birden, Bert Emanuel, Jeff George, Craig Heyward	2.00
3	Todd Collins, Bill Brooks, Jim Kelly, Bryce Paup	2.00
4	Mark Carrier, Kerry Collins, Willie Green, Derrick Moore	12.00
5	Curtis Conway, Robert Green, Erik Kramer, Kevin Miniefield	2.00
6	Eric Bieniemy, Jeff Blake, Harold Green, Tony McGee	2.00
7	Earnest Byner, Michael Jackson, Andre Rison, Eric Zeier	2.00
8	Michael Irvin, Jay Novacek, Deion Sanders, Kevin Williams	12.00
9	Terrell Davis, John Elway, Anthony Miller, Shannon Sharpe	20.00
10	Scott Mitchell, Herman Moore, Johnnie Morton, Brett Perriman	5.00
11	Edgar Bennett, Mark Chmura, Antonio Freeman, Reggie White	5.00
12	Chris Chandler, Steve McNair, Chris Sanders, Rodney Thomas	8.00
13	Zack Crockett, Sean Dawkins, Ken Dilger, Jim Harbaugh	2.00
14	Mark Brunell, Willie Jackson, Rob Johnson, James Stewart	10.00
15	Marcus Allen, Kimble Anders, Lake Dawson, Tamarick Vanover	5.00
16	Eric Green, Terry Kirby, O.J. McDuffie, Bernie Parmalee	2.00
17	Cris Carter, Warren Moon, Robert Smith, Chad May	5.00
18	Drew Bledsoe, Vincent Brisby, Ben Coates, Dave Meggett	12.00
19	Mario Bates, Jim Everett, Michael Haynes, Ray Zellars	2.00
20	Dave Brown, Chris Calloway, Rodney Hampton, Tyrone Wheatley	5.00
21	Kyle Brady, Wayne Chrebet, Adrian Murrell, Neil O'Donnell	2.00
22	Tim Brown, Jeff Hostetler, Raghib Ismail, Napoleon Kaufman	5.00
23	Charlie Garner, Rodney Peete, Ricky Watters, Calvin Williams	2.00
24	Andre Hastings, Ernie Mills, Kordell Stewart, Rod Woodson	10.00
25	Terrell Fletcher, Ronnie Harmon, Aaron Hayden, Junior Seau	5.00
26	William Floyd, Derek Loville, J.J. Stokes, Steve Young	10.00
27	Brian Blades, Christian Fauria, Joey Galloway, Rick Mirer	8.00
28	Mark Rypien, Isaac Bruce, Todd Kinchen, Steve Walsh	6.00
29	Horace Copeland, Trent Dilfer, Alvin Harper, Jackie Harris	5.00
30	Henry Ellard, Gus Frerotte, Heath Shuler, Michael Westbrook	5.00
31	Keyshawn Johnson, Kevin Hardy, Simeon Rice, Jonathan Ogden	8.00
32	Lawrence Phillips, Tim Biakabutuka, Terry Glenn, Rickey Dudley	8.00
33	Eddie George, Marvin Harrison, Eric Moulds, Eddie Kennison	20.00
34	Derrick Mayes, Karim Abdul-Jabbar, Alex Van Dyke, Bobby Engram	4.00
35	Leeland McElroy, Jason Dunn, Mike Alstott, Amani Toomer	6.00

A player's name in *italic* type indicates a rookie card.

1996 Playoff Absolute/ Prime Unsung Heroes

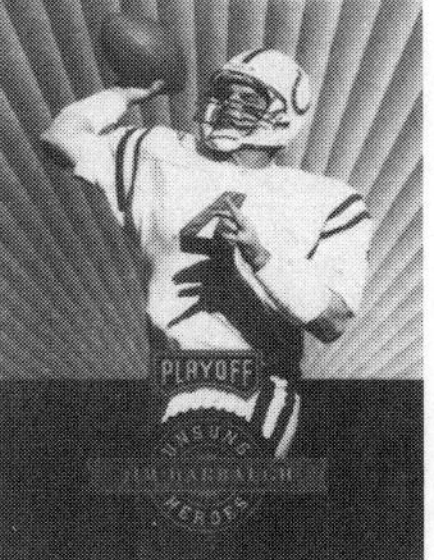

These cards were available in 1996 Playoff Absolute (#s 1- 15, NFC players) and 1996 Playoff Prime (#s 16-30, AFC players). The cards, which utilize a brand-new Tekchrome design, honor players long on desire and grit, but short on headlines. The players were chosen by fans in nationwide voting and were honored at the 23rd Annual NFLPA Banquet in March 1996 to benefit the Washington D.C. chapter of the Special Olympics. The cards were only available in Red packs, one in 24 packs. Fronts have a color action photo, with the brand/insert set logos and player's name toward the bottom.

		NM/M
Complete Set (30):		20.00
Complete Absolute Set (15):		8.00
Complete Prime Set (15):		12.00
Common Player:		.20
Minor Stars:		.50
Inserted 1:24		
1	Bill Bates	.20
2	Jeff Brady	.20
3	Ray Brown	.20
4	Isaac Bruce	2.00
5	Larry Centers	.50
6	Mark Chmura	.50
7	Keith Elias	.20
8	Robert Green	.20
9	Andy Harmon	.20
10	Rodney Holman	.20
11	Derek Loville	.50
12	J.J. McCleskey	.20
13	Sam Mills	.20
14	Hardy Nickerson	.50
15	Jessie Tuggle	.20
16	Eric Bieniemy	.20
17	Blaine Bishop	.20
18	Mark Brunell	3.00
19	Wayne Chrebet	1.50
20	Vince Evans	.20
21	Sam Gash	.20
22	Tim Grunhard	.20
23	Jim Harbaugh	.50
24	Dwayne Harper	.20
25	Bernie Parmalee	.20
26	Reggie Rivers	.20
27	Eugene Robinson	.20
28	Kordell Stewart	3.00
29	Steve Tasker	.20
30	Bennie Thompson	.20

1996 Playoff Absolute Xtreme Team

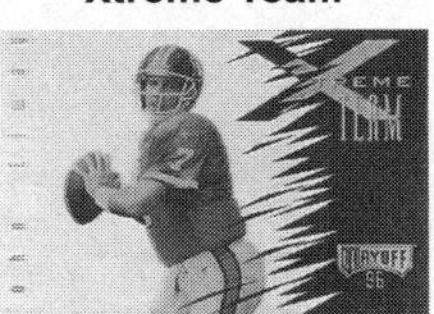

Thirty of the game's most coveted players appear to jump out at you on these 1996 Playoff Absolute cards. Each card is clear plastic, foil-enhanced, and available only in White inner packs (one in 24 packs). Fronts have a color action photo on one side against a clear background that has the player's name (along the left side) and a team logo showing through. The player's name is stamped in gold foil along the left side. The right side has a color panel with a gold-foil stamped brand logo. Gold foil is also used for part of the X in the insert set logo. The card back (numbered XT01, etc.) has a reverse angle of the photo from the front, plus a brief recap of the player's accomplishments.

	NM/M
Complete Set (30):	125.00
Common Player:	1.00
Minor Stars:	3.00

1	Troy Aikman	6.00
2	Emmitt Smith	8.00
3	Jerry Rice	6.00
4	Dan Marino	10.00
5	Brett Favre	10.00
6	Barry Sanders	8.00
7	Michael Irvin	3.00
8	John Elway	6.00
9	Joey Galloway	3.00
10	Steve Young	6.00
11	Deion Sanders	4.00
12	Terrell Davis	6.00
13	Herman Moore	3.00
14	Reggie White	1.00
15	Cris Carter	1.00
16	Rodney Hampton	1.00
17	Isaac Bruce	3.00
18	Brett Perriman	1.00
19	Curtis Conway	1.00
20	Scott Mitchell	1.00
21	Rashaan Salaam	1.00
22	Robert Brooks	1.00
23	Marshall Faulk	6.00
24	Curtis Martin	6.00
25	Harvey Williams	1.00
26	Yancey Thigpen	1.00
27	Chris Warren	1.00
28	Erict Rhett	1.00
29	Terry Allen	1.00
30	Carl Pickens	1.00

1996 Playoff Prime Promos

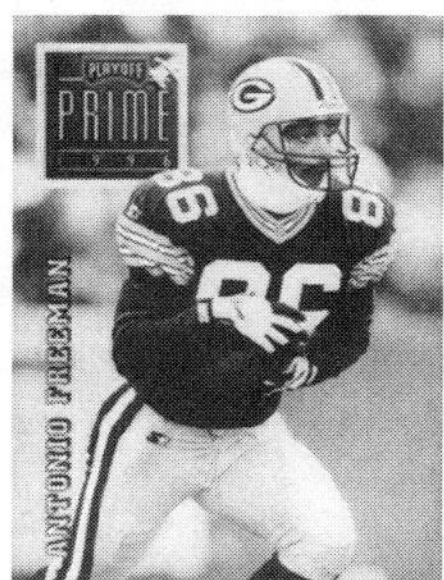

This six-card promo set gave collectors and dealers a sneak peak at the designs for 1996 Playoff Prime. The same six players were featured in 1996 Absolute Promos, but the photos and logos are different.

		NM/M
Complete Set (6):		20.00
Common Player:		1.50
	Terrell Davis	7.00
	Tamarick Vanover	3.00
	Rashaan Salaam	3.00
	J.J. Stokes	3.00
	Antonio Freeman	3.00
	Zack Crockett	1.50

1996 Playoff Prime

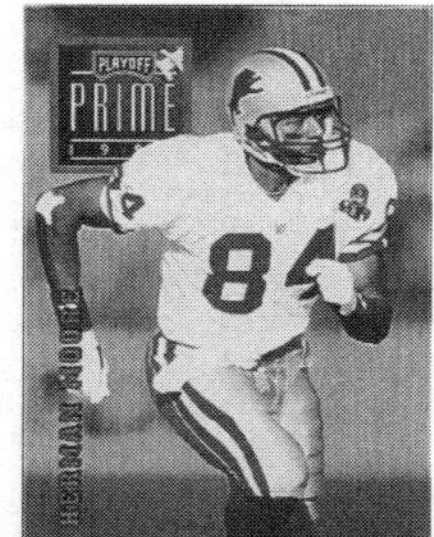

Playoff's 1996 Prime set is its 200-card retail version. The checklist order and card design are different than Prime's Absolute hobby version. Four insert sets are available; Prime Boss Hog is exclusive to Prime retail packs, while Metal XL and Unsung Heroes are in hobby and retail packs, with the retail versions picking up the numbering where the hobby versions ended. 1996 Playoff Prime also continues the pack-within-a-pack concept explained in the 1996 Playoff Absolute set introduction in this book.

		NM/M
Complete Set (200):		75.00
Common Bronze:		.10
Common Silver:		.40
Common Gold:		1.00
Pack (6):		1.50
Wax Box (24):		25.00
1	Brett Favre	4.00
2	Jerry Rice	1.50
3	Troy Aikman	1.50
4	Bruce Smith	.10
5	Marshall Faulk	1.25
6	Erik Kramer	.10
7	Carl Pickens	.20
8	Anthony Miller	.10
9	Cris Carter	.10
10	Todd Kinchen	.10
11	Stoney Case	.10
12	Chris Calloway	.10
13	Andre Rison	.10
14	Bill Brooks	.10
15	Shawn Jefferson	.10
16	Eric Zeier	.10
17	Yancey Thigpen	.30
18	Edgar Bennett	.10
19	Garrison Hearst	.20
20	Daryl Johnston	.10
21	Tyrone Wheatley	.10
22	Darick Holmes	.10
23	Dave Brown	.10
24	*Leeland McElroy*	.30
25	Craig Heyward	.10
26	*Kevin Hardy*	.30
27	Scott Mitchell	.10
28	Willie Green	.10
29	Vincent Brisby	.10
30	Mike Tomczak	.10
31	Luther Ellis	.10
32	Mike Pritchard	.10
33	Robert Green	.10
34	Jeff Graham	.10
35	Tamarick Vanover	.30
36	William Floyd	.10
37	Alvin Harper	.10
38	Stan Humphries	.10
39	Herman Moore	.40
40	Tony Martin	.10
41	Jonathan Ogden	.10
42	Randall Cunningham	.10
43	Chris Warren	.20
44	Bobby Hobert	.10
45	Jerome Bettis	.10
46	Joey Galloway	1.25
47	Ernie Mills	.10
48	Steve McNair	1.00
49	*Karim Abdul-Jabbar*	1.00
50	Chad May	.10
51	Jim Everett	.10
52	Robert Smith	.10
53	Tony Boselli	.10
54	William Henderson	.10
55	*Terry Glenn*	2.50
56	Neil O'Donnell	.10
57	Chris Chandler	.10
58	Michael Jackson	.10
59	*Jason Dunn*	.30
60	James Stewart	.10
61	Greg Hill	.10
62	Mark Carrier	.10
63	Bernie Parmalee	.10
64	Chris Sanders	.30
65	Jeff Hostetler	.10
66	*Eric Moulds*	4.00
67	James Jett	.10
68	Henry Ellard	.10
69	Mario Bates	.10
70	Natrone Means	.20
71	*Bobby Engram*	1.25
72	Christian Fauria	.10
73	Gus Frerotte	.10
74	Aaron Hayden	.30
75	Reggie White	.20
76	Dave Meggett	.10
77	Harvey Williams	.10
78	Terance Mathis	.10
79	Bam Morris	.10
80	Trent Dilfer	.10
81	Irving Fryar	.10
82	Quinn Early	.10
83	Lake Dawson	.10
84	Todd Collins	.10
85	Eric Metcalf	.10
86	*Tim Biakabutuka*	1.25
87	Rob Johnson	.10
88	Charlie Garner	.10
89	Mike Mamula	.10
90	Steve Walsh	.10
91	Charles Haley	.10
92	*Mike Alstott*	2.00
93	Wayne Chrebet	.10
94	Vinny Testaverde	.10
95	Fred Barnett	.10
96	Boomer Esiason	.10
97	Zack Crockett	.10
98	Kevin Williams	.10
99	Eric Bieniemy	.10
100	Bryan Cox	.10
101	Larry Centers	.40
102	Jeff George	.75
103	Bryce Paup	.40
104	Kerry Collins	1.00
105	Derrick Moore	.40
106	Adrian Murrell	.40
107	Harold Green	.40
108	Ki-Jana Carter	.75
109	Sherman Williams	.40
110	Deion Sanders	2.50
111	Emmitt Smith	6.00
112	Shannon Sharpe	.40
113	Johnnie Morton	.40
114	*Eddie Kennison*	1.50
115	*Marvin Harrison*	15.00
116	*Amani Toomer*	1.00
117	*Rickey Dudley*	1.00
118	*Alex Van Dyke*	1.00
119	Dorsey Levens	2.00
120	Antonio Freeman	.40
121	Willie Davis	.40
122	Lamont Warren	.40
123	Sean Dawkins	.40
124	Willie Jackson	.40
125	Kimble Anders	.40
126	Dan Marino	7.00
127	Terry Kirby	.40
128	Amp Lee	.40
129	Jake Reed	.40
130	Curtis Martin	4.00
131	Ray Zellars	.40
132	Herschel Walker	.40
133	Mike Sherrard	.40
134	Kyle Brady	.40
135	Raghib Ismail	.40
136	Ricky Watters	.40
137	Kordell Stewart	3.00
138	Andre Hastings	.40
139	Ronnie Harmon	.40
140	Terrell Fletcher	.40
141	J.J. Stokes	3.00
142	Brent Jones	.40
143	Tony McGee	.40
144	Brian Blades	.40
145	Isaac Bruce	.75
146	Errict Rhett	.75
147	Warren Sapp	.40
148	Horace Copeland	.40
149	Heath Shuler	.75
150	Michael Westbrook	.75
151	Frank Sanders	1.00
152	Rob Moore	1.00
153	Bert Emanuel	1.00
154	J.J. Birden	1.00
155	Thurman Thomas	2.00
156	Jim Kelly	2.00
157	Curtis Conway	2.00
158	Darnay Scott	2.00
159	Jeff Blake	2.00
160	Jay Novacek	1.00
161	Michael Irvin	2.00
162	John Elway	5.00
163	Terrell Davis	6.00
164	Barry Sanders	6.00
165	Brett Perriman	1.00
166	*Keyshawn Johnson*	10.00
167	*Eddie George*	14.00
168	*Derrick Mayes*	3.50
169	*Simeon Rice*	2.00
170	*Lawrence Phillips*	1.00
171	Robert Brooks	2.00
172	Mark Chmura	1.50
173	Rodney Thomas	1.00
174	Jim Harbaugh	1.00
175	Ken Dilger	1.00
176	Mark Brunell	4.00
177	Steve Bono	2.00
178	Marcus Allen	2.00
179	O.J. McDuffie	1.00
180	Eric Green	1.00
181	Warren Moon	2.00
182	Drew Bledsoe	5.00
183	Ben Coates	1.00
184	Michael Haynes	1.00
185	Rodney Hampton	1.00
186	Rashaan Salaam	2.00
187	Napoleon Kaufman	1.00
188	Tim Brown	1.00
189	Rodney Peete	1.00
190	Calvin Williams	1.00
191	Erric Pegram	1.00
192	Mark Bruener	1.00
193	Junior Seau	2.00
194	Steve Young	5.00
195	Derek Loville	1.00
196	Rick Mirer	2.00
197	Mark Rypien	1.00
198	Jackie Harris	1.00
199	Tracy Allen	1.00
200	Brian Mitchell	1.00

1996 Playoff Prime Boss Hogs

These cards were exclusive inserts in 1996 Playoff Prime retail packs.

		NM/M
Complete Set (18):		100.00
Common Player:		3.00
1	Curtis Martin	8.00
2	Chris Warren	3.00
3	Emmitt Smith	12.00
4	Barry Sanders	12.00
5	Rashaan Salaam	3.00
6	Marshall Faulk	8.00
7	Errict Rhett	3.00
8	Thurman Thomas	3.00
9	Kerry Collins	6.00
10	Dan Marino	15.00
11	Jerry Rice	10.00
12	Troy Aikman	10.00
13	Jeff George	3.00
14	Brett Favre	15.00
15	Robert Brooks	3.00
16	John Elway	10.00
17	Deion Sanders	6.00
18	Kordell Stewart	6.00

1996 Playoff Prime X's and O's

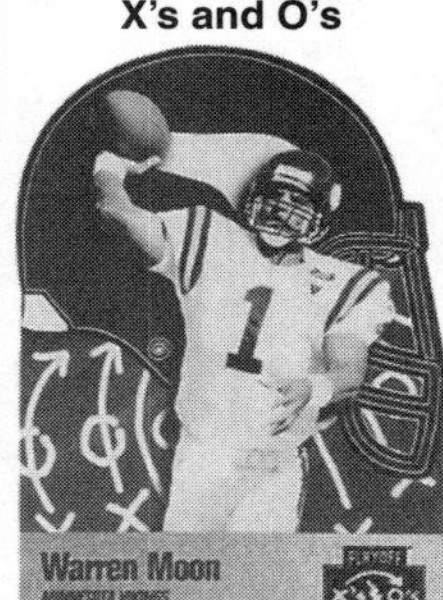

X's & O's is a 200-card parallel set of Prime, and was inserted one per 7.2 packs. It is considered a parallel set since it has an identical checklist to the base set, but X's & O's were printed on a die-cut plastic surface, with the player's team helmet in the background. There is a holographic strip on the bottom that includes the player's name, position and an X's & O's logo.

		NM/M
Complete Set (200):		250.00
Common Player:		.25
Minor Stars:		1.00
1	Brett Favre	15.00
2	Jerry Rice	10.00
3	Troy Aikman	10.00
4	Bruce Smith	.25
5	Marshall Faulk	8.00
6	Erik Kramer	.25
7	Carl Pickens	1.00
8	Anthony Miller	.25
9	Cris Carter	1.00
10	Todd Kinchen	.25
11	Stoney Case	.25
12	Chris Calloway	.25
13	Andre Rison	.25
14	Bill Brooks	.25
15	Shawn Jefferson	.25
16	Eric Zeier	.25
17	Yancey Thigpen	2.00
18	Edgar Bennett	.25
19	Garrison Hearst	1.00
20	Daryl Johnston	.25
21	Tyrone Wheatley	.25
22	Darick Holmes	1.00
23	Dave Brown	.25
24	Leeland McElroy	1.00
25	Craig Heyward	.25
26	Kevin Hardy	1.00
27	Scott Mitchell	.25
28	Willie Green	.25
29	Vincent Brisby	.25
30	Mike Tomczak	.25
31	Luther Ellis	.25
32	Mike Pritchard	.25
33	Robert Green	.25
34	Jeff Graham	.25
35	Tamarick Vanover	3.00
36	William Floyd	1.00
37	Alvin Harper	.25
38	Stan Humphries	.25
39	Herman Moore	3.00
40	Tony Martin	.25
41	Jonathan Ogden	.25
42	Randall Cunningham	.25
43	Chris Warren	1.00
44	Bobby Hobert	.25
45	Jerome Bettis	3.00
46	Joey Galloway	4.00
47	Ernie Mills	.25
48	Steve McNair	8.00
49	Karim Abdul-Jabbar	2.00
50	Chad May	.25
51	Jim Everett	.25
52	Robert Smith	1.00
53	Tony Boselli	.25
54	William Henderson	.25
55	Terry Glenn	6.00
56	Neil O'Donnell	1.00
57	Chris Chandler	.25
58	Michael Jackson	.25
59	Jason Dunn	1.00
60	James Stewart	.25
61	Greg Hill	.25
62	Mark Carrier	.25
63	Bernie Parmalee	.25
64	Chris Sanders	.25
65	Jeff Hostetler	.25
66	Eric Moulds	8.00
67	James Jett	.25
68	Henry Ellard	.25
69	Mario Bates	.25
70	Natrone Means	1.00
71	Bobby Engram	2.00
72	Christian Fauria	.25
73	Gus Frerotte	.25
74	Aaron Hayden	1.00
75	Reggie White	1.00
76	Dave Meggett	.25
77	Harvey Williams	.25
78	Terance Mathis	.25
79	Bam Morris	.25
80	Trent Dilfer	.25
81	Irving Fryar	.25
82	Quinn Early	.25
83	Lake Dawson	.25
84	Todd Collins	.25
85	Eric Metcalf	.25
86	Tim Biakabutuka	1.00
87	Rob Johnson	6.00
88	Charlie Garner	.25
89	Mike Mamula	.25
90	Steve Walsh	.25
91	Charles Haley	.25
92	Mike Alstott	6.00
93	Wayne Chrebet	.25
94	Vinny Testaverde	.25
95	Fred Barnett	.25
96	Boomer Esiason	.25
97	Zack Crockett	.25
98	Kevin Williams	.25
99	Eric Bieniemy	.25
100	Bryan Cox	.25
101	Larry Centers	.25
102	Jeff George	1.00
103	Bryce Paup	.25
104	Kerry Collins	6.00
105	Derrick Moore	.25
106	Adrian Murrell	.25
107	Harold Green	.25
108	Ki-Jana Carter	6.00
109	Sherman Williams	.25
110	Deion Sanders	5.00
111	Emmitt Smith	12.00
112	Shannon Sharpe	.25
113	Johnnie Morton	.25
114	Eddie Kennison	3.00
115	Marvin Harrison	8.00
116	Amani Toomer	6.00
117	Rickey Dudley	3.00
118	Alex Van Dyke	1.00
119	Dorsey Levens	2.00
120	Antonio Freeman	.25
121	Willie Davis	.25
122	Lamont Warren	.25
123	Sean Dawkins	.25
124	Willie Jackson	.25
125	Kimble Anders	.25
126	Dan Marino	15.00
127	Terry Kirby	.25
128	Amp Lee	.25
129	Jake Reed	.25
130	Curtis Martin	10.00
131	Ray Zellars	.25
132	Herschel Walker	.25
133	Mike Sherrard	.25
134	Kyle Brady	.25
135	Raghib Ismail	.25
136	Ricky Watters	1.00
137	Kordell Stewart	6.00
138	Andre Hastings	.25
139	Ronnie Harmon	.25
140	Terrell Fletcher	.25
141	J.J. Stokes	4.00
142	Brent Jones	.25
143	Tony McGee	.25
144	Brian Blades	.25
145	Isaac Bruce	6.00
146	Errict Rhett	3.00
147	Warren Sapp	.25
148	Horace Copeland	.25
149	Heath Shuler	1.00
150	Michael Westbrook	3.00
151	Frank Sanders	.25
152	Rob Moore	.25
153	Bert Emanuel	.25
154	J.J. Birden	.25
155	Thurman Thomas	1.00
156	Jim Kelly	1.00
157	Curtis Conway	1.00
158	Darnay Scott	1.00
159	Jeff Blake	2.00
160	Jay Novacek	.25
161	Michael Irvin	6.00
162	John Elway	10.00
163	Terrell Davis	12.00
164	Barry Sanders	12.00
165	Brett Perriman	.25
166	Keyshawn Johnson	5.00
167	Eddie George	8.00
168	Derrick Mayes	2.00
169	Simeon Rice	1.00
170	Lawrence Phillips	.50
171	Robert Brooks	1.00
172	Mark Chmura	1.00
173	Rodney Thomas	1.00
174	Jim Harbaugh	1.00
175	Ken Dilger	.25
176	Mark Brunell	8.00
177	Steve Bono	1.00
178	Marcus Allen	1.00
179	O.J. McDuffie	.25
180	Eric Green	.25
181	Warren Moon	1.00
182	Drew Bledsoe	10.00
183	Ben Coates	.25
184	Michael Haynes	.25
185	Rodney Hampton	.25
186	Rashaan Salaam	1.00
187	Napoleon Kaufman	1.00
188	Tim Brown	.25
189	Rodney Peete	.25
190	Calvin Williams	.25
191	Erric Pegram	.25
192	Mark Bruener	.25
193	Junior Seau	1.00
194	Steve Young	10.00
195	Derek Loville	.25
196	Rick Mirer	1.00
197	Mark Rypien	.25
198	Jackie Harris	.25
199	Terry Allen	.25
200	Brian Mitchell	.25

1996 Playoff Prime Surprise

This 14-card set was inserted in Prime at a rate of one in 288 packs.

		NM/M
Complete Set (14):		150.00
Common Player:		2.00
Minor Stars:		5.00
Inserted 1:288		
1	Dan Marino	15.00
2	Brett Favre	15.00
3	Emmitt Smith	12.00
4	Kordell Stewart	6.00
5	Jerry Rice	10.00
6	Troy Aikman	10.00
7	Barry Sanders	12.00
8	Curtis Martin	8.00
9	Marshall Faulk	8.00
10	Joey Galloway	5.00
11	Robert Brooks	2.00
12	Deion Sanders	6.00
13	Reggie White	2.00
14	Marcus Allen	4.00

A card number in parenthese ( ) indicates the set is unnumbered.

1996 Playoff Prime Playoff Honors

This 1996 Playoff Prime set features three of the NFL's brightest stars - Brett Favre, Emmitt Smith and Curtis Martin. The leather cards are seeded one per 7,200 packs.

		NM/M
Complete Set (3):		125.00
Common Player:		30.00
Inserted 1:7,200		
1	Emmitt Smith	50.00
2	Curtis Martin	30.00
3	Brett Favre	60.00

1996 Playoff Unsung Heroes Banquet

To honor the NFL's Unsung Heroes, Playoff produced this 30-card set which was handed out at the March 8, 1996 NFL Players Award Banquet in Washington, D.C. The card fronts have a color photo of the player over a purple striped background. At the bottom of the front, are "1996," and the Playoff and Unsung Heroes' logos. The card backs have a color photo of the player, his name and why he was named an Unsung Hero. The date of the banquet is also featured at the top of the horizontal card backs.

		NM/M
Complete Set (30):		20.00
Common Player:		.50
Minor Stars:		1.00
1	Bill Bates	.50
2	Jeff Brady	.50
3	Ray Brown	.50
4	Isaac Bruce	2.00
5	Larry Centers	1.00
6	Mark Chmura	1.00
7	Keith Elias	.50
8	Robert Green	.50
9	Andy Harmon	.50
10	Rodney Holman	.50
11	Derek Loville	1.00
12	J.J. McCleskey	.50
13	Sam Mills	.50
14	Hardy Nickerson	1.00
15	Jessie Tuggle	.50
16	Eric Bieniemy	.50
17	Blaine Bishop	.50
18	Mark Brunell	6.00
19	Wayne Chrebet	2.00
20	Vince Evans	.50
21	Sam Gash	.50
22	Tim Grunhard	.50
23	Jim Harbaugh	1.00
24	Dwayne Harper	.50
25	Bernie Parmalee	.50
26	Reggie Rivers	.50
27	Eugene Robinson	.50
28	Kordell Stewart	5.00
29	Steve Tasker	.50
30	Bennie Thompson	.50

1996 Playoff Contenders Leather

This 100-card base set lives up to its name, with a leather card front. The player's name, which can be printed in green, purple or red, is printed inside a black oval along the left side of the card. The Playoff Contenders' and Genuine Leather logos appear on the front. If the player's name is printed in green foil, it is a "Scarce" card, which was most frequently inserted. Purple foil is a "Rare" card, seeded one per 11 packs. Red foil is "Ultra Rare," and seeded one per 22 packs. The card backs include a full-bleed photo of the player. The card number is printed in the upper right.

NM/M
Common Player: .75
Pack (3): 3.50
Wax Box (12): 30.00
1 Brett Favre R 25.00
2 Steve Young P 15.00
3 Herman Moore P 5.00
4 Jim Harbaugh P 3.00
5 Curtis Martin R 15.00
6 Junior Seau .75
7 John Elway R 15.00
8 Troy Aikman R 15.00
9 Terry Allen .75
10 Kordell Stewart R 10.00
11 Drew Bledsoe R 15.00
12 Jim Kelly R 10.00
13 Dan Marino R 25.00
14 Andre Rison .75
15 Jeff Hostetler .75
16 Scott Mitchell .75
17 Carl Pickens .75
18 Larry Centers R 5.00
19 Craig Heyward .75
20 Barry Sanders R 20.00
21 Deion Sanders P 8.00
22 Emmitt Smith R 20.00
23 Rashaan Salaam P 1.00
24 Mario Bates .75
25 Lawrence Phillips R .50
26 Napoleon Kaufman P 1.00
27 Rodney Hampton .75
28 Marshall Faulk R 10.00
29 Trent Dilfer .75
30 Leeland McElroy 3.00
31 Marcus Allen 2.00
32 Ricky Watters R 10.00
33 Karim Abdul-Jabbar R 5.00
34 Herschel Walker .75
35 Thurman Thomas 2.00
36 Jerome Bettis 2.00
37 Gus Frerotte P 3.00
38 Neil O'Donnell P 3.00
39 Rick Mirer .75
40 Mike Alstott P 8.00
41 Vinny Testaverde P 3.00
42 Derek Loville .75
43 Ben Coates .75
44 Steve McNair 6.00
45 Bobby Engram 2.00
46 Yancey Thigpen .75
47 Lake Dawson .75
48 Terrell Davis 10.00
49 Kerry Collins P 6.00
50 Eric Metcalf .75
51 Stanley Pritchett P 3.00
52 Robert Brooks .75
53 Isaac Bruce R 10.00
54 Tim Brown .75
55 Edgar Bennett .75
56 Warren Moon .75
57 Jerry Rice R 20.00
58 Michael Westbrook 2.00
59 Keyshawn Johnson R 10.00
60 Steve Bono .75
61 Derrick Mayes 2.00
62 Erik Kramer .75
63 Rodney Peete .75
64 Eddie Kennison P 6.00
65 Derrick Thomas .75
66 Joey Galloway P 10.00
67 Amani Toomer 2.00
68 Reggie White P 7.00
69 Heath Shuler R 7.00
70 Dave Brown R 7.00
71 Tony Banks 6.00
72 Chris Warren R 7.00
73 J.J. Stokes R 8.00
74 Rickey Dudley 3.00
75 Stan Humphries .75
76 Jason Dunn .75
77 Tyrone Wheatley P 3.00
78 Jim Everett R 7.00
79 Cris Carter P 3.00
80 Alex Van Dyke 2.00
81 O.J. McDuffie .75
82 Mark Chmura .75
83 Terry Glenn 10.00
84 Boomer Esiason .75
85 Bruce Smith .75
86 Curtis Conway P 3.00
87 Ki-Jana Carter 2.00
88 Tamarick Vanover 2.00
89 Michael Jackson .75
90 Mark Brunell P 8.00
91 Tim Biakabutuka P 3.00
92 Anthony Miller P 3.00
93 Marvin Harrison P 10.00
94 Jeff George R 7.00
95 Jeff Blake P 6.00
96 Eddie George R 15.00
97 Eric Moulds 2.00
98 Mike Tomczak P 3.00
99 Chris Sanders P 3.00
100 Chris Chandler .75

1996 Playoff Contenders Pennants

This 100-card pennant-shaped base set includes a photo of the player, with the Playoff Pennants 1996 logo at the top. The player's name is printed in silver foil, also at the top. The felt-like material is coordinated with the player's team color. Three levels of this base set exist. If the "Pennants" logo is green it is a "Scarce" card, which was the most frequently inserted card. If it is purple, it is "Rare" and inserted one per eight packs. If it is red, it is "Ultra Rare" and inserted one per 16 packs. Card backs also have the felt-like surface, with the player's name in a colored bar in the middle.

NM/M
Complete Set (100): 150.00
Common Player: .50
1 Brett Favre R 20.00
2 Steve Young R 10.00
3 Herman Moore R 4.00
4 Jim Harbaugh R 2.00
5 Curtis Martin R 10.00
6 Junior Seau .50
7 John Elway R 12.00
8 Troy Aikman P 12.00
9 Terry Allen .50
10 Kordell Stewart R 6.00
11 Drew Bledsoe 8.00
12 Jim Kelly P 3.00
13 Dan Marino P 20.00
14 Andre Rison .50
15 Jeff Hostetler .50
16 Scott Mitchell .50
17 Carl Pickens R 1.00
18 Larry Centers P 1.00
19 Craig Heyward .50
20 Barry Sanders P 15.00
21 Deion Sanders R 8.00
22 Emmitt Smith R 20.00
23 Rashaan Salaam R 1.00
24 Mario Bates .50
25 Lawrence Phillips .50
26 Napoleon Kaufman .50
27 Rodney Hampton .50
28 Marshall Faulk P 5.00
29 Trent Dilfer .50
30 Leeland McElroy P .50
31 Marcus Allen P 2.00
32 Ricky Watters 2.00
33 Karim Abdul-Jabbar 1.00
34 Herschel Walker P 3.00
35 Thurman Thomas R 3.00
36 Jerome Bettis P 4.00
37 Gus Frerotte .50
38 Neil O'Donnell .50
39 Rick Mirer .50
40 Mike Alstott R 8.00
41 Vinny Testaverde R 1.00
42 Derek Loville .50
43 Ben Coates .50
44 Steve McNair R 8.00
45 Bobby Engram P 1.00
46 Yancey Thigpen .50
47 Lake Dawson .50
48 Terrell Davis P 10.00
49 Kerry Collins R 4.00
50 Eric Metcalf .50
51 Stanley Pritchett R 1.00
52 Robert Brooks R 1.00
53 Isaac Bruce 3.00
54 Tim Brown .50
55 Edgar Bennett P 3.00
56 Warren Moon .50
57 Jerry Rice R 15.00
58 Michael Westbrook 2.00
59 Keyshawn Johnson 2.00
60 Steve Bono R 1.00
61 Derrick Mayes P 1.00
62 Erik Kramer P 1.00
63 Rodney Peete .50
64 Eddie Kennison 2.00
65 Derrick Thomas .50
66 Joey Galloway R 5.00
67 Amani Toomer P 2.00
68 Reggie White 2.00
69 Heath Shuler .50
70 Dave Brown .50
71 Tony Banks P 1.00
72 Chris Warren .50
73 J.J. Stokes 2.00
74 Rickey Dudley P 2.00
75 Stan Humphries .50
76 Jason Dunn P .50
77 Tyrone Wheatley .50
78 Jim Everett .50
79 Cris Carter P 2.00
80 Alex Van Dyke P .50
81 O.J. McDuffie .50
82 Mark Chmura P 1.00
83 Terry Glenn P 5.00
84 Boomer Esiason R 3.00
85 Bruce Smith .50
86 Curtis Conway .50
87 Ki-Jana Carter 1.00
88 Tamarick Vanover 1.00
89 Michael Jackson .50
90 Mark Brunell 5.00
91 Tim Biakabutuka R 1.00
92 Anthony Miller .50
93 Marvin Harrison R 10.00
94 Jeff George P 2.00
95 Jeff Blake R 2.00
96 Eddie George 6.00
97 Eric Moulds P 6.00
98 Mike Tomczak .50
99 Chris Sanders .50
100 Chris Chandler .50

1996 Playoff Contenders Open Field

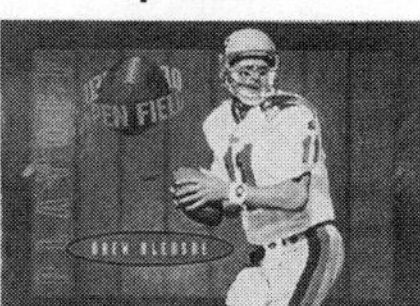

These mini-cards, which measure 3-1/8" x 2-1/4", were part of the Contenders base set. A color photo of the player is showcased, with a holographic background of a football field. The Open Field logo also is included in the hologram. Three levels of this base set exist. The "Scarce" cards, which have the player's name in a green oval, are the most frequently inserted. The "Rare" cards have the oval in purple and were inserted one per five packs. The "Ultra Rare" cards have the oval in red and are seeded one per nine packs. Card backs have a photo on the left, with a "Playoff The Wall Fact" on the right.

NM/M
Complete Set (100): 175.00
Common Player: .75
1 Brett Favre P 20.00
2 Steve Young R 15.00
3 Herman Moore P 4.00
4 Jim Harbaugh .75
5 Curtis Martin P 15.00
6 Junior Seau P 2.00
7 John Elway P 10.00
8 Troy Aikman R 18.00
9 Terry Allen .75
10 Kordell Stewart P 12.00
11 Drew Bledsoe 6.00
12 Jim Kelly 2.00
13 Dan Marino R 35.00
14 Andre Rison P 2.00
15 Jeff Hostetler .75
16 Scott Mitchell R 3.00
17 Carl Pickens .75
18 Larry Centers .75
19 Craig Heyward R 3.00
20 Barry Sanders R 20.00
21 Deion Sanders P 8.00
22 Emmitt Smith P 20.00
23 Rashaan Salaam R 6.00
24 Mario Bates P 2.00
25 Lawrence Phillips P 3.00
26 Napoleon Kaufman .75
27 Rodney Hampton .75
28 Marshall Faulk R 10.00
29 Trent Dilfer .75
30 Leeland McElroy R 1.00
31 Marcus Allen 2.00
32 Ricky Watters P 4.00
33 Karim Abdul-Jabbar P 2.00
34 Herschel Walker R 3.00
35 Thurman Thomas 2.00
36 Jerome Bettis 2.00
37 Gus Frerotte R 1.00
38 Neil O'Donnell .75
39 Rick Mirer .75
40 Mike Alstott 3.00
41 Vinny Testaverde .75
42 Derek Loville .75
43 Ben Coates .75
44 Steve McNair 3.00
45 Bobby Engram R 2.00
46 Yancey Thigpen .75
47 Lake Dawson P .75
48 Terrell Davis 8.00
49 Kerry Collins P 4.00
50 Eric Metcalf .75
51 Stanley Pritchett .75
52 Robert Brooks P 2.00
53 Isaac Bruce P 3.00
54 Tim Brown P 2.00
55 Edgar Bennett .75
56 Warren Moon P 2.00
57 Jerry Rice P 15.00
58 Michael Westbrook 2.00
59 Keyshawn Johnson P 8.00
60 Steve Bono .75
61 Derrick Mayes R 2.00
62 Erik Kramer .75
63 Rodney Peete .75
64 Eddie Kennison 2.00
65 Derrick Thomas .75
66 Joey Galloway R 10.00
67 Amani Toomer R 6.00
68 Reggie White R 2.00
69 Heath Shuler P 1.00
70 Dave Brown .75
71 Tony Banks R 2.00
72 Chris Warren .75
73 J.J. Stokes 2.00
74 Rickey Dudley R 2.00
75 Stan Humphries .75
76 Jason Dunn R .75
77 Tyrone Wheatley .75
78 Jim Everett .75
79 Cris Carter .75
80 Alex Van Dyke R 1.00
81 O.J. McDuffie P 2.00
82 Mark Chmura .75
83 Terry Glenn R 12.00
84 Boomer Esiason .75
85 Bruce Smith .75
86 Curtis Conway .75
87 Ki-Jana Carter R 3.00
88 Tamarick Vanover P 2.00
89 Michael Jackson R 3.00
90 Mark Brunell 6.00
91 Tim Biakabutuka 1.00
92 Anthony Miller .75
93 Marvin Harrison 4.00
94 Jeff George .75
95 Jeff Blake 1.00
96 Eddie George P 20.00
97 Eric Moulds R 12.00
98 Mike Tomczak R 1.00
99 Chris Sanders .75
100 Chris Chandler .75

1996 Playoff Contenders Leather Accents

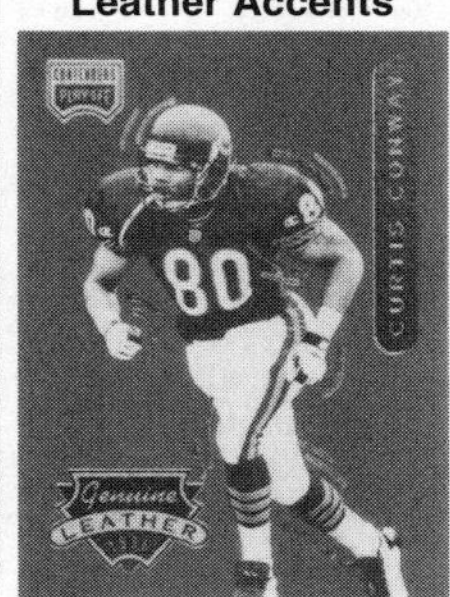

The difference between Genuine Leather and Genuine Leather Accents parallel set is Accents has the Genuine Leather and Playoff Contenders' logo and name oval in teal foil. Different scarcities also exist with the green, purple and red foils on the player's names. The card backs have a full-bleed photo, with the card number in the upper right. "Accent" is printed in teal foil in the lower center on the card back. One card was seeded per 216 packs.

NM/M
Common Player: 5.00
Minor Stars: 10.00
1 Brett Favre 75.00
2 Steve Young 50.00
3 Herman Moore 10.00
4 Jim Harbaugh 5.00
5 Curtis Martin 40.00
6 Junior Seau 10.00
7 John Elway 50.00
8 Troy Aikman 60.00
9 Terry Allen 5.00
10 Kordell Stewart 10.00
11 Drew Bledsoe 60.00
12 Jim Kelly 10.00
13 Dan Marino 75.00
14 Andre Rison 5.00
15 Jeff Hostetler 5.00
16 Scott Mitchell 5.00
17 Carl Pickens 10.00
18 Larry Centers 5.00
19 Craig Heyward 5.00
20 Barry Sanders 75.00
21 Deion Sanders 40.00
22 Emmitt Smith 75.00
23 Rashaan Salaam 10.00
24 Mario Bates 5.00
25 Lawrence Phillips 5.00
26 Napoleon Kaufman 5.00
27 Rodney Hampton 5.00
28 Marshall Faulk 30.00
29 Trent Dilfer 10.00
30 Leeland McElroy 5.00
31 Marcus Allen 10.00
32 Ricky Watters 10.00
33 Karim Abdul-Jabbar 10.00
34 Herschel Walker 10.00
35 Thurman Thomas 10.00
36 Jerome Bettis 10.00
37 Gus Frerotte 5.00
38 Neil O'Donnell 5.00
39 Rick Mirer 5.00
40 Mike Alstott 25.00
41 Vinny Testaverde 10.00
42 Derek Loville 5.00
43 Ben Coates 10.00
44 Steve McNair 40.00
45 Bobby Engram 5.00
46 Yancey Thigpen 5.00
47 Lake Dawson 5.00
48 Terrell Davis 50.00
49 Kerry Collins 10.00
50 Eric Metcalf 5.00
51 Stanley Pritchett 5.00
52 Robert Brooks 5.00
53 Isaac Bruce 25.00
54 Tim Brown 10.00
55 Edgar Bennett 5.00
56 Warren Moon 10.00
57 Jerry Rice 60.00
58 Michael Westbrook 10.00
59 Keyshawn Johnson 40.00
60 Steve Bono 5.00
61 Derrick Mayes 10.00
62 Erik Kramer 5.00
63 Rodney Peete 5.00
64 Eddie Kennison 5.00
65 Derrick Thomas 10.00
66 Joey Galloway 30.00
67 Amani Toomer 5.00
68 Reggie White 10.00
69 Heath Shuler 5.00
70 Dave Brown 5.00
71 Tony Banks 10.00
72 Chris Warren 5.00
73 J.J. Stokes 10.00
74 Rickey Dudley 5.00
75 Stan Humphries 5.00
76 Jason Dunn 5.00
77 Tyrone Wheatley 10.00
78 Jim Everett 5.00
79 Cris Carter 10.00
80 Alex Van Dyke 5.00
81 O.J. McDuffie 5.00
82 Mark Chmura 5.00
83 Terry Glenn 25.00
84 Boomer Esiason 5.00
85 Bruce Smith 5.00
86 Curtis Conway 5.00
87 Ki-Jana Carter 5.00
88 Tamarick Vanover 5.00
89 Michael Jackson 5.00
90 Mark Brunell 15.00
91 Tim Biakabutuka 5.00
92 Anthony Miller 5.00
93 Marvin Harrison 40.00
94 Jeff George 5.00
95 Jeff Blake 5.00
96 Eddie George 50.00
97 Eric Moulds 10.00
98 Mike Tomczak 5.00
99 Chris Sanders 5.00
100 Chris Chandler 5.00

1996 Playoff Contenders Ground Hogs

This insert set, which was seeded one per 44 packs, featured a leather front. A rainbow foil "swoosh" follows behind the player. The Ground Hogs logo appears in one of the lower corners. The player's name is in gold foil at the top of the card. The card back has the Playoff Contenders' logo in the upper left and the card number, prefixed by "GH," in the upper right. A color photo of the player is featured on the back, with the running back in focus and the background blurry.

NM/M
Complete Set (8): 60.00
Common Player: 5.00
1 Emmitt Smith 20.00
2 Barry Sanders 20.00
3 Marshall Faulk 12.00
4 Curtis Martin 12.00
5 Chris Warren 5.00
6 Ricky Watters 5.00
7 Thurman Thomas 5.00
8 Terrell Davis 15.00

1996 Playoff Contenders Pennant Flyers

This pennant-shaped insert set includes a felt-like surface on the right, with the player's last name embossed on the left in a gold-foil bar along the left border. The Playoff Pennant Flyer logo is pictured on the front, with "1996" embossed in a gold-foil oval. The player's team's main color is used for the felt on the front and back. The card backs include the player's full name embossed in the gold-foil band, team logo inside a circle and a gold-foil embossed Playoff Contenders' logo. These were seeded one per 48 packs. The card numbers are prefixed with "PF."

NM/M
Complete Set (8): 60.00
Common Player: 5.00
1 Jerry Rice 20.00
2 Joey Galloway 10.00
3 Isaac Bruce 10.00
4 Herman Moore 5.00
5 Carl Pickens 5.00
6 Yancey Thigpen 5.00
7 Deion Sanders 10.00
8 Robert Brooks 5.00

1996 Playoff Contenders Air Command

This insert set features a photograph of the player showcased over a hologram background comprised of jets and clouds. The Playoff Air Command '96 logo appears in the upper left. The player's name is printed in gold foil in the lower left. The card back has a silver and blue etched-foil background and a color photo of the player. The Playoff Contenders logo is in the upper left, with the card number, prefixed by "AC," in the upper right. Each card measures 3-1/8" x 2-1/4". The cards were inserted one per 96 packs.

NM/M
Complete Set (8): 60.00
Common Player: 5.00
1 Dan Marino 15.00
2 Brett Favre 15.00
3 Troy Aikman 10.00
4 Mike Tomczak 5.00
5 John Elway 10.00
6 Jeff George 5.00
7 Chris Chandler 5.00
8 Steve Bono 5.00

1996 Playoff Contenders Honors

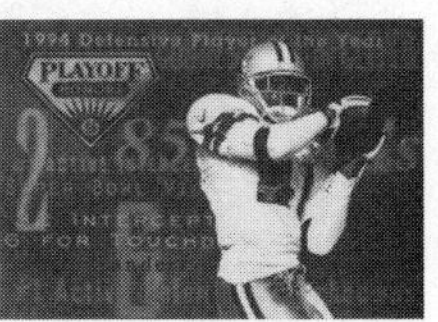

A continuation from Prime, this insert set had a new design that featured the Playoff Honors' logo and player's name in teal foil on the front of the card. The holographic background includes the various achievements of the player. The card back has a full-bleed photo of the player. The card numbers, prefixed by a "PH," are in the upper right. One card was seeded per 7,200 packs.

NM/M
Complete Set (3): 100.00
Common Player: 50.00
4 Dan Marino 50.00
5 Deion Sanders 25.00
6 Marcus Allen 25.00

1996 Playoff Illusions

The 120-card set's base cards are printed in different color schemes and graphics. The set features six different designs, each representing the six NFL divisions, as well as two levels of insertions. Cards #s 1-63 appeared approximately 3.5 cards per pack, while card #s 64-120 were found approximately one card per pack.

NM/M
Complete Set (120): 60.00
Common Player (1-63): .10
Common Player (64-120): .50

NM/M
Pack (5): 1.25
Wax Box (24): 20.00
1 Troy Aikman 2.00
2 Larry Centers .10
3 Terance Mathis .10
4 Calvin Williams .10
5 Jim Kelly .10
6 *Tim Biakabutuka* 1.50
7 Rashaan Salaam .75
8 Ki-Jana Carter .50
9 Anthony Miller .10
10 Deion Sanders 1.25
11 Scott Mitchell .10
12 Robert Brooks .10
13 Willie Davis .10
14 Zack Crockett .10
15 James Stewart .10
16 Tamarick Vanover .75
17 Stanley Pritchett .10
18 Warren Moon .10
19 Shawn Jefferson .10
20 Shannon Sharpe .10
21 Jim Everett .10
22 Dave Brown .10
23 Adrian Murrell .10
24 *Rickey Dudley* .75
25 Chris T. Jones .10
26 Andre Hastings .10
27 Stan Humphries .10
28 Steve Young 1.50
29 Joey Galloway 1.50
30 Jim Harbaugh .10
31 *Eddie Kennison* 1.00
32 *Mike Alstott* 2.50
33 Michael Westbrook .50
34 *Leeland McElroy* .75
35 Erik Kramer .10
36 Mark Chmura .10
37 Cris Carter .10
38 Ben Coates .10
39 Wayne Chrebet .10
40 Jerome Bettis .50
41 Tim Brown .10
42 Jason Dunn .10
43 William Henderson .10
44 Rick Mirer .10
45 J.J. Stokes .50
46 Rodney Peete .10
47 Neil O'Donnell .10
48 Tyrone Wheatley .10
49 *Terry Glenn* 2.50
50 Junior Seau .10
51 Jake Reed .10
52 O.J. McDuffie .10
53 Steve Bono .10
54 Steve McNair 2.00
55 Antonio Freeman .50
56 Johnnie Morton .10
57 Eric Metcalf .10
58 Andre Reed .10
59 *Bobby Engram* 1.00
60 Gus Frerotte .10
61 Jeff Blake .75
62 Erric Pegram .10
63 Jeff Hostetler .10
64 Edgar Bennett .50
65 *Eddie George* 10.00
66 *Marvin Harrison* 10.00
67 LeShon Johnson .50
68 *Jamal Anderson* 6.00
69 Thurman Thomas 1.00
70 Barry Sanders 5.00
71 *Muhsin Muhammad* 4.00
72 Robert Green .50
73 Garrison Hearst .50
74 John Elway 4.00
75 Herman Moore 1.00
76 Chris Chandler .50
77 Marshall Faulk 1.50
78 Mark Brunell 4.00
79 *Tony Banks* 3.00
80 Terrell Davis 8.00
81 Marcus Allen 1.00
82 Dan Marino 10.00
83 Robert Smith .50
84 Curtis Martin 7.00
85 *Amani Toomer* 1.00
86 Napoleon Kaufman .50
87 Ricky Watters 1.00
88 Kordell Stewart 5.00
89 *Keyshawn Johnson* 6.00
90 Emmitt Smith 10.00
91 Chris Warren .50
92 Isaac Bruce 1.50
93 Terry Allen .50
94 Trent Dilfer .50
95 Vinny Testaverde .50
96 Bruce Smith .50
97 Kerry Collins 2.00
98 Curtis Conway .50
99 *Karim Abdul-Jabbar* 2.00
100 Brett Favre 10.00
101 Carl Pickens .50
102 Brett Perriman .50
103 Keith Jackson .50
104 Drew Bledsoe 5.00
105 Rodney Hampton .50
106 Ray Zellars .50
107 Jeff Graham .50
108 Irving Fryar .50
109 *Lawrence Phillips* .50
110 Jerry Rice 5.00
111 Mike Tomczak .50
112 Tony Martin .50
113 Brian Blades .50
114 Bill Brooks .50
115 Rob Moore .50
116 Quinn Early .50
117 Darnay Scott .50
118 Ken Dilger .50
119 Derek Loville .50
120 Reggie White 1.00

1996 Playoff Illusions Spectralusion Elite

This 120-card parallel set utilizes Illusion printing technology and silver holographic foil background. It is one of four different parallel sets associated with the Illusion product, and is the easiest to get with a one per five packs insertion rate.

NM/M
Common Player: .40
Spectralusion Dominion: 3X-5X
XXXI Cards: 2X
XXXI Spectralusion Dominion: 2X-4X
1 Troy Aikman 10.00
2 Larry Centers .40
3 Terance Mathis .40
4 Calvin Williams .40
5 Jim Kelly 2.00
6 Tim Biakabutuka .50
7 Rashaan Salaam .50
8 Ki-Jana Carter 1.00
9 Anthony Miller .40
10 Deion Sanders 4.00
11 Scott Mitchell .40
12 Robert Brooks .40
13 Willie Davis .40
14 Zack Crockett .40
15 James Stewart .40
16 Tamarick Vanover 1.00
17 Stanley Pritchett .40
18 Warren Moon .40
19 Shawn Jefferson .40
20 Shannon Sharpe .40
21 Jim Everett .40
22 Dave Brown .40
23 Adrian Murrell .40
24 Rickey Dudley 2.00
25 Chris T. Jones .40
26 Andre Hastings .40
27 Stan Humphries .40
28 Steve Young 8.00
29 Joey Galloway 7.00
30 Jim Harbaugh .40
31 Eddie Kennison 6.00
32 Mike Alstott 8.00
33 Michael Westbrook 2.00
34 Leeland McElroy 2.00
35 Erik Kramer .40
36 Mark Chmura .40
37 Cris Carter .40
38 Ben Coates .40
39 Wayne Chrebet .40
40 Jerome Bettis 2.00
41 Tim Brown .40
42 Jason Dunn .40
43 William Henderson .40
44 Rick Mirer .40
45 J.J. Stokes 2.00
46 Rodney Peete .40
47 Neil O'Donnell .40
48 Tyrone Wheatley .40
49 Terry Glenn 6.00
50 Junior Seau .40
51 Jake Reed .40
52 O.J. McDuffie .40
53 Steve Bono .40
54 Steve McNair 5.00
55 Antonio Freeman .40
56 Johnnie Morton .40
57 Eric Metcalf .40
58 Andre Reed .40
59 Bobby Engram 2.00
60 Gus Frerotte .40
61 Jeff Blake 2.00
62 Erric Pegram .40
63 Jeff Hostetler .40
64 Edgar Bennett .40
65 Eddie George 12.00
66 Marvin Harrison 8.00
67 LeShon Johnson .40
68 Jamal Anderson 12.00
69 Thurman Thomas 2.00
70 Barry Sanders 12.00
71 Muhsin Muhammad 2.00
72 Robert Green .40
73 Garrison Hearst .40
74 John Elway 7.00
75 Herman Moore 3.00
76 Chris Chandler .40
77 Marshall Faulk 4.00
78 Mark Brunell 6.00
79 Tony Banks 2.00
80 Terrell Davis 12.00
81 Marcus Allen 2.00
82 Dan Marino 12.00
83 Robert Smith .40
84 Curtis Martin 8.00
85 Amani Toomer 2.00
86 Napoleon Kaufman 1.00
87 Ricky Watters 2.00
88 Kordell Stewart 4.00
89 Keyshawn Johnson 8.00
90 Emmitt Smith 10.00
91 Chris Warren .40
92 Isaac Bruce 5.00
93 Terry Allen .40
94 Trent Dilfer .40
95 Vinny Testaverde .40
96 Bruce Smith .40
97 Kerry Collins 3.00
98 Curtis Conway .40
99 Karim Abdul-Jabbar 2.00
100 Brett Favre 12.00
101 Carl Pickens .40
102 Brett Perriman .40
103 Keith Jackson .40
104 Drew Bledsoe 6.00
105 Rodney Hampton .40
106 Ray Zellars .40
107 Jeff Graham .40
108 Irving Fryar .40
109 Lawrence Phillips .50
110 Jerry Rice 8.00
111 Mike Tomczak .40
112 Tony Martin .40
113 Brian Blades .40
114 Bill Brooks .40
115 Rob Moore .40
116 Quinn Early .40
117 Darnay Scott .40
118 Ken Dilger .40
119 Derek Loville .40
120 Reggie White 2.00

1996 Playoff Illusions Spectralusion Dominion

Spectralusion Dominion was a 120-card parallel set that utilized Illusion printing technology and a gold holographic foil background. These parallel cards were inserted every 192 packs.

Spec. Dominion Cards: 3X-5X

1996 Playoff Illusions XXXI

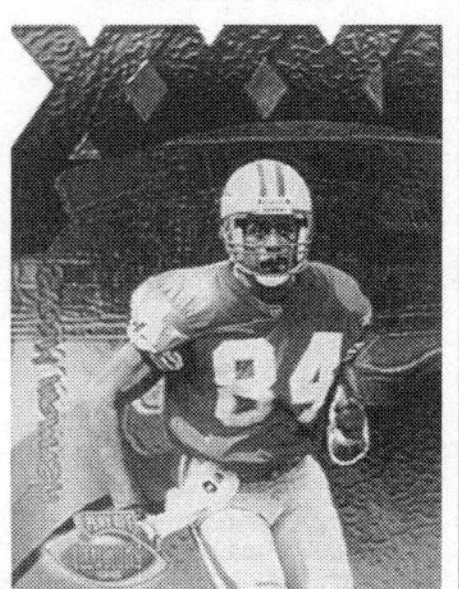

XXXI reprints all 120 cards in the base set in a die-cut, parallel that features the Roman numerals XXXI across the top of the card. This parallel set is inserted at a rate of one per 12 packs. These cards are also featured in a more difficult gold holographic parallel called Spectralusion Dominion.

XXXI Cards: 2X

1996 Playoff Illusions XXXI Spectralusion Dominion

XXXI Spectralusion Dominion reprints the die-cut XXXI cards and adds a gold holographic background. These parallel cards are found in every 96 packs.

XXXI Spec. Dominion: 2X-4X

1996 Playoff Illusions Optical Illusions

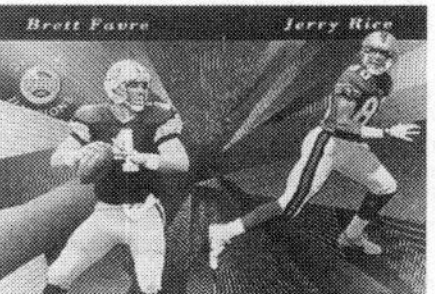

This 18-card chase set, found one per 96 packs, featured Troy Aikman handing off to Barry Sanders and Brett Favre passing to Jerry Rice.

NM/M
Complete Set (18): 200.00
Common Player: 5.00
1 Brett Favre, Jerry Rice 25.00
2 Troy Aikman, Barry Sanders 25.00
3 Dan Marino, Emmitt Smith 25.00
4 Warren Moon, Carl Pickens 5.00
5 John Elway, Herman Moore 20.00
6 Steve Young, Anthony Miller 15.00
7 Jim Harbaugh, Terrell Davis 15.00
8 Kordell Stewart, Kordell Stewart 10.00
9 Deion Sanders, Deion Sanders 10.00
10 Kerry Collins, Curtis Martin 15.00
11 Scott Mitchell, Robert Brooks 5.00
12 Jeff Blake, Tony Martin 5.00
13 Mark Brunell, Marshall Faulk 15.00
14 Drew Bledsoe, Jerome Bettis 15.00
15 Gus Frerotte, Karim Abdul-Jabbar 5.00
16 Steve Bono, Ricky Watters 5.00
17 Chris Chandler, Terry Allen 5.00
18 Tony Banks, Keyshawn Johnson 8.00

1996 Playoff Trophy Contenders

Playoff Trophy Contenders' regular 1996 football set puts a cap on the 1995 NFL season by highlighting members of the two teams in the Super Bowl - the Pittsburgh Steelers and Dallas Cowboys. Each regular card front has the player's name in a bar at the top. An action photo is in the center of the card; the Playoff and insert set logos are toward the bottom. The back has a color photo of the player, with the player's name and team at the top. A brief player profile and 1995 statistics are also included. The Steelers and Cowboys are featured in a 60-card mini parallel set called Back-to-Back. The first 11 cards in the set have an opposing player from each team on different card sides. Rookie Stallions and Playoff Zone cards are also included as inserts in packs, as are special cards redeemable for Wilson commemorative Super Bowl XXX footballs.

NM/M
Complete Set (120): 20.00
Common Player: .10
Minor Stars: .20
Pack (6): 1.75
Wax Box (24): 30.00
1 Brett Favre 3.00
2 Troy Aikman 1.50
3 Dan Marino 3.00
4 Emmitt Smith 3.00
5 Marshall Faulk 1.50
6 Jeff Blake 1.00
7 John Elway 1.00
8 Steve Young 1.50
9 Curtis Martin 4.00
10 Kordell Stewart 1.00
11 Drew Bledsoe 1.50
12 Jim Kelly .20
13 Steve Bono .20
14 Neil O'Donnell .20
15 Jeff Hostetler .10
16 Jim Harbaugh .10
17 Jim Everett .10
18 Erric Pegram .10
19 Tyrone Wheatley .20
20 Barry Sanders 1.50
21 Deion Sanders 1.00
22 Harvey Williams .10
23 Garrison Hearst .20
24 *Aaron Hayden* 1.00
25 Dorsey Levens .30
26 Napoleon Kaufman .50
27 Rodney Hampton .10
28 Scott Mitchell .10
29 Greg Hill .10
30 Charlie Garner .10
31 Rashaan Salaam .40
32 Errict Rhett .40
33 Bam Morris .20
34 Edgar Bennett .10
35 Jeff George .10
36 Rodney Peete .10
37 Stan Humphries .10
38 Kimble Anders .10
39 Natrone Means .25
40 Sherman Williams .10
41 Eric Metcalf .10
42 Chris Warren .10
43 Marcus Allen .10
44 Bill Brooks .10
45 Wayne Chrebet .10
46 Irving Fryar .10
47 Tony Martin .10
48 Daryl Johnston .10
49 O.J. McDuffie .10
50 Frank Sanders .50
51 Ken Norton .10
52 Jake Reed .10
53 Bert Emanuel .10
54 Floyd Turner .10
55 Junior Seau .10
56 Ernie Mills .10
57 Mark Pike .10
58 Warren Moon .10
59 Mike Mamula .10
60 Kerry Collins .50
61 Nate Newton .10
62 Terry Allen .10
63 Bernie Parmalee .10
64 James Stewart .10
65 Isaac Bruce 1.00
66 Lake Dawson .10
67 Terance Mathis .10
68 Chris Sanders .50
69 Anthony Miller .10
70 Jay Novacek .10
71 Sean Dawkins .10
72 J.J. Birden .10
73 Calvin Williams .10
74 Rick Mirer .10
75 Steve McNair 1.50
76 Lamont Warren .10
77 Rod Woodson .10
78 Larry Brown .10
79 Zack Crockett .10
80 Jerry Rice 1.50
81 Tim Brown .10
82 Yancey Thigpen .75
83 J.J. Stokes 1.00
84 Herman Moore .50
85 Kevin Williams .10
86 Gus Frerotte .10
87 Robert Brooks .10
88 Michael Irvin .50
89 Steve Tasker .10
90 Joey Galloway 1.50
91 Kevin Greene .10
92 Reggie White .10
93 Cris Carter .10
94 Charles Haley .10
95 Bryce Paup .10
96 Heath Shuler .10
97 Eric Zeier .20
98 Antonio Freeman .10
99 Erik Kramer .10
100 Derek Loville .10
101 Rodney Thomas .50
102 Terrell Davis 2.00
103 Ricky Watters .10
104 Craig Heyward .10
105 Terry Kirby .10
106 Bruce Smith .10
107 Curtis Conway .10
108 Charles Johnson .10
109 Brett Perriman .10
110 Carl Pickens .20
111 Michael Westbrook 1.00
112 Brent Jones .10
113 Ken Dilger .10
114 Fred Barnett .10
115 Mark Bruener .10
116 Tamarick Vanover .20
117 Quinn Early .10
118 Mark Chmura .10
119 Andre Hastings .10
120 Craig Newsome .10

1996 Playoff Trophy Contenders Mini Back-to-Backs

Eleven members from the Super Bowl participants, the Dallas Cowboys and Pittsburgh Steelers, are highlighted on the first 11 cards in this 1996 Playoff Trophy Contenders insert set. The mini cards form a 60-card parallel set to the main set, putting those 120 cards in a back-to-back format. These cards are seeded one per 17 packs.

NM/M
Complete Set (60): 225.00
Common Player: 2.00
Minor Stars: 5.00
1 Troy Aikman, Neil O'Donnell 10.00
2 Sherman Williams, Kordell Stewart 4.00
3 Deion Sanders, Andre Hastings 4.00
4 Emmitt Smith, Bam Morris 12.00
5 Daryl Johnston, Erric Pegram 2.00
6 Nate Newton, Kevin Greene 2.00
7 Larry Brown, Charles Johnson 2.00
8 Jay Novacek, Mark Bruener 2.00
9 Kevin Williams, Yancey Thigpen 3.00
10 Michael Irvin, Ernie Mills 5.00
11 Charles Haley, Rod Woodson 2.00
12 Brett Favre, Steve Young 15.00
13 Edgar Bennett, Derek Loville 2.00
14 Reggie White, Ken Norton 2.00
15 Robert Brooks, Jerry Rice 12.00
16 Dorsey Levens, J.J. Stokes 4.00
17 Mark Chmura, Brent Jones 2.00
18 Craig Newsome, Antonio Freeman 4.00
19 Dan Marino, Jim Kelly 15.00
20 Bernie Parmalee, Bruce Smith 2.00
21 Irving Fryar, Bill Brooks 2.00
22 O.J. McDuffie, Steve Tasker 2.00
23 Terry Kirby, Bryce Paup 2.00
24 Jim Harbaugh, Steve Bono 4.00
25 Marshall Faulk, Greg Hill 6.00
26 Lamont Warren, Marcus Allen 2.00
27 Floyd Turner, Kimble Anders 2.00
28 Sean Dawkins, Lake Dawson 2.00
29 Zack Crockett, Tamarick Vanover 3.00
30 Scott Mitchell, Rodney Peete 2.00
31 Barry Sanders, Ricky Watters 12.00
32 Brett Perriman, Calvin Williams 2.00
33 Herman Moore, Fred Barnett 3.00
34 Stan Humphries, Jeff George 3.00
35 Natrone Means, Craig Heyward 3.00
36 Aaron Hayden, Terance Mathis 2.00
37 Junior Seau, Bert Emanuel 2.00
38 Tony Martin, J.J. Birden 2.00
39 Jeff Blake, Carl Pickens 3.00
40 Erik Kramer, Curtis Conway 5.00
41 Garrison Hearst, Frank Sanders 5.00
42 John Elway, Anthony Miller 12.00
43 Steve McNair, Chris Sanders 8.00
44 Warren Moon, Cris Carter 5.00
45 Drew Bledsoe, Curtis Martin 14.00
46 Jim Everett, Quinn Early 2.00
47 Rodney Hampton, Tyrone Wheatley 2.00
48 Jeff Hostetler, Tim Brown 2.00
49 Rick Mirer, Joey Galloway 5.00
50 Gus Frerotte, Michael Westbrook 3.00
51 Heath Shuler, Terry Allen 3.00
52 Charlie Garner, Mike Mamula 2.00
53 Harvey Williams, Napoleon Kaufman 3.00
54 Errict Rhett, Rashaan Salaam 3.00
55 Mark Pike, Kerry Collins 5.00
56 Ken Dilger, Eric Zeier 3.00
57 Chris Warren, Terrell Davis 8.00
58 Isaac Bruce, Jake Reed 6.00
59 Eric Metcalf, Wayne Chrebet 2.00
60 James Stewart, Rodney Thomas 4.00

1996 Playoff Trophy Contenders Playoff Zone

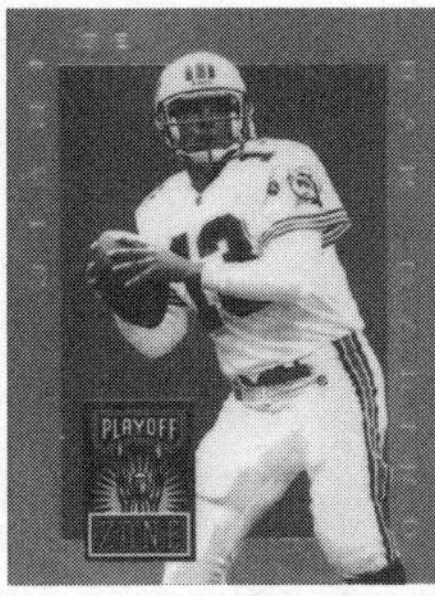

This 36-card insert set captures some of the top NFL players on gold and silver foil backgrounds. The player's name is written in the foil along the right side, while his team's name and position are in the upper left corner. The Playoff Zone logo, showing a referee signaling a touchdown, is in the lower left corner. Cards were seeded one per 24 packs of 1996 Playoff Trophy Contenders.

		NM/M
Complete Set (36):		100.00
Common Player:		1.00
Minor Stars:		3.00
1	Troy Aikman	10.00
2	Jeff Blake	3.00
3	John Elway	10.00
4	Brett Favre	15.00
5	Jeff George	3.00
6	Jim Harbaugh	3.00
7	Erik Kramer	1.00
8	Dan Marino	15.00
9	Scott Mitchell	1.00
10	Warren Moon	3.00
11	Neil O'Donnell	1.00
12	Steve Young	10.00
13	Marcus Allen	5.00
14	Terry Allen	3.00
15	Edgar Bennett	1.00
16	Marshall Faulk	10.00
17	Rodney Hampton	1.00
18	Craig Heyward	1.00
19	Errict Rhett	1.00
20	Barry Sanders	12.00
21	Emmitt Smith	12.00
22	Chris Warren	1.00
23	Ricky Watters	3.00
24	Harvey Williams	1.00
25	Robert Brooks	1.00
26	Isaac Bruce	3.00
27	Cris Carter	3.00
28	Curtis Conway	3.00
29	Michael Irvin	3.00
30	Anthony Miller	1.00
31	Herman Moore	3.00
32	Brett Perriman	1.00
33	Carl Pickens	1.00
34	Jerry Rice	10.00
35	Deion Sanders	6.00
36	Yancey Thigpen	1.00

1996 Playoff Trophy Contenders Rookie Stallions

The top 20 rookies from the 1995 season are featured on these 1996 Playoff Trophy Contenders insert cards. Cards, seeded one per 24 packs, are gold-foil etched, with "Stallions" etched into the background.

		NM/M
Complete Set (20):		75.00
Common Player:		1.00
Minor Stars:		2.00
1	Mark Bruener	1.00
2	Wayne Chrebet	2.00
3	Kerry Collins	5.00
4	Zack Crockett	1.00
5	Terrell Davis	12.00
6	Antonio Freeman	1.00
7	Joey Galloway	5.00
8	Napoleon Kaufman	2.00
9	Curtis Martin	10.00
10	Steve McNair	10.00
11	Rashaan Salaam	2.00
12	Chris Sanders	2.00
13	Frank Sanders	2.00
14	Kordell Stewart	6.00
15	J.J. Stokes	4.00
16	Rodney Thomas	2.00
17	Tamarick Vanover	3.00
18	Michael Westbrook	3.00
19	Tyrone Wheatley	2.00
20	Eric Zeier	2.00

1997 Playoff Absolute

The 200-card set showcases an action shot of the player with a map of his hometown serving as the background on the card front. Named "Absolute Beginnings," the backs include the player's bio at the top left and the card number in the upper right inside a shape of an NFL shield. A headshot of the player is featured in the left center, while his name, number, position and team, along with interesting facts regarding the player's hometown and his pre-collegiate years are included to the right of the photo. His 1996 and total stats are printed along the bottom. The base set has three levels of color coded insertion ratios: Green (card #s 1-100, 3.5 per pack), Blue (#s 101-150, 1 per pack) and Red (#s 151-200, 1 per every 2 packs). The backs for each colored card are identical. The cards are standard size.

		NM/M
Complete Set (200):		110.00
Comp. Green Set (100):		20.00
Comp. Blue Set (50):		40.00
Comp. Red Set (50):		110.00
Common Green (1-100):		.10
Minor Green Stars:		.20
Common Blue (101-150):		.40
Minor Blue Stars:		.75
Common Red (151-200):		.50
Minor Red Stars:		1.00
Pack (6):		3.00
Wax Box (24):		50.00
1	Marcus Allen	.20
2	Eric Bieniemy	.10
3	Jason Dunn	.10
4	Jim Harbaugh	.20
5	Michael Westbrook	.20
6	*Tiki Barber*	2.00
7	Frank Reich	.10
8	Irving Fryar	.10
9	Courtney Hawkins	.10
10	Eric Zeier	.10
11	Kent Graham	.10
12	Trent Dilfer	.20
13	Neil O'Donnell	.10
14	*Reidel Anthony*	2.00
15	Jeff Hostetler	.10
16	Lawrence Phillips	.20
17	Dave Brown	.10
18	Mike Tomczak	.10
19	Jake Reed	.10
20	Anthony Miller	.10
21	Eric Metcalf	.10
22	*Sedrick Shaw*	.50
23	Anthony Johnson	.10
24	Mario Bates	.10
25	Dorsey Levens	.30
26	Stan Humphries	.10
27	Ben Coates	.10
28	Tyrone Wheatley	.10
29	Adrian Murrell	.10
30	William Henderson	.10
31	*Warrick Dunn*	1.50
32	LeShon Johnson	.10
33	James Stewart	.10
34	Edgar Bennett	.10
35	Raymont Harris	.10
36	Leroy Butler	.10
37	Darren Woodson	.10
38	*Darnell Autry*	.40
39	Johnnie Morton	.10
40	William Floyd	.10
41	Terrell Fletcher	.10
42	Leonard Russell	.10
43	Henry Ellard	.10
44	Terrell Owens	.75
45	John Friesz	.10
46	*Antowain Smith*	2.00
47	Charles Johnson	.10
48	Rickey Dudley	.10
49	Lake Dawson	.10
50	Bert Emanuel	.10
51	Zach Thomas	.30
52	Ernest Byner	.10
53	*Yatil Green*	.75
54	Chris Spielman	.10
55	Muhsin Muhammad	.30
56	Bobby Engram	.20
57	Eric Bjornson	.10
58	Willie Green	.10
59	Derrick Mayes	.10
60	Chris Sanders	.10
61	Jimmy Smith	.10
62	*Tony Gonzalez*	.75
63	Rich Gannon	.10
64	Stanley Pritchett	.10
65	Brad Johnson	.10
66	Rodney Peete	.10
67	Sam Gash	.10
68	Chris Calloway	.10
69	Chris T. Jones	.10
70	*Will Blackwell*	.50
71	Mark Bruener	.10
72	Terry Kirby	.10
73	Brian Blades	.10
74	Craig Heyward	.10
75	Jamie Asher	.10
76	Terance Mathis	.10
77	*Troy Davis*	.50
78	Bruce Smith	.10
79	Simeon Rice	.10
80	Fred Barnett	.10
81	Tim Brown	.20
82	James Jett	.10
83	Mark Carrier	.10
84	Shawn Jefferson	.10
85	Ken Dilger	.10
86	*Rae Carruth*	1.00
87	Keenan McCardell	.10
88	Michael Irvin	.20
89	Mark Chmura	.20
90	Derrick Alexander	.10
91	Andre Reed	.10
92	Ed McCaffrey	.10
93	Erik Kramer	.10
94	Albert Connell	.10
95	Frank Wycheck	.10
96	Zach Crockett	.10
97	Jim Everett	.10
98	Michael Haynes	.10
99	Jeff Graham	.10
100	Brent Jones	.10
101	Troy Aikman	3.50
102	*Byron Hanspard*	.50
103	Robert Brooks	.50
104	Karim Abdul-Jabbar	1.00
105	Drew Bledsoe	3.50
106	Napoleon Kaufman	.40
107	Steve Young	2.50
108	Leeland McElroy	.40
109	Jamal Anderson	1.50
110	*David LaFleur*	.50
111	Vinny Testaverde	.40
112	Eric Moulds	.75
113	Tim Biakabutuka	.75
114	Rick Mirer	.75
115	Jeff Blake	.75
116	Jim Schwantz	.40
117	Herman Moore	1.00
118	*Ike Hilliard*	4.00
119	Reggie White	.75
120	Steve McNair	2.00
121	Marshall Faulk	1.25
122	Natrone Means	.75
123	Greg Hill	.40
124	O.J. McDuffie	.40
125	Robert Smith	.40
126	*Bryant Westbrook*	1.25
127	Ray Zellars	.40
128	Rodney Hampton	.40
129	Wayne Chrebet	.40
130	Desmond Howard	.75
131	Ty Detmer	.75
132	Erric Pegram	.40
133	Yancey Thigpen	.40
134	*Danny Wuerffel*	1.00
135	Charlie Jones	.40
136	Chris Warren	.75
137	Isaac Bruce	1.25
138	Errict Rhett	1.00
139	Gus Frerotte	.40
140	Frank Sanders	.40
141	Todd Collins	.40
142	*Jake Plummer*	4.00
143	Darnay Scott	.75
144	Rashaan Salaam	.75
145	Terrell Davis	4.00
146	Scott Mitchell	.40
147	Junior Seau	.75
148	Warren Moon	.40
149	Wesley Walls	.40
150	Daryl Johnston	.40
151	Brett Favre	14.00
152	Emmitt Smith	12.00
153	Dan Marino	12.00
154	Larry Centers	1.00
155	Michael Jackson	1.00
156	Kerry Collins	2.00
157	Curtis Conway	2.00
158	Peter Boulware	1.00
159	Carl Pickens	2.00
160	Shannon Sharpe	2.00
161	Brett Perriman	1.00
162	Eddie George	8.00
163	Mark Brunell	6.00
164	Tamarick Vanover	2.00
165	Cris Carter	1.00
166	*Corey Dillion*	10.00
167	Curtis Martin	7.00
168	Amani Toomer	1.00
169	Jeff George	1.00
170	Kordell Stewart	6.00
171	Garrison Hearst	1.00
172	Tony Banks	1.00
173	Mike Alstott	2.00
174	*Jim Druckenmiller*	1.00
175	Chris Chandler	.50
176	Bam Morris	.50
177	Billy Joe Hobert	.50
178	Ernie Mills	.50
179	Ki-Jana Carter	1.00
180	Deion Sanders	4.00
181	Ricky Watters	2.00
182	*Shawn Springs*	1.00
183	Barry Sanders	10.00
184	Antonio Freeman	3.00
185	Marvin Harrison	3.00
186	Elvis Grbac	1.00
187	Terry Glenn	5.00
188	Willie Roaf	1.00
189	Keyshawn Johnson	3.00
190	*Orlando Pace*	3.00
191	Jerome Bettis	2.00
192	Tony Martin	.50
193	Jerry Rice	6.00
194	Joey Galloway	1.00
195	Terry Allen	1.00
196	Eddie Kennison	1.00
197	Thurman Thomas	2.00
198	Darrell Russell	.50
199	Rob Moore	.50
200	John Elway	5.00

1997 Playoff Absolute Autographed Pennants

Measuring 3-1/2" x 5", one of the eight signed pennants were randomly inserted in boxes of Playoff Absolute. The cards are numbered with an "A" prefix.

		NM/M
Common Player:		20.00
1	Kordell Stewart	40.00
2	Eddie George	60.00
3	Karim Abdul-Jabbar	20.00
4	Mike Alstott	40.00
5	Terry Glenn	20.00
6	Napoleon Kaufman	20.00
7	Terry Allen	20.00
8	Tim Brown	40.00

1997 Playoff Absolute Chip Shots

Inserted one per pack, the Chip Shots resembled poker chips. The chips, which measure approximately 1-1/2" in diameter, were available in assorted colors. The plastic tokens were a 200-player parallel of the base set.

		NM/M
Complete Set (200):		75.00
Common Player:		.10
Minor Stars:		.25
1	Marcus Allen	.25
2	Eric Bieniemy	.10
3	Jason Dunn	.10
4	Jim Harbaugh	.10
5	Michael Westbrook	.10
6	Tiki Barber	2.00
7	Frank Reich	.10
8	Irving Fryar	.10
9	Courtney Hawkins	.10
10	Eric Zeier	.10
11	Kent Graham	.10
12	Trent Dilfer	.25
13	Neil O'Donnell	.10
14	Reidel Anthony	.50
15	Jeff Hostetler	.10
16	Lawrence Phillips	.10
17	Dave Brown	.10
18	Mike Tomczak	.10
19	Jake Reed	.10
20	Anthony Miller	.10
21	Eric Metcalf	.10
22	Sedrick Shaw	.10
23	Anthony Johnson	.10
24	Mario Bates	.10
25	Dorsey Levens	.50
26	Stan Humphries	.10
27	Ben Coates	.10
28	Tyrone Wheatley	.10
29	Adrian Murrell	.10
30	William Henderson	.10
31	Warrick Dunn	5.00
32	LeShon Johnson	.10
33	James Stewart	.10
34	Edgar Bennett	.10
35	Raymont Harris	.10
36	Leroy Butler	.10
37	Darren Woodson	.10
38	Darnell Autry	.50
39	Johnnie Morton	.10
40	William Floyd	.10
41	Terrell Fletcher	.10
42	Leonard Russell	.10
43	Henry Ellard	.10
44	Terrell Owens	4.00
45	John Friesz	.10
46	Antowain Smith	3.00
47	Charles Johnson	.10
48	Rickey Dudley	.10
49	Lake Dawson	.10
50	Bert Emanuel	.10
51	Zach Thomas	1.00
52	Ernest Byner	.10
53	Yatil Green	.50
54	Chris Spielman	.10
55	Muhsin Muhammad	.25
56	Bobby Engram	.25
57	Eric Bjornson	.10
58	Willie Green	.10
59	Derrick Mayes	.10
60	Chris Sanders	.10
61	Jimmy Smith	.10
62	Tony Gonzalez	1.00
63	Rich Gannon	.10
64	Stanley Pritchett	.10
65	Brad Johnson	.25
66	Rodney Peete	.10
67	Sam Gash	.10
68	Chris Calloway	.10
69	Chris T. Jones	.10
70	Will Blackwell	.25
71	Mark Bruener	.10
72	Terry Kirby	.10
73	Brian Blades	.10
74	Craig Heyward	.10
75	Jamie Asher	.10
76	Terance Mathis	.10
77	Troy Davis	.50
78	Bruce Smith	.10
79	Simeon Rice	.10
80	Fred Barnett	.10
81	Tim Brown	.10
82	James Jett	.10
83	Mark Carrier	.10
84	Shawn Jefferson	.10
85	Ken Dilger	.10
86	Rae Carruth	.10
87	Keenan McCardell	.25
88	Michael Irvin	.25
89	Mark Chmura	.10
90	Derrick Alexander	.10
91	Andre Reed	.10
92	Ed McCaffrey	.10
93	Erik Kramer	.10
94	Albert Connell	.10
95	Frank Wycheck	.10
96	Zach Crockett	.10
97	Jim Everett	.10
98	Michael Haynes	.10
99	Jeff Graham	.10
100	Brent Jones	.10
101	Troy Aikman	7.00
102	Byron Hanspard	2.00
103	Robert Brooks	.25
104	Karim Abdul-Jabbar	.50
105	Drew Bledsoe	7.00
106	Napoleon Kaufman	.25
107	Steve Young	4.00
108	Leeland McElroy	.10
109	Jamal Anderson	1.00
110	David LaFleur	1.50
111	Vinny Testaverde	.10
112	Eric Moulds	.25
113	Tim Biakabutuka	.25
114	Rick Mirer	.10
115	Jeff Blake	.40
116	Jim Schwantz	.10
117	Herman Moore	.40
118	Ike Hilliard	2.00
119	Reggie White	.25
120	Steve McNair	4.00
121	Marshall Faulk	1.00
122	Natrone Means	.25
123	Greg Hill	.10
124	O.J. McDuffie	.10
125	Robert Smith	.10
126	Bryant Westbrook	1.00
127	Ray Zellars	.10
128	Rodney Hampton	.10
129	Wayne Chrebet	.10
130	Desmond Howard	.10
131	Ty Detmer	.10
132	Erric Pegram	.10
133	Yancey Thigpen	.10
134	Danny Wuerffel	.50
135	Charlie Jones	.10
136	Chris Warren	.10
137	Isaac Bruce	1.00
138	Errict Rhett	.25
139	Gus Frerotte	.10
140	Frank Sanders	.10
141	Todd Collins	.10
142	Jake Plummer	4.00
143	Darnay Scott	.10
144	Rashaan Salaam	.25
145	Terrell Davis	6.00
146	Scott Mitchell	.10
147	Junior Seau	.25
148	Warren Moon	.10
149	Wesley Walls	.10
150	Daryl Johnston	.10
151	Brett Favre	10.00
152	Emmitt Smith	8.00
153	Dan Marino	10.00
154	Larry Centers	.10
155	Michael Jackson	.10
156	Kerry Collins	1.00
157	Curtis Conway	.25
158	Peter Boulware	.25
159	Carl Pickens	.10
160	Shannon Sharpe	.10
161	Brett Perriman	.10
162	Eddie George	5.00
163	Mark Brunell	4.00
164	Tamarick Vanover	.25
165	Cris Carter	.10
166	Corey Dillion	3.00
167	Curtis Martin	4.00
168	Amani Toomer	.10
169	Jeff George	.10
170	Kordell Stewart	3.00
171	Garrison Hearst	.10
172	Tony Banks	1.00
173	Mike Alstott	2.00
174	Jim Druckenmiller	.50
175	Chris Chandler	.10
176	Bam Morris	.10
177	Billy Joe Hobert	.10
178	Ernie Mills	.10
179	Ki-Jana Carter	.10
180	Deion Sanders	3.00
181	Ricky Watters	.25
182	Shawn Springs	.40
183	Barry Sanders	8.00
184	Antonio Freeman	1.00
185	Marvin Harrison	3.00
186	Elvis Grbac	.10
187	Terry Glenn	3.00
188	Willie Roaf	.10
189	Keyshawn Johnson	3.00
190	Orlando Pace	2.00
191	Jerome Bettis	.25
192	Tony Martin	.10
193	Jerry Rice	7.00
194	Joey Galloway	1.00
195	Terry Allen	.10
196	Eddie Kennison	1.00
197	Thurman Thomas	.25
198	Darrell Russell	.25
199	Rob Moore	.10
200	John Elway	4.00

1997 Playoff Absolute Leather Quads

The 18-card set, which was produced on leather, was inserted 1:144 packs. Each card included four players, with two appearing on each side. The player photos are superimposed over the leather background. The players' names are printed vertically in green along the left and right borders. "Leather Quad" is printed in white over a black stripe which runs diagonally between the two players' photos. The Playoff logo and "1997" are printed in green at the bottom center on both sides of the cards. The card numbers appear in the top center inside a green oval on both sides of the cards with a "LQ" prefix.

		NM/M
Complete Set (18):		300.00
Common Player:		5.00
Minor Stars:		10.00
1	Brett Favre, Jerry Rice, Dan Marino, Emmitt Smith	75.00
2	Barry Sanders, Terrell Davis, Eddie George, Curtis Martin	60.00
3	Kordell Stewart, Herman Moore, Elvis Grbac, Chris Warren	25.00
4	Troy Aikman, Leeland McElroy, Cris Carter, Zach Thomas	335.00
5	Drew Bledsoe, Jamal Anderson, Michael Jackson, Jim Harbaugh	35.00
6	John Elway, Reggie White, Warren Moon, Terrell Owens	40.00
7	Kerry Collins, Rashaan Salaam, Shannon Sharpe, Ricky Watters	25.00
8	Mark Brunell, Eric Moulds, Mario Bates, Larry Centers	25.00
9	Karim Abdul-Jabbar, Robert Brooks, Jerome Bettis, Carl Pickens	10.00
10	Steve Young, Tim Biakabutuka, Jeff George, Tony Martin	20.00
11	Terry Glenn, Jeff Blake, Mike Alstott, Curtis Conway	15.00
12	Joey Galloway, Antonio Freeman, Anthony Johnson, Rick Mirer	10.00
13	Steve McNair, Marshall Faulk, Jimmy Smith, Isaac Bruce	20.00
14	Deion Sanders, Tony Banks, Vinny Testaverde, Rodney Hampton	10.00
15	Marvin Harrison, Lawrence Phillips, Thurman Thomas, Chris Chandler	10.00
16	Keyshawn Johnson, Napoleon Kaufman, Gus Frerotte, Greg Hill	5.00
17	Eddie Kennison, Terry Allen, Scott Mitchell, Errict Rhett	5.00
18	Warrick Dunn, Orlando Pace, Jim Druckenmiller, Darrell Russell	10.00

1997 Playoff Absolute Pennants

Inserted one per box, the pennants measure 3-1/2" x 5". Each of the 192 pennants in the set have a felt-like feel to them. The pennant fronts have the player's name printed inside a rectangle in the upper left, while a cutout color action photo of the player is included in the center of the pennant. The Playoff Pennants 1997 logo is on the right of the front. The vertical backs have the player's name, appropriate logos and pennant number in a stripe at the top. The player's headshot is included inside a circle in the center of the back, which also has a felt-like feel to it. The Playoff Pennants' logo is on the bottom of the back.

NM/M
Common Player: 1.00
Minor Stars: 3.00
1 Marcus Allen 3.00
2 Eric Bieniemy 1.00
3 Jason Dunn 1.00
4 Jim Harbaugh (QBC) 1.00
5 Michael Westbrook 1.00
6 Tiki Barber 3.00
7 Frank Reich (QBC) 1.00
8 Irving Fryar 1.00
9 Courtney Hawkins 1.00
10 Eric Zeier 1.00
11 Kent Graham 1.00
12 Trent Dilfer (QBC) 3.00
13 Neil O'Donnell (QBC) 1.00
14 Reidel Anthony 1.00
15 Jeff Hostetler (QBC) 1.00
16 Lawrence Phillips 1.00
17 Dave Brown (QBC) 1.00
18 Mike Tomczak 1.00
19 Jake Reed 1.00
20 Anthony Miller 1.00
21 Eric Metcalf 1.00
22 Sedrick Shaw 1.00
23 Anthony Johnson 1.00
24 Mario Bates 1.00
25 Dorsey Levens 3.00
26 Stan Humphries 1.00
27 Ben Coates 1.00
28 Tyrone Wheatley 1.00
29 Adrian Murrell 1.00
30 William Henderson 1.00
31 Warrick Dunn 10.00
32 LeShon Johnson 1.00
33 James Stewart 1.00
34 Edgar Bennett 1.00
35 Raymont Harris 1.00
36 Leroy Butler 1.00
37 Darren Woodson 1.00
38 Darnell Autry 3.00
39 Johnnie Morton 1.00
40 William Floyd 3.00
41 Terrell Fletcher 1.00
42 Leonard Russell 1.00
43 Henry Ellard 1.00
44 Terrell Owens 10.00
45 John Friesz 1.00
46 Antowain Smith 8.00
47 Charles Johnson 1.00
48 Rickey Dudley 1.00
49 Lake Dawson 1.00
50 Bert Emanuel 1.00
51 Zach Thomas 6.00
52 Earnest Byner 1.00
53 Yatil Green 3.00
54 Chris Spielman 1.00
55 Muhsin Muhammad 1.00
56 Bobby Engram 1.00
57 Eric Bjornson 1.00
58 Willie Green 1.00
59 Derrick Mayes 1.00
60 Chris Sanders 1.00
61 Jimmy Smith 1.00
62 Tony Gonzalez 6.00
63 Rich Gannon 1.00
64 Stanley Pritchett 1.00
65 Brad Johnson 3.00
66 Rodney Peete (QBC) 1.00
67 Sam Gash 1.00
68 Chris Galloway 1.00
69 Chris T. Jones 1.00
70 Will Blackwell 1.00
71 Mark Bruener 1.00
72 Terry Kirby 1.00
73 Brian Blades 1.00
74 Craig Heyward 1.00
75 Jamie Asher 1.00
76 Terance Mathis 1.00
77 Troy Davis 1.00
78 Bruce Smith 1.00
79 Simeon Rice 1.00
80 Fred Barnett 1.00
81 Jerry Rice 30.00
82 James Jett 1.00
83 Mark Carrier 1.00
84 Shawn Jefferson 1.00
85 Ken Dilger 1.00
86 Rae Carruth 1.00
87 Keenan McCardell 3.00
88 Michael Irvin (QBC) 3.00
89 Mark Chmura 1.00
90 Derrick Alexander 1.00
91 Andre Reed 1.00
92 Ed McCaffrey 1.00
93 Erik Kramer (QBC) 1.00
94 Albert Connell 1.00
95 Frank Wycheck 1.00
96 Zach Crockett 1.00
97 Jim Everett (QBC) 3.00
98 Michael Haynes 1.00
99 Jeff Graham 1.00
100 Brent Jones 1.00
101 Troy Aikman (QBC) 20.00
102 Byron Hanspard 1.00
103 Robert Brooks 3.00
104 Joey Galloway 5.00
105 Drew Bledsoe (QBC) 20.00
106 Eddie Kennison 3.00
107 Steve Young (QBC) 20.00
108 Leeland McElroy 3.00
109 Jamal Anderson 5.00
110 David LaFleur 1.00
111 Vinny Testaverde 1.00
112 Eric Moulds 1.00
113 Tim Biakabutuka 3.00
114 Rick Mirer (QBC) 1.00
115 Jeff Blake (QBC) 3.00
116 Jim Schwantz 1.00
117 Herman Moore 15.00
118 Ike Hilliard 5.00
119 Reggie White 3.00
120 Steve McNair (QBC) 15.00
121 Marshall Faulk 3.00
122 Natrone Means 3.00
123 Greg Hill 1.00
124 O.J. McDuffie 1.00
125 Robert Smith 1.00
126 Bryant Westbrook 3.00
127 Ray Zellars 1.00
128 Rodney Hampton 1.00
129 Wayne Chrebet 1.00
130 Desmond Howard 1.00
131 Ty Detmer 1.00
132 Erric Pegram 1.00
133 Yancey Thigpen 1.00
134 Danny Wuerffel 3.00
135 Charlie Jones 1.00
136 Chris Warren 1.00
137 Isaac Bruce 6.00
138 Errict Rhett 3.00
139 Gus Frerotte (QBC) 1.00
140 Frank Sanders 1.00
141 Todd Collins 3.00
142 Jake Plummer 5.00
143 Darnay Scott 1.00
144 Rashaan Salaam 3.00
145 Terrell Davis 20.00
146 Scott Mitchell (QBC) 1.00
147 Junior Seau (QBC) 3.00
148 Warren Moon (QBC) 1.00
149 Wesley Walls 1.00
150 Daryl Johnston 1.00
151 Brett Favre (QBC) 45.00
152 Emmitt Smith (QBC) 40.00
153 Dan Marino (QBC) 45.00
154 Larry Centers 1.00
155 Michael Jackson 1.00
156 Kerry Collins (QBC) 3.00
157 Curtis Conway 3.00
158 Peter Boulware 1.00
159 Carl Pickens 3.00
160 Shannon Sharpe 1.00
161 Brett Perriman 1.00
162 Thurman Thomas 3.00
163 Mark Brunell (QBC) 12.00
164 Tamarick Vanover 3.00
165 Cris Carter 3.00
166 Corey Dillon 12.00
167 Curtis Martin 20.00
168 Amani Toomer 1.00
169 Jeff George (QBC) 1.00
170 Darrell Russell 1.00
171 Garrison Hearst 1.00
172 Tony Banks (QBC) 3.00
173 Rob Moore 1.00
174 Jim Druckenmiller 3.00
175 Chris Chandler 1.00
176 Bam Morris 1.00
177 Billy Joe Hobert 1.00
178 Ernie Mills 1.00
179 Ki-Jana Carter 3.00
180 Deion Sanders 10.00
181 Ricky Watters 3.00
182 Shawn Springs 1.00
183 Barry Sanders (QBC) 35.00
184 Antonio Freeman 3.00
185 Marvin Harrison 15.00
186 Elvis Grbac (QBC) 1.00
187 John Elway (QBC) 25.00
188 Willie Roaf 1.00
189 Keyshawn Johnson 12.00
190 Orlando Pace 3.00
191 Jerome Bettis 3.00
192 Tony Martin 1.00

1997 Playoff Absolute Playoff Honors

This three-card set, which was inserted 1:7,200 packs, was a continuation from the 1996 Playoff Prime and Contenders sets. The felt-like cards feature a player photo superimposed over a checkered background on the front. The Playoff Honors' logo appears in one of the upper corners of the card, with the player's name printed in a lower corner. The cards carry a prefix of "PF."

NM/M
Complete Set (3): 100.00
Common Player: 20.00
7 Jerry Rice 50.00
8 Reggie White 20.00
9 John Elway 50.00

1997 Playoff Absolute Reflex

The 200-card set is a parallel of the base set printed on mirror board. The card fronts have "Reflex" printed at the top, with the player's photo superimposed over a silver mirror background. "Playoff '97" is printed vertically along the left border, while his name is printed vertically along the right border. The cards were inserted 1:288 packs.

NM/M
Common Player: 5.00
Minor Stars: 10.00
1 Brett Favre 100.00
2 Dorsey Levens 10.00
3 Antonio Freeman 10.00
4 Robert Brooks 5.00
5 Mark Chmura 10.00
6 Reggie White 10.00
7 Drew Bledsoe 50.00
8 Curtis Martin 50.00
9 Ben Coates 5.00
10 Terry Glenn 20.00
11 Kerry Collins 25.00
12 Tim Biakabutuka 5.00
13 Anthony Johnson 5.00
14 Wesley Walls 5.00
15 Muhsin Muhammad 5.00
16 Mark Brunell 50.00
17 Natrone Means 10.00
18 Jimmy Smith 5.00
19 John Elway 75.00
20 Terrell Davis 75.00
21 Anthony Miller 5.00
22 Shannon Sharpe 5.00
23 Steve Young 75.00
24 Garrison Hearst 5.00
25 Jerry Rice 75.00
26 Troy Aikman 75.00
27 Deion Sanders 35.00
28 Emmitt Smith 90.00
29 Michael Irvin 10.00
30 Kordell Stewart 20.00
31 Jerome Bettis 10.00
32 Charles Johnson 5.00
33 Ty Detmer 5.00
34 Ricky Watters 10.00
35 Irving Fryar 5.00
36 Todd Collins 5.00
37 Thurman Thomas 10.00
38 Bruce Smith 5.00
39 Eric Moulds 5.00
40 Brad Johnson 10.00
41 Robert Smith 10.00
42 Cris Carter 10.00
43 Elvis Grbac 5.00
44 Greg Hill 5.00
45 Marcus Allen 10.00
46 Gus Frerotte 5.00
47 Terry Allen 5.00
48 Michael Westbrook 5.00
49 Jim Harbaugh 10.00
50 Marshall Faulk 10.00
51 Marvin Harrison 15.00
52 Jeff Blake 10.00
53 Ki-Jana Carter 5.00
54 Carl Pickens 5.00
55 Junior Seau 10.00
56 Tony Martin 5.00
57 Dan Marino 100.00
58 Karim Abdul-Jabbar 5.00
59 Stanley Pritchett 5.00
60 Zach Thomas 5.00
61 Steve McNair 35.00
62 Eddie George 35.00
63 Chris Sanders 5.00
64 Rick Mirer 5.00
65 Rashaan Salaam 10.00
66 Curtis Conway 5.00
67 Bobby Engram 5.00
68 Kent Graham 5.00
69 Leeland McElroy 5.00
70 Larry Centers 5.00
71 Frank Sanders 5.00
72 Jeff George 10.00
73 Napoleon Kaufman 5.00
74 Desmond Howard 5.00
75 Tim Brown 20.00
76 John Friesz 5.00
77 Chris Warren 5.00
78 Joey Galloway 10.00
79 Tony Banks 5.00
80 Lawrence Phillips 5.00
81 Isaac Bruce 15.00
82 Eddie Kennison 10.00
83 Errict Rhett 10.00
84 Mike Alstott 15.00
85 Rodney Hampton 5.00
86 Amani Toomer 5.00
87 Scott Mitchell 5.00
88 Barry Sanders 90.00
89 Herman Moore 10.00
90 Vinny Testaverde 5.00
91 Bam Morris 5.00
92 Michael Jackson 5.00
93 Chris Chandler 5.00
94 Eric Metcalf 5.00
95 Jamal Anderson 10.00
96 Jim Everett 5.00
97 Mario Bates 5.00
98 Wayne Chrebet 5.00
99 Adrian Murrell 10.00
100 Keyshawn Johnson 10.00
101 William Henderson 5.00
102 Edgar Bennett 5.00
103 LeRoy Butler 5.00
104 Derrick Mayes 5.00
105 Sedrick Shaw 10.00
106 Sam Gash 5.00
107 Shawn Jefferson 5.00
108 Mark Carrier 5.00
109 Rae Carruth 5.00
110 Ernie Mills 5.00
111 James Stewart 5.00
112 Keenan McCardell 5.00
113 Willie Green 5.00
114 Ed McCaffrey 5.00
115 William Floyd 5.00
116 Terrell Owens 25.00
117 Terry Kirby 5.00
118 Brent Jones 5.00
119 Jim Schwantz 5.00
120 Jim Druckenmiller 5.00
121 Darren Woodson 5.00
122 Eric Bjornson 5.00
123 David LaFleur 5.00
124 Daryl Johnston 5.00
125 Mike Tomczak 5.00
126 Will Blackwell 5.00
127 Mark Bruener 5.00
128 Erric Pegram 5.00
129 Yancey Thigpen 5.00
130 Jason Dunn 5.00
131 Chris T. Jones 5.00
132 Rodney Peete 5.00
133 Antowain Smith 20.00
134 Chris Spielman 5.00
135 Andre Reed 5.00
136 Billy Joe Hobert 5.00
137 Jake Reed 5.00
138 Tamarick Vanover 5.00
139 Lake Dawson 5.00
140 Tony Gonzalez 10.00
141 Rich Gannon 5.00
142 Henry Ellard 5.00
143 Jamie Asher 5.00
144 Albert Connell 5.00
145 Ken Dilger 5.00
146 Zack Crockett 5.00
147 Eric Bieniemy 5.00
148 Darnay Scott 5.00
149 Corey Dillon 35.00
150 Stan Humphries 5.00
151 Terrell Fletcher 5.00
152 Leonard Russell 5.00
153 Charlie Jones 5.00
154 Yatil Green 10.00
155 Fred Barnett 5.00
156 O.J. McDuffie 5.00
157 Frank Wycheck 5.00
158 Raymont Harris 5.00
159 Darnell Autry 10.00
160 Erik Kramer 5.00
161 LeShon Johnson 5.00
162 Simeon Rice 5.00
163 Jake Plummer 15.00
164 Rob Moore 5.00
165 Jeff Hostetler 5.00
166 Rickey Dudley 5.00
167 James Jett 5.00
168 Darrell Russell 5.00
169 Brian Blades 5.00
170 Warren Moon 10.00
171 Shawn Springs 5.00
172 Craig Heyward 5.00
173 Orlando Pace 10.00
174 Courtney Hawkins 5.00
175 Trent Dilfer 10.00
176 Reidel Anthony 10.00
177 Warrick Dunn 20.00
178 Tiki Barber 20.00
179 Dave Brown 5.00
180 Tyrone Wheatley 5.00
181 Chris Calloway 5.00
182 Ike Hilliard 12.00
183 Frank Reich 5.00
184 Johnnie Morton 5.00
185 Bryant Westbrook 5.00
186 Brett Perriman 5.00
187 Eric Zeier 5.00
188 Earnest Byner 5.00
189 Derrick Alexander 5.00
190 Peter Boulware 5.00
191 Bert Emanuel 5.00
192 Terance Mathis 5.00
193 Byron Hanspard 5.00
194 Troy Davis 5.00
195 Michael Haynes 5.00
196 Ray Zellars 5.00
197 Danny Wuerffel 10.00
198 Willie Roaf 5.00
199 Neil O'Donnell 5.00
200 Jeff Graham 5.00

1997 Playoff Absolute Unsung Heroes

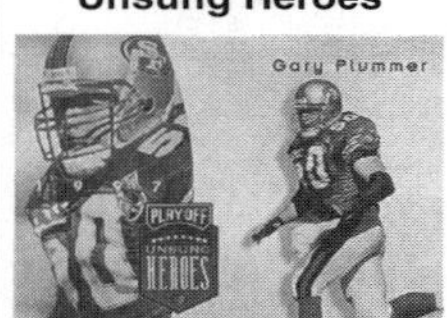

The 30-card set honors the players selected as the 1996 Playoff/Players Inc. Unsung Heroes, which were voted on by the fans and players. In its third year, the set includes a color photo of the player superimposed over a silver background on the right side of the front. His name is printed in the upper right. A black-and-white close-up photo, which is an enlarged version of the color photo, is printed on the left side of the card, with "1997" printed over the top of it. The Unsung Heroes logo is printed at the bottom. The backs are numbered inside a red box in the upper left. The player's name, bio and write-up are printed on the left side over a green background. Along the right side of the back is a color headshot of the player. The cards were inserted 1:12 packs.

NM/M
Complete Set (30): 25.00
Common Player: .50
Minor Stars: 1.00
Inserted 1:12
1 Larry Centers 1.25
2 Jessie Tuggle .50
3 Stevon Moore .50
4 Mark Pike .50
5 Anthony Johnson .50
6 Anthony Carter .50
7 Eric Bieniemy .50
8 Jim Schwantz .50
9 Tyrone Braxton .50
10 Bennie Blades .50
11 Don Beebe .50
12 Barron Wortham .50
13 Jason Belser .50
14 Mickey Washington .50
15 Dave Szott .50
16 Zach Thomas 2.50
17 Chris Walsh .50
18 Sam Gash .50
19 Willie Roaf 1.00
20 Charles Way .50
21 Wayne Chrebet 2.00
22 Russell Maryland .50
23 Michael Zordich .50
24 Tim Lester .50
25 Harold Green .50
26 Rodney Harrison .50
27 Gary Plummer .50
28 Winston Moss .50
29 Robb Thomas .50
30 Darrick Brownlow .50

1997 Playoff Contenders

Playoff Contenders includes a 150-card base set. Printed on 30 pt. stock, these cards feature player shots on each side, with foil etching and holographic technology. The player's name is added in silver on each side. A Blue Level parallel version was included in 1:4 packs, while a Red Level version was sequentially numbered to 25. Inserts include Playoff Clash, Leather Die-Cut Helmets, Playoff Plaques, Playoff Pennants and Playoff Rookie Wave Pennants.

NM/M
Complete Set (150): 40.00
Common Player: .20
Minor Stars: .50
Blue Cards: 2X-4X
Blue Rookies: 2X
Inserted 1:4
Red Cards: 10X-25X
Red Rookies: 5X-10X
Production 25 Sets
Pack (4): 4.75
Wax Box (12): 40.00
1 Kent Graham .20
2 Leeland McElroy .20
3 Rob Moore .20
4 Frank Sanders .20
5 *Jake Plummer* 4.00
6 Chris Chandler .20
7 Bert Emanuel .20
8 O.J. Santiago .20
9 *Byron Hanspard* .50
10 Vinny Testaverde .20
11 Michael Jackson .20
12 Ernest Byner .20
13 Jermaine Lewis .20
14 Derrick Alexander .20
15 *Jay Graham* .50
16 Todd Collins .50
17 Thurman Thomas .50
18 Bruce Smith .20
19 Andre Reed .20
20 Quinn Early .20
21 *Antowain Smith* 3.00
22 Kerry Collins 1.50
23 Tim Biakabutuka .20
24 Anthony Johnson .20
25 Wesley Johnson .20
26 *Fred Lane* .50
27 *Rae Carruth* .50
28 Raymont Harris .20
29 Rick Mirer .20
30 *Darnell Autry* 1.00
31 Jeff Blake .50
32 Ki-Jana Carter .50
33 Carl Pickens .50
34 Darnay Scott .20
35 *Corey Dillon* 8.00
36 Troy Aikman 4.00
37 Emmitt Smith 5.00
38 Michael Irvin .50
39 Deion Sanders 2.00
40 Anthony Miller .20
41 Eric Bjornson .20
42 *David LaFleur* .50
43 John Elway 4.00
44 Terrell Davis 4.00
45 Shannon Sharpe .20
46 Ed McCaffrey .20
47 Rod Smith .20
48 Scott Mitchell .20
49 Barry Sanders 5.00
50 Herman Moore 1.00
51 Brett Favre 6.00
52 Dorsey Levens .50
53 William Henderson .20
54 Derrick Mayes .20
55 Antonio Freeman .50
56 Robert Brooks .20
57 Mark Chmura .20
58 Reggie White .50
59 Darren Sharper .20
60 Jim Harbaugh .20
61 Marshall Faulk .50
62 Marvin Harrison 2.00
63 Mark Brunell 2.00
64 Natrone Means .50
65 Jimmy Smith .20
66 Keenan McCardell .20
67 Elvis Grbac .20
68 Greg Hill .20
69 Marcus Allen .50
70 Andre Rison .20
71 Kimble Anders .20
72 *Tony Gonzalez* 6.00
73 *Pat Barnes* .50
74 Dan Marino 6.00
75 Karim Abdul-Jabbar .75
76 Zach Thomas .50
77 O.J. McDuffie .20
78 *Brian Manning* .50
79 Brad Johnson .50
80 Cris Carter .50
81 Jake Reed .20
82 Robert Smith .50
83 Drew Bledsoe 3.00
84 Curtis Martin 3.00
85 Ben Coates .20
86 Terry Glenn 1.00
87 Shawn Jefferson .20
88 Heath Shuler .20
89 Mario Bates .20
90 Andre Hastings .20
91 *Troy Davis* 1.00
92 *Danny Wuerffel* 1.00
93 Dave Brown .20
94 Chris Calloway .20
95 *Tiki Barber* 8.00
96 Mike Cherry .20
97 Neil O'Donnell .20
98 Keyshawn Johnson 1.00
99 Adrian Murrell .50
100 Wayne Chrebet .20
101 Dedric Ward .20
102 Leon Johnson .20
103 Jeff George .50
104 Napoleon Kaufman .50
105 Tim Brown .50
106 James Jett .20
107 Ty Detmer .20
108 Ricky Watters .50
109 Irving Fryar .20
110 Michael Timpson .20
111 Chad Lewis .20
112 Kordell Stewart 2.00
113 Jerome Bettis .50
114 Charles Johnson .20
115 *George Jones* .50
116 *Will Blackwell* .50
117 Stan Humphries .20
118 Junior Seau .50
119 *Freddie Jones* .50
120 Steve Young 4.00
121 Jerry Rice 4.00
122 Garrison Hearst .20
123 William Floyd .20
124 Terrell Owens 2.00
125 J.J. Stokes .20
126 Marc Edwards .20
127 *Jim Druckenmiller* .75
128 Warren Moon .20
129 Chris Warren .20
130 Joey Galloway .50
131 *Shawn Springs* .50
132 Tony Banks .50
133 Lawrence Phillips .50
134 Isaac Bruce .50
135 Eddie Kennison 1.00
136 *Orlando Pace* .50
137 Trent Dilfer .50
138 Mike Alstott 2.00
139 Horace Copeland .20
140 Jackie Harris .20
141 *Warrick Dunn* 4.00
142 *Reidel Anthony* 1.00
143 Steve McNair 2.00
144 Eddie George 2.00
145 Chris Sanders .20
146 Gus Frerotte .20
147 Terry Allen .20
148 Henry Ellard .20
149 Leslie Shepherd .20
150 Michael Westbrook .20

1997 Playoff Contenders Clash

Clash is a 12-card insert highlighting some of the NFL's top match-ups. The cards feature two players with their team helmets die-cut in the background. Silver Level cards were inserted 1:48 and Blue Level cards were found 1:192.

NM/M
Complete Set (12): 200.00
Common Player: 5.00
Blue Cards: 3X
1 Brett Favre, Troy Aikman 40.00
2 Barry Sanders, Brad Johnson 30.00
3 Curtis Martin, Warrick Dunn 20.00
4 Steve Young, John Elway 25.00
5 Jerry Rice, Marcus Allen 25.00
6 Dan Marino, Drew Bledsoe 40.00
7 Terrell Davis, Napoleon Kaufman 15.00
8 Eddie George, Emmitt Smith 35.00
9 Mark Brunell, Tim Brown 15.00
10 Kerry Collins, Reggie White 5.00

11 Deion Sanders, Carl Pickens 5.00
12 Mike Alstott, Keyshawn Johnson 5.00

1997 Playoff Contenders Leather Helmets

This 18-card insert features a die-cut leather helmet. The Silver Level was found 1:24, Blue Level 1:216 and the Red Parallel was numbered to 25.

NM/M
Complete Set (18): 200.00
Common Player: 2.00
Minor Stars: 5.00
Inserted 1:24
Blue Cards: 2X-4X
Inserted 1:216
Red Cards: 3X-5X
Production 25 Sets
1 Dan Marino 25.00
2 Troy Aikman 15.00
3 Brett Favre 25.00
4 Barry Sanders 20.00
5 Drew Bledsoe 15.00
6 Deion Sanders 5.00
7 Curtis Martin 15.00
8 Warrick Dunn 10.00
9 Napoleon Kaufman 2.00
10 Eddie George 10.00
11 Antowain Smith 5.00
12 Emmitt Smith 20.00
13 John Elway 15.00
14 Steve Young 15.00
15 Mark Brunell 10.00
16 Terrell Davis 15.00
17 Terry Glenn 2.00
18 Terrell Owens 5.00

1997 Playoff Contenders Pennants

Pennants features player shots on a fuzzy pennant. The 36 cards came in Silver Level (1:12) and Blue Parallel (1:72) versions.

NM/M
Complete Set (36): 300.00
Common Player: 1.00
Minor Stars: 3.00
Blue Cards: 2X
1 Dan Marino 30.00
2 Kordell Stewart 10.00
3 Drew Bledsoe 15.00
4 Kerry Collins 10.00
5 John Elway 15.00
6 Trent Dilfer 3.00
7 Jerry Rice 20.00
8 Emmitt Smith 25.00
9 Jeff George 1.00
10 Eddie George 10.00
11 Terrell Davis 15.00
12 Mike Alstott 10.00
13 Jim Druckenmiller 1.00
14 Antowain Smith 5.00
15 Marcus Allen 3.00
16 Jerome Bettis 3.00
17 Terrell Owens 3.00
18 Gus Frerotte 1.00
19 Troy Aikman 15.00
20 Andre Rison 1.00
21 Mark Brunell 10.00
22 Antonio Freeman 3.00
23 Brett Favre 30.00
24 Steve McNair 10.00
25 Barry Sanders 20.00
26 Steve Young 15.00
27 Curtis Martin 15.00
28 Napoleon Kaufman 3.00
29 Deion Sanders 10.00
30 Terry Glenn 6.00
31 Warrick Dunn 6.00
32 Danny Wuerffel 1.00
33 Elvis Grbac 1.00
34 Cris Carter 1.00
35 Joey Galloway 3.00
36 Corey Dillon 6.00

1997 Playoff Contenders Plaques

These 45 die-cut cards feature a player shot on a card designed to resemble a plaque. Plaques were made in Silver Level (1:12) and Blue Parallel (1:36) versions.

NM/M
Complete Set (45): 200.00
Common Player: 1.00
Minor Stars: 3.00

NM/M
Blue Cards: 2X
1 Jim Druckenmiller 3.00
2 Danny Wuerffel 3.00
3 Antowain Smith 5.00
4 Warrick Dunn 8.00
5 Terrell Owens 3.00
6 Elvis Grbac 1.00
7 Andre Rison 1.00
8 Tim Brown 5.00
9 Trent Dilfer 3.00
10 Brad Johnson 1.00
11 Deion Sanders 6.00
12 Dan Marino 30.00
13 Kerry Collins 10.00
14 Steve McNair 10.00
15 Eddie George 10.00
16 Ricky Watters 3.00
17 Jerome Bettis 3.00
18 Robert Brooks 1.00
19 Keyshawn Johnson 3.00
20 Antonio Freeman 3.00
21 Eddie Kennison 3.00
22 Mike Alstott 6.00
23 Brett Favre 30.00
24 Troy Aikman 20.00
25 Emmitt Smith 25.00
26 Terrell Davis 20.00
27 John Elway 20.00
28 Barry Sanders 25.00
29 Steve Young 15.00
30 Curtis Martin 15.00
31 Cris Carter 3.00
32 Drew Bledsoe 15.00
33 Mark Brunell 15.00
34 Kordell Stewart 10.00
35 Tony Banks 3.00
36 Napoleon Kaufman 1.00
37 Marcus Allen 3.00
38 Terry Glenn 5.00
39 Herman Moore 3.00
40 Michael Irvin 3.00
41 Joey Galloway 3.00
42 Karim Abdul-Jabbar 3.00
43 Reggie White 3.00
44 Jerry Rice 20.00
45 Gus Frerotte 1.00

1997 Playoff Contenders Rookie Wave

Similar to the Pennants, except with a wavy design, this 27-card insert was only available in Silver Level (1:6).

NM/M
Complete Set (27): 80.00
Common Player: 1.00
Minor Stars: 2.00
1 Jim Druckenmiller 1.00
2 Antowain Smith 4.00
3 Will Blackwell 1.00
4 Tiki Barber 5.00
5 Rae Carruth 1.00
6 Jay Graham 1.00
7 Darnell Autry 2.00
8 David LaFleur 1.00
9 Tony Gonzalez 4.00
10 Chad Lewis 3.00
11 Freddie Jones 1.00
12 Shawn Springs 1.00
13 Danny Wuerffel 1.00
14 Warrick Dunn 15.00
15 Troy Davis 2.00
16 Reidel Anthony 5.00
17 Jake Plummer 15.00
18 Byron Hanspard 2.00
19 Fred Lane 4.00
20 Corey Dillon 20.00
21 Darren Sharper 4.00
22 Pat Barnes 1.00
23 Mike Cherry 1.00
24 Leon Johnson 1.00
25 George Jones 1.00
26 Marc Edwards 1.00
27 Orlando Pace 2.00

1997 Playoff Zone

Playoff Zone consists of a 150-card base set done on 24 pt. Tekchrome and 14 insert sets. The inserts include Prime Target, Prime Target Parallel, Sharp Shooters, Sharp Shooters Parallel, Rookies, Close-Ups, Frenzy and Treasures as well as a "1 of 5" parallel set of each insert. The parallels are limited to five each and are sequentially numbered.

NM/M
Complete Set (150): 20.00
Common Player: .10
Minor Stars: .20
Pack (10): 1.00
Wax Box (36): 30.00
1 Brett Favre 3.00
2 Dorsey Levens .20
3 William Henderson .10
4 Derrick Mayes .10
5 Antonio Freeman .20
6 Robert Brooks .10
7 Mark Chmura .10
8 Reggie White .20
9 Randall Cunningham .10
10 Brad Johnson .20
11 Robert Smith .10
12 Cris Carter .10
13 Jake Reed .10
14 Trent Dilfer .20
15 Errict Rhett .10
16 Mike Alstott .20
17 Scott Mitchell .10
18 Barry Sanders 2.00
19 Herman Moore .20
20 Erik Kramer .10
21 Rick Mirer .10
22 Rashaan Salaam .10
23 Troy Aikman 1.50
24 Deion Sanders .75
25 Emmitt Smith 2.50
26 Daryl Johnston .10
27 Anthony Miller .10
28 Eric Bjornson .10
29 Michael Irvin .20
30 Chris Jones .10
31 Ty Detmer .10
32 Ricky Watters .20
33 Irving Fryar .10
34 Rodney Peete .10
35 Jeff Hostetler .10
36 Terry Allen .20
37 Michael Westbrook .10
38 Gus Frerotte .10
39 Frank Sanders .10
40 Larry Centers .10
41 Kent Graham .10
42 Dave Brown .10
43 Rodney Hampton .10
44 Tyrone Wheatley .10
45 Chris Calloway .10
46 Ernie Mills .10
47 Tim Biakabutuka .10
48 Anthony Johnson .10
49 Wesley Walls .10
50 Muhsin Muhammad .10
51 Kerry Collins .30
52 Terrell Owens 1.00
53 Garrison Hearst .10
54 Jerry Rice 1.50
55 Steve Young 1.00
56 Lawrence Phillips .10
57 Isaac Bruce .20
58 Eddie Kennison .50
59 Tony Banks .75
60 Heath Shuler .10
61 Andre Hastings .10
62 Mario Bates .10
63 Chris Chandler .10
64 Jamal Anderson .10
65 Bert Emanuel .10
66 Drew Bledsoe 1.50
67 Curtis Martin 1.50
68 Ben Coates .10
69 Terry Glenn .40
70 Dan Marino 2.50
71 Karim Abdul-Jabbar .40
72 Fred Barnett .10
73 O.J. McDuffie .10
74 Jim Harbaugh .10
75 Marshall Faulk .20
76 Zack Crockett .10
77 Ken Dilger .10
78 Marvin Harrison .50
79 Keyshawn Johnson .50
80 Neil O'Donnell .10
81 Adrian Murrell .20
82 Wayne Chrebet .10
83 Todd Collins .10
84 Thurman Thomas .20
85 Bruce Smith .10
86 Eric Moulds .10
87 Rob Johnson .10
88 Mark Brunell 1.50
89 Natrone Means .20
90 Jimmy Smith .10
91 Keenan McCardell .10
92 Kordell Stewart 1.50
93 Jerome Bettis .20
94 Charles Johnson .10
95 Courtney Hawkins .10
96 Greg Lloyd .10
97 Ki-Jana Carter .10
98 Carl Pickens .10
99 Jeff Blake .20
100 Steve McNair 1.00
101 Chris Sanders .10
102 Eddie George 2.00
103 Vinny Testaverde .10
104 Michael Jackson .10
105 Derrick Alexander .10
106 Willie Green .10
107 Shannon Sharpe .10
108 Rod Smith .10
109 Terrell Davis 1.50
110 John Elway 1.00
111 Elvis Grbac .10
112 Greg Hill .10
113 Marcus Allen .20
114 Derrick Thomas .10
115 Brett Perriman .10
116 Andre Rison .10
117 Rickey Dudley .10
118 Tim Brown .10
119 Desmond Howard .10
120 Napoleon Kaufman .30
121 Jeff George .10
122 Warren Moon .10
123 John Friesz .10
124 Chris Warren .10
125 Joey Galloway .20
126 Stan Humphries .10
127 Tony Martin .10
128 Eric Metcalf .10
129 Jim Everett .10
130 *Warrick Dunn* 1.50
131 *Reidel Anthony* 1.00
132 *Derrick Mason* 1.00
133 *Joey Kent* .20
134 *Will Blackwell* .20
135 *Jim Druckenmiller* .40
136 *Byron Hanspard* .50
137 *John Allred* .10
138 *David LaFleur* 1.00
139 *Danny Wuerffel* .50
140 *Tiki Barber* 3.00
141 *Ike Hilliard* 1.50
142 *Troy Davis* .30
143 *Sedrick Shaw* .10
144 *Tony Gonzalez* 1.00
145 *Jake Plummer* 1.00
146 *Antowain Smith* 2.00
147 *Rae Carruth* 1.75
148 *Darnell Autry* 1.00
149 *Corey Dillon* 4.00
150 *Orlando Pace* .20

1997 Playoff Zone Close-Up

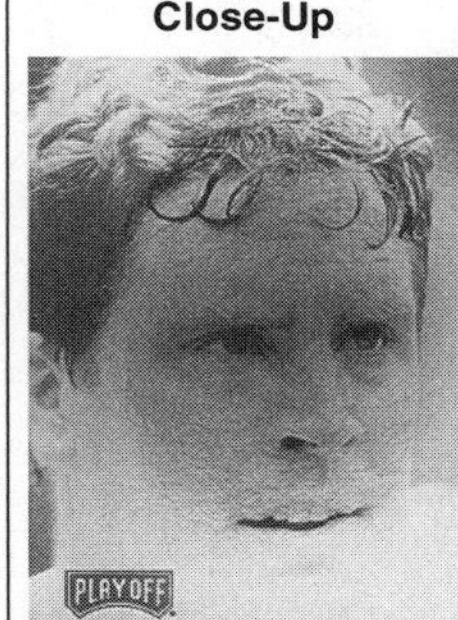

This 32-card insert features helmetless close-ups of top NFL players. The cards were inserted 1:6.

NM/M
Complete Set (32): 40.00
Common Player: .25
Minor Stars: .75
1 Brett Favre 6.00
2 Mark Brunell 2.00
3 Dan Marino 6.00
4 Kerry Collins 2.00
5 Troy Aikman 4.00
6 Drew Bledsoe 4.00
7 John Elway 4.00
8 Kordell Stewart 2.00
9 Steve Young 4.00
10 Steve McNair 3.00
11 Tony Banks 1.00
12 Emmitt Smith 5.00
13 Barry Sanders 5.00
14 Jerry Rice 5.00
15 Deion Sanders 2.00
16 Terrell Davis 3.00
17 Curtis Martin 3.00
18 Karim Abdul-Jabbar 1.00
19 Terry Glenn 2.00
20 Eddie George 4.00
21 Keyshawn Johnson .75
22 Marvin Harrison 2.00
23 Muhsin Muhammad .25
24 Joey Galloway .75
25 Terrell Owens 2.00
26 Antonio Freeman .75
27 Ricky Watters .75
28 Jeff Blake .75
29 Reggie White .75
30 Michael Irvin .75
31 Eddie Kennison .25
32 Robert Brooks .25

1997 Playoff Zone Frenzy

This 26-card insert set was done on etched foil cards and inserted 1:12.

NM/M
Complete Set (26): 75.00
Common Player: .40
Minor Stars: 1.00
1 Brett Favre 12.00
2 Dan Marino 12.00
3 Troy Aikman 8.00
4 Drew Bledsoe 6.00
5 John Elway 8.00
6 Kordell Stewart 4.00
7 Steve Young 6.00
8 Steve McNair 4.00
9 Tony Banks 1.00
10 Emmitt Smith 10.00
11 Barry Sanders 10.00
12 Deion Sanders 4.00
13 Terrell Davis 6.00
14 Curtis Martin 6.00
15 Karim Abdul-Jabbar 1.00
16 Terry Glenn 1.00
17 Eddie George 3.00
18 Keyshawn Johnson 1.00
19 Marvin Harrison 3.00
20 Joey Galloway 1.00
21 Antonio Freeman 1.00
22 Jeff Blake 1.00
23 Michael Irvin 1.00
24 Eddie Kennison 1.00
25 Reggie White 1.00
26 Robert Brooks .40

1997 Playoff Zone Prime Target

This 20-card insert features the NFL's top pass catchers backed by a blue and silver die-cut target design. This set had an insert rate of 1:24.

NM/M
Complete Set (20): 60.00
Common Player: 1.00
Minor Stars: 2.00
Red Cards: 2X
1 Emmitt Smith 10.00
2 Barry Sanders 10.00
3 Jerry Rice 8.00
4 Terrell Davis 8.00
5 Curtis Martin 8.00
6 Karim Abdul-Jabbar 2.00
7 Terry Glenn 3.00
8 Eddie George 5.00
9 Keyshawn Johnson 2.00
10 Joey Galloway 2.00
11 Antonio Freeman 2.00
12 Herman Moore 2.00
13 Tim Brown 4.00
14 Michael Irvin 2.00
15 Isaac Bruce 2.00
16 Eddie Kennison 2.00
17 Shannon Sharpe 1.00
18 Cris Carter 1.00
19 Napoleon Kaufman 1.00
20 Carl Pickens 1.00

1997 Playoff Zone Rookies

This insert features 24 rookies on etched foil cards. The cards were inserted 1:8.

NM/M
Complete Set (24): 25.00
Common Player: .25

NM/M
Minor Stars: 1.00
1 Jake Plummer 5.00
2 George Jones .25
3 Pat Barnes 1.00
4 Brian Manning .25
5 O.J. Santiago .25
6 Byron Hanspard 1.00
7 Antowain Smith 3.00
8 Rae Carruth .25
9 Darnell Autry 1.00
10 Corey Dillon 6.00
11 David LaFleur 1.00
12 Tony Gonzalez 4.00
13 Sedrick Shaw 1.00
14 Danny Wuerffel 1.00
15 Troy Davis 1.00
16 Ike Hilliard 3.00
17 Tiki Barber 6.00
18 Will Blackwell .25
19 Jim Druckenmiller 1.00
20 Orlando Pace 1.00
21 Warrick Dunn 5.00
22 Reidel Anthony 4.00
23 Derrick Mason 2.50
24 Joey Kent .50

1997 Playoff Zone Sharpshooters

The top NFL QBs are highlighted in this 18-card set with flaming graphics in the background. The cards were inserted 1:72.

NM/M
Complete Set (18): 60.00
Common Player: 1.00
Minor Stars: 2.00
Red Cards: 2X
1 Brett Favre 15.00
2 Dan Marino 15.00
3 John Elway 10.00
4 Troy Aikman 10.00
5 Drew Bledsoe 10.00
6 Todd Collins 1.00
7 Brad Johnson 2.00
8 Stan Humphries 1.00
9 John Friesz 1.00
10 Tony Banks 2.00
11 Ty Detmer 1.00
12 Steve McNair 6.00
13 Rob Johnson 1.00
14 Kordell Stewart 4.00
15 Danny Wuerffel 1.00
16 Jim Druckenmiller 1.00
17 Jake Plummer 5.00
18 Kerry Collins 4.00

1997 Playoff Zone Treasures

This 12-card insert features the top collectible NFL players. The cards were inserted 1:196.

NM/M
Complete Set (12): 125.00
Common Players: 5.00
1 Brett Favre 25.00
2 Dan Marino 25.00
3 Troy Aikman 15.00
4 Drew Bledsoe 15.00
5 Emmitt Smith 20.00
6 Barry Sanders 20.00
7 Warrick Dunn 6.00
8 Deion Sanders 5.00
9 Terrell Davis 15.00
10 Curtis Martin 15.00
11 Tiki Barber 5.00
12 Eddie George 10.00

1997 Playoff 1st & 10

The 250-card set features a color photo of a player superimposed over a purple "1st and 10" background on the front. The player's name is printed in light purple in the upper center and right, while "Nineteen Ninety Seven" appears vertically along the lower left border. The "1st and 10" logo appears in the lower right. The backs have the card number in the upper right, while the player's number, position, name, highlights, bio and stats all are printed along the left side over a purple "1st and 10" background. The player's head shot is printed on the right. In addition, a Kickoff parallel 250-card set was inserted 1:9 packs. The card fronts are identical to the base cards except they are printed on translucent lucite and a gold-foil Kickoff logo is stamped in the upper left. The only printing on the backs are the Players Inc., Play Football and the Playoff 1997 copyright tag line.

		NM/M
Complete Set (250):		15.00
Common Player:		.05
Minor Stars:		.20
Kickoff Cards:		3X-5X
Kickoff Rookies:		2X-4X
Inserted 1:9		
Pack (10):		1.00
Wax Box (36):		
1	Marcus Allen	.20
2	Eric Bieniemy	.05
3	Jason Dunn	.05
4	Jim Harbaugh	.05
5	Michael Westbrook	.05
6	*Tiki Barber*	1.00
7	Frank Reich	.05
8	Irving Fryar	.05
9	Courtney Hawkins	.05
10	Eric Zeier	.05
11	Kent Graham	.05
12	Trent Dilfer	.05
13	Neil O'Donnell	.05
14	*Reidel Anthony*	.50
15	Jeff Hostetler	.05
16	Lawrence Phillips	.20
17	Dave Brown	.05
18	Mike Tomczak	.05
19	Jake Reed	.05
20	Anthony Miller	.05
21	Eric Metcalf	.05
22	*Sedrick Shaw*	.50
23	Anthony Johnson	.05
24	Mario Bates	.05
25	Dorsey Levens	.25
26	Stan Humphries	.05
27	Ben Coates	.05
28	Tyrone Wheatley	.05
29	Adrian Murrell	.05
30	William Henderson	.05
31	*Warrick Dunn*	1.50
32	LeShon Johnson	.05
33	James Stewart	.05
34	Edgar Bennett	.05
35	Raymont Harris	.05
36	Leroy Butler	.05
37	Darren Woodson	.05
38	*Darnell Autry*	.75
39	Johnnie Morton	.05
40	William Floyd	.05
41	Terrell Fletcher	.05
42	Leonard Russell	.05
43	Henry Ellard	.05
44	Terrell Owens	.50
45	John Friesz	.05
46	*Antowain Smith*	1.25
47	Charles Johnson	.05
48	Rickey Dudley	.05
49	Lake Dawson	.05
50	Bert Emanuel	.05
51	Zach Thomas	.25
52	Earnest Byner	.05
53	*Yatil Green*	.75
54	Chris Spielman	.05
55	Muhsin Muhammad	.05
56	Bobby Engram	.05
57	Eric Bjornson	.05
58	Willie Green	.05
59	Derrick Mayes	.05
60	Chris Sanders	.05
61	Jimmy Smith	.05
62	*Tony Gonzalez*	.50
63	Rich Gannon	.05
64	Stanley Pritchett	.05
65	Brad Johnson	.05
66	Rodney Peete	.05
67	Sam Gash	.05
68	Chris Calloway	.05
69	Chris T. Jones	.05
70	*Will Blackwell*	.20
71	Mark Bruener	.05
72	Terry Kirby	.05
73	Brian Blades	.05
74	Craig Heyward	.05
75	Jamie Asher	.05
76	Terance Mathis	.05
77	*Troy Davis*	.30
78	Bruce Smith	.05
79	Simeon Rice	.05
80	Fred Barnett	.05
81	Tim Brown	.05
82	James Jett	.05
83	Mark Carrier	.05
84	Shawn Jefferson	.05
85	Ken Dilger	.05
86	*Rae Carruth*	.75
87	Keenan McCardell	.05
88	Michael Irvin	.20
89	Mark Chmura	.05
90	Derrick Alexander	.05
91	Andre Reed	.05
92	Ed McCaffrey	.05
93	Erik Kramer	.05
94	Albert Connell	.05
95	Frank Wycheck	.05
96	Zack Crockett	.05
97	Jim Everett	.05
98	Michael Haynes	.05
99	Jeff Graham	.05
100	Brent Jones	.05
101	Troy Aikman	1.00
102	*Byron Hanspard*	.75
103	Robert Brooks	.05
104	Karim Abdul-Jabbar	.75
105	Drew Bledsoe	1.00
106	Napoleon Kaufman	.05
107	Steve Young	.50
108	Leeland McElroy	.05
109	Jamal Anderson	.20
110	*David LaFleur*	.50
111	Vinny Testaverde	.05
112	Eric Moulds	.20
113	Tim Biakabutuka	.20
114	Rick Mirer	.05
115	Jeff Blake	.20
116	Jim Schwantz	.05
117	Herman Moore	.20
118	*Ike Hilliard*	1.00
119	Reggie White	.20
120	Steve McNair	.50
121	Marshall Faulk	.20
122	Natrone Means	.20
123	Greg Hill	.05
124	O.J. McDuffie	.05
125	Robert Smith	.05
126	*Bryant Westbrook*	.20
127	Ray Zellars	.05
128	Rodney Hampton	.05
129	Wayne Chrebet	.05
130	Desmond Howard	.05
131	Ty Detmer	.05
132	Erric Pegram	.05
133	Yancey Thigpen	.05
134	*Danny Wuerffel*	.75
135	Charlie Jones	.05
136	Chris Warren	.05
137	Isaac Bruce	.25
138	Errict Rhett	.20
139	Gus Frerotte	.05
140	Frank Sanders	.05
141	Todd Collins	.05
142	*Jake Plummer*	3.00
143	Darnay Scott	.05
144	Rashaan Salaam	.20
145	Terrell Davis	1.50
146	Scott Mitchell	.05
147	Junior Seau	.20
148	Warren Moon	.05
149	Wesley Walls	.05
150	Daryl Johnston	.05
151	Brett Favre	2.25
152	Emmitt Smith	2.00
153	Dan Marino	2.00
154	Larry Centers	.05
155	Michael Jackson	.05
156	Kerry Collins	.30
157	Curtis Conway	.20
158	*Peter Boulware*	.20
159	Carl Pickens	.05
160	Shannon Sharpe	.05
161	Brett Perriman	.05
162	Eddie George	1.50
163	Mark Brunell	1.00
164	Tamarick Vanover	.20
165	Cris Carter	.05
166	*Corey Dillon*	3.00
167	Curtis Martin	1.25
168	Amani Toomer	.05
169	Jeff George	.05
170	Kordell Stewart	.75
171	Garrison Hearst	.05
172	Tony Banks	.50
173	Mike Alstott	.20
174	*Jim Druckenmiller*	.75
175	Chris Chandler	.05
176	Bam Morris	.05
177	Billy Joe Hobert	.05
178	Ernie Mills	.05
179	Ki-Jana Carter	.05
180	Deion Sanders	.50
181	Ricky Watters	.20
182	*Shawn Springs*	.30
183	Barry Sanders	1.25
184	Antonio Freeman	.30
185	Marvin Harrison	.50
186	Elvis Grbac	.05
187	Terry Glenn	1.00
188	Willie Roaf	.05
189	Keyshawn Johnson	.50
190	*Orlando Pace*	.30
191	Jerome Bettis	.20
192	Tony Martin	.05
193	Jerry Rice	1.00
194	Joey Galloway	.30
195	Terry Allen	.05
196	Eddie Kennison	.50
197	Thurman Thomas	.20
198	*Darrell Russell*	.20
199	Rob Moore	.05
200	John Elway	.50
201	Quinn Early	.05
202	Kevin Greene	.05
203	Robert Green	.05
204	Tony Carter	.05
205	Michael Timpson	.05
206	Kevin Smith	.05
207	Herschel Walker	.05
208	Steve Atwater	.05
209	Tyrone Braxton	.05
210	Willie Davis	.05
211	Lamont Warren	.05
212	Sean Dawkins	.05
213	Dale Carter	.05
214	Kimble Anders	.05
215	Derrick Thomas	.05
216	Chris Penn	.05
217	Irving Spikes	.05
218	Amp Lee	.05
219	Qadry Ismail	.05
220	Dave Meggett	.05
221	Tyrone Hughes	.05
222	Haywood Jeffires	.05
223	Torrance Small	.05
224	Danny Kanell	.05
225	Thomas Lewis	.05
226	Kyle Brady	.05
227	Harvey Williams	.05
228	Bobby Hoying	.05
229	Charlie Garner	.05
230	Andre Hastings	.05
231	Heath Shuler	.05
232	J.J. Stokes	.05
233	Ken Norton	.05
234	Steve Walsh	.05
235	Harold Green	.05
236	Reggie Brooks	.05
237	Robb Thomas	.05
238	Brian Mitchell	.05
239	Bill Brooks	.05
240	Leslie Shepherd	.05
241	Jay Graham	.05
242	*Kevin Lockett*	.20
243	*Derrick Mason*	1.00
244	*Marc Edwards*	.20
245	*Joey Kent*	.40
246	*Pat Barnes*	.50
247	Sherman Williams	.05
248	Ray Brown	.05
249	Stephen Davis	.05
250	Lamar Smith	.05

1997 Playoff 1st & 10 Chip Shots

Similar to a poker chip, the 250 plastic Chip Shot tokens were inserted one per pack. The fronts have the player's name at the top, while his photo is in the center. The Playoff logo and team name are printed at the bottom, with the token number appearing on the left and right sides of the front. The backs have "Chip Shot" printed at the top, with the Playoff logo in the center. "'97" is printed on the left and right of the token. "NFL" appears at the bottom.

		NM/M
Complete Set (250):		75.00
Common Player:		.10
Minor Stars:		.25
1	Marcus Allen	.25
2	Eric Bieniemy	.10
3	Jason Dunn	.10
4	Jim Harbaugh	.10
5	Michael Westbrook	.10
6	Tiki Barber	3.00
7	Frank Reich	.10
8	Irving Fryar	.10
9	Courtney Hawkins	.10
10	Eric Zeier	.10
11	Kent Graham	.10
12	Trent Dilfer	.10
13	Neil O'Donnell	.10
14	Reidel Anthony	.75
15	Jeff Hostetler	.10
16	Lawrence Phillips	.25
17	Dave Brown	.10
18	Mike Tomczak	.10
19	Jake Reed	.10
20	Anthony Miller	.10
21	Eric Metcalf	.10
22	Sedrick Shaw	.75
23	Anthony Johnson	.10
24	Mario Bates	.10
25	Dorsey Levens	.10
26	Stan Humphries	.10
27	Ben Coates	.10
28	Tyrone Wheatley	.10
29	Adrian Murrell	.10
30	William Henderson	.10
31	Warrick Dunn	4.00
32	LeShon Johnson	.10
33	James Stewart	.10
34	Edgar Bennett	.10
35	Raymont Harris	.10
36	Leroy Butler	.10
37	Darren Woodson	.10
38	Darnell Autry	1.50
39	Johnnie Morton	.10
40	William Floyd	.10
41	Terrell Fletcher	.10
42	Leonard Russell	.10
43	Henry Ellard	.10
44	Terrell Owens	3.00
45	John Friesz	.10
46	Antowain Smith	2.00
47	Charles Johnson	.10
48	Rickey Dudley	.10
49	Lake Dawson	.10
50	Bert Emanuel	.10
51	Zach Thomas	.75
52	Earnest Byner	.10
53	Yatil Green	.50
54	Chris Spielman	.10
55	Muhsin Muhammad	.10
56	Bobby Engram	.10
57	Eric Bjornson	.10
58	Willie Green	.10
59	Derrick Mayes	.10
60	Chris Sanders	.10
61	Jimmy Smith	.10
62	Tony Gonzalez	.75
63	Rich Gannon	.10
64	Stanley Pritchett	.10
65	Brad Johnson	.10
66	Rodney Peete	.10
67	Sam Gash	.10
68	Chris Calloway	.10
69	Chris T. Jones	.10
70	Will Blackwell	.25
71	Mark Bruener	.10
72	Terry Kirby	.10
73	Brian Blades	.10
74	Craig Heyward	.10
75	Jamie Asher	.10
76	Terance Mathis	.10
77	Troy Davis	.40
78	Bruce Smith	.10
79	Simeon Rice	.10
80	Fred Barnett	.10
81	Tim Brown	.10
82	James Jett	.10
83	Mark Carrier	.10
84	Shawn Jefferson	.10
85	Ken Dilger	.10
86	Rae Carruth	.10
87	Keenan McCardell	.10
88	Michael Irvin	.25
89	Mark Chmura	.10
90	Derrick Alexander	.10
91	Andre Reed	.10
92	Ed McCaffrey	.10
93	Erik Kramer	.10
94	Albert Connell	.10
95	Frank Wycheck	.10
96	Zack Crockett	.10
97	Jim Everett	.10
98	Michael Haynes	.10
99	Jeff Graham	.10
100	Brent Jones	.10
101	Troy Aikman	4.00
102	Byron Hanspard	.40
103	Robert Brooks	.10
104	Karim Abdul-Jabbar	.40
105	Drew Bledsoe	4.00
106	Napoleon Kaufman	.10
107	Steve Young	3.00
108	Leeland McElroy	.10
109	Jamal Anderson	.25
110	David LaFleur	.75
111	Vinny Testaverde	.10
112	Eric Moulds	.25
113	Tim Biakabutuka	.25
114	Rick Mirer	.10
115	Jeff Blake	.25
116	Jim Schwantz	.10
117	Herman Moore	.25
118	Ike Hilliard	2.00
119	Reggie White	.25
120	Steve McNair	3.00
121	Marshall Faulk	.25
122	Natrone Means	.25
123	Greg Hill	.10
124	O.J. McDuffie	.10
125	Robert Smith	.10
126	Bryant Westbrook	.25
127	Ray Zellars	.10
128	Rodney Hampton	.10
129	Wayne Chrebet	.10
130	Desmond Howard	.10
131	Ty Detmer	.10
132	Erric Pegram	.10
133	Yancey Thigpen	.10
134	Danny Wuerffel	.50
135	Charlie Jones	.10
136	Chris Warren	.10
137	Isaac Bruce	.75
138	Errict Rhett	.25
139	Gus Frerotte	.10
140	Frank Sanders	.10
141	Todd Collins	.10
142	Jake Plummer	2.00
143	Darnay Scott	.10
144	Rashaan Salaam	.25
145	Terrell Davis	4.00
146	Scott Mitchell	.10
147	Junior Seau	.25
148	Warren Moon	.10
149	Wesley Walls	.10
150	Daryl Johnston	.10
151	Brett Favre	6.00
152	Emmitt Smith	5.00
153	Dan Marino	6.00
154	Larry Centers	.10
155	Michael Jackson	.10
156	Kerry Collins	1.00
157	Curtis Conway	.25
158	Peter Boulware	.25
159	Carl Pickens	.10
160	Shannon Sharpe	.10
161	Brett Perriman	.10
162	Eddie George	3.00
163	Mark Brunell	2.00
164	Tamarick Vanover	.25
165	Cris Carter	.10
166	Corey Dillon	3.00
167	Curtis Martin	3.00
168	Amani Toomer	.10
169	Jeff George	.10
170	Kordell Stewart	2.00
171	Garrison Hearst	.10
172	Tony Banks	1.00
173	Mike Alstott	1.00
174	Jim Druckenmiller	.75
175	Chris Chandler	.10
176	Bam Morris	.10
177	Billy Joe Hobert	.10
178	Ernie Mills	.10
179	Ki-Jana Carter	.10
180	Deion Sanders	2.00
181	Ricky Watters	.25
182	Shawn Springs	.25
183	Barry Sanders	5.00
184	Antonio Freeman	1.00
185	Marvin Harrison	2.50
186	Elvis Grbac	.10
187	Terry Glenn	1.00
188	Willie Roaf	.10
189	Keyshawn Johnson	2.50
190	Orlando Pace	.25
191	Jerome Bettis	.25
192	Tony Martin	.10
193	Jerry Rice	4.00
194	Joey Galloway	1.00
195	Terry Allen	.10
196	Eddie Kennison	1.00
197	Thurman Thomas	.25
198	Darrell Russell	.25
199	Rob Moore	.10
200	John Elway	3.00
201	Quinn Early	.10
202	Kevin Greene	.10
203	Robert Green	.10
204	Tony Carter	.10
205	Michael Timpson	.10
206	Kevin Smith	.10
207	Herschel Walker	.10
208	Steve Atwater	.10
209	Tyrone Braxton	.10
210	Willie Davis	.10
211	Lamont Warren	.10
212	Sean Dawkins	.10
213	Dale Carter	.10
214	Kimble Anders	.10
215	Derrick Thomas	.10
216	Chris Penn	.10
217	Irving Spikes	.10
218	Amp Lee	.10
219	Qadry Ismail	.10
220	Dave Meggett	.10
221	Tyrone Hughes	.10
222	Haywood Jeffires	.10
223	Torrance Small	.10
224	Danny Kanell	.10
225	Thomas Lewis	.10
226	Kyle Brady	.10
227	Harvey Williams	.10
228	Bobby Hoying	.10
229	Charlie Garner	.10
230	Andre Hastings	.10
231	Heath Shuler	.10
232	J.J. Stokes	.10
233	Ken Norton	.10
234	Steve Walsh	.10
235	Harold Green	.10
236	Reggie Brooks	.10
237	Robb Thomas	.10
238	Brian Mitchell	.10
239	Bill Brooks	.10
240	Leslie Shepherd	.10
241	Jay Graham	.10
242	Kevin Lockett	.25
243	Derrick Mason	.75
244	Marc Edwards	.25
245	Joey Kent	.75
246	Pat Barnes	.75
247	Sherman Williams	.10
248	Ray Brown	.10
249	Stephen Davis	.10
250	Lamar Smith	.10

1997 Playoff 1st & 10 Extra Point Autograph

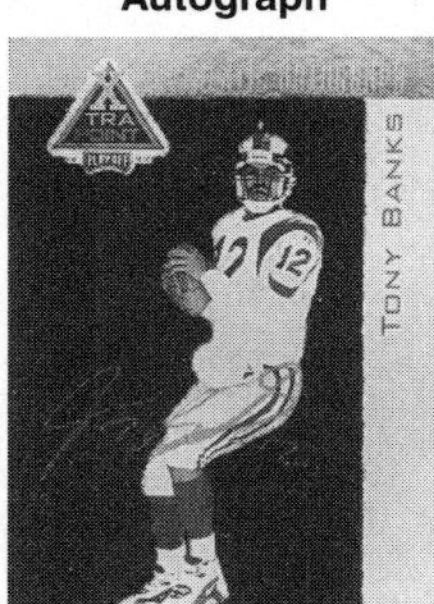

Inserted 1:444 packs, the autographed cards are signed by either Tony Banks or Terrell Davis. The cards have a gold-foil stripe at the top front with "Authentic Autograph" embossed on it. The Extra Point logo appears in the upper left. Black felt surrounds the photo of the respective player. The autograph is signed on the felt and into the photo. The player's name is listed inside a white stripe on the right border of the front. The backs, which are numbered with an "XPA" prefix, have a photo bordered in black. The number appears in an oval in the upper right.

		NM/M
Complete Set (2):		125.00
Common Player:		40.00
1	Tony Banks	40.00
2	Terrell Davis	100.00

1997 Playoff 1st & 10 Hot Pursuit

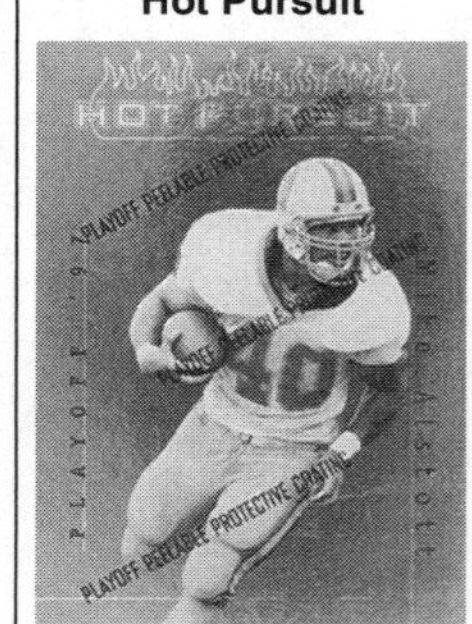

Inserted 1:180 packs, the 100-card set has the player photo superimposed on an orange background on the front. The Hot Pursuit logo is in the top center, while "Playoff '97" is printed vertically along the left border and the player's name is printed vertically along the right border. The card fronts did include a Playoff peelable protective coating. The backs featured a full-bleed photo of the player, with the card number in the upper right.

		NM/M
Compete Set (100):		250.00
Common Player:		1.00
Minor Stars:		2.00
1	Brett Favre	30.00
2	Dorsey Levens	5.00
3	Antonio Freeman	5.00
4	Robert Brooks	1.00
5	Mark Chmura	1.00
6	Reggie White	2.00
7	Drew Bledsoe	15.00
8	Curtis Martin	15.00
9	Ben Coates	2.00
10	Terry Glenn	5.00
11	Kerry Collins	2.00
12	Tim Biakabutuka	2.00
13	Anthony Johnson	1.00
14	Wesley Walls	2.00
15	Muhsin Muhammad	2.00
16	Mark Brunell	10.00
17	Natrone Means	2.00
18	Jimmy Smith	3.00
19	John Elway	20.00
20	Terrell Davis	20.00
21	Anthony Miller	1.00
22	Shannon Sharpe	2.00
23	Steve Young	20.00
24	Garrison Hearst	5.00
25	Jerry Rice	20.00
26	Troy Aikman	20.00
27	Deion Sanders	5.00
28	Emmitt Smith	25.00
29	Michael Irvin	5.00
30	Kordell Stewart	5.00
31	Jerome Bettis	5.00
32	Charles Johnson	1.00
33	Ty Detmer	1.00
34	Ricky Watters	2.00
35	Irving Fryar	1.00
36	Todd Collins	1.00
37	Thurman Thomas	2.00
38	Bruce Smith	2.00
39	Eric Moulds	5.00
40	Brad Johnson	5.00
41	Robert Smith	3.00
42	Cris Carter	5.00
43	Elvis Grbac	2.00
44	Greg Hill	2.00
45	Marcus Allen	5.00
46	Gus Frerotte	1.00
47	Terry Allen	2.00
48	Michael Westbrook	3.00
49	Jim Harbaugh	2.00
50	Marshall Faulk	10.00
51	Marvin Harrison	10.00
52	Jeff Blake	2.00
53	Ki-Jana Carter	2.00
54	Carl Pickens	2.00
55	Junior Seau	2.00
56	Tony Martin	2.00
57	Dan Marino	30.00
58	Karim Abdul-Jabbar	2.00
59	Stanley Pritchett	1.00
60	Zach Thomas	2.00
61	Steve McNair	10.00
62	Eddie George	10.00
63	Chris Sanders	1.00
64	Rick Mirer	1.00
65	Rashaan Salaam	1.00
66	Curtis Conway	2.00
67	Bobby Engram	1.00
68	Kent Graham	1.00
69	Leeland McElroy	1.00
70	Larry Centers	1.00
71	Frank Sanders	2.00
72	Jeff George	2.00
73	Napoleon Kaufman	2.00
74	Desmond Howard	1.00
75	Tim Brown	10.00
76	John Friesz	2.00
77	Chris Warren	2.00
78	Joey Galloway	8.00
79	Tony Banks	5.00
80	Lawrence Phillips	1.00
81	Isaac Bruce	10.00
82	Eddie Kennison	2.00
83	Errict Rhett	2.00
84	Mike Alstott	8.00
85	Rodney Hampton	1.00
86	Amani Toomer	2.00
87	Scott Mitchell	1.00
88	Barry Sanders	25.00
89	Herman Moore	5.00
90	Vinny Testaverde	5.00
91	Bam Morris	1.00
92	Michael Jackson	1.00
93	Chris Chandler	1.00
94	Eric Metcalf	1.00
95	Jamal Anderson	5.00
96	Jim Everett	1.00
97	Mario Bates	1.00
98	Wayne Chrebet	2.00
99	Adrian Murrell	1.00
100	Keyshawn Johnson	5.00

1997 Playoff 1st & 10 Xtra Point

The 10-card set was inserted 1:432 packs. The card fronts featured the Extra Point logo in the upper left, and a player photo in the center. Both were surrounded by felt. The player's name is printed inside a white stripe along the right border. The card backs, which featured a prefix of "XP," have the player photo surrounded by felt. The card's number is printed inside an oval in the upper right.

NM/M
Complete Set (10): 100.00
Common Player: 2.00
Inserted 1:432
Autographs 1:4,454
1 Kordell Stewart 5.00
2 Dan Marino 15.00
3 Brett Favre 15.00
4 Emmitt Smith 12.00
5 John Elway 10.00
6 Eddie George 8.00
7 Karim Abdul-Jabbar 2.00
8 Terry Glenn 5.00
9 Curtis Martin 10.00
10 Joey Galloway 5.00
A1 Tony Banks Auto 40.00
A2 Terrell Davis Auto 100.00

1997 Playoff Sports Cards Picks

Playoff produced this six-card set which was distributed to collectors who purchased a subscription to Sports Cards magazine at the 1997 National.

NM/M
Complete Set (6): 8.00
Common Player: 1.00
1 Brett Favre 3.00
2 Barry Sanders 2.00
3 Terrell Davis 1.50
4 Jerry Rice 1.50
5 Deion Sanders 1.00
6 Kordell Stewart 1.50

1997 Playoff Super Bowl Card Show

This set was available through wrapper redemption at the 1997 Super Bowl Card Show. Each card was available in exchange for three Playoff wrappers opened at the Playoff booth. The only exception is the Terrell Davis card, which could only be obtained by redeeming an entire box of wrappers for a complete seven-card set. The cards are not numbered.

NM/M
Complete Set (7): 20.00
Common Player: 2.00
1 Terry Allen 2.00
2 Jerome Bettis 3.00
3 Terrell Davis 5.00
4 Marshall Faulk 3.00
5 Eddie George 3.00
6 Deion Sanders 3.50
7 Reggie White 3.00

1998 Playoff Absolute Hobby

Absolute SSD was made for the hobby-only and contained 200 cards on super-thick 24-point stock. The horizontal cards featured brushed silver foil with a celluloid player image laminated between the front and back. Playoff also produced a retail version, called Absolute, which included all 200 cards, but on a thinner stock with a different twist to some of the inserts. The set was paralleled twice, in a Silver foil version and a Gold foil version numbered to 25 sets. Inserts include: Checklists, Draft Picks, Honors, Marino Milestones, Platinum Quads, Shields, Red Zone and Statistically Speaking.

NM/M
Complete Set (200): 75.00
Common Player: .50
Minor Stars: 1.00
Silver Cards: 3X
Silver Rookies: 2X
Inserted 1:3
Gold Cards: 50X-100X
Gold Rookies: 7X-14X
Production 25 Sets
Pack (5): 7.00
Wax Box (16): 80.00
1 John Elway 6.00
2 *Marcus Nash* 2.00
3 *Brian Griese* 6.00
4 Terrell Davis 4.00
5 Rod Smith 1.00
6 Shannon Sharpe 1.00
7 Ed McCaffrey .50
8 Brett Favre 12.00
9 Dorsey Levens 1.00
10 Derrick Mayes 1.00
11 Antonio Freeman 1.00
12 Robert Brooks .50
13 Mark Chmura 1.00
14 Reggie White 1.00
15 Kordell Stewart 5.00
16 *Hines Ward* 6.00
17 Jerome Bettis 1.00
18 Charles Johnson .50
19 Courtney Hawkins .50
20 Will Blackwell .50
21 Mark Bruener .50
22 Steve Young 4.00
23 Jim Druckenmiller .50
24 Garrison Hearst 1.00
25 *R.W. McQuarters* 2.00
26 Marc Edwards .50
27 Irv Smith .50
28 Jerry Rice 6.00
29 Terrell Owens 1.00
30 J.J. Stokes 1.00
31 Elvis Grbac 1.00
32 *Rashaan Shehee* .50
33 Donnell Bennett .50
34 Kimble Anders .50
35 Ted Popson .50
36 Derrick Alexander .50
37 Tony Gonzalez 1.00
38 Andre Rison 1.00
39 Brad Johnson 1.00
40 *Randy Moss* 15.00
41 Robert Smith 1.00
42 Leroy Hoard .50
43 Cris Carter 1.00
44 Jake Reed .50
45 Drew Bledsoe 6.00
46 *Tony Simmons* 1.00
47 *Chris Floyd* 1.00
48 *Robert Edwards* 4.00
49 Shawn Jefferson .50
50 Ben Coates .50
51 Terry Glenn 1.00
52 Trent Dilfer 1.00
53 *Jacquez Green* 3.00
54 Warrick Dunn 6.00
55 Mike Alstott 1.00
56 Reidel Anthony 1.00
57 Bert Emanuel .50
58 Warren Sapp .50
59 *Charlie Batch* 4.00
60 *Germane Crowell* 4.00
61 Scott Mitchell .50
62 Barry Sanders 8.00
63 Tommy Vardell .50
64 Herman Moore 1.00
65 Johnnie Morton .50
66 Mark Brunell 5.00
67 *Jonathan Quinn* 1.00
68 *Fred Taylor* 6.00
69 James Stewart .50
70 Jimmy Smith 1.00
71 Damon Jones .50
72 Keenan McCardell .50
73 Dan Marino 10.00
74 *Larry Shannon* 1.00
75 *John Avery* 4.00
76 Troy Drayton .50
77 Stanley Pritchett .50
78 Karim Abdul-Jabbar 1.00
79 O.J. McDuffie 1.00
80 Yatil Green 1.00
81 Danny Kanell .50
82 Tiki Barber 1.00
83 Tyrone Wheatley .50
84 Charles Way .50
85 Gary Brown .50
86 *Brian Alford* .50
87 *Joe Jurevicius* 2.00
88 Ike Hilliard 1.00
89 Troy Aikman 6.00
90 Deion Sanders 3.00
91 Emmitt Smith 10.00
92 Chris Warren 1.00
93 Daryl Johnston .50
94 Michael Irvin 1.00
95 David LaFleur .50
96 *Kevin Dyson* 4.00
97 Steve McNair 5.00
98 Eddie George 5.00
99 Yancey Thigpen .50
100 Frank Wycheck .50
101 Glenn Foley 1.00
102 Vinny Testaverde 1.00
103 Keyshawn Johnson 1.00
104 Curtis Martin 3.00
105 Keith Byars .50
106 *Scott Frost* .50
107 Wayne Chrebet .50
108 Warren Moon 1.00
109 *Ahman Green* 15.00
110 Steve Broussard .50
111 Ricky Watters 1.00
112 Joey Galloway 1.00
113 Mike Pritchard .50
114 Brian Blades .50
115 Gus Frerotte .50
116 *Skip Hicks* 4.00
117 Terry Allen .50
118 Michael Westbrook 1.00
119 Jamie Asher .50
120 Leslie Shepherd .50
121 Jeff Blake 1.00
122 Corey Dillon 4.00
123 Carl Pickens 1.00
124 Tony McGee .50
125 Darnay Scott .50
126 Kerry Collins 1.00
127 Fred Lane 1.00
128 William Floyd .50
129 Rae Carruth .50
130 Wesley Walls .50
131 Muhsin Muhammad .50
132 Jake Plummer 6.00
133 Adrian Murrell 1.00
134 *Michael Pittman* 1.00
135 Larry Centers .50
136 Frank Sanders .50
137 Rob Moore .50
138 *Andre Wadsworth* 3.00
139 Mario Bates .50
140 Chris Chandler .50
141 Byron Hanspard .50
142 Jamal Anderson 1.00
143 Terance Mathis .50
144 O.J. Santiago .50
145 Tony Martin .50
146 *Jammi German* 1.00
147 Jim Harbaugh .50
148 Errict Rhett .50
149 Michael Jackson .50
150 *Patrick Johnson* .50
151 Eric Green .50
152 Doug Flutie 4.00
153 Rob Johnson 1.00
154 Antowain Smith 3.00
155 Bruce Smith .50
156 Eric Moulds .50
157 Andre Reed .50
158 Erik Kramer .50
159 Darnell Autry .50
160 Edgar Bennett .50
161 *Curtis Enis* 4.00
162 Curtis Conway 1.00
163 *E.G. Green* 1.00
164 *Jerome Pathon* 2.00
165 *Peyton Manning* 20.00
166 Marshall Faulk 1.00
167 Zack Crockett .50
168 Ken Dilger .50
169 Marvin Harrison 1.00
170 Danny Wuerffel .50
171 Lamar Smith .50
172 Ray Zellars .50
173 Qadry Ismail .50
174 Sean Dawkins .50
175 Andre Hastings .50
176 Jeff George 1.00
177 *Charles Woodson* 5.00
178 Napoleon Kaufman 3.00
179 *Jon Ritchie* 1.00
180 Desmond Howard .50
181 Tim Brown .50
182 James Jett .50
183 Rickey Dudley .50
184 Bobby Hoying .50
185 Rodney Peete .50
186 Charlie Garner .50
187 Irving Fryar .50
188 Chris T. Jones .50
189 Jason Dunn .50
190 Tony Banks 1.00
191 *Robert Holcombe* 4.00
192 Craig Heyward .50
193 Isaac Bruce 1.00
194 *Az-Zahir Hakim* 1.00
195 Eddie Kennison 1.00
196 *Mikhael Ricks* 1.00
197 *Ryan Leaf* 4.00
198 Natrone Means 1.00
199 Junior Seau 1.00
200 Freddie Jones .50

1998 Playoff Absolute Hobby Silver/Gold

Two parallel versions of the 200-card Absolute SSD set exist. Silver foil versions were printed on a silver foil versus the team colored foil used on base cards. These were inserted one per three packs. Gold versions were printed on gold foil and sequentially numbered to 25 on the back.

Silver Cards: 2X
Silver Rookies: 2X
Gold Cards: 10X-25X
Gold Rookies: 3X-5X

1998 Playoff Absolute Hobby Checklist

This 30-card insert featured a horizontal shot of a key player from one of the NFL teams, with that team's home stadium in the background. On the back, each player card from that team is listed. Checklists were inserted one per 19 packs.

NM/M
Complete Set (30): 125.00
Common Player: 1.00
Inserted 1:19
1 Jake Plummer 5.00
2 Jamal Anderson 1.00
3 Jim Harbaugh 1.00
4 Rob Johnson 1.00
5 Fred Lane 1.00
6 Curtis Enis 3.00
7 Corey Dillon 5.00
8 Troy Aikman 8.00
9 Terrell Davis 8.00
10 Barry Sanders 10.00
11 Brett Favre 12.00
12 Peyton Manning 12.00
13 Mark Brunell 5.00
14 Elvis Grbac 1.00
15 Dan Marino 12.00
16 Cris Carter 1.00
17 Drew Bledsoe 8.00
18 Ray Zellars 1.00
19 Charles Way 1.00
20 Curtis Martin 8.00
21 Napoleon Kaufman 1.00
22 Irving Fryar 1.00
23 Kordell Stewart 3.00
24 Tony Banks 1.00
25 Ryan Leaf 1.00
26 Jerry Rice 10.00
27 Warren Moon 1.00
28 Warrick Dunn 5.00
29 Eddie George 5.00
30 Terry Allen 1.00

1998 Playoff Absolute Hobby Draft Picks

This 36-card insert set featured top players from the 1998 NFL Draft over a foil background. These were inserted one per 10 packs. In addition, Bronze versions of each card were available only through special three-card packs that contained only these Bronze versions. Those packs were inserted one per four boxes.

NM/M
Complete Set (36): 75.00
Common Player: 1.00
Minor Stars: 3.00
Inserted 1:10
1 Peyton Manning 12.00
2 Ryan Leaf 1.00
3 Andre Wadsworth 1.00
4 Charles Woodson 3.00
5 Curtis Enis 1.00
6 Fred Taylor 6.00
7 Kevin Dyson 5.00
8 Robert Edwards 2.00
9 Randy Moss 12.00
10 R.W. McQuarters 1.00
11 John Avery 1.00
12 Marcus Nash 3.00
13 Jerome Pathon 1.00
14 Jacquez Green 5.00
15 Robert Holcombe 4.00
16 Patrick Johnson 1.00
17 Germane Crowell 3.00
18 Tony Simmons 1.00
19 Joe Jurevicius 3.00
20 Mikhael Ricks 1.00
21 Charlie Batch 3.00
22 Jon Ritchie 1.00
23 Scott Frost 1.00
24 Skip Hicks 3.00
25 Brian Alford 1.00
26 E.G. Green 1.00
27 Jammi German 1.00
28 Ahman Green 8.00
29 Chris Floyd 1.00
30 Larry Shannon 1.00
31 Jonathan Quinn 1.00
32 Rashaan Shehee 3.00
33 Brian Griese 6.00
34 Hines Ward 8.00
35 Michael Pittman 1.00
36 Az-Zahir Hakim 1.00

1998 Playoff Absolute Hobby Marino Milestones

Playoff continued its 15-card Marino Milestones insert, with cards 6-10 inserted one per 397 packs of Absolute. Cards 1-5 were found in Prestige SSD and 11-15 were inserted into Momentum SSD. All versions were signed and featured a different record of Dan Marino's.

NM/M
Complete Set (5): 600.00
Common Player: 125.00
Inserted 1:397
6 Dan Marino (7,452) 125.00
7 Dan Marino (56/9) 125.00
8 Dan Marino (5,084) 125.00
9 Dan Marino (9) 125.00
10 Dan Marino (96.0) 125.00

1998 Playoff Absolute Hobby Platinum Quads

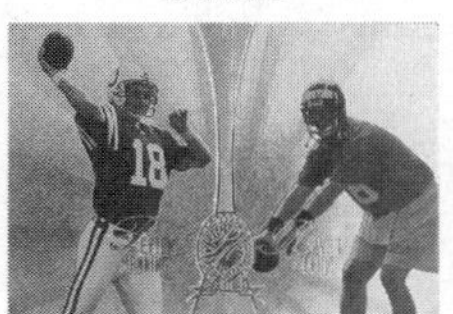

Platinum Quads was an 18-card insert that captured four players on a single card, with two per side. Cards were printed horizontally with the player's image appearing over foil with a "sunburst" etch. These were inserted one per 73 packs of Absolute SSD.

NM/M
Common Player: 10.00
Inserted 1:73
1 Brett Favre, John Elway, Barry Sanders, Warrick Dunn 75.00
2 Dan Marino, Terrell Davis, Napoleon Kaufman, Jerome Bettis 60.00
3 Jerry Rice, Brad Johnson, Marshall Faulk, Jimmy Smith 50.00
4 Troy Aikman, Herman Moore, Mark Chmura, Gus Frerotte 40.00
5 Steve Young, Mike Alstott, Tiki Barber, Keyshawn Johnson 40.00
6 Kordell Stewart, Robert Brooks, Karim Abdul-Jabbar, Shannon Sharpe 20.00
7 Mark Brunell, Dorsey Levens, Carl Pickens, Rob Moore 20.00
8 Drew Bledsoe, Joey Galloway, Tim Brown, Fred Lane 30.00
9 Eddie George, Rob Johnson, Irving Fryar, Andre Rison 15.00
10 Jake Plummer, Antonio Freeman, Steve McNair, Warren Moon 20.00
11 Emmitt Smith, Cris Carter, Junior Seau, Danny Kanell 50.00
12 Corey Dillon, Jake Reed, Curtis Martin, Bobby Hoying 15.00
13 Deion Sanders, Jim Druckenmiller, Reidel Anthony, Terry Allen 10.00
14 Antowain Smith, Wesley Walls, Isaac Bruce, Terry Glenn 10.00
15 Charlie Batch, Scott Frost, Jonathan Quinn, Brian Griese 15.00
16 Kevin Dyson, Randy Moss, Marcus Nash, Jerome Pathon 50.00
17 Curtis Enis, Fred Taylor, Robert Edwards, John Avery 25.00
18 Peyton Manning, Ryan Leaf, Andre Wadsworth, Charles Woodson 40.00

1998 Playoff Absolute Hobby Playoff Honors

This three-card insert continued Playoff's Honors insert through all of its products, and was numbered PH13-PH15. These die-cut cards showed the player's image over a large black Playoff logo with white letters. Honors were inserted one per 3,970 packs of Absolute SSD.

NM/M
Complete Set (3): 400.00
Common Player: 75.00
Inserted 1:3,970
13 John Elway 250.00
14 Jerome Bettis 75.00
15 Steve Young 100.00

1998 Playoff Absolute Hobby Red Zone

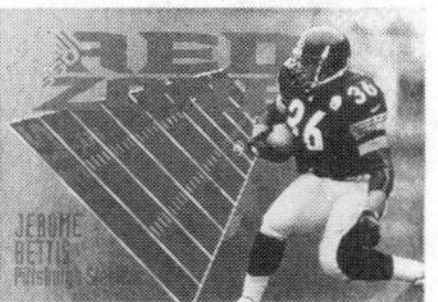

Red Zone featured 26 different players on a horizontal card with a mock-football field across the background. The insert name was printed in large letters in red foil, with his photo off to the right side. These were inserted one per 19 packs.

NM/M
Complete Set (26): 100.00
Common Player: 1.00
Inserted 1:19
1 Terrell Davis 5.00
2 Jerome Bettis 1.00
3 Mike Alstott 1.00
4 Brett Favre 10.00
5 Mark Brunell 3.00
6 Jeff George 1.00
7 John Elway 6.00
8 Troy Aikman 6.00
9 Steve Young 6.00
10 Kordell Stewart 3.00
11 Drew Bledsoe 6.00
12 James Jett 1.00
13 Dan Marino 10.00
14 Brad Johnson 1.00
15 Jake Plummer 3.00
16 Karim Abdul-Jabbar 1.00
17 Eddie George 4.00
18 Warrick Dunn 3.00
19 Cris Carter 1.00
20 Barry Sanders 8.00
21 Corey Dillon 5.00
22 Steve McNair 3.00
23 Herman Moore 1.00
24 Antonio Freeman 1.00
25 Dorsey Levens 1.00
26 James Stewart 1.00

1998 Playoff Absolute Hobby Shields

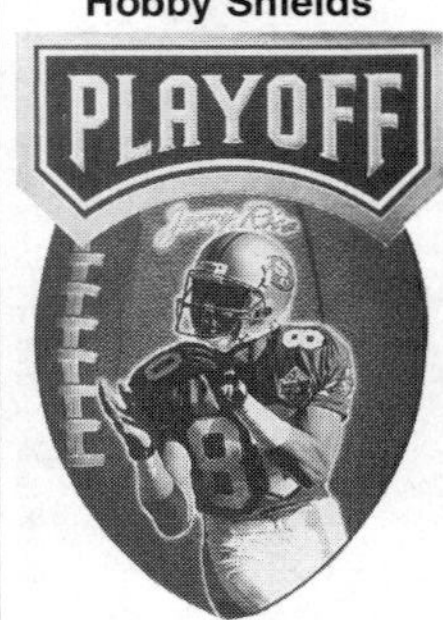

Shields was a 20-card insert that featured the player over a die-cut football with the Playoff logo cut across the top. These were inserted one per 37 packs.

NM/M
Complete Set (20): 100.00
Common Player: 2.00
Inserted 1:37
1 Terrell Davis 8.00
2 Corey Dillon 5.00
3 Dorsey Levens 2.00
4 Brett Favre 15.00
5 Warrick Dunn 5.00
6 Jerome Bettis 2.00
7 John Elway 10.00
8 Troy Aikman 10.00
9 Mark Brunell 5.00
10 Kordell Stewart 5.00
11 Eddie George 5.00
12 Jerry Rice 10.00
13 Dan Marino 15.00
14 Emmitt Smith 12.00
15 Napoleon Kaufman 2.00
16 Ryan Leaf 2.00
17 Curtis Martin 8.00
18 Peyton Manning 12.00
19 Cris Carter 2.00
20 Barry Sanders 12.00

A card number in parenthese ( ) indicates the set is unnumbered.

1998 Playoff Absolute Hobby Statistically Speaking

Statistically Speaking features 18 cards, with the player shown over a brushed foil background that highlights individual numbers of the featured player. These were inserted one per 55 packs.

		NM/M
Complete Set (18):		100.00
Common Player:		3.00
Inserted 1:55		
1	Jerry Rice	10.00
2	Barry Sanders	12.00
3	Deion Sanders	4.00
4	Brett Favre	15.00
5	Curtis Martin	6.00
6	Warrick Dunn	4.00
7	John Elway	10.00
8	Steve Young	10.00
9	Cris Carter	3.00
10	Kordell Stewart	4.00
11	Terrell Davis	10.00
12	Irving Fryar	3.00
13	Dan Marino	15.00
14	Tim Brown	6.00
15	Jerome Bettis	3.00
16	Troy Aikman	10.00
17	Napoleon Kaufman	3.00
18	Emmitt Smith	12.00

1998 Playoff Contenders Leather

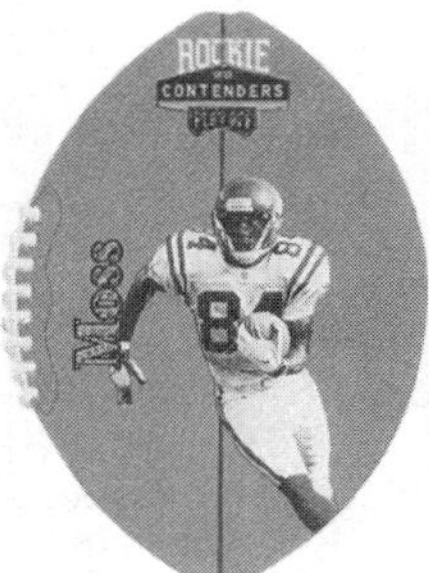

Leather cards are one of three base sets found in Contenders. Each Leather card is printed on actual leather with three different foil stamps and are found one-per-pack. The 100-card set includes 70 veterans and 30 rookies from 1998. The parallel Red set has the players last name in red foil. Singles from this insert were found 1:9 hobby packs.

		NM/M
Complete Set (100):		160.00
Common Player:		.50
Minor Stars:		1.00
Common Rookie:		1.00
Inserted 1:1		
Red Cards:		3X
Red Rookies:		2X
Inserted 1:9		
Gold Cards:		5X-25X
Pack (5):		10.50
Wax Box (16):		120.00
1	Adrian Murrell	.50
2	Michael Pittman	2.00
3	Jake Plummer	5.00
4	Andre Wadsworth	3.00
5	Jamal Anderson	2.00
6	Chris Chandler	1.00
7	Tim Dwight	4.00
8	Patrick Johnson	3.00
9	Jermaine Lewis	.50
10	Doug Flutie	1.00
11	Antowain Smith	2.00
12	Muhsin Muhammad	.50
13	Bobby Engram	.50
14	Curtis Enis	1.00
15	Alonzo Mayes	1.00
16	Corey Dillon	3.00
17	Carl Pickens	1.00
18	Troy Aikman	5.00
19	Michael Irvin	2.00
20	Deion Sanders	2.00
21	Emmitt Smith	7.00
22	Terrell Davis	4.00
23	John Elway	8.00
24	Brian Griese	8.00
25	Rod Smith	1.00
26	Charlie Batch	2.00
27	Germane Crowell	1.00
28	Terry Fair	1.00
29	Herman Moore	1.00
30	Barry Sanders	8.00
31	Brett Favre	10.00
32	Antonio Freeman	1.50
33	Vonnie Holliday	3.00
34	Reggie White	1.50
35	Marshall Faulk	1.50
36	Marvin Harrison	1.00
37	Peyton Manning	15.00
38	Jerome Pathon	3.00
39	Tavian Banks	3.00
40	Mark Brunell	4.00
41	Keenan McCardell	1.00
42	Fred Taylor	6.00
43	Elvis Grbac	.50
44	Andre Rison	1.00
45	Rashaan Shehee	2.00
46	Karim Abdul-Jabbar	1.00
47	John Avery	4.00
48	Dan Marino	8.00
49	O.J. McDuffie	1.00
50	Cris Carter	1.50
51	Brad Johnson	1.50
52	Randy Moss	15.00
53	Robert Smith	1.50
54	Drew Bledsoe	4.00
55	Ben Coates	1.00
56	Robert Edwards	7.00
57	Chris Floyd	2.00
58	Terry Glenn	1.50
59	Cameron Cleeland	4.00
60	Kerry Collins	1.00
61	Danny Kanell	.50
62	Charles Way	.50
63	Glenn Foley	1.00
64	Keyshawn Johnson	1.50
65	Curtis Martin	1.50
66	Tim Brown	1.00
67	Jeff George	1.00
68	Napoleon Kaufman	1.00
69	Charles Woodson	5.00
70	Irving Fryar	.50
71	Bobby Hoying	1.00
72	Jerome Bettis	1.00
73	Kordell Stewart	4.00
74	Hines Ward	3.00
75	Ryan Leaf	5.00
76	Natrone Means	1.00
77	Mikhael Ricks	1.00
78	Junior Seau	1.00
79	Garrison Hearst	1.00
80	Terrell Owens	1.50
81	Jerry Rice	5.00
82	Steve Young	3.00
83	Joey Galloway	1.50
84	Ahman Green	3.00
85	Warren Moon	1.00
86	Ricky Watters	1.00
87	Tony Banks	1.00
88	Isaac Bruce	1.00
89	Robert Holcombe	3.00
90	Mike Alstott	1.50
91	Trent Dilfer	1.00
92	Warrick Dunn	4.00
93	Jacquez Green	4.00
94	Kevin Dyson	4.00
95	Eddie George	4.00
96	Steve McNair	2.00
97	Yancey Thigpen	.50
98	Terry Allen	1.00
99	Skip Hicks	1.00
100	Michael Westbrook	.50

1998 Playoff Contenders Leather Gold

This insert parallel's the Leather set but each single is sequentially numbered to a player's featured stat. The cards look identical to the base Leather card except for the player's last name is in gold foil and the numbering is stamped on the back.

		NM/M
Gold		5X-25X
1	Adrian Murrell/27	30.00
2	Michael Pittman/32	30.00
3	Jake Plummer/53	100.00
4	Andre Wadsworth/29	50.00
5	Jamal Anderson/29	75.00
6	Chris Chandler/94	20.00
7	Tim Dwight/39	75.00
8	Patrick Johnson/55	20.00
9	Jermaine Lewis/42	20.00
10	Doug Flutie/48	75.00
11	Antowain Smith/28	75.00
12	Muhsin Muhammad/52	20.00
13	Bobby Engram/78	10.00
14	Curtis Enis/36	75.00
15	Alonzo Mayes/92	10.00
16	Corey Dillon/27	100.00
17	Carl Pickens/52	25.00
18	Troy Aikman/62	100.00
19	Michael Irvin/61	30.00
20	Deion Sanders/36	50.00
21	Emmitt Smith/40	200.00
22	Terrell Davis/35	275.00
23	John Elway/27	250.00
24	Brian Griese/33	125.00
25	Rod Smith/70	20.00
26	Charlie Batch/23	150.00
27	Germane Crowell/53	35.00
28	Terry Fair/42	30.00
29	Herman Moore/52	30.00
30	Barry Sanders/33	300.00
31	Brett Favre/35	300.00
32	Antonio Freeman/58	50.00
33	Vonnie Holliday/64	30.00
34	Reggie White/36	75.00
35	Marshall Faulk/47	50.00
36	Marvin Harrison/73	20.00
37	Peyton Manning/36	250.00
38	Jerome Pathon/69	20.00
39	Tavian Banks/33	45.00
40	Mark Brunell/52	85.00
41	Keenan McCardell/85	10.00
42	Fred Taylor/31	225.00
43	Elvis Grbac/29	35.00
44	Andre Rison/72	10.00
45	Rashaan Shehee/72	20.00
46	Karim Abdul-Jabbar/44	60.00
47	John Avery/26	60.00
48	Dan Marino/16	500.00
49	O.J. McDuffie/35	30.00
50	Cris Carter/89	20.00
51	Brad Johnson/37	50.00
52	Randy Moss/25	650.00
53	Robert Smith/90	20.00
54	Drew Bledsoe/28	175.00
55	Ben Coates/42	30.00
56	Robert Edwards/27	100.00
57	Chris Floyd/63	10.00
58	Terry Glenn/50	40.00
59	Cameron Cleeland/50	30.00
60	Kerry Collins/39	30.00
61	Danny Kanell/53	20.00
62	Charles Way/76	10.00
63	Glenn Foley/56	20.00
64	Keyshawn Johnson/70	25.00
65	Curtis Martin/41	40.00
66	Tim Brown/60	30.00
67	Jeff George/29	40.00
68	Napoleon Kaufman/40	50.00
69	Charles Woodson/27	120.00
70	Irving Fryar/75	10.00
71	Bobby Hoying/53	20.00
72	Jerome Bettis/31	65.00
73	Kordell Stewart/22	150.00
74	Hines Ward/55	30.00
75	Ryan Leaf/33	125.00
76	Natrone Means/78	20.00
77	Mikhael Ricks/47	25.00
78	Junior Seau/33	40.00
79	Garrison Hearst/74	25.00
80	Terrell Owens/60	35.00
81	Jerry Rice/16	325.00
82	Steve Young/19	175.00
83	Joey Galloway/72	25.00
84	Ahman Green/42	40.00
85	Warren Moon/25	85.00
86	Ricky Watters/56	25.00
87	Tony Banks/51	20.00
88	Isaac Bruce/56	30.00
89	Robert Holcombe/35	45.00
90	Mike Alstott/88	25.00
91	Trent Dilfer/38	45.00
92	Warrick Dunn/39	75.00
93	Jacquez Green/61	30.00
94	Kevin Dyson/60	30.00
95	Eddie George/30	150.00
96	Steve McNair/52	45.00
97	Yancey Thigpen/79	10.00
98	Terry Allen/58	30.00
99	Skip Hicks/48	45.00
100	Michael Westbrook/45	20.00

1998 Playoff Contenders Pennant

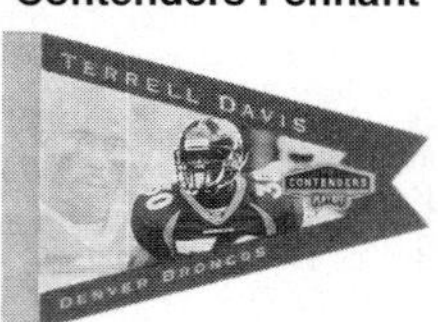

Pennant singles are printed on conventional stock with felt-like flocking and foil stamping. The 100-card set includes 70 veterans and 30 rookies from 1998. Pennant cards are found one-per-pack. Each player in the set has six different cards with each having a different color felt. The parallel Red singles are the same as the base except for the foil on the card is red. Singles are found 1:9 packs. The parallel Gold cards are in gold foil and are sequentially numbered to 98.

		NM/M
Complete Set (100):		75.00
Common Player:		.25
Minor Stars:		.50
Common Rookie:		.50
Each Card Issued In Six Colors		
Inserted 1:1		
Red Cards:		2X
Red Rookies:		2X
Inserted 1:9		
Gold Cards:		3X-5X
Gold Rookies:		2X-4X
Production 98 Sets		
1	Jake Plummer	1.00
2	Frank Sanders	.25
3	Jamal Anderson	2.00
4	Tim Dwight	2.00
5	Jammi German	.50
6	Tony Martin	.50
7	Jim Harbaugh	.50
8	Rod Woodson	.25
9	Rob Johnson	.50
10	Eric Moulds	1.50
11	Antowain Smith	1.50
12	Steve Beuerlein	.25
13	Fred Lane	.50
14	Curtis Enis	1.00
15	Corey Dillon	3.00
16	Neil O'Donnell	.25
17	Carl Pickens	.50
18	Darnay Scott	.25
19	Takeo Spikes	2.00
20	Troy Aikman	5.00
21	Michael Irvin	.50
22	Deion Sanders	1.50
23	Emmitt Smith	7.00
24	Chris Warren	.25
25	Terrell Davis	4.00
26	John Elway	6.00
27	Brian Griese	6.00
28	Ed McCaffrey	1.50
29	Marcus Nash	1.00
30	Shannon Sharpe	.50
31	Rod Smith	.50
32	Charlie Batch	1.00
33	Germane Crowell	1.00
34	Herman Moore	.50
35	Barry Sanders	8.00
36	Mark Chmura	.50
37	Brett Favre	10.00
38	Antonio Freeman	1.50
39	Reggie White	.50
40	Marshall Faulk	1.50
41	E.G. Green	2.50
42	Peyton Manning	10.00
43	Jerome Pathon	2.00
44	Mark Brunell	.50
45	Jonathan Quinn	2.00
46	Fred Taylor	5.00
47	Tony Gonzalez	.25
48	Andre Rison	.50
49	Karim Abdul-Jabbar	.50
50	John Avery	1.00
51	Dan Marino	7.00
52	Cris Carter	1.50
53	Randall Cunningham	1.00
54	Brad Johnson	1.50
55	Randy Moss	12.00
56	Robert Smith	.50
57	Drew Bledsoe	4.00
58	Robert Edwards	2.00
59	Terry Glenn	1.50
60	Tony Simmons	2.50
61	Tiki Barber	.50
62	Joe Jurevicius	2.00
63	Danny Kanell	.25
64	Keyshawn Johnson	1.50
65	Curtis Martin	1.50
66	Vinny Testaverde	.50
67	Tim Brown	.50
68	Jeff George	.50
69	Napoleon Kaufman	.50
70	Jon Ritchie	.50
71	Charles Woodson	5.00
72	Irving Fryar	.25
73	Duce Staley	.50
74	Jerome Bettis	1.50
75	Chris Fuamatu-Ma'afala	2.00
76	Kordell Stewart	2.00
77	Hines Ward	2.50
78	Ryan Leaf	1.00
79	Natrone Means	1.50
80	Mikhael Ricks	.50
81	Garrison Hearst	1.50
82	R.W. McQuarters	2.00
83	Jerry Rice	5.00
84	J.J. Stokes	.50
85	Steve Young	3.00
86	Joey Galloway	1.50
87	Ahman Green	3.00
88	Warren Moon	.50
89	Ricky Watters	.50
90	Isaac Bruce	.50
91	Robert Holcombe	2.50
92	Mike Alstott	1.50
93	Trent Dilfer	.50
94	Warrick Dunn	3.00
95	Jacquez Green	2.00
96	Kevin Dyson	3.00
97	Eddie George	4.00
98	Steve McNair	2.00
99	Terry Allen	.50
100	Skip Hicks	3.00

1998 Playoff Contenders Ticket

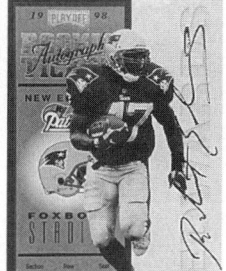

The 99-card Ticket set is made up 80 veterans and 19 rookies and was inserted one-per-pack. Each Ticket card was printed on conventional stock with foil stamping and has a ticket design to it. All of the rookie cards in this set are autographed. The quantities vary from player to player depending on how many they signed. A parallel Red and Gold insert was also produced. Red's were found 1:9 hobby packs and the Gold's were sequentially numbered to 25. The name on the fronts will either be in red or gold depending on which single you have.

		NM/M
Common Player:		.50
Minor Stars:		1.00
Common Rookie Autograph:		25.00
Inserted 1:1		
Red Cards:		3X
Red Rookies:		.2X
Inserted 1:9		
Gold Cards:		10X-25X
Gold Rookies:		2X
Production 25 Sets		
1	Rob Moore	1.00
2	Jake Plummer	1.00
3	Jamal Anderson	1.50
4	Terance Mathis	.50
5	Priest Holmes	75.00
6	Michael Jackson	.50
7	Eric Zeier	.50
8	Andre Reed	.50
9	Antowain Smith	1.50
10	Bruce Smith	.50
11	Thurman Thomas	1.00
12	Raghib Ismail	.50
13	Wesley Walls	.50
14	Curtis Conway	1.00
15	Jeff Blake	1.00
16	Corey Dillon	2.00
17	Carl Pickens	1.00
18	Troy Aikman	5.00
19	Michael Irvin	1.00
20	Ernie Mills	.50
21	Deion Sanders	1.50
22	Emmitt Smith	7.00
23	Terrell Davis	4.00
24	John Elway	6.00
25	Neil Smith	.50
26	Rod Smith	1.00
27	Herman Moore	1.00
28	Johnnie Morton	.50
29	Barry Sanders	10.00
30	Robert Brooks	.50
31	Brett Favre	10.00
32	Antonio Freeman	1.50
33	Dorsey Levens	1.00
34	Reggie White	1.00
35	Marshall Faulk	1.50
36	Mark Brunell	1.00
37	Jimmy Smith	1.00
38	James Stewart	.50
39	Donnell Bennett	.50
40	Andre Rison	1.00
41	Derrick Thomas	1.00
42	Karim Abdul-Jabbar	1.00
43	Dan Marino	7.00
44	Cris Carter	1.50
45	Brad Johnson	1.50
46	Robert Smith	1.00
47	Drew Bledsoe	4.00
48	Terry Glenn	1.50
49	Lamar Smith	.50
50	Ike Hilliard	.50
51	Danny Kanell	.50
52	Wayne Chrebet	1.50
53	Keyshawn Johnson	1.50
54	Curtis Martin	1.50
55	Tim Brown	1.00
56	Rickey Dudley	.50
57	Jeff George	1.00
58	Napoleon Kaufman	1.50
59	Irving Fryar	.50
60	Jerome Bettis	1.50
61	Charles Johnson	.50
62	Kordell Stewart	4.00
63	Natrone Means	1.00
64	Bryan Still	.50
65	Garrison Hearst	1.50
66	Jerry Rice	5.00
67	Steve Young	3.00
68	Joey Galloway	1.50
69	Warren Moon	1.00
70	Ricky Watters	1.00
71	Isaac Bruce	1.00
72	Mike Alstott	1.50
73	Reidel Anthony	1.00
74	Trent Dilfer	1.00
75	Warrick Dunn	3.00
76	Warren Sapp	.50
77	Eddie George	4.00
78	Steve McNair	2.00
79	Terry Allen	1.00
80	Gus Frerotte	.50
81	Andre Wadsworth AUTO	25.00
82	Tim Dwight AUTO	40.00
83	Curtis Enis AUTO/400	30.00
85	Charlie Batch AUTO	30.00
86	Germane Crowell AUTO	25.00
87	Peyton Manning AUTO/200	800.00
88	Jerome Pathon AUTO	30.00
89	Fred Taylor AUTO	125.00
90	Tavian Banks AUTO	25.00
92	Randy Moss AUTO/300	400.00
93	Robert Edwards AUTO	25.00
94	Hines Ward AUTO	125.00
95	Ryan Leaf AUTO/200	50.00
96	Mikhael Ricks AUTO	25.00
97	Ahman Green AUTO	150.00
98	Jacquez Green AUTO	25.00
99	Kevin Dyson AUTO	40.00
100	Skip Hicks AUTO	25.00
103	Chris FuamatuMa'afala AUTO	25.00

1998 Playoff Contenders Checklist

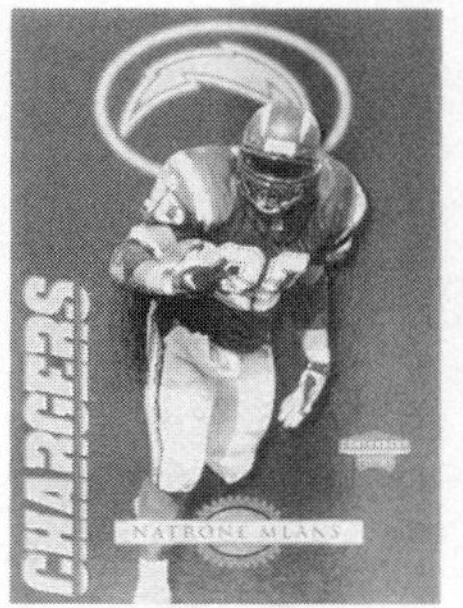

Each card in this 30-card set displays the top star from each club on the front and a checklist of each player from that team featured in our three base sets on the back. Each card measures 3" x 5" and was found one-per-box.

		NM/M
Complete Set (30):		75.00
Common Player:		1.00
Minor Stars:		2.00
Inserted 1:Box		
1	Jake Plummer	2.00
2	Jamal Anderson	2.00
3	Jermaine Lewis	1.00
4	Antowain Smith	2.00
5	Muhsin Muhammad	1.00
6	Curtis Enis	1.00
7	Corey Dillon	6.00
8	Deion Sanders	2.00
9	Terrell Davis	10.00
10	Barry Sanders	10.00
11	Brett Favre	12.00
12	Peyton Manning	15.00
13	Mark Brunell	8.00
14	Andre Rison	1.00
15	Dan Marino	12.00
16	Randy Moss	15.00
17	Drew Bledsoe	8.00
18	Kerry Collins	2.00
19	Danny Kanell	1.00
20	Curtis Martin	2.00
21	Tim Brown	1.00
22	Irving Fryar	1.00
23	Kordell Stewart	2.00
24	Natrone Means	2.00
25	Steve Young	6.00
26	Isaac Bruce	2.00
27	Warren Moon	2.00
28	Warrick Dunn	3.00
29	Eddie George	3.00
30	Terry Allen	2.00

1998 Playoff Contenders Honors

This is an insert that began with 1996 Playoff Prime and has continued throughout Playoff products over the past three years. Cards 19-21 can be found in this insert and are found 1:3,241 hobby packs.

		NM/M
Complete Set (3):		300.00
Common Player:		75.00
Inserted 1:3,241 Hobby		
19	Dan Marino	150.00
20	Jerry Rice	100.00
21	Mark Brunell	75.00

1998 Playoff Contenders MVP Contenders

This set showcases the players who are in contention for the league MVP. Each card is printed on holographic stock with an MVP graphic stamped in gold foil. Singles were inserted 1:19 hobby packs.

		NM/M
Complete Set (36):		75.00
Common Player:		1.00
Inserted 1:19		
1	Terrell Davis	8.00
2	Jerry Rice	8.00
3	Jerome Bettis	1.00
4	Brett Favre	12.00
5	Natrone Means	1.00
6	Steve Young	6.00
7	John Elway	8.00
8	Troy Aikman	8.00
9	Steve McNair	1.00
10	Kordell Stewart	2.00
11	Drew Bledsoe	6.00

12 Tim Brown 1.00
13 Dan Marino 12.00
14 Mark Brunell 3.00
15 Marshall Faulk 1.00
16 Jake Plummer 2.00
17 Corey Dillon 4.00
18 Carl Pickens 1.00
19 Keyshawn Johnson 1.00
20 Barry Sanders 10.00
21 Deion Sanders 1.00
22 Emmitt Smith 10.00
23 Antowain Smith 1.00
24 Curtis Martin 1.00
25 Cris Carter 1.00
26 Napoleon Kaufman 1.00
27 Eddie George 4.00
28 Warrick Dunn 4.00
29 Antonio Freeman 1.00
30 Joey Galloway 1.00
31 Herman Moore 1.00
32 Jamal Anderson 4.00
33 Terry Glenn 1.00
34 Garrison Hearst 1.00
35 Robert Smith 1.00
36 Mike Alstott 1.00

1998 Playoff Contenders Rookie of the Year

Playoff included the top 12 rookies from '98 who were battling for the rookie of the year award. Each card is printed on a wood-grain finish with two types of foil stamping. Singles were inserted 1:55 hobby packs.

NM/M
Complete Set (12): 75.00
Common Player: 3.00
Inserted 1:55
1 Tim Dwight 4.00
2 Curtis Enis 3.00
3 Charlie Batch 4.00
4 Peyton Manning 15.00
5 Fred Taylor 10.00
6 John Avery 3.00
7 Randy Moss 15.00
8 Robert Edwards 3.00
9 Charles Woodson 5.00
10 Ryan Leaf 3.00
11 Jacquez Green 4.00
12 Kevin Dyson 5.00

1998 Playoff Contenders Rookie Stallions

Only the top NFL draftees were featured in this 18-card set. Each card was printed on all micro-etched foil stock with silver foil stamping. Singles were inserted 1:19 hobby packs.

NM/M
Complete Set (18): 40.00
Common Player: 1.00
Minor Stars: 2.00
Inserted 1:19
1 Tim Dwight 3.00
2 Curtis Enis 2.00
3 Brian Griese 4.00
4 Charlie Batch 2.00
5 Germane Crowell 2.00
6 Peyton Manning 10.00
7 Tavian Banks 2.00
8 Fred Taylor 6.00
9 Rashaan Shehee 1.00
10 John Avery 2.00
11 Randy Moss 10.00
12 Robert Edwards 3.00
13 Charles Woodson 4.00
14 Ryan Leaf 2.00
15 Ahman Green 6.00
16 Jacquez Green 2.00
17 Kevin Dyson 4.00
18 Skip Hicks 2.00

1998 Playoff Contenders Super Bowl Leather

Each card in this set highlights a piece of an actual game-used football from Super Bowl XXXII. Each card back features a replica of the letter from the NFL verifying the authenticity of the ball. Cards are printed on conventional stock with foil stamping and were inserted 1:2,401 hobby packs.

NM/M
Common Player: 40.00
Inserted 1:2,401
1 Brett Favre 200.00
2 John Elway 150.00
3 Robert Brooks 40.00
4 Rod Smith 40.00
5 Antonio Freeman 40.00
6 Terrell Davis 150.00

1998 Playoff Contenders Touchdown Tandems

Two teammates from over 20 NFL franchises were paired on the front of each card in this debut insert set. These cards, printed on holographic foil stock with foil stamping, show the players known for carrying the scoring load for their respective clubs. Singles were found 1:19 hobby packs.

NM/M
Complete Set (24): 70.00
Common Player: 1.00
Inserted 1:19
1 Brett Favre, Antonio Freeman 15.00
2 Dan Marino, Karim Abdul-Jabbar 12.00
3 Emmitt Smith, Troy Aikman 12.00
4 Barry Sanders, Herman Moore 12.00
5 Eddie George, Steve McNair 6.00
6 Robert Edwards, Drew Bledsoe 6.00
7 Terrell Davis, Rod Smith 6.00
8 Mark Brunell, Fred Taylor 6.00
9 Jerry Rice, Steve Young 10.00
10 Jerome Bettis, Kordell Stewart 4.00
11 Curtis Martin, Keyshawn Johnson 1.00
12 Mike Alstott, Warrick Dunn 2.00
13 Isaac Bruce, Tony Banks 1.00
14 Adrian Murrell, Jake Plummer 2.00
15 Tim Brown, Napoleon Kaufman 2.00
16 Cris Carter, Randy Moss 10.00
17 Joey Galloway, Ricky Watters 2.00
18 Peyton Manning, Marshall Faulk 12.00
19 Ryan Leaf, Natrone Means 1.00
20 Carl Pickens, Corey Dillon 2.00
21 Doug Flutie, Antowain Smith 2.00
22 Randall Cunningham, Robert Smith 1.00
23 Chris Chandler, Jamal Anderson 1.00
24 John Elway, Ed McCaffrey 6.00

1998 Playoff Momentum Hobby

Each card in this 250-card set was printed on premium double-sided metalized mylar with double micro-etching on both sides. The shortprinted Rookie subset included 48 rising NFL stars and were inserted 1:6 packs. Each card also has a Red and Gold parallel version. The Reds were inserted 1:4 hobby packs while the Golds were sequentially numbered to 25.

NM/M
Complete Set (250): 175.00
Common Player: .30
Minor Stars: .60
Common Rookie: 1.00
Inserted 1:6
Red Cards: 2X-4X
Red Rookies: 1.2X
Inserted 1:4
Gold Cards: 15X-30X
Gold Rookies: 3X-6X
Production 25 Sets
Hobby Pack (5): 8.00
Hobby Wax Box (16): 90.00
1 Jake Plummer 1.00
2 Eric Metcalf .30
3 Adrian Murrell .30
4 Larry Centers .30
5 Frank Sanders .30
6 Rob Moore .60
7 *Andre Wadsworth* 1.00
8 Chris Chandler .60
9 Jamal Anderson 1.00
10 Tony Martin .30
11 Terrance Mathis .30
12 *Tim Dwight* 5.00
13 *Jammi German* 1.00
14 O.J. Santiago .30
15 Jim Harbaugh .60
16 Eric Zeier .30
17 *Duane Starks* 2.00
18 Rod Woodson .30
19 Errict Rhett .30
20 Jay Graham .30
21 Ray Lewis .30
22 Michael Jackson .30
23 Jermaine Lewis .30
24 *Patrick Johnson* 1.00
25 Eric Green .30
26 Doug Flutie 3.00
27 Rob Johnson .60
28 Antowain Smith 2.00
29 Thurman Thomas .60
30 *Jonathon Linton* 4.00
31 Bruce Smith .30
32 Eric Moulds .60
33 Kevin Williams .30
34 Andre Reed .30
35 Steve Beurlein .30
36 Kerry Collins .60
37 Anthony Johnson .30
38 Fred Lane .60
39 William Floyd .30
40 Raghib Ismail .30
41 Wesley Walls .30
42 Muhsin Muhammad .30
43 Rae Carruth .30
44 Kevin Greene .30
45 Greg Lloyd .30
46 *Moses Moreno* 2.00
47 Erik Kramer .30
48 Edgar Bennett .30
49 *Curtis Enis* 1.00
50 Curtis Conway .60
51 Bobby Engram .30
52 *Alonzo Mayes* 1.00
53 Jeff Blake .60
54 Neil O'Donnell .30
55 Corey Dillon 3.00
56 *Takeo Spikes* 4.00
57 Carl Pickens .60
58 Tony McGee .30
59 Darnay Scott .30
60 Troy Aikman 4.00
61 Deion Sanders 1.00
62 Emmitt Smith 8.00
63 Darren Woodson .30
64 Chris Warren .30
65 Daryl Johnston .30
66 Ernie Mills .30
67 Billy Davis .30
68 Michael Irvin .60
69 David LaFleur .30
70 John Elway 8.00
71 *Brian Griese* 10.00
72 Steve Atwater .30
73 Terrell Davis 4.00
74 Rod Smith .60
75 *Marcus Nash* 3.00
76 Shannon Sharpe .30
77 Ed McCaffrey .60
78 Neil Smith .30
79 *Charlie Batch* 4.00
80 *Germane Crowell* 4.00
81 Scott Mitchell .60
82 Barry Sanders 8.00
83 *Terry Fair* 2.00
84 Herman Moore 1.00
85 Johnnie Morton .30
86 Brett Favre 10.00
87 Rick Mirer .30
88 Dorsey Levens .60
89 William Henderson .30
90 Derrick Mayes .30
91 Antonio Freeman 1.00
92 Robert Brooks .30
93 Mark Chmura .30
94 *Vonnie Holliday* 2.00
95 Reggie White 1.00
96 *E.G. Green* 2.00
97 *Jerome Pathon* 4.00
98 *Peyton Manning* 30.00
99 Marshall Faulk 1.00
100 Zack Crockett .30
101 Ken Dilger .30
102 Marvin Harrison .60
103 Mark Brunell 3.00
104 *Jonathan Quinn* 4.00
105 *Tavian Banks* 4.00
106 *Fred Taylor* 10.00
107 James Stewart .30
108 Jimmy Smith .60
109 Keenan McCardell .30
110 Elvis Grbac .30
111 Rich Gannon .30
112 *Rashaan Shehee* 1.00
113 Donnell Bennett .30
114 Kimble Anders .30
115 Derrick Thomas .30
116 Kevin Lockett .30
117 Derrick Alexander .30
118 Tony Gonzalez .60
119 Andre Rison .30
120 Craig Erickson .30
121 Dan Marino 8.00
122 *John Avery* 4.00
123 Karim Abdul-Jabbar .60
124 Zach Thomas .60
125 O.J. McDuffie .30
126 Troy Drayton .30
127 Randall Cunningham 1.00
128 Brad Johnson .60
129 Robert Smith .60
130 Cris Carter 1.00
131 *Randy Moss* 25.00
132 Jake Reed .30
133 John Randle .30
134 Drew Bledsoe 3.00
135 *Tony Simmons* 2.00
136 Sedrick Shaw .30
137 *Chris Floyd* 4.00
138 *Robert Edwards* 5.00
139 *Rod Rutledge* 1.00
140 Shawn Jefferson .30
141 Ben Coates .60
142 Terry Glenn .60
143 Heath Shuler .30
144 Danny Wuerffel .30
145 Troy Davis .30
146 Qadry Ismail .30
147 Ray Zellars .30
148 Lamar Smith .30
149 *Cameron Cleeland* 2.00
150 Sean Dawkins .30
151 Andre Hastings .30
152 Danny Kanell .30
153 Tiki Barber .30
154 Tyrone Wheatley .30
155 Charles Way .30
156 Gary Brown .30
157 *Shaun Williams* 1.00
158 Chris Calloway .30
159 Amani Toomer .30
160 *Brian Alford* 1.00
161 *Joe Jurevicius* 4.00
162 Ike Hilliard .30
163 Michael Strahan .30
164 Glenn Foley .60
165 Vinny Testaverde .60
166 Keyshawn Johnson .60
167 Curtis Martin 1.00
168 Leon Johnson .30
169 Keith Byars .30
170 Wayne Chrebet .60
171 Kyle Brady .30
172 Dedric Ward .30
173 Jeff George .60
174 *Charles Woodson* 8.00
175 Napoleon Kaufman 1.00
176 *Jon Ritchie* 4.00
177 Tim Brown .60
178 James Jett .30
179 Rickey Dudley .30
180 Bobby Hoying .30
181 Duce Staley 3.00
182 Charlie Garner .30
183 Irvin Fryar .30
184 Jeff Graham .30
185 Jason Dunn .30
186 Kordell Stewart 3.00
187 Jerome Bettis 1.00
188 Andre Coleman .30
189 *Chris Fuamatu-Ma'afala* 4.00
190 Charles Johnson .30
191 *Hines Ward* 10.00
192 Mark Bruener .30
193 Courtney Hawkins .30
194 Will Blackwell .30
195 Levon Kirkland .30
196 *Mikhael Ricks* 3.00
197 *Ryan Leaf* 2.00
198 Natrone Means .60
199 Junior Seau .60
200 Bryan Still .30
201 Freddie Jones .30
202 Steve Young 2.00
203 Jim Druckenmiller 1.00
204 Garrison Hearst .60
205 *R.W. McQuarters* 3.00
206 Merton Hanks .30
207 Marc Edwards .30
208 Jerry Rice 4.00
209 Terrell Owens 1.50
210 J.J. Stokes .30
211 Tony Banks .60
212 *Robert Holcombe* 4.00
213 Greg Hill .30
214 Amp Lee .30
215 Jerald Moore .30
216 Isaac Bruce .60
217 *Az-Zahir Hakim* 4.00
218 Eddie Kennison .30
219 *Grant Wistrom* 4.00
220 Warren Moon .60
221 *Ahman Green* 25.00
222 Steve Broussard .30
223 Ricky Watters .60
224 James McKnight .30
225 Joey Galloway 1.00
226 Mike Pritchard .30
227 Trent Dilfer .60
228 Warrick Dunn 3.00
229 Mike Alstott 1.00
230 John Lynch .30
231 *Jacquez Green* 4.00
232 Reidel Anthony .60
233 Bert Emanuel .30
234 Warren Sapp .30
235 Steve McNair 1.50
236 Eddie George 3.00
237 Chris Sanders .30
238 Yancey Thigpen .30
239 Willie Davis .30
240 *Kevin Dyson* 4.00
241 Frank Wycheck .30
242 Trent Green .60
243 Gus Frerotte .30
244 *Skip Hicks* 5.00
245 Terry Allen .30
246 Stephen Davis .30
247 *Stephen Alexander* 4.00
248 Michael Westbrook .60
249 Dana Stubblefield .30
250 Dan Wilkinson .30

1998 Playoff Momentum Hobby Class Reunion Quads

Each card in this set includes stars from every draft class since the famous one in 1983. Four players drafted in the same year appear on each card (two on the front, two on the back). Cards are printed on doublesided mirror foil stock with micro-etching on each side as well as gold foil stamping. Singles were inserted 1:81 hobby packs.

NM/M
Complete Set (16): 200.00
Common Player: 5.00
Inserted 1:81
1 Dan Marino, John Elway, Bruce Matthews, Darrell Green 1983 30.00
2 Steve Young, Irving Fryar, Reggie White, Jeff Hostetler 1984 15.00
3 Jerry Rice, Bruce Smith, Andre Reed, Doug Flutie 1985 15.00
4 Keith Byars, Leslie O'Neal, Seth Joyner, Ray Brown 1986 5.00
5 Cris Carter, Vinny Testaverde, Jim Harbaugh, Rod Woodson 1987 5.00
6 Tim Brown, Chris Chandler, Michael Irvin, Neil Smith 1988 10.00
7 Troy Aikman, Barry Sanders, Deion Sanders, Andre Rison 1989 35.00
8 Emmitt Smith, Jeff George, Neil O'Donnell, Shannon Sharpe 1990 25.00
9 Brett Favre, Herman Moore, Yancey Thigpen, Ricky Watters 1991 30.00
10 Mark Chmura, Brad Johnson, Carl Pickens, Robert Brooks 1992 5.00
11 Drew Bledsoe, Jerome Bettis, Mark Brunell, Garrison Hearst 1993 20.00
12 Trent Dilfer, Dorsey Levens, Marshall Faulk, Isaac Bruce 1994 15.00
13 Terrell Davis, Kordell Stewart, Napoleon Kaufman, Curtis Martin 1995 20.00
14 Eddie George, Keyshawn Johnson, Karim Abdul-Jabbar, Terry Glenn 1996 10.00
15 Warrick Dunn, Corey Dillon, Jake Plummer, Antowain Smith 1997 10.00
16 Peyton Manning, Ryan Leaf, Curtis Enis, Randy Moss 1998 35.00

1998 Playoff Momentum Hobby EndZone Xpress

This 29-card set spotlights the NFL's best who have a knack for getting into the end zone. Each card is printed on die-cut clear plastic with holographic foil stamping. Singles were found 1:9 hobby packs.

NM/M
Complete Set (29): 60.00
Common Player: 1.00
Minor Stars: 2.00
Inserted 1:9
1 Jake Plummer 2.00
2 Herman Moore 1.00
3 Terrell Davis 5.00
4 Antowain Smith 2.00
5 Curtis Enis 1.00
6 Corey Dillon 3.00
7 Troy Aikman 6.00
8 John Elway 6.00
9 Barry Sanders 8.00
10 Brett Favre 10.00
11 Peyton Manning 10.00
12 Mark Brunell 3.00
13 Andre Rison 1.00
14 Dan Marino 10.00
15 Randy Moss 10.00
16 Drew Bledsoe 6.00
17 Jerome Bettis 2.00
18 Tim Brown 3.00
19 Antonio Freeman 1.00
20 Napoleon Kaufman 1.00
21 Emmitt Smith 8.00
22 Kordell Stewart 3.00
23 Curtis Martin 4.00
24 Ryan Leaf 1.00
25 Jerry Rice 6.00
26 Joey Galloway 2.00
27 Warrick Dunn 3.00
28 Eddie George 3.00
29 Steve McNair 3.00

1998 Playoff Momentum Hobby Headliners

These cards cover the events and milestones that made these players great. Each is printed on holographic stock with foil stamping. Singles were inserted 1:49 hobby packs.

NM/M
Complete Set (23): 75.00
Common Player: 2.00
Inserted 1:49
1 Brett Favre 12.00
2 Jerry Rice 8.00
3 Barry Sanders 10.00
4 Troy Aikman 40.00
5 Warrick Dunn 4.00
6 Dan Marino 12.00
7 John Elway 8.00
8 Drew Bledsoe 6.00
9 Kordell Stewart 3.00
10 Mark Brunell 3.00
11 Eddie George 3.00
12 Terrell Davis 8.00
13 Emmitt Smith 10.00
14 Steve McNair 4.00
15 Mike Alstott 2.00
16 Peyton Manning 12.00
17 Antonio Freeman 2.00
18 Curtis Martin 6.00
19 Terry Glenn 2.00
20 Brad Johnson 2.00
21 Karim Abdul-Jabbar 2.00

22	Ryan Leaf	2.00
23	Jerome Bettis	2.00

1998 Playoff Momentum Hobby Playoff Honors

This insert has appeared in most Playoff products since it debuted in 1996 Prime. These singles (#16-18) were inserted 1:3,841 hobby packs.

		NM/M
Complete Set (3):		400.00
Common Player:		100.00
Inserted 1:3,841		
PH16	Brett Favre	225.00
PH17	Kordell Stewart	100.00
PH18	Troy Aikman	125.00

1998 Playoff Momentum Hobby Marino Milestones

The final five cards (#11-15) of this chase set were inserted into Momentum packs at a ratio of 1:385. All cards are printed on premium card stock with film laminates and foil stamping designed to showcase the soon to be "Hall of Fame" autograph of Dan found on each.

	NM/M
Complete Set (11-15):	600.00
Common Player:	125.00
Inserted 1:385	

1998 Playoff Momentum Hobby NFL Rivals

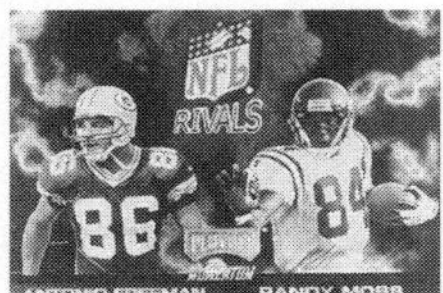

Top NFL stars and rookie rivals were paired together on the front of these tough inserts. Each card in this 22-card set is printed on premium mirror foil board stock with gold foil stamping. Each was inserted 1:49 packs.

		NM/M
Complete Set (22):		80.00
Common Player:		2.00
Inserted 1:49		
1	Mark Brunell, John Elway	8.00
2	Jerome Bettis, Eddie George	5.00
3	Barry Sanders, Emmitt Smith	12.00
4	Dan Marino, Drew Bledsoe	12.00
5	Troy Aikman, Jake Plummer	8.00
6	Terrell Davis, Napoleon Kaufman	6.00
7	Cris Carter, Herman Moore	2.00
8	Warrick Dunn, Dorsey Levens	4.00
9	Kordell Stewart, Steve McNair	6.00
10	Curtis Martin, Antowain Smith	6.00
11	Jerry Rice, Michael Irvin	10.00
12	Steve Young, Brett Favre	12.00
13	Corey Dillon, Fred Taylor	6.00
14	Tim Brown, Andre Rison	2.00
15	Mike Alstott, Robert Smith	2.00
16	Brad Johnson, Scott Mitchell	2.00
17	Robert Edwards, John Avery	4.00
18	Deion Sanders, Rob Moore	2.00
19	Antonio Freeman, Randy Moss	12.00
20	Peyton Manning, Ryan Leaf	12.00
21	Curtis Enis, Jacquez Green	2.00
22	Keyshawn Johnson, Terry Glenn	4.00

1998 Playoff Momentum Hobby Rookie Double Feature

Each card in this set was printed on doubleside foil board with three patterned micro-etches on each side. Two rookies with similar styles of play are matched in this 20-card chase set. One on the front and one on the back. Singles were inserted 1:17 hobby packs.

		NM/M
Complete Set (20):		50.00
Common Player:		1.00
Inserted 1:17		
1	Peyton Manning, Brian Griese	10.00
2	Ryan Leaf, Charlie Batch	2.00
3	Charles Woodson, Terry Fair	3.00
4	Curtis Enis, Tavian Banks	1.00
5	Fred Taylor, John Avery	5.00
6	Kevin Dyson, E.G. Green	3.00
7	Robert Edwards, Chris Fuamatu-Ma'afala	3.00
8	Randy Moss, Tim Dwight	10.00
9	Marcus Nash, Joe Jurevicius	2.00
10	Jerome Pathon, Az-Zahir Hakim	4.00
11	Jacquez Green, Tony Simmons	2.00
12	Robert Holcombe, Jon Ritchie	2.00
13	Cameron Cleeland, Alonzo Mayes	1.00
14	Patrick Johnson, Mikhael Ricks	1.00
15	Germane Crowell, Hines Ward	3.00
16	Skip Hicks, Chris Floyd	2.00
17	Brian Alford, Jammi German	1.00
18	Ahman Green, Rashaan Shehee	6.00
19	Jonathan Quinn, Moses Moreno	1.00
20	R.W. McQuarters, Duane Starks	1.00

1998 Playoff Momentum Hobby Team Threads

Each card in this 20-card set showcased authentic team jerseys that the pros use. All the Home jerseys were in color while the parallel Away jerseys were in white. Home jerseys could be found 1:33 hobby packs while the Away singles were tougher at 1:65.

		NM/M
Common Player:		4.00
Inserted 1:33		
Away Cards:		2X
Inserted 1:65		
1	Jerry Rice	20.00
2	Terrell Davis	20.00
3	Warrick Dunn	10.00
4	Brett Favre	40.00
5	Napoleon Kaufman	4.00
6	Corey Dillon	10.00
7	John Elway	20.00
8	Troy Aikman	20.00
9	Mark Brunell	10.00
10	Kordell Stewart	10.00
11	Drew Bledsoe	15.00
12	Curtis Martin	15.00
13	Dan Marino	40.00
14	Jerome Bettis	4.00
15	Eddie George	15.00
16	Ryan Leaf	4.00
17	Jake Plummer	8.00
18	Peyton Manning	40.00
19	Steve Young	15.00
20	Barry Sanders	30.00

1998 Playoff Momentum Retail

Each of the base cards in this set have a pigskin embossed style to them. Rookie cards are seeded at 1:3 retail packs. Each card has a parallel Red version with singles found 1:4 retail packs.

		NM/M
Complete Set (250):		75.00
Common Player:		.15
Minor Stars:		.30
Common Rookie:		1.00
Inserted 1:3		
Red Cards:		3X
Red Rookies:		1.5X
Inserted 1:4		
Wax Box:		50.00
1	Karim Abdul	.50
2	Troy Aikman	1.50
3	Derrick Alexander	.15
4	*Stephen Alexander*	3.00
5	*Brian Alford*	2.00
6	Terry Allen	.30
7	Mike Alstott	.50
8	Kimble Anders	.15
9	Jamal Anderson	.75
10	Reidel Anthony	.30
11	Steve Atwater	.15
12	*John Avery*	.50
13	*Tavian Banks*	.40
14	Tony Banks	.30
15	Tiki Barber	.15
16	*Charlie Batch*	2.00
17	Donnell Bennett	.15
18	Edgar Bennett	.15
19	Jerome Bettis	.50
20	Steve Beuerlein	.15
21	Will Blackwell	.15
22	Jeff Blake	.30
23	Drew Bledsoe	1.25
24	Kyle Brady	.15
25	Robert Brooks	.30
26	Steve Broussard	.15
27	Gary Brown	.15
28	Tim Brown	.30
29	Isaac Bruce	.30
30	Mark Bruener	.15
31	Mark Brunell	1.25
32	Keith Byars	.15
33	Chris Calloway	.15
34	Rae Carruth	.15
35	Cris Carter	.50
36	Larry Centers	.15
37	Chris Chandler	.50
38	Mark Chmura	.30
39	Wayne Chrebet	.50
40	*Cameron Cleeland*	.50
41	Ben Coates	.30
42	Kerry Collins	.30
43	Andre Coleman	.15
44	Curtis Conway	.30
45	Zack Crockett	.15
46	*Germane Crowell*	.50
47	Randall Cunningham	1.00
48	Billy Davis	.15
49	Stephen Davis	.15
50	Terrell Davis	2.50
51	Troy Davis	.15
52	Willie Davis	.15
53	Sean Dawkins	.15
54	Trent Dilfer	.30
55	Ken Dilger	.15
56	Corey Dillon	1.00
57	Troy Drayton	.15
58	Jim Druckenmiller	.30
59	Rickey Dudley	.15
60	Jason Dunn	.15
61	Warrick Dunn	1.25
62	*Tim Dwight*	4.00
63	*Kevin Dyson*	4.00
64	Marc Edwards	.15
65	*Robert Edwards*	7.00
66	John Elway	2.50
67	Bert Emanuel	.15
68	Bobby Engram	.15
69	*Curtis Enis*	1.00
70	Craig Erickson	.15
71	*Terry Fair*	.50
72	Marshall Faulk	.75
73	Brett Favre	3.00
74	*Chris Floyd*	1.00
75	William Floyd	.15
76	Doug Flutie	1.00
77	Glenn Foley	.30
78	Antonio Freeman	.50
79	Gus Frerotte	.30
80	Irving Fryar	.15
81	*Chris Fuamatu-Ma'afala*	2.00
82	Joey Galloway	.50
83	Rich Gannon	.15
84	Charlie Garner	.15
85	Eddie George	1.25
86	Jeff George	.30
87	*Jammi German*	.50
88	Terry Glenn	.50
89	Tony Gonzalez	.30
90	Jay Graham	.15
91	Jeff Graham	.15
92	Elvis Grbac	.30
93	*Ahman Green*	6.00
94	*E.G. Green*	3.00
95	Eric Green	.15
96	*Jacquez Green*	4.00
97	Trent Green	.50
98	Kevin Greene	.15
99	*Brian Griese*	6.00
100	*Az-Zahir Hakim*	3.00
101	Merton Hanks	.15
102	Jim Harbaugh	.30
103	Marvin Harrison	.30
104	Andre Hastings	.15
105	Courtney Hawkins	.15
106	Garrison Hearst	.50
107	William Henderson	.15
108	*Skip Hicks*	3.00
109	Greg Hill	.15
110	Ike Hilliard	.15
111	*Robert Holcombe*	3.00
112	*Vonnie Holliday*	1.00
113	Bobby Hoying	.30
114	Michael Irvin	.30
115	Qadry Ismail	.15
116	Raghib Ismail	.15
117	Michael Jackson	.15
118	Shawn Jefferson	.15
119	James Jett	.15
120	Anthony Johnson	.15
121	Brad Johnson	.50
122	Charles Johnson	.15
123	Keyshawn Johnson	.50
124	Leon Johnson	.15
125	*Patrick Johnson*	.50
126	Rob Johnson	.50
127	Daryl Johnston	.15
128	Freddie Jones	.15
129	*Joe Jurevicius*	3.00
130	Danny Kanell	.15
131	Napoleon Kaufman	.50
132	Eddie Kennison	.30
133	Levon Kirkland	.15
134	Erik Kramer	.15
135	David LaFleur	.15
136	Fred Lane	.30
137	*Ryan Leaf*	1.00
138	Amp Lee	.15
139	Dorsey Levens	.50
140	Jermaine Lewis	.30
141	Ray Lewis	.15
142	*Jonathon Linton*	3.00
143	Greg Lloyd	.15
144	Kevin Lockett	.15
145	John Lynch	.15
146	*Peyton Manning*	25.00
147	Dan Marino	2.00
148	Curtis Martin	.50
149	Tony Martin	.30
150	Terance Mathis	.15
151	*Alonzo Mayes*	1.00
152	Derrick Mayes	.15
153	Ed McCaffrey	.30
154	Keenan McCardell	.30
155	O.J. McDuffie	.30
156	Tony McGee	.15
157	James McKnight	.15
158	Steve McNair	.75
159	*R.W. McQuarters*	2.00
160	Natrone Means	.50
161	Eric Metcalf	.15
162	Ernie Mills	.15
163	Rick Mirer	.15
164	Scott Mitchell	.30
165	Warren Moon	.30
166	Herman Moore	.50
167	Jerald Moore	.15
168	Rob Moore	.30
169	*Moses Moreno*	2.00
170	Johnnie Morton	.15
171	*Randy Moss*	25.00
172	Eric Moulds	.75
173	Muhsin Muhammad	.15
174	Adrian Murrell	.30
175	*Marcus Nash*	4.00
176	Neil O'Donnell	.15
177	Terrell Owens	.75
178	*Jerome Pathon*	3.00
179	Carl Pickens	.50
180	Jake Plummer	1.25
181	Mike Pritchard	.15
182	*Jonathan Quinn*	3.00
183	John Randle	.15
184	Andre Reed	.30
185	Jake Reed	.30
186	Errict Rhett	.15
187	Jerry Rice	1.50
188	*Mikhael Ricks*	1.00
189	Andre Rison	.30
190	*John Ritchie*	2.00
191	*Rod Rutledge*	1.00
192	Barry Sanders	3.00
193	Chris Sanders	.15
194	Deion Sanders	.50
195	Frank Sanders	.15
196	O.J. Santiago	.30
197	Warren Sapp	.15
198	Darnay Scott	.15
199	Junior Seau	.30
200	Shannon Sharpe	.30
201	Sedrick Shaw	.15
202	*Rashaan Shehee*	.50
203	Heath Shuler	.15
204	*Tony Simmons*	4.00
205	Antowain Smith	.50
206	Bruce Smith	.15
207	Emmitt Smith	2.00
208	Jimmy Smith	.50
209	Lamar Smith	.15
210	Neil Smith	.15
211	Robert Smith	.30
212	Rod Smith	.30
213	*Takeo Spikes*	2.00
214	Duce Staley	1.00
215	*Duane Starks*	2.00
216	James Stewart	.15
217	Kordell Stewart	1.25
218	Bryan Still	.15
219	J.J. Stokes	.30
220	Michael Strahan	.15
221	Dana Stubblefield	.15
222	*Fred Taylor*	10.00
223	Vinny Testaverde	.30
224	Yancey Thigpen	.15
225	Derrick Thomas	.15
226	Thurman Thomas	.30
227	Zach Thomas	.30
228	Amani Toomer	.15
229	*Andre Wadsworth*	1.00
230	Wesley Walls	.15
231	Dedric Ward	.15
232	*Hines Ward*	6.00
233	Chris Warren	.30
234	Ricky Watters	.50
235	Charles Way	.15
236	Michael Westbrook	.15
237	Tyrone Wheatley	.15
238	Reggie White	.50
239	Dan Wilkinson	.15
240	Kevin Williams	.15
241	*Shaun Williams*	.50
242	*Grant Wistrom*	.50
243	*Charles Woodson*	7.00
244	Darren Woodson	.15
245	Rod Woodson	.15
246	Danny Wuerffel	.15
247	Frank Wycheck	.15
248	Steve Young	1.00
249	Eric Zeier	.15
250	Ray Zellars	.15

1998 Playoff Momentum Retail Class Reunion Tandems

The idea behind this insert was to pick two of the top players drafted from a specific season and picture one on the front and the other on the back. The set starts with the year 1983 and ends with 1998. Singles were inserted 1:121 retail packs.

		NM/M
Complete Set (16):		100.00
Common Player:		2.00
Minor Stars:		5.00
Inserted 1:121		
1	Dan Marino, John Elway	12.00
2	Steve Young, Reggie White	8.00
3	Jerry Rice, Bruce Smith	8.00
4	Keith Byars, Leslie O'Neal	2.00
5	Cris Carter, Vinny Testaverde	5.00
6	Tim Brown, Michael Irvin	5.00
7	Troy Aikman, Barry Sanders	12.00
8	Emmitt Smith, Jeff George	10.00
9	Brett Favre, Herman Moore	12.00
10	Brad Johnson, Carl Pickens	5.00
11	Drew Bledsoe, Mark Brunell	10.00
12	Dorsey Levens, Isaac Bruce	5.00
13	Terrell Davis, Kordell Stewart	8.00
14	Eddie George, Keyshawn Johnson	6.00
15	Warrick Dunn, Jake Plummer	5.00
16	Peyton Manning, Ryan Leaf	10.00

1998 Playoff Momentum Retail EndZone X-press

Each card in this set is similar to the hobby version except these singles aren't die cut. They are printed on plastic with gold foil and were inserted 1:13 retail packs.

		NM/M
Complete Set (29):		40.00
Common Player:		.50
Minor Stars:		1.00
Inserted 1:13		
1	Jake Plummer	1.00
2	Herman Moore	1.00
3	Terrell Davis	3.00
4	Antowain Smith	1.00
5	Curtis Enis	.50
6	Corey Dillon	3.00
7	Troy Aikman	4.00
8	John Elway	4.00
9	Barry Sanders	5.00
10	Brett Favre	6.00
11	Peyton Manning	6.00
12	Mark Brunell	3.00
13	Andre Rison	.50
14	Dan Marino	6.00
15	Randy Moss	6.00
16	Drew Bledsoe	3.00
17	Jerome Bettis	1.00
18	Tim Brown	1.00
19	Antonio Freeman	.50
20	Napoleon Kaufman	.50
21	Emmitt Smith	5.00
22	Kordell Stewart	2.00
23	Curtis Martin	3.00
24	Ryan Leaf	.50
25	Jerry Rice	5.00
26	Joey Galloway	1.00
27	Warrick Dunn	2.00
28	Eddie George	2.00
29	Steve McNair	2.00

1998 Playoff Momentum Retail Headliners

These red foil front cards highlight a record that the player had set in the past. Singles were found 1:73 retail packs.

		NM/M
Complete Set (23):		50.00
Common Player:		1.00
Inserted 1:73		
1	Brett Favre	10.00
2	Jerry Rice	20.00
3	Barry Sanders	8.00
4	Troy Aikman	6.00
5	Warrick Dunn	3.00
6	Dan Marino	10.00
7	John Elway	6.00
8	Drew Bledsoe	6.00
9	Kordell Stewart	4.00
10	Mark Brunell	4.00
11	Eddie George	4.00
12	Terrell Davis	6.00
13	Emmitt Smith	8.00
14	Steve McNair	4.00
15	Mike Alstott	1.00
16	Peyton Manning	10.00
17	Antonio Freeman	2.00
18	Curtis Martin	4.00
19	Terry Glenn	1.00
20	Brad Johnson	1.00
21	Karim Abdul	1.00
22	Ryan Leaf	1.00
23	Jerome Bettis	1.00

1998 Playoff Momentum Retail NFL Rivals

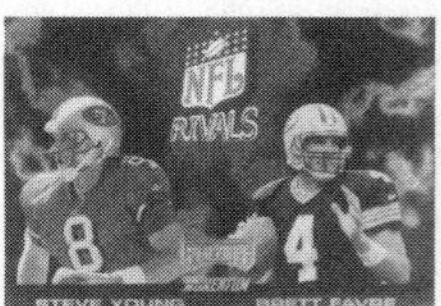

This set is identical to the hobby version except for the "R" prefix on these retail singles. Each card pictures two players who compete at the same position. Singles are found 1:73 retail packs.

	NM/M
Complete Set (22):	60.00
Common Player:	1.00
Inserted 1:73	

1	Mark Brunell, John Elway	5.00
2	Jerome Bettis, Eddie George	3.00
3	Barry Sanders, Emmitt Smith	10.00
4	Dan Marino, Drew Bledsoe	10.00
5	Troy Aikman, Jake Plummer	6.00
6	Terrell Davis, Napoleon Kaufman	4.00
7	Cris Carter, Herman Moore	1.00
8	Warrick Dunn, Dorsey Levens	2.00
9	Kordell Stewart, Steve McNair	3.00
10	Curtis Martin, Antowain Smith	1.00
11	Jerry Rice, Michael Irvin	8.00
12	Steve Young, Brett Favre	10.00
13	Corey Dillon, Fred Taylor	5.00
14	Tim Brown, Andre Rison	1.00
15	Mike Alstott, Robert Smith	1.00
16	Brad Johnson, Scott Mitchell	1.00
17	Robert Edwards, John Avery	2.00
18	Deion Sanders, Rob Moore	1.00
19	Antonio Freeman, Randy Moss	10.00
20	Peyton Manning, Ryan Leaf	10.00
21	Curtis Enis, Jacquez Green	2.00
22	Keyshawn Johnson, Terry Glenn	1.00

1998 Playoff Momentum Retail Rookie Double Feature

The hobby version of this set features two players on one card, where this set has the players on their own card. Each card also has the "R" prefix before the card number and were found 1:25 retail packs.

		NM/M
Complete Set (40):		35.00
Common Player:		.50
Minor Stars:		1.00
Inserted 1:25		
1	Peyton Manning	5.00
2	Ryan Leaf	1.00
3	Charles Woodson	2.00
4	Curtis Enis	1.00
5	Fred Taylor	4.00
6	Kevin Dyson	3.00
7	Robert Edwards	2.00
8	Randy Moss	5.00
9	Marcus Nash	1.00
10	Jerome Pathon	1.00
11	Jacquez Green	2.00
12	Robert Holcombe	2.00
13	Cameron Cleeland	.50
14	Patrick Johnson	.50
15	Germane Crowell	.50
16	Skip Hicks	1.00
17	Brian Alford	.50
18	Ahman Green	4.00
19	Jonathan Quinn	.50
20	R.W. McQuarters	1.00
21	Brian Griese	3.00
22	Charlie Batch	1.00
23	Terry Fair	.50
24	Tavian Banks	1.00
25	John Avery	.50
26	E.G. Green	.50
27	Chris Fuamatu-Ma'afala	1.00
28	Tim Dwight	2.00
29	Joe Jurevicius	1.00
30	Az-Zahir Hakim	2.00
31	Tony Simmons	.50
32	Jon Ritchie	1.00
33	Alonzo Mayes	.50
34	Mikhael Ricks	.50
35	Hines Ward	2.00
36	Chris Floyd	.50
37	Jammi German	.50
38	Rashaan Shehee	.50
39	Moses Moreno	.50
40	Duane Starks	.50

A player's name in *italic* type indicates a rookie card.

1998 Playoff Momentum Retail Team Jerseys

Team Jersey cards feature a photo of the player on the front and a piece of an authentic jersey on the back. It isn't an actual game worn but a jersey that the pros use. The Home versions carry a colored swatch and were inserted 1:49 retail packs. The parallel Away versions feature the white jerseys and were inserted 1:97 packs.

		NM/M
Common Player:		3.00
Inserted 1:49		
Away Cards:		1.5X
Inserted 1:97		
1	Jerry Rice	8.00
2	Terrell Davis	6.00
3	Warrick Dunn	4.00
4	Brett Favre	10.00
5	Napoleon Kaufman	3.00
6	Corey Dillon	3.00
7	John Elway	6.00
8	Troy Aikman	6.00
9	Mark Brunell	5.00
10	Kordell Stewart	4.00
11	Drew Bledsoe	5.00
12	Curtis Martin	5.00
13	Dan Marino	10.00
14	Jerome Bettis	3.00
15	Eddie George	5.00
16	Ryan Leaf	3.00
17	Jake Plummer	5.00
18	Peyton Manning	10.00
19	Steve Young	6.00
20	Barry Sanders	8.00

1998 Playoff Prestige

Prestige was a 200-card set that arrived with two different looks - one in hobby and one in retail. Prestige SSD cards are printed on 30-point etched silver foil stock. Retail versions are printed on thinner stock, with a foil strip across the bottom. While hobby cards are paralled in red and gold versions, retail cards are paralleled in red and green foil versus the silver foil used on base cards. Inserts include: Alma Mater (both retail and hobby), Award Winning Performers (both), Best of the NFL (both), Checklists (both), Draft Picks (both), Honors (hobby), Inside the Numbers (both) and Marino Milestones (hobby).

		NM/M
Complete Set (200):		75.00
Common Player:		.20
Minor Stars:		.60
Common Rookie (165-200):		.50
Red Cards:		2X-4X
Red Rookies:		2X
Gold Cards:		10X-20X
Gold Rookies:		3X-5X
Hobby Pack (5):		5.00
Hobby Wax Box (16):		75.00
Retail Pack (7):		4.00
Retail Wax Box (24):		70.00
1	John Elway	6.00
2	Steve Atwater	.20
3	Terrell Davis	6.00
4	Bill Romanowski	.20
5	Rod Smith	.20
6	Shannon Sharpe	.60
7	Ed McCaffrey	.20
8	Neil Smith	.20
9	Brett Favre	8.00
10	Dorsey Levens	.60
11	LeRoy Butler	.20
12	Antonio Freeman	.60
13	Robert Brooks	.20
14	Mark Chmura	.60
15	Gilbert Brown	.20
16	Kordell Stewart	3.00
17	Jerome Bettis	.60
18	Carnell Lake	.20
19	Dermontti Dawson	.20
20	Charles Johnson	.20
21	Greg Lloyd	.20
22	Levon Kirkland	.20
23	Steve Young	3.00
24	Jim Druckenmiller	.60
25	Garrison Hearst	.20
26	Merton Hanks	.20
27	Ken Norton	.20
28	Jerry Rice	5.00
29	Terrell Owens	.60
30	J.J. Stokes	.20
31	Trent Dilfer	.60
32	Warrick Dunn	4.00
33	Mike Alstott	.75
34	Reidel Anthony	.60
35	Warren Sapp	.20
36	Elvis Grbac	.20
37	Kimble Anders	.20
38	Ted Popson	.20
39	Derrick Thomas	.20
40	Tony Gonzalez	.60
41	Andre Rison	.20
42	Derrick Alexander	.20
43	Brad Johnson	.60
44	Robert Smith	.20
45	Randall McDaniel	.20
46	Cris Carter	.20
47	Jake Reed	.20
48	John Randle	.20
49	Drew Bledsoe	4.00
50	Willie Clay	.20
51	Chris Slade	.20
52	Willie McGinest	.20
53	Shawn Jefferson	.20
54	Ben Coates	.20
55	Terry Glenn	.60
56	Jason Hanson	.20
57	Scott Mitchell	.20
58	Barry Sanders	8.00
59	Herman Moore	.60
60	Johnnie Morton	.20
61	Mark Brunell	4.00
62	James Stewart	.20
63	Tony Boselli	.20
64	Jimmy Smith	.20
65	Keenan McCardell	.20
66	Dan Marino	8.00
67	Troy Drayton	.20
68	Bernie Parmalee	.20
69	Karim Abdul-Jabbar	.75
70	Zach Thomas	.20
71	O.J. McDuffie	.20
72	Tim Bowens	.20
73	Danny Kanell	.20
74	Tiki Barber	.60
75	Tyrone Wheatley	.20
76	Charles Way	.20
77	Jason Sehorn	.20
78	Ike Hilliard	.60
79	Michael Strahan	.20
80	Troy Aikman	4.00
81	Deion Sanders	2.00
82	Emmitt Smith	7.00
83	Darren Woodson	.20
84	Daryl Johnston	.20
85	Michael Irvin	.60
86	David LaFleur	.60
87	Glenn Foley	.20
88	Neil O'Donnell	.20
89	Keyshawn Johnson	.60
90	Aaron Glenn	.20
91	Wayne Chrebet	.20
92	Curtis Martin	2.00
93	Steve McNair	2.00
94	Eddie George	3.00
95	Bruce Matthews	.20
96	Frank Wycheck	.20
97	Yancey Thigpen	.20
98	Gus Frerotte	.20
99	Terry Allen	.20
100	Michael Westbrook	.20
101	Jamie Asher	.20
102	Marshall Faulk	.60
103	Zack Crockett	.20
104	Ken Dilger	.20
105	Marvin Harrison	.60
106	Chris Chandler	.20
107	Byron Hanspard	.60
108	Jamal Anderson	.60
109	Terance Mathis	.20
110	Peter Boulware	.20
111	Michael Jackson	.20
112	Jim Harbaugh	.60
113	Errict Rhett	.20
114	Antowain Smith	3.00
115	Thurman Thomas	.60
116	Bruce Smith	.20
117	Doug Flutie	1.00
118	Rob Johnson	.60
119	Kerry Collins	.75
120	Fred Lane	.20
121	Wesley Walls	.20
122	William Floyd	.20
123	Kevin Greene	.20
124	Erik Kramer	.20
125	Darnell Autry	.60
126	Curtis Conway	.20
127	Edgar Bennett	.20
128	Jeff Blake	.60
129	Corey Dillon	3.00
130	Carl Pickens	.20
131	Darnay Scott	.20
132	Jake Plummer	2.00
133	Larry Centers	.20
134	Frank Sanders	.20
135	Rob Moore	.20
136	Adrian Murrell	.60
137	Troy Davis	.60
138	Ray Zellars	.20
139	Willie Roaf	.20
140	Andre Hastings	.20
141	Jeff George	.60
142	Napoleon Kaufman	.75
143	Desmond Howard	.20
144	Tim Brown	.20
145	James Jett	.20
146	Rickey Dudley	.20
147	Bobby Hoying	.20
148	Duce Staley	2.00
149	Charlie Garner	.20
150	Irving Fryar	.20
151	Chris T. Jones	.20
152	Tony Banks	.60
153	Craig Heyward	.20
154	Isaac Bruce	.60
155	Eddie Kennison	.60
156	Junior Seau	.20
157	Tony Martin	.20
158	Freddie Jones	.20
159	Natrone Means	.60
160	Warren Moon	.60
161	Steve Broussard	.20
162	Joey Galloway	.60
163	Brian Blades	.20
164	Ricky Watters	.60
165	*Peyton Manning*	25.00
166	*Ryan Leaf*	4.00
167	*Andre Wadsworth*	3.00
168	*Charles Woodson*	5.00
169	*Curtis Enis*	3.00
170	*Fred Taylor*	8.00
171	*Kevin Dyson*	5.00
172	*Robert Edwards*	4.00
173	*Randy Moss*	15.00
174	*R.W. McQuarters*	1.50
175	*John Avery*	4.00
176	*Marcus Nash*	3.00
177	*Jerome Pathon*	3.00
178	*Jacquez Green*	4.00
179	*Robert Holcombe*	4.00
180	*Patrick Johnson*	1.50
181	*Germane Crowell*	4.00
182	*Tony Simmons*	3.00
183	*Joe Jurevicius*	3.00
184	*Mikhael Ricks*	1.50
185	*Charlie Batch*	3.00
186	*Jon Ritchie*	1.50
187	*Scott Frost*	.50
188	*Skip Hicks*	4.00
189	*Brian Alford*	.50
190	*E.G. Green*	2.00
191	*Jammi German*	.50
192	*Ahman Green*	15.00
193	*Chris Floyd*	1.50
194	*Larry Shannon*	1.50
195	*Jonathan Quinn*	2.00
196	*Rashaan Shehee*	3.00
197	*Brian Griese*	8.00
198	*Hines Ward*	8.00
199	*Michael Pittman*	1.50
200	*Az-Zahir Hakim*	5.00

1998 Playoff Prestige Red Hobby

All 200 cards in Prestige SSD were paralleled in this red foil version. Red parallels were seeded one per three packs.

Red Cards:	3X
Red Rookies:	2X

1998 Playoff Prestige Gold

All 200 cards in Prestige were available in a gold foil parallel version. These were sequentially numbered to 25 on the card back.

Gold Cards:	10X-20X
Gold Rookies:	3X-5X

1998 Playoff Prestige Alma Maters

This 28-card set featured three players from the same college on the silver foilboard. The back showed the same three players are gave a "Did you Know?" statistic about each. Silver versions were seeded one per 17 hobby packs, while Blue versions were seeded one per 25 retail packs.

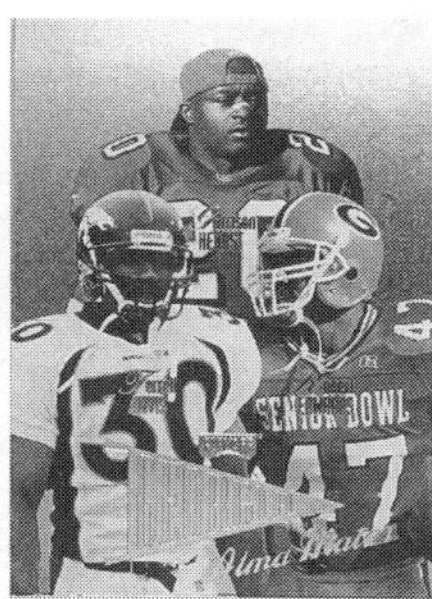

		NM/M
Complete Set (28):		160.00
Common Player:		1.00
1	Favre, Jackson, P. Carter	15.00
2	Irvin, Maryland, Testaverde	1.00
3	Dunn, Wadsworth, Boulware	3.00
4	D. Sanders, Bennett, B. Johnson	6.00
5	E. Smith, F. Taylor, Anthony	15.00
6	A. Smith, Anders, Lathon	3.00
7	Barry Sanders, R.J. McQuarters, Thurman Thomas	15.00
8	Leaf, Bledsoe, Hansen	10.00
9	Brunell, Moon, Shehee	5.00
10	Kaufman, Dillon, Pathon	5.00
11	Manning, Pickens, R. White	10.00
12	K. Stewart, Carruth, Westbrook	6.00
13	Enis, Collins, McDuffie	3.00
14	George, Hoying, Dudley	5.00
15	C. Carter, Glenn, Galloway	5.00
16	Grbac, Harbaugh, Woodson	4.00
17	Elway, McCaffrey, Milburn	8.00
18	T. Davis, Hearst, Edwards	8.00
19	Walker, Hastings, Ward	3.00
20	Marino, C. Martin, Heyward	15.00
21	Aikman, Stokes, Hicks	10.00
22	Seau, K. Johnson, Morton	4.00
23	Bettis, T. Brown, Watters	4.00
24	Faulk, Scott, Hakim	8.00
25	B. Smith, Druckenmiller, Freeman	3.00
26	Plummer, Woodson, Bates	6.00
27	H. Moore, Barber, Way	4.00
28	Avery, Walls, Bowens	1.00

1998 Playoff Prestige Award Winning Performers

This 22-card insert showcased top players on a large trophy, with the record they achieved and the Playoff logo near the top of the trophy. Hobby versions of this inserted were printed on silver foil, die-cut around the trophy and inserted one per 65 packs, while retail versions were printed on blue foil, not die-cut and inserted one per 97 packs.

		NM/M
Complete Set (22):		250.00
Common Player:		5.00
1	Terrell Davis	15.00
2	Troy Aikman	15.00
3	Brett Favre	25.00
4	Barry Sanders	20.00
5	Warrick Dunn	6.00
6	John Elway	15.00
7	Jerome Bettis	5.00
8	Jake Plummer	5.00
9	Corey Dillon	6.00
10	Jerry Rice	20.00
11	Steve Young	20.00
12	Mark Brunell	10.00
13	Drew Bledsoe	15.00
14	Dan Marino	25.00
15	Kordell Stewart	6.00
16	Emmitt Smith	20.00
17	Deion Sanders	6.00
18	Mike Alstott	5.00
19	Herman Moore	5.00
20	Cris Carter	5.00
21	Eddie George	10.00
22	Dorsey Levens	5.00

1998 Playoff Prestige Best of the NFL

Best in the NFL features 24 top players over a large NFL logo. Hobby versions of this insert were die-cut around the top of the NFL shield and inserted one per 33 hobby packs, while retail versions were not die-cut and inserted one per 49 retail packs.

		NM/M
Complete Set (24):		70.00
Common Player:		1.00
1	Terrell Davis	5.00
2	Troy Aikman	5.00
3	Brett Favre	8.00
4	Barry Sanders	6.00
5	Warrick Dunn	3.00
6	John Elway	5.00
7	Jerome Bettis	3.00
8	Jake Plummer	3.00
9	Corey Dillon	5.00
10	Jerry Rice	6.00
11	Steve Young	5.00
12	Mark Brunell	3.00
13	Drew Bledsoe	4.00
14	Dan Marino	6.00
15	Kordell Stewart	3.00
16	Emmitt Smith	5.00
17	Deion Sanders	3.00
18	Mike Alstott	2.00
19	Herman Moore	1.00
20	Cris Carter	2.00
21	Eddie George	3.00
22	Dorsey Levens	1.00
23	Peyton Manning	5.00
24	Ryan Leaf	1.00

1998 Playoff Prestige Checklist

This 30-card insert arrived in both retail and hobby packs, and contained a star player from each NFL team on the front and shots of each player on that team's cards on the back. Silver hobby versions were seeded one per 17 hobby packs, while gold retail versions were seeded one per 17 retail packs.

		NM/M
Complete Set (30):		75.00
Common Player:		1.00
1	Jake Plummer	3.00
2	Byron Hanspard	1.00
3	Michael Jackson	1.00
4	Antowain Smith	5.00
5	Wesley Walls	1.00
6	Erik Kramer	1.00
7	Corey Dillon	5.00
8	Troy Aikman	10.00
9	John Elway	10.00
10	Barry Sanders	12.00
11	Brett Favre	15.00
12	Peyton Manning	15.00
13	Mark Brunell	5.00
14	Andre Rison	1.00
15	Dan Marino	12.00
16	Cris Carter	2.00
17	Drew Bledsoe	8.00
18	Troy Davis	1.00
19	Danny Kanell	1.00

20	Glenn Foley	1.00
21	Napoleon Kaufman	1.00
22	Bobby Hoying	1.00
23	Kordell Stewart	4.00
24	Isaac Bruce	5.00
25	Ryan Leaf	2.00
26	Jerry Rice	10.00
27	Joey Galloway	4.00
28	Warrick Dunn	5.00
29	Eddie George	5.00
30	Gus Frerotte	1.00

1998 Playoff Prestige Draft Picks

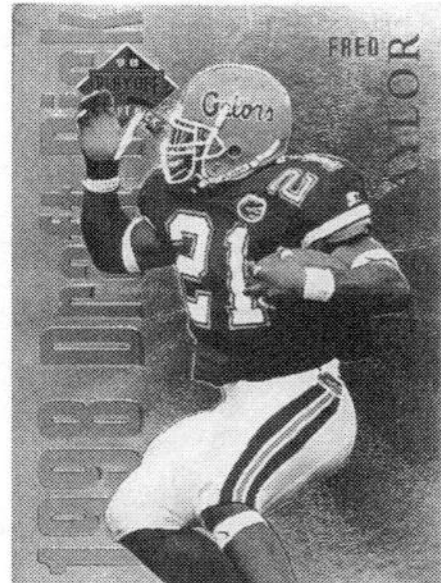

This 30-card insert featured the top draft picks from 1998. Silver versions were seeded one per nine hobby packs, while Silver Jumbos were inserted one per hobby box. Bronze standard sized cards were seeded one per nine retail packs, while Bronze Jumbos were inserted one per retail box. Green standard sized cards and Green Jumbos were also available, but only in special retail boxes, and both seeded one per box.

		NM/M
Complete Set (33):		60.00
Common Player:		1.00
Jumbos:		1X
1	Peyton Manning	10.00
2	Ryan Leaf	1.00
3	Andre Wadsworth	1.00
4	Charles Woodson	3.00
5	Curtis Enis	2.00
6	Fred Taylor	5.00
7	Kevin Dyson	4.00
8	Robert Edwards	3.00
9	Randy Moss	10.00
10	R.W. McQuarters	1.00
11	John Avery	1.00
12	Marcus Nash	2.00
13	Jerome Pathon	1.00
14	Jacquez Green	3.00
15	Robert Holcombe	3.00
16	Patrick Johnson	1.00
17	Germane Crowell	1.00
18	Tony Simmons	1.00
19	Joe Jurevicius	3.00
20	Mikhael Ricks	1.00
21	Charlie Batch	2.00
22	Jon Ritchie	1.00
23	Scott Frost	1.00
24	Skip Hicks	3.00
25	Brian Alford	1.00
26	E.G. Green	1.00
27	Jammi German	1.00
28	Ahman Green	7.00
29	Chris Floyd	1.00
30	Larry Shannon	1.00
31	Jonathan Quinn	1.00
32	Rashaan Shehee	1.00
33	Brian Griese	5.00

1998 Playoff Prestige Playoff Honors

This three-card insert was found only in hobby packs of Prestige. The cards were unnumbered and are listed alphabetically. The were inserted one per 3,200 packs.

		NM/M
Complete Set (3):		200.00
Common Player:		30.00
PH10	Terrell Davis	75.00
PH11	Barry Sanders	100.00
PH12	Warrick Dunn	30.00

Post-1980 cards in Near Mint condition will generally sell for about 75% of the quoted Mint value. Excellent-condition cards bring no more than 40%.

1998 Playoff Prestige Inside the Numbers

This 18-card insert set featured a player over some statistic that he has achieved. Hobby versions were die-cut and inserted one per 49 hobby packs, while retail not die-cut and inserted one per 72 retail packs.

		NM/M
Complete Set (18):		110.00
Common Player:		2.00
1	Barry Sanders	15.00
2	Terrell Davis	10.00
3	Jerry Rice	12.00
4	Kordell Stewart	6.00
5	Dan Marino	15.00
6	Warrick Dunn	6.00
7	Corey Dillon	5.00
8	Drew Bledsoe	10.00
9	Herman Moore	2.00
10	Troy Aikman	10.00
11	Brett Favre	15.00
12	Mark Brunell	5.00
13	Tim Brown	4.00
14	Jerome Bettis	2.00
15	Eddie George	4.00
16	Dorsey Levens	2.00
17	Napoleon Kaufman	2.00
18	John Elway	12.00

1998 Playoff Prestige Marino Milestones

The first five Marino Milestones cards were inserted into Prestige SSD at a rate of one per 321 packs. Each card highlighted a different record held by Marino, and no unautographed versions were available. Cards 6-10 were inserted into Absolute SSD and 11-15 were in Momentum SSD.

		NM/M
Complete Set (5):		600.00
Common Player:		125.00
1	Dan Marino 55,416	125.00
2	Dan Marino 13/4	125.00
3	Dan Marino 6	125.00
4	Dan Marino 48	125.00
5	Dan Marino 2.03	125.00

1998 Playoff Prestige Retail

Prestige Retail contained the same 200-card checklist that the hobby version had, but was printed on a thinner card stock and featured silver strip across the bottom with the player's name embossed in it. This set was paralleled in both a red (retail) and green (specail retail jumbos) foil set.

	NM/M
Common Player:	.20
Minor Stars:	.40
Red Stars:	3X
Red Rookies:	2X
Inserted 1:3	
Green Stars:	3X
Green Rookies:	2X
Inserted 1:1 Special Retail Pack	
Wax Box:	40.00

1998 Playoff Prestige Red/Green Retail

Each card in the Prestige retail set was paralleled in both red and green foil versions. The 200-card set contained either red foil (retail) or green foil (special retail) across the bottom instead of the silver used on base cards. Red foil versions were seeded one per three packs, while green foil versions were seeded one per Jumbo retail pack.

Red/Green Cards:	1.5X
Red/Green Rookies:	1X

1998 Playoff Super Bowl Show

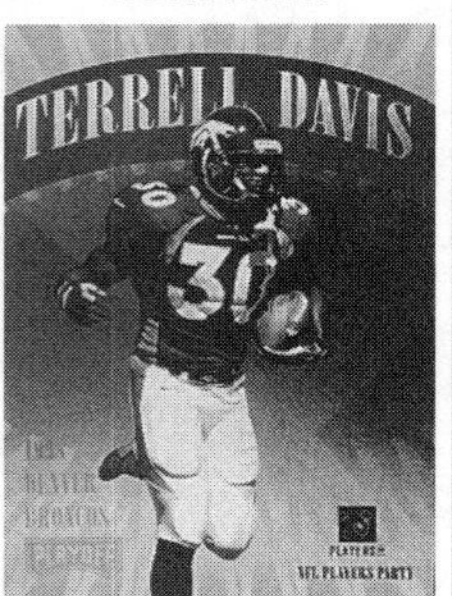

This seven-card set was available exclusively at the NFL Experience Show in conjunction with Super Bowl XXXII. The cards are horizontal with the player's image superimposed over Qualcomm Stadium and the player's last name running up the right side. The backs capture a superimposed shot of the player over San Diego scenery with the card number in the upper right.

		NM/M
Complete Set (7):		18.00
Common Player:		1.00
1	Trent Dilfer	2.00
2	Tony Martin	1.00
3	Terrell Davis	7.00
4	Antonio Freeman	2.00
5	Herschel Walker	1.00
6	Kordell Stewart	5.00
7	Drew Bledsoe	4.00

1999 Playoff Absolute EXP

This was a 200-card set that included 40 unseeded rookie cards. Each single was printed on 20-point stock with foil stamping. Inserts included: Tools of the Trade (parallel), Absolute Heroes, Absolute Rookies, Extreme Team, Terrell Davis Salute, Rookie Reflex, Barry Sanders Commemorative and Team Jersey Tandems. SRP was $2.99 for eight-card packs.

		NM/M
Complete Set (200):		40.00
Common Player:		.15
Minor Stars:		.30
Common Rookie:		.50
EXP Pack (8):		3.00
EXP Wax Box (24):		65.00
1	*Tim Couch*	2.50
2	*Donovan McNabb*	5.00
3	*Akili Smith*	1.50
4	*Edgerrin James*	5.00
5	*Ricky Williams*	3.00
6	*Torry Holt*	2.50
7	*Champ Bailey*	1.50
8	*David Boston*	2.50
9	*Chris Claiborne*	1.00
10	*Chris McAlister*	1.00
11	*Daunte Culpepper*	5.00
12	*Cade McNown*	1.50
13	*Troy Edwards*	1.50
14	*Kevin Johnson*	1.50
15	*James Johnson*	1.50
16	*Rob Konrad*	1.00
17	*Jim Kleinsasser*	1.00
18	*Kevin Faulk*	1.50
19	*Joe Montgomery*	1.50
20	*Shaun King*	1.00
21	*Peerless Price*	2.00
22	*Mike Cloud*	1.00
23	*Jermaine Fazande*	1.00
24	*D'Wayne Bates*	1.00
25	*Brock Huard*	1.50
26	*Marty Booker*	1.50
27	*Karsten Bailey*	1.00
28	*Shawn Bryson*	.50
29	*Jeff Paulk*	1.00
30	*Sedrick Irvin*	1.75
31	*Craig Yeast*	1.00
32	*Joe Germaine*	1.50
33	*Dameane Douglas*	.50
34	*Brandon Stokley*	.50
35	*Larry Parker*	.50
36	*Wane McGarity*	1.00
37	*Na Brown*	.50
38	*Cecil Collins*	1.00
39	*Darrin Chiaverini*	.50
40	*Madre Hill*	.50
41	Adrian Murrell	.30
42	Jake Plummer	1.50
43	Frank Sanders	.30
44	Rob Moore	.30
45	Andre Wadsworth	.30
46	Simeon Rice	.15
47	Eric Swann	.15
48	Terance Mathis	.15
49	Tim Dwight	.50
50	Jamal Anderson	.50
51	Chris Chandler	.30
52	Chris Calloway	.15
53	O.J. Santiago	.15
54	Jermaine Lewis	.15
55	Priest Holmes	1.00
56	Scott Mitchell	.15
57	Tony Banks	.30
58	Rod Woodson	.15
59	Andre Reed	.15
60	Thurman Thomas	.30
61	Bruce Smith	.15
62	Rob Johnson	.30
63	Eric Moulds	.50
64	Doug Flutie	1.00
65	Antowain Smith	.50
66	Tim Biakabutuka	.30
67	Muhsin Muhammad	.30
68	Steve Beuerlein	.30
69	Bobby Engram	.15
70	Curtis Conway	.30
71	Curtis Enis	.50
72	Edgar Bennett	.15
73	Jeff Blake	.30
74	Darnay Scott	.30
75	Carl Pickens	.30
76	Corey Dillon	.50
77	Ty Detmer	.15
78	Leslie Shepherd	.15
79	Sedrick Shaw	.15
80	Raghib Ismail	.15
81	Emmitt Smith	2.00
82	Michael Irvin	.30
83	Troy Aikman	1.50
84	Deion Sanders	.50
85	Darren Woodson	.15
86	Chris Warren	.15
87	John Elway	2.00
88	Brian Griese	1.25
89	Shannon Sharpe	.30
90	Terrell Davis	1.00
91	Bubby Brister	.30
92	Ed McCaffrey	.30
93	Rod Smith	.30
94	Germane Crowell	.30
95	Johnnie Morton	.15
96	Barry Sanders	2.00
97	Herman Moore	.50
98	Charlie Batch	1.00
99	Mark Chmura	.30
100	Derrick Mayes	.30
101	Dorsey Levens	.50
102	Brett Favre	3.00
103	Antonio Freeman	.50
104	Robert Brooks	.15
105	Desmond Howard	.15
106	Jerome Pathon	.15
107	Marvin Harrison	.50
108	Peyton Manning	2.00
109	E.G. Green	.15
110	Tavian Banks	.30
111	Keenan McCardell	.30
112	Jimmy Smith	.50
113	Mark Brunell	.75
114	Fred Taylor	.75
115	Bam Morris	.15
116	Andre Rison	.30
117	Elvis Grbac	.30
118	Warren Moon	.30
119	Tony Gonzalez	.30
120	Derrick Alexander	.15
121	Rashaan Shehee	.15
122	Zach Thomas	.30
123	Oronde Gadsden	.30
124	Dan Marino	2.00
125	Karim Abdul	.30
126	O.J. McDuffie	.30
127	Jake Reed	.30
128	John Randle	.15
129	Randy Moss	2.00
130	Cris Carter	.50
131	Randall Cunningham	.50
132	Robert Smith	.50
133	Terry Glenn	.50
134	Ben Coates	.30
135	Drew Bledsoe	1.25
136	Ty Law	.15
137	Tony Simmons	.30
138	Eddie Kennison	.15
139	Cam Cleeland	.30
140	Ike Hilliard	.15
141	Joe Jurevicius	.15
142	Gary Brown	.15
143	Kerry Collins	.30
144	Tiki Barber	.30
145	Jason Sehorn	.15
146	Dedric Ward	.15
147	Vinny Testaverde	.30
148	Wayne Chrebet	.50
149	Curtis Martin	.50
150	Keyshawn Johnson	.50
151	James Jett	.15
152	Napoleon Kaufman	.50
153	Tim Brown	.30
154	Charles Woodson	.50
155	Rickey Dudley	.30
156	Charles Johnson	.15
157	Duce Staley	.30
158	Chris Fuamatu-Ma'afala	.15
159	Jerome Bettis	.50
160	Kordell Stewart	.75
161	Levon Kirkland	.15
162	Hines Ward	.30
163	Mikhael Ricks	.15
164	Natrone Means	.30
165	Ryan Leaf	.50
166	Jim Harbaugh	.30
167	Junior Seau	.30
168	Steve Young	1.00
169	J.J. Stokes	.30
170	Terrell Owens	.50
171	Jerry Rice	1.50
172	Garrison Hearst	.50
173	Ricky Watters	.30
174	Jon Kitna	.75
175	Joey Galloway	.50
176	Ahman Green	.30
177	Isaac Bruce	.50
178	Marshall Faulk	.50
179	Trent Green	.50
180	Amp Lee	.15
181	Greg Hill	.15
182	Warren Sapp	.15
183	Hardy Nickerson	.15
184	Trent Dilfer	.30
185	Reidel Anthony	.30
186	Jacquez Green	.30
187	Warrick Dunn	.50
188	Mike Alstott	.50
189	Kevin Dyson	.30
190	Eddie George	.75
191	Yancey Thigpen	.30
192	Steve McNair	.75
193	Willie Davis	.15
194	Frank Wycheck	.15
195	Darrell Green	.15
196	Stephen Alexander	.15
197	Albert Connell	.15
198	Michael Westbrook	.30
199	Brad Johnson	.50
200	Skip Hicks	.30

1999 Playoff Absolute EXP Tools of the Trade

This was a 200-card parallel to the base set. Each single was printed on foil board with holographic foil stamping. Defensive players were sequentially numbered to 1,000, wide receivers to 750, running backs to 500 and quarterbacks to 250.

	NM/M
Defensive Cards:	3X-6X
Defensive Rookies:	2X
Production 1,000 Sets	
Receiver Cards:	3X-6X
Receiver Rookies:	3X
Production 750 Sets	
Running Back Cards:	5X-10X
Running Back Rookies:	4X
Production 500 Sets	
Quarterback Cards:	7X-14X
Quarterback Rookies:	6X
Production 250 Sets	

1999 Playoff Absolute EXP Absolute Heroes

This 24-card insert included superstars and highlighted them on mirror board with red foil stamping and silver borders. Singles were inserted 1:25 packs.

		NM/M
Complete Set (24):		25.00
Common Player:		.50
Inserted 1:25		
1	Terrell Owens	.50
2	Troy Aikman	2.00
3	Cris Carter	.50
4	Brett Favre	4.00
5	Jamal Anderson	.50
6	Doug Flutie	1.00
7	John Elway	3.00
8	Steve Young	3.00
9	Jerome Bettis	.50
10	Emmitt Smith	4.00
11	Drew Bledsoe	3.00
12	Fred Taylor	2.00
13	Dan Marino	4.00
14	Antonio Freeman	.50
15	Mark Brunell	1.00
16	Jake Plummer	1.00
17	Warrick Dunn	.50
18	Peyton Manning	4.00
19	Randy Moss	4.00
20	Barry Sanders	3.00
21	Keyshawn Johnson	.50
22	Eddie George	.50
23	Terrell Davis	2.00
24	Jerry Rice	3.00

1999 Playoff Absolute EXP Absolute Rookies

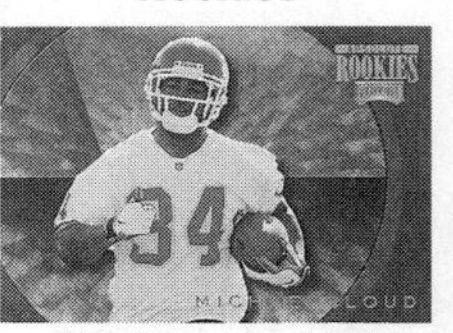

This 36-card insert included the hottest rookies from the '99 NFL Draft and pictured them on holographic board with bronze foil stamping. Each single had green borders. Cards were found 1:13 packs.

		NM/M
Complete Set (36):		25.00
Common Player:		.25
Inserted 1:13		
1	Champ Bailey	.50
2	Karsten Bailey	.25
3	D'Wayne Bates	.25
4	Marty Booker	.25
5	David Boston	2.00
6	Shawn Bryson	.25
7	Chris Claiborne	.25
8	Mike Cloud	.25
9	Cecil Collins	1.00
10	Tim Couch	4.00
11	Daunte Culpepper	5.00
12	Demeane Douglas	.25
13	Troy Edwards	3.00
14	Kevin Faulk	2.00
15	Jermaine Fazande	.25
16	Joe Germaine	1.50
17	Torry Holt	3.00
18	Brock Huard	1.50
19	Edgerrin James	6.00
20	James Johnson	2.00
21	Kevin Johnson	3.00
22	Shaun King	1.00
23	Jim Kleinsasser	.25
24	Rob Konrad	.25
25	Chris McAlister	.25
26	Travis McGriff	.25
27	Donovan McNabb	5.00
28	Cade McNown	1.00
29	Joe Montgomery	.50
30	Larry Parker	.25
31	Jeff Paulk	.25
32	Peerless Price	3.00
33	Akili Smith	2.00
34	Brandon Stokley	.25
35	Ricky Williams	6.00
36	Craig Yeast	.25

1999 Playoff Absolute EXP Extreme Team

This was a 36-card insert that highlighted the leaders of their team. Each was featured with holographic foil with foil stamping. Singles were inserted 1:25 packs.

		NM/M
Complete Set (36):		60.00
Common Player:		.50
Inserted 1:25		
1	Steve Young	2.00
2	Fred Taylor	2.00
3	Kordell Stewart	1.00
4	Emmitt Smith	4.00
5	Barry Sanders	4.00
6	Jerry Rice	3.00
7	Jake Plummer	1.00
8	Eric Moulds	.50
9	Randy Moss	4.00
10	Steve McNair	1.00
11	Curtis Martin	1.00
12	Dan Marino	5.00
13	Peyton Manning	4.00
14	Jon Kitna	1.00
15	Napoleon Kaufman	.50
16	Eddie George	2.00
17	Brett Favre	5.00
18	Marshall Faulk	1.00
19	John Elway	3.00
20	Corey Dillon	1.00
21	Terrell Davis	3.00
22	Randall Cunningham	1.00
23	Mark Brunell	2.00
24	Tim Brown	2.00
25	Drew Bledsoe	2.00
26	Jerome Bettis	1.00
27	Charlie Batch	.50
28	Jamal Anderson	1.00
29	Mike Alstott	1.00
30	Troy Aikman	3.00
31	Dorsey Levens	1.00
32	Joey Galloway	.50
33	Skip Hicks	.50
34	Terrell Owens	1.00
35	Keyshawn Johnson	1.00
36	Doug Flutie	.50

1999 Playoff Absolute EXP Terrell Davis Salute

This was a 5-card set that highlighted Davis' 1998 season. Singles were inserted 1:289 packs. The first 150 of each single was autographed and sequentially numbered.

		NM/M
Complete Set (5):		30.00
Common Player:		6.00
Inserted 1:289		
Autographed Cards:		8X
Production 150 Sets		
1	Terrell Davis	6.00
2	Terrell Davis	6.00
3	Terrell Davis	6.00
4	Terrell Davis	6.00
5	Terrell Davis	6.00

1999 Playoff Absolute EXP Rookie Reflex

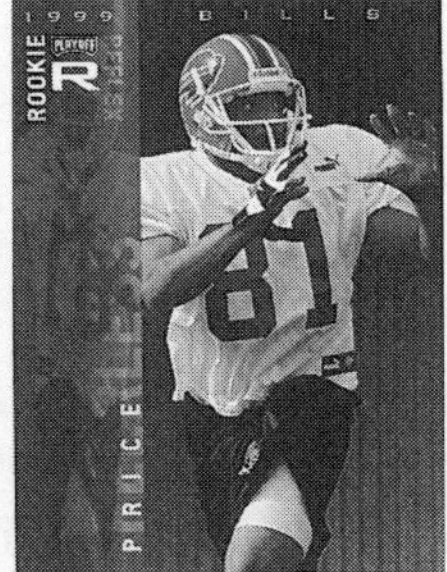

This was an 18-card set that highlighted the top rookies from 1999. Each single was printed on holographic foil board with micro-etching. Singles were found 1:49 packs.

		NM/M
Complete Set (18):		60.00
Common Player:		1.00
Inserted 1:49		
1	Peerless Price	4.00
2	Daunte Culpepper	6.00
3	Joe Montgomery	1.00
4	David Boston	4.00
5	Shaun King	1.00
6	Champ Bailey	1.00
7	Rob Konrad	1.00
8	Torry Holt	3.00
9	Kevin Faulk	1.00
10	Ricky Williams	8.00
11	James Johnson	1.00
12	Edgerrin James	6.00
13	Kevin Johnson	3.00
14	Akili Smith	2.00
15	Troy Edwards	3.00
16	Donovan McNabb	6.00
17	Cade McNown	2.00
18	Tim Couch	5.00

1999 Playoff Absolute EXP Barry Sanders Commemorative

This was a 5-card insert that commemorated the career of Barry Sanders. Singles were found 1:289 packs.

		NM/M
Complete Set (5):		50.00
Common Player:		10.00
Inserted 1:289		
2	Barry Sanders	10.00
3	Barry Sanders	10.00
4	Barry Sanders	10.00
5	Barry Sanders	10.00
6	Barry Sanders	10.00

1999 Playoff Absolute EXP Team Jersey Tandems

This was a 31-card insert that pictured a tandem with a swatch of a home and away authentic team jersey. One player was pictured on each side and singles were inserted 1:97 packs.

		NM/M
Common Player:		8.00
Inserted 1:97		
1	Jake Plummer, David Boston	10.00
2	Troy Aikman, Emmitt Smith	20.00
3	Skip Hicks, Brad Johnson	8.00
4	Joe Montgomery, Ike Hilliard	8.00
5	Charles Johnson, Donovan McNabb	12.00
6	Randy Moss, Cris Carter	20.00
7	Warrick Dunn, Mike Alstott	8.00
8	Barry Sanders, Charlie Batch	20.00
9	Antonio Freeman, Brett Favre	22.00
10	Curtis Enis, Cade McNown	8.00
11	Tim Biakabutuka, Muhsin Muhammad	8.00
12	Eddie Kennison, Ricky Williams	15.00
13	Steve Young, Jerry Rice	15.00
14	Marshall Faulk, Torry Holt	12.00
15	Jamal Anderson, Chris Chandler	8.00
16	Dan Marino, O.J. McDuffie	20.00
17	Drew Bledsoe, Terry Glenn	15.00
18	Eric Moulds, Doug Flutie	8.00
19	Peyton Manning, Edgerrin James	12.00
20	Keyshawn Johnson, Wayne Chrebet	8.00
21	Kordell Stewart, Jerome Bettis	10.00
22	Mark Brunell, Fred Taylor	10.00
23	Tim Couch, Kevin Johnson	12.00
24	Carl Pickens, Akili Smith	8.00
25	Jermaine Lewis, Tony Banks	8.00
26	Eddie George, Steve McNair	12.00
27	Napoleon Kaufman, Tim Brown	8.00
28	John Elway, Terrell Davis	15.00
29	Jon Kitna, Joey Galloway	8.00
30	Andre Rison, Elvis Grbac	8.00
31	Natrone Means, Mikhael Ricks	8.00

1999 Playoff Absolute SSD

This was a 200-card set that included 50 short printed singles. The 31 Checklist cards were found 1:9 packs and the 19 Canton Absolute cards were found 1:17. Each of the regular 150 base cards were found in five different colors. Blue, Green, Purple and Red were all found at equal ratios. The Orange singles were in shorter quanities and valued higher. Each base card featured the player in a cell window with foil stamping and wood grain embossing. Parallel sets included: Coaches Collection Gold and Coaches Collection Silver. Partial parallel sets included: Honor Red, Honor Gold and Honor Silver. Other insert sets included: Boss Hogs Autographs, Force, Heroes, Rookie Roundup, Rookies and Team Jersey Quads.

		NM/M
Complete Set (200):		160.00
Common Player:		.30
Minor Stars:		.60
Common Canton:		4.00
Inserted 1:17		
Common CL:		2.50
Inserted 1:9		
Common Rookie:		1.00
Blue,Green,Purple,Red:		1X
Orange Cards:		3X-5X
Orange Canton:		3X
Orange CL:		3X
Orange Rookies:		3X
Wax Box:		50.00
1	Rob Moore	.60
2	Frank Sanders	.30
3	Jake Plummer	1.00
4	Adrian Murrell	.30
5	Chris Chandler	.60
6	Jamal Anderson	1.00
7	Tim Dwight	1.00
8	Terance Mathis	.30
9	Priest Holmes	2.00
10	Jermaine Lewis	.30
11	Antowain Smith	.60
12	Doug Flutie	1.00
13	Eric Moulds	1.00
14	Muhsin Muhammad	.60
15	Tim Biakabutuka	.60
16	Curtis Enis	.40
17	Curtis Conway	.60
18	Bobby Engram	.30
19	Corey Dillon	1.00
20	Carl Pickens	.60
21	Darnay Scott	.60
22	Sedrick Shaw	.30
23	Leslie Shepherd	.30
24	Ty Detmer	.30
25	Deion Sanders	1.00
26	Troy Aikman	3.00
27	Michael Irvin	.60
28	Emmitt Smith	4.50
29	Raghib Ismail	.30
30	Rod Smith	.60
31	Ed McCaffrey	.60
32	Bubby Brister	.60
33	Terrell Davis	4.50
34	Shannon Sharpe	.60
35	Brian Griese	3.00
36	John Elway	4.50
37	Charlie Batch	2.00
38	Herman Moore	1.00
39	Barry Sanders	6.00
40	Johnnie Morton	.30
41	Antonio Freeman	1.00
42	Brett Favre	6.00
43	Dorsey Levens	1.00
44	Derrick Mayes	.60
45	Mark Chmura	.60
46	Peyton Manning	4.50
47	Marvin Harrison	1.00
48	Jerome Pathon	.30
49	Fred Taylor	2.00
50	Mark Brunell	2.00
51	Jimmy Smith	1.00
52	Keenan McCardell	.60
53	Elvis Grbac	.60
54	Andre Rison	.60
55	Bam Morris	.30
56	O.J. McDuffie	.60
57	Karim Abdul	.60
58	Dan Marino	4.50
59	Oronde Gadsden	.60
60	Robert Smith	1.00
61	Randall Cunningham	1.00
62	Cris Carter	1.00
63	Randy Moss	6.00
64	Drew Bledsoe	2.50
65	Ben Coates	.60
66	Terry Glenn	1.00
67	Cameron Cleeland	.60
68	Eddie Kennison	.60
69	Kerry Collins	.60
70	Gary Brown	.30
71	Joe Jurevicius	.30
72	Ike Hilliard	.30
73	Keyshawn Johnson	1.00
74	Curtis Martin	1.00
75	Wayne Chrebet	1.00
76	Tim Brown	.60
77	Napoleon Kaufman	1.00
78	James Jett	.30
79	Duce Staley	1.00
80	Charles Johnson	.30
81	Kordell Stewart	1.00
82	Jerome Bettis	1.00
83	Chris Fuamatu-Ma'afala	.30
84	Jim Harbaugh	.60
85	Ryan Leaf	1.00
86	Natrone Means	.60
87	Mikhael Ricks	.30
88	Garrison Hearst	.75
89	Jerry Rice	3.00
90	Terrell Owens	1.00
91	J.J. Stokes	.60
92	Steve Young	2.00
93	Joey Galloway	1.00
94	Jon Kitna	1.00
95	Ricky Watters	.60
96	Trent Green	.60
97	Marshall Faulk	1.00
98	Isaac Bruce	1.00
99	Mike Alstott	1.00
100	Warrick Dunn	1.00
101	Jacquez Green	.60
102	Reidel Anthony	.60
103	Trent Dilfer	.60
104	Steve McNair	1.25
105	Yancey Thigpen	.60
106	Eddie George	1.25
107	Kevin Dyson	.60
108	Skip Hicks	.60
109	Brad Johnson	1.00
110	Michael Westbrook	.60
111	Thurman Thomas CA	4.00
112	Andre Reed CA	4.00
113	Emmitt Smith CA	12.00
114	Troy Aikman CA	10.00
115	Deion Sanders CA	4.00
116	John Elway CA	12.00
117	Terrell Davis CA	8.00
118	Barry Sanders CA	12.00
119	Brett Favre CA	15.00
120	Warren Moon CA	4.00
121	Dan Marino CA	12.00
122	Cris Carter CA	6.00
123	Vinny Testaverde CA	4.00
124	Tim Brown CA	4.00
125	Jerome Bettis CA	4.00
126	Junior Seau CA	4.00
127	Jerry Rice CA	10.00
128	Steve Young CA	8.00
129	Eddie George CA	6.00
130	Dan Marino CL	8.00
131	Vinny Testaverde CL	2.50
132	Drew Bledsoe CL	6.00
133	Peyton Manning CL	8.00
134	Doug Flutie CL	6.00
135	Akili Smith CL	5.00
136	Tim Couch CL	8.00
137	Kordell Stewart CL	5.00
138	Fred Taylor CL	6.00
139	Steve McNair CL	5.00
140	Priest Holmes CL	2.50
141	Terrell Davis CL	8.00
142	Jon Kitna CL	5.00
143	Tim Brown CL	2.50
144	Natrone Means CL	2.50
145	Andre Rison CL	2.50
146	Troy Aikman CL	7.00
147	Kerry Collins CL	2.50
148	Jake Plummer CL	6.00
149	Brad Johnson CL	5.00
150	Donovan McNabb CL	5.00
151	Barry Sanders CL	10.00
152	Brett Favre CL	10.00
153	Cade McNown CL	5.00
154	Mike Alstott CL	2.50
155	Randy Moss CL	10.00
156	Ricky Williams CL	8.00
157	Muhsin Muhammad CL	2.50
158	Marshall Faulk CL	5.00
159	Jamal Anderson CL	2.50
160	Jerry Rice CL	6.00
161	*Tim Couch*	5.00
162	*Donovan McNabb*	12.00
163	*Akili Smith*	3.00
164	*Edgerrin James*	10.00
165	*Ricky Williams*	5.00
166	*Torry Holt*	5.00
167	*Champ Bailey*	3.00
168	*David Boston*	5.00
169	*Chris Claiborne*	1.00
170	*Chris McAlister*	1.00
171	*Daunte Culpepper*	10.00
172	*Cade McNown*	2.00
173	*Troy Edwards*	2.00
174	*Kevin Johnson*	2.00
175	*James Johnson*	1.00
176	*Rob Konrad*	1.00
177	*Jim Kleinsasser*	2.00
178	*Kevin Faulk*	3.00
179	*Joe Montgomery*	1.00
180	*Shaun King*	1.00
181	*Peerless Price*	4.00
182	*Mike Cloud*	1.00
183	*Jermaine Fazande*	2.00
184	*D'Wayne Bates*	1.00
185	*Brock Huard*	3.00
186	*Marty Booker*	1.00
187	*Karsten Bailey*	1.00
188	*Shawn Bryson*	1.00
189	*Jeff Paulk*	1.00
190	*Sedrick Irvin*	1.00
191	*Craig Yeast*	1.00
192	*Joe Germaine*	2.00
193	*Demeane Douglas*	1.00
194	*Brandon Stokley*	1.00
195	*Larry Parker*	1.00
196	*Wane McGarity*	1.00
197	*Na Brown*	1.00
198	*Cecil Collins*	2.00
199	*Darrin Chiaverini*	1.00
200	*Madre Hill*	1.00

1999 Playoff Absolute SSD Coaches Collection Gold

This was a 200-card parallel to the base set. Each single was sequentially numbered to 25.

Gold Cards:	10X-15X
Gold Canton:	8X-16X
Gold CL:	5X-10X
Gold Rookies:	8X-16X
Production 25 Sets	

1999 Playoff Absolute SSD Coaches Collection Silver

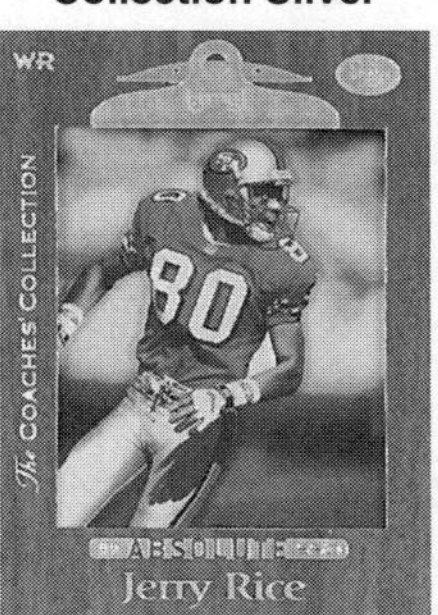

This was a 200-card parallel to the base set. Each of these singles was sequentially numbered to 500.

Silver Cards:	2X-4X
Silver Canton:	2X
Silver CL:	2X
Silver Rookies:	2X
Production 500 Sets	

1999 Playoff Absolute SSD Honors Red

This was a 150-card partial parallel to the base set. Each single had the Playoff logo in the background. Each card was sequentially numbered to 200.

Red Cards:	3X-5X
Red Rookies:	3X
Production 200 Sets	
Gold Cards:	10X-15X
Gold Rookies:	8X-16X
Production 25 Sets	
Silver Cards:	5X-10X
Silver Rookies:	3X-6X
Production 100 Sets	

1999 Playoff Absolute SSD Boss Hogs Autographs

This 10-card insert set included autographs of the top playmakers and each signed on real football leather. Each single was sequentially numbered to 400.

		NM/M
Common Player:		25.00
Production 400 Sets		
1	Ricky Williams	100.00
2	Terrell Davis	75.00
3	Mike Alstott	25.00
4	Jake Plummer	50.00
5	Vinny Testaverde	25.00
6	Cris Carter	25.00
7	Peyton Manning	125.00
8	Natrone Means	25.00
9	Eddie George	35.00
10	Barry Sanders	150.00

1999 Playoff Absolute SSD Force

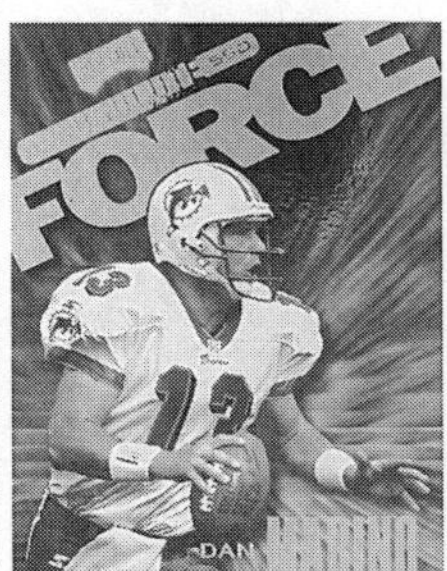

This 36-card insert included the hobby's hottest stars and featured them on a mirror board with gold foil stamping. Singles were found 1:19 packs.

		NM/M
Complete Set (36):		75.00
Common Player:		1.00
Inserted 1:19		
1	Steve Young	4.00
2	Fred Taylor	4.00
3	Kordell Stewart	1.00
4	Emmitt Smith	5.00
5	Barry Sanders	5.00
6	Jerry Rice	4.00
7	Jake Plummer	2.00
8	Eric Moulds	1.00
9	Randy Moss	5.00
10	Steve McNair	1.00
11	Curtis Martin	1.00
12	Dan Marino	5.00
13	Peyton Manning	5.00
14	Jon Kitna	1.00
15	Napoleon Kaufman	1.00
16	Keyshawn Johnson	1.00
17	Eddie George	2.00
18	Antonio Freeman	1.00
19	Doug Flutie	1.00
20	Brett Favre	6.00
21	Marshall Faulk	1.00
22	John Elway	4.00
23	Warrick Dunn	1.00
24	Corey Dillon	1.00
25	Terrell Davis	4.00
26	Randall Cunningham	1.00
27	Cris Carter	1.00
28	Mark Brunell	2.00
29	Tim Brown	1.00
30	Drew Bledsoe	3.00
31	Jerome Bettis	1.00
32	Charlie Batch	1.00
33	Jamal Anderson	1.00
34	Mike Alstott	1.00
35	Troy Aikman	4.00
36	Terrell Owens	1.00

1999 Playoff Absolute SSD Heroes

This 24-card insert included the top NFL superstars and highlighted them on a die-cut mirror board with red foil stamping and micro-etching. Singles were found 1:19 packs. A parallel Red (#'d to 100) and Jumbo (one per hobby box) version was also issued.

		NM/M
Complete Set (24):		60.00
Common Player:		1.00
Inserted 1:19		
Jumbo Cards:		1X
1:Box		
Red Cards:		4X-8X
Production 100 Sets		
1	Terrell Owens	1.00
2	Troy Aikman	4.00
3	Cris Carter	1.00
4	Brett Favre	6.00
5	Jamal Anderson	1.00
6	Doug Flutie	1.00
7	John Elway	4.00
8	Steve Young	4.00
9	Jerome Bettis	1.00
10	Emmitt Smith	5.00
11	Drew Bledsoe	4.00
12	Fred Taylor	3.00
13	Dan Marino	6.00
14	Antonio Freeman	1.00
15	Mark Brunell	3.00
16	Jake Plummer	2.00
17	Warrick Dunn	1.00
18	Peyton Manning	5.00
19	Randy Moss	5.00
20	Barry Sanders	5.00
21	Keyshawn Johnson	1.00
22	Eddie George	2.00
23	Terrell Davis	3.00
24	Jerry Rice	4.00

1999 Playoff Absolute SSD Rookie Roundup

This 18-card insert included both first and second round picks from the 1999 NFL Draft. First round pick cards were inserted 1:46 packs and second round picks were inserted 1:69. Each single was printed on mirror board with foil stamping.

		NM/M
Complete Set (18):		60.00
Common Player:		2.00
1st Rounders Inserted 1:46		
2nd Rounders Inserted 1:69		
1	Peerless Price	5.00
2	Daunte Culpepper	8.00
3	Joe Montgomery	2.00
4	David Boston	8.00
5	Shaun King	3.00
6	Champ Bailey	2.00
7	Rob Konrad	2.00
8	Torry Holt	5.00
9	Kevin Faulk	3.00
10	Ricky Williams	12.00
11	James Johnson	2.00
12	Edgerrin James	10.00

13 Kevin Johnson 3.00
14 Akili Smith 3.00
15 Troy Edwards 3.00
16 Donovan McNabb 6.00
17 Cade McNown 2.00
18 Tim Couch 5.00

1999 Playoff Absolute SSD Rookies

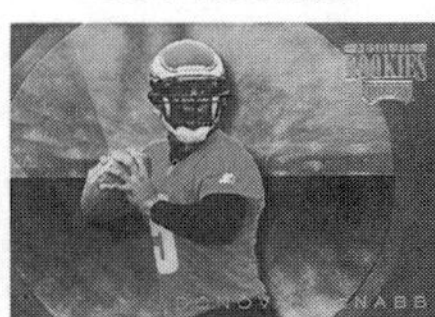

This 36-card insert included the hottest rookies from the '99 NFL Draft. Each was printed on holographic foil board with blue foil stamping. Singles were inserted 1:10 packs. A parallel Red version was also made and each of those singles were sequentially numbered to 100.

NM/M
Complete Set (36): 60.00
Common Player: .50
Minor Stars: 1.00
Inserted 1:10
Red Cards: 2X-4X
Production 100 Sets
1 Champ Bailey 2.00
2 Karsten Bailey .50
3 D'Wayne Bates .50
4 Marty Booker .50
5 David Boston 3.00
6 Shawn Bryson .50
7 Chris Claiborne 1.00
8 Mike Cloud 1.00
9 Cecil Collins 2.00
10 Tim Couch 5.00
11 Daunte Culpepper 6.00
12 Demeane Douglas .50
13 Troy Edwards 4.00
14 Kevin Faulk 3.00
15 Jermaine Fazande 1.00
16 Joe Germaine 1.00
17 Torry Holt 4.00
18 Brock Huard 2.50
19 Edgerrin James 8.00
20 James Johnson 2.50
21 Kevin Johnson 4.00
22 Shaun King 2.00
23 Jim Kleinsasser 1.00
24 Rob Konrad 1.00
25 Chris McAlister 1.00
26 Travis McGriff .50
27 Donovan McNabb 6.00
28 Cade McNown 2.00
29 Joe Montgomery 1.00
30 Larry Parker .50
31 Jeff Paulk .50
32 Peerless Price 4.00
33 Akili Smith 1.00
34 Brandon Stokley .50
35 Ricky Williams 10.00
36 Craig Yeast .50

1999 Playoff Absolute SSD Team Jersey Quads

This 31-card insert showcased an authentic team jersey and four superstars from each NFL team. Each was printed on a foil board with micro etching. Singles were inserted 1:73 packs.

NM/M
Common Player: 8.00
Minor Stars: 20.00
Inserted 1:73
1 David Boston, Adrian Murrell, Jake Plummer, Frank Sanders 15.00
2 Troy Aikman, Michael Irvin, Deion Sanders, Emmitt Smith 30.00
3 Champ Bailey, Skip Hicks, Brad Johnson, Michael Westbrook 15.00
4 Gary Brown, Kerry Collins, Ike Hilliard, Joe Montgomery 8.00
5 Na Brown, Charles Johnson, Donovan McNabb, Duce Staley 20.00
6 Cris Carter, Randall Cunningham, Randy Moss, Robert Smith 30.00
7 Mike Alstott, Reidel Anthony, Trent Dilfer, Warrick Dunn 15.00
8 Charlie Batch, Herman Moore, Johnnie Morton, Barry Sanders 30.00
9 Mark Chmura, Brett Favre, Antonio Freeman, Dorsey Levens 35.00
10 Curtis Conway, Bobby Engram, Curtis Enis, Cade McNown 15.00
11 Steve Beuerlein, Tim Biakabutuka, Muhsin Muhammad, Wesley Walls 8.00
12 Cam Cleeland, Eddie Kennison, Willie Roaf, Ricky Williams 25.00
13 Garrison Hearst, Terrell Owens, Jerry Rice, Steve Young 25.00
14 Isaac Bruce, Marshall Faulk, Trent Green, Torry Holt 20.00
15 Jamal Anderson, Chris Chandler, Tim Dwight, Terrance Mathis 8.00
16 Karim Abdul, Cecil Collins, Dan Marino, O.J. McDuffie 35.00
17 Drew Bledsoe, Ben Coates, Kevin Faulk, Terry Glenn 15.00
18 Doug Flutie, Eric Moulds, Peerless Price, Antowain Smith 20.00
19 Marvin Harrison, Edgerrin James, Peyton Manning, Jerome Pathon 35.00
20 Wayne Chrebet, Keyshawn Johnson, Curtis Martin, Vinny Testaverde 15.00
21 Jerome Bettis, Troy Edwards, Kordell Stewart, Hines Ward 20.00
22 Mark Brunell, Keenan McCardell, Jimmy Smith, Fred Taylor 20.00
23 Tim Couch, Kevin Johnson, Sedrick Shaw, Leslie Shepherd 20.00
24 Corey Dillon, Carl Pickens, Darnay Scott, Akili Smith 20.00
25 Tony Banks, Priest Holmes, Jermaine Lewis, Chris McAllister 15.00
26 Kevin Dyson, Eddie George, Steve McNair, Yancey Thigpen 15.00
27 Tim Brown, James Jett, Napoleon Kaufman, Charles Woodson 20.00
28 Terrell Davis, John Elway, Ed McCaffrey, Rod Smith 30.00
29 Joey Galloway, Ahman Green, Jon Kitna, Ricky Watters 20.00
30 Mike Cloud, Elvis Grbac, Bam Morris, Andre Rison 8.00
31 Ryan Leaf, Natrone Means, Mikhael Ricks, Junior Seau 8.00

1999 Playoff Contenders SSD

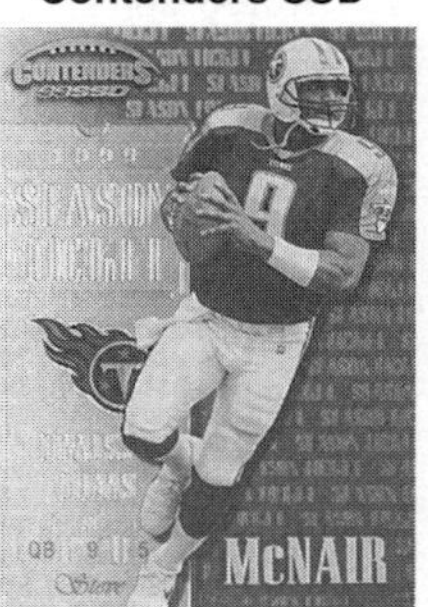

This was a 200-card base set that had 44 Rookie Tickets and 15 short-printed Playoff Tickets (1:7). Each card was printed on 30-point embossed holographic foil stock with foil stamping. Each of the Rookie Tickets were autographed by that player. Parallel sets included: Finesse Gold, Power Blue and Speed Red. Other inserts included: Game Day Souvenirs, MVP Contenders, Quads, Round Numbers Autographs, ROY Contenders, ROY Contenders Autographs, Touchdown Tandems and Triple Threat. SRP was $7.99 for four-card packs.

NM/M
Common Player: .30
Minor Stars: .60
Common Rookie Auto: 12.00
Common PT: 2.00
Inserted 1:7
Pack (4): 20.00
Wax Box (14): 220.00
1 Randy Moss 6.00
2 Randall Cunningham 1.00
3 Cris Carter 1.00
4 Robert Smith 1.00
5 Jake Reed .60
6 Albert Connell .60
7 Jeff George 1.00
8 Brett Favre 8.00
9 Antonio Freeman 1.00
10 Dorsey Levens 1.00
11 Mark Chmura .60
12 Mike Alstott 1.00
13 Warrick Dunn 1.00
14 Trent Dilfer .60
15 Jacquez Green .60
16 Reidel Anthony .60
17 Warren Sapp .60
18 Amani Toomer .30
19 Curtis Enis 1.00
20 Curtis Conway .60
21 Bobby Engram .30
22 Barry Sanders 6.00
23 Charlie Batch 2.50
24 Herman Moore 1.00
25 Johnnie Morton .30
26 Greg Hill .30
27 Germane Crowell .60
28 Kerry Collins .60
29 Ike Hilliard .30
30 Joe Jurevicius .30
31 Stephen Davis 1.00
32 Brad Johnson 1.00
33 Skip Hicks .60
34 Michael Westbrook .60
35 Jake Plummer 3.00
36 Adrian Murrell .30
37 Frank Sanders .60
38 Rob Moore .60
39 Gary Brown .30
40 Duce Staley 1.00
41 Charles Johnson .30
42 Emmitt Smith 6.00
43 Troy Aikman 4.00
44 Michael Irvin .60
45 Deion Sanders 1.00
46 Raghib Ismail .30
47 Jerry Rice 4.00
48 Terrell Owens 1.00
49 Steve Young 2.50
50 Garrison Hearst .60
51 J.J. Stokes .60
52 Lawrence Phillips .60
53 Jamal Anderson 1.00
54 Chris Chandler .60
55 Terance Mathis .30
56 Tim Dwight 1.00
57 Charlie Garner .60
58 Chris Calloway .30
59 Eddie Kennison .30
60 Billy Joe Hobert .30
61 Tim Biakabutuka .60
62 Muhsin Muhammad .60
63 *Olandis Gary 1825* 30.00
64 Wesley Walls .60
65 Isaac Bruce 1.00
66 Marshall Faulk 1.00
67 Kordell Stewart 1.00
68 Jerome Bettis 1.00
69 Hines Ward .60
70 Corey Dillon 1.00
71 Carl Pickens .60
72 Darnay Scott .30
73 Steve McNair 1.75
74 Eddie George 1.75
75 Yancey Thigpen .60
76 Kevin Dyson .60
77 Fred Taylor 1.00
78 Mark Brunell 1.00
79 Jimmy Smith 1.00
80 Keenan McCardell .60
81 James Stewart .60
82 Jermaine Lewis .30
83 Priest Holmes 1.00
84 Stoney Case .30
85 Errict Rhett .60
86 Bill Schroeder .60
87 Terry Kirby .30
88 Leslie Shepherd .30
89 *Terrence Wilkins 825* 30.00
90 Dan Marino 6.00
91 O.J. McDuffie .60
92 Karim Abdul .60
93 Zach Thomas .60
94 Terry Allen .60
95 Tony Martin .30
96 Drew Bledsoe 3.00
97 Terry Glenn 1.00
98 Ben Coates .60
99 Tony Simmons .60
100 Curtis Martin 1.00
101 Keyshawn Johnson 1.00
102 Vinny Testaverde .60
103 Wayne Chrebet 1.00
104 Peyton Manning 6.00
105 Marvin Harrison 1.00
106 E.G. Green .30
107 Doug Flutie 1.00
108 Thurman Thomas .60
109 Andre Reed .60
110 Eric Moulds 1.00
111 Antowain Smith 1.00
112 Bruce Smith .60
113 Terrell Davis 3.00
114 John Elway 6.00
115 Ed McCaffrey .75
116 Rod Smith .75
117 Shannon Sharpe .60
118 *Jeff Garcia 325* 300.00
119 Brian Griese 3.00
120 *Justin Watson 325* 30.00
121 Bubby Brister .60
122 Ryan Leaf 1.00
123 Natrone Means .75
124 Mikhael Ricks .30
125 Junior Seau .60
126 Jim Harbaugh .60
127 Andre Rison .60
128 Elvis Grbac .60
129 Bam Morris .60
130 Rashaan Shehee .30
131 Warren Moon .60
132 Tony Gonzalez .60
133 Derrick Alexander .30
134 Jon Kitna 1.50
135 Ricky Watters .60
136 Joey Galloway 1.00
137 Ahman Green .60
138 Derrick Mayes .60
139 Tyrone Wheatley .60
140 Napoleon Kaufman 1.00
141 Tim Brown .60
142 Charles Woodson 1.00
143 Rich Gannon .60
144 Rickey Dudley .60
145 Az-Zahir Hakim .60
146 *Kurt Warner 1825* 125.00
147 *Sean Bennett* 15.00
148 *Brandon Stokley* 12.00
149 *Amos Zereoue 1325* 50.00
150 *Brock Huard 1325* 20.00
151 *Tim Couch 1025* 100.00
152 *Ricky Williams 725* 200.00
153 *Donovan McNabb 525* 200.00
154 *Edgerrin James 525* 200.00
155 *Torry Holt 1025* 100.00
156 *Daunte Culpepper 1025* 125.00
157 *Akili Smith 1025* 25.00
158 *Champ Bailey 1725* 20.00
159 *Chris Claiborne* 12.00
160 *Chris McAlister* 12.00
161 *Troy Edwards 1225* 25.00
162 *Jevon Kearse 325* 75.00
163 *Darnell McDonald* 12.00
164 *David Boston 1025* 50.00
165 *Peerless Price 1325* 50.00
166 *Cecil Collins* 15.00
167 *Rob Konrad* 15.00
168 *Cade McNown 1025* 25.00
169 *Shawn Bryson* 12.00
170 *Kevin Faulk 1325* 25.00
171 *Corby Jones* 12.00
172 *James Johnson 1325* 25.00
173 *Autry Denson* 20.00
174 *Sedrick Irvin* 20.00
175 *Michael Bishop 1825* 25.00
176 *Joe Germaine 825* 30.00
177 *De'Mond Parker* 15.00
178 *Shaun King 1825* 30.00
179 *D'Wayne Bates* 12.00
180 *Tai Streets 1825* 40.00
181 *Na Brown* 12.00
182 *Desmond Clark* 12.00
183 *Jim Kleinsasser* 15.00
184 *Kevin Johnson 1325* 20.00
185 *Joe Montgomery* 20.00
186 John Elway PT 8.00
187 Dan Marino PT 8.00
188 Jerry Rice PT 6.00
189 Barry Sanders PT 10.00
190 Steve Young PT 4.00
191 Doug Flutie PT 4.00
192 Troy Aikman PT 6.00
193 Drew Bledsoe PT 5.00
194 Brett Favre PT 12.00
195 Randall Cunningham PT 2.00
196 Terrell Davis PT 6.00
197 Kordell Stewart PT 2.00
198 Keyshawn Johnson PT 2.00
199 Jake Plummer PT 5.00
200 Peyton Manning PT 8.00

1999 Playoff Contenders SSD Finesse Gold

This was a 200-card parallel insert that showcased each single with a gold background. Singles were sequentially numbered to 25.

NM/M
Gold Cards: 8X-15X
Gold Rookies: 3X
Gold PT Cards: 5X-10X
Production 25 Sets

1999 Playoff Contenders SSD Power Blue

This was a 200-card parallel insert that had each single printed with a blue background. Each card was sequentially numbered to 50.

Blue Cards: 3X-8X
Blue Rookies: 1.5X
Blue PT Cards: 2X-4X
Production 50 Sets

1999 Playoff Contenders SSD Speed Red

This was a 200-card parallel insert to the base set. Each of these singles were printed with a red background and were sequentially numbered to 100.

NM/M
Red Cards: 3X-5X
Red Rookies: 1.2X
Red PT Cards: 2X-4X
Production 100 Sets

1999 Playoff Contenders SSD Game Day Souvenirs

This 15-card insert included swatches of game-dated, game-used footballs from the 1998-99 season. Singles were found 1:308 packs.

NM/M
Common Player: 25.00
Inserted 1:308
1 Terrell Owens 25.00
2 Jerry Rice 75.00
3 Steve Young 75.00
4 Akili Smith 25.00
5 Tim Couch 50.00
6 Mark Brunell 40.00
7 Eddie George 40.00
8 Dorsey Levens 25.00
9 Brett Favre 100.00
10 Antonio Freeman 25.00
11 Ricky Williams 75.00
12 Steve McNair 30.00
13 Kurt Warner 60.00
14 John Elway 60.00
15 Terrell Davis 60.00

1999 Playoff Contenders SSD MVP Contenders

This 20-card insert included candidates for the NFL's MVP award. Each single was printed with actual leather in the background. Singles were inserted 1:43 packs.

NM/M
Complete Set (20): 75.00
Common Player: 2.00
Inserted 1:43
1 Jamal Anderson 2.00
2 Eddie George 3.00
3 Emmitt Smith 10.00
4 Jerry Rice 8.00
5 Barry Sanders 10.00
6 Keyshawn Johnson 2.00
7 Brett Favre 12.00
8 Randy Moss 8.00
9 Mark Brunell 5.00
10 Fred Taylor 5.00
11 Dan Marino 12.00
12 Peyton Manning 8.00
13 Drew Bledsoe 10.00
14 Antonio Freeman 2.00
15 Steve Young 6.00
16 Terrell Davis 6.00
17 Terrell Owens 2.00
18 Troy Aikman 6.00
19 Steve McNair 3.00
20 Jake Plummer 3.00

1999 Playoff Contenders SSD Quads

This 12-card insert featured two powerful, potential playoff opponents on each side of the card. Each card was printed on holographic board with micro-etching. Singles were found 1:57 packs.

NM/M
Complete Set (12): 140.00
Common Player: 5.00
Inserted 1:57
1 Jake Plummer, David Boston, Emmitt Smith, Troy Aikman 12.00
2 Jerry Rice, Steve Young, Jamal Anderson, Chris Chandler 10.00
3 Randy Moss, Cris Carter, Brett Favre, Antonio Freeman 20.00
4 Warrick Dunn, Mike Alstott, Stephen Davis, Brad Johnson 5.00
5 Cade McNown, Curtis Enis, Barry Sanders, Charlie Batch 12.00
6 Ricky Williams, Eddie Kennison, Marshall Faulk, Torry Holt 12.00
7 Kordell Stewart, Jerome Bettis, Eddie George, Steve McNair 8.00
8 Doug Flutie, Eric Moulds, Drew Bledsoe, Terry Glenn 6.00
9 Dan Marino, Cecil Collins, Keyshawn Johnson, Curtis Martin 15.00
10 Terrell Davis, Brian Griese, Mark Brunell, Fred Taylor 12.00
11 Jon Kitna, Joey Galloway, Napoleon Kaufman, Tim Brown 5.00
12 Peyton Manning, Edgerrin James, Tim Couch, Kevin Johnson 30.00

1999 Playoff Contenders SSD Round Numbers Autographs

This 10-card insert included autographs from one of ten pairs of rookies drafted from the same round. Both the player's image and autograph appeared on the front of the cards. Singles were inserted 1:109 packs.

NM/M
Common Player: 20.00
Inserted 1:109
1 Kevin Johnson, Peerless Price 50.00
2 Ricky Williams, Edgerrin James 275.00
3 Donovan McNabb, Akili Smith 75.00
4 Sean Bennett, Brandon Stokley 20.00
5 Tim Couch, Cade McNown 100.00
6 David Boston, Troy Edwards 50.00
7 Daunte Culpepper, Torry Holt 75.00
8 Kevin Faulk, James Johnson 40.00
9 Joe Montgomery, Rob Konrad 20.00
10 Cecil Collins, De'Mond Parker 20.00

1999 Playoff Contenders SSD ROY Contenders

This 12-card insert included rookies who would challenge for the Rookie of the Year Award. Each single was printed on actual wood and inserted 1:29 packs. A parallel autographed version was also issued with each of those singles sequentially numbered to 100.

NM/M
Complete Set (12): 60.00
Common Player: 2.00
Inserted 1:29
1 Tim Couch 12.00
2 Donovan McNabb 12.00
3 Akili Smith 5.00
4 Daunte Culpepper 12.00
5 Cade McNown 4.00
6 Edgerrin James 15.00
7 Ricky Williams 20.00
8 Cecil Collins 2.00
9 Torry Holt 8.00
10 David Boston 8.00
11 Troy Edwards 4.00
12 Champ Bailey 2.00

1999 Playoff Contenders SSD ROY Contenders Autographs

This was a 12-card parallel to the ROY Contenders insert. Each of these singles were printed on actual wood and sequentially numbered to 100.

NM/M
Common Player: 25.00
Production 100 Sets
1 Tim Couch 100.00
2 Donovan McNabb 100.00
3 Akili Smith 50.00
4 Daunte Culpepper 100.00
5 Cade McNown 100.00
6 Edgerrin James 150.00
7 Ricky Williams 150.00
8 Cecil Collins 25.00
9 Torry Holt 60.00
10 David Boston 50.00
11 Troy Edwards 50.00
12 Champ Bailey 25.00

1999 Playoff Contenders SSD Touchdown Tandems

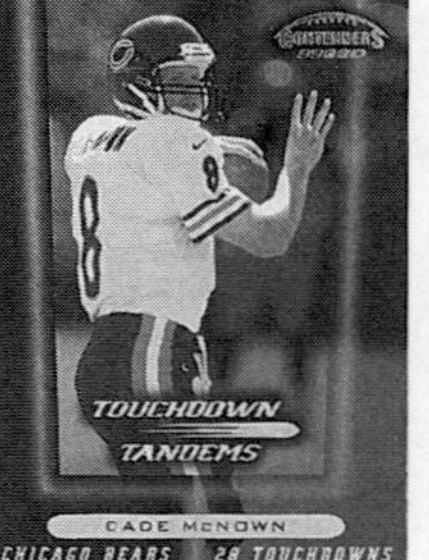

This was a 24-card insert that matched up two touchdown-scoring teammates and each was printed on dual-sided holographic foil board. Singles were inserted 1:15 packs. A parallel die-cut version was also issued with each of those singles sequentially numbered to the player's 1998 TD total.

		NM/M
Complete Set (24):		60.00
Common Player:		1.00
Minor Stars:		2.00
Inserted 1:15		
1	Keyshawn Johnson, Curtis Martin	2.00
2	Dan Marino, Tony Martin	8.00
3	Drew Bledsoe, Terry Glenn	5.00
4	Peyton Manning, Marvin Harrison	8.00
5	Doug Flutie, Thurman Thomas	2.00
6	Steve McNair, Eddie George	2.00
7	Kordell Stewart, Jerome Bettis	3.00
8	Akili Smith, Carl Pickens	2.00
9	Mark Brunell, Jimmy Smith	3.00
10	Jon Kitna, Joey Galloway	2.00
11	John Elway, Terrell Davis	10.00
12	Napoleon Kaufman, Tim Brown	2.00
13	Troy Aikman, Emmitt Smith	10.00
14	Jake Plummer, Rob Moore	2.00
15	Donovan McNabb, Charles Johnson	4.00
16	Brad Johnson, Michael Westbrook	1.00
17	Brett Favre, Antonio Freeman	10.00
18	Randall Cunningham, Randy Moss	8.00
19	Mike Alstott, Warrick Dunn	1.00
20	Cade McNown, Curtis Enis	1.00
21	Barry Sanders, Herman Moore	8.00
22	Steve Young, Jerry Rice	8.00
23	Chris Chandler, Jamal Anderson	1.00
24	Marshall Faulk, Isaac Bruce	2.00

1999 Playoff Contenders SSD Touchdown Tandems Die Cuts

This was a 24-card parallel to the Touchdown Tandem insert. Each of these singles were die-cut and sequentially numbered to the player's 1998 TD total.

		NM/M
Common Player:		15.00
1	Keyshawn Johnson, Curtis Martin 20	45.00
2	Dan Marino, Tony Martin 29	120.00
3	Drew Bledsoe, Terry Glenn 23	50.00
4	Peyton Manning, Marvin Harrison 33	120.00
5	Doug Flutie, Thurman Thomas 24	50.00
6	Steve McNair, Eddie George 25	45.00
7	Kordell Stewart, Jerome Bettis 16	45.00
8	Akili Smith, Carl Pickens 41	25.00
9	Mark Brunell, Jimmy Smith 28	50.00
10	Jon Kitna, Joey Galloway 18	35.00
11	John Elway, Terrell Davis 46	70.00
12	Napoleon Kaufman, Tim Brown 11	35.00
13	Troy Aikman, Emmitt Smith 29	85.00
14	Jake Plummer, Rob Moore 26	50.00
15	Donovan McNabb, Charles Johnson 37	40.00
16	Brad Johnson, Michael Westbrook 13	40.00
17	Brett Favre, Antonio Freeman 46	60.00
18	Randall Cunningham, Randy Moss 52	50.00
19	Mike Alstott, Warrick Dunn 11	45.00
20	Cade McNown, Curtis Enis 28	70.00
21	Barry Sanders, Herman Moore 9	225.00
22	Steve Young, Jerry Rice 51	35.00
23	Chris Chandler, Jamal Anderson 43	15.00
24	Marshall Faulk, Isaac Bruce 11	50.00

A card number in parenthese ( ) indicates the set is unnumbered.

1999 Playoff Contenders SSD Triple Threat

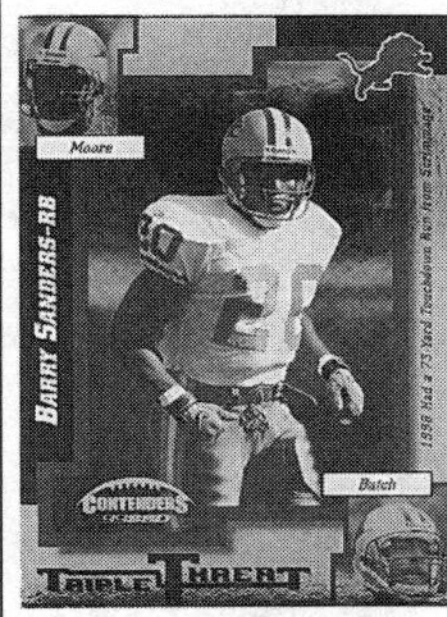

This was a 20-card insert that pictured three teammates on a mirror board with foil stamping. Singles were inserted 1:15 packs. A Triple Threat parallel was issued with one of the teammates on the front of each card for a total of 60 cards. Each was sequentially numbered to a player-specific stat.

		NM/M
Complete Set (20):		45.00
Common Player:		1.00
Inserted 1:15		
1	Jake Plummer, David Boston, Frank Sanders	2.00
2	Deion Sanders, Troy Aikman, Emmitt Smith	5.00
3	Terrell Owens, Jerry Rice, Steve Young	3.00
4	Dan Marino, O.J. McDuffie, Cecil Collins	5.00
5	Keyshawn Johnson, Wayne Chrebet, Curtis Martin	1.00
6	Jamal Anderson, Chris Chandler, Terance Mathis	1.00
7	Brian Griese, Terrell Davis, Shannon Sharpe	4.00
8	Fred Taylor, Mark Brunell, Keenan McCardell	3.00
9	Randy Moss, Cris Carter, Randall Cunningham	4.00
10	Antonio Freeman, Brett Favre, Dorsey Levens	5.00
11	Brad Johnson, Skip Hicks, Champ Bailey	1.00
12	Barry Sanders, Herman Moore, Charlie Batch	4.00
13	Eddie George, Steve McNair, Yancey Thigpen	2.00
14	Kordell Stewart, Jerome Bettis, Troy Edwards	2.00
15	Antowain Smith, Eric Moulds, Doug Flutie	1.00
16	Terry Glenn, Kevin Faulk, Drew Bledsoe	3.00
17	Mike Alstott, Warrick Dunn, Shaun King	1.00
18	Peyton Manning, Marvin Harrison, Edgerrin James	6.00
19	Corey Dillon, Akili Smith, Carl Pickens	2.00
20	Isaac Bruce, Torry Holt, Marshall Faulk	3.00

1999 Playoff Contenders SSD Triple Threat

This was a 60-card parallel to the Triple Threat insert. Each single featured one of the teammates on the front. Each was sequentially numbered to the player-specific stat.

		NM/M
Common Player:		8.00
1	Jake Plummer 17	25.00
2	Deion Sanders 16	35.00
3	Terrell Owens 14	45.00
4	Dan Marino 23	150.00
5	Keyshawn Johnson 10	60.00
6	Jamal Anderson 14	35.00
7	Brian Griese 33	40.00
8	Fred Taylor 14	60.00
9	Randy Moss 17	125.00
10	Antonio Freeman 14	35.00
11	Brad Johnson 48	15.00
12	Barry Sanders 73	45.00
13	Eddie George 37	35.00
14	Kordell Stewart 11	35.00
15	Antowain Smith 8	35.00
16	Terry Glenn 86	12.00
17	Mike Alstott 8	85.00
18	Peyton Manning 26	125.00
19	Corey Dillon 66	15.00
20	Isaac Bruce 80	12.00
21	David Boston 13	75.00
22	Troy Aikman 12	125.00
23	Jerry Rice 75	45.00
24	O.J. McDuffie 90	8.00
25	Wayne Chrebet 63	15.00
26	Chris Chandler 25	30.00
27	Terrell Davis 21	65.00
28	Mark Brunell 20	35.00
29	Cris Carter 12	35.00
30	Brett Favre 31	100.00
31	Skip Hicks 8	50.00
32	Herman Moore 82	8.00
33	Steve McNair 15	50.00
34	Jerome Bettis 4	100.00
35	Eric Moulds 84	12.00
36	Kevin Faulk 12	25.00
37	Warrick Dunn 50	20.00
38	Marvin Harrison 61	20.00
39	Akili Smith 32	25.00
40	Torry Holt 11	45.00
41	Frank Sanders 89	8.00
42	Emmitt Smith 13	125.00
43	Steve Young 36	55.00
44	Cecil Collins 28	25.00
45	Curtis Martin 60	15.00
46	Terance Mathis 11	25.00
47	Shannon Sharpe 10	25.00
48	Keenan McCardell 67	8.00
49	Randall Cunningham 34	225.00
50	Dorsey Levens 50	15.00
51	Champ Bailey 22	25.00
52	Charlie Batch 98	10.00
53	Yancey Thigpen 13	20.00
54	Troy Edwards 27	20.00
55	Doug Flutie 20	35.00
56	Drew Bledsoe 20	45.00
57	Shaun King 36	20.00
58	Edgerrin James 17	200.00
59	Carl Pickens 67	8.00
60	Marshall Faulk 78	15.00

1999 Playoff Momentum SSD

This was a 200-card base set that was divided into three tiers. Cards #1-100 were printed on foil board with micro- etching and inserted 4:1 packs. Cards #101-150 were printed on clear plastic with dual-sided holographic foil stamping and inserted 1:1. Rookie cards #151-200 were printed on clear plastic with clear holographic foil and micro-etching and inserted 1:5 packs. Parallel sets included O's and X's. Other inserts included: Chart Toppers, Terrell Davis Salute, Gridiron Force, Hog Heaven, Rookie Quads, Rookie Recall, Barry Sanders Commemorate, Star Gazing and Team Thread Checklists. SRP was $4.99 for five-card packs.

		NM/M
Complete Set (200):		275.00
Common Player:		.15
Minor Stars:		.30
Common Player (101-150):		.25
Minor Stars (101-150):		.50
Inserted 1:1		
Common Rookie:		2.50
Inserted 1:5		
Pack (5):		3.50
Wax Box (18):		45.00
1	Rob Moore	.30
2	Adrian Murrell	.15
3	Frank Sanders	.30
4	Andre Wadsworth	.15
5	Tim Dwight	.75
6	Terance Mathis	.15
7	Priest Holmes	.75
8	Jermaine Lewis	.15
9	Scott Mitchell	.15
10	Patrick Johnson	.30
11	Tony Banks	.30
12	Thurman Thomas	.30
13	Andre Reed	.30
14	Bruce Smith	.15
15	Tim Biakabutuka	.30
16	Muhsin Muhammad	.50
17	Wesley Walls	.30
18	Rae Carruth	.15
19	Curtis Conway	.30
20	Bobby Engram	.15
21	Jeff Blake	.30
22	Darnay Scott	.30
23	Ty Detmer	.15
24	Leslie Shepherd	.15
25	Sedrick Shaw	.15
26	Michael Irvin	.30
27	Raghib Ismail	.15
28	Ed McCaffrey	.50
29	Marcus Nash	.30
30	Shannon Sharpe	.30
31	Neil Smith	.15
32	Rod Smith	.50
33	Bubby Brister	.30
34	Germane Crowell	.30
35	Johnnie Morton	.15
36	Bill Schroeder	.15
37	Mark Chmura	.30
38	Marvin Harrison	.75
39	E.G. Green	.15
40	Jerome Pathon	.15
41	Keenan McCardell	.30
42	Jimmy Smith	.75
43	Kyle Brady	.15
44	Tavian Banks	.30
45	Warren Moon	.30
46	Derrick Alexander	.15
47	Elvis Grbac	.30
48	Andre Rison	.30
49	Bam Morris	.30
50	Rashaan Shehee	.30
51	Karim Abdul	.30
52	John Avery	.30
53	Tony Martin	.15
54	O.J. McDuffie	.30
55	Oronde Gadsden	.30
56	Robert Smith	.75
57	Jeff George	.75
58	Jake Reed	.30
59	Leroy Hoard	.30
60	Terry Allen	.30
61	Terry Glenn	.75
62	Ben Coates	.30
63	Tony Simmons	.30
64	Cameron Cleeland	.30
65	Eddie Kennison	.15
66	Billy Joe Hobert	.15
67	Amani Toomer	.30
68	Kerry Collins	.30
69	Ike Hilliard	.30
70	Gary Brown	.15
71	Joe Jurevicius	.15
72	Wayne Chrebet	.75
73	Vinny Testaverde	.30
74	Charles Woodson	.50
75	James Jett	.15
76	Charles Johnson	.15
77	Duce Staley	.50
78	Hines Ward	.30
79	Jim Harbaugh	.30
80	Ryan Leaf	.75
81	Junior Seau	.30
82	Mikhael Ricks	.15
83	Garrison Hearst	.50
84	J.J. Stokes	.30
85	Lawrence Phillips	.30
86	Derrick Mayes	.30
87	Mike Pritchard	.15
88	Ahman Green	.30
89	Ricky Watters	.50
90	Robert Holcombe	.30
91	Isaac Bruce	.75
92	Trent Dilfer	.50
93	Reidel Anthony	.30
94	Jacquez Green	.30
95	Warren Sapp	.30
96	Kevin Dyson	.30
97	Yancey Thigpen	.30
98	Stephen Davis	.75
99	Irving Fryar	.15
100	Michael Westbrook	.50
101	Jake Plummer	2.00
102	Jamal Anderson	1.00
103	Chris Chandler	.50
104	Doug Flutie	1.50
105	Eric Moulds	1.00
106	Antowain Smith	.50
107	Jonathon Linton	.50
108	Curtis Enis	1.00
109	Corey Dillon	1.00
110	Carl Pickens	.50
111	Emmitt Smith	3.00
112	Troy Aikman	2.00
113	Deion Sanders	1.00
114	John Elway	3.00
115	Terrell Davis	2.00
116	Brian Griese	2.00
117	Barry Sanders	3.00
118	Charlie Batch	.50
119	Herman Moore	1.00
120	Brett Favre	4.00
121	Antonio Freeman	.50
122	Dorsey Levens	.50
123	Peyton Manning	3.00
124	Fred Taylor	2.00
125	Mark Brunell	1.50
126	Dan Marino	3.00
127	Randy Moss	4.00
128	Cris Carter	1.00
129	Randall Cunningham	1.00
130	Drew Bledsoe	1.50
131	Keyshawn Johnson	1.00
132	Curtis Martin	1.00
133	Tim Brown	.75
134	Napoleon Kaufman	1.00
135	Kordell Stewart	1.00
136	Jerome Bettis	1.00
137	Natrone Means	.75
138	Jerry Rice	2.00
139	Steve Young	1.50
140	Terrell Owens	1.00
141	Joey Galloway	1.00
142	Jon Kitna	1.00
143	Marshall Faulk	1.00
144	*Kurt Warner*	15.00
145	Warrick Dunn	1.00
146	Mike Alstott	1.00
147	Eddie George	1.25
148	Steve McNair	1.25
149	Brad Johnson	1.00
150	Skip Hicks	.25
151	*Tim Couch*	8.00
152	*Donovan McNabb*	15.00
153	*Akili Smith*	4.00
154	*Edgerrin James*	15.00
155	*Ricky Williams*	8.00
156	*Torry Holt*	8.00
157	*Champ Bailey*	5.00
158	*David Boston*	8.00
159	*Chris Claiborne*	4.00
160	*Chris McAlister*	4.00
161	*Daunte Culpepper*	15.00
162	*Cade McNown*	4.00
163	*Troy Edwards*	4.00
164	*Jevon Kearse*	5.00
165	*Kevin Johnson*	4.00
166	*James Johnson*	4.00
167	*Reginald Kelly*	2.50
168	*Rob Konrad*	4.00
169	*Jim Kleinsasser*	4.00
170	*Kevin Faulk*	4.00
171	*Joe Montgomery*	3.00
172	*Shaun King*	3.00
173	*Peerless Price*	6.00
174	*Michael Cloud*	4.00
175	*Jermaine Fazande*	3.00
176	*D'Wayne Bates*	2.50
177	*Brock Huard*	4.00
178	*Marty Booker*	2.50
179	*Karsten Bailey*	2.50
180	*Shawn Bryson*	2.50
181	*Jeff Paulk*	2.50
182	*Travis McGriff*	2.50
183	*Amos Zereoue*	4.00
184	*Craig Yeast*	2.50
185	*Joe Germaine*	4.00
186	*Dameane Douglas*	2.50
187	*Sedrick Irvin*	4.00
188	*Brandon Stokley*	2.50
189	*Larry Parker*	2.50
190	*Sean Bennett*	2.50
191	*Wane McGarity*	2.50
192	*Olandis Gary*	4.00
193	*Na Brown*	2.50
194	*Aaron Brooks*	15.00
195	*Cecil Collins*	4.00
196	*Darrin Chiaverini*	4.00
197	*Kevin Daft*	2.50
198	*Darnell McDonald*	4.00
199	*Joel Makovicka*	4.00
200	*Michael Bishop*	4.00

1999 Playoff Momentum SSD O's

This was a 200-card parallel to the base set. Each single was printed on holographic foil board with foil stamping. Cards were sequentially numbered to 25.

	NM/M
O's Cards:	25X-60X
O's Cards (101-150):	15X-40X
O's Rookies (144,151-200):	3X-6X
Production 25 Sets	

1999 Playoff Momentum SSD X's

This was a 200-card parallel to the base set. Each was die cut in the shape of the letter "X" and was printed on holographic foil board with foil stamping. They were sequentially numbered to 300.

	NM/M
X's Cards:	6X-12X
X's Cards (101-150):	5X-10X
X's Rookies (144,151-200):	1.5X
Production 300 Sets	

1999 Playoff Momentum SSD Chart Toppers

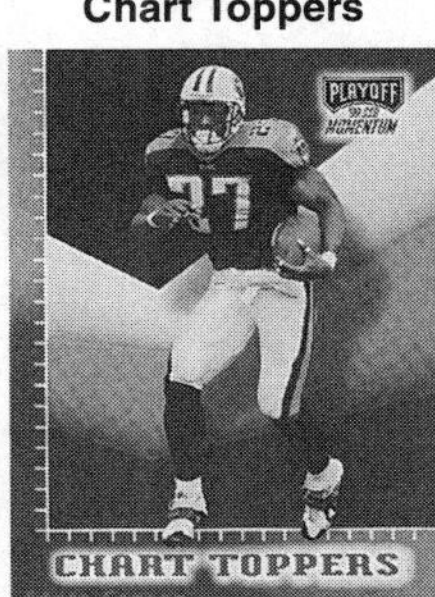

This 24-card insert included some of the top veteran and rookies in the NFL. Each was printed on holographic foil board with holographic foil stamping. Singles were found 1:33 packs.

		NM/M
Complete Set (24):		80.00
Common Player:		1.00
Inserted 1:33		
1	Donovan McNabb	5.00
2	Randy Moss	8.00
3	Cade McNown	2.00
4	Brett Favre	10.00
5	Edgerrin James	6.00
6	Dan Marino	10.00
7	Jamal Anderson	1.00
8	Barry Sanders	8.00
9	Kordell Stewart	1.00
10	John Elway	6.00
11	Eddie George	4.00
12	Terrell Davis	6.00
13	Ricky Williams	8.00
14	Peyton Manning	8.00
15	Tim Couch	6.00
16	Emmitt Smith	8.00
17	Doug Flutie	2.00
18	Troy Aikman	6.00
19	Steve Young	6.00
20	Jerry Rice	6.00
21	Mark Brunell	3.00
22	Fred Taylor	3.00
23	Jake Plummer	3.00
24	Drew Bledsoe	5.00

1999 Playoff Momentum SSD Terrell Davis Salute

This was a 5-card insert that covered Davis' career. Singles were numbered 11-15 and they were found 1:255 packs. The first 150 of each card were autographed and sequentially numbered.

		NM/M
Complete Set (5):		30.00
Common Player:		6.00
Inserted 1:255		
Common Autograph:		75.00
Production 150 Sets		
11	Terrell Davis	6.00
12	Terrell Davis	6.00
13	Terrell Davis	6.00
14	Terrell Davis	6.00
15	Terrell Davis	6.00

1999 Playoff Momentum SSD Gridiron Force

This 24-card insert included some of the top players in the NFL. Each was printed on holographic foil board with gold foil stamping. Singles were inserted 1:17 packs.

		NM/M
Complete Set (24):		60.00
Common Player:		1.00
Inserted 1:17		
1	Cris Carter	1.00
2	Brett Favre	8.00
3	Jamal Anderson	1.00
4	Dan Marino	8.00
5	Deion Sanders	1.00
6	Barry Sanders	6.00
7	Jerome Bettis	1.00
8	John Elway	5.00
9	Eddie George	3.00
10	Peyton Manning	6.00
11	Warrick Dunn	1.00
12	Troy Aikman	5.00
13	Keyshawn Johnson	1.00
14	Jerry Rice	6.00
15	Terrell Owens	1.00
16	Randy Moss	6.00
17	Fred Taylor	4.00
18	Mark Brunell	4.00
19	Steve Young	5.00
20	Drew Bledsoe	4.00
21	Kordell Stewart	1.00
22	Emmitt Smith	6.00
23	Terrell Davis	5.00
24	Jake Plummer	2.00

1999 Playoff Momentum SSD Hog Heaven

This 12-card insert pictured the players on a die-cut card with real football leather and foil stamping. Singles were inserted 1:81 packs.

		NM/M
Complete Set (12):		140.00
Common Player:		5.00
Inserted 1:81		
1	Ricky Williams	15.00
2	Terrell Davis	15.00
3	Emmitt Smith	20.00
4	Brett Favre	25.00

5 Fred Taylor 5.00
6 Tim Couch 15.00
7 John Elway 20.00
8 Dan Marino 25.00
9 Randy Moss 20.00
10 Barry Sanders 20.00
11 Jerry Rice 15.00
12 Jake Plummer 5.00

1999 Playoff Momentum SSD Rookie Quads

This was a 12-card insert that featured two rookies on each side of the card on a mirror board with micro-etching. Singles were inserted 1:97 packs. A parallel Gold version was also issued and each of those singles included holographic gold foil stamping and were sequentially numbered to 50.

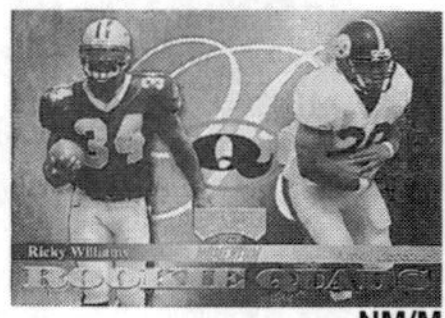

NM/M
Complete Set (12): 160.00
Common Player: 5.00
Inserted 1:97
Gold Cards: 2X
Production 50 Sets
1 Tim Couch, Aaron Brooks, Shaun King, Michael Bishop 25.00
2 Edgerrin James, Michael Cloud, Jeff Paulk, Joel Makovicka 30.00
3 Torry Holt, Reginald Kelly, Marty Booker, Dameane Douglas 15.00
4 Champ Bailey, Chris Claiborne, Chris McAlister, Anthony McFarland 5.00
5 David Boston, Jim Kleinsasser, Karsten Bailey, Brandon Stokley 10.00
6 Ricky Williams, Amos Zereoue, Cecil Collins, Olandis Gary 25.00
7 Donovan McNabb, Brock Huard, Daunte Culpepper, Scott Covington 25.00
8 James Johnson, Jermaine Fazande, Sedrick Irvin, Sean Bennett 5.00
9 Troy Edwards, Peerless Price, Travis McGriff, Larry Parker 20.00
10 Rob Konrad, Kevin Faulk, Joe Montgomery, Shawn Bryson 5.00
11 Cade McNown, Joe Germaine, Akili Smith, Chris Griesen 5.00
12 Kevin Johnson, D'Wayne Bates, Craig Yeast, Wane McGarity 5.00

1999 Playoff Momentum SSD Rookie Recall

This was a 30-card insert that featured photos of NFL stars on the front with their rookie photos on the back. Singles were found 1:49 packs.

NM/M
Complete Set (30): 110.00
Common Player: 2.00
Inserted 1:49
1 Jerome Bettis 2.00
2 Tim Brown 3.00
3 Cris Carter 2.00
4 Marshall Faulk 4.00
5 Doug Flutie 2.00
6 Randall Cunningham 2.00
7 Brett Favre 15.00
8 Dan Marino 15.00
9 Barry Sanders 12.00
10 John Elway 10.00
11 Emmitt Smith 12.00
12 Troy Aikman 10.00
13 Jerry Rice 10.00
14 Steve Young 8.00
15 Randy Moss 12.00
16 Peyton Manning 12.00
17 Fred Taylor 6.00
18 Jake Plummer 5.00
19 Drew Bledsoe 6.00
20 Mark Brunell 4.00
21 Charlie Batch 2.00
22 Antonio Freeman 2.00
23 Curtis Martin 4.00
24 Eddie George 4.00
25 Kordell Stewart 2.00
26 Jamal Anderson 2.00
27 Curtis Enis 2.00
28 Terrell Davis 10.00
29 Eric Moulds 3.00
30 Terrell Owens 4.00

1999 Playoff Momentum SSD Barry Sanders Commemorate

This was a five-card insert that covered the career of Barry Sanders. Singles were numbered 7 to 11 and found 1:275 packs.

NM/M
Complete Set (5): 40.00
Inserted 1:275
1 Barry Sanders 8.00
2 Barry Sanders 8.00
3 Barry Sanders 8.00
4 Barry Sanders 8.00
5 Barry Sanders 8.00

1999 Playoff Momentum SSD Star Gazing

This was a 45-card insert that was divided into three levels. The Red singles were the first eight cards in the set, each was autographed and found 1:185 packs. The next 22 cards were Blue and they were inserted 1:17 packs. The last 15 cards were Green and they were issued at 1:65 packs. Each single had a parallel Gold version and each of those singles were sequentially numbered to 50.

NM/M
Complete Set (45): 500.00
Common Red Auto. (1-8): 25.00
Inserted 1:185
Common Blue (9-30): 1.50
Inserted 1:17
Common Green (31-45): 5.00
Inserted 1:65
1 Terrell Davis (red) 75.00
2 Dan Marino (red) 100.00
3 Joey Galloway (red) 25.00
4 Steve McNair (red) 25.00
5 Doug Flutie (red) 35.00
6 Kordell Stewart (red) 25.00
7 Fred Taylor (red) 45.00
8 Jamal Anderson (red) 25.00
9 Karim Abdul (blue) 1.50
10 Mike Alstott (blue) 3.00
11 Jerome Bettis (blue) 1.50
12 Carl Pickens (blue) 1.50
13 Cris Carter (blue) 3.00
14 Randall Cunningham (blue) 3.00
15 Corey Dillon (blue) 3.00
16 Tim Dwight (blue) 1.50
17 Cade McNown (blue) 5.00
18 Marshall Faulk (blue) 3.00
19 Napoleon Kaufman (blue) 1.50
20 Antonio Freeman (blue) 1.50
21 Edgerrin James (blue) 15.00
22 Terrell Owens (blue) 3.00
23 Garrison Hearst (blue) 1.50
24 Keyshawn Johnson (blue) 3.00
25 Akili Smith (blue) 5.00
26 Curtis Martin (blue) 3.00
27 Dorsey Levens (blue) 1.50
28 Deion Sanders (blue) 3.00
29 Herman Moore (blue) 1.50
30 Eric Moulds (blue) 1.50
31 Randy Moss (green) 15.00
32 Eddie George (green) 5.00
33 Barry Sanders (green) 15.00
34 John Elway (green) 12.00
35 Peyton Manning (green) 12.00
36 Emmitt Smith (green) 12.00
37 Troy Aikman (green) 10.00
38 Jerry Rice (green) 10.00
39 Mark Brunell (green) 6.00
40 Steve Young (green) 6.00
41 Tim Couch (green) 15.00
42 Ricky Williams (green) 15.00
43 Donovan McNabb (green) 10.00
44 Drew Bledsoe (green) 6.00
45 Brett Favre (green) 15.00

1999 Playoff Momentum SSD Team Threads

This was a 31-card insert that featured swatches of authentic NFL team jerseys on the front and back of each card. Singles were inserted 1:17 packs.

NM/M
Complete Set (31): 200.00
Common Player: 2.00
Minor Stars: 5.00
Inserted 1:17
1 Dan Marino 15.00
2 Drew Bledsoe 10.00
3 Keyshawn Johnson 5.00
4 Eric Moulds 5.00
5 Peyton Manning 12.00
6 Natrone Means 2.00
7 Jon Kitna 2.00
8 Bam Morris 2.00
9 Tim Brown 5.00
10 Terrell Davis 12.00
11 Kordell Stewart 5.00
12 Fred Taylor 8.00
13 Tim Couch 10.00
14 Eddie George 8.00
15 Priest Holmes 8.00
16 Akili Smith 5.00
17 Emmitt Smith 12.00
18 Skip Hicks 2.00
19 Jake Plummer 6.00
20 Donovan McNabb 8.00
21 Ike Hilliard 2.00
22 Barry Sanders 12.00
23 Cade McNown 4.00
24 Randy Moss 12.00
25 Brett Favre 15.00
26 Mike Alstott 2.00
27 Marshall Faulk 8.00
28 Ricky Williams 12.00
29 Jamal Anderson 2.00
30 Jerry Rice 10.00
31 Tim Biakabutuka 2.00

1999 Playoff Prestige EXP

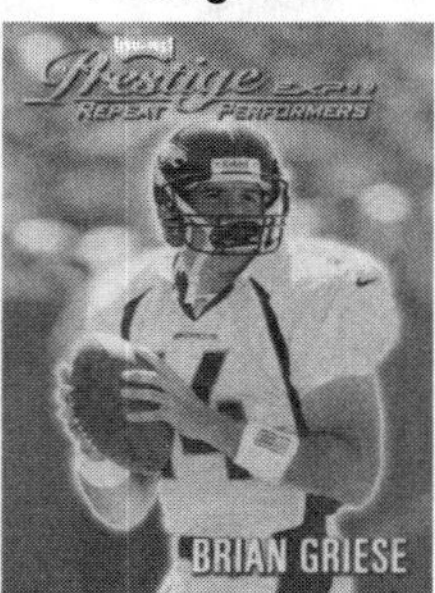

This 200-card set was a retail only release that included 40 unseeded rookie cards. It had two parallel sets with Reflections Gold and Reflections Silver. Other inserts include: Alma Maters, Checklists, Crowd Pleasers, Terrell Davis Salute, Draft Picks, Performers and Stars of the NFL.

NM/M
Complete Set (200): 40.00
Common Player: .10
Minor Stars: .40
Common Rookie: .50
SSD Pack (5): 7.00
SSD Wax Box (16): 100.00
EXP Pack (8): 2.00
EXP Wax Box (24): 45.00
1 *Anthony McFarland* 1.00
2 *Al Wilson* 1.00
3 *Jevon Kearse* 2.00
4 *Aaron Brooks* 6.00
5 *Travis McGriff* 1.00
6 *Jeff Paulk* 1.00
7 *Shawn Bryson* .50
8 *Karsten Bailey* 1.00
9 *Mike Cloud* 1.00
10 *James Johnson* 2.00
11 *Tai Streets* 1.00
12 *Jermaine Fazande* 1.00
13 *Ebenezer Ekuban* .50
14 *Joe Montgomery* .40
15 *Craig Yeast* .50
16 *Joe Germaine* .50
17 *Andy Katzenmoyer* 1.50
18 *Kevin Faulk* 2.00
19 *Chris McAlister* .50
20 *Sedrick Irvin* .50
21 *Brock Huard* 1.00
22 *Cade McNown* 1.00
23 *Shaun King* 1.00
24 *Amos Zereoue* 2.50
25 *Dameane Douglas* .50
26 *D'Wayne Bates* 1.00
27 *Kevin Johnson* 2.00
28 *Rob Konrad* 1.50
29 *Troy Edwards* 2.00
30 *Peerless Price* 2.50
31 *Daunte Culpepper* 6.00
32 *Akili Smith* 1.00
33 *David Boston* 3.00
34 *Chris Claiborne* .50
35 *Torry Holt* 3.00
36 *Champ Bailey* 2.00
37 *Edgerrin James* 6.00
38 *Donovan McNabb* 6.00
39 *Ricky Williams* 6.00
40 *Tim Couch* 3.00
41 Charles Woodson (Repeat Performers) .10
42 Skip Hicks (Repeat Performers) .10
43 Brian Griese (Repeat Performers) .75
44 Tim Dwight (Repeat Performers) .10
45 Ryan Leaf (Repeat Performers) .50
46 Curtis Enis (Repeat Performers) .10
47 Charlie Batch (Repeat Performers) .75
48 Fred Taylor (Repeat Performers) 1.00
49 Peyton Manning (Repeat Performers) 1.50
50 Randy Moss (Repeat Performers) 2.00
51 Jim Harbaugh (Trading Places) .10
52 Warren Moon (Trading Places) .75
53 Jeff George (Trading Places) .10
54 Rich Gannon (Trading Places) .10
55 Scott Mitchell (Trading Places) .10
56 Kerry Collins (Trading Places) .10
57 Brad Johnson (Trading Places) .75
58 Charles Johnson (Trading Places) .10
59 Chris Calloway (Trading Places) .10
60 Tyrone Wheatley (Trading Places) .10
61 Michael Westbrook .40
62 Skip Hicks .75
63 Terry Allen .10
64 Albert Connell .10
65 Kevin Dyson .40
66 Frank Wycheck .10
67 Yancey Thigpen .40
68 Steve McNair .75
69 Eddie George 1.00
70 Eric Zeier .10
71 Jacquez Green .40
72 Reidel Anthony .40
73 Warren Sapp .10
74 Mike Alstott .75
75 Warrick Dunn 1.00
76 Trent Dilfer .40
77 Ahman Green .40
78 Joey Galloway .75
79 Ricky Watters .40
80 Jon Kitna 1.00
81 Amp Lee .10
82 Isaac Bruce .40
83 Robert Holcombe .10
84 Greg Hill .10
85 Marshall Faulk .75
86 Trent Green .75
87 J.J. Stokes .40
88 Terrell Owens .75
89 Jerry Rice 2.00
90 Garrison Hearst .75
91 Steve Young 1.25
92 Junior Seau .40
93 Mikhael Ricks .10
94 Natrone Means .40
95 Ryan Leaf .75
96 Courtney Hawkins .10
97 Chris Fuamatu-Ma'afala .10
98 Jerome Bettis .75
99 Kordell Stewart .75
100 Bobby Hoying .40
101 Charlie Garner .40
102 Duce Staley .40
103 Charles Woodson .75
104 James Jett .10
105 Rickey Dudley .10
106 Tim Brown .50
107 Napoleon Kaufman .75
108 Wayne Chrebet .50
109 Keyshawn Johnson .75
110 Vinny Testaverde .40
111 Curtis Martin .75
112 Joe Jurevicius .10
113 Tiki Barber .10
114 Ike Hilliard .10
115 Kent Graham .10
116 Gary Brown .10
117 Lamar Smith .10
118 Eddie Kennison .10
119 Cameron Cleeland .10
120 Tony Simmons .10
121 Ben Coates .40
122 Darick Holmes .10
123 Terry Glenn .75
124 Drew Bledsoe 1.50
125 Leroy Hoard .10
126 Jake Reed .10
127 Randy Moss 4.00
128 Cris Carter .75
129 Robert Smith .75
130 Randall Cunningham .75
131 Lamar Thomas .10
132 John Avery .40
133 O.J. McDuffie .40
134 Dan Marino 3.00
135 Karim Abdul .40
136 Rashaan Shehee .10
137 Derrick Alexander .10
138 Bam Morris .10
139 Andre Rison .40
140 Elvis Grbac .40
141 Tavian Banks .10
142 Keenan McCardell .10
143 Jimmy Smith .40
144 Fred Taylor 2.00
145 Mark Brunell 1.50
146 Jerome Pathon .10
147 Marvin Harrison .40
148 Peyton Manning 3.00
149 Robert Brooks .10
150 Mark Chmura .40
151 Antonio Freeman .75
152 Dorsey Levens .75
153 Brett Favre 4.00
154 Johnnie Morton .10
155 Germane Crowell .40
156 Barry Sanders 4.00
157 Herman Moore .75
158 Charlie Batch 1.25
159 Marcus Nash .10
160 Shannon Sharpe .40
161 Rod Smith .40
162 Ed McCaffrey .40
163 Terrell Davis 3.00
164 John Elway 3.00
165 Ernie Mills .10
166 Michael Irvin .40
167 Deion Sanders .75
168 Emmitt Smith 3.00
169 Troy Aikman 2.00
170 Chris Spielman .10
171 Terry Kirby .10
172 Ty Detmer .10
173 Leslie Shepherd .10
174 Darnay Scott .10
175 Jeff Blake .40
176 Carl Pickens .40
177 Corey Dillon .75
178 Bobby Engram .10
179 Curtis Conway .40
180 Curtis Enis .75
181 Muhsin Muhammad .10
182 Steve Beuerlein .10
183 Tim Biakabutuka .10
184 Bruce Smith .10
185 Andre Reed .10
186 Thurman Thomas .40
187 Eric Moulds .75
188 Antowain Smith .75
189 Doug Flutie 1.25
190 Jermaine Lewis .10
191 Priest Holmes .75
192 O.J. Santiago .10
193 Tim Dwight .75
194 Terance Mathis .10
195 Chris Chandler .40
196 Jamal Anderson .75
197 Rob Moore .40
198 Frank Sanders .10
199 Adrian Murrell .10
200 Jake Plummer 1.50

1999 Playoff Prestige EXP Reflections Gold

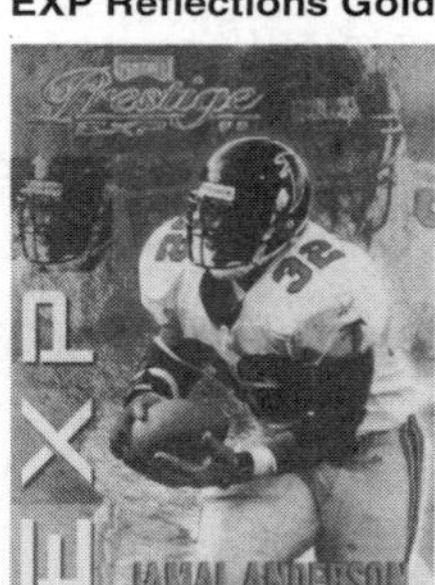

This is a parallel to the base set and each single is the same as the base card except for these singles are printed on a gold foil card and are sequentially numbered to 1,000.

Gold Cards: 3X-6X
Gold Rookies: 3X
Production 1,000 Sets

1999 Playoff Prestige EXP Reflections Silver

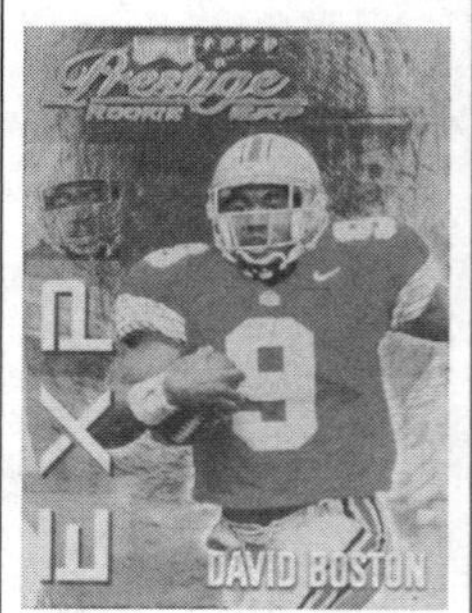

This is a parallel to the base set and is identical to the base card except each single is printed on a silver foil card and is sequentially numbered to 3,250.

Silver Cards: 2X
Silver Rookies: 1.5X
Production 3,250 Sets

1999 Playoff Prestige EXP Alma Maters

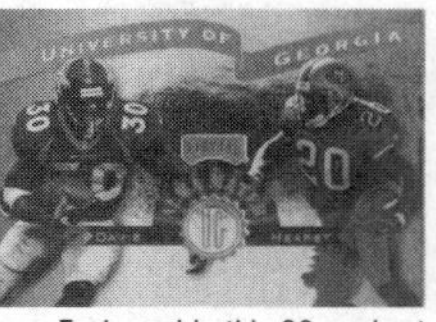

Each card in this 30-card set pictures two players that went to the same college. Singles were inserted 1:25 packs.

NM/M
Complete Set (30): 60.00
Common Player: 1.00
Minor Stars: 2.00
Inserted 1:25
1 Priest Holmes, Ricky Williams 8.00
2 Tim Couch, Dermonti Dawson 6.00
3 Terrell Davis, Garrison Hearst 6.00
4 Troy Brown, Randy Moss 6.00
5 Barry Sanders, Thurman Thomas 8.00
6 Emmitt Smith, Fred Taylor 8.00
7 Doug Flutie, Bill Romanowski 2.00
8 Brett Favre, Michael Jackson 8.00
9 Charlie Batch, Ron Rice 2.00
10 Mark Brunell, Chris Chandler 3.00
11 Warrick Dunn, Deion Sanders 2.00
12 Cris Carter, Eddie George 4.00
13 Drew Bledsoe, Ryan Leaf 4.00
14 Corey Dillon, Napoleon Kaufman 2.00
15 Jerome Bettis, Tim Brown 3.00
16 Marshall Faulk, Darnay Scott 2.00
17 Tiki Barber, Herman Moore 2.00
18 Jamal Anderson, Chris Fuamatu-Ma'afala 1.00
19 Troy Aikman, Cade McNown 4.00
20 Brian Griese, Charles Woodson 3.00
21 Charles Johnson, Kordell Stewart 2.00
22 Kevin Faulk, Eddie Kennison 1.00
23 Donovan McNabb, Rob Moore 5.00
24 Steve McNair, John Thierry 2.00
25 Michael Irvin, Vinny Testaverde 1.00
26 Randall Cunningham, Keenan McCardell 2.00
27 Keyshawn Johnson, Junior Seau 2.00
28 Karim Abdul, Skip Hicks 1.00
29 Curtis Enis, O.J. McDuffie 1.00
30 Joey Galloway, Robert Smith 1.00

1999 Playoff Prestige EXP Checklists

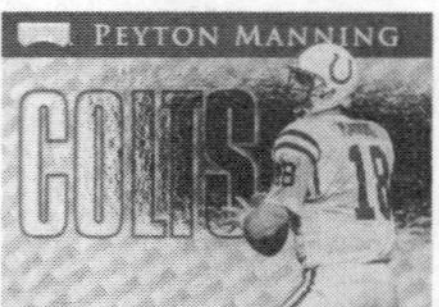

This 31-card set includes a card for each NFL team and highlights one player on the front of these silver foil singles. The backs include photos of each player on that team in the base set and includes their card number. Singles were inserted 1:25 packs.

NM/M
Complete Set (31): 45.00
Common Player: .50
Minor Stars: 1.00
Inserted 1:25
1 Jake Plummer 2.00
2 Chris Chandler .50
3 Priest Holmes 2.00

4	Doug Flutie	1.00
5	Wesley Walls	.50
6	Curtis Enis	.50
7	Corey Dillon	1.00
8	Kevin Johnson	1.00
9	Troy Aikman	4.00
10	Terrell Davis	6.00
11	Barry Sanders	8.00
12	Antonio Freeman	1.00
13	Peyton Manning	8.00
14	Fred Taylor	5.00
15	Andre Rison	.50
16	Dan Marino	10.00
17	Randy Moss	8.00
18	Kevin Faulk	4.00
19	Ricky Williams	8.00
20	Joe Montgomery	1.00
21	Vinny Testaverde	.50
22	Tim Brown	1.00
23	Duce Staley	.50
24	Jerome Bettis	1.00
25	Natrone Means	1.00
26	Terrell Owens	1.00
27	Joey Galloway	1.00
28	Isaac Bruce	1.00
29	Mike Alstott	1.00
30	Eddie George	4.00
31	Skip Hicks	1.00

1999 Playoff Prestige EXP Crowd Pleasers

Each card in this 30-card set highlights the hottest players who fill the stadiums. Singles were inserted 1:49 packs.

		NM/M
Complete Set (30):		110.00
Common Player:		1.00
Minor Stars:		2.00
Inserted 1:49		
1	Terrell Davis	8.00
2	Fred Taylor	5.00
3	Corey Dillon	5.00
4	Eddie George	4.00
5	Napoleon Kaufman	1.00
6	Jamal Anderson	3.00
7	Tim Couch	10.00
8	Emmitt Smith	12.00
9	Deion Sanders	5.00
10	Garrison Hearst	1.00
11	Peyton Manning	12.00
12	Ricky Williams	12.00
13	Barry Sanders	12.00
14	Jerry Rice	10.00
15	Jake Plummer	4.00
16	Tim Brown	3.00
17	Terrell Owens	5.00
18	Dan Marino	15.00
19	Chris Chandler	1.00
20	Drew Bledsoe	6.00
21	Charlie Batch	1.00
22	Mark Brunell	4.00
23	Troy Aikman	10.00
24	John Elway	10.00
25	Jon Kitna	1.00
26	Jerome Bettis	3.00
27	Brett Favre	15.00
28	Steve Young	6.00
29	Randy Moss	12.00
30	Antonio Freeman	2.00

1999 Playoff Prestige EXP Terrell Davis Salute

This 5-card set highlights 15 milestones in Davis' career. Each single is sequentially numbered to 750 and the first 150 of each single were autographed.

		NM/M
Complete Set (5):		30.00
Common Player:		6.00
Production 750 Sets		
Common Autographs:		85.00
First 150-cards were signed		
1	Terrell Davis	6.00
2	Terrell Davis	6.00
3	Terrell Davis	6.00
4	Terrell Davis	6.00
5	Terrell Davis	6.00

1999 Playoff Prestige EXP Draft Picks

This insert includes the top 30 players drafted in 1999. It pictures each player in their college uniform on a silver foil card. Singles were inserted 1:13 packs.

		NM/M
Complete Set (30):		35.00
Common Player:		.50
Minor Stars:		1.00
Inserted 1:13		
1	Tim Couch	6.00
2	Ricky Williams	10.00
3	Donovan McNabb	6.00
4	Edgerrin James	7.00
5	Champ Bailey	2.50
6	Torry Holt	4.00
7	Chris Claiborne	1.00
8	David Boston	4.00
9	Akili Smith	2.00
10	Daunte Culpepper	5.00
11	Peerless Price	4.00
12	Troy Edwards	4.00
13	Rob Konrad	.50
14	Kevin Johnson	2.00
15	D'Wayne Bates	1.00
16	Cecil Collins	2.00
17	Amos Zereoue	3.00
18	Shaun King	1.00
19	Cade McNown	2.00
20	Brock Huard	1.00
21	Sedrick Irvin	1.00
22	Chris McAlister	.50
23	Kevin Faulk	2.00
24	Jevon Kearse	2.50
25	Joe Germaine	1.00
26	Andy Katzenmoyer	1.00
27	Joe Montgomery	1.00
28	Al Wilson	.50
29	Jermaine Fazande	.50
30	Ebenezer Ekuban	.50

1999 Playoff Prestige EXP Performers

This 24-card insert includes the top performers from 1998. Singles were inserted 1:97 packs.

		NM/M
Complete Set (24):		125.00
Common Player:		1.00
Minor Stars:		2.00
Inserted 1:97		
1	Marshall Faulk	4.00
2	Jake Plummer	4.00
3	Antonio Freeman	2.00
4	Brett Favre	15.00
5	Troy Aikman	10.00
6	Randy Moss	12.00
7	John Elway	10.00
8	Mark Brunell	5.00
9	Jamal Anderson	2.00
10	Doug Flutie	2.00
11	Drew Bledsoe	8.00
12	Barry Sanders	12.00
13	Dan Marino	15.00
14	Randall Cunningham	2.00
15	Steve Young	8.00
16	Carl Pickens	1.00
17	Peyton Manning	10.00
18	Herman Moore	2.00
19	Eddie George	4.00
20	Fred Taylor	5.00
21	Garrison Hearst	2.00
22	Emmitt Smith	12.00
23	Jerry Rice	10.00
24	Terrell Davis	10.00

1999 Playoff Prestige EXP Barry Sanders Commemorative

This was a special insert found 1:289 packs that was commemorating Sanders run for the record.

		NM/M
Inserted 1:289		20.00
RR1	Barry Sanders	10.00

1999 Playoff Prestige EXP Stars of the NFL

Each card in this 20-card set is printed on clear plastic and is die cut. Singles were inserted 1:73 packs.

		NM/M
Complete Set (20):		90.00
Common Player:		2.00
Inserted 1:73		
1	Jerry Rice	8.00
2	Steve Young	8.00
3	Drew Bledsoe	8.00
4	Jamal Anderson	2.00
5	Eddie George	4.00
6	Keyshawn Johnson	2.00
7	Kordell Stewart	3.00
8	Barry Sanders	10.00
9	Tim Brown	2.00
10	Mark Brunell	4.00
11	Fred Taylor	4.00
12	Randy Moss	10.00
13	Peyton Manning	10.00
14	Emmitt Smith	10.00
15	Deion Sanders	2.00
16	Troy Aikman	8.00
17	Brett Favre	12.00
18	Dan Marino	12.00
19	Terrell Davis	8.00
20	John Elway	8.00

1999 Playoff Prestige SSD

Prestige SSD was a 200-card set that was a hobby-only product. It had 50 short prints with 40 rookies and 10 Repeat Performers that were inserted 1:2 packs. It has a parallel Spectrum insert in five different colors that include Blue, Gold, Green, Purple and Red. Other inserts include: Alma Maters, Checklists, Checklists Autographs, Draft Picks, For the Record, Gridiron Heritage, Inside the Numbers and Barry Sanders Run for the Record.

		NM/M
Complete Set (200):		125.00
Common Player:		.10
Minor Stars:		.50
Common RP (151-160):		1.00
Common Rookie:		2.00
Inserted 1:2		
Wax Box:		50.00
1	Jake Plummer	1.00
2	Adrian Murrell	.10
3	Frank Sanders	.50
4	Rob Moore	.50
5	Jamal Anderson	1.00
6	Chris Chandler	.50
7	Terrance Mathis	.50
8	Tim Dwight	1.00
9	O.J. Santiago	.10
10	Priest Holmes	1.50
11	Jermaine Lewis	.50
12	Doug Flutie	1.50
13	Antowain Smith	1.00
14	Eric Moulds	1.00
15	Thurman Thomas	.50
16	Andre Reed	.10
17	Bruce Smith	.10
18	Tim Biakabutuka	.50
19	Steve Beuerlein	.10
20	Muhsin Muhammed	.10
21	Curtis Enis	1.00
22	Curtis Conway	.50
23	Bobby Engram	.10
24	Corey Dillon	1.00
25	Carl Pickens	.50
26	Jeff Blake	.50
27	Darnay Scott	.10
28	Leslie Shepherd	.10
29	Ty Detmer	.10
30	Terry Kirby	.10
31	Chris Spielman	.10
32	Troy Aikman	2.50
33	Emmitt Smith	4.00
34	Deion Sanders	1.00
35	Michael Irvin	.50
36	Ernie Mills	.10
37	John Elway	4.00
38	Terrell Davis	2.00
39	Ed McCaffrey	.50
40	Rod Smith	.50
41	Shannon Sharpe	.50
42	Marcus Nash	.50
43	Charlie Batch	2.00
44	Herman Moore	1.00
45	Barry Sanders	5.00
46	Germane Crowell	.50
47	Johnnie Morton	.10
48	Brett Favre	5.00
49	Dorsey Levens	1.00
50	Antonio Freeman	1.00
51	Mark Chmura	.50
52	Robert Brooks	.10
53	Peyton Manning	4.00
54	Marvin Harrison	.50
55	Jerome Pathon	.10
56	Mark Brunell	2.00
57	Fred Taylor	2.50
58	Jimmy Smith	.50
59	Keenan McCardell	.10
60	Tavian Banks	.50
61	Elvis Grbac	.50
62	Andre Rison	.50
63	Bam Morris	.50
64	Derrick Alexander	.10
65	Rashaan Shehee	.10
66	Karim Abdul	.75
67	Dan Marino	4.00
68	O.J. McDuffie	.50
69	John Avery	.50
70	Lamar Thomas	.10
71	Randall Cunningham	1.00
72	Robert Smith	.75
73	Cris Carter	1.00
74	Randy Moss	6.00
75	Jake Reed	.10
76	Leroy Hoard	.10
77	Drew Bledsoe	2.00
78	Terry Glenn	.75
79	Darick Holmes	.10
80	Ben Coates	.50
81	Tony Simmons	.50
82	Cam Cleeland	.50
83	Eddie Kennison	.10
84	Lamar Smith	.10
85	Gary Brown	.10
86	Kent Graham	.10
87	Ike Hilliard	.50
88	Tiki Barber	.10
89	Joe Jurevicius	.10
90	Curtis Martin	1.00
91	Vinny Testaverde	.50
92	Keyshawn Johnson	1.00
93	Wayne Chrebet	1.00
94	Napoleon Kaufman	1.00
95	Tim Brown	.50
96	Rickey Dudley	.10
97	James Jett	.10
98	Charles Woodson	1.00
99	Duce Staley	.10
100	Charlie Garner	.10
101	Bobby Hoying	.10
102	Kordell Stewart	1.50
103	Jerome Bettis	1.00
104	Chris Fuamatu-Ma'afala	.10
105	Courtney Hawkins	.10
106	Ryan Leaf	1.50
107	Natrone Means	.75
108	Mikhael Ricks	.10
109	Junior Seau	.50
110	Steve Young	2.00
111	Garrison Hearst	1.00
112	Jerry Rice	2.50
113	Terrell Owens	1.00
114	J.J. Stokes	.50
115	Trent Green	1.00
116	Marshall Faulk	1.00
117	Greg Hill	.10
118	Robert Holcombe	.50
119	Isaac Bruce	.75
120	Amp Lee	.10
121	Jon Kitna	1.50
122	Ricky Watters	.75
123	Joey Galloway	1.00
124	Ahman Green	.50
125	Trent Dilfer	.75
126	Warrick Dunn	1.50
127	Mike Alstott	1.00
128	Warren Sapp	.10
129	Reidel Anthony	.50
130	Jacquez Green	.50
131	Eric Zeier	.10
132	Eddie George	1.50
133	Steve McNair	1.00
134	Yancey Thigpen	.50
135	Frank Wycheck	.10
136	Kevin Dyson	.50
137	Albert Connell	.10
138	Terry Allen	.50
139	Skip Hicks	1.00
140	Michael Westbrook	.50
141	Tyrone Wheatley (Trading Places)	.10
142	Chris Calloway (Trading Places)	.10
143	Charles Johnson (Trading Places)	.10
144	Brad Johnson (Trading Places)	.50
145	Kerry Collins (Trading Places)	.10
146	Scott Mitchel l (Trading Places)	.10
147	Rich Gannon (Trading Places)	.10
148	Jeff George (Trading Places)	.10
149	Warren Moon (Trading Places)	.10
150	Jim Harbaugh (Trading Places)	.10
151	Randy Moss (Repeat Performers)	8.00
152	Peyton Manning (Repeat Performers)	8.00
153	Fred Taylor (Repeat Performers)	6.00
154	Charlie Batch (Repeat Performers)	3.00
155	Curtis Enis (Repeat Performers)	1.00
156	Ryan Leaf (Repeat Performers)	2.00
157	Tim Dwight (Repeat Performers)	2.00
158	Brian Griese (Repeat Performers)	3.00
159	Skip Hicks (Repeat Performers)	1.00
160	Charles Woodson (Repeat Performers)	2.00
161	*Tim Couch*	6.00
162	*Ricky Williams*	12.00
163	*Donovan McNabb*	12.00
164	*Edgerrin James*	12.00
165	*Champ Bailey*	4.00
166	*Torry Holt*	6.00
167	*Chris Claiborne*	2.00
168	*David Boston*	6.00
169	*Akili Smith*	2.00
170	*Peerless Price*	5.00
171	*Troy Edwards*	4.00
172	*Rob Konrad*	2.00
173	*Kevin Johnson*	4.00
174	*D'Wayne Bates*	3.00
175	*Daunte Culpepper*	12.00
176	*Dameane Douglas*	1.00
177	*Amos Zereoue*	5.00
178	*Shaun King*	2.00
179	*Cade McNown*	2.00
180	*Brock Huard*	2.00
181	*Sedrick Irvin*	2.00
182	*Chris McAlister*	2.00
183	*Kevin Faulk*	4.00
184	*Andy Katzenmoyer*	4.00
185	*Joe Germaine*	2.00
186	*Craig Yeast*	2.00
187	*Joe Montgomery*	1.00
188	*Ebenezer Ekuban*	2.00
189	*Jermaine Fazande*	1.00
190	*Tai Streets*	2.00
191	*James Johnson*	4.00
192	*Mike Cloud*	1.00
193	*Karsten Bailey*	3.00
194	*Shawn Bryson*	2.00
195	*Jeff Paulk*	1.00
196	*Travis McGriff*	1.00
197	*Aaron Brooks*	12.00
198	*Jevon Kearse*	5.00
199	*Al Wilson*	1.00
200	*Anthony McFarland*	1.00

1999 Playoff Prestige SSD Spectrum Blue

This is a 200-card parallel to the base and is the same except for the background color is in blue and the foil on the fronts are also in blue. Each card is sequentially numbered on the back to 500. There is also a Gold, Green, Purple and Red version that are also numbered to 500 and are only different by the colors on the fronts of the cards.

Spectrum Blue Cards:	4X
Spectrum Blue Rookies:	1X
Production 500 Sets	

Prices and production are the same for Gold, Green, Purple and Red.

1999 Playoff Prestige SSD Alma Maters

Each of these horizontal cards picture two players that went to the same college and put them on a foil card. Singles were inserted 1:17 packs. A parallel Jumbo version was also produced and inserted as a box topper.

		NM/M
Complete Set (30):		110.00
Common Player:		2.00
Inserted 1:17		
Jumbos:		1X
One Per Box		
1	Priest Holmes, Ricky Williams	20.00
2	Tim Couch, Dermontti Dawson	12.00
3	Terrell Davis, Garrison Hearst	12.00
4	Troy Brown, Randy Moss	12.00
5	Barry Sanders, Thurman Thomas	12.00
6	Emmitt Smith, Fred Taylor	12.00
7	Doug Flutie, Bill Romanowski	4.00
8	Brett Favre, Michael Jackson	15.00
9	Charlie Batch, Ron Rice	2.00
10	Mark Brunell, Chris Chandler	4.00
11	Warrick Dunn, Deion Sanders	3.00
12	Cris Carter, Eddie George	4.00
13	Drew Bledsoe, Ryan Leaf	6.00
14	Corey Dillon, Napoleon Kaufman	2.00
15	Jerome Bettis, Tim Brown	4.00
16	Marshall Faulk, Darnay Scott	5.00
17	Tiki Barber, Herman Moore	2.00
18	Jamal Anderson, Chris Fuamatu-Ma'afala	2.00
19	Troy Aikman, Cade McNown	8.00
20	Brian Griese, Charles Woodson	6.00
21	Charles Johnson, Kordell Stewart	4.00
22	Kevin Faulk, Eddie Kennison	3.00
23	Donovan McNabb, Rob Moore	8.00
24	Steve McNair, John Thierry	6.00
25	Michael Irvin, Vinny Testaverde	2.00
26	Randall Cunningham, Keenan McCardell	2.00
27	Keyshawn Johnson, Junior Seau	4.00
28	Karim Abdul, Skip Hicks	2.00
29	Curtis Enis, O.J. McDuffie	2.00
30	Joey Galloway, Robert Smith	2.00

1999 Playoff Prestige SSD Checklist

Each NFL team has a card in this 31-card insert with a player from each team on the fronts of the foil singles. The backs have a small picture from each player on that team with their card number next to it. Singles were found 1:17 packs.

		NM/M
Complete Set (31):		110.00
Common Player:		1.00
Minor Stars:		2.00
Inserted 1:17		
1	Jake Plummer	2.00
2	Chris Chandler	1.00
3	Priest Holmes	6.00
4	Doug Flutie	2.00
5	Wesley Walls	1.00
6	Curtis Enis	1.00
7	Corey Dillon	4.00
8	Kevin Johnson	2.00
9	Troy Aikman	8.00
10	Terrell Davis	8.00
11	Barry Sanders	10.00
12	Antonio Freeman	2.00
13	Peyton Manning	10.00
14	Fred Taylor	6.00
15	Andre Rison	1.00
16	Dan Marino	12.00
17	Randy Moss	10.00
18	Kevin Faulk	3.00
19	Ricky Williams	12.00
20	Joe Montgomery	2.00
21	Vinny Testaverde	1.00
22	Tim Brown	4.00
23	Duce Staley	1.00
24	Jerome Bettis	2.00
25	Natrone Means	1.00
26	Terrell Owens	4.00
27	Joey Galloway	2.00
28	Isaac Bruce	2.00
29	Mike Alstott	2.00
30	Eddie George	6.00
31	Skip Hicks	2.00

1999 Playoff Prestige SSD Checklist Autographs

These cards are identical to the Checklist insert except for that each of these singles are autographed on the fronts. Each is sequentially numbered to 250.

		NM/M
Common Player:		20.00
Minor Stars:		40.00
Production 250 Sets		
1	Jake Plummer	40.00
2	Chris Chandler	20.00
3	Priest Holmes	40.00
4	Doug Flutie	40.00
5	Wesley Walls	20.00
6	Curtis Enis	20.00
7	Corey Dillon	40.00
8	Kevin Johnson	20.00
9	Troy Aikman	75.00
10	Terrell Davis	75.00
11	Barry Sanders	125.00
12	Antonio Freeman	40.00

13	Peyton Manning	125.00
14	Fred Taylor	75.00
15	Andre Rison	20.00
16	Dan Marino	125.00
17	Randy Moss	125.00
18	Kevin Faulk	20.00
19	Ricky Williams	150.00
20	Joe Montgomery	40.00
21	Vinny Testaverde	20.00
22	Tim Brown	40.00
23	Duce Staley	20.00
24	Jerome Bettis	40.00
25	Natrone Means	20.00
26	Terrell Owens	50.00
27	Joey Galloway	50.00
28	Isaac Bruce	40.00
29	Mike Alstott	40.00
30	Eddie George	50.00
31	Skip Hicks	40.00

1999 Playoff Prestige SSD Draft Picks

Each card in this 30-card set is printed on a silver-foiled card with a blue foil background. Singles were inserted 1:9 packs.

		NM/M
Complete Set (30):		90.00
Common Player:		1.00
Minor Stars:		2.00
Inserted 1:9		
1	Tim Couch	10.00
2	Ricky Williams	15.00
3	Donovan McNabb	10.00
4	Edgerrin James	12.00
5	Champ Bailey	5.00
6	Torry Holt	8.00
7	Chris Claiborne	2.00
8	David Boston	8.00
9	Akili Smith	5.00
10	Daunte Culpepper	10.00
11	Peerless Price	5.00
12	Troy Edwards	6.00
13	Rob Konrad	1.00
14	Kevin Johnson	2.00
15	D'Wayne Bates	1.00
16	Cecil Collins	2.00
17	Amos Zereoue	6.00
18	Shaun King	2.00
19	Cade McNown	2.00
20	Brock Huard	2.00
21	Sedrick Irvin	2.00
22	Chris McAlister	1.00
23	Kevin Faulk	2.00
24	Jevon Kearse	5.00
25	Joe Germaine	2.00
26	Andy Katzenmoyer	2.00
27	Joe Montgomery	2.00
28	Al Wilson	1.00
29	Jermaine Fazande	1.00
30	Ebenezer Ekuban	1.00

1999 Playoff Prestige SSD For the Record

Each card in this set has a player that broke a record in 1998 or projections for a player in 1999. They were printed on a holographic foil board with the name in gold foil. Singles were found 1:161 packs.

		NM/M
Common Player:		5.00
Inserted 1:161		
1	Mark Brunell	12.00
2	Jerry Rice	18.00
3	Peyton Manning	20.00
4	Barry Sanders	22.00
5	Deion Sanders	5.00
6	Eddie George	10.00
7	Corey Dillon	5.00
8	Jerome Bettis	5.00
9	Curtis Martin	5.00
10	Ricky Williams	20.00
11	Jake Plummer	10.00
12	Emmitt Smith	22.00
13	Dan Marino	25.00
14	Terrell Davis	20.00
15	Fred Taylor	15.00
16	Warrick Dunn	10.00
17	Steve McNair	5.00
18	Cris Carter	5.00
19	Mike Alstott	5.00
20	Steve Young	15.00
21	Charlie Batch	5.00
22	Tim Couch	15.00
23	Jamal Anderson	5.00
24	Randy Moss	20.00
25	Brett Favre	25.00
26	Drew Bledsoe	15.00
27	Troy Aikman	15.00
28	John Elway	15.00
29	Kordell Stewart	8.00
30	Keyshawn Johnson	5.00

1999 Playoff Prestige SSD Gridiron Heritage

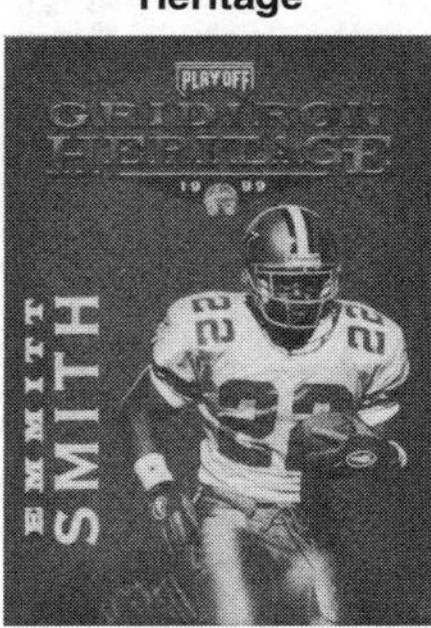

Each card in this 24-card set tracks the players career from high school to the NFL. Each is printed on actual leather and were inserted 1:33 packs.

		NM/M
Complete Set (24):		210.00
Common Player:		4.00
Inserted 1:33		
1	Randy Moss	20.00
2	Terrell Davis	15.00
3	Brett Favre	25.00
4	Barry Sanders	20.00
5	Peyton Manning	20.00
6	John Elway	15.00
7	Fred Taylor	10.00
8	Cris Carter	4.00
9	Jamal Anderson	4.00
10	Jake Plummer	6.00
11	Steve Young	15.00
12	Mark Brunell	8.00
13	Dan Marino	25.00
14	Emmitt Smith	20.00
15	Deion Sanders	4.00
16	Troy Aikman	15.00
17	Drew Bledsoe	15.00
18	Jerry Rice	15.00
19	Ricky Williams	15.00
20	Tim Couch	10.00
21	Jerome Bettis	4.00
22	Eddie George	6.00
23	Marshall Faulk	4.00
24	Terrell Owens	6.00

1999 Playoff Prestige SSD Inside the Numbers

Each card in this 20-card set is printed on clear plastic and each is sequentially numbered to a different number. Overall odds for these cards were 1:49 packs.

		NM/M
Complete Set (20):		140.00
Common Player:		3.00
Inserted 1:49		
1	Tim Brown 1012	5.00
2	Charlie Batch 2178	3.00
3	Deion Sanders 226	5.00
4	Eddie George 1294	6.00
5	Keyshawn Johnson 1131	5.00
6	Jamal Anderson 1846	3.00
7	Steve Young 4170	12.00
8	Tim Couch 4275	10.00
9	Ricky Williams 6279	12.00
10	Jerry Rice 1157	12.00
11	Randy Moss 1313	12.00
12	Edgerrin James 1416	12.00
13	Peyton Manning 3739	10.00
14	John Elway 2803	10.00
15	Terrell Davis 2008	10.00
16	Fred Taylor 1213	6.00
17	Brett Favre 4212	12.00
18	Jake Plummer 3737	5.00
19	Mark Brunell 2601	5.00
20	Barry Sanders 1491	10.00

A card number in parenthese ( ) indicates the set is unnumbered.

1999 Playoff Prestige SSD Barry Sanders

This is a 10-card set that celebrates Sanders ten years of pursuit for the rushing record. Singles were found 1:161 packs.

	NM/M
Complete Set (10):	300.00
Common Player:	30.00
Inserted 1:161	

2000 Playoff Absolute

		NM/M
Complete Set (250):		200.00
Common Player:		.15
Minor Stars:		.30
Common Rookies:		1.50
Production 3,000 Sets		
Pack (6):		3.50
Wax Box (20):		50.00
1	Frank Sanders	.30
2	Rob Moore	.30
3	Jake Plummer	.50
4	David Boston	.50
5	Chris Chandler	.30
6	Tim Dwight	.50
7	Terance Mathis	.15
8	Jamal Anderson	.30
9	Priest Holmes	.50
10	Tony Banks	.30
11	Jermaine Lewis	.15
12	Qadry Ismail	.15
13	Brandon Stokley	.30
14	Shannon Sharpe	.30
15	Trent Dilfer	.30
16	Eric Moulds	.50
17	Doug Flutie	.75
18	Antowain Smith	.30
19	Jonathon Linton	.30
20	Peerless Price	.30
21	Rob Johnson	.30
22	Muhsin Muhammad	.30
23	Wesley Walls	.30
24	Tim Biakabutuka	.30
25	Steve Beuerlein	.30
26	Patrick Jeffers	.50
27	Natrone Means	.30
28	Curtis Enis	.30
29	Bobby Engram	.15
30	Marcus Robinson	.50
31	Marty Booker	.15
32	Cade McNown	.50
33	Darnay Scott	.30
34	Carl Pickens	.30
35	Corey Dillon	.50
36	Akili Smith	.50
37	Michael Basnight	.15
38	Karim Abdul	.30
39	Tim Couch	1.25
40	Kevin Johnson	.50
41	Darrin Chiaverini	.15
42	Errict Rhett	.30
43	Emmitt Smith	1.75
44	Michael Irvin	.30
45	Raghib Ismail	.15
46	Troy Aikman	1.50
47	Jason Tucker	.30
48	Randall Cunningham	.30
49	Joey Galloway	.50
50	Ed McCaffrey	.50
51	Rod Smith	.30
52	Brian Griese	.75
53	John Elway	2.00
54	Terrell Davis	1.00
55	Olandis Gary	.50
56	Johnnie Morton	.30
57	Charlie Batch	.50
58	Barry Sanders	2.00
59	Germane Crowell	.50
60	Herman Moore	.50
61	James Stewart	.30
62	Corey Bradford	.15
63	Dorsey Levens	.50
64	Antonio Freeman	.50
65	Brett Favre	2.50
66	Bill Schroeder	.15
67	Marvin Harrison	.50
68	Peyton Manning	1.75
69	Terrence Wilkins	.30
70	Edgerrin James	2.00
71	Keenan McCardell	.30
72	Mark Brunell	1.00
73	Fred Taylor	1.00
74	Jimmy Smith	.50
75	Elvis Grbac	.30
76	Tony Gonzalez	.30
77	Donnell Bennett	.15
78	Warren Moon	.30
79	Kimble Anders	.15
80	Dan Marino	2.00
81	O.J. McDuffie	.30
82	Tony Martin	.15
83	James Johnson	.30
84	Thurman Thomas	.30
85	Randy Moss	2.00
86	Cris Carter	.50
87	Robert Smith	.50
88	Daunte Culpepper	1.25
89	Terry Glenn	.50
90	Drew Bledsoe	1.00
91	Kevin Faulk	.30
92	Ricky Williams	1.50
93	Jeff Blake	.30
94	Jake Reed	.30
95	Amani Toomer	.30
96	Kerry Collins	.30
97	Tiki Barber	.30
98	Ike Hilliard	.30
99	Curtis Martin	.50
100	Vinny Testaverde	.50
101	Wayne Chrebet	.50
102	Ray Lucas	.30
103	Tyrone Wheatley	.30
104	Napoleon Kaufman	.50
105	Tim Brown	.50
106	Rich Gannon	.30
107	Duce Staley	.50
108	Donovan McNabb	2.00
109	Kordell Stewart	.50
110	Jerome Bettis	.50
111	Troy Edwards	.50
112	Junior Seau	.30
113	Jim Harbaugh	.30
114	Ryan Leaf	.50
115	Jermaine Fazande	.30
116	Curtis Conway	.30
117	Terrell Owens	.50
118	Charlie Garner	.30
119	Jerry Rice	1.50
120	Steve Young	1.00
121	Jeff Garcia	.50
122	Derrick Mayes	.30
123	Ricky Watters	.50
124	Jon Kitna	.50
125	Sean Dawkins	.15
126	Az-Zahir Hakim	.30
127	Isaac Bruce	.50
128	Marshall Faulk	.60
129	Trent Green	.50
130	Kurt Warner	2.00
131	Torry Holt	.50
132	Jacquez Green	.30
133	Warren Sapp	.30
134	Mike Alstott	.50
135	Warrick Dunn	.50
136	Shaun King	.50
137	Keyshawn Johnson	.50
138	Eddie George	.60
139	Yancey Thigpen	.30
140	Steve McNair	.50
141	Kevin Dyson	.30
142	Frank Wycheck	.15
143	Jevon Kearse	.50
144	Stephen Davis	.50
145	Brad Johnson	.50
146	Michael Westbrook	.30
147	Albert Connell	.30
148	Bruce Smith	.30
149	Jeff George	.30
150	Deion Sanders	.50
151	*Peter Warrick*	3.00
152	*Courtney Brown*	3.00
153	*Plaxico Burress*	8.00
154	*Corey Simon*	4.00
155	*Thomas Jones*	5.00
156	*Travis Taylor*	4.00
157	*Shaun Alexander*	10.00
158	*Chris Redman*	4.00
159	*Chad Pennington*	15.00
160	*Jamal Lewis*	10.00
161	*Brian Urlacher*	8.00
162	*Bubba Franks*	5.00
163	*Dez White*	3.00
164	*Ahmed Plummer*	1.50
165	*Ron Dayne*	3.00
166	*Shaun Ellis*	1.50
167	*Sylvester Morris*	1.50
168	*Deltha O'Neal*	1.50
169	*R. Jay Soward*	2.50
170	*Sherrod Gideon*	1.50
171	*John Abraham*	1.50
172	*Travis Prentice*	4.00
173	*Darrell Jackson*	6.00
174	*Giovanni Carmazzi*	4.00
175	*Anthony Lucas*	1.50
176	*Danny Farmer*	2.50
177	*Dennis Northcutt*	3.00
178	*Troy Walters*	2.00
179	*Laveranues Coles*	4.00
180	*Kwame Cavil*	1.50
181	*Tee Martin*	4.00
182	*J.R. Redmond*	3.00
183	*Tim Rattay*	4.00
184	*Jerry Porter*	6.00
185	*Sebastian Janikowski*	2.50
186	*Michael Wiley*	2.50
187	*Reuben Droughns*	5.00
188	*Trung Canidate*	3.00
189	*Shyrone Stith*	2.00
190	*Ian Gold*	1.50
191	*Hank Poteat*	1.50
192	*Darren Howard*	1.50
193	*Rob Morris*	1.50
194	*Marc Bulger*	8.00
195	*Tom Brady*	30.00
196	*Doug Johnson*	3.00
197	*Todd Husak*	2.00
198	*Gari Scott*	1.50
199	*Erron Kinney*	1.50
200	*Nate Webster*	1.50
201	*Anthony Becht*	1.50
202	*Sammy Morris*	3.00
203	*Rondell Mealey*	2.00
204	*Doug Chapman*	1.50
205	*Rogers Beckett*	1.50
206	*Ron Dugans*	2.50
207	*Deon Dyer*	1.50
208	*Marcus Knight*	1.50
209	*Thomas Hamner*	1.50
210	*Joe Hamilton*	3.00
211	*Todd Pinkston*	3.00
212	*Chris Cole*	1.50
213	*Ron Dixon*	3.00
214	*JaJuan Dawson*	3.00
215	*Terrelle Smith*	1.50
216	*Curtis Keaton*	2.00
217	*Keith Bulluck*	1.50
218	*John Engelberger*	1.50
219	*Raynoch Thompson*	1.50
220	*Cornelius Griffin*	1.50
221	*William Bartee*	1.50
222	*Fred Robbins*	1.50
223	*Dwayne Goodrich*	1.50
224	*Deon Grant*	1.50
225	*Jacoby Shepherd*	1.50
226	*Ben Kelly*	1.50
227	*Corey Moore*	1.50
228	*Aaron Shea*	1.50
229	*Trevor Gaylor*	2.50
230	*Frank Moreau*	2.50
231	*Avion Black*	1.50
232	*Paul Smith*	1.50
233	*Dante Hall*	8.00
234	*Muneer Moore*	1.50
235	*James Whalen*	1.50
236	*Chad Morton*	2.50
237	*Frank Murphy*	1.50
238	*Mareno Philyaw*	1.50
239	*James Williams*	1.50
240	*Mike Anderson*	4.00
241	*Jarious Jackson*	2.50
242	*Demario Brown*	1.50
243	*Chris Coleman*	1.50
244	*Rashard Anderson*	1.50
245	*John Jones*	1.50
246	*Erik Flowers*	1.50
247	*JaJuan Seider*	1.50
248	*Leon Murray*	1.50
249	*Bashir Yamini*	1.50
250	*Na'il Diggs*	1.50

2000 Playoff Absolute Coaches Honors

Coaches Honors Cards:	2X-6X
Coaches Honors Rookies:	2X
Production 300 Sets	

2000 Playoff Absolute Players Honors

Production 10 Sets too limited to price

2000 Playoff Absolute Boss Hoggs

		NM/M
Complete Set (20):		600.00
Common Player:		12.00
Minor Stars:		20.00
Inserted 1:298		
Production 200 Sets		
1	Eric Moulds	20.00
2	Cade McNown	20.00
3	Tim Couch	35.00
4	Terrell Davis	45.00
5	Barry Sanders	75.00
6	Peyton Manning	75.00
7	Edgerrin James	65.00
8	Marvin Harrison	24.00
9	Mark Brunell	30.00
10	Fred Taylor	30.00
11	Dan Marino	85.00
12	Cris Carter	24.00
13	Drew Bledsoe	30.00
14	Ricky Williams	40.00
15	Curtis Martin	24.00
16	Kurt Warner	75.00
17	Isaac Bruce	24.00
18	Eddie George	30.00
19	Steve McNair	24.00
20	Brad Johnson	12.00

2000 Playoff Absolute Canton Absolutes

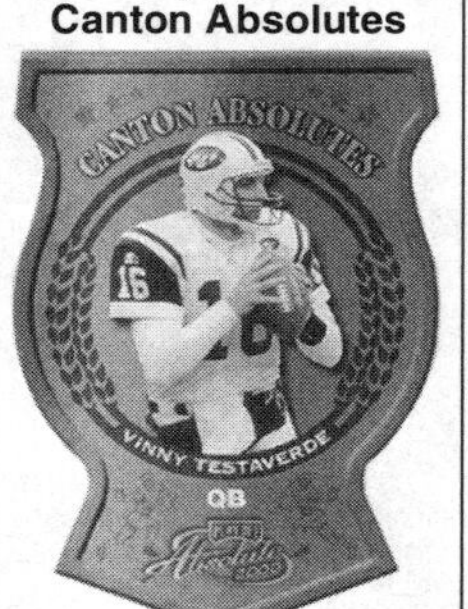

		NM/M
Complete Set (30):		110.00
Common Player:		1.00
Minor Stars:		2.00
Inserted 1:39		
1	Tim Couch	6.00
2	Emmitt Smith	10.00
3	Troy Aikman	8.00
4	John Elway	8.00
5	Terrell Davis	8.00
6	Barry Sanders	10.00
7	Brett Favre	12.00
8	Peyton Manning	8.00
9	Edgerrin James	8.00
10	Mark Brunell	4.00
11	Dan Marino	12.00
12	Randy Moss	8.00
13	Drew Bledsoe	6.00
14	Jerry Rice	8.00
15	Steve Young	5.00
16	Kurt Warner	6.00
17	Eddie George	5.00
18	Deion Sanders	2.00
19	Antonio Freeman	2.00
20	Warren Moon	1.00
21	Cris Carter	2.00
22	Randall Cunningham	2.00
23	Curtis Martin	2.00
24	Tim Brown	4.00
25	Marshall Faulk	5.00
26	Michael Irvin	2.00
27	Thurman Thomas	2.00
28	Vinny Testaverde	1.00
29	Ricky Watters	1.00
30	Jeff George	1.00

2000 Playoff Absolute Extreme Team

		NM/M
Complete Set (40):		90.00
Common Player:		1.00
Minor Stars:		2.00
Inserted 1:18		
1	Jake Plummer	2.00
2	Tim Couch	4.00
3	Terrell Davis	6.00
4	Brett Favre	10.00
5	Peyton Manning	8.00
6	Edgerrin James	6.00
7	Mark Brunell	4.00
8	Fred Taylor	4.00
9	Randy Moss	8.00
10	Drew Bledsoe	5.00
11	Ricky Williams	6.00
12	Kurt Warner	5.00
13	Eddie George	3.50
14	Cade McNown	2.00
15	Kevin Johnson	2.00
16	Joey Galloway	2.00
17	Olandis Gary	2.00
18	Dorsey Levens	2.00
19	Marvin Harrison	4.00
20	Daunte Culpepper	5.00
21	Duce Staley	2.00
22	Donovan McNabb	4.00
23	Marshall Faulk	3.50
24	Shaun King	2.00
25	Keyshawn Johnson	2.00
26	Steve McNair	2.00
27	Stephen Davis	2.00
28	Brad Johnson	1.00
29	Akili Smith	2.00
30	Brian Griese	2.00
31	Emmitt Smith	8.00
32	Isaac Bruce	2.00
33	Peter Warrick	2.00
34	Jamal Lewis	6.00
35	Thomas Jones	5.00
36	Plaxico Burress	6.00
37	Travis Taylor	4.00
38	Ron Dayne	3.00
39	Chad Pennington	10.00
40	Shaun Alexander	8.00

2000 Playoff Absolute Ground Hoggs

		NM/M
Common Player:		25.00
Inserted 1:188		
Production 135 Sets		
Autographs:		3X
#1,9,17,22 & 28 signed their first 25 cards.		
1	Jake Plummer	25.00
2	Muhsin Muhammad 75	25.00
3	Emmitt Smith	85.00
4	Ricky Watters	25.00
5	Terrell Davis	75.00
6	Brett Favre	100.00
7	Dorsey Levens	25.00
8	Antonio Freeman	25.00
9	Edgerrin James	85.00
10	Marvin Harrison	25.00
11	Mark Brunell	50.00
12	Fred Taylor	50.00
13	Jimmy Smith	25.00
14	James Johnson	25.00
15	Dan Marino	125.00
16	Jon Kitna	25.00
17	Ricky Williams	50.00
18	Curtis Martin	35.00
19	Wayne Chrebet	25.00
20	Steve Young	60.00
21	Junior Seau	25.00
22	Kurt Warner	125.00
23	Marshall Faulk	45.00
24	Eddie George	45.00
25	Steve McNair	25.00
26	Joey Galloway	25.00
27	Jerry Rice	85.00
28	Jevon Kearse	30.00
29	Stephen Davis	25.00
30	Albert Connell	25.00

2000 Playoff Absolute Hogg Heaven Points

		NM/M
Common Player:		10.00
500 points redeemable for autographed fb		
1	Cade McNown	10.00
2	Jim Harbaugh	10.00
3	Brad Johnson	10.00
4	Steve Young	20.00
5	Jake Plummer	15.00
6	Chris Chandler	10.00
7	Tony Banks	10.00

8 Bubby Brister 10.00
9 Kordell Stewart 15.00
10 Warren Moon 15.00
11 Donovan McNabb 20.00
12 Jim Kelly 15.00
13 Peyton Manning 35.00
14 Hogg Heaven 10.00

2000 Playoff Absolute Leather

NM/M
Common Player 350: 12.00
Common Player 175: 15.00
Laces Numbered to 20: 3X
Laces Numbered to 10: 4X
TA8 Troy Aikman 175 50.00
MA40 Mike Alstott 350 15.00
RA85 Reidel Anthony 175 15.00
MB35 Michael Basnight 175 15.00
JB36 Jerome Bettis 350 15.00
SB7 Steve Beuerlein 350 12.00
TB21 Tim Biakabutuka 350 12.00
JB18 Jeff Blake 175 15.00
DB11 Drew Bledsoe 350 30.00
DB89 David Boston 350 15.00
TB81 Tim Brown 350 15.00
IB80 Isaac Bruce 350 20.00
MB8A Mark Brunell 350 30.00
MB8B Mark Brunell 175 50.00
CC80 Cris Carter 175 20.00
DC84 Darren Chiaverini 175 15.00
WC80 WayneChrebet 175 20.00
BC85 Ben Coates 175 15.00
AC83 Albert Connell 175 15.00
CC80 Curtis Conway 175 15.00
TC2 Tim Couch 350 30.00
RC7 Randall Cunningham 175 15.00
SD48 Stephen Davis 175 20.00
TD30 Terrell Davis 175 60.00
TD7 Trent Dilfer 175 15.00
CD28 Corey Dillon 350 20.00
RD83 Rickey Dudley 175 15.00
WD28 Warrick Dunn 350 15.00
TD83 Tim Dwight 350 15.00
KD87 Kevin Dyson 175 15.00
TE81 Troy Edwards 350 15.00
JE7 John Elway 175 100.00
BE81 Bobby Engram 175 15.00
CE44 Curtis Enis 350 12.00
MF28A Marshall Faulk 175 30.00
MF28B Marshall Faulk 175 30.00
BF4A Brett Favre 350 60.00
BF4B Brett Favre 175 85.00
AF86A Antonio Freeman 350 15.00
AF86B Antonio Freeman 175 20.00
OG86 Oronde Gadsden 175 15.00
RG12 Rich Gannon 175 15.00
JG5 Jeff Garcia 350 25.00
CG25 Charlie Garner 350 12.00
EG27A Eddie George 350 25.00
EG27B Eddie George 175 40.00
JG87 Jami Germaine 175 15.00
TG88 Terry Glenn 175 20.00
JH4 Jim Harbaugh 175 15.00
MH88 Marvin Harrison 175 25.00
PH33 Priest Holmes 175 20.00
TH88 Torry Holt 175 20.00
DH11 Damon Huard 175 20.00
QI87 Qadry Ismail 175 15.00
RI81 Raghib Ismail 175 15.00
EJ32 Edgerrin James 175 65.00
BJ14 Brad Johnson 175 20.00
JJ32 James Johnson 350 12.00
KJ85 Kevin Johnson 350 15.00
KJ19 Keyshawn Johnson 175 20.00
RJ11 Rob Johnson 175 20.00
NK26 Napoleon Kaufman 175 20.00
JK90A Jevon Kearse 350 15.00
JK90B Jevon Kearse 175 20.00
LK99 LaVonne Kirkland 175 15.00
DL25A Dorsey Levens 350 15.00
DL25B Dorsey Levens 175 20.00
JL84 Jermaine Lewis 175 15.00
SM29 Sam Madison 175 15.00
PM18 Peyton Manning 350 70.00
DM13 Dan Marino 350 75.00
CM28 Curtis Martin 175 20.00
TM80 Tony Martin 175 15.00
TM81 Terance Mathis 175 15.00
BM74 Bruce Matthews 175 15.00
DM87 Derrick Mayes 175 15.00
EM87 Ed McCaffrey 175 20.00
KM87 Keenan McCardell 350 15.00
OM81 O.J. McDuffie 175 15.00
DM5 Donovan McNabb 350 25.00
SM9A Steve McNair 350 20.00
SM9B Steve McNair 175 25.00
NM20 Natrone Means 175 15.00
HM84 Herman Moore 175 20.00
RM85 Rob Moore 350 12.00
JM87 Johnnie Morton 175 15.00
RM84 Randy Moss 175 85.00
EM80 Eric Moulds 350 15.00
MM87 Muhsin Muhammad 350 12.00
NO14 Neil O'Donnell 175 15.00
TO81A Terrell Owens 175 25.00
TO81B Terrell Owens 175 25.00
CP81 Carl Pickens 175 15.00
JP16 Jake Plummer 350 20.00
PP81 Peerless Price 175 20.00
ER23 Errict Rhett 175 15.00
JR80A Jerry Rice 350 40.00
JR80B Jerry Rice 175 65.00
BS20 Barry Sanders 350 60.00
DS21 Deion Sanders 175 20.00
FS81 Frank Sanders 350 15.00
WS99 Warren Sapp 350 15.00
DS86 Darnay Scott 175 15.00
JS55 Junior Seau 175 20.00
AS11 Akili Smith 350 20.00
AS23 Antowain Smith 350 15.00
BS78 Bruce Smith 350 15.00
ES22 Emmitt Smith 175 70.00
JS82 Jimmy Smith 350 15.00
RS26 Robert Smith 175 20.00
RS80 Rod Smith 175 20.00
DS22 Duce Staley 350 15.00
JS33 James Stewart 350 15.00
KS10 Kordell Stewart 350 20.00
JS83 J.J. Stokes 175 20.00
FT28A Fred Taylor 350 25.00
FT28B Fred Taylor 175 40.00
VT16 Vinny Testaverde 175 20.00
YT82 Yancey Thigpen 175 20.00
TT34 Thurman Thomas 350 15.00
ZT54 Zach Thomas 175 20.00
HW86 Hines Ward 175 20.00
KW13A Kurt Warner 350 70.00
KW13B Kurt Warner 175 85.00
MW82 Michael Westbrook 175 20.00
TW47 Tyrone Wheatley 175 20.00
RW92 Reggie White 350 15.00
RW34 Ricky Williams 350 40.00
FW89 Frank Wycheck 175 15.00
SY8 Steve Young 350 30.00

2000 Playoff Absolute Rookie Reflex

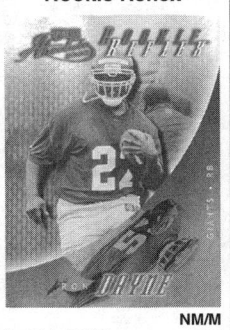

NM/M
Complete Set (30): 40.00
Common Player: 1.00
Minor Stars: 2.00
Inserted 1:10
Gold Cards: 2X-4X
Production 100 Sets
1 Peter Warrick 2.00
2 Jamal Lewis 6.00
3 Thomas Jones 5.00
4 Plaxico Burress 5.00
5 Travis Taylor 3.00
6 Ron Dayne 2.00
7 Bubba Franks 2.00
8 Chad Pennington 10.00
9 Shaun Alexander 6.00
10 Sylvester Morris 3.00
11 R. Jay Soward 2.00
12 Trung Canidate 1.00
13 Dennis Northcutt 2.00
14 Todd Pinkston 2.00
15 Jerry Porter 1.00
16 Travis Prentice 3.50
17 Giovanni Carmazzi 2.00
18 Ron Dugans 1.00
19 Erron Kinney 1.00
20 Dez White 1.00
21 Chris Cole 1.00
22 Doug Chapman 1.00
23 Chris Redman 4.00
24 J.R. Redmond 3.00
25 Laveranues Coles 5.00
26 JaJuan Dawson 2.00
27 Darrell Jackson 3.00
28 Reuben Droughns 1.00
29 Curtis Keaton 1.00
30 Gari Scott 1.00

2000 Playoff Absolute Tag Team Quads

NM/M
Complete Set (31): 300.00
Common Player: 10.00
Inserted 1:79
1 Jake Plummer, David Boston, Thomas Jones, Frank Sanders 12.00
2 Jamal Anderson, Tim Dwight, Chris Chandler, Terance Mathis 10.00
3 Tony Banks, Travis Taylor, Shannon Sharpe, Jamal Lewis 30.00
4 Rob Johnson, Eric Moulds, Antowain Smith, Peerless Price 10.00
5 Steve Beuerlein, Tim Biakabutuka, Patrick Jeffers, Muhsin Muhammad 10.00
6 Curtis Enis, Cade McNown, Marcus Robinson, Dez White 12.00
7 Corey Dillon, Akili Smith, Peter Warrick, Ron Dugans 25.00
8 Tim Couch, Errict Rhett, Kevin Johnson, Courtney Brown 15.00
9 Raghib Ismail, Emmitt Smith, Troy Aikman, Joey Galloway 25.00
10 Terrell Davis, Ed McCaffrey, Olandis Gary, Brian Griese 20.00
11 James Stewart, Charlie Batch, Herman Moore, Germane Crowell 10.00
12 Brett Favre, Bubba Franks, Dorsey Levens, Antonio Freeman 25.00
13 Peyton Manning, Marvin Harrison, Edgerrin James, Terrence Wilkins 30.00
14 Keenan McCardell, Mark Brunell, Jimmy Smith, Fred Taylor 15.00
15 Elvis Grbac, Sylvester Morris, Tony Gonzalez, Derrick Alexander 12.00
16 James Johnson, O.J. McDuffie, Tony Martin, Damon Huard 10.00
17 Randy Moss, Robert Smith, Cris Carter, Daunte Culpepper 30.00
18 Drew Bledsoe, Kevin Faulk, J.R. Redmond, Terry Glenn 15.00
19 Sherrod Gideon, Ricky Williams, Jeff Blake, Jake Reed 12.00
20 Kerry Collins, Amani Toomer, Ron Dayne, Ike Hilliard 20.00
21 Curtis Martin, Wayne Chrebet, Chad Pennington, Vinny Testaverde 15.00
22 Tim Brown, Napoleon Kaufman, Rich Gannon, Tyrone Wheatley 10.00
23 Donovan McNabb, Corey Simon, Todd Pinkston, Duce Staley 12.00
24 Plaxico Burress, Troy Edwards, Kordell Stewart, Jerome Bettis 12.00
25 Jim Harbaugh, Junior Seau, Curtis Conway, Jermaine Fazande 10.00
26 Charlie Garner, Jerry Rice, Terrell Owens, Steve Young 15.00
27 Derrick Mayes, Shaun Alexander, Ricky Watters, Jon Kitna 12.00
28 Kurt Warner, Torry Holt, Isaac Bruce, Marshall Faulk 30.00
29 Warrick Dunn, Keyshawn Johnson, Shaun King, Mike Alstott 12.00
30 Kevin Dyson, Eddie George, Steve McNair, Jevon Kearse 12.00
31 Albert Connell, Brad Johnson, Michael Westbrook, Stephen Davis 10.00

2000 Playoff Absolute Tools of the Trade

NM/M
Complete Set (60): 200.00
Common Player (#1-20): 2.00
Production 2,000 Sets
Die-Cut Cards (#1-20): 3X-8X
Production 25 Sets
Common Player (#21-40): 2.50
Production 1,500 Sets
Die-Cut Cards (#21-40): 2X-5X
Production 50 Sets
Common Player (#41-60): 3.00
Production 1,000 Sets
Die-Cut Cards (#41-60): 3X
Production 100 Sets
1 Jake Plummer 2.50
2 Tim Couch 4.00
3 Troy Aikman 7.00
4 John Elway 8.00
5 Charlie Batch 2.00
6 Brett Favre 12.00
7 Peyton Manning 10.00
8 Mark Brunell 4.00
9 Dan Marino 12.00
10 Drew Bledsoe 4.00
11 Steve Young 4.00
12 Kurt Warner 6.00
13 Cade McNown 2.50
14 Daunte Culpepper 4.00
15 Donovan McNabb 3.00
16 Jon Kitna 2.00
17 Steve McNair 2.00
18 Brad Johnson 2.00
19 Akili Smith 2.00
20 Chad Pennington 8.00
21 Emmitt Smith 10.00
22 Terrell Davis 8.00
23 Barry Sanders 10.00
24 Edgerrin James 8.00
25 Fred Taylor 4.00
26 Ricky Williams 6.00
27 Eddie George 4.00
28 Jamal Anderson 2.50
29 Corey Dillon 2.50
30 Dorsey Levens 2.50
31 Robert Smith 2.50
32 Curtis Martin 2.50
33 Jerome Bettis 2.50
34 Marshall Faulk 3.00
35 Stephen Davis 2.50
36 Jamal Lewis 15.00
37 Thomas Jones 6.00
38 Ron Dayne 5.00
39 Shaun Alexander 10.00
40 Trung Canidate 2.50
41 Randy Moss 10.00
42 Jerry Rice 10.00
43 Eric Moulds 4.00
44 Kevin Johnson 3.00
45 Joey Galloway 4.00
46 Antonio Freeman 4.00
47 Marvin Harrison 4.00
48 Cris Carter 4.00
49 Tim Brown 3.00
50 Terrell Owens 4.00
51 Keyshawn Johnson 4.00
52 Muhsin Muhammad 3.00
53 Patrick Jeffers 4.00
54 Marcus Robinson 4.00
55 Jimmy Smith 4.00
56 Amani Toomer 3.00
57 Isaac Bruce 4.00
58 Peter Warrick 3.00
59 Plaxico Burress 10.00
60 Travis Taylor 6.00

2000 Playoff Contenders

NM/M
Complete Set (200): 2,250
Common Player: .15
Minor Stars: .50
Common Rookie: 8.00
Common Europe Ticket: 5.00
Common Playoff Ticket: 20.00
Pack (5): 16.00
Wax Box (12): 145.00
1 David Boston .75
2 Jake Plummer .75
3 Chris Chandler .50
4 Jamal Anderson .75
5 Tim Dwight .75
6 Qadry Ismail .15
7 Tony Banks .50
8 Lamar Smith .50
9 Doug Flutie .50
10 Eric Moulds .75
11 Peerless Price .75
12 Rob Johnson .50
13 Muhsin Muhammad .50
14 Reggie White .50
15 Steve Beuerlein .50
16 Cade McNown .75
17 Derrick Alexander .15
18 Marcus Robinson .75
19 Akili Smith .75
20 Corey Dillon .75
21 Kevin Johnson .75
22 Tim Couch 1.50
23 Emmitt Smith 2.00
24 Joey Galloway .75
25 Raghib Ismail .15
26 Troy Aikman 1.50
27 Brian Griese 1.00
28 Ed McCaffrey .50
29 John Elway 2.00
30 Olandis Gary .75
31 Rod Smith .75
32 Terrell Davis 1.00
33 Charlie Batch .75
34 Germane Crowell .50
35 James Stewart .50
36 Barry Sanders 2.00
37 Antonio Freeman .75
38 Brett Favre 3.00
39 Dorsey Levens .75
40 Edgerrin James 2.50
41 Marvin Harrison .75
42 Peyton Manning 3.00
43 Fred Taylor 1.25
44 Jimmy Smith .75
45 Mark Brunell 1.25
46 Elvis Grbac .50
47 Tony Gonzalez .50
48 Dan Marino 2.00
49 Joe Horn .50
50 Jay Fiedler .50
51 Thurman Thomas .50
52 Cris Carter .75
53 Daunte Culpepper 1.50
54 Randy Moss 2.50
55 Robert Smith .75
56 Drew Bledsoe 1.25
57 Terry Glenn .75
58 Ricky Williams 1.50
59 Amani Toomer .50
60 Kerry Collins .50
61 Curtis Martin .75
62 Vinny Testaverde .50
63 Wayne Chrebet .75
64 Rich Gannon .50
65 Tim Brown .75
66 Tyrone Wheatley .50
67 Donovan McNabb 2.00
68 Duce Staley .75
69 Jerome Bettis .75
70 Jermaine Fazande .50
71 Junior Seau .50
72 Donald Hayes .50
73 Charlie Garner .50
74 Jeff Garcia .75
75 Jerry Rice 1.50
76 Steve Young 1.25
77 Terrell Owens .75
78 Tiki Barber .50
79 Tim Biakabutuka .50
80 Ricky Watters .50
81 Isaac Bruce .75
82 Kurt Warner 3.00
83 Marshall Faulk 1.00
84 Torry Holt .75
85 Keyshawn Johnson .75
86 Mike Alstott .75
87 Shaun King .75
88 Warren Sapp .50
89 Warrick Dunn .75
90 Eddie George 1.00
91 Jevon Kearse .75
92 Steve McNair .75
93 Carl Pickens .50
94 Albert Connell .50
95 Brad Johnson .50
96 Bruce Smith .50
97 Deion Sanders .75
98 Jeff George .50
99 Michael Westbrook .50
100 Stephen Davis .75
101 *Courtney Brown SP* 60.00
102 *Corey Simon* 20.00
103 *Brian Urlacher* 75.00
104 *Deon Grant* 8.00
105 *Peter Warrick* 50.00
106 *Jamal Lewis* 60.00
107 *Thomas Jones*
108 *Plaxico Burress* 50.00
109 *Travis Taylor* 20.00
110 *Ron Dayne* 20.00
111 *Bubba Franks* 35.00
112 *Chad Pennington* 150.00
113 *Shaun Alexander* 60.00
114 *Sylvester Morris* 8.00
115 *Mike Anderson* 25.00
116 *R. Jay Soward* 20.00
117 *Trung Canidate* 25.00
118 *Dennis Northcutt* 20.00
119 *Todd Pinkston* 20.00
120 *Jerry Porter* 50.00
121 *Travis Prentice* 20.00
122 *Giovanni Carmazzi* 20.00
123 *Ron Dugans* 15.00
124 *Dez White* 20.00
125 *Chris Cole* 12.00
126 *Ron Dixon* 15.00
127 *Chris Redman* 35.00
128 *J.R. Redmond* 15.00
129 *Laveranues Coles* 40.00
130 *JaJuan Dawson* 20.00
131 *Darrell Jackson* 25.00
132 *Reuben Droughns* 40.00
133 *Doug Chapman* 15.00
134 *Curtis Keaton* 12.00
135 *Gari Scott* 12.00
136 *Danny Farmer* 12.00
137 *Trevor Gaylor* 12.00
138 *Avion Black* 8.00
139 *Michael Wiley* 15.00
140 *Sammy Morris* 15.00
141 *Tee Martin* 15.00
142 *Troy Walters* 15.00
143 *Marc Bulger* 75.00
144 *Tom Brady* 300.00
145 *Todd Husak* 20.00
146 *Tim Rattay* 40.00
147 *Jarious Jackson* 25.00
148 *Joe Hamilton* 15.00
149 *Shyrone Stith* 12.00
150 *Kwame Cavil* 10.00
151 *Antonio Banks* 5.00
152 *Jonathan Brown* 5.00
153 *Ontiwaun Carter* 5.00
154 *Jeremaine Copeland* 5.00
155 *Ralph Dawkins* 5.00
156 *Marques Douglas* 5.00
157 *Kevin Drake* 5.00
158 *Damon Dunn* 5.00
159 *Todd Floyd* 5.00
160 *Tony Graziani* 8.00
161 *Derrick Ham* 5.00
162 *Duane Hawthorne* 5.00
163 *Alonzo Johnson* 5.00
164 *Mark Kacmarynski* 5.00
165 *Eric Kresser* 5.00
166 *Jim Kubiak* 5.00
167 *Blaine McElmurry* 5.00
168 *Scott Milanovich* 8.00
169 *Norman Miller* 5.00
170 *Sean Morey* 5.00
171 *Jeff Ogden* 8.00
172 *Pepe Pearson* 8.00
173 *Ron Powlus* 12.00
174 *Jason Shelley* 5.00
175 *Ben Snell* 5.00
176 *Aaron Stecker* 8.00
177 *L.C. Stevens* 5.00
178 *Mike Sutton* 5.00
179 *Damian Vaughn* 5.00
180 *Ted White* 5.00
181 *Marcus Crandell* 5.00
182 *Darryl Daniel* 5.00
183 *Jessie Haynes* 5.00
184 *Matt Lytle* 5.00
185 *Deon Mitchell* 5.00
186 *Kendrick Nord* 5.00
187 *Ronnie Powell* 5.00
188 *Selucio Sanford* 5.00
189 *Corey Thomas* 5.00
190 *Vershan Jackson* 5.00
191 Jake Plummer PT 20.00
192 Jim Kelly PT 30.00
193 Bernie Kosar PT 30.00
194 Marvin Harrison PT 25.00
195 Fred Taylor PT 30.00
196 Kerry Collins PT 25.00
197 Kurt Warner PT 75.00
198 Jevon Kearse PT 25.00
199 Brad Johnson PT 20.00
200 Jeff George PT 20.00

2000 Playoff Contenders Championship Ticket

NM/M
CT Cards: 4X-10X
CT European Ticket: 2X
CT Playoff Ticket: 1.5X
Production 100 Sets

2000 Playoff Contenders Championship Fabrics

NM/M
Common Player: 15.00
Single Jerseys #'d to 300
Single Pants #'d to 300
Single Jerseys/Pants #'d to 100
Double Jerseys #'d to 25
Double Pants #'d to 25
Double Jerseys/Pants #'d to 25
1 Az-Zahir Hakim P 20.00
2 Grant Wistrom P 15.00
3 Isaac Bruce P 25.00
4 Kevin Carter P 15.00
5 Kurt Warner P 45.00
6 Marshall Faulk P 25.00
7 Tony Horne P 15.00
8 Robert Holcombe P 15.00
9 Todd Collins P 15.00
10 Torry Holt P 25.00
11 Az-Zahir Hakim J 20.00
12 Grant Wistrom J 15.00
13 Isaac Bruce J 25.00
14 Kevin Carter J 15.00
15 Kurt Warner J 45.00
16 Marshall Faulk J 25.00
17 Tony Horne J 15.00
18 Robert Holcombe J 15.00
19 Todd Collins J 15.00
20 Torry Holt J 25.00
21 Az-Zahir Hakim PJ 40.00
22 Grant Wistrom PJ 30.00
23 Isaac Bruce PJ 85.00
24 Kevin Carter PJ 30.00
25 Kurt Warner PJ 100.00
26 Marshall Faulk PJ 85.00
27 Tony Horne PJ 30.00
28 Robert Holcombe PJ 30.00
29 Todd Collins PJ 30.00
30 Torry Holt PJ 40.00
31 Kurt Warner, Torry Holt P 150.00
32 Marshall Faulk, Isaac Bruce P 75.00
33 Tony Horne, Az-Zahir Hakim P 40.00
34 Grant Wistrom, Robert Holcombe P 30.00
35 Todd Collins, Kevin Carter P 30.00
36 Kurt Warner, Marshall Faulk J 150.00
37 Isaac Bruce, Torry Holt J 70.00
38 Kevin Carter, Az-Zahir Hakim J 40.00
39 Grant Wistrom, Robert Holcombe J 30.00
40 Todd Collins, Tony Horne J 40.00
41 Isaac Bruce, Kurt Warner PJ 150.00
42 Torry Holt, Marshall Faulk PJ 75.00
43 Az-Zahir Hakim, Robert Holcombe PJ 40.00
44 Kevin Carter, Tony Horne PJ 40.00
45 Grant Wistrom, Todd Collins PJ 40.00

A player's name in *italic* type indicates a rookie card.

2000 Playoff Contenders Hawaii Five-O

NM/M
Complete Set (50): 60.00
Common Player: .50
Minor Stars: 1.00
Inserted 1:11
1 Steve Beuerlein .50
2 Muhsin Muhammad 1.00
3 Jim Kelly 2.00
4 Doug Flutie 1.00
5 Reggie White 1.00
6 Corey Dillon 1.00
7 Emmitt Smith 6.00
8 Troy Aikman 5.00
9 Randall Cunningham 1.00
10 John Elway 5.00
11 Terrell Davis 5.00
12 Barry Sanders 6.00
13 Herman Moore .50
14 Brett Favre 7.00
15 Dorsey Levens .50
16 Antonio Freeman .50
17 Peyton Manning 5.00
18 Edgerrin James 5.00
19 Marvin Harrison 1.00
20 Mark Brunell 2.00
21 Jimmy Smith .50
22 Warren Moon 1.00
23 Dan Marino 7.00
24 Randy Moss 6.00
25 Cris Carter 1.00
26 Robert Smith 1.00
27 Drew Bledsoe 3.50
28 Tony Gonzalez .50
29 Rich Gannon .50
30 Curtis Martin 2.00
31 Vinny Testaverde .50
32 Frank Wycheck .50
33 Jerome Bettis 1.00
34 Junior Seau .50
35 Jerry Rice 5.00
36 Steve Young 3.50
37 Ricky Watters .50
38 Kurt Warner 5.00
39 Marshall Faulk 2.50
40 Isaac Bruce 1.00
41 Keyshawn Johnson 1.00
42 Mike Alstott 1.00
43 Warren Sapp .50
44 Eddie George 2.50
45 Jevon Kearse 1.00
46 Carl Pickens .50
47 Terry Glenn .50
48 Brad Johnson .50
49 Bruce Smith .50
50 Deion Sanders 1.00

2000 Playoff Contenders MVP Contenders

NM/M
Complete Set (30): 80.00
Common Player: 1.00
Minor Stars: 2.00
Inserted 1:35
1 Cade McNown 2.00
2 Tim Couch 5.00
3 Troy Aikman 7.00
4 Terrell Davis 7.00
5 Drew Bledsoe 7.00
6 Ricky Williams 7.00
7 Jerry Rice 10.00
8 Jamal Anderson 2.00
9 Dorsey Levens 2.00
10 Cris Carter 2.00
11 Emmitt Smith 12.00
12 Brett Favre 15.00
13 Peyton Manning 10.00
14 Edgerrin James 8.00
15 Fred Taylor 6.00
16 Randy Moss 10.00
17 Curtis Martin 2.00
18 Marshall Faulk 5.00
19 Steve McNair 2.00
20 Stephen Davis 2.00
21 Mark Brunell 7.00
22 Daunte Culpepper 7.00
23 Kurt Warner 8.00
24 Eddie George 5.00
25 Marvin Harrison 2.00
26 Isaac Bruce 2.00
27 Shaun King 5.00
28 Keyshawn Johnson 2.00
29 Brad Johnson 2.00
30 Jimmy Smith 2.00

2000 Playoff Contenders Quads

NM/M
Complete Set (15): 100.00
Common Player: 4.00
Inserted 1:59
1 Plaxico Burress, Jerome Bettis, Travis Prentice, Tim Couch 15.00
2 Troy Aikman, Emmitt Smith, Brad Johnson, Stephen Davis 12.00
3 Curtis Martin, Chad Pennington, Edgerrin James, Peyton Manning 18.00
4 Shaun King, Keyshawn Johnson, Daunte Culpepper, Randy Moss 12.00
5 Fred Taylor, Eddie George, Mark Brunell, Steve McNair 10.00
6 Ricky Watters, Jerry Porter, Tim Brown, Shaun Alexander 10.00
7 Antonio Freeman, Brett Favre, Marcus Robinson, Cade McNown 12.00
8 Donovan McNabb, Duce Staley, Kerry Collins, Ron Dayne 12.00
9 Jamal Lewis, Akili Smith, Peter Warrick, Travis Taylor 18.00
10 Jeff Blake, Ricky Williams, Thomas Jones, Jake Plummer 10.00
11 Jerry Rice, Terrell Owens, Marshall Faulk, Kurt Warner 15.00
12 Drew Bledsoe, Peerless Price, Terry Glenn, Eric Moulds 4.00
13 Terrell Davis, Brian Griese, Sylvester Morris, Elvis Grbac 12.00
14 Steve Beuerlein, Muhsin Muhammad, Jamal Anderson, Chris Chandler 4.00
15 Ryan Leaf, Jermaine Fazande, Jay Fiedler, Damon Huard 4.00

2000 Playoff Contenders Ultimate Quads

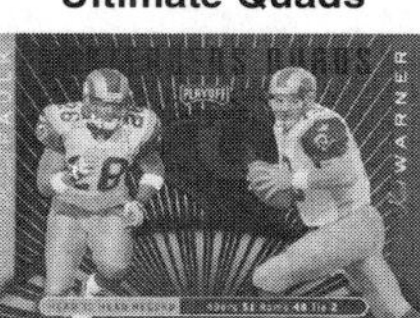

NM/M
Complete Set (15): 400.00
Common Player: 25.00
#'d to Stat
1 Plaxico Burress, Jerome Bettis, Travis Prentice, Tim Couch 94 30.00
2 Troy Aikman, Emmitt Smith, Brad Johnson, Stephen Davis 80 35.00
3 Curtis Martin, Chad Pennington, Edgerrin James, Peyton Manning 60 60.00
4 Shaun King, Keyshawn Johnson, Daunte Culpepper, Randy Moss 44 75.00
5 Fred Taylor, Eddie George, Mark Brunell, Steve McNair 10 75.00
6 Ricky Watters, Jerry Porter, Tim Brown, Shaun Alexander 44 40.00
7 Antonio Freeman, Brett Favre, Marcus Robinson, Cade McNown 159 30.00
8 Donovan McNabb, Duce Staley, Kerry Collins, Ron Dayne 131 30.00
9 Jamal Lewis, Akili Smith, Peter Warrick, Travis Taylor 8 150.00
10 Jeff Blake, Ricky Williams, Thomas Jones, Jake Plummer 22 45.00
11 Jerry Rice, Terrell Owens, Marshall Faulk, Kurt Warner 101 50.00
12 Drew Bledsoe, Peerless Price, Terry Glenn, Eric Moulds 80 25.00
13 Terrell Davis, Brian Griese, Sylvester Morris, Elvis Grbac 80 45.00
14 Steve Beuerlein, Muhsin Muhammad, Jamal Anderson, Chris Chandler 10 50.00
15 Ryan Leaf, Jermaine Fazande, Jay Fiedler, Damon Huard 21 25.00

A player's name in *italic* type indicates a rookie card.

2000 Playoff Contenders Round Numbers Autographs

NM/M
Common Player: 20.00
Inserted 1:173
1 Jamal Lewis, Travis Taylor 50.00
2 Thomas Jones, Shaun Alexander 50.00
3 Plaxico Burress, Chad Pennington 75.00
4 Sylvester Morris, R. Jay Soward 40.00
5 Todd Pinkston, Jerry Porter 20.00
6 J.R. Redmond, Doug Chapman 20.00
7 Giovanni Carmazzi, Chris Redman 35.00
8 Travis Prentice, JaJuan Dawson 25.00
9 Ron Dugans, Laveranues Coles 20.00
10 Corey Simon, Brian Urlacher 50.00
11 Marc Bulger, Tom Brady 60.00
12 Tim Rattay, Joe Hamilton 25.00
13 Trevor Gaylor, Avion Black 20.00
14 Chris Cole, Ron Dixon 20.00
15 Curtis Keaton, Gari Scott 20.00

2000 Playoff Contenders Round Numbers Autographs Gold

NM/M
Common Player: 30.00
Randomly Inserted
1 Jamal Lewis, Travis Taylor 10 125.00
2 Thomas Jones, Shaun Alexander 10 100.00
3 Plaxico Burress, Chad Pennington 10 175.00
4 Sylvester Morris, R. Jay Soward 10 85.00
5 Todd Pinkston, Jerry Porter 20 50.00
6 J.R. Redmond, Doug Chapman 30 40.00
7 Giovanni Carmazzi, Chris Redman 30 75.00
8 Travis Prentice, JaJuan Dawson 30 50.00
9 Ron Dugans, Laveranues Coles 30 50.00
10 Corey Simon, Brian Urlacher 10 100.00
11 Marc Bulger, Tom Brady 60 30.00
12 Tim Rattay, Joe Hamilton 70 40.00
13 Trevor Gaylor, Avion Black 40 30.00
14 Chris Cole, Ron Dixon 30 35.00
15 Curtis Keaton, Gari Scott 40 30.00

2000 Playoff Contenders ROY Contenders

NM/M
Complete Set (20): 40.00
Common Player: 1.00
Inserted 1:23
1 Thomas Jones 4.00
2 Jamal Lewis 6.00
3 Travis Taylor 3.00
4 Brian Urlacher 6.00
5 Peter Warrick 2.00
6 Travis Prentice 3.00
7 Courtney Brown 1.00
8 Bubba Franks 1.00
9 R. Jay Soward 1.00
10 Sylvester Morris 5.00
11 J.R. Redmond 3.00
12 Ron Dayne 2.00
13 Chad Pennington 8.00
14 Laveranues Coles 3.00
15 Jerry Porter 1.00
16 Todd Pinkston 1.00
17 Corey Simon 1.00
18 Plaxico Burress 5.00
19 Shaun Alexander 6.00
20 Darrell Jackson 3.00

2000 Playoff Contenders ROY Contenders Autographs

NM/M
Common Player: 25.00
Production 100 Sets
1 Thomas Jones 40.00
2 Jamal Lewis 75.00
3 Travis Taylor 30.00
4 Brian Urlacher 70.00
5 Peter Warrick 40.00
6 Travis Prentice 30.00
7 Courtney Brown 25.00
8 Bubba Franks 25.00
9 R. Jay Soward 25.00
10 Sylvester Morris 50.00
11 J.R. Redmond 30.00
12 Ron Dayne 30.00
13 Chad Pennington 125.00
14 Laveranues Coles 30.00
15 Jerry Porter 25.00
16 Todd Pinkston 25.00
17 Corey Simon 25.00
18 Plaxico Burress 50.00
19 Shaun Alexander 60.00
20 Darrell Jackson 30.00

2000 Playoff Contenders Touchdown Tandems

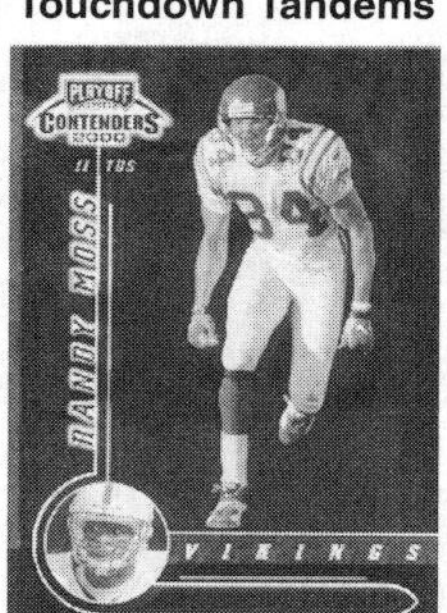

NM/M
Complete Set (30): 45.00
Common Player: .50
Minor Stars: 1.50
Inserted 1:11
1 Randy Moss, Marvin Harrison 5.00
2 Kurt Warner, Peyton Manning 5.00
3 Marshall Faulk, Edgerrin James 4.00
4 Eddie George, Fred Taylor 1.50
5 Emmitt Smith, Stephen Davis 5.00
6 Isaac Bruce, Jerry Rice 4.00
7 Antonio Freeman, Cris Carter .50
8 Drew Bledsoe, Mark Brunell 1.50
9 Jake Plummer, Steve McNair .50
10 Curtis Martin, Duce Staley .50
11 Keyshawn Johnson, Marcus Robinson .50
12 Dan Marino, Steve Young 6.00
13 Brett Favre, Troy Aikman 8.00
14 Tim Brown, Eric Moulds .50
15 Jerome Bettis, Mike Alstott .50
16 Dorsey Levens, James Stewart .50
17 Olandis Gary, Ricky Watters .50
18 Brian Griese, Charlie Batch 1.50
19 Terrell Owens, Torry Holt .50
20 Jimmy Smith, Joey Galloway .50
21 Kevin Johnson, Michael Westbrook .50
22 Corey Dillon, Ricky Williams 3.50
23 Donovan McNabb, Akili Smith 1.50
24 Tim Couch, Cade McNown 3.00
25 Shaun King, Jon Kitna 1.50
26 Peter Warrick, Plaxico Burress 5.00
27 Jamal Lewis, Shaun Alexander 5.00
28 Ron Dayne, Thomas Jones 3.00
29 Sylvester Morris, Travis Taylor 4.00
30 Chad Pennington, Chris Redman 8.00

2000 Playoff Contenders Touchdown Tandems Total

NM/M
Common Player: 20.00
Randomly Inserted
1 Randy Moss, Marvin Harrison 23 85.00
2 Kurt Warner, Peyton Manning 67 60.00
3 Marshall Faulk, Edgerrin James 20 75.00
4 Eddie George, Fred Taylor 15 35.00
5 Emmitt Smith, Stephen Davis 28 70.00
6 Isaac Bruce, Jerry Rice 17 85.00
7 Antonio Freeman, Cris Carter 19 20.00
8 Drew Bledsoe, Mark Brunell 33 35.00
9 Jake Plummer, Steve McNair 21 20.00
10 Curtis Martin, Duce Staley 9 45.00
11 Keyshawn Johnson, Marcus Robinson 17 35.00
12 Dan Marino, Steve Young 15 150.00
13 Brett Favre, roy Aikman 39 70.00
14 Tim Brown, Eric Moulds 13 20.00
15 Jerome Bettis, Mike Alstott 14 20.00
16 Dorsey Levens, James Stewart 22 20.00
17 Olandis Gary, Ricky Watters 12 35.00
18 Brian Griese, Charlie Batch 27 20.00
19 Terrell Owens, Torry Holt 10 45.00
20 Jimmy Smith, Joey Galloway 7 40.00
21 Kevin Johnson, Michael Westbrook 17 20.00
22 Corey Dillon, Ricky Williams 7 60.00
23 Donovan McNabb, Akili Smith 10 40.00
24 Tim Couch, Cade McNown 23 40.00
25 Shaun King, Jon Kitna 30 35.00
26 Peter Warrick, Plaxico Burress 20 50.00
27 Jamal Lewis, Shaun Alexander 26 65.00
28 Ron Dayne, Thomas Jones 35 45.00
29 Sylvester Morris, Travis Taylor 19 35.00
30 Chad Pennington, Chris Redman 67 35.00

2000 Playoff Momentum

NM/M
Complete Set (200): 300.00
Common Player: .10
Minor Stars: .40
Common Rookie: 2.00
Production 750 Sets
Pack (6): 6.75
Wax Box (16): 75.00
1 David Boston .50
2 Jake Plummer .50
3 Chris Chandler .10
4 Jamal Anderson .50
5 Tim Dwight .40
6 Qadry Ismail .10
7 Peerless Price .40
8 Antowain Smith .40
9 Eric Moulds .50
10 Rob Johnson .40
11 Natrone Means .40
12 Muhsin Muhammad .40
13 Steve Beuerlein .40
14 Patrick Jeffers .50
15 Curtis Enis .40
16 Cade McNown .50
17 Marcus Robinson .50
18 Corey Dillon .50
19 Akili Smith .50
20 Carl Pickens .40
21 Tim Couch 1.00
22 Kevin Johnson .40
23 Troy Aikman 1.25
24 Emmitt Smith 1.50
25 Joey Galloway .50
26 Raghib Ismail .10
27 Olandis Gary .50
28 John Elway 1.50
29 Brian Griese .60
30 Ed McCaffrey .40
31 Terrell Davis 1.00
32 Charlie Batch .50
33 James Stewart .40
34 Germane Crowell .40
35 Barry Sanders 1.50
36 Herman Moore .40
37 Antonio Freeman .50
38 Dorsey Levens .50
39 Brett Favre 2.50
40 Edgerrin James 2.00
41 Marvin Harrison .50
42 Peyton Manning 2.00
43 Fred Taylor .75
44 Keenan McCardell .40
45 Mark Brunell .75
46 Jimmy Smith .40
47 Elvis Grbac .40
48 Tony Gonzalez .40
49 James Johnson .40
50 Dan Marino 1.50
51 Thurman Thomas .40
52 Cris Carter .50
53 Robert Smith .40
54 Randy Moss 2.00
55 Daunte Culpepper 1.00
56 Terry Glenn .40
57 Kevin Faulk .40
58 Drew Bledsoe .75
59 Ricky Williams 1.00
60 Amani Toomer .40
61 Kerry Collins .40
62 Vinny Testaverde .40
63 Curtis Martin .50
64 Rich Gannon .40
65 Tyrone Wheatley .40
66 Napoleon Kaufman .40
67 Tim Brown .50
68 Duce Staley .50
69 Donovan McNabb .75
70 Kordell Stewart .50
71 Troy Edwards .40
72 Jerome Bettis .50
73 Jim Harbaugh .40
74 Jermaine Fazande .40
75 Steve Young .75
76 Charlie Garner .40
77 Terrell Owens .50
78 Jerry Rice 1.25
79 Jeff Garcia .50
80 Ricky Watters .50
81 Jon Kitna .40
82 Marshall Faulk .60
83 Isaac Bruce .50
84 Torry Holt .40
85 Kurt Warner 2.00
86 Keyshawn Johnson .50
87 Warrick Dunn .50
88 Mike Alstott .50
89 Warren Sapp .40
90 Shaun King .50
91 Eddie George .60
92 Steve McNair .50
93 Jevon Kearse .50
94 Bruce Smith .10
95 Deion Sanders .50
96 Albert Connell .40
97 Michael Westbrook .40
98 Brad Johnson .50
99 Jeff George .40
100 Stephen Davis .50
101 *Peter Warrick* 15.00
102 *Jamal Lewis* 25.00
103 *Thomas Jones* 12.00
104 *Plaxico Burress* 20.00
105 *Travis Taylor* 10.00
106 *Ron Dayne* 5.00
107 *Bubba Franks* 12.00
108 *Sebastian Janikowski* 8.00
109 *Chad Pennington* 40.00
110 *Shaun Alexander* 25.00
111 *Sylvester Morris* 5.00
112 *Anthony Becht* 6.00
113 *R. Jay Soward* 8.00
114 *Trung Canidate* 8.00
115 *Dennis Northcutt* 10.00
116 *Todd Pinkston* 10.00
117 *Jerry Porter* 15.00
118 *Travis Prentice* 8.00
119 *Giovanni Carmazzi* 5.00
120 *Ron Dugans* 5.00
121 *Erron Kinney* 4.00
122 *Dez White* 6.00
123 *Chris Cole* 4.00
124 *Ron Dixon* 8.00
125 *Chris Redman* 8.00
126 *J.R. Redmond* 8.00
127 *Laveranues Coles* 15.00
128 *JaJuan Dawson* 8.00
129 *Darrell Jackson* 15.00
130 *Reuben Droughns* 10.00
131 *Doug Chapman* 4.00
132 *Terrelle Smith* 2.00
133 *Curtis Keaton* 2.00
134 *Gari Scott* 2.00
135 *Courtney Brown* 5.00
136 *Corey Simon* 8.00
137 *Brian Urlacher* 20.00
138 *Shaun Ellis* 4.00
139 *John Abraham* 4.00
140 *Delthea O'Neal* 2.00
141 *Rashard Anderson* 2.00
142 *Ahmed Plummer* 4.00
143 *Chris Hovan* 4.00
144 *Erik Flowers* 2.00
145 *Rob Morris* 2.00
146 *Keith Bulluck* 2.00
147 *Darren Howard* 2.00
148 *John Engelberger* 2.00
149 *Ian Gold* 2.00
150 *Raynoch Thompson* 2.00
151 *Cornelius Griffin* 2.00

152	*Rogers Beckett*	2.00
153	*Dwayne Goodrich*	2.00
154	*Barrett Green*	2.00
155	*Kevin Thompson*	2.00
156	*Ben Kelly*	2.00
157	*Danny Farmer*	6.00
158	*Aaron Shea*	2.00
159	*Trevor Gaylor*	2.00
160	*Mike Brown*	4.00
161	*Frank Moreau*	2.00
162	*Deon Dyer*	2.00
163	*Avion Black*	2.00
164	*Spergon Wynn*	4.00
165	*Billy Volek*	8.00
166	*Michael Wiley*	3.00
167	*Dante Hall*	20.00
168	*Ronney Jenkins*	2.00
169	*Sammy Morris*	6.00
170	*Kevin McDougal*	2.00
171	*Tee Martin*	8.00
172	*Troy Walters*	2.00
173	*Chad Morton*	6.00
174	*Jamel White*	2.00
175	*Shockmain Davis*	2.00
176	*Mario Edwards*	2.00
177	*Brandon Short*	4.00
178	*James Williams*	4.00
179	*Mike Anderson*	12.00
180	*Tom Brady*	60.00
181	*Na'il Diggs*	4.00
182	*Todd Husak*	8.00
183	*JaJuan Seider*	2.00
184	*Tim Rattay*	12.00
185	*Jarious Jackson*	8.00
186	*Joe Hamilton*	8.00
187	*Shyrone Stith*	4.00
188	*Mondriel Fulcher*	2.00
189	*Bashir Yamini*	2.00
190	*Herbert Goodman*	2.00
191	*Mike Green*	2.00
192	*Demario Brown*	2.00
193	*Charles Lee*	2.00
194	*Doug Johnson*	4.00
195	*Windrell Hayes*	2.00
196	*Julian Peterson*	2.00
197	*Kwame Cavil*	2.00
198	*Hank Poteat*	2.00
199	*Clint Stoerner*	3.00
200	*Mark Simoneau*	2.00

2000 Playoff Momentum Game Day Souvenirs Jerseys

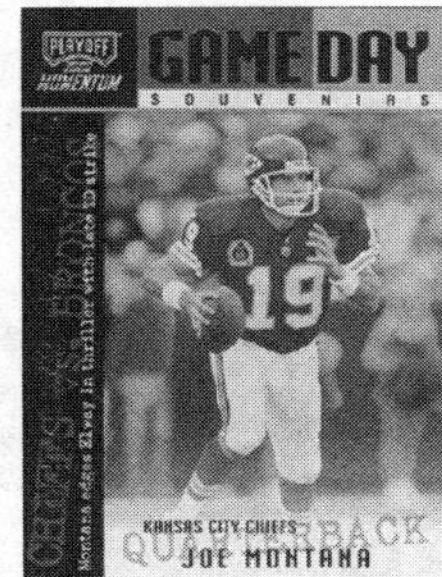

		NM/M
	Common Player:	25.00
1	Joe Montana	125.00
2	Dan Marino	100.00
3	Joe Montana	125.00
4	John Elway	100.00
5	Terry Bradshaw	100.00
6	Roger Staubach	100.00
7	Bob Griese	75.00
8	Fran Tarkenton	75.00
9	Phil Simms	75.00
10	Lawrence Taylor	75.00
11	Ronnie Lott	75.00
12	Boomer Esiason	75.00
13	Joe Namath	125.00
14	Don Maynard	25.00
15	Howie Long	75.00
16	Marcus Allen	75.00
17	Jim Kelly	25.00
18	Thurman Thomas	25.00
19	Fred Taylor	25.00
20	Mark Brunell	25.00
21	Randy Moss	75.00
22	Antonio Freeman	25.00
23	Ricky Williams	25.00
24	Tim Couch	25.00
25	Kurt Warner	50.00
26	Eddie George	25.00
27	Troy Aikman	75.00
28	Steve Young	75.00
29	Dorsey Levens	25.00
30	Barry Sanders	75.00
31	Joe Montana, Dan Marino	300.00
32	Joe Montana, John Elway	300.00
33	Terry Bradshaw, Roger Staubach	200.00
34	Bob Griese, Fran Tarkenton	150.00
35	Phil Simms, Lawrence Taylor	150.00
36	Ronnie Lott, Boomer Esiason	100.00
37	Joe Namath, Don Maynard	175.00
38	Howie Long, Marcus Allen	100.00
39	Jim Kelly, Thurman Thomas	100.00
40	Fred Taylor, Mark Brunell	100.00
41	Randy Moss, Antonio Freeman	100.00
42	Ricky Williams, Tim Couch	100.00
43	Kurt Warner, Eddie George	150.00
44	Troy Aikman, Steve Young	150.00
45	Dorsey Levens, Barry Sanders	150.00

2000 Playoff Momentum Generations

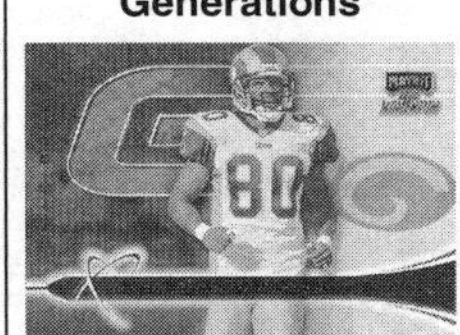

		NM/M
	Complete Set (50):	60.00
	Common Player:	.75
1	Jake Plummer	.75
2	Tim Couch	1.00
3	Emmitt Smith	2.00
4	Troy Aikman	2.00
5	John Elway	4.00
6	Terrell Davis	2.00
7	Barry Sanders	3.00
8	Brett Favre	4.00
9	Peyton Manning	3.00
10	Edgerrin James	3.00
11	Mark Brunell	2.00
12	Fred Taylor	1.00
13	Dan Marino	3.00
14	Randy Moss	3.00
15	Drew Bledsoe	2.00
16	Ricky Williams	2.00
17	Jerry Rice	4.00
18	Steve Young	2.00
19	Kurt Warner	4.00
20	Eddie George	2.00
21	Eric Moulds	1.00
22	Cade McNown	.75
23	Corey Dillon	1.00
24	Kevin Johnson	.75
25	Joey Galloway	.75
26	Dorsey Levens	.75
27	Antonio Freeman	.75
28	Marvin Harrison	2.00
29	Daunte Culpepper	3.00
30	Cris Carter	1.00
31	Curtis Martin	1.00
32	Tim Brown	1.00
33	Donovan McNabb	2.00
34	Terrell Owens	1.00
35	Peter Warrick	1.00
36	Jamal Lewis	3.00
37	Thomas Jones	2.00
38	Plaxico Burress	3.00
39	Travis Taylor	.75
40	Ron Dayne	2.00
41	Chad Pennington	3.00
42	Shaun Alexander	3.00
43	Marshall Faulk	2.00
44	Keyshawn Johnson	.75
45	Steve McNair	1.00
46	Stephen Davis	.75
47	Brad Johnson	.75
48	Akili Smith	.75
49	Brian Griese	1.00
50	Isaac Bruce	.75

2000 Playoff Momentum Rookie Quads

		NM/M
	Common Player:	5.00
1	Peter Warrick, Avion Black, Ron Dugans, Charles Lee	8.00
2	Plaxico Burress, Trevor Gaylor, JaJuan Dawson, Dez White	10.00
3	Travis Taylor, Danny Farmer, Jerry Porter, Laveranues Coles	5.00
4	Gari Scott, Sylvester Morris, Todd Pinkston, Ron Dixon	5.00
5	Darrell Jackson, R. Jay Soward, Dennis Northcutt, Chris Cole	5.00
6	Jamal Lewis, Ronney Jenkins, Doug Chapman, Reuben Droughns	10.00
7	Thomas Jones, Chad Morton, J.R. Redmond, Curtis Keaton	5.00
8	Ron Dayne, Sammy Morris, Travis Prentice, Frank Moreau	10.00
9	Shaun Alexander, Dante Hall, Trung Canidate, Michael Wiley	30.00
10	Chad Pennington, Todd Husak, Tee Martin, Billy Volek	12.00
11	Giovanni Carmazzi, Tim Rattay, Chris Redman, Tom Brady	30.00
12	Courtney Brown, Shaun Ellis, Corey Simon, Brian Urlacher	25.00

2000 Playoff Momentum Rookie Tandems

		NM/M
	Complete Set (24):	75.00
	Common Player:	2.00
1	Peter Warrick, Avion Black	5.00
2	Ron Dugans, Charles Lee	2.00
3	Plaxico Burress, Trevor Gaylor	5.00
4	Dez White, JaJuan Dawson	2.00
5	Travis Taylor, Danny Farmer	2.00
6	Jerry Porter, Laveranues Coles	4.00
7	Sylvester Morris, Gari Scott	2.00
8	Todd Pinkston, Ron Dixon	2.00
9	R. Jay Soward, Darrell Jackson	2.00
10	Dennis Northcutt, Chris Cole	2.00
11	Jamal Lewis, Ronney Jenkins	10.00
12	Reuben Droughns, Doug Chapman	2.00
13	Thomas Jones, Chad Morton	5.00
14	J.R. Redmond, Curtis Keaton	2.00
15	Ron Dayne, Sammy Morris	5.00
16	Travis Prentice, Frank Moreau	2.00
17	Shaun Alexander, Dante Hall	30.00
18	Trung Canidate, Michael Wiley	2.00
19	Chad Pennington, Todd Husak	20.00
20	Tee Martin, Billy Volek	3.00
21	Giovanni Carmazzi, Tim Rattay	2.00
22	Chris Redman, Tom Brady	20.00
23	Courtney Brown, Shaun Ellis	2.00
24	Corey Simon, Brian Urlacher	20.00

2000 Playoff Momentum Signing Bonus Quads

		NM/M
	Common Player:	100.00
1	Peter Warrick, R. Jay Soward, Sylvester Morris, Plaxico Burress	150.00
2	Jamal Lewis, Dez White, Shaun Alexander, Travis Taylor	100.00
3	Thomas Jones, Chris Redman, Chad Pennington, Ron Dayne	100.00

2000 Playoff Momentum Signing Bonus Tandems

		NM/M
	Common Player:	50.00
1	Peter Warrick, R. Jay Soward	100.00
2	Plaxico Burress, Sylvester Morris	125.00
3	Jamal Lewis, Dez White	100.00
4	Travis Taylor, Shaun Alexander	125.00
5	Thomas Jones, Chris Redman	50.00
6	Ron Dayne, Chad Pennington	100.00

2000 Playoff Prestige

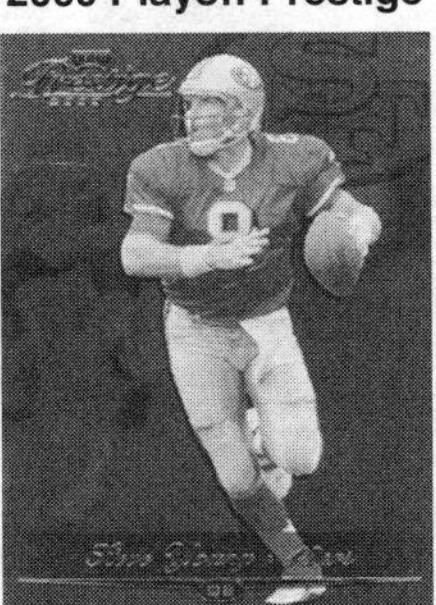

		NM/M
	Complete Set (300):	325.00
	Common Player:	.15
	Minor Stars:	.30
	Common Performer:	1.00
	Production 2,500 Sets	
	Common Rookie:	2.50
	Production 2,500 Sets	
	Pack (6):	5.25
	Wax Box (16):	60.00
1	Frank Sanders	.30
2	Rob Moore	.30
3	Michael Pittman	.15
4	Jake Plummer	.50
5	David Boston	.50
6	Chris Chandler	.30
7	Tim Dwight	.50
8	Shawn Jefferson	.15
9	Terance Mathis	.15
10	Jamal Anderson	.50
11	Byron Hanspard	.15
12	Ken Oxendine	.15
13	Priest Holmes	.50
14	Tony Banks	.30
15	Shannon Sharpe	.30
16	Rod Woodson	.30
17	Jermaine Lewis	.15
18	Qadry Ismail	.30
19	Eric Moulds	.50
20	Doug Flutie	.50
21	Jay Riemersma	.15
22	Antowain Smith	.30
23	Jonathon Linton	.30
24	Peerless Price	.30
25	Rob Johnson	.30
26	Muhsin Muhammad	.30
27	Wesley Walls	.15
28	Tim Biakabutuka	.30
29	Steve Beuerlein	.30
30	Patrick Jeffers	.50
31	Natrone Means	.30
32	Curtis Enis	.50
33	Bobby Engram	.15
34	Marcus Robinson	.50
35	Marty Booker	.15
36	Cade McNown	.75
37	Darnay Scott	.30
38	Carl Pickens	.30
39	Corey Dillon	.50
40	Akili Smith	.60
41	Michael Basnight	.15
42	Kareem Abdul Jabbar	.30
43	Tim Couch	1.25
44	Kevin Johnson	.50
45	Darrin Chiaverini	.15
46	Errict Rhett	.30
47	Emmitt Smith	1.50
48	Deion Sanders	.50
49	Michael Irvin	.30
50	Raghib Ismail	.15
51	Troy Aikman	1.00
52	Jason Tucker	.30
53	Joey Galloway	.50
54	David LaFleur	.15
55	Wane McGarity	.15
56	Ed McCaffrey	.30
57	Rod Smith	.30
58	Brian Griese	.60
59	John Elway	1.50
60	Gus Frerotte	.15
61	Neil Smith	.15
62	Terrell Davis	1.00
63	Olandis Gary	.60
64	Johnnie Morton	.15
65	Charlie Batch	.50
66	Barry Sanders	1.50
67	James Stewart	.50
68	Germane Crowell	.50
69	Sedrick Irvin	.15
70	Herman Moore	.30
71	Corey Bradford	.15
72	Dorsey Levens	.50
73	Antonio Freeman	.50
74	Brett Favre	2.00
75	De'Mond Parker	.15
76	Bill Schroeder	.15
77	Donald Driver	.15
78	E.G. Green	.15
79	Marvin Harrison	.50
80	Peyton Manning	1.75
81	Terrence Wilkins	.50
82	Edgerrin James	1.75
83	Keenan McCardell	.30
84	Mark Brunell	.75
85	Fred Taylor	.75
86	Jimmy Smith	.50
87	Derrick Alexander	.15
88	Andre Rison	.30
89	Elvis Grbac	.30
90	Tony Gonzalez	.30
91	Donnell Bennett	.15
92	Warren Moon	.30
93	Kimble Anders	.15
94	Tony Richardson	.15
95	Jay Fiedler	.50
96	Zach Thomas	.30
97	Oronde Gadsden	.15
98	Dan Marino	1.50
99	O.J. McDuffie	.30
100	Tony Martin	.15
101	James Johnson	.15
102	Rob Konrad	.15
103	Damon Huard	.50
104	Thurman Thomas	.30
105	Randy Moss	2.00
106	Cris Carter	.50
107	Robert Smith	.50
108	Randall Cunningham	.50
109	John Randle	.15
110	Leroy Hoard	.15
111	Daunte Culpepper	.75
112	Matthew Hatchette	.15
113	Troy Brown	.15
114	Tony Simmons	.30
115	Terry Glenn	.50
116	Ben Coates	.30
117	Drew Bledsoe	.75
118	Terry Allen	.15
119	Kevin Faulk	.15
120	Ricky Williams	1.00
121	*Jake Delhomme*	1.50
122	Jake Reed	.30
123	Jeff Blake	.30
124	Amani Toomer	.15
125	Kerry Collins	.30
126	Tiki Barber	.30
127	Ike Hilliard	.15
128	Joe Montgomery	.15
129	Sean Bennett	.15
130	Curtis Martin	.50
131	Vinny Testaverde	.50
132	Wayne Chrebet	.30
133	Ray Lucas	.30
134	Tyrone Wheatley	.30
135	Napoleon Kaufman	.30
136	Tim Brown	.30
137	Rickey Dudley	.15
138	James Jett	.15
139	Rich Gannon	.30
140	Charles Woodson	.50
141	Duce Staley	.50
142	Donovan McNabb	.75
143	Na Brown	.15
144	Kordell Stewart	.50
145	Jerome Bettis	.50
146	Hines Ward	.30
147	Troy Edwards	.50
148	Curtis Conway	.30
149	Junior Seau	.30
150	Jim Harbaugh	.30
151	Jermaine Fazande	.30
152	Terrell Owens	.50
153	J.J. Stokes	.30
154	Charlie Garner	.50
155	Jerry Rice	1.00
156	Garrison Hearst	.50
157	Steve Young	.75
158	Jeff Garcia	.50
159	Derrick Mayes	.30
160	Ahman Green	.30
161	Ricky Watters	.30
162	Jon Kitna	.30
163	Karsten Bailey	.15
164	Sean Dawkins	.15
165	Az-Zahir Hakim	.30
166	Isaac Bruce	.50
167	Marshall Faulk	.50
168	Trent Green	.50
169	Kurt Warner	2.00
170	Torry Holt	.50
171	Robert Holcombe	.15
172	Kevin Carter	.15
173	Keyshawn Johnson	.50
174	Jacquez Green	.30
175	Reidel Anthony	.30
176	Warren Sapp	.30
177	Mike Alstott	.50
178	Warrick Dunn	.50
179	Trent Dilfer	.30
180	Shaun King	.75
181	Neil O'Donnell	.15
182	Eddie George	.60
183	Yancey Thigpen	.15
184	Steve McNair	.60
185	Kevin Dyson	.30
186	Frank Wycheck	.15
187	Jevon Kearse	.60
188	Adrian Murrell	.15
189	Jeff George	.50
190	Stephen Davis	.50
191	Stephen Alexander	.15
192	Darrell Green	.15
193	Skip Hicks	.15
194	Brad Johnson	.50
195	Michael Westbrook	.30
196	Albert Connell	.30
197	Irving Fryar	.15
198	Bruce Smith	.15
199	Champ Bailey	.30
200	Larry Centers	.15
201	Jake Plummer	1.00
202	Doug Flutie	1.50
203	Eric Moulds	1.00
204	Muhsin Muhammad	1.00
205	Marcus Robinson	1.50
206	Cade McNown	2.00
207	Corey Dillon	1.00
208	Tim Couch	3.00
209	Kevin Johnson	1.00
210	Emmitt Smith	3.00
211	Troy Aikman	2.50
212	Brian Griese	1.50
213	Olandis Gary	1.50
214	Germane Crowell	1.00
215	Brett Favre	6.00
216	Charlie Batch	1.00
217	Antonio Freeman	1.00
218	Dorsey Levens	1.00
219	Peyton Manning	4.00
220	Edgerrin James	5.00
221	Marvin Harrison	1.00
222	Fred Taylor	2.00
223	Mark Brunell	2.00
224	Jimmy Smith	1.00
225	Dan Marino	4.00
226	Randy Moss	4.00
227	Cris Carter	1.00
228	Robert Smith	1.00
229	Drew Bledsoe	2.00
230	Terry Glenn	1.00
231	Ricky Williams	3.00
232	Amani Toomer	1.00
233	Keyshawn Johnson	1.00
234	Curtis Martin	1.00
235	Ray Lucas	1.00
236	Tim Brown	1.00
237	Duce Staley	1.00
238	Donovan McNabb	2.00
239	Jerry Rice	2.50
240	Jon Kitna	1.00
241	Isaac Bruce	1.00
242	Kurt Warner	4.00
243	Torry Holt	1.00
244	Mike Alstott	1.00
245	Marshall Faulk	1.00
246	Shaun King	2.00
247	Eddie George	1.50
248	Steve McNair	1.00
249	Stephen Davis	1.00
250	Brad Johnson	1.00
251	*Rondell Mealey*	3.00
252	*Peter Warrick*	8.00
253	*Courtney Brown*	5.00
254	*Plaxico Burress*	10.00
255	*Corey Simon*	4.00
256	*Thomas Jones*	6.00
257	*Travis Taylor*	6.00
258	*Shaun Alexander*	12.00
259	*Chris Redman*	6.00
260	*Chad Pennington*	20.00
261	*Jamal Lewis*	12.00
262	*Bubba Franks*	6.00
263	*Dez White*	6.00
264	*Ron Dayne*	5.00
265	*Sylvester Morris*	3.00
266	*R. Jay Soward*	4.00
267	*Sherrod Gideon*	3.00
268	*Travis Prentice*	6.00
269	*Darrell Jackson*	8.00
270	*Giovanni Carmazzi*	5.00
271	*Anthony Lucas*	3.00
272	*Danny Farmer*	4.00
273	*Dennis Northcutt*	5.00
274	*Troy Walters*	3.00
275	*Laveranues Coles*	8.00
276	*Tee Martin*	4.00
277	*J.R. Redmond*	6.00
278	*Jerry Porter*	8.00
279	*Sebastian Janikowski*	4.00
280	*Michael Wiley*	4.00
281	*Reuben Droughns*	5.00
282	*Trung Canidate*	4.00
283	*Shyrone Stith*	3.00
284	*Trevor Gaylor*	3.00
285	*Marc Bulger*	10.00
286	*Tom Brady*	25.00
287	*Todd Husak*	3.00
288	*Jarious Jackson*	3.00
289	*Terrelle Smith*	2.50
290	*Chad Morton*	5.00
291	*Chris Cole*	3.00
292	*Kwame Cavil*	2.50
293	*JuJuan Dawson*	4.00
294	*Curtis Keaton*	3.00
295	*Tim Rattay*	6.00
296	*Joe Hamilton*	4.00
297	*Gari Scott*	3.00
298	*Mike Anderson*	4.00
299	*Ron Dugans*	4.00
300	*Todd Pinkston*	4.00

2000 Playoff Prestige Spectrum Green

Green Cards:	25X-50X
Green Performers:	15X-30X
Green Rookies:	2X-4X
Production 25 Sets	

2000 Playoff Prestige Spectrum Red

Red Cards:	8X-20X
Red Performers:	4X-10X
Red Rookies:	1.5X
Production 100 Sets	

2000 Playoff Prestige Alma Mater Materials

		NM/M
	Complete Set (10):	475.00
	Common Player:	15.00
	Inserted 1:335	
	Patch Cards:	2X
	Inserted 1:2,005	
AM1	John Elway	100.00
AM2	Drew Bledsoe	60.00
AM3	Ricky Williams	75.00
AM4	Edgerrin James	85.00
AM5	Fred Taylor	70.00
AM6	J.J. Stokes	15.00
AM7	Eddie George	50.00
AM8	Frank Wycheck	15.00
AM9	Tim Biakabutuka	15.00
AM10	Ryan Leaf	15.00

2000 Playoff Prestige Award Winning Materials

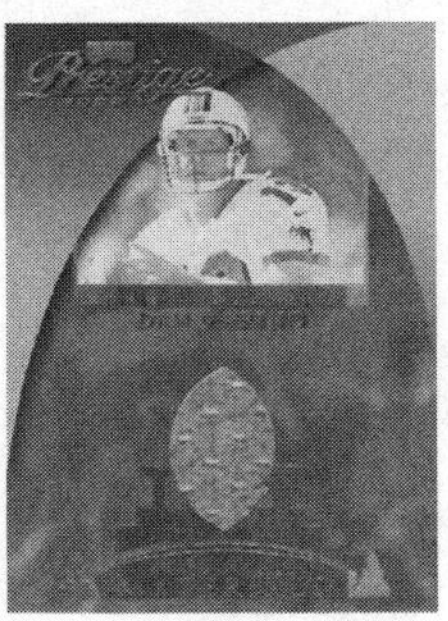

		NM/M
	Common Player:	25.00
	Inserted 1:429	
	Single Jerseys #'d to 75	
	Triple Jerseys #'d to 25	
AW1	Brett Favre	125.00
AW2	Barry Sanders	100.00
AW3	Thurman Thomas	25.00
AW4	Brett Favre, Barry Sanders, Thurman Thomas	175.00
AW5	Dan Marino	125.00
AW6	Steve Young	65.00
AW7	Kurt Warner	75.00
AW8	Dan Marino, Steve Young, Kurt Warner	175.00
AW9	John Elway	100.00
AW10	Terrell Davis	85.00
AW11	Phil Simms	25.00
AW12	John Elway, Terrell Davis, Phil Simms	175.00
AW13	Troy Aikman	85.00
AW14	Emmitt Smith	100.00
AW15	Jerry Rice	85.00
AW16	Troy Aikman, Emmitt Smith, Jerry Rice	200.00

AW17 Randy Moss 100.00
AW18 Eddie George 50.00
AW19 Jerome Bettis 25.00
AW20 Randy Moss, Eddie George, Jerome Bettis 150.00
AW21 Edgerrin James 75.00
AW22 Curtis Martin 25.00
AW23 Marshall Faulk 50.00
AW24 Edgerrin James, Curtis Martin, Marshall Faulk 125.00

2000 Playoff Prestige Award Winning Performers

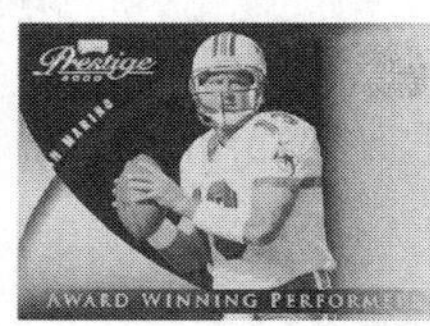

NM/M
Complete Set (24): 65.00
Common Player: 1.00
Minor Stars: 2.00
Inserted 1:31
AW1 Brett Favre 6.00
AW2 Barry Sanders 5.00
AW3 Thurman Thomas 1.00
AW4 Brett Favre, Barry Sanders, Thurman Thomas 5.00
AW5 Dan Marino 5.00
AW6 Steve Young 2.50
AW7 Kurt Warner 4.00
AW8 Dan Marino, Steve Young, Kurt Warner 5.00
AW9 John Elway 5.00
AW10 Terrell Davis 4.00
AW11 Phil Simms 1.00
AW12 John Elway, Terrell Davis, Phil Simms 4.00
AW13 Troy Aikman 4.00
AW14 Emmitt Smith 4.00
AW15 Jerry Rice 4.00
AW16 Troy Aikman, Emmitt Smith, Jerry Rice 4.00
AW17 Randy Moss 5.00
AW18 Eddie George 2.00
AW19 Jerome Bettis 1.00
AW20 Randy Moss, Eddie George, Jerome Bettis 4.00
AW21 Edgerrin James 4.00
AW22 Curtis Martin 1.00
AW23 Marshall Faulk 2.00
AW24 Edgerrin James, Curtis Martin, Marshall Faulk 3.00

2000 Playoff Prestige Award Winning Signatures

NM/M
Common Player: 45.00
Inserted 1:330
Single Autos #'d to 100
Triple Autos #'d to 25
AW1 Brett Favre 175.00
AW2 Barry Sanders 150.00
AW3 Thurman Thomas 45.00
AW4 Brett Favre, Barry Sanders, Thurman Thomas 350.00
AW5 Dan Marino 150.00
AW6 Steve Young 65.00
AW7 Kurt Warner 175.00
AW8 Dan Marino, Steve Young, Kurt Warner 425.00
AW9 John Elway 150.00
AW10 Terrell Davis 85.00
AW11 Phil Simms 45.00
AW12 John Elway, Terrell Davis, Phil Simms 350.00
AW13 Troy Aikman 100.00
AW14 Emmitt Smith 125.00
AW15 Jerry Rice 100.00
AW16 Troy Aikman, Emmitt Smith, Jerry Rice 425.00
AW17 Randy Moss 150.00
AW18 Eddie George 50.00
AW19 Jerome Bettis 45.00
AW20 Randy Moss, Eddie George, Jerome Bettis 300.00
AW21 Edgerrin James 150.00
AW22 Curtis Martin 45.00
AW23 Marshall Faulk 50.00
AW24 Edgerrin James, Curtis Martin, Marshall Faulk 275.00

2000 Playoff Prestige Draft Picks

NM/M
Complete Set (30): 60.00
Common Player: 1.00
Minor Stars: 2.00
Inserted 1:8
DP1 Joe Hamilton 2.00
DP2 Peter Warrick 2.00
DP3 Courtney Brown 3.00
DP4 Plaxico Burress 6.00
DP5 Thomas Jones 5.00
DP6 Travis Taylor 3.50
DP7 Shaun Alexander 5.00
DP8 Chris Redman 3.00
DP9 Chad Pennington 10.00
DP10 Jamal Lewis 5.00
DP11 Bubba Franks 2.00
DP12 Dez White 2.00
DP13 Ron Dayne 2.00
DP14 Sylvester Morris 3.00
DP15 R. Jay Soward 2.50
DP16 Travis Prentice 3.00
DP17 Darrell Jackson 2.50
DP18 Giovanni Carmazzi 3.00
DP19 Danny Farmer 1.00
DP20 Dennis Northcutt 2.50
DP21 Laveranues Coles 2.00
DP22 J.R. Redmond 2.50
DP23 Jerry Porter 2.00
DP24 Reuben Droughns 2.00
DP25 Trung Canidate 2.00
DP26 Trevor Gaylor 2.00
DP27 Chris Cole 1.00
DP28 Tim Rattay 2.50
DP29 Ron Dugans 2.00
DP30 Todd Pinkston 2.00

2000 Playoff Prestige Human Highlight Film

NM/M
Complete Set (70): 125.00
Common Player: 1.25
Minor Stars: 2.50
Inserted 1:15
Gold Cards: 4X-8X
Production 50 Sets
HH1 Randy Moss 6.00
HH2 Brett Favre 8.00
HH3 Dan Marino 8.00
HH4 Barry Sanders 8.00
HH5 John Elway 6.00
HH6 Peyton Manning 6.00
HH7 Terrell Davis 5.00
HH8 Emmitt Smith 6.00
HH9 Troy Aikman 6.00
HH10 Jerry Rice 6.00
HH11 Fred Taylor 4.00
HH12 Jake Plummer 2.50
HH13 Charlie Batch 2.50
HH14 Drew Bledsoe 3.50
HH15 Mark Brunell 3.50
HH16 Steve Young 3.50
HH17 Eddie George 3.00
HH18 Mike Alstott 2.50
HH19 Jamal Anderson 2.50
HH20 Jerome Bettis 2.50
HH21 Tim Brown 1.25
HH22 Cris Carter 2.50
HH23 Stephen Davis 2.50
HH24 Corey Dillon 2.50
HH25 Warrick Dunn 2.50
HH26 Curtis Enis 1.25
HH27 Marshall Faulk 2.50
HH28 Doug Flutie 3.00
HH29 Antonio Freeman 2.50
HH30 Joey Galloway 2.50
HH31 Terry Glenn 2.50
HH32 Marvin Harrison 2.50
HH33 Brad Johnson 2.50
HH34 Keyshawn Johnson 2.50
HH35 Jon Kitna 2.50
HH36 Dorsey Levens 2.50
HH37 Curtis Martin 2.50
HH38 Steve McNair 2.50
HH39 Eric Moulds 2.50
HH40 Terrell Owens 2.50
HH41 Deion Sanders 2.50
HH42 Antowain Smith 1.25
HH43 Robert Smith 2.50
HH44 Duce Staley 2.50
HH45 Kordell Stewart 2.50
HH46 Isaac Bruce 2.50
HH47 Germane Crowell 2.50
HH48 Michael Irvin 2.50
HH49 Ed McCaffrey 2.50
HH50 Muhsin Muhammad 2.50
HH51 Jimmy Smith 2.50
HH52 James Stewart 2.50
HH53 Amani Toomer 1.25
HH54 Ricky Watters 2.50
HH55 Michael Westbrook 2.50
HH56 Brian Griese 3.00
HH57 Marcus Robinson 2.50
HH58 Kurt Warner 5.00
HH59 Edgerrin James 5.00
HH60 Tim Couch 5.00
HH61 Ricky Williams 5.00
HH62 Donovan McNabb 3.00
HH63 Cade McNown 3.00
HH64 Daunte Culpepper 3.50
HH65 Akili Smith 3.00
HH66 Torry Holt 2.50
HH67 Peerless Price 2.50
HH68 Kevin Johnson 2.50
HH69 Shaun King 3.00
HH70 Olandis Gary 3.00

2000 Playoff Prestige Inside the Numbers

NM/M
Complete Set (100): 275.00
Common Player: 1.50
Minor Stars: 3.00
Inserted 1:15

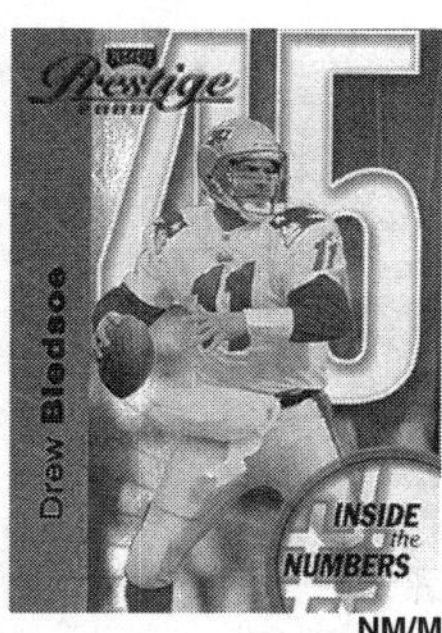

NM/M
IN1 Ricky Williams 6.00
IN2 Edgerrin James 6.00
IN3 Brett Favre 10.00
IN4 Donovan McNabb 5.00
IN5 James Stewart 1.50
IN6 Corey Dillon 3.00
IN7 Tim Couch 5.00
IN8 Doug Flutie 4.00
IN9 Jake Plummer 3.00
IN10 Akili Smith 4.00
IN11 Jerry Rice 8.00
IN12 Brian Griese 4.00
IN13 Peyton Manning 8.00
IN14 Fred Taylor 5.00
IN15 Brad Johnson 3.00
IN16 Courtney Brown 5.00
IN17 Randy Moss 8.00
IN18 Deion Sanders 3.00
IN19 Bruce Smith 1.50
IN20 Natrone Means 1.50
IN21 Dez White 4.00
IN22 Robert Smith 3.00
IN23 Jon Kitna 3.00
IN24 Duce Staley 3.00
IN25 Emmitt Smith 8.00
IN26 Dennis Northcutt 4.00
IN27 Antowain Smith 1.50
IN28 Mike Alstott 3.00
IN29 Ike Hilliard 1.50
IN30 Ed McCaffrey 3.00
IN31 Cade McNown 4.00
IN32 Jamal Lewis 6.00
IN33 Ron Dayne 3.00
IN34 Isaac Bruce 3.00
IN35 Tim Brown 1.50
IN36 Steve Beuerlein 1.50
IN37 Olandis Gary 3.00
IN38 Shyrone Stith 3.00
IN39 Jerome Bettis 3.00
IN40 Todd Pinkston 3.00
IN41 Kurt Warner 6.00
IN42 Peter Warrick 3.00
IN43 Steve Young 5.00
IN44 Corey Simon 3.00
IN45 Drew Bledsoe 5.00
IN46 Ron Dugans 4.00
IN47 Germane Crowell 3.00
IN48 Dan Marino 10.00
IN49 Eric Moulds 3.00
IN50 Peerless Price 3.00
IN51 Travis Taylor 6.00
IN52 Torry Holt 3.00
IN53 Charlie Batch 3.00
IN54 Shaun Alexander 6.00
IN55 John Elway 7.00
IN56 Amani Toomer 1.50
IN57 Thomas Jones 5.00
IN58 David Boston 3.00
IN59 Terrell Davis 7.00
IN60 Marvin Harrison 3.00
IN61 Priest Holmes 3.00
IN62 Troy Aikman 8.00
IN63 Chris Redman 6.00
IN64 Eddie George 4.00
IN65 Plaxico Burress 8.00
IN66 Kevin Johnson 3.00
IN67 Chad Pennington 15.00
IN68 Marshall Faulk 3.00
IN69 Sylvester Morris 6.00
IN70 Jimmy Smith 3.00
IN71 Dorsey Levens 3.00
IN72 Joey Galloway 3.00
IN73 Daunte Culpepper 4.50
IN74 Curtis Martin 3.00
IN75 Shaun King 4.00
IN76 Stephen Davis 3.00
IN77 Danny Farmer 3.00
IN78 Travis Prentice 6.00
IN79 Terrell Owens 3.00
IN80 Jamal Anderson 3.00
IN81 Antonio Freeman 3.00
IN82 Mark Brunell 5.00
IN83 Steve McNair 3.00
IN84 Marcus Robinson 3.00
IN85 Keenan McCardell 1.50
IN86 Jevon Kearse 3.00
IN87 Thurman Thomas 1.50
IN88 Patrick Jeffers 3.00
IN89 Keyshawn Johnson 3.00
IN90 Terry Glenn 3.00
IN91 Jerry Porter 4.00
IN92 J.R. Redmond 5.00
IN93 Yancey Thigpen 1.50
IN94 Troy Edwards 3.00
IN95 Cris Carter 3.00
IN96 Muhsin Muhammad 1.50
IN97 Ricky Watters 3.00
IN98 R. Jay Soward 4.00
IN99 Barry Sanders 8.00
IN100 James Johnson 1.50

2000 Playoff Prestige League Leader Quads

NM/M
Complete Set (12): 80.00
Common Player: 5.00
Inserted 1:159

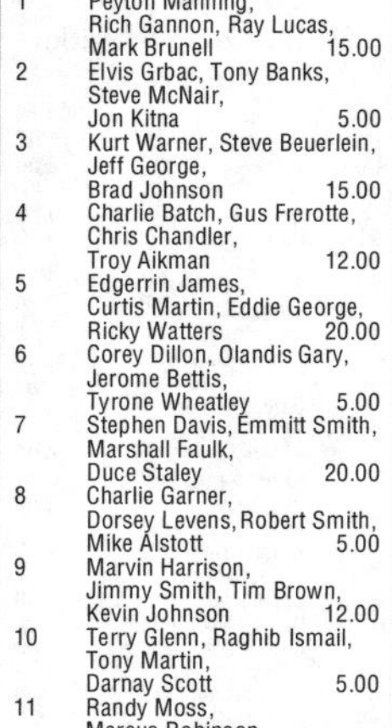

1 Peyton Manning, Rich Gannon, Ray Lucas, Mark Brunell 15.00
2 Elvis Grbac, Tony Banks, Steve McNair, Jon Kitna 5.00
3 Kurt Warner, Steve Beuerlein, Jeff George, Brad Johnson 15.00
4 Charlie Batch, Gus Frerotte, Chris Chandler, Troy Aikman 12.00
5 Edgerrin James, Curtis Martin, Eddie George, Ricky Watters 20.00
6 Corey Dillon, Olandis Gary, Jerome Bettis, Tyrone Wheatley 5.00
7 Stephen Davis, Emmitt Smith, Marshall Faulk, Duce Staley 20.00
8 Charlie Garner, Dorsey Levens, Robert Smith, Mike Alstott 5.00
9 Marvin Harrison, Jimmy Smith, Tim Brown, Kevin Johnson 12.00
10 Terry Glenn, Raghib Ismail, Tony Martin, Darnay Scott 5.00
11 Randy Moss, Marcus Robinson, Germane Crowell, Muhsin Muhammad 15.00
12 Amani Toomer, Cris Carter, Michael Westbrook, Isaac Bruce 12.00

2000 Playoff Prestige Team Checklist

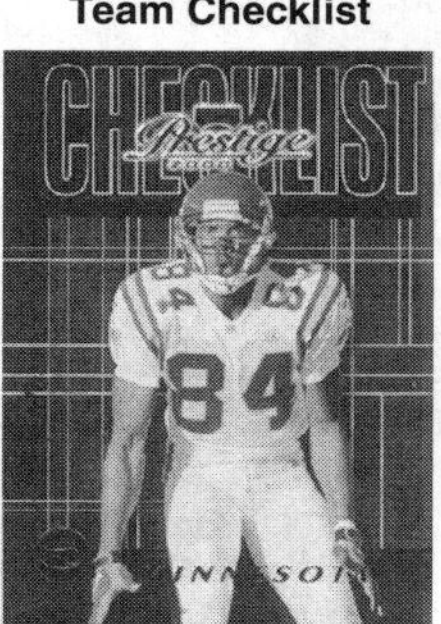

NM/M
Complete Set (93): 200.00
Common Player (1-31): 1.00
Inserted 1:15
Common Player (32-62): 1.50
Inserted 1:31
Common Player (63-93): 3.00
Inserted 1:63
CL1 Jake Plummer 1.00
CL2 Jamal Anderson 1.00
CL3 Jamal Lewis 3.50
CL4 Rob Johnson 1.00
CL5 Muhsin Muhammad 1.00
CL6 Marcus Robinson 1.00
CL7 Peter Warrick 5.00
CL8 Tim Couch 2.50
CL9 Emmitt Smith 3.50
CL10 Terrell Davis 3.50
CL11 Charlie Batch 1.00
CL12 Brett Favre 5.00
CL13 Peyton Manning 5.00
CL14 Mark Brunell 2.00
CL15 Elvis Grbac 1.00
CL16 Dan Marino 3.50
CL17 Randy Moss 5.00
CL18 Drew Bledsoe 2.00
CL19 Jeff Blake 1.00
CL20 Kerry Collins 1.00
CL21 Chad Pennington 8.00
CL22 Tim Brown 1.00
CL23 Duce Staley 1.00
CL24 Jerome Bettis 1.00
CL25 Jim Harbaugh 1.00
CL26 Jerry Rice 3.00
CL27 Jon Kitna 1.00
CL28 Kurt Warner 3.00
CL29 Keyshawn Johnson 1.00
CL30 Eddie George 1.50
CL31 Stephen Davis 1.00
CL32 Thomas Jones 3.00
CL33 Chris Chandler 1.50
CL34 Tony Banks 1.50
CL35 Eric Moulds 1.50
CL36 Tim Biakabutuka 1.50
CL37 Curtis Enis 1.50
CL38 Corey Dillon 1.50
CL39 Courtney Brown 3.00
CL40 Troy Aikman 4.00
CL41 Brian Griese 2.00
CL42 Herman Moore 1.50
CL43 Antonio Freeman 1.50
CL44 Edgerrin James 4.00
CL45 Fred Taylor 3.00
CL46 Derrick Alexander 1.50
CL47 James Johnson 1.50
CL48 Cris Carter 1.50
CL49 Terry Glenn 1.50
CL50 Sherrod Gideon 1.50
CL51 Ron Dayne 3.00
CL52 Curtis Martin 1.50
CL53 Rich Gannon 1.50
CL54 Todd Pinkston 2.00
CL55 Kordell Stewart 1.50
CL56 Junior Seau 1.50
CL57 Steve Young 3.00
CL58 Shaun Alexander 5.00
CL59 Marshall Faulk 1.50
CL60 Shaun King 2.50
CL61 Jevon Kearse 1.50
CL62 Brad Johnson 1.50
CL63 Frank Sanders 3.00
CL64 Tim Dwight 8.00
CL65 Qadry Ismail 3.00
CL66 Antowain Smith 3.00
CL67 Patrick Jeffers 8.00
CL68 Cade McNown 8.00
CL69 Akili Smith 8.00
CL70 Kevin Johnson 10.00
CL71 Joey Galloway 15.00
CL72 Olandis Gary 8.00
CL73 Germane Crowell 8.00
CL74 Dorsey Levens 8.00
CL75 Marvin Harrison 20.00
CL76 Jimmy Smith 10.00
CL78 Tony Martin 3.00
CL79 Daunte Culpepper 40.00
CL80 Kevin Faulk 3.00
CL81 Ricky Williams 50.00
CL82 Amani Toomer 3.00
CL83 Ray Lucas 5.00
CL84 Tyrone Wheatley 3.00
CL85 Donovan McNabb 30.00
CL86 Troy Edwards 10.00
CL87 Jermaine Fazande 5.00
CL88 Charlie Garner 10.00
CL89 Derrick Mayes 3.00
CL90 Isaac Bruce 20.00
CL91 Mike Alstott 15.00
CL92 Steve McNair 15.00
CL93 Albert Connell 3.00

2000 Playoff Prestige Xtra Points

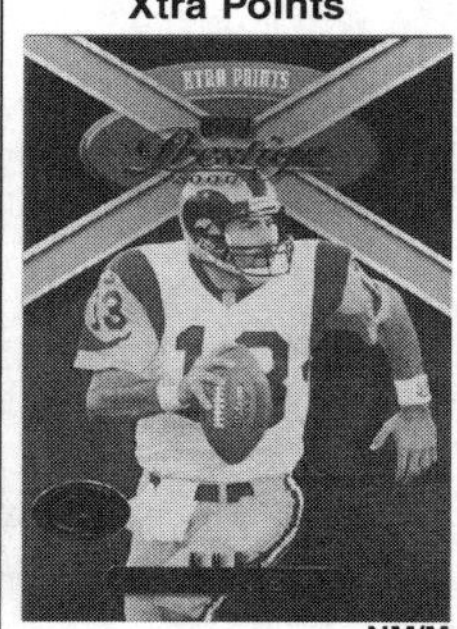

NM/M
Complete Set (40): 80.00
Common Player: 1.00
Minor Stars: 2.00
Inserted 1:47
XP1 Randy Moss 8.00
XP2 Brett Favre 12.00
XP3 Dan Marino 12.00
XP4 Peyton Manning 8.00
XP5 Emmitt Smith 10.00
XP6 Troy Aikman 8.00
XP7 Jerry Rice 8.00
XP8 Fred Taylor 5.00
XP9 Jake Plummer 2.00
XP10 Drew Bledsoe 5.00
XP11 Mark Brunell 5.00
XP12 Eddie George 2.00
XP13 Cris Carter 2.00
XP14 Stephen Davis 2.00
XP15 Corey Dillon 2.00
XP16 Marshall Faulk 2.00
XP17 Doug Flutie 2.00
XP18 Antonio Freeman 2.00
XP19 Terry Glenn 2.00
XP20 Marvin Harrison 2.00
XP21 Brad Johnson 2.00
XP22 Keyshawn Johnson 2.00
XP23 Jon Kitna 2.00
XP24 Dorsey Levens 2.00
XP25 Curtis Martin 2.00
XP26 Steve McNair 2.00
XP27 Isaac Bruce 2.00
XP28 Germane Crowell 2.00
XP29 Muhsin Muhammad 1.00
XP30 Jimmy Smith 2.00
XP31 Brian Griese 2.00
XP32 Marcus Robinson 2.00
XP33 Kurt Warner 7.00
XP34 Edgerrin James 7.00
XP35 Tim Couch 5.00
XP36 Ricky Williams 8.00
XP37 Torry Holt 2.00
XP38 Kevin Johnson 2.00
XP39 Shaun King 2.00
XP40 Olandis Gary 2.00

2001 Playoff Absolute Memorabilia

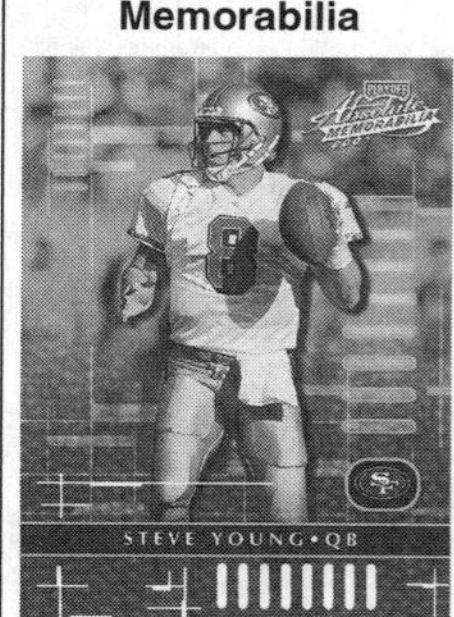

NM/M
Complete Set (185): 850.00
Common Player: .25
Minor Stars: .50
Common Rookie: 2.00
Rookie Production 1,750 Sets
Common RPM (151-185): 10.00
Production 850 Sets
Pack (6): 12.50
Wax Box (18): 165.00
1 David Boston 1.00
2 Jake Plummer 1.00
3 Thomas Jones .25
4 Jamal Anderson 1.00
5 Chris Redman .25
6 Jamal Lewis 2.50
7 Qadry Ismail .25
8 Ray Lewis .25
9 Shannon Sharpe .25
10 Travis Taylor .25
11 Trent Dilfer .25
12 Elvis Grbac .25
13 Eric Moulds .25
14 Rob Johnson .25
15 Muhsin Muhammad .25
16 Brian Urlacher 2.00
17 Cade McNown 1.00
18 Marcus Robinson 1.00
19 Akili Smith 1.00
20 Corey Dillon 1.00
21 Peter Warrick 2.00
22 Courtney Brown 1.00
23 Tim Couch 1.25
24 Emmitt Smith 3.00
25 Troy Aikman 2.00
26 Brian Griese 1.25
27 Ed McCaffrey 1.00
28 John Elway 3.00
29 Mike Anderson 3.00
30 Rod Smith .25
31 Terrell Davis 2.50
32 Barry Sanders 2.50
33 James Stewart .25
34 Ahman Green .25
35 Antonio Freeman 1.00
36 Brett Favre 4.00
37 Edgerrin James 2.50
38 Marvin Harrison 1.00
39 Peyton Manning 3.00
40 Fred Taylor 1.25
41 Jimmy Smith .25
42 Keenan McCardell .25
43 Mark Brunell 1.25
44 Sylvester Morris .25
45 Tony Gonzalez .25
46 Dan Marino 3.00
47 Jay Fiedler 1.00
48 Lamar Smith .25
49 Cris Carter 1.00
50 Daunte Culpepper 2.00
51 Randy Moss 3.00
52 Drew Bledsoe 1.25
53 Terry Glenn .25
54 Aaron Brooks 1.00
55 Joe Horn .25
56 Ricky Williams 1.00
57 Amani Toomer .25
58 Ike Hilliard .25
59 Kerry Collins .25
60 Ron Dayne 2.00
61 Tiki Barber .25
62 Chad Pennington 2.00
63 Curtis Martin 1.00
64 Laveranues Coles 1.00
65 Vinny Testaverde .25
66 Wayne Chrebet .25
67 Charles Woodson .25
68 Rich Gannon .25
69 Tim Brown 1.00
70 Tyrone Wheatley .25
71 Corey Simon .25
72 Donovan McNabb 1.50
73 Duce Staley 1.00
74 Jerome Bettis 1.00
75 Plaxico Burress 1.00
76 Doug Flutie 1.25
77 Junior Seau .25
78 Charlie Garner .25
79 Jeff Garcia 1.00
80 Jerry Rice 2.00
81 Steve Young 1.25
82 Terrell Owens 1.00
83 Darrell Jackson 1.00
84 Ricky Watters .25
85 Shaun Alexander 1.25
86 Isaac Bruce 1.00
87 Kurt Warner 3.00
88 Marshall Faulk 1.25
89 Torry Holt 1.00
90 Brad Johnson 1.00
91 Keyshawn Johnson 1.00
92 Mike Alstott 1.00
93 Shaun King 1.00
94 Warren Sapp .25
95 Warrick Dunn 1.00
96 Eddie George 1.25
97 Jevon Kearse 1.00
98 Steve McNair 1.00
99 Jeff George .25
100 Stephen Davis 1.00
101 *Jason McKinley* 2.00
102 *Bobby Newcombe* 5.00
103 *Cedrick Wilson* 5.00
104 *Ken-Yon Rambo* 5.00
105 *Kevin Kasper* 5.00
106 *Jamal Reynolds* 2.00
107 *Scotty Anderson* 2.00
108 *T.J. Houshmandzadeh* 4.00
109 *Chris Taylor* 4.00
110 *Vinny Sutherland* 4.00
111 *Jabari Holloway* 4.00
112 *Shad Meier* 4.00
113 *Correll Buckhalter* 6.00
114 *Dan Alexander* 4.00
115 *David Allen* 5.00
116 *LaMont Jordan* 6.00
117 *Nate Clements* 4.00

118 *Reggie White* 5.00
119 *Javon Green* 4.00
120 *Shaun Rogers* 2.00
121 *Heath Evans* 4.00
122 *Moran Norris* 2.00
123 *Ben Leard* 4.00
124 *David Rivers* 4.00
125 *A.J. Feely* 4.00
126 *Boo Williams* 4.00
127 *Ronney Daniels* 4.00
128 *Alge Crumpler* 5.00
129 *Todd Heap* 5.00
130 *Tim Hasselbeck* 5.00
131 *Josh Booty* 5.00
132 *Jamie Winborn* 4.00
133 *Brian Allen* 2.00
134 *Sedrick Hodge* 2.00
135 *Tommy Polley* 4.00
136 *Torrance Marshall* 4.00
137 *Damione Lewis* 4.00
138 *Marcus Stroud* 4.00
139 *Aaron Schobel* 2.00
140 *DeLawrence Grant* 2.00
141 *Fred Smoot* 5.00
142 *Jamar Fletcher* 5.00
143 *Ken Lucas* 4.00
144 *Will Allen* 4.00
145 *Adam Archuleta* 5.00
146 *Derrick Gibson* 2.00
147 *Jarrod Cooper* 2.00
148 *Eddie Berlin* 4.00
149 *Steve Smith* 4.00
150 *Willie Middlebrooks* 4.00
151 *Michael Vick* 100.00
152 *Drew Brees* 30.00
153 *Chris Weinke* 15.00
154 *Marques Tuiasosopo* 15.00
155 *Mike McMahon* 20.00
156 *Deuce McAllister* 65.00
157 *Leonard Davis* 10.00
158 *LaDainian Tomlinson* 85.00
159 *Anthony Thomas* 25.00
160 *Travis Henry* 30.00
161 *James Jackson* 20.00
162 *Michael Bennett* 30.00
163 *Kevan Barlow* 25.00
164 *Travis Minor* 25.00
165 *David Terrell* 20.00
166 *Santana Moss* 25.00
167 *Rod Gardner* 25.00
168 *Quincy Morgan* 15.00
169 *Freddie Mitchell* 15.00
170 *Reggie Wayne* 20.00
171 *Koren Robinson* 15.00
172 *Chad Johnson* 25.00
173 *Chris Chambers* 20.00
174 *Josh Heupel* 15.00
175 *Andre Carter* 15.00
176 *Justin Smith* 15.00
177 *Richard Seymour* 10.00
178 *Dan Morgan* 20.00
179 *Gerard Warren* 15.00
180 *Robert Ferguson* 15.00
181 *Sage Rosenfels* 15.00
182 *Rudi Johnson* 20.00
183 *Marvin "Snoop" Minnis* 15.00
184 *Jesse Palmer* 15.00
185 *Quincy Carter* 30.00

2001 Playoff Absolute Memorabilia Autograph Mini Helmet

NM/M
Common Helmet: 25.00
Inserted 1:Box
1 Alex Bannister 250 35.00
2 Barry Sanders 20 200.00
3 Cade McNown 1024 30.00
4 Chuck Foreman 600 35.00
5 Jake Plummer 1003 35.00
6 Jake Plummer CHR 19 125.00
7 Jevon Kearse 40 60.00
8 John Elway 40 200.00
9 Kurt Warner 119 130.00
10 Peyton Manning 287 125.00
11 Rich Gannon 1033 35.00
12 Trent Dilfer SB 100 60.00
13 Donovan McNabb 58 90.00
14 Dan Marino 80 180.00
15 Jim Kelly 20 170.00
16 Jim Kelly, Rob Johnson 18 185.00
17 Kerry Collins 18 85.00
18 Steve Young 20 200.00
19 Steve Young, Jeff Garcia 18 200.00
20 Troy Aikman 86 120.00
21 Troy Aikman CHR 34 175.00
22 Charlie Joiner 511 25.00
23 Charlie Taylor 485 25.00
24 Cliff Branch 554 35.00
25 Cliff Branch CHR 6 150.00
26 Jeff Garcia 1000 40.00
27 John Hannah 500 25.00
28 Kevin Greene 474 25.00
29 Kevin Greene CHR 24 85.00
30 Randall Cunningham 70 40.00
31 Ricky Williams 1046 40.00
32 Rob Johnson 501 35.00
33 Willie Brown 1005 25.00
34 Bob Lilly 600 40.00
35 Drew Pearson 600 35.00
36 Mike McMahon 289 35.00
37 Mike McMahon CHR 9 100.00
38 Drew Brees 273 120.00
39 Drew Brees CHR 24 225.00
40 Gerard Warren 250 30.00
41 James Jackson 238 35.00
42 James Jackson CHR 12 100.00
43 Ken-Yon Rambo 226 30.00
44 Ken-Yon Rambo CHR 24 85.00
45 LaDainian Tomlinson 226 120.00
46 LaDainian Tomlinson CHR 24 230.00
47 LaMont Jordan 237 35.00
48 Michael Bennett 251 100.00
49 Quincy Carter 236 75.00
50 Quincy Carter CHR 12 175.00
51 Quincy Morgan 238 45.00
52 Quincy Morgan CHR 12 120.00
53 Reggie Wayne 232 60.00
54 Reggie Wayne CHR 18 125.00
55 Sage Rosenfels 250 40.00
56 Santana Moss 238 65.00
57 Travis Minor 250 45.00
58 Rod Gardner 226 60.00
59 Chad Johnson 249 40.00
60 Chris Chambers 242 45.00
61 Chris Chambers CHR 12 180.00
62 Chris Weinke 226 75.00
63 Chris Weinke CHR 24 150.00
64 Deuce McAllister 224 80.00
65 Deuce McAllister CHR 24 150.00
66 Jesse Palmer 250 40.00
67 Justin Smith 239 35.00
68 Justin Smith CHR 11 100.00
69 Kevan Barlow 226 50.00
70 Kevan Barlow CHR 24 110.00
71 Robert Ferguson 226 50.00
72 Robert Ferguson CHR 24 110.00
73 Rudi Johnson 238 45.00
74 Rudi Johnson CHR 11 100.00
75 Anthony Thomas 238 60.00
76 Anthony Thomas CHR 12 125.00
77 Freddie Mitchell 217 50.00
78 Freddie Mitchell CHR 22 110.00
79 Koren Robinson 227 60.00
80 Koren Robinson CHR 23 120.00
81 Marvin "Snoop" Minnis 225 40.00
82 Marvin "Snoop" Minnis CHR 24 85.00
83 Michael Vick 226 150.00
84 Michael Vick CHR 24 300.00
85 Richard Seymour 228 25.00
86 Richard Seymour CHR 22 50.00
87 Todd Heap 225 35.00
88 Todd Heap CHR 22 70.00
89 Travis Henry 225 45.00
90 Travis Henry CHR 24 90.00
91 Will Allen 252 25.00
92 Harvey Martin 250 40.00

2001 Playoff Absolute Memorabilia Ground Hoggs

NM/M
Common Player: 15.00
Production 125 Sets
GH1 Amani Toomer 15.00
GH2 Antonio Freeman 20.00
GH3 Brett Favre 100.00
GH4 Bruce Mathews 15.00
GH5 Chad Pennington 40.00
GH6 Champ Bailey 20.00
GH7 Charles Woodson 20.00
GH8 Charlie Batch 15.00
GH9 Chris Samuels 15.00
GH10 Cris Carter 30.00
GH11 Curtis Martin 25.00
GH12 Dan Marino 125.00
GH13 Darrell Green 15.00
GH14 Darren Woodson 15.00
GH15 Daunte Culpepper 45.00
GH16 Deion Sanders 35.00
GH17 Derrick Mason 15.00
GH18 Eddie George 30.00
GH19 Edgerrin James 60.00
GH20 Emmitt Smith 70.00
GH21 Frank Wycheck 15.00
GH22 Fred Taylor 30.00
GH23 Ike Hilliard 15.00
GH24 Isaac Bruce 25.00
GH25 Jeff George 20.00
GH26 Jerry Rice 45.00
GH27 Jessie Armstead 15.00
GH28 Jevon Kearse 20.00
GH29 Jimmy Smith 15.00
GH30 Keyshawn Johnson 25.00
GH31 Lamar Smith 15.00
GH32 Laveranues Coles 15.00
GH33 Mark Brunell 30.00
GH34 Marshall Faulk 30.00
GH35 Marvin Harrison 25.00
GH36 Peerless Price 15.00
GH37 Peyton Manning 70.00
GH38 Raghib Ismail 15.00
GH39 Robert Smith 15.00
GH40 Ron Dayne 35.00
GH41 Stephen Davis 25.00
GH42 Terrell Owens 25.00
GH43 Terry Glenn 15.00
GH44 Tyrone Wheatley 15.00
GH45 Vinny Testaverde 15.00
GH46 Warren Moon 20.00
GH47 Warren Sapp 15.00
GH48 Wayne Chrebet 15.00
GH49 Willie McGinest 15.00
GH50 Zach Thomas 20.00

2001 Playoff Absolute Memorabilia Leather & Laces

NM/M
Common Player: 15.00
#1-16 Production 825 Sets
#17-34 Production 550 Sets
#35-50 Production 275 Sets
Combos: 3X
#1-16 Production 75 Sets

NM/M
#17-34 Production 50 Sets
#35-50 Production 25 Sets
LL1 David Boston 15.00
LL2 Thomas Jones 10.00
LL3 Akili Smith 15.00
LL4 Cris Carter 25.00
LL5 Tiki Barber 15.00
LL6 Jevon Kearse 15.00
LL7 Jamal Anderson 20.00
LL8 Corey Simon 10.00
LL9 Deion Sanders 25.00
LL10 Stephen Davis 15.00
LL11 Peter Warrick 20.00
LL12 Kerry Collins 15.00
LL13 Bruce Smith 15.00
LL14 Jake Plummer 15.00
LL15 Darren Woodson 10.00
LL16 Steve McNair 20.00
LL17 Brian Urlacher 30.00
LL18 Cade McNown 20.00
LL19 Marcus Robinson 20.00
LL20 Corey Dillon 25.00
LL21 Emmitt Smith 45.00
LL22 Brett Favre 60.00
LL23 Peyton Manning 60.00
LL24 Fred Taylor 20.00
LL25 Mark Brunell 20.00
LL26 Dan Marino 50.00
LL27 Daunte Culpepper 30.00
LL28 Randy Moss 50.00
LL29 Drew Bledsoe 25.00
LL30 Ron Dayne 20.00
LL31 Donovan McNabb 25.00
LL32 Jerome Bettis 20.00
LL33 Jerry Rice 35.00
LL34 Eddie George 25.00
LL35 Isaac Bruce 30.00
LL36 Ray Lewis 20.00
LL37 Tim Couch 40.00
LL38 Eric Moulds 20.00
LL39 Doug Flutie 30.00
LL40 Edgerrin James 50.00
LL41 Curtis Martin 20.00
LL42 Wayne Chrebet 20.00
LL43 Jamal Lewis 40.00
LL44 Kurt Warner 60.00
LL45 Barry Sanders 60.00
LL46 Marvin Harrison 25.00
LL47 Ricky Williams 25.00
LL48 Jimmy Smith 15.00
LL49 Tim Brown 25.00
LL50 Troy Aikman 50.00

2001 Playoff Absolute Memorabilia Tools of the Trade

NM/M
Common Player: 15.00
Glove Production 50 Sets
Pants Production 100 Sets
Facemask Production 125 Sets
Jersey Production 300 Sets
TT1 Antonio Freeman 20.00
TT2 Barry Sanders 50.00
TT3 Brett Favre 60.00
TT4 Brian Griese 25.00
TT5 Donovan McNabb 30.00
TT6 Daunte Culpepper 40.00
TT7 Drew Bledsoe 30.00
TT8 Emmitt Smith 50.00
TT9 Jamal Lewis 35.00
TT10 Jimmy Smith 15.00
TT11 Edgerrin James 45.00
TT12 Mike Anderson 30.00
TT13 Peyton Manning 60.00
TT14 Randy Moss 60.00
TT15 Rich Gannon 20.00
TT16 Ricky Williams 30.00
TT17 Steve McNair 25.00
TT18 Terrell Owens 25.00
TT19 Ricky Watters 15.00
TT20 Warren Sapp 25.00
TT21 Champ Bailey 40.00
TT22 Courtney Brown 25.00
TT23 Deion Sanders 40.00
TT24 Derrick Mason 25.00
TT25 Eddie George 50.00
TT26 Jevon Kearse 40.00
TT27 Keyshawn Johnson 35.00
TT28 Ron Dayne 40.00
TT29 Terry Glenn 25.00
TT30 Wayne Chrebet 35.00
TT31 Curtis Martin 30.00
TT32 Corey Dillon 30.00
TT33 Cris Carter 35.00
TT34 Junior Seau 30.00
TT35 Jerome Bettis 30.00
TT36 Warrick Dunn 30.00
TT37 Eric Moulds 30.00
TT38 Stephen Davis 25.00
TT39 Steve Young 45.00
TT40 Troy Aikman 60.00
TT41 Dan Marino 100.00
TT42 Isaac Bruce 25.00
TT43 Jerry Rice 50.00
TT44 John Elway 100.00
TT45 Kurt Warner 60.00
TT46 Mark Brunell 30.00
TT47 Marshall Faulk 30.00
TT48 Terrell Davis 50.00
TT49 Tim Couch 30.00
TT50 Torry Holt 20.00

A player's name in *italic* type indicates a rookie card.

2001 Playoff Absolute Memorabilia Signing Bonus

1 Alex Bannister
2 Anthony Thomas
3 Barry Sanders
4 Bob Lilly
5 Cade McNown
6 Chad Johnson
7 Charlie Joiner
8 Charley Taylor
9 Chris Chambers
10 Chris Weinke
11 Chuck Foreman
12 Cliff Branch
13 Dan Marino
14 Deuce McAllister
15 Donovan McNabb
16 Drew Brees
17 Drew Pearson
18 Freddie Mitchell
19 Gerald Warren
20 Harvey Martin
21 Jake Plummer
22 James Jackson
23 Jeff Garcia
24 Jesse Palmer
25 Jevon Kearse
26 Jim Kelly
27 Jim Kelly, Rob Johnson
28 John Elway
29 John Hannah
30 Justin Smith
31 Ken-Yon Rambo
32 Kerry Collins
33 Kevan Barlow
34 Kevin Green
35 Koren Robinson
36 Kurt Warner
37 LaDainian Tomlinson
38 LaMont Jordan
39 Marvin "Snoop" Minnis
40 Michael Bennett
41 Michael Vick
42 Mike McMahon
43 Peyton Manning
44 Quincy Carter
45 Quincy Morgan
46 Randall Cunningham
47 Reggie Wayne
48 Rich Gannon
49 Richard Seymour
50 Ricky Williams
51 Rob Johnson
52 Robert Ferguson
53 Rod Gardner
54 Rudi Johnson
55 Sage Rosenfels
56 Santana Moss
57 Steve Young
58 Steve Young, Jeff Garcia
59 Todd Heap
60 Travis Henry
61 Travis Minor
62 Trent Dilfer
63 Troy Aikman
64 Will Allen
65 Willie Brown

2001 Playoff Contenders

NM/M
Complete Set (100): 25.00
Common Player: .30
Minor Stars: .50
Common Rookie (101-200): 10.00
Pack (5): 18.00
Box (16): 200.00
1 David Boston .60
2 Jake Plummer .50
3 Jamal Anderson .50
4 Chris Chandler .30
5 Elvis Grbac .30
6 Brandon Stokley .30
7 Travis Taylor .50
8 Ray Lewis .50
9 Rob Johnson .50
10 Eric Moulds .50
11 Tim Biakabutuka .30
12 Muhsin Muhammad .30
13 James Allen .30
14 Brian Urlacher 1.25
15 Peter Warrick .60
16 Corey Dillon .60
17 Tim Couch .75
18 Kevin Johnson .50
19 Rickey Dudley .30
20 Emmitt Smith 2.00
21 Joey Galloway .50
22 Brian Griese 1.00
23 Terrell Davis 1.50
24 Mike Anderson 1.00
25 Ed McCaffrey .50
26 Rod Smith .50
27 Charlie Batch .50
28 James Stewart .50
29 Germane Crowell .30
30 Johnnie Morton .30
31 Brett Favre 3.00
32 Ahman Green .60
33 Antonio Freeman .50
34 Peyton Manning 2.00
35 Edgerrin James 2.00
36 Marvin Harrison .75
37 Jerome Pathon .30
38 Mark Brunell 1.00
39 Fred Taylor .75
40 Keenan McCardell .30
41 Jimmy Smith .50
42 Trent Green .50
43 Priest Holmes .50
44 Tony Gonzalez .50
45 Derrick Alexander .50
46 Jay Fiedler .50
47 Lamar Smith .50
48 Zach Thomas .30
49 Oronde Gadsden .30
50 Daunte Culpepper 1.50
51 Randy Moss 2.00
52 Cris Carter .60
53 Drew Bledsoe 1.00
54 J.R. Redmond .30
55 Troy Brown .50
56 Aaron Brooks 1.00
57 Ricky Williams 1.25
58 Joe Horn .30
59 Kerry Collins .60
60 Tiki Barber .50
61 Ron Dayne .50
62 Ike Hilliard .30
63 Vinny Testaverde .50
64 Curtis Martin .60
65 Wayne Chrebet .50
66 Laveranues Coles .50
67 Rich Gannon .60
68 Tyrone Wheatley .50
69 Tim Brown .75
70 Jerry Rice 2.00
71 Donovan McNabb 1.50
72 Duce Staley .50
73 Todd Pinkston .30
74 Kordell Stewart .75
75 Jerome Bettis .60
76 Plaxico Burress .75
77 Doug Flutie 1.00
78 Junior Seau .50
79 Jeff Garcia 1.00
80 Garrison Hearst .50
81 Terrell Owens .75
82 Matt Hasselbeck .60
83 Ricky Watters .50
84 Shaun Alexander 1.25
85 Darrell Jackson .50
86 Kurt Warner 2.00
87 Marshall Faulk 1.00
88 Isaac Bruce .75
89 Torry Holt .75
90 Brad Johnson .60
91 Keyshawn Johnson .75
92 Warrick Dunn .50
93 Warren Sapp .50
94 Steve McNair .60
95 Eddie George 1.00
96 Derrick Mason .50
97 Jevon Kearse .50
98 Stephen Davis .60
99 Bruce Smith .30
100 Michael Westbrook .50
101 *Adam Archuleta* 40.00
102 *Alex Bannister* 15.00
103 *Alge Crumpler* 10.00
104 *Andre Carter* 20.00
105 *Anthony Thomas* 50.00
106 *Ben Leard* 10.00
107 *Bobby Newcombe* 15.00
108 *Brian Allen* 10.00
109 *Carlos Polk* 10.00
110 *Casey Hampton* 25.00
111 *Cedric Scott* 10.00
112 *Cedrick Wilson* 12.00
113 *Chad Johnson* 40.00
114 *Chris Chambers* 150.00
115 *Chris Weinke* 25.00
116 *Correll Buckhalter* 30.00
117 *Damione Lewis* 25.00
118 *Dan Morgan* 30.00
119 *Daniel Guy* 12.00
120 *David Allen* 15.00
121 *David Terrell* 25.00
122 *Ken Lucas* 10.00
123 *Deuce McAllister* 120.00
124 *Drew Brees* 75.00
125 *Eddie Berlin* 25.00
126 *Eddie "Boo" Williams* 40.00
127 *Ennis Davis* 10.00
128 *Freddie Mitchell* 30.00
129 *Gary Baxter* 10.00
130 *Gerard Warren* 15.00
131 *Hakim Akbar* 10.00
132 *Heath Evans* 10.00
133 *Jabari Holloway* 12.00
134 *Jamal Reynolds* 15.00
135 *James Jackson* 20.00
136 *Jamie Winborn* 10.00
137 *Javon Green* 12.00
138 *Jesse Palmer* 30.00
139 *Dominic Rhodes* 40.00
140 *Josh Heupel* 25.00
141 *Justin Smith* 15.00
142 *Karon Riley* 10.00
143 *Keith Adams* 25.00
144 *Kendrell Bell* 50.00
145 *Kenny Smith* 10.00
146 *Kenyatta Walker* 60.00
147 *Ken-Yon Rambo* 15.00
148 *Kevan Barlow* 30.00
149 *Koren Robinson* 40.00
150 *LaDainian Tomlinson* 150.00
151 *LaMont Jordan* 60.00
152 *Leonard Davis* 25.00
153 *Marcus Stroud* 10.00
154 *Marques Tuiasosopo* 40.00
155 *Marvin "Snoop" Minnis* 30.00
156 *Michael Bennett* 75.00
157 *Michael Vick* 400.00
158 *Mike McMahon* 40.00
159 *Moran Norris* 10.00
160 *Morlon Greenwood* 10.00
161 *Nate Clements* 20.00
162 *Quincy Carter* 250.00
163 *Quincy Morgan* 20.00
164 *Jamar Fletcher* 25.00
165 *Reggie Germany* 25.00
166 *Reggie Wayne* 40.00
167 *Reggie White* 12.00
168 *Richard Seymour* 25.00
169 *Robert Carswell* 20.00
170 *Robert Ferguson* 20.00
171 *Rod Gardner* 200.00
172 *Ronney Daniels* 15.00
173 *Rudi Johnson* 50.00
174 *Sage Rosenfels* 25.00
175 *Santana Moss* 40.00
176 *Shaun Rogers* 10.00
177 *T.J. Houshmandzadeh* 10.00
178 *Tim Hasselbeck* 15.00
179 *Todd Heap* 80.00
180 *Tony Stewart* 12.00
181 *Torrance Marshall* 10.00
182 *Travis Henry* 100.00
183 *Travis Minor* 25.00
184 *Vinny Sutherland* 15.00
185 *Will Allen* 15.00
186 *Willie Howard* 10.00
187 *Willie Middlebrooks* 20.00
188 *Derrick Blaylock* 12.00
189 *A.J. Feeley* 40.00
190 *Steve Smith* 40.00
191 *Onome Ojo* 10.00
192 *Dee Brown* 12.00
193 *Kevin Kasper* 20.00
194 *Dave Dickenson* 20.00
195 *Chris Barnes* 12.00
196 *Scotty Anderson* 15.00
197 *Chris Taylor* 12.00
198 *Cedric James* 12.00
199 *Justin McCareins* 40.00
200 *Tommy Polley* 25.00

2001 Playoff Contenders MVP Contenders

NM/M
Complete Set (20): 50.00
Common Player: 1.00
Inserted 1:16
1 Brett Favre 8.00
2 Brian Griese 2.50
3 Corey Dillon 2.00
4 Cris Carter 2.00
5 Daunte Culpepper 4.00
6 Drew Bledsoe 2.50
7 Eddie George 2.50
8 Edgerrin James 5.00
9 Emmitt Smith 5.00
10 Isaac Bruce 2.00
11 Aaron Brooks 2.50
12 Jerry Rice 5.00
13 Kurt Warner 6.00
14 Mark Brunell 2.00
15 Marshall Faulk 2.50
16 Peyton Manning 6.00
17 Randy Moss 6.00
18 Ray Lewis 2.00
19 Ricky Williams 3.00
20 Stephen Davis 2.00

2001 Playoff Contenders MVP Contenders Autographs

1 Brett Favre
2 Brian Griese
3 Corey Dillon
4 Cris Carter
5 Daunte Culpepper
6 Drew Bledsoe
7 Eddie George
8 Edgerrin James
9 Emmitt Smith
10 Isaac Bruce
11 Aaron Brooks
12 Jerry Rice
13 Kurt Warner
14 Mark Brunell
15 Marshall Faulk
16 Peyton Manning
17 Randy Moss
18 Ray Lewis
19 Ricky Williams
20 Stephen Davis

2001 Playoff Contenders ROY Contenders

NM/M
Complete Set (20): 60.00
Common Player: 2.00
Inserted 1:32
1 Anthony Thomas 4.00
2 Chad Johnson 2.00
3 Chris Chambers 5.00
4 Chris Weinke 4.00
5 David Terrell 3.00
6 Deuce McAllister 4.00
7 Drew Brees 6.00
8 Freddie Mitchell 4.00
9 James Jackson 2.50
10 Kevan Barlow 3.00
11 Koren Robinson 4.00
12 LaDainian Tomlinson 8.00
13 Marvin "Snoop" Minnis 3.00
14 Michael Bennett 5.00
15 Michael Vick 10.00
16 Quincy Carter 5.00
17 Quincy Morgan 2.50
18 Reggie Wayne 4.00
19 Travis Henry 3.00
20 Travis Minor 2.50

2001 Playoff Contenders ROY Contenders Autographs

NM/M
Common Player: 40.00
Production 50 Sets
1 Anthony Thomas 50.00
2 Chad Johnson 40.00
3 Chris Chambers 75.00
4 Chris Weinke 60.00
5 David Terrell 75.00
6 Deuce McAllister 60.00
7 Drew Brees 90.00
8 Freddie Mitchell 50.00

9 James Jackson 40.00
10 Kevan Barlow 40.00
11 Koren Robinson 50.00
12 LaDainian Tomlinson 100.00
13 Marvin "Snoop" Minnis 40.00
14 Michael Bennett 75.00
15 Michael Vick 150.00
16 Quincy Carter 60.00
17 Quincy Morgan 40.00
18 Reggie Wayne 40.00
19 Travis Henry 40.00
20 Travis Minor 40.00

2001 Playoff Contenders Round Numbers Autographs

NM/M

Common Player: 25.00
1 Michael Vick, LaDainian Tomlinson 200.00
2 Deuce McAllister, Michael Bennett 60.00
3 David Terrell, Koren Robinson 60.00
4 Nate Clements, Will Allen 25.00
5 Todd Heap, Reggie Wayne 40.00
6 Richard Seymour, Justin Smith 25.00
7 Drew Brees, Quincy Carter 125.00
8 Anthony Thomas, Travis Henry 75.00
9 Chad Johnson, Quincy Morgan 25.00
10 Robert Ferguson, Chris Chambers 40.00
11 Shaun Rogers, Kendrell Bell 50.00
12 Kevan Barlow, Travis Minor 30.00
13 James Jackson, Marvin "Snoop" Minnis 30.00
14 Rudi Johnson, Correll Buckhalter 25.00
15 Chris Weinke, Jesse Palmer 40.00

2001 Playoff Contenders Round Numbers Gold

"Many cards too rare to price."

NM/M

1 Michael Vick/10, LaDainian Tomlinson/10
2 Deuce McAllister/10, Michael Bennett/10
3 David Terrell/10, Koren Robinson/10
4 Nate Clements/10, Will Allen/10
5 Todd Heap/10, Reggie Wayne/10
6 Richard Seymour/10, Justin Smith/10
7 Drew Brees/20, Quincy Carter/20 250.00
8 Anthony Thomas/20, Travis Henry/10
9 Chad Johnson/20, Quincy Morgan/20 75.00
10 Robert Ferguson/20, Chris Chambers/20 250.00
11 Shaun Rogers/20, Kendrell Bell/20 75.00
12 Kevan Barlow/30, Travis Minor/30 40.00
13 James Jackson/30, Marvin "Snoop" Minnis/30 40.00
14 Rudi Johnson/40, Correll Buckhalter/40 40.00
15 Chris Weinke/40, Jesse Palmer/40 100.00

2001 Playoff Honors

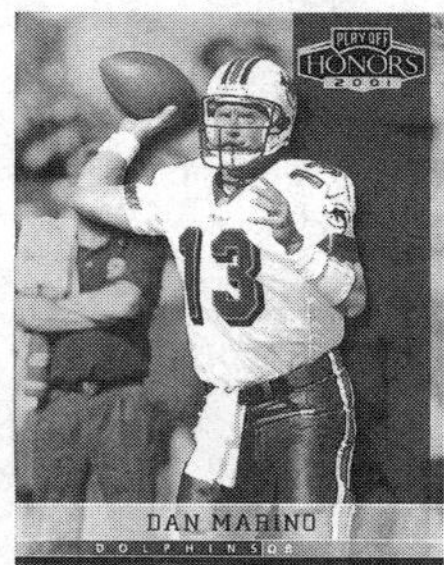

NM/M

Complete Set (235): 1,000
Common Player: .25
Minor Stars: .50
Common Rookie (#101-200): 3.00
Production 250 Sets
Common Rookie (#201-235): 5.00
Production 725 Sets
Cards #209, #211 & #221 Never Released
Pack (6): 8.00
Wax Box (16): 95.00
1 Rob Johnson .50
2 Eric Moulds .75
3 Marvin Harrison .75
4 Edgerrin James 2.00
5 Peyton Manning 2.50
6 Jay Fiedler .75
7 Lamar Smith .50
8 Zach Thomas .50
9 Dan Marino 3.00
10 Drew Bledsoe 1.00
11 Terry Glenn .50
12 Wayne Chrebet .75
13 Curtis Martin .75
14 Chad Pennington 1.25
15 Vinny Testaverde .50
16 Corey Dillon .75
17 Jon Kitna .75
18 Akili Smith .75
19 Peter Warrick 1.00
20 Kevin Johnson .75
21 Tim Couch 1.00
22 Eddie George 1.00
23 Steve McNair .75
24 Jevon Kearse .75
25 Jerome Bettis .75
26 Kordell Stewart .75
27 Plaxico Burress .75
28 Mark Brunell 1.00
29 Keenan McCardell .50
30 Jimmy Smith .75
31 Fred Taylor 1.00
32 Elvis Grbac .50
33 Jamal Lewis 2.00
34 Ray Lewis .75
35 Mike Anderson 2.00
36 Terrell Davis 1.50
37 John Elway 3.00
38 Brian Griese 1.00
39 Ed McCaffrey .75
40 Tony Gonzalez .75
41 Trent Green .75
42 Sylvester Morris .50
43 Tim Brown .75
44 Rich Gannon .50
45 Charlie Garner .50
46 Tyrone Wheatley .50
47 Charles Woodson .75
48 Tim Dwight .50
49 Doug Flutie 1.00
50 Junior Seau .50
51 Shaun Alexander 1.00
52 Matt Hasselbeck .75
53 Ricky Watters .50
54 Tony Banks .50
55 Joey Galloway .75
56 Emmitt Smith 2.00
57 Troy Aikman 1.50
58 Kerry Collins .50
59 Ron Dayne 1.25
60 Donovan McNabb 1.25
61 Duce Staley .75
62 David Boston .75
63 Thomas Jones .50
64 Jake Plummer .75
65 Stephen Davis .75
66 Jeff George .50
67 Michael Westbrook .50
68 Deion Sanders .75
69 James Allen .50
70 Cade McNown .75
71 Marcus Robinson .75
72 Brian Urlacher 1.50
73 Germane Crowell .75
74 Charlie Batch .75
75 James Stewart .50
76 Brett Favre 3.50
77 Antonio Freeman .75
78 Ahman Green .75
79 Cris Carter .75
80 Daunte Culpepper 1.50
81 Randy Moss 2.50
82 Mike Alstott .75
83 Warrick Dunn .75
84 Brad Johnson .50
85 Keyshawn Johnson .75
86 Warren Sapp .50
87 Jamal Anderson .75
88 Chris Chandler .50
89 Isaac Bruce .75
90 Marshall Faulk 1.00
91 Torry Holt .75
92 Kurt Warner 2.50
93 Aaron Brooks 1.00
94 Albert Connell .25
95 Ricky Williams 1.25
96 Jeff Garcia .75
97 Terrell Owens .75
98 Steve Young 1.00
99 Jerry Rice 1.75
100 Jeff Lewis .25
101 Rashard Casey 3.00
102 A.J. Feeley 3.00
103 Josh Booty 3.00
104 LaMont Jordan 5.00
105 Ben Leard 3.00
106 David Rivers 3.00
107 Tim Hasselbeck 5.00
108 Jason McKinley 3.00
109 Correll Buckhalter 15.00
110 Dan Alexander 5.00
111 Derrick Blaylock 3.00
112 Chris Barnes 5.00
113 Dadrian Brown 3.00
114 Derek Combs 3.00
115 David Allen 3.00
116 DeAngelo Evans 3.00
117 Reggie White 3.00
118 Heath Evans 3.00
119 George Layne 3.00
120 Moran Norris 3.00
121 Bhawoh Jue 3.00
122 Dustin McClintock 3.00
123 Ja'Mar Toombs 3.00
124 Steve Smith 8.00
125 Milton Wynn 3.00
126 Justin McCareins 8.00
127 Jarrod Cooper 3.00
128 Vinny Sutherland 5.00
129 Alex Bannister 5.00
130 Scotty Anderson 3.00
131 Onomo Ojo 3.00
132 Darnerian McCants 3.00
133 Eddie Berlin 3.00
134 Jonathan Carter 3.00
135 Bobby Newcombe 3.00
136 Cedrick Wilson 3.00
137 Kevin Kasper 8.00
138 Francis St. Paul 3.00
139 David Martin 5.00
140 T.J. Houshmandzadeh 3.00
141 John Capel 5.00
142 Reggie Germany 5.00
143 Chris Taylor 3.00
144 Ken-Yon Rambo 5.00
145 Richmond Flowers 3.00
146 Quentin McCord 3.00
147 Andre King 3.00
148 Eddie "Boo" Williams 5.00
149 Daniel Guy 3.00
150 Javon Green 3.00
151 Ronney Daniels 3.00
152 Alge Crumpler 8.00
153 Tony Driver 3.00
154 Shad Meier 3.00
155 Jabari Holloway 3.00
156 Ryan Pickett 3.00
157 Billy Baber 3.00
158 Tony Stewart 3.00
159 Arther Love 3.00
160 Orlando Huff 3.00
161 Nate Clements 3.00
162 Will Allen 5.00
163 Willie Middlebrooks 3.00
164 Jamar Fletcher 5.00
165 Ken Lucas 3.00
166 Fred Smoot 5.00
167 Michael Stone 3.00
168 Tony Dixon 3.00
169 Andre Dyson 3.00
170 Gary Baxter 3.00
171 Adam Archuleta 8.00
172 Derrick Gibson 3.00
173 Edgerton Hartwell 3.00
174 Jamal Reynolds 3.00
175 Richard Seymour 3.00
176 Aaron Schobel 3.00
177 Paul Toviessi 3.00
178 DeLawrence Grant 3.00
179 Karon Riley 3.00
180 Cedric Scott 3.00
181 Damione Lewis 3.00
182 Marcus Stroud 3.00
183 Casey Hampton 3.00
184 Willie Howard 3.00
185 Shaun Rogers 3.00
186 Kenny Smith 3.00
187 Marcus Bell 3.00
188 Mario Fatafehi 3.00
189 Kendrell Bell 25.00
190 Tommy Polley 3.00
191 Jamie Winborn 3.00
192 Sedrick Hodge 3.00
193 Torrance Marshall 3.00
194 Eric Westmoreland 3.00
195 Brian Allen 3.00
196 Morlon Greenwood 3.00
197 Brandon Spoon 3.00
198 Carlos Polk 3.00
199 Alex Lincoln 3.00
200 Keith Adams 3.00
201 Kevan Barlow 15.00
202 Michael Bennett 20.00
203 Drew Brees 25.00
204 Quincy Carter 12.00
205 Andre Carter 5.00
206 Chris Chambers 20.00
207 Robert Ferguson 5.00
208 Rod Gardner 20.00
210 Travis Henry 15.00
212 Chad Johnson 20.00
213 Rudi Johnson 15.00
214 Sage Rosenfels 10.00
215 Deuce McAllister 25.00
216 Mike McMahon 10.00
217 Marvin "Snoop" Minnis 10.00
218 Travis Minor 8.00
219 Freddie Mitchell 8.00
220 Quincy Morgan 8.00
222 Santana Moss 10.00
223 Jesse Palmer 10.00
224 Koren Robinson 8.00
225 Josh Heupel 10.00
226 Justin Smith 5.00
227 David Terrell 10.00
228 Anthony Thomas 20.00
229 LaDainian Tomlinson 30.00
230 Marques Tuiasosopo 12.00
231 Michael Vick 75.00
232 Gerard Warren 8.00
233 Reggie Wayne 10.00
234 Chris Weinke 12.00
235 Leonard Davis 5.00

2001 Playoff Honors Alma Mater Materials

NM/M

Common Player: 15.00
1 Shaun Alexander 20.00
2 Drew Bledsoe 20.00
3 Earl Campbell 25.00
4 Larry Csonka 15.00
5 Terrell Davis 20.00
6 Tony Dorsett 25.00
7 John Elway 75.00
8 Eddie George 20.00
9 Edgerrin James 40.00
10 Keyshawn Johnson 20.00
11 Jevon Kearse 15.00
12 Fred Taylor 15.00
13 Ricky Williams 15.00
14 Olandis Gary 15.00
15 E.G. Green 15.00

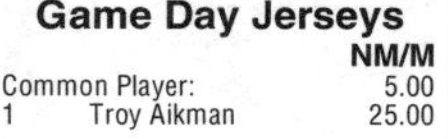

2001 Playoff Honors Game Day Jerseys

NM/M

Common Player: 5.00
1 Troy Aikman 25.00

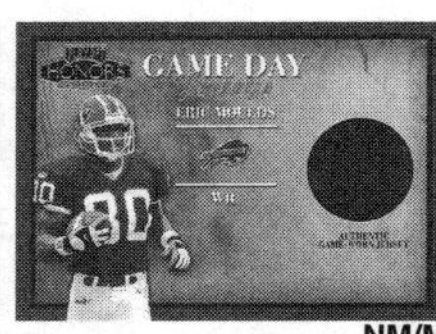

NM/M

2 Mike Anderson 10.00
3 Jerome Bettis 10.00
4 Drew Bledsoe 10.00
5 Aaron Brooks 10.00
6 Isaac Bruce 5.00
7 Tim Brown 10.00
8 Mark Brunell 10.00
9 Cris Carter 5.00
10 Kerry Collins 5.00
11 Tim Couch 10.00
12 Daunte Culpepper 15.00
13 Stephen Davis 10.00
14 Terrell Davis 15.00
15 Ron Dayne 15.00
16 Corey Dillon 10.00
17 Warrick Dunn 5.00
18 John Elway 30.00
19 Marshall Faulk 15.00
20 Brett Favre 40.00
21 Eddie George 10.00
22 Brian Griese 10.00
23 Marvin Harrison 5.00
24 Torry Holt 5.00
25 Edgerrin James 25.00
26 Keyshawn Johnson 5.00
27 Jevon Kearse 5.00
28 Jamal Lewis 25.00
29 Peyton Manning 15.00
30 Dan Marino 30.00
31 Curtis Martin 10.00
32 Donovan McNabb 10.00
33 Steve McNair 10.00
34 Joe Montana 30.00
35 Randy Moss 10.00
36 Eric Moulds 5.00
37 Jake Plummer 5.00
38 Jerry Rice 25.00
39 Barry Sanders 25.00
40 Deion Sanders 20.00
41 Warren Sapp 5.00
42 Junior Seau 5.00
43 Emmitt Smith 30.00
44 Fred Taylor 10.00
45 Zach Thomas 10.00
46 Brian Urlacher 40.00
47 Kurt Warner 30.00
48 Peter Warrick 10.00
49 Ricky Williams 10.00
50 Steve Young 30.00

2001 Playoff Honors Rookie Tandem/ Quad Materials

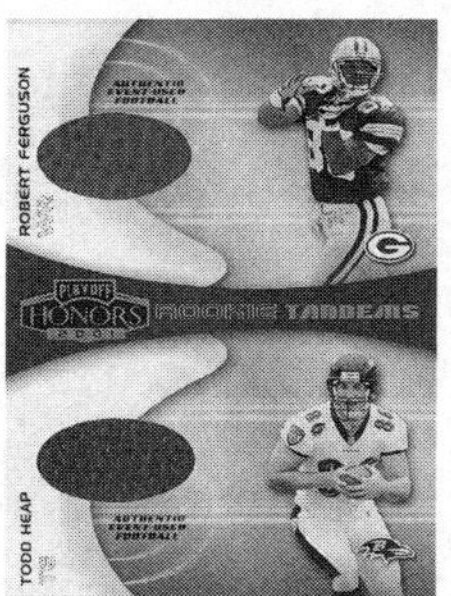

NM/M

Common Player: 10.00
1 Michael Vick, Quincy Carter 40.00
2 Chris Weinke, Mike McMahon 20.00
3 Drew Brees, LaDainian Tomlinson 30.00
4 Anthony Thomas, David Terrell 20.00
5 Sage Rosenfels, Rod Gardner 10.00
6 Rudi Johnson, Chad Johnson 10.00
7 Josh Heupel, Travis Minor 10.00
8 James Jackson, Quincy Morgan 10.00
9 Koren Robinson, Reggie Wayne 10.00
10 Freddie Mitchell, Santana Moss 20.00
11 Michael Bennett, Deuce McAllister 25.00
12 Travis Henry, Kevan Barlow 15.00
13 Chris Chambers, Marvin "Snoop" Minnis 15.00
14 Robert Ferguson, Todd Heap 10.00
15 Marques Tuiasosopo, Jesse Palmer 20.00
16 Justin Smith, Gerard Warren 10.00
17 Andre Carter, Dan Morgan 10.00
18 Michael Vick, Quincy Carter, Chris Weinke, Mike McMahon 75.00
19 Drew Brees, LaDainian Tomlinson, Anthony Thomas, David Terrell 75.00
20 Sage Rosenfels, Rod Gardner, Rudi Johnson, Chad Johnson 20.00
21 Josh Heupel, Travis Minor, James Jackson, Quincy Morgan 30.00
22 Koren Robinson, Reggie Wayne, Freddie Mitchell, Santana Moss 30.00
23 Michael Bennett, Deuce McAllister, Travis Henry, Kevan Barlow 50.00
24 Chris Chambers, Marvin "Snoop" Minnis, Robert Ferguson, Todd Heap 50.00
25 Marques Tuiasosopo, Jesse Palmer, Justin Smith, Gerard Warren 25.00

2001 Playoff NFL Players Award Banquet (Unsung Heroes)

NM/M

Complete Set (31): 12.00
Common Player: .50
1 Bob Christian .50
2 Ronald McKinnon .50
3 Trent Dilfer 1.00
4 Shawn Price .50
5 Mike Minter .50
6 Brian Urlacher 3.00
7 Takeo Spikes .50
8 Wali Rainer .50
9 Larry Allen .50
10 Howard Griffith .50
11 James Jones .50
12 Russell Maryland .50
13 Tarik Glenn .50
14 Daimon Shelton .50
15 Mike Maslowski .50
16 Brian Walker .50
17 Chris Walsh .50
18 Tedy Bruschi .50
19 La'Roi Glover .50
20 Greg Comella .50
21 Richie Anderson .50
22 Greg Biekert .50
23 Cecil Martin .50
24 John Fiala .50
25 John Parrella .50
26 Bryant Young .50
27 Fabien Bownes .50
28 Ray Agnew .50
29 John Lynch 1.00
30 Lorenzo Neal .50
31 James Thrash .50

2001 Playoff Preferred

NM/M

Common Player: .30
Rookies numbered to varying quantities
Unlisted Star: .75
Minor Star: .50
Rookies 201-225 include memorabilia
Box: 80.00
1 Elvis Grbac .30
2 Ray Lewis .50
3 Travis Taylor .30
4 Rob Johnson .30
5 Eric Moulds .30
6 Corey Dillon .75
7 Peter Warrick .50
8 Tim Couch 1.00
9 Kevin Johnson .30
10 Brian Griese .50
11 Mike Anderson .50
12 Rod Smith .30
13 Terrell Davis 1.00
14 Olandis Gary .30
15 Peyton Manning 2.00
16 Edgerrin James 1.50
17 Marvin Harrison .75
18 Terrence Wilkins .30
19 Mark Brunell .75
20 Fred Taylor .50
21 Keenan McCardell .30
22 Jimmy Smith .30
23 Stacey Mack .30
24 Trent Green .50
25 Priest Holmes 1.00
26 Tony Gonzalez .50
27 Jay Fiedler .30
28 Lamar Smith .30
29 Zach Thomas .30
30 Drew Bledsoe 1.25
31 Antowain Smith .30
32 Troy Brown .30
33 Tom Brady 8.00
34 Vinny Testaverde .50
35 Wayne Chrebet .50
36 Curtis Martin .75
37 Rich Gannon .75
38 Tyrone Wheatley .30
39 Jerry Rice 2.00
40 Tim Brown .75
41 Charles Woodson .50
42 Charlie Garner .30
43 Kordell Stewart .50
44 Jerome Bettis .50
45 Doug Flutie .50
46 Junior Seau .50
47 Matt Hasselbeck .30
48 Trent Dilfer .30
49 Shaun Alexander .75
50 Ricky Watters .50
51 Eddie George .75
52 Steve McNair .75
53 Jevon Kearse .30
54 David Boston .50
55 Jake Plummer .50
56 Chris Chandler .30
57 Maurice Smith .30
58 Muhsin Muhammad .30
59 Wesley Walls .30
60 James Allen .30
61 Marcus Robinson .50
62 Brian Urlacher 1.50
63 Clint Stoerner .30
64 Ryan Leaf .30
65 Emmitt Smith 2.00
66 Joey Galloway .30
67 Charlie Batch .30
68 James Stewart .30
69 Brett Favre 2.50
70 Ahman Green .75
71 Bill Schroeder .30
72 Bubba Franks .30
73 Daunte Culpepper 1.25
74 Randy Moss 2.00
75 Cris Carter .50
76 Aaron Brooks 1.00
77 Ricky Williams 1.00
78 Albert Connell .30
79 Kerry Collins .50
80 Ron Dayne .30
81 Jason Sehorn .30
82 Amani Toomer .30
83 Donovan McNabb 1.25
84 James Thrash .30
85 Duce Staley .30
86 Jeff Garcia .75
87 Garrison Hearst .50
88 Terrell Owens .75
89 Kurt Warner 2.00
90 Marshall Faulk 1.25
91 Torry Holt .75
92 Isaac Bruce .75
93 Brad Johnson .30
94 Warrick Dunn .50
95 Mike Alstott .50
96 Keyshawn Johnson .75
97 Warren Sapp .30
98 Tony Banks .30
99 Stephen Davis .30
100 Champ Bailey .30
101 Michael Vick 35.00
102 Drew Brees 15.00
103 Marques Tuiasosopo 8.00
104 Sage Rosenfels 3.00
105 Jesse Palmer 5.00
106 Mike McMahon 5.00
107 A.J. Feeley 5.00
108 Josh Booty 3.00
109 Josh Heupel 3.00
110 Henry Burris 3.00
111 Roderick Robinson 2.00
112 Tory Woodbury 2.00
113 Dave Dickenson 2.00
114 Deuce McAllister 20.00
115 Michael Bennett 15.00
116 Rudi Johnson 10.00
117 Derrick Blaylock 2.00
118 Dee Brown 2.00
119 Eric Kelly 2.00
120 Dominic Rhodes 6.00
121 Jason Brookins 3.00
122 Nick Goings 2.00
123 Markus Steele 2.00
124 Benjamin Gay 2.00
125 Tony Taylor 2.00
126 Elvis Joseph 2.00
127 Tay Cody 2.00
128 Heath Evans 2.00
129 George Layne 2.00
130 Moran Norris 2.00
131 Jameel Cook 2.00
132 Patrick Washington 2.00
133 Chad Johnson 12.00
134 Santana Moss 10.00
135 Reggie Wayne 10.00
136 Robert Ferguson 5.00
137 Steve Smith 10.00
138 Justin McCareins 5.00
139 Vinny Sutherland 2.00
140 Alex Bannister 2.00
141 Scotty Anderson 2.00
142 Onome Ojo 2.00
143 Darnerian McCants 2.00
144 Eddie Berlin 2.00
145 Cedrick Wilson 2.00
146 Kevin Kasper 2.00
147 T.J. Houshmandzadeh 5.00
148 Reggie Germany 2.00
149 Chris Taylor 2.00
150 Ken-Yon Rambo 3.00
151 Quentin McCord 2.00
152 Andre King 2.00
153 Arnold Jackson 2.00
154 Tim Baker 2.00
155 Drew Bennett 8.00
156 Cedric James 2.00
157 Todd Heap 5.00
158 Alge Crumpler 5.00
159 Sean Brewer 2.00
160 Shad Meier 2.00
161 Brandon Manumaleuna 2.00
162 Tony Stewart 2.00
163 David Martin 2.00
164 Matt Dominguez 2.00
165 Eddie "Boo" Williams 5.00
166 Justin Smith 2.00
167 Andre Carter 2.00
168 Jamal Reynolds 2.00
169 Ryan Pickett 2.00
170 Aaron Schobel 2.00
171 Derrick Burgess 2.00
172 DeLawrence Grant 2.00
173 Karon Riley 2.00
174 Richard Seymour 2.00
175 Marcus Stroud 2.00
176 Casey Hampton 2.00
177 Shaun Rogers 2.00

178 *Kris Jenkins* 2.00
179 *Eric Downing* 2.00
180 *Kenny Smith* 2.00
181 *Marcus Bell* 2.00
182 *Dan Morgan* 3.00
183 *Kendrell Bell* 12.00
184 *Tommy Polley* 2.00
185 *Jamie Winborn* 2.00
186 *Quinton Caver* 2.00
187 *Sedrick Hodge* 2.00
188 *Brian Allen* 2.00
189 *Torrance Marshall* 2.00
190 *Willie Middlebrooks* 2.00
191 *Jamar Fletcher* 3.00
192 *Ken Lucas* 2.00
193 *Fred Smoot* 2.00
194 *Andre Dyson* 2.00
195 *Anthony Henry* 3.00
196 *Adam Archuleta* 2.00
197 *Idrees Bashir* 2.00
198 *Adrian Wilson* 2.00
199 *Cory Bird* 2.00
200 *Jarrod Cooper* 2.00
201 *LaDainian Tomlinson* 35.00
202 *Chris Weinke* 10.00
203 *Anthony Thomas* 25.00
204 *Koren Robinson* 10.00
205 *James Jackson* 10.00
206 *Kevan Barlow* 10.00
207 *Quincy Morgan* 15.00
208 *Nate Clements* 10.00
209 *Travis Henry* 15.00
210 *Damione Lewis* 10.00
211 *Marvin "Snoop" Minnis* 10.00
212 *David Terrell* 10.00
213 *Gerard Warren* 8.00
214 *Chris Chambers* 15.00
215 *Will Allen* 8.00
216 *Leonard Davis* 8.00
217 *Travis Minor* 10.00
218 *Will Peterson* 5.00
219 *Rod Gardner* 10.00
220 *Freddie Mitchell* 8.00
221 *Derrick Gibson* 5.00
222 *Kyle Vanden Bosch* 5.00
223 *LaMont Jordan* 10.00
224 *Quincy Carter* 10.00
225 *Correll Buckhalter* .30

2001 Playoff Preferred Preferred Materials

NM/M
Common Player: 8.00
Minor Star: 12.00
1 Barry Sanders 40.00
2 Dan Marino 60.00
3 Warren Moon 12.00
4 Walter Payton 100.00
5 Brett Favre 60.00
6 Daunte Culpepper 15.00
7 Eddie George 15.00
8 Edgerrin James 15.00
9 Steve McNair 15.00
10 Terrell Owens 15.00
11 Troy Aikman 30.00
12 Randy Moss 30.00
13 Peyton Manning 30.00
14 Emmitt Smith 50.00
15 Marshall Faulk 15.00
16 Jevon Kearse 8.00
17 Jake Plummer 8.00
18 Jim Kelly 30.00
19 Boomer Esiason 8.00
20 John Elway 40.00
21 Brian Griese 8.00
22 Cris Carter 8.00
23 Isaac Bruce 8.00
24 Ricky Williams 15.00
25 Kurt Warner 20.00
26 Corey Dillon 8.00
27 Tyrone Wheatley 8.00
28 Rod Smith 8.00
29 Earl Campbell 15.00
30 Curtis Martin 12.00
31 Donovan McNabb 15.00
32 Lamar Smith 8.00
33 Tim Couch 12.00
34 Mark Brunell 8.00
35 Stephen Davis 8.00
36 Charles Woodson 12.00
37 Eric Moulds 8.00
38 Jay Fiedler 8.00
39 Jason Sehorn 8.00
40 Steve Young 15.00
41 Drew Bledsoe 15.00
42 Mike Alstott 12.00
43 Ron Dayne 8.00
44 Jeff Garcia 12.00
45 Torry Holt 8.00
46 Warren Sapp 8.00
47 Junior Seau 12.00
48 Wayne Chrebet 8.00
49 Jimmy Smith 8.00
50 David Boston 8.00

2001 Playoff Preferred Preferred Signatures

NM/M
Common Player: 8.00
Silver 1X to2X
Production 100 sets
Gold 2X to 5X
Production 25 sets
1 A.J. Feeley 15.00
2 Alan Page 25.00
3 Andre Carter 8.00
4 Archie Griffin 8.00
5 Archie Manning 15.00
6 Art Monk 15.00
7 Bart Starr
8 Bob Griese 35.00
9 Brian Griese 15.00
10 Cedric James 8.00
11 Charlie Batch 8.00
12 Chris Barnes 8.00
13 Chris Chambers 25.00
14 Chris Taylor 8.00
15 Chris Weinke 8.00
16 Corey Dillon 20.00
17 Damione Lewis 8.00
18 Dan Alexander 8.00
19 Dan Fouts 15.00
20 Daunte Culpepper 15.00
21 Dave Dickenson 8.00
22 Deacon Jones 20.00
23 Dee Brown 8.00
24 Derrick Blaylock 8.00
25 Don Maynard
26 Drew Pearson 8.00
27 Earl Campbell 30.00
28 Eddie "Boo" Williams 8.00
29 Edgerrin James 15.00
30 Eric Dickerson 15.00
31 Fran Tarkenton 20.00
32 Frank Gifford 25.00
33 Fred Biletnikoff 12.00
34 Freddie Mitchell 15.00
35 George Blanda 35.00
36 James Lofton 8.00
37 Jim Brown 45.00
38 Jim Plunkett 12.00
39 Joe Montana 150.00
40 Joe Namath 25.00
41 Joe Theismann 8.00
42 Johnny Unitas 100.00
43 Jonathan Carter 8.00
44 Josh Booty 8.00
45 Justin McCareins 8.00
46 Kellen Winslow 8.00
47 Kevin Kasper 8.00
48 LaMont Jordan 8.00
49 Lance Alworth 8.00
50 Larry Csonka 40.00
51 Lawrence Taylor 40.00
52 Marcus Allen 35.00
53 Marshall Faulk 15.00
54 Marvin Harrison 12.00
55 Mike Singletary 15.00
56 Onome Ojo 8.00
57 Otto Graham
58 Ozzie Newsome 8.00
59 Paul Hornung 35.00
60 Paul Warfield 12.00
61 Ray Lewis 35.00
62 Raymond Berry
63 Rod Gardner 8.00
64 Roger Craig 60.00
65 Roger Staubach 60.00
66 Ronnie Lott 12.00
67 Sammy Baugh
68 Scotty Anderson 8.00
69 Sonny Jurgensen
70 Steve Largent
71 Steve Smith 8.00
72 Terry Bradshaw 75.00
73 Tim Brown 20.00
74 Tommy Polley 8.00
75 Tony Dorsett 35.00
76 Tony Gonzalez 12.00
77 Torry Holt 12.00
78 Y.A. Tittle
79 Chad Pennington 35.00
80 Cris Carter 25.00
81 Laveranues Coles 8.00
82 Correll Buckhalter 8.00
83 Jamal Anderson 8.00
84 Jamal Lewis 12.00
85 Marcus Robinson 8.00
86 Mark Brunell 12.00
87 Wesley Walls 8.00
88 Terrell Owens 12.00
89 Thurman Thomas 15.00
90 Doug Johnson 8.00
91 Ron Dugans 8.00
92 Eddie George 12.00
93 Kenyatta Walker 8.00
94 Reggie Germany 8.00
95 Mike McMahon 8.00
96 Justin Smith 8.00
97 Heath Evans 8.00
98 Eddie Berlin 8.00
99 Jerome Bettis 12.00
100 Alge Crumpler 8.00
101 Shaun Rogers 8.00
102 Will Allen 8.00
103 Moran Norris 8.00
104 Travis Minor 8.00
105 Brian Allen 8.00
106 Emmitt Smith
107 Kurt Warner
108 Alex Bannister 8.00
109 Anthony Thomas 20.00
110 James Jackson 8.00

2002 Playoff Absolute Memorabilia

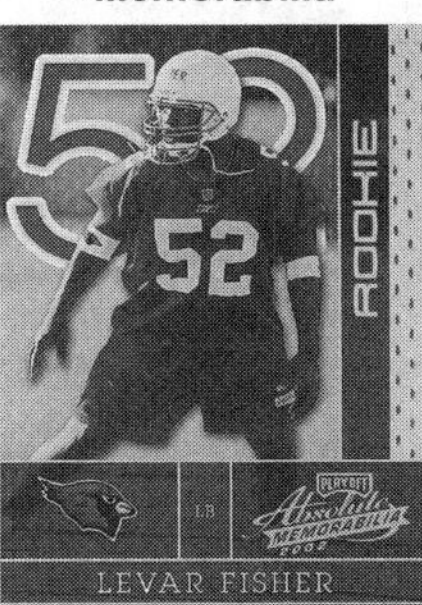

NM/M
Common Player (1-150): .25
Unlisted Stars: .75
Minor Stars: .50
Common Rookie (151-200): 1.00
Production 1500 sets
Common Rookie Premiere (201-232): 10.00
Production 825 sets
Pack (6): 6.00
Wax Box (18): 125.00
1 Aaron Brooks 1.50
2 Ahman Green .75
3 Alge Crumpler .25
4 Amani Toomer .50
5 Andre Carter .25
6 Anthony Thomas 2.50
7 Antonio Freeman .50
8 Antowain Smith .50
9 Az-Zahir Hakim .50
10 Bill Schroeder .25
11 Brad Johnson .50
12 Brett Favre 4.00
13 Brian Griese .75
14 Brian Urlacher 2.50
15 Chad Johnson .50
16 Chad Pennington .75
17 Champ Bailey .25
18 Charles Woodson .50
19 Charlie Batch .25
20 Charlie Garner .25
21 Chris Chambers .75
22 Chris Redman .50
23 Chris Weinke .75
24 Corey Dillon .75
25 Correll Buckhalter .25
26 Cris Carter .50
27 Curtis Martin .50
28 Darnay Scott .25
29 Darrell Jackson .50
30 Daunte Culpepper 2.00
31 David Boston .75
32 David Terrell .75
33 Derrick Alexander .25
34 Derrick Mason .50
35 Deuce McAllister 1.50
36 Dominic Rhodes .50
37 Donald Hayes .25
38 Donovan McNabb 2.00
39 Doug Flutie .25
40 Drew Bledsoe 2.00
41 Drew Brees 2.50
42 Duce Staley .50
43 Ed McCaffrey .50
44 Eddie George .75
45 Edgerrin James 2.50
46 Elvis Joseph .25
47 Emmitt Smith 3.00
48 Eric Moulds .25
49 Frank Sanders .25
50 Fred Taylor .25
51 Freddie Mitchell .50
52 Garrison Hearst .25
53 Gerard Warren .25
54 Germane Crowell .25
55 Isaac Bruce .50
56 Jake Plummer .50
57 Jamal Anderson .50
58 Jamal Lewis 1.50
59 James Allen .25
60 James Jackson .40
61 James Stewart .25
62 Jason Brookins .25
63 Jay Fiedler .50
64 Jeff Garcia .75
65 Jerome Bettis .50
66 Jerry Rice 3.00
67 Jevon Kearse .50
68 Jim Miller .25
69 Jimmy Smith .50
70 Joe Horn .25
71 Joey Galloway .25
72 Jon Kitna .25
73 Junior Seau .50
74 Keenan McCardell .25
75 Kendrell Bell .25
76 Kerry Collins .50
77 Kevan Barlow .25
78 Kevin Dyson .40
79 Kevin Johnson .25
80 Kevin Kasper .25
81 Keyshawn Johnson .50
82 Kordell Stewart .50
83 Koren Robinson .50
84 Kurt Warner 3.00
85 LaDainian Tomlinson 2.50
86 Lamar Smith .25
87 Laveranues Coles .25
88 MarTay Jenkins .25
89 Mark Brunell .75
90 Marshall Faulk 2.00
91 Marty Booker .25
92 Marvin Harrison .75
93 Marvin "Snoop" Minnis .50
94 Michael Bennett .75
95 Michael Strahan .50
96 Michael Vick 3.00
97 Mike Alstott .50
98 Mike Anderson 1.50
99 Mike McMahon .50
100 Muhsin Muhammad .50
101 Nate Clements .25
102 Oronde Gadsden .25
103 Peter Warrick .50
104 Peyton Manning 3.00
105 Plaxico Burress .75
106 Priest Holmes .75
107 Quincy Carter 2.00
108 Quincy Morgan .50
109 Raghib Ismail .25
110 Randy Moss 3.00
111 Ray Lewis .50
112 Reggie Wayne .25
113 Rich Gannon .50
114 Rickey Dudley .25
115 Ricky Watters .25
116 Ricky Williams 2.00
117 Rod Gardner .50
118 Rod Smith .50
119 Robert Ferguson .25
120 Santana Moss .25
121 Shaun Alexander .25
122 Stephen Davis .75
123 Steve McNair .75
124 Steve Smith .25
125 Terrell Davis 1.50
126 Terrell Owens .75
127 Terry Glenn .50
128 Thomas Jones .25
129 Tiki Barber .25
130 Tim Brown .75
131 Tim Couch 1.50
132 Todd Heap .50
133 Todd Pinkston .25
134 Tom Brady 3.00
135 Tony Boselli .25
136 Tony Gonzalez .50
137 Torry Holt .50
138 Travis Henry .50
139 Travis Taylor .25
140 Trent Dilfer .50
141 Trent Green .50
142 Troy Brown .75
143 Troy Hambrick .25
144 Trung Canidate .25
145 Vinny Testaverde .25
146 Warren Sapp .50
147 Warrick Dunn .50
148 Wayne Chrebet .50
149 Wesley Walls .25
150 Zach Thomas .50
151 *Quentin Jammer* 3.00
152 *Randy Fasani* 1.50
153 *Kurt Kittner* 2.50
154 *Chad Hutchinson* 1.50
155 *Major Applewhite* 2.00
156 *Wes Pate* 1.50
157 *J.T. O'Sullivan* 1.00
158 *Ryan Denney* 1.00
159 *Ronald Curry* 2.50
160 *Lamar Gordon* 2.50
161 *Brian Westbrook* 8.00
162 *Jonathan Wells* 3.00
163 *Ricky Williams* 1.50
164 *Verron Haynes* 1.00
165 *Josh Scobey* 1.00
166 *Larry Ned* 1.00
167 *Adrian Peterson* 1.50
168 *Chester Taylor* 1.00
169 *Luke Staley* 2.50
170 *Damien Anderson* 2.50
171 *Lee Mays* 1.00
172 *Deion Branch* 8.00
173 *Terry Charles* 1.00
174 *Woodrow Dantzler III* 1.00
175 *Jason McAddley* 1.50
176 *Kelly Campbell* 1.50
177 *Freddie Milons* 1.50
178 *Kahlil Hill* 1.00
179 *Brian Poli-Dixon* 1.00
180 *Mike Echols* 1.00
181 *Peter Rebstock* 1.00
182 *Dwight Freeney* 6.00
183 *Bryan Thomas* 1.00
184 *Charles Grant* 1.00
185 *Kalimba Edwards* 1.00
186 *Ryan Sims* 1.50
187 *John Henderson* 1.50
188 *Wendell Bryant* 1.50
189 *Albert Haynesworth* 1.50
190 *Larry Tripplett* 1.50
191 *Phillip Buchanon* 2.50
192 *Lito Sheppard* 2.50
193 *Mike Rumph* 1.00
194 *Levar Fisher* 1.00
195 *Ed Reed* 1.00
196 *Rocky Calmus* 2.50
197 *Michael Lewis* 1.00
198 *Napoleon Harris* 1.00
199 *Robert Thomas* 1.00
200 *Anthony Weaver* 1.00
201 *Ladell Betts* 8.00
202 *Antonio Bryant* 15.00
203 *Donald Reche Caldwell* 6.00
204 *David Carr* 50.00
205 *Tim Carter* 10.00
206 *Eric Crouch* 15.00
207 *Rohan Davey* 15.00
208 *Andre Davis* 15.00
209 *T.J. Duckett* 20.00
210 *DeShaun Foster* 10.00
211 *Jabar Gaffney* 15.00
212 *Daniel Graham* 12.00
213 *William Green* 15.00
214 *Joey Harrington* 40.00
215 *David Garrard* 10.00
216 *Ron Johnson* 10.00
217 *Ashley Lelie* 30.00
218 *Josh McCown* 15.00
219 *Maurice Morris* 15.00
220 *Julius Peppers* 20.00
221 *Clinton Portis* 50.00
222 *Patrick Ramsey* 20.00
223 *Antwann Randle El* 20.00
224 *Josh Reed* 15.00
225 *Cliff Russell* 10.00
226 *Jeremy Shockey* 30.00
227 *Donte Stallworth* 30.00
228 *Travis Stephens* 12.00
229 *Javon Walker* 25.00
230 *Marquise Walker* 12.00
231 *Roy Williams* 25.00
232 *Mike Williams* 10.00

2002 Playoff Absolute Memorabilia Spectrum

Stars: 3X-6X
1-150 Production 100 Sets
Rookies (151-200): 2X-4X
151-200 Production 50 Sets
201-232 Production 25 Sets

2002 Playoff Absolute Memorabilia Absolutely Ink

NM/M
Production 30 sets
1 Randy Moss 80.00
2 Brett Favre 325.00
3 Dan Marino
4 Tim Brown
5 Todd Heap
6 Correll Buckhalter 15.00
7 Mike McMahon 25.00
8 John Riggins
9 Aaron Brooks 50.00
10 David Terrell
11 Ray Lewis 100.00
12 Torry Holt
13 Stephen Davis 35.00
14 Mike Anderson 25.00
15 Jimmy Smith 25.00
16 Troy Aikman 125.00
17 Josh Heupel 30.00
18 Marcus Robinson 30.00
19 Kurt Warner 75.00
20 Shaun Rogers 15.00
21 LaMont Jordan 20.00
22 Peter Warrick 25.00
23 Santana Moss 25.00
24 Terrell Owens 55.00
25 Koren Robinson 20.00
26 Quincy Carter 35.00
27 Jamal Lewis
28 Ronnie Lott 60.00
29 Eric Moulds
30 Cade McNown
31 Isaac Bruce 50.00
32 Jesse Palmer 40.00
33 Travis Minor
34 Michael Irvin
35 Charlie Batch
36 Damione Lewis 15.00
37 Daunte Culpepper 50.00
39 Phil Simms 60.00
40 Deuce McAllister 50.00
41 Will Allen
42 Mark Brunell 40.00
43 Edgerrin James 60.00
44 Steve Young 70.00
45 Chris Weinke 30.00
46 Emmitt Smith 275.00
47 Sage Rosenfels
48 Kevan Barlow 25.00
49 Marshall Faulk 65.00
50 Thurman Thomas 45.00

2002 Playoff Absolute Memorabilia Boss Hoggs

NM/M
Common Player: 15.00
Production 125 sets
1 Edgerrin James 35.00
2 Eddie George 20.00
3 Curtis Martin 20.00
4 Stephen Davis 15.00
5 Lamar Smith 15.00
6 Emmitt Smith 60.00
7 Troy Aikman 60.00
8 Dan Marino 100.00
9 Drew Bledsoe 40.00
10 Zach Thomas 25.00
11 Michael Strahan 25.00
12 Troy Brown 35.00
13 Derrick Mason 15.00
14 Terrell Owens 30.00
15 Isaac Bruce 15.00

2002 Playoff Absolute Memorabilia Ground Hoggs

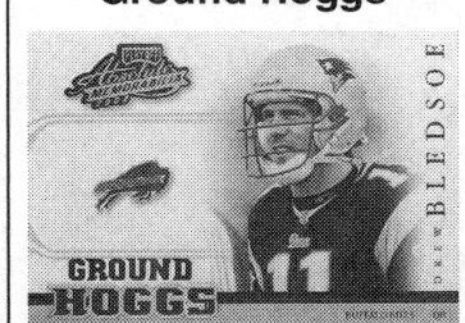

NM/M
Common Player: 2.00
Inserted 1:17
Gold versions: 2X
Inserted 1:85
1 Edgerrin James 4.00
2 Eddie George 2.00
3 Curtis Martin 2.00
4 Stephen Davis 2.00
5 Lamar Smith 2.00
6 Emmitt Smith 6.00
7 Troy Aikman 6.00
8 Dan Marino 8.00
9 Drew Bledsoe 4.00
10 Zach Thomas 2.00
11 Michael Strahan 2.00
12 Troy Brown 2.00
13 Derrick Mason 2.00
14 Terrell Owens 2.00
15 Isaac Bruce 2.00

2002 Playoff Absolute Memorabilia Leather & Laces

NM/M
Common Player: 10.00
LL1-LL25 Production 250 Sets
LL26-LL50 Production 500 Sets
Combos/25: 2X to 4X
Combos/50: 1.5X-3X

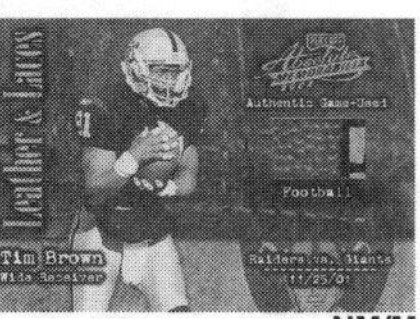

NM/M
1 Kurt Warner/250 15.00
2 Rod Smith/250 12.00
3 Curtis Martin/250 10.00
4 Ahman Green/250 15.00
5 Daunte Culpepper/250 25.00
6 David Boston/250 10.00
7 Brian Urlacher/250 30.00
8 Dominic Rhodes/250 10.00
9 Doug Flutie/250 10.00
10 Kordell Stewart/250 20.00
11 Antowain Smith/250 10.00
12 Torry Holt/250 10.00
13 Eric Moulds/250 10.00
14 Marvin Harrison/250 10.00
15 Troy Brown/250 20.00
16 Garrison Hearst/250 10.00
17 Mike Anderson/250 15.00
18 Priest Holmes/250 25.00
19 David Terrell/250 10.00
20 Peyton Manning/250 30.00
21 Isaac Bruce/250 10.00
22 Randy Moss/250 20.00
23 Kerry Collins/250 10.00
24 Shaun Alexander/250 20.00
25 Terrell Davis/250 10.00
26 Anthony Thomas/500 10.00
27 Keyshawn Johnson/500 10.00
28 Quincy Carter/500 20.00
29 Rich Gannon/500 15.00
30 Tom Brady/500 25.00
31 Aaron Brooks/500 15.00
32 Tim Brown/500 15.00
33 Chris Chambers/500 15.00
34 Stephen Davis/500 15.00
35 Cris Carter/500 10.00
36 Brett Favre/500 25.00
37 Eddie George/500 12.00
38 Travis Henry/500 10.00
39 Jerry Rice/500 30.00
40 Correll Buckhalter/500 10.00
41 Jeff Garcia/500 15.00
42 Emmitt Smith/500 30.00
43 Steve McNair/500 15.00
44 LaDainian Tomlinson/500 20.00
45 Ricky Williams/500 25.00
46 Brian Griese/500 20.00
47 Terrell Owens/500 15.00
48 Marshall Faulk/500 20.00
49 Jake Plummer/500 10.00
50 Donovan McNabb/500 15.00

2002 Playoff Absolute Memorabilia Signing Bonus

NM/M
Common Player 20.00
Inserted 1:Box
1 Troy Aikman Away/10
2 Troy Aikman Home/10
3 Mike Anderson/10
4 Jamal Anderson/125 30.00
5 Mike Anderson/50 50.00
6 Mike Anderson/150 25.00
7 Kevan Barlow/100 60.00
8 Kevan Barlow/300 30.00
9 Charlie Batch/150 30.00
10 Charlie Batch/250 20.00
11 Michael Bennett/50 50.00
12 Drew Bledsoe/5
13 Drew Bledsoe/50 100.00
14 Drew Bledsoe/100 75.00
15 David Boston/50 60.00
16 Drew Brees/200 40.00
17 Drew Brees/400 30.00
18 Aaron Brooks/5
19 Aaron Brooks/10
20 Aaron Brooks/100 75.00
21 Aaron Brooks/200 50.00
22 Tim Brown/50 75.00
23 Tim Brown/300 50.00
24 Isaac Bruce/5
25 Isaac Bruce/175 50.00
26 Isaac Bruce/300 40.00
27 Mark Brunell/15
28 Mark Brunell/150 50.00
29 Mark Brunell/350 30.00
30 Correll Buckhalter/150 40.00
31 Correll Buckhalter/350 20.00
32 Cris Carter/50 100.00
33 Cris Carter/100 80.00
34 Quincy Carter/10
35 Quincy Carter/250 50.00
36 Quincy Carter/350 40.00
37 Chris Chambers/10
38 Chris Chambers/125 75.00
39 Laveranues Coles/100 50.00
40 Kerry Collins/200 40.00
41 Kerry Collins/380 20.00
42 Daunte Culpepper/10
43 Daunte Culpepper/100 75.00

44 Stephen Davis/10
45 Stephen Davis/75 75.00
46 Stephen Davis/400 40.00
47 Terrell Davis/50 100.00
48 Terrell Davis/150 60.00
49 Corey Dillon/10
50 Corey Dillon/100 50.00
51 John Elway/10
52 Marshall Faulk/10
53 Marshall Faulk/50 100.00
54 Marshall Faulk/300 60.00
55 Brett Favre/5
56 Brett Favre/75 250.00
57 Robert Ferguson/150 40.00
58 RobertFerguson/250 25.00
59 Jeff Garcia/10
60 Jeff Garcia/40 125.00
61 Rob Gardner/50 50.00
62 Tony Gonzalez/50 60.00
63 Tony Gonzalez/150 40.00
64 Ahman Green/10
65 Ahman Green/100 80.00
66 Brian Griese/10
67 Brian Griese/25 100.00
68 Brian Griese/175 40.00
69 Marvin Harrison/50 100.00
70 Marvin Harrison/150 50.00
71 Todd Heap/150 50.00
72 Todd Heap/400 25.00
73 Torry Holt/100 75.00
74 Torry Holt/300 50.00
75 James Jackson/150 30.00
76 James Jackson/300 20.00
77 Edgerrin James/5
78 Edgerrin James/10
79 Edgerrin James/150 80.00
80 Edgerrin James/250 60.00
81 Chad Johnson/100 50.00
82 Chad Johnson/250 40.00
83 Jamal Lewis/100 60.00
84 Jamal Lewis/400 40.00
85 Ray Lewis/150 80.00
86 Ray Lewis/350 50.00
87 Dan Marino A/10
88 Dan Marino H/10
89 Deuce McAllister/200 60.00
90 Deuce McAllister/400 40.00
91 Mike McMahon/150 30.00
92 Mike McMahon/350 20.00
93 Quincy Morgan/200 30.00
94 Quincy Morgan/400 20.00
95 Santana Moss/200 40.00
96 Santana Moss/400 30.00
97 Eric Moulds/125 50.00
98 Eric Moulds/300 30.00
99 Terrell Owens/10
100 Terrell Owens/25 200.00
101 Terrell Owens/75 100.00
102 Chad Pennington/100 100.00
103 Chad Pennington/200 60.00
104 Jake Plummer/100 40.00
105 Jerry Rice/125 150.00
106 Barry Sanders/10
107 Junior Seau/25 125.00
108 Junior Seau/100 50.00
109 Emmitt Smith/5
110 Emmitt Smith/10
111 Emmitt Smith/75 250.00
112 Emmitt Smith/150 200.00
113 Jimmy Smith/300 30.00
114 Jimmy Smith/400 20.00
115 Michael Strahan/10
116 Michael Strahan/90 75.00
117 David Terrell/200 30.00
118 David Terrell/400 20.00
119 Vinny Testaverde/25 75.00
120 Vinny Testaverde/75 40.00
121 Anthony Thomas/10
122 Anthony Thomas/50 60.00
123 Anthony Thomas/150 40.00
124 Brian Urlacher/50 125.00
125 Brian Urlacher/200 80.00
126 Michael Vick/75 250.00
127 Kurt Warner/10
128 Kurt Warner/100 80.00
129 Kurt Warner/250 50.00
130 Peter Warrick/150 40.00
131 Peter Warrick/350 25.00
132 Ricky Watters/50 50.00
133 Ricky Watters/350 25.00
134 Reggie Wayne/75 40.00
135 Reggie Wayne/200 25.00
136 Chris Weinke/10
137 Chris Weinke/200 25.00
138 Chris Weinke/300 20.00
139 Ricky Williams/10
140 Ricky Williams/75 150.00
141 Steve Young/10

2002 Playoff Absolute Memorabilia Tools of the Trade

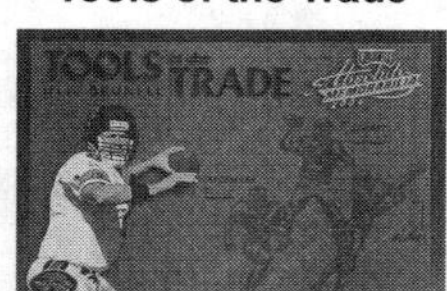

NM/M
Common Player: 2.00
Inserted 1:17
Gold versions: 2X
Inserted 1:85
1 Emmitt Smith 5.00
2 Brett Favre 5.00
3 Donovan McNabb 2.00
4 Brian Griese 2.00
5 Peyton Manning 3.00
6 Kurt Warner 3.00
7 Dan Marino 4.00
8 Shaun Alexander 2.00
9 Anthony Thomas 2.00
10 Troy Aikman 4.00
11 Barry Sanders 4.00
12 Mike Anderson 2.00
13 Jerry Rice 4.00
14 Daunte Culpepper 2.00
15 Chris Chambers 2.00
16 Marshall Faulk 2.00
17 Doug Flutie 2.00
18 Travis Henry 2.00
19 LaDainian Tomlinson 2.00
20 Eddie George 2.00
21 Aaron Brooks 2.00
22 Chris Weinke 2.00
23 Ricky Williams 2.00
24 Jerome Bettis 2.00
25 Ahman Green 2.00
26 Steve Young 2.00
27 Zach Thomas 2.00
28 Randy Moss 3.00
29 Quincy Carter 2.00
30 Jeff Garcia 2.00
31 Tim Brown 2.00
32 Jimmy Smith 2.00
33 Torry Holt 2.00
34 Todd Pinkston 2.00
35 Eric Moulds 2.00
36 Marvin Harrison 2.00
37 Derrick Mason 2.00
38 Troy Brown 2.00
39 Marty Booker 2.00
40 Wayne Chrebet 2.00
41 Darrell Green 2.00
42 Charles Woodson 2.00
43 Bruce Matthews 2.00
44 Tim Couch 2.00
45 Mark Brunell 2.00
46 Hines Ward 2.00
47 Corey Dillon 2.00
48 Edgerrin James 2.00
49 John Elway 4.00
50 Frank Wycheck 2.00

2002 Playoff Absolute Mem. Tools of the Trade Materials

NM/M
Common Player: 10.00
(1-30) Jersey
Production 150 sets
(31-42) Glove
Production 50 sets
(43-50) Facemask
Production 300 sets
1 Emmitt Smith 50.00
2 Brett Favre 40.00
3 Donovan McNabb 30.00
4 Brian Griese 30.00
5 Peyton Manning
6 Kurt Warner 25.00
7 Dan Marino 50.00
8 Shaun Alexander 25.00
9 Anthony Thomas 25.00
10 Troy Aikman 25.00
11 Barry Sanders
12 Mike Anderson 15.00
13 Jerry Rice 25.00
14 Daunte Culpepper 15.00
15 Chris Chambers 15.00
16 Marshall Faulk 15.00
17 Doug Flutie 10.00
18 Travis Henry 10.00
19 LaDainian Tomlinson 15.00
20 Eddie George 10.00
21 Aaron Brooks 10.00
22 Chris Weinke 10.00
23 Ricky Williams 15.00
24 Jerome Bettis 10.00
25 Ahman Green 15.00
26 Steve Young 15.00
27 Zach Thomas 25.00
28 Randy Moss 25.00
29 Quincy Carter 20.00
30 Jeff Garcia 10.00
31 Tim Brown
32 Jimmy Smith
33 Torry Holt
34 Todd Pinkston 10.00
35 Eric Moulds 10.00
36 Marvin Harrison 15.00
37 Derrick Mason 10.00
38 Troy Brown 20.00
39 Marty Booker 15.00
40 Wayne Chrebet 15.00
41 Darrell Green 20.00
42 Charles Woodson 30.00
43 Bruce Matthews 15.00
44 Tim Couch 20.00
45 Mark Brunell 10.00
46 Hines Ward 20.00
47 Corey Dillon 15.00
48 Edgerrin James 20.00
49 John Elway 50.00
50 Frank Wycheck 10.00

2002 Playoff Contenders

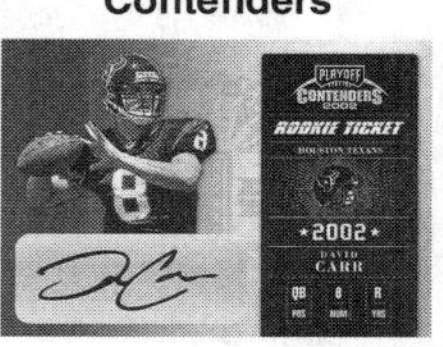

NM/M
Common Player: .25
Unlisted Star: .75
Minor Star: .50
Common Rookie (101-186): 15.00
Minor Rookie Star: 20.00
Pack (5): 5.00
Wax Box (20): 75.00
1 Drew Bledsoe 1.50
2 Travis Henry .50
3 Eric Moulds .50
4 Chris Chambers .75
5 Ricky Williams 1.50
6 Zach Thomas .50
7 Tom Brady 2.50
8 Antowain Smith .25
9 Troy Brown .50
10 Curtis Martin .75
11 Vinny Testaverde .25
12 Chad Pennington 1.25
13 Jeff Blake .25
14 Jamal Lewis 1.25
15 Ray Lewis .50
16 Michael Westbrook .25
17 Corey Dillon .75
18 Peter Warrick .25
19 Tim Couch 1.25
20 Quincy Morgan .50
21 Kevin Johnson .25
22 Kordell Stewart .50
23 Plaxico Burress .75
24 Jerome Bettis .50
25 James Allen .25
26 Corey Bradford .25
27 Mark Brunell .75
28 Fred Taylor .50
29 Jimmy Smith .25
30 Peyton Manning 2.50
31 Reggie Wayne .50
32 Marvin Harrison .75
33 Edgerrin James 2.00
34 Steve McNair .75
35 Eddie George .75
36 Jevon Kearse .50
37 Derrick Mason .50
38 Brian Griese .75
39 Terrell Davis 1.25
40 Ed McCaffrey .50
41 Rod Smith .50
42 Trent Green .50
43 Priest Holmes 1.25
44 Johnnie Morton .50
45 Tony Gonzalez .50
46 Rich Gannon .75
47 Tim Brown .75
48 Jerry Rice 2.50
49 Charlie Garner .50
50 Drew Brees 2.00
51 LaDainian Tomlinson 2.00
52 Junior Seau .50
53 Quincy Carter 1.25
54 Emmitt Smith 2.50
55 Joey Galloway .50
56 Kerry Collins .50
57 Tiki Barber .50
58 Michael Strahan .50
59 Donovan McNabb 1.50
60 Duce Staley .50
61 Antonio Freeman .25
62 Derrius Thompson .25
63 Stephen Davis .50
64 Rod Gardner .50
65 Anthony Thomas 1.25
66 Marty Booker .50
67 Brian Urlacher 2.00
68 James Stewart .50
69 Az-Zahir Hakim .50
70 Brett Favre 3.00
71 Ahman Green .75
72 Donald Driver .25
73 Daunte Culpepper 1.50
74 Michael Bennett .75
75 Randy Moss 2.50
76 Michael Vick 2.50
77 Warrick Dunn .50
78 Chris Weinke .25
79 Lamar Smith .25
80 Steve Smith .25
81 Aaron Brooks 1.25
82 Deuce McAllister 1.25
83 Joe Horn .50
84 Brad Johnson .50
85 Keyshawn Johnson .75
86 Mike Alstott .40
87 Warren Sapp .50
88 Jake Plummer .50
89 Thomas Jones .25
90 David Boston .75
91 Kurt Warner 2.50
92 Marshall Faulk 1.50
93 Isaac Bruce .50
94 Torry Holt .50
95 Jeff Garcia .75
96 Garrison Hearst .50
97 Kevan Barlow .50
98 Terrell Owens .75
99 Trent Dilfer .50
100 Shaun Alexander .75
101 *Adrian Peterson/360* 30.00
102 *Albert Haynesworth/ Redem* 20.00
103 *Alex Brown/410* 20.00
104 *Andra Davis/510* 15.00
105 *Andre Davis/360* 40.00
106 *Andre Lott/750* 15.00
107 *Anthony Weaver/450* 15.00
108 *Antonio Bryant/165* 120.00
109 *Antwann Randle El/ 135* 150.00
110 *Ashley Lelie/360* 100.00
111 *Brian Poli-Dixon/460* 15.00
112 *Brian Westbrook/ Redem* 60.00
113 *Bryant McKinnie/600* 20.00
114 *Chad Hutchinson/450* 30.00
115 *Charles Grant/450* 15.00
116 *Chester Taylor/315* 20.00
117 *Cliff Russell/545* 15.00
118 *Clinton Portis/360* 250.00
119 *Randy McMichael/ Redem* 50.00
120 *Damien Anderson/460* 15.00
121 *Daniel Graham/185* 50.00
122 *David Carr/250* 250.00
123 *David Garrard/310* 30.00
124 *Deion Branch/650* 50.00
125 *John Simon/400* 25.00
126 *DeShaun Foster/310* 50.00
127 *Donte Stallworth/302* 100.00
128 *Dwight Freeney/410* 30.00
129 *Ed Reed/550* 25.00
130 *Eric Crouch/280* 40.00
131 *Freddie Milons/380* 20.00
132 *Jabar Gaffney/315* 30.00
133 *Javon Walker/Redem* 60.00
134 *Jeremy Shockey/ Redem* 200.00
135 *Jerramy Stevens/250* 20.00
136 *Joey Harrington/250* 200.00
137 *John Henderson/560* 15.00
138 *Jonathan Wells/Redem* 40.00
139 *Josh McCown/595* 50.00
140 *Josh Reed/290* 60.00
141 *Josh Scobey/615* 15.00
142 *Julius Peppers/40* 300.00
143 *Kalimba Edwards/510* 15.00
144 *Kelly Campbell/360* 25.00
145 *Ken Simonton/650* 15.00
146 *Keyuo Craver/850* 15.00
147 *Kahlil Hill/850* 15.00
148 *Kurt Kittner/235* 25.00
149 *Ladell Betts/600* 40.00
150 *Lamar Gordon/600* 30.00
151 *Levar Fisher/760* 15.00
152 *Lito Sheppard/410* 20.00
153 *Luke Staley/360* 20.00
154 *Marquise Walker/330* 35.00
155 *Maurice Morris/153* 50.00
156 *Mike Rumph/510* 25.00
157 *Mike Williams/Redem* 15.00
158 *Najeh Davenport/460* 25.00
159 *Napoleon Harris/900* 15.00
160 *Patrick Ramsey/575* 60.00
161 *Phillip Buchanon/ Redem* 40.00
162 *Quentin Jammer/300* 40.00
163 *Randy Fasani/500* 20.00
164 *Donald Reche Caldwell/340* 25.00
165 *Robert Thomas/460* 15.00
166 *Rocky Calmus/385* 25.00
167 *Rohan Davey/295* 50.00
168 *Ron Johnson/385* 20.00
169 *Roy Williams/250* 100.00
170 *Ryan Sims/Redem* 20.00
171 *Tavon Mason/690* 15.00
172 *Terry Charles/750* 15.00
173 *T.J. Duckett/340* 60.00
174 *Tim Carter/600* 20.00
175 *Travis Stephens/170* 40.00
176 *Trev Faulk/600* 15.00
177 *Wendell Bryant/560* 15.00
178 *William Green/317* 60.00
179 *Woodrow Dantzler III/185* 40.00
180 *Tony Fisher/340* 40.00
181 *Javin Hunter/400* 15.00
182 *Daryl Jones/400* 20.00
183 *Jesse Chatman/Redem* 20.00
184 *J.T. O'Sullivan/340* 15.00
185 *Josh Norman/340* 20.00
186 *James Mungro/100* 100.00

2002 Playoff Contenders 10th Anniversary

Production 10 Sets

2002 Playoff Contenders Championship Ticket

NM/M
Stars: 3X-6X
1-100 Production 250 Sets
Common Rookie (101-186): 10.00
101-186 Production 50 Sets
101 Adrian Peterson 15.00
102 Albert Haynesworth 10.00
103 Alex Brown 12.00
104 Andra Davis 10.00
105 Andre Davis 30.00
106 Andre Lott 10.00
107 Anthony Weaver 10.00
108 Antonio Bryant 30.00
109 Antwaan Randle 40.00
110 Ashley Lelie 50.00
111 Brian Poli-Dixon 12.00
112 Brian Westbrook 25.00
113 Bryant McKinnie 12.00
114 Chad Hutchinson 15.00
115 Charles Grant 10.00
116 Chester Taylor 10.00
117 Cliff Russell 12.00
118 Clinton Portis 80.00
119 Randy McMichael 25.00
120 Damien Anderson 12.00
121 Daniel Graham 15.00
122 David Carr 80.00
123 David Garrard 15.00
124 Deion Branch 30.00
125 John Simon 10.00
126 DeShaun Foster 20.00
127 Donte Stallworth 50.00
128 Dwight Freeney 20.00
129 Ed Reed 20.00
130 Eric Crouch 25.00
131 Freddie Milons 12.00
132 Jabar Gaffney 25.00
133 Javon Walker 30.00
134 Jeremy Shockey 60.00
135 Jerramy Stevens 12.00
136 Joey Harrington 60.00
137 John Henderson 12.00
138 Jonathan Wells 15.00
139 Josh McCown 25.00
140 Josh Reed 30.00
141 Josh Scobey 10.00
142 Julius Peppers 30.00
143 Kalimba Edwards 10.00
144 Kelly Campbell 12.00
145 Ken Simonton 10.00
146 Keyuo Craver 10.00
147 Kahlil Hill 12.00
148 Kurt Kittner 15.00
149 Ladell Betts 20.00
150 Lamar Gordon 15.00
151 Levar Fisher 10.00
152 Lito Sheppard 12.00
153 Luke Staley 12.00
154 Marquise Walker 12.00
155 Maurice Morris 20.00
156 Mike Rumph 10.00
157 Mike Williams 10.00
158 Najeh Davenport 15.00
159 Napoleon Harris 12.00
160 Patrick Ramsey 30.00
161 Phillip Buchanon 15.00
162 Quentin Jammer 15.00
163 Randy Fasani 10.00
164 Reche Caldwell 12.00
165 Robert Thomas 10.00
166 Rocky Calmus 12.00
167 Rohan Davey 15.00
168 Ron Johnson 12.00
169 Roy Williams 40.00
170 Ryan Sims 12.00
171 Tavon Mason 10.00
172 Terry Charles 10.00
173 T.J. Duckett 30.00
174 Tim Carter 12.00
175 Travis Stephens 12.00
176 Trev Faulk 10.00
177 Wendell Bryant 12.00
178 William Green 30.00
179 Woodrow Dantzler III 15.00
180 Tony Fisher 15.00
181 Javin Hunter 10.00
182 Daryl Jones 10.00
183 Jesse Chatman 10.00
184 J.T. O'Sullivan 10.00
185 Josh Norman 20.00
186 James Mungro 20.00

2002 Playoff Contenders All-Time Contenders

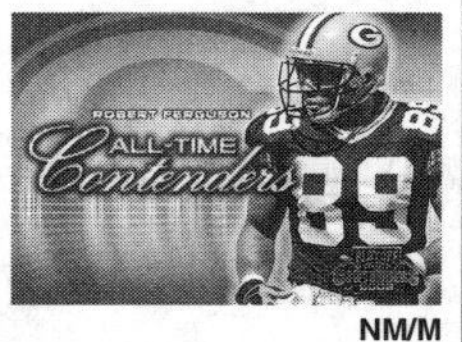

NM/M
Common Player: 1.00
Inserted 1:10
1 Corey Dillon 1.00
2 Ray Lewis 1.00
3 Mark Brunell 1.50
4 Eric Moulds 1.00
5 Tony Gonzalez 1.00
6 Marcus Robinson 1.00
7 Tim Brown 2.00
8 Brian Griese 1.50
9 Cris Carter 1.00
10 Tony Banks 1.00
11 Jamal Lewis 1.00
12 Jimmy Smith 1.00
13 Michael Strahan 1.00
14 David Boston 1.00
15 Marvin Harrison 1.50
16 Emmitt Smith 4.00
17 Robert Ferguson 1.00
18 Eddie "Boo" Williams 1.00
19 Mike Anderson 1.00
20 Isaac Bruce 1.00
21 Shaun Rogers 1.00
22 Jamal Anderson 1.00
23 Torry Holt 1.00
24 Aaron Brooks 2.00
25 Drew Bledsoe 3.00
26 Jake Plummer 1.00
27 Jevon Kearse 1.00
28 Kerry Collins 1.00
29 Terrell Davis 1.00
30 Jeff Blake 1.00
31 Randall Cunningham 1.50
32 Ricky Williams 2.00
33 Brett Favre 4.00

2002 Playoff Contenders All-Time Contenders Autos

NM/M
Common Player: 10.00
1 Corey Dillon/15 50.00
2 Ray Lewis/9
3 Mark Brunell/25 50.00
4 Eric Moulds/20
5 Tony Gonzalez/25 60.00
6 Marcus Robinson/135 10.00
7 Tim Brown/28 80.00
8 Brian Griese/25 50.00
9 Cris Carter/25 60.00
10 Tony Banks/10
11 Jamal Lewis/20
12 Jimmy Smith/50 15.00
13 Michael Strahan/25 50.00
14 David Boston/14
15 Marvin Harrison/25 100.00
16 Emmitt Smith/8
17 Robert Ferguson/9
18 Eddie "Boo" Williams/50 20.00
19 Mike Anderson/32 30.00
20 Isaac Bruce/57 40.00
21 Shaun Rogers/20 20.00
22 Jamal Anderson/8
23 Torry Holt/25 80.00
24 Aaron Brooks/15 100.00
25 Drew Bledsoe/10
26 Jake Plummer/15 40.00
27 Jevon Kearse/10
28 Kerry Collins/18 40.00
29 Terrell Davis/10
30 Jeff Blake/140 10.00
31 Randall Cunningham/140 25.00
32 Ricky Williams/125 100.00
33 Brett Favre/15 400.00

2002 Playoff Contenders Legendary Contenders

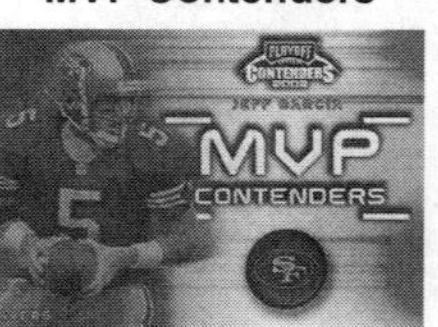

NM/M
Common Player: 2.00
Inserted 1:12
1 Boomer Esiason 2.00
2 Dan Marino 10.00
3 Jim Kelly 5.00
4 John Elway 10.00
5 Phil Simms 2.00
6 Steve Young 4.00
7 Troy Aikman 5.00
8 Warren Moon 2.00
9 Barry Sanders 10.00
10 Joe Montana 10.00
11 John Riggins 3.00
12 Ronnie Lott 2.00
13 Thurman Thomas 3.00
14 Ozzie Newsome 2.00
15 Jack Lambert 2.00

2002 Playoff Contenders Legendary Contenders Autos

NM/M
Common Player: 20.00
1 Boomer Esiason/17 150.00
2 Dan Marino/15 400.00
3 Jim Kelly/15 200.00
4 John Elway/15 400.00
5 Phil Simms/75 40.00
6 Steve Young/50 100.00
7 Troy Aikman/25 200.00
8 Warren Moon/10
9 Barry Sanders/19
10 Joe Montana/63 250.00
11 John Riggins/141 50.00
12 Ronnie Lott/11
13 Thurman Thomas/25 50.00
14 Ozzie Newsome/125 20.00
15 Jack Lambert/125 60.00

2002 Playoff Contenders MVP Contenders

NM/M
Common Player: 2.00
Inserted 1:12
1 Brett Favre 5.00
2 Jerry Rice 4.00
3 Ricky Williams 3.00
4 Edgerrin James 3.00
5 Emmitt Smith 4.00
6 Kurt Warner 3.00
7 Marshall Faulk 3.00
8 Randy Moss 4.00
9 Jeff Garcia 2.00
10 Ahman Green 2.00

2002 Playoff Contenders MVP Contenders Autos

NM/M
Production 25 sets
1 Brett Favre 350.00
2 Jerry Rice 225.00
3 Ricky Williams 100.00

4 Edgerrin James 75.00
5 Emmitt Smith 300.00
6 Kurt Warner 100.00
7 Marshall Faulk 40.00
8 Randy Moss 250.00
9 Jeff Garcia 75.00
10 Ahman Green 75.00

2002 Playoff Contenders Rookie Idols

NM/M
Common Player: 2.00
Inserted 1:12
1 Ladell Betts, Thurman Thomas 2.00
2 Antonio Bryant, Michael Irvin 2.00
3 David Garrard, Phil Simms 2.00
4 Eric Crouch, John Elway 3.00
5 Barry Sanders, William Green 5.00
6 Brett Favre, Josh McCown 5.00
7 Dan Marino, Joey Harrington 5.00
8 Donte Stallworth, Jerry Rice 4.00
9 Jabar Gaffney, Tim Brown 3.00
10 Daunte Culpepper, Rohan Davey 2.00

2002 Playoff Contenders Rookie Idols Autos

NM/M
Common Player: 50.00
Production 25 sets
1 Ladell Betts, Thurman Thomas 80.00
2 Antonio Bryant, Michael Irvin 100.00
3 David Garrard, Phil Simms 50.00
4 Eric Crouch, John Elway 250.00
5 Barry Sanders, William Green 200.00
6 Brett Favre, Josh McCown 350.00
7 Dan Marino, Joey Harrington 400.00
8 Donte Stallworth, Jerry Rice 200.00
9 Jabar Gaffney, Tim Brown 50.00
10 Daunte Culpepper, Rohan Davey 100.00

2002 Playoff Contenders ROY Contenders

NM/M
Common Player: 3.00
Inserted 1:12
1 Antonio Bryant 3.00
2 Ashley Lelie 4.00
3 David Carr 8.00
4 DeShaun Foster 3.00
5 Donte Stallworth 4.00
6 Joey Harrington 8.00
7 Quentin Jammer 3.00
8 Patrick Ramsey 4.00
9 T.J. Duckett 4.00
10 William Green 4.00

2002 Playoff Contenders ROY Contenders Autos

NM/M
Common Player: 40.00
Production 25 Sets
1 Antonio Bryant 50.00
2 Ashley Lelie 100.00
3 David Carr 200.00
4 DeShaun Foster 50.00
5 Donte Stallworth 100.00
6 Joey Harrington 150.00
7 Quentin Jammer 40.00
8 Patrick Ramsey 50.00
9 T.J. Duckett 60.00
10 William Green 60.00

2002 Playoff Contenders Round Numbers Autos

NM/M
Common Player: 15.00
Production 75 sets
1 David Carr, Joey Harrington 200.00
2 Quentin Jammer, Roy Williams 100.00
3 Donald Reche Caldwell, Jabar Gaffney 35.00
4 Antonio Bryant, Josh Reed 60.00
5 Eric Crouch, Josh McCown 50.00
6 Cliff Russell, Marquise Walker 20.00
7 Jonathan Wells, Travis Stephens/Redem 25.00
8 David Garrard, Rohan Davey 25.00
9 Kurt Kittner, Randy Fasani 20.00
10 Chester Taylor, Josh Scobey 15.00

2002 Playoff Contenders Round Numbers Autos Gold

NM/M
Common Player: 30.00
1 David Carr, Joey Harrington/10
2 Quentin Jammer, Roy Williams/10
3 Donald Reche Caldwell, Jabar Gaffney/20
4 Antonio Bryant, Josh Reed/20
5 Eric Crouch, Josh McCown/30 60.00
6 Cliff Russell, Marquise Walker/30 40.00
7 Jonathan Wells, Travis Stephens/40 40.00
8 David Garrard, Rohan Davey/40 40.00
9 Kurt Kittner, Randy Fasani/50 30.00
10 Chester Taylor, Josh Scobey/60 30.00

2002 Playoff Contenders Sophomore Contenders

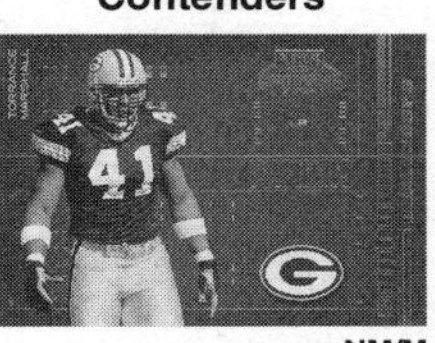

NM/M
Common Player: 1.00
Inserted 1:12
1 Chad Johnson 1.00
2 Chris Chambers 2.00
3 David Terrell 1.00
4 Jesse Palmer 1.00
5 Kevan Barlow 1.00
6 Koren Robinson 1.00
7 LaMont Jordan 1.00
8 Michael Bennett 2.00
9 Quincy Carter 1.50
10 Santana Moss 1.50
11 Mike McMahon 1.00
12 Ken-Yon Rambo 1.00
13 Will Allen 1.00
14 Todd Heap 1.00
15 T.J. Houshmandzadeh 1.00
16 Travis Henry 1.00
17 Sage Rosenfels 1.00
18 Torrance Marshall 1.00
19 Rudi Johnson 1.00
20 Travis Minor 1.00

2002 Playoff Contenders Sophmore Contenders Autos

NM/M
Common Player: 10.00
1 Chad Johnson/26 40.00
2 Chris Chambers/28 50.00
3 David Terrell/188 10.00
4 Jesse Palmer/300 10.00
5 Kevan Barlow/200 15.00
6 Koren Robinson/40 25.00
7 LaMont Jordan/250 15.00
8 Michael Bennett/34 50.00
9 Quincy Carter/300 20.00
10 Santana Moss/400 20.00
11 Mike McMahon/16 40.00
12 Ken-Yon Rambo/300 10.00
13 Will Allen/130 10.00
14 Todd Heap/61 20.00
15 T.J. Houshmandzadeh/220 10.00
16 Damione Lewis/400 10.00
17 Sage Rosenfels/70 20.00
18 Torrance Marshall/50 20.00
19 Rudi Johnson/350 30.00
20 Travis Minor/350 15.00

2002 Playoff Honors

NM/M
Common Player: .25
Unlisted Stars: .60
Minor Stars: .50
Common Rookie (101-200): 1.00
Production 1000 sets
Common Rookie Gems (201-232): 10.00
Production 650 sets

NM/M
Pack (6): 7.00
Wax Box Mini (12): 70.00
1 David Boston .60
2 Jake Plummer .50
3 Warrick Dunn .50
4 Michael Vick 2.00
5 Jamal Lewis 1.00
6 Chris Redman .50
7 Ray Lewis .50
8 Drew Bledsoe 1.25
9 Travis Henry .50
10 Eric Moulds .50
11 Lamar Smith .25
12 Steve Smith .25
13 Chris Weinke .60
14 Chris Chandler .25
15 David Terrell .60
16 Anthony Thomas 1.50
17 Brian Urlacher 1.50
18 Corey Dillon .60
19 Peter Warrick .50
20 Tim Couch 1.00
21 James Jackson .25
22 Kevin Johnson .25
23 Quincy Carter 1.25
24 Joey Galloway .50
25 Emmitt Smith 2.00
26 Terrell Davis 1.00
27 Brian Griese .60
28 Rod Smith .50
29 Germane Crowell .25
30 Az-Zahir Hakim .50
31 Mike McMahon .60
32 Brett Favre 2.50
33 Terry Glenn .50
34 Ahman Green .60
35 James Allen .25
36 Corey Bradford .25
37 Marvin Harrison .50
38 Peyton Manning 2.00
39 Edgerrin James 1.50
40 Reggie Wayne .25
41 Mark Brunell .60
42 Fred Taylor .25
43 Jimmy Smith .25
44 Tony Gonzalez .50
45 Trent Green .50
46 Priest Holmes .60
47 Marvin "Snoop" Minnis .50
48 Chris Chambers .60
49 Jay Fiedler .25
50 Ricky Williams 1.25
51 Zach Thomas .50
52 Randy Moss 2.00
53 Daunte Culpepper 1.25
54 Michael Bennett .60
55 Tom Brady 2.00
56 Troy Brown .60
57 Antowain Smith .50
58 Aaron Brooks 1.00
59 Deuce McAllister 1.00
60 Tiki Barber .50
61 Kerry Collins .50
62 Amani Toomer .50
63 Michael Strahan .50
64 Curtis Martin .50
65 Vinny Testaverde .50
66 Chad Pennington .50
67 Laveranues Coles .50
68 Tim Brown .60
69 Rich Gannon .50
70 Jerry Rice 2.00
71 Donovan McNabb 1.25
72 Freddie Mitchell .50
73 Duce Staley .50
74 Jerome Bettis .50
75 Plaxico Burress .60
76 Kordell Stewart .50
77 Drew Brees 1.50
78 Doug Flutie .60
79 LaDainian Tomlinson 1.50
80 Jeff Garcia .60
81 Garrison Hearst .50
82 Terrell Owens .60
83 Shaun Alexander .60
84 Trent Dilfer .50
85 Koren Robinson .50
86 Isaac Bruce .50
87 Marshall Faulk 1.25
88 Torry Holt .50
89 Kurt Warner 2.00
90 Mike Alstott .50
91 Brad Johnson .50
92 Keyshawn Johnson .50
93 Keenan McCardell .25
94 Steve McNair .60
95 Eddie George .60
96 Jevon Kearse .50
97 Derrick Mason .50
98 Stephen Davis .50
99 Sage Rosenfels .25
100 Rod Gardner .50
101 *Randy Fasani* 1.00
102 *Kurt Kittner* 1.00
103 *Brandon Doman* 3.00
104 *Craig Nall* 2.00
105 *J.T. O'Sullivan* 2.00
106 *Seth Burford* 5.00
107 *Jeff Kelly* 1.00
108 *Ronald Curry* 3.00
109 *Wes Pate* 1.00
110 *Chad Hutchinson* 2.00
111 *Major Applewhite* 2.00
112 *Preston Parsons* 1.00
113 *David Priestley* 4.00
114 *Lamar Gordon* 1.00
115 *Brian Westbrook* 8.00
116 *Jonathan Wells* 1.50
117 *Omar Easy* 1.00
118 *Verron Haynes* 1.00
119 *Josh Scobey* 3.00
120 *Larry Ned* 1.00
121 *Adrian Peterson* 1.00
122 *Brian Allen* 1.00
123 *Chester Taylor* 1.00
124 *Luke Staley* 1.50
125 *Antwoine Womack* 1.00
126 *Leonard Henry* 1.00
127 *Jesse Chatman* 1.00
128 *Damien Anderson* 1.00
129 *Eric McCoo* 10.00
130 *Tellis Redmon* 1.00
131 *Joe Burns* 1.00
132 *Delvon Flowers* 1.00
133 *Ken Simonton* 1.00
134 *Ricky Williams* 1.00
135 *Dicenzo Miller* 1.00
136 *James Mungro* 10.00
137 *Randy McMichael* 10.00
138 *Deion Branch* 10.00
139 *Terry Charles* 1.00
140 *Herb Haygood* 1.00
141 *Jason McAddley* 1.00
142 *Jake Schifino* 1.00
143 *Freddie Milons* 1.00
144 *Kahlil Hill* 1.00
145 *Lamont Brightful* 1.00
146 *Chris Luzar* 5.00
147 *Daryl Jones* 5.00
148 *Woodrow Dantzler III* 2.00
149 *Kelly Campbell* 2.00
150 *Brian Poli-Dixon* 1.00
151 *Atrews Bell* 2.00
152 *Jarrod Baxter* 1.00
153 *Eddie Drummond* 3.00
154 *Jerramy Stevens* 1.00
155 *Doug Jolley* 5.00
156 *Jamar Martin* 1.00
157 *Najeh Davenport* 3.00
158 *Dwight Freeney* 5.00
159 *Bryan Thomas* 1.00
160 *Charles Grant* 1.00
161 *Kalimba Edwards* 1.00
162 *Ryan Denney* 1.00
163 *Will Overstreet* 1.00
164 *Dennis Johnson* .25
165 *Alex Brown* 5.00
166 *Kenyon Coleman* 1.00
167 *Ryan Sims* 1.00
168 *John Henderson* 1.00
169 *Wendell Bryant* 1.00
170 *Albert Haynesworth* 1.00
171 *Larry Tripplett* 1.00
172 *Eddie Freeman* 1.00
173 *Anthony Weaver* 1.00
174 *Quentin Jammer* 1.00
175 *Phillip Buchanon* 3.00
176 *Lito Sheppard* 1.00
177 *Mike Rumph* 3.00
178 *Roosevelt Williams* 3.00
179 *Derek Ross* 1.00
180 *Mike Echols* 2.00
181 *Keyuo Craver* 1.00
182 *Edward Reed* 1.00
183 *Lamont Thompson* 1.00
184 *Tank Williams* 1.00
185 *Michael Lewis* 3.00
186 *Napoleon Harris* 2.00
187 *Robert Thomas* 1.00
188 *Raonall Smith* 3.00
189 *Levar Fisher* 4.00
190 *Rocky Calmus* 1.50
191 *Andra Davis* 1.00
192 *Nick Rolovich* 1.00
193 *Zak Kustok* 1.00
194 *Dusty Bonner* 2.00
195 *Tony Fisher* 4.00
196 *Sam Simmons* 2.00
197 *Lee Mays* 2.00
198 *Jamin Elliott* 1.00
199 *Javin Hunter* 1.00
200 *Kendall Newson* 1.00
201 *Ladell Betts JSY* 8.00
202 *Antonio Bryant JSY* 12.00
203 *Reche Caldwell JSY* 8.00
204 *David Carr JSY* 50.00
205 *Tim Carter JSY* 8.00
206 *Eric Crouch JSY* 15.00
207 *Rohan Davey JSY* 12.00
208 *Andre Davis JSY* 15.00
209 *T.J. Duckett JSY* 15.00
210 *DeShaun Foster JSY* 10.00
211 *Jabar Gaffney JSY* 12.00
212 *David Garrard JSY* 8.00
213 *Daniel Graham JSY* 10.00
214 *William Green JSY* 15.00
215 *Joey Harrington JSY* 40.00
216 *Ron Johnson JSY* 8.00
217 *Ashley Lelie JSY* 25.00
218 *Josh McCown JSY* 15.00
219 *Maurice Morris JSY* 12.00
220 *Julius Peppers JSY* 20.00
221 *Clinton Portis JSY* 50.00
222 *Patrick Ramsey JSY* 12.00
223 *Antwann Randle El JSY* 20.00
224 *Josh Reed JSY* 12.00
225 *Cliff Russell JSY* 10.00
226 *Jeremy Shockey JSY* 30.00
227 *Donte Stallworth JSY* 20.00
228 *Travis Stephens JSY* 8.00
229 *Javon Walker JSY* 20.00
230 *Marquise Walker JSY* 12.00
231 *Roy Williams JSY* 25.00
232 *Mike Williams JSY* 10.00
RWH1 Walter Payton, Emmitt Smith 125.00
RWH1A Walter Payton, Emmitt Smith 400.00

2002 Playoff Honors O's

Stars: 4X-8X
Production 100 Sets
101-200 Rookies: 1.5X-3X
101-200 Production 50 Sets
201-232 Production 25 Sets
Inserted in Retail Packs

2002 Playoff Honors X's

Stars: 4X-8X
Production 100 Sets
101-200 Rookies: 1.5X-3X
101-200 Production 50 Sets
201-232 Production 25 Sets
Inserted in Hobby Packs

2002 Playoff Honors Rookie Autos

NM/M
Common Players: 25.00
Production 50 Sets
201 Ladell Betts 40.00
202 Antonio Bryant 60.00
203 Reche Caldwell 30.00
204 David Carr 150.00
205 Tim Carter 25.00
206 Eric Crouch 50.00
207 Rohan Davey 40.00
208 Andre Davis 60.00
209 T.J. Duckett 75.00
210 DeShaun Foster 30.00
211 Jabar Gaffney 30.00
212 David Garrard 25.00
213 Daniel Graham 25.00
214 William Green 75.00
215 Joey Harrington 125.00
216 Ron Johnson 10.00
217 Ashley Lelie 100.00
218 Josh McCown 50.00
219 Maurice Morris 30.00
220 Julius Peppers 100.00
221 Clinton Portis 200.00
222 Patrick Ramsey 60.00
223 Antwaan Randle 75.00
224 Josh Reed 60.00
225 Cliff Russell 25.00
226 Jeremy Shockey 125.00
227 Donte Stallworth 100.00
228 Travis Stephens 25.00
229 Javon Walker 75.00
230 Marquise Walker 25.00
231 Roy Williams 75.00
232 Mike Williams 25.00

2002 Playoff Honors 10th Anniversary

NM/M
Production 10 Sets

2002 Playoff Honors Alma Mater Materials

NM/M
Production from 25 to 400 sets
Patch Production 25 Sets
1 Doug Flutie JSY/100 25.00
2 Ahman Green JSY/100 40.00
3 Travis Minor Shoe/100 15.00
4 Laveranues Coles JSY/250 10.00
5 Drew Brees Shoe/100 30.00
6 Terrell Davis HEL/75 40.00
7 Javon Walker Shoe/100 30.00
8 James Jackson JSY/250 10.00
9 Reggie Wayne JSY/400 10.00
10 Champ Bailey Hel/75 25.00
11 Snoop Minnis Glove/25 25.00
12 Dan Morgan JSY/25 20.00
13 Peyton Manning Hel/75 60.00
14 Santana Moss JSY/250 12.00
15 Peter Warrick Glove/25 40.00

2002 Playoff Honors Award Winning Materials

NM/M
Common Player: 20.00
Production 150 Sets
Auto Production 10 Sets
1 Anthony Thomas 20.00
2 Edgerrin James 30.00
3 Randy Moss 40.00
4 Curtis Martin 20.00
5 Eddie George 20.00
6 Marshall Faulk 25.00
7 Kurt Warner 20.00
8 Terrell Davis 25.00
9 Barry Sanders 50.00
10 Brett Favre 60.00
11 Emmitt Smith 50.00
12 Steve Young 40.00

2002 Playoff Honors Game Day Souvenirs

NM/M
Common Player: 15.00
Production 250 sets
1 Donovan McNabb 20.00
2 Emmitt Smith 40.00
3 Jerry Rice 30.00
4 Jeff Garcia 15.00
5 Brian Urlacher 25.00
6 Brett Favre 50.00

2002 Playoff Honors Honorable Signatures

NM/M
Common Player: 10.00
HS1 Barry Sanders SP 100.00
HS2 Joe Montana 125.00
HS3 Joe Namath 75.00
HS4 Jeff Blake 12.00
HS5 Kerry Collins 12.00
HS6 Randall Cunningham 20.00
HS7 Anthony Thomas 25.00
HS8 Damione Lewis 10.00
HS9 Dan Morgan 10.00
HS10 LaMont Jordan 15.00
HS11 Jesse Palmer 15.00
HS12 Eddie "Boo" Williams 10.00
HS13 Isaac Bruce 25.00
HS14 Jimmy Smith 15.00
HS15 Santana Moss 15.00
HS16 Quincy Carter 25.00
HS17 Sage Rosenfels 15.00
HS18 T.J. Houshmandzadeh 12.00
HS19 Robert Ferguson 15.00
HS20 Aaron Brooks SP 30.00
HS21 Brett Favre 200.00
HS22 Cade McNown 12.00
HS23 Drew Bledsoe 50.00
HS24 Jerry Rice 100.00
HS25 Junior Seau 40.00
HS26 Kordell Stewart 30.00
HS27 Tony Banks 12.00
HS28 Chris Chambers SP 40.00
HS29 David Terrell 12.00
HS30 Edgerrin James SP 50.00
HS31 Gerard Warren 10.00
HS32 Jamal Anderson 15.00
HS33 Jamal Lewis 25.00
HS34 Justin Smith 10.00
HS35 Ken-Yon Rambo 12.00
HS36 Kurt Warner 50.00
HS37 Marcus Robinson 15.00
HS38 Mark Brunell 20.00
HS39 Marshall Faulk 60.00
HS40 Mike McMahon 15.00
HS41 Peter Warrick 20.00
HS42 Quincy Morgan 15.00
HS43 Rudi Johnson 20.00
HS44 Shaun Rogers 15.00
HS45 Stephen Davis SP 25.00
HS46 Tim Brown SP 40.00
HS47 Travis Minor SP 15.00
HS48 Warren Moon SP 50.00
HS49 Dan Marino SP 200.00
HS50 John Elway SP 200.00

2002 Playoff Honors Player of the Week

NM/M
Common Player: .75
1 Priest Holmes 2.00
2 Drew Bledsoe 2.00
3 Tom Brady 2.00
4 Shaun Alexander .75
5 Rich Gannon 1.00
6 Drew Brees 1.00
7 Marshall Faulk 1.00
8 Michael Vick 6.00
9 Brad Johnson 1.00
10 Rich Gannon 1.00
11 Donovan McNabb 3.00
12 Priest Holmes 2.00
13 LaDainian Tomlinson 3.00
14 Ricky Williams 4.00
15 Clinton Portis 4.00
16 Amani Toomer .75
17 Clinton Portis 4.00
18 Jeff Garcia (Wild Card Week) 2.00
19 Steve McNair (Divisional Playoff Week) 2.00
20 Rich Gannon (Conference Championship) 1.00
21 Dexter Jackson (Super Bowl) .75

2002 Playoff Honors Rookie Class Jerseys

NM/M
Common Player: 30.00
Production 50 sets
1 Emmitt Smith, Junior Seau, Jeff George 60.00
2 Curtis Conway, Drew Bledsoe, Mark Brunell 40.00
3 Jerome Bettis, Michael Strahan, O.J. McDuffie 30.00

4 Trent Dilfer, Charlie Garner, Isaac Bruce 30.00
5 Kerry Collins, Curtis Martin, Terrell Davis 30.00
6 Keyshawn Johnson, Terrell Owens, Terry Glenn 30.00
7 Peyton Manning, Kevin Dyson, Ryan Leaf 50.00
8 Brian Griese, Randy Moss, Fred Taylor 60.00
9 Edgerrin James, Donovan McNabb, Jeff Garcia 75.00
10 Kurt Warner, Ricky Williams, Daunte Culpepper 40.00
11 Tom Brady, Brian Urlacher, Shaun Alexander 75.00
12 Michael Vick, LaDainian Tomlinson, Anthony Thomas 100.00

2002 Playoff Honors Rookie Stallions

NM/M
Common Player: 1.00
Inserted 1:12
1 Albert Haynesworth 1.00
2 Alex Brown 1.00
3 Andra Davis 1.00
4 Andre Lott 1.00
5 Antwann Randle El 3.00
6 Ashley Lelie 4.00
7 Brian Westbrook 1.00
8 Bryant McKinnie 1.00
9 Chad Hutchinson 1.00
10 Cliff Russell 1.00
11 Cortlen Johnson 1.00
12 Damien Anderson 1.00
13 David Garrard 1.00
14 Deion Branch 2.00
15 Mike Williams 1.00
16 Donte Stallworth 4.00
17 Edward Reed 1.00
18 Eric Crouch 2.00
19 Freddie Milons 1.00
20 Jabar Gaffney 1.50
21 Javon Walker 2.00
22 Jerramy Stevens 1.00
23 John Henderson 1.00
24 Jonathan Wells 1.50
25 Josh McCown 1.00
26 Josh Scobey 1.00
27 Levar Fisher 1.00
28 Kalimba Edwards 1.00
29 Ken Simonton 1.00
30 Keyuo Craver 1.00
31 Kurt Kittner 1.50
32 Lito Sheppard 1.00
33 Marquise Walker 1.00
34 Mike Rumph 1.00
35 Najeh Davenport 1.50
36 Patrick Ramsey 2.00
37 Randy Fasani 1.00
38 Robert Thomas 1.00
39 Rocky Calmus 1.50
40 Tavon Mason 1.00
41 Terry Charles 1.00
42 T.J. Duckett 4.00
43 Tim Carter 1.50
44 Trev Faulk 1.00
45 Wendell Bryant 1.00
46 William Green 3.00
47 Kahlil Hill 1.00
48 Ladell Betts 1.50
49 Lamar Gordon 1.50
50 Napoleon Harris 1.00

2002 Playoff Honors Rookie Stallions Autos

NM/M
Production 100 sets
1 Albert Haynesworth 10.00
2 Alex Brown 15.00
3 Andra Davis 10.00
4 Andre Lott 15.00
5 Antwann Randle El 40.00
6 Ashley Lelie 40.00
7 Brian Westbrook 25.00
8 Bryant McKinnie 15.00
9 Chad Hutchinson 12.00
10 Cliff Russell 15.00
11 Cortlen Johnson 10.00
12 Damien Anderson 10.00
13 David Garrard 15.00
14 Deion Branch 30.00
15 Mike Williams 12.00
16 Donte Stallworth 40.00
17 Edward Reed 15.00
18 Eric Crouch 25.00
19 Freddie Milons 15.00
20 Jabar Gaffney 20.00
21 Javon Walker 30.00
22 Jerramy Stevens 12.00
23 John Henderson 12.00
24 Jonathan Wells 15.00
25 Josh McCown 20.00
26 Josh Scobey 10.00
27 Levar Fisher 10.00
28 Kalimba Edwards 10.00
29 Ken Simonton 15.00
30 Keyuo Craver 10.00
31 Kurt Kittner 20.00
32 Lito Sheppard 10.00
33 Marquise Walker 12.00
34 Mike Rumph 10.00
35 Najeh Davenport 15.00
36 Patrick Ramsey 30.00
37 Randy Fasani 20.00
38 Robert Thomas 10.00
39 Rocky Calmus 15.00
40 Tavon Mason 10.00
41 Terry Charles 10.00
42 T.J. Duckett 40.00
43 Tim Carter 15.00
44 Trev Faulk 10.00
45 Wendell Bryant 12.00
46 William Green 30.00
47 Kahlil Hill 12.00
48 Ladell Betts 15.00
49 Lamar Gordon 15.00
50 Napoleon Harris 12.00

2002 Playoff Honors Rookie Tandems/ Quads

NM/M
Common Player (1-15): 8.00
Common Player (16-22): 20.00
16-22 Production 500 Sets
Tandems Gold: 1.5X
Production 250 Sets
Quad Gold Production 25 Sets
1 David Carr, Jabar Gaffney 20.00
2 Travis Stephens, Marquise Walker 8.00
3 Patrick Ramsey, Cliff Russell 10.00
4 Antonio Bryant, Roy Williams 15.00
5 Clinton Portis, Ashley Lelie 20.00
6 Maurice Morris, Andre Davis 10.00
7 DeShaun Foster, Julius Peppers 12.00
8 Eric Crouch, Antwann Randle El 15.00
9 Joey Harrington, David Garrard 15.00
10 Josh McCown, Rohan Davey 10.00
11 Donte Stallworth, Donald Reche Caldwell 12.00
12 Javon Walker, Ron Johnson 12.00
13 Josh Reed, Tim Carter 8.00
14 T.J. Duckett, Ladell Betts 10.00
15 Jeremy Shockey, Daniel Graham 15.00
16 David Carr, Jabar Gaffney, Travis Stephens, Marquise Walker 30.00
17 Patrick Ramsey, Cliff Russell, Antonio Bryant, Roy Williams 25.00
18 Clinton Portis, Ashley Lelie, Maurice Morris, Andre Davis 40.00
19 DeShaun Foster, Julius Peppers, Eric Crouch, Antwann Randle El 25.00
20 Joey Harrington, David Garrard, Josh McCown, Rohan Davey 25.00
21 Donte Stallworth, Donald Reche Caldwell, Javon Walker, Ron Johnson 20.00
22 Josh Reed, Tim Carter, T.J. Duckett, Ladell Betts 20.00

2002 Playoff Piece of the Game

NM/M
Common Player: .50
Unlisted Stars: 1.00
Minor Stars: .75
Common Rookie (76-100): 2.00
Common Rookie (101-132): 6.00
Production 500 sets
Pack (5): 13.00
Wax Box (6): 55.00
1 Daunte Culpepper 2.00
2 Tim Couch 1.50
3 Michael Vick 3.00
4 Brett Favre 4.00
5 Drew Bledsoe 2.00
6 Mark Brunell 1.00
7 Jake Plummer .75
8 Mike McMahon .75
9 Brian Griese 1.00
10 Aaron Brooks 1.50
11 Chris Weinke 1.00
12 Peyton Manning 3.00
13 Trent Green .75
14 Quincy Carter 2.00
15 Tom Brady 3.00
16 Vinny Testaverde .75
17 Drew Brees 2.50
18 Kordell Stewart .75
19 Kerry Collins .75
20 Kurt Warner 3.00
21 Rich Gannon .75
22 Jeff Garcia 1.00
23 Shaun Alexander 1.00
24 Doug Flutie 1.00
25 Donovan McNabb 2.00
26 Steve McNair 1.00
27 Michael Bennett 1.00
28 Jamal Lewis 1.50
29 Marshall Faulk 2.00
30 Curtis Martin .75
31 James Jackson .75
32 Terrell Davis 1.50
33 Travis Henry .75
34 Corey Dillon 1.00
35 Deuce McAllister 1.50
36 Priest Holmes 1.00
37 Antowain Smith .75
38 Anthony Thomas 2.50
39 Ricky Williams 2.00
40 Charlie Garner .75
41 Jerome Bettis .75
42 Ahman Green 1.00
43 Emmitt Smith 3.00
44 Edgerrin James 2.50
45 Warrick Dunn .75
46 LaDainian Tomlinson 2.50
47 Fred Taylor .75
48 Eddie George 1.00
49 Garrison Hearst .75
50 Stephen Davis .75
51 Marvin "Snoop" Minnis .75
52 Troy Brown .75
53 Cris Carter .75
54 Jerry Rice 3.00
55 Terry Glenn .75
56 Plaxico Burress 1.00
57 David Boston 1.00
58 Marvin Harrison .75
59 Randy Moss 3.00
60 Eric Moulds .75
61 Rod Smith .75
62 Freddie Mitchell .75
63 Chris Chambers 1.00
64 Keyshawn Johnson .75
65 Terrell Owens 1.00
66 Isaac Bruce .75
67 Tim Brown 1.00
68 Tony Gonzalez .75
69 Jevon Kearse .75
70 Warren Sapp .75
71 Junior Seau .75
72 Michael Strahan .75
73 Ray Lewis .75
74 Zach Thomas .75
75 Brian Urlacher 2.50
76 *Quentin Jammer* 3.00
77 *Kurt Kittner* 3.00
78 *Chad Hutchinson* 2.00
79 *Randy Fasani* 2.00
80 *Lamar Gordon* 3.00
81 *Brian Westbrook* 6.00
82 *Josh Scobey* 2.00
83 *Chester Taylor* 2.00
84 *Luke Staley* 3.00
85 *Deion Branch* 6.00
86 *Terry Charles* 2.00
87 *Kahlil Hill* 2.00
88 *Freddie Milons* 2.00
89 *Woodrow Dantzler III* 2.00
90 *Kelly Campbell* 2.50
91 *Dwight Freeney* 2.00
92 *Bryan Thomas* 2.00
93 *Ryan Sims* 2.50
94 *John Henderson* 2.50
95 *Wendell Bryant* 2.50
96 *Albert Haynesworth* 2.50
97 *Phillip Buchanon* 3.00
98 *Lito Sheppard* 2.50
99 *Edward Reed* 2.00
100 *Napoleon Harris* 2.00
101 *David Carr JSY* 50.00
102 *Rohan Davey JSY* 8.00
103 *Joey Harrington JSY* 30.00
104 *Josh McCown JSY* 15.00
105 *Patrick Ramsey JSY* 10.00
106 *Ladell Betts JSY* 6.00
107 *T.J. Duckett JSY* 10.00
108 *DeShaun Foster JSY* 8.00
109 *William Green JSY* 8.00
110 *Maurice Morris JSY* 8.00
111 *Clinton Portis JSY* 50.00
112 *Travis Stephens JSY* 6.00
113 *Antonio Bryant JSY* 8.00
114 *Donald Reche Caldwell JSY* 6.00
115 *Tim Carter JSY* 6.00
116 *Eric Crouch JSY* 6.00
117 *Andre Davis JSY* 8.00
118 *Jabar Gaffney JSY* 10.00
119 *Ron Johnson JSY* 6.00
120 *Ashley Lelie JSY* 15.00
121 *Antwann Randle El JSY* 15.00
122 *Josh Reed JSY* 8.00
123 *Cliff Russell JSY* 6.00
124 *Donte Stallworth JSY* 12.00
125 *Javon Walker JSY* 12.00
126 *Marquise Walker JSY* 6.00
127 *Jeremy Shockey JSY* 15.00
128 *Daniel Graham JSY* 6.00
129 *David Garrard JSY* 6.00
130 *Roy Williams JSY* 12.00
131 *Julius Peppers JSY* 15.00
132 *Mike Williams JSY* 6.00

2002 Playoff Piece of the Game Materials

NM/M
Common Player: 8.00
First Down/250: 1X
First Down/100: 1.5X
First Down/50: 2X
Second Down/150: 1.5X
Second Down/50: 2X
Second Down/25: 4X
Third Down/50: 2X
Third Down/25: 4X
Third Down/10 Not Priced
Fourth Down Not Priced
1F Ahman Green FB 12.00
1J Ahman Green JSY SP 20.00
2F Antonio Freeman FB 8.00
2J Antonio Freeman JSY 10.00
3J Barry Sanders JSY 20.00
4F Brett Favre FB 25.00
4J Brett Favre JSY 30.00
5F Brian Griese FB 8.00
5J Brian Griese JSY 10.00
6J Charles Woodson JSY 10.00
7F Chris Chambers FB 8.00
7J Chris Chambers JSY 10.00
8F Corey Dillon FB 8.00
8J Corey Dillon JSY 10.00
9J Cory Schlesinger JSY 8.00
10F Cris Carter FB 10.00
10J Cris Carter JSY 12.00
11F Curtis Martin FB SP 12.00
11J Curtis Martin JSY 12.00
11P Curtis Martin Pants 10.00
12J Dan Marino JSY 30.00
13J Darren Woodson JSY 10.00
14F Daunte Culpepper FB 8.00
14J Daunte Culpepper JSY 10.00
15F David Boston FB SP 10.00
15J David Boston JSY 10.00
15P David Boston Pants 8.00
16F Donovan McNabb FB SP 15.00
16J Donovan McNabb JSY 15.00
17J Ed McCaffrey JSY 10.00
18F Eddie George FB 8.00
18J Eddie George JSY 10.00
19F Edgerrin James FB 12.00
19J Edgerrin James JSY 15.00
20F Emmitt Smith FB SP 30.00
20J Emmitt Smith JSY 30.00
21P Frank Wycheck Pants SP 8.00
22J Fred Taylor JSY 10.00
23J Isaac Bruce JSY 10.00
24J Jake Plummer JSY 10.00
24P Jake Plummer Pants 8.00
25F Jeff Garcia FB SP 12.00
25J Jeff Garcia JSY 12.00
26J Jerome Bettis JSY SP 15.00
27J Jerry Rice JSY 20.00
28J Jevon Kearse JSY 10.00
29J Jim Kelly JSY 15.00
30J Jimmy Smith JSY SP 10.00
31J John Elway JSY 30.00
32J Junior Seau JSY 10.00
33J Kevin Johnson JSY 8.00
33P Kevin Johnson Pants 8.00
34J Kordell Stewart JSY 10.00
35F Kurt Warner FB SP 10.00
35J Kurt Warner JSY 10.00
35P Kurt Warner Pants 8.00
36F LaDainian Tomlinson FB 12.00
36J LaDainian Tomlinson JSY 15.00
37J Mark Brunell JSY 10.00
38J Marshall Faulk JSY 15.00
39F Marvin Harrison FB 10.00
39J Marvin Harrison JSY 12.00
40J Michael Irvin JSY 10.00
41J Mike Alstott JSY 10.00
42J Peyton Manning JSY SP 20.00
43F Randy Moss FB 12.00
43J Randy Moss JSY 15.00
44F Rich Gannon FB 8.00
44J Rich Gannon JSY 10.00
45F Ron Dayne FB SP 8.00
45J Ron Dayne JSY 8.00
46F Stephen Davis FB 8.00
46J Stephen Davis JSY 10.00
47F Steve McNair FB 8.00
47J Steve McNair JSY 10.00
48J Steve Young JSY 15.00
49F Terrell Davis FB 10.00
49J Terrell Davis JSY 12.00
50F Terrell Owens FB 8.00
50J Terrell Owens JSY 10.00
51J Thurman Thomas JSY 12.00
52F Tim Brown FB 10.00
52J Tim Brown JSY 12.00
53F Tim Couch FB SP 10.00
53J Tim Couch JSY 10.00
54F Tony Gonzalez FB 8.00
54J Tony Gonzalez JSY 10.00
55J Troy Aikman JSY 15.00
56F Vinny Testaverde FB 8.00
56J Vinny Testaverde JSY 10.00
57J Warren Sapp JSY 10.00
58J Zach Thomas JSY 10.00
59J Steve McNair, Eddie George JSY/500 15.00
60J Brian Griese, Terrell Davis JSY/500 15.00
61J Peyton Manning, Edgerrin James JSY/500 25.00
62J Kurt Warner, Marshall Faulk JSY/500 15.00
63J Troy Aikman, Emmitt Smith JSY/500 50.00
64J Cris Carter JSY/250 15.00
65J Jeff Garcia JSY/250 15.00
66J Emmitt Smith JSY/250 40.00
67J Kurt Warner JSY/250 12.00
68J Randy Moss JSY/250 20.00

2002 Playoff Prime Signatures

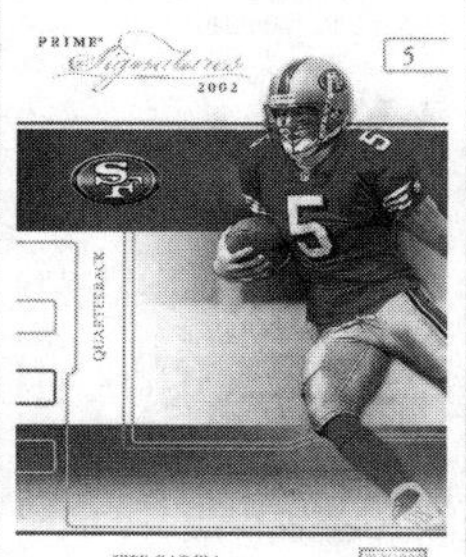

NM/M
Common Player: .40
Unlisted Star: .75
Minor Star: .60
Common Rookie (65-110): 5.00
Production 250 sets
Pack (4): 80.00
1 Aaron Brooks 1.25
2 Brett Favre 3.00
3 Drew Bledsoe 1.25
4 Jake Plummer .60
5 Jeff Blake .40
6 Jevon Kearse .60
7 Ricky Williams 1.00
8 Terrell Davis 1.25
9 Chris Chambers .75
10 Cris Carter .60
11 Emmitt Smith 2.50
12 Randall Cunningham .60
13 Corey Dillon .75
14 Brian Griese .75
15 Isaac Bruce .60
16 Koren Robinson .40
17 David Terrell .60
18 Mark Brunell .75
19 Eric Moulds .60
20 Kevan Barlow .60
21 David Boston .75
22 LaMont Jordan .40
23 Jimmy Smith .40
24 Marvin Harrison .75
25 Marcus Robinson .40
26 Ray Lewis .60
27 Mike Anderson .75
28 Randy Moss 2.50
29 Michael Bennett .75
30 Quincy Carter 1.25
31 Tim Brown .75
32 Michael Strahan .60
33 Tony Gonzalez .60
34 Santana Moss .60
35 Torry Holt .75
36 Anthony Thomas 1.50
37 Chris Weinke .40
38 Deuce McAllister 1.25
39 Drew Brees 2.00
40 Edgerrin James 2.00
41 Freddie Mitchell .60
42 James Jackson .60
43 Kendrell Bell .60
44 LaDainian Tomlinson 2.00
45 Mike McMahon .60
46 Quincy Morgan .60
47 Robert Ferguson .40
48 Steve Smith .40
49 Terrell Owens .75
50 Eddie George .75
51 Kurt Warner 2.50
52 Chad Johnson .40
53 Dan Marino 2.50
54 Jim Kelly 2.00
55 John Elway 2.50
56 Michael Irvin 1.00
57 Phil Simms .60
58 Steve Young .75
59 Troy Aikman 2.00
60 Warren Moon .60
61 Barry Sanders 2.50
62 Joe Montana 2.50
63 Joe Namath 2.00
64 Thurman Thomas 1.00
65 *T.J. Duckett* 30.00
66 *William Green* 25.00
67 *Travis Stephens* 6.00
68 *Tim Carter* 6.00
69 *Terry Charles* 5.00
70 *Roy Williams* 30.00
71 *Marquise Walker* 8.00
72 *Rohan Davey* 15.00
73 *Quentin Jammer* 8.00
74 *Donald Reche Caldwell* 8.00
75 *Maurice Morris* 10.00
76 *Woodrow Dantzler III* 6.00
77 *Patrick Ramsey* 25.00
78 *Tavon Mason* 6.00
79 *Ladell Betts* 15.00
80 *Kahlil Hill* 8.00
81 *Josh Scobey* 5.00
82 *Brian Westbrook* 20.00
83 *Javon Walker* 30.00
84 *DeShaun Foster* 12.00
85 *Kelly Campbell* 8.00
86 *Ashley Lelie* 40.00
87 *Donte Stallworth* 30.00
88 *David Carr* 75.00
89 *Kurt Kittner* 10.00
90 *Clinton Portis* 75.00
91 *Josh Reed* 15.00
92 *Joey Harrington* 50.00
93 *Antwann Randle El* 30.00
94 *Randy Fasani* 6.00
95 *Cliff Russell* 8.00
96 *John Henderson* 5.00
97 *Luke Staley* 8.00
98 *Antonio Bryant* 20.00
99 *Jonathan Wells* 10.00
100 *Chester Taylor* 6.00
101 *Lamar Gordon* 8.00
102 *Deion Branch* 25.00
103 *Josh McCown* 20.00
104 *Andre Davis* 20.00
105 *Freddie Milons* 5.00
106 *David Garrard* 8.00
107 *Chad Hutchinson* 12.00
108 *Jabar Gaffney* 15.00
109 *Eric Crouch* 15.00
110 *Albert Haynesworth* 5.00

2002 Playoff Prime Signatures Proofs

Stars: 1.5X-3X
1-64 Production 50 Sets
Rookie Production 25 Sets

A player's name in *italic* type indicates a rookie card.

2002 Playoff Prime Signatures Autographs

NM/M
Common Player: 10.00
Prime Cut Production 5 Sets
1 Aaron Brooks/58 30.00
2 Brett Favre/62 250.00
3 Drew Bledsoe/6
4 Jake Plummer/20 25.00
5 Jeff Blake/15 20.00
6 Jevon Kearse/6
7 Ricky Williams/116 55.00
8 Terrell Davis/21 40.00
9 Chris Chambers/223 20.00
10 Cris Carter/38 50.00
11 Emmitt Smith/40 250.00
12 Randall Cunningham/15
13 Corey Dillon/102 15.00
14 Brian Griese/81 20.00
15 Isaac Bruce/53 25.00
16 Koren Robinson/147 15.00
17 David Terrell/233 10.00
18 Mark Brunell/10
19 Eric Moulds/30 40.00
20 Kevan Barlow/210 15.00
21 David Boston/15
22 LaMont Jordan/115 10.00
23 Jimmy Smith/30 40.00
24 Marvin Harrison/94 40.00
25 Marcus Robinson/20 20.00
26 Ray Lewis/16
27 Mike Anderson/10
28 Randy Moss/195 60.00
29 Michael Bennett/250 20.00
30 Quincy Carter/95 20.00
31 Tim Brown/57 60.00
32 Michael Strahan/20 50.00
33 Tony Gonzalez/87 40.00
34 Santana Moss/115 15.00
35 Torry Holt/174 15.00
36 Anthony Thomas/131 15.00
37 Chris Weinke/99 12.00
38 Deuce McAllister/113 30.00
39 Drew Brees/57 30.00
40 Edgerrin James/28 60.00
41 Freddie Mitchell/126 10.00
42 James Jackson/126 10.00
43 Kendrell Bell/145 15.00
44 LaDainian Tomlinson/59 50.00
45 Mike McMahon/192 10.00
46 Quincy Morgan/160 12.00
47 Robert Ferguson/225 12.00
48 Steve Smith/209 15.00
49 Terrell Owens/98 30.00
50 Eddie George/22 40.00
51 Kurt Warner/176 30.00
52 Chad Johnson/216 15.00
53 Dan Marino/40 200.00
54 Jim Kelly/39 75.00
55 John Elway/68 200.00
56 Michael Irvin/143 40.00
57 Phil Simms/62 40.00
58 Steve Young/101 50.00
59 Troy Aikman/64 75.00
60 Warren Moon/5
61 Barry Sanders/38 150.00
62 Joe Montana/98 150.00
63 Joe Namath/216 75.00
64 Thurman Thomas/40 30.00
67 Travis Stephens/20 25.00
68 Tim Carter/120 15.00
69 Terry Charles/145 10.00
70 Roy Williams/70 100.00
71 Marquise Walker/95 12.00
72 Rohan Davey/20 50.00
73 Quentin Jammer/95 30.00
74 Donald Reche Caldwell/45 30.00
75 Maurice Morris/20 40.00
76 Woodrow Dantzler III/20 50.00
77 Patrick Ramsey/120 60.00
78 Tavon Mason/95 10.00
79 Ladell Betts/95 40.00
80 Kahlil Hill/45 20.00
81 Josh Scobey/145 12.00
82 Brian Westbrook/145 40.00
84 DeShaun Foster/70 30.00
85 Kelly Campbell/45 30.00
86 Ashley Lelie/120 60.00
87 Donte Stallworth/95 60.00
88 David Carr/70 200.00
89 Kurt Kittner/45 30.00
90 Clinton Portis/95 200.00
91 Josh Reed/120 30.00
92 Joey Harrington/95 125.00
93 Antwann Randle El/45 75.00
94 Randy Fasani/120 12.00
95 Cliff Russell/95 12.00
96 John Henderson/95 12.00
97 Luke Staley/95 12.00
98 Antonio Bryant/45 60.00
100 Chester Taylor/95 12.00
101 Lamar Gordon/45 30.00
102 Deion Branch/95 30.00
103 Josh McCown/95 25.00
104 Andre Davis/95 30.00
105 Freddie Milons/75 15.00
106 David Garrard/120 20.00
107 Chad Hutchinson/145 20.00
108 Jabar Gaffney/95 30.00
109 Eric Crouch/95 30.00

2002 Playoff Prestige

NM/M
Common Player: .25
Unlisted Stars: .75
Minor Stars: .50
Common Rookie (151-216): .75
Minor Rookie Stars: 1.00
Pack (5): 4.25
Wax Box (20): 60.00
1 David Boston .75
2 MarTay Jenkins .25
3 Jake Plummer .50

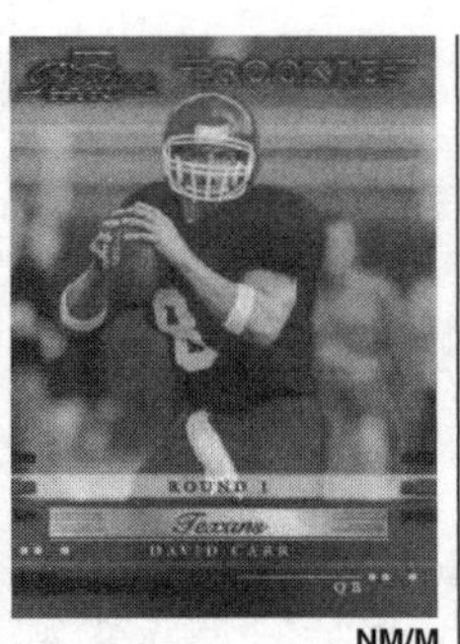

NM/M
4 Chris Chandler .25
5 Jamal Anderson .25
6 Michael Vick 3.00
7 Maurice Smith .25
8 Elvis Grbac .25
9 Jamal Lewis 1.50
10 Todd Heap .25
11 Qadry Ismail .25
12 Shannon Sharpe .50
13 Ray Lewis .50
14 Rod Woodson .50
15 Travis Henry .25
16 Rob Johnson .25
17 Eric Moulds .25
18 Nate Clements .25
19 Donald Hayes .25
20 Muhsin Muhammad .50
21 Steve Smith .25
22 Wesley Walls .25
23 Chris Weinke .75
24 James Allen .25
25 David Terrell .75
26 Anthony Thomas 2.50
27 Dez White .25
28 Brian Urlacher 2.50
29 Mike Brown .25
30 Corey Dillon .50
31 Chad Johnson .25
32 Peter Warrick .50
33 Justin Smith .25
34 Tim Couch 1.50
35 James Jackson .25
36 Quincy Morgan .50
37 Kevin Johnson .25
38 Gerard Warren .25
39 Anthony Henry .25
40 Quincy Carter 2.00
41 Joey Galloway .25
42 Raghib Ismail .25
43 Ryan Leaf .25
44 Emmitt Smith 3.00
45 Troy Hambrick .25
46 Mike Anderson 1.50
47 Terrell Davis 1.50
48 Brian Griese .75
49 Rod Smith .25
50 Ed McCaffrey .25
51 Charlie Batch .25
52 Johnnie Morton .25
53 Germane Crowell .25
54 James Stewart .50
55 Shaun Rogers .25
56 Brett Favre 4.00
57 Antonio Freeman .25
58 Ahman Green .75
59 Bill Schroeder .25
60 Kabeer Gbaja-Biamila .50
61 Marvin Harrison .75
62 Terrence Wilkins .25
63 Dominic Rhodes .25
64 Reggie Wayne .50
65 Edgerrin James 2.50
66 Mark Brunell .75
67 Keenan McCardell .25
68 Jimmy Smith .25
69 Fred Taylor .50
70 Derrick Alexander .25
71 Tony Gonzalez .25
72 Trent Green .50
73 Priest Holmes .75
74 Marvin "Snoop" Minnis .50
75 Chris Chambers .75
76 Jay Fiedler .50
77 Travis Minor .50
78 Lamar Smith .25
79 Zach Thomas .50
80 Michael Bennett .75
81 Cris Carter .50
82 Daunte Culpepper 2.00
83 Randy Moss 3.00
84 Drew Bledsoe 2.00
85 Tom Brady 3.00
86 Troy Brown .75
87 Antowain Smith .25
88 Aaron Brooks 1.50
89 Joe Horn .25
90 Deuce McAllister 1.50
91 Ricky Williams 1.50
92 Kerry Collins .50
93 Ron Dayne .50
94 Michael Strahan .50
95 Jason Sehorn .25
96 Wayne Chrebet .25
97 Laveranues Coles .25
98 LaMont Jordan .25
99 Curtis Martin .75
100 Santana Moss .75
101 Vinny Testaverde .25
102 Tim Brown .75
103 Jerry Porter .25
104 Jerry Rice 3.00
105 Charlie Garner .50
106 Tyrone Wheatley .25
107 Charles Woodson .75
108 Correll Buckhalter .50
109 Todd Pinkston .25
110 Freddie Mitchell .50
111 James Thrash .25
112 Duce Staley .50
113 Jerome Bettis .50
114 Plaxico Burress .75
115 Kordell Stewart .50
116 Hines Ward .25
117 Kendrell Bell .25
118 Drew Brees 2.50
119 Curtis Conway .25
120 Doug Flutie .75
121 LaDainian Tomlinson 2.50
122 Junior Seau .50
123 Kevan Barlow .25
124 Jeff Garcia .75
125 Garrison Hearst .50
126 Terrell Owens .50
127 Andre Carter .25
128 Shaun Alexander .75
129 Matt Hasselbeck .25
130 Koren Robinson .25
131 Ricky Watters .50
132 Isaac Bruce .50
133 Trung Canidate .25
134 Marshall Faulk 2.00
135 Torry Holt .25
136 Kurt Warner 3.00
137 Mike Alstott .50
138 Warrick Dunn .50
139 Brad Johnson .50
140 Keyshawn Johnson .50
141 Warren Sapp .50
142 Eddie George .75
143 Derrick Mason .25
144 Steve McNair .75
145 Jevon Kearse .50
146 Stephen Davis .50
147 Rod Gardner .50
148 Champ Bailey .50
149 Bruce Smith .25
150 Houston Texans 1.00
151 *David Carr* 15.00
152 *Julius Peppers* 4.00
153 *Joey Harrington* 10.00
154 *Quentin Jammer* 2.50
155 *Ryan Sims* 1.00
156 *Bryant McKinnie* 1.50
157 *Roy Williams* 4.00
158 *John Henderson* 1.00
159 *Dwight Freeney* 2.00
160 *Wendell Bryant* .75
161 *Donte Stallworth* 5.00
162 *Jeremy Shockey* 6.00
163 *Albert Haynesworth* 1.00
164 *William Green* 4.00
165 *Phillip Buchanon* 2.50
166 *T.J. Duckett* 5.00
167 *Ashley Lelie* 5.00
168 *Javon Walker* 6.00
169 *Daniel Graham* 2.00
170 *Napoleon Harris* 1.00
171 *Lito Sheppard* 1.50
172 *Robert Thomas* .75
173 *Patrick Ramsey* 3.00
174 *Jabar Gaffney* 3.00
175 *DeShaun Foster* 3.00
176 *Kalimba Edwards* 1.00
177 *Josh Reed* 3.00
178 *Larry Tripplett* 1.00
179 *Andre Davis* 3.00
180 *Donald Reche Caldwell* 2.50
181 *Levar Fisher* .75
182 *Clinton Portis* 15.00
183 *Anthony Weaver* .75
184 *Maurice Morris* 3.00
185 *Ladell Betts* 2.50
186 *Antwann Randle El* 4.00
187 *Antonio Bryant* 4.00
188 *Rocky Calmus* 2.50
189 *Josh McCown* 4.00
190 *Lamar Gordon* 2.50
191 *Marquise Walker* 2.50
192 *Cliff Russell* .75
193 *Eric Crouch* 3.00
194 *Dennis Johnson* 1.00
195 *Alex Brown* .75
196 *David Garrard* 1.00
197 *Rohan Davey* 3.00
198 *Alan Harper* .75
199 *Ron Johnson* .75
200 *Andra Davis* 1.00
201 *Kurt Kittner* 2.50
202 *Freddie Milons* 1.00
203 *Adrian Peterson* 2.50
204 *Luke Staley* 2.50
205 *Tracey Wistrom* .75
206 *Woodrow Dantzler III* .75
207 *Chad Hutchinson* 1.00
208 *Zak Kustok* 1.00
209 *Damien Anderson* 1.00
210 *James Mungro* .75
211 *Cortlen Johnson* .75
212 *Demontray Carter* .75
213 *Kelly Campbell* 1.00
214 *Brian Poli-Dixon* 1.00
215 *Mike Rumph* .75
216 *Najeh Davenport* 2.00

2002 Playoff Prestige X-tra Points

Stars: 2X-4X
1-150 Production 150 Sets
Rookies: 3X-6X
151-216 Production 25 Sets
Green Inserted Into Retail Packs
Purple Inserted Into Hobby Packs

2002 Playoff Prestige Banner Season

NM/M
Common Player: 1.00
Production to year of banner season
1 Archie Griffin 1.00
2 Archie Manning 2.00
3 Art Monk 1.00
4 Charley Taylor 1.00
5 Cris Collinsworth 1.00

NM/M
6 Craig Morton 1.00
7 Dick Butkus 3.00
8 Don Maynard 1.00
9 Drew Pearson 1.00
10 Dwight Clark 1.00
11 Eric Dickerson 4.00
12 Fran Tarkenton 3.00
13 Franco Harris 3.00
14 Frank Gifford 1.00
15 Fred Biletnikoff 1.00
16 Frenchy Fuqua 1.00
17 Gale Sayers 4.00
18 Henry Ellard 1.00
19 James Lofton 1.00
20 Jim Plunkett 1.00
21 Joe Greene 2.00
22 Joe Theismann 1.00
23 John Hadl 1.00
24 John Stallworth 2.00
25 Kellen Winslow 1.00
26 Ken Anderson 1.00
27 Lance Alworth 1.00
28 Mike Singletary 2.00
29 Otto Graham 1.50
30 Paul Hornung 2.00
31 Paul Warfield 1.00
32 Raymond Berry 1.00
33 Rocky Bleier 1.00
34 Ronnie Lott 2.00
35 Sammy Baugh 1.00
36 Sonny Jurgensen 1.50
37 Steve Largent 1.00
38 Terry Bradshaw 4.00
39 Todd Christensen 1.00
40 Y.A. Tittle 2.00

2002 Playoff Prestige Banner Season Ink

BS1 Archie Griffin
BS2 Archie Manning
BS3 Art Monk
BS4 Charley Taylor
BS5 Cris Collinsworth
BS6 Craig Morton
BS7 Dick Butkus
BS8 Don Maynard
BS9 Drew Pearson
BS10 Dwight Clark
BS11 Eric Dickerson
BS12 Fran Tarkenton
BS13 Franco Harris
BS14 Frank Gifford
BS15 Fred Biletnikoff
BS16 John Fuqua
BS17 Gale Sayers
BS18 Henry Ellard
BS19 James Lofton
BS20 Jim Plunkett
BS21 Joe Greene
BS22 Joe Theismann
BS23 John Hadl
BS24 John Stallworth
BS25 Kellen Winslow
BS26 Ken Anderson
BS27 Lance Alworth
BS28 Mike Singletary
BS29 Otto Graham
BS30 Paul Hornung
BS31 Paul Warfield
BS32 Raymond Berry
BS33 Rocky Bleier
BS34 Ronnie Lott
BS35 Sammy Baugh
BS36 Sonny Jurgensen
BS37 Steve Largent
BS38 Terry Bradshaw
BS39 Todd Christensen
BS40 Y.A. Tittle

2002 Playoff Prestige Connections

NM/M
Common Player: 10.00
Production 500 sets
1 Kurt Warner, Isaac Bruce 25.00
2 Cris Carter, Daunte Culpepper 20.00
3 Chris Chambers, Jay Fiedler 20.00
4 Tom Brady, Troy Brown 25.00
5 Ed McCaffrey, Brian Griese 10.00
6 Jeff Garcia, Terrell Owens 10.00
7 Muhsin Muhammad, Chris Weinke 15.00
8 David Boston, Jake Plummer 15.00
9 Vinny Testaverde, Laveranues Coles 10.00
10 Antonio Freeman, Brett Favre 35.00
11 Jimmy Smith, Mark Brunell 15.00
12 Rob Johnson, Eric Moulds 10.00
13 Tim Couch, Quincy Morgan 15.00
14 Kerry Collins, Amani Toomer 10.00
15 Tim Brown, Rich Gannon 15.00
16 Todd Pinkston, Donovan McNabb 10.00
17 Germane Crowell, Charlie Batch 10.00
18 Kurt Warner, Az-Zahir Hakim 25.00
19 Keyshawn Johnson, Brad Johnson 10.00
20 Mark Brunell, Keenan McCardell 15.00
21 Peyton Manning, Marvin Harrison 25.00
22 Rod Smith, Brian Griese 10.00
23 Steve McNair, Kevin Dyson 10.00
24 Kurt Warner, Torry Holt 25.00
25 Kevin Johnson, Tim Couch 15.00
26 Jake Plummer, Frank Sanders 10.00
27 Plaxico Burress, Kordell Stewart 15.00
28 Randy Moss, Daunte Culpepper 25.00
29 Vinny Testaverde, Wayne Chrebet 10.00
30 Jerry Rice, Rich Gannon 25.00

2002 Playoff Prestige Draft Picks

NM/M
Common Player: 1.00
Production 2002 sets
1 *David Carr* 8.00
2 *Joey Harrington* 6.00
3 *Kurt Kittner* 2.00
4 *Rohan Davey* 2.00
5 *Eric Crouch* 6.00
6 *William Green* 4.00
7 *T.J. Duckett* 4.00
8 *DeShaun Foster* 2.50
10 *Luke Staley* 1.50
11 *Clinton Portis* 5.00
12 *Antonio Bryant* 2.50
13 *Josh Reed* 3.00
14 *Marquise Walker* 2.00
15 *Andre Davis* 2.00
16 *Ashley Lelie* 4.00
17 *Jabar Gaffney* 2.50
18 *Donald Reche Caldwell* 2.00
19 *Daniel Graham* 1.00
20 *Jeremy Shockey* 1.00
21 *Julius Peppers* 3.00
22 *John Henderson* 1.00
24 *Roy Williams* 4.00
25 *Bryant McKinnie* 2.00

2002 Playoff Prestige Draft Picks Autographs

NM/M
Common Player: 25.00
Production 50 Sets
1 David Carr 120.00
2 Joey Harrington 100.00
3 Kurt Kittner 40.00
4 Rohan Davey 30.00
5 Eric Crouch 40.00
6 William Green 40.00
7 T.J. Duckett 40.00
8 DeShaun Foster 40.00
9 Travis Stephens 25.00
10 Luke Staley 40.00
11 Clinton Portis 120.00
12 Antonio Bryant 40.00
13 Josh Reed 40.00
14 Marquise Walker 25.00
15 Andre Davis 40.00
16 Ashley Lelie 50.00
17 Jabar Gaffney 40.00
18 Reche Caldwell 25.00
19 Daniel Graham 25.00
20 Jeremy Shockey 100.00
21 Julius Peppers 80.00
22 John Henderson 25.00
23 Ed Reed 30.00
24 Roy Williams 100.00
25 Bryant McKinnie 25.00

2002 Playoff Prestige Gridiron Heritage

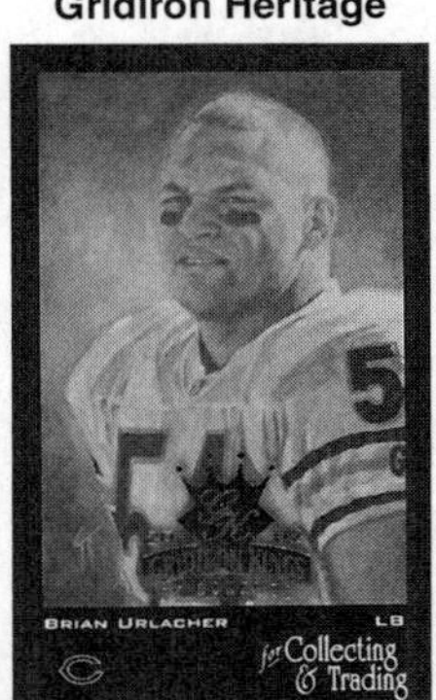

NM/M
Common Player: 20.00
Production 100 sets
1 Mike Anderson 25.00
2 Stephen Davis 20.00
3 Mark Brunell 20.00
4 Rich Gannon 25.00
5 Kordell Stewart 20.00
6 Curtis Martin 25.00
7 Michael Vick 100.00
8 Duce Staley 20.00
9 Troy Aikman 65.00
10 Warren Moon 20.00
11 Daunte Culpepper 45.00
12 Jerome Bettis 25.00
13 Junior Seau 20.00
14 Cris Carter 20.00
15 John Elway 125.00
16 Lamar Smith 20.00
17 Doug Flutie 45.00
18 Keyshawn Johnson 30.00
19 LaDainian Tomlinson 30.00
20 Aaron Brooks 20.00

2002 Playoff Prestige Inside the Numbers

NM/M
Common Player: 2.00
Inserted 1:18
1 Aaron Brooks 2.00
2 Mark Brunell 2.00
3 Daunte Culpepper 3.00
4 Brad Johnson 2.00
5 Steve McNair 2.00
6 Kurt Warner 4.00
7 Donovan McNabb 2.00
8 Brian Griese 2.00
9 Tom Brady 4.00
10 Marshall Faulk 3.00
11 Edgerrin James 3.00
12 LaDainian Tomlinson 3.00
13 Eddie George 2.00
14 Curtis Martin 2.00
15 Jerome Bettis 2.00
16 Shaun Alexander 2.00
17 Ricky Williams 2.00
18 Emmitt Smith 4.00
19 Randy Moss 4.00
20 Jimmy Smith 2.00
21 Troy Brown 2.00
22 Rod Smith 2.00
23 Chris Chambers 3.00
24 Terrell Owens 2.00
25 Marvin Harrison 2.00
26 Tim Brown 2.00
27 David Boston 2.00
28 Ray Lewis 2.00
29 Brian Urlacher 3.00
30 Zach Thomas 2.00

2002 Playoff Prestige Inside the Numbers Gold

NM/M
Common Player: 10.00
IN1 Aaron Brooks/2
IN2 Mark Brunell/8
IN3 Daunte Culpepper/11
IN4 Brad Johnson/14 15.00
IN5 Steve McNair/9
IN6 Kurt Warner/13
IN7 Donovan McNabb/5
IN8 Brian Griese/14 15.00
IN9 Tom Brady/12
IN10 Marshall Faulk/28 40.00
IN11 Edgerrin James/32 40.00
IN12 LaDainian Tomlinson/21 40.00
IN13 Eddie George/27 15.00
IN14 Curtis Martin/28 15.00
IN15 Jerome Bettis/36 15.00
IN16 Shaun Alexander/37 15.00
IN17 Ricky Williams/34 25.00
IN18 Emmitt Smith/22
IN29 Randy Moss/84 20.00
IN20 Jimmy Smith/82 10.00
IN21 Troy Brown/80 10.00
IN22 Rod Smith/80 10.00
IN23 Chris Chambers/84 12.00
IN24 Terrell Owens/81 12.00
IN25 Marvin Harrison/88 12.00
IN26 Tim Brown/81 12.00
IN27 David Boston/89 12.00
IN28 Ray Lewis/52 20.00
IN29 Brian Urlacher/54 30.00
IN30 Zach Thomas/54 12.00

2002 Playoff Prestige League Leader Tandems

NM/M
Common Player: 2.00
Inserted 1:18
Materials version 2X-4X
Production 250 sets
1 Kurt Warner, Brian Griese 6.00

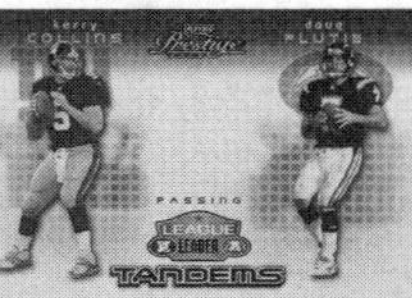

NM/M
2 Brett Favre, Peyton Manning 8.00
3 Daunte Culpepper, Rich Gannon 4.00
4 Doug Flutie, Kerry Collins 2.00
5 Jay Fiedler, Jake Plummer 2.00
6 Mark Brunell, Jeff Garcia 2.00
7 Kordell Stewart, Brad Johnson 2.00
8 Jerome Bettis, Ricky Williams 3.00
9 Ahman Green, Shaun Alexander 3.00
10 Marshall Faulk, Curtis Martin 4.00
11 Stephen Davis, LaDainian Tomlinson 4.00
12 Corey Dillon, Tiki Barber 2.00
13 Lamar Smith, Emmitt Smith 5.00
14 David Boston, Rod Smith 2.00
15 Terrell Owens, Marvin Harrison 2.00
16 Troy Brown, Keyshawn Johnson 2.00
17 Isaac Bruce, Tim Brown 3.00
18 Johnnie Morton, Jimmy Smith 2.00
19 Torry Holt, Kevin Johnson 2.00
20 Michael Strahan, Jevon Kearse 2.00

2002 Playoff Prestige Sophomore Signatures

NM/M
Common Player: 5.00
1 Mike McMahon SP 15.00
2 Alge Crumpler SP 10.00
3 Anthony Thomas 25.00
4 Carlos Polk 10.00
5 Cedric Scott 10.00
6 Cedrick Wilson 8.00
7 Chad Johnson 15.00
8 Chris Weinke 10.00
9 David Terrell 15.00
10 Deuce McAllister 25.00
11 Drew Brees 20.00
12 Ennis Davis 8.00
13 Hakim Akbar 8.00
14 Heath Evans 8.00
15 Jamal Reynolds 8.00
16 Jesse Palmer 12.00
17 Justin Smith 8.00
18 Karon Riley 8.00
19 Kendrell Bell SP 30.00
20 Kenny Smith 8.00
21 Kenyatta Walker 8.00
22 Ken-Yon Rambo 10.00
23 Kevan Barlow 15.00
24 Koren Robinson 15.00
25 Marcus Stroud 8.00
26 Marvin "Snoop" Minnis No Auto/100 10.00
27 Michael Bennett 15.00
28 Moran Norris SP 10.00
29 Morlon Greenwood SP 8.00
30 Nate Clements No Auto/100 8.00
31 Quincy Carter 40.00
32 Quincy Morgan 12.00
33 Reggie Germany 8.00
34 Robert Ferguson 12.00
35 Rudi Johnson 15.00
36 Santana Moss 15.00
37 T.J. Houshmandzadeh 8.00
38 Todd Heap 12.00
39 Travis Henry No Auto/100 10.00
40 Travis Minor 10.00

2002 Playoff Prestige Stars of the NFL

NM/M
Common Player: 10.00
Production 300 sets
1 Edgerrin James 20.00
2 Jerome Bettis 10.00
3 Shaun Alexander 10.00
4 Brett Favre 50.00
5 Donovan McNabb 15.00
6 Marshall Faulk 15.00
7 John Elway 40.00
8 Troy Aikman 20.00
9 Jeff Garcia 10.00
10 Randy Moss 30.00
11 Stephen Davis 10.00
12 Emmitt Smith 30.00
13 Dan Marino 40.00
14 Brian Urlacher 30.00
15 Mike Anderson 10.00
16 Jevon Kearse 10.00
17 Terrell Owens 10.00
18 Peyton Manning 30.00
19 Ricky Williams 10.00
20 Warren Sapp 10.00

2002 Playoff Prestige Stars of the NFL Autos

NM/M
Common Player: 40.00
SN4 Brett Favre/4
SN7 John Elway/7
SN8 Troy Aikman/8
SN11 Stephen Davis/48 50.00
SN13 Dan Marino/13
SN14 Brian Urlacher/54 120.00
SN15 Mike Anderson/38 50.00
SN16 Jevon Kearse/90 40.00
SN17 Terrell Owens/81 50.00
SN19 Ricky Williams/24 100.00

2003 Playoff Absolute

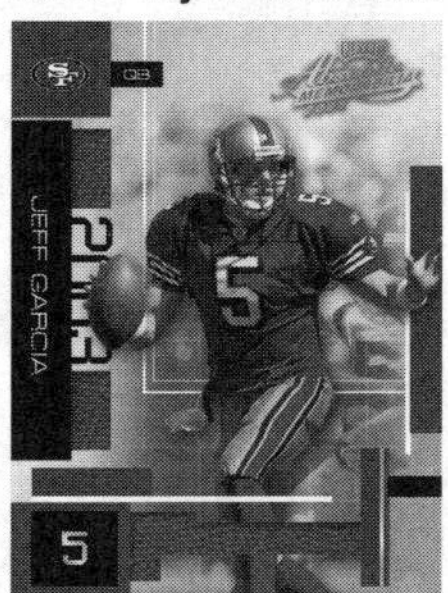

NM/M
Common Player (1-100): .40
Minor Stars: .75
Unlisted Stars: 1.00
Common Rookie (101-180): 4.00
Minor Rookies: 5.00
Unlisted Rookies: 6.00
101-150 Production 1100 Sets
151-180 Production 750 Sets
Pack (6): 6.00
Box (18): 75.00
1 Jamal Lewis 1.00
2 Ray Lewis .75
3 Todd Heap .40
4 Drew Bledsoe 1.50
5 Travis Henry .75
6 Peerless Price .75
7 Corey Dillon 1.00
8 Chad Johnson .75
9 Tim Couch .75
10 William Green 1.00
11 Andre Davis .75
12 Brian Griese .75
13 Ashley Lelie .75
14 Clinton Portis 3.00
15 Rod Smith .75
16 David Carr 2.50
17 Corey Bradford .40
18 Jonathan Wells .40
19 Peyton Manning 2.00
20 Edgerrin James 1.50
21 Marvin Harrison 1.00
22 Mark Brunell .75
23 Fred Taylor 1.00
24 Jimmy Smith .75
25 Trent Green .75
26 Priest Holmes 1.00
27 Tony Gonzalez .75
28 Jay Fiedler .75
29 Ricky Williams 2.00
30 Chris Chambers 1.00
31 Zach Thomas .40
32 Tom Brady 2.00
33 Troy Brown .75
34 Antowain Smith .40
35 Chad Pennington 1.50
36 Curtis Martin 1.00
37 Laveranues Coles .75
38 Rich Gannon .75
39 Charlie Garner .75
40 Jerry Rice 3.00
41 Tim Brown 1.00
42 Tommy Maddox 1.00
43 Jerome Bettis 1.00
44 Plaxico Burress 1.00
45 Hines Ward .75
46 Drew Brees 1.50
47 LaDainian Tomlinson 1.50
48 Junior Seau .75
49 Steve McNair 1.00
50 Eddie George 1.00
51 Jevon Kearse .75
52 Jake Plummer .75
53 David Boston 1.00
54 Marcel Shipp .75
55 Michael Vick 4.00
56 T.J. Duckett 1.00
57 Warrick Dunn .75
58 Muhsin Muhammad .40
59 Julius Peppers .75
60 Steve Smith .40
61 Anthony Thomas 1.00
62 Brian Urlacher 2.00
63 Marty Booker .75
64 Antonio Bryant .75
65 Chad Hutchinson 1.00
66 Roy Williams 1.00
67 Emmitt Smith 3.00
68 Joey Harrington 2.50
69 James Stewart .75
70 Az-Zahir Hakim .75
71 Brett Favre 4.00
72 Ahman Green 1.00
73 Donald Driver .75
74 Daunte Culpepper 1.00
75 Randy Moss 2.00
76 Michael Bennett 1.00
77 Aaron Brooks 1.00
78 Deuce McAllister 1.00
79 Donte Stallworth 1.00
80 Tiki Barber 1.00
81 Kerry Collins .75
82 Jeremy Shockey 2.50
83 Donovan McNabb 1.50
84 Duce Staley .75
85 Antonio Freeman .75
86 Jeff Garcia 1.00
87 Terrell Owens 1.00
88 Garrison Hearst .75
89 Matt Hasselbeck .75
90 Koren Robinson .75
91 Shaun Alexander 1.00
92 Kurt Warner 2.00
93 Marshall Faulk 1.50
94 Isaac Bruce .75
95 Brad Johnson .75
96 Keyshawn Johnson .75
97 Warren Sapp .75
98 Patrick Ramsey 1.00
99 Rod Gardner .75
100 Stephen Davis .75
101 *Jason Gesser* 5.00
102 *Brandon Lloyd* 6.00
103 *Ken Dorsey* 8.00
104 *Avon Cobourne* 6.00
105 *Cecil Sapp* 5.00
106 *Derek Watson* 4.00
107 *Dwone Hicks* 4.00
108 *Earnest Graham* 5.00
109 *LaBrandon Toefield* 5.00
110 *Quentin Griffin* 15.00
111 *Sultan McCullough* 4.00
112 *Lee Suggs* 8.00
113 *Talman Gardner* 5.00
114 *Arnaz Battle* 4.00
115 *Billy McMullen* 5.00
116 *Doug Gabriel* 4.00
117 *Justin Gage* 6.00
118 *Kareem Kelly* 4.00
119 *Paul Arnold* 4.00
120 *Sam Aiken* 4.00
121 *Shaun McDonald* 4.00
122 *Terrence Edwards* 5.00
123 *Walter Young* 4.00
124 *Ryan Hoag* 4.00
125 *Jason Witten* 8.00
126 *Bennie Joppru* 4.00
127 *George Wrighster* 5.00
128 *L.J. Smith* 4.00
129 *Robert Johnson* 5.00
130 *Chris Kelsay* 4.00
131 *Corey Redding* 4.00
132 *Dewayne White* 4.00
133 *Kenny Peterson* 4.00
134 *Jerome McDougal* 5.00
135 *Michael Haynes* 4.00
136 *Jimmy Kennedy* 6.00
137 *Kevin Williams* 4.00
138 *Jonathon Sullivan* 4.00
139 *Rien Long* 4.00
140 *Ty Warren* 4.00
141 *William Joseph* 6.00
142 *E.J. Henderson* 5.00
143 *Boss Bailey* 6.00
144 *Dennis Weathersby* 4.00
145 *Chris Simms* 10.00
146 *Rashean Mathis* 4.00
147 *Charles Rogers* 12.00
148 *Andre Woolfolk* 5.00
149 *Troy Polamalu* 10.00
150 *Mike Doss* 5.00
151 *Carson Palmer* 60.00
152 *Byron Leftwich* 60.00
153 *Kyle Boller* 35.00
154 *Rex Grossman* 40.00
155 *Dave Ragone* 15.00
156 *Kliff Kingsbury* 15.00
157 *Seneca Wallace* 15.00
158 *Larry Johnson* 35.00
159 *Willis McGahee* 40.00
160 *Justin Fargas* 30.00
161 *Onterrio Smith* 20.00
162 *Chris Brown* 20.00
163 *Musa Smith* 15.00
164 *Artose Pinner* 20.00
165 *Andre Johnson* 35.00
166 *Kelley Washington* 15.00
167 *Taylor Jacobs* 15.00
168 *Bryant Johnson* 20.00
169 *Tyrone Calico* 20.00
170 *Anquan Boldin* 30.00
171 *Bethel Johnson* 15.00
172 *Nate Burleson* 12.00
173 *Kevin Curtis* 12.00
174 *Dallas Clark* 20.00
175 *Teyo Johnson* 15.00
176 *Terrell Suggs* 20.00
177 *Dewayne Robertson* 12.00
178 *Brian St. Pierre* 12.00
179 *Terence Newman* 25.00
180 *Marcus Trufant* 12.00

2003 Playoff Absolute Spectrum

Stars: 3X-6X
1-100 Production 150 Sets
Rookies 101-150: 2X
101-150 Production 100 Sets
Rookies 151-180: 3X-6X
151-180 Production 25 Sets

2003 Playoff Absolute Absolutely Ink

Production 25
Not Priced Due to Scarcity
1 Marty Booker
2 Ahman Green
4 Deion Branch
6 Ed McCaffrey
7 Eric Moulds
8 Garrison Hearst
9 Jeff Garcia
10 Joe Horn
11 Jimmy Smith
12 Kurt Warner
13 Michael Vick
14 Patrick Ramsey
15 Randy Moss
16 Ricky Williams
17 Rod Smith
18 Tim Brown
19 Tom Brady

2003 Playoff Absolute Absolute Patches

Not Priced Due to Scarcity
Production 25 Sets
1 Brett Favre
2 Brian Urlacher
3 Clinton Portis
4 David Carr
5 Deuce McAllister
6 Donovan McNabb
7 Drew Bledsoe
8 Edgerrin James
9 Emmitt Smith
10 Priest Holmes
11 Jeremy Shockey
12 Jerry Rice
13 Joey Harrington
14 Kurt Warner
15 LaDainian Tomlinson
16 Marshall Faulk
17 Michael Vick
18 Peyton Manning
19 Randy Moss
20 Steve McNair

2003 Playoff Absolute Boss Hoggs

NM/M
Common Player: 15.00
Production 125 Sets
1 Amani Toomer 15.00
2 Chad Pennington 20.00
3 Curtis Martin 15.00
4 Daunte Culpepper 20.00
5 Eddie George 20.00
6 Edgerrin James 20.00
7 Emmitt Smith 75.00
8 Fred Taylor 20.00
9 Jerry Rice 60.00
10 Keyshawn Johnson 20.00
11 Marvin Harrison 20.00
12 Peyton Manning 30.00
13 Rich Gannon 15.00
14 Steve McNair 20.00
15 Terrell Owens 20.00

2003 Playoff Absolute Boss Hoggs Auto

Not Priced Due to Scarcity
Production 25 Sets
2 Chad Pennington
5 Eddie George
9 Jerry Rice
11 Marvin Harrison
13 Rich Gannon
14 Steve McNair
15 Terrell Owens

2003 Playoff Absolute Canton Absolutes

NM/M
Common Player: 10.00
Production 150 Sets
1 Ahman Green 12.00
2 Anthony Thomas 10.00
3 Brett Favre 50.00
4 Chris Chambers 10.00
5 Clinton Portis 10.00
6 Curtis Martin 10.00
7 Daunte Culpepper 15.00
8 David Carr 20.00
9 Donovan McNabb 20.00
10 Donte Stallworth 12.00
11 Drew Brees 10.00
12 Eddie George 12.00
13 Edgerrin James 15.00
14 Emmitt Smith 30.00
15 Garrison Hearst 10.00
16 Isaac Bruce 12.00
17 Jamal Lewis 12.00
18 Jeff Garcia 10.00
19 Jeremy Shockey 20.00
20 Jerry Rice 20.00
21 Jevon Kearse 10.00
22 Jimmy Smith 10.00
23 Joey Harrington 15.00
24 Julius Peppers 10.00
25 Junior Seau 10.00
26 Keyshawn Johnson 10.00
27 Kurt Warner 15.00
28 LaDainian Tomlinson 15.00
29 Marshall Faulk 15.00
30 Marvin Harrison 12.00
31 Michael Bennett 10.00
32 Michael Vick 50.00
33 Mike Alstott 10.00
34 Peyton Manning 20.00
35 Priest Holmes 15.00
36 Randy Moss 20.00
37 Ray Lewis 10.00
38 Rich Gannon 10.00
39 Ricky Williams 15.00
40 Rod Smith 10.00
41 Roy Williams 10.00
42 Shaun Alexander 12.00
43 Stephen Davis 10.00
44 Steve McNair 12.00
45 Terrell Owens 12.00
46 Tim Brown 10.00
47 T.J. Duckett 10.00
48 Tom Brady 12.00
49 Travis Henry 10.00
50 Zach Thomas 10.00

A player's name in *italic* type indicates a rookie card.

2003 Playoff Absolute Canton Absolute Auto

Not Priced Due to Scarcity
16 Isaac Bruce/25
17 Jamal Lewis/25
18 Jeff Garcia/25
27 Kurt Warner/50
32 Michael Vick/25

2003 Playoff Absolute Gridiron Force

1 A.J. Feeley
2 Amani Toomer
3 Brian Griese
4 Charles Woodson
5 Corey Dillon
6 Cory Schlesinger
7 Darren Woodson
8 David Boston
9 Derrick Mason
10 Duce Staley
11 Eric Moulds
12 Fred Taylor
13 Jake Plummer
14 Jerome Bettis
15 Donald Driver
16 Josh Reed
17 Kerry Collins
18 Kevin Johnson
19 Kordell Stewart
20 Koren Robinson
21 Muhsin Muhammed
22 Peerless Price
23 Peter Warrick
24 Randy McMichael
25 Rod Gardner
26 Ron Dayne
27 Santana Moss
28 Terry Glenn

2003 Playoff Absolute Leather and Laces

NM/M
Common Player: 8.00
1-20 Production 500 Sets
21-40 Production 250 Sets
1 Drew Brees 10.00
2 Jeremy Shockey 15.00
3 Antonio Bryant 10.00
4 Marc Bulger 10.00
5 Shaun Alexander 10.00
6 Koren Robinson 10.00
7 Jerry Porter 10.00
8 Joey Harrington 15.00
9 Kevan Barlow 8.00
10 Kurt Warner 12.00
11 Deuce McAllister 12.00
12 Eddie George 10.00
13 Donovan McNabb 15.00
14 Hines Ward 10.00
15 Michael Bennett 10.00
16 Steve McNair 12.00
17 Randy Moss 15.00
18 Mike Alstott 10.00
19 Curtis Martin 10.00
20 Ray Lewis 10.00
21 LaDainian Tomlinson 15.00
22 Marcel Shipp 12.00
23 Emmitt Smith 25.00
24 Marshall Faulk 12.00
25 Rich Gannon 20.00
26 Jerry Rice 25.00
27 Jeff Garcia 12.00
28 Priest Holmes 15.00
29 Michael Vick 40.00
30 Ahman Green 12.00
31 Brett Favre 40.00
32 Peyton Manning 20.00
33 Marvin Harrison 12.00
34 Travis Henry 10.00
35 Peerless Price 10.00
36 Rod Gardner 10.00
37 Terrell Owens 15.00
38 Charlie Garner 10.00
39 Daunte Culpepper 12.00
40 Anthony Thomas 10.00

2003 Playoff Absolute Pro Bowl Souvenirs

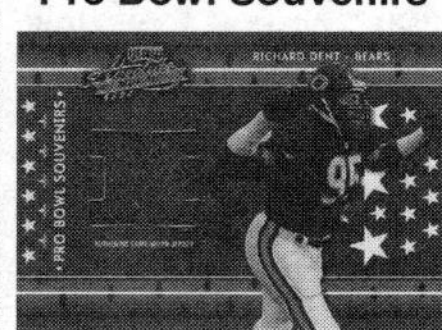

NM/M
Common Player: 10.00
Golds Not Priced Due to Scarcity
Gold Production 25 Sets
1 Eddie George/400 15.00
2 Edgerrin James/300 15.00
3 Tim Brown/600 15.00
4 Tom Brady/600 15.00
5 Jeff Garcia/600 10.00
6 Daunte Culpepper/300 15.00
7 Drew Bledsoe/600 20.00
8 Peyton Manning/250 25.00
9 Mark Brunell/400 10.00
10 Kevin Hardy/600 10.00
11 Jimmy Smith/250 12.00
12 Harvey Martin/500 12.00
13 John Elway/250 60.00
14 Terry Bradshaw/250 30.00
15 Richard Dent/600 12.00

2003 Playoff Absolute Pro Bowl Gold Auto

13 John Elway/15
14 Terry Bradshaw/15
15 Richard Dent/15

2003 Playoff Absolute Quad Series

NM/M
Complete Set (30): 140.00
Common Card: 4.00
Inserted 1:9
1 Drew Bledsoe, Travis Henry, Josh Reed, Eric Moulds 6.00
2 Tim Couch, William Green, Andre Davis, Quincy Morgan 5.00
3 Jake Plummer, Clinton Portis, Rod Smith, Ashley Lelie 6.00
4 David Carr, Jonathan Wells, Jabar Gaffney, Corey Bradford 6.00
5 Peyton Manning, Edgerrin James, James Mungro, Marvin Harrison 6.00
6 Mark Brunell, David Garrard, Fred Taylor, Jimmy Smith 4.00
7 Jay Fiedler, Ricky Williams, Chris Chambers, Zach Thomas 6.00
8 Tom Brady, Antowain Smith, Troy Brown, Deion Branch 4.00
9 Chad Pennington, Curtis Martin, LaMont Jordan, Santana Moss 5.00
10 Rich Gannon, Charlie Garner, Jerry Rice, Tim Brown 6.00
11 Tommy Maddox, Antwann Randle El, Plaxico Burress, Hines Ward 4.00
12 Drew Brees, LaDainian Tomlinson, Quentin Jammer, David Boston 5.00
13 Steve McNair, Eddie George, Derrick Mason, Jevon Kearse 4.00
14 Michael Vick, Warrick Dunn, T.J. Duckett, Peerless Price 8.00
15 Kordell Stewart, Anthony Thomas, David Terrell, Brian Urlacher 5.00
16 Chad Hutchinson, Terry Glenn, Antonio Bryant, Roy Williams 4.00
17 Joey Harrington, James Stewart, Az-Zahir Hakim, Bill Schroeder 5.00
18 Brett Favre, Ahman Green, Donald Driver, Javon Walker 8.00
19 Daunte Culpepper, Michael Bennett, Randy Moss, Byron Chamberlain 5.00
20 Aaron Brooks, Deuce McAllister, Donte Stallworth, Joe Horn 5.00
21 Kerry Collins, Tiki Barber, Amani Toomer, Michael Strahan 4.00
22 Donovan McNabb, A.J. Feeley, Duce Staley, James Thrash 5.00
23 Jeff Garcia, Garrison Hearst, Kevan Barlow, Terrell Owens 4.00
24 Matt Hasselbeck, Shaun Alexander, Koren Robinson, Darrell Jackson 4.00
25 Kurt Warner, Marshall Faulk, Isaac Bruce, Torry Holt 6.00
26 Brad Johnson, Mike Alstott, Keyshawn Johnson, Warren Sapp 5.00
27 Patrick Ramsey, Laveranues Coles, Rod Gardner, Champ Bailey 5.00
28 Carson Palmer, Byron Leftwich, Rex Grossman, Chris Simms 15.00
29 Larry Johnson, Lee Suggs, Chris Brown, Musa Smith 10.00
30 Andre Johnson, Taylor Jacobs, Charles Rogers, Kelley Washington 10.00

A player's name in *italic* type indicates a rookie card.

2003 Playoff Contenders

NM/M
Common Player (1-100): .20
Minor Stars: .40
Unlisted Stars: .60
Common Rookie (101-200): 8.00
Minor Rookie: 10.00
Unlisted Rookie: 12.00
Rookie Production Listed Below
Pack (5): 7.00
Box (24): 125.00
1 Roy Williams .60
2 Antonio Bryant .40
3 Jeremy Shockey 1.00
4 Kerry Collins .40
5 Tiki Barber .40
6 Michael Strahan .40
7 Donovan McNabb 1.00
8 Duce Staley .40
9 Todd Pinkston .40
10 Patrick Ramsey .60
11 Laveranues Coles .40
12 Rod Gardner .40
13 Drew Bledsoe .75
14 Travis Henry .40
15 Eric Moulds .40
16 Josh Reed .40
17 Ricky Williams 1.00
18 Jay Fiedler .40
19 Chris Chambers .60
20 Zach Thomas .40
21 Junior Seau .40
22 Tom Brady 1.00
23 Troy Brown .40
24 Chad Pennington .75
25 Curtis Martin .40
26 Santana Moss .40
27 Emmitt Smith 1.50
28 Jeff Garcia .40
29 Terrell Owens .60
30 Kevan Barlow .40
31 Shaun Alexander .60
32 Matt Hasselbeck .40
33 Koren Robinson .40
34 Kurt Warner .60
35 Marshall Faulk .75
36 Torry Holt .40
37 Isaac Bruce .40
38 Clinton Portis 1.50
39 Jake Plummer .40
40 Rod Smith .40
41 Ed McCaffrey .40
42 Ashley Lelie .40
43 Priest Holmes .60
44 Trent Green .40
45 Tony Gonzalez .40
46 Jerry Rice 1.50
47 Rich Gannon .40
48 Tim Brown .40
49 Jerry Porter .40
50 Charles Woodson .40
51 LaDainian Tomlinson .75
52 Drew Brees .60
53 David Boston .60
54 Brian Urlacher 1.00
55 Kordell Stewart .40
56 Marty Booker .40
57 Joey Harrington 1.00
58 Brett Favre 2.00
59 Ahman Green .60
60 Donald Driver .40
61 Javon Walker .40
62 Randy Moss 1.00
63 Daunte Culpepper .60
64 Michael Bennett .60
65 Jamal Lewis .60
66 Ray Lewis .40
67 Corey Dillon .60
68 Chad Johnson .40
69 William Green .60
70 Tim Couch .60
71 Quincy Morgan .40
72 Plaxico Burress .60
73 Tommy Maddox .40
74 Hines Ward .40
75 Antwann Randle El .40
76 Michael Vick 2.00
77 Peerless Price .40
78 Warrick Dunn .40
79 T.J. Duckett .60
80 Julius Peppers .40
81 Stephen Davis .40
82 Deuce McAllister .60
83 Aaron Brooks .60
84 Joe Horn .40
85 Donte Stallworth .40
86 Mike Alstott .40
87 Brad Johnson .40
88 Keyshawn Johnson .40
89 Warren Sapp .40
90 David Carr 1.25
91 Jabar Gaffney .40
92 Peyton Manning 1.00
93 Edgerrin James .75

94 Marvin Harrison .60
95 Mark Brunell .40
96 Fred Taylor .60
97 Jimmy Smith .40
98 Steve McNair .60
99 Eddie George .60
100 Jevon Kearse .40

2003 Playoff Contenders Playoff Ticket

NM/M
Stars: 4X-8X
Production 150 Sets
Common Rookie (101-200): 12.00
Minor Stars: 15.00
Unlisted Stars: 20.00
Production 30 Sets
101 Lee Suggs 40.00
102 Charles Rogers 50.00
103 Brandon Lloyd 25.00
104 Terrence Edwards 20.00
105 Mike Pinkard 12.00
106 Dewayne White 12.00
107 Jerome McDougle 12.00
108 Jimmy Kennedy 12.00
109 William Joseph 12.00
110 E.J. Henderson 12.00
111 Mike Doss 15.00
112 Chris Simms 40.00
113 Cecil Sapp 20.00
114 Justin Gage 30.00
115 Sam Aiken 20.00
116 Doug Gabriel 20.00
117 Jason Witten 25.00
118 Bennie Joppru 20.00
119 Chris Kelsay 12.00
120 Johnathan Sullivan 12.00
121 Kevin Williams 12.00
122 Rien Long 12.00
123 Kenny Peterson 12.00
124 Boss Bailey 25.00
125 Dennis Weathersby 12.00
126 Carson Palmer 80.00
127 Byron Leftwich 100.00
128 Kyle Boller 40.00
129 Rex Grossman 60.00
130 Dave Ragone 25.00
131 Brian St. Pierre 25.00
132 Kliff Kingsbury 25.00
133 Seneca Wallace 25.00
134 Larry Johnson 40.00
135 Willis McGahee 50.00
136 Justin Fargas 30.00
137 Onterrio Smith 40.00
138 Chris Brown 25.00
139 Musa Smith 20.00
140 Artose Pinner 20.00
141 Andre Johnson 60.00
142 Kelley Washington 25.00
143 Taylor Jacobs 20.00
144 Bryant Johnson 25.00
145 Tyrone Calico 30.00
146 Anquan Boldin 60.00
147 Bethel Johnson 30.00
148 Nate Burleson 25.00
149 Kevin Curtis 20.00
150 Dallas Clark 20.00
151 Teyo Johnson 20.00
152 Terrell Suggs 30.00
153 Dewayne Robertson 12.00
154 Terence Newman 30.00
155 Marcus Trufant 15.00
156 Tony Romo 20.00
157 Brooks Bollinger 25.00
158 Ken Dorsey 30.00
159 Kirk Farmer 20.00
160 Jason Gesser 25.00
161 Brock Forsey 30.00
162 Quentin Griffin 40.00
163 Avon Cobourne 25.00
164 Domanick Davis 40.00
165 Tony Hollings 25.00
166 LaBrandon Toefield 25.00
167 Arlen Harris 30.00
168 Sultan McCullough 20.00
169 Visanthe Shiancoe 12.00
170 L.J. Smith 15.00
171 LaTarence Dunbar 15.00
172 Walter Young 20.00
173 Bobby Wade 20.00
174 Zuriel Smith 15.00
175 Adrian Madise 15.00
176 Ken Hamlin 15.00
177 Carl Ford 20.00
178 Cortez Hankton 15.00
179 J.R. Tolver 20.00
180 Keenan Howry 20.00
181 Billy McMullen 15.00
182 Arnaz Battle 15.00
183 Shaun McDonald 15.00
184 Andre Woolfolk 15.00
185 Sammy Davis 15.00
186 Calvin Pace 15.00
187 Michael Haynes 15.00
188 Ty Warren 15.00
189 Nick Barnett 25.00
190 Troy Polamalu 25.00
191 Eric Parker 15.00
192 Justin Griffith 15.00
193 David Tyree 15.00
194 Pisa Tinoisamoa 25.00
195 Rashean Mathis 12.00
196 Mike Sherman 20.00
197 Dave Wannstedt 20.00
198 Dick Vermeil 20.00
199 Tony Dungy 25.00
200 Mike Martz 20.00

2003 Playoff Contenders Auto - Rookies

NM/M
101 Lee Suggs Auto/499 80.00
102 Charles Rogers Auto/204 150.00
103 Brandon Lloyd Auto Auto/589 50.00
104 Terrence Edwards Auto/399 20.00
105 Mike Pinkard Auto/849 8.00
106 Dewayne White Auto/524 8.00
107 Jerome McDougle Auto/339 12.00
108 Jimmy Kennedy Auto/514 12.00
109 William Joseph Auto/764 10.00
110 E.J. Henderson Auto/774 25.00
111 Mike Doss Auto/574 15.00
112 Chris Simms Auto/389 60.00
113 Cecil Sapp Auto/474 20.00
114 Justin Gage Auto/579 30.00
115 Sam Aiken Auto/664 10.00
116 Doug Gabriel Auto/389 20.00
117 Jason Witten Auto/599 30.00
118 Bennie Joppru Auto/449 15.00
119 Chris Kelsay Auto/864 8.00
120 Johnathan Sullivan Auto/924 12.00
121 Kevin Williams Auto/764 12.00
122 Rien Long Auto/849 8.00
123 Kenny Peterson Auto/674 20.00
124 Boss Bailey Auto/564 25.00
125 Dennis Weathersby Auto/774 8.00
126 Carson Palmer Auto/194 250.00
127 Byron Leftwich Auto/169 350.00
128 Kyle Boller Auto/439 80.00
129 Rex Grossman Auto/494 100.00
130 Dave Ragone Auto/344 30.00
131 Brian St. Pierre Auto/554 30.00
132 Kliff Kingsbury Auto/879 20.00
133 Seneca Wallace Auto/864 15.00
134 Larry Johnson Auto/344 50.00
135 Willis McGahee Auto/369 100.00
136 Justin Fargas Auto/354 60.00
137 Onterrio Smith Auto/414 60.00
138 Chris Brown Auto/279 80.00
139 Musa Smith Auto/379 20.00
140 Artose Pinner Auto/364 40.00
141 Andre Johnson Auto/199 175.00
142 Kelley Washington Auto/472 30.00
143 Taylor Jacobs Auto/349 25.00
144 Bryant Johnson Auto/389 25.00
145 Tyrone Calico Auto/499 40.00
146 Anquan Boldin Auto/524 100.00
147 Bethel Johnson Auto/484 40.00
148 Nate Burleson Auto/549 30.00
149 Kevin Curtis Auto/455 12.00
150 Dallas Clark Auto/539 30.00
151 Teyo Johnson Auto/389 25.00
152 Terrell Suggs Auto/564 25.00
153 Dewayne Robertson Auto/689 20.00
154 Terence Newman Auto/364 60.00
155 Marcus Trufant Auto/739 15.00
156 Tony Romo Auto/999 15.00
157 Brooks Bollinger Auto/974 15.00
158 Ken Dorsey Auto/774 40.00
159 Kirk Farmer Auto/999 8.00
160 Jason Gesser Auto/999 12.00
161 Brock Forsey Auto/999 20.00
162 Quentin Griffin Auto/999 60.00
163 Avon Cobourne Auto/974 12.00
164 Domanick Davis Auto/999 60.00
165 Tony Hollings Auto/974 15.00
166 LaBrandon Toefield Auto/799 25.00
167 Arlen Harris Auto/974 20.00
168 Sultan McCullough Auto/989 12.00
169 Visanthe Shiancoe Auto/999 8.00
170 L.J. Smith Auto/974 12.00
171 LaTarence Dunbar Auto/999 10.00
172 Walter Young Auto/889 10.00
173 Bobby Wade Auto/989 15.00
174 Zuriel Smith Auto/989 12.00
175 Adrian Madise Auto/999 10.00
176 Ken Hamlin Auto/989 12.00
177 Carl Ford Auto/999 15.00
178 Cortez Hankton Auto/989 8.00
179 J.R. Tolver Auto/889 10.00
180 Keenan Howry Auto/999 12.00
181 Billy McMullen Auto/899 10.00
182 Arnaz Battle Auto/989 15.00
183 Shaun McDonald Auto/899 10.00
184 Andre Woolfolk Auto/989 12.00
185 Sammy Davis Auto/999 8.00
186 Calvin Pace Auto/999 8.00
187 Michael Haynes Auto/999 12.00
188 Ty Warren Auto/999 20.00
189 Nick Barnett Auto/999 30.00
190 Troy Polamalu Auto/989 15.00
191 Eric Parker Auto/589 12.00
192 Justin Griffith Auto/589 10.00
193 David Tyree Auto/599 20.00
194 Pisa Tinoisamoa Auto/599 25.00
195 Rashean Mathis Auto/589 8.00
196 Mike Sherman Auto/574 25.00
197 Dave Wannstedt Auto/574 20.00
198 Dick Vermeil Auto/574 30.00
199 Tony Dungy Auto/574 30.00
200 Mike Martz Auto/574 15.00

2003 Playoff Contenders Legendary Contenders

NM/M
Common Player: 3.00
Inserted 1:24
Auto Production 25 Sets
LC-1 Barry Sanders 8.00
LC-2 Franco Harris 4.00
LC-3 Jim Brown 6.00
LC-4 Jim Kelly 5.00
LC-5 Joe Greene 3.00
LC-6 Larry Csonka 4.00
LC-7 Reggie White 3.00
LC-8 Roger Staubach 5.00
LC-9 Steve Largent 3.00
LC-10 Cris Carter 3.00

2003 Playoff Contenders MVP Contenders

NM/M
Common Player: 2.00
Inserted 1:24
Auto Production 25 Sets
MVP-1 Brett Favre 8.00
MVP-2 Brian Urlacher 4.00
MVP-3 Chad Pennington 3.00
MVP-4 Clinton Portis 5.00
MVP-5 Drew Bledsoe 3.00
MVP-6 Jeff Garcia 2.00
MVP-7 Jerry Rice 6.00
MVP-8 Joey Harrington 4.00
MVP-9 Kurt Warner 2.00
MVP-10 LaDainian Tomlinson 3.00
MVP-11 Marvin Harrison 2.00
MVP-12 Michael Vick 8.00
MVP-13 Randy Moss 5.00
MVP-14 Ricky Williams 4.00
MVP-15 Tom Brady 5.00

2003 Playoff Contenders Rookie Round-Up

NM/M
Common Player: 2.00
Production 375 Sets
RR-1 Anquan Boldin 6.00
RR-2 Bryant Johnson 3.00
RR-3 Kyle Boller 5.00
RR-4 Musa Smith 3.00
RR-5 Terrell Suggs 3.00
RR-6 Sam Aiken 2.00
RR-7 Willis McGahee 6.00
RR-8 Walter Young 3.00
RR-9 Rex Grossman 6.00
RR-10 Carson Palmer 8.00
RR-11 Kelley Washington 4.00
RR-12 Ken Hamlin 3.00
RR-13 Terence Newman 4.00
RR-14 Adrian Madise 2.00
RR-15 Artose Pinner 3.00

NM/M
RR-16 Boss Bailey 3.00
RR-17 Charles Rogers 5.00
RR-18 Eugene Wilson 2.00
RR-19 Nick Barnett 4.00
RR-20 Andre Johnson 6.00
RR-21 Dave Ragone 3.00
RR-22 Domanick Davis 5.00
RR-23 Tony Hollings 3.00
RR-24 Dallas Clark 3.00
RR-25 Mike Doss 3.00
RR-26 Byron Leftwich 10.00
RR-27 LaBrandon Toefield 3.00
RR-28 Larry Johnson 5.00
RR-29 J.R. Tolver 3.00
RR-30 Nate Burleson 3.00
RR-31 Onterrio Smith 5.00
RR-32 Bethel Johnson 4.00
RR-33 Cortez Hankton 2.00
RR-34 B.J. Askew 3.00
RR-35 Dewayne Robertson 2.00
RR-36 Justin Fargas 4.00
RR-37 Teyo Johnson 3.00
RR-38 Billy McMullen 3.00
RR-39 Jerome McDougle 2.00
RR-40 Troy Polamalu 3.00
RR-41 Sammy Davis 2.00
RR-42 Arnaz Battle 3.00
RR-43 Brandon Lloyd 3.00
RR-44 Marcus Trufant 3.00
RR-45 Seneca Wallace 3.00
RR-46 Kevin Curtis 3.00
RR-47 Shaun McDonald 3.00
RR-48 Chris Simms 5.00
RR-49 Tyrone Calico 4.00
RR-50 Taylor Jacobs 3.00

2003 Playoff Contenders ROY Contenders

NM/M
Common Player: 2.00
Inserted 1:24
Auto Production 25 Sets
ROY-1 Carson Palmer 6.00
ROY-2 Byron Leftwich 8.00
ROY-3 Charles Rogers 4.00
ROY-4 Andre Johnson 5.00
ROY-5 Dewayne Robertson 2.00
ROY-6 Terence Newman 3.00
ROY-7 Terrell Suggs 3.00
ROY-8 Kyle Boller 4.00
ROY-9 Rex Grossman 5.00
ROY-10 Larry Johnson 4.00

2003 Playoff Contenders Round Numbers Autos

NM/M
Common Player: 30.00
1-10 Production 100 Sets
11-15 Production 50 Sets
Gold Production 30 Or Less Sets
RN-1 Carson Palmer, Byron Leftwich 150.00
RN-2 Charles Rogers, Bryant Johnson 50.00
RN-3 Kyle Boller, Rex Grossman 80.00
RN-4 Willis McGahee, Larry Johnson 60.00
RN-5 Taylor Jacobs, Anquan Boldin 50.00
RN-6 Bethel Johnson, Tyrone Calico 40.00
RN-7 Dave Ragone, Chris Simms 40.00
RN-8 Musa Smith, Chris Brown 30.00
RN-9 Justin Fargas, Kevin Curtis 30.00
RN-10 Kelley Washington, Nate Burleson 30.00
RN-11 Carson Palmer, Byron Leftwich, Charles Rogers, Andre Johnson 300.00
RN-12 Kyle Boller, Rex Grossman, Willis McGahee, Larry Johnson 200.00
RN-13 Taylor Jacobs, Anquan Boldin, Bethel Johnson, Tyrone Calico 100.00
RN-14 Dave Ragone, Chris Simms, Musa Smith, Chris Brown 80.00
RN-15 Justin Fargas, Kevin Curtis, Kelley Washington, Nate Burleson 80.00

2003 Playoff Hogg Heaven

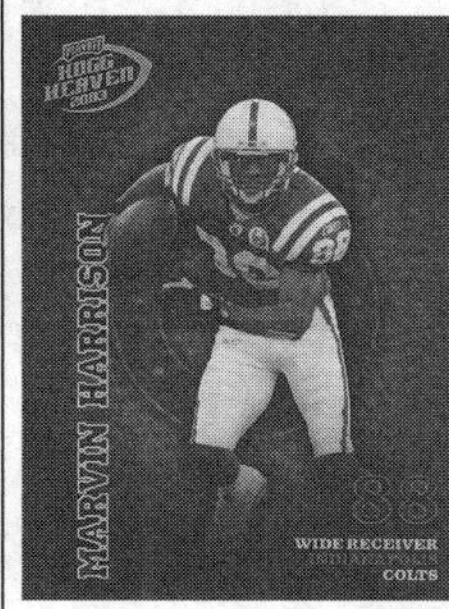

NM/M
Common Player (1-150): .30
Minor Stars: .60
Unlisted Stars: .75
Common Rookie (151-200): 2.00
Minor Rookies: 3.00
Unlisted Rookies: 4.00
Production 1000 Sets
Common Rookie Jsy (201-230): 6.00
Production 750 Sets
Pack (5): 4.25
Box (20): 60.00
1 Emmitt Smith 2.50
2 Marcel Shipp .60
3 Michael Vick 3.00
4 Warrick Dunn .60
5 T.J. Duckett .75
6 Peerless Price .60
7 Brian Finneran .30
8 Chris Redman .30
9 Jamal Lewis .75
10 Todd Heap .60
11 Travis Taylor .60
12 Ray Lewis .60
13 Peter Boulware .30
14 Ed Reed .30
15 Drew Bledsoe 1.00
16 Travis Henry .60
17 Eric Moulds .60
18 Josh Reed .60
19 Takeo Spikes .30
20 Julius Peppers .60
21 Stephen Davis .60
22 Muhsin Muhammad .30
23 Wesley Walls .30
24 Anthony Thomas .75
25 Brian Urlacher 1.50
26 Marty Booker .60
27 Mike Brown .30
28 Kordell Stewart .60
29 Dez White .60
30 Corey Dillon .75
31 Chad Johnson .60
32 Peter Warrick .60
33 Tim Couch .75
34 William Green .75
35 Andre Davis .60
36 Quincy Morgan .60
37 Kevin Johnson .60
38 Dennis Northcutt .30
39 Antonio Bryant .60
40 Terry Glenn .60
41 Joey Galloway .60
42 Roy Williams .75
43 Darren Woodson .30
44 Jake Plummer .60
45 Clinton Portis 2.50
46 Mike Anderson .60
47 Rod Smith .60
48 Ed McCaffrey .60
49 Ashley Lelie .75
50 Shannon Sharpe .60
51 Al Wilson .30
52 Joey Harrington 2.00
53 James Stewart .60
54 Brett Favre 3.00
55 Ahman Green .75
56 Darren Sharper .30
57 Donald Driver .60
58 Javon Walker .60
59 Robert Ferguson .60
60 David Carr 2.00
61 Jabar Gaffney .60
62 Stacey Mack .60
63 Marvin Harrison .75
64 Peyton Manning 2.50
65 Edgerrin James 1.00
66 Reggie Wayne .60
67 Fred Taylor .75
68 Mark Brunell .60
69 Jimmy Smith .60
70 Hugh Douglas .30
71 Priest Holmes .75
72 Trent Green .60
73 Tony Gonzalez .60
74 Marc Boerigter .30
75 Ricky Williams 1.50
76 Jay Fiedler .60
77 Chris Chambers .75
78 Zach Thomas .60
79 Jason Taylor .60
80 Junior Seau .60
81 Randy McMichael .30
82 Patrick Surtain .30
83 Randy Moss 1.50
84 Michael Bennett .75
85 Daunte Culpepper .75
86 Tom Brady 1.00
87 Troy Brown .60
88 Ty Law .30
89 Aaron Brooks .75
90 Deuce McAllister .75
91 Donte Stallworth .75
92 Joe Horn .60
93 Michael Strahan .60
94 Kerry Collins .60
95 Tiki Barber .60
96 Amani Toomer .60
97 Jeremy Shockey 1.50
98 Chad Pennington 1.00
99 Curtis Martin .75
100 Santana Moss .60
101 Rich Gannon .60
102 Jerry Rice 2.50
103 Tim Brown .60
104 Jerry Porter .60
105 Charlie Garner .60
106 Charles Woodson .60
107 Donovan McNabb 1.00
108 Duce Staley .60
109 James Thrash .60
110 Chad Lewis .30
111 Troy Vincent .30
112 Tommy Maddox .75
113 Plaxico Burress .75
114 Hines Ward .60
115 Antwann Randle El .60
116 Jerome Bettis .60
117 Kendrell Bell .60
118 LaDainian Tomlinson 1.00
119 Drew Brees 1.00
120 David Boston .75
121 Jeff Garcia .75
122 Terrell Owens .75
123 Tai Streets .60
124 Kevan Barlow .60
125 Matt Hasselbeck .60
126 Koren Robinson .60
127 Shaun Alexander .75
128 Kurt Warner 1.00
129 Marc Bulger .75
130 Marshall Faulk 1.00
131 Torry Holt .75
132 Isaac Bruce .60
133 Brad Johnson .60
134 Keyshawn Johnson .60
135 Warren Sapp .60
136 Derrick Brooks .60
137 John Lynch .30
138 Michael Pittman .60
139 Mike Alstott .60
140 Steve McNair .75
141 Eddie George .75
142 Jevon Kearse .60
143 Keith Bulluck .30
144 Derrick Mason .60
145 Patrick Ramsey .75
146 Ladell Betts .60
147 Laveranues Coles .60
148 Rod Gardner .60
149 Champ Bailey .60
150 Bruce Smith .60
151 *Ken Dorsey* 8.00
152 *Lee Suggs* 10.00
153 *Domanick Davis* 10.00
154 *Quentin Griffin* 10.00
155 *LaBrandon Toefield* 5.00
156 *B.J. Askew* 5.00
157 *Jason Witten* 8.00
158 *Bennie Joppru* 4.00
159 *L.J. Smith* 4.00
160 *Billy McMullen* 3.00
161 *Shaun McDonald* 3.00
162 *Brandon Lloyd* 8.00
163 *Sam Aiken* 3.00
164 *Bobby Wade* 4.00
165 *Justin Gage* 6.00
166 *Doug Gabriel* 3.00
167 *David Kircus* 3.00
168 *Arnaz Battle* 3.00
169 *Kareem Kelly* 3.00
170 *Talman Gardner* 3.00
171 *Ryan Hoag* 3.00
172 *LaTarence Dunbar* 3.00
173 *Johnathan Sullivan* 3.00
174 *Kevin Williams* 3.00
175 *Jimmy Kennedy* 4.00
176 *Ty Warren* 3.00
177 *William Joseph* 3.00
178 *Michael Haynes* 3.00
179 *Jerome McDougle* 3.00
180 *Calvin Pace* 2.00
181 *Tyler Brayton* 4.00
182 *Chris Kelsay* 3.00
183 *Dewayne White* 3.00
184 *E.J. Henderson* 3.00
185 *Charles Rogers* 12.00
186 *Terry Pierce* 3.00
187 *Nick Barnett* 5.00
188 *Boss Bailey* 5.00
189 *Pisa Tinoisamoa* 3.00
190 *Chaun Thompson* 2.00
191 *Andre Woolfolk* 3.00
192 *Sammy Davis* 3.00
193 *Eugene Wilson* 3.00
194 *Drayton Florence* 2.00
195 *Ricky Manning Jr.* 3.00
196 *Donald Strickland* 2.00
197 *Dennis Weathersby* 2.00
198 *Troy Polamalu* 6.00
199 *Ken Hamlin* 4.00
200 *Mike Doss* 4.00
201 *Carson Palmer* 20.00
202 *Byron Leftwich* 25.00
203 *Kyle Boller* 12.00
204 *Rex Grossman* 15.00
205 *Andre Johnson* 15.00
206 *Bryant Johnson* 8.00
207 *Larry Johnson* 10.00
208 *Taylor Jacobs* 6.00
209 *Bethel Johnson* 8.00
210 *Anquan Boldin* 12.00
211 *Tyrone Calico* 8.00
212 *Teyo Johnson* 8.00

213 *Kelley Washington* 8.00
214 *Musa Smith* 6.00
215 *Chris Brown* 12.00
216 *Justin Fargas* 8.00
217 *Artose Pinner* 6.00
218 *Onterrio Smith* 10.00
219 *Brian St. Pierre* 6.00
220 *Dave Ragone* 6.00
221 *Dallas Clark* 8.00
222 *Seneca Wallace* 6.00
223 *Terrell Suggs* 8.00
224 *Terence Newman* 10.00
225 *Dewayne Robertson* 5.00
226 *Marcus Trufant* 5.00
227 *Kliff Kingsbury* 6.00
228 *Kevin Curtis* 5.00
229 *Willis McGahee* 15.00
230 *Nate Burleson* 6.00

2003 Playoff Hogg Heaven Hogg Wild

Stars: 3X-6X
Production 150 Sets
Rookies 151-200: 1X-2X
Production 100 Sets

2003 Playoff Hogg Heaven Accent

Production 25 Sets
A1 Michael Vick
A2 Donovan McNabb
A3 Peyton Manning
A4 Brett Favre
A5 Rich Gannon
A6 Jeff Garcia
A7 LaDainian Tomlinson
A8 Marshall Faulk
A9 Emmitt Smith
A10 Edgerrin James
A11 Ricky Williams
A12 Deuce McAllister
A13 Priest Holmes
A14 Ahman Green
A15 Marvin Harrison
A16 Terrell Owens
A17 Randy Moss
A18 Jerry Rice
A19 Tim Brown
A20 Jeremy Shockey

2003 Playoff Hogg Heaven Branded

NM/M
Common Player: 2.00
Inserted 1:19
B1 Michael Vick 10.00
B2 Donovan McNabb 4.00
B3 Peyton Manning 5.00
B4 Brett Favre 10.00
B5 Drew Bledsoe 4.00
B6 Tom Brady 4.00
B7 LaDainian Tomlinson 4.00
B8 Edgerrin James 4.00
B9 Ricky Williams 5.00
B10 Deuce McAllister 3.00
B11 Ahman Green 3.00
B12 Marshall Faulk 4.00
B13 Priest Holmes 3.00
B14 Marvin Harrison 3.00
B15 Terrell Owens 3.00
B16 Randy Moss 5.00
B17 Jerry Rice 8.00
B18 David Boston 3.00
B19 Tony Gonzalez 3.00
B20 Jeremy Shockey 5.00
B21 Warren Sapp 2.00
B22 Brian Urlacher 5.00
B23 Zach Thomas 2.00
B24 Ray Lewis 2.00
B25 Charles Woodson 2.00

2003 Playoff Hogg Heaven Hogg of Fame

NM/M
Common Player: 2.00
Production 500 Sets
HF1 Dan Marino 10.00
HF2 John Riggins 3.00
HF3 Steve Young 5.00
HF4 Brett Favre 8.00
HF5 Jerry Rice 6.00
HF6 Emmitt Smith 8.00
HF7 Tim Brown 2.00
HF8 Cris Carter 2.00
HF9 Peyton Manning 5.00
HF10 Marvin Harrison 2.00
HF11 Edgerrin James 3.00
HF12 Randy Moss 5.00
HF13 Terrell Owens 2.00
HF14 Ricky Williams 3.00
HF15 Michael Vick 8.00
HF16 Donovan McNabb 4.00
HF17 Clinton Portis 5.00
HF18 Priest Holmes 4.00
HF19 Marshall Faulk 4.00
HF20 Brian Urlacher 4.00
HF21 Ray Lewis 2.00
HF22 Jeremy Shockey 3.00
HF23 LaDainian Tomlinson 2.00
HF24 Deuce McAllister 2.00
HF25 Kurt Warner 2.00
HF26 Tom Brady 4.00
HF27 Drew Bledsoe 3.00
HF28 Drew Brees 2.00

2003 Playoff Hogg Heaven Hoggs of Fame Materials Bronze

NM/M
Common Player: 10.00
Production 125 Sets
Silvers: 1.5X
Production 75 Sets
Gold Production 25 Sets
HF1 Dan Marino 60.00
HF2 John Riggins 25.00
HF3 Steve Young 15.00
HF4 Brett Favre 30.00
HF5 Jerry Rice 20.00
HF6 Emmitt Smith 30.00
HF7 Tim Brown 10.00
HF8 Cris Carter 10.00
HF9 Peyton Manning 20.00
HF10 Marvin Harrison 10.00
HF11 Edgerrin James 15.00
HF12 Randy Moss 15.00
HF13 Terrell Owens 10.00
HF14 Ricky Williams 15.00
HF15 Michael Vick 30.00
HF16 Donovan McNabb 15.00
HF17 Clinton Portis 15.00
HF18 Priest Holmes 15.00
HF19 Marshall Faulk 15.00
HF20 Brian Urlacher 15.00
HF21 Ray Lewis 10.00
HF22 Jeremy Shockey 12.00
HF23 LaDainian Tomlinson 10.00
HF24 Deuce McAllister 10.00
HF25 Kurt Warner 10.00
HF26 Tom Brady 12.00
HF27 Drew Bledsoe 12.00
HF28 Drew Brees 10.00

2003 Playoff Hogg Heaven Laces in Leather

LL1 Emmitt Smith
LL2 Donovan McNabb
LL3 Steve McNair
LL4 Drew Bledsoe
LL5 Kurt Warner
LL6 Aaron Brooks
LL7 Tom Brady
LL8 Marvin Harrison
LL9 Chad Pennington
LL10 Randy Moss
LL11 Carson Palmer
LL12 Byron Leftwich
LL13 Kyle Boller
LL14 Rex Grossman
LL15 Andre Johnson
LL16 Bryant Johnson
LL17 Larry Johnson
LL18 Taylor Jacobs
LL19 Bethel Johnson
LL20 Anquan Boldin
LL21 Tyrone Calico
LL22 Teyo Johnson
LL23 Kelley Washington
LL24 Musa Smith
LL25 Chris Brown
LL26 Justin Fargas
LL27 Artose Pinner
LL28 Onterrio Smith
LL29 Brian St. Pierre
LL30 Dave Ragone
LL31 Dallas Clark
LL32 Seneca Wallace
LL33 Terrell Suggs
LL34 Terence Newman
LL35 Dewayne Robertson
LL36 Marcus Trufant
LL37 Kliff Kingsbury
LL38 Kevin Curtis
LL39 Willis McGahee
LL40 Nate Burleson

2003 Playoff Hogg Heaven Leather in Leather

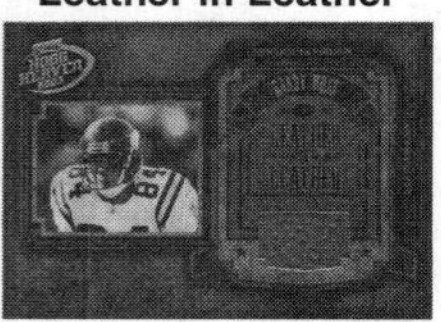

NM/M
Common Player: 5.00
Production 250 Sets
LL1 Emmitt Smith 20.00
LL2 Donovan McNabb 10.00
LL3 Steve McNair 8.00
LL4 Drew Bledsoe 10.00
LL5 Kurt Warner 10.00
LL6 Aaron Brooks 8.00
LL7 Tom Brady 10.00
LL8 Marvin Harrison 8.00
LL9 Chad Pennington 10.00
LL10 Randy Moss 12.00
LL11 Carson Palmer 20.00
LL12 Byron Leftwich 20.00
LL13 Kyle Boller 12.00
LL14 Rex Grossman 15.00
LL15 Andre Johnson 15.00
LL16 Bryant Johnson 8.00
LL17 Larry Johnson 12.00
LL18 Taylor Jacobs 6.00
LL19 Bethel Johnson 6.00
LL20 Anquan Boldin 12.00
LL21 Tyrone Calico 8.00
LL22 Teyo Johnson 8.00
LL23 Kelley Washington 8.00
LL24 Musa Smith 6.00
LL25 Chris Brown 6.00
LL26 Justin Fargas 8.00
LL27 Artose Pinner 6.00
LL28 Onterrio Smith 12.00
LL29 Brian St. Pierre 6.00
LL30 Dave Ragone 6.00
LL31 Dallas Clark 6.00
LL32 Seneca Wallace 6.00
LL33 Terrell Suggs 8.00
LL34 Terence Newman 10.00
LL35 Dewayne Robertson 5.00
LL36 Marcus Trufant 5.00
LL37 Kliff Kingsbury 6.00
LL38 Kevin Curtis 5.00
LL39 Willis McGahee 15.00
LL40 Nate Burleson 6.00

2003 Playoff Hogg Heaven Material Hoggs Bronze

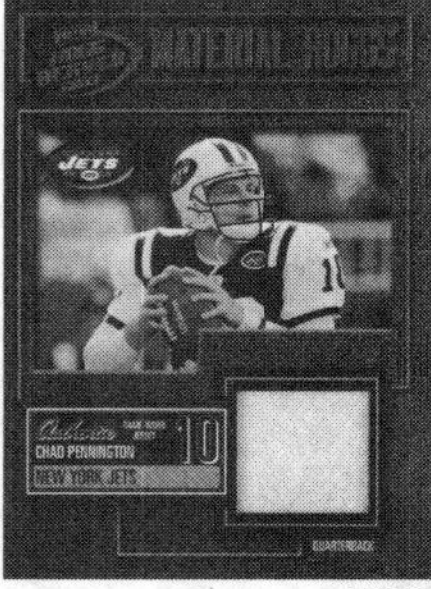

NM/M
Common Player: 5.00
Production 200 Sets
Silvers: 1.5X
Production 125 Sets
Gold Production 25 Sets
MH1 Emmitt Smith 20.00
MH2 Jerry Rice 15.00
MH3 Donovan McNabb 10.00
MH4 Peyton Manning 12.00
MH5 Brett Favre 20.00
MH6 Michael Vick 20.00
MH7 Aaron Brooks 8.00
MH8 Ahman Green 8.00
MH9 Antwann Randle El 6.00
MH10 Brian Urlacher 10.00
MH11 Chad Pennington 10.00
MH12 Chris Chambers 8.00
MH13 Clinton Portis 12.00
MH14 Corey Dillon 8.00
MH15 Curtis Martin 8.00
MH16 Daunte Culpepper 8.00
MH17 David Boston 8.00
MH18 David Carr 12.00
MH19 Deuce McAllister 8.00
MH20 Donald Driver 8.00
MH21 Donte Stallworth 8.00
MH22 Drew Bledsoe 10.00
MH23 Drew Brees 8.00
MH24 Ed McCaffrey 5.00
MH25 Eddie George 8.00
MH26 Edgerrin James 10.00
MH27 Eric Moulds 6.00
MH28 Fred Taylor 8.00
MH29 Garrison Hearst 6.00
MH30 Hines Ward 8.00
MH31 Isaac Bruce 8.00
MH32 Jake Plummer 6.00
MH33 Chris Redman 5.00
MH34 Jeff Garcia 6.00
MH35 Jeremy Shockey 10.00
MH36 Jerome Bettis 8.00
MH37 Jevon Kearse 6.00
MH38 Jimmy Smith 5.00
MH39 Joey Harrington 10.00
MH40 Julius Peppers 6.00
MH41 Kurt Warner 8.00
MH42 Laveranues Coles 6.00
MH43 Mark Brunell 6.00
MH44 Marshall Faulk 10.00
MH45 Marvin Harrison 8.00
MH46 Jamal Lewis 8.00
MH47 Plaxico Burress 8.00
MH48 Ricky Williams 10.00
MH49 Santana Moss 6.00
MH50 Terrell Davis 8.00

2003 Playoff Hogg Heaven Pig Pens

NM/M
Common Player: 10.00
PP1 Kurt Warner/200 25.00
PP2 Michael Vick/25
PP3 Dan Marino/50 150.00
PP4 John Riggins/100 40.00
PP5 Carson Palmer/50 100.00
PP6 Byron Leftwich/75 100.00
PP7 Kendrell Bell/25
PP8 Deuce McAllister/25
PP9 David Carr/25
PP10 Patrick Ramsey/25
PP11 Roy Williams/50 40.00
PP12 Joey Harrington/25
PP13 Anthony Thomas/50 20.00
PP14 Derrick Mason/70 20.00
PP15 Donald Driver/35 40.00
PP16 Marty Booker/30 30.00
PP17 Bethel Johnson/35 25.00
PP18 Antowain Smith/50 20.00
PP19 Garrison Hearst/75 10.00
PP20 Hines Ward/50 30.00
PP21 Jerome Bettis/50 25.00
PP22 Joe Horn/100 15.00
PP23 Deion Branch/75 15.00
PP24 Laveranues Coles/45 25.00
PP25 Marvin Harrison/45 40.00
PP26 Mike Alstott/50 40.00
PP27 Priest Holmes/25
PP28 Randy Moss/35
PP29 Rod Gardner/50 20.00
PP30 Sonny Jurgensen/141 20.00
PP31 Terrell Owens/25
PP32 Tommy Maddox/75 20.00
PP34 Charley Taylor/208 20.00
PP35 Jimmy Smith/75 15.00
PP36 E.J. Henderson/250 12.00
PP37 Musa Smith/250 15.00
PP38 Chris Brown/250 15.00
PP39 Dennis Weathersby/250 10.00
PP40 Kyle Boller/155 40.00
PP41 Marc Boerigter/250 15.00
PP42 Taylor Jacobs/200 15.00
PP43 Terrence Edwards/250 12.00
PP44 Dewayne White/250 10.00
PP45 Jerome McDougal/250 10.00
PP46 Kevin Curtis/250 10.00
PP47 Sam Aiken/250 10.00
PP48 Doug Gabriel/250 10.00
PP49 Chris Kelsay/250 15.00
PP50 Kevin Williams/250 12.00

2003 Playoff Hogg Heaven Rival Hoggs

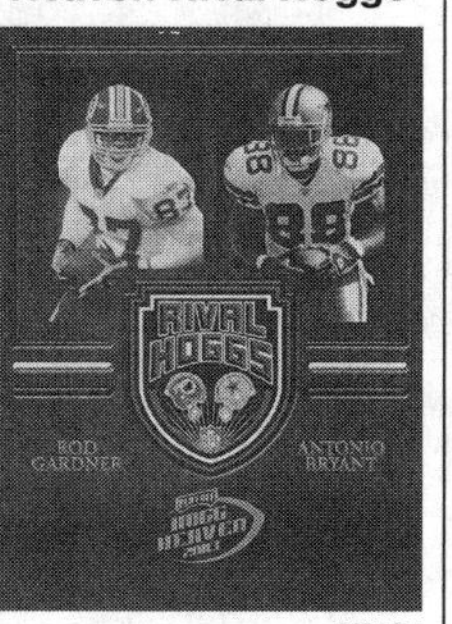

NM/M
Common Player: 2.00
Production 500 Sets
RH1 Brett Favre, Randy Moss 10.00
RH2 Joey Harrington, Brian Urlacher 6.00
RH3 Drew Bledsoe, Tom Brady 4.00
RH4 Ricky Williams, Deuce McAllister 3.00
RH5 Plaxico Burress, Ray Lewis 2.00
RH6 Michael Strahan, Warren Sapp 1.50
RH7 Emmitt Smith, Terrell Owens 8.00
RH8 LaDainian Tomlinson, Clinton Portis 4.00
RH9 Priest Holmes, Marshall Faulk 4.00
RH10 Peyton Manning, Steve McNair 4.00
RH11 William Green, Jerome Bettis 2.00
RH12 Travis Henry, Zach Thomas 2.00
RH13 Shaun Alexander, Ahman Green 3.00
RH14 Jevon Kearse, Julius Peppers 2.00
RH15 Michael Vick, Donovan McNabb 8.00
RH16 Antonio Bryant, Rod Gardner 2.00
RH17 Jamal Lewis, Kendrell Bell 3.00
RH18 Marvin Harrison, Jerry Rice 6.00
RH19 Jeremy Shockey, Tony Gonzalez 5.00
RH20 Kurt Warner, Jeff Garcia 3.00
RH21 Tim Brown, David Boston 2.00
RH22 Drew Brees, Rich Gannon 3.00
RH23 Daunte Culpepper, Kordell Stewart 3.00
RH24 Edgerrin James, Eddie George 4.00
RH25 David Carr, Mark Brunell 5.00
RH26 Walter Payton, Emmitt Smith 15.00
RH27 T.J. Duckett, Mike Alstott 2.00
RH28 Aaron Brooks, Brad Johnson 2.00
RH29 Hines Ward, Keyshawn Johnson 2.00
RH30 Michael Bennett, Anthony Thomas 3.00

2003 Playoff Hogg Heaven Rival Hoggs Materials

NM/M
Common Player: 12.00
Production 125 Sets
RH1 Brett Favre, Randy Moss 40.00
RH2 Joey Harrington, Brian Urlacher 20.00
RH3 Drew Bledsoe, Tom Brady 20.00
RH4 Ricky Williams, Deuce McAllister 15.00
RH5 Plaxico Burress, Ray Lewis 12.00
RH6 Michael Strahan, Warren Sapp 12.00
RH7 Emmitt Smith, Terrell Owens 40.00
RH8 LaDainian Tomlinson, Clinton Portis 20.00
RH9 Priest Holmes, Marshall Faulk 20.00
RH10 Peyton Manning, Steve McNair 20.00
RH11 William Green, Jerome Bettis 12.00
RH12 Travis Henry, Zach Thomas 12.00
RH13 Shaun Alexander, Ahman Green 15.00
RH14 Jevon Kearse, Julius Peppers 12.00
RH15 Michael Vick, Donovan McNabb 30.00
RH16 Antonio Bryant, Rod Gardner 12.00
RH17 Jamal Lewis, Kendrell Bell 12.00
RH18 Marvin Harrison, Jerry Rice 25.00
RH19 Jeremy Shockey, Tony Gonzalez 15.00
RH20 Kurt Warner, Jeff Garcia 12.00
RH21 Tim Brown, David Boston 12.00
RH22 Drew Brees, Rich Gannon 12.00
RH23 Daunte Culpepper, Kordell Stewart 12.00
RH24 Edgerrin James, Eddie George 15.00
RH25 David Carr, Mark Brunell 15.00
RH26 Walter Payton, Emmitt Smith 100.00
RH27 T.J. Duckett, Mike Alstott 12.00
RH28 Aaron Brooks, Brad Johnson 12.00
RH29 Hines Ward, Keyshawn Johnson 12.00
RH30 Michael Bennett, Anthony Thomas 12.00

2003 Playoff Hogg Heaven Rookie Hoggs

NM/M
Common Player: 3.00
Inserted 1:19
RCH1 Carson Palmer 12.00
RCH2 Byron Leftwich 12.00
RCH3 Kyle Boller 8.00
RCH4 Chris Simms 6.00
RCH5 Rex Grossman 10.00
RCH6 Willis McGahee 10.00
RCH7 Larry Johnson 8.00
RCH8 Lee Suggs 4.00
RCH9 Musa Smith 4.00
RCH10 Chris Brown 4.00
RCH11 Charles Rogers 10.00
RCH12 Andre Johnson 8.00
RCH13 Taylor Jacobs 3.00
RCH14 Kelley Washington 4.00
RCH15 Bryant Johnson 4.00
RCH16 Brandon Lloyd 3.00
RCH17 Tyrone Calico 4.00
RCH18 Jason Witten 4.00
RCH19 Dallas Clark 4.00
RCH20 Terrell Suggs 4.00
RCH21 Dewayne Robertson 3.00
RCH22 Jimmy Kennedy 3.00
RCH23 Boss Bailey 4.00
RCH24 Terence Newman 6.00
RCH25 Marcus Trufant 3.00

2003 Playoff Hogg Heaven National Previews

NM/M
Common Player: 1.00
1 Brett Favre 3.00
2 Jeff Garcia 1.00
3 Clinton Portis 2.00
4 Jeremy Shockey 1.00
5 Michael Vick 2.50
6 Ricky Williams 1.00

2003 Playoff Honors

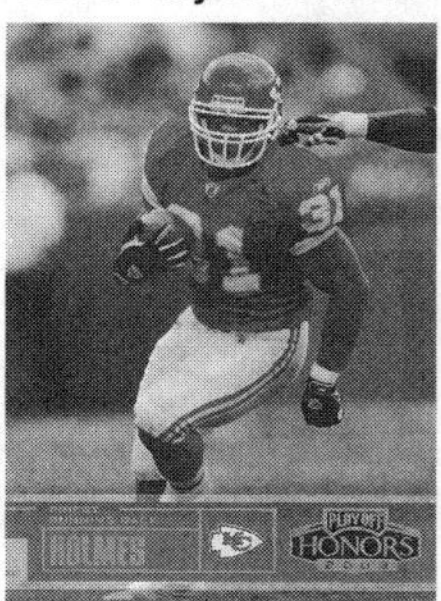

NM/M
Common Player (1-100): .30
Minor Stars: .60
Unlisted Stars: .75
Rookies (101-150): 2.00
Minor Rookies: 3.00
Unlisted Rookies: 4.00
101-150 Hobby Only
Rookies (151-200):
151-200 Retail Only
Rookies (201-230): 5.00
Production 700 Sets
Pack (6): 4.00
Box (20): 60.00
1 Aaron Brooks .75
2 Ahman Green .75
3 Amani Toomer .60
4 Anthony Thomas .75
5 Antonio Bryant .60
6 Antwann Randle El .60
7 Ashley Lelie .75
8 Brad Johnson .60
9 Brett Favre 3.00
10 Brian Urlacher 1.00
11 Bruce Smith .60
12 Chad Johnson .60
13 Chad Pennington 1.00
14 Charlie Garner .60
15 Chris Chambers .60
16 Clinton Portis 2.50
17 Corey Dillon .75
18 Curtis Martin .75
19 Daunte Culpepper .75
20 David Boston .75
21 David Carr 2.00
22 Deuce McAllister .75
23 Donald Driver .60
24 Donovan McNabb 1.00
25 Donte Stallworth .60
26 Drew Bledsoe 1.00
27 Drew Brees 1.00
28 Duce Staley .60
29 Ed McCaffrey .60
30 Eddie George .75
31 Edgerrin James 1.00
32 Emmitt Smith 2.50
33 Eric Moulds .60
34 Fred Taylor .75
35 Garrison Hearst .60
36 Hines Ward .60
37 Isaac Bruce .60
38 Jabar Gaffney .30
39 Jake Plummer .60
40 Jamal Lewis .75
41 Jay Fiedler .60
42 Jeff Garcia .75
43 Jeremy Shockey 1.50
44 Jerome Bettis .60
45 Jerry Porter .60
46 Jerry Rice 2.50
47 Jevon Kearse .60
48 Jimmy Smith .60
49 Joe Horn .60
50 Joey Harrington 2.00
51 Josh Reed .60
52 Julius Peppers .60
53 Kendrell Bell .60
54 Kerry Collins .60
55 Keyshawn Johnson .60
56 Kordell Stewart .60
57 Koren Robinson .60
58 Kurt Warner 1.00
59 LaDainian Tomlinson 1.00
60 Laveranues Coles .60
61 Mark Brunell .60
62 Marshall Faulk 1.00
63 Marvin Harrison .75
64 Matt Hasselbeck .60
65 Michael Bennett .75
66 Michael Strahan .30
67 Michael Vick 3.00
68 Mike Alstott .60
69 Patrick Ramsey .75
70 Peerless Price .60
71 Peyton Manning 1.50
72 Plaxico Burress .60
73 Priest Holmes .75
74 Randy Moss 1.50
75 Ray Lewis .60

76 Rich Gannon .60
77 Ricky Williams 1.50
78 Rod Gardner .60
79 Rod Smith .60
80 Roy Williams .60
81 Shaun Alexander .75
82 Stephen Davis .60
83 Steve McNair .75
84 T.J. Duckett .75
85 Terrell Owens .75
86 Tiki Barber .60
87 Tim Brown .60
88 Tim Couch .60
89 Todd Heap .60
90 Tom Brady 1.00
91 Tommy Maddox .60
92 Tony Gonzalez .60
93 Torry Holt .60
94 Travis Henry .60
95 Trent Green .60
96 Troy Brown .60
97 Warren Sapp .60
98 Warrick Dunn .60
99 William Green .75
100 Zach Thomas .30
101 *Chris Simms* 8.00
102 *Brooks Bollinger* 3.00
103 *Gibran Hamdan* 3.00
104 *Ken Dorsey* 5.00
105 *Jason Gesser* 3.00
106 *Brad Banks* 4.00
107 *Tony Romo* 4.00
108 *B.J. Askew* 4.00
109 *Domanick Davis* 8.00
110 *Lee Suggs* 8.00
111 *LaBrandon Toefield* 4.00
112 *Brock Forsey* 5.00
113 *Malaefou MacKenzie* 2.00
114 *Andrew Pinnock* 3.00
115 *Ahmaad Galloway* 3.00
116 *Tony Hollings* 4.00
117 *Charles Rogers* 8.00
118 *Billy McMullen* 3.00
119 *Shaun McDonald* 3.00
120 *Brandon Lloyd* 6.00
121 *Sam Aiken* 3.00
122 *Bobby Wade* 4.00
123 *Justin Gage* 6.00
124 *Adrian Madise* 3.00
125 *Jon Olinger* 2.00
126 *Doug Gabriel* 3.00
127 *J.R. Tolver* 3.00
128 *David Kircus* 3.00
129 *Zuriel Smith* 3.00
130 *LaTarence Dunbar* 3.00
131 *Arnaz Battle* 3.00
132 *Willie Ponder* 2.00
133 *Kareem Kelly* 3.00
134 *David Tyree* 3.00
135 *Keenan Howry* 4.00
136 *Taco Wallace* 3.00
137 *Walter Young* 3.00
138 *Talman Gardner* 3.00
139 *DeAndrew Rubin* 3.00
140 *Kevin Walter* 3.00
141 *Carl Ford* 4.00
142 *Travis Anglin* 3.00
143 *Ryan Hoag* 3.00
144 *Terrence Edwards* 3.00
145 *Bennie Joppru* 3.00
146 *L.J. Smith* 4.00
147 *Jason Witten* 6.00
148 *Andre Woolfolk* 3.00
149 *Nnamdi Asomugha* 3.00
150 *Troy Polamalu* 4.00
151 *Nate Hybl*
152 *Curt Anes*
153 *Avon Cobourne*
154 *Cecil Sapp*
155 *Casey Urlacher*
156 *Dwone Hicks*
157 *Jeremi Johnson*
158 *Kirk Farmer*
159 *James MacPherson*
160 *Chris Davis*
161 *Brandon Drumm*
162 *J.T. Wall*
163 *Casey Moore*
164 *Mike Seidman*
165 *Visanthe Shiancoe*
166 *George Wrighster*
167 *Dan Curley*
168 *Donald Lee*
169 *Aaron Walker*
170 *Trent Smith*
171 *Spencer Nead*
172 *Richard Angulo*
173 *Mike Pinkard*
174 *Johnathan Sullivan*
175 *Kevin Williams*
176 *Jimmy Kennedy*
177 *Ty Warren*
178 *William Joseph*
179 *Michael Haynes*
180 *Jerome McDougle*
181 *Calvin Pace*
182 *Tyler Brayton*
183 *Chris Kelsay*
184 *Osi Umenyiora*
185 *Alonzo Jackson*
186 *Dewayne White*
187 *Kenny Peterson*
188 *Nick Barnett*
189 *Boss Bailey*
190 *E.J. Henderson*
191 *Pisa Tinoisamoa*
192 *Sammy Davis*
193 *Charles Tillman*
194 *Eugene Wilson*
195 *Drayton Florence*
196 *Ricky Manning Jr.*
197 *Rashean Mathis*
198 *Ken Hamlin*
199 *Mike Doss*
200 *Julian Battle*

2003 Playoff Honors X's

Stars: 2X-4X
Production 250 Sets
Rookies (101-150): 1.5X-3X
Production 100 Sets
Rookies (201-230) Production 25 Sets

2003 Playoff Honors Rookie Autographs

NM/M
Common Player: 40.00
First 50 Cards Autographed
201 Andre Johnson Jsy 15 125.00
202 Anquan Boldin Jsy 12 100.00
203 Artose Pinner Jsy 5 40.00
204 Bethel Johnson Jsy 8 50.00
205 Brian St. Pierre Jsy 6 40.00
206 Bryant Johnson Jsy 8 60.00
207 Byron Leftwich Jsy 20 200.00
208 Carson Palmer Jsy 15 150.00
209 Chris Brown Jsy 8 50.00
210 Dallas Clark Jsy 6 50.00
211 Dave Ragone Jsy 5 40.00
212 Dewayne Robertson Jsy 5 40.00
213 Justin Fargas Jsy 10 60.00
214 Kelley Washington Jsy 8 50.00
215 Kevin Curtis Jsy 5 40.00
216 Kliff Kingsbury Jsy 5 40.00
217 Kyle Boller Jsy 12 80.00
218 Larry Johnson Jsy 10 80.00
219 Marcus Trufant Jsy 5 40.00
220 Musa Smith Jsy 6 40.00
221 Nate Burleson Jsy 6 40.00
222 Onterrio Smith Jsy 10 60.00
223 Rex Grossman Jsy 15 125.00
224 Seneca Wallace Jsy 6 40.00
225 Taylor Jacobs Jsy 5 40.00
226 Terrell Suggs Jsy 5 50.00
227 Terence Newman Jsy 8 60.00
228 Teyo Johnson Jsy 6 40.00
229 Tyrone Calico Jsy 8 50.00
230 Willis McGahee Jsy 15 100.00

2003 Playoff Honors Prime Signatures

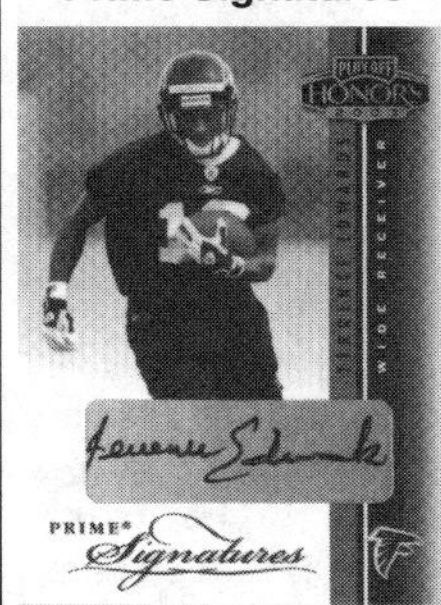

NM/M
Common Player: 10.00
Prime Cuts Versions Numbered to 5
Card #6 Does Not Exist
PS-1 Kurt Warner/300 20.00
PS-2 Eric Moulds/81 15.00
PS-3 Marc Boerigter/95 15.00
PS-4 Tim Brown/88 30.00
PS-5 Ahman Green/75 50.00
PS-7 Jimmy Smith/95 12.00
PS-8 Michael Vick/70 100.00
PS-9 Charlie Garner/75 20.00
PS-10 Corey Dillon/95 20.00
PS-11 Jamal Lewis/50 50.00
PS-12 Jerry Rice/40 120.00
PS-13 Randy Moss/1
PS-14 Shaun Alexander/70 25.00
PS-15 Steve McNair/59 50.00
PS-16 Tommy Maddox/70 25.00
PS-17 Chris Chambers/60 15.00
PS-18 Tom Jackson/55 20.00
PS-19 David Carr/50 50.00
PS-20 Deuce McAllister/50 25.00
PS-21 Jeff Garcia/50 25.00
PS-22 Torry Holt/50 25.00
PS-23 Zach Thomas/95 25.00
PS-24 Anthony Thomas/70 20.00
PS-25 Eddie George/45 30.00
PS-26 Marty Booker/45 20.00
PS-28 Peerless Price/70 15.00
PS-29 Ricky Williams/25
PS-30 Brett Favre/21
PS-31 Drew Bledsoe/20
PS-32 Hines Ward/3
PS-33 Jerome Bettis/45 25.00
PS-34 Joe Horn/3
PS-35 Kendrell Bell/20
PS-36 LaDainian Tomlinson/20
PS-37 Laveranues Coles/45 20.00
PS-38 Dan Marino/32 250.00
PS-39 Mike Alstott/45 25.00
PS-40 Rod Gardner/45 15.00
PS-41 Carson Palmer/20
PS-42 Byron Leftwich/20
PS-43 Kliff Kingsbury/300 15.00
PS-44 Seneca Wallace/300 15.00
PS-45 Anquan Boldin/300 50.00
PS-46 Bethel Johnson/300 25.00
PS-47 Nate Burleson/300 12.00
PS-48 Onterrio Smith/300 25.00
PS-49 Bryant Johnson/290 20.00
PS-50 Terrence Edwards/300 12.00
PS-51 Teyo Johnson/300 12.00
PS-52 Dewayne White/300 10.00
PS-53 Jerome McDougle/300 10.00
PS-54 Terrell Suggs/300 15.00
PS-55 Terence Newman/300 30.00
PS-56 Brian St. Pierre/300 15.00
PS-57 Artose Pinner/250 12.00
PS-58 Cecil Sapp/300 10.00
PS-59 Doug Gabriel/300 10.00
PS-60 Kenny Peterson/300 10.00

2003 Playoff Honors Alma Mater Materials

NM/M
Common Player: 6.00
AM-1 Fred Taylor/400 10.00
AM-2 Jevon Kearse/150 10.00
AM-3 Michael Pittman/400 6.00
AM-4 Ahman Green/250 20.00
AM-5 Eddie George/150 15.00
AM-6 Shaun Alexander/200 15.00
AM-7 Terrell Davis/150 12.00
AM-8 Frank Wycheck/400 6.00
AM-9 Laveranues Coles/250 10.00
AM-10 Edgerrin James/300 15.00
AM-11 Reggie Wayne/400 8.00
AM-12 Dan Morgan/400 6.00
AM-13 Santana Moss/300 10.00
AM-14 Jeremy Shockey/150 15.00
AM-15 Clinton Portis/50 30.00
AM-16 Tony Dorsett/25
AM-17 Earl Campbell/125 20.00
AM-18 Ricky Williams/150 20.00
AM-19 Drew Bledsoe/150 15.00
AM-20 Doug Flutie/250 12.00
AM-21 Curtis Martin/200 10.00
AM-22 Anquan Boldin/350 20.00
AM-23 Keyshawn Johnson/200 8.00
AM-24 Tyrone Calico/400 10.00
AM-25 Kyle Boller/200 12.00
AM-26 Fred Taylor, Jevon Kearse/100 15.00
AM-27 Ahman Green, Eddie George/100 20.00
AM-28 Shaun Alexander, Terrell Davis/100 15.00
AM-29 Edgerrin James, Clinton Portis/100 30.00
AM-30 Santana Moss, Jeremy Shockey/100 25.00
AM-31 Laveranues Coles, Reggie Wayne/100 20.00
AM-32 Earl Campbell, Ricky Williams/100 40.00
AM-33 Drew Bledsoe, Doug Flutie/100 20.00
AM-34 Curtis Martin, Anquan Boldin/100 20.00
AM-35 Keyshawn Johnson, Tyrone Calico/25 12.00
AM-36 Fred Taylor, Shaun Alexander, Terrell Davis/25
AM-37 Ahman Green, Earl Campbell, Ricky Williams/25
AM-38 Edgerrin James, Clinton Portis, Jeremy Shockey/25
AM-39 Drew Bledsoe, Doug Flutie, Kyle Boller/25
AM-40 Tony Dorsett, Curtis Martin, Eddie George/25
AM-16AU Tony Dorsett Auto 100.00
AM-17AU Earl Campbell Auto 80.00

2003 Playoff Honors Class Reunion Tandems

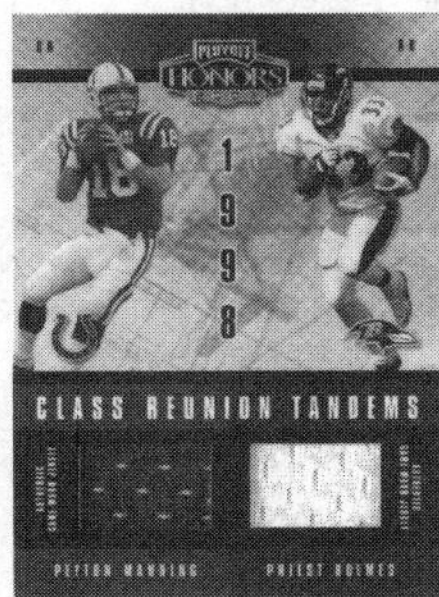

NM/M
Common Player: 6.00
Production 150 Sets
CRT-1 Emmitt Smith, Junior Seau 30.00
CRT-2 Brett Favre, Ed McCaffrey 30.00
CRT-3 Rod Smith, Jimmy Smith 6.00
CRT-4 Drew Bledsoe, Jerome Bettis 15.00
CRT-5 Marshall Faulk, Isaac Bruce 15.00
CRT-6 Terrell Davis, Curtis Martin 12.00
CRT-7 Steve McNair, Warren Sapp 10.00
CRT-8 Keyshawn Johnson, Eric Moulds 8.00
CRT-9 Terrell Owens, Marvin Harrison 12.00
CRT-10 Ray Lewis, Zach Thomas 10.00
CRT-11 Tony Gonzalez, Tiki Barber 10.00
CRT-12 Peyton Manning, Priest Holmes 25.00
CRT-13 Randy Moss, Hines Ward 20.00
CRT-14 Ahman Green, Fred Taylor 12.00
CRT-15 Edgerrin James, Ricky Williams 20.00
CRT-16 Donovan McNabb, Daunte Culpepper 6.00
CRT-17 Torry Holt, David Boston 10.00
CRT-18 Tim Brown, Sterling Sharpe 12.00
CRT-19 Aaron Brooks, Donald Driver 8.00
CRT-20 Laveranues Coles, Chad Pennington 20.00
CRT-21 Jamal Lewis, Shaun Alexander 15.00
CRT-22 Plaxico Burress, Brian Urlacher 15.00
CRT-23 Michael Vick, Drew Brees 20.00
CRT-24 LaDainian Tomlinson, Deuce McAllister 12.00
CRT-25 Koren Robinson, Rod Gardner 8.00
CRT-26 Michael Bennett, Travis Henry 8.00
CRT-27 Chris Chambers, Kendrell Bell 10.00
CRT-28 David Carr, Joey Harrington 15.00
CRT-29 Jeremy Shockey, Clinton Portis 15.00
CRT-30 Donte Stallworth, Antwann Randle El 8.00

2003 Playoff Honors Football Quads

NM/M
Common Player: 15.00
Production 50 Sets
FQ-1 Carson Palmer, Kelley Washington, Byron Leftwich, Dallas Clark 30.00
FQ-2 Larry Johnson, Artose Pinner, Nate Burleson, Onterrio Smith 20.00
FQ-3 Andre Johnson, Dave Ragone, Chris Brown, Tyrone Calico 20.00
FQ-4 Brian St. Pierre, Seneca Wallace, Rex Grossman, Taylor Jacobs 15.00
FQ-5 Bryant Johnson, Anquan Boldin, Willis McGahee, Kevin Curtis 20.00
FQ-6 Justin Fargas, Teyo Johnson, Kyle Boller, Musa Smith 15.00
FQ-7 Kliff Kingsbury, Bethel Johnson, Terrell Suggs, Terence Newman 15.00

2003 Playoff Honors Football Tandems

NM/M
Common Player: 6.00
Production 100 Sets
FT-1 Carson Palmer, Kelley Washington 15.00
FT-2 Byron Leftwich, Dallas Clark 15.00
FT-3 Larry Johnson, Artose Pinner 10.00
FT-4 Nate Burleson, Onterrio Smith 10.00
FT-5 Andre Johnson, Dave Ragone 12.00
FT-6 Chris Brown, Tyrone Calico 10.00
FT-7 Brian St. Pierre, Seneca Wallace 6.00
FT-8 Rex Grossman, Taylor Jacobs 12.00
FT-9 Bryant Johnson, Anquan Boldin 12.00
FT-10 Willis McGahee, Kevin Curtis 12.00
FT-11 Justin Fargas, Teyo Johnson 10.00
FT-12 Kyle Boller, Musa Smith 10.00
FT-13 Kliff Kingsbury, Bethel Johnson 6.00
FT-14 Dewayne Robertson, Terrell Suggs 6.00
FT-15 Terence Newman, Marcus Trufant 6.00

2003 Playoff Honors Game Day Souvenirs - Bronze

NM/M
Common Player: 8.00
Production 150 Sets
Silver Cards:
Production 75 Sets
Gold Cards: 1.5X-3X
Gold Production 25 Sets
GDS-1 Emmitt Smith 30.00
GDS-2 Donovan McNabb 15.00
GDS-3 Steve McNair 12.00
GDS-4 Curtis Martin 10.00
GDS-5 Edgerrin James 15.00
GDS-6 Rich Gannon 8.00
GDS-7 Kurt Warner 8.00
GDS-8 Aaron Brooks 10.00
GDS-9 LaDainian Tomlinson 12.00
GDS-10 Peyton Manning 20.00
GDS-11 David Boston 8.00
GDS-12 Michael Vick 30.00

2003 Playoff Honors Jersey Tandems

NM/M
Common Player: 6.00
JT-1 Carson Palmer, Kelley Washington 15.00
JT-2 Byron Leftwich, Dallas Clark 15.00
JT-3 Larry Johnson, Artose Pinner 10.00
JT-4 Nate Burleson, Onterrio Smith 10.00
JT-5 Andre Johnson, Dave Ragone 12.00
JT-6 Chris Brown, Tyrone Calico 6.00
JT-7 Brian St. Pierre, Seneca Wallace 12.00
JT-8 Rex Grossman, Taylor Jacobs 12.00
JT-9 Bryant Johnson, Anquan Boldin 12.00
JT-10 Willis McGahee, Kevin Curtis 10.00
JT-11 Justin Fargas, Teyo Johnson 10.00
JT-12 Kyle Boller, Musa Smith 6.00
JT-13 Kliff Kingsbury, Bethel Johnson 6.00
JT-14 Dewayne Robertson, Terrell Suggs 6.00
JT-15 Terence Newman, Marcus Trufant 6.00

2003 Playoff Honors Jersey Quads

NM/M
Common Player: 12.00
Production 250 Sets
JQ-1 Carson Palmer, Kelley Washington, Byron Leftwich, Dallas Clark 30.00
JQ-2 Larry Johnson, Artose Pinner, Nate Burleson, Onterrio Smith 15.00
JQ-3 Andre Johnson, Dave Ragone, Chris Brown, Tyrone Calico 15.00
JQ-4 Brian St. Pierre, Seneca Wallace, Rex Grossman, Taylor Jacobs 12.00
JQ-5 Bryant Johnson, Anquan Boldin, Willis McGahee, Kevin Curtis 15.00
JQ-6 Justin Fargas, Teyo Johnson, Kyle Boller, Musa Smith 15.00
JQ-7 Kliff Kingsbury, Bethel Johnson, Terrell Suggs, Terence Newman 12.00

2003 Playoff Honors Jersey/Football Tandems

NM/M
Common Player: 8.00
Production 75 Sets
JFT-1 Carson Palmer, Kelley Washington 20.00
JFT-2 Byron Leftwich, Dallas Clark 20.00
JFT-3 Larry Johnson, Artose Pinner 12.00
JFT-4 Nate Burleson, Onterrio Smith 12.00
JFT-5 Andre Johnson, Dave Ragone 15.00
JFT-6 Chris Brown, Tyrone Calico 12.00
JFT-7 Brian St. Pierre, Seneca Wallace 8.00
JFT-8 Rex Grossman, Taylor Jacobs 15.00
JFT-9 Bryant Johnson, Anquan Boldin 15.00
JFT-10 Willis McGahee, Kevin Curtis 15.00
JFT-11 Justin Fargas, Teyo Johnson 12.00
JFT-12 Kyle Boller, Musa Smith 12.00
JFT-13 Kliff Kingsbury, Bethel Johnson 8.00
JFT-14 Dewayne Robertson, Terrell Suggs 8.00
JFT-15 Terence Newman, Marcus Trufant 8.00

2003 Playoff Honors Jersey/Football Quads

JFQ-1 Carson Palmer, Kelley Washington, Byron Leftwich, Dallas Clark
JFQ-2 Larry Johnson, Artose Pinner, Nate Burleson, Onterrio Smith
JFQ-3 Andre Johnson, Dave Ragone, Chris Brown, Tyrone Calico
JFQ-4 Brian St. Pierre, Seneca Wallace, Rex Grossman, Taylor Jacobs
JFQ-5 Bryant Johnson, Anquan Boldin, Willis McGahee, Kevin Curtis
JFQ-6 Justin Fargas, Teyo Johnson, Kyle Boller, Musa Smith
JFQ-7 Kliff Kingsbury, Bethel Johnson, Terrell Suggs, Terence Newman

2003 Playoff Honors Patches

NM/M
Common Player: 12.00
Production 75 Sets
PP-1 Michael Vick 40.00
PP-2 Brett Favre 50.00
PP-3 Peyton Manning 30.00
PP-4 Donovan McNabb 25.00
PP-5 Daunte Culpepper 15.00
PP-6 Jeff Garcia 12.00
PP-7 David Carr 20.00
PP-8 Joey Harrington 15.00
PP-9 Kurt Warner 12.00
PP-10 Drew Brees 12.00
PP-11 Drew Bledsoe 15.00
PP-12 Tom Brady 30.00
PP-13 LaDainian Tomlinson 15.00
PP-14 Deuce McAllister 15.00
PP-15 Ricky Williams 20.00
PP-16 Marshall Faulk 15.00
PP-17 Edgerrin James 15.00
PP-18 Travis Henry 12.00
PP-19 Michael Bennett 12.00
PP-20 Emmitt Smith 40.00
PP-21 Priest Holmes 20.00
PP-22 Clinton Portis 20.00
PP-23 William Green 12.00
PP-24 T.J. Duckett 12.00
PP-25 Randy Moss 20.00
PP-26 Jerry Rice 30.00
PP-27 Terrell Owens 15.00
PP-28 David Boston 12.00
PP-29 Marvin Harrison 15.00
PP-30 Tim Brown 12.00
PP-31 Donte Stallworth 12.00
PP-32 Ashley Lelie 12.00
PP-33 Antwann Randle El 12.00
PP-34 Tony Gonzalez 12.00
PP-35 Jeremy Shockey 15.00
PP-36 Brian Urlacher 15.00
PP-37 Kendrell Bell 15.00
PP-38 Zach Thomas 15.00
PP-39 Warren Sapp 12.00
PP-40 Julius Peppers 12.00

2003 Playoff Honors Plates

PP-1 Michael Vick/23
PP-2 Brett Favre/29
PP-3 Peyton Manning/26
PP-4 Donovan McNabb/44
PP-5 Daunte Culpepper/41
PP-6 Jeff Garcia/35
PP-7 David Carr/32
PP-8 Joey Harrington/65
PP-9 Kurt Warner/55

PP-10 Drew Brees/30
PP-11 Drew Bledsoe/38
PP-12 Tom Brady/29
PP-13 LaDainian Tomlinson/36
PP-14 Deuce McAllister/38
PP-15 Ricky Williams/11
PP-16 Marshall Faulk/9
PP-17 Edgerrin James/1
PP-18 Travis Henry/48
PP-19 Michael Bennett/30
PP-20 Emmitt Smith/20
PP-21 Priest Holmes/14
PP-22 Clinton Portis/14
PP-23 William Green/29
PP-24 T.J. Duckett/10
PP-25 Randy Moss/22
PP-26 Jerry Rice/16
PP-27 Terrell Owens/31
PP-28 David Boston/31
PP-29 Marvin Harrison/40
PP-30 Tim Brown/25
PP-31 Donte Stallworth/57
PP-32 Ashley Lelie/16
PP-33 Antwann Randle El/52
PP-34 Tony Gonzalez/52
PP-35 Jeremy Shockey/42
PP-36 Brian Urlacher/49
PP-37 Kendrell Bell/12
PP-38 Zach Thomas/46
PP-39 Warren Sapp/10
PP-40 Julius Peppers/46

2003 Playoff Honors Plates & Patches

PP-1 Michael Vick/7
PP-2 Brett Favre/4
PP-3 Peyton Manning/18
PP-4 Donovan McNabb/5
PP-5 Daunte Culpepper/11
PP-6 Jeff Garcia/5
PP-7 David Carr/8
PP-8 Joey Harrington/3
PP-9 Kurt Warner/13
PP-10 Drew Brees/9
PP-11 Drew Bledsoe/11
PP-12 Tom Brady/12
PP-13 LaDainian Tomlinson/21
PP-14 Deuce McAllister/26
PP-15 Ricky Williams/34
PP-16 Marshall Faulk/28
PP-17 Edgerrin James/32
PP-18 Travis Henry/20
PP-19 Michael Bennett/23
PP-20 Emmitt Smith/22
PP-21 Priest Holmes/31
PP-22 Clinton Portis/26
PP-23 William Green/31
PP-24 T.J. Duckett/45
PP-25 Randy Moss/12
PP-26 Jerry Rice/8
PP-27 Terrell Owens/9
PP-28 David Boston/17
PP-29 Marvin Harrison/16
PP-30 Tim Brown/9
PP-31 Donte Stallworth/11
PP-32 Ashley Lelie/13
PP-33 Antwann Randle El/10
PP-34 Tony Gonzalez/16
PP-35 Jeremy Shockey/8
PP-36 Brian Urlacher/9
PP-37 Kendrell Bell/16
PP-38 Zach Thomas/9
PP-39 Warren Sapp/18
PP-40 Julius Peppers/9

2003 Playoff Honors Rookie Year Jerseys

NM/M
Common Player: 8.00
Production 100 Sets
RYJ-1 Curtis Martin 12.00
RYJ-2 Isaac Bruce 12.00
RYJ-3 Keyshawn Johnson 8.00
RYJ-4 Mark Brunell 8.00
RYJ-5 Peyton Manning 20.00
RYJ-6 Randy Moss 15.00
RYJ-7 Ricky Williams 15.00
RYJ-8 Tim Couch 10.00
RYJ-9 LaDainian Tomlinson 12.00
RYJ-10 Chris Chambers 8.00
RYJ-11 Koren Robinson 8.00
RYJ-12 Michael Vick 25.00
RYJ-13 Anthony Thomas 10.00
RYJ-14 David Terrell 8.00
RYJ-15 Joey Harrington 12.00
RYJ-16 Clinton Portis 15.00
RYJ-17 Jeremy Shockey 12.00
RYJ-18 David Carr 15.00
RYJ-19 Antwann Randle El 10.00
RYJ-20 Donte Stallworth 8.00

2003 Playoff Prestige

NM/M
Common Player: .20
Unlisted Star: .40
Minor Star: .60
Unlisted Rookie Star: 2.00
Minor Rookie Star: 1.00
Rookies Inserted 1:2
Pack (6): 3.00
Wax Box (24): 55.00
1 David Boston .60
2 Thomas Jones .20
3 Jake Plummer .20
4 Marcel Shipp .20
5 T.J. Duckett .60

NM/M
6 Warrick Dunn .40
7 Michael Vick 2.00
8 Jeff Blake .40
9 Todd Heap .40
10 Jamal Lewis .60
11 Ray Lewis .40
12 Drew Bledsoe 1.25
13 Travis Henry .60
14 Eric Moulds .40
15 Peerless Price .40
16 Josh Reed .60
17 DeShaun Foster .40
18 Muhsin Muhammad .40
19 Steve Smith .20
20 Julius Peppers .40
21 Marty Booker .40
22 David Terrell .40
23 Anthony Thomas .60
24 Brian Urlacher 1.50
25 Corey Dillon .60
26 Chad Johnson .20
27 Jon Kitna .20
28 Peter Warrick .20
29 Tim Couch 1.00
30 Andre Davis .40
31 William Green .60
32 Quincy Morgan .40
33 Dennis Northcutt .20
34 Antonio Bryant .60
35 Quincy Carter .60
36 Troy Hambrick .20
37 Chad Hutchinson .60
38 Emmitt Smith 2.00
39 Roy Williams .60
40 Brian Griese .60
41 Ashley Lelie 1.00
42 Ed McCaffrey .40
43 Clinton Portis 2.00
44 Rod Smith .60
45 Germane Crowell .20
46 Az-Zahir Hakim .40
47 Joey Harrington 1.50
48 James Stewart .40
49 Donald Driver .20
50 Brett Favre 2.50
51 Terry Glenn .40
52 Ahman Green .60
53 Javon Walker .60
54 Corey Bradford .40
55 David Carr 1.50
56 Jabar Gaffney .40
57 Jonathan Wells .60
58 Marvin Harrison .60
59 Edgerrin James 1.50
60 Peyton Manning 2.00
61 James Mungro .20
62 Reggie Wayne .40
63 Mark Brunell .60
64 David Garrard .40
65 Stacey Mack .20
66 Jimmy Smith .60
67 Fred Taylor .60
68 Marc Boerigter .20
69 Tony Gonzalez .60
70 Trent Green .40
71 Priest Holmes 1.00
72 Eddie Kennison .20
73 Cris Carter .40
74 Chris Chambers .60
75 Jay Fiedler .40
76 Randy McMichael .20
77 Zach Thomas .40
78 Ricky Williams 1.25
79 Michael Bennett .60
80 Todd Bouman .20
81 Daunte Culpepper 1.25
82 Randy Moss 2.00
83 Tom Brady 2.00
84 Deion Branch .40
85 Troy Brown .50
86 Kevin Faulk .40
87 Antowain Smith .40
88 Aaron Brooks 1.00
89 Joe Horn .40
90 Deuce McAllister 1.00
91 Donte Stallworth 1.00
92 Tiki Barber .40
93 Kerry Collins .40
94 Jeremy Shockey 1.50
95 Michael Strahan .40
96 Amani Toomer .40
97 Laveranues Coles .40
98 LaMont Jordan .20
99 Curtis Martin .60
100 Santana Moss .20
101 Chad Pennington 1.00
102 Tim Brown .60
103 Rich Gannon .60
104 Charlie Garner .40
105 Jerry Rice 2.00
106 Charles Woodson .40
107 Antonio Freeman .20
108 Dorsey Levens .20
109 Donovan McNabb 1.25
110 Duce Staley .40
111 James Thrash .20
112 Jerome Bettis .20
113 Plaxico Burress .60
114 Tommy Maddox .60
115 Antwann Randle El 1.25
116 Kordell Stewart .60
117 Hines Ward .60
118 Drew Brees 1.50
119 Curtis Conway .40
120 Junior Seau .40
121 LaDainian Tomlinson 1.50
122 Kevan Barlow .20
123 Jeff Garcia .60
124 Garrison Hearst .40
125 Terrell Owens .60
126 Shaun Alexander .60
127 Trent Dilfer .40
128 Darrell Jackson .20
129 Maurice Morris .40
130 Koren Robinson .40
131 Isaac Bruce .60
132 Marc Bulger .60
133 Marshall Faulk 1.25
134 Torry Holt .60
135 Kurt Warner 1.50
136 Mike Alstott .40
137 Brad Johnson .40
138 Keyshawn Johnson .40
139 Dexter Jackson .20
140 Warren Sapp .40
141 Kevin Dyson .40
142 Eddie George .60
143 Jevon Kearse .40
144 Derrick Mason .40
145 Steve McNair .60
146 Stephen Davis .60
147 Rod Gardner .40
148 Shane Matthews .20
149 Patrick Ramsey .60
150 Derrius Thompson .20
151 *Byron Leftwich* 12.00
152 *Carson Palmer* 10.00
153 *Chris Simms* 6.00
154 *Kliff Kingsbury* 2.00
155 *Dave Ragone* 3.00
156 *Jason Gesser* 2.00
157 *Ken Dorsey* 4.00
158 *Kyle Boller* 7.00
159 *Brad Banks* 3.00
160 *Rex Grossman* 8.00
161 *Seneca Wallace* 3.00
162 *Brian St. Pierre* 2.00
163 *Larry Johnson* 4.00
164 *Earnest Graham* 2.00
165 *Musa Smith* 2.00
166 *Lee Suggs* 8.00
167 *Willis McGahee* 8.00
168 *Onterrio Smith* 5.00
169 No Card .20
170 *Sultan McCullough* 1.00
171 *Chris Brown* 5.00
172 *Justin Fargas* 2.00
173 *Avon Cobourne* 1.00
174 *Dahrran Diedrick* 2.00
175 *LaBrandon Toefield* 1.00
176 *Artose Pinner* 2.00
177 *Quentin Griffin* 4.00
178 *Reshard Lee* 1.00
179 *Andrew Pinnock* 2.00
180 *B.J. Askew* 1.00
181 *Andre Johnson* 8.00
182 *Brandon Lloyd* 2.00
183 *Bryant Johnson* 2.00
184 *Charles Rogers* 6.00
185 *Doug Gabriel* 2.00
186 *Justin Gage* 3.00
187 *Kareem Kelly* 2.00
188 *Kelley Washington* 2.00
189 *Taylor Jacobs* 3.00
190 *Terrence Edwards* 2.00
191 *Anquan Boldin* 8.00
192 *Billy McMullen* 2.00
193 *Talman Gardner* 2.00
194 *Arnaz Battle* 2.00
195 *Sam Aiken* 2.00
196 *Bobby Wade* 1.00
197 *Mike Bush* 1.00
198 *Keenan Howry* 1.00
199 *Jerel Meyers* 1.00
200 *Dallas Clark* 4.00
201 *Mike Pinkard* 1.00
202 *Teyo Johnson* 1.00
203 *Trent Smith* 1.00
204 *George Wrighster* 1.00
205 *Jason Witten* 4.00
206 *Corey Redding* 2.00
207 *Dewayne White* 1.00
208 *Jerome McDougal* 1.00
209 *Michael Haynes* 2.00
210 *Chris Kelsay* 2.00
211 *Calvin Pace* 1.00
212 *Kenny King* 1.00
213 *Jimmy Kennedy* 2.00
214 *William Joseph* 2.00
215 *Dewayne Robertson* 2.00
216 *Jarret Johnson* 1.00
217 *Rien Long* 1.00
218 *Boss Bailey* 3.00
219 *Terrell Suggs* 4.00
220 *Terry Pierce* 2.00
221 *Bradie James* 1.00
222 *Angelo Crowell* 1.00
223 *Andre Woolfolk* 1.00
224 *Dennis Weathersby* 1.00
225 *Marcus Trufant* 2.00
226 *Terence Newman* 4.00
227 *Ricky Manning* 1.00
228 *Mike Doss* 2.00
229 *Julian Battle* 1.00
230 *Rashean Mathis* 2.00

2003 Playoff Prestige Backfield Tandems

NM/M
Common Player: 10.00
Production 400 sets
1 Jake Plummer, Marcel Shipp 10.00
2 Drew Bledsoe, Travis Henry 25.00
3 Tim Couch, William Green 12.00
4 Brian Griese, Clinton Portis 15.00
5 Brett Favre, Ahman Green 35.00
6 David Carr, Jonathan Wells
7 Peyton Manning, Edgerrin James 25.00
8 Mark Brunell, Fred Taylor 10.00
9 Trent Green, Priest Holmes 15.00
10 Jay Fiedler, Ricky Williams 15.00
11 Daunte Culpepper, Michael Bennett 18.00
12 Tom Brady, Antowain Smith 15.00
13 Aaron Brooks, Deuce McAllister 20.00
14 Chad Pennington, Curtis Martin 25.00
15 Donovan McNabb, Duce Staley 12.00
16 Tommy Maddox, Jerome Bettis
17 Drew Brees, LaDainian Tomlinson 10.00
18 Jeff Garcia, Garrison Hearst 15.00
19 Kurt Warner, Marshall Faulk 25.00
20 Steve McNair, Eddie George 12.00

2003 Playoff Prestige Draft Picks

NM/M
Common Player: 1.00
Production 2003 sets
1 Byron Leftwich 6.00
2 Carson Palmer 6.00
3 Dave Ragone 2.00
4 Larry Johnson 2.50
5 Musa Smith 1.50
6 Lee Suggs 2.50
7 Onterrio Smith 1.00
8 Chris Brown 1.00
9 Andre Johnson 4.00
10 Brandon Lloyd 1.00
11 Bryant Johnson 2.50
12 Charles Rogers 4.00
13 Kelley Washington 1.50
14 Taylor Jacobs 2.00
15 Terrence Edwards 1.00
16 Mike Pinkard 1.00
17 Teyo Johnson 1.50
18 Dewayne White 1.00
19 Jerome McDougal 1.50
20 Jimmy Kennedy 1.50
21 William Joseph 1.50
23 Terrell Suggs 2.50
24 Terence Newman 2.50
25 Mike Doss 1.00

2003 Playoff Prestige Draft Picks Rights

NM/M
Common Player: 15.00
Production 50 sets
1 Byron Leftwich 110.00
2 Carson Palmer 110.00
4 Larry Johnson 75.00
5 Musa Smith 40.00
6 John Sullivan 15.00
7 Onterrio Smith 40.00
8 Chris Brown 20.00
9 Andre Johnson 50.00
10 Brandon Lloyd 15.00
12 Charles Rogers 75.00
13 Kelley Washington 25.00
14 Taylor Jacobs 25.00
15 Terrence Edwards 15.00
17 Teyo Johnson 20.00
18 Dewayne White 25.00
19 Jerome McDougal 30.00
20 Jimmy Kennedy 35.00
23 Terrell Suggs 45.00
24 Terence Newman 65.00
25 Mike Doss 40.00

2003 Playoff Prestige Game Day Jerseys - Hobby

NM/M
Common Player: 8.00
Inserted 1:34
1 Aaron Brooks 12.00
2 Brett Favre 25.00
3 Brian Griese 10.00
4 Daunte Culpepper 10.00
5 Emmitt Smith 20.00
6 Isaac Bruce 8.00
7 Jevon Kearse 8.00
8 Joe Horn 8.00
9 Kordell Stewart 10.00
10 Kurt Warner 12.00
11 Marshall Faulk 12.00
12 Marvin Harrison 10.00
13 Mike Alstott 8.00
14 Peyton Manning 15.00
15 Randy Moss 15.00
16 Rod Smith 8.00
17 Terry Glenn 8.00
18 Tiki Barber 8.00
19 Tim Brown 12.00
20 Torry Holt 8.00

2003 Playoff Prestige Game Day Jerseys - Retail

NM/M
Common Player: 6.00
Inserted 1:28
21 Akili Smith 6.00
22 Amani Toomer 6.00
23 Corey Simon 6.00
24 Curtis Martin 10.00
25 Dennis Northcutt 6.00
26 Duce Staley 8.00
27 Frank Sanders 6.00
28 Freddie Mitchell 6.00
29 Ike Hilliard 6.00
30 Jamel White 6.00
31 Jason Sehorn 8.00
32 Jimmy Smith 6.00
33 J.J. Stokes 6.00
34 Junior Seau 6.00
35 Kevin Johnson 6.00
36 Marcel Shipp 6.00
37 Mark Brunell 10.00
38 Samari Rolle 6.00
39 Shaun King 6.00
40 Stephen Davis 6.00

2003 Playoff Prestige Game Day Jersey Auto.

NM/M
Production 25 sets
8 Joe Horn 45.00
10 Kurt Warner 100.00
15 Randy Moss 100.00
16 Rod Smith 35.00

2003 Playoff Prestige Gridiron Heritage

NM/M
Common Player: 1.00
Inserted 1:17
1 Randy Moss 4.00
2 Ray Lewis 1.00
3 Cris Carter 1.00
4 Corey Dillon 1.00
5 Marvin Harrison 2.00
6 Jake Plummer 1.00
7 Tim Couch 2.00
8 Hines Ward 1.00
9 Edgerrin James 2.50
10 Jevon Kearse 1.00
11 Garrison Hearst 1.00
12 Anthony Thomas 2.00
13 Brett Favre 5.00
14 Junior Seau 1.00
15 Emmitt Smith 4.00
16 Kurt Warner 3.00
17 Donovan McNabb 2.00
18 Terrell Owens 1.50
19 Chad Pennington 2.00
20 Eric Moulds 1.00
21 Jeff Garcia 1.00
22 David Boston 1.00
23 Derrick Mason 1.00
24 Fred Taylor 1.00
25 Thomas Jones 1.00

2003 Playoff Prestige Gridiron Heritage Matieral

NM/M
Common Player: 5.00
Production 100 for 1-10 (Helmet)
Production 250 for 11-25 (Jersey)
1 Randy Moss 50.00
2 Ray Lewis 35.00
3 Cris Carter 20.00
4 Corey Dillon
5 Marvin Harrison 35.00
6 Jake Plummer 15.00
7 Tim Couch 20.00
8 Hines Ward
9 Edgerrin James 30.00
10 Jevon Kearse 20.00
11 Garrison Hearst 8.00
12 Anthony Thomas 8.00
13 Brett Favre 25.00
14 Junior Seau 5.00
15 Emmitt Smith 25.00
16 Kurt Warner 10.00
17 Donovan McNabb 10.00
18 Terrell Owens 8.00
19 Chad Pennington 18.00
20 Eric Moulds 6.00
21 Jeff Garcia 10.00
22 David Boston 8.00
23 Derrick Mason 5.00
24 Fred Taylor 8.00
25 Thomas Jones 5.00

2003 Playoff Prestige Inside the Numbers

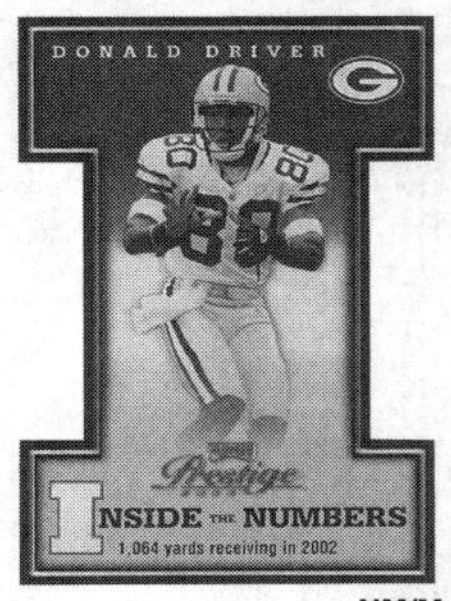

NM/M
Common Player: 1.00
Production 2002 sets
1 Brett Favre 5.00
2 Rich Gannon 2.00
3 Tommy Maddox 2.00
4 Drew Bledsoe 2.50
5 Chad Pennington 2.00
6 Jeff Garcia 1.50
7 Aaron Brooks 2.00
8 Michael Vick 4.00
9 LaDainian Tomlinson 3.00
10 Priest Holmes 2.00
11 Deuce McAllister 2.00
12 Marshall Faulk 2.00
13 Ricky Williams 3.00
14 Jamal Lewis 1.50
15 Travis Henry 1.50
16 Michael Bennett 2.00
17 Marvin Harrison 2.00
18 Eric Moulds 1.00
19 Peerless Price 1.50
20 Jerry Rice 4.00
21 Donald Driver 2.00
22 Plaxico Burress 2.00
23 Terrell Owens 2.00
24 Julius Peppers 2.00
25 Andre Carter 1.50

2003 Playoff Prestige Inside the Numbers DC

Production to jersey number
1 Brett Favre
2 Rich Gannon
3 Tommy Maddox
4 Drew Bledsoe
5 Chad Pennington
6 Jeff Garcia
7 Aaron Brooks
8 Michael Vick
9 LaDainian Tomlinson
10 Priest Holmes
11 Deuce McAllister
12 Marshall Faulk
13 Ricky Williams
14 Jamal Lewis
15 Travis Henry
16 Michael Bennett
17 Marvin Harrison
18 Eric Moulds
19 Peerless Price
20 Jerry Rice
21 Donald Driver
22 Plaxico Burress
23 Terrell Owens
24 Julius Peppers
25 Andre Carter

2003 Playoff Prestige League Leader Tandems

NM/M
Common Player: 1.00
Production 2002 sets
1 Jeff Garcia, Rich Gannon 2.00
2 Brett Favre, Chad Pennington 6.00
3 Steve McNair, Brad Johnson 2.00
4 Drew Bledsoe, Aaron Brooks 3.00
5 Peyton Manning, Michael Vick 6.00
6 Tom Brady, Kerry Collins 3.00
7 LaDainian Tomlinson, Marshall Faulk 3.00
8 Priest Holmes, Deuce McAllister 3.00
9 Ricky Williams, Ahman Green 4.00
10 Corey Dillon, Michael Bennett 2.00
11 Clinton Portis, James Stewart 5.00
12 Fred Taylor, Emmitt Smith 5.00
13 Marvin Harrison, Joe Horn 2.00
14 Eric Moulds, Keyshawn Johnson 1.00
15 Peerless Price, Torry Holt 1.00
16 Jerry Rice, Terrell Owens 4.00
17 Plaxico Burress, Donald Driver 3.00
18 Hines Ward, Randy Moss 5.00
19 Julius Peppers, Zach Thomas 2.00
20 Warren Sapp, Keith Bulluck 1.00

2003 Playoff Prestige LL Tandems Materials

Production 250 sets
1 Jeff Garcia, Rich Gannon
2 Brett Favre, Chad Pennington
3 Steve McNair, Brad Johnson
4 Drew Bledsoe, Aaron Brooks
5 Peyton Manning, Michael Vick
6 Tom Brady, Kerry Collins
7 LaDainian Tomlinson, Marshall Faulk
8 Priest Holmes, Deuce McAllister
9 Ricky Williams, Ahman Green
10 Corey Dillon, Michael Bennett
11 Clinton Portis, James Stewart
12 Fred Taylor, Emmitt Smith
13 Marvin Harrison, Joe Horn
14 Eric Moulds, Keyshawn Johnson
15 Peerless Price, Torry Holt
16 Jerry Rice, Terrell Owens
17 Plaxico Burress, Donald Driver
18 Hines Ward, Randy Moss
19 Julius Peppers, Zach Thomas
20 Warren Sapp, Keith Bulluck

2003 Playoff Prestige League Leaders Quads

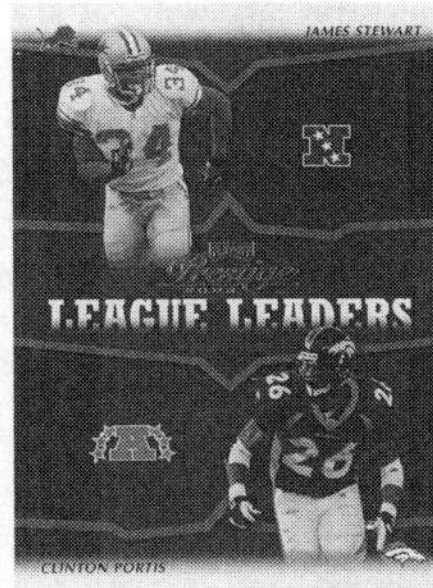

NM/M
Common Player: 3.00
Production 500 sets
1 Jeff Garcia, Rich Gannon, Brett Favre, Chad Pennington 8.00
2 Steve McNair, Brad Johnson, Drew Bledsoe, Aaron Brooks 4.00
3 Peyton Manning, Michael Vick, Tom Brady, Kerry Collins 8.00
4 LaDainian Tomlinson, Marshall Faulk, Priest Holmes, Deuce McAllister 5.00
5 Ricky Williams, Ahman Green, Corey Dillon, Michael Bennett 5.00
6 Clinton Portis, James Stewart, Fred Taylor, Emmitt Smith 8.00
7 Marvin Harrison, Joe Horn, Eric Moulds, Keyshawn Johnson 3.00
8 Peerless Price, Torry Holt, Jerry Rice, Terrell Owens 5.00
9 Plaxico Burress, Donald Driver, Hines Ward, Randy Moss 6.00
10 Julius Peppers, Zach Thomas, Warren Sapp, Keith Bulluck 3.00

2003 Playoff Prestige LL Quads Materials

NM/M
Common Player: 50.00
Production 25 sets
1 Jeff Garcia, Rich Gannon, Brett Favre, Chad Pennington 150.00
2 Steve McNair, Brad Johnson, Drew Bledsoe, Aaron Brooks 95.00
3 Peyton Manning, Michael Vick, Tom Brady, Kerry Collins
4 LaDainian Tomlinson, Marshall Faulk, Priest Holmes, Deuce McAllister 75.00
5 Ricky Williams, Ahman Green, Corey Dillon, Michael Bennett
6 Clinton Portis, James Stewart, Fred Taylor, Emmitt Smith 125.00
7 Marvin Harrison, Joe Horn, Eric Moulds, Keyshawn Johnson 50.00
8 Peerless Price, Torry Holt, Jerry Rice, Terrell Owens 90.00
9 Plaxico Burress, Donald Driver, Hines Ward, Randy Moss 90.00
10 Julius Peppers, Zach Thomas, Warren Sapp, Keith Bulluck

2003 Playoff Prestige Patches of the NFL

NM/M
Common Player: 15.00
Production 50 sets
1 Anthony Thomas 25.00
2 Chris Chambers 30.00
3 Donte Stallworth 30.00
4 Eddie George 30.00
5 Eric Moulds 15.00
6 Isaac Bruce 20.00
7 Jeff Garcia 25.00
8 Jerome Bettis 15.00
9 Jerry Rice 45.00
10 Joey Harrington 50.00
11 Koren Robinson
12 Kurt Warner 25.00
13 Mark Brunell 20.00
14 Michael Bennett 20.00
15 Michael Strahan 15.00
16 Plaxico Burress 25.00
17 Rich Gannon 20.00
18 Rod Smith 20.00
19 Steve McNair 40.00
20 Terrell Owens 20.00

2003 Playoff Prestige Patches of the NFL Auto.

NM/M
Production 25 sets
1 Anthony Thomas 50.00
5 Eric Moulds 50.00
12 Kurt Warner 150.00
17 Rich Gannon
19 Steve McNair 75.00

2003 Playoff Prestige Signature Impressions

NM/M
Common Player: 15.00
Production 50 sets
1 Antowain Smith 15.00
2 Brian Urlacher 60.00
3 Deion Branch 25.00
4 Derrick Mason 35.00
5 Donald Driver 40.00
6 Drew Bledsoe 55.00
7 Eddie George 50.00
8 Garrison Hearst 35.00
9 Jeff Garcia 35.00
10 Jerome Bettis 45.00
11 LaDainian Tomlinson 50.00
12 Mike Alstott 25.00
13 Priest Holmes 35.00
14 Ricky Williams 60.00
15 Rod Gardner 20.00
16 Hines Ward 45.00
17 Zach Thomas
18 Charlie Garner/Redem 15.00
19 Ed McCaffrey
20 Laveranues Coles
21 Marty Booker
22 Terrell Owens
23 Tommy Maddox 30.00
24 Kurt Warner 40.00
25 Michael Vick 150.00

2003 Playoff Prestige Stars of the NFL

NM/M
Common Player: 5.00
Production 250 sets
1 Anthony Thomas 8.00
2 Chris Chambers 8.00
3 Donte Stallworth 6.00
4 Eddie George 8.00
5 Eric Moulds 5.00
6 Isaac Bruce 5.00
7 Jeff Garcia 8.00
8 Jerome Bettis 8.00
9 Jerry Rice 15.00
10 Joey Harrington 15.00
11 Koren Robinson 5.00
12 Kurt Warner 12.00
13 Mark Brunell 5.00
14 Michael Bennett 10.00
15 Michael Strahan 5.00
16 Plaxico Burress 10.00
17 Rich Gannon 8.00
18 Rod Smith 5.00
19 Steve McNair 5.00
20 Terrell Owens 10.00

2003 Playoff Prestige 2002 Reunion

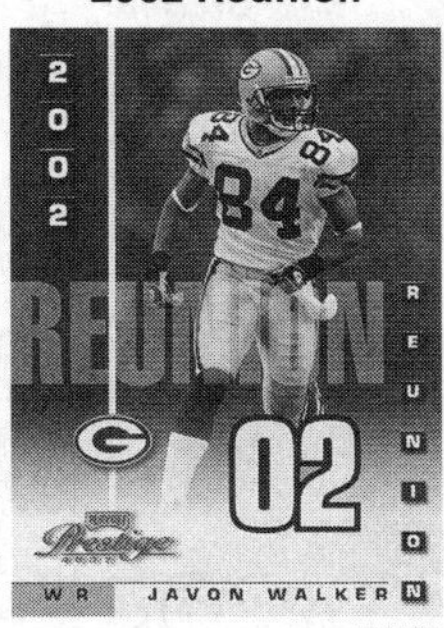

NM/M
Common Player: 1.00
Production 2002 sets
1 David Carr 3.00
2 Joey Harrington 3.00
3 Patrick Ramsey 2.00
4 William Green 2.00
5 T.J. Duckett 2.00
6 DeShaun Foster 1.50
7 Jonathan Wells 1.50
8 Clinton Portis 4.00
9 Brian Westbrook 1.00
10 Donte Stallworth 1.00
11 Ashley Lelie 2.00
12 Javon Walker 2.00
13 Jabar Gaffney 1.00
14 Josh Reed 1.00
15 Andre Davis 1.00
16 Antwann Randle El 3.00
17 Antonio Bryant 2.00
18 Deion Branch 1.00
19 Jeremy Shockey 3.00
20 Daniel Graham 1.00
21 Randy McMichael 1.00
22 Julius Peppers 2.00
23 Dwight Freeney 1.00
24 John Henderson 1.00
25 Quentin Jammer 1.00
26 Phillip Buchanon 1.00
27 Roy Williams 3.00
28 Ed Reed 1.00
29 Coy Wire 1.00
30 Napoleon Harris 1.00

2003 Playoff Prestige 2002 Reunion Materials

NM/M
Common Player: 10.00
Production 150 sets
1 David Carr 18.00
2 Joey Harrington 18.00
4 William Green 10.00
5 T.J. Duckett 10.00
8 Clinton Portis 18.00
10 Donte Stallworth 10.00
14 Josh Reed 10.00
19 Jeremy Shockey 15.00
22 Julius Peppers 10.00
27 Roy Williams 12.00

2003 Playoff Prestige Turning Pro

NM/M
Common Player: 12.00
Production 250 sets
1 Drew Bledsoe 25.00
2 Curtis Martin 12.00
3 Fred Taylor 12.00
4 Jevon Kearse 15.00
5 Ahman Green 25.00
6 Eddie George 20.00
7 Shaun Alexander 12.00
8 Edgerrin James 20.00
9 Keyshawn Johnson 12.00
10 Ricky Williams 35.00

2004 Playoff Absolute Memorabilia

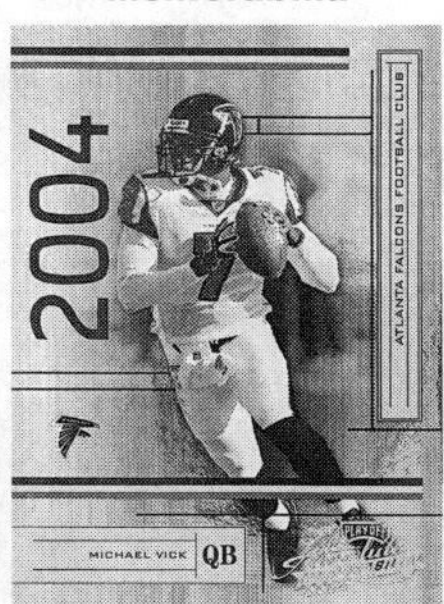

NM/M
Common Player (1-150): .50
Minor Stars (1-150): .75
Unlisted Stars (1-150): 1.50
Production 1150 Sets
Common Rookie (151-200): 3.00
Production 750 Sets
Common RY Premiere Materials (201-233): 8.00
Production 75 Sets
Pack: 42.00
Box (6): 180.00
1 Anquan Boldin 1.50
2 Emmitt Smith 4.00
3 Josh McCown .50
4 Marcel Shipp .50
5 Michael Vick 4.00
6 Peerless Price .75
7 T.J. Duckett .75
8 Warrick Dunn .50
9 Jamal Lewis 1.50
10 Kyle Boller 1.50
11 Ray Lewis .75
12 Terrell Suggs .50
13 Drew Bledsoe 1.50
14 Eric Moulds .50
15 Josh Reed .75
16 Travis Henry .50
17 DeShaun Foster .50
18 Jake Delhomme 1.50
19 Julius Peppers .25
20 Muhsin Muhammad .75
21 Stephen Davis .75
22 Steve Smith .25
23 Anthony Thomas .75
24 Brian Urlacher 1.50
25 Marty Booker .75
26 Rex Grossman 1.50
27 Carson Palmer 2.00
28 Chad Johnson .75
29 Corey Dillon .75
30 Peter Warrick .75
31 Rudi Johnson .75
32 Andre Davis .75
33 Dennis Northcutt .50
34 Lee Suggs .50
35 Tim Couch .75
36 Jeff Garcia 1.50
37 Willie Green .75
38 Antonio Bryant .75
39 Quincy Carter 1.50
40 Roy Williams .75
41 Terence Newman .50
42 Keyshawn Johnson .75
43 Garrison Hearst .50
44 Champ Bailey .75
45 Ashley Lelie .75
46 Jake Plummer .75
47 Rod Smith .50
48 Shannon Sharpe .75
49 Charles Rogers 1.50
50 Joey Harrington 1.50
51 Ahman Green 1.50
52 Brett Favre 5.00
53 Donald Driver .50
54 Javon Walker .75
55 Robert Ferguson .50
56 Andre Johnson 1.50
57 David Carr 2.00
58 Domanick Davis 1.50
59 Edgerrin James 2.00
60 Marvin Harrison 1.50
61 Peyton Manning 3.00
62 Reggie Wayne .50
63 Byron Leftwich 3.00
64 Fred Taylor 1.50
65 Jimmy Smith .50
66 Dante Hall .50
67 Priest Holmes 2.00
68 Tony Gonzalez .75
69 Trent Green .75
70 Chris Chambers 1.50
71 Jay Fiedler .75
72 David Boston .75
73 Ricky Williams 1.50
74 Zach Thomas .50
75 Daunte Culpepper 1.50
76 Michael Bennett 1.50
77 Moe Williams .50
78 Randy Moss 3.00
79 David Givens .50
80 Deion Branch .50
81 Kevin Faulk .50
82 Richard Seymour .50
83 Tom Brady 3.00
84 Troy Brown .50
85 Ty Law .50
86 Aaron Brooks 1.50
87 Deuce McAllister 1.50
88 Donte Stallworth .75
89 Joe Horn .50
90 Amani Toomer .75
91 Jeremy Shockey 1.50
92 Kerry Collins .50
93 Michael Strahan .50
94 Tiki Barber .50
95 Chad Pennington 2.00
96 Curtis Martin 1.50
97 Santana Moss .50
98 Wayne Chrebet .50
99 Justin McCareins .50
100 Charles Woodson .50
101 Jerry Porter .50
102 Jerry Rice 4.00
103 Rich Gannon .75
104 Tim Brown 1.50
105 Warren Sapp .50
106 A.J. Feeley .50
107 Brian Westbrook .50
108 Correll Buckhalter .50
109 Donovan McNabb 2.00
110 Freddie Mitchell .50
111 Terrell Owens 1.50
112 Jevon Kearse .50
113 Todd Pinkston .50
114 Antwann Randle El .75
115 Hines Ward .75
116 Jerome Bettis .75
117 Kendrell Bell .50
118 Plaxico Burress 1.50
119 Tommy Maddox .75
120 Duce Staley .50
121 Drew Brees .75
122 LaDainian Tomlinson 2.00
123 Kevan Barlow .50
124 Tai Streets .50
125 Tim Rattay .50
126 Darrell Jackson .50
127 Koren Robinson .50
128 Matt Hasselbeck .75
129 Shaun Alexander 1.50
130 Isaac Bruce .75
131 Kurt Warner 1.50
132 Marc Bulger .75
133 Marshall Faulk 2.00
134 Torry Holt 1.50
135 Derrick Brooks .50
136 Keenan McCardell .50
137 Mike Alstott .50
138 Thomas Jones .50
139 Charlie Garner .50
140 Derrick Mason .50
141 Drew Bennett .50
142 Eddie George 1.50
143 Keith Bulluck .50
144 Steve McNair 1.50
145 LaVar Arrington 1.50
146 Laveranues Coles .75
147 Patrick Ramsey .75
148 Rod Gardner .50
149 Clinton Portis 3.00
150 Mark Brunell .75
151 *Craig Krenzel/Auto.* 12.00
152 *Andy Hall/Auto.* 10.00
153 *Josh Harris* 3.00
154 *Jim Sorgi/Auto.* 8.00
155 *Jeff Smoker/Auto.* 15.00
156 *John Navarre/Auto.* 12.00
157 *Jared Lorenzen/Auto.* 8.00
158 *Cody Pickett/Auto.* 12.00
159 *Casey Bramlet* 3.00
160 *Matt Mauck/Auto.* 15.00
161 *B.J. Symons/Auto.* 10.00
162 *Bradlee Van Pelt* 6.00
163 *Ryan Dinwiddie* 3.00
164 *Michael Turner* 3.00
165 *Drew Henson* 15.00
166 *Troy Fleming* 3.00
167 *Adimchinobe Echemandu* 3.00
168 *Quincy Wilson* 3.00
169 *Derrick Ward* 3.00
170 *Bruce Perry* 3.00
171 *Brandon Miree* 4.00
172 *Jarrett Payton/Auto.* 12.00
173 *Ran Carthon* 3.00
174 *Carlos Francis/Auto.* 3.00
175 *Samie Parker* 3.00
176 *Jerricho Cotchery* 3.00
177 *Ernest Wilford* 3.00
178 *Johnnie Morant* 3.00
179 *Maurice Mann/Auto.* 8.00
180 *D.J. Hackett* 4.00
181 *Drew Carter* 4.00
182 *P.K. Sam* 8.00
183 *Jamaar Taylor* 3.00
184 *Ryan Krause* 3.00
185 *Triandos Luke* 6.00
186 *Jeris McIntyre* 3.00
187 *Clarence Moore/Auto.* 8.00
188 *Mark Jones* 3.00
189 *Sloan Thomas/Auto.* 8.00
190 *Sean Taylor* 12.00
191 *Derek Abney* 4.00
192 *Jonathan Vilma* 8.00
193 *Tommie Harris* 8.00
194 *D.J. Williams* 4.00
195 *Will Smith* 6.00
196 *Kenechi Udeze* 4.00
197 *Vince Wilfork* 8.00
198 *Ahmad Carroll* 3.00
199 *Jason Babin* 8.00
200 *Chris Gamble* 6.00
201 *Larry Fitzgerald* 30.00
202 *DeAngelo Hall* 15.00
203 *Matt Schaub* 10.00
204 *Michael Jenkins/Auto.* 20.00
205 *Devard Darling/Auto.* 15.00
206 *J.P. Losman* 18.00
207 *Lee Evans* 15.00
208 *Keary Colbert/Auto.* 30.00
209 *Bernard Berrian/Auto.* 20.00
210 *Chris Perry* 12.00
211 *Kellen Winslow Jr.* 12.00
212 *Luke McCown* 10.00
213 *Julius Jones* 20.00
214 *Darius Watts* 10.00
215 *Tatum Bell/Auto.* 40.00
216 *Kevin Jones* 20.00
217 *Roy Williams* 30.00
218 *Dunta Robinson* 10.00
219 *Greg Jones/Auto.* 25.00
220 *Reggie Williams* 15.00
221 *Mewelde Moore* 8.00
222 *Ben Watson* 8.00
223 *Cedric Cobbs* 10.00
224 *Devery Henderson/Auto.* 10.00
225 *Eli Manning* 60.00
226 *Robert Gallery* 10.00
227 *Ben Roethlisberger* 80.00
228 *Philip Rivers* 25.00
229 *Derrick Hamilton* 8.00
230 *Rashaun Woods* 15.00
231 *Steven Jackson* 20.00
232 *Michael Clayton* 15.00
233 *Ben Troupe* 8.00

2004 Playoff Absolute Memorabilia Spectrum

Veterans (1-150):
Production 100 Sets
Rookies (151-200): .75X-1.5X
Rookies (151-200): .25X-.5X
Auto cards
Production 100 Sets
Rookies (201-233): .75X-1.5X
Rookies (201-233): .25X-.5X
Auto cards
Production 75 Sets

2004 Playoff Absolute Memorabilia Platinum Spectrum

No Pricing
Production 1 Set

2004 Playoff Absolute Memorabilia Absolute Patches

No Pricing
Production 25 Sets
Spectrum: No Pricing
Production 1 Set
AP-1 Anquan Boldin
AP-2 Barry Sanders
AP-3 Brett Favre
AP-4 Brian Urlacher
AP-5 Chad Pennington
AP-6 Clinton Portis
AP-7 Dan Marino
AP-8 Daunte Culpepper
AP-9 David Carr
AP-10 Deuce McAllister
AP-11 Donovan McNabb
AP-12 Drew Bledsoe
AP-13 Edgerrin James
AP-14 Emmitt Smith
AP-15 Jeremy Shockey
AP-16 Jerry Rice
AP-17 John Elway
AP-18 Joey Harrington
AP-19 LaDainian Tomlinson
AP-20 Michael Vick
AP-21 Peyton Manning
AP-22 Priest Holmes
AP-23 Randy Moss
AP-24 Ricky Williams
AP-25 Tom Brady

2004 Playoff Absolute Memorabilia Boss Hogs

NM/M
Common Player: 1.50
Production 1,000 Sets
Boss Hoggs Materials: 5X-8X

Production 125 Sets
Materials Prime
Spectrum: No Pricing
Production 1 Set
BH-1 Amani Toomer 1.50
BH-2 Brett Favre 6.00
BH-3 Charles Woodson 1.50
BH-4 Curtis Martin 2.00
BH-5 Eddie George 2.00
BH-6 Edgerrin James 3.00
BH-7 Emmitt Smith 5.00
BH-8 Jeff Garcia 2.00
BH-9 Jerry Rice 5.00
BH-10 Jevon Kearse 1.50
BH-11 Jimmy Smith 1.50
BH-12 Keith Bulluck 1.50
BH-13 Kurt Warner 2.00
BH-14 Laveranues Coles 1.50
BH-15 Mark Brunell 1.50
BH-16 Marshall Faulk 3.00
BH-17 Marvin Harrison 2.00
BH-18 Michael Strahan 1.50
BH-19 Michael Vick 5.00
BH-20 Peyton Manning 4.00
BH-21 Rich Gannon 1.50
BH-22 Samari Rolle 1.50
BH-23 Steve McNair 2.00
BH-24 Tim Brown 2.00
BH-25 Wayne Chrebet 1.50

2004 Playoff Abs. Mem. Canton Absolutes Jersey Bronze

NM/M
Common Player: 12.00
Production 100 Sets
Silver: .75X-1.5X
Production 50 Sets
Gold: No Pricing
Production 25 Sets
Platinum: No Pricing
Production 1 Set
CA-1 Barry Sanders 40.00
CA-2 Brett Favre 25.00
CA-3 Brian Urlacher 12.00
CA-4 Clinton Portis 18.00
CA-5 Dan Marino 40.00
CA-6 Daunte Culpepper 15.00
CA-7 Deuce McAllister 12.00
CA-8 Donovan McNabb 12.00
CA-9 Earl Campbell 15.00
CA-10 Edgerrin James 12.00
CA-11 Emmitt Smith 20.00
CA-12 Jerry Rice 20.00
CA-13 Jim Kelly 15.00
CA-14 John Elway 40.00
CA-15 LaDainian Tomlinson 15.00
CA-16 Marshall Faulk 15.00
CA-17 Marcus Allen 12.00
CA-18 Michael Vick 20.00
CA-19 Peyton Manning 18.00
CA-20 Priest Holmes 15.00
CA-21 Randy Moss 18.00
CA-22 Ricky Williams 12.00
CA-23 Steve McNair 12.00
CA-24 Tom Brady 18.00
CA-25 Warren Moon 12.00

2004 Playoff Absolute Memorabilia Fans of the Game

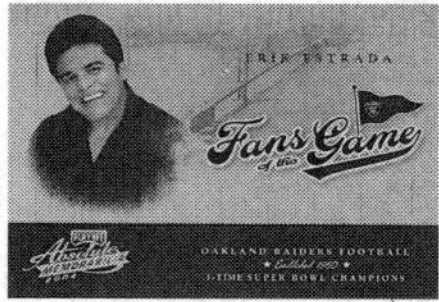

NM/M
234 Erik Estrada 2.00
236 Chris Berman 3.00
237 Rich Eisen 2.00
238 John Clayton 2.00

2004 Playoff Absolute Memorabilia Fans of the Game Auto

NM/M
Production 300 Sets (Hobby)
234 Erik Estrada 25.00
236 Chris Berman 40.00
237 Rich Eisen 30.00
238 John Clayton 20.00

2004 Playoff Absolute Memorabilia Gridiron Force

NM/M
Common Player: 1.50
Production 1,000 Sets
Bronze: 5X-8X
Production 100 Sets
Silver: 5X-8X
Production 50 Sets
Gold: No Pricing
Production 25 Sets
Platinum: No Pricing
Production 10 Sets
GF-1 Aaron Brooks 2.00
GF-2 Anquan Boldin 2.00
GF-3 Brian Urlacher 2.00
GF-4 Byron Leftwich 4.00
GF-5 Chad Johnson 1.50
GF-6 Chad Pennington 3.00
GF-7 Clinton Portis 4.00
GF-8 Daunte Culpepper 2.00
GF-9 David Carr 3.00
GF-10 Deuce McAllister 2.00
GF-11 Donovan McNabb 3.00
GF-12 Edgerrin James 3.00
GF-13 Emmitt Smith 5.00
GF-14 Jamal Lewis 2.00
GF-15 Jeff Garcia 2.00
GF-16 Jeremy Shockey 2.00
GF-17 Joey Harrington 2.00
GF-18 Koren Robinson 1.50
GF-19 LaDainian Tomlinson 3.00
GF-20 Plaxico Burress 2.00
GF-21 Priest Holmes 3.00
GF-22 Ricky Williams 2.00
GF-23 Shaun Alexander 2.00
GF-24 Terrell Owens 2.00
GF-25 Tom Brady 4.00

2004 Playoff Absolute Memorabilia Ground Hoggs

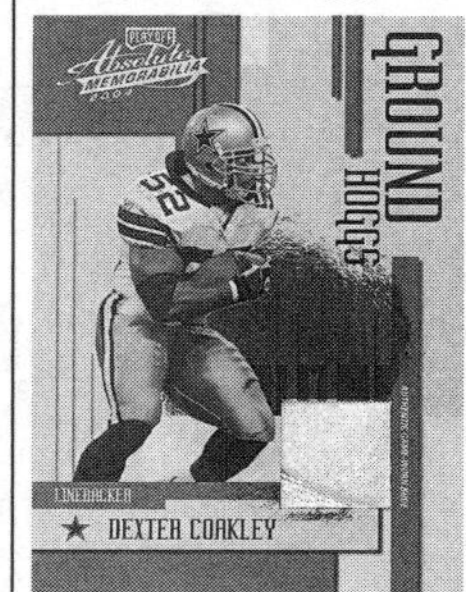

NM/M
Common Player: 10.00
Production 125 Sets
GH-1 Amani Toomer 10.00
GH-2 Brett Favre 30.00
GH-3 Curtis Martin 12.00
GH-4 Derrick Brooks 10.00
GH-5 Derrick Mason 10.00
GH-6 Dexter Coakley 10.00
GH-7 Eddie George 12.00
GH-8 Edgerrin James 15.00
GH-9 Emmitt Smith 25.00
GH-10 Jason Taylor 10.00
GH-11 Jerry Rice 25.00
GH-12 Jevon Kearse 10.00
GH-13 Joey Galloway 10.00
GH-14 Junior Seau 10.00
GH-15 Keyshawn Johnson 10.00
GH-16 Kurt Warner 12.00
GH-17 Laveranues Coles 10.00
GH-18 Marvin Harrison 12.00
GH-19 Patrick Surtain 10.00
GH-20 Peyton Manning 20.00
GH-21 Rich Gannon 10.00
GH-22 Samari Rolle 10.00
GH-23 Steve McNair 12.00
GH-24 Terry Glenn 10.00
GH-25 Wayne Chrebet 10.00

2004 Playoff Absolute Memorabilia Leather & Lace

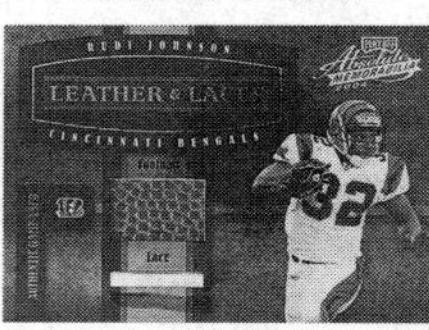

NM/M
Common Player: 10.00
Production 250 Sets
Football & Lace: No Pricing
Production 25 Sets
LL-1 Ahman Green 12.00
LL-2 Anquan Boldin 12.00
LL-3 Brett Favre 25.00
LL-4 Chad Johnson 10.00
LL-5 Chad Pennington 15.00
LL-6 Curtis Martin 12.00
LL-7 Daunte Culpepper 12.00
LL-8 Donovan McNabb 15.00
LL-9 Emmitt Smith 20.00
LL-10 Jake Delhomme 12.00
LL-11 Jamal Lewis 12.00
LL-12 Kevan Barlow 10.00
LL-13 Koren Robinson 10.00
LL-14 Marc Bulger 10.00
LL-15 Marshall Faulk 15.00
LL-16 Matt Hasselbeck 10.00
LL-17 Randy Moss 18.00
LL-18 Ricky Williams 12.00
LL-19 Rudi Johnson 10.00
LL-20 Shaun Alexander 12.00
LL-21 Stephen Davis 10.00
LL-22 Steve McNair 12.00
LL-23 Steve Smith 10.00
LL-24 Terrell Owens 12.00
LL-25 Torry Holt 12.00

2004 Playoff Absolute Memorabilia Marks of Fame

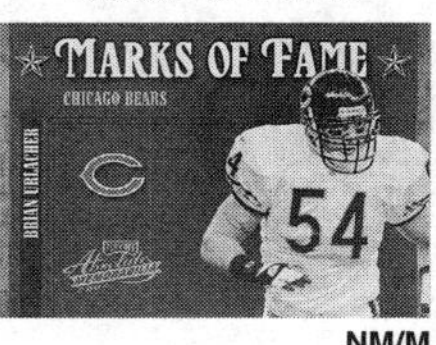

NM/M
Common Player: 3.00
Production 1,000 Sets
Marks of Fame Materials: 3X-5X
Production 75 Sets
Marks of Fame Materials
Prime: No Pricing
Production 25 Sets
Materials Prime
Spectrum: No Pricing
Production 1 Set
MOF-1 Aaron Brooks 3.00
MOF-2 Anquan Boldin 3.00
MOF-3 Brett Favre 8.00
MOF-4 Brian Urlacher 3.00
MOF-5 Chad Pennington 4.00
MOF-6 Clinton Portis 5.00
MOF-7 Daunte Culpepper 3.00
MOF-8 David Carr 4.00
MOF-9 Deuce McAllister 3.00
MOF-10 Donovan McNabb 4.00
MOF-11 Emmitt Smith 6.00
MOF-12 Jamal Lewis 3.00
MOF-13 Jeremy Shockey 3.00
MOF-14 Jerry Rice 6.00
MOF-15 Joey Harrington 3.00
MOF-16 LaDainian Tomlinson 4.00
MOF-17 Marvin Harrison 3.00
MOF-18 Michael Vick 6.00
MOF-19 Peyton Manning 5.00
MOF-20 Priest Holmes 4.00
MOF-21 Ricky Williams 3.00
MOF-22 Steve McNair 3.00
MOF-23 Terrell Owens 3.00
MOF-24 Tom Brady 5.00
MOF-25 Torry Holt 3.00

2004 Playoff Absolute Memorabilia Signature Materials

NM/M
Common Player: 15.00
Numbered to varying quantities
Prime: No Pricing
Production 5 Sets
Prime Spectrum: No Pricing
Production 1 Set
SM-1 Ahman Green/194 40.00
SM-2 Antwann Randle El/119 30.00
SM-3 Chris Chambers/94 20.00
SM-4 Deuce McAllister/94 25.00
SM-5 Joe Horn/94 20.00
SM-6 Roy Williams/194 30.00
SM-7 Shaun Alexander/144 30.00
SM-8 Stephen Davis/144 20.00
SM-9 Tom Brady/194 125.00
SM-10 Joe Namath/94 100.00
SM-11 Terry Bradshaw/19
SM-12 Jim Kelly/19
SM-13 Cedric Cobbs/300 20.00
SM-14 Chris Perry/280 20.00
SM-15 Devery Henderson/280 15.00
SM-16 Julius Jones/300 50.00
SM-17 Keary Colbert/300 30.00
SM-18 Kevin Jones/280 40.00
SM-19 Lee Evans/300 25.00
SM-20 Matt Schaub/280 30.00
SM-21 Michael Clayton/300 30.00
SM-22 Philip Rivers/300 60.00
SM-23 Reggie Williams/280 25.00
SM-24 Steven Jackson/280 50.00
SM-25 Tatum Bell/300 50.00

2004 Playoff Absolute Memorabilia Spectrum Signatures

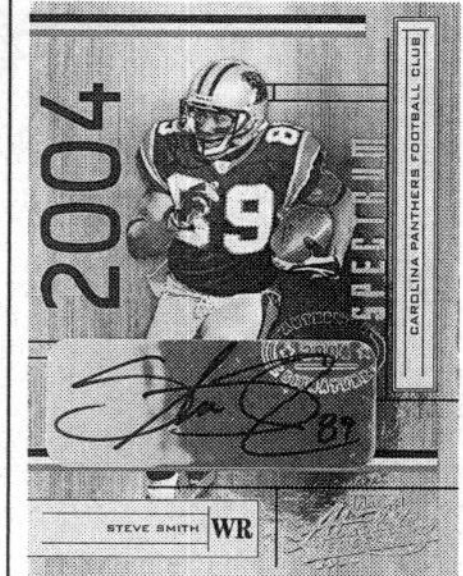

NM/M
Numbered to varying quantities
3 Josh McCown/300 15.00
10 Kyle Boller/225 20.00
18 Jake Delhomme/150 20.00
21 Stephen Davis/50 25.00
22 Steve Smith/300 15.00
26 Rex Grossman/50 30.00
31 Rudi Johnson/300 20.00
58 Domanick Davis/300 20.00
60 Marvin Harrison/25 40.00
65 Jimmy Smith/125 15.00
83 Tom Brady/50 125.00
89 Joe Horn/50 20.00
93 Michael Strahan/25 25.00
117 Kendrell Bell/25 40.00
128 Matt Hasselbeck/125 25.00
134 Torry Holt/50 30.00
140 Derrick Mason/125 15.00
146 Laveranues Coles/25 30.00
153 Josh Harris/50
164 Michael Turner/50 20.00
165 Drew Henson/300 30.00
168 Quincy Wilson/50 20.00
175 Samie Parker/50
176 Jerricho Cotchery/50
177 Ernest Wilford/50
178 Johnnie Morant/75 20.00
180 D.J. Hackett/50
182 P.K. Sam/50 20.00
190 Sean Taylor/50
192 Jonathan Vilma/50
193 Tommie Harris/50
194 D.J. Williams/25
195 Will Smith/25 30.00
196 Kenechi Udeze/25
197 Vince Wilfork/25
198 Ahmad Carroll/25 30.00
200 Chris Gamble/25

2004 Playoff Absolute Memorabilia Team Tandems

NM/M
Common Player: 1.50
Production 1,000 Sets
Spectrum: 3X-5X
Production 25 Sets
Materials Jersey: 5X-10X
Production 125 Sets
Materials Prime: No Pricing
Production 25 Sets
Materials Prime
Spectrum: No Pricing
Production 1 Set
TT-1 Anquan Boldin, Emmitt Smith 4.00
TT-2 Michael Vick, Peerless Price 4.00
TT-3 Jamal Lewis, Ray Lewis 1.50
TT-4 Stephen Davis, Julius Peppers 1.50
TT-5 Brian Urlacher, Anthony Thomas 1.50
TT-6 Clinton Portis, Rod Smith 3.00
TT-7 Charles Rogers, Joey Harrington 1.50
TT-8 Ahman Green, Brett Favre 5.00
TT-9 Andre Johnson, David Carr 2.00
TT-10 Edgerrin James, Peyton Manning 3.00
TT-11 Byron Leftwich, Fred Taylor 3.00
TT-12 Priest Holmes, Trent Green 2.00
TT-13 Chris Chambers, Ricky Williams 1.50
TT-14 Daunte Culpepper, Randy Moss 3.00
TT-15 Tom Brady, Troy Brown 3.00
TT-16 Aaron Brooks, Deuce McAllister 1.50
TT-17 Jeremy Shockey, Kerry Collins 1.50
TT-18 Chad Pennington, Curtis Martin 2.00
TT-19 Jerry Rice, Tim Brown 4.00
TT-20 Donovan McNabb, Correll Buckhalter 2.00
TT-21 Drew Brees, LaDainian Tomlinson 2.00
TT-22 Matt Hasselbeck, Shaun Alexander 1.50
TT-23 Kurt Warner, Marshall Faulk 2.00
TT-24 Eddie George, Steve McNair 1.50
TT-25 Patrick Ramsey, Laveranues Coles 1.50

2004 Playoff Absolute Memorabilia Team Trios

NM/M
Common Player: 3.00
Production 500 Sets
Spectrum: No Pricing
Production 10 Sets
Team Trios Materials: 2X-4X
Production 100 Sets
Materials Prime: No Pricing
Production 10 Sets
Materials Prime
Spectrum: No Pricing
Production 1 Set
TTR-1 Anquan Boldin, Emmitt Smith, Josh McCown 8.00
TTR-2 Michael Vick, Peerless Price, T.J. Duckett 8.00
TTR-3 Jamal Lewis, Ray Lewis, Terrell Suggs 4.00
TTR-4 Drew Bledsoe, Eric Moulds, Travis Henry 4.00
TTR-5 Anthony Thomas, Brian Urlacher, Rex Grossman 4.00
TTR-6 Chad Johnson, Corey Dillon, Peter Warrick 3.00
TTR-7 Quincy Carter, Roy Williams, Terence Newman 4.00
TTR-8 Clinton Portis, Rod Smith, Jake Plummer 6.00
TTR-9 Charles Rogers, Joey Harrington, James Stewart 4.00
TTR-10 Ahman Green, Brett Favre, Javon Walker 10.00
TTR-11 Edgerrin James, Peyton Manning, Marvin Harrison 6.00
TTR-12 Byron Leftwich, Fred Taylor, Jimmy Smith 6.00
TTR-13 Priest Holmes, Trent Green, Tony Gonzalez 5.00
TTR-14 Chris Chambers, Ricky Williams, Zach Thomas 4.00
TTR-15 Daunte Culpepper, Randy Moss, Michael Bennett 6.00
TTR-16 Aaron Brooks, Deuce McAllister, Joe Horn 4.00
TTR-17 Jeremy Shockey, Kerry Collins, Michael Strahan 4.00
TTR-18 Chad Pennington, Curtis Martin, Santana Moss 5.00
TTR-19 Jerry Rice, Tim Brown, Rich Gannon 8.00
TTR-20 Hines Ward, Jerome Bettis, Antwann Randle El 3.00
TTR-21 Drew Brees, LaDainian Tomlinson, Doug Flutie 5.00
TTR-22 Matt Hasselbeck, Shaun Alexander, Koren Robinson 4.00
TTR-23 Kurt Warner, Marshall Faulk, Marc Bulger 5.00
TTR-24 Eddie George, Steve McNair, Jevon Kearse 4.00
TTR-25 Laveranues Coles, Patrick Ramsey, LaVar Arrington 5.00

2004 Playoff Absolute Memorabilia Team Quads

NM/M
Common Player: 4.00
Production 250 Sets
Spectrum: No Pricing
Production 5 Sets
Team Quads Materials
Jersey: 4X-6X
Production 50 Sets
Materials Prime Jersey: No Pricing
Production 5 Sets
Mat. Prime Spectrum
Jersey: No Pricing
Production 1 Set
TQ-1 Anquan Boldin, Emmitt Smith, Josh McCown, Marcel Shipp 8.00
TQ-2 Jamal Lewis, Ray Lewis, Terrell Suggs, Kyle Boller 5.00
TQ-3 Drew Bledsoe, Eric Moulds, Travis Henry, Josh Reed 5.00
TQ-4 Anthony Thomas, Brian Urlacher, Rex Grossman, David Terrell 5.00
TQ-5 Clinton Portis, Rod Smith, Jake Plummer, Ashley Lelie 8.00
TQ-6 Brett Favre, Ahman Green, Javon Walker, Donald Driver 12.00
TQ-7 Edgerrin James, Peyton Manning, Marvin Harrison, Reggie Wayne 8.00
TQ-8 Priest Holmes, Trent Green, Tony Gonzalez, Dante Hall 6.00
TQ-9 Chris Chambers, Ricky Williams, Zach Thomas, Jason Taylor 5.00
TQ-10 Jeremy Shockey, Kerry Collins, Michael Strahan, Tiki Barber 4.00
TQ-11 Chad Pennington, Curtis Martin, Santana Moss, John Abraham 6.00
TQ-12 Jerry Rice, Tim Brown, Rich Gannon, Charles Woodson 10.00
TQ-13 Hines Ward, Jerome Bettis, Antwann Randle El, Plaxico Burress 5.00
TQ-14 Kurt Warner, Marshall Faulk, Marc Bulger, Torry Holt 6.00
TQ-15 Eddie George, Steve McNair, Jevon Kearse, Derrick Mason 5.00

2004 Playoff Absolute Memorabilia Tools of the Trade

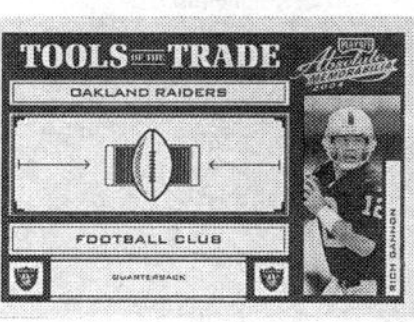

NM/M
Common Player: 2.00
Production 250 Sets
Spectrum: No Pricing
Production 10 Sets
TT-1 Aaron Brooks 4.00
TT-2 Ahman Green 4.00
TT-3 Andre Johnson 4.00
TT-4 Anquan Boldin 4.00
TT-5 Anthony Thomas 3.00
TT-6 Antwann Randle El 3.00
TT-7 Ashley Lelie 3.00
TT-8 Brad Johnson 2.00
TT-9 Brett Favre 10.00
TT-10 Brian Urlacher 4.00
TT-11 Byron Leftwich 6.00
TT-12 Chad Johnson 3.00
TT-13 Chad Pennington 5.00
TT-14 Charles Rogers 4.00
TT-15 Charles Woodson 2.00
TT-16 Chris Chambers 4.00
TT-17 Clinton Portis 6.00
TT-18 Corey Dillon 3.00
TT-19 Curtis Martin 4.00
TT-20 Dante Hall 2.00
TT-21 Daunte Culpepper 4.00
TT-22 David Boston 3.00
TT-23 David Carr 5.00
TT-24 Deuce McAllister 4.00
TT-25 Donovan McNabb 5.00
TT-26 Donte Stallworth 3.00
TT-27 Drew Bledsoe 4.00
TT-28 Eddie George 4.00
TT-29 Edgerrin James 5.00
TT-30 Emmitt Smith 8.00
TT-31 Eric Moulds 2.00
TT-32 Fred Taylor 4.00
TT-33 Hines Ward 3.00
TT-34 Isaac Bruce 3.00
TT-35 Jake Plummer 3.00
TT-36 Jamal Lewis 4.00
TT-37 Javon Walker 3.00
TT-38 Jeff Garcia 4.00
TT-39 Jeremy Shockey 4.00
TT-40 Jerome Bettis 3.00
TT-41 Jerry Rice 8.00
TT-42 Jevon Kearse 2.00
TT-43 Joey Harrington 4.00
TT-44 Josh McCown 2.00
TT-45 Julius Peppers 2.00
TT-46 Kendrell Bell 2.00
TT-47 Kerry Collins 2.00
TT-48 Keyshawn Johnson 3.00
TT-49 Koren Robinson 2.00
TT-50 Kurt Warner 4.00
TT-51 Kyle Boller 4.00
TT-52 LaDainian Tomlinson 5.00
TT-53 LaVar Arrington 4.00
TT-54 Laveranues Coles 3.00
TT-55 Marc Bulger 3.00
TT-56 Marcel Shipp 2.00
TT-57 Mark Brunell 3.00
TT-58 Marshall Faulk 5.00
TT-59 Marvin Harrison 4.00
TT-60 Matt Hasselbeck 3.00
TT-61 Michael Bennett 4.00
TT-62 Michael Strahan 2.00
TT-63 Michael Vick 8.00
TT-64 Patrick Ramsey 3.00
TT-65 Peerless Price 3.00
TT-66 Peter Warrick 3.00
TT-67 Peyton Manning 6.00
TT-68 Plaxico Burress 4.00
TT-69 Priest Holmes 5.00
TT-70 Quincy Carter 4.00
TT-71 Randy Moss 6.00
TT-72 Ray Lewis 3.00
TT-73 Reggie Wayne 2.00
TT-74 Rex Grossman 4.00
TT-75 Rich Gannon 3.00
TT-76 Ricky Williams 4.00
TT-77 Rod Smith 2.00
TT-78 Roy Williams 3.00
TT-79 Santana Moss 2.00
TT-80 Shaun Alexander 4.00
TT-81 Stephen Davis 3.00
TT-82 T.J. Duckett 3.00
TT-83 Terence Newman 2.00
TT-84 Terrell Owens 4.00
TT-85 Terrell Suggs 2.00
TT-86 Tiki Barber 2.00
TT-87 Tim Brown 4.00
TT-88 Tom Brady 6.00
TT-89 Tony Gonzalez 3.00
TT-90 Torry Holt 4.00
TT-91 Travis Henry 2.00
TT-92 Trent Green 2.00
TT-93 Warrick Dunn 2.00
TT-94 Zach Thomas 2.00

TT-95 Barry Sanders 8.00
TT-96 Dan Marino 10.00
TT-97 Deion Sanders 4.00
TT-98 Joe Montana 10.00
TT-99 John Elway 10.00
TT-100 Warren Moon 4.00

2004 Playoff Abs. Mem. Tools/Trade Materials Jersey

NM/M
Common Player: 8.00
Production 100 Sets
Spectrum Jersey: No Pricing
Production 10 Sets
Prime Jersey: No Pricing
Production 25 Sets
Prime Spectrum Jersey: No Pricing
Production 1 Sets
TT-1 Aaron Brooks 10.00
TT-2 Ahman Green 10.00
TT-3 Andre Johnson 10.00
TT-4 Anquan Boldin 10.00
TT-5 Anthony Thomas 8.00
TT-6 Antwann Randle El 8.00
TT-7 Ashley Lelie 8.00
TT-8 Brad Johnson 8.00
TT-9 Brett Favre 25.00
TT-10 Brian Urlacher 10.00
TT-11 Byron Leftwich/50 20.00
TT-11 Byron Leftwich/50 Auto.
TT-12 Chad Johnson/Auto. 25.00
TT-13 Chad Pennington 12.00
TT-14 Charles Rogers 10.00
TT-15 Charles Woodson 8.00
TT-16 Chris Chambers/Auto. 25.00
TT-17 Clinton Portis 15.00
TT-18 Corey Dillon 8.00
TT-19 Curtis Martin 10.00
TT-20 Dante Hall 8.00
TT-21 Daunte Culpepper 10.00
TT-22 David Boston 8.00
TT-23 David Carr/75 20.00
TT-23 David Carr/25 Auto.
TT-24 Deuce McAllister 10.00
TT-25 Donovan McNabb 12.00
TT-26 Donte Stallworth 8.00
TT-27 Drew Bledsoe 10.00
TT-28 Eddie George 10.00
TT-29 Edgerrin James 12.00
TT-30 Emmitt Smith 20.00
TT-31 Eric Moulds 8.00
TT-32 Fred Taylor 10.00
TT-33 Hines Ward/Auto. 30.00
TT-34 Isaac Bruce 8.00
TT-35 Jake Plummer 8.00
TT-36 Jamal Lewis 10.00
TT-37 Javon Walker 8.00
TT-38 Jeff Garcia 10.00
TT-39 Jeremy Shockey 10.00
TT-40 Jerome Bettis 8.00
TT-41 Jerry Rice 20.00
TT-42 Jevon Kearse 8.00
TT-43 Joey Harrington 10.00
TT-44 Josh McCown 8.00
TT-45 Julius Peppers 8.00
TT-46 Kendrell Bell 8.00
TT-47 Kerry Collins 8.00
TT-48 Keyshawn Johnson 8.00
TT-49 Koren Robinson 8.00
TT-50 Kurt Warner 10.00
TT-51 Kyle Boller/Auto. 30.00
TT-52 LaDainian Tomlinson 12.00
TT-53 LaVar Arrington 15.00
TT-54 Laveranues Coles 8.00
TT-55 Marc Bulger 10.00
TT-56 Marcel Shipp 8.00
TT-57 Mark Brunell 8.00
TT-58 Marshall Faulk 12.00
TT-59 Marvin Harrison 10.00
TT-60 Matt Hasselbeck/Auto. 30.00
TT-61 Michael Bennett 10.00
TT-62 Michael Strahan 8.00
TT-63 Michael Vick 20.00
TT-64 Patrick Ramsey 8.00
TT-65 Peerless Price 8.00
TT-66 Peter Warrick 8.00
TT-67 Peyton Manning 15.00
TT-68 Plaxico Burress 10.00
TT-69 Priest Holmes 12.00
TT-70 Quincy Carter 8.00
TT-71 Randy Moss 15.00
TT-72 Ray Lewis 8.00
TT-73 Reggie Wayne 8.00
TT-74 Rex Grossman/Auto. 30.00
TT-75 Rich Gannon 8.00
TT-76 Ricky Williams 10.00
TT-77 Rod Smith 8.00
TT-78 Roy Williams/Auto. 40.00
TT-79 Santana Moss 8.00
TT-80 Shaun Alexander/50 12.00
TT-80 Shaun Alexander/50 Auto.
TT-81 Stephen Davis 8.00
TT-82 T.J. Duckett 8.00
TT-83 Terence Newman 8.00
TT-84 Terrell Owens 10.00
TT-85 Terrell Suggs 8.00
TT-86 Tiki Barber 8.00
TT-87 Tim Brown 10.00
TT-88 Tom Brady 15.00
TT-89 Tony Gonzalez 8.00
TT-90 Torry Holt/50 12.00
TT-90 Torry Holt/50 Auto.
TT-91 Travis Henry 8.00
TT-92 Trent Green/25 8.00
TT-92 Trent Green/75 Auto.
TT-93 Warrick Dunn 8.00
TT-94 Zach Thomas 8.00
TT-95 Barry Sanders 30.00
TT-96 Dan Marino 40.00
TT-97 Deion Sanders 15.00
TT-98 Joe Montana/50 50.00
TT-98 Joe Montana/50 Auto.
TT-99 John Elway 40.00
TT-100 Warren Moon/50 40.00
TT-100 Warren Moon/50 Auto.

2004 Playoff Abs. Mem. Tools/the Trade Materials Combo

NM/M
Common Player: 12.00
Production 75 Sets
Combos Prime: No Pricing
Production 10 Sets
TT-1 Aaron Brooks 15.00
TT-4 Anquan Boldin 15.00
TT-5 Anthony Thomas 12.00
TT-8 Brad Johnson 12.00
TT-9 Brett Favre 40.00
TT-10 Brian Urlacher 15.00
TT-13 Chad Pennington/50 20.00
TT-13 Chad Pennington/25 Auto.
TT-19 Curtis Martin 15.00
TT-20 Dante Hall/Auto. 25.00
TT-21 Daunte Culpepper 15.00
TT-23 David Carr/50 20.00
TT-23 David Carr/25 Auto.
TT-25 Donovan McNabb 20.00
TT-27 Drew Bledsoe/25 25.00
TT-27 Drew Bledsoe/50 Auto.
TT-28 Eddie George/50 15.00
TT-28 Eddie George/25 Auto.
TT-30 Emmitt Smith 30.00
TT-32 Fred Taylor 15.00
TT-34 Isaac Bruce 12.00
TT-38 Jeff Garcia 15.00
TT-41 Jerry Rice 30.00
TT-42 Jevon Kearse 12.00
TT-43 Joey Harrington 15.00
TT-44 Josh McCown/Auto. 25.00
TT-45 Julius Peppers 12.00
TT-48 Keyshawn Johnson/Auto. 25.00
TT-50 Kurt Warner 15.00
TT-52 LaDainian Tomlinson 20.00
TT-56 Marcel Shipp 12.00
TT-57 Mark Brunell 12.00
TT-58 Marshall Faulk 20.00
TT-59 Marvin Harrison 15.00
TT-62 Michael Strahan 12.00
TT-63 Michael Vick 30.00
TT-67 Peyton Manning 25.00
TT-69 Priest Holmes 20.00
TT-75 Rich Gannon 12.00
TT-77 Rod Smith 12.00
TT-79 Santana Moss/Auto. 25.00
TT-86 Tiki Barber/Auto. 25.00
TT-87 Tim Brown 15.00
TT-88 Tom Brady 25.00
TT-89 Tony Gonzalez 12.00
TT-90 Torry Holt/25 25.00
TT-90 Torry Holt/50 Auto.
TT-91 Travis Henry 12.00
TT-94 Zach Thomas 12.00
TT-95 Barry Sanders 40.00
TT-96 Dan Marino 50.00
TT-97 Deion Sanders 20.00
TT-98 Joe Montana/50 60.00
TT-98 Joe Montana/25 Auto.
TT-99 John Elway 50.00
TT-100 Warren Moon 40.00

2004 Playoff Abs. Mem. Tools of/Trade Materials Trios

NM/M
Common Player: 12.00
Production 50 Sets
Trios Prime: No Pricing
Production 5 Sets
TT-4 Anquan Boldin 15.00
TT-10 Brian Urlacher 30.00
TT-13 Chad Pennington 20.00
TT-21 Daunte Culpepper 15.00
TT-25 Donovan McNabb 20.00
TT-28 Eddie George 15.00
TT-29 Edgerrin James 20.00
TT-30 Emmitt Smith 30.00
TT-41 Jerry Rice 30.00
TT-49 Koren Robinson 12.00
TT-50 Kurt Warner 15.00
TT-58 Marshall Faulk 20.00
TT-59 Marvin Harrison 15.00
TT-63 Michael Vick 30.00
TT-67 Peyton Manning 25.00
TT-69 Priest Holmes 20.00
TT-88 Tom Brady 25.00
TT-90 Torry Holt 15.00
TT-92 Trent Green 12.00
TT-95 Barry Sanders 50.00
TT-96 Dan Marino 60.00
TT-97 Deion Sanders 25.00
TT-98 Joe Montana 75.00
TT-99 John Elway 60.00
TT-100 Warren Moon 40.00

2004 Playoff Abs. Mem. Tools of/Trade Materials Quads

No Pricing
Production 25 Sets
Quads Prime: No Pricing
Production 1 Set
TT-4 Anquan Boldin
TT-10 Brian Urlacher
TT-13 Chad Pennington
TT-19 Curtis Martin
TT-21 Daunte Culpepper
TT-25 Donovan McNabb
TT-28 Eddie George
TT-29 Edgerrin James
TT-30 Emmitt Smith
TT-34 Isaac Bruce
TT-38 Jeff Garcia
TT-41 Jerry Rice
TT-44 Josh McCown/Auto.
TT-50 Kurt Warner
TT-58 Marshall Faulk
TT-59 Marvin Harrison
TT-63 Michael Vick
TT-67 Peyton Manning
TT-69 Priest Holmes
TT-79 Santana Moss/Auto.
TT-88 Tom Brady
TT-90 Torry Holt
TT-96 Dan Marino/Auto.
TT-97 Deion Sanders
TT-99 John Elway

2004 Playoff Contenders

NM/M
Common Player (1-100): .40
Minor Stars (1-100): .60
Unlisted Stars (1-100): 1.00
Common Rookie Auto. (101-195): 10.00
Minor Rookie Auto. (101-195): 15.00
Common Coach Auto. (196-200): 20.00
Pack (5): 8.00
Box (24): 200.00
1 Anquan Boldin 1.00
2 Emmitt Smith 2.50
3 Josh McCown .40
4 Michael Vick 2.50
5 Peerless Price .60
6 T.J. Duckett .60
7 Warrick Dunn .40
8 Jamal Lewis 1.00
9 Kyle Boller 1.00
10 Ray Lewis .60
11 Drew Bledsoe 1.00
12 Eric Moulds .40
13 Travis Henry .40
14 Willis McGahee 1.00
15 DeShaun Foster .40
16 Jake Delhomme 1.00
17 Stephen Davis .60
18 Steve Smith .40
19 Brian Urlacher 1.00
20 Rex Grossman 1.00
21 Thomas Jones .60
22 Carson Palmer 1.50
23 Chad Johnson .60
24 Rudi Johnson .60
25 Jeff Garcia 1.00
26 Lee Suggs .40
27 William Green .40
28 Keyshawn Johnson .60
29 Roy Williams .60
30 Eddie George 1.00
31 Ashley Lelie .60
32 Jake Plummer .60
33 Quentin Griffin .60
34 Rod Smith .40
35 Charles Rogers 1.00
36 Joey Harrington 1.00
37 Ahman Green 1.00
38 Brett Favre 3.00
39 Javon Walker .60
40 Andre Johnson 1.00
41 David Carr 1.50
42 Domanick Davis 1.00
43 Edgerrin James 1.50
44 Marvin Harrison 1.00
45 Peyton Manning 2.00
46 Byron Leftwich 2.00
47 Fred Taylor 1.00
48 Jimmy Smith .25
49 Priest Holmes 1.50
50 Tony Gonzalez .60
51 Trent Green .40
52 A.J. Feeley .40
53 Chris Chambers 1.00
54 Deion Sanders 1.00
55 Daunte Culpepper 1.00
56 Michael Bennett 1.00
57 Randy Moss 2.00
58 Corey Dillon 1.00
59 Deion Branch .40
60 Tom Brady 2.00
61 Aaron Brooks 1.00
62 Deuce McAllister 1.00
63 Donte Stallworth .60
64 Joe Horn .40
65 Amani Toomer .60
66 Jeremy Shockey 1.00
67 Michael Strahan .40
68 Tiki Barber .40
69 Chad Pennington 1.50
70 Curtis Martin 1.00
71 Santana Moss .40
72 Jerry Porter .40
73 Jerry Rice 2.50
74 Warren Sapp .40
75 Brian Westbrook .40
76 Donovan McNabb 1.50
77 Jevon Kearse .40
78 Terrell Owens 1.00
79 Antwann Randle El .60
80 Hines Ward .60
81 Jerome Bettis .60
82 LaDainian Tomlinson 1.50
83 Kevan Barlow .40
84 Tim Rattay .60
85 Koren Robinson .40
86 Matt Hasselbeck .60
87 Shaun Alexander 1.00
88 Isaac Bruce .60
89 Marc Bulger .60
90 Marshall Faulk 1.50
91 Torry Holt 1.00
92 Brad Johnson .40
93 Mike Alstott .40
94 Chris Brown .60
95 Derrick Mason .40
96 Steve McNair 1.00
97 Clinton Portis 2.00
98 LaVar Arrington 1.00
99 Laveranues Coles .60
100 Mark Brunell .60
101 *Adimchinobe Echemandu* 10.00
102 *Ahmad Carroll* 20.00
103 *Andy Hall* 15.00
104 *B.J. Johnson* 15.00
105 *B.J. Symons* 15.00
106 *Ben Roethlisberger SP* 400.00
107 *Ben Troupe SP* 20.00
108 *Ben Watson* 20.00
109 *Bernard Berrian* 15.00
110 *Brandon Miree* 10.00
111 *Bruce Perry* 15.00
112 *Carlos Francis* 15.00
113 *Casey Bramlet* 15.00
114 *Cedric Cobbs* 20.00
115 *Chris Gamble SP* 30.00
116 *Chris Perry SP* 50.00
117 *Clarence Moore* 10.00
118 *Cody Pickett* 20.00
119 *Craig Krenzel* 20.00
120 *D.J. Hackett SP* 30.00
121 *D.J. Williams SP* 30.00
122 *Darius Watts* 30.00
123 *DeAngelo Hall* 25.00
124 *Derrick Hamilton SP* 30.00
125 *Derrick Ward* 10.00
126 *Devard Darling SP* 25.00
127 *Devery Henderson SP* 25.00
128 *Drew Carter* 10.00
129 *Drew Henson SP* 75.00
130 *Dunta Robinson* 25.00
131 *Eli Manning SP* 300.00
132 *Ernest Wilford SP* 30.00
133 *Greg Jones* 30.00
134 *J.P. Losman SP* 150.00
135 *Jamaar Taylor* 10.00
136 *Jared Lorenzen* 10.00
137 *Jarrett Payton* 15.00
138 *Jason Babin* 15.00
139 *Jeff Smoker* 25.00
140 *Jerricho Cotchery SP* 30.00
141 *Jim Sorgi* 15.00
142 *John Navarre* 20.00
143 *Johnnie Morant SP* 40.00
144 *Jonathan Vilma* 30.00
145 *Josh Harris* 20.00
146 *Julius Jones SP* 275.00
147 *Keary Colbert SP* 50.00
148 *Kellen Winslow Jr. SP*
149 Kenechi Udeze SP 20.00
150 *Kevin Jones SP* 200.00
151 *Larry Fitzgerald SP* 200.00
152 *Lee Evans SP* 100.00
153 *Luke McCown* 30.00
154 *Matt Mauck* 15.00
155 *Matt Schaub SP* 80.00
156 *Maurice Mann* 10.00
157 *Mewelde Moore SP* 40.00
158 *Michael Clayton SP* 120.00
159 *Michael Jenkins SP* 40.00
160 *Michael Turner SP* 30.00
161 *P.K. Sam SP* 30.00
162 *Philip Rivers* 120.00
163 *Quincy Wilson SP* 30.00
164 *Ran Carthon* 10.00
165 *Rashaun Woods* 25.00
166 *Reggie Williams SP* 80.00
167 *Ricardo Colclough* 20.00
168 *Robert Gallery SP* 50.00
169 *Roy Williams* 150.00
170 *Samie Parker SP* 40.00
171 *Sean Jones* 10.00
172 *Sean Taylor* 40.00
173 *Sloan Thomas* 10.00
174 *Steven Jackson SP* 200.00
175 *Tatum Bell SP* 120.00
176 *Tommie Harris SP* 40.00
177 *Triandos Luke* 10.00
178 *Troy Fleming* 10.00
179 *Vince Wilfork SP* 20.00
180 *Will Smith* 10.00
181 *Marcus Tubbs* 10.00
182 *Michael Boulware* 15.00
183 *Kris Wilson* 10.00
184 *Richard Smith* 10.00
185 *Teddy Lehman* 10.00
186 *Chris Cooley* 15.00
187 *Thomas Tapeh* 10.00
188 *Willie Parker* 20.00
189 *Patrick Crayton* 10.00
190 *Kendrick Starling* 10.00
191 *B.J. Sams* 10.00
192 *Derick Armstrong* 10.00
193 *Wes Welker* 15.00
194 *Erik Coleman* 10.00
195 *Gibril Wilson* 10.00
196 Andy Reid SP 30.00
197 Brian Billick 20.00
198 Jeff Fisher 20.00
199 Jon Gruden 20.00
200 Marvin Lewis 25.00

2004 Playoff Contenders Playoff Tickets

Veterans (1-100): .75X-2X
Production 150 Sets
Rookies (101-195): .25X-.75X
Production 50 Sets
Coaches (196-200): .25X-.75X
Production 50 Sets

2004 Playoff Contenders Championship Tickets

Cards 1-200: No Pricing
Production 1 Set

2004 Playoff Contenders Legendary Contenders

NM/M
Common Player: 3.00
Production 2,000 Sets
Red: .5X-1.25X
Production 750 Sets
Blue: .75X-2X
Production 250 Sets
Green:
Production 100 Sets
LC-1 Barry Sanders 8.00
LC-2 Don Shula 4.00
LC-3 Gale Sayers 6.00
LC-4 Herman Edwards 3.00
LC-5 Joe Montana 10.00
LC-6 Joe Namath 8.00
LC-7 Larry Csonka 4.00
LC-8 Mark Bavaro 3.00
LC-9 Michael Irvin 5.00
LC-10 Roger Staubach 8.00

2004 Playoff Contenders Legendary Contenders Autos

NM/M
Production 25 Sets
LC-1 Barry Sanders 300.00
LC-2 Don Shula 75.00
LC-3 Gale Sayers
LC-4 Herman Edwards 20.00
LC-5 Joe Montana
LC-6 Joe Namath
LC-7 Larry Csonka 100.00
LC-8 Mark Bavaro 60.00
LC-9 Michael Irvin
LC-10 Roger Staubach

2004 Playoff Contenders MVP Contenders

NM/M
Common Player: 3.00
Production 1,250 Sets
Orange: .5X-1.5X
Production 500 Sets
Green: 1X-2X
Production 250 Sets
Blue: 1.5X-3X
Production 100 Sets
MC-1 Ahman Green 4.00
MC-2 Brett Favre 10.00
MC-3 Clinton Portis 6.00
MC-4 Deuce McAllister 4.00
MC-5 Donovan McNabb 5.00
MC-6 LaDainian Tomlinson 5.00
MC-7 Matt Hasselbeck 3.00
MC-8 Priest Holmes 5.00
MC-9 Brian Urlacher 4.00
MC-10 Jake Delhomme 4.00
MC-11 Shaun Alexander 4.00
MC-12 Stephen Davis 3.00
MC-13 Steve McNair 4.00
MC-14 Tom Brady 6.00
MC-15 Torry Holt 4.00

2004 Playoff Contenders MVP Contenders Autos

NM/M
Production 25 Sets
MC-1 Ahman Green
MC-2 Brett Favre 250.00
MC-3 Clinton Portis 100.00
MC-4 Deuce McAllister
MC-5 Donovan McNabb
MC-6 LaDainian Tomlinson 80.00
MC-7 Matt Hasselbeck
MC-8 Priest Holmes
MC-9 Brian Urlacher
MC-10 Jake Delhomme
MC-11 Shaun Alexander
MC-12 Stephen Davis
MC-13 Steve McNair 120.00
MC-14 Tom Brady 250.00
MC-15 Torry Holt 60.00

2004 Playoff Contenders Rookie of the Year Contenders

NM/M
Common Player: 2.50
Production 2, 000 Sets
Blue: .5X-1.25X
Production 750 Sets
Red: 1X-2X
Production 250 Sets
Orange: 1.5X-3X
Production 100 Sets
ROY-1 Ben Roethlisberger 15.00
ROY-2 DeAngelo Hall 2.50
ROY-3 Drew Henson 4.00
ROY-4 Eli Manning 8.00
ROY-5 Kellen Winslow Jr. 4.00
ROY-6 Kevin Jones 4.00
ROY-7 Philip Rivers 6.00
ROY-8 Reggie Williams 3.00
ROY-9 Roy Williams 5.00
ROY-10 Steven Jackson 4.00

2004 Playoff Contenders ROY Contenders Autos

NM/M
Production 25 Sets
ROY-1 Ben Roethlisberger 600.00
ROY-2 DeAngelo Hall 50.00
ROY-3 Drew Henson 80.00
ROY-4 Eli Manning
ROY-5 Kellen Winslow Jr. 120.00
ROY-6 Kevin Jones
ROY-7 Philip Rivers
ROY-8 Reggie Williams
ROY-9 Roy Williams
ROY-10 Steven Jackson 150.00

2004 Playoff Contenders Rookie Round-Up

NM/M
Common Player: 1.50
Production 375 Sets
RRU-1 Eli Manning 10.00
RRU-2 Robert Gallery 2.50
RRU-3 Larry Fitzgerald 8.00
RRU-4 Philip Rivers 8.00
RRU-5 Sean Taylor 4.00
RRU-6 Kellen Winslow Jr. 4.00
RRU-7 Roy Williams 6.00
RRU-8 DeAngelo Hall 3.00
RRU-9 Reggie Williams 4.00
RRU-10 Dunta Robinson 2.00
RRU-11 Ben Roethlisberger 20.00
RRU-12 Jonathan Vilma 2.50
RRU-13 Lee Evans 4.00
RRU-14 Tommie Harris 2.50
RRU-15 Michael Clayton 4.00
RRU-16 D.J. Williams 2.50
RRU-17 Will Smith 2.00
RRU-18 Kenechi Udeze 1.50
RRU-19 Vince Wilfork 2.50
RRU-20 J.P. Losman 5.00
RRU-21 Marcus Tubbs 1.50
RRU-22 Steven Jackson 5.00
RRU-23 Ahmad Carroll 1.50
RRU-24 Chris Perry 3.00
RRU-25 Jason Babin 1.50
RRU-26 Chris Gamble 1.50
RRU-27 Michael Jenkins 3.00
RRU-28 Kevin Jones 5.00
RRU-29 Rashaun Woods 4.00
RRU-30 Ben Watson 1.50
RRU-31 Karlos Dansby 1.50
RRU-32 Teddy Lehman 2.00
RRU-33 Ricardo Colclough 1.50
RRU-34 Daryl Smith 1.50
RRU-35 Ben Troupe 1.50
RRU-36 Tatum Bell 3.00
RRU-37 Julius Jones 8.00
RRU-38 Erik Coleman 1.50
RRU-39 Dontarrious Thomas 1.50
RRU-40 Keiwan Ratliff 1.50
RRU-41 Devery Henderson 2.00
RRU-42 Michael Boulware 1.50
RRU-43 Darius Watts 2.00
RRU-44 Greg Jones 2.50
RRU-45 Madieu Williams 1.50
RRU-46 Shawntae Spencer 1.50
RRU-47 Courtney Watson 1.50
RRU-48 Keary Colbert 2.50
RRU-49 Cedric Cobbs 1.50
RRU-50 Drew Henson 5.00

2004 Playoff Contenders Round #s

NM/M
Common Player: 2.00
Cards 1-10: Production 1,500 Sets
Cards 11-15: Production 1,000 Sets
Green: .75X-1.5X
Cards 1-10: Production 750 Sets
Cards 11-15: Production 500 Sets
Orange: 1X-2X
Cards 1-10: Production 500 Sets
Cards 11-15: Production 250 Sets
Red: 2X-5X
Cards 1-10: Production 250 Sets
Cards 11-15: Production 100 Sets
RN-1 Eli Manning, Philip Rivers 10.00
RN-2 Ben Roethlisberger, J.P. Losman 15.00
RN-3 Roy Williams, Reggie Williams 6.00
RN-4 Michael Clayton, Michael Jenkins 4.00
RN-5 Steven Jackson, Kevin Jones 5.00
RN-6 Ben Troupe, Greg Jones 2.50
RN-7 Tatum Bell, Julius Jones 8.00
RN-8 Darius Watts, Keary Colbert 2.00
RN-9 Derrick Hamilton, Matt Schaub 2.00
RN-10 Bernard Berrian, Devard Darling 2.00
RN-11 Eli Manning, Philip Rivers, Ben Roethlisberger, J.P. Losman 20.00
RN-12 Reggie Williams, Chris Perry, Steven Jackson, Kevin Jones 15.00
RN-13 Roy Williams, Lee Evans, Michael Clayton, Michael Jenkins 12.00
RN-14 Tatum Bell, Julius Jones, Greg Jones, Keary Colbert 15.00
RN-15 Derrick Hamilton, Matt Schaub, Bernard Berrian, Devard Darling 10.00

2004 Playoff Contenders Rounds #s Autos

NM/M
Common Card: 30.00
Cards 1-10: Production 100 Sets
Cards 11-15: Production 50 Sets
Autos Gold: No Pricing
Sequentially numbered to 10, 20 or 30

RN-1 Eli Manning, Philip Rivers 150.00
RN-2 Ben Roethlisberger, J.P. Losman 350.00
RN-3 Roy Williams, Reggie Williams 75.00
RN-4 Michael Clayton, Michael Jenkins 60.00
RN-5 Steven Jackson, Kevin Jones 125.00
RN-6 Ben Troupe, Greg Jones 30.00
RN-7 Tatum Bell, Julius Jones 125.00
RN-8 Darius Watts, Keary Colbert 50.00
RN-9 Derrick Hamilton, Matt Schaub 30.00
RN-10 Bernard Berrian, Devard Darling 25.00
RN-11 Eli Manning, Philip Rivers, Ben Roethlisberger, J.P. Losman 500.00
RN-12 Reggie Williams, Chris Perry, Steven Jackson, Kevin Jones 200.00
RN-13 Roy Williams, Lee Evans, Michael Clayton, Michael Jenkins 200.00
RN-14 Tatum Bell, Julius Jones, Greg Jones, Keary Colbert 200.00
RN-15 Derrick Hamilton, Matt Schaub, Bernard Berrian, Devard Darling 75.00

2004 Playoff Contenders Toe to Toe

NM/M
Common Card: 1.50
Production 375 Sets

TT-1 Anquan Boldin, Torry Holt 3.00
TT-2 Marc Bulger, Matt Hasselbeck 2.50
TT-3 Shaun Alexander, Kevan Barlow 3.00
TT-4 Emmitt Smith, Marshall Faulk 6.00
TT-5 Brett Favre, Rex Grossman 8.00
TT-6 Isaac Bruce, Koren Robinson 2.50
TT-7 Joey Harrington, Daunte Culpepper 3.00
TT-8 Michael Bennett, Ahman Green 3.00
TT-9 Randy Moss, Roy Williams 5.00
TT-10 Kevin Jones, Brian Urlacher 4.00
TT-11 Aaron Brooks, Michael Vick 6.00
TT-12 Deuce McAllister, Stephen Davis 3.00
TT-13 Brad Johnson, Jake Delhomme 3.00
TT-14 Joe Horn, Steve Smith 1.50
TT-15 Michael Clayton, Michael Jenkins 2.00
TT-16 Julius Jones, Tiki Barber 5.00
TT-17 Eli Manning, Mark Brunell 6.00
TT-18 Laveranues Coles, Amani Toomer 2.50
TT-19 Terrell Owens, Keyshawn Johnson 3.00
TT-20 Roy Williams, Sean Taylor 3.00
TT-21 Brian Westbrook, Clinton Portis 5.00
TT-22 Donovan McNabb, Eddie George 4.00
TT-23 Jevon Kearse, Michael Strahan 1.50
TT-24 Jeremy Shockey, LaVar Arrington 3.00
TT-25 LaDainian Tomlinson, Priest Holmes 4.00
TT-26 Philip Rivers, Trent Green 6.00
TT-27 Rod Smith, Jerry Rice 6.00
TT-28 Antonio Gates, Tony Gonzalez 2.50
TT-29 Charles Woodson, Champ Bailey 1.50
TT-30 Jamal Lewis, Rudi Johnson 3.00
TT-31 Jeff Garcia, Carson Palmer 4.00
TT-32 Kyle Boller, Ben Roethlisberger 10.00
TT-33 Kendrell Bell, Ray Lewis 2.50
TT-34 Todd Heap, Kellen Winslow Jr. 3.00
TT-35 Hines Ward, Chad Johnson 2.50
TT-36 Peter Warrick, Antwann Randle El 2.50
TT-37 Andre Johnson, Marvin Harrison 3.00
TT-38 David Carr, Byron Leftwich 5.00
TT-39 Peyton Manning, Steve McNair 5.00
TT-40 Edgerrin James, Fred Taylor 4.00
TT-41 Domanick Davis, Chris Brown 3.00
TT-42 Tyrone Calico, Reggie Williams 1.50
TT-43 Tom Brady, Drew Bledsoe 5.00
TT-44 Chad Pennington, A.J. Feeley 4.00
TT-45 Willis McGahee, Curtis Martin 3.00
TT-46 Corey Dillon, Travis Henry 2.50
TT-47 Santana Moss, Chris Chambers 3.00
TT-48 Zach Thomas, Tedy Bruschi 1.50
TT-49 Deion Branch, Lee Evans 3.00
TT-50 Justin McCareins, Eric Moulds 1.50

2004 Playoff Hogg Heaven

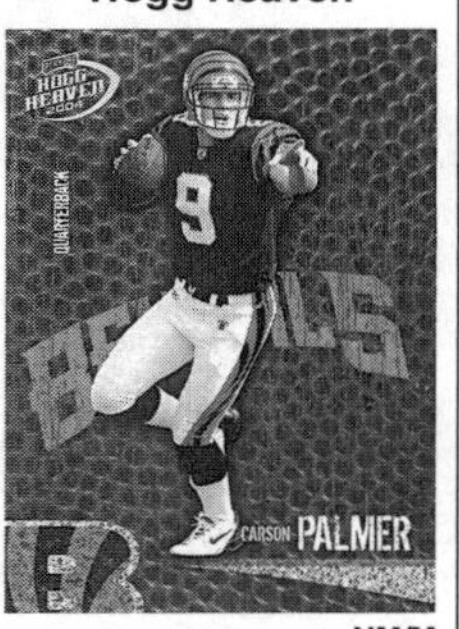

NM/M
Common Player (1-100): .30
Minor Stars (1-100): .60
Unlisted Stars (1-100): 1.00
Common Rookie (101-150): 3.00
Production 750 Sets
Common Rookie (151-180): 6.00
Production 750 Sets
Pack: 6.50
Box (12): 55.00

1 Anquan Boldin 1.00
2 Emmitt Smith 2.50
3 Josh McCown .30
4 Michael Vick 2.50
5 Peerless Price .60
6 T.J. Duckett .60
7 Jamal Lewis 1.00
8 Kyle Boller 1.00
9 Ray Lewis .60
10 Terrell Owens 1.00
11 Drew Bledsoe 1.00
12 Eric Moulds .30
13 Travis Henry .30
14 Jake Delhomme 1.00
15 Stephen Davis .60
16 Steve Smith .30
17 Anthony Thomas .60
18 Brian Urlacher 1.00
19 Rex Grossman 1.00
20 Carson Palmer 1.50
21 Chad Johnson .60
22 Peter Warrick .60
23 Rudi Johnson .60
24 Andre Davis .60
25 Lee Suggs .30
26 Keyshawn Johnson .60
27 Quincy Carter 1.00
28 Roy Williams .60
29 Ashley Lelie .60
30 Jake Plummer .60
31 Rod Smith .30
32 Charles Rogers 1.00
33 Joey Harrington 1.00
34 Ahman Green 1.00
35 Brett Favre 3.00
36 Javon Walker .60
37 Andre Johnson 1.00
38 David Carr 1.50
39 Domanick Davis 1.00
40 Edgerrin James 1.50
41 Marvin Harrison 1.00
42 Peyton Manning 2.00
43 Reggie Wayne .30
44 Byron Leftwich 2.00
45 Fred Taylor 1.00
46 Jimmy Smith .30
47 Priest Holmes 1.50
48 Tony Gonzalez .60
49 Trent Green .30
50 A.J. Feeley .30
51 Chris Chambers 1.00
52 Ricky Williams 1.00
53 Zach Thomas .30
54 Daunte Culpepper 1.00
55 Michael Bennett 1.00
56 Randy Moss 2.00
57 Deion Branch .30
58 Tom Brady 2.00
59 Ty Law .30
60 Aaron Brooks 1.00
61 Deuce McAllister 1.00
62 Joe Horn .30
63 Jeremy Shockey 1.00
64 Kerry Collins .30
65 Michael Strahan .30
66 Tiki Barber .30
67 Chad Pennington 1.50
68 Curtis Martin 1.00
69 Santana Moss .30
70 Jerry Rice 2.50
71 Rich Gannon .60
72 Tim Brown 1.00
73 Brian Westbrook .30
74 Donovan McNabb 1.50
75 Jevon Kearse .30
76 Hines Ward .60
77 Jerome Bettis .60
78 Kendrell Bell .30
79 David Boston 1.00
80 Drew Brees .60
81 LaDainian Tomlinson 1.50
82 Jeff Garcia 1.00
83 Kevan Barlow .30
84 Tim Rattay .30
85 Koren Robinson .30
86 Matt Hasselbeck .60
87 Shaun Alexander 1.00
88 Isaac Bruce .60
89 Marc Bulger .60
90 Marshall Faulk 1.50
91 Torry Holt 1.00
92 Brad Johnson .30
93 Keenan McCardell .30
94 Warren Sapp .30
95 Derrick Mason .30
96 Steve McNair 1.00
97 Eddie George 1.00
98 Clinton Portis 2.00
99 Laveranues Coles .60
100 Mark Brunell .60
101 *Adimchinobe Echemandu* 3.00
102 *Ahmad Carroll* 5.00
103 *Andy Hall* 3.00
104 *B.J. Symons* 3.00
105 *Bradlee Van Pelt* 3.00
106 *Brandon Miree* 3.00
107 *Bruce Perry* 3.00
108 *Carlos Francis* 3.00
109 *Casey Bramlet* 5.00
110 *Chris Gamble* 5.00
111 *Clarence Moore* 3.00
112 *Cody Pickett* 3.00
113 *Craig Krenzel* 8.00
114 *D.J. Hackett* 3.00
115 *D.J. Williams* 8.00
116 *Derrick Ward* 3.00
117 *Drew Carter* 3.00
118 *Ernest Wilford* 5.00
119 *Drew Henson* 12.00
120 *Jamaar Taylor* 3.00
121 *Jared Lorenzen* 5.00
122 *Jarrett Payton* 8.00
123 *Jason Babin* 5.00
124 *Jeff Smoker* 8.00
125 *Jeris McIntyre* 3.00
126 *Jerricho Cotchery* 5.00
127 *Jim Sorgi* 3.00
128 *John Navarre* 8.00
129 *Johnnie Morant* 5.00
130 *Sean Taylor* 10.00
131 *Jonathan Vilma* 8.00
132 *Josh Harris* 5.00
133 *Kenechi Udeze* 5.00
134 *Marcus Tubbs* 3.00
135 *Mark Jones* 3.00
136 *Matt Mauck* 3.00
137 *Maurice Mann* 3.00
138 *Michael Turner* 3.00
139 *P.K. Sam* 5.00
140 *Patrick Crayton* 3.00
141 *Quincy Wilson* 5.00
142 *Ran Carthon* 3.00
143 *Ryan Krause* 3.00
144 *Samie Parker* 3.00
145 *Sloan Thomas* 3.00
146 *Tommie Harris* 5.00
147 *Triandos Luke* 3.00
148 *Troy Fleming* 3.00
149 *Vince Wilfork* 5.00
150 *Will Smith* 5.00
151 *Larry Fitzgerald* 20.00
152 *DeAngelo Hall* 10.00
153 *Matt Schaub* 6.00
154 *Michael Jenkins* 10.00
155 *Devard Darling* 6.00
156 *J.P. Losman* 15.00
157 *Lee Evans* 12.00
158 *Keary Colbert* 6.00
159 *Bernard Berrian* 6.00
160 *Chris Perry* 10.00
161 *Kellen Winslow Jr.* 12.00
162 *Luke McCown* 6.00
163 *Julius Jones* 15.00
164 *Darius Watts* 6.00
165 *Tatum Bell* 10.00
166 *Kevin Jones* 15.00
167 *Roy Williams* 20.00
168 *Greg Jones* 8.00
169 *Reggie Williams* 12.00
170 *Ben Watson* 6.00
171 *Cedric Cobbs* 6.00
172 *Devery Henderson* 6.00
173 *Eli Manning* 30.00
174 *Ben Roethlisberger* 40.00
175 *Philip Rivers* 25.00
176 *Derrick Hamilton* 6.00
177 *Rashaun Woods* 12.00
178 *Steven Jackson* 15.00
179 *Michael Clayton* 12.00
180 *Ben Troupe* 6.00

2004 Playoff Hogg Heaven Hogg Wild

Current (1-100): 3X-5X
Production 250 Sets
Rookies (101-150): 1X-3X
Production 125 Sets
Rookies (151-180): No Pricing
Production 25 Sets

A player's name in *italic* type indicates a rookie card.

2004 Playoff Hogg Heaven Accent

No Pricing
Production 25 Sets

A-1 Andre Johnson
A-2 Brian Urlacher
A-3 Byron Leftwich
A-4 Carson Palmer
A-5 Clinton Portis
A-6 Daunte Culpepper
A-7 David Carr
A-8 Deuce McAllister
A-9 Edgerrin James
A-10 Emmitt Smith
A-11 Jake Delhomme
A-12 Jeremy Shockey
A-13 Jerry Rice
A-14 Joey Harrington
A-15 LaDainian Tomlinson
A-16 Marvin Harrison
A-17 Matt Hasselbeck
A-18 Michael Vick
A-19 Peyton Manning
A-20 Priest Holmes
A-21 Randy Moss
A-22 Roy Williams
A-23 Santana Moss
A-24 Stephen Davis
A-25 Tom Brady

2004 Playoff Hogg Heaven Branded

NM/M
Common Player: 1.50
Production 1250 Sets

B-1 Ahman Green 2.00
B-2 Andre Johnson 2.00
B-3 Anquan Boldin 2.00
B-4 Brian Urlacher 2.00
B-5 Byron Leftwich 4.00
B-6 Carson Palmer 3.00
B-7 Clinton Portis 4.00
B-8 Daunte Culpepper 2.00
B-9 David Carr 3.00
B-10 Deuce McAllister 2.00
B-11 Edgerrin James 3.00
B-12 Jake Delhomme 2.00
B-13 Jeremy Shockey 2.00
B-14 Joey Harrington 2.00
B-15 LaDainian Tomlinson 3.00
B-16 Marvin Harrison 2.00
B-17 Matt Hasselbeck 1.50
B-18 Priest Holmes 3.00
B-19 Randy Moss 3.00
B-20 Roy Williams 1.50
B-21 Santana Moss 1.50
B-22 Shaun Alexander 2.00
B-23 Stephen Davis 1.50
B-24 Tom Brady 4.00
B-25 Torry Holt 2.00

2004 Playoff Hogg Heaven Hogg of Fame

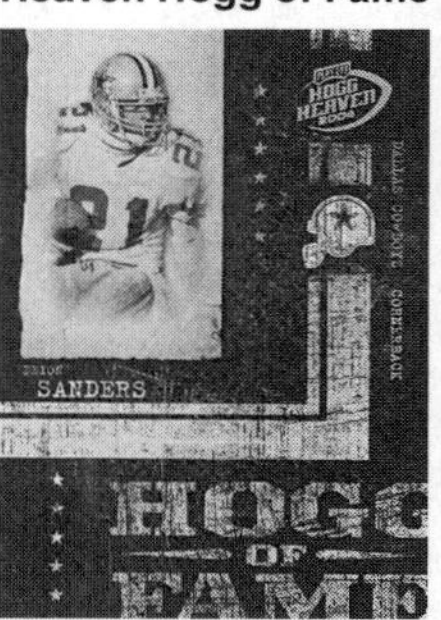

NM/M
Common Player: 1.50
Inserted 1:12
Materials Bronze: 4X-6X
Production 150 Sets
Materials Silver: 5X-8X
Production 75 Sets
Production 25 Sets
Materials Platinum: No Pricing
Production 1 Set

HF-1 Brett Favre 5.00
HF-2 Chad Pennington 2.00
HF-3 Clinton Portis 3.00
HF-4 David Carr 2.00
HF-5 Deion Sanders 1.50
HF-6 Donovan McNabb 2.00
HF-7 Drew Bledsoe 1.50
HF-8 Emmitt Smith 4.00
HF-9 Jamal Lewis 1.50
HF-10 Jerry Rice 4.00
HF-11 Jim Kelly 2.00
HF-12 Joe Montana 5.00
HF-13 Joey Harrington 1.50
HF-14 Marshall Faulk 2.00
HF-15 Marvin Harrison 1.50
HF-16 Michael Irvin 1.50
HF-17 Michael Vick 4.00
HF-18 Michael Singletary 1.50
HF-19 Peyton Manning 2.00
HF-20 Ricky Williams 1.50
HF-21 Steve McNair 1.50
HF-22 Terrell Davis 1.50
HF-23 Terrell Owens 1.50
HF-24 Tom Brady 3.00
HF-25 Warren Moon 1.50

2004 Playoff Hogg Heaven Leather in Leather

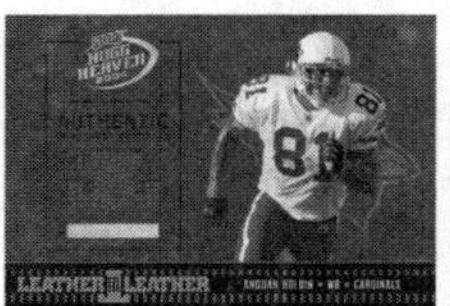

NM/M
Common Player: 6.00
Production 250 Sets
Laces in Leather: No Pricing
Production 25 Sets

LL-1 Ahman Green 10.00
LL-2 Anquan Boldin 10.00
LL-3 Chad Johnson 8.00
LL-4 Donovan McNabb 12.00
LL-5 Emmitt Smith 20.00
LL-6 Jamal Lewis 10.00
LL-7 Jeff Garcia 10.00
LL-8 Kevan Barlow 6.00
LL-9 Koren Robinson 6.00
LL-10 Marc Bulger 8.00
LL-11 Matt Hasselbeck 8.00
LL-12 Randy Moss 15.00
LL-13 Ray Lewis 8.00
LL-14 Ricky Williams 10.00
LL-15 Rudi Johnson 8.00
LL-16 Shaun Alexander 10.00
LL-17 Steve McNair 10.00
LL-18 Steve Smith 6.00
LL-19 Terrell Owens 10.00
LL-20 Terrell Suggs 6.00
LL-21 Eli Manning 20.00
LL-22 Philip Rivers 15.00
LL-23 Ben Roethlisberger 20.00
LL-24 J.P. Losman 8.00
LL-25 Larry Fitzgerald 12.00
LL-26 Roy Williams 12.00
LL-27 Reggie Williams 8.00
LL-28 Lee Evans 8.00
LL-29 Steven Jackson 10.00
LL-30 Chris Perry 6.00
LL-31 Kevin Jones 10.00
LL-32 Tatum Bell 6.00
LL-33 Michael Clayton 8.00
LL-34 Kellen Winslow Jr. 10.00
LL-35 Michael Jenkins 6.00
LL-36 Julius Jones 8.00
LL-37 Matt Schaub 6.00
LL-38 Luke McCown 6.00
LL-39 Rashaun Woods 8.00
LL-40 Greg Jones 6.00

2004 Playoff Hogg Heaven Leather Quads

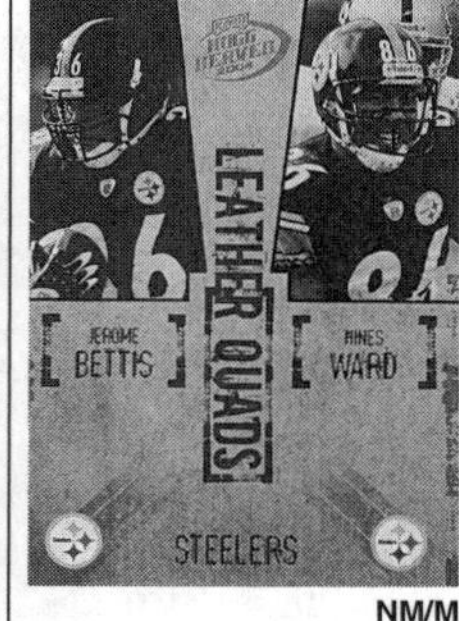

NM/M
Common Card: 1.50
Production 1,250 Sets
Single Material: 3X-5X
Production 150 Sets
Double Material: 3X-6X
Production 100 Sets
Triple Material: 5X-8X
Production 50 Sets
Quad Material: No Pricing
Production 25 Sets

LQ-1 Josh McCown, Anquan Boldin, Bryant Johnson, Marcel Shipp 2.00
LQ-2 Michael Vick, Peerless Price, T.J. Duckett, Warrick Dunn 5.00
LQ-3 Kyle Boller, Jamal Lewis, Ray Lewis, Todd Heap 2.00
LQ-4 Drew Bledsoe, Travis Henry, Eric Moulds, Josh Reed 2.00
LQ-5 Rex Grossman, Anthony Thomas, Brian Urlacher, David Terrell 2.00
LQ-6 Tim Couch, William Green, Kelly Holcomb, Dennis Northcutt 1.50
LQ-7 Brett Favre, Ahman Green, Donald Driver, Javon Walker 6.00
LQ-8 Peyton Manning, Edgerrin James, Marvin Harrison, Reggie Wayne 4.00
LQ-9 Trent Green, Priest Holmes, Dante Hall, Tony Gonzalez 3.00
LQ-10 Jay Fiedler, Ricky Williams, Chris Chambers, Zach Thomas 2.00
LQ-11 Aaron Brooks, Deuce McAllister, Donte Stallworth, Joe Horn 2.00
LQ-12 Kerry Collins, Tiki Barber, Amani Toomer, Jeremy Shockey 2.00
LQ-13 Chad Pennington, Curtis Martin, John Abraham, Shaun Ellis 3.00
LQ-14 Rich Gannon, Jerry Rice, Tim Brown, Charles Woodson 5.00
LQ-15 Donovan McNabb, Correll Buckhalter, Freddie Mitchell, Todd Pinkston 3.00
LQ-16 Jerome Bettis, Hines Ward, Kendrell Bell, Plaxico Burress 2.00
LQ-17 Doug Flutie, LaDainian Tomlinson, Drew Brees, David Boston 3.00
LQ-18 Kurt Warner, Marshall Faulk, Isaac Bruce, Torry Holt 3.00
LQ-19 Brad Johnson, Mike Alstott, Keyshawn Johnson, Warren Sapp 1.50
LQ-20 Steve McNair, Eddie George, Jevon Kearse, Derrick Mason 2.00
LQ-21 Patrick Ramsey, Laveranues Coles, Rod Gardner, LaVar Arrington 2.00
LQ-22 Eli Manning, Philip Rivers, Ben Roethlisberger, J.P. Losman 10.00
LQ-23 Larry Fitzgerald, Roy Williams, Reggie Williams, Lee Evans 8.00
LQ-24 Steven Jackson, Chris Perry, Kevin Jones, Tatum Bell 6.00
LQ-25 Michael Clayton, Kellen Winslow Jr., Michael Jenkins, Julius Jones 8.00

2004 Playoff Hogg Heaven Material Hoggs Bronze

NM/M
Common Player: 6.00
Production 150
Silver: .75X-1.5X
Production 75 Sets
Gold: No Pricing
Production 25 Sets
Platinum: No Pricing
Production 1 Set

MH-1 Aaron Brooks 10.00
MH-2 Anquan Boldin 10.00
MH-3 Brett Favre 25.00
MH-4 Brian Urlacher 10.00
MH-5 Bruce Smith 8.00
MH-6 Byron Leftwich 15.00
MH-7 Chad Johnson 8.00
MH-8 Chad Pennington 12.00
MH-9 Charles Rogers 10.00
MH-10 Clinton Portis 15.00
MH-11 Curtis Martin 10.00
MH-12 Daunte Culpepper 10.00
MH-13 David Carr 15.00
MH-14 Deuce McAllister 10.00
MH-15 Donovan McNabb 12.00
MH-16 Eddie George 10.00
MH-17 Edgerrin James 12.00
MH-18 Emmitt Smith 20.00
MH-19 Fred Taylor 10.00
MH-20 Jamal Lewis 10.00
MH-21 Jeff Garcia 10.00
MH-22 Jeremy Shockey 10.00
MH-23 Jerome Bettis 8.00

MH-24 Jerry Rice 20.00
MH-25 Jevon Kearse 8.00
MH-26 Joey Harrington 10.00
MH-27 Josh McCown 8.00
MH-28 Kendrell Bell 8.00
MH-29 Keyshawn Johnson 8.00
MH-30 Kurt Warner 10.00
MH-31 LaDainian Tomlinson 12.00
MH-32 Mark Brunell 8.00
MH-33 Marshall Faulk 12.00
MH-34 Marvin Harrison 10.00
MH-35 Michael Bennett 10.00
MH-36 Michael Vick 20.00
MH-37 Patrick Ramsey 8.00
MH-38 Peyton Manning 15.00
MH-39 Priest Holmes 12.00
MH-40 Randy Moss 15.00
MH-41 Ricky Williams 10.00
MH-42 Roy Williams 8.00
MH-43 Santana Moss 8.00
MH-44 Shaun Alexander 10.00
MH-45 Steve McNair 10.00
MH-46 Terrell Owens 10.00
MH-47 Terrell Davis 10.00
MH-48 Tiki Barber 8.00
MH-49 Tim Brown 10.00
MH-50 Torry Holt 10.00

2004 Playoff Hogg Heaven Pig Pals

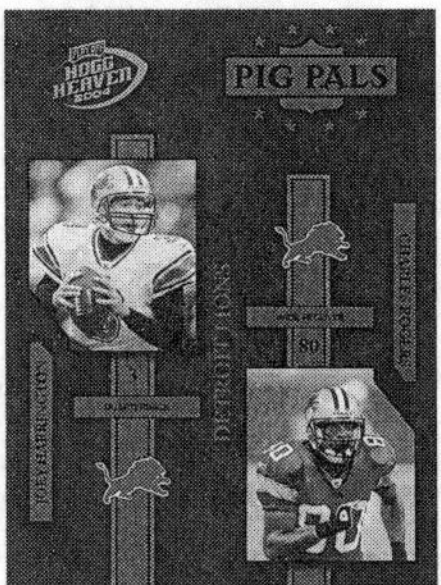

NM/M
Production 1,050 Sets
Materials: 4X-6X
Production 100 Sets
Materials Prime: No Pricing
Production 1 Set
PP-1 Anquan Boldin, Emmitt Smith 6.00
PP-2 Michael Vick, Peerless Price 6.00
PP-3 Jamal Lewis, Ray Lewis 3.00
PP-4 Drew Bledsoe, Eric Moulds 3.00
PP-5 Stephen Davis, Julius Peppers 2.50
PP-6 Brian Urlacher, Rex Grossman 3.00
PP-7 Chad Johnson, Peter Warrick 2.50
PP-8 Roy Williams, Terence Newman 2.50
PP-9 Jake Plummer, Clinton Portis 5.00
PP-10 Joey Harrington, Charles Rogers 3.00
PP-11 Brett Favre, Ahman Green 8.00
PP-12 David Carr, Andre Johnson 4.00
PP-13 Peyton Manning, Edgerrin James 5.00
PP-14 Byron Leftwich, Jimmy Smith 5.00
PP-15 Priest Holmes, Tony Gonzalez 4.00
PP-16 Ricky Williams, Zach Thomas 3.00
PP-17 Randy Moss, Michael Bennett 5.00
PP-18 Tom Brady, Ty Law 5.00
PP-19 Aaron Brooks, Deuce McAllister 3.00
PP-20 Kerry Collins, Michael Strahan 2.50
PP-21 Chad Pennington, Curtis Martin 4.00
PP-22 Jerry Rice, Tim Brown 6.00
PP-23 Donovan McNabb, Correll Buckhalter 4.00
PP-24 Jerome Bettis, Hines Ward 2.50
PP-25 Drew Brees, LaDainian Tomlinson 4.00
PP-26 Matt Hasselbeck, Koren Robinson 2.50
PP-27 Marc Bulger, Isaac Bruce 2.50
PP-28 Steve McNair, Eddie George 3.00
PP-29 Brad Johnson, Warren Sapp 2.50
PP-30 Patrick Ramsey, Laveranues Coles 2.50

2004 Playoff Hogg Heaven Pig Pens Autographs

NM/M
Common Player: 20.00
Numbered to indicated quantity
PP-1 Aaron Brooks 25.00
PP-2 Ahman Green 30.00
PP-3 Anquan Boldin 25.00
PP-4 Dante Hall 25.00
PP-5 Deuce McAllister 30.00
PP-6 Domanick Davis 20.00
PP-7 George Blanda 25.00
PP-8 Ickey Woods 20.00
PP-9 James Lofton 20.00
PP-10 Jim Brown 75.00
PP-11 Jim Plunkett 25.00
PP-12 Joe Greene 40.00
PP-13 Joe Namath 80.00
PP-14 John Riggins 50.00
PP-15 Josh McCown 20.00
PP-16 Kyle Boller 20.00
PP-17 Matt Hasselbeck 25.00
PP-18 Mel Blount 50.00
PP-19 Ozzie Newsome 25.00
PP-20 Patrick Ramsey 20.00
PP-21 Priest Holmes 50.00
PP-22 Rex Grossman 40.00
PP-23 Roy Williams 50.00
PP-24 Rudi Johnson 20.00
PP-25 Sammy Baugh 50.00
PP-26 Shaun Alexander 30.00
PP-27 Steve Smith 20.00
PP-28 Terence Newman 20.00
PP-29 Todd Heap 25.00
PP-30 Warren Moon 30.00
PP-31 Ahmad Carroll 25.00
PP-32 Bernard Berrian 25.00
PP-33 Cedric Cobbs 25.00
PP-34 D.J. Hackett 25.00
PP-35 D.J. Williams 25.00
PP-36 Devard Darling 25.00
PP-37 Dunta Robinson 25.00
PP-38 Ernest Wilford 25.00
PP-39 Jerricho Cotchery 25.00
PP-40 Johnnie Morant 25.00
PP-41 Jonathan Vilma 25.00
PP-42 Josh Harris 25.00
PP-43 Julius Jones 50.00
PP-44 Luke McCown 30.00
PP-45 Mewelde Moore 25.00
PP-46 Michael Jenkins 25.00
PP-47 Philip Rivers 80.00
PP-48 Ricardo Colclough 25.00
PP-49 Tatum Bell 40.00
PP-50 Tommie Harris 25.00

2004 Playoff Hogg Heaven Rookie Hoggs

NM/M
Common Player: 2.00
Production 750 Sets
RH-1 Eli Manning 15.00
RH-2 Robert Gallery 4.00
RH-3 Larry Fitzgerald 10.00
RH-4 Philip Rivers 12.00
RH-5 Sean Taylor 6.00
RH-6 Kellen Winslow Jr. 8.00
RH-7 Roy Williams 10.00
RH-8 DeAngelo Hall 5.00
RH-9 Reggie Williams 6.00
RH-10 Dunta Robinson 3.00
RH-11 Ben Roethlisberger 20.00
RH-12 Jonathan Vilma 4.00
RH-13 Lee Evans 6.00
RH-14 Tommie Harris 4.00
RH-15 Michael Clayton 6.00
RH-16 D.J. Williams 4.00
RH-17 Will Smith 3.00
RH-18 Kenechi Udeze 2.00
RH-19 Vince Wilfork 4.00
RH-20 J.P. Losman 6.00
RH-21 Marcus Tubbs 2.00
RH-22 Steven Jackson 8.00
RH-23 Ahmad Carroll 2.00
RH-24 Chris Perry 5.00
RH-25 Jason Babin 2.00
RH-26 Chris Gamble 3.00
RH-27 Michael Jenkins 5.00
RH-28 Kevin Jones 8.00
RH-29 Rashaun Woods 6.00
RH-30 Ben Watson 2.00
RH-31 Ben Troupe 2.00
RH-32 Tatum Bell 5.00
RH-33 Julius Jones 5.00
RH-34 Ernest Wilford 2.00
RH-35 Devery Henderson 3.00
RH-36 Darius Watts 3.00
RH-37 Greg Jones 4.00
RH-38 Sean Jones 2.00
RH-39 Keary Colbert 3.00
RH-40 Derrick Hamilton 2.00
RH-41 Bernard Berrian 3.00
RH-42 Devard Darling 3.00
RH-43 Matt Schaub 3.00
RH-44 Carlos Francis 2.00
RH-45 Samie Parker 2.00
RH-46 Luke McCown 3.00
RH-47 Jerricho Cotchery 2.00
RH-48 Mewelde Moore 2.00
RH-49 Cedric Cobbs 3.00
RH-50 Drew Henson 8.00

2004 Playoff Hogg Heaven Rookie Hoggs Signatures

NM/M
Common Player: 20.00
Production 150 Sets
RH-2 Robert Gallery 30.00
RH-4 Philip Rivers 60.00
RH-7 Roy Williams 100.00
RH-8 DeAngelo Hall 30.00
RH-10 Dunta Robinson 30.00
RH-13 Lee Evans 40.00
RH-15 Michael Clayton 40.00
RH-20 J.P. Losman 50.00
RH-24 Chris Perry 30.00
RH-27 Michael Jenkins 25.00
RH-30 Ben Watson 25.00
RH-31 Ben Troupe 20.00
RH-32 Tatum Bell 30.00
RH-33 Julius Jones 40.00
RH-35 Devery Henderson 25.00
RH-36 Darius Watts 20.00
RH-37 Greg Jones 25.00
RH-39 Keary Colbert 30.00
RH-40 Derrick Hamilton 25.00
RH-41 Bernard Berrian 25.00
RH-42 Devard Darling 20.00
RH-46 Luke McCown 20.00
RH-48 Mewelde Moore 30.00
RH-49 Cedric Cobbs 25.00

2004 Playoff Hogg Heaven Unsung Heroes

NM/M
Production 1,250
UH-1 Keith Brooking 2.00
UH-2 Ed Reed 2.00
UH-3 Takeo Spikes 3.00
UH-4 Kris Jenkins 2.00
UH-5 Marty Booker 3.00
UH-6 Quincy Morgan 2.00
UH-7 Dat Nguyen 3.00
UH-8 Al Wilson 2.00
UH-9 Kabeer Gbaja-Biamila 2.00
UH-10 Dwight Freeney 2.00
UH-11 Marcus Stroud 2.00
UH-12 Tony Richardson 2.00
UH-13 Patrick Surtain 2.00
UH-14 Jim Kleinsasser 2.00
UH-15 Tedy Bruschi 4.00
UH-16 Michael Lewis 2.00
UH-17 Tyrone Wheatley 2.00
UH-18 Brian Dawkins 2.00
UH-19 Joey Porter 2.00
UH-20 Julian Peterson 2.00
UH-21 Darrell Jackson 3.00
UH-22 Keenan McCardell 2.00
UH-23 Joe Jurevicius 2.00
UH-24 Keith Bulluck 2.00
UH-25 Darnerian McCants 2.00

2004 Playoff Honors

NM/M
Common Player (1-100): .40
Minor Stars (1-100): .60
Unlisted Stars (1-100): 1.00
Common Rookie (101-150): 3.00
Unlisted Rookie (101-150): 4.00
Production 750 Sets (hobby only)
Common Rookie (151-200): 3.00
Production 425 Sets (retail only)
Common Rookie (201-233): 5.00
Production 750 Sets
Pack (6): 7.00
Box (12): 60.00
1 Anquan Boldin 1.00
2 Emmitt Smith 2.50
3 Josh McCown .40
4 Michael Vick 2.50
5 Peerless Price .60
6 T.J. Duckett .60
7 Warrick Dunn .40
8 Jamal Lewis 1.00
9 Kyle Boller 1.00
10 Ray Lewis .60
11 Drew Bledsoe 1.00
12 Eric Moulds .40
13 Travis Henry .40
14 DeShaun Foster .40
15 Jake Delhomme 1.00
16 Steve Smith .40
17 Stephen Davis .60
18 Brian Urlacher 1.00
19 Rex Grossman 1.00
20 Thomas Jones .60
21 Carson Palmer 1.50
22 Chad Johnson .60
23 Rudi Johnson .60
24 Jeff Garcia 1.00
25 Lee Suggs .40
26 Keyshawn Johnson .60
27 Quincy Carter 1.00
28 Roy Williams .60
29 Jake Plummer .60
30 Quentin Griffin .40
31 Rod Smith .40
32 Charles Rogers 1.00
33 Joey Harrington 1.00
34 Ahman Green 1.00
35 Brett Favre 3.00
36 Javon Walker .60
37 Andre Johnson 1.00
38 David Carr 1.50
39 Domanick Davis 1.00
40 Edgerrin James 1.50
41 Marvin Harrison 1.00
42 Peyton Manning 2.00
43 Byron Leftwich 2.00
44 Fred Taylor 1.00
45 Jimmy Smith .40
46 Priest Holmes 1.50
47 Tony Gonzalez .60
48 Trent Green .40
49 A.J. Feeley .40
50 Chris Chambers 1.00
51 Ricky Williams 1.00
52 Daunte Culpepper 1.00
53 Michael Bennett 1.00
54 Randy Moss 2.00
55 Corey Dillon .60
56 Deion Branch .40
57 Tom Brady 2.00
58 Aaron Brooks 1.00
59 Deuce McAllister 1.00
60 Joe Horn .40
61 Jeremy Shockey 1.00
62 Michael Strahan .40
63 Tiki Barber .40
64 Chad Pennington 1.50
65 Curtis Martin 1.00
66 Santana Moss .40
67 Jerry Rice 2.50
68 Justin Fargas .40
69 Kerry Collins .40
70 Tim Brown 1.00
71 Brian Westbrook .40
72 Donovan McNabb 1.50
73 Jevon Kearse .40
74 Terrell Owens 1.00
75 Duce Staley .40
76 Hines Ward .40
77 Jerome Bettis .60
78 Tommy Maddox .60
79 Drew Brees .60
80 LaDainian Tomlinson 1.50
81 Kevan Barlow .40
82 Tim Rattay .40
83 Koren Robinson .40
84 Matt Hasselbeck .60
85 Shaun Alexander 1.00
86 Isaac Bruce .60
87 Marc Bulger .60
88 Marshall Faulk 1.50
89 Torry Holt 1.00
90 Brad Johnson .40
91 Charlie Garner .40
92 Keenan McCardell .40
93 Chris Brown .60
94 Derrick Mason .40
95 Eddie George 1.00
96 Steve McNair 1.00
97 Clinton Portis 2.00
98 LaVar Arrington 1.00
99 Laveranues Coles .60
100 Mark Brunell .60
101 *Drew Henson* 12.00
102 *Craig Krenzel* 5.00
103 *Andy Hall* 4.00
104 *Josh Harris* 4.00
105 *Jim Sorgi* 3.00
106 *Jeff Smoker* 6.00
107 *John Navarre* 6.00
108 *Cody Pickett* 5.00
109 *Casey Bramlet* 5.00
110 *Matt Mauck* 3.00
111 *B.J. Symons* 3.00
112 *Bradlee Van Pelt* 5.00
113 *Michael Turner* 3.00
114 *Troy Fleming* 3.00
115 *Adimchinobe Echemandu* 4.00
116 *Quincy Wilson* 6.00
117 *Derrick Ward* 3.00
118 *Bruce Perry* 4.00
119 *Brandon Miree* 3.00
120 *Carlos Francis* 3.00
121 *Samie Parker* 4.00
122 *Jerricho Cotchery* 5.00
123 *Ernest Wilford* 4.00
124 *Johnnie Morant* 4.00
125 *Maurice Mann* 4.00
126 *D.J. Hackett* 4.00
127 *Drew Carter* 4.00
128 *P.K. Sam* 6.00
129 *Jamaar Taylor* 4.00
130 *Ryan Krause* 4.00
131 *Triandos Luke* 4.00
132 *Jeris McIntyre* 3.00
133 *Clarence Moore* 3.00
134 *Mark Jones* 3.00
135 *Sloan Thomas* 4.00
136 *Jonathan Smith* 4.00
137 *Patrick Crayton* 4.00
138 *Derek Abney* 3.00
139 *Kris Wilson* 4.00
140 *Sean Taylor* 10.00
141 *Jonathan Vilma* 6.00
142 *Tommie Harris* 6.00
143 *D.J. Williams* 6.00
144 *Will Smith* 5.00
145 *Kenechi Udeze* 5.00
146 *Vince Wilfork* 6.00
147 *Marcus Tubbs* 4.00
148 *Ahmad Carroll* 5.00
149 *Jason Babin* 4.00
150 *Chris Gamble* 5.00
151 *Willie Parker* 3.00
152 *Darnell Dockett* 3.00
153 *Nate Poole* 3.00
154 *Matt Kegel* 3.00
155 *Kendrick Starling* 3.00
156 *Tramon Douglas* 3.00
157 *Ryan Dinwiddie* 3.00
158 *Brian Gaither* 3.00
159 *Ran Carthon* 3.00
160 *Derick Armstrong* 3.00
161 *Chris Cooley* 4.00
162 *Casey Clausen* 4.00
163 *Omar Jenkins* 8.00
164 *Justin Jenkins* 3.00
165 *Wes Welker* 8.00
166 *Terrance Copper* 8.00
167 *Jarrett Payton* 6.00
168 *Zamir Cobb* 3.00
169 *Derrick Knight* 3.00
170 *Romby Bryant* 3.00
171 *Larry Croom* 3.00
172 *Thomas Tapeh* 3.00
173 *Brock Lesnar* 10.00
174 *Richard Smith* 4.00
175 *Ricky Ray* 3.00
176 *John Booth* 3.00
177 *Huey Whittaker* 3.00
178 *Fred Russell* 3.00
179 *Ben Hartsock* 3.00
180 *Tim Euhus* 8.00
181 *Ricardo Colclough* 4.00
182 *Keiwan Ratliff* 3.00
183 *Shawntae Spencer* 3.00
184 *Joey Thomas* 3.00
185 *Keith Smith* 3.00
186 *Derrick Strait* 3.00
187 *Jeremy LeSueur* 3.00
188 *Matt Ware* 3.00
189 *Rich Gardner* 3.00
190 *Daryl Smith* 3.00
191 *Dontarrious Thomas* 3.00
192 *Courtney Watson* 3.00
193 *Karlos Dansby* 4.00
194 *Teddy Lehman* 5.00
195 *Michael Boulware* 5.00
196 *Bob Sanders* 3.00
197 *Travis LaBoy* 3.00
198 *Antwan Odom* 3.00
199 *Marquise Hill* 3.00
200 *Terry Johnson* 3.00
201 *Larry Fitzgerald Jersey* 15.00
202 *DeAngelo Hall Jersey* 8.00
203 *Matt Schaub Jersey* 5.00
204 *Michael Jenkins Jersey* 8.00
205 *Devard Darling Jersey* 5.00
206 *J.P. Losman Jersey* 12.00
207 *Lee Evans Jersey* 10.00
208 *Keary Colbert Jersey* 5.00
209 *Bernard Berrian Jersey* 5.00
210 *Chris Perry Jersey* 8.00
211 *Kellen Winslow Jr. Jersey* 10.00
212 *Luke McCown Jersey* 5.00
213 *Julius Jones Jersey* 15.00
214 *Darius Watts Jersey* 5.00
215 *Tatum Bell Jersey* 8.00
216 *Kevin Jones Jersey* 15.00
217 *Roy Williams Jersey* 15.00
218 *Dunta Robinson Jersey* 5.00
219 *Greg Jones Jersey* 6.00
220 *Reggie Williams Jersey* 10.00
221 *Mewelde Moore Jersey* 5.00
222 *Ben Watson Jersey* 5.00
223 *Cedric Cobbs Jersey* 5.00
224 *Devery Henderson Jersey* 5.00
225 *Eli Manning Jersey* 30.00
226 *Robert Gallery Jersey* 8.00
227 *Ben Roethlisberger Jersey* 60.00
228 *Philip Rivers Jersey* 15.00
229 *Derrick Hamilton Jersey* 5.00
230 *Rashaun Woods Jersey* 10.00
231 *Steven Jackson Jersey* 12.00
232 *Michael Clayton Jersey* 10.00
233 *Ben Troupe Jersey* 5.00

2004 Playoff Honors Os

Veterans (1-100): 2X-4X
Production 175 Sets (retail)
Rookies (151-200): 1X-3X
Production 100 Sets (retail)
Rookies (201-233): No Pricing
Production 25 Sets (retail)

2004 Playoff Honors Xs

Veterans (1-100): 2X-5X
Production 199 Sets (hobby)
Rookies (101-150): 1X-2X
Production 99 Sets (hobby)
Rookies (201-233): No Pricing
Production 25 Sets (hobby)

2004 Playoff Honors Accolades

NM/M
Common Player: 3.00
Production 1,000 Sets
Die-Cut: No Pricing
Production 5 Sets
A-1 Aaron Brooks 4.00
A-2 Ahman Green 4.00
A-3 Andre Johnson 4.00
A-4 Anquan Boldin 4.00
A-5 Barry Sanders 10.00
A-6 Brett Favre 10.00
A-7 Brian Urlacher 4.00
A-8 Byron Leftwich 6.00
A-9 Carson Palmer 5.00
A-10 Chad Johnson 3.00
A-11 Chad Pennington 5.00
A-12 Chris Chambers 4.00
A-13 Clinton Portis 6.00
A-14 Daunte Culpepper 4.00
A-15 David Carr 5.00
A-16 Deuce McAllister 4.00
A-17 Domanick Davis 4.00
A-18 Donovan McNabb 5.00
A-19 Drew Bledsoe 4.00
A-20 Edgerrin James 5.00
A-21 Emmitt Smith 8.00
A-22 Fred Taylor 4.00
A-23 Jack Lambert 6.00
A-24 Jake Delhomme 4.00
A-25 Jake Plummer 3.00
A-26 Jamal Lewis 4.00
A-27 Jeremy Shockey 4.00
A-28 Jerry Rice 8.00
A-29 Jim Brown 6.00
A-30 Joe Namath 8.00
A-31 Joey Harrington 4.00
A-32 John Riggins 4.00
A-33 LaDainian Tomlinson 5.00
A-34 Marc Bulger 3.00
A-35 Marshall Faulk 5.00
A-36 Marvin Harrison 4.00
A-37 Matt Hasselbeck 3.00
A-38 Michael Vick 8.00
A-39 Peyton Manning 6.00
A-40 Priest Holmes 5.00
A-41 Randy Moss 6.00
A-42 Ray Lewis 3.00
A-43 Rex Grossman 4.00
A-44 Ricky Williams 4.00
A-45 Shaun Alexander 4.00
A-46 Steve McNair 4.00
A-47 Terrell Owens 4.00
A-48 Tom Brady 6.00
A-49 Torry Holt 4.00
A-50 Travis Henry 3.00

2004 Playoff Honors Alma Mater Materials

NM/M
Common Card: 8.00
Cards 26-35: Production 100 Sets
Cards 36-40: No Pricing
Production 25 Sets
AM-1 Aaron Brooks 10.00
AM-2 Anquan Boldin 10.00
AM-3 Laveranues Coles 8.00
AM-4 Ahman Green 12.00
AM-5 Barry Sanders 30.00
AM-6 Ricky Williams 12.00
AM-7 Drew Bledsoe 12.00
AM-8 Reggie Williams 8.00
AM-9 Marshall Faulk 12.00
AM-10 Steven Jackson 15.00
AM-11 DeShaun Foster 8.00
AM-12 Keyshawn Johnson 8.00
AM-13 Carson Palmer 12.00
AM-14 Kyle Boller 10.00
AM-15 Doug Flutie 15.00
AM-16 Edgerrin James 15.00
AM-17 Clinton Portis 15.00
AM-18 Jeremy Shockey 10.00
AM-19 Santana Moss 8.00
AM-20 Curtis Martin 10.00
AM-21 Andre Johnson 10.00
AM-22 Herschel Walker 20.00
AM-23 Shaun Alexander 12.00
AM-24 Fred Taylor 10.00
AM-25 Eddie George 10.00
AM-26 Anquan Boldin, Aaron Brooks 15.00
AM-27 Barry Sanders, Ahman Green 40.00
AM-28 Drew Bledsoe, Reggie Williams 20.00
AM-29 Marshall Faulk, Steven Jackson 30.00
AM-30 Dan Morgan, DeShaun Foster 15.00
AM-31 Carson Palmer, Kyle Boller 20.00
AM-32 Edgerrin James, Andre Johnson 20.00
AM-33 Laveranues Coles, Clinton Portis 20.00
AM-34 Jeremy Shockey, Santana Moss 20.00
AM-35 Herschel Walker, Shaun Alexander 25.00
AM-36 Aaron Brooks, Anquan Boldin, Laveranues Coles
AM-37 Barry Sanders, Ahman Green, Ricky Williams
AM-38 Drew Bledsoe, Reggie Williams, Steven Jackson
AM-39 Carson Palmer, Kyle Boller, Doug Flutie
AM-40 Edgerrin James, Jeremy Shockey, Clinton Portis

2004 Playoff Honors Class Reunion

NM/M
Common Card: 2.00
Production 1,500 Sets
Class Reunion Materials: 2X-4X
Production 150 Sets
CR-1 Emmitt Smith, Shannon Sharpe 6.00
CR-2 Brett Favre, Keenan McCardell 6.00
CR-3 Jerome Bettis, Mark Brunell 2.00
CR-4 Marshall Faulk, Charlie Garner 4.00
CR-5 Steve McNair, Ty Law 3.00
CR-6 Terrell Owens, Ray Lewis 3.00
CR-7 Marvin Harrison, Eric Moulds 3.00
CR-8 Eddie George, Stephen Davis 3.00
CR-9 Ahman Green, Matt Hasselbeck 3.00
CR-10 Priest Holmes, Charles Woodson 4.00
CR-11 Peyton Manning, Fred Taylor 5.00
CR-12 Randy Moss, Hines Ward 5.00
CR-13 Ricky Williams, David Boston 3.00
CR-14 Donovan McNabb, Jevon Kearse 4.00
CR-15 Daunte Culpepper, Aaron Brooks 3.00
CR-16 Edgerrin James, Torry Holt 4.00
CR-17 Tom Brady, Chad Pennington 5.00
CR-18 Marc Bulger, Shaun Alexander 3.00
CR-19 LaVar Arrington, Laveranues Coles 3.00
CR-20 Jamal Lewis, Keith Bulluck 3.00
CR-21 Brian Urlacher, Thomas Jones 3.00

CR-22 Michael Vick, Deuce McAllister 6.00
CR-23 LaDainian Tomlinson, Travis Henry 4.00
CR-24 Clinton Portis, Jeremy Shockey 5.00
CR-25 Joey Harrington, Javon Walker 3.00
CR-26 David Carr, Josh McCown 4.00
CR-27 Andre Johnson, Charles Rogers 3.00
CR-28 Anquan Boldin, Terrell Suggs 3.00
CR-29 Byron Leftwich, Tyrone Calico 5.00
CR-30 Kyle Boller, Rex Grossman 3.00

2004 Playoff Honors Fans of the Game

NM/M
Common Card: 2.00
234 Ray Romano Giants 3.00
234 Ray Romano Jets 3.00
235 Darius Rucker 3.00
236 Mel Kiper 2.00
237 Chris Mortensen 2.00
238 John O'Hurley 2.00

2004 Playoff Honors Fans of the Game Autographs

NM/M
Common Card: 20.00
234 Ray Romano Giants 20.00
234 Ray Romano Jets 20.00
235 Darius Rucker 60.00
236 Mel Kiper 30.00
237 Chris Mortensen 20.00
238 John O'Hurley 40.00

2004 Playoff Honors Game Day

NM/M
Common Player: 1.50
Production 1,750 Sets
Game Day Souvenirs: 2X-5X
Production 250 Sets
Souvenirs Prime: No Pricing
Production 25 Sets
GS-1 Ahman Green 2.00
GS-2 Anquan Boldin 2.00
GS-3 Brett Favre 6.00
GS-4 Chad Johnson 1.50
GS-5 Daunte Culpepper 2.00
GS-6 Donovan McNabb 3.00
GS-7 Eddie George 2.00
GS-8 Emmitt Smith 5.00
GS-9 Jamal Lewis 2.00
GS-10 Jerry Rice 5.00
GS-11 Koren Robinson 1.50
GS-12 LaDainian Tomlinson 3.00
GS-13 LaVar Arrington 2.00
GS-14 Marc Bulger 1.50
GS-15 Marshall Faulk 3.00
GS-16 Matt Hasselbeck 1.50
GS-17 Michael Vick 5.00
GS-18 Randy Moss 4.00
GS-19 Ray Lewis 1.50
GS-20 Ricky Williams 2.00
GS-21 Shaun Alexander 2.00
GS-22 Stephen Davis 1.50
GS-23 Steve McNair 2.00
GS-24 Terrell Suggs 1.50
GS-25 Torry Holt 2.00

2004 Playoff Honors Patches

NM/M
Common Player: 12.00
Production 75 Sets
Plates
Cards #'d from 31-50: .75X-1.5X
Cards #'d 25 or less: No Pricing
Plates and Patches: No Pricing
Production 10 Sets
PP-1 Anquan Boldin 15.00
PP-2 Brett Favre 40.00
PP-3 Brian Urlacher 15.00
PP-4 Chad Johnson 12.00
PP-5 Chad Pennington 20.00
PP-6 Clinton Portis 25.00
PP-7 Daunte Culpepper 15.00
PP-8 Deuce McAllister 15.00
PP-9 Donovan McNabb 20.00
PP-10 Drew Bledsoe 15.00
PP-11 Edgerrin James 20.00
PP-12 Emmitt Smith 30.00
PP-13 Jerry Rice 30.00
PP-14 LaDainian Tomlinson 20.00
PP-15 LaVar Arrington 50.00
PP-16 Marc Bulger 12.00
PP-17 Marshall Faulk 20.00
PP-18 Matt Hasselbeck 12.00
PP-19 Peyton Manning 25.00
PP-20 Priest Holmes 20.00
PP-21 Randy Moss 25.00
PP-22 Ricky Williams 15.00
PP-23 Shaun Alexander 15.00
PP-24 Steve McNair 15.00
PP-25 Tom Brady 25.00

2004 Playoff Honors Prime Signature Previews

NM/M
Common Player: 2.00
Production 999 Sets
PS-1 Aaron Brooks 2.50
PS-2 Adam Vinatieri 2.00
PS-3 Deacon Jones 2.00
PS-4 Domanick Davis 2.50
PS-5 Don Maynard 2.50
PS-6 George Blanda 2.50
PS-7 Herschel Walker 2.50
PS-8 Jack Lambert 3.00
PS-9 Jim Brown 4.00
PS-10 Jim Plunkett 2.50
PS-11 Joe Greene 3.00
PS-12 Joe Namath 5.00
PS-13 L.C. Greenwood 2.50
PS-14 Laveranues Coles 2.00
PS-15 Leroy Kelly 2.00
PS-16 Mel Blount 2.00
PS-17 Michael Strahan 2.00
PS-18 Paul Warfield 2.50
PS-19 Richard Dent 2.00
PS-20 Sonny Jurgensen 2.50
PS-21 Steve Smith 2.00
PS-22 Tom Brady 4.00
PS-23 Ernest Wilford 2.00
PS-24 Philip Rivers 5.00
PS-25 Samie Parker 2.00

2004 Playoff Honors Prime Signature Previews Autographs

NM/M
Common Player: 15.00
Sequentially #'d to indicated quantity
cards #'d to 25 or less: No Priced
PS-1 Aaron Brooks/25
PS-2 Adam Vinatieri/200 40.00
PS-3 Deacon Jones/125 25.00
PS-4 Domanick Davis/300 15.00
PS-5 Don Maynard/100 20.00
PS-6 George Blanda/25
PS-7 Herschel Walker/25
PS-8 Jack Lambert/25
PS-9 Jim Brown/34 125.00
PS-10 Jim Plunkett/25
PS-11 Joe Greene/25
PS-12 Joe Namath/70 75.00
PS-13 L.C. Greenwood/25
PS-14 Laveranues Coles/100 15.00
PS-15 Leroy Kelly/206 20.00
PS-16 Mel Blount/25
PS-17 Michael Strahan/25
PS-18 Paul Warfield/25
PS-19 Richard Dent/25
PS-20 Sonny Jurgensen/25
PS-21 Steve Smith/300 15.00
PS-22 Tom Brady/25
PS-23 Ernest Wilford/300 15.00
PS-24 Philip Rivers/300 40.00
PS-25 Samie Parker/300 15.00

2004 Playoff Honors Rookie Hidden Gems Autographs

NM/M
Common Player: 40.00
Production 50 Sets
201 Larry Fitzgerald 120.00
202 DeAngelo Hall 50.00
203 Matt Schaub 75.00
204 Michael Jenkins 50.00
205 Devard Darling/25 60.00
206 J.P. Losman 100.00
207 Lee Evans 80.00
208 Keary Colbert 40.00
209 Bernard Berrian 40.00
210 Chris Perry 50.00
211 Kellen Winslow Jr. 60.00
212 Luke McCown 50.00
213 Julius Jones 120.00
214 Darius Watts 40.00
215 Tatum Bell 100.00
216 Kevin Jones 80.00
217 Roy Williams 120.00
218 Dunta Robinson 40.00
219 Greg Jones 40.00
220 Reggie Williams 50.00
221 Mewelde Moore 60.00
222 Ben Watson 40.00
223 Cedric Cobbs 40.00
224 Devery Henderson 40.00
225 Eli Manning 200.00
226 Robert Gallery 40.00
227 Ben Roethlisberger 400.00
228 Philip Rivers 120.00
229 Derrick Hamilton 40.00
230 Rashaun Woods 75.00
231 Steven Jackson 80.00
232 Michael Clayton 40.00
233 Ben Troupe 40.00

2004 Playoff Honors Rookie Tandems

NM/M
Common Card: 3.00
Inserted 1:12
Jersey: 1X-3X
Inserted 1:91
Football: 2X-4X
Production 125 Sets
Jersey/Football: 2X-5X
Production 50 Sets
RT-1 Eli Manning, Julius Jones 12.00
RT-2 Michael Clayton, Keary Colbert 3.00
RT-3 Larry Fitzgerald, DeAngelo Hall 5.00
RT-4 Michael Jenkins, Matt Schaub 3.00
RT-5 Philip Rivers, Devery Henderson 5.00
RT-6 Tatum Bell, Darius Watts 4.00
RT-7 Ben Roethlisberger, Devard Darling 15.00
RT-8 Kellen Winslow Jr., Luke McCown 5.00
RT-9 Kevin Jones, Roy Williams 8.00
RT-10 Bernard Berrian, Mewelde Moore 3.00
RT-11 Greg Jones, Reggie Williams 3.00
RT-12 Dunta Robinson, Ben Troupe 3.00
RT-13 J.P. Losman, Lee Evans 5.00
RT-14 Cedric Cobbs, Ben Watson 3.00
RT-15 Steven Jackson, Chris Perry 5.00
RT-16 Rashaun Woods, Derrick Hamilton 3.00

2004 Playoff Honors Rookie Quads

NM/M
Common Card: 5.00
Production 1,250 Sets
Jersey: 3X-5X
Production 250 Sets
Football: 3X-6X
Production 75 Sets
Jersey/Football: No Pricing
Production 25 Sets
RQ-1 Eli Manning, Julius Jones, Michael Clayton, Keary Colbert 10.00
RQ-2 Larry Fitzgerald, DeAngelo Hall, Michael Jenkins, Matt Schaub 8.00
RQ-3 Philip Rivers, Devery Henderson, Tatum Bell, Darius Watts 8.00
RQ-4 Ben Roethlisberger, Devard Darling, Kellen Winslow Jr., Luke McCown 15.00
RQ-5 Kevin Jones, Roy Williams, Bernard Berrian, Mewelde Moore 8.00
RQ-6 Greg Jones, Reggie Williams, Dunta Robinson, Ben Troupe 5.00
RQ-7 J.P. Losman, Lee Evans, Cedric Cobbs, Ben Watson 6.00
RQ-8 Steven Jackson, Chris Perry, Rashaun Woods, Derrick Hamilton 8.00

2004 Playoff Honors Rookie Year

NM/M
Common Player: 2.00
Inserted 1:12
Rookie Year Jerseys: 2X-5X
Production 150 Sets
RY-1 Curtis Martin 3.00
RY-2 David Carr 4.00
RY-3 Jeremy Shockey 3.00
RY-4 Joey Harrington 3.00
RY-5 John Riggins 3.00
RY-6 Koren Robinson 2.00
RY-7 LaDainian Tomlinson 4.00
RY-8 Mark Brunell 2.00
RY-9 Keyshawn Johnson 2.00
RY-10 Peyton Manning 5.00
RY-11 Randy Moss 5.00
RY-12 Ricky Williams 3.00
RY-13 Roy Williams 2.00
RY-14 Quincy Carter 2.00
RY-15 Andre Johnson 3.00
RY-16 Anquan Boldin 2.00
RY-17 Byron Leftwich 5.00
RY-18 Kyle Boller 3.00
RY-19 Rex Grossman 3.00
RY-20 Terrell Suggs 2.00

2004 Playoff Prestige

NM/M
Common Player (1-150): .30
Minor Stars: .50
Unlisted Stars: .75
Common Rookie (151-227): 1.00
Minor Rookies: 1.50
Unlisted Rookies: 2.00
Common Rookie SP: 15.00
SP Inserted 1:144
Pack (6): 6.00
Box (24): 115.00
1 Anquan Boldin .75
2 Emmitt Smith 1.50
3 Jeff Blake .50
4 Marcel Shipp .30
5 Michael Vick 1.50
6 Peerless Price .50
7 T.J. Duckett .50
8 Warrick Dunn .50
9 Ed Reed .50
10 Jamal Lewis .75
11 Kyle Boller .75
12 Ray Lewis .50
13 Todd Heap .50
14 Drew Bledsoe .75
15 Eric Moulds .50
16 Josh Reed .50
17 Travis Henry .50
18 DeShaun Foster .50
19 Stephen Davis .50
20 Jake Delhomme .75
21 Julius Peppers .50
22 Steve Smith .50
23 Anthony Thomas .50
24 Brian Urlacher .75
25 Marty Booker .50
26 Rex Grossman .75
27 Chad Johnson .50
28 Corey Dillon .50
29 Carson Palmer 1.00
30 Peter Warrick .50
31 Rudi Johnson .50
32 Andre Davis .50
33 Quincy Morgan .50
34 William Green .50
35 Kelly Holcomb .30
36 Antonio Bryant .50
37 Quincy Carter .75
38 Roy Williams .50
39 Terence Newman .50
40 Terry Glenn .50
41 Troy Hambrick .30
42 Ashley Lelie .50
43 Clinton Portis 1.25
44 Rod Smith .50
45 Shannon Sharpe .50
46 Mike Anderson .50
47 Jake Plummer .50
48 Charles Rogers .75
49 Joey Harrington .75
50 Ahman Green .75
51 Brett Favre 2.00
52 Donald Driver .50
53 Javon Walker .50
54 Robert Ferguson .50
55 Andre Johnson .75
56 David Carr 1.00
57 Domanick Davis .75
58 Jabar Gaffney .50
59 Dwight Freeney .50
60 Dallas Clark .50
61 Edgerrin James 1.00
62 Marvin Harrison .75
63 Peyton Manning 1.25
64 Reggie Wayne .50
65 Byron Leftwich 1.25
66 Fred Taylor .75
67 Jimmy Smith .50
68 Johnnie Morton .30
69 Priest Holmes 1.00
70 Tony Gonzalez .50
71 Trent Green .50
72 Chris Chambers .75
73 Jay Fiedler .50
74 Randy McMichael .30
75 Ricky Williams 1.00
76 Zach Thomas .50
77 Daunte Culpepper .75
78 Kelly Campbell .30
79 Michael Bennett .75
80 Moe Williams .30
81 Nate Burleson .50
82 Randy Moss 1.25
83 Deion Branch .30
84 Kevin Faulk .30
85 Tom Brady 1.25
86 Troy Brown .30
87 Tedy Bruschi .30
88 Aaron Brooks .75
89 Deuce McAllister .75
90 Donte Stallworth .50
91 Joe Horn .50
92 Amani Toomer .50
93 Ike Hilliard .50
94 Jeremy Shockey .75
95 Kerry Collins .50
96 Michael Strahan .50
97 Tiki Barber .50
98 Chad Pennington 1.00
99 Curtis Martin .75
100 LaMont Jordan .30
101 Santana Moss .50
102 Charlie Garner .50
103 Jerry Porter .50
104 Jerry Rice 1.50
105 Justin Fargas .50
106 Rich Gannon .50
107 Rod Woodson .50
108 Tim Brown .75
109 Brian Westbrook .50
110 Correll Buckhalter .50
111 Donovan McNabb 1.00
112 Freddie Mitchell .30
113 James Thrash .30
114 Amos Zereoue .30
115 Antwann Randle El .50
116 Hines Ward .30
117 Joey Porter .30
118 Kendrell Bell .30
119 Plaxico Burress .75
120 David Boston .50
121 Drew Brees .50
122 LaDainian Tomlinson 1.00
123 Jeff Garcia .75
124 Kevan Barlow .75
125 Tai Streets .50
126 Terrell Owens .75
127 Tim Rattay .50
128 Darrell Jackson .50
129 Koren Robinson .50
130 Matt Hasselbeck .50
131 Shaun Alexander .75
132 Isaac Bruce .50
133 Marc Bulger .50
134 Marshall Faulk 1.00
135 Torry Holt .75
136 Brad Johnson .50
137 Derrick Brooks .50
138 Keenan McCardell .50
139 Keyshawn Johnson .50
140 Mike Alstott .50
141 Derrick Mason .50
142 Drew Bennett .30
143 Jevon Kearse .50
144 Justin McCareins .50
145 Steve McNair .75
146 Tyrone Calico .50
147 Bruce Smith .50
148 Laveranues Coles .50
149 Patrick Ramsey .50
150 LaVar Arrington .75
151 *Eli Manning* 10.00
152 *Larry Fitzgerald* 6.00
153 *Philip Rivers* 6.00
154 *Sean Taylor* 4.00
155 *Kellen Winslow* 4.00
156 *Roy Williams* 6.00
157 *DeAngelo Hall* 3.00
158 *Reggie Williams* 4.00
159 *Ben Roethlisberger* 15.00
160 *Jonathan Vilma* 2.50
161 *Lee Evans* 4.00
162 *Tommie Harris* 2.50
163 *Michael Clayton* 4.00
164 *DJ Williams SP* 30.00
165 *Will Smith* 2.00
166 *Kenechi Udeze* 2.00
167 *Vince Wilfork SP* 25.00
168 *J.P. Losman* 5.00
169 *Steven Jackson SP* 60.00
170 *Ahmad Carroll* 2.00
171 *Chris Perry* 3.00
172 *Jason Babin SP* 40.00
173 *Chris Gamble* 2.00
174 *Michael Jenkins* 3.00
175 *Kevin Jones* 5.00
176 *Rashaun Woods* 4.00
177 *Ben Watson* 1.50
178 *Karlos Dansby* 1.50
179 *Teddy Lehman* 2.00
180 *Ricardo Colclough SP* 25.00
181 *Daryl Smith* 1.50
182 *Ben Troupe* 1.50
183 *Tatum Bell* 3.00
184 *Julius Jones* 10.00
185 *Bob Sanders* 1.50
186 *Devery Henderson* 2.00
187 *Dwan Edwards* 1.50
188 *Michael Boulware* 1.50
189 *Darius Watts* 2.00
190 *Greg Jones* 2.50
191 *Antwan Odom* 1.50
192 *Sean Jones SP* 15.00
193 *Courtney Watson* 1.50
194 *Keary Colbert* 2.00
195 *Keith Smith* 1.50
196 *Derrick Strait* 2.00
197 *Bernard Berrian* 2.00
198 *Devard Darling* 2.00
199 *Matt Schaub* 2.00
200 *Will Poole* 1.50
201 *Samie Parker* 1.50
202 *Luke McCown SP* 20.00
203 *Jerricho Cotchery* 1.50
204 *Mewelde Moore* 2.00
205 *Ernest Wilford* 1.50
206 *Cedric Cobbs SP* 25.00
207 *Johnnie Morant* 1.50
208 *Craig Krenzel* 1.50
209 *Michael Turner* 1.50
210 *D.J. Hackett* 1.50
211 *P.K. Sam* 2.50
212 *Josh Harris* 1.50
213 *Drew Henson* 5.00
214 *Jeff Smoker* 2.50
215 *John Navarre* 2.50
216 *Cody Pickett* 2.00
217 *Quincy Wilson* 2.50
218 *Derek Abney* 1.00
219 *Maurice Clarett SP* 50.00
220 *Mike Williams SP* 100.00
221 *B. Johnson* 1.00
222 *Brandon Everage* 1.00
223 *Derek McCoy* 1.00
224 *Jared Lorenzen* 1.00
225 *Jarrett Payton* 3.00
226 *Jason Fife* 1.00
227 *Robert Kent* 1.00

2004 Playoff Prestige Xtra Point Black

NM/M
Stars: 10X-20X
Rookies: 5X-10X
Rookie SPs: 1X-1.5X
Production 25 Hobbys Sets
19 Stephen Davis Auto 40.00
38 Roy Williams Auto 80.00
57 Domanick Davis Auto 50.00
67 Jimmy Smith Auto 25.00
72 Chris Chambers Auto 50.00
88 Aaron Brooks Auto 40.00
91 Joe Horn Auto 30.00
97 Tiki Barber Auto 40.00
116 Hines Ward Auto 80.00
141 Derrick Mason Auto 30.00
213 Drew Henson Auto 200.00

Values quoted in this guide reflect the retail price of a card—the price a collector can expect to pay when buying a card from a dealer. The wholesale price—that which a collector can expect to receive from a dealer when selling cards—will be significantly lower, depending on desirability and condition.

2004 Playoff Prestige Xtra Points Purple

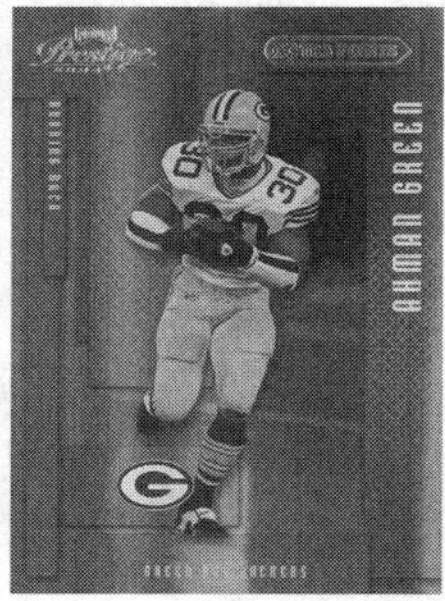

Stars: 5X-10X
Rookies: 2X-4X
Rookie SPs: 1X
Production 75 Hobby Sets

2004 Playoff Prestige Achievements

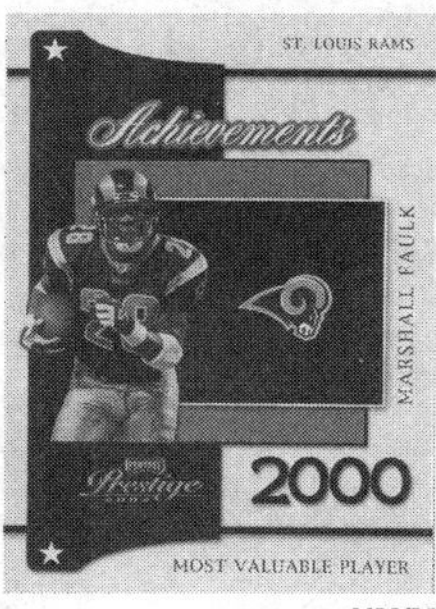

NM/M
Common Player: 1.50
A1 Brian Urlacher 2.00
A2 Emmitt Smith 4.00
A3 Clinton Portis 3.00
A4 Brett Favre 5.00
A5 Peyton Manning 2.50
A6 Ricky Williams 2.50
A7 Randy Moss 2.50
A8 Tom Brady 2.50
A9 LaDainian Tomlinson 2.00
A10 Marshall Faulk 2.00
A11 Jamal Lewis 1.50
A12 Steve McNair 1.50
A13 Rich Gannon 1.50
A14 Kurt Warner 1.50
A15 Torry Holt 1.50

2004 Playoff Prestige Achievements Materials

NM/M
Common Player: 8.00
Inserted Hobby Only
A1 Brian Urlacher/100 15.00
A2 Emmitt Smith/93 30.00
A3 Clinton Portis/102 20.00
A4 Brett Favre/97 40.00
A5 Peyton Manning/103 20.00
A6 Ricky Williams/102 15.00
A7 Randy Moss/98 15.00
A8 Tom Brady/101 15.00
A9 LaDainianTomlinson/102 12.00
A10 Marshall Faulk/100 12.00
A11 Jamal Lewis/103 10.00
A12 Steve McNair/103 10.00
A13 Rich Gannon/102 8.00
A14 Kurt Warner/99 10.00
A15 Torry Holt/103 10.00

2004 Playoff Prestige Changing Stripes

NM/M
Common Player: 12.00
Production 225 Sets
Prime Production 25 Sets
CS1 David Boston 12.00
CS2 Priest Holmes 20.00
CS3 Trent Green 12.00
CS4 Jerry Rice 30.00
CS5 Jake Plummer 12.00

CS6 Emmitt Smith 50.00
CS7 Laveranues Coles 12.00
CS8 Brad Johnson 12.00
CS9 Junior Seau 12.00
CS10 Stephen Davis 12.00

2004 Playoff Prestige Draft Picks

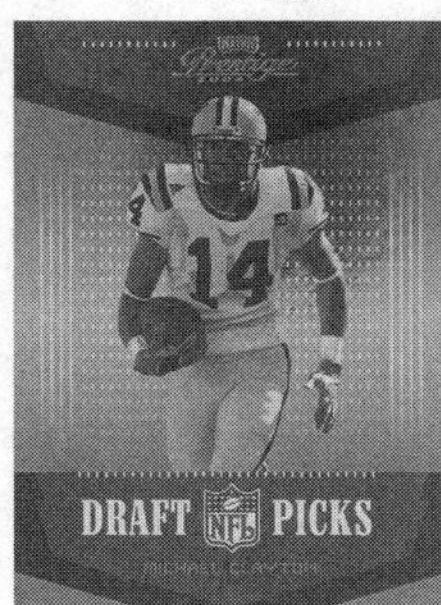

NM/M
Common Player: 1.50
DP1 Ben Roethlisberger 10.00
DP2 Eli Manning 10.00
DP3 J.P. Losman 4.00
DP4 Philip Rivers 8.00
DP5 Steven Jackson 5.00
DP6 Kevin Jones 5.00
DP7 Chris Perry 3.00
DP8 Greg Jones 2.50
DP9 Michael Turner 1.50
DP10 Roy Williams 6.00
DP11 Rashaun Woods 4.00
DP12 Reggie Williams 4.00
DP13 Michael Clayton 4.00
DP14 Lee Evans 4.00
DP15 Kellen Winslow 5.00
DP16 Matt Schaub 2.00
DP17 Quincy Wilson 2.50
DP18 Julius Jones 4.00
DP19 Larry Fitzgerald 6.00
DP20 Ernest Wilford 2.50
DP21 Keary Colbert 2.00
DP22 Tommie Harris 2.50
DP23 Jonathan Vilma 2.50
DP24 Chris Gamble 2.00
DP25 Sean Taylor 4.00

2004 Playoff Prestige Draft Picks Autos

NM/M
Common Player: 20.00
Production 50 Sets
DP1 Ben Roethlisberger 400.00
DP2 Eli Manning 300.00
DP3 J.P. Losman 80.00
DP4 Philip Rivers 150.00
DP5 Steven Jackson 100.00
DP6 Kevin Jones 100.00
DP7 Chris Perry 60.00
DP8 Greg Jones 50.00
DP9 Michael Turner 20.00
DP10 Roy Williams
DP11 Rashaun Woods 60.00
DP12 Reggie Williams 60.00
DP13 Michael Clayton 60.00
DP14 Lee Evans 80.00
DP15 Kellen Winslow 100.00
DP16 Matt Schaub 30.00
DP17 Quincy Wilson 40.00
DP18 Julius Jones 100.00
DP19 Larry Fitzgerald 150.00
DP20 Ernest Wilford 30.00
DP21 Keary Colbert 30.00
DP22 Tommie Harris 40.00
DP23 Jonathan Vilma 40.00
DP24 Chris Gamble 30.00
DP25 Sean Taylor 100.00

2004 Playoff Prestige Game Day Jerseys

NM/M
Common Player: 6.00
1-20 Inserted Hobby Only
21-40 Inserted Retail Only
GJ1 Anquan Boldin 10.00
GJ2 Marcel Shipp 6.00
GJ3 Peerless Price 8.00
GJ4 Travis Henry 8.00
GJ5 Jimmy Smith 6.00
GJ6 Amani Toomer 8.00
GJ7 Tim Brown 8.00
GJ8 Correll Buckhalter 6.00
GJ9 Donovan McNabb 10.00
GJ10 Jerome Bettis 8.00
GJ11 Jeff Garcia 8.00

NM/M
GJ12 Isaac Bruce 8.00
GJ13 Warren Sapp 8.00
GJ14 Steve McNair 8.00
GJ15 Jamal Lewis 8.00
GJ16 Roy Williams 8.00
GJ17 David Carr 12.00
GJ18 Peyton Manning 15.00
GJ19 Chris Chambers 8.00
GJ20 Michael Bennett 8.00
GJ21 Jason McAddley
GJ22 Muhsin Muhammad
GJ23 David Terrell
GJ24 Dennis Northcutt
GJ25 William Green
GJ26 Tim Couch
GJ27 Rod Smith
GJ28 Scott Anderson
GJ29 Antonio Freeman
GJ30 Fred Taylor
GJ31 Mark Brunell
GJ32 Byron Chamberlain
GJ33 Antowain Smith
GJ34 Tedy Bruschi
GJ35 Ike Hilliard
GJ36 Ron Dayne
GJ37 Wayne Chrebet
GJ38 Josh McCown
GJ39 Duce Staley
GJ40 Jeremy Shockey

2004 Playoff Prestige Gamers

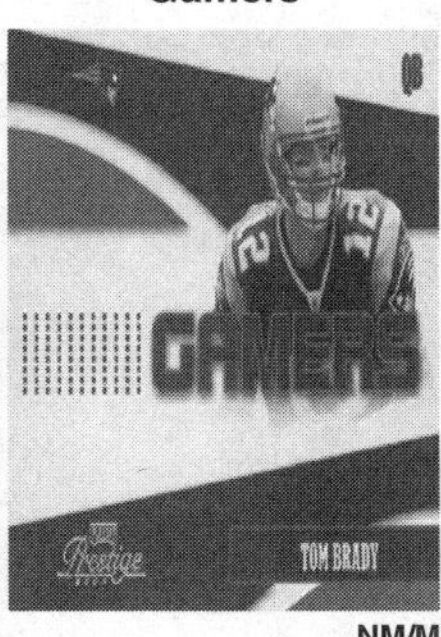

NM/M
Common Player: 2.00
Production 750 Hobby Sets
Jerseys: 2X-4X
Jersey Production 100 Sets
G1 Michael Vick 6.00
G2 Jamal Lewis 2.00
G3 Ray Lewis 2.00
G4 Travis Henry 2.00
G5 Brian Urlacher 2.50
G6 Clinton Portis 4.00
G7 Brett Favre 6.00
G8 Ahman Green 2.00
G9 David Carr 3.00
G10 Marvin Harrison 2.00
G11 Peyton Manning 3.00
G12 Priest Holmes 2.50
G13 Ricky Williams 3.00
G14 Daunte Culpepper 2.00
G15 Randy Moss 3.00
G16 Tom Brady 3.00
G17 Deuce McAllister 2.00
G18 Jeremy Shockey 2.50
G19 Chad Pennington 2.50
G20 Jerry Rice 5.00
G21 Donovan McNabb 2.50
G22 LaDainian Tomlinson 2.50
G23 Terrell Owens 2.00
G24 Torry Holt 2.00
G25 Steve McNair 2.00

2004 Playoff Prestige Gridiron Heritage

NM/M
Common Player: 1.50
Inserted 1:24
Jerseys: 2X-4X
Jerseys 1:48 Hobby
GH1 Marcel Shipp 1.50
GH2 Eric Moulds 1.50
GH3 Anthony Thomas 1.50
GH4 Corey Dillon 2.00
GH5 Kelly Holcomb 1.50
GH6 Rod Smith 1.50
GH7 Joey Harrington 2.50
GH8 Brett Favre 6.00
GH9 Edgerrin James 2.50
GH10 Fred Taylor 2.00
GH11 Zach Thomas 1.50
GH12 Aaron Brooks 2.00
GH13 Tiki Barber 1.5

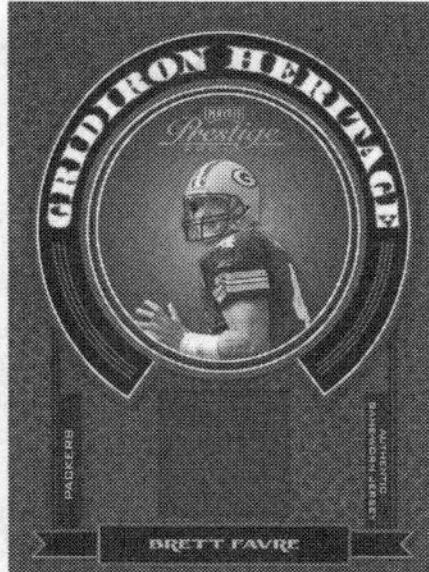

NM/M
GH14 Curtis Martin 2.00
GH15 Tim Brown 2.00
GH16 Correll Buckhalter 1.50
GH17 Hines Ward 1.50
GH18 Jeff Garcia 2.00
GH19 Mike Alstott 1.50
GH20 Eddie George 2.00

2004 Playoff Prestige League Leaders

NM/M
Common Player: 1.50
Jerseys: 3X-6X
Jersey Production 250 Sets
LL1 Peyton Manning, Trent Green 3.00
LL2 Aaron Brooks, Daunte Culpepper 2.00
LL3 Brett Favre, Quincy Carter 5.00
LL4 Donovan McNabb, Kerry Collins 2.00
LL5 Brad Johnson, Marc Bulger 1.50
LL6 Steve McNair, Tom Brady 2.50
LL7 Jamal Lewis, Ricky Williams 2.50
LL8 Deuce McAllister, Stephen Davis 2.00
LL9 Clinton Portis, Curtis Martin 3.00
LL10 Fred Taylor, Priest Holmes 2.00
LL11 Ahman Green, Shaun Alexander 2.00
LL12 LaDainian Tomlinson, Travis Henry 2.00
LL13 Eddie George, Edgerrin James 2.00
LL14 Anthony Thomas, Tiki Barber 1.50
LL15 Laveranues Coles, Torry Holt 1.50
LL16 Anquan Boldin, Randy Moss 3.00
LL17 Chad Johnson, Derrick Mason 1.50
LL18 Hines Ward, Marvin Harrison 2.00
LL19 Andre Johnson, Santana Moss 2.00
LL20 Amani Toomer, Terrell Owens 2.00

2004 Playoff Prestige Stars of the NFL

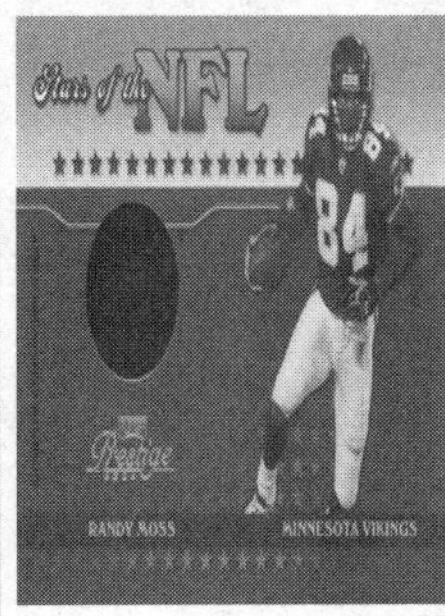

NM/M
Common Player: 10.00
Production 150 Sets
Prime Production 25 Sets
Cards 7, 15, 16, 18 Auto Prime Versions
NFL1 Michael Vick 20.00
NFL2 Jamal Lewis 10.00
NFL3 Drew Bledsoe 10.00
NFL4 Brian Urlacher 10.00
NFL5 Clinton Portis 12.00
NFL6 Emmitt Smith 30.00
NFL7 Ahman Green 12.00
NFL8 Brett Favre 30.00
NFL9 David Carr 12.00
NFL10 Edgerrin James 12.00
NFL11 Peyton Manning 15.00
NFL12 Priest Holmes 12.00
NFL13 Ricky Williams 12.00
NFL14 Randy Moss 12.00
NFL15 Tom Brady 15.00
NFL16 Deuce McAllister 10.00
NFL17 Jeremy Shockey 10.00
NFL18 Chad Pennington 10.00
NFL19 Jerry Rice 20.00
NFL20 Donovan McNabb 12.00
NFL21 LaDainian Tomlinson 10.00
NFL22 Jeff Garcia 10.00
NFL23 LaVar Arrington 50.00
NFL24 Marshall Faulk 10.00
NFL25 Steve McNair 10.00

2004 Playoff Prestige Super Bowl Heroes

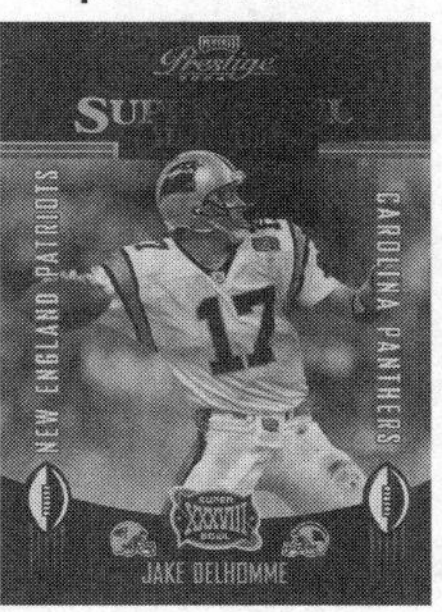

NM/M
Inserted 1:24
SB1 Tom Brady 5.00
SB2 Deion Branch 3.00
SB3 Adam Vinatieri 2.00
SB4 Mike Vrabel
SB5 Antowain Smith 2.00
SB6 David Givens 1.00
SB7 Troy Brown 2.00
SB8 Kevin Faulk 2.00
SB9 Jake Delhomme 3.00
SB10 Muhsin Mohammed 2.00

2004 Playoff Prestige Turning Pro

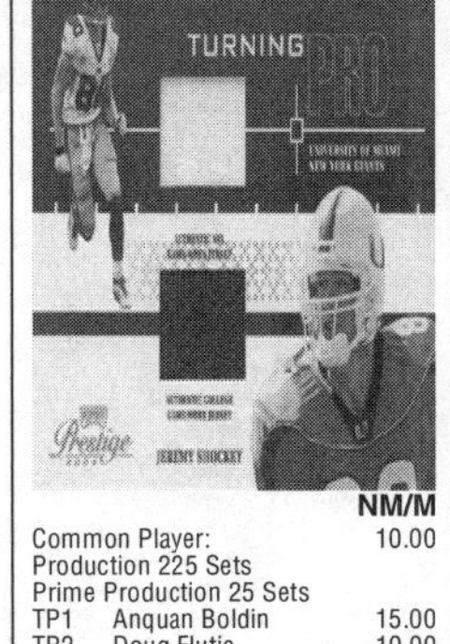

NM/M
Common Player: 10.00
Production 225 Sets
Prime Production 25 Sets
TP1 Anquan Boldin 15.00
TP2 Doug Flutie 10.00
TP3 Clinton Portis 20.00
TP4 Ahman Green 25.00
TP5 Edgerrin James 20.00
TP6 Reggie Wayne 10.00
TP7 Jeremy Shockey 15.00
TP8 Marshall Faulk 15.00
TP9 Tyrone Calico 10.00
TP10 Andre Johnson 15.00

2004 Playoff Prime Signatures

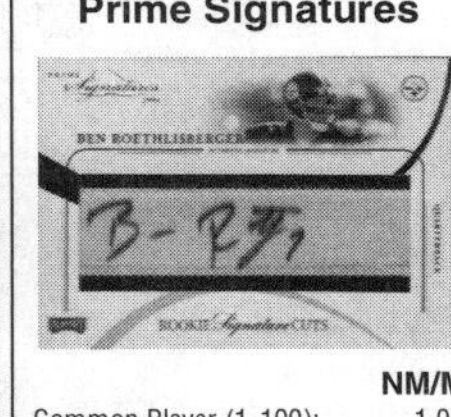

NM/M
Common Player (1-100): 1.00
Minor Stars (1-100): 2.00
Unlisted Stars (1-100): 3.00
Production 999 Sets
Common Rookie (101-125): 15.00
Production 199 Sets
Sean Taylor & Teddy Lehman did not sign their cards
Common Rookie (126-158): 30.00
Production 99 Sets
1 Anquan Boldin 3.00
2 Josh McCown 1.00
3 Alge Crumpler 1.00
4 Michael Vick 6.00
5 Jamal Lewis 3.00
6 Todd Heap 2.00
7 Jim Kelly 5.00
8 Thurman Thomas 3.00
9 Travis Henry 1.00
10 Jake Delhomme 3.00
11 Stephen Davis 2.00
12 Steve Smith 1.00
13 Brian Urlacher 3.00
14 Dick Butkus 4.00
15 Gale Sayers 5.00
16 Mike Ditka 3.00
17 Mike Singletary 3.00
18 Rex Grossman 3.00
19 Richard Dent 2.00
20 Chad Johnson 2.00
21 Rudi Johnson 2.00
22 Jim Brown 6.00
23 Lee Suggs 1.00
24 Ozzie Newsome 2.00
25 Paul Warfield 3.00
26 Quincy Morgan 1.00
27 Willie Green 2.00
28 Antonio Bryant 2.00
29 Herschel Walker 2.00
30 Jimmy Johnson 2.00
31 Keyshawn Johnson 2.00
32 Roger Staubach 6.00
33 Terence Newman 1.00
34 Tony Dorsett 4.00
35 Terrell Davis 3.00
36 Joey Harrington 3.00
37 Ahman Green 3.00
38 Javon Walker 2.00
39 Paul Hornung 5.00
40 Reggie White 4.00
41 Robert Ferguson 1.00
42 Sterling Sharpe 3.00
43 David Carr 4.00
44 Domanick Davis 3.00
45 Earl Campbell 3.00
46 Peyton Manning 5.00
47 Reggie Wayne 1.00
48 Dante Hall 1.00
49 Priest Holmes 4.00
50 Trent Green 1.00
51 A.J. Feeley 1.00
52 Don Shula 3.00
53 Chris Chambers 3.00
54 Travis Minor 1.00
55 Fran Tarkenton 4.00
56 Bill Belichick 2.00
57 Tom Brady 5.00
58 Aaron Brooks 3.00
59 Deuce McAllister 3.00
60 Eddie "Boo" Williams 1.00
61 Joe Horn 1.00
62 Lawrence Taylor 4.00
63 Mark Bavaro 2.00
64 Michael Strahan 2.00
65 Tiki Barber 6.00
66 Herman Edwards 1.00
67 Joe Namath 1.00
68 Justin McCareins 1.00
69 LaMont Jordan 1.00
70 Santana Moss 1.00
71 Bo Jackson 6.00
72 Fred Biletnikoff 3.00
73 George Blanda 3.00
74 Jim Plunkett 2.00
75 Marcus Allen 4.00
76 Barry Switzer 2.00
77 Correll Buckhalter 1.00
78 Donovan McNabb 4.00
79 Antwann Randle El 2.00
80 Bill Cowher 2.00
81 Franco Harris 4.00
82 Jack Lambert 3.00
83 Joe Greene 3.00
84 Kendrell Bell 1.00
85 L.C. Greenwood 3.00
86 Mel Blount 2.00
87 Terry Bradshaw 8.00
88 LaDainian Tomlinson 4.00
89 Andre Carter 1.00
90 Bill Walsh 2.00
91 Shaun Alexander 3.00
92 Steve Largent 4.00
93 Matt Hasselbeck 2.00
94 Torry Holt 3.00
95 Clinton Portis 5.00
96 Laveranues Coles 1.00
97 Mark Brunell 2.00
98 Patrick Ramsey 2.00
99 Reuben Droughns 2.00
100 Sonny Jurgensen 3.00
101 *Matt Mauck, Triandos Luke* 20.00
102 *D.J. Williams, Brandon Miree* 15.00
103 *Carlos Francis, Johnnie Morant* 15.00
104 *Jonathan Vilma, Derrick Ward* 20.00
105 *Vince Wilfork, P.K. Sam* 20.00
106 *Jim Sorgi, Ran Carthon* 20.00
107 *Troy Fleming, Jarrett Payton* 30.00
108 *Jason Babin, B.J. Symons* 15.00
109 *Josh Harris, Clarence Moore* 25.00
110 *Maurice Mann, Casey Bramlet* 20.00
111 *Sean Jones, Adimchinobe Echemandu* 15.00
112 *Andy Hall, Bruce Perry* 15.00
113 *Jamaar Taylor, Jared Lorenzen* 15.00
114 *Chris Gamble, Drew Carter* 20.00
115 *Drew Henson, Craig Krenzel* 30.00
116 *Tommie Harris, Ahmad Carroll* 30.00
117 *Jeff Smoker, D.J. Hackett* 15.00
118 *Ernest Wilford, Jerricho Cotchery* 15.00
119 *Will Smith, Kenechi Udeze* 15.00
120 *Samie Parker, Michael Turner* 15.00
121 *Sloan Thomas, B.J. Johnson* 15.00
122 *John Navarre, Cody Pickett* 20.00
123 *Ricardo Colclough, Quincy Wilson* 20.00
124 *Sean Taylor, Chris Cooley* 20.00
125 *Michael Boulware, Teddy Lehman* 15.00
126 *J.P. Losman* 120.00
127 *Lee Evans* 75.00
128 *Ben Watson* 40.00
129 *Cedric Cobbs* 30.00
130 *Devard Darling* 30.00
131 *Chris Perry* 60.00
132 *Kellen Winslow Jr.* 75.00
133 *Luke McCown* 50.00
134 *Ben Roethlisberger* 500.00
135 *Dunta Robinson* 60.00
136 *Greg Jones* 75.00
137 *Reggie Williams* 40.00
138 *Ben Troupe* 30.00
139 *Tatum Bell* 100.00
140 *Darius Watts* 40.00
141 *Robert Gallery* 40.00
142 *Philip Rivers* 150.00
143 *Julius Jones* 175.00
144 *Eli Manning* 300.00
145 *Bernard Berrian* 40.00
146 *Roy Williams* 150.00
147 *Kevin Jones* 175.00
148 *Mewelde Moore* 60.00
149 *DeAngelo Hall* 50.00
150 *Michael Jenkins* 40.00
151 *Matt Schaub* 50.00
152 *Keary Colbert* 60.00
153 *Devery Henderson* 40.00
154 *Michael Clayton* 100.00
155 *Larry Fitzgerald* 150.00
156 *Rashaun Woods* 50.00
157 *Derrick Hamilton* 40.00
158 *Steven Jackson* 150.00

2004 Playoff Prime Signatures Bronze Proofs

Cards 1-100: 1X-3X
Production 50 Sets

2004 Playoff Prime Signatures Silver Proofs

Cards 1-100: No Pricing
Production 25 Sets

2004 Playoff Prime Signatures Gold Proofs

Cards 1-100: No Pricing
Production 5 Sets
Rookies (101-125): .75X-1.5X
Production 50 Sets
Rookies (126-158): No Pricing
Production 5 Sets

2004 Playoff Prime Signatures Platinum Proofs

Cards 1-100: No Pricing
Production 1 Set
Rookies (101-158): No Pricing
Production 1 Set

2004 Playoff Prime Signatures Prime Cuts

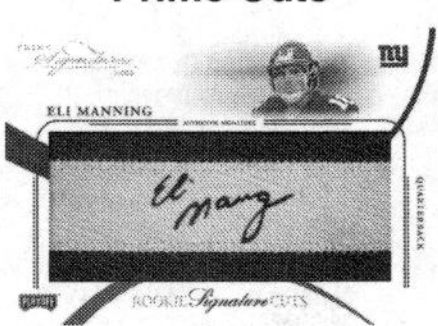

Cards 1-100: No Pricing
Production 1 Set

2004 Playoff Prime Signatures Prime Pairings

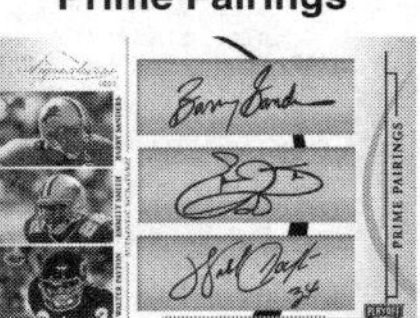

NM/M
Sequentially #'d to indicated quantity
Cards #'d 25 or less: No Pricing
Prime Cuts: No Pricing

Production 1 Set
PP-1 Brett Favre, Daunte Culpepper, Kyle Boller/42 200.00
PP-2 Byron Leftwich, Chad Pennington, Jake Delhomme/50 100.00
PP-3 Archie Manning, Matt Hasselbeck, Steve McNair/18
PP-4 Joe Montana, Ken Stabler, Carson Palmer, Jeff Garcia/28 400.00
PP-5 Barry Sanders, Chris Perry, Marshall Faulk, Kevan Barlow/31 200.00
PP-6 Jerry Rice, Michael Clayton, Marvin Harrison, Andre Johnson/31 250.00
PP-7 Ray Lewis, Kendrell Bell, Dan Morgan, Jonathan Vilma/24
PP-8 Tony Gonzalez, Dallas Clark, Alge Crumpler, Todd Heap/26 150.00
PP-9 Troy Aikman, Michael Irvin, Drew Henson, Julius Jones/26 450.00
PP-10 J.P. Losman, Willis McGahee, James Lofton, Lee Evans/39 120.00
PP-11 Dan Marino, Bob Griese, Larry Csonka, Ricky Williams/28 300.00
PP-12 Ben Roethlisberger, Hines Ward, Kendrell Bell, Jerome Bettis/17
PP-13 Deuce McAllister, T.J. Duckett, Eddie George, Domanick Davis/50 80.00
PP-14 Marvin Harrison, Andre Johnson, Michael Irvin, Michael Clayton/3
PP-15 Dan Marino, Chad Pennington, Eli Manning, Roy Williams/4
PP-16 Edgerrin James, Ricky Williams, Kevin Jones, DeShaun Foster/4
PP-17 Bart Starr, Sammy Baugh, Archie Manning, Troy Aikman, Randall Cunningham, Drew Bledsoe/33 400.00
PP-18 John Riggins, Steven Jackson, Ickey Woods, Quentin Griffin, Tatum Bell, Onterrio Smith/49 120.00
PP-19 Johnny Unitas, Bart Starr, Joe Montana, John Elway, Dan Marino, Brett Favre/15
PP-20 Deacon Jones, Deion Sanders, Ed Reed, Julius Peppers, Adam Vinatieri, Dan Morgan/33 120.00
PP-21 Reggie Williams, Steve Smith, Jimmy Smith, Reggie Wayne, Kelley Washington, Brandon Lloyd/50 100.00
PP-22 Edgerrin James, Corey Dillon, Travis Henry, Julius Jones, Brian Westbrook, Michael Bennett/20
PP-23 Deion Branch, Peter Warrick, Bethel Johnson, Keary Colbert, Rod Gardner, Bernard Berrian/41 120.00
PP-24 Deuce McAllister, Greg Jones, Archie Manning, Drew Henson, Ed Reed, Reggie Wayne/6
PP-25 Michael Irvin, Charles Rogers, Laveranues Coles, Don Maynard, Ashley Lelie, Derrick Mason/24
PP-26 Ben Roethlisberger, Byron Leftwich, Kendrell Bell, Eddie George, Adam Vinatieri, Koren Robinson/10
PP-27 Hines Ward, Kyle Boller, Randall Cunningham, Isaac Bruce, Jimmy Smith, T.J. Duckett/12
PP-28 Eli Manning, Philip Rivers, Ben Roethlisberger, J.P. Losman, Matt Schaub, Luke McCown/9
PP-29 Steven Jackson, Chris Perry, Kevin Jones, Tatum Bell, Julius Jones, Greg Jones/9
PP-30 Roy Williams, Reggie Williams, Lee Evans, Michael Clayton, Rashaun Woods, Michael Jenkins/9
PP-31 Mike Alstott, Chad Johnson, Steve Smith, Lee Evans, Terrell Suggs, Brandon Lloyd/9
PP-32 Bob Griese, Quentin Griffin, Tim Brown, Eric Moulds, Ashley Lelie, Peerless Price/8
PP-33 Eli Manning, Reggie Williams, Kevin Jones, Michael Jenkins, Greg Jones, Matt Schaub/9
PP-34 Philip Rivers, Roy Williams, Steven Jackson, Rashaun Woods, Tatum Bell, Luke McCown/9
PP-35 Ben Roethlisberger, Lee Evans, Michael Clayton, J.P. Losman, Chris Perry/9

A card number in parenthese ( ) indicates the set is unnumbered.

PP-37 Byron Leftwich, Deuce McAllister, Ben Roethlisberger, Eddie George, Greg Jones, Koren Robinson/3
PP-38 Dan Marino, Charles Rogers, Archie Manning, Hines Ward, Donte Stallworth, Kelley Washington/2
PP-39 Joe Montana, Bart Starr, Carson Palmer, Matt Hasselbeck, Drew Henson, Drew Bledsoe/1
PP-40 Jerry Rice, Marvin Harrison, Randy Moss, Hines Ward, Chad Johnson, Koren Robinson/13
PP-41 Joe Montana, Dan Marino, Jerry Rice, Barry Sanders, Brett Favre, Steve McNair/3
PP-42 Walter Payton, Barry Sanders, Emmitt Smith, Jim Brown, Tony Dorsett, Marcus Allen/3
PP-42 Walter Payton, Barry Sanders, Emmitt Smith, Jim Brown, Tony Dorsett, Marcus Allen/3

2004 Playoff Prime Signatures Signature Proofs Bronze

NM/M
Common Player: 15.00
Sequentially #'d to indicated quantity
Cards #'d 25 or less: No Pricing
1 Anquan Boldin/125 15.00
2 Josh McCown/65 15.00
3 Alge Crumpler/150 15.00
4 Michael Vick/85 15.00
5 Jamal Lewis/31
6 Todd Heap/150 15.00
7 Jim Kelly/44 50.00
8 Thurman Thomas/46 20.00
9 Travis Henry/81 15.00
10 Jake Delhomme/150 20.00
11 Stephen Davis/125 15.00
12 Steve Smith/150 15.00
13 Brian Urlacher/3
14 Dick Butkus/51 75.00
15 Gale Sayers/51 60.00
16 Mike Ditka/89 40.00
17 Mike Singletary/110 30.00
18 Rex Grossman/150 20.00
19 Richard Dent/50 15.00
20 Chad Johnson/85 20.00
21 Rudi Johnson/150 15.00
22 Jim Brown/150 80.00
23 Lee Suggs/20
24 Ozzie Newsome/82 15.00
25 Paul Warfield/125 20.00
26 Quincy Morgan/109 15.00
27 Willie Green/87 15.00
28 Antonio Bryant/59 15.00
29 Herschel Walker/134 25.00
30 Jimmy Johnson/45 30.00
31 KeyshawnJohnson/64 15.00
32 Roger Staubach/75 80.00
33 Terence Newman/83 15.00
34 Tony Dorsett/75 40.00
35 Terrell Davis/68 25.00
36 Joey Harrington/83 20.00
37 Ahman Green/14
38 Javon Walker/133 25.00
39 Paul Hornung/99 30.00
40 Reggie White/92 100.00
41 Robert Ferguson/112 15.00
42 Sterling Sharpe/125 20.00
43 David Carr/65 30.00
44 Domanick Davis/150 15.00
45 Earl Campbell/65 30.00
46 Peyton Manning/75 100.00
47 Reggie Wayne/87 25.00
48 Dante Hall/82 15.00
49 Priest Holmes/57 40.00
50 Trent Green/89 30.00
51 A.J. Feeley/94 15.00
52 Don Shula/40 30.00
53 Chris Chambers/63 20.00
55 Fran Tarkenton/86 40.00
56 Bill Belichick/125 80.00
57 Tom Brady/86 150.00
58 Aaron Brooks/99 15.00
59 Deuce McAllister/125 20.00
61 Joe Horn/49 20.00
62 Lawrence Taylor/65 40.00
63 Mark Bavaro/8
64 Michael Strahan/125 15.00
65 Tiki Barber/139 20.00
66 Herman Edwards/65 25.00
67 Joe Namath/99 80.00
68 Justin McCareins/49 15.00
70 Santana Moss/81 15.00
71 Bo Jackson/49 100.00
72 Fred Biletnikoff/75 30.00
73 George Blanda/150 30.00
74 Jim Plunkett/143 20.00
75 Marcus Allen/150 30.00
76 Barry Switzer/125 60.00
77 Donovan McNabb/50 100.00
79 Antwan Randle El/82 30.00
80 Bill Cowher/125 30.00
81 Franco Harris/60 60.00
82 Jack Lambert/58 100.00
83 Joe Greene/75 50.00
84 Kendrell Bell/150 15.00
85 L.C. Greenwood/96 40.00
86 Mel Blount/87 25.00
87 Terry Bradshaw/94 80.00
88 LaDainian Tomlinson/68 40.00
90 Bill Walsh/125 30.00
91 Shaun Alexander/99 25.00
92 Steve Largent/150 30.00
93 Matt Hasselbeck/108 25.00
94 Torry Holt/69 20.00
95 Clinton Portis/65 25.00
96 Laveranues Coles/150 15.00
97 Mark Brunell/49 20.00
98 Patrick Ramsey/99 15.00
99 Reuben Droughns/150 15.00
100 Sonny Jurgensen/150 30.00

2004 Playoff Prime Signatures Signature Proofs Silver

NM/M
Common Player: 15.00
Sequentially #'d to indicated quantity
Cards #'d less than 25: No Pricing
1 Anquan Boldin/81 15.00
2 Josh McCown/44 15.00
3 Alge Crumpler/100 15.00
4 Michael Vick/50 120.00
5 Jamal Lewis/20
6 Todd Heap/100 15.00
7 Jim Kelly/25 60.00
8 Thurman Thomas/34 25.00
9 Travis Henry/50 15.00
10 Jake Delhomme/100 30.00
11 Stephen Davis/48 20.00
12 Steve Smith/100 20.00
13 Brian Urlacher/2
14 Dick Butkus/45 75.00
15 Gale Sayers/40 60.00
16 Mike Ditka/35 40.00
17 Mike Singletary/50 40.00
18 Rex Grossman/100 20.00
19 Richard Dent/35 30.00
20 Chad Johnson/30 25.00
21 Rudi Johnson/100 15.00
22 Jim Brown/100 80.00
23 Lee Suggs/15
24 Ozzie Newsome/55 15.00
25 Paul Warfield/89 20.00
26 Quincy Morgan/81 15.00
27 Willie Green/50 20.00
28 Antonio Bryant/40 15.00
29 Herschel Walker/99 30.00
30 Jimmy Johnson/20
31 Keyshawn Johnson/40 15.00
32 Roger Staubach/53 80.00
33 Terence Newman/41 20.00
34 Tony Dorsett/57 40.00
35 Terrell Davis/30 25.00
36 Joey Harrington/50 20.00
37 Ahman Green/8
38 Javon Walker/84 25.00
39 Paul Hornung/50 40.00
40 Reggie White/38 120.00
41 Robert Ferguson/89 20.00
42 Sterling Sharpe/84 25.00
43 David Carr/39 40.00
44 Domanick Davis/100 15.00
45 Earl Campbell/50 30.00
46 Peyton Manning/63 100.00
47 Reggie Wayne/48 30.00
48 Dante Hall/52 20.00
49 Priest Holmes/31 60.00
50 Trent Green/58 30.00
51 A.J. Feeley/67 20.00
52 Don Shula/25 40.00
53 Chris Chambers/49 25.00
55 Fran Tarkenton/48 50.00
56 Bill Belichick/99 80.00
57 Tom Brady/55 150.00
58 Aaron Brooks/79 20.00
59 Deuce McAllister/96 20.00
61 Joe Horn/35 20.00
62 Lawrence Taylor/56 50.00
63 Mark Bavaro/6
64 Michael Strahan/92 20.00
65 Tiki Barber/97 20.00
66 Herman Edwards/49 40.00
67 Joe Namath/54 100.00
68 Justin McCareins/35 20.00
69 LaMont Jordan/50 15.00
70 Santana Moss/60 15.00
71 Bo Jackson/34 100.00
72 Fred Biletnikoff/40 50.00
73 George Blanda/110 30.00
74 Jim Plunkett/88 30.00
75 Marcus Allen/100 30.00
76 Barry Switzer/83 60.00
77 Correll Buckhalter/100 15.00
78 Donovan McNabb/30 100.00
79 Antwann Randle El/59 30.00
80 Bill Cowher/99 50.00
81 Franco Harris/32 60.00
82 Jack Lambert/42 100.00
83 Joe Greene/59 50.00
84 Kendrell Bell/97 15.00
85 L.C. Greenwood/68 40.00
86 Mel Blount/65 50.00
87 Terry Bradshaw/49 100.00
88 LaDainian Tomlinson/49 50.00
90 Bill Walsh/83 30.00
91 Shaun Alexander/54 30.00
92 Steve Largent/80 40.00
93 Matt Hasselbeck/100 25.00
94 Torry Holt/50 20.00
95 Clinton Portis/39 40.00
96 Laveranues Coles/100 15.00
97 Mark Brunell/30 20.00
98 Patrick Ramsey/59 25.00
99 Reuben Droughns/100 15.00
100 Sonny Jurgensen/99 30.00

2004 Playoff Prime Signatures Signature Proofs Gold

NM/M
Common Player: 15.00
Sequentially #'d to indicated quantity
Cards #'d 25 or less: No Pricing
1 Anquan Boldin/45 20.00
2 Josh McCown/12
3 Alge Crumpler/50 15.00
4 Michael Vick/7
5 Jamal Lewis/7
6 Todd Heap/50 20.00
7 Jim Kelly/12
8 Thurman Thomas/15
9 Travis Henry/20
10 Jake Delhomme/50 30.00
11 Stephen Davis/30 20.00
12 Steve Smith/50 20.00
13 Brian Urlacher/2
14 Dick Butkus/36 100.00
15 Gale Sayers/21
16 Mike Ditka/23
17 Mike Singletary/33 60.00
18 Rex Grossman/8
19 Richard Dent/14
20 Chad Johnson/14
21 Rudi Johnson/49 20.00
22 Jim Brown/32 100.00
23 Lee Suggs/7
24 Ozzie Newsome/40 20.00
25 Paul Warfield/42 40.00
26 Quincy Morgan/30 15.00
27 Willie Green/31 20.00
28 Antonio Bryant/15
29 Herschel Walker/34 40.00
30 Jimmy Johnson/10
31 Keyshawn Johnson/19
32 Roger Staubach/12
33 Terence Newman/25
34 Tony Dorsett/24
35 Terrell Davis/10
36 Joey Harrington/3
37 Ahman Green/5
38 Javon Walker/49 30.00
39 Paul Hornung/5
40 Reggie White/25
41 Robert Ferguson/25
42 Sterling Sharpe/50 25.00
43 David Carr/8
44 Domanick Davis/50 25.00
45 Earl Campbell/34 40.00
46 Peyton Manning/18
47 Reggie Wayne/15
48 Dante Hall/34 25.00
49 Priest Holmes/20
50 Trent Green/10
51 A.J. Feeley/14
52 Don Shula/10
53 Chris Chambers/23
54 Travis Minor/50 15.00
55 Fran Tarkenton/10
56 Bill Belichick/45 100.00
57 Tom Brady/12
58 Aaron Brooks/2
59 Deuce McAllister/49 25.00
60 Eddie "Boo" Williams/23
61 Joe Horn/20
62 Lawrence Taylor/22
63 Mark Bavaro/3
64 Michael Strahan/37 25.00
65 Tiki Barber/21
66 Herman Edwards/15
67 Joe Namath/12
68 Justin McCareins/13
69 LaMont Jordan/34 20.00
70 Santana Moss/37 20.00
71 Bo Jackson/21
72 Fred Biletnikoff/25
73 George Blanda/16
74 Jim Plunkett/14
75 Marcus Allen/32 50.00
76 Barry Switzer/49 60.00
77 Correll Buckhalter/50 15.00
78 Donovan McNabb/5
79 Antwann Randle El/33 30.00
80 Bill Cowher/49 80.00
81 Franco Harris/25
82 Jack Lambert/25
83 Joe Greene/42 50.00
84 Kendrell Bell/50 20.00
85 L.C. Greenwood/20
86 Mel Blount/47 60.00
87 Terry Bradshaw/12
88 LaDainian Tomlinson/21
89 Andre Carter/21
90 Bill Walsh/49 40.00
91 Shaun Alexander/37 30.00
92 Steve Largent/50 40.00
93 Matt Hasselbeck/50 25.00
94 Torry Holt/10
95 Clinton Portis/26 40.00
96 Laveranues Coles/50 15.00
97 Mark Brunell/8
98 Patrick Ramsey/11
99 Reuben Droughns/50 30.00
100 Sonny Jurgensen/9

2005 Playoff Prestige

NM/M
Common Player (1-150): .25
Minor Stars (1-150): .50
Unlisted Stars (1-150): .75
Common Rookie (151-244): 1.00
Minor Rookie (151-244): 2.00
Unlisted Rookie (151-244): 3.00
Common Rookie SP: 30.00
Pack (8): 5.00
Box (24): 80.00
1 Anquan Boldin .75
2 Emmitt Smith 2.00
3 Josh McCown .25
4 Larry Fitzgerald .75
5 Michael Vick 2.00
6 Peerless Price .50
7 Alge Crumpler .25
8 T.J. Duckett .50
9 Warrick Dunn .25
10 Ed Reed .25
11 Jamal Lewis .75
12 Kyle Boller .75
13 Ray Lewis .50
14 Todd Heap .25
15 Drew Bledsoe .75
16 Eric Moulds .25
17 Lee Evans .50
18 Travis Henry .25
19 Willis McGahee .75
20 Anthony Thomas .50
21 Brian Urlacher .75
22 Rex Grossman .75
23 David Terrell .25
24 Thomas Jones .50
25 Carson Palmer 1.00
26 Chad Johnson .50
27 Peter Warrick .50
28 Rudi Johnson .50
29 Antonio Bryant .50
30 William Green .50
31 Jeff Garcia .75
32 Kellen Winslow Jr. .50
33 Lee Suggs .25
34 Drew Henson .75
35 Julius Jones 1.00
36 Jason Witten .25
37 Keyshawn Johnson .50
38 Roy Williams-S .50
39 Ashley Lelie .50
40 Champ Bailey .25
41 Jake Plummer .50
42 Reuben Droughns .25
43 Rod Smith .25
44 Charles Rogers .75
45 Joey Harrington .75
46 Kevin Jones .75
47 Roy Williams-WR .75
48 Ahman Green .75
49 Donald Driver .25
50 Javon Walker .50
51 Brett Favre 2.50
52 Andre Johnson .75
53 David Carr 1.00
54 Domanick Davis .75
55 Jabar Gaffney .25
56 Edgerrin James 1.00
57 Marvin Harrison .75
58 Brandon Stokley .25
59 Peyton Manning 1.50
60 Reggie Wayne .25
61 Byron Leftwich 1.50
62 Fred Taylor .75
63 Jimmy Smith .25
64 Priest Holmes 1.00
65 Tony Gonzalez .50
66 Johnnie Morton .25
67 Trent Green .25
68 Chris Chambers .75
69 Randy McMichael .25
70 A.J. Feeley .25
71 Zach Thomas .25
72 Daunte Culpepper .75
73 Marcus Robinson .25
74 Mewelde Moore .25
75 Nate Burleson .25
76 Onterrio Smith .25
77 Randy Moss 1.50
78 Corey Dillon .50
79 Tom Brady 1.50
80 Deion Branch .25
81 Tedy Bruschi .25
82 David Givens .25
83 David Patten .25
84 Aaron Brooks .75
85 Deuce McAllister .25
86 Donte Stallworth .50
87 Joe Horn .25
88 Eli Manning 1.00
89 Jeremy Shockey .75
90 Kurt Warner .75
91 Michael Strahan .25
92 Tiki Barber .25
93 Amani Toomer .50
94 Chad Pennington 1.00
95 Curtis Martin .75
96 Santana Moss .25
97 Justin McCareins .25
98 Charles Woodson .25
99 Kerry Collins .25
100 Warren Sapp .25
101 Jerry Porter .25
102 Donovan McNabb 1.00
103 Jevon Kearse .25
104 Terrell Owens .75
105 Brian Westbrook .25
106 Todd Pinkston .25
107 Duce Staley .25
108 Hines Ward .50
109 Jerome Bettis .50
110 Joey Porter .25
111 Plaxico Burress .75
112 Ben Roethlisberger 1.50
113 Drew Brees .50
114 LaDainian Tomlinson 1.00
115 Keenan McCardell .25
116 Philip Rivers 1.00
117 Antonio Gates .50
118 Eric Johnson .25
119 Kevan Barlow .25
120 Brandon Lloyd .25
121 Tim Rattay .25
122 Darrell Jackson .25
123 Koren Robinson .25
124 Jerry Rice 2.00
125 Matt Hasselbeck .50
126 Shaun Alexander .75
127 Isaac Bruce .50
128 Marc Bulger .50
129 Marshall Faulk 1.00
130 Steven Jackson 1.00
131 Torry Holt .75
132 Derrick Brooks .25
133 Michael Clayton .50
134 Michael Pittman .25
135 Chris Simms .25
136 Chris Brown .50
137 Derrick Mason .25
138 Drew Bennett .25
139 Steve McNair .75
140 Clinton Portis 1.50
141 LaVar Arrington .75
142 Laveranues Coles .50
143 Patrick Ramsey .50
144 Rod Gardner .25
145 DeShaun Foster .25
146 Stephen Davis .50
147 Jake Delhomme .75
148 Muhsin Muhammad .50
149 Steve Smith .25
150 Keary Colbert .25
151 *Aaron Rodgers-SP* .25
152 *Adrian McPherson-SP* .25
153 *Alex Smith* .25
154 *Andrew Walter* .25
155 *Brock Berlin* 1.00
156 *Charlie Frye-SP* 50.00
157 *Chris Rix* 2.00
158 *Dan Orlovsky* 3.00
159 *Darian Durant* 1.00
160 *David Greene* 3.00
161 *Derek Anderson* 2.00
162 *Gino Guidugli* 1.00
163 *Jason Campbell* 6.00
164 *Jason White* 4.00
165 *Kyle Orton* 4.00
166 *Matt Jones-SP* 60.00
167 *Ryan Fitzpatrick* 1.00
168 *Stefan LeFors* 3.00
169 *Timmy Chang* 2.00
170 *Alvin Pearman* 2.00
171 *Anthony Davis* 2.00
172 *Brandon Jacobs* 1.00
173 *Carnell Williams* 6.00
174 *Cedric Benson* 6.00
175 *Cedric Houston* 1.00
176 *Ciatrick Fason* 3.00
177 *Damien Nash* 1.00
178 *Darren Sproles* 3.00
179 *Eric Shelton-SP* 30.00
180 *Frank Gore-SP* 50.00
181 *J.J. Arrington-SP* 40.00
182 *Kay-Jay Harris* 2.00
183 *Marion Barber III* 2.00
184 *Ronnie Brown* 6.00
185 *Ryan Moats* 2.00
186 *T.A. McLendon* 2.00
187 *Vernand Morency* 2.00
188 *Walter Reyes* 1.00
189 *Braylon Edwards* 6.00
190 *Charles Frederick* 1.00
191 *Chris Henry* 1.00
192 *Courtney Roby* 1.00
193 *Craig Bragg* 1.00
194 *Craphonso Thorpe-SP* 40.00
195 *Dante Ridgeway* 1.00
196 *Fred Amey* 1.00
197 *Fred Gibson* 3.00
198 *J.R. Russell* 1.00
199 *Jerome Mathis-SP* 30.00
200 *Josh Davis* 1.00
201 *Larry Brackins* 1.00
202 *Mark Bradley* 4.00
203 *Mark Clayton-SP* 50.00
204 *Mike Williams* 6.00
205 *Reggie Brown* 1.00
206 *Roddy White* 3.00
207 *Roscoe Parrish* 3.00
208 *Roydell Williams* 1.00
209 *Steve Savoy* 1.00
210 *Tab Perry* 1.00
211 *Taylor Stubblefield* 1.00
212 *Terrence Murphy* 2.00
213 *Troy Williamson* 5.00
214 *Vincent Jackson* 1.00
215 *Alex Smith* 3.00
216 *Heath Miller* 4.00
217 *Dan Cody* 3.00
218 *David Pollack* 4.00
219 *Erasmus James* 3.00
220 *Justin Tuck* 1.00
221 *Marcus Spears* 1.00
222 *Mike Roth* 2.00
223 *Anttaj Hawthorne* 1.00
224 *Mike Patterson* 2.00
225 *Shaun Cody* 1.00
226 *Travis Johnson* 1.00
227 *Channing Crowder* 2.00
228 *Darryl Blackstock* 1.00
229 *Demarcus Ware* 3.00
230 *Derrick Johnson* 4.00
231 *Kevin Burnett* 1.00
232 *Shawne Merriman* 1.00
233 *Adam Jones* 4.00
234 *Antrel Rolle* 4.00
235 *Brandon Browner* 1.00
236 *Bryant McFadden* 1.00
237 *Carlos Rogers* 3.00
238 *Corey Webster* 2.00
239 *Fabian Washington* 1.00
240 *Justin Miller* 2.00
241 *Marlin Jackson* 2.00
242 *Ernest Shazor* 1.00
243 *Josh Bullocks* 1.00
244 *Thomas Davis* 1.00

2005 Playoff Prestige Extra Points Red

Stars (1-150): 3X-5X
Rookies (151-244): 1X-2X
Rookie SPs: 1X
Production 125 Sets

2005 Playoff Prestige Extra Points Purple

Stars (1-150): 3X-6X
Rookies (151-244): 1X-3X
Rookie SPs: 1X-2X
Production 100 Sets

2005 Playoff Prestige Extra Points Green

Stars (1-150): 6X-12X
Rookies (151-244): 3X-6X
Rookie SPs: 2X-4X
Production 50 Sets

2005 Playoff Prestige Extra Points Black

Stars (1-150): 10X-20X
Rookies (151-244): 6X-12X
Rookie SPs: 4X-8X
Production 25 Sets

2005 Playoff Prestige Changing Stripes Materials

NM/M
Common Player: 8.00
Production 250 Sets
Prime: No Pricing
Production 25 Sets
1 Ahman Green 12.00
2 Clinton Portis 15.00
3 Duce Staley 12.00
4 Jevon Kearse 8.00
5 Terrell Owens 12.00
6 Jeff Garcia 8.00
7 Keyshawn Johnson 10.00
8 Drew Bledsoe 12.00
9 Jake Plummer 10.00
10 Marshall Faulk 12.00

2005 Playoff Prestige Draft Picks

NM/M
Common Player: 2.00
Inserted 1:24
Foil: 2X-4X
Production 100 Sets
Holo-Foil: No Pricing
Production 25 Sets
1 Alex Smith 10.00
2 Aaron Rodgers 8.00
3 Charlie Frye 4.00
4 Cedric Benson 6.00
5 Ronnie Brown 6.00
6 Carnell Williams 6.00
7 Vernand Morency 2.00
8 Braylon Edwards 6.00
9 Troy Williamson 5.00
10 Roddy White 3.00

2005 Playoff Prestige Draft Picks Rights

NM/M
Production 50 Sets
1 Alex Smith 275.00
2 Aaron Rodgers 225.00
3 Charlie Frye
4 Cedric Benson 225.00
5 Ronnie Brown 200.00
6 Carnell Williams 200.00
7 Vernand Morency
8 Braylon Edwards
9 Troy Williamson
10 Roddy White

2005 Playoff Prestige Game Day Jerseys

NM/M
Common Player: 6.00
Inserted 1:49
1 David Carr 12.00
2 Peyton Manning 15.00
3 Randy Moss 15.00
4 Donovan McNabb 12.00
5 Tom Brady 20.00
6 Larry Fitzgerald 10.00
7 Shaun Alexander 10.00
8 Anquan Boldin 10.00
9 Daunte Culpepper 10.00
10 Chris Brown 8.00
11 Isaac Bruce 8.00
12 Rod Smith 6.00
13 Roy Williams-S 8.00
14 Tony Gonzalez 8.00
15 Torry Holt 10.00
16 John Abraham 6.00
17 Ike Hilliard 6.00
18 Jimmy Smith 6.00
19 Byron Leftwich 15.00
20 Stephen Davis 8.00
21 T.J. Duckett 8.00
22 Travis Henry 6.00
23 Julius Peppers 6.00
24 Charles Rogers 8.00
25 Eric Moulds 6.00
26 Freddie Mitchell 6.00
27 Anthony Thomas 8.00
28 Steve McNair 10.00
29 Brian Urlacher 10.00
30 Donte Stallworth 8.00

2005 Playoff Prestige Gridiron Heritage

NM/M
Common Player: 2.00
Inserted 1:24
Foil: 1X-3X
Production 100 Sets
Materials: 2X-4X
Inserted 1:60
1 Brett Favre 8.00
2 Edgerrin James 4.00
3 Byron Leftwich 5.00
4 Peyton Manning 5.00
5 Larry Fitzgerald 3.00
6 Shaun Alexander 3.00
7 Daunte Culpepper 3.00
8 Marshall Faulk 4.00
9 Steve McNair 3.00
10 Zach Thomas 2.00
11 Mike Alstott 2.00
12 Jeremiah Trotter 2.00
13 Drew Brees 2.50
14 Isaac Bruce 2.50
15 Chris Chambers 3.00
16 Santana Moss 2.00
17 Peerless Price 2.50
18 Donald Driver 2.00
19 Amani Toomer 2.50
20 Todd Pinkston 2.00
21 Derrick Mason 2.00
22 Jimmy Smith 2.00
23 Michael Vick 6.00
24 Andre Johnson 3.00
25 Josh McCown 2.00

2005 Playoff Prestige Fans of the Game

NM/M
Common Card: 2.00
Inserted 1:24
1 Rick Reilly 3.00
2 Heather Mitts 3.00
3 Rulon Gardner 2.00
4 Sue Bird 3.00

2005 Playoff Prestige Fans of the Game Signatures

NM/M
Common Card: 40.00
1 Rick Reilly 50.00
2 Heather Mitts 75.00
3 Rulon Gardner 40.00
4 Sue Bird 80.00

2005 Playoff Prestige League Leaders

NM/M
Common Card: 2.50
Inserted 1:24
Foil: 2X-4X
Production 100 Sets
Holo-Foil: No Pricing
Production 25 Sets
Materials: 3X-6X
Production 250 Sets
Materials Prime: No Pricing
Production 25 Sets
1 Peyton Manning, Trent Green 5.00
2 Daunte Culpepper, Brett Favre 8.00
3 Donovan McNabb, Aaron Brooks 4.00
4 Jake Plummer, Drew Bledsoe 3.00
5 Tom Brady, David Carr 5.00
6 Marc Bulger, Matt Hasselbeck 2.50
7 Carson Palmer, Byron Leftwich 5.00
8 Shaun Alexander, Clinton Portis 5.00
9 Edgerrin James, Corey Dillon 4.00
10 Curtis Martin, LaDainian Tomlinson 4.00
11 Tiki Barber, Ahman Green 3.00
12 Rudi Johnson, Fred Taylor 3.00
13 Willis McGahee, Domanick Davis 3.00
14 Kevin Jones, Deuce McAllister 3.00
15 Keyshawn Johnson, Laveranues Coles 2.50
16 Javon Walker, Torry Holt 3.00
17 Chad Johnson, Drew Bennett 2.50
18 Isaac Bruce, Terrell Owens 3.00
19 Rod Smith, Plaxico Burress 3.00
20 Michael Clayton, Darrell Jackson 2.50
21 Curtis Martin, Corey Dillon, Shaun Alexander, Tiki Barber 3.00
22 Edgerrin James, LaDainian Tomlinson, Clinton Portis, Ahman Green 5.00
23 Rudi Johnson, Fred Taylor, Kevin Jones, Deuce McAllister 3.00
24 Trent Green, Peyton Manning, Brett Favre, Daunte Culpepper 8.00
25 Jake Plummer, Tom Brady, Jake Delhomme, Donovan McNabb 5.00
26 David Carr, Carson Palmer, Marc Bulger, Aaron Brooks 4.00
27 Chad Johnson, Drew Bennett, Keyshawn Johnson, Laveranues Coles 2.50
28 Tony Gonzalez, Plaxico Burress, Javon Walker, Torry Holt 3.00
29 Jimmy Smith, Rod Smith, Isaac Bruce, Donald Driver 2.50
30 Derrick Mason, Andre Johnson, Terrell Owens, Michael Clayton 3.00

2005 Playoff Prestige Prestigious Pros - Orange

NM/M
Common Card: 2.50
Production 500 Sets
Blue: 1X-2X
Production 250 Sets
Red: 1X-2X
Production 150 Sets
Purple: 1X-3X
Production 100 Sets
Green: 1.5X-3X
Production 75 Sets
Silver: 2X-4X
Production 50 Sets
Gold: No Pricing
Production 25 Sets
Platinum: No Pricing
Production 10 Sets
1 Aaron Brooks 3.00
2 Andre Johnson 3.00
3 Ben Roethlisberger 5.00
4 Brett Favre 8.00
5 Brian Urlacher 3.00
6 Byron Leftwich 5.00
7 Carson Palmer 4.00
8 Chad Pennington 4.00
9 Corey Dillon 2.50
10 Daunte Culpepper 3.00
11 David Carr 4.00
12 Deuce McAllister 3.00
13 Donovan McNabb 4.00
14 Drew Bledsoe 3.00
15 Drew Brees 2.50
16 Duce Staley 2.50
17 Edgerrin James 4.00
18 Hines Ward 2.50
19 Isaac Bruce 2.50
20 Jake Plummer 2.50
21 Jamal Lewis 3.00
22 Javon Walker 2.50
23 Jeff Garcia 3.00
24 Jeremy Shockey 3.00
25 Jevon Kearse 2.50
26 Joey Harrington 3.00
27 Keyshawn Johnson 2.50
28 LaDainian Tomlinson 4.00
29 LaVar Arrington 3.00
30 Lee Suggs 2.50
31 Marc Bulger 2.50
32 Marshall Faulk 4.00
33 Marvin Harrison 3.00
34 Matt Hasselbeck 2.50
35 Michael Vick 6.00
36 Peyton Manning 5.00
37 Plaxico Burress 3.00
38 Priest Holmes 4.00
39 Randy Moss 5.00
40 Ray Lewis 2.50
41 Rex Grossman 3.00
42 Rudi Johnson 2.50
43 Shaun Alexander 3.00
44 Steve McNair 3.00
45 Terrell Owens 3.00
46 Tiki Barber 2.50
47 Tom Brady 5.00
48 Tony Gonzalez 2.50
49 Torry Holt 3.00
50 Trent Green 2.50

2005 Playoff Pres. Prestigious Pros Mat. Gold-Jerseys

NM/M
Common Card: 8.00
Production 100 Sets
Patches-Platinum: No Pricing
Production 10 Sets
1 Aaron Brooks 10.00
2 Andre Johnson 10.00
3 Ben Roethlisberger 15.00
4 Brett Favre 20.00
5 Brian Urlacher 10.00
6 Byron Leftwich 15.00
7 Carson Palmer 12.00
8 Chad Pennington 12.00
9 Corey Dillon 8.00
10 Daunte Culpepper 10.00
11 David Carr 12.00
12 Deuce McAllister 10.00
13 Donovan McNabb 12.00
14 Drew Bledsoe 10.00
15 Drew Brees 8.00
16 Duce Staley 8.00
17 Edgerrin James 12.00
18 Hines Ward 8.00
19 Isaac Bruce 8.00
20 Jake Plummer 8.00
21 Jamal Lewis 10.00
22 Javon Walker 8.00
23 Jeff Garcia 10.00
24 Jeremy Shockey 10.00
25 Jevon Kearse 8.00
26 Joey Harrington 10.00
27 Keyshawn Johnson 8.00
28 LaDainian Tomlinson 12.00
29 LaVar Arrington 10.00
30 Lee Suggs 8.00
31 Marc Bulger 8.00
32 Marshall Faulk 12.00
33 Marvin Harrison 10.00
34 Matt Hasselbeck 8.00
35 Michael Vick 18.00
36 Peyton Manning 15.00
37 Plaxico Burress 10.00
38 Priest Holmes 12.00
39 Randy Moss 15.00
40 Ray Lewis 8.00
41 Rex Grossman 10.00
42 Rudi Johnson 8.00
43 Shaun Alexander 10.00
44 Steve McNair 10.00
45 Terrell Owens 10.00
46 Tiki Barber 8.00
47 Tom Brady 15.00
48 Tony Gonzalez 8.00
49 Torry Holt 10.00
50 Trent Green 8.00

2005 Playoff Prestige Stars of the NFL

NM/M
Common Player: 2.50
Inserted 1:24
Foil: 1X-3X
Production 100 Sets
1 Aaron Brooks 3.00
2 Andre Johnson 3.00
3 Brett Favre 8.00
4 Brian Urlacher 3.00
5 Byron Leftwich 5.00
6 Chad Johnson 2.50
7 Chad Pennington 4.00
8 Chris Brown 2.50
9 Daunte Culpepper 3.00
10 David Carr 4.00
11 Donovan McNabb 4.00
12 Drew Bledsoe 3.00
13 Edgerrin James 4.00
14 Isaac Bruce 2.50
15 Jake Delhomme 3.00
16 Javon Walker 2.50
17 Jeremy Shockey 3.00
18 LaDainian Tomlinson 4.00
19 Marvin Harrison 3.00
20 Matt Hasselbeck 2.50
21 Michael Vick 6.00
22 Peyton Manning 5.00
23 Randy Moss 5.00
24 Priest Holmes 4.00
25 Tom Brady 5.00

2005 Playoff Prestige Stars of the NFL Holo-Foil

No Pricing
Production 25 Sets
Materials-Jerseys Prime: No Pricing
Production 25 Sets
1 Aaron Brooks
2 Andre Johnson
3 Brett Favre
4 Brian Urlacher
5 Byron Leftwich
6 Chad Johnson
7 Chad Pennington
8 Chris Brown
9 Daunte Culpepper
10 David Carr
11 Donovan McNabb
12 Drew Bledsoe
13 Edgerrin James
14 Isaac Bruce
15 Jake Delhomme
16 Javon Walker
17 Jeremy Shockey
18 LaDainian Tomlinson
19 Marvin Harrison
20 Matt Hasselbeck
21 Michael Vick
22 Peyton Manning
23 Randy Moss
24 Priest Holmes
25 Tom Brady

2005 Playoff Prestige Super Bowl Heroes

NM/M
Common Player: 2.00
Inserted 1:24
Foil: 1X-2X
Production 100 Sets
Holo-Foil: No Pricing
Production 25 Sets
Some Holo-Foil Cards are autographed
1 Tom Brady 5.00
2 Deion Branch 2.00
3 Corey Dillon 2.50
4 David Givens 2.00
5 Mike Vrabel 2.00
6 Tedy Bruschi 2.00
7 Rodney Harrison 2.00
8 Adam Vinatieri 2.00
9 Donovan McNabb 4.00
10 Terrell Owens 3.00

2005 Playoff Prestige Turning Pro

NM/M
Common Card: 6.00
Production 250 Sets
Prime: No Pricing
Production 25 Sets
1 Lee Suggs 6.00
2 Barry Sanders 25.00
3 Andre Johnson 10.00
4 Kyle Boller 10.00
5 Carson Palmer 12.00
6 Michael Vick 20.00
7 Laveranues Coles 6.00
8 Clinton Portis 15.00
9 Edgerrin James 12.00
10 Marshall Faulk 12.00

2004 Playoff Super Bowl XXXVIII Jerseys

NM/M
Common Player: 15.00
SB1 David Carr 15.00
SB2 Warren Moon 15.00
SB3 David Carr, Warren Moon 25.00

1985 Police Raiders/Rams

Broken down into two 15-card subsets for each team, the cards are not numbered, except with the player's uniform numerals. It was sponsored by KIIS Radio, the Rams and Raiders and the Los Angeles County Sheriff's Department. Card fronts include a photo of the player, with his name underneath, along with his team's helmet and sponsor logo. Card backs have the player's name, uniform number, position, bio and a safety message printed in black. The cards measure 2-13/16 x 4-1/8".

NM/M
Complete Set (30): 20.00
Common Raiders (1-15): .75
Common Rams (16-30): .50
1 Marcus Allen 4.00
2 Lyle Alzado 1.50
3 Todd Christensen 1.00
4 Dave Dalby .75
5 Mike Davis .75
6 Ray Guy 1.00
7 Frank Hawkins .75
8 Lester Hayes 1.00
9 Mike Haynes 1.00
10 Howie Long 2.00
11 Rod Martin .75
12 Mickey Marvin .75
13 Jim Plunkett 1.25
14 Brad Van Pelt .75
15 Dokie Williams .75
16 Bill Bain .50
17 Mike Barber .50
18 Dieter Brock .75
19 Nolan Cromwell .75
20 Eric Dickerson 3.00
21 Reggie Doss .50
22 Carl Ekern .50
23 Kent Hill .50
24 LeRoy Irvin .75
25 Johnnie Johnson .50
26 Jeff Kemp .50
27 Mike Lansford .50
28 Mel Owens .50
29 Barry Redden .50
30 Mike Wilcher .50

1986 Police Bears/ Patriots

Featuring the two teams from Super Bowl XX, this 17-card set measures 2-5/8" x 4-1/4". The card fronts boast a photo of the player, with his name, uniform number and position at the bottom. The card backs have "Super Bowl Superstars 1986 presents" at the top, with a safety tip listed at the bottom of the card. The card number is located in the lower right. Chicago players are on card #s 2-9, while New England players are highlighted on #s 10-17.

NM/M
Complete Set (17): 15.00
Common Player: .50
1 Title Card (Checklist on back of card) .75
2 Richard Dent 2.00
3 Walter Payton 6.00
4 William Perry 1.00
5 Jim McMahon 1.50
6 Dave Duerson .75
7 Gary Fencik .75
8 Otis Wilson .75
9 Willie Gault 1.00
10 Craig James 1.00
11 Fred Marion .50
12 Ronnie Lippett .50
13 Stanley Morgan 1.00
14 John Hannah 1.00
15 Andre Tippett 1.00
16 Tony Franklin .50
17 Tony Eason 1.00

1976 Popsicle Teams

Each NFL team is represented in this 28-card set, which features a color action shot on the front of each card, plus the corresponding team's helmet. The back provides a historical overview of the team. The cards, which are unnumbered, are listed below alphabetically. Each one is 3-3/8" x 2-1/8" and resembles a thin plastic credit card with rounded corners. A title card, which says "Pro Quarterback, Pro Football's Leading Magazine," was also produced.

NM/M
Complete Set (30): 40.00
Common Player: 2.50
(1) Atlanta Falcons 2.50
(2) Baltimore Colts 2.50
(3) Buffalo Bills 2.50
(4) Chicago Bears 2.50
(5) Cincinnati Bengals 2.50
(6) Cleveland Browns 2.50
(7) Dallas Cowboys 4.00
(8) Denver Broncos 2.50
(9) Detriot Lions 2.50
(10) Green Bay Packers 2.50
(11) Houston Oilers 2.50
(12) Kansas City Chiefs 2.50
(13) Los Angeles Rams 2.50
(14) Miami Dolphins 4.00
(15) Minnesota Vikings 2.50
(16) New England Patriots 2.50
(17) New Orleans Saints 2.50
(18A) New York Giants (Giants on helmet) 3.50
(18B) New York Giants (New York on helmet) 4.50
(19) New York Jets 2.50
(20) Oakland Raiders 4.00
(21) Philadelphia Eagles 2.50
(22) Pittsburgh Steelers 4.00
(23) St. Louis Cardinals 2.50
(24) San Diego Chargers 2.50
(25) San Francisco 49ers 3.00
(26) Seattle Seahawks 2.50
(27) Tampa Bay Buccaneers 2.50
(28) Washington Redskins 3.50
---- Title Card, Pro Quarterback 30.00

1962 Post Cereal

Post Cereal's only U.S. football issue, the 1962 set is complete at 200 cards. The blank-backed cards were printed on the back panels of various Post cereals and measure the standard 2-1/2" x 3-1/2" when properly cut. Like the Post Cereal baseball issues from the same period, the cards must be very carefully cut from the boxes to be considered in top condition. Players who were pictured on boxes of the less-popular cereals are scarcer and more valuable, explaining the higher prices on about two dozen of the cards listed below.

NM/M
Complete Set (200): 2,500
Common Player: 3.50
1 Dan Currie 3.50
2 Boyd Dowler 3.50
3 Bill Forester 3.50
4 Forrest Gregg 4.00
5 Dave Hanner 3.50
6 Paul Hornung 14.00
7 Henry Jordan 3.50
8 Jerry Kramer 12.00
9 Max McGee 3.50
10 Tom Moore 100.00
11 Jim Ringo 6.00
12 Bart Starr 20.00
13 Jim Taylor 12.00
14 Fred Thurston 3.50
15 Kess Whittenton 3.50
16 Erich Barnes 3.50
17 Roosevelt Grier 5.00
18 Bob Gaiters 3.50
19 Roosevelt Brown 3.50
20 Sam Huff 8.00
21 Jim Katcavage 3.50
22 Cliff Livingston 3.50
23 Dick Lynch 3.50
24 Joe Morrison 20.00
25 Dick Nolan 18.00
26 Andy Robustelli 5.00
27 Kyle Rote 7.00
28 Del Shofner 25.00
29 Y.A. Tittle 60.00
30 Alex Webster 3.50
31 Bill Barnes 3.50
32 Maxie Baughan 3.50
33 Chuck Bednarik 8.00
34 Tom Brookshier 6.00
35 Jimmy Carr 3.50
36 Ted Dean 3.50
37 Sonny Jurgensen 12.00
38 Tommy McDonald 3.50
39 Clarence Peaks 3.50
40 Pete Retzlaff 3.50
41 Jesse Richardson 30.00
42 Leo Sugar 3.50
43 Bobby Walston 40.00
44 Chuck Weber 3.50
45 Ed Khayat 3.50
46 Howard Cassady 3.50
47 Gail Cogdill 3.50
48 Jim Gibbons 3.50
49 Bill Glass 3.50
50 Alex Karras 3.50
51 Dick "Night Train" Lane 3.50
52 Yale Lary 3.50
53 Dan Lewis 3.50
54 Darris McCord 50.00
55 Jim Martin 3.50
56 Earl Morrall 3.50
57 Jim Ninowski 3.50
58 Nick Pietrosante 3.50
59 Joe Schmidt 50.00
60 Harley Sewell 3.50
61 Jim Brown 60.00
62 Galen Fiss 40.00
63 Bob Gain 3.50
64 Jim Houston 3.50
65 Mike McCormack 3.50
66 Gene Hickerson 3.50
67 Bob Mitchell 3.50
68 John Morrow 3.50
69 Bernie Parrish 3.50
70 Milt Plum 3.50
71 Ray Renfro 3.50
72 Dick Schafrath 3.50
73 Jim Ray Smith 3.50
74 Sam Baker 220.00
75 Paul Wiggin 3.50
76 Raymond Berry 3.50
77 Bob Boyd 3.50
78 Ordell Braase 3.50
79 Art Donovan 3.50
80 Dee Mackey 3.50
81 Gino Marchetti 3.50
82 Lenny Moore 3.50
83 Jim Mutscheller 3.50
84 Steve Myhra 3.50
85 Jimmy Orr 3.50
86 Jim Parker 3.50
87 Bill Pellington 3.50
88 Alex Sandusky 3.50
89 Dick Szymanski 3.50
90 Johnny Unitas 25.00
91 Bruce Bosley 3.50
92 John Brodie 12.00
93 Dave Baker 125.00
94 Tommy Davis 3.50
95 Bob Harrison 3.50

96 Matt Hazeltine 3.50
97 Jim Johnson 50.00
98 Bill Kilmer 8.00
99 Jerry Mertens 3.50
100 Frank Morze 3.50
101 R.C. Owens 3.50
102 J.D. Smith 3.50
103 Bob St. Clair 60.00
104 Monty Stickles 3.50
105 Abe Woodson 3.50
106 Doug Atkins 3.50
107 Ed Brown 3.50
108 J.C. Caroline 3.50
109 Rick Casares 3.50
110 Angelo Coia 175.00
111 Mike Ditka 20.00
112 Joe Fortunato 3.50
113 Willie Galimore 3.50
114 Bill George 5.50
115 Stan Jones 3.50
116 Johnny Morris 5.50
117 Larry Morris 40.00
118 Rich Pettibon 3.50
119 Bill Wade 4.00
120 Maury Youmans 3.50
121 Preston Carpenter 3.50
122 Buddy Dial 3.50
123 Bobby Joe Green 3.50
124 Mike Henry 3.50
125 John Henry Johnson 5.50
126 Bobby Layne 15.00
127 Gene Lipscomb 5.50
128 Lou Michaels 3.50
129 John Nisby 3.50
130 John Reger 3.50
131 Mike Sandusky 3.50
132 George Tarasovic 3.50
133 Tom Tracy 40.00
134 Glynn Gregory 3.50
135 Frank Clarke 40.00
136 Mike Connelly 40.00
137 L.G. Dupre 3.50
138 Bob Fry 3.50
139 Allen Green 60.00
140 Bill Howton 3.50
141 Bob Lilly 12.00
142 Don Meredith 16.00
143 Dick Moegle 3.50
144 Don Perkins 5.50
145 Jerry Tubbs 60.00
146 J.W. Lockett 3.50
147 Ed Cook 3.50
148 John David Crow 5.50
149 Sam Etcheverry 5.50
150 Frank Fuller 3.50
151 Prentice Gautt 3.50
152 Jimmy Hill 3.50
153 Bill Koman 40.00
154 Larry Wilson 5.50
155 Dale Meinert 3.50
156 Ed Henke 3.50
157 Sonny Randle 3.50
158 Ralph Guglielmi 40.00
159 Joe Childress 3.50
160 Jon Arnett 5.50
161 Dick Bass 3.50
162 Zeke Bratkowski 5.50
163 Carroll Dale 3.50
164 Art Hunter 3.50
165 John Lovetere 3.50
166 Lamar Lundy 3.50
167 Ollie Matson 8.00
168 Ed Meador 3.50
169 Jack Pardee 60.00
170 Jim Phillips 3.50
171 Les Richter 3.50
172 Frank Ryan 3.50
173 Frank Varrichione 3.50
174 Grady Alderman 3.50
175 Rip Hawkins 3.50
176 Don Joyce 60.00
177 Bill Lapham 3.50
178 Tommy Mason 3.50
179 Hugh McElhenny 3.50
180 Dave Middleton 3.50
181 Dick Pesonen 3.50
182 Karl Rubke 3.50
183 George Shaw 3.50
184 Fran Tarkenton 35.00
185 Mel Triplett 3.50
186 Frank Youso 40.00
187 Bill Bishop 3.50
188 Bill Anderson 40.00
189 Don Bosseler 3.50
190 Fred Hageman 3.50
191 Sam Horner 3.50
192 Jim Kerr 3.50
193 Joe Krakoski 150.00
194 Fred Dugan 3.50
195 John Paluck 3.50
196 Vince Promuto 3.50
197 Joe Rutgens 3.50
198 Norm Snead 5.50
199 Andy Stynchula 3.50
200 Bob Toneff 3.50

1962 Post Booklets

Measuring 5" x 3", each of the four booklets included 15 pages. The booklet covers include a drawing of the player, with his name, position and team, along with the title. The book covers are numbered in the upper right with a prefix of "book."

NM/M
Complete Set (4): 65.00
Common Player: 10.00
1 Jon Arnett Football Formations To Watch (Important Rules of the Game) 10.00
2 Paul Hornung Fundamentals of Football 25.00
3 Sonny Jurgensen How To Play On Offense (How To Call Signals And Key Plays) 20.00
4 Sam Huff How To Play Defense 15.00

1977 Pottsville Maroons

This 1977 17-card set commemorates the 1925 NFL champion team with photos of the players on the front. The player's name, number and team are printed at the bottom of the card front. The back include the player's name, number, bio, position and career highlights. At the bottom of the card back is the 1977 copyright line, which attributes the set to the estate of Joseph C. Zacko Sr. and executor Russel F. Zacko.

NM/M
Complete Set (17): 25.00
Common Player: 1.50
1 Team History 1.50
2 The Symbolic Shoe 1.50
3 Jack Ernst 1.50
4 Tony Latone 1.50
5 Duke Osborn 1.50
6 Frank Bucher 1.50
7 Frankie Racis 1.50
8 Russ Hathaway 1.50
9 W.H. Flanagan 1.50
10 Charlie Berry 3.00
11 Russ Stein, Herb Stein 1.50
12 Howard Lebengood 1.50
13 Denny Hughes 1.50
14 Barney Wentz 1.50
15 Eddie Doyle (UER) (Bio says American troops landed in Africa 1943; should be 1942) 1.50
16 Walter French 1.50
17 Dick Rauch 3.00

1994 Predators Arena Team Issue

This set was issued by the Orlando Predators of the Arena Football League and sold through their concession stands and gift shop. The cards are unnumbered.

NM/M
Complete Set (27): 7.00
Common Player: .25
1 Ben Bennett .25
2 Henry Brown .25
3 Webbie Burnett .25
4 Jorge Cimadevilla .25
5 Bernard Clark .25
6 Wayne Dickson .25
7 Eric Drakes .25
8 Chris Ford .25
9 Victor Hall .25
10 Paul McGowan .25
11 Perry Moss CO .25
12 Jerry Odom .25
13 Billy Owens .25
14 Marshall Roberts .25
15 Durwood Roquemore .25
16 Rusty Russell DL .25
17 Tony Scott .25
18 Ricky Shaw .25
19 Alex Shell .25
20 Bill Stewart .25
21 Duke Tobin .25
22 Barry Wagner .25
23 Jackie Walker .25
24 Herkie Walls .25
25 Isaac Williams .25
26 Coaches .25
27 The Klaw (mascot) .25

1994 Press Pass SB Photo Board

Measuring 10" x 14", these Photo Boards showcased color photos of both Buffalo and Dallas players on the front, along with the Super Bowl logo in gold foil. Each of the boards are individually numbered of 50,000. The product was sold at the Super Bowl Card Show in Atlanta. The backs include photos and statistic leaders in both conferences.

NM/M
1 John Elway, Rick Mirer, Reggie Langhorne, Neil Smith, Nate Odomes, Thurman Thomas, Steve Young, Jerome Bettis, Sterling Sharpe, Reggie White, Deion Sanders, Emmitt Smith SB XXVIII Photo Board 10.00

1996 Press Pass

Top rookies slated to make NFL debuts in 1996 are featured in this 55-card 1996 Press Pass Football Draft Picks set, the company's first devoted to football. Each card front has a pair of color action photos on it, along with gold foil stamping which is used for the player's name at the bottom and the brand logo in the upper left corner. The back has the player's name, college and card number at the top, with a box below with information about his college career. In the center is a circle with statistics around the diameter and a color photo in the center. Another box below the photo has biographical information in it. Three parallel sets were also created. First, autographed versions of all 55 cards are available at a rate of one per every 72 packs. Next, Emerald Proofs were limited to only 380 of each card, with an insertion rate of one per every 36 packs. Last, each pack includes a Holofoil version of the set, which features a holographic finish on the front. Insert sets include Crystal Ball, and four different denominations of Prime Time Phone cards of nine different players.

NM/M
Complete Set (55): 12.00
Common Player: .10
Comp. Holofoil Set (55):
Holofoil Cards: 1X-2X
Comp. Emerald Proof (55):
Emerald Proof Cards: 3X-5X
1 Keyshawn Johnson 3.00
2 Jonathan Ogden .10
3 Duane Clemons .10
4 Kevin Hardy .10
5 Eddie George 5.00
6 Karim Abdul-Jabbar 1.50
7 Terry Glenn 1.50
8 Leeland McElroy 1.00
9 Simeon Rice .10
10 Roman Oben .10
11 Daryl Gardener .10
12 Marcus Coleman .10
13 Christian Peter .10
14 Tim Biakabutuka 1.00
15 Eric Moulds .75
16 Chris Darkins .50
17 Andre Johnson .10
18 Lawyer Milloy .10
19 Jon Runyan .10
20 Mike Alstott .50
21 Jeff Hartings .10
22 Amani Toomer .75
23 Danny Kanell .75
24 Marco Battaglia .50
25 Stephen Davis .75
26 Johnny McWilliams .50
27 Israel Ifeanyi .10
28 Scott Slutzker .50
29 Bryant Mix .10
30 Brian Roche .10
31 Stanley Pritchett .10
32 Jerome Woods .10
33 Tommie Frazier .10
34 Stepfret Williams .10
35 Ray Mickens .10
36 Alex Van Dyke .50
37 Bobby Hoying .50
38 Tony Brackens .10
39 Dietrich Jells .10
40 Jason Odom .10
41 Randall Godfrey .10
42 Willie Anderson .10
43 Tony Banks .10
44 Michael Cheever .10
45 Jerod Cherry .10
46 Chris Doering .10
47 Steve Taneyhill .10
48 Kyle Wachholz .10
49 Dusty Zeigler .10
50 Derrick Mayes .50
51 Orpheus Roye .10
52 Sedric Clark .10
53 Richard Huntley .10
54 Donnie Edwards .10
55 Zach Thomas .10

1996 Press Pass Holofoil

The 55-card, standard-size set was issued as a parallel to the base Press Pass set. The cards were inserted in each pack and featured holofoil stock.

NM/M
Common Player: .30
Stars: 2X

1996 Press Pass Holofoil Emerald Proofs

The 55-card, standard-size set was a parallel issue to the base set. Inserted every 36 packs, the cards feature holofoil stock with "Emerald Proof" printed on each card front. Production of each card was limited to just 280.

NM/M
Common Player: 1.00
Stars: 3X-5X

1996 Press Pass Autographs

The 12-card, standard-size set, inserted every 72 packs, is similar to the base cards, except with the player's autograph on the card front. The card backs inform the collector that he/she has received a "limited edition" signed card.

NM/M
Common Player: 10.00
1 Karim Abdul-Jabbar 15.00
2 Tony Banks 18.00
3 Tim Biakabutuka 12.00
4 Duane Clemons 10.00
5 Stephen Davis 30.00
6 Chris Doering 10.00
7 Bobby Hoying 15.00
8 Keyshawn Johnson 45.00
9 Danny Kanell 15.00
10 Leeland McElroy 20.00
11 Jonathan Ogden 10.00
12 Steve Taneyhill 10.00

1996 Press Pass Crystal Ball

These 1996 Press Pass inserts were seeded one per 18 packs. The die-cut cards, numbered using a "CB" prefix, have a crystal ball on the front with a player photo inside. His name is written along the base of the crystal ball. The back has the player's name inside the ball with an analysis of the player's talents. The card number is in a circle in the lower left corner.

NM/M
Complete Set (12): 50.00
Common Player: 2.00
1 Lawyer Milloy 2.00
2 Terry Glenn 5.00
3 Duane Clemons 2.00
4 Kevin Hardy 2.00
5 Eddie George 12.00
6 Jonathan Ogden 2.00
7 Karim Abdul-Jabbar 3.00
8 Tim Biakabutuka 2.00
9 Eric Moulds 8.00
10 Danny Kanell 2.00
11 Israel Ifeanyi 2.00
12 Keyshawn Johnson 15.00

1996 Press Pass Prime Time Phone Cards

Four different denominations - $5, $10, $20 and $1,996 - are used for these Prime Time Phone cards, found one every 36 packs of 1996 Press Pass Football Draft Picks product. Nine players are featured on the cards, which have a color action photo on the front, plus the denomination. The back, numbered using a "PT" prefix, has instructions on how to use the card.

NM/M
Complete Set (9): 120.00
Common Player: 10.00
Ten Dollar Cards: 2X-4X
Twenty Dollar Cards: 3X-6X
1 Keyshawn Johnson 30.00
2 Jonathan Ogden 10.00
3 Tommie Frazier 12.00
4 Eddie George 20.00
5 Karim Abdul-Jabbar 15.00
6 Terry Glenn 15.00
7 Leeland McElroy 12.00
8 Tim Biakabutuka 18.00
9 Kevin Hardy 10.00

1996 Press Pass Paydirt

The 75-card, standard-size set was issued in five-card packs. The set is the retail version and includes inserts such as: Paydirt Holofoil, Paydirt Red Foil, Paydirt Autographs and Paydirt Eddie George.

NM/M
Complete Set (75): 20.00
Common Player: .10
1 Keyshawn Johnson 4.00
2 Jonathan Ogden .25
3 Duane Clemons .40
4 Kevin Hardy .50
5 Eddie George 3.50
6 Karim Abdul-Jabbar 2.00
7 Terry Glenn 3.00
8 Leeland McElroy 2.00
9 Simeon Rice .40
10 Roman Oben .10
11 Daryl Gardener .40
12 Marcus Coleman .10
13 Christian Peter .10
14 Tim Biakabutuka 3.00
15 Eric Moulds 1.25
16 Chris Darkins 1.00
17 Andre Johnson .10
18 Lawyer Milloy .25
19 Jon Runyan .10
20 Mike Alstott 1.50
21 Jeff Hartings .10
22 Amani Toomer 1.25
23 Danny Kanell 1.25
24 Marco Battaglia .60
25 Stephen Davis 1.00
26 Johnny McWilliams .40
27 Israel Ifeanyi .10
28 Scott Slutzker .10
29 Bryant Mix .10
30 Brian Roche .10
31 Stanley Pritchett .40
32 Jerome Woods .10
33 Tommie Frazier 1.50
34 Stepfret Williams .75
35 Ray Mickens .10
36 Alex Van Dyke 1.00
37 Bobby Hoying 1.25
38 Tony Brackens .10
39 Dietrich Jells .10
40 Jason Odom .10
41 Randall Godfrey .25
42 Willie Anderson .25
43 Tony Banks .75
44 Michael Cheever .10
45 Je'Rod Cherry .25
46 Chris Doering .25
47 Steve Taneyhill .40
48 Kyle Wachholz .40
49 Dusty Zeigler .10
50 Derrick Mayes 1.25
51 Orpheus Roye .10
52 Sedric Clark .10
53 Richard Huntley .10
54 Donnie Edwards .25
55 Zach Thomas .10
56 Alex Molden .30
57 Jimmy Herndon .10
58 Mike Alstott 1.50
59 Scott Greene .40
60 Danny Kanell 1.25
61 Jonathan Ogden .25
62 Simeon Rice .40
63 Kevin Hardy .50
64 Jon Runyan .10
65 Stephen Davis 1.00
66 Tim Biakabutuka 3.00
67 Terry Glenn 3.00
68 Leeland McElroy 2.00
69 Eric Moulds 1.25
70 Karim Abdul-Jabbar 2.00
71 Lawyer Milloy .25
72 Derrick Mayes 1.25
73 Tommie Frazier 1.50
74 Bobby Hoying 1.25
75 Kyle Wachholz (CL) .10

1996 Press Pass Paydirt Holofoil

The 75-card, standard-size set, a parallel to the base set with holofoil paper, was inserted every four packs.

NM/M
Complete Set (75): 125.00
Common Player: .40
Stars: 2X-4X

1996 Press Pass Paydirt Red Foil

The 75-card, regular-size set was inserted in each pack of Paydirt and was also known as Torquers. The foil wrappers incorrectly describe the parallel set as having "blue foil."

NM/M
Common Player: .20
Stars: 1X-2X

1996 Press Pass Paydirt Autographs

The 16-card, standard-size set was inserted every 72 packs of Paydirt. The card fronts contain the player's autograph while the backs inform the collectors of his/her pull. The cards are unnumbered.

NM/M
Common Player: 10.00
1 Karim Abdul-Jabbar 15.00
2 Tony Banks 30.00
3 Tim Biakabutuka 12.00
4 Duane Clemons 10.00
5 Stephen Davis 30.00
6 Chris Doering 10.00
7 Bobby Hoying 25.00
8 Keyshawn Johnson 30.00
9 Danny Kanell 15.00
10 Derrick Mayes 15.00
11 Leeland McElroy 20.00
12 Lawyer Milloy 10.00
13 Eric Moulds 15.00
14 Jonathan Ogden 10.00
15 Steve Taneyhill 10.00
16 Alex Van Dyke 15.00

1996 Press Pass Paydirt Eddie George

The four-card, standard-size set features the 1995 Heisman Trophy winner. The cards were inserted into packs at a progressive rate. Card No. 1 was every 36 packs; card No. 2 was every 72; card No. 3 every 216, and card No. 4 every 864 packs. The cards are numbered with the "EG" prefix.

NM/M
Complete Set (4): 40.00
Common Player: 3.00
1 Eddie George 3.00
2 Eddie George 6.00
3 Eddie George 12.00
4 Eddie George 25.00

1996 Press Pass Paydirt Game Breakers

The 12-card, standard-size set was inserted every 18 packs and features players who excelled in college. The cards are numbered with the "GB" prefix.

NM/M
Complete Set (12): 30.00
Common Player: 1.00
1 Lawyer Milloy 1.00
2 Terry Glenn 4.00
3 Duane Clemons 1.00
4 Kevin Hardy 2.00
5 Eddie George 7.00
6 Jonathan Ogden 1.00

7 Karim Abdul-Jabbar 2.00
8 Tim Biakabutuka 2.00
9 Eric Moulds 6.00
10 Danny Kanell 2.00
11 Leeland McElroy 2.00
12 Keyshawn Johnson 10.00

1997 Press Pass

The 55-card set features full-bleed fronts, with the player's name, position and Press Pass logo at the bottom in gold foil. The backs have a player photo on the left over a "groovy" multicolored background. The player's name, bio, highlights and stats are printed on the right side. Red Zone is a red-foil parallel which was inserted 1:1 hobby packs. Torquers, which is a blue-foil parallel, was inserted 1:1 mass market packs. In addition, a 50-card all-foil die-cut "set within a set" was inserted 1:1 pack.

		NM/M
Complete Set (50):		15.00
Common Player:		.10
Minor Stars:		.20
Combine Cards:		2X
Red Zone Cards:		2X
1	Orlando Pace	1.00
2	Warrick Dunn	2.00
3	Danny Wuerffel	2.00
4	Darnell Autry	.75
5	Troy Davis	1.25
6	Jake Plummer	.75
7	Corey Dillon	.50
8	Reidel Anthony	1.25
9	Byron Hanspard	.75
10	Tiki Barber	.75
11	Ike Hilliard	1.25
12	Rae Carruth	1.00
13	Yatil Green	1.25
14	Peter Boulware	.10
15	Jim Druckenmiller	1.50
16	Pat Barnes	.20
17	Trevor Pryce	.10
18	Kevin Lockett	.10
19	Koy Detmer	.20
20	Bryant Westbrook	.40
21	Darrell Russell	.20
22	Tony Gonzalez	.30
23	Shawn Springs	.50
24	Chris Canty	.10
25	David LaFleur	.50
26	Dwayne Rudd	.10
27	Bob Sapp	.10
28	Mike Vrabel	.10
29	Antowain Smith	.50
30	Keith Poole	.10
31	Sedrick Shaw	.10
32	Tremain Mack	.10
33	Matt Russell	.10
34	Reinard Wilson	.10
35	Marc Edwards	.10
36	Greg Jones	.10
37	Michael Booker	.10
38	James Farrior	.10
39	Danny Wuerffel	.75
40	Troy Davis	.50
41	Corey Dillon	.10
42	Jake Plummer	.30
43	Peter Boulware, Reinard Wilson	.10
44	Eddie Robinson	.20
45	Bobby Bowden	.75
46	Steve Spurrier	1.00
47	Gary Barnett	.10
49	Tom Osborne Checklist	.50
50	Jarrett Irons Checklist	.10

1997 Press Pass Combine

Combine was a 50-card parallel set to the Press Pass Draft Picks set that was included one per pack. These die-cut cards were printed on silver foil and include towers up both sides. The word "Combine" and the player's name is printed in red letters across the bottom.

Combine Cards: 2X

1997 Press Pass Red Zone

Red Zone was another parallel set to the 50-card Press Pass Draft Picks. These parallels were identical to base cards except they were printed with red foil on the front instead of the gold foil used on base cards. Red Zone parallels were inserted one per pack.

Red Zone Cards: 2X

1997 Press Pass Big 12

Inserted 1:12 packs, the 12-card set features a player photo superimposed over an etched foil background. The player's name, chase set name and Press Pass logo are printed at the bottom of the card front. The backs include a player photo over a "sun ray" background. The player's name and highlights are printed inside a box along the right side. The cards are numbered with a prefix of "B".

		NM/M
Complete Set (12):		18.00
Common Player:		1.00
1	Orlando Pace	2.00
2	Peter Boulware	1.00
3	Shawn Springs	1.00
4	Warrick Dunn	5.00
5	Dwayne Rudd	1.00
6	Rae Carruth	1.00
7	Bryant Westbrook	4.00
8	Darrell Russell	1.00
9	Yatil Green	3.00
10	David LaFleur	1.00
11	Jim Druckenmiller	1.00
12	Reidel Anthony	2.00

1997 Press Pass Can't Miss

The six-card foil set was inserted on a progressive scale. Card No. 1 was inserted 1:720, while No. 2 was seeded at 1:360. The rest were as follows: No. 3 1:180, No. 4 1:90, No. 5 1:45 and No. 6 1:36. The player's photo is superimposed over a foil background. A football field and X's and O's also appear on the front. The Can't Miss logo and the player's name are printed at the bottom. The backs have a photo of each of the six players. The numbers have a prefix of "CM".

		NM/M
Complete Set (6):		35.00
Common Player:		3.00
1	Warrick Dunn	15.00
2	Jim Druckenmiller	3.00
3	Yatil Green	5.00
4	Orlando Pace	5.00
5	Rae Carruth	3.00
6	Peter Boulware	3.00

1997 Press Pass Head-Butt

Inserted 1:18 packs, the nine-card set features the player's photo superimposed over the player's college helmet. The Head Butt logo is in gold foil at the bottom, while the player's name is printed inside a gold-foil stripe at the bottom center. The backs have the player's photo printed over his college helmet. The bottom of the card back has the player's name and his highlights. The card numbers carry a prefix of "HB". A die-cut parallel version is randomly seeded 1:36 packs.

		NM/M
Complete Set (9):		15.00
Common Player:		1.00
Die Cuts:		2X
1	Warrick Dunn	7.00
2	Orlando Pace	3.00
3	Troy Davis	3.00
4	Reidel Anthony	2.00
5	Rae Carruth	1.00
6	Yatil Green	2.00
7	Corey Dillon	5.00
8	Danny Wuerffel	2.00
9	Darnell Autry	2.00

1997 Press Pass Marquee Matchups

Inserted 1:18 packs, the nine-card set features two players on the front, with their names printed at the bottom in prism foil. "Marquee Matchup" is printed in black inside a prism stripe at the bottom of the front. The backs have two player photos, their names and highlights. The card numbers are prefixed by "MM".

		NM/M
Complete Set (9):		15.00
Common Player:		1.00
1	Jim Druckenmiller, Danny Wuerffel	2.00
2	Warrick Dunn, Corey Dillon	6.00
3	Darnell Autry, Troy Davis	2.00
4	Byron Hanspard, Tiki Barber	3.00
5	Reidel Anthony, Bryant Westbrook	3.00
6	Orlando Pace, Peter Boulware	2.00
7	Rae Carruth, Ike Hilliard	3.00
8	Yatil Green, Shawn Springs	1.00
9	David LaFleur, Tony Gonzalez	3.00

1998 Press Pass

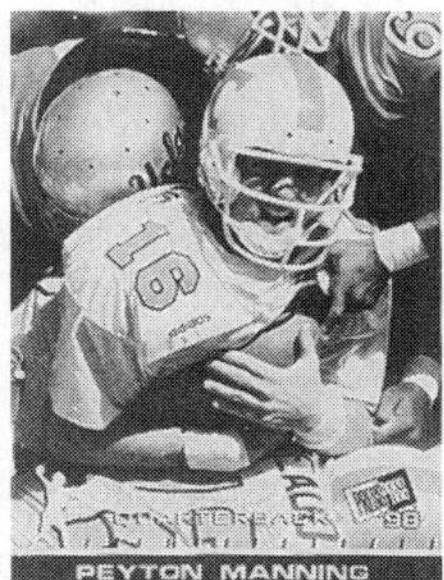

Press Pass Draft Picks Football contained 50 cards in 1998, with 45 players eligible for the 1998 NFL Draft, four coaches and a checklist card featuring Peyton Manning. Cards featured a black strip across the bottom identifying the player, with his position and several logo above over the bottom of the player photograph. The set was paralleled in Paydirt (hobby), Pickoffs (retail), Reflectors and Reflector Solos sets. Inserts include: Fields of Fury, Head Butt, Jerseys, Kick-off, Triple Threat and Trophy Case.

		NM/M
Complete Set (50):		18.00
Common Player:		.10
Minor Stars:		.20
Paydirt Cards:		2X
Pickoff Cards:		2X
Reflectors:		10X-20X
Wax Box:		60.00
1	Peyton Manning	4.00
2	Ryan Leaf	1.00
3	Charles Woodson	1.50
4	Andre Wadsworth	.75
5	Randy Moss	4.00
6	Curtis Enis	1.50
7	T. Thomas	.10
8	Flozell Adams	.10
9	Jason Peter	.10
10	Brian Simmons	.10
11	Takeo Spikes	.10
12	Michael Myers	.10
13	Kevin Dyson	.75
14	Grant Wistrom	.10
15	Fred Taylor	2.00
16	Germane Crowell	.75
17	Sam Cowart	.10
18	Anthony Simmons	.10
19	Robert Edwards	1.50
20	Shaun Williams	.10
21	Phil Savoy	.10
22	Leonard Little	.10
23	Saladin McCullough	.10
24	Duane Starks	.10
25	John Avery	.75
26	Vonnie Holliday	.50
27	Tim Dwight	.50
28	Donovin Darius	.10
29	Alonzo Mayes	.30
30	Jerome Pathon	.30
31	Brian Kelly	.10
32	Hines Ward	.50
33	Jacquez Green	.75
34	Marcus Nash	.75
35	Ahman Green	3.00
36	Joe Jurevicius	.50
37	Tavian Banks	1.00
38	Donald Hayes	.30
39	Robert Holcombe	.75
40	Eric Green	.50
41	John Dutton	.30
42	Skip Hicks	.75
43	Patrick Johnson	.10
44	Keith Brooking	.10
45	Alan Faneca	.10
46	Steve Spurrier	1.00
47	Mike Price	.10
48	Bobby Bowden	.75
49	Tom Osborne	1.00
50	Manning - Checklist	1.50

1998 Press Pass Paydirt

Paydirt included all 50 cards, but were distinguised by red foil stamping versus the gold used on base cards. These were found in hobby packs only and inserted one per pack.

Paydirt Cards: 2X

1998 Press Pass Pickoff

Pickoff included parallel versions of all 50 cards, but were distinguished by silver foil stamping on the front versus the gold foil used on base cards. These were retail exclusive and inserted one per pack.

	NM/M
Pickoff Cards:	2X

1998 Press Pass Reflectors

This 50-card parallel set was seeded one per 180 packs and arrived with a protective covering over the card. This covering could be peeled back to reveal a holofoil finish. Reflectors were numbered with a "R" prefix. In addition, Solos versions of Reflectors were also available, with only one existing set. These were distinguised by a "Solos 1 of 1" stamp on the card back.

Reflector Cards: 10X-20X

1998 Press Pass Autographs

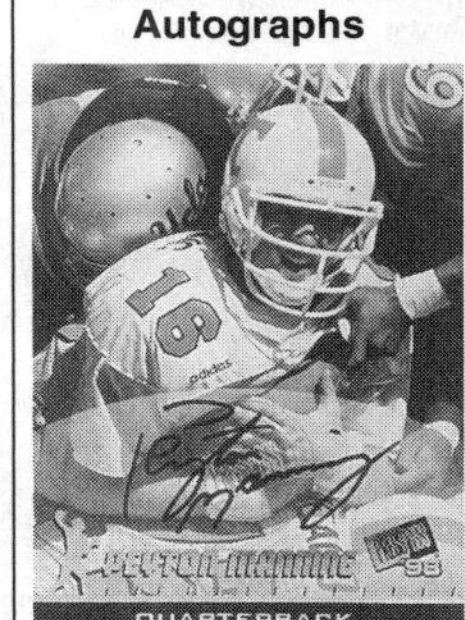

Autographed versions of Press Pass cards were seeded one per 18 hobby packs and one per 36 retail packs. They were similar to base cards, except for a faded area across the bottom of the photograph that included the player's signature. Backs were green, with the word "Autograph" in large white letters and a paragraph that congratulated the collector and certified the card. Autographs were unnumbered and are listed in alphabetical order.

		NM/M
Complete Set (38):		300.00
Common Player:		8.00
Minor Stars:		12.00
1	John Avery	12.00
2	Tavian Banks	20.00
3	Bobby Bowden	20.00
4	Germane Crowell	20.00
5	Donovin Darius	8.00
6	Tim Dwight	15.00
7	Kevin Dyson	20.00
8	Robert Edwards	30.00
9	Curtis Enis	30.00
10	Alan Faneca	8.00
11	Ahman Green	50.00
12	Jacquez Green	25.00
13	Donald Hayes	12.00
14	Skip Hicks	15.00
15	Robert Holcombe	12.00
16	Vonnie Holliday	15.00
17	Patrick Johnson	8.00
18	Joe Jurevicius	15.00
19	Brian Kelly	8.00
20	Ryan Leaf	20.00
21	Peyton Manning	100.00
22	Alonzo Mayes	12.00
23	Randy Moss	100.00
24	Michael Myers	8.00
25	Marcus Nash	15.00
26	Tom Osborne	25.00
27	Jason Peter	8.00
28	Mike Price	8.00
29	Phil Savoy	12.00
30	Anthony Simmons	8.00
31	Brian Simmons	8.00
32	Takeo Spikes	12.00
33	Steve Spurrier	25.00
34	Fred Taylor	40.00
35	Andre Wadsworth	15.00
36	Hines Ward	15.00
37	Shaun Williams	8.00
38	Grant Wistrom	8.00

1998 Press Pass Fields of Fury

This horizontal, nine-card set featured the player off to the right side, with a game highlight of him roughly bordered in black across the majority of the card. Fields of Fury were numbered with a "FF" prefix and inserted one per 36 packs.

		NM/M
Complete Set (9):		35.00
Common Player:		3.00
1	Peyton Manning	10.00
2	Marcus Nash	3.00
3	Ryan Leaf	3.00
4	Randy Moss	10.00
5	Robert Edwards	4.00
6	Curtis Enis	3.00
7	Kevin Dyson	4.00
8	Fred Taylor	5.00
9	Jacquez Green	3.00

1998 Press Pass Head Butt

Head Butt was a nine-card insert that included a film-like shot of the player over a black background, with his embossed college team helmet at the bottom center. These were numbered with a "HB" prefix and inserted one per 18 packs. Die-cut versions were seeded one per 36 packs.

		NM/M
Complete Set (9):		25.00
Common Player:		1.00
Die-Cut Cards:		2X
1	Peyton Manning	8.00
2	Charles Woodson	4.00
3	Ryan Leaf	1.00
4	Curtis Enis	1.00
5	Jacquez Green	2.00
6	Ahman Green	5.00
7	Randy Moss	8.00
8	Tavian Banks	2.00
9	Robert Edwards	3.00

1998 Press Pass Jerseys

Jerseys was a four-card insert that featured a swatch of the player's game-used college jersey embedded in the front. These were sequentially numbered to 425 sets, numbered with a "JC" prefix and inserted one per 720 packs.

		NM/M
Complete Set (4):		200.00
Common Player:		25.00
PM	Peyton Manning	150.00
RL	Ryan Leaf	25.00
KD	Kevin Dyson	25.00
TB	Tavian Banks	25.00

1998 Press Pass Kick-Off

Kick-Off included 36 of the players from the base set on a die-cut, football-shaped card. The player's image and the football were both embossed. These were numbered with a "KO" prefix and inserted one per pack in both hobby and retail.

		NM/M
Complete Set (36):		15.00
Common Player:		.20
Minor Stars:		.40
1	Peyton Manning	4.00
2	Ryan Leaf	.50
3	Charles Woodson	2.00
4	Andre Wadsworth	1.00
5	Randy Moss	4.00
6	Curtis Enis	1.00
7	Donald Hayes	.20
8	Flozell Adams	.20
9	Jason Peter	.20
10	Brian Simmons	.20
11	Takeo Spikes	.20
12	Germane Crowell	.20
13	Donovin Darius	.20
14	Grant Wistrom	.20
15	Alonzo Mayes	.20
16	Kevin Dyson	1.50
17	John Avery	.50
18	Anthony Simmons	.20
19	Robert Edwards	1.50
20	Shaun Williams	.20
21	Leonard Little	.20
22	Skip Hicks	1.50
23	Phil Savoy	.20
24	Tavian Banks	1.00
25	Robert Holcombe	1.00
26	Eric Green	1.00
27	Tim Dwight	.20
28	Saladin McCullough	.20
29	Fred Taylor	1.50
30	Jerome Pathon	.20
31	Brian Kelly	.20
32	Hines Ward	2.00
33	Jacquez Green	1.00
34	Marcus Nash	1.50
35	Ahman Green	2.50
36	Joe Jurevicius	.20

1998 Press Pass Triple Threat

This nine-card insert featured three different players, with each having three different fit-together cards to form a three-card panel. They were numbered with a "TT" prefix and inserted one per 12 packs.

		NM/M
Complete Set (9):		20.00
Common Player:		1.00
1	Peyton Manning	5.00
2	Peyton Manning	5.00
3	Peyton Manning	5.00
4	Ryan Leaf	1.00
5	Ryan Leaf	1.00
6	Ryan Leaf	1.00
7	Charles Woodson	2.00
8	Charles Woodson	2.00
9	Charles Woodson	2.00

1998 Press Pass Trophy Case

This 12-card insert was printed on silver foilboard, with the player's name across the top and the insert name across the bottom. Trophy Case cards are numbered with a "TC" prefix and inserted one per nine packs.

		NM/M
Complete Set (12):		25.00
Common Player:		1.00
1	Peyton Manning	6.00
2	Ryan Leaf	1.00
3	Charles Woodson	2.00
4	Randy Moss	6.00
5	Curtis Enis	1.00
6	Grant Wistrom	1.00
7	Kevin Dyson	3.00
8	Fred Taylor	3.00
9	Tavian Banks	1.00
10	Ahman Green	4.00
11	Skip Hicks	1.00
12	Andre Wadsworth	1.00

1999 Press Pass

This 45-card set includes all of the top draft picks from 1999. Each is pictured in his college uniform and each name is in gold foil. Three parallel sets were made with Paydirt, Torquers and Reflectors. Other inserts include: Autographs, Big Numbers, Game Jerseys, Goldenarm, Hardware and X's and O's.

		NM/M
Complete Set (45):		15.00
Common Player:		.10
Minor Stars:		.20
Paydirt Cards:		1.5X
Inserted 1:1 Hobby		
Torquer Cards:		1.5X
Inserted 1:1 Mass		
Reflector Cards:		5X-8X
Inserted 1:180		
Pack (4):		2.75
Wax Box (32):		60.00
1	Ricky Williams	3.00
2	Tim Couch	3.00
3	Champ Bailey	.50
4	Chris Claiborne	.20
5	Donovan McNabb	2.00
6	Edgerrin James	3.00
7	Akili Smith	.75
8	John Tait	.10
9	Jevon Kearse	1.00
10	Torry Holt	1.25
11	Troy Edwards	1.25
12	Chris McAlister	.20
13	Daunte Culpepper	2.00
14	Andy Katzenmoyer	.20
15	David Boston	1.25
16	Ebenezer Ekuban	.10
17	Peerless Price	.75
18	Shaun King	.75
19	Joe Germaine	.30
20	Brock Huard	.50
21	Michael Bishop	.50
22	Amos Zereoue	.30
23	Sedrick Irvin	.50
24	Autry Denson	.20
25	Kevin Faulk	.50
26	James Johnson	.50
27	D'Wayne Bates	.20
28	Kevin Johnson	.75
29	Tai Streets	.30
30	Craig Yeast	.20
31	Dre' Bly	.10
32	Anthony Poindexter	.10
33	Jared DeVries	.10
34	Rob Konrad	.20
35	Dat Nguyen	.10
36	Cade McNown	.75
37	Scott Covington	.20
38	Jon Jansen	.10
39	Rufus French	.10
40	Mike Rucker	.10
41	Aaron Gibson	.10
42	Kris Farris	.10
43	Anthony McFarland	.10
44	Matt Stinchcomb	.10
45	Dee Miller Checklist	.10

1999 Press Pass Autographs

Each autographed card in this set has the same photo as his base card but the name is in smaller type and the autograph is above it. Singles were inserted 1:16 packs.

	NM/M
Common Player:	6.00
Minor Stars:	12.00
Inserted 1:16 Hobby	
Inserted 1:36 Retail	
Champ Bailey	15.00
D'Wayne Bates	12.00
Michael Bishop	15.00
Dre' Bly	6.00
David Boston	25.00
Chris Claiborne	12.00
Mike Cloud	12.00
Tim Couch	50.00
Scott Covington	12.00
Daunte Culpepper	35.00
Autry Denson	12.00
Jared DeVries	6.00
Antwan Edwards	12.00
Troy Edwards	25.00
Ebenezer Ekuban	6.00
Kris Farris	6.00
Kevin Faulk	15.00
Rufus French	6.00
Joe Germaine	12.00
Aaron Gibson	6.00
Torry Holt	25.00
Brock Huard	15.00
Sedrick Irvin	15.00
Edgerrin James	60.00
Jon Jansen	6.00
James Johnson	15.00
Kevin Johnson	25.00
Andy Katzenmoyer	12.00
Jevon Kearse	20.00
Shaun King	25.00
Rob Konrad	12.00
Chris McAlister	12.00
Darnell McDonald	12.00
Anthony McFarland	6.00
Donovan McNabb	35.00
Cade McNown	35.00
Dee Miller	6.00
Dat Nguyen	6.00
Mike Peterson	6.00
Anthony Poindexter	6.00
Peerless Price	20.00
Mike Rucker	6.00
Akili Smith	35.00
Matt Stinchcomb	6.00
Tai Streets	12.00
John Tait	6.00
Jerame Tuman	6.00
Ricky Williams	75.00
Craig Yeast	6.00
Amos Zereoue	12.00

1999 Press Pass Big Numbers

Each card in this 9-card set is printed on foil board with a photo of the player and the number that he was drafted in the background. Singles were inserted 1:16 packs. A parallel Die Cut version was also made with each single the same except for die cut. Those were found 1:32 packs.

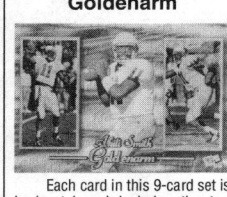

		NM/M
Complete Set (9):		20.00
Common Player:		2.00
Inserted 1:16		
Die-Cut Cards:		2X
Inserted 1:32		
1	Tim Couch	4.00
2	Ricky Williams	6.00
3	Donovan McNabb	5.00
4	Edgerrin James	5.00
5	Peerless Price	3.00
6	Amos Zereoue	2.00
7	Daunte Culpepper	5.00
8	Tai Streets	2.00
9	Akili Smith	5.00

1999 Press Pass Goldenarm

Each card in this 9-card set is horizontal and includes the top quarterbacks drafted in 1999. They were printed on foil board and were inserted 1:10 packs.

		NM/M
Complete Set (9):		15.00
Common Player:		1.00
Inserted 1:10		
1	Tim Couch	5.00
2	Donovan McNabb	5.00
3	Akili Smith	2.00
4	Daunte Culpepper	4.00
5	Cade McNown	2.00
6	Brock Huard	1.00
7	Joe Germaine	1.00
8	Shaun King	1.00
9	Michael Bishop	2.00

1999 Press Pass Hardware

Only the top rookies were included in this 12-card insert that was inserted 1:8 packs.

		NM/M
Complete Set (12):		20.00
Common Player:		1.00
Inserted 1:8		
1	Cade McNown	2.00
2	Ricky Williams	6.00
3	Torry Holt	2.00
4	Tim Couch	4.00
5	David Boston	2.00
6	Troy Edwards	2.00
7	Michael Bishop	1.00
8	Mike Cloud	1.00
9	Champ Bailey	1.00
10	Kevin Faulk	1.00
11	Autry Denson	1.00
12	Donovan McNabb	4.00

1999 Press Pass Jersey Cards

Each single in this 6-card set features a piece of game-used jersey on the card. Singles were found 1:640 packs.

		NM/M
Common Player:		20.00
Inserted 1:640 Hobby		
Inserted 1:720 Mass		
TC	Tim Couch (redemption)	75.00
DC	Daunte Culpepper	75.00
TH	Torry Holt	60.00
AS	Akili Smith	20.00
CM	Cade McNown	20.00
PP	Peerless Price	40.00

1999 Press Pass "X's and O's"

The top 36 players from the base set were included in this insert that was found one-per-pack. Each is die cut and embossed on extra thick stock.

		NM/M
Complete Set (36):		20.00
Common Player:		.25
Minor Stars:		.50
Inserted 1:1		
1	Ricky Williams	4.00
2	Tim Couch	3.00
3	Champ Bailey	.75
4	Donovan McNabb	2.00
5	Edgerrin James	3.00
6	Akili Smith	2.00
7	Torry Holt	1.25
8	Troy Edwards	1.25
9	Daunte Culpepper	2.00
10	Andy Katzenmoyer	.50
11	David Boston	1.25
12	Peerless Price	.75
13	Shaun King	2.00
14	Joe Germaine	.50
15	Brock Huard	.75
16	Michael Bishop	.75
17	Amos Zereoue	.50
18	Sedrick Irvin	.75
19	Autry Denson	.50
20	Kevin Faulk	.75
21	James Johnson	.75
22	D'Wayne Bates	.50
23	Kevin Johnson	1.25
24	Tai Streets	.50
25	Cade McNown	2.00
26	Scott Covington	.50
27	Chris Claiborne	.50
28	Jevon Kearse	1.00
29	Rob Konrad	.25
30	Dat Nguyen	.25
31	Chris McAlister	.50
32	Craig Yeast	.25
33	Anthony Poindexter	.25
34	Dre' Bly	.25
35	Mike Rucker	.25
36	Tim Couch Checklist	2.00

2000 Press Pass

		NM/M
Complete Set (45):		20.00
Common Player:		.20
Minor Stars:		.40
Pack (5):		4.00
Wax Box (24):		65.00
1	Peter Warrick	1.00
2	Travis Claridge	.20
3	Courtney Brown	.75
4	Plaxico Burress	2.00
5	Chad Pennington	2.00
6	Thomas Jones	1.00
7	Ron Dayne	1.00
8	Brian Urlacher	2.50
9	Corey Simon	.40
10	Chris Samuels	.20
11	Stockar McDougle	.20
12	Deon Grant	.20
13	Cosey Coleman	.20
14	Sylvester Morris	1.00
15	Shyrone Stith	.40
16	Shaun Alexander	1.50
17	Dez White	.75
18	John Engelberger	.40
19	Tim Rattay	.60
20	Todd Pinkston	.60
21	John Abraham	.40
22	R. Jay Soward	.40
23	Shaun Ellis	.40
24	Keith Bullock	.40
25	Jerry Porter	1.00
26	Darren Howard	.40
27	Joe Hamilton	.60
28	Delthea O'Neal	.40
29	Chris Redman	.75
30	Deon Dyer	.40
31	Jamal Lewis	1.50
32	Chris Hovan	.40
33	Raynoch Thompson	.40
34	Travis Taylor	1.00
35	Sebastian Janikowski	.75
36	Travis Prentice	1.00
37	Tom Brady	3.00
38	Tee Martin	.75
39	JR Redmond	1.00
40	Dennis Northcutt	.40
41	Laveranues Coles	.40
42	Danny Farmer	.60
43	Darrell Jackson	.50
44	Chris McIntosh	.20
45	Peter Warrick CL Checklist	.75

2000 Press Pass Gold

	NM/M
Gold Cards:	1.2X
Inserted 1:1 Hobby	

2000 Press Pass Reflectors

	NM/M
Reflector Cards:	2X-5X
Inserted 1:72	
Production 500 Sets	

2000 Press Pass Torquers

	NM/M
Torquers Cards:	1.5X
Inserted 1:1 Retail	

2000 Press Pass Autographs

	NM/M
Common Player:	5.00
Minor Stars:	10.00
Inserted 1:8	
Holofoil Cards:	2X
Production 100 Sets	

	NM/M
John Abraham	5.00
Shaun Alexander	30.00
Tom Brady	40.00
Courtney Brown	15.00
Keith Bulluck	5.00
Plaxico Burress	30.00
Giovanni Carmazzi	10.00
Kwame Cavil	5.00
Travis Claridge	5.00
Cosey Coleman	5.00
Laveranues Coles	12.00
Ron Dayne	20.00
Na'il Diggs	10.00
Ron Dugans	5.00
Deon Dyer	5.00
Shaun Ellis	5.00
John Engelberger	5.00
Danny Farmer	12.00
Deon Grant	5.00
Joe Hamilton	10.00
Chris Hovan	10.00
Darren Howard	5.00
Darrell Jackson	5.00
Sebastian Janikowski	10.00
Thomas Jones	20.00
Jamal Lewis	30.00
Tee Martin	10.00
Stockar McDougle	5.00
Chris McIntosh	5.00
Corey Moore	5.00
Rob Morris	5.00
Sylvester Morris	12.00
Dennis Northcutt	5.00
Delthea O'Neal	10.00
Chad Pennington	40.00
Todd Pinkston	12.00
Jerry Porter	12.00
Travis Prentice	12.00
Tim Rattay	8.00
Chris Redman	12.00
J.R. Redmond	10.00
Chris Samuels	5.00
Corey Simon	10.00
Marvel Smith	5.00
Shyrone Stith	5.00
Travis Taylor	12.00
Raynoch Thompson	5.00
Brian Urlacher	35.00
Todd Wade	5.00
Peter Warrick	15.00
Dez White	15.00

2000 Press Pass Autographs Holofoils

Holofoil Cards:	2X
Production 100 Sets	

2000 Press Pass Big Numbers

		NM/M
Complete Set (8):		15.00
Common Player:		2.00
Inserted 1:12		
Die-Cut Cards:		2X
Inserted 1:24		
BN1	Peter Warrick	1.00
BN2	Ron Dayne	1.00
BN3	Courtney Brown	1.00
BN4	Plaxico Burress	3.00
BN5	Shaun Alexander	3.00
BN6	Thomas Jones	2.00
BN7	Chad Pennington	5.00
BN8	Chris Redman	2.00

2000 Press Pass Breakout

		NM/M
Complete Set (35):		20.00
Common Player:		.25
Minor Stars:		.50
Inserted 1:1		
BO1	Peter Warrick	1.00

B02 Sebastian Janikowski .50
B03 Courtney Brown .75
B04 Plaxico Burress 2.00
B05 Chad Pennington 2.00
B06 Thomas Jones 1.00
B07 Ron Dayne 1.00
B08 Brian Urlacher 3.00
B09 Deon Dyer .50
B010 Chris Samuels .50
B011 Stockar McDougle .25
B012 Deon Grant .50
B013 Cosey Coleman .25
B014 Shyrone Stith .50
B015 Tim Rattay .75
B016 Shaun Alexander 1.50
B017 Dez White .75
B018 John Engelberger .50
B019 Laveranues Coles .75
B020 J.R. Redmond 1.00
B021 R. Jay Soward 1.00
B022 Chris McIntosh .25
B023 Shaun Ellis .50
B024 Keith Bulluck .50
B025 Jerry Porter 1.00
B026 Darren Howard .50
B027 Tee Martin 1.00
B028 Delthea O'Neal .50
B029 Chris Redman 1.00
B030 Danny Farmer .75
B031 Jamal Lewis 2.00
B032 Chris Hovan .50
B033 Corey Simon .50
B034 Travis Taylor 1.25
B035 Ron Dayne CL Checklist .40

2000 Press Pass Game Jerseys

NM/M
Common Player: 30.00
Inserted 1:380 Hobby
Inserted 1:720 Retail
Production 475 Sets
JC1 Ron Dayne 40.00
JC2 Thomas Jones 50.00
JC3 Chad Pennington 60.00
JC4 Chris Redman 10.00
JC5 Corey Simon 10.00
JC6 Peter Warrick 25.00

2000 Press Pass Gridiron

NM/M
Complete Set (3): 6.00
Common Player: 2.00
Inserted 1:1 Special Retail Box
1 Peter Warrick 2.00
2 Chad Pennington 5.00
3 Ron Dayne 2.00

2000 Press Pass Paydirt

NM/M
Complete Set (12): 25.00
Common Player: .75
Minor Stars: 1.50
Inserted 1:16
PD1 Peter Warrick 2.00
PD2 Plaxico Burress 4.00
PD3 Chad Pennington 6.00
PD4 Thomas Jones 3.00
PD5 Ron Dayne 2.00
PD6 Shyrone Stith .75
PD7 Shaun Alexander 3.00
PD8 Chris Redman 1.00
PD9 Dez White 2.00
PD10 Jamal Lewis 4.00
PD11 J.R. Redmond 1.00
PD12 Travis Taylor 1.00

2000 Press Pass Power Picks

NM/M
Complete Set (10): 12.00
Common Player: .50
Minor Stars: 1.00
Inserted 1:12
PP1 Peter Warrick 1.00
PP2 Courtney Brown 1.00
PP3 Plaxico Burress 2.00
PP4 Chad Pennington 4.00
PP5 Thomas Jones 1.00
PP6 Ron Dayne 1.00
PP7 Corey Simon 1.00
PP8 Shaun Alexander 1.50
PP9 Brian Urlacher 3.00
PP10 Chris Samuels .50

A card number in parenthese ( ) indicates the set is unnumbered.

2000 Press Pass Showbound

NM/M
Complete Set (8): 10.00
Common Player: .50
Inserted 1:8
SB1 Peter Warrick 1.00
SB2 Dez White 1.00
SB3 Courtney Brown 1.00
SB4 Plaxico Burress 2.00
SB5 Chad Pennington 4.00
SB6 Thomas Jones 1.50
SB7 Ron Dayne 1.00
SB8 Shaun Alexander 1.50

2001 Press Pass

NM/M
Complete Set (50): 30.00
Common Player: .20
Minor Stars: .40
Common Power Pick (46-50): 3.00
Inserted 1:16
Pack (5): 3.50
Wax Box (24): 65.00
1 Michael Vick 2.50
2 Drew Brees 4.00
3 Michael Vick 5.00
4 Chris Weinke 2.00
5 Marques Tuiasosopo 1.25
6 Josh Booty 1.25
7 Josh Heupel 1.50
8 Sage Rosenfels .50
9 Mike McMahon .50
10 Deuce McAllister 2.00
11 LaDainian Tomlinson 2.50
12 LaMont Jordan 1.25
13 James Jackson .75
14 Travis Henry 1.25
15 Anthony Thomas 1.00
16 Travis Minor .75
17 Michael Bennett 2.00
18 Kevan Barlow .75
19 Rudi Johnson 1.00
20 Santana Moss 2.00
21 Quincy Morgan 1.25
22 Rod Gardner 2.00
23 David Terrell 2.00
24 Chris Chambers 1.00
25 Reggie Wayne 2.00
26 Ken-Yon Rambo .60
27 Chad Johnson .60
28 Marvin "Snoop" Minnis .60
29 Freddie Mitchell .75
30 Koren Robinson 2.00
31 Bobby Newcombe .60
32 Robert Ferguson .75
33 Todd Heap .20
34 Steve Hutchinson .20
35 Leonard Davis .20
36 Kenyatta Walker .20
37 Justin Smith .20
38 Jamal Reynolds .20
39 Richard Seymour .20
40 Shaun Rogers .20
41 Gerard Warren .20
42 Jamar Fletcher .40
43 Gary Baxter .20
44 Nate Clements .20
45 Derrick Gibson .40
46 Drew Brees PP 5.00
47 Michael Vick PP 8.00
48 Deuce McAllister PP 3.00
49 LaDainian Tomlinson PP 4.00
50 David Terrell PP 3.00

2001 Press Pass Gold

Gold Cards: 1.2X
Inserted 1:1

2001 Press Pass Reflectors

Reflector Cards: 5X-10X
Inserted 1:60
Production 500 Sets

2001 Press Pass Autograph Cards

NM/M
Common Player: 5.00
Inserted 1:8
1 Michael Vick 75.00
2 Drew Brees 60.00
3 Marques Tuiasosopo 25.00
4 Chris Weinke 20.00
5 Sage Rosenfels 5.00
6 Jesse Palmer 5.00
7 Mike McMahon 5.00
8 Josh Booty 5.00
9 LaDainian Tomlinson 45.00
10 Deuce McAllister 35.00
11 Michael Bennett 30.00
12 Anthony Thomas 10.00
13 LaMont Jordan 20.00
14 Travis Henry 15.00
15 James Jackson 10.00
16 Rudi Johnson 12.00
17 David Terrell 35.00
18 Koren Robinson 35.00
19 Rod Gardner 35.00
20 Santana Moss 35.00
21 Reggie Wayne 25.00
22 Quincy Morgan 15.00
23 Chad Johnson 8.00
24 Robert Ferguson 10.00
25 Chris Chambers 12.00
26 Marvin "Snoop" Minnis 5.00
27 Bobby Newcombe 5.00
28 Ken-Yon Rambo 5.00
29 Todd Heap 5.00
30 Jabari Holloway 5.00
31 Nate Clements 5.00
32 Jamar Fletcher 5.00
33 Kenyatta Walker 5.00
34 Jeff Bakus 5.00
35 Steve Hutchinson 5.00
36 Chad Ward 5.00
37 Jamal Reynolds 5.00
38 Justin Smith 5.00
39 Gerard Warren 5.00
40 Casey Hampton 5.00
41 Ennis Davis 5.00
42 Moran Norris 5.00
43 Tommy Polley 5.00
44 Quinton Caver 5.00
45 Torrance Marshall 5.00
46 Brian Allen 5.00
47 Dominic Raiola 5.00

2001 Press Pass Big Numbers

NM/M
Complete Set (9): 12.00
Common Player: 1.25
Inserted 1:12
Die-Cut Cards: 1.5X
Inserted 1:24
BN1 Drew Brees 3.00
BN2 Michael Vick 4.00
BN3 Deuce McAllister 1.50
BN4 LaDainian Tomlinson 2.00
BN5 Santana Moss 1.50
BN6 David Terrell 1.50
BN7 Freddie Mitchell 1.25
BN8 Koren Robinson 1.50
BN9 Chad Johnson 1.25

2001 Press Pass Breakout

NM/M
Complete Set (36): 25.00
Common Player: .25
Minor Stars: .50
Inserted 1:1
B1 Drew Brees 3.00
B2 Michael Vick 4.00
B3 Chris Weinke 1.50
B4 Marques Tuiasosopo 1.00
B5 Josh Heupel 1.00
B6 Sage Rosenfels .50
B7 Mike McMahon .50
B8 Deuce McAllister 1.50
B9 LaDainian Tomlinson 2.00
B10 LaMont Jordan 1.00
B11 James Jackson .50
B12 Travis Henry .75
B13 Anthony Thomas .75
B14 Michael Bennett 1.25
B15 Kevan Barlow .50
B16 Rudi Johnson .75
B17 Travis Minor .50
B18 Ken-Yon Rambo .50
B19 Santana Moss 1.50
B20 Quincy Morgan 1.00
B21 Rod Gardner 1.50
B22 David Terrell 1.50
B23 Chris Chambers .75
B24 Reggie Wayne 1.50
B25 Chad Johnson .50
B26 Marvin "Snoop" Minnis .50
B27 Freddie Mitchell .75
B28 Koren Robinson 1.50
B29 Todd Heap .25
B30 Leonard Davis .25
B31 Kenyatta Walker .25
B32 Jamal Reynolds .25
B33 Richard Seymour .25
B34 Justin Smith .25
B35 Jamar Fletcher .50
B36 David Terrell 1.50

2001 Press Pass Jersey Cards

NM/M
Common Player: 30.00
Inserted 1:320
JC/MB Michael Bennett 35.00
JC/DB Drew Brees 75.00
JC/JS Justin Smith 30.00
JC/LT LaDainian Tomlinson 50.00
JC/MV Michael Vick 125.00
JC/CW Chris Weinke 40.00

2001 Press Pass Paydirt

NM/M
Complete Set (6): 15.00
Common Player: 1.50
Inserted 1:24
PD1 Drew Brees 4.00
PD2 Michael Vick 5.00
PD3 Deuce McAllister 2.00
PD4 LaDainian Tomlinson 3.00
PD5 Santana Moss 1.50
PD6 David Terrell 1.50

2001 Press Pass Power Pick Autographs

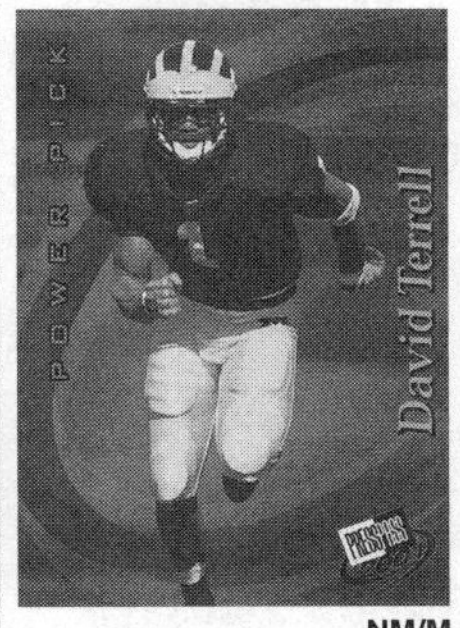

NM/M
Common Player: 35.00
Inserted 1:320
Production 250 Sets
1 Michael Vick 125.00
2 LaDainian Tomlinson 50.00
3 David Terrell 45.00
4 Koren Robinson 45.00
5 Santana Moss 45.00
6 Deuce McAllister 45.00
7 Michael Bennett 35.00
8 Drew Brees 75.00
9 Chris Weinke 40.00

2001 Press Pass Showbound

NM/M
Complete Set (12): 15.00
Common Player: .75
Inserted 1:12
SB1 Drew Brees 3.00
SB2 Michael Vick 4.00
SB3 Chris Weinke 1.50
SB4 Koren Robinson 1.50
SB5 Deuce McAllister 1.50
SB6 Michael Bennett 1.25
SB7 LaDainian Tomlinson 2.00

NM/M
SB8 Santana Moss 1.50
SB9 Rod Gardner 1.50
SB10 David Terrell 1.50
SB11 Chris Chambers .75
SB12 Chad Johnson .75

2001 Press Pass Signature Edition

NM/M
Complete Set (45): 45.00
Common Player: .30
Minor Stars: .60
Pack (4): 14.50
Wax Box (12): 125.00
1 Michael Vick 6.00
2 Drew Brees 4.50
3 Quincy Carter 1.75
4 Marques Tuiasosopo 1.50
5 Chris Weinke 2.50
6 Sage Rosenfels 1.00
7 Jesse Palmer .75
8 Mike McMahon .75
9 Josh Booty .75
10 Josh Heupel 2.50
11 LaDainian Tomlinson 3.50
12 Deuce McAllister 2.50
13 Michael Bennett 3.00
14 Anthony Thomas 2.00
15 LaMont Jordan 1.25
16 Travis Henry 1.50
17 James Jackson 1.25
18 Kevan Barlow 1.00
19 Travis Minor 1.25
20 Rudi Johnson 1.00
21 David Terrell 3.00
22 Koren Robinson 2.50
23 Rod Gardner 2.50
24 Santana Moss 3.00
25 Freddie Mitchell 1.50
26 Reggie Wayne 1.75
27 Quincy Morgan 1.00
28 Chris Chambers 1.25
29 Robert Ferguson 1.25
30 Chad Johnson 1.25
31 Marvin "Snoop" Minnis 1.25
32 Todd Heap .75
33 Steve Hutchinson .60
34 Leonard Davis .30
35 Kenyatta Walker .30
36 Justin Smith .75
37 Andre Carter .75
38 Jamal Reynolds .75
39 Gerard Warren .75
40 Richard Seymour .30
41 Damione Lewis .75
42 Jamar Fletcher .75
43 Nate Clements .60
44 Derrick Gibson .30
45 David Terrell CL 1.50

2001 Press Pass Signature Edition Autographs

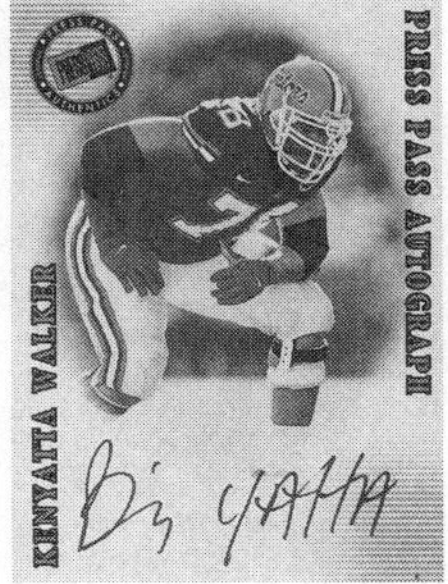

NM/M
Common Player: 4.00
Minor Stars: 8.00
Inserted 1:1
1 Anthony Thomas 15.00
2 Ben Leard 8.00
3 Bobby Newcombe 8.00
4 Brian Allen 4.00
5 Chad Johnson 10.00
6 Chad Ward 4.00
7 Chris Chambers 10.00
8 Chris Weinke 20.00
9 Dan Alexander 8.00
10 David Terrell 25.00
11 Deuce McAllister 20.00
12 Dominic Raiola 4.00
13 Drew Brees 30.00
14 Ennis Davis 4.00
15 Freddie Mitchell 12.00
16 Gerard Warren 8.00
17 Jabari Holloway 4.00
18 Jamal Reynolds 8.00
19 James Jackson 10.00
20 Jamie Winborn 4.00
21 Jeff Backus 4.00
22 Jesse Palmer 8.00
23 Josh Booty 8.00
24 Josh Heupel 20.00
25 Justin Smith 8.00
26 Kenyatta Walker 4.00
27 Ken-Yon Rambo 8.00
28 Kevan Barlow 10.00
29 Koren Robinson 10.00
30 LaDainian Tomlinson 30.00
31 LaMont Jordan 12.00
32 Marques Tuiasosopo 12.00
33 Maurice Williams 4.00
34 Michael Bennett 25.00
36 Mike McMahon 8.00
37 Moran Norris 4.00
38 Quincy Morgan 10.00
39 Reggie Wayne 12.00
40 Richard Seymour 4.00
41 Robert Ferguson 10.00
42 Rod Gardner 15.00
43 Rudi Johnson 10.00
44 Sage Rosenfels 10.00
45 Santana Moss 25.00
46 Marvin "Snoop" Minnis 12.00
47 Steve Hutchinson 4.00
48 Todd Heap 8.00
49 Tommy Polley 4.00
50 Travis Henry 12.00
51 Travis Minor 10.00
52 Willie Howard 4.00

2001 Press Pass Signature Edition Autographs Silver

NM/M
Silver Cards: 1.5X
Production 250 Sets
Blue Cards: 3X
Production 25 Sets
Michael Vick 100.00

2001 Press Pass Signature Edition Class of 2001

NM/M
Complete Set (9): 25.00
Common Player: 2.00
Inserted 1:6
CL1 Michael Vick 8.00
CL2 LaDainian Tomlinson 5.00
CL3 David Terrell 4.00
CL4 Koren Robinson 3.00
CL5 Santana Moss 4.00
CL6 Deuce McAllister 3.50
CL7 Freddie Mitchell 2.00
CL8 Drew Brees 6.00
CL9 Chris Weinke 3.00

2001 Press Pass Signature Edition Game Jersey

NM/M
Complete Set (6): 400.00
Common Player: 25.00
Inserted 1:96
Production 250 Sets
J/MB Michael Bennett 60.00
J/DB Drew Brees 85.00
J/JS Justin Smith 25.00
J/LT LaDainian Tomlinson 75.00
J/MV Michael Vick 125.00
J/CW Chris Weinke 40.00
Michael Vick, Drew Brees 125.00

A card number in parenthese ( ) indicates the set is unnumbered.

2001 Press Pass Signature Edition Game Jersey Autograph

		NM/M
Production 25 Sets		
AJC/MB	Michael Bennett	150.00
AJC/DB	Drew Brees	200.00
AJC/LT	LaDainian Tomlinson	175.00
AJC/MV	Michael Vick 15	350.00
AJC/CW	Chris Weinke	125.00

2001 Press Pass Signature Edition Game Jersey Uniform

		NM/M
Production 25 Sets		
JN/MB	Michael Bennett	150.00
JN/DB	Drew Brees	200.00
JN/JS	Justin Smith	50.00
JN/LT	LaDainian Tomlinson	175.00
JN/MV	Michael Vick	250.00
JN/CW	Chris Weinke	125.00

2001 Press Pass Signature Edition Jersey Patch Swatch

		NM/M
Common Player:		50.00
JP/MB	Michael Bennett	150.00
JP/DB	Drew Brees	200.00
JP/JS	Justin Smith	50.00
JP/LT	LaDainian Tomlinson	175.00
JP/MV	Michael Vick	250.00
JP/CW	Chris Weinke	125.00

2001 Press Pass Signature Edition Old School

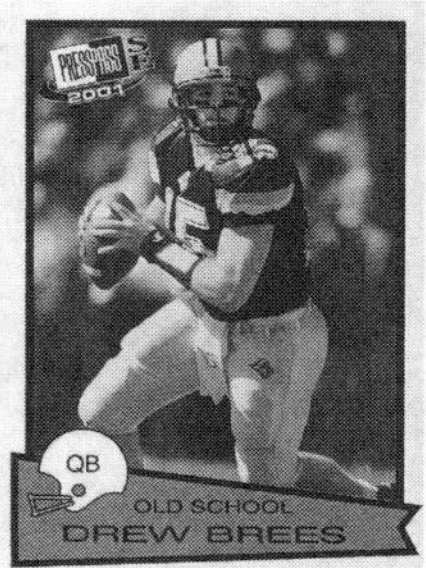

		NM/M
Complete Set (27):		45.00
Common Player:		.50
Minor Stars:		1.00
Inserted 1:2		
OS1	Michael Vick	8.00
OS2	Drew Brees	6.00
OS3	Chris Weinke	3.00
OS4	LaDainian Tomlinson	5.00
OS5	Deuce McAllister	3.00
OS6	Michael Bennett	4.00
OS7	Anthony Thomas	2.50
OS8	LaMont Jordan	1.50
OS9	Travis Henry	2.00
OS10	James Jackson	1.25
OS11	Kevan Barlow	1.00
OS12	David Terrell	4.00
OS13	Koren Robinson	2.50
OS14	Rod Gardner	2.50
OS15	Santana Moss	4.00
OS16	Freddie Mitchell	1.75
OS17	Reggie Wayne	2.00
OS18	Quincy Morgan	1.25
OS19	Chad Johnson	1.25
OS20	Chris Chambers	1.25
OS21	Todd Heap	1.00
OS22	Justin Smith	1.00
OS23	Andre Carter	1.00
OS24	Leonard Davis	.50
OS25	Kenyatta Walker	.50
OS26	Richard Seymour	.50
OS27	Michael Vick CL	4.00

2001 Press Pass Signature Edition Rookievision

		NM/M
Complete Set (12):		30.00
Common Player:		1.00
Inserted 1:3		
RV1	Michael Vick	8.00
RV2	LaDainian Tomlinson	5.00
RV3	David Terrell	4.00
RV4	Koren Robinson	2.50
RV5	Rod Gardner	2.50
RV6	Deuce McAllister	3.50
RV7	Santana Moss	4.00
RV8	Michael Bennett	4.00
RV9	Freddie Mitchell	2.00
RV10	Todd Heap	1.00
RV11	Drew Brees	6.00
RV12	Chad Johnson	1.75

2001 Press Pass Signature Edition Up Close

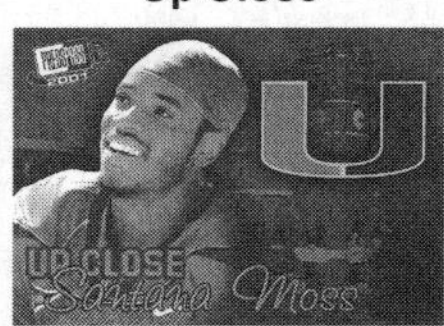

		NM/M
Complete Set (6):		20.00
Common Player:		2.50
Inserted 1:9		
UC1	Michael Vick	8.00
UC2	Drew Brees	6.00
UC3	LaDainian Tomlinson	5.00
UC4	David Terrell	4.00
UC5	Deuce McAllister	2.50
UC6	Santana Moss	4.00

2002 Press Pass

		NM/M
Complete Set (50):		40.00
Common Player:		.75
Minor Star:		
Cards 46-50 Power Pick Inserted 1:14		
Gold Zone Parallel (hobby)		1X to 2X
Torquers Parallel (retail)		1X to 2X
Pack (5):		3.50
Box (24):		60.00
1	*David Carr*	5.00
2	*Eric Crouch*	1.50
3	*Rohan Davey*	1.50
4	*David Garrard*	.75
5	*Joey Harrington*	5.00
6	*Kurt Kittner*	1.00
7	*David Neill*	.75
8	*Patrick Ramsey*	1.50
9	*Antwann Randle El*	2.00
10	*Damien Anderson*	.75
11	*T.J. Duckett*	3.00
12	*DeShaun Foster*	1.50
13	*Lamar Gordon*	1.00
14	*William Green*	2.00
15	*Leonard Henry*	.75
16	*Adrian Peterson*	.75
17	*Clinton Portis*	4.00
18	*Jonathan Wells*	1.25
19	*Brian Westbrook*	1.00
20	*Antonio Bryant*	2.00
21	*Donald Reche Caldwell*	1.00
22	*Kelly Campbell*	.75
23	*Andre Davis*	1.50
24	*Jabar Gaffney*	1.50
25	*Ron Johnson*	.75
26	*Ashley Lelie*	3.00
27	*Josh Reed*	1.50
28	*Cliff Russell*	.75
29	*Donte Stallworth*	3.00
30	*Javon Walker*	2.00
31	*Marquise Walker*	1.00
32	*Daniel Graham*	1.00
33	*Jeremy Shockey*	2.00
34	*Bryant McKinnie*	.75
35	*Mike Pearson*	.75
36	*Mike Williams*	.75
37	*Phillip Buchanon*	1.00
38	*Quentin Jammer*	1.00
39	*Kalimba Edwards*	.75
40	*Julius Peppers*	2.00
41	*Wendell Bryant*	.75
42	*John Henderson*	.75
43	*Ryan Sims*	.75
44	*Roy Williams*	2.00
45	*David Carr*	2.00
46	*David Carr*	6.00
47	*Joey Harrington*	6.00
48	*T.J. Duckett*	3.00
49	*Donte Stallworth*	3.00
50	*William Green*	2.00

A card number in parenthese ( ) indicates the set is unnumbered.

2002 Press Pass Autographed

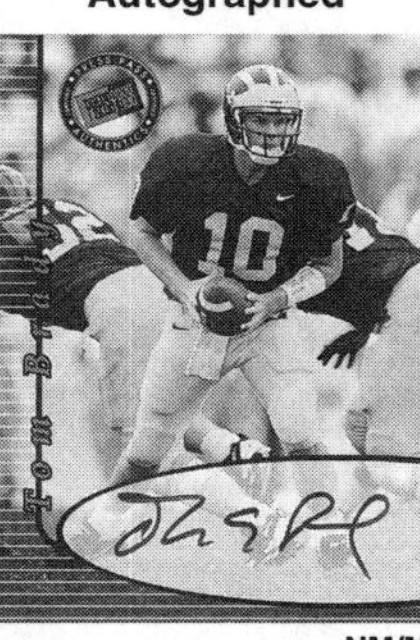

		NM/M
Common Player:		10.00
Inserted 1:8		
1	Damien Anderson	10.00
2	Antonio Bryant	25.00
3	Phillip Buchanon	10.00
4	Donald Reche Caldwell	15.00
5	Rocky Calmus	10.00
6	Kelly Campbell	10.00
7	David Carr	60.00
8	Eric Crouch	40.00
9	Rohan Davey	25.00
10	Andre Davis	15.00
11	T.J. Duckett	40.00
12	Kalimba Edwards	10.00
13	DeShaun Foster	25.00
14	Jabar Gaffney	25.00
15	David Garrard	10.00
16	Lamar Gordon	15.00
17	Daniel Graham	10.00
18	William Green	40.00
19	Joey Harrington	60.00
20	John Henderson	10.00
21	Leonard Henry	10.00
22	Ron Johnson	15.00
23	Kyle Johnson	10.00
24	Levi Jones	10.00
25	Kurt Kittner	15.00
26	Ashley Lelie	40.00
27	Josh McCown	15.00
28	Freddie Millons	10.00
29	Maurice Morris	15.00
30	David Neill	10.00
31	Mike Pearson	10.00
32	Adrian Peterson	10.00
33	Patrick Ramsey	25.00
34	Antwann Randle El	30.00
35	Josh Reed	30.00
36	Cliff Russell	10.00
37	Ryan Sims	10.00
38	Luke Staley	10.00
39	Donte Stallworth	40.00
40	Marquise Walker	15.00
41	Anthony Weaver	10.00
42	Jonathan Wells	10.00
43	Brian Westbrook	15.00
44	Roy Williams	30.00

2002 Press Pass Big Numbers

		NM/M
Complete Set (36):		20.00
Common Player:		.40
Inserted 1:1		
BN1	David Carr	3.00
BN2	Eric Crouch	1.00
BN3	Rohan Davey	.75
BN4	Joey Harrington	3.00
BN5	Kurt Kittner	.40
BN6	Patrick Ramsey	.75
BN7	Antwann Randle El	1.00
BN8	T.J. Duckett	2.00
BN9	DeShaun Foster	.75
BN10	Lamar Gordon	.40
BN11	William Green	2.00
BN12	Adrian Peterson	.40
BN13	Clinton Portis	2.00
BN14	Javon Walker	1.00
BN15	Brian Westbrook	.40
BN16	Antonio Bryant	.40
BN17	Donald Reche Caldwell	.40
BN18	Kelly Campbell	.40
BN19	Andre Davis	.40
BN20	Jabar Gaffney	.75
BN21	Ashley Lelie	2.00
BN22	Josh Reed	1.00
BN23	Donte Stallworth	2.00
BN24	Marquise Walker	.40
BN25	Daniel Graham	.40
BN26	Jeremy Shockey	.40
BN27	Bryant McKinnie	.40
BN28	Mike Pearson	.40
BN29	Phillip Buchanon	.40
BN30	Quentin Jammer	.40
BN31	Kalimba Edwards	.40
BN32	Julius Peppers	1.00
BN33	Wendell Bryant	.40
BN34	John Henderson	.40
BN35	Roy Williams	1.00
BN36	Joey Harrington	3.00

2002 Press Pass Jersey Cards

		NM/M
Common Player:		15.00
Inserted 1:160		
JC/DC	David Carr	90.00
JC/EC	Eric Crouch	50.00
JC/DF	DeShaun Foster	20.00
JC/DG	David Garrard	15.00
JC/WG	William Green	50.00
JC/JH	Joey Harrington	90.00
JC/LH	Leonard Henry	15.00
JC/KK	Kurt Kittner	20.00
JC/JM	Josh McCown	15.00
JC/AP	Adrian Peterson	15.00
JC/JR	Josh Reed	25.00
JC/LS	Luke Staley	15.00
JC/RW	Roy Williams	25.00

2002 Press Pass Paydirt

		NM/M
Complete Set (9):		12.00
Common Player:		1.00
Die Cut:		2X
Inserted 1:12 Die-Cut 1:24		
PD1	David Carr	4.00
PD2	Joey Harrington	4.00
PD3	Kurt Kittner	1.00
PD4	T.J. Duckett	2.00
PD5	William Green	3.00
PD6	Clinton Portis	2.00
PD7	Antonio Bryant	1.00
PD8	DeShaun Foster	1.00
PD9	Donte Stallworth	3.00

2002 Press Pass Power Pick Autographs

		NM/M
Common Player:		20.00
Production 250 sets		
1	Antonio Bryant	30.00
2	David Carr	75.00
3	Eric Crouch	60.00
4	Andre Davis	20.00
5	T.J. Duckett	60.00
6	DeShaun Foster	40.00
7	William Green	60.00
8	Joey Harrington	75.00
9	Kurt Kittner	20.00
10	Ashley Lelie	60.00
11	Josh Reed	40.00
12	Marquise Walker	20.00

2002 Press Pass Prime Time

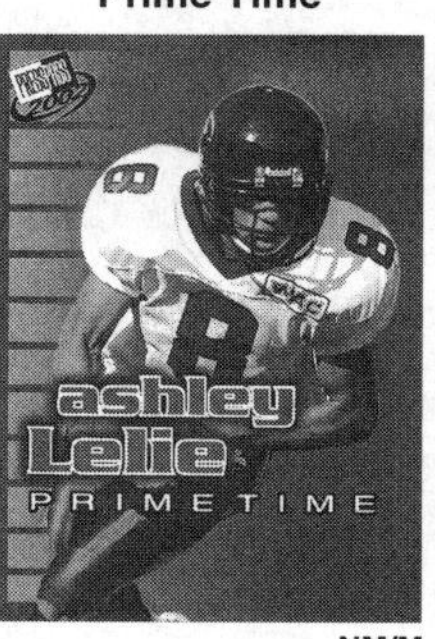

		NM/M
Complete Set (12):		16.00
Common Player:		.75
Inserted 1:8		
PT1	David Carr	4.00
PT2	Joey Harrington	4.00
PT3	T.J. Duckett	2.00
PT4	William Green	2.00
PT5	DeShaun Foster	.75
PT6	Clinton Portis	2.00
PT7	Antonio Bryant	.75
PT8	Jabar Gaffney	.75
PT9	Ashley Lelie	2.00
PT10	Josh Reed	1.00
PT11	Donte Stallworth	2.00
PT12	Julius Peppers	1.00

2002 Press Pass Rookie Chase

		NM/M
Complete Set (12):		50.00
Common Player:		2.00
Inserted 1:24		
RC1	David Carr	15.00
RC2	Joey Harrington	15.00
RC3	William Green	8.00
RC4	T.J. Duckett	8.00
RC5	Jabar Gaffney	4.00
RC6	Donte Stallworth	8.00
RC7	Antonio Bryant	2.00
RC8	Jeremy Shockey	2.00
RC9	Julius Peppers	6.00
RC10	Josh Reed	6.00
RC11	DeShaun Foster	4.00
RC12	Field Card	15.00

2002 Press Pass Showbound

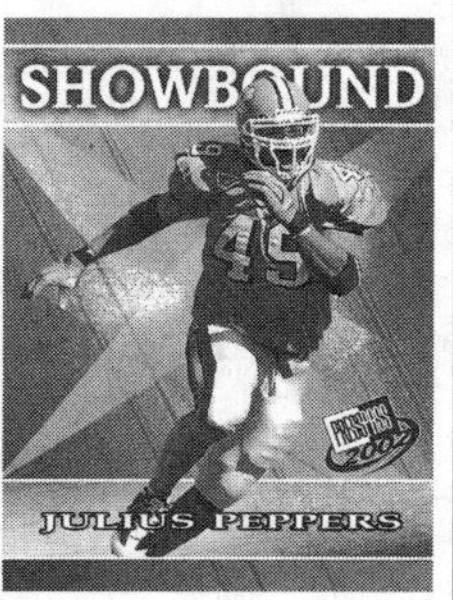

		NM/M
Complete Set (6):		22.00
Inserted 1:24		
SB1	David Carr	8.00
SB2	Joey Harrington	8.00
SB3	William Green	5.00
SB4	T.J. Duckett	5.00
SB5	Antonio Bryant	2.00
SB6	Julius Peppers	3.00

2002 Press Pass Jersey Edition

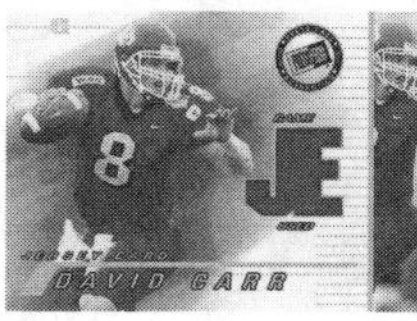

		NM/M
Complete Set (45):		45.00
Common Player:		.40
Minor Stars:		
First Down Gold retail		1X to 2X
Pack (4):		4.00
Wax Box (24):		65.00
1	*David Carr*	5.00
2	*Julius Peppers*	2.00
3	*Joey Harrington*	5.00
4	*Mike Williams*	.40
5	*Quentin Jammer*	1.00
6	*Ryan Sims*	.75
7	*Bryant McKinnie*	.40
8	*Roy Williams*	2.00
9	*John Henderson*	.75
10	*Wendell Bryant*	.75
11	*Donte Stallworth*	3.00
12	*Jeremy Shockey*	2.00
13	*William Green*	2.00
14	*Phillip Buchanon*	1.00
15	*T.J. Duckett*	3.00
16	*Ashley Lelie*	3.00
17	*Javon Walker*	2.00
18	*Daniel Graham*	1.00
19	*Jerramy Stevens*	.40
20	*Patrick Ramsey*	1.50
21	*Jabar Gaffney*	1.50
22	*DeShaun Foster*	1.50
23	*Kalimba Edwards*	.40
24	*Josh Reed*	1.00
25	*Mike Pearson*	.40
26	*Andre Davis*	1.00
27	*Donald Reche Caldwell*	1.00
28	*Clinton Portis*	4.00
29	*Maurice Morris*	1.00
30	*Ladell Betts*	1.00
31	*Antwann Randle El*	2.00
32	*Antonio Bryant*	2.00
33	*Josh McCown*	1.00
34	*Lamar Gordon*	1.00
35	*Marquise Walker*	1.00
36	*Cliff Russell*	.40
37	*Brian Westbrook*	1.00
38	*Eric Crouch*	1.00
39	*Jonathan Wells*	.40
40	*David Garrard*	.40
41	*Rohan Davey*	1.50
42	*Ron Johnson*	1.00
43	*Kurt Kittner*	1.00
44	*Adrian Peterson*	.40
45	*David Carr*	2.00

2002 Press Pass Jersey Edition Autograph Cards

		NM/M
Common Player:		5.00
1	Damien Anderson	5.00
2	Antonio Bryant	20.00
3	Phillip Buchanon	12.00
4	Donald Reche Caldwell	16.00
5	Rocky Calmus	5.00
7	David Carr	60.00
8	Eric Crouch	30.00
9	Rohan Davey	20.00
10	Andre Davis	16.00
11	Kalimba Edwards	5.00
12	Jabar Gaffney	20.00
13	David Garrard	5.00
14	Lamar Gordon	16.00
15	Daniel Graham	12.00
16	William Green	30.00
17	Joey Harrington	60.00
18	John Henderson	12.00
19	Leonard Henry	5.00
20	Quentin Jammer	16.00
21	Ron Johnson	16.00
22	Kyle Johnson	5.00
23	Levi Jones	12.00
24	Kurt Kittner	16.00
25	Josh McCown	16.00
26	Freddie Milons	5.00
27	Maurice Morris	16.00
28	Mike Pearson	5.00
29	Adrian Peterson	5.00
30	Patrick Ramsey	20.00
31	Antwann Randle El	24.00
32	Josh Reed	24.00
33	Cliff Russell	5.00
34	Ryan Sims	12.00
35	Luke Staley	12.00
36	Donte Stallworth	30.00
37	Marquise Walker	16.00
38	Anthony Weaver	5.00
39	Jonathan Wells	5.00
40	Roy Williams	24.00

2002 Press Pass Jersey Edition Class 2002

		NM/M
Complete Set (9):		20.00
Common Player:		.50
CL1	David Carr	6.00
CL2	T.J. Duckett	3.00
CL3	Jabar Gaffney	2.00

CL4 William Green 3.00
CL5 Joey Harrington 5.00
CL6 Ashley Lelie 3.00
CL7 Julius Peppers 2.00
CL8 Jeremy Shockey .50
CL9 Donte Stallworth 3.00

2002 Press Pass Jersey Edition Class 2002 Autographs

NM/M
Common Player: 5.00
ACL/AB Antonio Bryant 12.00
ACL/DRC Donald Reche Caldwell 10.00
ACL/DC David Carr 40.00
ACL/AD Andre Davis 10.00
ACL/JG Jabar Gaffney 12.00
ACL/WG William Green 20.00
ACL/JH Joey Harrington 40.00
ACL/KK Kurt Kittner 10.00
ACL/JR Josh Reed 15.00
ACL/DS Donte Stallworth 20.00

2002 Press Pass Jersey Edition Jersey Cards

NM/M
Common Player: 5.00
JE/DC David Carr 50.00
JE/EC Eric Crouch 50.00
JE/AD Andre Davis 10.00
JE/DF DeShaun Foster 12.00
JE/DGa David Garrard 5.00
JE/WG William Green 40.00
JE/JH Joey Harrington 50.00
JE/LH Leonard Henry 5.00
JE/KK Kurt Kittner 20.00
JE/AL Ashley Lelie 40.00
JE/JM Josh McCown 10.00
JE/MM Maurice Morris 10.00
JE/DN David Neill 5.00
JE/AP Adrian Peterson 15.00
JE/PR Patrick Ramsey 30.00
JE/JR Josh Reed 30.00
JE/LS Luke Staley 10.00
JE/BW Brian Westbrook 10.00
JE/RW Roy Williams 30.00

2002 Press Pass Jersey Edition Autograph Jersey Cards

NM/M
Common Player: 50.00
AJE/DC David Carr 200.00
AJE/WG William Green 100.00
AJE/JH Joey Harrington 200.00
AJE/JM Josh McCown 50.00
AJE/JR Josh Reed 100.00
AJE/RW Roy Williams 100.00

2002 Press Pass Jersey Edition Jersey Name Cards

NM/M
Common Player: 25.00
JN/DC David Carr 200.00
JN/EC Eric Crouch 150.00
JN/AD Andre Davis 50.00
JN/DF DeShaun Foster 50.00
JN/DG David Garrard 25.00
JN/WG William Green 100.00
JN/JH Joey Harrington 200.00
JN/LH Leonard Henry 25.00
JN/KK Kurt Kittner 50.00
JN/AL Ashley Lelie 150.00
JN/JM Josh McCown 50.00
JN/MM Maurice Morris 50.00
JN/DN David Neill 25.00
JN/AP Adrian Peterson 50.00
JN/PR Patrick Ramsey 75.00
JN/JR Josh Reed 100.00
JN/LS Luke Staley 25.00
JN/BW Brian Westbrook 50.00
JN/RW Roy Williams 100.00

2002 Press Pass Jersey Edition Jersey Patch Cards

JP/DC David Carr
JP/EC Eric Crouch
JP/AD Andre Davis
JP/DF DeShaun Foster
JP/DG David Garrard
JP/WG William Green
JP/JH Joey Harrington
JP/LH Leonard Henry
JP/KK Kurt Kittner
JP/AL Ashley Lelie
JP/PR Patrick Ramsey
JP/JR Josh Reed
JP/BW Brian Westbrook

2002 Press Pass Jersey Edition Old School

NM/M
Complete Set (27): 30.00
Common Player: .50
OS1 David Carr 5.00
OS2 Julius Peppers 2.00
OS3 Joey Harrington 4.00
OS4 Mike Williams 1.00
OS5 Quentin Jammer 1.00
OS6 Ryan Sims 1.00
OS7 Bryant McKinnie .50
OS8 Roy Williams 4.00
OS9 Donte Stallworth 3.00
OS10 Jeremy Shockey .50
OS11 William Green 3.00
OS12 T.J. Duckett 3.00
OS13 Ashley Lelie 3.00
OS14 Javon Walker 2.00
OS15 Daniel Graham .50
OS16 Patrick Ramsey 1.50
OS17 Jabar Gaffney 1.50
OS18 DeShaun Foster 1.50
OS19 Josh Reed 2.00
OS20 Andre Davis 1.00
OS21 Donald Reche Caldwell 1.00
OS22 Clinton Portis 2.00
OS23 Antwann Randle El 2.00
OS24 Antonio Bryant 1.50
OS25 Marquise Walker 1.00
OS26 Eric Crouch 4.00
OS27 Joey Harrington Checklist 1.00

2002 Press Pass Jersey Edition Rookie Vision

NM/M
Complete Set (12): 25.00
Common Player: .50
RV1 David Carr 10.00
RV2 T.J. Duckett 5.00
RV3 DeShaun Foster 2.00
RV4 Jabar Gaffney .50
RV5 William Green 5.00
RV6 Joey Harrington 5.00
RV7 Ashley Lelie 5.00
RV8 Julius Peppers 4.00
RV9 Patrick Ramsey 2.00
RV10 Jeremy Shockey 1.00
RV11 Donte Stallworth 5.00
RV12 Javon Walker 4.00

2002 Press Pass Jersey Edition Up Close

NM/M
Complete Set (6): 15.00
Common Player: 2.00
UC1 David Carr 5.00
UC2 Jabar Gaffney 2.00
UC3 William Green 3.00
UC4 Joey Harrington 5.00
UC5 Julius Peppers 2.00
UC6 T.J. Duckett 3.00

2003 Press Pass

NM/M
Complete Set (50): 50.00
Common Player: .25
Unlisted Rookie Star:
Gold Zone parallel Hobby (1-45) 1X to 2X
Torquers parallel Retail (1-45) 1X to 2X

NM/M
Cards 46-50 Power Picks Inserted 1:14
Reflectors 1X to 3X
Production 500 sets
Reflectors Proof Edition
Production 100 sets 2X to5X
Pack (5): 3.00
Wax Box (28): 65.00
1 Brad Banks 1.00
2 Kyle Boller 3.00
3 Ken Dorsey 2.00
4 Jason Gesser .75
5 Rex Grossman 2.00
6 Kliff Kingsbury .75
7 Byron Leftwich 4.00
8 Carson Palmer 4.00
9 Dave Ragone 2.00
10 Chris Simms 2.00
11 Brian St. Pierre .25
12 Chris Brown .75
13 Avon Cobourne .75
14 Daharran Diedrick .75
15 Justin Fargas .75
16 Earnest Graham .75
17 Larry Johnson 2.00
18 Willis McGahee 3.00
19 Musa Smith .75
20 Onterrio Smith .75
21 Lee Suggs 2.00
22 Anquan Boldin 1.00
23 Talman Gardner .75
24 Taylor Jacobs 1.00
25 Andre Johnson 3.00
26 Bryant Johnson 2.00
27 Brandon Lloyd .50
28 Charles Rogers 3.00
29 Kelley Washington .75
30 Teyo Johnson .75
31 Bennie Joppru .75
32 Jason Witten .75
33 Andrew Pinnock .25
34 Jordan Gross .25
35 Kwame Harris .25
36 Eric Steinbach .25
37 Brett Williams .25
38 Terence Newman 2.00
39 Marcus Trufant .75
40 Andre Woolfolk .50
41 Terrell Suggs 2.00
42 Jimmy Kennedy .75
43 Boss Bailey 1.00
44 Mike Doss .50
45 Carson Palmer 1.00
46 Carson Palmer 6.00
47 Byron Leftwich 6.00
48 Charles Rogers 4.50
49 Kyle Boller 4.50
50 Andre Johnson 4.50

2003 Press Pass Certified Auth. Autographed Cards

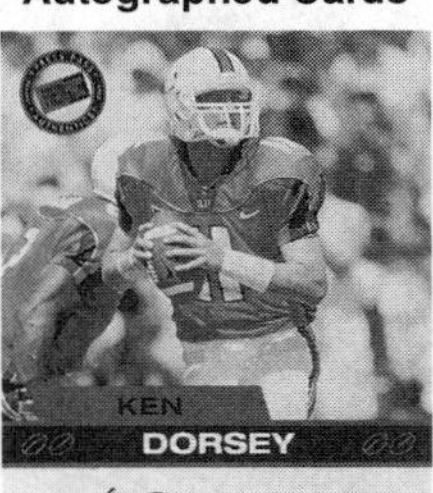

NM/M
Common Player: 8.00
Bronze not numbered
Silver 1X to 2X
Production 200 sets
Gold 1.5X to 3X
Production 100 sets
All 3 versions not found for all players
1 Boss Bailey 15.00
2 Brad Banks 15.00
3 Anquan Boldin 15.00
4 Kyle Boller 30.00
5 Chris Brown 15.00
6 Mike Bush 8.00
7 Avon Cobourne 15.00
8 Angelo Crowell 8.00
9 Chris Davis 8.00
10 Domanick Davis 8.00
11 Ken Dorsey 25.00
12 Justin Fargas 15.00
13 Talman Gardner 15.00
14 Jason Gesser 15.00
15 Earnest Graham 15.00
16 Justin Griffith 8.00
17 DeJuan Groce 8.00
18 Jordan Gross 8.00
19 Kwame Harris 8.00
20 Michael Haynes 15.00
21 Wayne Hunter 8.00
22 Taylor Jacobs 15.00
23 Larry Johnson 25.00
24 Teyo Johnson 12.00
25 Ben Johnson 8.00
26 Bennie Joppru 15.00
27 Kareem Kelly 8.00
28 Kliff Kingsbury 15.00
29 Byron Leftwich 40.00
30 Brandon Lloyd 8.00
31 Vincent Manuwai 8.00
32 Rashean Mathis 8.00
33 Sultan McCullough 8.00
34 Willis McGahee 30.00
35 Terence Newman 20.00
36 Tony Pashos 8.00
37 Carson Palmer 40.00
38 Andrew Pinnock 8.00
39 Dave Ragone 20.00
40 Dewayne Robertson 8.00
41 Steve Sciullo 8.00
42 Musa Smith 12.00
43 Brian St. Pierre 8.00
44 Jon Stinchcomb 8.00
45 LaBrandon Toefield 8.00
46 Marcus Trufant 15.00
47 Seneca Wallace 15.00
48 Shane Walton 8.00
49 Kelley Washington 15.00
50 Dennis Weathersby 8.00
51 Dewayne White 8.00
52 Brett Williams 8.00
53 Juston Wood 8.00

2003 Press Pass Big Numbers

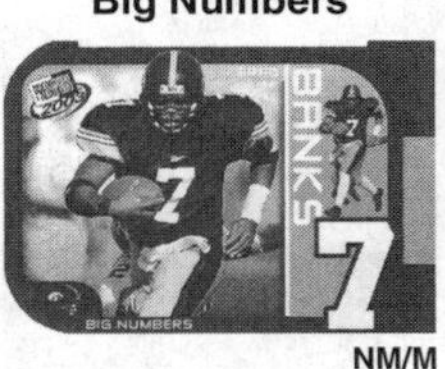

NM/M
Common Player: .50
Inserted 1:1
BN1 Brad Banks 1.00
BN2 Anquan Boldin 1.00
BN3 Kyle Boller 3.00
BN4 Chris Brown .75
BN5 Avon Cobourne .75
BN6 Ken Dorsey 2.00
BN7 Mike Doss .50
BN8 Justin Fargas .75
BN9 Talman Gardner .75
BN10 Earnest Graham .75
BN11 Rex Grossman 2.00
BN12 Taylor Jacobs 1.00
BN13 Andre Johnson 3.00
BN14 Bryant Johnson 2.00
BN15 Larry Johnson 2.00
BN16 Teyo Johnson .75
BN17 Bennie Joppru .75
BN18 Jimmy Kennedy .75
BN19 Byron Leftwich 4.00
BN20 Brandon Lloyd .50
BN21 Jerome McDougle .50
BN22 Willis McGahee 2.50
BN23 Terence Newman 1.00
BN24 Carson Palmer 4.00
BN25 Dave Ragone 2.00
BN26 Charles Rogers 3.00
BN27 Chris Simms 1.00
BN28 Musa Smith .75
BN29 Onterrio Smith .75
BN30 Brian St. Pierre .50
BN31 Lee Suggs 2.00
BN32 Terrell Suggs 2.00
BN33 Kelley Washington .75
BN34 Jason Witten .75
BN35 Andre Woolfolk .50
BN36 Byron Leftwich 4.00

2003 Press Pass Jersey Cards

NM/M
Common Player: 15.00
Three Levels of Production
Gold Production 475 sets
Silver Production 225 sets 1X to 2X
Holofoil Production 150 sets 1X to 3X
JC/KD Ken Dorsey 30.00
JC/EG Earnest Graham 15.00
JC/TJ Teyo Johnson 15.00
JC/BJ Bennie Joppru 15.00
JC/KK Kareem Kelly 15.00
JC/BL Byron Leftwich 45.00
JC/CP Carson Palmer 45.00
JC/SW Seneca Wallace 25.00

2003 Press Pass Paydirt

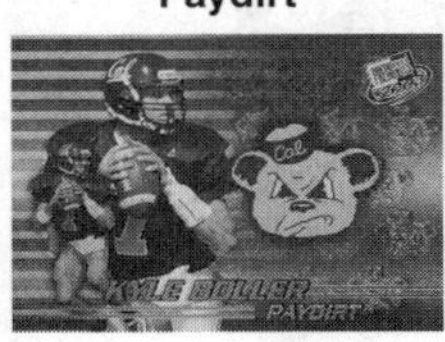

NM/M
Common Player: 1.00
Inserted 1:14
PD1 Kyle Boller 2.00
PD2 Andre Johnson 2.00
PD3 Larry Johnson 1.00
PD4 Byron Leftwich 3.00
PD5 Carson Palmer 3.00
PD6 Rex Grossman 1.00
PD7 Charles Rogers 2.00

2003 Press Pass Power Pick Autographs

NM/M
Common Player: 12.00
Production 250 sets
Brad Banks 25.00
Anquan Boldin 15.00
Kyle Boller 35.00
Taylor Jacobs 15.00
Larry Johnson 30.00
Byron Leftwich 45.00
Brandon Lloyd 12.00
Carson Palmer 45.00
Dave Ragone 25.00

2003 Press Pass Prime Time

NM/M
Common Player: 1.00
Inserted 1:9
PT1 Kyle Boller 2.00
PT2 Rex Grossman 1.50
PT3 Larry Johnson 1.50
PT4 Andre Johnson 2.00
PT5 Byron Leftwich 3.00
PT6 Carson Palmer 3.00
PT7 Dave Ragone 1.50
PT8 Charles Rogers 2.00
PT9 Chris Simms 1.50
PT10 Onterrio Smith 1.00

2003 Press Pass Rookie Chase

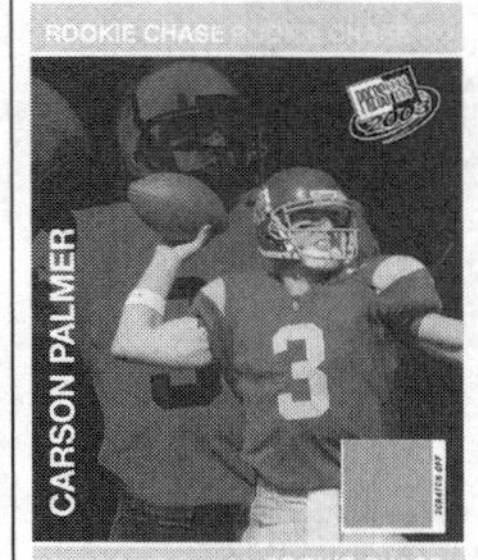

NM/M
Common Player: 4.00
Inserted 1:28
RC1 Taylor Jacobs 4.00
RC2 Larry Johnson 6.00
RC3 Andre Johnson 8.00
RC4 Byron Leftwich 10.00
RC5 Carson Palmer 10.00
RC6 Dave Ragone 6.00
RC7 Charles Rogers 8.00
RC8 Onterrio Smith 4.00
RC9 Terrell Suggs 6.00

2003 Press Pass Showbound

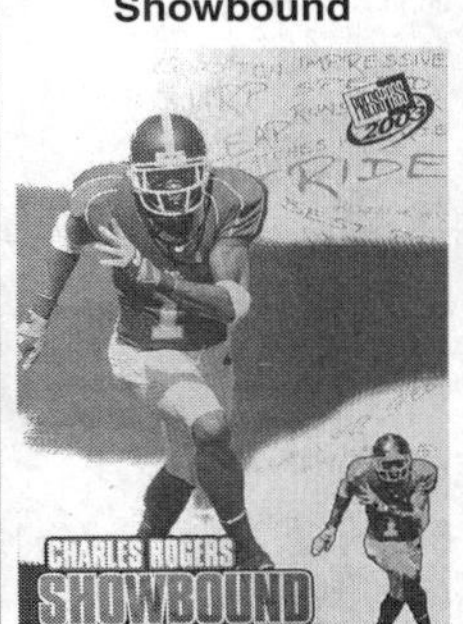

NM/M
Common Player: 1.50
Inserted 1:28
SB1 Byron Leftwich 3.00
SB2 Carson Palmer 3.00
SB3 Dave Ragone 1.50
SB4 Larry Johnson 1.50
SB5 Charles Rogers 2.00
SB6 Andre Johnson 2.00
SB7 Kyle Boller 2.00

2003 Press Pass Jersey Edition

NM/M
Complete Set (45): 25.00
Common Player: .25
1st Down Parallel (retail) 1X to 2X
Wax Pack (4): 3.25
Wax Box (28): 65.00
1 Boss Bailey 1.00
2 Brad Banks 1.00
3 Anquan Boldin 1.00
4 Kyle Boller 3.00
5 Chris Brown .25
6 Avon Cobourne .75
7 Ken Dorsey 2.00
8 Justin Fargas .75
9 Talman Gardner .75
10 Jason Gesser .75
11 Earnest Graham .75
12 Jordan Gross .25
13 Rex Grossman 2.50
14 Kwame Harris .25
15 Taylor Jacobs 1.00
16 Larry Johnson 2.00
17 Bryant Johnson 2.00
18 Andre Johnson 3.00
19 Teyo Johnson .75
20 William Joseph .75
21 Bennie Joppru .75
22 Jimmy Kennedy .75
23 Kliff Kingsbury .75
24 Byron Leftwich 4.00
25 Brandon Lloyd .25
26 Jerome McDougle .25
27 Willis McGahee 3.00
28 Terence Newman 2.00
29 Carson Palmer 4.00
30 Terry Pierce .25
31 Dave Ragone 2.00
32 Dewayne Robertson .50
33 Charles Rogers 3.00
34 Chris Simms 2.00
35 Musa Smith .75
36 Onterrio Smith .75
37 Brian St. Pierre .75
38 Lee Suggs 2.00
39 Terrell Suggs 2.00
40 Marcus Trufant .75
41 Seneca Wallace 1.00
42 Kelley Washington .75
43 Jason Witten .75
44 Andre Woolfolk .25
45 Byron Leftwich Checklist 1.00

2003 Press Pass Jersey Edition 1st Down

Common Player:
Retail Only 1X to 2X

2003 Press Pass Jersey Edition Autograph Cards

NM/M
Common Player: 8.00
Inserted 1:4
Silver 1X to 2X
Production 200 sets
Gold
Production 100 sets 1.5X to 3X

1 Boss Bailey 15.00
2 Brad Banks 15.00
3 Anquan Boldin 15.00
4 Kyle Boller 30.00
5 Chris Brown 8.00
6 Mike Bush 8.00
7 Tyrone Calico 8.00
8 Avon Cobourne 12.00
9 Angelo Crowell 8.00
10 Chris Davis 8.00
11 Domanick Davis 8.00
12 Dahrran Diedrick 12.00
13 Ken Dorsey 15.00
14 Mike Doss 8.00
15 Justin Fargas 12.00
16 Talman Gardner 12.00
17 Jason Gesser 12.00
18 Earnest Graham 12.00
19 Justin Griffith 8.00
20 DeJuan Groce 8.00
21 Jordan Gross 8.00
22 Kwame Harris 8.00
23 Michael Haynes 12.00
24 Wayne Hunter 8.00
25 Taylor Jacobs 15.00
26 Larry Johnson 20.00
27 Teyo Johnson 12.00
28 Ben Johnson 8.00
29 Bryant Johnson 20.00
30 Bennie Joppru 12.00
31 Kareem Kelly 8.00
32 Chris Kelsay 8.00
33 Jimmy Kennedy 12.00
34 Kliff Kingsbury 12.00
35 Byron Leftwich 40.00
36 Brandon Lloyd 8.00
37 Vincent Manuwai 8.00
38 Rashean Mathis 8.00
39 Sultan McCullough 8.00
40 Jerome McDougle 8.00
41 Willis McGahee 30.00
42 Terence Newman 20.00
43 Tony Pashos 8.00
44 Carson Palmer 40.00
45 Andrew Pinnock 8.00
46 Dave Ragone 20.00
47 Dewayne Robertson 8.00
48 Steve Sciullo 8.00
49 Musa Smith 12.00
50 Brian St. Pierre 12.00
51 Eric Steinbach 8.00
52 Jon Stinchcomb 8.00
53 Terrell Suggs 20.00
54 LaBrandon Toefield 8.00
55 Marcus Trufant 12.00
56 Bobby Wade 8.00
57 Seneca Wallace 20.00
58 Shane Walton 8.00
59 Kelley Washington 12.00
60 Dennis Weathersby 8.00
61 Dewayne White 8.00
62 Brett Williams 8.00
63 Juston Wood 8.00
64 Andre Woolfolk 8.00

2003 Press Pass Jersey Edition Class of 2003

NM/M
Common Player: 1.50
Inserted 1:9
CL1 Kyle Boller 2.00
CL2 Rex Grossman 1.50
CL3 Larry Johnson 1.50
CL4 Andre Johnson 2.00
CL5 Byron Leftwich 3.00
CL6 Carson Palmer 3.00
CL7 Dave Ragone 1.50
CL8 Charles Rogers 2.00
CL9 Chris Simms 1.50

2003 Press Pass Jersey Edition Class of 2003 Autographs

NM/M
Common Player: 15.00
Production 200 sets
Brad Banks 20.00
Anquan Boldin 20.00
Kyle Boller 40.00
Chris Brown 15.00
Justin Fargas 15.00
Taylor Jacobs 20.00
Byron Leftwich 60.00
Carson Palmer 60.00
Dave Ragone 25.00

2003 Press Pass Jersey Edition Jersey Cards

NM/M
Common Player: 6.00
Inserted 1:28
Gold numbered from 450-575
Not all players have a gold version
Silver numbered from 200-375 1X to 2X
Holofoil numbered from 100-150 1X to 3X
Patch Version numbered from 4-10
Patch version too uncommon to price
JC/AC Avon Cobourne 6.00
JC/DD Dahrran Diedrick 6.00
JC/KD Ken Dorsey 12.00
JC/EG Earnest Graham 8.00
JC/TJ Teyo Johnson 10.00
JC/BJ Bennie Joppru 10.00
JC/KK Kareem Kelly 6.00
JC/BL Byron Leftwich 35.00
JC/BLI Brandon Lloyd 12.00
JC/JM Jerome McDougle 6.00
JC/CP Carson Palmer 35.00
JC/SW Seneca Wallace 15.00
JC/JW Jason Witten 12.00
JC/AW Andre Woolfolk 10.00

2003 Press Pass Jersey Edition Autograph Jersey Cards

NM/M
Production 25 sets
Most too uncommon to price at this time
AJC/TJ Teyo Johnson
AJC/BJ Bennie Joppru 40.00
AJC/BL Byron Leftwich 225.00
AJC/CP Carson Palmer
AJC/AW Andre Woolfolk

2003 Press Pass Jersey Edition Jersey Name Cards

NM/M
Production 25 sets
Too uncommon to price at this time
JC/AC Avon Cobourne
JC/DD Dahrran Diedrick
JC/KD Ken Dorsey
JC/EG Earnest Graham
JC/TJ Teyo Johnson
JC/BJ Bennie Joppru
JC/KK Kareem Kelly
JC/BL Byron Leftwich
JC/BLI Brandon Lloyd
JC/JM Jerome McDougle
JC/CP Carson Palmer
JC/SW Seneca Wallace
JC/JW Jason Witten
JC/AW Andre Woolfolk

2003 Press Pass Jersey Edition Jersey Patch Cards

Production 10 sets
Too uncommon to price
JC/AC Avon Cobourne
JC/DD Dahrran Diedrick
JC/KD Ken Dorsey
JC/EG Earnest Graham
JC/TJ Teyo Johnson
JC/BJ Bennie Joppru
JC/KK Kareem Kelly
JC/BL Byron Leftwich
JC/BLI Brandon Lloyd
JC/JM Jerome McDougle
JC/CP Carson Palmer
JC/SW Seneca Wallace
JC/JW Jason Witten
JC/AW Andre Woolfolk

2003 Press Pass Jersey Edition Old School

NM/M
Common Player: .50
Inserted 1:1
OS1 Brad Banks .75
OS2 Anquan Boldin .75
OS3 Kyle Boller 2.00
OS4 Chris Brown .50
OS5 Avon Cobourne .50

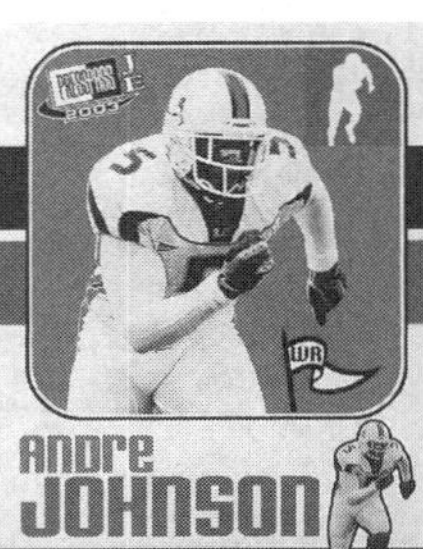

NM/M
OS6 Ken Dorsey 1.00
OS7 Rex Grossman 1.00
OS8 Taylor Jacobs .75
OS9 Andre Johnson 2.00
OS10 Bryant Johnson 1.00
OS11 Larry Johnson 1.00
OS12 Jimmy Kennedy .50
OS13 Byron Leftwich 2.50
OS14 Brandon Lloyd .50
OS15 Willis McGahee 1.75
OS16 Terence Newman .75
OS17 Carson Palmer 2.50
OS18 Dave Ragone 1.00
OS19 Charles Rogers 2.00
OS20 Chris Simms 1.00
OS21 Musa Smith .50
OS22 Onterrio Smith .50
OS23 Terrell Suggs 1.00
OS24 Lee Suggs 1.00
OS25 Kelley Washington .50
OS26 Andre Woolfolk .50
OS27 Carson Palmer Checklist 1.00

2003 Press Pass Jersey Edition Rookie Vision

NM/M
Common Player: .75
Inserted 1:4
RV1 Kyle Boller 2.00
RV2 Justin Fargas .75
RV3 Rex Grossman 1.00
RV4 Taylor Jacobs .75
RV5 Larry Johnson 2.00
RV6 Andre Johnson 2.00
RV7 Byron Leftwich 2.50
RV8 Carson Palmer 2.50
RV9 Dave Ragone 1.00
RV10 Charles Rogers 2.00
RV11 Chris Simms 1.00
RV12 Lee Suggs 1.00

2003 Press Pass Jersey Edition Up Close

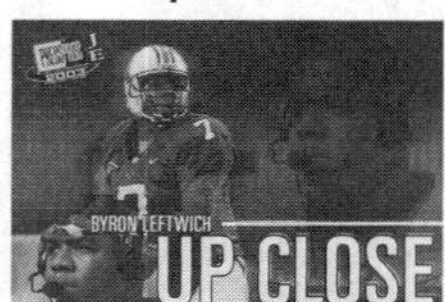

NM/M
Common Player: 1.00
Inserted 1:14
UC1 Carson Palmer 3.00
UC2 Byron Leftwich 3.00
UC3 Chris Simms 1.00
UC4 Charles Rogers 2.00
UC5 Dave Ragone 1.00
UC6 Larry Johnson 1.00

2004 Press Pass

NM/M
Complete Set (50): 50.00
Common Player: .75
Minor Stars: 1.00
Unlisted Stars: 1.25
Common Player Pick (46-50): 4.00
46-50 Inserted 1:14
Pack (5): 7.25
Box (24): 125.00
1 Casey Clausen 1.00
2 Craig Krenzel 1.00
3 J.P. Losman 2.00
4 Eli Manning 5.00

NM/M
5 Luke McCown 1.00
6 John Navarre 1.25
7 Cody Pickett 1.00
8 Philip Rivers 4.00
9 Ben Roethlisberger 5.00
10 Matt Schaub 1.00
11 Cedric Cobbs 1.00
12 Steven Jackson 2.50
13 Kevin Jones 2.50
14 Greg Jones 1.25
15 Julius Jones 2.50
16 Jarrett Payton 1.50
17 Chris Perry 1.50
18 Michael Turner .75
19 Quincy Wilson 1.25
20 Jason Wright .75
21 Bernard Berrian 1.00
22 Michael Clayton 2.00
23 Devard Darling 1.00
24 Lee Evans 2.00
25 Larry Fitzgerald 3.00
26 Devery Henderson 1.00
27 Michael Jenkins 1.50
28 Darius Watts 1.00
29 Mike Williams 3.00
30 Roy Williams 3.00
31 Rashaun Woods 2.00
32 Ben Troupe .75
33 Shawn Andrews .75
34 Robert Gallery 1.25
35 Tommie Harris 1.25
36 Vince Wilfork 1.25
37 Will Smith 1.00
38 Teddy Lehman 1.00
39 Jonathan Vilma 1.25
40 DJ Williams 1.25
41 DeAngelo Hall 1.50
42 Dunta Robinson 1.00
43 Derrick Strait 1.00
44 Keith Smith .75
45 Eli Manning 2.50
46 Eli Manning 8.00
47 Ben Roethlisberger 8.00
48 Larry Fitzgerald 4.00
49 Roy Williams 4.00
50 Philip Rivers 6.00

2004 Press Pass Gold

NM/M
Singles (1-45): 1X-1.5X

2004 Press Pass Reflectors

Singles (1-45): 2X-4X
Production 500 Sets

2004 Press Pass Reflectors Proofs

Singles (1-45): 5X-10X
Production 100 Sets

2004 Press Pass Autographs

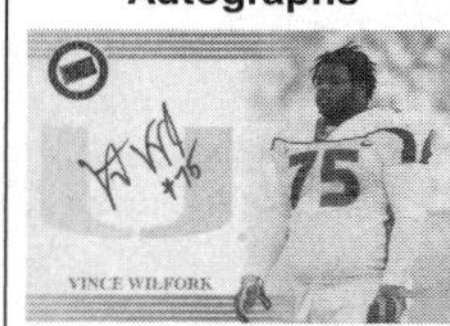

NM/M
Common Player: 8.00
Inserted 1:7
1 Casey Clausen12.002
Michael Clayton 15.00
3 Cedric Cobbs 12.00
4 Ricardo Colclough 12.00
5 Devard Darling 10.00
6 Dwan Edwards 10.00
7 Lee Evans 20.00
8 Larry Fitzgerald
9 Robert Gallery 25.00
10 DeAngelo Hall 20.00
11 Tommie Harris 15.00
12 Ben Hartsock 10.00
13 Devery Henderson 10.00
14 Steven Jackson 40.00
15 Michael Jenkins 15.00
16 Greg Jones 15.00
17 Julius Jones 30.00
18 Sean Jones 10.00
19 Nate Kaeding 10.00
20 Robert Kent 8.00
21 Teddy Lehman 12.00
22 Jared Lorenzen 10.00
23 Eli Manning 100.00
24 Luke McCown 10.00
25 Mewelde Moore 10.00
26 John Navarre 12.00
27 James Newson 10.00
28 Tony Pape 10.00
29 Jarrett Payton 20.00
30 Chris Perry 20.00
31 Cody Pickett 10.00
32 Philip Rivers 40.00
33 Ben Roethlisberger 60.00
34 P K Sam 12.00
35 Matt Schaub 10.00
36 Justin Smiley 10.00
37 Keith Smith 8.00
38 Will Smith 10.00
39 Jeff Smoker 15.00
40 Derrick Strait 12.00
41 Ben Troupe 10.00
42 Michael Turner 10.00
43 Jonathan Vilma 15.00
44 Ben Watson 12.00
45 Darius Watts 15.00
46 Vince Wilfork 12.00
47 DJ Williams 12.00
48 Mike Williams 80.00
49 Quincy Wilson 12.00
50 Kellen Winslow 80.00
51 Rashaun Woods 20.00
52 Jason Wright 8.00

2004 Press Pass Autographs Gold

Golds: 1X-1.5X
Production 100 Sets
8 Larry Fitzgerald/75

2004 Press Pass Autographs Silver

Silvers: 1X-1.2X
Production 200 Sets
8 Larry Fitzgerald/50

2004 Press Pass Big Numbers

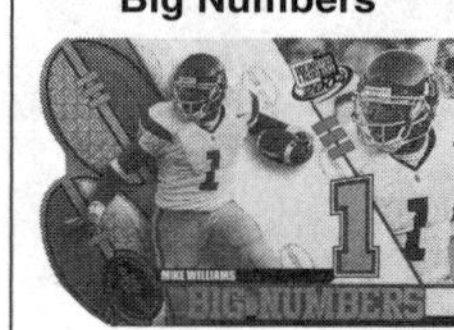

NM/M
Common Player: 1.00
Inserted 1:1
BN 1 Casey Clausen 1.00
BN 2 Michael Clayton 2.00
BN 3 Cedric Cobbs 1.00
BN 4 Devard Darling 1.00
BN 5 Lee Evans 2.00
BN 6 Larry Fitzgerald 3.00
BN 7 Robert Gallery 1.25
BN 8 DeAngelo Hall 1.50
BN 9 Steven Jackson 2.50
BN10 Michael Jenkins 1.50
BN11 Greg Jones 1.25
BN12 Kevin Jones 2.50
BN13 Craig Krenzel 1.00
BN14 J.P. Losman 2.00
BN15 Eli Manning 5.00
BN16 John Navarre 1.25
BN17 Jarrett Payton 1.50
BN18 Chris Perry 1.50
BN19 Cody Pickett 1.00
BN20 Philip Rivers 4.00
BN21 Ben Roethlisberger 4.00
BN22 Matt Schaub 1.00
BN23 Will Smith 1.00
BN24 Ben Troupe .75
BN25 Michael Turner .75
BN26 Jonathan Vilma 1.25
BN27 Vince Wilfork 1.25
BN28 Quincy Wilson 1.25
BN29 DJ Williams 1.25
BN30 Mike Williams 3.00
BN31 Roy Williams 3.00
BN32 Rashaun Woods 2.00
BN33 Eli Manning 5.00

2004 Press Pass Jersey Cards

NM/M
Common Player: 10.00
Production 300 Sets
Golds: 1X-1.5X
Gold Production 100 Sets
Holofoils: 1.5X-2.5X
Holofoil Production 50 Sets
JC/DD Devard Darling 10.00
JC/JG Jermaine Green 10.00
JC/SJ Steven Jackson 20.00
JC/JL Jared Lorenzen 10.00
JC/EM Eli Manning 50.00
JC/LM Luke McCown 10.00
JC/MM Mewelde Moore 10.00

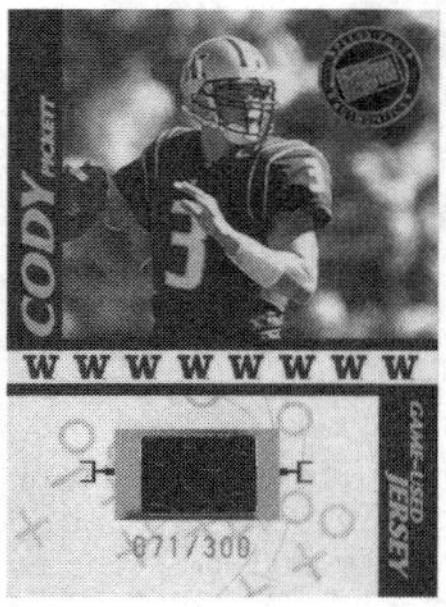

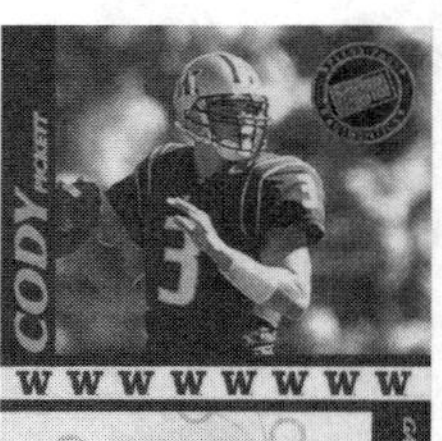

NM/M
JC/JP Jarrett Payton 20.00
JC/CP Cody Pickett 10.00
JC/BR Ben Roethlisberger 30.00
JC/MS Matt Schaub 10.00
JC/DW Darius Watts 12.00

2004 Press Pass Paydirt

NM/M
Common Player: 1.25
Inserted 1:6
PD 1 Eli Manning 5.00
PD 2 Roy Williams 3.00
PD 3 Kevin Jones 2.50
PD 4 Philip Rivers 4.00
PD 5 Rashaun Woods 2.00
PD 6 Ben Roethlisberger 4.00
PD 7 Ben Troupe 1.00
PD 8 Steven Jackson 2.50
PD 9 Michael Clayton 2.00
PD10 Chris Perry 1.50
PD11 Larry Fitzgerald 3.00
PD12 Greg Jones 1.25

2004 Press Pass Showbound

NM/M
Common Player: 2.00
Inserted 1:12
SB 1 Steven Jackson 3.00
SB 2 Larry Fitzgerald 4.00
SB 3 Eli Manning 8.00
SB 4 Kevin Jones 3.00
SB 5 Roy Williams 4.00
SB 6 Ben Roethlisberger 6.00
SB 7 Philip Rivers 6.00
SB 8 Chris Perry 2.00
SB 9 J.P. Losman 3.00

2004 Press Pass SE

NM/M
Complete Set (40): 25.00
Common Player: .75
Minor Stars: 1.00
Unlisted Stars: 1.25
Pack (5): 25.00
Box (12): 250.00
1 Shawn Andrews .75
2 Casey Clausen 1.00
3 Michael Clayton 2.00
4 Cedric Cobbs 1.00
5 Devard Darling 1.00
6 Lee Evans 2.00
7 Larry Fitzgerald 3.00
8 Robert Gallery 1.25
9 DeAngelo Hall 1.50
10 Tommie Harris 1.25
11 Ben Hartsock 1.00
12 Devery Henderson 1.00
13 Steven Jackson 2.50
14 Michael Jenkins 1.50
15 Greg Jones 1.25

16 Kevin Jones 2.50
17 Teddy Lehman 1.00
18 J.P. Losman 2.00
19 Eli Manning 5.00
20 Mewelde Moore 1.00
21 John Navarre 1.25
22 Jarrett Payton 1.50
23 Chris Perry 1.50
24 Cody Pickett 1.00
25 Philip Rivers 4.00
26 Ben Roethlisberger 10.00
27 Matt Schaub 1.00
28 Will Smith 1.00
29 Ben Troupe .75
30 Michael Turner .75
31 Ben Watson .75
32 Darius Watts 1.00
33 Vince Wilfork 1.25
34 Mike Williams 3.00
35 Reggie Williams 2.00
36 Roy Williams 3.00
37 Quincy Wilson 1.25
38 Rashaun Woods 2.00
39 Jason Wright .75
40 Eli Manning 2.50
NNO Eli Manning Mini Helmet 150.00

2004 Press Pass SE 1st Down

Singles: 1X-1.5X
Inserted 1:1

2004 Press Pass SE Autographs Blue

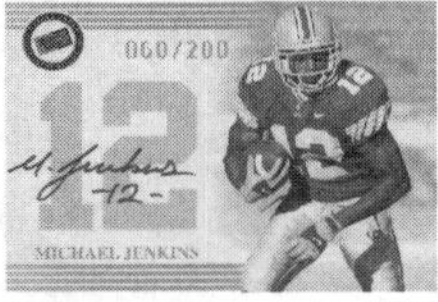

Blues: 1X-2X
Production 50 Sets

2004 Press Pass SE Class of 2004

NM/M
Common Player: 2.00
Inserted 1:3
CL1 Eli Manning 5.00
CL2 Ben Roethlisberger 4.00
CL3 Philip Rivers 4.00
CL4 Mike Williams 3.00
CL5 Kevin Jones 2.50
CL6 Rashaun Woods 2.00
CL7 Steven Jackson 2.50
CL8 Larry Fitzgerald 3.00
CL9 Roy Williams 3.00

2004 Press Pass SE Class of 2004 Autos

NM/M
Common Player: 15.00
1 Steven Jackson/50 60.00
2 Kevin Jones/50 60.00
3 Eli Manning/200 150.00
4 Chris Perry/200 20.00
5 Philip Rivers/200 60.00
6 Ben Roethlisberger/25 300.00
7 Ben Troupe/200 15.00
8 Mike Williams/200 80.00
9 Rashaun Woods/200 20.00

2004 Press Pass SE Jerseys

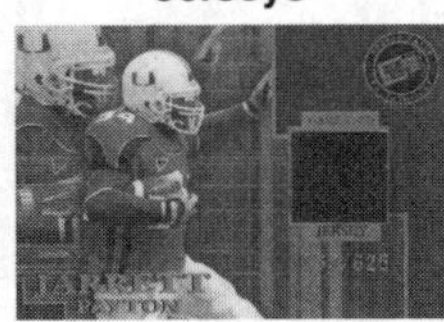

NM/M
Bronze Production 700 Sets
Silvers: 1X-1.2X
Silver Production 400 Sets
Golds: 1X-2X
Gold Production 100 Sets
Numbers: 2X-4X
Number Production 25 Sets
Patch Production 10 Sets
JCBB Bernard Berrian 8.00
JCBH Ben Hartsock 8.00
JCBR Ben Roethlisberger 30.00
JCCC Casey Clausen 8.00
JCCP Cody Pickett 8.00
JCDD Devard Darling 8.00
JCDW Darius Watts 8.00
JCEM Eli Manning 30.00
JCJG Jermaine Green 6.00
JCJL Jared Lorenzen 8.00
JCJP Jarrett Payton 12.00
JCLM Luke McCown 8.00
JCMM Mewelde Moore 8.00
JCMS Matt Schaub 8.00
JCPR Philip Rivers 20.00
JCSJ Steven Jackson 12.00
AU1 Eli Manning Auto/25 350.00
AU2 Ben Roethlisberger Auto/25

2004 Press Pass SE Old School

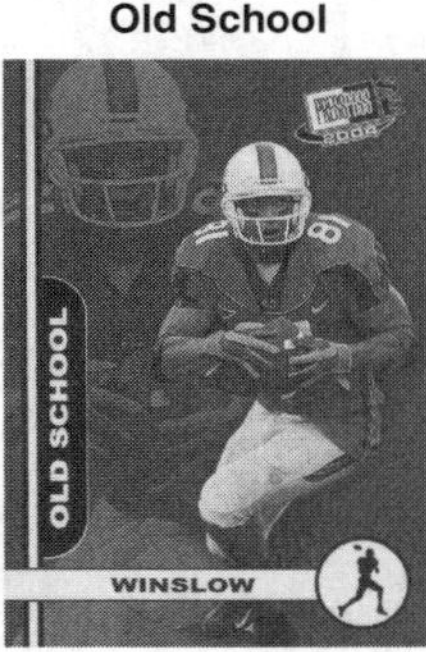

NM/M
Common Player: .75
Inserted 1:1
OS1 Casey Clausen 1.00
OS2 J.P. Losman 2.00
OS3 Eli Manning 5.00
OS4 John Navarre 1.25
OS5 Cody Pickett 1.00
OS6 Philip Rivers 4.00
OS7 Ben Roethlisberger 4.00
OS8 Matt Schaub 1.00
OS9 Steven Jackson 2.50
OS10 Greg Jones 1.25
OS11 Kevin Jones 2.50
OS12 Chris Perry 1.50
OS13 Michael Clayton 2.00
OS14 Lee Evans 2.00
OS15 Larry Fitzgerald 3.00
OS16 Michael Jenkins 1.50
OS17 Mike Williams 3.00
OS18 Roy Williams 3.00
OS19 Rashaun Woods 2.00
OS20 Ben Troupe .75
OS21 Ben Watson .75
OS22 Kellen Winslow 2.50
OS23 Robert Gallery 1.25
OS24 Will Smith 1.00
OS25 Tommie Harris 1.25
OS26 Vince Wilfork 1.25
OS27 Eli Manning 2.50

2004 Press Pass SE Up Close

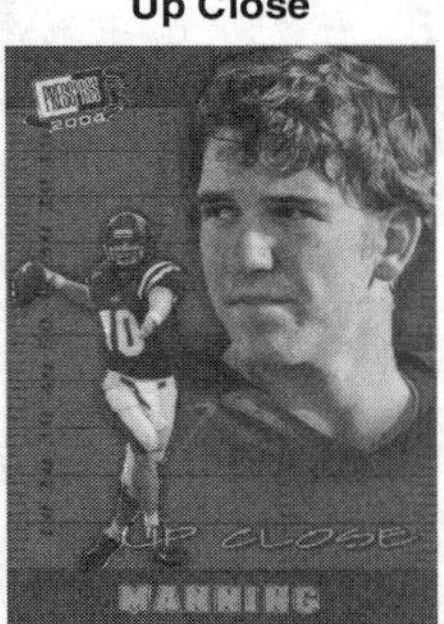

NM/M
Common Player: 2.50
Inserted 1:4
UC1 Eli Manning 5.00
UC2 Larry Fitzgerald 3.00
UC3 Roy Williams 3.00
UC4 Ben Roethlisberger 4.00
UC5 Philip Rivers 4.00
UC6 Kevin Jones 2.50

2005 Press Pass

NM/M
Common Player (1-45): .50
Minor Stars: .75
Unlisted Stars: 1.00
Common PP (46-50): 5.00
Pack (4): 4.00
Box (24): 70.00
1 Derek Anderson .75
2 Brock Berlin .75
3 Charlie Frye 1.50
4 Gino Guidugli .50
5 David Greene 1.00
6 Stefan LeFors 1.00
7 Dan Orlovsky 1.00
8 Kyle Orton 1.50
9 Aaron Rodgers 4.00
10 Alex Smith QB 5.00
11 Andrew Walter 1.00
12 Jason White 1.50
13 J.J. Arrington 1.50
14 Ronnie Brown 3.00
15 Anthony Davis .75
16 Kay-Jay Harris .75
17 T.A. McLendon .75
18 Ryan Moats .75
19 Vernand Morency .75
20 Carnell Williams 3.00
21 Mark Bradley 1.50
22 Reggie Brown .75
23 Mark Clayton 1.50
24 Braylon Edwards 3.00
25 Fred Gibson 1.00
26 Terrence Murphy .50
27 J.R. Russell .50
28 Craphonso Thorpe .75
29 Roddy White 1.00
30 Mike Williams 3.00
31 Troy Williamson 2.00
32 Heath Miller 1.50
33 Alex Smith TE 1.00
34 Khalif Barnes .50
35 Jammal Brown .75
36 Brandon Browner .50
37 Marlin Jackson .75
38 Carlos Rogers 1.00
39 Antrel Rolle 1.50
40 Dan Cody 1.00
41 Erasmus James 1.00
42 David Pollack 1.50
43 Anttaj Hawthorne .50
44 Derrick Johnson 1.50
45 Ronnie Brown CL 1.50
46 Carnell Williams PP 5.00
47 Aaron Rodgers PP 6.00
48 Alex Smith QB PP 8.00
49 Braylon Edwards PP 5.00
50 Mike Williams PP 5.00

2005 Press Pass Blue

Singles: 1X-2X
Inserted 1:1 Retail

2005 Press Pass Reflectors

Singles: 3X-6X
Production 500 Sets
Proofs: 5X-10X
Proof Production 100 Sets

2005 Press Pass Autographs Bronze

NM/M
Common Player: 8.00
Inserted 1:7 Hobby
1 Derek Anderson 8.00
2 J.J. Arrington 12.00
3 Marion Barber 10.00
4 Khalif Barnes 8.00
5 Brock Berlin 10.00
6 Mark Bradley 15.00
7 Elton Brown 8.00
8 Reggie Brown 10.00
9 Ronnie Brown SP 60.00
10 Luis Castillo 8.00
11 Dan Cody 20.00
12 Jerome Collins 8.00
13 Sean Considine 8.00
14 Anthony Davis 10.00
15 Thomas Davis 10.00
16 Braylon Edwards SP 125.00
17 Ciatrick Fason 12.00
18 Diamond Ferri 8.00
19 Charlie Frye SP 25.00
20 Fred Gibson 12.00
21 David Greene 15.00
22 Gino Guidugli 8.00
23 Kay-Jay Harris 10.00
24 Anttaj Hawthorne 8.00
25 Chris Henry 15.00
26 Keron Henry 8.00
27 Noah Herron 8.00
28 Marlin Jackson 10.00
29 Derrick Johnson 20.00
30 Stefan LeFors 15.00
31 T.A. McLendon 8.00
32 Heath Miller 30.00
33 Ryan Moats 12.00
34 Vernand Morency 10.00
35 Terrence Murphy 8.00
36 Dan Orlovsky 15.00
37 Kyle Orton 15.00
38 David Pollack 20.00
39 Walter Reyes 8.00
40 Aaron Rodgers SP 80.00
41 Antrel Rolle 20.00
42 J.R. Russell 8.00
43 Barrett Ruud 20.00
44 Eric Shelton 10.00
45 Alex Smith TE 10.00
46 Craphonso Thorpe 10.00
47 Andrew Walter 15.00
48 Jason White 15.00
49 Roddy White 10.00
50 Mike Williams SP 100.00
51 Troy Williamson 25.00
52 Stanley Wilson 8.00

2005 Press Pass Autographs Gold

NM/M
Gold: 1X-1.5X
Gold SP: 1X-1.2X
Ronnie Brown/50 100.00
Mike Williams/50 150.00
Production 100 Hobby Sets

2005 Press Pass Autographs Silver

NM/M
Silver: 1X-1.2X
Silver SP: 1X
Ronnie Brown/75 80.00
Mike Williams/75 120.00
Production 200 Sets

2005 Press Pass Autograph Power Picks

NM/M
Common Player: 25.00
1 Ronnie Brown/100 100.00
2 Braylon Edwards/50
3 Charlie Frye/250 25.00
4 Heath Miller/50 80.00
5 Aaron Rodgers/250 60.00
6 Andrew Walter/250 25.00
7 Mike Williams/100 120.00
8 Troy Williamson/250 40.00

2005 Press Pass Big Numbers

NM/M
Common Player: .50
Inserted 1:1
BN1 Reggie Brown .75
BN2 Ronnie Brown 3.00
BN3 Mark Clayton 1.50
BN4 Dan Cody 1.00
BN5 Anthony Davis .75
BN6 Braylon Edwards 3.00
BN7 Charlie Frye 1.50
BN8 Fred Gibson 1.00
BN9 David Greene 1.00
BN10 Gino Guidugli .50
BN11 Derrick Johnson 1.50
BN12 T.A. McLendon .75
BN13 Heath Miller 1.50
BN14 Vernand Morency .75
BN15 Dan Orlovsky 1.00
BN16 Kyle Orton 1.50
BN17 Aaron Rodgers 4.00
BN18 J.R. Russell .50
BN19 Alex Smith QB 5.00
BN20 Andrew Walter 1.00
BN21 Jason White 1.50
BN22 Carnell Williams 3.00
BN23 Mike Williams 3.00
BN24 Troy Williamson 2.00
BN25 Aaron Rodgers CL 2.00

2005 Press Pass Jerseys Silver

NM/M
Common Player: 8.00
Silver Production 300 Sets
Gold: 1X-1.5X
Gold Production 125 Sets
Holofoil: 1.5X-3X
Holofoil Production 50 Sets
JCMB Mark Bradley 15.00
JCJC Jerome Collins 8.00
JCMJ Marlin Jackson 10.00
JCSL Stefan LeFors 12.00
JCTM Terrence Murphy 8.00
JCDO Dan Orlovsky 10.00
JCKO Kyle Orton 15.00
JCAS Alex Smith TE 8.00
JCCT Craphonso Thorpe 10.00
JCJW Jason White 15.00
JCRW Roddy White 12.00

2005 Press Pass Paydirt

NM/M
Common Player: 2.00
Inserted 1:6
PD1 Carnell Williams 5.00
PD2 Charlie Frye 3.00
PD3 Mike Williams 5.00
PD4 Braylon Edwards 5.00
PD5 Alex Smith QB 8.00
PD6 Dan Orlovsky 2.00
PD7 Andrew Walter 3.00
PD8 Ronnie Brown 5.00
PD9 Heath Miller 3.00
PD10 Troy Williamson 4.00
PD11 Aaron Rodgers 6.00
PD12 Mark Clayton 3.00

2005 Press Pass Showbound

NM/M
Common Player: 3.00
Inserted 1:12
SB1 Alex Smith QB 8.00
SB2 Ronnie Brown 5.00
SB3 Aaron Rodgers 6.00
SB4 Carnell Williams 5.00
SB5 Heath Miller 3.00
SB6 Braylon Edwards 5.00
SB7 Mark Clayton 3.00
SB8 Mike Williams 5.00
SB9 Troy Williamson 4.00

2005 Press Pass SE

NM/M
Common Player (1-40): .75
Minor Stars: 1.00
Unlisted Stars: 1.25
Pack (5): 12.00
Box (12): 120.00
1 Charlie Frye 1.50
2 David Greene 1.25
3 Gino Guidugli 1.00
4 Stefan LeFors 1.25
5 Dan Orlovsky 1.25
6 Kyle Orton 1.50
7 Aaron Rodgers 4.00
8 Alex Smith 5.00
9 Andrew Walter 1.25
10 Jason White 1.50
11 J.J. Arrington 1.50
12 Marion Barber III 1.00
13 Ronnie Brown 3.00
14 Anthony Davis 1.00
15 Ciatrick Fason 1.00
16 T.A. McLendon 1.00
17 Vernand Morency 1.25
18 Walter Reyes .75
19 Carnell Williams 3.00
20 Mark Bradley 1.50
21 Reggie Brown 1.25
22 Mark Clayton 1.50
23 Braylon Edwards 3.00
24 Fred Gibson 1.25
25 Chris Henry 1.00
26 Terrence Murphy 1.00
27 J.R. Russell .75
28 Craphonso Thorpe 1.00
29 Roddy White 1.25
30 Mike Williams 3.00
31 Troy Williamson 2.00
32 Heath Miller 1.50
33 Alex Smith TE 1.00
34 Jammal Brown 1.00
35 Marlin Jackson 1.00
36 Antrel Rolle 1.50
37 Dan Cody 1.00
38 Derrick Johnson 1.50
39 Thomas Davis 1.25
40 Aaron Rodgers 2.00

2005 Press Pass SE Autographs

NM/M
Common Bronze: 8.00
Silver Autos: 1X-2X
Silver Production 200 Sets
Gold Autos: 1X-1.5X
Gold Production 100 Sets
Blue Autos: 1X-2X
Blue Production 50 Sets
1 Derek Anderson 8.00
2 J.J. Arrington 12.00
3 Marion Barber III 10.00
4 Khalif Barnes 8.00
5 Brock Berlin 10.00
6 Mark Bradley 15.00
7 Elton Brown 8.00
8 Jammal Brown 8.00
9 Reggie Brown 10.00
10 Ronnie Brown SP 60.00
11 Brandon Browner 8.00
12 Luis Castillo 8.00
13 Mark Clayton 20.00
14 Dan Cody 20.00
15 Jerome Collins 8.00
16 Sean Considine 8.00
17 Anthony Davis 10.00
18 Thomas Davis 10.00
19 Braylon Edwards SP 125.00
20 Ciatrick Fason 12.00
21 Diamond Ferri 8.00
22 Charlie Frye SP 25.00
23 Fred Gibson 12.00
24 David Greene 15.00
25 Gino Guidugli 8.00
26 Kay-Jay Harris 10.00
27 Anttaj Hawthorne 8.00
28 Chris Henry 15.00
29 Keron Henry 8.00
30 Noah Herron 8.00
31 Marlin Jackson 10.00
32 Erasmus James 12.00
33 Derrick Johnson 20.00
34 Stefan LeFors 15.00
35 T.A. McLendon 8.00
36 Heath Miller 30.00
37 Ryan Moats 12.00
38 Vernand Morency 10.00
39 Terrence Murphy 8.00
40 Dan Orlovsky 15.00
41 Kyle Orton 15.00
42 David Pollack 20.00
43 Walter Reyes 8.00
44 Aaron Rodgers SP 80.00
45 Carlos Rogers 12.00
46 Antrel Rolle 20.00
47 J.R. Russell 8.00
48 Barrett Ruud 20.00
49 Eric Shelton 8.00
50 Alex Smith TE 10.00
51 Craphonso Thorpe 10.00
52 Andrew Walter 15.00
53 Jason White 15.00
54 Roddy White 10.00
55 Carnell Williams SP
56 Mike Williams SP 100.00
57 Troy Williamson 25.00
58 Stanley Wilson 8.00

2005 Press Pass SE Class of 2005

NM/M
Common Player: 2.00
Inserted 1:3
CL1 Aaron Rodgers 5.00
CL2 Braylon Edwards 4.00
CL3 Charlie Frye 2.50
CL4 Heath Miller 2.00
CL5 Troy Williamson 3.00
CL6 Alex Smith 6.00
CL7 Ronnie Brown 4.00
CL8 Andrew Walter 2.00
CL9 Carnell Williams 4.00

2005 Press Pass SE Class of 2005 Autographs

NM/M
Common Player: 25.00
Production 200 Sets
Ronnie Brown/23
Braylon Edwards/50 140.00
Heath Miller 40.00
Dan Orlovsky 25.00
Aaron Rodgers 80.00
Carnell Williams 60.00
Troy Williamson 40.00

2005 Press Pass SE Jerseys

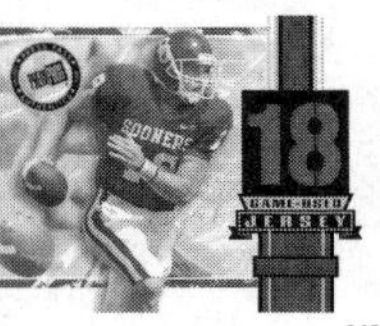

NM/M
Common Player: 6.00
Production 450-700 Sets
Gold: 1X-2X
Gold Production 450-550 Sets
Holofoil: 1X-2X
Holofoil Production 100 Sets
Numbers: 2X-4X
Number Production 25 Sets
Patches Unpriced
Patch Production 1-10 Sets
JC/DA Derek Anderson 6.00
JC/BB Brock Berlin 6.00
JC/MB Mark Bradley 8.00
JC/RB Reggie Brown 6.00
JC/JC Jerome Collins 6.00
JC/DG David Green 8.00
JC/MJ Marlin Jackson 6.00
JC/SL Stefan LeFors 8.00
JC/VM Vernand Morency 8.00
JC/TM Terrence Murphy 6.00
JC/DO Dan Orlovsky 8.00
JC/KO Kyle Orton 10.00
JC/AS Alex Smith 6.00
JC/CT Craphonso Thorpe 6.00
JC/AW Andrew Walter 8.00
JC/JW Jason White 10.00
JC/RW Roddy White 8.00

2005 Press Pass SE Jersey Autographs

NM/M
Common Player: 50.00
Production 25 Sets
JC/RB Reggie Brown 60.00
JC/DG David Green 50.00
JC/DO Dan Orlovsky 50.00
JC/KO Kyle Orton 60.00
JC/AW Andrew Walter 50.00
JC/JW Jason White 100.00

2005 Press Pass SE Old School

NM/M
Common Player: 1.00
Inserted 1:1
OS1 Marion Barber III 1.00
OS2 Reggie Brown 1.50
OS3 Ronnie Brown 3.00
OS4 Mark Clayton 1.50
OS5 Dan Cody 1.00
OS6 Anthony Davis 1.00
OS7 Braylon Edwards 3.00
OS8 Ciatrick Fason 1.00
OS9 Charlie Frye 1.50
OS10 David Greene 1.25
OS11 Gino Guidugli 1.00
OS12 Derrick Johnson 1.50
OS13 Heath Miller 1.50
OS14 Vernand Morency 1.25
OS15 Dan Orlovsky 1.25
OS16 Kyle Orton 1.50
OS17 Aaron Rodgers 4.00
OS18 Antrel Rolle 1.50
OS19 Eric Shelton 1.25
OS20 Alex Smith 5.00
OS21 Andrew Walter 1.25
OS22 Jason White 1.50
OS23 Roddy White 1.25
OS24 Carnell Williams 3.00
OS25 Mike Williams 3.00
OS26 Troy Williamson 2.00
OS27 Braylon Edwards Checklist 1.50

2005 Press Pass SE Up Close

NM/M
Common Player: 2.00
Inserted 1:4
UC1 Carnell Williams 4.00
UC2 Aaron Rodgers 3.00
UC3 Mike Williams 4.00
UC4 Ronnie Brown 4.00
UC5 Braylon Edwards 4.00
UC6 Dan Orlovsky 2.00

1993-94 Pro Athletes Outreach

Measuring 7-1/8" x 4-1/8", the 12-card set was made up of triple-fold cards, which showcased a player photo on the right panel. Beneath the photo is the PAO logo, player's name and position. The player's career highlights and his Christian philosophy also are featured on the unnumbered card.

NM/M
Complete Set (12): 6.00
Common Player: .50
1 Mark Boyer .50
2 Gill Byrd .50

3 Darren Carrington .50
4 Paul Coffman .50
5 Burnell Dent .50
6 Johnny Holland .50
7 Jeff Kemp 1.00
8 Steve Largent 3.00
9 John Offerdahl .50
10 Stephone Paige .50
11 Doug Smith .50
12 Rob Taylor .50

1990 Pro Line Samples

These Pro Line samples can be identified from the regular set's card by several factors, including having the word SAMPLE written on the card back next to a player head shot. The card fronts have photos which are entirely different, or cropped differently, than their regular counterparts. The front also has a silver border; the regular cards are full-bleed. Some backs also have different photos than those used in the regular set and quotes. Card numbers are from 1-37, using all the odd numbers except 15.

NM/M
Complete Set (18): 45.00
Common Player: 2.00
1 Charles Mann 2.00
3 Troy Aikman 10.00
5 Boomer Esiason 5.00
7 Warren Moon 5.00
9 Bill Fralic 2.00
11 Lawrence Taylor 5.00
13 George Seifert 2.00
17 Dan Marino 10.00
19 Jim Everett 3.00
21 John Elway 6.00
23 Jeff George 2.00
25 Lindy Infante 2.00
27 Dan Reeves 2.00
29 Steve Largent 5.00
31 Roger Craig 4.00
33 Marty Schottenheimer 2.00
35 Mike Ditka 5.00
37 Sam Wyche 2.00

1991 Pro Line Portraits

This set of high-end cards issued by NFL Properties shows a number of past and present NFL players in posed shots, wearing team apparel without football equipment. These cards were issued in August 1991 in 12-card wax packs. Some 250,000 autographed, embossed and unnumbered were randomly packed. Cards are not licensed by the NFL Players Association, so non-association members such as Eric Dickerson, Michael Dean Perry, Jim Kelly, Bernie Kosar, Webster Slaughter and Cornelius Bennett appear here while they don't appear in any other 1991 sets. A subset, Spirit Collectibles, shows seven player wives. Two other cards, Pro Line Portraits Collectible #1 (Ahmad Rashad and family) and #2 (Payne Stewart), were limited to 10,000 randomly issued cards. Each card in the regular set was also autographed.

NM/M
Complete Set (300): 4.50
Common Player: .03
Pack (12): .40
Wax Box (36): 12.00
1 Jim Kelly .20
2 Carl Banks .03
3 Neal Anderson .03
4 James Brooks .03
5 Reggie Langhorne .03
6 Robert Awalt .03
7 Greg Kragen .03
8 Steve Young .50
9 *Nick Bell* .10
10 Ray Childress .03
11 Albert Bentley .03
12 Albert Lewis .03
13 Howie Long .03
14 Willie Anderson .03
15 Mark Clayton .03
16 *Jarrod Bunch* .10
17 Bruce Armstrong .03
18 *Vinnie Clark* .10
19 Rob Moore .10
20 Eric Allen .03
21 Timm Rosenbach .03
22 Gary Anderson .03
23 Martin Bayless .03
24 Kevin Fagan .03
25 Brian Blades .03
26 Gary Anderson .03
27 Earnest Bymer .03
28 O.J. Simpson 1.00
29 Dan Henning .03
30 Sean Landeta .03
31 James Lofton .03
32 Mike Singletary .03
33 David Fulcher .03
34 Mark Murphy .03
35 Issiac Holt .03
36 Dennis Smith .03
37 Lomas Brown .03
38 Ernest Givins .03
39 Duane Bickett .03
40 Barry Word .03
41 Tony Mandarich .03
42 Cleveland Gary .03
43 Ferrell Edmunds .03
44 *Randal Hill* .25
45 Irving Fryar .03
46 *Henry Jones* .10
47 Blair Thomas .03
48 Andre Waters .03
49 J.T. Smith .03
50 Thomas Everett .03
51 Marion Butts .03
52 Tom Rathman .03
53 Vann McElroy .03
54 Mark Carrier (T.B.) .03
55 Jim Lachey .03
56 Joe Theismann .03
57 Jerry Glanville .03
58 Doug Riesenberg .03
59 Cornelius Bennett .03
60 Mark Carrier (Chi.) .03
61 Rodney Holman .03
62 Leroy Hoard .03
63 Michael Irvin .65
64 Bobby Humphrey .03
65 Mel Gray .03
66 Brian Noble .03
67 Al Smith .03
68 Eric Dickerson .10
69 Steve DeBerg .03
70 Jay Schroeder .03
71 Irv Pankey .03
72 Reggie Roby .03
73 Wade Wilson .03
74 Reggie Rembert .03
75 *Russell Maryland* .40
76 Al Toon .03
77 Randall Cunningham .10
78 Lonnie Young .03
79 Carnell Lake .03
80 Brut Grossman .03
81 Jim Mora .03
82 Dave Krieg .03
83 Bruce Hill .03
84 Ricky Sanders .03
85 Roger Staubach .10
86 Richard Williamson .03
87 Everson Walls .03
88 Shane Conlan .03
89 Mike Ditka .10
90 Mark Bortz .03
91 Tim McGee .03
92 Michael Dean Perry .10
93 Danny Noonan .03
94 Mark Jackson .03
95 Chris Miller .03
96 *Ed McCaffrey* .50
97 Lorenzo White .10
98 Ray Donaldson .03
99 Nick Lowery .03
100 Steve Smith .03
101 Jackie Slater .03
102 Louis Oliver .03
103 *Kanavis McGhee* .10
104 Ray Agnew .03
105 Sam Mills .03
106 Bill Pickel .03
107 Keith Byars .03
108 Ricky Proehl .10
109 Merril Hoge .03
110 Rod Berstine .03
111 Andy Heck .03
112 Broderick Thomas .03
113 Andre Reed .03
114 Paul Warfield .03
115 Bill Belichick .03
116 Ottis Anderson .03
117 Andre Reed .10
118 Andre Rison .20
119 Dexter Carter .03
120 Anthony Munoz .03
121 Bernie Kosar .03
122 Alonzo Highsmith .03
123 David Treadwell .03
124 Rodney Peete .03
125 Haywood Jeffires .15
126 Clarence Verdin .03
127 Christian Okoye .03
128 Greg Townsend .03
129 Tom Newberry .03
130 Keith Sims .03
131 Myron Guyton .03
132 Andre Tippett .03
133 Steve Walsh .03
134 Erik McMillan .03
135 Jim McMahon .03
136 Derek Hill .03
137 David Johnson .03
138 Leslie O'Neal .03
139 Pierce Holt .03
140 Cortez Kennedy .20
141 Danny Peebles .03
142 Alvin Walton .03
143 Drew Pearson .03
144 Dick MacPherson .03
145 Erik Howard .03
146 Steve Tasker .03
147 Bill Fralic .03
148 Don Warren .03
149 Eric Thomas .03
150 Jack Pardee .03
151 Gary Zimmerman .03
152 Leonard Marshall .03
153 Chris Spielman .03
154 Sam Wyche .03
155 Rohn Stark .03
156 Stephone Paige .03
157 Lionel Washington .03
158 Henry Ellard .03
159 Dan Marino .75
160 Lindy Infante .03
161 *Dan McGwire* .10
162 Ken O'Brien .03
163 Tim McDonald .03
164 Louis Lipps .03
165 Billy Joe Tolliver .03
166 Harris Barton .03
167 Tony Woods .03
168 Matt Millen .03
169 Gale Sayers .03
170 Ron Meyer .03
171 William Roberts .03
172 Thurman Thomas .25
173 Steve McMichael .03
174 Ickey Woods .03
175 Eugene Lockhart .03
176 George Seifert .03
177 Keith Jones .03
178 Jack Trudeau .03
179 Kevin Porter .03
180 Ronnie Lott .10
181 Marty Schottenheimer .03
182 Morten Andersen .03
183 Anthony Thompson .03
184 Tim Worley .03
185 Billy Ray Smith .03
186 David Whitmore .03
187 Jacob Green .03
188 *Browning Nagle* .15
189 Franco Harris .10
190 Art Shell .03
191 Bart Oates .03
192 William Perry .03
193 Chuck Noll .03
194 Troy Aikman 1.00
195 Jeff George .15
196 Derrick Thomas .15
197 Roger Craig .03
198 John Fourcade .03
199 Rod Woodson .03
200 Anthony Miller .03
201 Jerry Rice .75
202 Eugene Robinson .03
203 Charles Mann .03
204 Mel Blount .03
205 Don Shula .03
206 John Elliott .03
207 Jay Hilgenberg .03
208 Deron Cherry .03
209 Dan Reeves .03
210 *Roman Phifer* .10
211 David Little .03
212 Lee Williams .03
213 John Taylor .10
214 Monte Coleman .03
215 Walter Payton .10
216 John Robinson .03
217 Pepper Johnson .03
218 Tom Thayer .03
219 Dan Saleumua .03
220 Ernest Spears .03
221 Bubby Brister .03
222 Junior Seau .20
223 Brent Jones .03
224 Rufus Porter .03
225 Jack Kemp .10
226 Wayne Fontes .03
227 Phil Simms .10
228 Shaun Gayle .03
229 Bill Maas .03
230 Renaldo Turnbull .03
231 Bryan Hinkle .03
232 Gary Plummer .03
233 Jerry Burns .03
234 Lawrence Taylor .10
235 Joe Gibbs .03
236 Neil Smith .03
237 Rich Kotite .03
238 Jim Covert .03
239 Tim Grunhard .03
240 Joe Bugel .03
241 Dave Wyman .03
242 Maruy Buford .03
243 Kevin Ross .03
244 Jimmy Johnson .03
245 Jim Morrissey .03
246 Jeff Hostetler .20
247 Andre Ware .10
248 Steve Largent .10
249 Chuck Knox .03
250 Boomer Esiason .10
251 Kevin Butler .03
252 Bruce Smith .03
253 Webster Slaughter .03
254 Mike Sherrard .03
255 Steve Broussard .03
256 Warren Moon .15
257 John Elway .25
258 Bob Golic .03
259 Jim Everett .03
260 Bruce Coslet .03
261 James Francis .03
262 Eric Dorsey .03
263 Marcus Dupree .03
264 Hart Lee Dykes .03
265 Vinny Testaverde .03
266 Chip Lohmiller .03
267 John Riggins .03
268 Mike Schad .03
269 Kevin Greene .03
270 Dean Biasucci .03
271 *Mike Pritchard* .40
272 *Ted Washington* .10
273 *Alfred Williams* .10
274 *Chris Zorich* .15
275 Reggie Barrett .03
276 Chris Hinton .03
277 Tracy Johnson .10
278 Jim Harbaugh .03
279 John Roper .03
280 Mike Dumas .03
281 *Herman Moore* 3.50
282 *Eric Turner* .15
283 Steve Atwater .03
284 Michael Cofer (Det.) .03
285 Darion Conner .03
286 Darryl Talley .03
287 Donnell Woolford .03
288 Keith McCants .03
289 Ray Handley .03
290 Ahmad Rashad .03
291 *Eric Swann* .15
292 Dalton Hilliard .03
293 Rickey Jackson .03
294 Vaughan Johnson .03
295 Eric Martin .03
296 Pat Swilling .03
297 Anthony Carter .03
298 Guy McIntyre .03
299 Bennie Blades .03
300 Paul Farren .03

1991 Pro Line Portraits Autographs

Each card in the regular set was also autographed. The card is the same as the regular one, except it is not numbered. These cards command premium prices and were random inserts in packs, about one every three boxes.

NM/M
Complete Set (301): 5,250
Common Player: 6.00
Minor Stars: 12.00
1A Jim Kelly (Autopenned) 20.00
1B Jim Kelly (Real Signature) 250.00
2 Carl Banks 6.00
3 Neal Anderson 6.00
4 James Brooks 6.00
5 Reggie Langhorne 60.00
6 Robert Awalt 6.00
7 Greg Kragen 6.00
8 Steve Young 125.00
9 Nick Bell 6.00
10 Ray Childress 12.00
11 Albert Bentley 6.00
12 Albert Lewis (Most signatures are cut off) 60.00
13 Howie Long 35.00
14 Flipper Anderson 12.00
15 Mark Clayton 12.00
16 Jarrod Bunch 6.00
17 Bruce Armstrong 6.00
18 Vinnie Clark 6.00
19 Rob Moore 20.00
20 Eric Allen 6.00
21 Timm Rosenbach 6.00
22 Gary Anderson (K) 6.00
23 Martin Bayless 6.00
24 Kevin Fagan 6.00
25 Brian Blades 12.00
26 Gary Anderson (RB) 6.00
27 Earnest Byner 6.00
28 O.J. Simpson (RET) 300.00
29 Dan Henning (CO) 6.00
30 Sean Landeta 6.00
31 James Lofton 25.00
32 Mike Singletary 40.00
33 David Fulcher 6.00
34 Mark Murphy 6.00
35 Issiac Holt 6.00
36 Dennis Smith 6.00
37 Lomas Brown 6.00
38 Ernest Givins 12.00
39 Duane Bickett 6.00
40 Barry Word 6.00
41 Tony Mandarich 12.00
42 Cleveland Gary 12.00
43 Ferrell Edmunds 6.00
44 Randal Hill 12.00
45 Irving Fryar 12.00
46 Henry Jones 6.00
47 Blair Thomas 6.00
48 Andre Waters 6.00
49 J.T. Smith 6.00
50 Thomas Everett 6.00
51 Marion Butts 6.00
52 Tom Rathman 12.00
53 Vann McElroy 6.00
54 Mark Carrier (WR) 6.00
55 Jim Lachey 6.00
56 Joe Theismann (RET) 30.00
57 Jerry Glanville (CO) 12.00
58 Doug Riesenberg 6.00
59 Cornelius Bennett 12.00
60 Mark Carrier (DB) 100.00
61 Rodney Holman 225.00
62 Leroy Hoard 12.00
63 Michael Irvin 35.00
64 Bobby Humphrey 6.00
65 Mel Gray 12.00
66 Brian Noble 6.00
67 Al Smith 6.00
68 Eric Dickerson 30.00
69 Steve DeBerg 12.00
70 Jay Schroeder 12.00
71 Irv Pankey 6.00
72 Reggie Roby 12.00
73 Wade Wilson 12.00
74 Johnny Rembert 6.00
75 Russell Maryland 12.00
76 Al Toon 12.00
77 Randall Cunningham 30.00
78 Lonnie Young 6.00
79 Carnell Lake 12.00
80 Brut Grossman 6.00
81 Jim Mora (CO) 6.00
82 Dave Krieg 12.00
83 Bruce Hill 6.00
84 Ricky Sanders 12.00
85 Roger Staubach (RET) 150.00
86 Richard Williamson (CO) 6.00
87 Everson Walls 12.00
88 Shane Conlan 6.00
89 Mike Ditka (CO) 40.00
90 Mark Bortz 6.00
91 Tim McGee 6.00
92 Michael Dean Perry 12.00
93 Danny Noonan 6.00
94 Mark Jackson 12.00
95 Chris Miller 12.00
96 Ed McCaffrey 25.00
97 Lorenzo White 12.00
98 Ray Donaldson 6.00
99 Nick Lowery (May be autopenned) 6.00
100 Steve Smith 6.00
101 Jackie Slater 12.00
102 Louis Oliver 6.00
103 Kanavis McGhee 6.00
104 Ray Agnew 6.00
105 Sam Mills 12.00
106 Bill Pickel 12.00
107 Keith Byars 12.00
108 Ricky Proehl 12.00
109 Merril Hoge 6.00
110 Rod Berstine 6.00
111 Andy Heck 6.00
112 Broderick Thomas 6.00
113 Andre Collins 6.00
114 Paul Warfield (RET) 25.00
115 Bill Belichick (CO) 12.00
116 Ottis Anderson 12.00
117 Andre Reed 25.00
118A Andre Rison (Ball-point pen) 15.00
118B Andre Rison (Signed in Sharpie) 30.00
119 Dexter Carter 12.00
120 Anthony Munoz 12.00
121 Bernie Kosar 15.00
122 Alonzo Highsmith 60.00
123 David Treadwell 6.00
124 Rodney Peete 12.00
125 Haywood Jeffires 12.00
126 Clarence Verdin 6.00
127 Christian Okoye 12.00
128 Greg Townsend 125.00
129 Tom Newberry 6.00
130 Keith Sims 6.00
131 Myron Guyton 6.00
132 Andre Tippett 6.00
133 Steve Walsh 12.00
134 Erik McMillan 6.00
135 Jim McMahon 280.00
136 Derek Hill 6.00
137 D.J. Johnson 6.00
138 Leslie O'Neal 12.00
139 Pierce Holt 6.00
140 Cortez Kennedy 12.00
141 Danny Peebles 6.00
142 Alvin Walton 6.00
143 Drew Pearson (RET) 12.00
144 Dick MacPherson (CO) 6.00
145 Erik Howard 6.00
146 Steve Tasker 6.00
147 Bill Fralic 6.00
148 Don Warren 6.00
149 Eric Thomas 6.00
150 Jack Pardee (CO) 6.00
151 Gary Zimmerman 6.00
152 Leonard Marshall (Frequently miscut) 12.00
153 Chris Spielman 12.00
154 Sam Wyche (CO) 6.00
155 Rohn Stark 6.00
156 Stephone Paige 6.00
157 Lionel Washington (Most signatures are cut off) 120.00
158 Henry Ellard 12.00
159 Dan Marino 200.00
160 Lindy Infante (CO) 6.00
161 Dan McGwire 6.00
162 Ken O'Brien 12.00
163 Tim McDonald 6.00
164 Louis Lipps 6.00
165 Billy Joe Tolliver 12.00
166 Harris Barton 6.00
167 Tony Woods 6.00
168 Matt Millen 12.00
169 Gale Sayers (RET) 35.00
170 Ron Meyer (CO) 12.00
171 William Roberts 6.00
172 Thurman Thomas 30.00
173 Steve McMichael 6.00
174 Ickey Woods 6.00
175 Eugene Lockhart 6.00
176 George Seifert (CO) 12.00
177 Keith Jones 6.00
178 Jack Trudeau 6.00
179 Kevin Porter 6.00
180 Ronnie Lott 15.00
181 Marty Schottenheimer (CO) 12.00
182 Morten Andersen 12.00
183 Anthony Thompson 6.00
184 Tim Worley 6.00
185 Billy Ray Smith 6.00
186 David Whitmore 6.00
187 Jacob Green 6.00
188 Browning Nagle 6.00
189 Franco Harris (RET) (Most signatures are cut off) 45.00
190 Art Shell (CO) 15.00
191 Bart Oates 6.00
192 William Perry 12.00
193 Chuck Noll (CO) 30.00
194 Troy Aikman 100.00
195 Jeff George 25.00
196 Derrick Thomas 40.00
197 Roger Craig 12.00
198 John Fourcade 6.00
199 Rod Woodson 12.00
200 Anthony Miller 12.00
201 Jerry Rice 150.00
202 Eugene Robinson 6.00
203 Charles Mann 6.00
204 Mel Blount (RET) 12.00
205 Don Shula (CO) 45.00
206 John Elliott 6.00
207 Jay Hilgenberg 6.00
208 Deron Cherry 6.00
209 Dan Reeves (CO) 12.00
210 Roman Phifer 6.00
211 David Little 6.00
212 Lee Williams 6.00
213 John Taylor 12.00
214 Monte Coleman 6.00
215 Walter Payton (RET) 150.00
216 John Robinson (CO) 6.00
217 Pepper Johnson 6.00
218 Tom Thayer 6.00
219 Dan Saleumua 6.00
220 Ernest Spears 6.00
221 Bubby Brister (Signed Bubby 6) 12.00
222 Junior Seau 20.00
223 Brent Jones 12.00
224 Rufus Porter 6.00
225 Jack Kemp (RET) (Autopenned) 30.00
226 Wayne Fontes (CO) 6.00
227 Phil Simms 30.00
228 Shaun Gayle 6.00
229 Bill Maas 6.00
230 Renaldo Turnbull 6.00
231 Bryan Hinkle 6.00
232 Gary Plummer 6.00
233 Jerry Burns (CO) 6.00
234 Lawrence Taylor 40.00
235 Joe Gibbs (CO) 20.00
236 Neil Smith (Most signatures are cut off) 60.00
237 Rich Kotite (CO) 6.00
238 Jim Covert 6.00
239 Tim Grunhard (Two different signatures known for this card) 6.00
240 Joe Bugel (CO) 6.00
241 Dave Wyman 6.00
242 Maruy Buford 6.00
243 Kevin Ross 6.00
244 Jimmy Johnson (CO) 40.00
245 Jim Morrissey 6.00
246 Jeff Hostetler 12.00
247 Andre Ware 12.00
248 Steve Largent (RET) 40.00
249 Chuck Knox (CO) 12.00
250 Boomer Esiason 12.00
251 Kevin Butler 6.00
252 Bruce Smith 12.00
253 Webster Slaughter 6.00
254 Mike Sherrard 6.00
255 Steve Broussard 6.00
256 Warren Moon 35.00
257 John Elway 100.00
258 Bob Golic 6.00
259 Jim Everett 12.00
260 Bruce Coslet (CO) 6.00
261 James Francis 280.00
262 Eric Dorsey 6.00
263 Marcus Dupree 6.00
264 Hart Lee Dykes 6.00
265 Vinny Testaverde 15.00
266 Chip Lohmiller 6.00
267 John Riggins (RET) 50.00
268 Mike Schad 6.00
269 Kevin Greene 12.00
270 Dean Biasucci 6.00
271 Mike Pritchard 6.00
272 Ted Washington 6.00
273 Alfred Williams 6.00
274 Chris Zorich 6.00
275 Reggie Barrett 6.00
276 Chris Hinton 6.00
277 Tracy Johnson 6.00
278 Jim Harbaugh 12.00
279 John Roper 6.00
280 Mike Dumas 6.00
281 Herman Moore 60.00
282 Eric Turner 6.00
283 Steve Atwater 6.00
284 Michael Cofer 6.00
285 Darion Conner 6.00
286 Darryl Talley 6.00
287 Donnell Woolford 6.00
288 Keith McCants 6.00
289 Ray Handley (CO) 6.00
290 Ahmad Rashad (RET) 175.00
291 Eric Swann 12.00
292 Dalton Hilliard (Signatures usually miscut) 25.00
293 Rickey Jackson 6.00
294 Vaughan Johnson 6.00
295 Eric Martin 6.00
296 Pat Swilling 12.00
297 Anthony Carter (Signatures usually miscut) 25.00
298 Guy McIntyre 75.00
299 Bennie Blades 6.00
300 Paul Farren 6.00
PLC2 Payne Stewart (Golfer) 85.00
NNO Santa Claus Sendaway (Signed) 30.00
Santa Claus Sendaway (Signed and numbered) 60.00

1991 Pro Line Portraits Collectibles

These two cards were randomly inserted in 1991 Pro Line foil packs and feature NBC sports commentator Ahmad Rashad and pro golfer Payne Stewart. The Stewart card shows him kissing a trophy and offers a tip on the back on how to approach the game. The card, like the Rashad card, has a number on the back, along with the words "Pro Line Portraits Collectible." The Rashad card pictures him and his family on the front, including his wife, TV actress, Phylicia. The back, in a horizontal format, has a quote from Rashad about the importance of family life.

		NM/M
	Complete Set (2):	8.00
	Common Player:	4.00
1	Ahmad Rashad Rashad Family	4.00
2	Payne Stewart Golfer	4.00

1991 Pro Line Portraits Wives

Wives of some of the most popular NFL players are featured in this seven-card "Spirit" set. The cards are numbered on the back and were included in the 1991 Pro Line Portraits set.

		NM/M
	Common Wife:	.05
1	Jennifer Montana	.25
2	Babette Kosar	.05
3	Janet Elway	.05
4	Michelle Oates	.05
5	Toni Lipps	.05
6	Stacey O'Brien	.05
7	Phylicia Rashad	.20

1991 Pro Line Portraits Wives Autographs

The seven-card, standard-size set featured wives of top NFL players and was inserted in packs of 1991 NFL Pro Line. The Rashad signed card was limited to 15, thus giving it its high value. The cards are identical to the seven wives featured in the base set, except with signatures.

		NM/M
	Complete Set (7):	550.00
	Common Player:	15.00
1	Jennifer Montana	75.00
2	Babette Kosar	15.00
3	Janet Elway	15.00
4	Michelle Oates	15.00
5	Toni Lipps	15.00
6	Stacey O'Brien	15.00
7	Phylicia Rashad	450.00

1991 Pro Line Punt, Pass and Kick

Eleven NFL quarterbacks are featured in this 12-card set issued to promote nationwide Punt, Pass and Kick competitions. Each card front has a full bleed posed shot of the player, along with Pro Line Portraits and Punt, Pass and Kick logos. The card back is numbered and includes a player head shot and a quote from him about being a successful NFL quarterback. A checklist card was also produced.

		NM/M
	Complete Set (11):	50.00
	Common Player:	3.00
1	Troy Aikman	10.00
2	Bubby Brister	3.00
3	Randall Cunningham	5.00
4	John Elway	8.00
5	Boomer Esiason	5.00
6	Jim Everett	3.00
7	Jim Kelly	5.00
8	Bernie Kosar	7.00
9	Dan Marino	12.00
10	Warren Moon	5.00
11	Phil Simms	4.00
	Punt, Pass & Kick Checklist:	3.00

A card number in parenthese ( ) indicates the set is unnumbered.

1991 Pro Line Profiles Anthony Munoz

Cincinnati Bengals lineman Anthony Munoz is profiled in this set of cards, which was included inside Super Bowl XXVI programs. The cards chronicle Munoz's career and are listed below according to the topic presented on the card back. Each back is also numbered. A full-color photo appears on the card front, along with the Pro Line Profiles logo. The back has a smaller photo and provides information and quotes from Munoz about his life, community service projects, his family and his NFL career.

		NM/M
	Complete Set (9):	4.00
	Common Player:	.50
1	1991 NFL Man of Year	.50
2	Little League player	.50
3	1980 Rose Bowl	.50
4	Community Service	.50
5	Portrait	.50
6	1981 AFC Championship Game	.50
7	1992 Pro Bowl	.50
8	Super Bowl XVI and XXIII	.50
9	Physical Fitness Video	.50

1992 Pro Line Draft Day

The two-card, regular-size set features top pick Steve Emtman on one card with NFL coaches on the other. The card back features Emtman on No. 1 with a quote, an ESPN announcer Chris Berman on No. 2, also with a quote.

		NM/M
	Complete Set (2):	4.00
	Common Player:	2.00
1	Steve Emtman	2.00
2	Coaches Photo	2.00

1992 Pro Line Mobil

This 72-card set was available in nine-card packs in an eight-week promotion in Southern California. It could be obtained by purchasing eight or more gallons of Mobil Super Unleaded Plus. The first nine cards are from 1991 Portraits, while the final 63 cards are from 1992 Portraits, both of which are produced by NFL Properties. The first pack included a checklist card, a title card and a card for each of the seven players featured, with the dates that their nine-card packs would be available. Card number nine of Eric Dickerson in a Raiders' uniform is an exclusive to the set. Only one player is featured per pack, with cards numbered "X of 9."

		NM/M
	Complete Set (72):	8.00
	Common Player:	.10
1	Title Card (October 3-9)	.10
2	Checklist	.10
3	Ronnie Lott	.15
4	Junior Seau	.40
5	Jim Everett	.10
6	Howie Long	.15
7	Jerry Rice	1.00
8	Art Shell (CO)	.15
9	Eric Dickerson	.25
10	Ronnie Lott (October 10-16) (Making Hit)	.15
11	Ronnie Lott (Little Leaguer)	.15
12	Ronnie Lott (Playing for USC)	.15
13	Ronnie Lott (Exultation)	.15
14	Ronnie Lott (Portrait)	.15
15	Ronnie Lott (Behind Bar)	.15
16	Ronnie Lott(With Family)	.15
17	Ronnie Lott (Catching Ball)	.15
18	Ronnie Lott (Tuxedo)	.15
19	Junior Seau (October 17-23) (With Ball)	.25
20	Junior Seau (Young Junior)	.25
21	Junior Seau (Pointing)	.25
22	Junior Seau (Over Fallen Opponent)	.25
23	Junior Seau (Portrait)	.25
24	Junior Seau (With Wife)	.25
25	Junior Seau (Running in Surf)	.25
26	Junior Seau (Weightlifting)	.25
27	Junior Seau (Seaweed Boa)	.25
28	Jim Everett (October 24-30) (Looking for Receiver)	.10
29	Jim Everett (Young Jim)	.10
30	Jim Everett (Playing for Purdue)	.10
31	Jim Everett (With Parents, Sister)	.10
32	Jim Everett (Portrait)	.10
33	Jim Everett (Eluding Rush)	.10
34	Jim Everett (Fishing)	.10
35	Jim Everett (Handing Off)	.10
36	Jim Everett (Studio Photo)	.10
37	Howie Long (October 31-November 6) (Hand Up to Block Pass)	.15
38	Howie Long (High School Footballer)	.15
39	Howie Long (Closing in for Sack)	.15
40	Howie Long (With Family)	.15
41	Howie Long (Portrait)	.15
42	Howie Long (Fundraising for Kids)	.15
43	Howie Long (Hitting the Heavy Bag)	.15
44	Howie Long (Taking Swipe at Ball)	.15
45	Howie Long (Studio Photo)	.15
46	Jerry Rice (November 7-13) (With Trophy)	.50
47	Jerry Rice (Avoiding Block)	.50
48	Jerry Rice (Eluding Steeler)	.50
49	Jerry Rice (With Family)	.50
50	Jerry Rice (Portrait)	.50
51	Jerry Rice (With Toddler)	.50
52	Jerry Rice (Playing Tennis)	.50
53	Jerry Rice (Scoring TD)	.50
54	Jerry Rice (Studio Photo)	.50
55	Art Shell (CO) (November 14-20) (In Front of his Team)	.15
56	Art Shell (CO) (At Maryland State)	.15
57	Art Shell (CO) (Blocking Viking)	.15
58	Art Shell (CO) (Playing Basketball)	.15
59	Art Shell (CO) (Portrait)	.15
60	Art Shell (CO) (Talking to Player)	.15
61	Art Shell (CO) (In Front of TV)	.15
62	Art Shell (CO) (Blocking for Raiders)	.15
63	Art Shell (CO) (With Teddy Bear)	.15
64	Eric Dickerson (November 21-30) (Studio Suit Up)	.15
65	Eric Dickerson (Running for SMU)	.15
66	Eric Dickerson (With Mom)	.15
67	Eric Dickerson (49ers in Pursuit)	.15
68	Eric Dickerson (Portrait)	.15
69	Eric Dickerson (Running for Colts)	.15
70	Eric Dickerson (On Training Ramp)	.15
71	Eric Dickerson (Running Against Rams)	.15
72	Eric Dickerson (Posed With Football)	.15

1992 Pro Line Prototypes

The 13-card, regular-size set was distributed by Pro Line to sample its upcoming releases. Featured in the sample set are Profiles, Spirit and Portraits. The Profiles backs have "Prototype" printed while Portraits backs have "Sample."

		NM/M
	Complete Set (13):	8.00
	Common Player:	.50
12	Kathie Lee Gifford	1.00
28	Thurman Thomas (Bills' uniform, action shot)	.75
29	Thurman Thomas (With his mother)	.75
30	Thurman Thomas (OSU Cowboy uniform, action shot)	.75
31	Thurman Thomas (With family)	.75
32	Thurman Thomas (Color portrait)	.75
33	Thurman Thomas (Action shot, Super Bowl XXV)	.75
34	Thurman Thomas (Fishing)	.75
35	Thurman Thomas (Stretching on track)	.75
36	Thurman Thomas (Close-up photo)	.75
379	Jessie Tuggle	.50
386	Neil O'Donnell	.50
NNO	Advertisement Card	.50

1992 Pro Line Portraits

This 1992 Pro Line Portraits set continues numbering where the 1991 set ended, starting at #301. The front has a full-bleed color non-action photo; the back has a mug shot and player information. CO means coach; RET means retired. There were also cards autographed by the players. These command premium prices. They are identical to those in the regular set, except they are unnumbered. Cards 349, 370, 417, 428, 451 and 462 were never signed, however.

		NM/M
	Complete Set (167):	7.00
	Common Player:	.04
	Pack (12):	.40
	Wax Box (36):	12.00
301	*Steve Emtman*	.15
302	Al Edwards	.04
303	Wendell Davis	.05
304	Lewis Billups	.04
305	Brian Brennan	.04
306	John Gesek	.04
307	*Terrell Buckley*	.25
308	*Johnny Mitchell*	.60
309	LeRoy Butler	.04
310	William Fuller	.04
311	Bill Brooks	.06
312	Dino Hackett	.04
313	Willie Gault	.06
314	Aaron Cox	.04
315	Jeff Cross	.04
316	Emmitt Smith	2.00
317	Marv Cook	.06
318	Gill Fenerty	.06
319	*Jeff Carlson*	.20
320	Brad Baxter	.06
321	Fred Barnett	.10
322	Kurt Barber	.10
323	Eric Green	.06
324	Greg Clark	.10
325	Keith DeLong	.04
326	Patrick Hunter	.04
327	*Troy Vincent*	.10
328	Gary Clark	.08
329	Joe Montana	1.75
330	Michael Haynes	.25
331	*Edgar Bennett*	.50
332	Darren Lewis	.15
333	Derrick Fenner	.06
334	Rob Burnett	.04
335	Alvin Harper	.40
336	Vance Johnson	.06
337	William White	.04
338	Sterling Sharpe	.50
339	Sean Jones	.04
340	Jeff Herrod	.04
341	Chris Martin	.04
342	Ethan Horton	.04
343	Robert Delpino	.06
344	Mark Higgs	.15
345	Chris Doleman	.06
346	Tom Hodson	.06
347	Craig Heyward	.06
348	Cary Conklin	.08
349	James Hasty	.04
350	Antone Davis	.04
351	Ernie Jones	.04
352	Greg Lloyd	.04
353	John Friesz	.06
354	Charles Haley	.06
355	*Tracy Scroggins*	.20
356	Paul Gruber	.06
357	Ricky Ervins	.10
358	Brad Muster	.06
359	Deion Sanders	.20
360	*Mitch Frerotte*	.10
361	Stan Thomas	.04
362	Harold Green	.08
363	Eric Metcalf	.06
364	Ken Norton Jr.	.06
365	Dave Widell, Doug Widell	.04
366	Mike Tomczak	.06
367	Bubba McDowell	.04
368	Jessie Hester	.04
369	Ervin Randle	.04
370	Tony Smith	.04
371	Pat Terrell	.04
372	Jim C. Jensen	.04
373	Mike Merriweather	.06
374	Chris Singleton	.04
375	Floyd Turner	.04
376	Jim Sweeney	.04
377	Keith Jackson	.15
378	Walter Reeves	.04
379	Neil O'Donnell	.50
380	Nate Lewis	.12
381	Keith Henderson	.04
382	Kelly Stouffer	.04
383	Ricky Reynolds	.04
384	Joe Jacoby	.04
385	Fred Biletnikoff (RET)	.10
386	Jessie Tuggle	.04
387	Tom Waddle	.12
388	Dave Shula (CO)	.10
389	*Van Waiters*	.10
390	Jay Novacek	.12
391	Michael Young	.04
392	Mike Holmgren	.08
393	Doug Smith	.04
394	Mike Prior	.04
395	Harvey Williams	.10
396	Aaron Wallace	.04
397	Tony Zendejas	.04
398	Sammie Smith	.06
399	Henry Thomas	.04
400	Jon Vaughn	.12
401	Brian Washington	.04
402	*Leon Searcy*	.10
403	Lance Smith	.04
404	Warren Williams	.04
405	Bobby Ross (CO)	.10
406	Harry Sydney	.04
407	John L. Williams	.06
408	Ken Willis	.04
409	Brian Mitchell	.06
410	Dick Butkus (RET)	.10
411	Chuck Knox (CO)	.04
412	*Robert Porcher*	.25
413	Calvin Williams	.10
414	Bill Cowher (CO)	.10
415	Eric Moore	.04
416	*Derek Brown*	.20
417	Dennis Greene (CO)	.10
418	Tom Flores (CO)	.04
419	*Dale Carter*	.30
420	Tony Dorsett (RET)	.10
421	*Marco Coleman*	.40
422	Sam Wyche (CO)	.04
423	Ray Crockett	.04
424	Dan Fouts (RET)	.10
425	Hugh Millen	.15
426	*Quentin Coryatt*	.40
427	Brian Jordan	.06
428	Frank Gifford (RET)	.10
429	*Toby Caston*	.10
430	Ted Marchibroda (CO)	.04
431	Cris Carter	.06
432	Tim Krumrie	.04
433	Otto Graham (CO)	.10
434	*Vaughn Dunbar*	.25
435	*John Fina*	.10
436	Sonny Jurgensen (RET)	.10
437	*Robert Jones*	.15
438	Steve DeOssie	.04
439	Eddie LeBaron (RET)	.04
440	*Chester McGlockton*	.15
441	Ken Stabler (RET)	.10
442	Joe DeLamielleure (RET)	.04
443	Charley Taylor (RET)	.10
444	*Greg Skrepenak*	.10
445	Y.A. Tittle (RET)	.10
446	*Chuck Smith*	.10
447	Kellen Winslow (RET)	.10
448	*Kevin Smith*	.30
449	*Phillippi Sparks*	.12
450	*Alonzo Spellman*	.20
451	Mark Rypien	.10
452	*Darryl Williams*	.15
453	*Tommy Vardell*	.20
454	*Tommy Maddox*	.30
455	*Steve Israel*	.12
456	*Marquez Pope*	.12
457	*Eugene Chung*	.10
458	Lynn Swann (RET)	.10
459	*Sean Gilbert*	.40
460	*Chris Mims*	.30
461	Al Davis	.04
462	Richard Todd	.04
463	Mike Fox	.04
464	*David Klingler*	.40
465	*Darren Woodson*	.12
466	*Jason Hanson*	.12
467	Lem Barney (RET)	.10
1NNO	Santa Sendaway	5.00
2NNO	Mrs. Claus Sendaway	7.00

1992 Pro Line Portraits Checklists

These checklist cards were randomly included in 1992 Pro Line Portraits foil packs. The cards use letters instead of card numbers. The card fronts form a 3x3 puzzle which shows the Pro Line Collection emblem on a screened background with NFL logos. The backs include checklists for the 1991-92 Portraits series, 1992 Profiles series and collectible series.

		NM/M
	Complete Set (9):	1.00
	Common Checklists:	.15
A	Introduction Card	.15
B	Checklist 1-75	.15
C	Checklist 76-150	.15
D	Checklist 151-225	.15
E	Checklist 226-300	.15
F	Checklist 301-375	.15
G	Checklist 376-450	.15
H	Checklist 451-467 and inserts	.15
I	Checklist Profiles	.15

1992 Pro Line Portraits Autographs

This 1992 Pro Line Portraits set was autographed by the players. These command premium prices. They are identical to those in the regular set, except they are unnumbered. Cards 349, 370, 417, 428, 451 and 462 were never signed, however.

		NM/M
	Complete Set (161):	1,200
	Common Player:	4.00
	Minor Stars:	8.00
301	Steve Emtman	4.00
302	Al Edwards	4.00
303	Wendell Davis	4.00
304	Lewis Billups	8.00
305	Brian Brennan	4.00
306	John Gesek	4.00
307	Terrell Buckley	8.00
308	Johnny Mitchell	4.00
309	LeRoy Butler	4.00
310	William Fuller	4.00
311	Bill Brooks	4.00
312	Dino Hackett	4.00
313	Willie Gault	8.00
314	Aaron Cox	4.00
315	Jeff Cross	4.00
316	Emmitt Smith	85.00
317	Marv Cook	4.00
318	Gill Fenerty	4.00
319	Jeff Carlson	4.00
320	Brad Baxter	4.00
321	Fred Barnett	8.00
322	Kurt Barber	4.00
323	Eric Green	4.00
324	Greg Clark	4.00
325	Keith DeLong	4.00
326	Patrick Hunter	4.00
327	Troy Vincent	8.00
328	Gary Clark	8.00
329	Joe Montana	120.00
330	Michael Haynes	8.00
331	Edgar Bennett	8.00
332	Darren Lewis	4.00
333	Derrick Fenner	4.00
334	Rob Burnett	4.00
335	Alvin Harper	8.00
336	Vance Johnson	4.00
337	William White	4.00
338	Sterling Sharpe	20.00
339	Sean Jones	4.00
340	Jeff Herrod	4.00
341	Chris Martin	4.00
342	Ethan Horton	4.00
343	Robert Delpino	4.00
344	Mark Higgs	4.00
345	Chris Doleman	4.00
346	Tom Hodson	4.00
347	Craig Heyward	4.00
348	Cary Conklin	4.00
349	James Hasty	4.00
350	Antone Davis	4.00
351	Ernie Jones	4.00
352	Greg Lloyd	8.00
353	John Friesz	8.00
354	Charles Haley	8.00
355	Tracy Scroggins	4.00
356	Paul Gruber	4.00
357	Ricky Ervins	4.00
358	Brad Muster	4.00
359	Deion Sanders (Deion also signed and numbered 200 cards from his personal stock; these are worth double)	40.00
360	Mitch Frerotte	4.00
361	Stan Thomas	4.00
362	Harold Green	4.00
363	Eric Metcalf	8.00
364	Ken Norton Jr.	8.00
365	Dave Widell, Doug Widell	8.00
366	Mike Tomczak	8.00
367	Bubba McDowell	4.00
368	Jessie Hester (Signed in ballpoint pen)	4.00
369	Ervin Randle	4.00
370	Tony Smith	4.00
371	Pat Terrell	4.00
372	Jim C. Jensen	4.00
373	Mike Merriweather	4.00
374	Chris Singleton	4.00
375	Floyd Turner	4.00
376	Jim Sweeney	4.00
377	Keith Jackson	8.00
378	Walter Reeves	4.00
379	Neil O'Donnell	8.00
380	Nate Lewis	4.00
381	Keith Henderson	4.00
382	Kelly Stouffer	4.00
383	Ricky Reynolds	4.00
384	Joe Jacoby	4.00
385	Fred Biletnikoff (RET)	180.00
386	Jessie Tuggle	4.00
387	Tom Waddle	4.00
388	Dave Shula (CO)	4.00
389	Van Waiters	4.00
390	Jay Novacek	8.00
391	Michael Young	4.00
392	Mike Holmgren (CO)	25.00
393	Doug Smith	4.00
394	Mike Prior	4.00
395	Harvey Williams	8.00
396	Aaron Wallace	4.00
397	Tony Zendejas	4.00
398	Sammie Smith	4.00
399	Henry Thomas	4.00
400	Jon Vaughn	4.00
401	Brian Washington	4.00
402	Leon Searcy	4.00
403	Lance Smith	4.00
404	Warren Williams	4.00
405	Bobby Ross (CO)	4.00
406	Harry Sydney	4.00
407	John L. Williams	4.00
408	Ken Willis	4.00
409	Brian Mitchell	4.00
410	Dick Butkus (RET)	25.00
411	Chuck Knox (CO)	4.00
412	Robert Porcher	4.00
413	Calvin Williams	4.00
414	Bill Cowher (CO)	15.00
415	Eric Moore	4.00
416	Derek Brown (TE)	4.00

417 Dennis Greene (CO) 8.00
418 Tom Flores (CO) 4.00
419 Dale Carter 4.00
420 Tony Dorsett (RET) 25.00
421 Marco Coleman 4.00
422 Sam Wyche (CO) 4.00
423 Ray Crockett 4.00
424 Dan Fouts (RET) 15.00
425 Hugh Millen 4.00
426 Quentin Coryatt 8.00
427 Brian Jordan 8.00
428 Frank Gifford (RET) 12.00
429 Toby Caston 4.00
430 Ted Marchibroda (CO) 4.00
431 Cris Carter 35.00
432 Tim Krumrie 4.00
433 Otto Graham (CO) 25.00
434 Vaughn Dunbar 4.00
435 John Fina 4.00
436 Sonny Jurgensen (RET) 20.00
437 Robert Jones 4.00
438 Steve DeOssie 4.00
439 Eddie LeBaron (RET) 8.00
440 Chester McGlockton 8.00
441 Ken Stabler (RET) 25.00
442 Joe DeLamielleure (RET) 4.00
443 Charley Taylor (RET) 8.00
444 Greg Skrepenak 4.00
445 Y.A. Tittle (RET) 25.00
446 Chuck Smith 4.00
447 Kellen Winslow (RET) 8.00
448 Kevin Smith 4.00
449 Phillippi Sparks 4.00
450 Alonzo Spellman 4.00
451 Mark Rypien 4.00
452 Darryl Williams 4.00
453 Tommy Vardell 4.00
454 Tommy Maddox 4.00
455 Steve Israel 4.00
456 Marquez Pope 4.00
457 Eugene Chung 4.00
458 Lynn Swann (RET) 75.00
459 Sean Gilbert 8.00
460 Chris Mims 4.00
461 Al Davis (OWN) 325.00
462 Richard Todd 4.00
463 Mike Fox 4.00
464 David Klingler 4.00
465 Darren Woodson 8.00
466 Jason Hanson 4.00
467 Lem Barney (RET) 8.00
NNO Santa Claus 8.00
NNO Mrs. Santa Claus 8.00

1992 Pro Line Portraits Collectibles

These cards continue numbering where two prior special insert cards left off the preceding year. Each card front has a full-color photo and the set logo; the back has the card number with a "PLC" suffix and a quote on a silver background. Cards were random inserts in 1992 Pro Line foil packs.

NM/M
Complete Set (6): 12.00
Common Player: 2.00
3 Chris Berman Coaches Photo 2.00
4 Joe Gibbs CO (Racing) 2.00
5 Gifford Family (Frank, Kathie Lee, Cody) 2.00
6 Dale Jarrett (NASCAR driver) 4.00
7 Paul Tagliabue COM (Autographed) 2.00
8 Don Shula, Dave Shula (CO) 3.00

1992 Pro Line Portraits Collectibles Autographs

Randomly seeded in 1992 Pro Line foil packs, the cards are anchored by a borderless photo on the front, with the Pro Line logo at the bottom. The card backs, which are unnumbered, have a quote from the featured person in a silver-colored area. His autograph is signed over his photo on the bottom of the card back.

NM/M
Complete Set (4): 160.00
Common Player: 5.00
3 Chris Berman Coaches Photo 25.00
6 Dale Jarrett (NASCAR driver) 40.00
7 Paul Tagliabue (COM) (Autopenned) 5.00
8 Don Shula CO, Dave Shula CO 100.00

1992 Pro Line Portraits QB Gold

These 18 insert cards, randomly included in 1992 Pro Line foil packs, feature some of the top quarterbacks in the NFL. Each card front has a color action photo on it, with gold foil stripes on the left and right borders. The player's name and "Quarterback Gold" are printed in black in the foil stripes. The backs also have gold stripes for borders; they are at the top and bottom. Statistics are given against a white background. The cards are also numbered on the back. Pro Line stated it put an average of three of these insert cards in each box it made. The company also sent a complete set to dealers who ordered a hobby case of the cards.

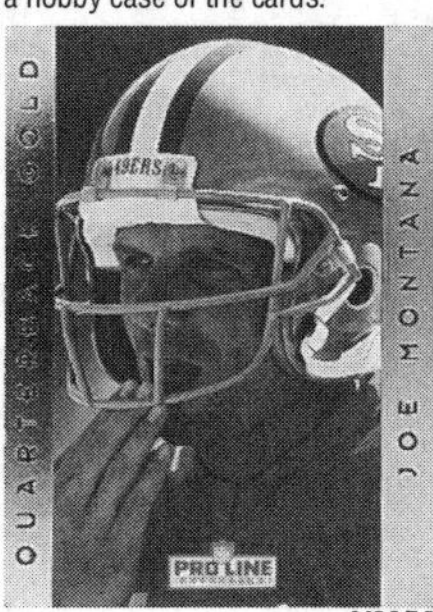

NM/M
Complete Set (18): 10.00
Common Player: .25
Minor Stars: .50
1 Troy Aikman 1.50
2 Bubby Brister .25
3 Randall Cunningham .25
4 John Elway 1.00
5 Boomer Esiason .25
6 Jim Everett .25
7 Jeff George .50
8 Jim Harbaugh .25
9 Jeff Hostetler .25
10 Jim Kelly .50
11 Bernie Kosar .25
12 Dan Marino 3.00
13 Chris Miller (Birthdate incorrectly listed as 8-91-65) .25
14 Joe Montana 1.50
15 Warren Moon .50
16 Mark Rypien .25
17 Phil Simms .25
18 Steve Young 1.50

1992 Pro Line Portraits Rookie Gold

These insert cards, randomly included one per every 1992 Pro Line jumbo pack, feature some of the top rookies in the NFL. Each card front shows a color action photo, with gold foil stripes creating borders on the right and left sides. The player's name and "Rookie Gold" are printed in black in the stripes. The backs have white backgrounds with collegiate statistics in black, plus a card number. Gold foil stripes appear at the top and bottom of the card, too. A complete set of the cards was sent to every dealer for each hobby case they ordered.

NM/M
Complete Set (28): 12.00
Common Player: .30
1 Tony Smith .50
2 John Fina .30
3 Alonzo Spellman .50
4 David Klinger 1.75
5 Tommy Vardell .60
6 Kevin Smith .60
7 Tommy Maddox 1.25
8 Robert Porcher .50
9 Terrell Buckley .60
10 Eddie Robinson .30
11 Steve Emtman .30
12 Quentin Coryatt .75
13 Dale Carter .50
14 Chester McGlockton .30
15 Sean Gilbert .75
16 Troy Vincent .50
17 Robert Harris .30
18 Eugene Chung .30
19 Vaughn Dunbar .60
20 Derek Brown .30
21 Johnny Mitchell 1.50
22 Siran Stacy .50
23 Tony Sacca .50
24 Leon Searcy .30
25 Chris Mims .60
26 Dana Hall .50
27 Courtney Hawkins .75
28 Shane Collins .30

1992 Pro Line Portraits Team NFL

Celebrities and entertainers from outside the sporting world are featured on these five insert cards. Each card front shows the entertainer/celebrity wearing his favorite team's apparel. The backs, done in a horizontal format, have a silver panel which contains a quote from the person. The back is numbered with a "TNC" prefix and has team color-coded stripes at the top.

NM/M
Complete Set (5): 10.00
Common Player: 1.50
1 Muhammad Ali 5.00
2 Milton Berle 2.50
3 Don Mattingly 3.00
4 Martin Mull 1.50
5 Isiah Thomas 2.50

1992 Pro Line Portraits Team NFL Autographs

This five-card set features stars from other sports and celebrities, with each personality pictured on the card front in their favorite team's attire. This unnumbered set marks the debut of Pro Line's Team Collectible cards, and includes a very limited number of signed Muhammad Ali cards, with his birth name Cassius Clay.

NM/M
Complete Set (5): 200.00
Common Player: 20.00
1A Muhammad Ali 150.00
1B Muhammad Ali 475.00
2 Milton Berle 30.00
3 Don Mattingly 50.00
4 Martin Mull 20.00
5 Isiah Thomas 25.00

1992 Pro Line Portraits Wives

These insert cards, included in 1992 Pro Line Portraits packs, continue with numbers from where a similar set ended in 1991. The cards feature full-bleed photos of wives whose husbands are star coaches or players in the NFL. The card back has a profile shot of the wife, plus a quote from her. A card number is also included on the back. Each of the wives, except Kathie Lee Gifford, autographed her cards, too. They are identical to the regular cards, except they are unnumbered with a "SC" prefix and command premium prices.

NM/M
Complete Set (16): 1.00
Common Wives: .10
8 Ortancis Carter .10
9 Faith Cherry .10
10 Kaye Cowher .10
11 Dainnese Gault .10
12 Kathie Lee Gifford .20
13 Carole Hinton .10
14 Diane Long .10
15 Karen Lott .10
16 Felicia Moon .10
17 Cindy Noble .10
18 Line Seifert .10
19 Mitzi Testaverde .10
20 Robin Swilling .10
21 Lesley Visser (ANN) .20
22 Toni Doleman .10
23 Diana Ditka (with Mike Ditka) .20

1992 Pro Line Portraits Wives Autographs

These insert cards, included in 1992 Pro Line Portraits packs, continue with numbers from where a similar set ended in 1991. Each of the wives, except Kathie Lee Lee Gifford, autographed her cards. They are identical to the regular cards, except they are unnumbered and command premium prices.

NM/M
Complete Set (16): 90.00
Common Wives: 6.00
8 Ortancis Carter 6.00
9 Faith Cherry 6.00
10 Kaye Cowher 6.00
11 Dainnese Gault 6.00
12 Kathie Lee Gifford 6.00
13 Carole Hinton 6.00
14 Diane Long 6.00
15 Karen Lott 6.00
16 Felicia Moon 6.00
17 Cindy Noble 6.00
18 Line Seifert 6.00
19 Mitzi Testaverde 6.00
20 Robin Swilling 6.00
21 Lesley Visser (ANN) 20.00
22 Toni Doleman 6.00
23 Diana Ditka (with Mike Ditka) 6.00

1992 Pro Line Profiles

This set features nine-card sets for 55 pro football players. Each card set traces the player's progress from his collegiate days to his professional career and life off the field. The card front has a full-bleed color action shot; the back has an action shot and a quote from the player. A 10-card Art Monk set was also offered by a mail-in exchange.

NM/M
Complete Set (504): 12.00
Common Player: .04
Pack (12): .35
Wax Box (36): 10.00
NNO Art Monk (Collection Bonus Set title card) 1.00
1 Ronnie Lott (Tackling opponent (1-9)) .06
2 Ronnie Lott (As youth, in baseball uniform) .06
3 Ronnie Lott (Playing for USC) .06
4 Ronnie Lott (Arms raised in triumph) .06
5 Ronnie Lott (Portrait by Chris Hopkins) .06
6 Ronnie Lott (At the Sports City Cafe) .06
7 Ronnie Lott (With family) .06
8 Ronnie Lott (Catching) .06
9 Ronnie Lott (In tuxedo) .06
10 Rodney Peete (Right arm raised (10-18)) .10
11 Rodney Peete (As youth, in football uniform) .10
12 Rodney Peete (Playing baseball) .10
13 Rodney Peete (In sweats with ball) .10
14 Rodney Peete (Portrait by Merv Corning) .10
15 Rodney Peete (Looking for receiver) .10
16 Rodney Peete (Playing pool) .10
17 Rodney Peete (Passing) .10
18 Rodney Peete (Injured) .10
19 Carl Banks (In action on field (19-27)) .04
20 Carl Banks (Playing basketball at Beecher High School) .04
21 Carl Banks (In Michigan State uniform) .04
22 Carl Banks (With family) .04
23 Carl Banks (Portrait by Merv Corning) .04
24 Carl Banks (Talking, wearing suit) .04
25 Carl Banks (Tackling opponent) .04
26 Carl Banks (On the air) .04
27 Carl Banks (Close-up) .04
28 Thurman Thomas (Running with ball, blue jersey (28-36)) .40
29 Thurman Thomas (With mother, Terlisha Cockrell) .25
30 Thurman Thomas (At Oklahoma State) .25
31 Thurman Thomas (With family) .25
32 Thurman Thomas (Portrait by Gary Kelley) .25
33 Thurman Thomas (Running with ball, white jersey) .25
34 Thurman Thomas (Fishing) .25
35 Thurman Thomas (Stretching) .25
36 Thurman Thomas (Close-up) .25
37 Roger Staubach (With Heisman Trophy (37-45)) .15
38 Roger Staubach (At Naval Academy) .15
39 Roger Staubach (In Navy dress whites) .15
40 Roger Staubach (Front view, running with ball) .15
41 Roger Staubach (Portrait by John Collier) .15
42 Roger Staubach (Passing, side view) .15
43 Roger Staubach (With family) .15
44 Roger Staubach (With young person at Daytop, substance abuse recovery facility) .15
45 Roger Staubach (Calling the play) .15
46 Jerry Rice (With MVP trophy (46-54)) .50
47 Jerry Rice (At Mississippi Valley State) .50
48 Jerry Rice (Running with ball) .50
49 Jerry Rice (With family) .50
50 Jerry Rice (Portrait by Gary Kelley) .50
51 Jerry Rice (With March of Dimes Ambassador, Ashley Johnson) .50
52 Jerry Rice (Playing tennis) .50
53 Jerry Rice (Arms raised in triumph) .50
54 Jerry Rice (Close-up) .50
55 Vinny Testaverde (Posed with Heisman (55-63)) .04
56 Vinny Testaverde (At Fork Union Military Academy) .04
57 Vinny Testaverde (Playing for the University of Miami) .04
58 Vinny Testaverde (Passing) .04
59 Vinny Testaverde (Portrait by Merv Corning) .04
60 Vinny Testaverde (Running with ball) .04
61 Vinny Testaverde (With family) .04
62 Vinny Testaverde (View from hips up, fist raised in triumph) .04
63 Vinny Testaverde (With Vince Hanley) .04
64 Anthony Carter (Manuevering around opponent, with ball 64-72)) .06
65 Anthony Carter (In high school football game, black-and-white) .06
66 Anthony Carter (At Michigan, running with ball) .06
67 Anthony Carter (Fishing) .06
68 Anthony Carter (Portrait by John Collier) .06
69 Anthony Carter (Running, looking over shoulder) .06
70 Anthony Carter (With family) .06
71 Anthony Carter (Catching pass) .06
72 Anthony Carter (Close-up) .06
73 Sterling Sharpe (Catching (73-81)) .35
74 Sterling Sharpe (Passing, in high school) .35
75 Sterling Sharpe (Walking on field at South Carolina) .35
76 Sterling Sharpe (With books on SC campus) .35
77 Sterling Sharpe (Portrait by Chris Hopkins) .35
78 Sterling Sharpe (Running with ball against Rams) .35
79 Sterling Sharpe (At the piano) .35
80 Sterling Sharpe (Running with ball against Lions) .35
81 Sterling Sharpe (In brick arch with football) .35
82 Anthony Munoz (With NFL Man of the Year award (82-90)) .04
83 Anthony Munoz (As youth, batting) .04
84 Anthony Munoz (Playing for USC) .04
85 Anthony Munoz (With child at Children's Hospital) .04
86 Anthony Munoz (Portrait by Merv Corning) .04
87 Anthony Munoz (Blocking opponent) .04
88 Anthony Munoz (Holding baby, with fellow players and children) .04
89 Anthony Munoz (In action for Bengals) .04
90 Anthony Munoz (Close-up) .04
91 Bubby Brister (Passing, white jersey (91-99)) .04
92 Bubby Brister (NLU uniform) .04
93 Bubby Brister (Baseball unform) .04
94 Bubby Brister (With kids at Ronald McDonald House) .04
95 Bubby Brister (Portrait by Greg Spalenka) .04
96 Bubby Brister (Wearing western attire) .04
97 Bubby Brister (Running with ball, white jersey) .04
98 Bubby Brister (Passing, black jersey) .04
99 Bubby Brister (Close-up) .04
100 Bernie Kosar (Passing, white jersey (100-108)) .10
101 Bernie Kosar (In high school) .10
102 Bernie Kosar (Playing for Miami) .10
103 Bernie Kosar (Being tackled) .10
104 Bernie Kosar (Portrait by Greg Spalenka) .10
105 Bernie Kosar (With family) .10
106 Bernie Kosar (Playing golf) .10
107 Bernie Kosar (Looking for receiver) .10
108 Bernie Kosar (Close-up) .10
109 Art Shell (On sidelines (109-117)) .06
110 Art Shell (At Maryland State) .06
111 Art Shell (Playing for Raiders) .06
112 Art Shell (Playing basketball with sons) .06
113 Art Shell (Portrait by Chris Hopkins) .06
114 Art Shell (Talking to player on sidelines) .06
115 Art Shell (In front of big screen TV) .06
116 Art Shell (In line of scrimmage) .06
117 Art Shell (With teddy bear) .06
118 Don Shula (With players) .06
119 Don Shula (At John Carroll University) .06
120 Don Shula (Coaching Baltimore Colts) .06
121 Don Shula (With son, Mike) .06
122 Don Shula (Portrait by Merv Corning) .06
123 Don Shula (With daughters) .06
124 Don Shula (With Dan Marino) .06
125 Don Shula (With doctor at the Don Shula Foundation) .06
126 Don Shula (With Super Bowl trophies) .06
127 Joe Gibbs (Writing out play) .06
128 Joe Gibbs (Playing for San Diego State) .06
129 Joe Gibbs (Coaching on sidelines) .06
130 Joe Gibbs (With sons) .06
131 Joe Gibbs (Portrait by John Collier) .06
132 Joe Gibbs (Reading in office) .06
133 Joe Gibbs (With Youth For Tomorrow group) .06
134 Joe Gibbs (In front of race car) .06
135 Joe Gibbs (In front of Church) .06
136 Junior Seau (Holding ball (136-144)) .15
137 Junior Seau (As youth, in football uniform) .15
138 Junior Seau (At USC) .15
139 Junior Seau (Finger pointing up) .15
140 Junior Seau (Portrait by Merv Corning) .15
141 Junior Seau (With wife, Gina) .15
142 Junior Seau (Running on beach) .15
143 Junior Seau (Lifting weights) .15
144 Junior Seau (In swim trunks with seaweed) .15
145 Al Toon (Running with ball, white jersey 145-153)) .06
146 Al Toon (During Pee-Wee football days) .06
147 Al Toon (On the field at Wisconsin) .06
148 Al Toon (With family) .06
149 Al Toon (Portrait by Gary Kelley) .06
150 Al Toon (Catching) .06
151 Al Toon (Working out) .06
152 Al Toon (Running with ball, green jersey) .06
153 Al Toon (Close-up) .06
154 Jack Kemp (In office (154-162)) .10
155 Jack Kemp (Portrait from Occidental College) .10
156 Jack Kemp (Playing for Chargers) .10
157 Jack Kemp (With family) .10
158 Jack Kemp (Portrait by Merv Corning) .10
159 Jack Kemp (Playing for Buffalo) .10
160 Jack Kemp (Passing) .10
161 Jack Kemp (With son, Jeff) .10
162 Jack Kemp (In Washington) .10
163 Jim Harbaugh (Passing, blue jersey (163-171)) .10

164 Jim Harbaugh (Playing in high school) .10
165 Jim Harbaugh (Playing for Michigan) .10
166 Jim Harbaugh (Passing, white jersey) .10
167 Jim Harbaugh (Portrait by Gary Kelley) .10
168 Jim Harbaugh (With children in children's home) .10
169 Jim Harbaugh (Working out) .10
170 Jim Harbaugh (Calling play) .10
171 Jim Harbaugh (Close-up) .10
172 Dan McGwire (From waist up (172-180)) .15
173 Dan McGwire (At Purdue) .15
174 Dan McGwire (At San Diego) .15
175 Dan McGwire (From waist down) .15
176 Dan McGwire (Portrait by Chris Hopkins) .15
177 Dan McGwire (Passing, blue jersey) .15
178 Dan McGwire (Passing, white jersey) .15
179 Dan McGwire (Working out) .15
180 Dan McGwire (With wife, Dana) .15
181 Troy Aikman (Passing, wearing blue jersey (181-189)) .75
182 Troy Aikman (As youth) .75
183 Troy Aikman (Passing, at UCLA) .75
184 Troy Aikman (Preparing to pass, with Cowboys) .75
185 Troy Aikman (Portrait by Greg Spalenka) .75
186 Troy Aikman (Golfing) .75
187 Troy Aikman (Looking for opening, front view) .75
188 Troy Aikman (In sweats, passing) .75
189 Troy Aikman (In cowboy hat) .75
190 Keith Byars (With little brother (190-198)) .06
191 Keith Byars (Childhood picture) .06
192 Keith Byars (High School football photo) .06
193 Keith Byars (Ohio State photo, red jersey) .06
194 Keith Byars (Portrait by Chris Hopkins) .06
195 Keith Byars (Working out) .06
196 Keith Byars (Running, green jersey) .06
197 Keith Byars (Running, white jersey) .06
198 Keith Byars (Close-up) .06
199 Timm Rosenbach (Running with ball, red jersey 199-207)) .04
200 Timm Rosenbach (In high school football uniform) .04
201 Timm Rosenbach (At Washington State) .04
202 Timm Rosenbach (With wife, Kerry) .04
203 Timm Rosenbach (Portrait by John Collier) .04
204 Timm Rosenbach (Passing, white jersey) .04
205 Timm Rosenbach (Roping a calf) .04
206 Timm Rosenbach (Working out) .04
207 Timm Rosenbach (Seated on hay, in western attire) .04
208 Gary Clark (In the end zone (208-216)) .12
209 Gary Clark (Playing for James Madison University) .12
210 Gary Clark (Catching ball in end zone) .12
211 Gary Clark (With daughter) .12
212 Gary Clark (Portrait by John Collier) .12
213 Gary Clark (Running, slouched position) .12
214 Gary Clark (Playing basketball) .12
215 Gary Clark (Lifted by teammates) .12
216 Gary Clark (Close-up) .12
217 Chris Doleman (Playing for Vikings, white jersey 217-225)) .04
218 Chris Doleman (In Pittsburgh uniform) .04
219 Chris Doleman (With wife, Toni, and dog) .04
220 Chris Doleman (Playing for Vikings, blue jersey) .04
221 Chris Doleman (Portrait by John Collier) .04
222 Chris Doleman (Working out) .04
223 Chris Doleman (Leaping over opponent) .04
224 Chris Doleman (Playing golf) .04
225 Chris Doleman (Close-up) .04
226 John Elway (Passing, orange jersey (226-234)) .25
227 John Elway (Playing for Stanford) .25
228 John Elway (Passing, white jersey) .25
229 John Elway (With family) .25
230 John Elway (Portrait by Greg Spalenka) .25
231 John Elway (Working out) .25
232 John Elway (Sitting on car) .25
233 John Elway (Running with ball) .25
234 John Elway (Close-up) .25
235 Boomer Esiason (Calling play (235-243)) .15
236 Boomer Esiason (In high school) .15
237 Boomer Esiason (In Terps uniform) .15
238 Boomer Esiason (Passing) .15
239 Boomer Esiason (Portrait by Greg Spalenka) .15
240 Boomer Esiason (With dogs) .15
241 Boomer Esiason (With Kinny McQuade) .15
242 Boomer Esiason (Looking for pass receiver) .15
243 Boomer Esiason (Close-up) .15
244 Jim Everett (Passing, white jersey (244-252)) .10
245 Jim Everett (In high school uniform) .10
246 Jim Everett (Playing for Purdue) .10
247 Jim Everett (With family) .10
248 Jim Everett (Portrait by Greg Spalenka) .10
249 Jim Everett (Running with ball, blue jersey) .10
250 Jim Everett (Fishing) .10
251 Jim Everett (Handing off ball) .10
252 Jim Everett (Close-up) .10
253 Eric Green (Running with ball (253-261)) .04
254 Eric Green (With coach Sam Rutigliano) .04
255 Eric Green (Being blocked by opponent) .04
256 Eric Green (Playing basketball) .04
257 Eric Green (Portrait by Merv Corning) .04
258 Eric Green (In locker room) .04
259 Eric Green (Blocking opponent) .04
260 Eric Green (Catching) .04
261 Eric Green (Close-up) .04
262 Jerry Glanville (On motorcycle (262-270)) .04
263 Jerry Glanville (With Lions coaching staff) .04
264 Jerry Glanville (Coaching, clapping) .04
265 Jerry Glanville (With family) .04
266 Jerry Glanville (Portrait by Gary Kelley) .04
267 Jerry Glanville (Coaching, with players) .04
268 Jerry Glanville (In race car) .04
269 Jerry Glanville (With country music stars) .04
270 Jerry Glanville (In black western attire) .04
271 Jeff Hostetler (Passing, blue jersey (271-279)) .12
272 Jeff Hostetler (Playing for West Virginia) .12
273 Jeff Hostetler (Lifting weights) .12
274 Jeff Hostetler (With family) .12
275 Jeff Hostetler (Portrait by John Collier) .12
276 Jeff Hostetler (Passing, white jersey) .12
277 Jeff Hostetler (At Ronald McDonald house) .12
278 Jeff Hostetler (With father-in-law) .12
279 Jeff Hostetler (Close-up) .12
280 Haywood Jeffires (Catching, Houston uniform (280-288)) .15
281 Haywood Jeffires (Playing for North Carolina) .15
282 Haywood Jeffires (With wife, Robin) .15
283 Haywood Jeffires (Pushing past opponent) .15
284 Haywood Jeffires (Portrait by John Collier) .15
285 Haywood Jeffires (With car) .15
286 Haywood Jeffires (With Boy and Girls Club members) .15
287 Haywood Jeffires (Being tackled) .15
288 Haywood Jeffires (Close-up) .15
289 Michael Irvin (Running with ball (289-297)) .40
290 Michael Irvin (Playing basketball) .40
291 Michael Irvin (In Miami uniform) .40
292 Michael Irvin (With wife, Sandy) .40
293 Michael Irvin (Portrait by Gary Kelley) .40
294 Michael Irvin (Catching) .40
295 Michael Irvin (With student, Nyna Sherte) .40
296 Michael Irvin (Playing in Pro Bowl) .40
297 Michael Irvin (Close-up) .40
298 Steve Largent (Catching, blue jersey (298-306)) .10
299 Steve Largent (Playing for Tulsa) .10
300 Steve Largent (With family) .10
301 Steve Largent (At school for disabled children) .10
302 Steve Largent (Portrait by Chris Hopkins) .10
303 Steve Largent (Catching, white jersey) .10
304 Steve Largent (In dress attire) .10
305 Steve Largent (Running, white jersey) .10
306 Steve Largent (Close-up) .10
307 Ken O'Brien (Passing, side view (307-315)) .04
308 Ken O'Brien (With University of California-Davis) .04
309 Ken O'Brien (With family) .04
310 Ken O'Brien (Passing, front view) .04
311 Ken O'Brien (Portrait by Chris Hopkins) .04
312 Ken O'Brien (Shaking hands with Tony Eason) .04
313 Ken O'Brien (Playing golf) .04
314 Ken O'Brien (Handing off the ball) .04
315 Ken O'Brien (Close-up) .04
316 Christian Okoye (Running with ball, red jersey 316-324)) .06
317 Christian Okoye (Close-up at Asuza Pacific Univ.) .06
318 Christian Okoye (Cooking) .06
319 Christian Okoye (Running with ball, white jersey) .06
320 Christian Okoye (Portrait by Chris Hopkins) .06
321 Christian Okoye (In Nigerian attire) .06
322 Christian Okoye (With daughter, Christiana) .06
323 Christian Okoye (Withstanding an opponent) .06
324 Christian Okoye (In casual attire) .06
325 Michael Dean Perry (Blocking opponent, white jersey 325-333)) .12
326 Michael Dean Perry (Playing for Clemson) .12
327 Michael Dean Perry (Blocking opponent, brown jersey) .12
328 Michael Dean Perry (With family) .12
329 Michael Dean Perry (Portrait by Merv Corning) .12
330 Michael Dean Perry (At Children's Hospital) .12
331 Michael Dean Perry (Playing basketball) .12
332 Michael Dean Perry (Blocking opponent, horizontal shot) .12
333 Michael Dean Perry (With AFC Player of the Year trophy) .12
334 Chris Miller (Passing, black jersey (334-342)) .10
335 Chris Miller (As youth, fishing) .10
336 Chris Miller (Playing for Oregon) .10
337 Chris Miller (In baseball uniform) .10
338 Chris Miller (Portrait by Greg Spalenka) .10
339 Chris Miller (Running with ball) .10
340 Chris Miller (With wife, Jennifer) .10
341 Chris Miller (In the Pro Bowl) .10
342 Chris Miller (Close-up) .10
343 Phil Simms (Passing, blue jersey (343-351)) .10
344 Phil Simms (Calling the play) .10
345 Phil Simms (With family) .10
346 Phil Simms (Playing pool) .10
347 Phil Simms (Portrait by Greg Spalenka) .10
348 Phil Simms (Running with ball) .10
349 Phil Simms (With young man from the Eastern Christian School for handicapped children) .10
350 Phil Simms (Passing, white jersey) .10
351 Phil Simms (Close-up) .10
352 Bruce Smith (Tackling opponent, white jersey 352-360)) .06
353 Bruce Smith (At Virginia Tech) .06
354 Bruce Smith (Close-up in game) .06
355 Bruce Smith (With wife, Carmen) .06
356 Bruce Smith (Portrait by John Collier) .06
357 Bruce Smith (In Pro Bowl) .06
358 Bruce Smith (Working out) .06
359 Bruce Smith (Blocking, blue jersey) .06
360 Bruce Smith (Close-up) .06
361 Derrick Thomas (Running, red jersey (361-369)) .15
362 Derrick Thomas (At the University of Alabama) .15
363 Derrick Thomas (With his father's Air Force momentos) .15
364 Derrick Thomas (Seated on helmet) .15
365 Derrick Thomas (Portrait by Merv Corning) .15
366 Derrick Thomas (With motivational program participants) .15
367 Derrick Thomas (Posed with Limo) .15
368 Derrick Thomas (In Pro Bowl) .15
369 Derrick Thomas (Close-up) .15
370 Pat Swilling (Relaxed against tree (370-378)) .06
371 Pat Swilling (At Georgia Tech) .06
372 Pat Swilling (With family) .06
373 Pat Swilling (Running on field) .06
374 Pat Swilling (Portrait by John Collier) .06
375 Pat Swilling (Working out) .06
376 Pat Swilling (Tackling opponent on icy field) .06
377 Pat Swilling (With underprivileged children) .06
378 Pat Swilling (Relaxed at home) .06
379 Eric Dickerson (Close-up in Rams football gear 379-387)) .10
380 Eric Dickerson (Playing for SMU) .10
381 Eric Dickerson (With great aunt Viola) .10
382 Eric Dickerson (Running with ball, Rams uniform) .10
383 Eric Dickerson (Portrait by Merv Corning) .10
384 Eric Dickerson (Running with ball, Colts uniform) .10
385 Eric Dickerson (Working out) .10
386 Eric Dickerson (Leaping over other players, Colts uniform) .10
387 Eric Dickerson (Close-up) .10
388 Howie Long (Being blocked by opponent (388-396)) .06
389 Howie Long (At Villanova) .06
390 Howie Long (Rushing quarterback) .06
391 Howie Long (With family) .06
392 Howie Long (Portrait by Chris Hopkins) .06
393 Howie Long (On sidelines) .06
394 Howie Long (Boxing) .06
395 Howie Long (Blocking pass) .06
396 Howie Long (Close-up) .06
397 Mike Singletary (Crouched, ready for play) .06
398 Mike Singletary (At Baylor) .06
399 Mike Singletary (With children) .06
400 Mike Singletary (In the gym) .06
401 Mike Singletary (Portrait by Gary Kelley) .06
402 Mike Singletary (Rushing, white jersey) .06
403 Mike Singletary (With Man of the Year Award) .06
404 Mike Singletary (Tackling, blue jersey) .06
405 Mike Singletary (In sweatshirt) .06
406 John Taylor (Celebrating on the field (406-414)) .10
407 John Taylor (In high school) .10
408 John Taylor (Playing for Delaware State) .10
409 John Taylor (Posed with bowling ball and pins) .10
410 John Taylor (Portrait by John Collier) .10
411 John Taylor (With family) .10
412 John Taylor (With kids from Northern Light School) .10
413 John Taylor (Catching) .10
414 John Taylor (Close-up) .10
415 Andre Tippett (Blocking opponent, arms outspread) .04
416 Andre Tippett (At Iowa State (416-423)) .04
417 Andre Tippett (With daughter, Janea Lynn) .04
418 Andre Tippett (In Okinawa with karate masters) .04
419 Andre Tippett (Portrait by Gary Kelley) .04
420 Andre Tippett (Running on the field) .04
421 Andre Tippett (Performing karate move) .04
422 Andre Tippett (In action, from knees up) .04
423 Andre Tippett (Close-up) .04
424 Jim Kelly (Passing, white jersey (424-432)) .25
425 Jim Kelly (With Punt, Pass, and Kick trophy) .25
426 Jim Kelly (Passing for Miami) .25
427 Jim Kelly (With family) .25
428 Jim Kelly (Portrait by Greg Spalenka) .25
429 Jim Kelly (With sports jersey collection) .25
430 Jim Kelly (With young cancer patients) .25
431 Jim Kelly (Calling play) .25
432 Jim Kelly (Close-up) .25
433 Mark Rypien (Passing, horizontal shot (433-441) .10
434 Mark Rypien (In high school football uniform) .10
435 Mark Rypien (At Washington State) .10
436 Mark Rypien (Playing golf) .10
437 Mark Rypien (Portrait by Merv Corning) .10
438 Mark Rypien (With family) .10
439 Mark Rypien (Passing, vertical shot) .10
440 Mark Rypien (With young cystic fibrosis patients) .10
441 Mark Rypien (Close-up) .10
442 Warren Moon (Passing, white jersey (442-450)) .20
443 Warren Moon (As youth, in football uniform) .20
444 Warren Moon (Playing for Washington) .20
445 Warren Moon (With Edmonton Eskimos) .20
446 Warren Moon (Portrait by Greg Spalenka) .20
447 Warren Moon (With family) .20
448 Warren Moon (Calling the play) .20
449 Warren Moon (In his office) .20
450 Warren Moon (Posed with football and helmet) .20
451 Deion Sanders (In position for a play (451-459)) .15
452 Deion Sanders (As youth, in football uniform) .15
453 Deion Sanders (With Florida State) .15
454 Deion Sanders (Playing baseball) .15
455 Deion Sanders (Portrait by Gary Kelley) .15
456 Deion Sanders (Running with ball) .15
457 Deion Sanders (With family) .15
458 Deion Sanders (Walking on field) .15
459 Deion Sanders (Close-up) .15
460 Lawrence Taylor (Facing opponent, blue jersey (460-468)) .10
461 Lawrence Taylor (At North Carolina State) .10
462 Lawrence Taylor (Side view, white jersey) .10
463 Lawrence Taylor (Playing golf on football field) .10
464 Lawrence Taylor (Portrait by Chris Hopkins) .10
465 Lawrence Taylor (In Honolulu) .10
466 Lawrence Taylor (In front of his restaurant) .10
467 Lawrence Taylor (Steping over Jets player) .10
468 Lawrence Taylor (Close-up) .10
469 Randall Cunningham (Looking for receiver) .10
470 Randall Cunningham (In Pop Warner team uniform) .15
471 Randall Cunningham (Playing for UNLV) .15
472 Randall Cunningham (Running with ball) .15
473 Randall Cunningham (Portrait by Greg Spalenka) .15
474 Randall Cunningham (Playing golf) .15
475 Randall Cunningham (Passing) .15
476 Randall Cunningham (Working out) .15
477 Randall Cunningham (In dress attire) .15
478 Earnest Byner (Redskins uniform, running, side view 478-486)) .06
479 Earnest Byner (At East Carolina, black and white) .06
480 Earnest Byner (Browns, brown jersey) .06
481 Earnest Byner (With family) .06
482 Earnest Byner (Portrait by Chris Hopkins) .06
483 Earnest Byner (Browns, white jersey) .06
484 Earnest Byner (Fishing) .06
485 Earnest Byner (Redskins, uniform, running, front view) .06
486 Earnest Byner (In workout attire) .06
487 Mike Ditka (On sideline, in shirt and tie 487-495)) .10
488 Mike Ditka (Playing for Bears) .10
489 Mike Ditka (With family) .10
490 Mike Ditka (Playing for Cowboys) .10
491 Mike Ditka (Portrait by Garry Kelley) .10
492 Mike Ditka (With antique car) .10
493 Mike Ditka (Playing golf) .10
494 Mike Ditka (Eating) .10
495 Mike Ditka (Close-up) .10
496 Art Monk (Catching, close-up (496-504)) .75
497 Art Monk (Running hurdles in high school) .75
498 Art Monk (Running with ball, front view) .75
499 Art Monk (With family) .75
500 Art Monk (Portrait by Gary Kelley) .75
501 Art Monk (With youth at his football camp) .75
502 Art Monk (Running with ball, side view) .75
503 Art Monk (Working out) .75
504 Art Monk (Ready to catch ball, hands extended) .75

1992 Pro Line Profiles Autographs

Profiles Autographs run parallel to the Profiles set and were inserted in Pro Line foil packs at a rate of one per box. The cards were signed in black Sharpies, embossed with an NFL seal and are missing the card number to distinguish them from regular cards. Cards signed by Jack Kemp, Chris Miller and Mark Rypien do not exist, as well as cards 46-49, 56, 58, 356, 376, 383, 457-459 and 504. Art Monk's autographed cards were the first ones sent to wrapper redemption offers and do not have the card numbers removed and are not considered part of the set. Prices below are for the entire set of that player.

	NM/M
Complete Set (457):	3,200
Troy Aikman (181-189):	45.00
Carl Banks (19-27):	4.00
Bubby Brister (91-99):	4.00
Keith Byars (190-198):	4.00
Earnest Byner (478-486):	4.00
Anthony Carter (64-72):	4.00
Gary Clark (208-216):	4.00
Randall Cunningham (469-477):	20.00
Eric Dickerson (379-387):	10.00
Mike Ditka (487-495):	20.00
Chris Doleman (217-225):	4.00
John Elway (226-234):	45.00
Boomer Esiason (235-243):	8.00
Jim Everett (244-252):	25.00
Joe Gibbs (127-135):	8.00
Jerry Glanville (262-270):	4.00
Eric Green (253-261):	4.00
Jim Harbaugh (163-171):	4.00
Jeff Hostetler (271-279):	4.00
Michael Irvin (289-297):	20.00
Haywood Jeffires (280-288):	4.00
Jim Kelly (424-432):	20.00
Jack Kemp (154-162):	25.00
Bernie Kosar (100-108):	4.00
Steve Largent (298-306):	25.00
Howie Long (388-396):	20.00
Ronnie Lott (1-9):	8.00
Dan McGwire (172-180):	4.00
Art Monk (496-504):	35.00
Warren Moon (442-450):	10.00
Anthony Munoz (82-90):	8.00
Ken O'Brien (307-315):	4.00
Christian Okoye (316-324):	4.00
Rodney Peete (10-18):	4.00
Michael D. Perry (325-333):	4.00
Jerry Rice (46-54):	50.00
Timm Rosenbach (199-207):	4.00
Deion Sanders (451-459):	30.00
Junior Seau (136-144):	8.00
Sterling Sharpe (73-81):	10.00

Art Shell (109-117):	8.00
Don Shula (118-126):	20.00
Phil Simms (343-351):	15.00
Mike Singletary (397-405):	15.00
Bruce Smith (352-360):	8.00
Roger Staubach (37-45):	25.00
Pat Swilling (370-378):	4.00
John Taylor (406-414):	4.00
Lionel Taylor (460-468):	10.00
Vinny Testaverde (55-63):	8.00
Derrick Thomas (361-369):	35.00
Thurman Thomas (28-36):	12.00
Andre Tippett (415-423):	4.00
Al Toon (145-153):	4.00

1992-93 Pro Line SB Program

Numbered "of 9," the nine-card set chronicles the career of Steve Young from BYU to the L.A. Express to Tampa Bay and San Francisco. Showcased on the front are borderless photos, with his name in a strip at the top and the Pro Line logo at the bottom. The card back includes a photo, along with highpoints of his life and football career. A promo card was included with copies of the 1993 Super Bowl program.

		NM/M
Complete Set (9):		8.00
Common Player:		1.00
1	Steve Young (Just after release of ball)	1.00
2	Steve Young (Posed beside statue of Brigham Young)	1.00
3	Steve Young (in BYU uniform)	1.00
4	Steve Young (in Los Angeles Express uniform USFL)	1.00
5	Steve Young (Portrait)	1.00
6	Steve Young (in Tampa Bay Buccaneers uniform)	1.00
7	Steve Young (Posed with children for the Children's Miracle Network)	1.00
8	Steve Young (in San Francisco 49ers uniform)	1.00
9	Steve Young (Close-up shot, posed in law library)	1.00

1993 Pro Line Live Draft Day NYC

This 10-card set included cards which featured the four possible top draft picks of the 1993 draft with different teams. The set was housed in a cellophane pack and given to attendees at the NFL Draft in New York. The fronts include a photo, with a colored stripe down the right side which includes the player's name and possible team, along with the NFL Draft logo. The Classic Pro Line Live logo is in the lower left. The card backs have a photo at the top, with a write-up, stats and the card number printed below. To add to the confusion, each card was No. 1. Classic produced 1,000 sets.

		NM/M
Complete Set (10):		75.00
Common Player:		2.50
1A	Drew Bledsoe	20.00
1B	Drew Bledsoe	20.00
1C	Drew Bledsoe	20.00
1D	Eric Curry	2.50
1E	Eric Curry	2.50
1F	Marvin Jones	2.50
1G	Marvin Jones	2.50
1H	Rick Mirer	7.00
1I	Rick Mirer	7.00
1J	Rick Mirer	7.00

1993 Pro Line Live Draft Day QVC

Resembling the Draft Day New York City set on the front, the backs of the 10-card set included the Classic Pro Line Live logo, draft date and set number "of 9,300" printed over a continuous background of "Draft Day 1993." The cards also featured different versions with the players on different teams. The set was produced for sale on the QVC television network.

		NM/M
Complete Set (10):		20.00
Common Player:		1.00
1A	Drew Bledsoe	4.00
1B	Drew Bledsoe	4.00
1C	Drew Bledsoe	4.00
1D	Eric Curry	1.00
1E	Eric Curry	1.00
1F	Marvin Jones	1.00
1G	Marvin Jones	1.00
1H	Rick Mirer	2.00
1I	Rick Mirer	2.00
1J	Rick Mirer	2.00

1993 Pro Line Previews

Randomly seeded in 1993 Classic Football Draft Picks foil packs, the five-card set focused on the previous five No. 1 NFL Draft picks. According to Classic, 12,000 of each card was produced. Versions of Pro Line Live, Portraits and Profiles are on the card fronts, while the backs for each card are identical, listing the season and the player's name. The cards carry a "PL" prefix.

		NM/M
Complete Set (5):		45.00
Common Player:		4.00
1	Troy Aikman (Live)	20.00
2	Jeff George (Profile)	6.00
3	Russell Maryland (Live)	4.00
4	Steve Emtman	4.00
5	Drew Bledsoe (Portrait)	20.00

1993 Pro Line Live

This premiere edition features 285 Classic Pro Line Live cards, 48 Portraits cards and 13 nine-card Profiles sets. The card front has a full-bleed color action photo with the team and player's name on the right in its corresponding color. The back has an action photo and player information. Randomly inserted autographed cards were also issued, two per case. Players (35) signed between 900-1,050 cards; the autograph and the limited-edition card number appear on the card front. The card front is basically the same design as those in the regular set. The card back indicates the card is a limited-edition autographed card. The players who signed cards are #s 7, 16, 23, 34, 46, 51, 67, 70, 76, 79, 87, 88, 91, 96, 99, 107, 108, 109, 119, 120, 121, 124, 129, 131, 146, 151, 158, 160, 188, 199, 201, 217, 227, 231, and 242. These command premium prices.

		NM/M
Complete Set (285):		15.00
Common Player:		.05
Minor Stars:		.10
Pack (12):		.50
Wax Box (36):		15.00
1	Michael Haynes	.10
2	Chris Hinton	.05
3	Pierce Holt	.05
4	Chris Miller	.10
5	Mike Pritchard	.05
6	Andre Rison	.20
7	Deion Sanders	.50
8	Jessie Tuggle	.05
9	*Lincoln Kennedy*	.10
10	*Roger Harper*	.10
11	Cornelius Bennett	.05
12	Henry Jones	.05
13	Jim Kelly	.20
14	Bill Brooks	.05
15	Nate Odomes	.05
16	Andre Reed	.10
17	Frank Reich	.05
18	Bruce Smith	.05
19	Steve Tasker	.05
20	Thurman Thomas	.20
21	*Thomas Smith*	.10
22	*John Parrella*	.10
23	Neal Anderson	.05
24	Mark Carrier	.05
25	Jim Harbaugh	.10
26	Darren Lewis	.05
27	Steve McMichael	.05
28	Alonzo Spellman	.05
29	Tom Waddle	.05
30	*Curtis Conway*	.50
31	Carl Simpson	.05
32	David Fulcher	.05
33	Harold Green	.05
34	David Klingler	.10
35	Tim Krumrie	.05
36	Carl Pickens	.50
37	Alfred Williams	.05
38	Darryl William	.05
39	*John Copeland*	.10
40	*Tony McGee*	.10
41	Bernie Kosar	.05
42	Kevin Mack	.05
43	Clay Mathews	.05
44	Eric Metcalf	.05
45	Michael Dean Perry	.05
46	Vinny Testaverde	.20
47	Jerry Ball	.05
48	Tommy Vardell	.05
49	*Steve Everitt*	.10
50	*Dan Footman*	.10
51	Troy Aikman	.75
52	Daryl Johnston	.05
53	Tony Casillas	.05
54	Charles Haley	.05
55	Alvin Harper	.10
56	Michael Irvin	.20
57	Robert Jones	.05
58	Russell Maryland	.05
59	Nate Newton	.05
60	Ken Norton	.05
61	Jay Novacek	.05
62	Emmitt Smith	1.50
63	Kevin Smith	.05
64	*Kevin Williams*	.20
65	*Darrin Smith*	.10
66	Steve Atwater	.05
67	Rod Bernstine	.05
68	Mike Croel	.05
69	John Elway	1.00
70	Tommy Maddox	.10
71	Karl Mecklenburg	.05
72	Shannon Sharpe	.20
73	Dennis Smith	.05
74	*Dan Williams*	.10
75	*Glyn Milburn*	.20
76	Pat Swilling	.05
77	Bernie Blades	.05
78	Herman Moore	.50
79	Rodney Peete	.05
80	Brett Perriman	.05
81	Barry Sanders	2.00
82	Chris Spielman	.05
83	Andre Ware	.05
84	*Ryan McNeil*	.10
85	*Antonio London*	.10
86	Tony Bennett	.05
87	Terrell Buckley	.10
88	Brett Favre	2.00
89	Brian Noble	.05
90	Ken O'Brien	.05
91	Sterling Sharpe	.20
92	Reggie White	.20
93	John Stephens	.05
94	*Wayne Simmons*	.10
95	*George Teague*	.10
96	Ray Childress	.05
97	Curtis Duncan	.05
98	Ernest Givins	.05
99	Haywood Jeffires	.10
100	Bubba McDowell	.05
101	Warren Moon	.20
102	Al Smith	.05
103	Lorenzo White	.05
104	*Brad Hopkins*	.10
105	*Micheal Barrow*	.10
106	Duane Bickett	.05
107	Quentin Coryatt	.10
108	Steve Emtman	.10
109	Jeff George	.20
110	Anthony Johnson	.05
111	Reggie Langhorne	.05
112	Jack Trudeau	.05
113	Clarence Verdin	.05
114	Sean Dawkins	.05
115	*Roosevelt Potts*	.10
116	Dale Carter	.05
117	Dave Krieg	.05
118	Nick Lowery	.05
119	Christian Okoye	.05
120	Neil Smith	.05
121	Derrick Thomas	.20
122	Harvey Williams	.05
123	Barry Word	.05
124	Joe Montana	1.00
125	Marcus Allen	.20
126	James Lofton	.05
127	Nick Bell	.05
128	Tim Brown	.20
129	Eric Dickerson	.10
130	Jeff Hostetler	.10
131	Howie Long	.10
132	Todd Marinovich	.05
133	Greg Townsend	.05
134	*Patrick Bates*	.10
135	Billy Joe Hobart	.05
136	Willie Anderson	.05
137	Shane Conlan	.05
138	Henry Ellard	.05
139	Jim Everett	.10
140	Cleveland Gary	.05
141	Sean Gilbert	.05
142	Todd Lyght	.05
143	*Jerome Bettis*	1.50
144	*Troy Drayton*	.20
145	Louis Oliver	.05
146	Marco Coleman	.05
147	Bryan Cox	.05
148	Mark Duper	.05
149	Irving Fryar	.05
150	Mark Higgs	.05
151	Keith Jackson	.10
152	Dan Marino	1.50
153	Troy Vincent	.10
154	Richmond Webb	.05
155	*O.J. McDuffie*	.75
156	*Terry Kirby*	.20
157	Terry Allen	.20
158	Anthony Carter	.05
159	Cris Carter	.50
160	Chris Doleman	.05
161	Randall McDaniel	.05
162	Audray McMillian	.05
163	Henry Thomas	.05
164	Gary Zimmerman	.05
165	*Robert Smith*	1.00
166	*Qadry Ismail*	.20
167	Vincent Brown	.05
168	Marv Cook	.05
169	Greg McMurtry	.05
170	Jon Vaughn	.05
171	Leonard Russell	.10
172	Andre Tippett	.05
173	Scott Zolak	.05
174	*Drew Bledsoe*	3.00
175	*Chris Slade*	.10
176	Morten Andersen	.05
177	Vaughn Dunbar	.05
178	Rickey Jackson	.05
179	Vaughan Johnson	.05
180	Eric Martin	.05
181	Sam Mills	.05
182	Brad Muster	.05
183	*Willie Roaf*	.10
184	*Irv Smith*	.20
185	*Reggie Freeman*	.10
186	Michael Brooks	.05
187	*Dave Brown*	.20
188	Rodney Hampton	.10
189	Pepper Johnson	.05
190	Ed McCaffrey	.30
191	David Meggett	.05
192	Bart Oates	.05
193	Phil Simms	.10
194	Lawrence Taylor	.20
195	Michael Strahan	.05
196	Brad Baxter	.05
197	Johnny Johnson	.10
198	Boomer Esiason	.10
199	Ronnie Lott	.10
200	Johnny Mitchell	.10
201	Rob Moore	.20
202	Browning Nagle	.05
203	Blair Thomas	.05
204	*Marvin Jones*	.10
205	*Coleman Rudolph*	.10
206	Eric Allen	.05
207	Fred Barnett	.10
208	Tim Harris	.05
209	Randall Cunningham	.20
210	Seth Joyner	.05
211	Clyde Simmons	.05
212	Herschel Walker	.10
213	Calvin Williams	.05
214	*Lester Holmes*	.10
215	*Leonard Renfro*	.10
216	Chris Chandler	.20
217	Gary Clark	.05
218	Ken Harvey	.05
219	Randal Hill	.05
220	Steve Beuerlein	.10
221	Ricky Proehl	.05
222	Timm Rosenbach	.05
223	*Garrison Hearst*	1.00
224	*Ernest Dye*	.10
225	Bubby Brister	.05
226	Dermontti Dawson	.05
227	Barry Foster	.05
228	Kevin Greene	.05
229	Merril Hoge	.05
230	Greg Lloyd	.05
231	Neil O'Donnell	.20
232	Rod Woodson	.10
233	*Deon Figures*	.10
234	*Chad Brown*	.20
235	Marion Butts	.05
236	Gill Byrd	.05
237	Ronnie Harmon	.05
238	Stan Humphries	.10
239	Anthony Miller	.05
240	Leslie O'Neil	.05
241	Stanley Richard	.05
242	Junior Seau	.20
243	*Darrien Gordon*	.20
244	*Natrone Means*	1.00
245	Dana Hall	.05
246	Brent Jones	.05
247	Tim McDonald	.05
248	Steve Bono	.20
249	Jerry Rice	1.00
250	John Taylor	.10
251	Ricky Watters	.20
252	Steve Young	.75
253	*Dana Stubblefield*	.20
254	*Todd Kelly*	.10
255	Brian Blades	.05
256	Ferrell Edmunds	.05
257	Stan Gelbaugh	.05
258	Cortez Kennedy	.10
259	Dan McGwire	.10
260	Chris Warren	.10
261	John L. Williams	.05
262	David Wyman	.05
263	*Rick Mirer*	.25
264	*Carlton Gray*	.10
265	Marty Carter	.05
266	Reggie Cobb	.05
267	Lawrence Dawsey	.05
268	Santana Dotson	.05
269	Craig Erickson	.10
270	Paul Gruber	.05
271	Keith McCants	.05
272	Broderick Thomas	.05
273	*Eric Curry*	.10
274	*Demetrius Duboise*	.10
275	Earnest Byner	.05
276	Ricky Ervins	.05
277	Brad Edwards	.05
278	Jim Lachey	.05
279	Charles Mann	.05
280	Carl Banks	.05
281	Art Monk	.10
282	Mark Rypien	.10
284	*Tom Carter*	.10
285	*Reggie Brooks*	.20

1993 Pro Line Live Autographs

Randomly seeded two per 10-box case, the card fronts carry the same design as the regular cards, with the autograph signed over the photo. The backs congratulate the winner of the autograph. The Classic, NFL and NFLPA logos appear at the bottom. The cards are unnumbered, but are listed below respective of the player's regular card.

		NM/M
Complete Set (38):		1,200
Common Player:		10.00
Minor Stars:		20.00
7	Deion Sanders (900)	75.00
16	Andre Reed (1050)	20.00
23	Neal Anderson (1050)	10.00
34	David Klingler (1200)	10.00
46	Vinny Testaverde (900)	30.00
51	Troy Aikman (700)	80.00
67	Rod Bernstine (1000)	10.00
70	Tommy Maddox (1050)	10.00
76	Pat Swilling (950)	10.00
79	Rodney Peete (1000)	10.00
87	Terrell Buckley (1050)	20.00
88	Brett Favre (650)	200.00
91	Sterling Sharpe (1050)	20.00
96	Ray Childress (950)	10.00
99	Haywood Jeffires (950)	10.00
107	Quentin Coryatt (900)	10.00
108	Steve Emtman (800)	10.00
109	Jeff George (1050)	20.00
119	Christian Okoye (900)	10.00
120	Neil Smith (1050)	20.00
121	Derrick Thomas (550)	35.00
124	Joe Montana (600)	200.00
129	Eric Dickerson (900)	20.00
131	Howie Long (950)	20.00
146	Marco Coleman (1000)	10.00
151	Keith Jackson (650)	10.00
158	Anthony Carter (950)	10.00
160	Chris Doleman (1000)	10.00
188	Rodney Hampton (650)	20.00
199	Ronnie Lott (1050)	20.00
201	Rob Moore (950)	30.00
212	Herschel Walker (400)	20.00
217	Gary Clark (1050)	10.00
227	Barry Foster (750)	10.00
231	Neil O'Donnell (1050)	20.00
242	Junior Seau (900)	20.00
275	Earnest Byner (750)	10.00
281	Art Monk (750)	20.00

1993 Pro Line Live Future Stars

The 28-card set was seeded one per Pro Line Live jumbo pack. The fronts are anchored with a photo, with a colored stripe running along the right side of the card. The player's name and team appears in the stripe. The Pro Line Live logo is located in the lower left. The backs have the photo at the top, with his name and position in the upper left. His highlights and stats are printed in a colored rectangle at the bottom of the card. The card fronts also boast a gold-foil stamp of "1 of 22,000" printed to the inside of the stripe on the right side. The cards are numbered with "FS."

		NM/M
Complete Set (28):		15.00
Common Player:		.25
Minor Stars:		.50
1	Patrick Bates	.25
2	Jerome Bettis	2.00
3	Drew Bledsoe	4.50
4	Tom Carter	.25
5	Curtis Conway	.75
6	Steve Everitt	.25
7	Deon Figures	.25
8	Darrien Gordon	.25
9	Lester Holmes	.25
10	Brad Hopkins	.25
11	Marvin Jones	.50
12	Lincoln Kennedy	.25
13	O.J. McDuffie	1.00
14	Rick Mirer	.50
15	Willie Roaf	.50
16	Will Shields	.25
17	Wayne Simmons	.25
18	Robert Smith	2.00
19	Thomas Smith	.25
20	Michael Strahan	.25
21	Dana Stubblefield	.50
22	Dan Williams	.25
23	Kevin Williams (WR)	.50
24	Garrison Hearst	2.00
25	John Copeland	.25
26	Ryan McNeil	.25
27	Eric Curry	.25
28	Roosevelt Potts	.25

1993 Pro Line Live Illustrated

Artwork was the main feature of this six-card set, created by artist Neal Adams. The fronts showcase artwork on the left, with the player's name and team in a colored stripe on the right side. The Pro Line logo is in the lower left. "One of 10,000" is printed along the inside of the stripe on the right side. The backs carry the same design as the base cards, but are numbered with a prefix of "SP." The cards were seeded three per case. Classic produced 10,000 of each card.

		NM/M
Complete Set (6):		20.00
Common Player:		2.00
1	Troy Aikman	4.50
2	Jerry Rice	6.00
3	Michael Irvin	2.00
4	Thurman Thomas	2.00
5	Lawrence Taylor	2.00
6	Deion Sanders	3.00

1993 Pro Line Live LPs

Randomly seeded in packs, the 20-card set included a large photo on the front, with the player's name in a colored stripe on the right side. The Pro Line logo is in the lower left corner, while a "one of 40,000" gold-foil seal is on the right corner. The backs, prefixed with an "LP," have the player's name in the upper left of the photo. The player's write-up is included beneath the photo, with the card number in the lower right.

		NM/M
Complete Set (20):		30.00
Common Player:		.75
Minor Stars:		1.50
1	Chris Webber (Dunking football)	2.00
2	Shaquille O'Neal (Wearing street clothes)	5.00
3	Jamal Mashburn (Wearing ProLine apparel)	1.50
4	Marcus Allen	1.50
5	Neal Anderson	.75
6	Reggie Cobb	.75
7	Rod Bernstine	.75
8	Barry Word	.75
9	Troy Aikman	3.00
10	Brett Favre	6.00
11	Ricky Watters	1.50
12	Terry Allen	1.50
13	Rodney Hampton	.75
14	Garrison Hearst	1.50
15	Jerome Bettis	1.50
16	Barry Foster	.75
17	Harold Green	.75
18	Tommy Vardell	.75
19	Lorenzo White	.75
20	Marion Butts	.75

1993 Pro Line Live Tonx

Randomly seeded in packs, the six-milk cap set previewed the NFL Tonx set. The milk cap, which measures 1-5/8 inches in diameter, could be removed from the standard size card. The front of the disc features a full-bleed photo, while the back has the team's helmet, player name and Tonx logo. The card front announces that Tonx is coming in the fall, while the card back explains the Tonx set. Each card is unnumbered.

		NM/M
Complete Set (6):		6.00
Common Player:		.50
1	Troy Aikman	2.00
2	Michael Irvin	.50
3	Jerry Rice	1.50
4	Deion Sanders	1.00
5	Lawrence Taylor	.50
6	Thurman Thomas	.50

1993 Pro Line Portraits

These cards continue where the numbers from the 1992 Pro Line Portraits left off, at #468. The players are featured in non-game photos on the front, with a small mug shot on the card back. A quote from the player also appears on the back.

		NM/M
Complete Set (44):		7.50
Common Player:		.05
468	*Willie Roaf*	.15
469	Terry Allen	.15
470	Jerry Ball	.05
471	Patrick Bates	.15
472	Ray Bentley	.05
473	*Jerome Bettis*	.50
474	Steve Beuerlein	.10
475	*Drew Bledsoe*	3.00
476	*Dave Brown*	.10
477	Gill Byrd	.05
478	Tony Casillas	.05
479	Chuck Cecil	.05
480	Reggie Cobb	.05
481	Pat Harlow	.05
482	*John Copeland*	.25
483	Bryan Cox	.05
484	*Eric Curry*	.25
485	Jeff Lageman	.05
486	Brett Favre	.75
487	Barry Foster	.25
488	Gaston Green	.05
489	Rodney Hampton	.25
490	Tim Harris	.05
491	*Garrison Hearst*	1.00
492	Tony Smith	.05
493	*Marvin Jones*	.20
494	*Lincoln Kennedy*	.25
495	Wilber Marshall	.05
496	Terry McDaniel	.05
497	*Rick Mirer*	.50
498	Art Monk	.08
499	Mike Munchak	.05
500	Frank Reich	.05
501	Barry Sanders	1.00
502	Shannon Sharpe	.05
503	*Gino Torretta*	.25
504	Ricky Watters	.40
505	Richmond Webb	.05
506	Reggie White	.25
507	Bert Jones	.05
508	Billy Kilmer	.05
509	John Mackey	.05
510	Archie Manning	.05
511	Harvey Martin	.05

1993 Pro Line Portraits Autographs

The 26-card set includes a full-bleed photo on the front, with the Pro Line logo in the bottom center. The card front is autographed. The back has the player's name in the upper left, team in the upper right and a quote in the center of the card. His photo is at the bottom center.

		NM/M
Complete Set (26):		750.00
Common Player:		20.00
468	Willie Roaf	20.00
471	Patrick Bates	20.00
473	Jerome Bettis	45.00
474	Steve Beuerlein	20.00
478	Tony Casillas	20.00
479	Chuck Cecil	20.00
480	Reggie Cobb	20.00
481	Pat Harlow	20.00
482	John Copeland	20.00
484	Eric Curry	20.00
485	Jeff Lageman	20.00
486	Brett Favre	250.00
488	Gaston Green	20.00
489	Rodney Hampton	25.00
492	Tony Smith	20.00
493	Marvin Jones	20.00
494	Lincoln Kennedy	20.00
496	Terry McDaniel	20.00
499	Mike Munchak	20.00
500	Frank Reich	25.00
502	Shannon Sharpe	35.00
503	Gino Torretta	20.00
507	Bert Jones (TB)	20.00
508	Billy Kilmer (TB)	30.00
510	Archie Manning (TB)	30.00
511	Harvey Martin (TB)	20.00

1993 Pro Line Portraits Wives

This four-card set features wives of NFL players and was inserted into packs of 1993 Pro Line. The cards are numbered SC25-SC28 in a continuation from 1992 Pro Line Wives, however card number SC24 was never produced.

		NM/M
Complete Set (4):		.50
Common Player:		.15
25	Annette Rypien	.15
26	Ann Stark	.15
27	Cindy Walker	.15
28	Cindy Reed	.15

1993 Pro Line Portraits Wives Autographs

The set features the same design as the Portraits Wives set, except these are autographed. Three of the four wives featured in the basic set signed cards, with the exception of Cindy Walker.

		NM/M
Complete Set (3):		75.00
Common Player:		25.00
25	Annette Rypien	25.00
26	Ann Stark	25.00
28	Cindy Reed	25.00

1994 Pro Line Live Draft Day Prototypes

The 1994 Draft was previewed by this 13-card set. The fronts are anchored with a borderless photo, with the NFL Draft logo in the upper right and the player's name and possible team at the bottom. The backs showcase a cutout of a portion of a photo, with the rest of the photo grayed out. The cards are numbered by a prefix of "FD" in the upper right. The backs state, "1994 NFL Draft Day prototype set April 24, 1994, limited edition 1 of 19,940."

		NM/M
Complete Set (13):		25.00
Common Player:		1.00
1	Dan Wilkinson	1.00
2	Dan Wilkinson	1.00
3	Marshall Faulk	5.00
4	Marshall Faulk	5.00
5	Marshall Faulk	5.00
6	Troy Aikman 1989 First Pick	3.00
7	Trent Dilfer	2.00
8	Trent Dilfer	2.00
9	Heath Shuler	3.00
10	Heath Shuler	3.00
11	Aaron Glenn	1.00
12	Aaron Glenn	1.00
13	Dan Wilkinson	1.00

1994 Pro Line Live Previews

This five-card set boasts a full-bleed photo on the front, with the Classic Pro Line Preview logo in the upper left and player's name and team at the bottom. The backs, numbered in the lower left with a prefix of "PL," have the player's name and position in the upper left and his highlights and bio in a stripe along the left side of the card. An action shot and his stats are printed over his photo. The back also has a tagline which says the card is one of 12,000.

		NM/M
Complete Set (5):		45.00
Common Player:		7.00
1	Troy Aikman	12.00
2	Jerry Rice	12.00
3	Steve Young	10.00
4	Rick Mirer	7.00
5	Drew Bledsoe	12.00

1994 Pro Line Live

Classic Games Inc. produced the 405-card 1994 Pro Line Live set. The set includes 327 NFL veterans and 62 rookies. Each card front has a borderless color action photo on the front, along with the player's name and team and set logo. The back has another color photo of the player, with statistics, biographical information and a brief career summary. More than 150 players also autographed their cards; these cards, issued one per box, command premium values. Two subsets were also made, featuring the league's two new expansion teams (the Jacksonville Jaguars and Carolina Panthers), and the player illustrations of comic book artist Neal Adams (#s 401-405). There were also three insert sets produced. Emmitt Smith is honored with 15,000 sequentially-numbered inserts, while another set honors 45 players who were MVP candidates. Collectors who obtained one of the 2,083 cards of the 1994 NFL MVP could redeem it for a limited, uncut sheet of the 45 cards. The other insert series previews the company's 1994 Basketball Draft Pick series.

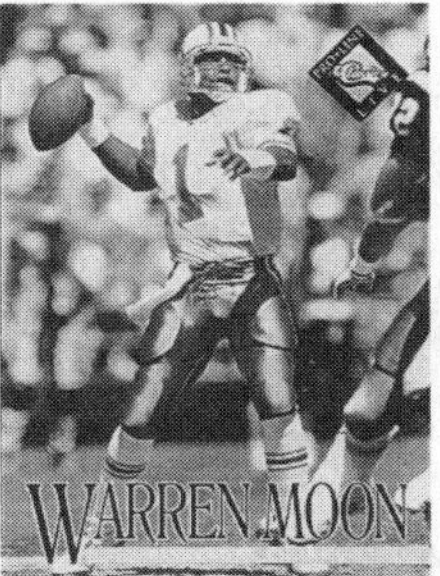

		NM/M
Complete Set (405):		20.00
Common Player:		.05
Minor Stars:		.10
Pack (10):		1.50
Wax Box (36):		40.00
1	Emmitt Smith	1.50
2	Andre Rison	.10
3	Deion Sanders	.50
4	Jeff George	.10
5	Cornelius Bennett	.05
6	Jim Kelly	.25
7	Andre Reed	.10
8	Bruce Smith	.05
9	Thurman Thomas	.25
10	Mark Carrier	.05
11	Curtis Conway	.25
12	Donnell Woolford	.05
13	Chris Zorich	.05
14	Erik Kramer	.10
15	John Copeland	.05
16	Harold Green	.05
17	David Klingler	.10
18	Tony McGee	.05
19	Carl Pickens	.25
20	Michael Jackson	.10
21	Eric Metcalf	.10
22	Michael Dean Perry	.05
23	Vinny Testaverde	.25
24	Eric Turner	.05
25	Tommy Vardell	.05
26	Troy Aikman	1.00
27	Charles Haley	.05
28	Michael Irvin	.25
29	Pierce Holt	.05
30	Russell Maryland	.05
31	Eric Williams	.05
32	Thomas Everett	.05
33	Steve Atwater	.10
34	John Elway	1.50
35	Glyn Milburn	.10
36	Shannon Sharpe	.25
37	Anthony Miller	.05
38	Barry Sanders	2.00
39	Chris Spielman	.05
40	Pat Swilling	.05
41	Brett Perriman	.05
42	Herman Moore	.30
43	Scott Mitchell	.10
44	Edgar Bennett	.05
45	Terrell Buckley	.05
46	LeRoy Butler	.05
47	Brett Favre	2.00
48	Jackie Harris	.05
49	Sterling Sharpe	.25
50	Reggie White	.25
51	Gary Brown	.10
52	Cody Carlson	.05
53	Ray Childress	.05
54	Ernest Givins	.05
55	Bruce Matthews	.05
56	Quentin Coryatt	.05
57	Steve Emtman	.05
58	Roosevelt Potts	.05
59	Tony Bennett	.05
60	Marcus Allen	.25
61	Joe Montana	1.00
62	Neil Smith	.05
63	Derrick Thomas	.10
64	Dale Carter	.05
65	Tim Brown	.25
66	Jeff Hostetler	.05
67	Terry McDaniel	.05
68	Chester McGlockton	.05
69	Anthony Smith	.05
70	Albert Lewis	.05
71	Jerome Bettis	.50
72	Shane Conlan	.05
73	Troy Drayton	.10
74	Sean Gilbert	.05
75	Chris Miller	.05
76	Bryan Cox	.05
77	Irving Fryar	.05
78	Keith Jackson	.05
79	Terry Kirby	.10
80	Dan Marino	1.50
81	O.J. McDuffie	.25
82	Terry Allen	.25
83	Cris Carter	.50
84	Chris Doleman	.05
85	Randall McDaniel	.05
86	John Randle	.10
87	Robert Smith	.50
88	Jason Belser	.05
89	Jack Del Rio	.05
90	Vincent Brown	.05
91	Ben Coates	.10
92	Chris Slade	.05
93	Derek Brown	.05
94	Morten Andersen	.05
95	Willie Roaf	.05
96	Irv Smith	.05
97	Tyrone Hughes	.05
98	Michael Haynes	.05
99	Jim Everett	.05
100	Michael Brooks	.05
101	Leroy Thompson	.05
102	Rodney Hampton	.10
103	David Meggett	.05
104	Phil Simms	.10
105	Boomer Esiason	.10
106	Johnny Johnson	.05
107	Gary Anderson	.05
108	Mo Lewis	.05
109	Ronnie Lott	.10
110	Johnny Mitchell	.05
111	Howard Cross	.05
112	Victor Bailey	.05
113	Fred Barnett	.05
114	Randall Cunningham	.25
115	Calvin Williams	.05
116	Steve Beuerlein	.05
117	Gary Clark	.05
118	Ron Moore	.05
119	Ricky Proehl	.05
120	Eric Swann	.05
121	Barry Foster	.05
122	Kevin Greene	.05
123	Greg Lloyd	.05
124	Neil O'Donnell	.10
125	Rod Woodson	.05
126	Ronnie Harmon	.05
127	Mark Higgs	.05
128	Stan Humphries	.10
129	Leslie O'Neal	.05
130	Chris Mims	.05
131	Stanley Richard	.05
132	Junior Seau	.10
133	Brent Jones	.05
134	Tim McDonald	.05
135	Jerry Rice	1.00
136	Dana Stubblefield	.10
137	Ricky Watters	.25
138	Steve Young	.75
139	Cortez Kennedy	.05
140	Rick Mirer	.10
141	Eugene Robinson	.05
142	Chris Warren	.10
143	Nate Odomes	.05
144	Howard Ballard	.05
145	Willie Anderson	.05
146	Chris Jacke	.05
147	Santana Dotson	.05
148	Craig Erickson	.05
149	Hardy Nickerson	.05
150	Lawrence Dawsey	.05
151	Terry Wooden	.05
152	Ethan Horton	.05
153	John Kasay	.05
154	Desmond Howard	.05
155	Ken Harvey	.05
156	William Fuller	.05
157	Clyde Simmons	.05
158	Randal Hill	.05
159	Garrison Hearst	.50
160	Mike Pritchard	.05
161	Jessie Tuggle	.05
162	Erric Pegram	.05
163	Kevin Ross	.05
164	Bill Brooks	.05
165	Darryl Talley	.05
166	Steve Tasker	.05
167	Pete Stoyanovich	.05
168	Dante Jones	.05
169	Vencie Glenn	.05
170	Tom Waddle	.05
171	Harlon Barnett	.05
172	Trace Armstrong	.05
173	Tim Worley	.05
174	Alfred Williams	.05
175	Louis Oliver	.05
176	Darryl Williams	.05
177	Clay Matthews	.05
178	Kyle Clifton	.05
179	Alvin Harper	.05
180	Jay Novacek	.05
181	Ken Norton	.05
182	Kevin Williams	.10
183	Daryl Johnson	.05
184	Rod Bernstine	.05
185	Karl Mecklenburg	.05
186	Dennis Smith	.05
187	Robert Delpino	.05
188	Bennie Blades	.05
189	Jason Hanson	.05
190	Derrick Moore	.05
191	Mark Clayton	.05
192	Webster Slaughter	.05
193	Haywood Jeffires	.05
194	Bubba McDowell	.05
195	Warren Moon	.25
196	Al Smith	.05
197	Bill Romanowski	.05
198	John Carney	.05
199	Kerry Cash	.05
200	Darren Carrington	.05
201	Jeff Lageman	.05
202	Tracy Simien	.05
203	Willie Davis	.05
204	Dan Saleaumua	.05
205	Raghib Ismail	.05
206	James Jett	.10
207	Todd Lyght	.05
208	Roman Phifer	.05
209	Jimmie Jones	.10
210	Jeff Cross	.05
211	Eric Davis	.05
212	Keith Byars	.05
213	Richmond Webb	.05
214	Anthony Carter	.05
215	Henry Thomas	.05
216	Andre Tippett	.05
217	Rickey Jackson	.05
218	Vaughan Johnson	.05
219	Eric Martin	.05
220	Sam Mills	.05
221	Renaldo Turnbull	.05
222	Mark Collins	.05
223	Mike Johnson	.05
224	Rob Moore	.25
225	Seth Joyner	.05
226	Herschel Walker	.10
227	Eric Green	.05
228	Marion Butts	.05
229	John Friesz	.10
230	John Taylor	.05
231	Dexter Carter	.05
232	Brian Blades	.05
233	Reggie Cobb	.05
234	Paul Gruber	.05
235	Ricky Reynolds	.05
236	Vince Workman	.05
237	Darrell Green	.05
238	Jim Lachey	.05
239	James Hasty	.05
240	Howie Long	.10
241	Aeneas Williams	.05
242	Mike Kenn	.05
243	Henry Jones	.05
244	Kenneth Davis	.05
245	Tim Krumrie	.05
246	Derrick Fenner	.05
247	Mark Carrier	.05
248	Robert Porcher	.05
249	Darren Woodson	.05
250	Kevin Smith	.05
251	Mark Stepnoski	.05
252	Simon Fletcher	.05
253	Derek Russell	.05
254	Mike Croel	.05
255	Johnny Holland	.05
256	Bryce Paup	.05
257	Cris Dishman	.05
258	Sean Jones	.05
259	Marcus Robertson	.05
260	Steve Jackson	.05
261	Jeff Herrod	.05
262	John Alt	.05
263	Nick Lowery	.05
264	Greg Robinson	.05
265	Alexander Wright	.05
266	Steve Wisniewski	.05
267	Henry Ellard	.05
268	Tracy Scroggins	.05
269	Jackie Slater	.05
270	Troy Vincent	.05
271	Qadry Ismail	.10
272	Steve Jordan	.05
273	Leonard Russell	.05
274	Maurice Hurst	.05
275	*Scottie Graham*	.10
276	Carlton Bailey	.05
277	John Elliott	.05
278	Corey Miller	.05
279	Brad Baxter	.05
280	Brian Washington	.05
281	Tim Harris	.05
282	Byron Evans	.05
283	Dermontti Dawson	.05
284	Carnell Lake	.05
285	Jeff Graham	.05
286	Merton Hanks	.05
287	Harris Barton	.05
288	Guy McIntyre	.05
289	Kelvin Martin	.05
290	John Williams	.05
291	Courtney Hawkins	.05
292	Vaughn Hebron	.05
293	Brian Mitchell	.05
294	Andre Collins	.05
295	Art Monk	.10
296	Mark Rypien	.10
297	Ricky Sanders	.05
298	Eric Hill	.05
299	Larry Centers	.05
300	Norm Johnson	.05
301	Pete Metzelaars	.05
302	Ricardo McDonald	.05
303	Stevon Moore	.05
304	Mike Sherrard	.05
305	Andy Harmon	.05
306	Anthony Johnson	.05
307	J.J. Birden	.05
308	Neal Anderson	.05
309	Lewis Tillman	.05
310	Richard Dent	.10
311	Nate Newton	.05
312	*Sean Dawkins*	.25
313	Lawrence Taylor	.25
314	Wilber Marshall	.05
315	Tim Carter	.05
316	Reggie Brooks	.10
317	Eric Curry	.05
318	Horace Copeland	.05
319	Natrone Means	.50
320	Eric Allen	.05
321	Marvin Jones	.05
322	Keith Hamilton	.05
323	Vincent Brisby	.10
324	Drew Bledsoe	1.00
325	Tom Rathman	.05
326	Ed McCaffrey	.30
327	Steve Israel	.05
328	*Dan Wilkinson*	.25
329	*Marshall Faulk*	4.00
330	*Heath Shuler*	.50
331	*Willie McGinest*	.25
332	*Trev Alberts*	.25
333	*Trent Dilfer*	2.50
334	*Bryant Young*	.50
335	*Sam Adams*	.25
336	*Antonio Langham*	.25
337	*Jamir Miller*	.25
338	*John Thierry*	.25
339	*Aaron Glenn*	.25
340	*Joe Johnson*	.10
341	*Bernard Williams*	.10
342	*Wayne Gandy*	.10
343	*Aaron Taylor*	.10
344	*Charles Johnson*	.25
345	*DeWayne Washington*	.10
346	*Todd Steussie*	.25
347	*Tim Bowens*	.10
348	*Johnnie Morton*	.40
349	*Rob Fredrickson*	.10
350	*Shante Carver*	.10
351	*Thomas Lewis*	.10
352	*Greg Hill*	.50
353	*Henry Ford*	.10
354	*Jeff Burris*	.10
355	*William Floyd*	.50
356	*Derrick Alexander*	.25
357	*Darnay Scott*	.75
358	*Isaac Bruce*	4.00
359	*Errict Rhett*	.50
360	*Kevin Lee*	.10
361	*Chuck Levy*	.25
362	*David Palmer*	.50
363	*Ryan Yarborough*	.10
364	*Charlie Garner*	2.50
365	*Isaac Davis*	.10
366	*Mario Bates*	.25
367	*Bert Emanuel*	.75
368	*Thomas Randolph*	.10
369	*Bucky Brooks*	.10
370	*Allen Aldridge*	.10
371	*Charlie Ward*	.50
372	*Audrey Beavers*	.10
373	*Donnell Bennett*	.50
374	*Jason Sehorn*	.25
375	*Lonnie Johnson*	.25
376	*Tyronne Drakeford*	.10
377	*Andre Coleman*	.10
378	*Lamar Smith*	2.50
379	*Calvin Jones*	.10
380	*LeShon Johnson*	.10
381	*Byron Morris*	.50
382	*Lake Dawson*	.25
383	*Corey Sawyer*	.10
384	*Willie Jackson*	.10
385	*Perry Klein*	.10
386	*Ronnie Woolfork*	.10
387	*Doug Nussmeier*	.10
388	*Rob Waldrop*	.10
389	*Glenn Foley*	.50
390	Aikman, Irvin	.50
391	Young, Rice	.50
392	Favre, Sharpe	1.00
393	Kelly, Reed	.10
394	Elway, Sharpe	.75
395	Carolina Panthers	.05
396	Jacksonville Jaguars	.05
397	Checklist #1	.05
398	Checklist #2	.05
399	Checklist #3	.05
400	Checklist #4	.05
401	Sterling Sharpe	.10
402	Derrick Thomas	.05
403	Joe Montana	.50
404	Emmitt Smith	.75
405	Barry Sanders	1.00

1994 Pro Line Live Autographs

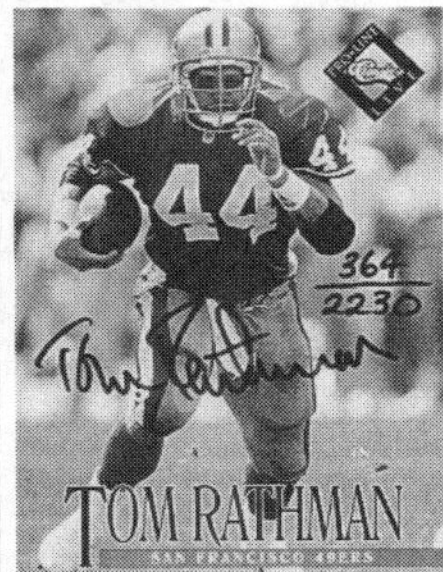

This 132-card autographed set showcases the same design as the base cards, except they are signed and numbered on the front. The card backs congratulate the collector on receiving an autographed card. The Pro Line Live logo is in the center of the unnumbered card back. The cards are numbered below according to the player's base card number.

		NM/M
Complete Set (132):		2,750
Common Player:		10.00
Minor Stars:		20.00
Inserted 1:36		
1	Emmitt Smith (925)	125.00
4	Jeff George (2140)	20.00
12	Donnell Woolford (1000)	10.00
14	Eric Kramer (1020)	10.00
17	David Klingler (2140)	10.00
20	Michael Jackson (1490)	10.00

24 Eric Turner (1030) 10.00
25 Tommy Vardell (1000) 10.00
26 Troy Aikman (340) 125.00
28 Michael Irvin (450) 25.00
29 Pierce Holt (2020) 10.00
30 Russell Maryland (1945) 10.00
33 Steve Atwater (1040) 10.00
34 John Elway (1000) 100.00
35 Glyn Milburn (440) 20.00
36 Shannon Sharpe (1020) 20.00
37 Anthony Miller (2070) 10.00
47 Brett Favre (1130) 100.00
49 Sterling Sharpe (450) 35.00
51 Gary Brown (950) 20.00
53 Ray Childress (2240) 10.00
56 Quentin Coryatt (970) 10.00
57 Steve Emtman (1900) 10.00
61 Joe Montana (920) 150.00
62 Neil Smith (1000) 20.00
63 Derrick Thomas (1087) 50.00
64 Dale Carter (1031) 10.00
65 Tim Brown (1920) 20.00
66 Jeff Hostetler (955) 10.00
67 Terry McDaniel (1980) 10.00
72 Shane Conlan (1110) 10.00
73 Troy Drayton (450) 20.00
77 Irving Fryar (1040) 10.00
78 Keith Jackson (1020) 10.00
93 Derek Brown (RB/449) 10.00
96 Irv Smith (470) 20.00
97 Tyrone Hughes (470) 10.00
99 Jim Everett (1265) 10.00
102 Rodney Hampton (1090) 20.00
105 Boomer Esiason (920) 20.00
109 Ronnie Lott (910) 20.00
112 Victor Bailey (450) 20.00
116 Steve Beuerlein (970) 20.00
119 Ricky Proehl (1020) 10.00
121 Barry Foster (1080) 10.00
127 Mark Higgs (980) 10.00
129 Leslie O'Neal (2050) 10.00
133 Brent Jones (1880) 10.00
134 Tim McDonald (2040) 10.00
138 Steve Young (925) 75.00
149 Hardy Nickerson (1175) 10.00
159 Garrison Hearst (1435) 25.00
162 Eric Pegram (1020) 10.00
164 Bill Brooks (1030) 10.00
177 Clay Matthews (2000) 10.00
184 Rod Bernstine (1010) 10.00
187 Robert Delpino (1030) 10.00
208 Roman Phifer (2140) 10.00
212 Keith Byars (1020) 10.00
213 Richmond Webb (1020) 10.00
214 Anthony Carter (1020) 10.00
216 Andre Tippett (1090) 10.00
220 Sam Mills (1115) 10.00
221 Renaldo Turnbull (945) 10.00
224 Rob Moore (1025) 20.00
228 Marion Butts (2040) 10.00
229 John Friesz (2150) 20.00
230 John Taylor (1030) 10.00
238 Jim Lachey (1850) 10.00
244 Kenneth Davis (1170) 10.00
266 Steve Wisniewski (2150) 10.00
269 Jackie Slater (1110) 10.00
271 Qadry Ismail (450) 20.00
277 John Elliott (2150) 10.00
279 Brad Baxter (1070) 10.00
284 Carnell Lake (1985) 10.00
287 Harris Barton (2120) 10.00
294 Andre Collins (1100) 10.00
315 Tom Carter (460) 10.00
316 Reggie Brooks (460) 20.00
318 Horace Copeland (450) 10.00
319 Natrone Means (445) 40.00
320 Eric Allen (1980) 10.00
324 Drew Bledsoe (1150) 65.00
325 Tom Rathman (2230) 10.00
326 Ed McCaffrey (2030) 25.00
327 Steve Israel (2020) 10.00
328 Dan Wilkinson (1960) 10.00
329 Marshall Faulk (2230) 50.00
330 Heath Shuler (2020) 20.00
331 Willie McGinest (3520) 10.00
333 Trent Dilfer (2680) 20.00
336 Antonio Langham (1240) 10.00
338 John Thierry (1150) 10.00
339 Aaron Glenn (1140) 10.00
342 Wayne Gandy (1040) 10.00
343 Aaron Taylor (950) 10.00
344 Charles Johnson 10.00
345 DeWayne Washington (1040) 10.00
348 Johnnie Morton (2945) 10.00
349 Rob Fredrickson (1160) 10.00
350 Shante Carver (1160) 10.00
351 Thomas Lewis (1140) 10.00
352 Greg Hill (1145) 20.00
353 Henry Ford (1110) 10.00
354 Jeff Burris (1140) 10.00
355 William Floyd (950) 20.00
356 Derrick Alexander (WR/950) 20.00
357 Darnay Scott (1400) 20.00
359 Errict Rhett (1120) 20.00
360 Kevin Lee (1190) 10.00
361 Chuck Levy (950) 10.00
362 David Palmer (950) 20.00
364 Charlie Garner (1130) 20.00
365 Isaac Davis (1150) 10.00
366 Mario Bates (1145) 10.00
368 Thomas Randolph (1100) 10.00
369 Bucky Brooks (1090) 10.00
372 Aubrey Beavers (1150) 10.00
373 Donnell Bennett (1130) 20.00
374 Jason Sehorn (950) 20.00
377 Andre Coleman (1000) 10.00
378 Lamar Smith (1130) 10.00
379 Calvin Jones (960) 10.00
381 Byron "Bam" Morris (1130) 20.00
382 Lake Dawson (1100) 10.00
384 Willie Jackson (1140) 10.00
385 Perry Klein (1000) 10.00
386 Ronnie Woolfork(360) 20.00
387 Doug Nussmeier (1150) 10.00
389 Glenn Foley (890) 20.00
390 Troy Aikman, Michael Irvin (Combo/345) 225.00
391 Steve Young, Jerry Rice (Combo/450) 275.00

1994 Pro Line Live MVP Sweepstakes

This 45-card insert set contains candidates to win the 1994 NFL MVP Award. Collectors who obtain one of the 2,083 cards of the eventual 1994 NFL MVP could redeem the card for a limited-edition uncut sheet of the 45 cards. Each card front has four player photos on it. Card backs are numbered with an "MVP" prefix.

		NM/M
Complete Set (45):		75.00
Common Player:		1.00
Minor Stars:		2.00
Inserted 1:72		
1	Jeff George	1.00
2	Andre Rison	2.00
3	Jim Kelly	2.00
4	Thurman Thomas	2.00
5	Troy Aikman	8.00
6	Emmitt Smith	10.00
7	Michael Irvin	2.00
8	John Elway	8.00
9	Brett Favre	10.00
10	Sterling Sharpe	2.00
11	Barry Sanders	8.00
12	Scott Mitchell	1.00
13	Gary Brown	1.00
14	Warren Moon	2.00
15	Marcus Allen	2.00
16	Joe Montana	10.00
17	Tim Brown	2.00
18	Jeff Hostetler	1.00
19	Dan Marino	10.00
20	Terry Kirby	1.00
21	Terry Allen	2.00
22	Drew Bledsoe	6.00
23	Chris Miller	1.00
24	Jerome Bettis	2.00
25	Derek Brown	1.00
26	Rodney Hampton	1.00
27	Phil Simms	1.00
28	Randall Cunningham	2.00
29	Barry Foster	1.00
30	Neil O'Donnell	1.00
31	Boomer Esiason	1.00
32	Johnny Johnson	1.00
33	Garrison Hearst	4.00
34	Ron Moore	1.00
35	Natrone Means	2.00
36	Steve Young	8.00
37	Ricky Watters	2.00
38	Jerry Rice	10.00
39	Rick Mirer	2.00
40	Chris Warren	1.00
41	Reggie Brooks	1.00
42	Marshall Faulk	7.00
43	Heath Shuler	2.00
44	Trent Dilfer	4.00
45	Field Card	1.00

1994 Pro Line Live Spotlight

The chromium cards have the player's name and the Spotlight logo inside a border on the left side of the card. The Classic Pro Line logo is in the upper left. The cards were seeded one per 16-card pack. The card backs, numbered in the lower left with a prefix of "PB," have the player's name, position, team and bio inside a stripe on the left side. A photo is anchored on the right side of the card, with his stats printed toward the bottom.

		NM/M
Complete Set (25):		25.00
Common Player:		.25
Minor Stars:		.50
1	Trent Dilfer	1.00
2	Heath Shuler	.50
3	Marshall Faulk	2.00
4	Troy Aikman	1.50
5	Emmitt Smith	2.00
6	Thurman Thomas	.50
7	Andre Rison	.50
8	Jerry Rice	1.50
9	Sterling Sharpe	.50
10	Brett Favre	3.00
11	Steve Young	1.00
12	Drew Bledsoe	1.50
13	Rick Mirer	.50
14	Barry Sanders	3.00
15	Joe Montana	2.00
16	Jerome Bettis	.50
17	Ricky Watters	.50
18	Rodney Hampton	.25
19	Tim Brown	.50
20	Reggie Brooks	.25
21	Natrone Means	.50
22	Marcus Allen	.50
23	Gary Brown	.25
24	Barry Foster	.25
25	Dan Marino	2.00

1995 Pro Line Previews

These five cards preview the design of Classic's micro-lined insert cards from its 1995 NFL Pro Line set. The Game Breakers, seeded one per box of 1995 Classic NFL Rookies product, feature players who have the ability to change the course of a game at any moment. The insert set logo is in the lower left corner; the Classic Pro Line brand logo is in the upper left corner. The player's name and position are in a black band at the bottom. The card back is numbered using a "GP" prefix.

		NM/M
Complete Set (5):		20.00
Common Player:		2.00
1	Dan Marino	10.00
2	Natrone Means	2.00
3	Joe Montana	8.00
4	Barry Sanders	8.00
5	Deion Sanders	4.00

1995 Pro Line Previews Phone Cards $2

These four cards were random inserts in 1995 Classic Basketball Rookies packs, one per two boxes of the product. The cards preview 1995 Classic Pro Line Series II $2 phone cards.

		NM/M
Complete Set (4):		10.00
Common Player:		2.00
1	Troy Aikman	4.00
2	Drew Bledsoe	4.00
3	Ki-Jana Carter	2.00
4	Marshall Faulk	3.00

1995 Pro Line Previews Phone Cards $5

These four cards were random inserts in 1995 Classic Basketball Rookies packs, seeded one per case of the product. The cards preview the 1995 Classic NFL Pro Line Series II $5 phone cards.

		NM/M
Complete Set (4):		12.00
Common Player:		3.00
1	Troy Aikman	5.00
2	Drew Bledsoe	5.00
3	Ki-Jana Carter	2.00
4	Marshall Faulk	4.00

1995 Pro Line

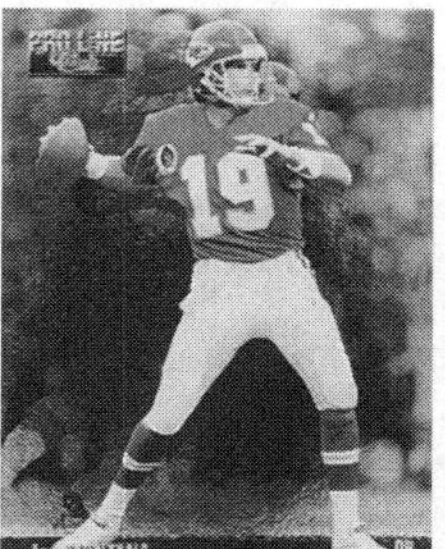

Only in Classic's 1995 NFL Pro Line will collectors find cards autographed by some of the NFL's marquee players, including Steve Young, Emmitt Smith and Drew Bledsoe. The complete Pro Line series has 400 cards from all 30 NFL teams, including the expansion Jacksonville Jaguars and Carolina Panthers. Forty rookies, including the first 32 selected in the draft, are also included in the set. Each card, which has 29 percent thicker stock than before, has a full-bleed color action photo on the front. The player's name is in the lower left corner; the player's team is in a bar along the bottom, with his position above the bar. The Pro Line logo is in the upper left corner. The card back has a color photo on one side, with a recap of the previous season, biographical information and stats on the other. The card number is in the upper left corner in a box. As a bonus, more than 100 top NFL players personally signed a maximum of 2,500 cards each. One autographed card was guaranteed to be in every box. Pro Line also continued its Hot Boxes program. Each pack in a Hot Box contains 40 percent inserts. Hot Boxes were randomly inserted one in every 10 cases. Exclusive to Hot Boxes are 10 Team Record Breaker acetate cards sequentially numbered to 350. Other insert sets include Pro Line Impact, MVP Interactive cards, Game Breaker cards, Pro Line Silver cards and Basketball Rookies Preview cards. A parallel insert set of the regular cards printed on silver foil board was also produced; these cards were included one per pack.

		NM/M
Complete Set (400):		20.00
Common Player:		.05
Minor Stars:		.10
Comp. Silver Set (400):		80.00
Silver Cards:		2X-4X
Comp. Print. Proof (400):		700.00
Print. Proof Cards:		3X-5X
Comp. PP Silver Set (400):		1,400
PP Silver Cards:		2X PP
Series 1 Pack (10):		1.50
Series 1 Wax Box (36):		45.00
Series 2 Pack (6):		3.50
Series 2 Wax Box (18):		55.00
1	Garrison Hearst	.10
2	Anthony Miller	.05
3	Brett Favre	1.50
4	Jessie Hester	.05
5	Mike Fox	.05
6	*Jeff Blake*	1.00
7	J.J. Birden	.05
8	Greg Jackson	.05
9	Leon Lett	.05
10	Bruce Matthews	.05
11	Andre Reed	.05
12	Joe Montana	1.00
13	Craig Heyward	.05
14	Henry Ellard	.05
15	Chris Spielman	.05
16	Tony Woods	.05
17	Carl Banks	.05
18	*Eric Zeier*	.75
19	Michael Brooks	.05
20	Kevin Ross	.05
21	Qadry Ismail	.05
22	Mel Gray	.05
23	Ty Law	.15
24	Mark Collins	.05
25	Neil O'Donnell	.10
26	Ellis Johnson	.15
27	Rick Mirer	.40
28	Fred Barnett	.05
29	*Mike Mamula*	.10
30	Jim Jeffcoat	.05
31	Reggie Cobb	.05
32	Mark Carrier	.05
33	Darnay Scott	.40
34	Michael Jackson	.05
35	Terrell Buckley	.05
36	Nolan Harrison	.05
37	Thurman Thomas	.20
38	Anthony Smith	.05
39	Phillippi Sparks	.05
40	Cornelius Bennett	.05
41	Robert Young	.05
42	Pierce Holt	.05
43	Greg Lloyd	.05
44	*Chad May*	.10
45	Darrien Gordon	.05
46	Bryan Cox	.05
47	Junior Seau	.10
48	Al Smith	.05
49	Chris Slade	.05
50	Hardy Nickerson	.05
51	Brad Baxter	.05
52	Darryl Lewis	.05
53	Bryant Young	.05
54	Chris Warren	.05
55	Darion Conner	.05
56	Thomas Everett	.05
57	Charles Haley	.05
58	Chris Mims	.05
59	Sean Jones	.05
60	*Tamarick Vanover*	1.00
61	Daryl Johnston	.05
62	*Rashaan Salaam*	1.00
63	James Hasty	.05
64	Dante Jones	.05
65	Darren Perry	.05
66	Troy Drayton	.05
67	Mark Fields	.10
68	Brian Williams	.10
69	Steve Bono	.15
70	Eric Allen	.05
71	Chris Zorich	.05
72	Dave Brown	.05
73	Ken Norton	.05
74	Wayne Martin	.05
75	Mo Lewis	.05
76	Johnny Mitchell	.05
77	Todd Lyght	.05
78	Erric Pegram	.05
79	Kevin Greene	.05
80	Randal Hill	.05
81	Brett Perriman	.05
82	Mike Sherrard	.05
83	Curtis Conway	.05
84	Mark Tuinei	.05
85	Mark Seay	.05
86	Randy Baldwin	.05
87	Ricky Ervins	.05
88	Chester McGlockton	.05
89	*Tyrone Wheatley*	.50
90	Micheal Barrow	.05
91	Kenneth Davis	.05
92	*Napoleon Kaufman*	2.00
93	Webster Slaughter	.05
94	Darren Woodson	.05
95	Pete Stoyanovich	.05
96	Jimmie Jones	.05
97	Craig Erickson	.05
98	*Michael Westbrook*	1.00
99	*Steve McNair*	2.50
100	Errict Rhett	.50
101	Devin Bush	.15
102	Dewayne Washington	.05
103	Bart Oates	.05
104	Aaron Pierce	.05
105	*Warren Sapp*	.50
106	Eric Green	.05
107	Glyn Milburn	.05
108	Johnny Johnson	.05
109	Marshall Faulk	.75
110	William Thomas	.05
111	George Koonce	.05
112	Dana Stubblefield	.05
113	Steve Tovar	.05
114	Steve Israel	.05
115	Brent Williams	.05
116	Shane Conlan	.05
117	Winston Moss	.05
118	Nate Newton	.05
119	Michael Irvin	.20
120	Jeff Lageman	.05
121	*Ki-Jana Carter*	2.00
122	Dan Marino	1.50
123	Tony Casillas	.05
124	*Kevin Carter*	.20
125	Warren Moon	.10
126	Byron Morris	.40
127	Ben Coates	.10
128	Michael Bankston	.05
129	Anthony Parker	.05
130	LeRoy Butler	.05
131	Tony Bennett	.05
132	Alvin Harper	.05
133	Tim Brown	.10
134	Tom Carter	.05
135	Lorenzo White	.05
136	Shane Dronett	.05
137	John Elliott	.05
138	Korey Stringer	.05
139	Jerry Rice	.50
140	*Sherman Williams*	.10
141	Kevin Turner	.05
142	Randall Cunningham	.10
143	Vinny Testaverde	.05
144	Tim Bowens	.05
145	Russell Maryland	.05
146	Chris Miller	.05
147	Vince Buck	.05
148	Willie Clay	.05
149	Jeff Graham	.05
150	Shannon Sharpe	.10
151	Carnell Lake	.05
152	*Mark Bruener*	.30
153	James Washington	.05
154	Pepper Johnson	.05
155	Bert Emanuel	.20
156	Mark Stepnoski	.05
157	Robert Jones	.05
158	Cris Dishman	.05
159	Henry Jones	.05
160	Henry Thomas	.05
161	John L. Williams	.05
162	Joe Cain	.05
163	Mike Johnson	.05
164	Merton Hanks	.05
165	Deion Sanders	.35
166	William Floyd	.25
167	Leroy Thompson	.05
168	Ray Childress	.05
169	Donnell Woolford	.05
170	Tony Siragusa	.05
171	Chad Brown	.05
172	Stanley Richard	.05
173	*Rob Johnson*	2.00
174	Derrick Brooks	.10
175	Drew Bledsoe	.75
176	Maurice Hurst	.05
177	Ricky Watters	.10
178	Myron Guyton	.05
179	Ricky Proehl	.05
180	Haywood Jeffires	.05
181	Michael Strahan	.05
182	Charles Wilson	.05
183	Mark Carrier	.05
184	*James Stewart*	1.25
185	Andy Harmon	.05
186	Ronnie Lott	.05
187	Clay Matthews	.05
188	John Carney	.05
189	Andre Rison	.10
190	Aeneas Williams	.05
191	Alexander Wright	.05
192	Desmond Howard	.05
193	Herman Moore	.10
194	Alfred Williams	.05
195	Tyrone Poole	.10
196	Darren Mickell	.05
197	Steve Young	.50
198	Roman Phifer	.05
199	Darrell Green	.05
200	Terry Wooden	.05
201	Chris Calloway	.05
202	Lewis Tillman	.05
203	Cris Carter	.10
204	Jim Everett	.05
205	Adrian Murrell	.05
206	Barry Sanders	1.25
207	Mario Bates	.25
208	Shawn Lee	.05
209	Charles Mincy	.05
210	*Kerry Collins*	2.00
211	Steve Walsh	.05
212	Chris Chandler	.05
213	Bennie Blades	.05
214	Kevin Williams	.05
215	Jim Kelly	.10
216	Marion Butts	.05
217	Jay Novacek	.05
218	Shawn Jefferson	.05
219	O.J. McDuffie	.05
220	Ray Seals	.05
221	Arthur Marshall	.05
222	Karl Mecklenburg	.05
223	Terance Mathis	.05
224	David Klinger	.05
225	Rod Woodson	.05
226	Quentin Coryatt	.05
227	Leroy Hoard	.05
228	Brian Blades	.05
229	Rob Moore	.05
230	Boomer Esiason	.05
231	Dave Krieg	.05
232	Sterling Sharpe	.10
233	Marcus Allen	.10
234	John Randle	.05
235	Craig Powell	.05
236	John Elway	.25
237	Mark Ingram	.05
238	Cortez Kennedy	.05
239	Brent Jones	.05
240	Ken Harvey	.05
241	Keenan McCardell	.05
242	Dan Wilkinson	.05
243	Don Beebe	.05
244	Jack Del Rio	.05
245	Byron Evans	.05
246	Ron Moore	.05
247	Edgar Bennett	.05
248	William Fuller	.05
249	James Williams	.05
250	Neil Smith	.05
251	Sam Mills	.05
252	Willie McGinest	.05
253	Howard Cross	.05
254	Troy Aikman	.60
255	Herschel Walker	.05
256	Dale Carter	.05
257	Sean Dawkins	.15
258	Greg Hill	.25
259	Stan Humphries	.10
260	Erik Kramer	.05
261	Leslie O'Neal	.05
262	Trezelle Jenkins	.10
263	Antonio Langham	.05
264	Bryce Paup	.05
265	Jake Reed	.05
266	Richmond Webb	.05
267	Eric Davis	.05
268	Mark McMillian	.05
269	*John Walsh*	.25
270	Irving Fryar	.05
271	Raghib Ismail	.05
272	Phil Hansen	.05
273	*J.J. Stokes*	1.00
274	*Craig Newsome*	.10
275	Leonard Russell	.05
276	Derrick Deese	.05
277	Broderick Thomas	.05
278	Bobby Houston	.05
279	Lamar Lathon	.05
280	Eugene Robinson	.05
281	Dan Saleaumua	.05
282	*Kyle Brady*	.10
283	John Taylor	.05
284	*Tony Boselli*	.10
285	Seth Joyner	.05
286	Steve Beuerlein	.05
287	Sam Adams	.05
288	Frank Reich	.05
289	Patrick Hunter	.05
290	Sean Gilbert	.05
291	Dermontti Dawson	.05
292	Shaun Gayle	.05
293	Vincent Brown	.05
294	Terry Kirby	.05
295	Courtney Hawkins	.05
296	Carl Pickens	.05
297	Luther Elliss	.10
298	Steve Atwater	.05
299	James Francis	.05
300	Rob Burnett	.05
301	Keith Hamilton	.05
302	Rob Fredrickson	.05
303	Jerome Bettis	.30
304	Emmitt Smith	1.50
305	Clyde Simmons	.05
306	Reggie White	.10
307	Rodney Hampton	.05
308	Steve Emtman	.05
309	*Hugh Douglas*	.10
310	Bernie Parmalee	.20
311	Trent Dilfer	.40
312	Willie Anderson	.05
313	Heath Shuler	.75
314	Rod Smith	.05
315	*Ray Zellars*	.10
316	Robert Brooks	.05
317	Lee Woodall	.05
318	Robert Porcher	.05
319	*Todd Collins*	.10
320	Willie Roaf	.05
321	Eric Williams	.05
322	Steve Wisniewski	.05
323	Derrick Alexander	.20
324	Frank Warren	.05
325	Kelvin Pritchett	.05
326	Dennis Gibson	.05
327	Jason Belser	.05
328	Vincent Brisby	.05
329	Calvin Williams	.05
330	Derek Brown	.05
331	Blake Brockermeyer	.05
332	Jeff Herrod	.05
333	Darryl Williams	.05
334	Aaron Glenn	.05
335	Eric Metcalf	.05
336	Billy Milner	.05
337	Terry McDaniel	.05

338 Trace Armstrong .05
339 *Yancey Thigpen* 1.00
340 Jackie Harris .05
341 Jeff George .10
342 Darryl Talley .05
343 Marcus Robertson .05
344 Robert Massey .05
345 Jessie Tuggle .05
346 Scott Mitchell .05
347 Harvey Williams .05
348 *Jack Jackson* .10
349 Brian Mitchell .05
350 Lawrence Dawsey .05
351 Erik Howard .05
352 Quinn Early .05
353 Terry Allen .05
354 Simon Fletcher .05
355 Eric Turner .05
356 Natrone Means .40
357 *Frank Sanders* .20
358 Michael Timpson .05
359 Michael Haynes .05
360 Ruben Brown .05
361 Troy Vincent .05
362 Floyd Turner .05
363 Larry Centers .05
364 Eric Swann .05
365 Albert Lewis .05
366 Barry Foster .05
367 Michael Dean Perry .05
368 Jumpy Geathers .05
369 *Kordell Stewart* 4.00
370 Chuck Smith .05
371 Lake Dawson .20
372 Terry Hoage .05
373 Jeff Cross .05
374 Tony McGee .05
375 Eric Curry .05
376 Harold Green .05
377 Eric Hill .05
378 Ray Buchanan .05
379 Willie Davis .05
380 *Chris Jones* .20
381 Martin Mayhew .05
382 Anthony Pleasant .05
383 *Joey Galloway* 2.00
384 Anthony Morgan .05
385 Harlon Barnett .05
386 Bruce Smith .05
387 Jeff Hostetler .05
388 Randall McDaniel .05
389 David Meggett .05
390 Bill Romanowski .05
391 Gary Brown .05
392 Charles Johnson .20
393 Chris Doleman .05
394 Tony Martin .05
395 Raymont Harris .15
396 John Copeland .05
397 Emmitt Smith Checklist #1 .40
398 Steve Young Checklist #2 .25
399 Marshall Faulk Checklist #3 .40
400 Ki-Jana Carter Checklist #4 .40

1995 Pro Line Printer's Proofs

Packaged two per hobby box, this set is a parallel to the base set. "Printer's Proof" is printed near the bottom of the card front. Overall, 400 of each card were printed.

Common Player: 1.25
Veteran Stars: 3X-5X
Young Stars: 3X-5X
RCs: 2X-4X

1995 Pro Line Printer's Proof Silver

Randomly seeded one per hobby box, this set is a parallel to the 400-card base set. "Printer's Proof" is printed on the front over silver foil. Overall, 175 of each card were produced.

NM/M
Common Player: 2.50
Semistars 4.00
Veteran Stars: 2X
Young Stars: 2X
RCs: 2X

1995 Pro Line Silver

Randomly seeded one per hobby and retail pack, this is a 400-card parallel to the base set. A silver-foil background is the distinguishing feature of this set.

NM/M
Complete Set (400): 80.00
Common Player: .20
Veteran Stars: 2X-4X
Young Stars: 1.5X-3X
RCs: 2X

1995 Pro Line Autographs

Randomly seeded one per box, the 128-card set was signed by NFL players, who signed less than 2,500 cards each. The card fronts have the identical design to the base cards, while the backs offer congratulations to the card holder for picking up an autographed card.

NM/M
Complete Set (128): 2,200
Common Player: 10.00
1 Garrison Hearst (1460) 25.00
2 Anthony Miller (2385) 12.00
5 Mike Fox (1445) 10.00
6 Jeff Blake (1200) 40.00
7 J.J. Birden (775) 12.00
9 Leon Lett (1550) 12.00
11 Andre Reed (1440) 12.00
13A Craig Heyward (1200) 12.00
13B Craig Heyward (265AP) 12.00
14 Henry Ellard (1440) 12.00
18 Eric Zeier (500) 30.00
21 Qadry Ismail (1170) 12.00
23 Ty Law (1460) 10.00
24 Mark Collins (1430) 10.00
29 Mike Mamula (1250) 10.00
34 Michael Jackson (1200) 12.00
40A Cornelius Bennett (1200) 12.00
40B Cornelius Bennett (255AP) 12.00
42 Pierce Holt (1440) 10.00
44A Chad May (1180) 12.00
44B Chad May (2410AP) 12.00
45 Darrien Gordon (2400) 10.00
48 Al Smith (1360) 10.00
49A Chris Slade (1100) 10.00
49B Chris Slade (2417AP) 10.00
57 Charles Haley (1420) 12.00
59 Sean Jones (2385) 12.00
60 Tamarick Vanover (1155) 30.00
62 Rashaan Salaam (1320) 30.00
66 Troy Drayton (1375) 10.00
68A Brian Williams (1175) 10.00
68B Brian Williams (2670AP) 10.00
68C Brian Williams (865AP) 10.00
70A Eric Allen (1225) 10.00
70B Eric Allen (2398AP) 10.00
70C Eric Allen (745AP) 10.00
81A Brett Perriman (1380) 12.00
81B Brett Perriman (935) 12.00
82 Mike Sherrard (1450) 12.00
83 Curtis Conway (1200) 15.00
86A Randy Baldwin (1435) 10.00
86B Randy Baldwin (2405AP) 10.00
86C Randy Baldwin (760AP) 10.00
88 Chester McGlockton (1280) 12.00
97A Craig Erickson (630) 12.00
97B Craig Erickson (890AP) 12.00
99 Steve McNair (3490) 40.00
100 Errict Rhett (1400) 45.00
106 Eric Green (1460) 12.00
109 Marshall Faulk (1030) 75.00
114A Steve Israel (1200) 10.00
114B Steve Israel (2413AP) 10.00
114C Steve Israel (750AP) 10.00
119 Michael Irvin (1490) 15.00
126 Byron "Bam" Morris (1430) 12.00
127 Ben Coates (1175) 15.00
131 Tony Bennett (1475) 12.00
133 Tim Brown (2410) 15.00
137 John Elliott (2380) 10.00
140 Sherman Williams (1460) 12.00
142 Randall Cunningham (470) 30.00
143 Vinny Testaverde (1020) 12.00
145 Russell Maryland (1250) 12.00
149 Jeff Graham (1465) 12.00
155 Bert Emanuel (1445) 15.00
156 Mark Stepnoski (1500) 10.00
160 Henry Thomas (1420) 10.00
168A Ray Childress (1200) 10.00
168B Ray Childress (235AP) 10.00
173A Rob Johnson (2815) 15.00
173B Rob Johnson (500) 15.00
174 Derrick Brooks (1470) 12.00
175 Drew Bledsoe (515) 125.00
179 Ricky Proehl (1475) 10.00
180 Haywood Jeffires (1470) 12.00
185 Andy Harmon (1200) 10.00
186 Ronnie Lott (1900) 15.00
187 Clay Matthews (2385) 12.00
193 Herman Moore (2070) 20.00
197 Steve Young (500) 100.00
198 Roman Phifer (2395) 10.00
202 Lewis Tillman (1170) 12.00
207 Mario Bates (1480) 15.00
210 Kerry Collins (3300) 45.00
211A Steve Walsh (1185) 12.00
211B Steve Walsh (1015AP) 12.00
215 Jim Kelly (470) 40.00
217 Jay Novacek (1195) 12.00
218A Shawn Jefferson (1200) 12.00
218B Shawn Jefferson (240AP) 12.00
221A Arthur Marshall (1165) 10.00
221B Arthur Marshall (2400AP) 10.00
221C Arthur Marshall (870AP) 10.00
226 Quentin Coryatt (1400) 12.00
228 Brian Blades (1465) 12.00
230 Boomer Esiason (1700) 12.00
231 Dave Krieg (1470) 12.00
234A John Randle (1170) 12.00
234B John Randle (2400AP) 12.00
234C John Randle (757AP) 12.00
238 Cortez Kennedy (1380) 12.00
241A Keenan McCardell (1235) 12.00
241B Keenan McCardell (2403AP) 12.00
243A Don Beebe (1200) 12.00
243B Don Beebe (275AP) 12.00
244A Jack Del Rio (1480) 10.00
244B Jack Del Rio (930AP) 10.00
247 Edgar Bennett (1475) 12.00
250 Neil Smith (1465) 12.00
251 Sam Mills (1470) 12.00
252A Willie McGinest (1160) 12.00
252B Willie McGinest (2407AP) 12.00
252C Willie McGinest (754AP) 12.00
254 Troy Aikman (500) 125.00
256 Dale Carter (1400) 12.00
258 Greg Hill (1455) 12.00
262 Trezelle Jenkins (1470) 10.00
263A Antonio Langham (1200) 10.00
263B Antonio Langham (1200) 10.00
265 Jake Reed (1470) 12.00
268A Mark McMillian (1175) 10.00
268B Mark McMillian (2400AP) 10.00
268C Mark McMillian (1175) 10.00
269 John Walsh (3340) 12.00
270 Irving Fryar (1500) 12.00
273 J.J. Stokes (1435) 35.00
276A Derrick Deese (1200) 10.00
276B Derrick Deese (2375AP) 10.00
276C Derrick Deese (735AP) 10.00
285 Seth Joyner (1480) 10.00
286 Steve Beuerlein (1465) 12.00
289 Patrick Hunter (2375) 10.00
292A Shaun Gayle 10.00
292B Shaun Gayle (265AP) 10.00
294 Terry Kirby (1450) 12.00
295 Courtney Hawkins (1445) 12.00
297 Luther Elliss (1470) 12.00
304 Emmitt Smith (500) 200.00
305 Clyde Simmons (735) 12.00
307 Rodney Hampton (1120) 15.00
308 Steve Emtman (2365) 10.00
311A Trent Dilfer (2010) 15.00
311B Trent Dilfer (306AP) 15.00
312 Flipper Anderson (1140) 12.00
313A Heath Shuler (2000) 25.00
313B Heath Shuler (366AP) 35.00
320A Willie Roaf (1200) 12.00
320B Willie Roaf (245AP) 12.00
329 Calvin Williams (1200) 12.00
331A Blake Brockermeyer (1445) 12.00
331B Blake Brockermeyer (2315AP) 12.00
337 Terry McDaniel (2340) 10.00
341 Jeff George (1295) 15.00
345A Jessie Tuggle (1200) 10.00
345B Jessie Tuggle (195AP) 10.00
348 Jack Jackson (1475) 12.00
352 Quinn Early (1200) 12.00
356 Natrone Means (1058) 15.00
359 Michael Haynes (1180) 12.00
361 Troy Vincent (1490) 10.00
366 Barry Foster (1455) 12.00
367A Michael Dean Perry (1200) 12.00
367B Michael Dean Perry (295AP) 12.00
374 Tony McGee (1385) 12.00
379 Willie Davis (1500) 12.00
383 Joey Galloway (1445) 45.00
390 Bill Romanowski (1450) 10.00

1995 Pro Line Bonus Card Jumbos

This complete set of 14 oversized cards was issued in four series. Cards 1-3 were inserted in 1995 Classic NFL Rookies cases (one per hobby case); cards 4-8 were inserted in 1995 Classic Pro Line cases (one per case); cards 9-11 were inserted in 1995 Classic NFL Pro Line Series II cases (one per case); cards 13-15 were inserted in 1996 Classic NFL Experience (one per case). Cards are sequentially numbered up to 2,500 and measure 4-3/4" x 2-1/2". There was no #12 card made.

NM/M
Complete Set (14): 35.00
Comp. Series 1 (3): 7.00
Comp. Series 2 (5): 15.00
Comp. Series 3 (3): 5.00
Comp. Series 4 (3): 12.00
Common Player: 1.00
1 Ki-Jana Carter 1.00
2 Steve McNair 5.00
3 Kerry Collins 3.00
4 Deion Sanders 3.00
5 Steve Young 4.00
6 Emmitt Smith 6.00
7 Natrone Means 1.00
8 Drew Bledsoe 5.00
9 Troy Aikman 6.00
10 Marshall Faulk 1.00
11 J.J. Stokes 1.00
13 Emmitt Smith 10.00
14 Rashaan Salaam 1.00

1995 Pro Line Field Generals

These 10 insert cards were randomly included one per every 60 packs of 1995 Classic NFL Pro Line Series II product. The acetate cards, featuring some of the NFL's leaders on the field, are sequentially numbered to 1,700. Card backs are numbered using a "G" prefix.

NM/M
Complete Set (10): 35.00
Common Player: 2.00
1 Marshall Faulk 4.00
2 Emmitt Smith 10.00
3 Steve Young 5.00
4 Ki-Jana Carter 2.00
5 Rashaan Salaam 2.00
6 Dan Marino 12.00
7 J.J. Stokes 2.00
8 Drew Bledsoe 8.00
9 Brett Favre 12.00
10 Barry Sanders 10.00

1995 Pro Line Game of the Week

The 60-card interactive game set showcased two teams in a key game from the 1995 season. "H" or "V" prefixes are listed on the back and stand for home or visitor. A set of 30 NFL Pro Line silver-foil winning cards with the final score printed on the card was given to the first 1,000 collectors who redeemed 21-30 different game cards. In addition, 2,500 collectors who redeemed 10-20 winning game cards received a set of 30 Pro Line winning cards with the score stamped on them. Those who redeemed 30 winning cards were entered into a drawing for a Steve Young or Jerry Rice game-used jersey.

NM/M
Complete Set (60): 25.00
Common Player: .40
1 Barry Sanders, Reggie White 1.50
2 Jeff Hostetler, John Elway .75
3 Michael Westbrook, Ricky Watters .75
4 Jim Kelly, Mo Lewis .60
5 Marshall Faulk, Jerome Bettis 1.00
6 Natrone Means, Bam Morris .60
7 Seth Joyner, Michael Irvin .60
8 Errict Rhett, Heath Shuler 1.00
9 Junior Seau, Randall Cunningham .60
10 Drew Bledsoe, Steve Young 1.00
11 Dave Krieg, Kerry Collins 1.50
12 Steve Beuerlein, Alvin Harper .40
13 Ben Coates, Troy Vincent .60
14 Jerry Rice, Michael Irvin 1.50
15 Rodney Hampton, Cortez Kennedy .60
16 Ray Childress, Leroy Hoard .40
17 Thurman Thomas, Irving Fryar .60
18 Andre Rison, Ki-Jana Carter .75
19 Dan Marino, Boomer Esiason 2.00
20 Brett Favre, Warren Moon 2.00
21 Anthony Miller, Tim Brown .40
22 Chris Warren, Steve Bono .60
23 Shannon Sharpe, Neil Smith .40
24 John Randle, Dana Stubblefield .40
25 Jim Everett, Terance Mathis .40
26 Troy Aikman, Mike Mamula 1.50
27 Trent Dilfer, Cris Carter .60
28 Steve Walsh, Scott Mitchell .40
29 Greg Lloyd, Vinny Testaverde .60
30 Jeff George, Garrison Hearst .60

1995 Pro Line Game Breakers

These 1995 Classic NFL Pro Line insert cards use an attention-grabbing micro-lined foil-board for the cards. The cards, featuring players who can break a game open at any moment, were randomly seeded one per box of the football product. Cards are numbered using a "GB" prefix. Printer's Proof cards were also made for these inserts.

NM/M
Complete Set (30): 25.00
Common Player: .50
Minor Stars: 1.00
Comp. Prin. Proof Set (30): 800.00
Printer's Proofs: 2X-4X
1 Troy Aikman 4.00
2 Drew Bledsoe 4.00
3 Tim Brown 2.00
4 Cris Carter 1.00
5 Ki-Jana Carter 1.00
6 Kerry Collins 2.00
7 John Elway 5.00
8 Marshall Faulk 2.00
9 Brett Favre 6.00
10 Garrison Hearst 1.00
11 Michael Irvin 1.00
12 Jim Kelly 1.00
13 Dan Marino 6.00
14 Natrone Means 1.00
15 Eric Metcalf .50
16 J.J. Stokes 1.00
17 Carl Pickens .50
18 Jerry Rice 5.00
19 Andre Rison 1.00
20 Barry Sanders 5.00
21 Deion Sanders 2.00
22 Junior Seau 1.00
23 Emmitt Smith 5.00
24 Thurman Thomas 1.00
25 Ricky Watters 1.00
26 Reggie White 1.00
27 Rod Woodson .50
28 Steve Young 4.00
29 Rashaan Salaam 1.00
30 Michael Westbrook 1.00

1995 Pro Line Grand Gainers

The 30-card retail-only set has an action photo, with white mesh in the background on the top half of the card front, while the bottom half included the photo background. The player's name and position are printed in a box in the lower right, with the Grand Gainers' logo in the lower left. The backs include an action photo of the player, his name, position and write-up on the left. The player's yardage is printed inside a stripe on the right side of the card back, which are numbered with a "G" prefix.

NM/M
Complete Set (30): 10.00
Common Player: .20
1 Barry Sanders 2.00
2 Emmitt Smith 2.00
3 Natrone Means .60
4 Marshall Faulk 1.00
5 Errict Rhett .40
6 Jerry Rice 1.50
7 Tim Brown .60
8 Cris Carter .60
9 Irving Fryar .20
10 Ben Coates .20
11 Fred Barnett .20
12 Andre Rison .20
13 Drew Bledsoe 1.00
14 Dan Marino 2.00
15 Warren Moon .60
16 Steve Young 1.00
17 Brett Favre 3.00
18 John Elway 1.00
19 Randall Cunningham .20
20 Stan Humphries .60
21 Jim Kelly .60
22 Ki-Jana Carter .40
23 Rodney Hampton .60
24 Tyrone Wheatley .60
25 J.J. Stokes .40
26 Michael Irvin .20
27 Herman Moore .75
28 Kerry Collins 1.00
29 Steve McNair 1.00
30 Rob Johnson .60

1995 Pro Line Images Previews

This five-card preview of the 1995 Images series was inserted one per 18 packs of Series Two.

NM/M
Complete Set (5): 15.00
Common Player: 2.00
1 Emmitt Smith 6.00
2 Steve Young 4.00
3 Drew Bledsoe 4.00
4 Kerry Collins 2.00
5 Marshall Faulk 4.00

1995 Pro Line Impact

These 30 exclusive cards of Impact NFL superstars are each sequentially numbered to only 4,500. The horizontal cards were seeded at a rate of one per every box of 1995 Classic Pro Line football product. A rarer version, Pro Line Golden Impact was also created. These cards, each sequentially numbered to 1,750, were seeded one per 90 packs.

NM/M
Complete Set (30): 25.00
Common Player: .50
Minor Stars: 1.00
Comp. Golden Set (30): 375.00
Gold Cards: 2X-4X
1 Jim Kelly 1.00
2 Thurman Thomas 1.00
3 Troy Aikman 4.00
4 Michael Irvin 2.00
5 Emmitt Smith 5.00
6 John Elway 4.00
7 Barry Sanders 5.00
8 Brett Favre 6.00
9 Reggie White 1.00
10 Marshall Faulk 2.00
11 Ki-Jana Carter 1.00
12 Tim Brown 2.00
13 Jeff Hostetler .50
14 Dan Marino 6.00
15 Drew Bledsoe 4.00
16 Ben Coates .50
17 Rodney Hampton .50
18 Randall Cunningham 1.00
19 Ricky Watters 1.00
20 Bam Morris 1.00
21 Natrone Means 1.00
22 Junior Seau 1.00
23 Jerry Rice 5.00
24 Steve Young 4.00
25 William Floyd 1.00
26 Rick Mirer 1.00
27 Chris Warren .50
28 Jerome Bettis 1.00
29 Alvin Harper 1.00
30 Heath Shuler 1.00

1995 Pro Line MVP Redemption

These 1995 Classic NFL Pro Line inserts feature foil-board cards of the top 34 candidates for the Associated Press' 1995 Offensive MVP Award, plus one field card. Cards which depicted the MVP winner were winners and were redeemable for one of the following prizes: winner cards stamped 1 of 4,000 were redeemable for a prepaid $50 phone card of the player; winner cards hand-numbered to 200 were redeemable for a $100 phone card of the player; the winner card hand-numbered "1/200" was redeemable for the $100 phone card and a complete 1995 Pro Line autographed set of more than 100 cards. The MVP Interactive cards were seeded an average of one per two boxes.

NM/M
Complete Set (35): 40.00
Common Player: .50
1 Garrison Hearst 1.00
2 Terance Mathis .50
3 Jim Kelly 1.00
4 Thurman Thomas 1.00
5 Kerry Collins 2.00
6 Rashaan Salaam .50
7 Ki-Jana Carter 1.00
8 Andre Rison .50

9 Troy Aikman 4.00
10 Michael Irvin .50
11 Emmitt Smith 5.00
12 John Elway 4.00
13 Barry Sanders 4.00
14 Brett Favre 5.00
15 Marshall Faulk 2.00
16 Marcus Allen .50
17 Jeff Hostetler .50
18 Dan Marino 5.00
19 Cris Carter .50
20 Warren Moon 1.00
21 Drew Bledsoe 4.00
22 Ben Coates .50
23 Rodney Hampton .50
24 Boomer Esiason .50
25 Ricky Watters 1.00
26 Barry Foster .50
27 Natrone Means .50
28 Rick Mirer .50
29 Chris Warren .50
30 Jerry Rice 4.00
31 Steve Young 3.00
32 Jerome Bettis 1.00
33 Errict Rhett 1.00
34 Heath Shuler .50
35 Field Card 1.00

1995 Pro Line National Attention

Randomly seeded in Pro Line National boxes sold by dealers who had a booth at the National Convention in St. Louis, Mo., the 10-card set is numbered with a prefix of "NA".

NM/M
Complete Set (10): 25.00
Common Player: 1.00
1 Jerome Bettis 2.00
2 Sean Gilbert 1.00
3 Chris Miller 1.00
4 Troy Aikman 5.00
5 Kevin Carter 1.00
6 Marshall Faulk 4.00
7 Drew Bledsoe 5.00
8 Shane Conlan 1.00
9 Emmitt Smith 7.00
10 Steve Young 5.00

1995 Pro Line Phone Cards $1

Phone cards were randomly inserted into 1995 Classic NFL Series II packs at a ratio of one per pack, and at least three $2 cards and a $5 card per box. Printer's Proof versions were also made of these $1 cards. They are stamped with a printer's proof logo and are numbered 1 of 699. The proof cards were seeded at a ratio of one per 44 packs.

NM/M
Complete Set (30): 10.00
Common Player: .25
Artist Proofs Cards: 2X-4X
1 Kerry Collins .50
2 Barry Foster .25
3 Jeff Blake .25
4 Troy Aikman 1.00
5 Reggie White .25
6 Marshall Faulk 1.00
7 Steve Bono .25
8 Drew Bledsoe 1.00
9 Byron Morris .25
10 Rodney Hampton .25
11 Trent Dilfer .40
12 Errict Rhett .40
13 Heath Shuler .25
14 Mike Mamula .25
15 Ricky Watters .25
16 Stan Humphries .25
17 Natrone Means .25
18 William Floyd .25
19 Joey Galloway 1.00
20 Ki-Jana Carter .40
21 Andre Rison .25
22 Steve McNair 1.00
23 Napoleon Kaufman .25
24 Kyle Brady .25
25 Desmond Howard .25
26 Ben Coates .25
27 Eric Metcalf .25
28 Steve Beurlein .25
29 Deion Sanders .50
30 J.J. Stokes .40

A player's name in *italic* type indicates a rookie card.

1995 Pro Line Phone Cards $2

Phone cards were randomly inserted into 1995 Classic NFL Pro Line Series II packs at a ratio of one per pack, and at least three $2 cards and one $5 card in every box. Printer's proof versions were also made of these $2 cards. They are stamped with a printer's proof logo and are numbered 1 of 494. The proof cards are seeded at a ratio of one per 75 packs.

NM/M
Complete Set (25): 15.00
Common Player: .40
Artist Proofs Cards: 2X-4X
1 Troy Aikman 2.00
2 Marshall Faulk 1.00
3 Drew Bledsoe 1.00
4 Byron Morris .40
5 Rodney Hampton .40
6 Errict Rhett .40
7 Heath Shuler .40
8 Mike Mamula .40
9 Ricky Watters .40
10 Stan Humphries .40
11 Natrone Means .40
12 William Floyd .40
13 Kerry Collins .50
14 Barry Foster .40
15 Ki-Jana Carter .50
16 Andre Rison .40
17 Steve McNair 1.00
18 Kyle Brady .40
19 Deion Sanders 1.00
20 J.J. Stokes .50
21 Jeff Blake .50
22 Eric Metcalf .40
23 Steve Beuerlein .40
24 Eric Green .40
25 Steve Bono .40

1995 Pro Line Phone Cards $5

Phone cards were randomly inserted into 1995 Classic NFL Pro Line Series II packs at a ratio of one per pack, and at least three $2 cards and a $5 card in every box. Printer's proof versions were also made of these $5 cards. They are stamped with a printer's proof logo and are numbered 1 of 297. The proof cards were seeded at a ratio of one per 210 packs.

NM/M
Complete Set (15): 20.00
Common Player: .75
1 Marshall Faulk 3.00
2 Troy Aikman 4.00
3 Drew Bledsoe 4.00
4 Deion Sanders 1.00
5 Kerry Collins 1.00
6 Steve McNair 2.00
7 Kyle Brady .75
8 J.J. Stokes 1.00
9 Ki-Jana Carter 1.00
10 Emmitt Smith 4.00
11 William Floyd .75
12 Ricky Watters .75
13 Reggie White .75
14 Warren Sapp .75
15 Steve Young 2.00

1995 Pro Line Phone Cards $20

Phone cards were randomly inserted into 1995 Classic NFL Pro Line Series II packs at a ratio of one per pack, and at least three $2 cards and a $5 card in every box. The higher denominations were seeded at scarcer rates.

NM/M
Complete Set (5): 35.00
Common Player: 2.00
1 Steve Young 10.00
2 Drew Bledsoe 10.00
3 Marshall Faulk 10.00
4 Ki-Jana Carter 2.00
5 Kerry Collins 5.00

1995 Pro Line Phone Cards $100

One phone card is seeded in each pack of 1995 Classic Pro Line Series II packs; at least three $2 cards and a $5 card are in every box. These $100 phone cards, featuring four NFL stars and a promising rookie, were fairly scarce.

NM/M
Complete Set (5): 45.00
Common Player: 4.00
1 Emmitt Smith 15.00
2 Steve Young 10.00
3 Drew Bledsoe 10.00
4 Ki-Jana Carter 4.00
5 Troy Aikman 10.00

1995 Pro Line Phone Cards $1,000

Phone cards were randomly inserted into 1995 Classic NFL Pro Line Series II packs, one per every pack, and at least three $2 cards and one $5 card in every box. The higher the denomination, the more exclusive the number made.

NM/M
Complete Set (4):
Common Player: 50.00
1 Steve Young 100.00
2 Drew Bledsoe 75.00
3 Ki-Jana Carter 50.00
4 Troy Aikman 100.00

1995 Pro Line Phone Cards $1,500

Dallas Cowboys' star running back Emmitt Smith is featured on this 1995 Classic NFL Pro Line Series II phone card insert. This card is the scarcest of the phone card inserts.

NM/M
Complete Set (1): 2,000
Common Player: 2,000
1 Emmitt Smith 400.00

1995 Pro Line Pogs

The 30-card retail-only set included an action photo on the front, with two Pogs punched out on the card. The backs have the player's name and stats. The cards carry a "C" prefix.

NM/M
Complete Set (30): 8.00
Common Player: .25
1 Steve Walsh, Rashaan Salaam .35
2 Kerry Collins, Barry Foster .75
3 Jim Kelly, Thurman Thomas .35
4 Terance Mathis, Jeff George .25
5 Garrison Hearst, Seth Joyner .25
6 Barry Sanders, Herman Moore .75
7 John Elway, Shannon Sharpe .50
8 Troy Aikman, Emmitt Smith 1.50
9 Leroy Hoard, Andre Rison .25
10 Jeff Blake, Ki-Jana Carter .50
11 Marcus Allen, Steve Bono .35
12 Tony Boselli, Steve Beuerlein .25
13 Marshall Faulk, Quentin Coryatt .35
14 Steve McNair, Gary Brown .35
15 Brett Favre, Reggie White 1.50
16 Jim Everett, Michael Bates .35
17 Drew Bledsoe, Ben Coates .75
18 Warren Moon, Cris Carter .35
19 Dan Marino, Irving Fryar 1.50
20 Jeff Hostetler, Tim Brown .35
21 Kevin Greene, Bam Morris .35
22 Derek Brown, Rodney Hampton .25
23 Boomer Esiason, Mo Lewis .25
24 Randall Cunningham, Ricky Watters .25
25 Natrone Means, Junior Seau .25
26 Heath Shuler, Michael Westbrook .35
27 Trent Dilfer, Errict Rhett .35
28 Jerome Bettis, Ki-Jana Carter .35
29 Steve Young, Jerry Rice 1.00
30 Rick Mirer, Chris Warren .35

1995 Pro Line Precision Cuts

These 20 die-cut cards feature NFL superstars on silver foil board. The cards were exclusive inserts in 1995 Classic Pro Line Series II cases, one per 45 packs. The cards are sequentially numbered up to 1,250.

NM/M
Complete Set (20): 60.00
Common Player: 1.00
1 Jim Kelly 2.00
2 John Elway 4.00
3 Kerry Collins 2.00
4 Ki-Jana Carter 1.00
5 Andre Rison 1.00
6 Troy Aikman 4.00
7 Emmitt Smith 6.00
8 Barry Sanders 5.00
9 Warren Moon 2.00
10 Jeff Hostetler 1.00
11 Dan Marino 6.00
12 Drew Bledsoe 4.00
13 Rodney Hampton 1.00
14 Ricky Watters 1.00
15 Byron Morris 1.00
16 Natrone Means 1.00
17 Steve Young 4.00
18 Jerry Rice 5.00
19 J.J. Stokes 2.00
20 Errict Rhett 1.00

1995 Pro Line Pro Bowl

The 30-card set was seeded one per box in $1.99 retail packs. The ticket-shaped die-cut fronts have an action photo of the player on a silver-foil background. Every card showcases the number "250392" on the top and bottom. The card backs, numbered with a "PB" prefix, have another action shot, with the player's name, position and write-up included.

NM/M
Complete Set (30): 10.00
Common Player: .25
1 Seth Joyner .25
2 Andre Reed .25
3 Bruce Smith .50
4 Michael Irvin .50
5 Troy Aikman 2.00
6 Emmitt Smith 3.00
7 Charles Haley .25
8 Shannon Sharpe .25
9 John Elway 2.00
10 Barry Sanders 2.00
11 Reggie White .50
12 Marshall Faulk 1.00
13 Tim Brown 1.25
14 Chester McGlockton .25
15 Dan Marino 4.00
16 Cris Carter .50
17 Warren Moon .50
18 Ben Coates .50
19 Drew Bledsoe 1.00
20 Rod Woodson .50
21 Natrone Means .50
22 Leslie O'Neal .25
23 Junior Seau .50
24 Jerry Rice 2.00
25 Chris Warren .40
26 Brent Jones .25
27 Steve Young 2.00
28 Dana Stubblefield .25
29 Deion Sanders 1.00
30 Jerome Bettis 1.00

1995 Pro Line Record Breakers

These Record Breaker acetate cards were exclusive inserts in 1995 Classic NFL Pro Line Hot Boxes. Each pack in a Hot Box contains 40 percent inserts. Hot Boxes were randomly inserted one per 10 cases of 1995 Classic NFL Pro Line cases. Cards 1-5 were hobby inserts; 6-10 were retail inserts. They carried a "RB" prefix. Cards were sequentially numbered up to 350.

NM/M
Complete Set (10): 50.00
Common Player: 3.00
1 Drew Bledsoe 6.00
2 Cris Carter 3.00
3 Jerry Rice 8.00
4 Steve Young 6.00

NM/M
5 Marshall Faulk 6.00
6 Emmitt Smith 12.00
7 Barry Sanders 12.00
8 Natrone Means 3.00
9 Ben Coates 3.00
10 Bruce Smith 3.00

1995 Pro Line Series II

Classic's 1995 NFL Pro Line Series II contains 75 cards, including the NFL's top stars, most promising rookies and traded veterans in their new uniforms. The basic format for the cards is similar to the Series I cards, but the cards can be distinguished because they say Series II on the front. Exclusive to hobby cases is a 75-card parallel set of Printer's Proofs cards, which feature holographic foil-stamped logos. These cards are seeded one per 18 packs in hobby cases. Phone cards have a dominant presence in Series II, with denominations of $1, $2, $5, $20, $100 and $1,000. One phone card appears in each pack and at least three $2 cards and one $5 phone card are in a box. Printer's Proof versions of the $1 (one per 44 packs), $2 (one per 75) and $5 (one per 210) also exist. The $1 phone cards are stamped with the printer's proof logo and are numbered 1 of 699. The $2 cards are also stamped with the logo and are numbered 1 of 494, while the $5 cards are stamped and numbered 1 of 297. Other inserts include Precision Cut, NFL Images Preview cards, Field Generals, and a continuation of Classic's oversized bonus cards program. These micro-lined cards are numbered 9-11 in the bonus series and are sequentially numbered to 1,250. One oversized bonus card is packed in every case of 1995 Pro Line Series II product.

NM/M
Complete Set (75): 15.00
Common Player: .05
Minor Stars: .10
Comp. Prin. Proof Set (75): 250.00
Printers Proof Cards: 3X-8X
1 Jim Kelly .10
2 Steve Walsh .05
3 Jeff Blake 1.00
4 Vinny Testaverde .05
5 Jeff Hostetler .05
6 Dan Marino 1.50
7 Cris Carter .10
8 Drew Bledsoe 1.00
9 Jim Everett .05
10 Neil O'Donnell .05
11 Rodney Hampton .05
12 Troy Aikman .75
13 John Elway .50
14 Barry Sanders 1.25
15 Reggie White .10
16 Marshall Faulk .50
17 Marcus Allen .10
18 James Stewart .10
19 Randall Cunningham .10
20 Natrone Means .50
21 Rick Mirer .40
22 Jerry Rice .75
23 Errict Rhett .50
24 Heath Shuler .50
25 Jerome Bettis .25
26 Garrison Hearst .10
27 Jeff George .10
28 Andre Reed .05
29 Warren Moon .10
30 Ben Coates .05
31 Mario Bates .20
32 Byron Morris .40
33 Dave Brown .05
34 Emmitt Smith 1.50
35 Anthony Miller .05
36 Herman Moore .10
37 Brett Favre 1.50
38 Steve Bono .20
39 Stan Humphries .05
40 Steve Young .75
41 Trent Dilfer .30
42 Chris Miller .05
43 Herschel Walker .05
44 Michael Irvin .20
45 Junior Seau .10
46 Deion Sanders .40
47 William Floyd .30
48 Ki-Jana Carter .75
49 Kerry Collins 1.00
50 Steve McNair 1.00
51 Tony Boselli .10
52 Kyle Brady .10
53 Mike Mamula .05
54 Warren Sapp .10
55 J.J. Stokes .75
56 Joey Galloway 1.00
57 Hugh Douglas .05
58 Michael Westbrook .50
59 Napoleon Kaufman .50
60 Rashaan Salaam 1.00
61 Tyrone Wheatley .50
62 *Terrell Fletcher* .50
63 Eric Metcalf .05
64 Kevin Carter .05
65 Andre Rison .05
66 Eric Green .05
67 Dave Meggett .05
68 Ricky Watters .10
69 Steve Beuerlein .05
70 Craig Erickson .05
71 Michael Dean Perry .05
72 Alvin Harper .05
73 Rob Moore .05
74 Frank Reich .05
75 Checklist .05

1995 Pro Line Series II Printer's Proofs

The 75-card set is a parallel to the Series II cards. Seeded one per 18 packs, the cards have a printer's proof logo on the front.

NM/M
Complete Set (75): 300.00
Common Player: 1.50
PP Veteran Stars: 3X-8X
PP Young Stars: 3X-6X
PP RCs: 2X-4X

1996 Pro Line

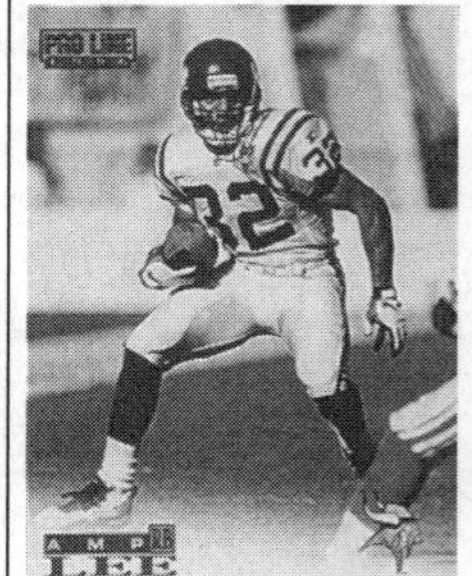

Pro Line's 1996 football offers one autographed card in every box and cards of newly-signed free agents and rookies. Each regular card front has a full-bleed color action photo on it, with the Pro Line logo at the top. The player's name and position are in the lower left corner, opposite his team's logo. The card back has a color photo on the right, flanked by a recap of some of the player's accomplishments. The player's name, position and card number are at the top; a team logo, biographical information and statistics are along the bottom. The autographed cards of players are available in blue and gold foil-stamped versions, with gold ones limited to a maximum of 250 cards. One autographed card is seeded in every 25th pack. Five cards are jointly autographed by a quarterback/wide receiver combination. Other inserts include Cels, Cover Story, Rivalries and Touchdown Performers.

NM/M
Complete Set (350): 25.00
Common Player: .05
Minor Stars: .10

Complete PP Set (350): 500.00
Printer's Proof Cards: 3X-8X
Pack (10): 1.75
Wax Box (36): 50.00
1 Troy Aikman 1.00
2 Steve Young 1.00
3 John Elway .50
4 Jim Kelly .10
5 Dan Marino 2.00
6 Brett Favre 2.00
7 Kerry Collins 1.25
8 Jeff Blake .50
9 Stan Humphries .05
10 Steve Bono .05
11 Jeff George .10
12 Mark Brunell .75
13 Scott Mitchell .05
14 Steve McNair 1.00
15 Jeff Hostetler .05
16 Jim Everett .05
17 Rick Mirer .05
18 Boomer Esiason .05
19 Neil O'Donnell .05
20 Dave Brown .05
21 Erik Kramer .05
22 Trent Dilfer .05
23 Jim Harbaugh .05
24 Vinny Testaverde .05
25 Thurman Thomas .10
26 Rodney Peete .05
27 Gus Frerotte .05
28 Warren Moon .05
29 Eric Zeier .05
30 Randall Cunningham .05
31 Heath Shuler .40
32 John Friesz .05
33 Tommy Maddox .05
34 Glenn Foley .05
35 Drew Bledsoe .75
36 Kordell Stewart 1.25
37 Natrone Means .15
38 Errict Rhett .30
39 Rashaan Salaam .30
40 Emmitt Smith 2.00
41 Larry Centers .05
42 Terrell Davis 1.00
43 Marshall Faulk .50
44 Rodney Hampton .05
45 Byron Morris .05
46 Chris Warren .15
47 Curtis Martin 2.00
48 Ricky Watters .05
49 Marcus Allen .05
50 Barry Sanders 1.25
51 Edgar Bennett .05
52 Adrian Murrell .05
53 James Stewart .05
54 Leroy Hoard .05
55 Jerome Bettis .05
56 Craig Heyward .05
57 Harvey Williams .05
58 Bernie Parmalee .05
59 Garrison Hearst .05
60 Terry Allen .05
61 Charlie Garner .05
62 Dorsey Levens .10
63 Derek Loville .05
64 Greg Hill .05
65 Derrick Moore .05
66 Rodney Thomas .40
67 Daryl Johnston .05
68 Mario Bates .05
69 *Aaron Hayden* .10
70 Napoleon Kaufman .05
71 Terry Kirby .05
72 Glyn Milburn .05
73 Robert Smith .05
74 Ki-Jana Carter .40
75 Tyrone Wheatley .05
76 Erric Pegram .05
77 Brian Mitchell .05
78 Vaughn Dunbar .05
79 Dave Meggett .05
80 Scottie Graham .05
81 Darick Holmes .05
82 Marion Butts .05
83 Harold Green .05
84 Zack Crockett .05
85 Amp Lee .05
86 Lamont Warren .05
87 Mark Chmura .25
88 Irving Fryar .05
89 Tim Brown .05
90 Michael Irvin .05
91 Tony Martin .05
92 Alvin Harper .05
93 Darnay Scott .05
94 Eric Metcalf .05
95 Michael Timpson .05
96 Sean Dawkins .05
97 Qadry Ismail .05
98 Yancey Thigpen .50
99 Joey Galloway 1.00
100 Herman Moore .25
101 J.J. Stokes .10
102 Wayne Chrebet .05
103 Ernest Givins .05
104 Michael Jackson .05
105 Henry Ellard .05
106 Thomas Lewis .05
107 Anthony Miller .05
108 Terance Mathis .05
109 Horace Copeland .05
110 Raghib Ismail .05
111 Quinn Early .05
112 Haywood Jeffires .05
113 Mark Carrier .05
114 Brent Jones .05
115 Ben Coates .05
116 Ken Dilger .05
117 Irv Smith .05
118 Jay Novacek .05
119 Tony McGee .05
120 Troy Drayton .05
121 Johnny Mitchell .05
122 Rob Moore .05
123 Kevin Williams .05
124 O.J. McDuffie .05
125 Carl Pickens .10
126 Curtis Conway .05
127 Ed McCaffery .05
128 Arthur Marshall .05
129 Ernie Mills .05
130 Cris Carter .05
131 Isaac Bruce .50
132 Brian Blades .05
133 Michael Westbrook .10
134 Andre Reed .05
135 Andre Rison .05
136 Brett Perriman .05
137 Willie Jackson .05
138 Ryan Yarborough .05
139 Chris T. Jones .05
140 Jerry Rice 1.00
141 Lake Dawson .05
142 Robert Brooks .05
143 Vincent Brisby .05
144 Desmond Howard .05
145 Johnnie Morton .05
146 Steve Tasker .05
147 Ty Detmer .05
148 Todd Kinchen .05
149 Mike Sherrard .05
150 Eric Green .05
151 Mark Bruener .05
152 Kyle Brady .05
153 Frank Sanders .05
154 Willie Green .05
155 Jeff Graham .05
156 Bert Emanuel .05
157 Courtney Hawkins .05
158 Mark Seay .05
159 Chris Calloway .05
160 John Taylor .05
161 Fred Barnett .05
162 Tamarick Vanover .60
163 Keenan McCardell .05
164 Bill Brooks .05
165 Alexander Wright .05
166 Jake Reed .05
167 Floyd Turner .05
168 Mike Pritchard .05
169 Lawrence Dawsey .05
170 Shawn Jefferson .05
171 Michael Haynes .05
172 Shannon Sharpe .05
173 Jackie Harris .05
174 Daryl Hobbs .05
175 Chris Sanders .25
176 Willie Davis .05
177 Marco Coleman .05
178 Pat Swilling .05
179 Alonzo Spellman .05
180 Simon Fletcher .05
181 Sean Gilbert .05
182 Tracy Scroggins .05
183 Hugh Douglas .05
184 Eric Swann .05
185 Russell Maryland .05
186 Warren Sapp .05
187 Jim Flanigan .05
188 Cortez Kennedy .05
189 Andy Harmon .05
190 Dan Saleaumua .05
191 Kelvin Pritchett .05
192 John Randle .05
193 Dan Wilkinson .05
194 Chester McGlockton .05
195 Leon Lett .05
196 Neil Smith .05
197 Mike Mamula .05
198 Mike Jones .05
199 Reggie White .05
200 Anthony Pleasant .05
201 Phil Hansen .05
202 Ray Seals .05
203 Tony Bennett .05
204 Leslie O'Neal .05
205 Jeff Cross .05
206 Anthony Cook .05
207 Clyde Simmons .05
208 Renaldo Turnbull .05
209 Charles Haley .05
210 John Copeland .05
211 John Thierry .05
212 Michael Strahan .05
213 Jeff Lageman .05
214 William Fuller .05
215 Rickey Jackson .05
216 Wayne Martin .05
217 Steve Emtman .05
218 Shawn Lee .05
219 Chris Zorich .05
220 Henry Thomas .05
221 Dana Stubblefield .05
222 D'Marco Farr .05
223 Pierce Holt .05
224 Sean Jones .05
225 Robert Porcher .05
226 Kevin Carter .05
227 Chris Doleman .05
228 Tony Tolbert .05
229 Bruce Smith .05
230 Marvin Washington .05
231 Blaine Bishop .05
232 Bryant Young .05
233 Rob Burnett .05
234 *Lawrence Phillips* .50
235 Trev Alberts .05
236 Eric Curry .05
237 Anthony Smith .05
238 Sam Mills .05
239 Seth Joyner .05
240 Quentin Coryatt .05
241 Levon Kirkland .05
242 Cornelius Bennett .05
243 Chris Spielman .05
244 Mo Lewis .05
245 Lee Woodall .05
246 Derrick Thomas .05
247 Willie McGinest .05
248 Terry Wooden .05
249 Greg Lloyd .05
250 Jack Del Rio .05
251 Hardy Nickerson .05
252 Micheal Barrow .05
253 Lamar Lathon .05
254 Bryan Cox .05
255 Randy Kirk .05
256 Jessie Tuggle .05
257 Roman Phifer .05
258 Ken Harvey .05
259 Junior Seau .05
260 Pepper Johnson .05
261 Chris Slade .05
262 Gary Plummer .05
263 Wayne Simmons .05
264 Bryce Paup .05
265 William Thomas .05
266 Kevin Greene .05
267 *Bobby Engram* 1.00
268 Ken Norton .05
269 Eric Hill .05
270 Darion Conner .05
271 Tyrone Poole .05
272 Cris Dishman .05
273 Marcus Jones .05
274 Rod Woodson .05
275 Mark McMillian .05
276 Dale Carter .05
277 Darrell Green .05
278 Donnell Woolford .05
279 Troy Vincent .05
280 Larry Brown .05
281 Aeneas Williams .05
282 Eric Allen .05
283 Ray Buchanan .05
284 Ty Law .05
285 Eric Davis .05
286 Todd Lyght .05
287 Terry McDaniel .05
288 Darryl Lewis .05
289 Deion Sanders .50
290 Phillippi Sparks .05
291 Bobby Taylor .05
292 Mark Collins .05
293 Steve Atwater .05
294 Stanley Richard .05
295 Stevon Moore .05
296 Bennie Blades .05
297 Tim McDonald .05
298 Shaun Gayle .05
299 Darren Woodson .05
300 Mark Carrier .05
301 Carnell Lake .05
302 James Washington .05
303 LeRoy Butler .05
304 Henry Jones .05
305 Darryl Williams .05
306 Darren Perry .05
307 Merton Hanks .05
308 Orlando Thomas .05
309 Eric Turner .05
310 Nate Newton .05
311 Steve Wisniewski .05
312 Derrick Deese .05
313 Larry Allen .05
314 Aaron Taylor .05
315 Blake Brockermeyer .05
316 William Roaf .05
317 John Elliott .05
318 *Keyshawn Johnson* 2.00
319 *Karim Abdul-Jabbar* 1.00
320 *Kevin Hardy* .30
321 Duane Clemons .05
322 Jevon Langford .05
323 *Mike Alstott* 1.50
324 Scott Greene .05
325 *Derrick Mayes* .75
326 Chris Doering .05
327 *Amani Toomer* .10
328 *Eric Moulds* 1.50
329 Alex Molden .05
330 Lawyer Milloy .05
331 Daryl Gardener .05
332 Randall Godfrey .05
333 Willie Anderson .05
334 *Tony Banks* .50
335 *Jeff Lewis* .50
336 Roman Oben .05
337 Andre Johnson .05
338 Brian Roche .05
339 Johnny McWilliams .05
340 *Alex Van Dyke* .10
341 Ray Mickens .05
342 *Marvin Harrison* 2.00
343 *Terry Glenn* 1.75
344 *Tim Biakabutuka* 1.00
345 *Simeon Rice* .30
346 Cedric Jones .05
347 *Eddie George* 3.50
348 Checklist 1 .05
349 Checklist 2 .30
350 Checklist 3 .30

1996 Pro Line National

This 350-card parallel set was inserted 1:1 in 1996 Pro Line National packs. The card fronts feature the 1996 National logo printed in silver foil. Each card is numbered one of 499.

NM/M
Complete Set (350): 400.00
Common Player: .50
National Stars: 3X-5X
National RCs: 2X-4X

1996 Pro Line Printer's Proof

Inserted at a rate of one per 10 packs, this 350-card set parallels the regular-issue set. Printer's Proof cards are distinguished by a large red foil "Printer's Proof" stamp.

NM/M
Complete Set (350): 500.00
Printer's Proof Cards: 3X-8X

1996 Pro Line Autographs

This 73-card insert features authentic player autographs printed in gold foil. The cards were inserted 1:170 in hobby and retail packs and 1:200 in jumbo packs. The cards in this insert are not numbered. Blue foil versions were inserted 1:25 hobby and retail and 1:90 jumbo.

NM/M
Common Gold Foil: 10.00
Common Blue Foil: 5.00
Blue Cards: .5X
1 Troy Aikman, Emmitt Smith (Gold only) 250.00
2 Eric Allen 10.00
3 Mike Alstott 40.00
4 Tony Banks 40.00
5 Blaine Bishop 10.00
6 Drew Bledsoe 75.00
7 Tim Brown 25.00
8 Marion Butts 10.00
9 Sedric Clark 10.00
10 Duane Clemons 10.00
11 Marco Coleman 10.00
12 Eric Davis 10.00
13 Derrick Deese 10.00
14 Jack Del Rio 10.00
15 Ty Detmer 30.00
16 Chris Doering 10.00
17 Jumbo Elliott 10.00
18 Marshall Faulk 60.00
19 Glenn Foley 10.00
20 John Friesz 10.00
21 Daryl Gardener 10.00
22 Randall Godfrey 10.00
23 Scott Greene 10.00
24 Rhett Hall 10.00
25 Merton Hanks 10.00
26 Kevin Hardy 10.00
27 Richard Huntley 10.00
28 Michael Jackson 10.00
29 Ron Jaworski 25.00
30 Andre Johnson 10.00
31 Keyshawn Johnson 75.00
32 Keyshawn Johnson, Neil O'Donnell (Gold only) 75.00
33 Mike Jones 10.00
34 Jim Kiick 10.00
35 Jeff Lewis 25.00
36 Tommy Maddox 10.00
37 Arthur Marshall 10.00
38 Russell Maryland 10.00
39 Derrick Mayes 40.00
40 Ed McCaffrey 10.00
41 Keenan McCardell 25.00
42 Terry McDaniel 10.00
43 Tim McDonald 10.00
44 Willie McGinest 10.00
45 Mark McMillian 10.00
46 Johnny McWilliams 10.00
47 Ray Mickens 10.00
48 Anthony Miller 10.00
49 Rick Mirer 10.00
50 Alex Molden 10.00
51 Johnnie Morton 25.00
52 Eric Moulds 30.00
53 Roman Oben 10.00
54 Neil O'Donnell (Gold only) 25.00
55 Leslie O'Neal 10.00
56 Roman Phifer 10.00
57 Gary Plummer 10.00
58 Jim Plunkett 10.00
59 Stanley Pritchett 10.00
60 John Randle 10.00
61 Brian Roche 10.00
62 Orpheus Roye 10.00
63 Mark Seay 10.00
64 Mike Sherrard 10.00
65 Chris Slade 10.00
66 Scott Slutzker 10.00
67 Emmitt Smith (Gold only) 175.00
68 Steve Taneyhill 10.00
69 Robb Thomas 10.00
70 William Thomas 10.00
71 Alex Van Dyke 10.00
72 Randy White 30.00
73 Steve Young (Gold only) 75.00

1996 Pro Line Cels

Each of these 1996 Pinnacle inserts features a top NFL veteran or rookie on an acetate card and contains two foil stamps on it. The cards were seeded exclusively in hobby packs, one per 75 packs. They are numbered with a "C" prefix.

NM/M
Complete Set (20): 125.00
Common Player: 2.00
1 Bryce Paup 2.00
2 Kerry Collins 4.00
3 Troy Aikman 8.00
4 Deion Sanders 4.00
5 Emmitt Smith 10.00
6 Steve McNair 6.00
7 Drew Bledsoe 8.00
8 Kordell Stewart 5.00
9 Ricky Watters 2.00
10 Jerry Rice 10.00
11 Steve Young 8.00
12 Errict Rhett 4.00
13 Brett Favre 12.00
14 Jeff Blake 3.00
15 Joey Galloway 4.00
16 Herman Moore 2.00
17 Curtis Martin 8.00
18 Keyshawn Johnson 4.00
19 Eddie George 6.00
20 Simeon Rice 2.00

1996 Pro Line Rivalries

This 30-card 1996 Pro Line insert set provides an in-depth look at some of the NFL's most heated battles. Each card side features an action shot of one of two players along with a decorative foil stamp, used for the player's name. His team logo and highlights from the two team's rivalries are also on each side. The metallic background shows a ghosted image of the player's opponent. A card number, using an "R" prefix, is on one side only. Cards were seeded one per every 10 packs.

NM/M
Complete Set (20): 60.00
Common Player: 1.00
1 Drew Bledsoe, Jim Kelly 4.00
2 Dan Marino, Greg Lloyd 6.00
3 Kordell Stewart, Mark Brunell 3.00
4 Tamarick Vanover, Napoleon Kaufman 1.00
5 John Elway, Jeff Blake 4.00
6 Emmitt Smith, Ricky Watters 5.00
7 Troy Aikman, Steve Young 5.00
8 Deion Sanders, Gus Frerotte 2.00
9 Brett Favre, Errict Rhett 6.00
10 Rashaan Salaam, Warren Moon 2.00
11 Kerry Collins, Ken Norton Jr. 2.00
12 Jeff George, Isaac Bruce 2.00
13 Rod Woodson, Rodney Thomas 1.00
14 Herman Moore, Reggie White 1.00
15 Marshall Faulk, Curtis Martin 5.00
16 Keyshawn Johnson, Marvin Harrison 4.00
17 Kevin Hardy, Alex Molden 1.00
18 Terry Glenn, Simeon Rice 2.00
19 Eddie George, Tim Biakabutuka 4.00
20 Karim Abdul-Jabbar, Cedric Jones 1.00

1996 Pro Line Cover Story

This 20-card set was inserted one per 30 periodical packs. The cards feature a newspaper design and carry a "CS" prefix on the card number. The insert is made up of a mix of top 1995 players as well as some of the top rookies from 1996.

NM/M
Complete Set (20): 35.00
Common Player: 1.00
1 Bryce Paup 1.00
2 Kerry Collins 3.00
3 Rashaan Salaam 1.00
4 Troy Aikman 4.00
5 Emmitt Smith 6.00
6 Herman Moore 2.00
7 Curtis Martin 4.00
8 Kordell Stewart 2.00
9 Ricky Watters 1.00
10 Carl Pickens 1.00
11 Joey Galloway 2.00
12 Errict Rhett 1.00
13 Deion Sanders 2.00
14 Reggie White 1.00
15 Hugh Douglas 1.00
16 Tamarick Vanover 1.00
17 Derrick Mayes 1.00
18 Marvin Harrison 3.00
19 Tim Biakabutuka 1.00
20 Terry Glenn 4.00

1996 Pro Line Touchdown Performers

Touchdown Performers is a 20-card insert that was found every 75 retail packs. The cards are numbered TD1-TD20.

NM/M
Complete Set (20): 75.00
Common Player: 1.00
1 Kerry Collins 3.00
2 Troy Aikman 5.00
3 Deion Sanders 2.00
4 Emmitt Smith 6.00
5 Mark Brunell 3.00
6 Steve McNair 3.00
7 Marshall Faulk 4.00
8 Dan Marino 8.00
9 Cris Carter 1.00
10 Drew Bledsoe 4.00
11 Yancey Thigpen 1.00
12 Jerry Rice 6.00
13 J.J. Stokes 2.00
14 Terrell Davis 5.00
15 Carl Pickens 1.00
16 Joey Galloway 3.00
17 Kordell Stewart 2.00
18 Isaac Bruce 3.00
19 Keyshawn Johnson 3.00
20 Amani Toomer 1.00

1996 Pro Line II Intense

Pro Line II Intense features 100 cards, a parallel set and four insert sets. Each regular card has a full-bleed color photo on the front, with the Intense logo at the top. The player's name and position are in a bar along the bottom, flanked by a team helmet in the lower left corner. The back has a card number and the player's name at the top, with a photo on one side and statistics on the other. A box with biographical information is in the lower left corner. There were also parallel Double Intensity cards made; they were seeded one per five packs and are stamped in bronze on the front. Three other insert sets were also made - Determined and $3 and $5 Sprint Foncards. There's an average of $11 in phone time in every box.

NM/M
Complete Set (100): 20.00
Common Player: .05
Minor Stars: .10
Double Intensity: 2X-4X
Pack (5): 1.25
Wax Box (36): 35.00
1 Kerry Collins 1.25
2 Jeff George .05
3 Mark Brunell 1.00
4 Steve McNair .75
5 Rick Mirer .05
6 Dave Brown .05
7 Rashaan Salaam .50
8 Marshall Faulk .50
9 Erric Pegram .05
10 Cris Carter .05
11 Eric Allen .05
12 Jim Kelly .05
13 Jeff Blake .50
14 Stan Humphries .05
15 Scott Mitchell .05
16 Jeff Hostetler .05
17 Rodney Peete .05
18 Warren Moon .05
19 Errict Rhett .40
20 Terrell Davis 2.00
21 J.J. Stokes .10
22 Marco Coleman .05
23 Heath Shuler .05
24 Duane Clemons .05
25 *Amani Toomer* .10
26 Leslie O'Neal .05
27 Tamarick Vanover .50
28 Steve Bono .05
29 Jim Everett .05
30 Erik Kramer .05
31 Trent Dilfer .10
32 Jim Harbaugh .05
33 Vinny Testaverde .05
34 Rodney Hampton .05
35 Chris Warren .10
36 Curtis Martin 2.00
37 *Eddie Kennison* .50
38 Herman Moore .40
39 Terance Mathis .05
40 Carl Pickens .05
41 Isaac Bruce .50
42 Reggie White .10
43 Junior Seau .05
44 Bryce Paup .05
45 Deion Sanders .50
46 Thurman Thomas .10
47 Gus Frerotte .05
48 Jerome Bettis .10
49 Michael Irvin .10
50 Wayne Chrebet .05
51 *Bobby Engram* .75
52 Marcus Jones .05
53 Daryl Gardener .05
54 *Alex Van Dyke* .10
55 Cedric Jones .05
56 Regan Upshaw .05
57 *Jason Dunn* .30
58 Mark Chmura .25
59 Ray Lewis .25
60 *Rickey Dudley* .20
61 *Leeland McElroy* .20
62 Derrick Thomas .05
63 *Bobby Hoying* .75
64 Robert Brooks .05
65 Tim Brown .05
66 Michael Westbrook .40
67 Jim Miller .05
68 Aaron Hayden .05
69 Marcus Allen .05
70 Troy Aikman 1.00
71 Steve Young .75
72 Neil O'Donnell .05
73 Drew Bledsoe .75
74 Emmitt Smith 2.00
75 Ki-Jana Carter .30
76 Irving Fryar .05
77 Joey Galloway .75
78 Russell Maryland .05
79 Kordell Stewart 1.00
80 Barry Sanders 1.25
81 Bryan Cox .05
82 *Keyshawn Johnson* 1.50
83 *Karim Abdul-Jabbar* 1.75
84 *Kevin Hardy* .30
85 Rodney Thomas .05
86 John Elway .50
87 Dan Marino 2.00
88 Brett Favre 2.00
89 John Mobley .05
90 Jonathan Ogden .05
91 *Eddie George* 2.50
92 *Simeon Rice* .25
93 *Tim Biakabutuka* 1.00
94 *Terry Glenn* 1.75
95 *Marvin Harrison* 1.00
96 *Lawrence Phillips* .50
97 Natrone Means .10
98 Jerry Rice .75
99 Ricky Watters .10
100 Checklist .05

A card number in parenthese ( ) indicates the set is unnumbered.

1996 Pro Line II Intense Double Intensity

Pro Line II Intense Double Intensity was a 100-card parallel set that included the words "Double Intensity" on the front in foil. These parallel cards were inserted at a rate of one per five packs.

Double Intensity Cards: 2X-4X

1996 Pro Line II Intense Determined

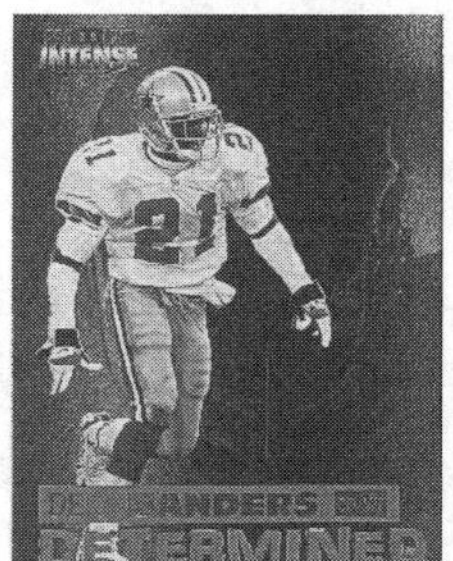

These 1996 Pro Line II inserts offer an in-depth view of the look and determination of 20 of the NFL's fiercest competitors. Each card front has an action photo of the player against a metallic ghosted close-up image of him as the background. The Pro Line II logo is at the top of the card; the player's name and position are in a bar at the bottom, above the word "Determined." The card back, numbered 1 of 20, etc., has a full-bleed color action photo on it, with an oval toward the bottom which recaps some of the player's achievements.

NM/M
Complete Set (20): 30.00
Common Player: 1.00
1 Kerry Collins 2.00
2 Troy Aikman 4.00
3 Herman Moore 1.00
4 Mark Brunell 2.00
5 Dan Marino 6.00
6 Kordell Stewart 2.00
7 Junior Seau 1.00
8 Steve Young 4.00
9 John Elway 4.00
10 Emmitt Smith 5.00
11 Steve McNair 3.00
12 Drew Bledsoe 3.00
13 Joey Galloway 2.00
14 Deion Sanders 2.00
15 Kevin Hardy 1.00
16 Keyshawn Johnson 2.00
17 Marvin Harrison 3.00
18 Tim Biakabutuka 1.00
19 Eddie George 3.00
20 Terry Glenn 2.00

1996 Pro Line II Intense $3 Phone Cards

Fifty top players are featured in this 1996 Pro Line II insert set, which is licensed by the NFL and sponsored by Sprint. The cards, randomly inserted one per 18 packs, contain $3 worth of prepaid Sprint long-distance calling. The card front has the brand and Sprint logos at the top; the player's name, position and a team helmet are at the bottom. The card back explains how to use the card and when it expires.

NM/M
Complete Set (50): 25.00
Common Player: .25
1 Jim Kelly .50
2 Kerry Collins .50
3 Jeff George .25
4 Troy Aikman 1.00
5 John Elway 1.00
6 Herman Moore .50
7 Barry Sanders 2.00
8 Brett Favre 3.00
9 Jim Harbaugh .25
10 Steve Bono .25
11 Dan Marino 3.00
12 Drew Bledsoe 1.00
13 Jim Everett .25
14 Neil O'Donnell .25
15 Ricky Watters .25
16 Junior Seau .25
17 Jerry Rice 2.00
18 Errict Rhett .25
19 Joey Galloway .50
20 Steve Young 1.00
21 Kordell Stewart .50
22 Rodney Hampton .25
23 Curtis Martin 1.00
24 Mark Brunell 1.00
25 Steve McNair 1.00
26 Deion Sanders .50
27 Carl Pickens .25
28 Michael Irvin .25
29 Tamarick Vanover .25
30 Emmitt Smith 2.00
31 Chris Warren .25
32 Stan Humphries .50
33 J.J. Stokes .50
34 Tim Biakabutuka .25
35 Keyshawn Johnson 1.00
36 Simeon Rice .25
37 Jonathan Ogden .25
38 Rashaan Salaam .25
39 Bobby Engram .25
40 John Mobley .25
41 Derrick Mayes .25
42 Eddie George 1.00
43 Marvin Harrison 1.00
44 Kevin Hardy .25
45 Karim Abdul-Jabbar .25
46 Duane Clemons .25
47 Terry Glenn .50
48 Cedric Jones .25
49 Rickey Dudley .25
50 Lawrence Phillips .25

1996 Pro Line II Intense $5 Phone Cards

Twenty top players are featured in this 1996 Pro Line II insert set, which is licensed by the NFL and sponsored by Sprint. The cards, randomly inserted one per 35 packs, contain $5 worth of prepaid Sprint long-distance calling. The card front has the brand logo at the top; the Sprint logo, denomination and player's name and team are at the bottom. The card back explains how to use the card and when it expires.

NM/M
Complete Set (20): 35.00
Common Player: .40
1 Kerry Collins 1.00
2 Troy Aikman 3.00
3 Herman Moore .40
4 Mark Brunell 2.00
5 Dan Marino 4.00
6 Kordell Stewart 2.00
7 Junior Seau .40
8 Steve Young 2.00
9 John Elway 2.00
10 Emmitt Smith 5.00
11 Steve McNair .40
12 Drew Bledsoe 3.00
13 Joey Galloway 1.00
14 Deion Sanders 1.00
15 Kevin Hardy .40
16 Keyshawn Johnson 1.00
17 Marvin Harrison 2.00
18 Tim Biakabutuka .50
19 Eddie George 1.00
20 Terry Glenn .75

1996 Pro Line Memorabilia

Pro Line Memorabilia was the third installment of Pro Line Football in 1996. The same 100 players from Intense were used, but with different designs. Memorabilia included one autographed memorabilia redemption card, two autographed cards, with one of a 1996 NFL first-round pick, as well as two inserts - Down the Stretch and Producers.

NM/M
Complete Set (100): 25.00
Common Player: .10
Minor Stars: .20
Pack (5): 1.25
Box (24): 100.00
1 Kerry Collins 1.50
2 Jeff George .10
3 Mark Brunell 1.50
4 Steve McNair 1.00
5 Rick Mirer .20
6 Dave Brown .10
7 Rashaan Salaam .30
8 Marshall Faulk .30
9 Erric Pegram .10
10 Cris Carter .10
11 Eric Allen .10
12 Jim Kelly .20
13 Jeff Blake .30
14 Stan Humphries .10
15 Scott Mitchell .10
16 Jeff Hostetler .10
17 Rodney Peete .10
18 Warren Moon .20
19 Errict Rhett .30
20 Terrell Davis 1.75
21 J.J. Stokes .20
22 Marco Coleman .10
23 Heath Shuler .20
24 Duane Clemons .10
25 Amani Toomer .20
26 Leslie O'Neal .10
27 Tamarick Vanover .20
28 Steve Bono .10
29 Jim Everett .10
30 Erik Kramer .10
31 Trent Dilfer .20
32 Jim Harbaugh .10
33 Vinny Testaverde .10
34 Rodney Hampton .10
35 Chris Warren .10
36 Curtis Martin 1.75
37 Eddie Kennison 1.50
38 Herman Moore .30
39 Terance Mathis .10
40 Carl Pickens .20
41 Isaac Bruce .30
42 Reggie White .20
43 Junior Seau .20
44 Bryce Paup .10
45 Deion Sanders .75
46 Thurman Thomas .20
47 Gus Frerotte .10
48 Tony Mandarich .10
49 Michael Irvin .20
50 Wayne Chrebet .10
51 Bobby Engram 1.00
52 Marcus Jones .10
53 Daryl Gardener .10
54 Alex Van Dyke .20
55 Andre Rison .10
56 Regan Upshaw .10
57 Jason Dunn .10
58 Mark Chmura .20
59 Ray Lewis .25
60 Rickey Dudley .30
61 Leeland McElroy .20
62 Derrick Thomas .10
63 Bobby Hoying .20
64 Robert Brooks .20
65 Tim Brown .20
66 Michael Westbrook .20
67 Jim Miller .10
68 Aaron Hayden .10
69 Marcus Allen .20
70 Troy Aikman 1.50
71 Steve Young 1.00
72 Neil O'Donnell .10
73 Drew Bledsoe 1.50
74 Emmitt Smith 3.00
75 Ki-Jana Carter .20
76 Irving Fryar .10
77 Joey Galloway .50
78 Russell Maryland .10
79 Kordell Stewart 1.50
80 Barry Sanders 1.50
81 Bryan Cox .10
82 Keyshawn Johnson 1.50
83 Karim Abdul-Jabbar 2.00
84 Kevin Hardy .20
85 Rodney Thomas .10
86 John Elway 1.00
87 Dan Marino 3.00
88 Brett Favre 3.00
89 Eric Metcalf .10
90 Jonathan Ogden .20
91 Eddie George 3.00
92 Simeon Rice .20
93 Tim Biakabutuka .30
94 Terry Glenn 2.50
95 Marvin Harrison 1.50
96 Lawrence Phillips .30
97 Natrone Means .20
98 Jerry Rice 1.50
99 Ricky Watters .20
100 Emmitt Smith Checklist .50

1996 Pro Line Memorabilia Stretch Drive

Stretch Drive featured 30 top players on a foil background, with cards numbered DS1-DS30. Regular versions were inserted every three packs, while Signature Series versions, which had facsimile signatures, were inserted every 25 packs.

NM/M
Complete Set (30): 35.00
Common Player: .50
Minor Stars: 1.00
1 Jim Kelly 1.00
2 Kerry Collins 1.00
3 Rashaan Salaam .50
4 Jeff Blake 1.00
5 Deion Sanders 1.00
6 Troy Aikman 3.00
7 Emmitt Smith 5.00
8 John Elway 4.00
9 Terrell Davis 4.00
10 Barry Sanders 5.00
11 Herman Moore 1.00
12 Brett Favre 6.00
13 Steve McNair 2.00
14 Eddie George 2.00
15 Marshall Faulk 2.00
16 Marvin Harrison 2.00
17 Dan Marino 6.00
18 Curtis Martin 3.00
19 Drew Bledsoe 3.00
20 Terry Glenn 1.00
21 Neil O'Donnell .50
22 Keyshawn Johnson 2.00
23 Ricky Watters 1.00
24 Kordell Stewart 2.00
25 J.J. Stokes .50
26 Steve Young 3.00
27 Joey Galloway 1.00
28 Lawrence Phillips .50
29 Isaac Bruce 1.00
30 Errict Rhett 1.00

1996 Pro Line Memorabilia Producers

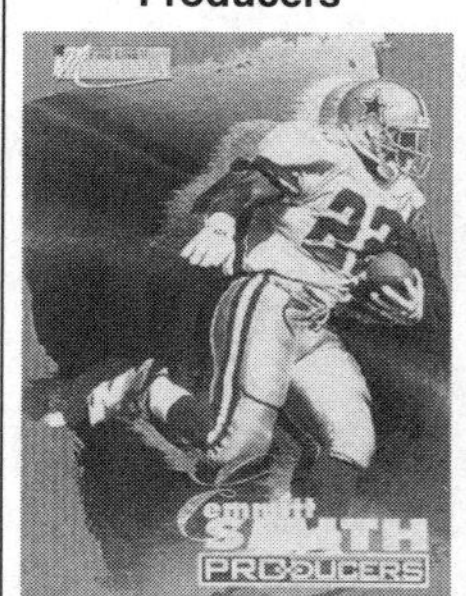

Producers was a 10-card insert found in every six packs of Memorabilia. Cards in this insert were numbered P1-P10. There are also Signature Series Producers, which have facsimile signatures, inserted every 100 packs.

NM/M
Complete Set (10): 15.00
Common Player: .50
Minor Stars: 1.00
Silver Signatures: 2X-4X
1 Keyshawn Johnson 1.00
2 Barry Sanders 3.00
3 Eddie George 1.00
4 Emmitt Smith 3.00
5 Jerry Rice 2.00
6 Brett Favre 4.00
7 Marshall Faulk .50
8 Dan Marino 4.00
9 Deion Sanders 1.00
10 Ricky Watters .50

1996 Pro Line Memorabilia Rookie Autographs

This 15-card insert features autographs of NFL rookies from 1996 and was inserted 1:12. Each card is limited to a different production number and sequentially numbered. The cards are not numbered within the insert set.

NM/M
Common Player: 10.00
1 Tim Biakabutuka/210 25.00
2 Tim Biakabutuka/600, Eddie George 75.00
3 Duane Clemons/1255 10.00
4 Daryl Gardener/1390 10.00
5 Eddie George/395 75.00
6 Terry Glenn/600, Keyshawn Johnson 75.00
7 Kevin Hardy/940 20.00
8 Jeff Hartings/1370 10.00
9 Andre Johnson/1370 10.00
10 Keyshawn Johnson/195 60.00
11 Pete Kendall/1495 10.00
12 Alex Molden/1320 10.00
13 Eric Moulds/1010 30.00
14 Jamain Stephens/795 10.00
15 Jerome Woods/1375 10.00

1996 Pro Line DC III

Pro Line III DC, by Classic, follows the hobby trend with all 100 cards printed on a die-cut design. Every card is printed on 24-point stock, die-cut around the top. The back has final statistics from the 1995 season, plus career totals, biographical information, a color action photo, and trivial notes about the player. There were also insert sets created for the set: Road to the Super Bowl and All-Pro/All-Pro Rookies.

NM/M
Complete Set (100): 15.00
Common Player: .05
Minor Stars: .40
Pack (5): 2.00
Wax Box (24): 40.00
1 Emmitt Smith 4.00
2 Larry Centers .05
3 Jeff George .40
4 Jim Kelly .40
5 Kerry Collins 2.00
6 Erik Kramer .05
7 Jeff Blake 1.00
8 Andre Rison .05

9 John Elway 1.50
10 Herman Moore .75
11 Robert Brooks .50
12 Steve McNair 3.00
13 Jim Harbaugh .05
14 Mark Brunell 1.00
15 Steve Bono .40
16 Dan Marino 5.00
17 Warren Moon .40
18 Drew Bledsoe 3.00
19 Jim Everett .05
20 Rodney Hampton .05
21 Kyle Brady .05
22 Jeff Hostetler .05
23 Neil O'Donnell .40
24 Ricky Watters .05
25 Isaac Bruce 1.50
26 Steve Young 3.00
27 Stan Humphries .05
28 Joey Galloway 1.00
29 Errict Rhett 1.00
30 Terry Allen .05
31 Eric Swann .05
32 Craig Heyward .05
33 Bryce Paup .05
34 Sam Mills .05
35 Jim Flanigan .05
36 Carl Pickens .40
37 Pepper Johnson .05
38 Troy Aikman 3.00
39 Terrell Davis 3.00
40 Scott Mitchell .05
41 Brett Favre 5.00
42 Chris Sanders 1.00
43 Marshall Faulk 3.00
44 James Stewart .05
45 Marcus Allen .05
46 Bernie Parmalee .05
47 Cris Carter .05
48 Ben Coates .05
49 Quinn Early .05
50 Tyrone Wheatley .40
51 Adrian Murrell .05
52 Tim Brown .05
53 Yancey Thigpen 1.50
54 Andy Harmon .05
55 Jerome Bettis .05
56 Jerry Rice 3.00
57 Natrone Means .50
58 Chris Warren .40
59 Warren Sapp .05
60 Michael Westbrook 2.00
61 Aeneas Williams .05
62 Eric Metcalf .05
63 Bruce Smith .05
64 Rashaan Salaam .50
65 Michael Irvin .75
66 Anthony Miller .05
67 Barry Sanders 3.00
68 Reggie White .40
69 Rodney Thomas .40
70 Zack Crockett .05
71 Neil Smith .05
72 Bryan Cox .05
73 Curtis Martin 3.00
74 Eric Allen .05
75 Hugh Douglas .05
76 Napoleon Kaufman .75
77 Greg Lloyd .05
78 Charlie Garner .05
79 Lee Woodall .05
80 Tony Martin .05
81 Cortez Kennedy .05
82 Gus Frerotte .40
83 Darick Holmes .50
84 Jay Novacek .05
85 Brett Perriman .05
86 Mark Chmura .40
87 Chester McGlockton .05
88 Dave Brown .05
89 William Thomas .05
90 Ken Norton .05
91 Junior Seau .40
92 Deion Sanders 2.00
93 J.J. Stokes 2.00
94 Kordell Stewart 1.00
95 Tamarick Vanover .50
96 Ken Harvey .05
97 John Randle .05
98 Lamont Warren .05
99 Dorsey Levens .40
100 Frank Sanders .50

1996 Pro Line DC III All-Pros

These cards, printed on 24-point fabric stock, were inserted one per 100 packs of 1996 Pro Line III DC product. The card back is numbered using an "AP" prefix.

NM/M
Complete Set (20): 100.00
Common Player: 2.00
1 Bryce Paup 2.00
2 Kerry Collins 6.00
3 Rashaan Salaam 2.00
4 Emmitt Smith 12.00
5 Terrell Davis 8.00
6 Herman Moore 2.00
7 Barry Sanders 12.00
8 Brett Favre 15.00
9 Marshall Faulk 8.00
10 Dan Marino 15.00
11 Cris Carter 2.00
12 Curtis Martin 8.00
13 Hugh Douglas 2.00
14 Kordell Stewart 4.00
15 Jerry Rice 10.00
16 J.J. Stokes 4.00
17 Joey Galloway 5.00
18 Isaac Bruce 5.00
19 Steve McNair 8.00
20 Tim Brown 5.00

A player's name in *italic* type indicates a rookie card.

1996 Pro Line DC III Road to the Super Bowl

The key members and moments in the 1995 season are captured in this 30-card Road to the Super Bowl set. The cards, which were inserted one per 15 packs of 1996 Pro Line III DC product, have the player's name at the top, with "Road to the Super Bowl" written along the bottom. The back has statistics or a brief box score of the game being recalled, plus a photo of the player inside a circle. A map of Phoenix is used as a background motif on both sides of the card. The card number is listed as 1 of 30, etc..

NM/M
Complete Set (30): 50.00
Common Player: .50
Minor Stars: 8.00
1 Larry Centers .50
2 Eric Metcalf .50
3 Jim Kelly 2.00
4 Bryce Paup .50
5 Kerry Collins 3.00
6 Carl Pickens 1.00
7 Emmitt Smith 6.00
8 Michael Irvin 2.00
9 Troy Aikman 5.00
10 Terrell Davis 5.00
11 Barry Sanders 6.00
12 Herman Moore 1.00
13 Brett Favre 6.00
14 Robert Brooks 1.00
15 Jim Harbaugh .50
16 Tony Bennett .50
17 Steve Bono 1.00
18 Dan Marino 6.00
19 Cris Carter .50
20 Curtis Martin 3.00
21 Tim Brown 2.00
22 Ricky Watters .50
23 Yancey Thigpen 1.00
24 Neil O'Donnell .50
25 Kordell Stewart 2.00
26 Isaac Bruce 2.00
27 Tony Martin .50
28 Steve Young 3.00
29 Jerry Rice 4.00
30 Chris Warren .50

1997 Pro Line

The 300-card set featured a full-bleed photo with a stripe at the bottom that included the player's name, team and position. The team's logo is included inside a circle at the bottom center. The Pro Line logo is in the upper left.

NM/M
Complete Set (300): 15.00
Common Player: .05
Minor Stars: .10
Pack (8): 1.00
Wax Box (28): 25.00
1 Larry Centers .05
2 Kent Graham .05
3 LeShon Johnson .05
4 Leeland McElroy .10
5 Rob Moore .05
6 Simeon Rice .05
7 Frank Sanders .05
8 Eric Swann .05
9 Aeneas Williams .05
10 Jamal Anderson .15
11 Cornelius Bennett .05
12 Ray Buchanan .05
13 Bert Emanuel .05
14 Terance Mathis .05
15 Eric Metcalf .05
16 Jessie Tuggle .05
17 Derrick Alexander .05
18 Earnest Byner .05
19 Michael Jackson .05
20 Antonio Langham .05
21 Ray Lewis .05
22 Bam Morris .05
23 Jonathan Ogden .05
24 Vinny Testaverde .05
25 Eric Moulds .10
26 Todd Collins .05
27 Quinn Early .05
28 Phil Hansen .05
29 Darick Holmes .10
30 Bryce Paup .05
31 Andre Reed .05
32 Bruce Smith .05
33 Chris Spielman .05
34 Matt Stevens .05
35 Steve Tasker .05
36 Thurman Thomas .10
37 Mark Carrier .05
38 Kerry Collins .25
39 Tim Biakabutuka .25
40 Eric Davis .05
41 Kevin Greene .05
42 Anthony Johnson .05
43 Lamar Lathon .05
44 Sam Mills .05
45 Wesley Walls .05
46 Muhsin Muhammad .10
47 Mark Carrier .05
48 Curtis Conway .10
49 Bryan Cox .05
50 Bobby Engram .05
51 Raymont Harris .05
52 Walt Harris .05
53 Rick Mirer .05
54 Rashaan Salaam .10
55 Alonzo Spellman .05
56 Ashley Ambrose .05
57 Jeff Blake .15
58 Ki-Jana Carter .10
59 John Copeland .05
60 James Francis .05
61 Tony McGee .05
62 Carl Pickens .10
63 Darnay Scott .05
64 Steve Tovar .05
65 Dan Wilkinson .05
66 Troy Aikman 1.00
67 Eric Bjornson .05
68 Michael Irvin .10
69 Daryl Johnston .05
70 Nate Newton .05
71 Deion Sanders .40
72 Emmitt Smith 2.00
73 Kevin Smith .05
74 Kevin Williams .05
75 Darren Woodson .05
76 Mark Tuinei .05
77 Steve Atwater .05
78 Terrell Davis 1.25
79 John Elway .75
80 Ed McCaffrey .05
81 Anthony Miller .05
82 John Mobley .05
83 Michael Dean Perry .05
84 Shannon Sharpe .05
85 Alfred Williams .05
86 Reggie Brown .05
87 Luther Elliss .05
88 Scott Mitchell .05
89 Herman Moore .15
90 Johnnie Morton .05
91 Brett Perriman .05
92 Robert Porcher .05
93 Barry Sanders 1.25
94 Henry Thomas .05
95 Edgar Bennett .05
96 Robert Brooks .10
97 Gilbert Brown .05
98 LeRoy Butler .05
99 Mark Chmura .05
100 Brett Favre 2.25
101 Santana Dotson .05
102 Antonio Freeman .20
103 Dorsey Levens .20
104 Wayne Simmons .05
105 Reggie White .10
106 Willie Davis .05
107 Eddie George 1.50
108 Darryll Lewis .05
109 Steve McNair .30
110 Marcus Robertson .05
111 Chris Sanders .05
112 Al Smith .05
113 Tony Bennett .05
114 Quentin Coryatt .05
115 Ken Dilger .05
116 Sean Dawkins .05
117 Marshall Faulk .20
118 Jim Harbaugh .05
119 Marvin Harrison .30
120 Jeff Herrod .05
121 Tony Boselli .05
122 Tony Brackens .05
123 Mark Brunell 1.00
124 Kevin Hardy .05
125 Jeff Lageman .05
126 Keenan McCardell .05
127 Natrone Means .10
128 Eddie Robinson .05
129 Jimmy Smith .05
130 James Stewart .05
131 Marcus Allen .10
132 Dale Carter .05
133 Mark Collins .05
134 Lake Dawson .05
135 Greg Hill .05
136 Sean LaChapelle .05
137 Chris Penn .05
138 Derrick Thomas .05
139 Tamarick Vanover .10
140 Elvis Grbac .05
141 Karim Abdul-Jabbar .30
142 Fred Barnett .05
143 Terrell Buckley .05
144 Daryl Gardener .05
145 Randal Hill .05
146 Dan Marino 2.00
147 O.J. McDuffie .05
148 Jerris McPhail .05
149 Zach Thomas .20
150 Cris Carter .05
151 Dixon Edwards .05
152 Leroy Hoard .05
153 Qadry Ismail .05
154 Brad Johnson .05
155 John Randle .05
156 Jake Reed .05
157 Robert Smith .05
158 Orlando Thomas .05
159 DeWayne Washington .05
160 Drew Bledsoe 1.00
161 Tedy Bruschi .05
162 Willie Clay .05
163 Ben Coates .05
164 Terry Glenn .25
165 Shawn Jefferson .05
166 Ty Law .05
167 Curtis Martin 1.25
168 Willie McGinest .05
169 Chris Slade .05
170 Eric Allen .05
171 Mario Bates .05
172 Jim Everett .05
173 Michael Haynes .05
174 Wayne Martin .05
175 Torrance Small .05
176 Dave Brown .05
177 Chris Calloway .05
178 Rodney Hampton .05
179 Danny Kanell .05
180 Thomas Lewis .05
181 Jason Sehorn .05
182 Amani Toomer .05
183 Charles Way .05
184 Tyrone Wheatley .05
185 Wayne Chrebet .05
186 Hugh Douglas .05
187 Aaron Glenn .05
188 Jeff Graham .05
189 Keyshawn Johnson .30
190 Mo Lewis .05
191 Adrian Murrell .05
192 Neil O'Donnell .05
193 Tim Brown .05
194 Rickey Dudley .10
195 Jeff George .10
196 Napoleon Kaufman .05
197 Russell Maryland .05
198 Terry McDaniel .05
199 Chester McGlockton .05
200 Pat Swilling .05
201 Desmond Howard .05
202 Ty Detmer .05
203 Jason Dunn .05
204 Ray Farmer .05
205 Irving Fryar .05
206 Chris T. Jones .05
207 Bobby Taylor .05
208 William Thomas .05
209 Hollis Thomas .05
210 Kevin Turner .05
211 Ricky Watters .10
212 Jerome Bettis .10
213 Andre Hastings .05
214 Charles Johnson .05
215 Levon Kirkland .05
216 Carnell Lake .05
217 Greg Lloyd .05
218 Darren Perry .05
219 Kordell Stewart .75
220 Rod Woodson .05
221 Andre Coleman .05
222 Marco Coleman .05
223 Leonard Russell .05
224 Stan Humphries .05
225 Shawn Lee .05
226 Tony Martin .05
227 Chris Mims .05
228 Junior Seau .10
229 Chris Doleman .05
230 William Floyd .05
231 Merton Hanks .05
232 Brent Jones .05
233 Terry Kirby .05
234 Ken Norton .05
235 Terrell Owens .75
236 Jerry Rice 1.00
237 Bryant Young .05
238 Steve Young .75
239 Garrison Hearst .05
240 Brian Blades .05
241 Chad Brown .05
242 John Friesz .05
243 Joey Galloway .30
244 Cortez Kennedy .05
245 Chris Warren .05
246 Darryl Williams .05
247 Tony Banks .30
248 Isaac Bruce .15
249 Kevin Carter .05
250 Eddie Kennison .10
251 Todd Lyght .05
252 Leslie O'Neal .05
253 Anthony Parker .05
254 Roman Phifer .05
255 Lawrence Phillips .10
256 Mike Alstott .15
257 Derrick Brooks .05
258 Trent Dilfer .10
259 Jackie Harris .05
260 Hardy Nickerson .05
261 Errict Rhett .10
262 Warren Sapp .05
263 Terry Allen .05
264 Jamie Asher .05
265 Henry Ellard .05
266 Gus Frerotte .05
267 Sean Gilbert .05
268 Darrell Green .05
269 Ken Harvey .05
270 Brian Mitchell .05
271 Michael Westbrook .05
272 *Koy Detmer* .30
273 *Yatil Green* .40
274 *Troy Davis* .30
275 *Darrell Russell* .05
276 *Warrick Dunn* 1.00
277 *David LaFleur* .30
278 *Tony Gonzalez* .30
279 *Jake Plummer* 2.50
280 *Antowain Smith* 1.25
281 *Peter Boulware* .05
282 *Shawn Springs* .25
283 *Bryant Westbrook* .10
284 *Rae Carruth* .30
285 *Corey Dillon* 2.00
286 *Byron Hanspard* .30
287 *Greg Jones* .05
288 *Trevor Pryce* .05
289 *Michael Booker* .05
290 *Orlando Pace* .40
291 *James Farrior* .05
292 *Walter Jones* .05
293 *Reinard Wilson* .05
294 *Ike Hilliard* 1.00
295 *Kenard Lang* .05
296 *Reidel Anthony* 1.00
297 Brett Favre CL .75
298 Kerry Collins CL .30
299 Drew Bledsoe CL .30
300 Terrell Davis CL .50

1997 Pro Line Board Members

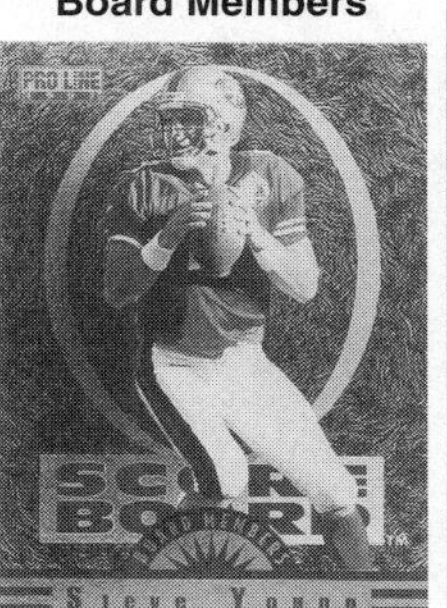

This 15-card set was inserted 1:112 packs. It includes an inside look at the NFL Players that Score Board has signed to exclusive spokesman contracts. The cards are numbered with a "B" prefix.

NM/M
Complete Set (15): 60.00
Common Player: 1.00
1 Troy Aikman 6.00
2 Kerry Collins 2.00
3 Terrell Davis 6.00
4 Brett Favre 8.00
5 Gus Frerotte 1.00
6 Emmitt Smith 7.00
7 Kordell Stewart 2.00
8 Steve Young 5.00
9 Eddie George 3.00
10 Terry Glenn 2.00
11 Troy Davis 1.00
12 Darrell Russell 1.00
13 Peter Boulware 1.00
14 Warrick Dunn 3.00
15 Rae Carruth 1.00

1997 Pro Line Brett Favre

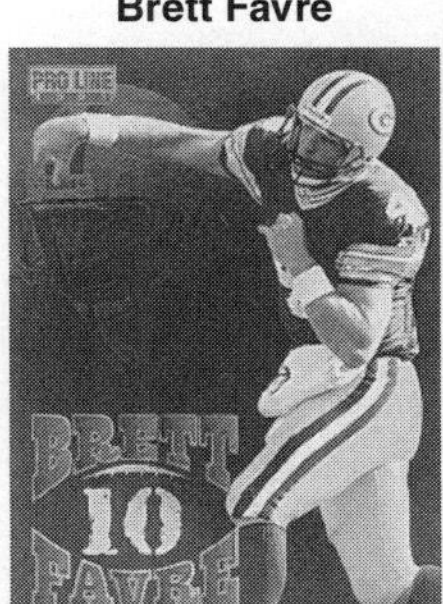

This 10-card set, which was inserted 1:28 packs, is an interactive insert series that focuses on Brett Favre. All 10 cards could be redeemed for autographed memorabilia. All sets redeemed won either an autographed jersey or a Super Bowl XXXI autographed plaque.

NM/M
Complete Set (10): 50.00
Common Player: 5.00
1 Brett Favre 5.00
2 Brett Favre 5.00
3 Brett Favre 5.00
4 Brett Favre 5.00
5 Brett Favre 5.00
6 Brett Favre 5.00
7 Brett Favre 5.00
8 Brett Favre 5.00
9 Brett Favre 5.00
10 Brett Favre 75.00

1997 Pro Line Rivalries

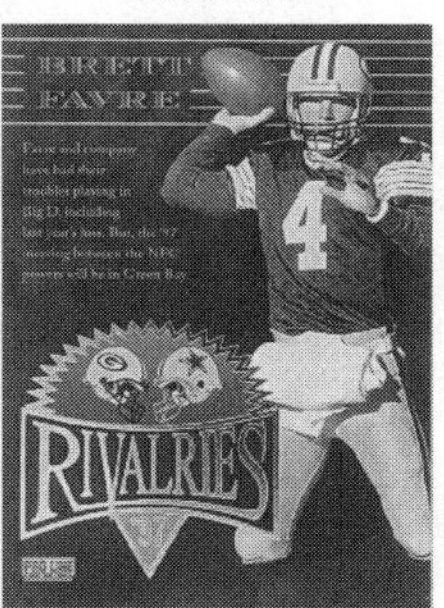

The 20-card set, which is numbered with an "R" prefix, was inserted 1:35 packs. The double-front cards provide insight into the top games of the 1997 campaign.

NM/M
Complete Set (20): 60.00
Common Player: 1.00
1 John Elway, Derrick Thomas 5.00
2 Jeff Blake, Vinny Testaverde 1.00
3 Emmitt Smith, Ricky Watters 7.00
4 Jim Harbaugh, Thurman Thomas 1.00
5 Barry Sanders, Reggie White 6.00
6 Desmond Howard, Junior Seau 1.00
7 Dan Marino, Hugh Douglas 7.00
8 Jerome Bettis, Carl Pickens 1.00
9 Mark Brunell, Kordell Stewart 3.00
10 Karim Abdul-Jabbar, Bruce Smith 1.00
11 Rashaan Salaam, Brad Johnson 1.00
12 Steve Young, Kerry Collins 4.00
13 Brett Favre, Troy Aikman 8.00
14 Drew Bledsoe, Marshall Faulk 5.00
15 Steve McNair, Ki-Jana Carter 3.00
16 Jerry Rice, Terrell Davis 6.00
17 Deion Sanders, Dave Brown 2.00
18 Darrell Russell, Orlando Pace 1.00
19 Warrick Dunn, Bryant Westbrook 2.00
20 Yatil Green, Reidel Anthony 1.00

1997 Pro Line Gems

The 100-card base set consists of three subsets. Veterans is a 60-card set on blue foil-stamped cards, Rookies features 30 black foil-stamped cards and Leaders is a 10-card set with black and blue foil-stamping. The insert sets include Gems of the NFL, Championship Ring and Through the Years.

NM/M
Complete Set (100): 10.00
Common Player: .05
Minor Stars: .20
Pack (4): 1.00
Wax Box (24): 20.00
1 Brett Favre 3.00
2 Robert Brooks .05
3 Reggie White .20
4 Drew Bledsoe 1.50
5 Curtis Martin 1.50
6 Terry Glenn .30
7 Kerry Collins .30
8 Kevin Greene .05
9 Troy Aikman 1.50

10 Emmitt Smith 3.00
11 Deion Sanders .75
12 John Elway 1.00
13 Terrell Davis 1.50
14 Kordell Stewart 1.50
15 Jerome Bettis .20
16 Steve Young 1.00
17 Jerry Rice 1.50
18 Bruce Smith .05
19 Thurman Thomas .20
20 Jim Harbaugh .05
21 Marshall Faulk .20
22 Marvin Harrison .50
23 Ricky Watters .20
24 Seth Joyner .05
25 Mark Brunell 1.50
26 Natrone Means .20
27 Dan Marino 3.00
28 Zach Thomas .50
29 Karim Abdul-Jabbar .30
30 Isaac Bruce .20
31 Eddie Kennison .30
32 Tony Banks .50
33 Tony Martin .05
34 Junior Seau .20
35 Barry Sanders 1.50
36 Herman Moore .20
37 Leeland McElroy .05
38 Jamal Anderson .20
39 Rick Mirer .05
40 Rashaan Salaam .20
41 Vinny Testaverde .05
42 Elvis Grbac .05
43 Cris Carter .05
44 Brad Johnson .20
45 Keyshawn Johnson .50
46 Adrian Murrell .05
47 Joey Galloway .30
48 Trent Dilfer .20
49 Gus Frerotte .05
50 Terry Allen .05
51 Tim Brown .05
52 Desmond Howard .05
53 Jeff George .05
54 Heath Shuler .05
55 Steve McNair 1.00
56 Eddie George 1.00
57 Jeff Blake .20
58 Carl Pickens .05
59 Dave Brown .05
60 Brett Favre 1.50
61 Antowain Smith .75
62 Emmitt Smith 1.25
63 Terry Glenn .50
64 Herman Moore .05
65 Barry Sanders .50
66 Derrick Thomas .05
67 Brett Favre 1.50
68 Warrick Dunn 1.00
69 Emmitt Smith 1.25
70 Brett Favre 1.50
71 Orlando Pace .05
72 Darrell Russell .05
73 Shawn Springs .05
74 Warrick Dunn 1.00
75 Tiki Barber .30
76 Tom Knight .05
77 Peter Boulware .05
78 David LaFleur .50
79 Tony Gonzalez .50
80 Yatil Green .30
81 Ike Hilliard .30
82 James Farrior .05
83 Jim Druckenmiller .40
84 Jon Harris .05
85 Walter Jones .05
86 Reidel Anthony .40
87 Jake Plummer 1.00
88 Reinard Wilson .05
89 Kevin Lockett .05
90 Rae Carruth .05
91 Byron Hanspard .50
92 Renaldo Wynn .05
93 Troy Davis .75
94 Duce Staley .75
95 Kenard Lang .05
96 Freddie Jones .75
97 Corey Dillon 2.00
98 Antowain Smith 1.50
99 Dwayne Rudd .05
100 Warrick Dunn .75

1997 Pro Line Gems Gems of the NFL

This 15-card insert features either a sapphire or emerald gemstone on a 23-karat gold card. These cards were seeded one per box (24 packs per box). The cards are numbered with a "G" prefix.

NM/M
Complete Set (15): 75.00
Common Player: 1.00
1 Kerry Collins 2.00
2 Troy Aikman 5.00
3 Emmitt Smith 6.00
4 Terrell Davis 5.00
5 Barry Sanders 6.00
6 Brett Favre 7.00
7 Eddie George 3.00
8 Mark Brunell 3.00
9 Dan Marino 7.00
10 Curtis Martin 4.00
11 Terry Glenn 2.00
12 Jerome Bettis 1.00
13 Steve Young 5.00
14 Jerry Rice 6.00
15 Warrick Dunn 2.00

1997 Pro Line Gems Championship Ring

This card featured Brett Favre and his Super Bowl XXXI championship ring. The card contains a real diamond and was inserted one per case (10 boxes per case, 24 packs per box).

NM/M
Complete Set (1): 50.00
CR1 Brett Favre 50.00

1997 Pro Line Gems Through the Years

This 20-card insert features 10 veterans and 10 rookies. The cards are die-cut to fit one of the rookies' cards with one of the veterans'. The cards were inserted 1:12. The cards are numbered with a "TY" prefix.

NM/M
Complete Set (20): 30.00
Common Player: .50
Minor Stars: 1.00
1 Emmitt Smith 5.00
2 Brett Favre 6.00
3 Deion Sanders 1.00
4 Dan Marino 6.00
5 Barry Sanders 5.00
6 Herman Moore 1.00
7 Curtis Martin 3.00
8 Jerome Bettis 1.00
9 Mark Brunell 3.00
10 Jerry Rice 5.00
11 Warrick Dunn 2.00
12 Jim Druckenmiller .50
13 Shawn Springs .50
14 Tony Banks 1.00
15 Byron Hanspard .50
16 Ike Hilliard 1.00
17 Antowain Smith 2.00
18 Eddie George 3.00
19 Jake Plummer 2.00
20 Terry Glenn 1.00

1997 Pro Line DC III

The 100-card, regular-sized, die-cut set includes two subsets: Rewind and DC Top Ten. The first 67 cards in the set are die-cut in a circular pattern with a rectangular base. Cards 68-89 are die-cut with wave outlines on the sides (Rewind) while cards 90-100 are horizontal with the top die-cut in the shape of a football. All cards have gold foil.

NM/M
Complete Set (100): 15.00
Common Player: .05
Minor Stars: .40
Pack (4): 2.00
Wax Box (24): 45.00
1 Emmitt Smith 4.00
2 Rod Woodson .05
3 Eddie George 2.00
4 Ty Detmer .05
5 Zach Thomas 1.00
6 Kevin Greene .05
7 Michael Jackson .05
8 Isaac Bruce 1.00
9 Joey Galloway 1.50
10 Bryant Young .05
11 Terrell Davis 2.00
12 Mark Brunell 1.00
13 Marvin Harrison 1.50
14 Jake Reed .05
15 Terry Allen .05
16 Kordell Stewart 1.00
17 Reggie White .40
18 Michael Irvin .40
19 Tony Martin .05
20 Barry Sanders 2.50
21 Tony Boselli .05
22 Carl Pickens .05
23 Simeon Rice .05
24 Adrian Murrell .05
25 Lamar Lathon .05
26 Thurman Thomas .40
27 Tim Brown .05
28 Karim Abdul-Jabbar .75
29 Brad Johnson .05
30 Keenan McCardell .05
31 Keyshawn Johnson 1.50
32 Ricky Watters .40
33 Michael McCrary .05
34 Brett Favre 4.00
35 Steve McNair 2.00
36 Herman Moore .40
37 Tony Banks 1.00
38 Deion Sanders 1.75
39 Kerry Collins .75
40 Shannon Sharpe .05
41 Drew Bledsoe 2.50
42 Jim Everett .05
43 Jamal Anderson .40
44 Irving Fryar .05
45 Terry Glenn .75
46 Jerry Rice 2.50
47 Curtis Martin 2.00
48 Curtis Conway .05
49 Jerome Bettis .40
50 Vinny Testaverde .05
51 Mike Alstott .75
52 Anthony Johnson .05
53 Dan Marino 4.00
54 Junior Seau .05
55 Steve Young 1.75
56 Troy Aikman 2.50
57 Jimmy Smith .05
58 Cris Carter .05
59 Gus Frerotte .05
60 Marcus Allen .40
61 Rodney Hampton .05
62 Bruce Smith .05
63 Leroy Butler .05
64 Jeff Blake .75
65 Antonio Freeman .05
66 John Elway 1.75
67 Checklist .05
68 Barry Sanders 1.50
69 Troy Aikman 1.00
70 Jerome Bettis .05
71 Mark Brunell 1.00
72 Junior Seau .05
73 John Elway .75
74 Chad Brown .05
75 Irving Fryar .05
76 Drew Bledsoe 1.00
77 Jerry Rice 1.00
78 Larry Centers .05
79 Terrell Davis 1.50
80 Carl Pickens .05
81 Emmitt Smith 2.00
82 Kerry Collins 1.00
83 Eddie Kennison .05
84 Kordell Stewart 1.00
85 Natrone Means .05
86 Curtis Martin 1.50
87 Dorsey Levens .05
88 Desmond Howard .05
89 Brett Favre MVP Checklist 2.00
90 Brett Favre 2.00
91 Terrell Davis 1.50
92 Kevin Greene .05
93 Terry Allen .05
94 Barry Sanders 1.50
95 John Elway .75
96 Ricky Watters .05
97 Reggie White .05
98 Jerome Bettis .05
99 Jerry Rice 1.00
100 Brett Favre CL Checklist 2.00

1997 Pro Line DC III Perennial/Future All-Pros

The 20-card, regular-sized, die-cut set was inserted every 24 packs of Pro Line III DC football. The cards feature the same die-cut design as the Rewind subset in the base set, except the cards in Perennial/Future All-Pros are vertical, making the wave cut design on the card's top and bottom. The cards feature bronze foil on the top and bottom and the backs are numbered as "x of 20." The backs have a color action shot imaged over a white background with a black-and-white closeup behind a brief statistical analysis. The cards are numbered with an "AP" prefix.

NM/M
Complete Set (20): 100.00
Common Player: 1.00
1 Emmitt Smith 10.00
2 Brett Favre 12.00
3 Jerry Rice 8.00
4 Steve Young 8.00
5 Barry Sanders 10.00
6 Reggie White 2.00
7 Ricky Watters 1.00
8 Lawrence Phillips 1.00
9 Kerry Collins 2.00
10 Mark Brunell 4.00
11 John Elway 8.00
12 Dan Marino 12.00
13 Drew Bledsoe 6.00
14 Curtis Martin 6.00
15 Terrell Davis 6.00
16 Karim Abdul-Jabbar 1.00
17 Marvin Harrison 4.00
18 Keyshawn Johnson 4.00
19 Terry Glenn 2.00
20 Eddie George 5.00

1997 Pro Line DC III Road to the Super Bowl

The 30-card, regular-sized, die-cut set was inserted every 12 packs of Pro Line III DC. The cards feature the same die-cut design as the DC Top Ten subset in the base set. The cards are numbered with a "SB" prefix.

NM/M
Complete Set (30): 75.00
Common Player: 1.00
1 Ricky Watters 2.00
2 Ty Detmer 1.00
3 Emmitt Smith 8.00
4 Troy Aikman 6.00
5 Kerry Collins 2.00
6 Kevin Greene 1.00
7 Steve Young 6.00
8 Jerry Rice 6.00
9 Brett Favre 10.00
10 Reggie White 2.00
11 Cris Carter 1.00
12 Brad Johnson 1.00
13 Drew Bledsoe 5.00
14 Curtis Martin 5.00
15 Bruce Smith 1.00
16 Thurman Thomas 1.00
17 Jim Harbaugh 1.00
18 Marshall Faulk 5.00
19 Mark Brunell 3.00
20 Natrone Means 1.00
21 John Elway 6.00
22 Terrell Davis 6.00
23 Kordell Stewart 3.00
24 Jerome Bettis 3.00
25 Eddie George 4.00
26 Dan Marino 10.00
27 Terry Glenn 3.00
28 Antonio Freeman 1.00
29 Anthony Johnson 1.00
30 Kevin Hardy 1.00

1998 Pro Line DC III

Pro Line DC III was a 100-card, all die-cut set that included 20 DC Rewind subset cards and 10 Rookie Uprising subset cards. The primary base cards feature the player in an oval shot with gold foil extended and squared off on all four corners, with the Pro Line DC logo in the upper right corner. Inserts in the product included: Clear Cuts, X-Tra Effort, Decade Draft, SB Team Totals and Choice Cuts. Each card and insert was also included in a Perfect Cut 1 of 1 set that was encapsulated in a PSA container and graded Mint. This included 170 total cards and these were available through redemptions.

NM/M
Complete Set (100): 20.00
Common Player: .20
Minor Stars: .60
Gold Version 1X-2X
Pack (4): 2.00
Wax Box (24): 40.00
1 Drew Bledsoe 2.00
2 Emmitt Smith 3.00
3 Dana Stubblefield .20
4 Brett Favre 4.00
5 Derrick Alexander .20
6 Bert Emanuel .20
7 Joey Galloway .60
8 Terrell Davis 2.00
9 Mark Brunell 2.00
10 Marshall Faulk .60
11 Jake Reed .20
12 Terry Allen .20
13 Kordell Stewart 2.00
14 Reggie White .60
15 Michael Irvin .60
16 Tony Martin .20
17 Barry Sanders 3.00
18 Carl Pickens .20
19 Bobby Hoying .20
20 Adrian Murrell .60
21 Jeff George .60
22 Tim Brown .20
23 Karim Abdul-Jabbar .60
24 Robert Smith .20
25 Eddie George 2.50
26 Corey Dillon 1.50
27 Keyshawn Johnson .60
28 Ricky Watters .60
29 Robert Brooks .20
30 Antonio Freeman .60
31 Danny Kanell .20
32 Steve McNair 1.50
33 Antowain Smith 1.50
34 Warrick Dunn 3.00
35 Napoleon Kaufman .60
36 Trent Dilfer .60
37 Herman Moore .60
38 Brad Johnson .20
39 Deion Sanders 1.00
40 Kerry Collins 1.25
41 Shannon Sharpe .20
42 Irving Fryar .20
43 Dorsey Levens .60
44 Jerry Rice 2.00
45 Curtis Martin 2.00
46 Jerome Bettis .60
47 Raymont Harris .20
48 Vinny Testaverde .20
49 Dan Marino 3.00
50 Junior Seau .20
51 Steve Young 1.50
52 Troy Aikman 2.00
53 Jimmy Smith .20
54 Ben Coates .20
55 Gus Frerotte .20
56 Marcus Allen .60
57 Bruce Smith .20
58 Jeff Blake .60
59 John Elway 1.50
60 Rod Smith .20
61 Andre Rison .20
62 Isaac Bruce .60
63 Cris Carter .20
64 Danny Wuerffel 1.00
65 Rob Moore .20
66 Garrison Hearst .20
67 Warren Moon .20
68 Jerome Bettis Checklist .20
69 Marcus Allen (DC Rewind) .20
70 James Stewart (DC Rewind) .20
71 Karim Abdul-Jabbar (DC Rewind) .20
72 Joey Galloway (DC Rewind) .20
73 Corey Dillon (DC Rewind) 1.50
74 Andre Rison (DC Rewind) .20
75 Napoleon Kaufman (DC Rewind) .20
76 Dorsey Levens (DC Rewind) .20
77 Irving Fryar (DC Rewind) .20
78 Eric Metcalf (DC Rewind) .20
79 Darrien Gordon (DC Rewind) .20
80 Neil O'Donnel l (DC Rewind) .20
81 Rod Woodson (DC Rewind) .20
82 Rob Johnson (DC Rewind) .20
83 Michael Westbrook (DC Rewind) .20
84 Jake Plummer (DC Rewind) 1.50
85 Bobby Hoying (DC Rewind) .20
86 Adrian Murrell (DC Rewind) .20
87 Jim Druckenmiller (DC Rewind) 1.50
88 Warren Moon (DC Rewind) .20
89 Dorsey Levens Checklist (DC Rewind) .20
90 Tony Gonzalez (Rookie Uprising) .20
91 Jim Druckenmiller (Rookie Uprising) 1.50
92 Corey Dillon (Rookie Uprising) 1.50
93 Darrell Russell (Rookie Uprising) .20
94 Byron Hanspard (Rookie Uprising) 1.00
95 Rae Carruth (Rookie Uprising) 1.00
96 Peter Boulware (Rookie Uprising) .20
97 Troy Davis (Rookie Uprising) 1.00
98 Reidel Anthony (Rookie Uprising) 1.25
99 Tiki Barber (Rookie Uprising) 1.25
100 Jake Plummer Checklist (Rookie Uprising) .20

1998 Pro Line DC III Choice Cuts

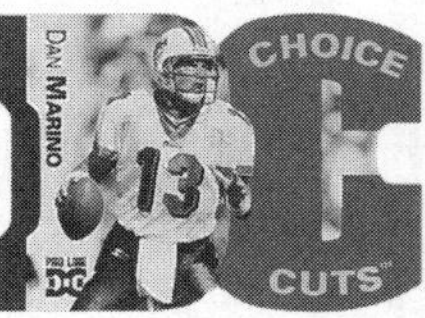

Choice Cuts were randomly inserted into packs of Pro Line DC III. The cards are horizontal and die-cut in design, with the player featured on the left side, and a large blue "C" die-cut out of the right side. The insert name is included in the blue "C" with "Choice" on the top and "Cuts" across the bottom. Choice Cuts are numbered on the back with a "CHC" prefix, with 10 cards in the set.

NM/M
Complete Set (10): 30.00
Common Player: 1.00
1 Deion Sanders 2.00
2 Jerome Bettis 2.00
3 Troy Aikman 4.00
4 Jerry Rice 5.00
5 Mark Brunell 3.00
6 Curtis Martin 3.00
7 Cris Carter 1.00
8 Steve Young 4.00
9 Reggie White 1.00
10 Dan Marino 6.00

1998 Pro Line DC III Clear Cuts

This 10-card set was printed on horizontal plastic that was die-cut. Clear Cuts were hobby exclusive, inserted one per 95 packs and sequentially numbered to 500. Cards featured the insert name printed across the top, with a gold foil finish. A color shot of the player was centered on the card, with his name and team logo off to the right. Clear Cuts inserts were numbered on the back with a "CLC" prefix.

NM/M
Complete Set (10): 125.00
Common Player: 5.00
1 John Elway 15.00
2 Drew Bledsoe 12.00
3 Terrell Davis 12.00
4 Brett Favre 20.00
5 Cris Carter 5.00
6 Eddie George 12.00
7 Kordell Stewart 8.00
8 Warrick Dunn 8.00
9 Tim Brown 10.00
10 Barry Sanders 15.00

1998 Pro Line DC III Decade Draft

Decade Draft was a 10-card insert that was inserted at a rate of one per 24 packs in Pro Line DC III. The cards are die-cut in the shape of a "D" with foil etched around the edge. An action shot of the player is shown on the right side of the card with a closer shot on the left. Decade Draft inserts are numbered with a "DD" prefix on the back.

		NM/M
Complete Set (10):		60.00
Common Player:		1.00
Gold		1X-2X
1	T. Aikman, B. Sanders	10.00
2	J. George, E. Smith	10.00
3	R. Maryland, B. Favre	10.00
4	S. Emtman, C. Pickens	1.00
5	D. Bledsoe, D. Bledsoe	5.00
6	D. Wilkinson, M. Faulk	5.00
7	K. Carter, T. Davis	5.00
8	K. Johnson, E. George	5.00
9	O. Pace, W. Dunn	4.00
10	1998 Top Draft Pick	8.00

1998 Pro Line DC III Team Totals

Team Totals was a 30-card insert that was found in packs of Pro Line DC III at a rate of one per eight packs. The cards were die-cut in the shape of a crystal ball, with the insert name across the bottom in gold foil and two shots of the player in the ball part - an action shot on the right and a close-up on the left. Team Totals inserts are numbered on the back with a "TT" prefix.

		NM/M
Complete Set (30):		40.00
Common Player:		.50
Minor Stars:		1.00
1	Ben Coates, Willie McGinest	.50
2	Michael Irvin, Deion Sanders	2.00
3	Carl Pickens, Dan Wilkinson	.50
4	LeRoy Butler, Antonio Freeman	1.00
5	Adrian Murrell, Hugh Douglas	1.00
6	Raymont Harris, Bryan Cox	.50
7	Ricky Watters, William Thomas	1.00
8	Neil Smith, Shannon Sharpe	2.00
9	Dana Stubblefield, Garrison Hearst	2.00
10	Keenan McCardell, Jeff Lageman	.50
11	Rae Carruth, Lamar Lathon	.50
12	Yancey Thigpen, Greg Lloyd	.50
13	Chris Calloway, Michael Strahan	.50
14	Troy Davis, Wayne Martin	.50
15	Warren Moon, Cortez Kennedy	1.00
16	Rob Moore, Simeon Rice	.50
17	O.J. McDuffie, Zach Thomas	1.00
18	John Randle, Robert Smith	1.00
19	Derrick Thomas, Elvis Grbac	1.00
20	Antowain Smith, Bruce Smith	3.00
21	Jeff George, Darrell Russell	.50
22	Steve McNair, Darryll Lewis	3.00
23	Isaac Bruce, Leslie O'Neal	1.00
24	Junior Seau, Tony Martin	2.00
25	Warren Sapp, Mike Alstott	1.00
26	Jessie Tuggle, Jamal Anderson	.50
27	Michael Jackson, Peter Boulware	.50
28	Quentin Coryatt, Marvin Harrison	2.00
29	Bryant Westbrook, Scott Mitchell	.50
30	Michael Westbrook, Darrell Green	1.00

A card number in parenthese ( ) indicates the set is unnumbered.

1998 Pro Line DC III X-Tra Effort

X-Tra Effort inserts are die-cut in the shape of an "X" on a horizontal format. Card fronts have the player's first name in the top left corner, his last name in the top right corner, a Pro Line DC logo in the bottom left and the insert name in the bottom right corner. The player is centered in the card with lightning bolts coming out on all sides. In addition, the front bears gold foil on all sides of the "X" as if a gold oval was set in back of the card to form a second layer. X-Tra Effort was a 20-card insert that was found one per 24 hobby packs and sequentially numbered to 1,000 sets. Cards carried an "XE" prefix on the back card number.

		NM/M
Complete Set (20):		125.00
Common Player:		1.00
1	Reggie White	2.00
2	Emmitt Smith	10.00
3	Junior Seau	3.00
4	Brett Favre	12.00
5	Warrick Dunn	5.00
6	Keyshawn Johnson	4.00
7	Dan Marino	12.00
8	Thurman Thomas	3.00
9	Steve Young	6.00
10	Curtis Martin	5.00
11	Karim Abdul-Jabbar	1.00
12	John Elway	8.00
13	Marcus Allen	3.00
14	Napoleon Kaufman	1.00
15	Irving Fryar	1.00
16	Mark Brunell	4.00
17	Andre Rison	1.00
18	Herman Moore	3.00
19	Jerry Rice	8.00
20	Kordell Stewart	4.00

1988 Pro Set Test Designs

Philadelphia Eagles quarterback Randall Cunningham is featured on these five prototype cards, used to preview Pro Set's 1989 debut set. The card numbers are the same on each card, but five different designs were used for the fronts. These are indicated with the corresponding card. Each card back is designed horizontally, with a mug shot, statistics, player profile and biographical information provided.

		NM/M
Complete Set (5):		160.00
Common Player:		40.00
315A	Randall Cunningham (No team or name listed on card front; borderless; logo is vertical)	40.00
315B	Randall Cunningham (No team or name listed on card front; border is silver; logo is vertical)	40.00
315C	Randall Cunningham (Name and team are listed on card front; borderless; logo is horizontal)	40.00
315D	Randall Cunningham (Team and name listed on card front; border is black; logo is horizontal)	40.00
315E	Randall Cunningham (Team and name listed on card front; border is gray; logo is horizontal)	40.00

1988 Pro Set Test

These promotional cards, used to preview Pro Set's debut set in 1989, can be distinguished from regular cards in several manners. First, each of the card backs is designed in a vertical fashion; the regular cards use a horizontal format. Also, the card number includes a # symbol before it. Plus, all the photos used for the fronts, except for the Jerry Rice photo, are different than those used on the regular cards.

		NM/M
Complete Set (8):		200.00
Common Player:		10.00
1	Dan Marino	80.00
2	Jerry Rice	65.00
3	Eric Dickerson	25.00
4	Reggie White	25.00
5	Mike Singletary	15.00
6	Frank Minnifield	10.00
7	Phil Simms	25.00
8	Jim Kelly	45.00

1989 Pro Set Promos

These five cards preview Pro Set's 1989 card design. The Santa Claus card was given to dealers, NFL representatives and members of the hobby press in December 1989. The Super Bowl card was given to those who attended the card show at Super Bowl XXIV in New Orleans in January 1990. The three player cards were samples which were mistakenly handed out at card shows in San Francisco and Chicago. The Bush and Lofton cards were intended to be included in Pro Set's Series II cards, but were bumped for Eric Dickerson and Greg Townsend. Sanders was given #446.

		NM/M
Complete Set (5):		45.00
Common Player:		5.00
445	Thomas Sanders	10.00
455	Blair Bush	5.00
463	James Lofton	15.00
1989	Santa Claus	15.00
Super Bowl Show I		10.00

1989 Pro Set

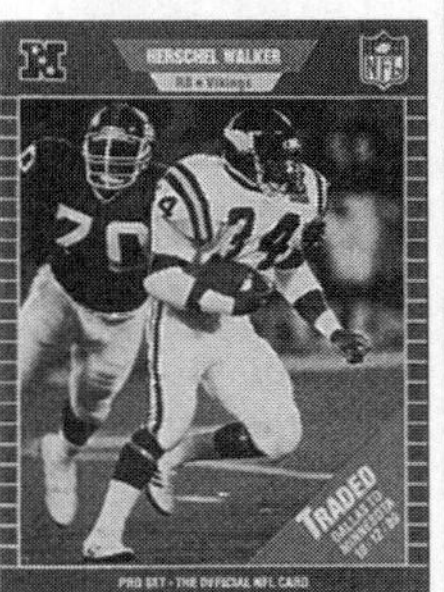

Pro Set's premier football issue was released in two series in the summer and fall of 1989. Printed on heavy white cardboard stock, the standard-size cards come in a variety of colors and feature full-color action shots on the front, full-color head shots on the back, and biographical notes and statistics on the back. The 615-card set (541 player/coach cards, 23 Super Bowl cards, 30 announcer cards, 20 Final Update cards, one commissioner card) was not released in factory-issued sets. Pro Set is the only one of the three 1989 football card sets featuring coaches cards. Pro Set released its first series in late July 1989, and its second series in September 1989. The third series, labeled "Final Update" on the boxes only, contained 20 additional cards of traded players, rookies and players not previously included in the set. Along with the re-released Art Shell card, these blue-bordered cards were included with Series I and II cards. Art Shell cards were printed on separate sheets and were inserted into late Series II and all Final Update print runs; the card was usually found on top of the pack.

		NM/M
Complete Set (561):		30.00
Complete Series 1 (440):		8.00
Complete Series 2 (100):		20.00
Complete Series 3 (21):		2.00
Common Player:		.03
Minor Stars:		.10
Series 1 Pack (14):		.45
Series 1 Box (36):		8.50
Series 2 or 3 Pack (14):		1.00
Series 2 or 3 Wax Box (36):		24.00
1	Stacey Bailey	.03
2	*Aundray Bruce*	.03
3	Rick Bryan	.03
4	Bobby Butler	.03
5	*Scott Case*	.10
6	Tony Casillas	.03
7	Floyd Dixon	.03
8	Rick Donnelly	.03
9	Bill Fralic	.03
10	Mike Gann	.03
11	Mike Kenn	.03
12	*Chris Miller*	.25
13	John Rade	.03
14	Gerald Riggs	.03
15	*John Settle*	.10
16	Marion Campbell	.03
17	Cornelius Bennett	.10
18	Derrick Burroughs	.03
19	Shane Conlan	.03
20	Ronnie Harmon	.03
21	*Kent Hull*	.10
22	Jim Kelly	.50
23	Mark Kelso	.03
24	Pete Metzelaars	.03
25	Scott Norwood	.03
26	Andre Reed	.10
27	Fred Smerlas	.03
28	Bruce Smith	.10
29	Leonard Smith	.03
30	Art Still	.03
31	Darryl Talley	.03
32	*Thurman Thomas*	1.50
33	Will Wolford	.03
34	Marv Levy (C)	.03
35	Neal Anderson	.03
36	Kevin Butler	.03
37	Jim Covert	.03
38	Richard Dent	.10
39	Dave Duerson	.03
40	Dennis Gentry	.03
41	Dan Hampton	.03
42	Jay Hilgenberg	.03
43	Dennis McKinnon	.03
44	Jim McMahon	.10
45	Steve McMichael	.03
46	*Brad Muster*	.10
47	William Perry ERR	3.00
48	Ron Rivera	.03
49	*Vestee Jackson*	.03
50	Mike Singletary	.10
51	Mike Tomczak	.03
52	*Keith Van Horne*	.03
53	Mike Ditka (C HOF stripe)	.10
54	Lewis Billups	.03
55	James Brooks	.03
56	Eddie Brown	.03
57	*Jason Buck*	.03
58	Boomer Esiason	.10
59	David Fulcher	.03
60	*Rodney Holman*	.10
61	Reggie Williams	.03
62	*Joe Kelly*	.03
63	Tim Krumrie	.03
64	Tim McGee	.03
65	Max Montoya	.03
66	Anthony Munoz	.10
67	Jim Skow	.03
68	*Eric Thomas*	.03
69	Leon White	.03
70	Ickey Woods	.03
71	Carl Zander	.03
72	Sam Wyche (C)	.03
73	Brian Brennan	.03
74	Earnest Byner	.03
75	Hanford Dixon	.03
76	Mike Pagel	.03
77	Bernie Kosar	.10
78	*Reggie Langhorne*	.10
79	Kevin Mack	.03
80	Clay Matthews	.03
81	Gerald McNeil	.03
82	Frank Minnifield	.03
83	Cody Risien	.03
84	Webster Slaughter	.10
85	Felix Wright	.03
86	Bud Carson (C)	.03
87	Bill Bates	.03
88	Kevin Brooks	.03
89	*Michael Irvin*	1.00
90	Jim Jeffcoat	.03
91	Too Tall Jones	.03
92	Eugene Lockhart	.03
93	*Nate Newton*	.20
94	Danny Noonan	.03
95	Steve Pelluer	.03
96	Herschel Walker	.10
97	Everson Walls	.03
98	Jimmy Johnson (C)	.10
99	Keith Bishop	.03
100	John Elway DRAFT	4.00
100a	John Elway TRADE	2.00
101	*Simon Fletcher*	.10
102	Mike Harden	.03
103	Mike Horan	.03
104	Mark Jackson	.03
105	Vance Johnson	.03
106	Rulon Jones	.03
107	Clarence Kay	.03
108	Karl Mecklenburg	.03
109	Ricky Nattiel	.03
110	*Steve Sewell*	.10
111	Dennis Smith	.03
112	Gerald Willhite	.03
113	Sammy Winder	.03
114	Dan Reeves	.10
115	Jim Arnold	.03
116	*Jerry Ball*	.10
117	*Bennie Blades*	.10
118	Lomas Brown	.03
119	Michael Cofer	.03
120	Garry James	.03
121	James Jones	.03
122	Chuck Long	.03
123	Pete Mandley	.03
124	Eddie Murray	.03
125	*Chris Spielman*	.10
126	Dennis Gibson	.03
127	Wayne Fontes (C)	.03
128	John Anderson	.03
129	Brent Fullwood	.03
130	Mark Cannon	.03
131	Tim Harris	.03
132	Mark Lee	.03
133	*Don Majkowski*	.10
134	Mark Murphy	.03
135	Brian Noble	.03
136	*Ken Ruettgers*	.03
137	Johnny Holland	.03
138	Randy Wright	.03
139	Lindy Infante (C)	.03
140	Steve Brown	.03
141	Ray Childress	.03
142	Jeff Donaldson	.03
143	Ernest Givins	.10
144	John Grimsley	.03
145	Alonzo Highsmith	.03
146	Drew Hill	.03
147	Robert Lyles	.03
148	*Bruce Matthews*	.10
149	Warren Moon	.25
150	Mike Munchak	.03
151	*Allen Pinkett*	.10
152	Mike Rozier	.03
153	Tony Zendejas	.03
154	Jerry Glanville (C)	.10
155	Albert Bentley	.03
156	Dean Biasucci	.03
157	Duane Bickett	.03
158	Bill Brooks	.03
159	*Chris Chandler*	2.00
160	Pat Beach	.03
161	Ray Donaldson	.03
162	Jon Hand	.03
163	Chris Hinton	.03
164	Rohn Stark	.03
165	Fredd Young	.03
166	Ron Meyer (C)	.03
167	Lloyd Burruss	.03
168	Carlos Carson	.03
169	Deron Cherry	.03
170	Irv Eatman	.03
171	Dino Hackett	.03
172	Steve DeBerg	.03
173	Albert Lewis	.03
174	Nick Lowery	.03
175	Bill Maas	.03
176	Christian Okoye	.10
177	Stephone Paige	.03
178	Mark Addickes	.03
179	*Kevin Ross*	.10
180	*Neil Smith*	.50
181	Marty Schottenheimer (C)	.03
182	Marcus Allen	.25
183	*Tim Brown*	1.50
184	Willie Gault	.03
185	Bo Jackson	.25
186	Howie Long	.10
187	Vann McElroy	.03
188	Matt Millen	.10
189	*Don Mosebar*	.03
190	Bill Pickel	.03
191	Jerry Robinson	.03
192	Jay Schroeder	.03
193	Stacey Toran	.10
193a	Stacey Toran (1961-1989)	.50
194	Mike Shanahan (C)	.10
195	Greg Bell	.03
196	Ron Brown	.03
197	*Aaron Cox*	.03
198	Henry Ellard	.03
199	Jim Everett	.10
200	Jerry Gray	.03
201	Kevin Greene	.10
202	Pete Holohan	.03
203	LeRoy Irvin	.03
204	Mike Lansford	.03
205	*Tom Newberry*	.10
206	Mel Owens	.03
207	Jackie Slater	.03
208	Doug Smith	.03
209	Mike Wilcher	.03
210	John Robinson (C)	.03
211	John Bosa	.03
212	Mark Brown	.03
213	Mark Clayton	.03
214	*Ferrell Edmunds* (corrected)	.10
214a	*Ferrell Edmonds* (error)	.50
215	Roy Foster	.03
216	Lorenzo Hampton	.03
217	Jim Jensen	.03
218	William Judson	.03
219	*Eric Kumerow*	.03
220	Dan Marino	2.00
221	John Offerdahl	.03
222	Fuad Reveiz	.03
223	Reggie Roby	.03
224	Brian Sochia	.03
225	Don Shula (C)	.20
226	Alfred Anderson	.03
227	Joey Browner	.03
228	Anthony Carter	.03
229	Chris Doleman	.03
230	*Hassan Jones*	.03
231	Steve Jordan	.03
232	Tommy Kramer	.03
233	*Carl Lee*	.03
234	*Kirk Lowdermilk*	.10
235	*Randall McDaniel*	.10
236	Doug Martin	.03
237	Keith Millard	.03
238	Darrin Nelson	.03
239	Jesse Solomon	.03
240	Scott Studwell	.03
241	Wade Wilson	.03
242	Gary Zimmerman	.03
243	Jerry Burns (C)	.03
244	*Bruce Armstrong*	.10
245	Raymond Clayburn	.03
246	Reggie Dupard	.03
247	Tony Eason	.03
248	Sean Farrell	.03
249	Doug Flutie	.75
250	*Brent Williams*	.03
251	Roland James	.03
252	Ronnie Lippett	.03
253	Fred Marion	.03
254	Lawrence McGrew	.03
255	Stanley Morgan	.03
256	*Johnny Rembert*	.03
257	*John Stephens*	.10
258	Andre Tippett	.03
259	Garin Veris	.03
260	Ray Berry (C HOF stripe)	.10
261	Morten Andersen	.10
262	Hoby Brenner	.03
263	Stan Brock	.03
264	Brad Edelmann	.03
265	James Geathers	.03
266	Bobby Hebert ("touchdown passers")	.50
266a	Bobby Hebert ("touchdown passes")	.10
267	*Craig Heyward*	.10
268	Lonzell Hill	.03
269	Dalton Hilliard	.03
270	Rickey Jackson	.03
271	Steve Korte	.03
272	Eric Martin	.03
273	Reuben Mayes	.03
274	Sam Mills	.03
275	*Brett Perriman*	.25
276	Pat Swilling	.10
277	John Tice	.03
278	Jim Mora (C)	.03
279	Eric Moore	.03
280	Carl Banks	.03
281	Mark Bavaro	.03
282	Maurice Carthon	.03
283	*Mark Collins*	.10
284	Erik Howard	.03
285	Terry Kinard	.03
286	Sean Landeta	.03
287	Lionel Manuel	.03
288	Leonard Marshall	.03
289	Joe Morris	.03
290	Bart Oates	.03
291	Phil Simms	.10
292	Lawrence Taylor	.20
293	Bill Parcells (C)	.10
294	Dave Cadigan	.03
295	*Kyle Clifton*	.10
296	Alex Gordon	.03
297	*James Hasty*	.10
298	Johnny Hector	.03
299	Bobby Humphery	.03
300	Pat Leahy	.03
301	Marty Lyons	.03
302	*Reggie McElroy*	.10
303	*Erik McMillan*	.10
304	Freeman McNeil	.03
305	Ken O'Brien	.03
306	Pat Ryan	.03
307	Mickey Shuler	.03
308	Al Toon	.03
309	JoJo Townsell	.03
310	Roger Vick	.03
311	Joe Walton (C)	.03
312	Jerome Brown	.03
313	Keith Byars	.03
314	*Cris Carter*	2.00
315	Randall Cunningham	.40
316	Terry Hoage	.03
317	Wes Hopkins	.03
318	*Keith Jackson*	.20
319	Mike Quick	.03
320	Mike Reichenbach	.03
321	Dave Rimington	.03
322	John Teltschik	.03
323	Anthony Toney	.03
324	Andre Waters	.03
325	Reggie White	.25
326	Luis Zendejas	.03
327	Buddy Ryan (C)	.03
328	Robert Awalt	.03
329	*Tim McDonald*	.10
330	Roy Green	.03
331	Neil Lomax	.03
332	Cedric Mack	.03
333	Stump Mitchell	.03
334	Niko Noga	.03
335	*Jay Novacek*	.25
336	Freddie Joe Nunn	.03
337	Luis Sharpe	.03
338	Vai Sikahema	.03
339	J.T. Smith	.03
340	Ron Wolfley	.03
341	Gene Stallings (C)	.03
342	Gary Anderson (Pit.)	.03
343	*Bubby Brister*	.75
344	*Dermontti Dawson*	.10
345	*Thomas Everett*	.10
346	Delton Hall	.03
347	*Bryan Hinkle*	.10
348	*Merril Hoge*	.10
349	Tunch Ilken	.03
350	*Aaron Jones*	.10
351	Louis Lipps	.03
352	David Little	.03
353	*Hardy Nickerson*	.20
354	*Rod Woodson*	.75
355	Chuck Noll ("One of the only three") (C)	.15
355a	Chuck Noll ("One of only two") (C)	.15
356	Gary Anderson (S.D.)	.03
357	*Rod Berstine*	.10
358	Gill Byrd	.03
359	Vencie Glenn	.03
360	Dennis McKnight	.03
361	Lionel James	.03
362	Mark Malone	.03
363	*Anthony Miller 14.8*	.40
363a	*Anthony Miller 3*	.40
364	Ralf Mojsiejenko	.03
365	Leslie O'Neal	.03
366	Jamie Holland	.03
367	Lee Williams	.03
368	Dan Henning	.03
369	*Harris Barton*	.10
370	Michael Carter	.03
371	*Mike Cofer* (S.F.)	.10
372	Roger Craig	.10
373	Riki Ellison	.03
374	Jim Fahnhorst	.03
375	John Frank	.03
376	Jeff Fuller	.03
377	Don Griffin	.03
378	Charles Haley	.10
379	Ronnie Lott	.10
380	Tim McKyer	.03
381	Joe Montana	2.00
382	Tom Rathman	.03
383	Jerry Rice	1.50
384	*John Taylor*	.25
385	Keena Turner	.03
386	Michael Walter	.03
387	Bubba Paris	.03
388	Steve Young	1.00
389	*George Siefert* (C)	.10
390	*Brian Blades*	.20
391	Brian Bosworth (Seahawks)	.10
391a	Brian Bosworth (Seattle)	.10

392	Jeff Bryant	.03
393	Jacob Green	.03
394	Norm Johnson	.03
395	Dave Krieg	.03
396	Steve Largent	.15
397	Bryan Millard	.03
398	Paul Moyer	.03
399	Joe Nash	.03
400	Rufus Porter	.03
401	*Eugene Robinson*	.20
402	Bruce Scholtz	.03
403	*Kelly Stouffer*	.10
404	Curt Warner 1455 (yards 1,455)	1.00
404a	Curt Warner (yards 6,074)	.15
405	John L. Williams	.03
406	*Tony Woods*	.10
407	David Wyman	.03
408	Chuck Knox (C)	.03
409	*Mark Carrier*	.50
410	Randy Grimes	.03
411	*Paul Gruber*	.10
412	Harry Hamilton	.03
413	Ron Holmes	.03
414	Donald Igwebuike	.03
415	Dan Turk	.03
416	Ricky Reynolds	.03
417	Bruce Hill	.03
418	Lars Tate	.03
419	Vinny Testaverde	.30
420	James Wilder	.03
421	Ray Perkins (C)	.03
422	Jeff Bostic	.03
423	Kelvin Bryant	.03
424	Gary Clark	.10
425	Monte Coleman	.03
426	Darrell Green	.03
427	Joe Jacoby	.03
428	Jim Lachey	.03
429	Charles Mann	.03
430	Dexter Manley	.03
431	Darryl Grant	.03
432	*Mark May*	.10
433	Art Monk	.15
434	*Mark Rypien*	.20
435	Ricky Sanders	.03
436	*Alvin Walton*	.10
437	Don Warren	.03
438	Jamie Morris	.03
439	Doug Williams	.03
440	Joe Gibbs (C)	.10
441	Marcus Cotton	.03
442	Joel Williams	.03
443	Joe Devlin	.03
444	Robb Riddick	.03
445	William Perry	.03
446	*Thomas Sanders*	.03
447	Brian Blades	.03
448	Cris Collinsworth	.10
449	Stanford Jennings	.03
450	Barry Krauss	.03
451	Ozzie Newsome	.10
452	Mike Oliphant	.03
453	Tony Dorsett	.15
454	Bruce McNorton	.03
455	Eric Dickerson	.20
456	Keith Bostic	.03
457	Sam Clancy	.03
458	Jack Del Rio	.03
459	Mike Webster	.03
460	Bob Golic	.03
461	Otis Wilson	.03
462	Mike Haynes	.03
463	Greg Townsend	.03
464	Mark Duper	.03
465	E.J. Junior	.03
466	Troy Stradford	.03
467	Mike Merriweather	.03
468	Irving Fryar	.10
469	*Vaughan Johnson*	.10
470	Pepper Johnson	.03
471	Gary Reasons	.03
472	*Perry Williams*	.10
473	Wesley Walker	.03
474	Anthony Bell	.03
475	Earl Ferrell	.03
476	Craig Wolfley	.03
477	Billy Ray Smith	.03
478	Jim McMahon	.10
478a	Jim McMahon (traded)	.40
479	Eric Wright	.03
480	Earnest Byner	.10
480a	Earnest Byner (traded)	.30
481	Russ Grimm	.03
482	Wilber Marshall	.03
483	Gerald Riggs	.03
484	*Brian Davis*	.10
485	*Shawn Collins*	.10
486	*Deion Sanders*	2.00
487	*Trace Armstrong*	.10
488	*Donnell Woolford*	.20
489	*Eric Metcalf*	.25
490	*Troy Aikman*	3.00
491	*Steve Walsh*	.20
492	*Steve Atwater*	.30
493	*Bobby Humphrey*	.10
494	*Barry Sanders*	15.00
495	*Tony Mandarich*	.20
496	*David Williams*	.10
497	*Andre Rison*	1.00
498	*Derrick Thomas*	1.00
499	*Cleveland Gary*	.20
500	*Bill Hawkins*	.10
501	*Louis Oliver*	.10
502	*Sammie Smith*	.10
503	*Hart Lee Dykes*	.10
504	*Wayne Martin*	.10
505	*Brian Williams*	.10
506	*Jeff Lageman*	.10
507	*Eric Hill*	.10
508	*Joe Wolf*	.10
509	*Timm Rosenbach*	.10
510	*Tom Ricketts*	.10
511	*Tim Worley*	.10
512	*Burt Grossman*	.10
513	*Keith DeLong*	.10
514	*Andy Heck*	.10
515	*Broderick Thomas*	.10
516	*Don Beebe*	.25
517	*James Thornton*	.10
518	*Eric Kattus*	.10
519	*Bruce Kozerski*	.10
520	*Brian Washington*	.10
521	*Rodney Peete*	.25
522	*Erik Affholter*	.10
523	*Anthony Dilweg*	.10
524	*O'Brien Alston*	.10
525	*Mike Elkins*	.10
526	*Jonathan Hayes*	.10
527	*Terry McDaniel*	.10
528	*Frank Stams*	.10
529	*Darryl Ingram*	.10
530	*Henry Thomas*	.10
531	*Eric Coleman*	.10
532	*Sheldon White*	.10
533	*Eric Allen*	.20
534	Robert Drummond	.03
535	Gizmo Williams ("Scouting Photo")	10.00
535a	Gizmo Williams (no "Scouting Photo")	.25
535b	Gizmo Williams (no "Scouting Photo," "Canadian Football" on back)	.15
536	*Billy Joe Tolliver*	.20
537	*Danny Stubbs*	.10
538	*Wesley Walls*	.40
539	James Jefferson (no stripe)	.30
539a	James Jefferson (Pro Set Prospect stripe)	.10
540	Tracy Rocker	.03
541	Art Shell (C)	.10
542	*Lemuel Stinson*	.15
543	*Tyrone Braxton*	.10
543a	*Tyrone Braxton* (back photo actually Ken Bell)	.10
544	*David Treadwell*	.10
545	*Willie Anderson*	.20
546	*Dave Meggett*	.25
547	*Lewis Tillman*	.20
548	*Carnell Lake*	.20
549	*Marion Butts*	.20
550	*Sterling Sharpe*	1.00
551	Ezra Johnson	.03
552	*Clarence Verdin*	.10
553	Mervyn Fernandez	.03
554	Ottis Anderson	.10
555	Gary Hogeboom	.03
556	Paul Palmer	.03
557	Jesse Solomon	.03
558	Chip Banks	.03
559	Steve Pelluer	.03
560	Darrin Nelson	.03
561	Herschel Walker	.10
CC1	Pete Rozelle	.50

1989 Pro Set Announcer Inserts

This set of 30 cards was issued in Pro Set's Series II wax packs, one per pack. Like the Super Bowl inserts, the glossy cards are standard size. They feature color photos (bordered in bright orange) of the announcer on the front and back - if the announcer is a former player, a shot of him in action is shown. If the announcer made it to the Hall of Fame as a player (Terry Bradshaw, O.J. Simpson), a yellow stripe bearing a "Hall of Fame" label is in the lower left corner of his action picture. Pro Set had announced the names of the players of its first 20 cards in its premier issue of Pro Set Gazette. Since the initial announcement, Pro Set acquired the rights to NBC announcers and added them shortly before the presses began to roll. Verne Lundquist was apparently substituted for Dan Jiggetts just before the print run began.

		NM/M
Complete Set (30):		5.00
Common Player:		.08
1	Dan Dierdorf	.25
2	Frank Gifford	.75
3	Al Michaels	.15
4	Pete Axthelm	.08
5	Chris Berman	.25
6	Tom Jackson	.15
7	Mike Patrick	.08
8	John Saunders	.08
9	Joe Theismann	.30
10	Steve Sabol	.08
11	Jack Buck	.08
12	Terry Bradshaw	.50
13	James Brown	.08
14	Dan Fouts	.30
15	Dick Butkus	.50
16	Irv Cross	.08
17	Brent Musberger	.15
18	Ken Stabler	.25
19	Dick Stockton	.08
20	Hank Stram	.08
21	Verne Lundquist	.08
22	Will McDonough	.08
23	Bob Costas	.25
24	Dick Enberg	.15
25	Joe Namath	.65
26	Bob Trumpy	.08
27	Merlin Olsen	.25
28	Ahmad Rashad	.30
29	O.J. Simpson	2.00
30	Bill Walsh	.30

1989 Pro Set Super Bowl Inserts

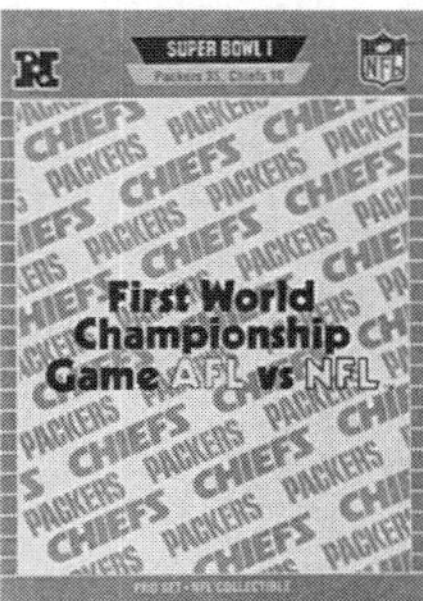

Pro Set included a glossy Super Bowl card (1 through 23) in each wax pack of its 1989 Series I cards. The standard-size cards show the official logo of each Super Bowl surrounded by a bright orange border on the front of the card, with the stylized names of the two participating teams in the background. Card backs include a recap of the game and a line score.

		NM/M
Complete Set (23):		5.00
Common Player:		.25
1	Super Bowl I	.25
2	Super Bowl II	.25
3	Super Bowl IV	.25
4	Super Bowl IV	.25
5	Super Bowl V	.25
6	Super Bowe VI	.25
7	Super Bowl VII	.25
8	Super Bowl VIII	.25
9	Super Bowl IX	.25
10	Super Bowl X	.25
11	Super Bowl XI	.25
12	Super Bowl XII	.25
13	Super Bowl XIII	.25
14	Super Bowl XIV	.25
15	Super Bowl XV	.25
16	Super Bowl XVI	.25
17	Super Bowl XVII	.25
18	Super Bowl XVIII	.25
19	Super Bowl XIX	.25
20	Super Bowl XX	.25
21	Super Bowl XXI	.25
22	Super Bowl XXII	.25
23	Super Bowl XXIII	.25

1989 Pro Set GTE SB Album

This 40-card set was made available to those who attended the Super Bowl XXIV game in New Orleans in 1990. Players from the participants in the game, the San Francisco 49ers and Denver Broncos, are represented in the set. The card numbers are identical to those in the regular set, but these cards can be distinguished from the regulars by the NFC or AFC Champs designation on the card front, along with the Super Bowl logo. GTE issued the cards in conjunction with Pro Set, and created a card album to hold the set.

		NM/M
Complete Set (40):		30.00
Common Player:		.40
99	Keith Bishop	.40
100	John Elway	6.00
101	Simon Fletcher	.60
103	Mike Horan	.40
104	Mark Jackson	.70
105	Vance Johnson	.60
107	Clarence Kay	.40
108	Karl Mecklenburg	.60
109	Ricky Nattiel	.60
110	Steve Sewell	.50
111	Dennis Smith	.50
113	Sammy Winder	.50
114	Dan Reeves CO	.60
369	Harris Barton	.40
370	Michael Carter	.60
371	Mike Cofer	.40
372	Roger Craig	1.75
374	Jim Fahnhorst	.40
377	Don Griffin	.50
378	Charles Haley	.60
379	Ronnie Lott	2.50
380	Tim McKyer	.50
381	Joe Montana	11.00
382	Tom Rathman	.75
383	Jerry Rice	8.00
384	John Taylor	2.00
385	Keena Turner	.50
386	Michael Walter	.40
387	Bubba Paris	.40
388	Steve Young	4.00
389	George Seifert CO	.50
479	Eric Wright	.60
492	Steve Atwater	1.00
493	Bobby Humphrey	.75
537	Danny Stubbs	.40
543	Tyrone Braxton	.50
544	David Treadwell	.40
----	AFC Logo XXIV Collectible	.60
----	NFC logo XXIV Collectible	.60
----	Superdome XXIV Collectible	.60

1990 Pro Set Draft Day

Each of these cards, numbered 669, was issued by Pro Set on the day of the 1990 NFL draft to present various scenarios for the draft. The card fronts preview Pro Set's 1990 main set design; each back uses a horizontal format and includes a mug shot, biographical information and a player profile.

		NM/M
Complete Set (3):		5.00
Common Player:		1.00
669A	Jeff George	2.00
669B	Jeff George	2.00
669D	Keith McCants	1.00

1990 Pro Set

Pro Set's Series I was issued in late May of 1990. The sophomore set for the Dallas-based company was its first using its own printing press, and that allowed Pro Set to create die-cut borderless cards. Again, several insert cards were included throughout Series I: Paul Tagliabue was randomly included in early Series I wax packs; golfer Payne Stewart was added to the rotation; and Jeff George completed the rotating triumverate in late Series I printings. Because of a squabble over what card companies he wanted to appear with, Eric Dickerson was not to appear in any 1990 card sets. Pro Set already had a card of him created, however, and was forced to pull them by hand from Series I. Some, however, did get through to the hobby. Issued in November 1990, the second series of Pro Set was, unlike the year before, not included in Series I wax boxes. In addition, space was saved in the middle of the set for the mail-in Final Update offer. Five cards were inserted on a rotating basis in every 50th pack: Paul Tagliabue (carried over from Series I), Payne Stewart (same), Santa Claus, Joe Robbie, and Marvel Comics Super Pro. The Final Update was available in late January through a mail-in offer. It included 28 cards, plus three other special cards: card 799, which featured Ronnie Lott in his role as a spokesman for the NFL's "Stay in School" program; the Series I Andre Rison card with a traded stripe; and cards 800, Emmitt Smith and Mark Carrier, the 1990 NFL Pro Set Rookies of the Year in the 1991 Pro Set design. One correction was made very early in the print run. The text on the back of card 772, Dexter Manley, originally read, "Reinstated by Paul Tagliabue 11 weeks into the 1990 season after suspension for violating the league's substance-abuse policy." According to reports, Manley's agent objected to the wording, and it was changed to "After missing the first 10 weeks of the 1990 season, Dexter returned to the NFL." Very few of the original cards were issued.

		NM/M
Complete Set (801):		15.00
Complete Series 1 (377):		6.00
Complete Series 2 (392):		6.00
Complete Series 3 (32):		3.00
Common Player:		.03
Series 1 Pack (14+1):		.50
Series 1 Wax Box (36):		10.00
Series 2 Pack (14+1):		.50
Series 2 Wax Box (36):		10.00
1	Barry Sanders (ROY)	.75
2	Joe Montana (SPL) (back reads "Kelly-3,521 yards")	.50
2a	Joe Montana (SPL) (back corrected to "Kelly: 3,130 yards")	.75
3	Lindy Infante (SPL)	.03
4	Warren Moon (SPL)	.10
5	Keith Millard (SPL)	.03
6	Derrick Thomas (SPL)	.10
7	Ottis Anderson (SPL)	.03
8	Joe Montana (LL)	.50
9	Christian Okoye (SPL)	.03
10	Thurman Thomas	.25
11	Mike Cofer (SPL)	.03
12	Dalton Hilliard (SPL)	.03
13	Sterling Sharpe (LL)	.20
14	Rich Camarillo (LL)	.03
15	Walter Stanley (SPL) (#8 on back)	.10
15a	Walter Stanley (SPL) (#86 on back)	.10
16	Rod Woodson (LL)	.03
17	Felix Wright (LL)	.03
18	Chris Doleman (SPL) (error back)	.10
18a	Chris Doleman (SPL) (back corrected to 104.5 sacks for Taylor; "Townsent" corrected to "Townsend")	.10
19	Andre Ware (SPL)	.10
19a	Andre Ware (SPL) (drafted stripe added)	.10
20	Mohammed Elewonibi (SPL)	.05
20a	Mohammed Elewonibi (SPL) (drafted stripe added)	.05
21	Percy Snow (SPL)	.05
21a	Percy Snow (SPL) (drafted stripe added)	.05
22	Anthony Thompson (SPL)	.10
22a	Anthony Thompson (SPL) (drafted stripe added)	.10
23	Buck Buchanan (HOF)	.03
24	Bob Griese (HOF)	.03
25	Franco Harris (HOF)	.05
25a	Franco Harris (HOF) (corrected birthdate: 3/7/50)	.05
26	Ted Hendricks (HOF)	.03
27	Jack Lambert (HOF)	.08
27a	Jack Lambert (HOF) (corrected birthdate 7/8/52)	.08
28	Tom Landry (HOF)	.06
29	Bob St. Clair (HOF)	.03
30	Aundray Bruce	.06
31	Tony Casillas	.03
32	Shawn Collins	.03
33	Marcus Cotton	.03
34	Bill Fralic	.03
35	Chris Miller	.06
36	Deion Sanders	.30
37	John Settle	.03
38	Jerry Glanville	.03
39	Cornelius Bennett	.03
40	Jim Kelly	.35
41	Mark Kelso	.03
42	Scott Norwood	.03
43	*Nate Odomes*	.30
44	Scott Radecic	.03
45	Jim Ritcher	.03
46	Leonard Smith	.03
47	Darryl Talley	.03
48	Marv Levy (C)	.03
49	Neal Anderson	.03
50	Kevin Butler	.03
51	Jim Covert	.03
52	Richard Dent	.03
53	Jay Hilgenberg	.03
54	Steve McMichael	.03
55	Ron Morris	.03
56	John Roper	.03
57	Mike Singletary	.03
59	Mike Ditka (C)	.03
60	Lewis Billups	.03
61	Eddie Brown	.03
62	Jason Buck	.03
63	Rickey Dixon (no bio notes under photo)	.10
63a	Rickey Dixon (with bio notes)	.10
64	Tim McGee	.03
65	Eric Thomas	.03
66	Ickey Woods	.03
67	Carl Zander	.03
68	Sam Wyche (C) (no bio notes under photo)	.05
68a	Sam Wyche (C) (correction)	.05
69	Paul Farren	.03
70	Thane Gash	.03
71	David Grayson	.03
72	Bernie Kosar	.03
73	Reggie Langhorne	.03
74	Eric Metcalf	.03
75	Ozzie Newsome	.10
75a	Ozzie Newsome (corrected hometown: Muscle Shoals, AL)	.10
75	Cody Risien (SP)	.10
76	Felix Wright	.03
77	Bud Carson (C)	.03
78	Troy Aikman	1.00
79	Michael Irvin	.30
80	Jim Jeffcoat	.03
81	Crawford Ker	.03
82	Eugene Lockhart	.03
83	*Kelvin Martin*	.25
84	*Ken Norton Jr.*	.50
85	Jimmy Johnson (C)	.03
86	Steve Atwater	.03
87	Tyrone Braxton	.03
88	John Elway	.40
89	Simon Fletcher	.03
90	Ron Holmes	.03
91	Bobby Humphrey	.03
92	Vance Johnson	.03
93	Ricky Nattiel	.03
94	Dan Reeves	.03
95	Jim Arnold	.03
96	Jerry Ball	.03
97	Bennie Blades	.03
98	Lomas Brown	.03
99	Michael Cofer	.03
100	Richard Johnson	.03
101	Eddie Murray	.03
102	Barry Sanders	1.25
103	Chris Spielman	.03
104	*William White*	.08
105	*Eric Williams*	.08
106	Wayne Fontes (C)	.03
107	Brent Fullwood	.03
108	*Ron Hallstrom*	.08
109	Tim Harris	.03
110	Johnny Holland (no name, number on back)	1.00
110a	Johnny Holland (corrected)	.15
111	Perry Kemp (Ken Stills photo on back)	.10
111a	Perry Kemp (corrected)	.10
112	Don Majkowski	.03
113	Mark Murphy	.03
114	Sterling Sharpe	.20
114a	Sterling Sharpe (corrected birthplace: Chicago, IL)	.20
115	Ed West	.03
116	Lindy Infante (C)	.03
117	Steve Brown	.03
118	Ray Childress	.03
119	Ernest Givins	.03
120	John Grimsley	.03
121	Alonzo Highsmith	.03
122	Drew Hill	.03
123	Bubba McDowell	.03
124	Dean Steinkuhler	.03
125	Lorenzo White	.10
126	Tony Zendejas	.03
127	Jack Pardee (C)	.03
128	Albert Bentley	.03
129	Dean Biasucci	.03
130	Duane Bickett	.03
131	Bill Brooks	.03
132	John Hand	.03
133	Mike Prior	.03
134	Andre Rison (no stripe)	.25
134a	Andre Rison (with stripe)	.50
135	Rohn Stark	.03
136	Donnell Thompson	.03
137	Clarence Verdin	.03
138	Fredd Young	.03
139	Ron Meyer (C)	.03
140	*John Alt*	.08
141	Steve DeBerg	.03
142	Irv Eatman	.03
143	Dino Hackett	.03
144	Nick Lowery	.03
145	Bill Maas	.03
146	Stephone Paige	.03
147	Neil Smith	.25
148	Marty Schottenheimer (C)	.03
149	Steve Beuerlein	.25
150	Tim Brown	.35
151	Mike Dyal	.03
152	Mervyn Fernandez	.10
152a	Mervyn Fernandez (status corrected to "Drafted 10th round '83")	.10
153	Willie Gault	.03
154	Bob Golic	.03
155	Bo Jackson	.40
156	Don Mosebar	.03
157	Steve Smith	.03
158	Greg Townsend	.03
159	*Bruce Wilkerson*	.08
160	Steve Wisniewski	.03
161	Art Shell (C)	.10
161a	Art Shell (C)(birthdate corrected to 11/26/46)	.10
162	Willie Anderson	.10
163	Greg Bell	.03
164	Henry Ellard	.03
165	Jim Everett	.03
166	Jerry Gray	.03
167	Kevin Greene	.03
168	Pete Holohan	.03
169	*Larry Kelm*	.08
170	Tom Newberry	.03
171	Vince Newsome	.03
172	Irv Pankey	.03
173	Jackie Slater	.03
174	*Fred Strickland*	.08
175	Mike Wilcher	.03
176	John Robinson (C)	.03
177	Mark Clayton	.03
178	Roy Foster	.03

No.	Player	Price
179	*Harry Galbreath*	.08
180	Jim Jensen	.03
181	Dan Marino	.75
182	Louis Oliver	.03
183	Sammie Smith	.03
184	Brian Sochia	.03
185	Don Shula (C)	.03
186	Joey Browner	.03
187	Anthony Carter	.03
188	Chris Doleman	.03
189	Steve Jordan	.03
190	Carl Lee	.03
191	Randall McDaniel	.03
192	Mike Merriweather	.03
193	Keith Millard	.03
194	Al Noga	.03
195	Scott Studwell	.03
196	Henry Thomas	.03
197	Herschel Walker	.03
198	Wade Wilson	.03
199	Gary Zimmerman	.03
200	Jerry Burns (C)	.03
201	*Vincent Brown*	.15
202	Hart Lee Dykes	.03
203	Sean Farrell	.03
204	Fred Marion (49er with belt)	.05
204a	Fred Marion (corrected)	.05
205	Stanley Morgan	.03
206	Eric Sievers	.03
207	John Stephens	.03
208	Andre Tippett	.03
209	Rod Rust (C)	.03
210	Morten Andersen (name in white on back)	.10
210a	Morten Andersen (corrected)	.10
211	Brad Edelman	.03
212	John Fourcade	.03
213	Dalton Hilliard	.03
214	Rickey Jackson	.03
215	Vaughan Johnson	.03
216	Eric Martin (name in white on back)	.05
216a	Eric Martin (corrected)	.05
217	Sam Mills	.03
218	Pat Swilling	.03
219	*Frank Warren*	.08
220	Jim Wilks	.03
221	Jim Mora (C) (name in white on back)	.03
221a	Jim Mora (C) (corrected)	.03
222	Raul Allegre	.03
223	Carl Banks	.03
224	John Elliot	.03
225	Erik Howard	.03
226	Pepper Johnson	.03
227	Leonard Marshall	.03
228	David Meggett	.10
229	Bart Oates	.03
230	Phil Simms	.10
231	Lawrence Taylor	.10
232	Bill Parcells (C)	.03
233	Troy Benson	.03
234	Kyle Clifton	.03
235	Johnny Hector	.03
236	Jeff Lageman	.03
237	Pat Leahy	.03
238	Freeman McNeil	.03
239	Ken O'Brien	.03
240	Al Toon	.03
241	JoJo Townsell	.03
242	Bruce Coslet (C)	.03
243	Eric Allen	.03
244	Jerome Brown	.03
245	Keith Byars	.03
246	Cris Carter	.35
247	Randall Cunningham	.15
248	Keith Jackson	.25
249	Mike Quick	.03
250	Clyde Simmons	.03
251	Andre Waters	.03
252	Reggie White	.15
253	Buddy Ryan (C)	.03
254	Rich Camarillo	.03
255	Earl Ferrell	.03
256	Roy Green	.03
257	*Ken Harvey*	.08
258	*Ernie Jones*	.10
259	Tim McDonald	.03
260	Timm Rosenbach	.03
261	Luis Sharpe	.03
262	Vai Sikahema	.03
263	J.T. Smith	.03
264	Ron Wolfley	.03
265	Joe Bugel (C)	.03
266	Gary Anderson	.03
267	Bubby Brister	.10
268	Merril Hoge	.03
269	Carnell Lake	.03
270	Louis Lipps	.03
271	David Little	.03
272	Greg Lloyd	.03
273	Keith Willie	.03
274	Tim Worley	.03
275	Chuck Noll (C)	.03
276	Marion Butts	.06
277	Gill Byrd	.03
278	Vencie Glenn	.03
279	Burt Grossman	.03
280	Gary Plummer	.03
281	Billy Ray Smith	.03
282	Billy Joe Tolliver	.03
283	Dan Henning (C)	.03
284	Harris Barton	.03
285	Michael Carter	.03
286	Mike Cofer	.03
287	Roger Craig	.03
288	Don Griffin	.03
289	Charles Haley	.05
289a	Charles Haley (stats corrected to 5 total fumble recoveries)	.05
290	*Pierce Holt*	.10
291	Ronnie Lott	.10
292	Guy McIntyre	.03
293	Joe Montana	1.00
294	Tom Rathman	.03
295	Jerry Rice	.75
296	*Jesse Sapolu*	.05
297	John Taylor	.20
298	Michael Walter	.03
299	George Seifert (C)	.03
300	Jeff Bryant	.03
301	Jacob Green	.03
302	Norm Johnson	.03
303	Bryan Millard	.03
304	Joe Nash	.03
305	Eugene Robinson	.03
306	John L. Williams	.03
307	Dave Wyman	.03
308	Chuck Knox (C)	.03
309	Mark Carrier	.03
310	Paul Gruber	.03
311	Harry Hamilton	.03
312	Bruce Hill	.03
313	Donald Igwebuike	.03
314	Kevin Murphy	.03
315	Ervin Randle	.03
316	Mark Robinson	.03
317	Lars Tate	.03
318	Vinny Testaverde	.08
319	Ray Perkins (C) (no name, number on back)	.05
319a	Ray Perkins (C) (corrected)	.05
320	Earnest Byner	.03
321	Gary Clark	.15
322	Darryl Grant	.03
323	Darrell Green	.03
324	Jim Lachey	.03
325	Charles Mann	.03
326	Wilber Marshall	.03
327	Ralf Mojsienjenko	.03
328	Art Monk	.03
329	Gerald Riggs	.03
330	Mark Rypien	.10
331	Ricky Sanders	.03
332	Alvin Walton	.03
333	Joe Gibbs (C)	.03
334	Aloha Stadium - PB	.03
335	Brian Blades (PB)	.03
336	James Brooks (PB)	.03
337	Shane Conlan (PB)	.03
338	Eric Dickerson	4.00
339	Ray Donaldson (PB)	.03
340	Ferrell Edmunds	.03
341	Boomer Esiason (PB)	.06
342	David Fulcher (PB)	.03
343	Chris Hinton (PB) (no traded stripe)	.05
343a	Chris Hinton (PB) (traded)	.05
344	Rodney Holman (PB)	.06
345	Kent Hull (PB)	.03
346	Tunch Ilkin (PB)	.03
347	Mike Johnson (PB)	.03
348	Greg Kragen (PB)	.03
349	Dave Krieg (PB)	.03
350	Albert Lewis (PB)	.03
351	Howie Long (PB)	.03
352	Bruce Matthews	.03
353	Clay Matthews (PB)	.03
354	Erik McMillan (PB)	.03
355	Karl Mecklenberg (PB)	.03
356	Anthony Miller (PB)	.25
357	Frank Minnifield (PB)	.03
358	Max Montoya (PB)	.03
359	Warren Moon (PB)	.08
360	Mike Munchak (PB)	.03
361	Anthony Munoz (PB)	.03
362	John Offerdahl (PB)	.03
363	Christian Okoye (PB)	.03
364	Leslie O'Neal (PB)	.06
365	Rufus Porter (PB)	.03
366	Andre Reed (PB)	.06
367	Johnny Rembert (PB)	.03
368	Reggie Roby (PB)	.03
369	Kevin Ross (PB)	.03
370	Webster Slaughter (PB)	.03
371	Bruce Smith (PB)	.06
372	Dennis Smith	.03
373	Derrick Thomas (PB)	.06
374	Thurman Thomas	.25
375	David Treadwell (PB)	.03
376	Lee Williams (PB)	.03
377	Rod Woodson (PB)	.03
378	Bud Carson (PB)	.03
379	Eric Allen (PB)	.03
380	Neal Anderson (PB)	.03
381	Jerry Ball (PB)	.03
382	Joey Browner (PB)	.03
383	Rich Camarillo (PB)	.03
384	Mark Carrier (PB)	.03
385	Roger Craig (PB)	.03
386	Randall Cunningham (PB)	.10
387	Chris Doleman (PB)	.03
388	Henry Ellard (PB)	.03
389	Bill Fralic (PB)	.03
390	Brent Fullwood (PB)	.03
391	Jerry Gray (PB)	.03
392	Kevin Greene (PB)	.03
393	Tim Harris (PB)	.03
394	Jay Hilgenberg (PB)	.03
395	Dalton Hilliard (PB)	.03
396	Keith Jackson (PB)	.08
397	Vaughan Johnson (PB)	.03
398	Steve Jordan (PB)	.03
399	Carl Lee (PB)	.03
400	Ronnie Lott (PB)	.06
401	Don Majkowski (PB)	.03
402	Charles Mann (PB)	.03
403	Randall McDaniel (PB)	.03
404	Tim McDonald (PB)	.03
405	Guy McIntyre (PB)	.03
406	Dave Meggett (PB)	.03
407	Keith Millard (PB)	.03
408	Joe Montana (PB)	.50
409	Eddie Murray	.03
410	Tom Newberry (PB)	.03
411	Jerry Rice (PB)	.40
412	Mark Rypien (PB)	.03
413	Barry Sanders (PB)	.75
414	Luis Sharpe (PB)	.03
415	Sterling Sharpe (PB)	.20
416	Mike Singletary (PB)	.03
417	Jackie Slater (PB)	.03
418	Doug Smith (PB)	.03
419	Chris Spielman (PB)	.03
420	Pat Swilling (PB)	.03
421	John Taylor (PB)	.10
422	Lawrence Taylor (PB)	.10
423	Reggie White (PB)	.08
424	Ron Wolfley (PB)	.03
425	Gary Zimmerman (PB)	.03
426	John Robinson (PB)	.03
427	Scott Case	.03
428	Mike Kenn	.03
429	Mike Gann	.03
430	*Tim Green*	.08
431	*Michael Haynes*	.30
432	*Jessie Tuggle*	.20
433	John Rade	.03
434	Andre Rison	.25
435	Don Beebe	.03
436	Ray Bentley	.03
437	Shane Conlan	.03
438	Kent Hull	.03
439	Pete Metzelaars	.03
440	Andre Reed	.15
441	Frank Reich	.15
442	Leon Seals	.08
443	Bruce Smith	.03
444	Thurman Thomas	.40
445	Will Wolford	.03
446	Trace Armstrong	.03
447	*Mark Bortz*	.10
448	*Tom Thayer*	.10
449	Dan Hampton (DE back)	.05
449a	Dan Hampton (DT back)	.05
451	Dennis Gentry	.03
452	Jim Harbaugh	.10
453	Vestee Jackson	.03
454	Brad Muster	.03
455	William Perry	.03
456	Ron Rivera	.03
457	James Thornton	.03
458	Mike Tomczak	.03
459	Donnell Woolford	.03
460	Eric Ball	.03
461	James Brooks	.03
462	David Fulcher	.03
463	Boomer Esiason	.10
464	Rodney Holman	.03
465	Bruce Kozerski	.03
466	Tim Krumrie	.03
467	Anthony Munoz	.03
468	Brian Blados	.03
469	Mike Baab	.03
470	Brian Brennan	.03
471	Raymond Clayborn	.03
472	Mike Johnson	.03
473	Kevin Mack	.03
474	Clay Matthews	.03
475	Frank Minnifield	.03
476	Gregg Rakoczy	.03
477	Webster Slaughter	.03
478	James Dixon	.03
479	Robert Awalt	.03
480	Dennis McKinnon	.03
481	Danny Noonan	.03
482	Jesse Soloman	.03
483	Danny Stubbs	.03
484	Steve Walsh	.03
485	*Michael Brooks*	.25
486	Mark Jackson	.03
487	Greg Kragen	.03
488	*Ken Lanier*	.08
489	Karl Mecklenburg	.03
490	Steve Sewell	.03
491	Dennis Smith	.03
492	David Treadwell	.03
493	*Michael Young*	.08
494	*Robert Clark*	.10
495	Dennis Gibson	.03
496	*Kevin Glover* (C-G back)	.15
496a	*Kevin Glover* (G back)	.10
497	Mel Gray	.03
498	Rodney Peete	.10
499	Dave Brown	.03
500	Jerry Holmes	.03
501	Chris Jacke	.03
502	Alan Veingrad	.03
503	Mark Lee	.03
504	Tony Mandarich	.03
505	Brian Noble	.03
506	Jeff Query	.03
507	Ken Ruettgers	.03
508	Patrick Allen	.03
509	Curtis Duncan	.03
510	William Fuller	.03
511	*Haywood Jeffires*	.50
512	Sean Jones	.03
513	Terry Kinard	.03
514	Bruce Matthews	.03
515	Gerald McNeil	.03
516	*Greg Montgomery*	.08
517	Warren Moon	.20
518	Mike Munchak	.03
519	Allen Pinkett	.03
520	Pat Beach	.03
521	Eugene Daniel	.03
522	Kevin Call	.03
523	Ray Donaldson	.03
524	*Jeff Herrod*	.08
525	Keith Taylor	.03
526	Jack Trudeau	.03
527	Deron Cherry	.03
528	Jeff Donaldson	.03
529	Albert Lewis	.03
530	Pete Mandley	.03
531	*Chris Martin*	.08
532	Christian Okoye	.03
533	Steve Pelluer	.03
534	Kevin Ross	.03
535	Dan Saleaumua	.03
536	Derrick Thomas	.25
537	Mike Webster	.03
538	Marcus Allen	.03
539	Greg Bell	.03
540	Thomas Benson	.03
541	Ron Brown	.03
542	Scott Davis	.03
543	Riki Ellison	.03
544	Jamie Holland	.03
545	Howie Long	.03
546	Terry McDaniel	.03
547	Max Montoya	.03
548	Jay Schroeder	.03
549	Lionel Washington	.03
550	Robert Delpino	.03
551	Bobby Humphery	.03
552	Mike Lansford	.03
553	*Michael Stewart*	.08
554	Doug Smith	.03
555	Curt Warner	.03
556	Alvin Wright	.03
557	Jeff Cross	.03
558	*Jeff Dellenbach*	.08
559	Mark Duper	.03
560	Ferrell Edmunds	.03
561	Tim McKyer	.03
562	John Offerdahl	.03
563	Reggie Roby	.03
564	Pete Stoyanovich	.03
565	Alfred Anderson	.03
566	Ray Berry	.03
567	Rick Fenney	.03
568	*Rich Gannon*	2.00
569	Tim Irwin	.03
570	Hassan Jones	.03
571	Cris Carter	.30
572	Kirk Lowdermilk	.03
573	*Reggie Rutland*	.08
574	Ken Stills	.03
575	Bruce Armstrong	.03
576	Irving Fryar	.03
577	Roland James	.03
578	Robert Perryman	.03
579	Cedric Jones	.03
580	Steve Grogan	.03
581	Johnny Rembert	.03
582	Ed Reynolds	.03
583	Brent Williams	.03
584	Marc Wilson	.03
585	Hoby Brenner	.03
586	Stan Brock	.03
587	*Jim Dombrowski*	.08
588	*Joel Hilgenberg*	.10
589	Robert Massey	.03
590	Floyd Turner	.10
591	Ottis Anderson	.03
592	Mark Bavaro	.03
593	Maurice Carthon	.03
594	*Eric Dorsey*	.10
595	Myron Guyton	.03
596	*Jeff Hostetler*	.75
597	Sean Landeta	.03
598	Lionel Manuel	.03
599	*Odessa Turner*	.10
600	Perry Williams	.03
601	James Hasty	.03
602	Erik McMillan	.03
603	Alex Gordon	.03
604	Ron Stallworth	.03
605	*Byron Evans*	.10
606	*Ron Heller*	.10
607	Wes Hopkins (black, red fumble/ interceptions head)	.10
607a	Wes Hopkins (red fumble/ interceptions head)	.10
608	Mickey Shuler	.03
609	Seth Joyner	.03
610	Jim McMahon	.03
611	Mike Pitts	.03
612	Izel Jenkins	.03
613	Anthony Bell	.03
614	David Galloway	.03
615	Eric Hill	.03
616	Cedric Mack	.03
617	Freddie Joe Nunn	.03
618	Tootie Robbins	.03
619	*Tom Tupa*	.10
620	Joe Wolf	.03
621	Dermontti Dawson	.03
622	Thomas Everett	.03
623	Tunch Ilken	.03
624	Hardy Nickerson	.03
625	*Gerald Williams*	.08
626	Rod Woodson (black, red fumbles/ interceptions head)	.25
626a	Rod Woodson (red fumbles/ interceptions head)	.25
627	Rod Bernstine (error TE)	.25
627a	Rod Bernstine (corrected RB)	.15
628	Courtney Hall	.03
629	Ronnie Harmon	.03
630	Anthony Miller (WR back)	.25
630a	Anthony Miller (WR-KR back)	.20
630b	Anthony Miller (WR-KR back, front)	.20
631	Joe Philips	.03
632	Leslie O'Neal (LB-DE front)	.20
632a	Leslie O'Neal (LB front)	.15
633	David Richards (G-T back)	.05
633a	David Richards (G back)	.05
634	Mark Vlasic	.08
635	Lee Williams	.03
636	Chet Brooks	.03
637	Keena Turner	.03
638	Kevin Fagan	.03
639	*Brent Jones*	.70
640	Matt Millen	.03
641	Bubba Paris	.03
642	*Bill Romanowski*	.10
643	Fred Smerlas	.03
644	Dave Waymer	.03
645	Steve Young	.40
646	Brian Blades	.03
647	Andy Heck	.03
648	Dave Krieg	.03
649	Rufus Porter	.03
650	Kelly Stouffer	.03
651	Tony Woods	.03
652	Gary Anderson	.03
653	Reuben Davis	.03
654	Randy Grimes	.03
655	Ron Hall	.03
656	Eugene Marve	.03
657	Curt Jarvis (no "Official NFL card")	.05
657a	Curt Jarvis ("Official NFL card" added)	.05
658	Ricky Reynolds	.03
659	Broderick Thomas	.03
660	Jeff Bostic	.03
661	*Todd Bowles*	.10
662	Ravin Caldwell	.03
663	Russ Grimm	.03
664	Joe Jacoby	.03
665	Mark May	.03
666	Walter Stanley	.03
667	Don Warren	.03
668	*Stan Humphries*	.75
669	*Jeff George* (Illinois)	1.00
670	*Blair Thomas* (R1)	.10
671	*Cortez Kennedy*	.25
672	*Keith McCants* (R1)	.08
673	*Junior Seau*	1.00
674	*Mark Carrier*	.25
675	*Andre Ware* (R1)	.10
676	*Chris Singleton* (R1)	.10
677	*Richmond Webb* (R1)	.15
678	*Ray Agnew* (R1)	.08
679	*Anthony Smith*	.30
680	*James Francis* (R1)	.10
681	Percy Snow (R1)	.03
682	*Renaldo Turnbull*	.35
683	*Lamar Lathon* (R1)	.10
684	*James Williams* (R1)	.10
685	*Emmitt Smith*	6.00
686	*Tony Bennett*	.25
687	*Darrell Thompson*	.20
688	Steve Broussard (R1)	.08
689	*Eric Green*	.25
690	*Ben Smith* (R1)	.08
691	*Bern Brostek* (R1)	.08
692	*Rodney Hampton*	1.25
693	*Dexter Carter* (R1)	.10
694	*Rob Moore*	1.50
695	*Alexander Wright* (R2)	.20
696	*Darion Conner* (R2)	.10
697	Reggie Rembert (R2)	.03
698	*Terry Wooden* (R2) (back number 51)	.05
698a	*Terry Wooden* (R2) (back number 90)	.05
699	*Reggie Cobb*	.60
700	Anthony Thompson (R2)	.03
701	Fred Washington (R2)	.05
701a	Fred Washington (Final Update memorial)	.05
702	*Ron Cox* (R2)	.10
703	*Robert Blackmon* (R2)	.10
704	*Dan Owens* (R2)	.10
705	*Anthony Johnson* (R2)	.15
706	*Aaron Wallace* (R2)	.15
707	*Harold Green*	.35
708	*Keith Sims* (R2)	.10
709	*Tim Grunhard* (R2)	.10
710	Jeff Alm (R2)	.03
711	*Carwell Gardner*	.10
712	*Ken Davidson* (R2)	.10
713	*Vince Buck* (R2)	.10
714	*Leroy Hoard* (R2)	.50
715	*Andre Collins* (R2)	.08
716	*Dennis Brown* (R2)	.08
717	*Leroy Butler*	.20
718	*Pat Terrell* (R2) (back number 41)	.20
718a	*Pat Terrell* (R2) (back number 37)	.10
719	Mike Bellamy (R2)	.03
720	*Mike Fox* (R2)	.08
721	*Alton Montgomery* (R2)	.08
722	*Eric Davis* (R2)	.08
723	*Oliver Barnett* (PR) (DT front)	.30
723a	*Oliver Barnett* (PR) (NT front)	.10
724	*Houston Hoover* (PR)	.08
725	*Howard Ballard* (PR)	.08
726	*Keith McKeller* (PR)	.08
727	*Wendell Davis*	.10
728	*Peter Tom Willis* (PR)	.10
729	Bernard Clark (PR)	.03
730	*Doug Widell* (PR)	.10
731	Eric Andolsek (PR)	.03
732	*Jeff Campbell* (PR)	.08
733	*Marc Spindler* (PR)	.08
734	Keith Woodside (PR)	.03
735	*Willis Peguese* (PR)	.08
736	Frank Stams (PR)	.03
737	Jeff Uhlenhake (PR)	.03
738	Todd Kalis (PR)	.03
739	Tom Hodson (PR)	.03
740	Greg McMurtry (PR)	.03
741	Mike Buck (PR)	.03
742	Kevin Haverdink (PR)	.03
743	*Johnny Bailey* (PR) (back number 46)	.50
743a	*Johnny Bailey* (PR) (back number 22)	.25
744	*Eric Moore* (PR) (no prospect stripe)	.10
744a	*Eric Moore* (PR) (stripe added)	.10
745	*Tony Stargell* (PR)	.08
746	*Fred Barnett*	.60
747	Walter Reeves (PR)	.03
748	Derek Hill (PR)	.03
749	*Quinn Early* (PR)	.35
750	*Ronald Lewis* (PR)	.05
751	*Ken Clark* (PR)	.05
752	Garry Lewis (PR)	.03
753	James Lofton	.03
754	Jim Morrissey	.03
755	Jim Shofner	.03
756	*Jimmie Jones*	.10
757	Jay Novacek	.40
758	*Jessie Hester*	.20
759	*Barry Word*	.30
760	*Eddie Anderson*	.08
761	Cleveland Gary	.08
762	Marcus Dupree	.03
763	*David Griggs*	.08
764	Rueben Mayes	.03
765	Stephen Baker	.08
766	Reyna Thompson	.03
767	Everson Walls	.03
768	*Brad Baxter*	.25
769	Steve Walsh	.03
770	*Heath Sherman*	.20
771	*Johnny Johnson*	.10
772	Dexter Manley	.03
773	*Ricky Proehl*	.50
774	Frank Cornish	.03
775	*Tommy Kane*	.10
776	*Derrick Fenner*	.10
777	*Steve Christie*	.10
778	*Wayne Haddix*	.08
779	Richard Williamson	.03
780	*Brian Mitchell*	.50
781	American Bowl London	.03
782	American Bowl Berlin	.03
783	American Bowl Tokyo	.03
784	American Bowl Montreal	.03
785	Paul Tagliabue (NR)("peered through the Berlin Wall")	.05
785a	Paul Tagliabue (NR) ("posed at the Berlin Wall")	.05
786	Al Davis (NR)	.10
787	Jerry Glanville (NR)	.03
788	WLF (NR)	.03
789	Overseas (NR)	.03
790	Mike Mularkey (PC)	.03
791	Gary Reasons (PC)	.03
792	Maurice Hurst, Drew Hill (PC)	.03
793	Ronnie Lott (PC)	.03
794	Barry Sanders, Felix Wright (PC)	.75
795	George Seifert (PC)	.03
796	Doug Smith (PC)	.03
797	Doug Widell (PC)	.03
798	Cris Carter, Todd Bowles (PC)	.03
799	Ronnie Lott (Stay in School)	.03
800	Mark Carrier, Emmitt Smith (ROY)	1.00
SC3	Joe Robbie Stadium	1.00
CC2	Paul Tagliabue	1.00
NNO	Lombardi Trophy (2-9,999)	50.00
SC2	Santa Claus	1.00
SC	Super Pro	1.00
NNO	Super Bowl XXIVB logo	.30
SP1	Payne Stewart	1.00

1990 Pro Set Super Bowl MVPs

These 1990 Pro Set Series II inserts feature the 24 players who were named MVP of a Super Bowl. Each card front has a portrait of the player done by artist Merv Corning. Two silver panels are also on the front, one on top, the other at the bottom. The player's name is in the bottom panel, which is bordered by two stripes featuring the player's team colors. The horizontal card back has a color action photo and summary of the player's Super Bowl achievement. The cards are numbered on the back in a chronological manner, beginning with Super Bowl I.

		NM/M
Complete Set (24):		4.00
Common Player:		.10
1	Bart Starr Super Bowl I	.30
2	Bart Starr Super Bowl II	.30
3	Joe Namath Super Bowl III	.50
4	Len Dawson Super Bowl IV	.20
5	Chuck Howley Super Bowl V	.10
6	Roger Staubach Super Bowl VI	.50
7	Jake Scott Super Bowl VII	.10
8	Larry Csonka Super Bowl VIII	.30
9	Franco Harris Super Bowl IX	.30
10	Lynn Swann Super Bowl X	.20
11	Fred Biletnikoff Super Bowl XI	.20
12	Harvey Martin Super Bowl XII	.10
13	Terry Bradshaw Super Bowl XIII	.40
14	Terry Bradshaw Super Bowl XIV	.40
15	Jim Plunkett Super Bowl XV	.20
16	Joe Montana Super Bowl XVI	.50
17	John Riggins Super Bowl XVII	.20
18	Marcus Allen Super Bowl XVIII	.20
19	Joe Montana Super Bowl XIX	.50
20	Richard Dent Super Bowl XX	.10
21	Phil Simms Super Bowl XXI	.20
22	Doug Williams Super Bowl XXII	.10

23 Jerry Rice Super Bowl XXIII .30
24 Joe Montana Super Bowl XXIV .50

1990 Pro Set Theme Art

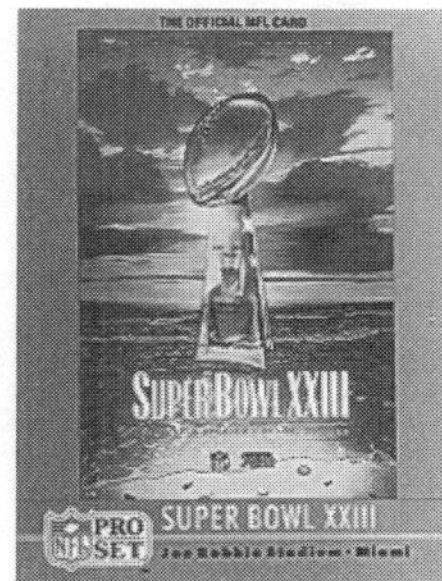

The 25-card set spotlights Super Bowl theme art on the front, which resembles the cover art of Super Bowl programs. The Pro Set logo is in the lower left, with the Super Bowl listed in the lower right, with the site and city name listed beneath. Card backs include a photo of the winning team's championship ring. The Super Bowl number and date, along with the score, are listed at the top, with background text also included. The cards were seeded one per 1990 Pro Set Series I pack.

NM/M
Complete Set (24): 3.00
Common Player: .15
1 Super Bowl I .15
2 Super Bowl II .15
3 Super Bowl III .15
4 Super Bowl IV .15
5 Super Bowl V .15
6 Super Bowl VI .15
7 Super Bowl VII .15
8 Super Bowl VIII .15
9 Super Bowl IX .15
10 Super Bowl X .15
11 Super Bowl XI .15
12 Super Bowl XII .15
13 Super Bowl XIII UER (Colgate University 7, should be Colgate 13) .15
14 Super Bowl XIV .15
15 Super Bowl XV .15
16 Super Bowl XVI .15
17 Super Bowl XVII .15
18 Super Bowl XVIII .15
19 Super Bowl XIX .15
20 Super Bowl XX .15
21 Super Bowl XXI .15
22A Super Bowl XXII ERR (Jan. 31, 1989 on back) .50
22B Super Bowl XXII COR (Jan. 31, 1988 on back) .15
23 Super Bowl XXIII .15
24 Super Bowl XXIV Theme Art .15

1990 Pro Set Collect-A-Books

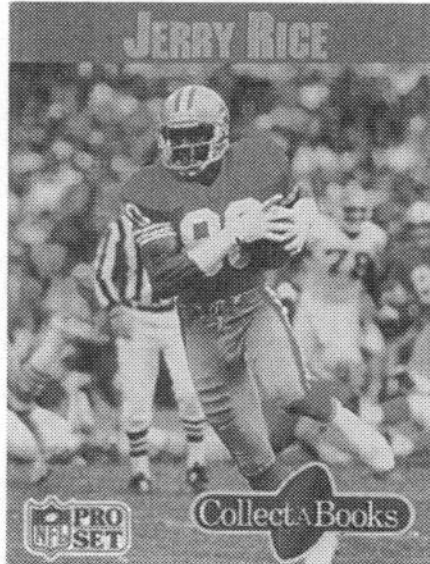

These 2-1/2" x 3-1/2" 8-page booklets were issued in three series of 12. Each series came in its own box, and included one player who was a rookie. The front of the booklet has an action photo of the player, along with his name, and set logos. Page two has a color mug shot of the player; pages 3-4 provide a career summary in text form. Pages 6-7 are a double-page action photo of the player; page 8 has statistics and trademark information. Two players who have booklets - Eric Dickerson and Michael Dean Perry - were not included in Pro Set's regular 1990 card set.

NM/M
Complete Set (36): 7.50
Common Player: .15
1 Jim Kelly .50
2 Andre Ware .20
3 Phil Simms .25
4 Bubby Brister .20
5 Bernie Kosar .25
6 Eric Dickerson .25
7 Barry Sanders .75
8 Jerry Rice 1.00
9 Keith Millard .15
10 Erik McMillan .15
11 Ickey Woods .15
12 Mike Singletary .25
13 Randall Cunningham .30
14 Boomer Esiason .25
15 John Elway .25
16 Wade Wilson .20
17 Troy Aikman 1.50
18 Dan Marino 1.50
19 Lawrence Taylor .35
20 Roger Craig .25
21 Merril Hoge .15
22 Christian Okoye .15
23 Blair Thomas .15
24 William Perry .20
25 Bill Fralic .15
26 Warren Moon .30
27 Jim Everett .20
28 Jeff George .50
29 Shane Conlan .15
30 Carl Banks .15
31 Charles Mann .15
32 Anthony Munoz .25
33 Dan Hampton .25
34 Michael Dean Perry .15
35 Joey Browner .15
36 Ken O'Brien .20

1990 Pro Set Pro Bowl 106

Participants in the annual Pro Bowl game are honored in this 106-card set produced by Pro Set. The set includes a white binder which features the Pro Bowl game logo on the front cover. The cards, except for four, are identical to their corresponding numbered counterparts in the regular set; there is no indication they were in the Pro Bowl set. However, four players who are featured in the Final Update set have "1990 Final Update" on the front (#s 754, 766, 771 and 778). This is not written on the fronts of the regular update cards.

NM/M
Complete Set (106): 10.00
Common Player: .03
39 Cornelius Bennett .10
40 Jim Kelly .25
49 Neal Anderson .05
52 Richard Dent .05
53 Jay Hilgenberg .03
57 Mike Singletary .08
86 Steve Atwater .05
91 Bobby Humphrey .03
96 Jerry Ball .03
98 Lomas Brown .03
102 Barry Sanders 1.00
114 Sterling Sharpe .75
118 Ray Childress .05
119 Ernest Givins .05
122 Drew Hill .05
135 Rohn Stark .03
137 Clarence Verdin .03
144 Nick Lowery .03
155 Bo Jackson .40
156 Don Mosebar .03
158 Greg Townsend .05
160 Steve Wisniewski .03
173 Jackie Slater .05
186 Joey Browner .05
188 Chris Doleman .05
189 Steve Jordan .03
190 Carl Lee .03
191 Randall McDaniel .05
210 Morten Andersen .05
215 Vaughan Johnson .03
218 Pat Swilling .05
226 Pepper Johnson .03
229 Bart Oates .03
231 Lawrence Taylor .15
244 Jerome Brown .03
247 Randall Cunningham .15
248 Keith Jackson .15
252 Reggie White .25
271 David Little .03
276 Marion Butts .10
289 Charles Haley .05
291 Ronnie Lott .10
292 Guy McIntyre .03
293 Joe Montana 1.00
295 Jerry Rice .75
320 Earnest Byner .03
321 Gary Clark .05
323 Darrell Green .05
324 Jim Lachey .03
334 Pro Bowl Aloha Stadium .03
436 Andre Rison .25
438 Kent Hull .03
440 Andre Reed .15
443 Bruce Smith .10
444 Thurman Thomas .25
447 Mark Bortz .03
462 David Fulcher .03
464 Rodney Holman .03
467 Anthony Munoz .10
491 Dennis Smith .03
497 Mel Gray .03
514 Bruce Matthews .03
517 Warren Moon .25
529 Albert Lewis .05
534 Kevin Ross .03
536 Derrick Thomas .20
557 Jeff Cross .03
560 Ferrell Edmunds .03
562 John Offerdahl .05
575 Bruce Armstrong .03
597 Sean Landeta .03
626 Rod Woodson .20
630 Anthony Miller .10
632 Leslie O'Neal .05
677 Richmond Webb .05
754 Steve Tasker 8.00
766 Reyna Thompson 8.00
771 Johnny Johnson 12.00
778 Wayne Haddix 8.00
800 Mark Carrier .10
SB1 Super Bowl I .15
SB2 Super Bowl II .15
SB3 Super Bowl III .15
SB4 Super Bowl IV .15
SB5 Super Bowl V .15
SB6 Super Bowl VI .15
SB7 Super Bowl VII .15
SB8 Super Bowl VIII .15
SB9 Super Bowl IX .15
SB10 Super Bowl X .15
SB11 Super Bowl XI .15
SB12 Super Bowl XII .15
SB13 Super Bowl XIII .15
SB14 Super Bowl XIV .15
SB15 Super Bowl XV .15
SB16 Super Bowl XVI .15
SB17 Super Bowl XVII .15
SB18 Super Bowl XVIII .15
SB19 Super Bowl XIX .15
SB20 Super Bowl XX .15
SB21 Super Bowl XXI .15
SB22 Super Bowl XXII .15
SB23 SUper Bowl XXIII .15
SB24 Super Bowl XXIV .15

1990 Pro Set Super Bowl 160

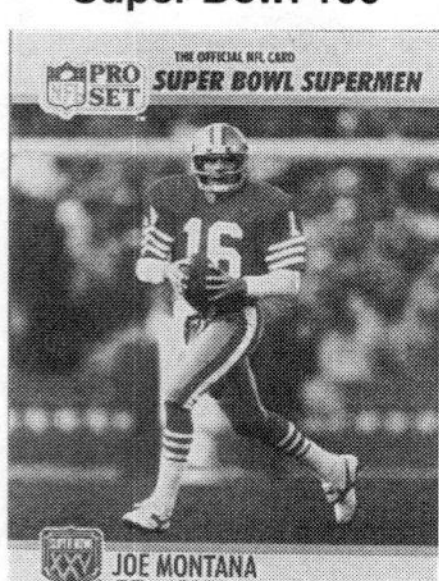

This set was issued in its own commemorative box and traces the history of the Super Bowl in four categories - Super Bowl Tickets, Super Bowl Supermen, Super Bowl Super Moments, and puzzle cards, which make up art for Super Bowl XXV. Cards were also sold in packs of eight and were originally given away at Texas Stadium during the Dallas Cowboys Pro Set Sports Collectors Show.

NM/M
Complete Set (160): 5.00
Common Player: .05
Common Puzzle: .03
1 SB 1 Ticket .10
2 SB II Ticket .05
3 SB III Ticket .05
4 SB IV Ticket .05
5 SB V Ticket .05
6 SB VI Ticket .05
7 SB VII Ticket .05
8 SB VIII Ticket .05
9 SB IV Ticket .05
10 SB X Ticket .05
11 SB XI Ticket .05
12 SB XII Ticket .05
13 SB XIII Ticket .05
14 SB XIV Ticket .05
15 SB XV Ticket .05
16 SB XVI Ticket .05
17 SB XVII Ticket .05
18 SB XVIII Ticket .05
19 SB XIX Ticket .05
20 SB XX Ticket .05
21 SB XXI Ticket .05
22 SB XXII Ticket .05
23 SB XXIII Ticket .05
24 SB XXIV Ticket .05
25 Tom Flores (CO) .05
26 Joe Gibbs (CO) .05
27 Tom Landry (CO) .15
28 Vince Lombardi (CO) .15
29 Chuck Noll (CO) .10
30 Don Shula (CO) .15
31 Bill Walsh (CO) .15
32 Terry Bradshaw .25
33 Joe Montana .50
34 Joe Namath .35
35 Jim Plunkett .10
36 Bart Starr .20
37 Roger Staubach .35
38 Marcus Allen .20
39 Roger Craig .10
40 Larry Csonka .10
41 Franco Harris .10
42 John Riggins .10
43 Timmy Smith .05
44 Matt Snell .05
45 Fred Biletnikoff .10
46 Cliff Branch .05
47 Max McGee .10
48 Jerry Rice .50
49 Ricky Sanders .05
50 George Sauer .05
51 John Stallworth .10
52 Lynn Swann .15
53 Dave Casper .05
54 Marv Fleming .05
55 Dan Ross .05
56 Forrest Gregg .10
57 Winston Hill .05
58 Joe Jacoby .05
59 Anthony Munoz .10
60 Art Shell .10
61 Rayfield Wright .05
62 Ron Yary .05
63 Randy Cross .05
64 Jerry Kramer .10
65 Bob Kuechenberg .05
66 Larry Little .05
67 Gerry Mullins .05
68 John Niland .05
69 Gene Upshaw .10
70 Dave Dalby .05
71 Jim Langer .05
72 Dwight Stephenson .05
73 Mike Webster .10
74 Ross Browner .05
75 Willie Davis .10
76 Richard Dent .10
77 L.C. Greenwood .10
78 Ed "Too Tall" Jones .10
79 Harvey Martin .05
80 Dwight White .05
81 Buck Buchanan .10
82 Curley Culp .05
83 Manny Fernandez .05
84 Joe Greene .15
85 Bob Lilly .15
86 Alan Page .15
87 Randy White .10
88 Nick Buoniconti .10
89 Lee Roy Jordan .10
90 Jack Lambert .15
91 Willie Lanier .10
92 Ray Nitschke .15
93 Mike Singletary .15
94 Carl Banks .05
95 Charles Haley .05
96 Jack Ham .10
97 Ted Hendricks .10
98 Chuck Howley .05
99 Rod Martin .05
100 Herb Adderley .10
101 Mel Blount .10
102 Willie Brown .10
103 Lester Hayes .05
104 Mike Haynes .05
105 Ronnie Lott .15
106 Mel Renfro .05
107 Eric Wright .05
108 Dick Anderson .05
109 David Fulcher .05
110 Cliff Harris .05
111 Johnny Robinson .05
112 Jake Scott .05
113 Donnie Shell .05
114 Mike Wagner .05
115 Willie Wood .10
116 Ray Guy .10
117 Lee Johnson .05
118 Larry Seiple .05
119 Jerrel Wilson .05
120 Kevin Butler .05
121 Don Chandler .05
122 Jan Stenerud .10
123 Jim Turner .05
124 Ray Wersching .05
125 Larry Anderson .05
126 Stanford Jennings .05
127 Mike Nelms .05
128 John Taylor .10
129 Fulton Walker .05
130 E.J. Holub .05
131 George Siefert CO .05
132 Jim Taylor .10
133 Joe Theismann .15
134 Johnny Unitas .25
135 Reggie Williams .05
136 Paul Christman, Frank Gifford Two Networks .05
137 First Fly-Over (Military jets) .05
138 Weeb Ewbank (Super Bowl Super Moment) .05
139 Otis Taylor (Super Bowl Super Moment) .05
140 Jim O'Brien (Super Bowl Super Moment) .05
141 Garo Yepremian (Super Bowl Super Moment) .05
142 Pete Rozelle, Art Rooney .05
143 Percy Howard (Super Bowl Super Moment) .05
144 Jackie Smith (Super Bowl Super Moment) .05
145 Record Crowd (Super Bowl Super Moment) .05
146 Yellow Ribbon UER (Fourth line says more than year, should say more than a year) .05
147 Dan Bunz, Charles Alexander (Super Bowl Super Moment) .05
148 Smurfs (Redskins) (Super Bowl Super Moment) .05
149 William "The Fridge" Perry (Scores)(Super Bowl Super Moment) .05
150 Phil McConkey (Super Bowl Super Moment) .05
151 Doug Williams (Super Bowl Super Moment) .05
152 Top row left .03
153 Top row middle XXV Theme Art Puzzle .03
154 Top row left XXV Theme Art Puzzle .03
155 Center row left XXV Theme Art Puzzle .03
156 Center row right XXV Theme Art Puzzle .03
157 Center row right XXV Theme Art Puzzle .03
158 Bottom row left VVX Theme Art Puzzle .03
159 Bottom row right XXV Theme Art Puzzle .03
160 Bottom row right XXV Theme Art Puzzle .03
Special Offer Card .10

1990 Pro Set Super Bowl Binder

This 56-card set, with Buick as its sponsor, was given to those who attended Super Bowl XXV between the New York Giants and Buffalo Bills. Included within the set are a cover card for Buick, a commemorative card for the 2-millionth Super Bowl fan, cards for the NFC and AFC Championship trophies, and a Ronnie Lott Stay in School card from Pro Set's Final Update set. Players from the two participating Super Bowl teams are featured in the set, along with 27 cards featuring fans' choices for the Silver Anniversary Super Bowl Team. Super Bowl participants' cards have the same photos as their counterparts in the regular set, but have NFC or AFC Champions designated on the front. A binder with pages that hold four cards per page was also issued to store the cards in.

NM/M
Complete Set (56): 25.00
Common Player: .25
1 Vince Lombardi .35
2 Joe Montana 4.00
3 Larry Csonka .50
4 Franco Harris .50
5 Jerry Rice 3.00
6 Lynn Swann .50
7 Forrest Gregg .35
8 Art Shell .35
9 Jerry Kramer .25
10 Gene Upshaw .35
11 Mike Webster .35
12 Dave Casper .25
13 Jan Stenerud .35
14 John Taylor .35
15 L.C. Greenwood .25
16 Ed "Too Tall" Jones .35
17 Joe Greene .50
18 Randy White .50
19 Jack Lambert .50
20 Mike Singletary .35
21 Jack Ham .35
22 Ted Hendricks .35
23 Mel Blount .35
24 Ronnie Lott .50
25 Donnie Shell .25
26 Willie Wood .35
27 Ray Guy .35
SC1 2,000,000th Fan .50
SC2 Buick Checklist Card .50
SC3 Lamar Hunt Trophy .50
SC4 George Halas Trophy .50
799 Ronnie Lott Education .35
39 Cornelius Bennett .50
40 Jim Kelly 1.50
47 Darryl Talley .25
48 Marv Levy (CO) .25
437 Shane Conlan .25
438 Kent Hull .25
440 Andre Reed 1.00
443 Bruce Smith 1.00
444 Thurman Thomas 2.50
725 Howard Ballard .25
753 James Lofton .50
754 Steve Tasker .25
223 Carl Banks .25
226 Pepper Johnson .25
228 Dave Meggett .25
230 Phil Simms .50
231 Lawrence Taylor .75
232 Bill Parcells (CO) .35
591 Ottis Anderson .50
592 Mark Bavaro .25
596 Jeff Hostetler .35
692 Rodney Hampton 1.00
765 Stephen Baker .25
766 Reyna Thompson .25

1991 Pro Set Draft Day

These cards, issued in conjunction with the 1991 NFL draft, create different scenarios regarding the first selection in the draft. Each card is numbered 694 and features the player in his collegiate uniform. The card back is in a horizontal format and has another player photo on it, plus biographical information and statistics.

NM/M
Complete Set (8): 50.00
Common Player: 5.00
694A Nick Bell 5.00
694B Mike Croel 5.00
694C Raghib (Rocket) Ismail (Cowboys) 15.00
694D Raghib (Rocket) Ismail (Falcons) 15.00
694E Raghib (Rocket) Ismail (Patriots) 15.00
694F Todd Lyght 5.00
694G Russell Maryland 5.00
694H Dan McGwire 5.00

1991 Pro Set Promos

These six promotional cards were distributed in various manners. Each is unnumbered. The Kids on the Block card was given away during the Super Bowl XXV Football Clinic, which featured NFL stars talking about drug education. The card was sponsored by Pro Set, Sports Illustrated for Kids and The Learning Channel, which broadcast the clinic. The Super Bowl XXV Card Show II card is similiar to the Card Show I issued in 1989, except the front gives the date of the second card show, which occurred Jan. 24-27, 1991. The cards for William Roberts and Michael Dean Perry (there were two versions for the Perry card) were intended to be in the previously issued Pro Bowl set, but were withdrawn. The Emmitt Smith card was a mail-in offer through the Pro Set Gazette, a quarterly publication designed to provide an overview of the hobby to young collectors.

NM/M
Complete Set (6): 25.00
Common Player: .50
NNO NLF Kids on the Block (Teleclinic) .50
NNO Super Bowl XXV (Card Show II) 5.00
NNO Michael Dean Perry Pro Bowl (unnumbered, with Pro Set logo) 6.00
NNO Michael Dean Perry Pro Bowl (unnumbered, without Pro Set logo) 6.00
NNO William Roberts Pro Bowl (unnumbered) 6.00
NNO Emmitt Smith Gazette (Pro Set Gazette) 4.00

1991 Pro Set

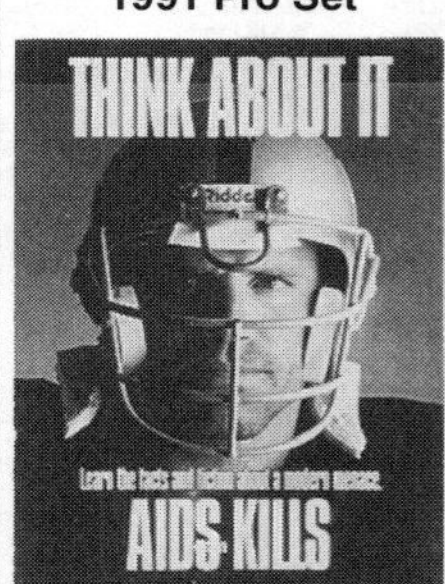

Released in late April, Pro Set's third annual football set was again divided into two series. Subsets added this year to Series I include Heisman Heroes, Super Bowl XXV Replay, NFL Officials, and Think About It messages. World League of American Football cards made their debut in Series I as well. Again, randomly-packed insert cards were included in Series I: Super Bowl XXV logo, Walter Payton and Team 34, a mini Pro Set Gazette, Red Grange, Russell Maryland 31 Draft Pick (only in Series I), and 1,000 autographed Lawrence Taylor cards. (Key: L - leader, M - milestone, HOF - Hall of Fame, AW - college award winner, HH - Heisman hero, SBR - Super Bowl XXV replay, R - 1990 replay, NR - newsreel, O - official, M - NFL message, NFC - all-NFC team, C - coach).

NM/M
Complete Set (850): 18.00
Complete Series 1 (405): 7.00
Complete Series 2 (407): 7.00
Complete Final (38): 4.00
Common Player: .03
Series 1 Pack (14): .20
Series 1 Wax Box (36): 10.00
Series 2 Pack (14): .30
Series 2 Wax Box (36): 15.00
1 Emmitt Smith (LL) 1.00
2 Mark Carrier (LL) .25
3 Joe Montana (LL) .50
4 Art Shell (LL) .03
5 Mike Singletary (LL) .03
6 Bruce Smith (LL) .04
7 Barry Word (LL) .03
8 Jim Kelly (LL) (with NFLPA logo) .25

8a Jim Kelly (LL) (without NFLPA logo) .20
8b Jim Kelly (LL) (without NFLPA logo, with registered symbol) 6.00
9 Warren Moon (LL) .08
10 Barry Sanders (LL) .50
11 Jerry Rice (LL) .40
12 Jay Novacek (LL) .05
13 Thurman Thomas (LL) .20
14 Nick Lowery (LL) .03
15 Mike Horan (LL) .03
16 Clarence Verdin (LL) .03
17 Kevin Clark (LL) .03
18 Mark Carrier (LL) .03
19 Derrick Thomas (LL) (error: Bills helmet on front) 15.00
19a Derrick Thomas (LL) (corrected: Chiefs helmet on front) .25
20 Ottis Anderson (M) .03
21 Roger Craig (M) .03
22 Art Monk (M) .05
23 Chuck Noll (M) .03
24 Randall Cunningham (M) .08
25 Dan Marino (M) .40
26 Charles Haley (M) .03
27 Earl Campbell (HOF) .10
28 John Hannah (HOF) .03
29 Stan Jones (HOF) .03
30 Tex Schramm (HOF) .03
31 Jan Stenerud (HOF) .03
32 *Russell Maryland* (AW) .40
33 *Chris Zorich* (AW) .15
34 *Darryl Lewis* (AW) .03
35 *Alfred Williams* (AW) .08
36 *Raghib Ismail* (AW) 1.00
37 *Ty Detmer* (HH) 1.00
38 Andre Ware (HH) .05
39 Barry Sanders (HH) .50
40 Tim Brown (HH) .05
41 Vinny Testaverde (HH) .03
42 Bo Jackson (HH) .15
43 Mike Rozier (HH) .03
44 Herschel Walker (HH) .03
45 Marcus Allen (HH) .04
46 James Lofton (SBR) (with NFLPA logo) .05
46a James Lofton (SBR) (NFLPA logo removed) .08
47 Bruce Smith (SBR)("Official NFL Card" in white) .15
47a Bruce Smith (SBR)("Official NFL Card" in black) .10
48 Myron Guyton (SBR) .03
49 Stephen Baker (SBR) .03
50 Mark Ingram (SBR) .03
51 O.J. Anderson (SBR) .03
52 Thurman Thomas .20
53 Matt Bahr (SBR) .03
54 Scott Norwood (SBR) .03
55 Stephen Baker .03
56 Carl Banks .03
57 Mark Collins .03
58 Steve DeOssie .03
59 Eric Dorsey .03
60 John Elliott .03
61 Myron Guyton .03
62 Rodney Hampton .50
63 Jeff Hostetler .15
64 Erik Howard .03
65 Mark Ingram .03
66 *Greg Jackson* .08
67 Leonard Marshall .03
68 David Meggett .03
69 Eric Moore .03
70 Bart Oates .03
71 Gary Reasons .03
72 Bill Parcells (C) .03
73 Howard Ballard .03
74 Cornelius Bennett (with NFLPA logo) .25
74a Cornelius Bennett (NFLPA logo removed) .10
75 Shane Conlan .03
76 Kent Hull .03
77 Kirby Jackson .03
78 Jim Kelly (w/o logo) .35
79 Mark Kelso .03
80 Nate Odomes .03
81 Andre Reed .08
82 Jim Ritcher .03
83 Bruce Smith .03
84 Darryl Talley .03
85 Steve Tasker .03
86 Thurman Thomas .35
87 James Williams .03
88 Will Wolford .03
89 Jeff Wright .03
90 Marv Levy (C) .03
91 Steve Broussard .03
92 Darion Conner (error: "Drafted 1st Round '99") 6.00
92a Darion Conner (corrected: "Drafted 2nd Round '90") .15
93 Bill Fralic .03
94 Tim Green .03
95 Michael Haynes .03
96 Chris Hinton .03
97 Chris Miller .03
98 Deion Sanders .20
99 Jerry Glanville (C) .03
100 Kevin Butler .03
101 Mark Carrier (Chi.) .03
102 Jim Covert .03
103 Richard Dent .03
104 Jim Harbaugh .08
105 Brad Muster .03
106 Lemuel Stinson .03
107 Keith Van Horne .03
108 Mike Ditka (C) .05
109 Lewis Billups .03
110 James Brooks .03
111 Boomer Esiason .10
112 James Francis .03
113 David Fulcher .03
114 Rodney Holman .03
115 Tim McGee .03
116 Anthony Munoz .03
117 Sam Wyche (C) .03
118 Paul Farren .03
119 Thane Gash .03
120 Mike Johnson .03
121 Bernie Kosar (with NFLPA logo) .05
121a Bernie Kosar (NFLPA logo removed) .10
122 Clay Matthews .03
123 Eric Metcalf .03
124 Frank Minnifield .03
125 Webster Slaughter (with NFLPA logo) .05
125a Webster Slaughter (NFLPA logo removed) .05
126 Bill Belichick (C) .03
127 Tommie Agee .03
128 Troy Aikman 1.00
129 Jack Del Rio .03
130 *John Gesek* .06
131 Issiac Holt .03
132 Michael Irvin .55
133 Ken Norton .03
134 Daniel Stubbs .03
135 Jimmy Johnson (C) .05
136 Steve Atwater (AW) .03
137 Michael Brooks .03
138 John Elway .35
139 Wymon Henderson .03
140 Bobby Humphery .03
141 Mark Jackson .03
142 Karl Mecklenburg .03
143 Doug Widell .03
144 Dan Reeves (C) .03
145 Eric Andolsek .03
146 Jerry Ball .03
147 Bennie Blades .03
148 Lomas Brown .03
149 Robert Clark .03
150 Michael Cofer .03
151 Dan Owens .03
152 Rodney Peete .03
153 Wayne Fontes (C) .03
154 Tim Harris .03
155 Johnny Holland .03
156 Don Majkowski .03
157 Tony Mandarich .03
158 Mark Murphy .03
159 Brian Noble .03
160 Jeff Query .03
161 Sterling Sharpe .20
162 Lindy Infante (C) .03
163 Ray Childress .03
164 Ernest Givins .03
165 Richard Johnson .03
166 Bruce Matthews .03
167 Warren Moon .15
168 Mike Munchak .03
169 Al Smith .03
170 Lorenzo White .08
171 Jack Pardee (C) .03
172 Albert Bentley .03
173 Duane Bickett .03
174 Bill Brooks .03
175 Eric Dickerson (with NFLPA logo)(error text: 667) .50
175a Eric Dickerson (NFLPA logo removed) (error text: 667) 1.25
175b Eric Dickerson (NFLPA logo removed) (corrected text: 677)) .25
176 Ray Donaldson .03
177 Jeff George .20
178 Jeff Herrod .03
179 Clarence Verdin .03
180 Ron Meyer (C) .03
181 John Alt .03
182 Steve DeBerg .03
183 Albert Lewis .03
184 Nick Lowery .03
185 Christian Okoye .03
186 Stephone Paige .03
187 Kevin Porter .03
188 Derrick Thomas .15
189 Marty Schottenheimer (C) .03
190 Willie Gault .03
191 Howie Long .03
192 Terry McDaniel .03
193 Jay Schroeder .03
194 Steve Smith .03
195 Greg Townsend .03
196 Lionel Washington .03
197 Steve Wisniewski .03
198 Art Shell (C) .03
199 Henry Ellard .03
200 Jim Everett .03
201 Jerry Gray .03
202 Kevin Greene .03
203 Buford McGee .03
204 Tom Newberry .03
205 Frank Stams, David Wyman .03
206 Alvin Wright .03
207 John Robinson (C) .03
208 Jeff Gross .03
209 Mark Duper .03
210 Dan Marino .75
211 Tim McKyer .05
211a Tim McKyer (traded stripe added) .05
212 John Offerdahl .03
213 Sammie Smith .03
214 Richmond Webb .03
215 Jarvis Williams .03
216 Don Shula (C) .03
217 Darrell Fullington (missing registered symbol by NFLPA logo) .05
217a Darrell Fullington (corrected) .05
218 Tim Irwin .03
219 Mike Merriweather .03
220 Keith Millard .03
221 Al Noga .03
222 Henry Thomas .03
223 Wade Wilson .03
224 Gary Zimmerman .03
225 Jerry Burns (C) .03
226 Bruce Armstrong .03
227 Marv Cook .03
228 Hart Lee Dykes .03
229 Tom Hodson .03
230 Ronnie Lippett .03
231 Ed Reynolds .03
232 Chris Singleton .03
233 John Stephens .03
234 Dick MacPherson (C) .03
235 Stan Brock .03
236 Craig Heyward .03
237 Vaughan Johnson .03
238 Robert Massey .03
239 Brett Maxie .03
240 Rueben Mayes .03
241 Pat Swilling .03
242 Renaldo Turnbull .03
243 Jim Mora (C) .03
244 Kyle Clifton .03
245 Jeff Criswell .03
246 James Hasty .03
247 Erik McMillan .03
248 *Scott Mersereau* .05
249 Ken O'Brien .03
250 Blair Thomas (with NFLPA logo) .30
250a Blair Thomas (NFLPA logo removed) .10
251 Al Toon .03
252 Bruce Coslet (C) .03
253 Eric Allen (AW)(FC) .03
254 Fred Barnett .10
255 Keith Byars .03
256 Randall Cunningham .10
257 Seth Joyner .03
258 Clyde Simmons .03
259 Jessie Small .03
260 Andre Waters .03
261 Rich Kotite (C) .03
262 Roy Green .03
263 Ernie Jones .03
264 Tim McDonald .03
265 Timm Rosenbach .03
266 Rod Saddler .03
267 Luis Sharpe .03
268 Anthony Thompson .03
269 *Marcus Turner* .08
270 Joe Bugel (C) .03
271 Gary Anderson (Pit.) .03
272 Dermontti Dawson .03
273 Eric Green .10
274 Merril Hoge .03
275 Tunch Ilkin .03
276 David Johnson .03
277 Louis Lipps .03
278 Rod Woodson .05
279 Chuck Noll (C) .03
280 Martin Bayless .03
281 Marion Butts .05
282 Gill Byrd .03
283 Burt Grossman .03
284 Courtney Hall .03
285 Anthony Miller .03
286 Leslie O'Neal .03
287 Billy Joe Tolliver .03
288 Dan Henninng (C) .03
289 Dexter Carter .03
290 Michael Carter .03
291 Kevin Fagan .03
292 Pierce Holt .03
293 Guy McIntyre .03
294 Tom Rathman .03
295 John Taylor .08
296 Steve Young .50
297 George Seifert (C) .03
298 Brian Blades .03
299 Jeff Bryant .03
300 Norm Johnson .03
301 Tommy Kane .03
302 Cortez Kennedy .20
303 Bryan Millard .03
304 John L. Williams .03
306 Chuck Knox (C) (with NFLPA logo) .10
306a Chuck Knox (NFLPA logo removed) .40
307 Gary Anderson (T.B.) .03
308 Reggie Cobb .10
309 Randy Grimes .03
310 Harry Hamilton .03
311 Bruce Hill .03
312 Eugene Marve .03
313 Ervin Randle .03
314 Vinny Testaverde .08
315 Richard Williamson (C) .03
316 Ernest Byner .03
317 Gary Clark .08
318 Andre Collins (with NFLPA logo) .05
318a Andre Collins (NFLPA logo removed) .05
319 Darryl Grant .03
320 Chip Lohmiller .03
321 Martin Mayhew .03
322 Mark Rypien .08
323 Alvin Walton .03
324 Joe Gibbs .03
325 Jerry Glanville (R) .03
326 Nate Odomes (with NFLPA logo) .05
326a Nate Odomes (NFLPA logo removed) .05
327 Boomer Esiason .03
328 Steve Tasker (with NFLPA logo) .05
328a Steve Tasker (NFLPA logo removed) .05
329 Jerry Rice .25
330 Jeff Rutledge .03
331 KC defense (R) .03
332 Rams (R) .03
333 John Taylor (R) .03
334 Randall Cunningham (with NFLPA logo) .10
334a Randall Cunningham (NFLPA logo removed) .10
335 Bo Jackson .10
336 Lawrence Taylor .08
337 Warren Moon .10
338 Alan Grant .03
339 Steve DeBerg .03
340 Mark Clayton Playoff (TM on Chief #27's shoulder) .05
340a Mark Clayton Playoff (TM away from Chief #27) .05
341 Jim Kelly Playoff (with NFLPA logo) .05
341a Jim Kelly Playoff (NFLPA logo removed) .05
342 Matt Bahr NFC Championship (R) .03
343 *Robert Tisch* .08
344 Sam Jankovich .03
345 John Elway .08
346 Bo Jackson .08
347 Paul Tagliabue .03
348 Ronnie Lott .05
349 Super Bowl XXV Teleclinic .03
350 Whitney Houston .08
351 U.S. Troops .03
352 Art McNally (O) .03
353 Dick Jorgensen (O) .03
354 Jerry Seeman (O) .03
355 Jim Tunney (O) .03
356 Gerry Austin (O) .03
357 Gene Barth (O) .03
358 Red Cashion (O) .03
359 Tom Dooley (O) .03
360 Johnny Grier (O) .03
361 Pat Haggerty (O) .03
362 Dale Hamer (O) .03
363 Dick Hantak (O) .03
364 Jerry Markbreit (O) .03
365 Gordon McCarter (O) .03
366 Bob McElwee (O) .03
367 Howard Roe (O) .03
368 Tom White (O) .03
369 Norm Schachter (O) .03
370 Warren Moon (small type) .12
370a Warren Moon (large type) .10
371 Boomer Esiason (small type) .05
371a Boomer Esiason (large type) .05
372 Troy Aikman (small type) .50
372a Troy Aikman (large type) .50
373 Carl Banks (small type) .05
373a Carl Banks (large type) .05
374 Jim Everett (small type) .05
374a Jim Everett (large type) .05
375 Anthony Munoz (small type)(error back: "dificul", "latrapar")(error front: "Quadante," "Antony") .05
375a Anthony Munoz (small type)(corrected back: "dicifil", "atrapar") (error front: "Quadante," "Antony") .05
375b Anthony Munoz (large type) (error front: "Quadante," "Antony") .05
375c Anthony Munoz (large type)(corrected front: "Quedate," "Anthony") .05
376 Ray Childress (small type) .05
376a Ray Childress (large type) .05
377 Charles Mann (small type) .05
377a Charles Mann (large type) .05
378 Jackie Slater (small type) .05
378a Jackie Slater (large type) .05
379 Jerry Rice (NFC) .25
380 Andre Rison (NFC) .10
381 Jim Lachey (NFC) .03
382 Jackie Slater (NFC) .03
383 Randall McDaniel (NFC) .03
384 Mark Bortz (NFC) .03
385 Jay Hilgenberg (NFC) .03
386 Keith Jackson (NFC) .05
387 Joe Montana (NFC) .50
388 Barry Sanders (NFC) .50
389 Neal Anderson (NFC) .05
390 Reggie White (NFC) .05
391 Chris Doleman (NFC) .03
392 Jerome Brown (NFC) .03
393 Charles Haley (NFC) .03
394 Lawrence Taylor (NFC) .05
395 Pepper Johnson (NFC) .03
396 Mike Singletary (NFC) .03
397 Darrell Green (NFC) .03
398 Carl Lee (NFC) .03
399 Joey Browner (NFC) .03
400 Ronnie Lott (NFC) .05
401 Sean Landeta (NFC) .03
402 Morten Andersen (NFC) .03
403 Mel Gray (NFC) .03
404 Reyna Thompson (NFC) .03
405 Jimmy Johnson (NFC) .03
406 Andre Reed .05
407 Anthony Miller .03
408 Anthony Munoz .03
409 Bruce Armstrong .03
410 Bruce Matthews .03
411 Mike Munchak .03
412 Kent Hull .03
413 Rodney Holman .03
414 Warren Moon .10
415 Thurman Thomas .15
416 Marion Butts .05
417 Bruce Smith .08
418 Greg Townsend .03
419 Ray Childress .03
420 Derrick Thomas .08
421 Leslie O'Neal .03
422 John Offerdahl .03
423 Shane Conlan .03
424 Rod Woodson .04
425 Albert Lewis .03
426 Steve Atwater .03
427 David Fulcher .03
428 Rohn Stark .03
429 Nick Lowery .03
430 Clarence Verdin .03
431 Steve Tasker .03
432 Art Shell .03
433 Scott Case .03
434 Tory Epps .03
435 Mike Gann .03
436 Brian Jordan .03
437 Mike Kenn .03
438 John Rade .03
439 Andre Rison .30
440 Mike Rozier .03
441 Jessie Tuggle .03
442 Don Beebe .03
443 *John Davis* .08
444 James Lofton .03
445 Keith McKeller .03
446 Frank Reich .03
447 Scott Norwood .03
448 Frank Reich .03
449 Leon Seals .03
450 Leonard Smith .03
451 Neal Anderson .03
452 Trace Armstrong .03
453 Mark Bortz .03
454 Wendell Davis .05
455 Shaun Gayle .03
456 Jay Hilgenberg .03
457 Steve McMichael .03
458 Mike Singletary .05
459 Donnell Woolford .03
460 Jim Breech .03
461 Eddie Brown .03
462 Barney Bussey .03
463 Bruce Kozerski .03
464 Tim Krumrie .03
465 Bruce Reimers .03
466 *Kevin Walker* .08
467 Ickey Woods .03
468 Carl Zander .03
469 Mike Baab .03
470 Brian Brennan .03
471 *Rob Burnett* .08
472 Raymond Clayborn .03
473 Reggie Langhorne .03
474 Kevin Mack .03
475 Anthony Pleasant .03
476 Joe Morris .03
477 Dan Fike .03
478 Ray Horton .03
479 Jim Jeffcoat .03
480 Jimmie Jones .03
481 Kelvin Martin .03
482 Nate Newton .03
483 Danny Noonan .03
484 Jay Novacek .10
485 Emmitt Smith 2.00
486 *James Washington* .08
487 Simon Fletcher .03
488 Ron Holmes .03
489 Mike Horan .03
490 Vance Johnson .03
491 Keith Kartz .03
492 Greg Kragen .03
493 Ken Lanier .03
494 Warren Powers .03
495 Dennis Smith .03
496 Jeff Campbell .03
497 Ken Dallafior .03
498 Dennis Gibson .03
499 Kevin Glover .03
500 Mel Gray .03
501 Eddie Murray .03
502 Barry Sanders 1.25
503 Chris Spielman .03
504 William White .03
505 *Matt Brock* .08
506 Robert Brown .03
507 LeRoy Butler .03
508 James Campen .03
509 Jerry Holmes .03
510 Perry Kemp .03
511 Ken Ruettgers .03
512 Scott Stephen .03
513 Ed West .03
514 *Cris Dishman* .08
515 Curtis Duncan .03
516 Drew Hill .03
517 Haywood Jeffires .10
518 Sean Jones .03
519 Lamar Lathon .03
520 Don Maggs .03
521 Bubba McDowell .03
522 Johnny Meads .03
523 Chip Banks (error no text) .03
523a Chip Banks (corrected) .03
524 Pat Beach .03
525 Sam Clancy .03
526 Eugene Daniel .03
527 Jon Hand .03
528 Jessie Hester .03
529 Mike Prior (error no textual information) .08
529a Mike Prior (corrected) .03
530 Keith Taylor .03
531 Donnell Thompson .03
532 Dino Hackett .05
533 David Lutz .03
534 Chris Martin .03
535 Kevin Ross .03
536 Dan Saleaumua .03
537 Neil Smith .05
538 Percy Snow .05
539 Robb Thomas .03
540 Barry Word .08
541 Marcus Allen .03
542 Eddie Anderson .03
543 Scott Davis .03
544 Mervyn Fernandez .03
545 Ethan Horton .03
546 Ronnie Lott .08
547 Don Mosebar .03
548 Jerry Robinson .03
549 Aaron Wallace .03
550 Flipper Anderson .05
551 Cleveland Gary .03
552 Damone Johnson .03
553 Duval Love .03
554 Irv Pankey .03
555 Mike Piel .03
556 Jackie Slater .03
557 Michael Stewart .03
558 Pat Terrell .03
559 J.B. Brown .03
560 Mark Clayton .03
561 Ferrell Edmunds .03
562 Harry Galbreath .03
563 David Griggs .03
564 Jim C. Jensen .03
565 Louis Oliver .03
566 Tony paige .05
567 Keith Sims .03
568 Joey Browner .03
569 Anthony Carter .05
570 Chris Doleman .05
571 Rich Gannon .05
572 Hassan Jones .03
573 Steve Jordan .03
574 Carl Lee .03
575 Randall McDaniel .03
576 Herschel Walker .05
577 Ray Agnew .03
578 Vincent Brown .03
579 Irving Fryar .05
580 Tim Goad .03
581 Maurice Hurst .03
582 Fred Marion .03
583 Johnny Rembert .03
584 Andre Tippett .03
585 Brent Williams .03
586 Morten Andersen .03
587 *Toi Cook* .08
588 Jim Dombrowski .03
589 Dalton Hilliard .05
590 Rickey Jackson .03
591 Eric Martin .03
592 Sam Mills .03
593 Bobby Hebert .03
594 Steve Walsh .03
595 Ottis Anderson .03
596 Pepper Johnson .03
597 *Bob Kratch* .05
598 Sean Landeta .03
599 Doug Riesenberg .03
600 William Roberts .03
601 Phil Simms .05
602 Lawrence Taylor .08
603 Everson Walls .03
604 Brad Baxter .05
605 Dennis Byrd .03
606 Jeff Lageman .03
607 Pat Leahy .03
608 Rob Moore .08
609 Joe Mott .03
610 Tony Stargell .03
611 Brian Washington .03
612 *Marvin Washington* .15
613 David Alexander .03
614 Jerome Brown .03
615 Byron Evans .03
616 Ron Heller .03
617 Wes Hopkins .03
618 Keith Jackson .10
619 Heath Sherman .03
620 Reggie White .10
621 Calvin Williams .10
622 Ken Harvey .03
623 Eric Hill .03
624 Johnny Johnson .20
625 Freddie Joe Nunn .03
626 Ricky Proehl .08
627 Tootie Robbins .03
628 Jay Taylor .03
629 Tom Tupa .03
630 *Jim Wahler* .08
631 Bubby Brister .03
632 Thomas Everett .03
633 Bryan Hinkle .03
634 Carnell Lake .03
635 David Little .03
636 Hardy Nickerson .03
637 Gerald Williams .03
638 Keith Willis .03
639 Tim Worley .03
640 Rod Bernstine .03
641 Frank Cornish .03
642 Gary Plummer .03
643 *Henry Rolling* .08
644 Sam Seale .03
645 Junior Seau .20
646 Billy Ray Smith .03
647 Broderick Thompson .03
648 *Derrick Walker* .08
649 Todd Bowles .03
650 Don Griffin .03
651 Charles Haley .03
652 Brent Jones .03
653 Joe Montana 1.00
654 Jerry Rice .75
655 Bill Romanowski .03
656 Michael Walter .03
657 Dave Waymer .03
658 Jeff Chadwick .03
659 Derrick Fenner .03
660 Nesby Glasgow .03
661 Jacob Green .03
662 *Dwayne Harper* .08
663 Andy Heck .03
664 Dave Krieg .03
665 Rufus Porter .03
666 Eugene Robinson .03
667 Mark Carrier .03
668 Steve Christie .03
669 Reuben Davis .03
670 Paul Gruber .03
671 Wayne Haddix .03
672 Ron Hall .03
673 Keith McCants .03

674 Ricky Reynolds .03
675 Mark Robinson .03
676 Jeff Bostic .03
677 Darrell Green .05
678 Markus Koch .03
679 Jim Lachey .03
680 Charles Mann .03
681 Wilber Marshall .03
682 Art Monk .05
683 Gerald Riggs .03
684 Ricky Sanders .03
685 Ray Handley replaces Bill Parcels .03
686 NFL Announces Expansion .03
687 Miami Gets Super Bowl XXIX .03
688 George Young named NFL Executive of yea .03
689 Five-millionth fan visits Pro FB HOF .03
690 Sports Illustrated poll pro football #1 .03
691 American Bowl London .03
692 American Bowl Berlin .03
693 American Bowl Tokyo .03
694 Joe Ferguson (LEG) .03
695 Carl Hairston (LEG) .03
696 Dan Hampton (LEG) .03
697 Mike Haynes (LEG) .03
698 Marty Lyons (LEG) .03
699 Ozzie Newsome (LEG) .08
700 Scott Studwell (LEG) .03
701 Mike Webster (LEG) .04
702 Dwayne Woodruff (LEG) .03
703 Larry Kennan (CO) .03
704 *Stan Gelbaugh* .08
705 John Brantley .03
706 Danny Lockett .03
707 *Anthony Parker* .08
708 Dan Crossman .03
709 Eric Wilkerson .03
710 *Judd Garrett* .08
711 Tony Baker .03
712 Randall Cunningham 1st Place BW .06
713 Mark Ingram 2nd Place BW .03
714 Pete Holohan, Barney Bussey, Carl Carter 3rd Place BW .03
715 Sterling Sharpe 1st Place Color Action .08
716 Jim Harbaugh 2nd Place Color Action .04
717 Anthony Miller, David Fulcher 3rd Place Color Action .03
718 Bill Parcells, Lawrence Taylor 1st Place Color Feature (CO) .03
719 Patriotic Crowd (2nd Place Color Feature) .03
720 Alfredo Roberts 3rd Place Color Feature .03
721 Ray Bentley Read And Study .03
722 Earnest Byner Never Give Up .03
723 Bill Fralic Steroids Destroy .03
724 Joe Jacoby Don't Polute .03
725 Howie Long AIDS Kills .03
726 Dan Marino School's The Ticket .40
727 Ron Rivera Leer Y Estudiar .03
728 Mike Singletary Be The Best .05
729 Cornelius Bennett Chill .03
730 Russell Maryland .20
731 *Eric Turner* .20
732 *Bruce Pickens* .08
733 *Mike Croel* .15
734 *Todd Lyght* .15
735 *Eric Swann* .10
736 *Charles McRae* .10
737 *Antone Davis* .10
738 *Stanley Richard* .30
739 *Herman Moore* 2.50
740 *Pat Harlow* .08
741 *Alvin Harper* .30
742 *Mike Pritchard* .50
743 *Leonard Russell* .15
744 *Huey Richardson* .04
745 *Dan McGwire* .10
746 *Bobby Wilson* .08
747 *Alfred Williams* .10
748 *Vinnie Clark* .08
749 *Kelvin Pritchett* .10
750 *Harvey Williams* 1.00
751 *Stan Thomas* .05
752 *Randal Hill* .35
753 *Todd Marinovich* .08
754 *Ted Washington* .08
755 *Henry Jones* .20
756 *Jarrod Bunch* .10
757 *Mike Dumas* .05
758 *Ed King* .08
759 *Reggie Johnson* .08
760 *Roman Phifer* .10
761 *Mike Jones* .10
762 *Brett Favre* 5.00
763 *Browning Nagle* .20
764 *Esera Tuaolo* .05
765 George Thornton .03
766 *Dixon Edwards* .05
767 Darryll Lewis .03
768 *Eric Bieniemy* .05
769 *Shane Curry* .05
770 *Jerome Henderson* .06
771 *Wesley Carroll* .10
772 *Nick Bell* .15
773 John Flannery .03
774 *Ricky Watters* 1.50
775 *Jeff Graham* .75
776 *Eric Moten* .08
777 *Jesse Campbell* .08
778 *Chris Zorich* .10
779 Joe Valerio .03
780 *Doug Thomas* .08
781 Lamar Rogers .04
782 *John Johnson* .08
783 *Phil Hansen* .08
784 *Kanavis McGhee* .05
785 *Calvin Stephens* .05
786 *James Jones* .10
787 Reggie Barrett .03
788 *Aeneas Williams* .10
789 *Aaron Craver* .10
790 *Keith Traylor* .08
791 *Godfrey Myles* .08
792 *Mo Lewis* .08
793 James Richard .03
794 *Carlos Jenkins* .20
795 *Lawrence Dawsey* .25
796 *Don Davey* .04
797 *Jake Reed* 1.00
798 Dave McCloughan .03
799 *Eric Williams* .15
800 *Steve Jackson* .10
801 Bob Dahl .03
802 *Ernie Mills* .10
803 David Daniels .03
804 Rob Selby .03
805 *Ricky Ervins* .20
806 *Tim Barnett* .20
807 *Chris Gardocki* .04
808 *Kevin Donnalley* .04
809 *Robert Wilson* .04
810 *Chuck Webb* .04
811 *Darryl Wren* .08
812 *Ed McCaffrey* 3.00
813 Shula's 300th Victory .05
814 Raiders-49ers Sell Out Coliseum .03
815 NFL International .03
816 *Moe Gardner* .08
817 *Tim McKyer* .05
818 *Tom Waddle* .50
819 *Michael Jackson* .75
820 Tony Casillas .03
821 Gaston Green .03
822 *Kenny Walker* .08
823 *Willie Green* .30
824 *Erik Kramer* 1.00
825 *William Fuller* .05
826 *Allen Pinkett* .04
827 *Rick Venturi* .04
828 *Bill Maas* .04
829 *Jeff Jaeger* .04
830 Robert Delpino .04
831 *Mark Higgs* .50
832 Reggie Roby .03
833 *Terry Allen* 1.50
834 Cris Carter .25
835 John Randle .40
836 *Hugh Millen* .25
837 *Jon Vaughn* .25
838 Gill Fenerty .03
839 Floyd Turner .03
840 Irv Eatman .03
841 Lonnie Young .03
842 Jim McMahon .05
843 Randal Hill .05
844 Barry Foster .45
845 *Neil O'Donnell* 1.50
846 John Friesz .10
847 Broderick Thomas .03
848 Brian Mitchell .10
849 *Mike Utley* .15
850 Mike Croel .08
Super Bowl XXV logo .03
Super Bowl XXV ART .03
Walter Payton .03
Pro Set Gazette .03
Harold "Red" Grange .03

1991 Pro Set WLAF Helmets

Each of these 10 cards features a helmet for a team in the World League of American Football in its initial season. The cards, random inserts in 1991 Pro Set Series I packs, are numbered on the back and include information about the team depicted on the front, plus a schedule.

NM/M
Complete Set (10): 3.00
Common Helmet: .30
1 Barcelona Dragons .30
2 Birmingham Fire .30
3 Frankfurt Galaxy .30
4 London Monarchs .30
5 Montreal Machine .30
6 NY-NJ Knights .30
7 Orlando Thunder .30
8 Raleigh-Durham Skyhawks .30
9 Sacramento Surge .30
10 San Antonio Riders .30

1991 Pro Set WLAF Inserts

These cards, featuring players from each of the 10 teams in the World League of American Football during its initial season in 1991, were random inserts in 1991 Pro Set Series I packs. Each team is represented by its quarterback and head coach, at least. The card front has the set's logo in an upper corner and indicates it is an official World League card. The back also has the set logo, plus a player profile and head shot. Card numbering includes "World League Collectible" above the number.

NM/M
Complete Set (32): 6.00
Common Player: .10
1 Mike Lynn .35
2 Larry Kennan .10
3 Jack Bicknell .10
4 Scott Erney .20
5 A.J. Green .25
6 Chan Gailey .10
7 Paul McGowan .15
8 Brent Pease .20
9 Jack Elway .30
10 Mike Perez .30
11 Mike Tetter .10
12 Larry Kennan .10
13 Corris Ervin .10
14 John Witkowski .25
15 Jacques Dussault .10
16 Ray Savage .10
17 Kevin Sweeney .50
18 Mouse Davis .50
19 Todd Hammel .20
20 Anthony Parker .30
21 Don Matthews .15
22 Kerwin Bell .30
23 Wayne Davis .10
24 Roman Gabriel .60
25 John Carter .20
26 Mark Maye .20
27 Kay Stephenson .20
28 Ben Bennett .50
29 Shawn Knight .20
30 Mike Riley .10
31 Jason Garrett .15
32 Greg Gilbert .20

1991 Pro Set Cinderella Story

This nine-card perforated sheet was available inside The Official NFL Pro Set Card Book. The card fronts are similar to the design Pro Set used for its 1991 set, except there are four cards which have black-and-white photos instead of color ones. Each card back is numbered indicating it is in the Cinderella Story set, which profiles players who have achieved success in the NFL despite formidable roadblocks in their paths. If a card is perforated from the sheet, it measures the standard 2-1/2" x 3-1/2".

NM/M
Complete Set (9): 8.00
Common Player: .60
1 Rocky Bleier 1.00
2 Tom Dempsey .60
3 Dan Hampton .75
4 Charlie Hennigan .60
5 Dante Lavelli .75
6 Jim Plunkett .75
7 1968 New York Jets (Joe Namath Handing Off) 1.50
8 1981 San Francisco 49ers (Joe Montana Passing) 3.00
9 1979 Tampa Bay Bucs (Ricky Bell Running) .60

1991 Pro Set National Banquet

Each of these cards can be identified by the National Sports Collectors Convention logo on the front. The cards, which feature full-bleed color photos, were given away during the convention, held in Anaheim, Calif. Each card back is numbered and includes a player profile, biographical information and a mug shot.

NM/M
Complete Set (5): 5.00
Common Player: .50
1 Ronnie Lott 1.50
2 Roy Firestone (Television celebrity) 1.25
3 Roger Craig 1.25
4 Craig James, Tim Brant ProFiles Television Show 1.00
5 Title Card .50

1991 Pro Set Platinum

Pro Set issued this 315-card set in two series - 150 and 165 cards each. The glossy cards have full-bleed color action photos on the front, along with the Pro Set Platinum logo. The card backs use a horizontal format and include another action photo, plus the player's name, team and position. A "Platinum Performer" feature is also included, highlighting an outstanding performance by the player. Each series is numbered alphabetically by team, beginning with Atlanta. Subsets include "Special Teams" (#s 128-135), "Platinum Performance" (#s 136-150) and "Platinum Prospects" (#s 286-315). Random insert cards include "Special Collectibles" (numbered PC1-PC10) and redemption cards for a limited-edition Platinum card of Paul Brown or Emmitt Smith.

NM/M
Complete Set (315): 12.00
Complete Series 1 (150): 5.00
Complete Series 2 (165): 7.00
Common Player: .05
Pack (16): .20
Wax Box (36): 6.00
1 Chris Miller .05
2 Andre Rison .25
3 Tim Green .05
4 Jessie Tuggle .05
5 Thurman Thomas .40
6 Darryl Talley .05
7 Kent Hull .05
8 Bruce Smith .05
9 Shane Conlan .05
10 Jim Harbaugh .08
11 Neal Anderson .08
12 Mark Bortz .05
13 Richard Dent .05
14 Steve McMichael .05
15 James Brooks .05
16 Boomer Esiason .08
17 Tim Krumrie .05
18 James Francis .05
19 Lewis Billups .05
20 Eric Metcalf .05
21 Kevin Mack .05
22 Clay Matthews .05
23 Mike Johnson .05
24 Troy Aikman 1.00
25 Emmitt Smith 2.00
26 Daniel Stubbs .05
27 Ken Norton .05
28 John Elway .40
29 Bobby Humphrey .05
30 Simon Fletcher .05
31 Karl Mecklenburg .05
32 Rodney Peete .05
33 Barry Sanders 1.00
34 Michael Cofer .05
35 Jerry Ball .05
36 Sterling Sharpe .20
37 Tony Mandarich .05
38 Brian Noble .05
39 Tim Harris .05
40 Warren Moon .15
41 Ernest Givins .05
42 Mike Munchak .05
43 Sean Jones .05
44 Ray Childress .05
45 Jeff George .30
46 Albert Bentley .05
47 Duane Bickett .05
48 Steve DeBerg .05
49 Christian Okoye .05
50 Neil Smith .05
51 Derrick Thomas .25
52 Willie Gault .05
53 Don Mosebar .05
54 Howie Long .05
55 Greg Townsend .05
56 Terry McDaniel .05
57 Jackie Slater .05
58 Jim Everett .05
59 Cleveland Gary .05
60 Mike Piel .05
61 Jerry Gray .05
62 Dan Marino .75
63 Sammie Smith .05
64 Richmond Webb .05
65 Louis Oliver .05
66 Ferrell Edmunds .05
67 Jeff Cross .05
68 Wade Wilson .05
69 Chris Doleman .05
70 Joey Browner .05
71 Keith Millard .05
72 John Stephens .05
73 Andre Tippett .05
74 Brent Williams .05
75 Craig Heyward .05
76 Eric Martin .05
77 Pat Swilling .05
78 Sam Mills .05
79 Jeff Hostetler .25
80 Ottis Anderson .05
81 Lawrence Taylor .10
82 Pepper Johnson .05
83 Blair Thomas .05
84 Al Toon .05
85 Ken O'Brien .05
86 Erik McMillan .05
87 Dennis Byrd .05
88 Randall Cunningham .10
89 Fred Barnett .15
90 Seth Joyner .05
91 Reggie White .15
92 Timm Rosenbach .05
93 Johnny Johnson .25
94 Tim McDonald .05
95 Freddie Joe Nunn .05
96 Bubby Brister .08
97 Gary Anderson .05
98 Merril Hoge .05
99 Keith Willis .05
100 Rod Woodson .08
101 Billy Joe Tolliver .05
102 Marion Butts .08
103 Rod Benstine .05
104 Lee Williams .05
105 Burt Grossman .05
106 Tom Rathman .05
107 John Taylor .10
108 Michael Carter .05
109 Guy McIntyre .05
110 Pierce Holt .05
111 John L. Williams .05
112 Dave Krieg .05
113 Bryan Millard .05
114 Cortez Kennedy .30
115 Derrick Fenner .05
116 Vinny Testaverde .08
117 Reggie Cobb .25
118 Gary Anderson .05
119 Bruce Hill .05
120 Wayne Haddix .05
121 Broderick Thomas .05
122 Keith McCants .05
123 Andre Collins .05
124 Earnest Byner .05
125 Jim Lachey .05
126 Mark Rypien .10
127 Charles Mann .05
128 Nick Lowery .05
129 Chip Lohmiller .05
130 Mike Horan .05
131 Rohn Stark .05
132 Sean Landeta .05
133 Clarence Verdin .05
134 Johnny Bailey .05
135 Herschel Walker .05
136 Bo Jackson .40
137 Dexter Carter .05
138 Warren Moon .10
139 Joe Montana 1.00
140 Jerry Rice .75
141 Deion Sanders .30
142 Ronnie Lippett .05
143 Terance Mathis .05
144 Gaston Green .05
145 Dean Biasucci .05
146 Charles Haley .05
147 Derrick Thomas .25
148 Lawrence Taylor .10
149 Art Shell .05
150 Bill Parcells .05
151 Steve Broussard .05
152 Darion Conner .05
153 Bill Fralic .05
154 Mike Gann .05
155 Tim McKyer .05
156 Don Beebe .05
157 Cornelius Bennett .05
158 Andre Reed .10
159 Leonard Smith .05
160 Will Wolford .05
161 Mark Carrier .05
162 Wendell Davis .10
163 Jay Hilgenberg .05
164 Brad Muster .05
165 Mike Singletary .05
166 Eddie Brown .05
167 David Fulcher .05
168 Rodney Holman .05
169 Anthony Munoz .05
170 Craig Taylor .05
171 Mike Baab .05
172 David Grayson .05
173 Reggie Langhorne .05
174 Joe Morris .05
175 Kevin Gogan .10
176 Jack Del Rio .05
177 Issiac Holt .05
178 Michael Irvin .60
179 Jay Novacek .15
180 Steve Atwater .05
181 Mark Jackson .05
182 Ricky Nattiel .05
183 Warren Powers .05
184 Dennis Smith .05
185 Bennie Blades .05
186 Lomas Brown .05
187 Robert Clark .05
188 Mel Gray .05
189 Chris Spielman .05
190 Johnny Holland .05
191 Don Majkowski .05
192 *Bryce Paup* .50
193 Darrell Thompson .15
194 Ed West .05
195 Cris Dishman .15
196 Drew Hill .05
197 Bruce Matthews .05
198 Bubba McDowell .05
199 Allen Pinkett .05
200 Bill Brooks .05
201 Jeff Herrod .05
202 Anthony Johnson .10
203 Mike Prior .05
204 John Alt .05
205 Stephone Paige .05
206 Kevin Ross .05
207 Dan Saleaumua .05
208 Barry Word .10
209 Marcus Allen .10
210 Roger Craig .05
211 Ronnie Lott .10
212 Winston Moss .05
213 Jay Schroeder .05
214 Robert Delpino .05
215 Henry Ellard .05
216 Kevin Greene .05
217 Tom Newberry .05
218 Michael Stewart .05
219 Mark Duper .05
220 *Mark Higgs* .30
221 John Offerdahl .05
222 Keith Sims .05
223 Anthony Carter .05
224 Cris Carter .05
225 Steve Jordan .05
226 Randall McDaniel .05
227 Al Noga .05
228 Ray Agnew .05
229 Bruce Armstrong .05
230 Bruce Armstrong .05
231 Greg McMurtry .05
232 Chris Singleton .05
233 Morten Andersen .05
234 Vince Buck .05
235 Gill Fenerty .05
236 Rickey Jackson .05
237 Vaughan Johnson .05
238 Carl Banks .05
239 Mark Collins .05
240 Rodney Hampton .50
241 David Meggett .05
242 Bart Oates .05
243 Kyle Clifton .05
244 Jeff Lageman .05
245 Freeman McNeil .05
246 Rob Moore .20
247 Eric Allen .05
248 Keith Byars .05
249 Keith Jackson .10
250 Jim McMahon .05
251 Andre Waters .05
252 Ken Harvey .05
253 Ernie Jones .05
254 Luis Sharpe .05
255 Anthony Thompson .05
256 Tom Tupa .05
257 Eric Green .10
258 Barry Foster .50
259 Bryan Hinkle .05
260 Tunch Ilkin .05
261 Louis Lipps .05
262 Gill Byrd .05
263 John Friesz .10
264 Anthony Miller .05
265 Junior Seau .25
266 Ronnie Harmon .05
267 Harris Barton .05
268 Todd Bowles .05
269 Don Griffin .05
270 Bill Romanowski .05
271 Steve Young .50
272 Brian Blades .05
273 Jacob Green .05
274 Rufus Porter .05
275 Eugene Robinson .05
276 Mark Carrier .05
277 Reuben Davis .05
278 Paul Gruber .05
279 Gary Clark .10
280 Darrell Green .05
281 Wilber Marshall .05
282 Matt Millen .05
283 Alvin Walton .05
284 Joe Gibbs .05
285 Don Shula .15
286 *Larry Brown* .15
287 *Mike Croel* .30
288 *Antone Davis* .10
289 *Ricky Ervins* .25
290 *Brett Favre* 5.00
291 *Pat Harlow* .10
292 *Michael Jackson* .60
293 *Henry Jones* .25
294 *Aaron Craver* .10
295 *Nick Bell* .25
296 *Todd Lyght* .15
297 *Todd Marinovich* .10
298 *Russell Maryland* .35
299 *Kanavis McGhee* .10
300 *Dan McGwire* .15
301 Charles McRae .10
302 Eric Moten .10
303 Jerome Henderson .10
304 *Browning Nagle* .25
305 *Mike Pritchard* .35
306 *Stanley Richard* .30
307 *Randal Hill* .25
308 *Leonard Russell* 1.00
309 *Eric Swann* .15
310 *Phil Hansen* .15
311 *Moe Gardner* .15
312 *Jon Vaughn* .15
313 *Aeneas Williams* .10
314 *Alfred Williams* .15
315 *Harvey Williams* .35

1991 Pro Set Platinum PC

These 10 insert cards were randomly included in Series II Platinum packs. Each is numbered on the card back using a "PC" prefix. The card front has a full-bleed color action photo, plus the set logo. The back has another photo and player summary, all designed in a horizontal format. The cards were divided into three subsets - Platinum Profile, Platinum Photo and Platinum Game Breaker.

		NM/M
Complete Set (10):		10.00
Common Player:		.50
1	Bobby Hebert	.50
2	Art Monk	.50
3	Kenny Walker	.50
4	Low Fives	.50
5	Kevin Mack	.50
6	Neal Anderson	.50
7	Gaston Green	.50
8	Barry Sanders	3.00
9	Emmitt Smith	5.00
10	Thurman Thomas	1.50

1991 Pro Set Spanish

These cards have the same photos on them as their regular 1991 Pro Set counterparts, but the card numbers have been changed. Also, the big difference is that all text and information on the card is in Spanish. Five insert cards (ES1-ES5) were also randomly included in packs.

		NM/M
Complete Set (300):		10.00
Common Player:		.03
1	Steve Broussard	.03
2	Darion Conner	.03
3	Tory Epps	.03
4	Bill Fralic	.03
5	Mike Gann	.03
6	Chris Miller	.15
7	Andre Rison	.20
8	Deion Sanders	.25
9	Jessie Tuggle	.03
10	Cornelius Bennett	.10
11	Shane Conlan	.05
12	Kent Hull	.03
13	Kirby Jackson	.03
14	James Lofton	.15
15	Andre Reed	.15
16	Bruce Smith	.15
17	Darryl Talley	.05
18	Thurman Thomas	.50
19	Neal Anderson	.15
20	Trace Armstrong	.03
21	Mark Carrier	.07
22	Wendell Davis	.03
23	Richard Dent	.15
24	Jim Harbaugh	.10
25	Ron Rivera	.03
26	Mike Singletary	.15
27	Lemuel Stinson	.03
28	James Brooks	.03
29	Eddie Brown	.03
30	Boomer Esiason	.15
31	James Francis	.03
32	David Fulcher	.03
33	Rodney Holman	.03
34	Anthony Munoz	.10
35	Bruce Reimers	.03
36	Ickey Woods	.05
37	Mike Baab	.03
38	Brian Brennan	.03
39	Raymond Clayborn	.03
40	Mike Johnson	.03
41	Clay Matthews	.03
42	Eric Metcalf	.07
43	Frank Minnifield	.03
44	Joe Morris	.05
45	Anthony Pleasant	.03
46	Troy Aikman	1.00
47	Jack Del Rio	.03
48	Issiac Holt	.03
49	Michael Irvin	.50
50	Jimmie Jones	.03
51	Nate Newton	.03
52	Danny Noonan	.03
53	Jay Novacek	.07
54	Emmitt Smith	2.00
55	Steve Atwater	.05
56	Michael Brooks	.05
57	John Elway	.25
58	Mike Horan	.03
59	Mark Jackson	.03
60	Karl Mecklenburg	.03
61	Warren Powers	.03
62	Dennis Smith	.03
63	Doug Widell	.03
64	Jerry Ball	.05
65	Bennie Blades	.05
66	Robert Clark	.03
67	Ken Dallafior	.03
68	Mel Gray	.07
69	Eddie Murray	.05
70	Rodney Peete	.05
71	Barry Sanders	.75
72	Chris Spielman	.07
73	Robert Brown	.03
74	LeRoy Butler	.07
75	Perry Kemp	.03
76	Don Majkowski	.05
77	Tony Mandarich	.03
78	Mark Murphy	.03
79	Brian Noble	.03
80	Sterling Sharpe	.50
81	Ed West	.03
82	Ray Childress	.03
83	Cris Dishman	.03
84	Ernest Givins	.07
85	Drew Hill	.05
86	Haywood Jeffires	.07
87	Lamar Lathon	.03
88	Bruce Matthews	.07
89	Bubba McDowell	.03
90	Warren Moon	.25
91	Chip Banks	.03
92	Albert Bentley	.05
93	Duane Bickett	.03
94	Bill Brooks	.03
95	Sam Clancy	.03
96	Ray Donaldson	.03
97	Jeff George	.25
98	Mike Prior	.03
99	Clarence Verdin	.03
100	Steve DeBerg	.05
101	Albert Lewis	.03
102	Christian Okoye	.05
103	Kevin Ross	.03
104	Stephone Paige	.03
105	Kevin Porter	.03
106	Percy Snow	.03
107	Derrick Thomas	.20
108	Barry Word	.05
109	Marcus Allen	.20
110	Mervyn Fernandez	.03
111	Howie Long	.07
112	Ronnie Lott	.15
113	Terry McDaniel	.03
114	Max Montoya	.03
115	Don Mosebar	.03
116	Jay Schroeder	.10
117	Greg Townsend	.03
118	Flipper Anderson	.07
119	Henry Ellard	.07
120	Jim Everett	.10
121	Kevin Greene	.07
122	Damone Johnson	.03
123	Buford McGee	.03
124	Tom Newberry	.05
125	Michael Stewart	.03
126	Alvin Wright	.03
127	Mark Clayton	.05
128	Jeff Cross	.03
129	Mark Duper	.05
130	Ferrell Edmunds	.03
131	Dan Marino	.75
132	Tim McKyer	.03
133	John Offerdahl	.05
134	Louis Oliver	.03
135	Sammie Smith	.03
136	Joey Browner	.05
137	Anthony Carter	.10
138	Chris Doleman	.05
139	Hassan Jones	.03
140	Steve Jordan	.05
141	Carl Lee	.03
142	Al Noga	.03
143	Henry Thomas	.03
144	Herschel Walker	.15
145	Ray Agnew	.03
146	Bruce Armstrong	.03
147	Marv Cook	.05
148	Irving Fryar	.07
149	Tommy Hodson	.07
150	Fred Marion	.03
151	Johnny Rembert	.03
152	Chris Singleton	.03
153	Andre Tippett	.07
154	Morten Andersen	.10
155	Toi Cook	.03
156	Craig Heyward	.05
157	Dalton Hilliard	.03
158	Rickey Jackson	.07
159	Vaughan Johnson	.07
160	Rueben Mayes	.03
161	Pat Swilling	.07
162	Bobby Hebert	.07
163	Ottis Anderson	.10
164	Carl Banks	.05
165	Rodney Hampton	.25
166	Jeff Hostetler	.15
167	Mark Ingram	.05
168	Leonard Marshall	.03
169	David Meggett	.05
170	Lawrence Taylor	.25
171	Everson Walls	.03
172	Brad Baxter	.03
173	Jeff Lageman	.03
174	Pat Leahy	.03
175	Erik McMillan	.03
176	Scott Mersereau	.03
177	Rob Moore	.10
178	Ken O'Brien	.07
179	Blair Thomas	.10
180	Al Toon	.07
181	Eric Allen	.03
182	Jerome Brown	.03
183	Keith Byars	.05
184	Randall Cunningham	.15
185	Byron Evans	.03
186	Keith Jackson	.05
187	Heath Sherman	.03
188	Clyde Simmons	.05
189	Reggie White	.20
190	Rich Camarillo	.03
191	Johnny Johnson	.15
192	Ernie Jones	.03
193	Tim McDonald	.03
194	Freddie Joe Nunn	.03
195	Luis Sharpe	.03
196	Jay Taylor	.03
197	Anthony Thompson	.03
198	Tom Tupa	.03
199	Gary Anderson	.03
200	Bubby Brister	.10
201	Eric Green	.07
202	Bryan Hinkle	.03
203	Merril Hoge	.03
204	Carnell Lake	.03
205	Louis Lipps	.03
206	Keith Willis	.03
207	Rod Woodson	.10
208	Rod Bernstine	.05
209	Marion Butts	.07
210	Anthony Miller	.10
211	Leslie O'Neal	.03
212	Henry Rolling	.03
213	Junior Seau	.15
214	Billy Ray Smith	.03
215	Broderick Thompson	.03
216	Derrick Walker	.03
217	Dexter Carter	.03
218	Don Griffin	.03
219	Charles Haley	.05
220	Pierce Holt	.03
221	Joe Montana	1.00
222	Jerry Rice	.75
223	John Taylor	.10
224	Michael Walter	.03
225	Steve Young	.25
226	Brian Blades	.05
227	Jeff Bryant	.03
228	Jacob Green	.03
229	Tommy Kane	.03
230	Dave Krieg	.07
231	Bryan Millard	.03
232	Rufus Porter	.03
233	Eugene Robinson	.03
234	John L. Williams	.03
235	Gary Anderson	.05
236	Mark Carrier	.05
237	Reggie Cobb	.05
238	Rueben Davis	.03
239	Paul Gruber	.05
240	Harry Hamilton	.03
241	Keith McCants	.03
242	Ricky Reynolds	.03
243	Vinny Testaverde	.10
244	Earnest Byner	.05
245	Gary Clark	.10
246	Andre Collins	.03
247	Darrell Green	.07
248	Jim Lachey	.03
249	Charles Mann	.03
250	Wilber Marshall	.05
251	Art Monk	.10
252	Mark Rypien	.10
253	Russell Maryland	.15
254	Mike Croel	.03
255	Stanley Richard	.03
256	Leonard Russell	.03
257	Dan McGwire	.10
258	Todd Marinovich	.05
259	Eric Swann	.03
260	Mike Pritchard	.05
261	Alfred Williams	.03
262	Brett Favre	5.00
263	Browning Nagle	.07
264	Darryll Lewis	.03
265	Nick Bell	.03
266	Jeff Graham	.05
267	Eric Moten	.03
268	Roman Phifer	.03
269	Eric Bieniemy	.03
270	Phil Hansen	.03
271	Reggie Barrett	.03
272	Aeneas Williams	.07
273	Aaron Craver	.03
274	Lawrence Dawsey	.03
275	Ricky Ervins	.03
276	Jake Reed	.05
277	Eric Williams	.10
278	Tim Barnett	.10
279	Keith Traylor	.03
280	Jerry Rice	.25
281	Jim Lachey	.03
282	Barry Sanders	.50
283	Neal Anderson	.07
284	Reggie White	.15
285	Lawrence Taylor	.15
286	Mike Singletary	.10
287	Joey Browner	.05
288	Morten Andersen	.05
289	Andre Reed	.10
290	Anthony Munoz	.07
291	Warren Moon	.20
292	Thurman Thomas	.25
293	Ray Childress	.05
294	Derrick Thomas	.15
295	Rod Woodson	.10
296	Steve Atwater	.05
297	David Fulcher	.03
298	Anthony Munoz	.10
299	Ron Rivera	.03
300	Cornelius Bennett	.10
E1	Tom Flores	2.00
E2	Anthony Munoz	2.00
E3	Tony Casillas	2.00
E4	Super Bowl XXVI	2.00
E5	Felicidades	2.00

1991 Pro Set UK Sheets

Measuring 5-1/8" x 11-3/4", the five six-card strips were used as a promotion in a Middlesex, England, newspaper called Today. Released one strip per week in Sunday papers during Fall 1991, the unperforated strips were numbered 1-5. Each player card is numbered identically to his 1991 regular-issue cards.

		NM/M
Complete Set (5):		25.00
Common Player:		2.00
1	200 Jim Everett, 167 Warren Moon, 111 Boomer Esiason, 128 Troy Aikman, 726 Dan Marino, 138 John Elway Quarterbacks	10.00
2	576 Herschel Walker, 213 Sammie Smith, 722 Earnest Byner, 123 Eric Metcalf, 485 Emmitt Smith Running Backs	10.00
3	209 Mark Duper, 654 Jerry Rice, 251 Al Toon, 161 Sterling Sharpe, 618 Keith Jackson, 115 Tim McGee Receivers	6.00
4	460 Jim Breech, 447 Scott Norwood, 489 Mike Horan, 300 Norm Johnson, 184 Nick Lowery, 401 Sean Landeta Kickers	2.00
5	728 Mike Singletary, 56 Carl Banks, 98 Deion Sanders, 191 Howie Long, 131 Issiac Holt, 241 Pat Swilling Defensive	3.00

1991 Pro Set WLAF

These cards feature players from the World League of American Football. This logo and a notation that the card is an "Official World League Card" are on the front, which has a full-bleed color action photo. The back has a card number, player profile, biographical information and a mug shot. Each back is designed in a horizontal format.

		NM/M
Complete Set (150):		5.00
Common Player:		.05
1	World League Logo	.15
2	Mike Lynn	.15
3	First Weekend	.15
4	World Bowl Trophy	.30
5	Jon Horton	.05
6	Stan Gelbaugh	.50
7	Dan Crossman	.05
8	Marlon Brown	.10
9	Judd Garrett	.25
10	Barcelona Dragons	.05
11	Birmingham Fire	.05
12	Frankfurt Galaxy	.05
13	London Monarchs	.05
14	Montreal Machine	.05
15	NY-NJ Knights	.05
16	Orlando Thunder	.05
17	Raleigh-Durham Skyhawks	.05
18	Sacramento Surge	.05
19	San Antonio Riders	.05
20	Eric Wilkerson	.05
21	Stan Gelbaugh	.35
22	Judd Garrett	.15
23	Tony Baker	.05
24	Byron Williams	.05
25	Chris Mohr	.10
26	Errol Tucker	.05
27	Carl Painter	.05
28	Anthony Parker	.10
29	Danny Lockett	.10
30	Scott Adams	.05
31	Jim Bell	.05
32	Lydell Carr	.15
33	Bruce Clark	.15
34	Demetrius Davis	.10
35	Scott Erney	.10
36	Ron Goetz	.05
37	Xisco Marcos	.05
38	Paul Palmer	.15
39	Tony Rice	.40
40	Bobby Sign	.05
41	Gene Taylor	.05
42	Barry Voorhees	.05
43	Jack Bicknell	.10
44	Kenny Bell	.05
45	Willie Bouyer	.05
46	John Brantley	.10
47	Elroy Harris	.05
48	James Henry	.05
49	John Holland	.10
50	Arhur Hunter	.05
51	Eric Jones	.05
52	Kirk Maggio	.05
53	Paul McGowan	.05
54	John Miller	.10
55	Maurice Oliver	.05
56	Darrel Phillips	.05
57	Chan Gailey	.05
58	Tony Baker	.10
59	Tim Broady	.05
60	Garry Frank	.05
61	Jason Johnson	.05
62	Stefan Maslo	.05
63	Mark Mraz	.05
64	Yepi Pau'u	.05
65	Mike Perez	.25
66	Mike Teeter	.05
67	Chris Williams	.05
68	Jack Elway	.20
69	Theo Adams	.05
70	Jeff Alexander	.05
71	Phillip Alexander	.05
72	Paul Berardelli	.10
73	Dana Brinson	.05
74	Marlon Brown	.05
75	Dedrick Dodge	.05
76	Victor Ebubedike	.05
77	Corris Ervin	.10
78	Steve Gabbard	.05
79	Judd Garrett	.15
80	Stan Gelbaugh	.75
81	Roy Hart	.05
82	Jon Horton	.05
83	Danny Lockett	.15
84	Doug Marrone	.05
85	Ken Sale	.05
86	Larry Kennan	.05
87	Mike Cadore	.05
88	K.D. Dunn	.05
89	Ricky Johnson	.05
90	Chris Mohr	.05
91	Bjorn Nittmo	.10
92	Michael Proctor	.05
93	Richard Shelton	.15
94	Tracy Simien	.30
95	Jacques Dussault	.05
96	Cornell Burbage	.10
97	Joe Campbell	.05
98	Monty Gilbreath	.05
99	Jeff Graham	.25
100	Kip Lewis	.05
101	Bob Lilljedahl	.05
102	Falanda Newton	.10
103	Anthony Parker	.10
104	Caesar Rentie	.05
105	Ron Sancho	.10
106	Craig Schlicting	.10
107	Lonnie Turner	.05
108	Eric Wilkerson	.05
109	Tony Woods	.10
110	Darrell "Mouse" Davis	.15
111	Kerwin Bell	.30
112	Wayne Davis	.05
113	John Guerrero	.05
114	Myron Jones	.05
115	Eric Mitchel	.20
116	Billy Owens	.05
117	Carl Painter	.10
118	Rob Sterling	.05
119	Errol Tucker	.05
120	Byron Williams	.05
121	Mike Withycombe	.05
122	Don Matthews	.05
123	Jon Carter	.05
124	Marvin Hargrove	.05
125	Clarkston Hines	.05
126	Ray Jackson	.05
127	Bobby McAllister	.25
128	Darryl McGill	.05
129	Pat McGuirk	.10
130	Shawn Woodson	.05
131	Roman Gabriel	.25
132	Greg Coauette	.05
133	Mike Eklins	.15
134	Victor Floyd	.05
135	Shawn Knight	.10
136	Pete Najarian	.05
137	Carl Parker	.10
138	Richard Stephens	.05
139	Curtis Wilson	.05
140	Kay Stephenson	.10
141	Ricky Blake	.25
142	Donnie Gardner	.05
143	Jason Garrett	.25
144	Mike Johnson	.05
145	Undra Johnson	.10
146	John Layfield	.05
147	Mark Ledbetter	.05
148	Gary Richard	.05
149	Tim Walton	.05
150	Mike Riley	.05

1991 Pro Set WLAF World Bowl Combo 43

This set combines Pro Set's helmet and 32-card insert sets into one issue. Fans who attended the World Bowl Game in Wembley Stadium in London, England, received the set. The cards have been renumbered from the original sets, and the helmet cards can be identified by the chronological text which is on the back instead of a team schedule.

		NM/M
Complete Set (43):		15.00
Common Player:		.25
1	Mike Lynn PRES	.75
2	League Opener London 24, Frankfurt 11	.50
3	Jack Bicknell	.50
4	Scott Erney	.40
5	Anthony Greene	.50
6	Chan Gailey	.50
7	Paul McGowan	.25
8	Brent Pease	.50
9	Jack Elway	.80
10	Mike Perez	.75
11	Mike Teeter	.25
12	Larry Kennan	.25
13	Corris Ervin	.25
14	John Witkowski	.50
15	Jacques Dussault	.25
16	Ray Savage	.35
17	Kevin Sweeney	.65
18	Mouse Davis	.65
19	Todd Hammel	.50
20	Anthony Parker	.50
21	Don Matthews	.25
22	Kerwin Bell	.75
23	Wayne Davis	.25
24	Roman Gabriel	.75
25	Jon Carter	.50
26	Bobby McAllister	1.00
27	Kay Stephenson	.25
28	Mike Elkins	1.00
29	Shawn Knight	.50
30	Mike Riley	.25
31	Jason Garrett	.75
32	Greg Gilbert	.50
33	World Bowl Trophy	4.00
34	Barcelona Dragons Helmet	.60
35	Birmingham Fire Helmet	.60
36	Frankfurt Galaxy Helmet	.60
37	London Monarchs Helmet	.60
38	Montreal Machine Helmet	.60
39	NY-NJ Knights Helmet	.60
40	Orlando Thunder Helmet	.60
41	Ral.-Durham Skyhawks Helmet	.60
42	Sacramento Surge Helmet	.60
43	San Antonio Riders Helmet	.60

1991 Pro Set Super Bowl XXVI AMEX Binder

American Express sponsored this 49-card set which was sold to commemorate Super Bowl XXVI in Minneapolis. The cards were included in an album, which holds four cards per page. Representatives from the Super Bowl teams - the Buffalo Bills and Washington Redskins - are included in the set. The cards have the same photos and numbers as their regular set counterparts, except these are marked with an AFC or NFC Champs logo on the front.

		NM/M
Complete Set (49):		25.00
Common Player:		.40
1	The NFL Experience	1.00
2	Super Bowl XXVI	.50
3	AFC Standings	.50
4	NFC Standings	.50
5	The Metrodome	.50
73	Howard Ballard	.40
74	Cornelius Bennett	.75
75	Shane Conlan	.50
76	Kent Hull	.50
77	Kirby Jackson	.40
79	Mark Kelso	.40
80	Nate Odomes	.40
81	Andre Reed	.90
82	Jim Ritcher	.40
83	Bruce Smith	.75
84	Darryl Talley	.50
86	Thurman Thomas	3.00
88	Will Wolford	.40
89	Jeff Wright	.40
90	Marv Levy	.40
300	Cornelius Bennett	.50
316	Earnest Byner	.60
317	Gary Clark	.90
318	Andre Collins	.50
320	Chip Lohmiller	.40
321	Martin Mayhew	.40
322	Mark Rypien	.75
323	Alvin Walton	.40
324	Joe Gibbs	.50
370	Warren Moon	.75
444	James Lofton	.75
445	Keith McKeller	.50
449	Leon Seals	.40
450	Leonard Smith	.40
676	Jeff Bostic	.40
677	Darrell Green	.75
678	Markus Koch	.40
679	Jim Lachey	.50
680	Charles Mann	.50
681	Wilber Marshall	.50
682	Art Monk	.75
683	Gerald Riggs	.50
684	Ricky Sanders	.75
725	Howie Long	.75
726	Dan Marino	2.00
746	Bobby Wilson	.50
805	Ricky Ervins	.75
848	Brian Mitchell	.75
(1)	Jim Kelly	20.00

1992 Pro Set

Pro Set issued its 700-card 1992 set in two series - 400 and 300 cards. The fronts have full-bleed color action photos and the player's name and NFL/Pro Set logos at the bottom. The backs, using a horizontal format, offer statistics, a biography, career highlights and a close-up shot of the player. Subsets include Statistical Leaders, Milestones, Draft Day, Innovators, 1991 Replays, Pro Set Super Bowl XXVI Replays, Pro Set Newsreel, Magic Numbers, Play Smart,

NFC Spirit of the Game, AFC Pro Bowl Stars, NFC Pro Bowl Stars, and six miscellaneous cards. Insert cards include an Emmitt Smith hologram set of four cards (ES1-ES4), Hall of Fame 2000 (10 cards), Team MVPs (30 gold-foil stamped cards), a Santa Claus card, Ground Force, Hall of Fame Inductees and a Pro Set Emmitt Smith Power Preview special offer card.

	NM/M
Complete Set (700):	20.00
Complete Series 1 (400):	10.00
Complete Series 2 (300):	10.00
Common Player:	.05
Minor Stars:	.10
Series 1 Pack (14):	.25
Series 1 Wax Box (36):	8.00
Series 2 Pack (14):	.40
Series 2 Wax Box (36):	12.00

1 Mike Croel (LL) .05
2 Thurman Thomas (LL) .10
3 Wayne Fontes (CO) (LL) .05
4 Anthony Munoz (LL) .05
5 Steve Young (LL) .25
6 Warren Moon (LL) .10
7 Emmitt Smith (LL) .50
8 Haywood Jeffires (LL) .05
9 Marv Cook (LL) .05
10 Michael Irvin (LL) .10
11 Thurman Thomas (LL) .10
12 Chip Lohmiller (LL) .05
13 Barry Sanders (LL) .75
14 Reggie Roby (LL) .05
15 Mel Gray (LL) .05
16 Ronnie Lott (LL) .05
17 Pat Swilling (LL) .05
18 Reggie White (LL) .10
19 Haywood Jeffires (ML) .05
20 Pat Leahy (ML) .05
21 James Lofton (ML) .05
22 Art Monk (ML) .10
23 Don Shula (ML) .05
24 Nick Lowery (ML) .05
25 John Elway (ML) .50
26 Chicago Bears (ML) .05
27 Marcus Allen (ML) .10
28 *Terrell Buckley* .20
29 *Amp Lee* .10
30 *Chris Mims* .10
31 *Leon Searcy* .10
32 *Jimmy Smith* 2.00
33 *Siran Stacy* .10
34 Pete Gogolak .05
35 Cheerleaders .05
36 Houston Astrodome .05
37 Christian Okoye (Week 1) .05
38 Don Beebe (Week 2) .05
39 Wendell Davis (Week 3) .05
40 Don Shula (CO) (Week 4) .05
41 Ronnie Lott (Week 5) .05
42 Art Monk (Week 6) .10
43 Thurman Thomas (Week 7) .10
44 John Stephens (Week 8) .05
45 Herschel Walker (Week 9) .05
46 Chris Burkett (Week 10) .05
47 Line Play (Week 11) .05
48 Andre Rison (Week 12) .10
49 Steve Beuerlein, Michael Irvin (Week 13) .10
50 Irving Fryar (Week 14) .05
51 Bill's Defense (Week 15) .05
52 Kelvin Martin (Week 16) .05
53 Bruce Coslet (CO) (Week 17) .05
54 Fred Jones (AFC Wild Card) .05
55 Oilers' Run-and-Shoot (AFC Wild Card) .05
56 Bill Bates (NFC Wild Card) .05
57 Michael Haynes (NFC Wild Card) .05
58 Bronco Interception (AFC Divisional Playoff) .05
59 Thurman Thomas (AFC Divisional Playoff) .10
60 Erik Kramer (NFC Divisional Playoff) .05
61 Darrell Green (NFC Divisional Playoff) .05
62 Carlton Bailey (AFC Championship) .05
63 Mark Rypien (NFC Championship) .05
64 TD Reversed, FG Blocked .05
65 Brad Edwards (Picks Off First of Two) .05
66 Rypien to Byner, Rypien to Byner .05
67 Riggs Puts Redskins Up .05
68 Gouvela Interceptions Buries Bills .05
69 Thurman Thomas .20
70 Clark Catches Rypien's Second TD .05
71 Bills Convert Late Break .05
72 Redskins Run Out the Clock .05
73 Jeff Bostic .05
74 Earnest Byner .05
75 Gary Clark .05
76 Andre Collins .05
77 Darrell Green .05
78 Joe Jacoby .05
79 Jim Lachey .05
80 Chip Lohmiller .05
81 Charles Mann .05
82 Martin Mayhew .05
83 Matt Millen .05
84 Brian Mitchell .05
85 Art Monk .10
86 Gerald Riggs .05
87 Mark Rypien .05
88 Fred Stokes .05
89 Bobby Wilson .05
90 Joe Gibbs .05
91 Howard Ballard .05
92 Cornelius Bennett .10
93 Kenneth Davis .05
94 Al Edwards .05
95 Kent Hull .05
96 Kirby Jackson .05
97 Mark Kelso .05
98 James Lofton .10
99 Keith McKeller .05
100 Nate Odomes .05
101 Jim Ritcher .05
102 Leon Seals .05
103 Steve Tasker .05
104 Darryl Talley .05
105 Thurman Thomas .20
106 Will Wolford .05
107 Jeff Wright .05
108 Marv Levy .05
109 Darion Conner .05
110 Bill Fralic .05
111 Moe Gardner .05
112 Michael Haynes .05
113 Chris Miller .05
114 Erric Pegram .05
115 Bruce Pickens .05
116 Andre Rison .20
117 Jerry Glanville .05
118 Neal Anderson .05
119 Trace Armstrong .05
120 Wendell Davis .05
121 Richard Dent .10
122 Jay Hilgenberg .05
123 Lemuel Stinson .05
124 Stan Thomas .05
125 Tom Waddle .05
126 Mike Ditka .10
127 James Brooks .05
128 Eddie Brown .05
129 David Fulcher .05
130 Harold Green .05
131 Tim Krumrie .05
132 Anthony Munoz .05
133 Craig Taylor .05
134 Eric Thomas .05
135 David Shula .05
136 Mike Baab .05
137 Brian Brennan .05
138 Michael Jackson .10
139 James Jones .05
140 Ed King .05
141 Clay Matthews .05
142 Eric Metcalf .05
143 Joe Morris .05
144 Bill Belichick .05
145 Steve Beuerlein .05
146 Larry Brown .05
147 Ray Horton .05
148 Ken Norton .05
149 Jeff Jaeger .05
150 Emmitt Smith 1.50
151 Mark Stepnoski .05
152 Alexander Wright .05
153 Jimmy Johnson .10
154 Mike Croel .05
155 John Elway .75
156 Gaston Green .05
157 Wymon Henderson .05
158 Karl Mecklenburg .05
159 Warren Powers .05
160 Steve Sewell .05
161 Doug Widell .05
162 Dan Reeves .05
163 Eric Andolsek .05
164 Jerry Ball .05
165 Bennie Blades .05
166 Ray Crockett .05
167 Willie Green .05
168 Erik Kramer .05
169 Barry Sanders 2.00
170 Chris Spielman .05
171 Wayne Fontes .05
172 Vinnie Clark .05
173 Tony Mandarich .05
174 Brian Noble .05
175 Bryce Paup .05
176 Sterling Sharpe .20
177 Darrell Thompson .05
178 Esera Tuaolo .05
179 Ed West .05
180 Mike Holmgren .20
181 Ray Childress .05
182 Cris Dishman .05
183 Curtis Duncan .05
184 William Fuller .05
185 Lamar Lathon .05
186 Warren Moon .20
187 *Bo Orlando* .10
188 Lorenzo White .05
189 Jack Pardee .05
190 Chip Banks .05
191 Dean Biasucci .05
192 Bill Brooks .05
193 Ray Donaldson .05
194 Jeff Herrod .05
195 Mike Prior .05
196 Mark Vander Poel .05
197 Clarence Verdin .05
198 Ted Marchibroda .05
199 John Alt .05
200 Deron Cherry .05
201 Steve DeBerg .05
202 Nick Lowery .05
203 Neil Smith .05
204 Derrick Thomas .20
205 Joe Valerio .05
206 Barry Word .05
207 Marty Schottenheimer .05
208 Marcus Allen .20
209 Nick Bell .05
210 Tim Brown .20
211 Howie Long .10
212 Ronnie Lott .10
213 Todd Marinovich .05
214 Greg Townsend .05
215 Steve Wright .05
216 Art Shell .05
217 Flipper Anderson .05
218 Robert Delpino .05
219 Henry Ellard .05
220 Kevin Greene .05
221 Todd Lyght .05
222 Tom Newberry .05
223 Roman Phifer .05
224 Michael Stewart .05
225 Chuck Knox .05
226 Aaron Craver .05
227 Jeff Cross .05
228 Mark Duper .05
229 Ferrell Edmunds .05
230 Jim C. Jensen .05
231 Louis Oliver .05
232 Reggie Roby .05
233 Sammie Smith .05
234 Don Shula .10
235 Joey Browner .05
236 Anthony Carter .05
237 Chris Doleman .05
238 Steve Jordan .05
239 Kirk Lowdermilk .05
240 Henry Thomas .05
241 Herschel Walker .10
242 Felix Wright .05
243 Dennis Green .10
244 Ray Agnew .05
245 Marv Cook .05
246 Irving Fryar .10
247 Pat Harlow .05
248 Hugh Millen .05
249 Leonard Russell .10
250 Andre Tippett .05
251 Jon Vaughn .05
252 Dick MacPherson .05
253 Morten Andersen .10
254 Bobby Hebert .05
255 Joel Hilgenberg .05
256 Vaughan Johnson .05
257 Sam Mills .05
258 Pat Swilling .05
259 Floyd Turner .05
260 Steve Walsh .05
261 Jim Mora .05
262 Stephen Baker .05
263 Mark Collins .05
264 Rodney Hampton .10
265 Jeff Hostetler .10
266 Erik Howard .05
267 Sean Landeta .05
268 Gary Reasons .05
269 Everson Walls .05
270 Ray Handley .05
271 *Louis Aguiar* .10
272 Brad Baxter .05
273 Chris Burkett .05
274 Irv Eatman .05
275 Jeff Lageman .05
276 Freeman McNeil .05
277 Rob Moore .20
278 Lonnie Young .05
279 Bruce Coslet .05
280 Jerome Brown .05
281 Keith Byars .05
282 Bruce Collie .05
283 Keith Jackson .10
284 James Joseph .05
285 Seth Joyner .05
286 Andre Waters .05
287 Reggie White .20
288 Rich Kotite .05
289 Rich Camarillo .05
290 Garth Jax .05
291 Ernie Jones .05
292 Tim McDonald .05
293 Rod Saddler .05
294 Anthony Thompson .05
295 Tim Tupa .05
296 Ron Wolfley .05
297 Joe Bugel .05
298 Gary Anderson .05
299 Jeff Graham .10
300 Eric Green .05
301 Bryan Hinkle .05
302 Tunch Ilkin .05
303 Louis Lipps .05
304 Neil O'Donnell .10
305 Rod Woodson .05
306 Bill Cowher .05
307 Eric Bieniemy .05
308 Marion Butts .05
309 John Friesz .10
310 Courtney Hall .05
311 Ronnie Harmon .05
312 Henry Rolling .05
313 Billy Ray Smith .05
314 George Thornton .05
315 Bobby Ross .05
316 Todd Bowles .05
317 Michael Carter .05
318 Don Griffin .05
319 Charles Haley .10
320 Brent Jones .05
321 John Taylor .10
322 Ted Washington .05
323 Steve Young .50
324 George Seifert .10
325 Brian Blades .05
326 Jacob Green .05
327 Patrick Hunter .05
328 Tommy Kane .05
329 Cortez Kennedy .10
330 Dave Krieg .05
331 Rufus Porter .05
332 John L. Williams .05
333 Tom Flores .05
334 Gary Anderson .05
335 Mark Carrier .05
336 Reuben Davis .05
337 Lawrence Dawsey .05
338 Keith McCants .05
339 Vinny Testaverde .20
340 Broderick Thomas .05
341 Robert Wilson .05
342 Sam Wyche .05
343 1991 Teacher of the Year .05
344 Owners Reject Instant Replay .05
345 NFL Experience Unveiled .05
346 Noll Retires Tosses Coin .05
347 Isaac Curtis, Tim McGee .05
348 Drew Pearson, Michael Irvin .10
349 Billy Sims, Barry Sanders .50
350 Kenny Stabler, Todd Marinovich .05
351 Craig James, Leonard Russell .05
352 Bob Golic (Graffiti It's a Sign of Ignorance) .05
353 Pat Harlow (Vote, Let Your Choice Be Heard) .05
354 Esera Tuaolo (Stand Tall, Be Proud of Your Heritage) .05
355 Mark Schlereth (Save the Environment Be a Team Player) .05
356 Trace Armstrong (Drug Abuse Stay in Control) .05
357 Eric Bieniemy (Save a Life Buckle Up) .05
358 Bill Romanowski (Education Stay in School) .05
359 Irv Eatman (Exercise Be Active) .05
360 Jonathan Hayes (Diabetes Be Your Best) .05
361 Atlanta Falcons .05
362 Chicago Bears .05
363 Dallas Cowboys .05
364 Detroit Lions .05
365 Green Bay Packers .05
366 Los Angeles Rams .05
367 Minnesota Vikings .05
368 New Orleans Saints .05
369 New York Giants .05
370 Philadelphia Eagles .05
371 Phoenix Cardinals .05
372 San Francisco 49ers .05
373 Tampa Bay Buccaneers .05
374 Washington Redskins .05
375 Steve Atwater .05
376 Cornelius Bennett .05
377 Tim Brown .10
378 Marion Butts .05
379 Ray Childress .05
380 Mark Clayton .05
381 Marv Cook .05
382 Cris Dishman .05
383 William Fuller .05
384 Gaston Green .05
385 Jeff Jaeger .05
386 Haywood Jeffires .05
387 James Lofton .05
388 Ronnie Lott .05
389 Karl Mecklenburg .05
390 Warren Moon .10
391 Anthony Munoz .05
392 Dennis Smith .05
393 Neil Smith .05
394 Darryl Talley .05
395 Derrick Thomas .10
396 Thurman Thomas .20
397 Greg Townsend .05
398 Richmond Webb .05
399 Rod Woodson .05
400 Dan Reeves .05
401 Troy Aikman (PB) .30
402 Eric Allen PB .05
403 Bennie Blades PB .05
404 Lomas Brown PB .05
405 Mark Carrier PB .05
406 Gary Clark PB .05
407 Mel Gray PB .05
408 Darrell Green PB .05
409 Michael Irvin PB .10
410 Vaughan Johnson PB .05
411 Seth Joyner PB .05
412 Jim Lachey PB .05
413 Chip Lohmiller PB .05
414 Charles Mann PB .05
415 Chris Miller PB .05
416 Sam Mills PB .05
417 Bart Oates PB .05
418 Jerry Rice PB .30
419 Andre Rison PB .10
420 Mark Rypien PB .05
421 Barry Sanders PB .75
422 Deion Sanders PB .10
423 Mark Schlereth PB .05
424 Mike Singletary PB .05
425 Emmitt Smith PB .50
426 Pat Swilling PB .05
427 Reggie White PB .10
428 Rick Bryan .05
429 Tim Green .05
430 Drew Hill .05
431 Norm Johnson .05
432 Keith Jones .05
433 Mike Pritchard .10
434 Deion Sanders .50
435 *Tony Smith* .10
436 Jessie Tuggle .05
437 Steve Christie .05
438 Shane Conlan .05
439 *Matt Darby* .10
440 *John Fina* .05
441 Henry Jones .05
442 Jim Kelly .20
443 Pete Metzelaars .05
444 Andre Reed .10
445 Bruce Smith .05
446 *Troy Auzenne* .10
447 Mark Carrier .05
448 *Will Furrer* .10
449 Jim Harbaugh .10
450 Brad Muster .05
451 Darren Lewis .05
452 Mike Singletary .10
453 *Alonzo Spellman* .20
454 Chris Zorich .05
455 Jim Breech .05
456 Boomer Esiason .10
457 James Francis .05
458 Derrick Fenner .05
459 *David Klingler* .20
460 Tim McGee .05
461 *Carl Pickens* 1.00
462 Alfred Williams .05
463 *Darryl Williams* .10
464 Mark Bavaro .05
465 Jay Hilgenberg .05
466 Leroy Hoard .10
467 Bernie Kosar .10
468 Michael Dean Perry .10
469 *Todd Philcox* .10
470 *Patrick Rowe* .10
471 *Tommy Vardell* .20
472 Everson Walls .05
473 Troy Aikman .75
474 *Kenneth Gant* .10
475 Charles Haley .05
476 Michael Irvin .20
477 *Robert Jones* .10
478 Russell Maryland .10
479 Jay Novacek .10
480 *Kevin Smith* .10
481 Tony Tolbert .05
482 Steve Atwater .05
483 *Shane Dronett* .10
484 Simon Fletcher .05
485 Greg Lewis .05
486 *Tommy Maddox* .20
487 Shannon Sharpe .20
488 Dennis Smith .05
489 Sammie Smith .05
490 Kenny Walker .05
491 Lomas Brown .05
492 Mike Farr .05
493 Mel Gray .05
494 *Jason Hanson* .10
495 Herman Moore .75
496 Rodney Peete .05
497 *Robert Porcher* .10
498 Kelvin Pritchett .05
499 Andre Ware .05
500 *Sanjay Beach* .10
501 *Edgar Bennett* .20
502 Lewis Billups .05
503 Terrell Buckley .20
504 Ty Detmer .10
505 Brett Favre 2.50
506 Johnny Holland .05
507 *Dexter McNabb* .10
508 Vince Workman .05
509 Cody Carlson .05
510 Ernest Givins .05
511 Jerry Gray .05
512 Haywood Jeffires .10
513 Bruce Matthews .05
514 Bubba McDowell .05
515 *Bucky Richardson* .10
516 Webster Slaughter .05
517 Al Smith .05
518 Mel Agee .05
519 *Ashley Ambrose* .10
520 Kevin Call .05
521 Ken Clark .05
522 *Quentin Coryatt* .20
523 *Steve Emtman* .10
524 Jeff George .20
525 Jessie Hester .05
526 Anthony Johnson .05
527 Tim Barnett .05
528 Martin Bayless .05
529 J.J. Birden .05
530 *Dale Carter* .20
531 Dave Krieg .05
532 Albert Lewis .05
533 Nick Lowery .05
534 Christian Okoye .05
535 Harvey Williams .10
536 Aundray Bruce .05
537 Eric Dickerson .10
538 Willie Gault .05
539 Ethan Horton .05
540 Jeff Jaeger .05
541 Napoleon McCallum .05
542 *Chester McGlockton* .10
543 Steve Smith .05
544 Steve Wisniewski .05
545 Marc Boutte .05
546 Pat Carter .05
547 Jim Everett .05
548 Cleveland Gary .05
549 *Sean Gilbert* .20
550 Steve Israel .05
551 *Todd Kinchen* .20
552 Jackie Slater .05
553 Tony Zendejas .05
554 Robert Clark .05
555 Mark Clayton .05
556 *Marco Coleman* .10
557 Bryan Cox .05
558 Keith Jackson (Card says drafted in '88, but acquired as free agent in '92) .05
559 Dan Marino 1.25
560 John Offerdahl .05
561 *Troy Vincent* .20
562 Richmond Webb .05
563 Terry Allen .20
564 Cris Carter .50
565 Roger Craig .10
566 Rich Gannon .10
567 Hassan Jones .05
568 Randall McDaniel .05
569 Al Noga .05
570 Todd Scott .05
571 *Van Walters* .10
572 Bruce Armstrong .05
573 *Gene Chilton* .10
574 *Eugene Chung* .10
575 *Todd Collins* .10
576 Hart Lee Dykes .05
577 *David Howard* .10
578 Eugene Lockhart .05
579 Greg McMurtry .05
580 *Rodney Smith* .05
581 Gene Atkins .05
582 Vince Buck .05
583 Wesley Carroll .05
584 Jim Dombrowski .05
585 *Vaughn Dunbar* .10
586 Craig Heyward .05
587 Dalton Hilliard .05
588 Wayne Martin .05
589 Renaldo Turnbull .05
590 Carl Banks .05
591 *Derek Brown* .10
592 Jarrod Bunch .05
593 Mark Ingram .05
594 Ed McCaffrey .30
595 Phil Simms .10
596 *Phillippi Sparks* .10
597 Lawrence Taylor .20
598 Lewis Tillman .05
599 Kyle Clifton .05
600 Mo Lewis .05
601 Terance Mathis .05
602 Scott Mersereau .05
603 *Johnny Mitchell* .20
604 Browning Nagle .10
605 Ken O'Brien .05
606 Al Toon .05
607 Marvin Washington .05
608 Eric Allen .05
609 Fred Barnett .05
610 John Booty .05
611 Randall Cunningham .20
612 Rich Miano .05
613 Clyde Simmons .05
614 Siran Stacy .05
615 Herschel Walker .10
616 Calvin Williams .05
617 Chris Chandler .20
618 Randal Hill .10
619 Johnny Johnson .10
620 Lorenzo Lynch .05
621 Robert Massey .05
622 Ricky Proehl .05
623 Timm Rosenbach .05
624 *Tony Sacca* .10
625 Aeneas Williams (name misspelled Aaneas) .10
626 Bubby Brister .05
627 Barry Foster .05
628 Merril Hoge .05
629 David Johnson .05
630 David Little .05
631 Greg Lloyd .05
632 Ernie Mills .05
633 *Leon Searcy* .10
634 Dwight Stone .05
635 *Sam Anno* .10
636 Burt Grossman .05
637 Stan Humphries .10
638 Nate Lewis .05
639 Anthony Miller .05
640 Chris Mims .05
641 *Marquez Pope* .20
642 Stanley Richard .05
643 Junior Seau .20
644 *Brian Bollinger* .05
645 *Steve Bono* .30
646 Dexter Carter .10
647 *Dana Hall* .05
648 Amp Lee .10
649 Joe Montana 1.25
650 Tom Rathman .05
651 Jerry Rice .75
652 Ricky Watters .20
653 Robert Blackmon .05
654 John Kasay .05
655 *Ronnie Lee* .10
656 Dan McGwire .10
657 *Ray Roberts* .10
658 Kelly Stouffer .05
659 Chris Warren .20
660 Tony Woods .05
661 David Wyman .05
662 *Reggie Cobb* .05
663A Steve DeBerg (incorrect career yardage 1,455; found in foil packs) .05
663B Steve DeBerg (correct career yardage 31,455; found in jumbo packs) .05
664 *Santana Dotson* .20
665 Craig Erickson .10
666 Paul Gruber .05
667 Ron Hall .05
668 *Courtney Hawkins* .10
669 Charles McRae .05
670 Ricky Reynolds .05
671 Monte Coleman .05
672 Brad Edwards .05

673	James Geathers (card says played in New Orleans '89; should say Washington)	.05
674	Kelly Goodburn	.05
675	Kurt Gouveia	.05
676	*Chris Hakel*	.10
677	Wilber Marshall	.05
678	Ricky Sanders	.05
679	Mark Schlereth	.05
680	Spirit of the Game (Rich Stadium)	.05
681	Boomer Esiason Spirit of the Game (with tiger cub)	.05
682	Spirit of the Game (The Dog Pound)	.05
683	Spirit of the Game (Bronco Statue)	.05
684	Spirit of the Game ("Luv Ya Blue")	.05
685	Spirit of the Game (Hoosier Dome)	.05
686	Mack Lee Hill, Tracy Simien Spirit of the Game (Mack Lee Hill Award)	.05
687	Spirit of the Game (The Team of the Decades)	.05
688	Spirit of the Game (Dolphins' helmet)	.05
689	Francis J. Kilroy Spirit of the Game (VP)	.05
690	Spirit of the Game (Team mascot)	.05
691	Spirit of the Game (Steelers' helmet)	.05
692	Spirit of the Game (Charger in parachute)	.05
693	Spirit of the Game (Kingdome)	.05
694	Stephen Baker Play Smart	.05
695	Hank Williams Jr.	.20
696	Brian Baldinger, Gary Baldinger, Rich Baldinger NEW (3 Brothers in NFL)	.05
697	NEW (Japan Bowl August 2, 1992)	.05
698	NEW (Georgia Dome)	.05
699	NEW (Theme Art Super Bowl XXVII)	.05
700	Mark Rypien Super Bowl XXVI MVP	.10
AU150	Emmitt Smith AUTO (Certified Autograph)	200.00
AU168	Erik Kramer AUTO (Certified Autograph)	40.00
NNO	Emmitt Smith Power Preview	1.00
NNO	Santa Claus (Spirit of the Game)	.50

1992 Pro Set Emmitt Smith Holograms

Dallas Cowboys' star running back Emmitt Smith is featured on these four insert holograms offered randomly in 1992 Pro Set foil packs. Each card front represents a different part of Smith's career. The red, white and blue backs have player profile information, 1991 and projected stats and a career summary. Cards are numbered ES1-ES4, with those numbered ES1 being the easiest to find, while the ES4 cards were the most difficult to find.

		NM/M
Complete Set (4):		60.00
Common Smith:		7.00
1	Stats 1990-1999	7.00
2	Drafted by Cowboys	10.00
3	Rookie of the Year	20.00
4	NFL Rushing Leader	30.00

1992 Pro Set Gold MVPs

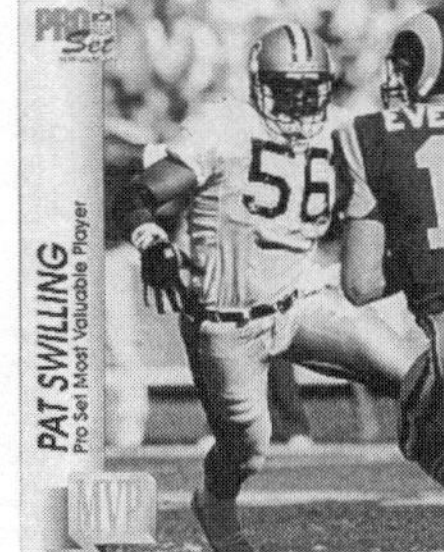

A most valuable player from each of the 28 NFL teams has been selected for this insert set. Two coaches were also selected. Cards 1-15, Series I jumbo pack inserts, have full-bleed action photos, plus a diamond-shaped "92 MVP" emblem on the front. The player's name is stamped in gold foil near the Pro Set/NFL logo. The horizontal card backs have statistics, a career summary and close-up shot. Series II pack inserts, cards 16-30, have a two-toned stripe on the left, plus a gray box in the lower left corner which has "MVP" stamped in gold foil. The backs are screened and have career information and a close-up shot of the player. All cards are numbered with an "MVP" prefix; AFC players are cards 1-14; NFC cards are 16-29. Coaches' cards are Don Shula (15) and Jimmy Johnson (30).

		NM/M
Complete Set (30):		15.00
Common Player:		.10
Minor Stars:		.20
1	Thurman Thomas	.40
2	Anthony Munoz	.10
3	Clay Matthews	.10
4	John Elway	2.00
5	Warren Moon	.40
6	Bill Brooks	.10
7	Derrick Thomas	.20
8	Todd Marinovich	.10
9	Mark Higgs	.10
10	Leonard Russell	.20
11	Rob Moore	.40
12	Rod Woodson	.20
13	Marion Butts	.10
14	Brian Blades	.10
15	Don Shula	.20
16	Deion Sanders	1.00
17	Neal Anderson	.10
18	Emmitt Smith	3.00
19	Barry Sanders	4.00
20	Brett Favre	5.00
21	Kevin Greene	.10
22	Terry Allen	.40
23	Pat Swilling	.10
24	Rodney Hampton	.20
25	Randall Cunningham	.50
26	Randall Hill	.10
27	Jerry Rice	1.50
28	Vinny Testaverde	.40
29	Mark Rypien	.20
30	Jimmy Johnson	.20

1992 Pro Set Ground Force

These cards are identical to their counterparts in the regular 1992 Pro Set issue, except they are stamped with a "Ground Force" logo in gold foil on the front. They share the same number as their counterparts in the regular issue's Ground Force subset. The gold-foiled inserts were included in foil packs of numbered hobby cases only.

		NM/M
Complete Set (6):		20.00
Common Player:		1.00
86	Gerald Riggs	1.00
105	Thurman Thomas	5.00
118	Neal Anderson	1.00
150	Emmitt Smith	12.00
206	Barry Word	1.00
249	Leonard Russell	1.00

1992 Pro Set HOF Inductees

These cards, numbered with an "SC" prefix, are a "Special Collectibles" subset that features the 1992 Pro Football Hall of Fame Inductees. The cards, random inserts in 1992 Pro Set packs, have the Hall of Fame's logo on the front, along with the Pro Set logo, and show an action photo of the player. The card back has a career summary and a portrait shot.

		NM/M
Complete Set (4):		1.50
Common Player:		.40
1	Lem Barney	.40
2	Al Davis	.40
3	John Mackey	.40
4	John Riggins	.50

1992 Pro Set HOF 2000

Randomly inserted in Series II foil packs, the 10-card set honors players which Pro Set said would be inducted into the Hall of Fame shortly after the year 2000. The card fronts are identical to the base cards, with the player's name in a white stripe along the left and his team name listed beneath it. The HOF-2000 logo appears on a 3-D band in the lower left. Card backs have HOF-2000 listed at the top, with the player's name, position and team printed below it. Inside a 3-D text box is a write-up on the player's career. The cards are numbered inside a small rectangle in the lower right.

		NM/M
Complete Set (10):		20.00
Common Player:		1.50
Minor Stars:		3.00
1	Marcus Allen	3.00
2	Richard Dent	1.50
3	Eric Dickerson	3.00
4	Ronnie Lott	1.50
5	Art Monk	1.50
6	Joe Montana	8.00
7	Warren Moon	3.00
8	Anthony Munoz	1.50
9	Mike Singletary	3.00
10	Lawrence Taylor	3.00

1992 Pro Set Club

This nine-card set was used as a football practice educational tool. The full-bleed card fronts include photos which deal with various football skills. The bottom of each card includes the card's caption inside a purple stripe. The Pro Set Club logo is located on the left side of the stripe. The card backs include details on the skill highlighted on the front. The text is printed inside a yellow box. Card numbers are printed inside an oval in the lower right.

		NM/M
Complete Set (9):		5.00
Common Player:		.75
1	Quarterback Throwing Pass	.75
2	Coach Reviewing Play Strategy	.75
3	Team Stretching	.75
4	Offensive Play	.75
5	Kickoff	.75
6	Player's Stance	.75
7	Football Is a Spectator Sport	.75
8	Defensive Practice	.75
9	Play in Motion	.75

1992 Pro Set Emmitt Smith Promo Sheet

Measuring 7" x 13" and numbered to 2,000, this five-card sheet was used to promote the signing of Emmitt Smith as the Pro Set spokesman. Showcased on the sheet are his 1990, 1991, 1991 Platinum, 1991 Platinum Game Breaker and 1992 cards with a checklist back.

		NM/M
Complete Set (1):		10.00
Common Sheet:		10.00
NNO	Emmitt Smith Sheet (five cards featured numberd of 2000)	10.00

1992 Pro Set Power

This 330-card UV-coated set features action photos on the fronts with a semi-ghosted background. The player's name is in red letters at the bottom. The backs are in a horizontal format and feature the team and player name printed in the team's colors. A player profile is also included. A 10-card insert set, "Power Combos," was also made and features pairs of teammates. The cards were random inserts in foil packs.

		NM/M
Complete Set (330):		15.00
Common Player:		.05
Wax Box:		15.00
1	Warren Moon	.30
2	Mike Horan	.05
3	Bobby Hebert	.05
4	Jim Harbaugh	.05
5	Sean Landeta	.05
6	Bubby Brister	.05
7	John Elway	.50
8	Troy Aikman	1.00
9	Rodney Peete	.05
10	Dan McGwire	.05
11	Mark Rypien	.10
12	Randall Cunningham	.20
13	Dan Marino	1.50
14	Vinny Testaverde	.05
15	Jeff Hostetler	.35
16	Joe Montana	1.00
17	Dave Krieg	.05
18	Jeff Jaeger	.05
19	Bernie Kosar	.05
20	Barry Sanders	1.00
21	Deion Sanders	.40
22	Emmitt Smith	2.00
23	Mel Gray	.05
24	Stanley Richard	.05
25	Brad Muster	.05
26	Rod Woodson	.10
27	Rodney Hampton	.50
28	Darrell Green	.05
29	Barry Foster	.50
30	Dave Meggett	.05
31	Lonnie Young	.05
32	Marcus Allen	.05
33	Merril Hoge	.05
34	Thurman Thomas	.25
35	Neal Anderson	.10
36	Bennie Blades	.05
37	Pat Terrell	.05
38	Nick Bell	.20
39	Johnny Johnson	.20
40	Bill Bates	.05
41	Keith Byars	.05
42	Ronnie Lott	.05
43	Elvis Patterson	.05
44	Lorenzo White	.05
45	Tony Stargell	.05
46	Tim McDonald	.05
47	Kirby Jackson	.05
48	Lionel Washington	.05
49	Dennis Smith	.05
50	Mike Singletary	.05
51	Mike Croel	.05
52	Pepper Johnson	.05
53	Vaughn Johnson	.05
54	Chris Spielman	.05
55	Junior Seau	.10
56	Lawrence Taylor	.15
57	Clay Matthews	.05
58	Derrick Thomas	.20
59	Seth Joyner	.05
60	Stan Thomas	.05
61	Nate Newton	.05
62	Matt Brock	.05
63	*Gene Chilton*	.15
64	Randall McDaniel	.05
65	Max Montoya	.05
66	Joe Jacoby	.05
67	Russell Maryland	.25
68	Ed King	.05
69	*Mark Schlereth*	.15
70	Charles McRae	.05
71	Charles Mann	.05
72	William Perry	.05
73	Simon Fletcher	.05
74	Paul Gruber	.05
75	Howie Long	.05
76	Steve McMichael	.05
77	Karl Mecklenberg	.05
78	Anthony Munoz	.05
79	Ray Childress	.05
80	Jerry Rice	1.00
81	Art Monk	.10
82	John Taylor	.10
83	Andre Reed	.25
84	Haywood Jeffires	.25
85	Mark Duper	.05
86	Fred Barnett	.25
87	Tom Waddle	.15
88	Michael Irvin	.25
89	Brian Blades	.05
90	Neil Smith	.05
91	*Reggie Greene*	.05
92	Reggie White	.30
93	Jerry Ball	.05
94	Charles Haley	.05
95	Richard Dent	.05
96	Clyde Simmons	.05
97	Cornelius Bennett	.05
98	Eric Swann	.05
99	Doug Smith	.05
100	Jim Kelly	.40
101	Michael Jackson	.30
102	Steve Christie	.05
103	Timm Rosenbach	.05
104	Brett Favre	1.25
105	Jeff Feagles	.05
106	Kevin Butler	.10
107	Boomer Esiason	.25
108	Steve Young	1.00
109	Norm Jackson	.05
110	Jay Schroeder	.05
111	Jeff George	.40
112	Chris Miller	.05
113	*Steve Bono*	1.00
114	Neil O'Donnell	.50
115	*David Klingler*	.35
116	Rich Gannon	.10
117	Chris Chandler	.05
118	Stan Gelbaugh	.05
119	Scott Mitchell	.50
120	Mark Carrier	.05
121	Terry Allen	.55
122	Tim McKyer	.05
123	Barry Wood	.20
124	Freeman McNeil	.05
125	Louis Oliver	.05
126	Jarvis Williams	.05
127	Steve Atwater	.05
128	Cris Dishman	.05
129	Eric Dickerson	.05
130	Brad Baxter	.05
131	Frank Minnifield	.05
132	Ricky Watters	.50
133	David Fulcher	.05
134	Herschel Walker	.05
135	Christian Okoye	.05
136	Jerome Henderson	.05
137	Nate Odomes	.05
138	Todd Scott	.05
139	Robert Delpino	.05
140	Gary Anderson	.05
141	Todd Lyght	.05
142	Chris Warren	.30
143	*Mike Brim*	.15
144	Tom Rathman	.05
145	*Dexter McNabb*	.10
146	Vince Workman	.05
147	Anthony Jackson	.05
148	Brian Washington	.05
149	David Tate	.05
150	Johnny Holland	.05
151	Monte Coleman	.05
152	Keith McCants	.05
153	*Eugene Seale*	.10
154	Al Smith	.05
155	Andre Collins	.05
156	Pat Swilling	.05
157	Rickey Jackson	.05
158	Wilbur Marshall	.05
159	Kyle Clifton	.05
160	Fred Stokes	.05
161	Lance Smith	.05
162	Guy McIntyre	.05
163	Bill Maas	.05
164	Gerald Perry	.05
165	Bart Oates	.05
166	Tony Jones	.05
167	Moe Gardner	.05
168	Joe Wolf	.05
169	Tim Krumrie	.05
170	Leonard Marshall	.05
171	Kevin Call	.05
172	Keith Kartz	.05
173	Ron Heller	.05
174	Steve Wallace	.05
175	Tony Casillas	.05
176	Tim Irwin	.05
177	Pat Harlow	.05
178	Bruce Smith	.05
179	Jim Lachey	.05
180	Andre Rison	.50
181	Michael Haynes	.60
182	Rod Bernstine	.05
183	Mark Clayton	.05
184	Jay Novacek	.25
185	Rob Moore	.05
186	Willie Green	.20
187	Ricky Proehl	.05
188	Al Toon	.05
189	Webster Slaughter	.05
190	Tony Bennett	.05
191	Jeff Cross	.05
192	Michael Dean Perry	.05
193	Greg Townsend	.05
194	Alfred Williams	.05
195	William Fuller	.05
196	Cortez Kennedy	.05
197	Henry Thomas	.05
198	Esera Tuaolo	.05
199	Tim Green	.05
200	Keith Jackson	.15
201	Don Majkowski	.05
202	Steve Beuerlein	.40
203	Hugh Millen	.05
204	Browning Nagel	.15
205	Chip Lohmiller	.05
206	Phil Simms	.15
207	Jim Everett	.05
208	Erik Kramer	.05
209	Todd Marinovich	.05
210	Henry Jones	.15
211	Dwight Stone	.05
212	Andre Waters	.05
213	Darryl Henley	.05
214	Mark Higgs	.15
215	Dalton Hilliard	.05
216	Earnest Byner	.05
217	Eric Metcalf	.05
218	Gill Byrd	.05
219	*Robert Williams*	.10
220	Kenneth Davis	.05
221	Larry Brown	.05
222	Mark Collins	.05
223	Vinnie Clark	.05
224	Patrick Hunter	.05
225	Gaston Green	.05
226	Everson Walls	.05
227	Harold Green	.05
228	Albert Lewis	.05
229	Don Griffin	.05
230	Lorenzo Lynch	.05
231	Brian Mitchell	.05
232	Thomas Everett	.05
233	Leonard Russell	.50
234	Eric Bieniemy	.05
235	John L. Williams	.05
236	Leroy Hoard	.05
237	Darren Lewis	.05
238	Reggie Cobb	.15
239	Steve Broussard	.05
240	Marion Butts	.05
241	Mike Pritchard	.25
242	Dexter Carter	.05
243	Aeneas Williams	.05
244	Bruce Pickens	.05
245	Harvey Williams	.15
246	Bobby Humphrey	.05
247	Duane Bickett	.05
248	James Francis	.05
249	Broderick Thomas	.05
250	Chip Banks	.05
251	Bryan Cox	.05
252	Sam Mills	.05
253	Ken Norton	.05
254	Jeff Harrod	.05
255	John Roper	.05
256	Darryl Talley	.05
257	Andre Tippett	.05
258	Jeff Lageman	.05
259	Chris Doleman	.05
260	Shane Conlan	.05
261	Jessie Tuggle	.05
262	Eric Hill	.05
263	Bruce Armstrong	.05
264	Bill Fralic	.05
265	Alvin Harper	.60
266	Bill Brooks	.05
267	Henry Ellard	.05
268	Cris Carter	.05
269	Irving Fryar	.05
270	Lawrence Dawsey	.05
271	James Lofton	.05
272	Ernest Givins	.05
273	Terance Mathis	.05
274	Randal Hill	.15
275	Eddie Brown	.05
276	Tim Brown	.50
277	Anthony Carter	.05
278	Wendell Davis	.05
279	Mark Ingram	.05
280	Anthony Miller	.05
281	Clarence Verdin	.05
282	Willie Anderson	.05
283	Ricky Sanders	.05
284	Shane Jordan	.05
285	Gary Clark	.05
286	Sterling Sharpe	.20
287	Herman Moore	.65
288	Stephen Baker	.05
289	Marv Cook	.05
290	Ernie Jones	.05
291	Eric Green	.05
292	Mervyn Fernandez	.05
293	Greg McMurty	.05
294	Quinn Early	.05
295	Tim Harris	.05
296	*Will Furrer*	.25
297	*Jason Hanson*	.15
298	*Chris Hakel*	.15
299	*Ty Detmer*	.20
300	David Klingler	.30
301	*Amp Lee*	.30
302	*Troy Vincent*	.30
303	*Kevin Smith*	.30
304	*Terrell Buckley*	.20
305	*Dana Hall*	.25
306	*Tony Smith*	.20
307	*Steve Israel*	.25
308	*Vaughn Dunbar*	.20
309	*Ashley Ambrose*	.10
310	*Edgar Bennett*	.50
311	*Dale Carter*	.40
312	*Rodney Culver*	.25
313	*Matt Darby*	.15
314	*Tommy Vardell*	.30
315	*Quentin Coryatt*	.40
316	*Robert Jones*	.25
317	*Joe Bowden*	.10
318	*Eugene Chung*	.10
319	*Troy Auzenne*	.10
320	*Santana Dotson*	.25
321	*Greg Skrepenak*	.10
322	*Steve Emtman*	.20
323	*Carl Pickens*	2.00
324	*Johnny Mitchell*	.75
325	*Patrick Rowe*	.25
326	*Alonzo Spellman*	.35
327	*Robert Porcher*	.30
328	*Chris Mims*	.30
329	*Marc Boutte*	.10
330	*Shane Dronett*	.35

1992 Pro Set Power Power Combos

These cards feature top offensive and defensive combinations from the same team. The front of each card has a color photo of the two players together, with a ghosted background. "Combos" and "Power" are written at the top of the card in holographic letters. The cards are numbered on the back and have a purple background which contains player biographical information and a summary of their roles with their team. This information is framed by a marble-like border all the way around the card. The cards were randomly included in Pro Set Power foil packs.

		NM/M
Complete Set (10):		20.00
Common Player:		1.00
1	Steve Emtman, Quentin Coryatt	1.00
2	Barry Word, Christian Okoye	1.00
3	Sam Mills, Vaughan Johnson	1.00
4	Broderick Thomas, Keith McCants	1.00
5	Michael Irvin, Emmitt Smith	12.00
6	Jerry Ball, Chris Spielman	1.00
7	Rickey Sanders, Gary Clark, Art Monk	4.00
8	Dave Johnson, Rod Woodson	3.00
9	Bill Fralic, Chris Hinton	1.00
10	Irving Fryar, Marv Cook	1.00

1992-93 Pro Set Super Bowl XXVII

Inserted into Super Bowl XXVII GTE seat cushions at the Super Bowl and available by mail - with either a Bills or Cowboys mini-binder - for $22, the 38-card set was packaged in two cello packs. Reports have said 7,000 sets were issued for the mail-in offer. The cards are identical to the regular-issue cards, with the exception of the Super Bowl XXVII logo and AFC or NFC Champions listed under the player's name on the card fronts. Card backs are numbered "XXVII," except Marco Coleman who was named Pro Set Rookie of the Year. There are NFC and AFC logo cards and a Newsreel card included in the set.

		NM/M
Complete Set (38):		10.00
Common Player:		.20
1	AFC Logo	.20
2	Cornelius Bennett	.30
3	Steve Christie	.20
4	Shane Conlan	.20
5	Matt Darby	.20
6	Kenneth Davis	.20
7	John Fina	.20
8	Henry Jones	.30
9	Jim Kelly	.50
10	Marv Levy (CO)	.20
11	James Lofton	.30
12	Pete Metzelaars	.20
13	Nate Odomes	.20
14	Andre Reed	.40
15	Bruce Smith	.40
16	Darryl Talley	.20
17	Steve Tasker	.30
18	Thurman Thomas	.75
19	NFC Logo	.20
20	Troy Aikman	2.00
21	Steve Beuerlein	.30
22	Tony Casillas	.20
23	Kenneth Gant	.30
24	Charles Haley	.30
25	Alvin Harper	.30
26	Michael Irvin	.75
27	Jimmy Johnson (CO)	.30
28	Robert Jones	.20
29	Russell Maryland	.30
30	Nate Newton	.30
31	Ken Norton	.30
32	Jay Novacek	.40
33	Emmitt Smith	4.00
34	Kevin Smith	.30
35	Mark Stepnoski	.20
36	Tony Tolbert	.20
37	Newsreel Art, Super Bowl XXVII	.20
38	Marco Coleman (PS-ROY)	.30

1992-93 Pro Set Power Emmitt Smith

Produced as a premium for Pro Set Series II, the 10-card set honors Emmitt Smith's career. The set was offered through a chase card which was randomly seeded in Series II foil packs. The set was available through the mail in exchange for 10 1992 Pro Set first or second series wrappers and 10 1992 Pro Set Power wrappers, in addition to $7.50 for shipping. Those collectors who paid $20 more would receive one of 7,500 Smith-autographed cards. The card fronts have a borderless photo, with Pro Set Power printed in one of the upper corners. A blue stripe at the bottom includes Smith's name and card caption. The backs, numbered "of 10," include a "Report Card" and highlights.

		NM/M
Complete Set (10):		20.00
Common Player:		2.50
1	Emmitt Smith Title Card	2.50
2	Emmitt Smith Drafted by the Cowboys	2.50
3	Emmitt Smith Emmitt Scores Four Touchdowns	2.50
4	Emmitt Smith Pro Set Offensive Rookie of the Year	2.50
5	Emmitt Smith Cowboys Beat Undefeated Redskins	2.50
6	Emmitt Smith Cowboys Beat Chicago In Playoffs	2.50
7	Emmitt Smith Back-to-Back Rushing Titles	2.50
8	Emmitt Smith Emmitt's Three Pro Bowls	2.50
9	Emmitt Smith Emmitt's Super Day	2.50
10	Emmitt Smith Running Back of the 90's	2.50

1993 Pro Set Promos

Measuring 8" x 13-1/2", the 10-card unperforated sheets featuring six different cards were given to dealers, card show attendees and promoters. In addition, single cards were also handed out. The sheet included a bottom row of five Emmitt Smith cards. The card fronts have a full-bleed photo, with the player's name, team logo and 1993 Pro Set logo printed inside "a ripped away" area. Card backs feature a player photo at the top, with the player's name, position and team in the "ripped away" area along the left border. The player's bio, highlights and stats are printed underneath the photo.

		NM/M
Complete Set (6):		8.00
Common Player:		.75
1	Jerome Bettis	2.00
2	Reggie Brooks	1.00
3	Cortez Kennedy	1.00
4	Junior Seau	1.00
5	Emmitt Smith	4.00
6	Wade Wilson	.75

1993 Pro Set

Pro Set's 1993 set consists of one series of 449 cards featuring full-bleed photos on the fronts and backs. The player's name and team logo appear at the bottom of the card over a gray slate panel that stretches along the left side of the back of the card. The backs include statistics for the past three years and lifetime totals, plus biographical information. Insert sets include prism cards for "All Rookie Forecast" (27 cards) and "Rookie Running Backs" (14); "College Connections" (10 cards, each featuring a pair of players from the same college) and "Rookie Quarterbacks" (6 cards).

		NM/M
Complete Set (449):		15.00
Common Player:		.05
Minor Stars:		.10
Pack (15):		.60
Wax Box (36):		15.00
1	Marco Coleman (LL)	.05
2	Steve Young (LL)	.25
3	Mike Holmgren (LL)	.10
4	John Elway (LL)	.40
5	Steve Young (LL)	.25
6	Dan Marino (LL)	.75
7	Emmitt Smith (LL)	.75
8	Sterling Sharpe (LL)	.10
9	Jay Novacek (LL)	.05
10	Sterling Sharpe (LL)	.10
11	Thurman Thomas (LL)	.10
12	Pete Stoyanovich (LL)	.05
13	Greg Montgomery (LL)	.05
14	Johnny Bailey (LL)	.05
15	Jon Vaughn (LL)	.05
16	Jones/McMillan, Jones/McMillan (LL)	.05
17	Clyde Simmons (LL)	.05
18	Cortez Kennedy (LL)	.05
19	AFC Wildcard	.05
20	AFC Wildcard	.05
21	NFC Wildcard	.05
22	NFC Wildcard	.05
23	AFC Divisional	.05
24	AFC Divisional	.75
25	NFC Divisional	.50
26	Watters NFC Divisional	.10
27	AFC Championship	.05
28	NFC Championship	.05
29	SB 28 Theme Art	.05
30	Troy Aikman	.75
31	Thomas Everett	.05
32	Charles Haley	.05
33	Alvin Harper	.10
34	Michael Irvin	.20
35	Robert Jones	.05
36	Russell Maryland	.05
37	Ken Norton	.05
38	Jay Novacek	.05
39	Emmitt Smith	1.75
40	*Darrin Smith*	.20
41	Mark Stepnoski	.05
42	*Kevin Williams*	.20
43	Daryl Johnston	.05
44	*Derrick Lassic*	.10
45	Don Beebe	.05
46	Cornelius Bennett	.05
47	Bill Brooks	.05
48	Kenneth Davis	.05
49	Jim Kelly	.20
50	Andre Reed	.10
51	Bruce Smith	.05
52	*Thomas Smith*	.10
53	Darryl Talley	.05
54	Thurman Thomas	.10
55	*Reggie Copeland*	.20
56	Scott Christie	.05
57	Pete Metzelaars	.05
58	Frank Reich	.05
59	Henry Jones	.05
60	Vinny Clark	.05
61	Eric Dickerson	.05
62	Jumpy Geathers	.05
63	*Roger Harper*	.10
64	Michael Haynes	.05
65	Bobby Hebert	.05
66	*Lincoln Kennedy*	.10
67	Chris Miller	.10
68	Andre Rison	.10
69	Deion Sanders	.50
70	Jessie Tuggle	.05
71	*Ron George*	.10
72	Erric Pegram	.05
73	Melvin Jenkins	.05
74	Pierce Holt	.05
75	Neal Anderson	.05
76	Mark Carrier	.05
77	*Curtis Conway*	.75
78	Richard Dent	.05
79	Jim Harbaugh	.10
80	Craig Heyward	.05
81	Darren Lewis	.05
82	Alonzo Spellman	.05
83	Tom Waddle	.05
84	Wendall Davis	.05
85	Chris Zorich	.05
86	*Carl Simpson*	.10
87	*Chris Gedney*	.20
88	Trace Armstrong	.05
89	Peter Tom Willis	.05
90	*John Copeland*	.10
91	Derrick Fenner	.05
92	James Francis	.05
93	Harold Green	.05
94	David Klingler	.10
95	Tim Krumrie	.05
96	*Tony McGee*	.10
97	Carl Pickens	.75
98	Alfred Williams	.05
99	Doug Pelrey	.10
100	*Lance Gunn*	.10
101	Jay Schroeder	.05
102	*Steve Tovar*	.10
103	Jeff Query	.05
104	*Ty Parten*	.10
105	Jerry Ball	.05
106	Mark Carrier	.05
107	Rob Burnett	.05
108	Michael Jackson	.10
109	Mike Johnson	.05
110	Bernie Kosar	.10
111	Clay Matthews	.05
112	Eric Metcalf	.05
113	Michael Dean Perry	.05
114	Vinny Testaverde	.20
115	Eric Turner	.05
116	Tommy Vardell	.05
117	Leroy Hoard	.05
118	*Steve Everitt*	.10
119	Everson Walls	.05
120	Steve Atwater	.05
121	Rod Bernstine	.05
122	Mike Croel	.05
123	John Elway	1.00
124	Simon Fletcher	.05
125	*Glyn Milburn*	.20
126	*Reggie Rivers*	.10
127	Shannon Sharpe	.20
128	Dennis Smith	.05
129	*Dan Williams*	.10
130	*Rondell Jones*	.10
131	*Jason Elam*	.20
132	*Arthur Marshall*	.10
133	Gary Zimmerman	.05
134	Karl Mecklenberg	.05
135	Bennie Blades	.05
136	Lomas Brown	.05
137	Bill Fralic	.05
138	Mel Gray	.05
139	Willie Green	.05
140	*Ryan McNeil*	.10
141	Rodney Peete	.05
142	Barry Sanders	2.00
143	Chris Spielman	.05
144	Pat Swilling	.05
145	Andre Ware	.05
146	Herman Moore	.50
147	Tim McKyer	.05
148	Brett Perriman	.05
149	*Antonio London*	.10
150	Edgar Bennett	.10
151	Terrell Buckley	.05
152	Brett Favre	2.00
153	Jackie Harris	.05
154	Johnny Holland	.05
155	Sterling Sharpe	.10
156	*Tim Hauck*	.10
157	*George Teague*	.25
158	Reggie White	.20
159	Mark Clayton	.05
160	Ty Detmer	.10
161	*Wayne Simmons*	.10
162	*Mark Brunell*	3.00
163	Tony Bennett	.05
164	Brian Noble	.05
165	Cody Carlson	.05
166	Ray Childress	.05
167	Cris Dishman	.05
168	Curtis Duncan	.05
169	*Brad Hopkins*	.10
170	Haywood Jeffires	.05
171	Wilber Marshall	.05
172	*Micheal Barrow*	.10
173	Bubba McDowell	.05
174	Warren Moon	.20
175	Webster Slaughter	.05
176	*Travis Hannah*	.10
177	Lorenzo White	.05
178	Ernest Givins	.05
179	Keith McCants	.05
180	Kerry Cash	.05
181	Quentin Coryatt	.05
182	Kirk Lowdermilk	.05
183	Rodney Culver	.05
184	Rohn Stark	.05
185	Steve Emtman	.05
186	Jeff George	.20
187	Jeff Herrod	.05
188	Reggie Langhorne	.05
189	*Roosevelt Potts*	.10
190	Jack Trudeau	.05
191	Will Wolford	.05
192	Jessie Hester	.05
193	Anthony Johnson	.10
194	*Ray Buchanan*	.10
195	Dale Carter	.05
196	Willie Davis	.05
197	John Alt	.05
198	Joe Montana	1.00
199	*Will Shields*	.10
200	Neil Smith	.05
201	Derrick Thomas	.10
202	Harvey Williams	.05
203	Marcus Allen	.20
204	J.J. Birden	.05
205	Tim Barnett	.05
206	Albert Lewis	.05
207	Nick Lowery	.05
208	Dave Krieg	.05
209	Keith Cash	.05
210	*Patrick Bates*	.10
211	Nick Bell	.05
212	Tim Brown	.20
213	Willie Gault	.05
214	Ethan Horton	.05
215	Jeff Hostetler	.10
216	Howie Long	.05
217	Greg Townsend	.05
218	Rocket Ismail	.10
219	Alexander Wright	.05
220	*Greg Robinson*	.10
221	*Billy Joe Hobert*	.20
222	Steve Wisenienski	.05
223	Steve Smith	.05
224	Vince Evans	.05
225	Willie Anderson	.05
226	*Jerome Bettis*	1.50
227	*Troy Drayton*	.25
228	Henry Ellard	.05
229	Jim Everett	.10
230	Tony Zendejas	.05
231	Todd Lyght	.05
232	Todd Kinchen	.10
233	Jackie Slater	.05
234	Fred Stokes	.05
235	*Russell White*	.10
236	Cleveland Gary	.05
237	*Sean Lachapelle*	.20
238	Steve Israel	.05
239	Shane Conlan	.05
240	Keith Byars	.05
241	Marco Coleman	.05
242	Bryan Cox	.05
243	Irving Fryar	.05
244	Richmond Webb	.05
245	Mark Higgs	.05
246	*Terry Kirby*	.30
247	Mark Ingram	.05
248	John Offerdahl	.05
249	Keith Jackson	.05
250	Dan Marino	2.00
251	*O.J. McDuffie*	.75
252	Louis Oliver	.05
253	Pete Stoyanovich	.05
254	Troy Vincent	.10
255	Anthony Carter	.05
256	Cris Carter	.20
257	Roger Craig	.10
258	Jack Del Rio	.05
259	Chris Doleman	.05
260	Barry Word	.05
261	*Qadry Ismail*	.25
262	Jim McMahon	.05
263	*Robert Smith*	1.25
264	Fred Strickland	.05
265	Randall McDaniel	.05
266	Carl Lee	.05
267	*Orlanda Truitt*	.10
268	Terry Allen	.10
269	Audray McMillan	.05
270	*Drew Bledsoe*	4.00
271	Eugene Chug	.05
272	Marv Cook	.05
273	Pat Harlow	.05
274	Greg McMurty	.05
275	Leonard Russell	.05
276	*Chris Slade*	.10
277	Andre Tippett	.05
278	*Vincent Brisby*	.25
279	Ben Coates	.30
280	*Sam Gash*	.10
281	Bruce Armstrong	.05
282	Rod Smith	.20
283	Michael Timpson	.05
284	*Scott Sisson*	.10
285	Morten Anderson	.05
286	*Reggie Freeman*	.10
287	Dalton Hilliard	.05
288	Rickey Jackson	.05
289	Vaughan Johnson	.05
290	Eric Martin	.05
291	Sam Mills	.05
292	Brad Muster	.05
293	*Willie Roaf*	.20
294	*Irv Smith*	.20
295	Wade Wilson	.05
296	*Derek Brown*	.10
297	Quinn Early	.05
298	Steve Walsh	.05
299	Renaldo Turnbull	.05
300	*Jessie Armstead*	.10
301	Carlton Bailey	.05
302	Michael Brooks	.05
303	Rodney Hampton	.10
304	Ed McCaffrey	.10
305	Dave Meggett	.05
306	Bart Oates	.05
307	Mike Sherrard	.05
308	Phil Simms	.10
309	Lawrence Taylor	.10
310	Mark Jackson	.05
311	Jarrod Bunch	.05
312	Howard Cross	.05
313	Michael Strahan	.05
314	Marcus Buckley	.05
315	Brad Baxter	.05
316	*Adrian Murrell*	1.00
317	Boomer Esiason	.10
318	Johnny Johnson	.05
319	*Marvin Jones*	.20
320	Jeff Lageman	.05
321	Ronnie Lott	.10
322	Leonard Marshall	.05
323	Johnny Mitchell	.05
324	Rob Moore	.10
325	Browning Nagle	.05
326	Blair Thomas	.05
327	Brian Washington	.05
328	Terrance Mathis	.10
329	Kyle Clifton	.05
330	Eric Allen	.05
331	*Victor Bailey*	.10
332	Fred Barnett	.05
333	Mark Bavaro	.05
334	Randall Cunningham	.10
335	Ken O'Brien	.05
336	Seth Joyner	.05
337	*Leonard Renfro*	.10
338	Heath Sherman	.05
339	Clyde Simmons	.05
340	Herschel Walker	.10
341	Calvin Williams	.05
342	Bubby Brister	.05
343	*Vaughn Hebron*	.10
344	Keith Millard	.05
345	Johnny Bailey	.05
346	Steve Beuerlein	.10
347	Chuck Cecil	.05
348	*Larry Centers*	.20
349	Chris Chandler	.10
350	*Ernest Dye*	.10
351	*Garrison Hearst*	1.00
352	Randal Hill	.05
353	John Booty	.05
354	Gary Clark	.05
355	*Ron Moore*	.10
356	Ricky Proehl	.05
357	Eric Swann	.05
358	Ken Harvey	.05
359	*Ben Coleman*	.10
360	*Deon Figures*	.20
361	Barry Foster	.05
362	Jeff Graham	.05
363	Eric Green	.05
364	Kevin Greene	.05
365	*Andre Hastings*	.10
366	Greg Lloyd	.05
367	Neil O'Donnell	.10
368	Dwight Stone	.05
369	Mike Tomczak	.05
370	Rod Woodson	.10
371	*Chad Brown*	.20
372	Ernie Mills	.05
373	Darren Perry	.05
374	Leon Searcy	.05
375	Marion Butts	.05
376	John Carney	.05
377	Ronnie Harmon	.05
378	Stan Humphries	.10
379	Nate Lewis	.05
380	*Natrone Means*	1.00
381	Anthony Miller	.05
382	Chris Mims	.05
383	Leslie O'Neal	.05
384	*Joe Coccozzo*	.10
385	Junior Seau	.10
386	Jerrol Williams	.05
387	John Friesz	.05
388	*Darrien Gordon*	.10
389	Derrick Walker	.05
390	Dana Hall	.05
391	Brent Jones	.05
392	*Todd Kelly*	.10
393	Amp Lee	.10
394	Tim McDonald	.05
395	Jerry Rice	1.00
396	*Dana Stubblefield*	.40
397	John Taylor	.05
398	Ricky Watters	.20
399	Steve Young	.75
400	Steve Bono	.30
401	*Adrian Hardy*	.10
402	Tom Rathman	.05
403	*Elvis Grbac*	1.50
404	Bill Romanowski	.05
405	Brian Blades	.05
406	Ferrell Edmunds	.05
407	*Carlton Gray*	.10
408	Cortez Kennedy	.10
409	Kelvin Martin	.05
410	Dan McGwire	.05
411	*Rick Mirer*	.30
412	Rufus Porter	.05
413	Chris Warren	.20
414	Jon Vaughn	.05
415	John L. Williams	.05
416	Eugene Robinson	.05
417	*Michael McCrary*	.10
418	*Michael Bates*	.20
419	Stan Gelbaugh	.05
420	Reggie Cobb	.05
421	*Eric Curry*	.10
422	Lawrence Dawsey	.05
423	Santana Dotson	.05
424	Craig Erickson	.10
425	Ron Hall	.05
426	Courtney Hawkins	.05
427	Broderick Thomas	.05
428	Vince Workman	.05
429	*Demetrius DuBose*	.10
430	*Lamar Thomas*	.10
431	*John Lynch*	.20
432	Hardy Nickerson	.05
433	*Horace Copeland*	.20
434	Steve DeBerg	.05
435	Joe Jacoby	.05
436	*Tom Carter*	.10
437	Andre Collins	.05
438	Darrell Green	.05
439	Desmond Howard	.10
440	Chip Lohmiller	.05
441	Charles Mann	.05
442	Tim McGee	.05
443	Art Monk	.10
444	Mark Rypien	.05
445	Ricky Sanders	.05
446	Brian Mitchell	.05
447	*Reggie Brooks*	.10
448	Carl Banks	.05
449	Cary Conklin	.05

1993 Pro Set All-Rookies

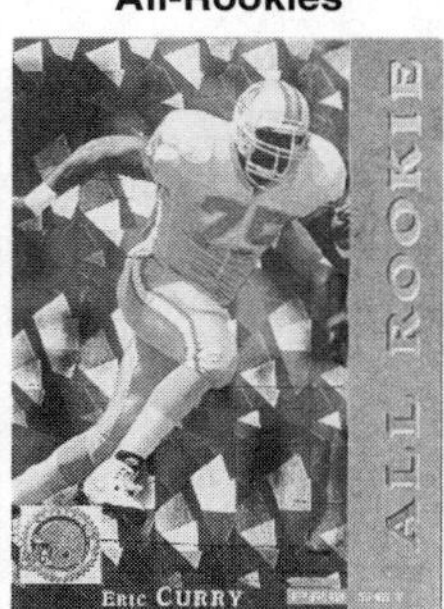

These cards feature color action shots against a prism-like background. Twenty-seven of the NFL's top rookie prospects are featured on these cards, which were random inserts in 1993 Pro Set foil packs. The player's name is at the bottom of the card, while the set's name is in a brown stripe along the right side. The numbered card back is green and has a football field ghosted over it. A player biography and team logo are also included. The player's name and card number are inside a gray stripe running along the left side of the card.

		NM/M
Complete Set (27):		10.00
Common Player:		.20
Minor Stars:		.40
1	Rick Mirer	.40
2	Garrison Hearst	1.75
3	Jerome Bettis	1.75
4	Vincent Brisby	.20
5	O.J. McDuffie	.75
6	Curtis Conway	.75
7	Raghib Ismail	.20
8	Steve Everitt	.20
9	Ernest Dye	.20
10	Todd Rucci	.20
11	Willie Roaf	.40
12	Lincoln Kennedy	.20
13	Irv Smith	.20
14	Jason Elam	.20
15	Derrick Alexander	.20
16	John Copeland	.20
17	Eric Curry	.20
18	Dana Stubblefield	.40
19	Leonard Renfro	.20
20	Marvin Jones	.20
21	Demetrius DuBose	.20
22	Chris Slade	.20
23	Darrin Smith	.20
24	Deon Figures	.20
25	Darrien Gordon	.20
26	Patrick Bates	.20
27	George Teague	.20

1993 Pro Set College Connections

College teammates who've become stars in the NFL are featured on these insert cards, randomly included in 1993 jumbo packs. Each card front is horizontal and features two small color action photos of the teammates against a silver prism-like background. A gray stripe at the bottom has the set's name. Each back has two panels which compare the players and give biographical information about them. The cards are numbered with a "CC" prefix.

		NM/M
Complete Set (10):		20.00
Common Player:		.50
Minor Stars:		2.00
1	Barry Sanders, Thurman Thomas	5.00
2	Jerome Bettis, Reggie Brooks	2.00
3	Neal Anderson, Emmitt Smith	4.00
4	Raghib Ismail, Tim Brown	1.00
5	Rodney Hampton, Garrison Hearst	1.00
6	Derrick Thomas, Cornelius Bennett	.50
7	Steve Young, Jim McMahon	2.00
8	Rick Mirer, Joe Montana	5.00
9	Terrell Buckley, Deion Sanders	1.00
10	Drew Bledsoe, Mark Rypien	3.00

1993 Pro Set Rookie Quarterbacks

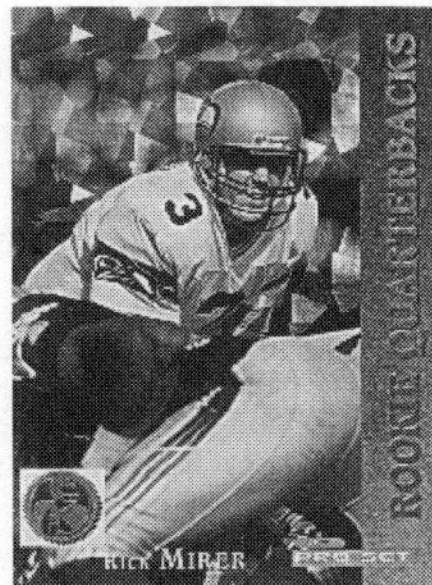

These cards, randomly inserted in 1993 Pro Set jumbo packs, have color action shots on them against a prism-like background. The set name is in a gray stripe along the right side; the player's name is at the bottom of the card. The pink backs have a team logo and career highlights and are numbered with a "RQ" prefix. The player's name is in a purple stripe which runs along the left side of the card.

		NM/M
Complete Set (6):		6.00
Common Player:		.20
1	Drew Bledsoe	3.00
2	Rick Mirer	.40
3	Mark Brunell	3.00
4	Billy Joe Hobert	.20
5	Trent Green	2.00
6	Elvis Grbac	1.00

1993 Pro Set Rookie Running Backs

Fourteen promising rookie running backs are featured on these cards, which were random inserts in 1993 Pro Set foil packs. Each card front has a color action shot against a prism background. The player's name is at the bottom of the card; the set name runs along the right side in a brown stripe. The backs, numbered with a "RRB" prefix, are gray and have a light brown stripe along the left side containing the player's name. His career highlights, team, position and biography are also given.

		NM/M
Complete Set (14):		8.00
Common Player:		.20
Minor Stars:		.40
1	Derrick Lassic	.20
2	Reggie Brooks	.20
3	Garrison Hearst	1.00
4	Ron Moore	.20
5	Robert Smith	1.00
6	Jerome Bettis	2.00
7	Russell White	.20
8	Derek Brown	.20
9	Roosevelt Potts	.20
10	Terry Kirby	.40
11	Glyn Milburn	.40
12	Greg Robinson	.20
13	Natrone Means	.50
14	Vaughn Hebron	.20

1993 Pro Set Power Prototypes

The 10-card set previewed the 1993 Pro Set Power series. The card fronts have the Pro Set Power logo in one of the upper corners, with the player's name and team listed in a red, white and blue box at the bottom of the full-bleed cards. The backs include a horizontal photo, along with a rating system and career highlights. The cards are numbered in the upper left. "Prototype" is printed at the bottom center.

		NM/M
Complete Set (10):		10.00
Common Player:		.50
20	Barry Sanders	2.00
22	Emmitt Smith	4.00
26	Rod Woodson	.50
32	Ricky Watters	.75
37	Larry Centers	.50
71	Santana Dotson	.50
80	Jerry Rice	2.00
138	Reggie Rivers	.50
193	Trace Armstrong	.50
NNO	Title/Ad Card	.50

1993 Pro Set Power

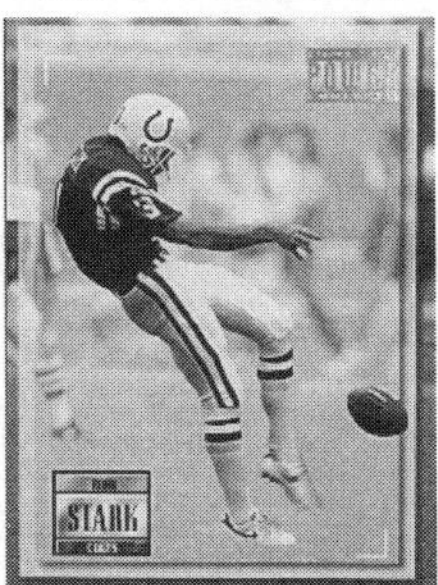

Pro Set Power's 1993 set has 200 cards. The fronts are similar to the 1992 look; the player is featured in a color action shot against a ghosted background. The player's name and team are at the bottom left; the foil-stamped Pro Set Power logo is in the upper right. The card back has a summary of the player's 1992 season, including statistics and a rating guide. His name appears at the top between team color-coded bars. Below that is an action photo. Insert sets include All-Power Defense (25 cards), Power Moves (30), Draft Picks (30), and Power Combos (10).

		NM/M
Complete Set (200):		7.00
Common Player:		.05
Minor Stars:		.10
Comp. Gold Set (200):		16.00
Gold Cards:		1X-2X
Wax Box:		15.00
1	Warren Moon	.20
2	Steve Christie	.05
3	Jim Breech	.05
4	Brett Favre	1.00
5	Sean Landeta	.05
6	Jim Arnold	.05
7	John Elway	.50
8	Troy Aikman	1.00
9	Rodney Peete	.10
10	Pete Stoyanovich	.05
11	Mark Rypien	.05
12	Jim Kelly	.20
13	Dan Marino	1.25
14	Neil O'Donnell	.10
15	David Klingler	.10
16	Rich Gannon	.05
17	Dave Krieg	.05
18	Jeff Jaeger	.05
19	Bernie Kosar	.05
20	Barry Sanders	1.00
21	Deion Sanders	.40
22	Emmitt Smith	1.25
23	Barry Word	.05
24	Stanley Richard	.05
25	Louis Oliver	.05
26	Rod Woodson	.10
27	Rodney Hampton	.20
28	Cris Dishman	.05
29	Barry Foster	.10
30	Dave Meggett	.05
31	Kevin Ross	.05
32	Ricky Watters	.20
33	Darren Lewis	.05
34	Thurman Thomas	.20
35	Rodney Culver	.05
36	Bennie Blades	.05
37	*Larry Centers*	.20
38	Todd Scott	.05
39	Darren Perry	.05
40	Robert Massey	.05
41	Keith Byars	.05
42	Chris Warren	.10
43	Cleveland Gary	.05
44	Lorenzo White	.05
45	Tony Stargell	.05
46	Bennie Thompson	.05
47	A.J. Johnson	.05
48	Daryl Johnston	.05
49	Dennis Smith	.05
50	Johnny Holland	.05
51	Ken Norton Jr.	.05
52	Pepper Johnson	.05
53	Vaughn Johnson	.05
54	Chris Spielman	.05
55	Junior Seau	.20
56	Chris Doleman	.05
57	Rickey Jackson	.05
58	Derrick Thomas	.10
59	Seth Joyner	.05
60	Stan Thomas	.05
61	Nate Newton	.05
62	Matt Brock	.05
63	Mike Munchak	.05
64	Randall McDaniel	.05
65	Ron Hallstrom	.05
66	Andy Heck	.05
67	Russell Maryland	.05
68	Bruce Wilkerson	.05
69	Mark Schlereth	.05
70	John Fina	.05
71	Santana Dotson	.05
72	Don Mosebar	.05
73	Simon Fletcher	.05
74	Paul Gruber	.05
75	Howard Ballard	.05
76	John Alt	.05
77	Carlton Hasselrig	.05
78	Bruce Smith	.05
79	Ray Childress	.05
80	Jerry Rice	.75
81	Art Monk	.10
82	John Taylor	.05
83	Andre Reed	.10
84	Sterling Sharpe	.10
85	Sam Graddy	.05
86	Fred Barnett	.05
87	Ricky Proehl	.05
88	Michael Irvin	.25
89	Webster Slaughter	.05
90	Tony Bennett	.05
91	Leslie O'Neal	.05
92	Michael Dean Perry	.05
93	Greg Townsend	.05
94	Anthony Smith	.05
95	Richard Dent	.05
96	Clyde Simmons	.05
97	Cornelius Bennett	.05
98	Eric Swann	.05
99	Cortez Kennedy	.05
100	Emmitt Smith	.75
101	Michael Jackson	.05
102	Lin Elliott	.05
103	Rohn Stark	.05
104	Jim Harbaugh	.05
105	Greg Davis	.05
106	Mike Cofer	.05
107	Morten Andersen	.05
108	Steve Young	.75
109	Norm Johnson	.05
110	Dan McGwire	.05
111	Jim Everett	.05
112	Randall Cunningham	.10
113	Steve Bono	.20
114	Cody Carlson	.05
115	Jeff Hostetler	.10
116	Rich Camarillo	.05
117	Chris Chandler	.05
118	Stan Gelbaugh	.05
119	Tony Sacca	.05
120	Henry Jones	.05
121	Terry Allen	.05
122	Amp Lee	.05
123	Mel Gray	.05
124	Jon Vaughn	.05
125	Bubba McDowell	.05
126	Audray McMilliam	.05
127	Terrell Buckley	.05
128	Dana Hall	.05
129	Eric Dickerson	.05
130	Martin Bayless	.05
131	Steve Israel	.05
132	Vaughn Dunbar	.05
133	Ronnie Harmon	.05
134	Dale Carter	.05
135	Neal Anderson	.05
136	Merton Hanks	.05
137	James Washington	.05
138	*Reggie Rivers*	.05
139	Bruce Pickens	.05
140	Gary Anderson	.05
141	Eugene Robinson	.05
142	*Charles Mincy*	.10
143	Matt Darby	.05
144	Tom Rathman	.05
145	Mike Prior	.05
146	Sean Lumpkin	.05
147	Greg Jackson	.05
148	Wes Hopkins	.05
149	David Tate	.05
150	James Francis	.05
151	Brian Cox	.05
152	Keith McCants	.05
153	Mark Stepnoski	.05
154	Al Smith	.05
155	Robert Jones	.05
156	Lawrence Taylor	.10
157	Clay Matthews	.05
158	Wilber Marshall	.05
159	Mike Johnson	.05
160	Adam Schreiber	.05
161	Tim Grunhard	.05
162	Mark Bortz	.05
163	Gene Chilton	.05
164	Jamie Dukes	.05
165	Bart Oates	.05
166	Kevin Gogan	.05
167	Kent Hull	.05
168	Ed King	.05
169	Eugene Chung	.05
170	Troy Auzenne	.05
171	Charles Mann	.05
172	William Perry	.05
173	Mike Lodish	.05
174	Bruce Matthews	.05
175	Tony Casillas	.05
176	Steve Wisenewski	.05
177	Karl Mecklenberg	.05
178	Richmond Webb	.05
179	Eric Williams	.05
180	Andre Rison	.10
181	Michael Haynes	.05
182	Don Beebe	.05
183	Anthony Miller	.05
184	Jay Novacek	.05
185	Rob Moore	.05
186	Willie Green	.05
187	Tom Waddle	.05
188	Keith Jackson	.05
189	Steve Tasker	.05
190	Marco Coleman	.05
191	Jeff Wright	.05
192	Burt Grossman	.05
193	Trace Armstong	.05
194	Charles Haley	.05
195	Greg Lloyd	.05
196	Marc Boutte	.05
197	Rufus Porter	.05
198	Dennis Gibson	.05
199	Shane Dronett	.05
200	Joe Montana	1.00
H1	Emmitt Smith HOLO	25.00
H2	Emmitt Smith HOLO	25.00

1993 Pro Set Power Gold

Inserted one per pack, this set was a parallel to the Power base cards. The Power logo is printed in gold foil, which is very similar to the silver foil. If the card is held at the correct angle, the gold foil can be differentiated.

	NM/M
Complete Set (200):	20.00
Common Player:	.10
Gold Cards:	1X-2X

1993 Pro Set Power All-Power Defense

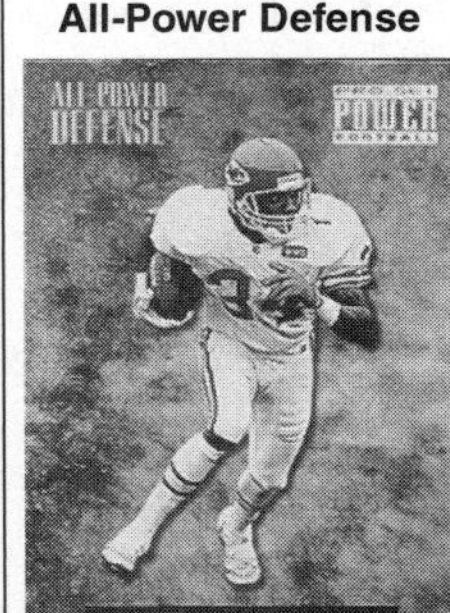

Twenty-five top NFL defensive players are featured on these cards, which were randomly inserted at a rate of two per jumbo pack. Each card front has a borderless color photo against a brown background. A black rectangle at the bottom includes the player's name in yellow letters. The back is also in brown, and includes the player's name, team, position and biography in a yellow box in the upper left corner. A career summary is also given in red lettering. Cards are numbered with an "APD" prefix. Scarcer gold-foil versions were also made for each card.

		NM/M
Complete Set (25):		5.00
Common Player:		.20
Minor Stars:		.40
Comp. Gold Set (25):		10.00
Gold Cards:		1X-2X
1	Clyde Simmons	.20
2	Anthony Smith	.20
3	Ray Childress	.20
4	Michael Dean Perry	.40
5	Bruce Smith	.40
6	Cortez Kennedy	.40
7	Charles Haley	.20
8	Marco Coleman	.20
9	Alonzo Spellman	.20
10	Junior Seau	.75
11	Ken Norton	.20
12	Derrick Thomas	.40
13	Wilber Marshall	.20
14	Chris Doleman	.20
15	Seth Joyner	.20
16	Al Smith	.20
17	Deion Sanders	.75
18	Rod Woodson	.40
19	Audray McMillian	.20
20	Dale Carter	.20
21	Terrell Buckley	.20
22	Bennie Thompson	.20
23	Chris Spielman	.20
24	Lawrence Taylor	.40
25	Tony Bennett	.20

1993 Pro Set Power Combos

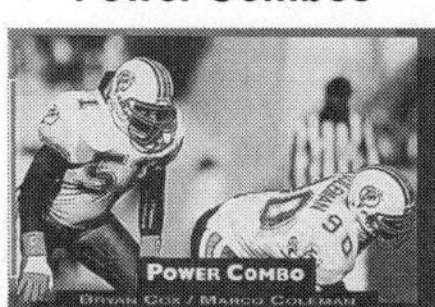

Two players are featured on the front of each card in this Pro Set Power insert set. Cards were random inserts in foil packs. Each card front has a black, blue and purple border, along with the players' names in red in a black bar at the bottom. The card back has a purple rectangle at the top, which has the players' team name in it in yellow lettering. Their names, positions, uniform numbers, career summaries and highlights are featured on the back against a green background with borders in the same color as those on the front. Gold versions and prism versions, were also made for each card.

		NM/M
Complete Set (10):		6.00
Common Player:		.50
Minor Stars:		1.00
Comp. Gold Set (10):		12.00
Gold Cards:		1X-2X
Comp. Prism Set (10):		18.00
Prism Cards:		1X-3X
1	Emmitt Smith, Barry Sanders	3.00
2	Terrell Buckley, Sterling Sharpe	1.00
3	Junior Seau, Gary Plummer	1.00
4	Deion Sanders, Tim McKyer	1.00
5	Bruce Smith, Darryl Talley	.50
6	Warren Moon, Webster Slaughter	.50
7	Chris Doleman, Henry Thomas	.50
8	Karl Mecklenberg, Michael Brooks	.50
9	Ken Norton, Robert Jones	.50
10	Bryan Cox, Marco Coleman	.50

1993 Pro Set Power Draft Picks

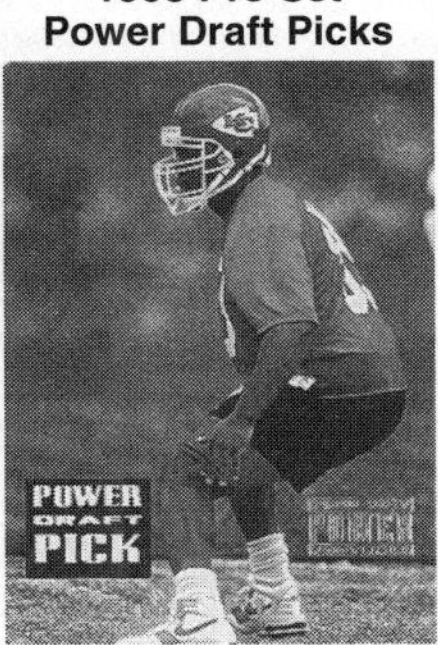

These cards feature color action photos on the front against a black-and-white background. The cards, random inserts in 1993 Pro Set Power packs, feature top rookies in the NFL for the 1993 season; the player's name is in red at the bottom. The card back also has the player's name in red at the top, and is in a horizontal format. The player's name and player biography are also included. Cards are numbered with a "PDP" prefix. Gold foil versions were also made for each card.

		NM/M
Complete Set (30):		8.00
Common Player:		.10
Minor Stars:		.20
Comp. Gold Set (30):		16.00
Gold Cards:		1X-2X
1	Lincoln Kennedy	.10
2	Thomas Smith	.10
3	Robert Smith	1.00
4	John Copeland	.20
5	Dan Footman	.10
6	Darrin Smith	.20
7	Qadry Ismail	.50
8	Ryan McNeil	.10
9	George Teague	.20
10	Brad Hopkins	.10
11	Ernest Dye	.10
12	Jaime Fields	.10
13	Patrick Bates	.10
14	Jerome Bettis	1.00
15	O.J. McDuffie	.75
16	Gino Torretta	.10
17	Drew Bledsoe	2.50
18	Irv Smith	.10
19	Marcus Buckley	.10
20	Coleman Rudolph	.10
21	Leonard Renfro	.10
22	Garrison Hearst	1.00
23	Deon Figures	.20
24	Natrone Means	1.00
25	Todd Kelly	.10
26	Carlton Gray	.10
27	Eric Curry	.10
28	Tom Carter	.20
29	AFC Stars	.10
30	NFC Stars	.10

1993 Pro Set Power Moves

These insert cards feature borderless color action photos on the front, with a ghosted version of the same photo on the back. The front has a red frame for a border, with the player's name in red at the bottom. The back has the set name in white in a black stripe along the left side, with the player's name and his team name in black in a gray plaque at the top. Cards are numbered with a "PM" prefix. Card numbers 1-30 were randomly inserted in 1993 Pro Set Power packs; cards 31-40 were random inserts in 1993 Pro Set Power jumbo packs. Scarcer gold-foil versions were also made for each card.

		NM/M
Complete Set (40):		5.00
Common Player:		.10
Minor Stars:		.20
Comp. Gold Set (40):		10.00
Gold Cards:		1X-2X
1	Bobby Hebert	.20
2	Billy Brooks	.10
3	Vinny Testaverde	.20
4	Hugh Millen	.10
5	Rod Berstine	.10
6	Robert Delpino	.10
7	Pat Swilling	.10
8	Reggie White	.30
9	Aaron Cox	.10
10	Joe Montana	2.00
11	Gaston Green	.10
12	Jeff Hostetler	.20
13	Shane Conlan	.10
14	Irv Eatman	.10
15	Mark Ingram	.10
16	Irving Fryar	.10
17	Don Majkowski	.10
18	Will Wolford	.10
19	Boomer Esiason	.20
20	Ronnie Lott	.10
21	Johnny Johnson	.10
22	Steve Beuerlein	.10
23	Chuck Cecil	.10
24	Gary Clark	.10
25	Kevin Greene	.10
26	Jerrol Williams	.10
27	Tim McDonald	.10
28	Ferrell Edmunds	.10
29	Kelvin Martin	.10
30	Hardy Nickerson	.10
31	Jerry Ball	.10
32	Jim McMahon	.10
33	Marcus Allen	.30
34	John Stephens	.10
35	John Booty	.10

36 Wade Wilson .10
37 Mark Bavaro .10
38 Bill Fralic .10
39 Mark Clayton .10
40 Mike Sherrard .10

1993 Pro Set Power Update Power Moves

These insert cards feature color action photos on the front, with a purple border framed with blue and red lines. The player's name is at the bottom in yellow letters. The card backs, numbered with a "PMVD" prefix, have a biography and season highlights, plus a date when he was traded. Helmets for his old and new team appear at the top, too. The background has shades of purple and white. These inserts shared packs with 1993 Pro Set Power Update Power Prospects cards.

	NM/M
Complete Set (50):	4.00
Common Player:	.10
Minor Stars:	.20
Comp. Gold Set (50):	8.00
Gold Cards:	1X-2X
1 Bobby Hebert	.20
2 Bill Brooks	.10
3 Vinny Testaverde	.20
4 Hugh Millen	.10
5 Rod Bernstine	.10
6 Robert Delpino	.10
7 Pat Swilling	.10
8 Reggie White	.30
9 Aaron Cox	.10
10 Joe Montana	2.00
11 Vinnie Clark (Name misspelled Vinny on card)	.10
12 Jeff Hostetler	.20
13 Shane Conlan	.10
14 Irv Eatman	.10
15 Mark Ingram	.10
16 Irving Fryar	.10
17 Don Majkowski	.10
18 Will Wolford	.10
19 Boomer Esiason	.20
20 Ronnie Lott	.10
21 Johnny Johnson	.10
22 Steve Beuerlein	.10
23 Chuck Cecil	.10
24 Gary Clark	.10
25 Kevin Greene	.10
26 Jerrol Williams	.10
27 Tim McDonald	.10
28 Ferrell Edmunds	.10
29 Kelvin Martin	.10
30 Hardy Nickerson	.10
31 Jumpy Geathers	.10
32 Craig Heyward	.10
33 Tim McKyer	.10
34 Mark Carrier	.10
35 Gary Zimmerman	.10
36 Jay Schroeder	.10
37 Keith Millard	.10
38 Vince Workman	.10
39 Kirk Lowdermilk	.10
40 Fred Stokes	.10
41 Ernie Jones	.10
42 Keith Byars	.10
43 Carlton Bailey	.10
44 Michael Brooks	.10
45 Tim McGee	.10
46 Leonard Marshall	.10
47 Bubby Brister	.10
48 Mike Tomczak	.10
49 Mark Jackson	.10
50 Wade Wilson	.10

1993 Pro Set Power Update Power Prospects

These cards were included in packs containing 1993 Pro Set Power Update Power Moves cards. Each card has a color action photo framed by gray borders. A horizontally-patterned background is also used on the front. The player's name is in yellow at the bottom on the front, while it and his team helmet appear at the top in a panel on the back. The back is gray and contains a career summary and a number, which uses a "PP" prefix. Gold versions were also made for each card.

	NM/M
Complete Set (60):	10.00
Common Player:	.10
Minor Stars:	.20
Comp. Gold Set (60):	20.00
Gold Cards:	1X-2X
1 *Drew Bledsoe*	2.50
2 *Rick Mirer*	.25
3 *Trent Green*	2.00
4 *Mark Brunell*	3.00
5 *Billy Joe Hobert*	.20
6 *Ron Moore*	.40
7 *Elvis Grbac*	.50
8 *Garrison Hearst*	1.00
9 *Jerome Bettis*	1.00
10 *Reggie Brooks*	.25
11 *Robert Smith*	1.00
12 *Vaughn Hebron*	.10
13 *Derek Brown*	.25
14 *Roosevelt Potts*	.20
15 *Terry Kirby*	.30
16 *Glyn Milburn*	.30
17 *Greg Robinson*	.10
18 *Natrone Means*	1.00
19 *Curtis Conway*	.50
20 *James Jett*	.75
21 *O.J. McDuffie*	.50
22 Raghib Ismail	.20
23 *Qadry Ismail*	.40
24 *Kevin Williams*	.60
25 *Victor Bailey*	.20
26 *Vincent Brisby*	.60
27 *Irv Smith*	.10
28 *Troy Drayton*	.40
29 Wayne Simmons	.10
30 *Marvin Jones*	.10
31 *Demetrius DuBase*	.10
32 *Chad Brown*	.40
33 *Micheal Barrow*	.10
34 *Darrin Smith*	.20
35 *Deon Figures*	.20
36 *Darrien Gordon*	.20
37 Patrick Bates	.10
38 *George Teague*	.20
39 *Lance Gunn*	.10
40 *Tom Carter*	.20
41 *Carlton Gray*	.20
42 *John Copeland*	.20
43 *Eric Curry*	.25
44 *Dana Stubblefield*	.40
45 *Leonard Renfro*	.10
46 *Dan Williams*	.10
47 *Todd Kelly*	.10
48 *Chris Slade*	.40
49 *Carl Simpson*	.10
50 *Coleman Rudolph*	.10
51 *Michael Strahan*	.10
52 *Dan Footman*	.10
53 *Steve Everitt*	.10
54 *Will Shields*	.10
55 *Ben Coleman*	.10
56 *William Roaf*	.10
57 *Lincoln Kennedy*	.10
58 *Brad Hopkins*	.10
59 *Ernest Dye*	.10
60 *Jason Elam*	.10

1993 Pro Set Power Update Prospects Gold

Featuring a gold-foil stamp on the card fronts, this 60-card set is a parallel to the Power Update base set.

	NM/M
Complete Set (60):	25.00
Common Player:	.10
Gold Cards:	1X-2X

1993 Pro Set Power Update Combos

These inserts were randomly included in 1993 Pro Set Power Update packs. Each card front features two players on it, in a horizontal format. Their names are at the bottom in red letters. The backs are horizontal too, and include the players' names at the top, along with career highlights for them against a turf-like background. Cards are numbered with a "PC" prefix. Gold versions and prism versions.

	NM/M
Complete Set (10):	10.00
Common Player:	.50
Minor Stars:	1.00
Comp. Gold Set (10):	20.00
Gold Cards:	1X-2X
Comp. Prism Set (10):	30.00
Prism Cards:	1X-3X
1 Andre Rison, Michael Haynes, Mike Pritchard, Drew Hill	.50
2 Steve Young, Jerry Rice	3.00
3 Jim Kelly, Frank Reich	1.00
4 Alvin Harper, Michael Irvin	1.50
5 Rod Woodson, Deon Figures	.50
6 Bruce Smith, Cornelius Bennett	.50
7 Bryan Cox, Marco Coleman	.50
8 Troy Aikman, Emmitt Smith	4.00
9 Tim Brown, Raghib Ismail	1.00
10 Art Monk, Desmond Howard, Ricky Sanders	.50

1993 Pro Set Power Update Impact Rookies

These cards feature top rookies entering the 1993 season. Each card front has an action photo framed by a gold border. The player's name is in yellow at the bottom. The back is gray and includes the player's team name and helmet at the top, along with the college he attended, position and collegiate highlights underneath. Cards were numbered with an "IR" prefix.

	NM/M
Complete Set (15):	10.00
Common Player:	.25
Minor Stars:	.50
1 Rick Mirer	2.00
2 Drew Bledsoe	3.00
3 Jerome Bettis	1.00
4 Derek Brown	.50
5 Roosevelt Potts	.25
6 Glyn Milburn	.50
7 Adrian Murrell	.50
8 Victor Bailey	.25
9 Vincent Brisby	.50
10 O.J. McDuffie	1.00
11 James Jett	.50
12 Eric Curry	.25
13 Dana Stubblefield	.50
14 William Roaf	.25
15 Patrick Bates	.25

1994 Pro Set National Promos

Six of eight cards were handed out at the Pro Set booth at the 1994 National Sports Collectors Convention. The cards, numbered by a letter, were promos from either Pro Set football, Power football or Power racing. A title card, which was unnumbered, featured the National logo and was individually numbered "of 10,000." The Garrison Hearst and Richmond Webb cards were inserts in "Tuff Stuff" magazine. The card backs have "proto" printed inside a strip at the bottom.

	NM/M
Complete Set (8):	14.00
Common Player:	1.00
1 Jerome Bettis Fire Power	2.00
2 Drew Bledsoe	3.00
3 Brett Favre, Sterling Sharpe Green Bay Packers, Air Power	5.00
4 Ronald Moore	1.00
5 Willie Roaf Power Line	1.00
6 Garrison Hearst	1.50
7 Richmond Webb	1.00
NNO Title Card (1994 National)	1.00

Q

1991 Quarterback Legends

This 50-card set, produced by NFL Quarterback Legends, comes in a special commemorative box. Each card front has a full-bleed color action photo, with the set logo and name given at the bottom of the card in a checkerboard pattern. The card back has the sponsors' logos, a card number, a color photo, statistics and a career summary. The design is horizontal. Cards were released at the Quarterback Legends Show in Nashville, Tenn., in January 1992.

	NM/M
Complete Set (50):	20.00
Common Player:	.25
1 Ken Anderson	.75
2 Steve Bartkowski	.35
3 George Blanda	1.50
4 Terry Bradshaw	2.00
5 Zeke Bratkowski	.25
6 John Brodie	.50
7 Charley Conerly	.50
8 Len Dawson	.50
9 Lynn Dickey	.25
10 Joe Ferguson	.25
11 Vince Ferragamo	.25
12 Tom Flores	.35
13 Dan Fouts	1.00
14 Roman Gabriel	.35
15 Otto Graham	.75
16 Bob Griese	1.25
17 Steve Grogan	.35
18 John Hadl	.35
19 James Harris	.25
20 Jim Hart	.25
21 Ron Jaworski	.25
22 Charlie Johnson	.25
23 Bert Jones	.35
24 Sonny Jurgensen	.75
25 Joe Kapp	.25
26 Billy Kilmer	.50
27 Daryle Lamonica	.35
28 Greg Landry	.25
29 Neil Lomax	.25
30 Archie Manning	.40
31 Earl Morrall	.35
32 Craig Morton	.35
33 Gifford Nielsen	.25
34 Dan Pastorini	.25
35 Jim Plunkett	.35
36 Norm Snead	.25
37 Ken Stabler	.75
38 Bart Starr	1.50
39 Roger Staubach	3.00
40 Joe Theismann	.75
41 Y.A. Tittle	.75
42 Johnny Unitas	1.50
43 Bill Wade	.25
44 Danny White	.35
45 Doug Williams	.25
46 Jim Zorn	.35
47 Otto Graham Legendary Feats	1.00
48 Johnny Unitas Legendary Feats	1.00
49 Bart Starr Legendary Feats	1.00
50 Terry Bradshaw Legendary Feats	1.75

1992 Quarterback Greats GE

Members of the Quarterback Club are represented in this 12-card set sponsored by General Electric. The QB Club, GE and NFL Team Players logos all appear on the card back, which is numbered. The card front has a color action photo against a red background. The player's name is at the top of the card in white letters. Quarterback Greats is also written on the card front. The back has a career summary and player statistics. Cards were available through a mail-in offer utilizing proofs of purchase seals. An unnumbered checklist card was also produced for the set.

	NM/M
Complete Set (12):	10.00
Common Player:	.50
1 Troy Aikman	5.00
2 Bubby Brister	.75
3 Randall Cunningham	1.00
4 John Elway	2.00
5 Boomer Esiason	.75
6 Jim Everett	.75
7 Jim Kelly	1.50
8 Bernie Kosar	.50
9 Dan Marino	4.00
10 Warren Moon	1.00
11 Phil Simms	.50
NNO Title Card (Checklist)	.25

1993 Quarterback Legends

These cards feature color photos of some of the NFL's best quarterbacks, against a sepia-toned background. The set name runs vertically along the left side of the card, written in bronze letters. The card back is numbered and includes a career summary and closeup shot of the player.

	NM/M
Complete Set (50):	15.00
Common Player:	.20
1 Checklist Card	.25
2 Ken Anderson	.50
3 Steve Bartkowski	.25
4 George Blanda	1.00
5 Terry Bradshaw	1.50
6 Zeke Bratkowski	.20
7 John Brodie	.50
8 Charley Conerly	.50
9 Len Dawson	.50
10 Lynn Dickey	.20
11 Joe Ferguson	.20
12 Vince Ferragamo	.20
13 Tom Flores	.25
14 Dan Fouts	.75
15 Roman Gabriel	.25
16 Otto Graham	.75
17 Bob Griese	1.00
18 Steve Grogan	.25
19 John Hadl	.25
20 James Harris	.20
21 Jim Hart	.20
22 Ron Jaworski	.20
23 Charlie Johnson	.20
24 Bert Jones	.25
25 Sonny Jurgensen	.50
26 Joe Kapp	.20
27 Billy Kilmer	.20
28 Daryle Lamonica	.20
29 Greg Landry	.20
30 Neil Lomax	.20
31 Archie Manning	.50
32 Earl Morrall	.25
33 Craig Morton	.25
34 Gifford Nielsen	.20
35 Dan Pastorini	.20
36 Jim Plunkett	.25
37 Norm Snead	.20
38 Ken Stabler	.75
39 Bart Starr	1.00
40 Roger Staubach	2.00
41 Joe Theismann	.75
42 Y.A. Tittle	.75
43 Johnny Unitas	1.00
44 Bill Wade	.20
45 Danny White	.25
46 Doug Williams	.20
47 Jim Zorn	.20
48 George Blanda Miracle Streak	.75
49 Bob Griese, Earl Morrall Perfect Season	.50
50 Doug Williams Record Setting Super Bowl XXII	.25

R

1935 R311-2 Premium Photos

Measuring 6" x 8", these 17 photos feature both collegiate and professional players. The black-and-white photos have blank backs. The photos could be ordered from National Chicle in exchange for 20 wrappers given to the retailer. The photos are listed in alphabetical order by the player's name or team.

	NM/M
Complete Set (17):	3,000
Common Player:	175.00
1 Joe Bach	175.00
2 Eddie Casey	175.00
3 George Christensen	175.00
4 Harold "Red" Grange	525.00
5 Stan Kostka TD Next Stop	175.00
6 Joe Maniaci Fordham Back (26 with ball, shown trying to gain around left end)	175.00
7 Harry Newman	175.00
8 Walter Switzer (Cornell quarterback)	175.00
9 Chicago Bears, 1934 Western Champs	300.00
10 New York Giants, 1934 World's Champs	350.00
11 1934	220.00
12 Navy 1945	175.00
13 Pittsburgh Pirates, 1935 Football Club	250.00
14 Touchdown: Morton of Yale	175.00
15 A Tight Spot	175.00
16 Cotton Goes Places	175.00
17 Ace Gutowky, Steve Hokuf Picture Ever Photographed	220.00

1985 Raiders Shell Oil Posters

Measuring 11-5/8" x 18", the five posters were available at participating Southern California Shell gas stations during the 1985 season. Color artwork of Raider players in action are included on the poster fronts. The backs are blank, except for the Pro Bowl poster which has the Raiders and Shell logos and the release schedule of the posters.

	NM/M
Complete Set (5):	25.00
Common Player:	5.00
1 Pro Bowl (No release date)	6.00
2 Defensive Front (September)	6.00
3 Deep Secondary (October)	5.00
4 Big Offensive Line (November)	5.00
5 Scores (December)	5.00

1985 Raiders Smokey

Measuring 2-5/8" x 4-1/8", the four-card set is anchored by a photo on the front, with the player's name, position and team at the bottom. The Raiders' logo and Kodak logo are printed on the lower left and right, respectively. The card backs have the player's name and his highlights on the left. A fire safety tip and cartoon are included on the right. The cards are numbered on the backs. The sponsors and Kodak logos are printed at the bottom of the card backs.

	NM/M
Complete Set (4):	3.00
Common Player:	.35
1 Marcus Allen	1.50
2 Tom Flores (CO)	.50
3 Howie Long	1.25
4 Rod Martin	.35

1987 Raiders Smokey Color-Grams

This 14-page booklet includes 13 player drawings and one of Smokey and Huddles. Featured on a page are a 5-5/8" x 3-11/16" postcard and a perforated card which measures 2-1/2" x 3-11/16". Each booklet measures 8-1/8" x 3-11/16". The postcard fronts have "Arsonbusters" printed at the top, with a Smokey the Bear and two Raiders logos printed at the bottom. The cards, which are unnumbered, are listed by page number.

	NM/M
Complete Set (14):	25.00
Common Player:	1.25
1 Smokey and Huddles	1.25
2 Matt Millen	1.50
3 Rod Martin	1.50
4 Sean Jones	2.50
5 Dokie Williams	1.25
6 Don Mosebar	1.50
7 Todd Christensen	2.50
8 Bill Pickel	1.25
9 Marcus Allen	8.00
10 Charley Hannah	1.25
11 Howie Long	3.00
12 Vann McElroy	1.50
13 Reggie McKenzie	1.25
14 Mike Haynes	2.00

1988 Raiders Police

Measuring 2-3/4" x 4-1/8", the 12-card set is anchored by a large photo on the front, with "Los Angeles Raiders," Texaco logo and Raiders' logo printed at the top. The player's number, name and position are listed beneath the photo. The card backs, which are numbered, have the player's name, number, position, bio, safety tip and L.A.P.D. shield.

	NM/M
Complete Set (12):	8.00
Common Player:	.40
1 Vann McElroy	.40
2 Bill Pickel	.40
3 Marcus Allen	2.00
4 Rod Martin	.50
5 Lionel Washington	.50
6 Don Mosebar	.50
7 Reggie McKenzie	.40
8 Todd Christensen	.75
9 Bo Jackson	2.50
10 James Lofton	1.25
11 Howie Long	1.00
12 Mike Shanahan (CO)	.75

1988 Raiders Smokey

Measuring 3" x 5", the 14-card set showcases "Arsonbusters" at the top of the photo. The player's name and position are printed at the bottom of the photo. The Smokey the Bear and Raiders' logos are printed at the bottom of the black-bordered card fronts. The unnumbered card backs have the player's name, position, bio and safety tip cartoon.

	NM/M
Complete Set (14):	10.00
Common Player:	.75
1 Marcus Allen	4.00
2 Todd Christensen	1.00
3 Bo Jackson	4.00
4 James Lofton	2.00
5 Howie Long	1.50
6 Rod Martin	1.00
7 Vann McElroy	.75
8 Don Mosebar	1.00
9 Bill Pickel	.75
10 Jerry Robinson	.75
11 Mike Shanahan (CO)	1.50
12 Smokey Bear	.75
13 Stacey Toran	.75
14 Greg Townsend	1.00

1989 Raiders Swanson

The three cards were printed on a perforated strip, which also included two Swanson Hungry-Man dinner coupons. The cards measure 2-1/2" x 3-3/4". The card fronts have a black-and-white player photo inside an oval, with "Hungry Man" printed in a stripe in the upper left corner. The player's name is printed at the bottom. The card backs, which are unnumbered, showcase the player's name, bio and highlights. The Swanson Hungry-Man logo is printed at the top of the horizontal card backs.

		NM/M
Complete Set (3):		8.00
Common Player:		2.50
1	Marcus Allen	5.00
2	Howie Long	3.00
3	Jim Plunkett	2.50

1990 Raiders Smokey

The 16-card set is anchored on the front with a large photo. "Los Angeles Raiders" is printed above the photo, while the player's name and number are printed beneath the photo. The Smokey the Bear logo is in the lower left. The card fronts are bordered in black. The unnumbered card backs have the player's name, position, bio, Raiders' logos and safety tip cartoon.

		NM/M
Complete Set (16):		10.00
Common Player:		.75
1	Eddie Anderson	1.00
2	Tom Benson	.75
3	Mervyn Fernandez	1.25
4	Bob Golic	1.00
5	Jeff Gossett	.75
6	Rory Graves	.75
7	Jeff Jaeger	.75
8	Howie Long	2.00
9	Don Mosebar	1.00
10	Jay Schroeder	1.25
11	Art Shell (CO)	2.00
12	Greg Townsend	1.25
13	Lionel Washington	1.00
14	Steve Wisniewski	1.25
15	Commitment to Excellence (Helmet and Super Bowl trophies)	.75
16	Denise Franzen (Cheerleader)	.75

1990-91 Raiders Main Street Dairy

The six half-pint milk cartons have the Raiders logo, player head shot, his name, position, team and safety tip printed on a panel. The cartons measure 4-1/2" x 6" when they are collapsed. Released in the Los Angeles metro area, the cartons were produced in three colors -- brown (chocolate lowfat), red (vitamin D) and blue (two percent lowfat).

		NM/M
Complete Set (6):		15.00
Common Player:		2.50
1	Bob Golic (Blue)	3.50
2	Terry McDaniel (Brown)	2.50
3	Don Mosebar (Red)	2.50
4	Jay Schroeder (Blue)	3.50
5	Art Shell (CO) (Red)	5.00
6	Steve Wisniewski (Brown)	2.50

1991 Raiders Police

The 12-card set showcases a color action photo on the front, with the player's name printed in a gray stripe above the photo. The Raiders and sponsor logos are printed at the bottom of the card front. The card backs are numbered, have the player's name, position, bio and safety tip. The sponsors are listed at the bottom, while the card number is printed inside a football in the upper right.

		NM/M
Complete Set (12):		15.00
Common Player:		1.00
1	Art Shell (CO)	3.00
2	Marcus Allen	3.00
3	Mervyn Fernandez	1.50
4	Willie Gault	1.50
5	Howie Long	2.00
6	Don Mosebar	1.25
7	Winston Moss	1.00
8	Jay Schroeder	1.50
9	Steve Wisniewski	1.25
10	Ethan Horton	1.00
11	Lionel Washington	1.25
12	Greg Townsend	1.50

1991 Raiders Adohr Farms Dairy

These 10 half-pint milk cartons have the Raiders' logo, player headshot, safety tip, player's name, position and team printed on one of the panels. The cartons measure 4-1/2" x 6" when collapsed. The cartons were printed in two colors -- blue (two percent lowfat) and red (vitamin D). The Greg Townsend carton was the only one to be released in both colors. The cartons are unnumbered.

		NM/M
Complete Set (10):		25.00
Common Player:		2.50
1	Jeff Gossett (Red)	2.50
2	Ethan Horton (Blue)	2.50
3	Jeff Jaeger (Red)	2.50
4	Ronnie Lott (Blue)	5.00
5	Terry McDaniel (Red)	2.50
6	Don Mosebar (Red)	2.50
7	Jay Schroeder (Red)	3.50
8	Art Shell (CO) (Red)	5.00
9	Greg Townsend (Red or blue)	3.50
10	Steve Wisniewski (Red)	2.50

1993-94 Raiders Adohr Farms Dairy

The six half-pint milk cartons have the Raiders' logo, player headshot, safety tip, player's name and position printed on one of the panels. The cartons measure 4-1/2" x 6" when collapsed. According to reports, 2 million cartons were sold through Los Angeles area schools and hospitals during a two-week period. The cartons are unnumbered.

		NM/M
Complete Set (6):		15.00
Common Player:		2.50
1	Jeff Gossett	2.50
2	Ethan Horton	2.50
3	Terry McDaniel	2.50
4	Don Mosebar	2.50
5	Art Shell (CO)	5.00
6	Steve Wisniewski	2.50

1994-95 Raiders Adohr Farms Dairy

The four half-pint milk cartons showcase the Raiders' logo, player headshot, safety tip, player's name and position on one of the carton's panels. The cartons measure 4-1/2" x 6" when collapsed. Five million sets were distributed during a three-week period to hospitals, schools, airlines and the general public. The cartons are not numbered.

		NM/M
Complete Set (4):		15.00
Common Player:		3.50
1	Jeff Jaeger	3.50
2	Terry McDaniel	3.50
3	Art Shell (CO)	6.00
4	Steve Wisniewski	3.50

1950 Rams Admiral

Measuring 3-1/2" x 5-1/2", the 35-card set features a posed black-and-white photo on the front of the card, with "Your Admiral dealer presents..." and the player's name printed in a black area at the top. Beneath the photo are the card number and player bio. The backs have a Rams schedule on one half, while the other half is blank. Card Nos. 26-35 are blank-backed and are a bit smaller than the other cards in the set.

		NM/M
Complete Set (35):		110.00
Common Player:		20.00
1	Joe Stydahar (CO)	30.00
2	Hampton Pool (CO)	20.00
3	Fred Naumetz	20.00
4	Jack Finlay	20.00
5	Gil Bouley	20.00
6	Bob Reinhard	20.00
7	Bob Boyd	25.00
8	Bob Waterfield	100.00
9	Mel Hein (CO)	40.00
10	Howard Hickey (CO)	25.00
11	Ralph Pasquariello	20.00
12	Jack Zilly	20.00
13	Tom Kalmanir	20.00
14	Norm Van Brocklin	125.00
15	Woodley Lewis	25.00
16	Glenn Davis	50.00
17	Dick Hoerner	20.00
18	Bob Kelley (ANN)	20.00
19	Paul (Tank) Younger	30.00
20	George Sims	20.00
21	Dick Huffman	20.00
22	Tom Fears	50.00
23	Vitamin Smith	25.00
24	Elroy Hirsch	75.00
25	Don Paul	25.00
26	Bill Lange	20.00
27	Paul Barry	20.00
28	Deacon Dan Towler	30.00
29	Vic Vasicek	20.00
30	Bill Smyth	20.00
31	Larry Brink	20.00
32	Jerry Williams	20.00
33	Stan West	20.00
34	Art Statuto	20.00
35	Ed Champagne	20.00

1953 Rams Black Border

Measuring 4-1/4" x 6-3/8", the 36-card set is anchored by a large photo and bordered in black. A facsimile autograph is printed near the bottom of the photo. The unnumbered card backs have the player's name, bio and highlights. The set was available from the Rams. Some cards from the 1953-55 and 1957 Rams Black Border sets are very similar, with the excepton of different information on the card backs.

		NM/M
Complete Set (36):		175.00
Common Player:		3.00
1	Ben Agajanian	3.00
2	Bob Boyd (Born in Riverside)	3.00
3	Larry Brink	3.00
4	Rudy Bukich	5.00
5	Tom Dahms (4 text lines)	3.00
6	Dick Daugherty (Regular Ram ...)	3.00
7	Jack Dwyer (Played 1951 ...)	3.00
8	Tom Fears (1952 stats)	10.00
9	Bob Fry (Was sprinter)	3.00
10	Frank Fuller (Attended ...)	3.00
11	Norbert Hecker	3.00
12	Elroy Hirsch (1952 stats)	12.00
13	John Hock (Just completed ...)	3.00
14	Bob Kelley (ANN) (Signature in upperleft of photo)	3.00
15	Dick "Night Train"Lane	12.00
16	Woodley Lewis (Ram utility ...)	4.00
17	Tom McCormick (Set three ...)	3.00
18	Lewis Bud McFadin (Came to Rams ...)	3.00
19	Leon McLaughlin (Played every ...)	3.00
20	Brad Myers	3.00
21	Don Paul (A five year ...)	4.00
22	Hampton Pool (CO) (Hampton Pool ...)	3.00
23	Duane Putnam (As rookie ...)	4.00
24	Volney Quinlan (Nickname ...)	4.00
25	Herb Rich	3.00
26	Andy Robustelli (Rams' regular ...)	10.00
27	Vitamin Smith	4.00
28	Harland Svare (Attended ...)	3.00
29	Len Teeuws	3.00
30	Harry Thompson (Used at ...)	3.00
31	Charley Toogood (Been defensive ...)	3.00
32	Deacon Dan Towler (National football)	7.00
33	Norm Van Brocklin (1952 stats)	20.00
34	Stan West (Rams' regular)	3.00
35	Paul (Tank) Younger (1952 stats)	6.00
36	John Sauer, William Battles, Howard (Red) Hickey Coaches	4.00

1954 Rams Black Border

Measuring 4-1/4" x 6-3/8", the front is anchored by a large black-and-white photo, bordered in black. A facsimile autograph also appears near the bottom of the photo. The unnumbered backs have the player's name, bio and career highlights. The 36-card set was available from the Rams.

		NM/M
Complete Set (36):		175.00
Common Player:		3.00
1	Bob Boyd (One of fastest ...)	3.00
2	Bob Carey	3.00
3	Bobby Cross	3.00
4	Tom Dahms (5 text lines)	3.00
5	Don Doll	3.00
6	Jack Dwyer (Regular defensive ...)	3.00
7	Tom Fears (1953 stats)	20.00
8	Bob Griffin (All American ...)	3.00
9	Art Hauser (Was fastest ...)	3.00
10	Hall Haynes	3.00
11	Elroy Hirsch (1953 stats)	12.00
12	Ed Hughes	3.00
13	Bob Kelley (ANN) (Signature across photo)	3.00
14	Woodley Lewis (Established ...)	4.00
15	Gene Lipscomb	10.00
16	Tom McCormick (Rams' regular)	3.00
17	Bud McFadin (Although ...)	3.00
18	Leon McLaughlin (Started every ...)	3.00
19	Paul Miller (Lettered at ...)	3.00
20	Don Paul (One of two ...)	4.00
21	Hampton Pool (CO) (Since taking ...)	3.00
22	Duane Putnam (Offensive guard)	4.00
23	Volney Quinlan (Had best ...)	4.00
24	Les Richter (Rated one ...)	7.00
25	Andy Robustelli (L.A.'s regular ...)	10.00
26	Willard Sherman (Played at ...)	4.00
27	Harland Svare (An outside ...)	3.00
28	Harry Thompson (Played offensive ...)	3.00
29	Charley Toogood	3.00
30	Deacon Dan Towler (Since becoming ...)	7.00
31	Norm Van Brocklin (1953 stats)	20.00
32	Bill Wade (Selected as)	8.00
33	Duane Wardlow	3.00
34	Stan West (Virtually ...)	3.00
35	Paul (Tank) Younger (1953 stats)	7.00
36	Bill Battles, Howard Hickey, John Sauer, Dick Voris, Buck Weaver, Hampton Pool Coaches	4.00

1955 Rams Black Border

Measuring 4-1/4" x 6-3/8", the 37-card set is anchored by a large black-and-white photo on the front and bordered in black. A facsimile autograph appears near the bottom of the photo. The backs include the player's name, bio and career highlights. The cards are unnumbered and were available as a set from the Rams.

		NM/M
Complete Set (37):		175.00
Common Player:		3.00
1	Jack Bighead	3.00
2	Bob Boyd	3.00
3	Don Burroughs	3.00
4	Jim Cason	3.00
5	Bobby Cross	3.00
6	Jack Ellena	3.00
7	Tom Fears	10.00
8	Sid Fournet	3.00
9	Frank Fuller	4.00
10	Sid Gillman (and staff)	7.00
11	Bob Griffin	3.00
12	Art Hauser	3.00
13	Hall Haynes	3.00
14	Elroy Hirsch	12.00
15	John Hock	3.00
16	Glenn Holtzman	3.00
17	Ed Hughes	3.00
18	Woodley Lewis	4.00
19	Gene Lipscomb	10.00
20	Tom McCormick	3.00
21	Bud McFadin	3.00
22	Leon McLaughlin	3.00
23	Paul Miller	3.00
24	Larry Morris	3.00
25	Don Paul	4.00
26	Duane Putnam	4.00
27	Volney Quinlan	4.00
28	Les Richter	7.00
29	Andy Robustelli	10.00
30	Willard Sherman	4.00
31	Corky Taylor	3.00
32	Charley Toogood	3.00
33	Deacon Dan Towler	7.00
34	Norm Van Brocklin	20.00
35	Bill Wade	8.00
36	Ron Waller	3.00
37	Paul (Tank) Younger	7.00

1956 Rams White Border

Measuring 4-1/4" x 6-3/8", the 37-card set is anchored by a black-and-white photo on the front and bordered in white. A facsimile autograph appears near the bottom of the photo. The unnumbered card backs have the player's name, bio and career highlights. The set was available from the Rams.

		NM/M
Complete Set (37):		175.00
Common Player:		3.00
1	Bob Boyd	3.00
2	Rudy Bukich	5.00
3	Don Burroughs	3.00
4	Jim Cason	3.00
5	Leon Clarke	3.00
6	Dick Daugherty	3.00
7	Jack Ellena	3.00
8	Tom Fears	10.00
9	Sid Fournet	3.00
10	Bob Fry	3.00
11	Sid Gillman, Joseph Madro, Jack Faulkner, Joe Thomas, Lowell Storm (Coaches)	7.00
12	Bob Griffin	3.00
13	Art Hauser	3.00
14	Elroy Hirsch	12.00
15	John Hock	3.00
16	Bobby Holladay	3.00
17	Glenn Holtzman	3.00
18	Bob Kelley (ANN)	3.00
19	Joe Marconi	4.00
20	Bud McFadin	3.00
21	Paul Miller	3.00
22	Ron Miller	3.00
23	Larry Morris	3.00
24	John Morrow	3.00
25	Brad Myers	3.00
26	Hugh Pitts	3.00
27	Duane Putnam	3.00
28	Les Richter	7.00
29	Willard Sherman	4.00
30	Charley Toogood	3.00
31	Norm Van Brocklin	20.00
32	Bill Wade	7.00
33	Ron Waller	4.00
34	Duane Wardlow	3.00
35	Jesse Whittenton	4.00
36	Tom Wilson	4.00
37	Paul (Tank) Younger	7.00

1957 Rams Black Border

Measuring 4-1/4" x 6-3/8", the 38-card set is anchored by a large photo on the front bordered in black. A facsimile autograph appears near the bottom of the photo. The card backs include the player's name, bio and career highlights. The cards are unnumbered and were sold as a set by the Rams.

		NM/M
Complete Set (38):		175.00
Common Player:		3.00
1	Jon Arnett	8.00
2	Bob Boyd (Frequently called ...)	4.00
3	Alex Bravo	3.00
4	Bill Brundige (ANN)	3.00
5	Don Burroughs	3.00
6	Jerry Castete	3.00
7	Leon Clarke	4.00
8	Paige Cothren	3.00
9	Dick Daugherty (Has the ...)	3.00
10	Bob Dougherty	3.00
11	Bob Fry (One of the ...)	3.00
12	Frank Fuller (One of the ...)	3.00
13	Sid Gillman, Joseph Madro, George Allen, Jack Faulkner, Lowell Storm Coaches	10.00
14	Bob Griffin (After four ...)	3.00
15	Art Hauser (One of the ...)	3.00
16	Elroy Hirsch (A legendary ...)	12.00
17	John Hock (Teamed with ...)	3.00
18	Glenn Holtzman	3.00
19	John Houser	3.00
20	Bob Kelley (ANN) (Signature near right border of photo)	3.00
21	Lamar Lundy	8.00
22	Joe Marconi	3.00
23	Paul Miller (From a ...)	3.00
24	Larry Morris	3.00
25	Ken Panfil	3.00
26	Jack Pardee	12.00
27	Duane Putnam (Named to a ...)	4.00
28	Les Richter (One of the ...)	7.00
29	Willard Sherman (One of the ...)	4.00
30	Del Shofner	8.00
31	Bill Ray Smith	6.00
32	George Strugar	3.00
33	Norm Van Brocklin (When Van Brocklin ...)	25.00
34	Bill Wade (In the first ...)	7.00
35	Ron Waller	3.00
36	Jesse Whittenton	4.00
37	Tom Wilson	4.00
38	Paul (Tank) Younger (One of a ...)	7.00

1959 Rams Bell Brand

The 40-card set is anchored by a color photo on the front, with the player's name, position and team at the bottom. The numbered card backs have the player's name, position, bio and career highlights, along with an advertisement for Bell Snacks on the left side. The right side has an ad for fans to buy L.A. Rams' Signature Merchandise. The card number is located in the upper left corner. The cards were included in specially marked bags of Bell's potato chips and corn chips.

		NM/M
Complete Set (40):		1,500
Common Player:		30.00
1	Bill Wade	45.00
2	Buddy Humphrey	30.00
3	Frank Ryan	50.00
4	Ed Meador	40.00
5	Tom Wilson	30.00
6	Don Burroughs	30.00
7	Jon Arnett	45.00
8	Del Shofner	45.00
9	Jack Pardee	50.00
10	Ollie Matson	75.00
11	Joe Marconi	30.00
12	Jim Jones	30.00
13	Jack Morris	30.00
14	Willard Sherman	40.00
15	Clendon Thomas	40.00
16	Les Richter	40.00
17	John Morrow	30.00
18	Lou Michaels	40.00
19	Bob Reifsnyder	30.00
20	John Guzik	30.00
21	Duane Putnam	30.00
22	John Houser	30.00
23	Buck Lansford	30.00
24	Gene Selawski	30.00
25	John Baker	30.00
26	Bob Fry	30.00
27	John Lovetere	30.00
28	George Strugar	30.00
29	Roy Wilkins	30.00
30	Charley Bradshaw	30.00
31	Gene Brito	40.00
32	Jim Phillips	40.00
33	Leon Clarke	40.00
34	Lamar Lundy	45.00
35	Sam Williams	30.00
36	Sid Gillman (CO)	60.00
37	Jack Faulkner (CO)	30.00
38	Joseph Madro (CO)	30.00
39	Don Paul (CO)	30.00
40	Lou Rymkus (CO)	40.00

1960 Rams Bell Brand

The 39-card standard sized set features the identical design on the front and back as the 1959 set, except the fronts of the 1960 set has yellow borders (the 1959 set had white borders). Card Nos. 1-18, with the exception of No. 2, are duplicate photos from the 1959 set. These cards were also inserted into specially marked bags of Bell's Snacks. Card No. 2 of Gene Selawski was pulled from the set early in the season because he was waived from the team. However, the card was available from the company.

		NM/M
Complete Set (39):		2,000
Common Player (1-18):		25.00
Common Player (19-39):		50.00
1	Joe Marconi	25.00
2	Gene Selawski (SP)	1,200
3	Frank Ryan	40.00
4	Ed Meador	30.00
5	Tom Wilson	25.00
6	Gene Brito	30.00
7	Jon Arnett	35.00
8	Buck Lansford	25.00
9	Jack Pardee	45.00
10	Ollie Matson	65.00
11	John Lovetere	25.00
12	Bill Jolko	25.00
13	Jim Phillips	30.00
14	Lamar Lundy	35.00
15	Del Shofner	40.00
16	Les Richter	30.00
17	Bill Wade	35.00
18	Lou Michaels	30.00
19	Dick Bass	60.00
20	Charley Britt	50.00
21	Willard Sherman	60.00
22	George Strugar	50.00
23	Bob Long	50.00
24	Danny Villanueva	60.00
25	Jim Boeke	50.00
26	Clendon Thomas	50.00
27	Art Hunter	50.00
28	Carl Karilivacz	50.00
29	John Baker	50.00
30	Charley Bradshaw	50.00
31	John Guzik	50.00
32	Buddy Humphrey	50.00
33	Carroll Dale	60.00
34	Don Ellensick	50.00
35	Ray Hord	50.00
36	Charles Janerette	50.00
37	John Kenerson	50.00
38	Jerry Stalcup	50.00
39	Bob Waterfield (CO)	125.00

1973 Rams Team Issue

Measuring 7" x 8-3/4", the six sheets are anchored on the front by color photos. Bordered in white, the fronts have the player's name and team listed beneath the photo. The blank-backed cards are unnumbered.

		NM/M
Complete Set (6):		32.00
Common Player:		2.50
1	Jim Bertelsen	2.50
2	John Hadl	7.00
3	Harold Jackson	5.00
4	Merlin Olsen	10.00
5	Isiah Robertson	3.50
6	Jack Snow	3.50

1980 Rams Police

Measuring 2-5/8" x 4-1/8", the 14-card set is anchored by a large photo. The player's name, number, position and team are printed beneath the photo. The Rams' and Kiwanis' logos appear in the lower left and right, respectively, on the card fronts. The backs have Rams' tips inside a box, with the sponsors listed at the bottom. The cards are unnumbered. The cards were handed out by police officers for 14 weeks.

		NM/M
Complete Set (14):		20.00
Common Player:		1.00
11	Pat Haden	3.50
15	Vince Ferragamo	2.50
21	Nolan Cromwell	2.50
26	Wendell Tyler	2.50
32	Cullen Bryant	1.25
53	Jim Youngblood	1.25
59	Bob Brudzinski	1.00
61	Rich Saul	1.00
77	Doug France	1.00
82	Willie Miller	1.00
85	Jack Youngblood	4.00
88	Preston Dennard	1.00
90	Larry Brooks	1.00
xx0	Ray Malavasi (CO)	1.00

1985 Rams Smokey

Measuring 4" x 6", the 24-card set showcases the player's last name at the top of the card, with a photo of the player standing with Smokey the Bear printed in the center of the card front. The Rams' logo, helmet and Smokey the Bear logo are printed beneath the photo on the front. The backs include the card number, player name, position and bio, along with a safety tip cartoon.

		NM/M
Complete Set (24):		15.00
Common Player:		.50
1	George Andrews	.50
2	Bill Bain	.50
3	Russ Bolinger	.50
4	Jim Collins	.50
5	Nolan Cromwell	1.00
6	Reggie Doss	.50
7	Carl Ekern	.50
8	Vince Ferragamo	1.00
9	Gary Green	.50
10	Mike Guman	.50
11	David Hill	.50
12	LeRoy Irvin (SP)	4.00
13	Mark Jerue	.50
14	Johnnie Johnson	.75
15	Jeff Kemp	1.00
16	Mel Owens	.50
17	Irv Pankey	.50
18	Doug Smith	.75
19	Ivory Sully	.50
20	Jack Youngblood	1.50
21	Mike McDonald	.50
22	Norwood Vann	.50
23	Smokey Bear (Unnumbered)	.50
24	Reggie Doss, Gary Green, Johnnie Johnson, Carl Ekern Smokey Bear (Unnumbered)	.75

1987 Rams Jello/General Foods

Jello and Bird's Eye sponsored this 10-card set, which features a large photo, with the Rams' helmet in the upper left and the NFL shield in the upper right. The Jello and Bird's Eye logos are in the lower left and right, respectively, with the player's name and position printed in the bottom center of the card front. The card backs have the player's name and number at the top, with his bio inside an oval in the center. His career highlights are listed at the bottom of the card, along with the Jello and Bird's Eye logos. The cards are unnumbered.

		NM/M
Complete Set (10):		5.00
Common Player:		.35
1	Ron Brown	.50
2	Nolan Cromwell	.60
3	Eric Dickerson	2.00
4	Carl Ekern	.35
5	Jim Everett	2.00
6	Dennis Harrah	.35
7	LeRoy Irvin	.50
8	Mike Lansford	.35
9	Jackie Slater	.60
10	Doug Smith	.50

1987 Rams Oscar Mayer

This 19-card set celebrated the Rams Special Teams Player of the Week. The player's photo appears inside a ripped-out hole in the center of the card. The Rams' helmet and Oscar Mayer logo are on the lower left and right, respectively. The player's name and position are listed beneath the photo. The fronts have a baby blue background. The unnumbered card backs have the player's name, bio Rams' helmet and Oscar Mayer logo.

		NM/M
Complete Set (19):		14.00
Common Player:		.75
1	Sam Anno	.75
2	Ron Brown	1.00
3	Nolan Cromwell	1.25
4	Henry Ellard	1.50
5	Jerry Gray	1.00
6	Kevin Greene	3.00
7	Mike Guman	.75
8	Dale Hatcher	.75
9	Clifford Hicks	.75
10	Mark Jerue	.75
11	Johnnie Johnson	1.00
12	Larry Kelm	.75
13	Mike Lansford	.75
14	Vince Newsome	.75
15	Michael Stewart	.75
16	Mickey Sutton	.75
17	Tim Tyrrell	.75
18	Norwood Vann	.75
19	Charles White	1.25

1989 Rams Police

Released as a 16-card perforated sheet, the cards have a photo of the player, with his name and position, along with the Rams' helmet and Frito-Lay logos beneath the helmet. The card backs, numbered "of 16," have the Rams' helmet and Frito-Lay logo in the upper corners, followed by the player's name, position and quote. McGruff the Crime Dog's safety tip is also included on the back. The 7-11 and police badge logos are in the lower corners, with the card number centered at the bottom.

		NM/M
Complete Set (16):		10.00
Common Player:		1.00
1	John Robinson	2.00
2	Jim Everett	2.50
3	Doug Smith	1.25
4	Duval Love	1.00
5	Henry Ellard	2.00
6	Mel Owens	1.00
7	Jerry Gray	1.25
8	Kevin Greene	2.00
9	Vince Newsome	1.00
10	Irv Pankey	1.00
11	Tom Newberry	1.25
12	Pete Holohan	1.00
13	Mike Lansford	1.00
14	Greg Bell	1.25
15	Jackie Slater	1.25
16	Dale Hatcher	1.00

1990 Rams Smokey

Full-bleed photos are on the fronts of this 12-card set, while the backs have a black-and-white photo of the player and his bio. The cards are unnumbered and sponsored by local fire departments. The cards measure 3-3/4" x 5-3/4".

		NM/M
Complete Set (12):		8.00
Common Player:		.75
1	Aaron Cox	.75
2	Henry Ellard	1.25
3	Jim Everett	1.50
4	Jerry Gray	1.00
5	Kevin Greene	1.50
6	Pete Holohan	.75
7	Mike Lansford	.75
8	Vince Newsome	.75
9	Doug Reed	.75
10	Jackie Slater	1.00
11	Fred Strickland	.75
12	Mike Wilcher	.75

1992 Rams Carl's Jr.

The 21-card set is anchored on the front with a photo, with the Rams' helmet in the lower left, player's name, position and number in the lower center and "Drug abuse is life abuse" in the bottom right. The card backs include a photo of the player in the upper left, with his name, position, number and bio printed beneath it. A safety message is printed to the right of the photo, with the card number printed inside a black box in the upper right. The player's stats and highlights are listed on the right side, along with Carl's Jr.'s logo and the other sponsors' logos. Reportedly, 80,000 sets were distributed.

		NM/M
Complete Set (21):		10.00
Common Player:		.60
1	Carl Karcher (Founder)	.60
2	Happy Star (Carl's Jr. symbol)	.75
3	Tony Zendejas	.60
4	Henry Ellard	1.25
5	Jackie Slater	.75
6	Bern Brostek	.60
7	Cleveland Gary	.75
8	Larry Kelm	.60
9	Roman Phifer	.75
10	Jim Everett	1.25
11	Anthony Newman	.60
12	Steve Israel	.60
13	Marc Boutte	.75
14	Darryl Henley	.60
15	Michael Stewart	.60
16	Flipper Anderson	1.25
17	Kevin Greene	1.25
18	Sean Gilbert	1.25
NNOO	Skippy (Be Drug Free)	.75
NNOO	Spike (Be Drug Free)	.75
NNOO	Wise Owl Mike (Be Drug Free)	.75

1994 Rams L.A. Times

Measuring 5-1/2" x 8-1/2", the 32-sheet set was printed by the Los Angeles Times on semi-gloss stock. Showcased on the fronts is a large color photo, with the player's last name printed along the right side. The "Collector Series" logo is located in the upper left, while the L.A. Rams' logo and helmet are printed inside a yellow stripe at the bottom of the card front. The sheets are numbered "of 32" on the fronts. The backs have the player's name in a stripe at the top, with his jersey number, position, bio, headshot, career highlights and 1994 Rams' schedule following underneath. The sheets were included in weekend editions of the L.A. Times.

		NM/M
Complete Set (32):		10.00
Common Player:		.40
1	Toby Wright	.40
2	Tim Lester	.40
3	Shane Conlan	.50
4	Troy Drayton	.50
5	Fred Stokes	.40
6	Jerome Bettis	1.25
7	Jimmie Jones	.40
8	Henry Rolling	.40
9	Anthony Newman	.40
10	Flipper Anderson	.75
11	Steve Israel	.40
12	Johnny Bailey	.40
13	Jackie Slater	.50
14	Chris Chandler	.50
15	Sean Landeta	.40
16	Bern Brostek	.40
17	Roman Phifer	.40
18	Robert Young	.50
19	Leo Goeas	.40
20	Chris Miller	.75
21	Darryl Ashmore	.40
22	Joe Kelly	.40
23	Wayne Gandy	.50
24	Tony Zendejas	.40
25	Tom Newberry	.40
26	David Lang	.40
27	Sean Gilbert	.50
28	Chris Martin	.40
29	Thomas Homco	.40
30	Chuck Knox (CO)	.50
31	Todd Lyght	.50
32	Jerome Bettis, Sean Gilbert	.75

1995 Rams Upper Deck McDonald's

Sold in five-card packs for 79 cents at St. Louis area McDonald's restaurants, the 26-card set featured the Upper Deck logo in the upper left and McDonald's logo in top right. The player's name is in the lower left, with the team name and his position at the bottom right. Printed along the left side of the photo is "Special Edition" and "Premiere Season." The backs, prefixed with "McD," have the player's name, team, position and bio at the top above the photo, while the player's stats are printed beneath the photo. Proceeds from the sales of this set went to the Ronald McDonald Children's Charities.

		NM/M
Complete Set (26):		8.00
Common Player:		.25
1	Johnny Bailey	.25
2	Jerome Bettis	.50
3	Isaac Bruce	2.00
4	Kevin Carter	.50
5	Shane Conlan	.25
6	Troy Drayton	.35
7	Wayne Gandy	.35
8	Sean Gilbert	.35
9	Jessie Hester	.25
10	Bern Brostek	.25
11	Jimmie Jones	.25
12	Todd Kinchen	.35
13	Sean Landeta	.25
14	Thomas Homco	.25
15	Todd Lyght	.25
16	Keith Lyle	.25
17	Chris Miller	.35
18	Toby Wright	.25
19	Anthony Parker	.25
20	Roman Phifer	.25
21	Leonard Russell	.25
22	Jackie Slater	.35
23	Fred Stokes	.25
24	Alexander Wright	.25
25	Robert Young	.35
NNO	Checklist Card	.35

1996 Ravens Score Board/Exxon

Score Board produced this set which was distributed at Baltimore-area Exxon stations. The nine-card set was sold in four-card packs (three players and a checklist) and carried a "BR" prefix.

		NM/M
Complete Set (9):		2.50
Common Player:		.25
1	Vinny Testaverde	.40
2	Eric Zeier	.40
3	Earnest Byner	.25
4	Derrick Alexander	.75
5	Michael Jackson	.40
6	Jonathan Ogden	.25
7	Ray Lewis	.25
8	Eric Turner	.25
9	Ravens Checklist	.25

1939 Redskins Matchbooks

Measuring 1-1/2" x 4-1/2" when folded out, the 20 matchbooks have a black-and-white headshot of the player at the top, with his facsimile autograph, position, college and bio listed underneath. The backside says, "This is one of 20 autographed pictures of the Washington Redskins. Compliments of The Ross Jewelry Co." The inside of the matchbook has the official 1939 Redskins schedule. The matchbooks are unnumbered.

		NM/M
Complete Set (20):		525.00
Common Matchbook:		10.00
1	Jim Barber (SP)	125.00
2	Sammy Baugh	65.00
3	Hal Bradley	10.00
4	Vic Carroll	10.00
5	Bud Erickson	10.00
6	Andy Farkas	12.00
7	Frank Filchock	12.00
8	Ray Flaherty (CO)	18.00
9	Don Irwin	10.00
10	Ed Justice	10.00
11	Jim Karcher	10.00
12	Max Krause	10.00
13	Charley Malone	10.00
14	Bob Masterson	10.00
15	Wayne Millner	20.00
16	Mickey Parks	10.00
17	Ernie Pinckert	12.00
18	Steve Slivinski (SP)	125.00
19	Clem Stralka	10.00
20	Jay Turner	10.00

1940 Redskins Matchbooks

This 20-matchbook set is very similar in design to the 1939 set. The 1940 set has a headshot of the player, a facsimile autograph, his position, college and bio showcased on the front. The backside of the matchbook states, "This is one of 20 autographed pictures of the Washington Redskins. Compliments of Ross Jewelry Co." The inside of the matchbooks have the official 1940 Redskins' schedule. Prices listed here are for matchbooks missing the matches, but with the strikers intact.

		NM/M
Complete Set (20):		225.00
Common Player:		10.00
1	Jim Barber	10.00
2	Sammy Baugh	45.00
3	Vic Carroll	10.00
4	Glen Edwards	25.00
5	Andy Farkas	12.00
6	Dick Farman	10.00
7	Bob Hoffman	10.00
8	Don Irwin	10.00
9	Charley Malone	10.00
10	Bob Masterson	10.00
11	Wayne Millner	20.00
12	Mickey Parks	10.00
13	Ernie Pinckert	12.00
14	Bo Russell	10.00
15	Clyde Shugart	10.00
16	Steve Slivinski	10.00
17	Clem Stralka	10.00
18	Dick Todd	12.00
19	Bill Young	10.00
20	Roy Zimmerman	10.00

1941 Redskins Matchbooks

Measuring 1-1/2" x 4-1/2" when folded out, the 20 matchbooks have a headshot of the player at the top of the front, with his facsimile autograph, position, college and bio listed beneath. The backside of the cover states, "This is one of 20 autographed pictures of the Washington Redskins. Compliments of Home Laundry." The phone number Atlantic 2400 is also included. The inside features the 1941 official Redskins' schedule.

		NM/M
Complete Set (20):		195.00
Common Player:		8.00
1	Ki Aldrich	10.00
2	Jim Barber	8.00
3	Sammy Baugh	40.00
4	Vic Carroll	8.00
5	Fred Davis	8.00
6	Andy Farkas	10.00
7	Dick Farman	8.00
8	Frank Filchock	10.00
9	Ray Flaherty (CO)	12.00
10	Bob Masterson	8.00
11	Bob McChesney	8.00
12	Wayne Millner	15.00
13	Wilbur Moore	10.00
14	Bob Seymour	8.00
15	Clyde Shugart	8.00
16	Clem Stralka	8.00
17	Robert Titchenal	8.00
18	Dick Todd	10.00
19	Bill Young	8.00
20	Roy Zimmerman	8.00

1942 Redskins Matchbooks

Measuring 1-1/2" x 4-1/2" when folded out, the 20 matchbooks follow the same design as the previous sets. A player headshot is showcased on the front, with his facsimile signature, position, college and bio printed beneath. The back of the cover states, "This is one of 20 autographed pictures of the Washington Redskins. Compliments of Home Laundry Atlantic 2400." The inside of the covers have the official 1942 Redskins' schedule, plus an ad for Home Laundry.

		NM/M
Complete Set (20):		195.00
Common Player:		8.00
1	Ki Aldrich	10.00
2	Sammy Baugh	45.00
3	Joe Beinor	8.00
4	Vic Carroll	8.00
5	Ed Cifers	8.00
6	Fred Davis	8.00
7	Glen Edwards	16.00
8	Andy Farkas	10.00
9	Dick Farman	8.00
10	Ray Flaherty (CO)	12.00
11	Al Krueger	8.00
12	Bob Masterson	8.00
13	Bob McChesney	8.00
14	Wilbur Moore	10.00
15	Bob Seymour	8.00
16	Clyde Shugart	8.00
17	Clem Stralka	8.00
18	Dick Todd	10.00
19	Willie Wilkin	8.00
20	Bill Young	8.00

1951-52 Redskins Matchbooks

Measuring 1-1/2" x 4-1/2" when folded out, the 20 matchbooks have the player headshot on the front, followed by a facsimile signature, position, college and bio. The backs state, "This is one of 20 autographed pictures of the Washington Redskins. Compliments of Jack Blank, President, Arcade Pontiac Co. ADams 8500." The outside of the matchbooks have the Redskins' logo on black and gold. An advertisement for Arcade Pontiac is printed on the back, also in color. The matchbooks are unnumbered.

		NM/M
Complete Set (25):		225.00
Common Player:		8.00
1	John Badaczewski	8.00
2A	Herman Ball Head Coach (CO)	8.00
2B	Herman Ball Assistant Coach (CO)	8.00
3	Sammy Baugh	40.00
4	Ed Berrang (1951)	10.00
5	Dan Brown (1951)	10.00
6	Al DeMao	8.00
7	Harry Dowda (1952)	10.00
8	Chuck Drazenovich	8.00
9	Bill Dudley (1951)	15.00
10	Harry Gilmer	12.00
11	Robert Goode (1951)	10.00
12	Leon Heath (1952)	10.00
13	Charlie Justice (1952)	15.00
14	Lou Karras	8.00
15	Eddie LeBaron (1952)	12.00
16	Paul Lipscomb	8.00
17	Laurie Niemi	8.00
18	John Papit (1952)	10.00
19	James Peebles (1951)	10.00
20	Ed Quirk	8.00
21	Jim Ricca (1952)	10.00
22	James Staton (1951)	10.00
23	Hugh Taylor	10.00
24	Joe Tereshinski	8.00
25	Dick Todd (CO) (1952)	10.00

1958-59 Redskins Matchbooks

Measuring 1-1/2" x 4-1/2" when folded out, the 20 matchbooks went with a totally different design than in years past. This set features a cutout of a player headshot printed below the Redskins' logo and "Famous Redskins." The years he played with the Redskins are listed to the left of the headshot. The back of the cover has an ad for First Federal Savings. The inside includes the player's name and bio, along with an ad for First Federal Savings. The matchbooks, which are unnumbered, are printed on gray cardboard.

		NM/M
Complete Set (20):		195.00
Common Player:		8.00
1	Steve Bagarus (58)	8.00
2	Cliff Battles (58)	15.00
3	Sammy Baugh (58)	40.00
4	Gene Brito (58)	10.00
5	Jim Castiglia (58)	8.00
6	Al DeMao (58)	8.00
7	Chuck Drazenovich (59)	10.00
8	Bill Dudley (59)	18.00
9	Al Fiorentino (59)	8.00
10	Don Irwin (59)	8.00
11	Eddie LeBaron (58)	10.00
12	Wayne Millner (58)	12.00
13	Wilbur Moore (58)	10.00
14	Jim Schrader (59)	8.00
15	Riley Smith (59)	8.00
16	Mike Sommer (59)	8.00
17	Joe Tereshinski (58)	8.00
18	Dick Todd (59)	10.00
19	Willie Wilkin (59)	8.00
20	Casimir Witucki	8.00

1960-61 Redskins Matchbooks

Measuring 1-1/2" x 4-1/2" when folded out, the 20 matchbooks are very similar in design to the 1958-59 set except this 1960-61 set is printed on off-white cardboard. The front has a headshot of the player, along with the Redskins' logo and "Famous Redskins." The player's bio is printed on the back, along with "This is one of twenty famous Redskins presented for you by your 1st Federal Savings and Loan Association of Washington, Bethesda Branch." The matchbooks are not numbered.

		NM/M
Complete Set (20):		175.00
Common Player:		8.00
1	Bill Anderson (61)	10.00
2	Don Bosseler (60)	10.00
3	Glen Edwards (60)	15.00
4	Ralph Guglielmi (61)	10.00
5	Bill Hartman (60)	8.00
6	Norbert Hecker (61)	8.00
7	Dick James (61)	10.00
8	Charlie Justice (60)	15.00
9	Ray Krause (61)	8.00
10	Ray Lemek (61)	8.00
11	Tommy Mont (60)	8.00
12	John Olszewski (61)	10.00
13	John Paluck (61)	8.00
14	Jim Peebles (60)	8.00
15	Bo Russell (60)	8.00
16	Jim Schrader (61)	8.00
17	Louis Stephens (61)	8.00
18	Ed Sutton (60)	8.00
19	Bob Toneff (60)	10.00
20	Lavern Torgeson (60)	10.00

1960 Redskins Jay Publishing

Measuring 5" x 7", the 12-card set is anchored by a black-and-white posed photo on the front. The cards are unnumbered and blank-backed. Originally, the cards were sold for 25 cents in 12-photo packs.

		NM/M
Complete Set (12):		50.00
Common Player:		5.00
1	Sam Baker	6.00
2	Don Bosseler	6.00
3	Gene Brito	5.00
4	Johnny Carson	5.00
5	Chuck Drazenovich	5.00
6	Ralph Guglielmi	6.00
7	Dick James	6.00
8	Eddie LeBaron	7.50
9	Jim Podoley	5.00
10	Jim Schrader	5.00
11	Ed Sutton	5.00
12	Albert Zagers	5.00

1969 Redskins High's Dairy

Measuring 8" x 10", the eight-card set includes Alex Fournier artwork on the front. The player's facsimile signature is printed near the bottom of the artwork. On the left side of the unnumbered card backs is the player's name, bio and stats, while on the right side is data on Fournier. The portraits were available two ways - they could be purchased at High's Dairy Stores or consumers could purchase two half gallons of milk and recieve a free portrait.

NM/M
Complete Set (8): 100.00
Common Player: 6.00
1 Chris Hanburger 10.00
2 Len Hauss 8.00
3 Sam Huff 15.00
4 Sonny Jurgensen 25.00
5 Carl Kammerer 6.00
6 Brig Owens 6.00
7 Pat Richter 8.00
8 Charley Taylor 20.00

1972 Redskins Caricature

Dick Shuman and Compu-Set, Inc. produced this 15-card set. The 8" x 10" cards feature a caricature of a Washington Redskin player. The cards are unnumbered and blank-backed.

NM/M
Complete Set (16): 130.00
Common Player: 8.00
1 Mike Bass 10.00
2 Verlon Biggs 8.00
3 Mike Bragg 8.00
4 Speedy Duncan 10.00
5 Pat Fischer 10.00
6 Chris Hanburger 10.00
7 Curt Knight 8.00
8 Ron McDole 8.00
9 Brig Owens 8.00
10 Jack Pardee 10.00
11 Richie Petibon 10.00
12 Myron Pottios 8.00
13 Manny Sistrunk 8.00
14 Diron Talbert 8.00
15 Ted Vactor 8.00
16 Jack Pardee, Mike Bass, Manny Sistrunk, Chris Hanburger Cover Card 10.00

1981 Redskins Frito-Lay Schedules

Measuring 3-1/2" x 7-1/2", the 30 schedules are anchored by a color photo on the inside. Included on the collectibles are the 1981 Redskins' schedule, player photo and his name and bio, along with sponsor logos. The schedules are unnumbered.

NM/M
Complete Set (30): 22.00
Common Player: .40
1 Coy Bacon .60
2 Perry Brooks .40
3 Dave Butz .60
4 Rickey Claitt .40
5 Monte Coleman .60
6 Mike Connell .40
7 Brad Dusek .60
8 Ike Forte .40
9 Clarence Harmon .40
10 Terry Hermeling .40
11 Wilbur Jackson .40
12 Mike Kruczek .40
13 Bob Kuziel .40
14 Joe Lavender .60
15 Karl Lorch .40
16 LeCharls McDaniel .40
17 Rich Milot .40
18 Art Monk 2.25
19 Mark Moseley .70
20 Mark Murphy .60
21 Mike Nelms .40
22 Neal Olkewicz .40
23 Lemar Parrish .60
24 Tony Peters .40
25 Ron Saul .40
26 George Starke .40
27 Joe Theismann 1.50
28 Ricky Thompson .40
29 Don Warren .60
30 Jeris White .40

1982 Redskins Frito-Lay Schedules

Measuring 3-1/2" x 7-1/2", the 15 schedule set boasts a color photo of the player on the inside, with "Redskins' '82 Schedule" printed on another panel. The player's name and bio are also included on the schedules.

NM/M
Complete Set (15): 15.00
Common Player: .50
1 Dave Butz .75
2 Monte Coleman .75
3 Brad Dusek .50
4 Joe Lavender .75
5 Art Monk 2.00
6 Mark Moseley 1.00
7 Mark Murphy .75
8 Mike Nelms .50
9 Neal Olkewicz .50
10 Tony Peters .50
11 John Riggins 3.00
12 George Starke .50
13 Joe Theismann 2.00
14 Don Warren .75
15 Joe Washington 1.00

1982 Redskins Police

Measuring 2-5/8" x 4-1/8", the 15-card set includes a photo of the player on the front, with the Redskins' helmet on the lower left. On the bottom right are the player's number, name, position and team. The backs have a boxed-in "Redskins/PACT Tips." The Frito-Lay and PACT logos appear at the bottom corners. The cards are numbered.

NM/M
Complete Set (15): 10.00
Common Player: .50
1 Dave Butz .75
2 Art Monk 2.50
3 Mark Murphy .50
4 Monte Coleman .75
5 Mark Moseley .75
6 George Starke .50
7 Perry Brooks .50
8 Joe Washington .75
9 Don Warren .75
10 Joe Lavender .50
11 Joe Theismann 2.00
12 Tony Peters .50
13 Neal Olkewicz .50
14 Mike Nelms .50
15 John Riggins 2.00

1983 Redskins Frito-Lay Schedules

Measuring 2-1/2" x 3-1/2", the 15-schedule set showcases an action photo, along with the player's name and bio. The schedules are unnumbered.

NM/M
Complete Set (15): 15.00
Common Player: .50
1 Charlie Brown .75
2 Dave Butz .75
3 The Hogs .75
4 Dexter Manley .75
5 Rich Milot .50
6 Art Monk 1.50
7 Mark Moseley .75
8 Mark Murphy .50
9 Mike Nelms .50
10 Neal Olkewicz .50
11 Tony Peters .50
12 John Riggins 2.00
13 Joe Theismann 2.00
14 Joe Washington .75
15 Jeris White .50

1983 Redskins Police

Measuring 2-5/8" x 4-1/8", the 16-card set was handed out one per week by police officers. The card fronts are anchored by a large photo, with the player's number, position, name and bio beneath it. The Redskins' helmet is in the lower left corner, with "Washington Redskins, Super Bowl XVII Champions" printed at the bottom right. The backs, numbered "of 16," have a boxed-in "Redskins PACT Tips" and the player's bio and highlights. The Frito-Lay and PACT logos are printed in the lower left and right corners, respectively. Jeris White's card is tough to locate, as his card was never handed out because he held out during the season.

NM/M
Complete Set (16): 10.00
Common Player: .50
1 Joe Washington 1.00
2 The Hogs (Offensive Line) .75
3 Mark Moseley 1.00
4 Monte Coleman .50
5 Mike Nelms .50
6 Neal Olkewicz .50
7 Joe Theismann 3.00
8 Charlie Brown .75
9 Dave Butz .75
10 Jeris White (SP) 1.50
11 Mark Murphy .50
12 Dexter Manley .75
13 Art Monk 3.00
14 Rich Milot .50
15 Vernon Dean .50
16 John Riggins 2.00

1984 Redskins Frito-Lay Schedules

Measuring 3-1/2" x 7-1/2", the 15 schedules boast a color photo of the player, along with his name and bio. The schedules are unnumbered.

NM/M
Complete Set (15): 15.00
Common Player: .50
1 Charlie Brown .75
2 Dave Butz .75
3 Ken Coffey .50
4 Clint Didier .50
5 Darryl Grant .50
6 Darrell Green 1.00
7 Jeff Hayes .50
8 The Hogs .75
9 Rich Milot .50
10 Art Monk 1.50
11 Mark Murphy .50
12 John Riggins 1.50
13 Joe Theismann 1.50
14 Don Warren .75
15 Joe Washington .75

1984 Redskins Police

Measuring 2-5/8" x 4-1/8", the 16-card set showcases a color photo on the front, with the player's name, number and position printed beneath the photo. The player's facsimile signature and "NFC Champion Redskins" is printed in the lower right. The Redskins' helmet is located in the lower left. The card backs, numbered "of 16," have the "Redskins/PACT Tip" at the top, while the player's name, number, bio and highlights are printed below. The Frito-Lay and PACT logos are printed in the lower left and right, respectively.

NM/M
Complete Set (16): 8.00
Common Player: .35
1 John Riggins 1.25
2 Darryl Grant .35
3 Art Monk 1.50
4 Neal Olkewicz .35
5 The Hogs .50
6 Jeff Hayes .35
7 Joe Theismann 1.25
8 Clint Didier .35
9 Mark Murphy .35
10 Don Warren .50
11 Darrell Green 1.00
12 Dave Butz .50
13 Ken Coffey .35
14 Rich Milot .35
15 Charlie Brown .50
16 Joe Washington .50

1985 Redskins Frito-Lay Schedules

Measuring 3-1/2" x 7-1/2", the 16 schedules showcase a photo of a legendary Washington Redskins' player. The schedules are unnumbered.

NM/M
Complete Set (16): 15.00
Common Player: .50
1 Cliff Battles .75
2 Sammy Baugh 1.50
3 Larry Brown .75
4 Bill Dudley .75
5 Turk Edwards .75
6 Pat Fischer .50
7 Chris Hanburger .50
8 Len Hauss .50
9 Ken Houston .75
10 Sam Huff 1.00
11 Sonny Jurgenson 1.00
12 Billy Kilmer .50
13 Wayne Millner .50
14 Bobby Mitchell .75
15 Brig Owens .50
16 Charley Taylor 1.00

1985 Redskins Police

Measuring 2-5/8" x 4-1/8", the 16-card set has the Washington Redskins' logo at the top of the card front, with the player photo in the center. Beneath the photo are the player's number, position and name. The backs, numbered "of 16," have "Redskins/PACT Tips" at the top. Printed in the center of the back are the player's name, number, position, bio and career highlights. The Frito-Lay and PACT logos are located in the lower left and right, respectively.

NM/M
Complete Set (16): 5.00
Common Player: .35
1 Darrell Green .75
2 Clint Didier .35
3 Neal Olkewicz .35
4 Darryl Grant .35
5 Joe Jacoby .50
6 Vernon Dean .35
7 Joe Theismann 1.00
8 Mel Kaufman .35
9 Calvin Muhammad .35
10 Dexter Manley .50
11 John Riggins 1.00
12 Mark May .50
13 Dave Butz .35
14 Art Monk 1.25
15 Russ Grimm .50
16 Charles Mann .50

1986 Redskins Frito-Lay Schedules

These 16 schedules feature the Redskins' 50th Anniversary logo on the front and Frito-Lay's logos on the back. When opened, the left panel contains the preseason and postseason schedules, the center panel has a player photo and the right panel features the regular season schedule. The other panel has basic player information. The schedules are unnumbered.

NM/M
Complete Set (16): 20.00
Common Player: 1.00
1 Cliff Battles 1.50
2 Sammy Baugh 2.00
3 Larry Brown 1.00
4 Bill Dudley 1.50
5 Turk Edwards 1.00
6 Pat Fischer 1.00
7 Chris Hanburger 1.00
8 Len Hauss 1.00
9 Sam Huff 2.00
10 Ken Houston 1.50
11 Sonny Jurgenson 2.00
12 Billy Kilmer 1.50
13 Wayne Millner 1.50
14 Bobby Mitchell 2.00
15 Brig Owens 1.00
16 Charley Taylor 2.00

1986 Redskins Police

Measuring 2-5/8" x 4-1/8", the 16-card set has a Washington Redskins' pennant in the upper left corner of the front. Inside the pennant is a facsimile signature of the player. His number, name and position is printed to the right of the pennant. The photo fills up the bottom portion of the card front. The backs, numbered "of 16," have the player's name inside a pennant at the top, with his number, position, bio and career highlights printed beneath it. Quick quiz and crime prevention tips are also included on the back. The Frito-Lay, PACT and WMAL radio logos are printed at the bottom.

NM/M
Complete Set (16): 5.00
Common Player: .35
1 Darrell Green .75
2 Joe Jacoby .50
3 Charles Mann .50
4 Jay Schroeder .50
5 Raphel Cherry .35
6 Russ Grimm .50
7 Mel Kaufman .35
8 Gary Clark 1.25
9 Vernon Dean .35
10 Mark May .50
11 Dave Butz .50
12 Jeff Bostic .35
13 Dean Hamel .35
14 Dexter Manley .50
15 George Rogers .50
16 Art Monk 1.00

1987 Redskins Frito-Lay Schedules

Measuring 3-1/2" x 7-1/2", the 16 schedule set includes an action photo of the player. The schedules are unnumbered.

NM/M
Complete Set (16): 15.00
Common Player: .50
1 Jeff Bostic .75
2 Kelvin Bryant .75
3 Dave Butz .75
4 Gary Clark 1.00
5 Steve Cox .50
6 Clint Didier .50
7 Darryl Grant .50
8 Darrell Green .75
9 Joe Jacoby .75
10 Dexter Manley .75
11 Charles Mann .75
12 Mark May .75
13 Art Monk 1.00
14 Jay Schroeder .75
15 Alvin Walton .50
16 Don Warren .75

1987 Redskins Police

Measuring 2-5/8" x 4-1/8", the 16-card set has the Washington Redskins' logo at the top, with the player photo anchoring the middle. The player's name is printed at the bottom of the card front. The backs, numbered "Week X of 16," have the player's number inside a football in the upper left. The player's name, position, bio and career highlights are also listed on the back. "Did you know?" and a tip from McGruff the Crime Dog round out the back, along with Frito-Lay and PACT logos at the bottom right.

NM/M
Complete Set (16): 5.00
Common Player: .30
1 Joe Jacoby .40
2 Gary Clark .75
3 Dexter Manley .40
4 Darrell Green .40
5 Alvin Walton .30
6 Clint Didier .30
7 Art Monk 1.00
8 Darryl Grant .30
9 Kelvin Bryant .40
10 Jay Schroeder .40
11 Don Warren .40
12 Steve Cox .30
13 Mark May .40
14 Jeff Bostic .40
15 Charles Mann .40
16 Dave Butz .40

1988 Redskins Frito-Lay Schedules

Measuring 3-1/2" x 7-1/2", the 16 schedules boast an action photo of a player, with his name and bio. A photo of the Super Bowl trophy is showcased on these schedules, which are unnumbered.

NM/M
Complete Set (16): 15.00
Common Player: .50
1 Jeff Bostic .75
2 Dave Butz .75
3 Gary Clark 1.00
4 Brian Davis .50
5 Joe Jacoby .75
6 Markus Koch .50
7 Charles Mann .75
8 Wilbur Marshall .75
9 Mark May .75
10 Raleigh McKenzie .50
11 Art Monk 1.00
12 Ricky Sanders .75
13 Alvin Walton .50
14 Don Warren .75
15 Barry Wilburn .50
16 Doug Williams 1.00

1988 Redskins Police

Measuring 2-5/8" x 4-1/8", the 16-card set has the Washington Redskins' logo (with the Vince Lombardi Super Bowl Trophy printed where the "i" in Redskins would appear) located in the upper left. The player's number and name are printed in the upper right. A color photo covers the remaining portion of the card front. The backs, numbered with a "Week X," have the player's name and number at the top, followed by his bio, career highlights and a safety tip. The logos printed at the bottom from left to right are Mobil, PACT and Jello.

NM/M
Complete Set (16): 5.00
Common Player: .30
1 Jeff Bostic .40
2 Dave Butz .40
3 Gary Clark .75
4 Brian Davis .30
5 Joe Jacoby .40
6 Markus Koch .30
7 Charles Mann .40
8 Wilber Marshall .40
9 Mark May .40
10 Raleigh McKenzie .30
11 Art Monk 1.00
12 Ricky Sanders .75
13 Alvin Walton .30
14 Don Warren .40
15 Barry Wilburn .30
16 Doug Williams .75

1989 Redskins Mobil Schedules

Measuring 3-1/2" x 7-1/2", the 16 schedules showcase a color player photo, along with the 1989 schedule. These schedules are unnumbered.

NM/M
Complete Set (16): 10.00
Common Player: .40
1 Ravin Caldwell .40
2 Gary Clark 1.00
3 Monte Coleman .60
4 Brian Davis .40
5 Joe Jacoby .60
6 Jim Lachey .60
7 Chip Lohmiller .60
8 Charles Mann .60
9 Wilbur Marshall .60
10 Mark May .60
11 Raleigh McKenzie .40
12 Art Monk 1.00
13 Mark Rypien .60
14 Ricky Sanders .60
15 Don Warren .60
16 Doug Williams .75

1989 Redskins Police

Measuring 2-5/8" x 4-1/8", the 16-card set has "Washington" in a stripe at the top of the card front, with "Redskins" printed beneath it. The player photo has the player's name and number inside a stripe near the bottom. The unnumbered card backs have the player's number and name at the top, along with his bio, career highlights, safety tip and "Did you know?" The Mobil, PACT and Fox-TV 5 logos are printed at the bottom of the card backs.

NM/M
Complete Set (16): 5.00
Common Player: .30
11 Mark Rypien .60
17 Doug Williams .60
21 Earnest Byner .40
22 Jamie Morris .30
28 Darrell Green .40
34 Brian Davis .30
37 Gerald Riggs .40
50 Ravin Caldwell .30
52 Neal Olkewicz .30
58 Wilber Marshall .40
73 Mark May .40
74 Markus Koch .30
81 Art Monk 1.00
83 Ricky Sanders .60
84 Gary Clark .75
85 Don Warren .40

1990 Redskins Mobil Schedules

Measuring 3-1/2" x 7-1/2", the 16 pocket schedules boast a color action photo of the player. The schedules are unnumbered.

NM/M
Complete Set (16): 10.00
Common Player: .40
1 Jeff Bostic .60
2 Earnest Byner .60
3 Gary Clark .75
4 Darryl Grant .40
5 Darrell Green .60
6 Jim Lachey .60
7 Chip Lohmiller .60
8 Charles Mann .60
9 Wilbur Marshall .60
10 Ralf Mojsiejenko .40
11 Art Monk 1.00
12 Gerald Riggs .60
13 Mark Rypien .60
14 Ricky Sanders .60
15 Alvin Walton .40
16 Don Warren .60

1990 Redskins Police

Measuring 3-1/2" x 7-1/2", the 16-card set includes a Washington Redskins' logo at the top, with the player's name and number at the bottom of the card front. The unnumbered card backs have the player's name, number, bio, career highlights, safety tip and "Did you know?" Printed at the bottom of the card backs are the Mobil, PACT and Fox-TV 5 logos.

NM/M
Complete Set (16): 5.00
Common Player: .25
1 Todd Bowles .25
2 Earnest Byner .35
3 Ravin Caldwell .25
4 Gary Clark .60
5 Darrell Green .35
6 Jimmie Johnson .25
7 Jim Lachey .35
8 Chip Lohmiller .35
9 Charles Mann .35
10 Greg Manusky .25
11 Wilber Marshall .35
12 Art Monk .75
13 Gerald Riggs .35
14 Mark Rypien .35
15 Alvin Walton .25
16 Don Warren .35

1991 Redskins Mobil Schedules

Measuring 2-1/2" x 3-1/2", the 16 pocket schedules boast a photo of the player on the front. The player's name and bio also are printed on the unnumbered schedule.

		NM/M
Complete Set (16):		10.00
Common Player:		.40
1	Earnest Byner	.60
2	Gary Clark	.75
3	Andre Collins	.60
4	Kurt Gouveia	.40
5	Darrell Green	.60
6	Jimmie Johnson	.40
7	Markus Koch	.40
8	Jim Lachey	.60
9	Chip Lohmiller	.40
10	Charles Mann	.60
11	Martin Mayhew	.40
12	Art Monk	1.00
13	Mark Rypien	.60
14	Mark Schlereth	.40
15	Ed Simmons	.40
16	Eric Williams	.40

1991 Redskins Police

Measuring 2-5/8" x 4-1/8", the 16-card set has "Washington" printed inside a gold stripe at the top, while "Redskins" is printed vertically along the left side. The player photo is to the right of "Redskins." The player's number is printed inside a circle at the bottom, with his name inside a black stripe at the bottom. The backs have the player's name, number, bio, career highlights, safety tip and "Did you know?" The logos printed on the bottom, from left to right, are Mobil, PACT and Fox-TV 5. The cards are unnumbered.

		NM/M
Complete Set (16):		5.00
Common Player:		.25
1	John Brandes	.25
2	Earnest Byner	.35
3	Gary Clark	.60
4	Andre Collins	.35
5	Darrell Green	.35
6	Joey Howard	.25
7	Tim Johnson	.25
8	Jim Lachey	.35
9	Chip Lohmiller	.25
10	Charles Mann	.35
11	Art Monk	.75
12	Mark Rypien	.35
13	Mark Schlereth	.25
14	Fred Stokes	.25
15	Don Warren	.35
16	Eric Williams	.25

1992 Redskins Mobil Schedules

Measuring 2-1/2" x 3-1/2", the 16 pocket schedules have a color action photo of the player, along with his name and bio. The schedules are unnumbered.

		NM/M
Complete Set (16):		10.00
Common Player:		.40
1	Gary Clark	.75
2	Brad Edwards	.40
3	Ricky Ervins	.75
4	Jumpy Geathers	.40
5	Darrell Green	.60
6	Joe Jacoby	.60
7	Tim Johnson	.40
8	Charles Mann	.60
9	Wilber Marshall	.60
10	Ron Middleton	.40
11	Brian Mitchell	.75
12	Art Monk	1.00
13	Jim Lachey	.60
14	Chip Lohmiller	.40
15	Mark Rypien	.60
16	Fred Stokes	.40

1992 Redskins Police

Measuring 2-1/2" x 4-1/8", the 16-card set has "Washington Redskins" printed in the upper right, with the Vince Lombardi Trophy in the upper left of the photo. The player's number is printed inside a circle on the lower left of the photo, while the player's name is printed inside the border at the bottom of the card front. The card backs, which are unnumbered, have the player's number, name, bio, career highlights and tip. The sponsor logos, from left to right, are Mobil, PACT and Fox-TV 5.

		NM/M
Complete Set (16):		5.00
Common Player:		.30
1	Jeff Bostic	.40
2	Earnest Byner	.40
3	Gary Clark	.60
4	Monte Coleman	.40
5	Andre Collins	.40
6	Danny Copeland	.30
7	Kurt Gouveia	.30
8	Darrell Green	.40
9	Jim Lachey	.40
10	Charles Mann	.40
11	Wilber Marshall	.40
12	Raleigh McKenzie	.30
13	Art Monk	1.00
14	Mark Rypien	.40
15	Mark Schlereth	.30
16	Eric Williams	.30

1993 Redskins Mobil Schedules

Measuring 2-1/2" x 3-1/2", the 16 pocket schedules have an action photo on the front, along with the player's name and bio. The schedules are unnumbered.

		NM/M
Complete Set (16):		10.00
Common Player:		.40
1	Todd Bowles	.40
2	Earnest Byner	.60
3	Monte Coleman	.60
4	Andre Collins	.60
5	Shane Collins	.40
6	Danny Copeland	.40
7	Kurt Gouveia	.40
8	Darrell Green	.60
9	A.J. Johnson	.40
10	Jim Lachey	.40
11	Ron Middleton	.40
12	Brian Mitchell	.75
13	Mark Rypien	.60
14	Ricky Sanders	.60
15	Mark Schlereth	.40
16	Ed Simmons	.40

1993 Redskins Police

Measuring 2-3/4" x 4-1/8", the 16-card set has "Washington Redskins" printed at the top, with a photo in the middle. The Redskins' helmet is in the lower left, with the player's name and number printed beneath the photo to the right of the helmet. The unnumbered card backs have the player's name, number, bio, career highlights and safety tip. The sponsor logos printed at the bottom, from left to right, are Mobil, PACT and Cellular One.

		NM/M
Complete Set (16):		5.00
Common Player:		.30
1	Ray Brown	.30
2	Andre Collins	.40
3	Brad Edwards	.30
4	Matt Elliott	.30
5	Ricky Ervins	.40
6	Darrell Green	.40
7	Desmond Howard	.60
8	Joe Jacoby	.40
9	Tim Johnson	.30
10	Jim Lachey	.40
11	Chip Lohmiller	.30
12	Charles Mann	.40
13	Raleigh McKenzie	.30
14	Brian Mitchell	.50
15	Terry Orr	.30
16	Mark Rypien	.40

1994 Redskins Mobil Schedules

Measuring 2-1/2" x 3-1/2", the 16 pocket schedules showcase an action photo of the player, along with his name and bio. The schedules are unnumbered.

		NM/M
Complete Set (16):		10.00
Common Player:		.40
1	Reggie Brooks	.60
2	Ray Brown	.40
3	Tom Carter	.60
4	Shane Collins	.40
5	Darrell Green	.60
6	Ken Harvey	.60
7	Lamont Hollinquest	.40
8	Desmond Howard	.60
9	Tim Johnson	.40
10	Jim Lachey	.60
11	Chip Lohmiller	.40
12	Chip Lohmiller	.60
13	Sterling Palmer	.40
14	Heath Shuler	1.50
15	Bobby Wilson	.40
16	Frank Wycheck	.40

1995 Redskins Program Sheets

Measuring 8" x 10", the eight sheets were inserted into Redskins' GameDay programs during the regular season. The sheets showcase stadium photographs taken during championship games. The sheets are unnumbered.

		NM/M
Complete Set (8):		20.00
Common Player:		3.00
1	Bears, 1937, 1943. (Wrigley Field)	3.00
2	Bears, 1940, 1942. (Griffith Stadium)	3.00
3	1945. (Cleveland Stadium)	3.00
4	Dolphins, S.B. VII. (L.A. Coliseum)	3.00
5	Dolphins, S.B. XVII. (Rose Bowl)	3.00
6	Raiders, S.B. XVIII. (Tampa Stadium)	3.00
7	S.B. XXII. (Jack Murphy Stadium)	3.00
8	Bills, S.B. XXVI. (H.H.H. Metrodome)	3.00

1996 Redskins Score Board/Exxon

This nine-card set was produced by Score Board and distributed by Washington D.C. area Exxon stations. The cards were sold in four-card packs, which contained three player cards and one checklist. They have a "WR" prefix.

		NM/M
Complete Set (9):		3.00
Common Player:		.25
1	Gus Frerotte	.75
2	Terry Allen	.50
3	Henry Ellard	.50
4	Michael Westbrook	1.00
5	Brian Mitchell	.25
6	Sean Gilbert	.25
7	Ken Harvey	.25
8	Darrell Green	.50
9	Redskins Checklist	.25

1993 Rice Council

Athletes from football, baseball, swimming, bobsledding and tennis are honored in this 10-card set produced by the USA Rice Council in Houston, Texas. Troy Aikman and Warren Moon are the two football players featured in the set. Showcased on the fronts are a color photo, player's name and USA Rice Council logo. The fronts are bordered in red or blue. The backs, which are numbered in the upper right corner, have the player's name, team and position, along with his bio. A recipe also is included on the back.

		NM/M
Complete Set (10):		10.00
Common Player:		.25
1	Steve Sax	.50
2	Troy Aikman	4.00
3	Roger Clemens	1.50
4	Zina Garrison	.75
5	Warren Moon	1.50
6	Summer Sanders	.75
7	Steve Sax	.50
8	Brian Shimer	.25
9	Food Guide Pyramid	.25
10	Ten Tips to Healthy Eating for Kids	.25

1976 Saga Discs

Cards from this set parallel the 1976 Crane Disk singles. Instead of having the Crane logo on the back they have the Saga logo. Cards from this set are much tougher to find than the Crane singles.

		NM/M
Complete Set (30):		750.00
Common Player:		9.00
1	Ken Anderson	9.00
2	Otis Armstrong	9.00
3	Steve Barkowski	9.00
4	Terry Bradshaw	9.00
5	John Brockington	9.00
6	Doug Buffone	9.00
7	Wally Chambers	9.00
8	Isaac Curtis	9.00
9	Chuck Foreman	9.00
10	Roman Gabriel	9.00
11	Mel Gray	9.00
12	Joe Greene	9.00
13	James Harris	9.00
14	Jim Hart	9.00
15	Billy Kilmer	9.00
16	Greg Landry	9.00
17	Ed Marinaro	9.00
18	Lawrence McCutcheon	9.00
19	Terry Metcalf	9.00
20	Lydell Mitchell	9.00
21	Jim Otis	9.00
22	Alan Page	9.00
23	Walter Payton	9.00
24	Greg Pruitt	9.00
25	Charlie Sanders	9.00
26	Ron Shanklin	9.00
27	Roger Staubach	9.00
28	Jan Stenerud	9.00
29	Charley Taylor	9.00
30	Roger Wehrli	9.00

1999 Sage

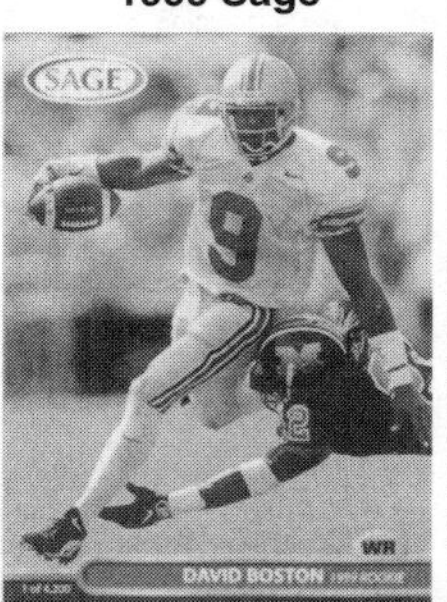

This was the premiere issue of Sage Football. It released a 50-card prospect set that included all of the top picks from 1999 except for Ricky Williams. Only 4,200 of each player was produced. Inserts included five different levels of autographs with Red, Bronze, Silver, Gold and Platinum.

		NM/M
Complete Set (50):		35.00
Common Player:		.25
Minor Stars:		.50
Pack (3):		14.00
Wax Box (12):		120.00
1	Rahim Abdullah	.25
2	Jerry Azumah	.25
3	Champ Bailey	1.00
4	D'Wayne Bates	.50
5	Michael Bishop	1.00
6	David Boston	1.50
7	Fernando Bryant	.25
8	Tony Bryant	.25
9	Chris Claiborne	.50
10	Mike Cloud	.50
11	Cecil Collins	.50
12	Tim Couch	4.00
13	Daunte Culpepper	2.50
14	Jared DeVries	.25
15	Adrian Dingle	.25
16	Antwan Edwards	.50
17	Troy Edwards	.75
18	Kevin Faulk	.75
19	Rufus French	.25
20	Martin Gramatica	.50
21	Torry Holt	1.50
22	Sedrick Irvin	.75
23	Edgerrin James	5.00
24	Jon Jansen	.25
25	Andy Katzenmoyer	.50
26	Jevon Kearse	1.50
27	Patrick Kerney	.25
28	Lamar King	.25
29	Shaun King	.75
30	Jim Kleinsasser	.50
31	Rob Konrad	.50
32	Brian Kuklick	.25
33	Chris McAlister	.50
34	Darnell McDonald	.50
35	Reggie McGrew	.25
36	Donovan McNabb	2.50
37	Cade McNown	.75
38	Dat Nguyen	.50
39	Solomon Page	.25
40	Mike Peterson	.25
41	Anthony Poindexter	.25
42	Peerless Price	.75
43	Michael Rucker	.25
44	L.J. Shelton	.25
45	Akili Smith	2.50
46	John Tait	.25
47	Fred Vinson	.25
48	Al Wilson	.25
49	Antoine Winfield	.25
50	Damien Woody	.25

A player's name in *italic* type indicates a rookie card.

1999 Sage Autographs

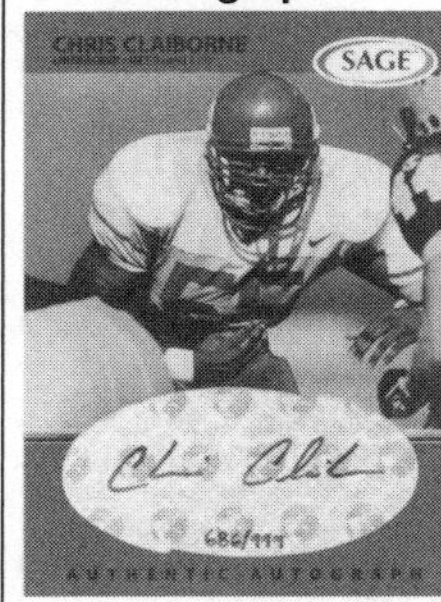

This is a 50-card Autograph insert that has red borders and a hologram on the front with the player's autograph and sequentially numbered. Most players signed a total of 999 except for ten players.

		NM/M
Complete Set (50):		550.00
Common Player:		4.00
Minor Stars:		8.00
1	Rahim Abdullah 999	4.00
2	Jerry Azumah 999	4.00
3	Champ Bailey 999	12.00
4	D'Wayne Bates 999	8.00
5	Michael Bishop 999	12.00
6	David Boston 869	20.00
7	Fernando Bryant 999	4.00
8	Tony Bryant 999	4.00
9	Chris Claiborne 999	8.00
10	Mike Cloud 434	15.00
11	Cecil Collins 999	15.00
12	Tim Couch 999	40.00
13	Daunte Culpepper 419	40.00
14	Jared DeVries 887	4.00
15	Adrian Dingle 999	4.00
16	Antwan Edwards 999	8.00
17	Troy Edwards 999	20.00
18	Kevin Faulk 999	12.00
19	Rufus French 999	4.00
20	Martin Gramatica 999	8.00
21	Torry Holt 999	20.00
22	Sedrick Irvin 999	12.00
23	Edgerrin James 859	50.00
24	Jon Jansen 999	4.00
25	Andy Katzenmoyer 209	35.00
26	Jevon Kearse 999	15.00
27	Patrick Kerney 879	4.00
28	Lamar King 999	4.00
29	Shaun King 999	25.00
30	Jim Kleinsasser 999	8.00
31	Rob Konrad 999	8.00
32	Brian Kuklick 999	4.00
33	Chris McAlister 999	8.00
34	Darnell McDonald 999	15.00
35	Reggie McGrew 999	4.00
36	Donovan McNabb 999	30.00
37	Cade McNown 209	25.00
38	Dat Nguyen 999	8.00
39	Solomon Page 999	4.00
40	Mike Peterson 999	4.00
41	Anthony Poindexter 999	4.00
42	Peerless Price 232	30.00
43	Michael Rucker 999	4.00
44	L.J. Shelton 999	4.00
45	Akili Smith 419	20.00
46	John Tait 999	4.00
47	Fred Vinson 999	4.00
48	Al Wilson 999	4.00
49	Antoine Winfield 999	4.00
50	Damien Woody 999	4.00

1999 Sage Autographs Bronze

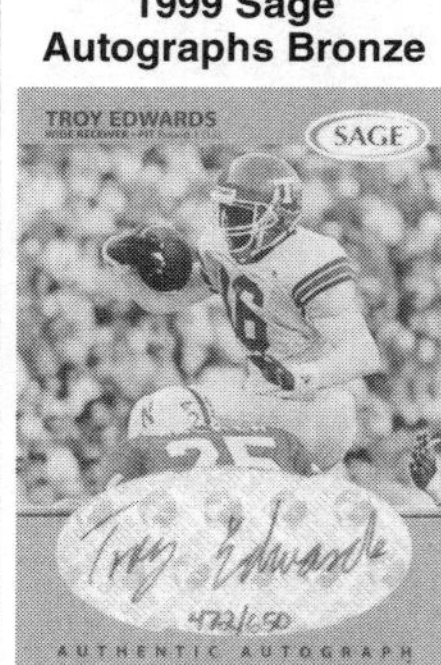

This insert is the same as the Red Autographs except for the borders are Bronze and the players only signed a total of 650. A few of the players signed less.

		NM/M
Common Player:		6.00
Minor Stars:		12.00
1	Rahim Abdullah 650	6.00
2	Jerry Azumah 650	6.00
3	Champ Bailey 650	15.00
4	D'Wayne Bates 650	12.00
5	Michael Bishop 650	15.00
6	David Boston 565	30.00
7	Fernando Bryant 650	6.00
8	Tony Bryant 650	6.00
9	Chris Claiborne 650	12.00
10	Mike Cloud 280	20.00
11	Cecil Collins 650	18.00
12	Tim Couch 650	45.00
13	Daunte Culpepper 285	45.00
14	Jared DeVries 575	6.00
15	Adrian Dingle 650	6.00
16	Antwan Edwards 650	12.00
17	Troy Edwards 650	20.00
18	Kevin Faulk 650	15.00
19	Rufus French 650	6.00
20	Martin Gramatica 650	12.00
21	Torry Holt 650	20.00
22	Sedrick Irvin 650	15.00
23	Edgerrin James 570	55.00
24	Jon Jansen 650	6.00
25	Andy Katzenmoyer 140	45.00
26	Jevon Kearse 650	20.00
27	Patrick Kerney 585	12.00
28	Lamar King 650	6.00
29	Shaun King 650	30.00
30	Jim Kleinsasser 650	12.00
31	Rob Konrad 650	12.00
32	Brian Kuklick 650	6.00
33	Chris McAlister 650	12.00
34	Darnell McDonald 650	15.00
35	Reggie McGrew 650	6.00
36	Donovan McNabb 650	30.00
37	Cade McNown 140	30.00
38	Dat Nguyen 650	6.00
39	Solomon Page 650	6.00
40	Mike Peterson 650	6.00
41	Anthony Poindexter 650	6.00
42	Peerless Price 150	35.00
43	Michael Rucker 650	6.00
44	L.J. Shelton 650	6.00
45	Akili Smith 285	25.00
46	John Tait 650	6.00
47	Fred Vinson 650	6.00
48	Al Wilson 650	6.00
49	Antoine Winfield 650	6.00
50	Damien Woody 650	6.00

1999 Sage Autographs Gold

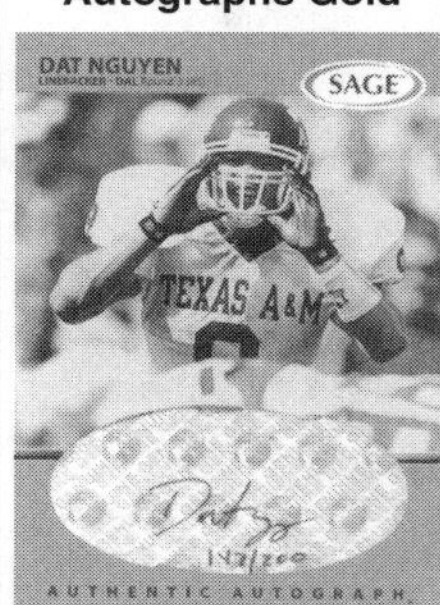

This insert is the same as the Red set except for the borders are in gold and most players in the set signed only 200.

		NM/M
Common Player:		8.00
Minor Stars:		20.00
1	Rahim Abdullah 200	8.00
2	Jerry Azumah 200	8.00
3	Champ Bailey 200	25.00
4	D'Wayne Bates 200	20.00
5	Michael Bishop 200	25.00
6	David Boston 174	45.00
7	Fernando Bryant 200	8.00
8	Tony Bryant 200	8.00
9	Chris Claiborne 200	20.00
10	Mike Cloud 88	35.00
11	Cecil Collins 200	30.00
12	Tim Couch 200	60.00
13	Daunte Culpepper 90	75.00
14	Jared DeVries 185	20.00
15	Adrian Dingle 200	8.00
16	Antwan Edwards 200	20.00
17	Troy Edwards 200	35.00
18	Kevin Faulk 200	25.00
19	Rufus French 200	8.00
20	Martin Gramatica 200	20.00
21	Torry Holt 200	35.00
22	Sedrick Irvin 200	25.00
23	Edgerrin James 175	75.00
24	Jon Jansen 200	8.00
25	Andy Katzenmoyer 45	60.00
26	Jevon Kearse 200	30.00
27	Patrick Kerney 175	8.00
28	Lamar King 200	8.00
29	Shaun King 200	35.00
30	Jim Kleinsasser 200	20.00
31	Rob Konrad 200	20.00
32	Brian Kuklick 200	8.00
33	Chris McAlister 200	20.00
34	Darnell McDonald 200	25.00
35	Reggie McGrew 200	8.00
36	Donovan McNabb 200	50.00
37	Cade McNown 45	45.00
38	Dat Nguyen 200	8.00
39	Solomon Page 200	8.00
40	Mike Peterson 200	8.00
41	Anthony Poindexter 200	8.00
42	Peerless Price 46	60.00
43	Michael Rucker 200	8.00
44	L.J. Shelton 200	8.00
45	Akili Smith 90	35.00
46	John Tait 200	8.00
47	Fred Vinson 200	8.00
48	Al Wilson 200	8.00
49	Antoine Winfield 200	8.00
50	Damien Woody 200	8.00

1999 Sage Autographs Platinum

This insert is the same as the Red Autographs except most of the players only signed 50 cards and the borders are in platinum.

NM/M
Common Player: 10.00
Minor Stars: 30.00
1 Rahim Abdullah 50 10.00
2 Jerry Azumah 50 10.00
3 Champ Bailey 50 35.00
4 D'Wayne Bates 50 30.00
5 Michael Bishop 50 35.00
6 David Boston 43 60.00
7 Fernando Bryant 50 10.00
8 Tony Bryant 50 10.00
9 Chris Claiborne 50 30.00
10 Mike Cloud 22 45.00
11 Cecil Collins 50 40.00
12 Tim Couch 50 100.00
13 Daunte Culpepper 25 130.00
14 Jared DeVries 47 10.00
15 Adrian Dingle 50 10.00
16 Antwan Edwards 50 40.00
17 Troy Edwards 50 55.00
18 Kevin Faulk 50 60.00
19 Rufus French 50 10.00
20 Martin Gramatica 50 10.00
21 Torry Holt 50 60.00
22 Sedrick Irvin 50 40.00
23 Edgerrin James 45 125.00
24 Jon Jansen 50 10.00
25 Andy Katzenmoyer 15 60.00
26 Jevon Kearse 50 45.00
27 Patrick Kerney 45 10.00
28 Lamar King 50 10.00
29 Shaun King 50 45.00
30 Jim Kleinsasser 50 10.00
31 Rob Konrad 50 40.00
32 Brian Kuklick 50 40.00
33 Chris McAlister 50 40.00
34 Darnell McDonald 50 40.00
35 Reggie McGrew 50 40.00
36 Donovan McNabb 50 80.00
37 Cade McNown 15 55.00
38 Dat Nguyen 50 40.00
39 Solomon Page 50 10.00
40 Mike Peterson 50 10.00
41 Anthony Poindexter 50 10.00
42 Peerless Price 13 100.00
43 Michael Rucker 50 10.00
44 L.J. Shelton 50 10.00
45 Akili Smith 25 65.00
46 John Tait 50 10.00
47 Fred Vinson 50 10.00
48 Al Wilson 50 10.00
49 Antoine Winfield 50 10.00
50 Damien Woody 50 10.00

1999 Sage Autographs Silver

This insert is the same as the Red Autographs except most of the players signed a total of 400 cards and the borders are in silver.

NM/M
Common Player: 8.00
Minor Stars: 15.00
1 Rahim Abdullah 400 8.00
2 Jerry Azumah 400 8.00
3 Champ Bailey 400 20.00
4 D'Wayne Bates 400 15.00
5 Michael Bishop 400 30.00
6 David Boston 348 45.00
7 Fernando Bryant 400 15.00
8 Tony Bryant 400 8.00
9 Chris Claiborne 400 20.00
10 Mike Cloud 175 30.00
11 Cecil Collins 400 30.00
12 Tim Couch 400 55.00
13 Daunte Culpepper 180 75.00
14 Jared DeVries 355 8.00
15 Adrian Dingle 400 8.00
16 Antwan Edwards 400 15.00
17 Troy Edwards 400 30.00
18 Kevin Faulk 400 35.00
19 Rufus French 400 8.00
20 Martin Gramatica 400 8.00
21 Torry Holt 400 35.00
22 Sedrick Irvin 400 20.00
23 Edgerrin James 350 65.00
24 Jon Jansen 400 8.00
25 Andy Katzenmoyer 90 35.00
26 Jevon Kearse 400 25.00
27 Patrick Kerney 365 8.00
28 Lamar King 400 8.00
29 Shaun King 400 20.00
30 Jim Kleinsasser 400 8.00
31 Rob Konrad 400 15.00
32 Brian Kuklick 400 15.00
33 Chris McAlister 400 15.00
34 Darnell McDonald 400 20.00
35 Reggie McGrew 400 15.00
36 Donovan McNabb 400 50.00
37 Cade McNown 90 35.00
38 Dat Nguyen 400 15.00
39 Solomon Page 400 8.00
40 Mike Peterson 400 8.00
41 Anthony Poindexter 400 8.00
42 Peerless Price 93 50.00
43 Michael Rucker 400 8.00
44 L.J. Shelton 400 8.00
45 Akili Smith 180 25.00
46 John Tait 400 8.00
47 Fred Vinson 400 8.00
48 Al Wilson 400 8.00
49 Antoine Winfield 400 8.00
50 Damien Woody 400 8.00

2000 Sage Autographed

NM/M
Complete Set (50): 20.00
Common Player: .20
Minor Stars: .50
Pack (3): 16.00
Wax Box (12): 140.00
1 John Abraham .20
2 Shaun Alexander 2.00
3 LaVar Arrington 1.00
4 Courtney Brown 1.25
5 Keith Bulluck .20
6 Plaxico Burress 3.50
7 Giovanni Carmazzi 1.00
8 Kwame Cavil .50
9 Cosey Coleman .20
10 Laveranues Coles 2.00
11 Tim Couch 2.00
12 Ron Dayne 1.00
13 Reuben Droughns 1.00
14 Shaun Ellis .20
15 John Engelberger .20
16 Danny Farmer .75
17 Dwayne Goodrich .20
18 Deon Grant .20
19 Chris Hovan .20
20 Darren Howard .20
21 Todd Husak .75
22 Thomas Jones 1.00
23 Curtis Keaton .75
24 Jamal Lewis 2.50
25 Anthony Lucas .50
26 Tee Martin 1.25
27 Stockar McDougle .20
28 Corey Moore .20
29 Rob Morris .20
30 Sammy Morris .20
31 Sylvester Morris 1.25
32 Chad Pennington 4.00
33 Todd Pinkston .75
34 Ahmed Plummer .75
35 Jerry Porter 1.25
36 Travis Prentice 1.25
37 Tim Rattay 1.25
38 Chris Redman 1.50
39 J.R. Redmond 1.50
40 Chris Samuels .75
41 Brandon Short .20
42 Corey Simon .50
43 R. Jay Soward 1.25
44 Shyrone Stith .20
45 Raynoch Thompson .20
46 Brian Urlacher 3.00
47 Todd Wade .20
48 Troy Walters .50
49 Dez White 1.00
50 Michael Wiley .75
51 Ron Dayne AUTO SP 20.00

2000 Sage Autographed Red Autographs

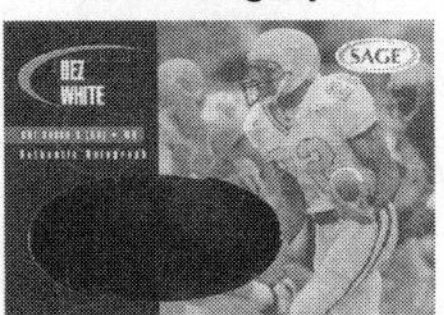

NM/M
Common Player: 4.00
Minor Stars: 8.00
Inserted 1:2
Production 999 Sets
1 John Abraham 999 4.00
2 Shaun Alexander 999 20.00
3 LaVar Arrington 514 30.00
4 Courtney Brown 514 20.00
6 Plaxico Burress 999 35.00
7 Giovanni Carmazzi 999 18.00
8 Kwame Cavil 999 8.00
9 Cosey Coleman 999 4.00
10 Laveranues Coles 999 10.00
11 Tim Couch 339 50.00
12 Ron Dayne 309 45.00
13 Reuben Droughns 999 10.00
14 Shaun Ellis 999 4.00
15 John Engelberger 999 4.00
16 Danny Farmer 999 10.00
17 Dwayne Goodrich 999 4.00
18 Deon Grant 999 4.00
19 Chris Hovan 999 4.00
20 Darren Howard 999 4.00
21 Todd Husak 999 8.00
22 Thomas Jones 999 30.00
23 Curtis Keaton 999 8.00
24 Jamal Lewis 999 25.00
25 Anthony Lucas 999 4.00
26 Tee Martin 999 15.00
28 Corey Moore 999 4.00
29 Rob Morris 999 4.00
30 Sammy Morris 999 4.00
31 Sylvester Morris 999 15.00
32 Chad Pennington 689 50.00
33 Todd Pinkston 999 8.00
34 Ahmed Plummer 999 8.00
35 Jerry Porter 999 12.00
36 Travis Prentice 999 15.00
37 Tim Rattay 999 12.00
38 Chris Redman 999 15.00
39 J.R. Redmond 999 15.00
40 Chris Samuels 999 10.00
41 Brandon Short 999 4.00
43 R. Jay Soward 999 12.00
44 Shyrone Stith 999 4.00
45 Raynoch Thompson 999 4.00
46 Brian Urlacher 999 10.00
47 Todd Wade 999 4.00
48 Troy Walters 999 4.00
49 Dez White 999 10.00
50 Michael Wiley 999 8.00

2000 Sage Autographed Bronze Autographs

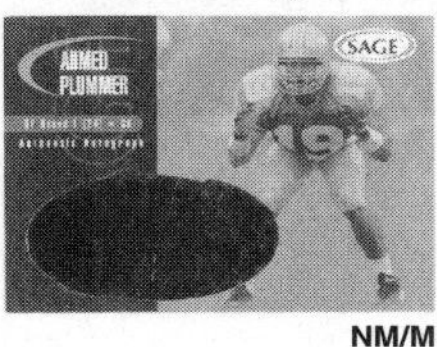

NM/M
Common Player: 5.00
Minor Stars: 10.00
Inserted 1:4
Production 650 Sets
1 John Abraham 650 5.00
2 Shaun Alexander 650 30.00
3 LaVar Arrington 340 30.00
4 Courtney Brown 340 30.00
6 Plaxico Burress 650 45.00
7 Giovanni Carmazzi 650 25.00
8 Kwame Cavil 650 10.00
9 Cosey Coleman 650 5.00
10 Laveranues Coles 650 20.00
11 Tim Couch 230 60.00
12 Ron Dayne 215 50.00
13 Reuben Droughns650 15.00
14 Shaun Ellis 650 5.00
15 John Engelberger 650 5.00
16 Danny Farmer 650 12.00
17 Dwayne Goodrich 650 5.00
18 Deon Grant 650 5.00
19 Chris Hovan 650 5.00
20 Darren Howard 650 5.00
21 Todd Husak 650 10.00
22 Thomas Jones 650 35.00
23 Curtis Keaton 650 10.00
24 Jamal Lewis 650 30.00
25 Anthony Lucas 650 10.00
26 Tee Martin 650 15.00
27 Stockar McDougle 650 5.00
28 Corey Moore 650 5.00
29 Rob Morris 650 5.00
30 Sammy Morris 650 5.00
31 Sylvester Morris 650 20.00
32 Chad Pennington 455 60.00
33 Todd Pinkston 650 10.00
34 Ahmed Plummer 650 10.00
35 Jerry Porter 650 15.00
36 Travis Prentice 650 15.00
37 Tim Rattay 650 15.00
38 Chris Redman 650 20.00
39 J.R. Redmond 650 20.00
40 Chris Samuels 650 10.00
41 Brandon Short 650 5.00
43 R. Jay Soward 650 18.00
44 Shyrone Stith 650 5.00
45 Raynoch Thompson 650 5.00
46 Brian Urlacher 650 15.00
47 Todd Wade 650 5.00
48 Troy Walters 650 10.00
49 Dez White 650 12.00
50 Michael Wiley 650 10.00

2000 Sage Autographed Gold Autographs

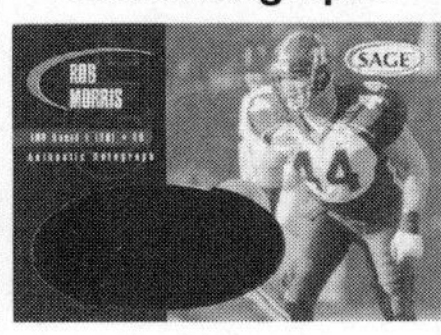

NM/M
Common Player: 8.00
Minor Stars: 16.00
Inserted 1:12
Production 200 Sets
1 John Abraham 200 8.00
2 Shaun Alexander 200 50.00
3 LaVar Arrington 105 45.00
4 Courtney Brown 105 50.00
6 Plaxico Burress 200 70.00
7 Giovanni Carmazzi 200 40.00
8 Kwame Cavil 200 16.00
9 Cosey Coleman 200 8.00
10 Laveranues Coles 200 20.00
11 Tim Couch 70 100.00
12 Ron Dayne 70 50.00
13 Reuben Droughns 200 20.00
14 Shaun Ellis 200 8.00
15 John Engelberger 200 8.00
16 Danny Farmer 200 18.00
17 Dwayne Goodrich 200 8.00
18 Deon Grant 200 8.00
19 Chris Hovan 200 8.00
20 Darren Howard 200 8.00
21 Todd Husak 200 16.00
22 Thomas Jones 200 60.00
23 Curtis Keaton 200 16.00
24 Jamal Lewis 200 50.00
25 Anthony Lucas 200 16.00
26 Tee Martin 200 25.00
27 Stockar McDougle 200 8.00
28 Corey Moore 200 8.00
29 Rob Morris 200 8.00
30 Sammy Morris 200 8.00
31 Sylvester Morris 200 30.00
32 Chad Pennington 140 85.00
33 Todd Pinkston 200 16.00
34 Ahmed Plummer 200 16.00
35 Jerry Porter 200 25.00
36 Travis Prentice 200 30.00
37 Tim Rattay 200 30.00
38 Chris Redman 200 30.00
39 J.R. Redmond 200 30.00
40 Chris Samuels 200 16.00
41 Brandon Short 200 8.00
43 R. Jay Soward 200 30.00
44 Shyrone Stith 200 8.00
45 Raynoch Thompson 200 8.00
46 Brian Urlacher 200 20.00
47 Todd Wade 200 8.00
48 Troy Walters 200 16.00
49 Dez White 200 20.00
50 Michael Wiley 200 16.00

2000 Sage Autographed Platinum Autographs

NM/M
Common Player: 10.00
Minor Stars: 20.00
Inserted 1:46
Production 50 Sets
1 John Abraham 50 10.00
2 Shaun Alexander 50 65.00
3 LaVar Arrington 30 60.00
4 Courtney Brown 30 75.00
6 Plaxico Burress 50 100.00
7 Giovanni Carmazzi 50 50.00
8 Kwame Cavil 50 20.00
9 Cosey Coleman 50 10.00
10 Laveranues Coles 50 30.00
11 Tim Couch 20 100.00
12 Ron Dayne 20 75.00
13 Reuben Droughns 50 30.00
14 Shaun Ellis 50 10.00
15 John Engelberger 50 10.00
16 Danny Farmer 50 25.00
17 Dwayne Goodrich 50 10.00
18 Deon Grant 50 10.00
19 Chris Hovan 50 10.00
20 Darren Howard 50 10.00
21 Todd Husak 50 20.00
22 Thomas Jones 50 85.00
23 Curtis Keaton 50 20.00
24 Jamal Lewis 50 75.00
25 Anthony Lucas 50 20.00
26 Tee Martin 50 40.00
27 Corey Moore 50 10.00
28 Rob Morris 50 10.00
29 Rob Morris 50 10.00
30 Sammy Morris 50 10.00
31 Sylvester Morris 50 40.00
32 Chad Pennington 35 150.00
33 Todd Pinkston 50 20.00
34 Ahmed Plummer 50 25.00
35 Jerry Porter 50 40.00
36 Travis Prentice 50 45.00
37 Tim Rattay 50 45.00
38 Chris Redman 50 50.00
39 J.R. Redmond 50 50.00
40 Chris Samuels 50 25.00
41 Brandon Short 50 10.00
43 R. Jay Soward 50 40.00
44 Shyrone Stith 50 10.00
45 Raynoch Thompson 50 10.00
46 Brian Urlacher 50 30.00
47 Todd Wade 50 10.00
48 Troy Walters 50 20.00
49 Dez White 50 30.00
50 Michael Wiley 50 25.00

2000 Sage Autographed Silver Autographs

NM/M
Common Player: 6.00
Minor Stars: 12.00
Inserted 1:6
Production 400 Sets
1 John Abraham 400 6.00
2 Shaun Alexander 400 40.00
3 LaVar Arrington 210 40.00
4 Courtney Brown 210 40.00
6 Plaxico Burress 400 55.00
7 Giovanni Carmazzi 400 20.00
8 Kwame Cavil 400 12.00
9 Cosey Coleman 400 6.00
10 Laveranues Coles 400 15.00
11 Tim Couch 140 60.00
12 Ron Dayne 135 65.00
13 Reuben Droughns 400 20.00
14 Shaun Ellis 400 6.00
15 John Engelberger 400 6.00
16 Danny Farmer 400 12.00
17 Dwayne Goodrich 400 6.00
18 Deon Grant 400 6.00
19 Chris Hovan 400 6.00
20 Darren Howard 400 6.00
21 Todd Husak 400 12.00
22 Thomas Jones 400 40.00
23 Curtis Keaton 400 12.00
24 Jamal Lewis 400 40.00
25 Anthony Lucas 400 12.00
26 Tee Martin 400 20.00
27 Stockar McDougle 400 6.00
28 Corey Moore 400 6.00
29 Rob Morris 400 6.00
30 Sammy Morris 400 6.00
31 Sylvester Morris 400 20.00
32 Chad Pennington 280 75.00
33 Todd Pinkston 400 12.00
34 Ahmed Plummer 400 12.00
35 Jerry Porter 400 20.00
36 Travis Prentice 400 20.00
37 Tim Rattay 400 20.00
38 Chris Redman 400 25.00
39 J.R. Redmond 400 25.00
40 Chris Samuels 400 12.00
41 Brandon Short 400 6.00
42 Corey Simon 400 12.00
43 R. Jay Soward 400 20.00
44 Shyrone Stith 400 6.00
45 Raynoch Thompson 400 6.00
46 Brian Urlacher 400 15.00
47 Todd Wade 400 6.00
48 Troy Walters 400 12.00
49 Dez White 400 15.00
50 Michael Wiley 400 15.00

2000 Sage Hit

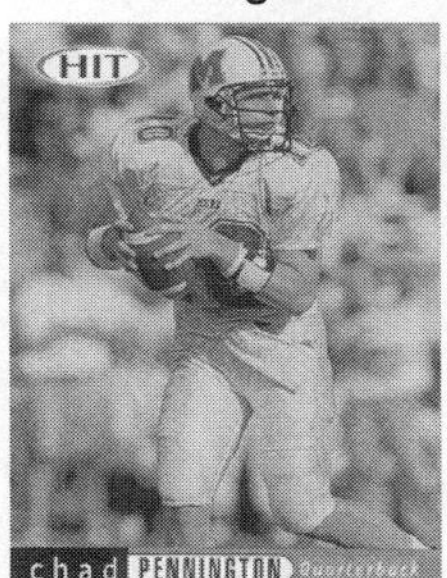

NM/M
Complete Set (50): 25.00
Common Player: .25
Minor Stars: .50
Pack (5): 3.25
Wax Box (24): 55.00
1 Jerry Porter 2.00
2 Tim Couch 1.00
3 Chris Samuels .50
4 Plaxico Burress 2.50
5 Michael Wiley .75
6 Thomas Jones 2.50
7 Chris Redman 1.50
8 Anthony Lucas .75
9 Kwame Cavil .50
10 Chad Pennington 4.00
11 LaVar Arrington 2.00
12 Giovanni Carmazzi 1.50
13 Tim Rattay 1.00
14 Laveranues Coles .75
15 Mario Edwards .25
16 John Engelberger .25
17 Tee Martin 1.25
18 R. Jay Soward 1.25
19 Ahmed Plummer .50
20 Na'il Diggs .50
21 J.R. Redmond 1.25
22 Dez White .75
23 Reuben Droughns .75
24 Sylvester Morris 1.25
25 Cosey Coleman .25
26 Corey Moore .50
27 Curtis Keaton .50
28 Danny Farmer .75
29 Travis Claridge .25
30 Troy Walters .50
31 Jamal Lewis 2.50
32 Shaun King 1.25
33 Ron Dayne 2.00
34 Keith Bulluck .50
35 Corey Simon .50
36 Deon Dyer .50
37 Shaun Alexander 2.00
38 Shyrone Stith .50
39 Shaun Ellis .50
40 Todd Pinkston .75
41 Travis Prentice 1.25
42 Chris Hovan .50
43 Brandon Short .50
44 Brian Urlacher 1.00
45 Rob Morris .50
46 Raynoch Thompson .50
47 Deon Grant .50
48 Stockar McDougle .25
49 Darren Howard .50
50 Courtney Brown 1.25

2000 Sage Hit NGR

NM/M
Complete Set (50): 40.00
NGR Cards: 1.5X
Inserted 1:1.5

2000 Sage Hit Autographs Emerald

NM/M
Common Player: 5.00
Minor Stars: 10.00
Inserted 1:12
Emerald Die Cuts: 2X
Inserted 1:40
Diamond Cards: 1.5X
Inserted 1:20
Diamond Die Cuts: 3X
Inserted 1:100
1 Jerry Porter 30.00
2 Tim Couch 30.00
3 Chris Samuels 10.00
4 Plaxico Burress 40.00
5 Michael Wiley 10.00
6 Thomas Jones 30.00
7 Chris Redman 20.00
8 Anthony Lucas 10.00
9 Kwame Cavil 10.00
10 Chad Pennington 65.00
11 LaVar Arrington 25.00
12 Giovanni Carmazzi 25.00
13 Tim Rattay 10.00
14 Laveranues Coles 10.00
15 Mario Edwards 5.00
16 John Engelberger 5.00
17 Tee Martin 20.00
18 R. Jay Soward 15.00
19 Ahmed Plummer 10.00
20 Na'il Diggs 10.00
21 J.R. Redmond 15.00
22 Dez White 10.00
23 Reuben Droughns 10.00
24 Sylvester Morris 15.00
25 Cosey Coleman 10.00
26 Corey Moore 10.00
27 Curtis Keaton 10.00
28 Danny Farmer 10.00
29 Travis Claridge 5.00
30 Troy Walters 10.00
31 Jamal Lewis 35.00
32 Shaun King 20.00
33 Ron Dayne 25.00
35 Corey Simon 10.00
36 Deon Dyer 10.00
37 Shaun Alexander 30.00
38 Shyrone Stith 10.00
39 Shaun Ellis 10.00
40 Todd Pinkston 10.00
41 Travis Prentice 10.00
42 Chris Hovan 10.00
43 Brandon Short 10.00
44 Brian Urlacher 12.00
45 Rob Morris 10.00
46 Raynoch Thompson 10.00
47 Deon Grant 10.00
48 Stockar McDougle 10.00
49 Darren Howard 10.00
50 Courtney Brown 25.00

Post-1980 cards in Near Mint condition will generally sell for about 75% of the quoted Mint value. Excellent-condition cards bring no more than 40%.

2000 Sage Hit Autographs Emerald Die Cut

NM/M
Emerald Die Cuts: 2X
Inserted 1:40

2000 Sage Hit Autographs Diamond

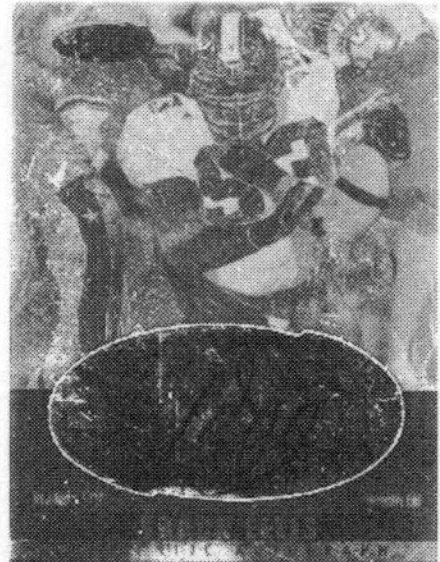

NM/M
Diamond Cards: 1.5X
Inserted 1:20

2000 Sage Hit Autographs Diamond Die Cut

NM/M
Diamond Die Cuts: 3X
Inserted 1:100

2000 Sage Hit Prospectors Emerald

NM/M
Complete Set (20): 45.00
Common Player: 1.00
Production 999 Sets
Inserted 1:24
Emerald Die Cuts: 2X
Production 300 Sets
Inserted 1:80
Diamond Cards: 1.5X
Production 600 Sets
Inserted 1:40
Diamond Die Cuts: 2X-4X
Production 100 Sets
Inserted 1:240
P1 Shaun Alexander 5.00
P2 LaVar Arrington 2.00
P3 Courtney Brown 2.00
P4 Plaxico Burress 8.00
P5 Giovanni Carmazzi 2.00
P6 Tim Couch 6.00
P7 Ron Dayne 2.00
P8 Thomas Jones 2.00
P9 Shaun King 2.00
P10 Jamal Lewis 5.00
P11 Tee Martin 4.00
P12 Sylvester Morris 4.00
P13 Chad Pennington 10.00
P14 Jerry Porter 4.00
P15 Travis Prentice 4.00
P16 Tim Rattay 1.00
P17 Chris Redman 4.00
P18 R. Jay Soward 1.00
P19 Dez White 1.00
P20 Michael Wiley 1.00

2000 Sage Hit Prospectors Emerald Die Cut

NM/M
Emerald Die Cuts: 2X
Production 300 Sets
Inserted 1:80

2000 Sage Hit Prospectors Diamond

NM/M
Diamond Cards: 1.5X
Production 600 Sets
Inserted 1:40

2000 Sage Hit Prospectors Diamond Die Cut

NM/M
Diamond Die Cuts: 2X-4X
Production 100 Sets
Inserted 1:240

2001 Sage HIT

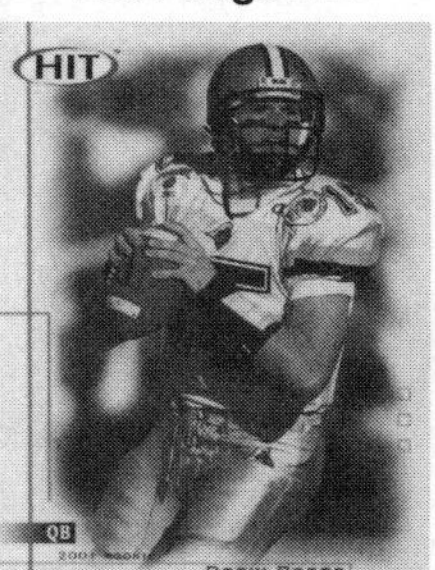

NM/M
Complete Set (50): 25.00
Common Player: .25
Minor Stars: .50
Pack (5): 4.75
Wax Box (24): 80.00
1 David Terrell 3.00
2 Jamar Fletcher .50
3 Koren Robinson 2.00
4 Ken-Yon Rambo .75
5 LaDainian Tomlinson 4.00
6 Santana Moss 3.00
7 Michael Vick 6.00
8 Steve Hutchinson .50
9 Robert Ferguson 1.00
10 Torrance Marshall .50
11 Scotty Anderson .50
12 Derrick Gibson .50
13 Marcus Stroud .50
14 Josh Heupel 2.00
15 Drew Brees 4.00
16 Gerard Warren 1.00
17 Quincy Carter 1.50
18 Gary Baxter .50
19 Alex Bannister 1.25
20 Travis Henry 1.75
21 Andre Dyson .25
22 Deuce McAllister 3.00
23 Rod Gardner 2.00
24 Jamie Winborn .50
25 Will Allen .50
26 Kenyatta Walker .25
27 Tim Hasselbeck .75
28 Alge Crumpler .75
29 Michael Bennett 3.00
30 LaMont Jordan 1.25
31 Jeff Backus .50
32 Rudi Johnson 1.25
33 Willie Howard .50
34 Josh Booty .75
35 Todd Heap .75
36 Correll Buckhalter 1.00
37 Jesse Palmer .75
38 Carlos Polk .50
39 Richard Seymour .50
40 Adam Archuleta .50
41 James Jackson 1.00
42 Willie Middlebrooks .50
43 Ja'Mar Toombs .50
44 Chris Chambers 1.50
45 Reggie Germany .50
46 Casey Hampton .50
47 Reggie Wayne 1.50
48 Jamal Reynolds .75
49 Justin Smith .75
50 Quincy Morgan 1.00

A player's name in *italic* type indicates a rookie card.

2001 Sage HIT A-Game

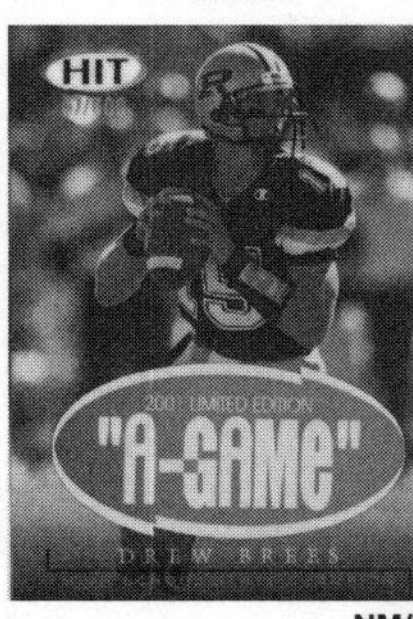

NM/M
Complete Set (9): 75.00
Common Player: 10.00
Inserted 1:42
Production 600 Sets
1 Drew Brees 12.00
2 Drew Brees 12.00
3 Drew Brees 12.00
4 David Terrell 10.00
5 David Terrell 10.00
6 David Terrell 10.00
7 Michael Vick 15.00
8 Michael Vick 15.00
9 Michael Vick 15.00

2001 Sage HIT Autographs

NM/M
Common Player: 7.00
Inserted 1:9
Die-Cut Cards: 2X
Inserted 1:26
Production 250 Sets
Foilboard Cards: 2X
Inserted 1:13
Foilboard Die-Cut Cards: 3X
Inserted 1:64
Production 100 Sets
Overall inserted 1:4
1 David Terrell 25.00
2 Jamar Fletcher
3 Koren Robinson 20.00
4 Ken-Yon Rambo 7.00
5 LaDainian Tomlinson 40.00
6 Santana Moss 30.00
7 Michael Vick 75.00
8 Steve Hutchinson 7.00
9 Robert Ferguson 12.00
10 Torrance Marshall 10.00
11 Scotty Anderson 7.00
12 Derrick Gibson
13 Marcus Stroud 7.00
14 Josh Heupel 30.00
15 Drew Brees 50.00
16 Gerard Warren
17 Quincy Carter 15.00
18 Gary Baxter 7.00
19 Alex Bannister 12.00
20 Travis Henry 20.00
21 Andre Dyson 7.00
22 Deuce McAllister 25.00
23 Rod Gardner 20.00
24 Jamie Winborn 7.00
25 Will Allen 10.00
26 Kenyatta Walker 7.00
27 Tim Hasselbeck 12.00
28 Alge Crumpler 7.00
29 Michael Bennett 25.00
30 LaMont Jordan 12.00
31 Jeff Backus 7.00
32 Rudi Johnson 12.00
33 Willie Howard 7.00
34 Josh Booty 10.00
35 Todd Heap 10.00
36 Correll Buckhalter 10.00
37 Jesse Palmer 12.00
38 Carlos Polk 7.00
39 Richard Seymour 7.00
40 Adam Archuleta 10.00
41 James Jackson
42 Willie Middlebrooks 7.00
43 Ja'Mar Toombs
44 Chris Chambers 12.00
45 Reggie Germany 7.00
46 Casey Hampton
47 Reggie Wayne 15.00
48 Jamal Reynolds 10.00
49 Justin Smith 10.00
50 Quincy Morgan 10.00

2001 Sage HIT Jerseys

NM/M
Complete Set (9): 500.00
Common Player: 20.00
Inserted 1:205
Production 175 Sets
1 Michael Vick 100.00
2 Michael Vick 100.00
3 Michael Vick 100.00
4 Drew Brees 50.00
5 Drew Brees 50.00
6 Drew Brees 50.00
7 David Terrell 20.00
8 David Terrell 20.00
9 David Terrell 20.00

2001 Sage HIT Prospector Emerald

NM/M
Complete Set (15): 85.00
Common Player: 3.00
Inserted 1:19
Production 999 Sets
Emerald Die-Cut Cards: 2X
Inserted 1:63
Production 299 Sets
Diamond Cards: 1.5X
Inserted 1:32
Production 599 Sets
Diamond Die-Cut Cards: 4X
Inserted 1:190
Production 99 Sets
1 Michael Bennett 8.00
2 Drew Brees 10.00
3 Quincy Carter 4.00
4 Chris Chambers 4.00
5 Rod Gardner 7.00
6 Josh Heupel 7.00
7 LaMont Jordan 4.00
8 Deuce McAllister 10.00
9 Quincy Morgan 3.00
10 Santana Moss 6.00
11 Koren Robinson 8.00
12 David Terrell 6.00
13 LaDainian Tomlinson 12.00
14 Michael Vick 20.00
15 Reggie Wayne 4.00

2001 Sage HIT Rarefied

NM/M
Complete Set (50): 75.00
Common Player: .75
Minor Stars: 1.50
Inserted 1:3
Production 2,001 Sets
Silver Cards: 2X
Inserted 1:6
Production 999 Sets
Gold Cards: 3X
Inserted 1:11
Production 500 Sets
R1 Will Allen .75
R2 Adam Archuleta 1.50
R3 Jeff Backus .75
R4 Alex Bannister 2.00
R5 Gary Baxter .75
R6 Michael Bennett 5.00
R7 Josh Booty 1.50
R8 Drew Brees 6.00
R9 Correll Buckhalter 2.00
R10 Quincy Carter 2.50
R11 Chris Chambers 2.00
R12 Alge Crumpler .75
R13 Andre Dyson .75
R14 Robert Ferguson 2.50
R15 Jamar Fletcher 1.50
R16 Rod Gardner 4.00
R17 Reggie Germany .75
R18 Derrick Gibson .75
R19 Casey Hampton .75
R20 Tim Hasselbeck 1.50
R21 Todd Heap .75
R22 Travis Henry 3.00
R23 Josh Heupel 4.50
R24 Willie Howard .75
R25 Steve Hutchinson .75
R26 James Jackson 2.00
R27 Rudi Johnson 2.00
R28 LaMont Jordan 2.00
R29 Torrance Marshall .75
R30 Deuce McAllister 5.00
R31 Willie Middlebrooks .75
R32 Quincy Morgan 2.00
R33 Santana Moss 3.00
R34 Jesse Palmer .75
R35 Carlos Polk .75
R36 Ken-Yon Rambo 1.50
R37 Jamal Reynolds .75
R38 Koren Robinson 2.00
R39 Richard Seymour .75
R40 Justin Smith 1.50
R41 Fred Smoot .75
R42 Marcus Stroud .75
R43 David Terrell 6.00
R44 LaDainian Tomlinson 8.00
R45 Ja'Mar Toombs .75
R46 Michael Vick 12.00
R47 Kenyatta Walker .75
R48 Gerard Warren 1.50
R49 Reggie Wayne 3.00
R50 Jamie Winborn .75

2001 Sage Autographed

NM/M
Complete Set (50): 20.00
Common Player: .25
Minor Stars: .50
Production 4,500 Sets
Pack (3): 18.00
Wax Box (12): 160.00
A1 Will Allen .25
A2 Adam Archuleta .75
A3 Jeff Backus .50
A4 Alex Bannister .75
A5 Gary Baxter .25
A6 Michael Bennett 3.00
A7 Josh Booty .50
A8 Drew Brees 3.00
A9 Correll Buckhalter .75
A10 Quincy Carter 1.50
A11 Chris Chambers 1.00
A12 Alge Crumpler .50
A13 Andre Dyson .25
A14 Robert Ferguson 1.50
A15 Jamar Fletcher .75
A16 Rod Gardner 2.00
A17 Reggie Germany 1.25
A18 Derrick Gibson .50
A19 Casey Hampton .25
A20 Tim Hasselbeck .75
A21 Todd Heap .50
A22 Travis Henry 1.50
A23 Josh Heupel 2.50
A24 Willie Howard .25
A25 Steve Hutchinson .50
A26 James Jackson 1.25
A27 Rudi Johnson 1.00
A28 LaMont Jordan 1.00
A29 Torrance Marshall .50
A30 Deuce McAllister 2.50
A31 Willie Middlebrooks .25
A32 Quincy Morgan 1.00
A33 Santana Moss 2.50
A34 Jesse Palmer .75
A35 Carlos Polk .25
A36 Ken-Yon Rambo .50
A37 Jamal Reynolds .50
A38 Koren Robinson 2.00
A39 Richard Seymour .25
A40 Justin Smith .75
A41 Fred Smoot .50
A42 Marcus Stroud .50
A43 David Terrell 2.75
A44 LaDainian Tomlinson 3.50
A45 Ja'Mar Toombs .25
A46 Michael Vick 6.00
A47 Kenyatta Walker .50
A48 Gerard Warren 1.00
A49 Reggie Wayne 1.75
A50 Jamie Winborn .50

2001 Sage Autographed Bronze

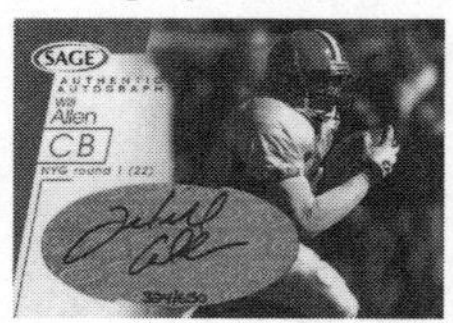

NM/M
Common Player: 6.00
Inserted 1:4
Production 650 Sets
A1 Will Allen 650 6.00
A2 Adam Archuleta 650 6.00
A3 Jeff Backus 600 6.00
A4 Alex Bannister 650 8.00
A5 Gary Baxter 650 6.00
A6 Michael Bennett 650 30.00
A7 Josh Booty 600 6.00
A8 Drew Brees 500 50.00
A9 Correll Buckhalter 650 12.00
A10 Quincy Carter 650 15.00
A11 Chris Chambers 650 10.00
A12 Alge Crumpler 650 6.00
A13 Andre Dyson 650 6.00
A14 Robert Ferguson 650 12.00
A16 Rod Gardner 650 18.00
A17 Reggie Germany 650 12.00
A18 Derrick Gibson 650 6.00
A19 Casey Hampton 650 6.00
A20 Tim Hasselbeck 600 7.00
A21 Todd Heap 650 6.00
A22 Travis Henry 600 18.00
A23 Josh Heupel 650 25.00
A24 Willie Howard 600 6.00
A25 Steve Hutchinson 650 6.00
A26 James Jackson 650 10.00
A27 Rudi Johnson 650 8.00
A28 LaMont Jordan 650 10.00
A29 Torrance Marshall 650 6.00
A30 Deuce McAllister 500 30.00
A31 Willie Middlebrooks 650 6.00
A32 Quincy Morgan 650 10.00
A33 Santana Moss 650 30.00
A34 Jesse Palmer 650 7.00
A35 Carlos Polk 650 6.00
A36 Ken-Yon Rambo 500 6.00
A37 Jamal Reynolds 650 6.00
A38 Koren Robinson 650 18.00
A39 Richard Seymour 650 6.00
A40 Justin Smith 650 8.00
A41 Fred Smoot 650 6.00
A42 Marcus Stroud 600 6.00
A43 David Terrell 425 25.00
A44 LaDainian Tomlinson 650 35.00
A45 Ja'Mar Toombs 650 6.00
A46 Michael Vick 325 85.00
A47 Kenyatta Walker 650 6.00
A49 Reggie Wayne 650 15.00
A50 Jamie Winborn 650 6.00

2001 Sage Autographed Gold

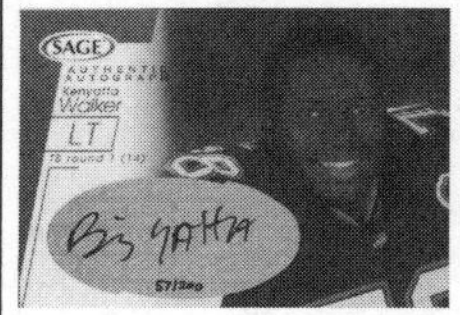

NM/M
Common Player: 10.00
Inserted 1:12
Production 200 Sets
A1 Will Allen 200 10.00
A2 Adam Archuleta 200 12.00
A3 Jeff Backus 200 10.00
A4 Alex Bannister 200 15.00
A5 Gary Baxter 200 10.00
A6 Michael Bennett 200 50.00
A7 Josh Booty 200 10.00
A8 Drew Brees 150 85.00
A9 Correll Buckhalter 200 20.00
A10 Quincy Carter 200 25.00
A11 Chris Chambers 200 18.00
A12 Alge Crumpler 200 10.00
A13 Andre Dyson 200 10.00
A14 Robert Ferguson 200 20.00
A16 Rod Gardner 200 30.00
A17 Reggie Germany 200 25.00
A18 Derrick Gibson 200 10.00
A19 Casey Hampton 200 10.00
A20 Tim Hasselbeck 200 12.00
A21 Todd Heap 200 10.00
A22 Travis Henry 200 30.00
A23 Josh Heupel 200 40.00
A24 Willie Howard 200 10.00
A25 Steve Hutchinson 200 10.00
A26 James Jackson 200 16.00
A27 Rudi Johnson 200 15.00
A28 LaMont Jordan 200 16.00
A29 Torrance Marshall 200 10.00
A30 Deuce McAllister 150 50.00
A31 Willie Middlebrooks 200 10.00
A32 Quincy Morgan 200 15.00
A33 Santana Moss 200 45.00
A34 Jesse Palmer 200 12.00
A35 Carlos Polk 200 10.00
A36 Ken-Yon Rambo 150 10.00
A37 Jamal Reynolds 200 10.00
A38 Koren Robinson 200 20.00
A39 Richard Seymour 200 10.00
A40 Justin Smith 200 12.00
A41 Fred Smoot 200 10.00
A42 Marcus Stroud 200 10.00
A43 David Terrell 130 40.00
A44 LaDainian Tomlinson 200 60.00
A45 Ja'Mar Toombs 200 10.00
A46 Michael Vick 100 150.00
A47 Kenyatta Walker 200 10.00
A49 Reggie Wayne 200 25.00
A50 Jamie Winborn 200 10.00

2001 Sage Autographed Platinum

NM/M
Common Player: 20.00
Inserted 1:46
Production 50 Sets
A1 Will Allen 50 20.00
A2 Adam Archuleta 50 20.00
A3 Jeff Backus 50 20.00
A4 Alex Bannister 50 25.00
A5 Gary Baxter 50 20.00
A6 Michael Bennett 50 100.00
A7 Josh Booty 50 20.00
A8 Drew Brees 40 150.00
A9 Correll Buckhalter 50 35.00
A10 Quincy Carter 50 45.00
A11 Chris Chambers 50 30.00
A12 Alge Crumpler 50 20.00
A13 Andre Dyson 50 20.00
A14 Robert Ferguson 50 40.00
A16 Rod Gardner 50 60.00
A17 Reggie Germany 50 45.00
A18 Derrick Gibson 50 20.00

A19 Casey Hampton 50 20.00
A20 Tim Hasselbeck 50 25.00
A21 Todd Heap 50 20.00
A22 Travis Henry 50 60.00
A23 Josh Heupel 50 75.00
A24 Willie Howard 50 20.00
A25 Steve Hutchinson 50 20.00
A26 James Jackson 50 30.00
A27 Rudi Johnson 50 25.00
A28 LaMont Jordan 50 35.00
A29 Torrance Marshall 50 20.00
A30 Deuce McAllister 40 100.00
A31 Willie Middlebrooks 50 20.00
A32 Quincy Morgan 50 35.00
A33 Santana Moss 50 90.00
A34 Jesse Palmer 50 25.00
A35 Carlos Polk 50 20.00
A36 Ken-Yon Rambo 40 20.00
A37 Jamal Reynolds 50 20.00
A38 Koren Robinson 50 60.00
A39 Richard Seymour 50 20.00
A40 Justin Smith 50 25.00
A41 Fred Smoot 50 20.00
A42 Marcus Stroud 50 20.00
A43 David Terrell 35 80.00
A44 LaDainian Tomlinson 50 125.00
A45 Ja'Mar Toombs 50 20.00
A46 Michael Vick 25 275.00
A47 Kenyatta Walker 50 20.00
A49 Reggie Wayne 50 50.00
A50 Jamie Winborn 50 20.00

2001 Sage Autographed Red

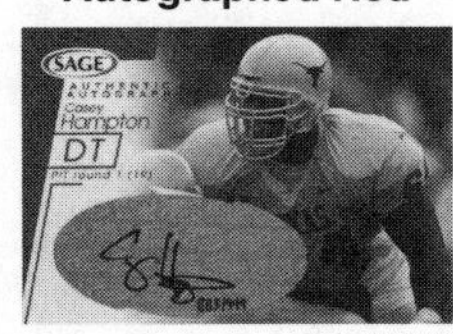

NM/M
Common Player: 5.00
Inserted 1:2
Production 999 Sets
A1 Will Allen 999 5.00
A2 Adam Archuleta 999 5.00
A3 Jeff Backus 900 6.00
A4 Alex Bannister 999 7.00
A5 Gary Baxter 999 5.00
A6 Michael Bennett 999 25.00
A7 Josh Booty 900 6.00
A8 Drew Brees 749 40.00
A9 Correll Buckhalter 999 10.00
A10 Quincy Carter 999 12.00
A11 Chris Chambers 999 8.00
A12 Alge Crumpler 999 5.00
A13 Andre Dyson 999 5.00
A14 Robert Ferguson 999 10.00
A16 Rod Gardner 999 15.00
A17 Reggie Germany 999 10.00
A18 Derrick Gibson 999 5.00
A19 Casey Hampton 999 5.00
A20 Tim Hasselbeck 900 6.00
A21 Todd Heap 999 6.00
A22 Travis Henry 800 15.00
A23 Josh Heupel 999 18.00
A24 Willie Howard 900 5.00
A25 Steve Hutchinson 999 5.00
A26 James Jackson 999 8.00
A27 Rudi Johnson 999 7.00
A28 LaMont Jordan 999 8.00
A29 Torrance Marshall 999 5.00
A30 Deuce McAllister 749 30.00
A31 Willie Middlebrooks 999 5.00
A32 Quincy Morgan 999 8.00
A33 Santana Moss 999 25.00
A34 Jesse Palmer 999 6.00
A35 Carlos Polk 999 5.00
A36 Ken-Yon Rambo 749 5.00
A37 Jamal Reynolds 999 5.00
A38 Koren Robinson 999 15.00
A39 Richard Seymour 999 5.00
A40 Justin Smith 999 7.00
A41 Fred Smoot 999 5.00
A42 Marcus Stroud 900 5.00
A43 David Terrell 649 25.00
A44 LaDainian Tomlinson 999 30.00
A45 Ja'Mar Toombs 999 5.00
A46 Michael Vick 499 75.00
A47 Kenyatta Walker 999 5.00
A49 Reggie Wayne 999 12.00
A50 Jamie Winborn 999 5.00

2001 Sage Autographed Silver

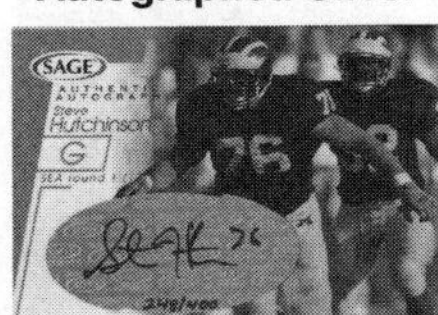

NM/M
Common Player: 7.50
Inserted 1:6
Production 400 Sets
A1 Will Allen 400 7.50
A2 Adam Archuleta 400 7.50
A3 Jeff Backus 400 7.50
A4 Alex Bannister 400 10.00
A5 Gary Baxter 400 7.50
A6 Michael Bennett 400 40.00
A7 Josh Booty 400 7.50
A8 Drew Brees 300 60.00
A9 Correll Buckhalter 400 15.00
A10 Quincy Carter 400 18.00
A11 Chris Chambers 400 12.00
A12 Alge Crumpler 400 7.50
A13 Andre Dyson 400 7.50
A14 Robert Ferguson 400 15.00
A16 Rod Gardner 400 25.00
A17 Reggie Germany 400 18.00
A18 Derrick Gibson 400 7.50
A19 Casey Hampton 400 7.50
A20 Tim Hasselbeck 400 10.00
A21 Todd Heap 400 7.50
A22 Travis Henry 400 25.00
A23 Josh Heupel 400 30.00
A24 Willie Howard 400 7.50
A25 Steve Hutchinson 400 7.50
A26 James Jackson 400 12.00
A27 Rudi Johnson 400 10.00
A28 LaMont Jordan 400 12.00
A29 Torrance Marshall 400 7.50
A30 Deuce McAllister 300 40.00
A31 Willie Middlebrooks 400 7.50
A32 Quincy Morgan 400 12.00
A33 Santana Moss 400 35.00
A34 Jesse Palmer 400 10.00
A35 Carlos Polk 400 7.50
A36 Ken-Yon Rambo 300 7.50
A37 Jamal Reynolds 400 7.50
A38 Koren Robinson 400 25.00
A39 Richard Seymour 400 7.50
A40 Justin Smith 400 10.00
A41 Fred Smoot 400 7.50
A42 Marcus Stroud 400 7.50
A43 David Terrell 260 30.00
A44 LaDainian Tomlinson 400 45.00
A45 Ja'Mar Toombs 400 7.50
A46 Michael Vick 200 100.00
A47 Kenyatta Walker 400 7.50
A49 Reggie Wayne 400 18.00
A50 Jamie Winborn 400 7.50

2001 Sage Autographed Jerseys

NM/M
Complete Set (3): 160.00
Common Player: 25.00
Inserted 1:205
Production 175 Sets
J1 Michael Vick 100.00
J2 Drew Brees 50.00
J3 David Terrell 25.00

2001 Sage Autographed Michael Vick Specials

NM/M
Complete Set (2): 125.00
Common Player: 60.00
MV1 Vick Authentic Jersey 60.00
MV2 Vick Authentic Autograph 75.00

2002 Sage

NM/M
Complete Set (45): 30.00
Common Player: .50
Minor Stars:
Pack (3): 12.00
Wax Box (12): 100.00
1 Ladell Betts 1.00
2 Antonio Bryant 2.00
3 Donald Reche Caldwell 1.00
4 Kelly Campbell 1.00
5 David Carr 5.00
6 Tim Carter 1.00
7 Eric Crouch 2.00
8 Ronald Curry 1.00
9 Rohan Davey 1.50
10 Andre Davis 1.50
11 T.J. Duckett 3.00
12 Randy Fasani .50
13 DeShaun Foster 2.00
14 Dwight Freeney .50
15 Jabar Gaffney 1.00
16 Lamar Gordon 1.00
17 Daniel Graham 1.00
18 Joey Harrington 5.00
19 Napoleon Harris .75
20 Albert Haynesworth .50
21 John Henderson 1.00
22 Chad Hutchinson 1.00
23 Quentin Jammer 1.50
24 Ron Johnson .50
25 Kurt Kittner 1.50
26 Ashley Lelie 3.00
27 Bryant McKinnie 1.00
28 Maurice Morris 1.00
29 David Neill 1.00
30 J.T. O'Sullivan .50
31 Brian Poli-Dixon 1.00
32 Clinton Portis 4.00
33 Patrick Ramsey 2.00
34 Josh Reed 1.00
35 Cliff Russell .50
36 Lito Sheppard 1.00
37 Jeremy Shockey 2.00
38 Luke Staley 1.00
39 Donte Stallworth 3.00
40 Travis Stephens 2.00
41 Chester Taylor .50
42 Larry Tripplett 1.00
43 Javon Walker 2.00
44 Marquise Walker 1.50
45 Jonathan Wells 2.00

2002 Sage Autographed

NM/M
Common Player: 5.00
Prices for Red version
Bronze version 1X to2X
Silver version 1X to2X
Gold version 1X to3X
Platinum version 1X to4X
A1 Ladell Betts/40 40.00
A2 Antonio Bryant/740 15.00

NM/M
A3 Donald Reche Caldwell/630 10.00
A4 Kelly Campbell/750 10.00
A5 David Carr/220 75.00
A6 Tim Carter/720 5.00
A7 Eric Crouch/220 3.00
A8 Ronald Curry 60.00
A9 Rohan Davey/650 10.00
A10 Andre Davis/650 15.00
A11 T.J. Duckett/860 25.00
A12 Randy Fasani/700 5.00
A13 DeShaun Foster/500 30.00
A14 Dwight Freeney/800 5.00
A15 Jabar Gaffney/700 15.00
A16 Lamar Gordon/700 15.00
A17 Daniel Graham/650 15.00
A18 Joey Harrington/170 60.00
A19 Napoleon Harris/770 5.00
A20 Albert Haynesworth/100 12.00
A21 John Henderson/625 10.00
A22 Chad Hutchinson/600 5.00
A23 Quentin Jammer/300 20.00
A24 Ron Johnson/720 10.00
A25 Kurt Kittner/500 15.00
A26 Ashley Lelie/700 30.00
A27 Bryant McKinnie/720 10.00
A28 Maurice Morris/720 12.00
A29 David Neill/770 5.00
A30 J.T. O'Sullivan/660 5.00
A31 Brian Poli-Dixon/700 10.00
A32 Clinton Portis/70 75.00
A33 Patrick Ramsey/720 15.00
A34 Josh Reed/720 30.00
A35 Cliff Russell/720 10.00
A36 Lito Sheppard/670 12.00
A37 Jeremy Shockey/700 35.00
A38 Luke Staley/750 12.00
A39 Donte Stallworth/800 30.00
A40 Travis Stephens/660 20.00
A41 Chester Taylor/700 5.00
A42 Larry Tripplett/650 10.00
A43 Javon Walker/650 25.00
A44 Marquise Walker/600 15.00
A45 Jonathan Wells/680 15.00
VS Michael Vick/110 50.00

2002 Sage Jersey

NM/M
Common Player: 15.00
Inserted 1:35
Prices for red version
Production 99 sets
Bronze version 1X to2X
Silver version 1X to2X
Gold version 1X to3X
Jersey/auto combo
Production 10 sets
1 David Carr 75.00
2 Eric Crouch 50.00
3 Rohan Davey 15.00
4 T.J. Duckett 40.00
5 DeShaun Foster 40.00
6 Joey Harrington 60.00
7 Kurt Kittner 25.00
8 Clinton Portis 40.00
9 Patrick Ramsey 20.00
10 Michael Vick 40.00

2002 Sage Jersey Combination

Production 10 sets
David Carr, Michael Vick
David Carr, Joey Harrington
Joey Harrington, Clinton Portis
Clinton Portis, Eric Crouch

2002 Sage Hit

NM/M
Complete Set (48): 35.00
Common Player: .75
Minor Stars:
Rarefied Emerald: 1.5X
Rarefied Silver 2X
Pack (5): 4.75
Wax Box (24): 80.00
1 John Henderson .75
2 Tim Carter .75
3 Joey Harrington 5.00
4 Marquise Walker 1.00
5 Quentin Jammer 1.00
6 Rohan Davey 1.50
7a Eric Crouch QB 2.00
7b Eric Crouch RB 2.00
8 David Carr 5.00
9 Maurice Morris 1.50
10 Jabar Gaffney 1.50
11 David Neill .75
12 Randy Fasani .75
13 Alex Brown .75
14 J.T. O'Sullivan 1.00
15 Kurt Kittner 1.50
16 Ashley Lelie 3.00
17 Reche Caldwell 1.00
18 T.J. Duckett 3.00
19 Chester Taylor .75
20 Jonathan Wells .75
21 Kelly Campbell .75
22 Bryant McKinnie .75
23 Lito Sheppard 1.00
24 Donte Stallworth 3.00
25 Josh Reed 1.50
26 DeShaun Foster 1.50
27 Patrick Ramsey 1.50
28 Clinton Portis 4.00
29 Albert Haynesworth .75
30 Ronald Curry (has no base card) .75
31 Cliff Russell .75
32 Luke Staley .75
33 Ron Johnson .75
34 Travis Stephens .75
35 Chad Hutchinson .75
36 Lamar Gordon 1.00
37 Larry Tripplett .75
38 Napoleon Harris .75
39 Daniel Graham 1.00
40 Antonio Bryant 2.00
41 Javon Walker 2.00
42 Brian Poli-Dixon .75
43 Jeremy Shockey 2.00
44 Andre Davis 1.50
45 Ladell Betts 1.00
46 Michael Vick 1.00
-- David Carr/Checklist 2.00

2002 Sage Hit Autographs

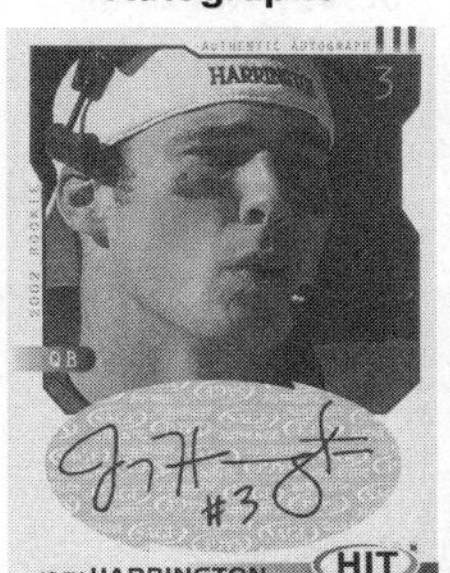

NM/M
Common Player: 7.50
Emerald:
Silver: 1.5X
Gold: 2X
Rarefied Gold: 3X
Inserted 1:16
1 John Henderson 7.50
2 Tim Carter 7.50
3 Joey Harrington 50.00
4 Marquise Walker 10.00
5 Quentin Jammer 10.00
6 Rohan Davey 15.00
7a Eric Crouch QB 25.00
7b Eric Crouch RB 25.00
8 David Carr 50.00
9 Maurice Morris 10.00
10 Jabar Gaffney 15.00
11 David Neill 7.50
12 Randy Fasani 7.50
13 Alex Brown 7.50
14 J.T. O'Sullivan 7.50
15 Kurt Kittner 10.00
16 Ashley Lelie 30.00
17 Reche Caldwell 10.00
18 T.J. Duckett 30.00
19 Chester Taylor 7.50
20 Jonathan Wells 7.50
21 Kelly Campbell 7.50
22 Bryant McKinnie 7.50
23 Lito Sheppard 10.00
24 Donte Stallworth 7.50
25 Josh Reed 20.00
26 DeShaun Foster 15.00
27 Patrick Ramsey 15.00
28 Clinton Portis 15.00
29 Albert Haynesworth 7.50
30 Ronald Curry (has no base card) 7.50
31 Cliff Russell 7.50
32 Luke Staley 7.50
33 Ron Johnson 7.50
34 Travis Stephens 7.50
35 Chad Hutchinson 7.50
36 Lamar Gordon 10.00
37 Larry Tripplett 7.50
38 Napoleon Harris 7.50
39 Daniel Graham 7.50
40 Antonio Bryant 15.00
41 Javon Walker 20.00
42 Brian Poli-Dixon 7.50
43 Jeremy Shockey 7.50
44 Andre Davis 10.00
45 Ladell Betts 10.00
46 Michael Vick 10.00
-- David Carr/Checklist 20.00

A card number in parenthese ( ) indicates the set is unnumbered.

2002 Sage Hit Authentic Jersey Cards

NM/M
Complete Set (9):
Inserted 1:80
J1 David Carr 60.00
J2 Eric Crouch 30.00
J3 Rohan Davey 25.00
J4 T.J. Duckett 40.00
J5 DeShaun Foster 25.00
J6 Joey Harrington 60.00
J7 Kurt Kittner 15.00
J8 Clinton Portis 25.00
J9 Patrick Ramsey 25.00

2002 Sage Hit The Write Stuff

NM/M
Complete Set (15): 50.00
Inserted 1:20
1 Antonio Bryant 3.00
2 David Carr 12.00
3 Eric Crouch 6.00
4 Rohan Davey 3.00
5 T.J. Duckett 6.00
6 DeShaun Foster 3.00
7 Jabar Gaffney 3.00
8 Joey Harrington 12.00
9 Chad Hutchinson 2.00
10 Kurt Kittner 2.00
11 Ashley Lelie 6.00
12 Clinton Portis 3.00
13 Patrick Ramsey 2.00
14 Josh Reed 4.00
15 Michael Vick 2.00

2003 Sage Autographed

NM/M
Complete Set (45): 25.00
Common Player: .25
Unlisted Star: .75
Minor Star: .50
Pack (3): 12.00
Wax Box (12): 100.00
A1 Sam Aiken .75
A2 Boss Bailey 1.00
A3 Brad Banks 1.00
A4 Tully Banta-Cain .25
A5 Arnaz Battle .75
A6 Ronald Bellamy .75
A7 Kyle Boller 3.00
A8 Chris Brown .75
A9 Tyrone Calico .75
A10 Dallas Clark .75
A11 Kevin Curtis .75
A12 Sammy Davis .75
A13 Dahrran Diedrick .75
A14 Ken Dorsey 2.00
A15 Justin Fargas .75
A16 Justin Gage .75
A17 Jason Gesser .75
A18 Cie Grant .75
A19 Rex Grossman 2.50
A20 E.J. Henderson 1.00
A21 Taylor Jacobs 1.00
A22 Bryant Johnson 2.00
A23 Larry Johnson 2.00
A24 Teyo Johnson .75
A25 Kliff Kingsbury .75
A26 Brandon Lloyd .75
A27 Rashean Mathis .50
A28 Jerome McDougle .75
A29 Willis McGahee 3.00
A30 Billy McMullen .75
A31 Terence Newman 2.00
A32 Donnie Nickey .75
A33 Terry Pierce .50
A34 Dave Ragone 1.00
A35 Charles Rogers 3.00
A36 Chris Simms 2.00
A37 Musa Smith .75
A38 Lee Suggs 2.00
A39 Terrell Suggs 2.00
A40 Marcus Trufant .75
A41 Seneca Wallace 1.00
A42 Kelley Washington 1.00
A43 Matt Wilhelm .75
A44 Jason Witten .75
A45 George Wrighster .75

2003 Sage Autographed Autographed Bronze

Production to varying quantities 55-650
A1 Sam Aiken 260
A2 Boss Bailey 250
A3 Brad Banks 360
A4 Tully Banta-Cain 410
A5 Arnaz Battle 600
A6 Ronald Bellamy 540
A7 Kyle Boller 490
A8 Chris Brown 650
A9 Tyrone Calico 500
A10 Dallas Clark 450
A11 Kevin Curtis 650
A12 Sammy Davis 520
A13 Dahrran Diedrick 95
A14 Ken Dorsey 225
A15 Justin Fargas 650
A16 Justin Gage 460
A17 Jason Gesser 520
A19 Rex Grossman 220
A20 E.J. Henderson 420
A21 Taylor Jacobs 450
A22 Bryant Johnson 250
A23 Larry Johnson 250
A24 Teyo Johnson 460
A25 Kliff Kingsbury 450
A26 Brandon Lloyd 520
A27 Rashean Mathis 280
A28 Jerome McDougle 650
A29 Willis McGahee 240
A30 Billy McMullen 460
A31 Terence Newman 420
A32 Donnie Nickey 200
A33 Terry Pierce 650
A34 Dave Ragone 155
A35 Charles Rogers 160
A36 Chris Simms 250
A37 Musa Smith 250
A38 Lee Suggs 250
A39 Terrell Suggs 230
A40 Marcus Trufant 650
A41 Seneca Wallace 525
A42 Kelley Washington 55
A43 Matt Wilhelm 425
A44 Jason Witten 650
A45 George Wrighster 450

2003 Sage Autographed Autographed Gold

Production to varying quantities 20-200
A1 Sam Aiken 80
A2 Boss Bailey 80
A3 Brad Banks 120
A4 Tully Banta-Cain 130
A5 Arnaz Battle 170
A6 Ronald Bellamy 170
A7 Kyle Boller 150
A8 Chris Brown 200
A9 Tyrone Calico 150
A10 Dallas Clark 140
A11 Kevin Curtis 200
A12 Sammy Davis 160
A13 Dahrran Diedrick 30
A14 Ken Dorsey 70
A15 Justin Fargas 200
A16 Justin Gage 140
A17 Jason Gesser 160
A19 Rex Grossman 70
A20 E.J. Henderson 130
A21 Taylor Jacobs 140
A22 Bryant Johnson 80
A23 Larry Johnson 80
A24 Teyo Johnson 140
A25 Kliff Kingsbury 160
A26 Brandon Lloyd 160
A27 Rashean Mathis 90
A28 Jerome McDougle 200
A29 Willis McGahee 80
A30 Billy McMullen 140
A31 Terence Newman 130
A32 Donnie Nickey 60
A33 Terry Pierce 200
A34 Dave Ragone 50
A35 Charles Rogers 50
A36 Chris Simms 80
A37 Musa Smith 80
A38 Lee Suggs 80
A39 Terrell Suggs 75
A40 Marcus Trufant 200
A41 Seneca Wallace 160
A42 Kelley Washington 20
A43 Matt Wilhelm 130
A44 Jason Witten 200
A45 George Wrighster 140

2003 Sage Autographed Autographed M.E.

Production 1 set
A1 Sam Aiken 1

A2 Boss Bailey 1
A3 Brad Banks 1
A4 Tully Banta-Cain 1
A5 Arnaz Battle 1
A6 Ronald Bellamy 1
A7 Kyle Boller 1
A8 Chris Brown 1
A9 Tyrone Calico 1
A10 Dallas Clark 1
A11 Kevin Curtis 1
A12 Sammy Davis 1
A13 Dahrran Diedrick 1
A14 Ken Dorsey 1
A15 Justin Fargas 1
A16 Justin Gage 1
A17 Jason Gesser 1
A18 Cie Grant 1
A19 Rex Grossman 1
A20 E.J. Henderson 1
A21 Taylor Jacobs 1
A22 Bryant Johnson 1
A23 Larry Johnson 1
A24 Teyo Johnson 1
A25 Kliff Kingsbury 1
A26 Brandon Lloyd 1
A27 Rashean Mathis 1
A28 Jerome McDougle 1
A29 Willis McGahee 1
A30 Billy McMullen 1
A31 Terence Newman 1
A32 Donnie Nickey 1
A33 Terry Pierce 1
A34 Dave Ragone 1
A35 Charles Rogers 1
A36 Chris Simms 1
A37 Musa Smith 1
A38 Lee Suggs 1
A39 Terrell Suggs 1
A40 Marcus Trufant 1
A41 Seneca Wallace 1
A42 Kelley Washington 1
A43 Matt Wilhelm 1
A44 Jason Witten 1
A45 George Wrighster 1

2003 Sage Autographed Autographed Platinum

Production to varying quantities 5-50
A1 Sam Aiken 20
A2 Boss Bailey
A3 Brad Banks 30
A4 Tully Banta-Cain 35
A5 Arnaz Battle 50
A6 Ronald Bellamy 45
A7 Kyle Boller 40
A8 Chris Brown 50
A9 Tyrone Calico 40
A10 Dallas Clark 40
A11 Kevin Curtis 50
A12 Sammy Davis 40
A13 Dahrran Diedrick 10
A14 Ken Dorsey 20
A15 Justin Fargas 50
A16 Justin Gage 40
A17 Jason Gesser 40
A19 Rex Grossman 20
A20 E.J. Henderson 35
A21 Taylor Jacobs 40
A22 Bryant Johnson 20
A23 Larry Johnson 20
A24 Teyo Johnson 40
A25 Kliff Kingsbury 40
A26 Brandon Lloyd 40
A27 Rashean Mathis 30
A28 Jerome McDougle 50
A29 Willis McGahee 20
A30 Billy McMullen 40
A31 Terence Newman 35
A32 Donnie Nickey 15
A33 Terry Pierce 50
A34 Dave Ragone 15
A35 Charles Rogers 20
A36 Chris Simms 20
A37 Musa Smith 20
A38 Lee Suggs 20
A39 Terrell Suggs 20
A40 Marcus Trufant 50
A41 Seneca Wallace 45
A42 Kelley Washington 5
A43 Matt Wilhelm 35
A44 Jason Witten 50
A45 George Wrighster 40

2003 Sage Autographed Autographed Red

	NM/M
Common Player:	7.00
Production to varying quantities (95-999)	
Bronze (55-650)	1X-1.5X
Silver (35-400)	1X-2X
Gold (20-200)	2X-3X
Platinum (5-50)	3X-4X
A1 Sam Aiken 379	7.00
A2 Boss Bailey 370	10.00
A3 Brad Banks 540	9.00
A4 Tully Banta-Cain 620	7.00
A5 Arnaz Battle 910	7.00
A6 Ronald Bellamy 810	7.00
A7 Kyle Boller 750	25.00
A8 Chris Brown 999	7.00
A9 Tyrone Calico 670	7.00
A10 Dallas Clark 670	7.00
A11 Kevin Curtis 999	7.00
A12 Sammy Davis 799	7.00
A13 Dahrran Diedrick 139	7.00
A14 Ken Dorsey 335	18.00
A15 Justin Fargas 999	8.00
A16 Justin Gage 690	7.00
A17 Jason Gesser 799	8.00
A19 Rex Grossman 320	7.00
A20 E.J. Henderson 640	8.00
A21 Taylor Jacobs 700	8.00
A22 Bryant Johnson 360	15.00
A23 Larry Johnson 360	18.00
A24 Teyo Johnson 679	8.00
A25 Kliff Kingsbury 675	8.00
A26 Brandon Lloyd 779	7.00
A27 Rashean Mathis 400	7.00
A28 Jerome McDougle 930	7.00
A29 Willis McGahee 360	25.00
A30 Billy McMullen 690	7.00
A31 Terence Newman 640	15.00
A32 Donnie Nickey 290	7.00
A33 Terry Pierce 930	7.00
A34 Dave Ragone 210	10.00
A35 Charles Rogers 220	25.00
A36 Chris Simms 350	15.00
A37 Musa Smith 360	7.00
A38 Lee Suggs 355	15.00
A39 Terrell Suggs 350	15.00
A40 Marcus Trufant 930	10.00
A41 Seneca Wallace 799	10.00
A42 Kelley Washington 75	15.00
A43 Matt Wilhelm 650	8.00
A44 Jason Witten 950	8.00
A45 George Wrighster 670	7.00

2003 Sage Autographed Autographed Silver

Production to varying quantities 60-400
A1 Sam Aiken 160
A2 Boss Bailey 160
A3 Brad Banks 240
A4 Tully Banta-Cain 255
A5 Arnaz Battle 370
A6 Ronald Bellamy 333
A7 Kyle Boller 300
A8 Chris Brown 400
A9 Tyrone Calico 300
A10 Dallas Clark 280
A11 Kevin Curtis 400
A12 Sammy Davis 320
A13 Dahrran Diedrick 60
A14 Ken Dorsey 140
A15 Justin Fargas 400
A16 Justin Gage 290
A17 Jason Gesser 320
A19 Rex Grossman 140
A20 E.J. Henderson 260
A21 Taylor Jacobs 270
A22 Bryant Johnson 160
A23 Larry Johnson 160
A24 Teyo Johnson 290
A25 Kliff Kingsbury 275
A26 Brandon Lloyd 320
A27 Rashean Mathis 180
A28 Jerome McDougle 400
A29 Willis McGahee 150
A30 Billy McMullen 290
A31 Terence Newman 260
A32 Donnie Nickey 120
A33 Terry Pierce 400
A34 Dave Ragone 100
A35 Charles Rogers 100
A36 Chris Simms 160
A37 Musa Smith 160
A38 Lee Suggs 160
A39 Terrell Suggs 150
A40 Marcus Trufant 400
A41 Seneca Wallace 320
A42 Kelley Washington 35
A43 Matt Wilhelm 260
A44 Jason Witten 400
A45 George Wrighster 280

2003 Sage Autographed Jersey Bronze

Production 75 sets
SJ1 Brad Banks
SJ2 Arnaz Battle
SJ3 Kyle Boller
SJ4 Chad Brown
SJ5 David Carr
SJ6 Ken Dorsey
SJ7 Rex Grossman
SJ8 Taylor Jacobs
SJ9 Bryant Johnson
SJ10 Larry Johnson
SJ11 Willis McGahee
SJ12 Dave Ragone
SJ13 Charles Rogers
SJ14 Chris Simms
SJ15 Musa Smith
SJ16 Lee Suggs
SJ17 Seneca Wallace
SJ18 Kelley Washington

2003 Sage Autographed Jersey Combination

Production 10 sets
Too limited to price
Willis McGahee, Ken Dorsey
Rex Grossman, Taylor Jacobs
Larry Johnson,
Bryant Johnson
David Carr, Dave Ragone
Kyle Boller, Musa Smith
Willis McGahee,
Larry Johnson
Kyle Boller, Rex Grossman
Jay Williams, Brad Banks
Amare Stoudemire,
Bryant Johnson
Jay Ming, Rex Grossman
Yao Ming, Dave Ragone
Yao Ming, David Carr

2003 Sage Autographed Jersey Gold

Production 25 sets
SJ1 Brad Banks
SJ2 Arnaz Battle
SJ3 Kyle Boller
SJ4 Chad Brown
SJ5 David Carr
SJ6 Ken Dorsey
SJ7 Rex Grossman
SJ8 Taylor Jacobs
SJ9 Bryant Johnson
SJ10 Larry Johnson
SJ11 Willis McGahee
SJ12 Dave Ragone
SJ13 Charles Rogers
SJ14 Chris Simms
SJ15 Musa Smith
SJ16 Lee Suggs
SJ17 Seneca Wallace
SJ18 Kelley Washington

2003 Sage Autographed Jersey/Aut Combo

Production 10 sets
SJ1 Brad Banks
SJ2 Arnaz Battle
SJ3 Kyle Boller
SJ4 Chad Brown
SJ5 David Carr
SJ6 Ken Dorsey
SJ7 Rex Grossman
SJ8 Taylor Jacobs
SJ9 Bryant Johnson
SJ10 Larry Johnson
SJ11 Willis McGahee
SJ12 Dave Ragone
SJ13 Charles Rogers
SJ14 Chris Simms
SJ15 Musa Smith
SJ16 Lee Suggs
SJ17 Seneca Wallace
SJ18 Kelley Washington

2003 Sage Autographed Jersey M.E.

Production 1 set
SJ1 Brad Banks
SJ2 Arnaz Battle
SJ3 Kyle Boller
SJ4 Chad Brown
SJ5 David Carr
SJ6 Ken Dorsey
SJ7 Rex Grossman
SJ8 Taylor Jacobs
SJ9 Bryant Johnson
SJ10 Larry Johnson
SJ11 Willis McGahee
SJ12 Dave Ragone
SJ13 Charles Rogers
SJ14 Chris Simms
SJ15 Musa Smith
SJ16 Lee Suggs
SJ17 Seneca Wallace
SJ18 Kelley Washington

2003 Sage Autographed Jersey Platinum

Production 10 sets
SJ1 Brad Banks
SJ2 Arnaz Battle
SJ3 Kyle Boller
SJ4 Chad Brown
SJ5 David Carr
SJ6 Ken Dorsey
SJ7 Rex Grossman
SJ8 Taylor Jacobs
SJ9 Bryant Johnson
SJ10 Larry Johnson
SJ11 Willis McGahee
SJ12 Dave Ragone
SJ13 Charles Rogers
SJ14 Chris Simms
SJ15 Musa Smith
SJ16 Lee Suggs
SJ17 Seneca Wallace
SJ18 Kelley Washington

2003 Sage Autographed Jersey Player Proof

Production 20 sets
SJ1 Brad Banks
SJ2 Arnaz Battle
SJ3 Kyle Boller
SJ4 Chad Brown
SJ5 David Carr
SJ6 Ken Dorsey
SJ7 Rex Grossman
SJ8 Taylor Jacobs
SJ9 Bryant Johnson
SJ10 Larry Johnson
SJ11 Willis McGahee
SJ12 Dave Ragone
SJ13 Charles Rogers
SJ14 Chris Simms
SJ15 Musa Smith
SJ16 Lee Suggs
SJ17 Seneca Wallace
SJ18 Kelley Washington

2003 Sage Autographed Jersey Red

	NM/M
Common Player:	8.00
Production 99 sets	
Bronze	1X-1.5X
Production 75 sets	
Silver	1X-2X
Production 50 sets	
Gold	1X-3X
Production 25 sets	
Player Proof	2X-5X
Production 20 sets	
Platinum	2X-6x
Production 10 sets	
Jersey/Auto Combo	3X-15X
Production 10 sets	
SJ1 Brad Banks	10.00
SJ2 Arnaz Battle	8.00
SJ3 Kyle Boller	20.00
SJ4 Chad Brown	10.00
SJ5 David Carr	15.00
SJ6 Ken Dorsey	15.00
SJ7 Rex Grossman	18.00
SJ8 Taylor Jacobs	15.00
SJ9 Bryant Johnson	15.00
SJ10 Larry Johnson	15.00
SJ11 Willis McGahee	20.00
SJ12 Dave Ragone	12.00
SJ13 Charles Rogers	20.00
SJ14 Chris Simms	15.00
SJ15 Musa Smith	10.00
SJ16 Lee Suggs	12.00
SJ17 Seneca Wallace	12.00
SJ18 Kelley Washington	12.00

2003 Sage Hit

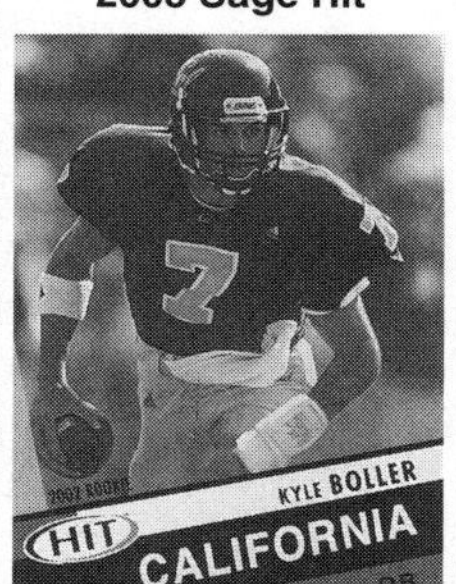

	NM/M
Complete Set (48):	25.00
Common Player:	.25
Unlisted Star:	.75
Pack (5):	4.75
Wax Box (30):	100.00
1 Charles Rogers	3.00
2 Willis McGahee	3.00
3 Arnaz Battle	.50
4 Terence Newman	1.00
5 Larry Johnson	2.00
6 Taylor Jacobs	1.00
7 Kyle Boller	3.00
8 Rex Grossman	2.50
9 Jerome McDougle	.50
10 Jason Witten	.75
11 Ken Dorsey	2.00
12 Justin Gage	.50
13 Andy Groom	.25
14 Seneca Wallace	1.00
15 Dave Ragone	1.00
16 Kliff Kingsbury	.75
17 Jason Gesser	.75
18 George Wrighster	.50
19 Ronald Bellamy	.50
20 Donnie Nickey	.50
21 Billy McMullen	.50
22 Lee Suggs	2.00
23 Chris Brown	.75
24 Bryant Johnson	2.00
25 Justin Fargas	.75
26 Brandon Lloyd	.50
27 Tyrone Calico	.50
28 Sam Aiken	.50
29 Cie Grant	.50
30 Dahrran Diedrick	.75
31 Kelley Washington	.75
32 Musa Smith	.75
33 Kevin Curtis	.50
34 Terry Pierce	.50
35 Matt Wilhelm	.50
36 Rashean Mathis	.50
37 Brad Banks	1.00
38 Tully Banta-Cain	.50
39 Sammy Davis	.50
40 Teyo Johnson	.75
41 Chris Simms	2.00
42 E.J. Henderson	1.00
43 Terrell Suggs	2.00
44 Dallas Clark	.50
45 Marcus Trufant	.75
46 Boss Bailey	1.00
47 David Carr	.75
no # Checklist/Rogers	2.00

2003 Sage Hit Emerald Autograph

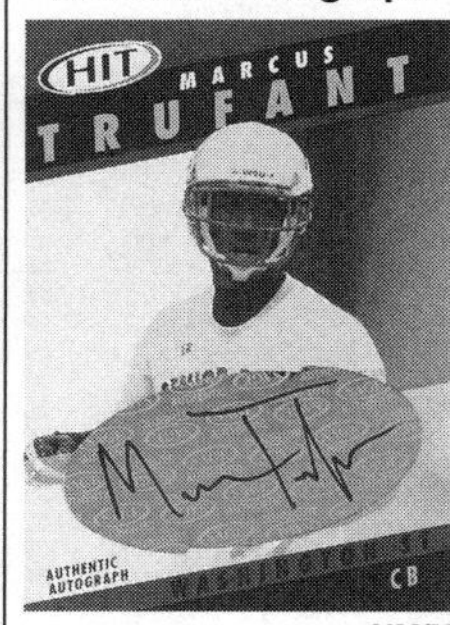

	NM/M
Common Player:	8.00
Inserted 1:6	
Silver Level	
Inserted 1:9	
Gold Level	
Production 250 sets	
1 Charles Rogers	30.00
2 Willis McGahee	30.00
3 Arnaz Battle	8.00
4 Terence Newman	15.00
5 Larry Johnson	20.00
6 Taylor Jacobs	15.00
7 Kyle Boller	30.00
8 Rex Grossman	25.00
9 Jerome McDougle	8.00
10 Jason Witten	8.00
11 Ken Dorsey	20.00
12 Justin Gage	8.00
13 Andy Groom	8.00
14 Seneca Wallace	15.00
15 Dave Ragone	20.00
16 Kliff Kingsbury	12.00
17 Jason Gesser	12.00
18 George Wrighster	8.00
19 Ronald Bellamy	12.00
20 Donnie Nickey	8.00
21 Billy McMullen	8.00
22 Lee Suggs	20.00
23 Chris Brown	12.00
24 Bryant Johnson	20.00
25 Justin Fargas	12.00
26 Brandon Lloyd	8.00
27 Tyrone Calico	8.00
28 Sam Aiken	8.00
29 Cie Grant	8.00
30 Dahrran Diedrick	12.00
31 Kelley Washington	12.00
32 Musa Smith	12.00
33 Kevin Curtis	8.00
34 Terry Pierce	8.00
35 Matt Wilhelm	12.00
36 Rashean Mathis	8.00
37 Brad Banks	15.00
38 Tully Banta-Cain	8.00
39 Sammy Davis	12.00
40 Teyo Johnson	12.00
41 Chris Simms	20.00
42 E.J. Henderson	15.00
43 Terrell Suggs	20.00
44 Dallas Clark	12.00
45 Marcus Trufant	12.00
46 Boss Bailey	15.00

2003 Sage Hit Class of 2003

	NM/M
Common Player:	.25
Emerald Level Inserted 1:3	
Silver Level	1X
Inserted 1:5	
Gold/Autographed Level	
Production 100 sets	
Autographs not priced at this time	
1 Charles Rogers	2.00
2 Willis McGahee	1.75
3 Arnaz Battle	.50
4 Terence Newman	1.00
5 Larry Johnson	1.50
6 Taylor Jacobs	1.00
7 Kyle Boller	2.00
8 Rex Grossman	1.50
9 Jerome McDougle	.50
10 Jason Witten	.50
11 Ken Dorsey	1.50
12 Justin Gage	.50
13 Andy Groom	.25
14 Seneca Wallace	1.00
15 Dave Ragone	1.50
16 Kliff Kingsbury	.50
17 Jason Gesser	.50
18 George Wrighster	.25
19 Ronald Bellamy	.25
20 Donnie Nickey	.25
21 Billy McMullen	.25
22 Lee Suggs	1.50
23 Chris Brown	.50
24 Bryant Johnson	1.50
25 Justin Fargas	.50
26 Brandon Lloyd	.25
27 Tyrone Calico	.25
28 Sam Aiken	.25
29 Cie Grant	.25
30 Dahrran Diedrick	.50
31 Kelley Washington	.50
32 Musa Smith	.50
33 Kevin Curtis	.25
34 Terry Pierce	.25
35 Matt Wilhelm	.25
36 Rashean Mathis	.25
37 Brad Banks	1.00
38 Tully Banta-Cain	.25
39 Sammy Davis	.25
40 Teyo Johnson	.50
41 Chris Simms	1.50
42 E.J. Henderson	1.00
43 Terrell Suggs	1.50
44 Dallas Clark	.25
45 Marcus Trufant	.50
46 Boss Bailey	1.00

2003 Sage Hit Class of 2003 Gold Autograph

	NM/M
Common Player:	12.00
Production 100 sets	
1 Charles Rogers	60.00
2 Willis McGahee	50.00
3 Arnaz Battle	12.00
4 Terence Newman	30.00
5 Larry Johnson	30.00
6 Taylor Jacobs	20.00
7 Kyle Boller	40.00
8 Rex Grossman	35.00
9 Jerome McDougle	12.00
10 Jason Witten	15.00
11 Ken Dorsey	30.00
12 Justin Gage	12.00
13 Andy Groom	12.00
14 Seneca Wallace	20.00
15 Dave Ragone	30.00
16 Kliff Kingsbury	15.00
17 Jason Gesser	15.00
18 George Wrighster	12.00
19 Ronald Bellamy	20.00
20 Donnie Nickey	12.00
21 Billy McMullen	12.00
22 Lee Suggs	30.00
23 Chris Brown	12.00
24 Bryant Johnson	30.00
25 Justin Fargas	15.00
26 Brandon Lloyd	12.00
27 Tyrone Calico	12.00
28 Sam Aiken	12.00
29 Cie Grant	12.00
30 Dahrran Diedrick	15.00
31 Kelley Washington	15.00
32 Musa Smith	15.00
33 Kevin Curtis	12.00
34 Terry Pierce	12.00
35 Matt Wilhelm	12.00
36 Rashean Mathis	12.00
37 Brad Banks	20.00
38 Tully Banta-Cain	12.00
39 Sammy Davis	12.00
40 Teyo Johnson	15.00
41 Chris Simms	30.00
42 E.J. Henderson	20.00
43 Terrell Suggs	30.00
44 Dallas Clark	12.00
45 Marcus Trufant	15.00
46 Boss Bailey	20.00

2003 Sage Hit Authentic Jersey Cards

	NM/M
Common Player:	15.00
Inserted 1:35	
Premium Swatches	
Production 50 sets	1X to 3X
J1 Brad Banks	15.00
J2 Kyle Boller	30.00
J3 Ken Dorsey	20.00
J4 Rex Grossman	25.00
J5 Taylor Jacobs	15.00

J6 Larry Johnson 20.00
J7 Willis McGahee 35.00
J8 Dave Ragone 20.00
J9 Charles Rogers 30.00
J10 Chris Simms 20.00
J11 Lee Suggs 20.00
J12 Kelley Washington 15.00

2003 Sage Hit Write Stuff

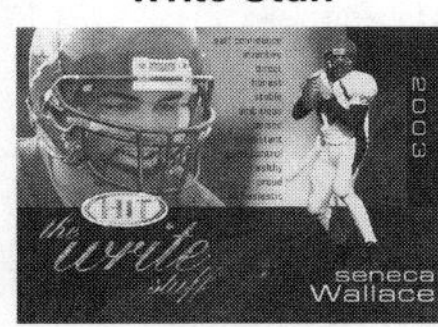

NM/M
Common Player: 1.00
Inserted 1:15
Autographed Version
Production 25 sets
(also includes Carr)
Autographs not priced at this time
1 Charles Rogers 3.00
2 Willis McGahee 2.50
3 Justin Fargas 1.00
4 Lee Suggs 2.00
5 Larry Johnson 2.00
6 Kliff Kingsbury 1.00
7 Kyle Boller 3.00
8 Rex Grossman 2.00
9 Seneca Wallace 1.50
10 Chris Simms 2.00
11 Ken Dorsey 2.00
12 Chris Brown 1.50
13 Musa Smith 1.00
14 Brad Banks 1.50
15 Dave Ragone 2.00

2003 Sage Hit Write Stuff Autographed

NM/M
Common Player: 20.00
Inserted 1:585 Production 25 sets
Too uncommon to price at this time
1 Charles Rogers 110.00
2 Willis McGahee 110.00
3 Justin Fargas 40.00
4 Lee Suggs 60.00
5 Larry Johnson 60.00
6 Kliff Kingsbury 30.00
7 Kyle Boller 110.00
8 Rex Grossman 95.00
9 Seneca Wallace 30.00
10 Chris Simms 60.00
11 Ken Dorsey 60.00
12 Chris Brown 20.00
13 Musa Smith 30.00
14 Brad Banks 40.00
15 Dave Ragone 60.00
16 David Carr 40.00

2003 Sage First Cards

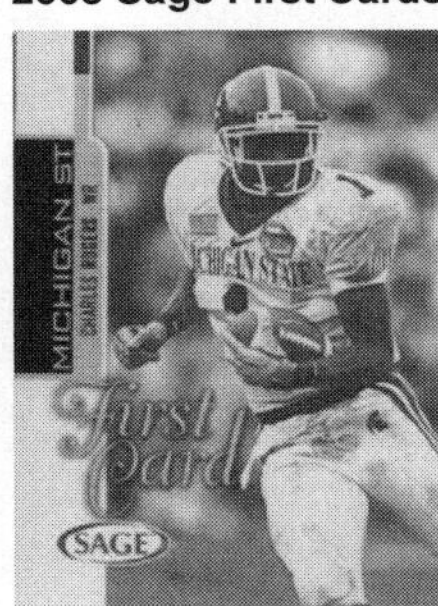

NM/M
Common Player: 8.00
Brad Banks 8.00
Arnaz Battle 8.00
Kyle Boller 12.00
Chris Brown 12.00
Ken Dorsey 12.00
Justin Fargas 12.00
Jason Gesser 12.00
Rex Grossman 12.00
Taylor Jacobs 12.00
Bryant Johnson 12.00
Larry Johnson 12.00
Teyo Johnson 8.00
Kliff Kingsbury 12.00
Willis McGahee 12.00
Terence Newman 8.00
Dave Ragone 12.00
Charles Rogers 12.00
Chris Simms 12.00
Musa Smith 12.00
Lee Suggs 12.00
Terrell Suggs 8.00
Seneca Wallace 12.00
Kelley Washington 12.00
Jason Witten 8.00

2004 Sage

NM/M
Common Player: .75
Minor Stars: 1.00
Unlisted Stars: 1.50
Pack (3): 20.00
Box (12): 200.00
1 Tatum Bell 2.50
2 Bernard Berrian 1.50
3 Michael Boulware 1.00
4 Drew Carter 1.00
5 Maurice Clarett 3.00
6 Casey Clausen 1.50
7 Michael Clayton 3.00
8 Chris Collins 1.00
9 Karlos Dansby 1.00
10 Devard Darling 1.50
11 Lee Evans 3.00
12 Clarence Farmer 1.00
13 Chris Gamble 1.50
14 Jake Grove 1.00
15 DeAngelo Hall 2.50
16 Josh Harris 1.00
17 Tommie Harris 2.00
18 Devery Henderson 1.50
19 Steven Jackson 4.00
20 Michael Jenkins 2.50
21 Greg Jones 2.00
22 Kevin Jones 4.00
23 Sean Jones 1.00
24 Derrick Knight 1.00
25 Craig Krenzel 1.50
26 Jared Lorenzen 1.00
27 Eli Manning 8.00
28 John Navarre 2.00
29 Chris Perry 2.50
30 Cody Pickett 1.50
31 Will Poole 1.00
32 Philip Rivers 6.00
33 Eli Roberson 2.00
34 Dunta Robinson 1.50
35 Ben Roethlisberger 12.00
36 Rod Rutherford 1.50
37 P.K. Sam 2.00
38 Matt Schaub 1.50
39 Will Smith 1.50
40 Jeff Smoker 2.00
41 Ben Troupe 1.00
42 Ernest Wilford 1.50
43 Reggie Williams 3.00
44 Roy Williams 5.00
45 Quincy Wilson 2.00
46 Rashaun Woods 3.00

2004 Sage Autographs Red

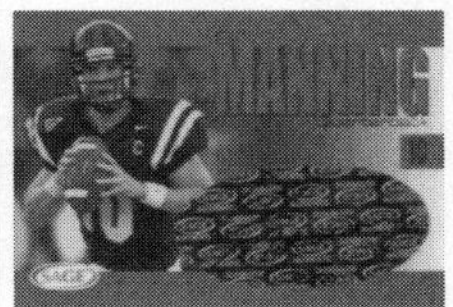

NM/M
Common Player: 6.00
Bronze: 1X-1.2X
Silver: 1X-1.5X
Gold: 1X-2X
Platinum: 2X-4X
Player Proof Production 20 Sets
Master Edition Production 1 Set
A1 Tatum Bell/500 12.00
A2 Bernard Berrian/850 6.00
A3 Michael Boulware/600 6.00
A4 Drew Carter/700 6.00
A5 Maurice Clarett/350 25.00
A6 Casey Clausen/999 6.00
A7 Michael Clayton/970 10.00
A8 Chris Collins/300 8.00
A9 Karlos Dansby/770 6.00
A10 Devard Darling/550 6.00
A11 Lee Evans/770 10.00
A13 Chris Gamble/750 8.00
A14 Jake Grove/650 8.00
A15 DeAngelo Hall/470 10.00
A16 Josh Harris/770 6.00
A17 Tommie Harris/500 8.00
A18 Devery Henderson/700 6.00
A20 Michael Jenkins/850 8.00
A21 Greg Jones/750 8.00
A22 Kevin Jones/750 15.00
A23 Sean Jones/999 6.00
A24 Derrick Knight/550 6.00
A26 Jared Lorenzen/800 6.00
A27 Eli Manning/400 80.00
A28 John Navarre/440 8.00
A29 Chris Perry/750 10.00
A30 Cody Pickett/600 6.00
A31 Will Poole/420 6.00
A32 Philip Rivers/500 30.00
A33 Eli Roberson/999 6.00
A34 Dunta Robinson/720 6.00
A35 Ben Roethlisberger/300 100.00
A36 Rod Rutherford/500 6.00
A37 P Sam/850 6.00
A38 Matt Schaub/600 6.00
A39 Will Smith/770 6.00
A40 Jeff Smoker/500 12.00
A41 Ben Troupe/999 6.00
A42 Ernest Wilford/350 6.00
A43 Reggie Williams/600 10.00
A44 Roy Williams/350 25.00
A45 Quincy Wilson/850 6.00
A46 Rashaun Woods/777 10.00

2004 Sage Jerseys Autographs

Production 10 Sets
J1 Tatum Bell
J2 Maurice Clarett
J3 Casey Clausen
J4 Lee Evans
J5 Josh Harris
J6 Devery Henderson
J7 Michael Jenkins
J8 Greg Jones
J9 Kevin Jones
J10 Jared Lorenzen
J11 Eli Manning
J12 John Navarre
J13 Chris Perry
J14 Cody Pickett
J15 Philip Rivers
J16 Eli Roberson
J17 Ben Roethlisberger
J19 Matt Schaub
J21 Reggie Williams
J22 Roy Williams
J24 Rashaun Woods

2004 Sage Jerseys Combos

Production 10 Sets
JJ1 Cody Pickett, Reggie Williams
JJ2 Chris Perry, John Navarre
JJ3 Tatum Bell, Rashaun Woods
JJ4 Maurice Clarett, Michael Jenkins
JJ5 Kevin Jones, Roy Williams
JJ6 Eli Manning, Philip Rivers
JJ7 Willis McGahee, Lee Evans
JJ8 Charles Rogers, Roy Williams
JJ9 Chris Simms, Roy Williams
JJ11 Ben Roethlisberger, Eli Manning
JJ12 Ben Roethlisberger, Philip Rivers
JJ13 Roy Williams, Reggie Williams
JJ14 Kevin Jones, Greg Jones
JJ15 Kevin Jones, Chris Perry
JJ16 Josh Harris, Kyle Boller
JJ17 Lee Suggs, Kevin Jones
JJ18 Maurice Clarett, Eli Manning

2004 Sage Jerseys Red

NM/M
Common Player: 12.00
Red Production 99 Sets
Bronze: 1X-1.2X
Bronze Production 75 Sets
Silver: 1X-1.5X
Silver Production 50 Sets
Gold: 1X-2X
Gold Production 25 Sets
Player Proofs: 1X-2X
Proof Production 20 Sets
Platinum Production 10 Sets
Master Edition Production 1 Set
J1 Tatum Bell 15.00
J2 Maurice Clarett 25.00
J3 Casey Clausen 15.00
J4 Lee Evans 25.00
J5 Josh Harris 12.00
J6 Devery Henderson 10.00
J7 Michael Jenkins 20.00
J8 Greg Jones 15.00
J9 Kevin Jones 30.00
J10 Jared Lorenzen 15.00
J11 Eli Manning 60.00
J12 John Navarre 15.00
J13 Chris Perry 15.00
J14 Cody Pickett 12.00
J15 Philip Rivers 40.00
J16 Eli Roberson 12.00
J17 Ben Roethlisberger 60.00
J19 Matt Schaub 12.00
J21 Reggie Williams 15.00
J22 Roy Williams 25.00
J24 Rashaun Woods 20.00

2004 Sage First Card

NM/M
Common Player: 10.00
1 Maurice Clarett/250 15.00
2 Casey Clausen/99 10.00
3 Michael Clayton/99 12.00
4 Lee Evans/99 12.00
5 Tommie Harris/99 10.00
6 Steven Jackson/150 15.00
7 Michael Jenkins/99 12.00
8 Greg Jones/99 10.00
9 Kevin Jones/150 15.00
10 Eli Manning/250 25.00
11 John Navarre/99 10.00
12 Chris Perry/150 15.00
13 Philip Rivers/150 20.00
14 Eli Roberson/99 10.00
15 Ben Roethlisberger/250 30.00
16 Reggie Williams/99 10.00
17 Roy Williams WR/150 12.00
18 Rashaun Woods/99 12.00

2004 Sage First Card Autographs

NM/M
AMC Maurice Clarett/99 75.00
AEM Eli Manning/99 125.00
APR Philip Rivers/99 100.00
ABR Ben Roethlisberger/99 150.00

2004 Sage Hit

NM/M
Complete Set (46): 30.00
Common Player: .75
Minor Stars: 1.00
Unlisted Stars: 1.25
Pack (5): 4.75
Box (30): 100.00
1 Reggie Williams 2.00
2 Bernard Berrian 1.00
3 Lee Evans 2.00
4 Roy Williams 3.00
5 Josh Harris 1.00
6 Greg Jones 1.25
7 Ben Roethlisberger 10.00
8 Drew Carter 1.00
9 Devery Henderson 1.00
10 Eli Manning 5.00
11 Karlos Dansby 1.00
12 Michael Jenkins 1.50
13 Maurice Clarett 2.00
14 Michael Clayton 2.00
15 Casey Clausen 1.00
16 John Navarre 1.25
17 Philip Rivers 4.00
18 Jeff Smoker 1.25
19 Ernest Wilford 1.00
20 Derrick Knight .75
21 Chris Gamble 1.00
22 Jared Lorenzen 1.00
23 Chris Perry 1.50
24 Rod Rutherford 1.00
25 Kevin Jones 2.50
26 Michael Boulware 1.00
27 Tatum Bell 1.50
28 Will Poole .75
29 Jake Grove .75
30 Eli Roberson 1.25
31 Devard Darling 1.00
32 Dunta Robinson 1.00
33 Cody Pickett 1.00
34 Steven Jackson 2.50
35 Matt Schaub 1.00
36 Sean Jones .75
37 Tommie Harris 1.25
38 Chris Collins .75
39 Will Smith 1.00
40 DeAngelo Hall 1.50
41 Rashaun Woods 2.00
42 Ben Troupe .75
43 Quincy Wilson 1.25
44 P K Sam 1.25
45 Clarence Farmer 1.00
NNO Eli Manning CL 2.50
EM1 Eli Manning SEC/30 60.00

2004 Sage Hit Autographs Emerald

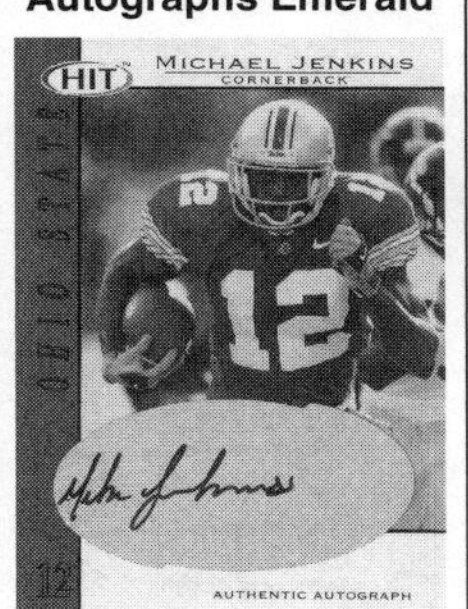

NM/M
Common Player: 8.00
Inserted 1:10
Silvers: 1X-1.2X
Silvers Inserted 1:18
Golds: 1X-1.5X
Golds Production 250 Sets
A1 Reggie Williams 15.00
A2 Bernard Berrian 10.00
A3 Lee Evans 15.00
A4 Roy Williams SP 40.00
A5 Josh Harris 10.00
A6 Greg Jones 12.00
A7 Ben Roethlisberger 100.00
A8 Drew Carter 10.00
A9 Devery Henderson 10.00
A10 Eli Manning 80.00
A11 Karlos Dansby 10.00
A12 Michael Jenkins 12.00
A13 Maurice Clarett SP 40.00
A14 Michael Clayton 15.00
A15 Casey Clausen 10.00
A16 John Navarre 12.00
A17 Philip Rivers 30.00
A18 Jeff Smoker 12.00
A19 Ernest Wilford 10.00
A20 Derrick Knight 8.00
A21 Chris Gamble 12.00
A22 Jared Lorenzen 10.00
A23 Chris Perry 15.00
A24 Rod Rutherford 12.00
A25 Kevin Jones 20.00
A26 Michael Boulware 10.00
A27 Tatum Bell 15.00
A28 Will Poole 10.00
A29 Jake Grove 8.00
A30 Eli Roberson SP
A31 Devard Darling 10.00
A32 Dunta Robinson 10.00
A33 Cody Pickett 10.00
A35 Matt Schaub 10.00
A36 Sean Jones 8.00
A37 Tommie Harris 12.00
A38 Chris Collins 8.00
A39 Will Smith 10.00
A40 DeAngelo Hall 12.00
A41 Rashaun Woods 15.00
A42 Ben Troupe 8.00
A43 Quincy Wilson 10.00
A44 P K Sam 10.00
A46 Craig Krenzel SP
A47 Rex Grossman 15.00

2004 Sage Hit Inside the Numbers

NM/M
Common Player: 3.00
Inserted 1:14
1 Pittsburgh Wide Receiver 3.00
2 USC Wide Receiver 3.00
3 Mississippi Quarterback 5.00
4 USC Quarterback 3.00
5 Ohio St. Running Back 3.00
6 Oklahoma Quarterback 3.00
7 Auburn Running Back 3.00
8 Texas Running Back 3.00
9 Kansas St. Running Back 3.00

2004 Sage Hit Jerseys

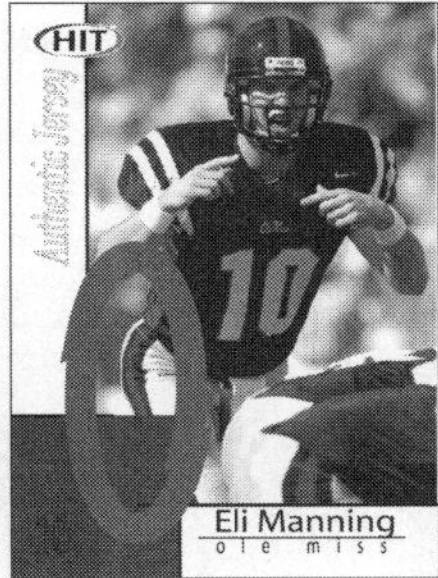

NM/M
Common Player: 10.00
Inserted 1:31
Patch Versions: 1.5X-3X
Patch Production 50 Sets
JTB Tatum Bell 12.00
JMC Maurice Clarett 20.00
JCC Casey Clausen 10.00
JLE Lee Evans 15.00
JMJ Michael Jenkins 12.00
JGJ Greg Jones 12.00
JKJ Kevin Jones 20.00
JJL Jared Lorenzen 10.00
JEM Eli Manning 50.00
JJN John Navarre 12.00
JCP Chris Perry 15.00
JPR Philip Rivers 30.00
JER Eli Roberson 10.00
JBR Ben Roethlisberger 50.00
JRE Reggie Williams 12.00
JRO Roy Williams 20.00
JRW Rashaun Woods 15.00

2004 Sage Hit Ohio State Autographs

NM/M
Common Player: 20.00
Production 50 Sets
OA1 Drew Carter 20.00
OA2 Maurice Clarett 80.00
OA3 Chris Gamble 20.00
OA4 Michael Jenkins 30.00
OA5 Craig Krenzel 40.00
OA6 Will Smith 25.00

2004 Sage Hit Q&A

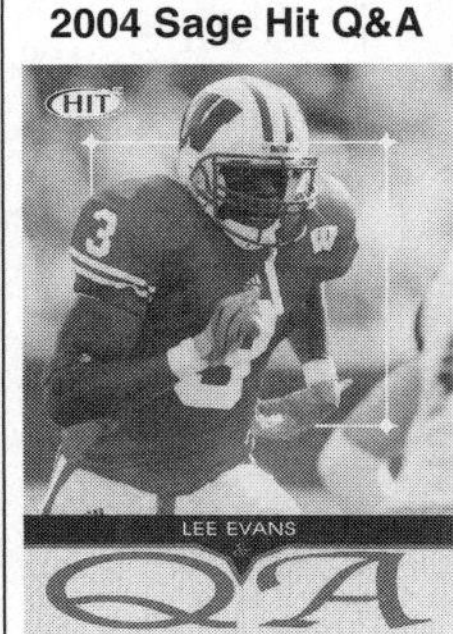

Singles: Same As Base Set
Emerald Inserted 1:2
Silver: 1X-1.2X
Silver Inserted 1:5

2004 Sage Hit Q&A Autographs

NM/M
Common Player: 12.00
Production 100 Sets
QA34 & QA45 Not Issued
QA1 Reggie Williams 30.00
QA2 Bernard Berrian 15.00
QA3 Lee Evans 40.00
QA4 Roy Williams 50.00
QA5 Josh Harris 15.00
QA6 Greg Jones 20.00
QA7 Ben Roethlisberger 150.00
QA8 Drew Carter 12.00
QA9 Devery Henderson 12.00
QA10 Eli Manning 120.00
QA11 Karlos Dansby 12.00
QA12 Michael Jenkins 20.00
QA13 Maurice Clarett
QA14 Michael Clayton 30.00
QA15 Casey Clausen 20.00
QA16 John Navarre 15.00
QA17 Philip Rivers 60.00
QA18 Jeff Smoker 25.00
QA19 Ernest Wilford 12.00
QA20 Derrick Knight 12.00
QA21 Chris Gamble 80.00
QA22 Jared Lorenzen 12.00
QA23 Chris Perry 25.00
QA24 Rod Rutherford 12.00
QA25 Kevin Jones 30.00
QA26 Michael Boulware 12.00
QA27 Tatum Bell 30.00
QA28 Will Poole 12.00
QA29 Jake Grove 12.00
QA30 Eli Roberson SP
QA31 Devard Darling 12.00
QA32 Dunta Robinson 20.00
QA33 Cody Pickett 20.00
QA35 Matt Schaub 20.00
QA36 Sean Jones 12.00
QA37 Tommie Harris 20.00
QA38 Chris Collins 15.00
QA39 Will Smith 15.00
QA40 DeAngelo Hall 25.00
QA41 Rashaun Woods 25.00
QA42 Ben Troupe 12.00
QA43 Quincy Wilson 20.00
QA44 P K Sam 15.00
QA46 Craig Krenzel 25.00

2004 Sage Hit Write Stuff

NM/M
Common Plaer: 1.25
Inserted 1:15
1 Eli Manning 5.00
2 Ben Roethlisberger 4.00
3 Philip Rivers 4.00
4 Matt Schaub 1.00
5 John Navarre 1.25
6 Cody Pickett 1.00
7 Roy Williams 3.00
8 Reggie Williams 2.00
9 Lee Evans 2.00
10 Rashaun Woods 2.00
11 Michael Clayton 2.00
12 Greg Jones 1.25
13 Maurice Clarett 2.00
14 Chris Perry 1.50
15 Kevin Jones 2.50

2004 Sage Hit Write Stuff Autographs

Production 25 Sets
WSA1 Eli Manning
WSA2 Ben Roethlisberger
WSA3 Philip Rivers
WSA4 Matt Schaub
WSA5 John Navarre
WSA6 Cody Pickett
WSA7 Roy Williams
WSA8 Reggie Williams
WSA9 Lee Evans
WSA10 Rashaun Woods
WSA11 Michael Clayton
WSA12 Greg Jones
WSA13 Maurice Clarett
WSA14 Chris Perry
WSA15 Kevin Jones

2004 Sage Jersey Update

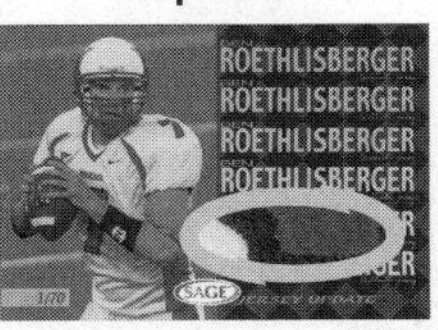

NM/M
Common Player (J1-J24): 5.00
Minor Stars (J1-J24): 6.00
Unlisted Stars (J1-J24): 8.00
Pack (1): 15.00
Box (6): 70.00
J1 Tatum Bell 10.00
J2 Maurice Clarett 12.00
J3 Casey Clausen 6.00

J4 Lee Evans 12.00
J5 Josh Harris 5.00
J6 Devery Henderson 6.00
J7 Michael Jenkins 10.00
J8 Greg Jones 8.00
J9 Kevin Jones 15.00
J10 Jared Lorenzen 5.00
J11 Eli Manning 25.00
J12 John Navarre 8.00
J13 Chris Perry 10.00
J14 Cody Pickett 6.00
J15 Philip Rivers 20.00
J16 Eli Roberson 5.00
J17 Ben Roethlisberger 30.00
J18 Rod Rutherford 5.00
J19 Matt Schaub 6.00
J20 Jeff Smoker 8.00
J21 Reggie Williams 12.00
J22 Roy Williams-WR 20.00
J23 Quincy Wilson 8.00
J24 Rashaun Woods 12.00

2004 Sage Jersey Update Autographs

No Pricing
Production to 5
AJ1 Eli Manning
AJ2 Philip Rivers
AJ3 Roy Williams
AJ4 Ben Roethlisberger
AJ5 Lee Evans
AJ6 Kevin Jones

2004 Sage Jersey Update Premium Swatch/Jersey

No Pricing
Production 10 Sets
J1 Tatum Bell
J2 Maurice Clarett
J3 Casey Clausen
J4 Lee Evans
J5 Josh Harris
J6 Devery Henderson
J7 Michael Jenkins
J8 Greg Jones
J9 Kevin Jones
J10 Jared Lorenzen
J11 Eli Manning
J12 John Navarre
J13 Chris Perry
J14 Cody Pickett
J15 Philip Rivers
J16 Eli Roberson
J17 Ben Roethlisberger
J18 Rod Rutherford
J19 Matt Schaub
J20 Jeff Smoker
J21 Reggie Williams
J22 Roy Williams
J23 Quincy Wilson
J24 Rashaun Woods

2004 Sage Jersey Update Roethlisberger

NM/M
Sequentially Numbered
1B Ben Roethlisberger 60.00
1W Ben Roethlisberger 40.00
BR1 Ben Roethlisberger 30.00

2005 Sage Hit

NM/M
Common Player (1-50): .50
Minor Star (1-50): .75
Unlisted Star (1-50): 1.00
Pack (5): 4.00
Box (30): 125.00
1 Craphonso Thorpe .50
2 Derrick Johnson 1.50
3 Frank Gore 1.00
4 Ciatrick Fason 1.00
5 Charlie Frye 1.50
6 Antrel Rolle 1.50
7 Dan Orlovsky 1.00
8 Aaron Rodgers 4.00
9 Mark Clayton 1.50
10 Thomas Davis .50
11 Alex Smith QB 5.00
12 Fred Gibson 1.00
13 Maurice Clarett 2.00
14 David Greene 1.00
15 Carlos Rogers 1.00
16 Andrew Walter 1.00
17 Jason Campbell 3.00
18 Jason White 1.50
19 Matt Jones 2.00
20 Marion Barber .75
21 Taylor Stubblefield .50
22 Jammal Brown .75
23 Ronnie Brown 3.00
24 Carnell Williams 3.00
25 Kay-Jay Harris .75
26 Reggie Brown .75
27 Troy Williamson 2.00
28 Anthony Davis .75
29 Josh Davis .50
30 J.J. Arrington 1.50
31 Alex Smith TE 1.00
32 Corey Webster .75
33 Vernand Morency .75
34 Derek Anderson .75
35 Demarcus Ware 1.00
36 Kyle Orton 1.50
37 Brock Berlin .75
38 Marlin Jackson .75
39 Channing Crowder .75
40 Roddy White 1.00
41 Roscoe Parrish 1.00
42 Adrian McPherson 1.50
43 Brodney Pool .75
44 T.A. McLendon .75
45 Terrence Murphy .50
46 Chris Rix .75
47 Ben Roethlisberger 5.00
48 Dante Ridgeway .50
49 Justin Miller .75
50 Jonathan Goddard .50
BRJ Ben Roethlisberger MAC Jsy/7
EMJ Eli Manning SEC Jsy/10
PRJ Philip Rivers AAC Jsy/17
ROY Ben Roethlisberger ROY/100 20.00

2005 Sage Hit Reflect Blue

Cards 1-50: .75X-2X
Inserted 1:1.5

2005 Sage Hit Reflect Silver

Cards 1-50: .75X-2X
Inserted 1:1.5

2005 Sage Hit Reflect Gold Autographs

Cards 1-50: 15X-25X
Production 100 Sets

2005 Sage Hit ACC Autographs

NM/M
Common Player: 20.00
Production 50 Sets
ACC1 Philip Rivers/7
ACC2 T.A. McLendon 20.00
ACC3 Frank Gore 30.00
ACC4 Roscoe Parrish 50.00
ACC5 Brock Berlin 20.00
ACC6 Justin Miller 20.00
ACC7 Chris Rix 20.00
ACC8 Craphonso Thorpe 20.00
ACC9 Adrian McPherson 50.00

2005 Sage Hit Autographs Blue

NM/M
Common Player: 8.00
Inserted 1:10
Silver: .75X-1.25X
Inserted 1:18
Gold: 1X-2X
Production 250 Sets
1 Craphonso Thorpe 8.00
2 Derrick Johnson 15.00
3 Frank Gore 12.00
4 Ciatrick Fason 12.00
5 Charlie Frye 15.00
7 Dan Orlovsky 12.00
8 Aaron Rodgers 50.00
9 Mark Clayton 15.00
10 Thomas Davis 8.00
11 Alex Smith QB 75.00
12 Fred Gibson 12.00
14 David Greene 12.00
15 Carlos Rogers 12.00
16 Andrew Walter 12.00
17 Jason Campbell 25.00
18 Jason White 15.00
19 Matt Jones 20.00
20 Marion Barber 10.00
21 Taylor Stubblefield 10.00
22 Jammal Brown 10.00
23 Ronnie Brown 25.00
24 Carnell Williams 25.00
25 Kay-Jay Harris 10.00
26 Reggie Brown 10.00
27 Troy Williamson 20.00
28 Anthony Davis 10.00
29 Josh Davis 8.00
30 J.J. Arrington 8.00
31 Alex Smith TE 15.00
32 Corey Webster 12.00
33 Vernand Morency 10.00
34 Derek Anderson 10.00
35 Demarcus Ware 12.00
36 Kyle Orton 15.00
37 Brock Berlin 10.00
38 Marlin Jackson 10.00
39 Channing Crowder 10.00
41 Roscoe Parrish 12.00
42 Adrian McPherson 15.00
43 Brodney Pool 10.00
44 T.A. McLendon 10.00
45 Terrence Murphy 8.00
46 Chris Rix 10.00
48 Dante Ridgeway 8.00
49 Justin Miller 10.00
50 Jonathan Goddard 8.00

2005 Sage Hit Ben Roethlisberger

NM/M
Roethlisberger Card: 2.00
Inserted 1:MAC pack
1 Ben Roethlisberger 2.00
2 Ben Roethlisberger 2.00
3 Ben Roethlisberger 2.00
4 Ben Roethlisberger 2.00
5 Ben Roethlisberger 2.00
6 Ben Roethlisberger 2.00
7 Ben Roethlisberger 2.00
8 Ben Roethlisberger 2.00
9 Ben Roethlisberger 2.00
10 Ben Roethlisberger 2.00
11 Ben Roethlisberger 2.00
12 Ben Roethlisberger 2.00
13 Ben Roethlisberger 2.00
14 Ben Roethlisberger 2.00
15 Ben Roethlisberger 2.00
16 Ben Roethlisberger 2.00
17 Ben Roethlisberger 2.00
18 Ben Roethlisberger 2.00
19 Ben Roethlisberger 2.00
20 Ben Roethlisberger 2.00
21 Ben Roethlisberger 2.00
22 Ben Roethlisberger 2.00
23 Ben Roethlisberger 2.00
24 Ben Roethlisberger 2.00
25 Ben Roethlisberger 2.00
26 Ben Roethlisberger 2.00
27 Ben Roethlisberger 2.00
28 Ben Roethlisberger 2.00
29 Ben Roethlisberger 2.00
30 Ben Roethlisberger 2.00
31 Ben Roethlisberger 2.00
32 Ben Roethlisberger 2.00
33 Ben Roethlisberger 2.00
34 Ben Roethlisberger 2.00
35 Ben Roethlisberger 2.00
36 Ben Roethlisberger 2.00

2005 Sage Hit Jerseys

NM/M
Common Player: 8.00
Inserted 1:31
Premium Swatches: 1X-2X
Production 50 Sets
JA J.J. Arrington 12.00
RB Ronnie Brown 20.00
JC Jason Campbell 20.00
MO Maurice Clarett 15.00
MC Mark Clayton 12.00
AD Anthony Davis 8.00
CF Ciatrick Fason 10.00
DG David Greene 10.00
AM Adrian McPherson 12.00
VM Vernand Morency 8.00
DO Dan Orlovsky 10.00
KO Kyle Orton 12.00
RP Roscoe Parrish 10.00
CR Chris Rix 8.00
AR Aaron Rodgers 25.00
BR Ben Roethlisberger 30.00
AS Alex Smith QB 30.00
AW Andrew Walter 10.00
JW Jason White 12.00
CW Carnell Williams 20.00

2005 Sage Hit MAC Autographs

NM/M
Common Player: 20.00
Production 50 Sets
MAC1 Ben Roethlisberger/7
MAC2 Charlie Frye 40.00
MAC3 Jonathan Goddard 20.00
MAC4 Josh Davis 20.00
MAC5 Dante Ridgeway 25.00

2005 Sage Hit SEC Autographs

NM/M
Common Player: 25.00
Production 50 Sets
SEC1 Eli Manning/10
SEC2 Carnell Williams 100.00
SEC3 Ronnie Brown 100.00
SEC4 Jason Campbell 50.00
SEC5 Carlos Rogers 25.00
SEC6 David Greene 25.00
SEC7 Reggie Brown 25.00
SEC8 Fred Gibson 25.00
SEC9 Thomas Davis 30.00
SEC10 Troy Williamson 50.00
SEC11 Matt Jones 100.00
SEC12 Corey Webster 25.00
SEC13 Ciatrick Fason 30.00
SEC14 Channing Crowder 40.00

2005 Sage Hit Write Staff

NM/M
Common Player: 3.00
Inserted 1:15
Autographs: 12X-15X
Production 25 Sets
1 Ronnie Brown 6.00
2 Jason Campbell 6.00
3 Mark Clayton 4.00
4 Ciatrick Fason 3.00
5 Charlie Frye 4.00
6 David Greene 3.00
7 Derrick Johnson 4.00
8 Dan Orlovsky 3.00
9 Kyle Orton 4.00
10 Aaron Rodgers 8.00
11 Alex Smith QB 10.00
12 Andrew Walter 3.00
13 Jason White 4.00
14 Carnell Williams 6.00
15 Troy Williamson 5.00

1968-69 Saints 8x10

Measuring 8" x 10", the 35 black-and-white photo cards feature members of the 1968-69 Saints teams. The backs are unnumbered and blank.

NM/M
Complete Set (35): 120.00
Common Player: 3.00
1 Dan Abramowicz 6.00
2 Doug Atkins 7.50
3 Tom Barrington 4.00
4 Jim Boeke 3.00
5 Johnny Brewer 4.00
6 Bo Burris 3.00
7 Bill Cody 3.00
8 Ted Davis 3.00
9 John Douglas 3.00
10 Charles Durkee 3.00
11 John Gilliam 4.00
12 Jim Hester 3.00
13 Gene Howard 3.00
14 Les Kelley 3.00
15 Jake Kupp 4.00
16 Earl Leggett 3.00
17 Archie Manning 20.00
18 Don McCall 3.00
19 Tom McNeill 3.00
20 Richard Neal 3.00
21 Dave Parks 4.00
22 Dave Parks (with small inset photo) 4.00
23 Ray Poage 3.00
24 David Rowe 3.00
25 Roy Schmidt 3.00
26 Randy Schultz 3.00
27 Brian Schweda 3.00
28 Monty Stickles 3.00
29 Steve Stonebreaker 4.00
30 Jerry Sturm 3.00
31 Mike Tilleman 3.00
32 Joe Wendryhoski 3.00
33 Ernie Wheelwright 4.00
34 Fred Whittingham 3.00
35 Del Williams 3.00

1974 Saints Circle Inset

Measuring 8" x 10", the 22 photos showcase a black-and-white action photo on the front, with a player headshot pictured inside a circle inset. Printed at the bottom of the card are the player's name, position and team name. The backs are unnumbered and blank.

NM/M
Complete Set (22): 120.00
Common Player: 5.00
1 John Beasley 5.00
2 Tom Blanchard 6.00
3 Larry Cipa 5.00
4 Don Coleman 5.00
5 Wayne Colman 5.00
6 Jack DeGrenier 5.00
7 Rick Kingrea 5.00
8 Phil LaPorta 5.00
9 Odell Lawson 5.00
10 Archie Manning 20.00
11 Alvin Maxson 6.00
12 Bill McClard 5.00
13 Bill McNeill 5.00
14 Jim Merlo 6.00
15 Rick Middleton 5.00
16 Derland Moore 5.00
17 Jerry Moore 5.00
18 Joel Parker 5.00
19 Jess Phillips 5.00
20 Terry Schmidt 5.00
21 Paul Seal 5.00
22 Dave Thompson 5.00

1979 Saints Coke

The 45 cards are anchored by a black-and-white player headshot, with the Coca-Cola logo in an oval in the upper right. The Saints logo is in the lower left and the player's name is printed in the lower right. The fronts of the cards are bordered in red. The card backs have the card number inside a helmet in the upper left, while the player's name is to the right of the helmet. His position is printed inside a banner. Beneath the banner is the player's bio. The Coca-Cola logo is located at the bottom center.

NM/M
Complete Set (45): 60.00
Common Player: 1.00
1 Archie Manning 8.00
2 Ed Burns 1.00
3 Bobby Scott 1.50
4 Russell Erxleben 1.50
5 Eric Felton 1.00
6 David Gray 1.00
7 Ricky Ray 1.00
8 Clarence Chapman 1.00
9 Kim Jones 1.00
10 Mike Strachan 1.00
11 Tony Galbreath 2.00
12 Tom Myers 1.50
13 Chuck Muncie 3.00
14 Jack Holmes 1.00
15 Don Schwartz 1.00
16 Ralph McGill 1.00
17 Ken Bordelon 1.00
18 Jim Kovach 1.00
19 Pat Hughes 1.00
20 Reggie Mathis 1.00
21 Jim Merlo 1.00
22 Joe Federspiel 1.00
23 Don Reese 1.00
24 Roger Finnie 1.00
25 John Hill 1.00
26 Barry Bennett 1.00
27 Dave Lafary 1.00
28 Robert Woods 1.00
29 Conrad Dobler 1.50
30 John Watson 1.00
31 Fred Sturt 1.00
32 J.T. Taylor 1.00
33 Mike Fultz 1.00
34 Joe Campbell 1.00
35 Derland Moore 1.00
36 Elex Price 1.00
37 Elois Grooms 1.00
38 Emanuel Zanders 1.00
39 Ike Harris 1.00
40 Tinker Owens 1.50
41 Rich Mauti 1.00
42 Henry Childs 1.50
43 Larry Hardy 1.00
44 Brooks Williams 1.00
45 Wes Chandler 3.50
--- Cover Card 3.00

1992 Saints McDag

Showcased on the front of the 32-card set is "Saints '92" inside a brown border on the left side. The photo is located on the right, with the Saints' logo in the lower left of the photo. The player's name is printed in a gold stripe at the bottom of the front. The backs, which are unnumbered, have the player's name, position, bio, number, career highlights and safety tips. The Behavioral Health and Saints logos are printed on the lower left and right, respectively. The cards were produced by McDag Productions.

NM/M
Complete Set (32): 12.00
Common Player: .25
1 Morten Andersen .50
2 Gene Atkins .40
3 Toi Cook .25
4 Tommy Barnhardt .25
5 Hoby Brenner .40
6 Stan Brock .40
7 Vince Buck .40
8 Wesley Carroll .40
9 Jim Dombrowski .25
10 Vaughn Dunbar .50
11 Quinn Early .75
12 Bobby Hebert .50
13 Craig Heyward .60
14 Joel Hilgenberg .25
15 Dalton Hilliard .40
16 Rickey Jackson .40
17 Vaughan Johnson .25
18 Reginald Jones .25
19 Eric Martin .40
20 Wayne Martin .40
21 Brett Maxie .25
22 Fred McAfee .25
23 Sam Mills .40
24 Jim Mora (CO) .40
25 Pat Swilling .50
26 John Tice .25
27 Renaldo Turnbull .50
28 Floyd Turner .40
29 Steve Walsh .50
30 Frank Warren .25
31 Jim Wilks .25
32 Saints Cheerleaders .40

1962 Salada Coins

These coins, featuring 154 pro football players, are color-color-coded according to the team the player plays for; each team has a specific rim color. The fronts feature a color head-and-shoulders shot of the player without his helmet on. The backs are numbered and contain advertising for Salada Tea and Junket brand desserts. Brief biographical information, including the collegiate school the player attended, is also given. Each coin measures 1-1/2" diameter. The set can sometimes be found as a complete set in its own custom box. Double- and triple-printed coins are indicated by (DP) and (TP) and are easier to find than the others.

NM/M
Complete Set (154): 3,000
Common Player DP: 7.50
Common Player SP: 25.00
1 Johnny Unitas 175.00
2 Lenny Moore 85.00
3 Jim Parker 50.00
4 Gino Marchetti 60.00
5 Dick Szymanski 25.00
6 Alex Sandusky 25.00
7 Raymond Berry 90.00
8 Jimmy Orr 30.00
9 Ordell Braase 25.00
10 Bill Pellington 25.00
11 Bob Boyd 25.00
12 Paul Hornung (DP) 25.00
13 Jim Taylor (DP) 20.00
14 Henry Jordan (DP) 8.00
15 Dan Currie (DP) 8.00
16 Bill Forester (DP) 8.00
17 Dave Hanner (DP) 8.00
18 Bart Starr (DP) 30.00
19 Max McGee (DP) 7.50
20 Jerry Kramer (DP) 9.00
21 Forrest Gregg (DP) 15.00
22 Jim Ringo (DP) 15.00
23 Billy Kilmer 55.00
24 Charlie Krueger 25.00
25 Bob St. Clair 50.00
26 Abe Woodson 25.00
27 Jimmy Johnson 65.00
28 Matt Hazeltine 25.00
29 Bruce Bosley 25.00
30 Dan Conners 25.00
31 John Brodie 80.00
32 J.D. Smith 25.00
33 Monty Stickles 25.00
34 Johnny Morris (DP) 9.00
35 Stan Jones (DP) 15.00
36 J.C. Caroline (DP) 8.00
37 Richie Petitbon (DP) 9.00
38 Joe Fortunato (DP) 9.00
39 Larry Morris (DP) 6.00
40 Doug Atkins (DP) 12.00
41 Billy Wade (DP) 7.50
42 Rick Casares (DP) 9.00
43 Willie Galimore (DP) 9.00
44 Angelo Coia (DP) 8.00
45 Ollie Matson 65.00
46 Carroll Dale 30.00
47 Ed Meador 30.00
48 Jon Arnett 35.00
49 Joe Marconi 25.00
50 John LoVetere 25.00
51 Red Phillips 25.00
52 Zeke Bratkowski 35.00
53 Dick Bass 30.00
54 Les Richter 30.00
55 Art Hunter (DP) 8.00
56 Jim Brown (TP) 65.00
57 Mike McCormack (DP) 12.00
58 Bob Gain (DP) 8.00
59 Paul Wiggin (DP) 7.50
60 Jim Houston (DP) 7.50
61 Ray Renfro (DP) 7.50
62 Galen Fiss (DP) 8.00
63 J.R. Smith (DP) 8.00
64 John Morrow (DP) 8.00
65 Gene Hickerson (DP) 8.00
66 Jim Ninowski (DP) 7.50
67 Tom Tracy 30.00
68 Buddy Dial 30.00
69 Mike Sandusky 30.00
70 Lou Michaels 30.00
71 Preston Carpenter 25.00
72 John Reger 25.00
73 John Henry Johnson 65.00
74 Gene Lipscomb 40.00
75 Mike Henry 30.00
76 George Tarasovic 25.00
77 Bobby Layne 70.00
78 Harley Sewell (DP) 8.00
79 Darris McCord (DP) 8.00
80 Yale Lary (DP) 12.00
81 Jim Gibbons (DP) 8.00
82 Gail Codgill (DP) 8.00
83 Nick Pietrosante (DP) 9.00
84 Alex Karras (DP) 15.00
85 Dick "Night Train" Lane (DP) 12.00
86 Joe Schmidt (DP) 15.00
87 John Gordy (DP) 8.00
88 Milt Plum (DP) 7.50
89 Andy Stynchula 25.00
90 Bob Toneff 25.00
91 Bill Anderson 30.00
92 Sam Horner 25.00
93 Norm Snead 30.00
94 Bobby Mitchell 65.00
95 Billy Barnes 25.00
96 Rod Breedlove 25.00
97 Fred Hageman 25.00
98 Vince Promuto 25.00
99 Joe Rutgens 25.00
100 Maxie Baughan (DP) 9.00
101 Pete Retzlaff (DP) 7.50
102 Tom Brookshier (DP) 9.00
103 Sonny Jurgensen (DP) 25.00
104 Ed Khayat (DP) 6.00
105 Chuck Bednarik (DP) 15.00
106 Tommy McDonald (DP) 9.00
107 Bobby Walston (DP) 8.00
108 Ted Dean (DP) 8.00
109 Clarence Peaks (DP) 8.00
110 Jimmy Carr (DP) 8.00
111 Sam Huff (DP) 15.00
112 Erich Barnes (DP) 7.50
113 Del Shofner (DP) 9.00
114 Bob Gaiters (DP) 8.00
115 Alex Webster (DP) 9.00
116 Dick Modzelewski (DP) 7.50
117 Jim Katcavage (DP) 7.50
118 Roosevelt Brown (DP) 15.00
119 Y.A. Tittle (DP) 25.00
120 Andy Robustelli (DP) 12.00
121 Dick Lynch (DP) 7.50
122 Don Webb (DP) 8.00
123 Larry Eisenhauer (DP) 8.00
124 Babe Parilli (DP) 7.50
125 Charles Long (DP) 8.00
126 Billy Lott (DP) 8.00
127 Harry Jacobs (DP) 8.00
128 Bob Dee (DP) 8.00
129 Ron Burton (DP) 7.50
130 Jim Colclough (TP) 3.00
131 Gino Cappelletti (DP) 9.00
132 Tommy Addison (DP) 8.00
133 Larry Grantham (DP) 7.50
134 Dick Christy (DP) 8.00
135 Bill Mathis (DP) 7.50
136 Butch Songin (DP) 8.00
137 Dainard Paulson (DP) 8.00
138 Roger Ellis (DP) 8.00
139 Mike Hudock (DP) 8.00
140 Don Maynard (DP) 20.00
141 Al Dorow (DP) 7.50
142 Jack Klotz (DP) 8.00
143 Lee Riley (DP) 8.00
144 Bill Atkins (DP) 8.00
145 Art Baker (DP) 8.00
146 Stew Barber (DP) 8.00
147 Glen Bass (DP) 8.00
148 Al Bemiller (DP) 8.00
149 Richie Lucas (DP) 7.50
150 Archie Matsos (DP) 8.00
151 Warren Rabb (DP) 8.00
152 Ken Rice (DP) 8.00
153 Billy Shaw (DP) 7.50
154 Laverne Torczon (DP) 8.00

1959 San Giorgio Flipbooks

Measuring 5-3/4" x 3-9/16", the 17 flipbooks showcase movement of a player on 14 different photos. When the photos are separated and sorted, the photos go into motion when they are flipped. Players from the Washington Redskins, Philadelphia Eagles and Pittsburgh Steelers are pictured in the set. Many collectors prefer the flipbooks to be intact and uncut.

		NM/M
Complete Set (17):		2,500
Common Player:		150.00
1	Sam Baker	175.00
2	Bill Barnes	150.00
3	Chuck Bednarik	300.00
4	Don Bosseler	150.00
5	Darrell Brewster	150.00
6	Jack Butler	150.00
7	Proverb Jacobs	150.00
8	Eddie LeBaron	200.00
9	Tommy McDonald	175.00
10	Ed Meadows	150.00
11	Gern Nagler	150.00
12	Clarence Peaks	150.00
13	Pete Retzlaff	175.00
14	Mike Sommer	150.00
15	Tom Tracy	175.00
16	Bobby Walston	150.00
17	Chuck Weber	150.00

1989 Score Promos

These cards were used to promote Score's debut football set. They are basically identical to the 1989 regular issue, but these six promo cards can be distinguished from the regular set by the use of a registered symbol on them instead of a trademark symbol. Also, the stats on these promo cards are carried out to only one decimal place on the card back; the regular cards carry out the stats to two places. These cards were sent to dealers along with order forms for the 1989 set.

		NM/M
Complete Set (6):		75.00
Common Player:		5.00
1	Joe Montana	35.00
2	Bo Jackson	15.00
3	Boomer Esiason	12.00
4	Roger Craig	8.00
5	Too Tall Jones (Registered seven sacks, regular card issue has registered 7.0 sacks)	5.00
6	Phil Simms (Moorehead State, should say Morehead State; photo cropping has Score logo blocking part of the ball)	8.00

1989 Score

Score's premier set of football cards, a 330-card edition, was released in August 1989. An additional 110 cards were released as a boxed updated set to hobby shops in January 1990 and were numbered 331-440 with an "S" following the number. Score expanded its print run and corrected several errors in the regular set: #101, Keith Jackson (wrong uniform number on back); #122, Ricky Sanders (wrong uniform number on back); #126, Ron Hall (wrong photos on front and back); #188 Mark Carrier (wrong photo -- original back showed Bruce Hill); #218, Willie Gault (photo showed Greg Townsend); #293, Keith Jackson's All Pro card (wrong uniform number on back); #305, Tim Brown (photo showed James Lofton); and #316, Eric Thomas (wrong uniform number on back). The corrected cards were issued in both wax boxes and in factory sets, a Score spokesman said. The corrected cards are scarcer than the error cards. Score was the first set to include the same year's first-round draft picks. Rookies in this set include Barry Sanders, Deion Sanders, Troy Aikman, Louis Oliver, Dave Meggett, Erik McMillan and Don Majkowski.

		NM/M
Complete Set (330):		100.00
Comp. Factory Set (330):		125.00
Common Player:		.10
Minor Stars:		.20
Pack (15):		8.00
Wax Box (36):		200.00
1	Joe Montana	3.00
2	Bo Jackson	1.00
3	Boomer Esiason	.20
4	Roger Craig	.10
5	Ed Jones	.10
6	Phil Simms	.20
7	Dan Hampton	.10
8	*John Settle*	.10
9	Bernie Kosar	.20
10	Al Toon	.10
11	*Bubby Brister*	3.00
12	Mark Clayton	.10
13	Dan Marino	4.00
14	Joe Morris	.10
15	Warren Moon	1.00
16	Chuck Long	.10
17	Mark Jackson	.10
18	*Michael Irvin*	5.00
19	Bruce Smith	.10
20	Anthony Carter	.10
21	Charles Haley	.20
22	Dave Duerson	.10
23	Troy Stradford	.10
24	Freeman McNeil	.10
25	Jerry Gray	.10
26	Bill Maas	.10
27	*Chris Chandler*	6.00
28	*Tom Newberry*	.10
29	Albert Lewis	.10
30	Jay Schroeder	.10
31	Dalton Hilliard	.10
32	Tony Eason	.10
33	Rick Donnelly	.10
34	Herschel Walker	.20
35	Wesley Walker	.10
36	Chris Doleman	.20
37	Pat Swilling	.20
38	Joey Browner	.10
39	Shane Conlan	.10
40	Mike Tomczak	.10
41	Webster Slaughter	.10
42	Ray Donaldson	.10
43	Christian Okoye	.10
44	Jon Bosa	.10
45	*Aaron Cox*	.10
46	Bobby Hebert	.10
47	Carl Banks	.10
48	Jeff Fuller	.10
49	Gerald Willhite	.10
50	Mike Singletary	.10
51	Stanley Morgan	.10
52	Mark Bavaro	.10
53	Mickey Shuler	.10
54	Keith Millard	.10
55	Andre Tippett	.10
56	Vance Johnson	.10
57	*Bennie Blades*	.20
58	Tim Harris	.10
59	Hanford Dixon	.10
60	*Chris Miller*	1.50
61	Cornelius Bennett	.75
62	Neal Anderson	.10
63	Ickey Woods	.10
64	Gary Anderson	.10
65	*Vaughan Johnson*	.20
66	Ronnie Lippett	.10
67	Mike Quick	.10
68	Roy Green	.10
69	Tim Krumrie	.10
70	Mark Malone	.10
71	James Jones	.10
72	*Cris Carter*	15.00
73	Ricky Nattiel	.10
74	Jim Arnold	.10
75	Randall Cunningham	1.00
76	John L. Williams	.10
77	*Paul Gruber*	.10
78	*Rod Woodson*	4.00
79	Ray Childress	.10
80	Doug Williams	.10
81	Deron Cherry	.10
82	John Offerdahl	.10
83	Louis Lipps	.10
84	Neil Lomax	.10
85	Wade Wilson	.10
86	*Tim Brown*	16.00
87	Chris Hinton	.10
88	Stump Mitchell	.10
89	Tunch Ilkin	.10
90	Steve Pelluer	.10
91	Brian Noble	.10
92	Reggie White	1.00
93	*Aundray Bruce*	.10
94	Garry James	.10
95	Drew Hill	.10
96	Anthony Munoz	.10
97	James Wilder	.10
98	Dexter Manley	.10
99	Lee Williams	.10
100	Dave Krieg	.10
101	*Keith Jackson ERR* (incorrect number 84)	1.00
101a	*Keith Jackson COR* (correct number 88)	1.00
102	Luis Sharpe	.10
103	Kevin Greene	.20
104	Duane Bickett	.10
105	*Mark Rypien*	.75
106	Curt Warner	.10
107	Jacob Green	.10
108	Gary Clark	.20
109	*Bruce Matthews*	1.00
110	Bill Fralic	.10
111	Bill Bates	.10
112	Jeff Bryant	.10
113	Charles Mann	.10
114	Richard Dent	.10
115	Bruce Hill	.10
116	*Mark May*	.10
117	*Mark Collins*	.10
118	Ron Holmes	.10
119	*Scott Case*	.20
120	Tom Rathman	.10
121	Dennis McKinnon	.10
122	Ricky Sanders ERR (incorrect number 46)	.25
122a	Ricky Sanders COR (correct number 83)	.50
123	Michael Carter	.10
124	Ozzie Newsome	.10
125	Irving Fryar	.10
126	*Ron Hall ERR* (wrong photo)	.25
126a	*Ron Hall COR* (corrected photo)	.50
127	Clay Matthews	.10
128	Leonard Marshall	.10
129	Kevin Mack	.10
130	Art Monk	.20
131	Garin Veris	.10
132	Steve Jordan	.10
133	Frank Minnifield	.10
134	Eddie Brown	.10
135	Stacey Bailey	.10
136	Rickey Jackson	.10
137	Henry Ellard	.10
138	Jim Burt	.10
139	Jerome Brown	.10
140	*Rodney Holman*	.20
141	Sammy Winder	.10
142	Marcus Cotton	.10
143	Jim Jeffcoat	.10
144	Reuben Mayes	.10
145	Jim McMahon	.10
146	Reggie Williams	.10
147	John Anderson	.10
148	*Harris Barton*	.20
149	Philip Epps	.10
150	Jay Hilgenberg	.10
151	Earl Ferrell	.10
152	Andre Reed	.50
153	Dennis Gentry	.10
154	Max Montoya	.10
155	Darrin Nelson	.10
156	Jeff Chadwick	.10
157	James Brooks	.10
158	Keith Bishop	.10
159	Robert Awalt	.10
160	Marty Lyons	.10
161	Johnny Hector	.10
162	Tony Casillas	.10
163	*Kyle Clifton*	.20
164	Cody Risien	.10
165	Jamie Holland	.10
166	*Merril Hoge*	.10
167	*Chris Spielman*	1.50
168	Carlos Carson	.10
169	*Jerry Ball*	.20
170	*Don Majkowski*	.20
171	Everson Walls	.10
172	Mike Rozier	.10
173	Matt Millen	.10
174	Karl Mecklenberg	.10
175	Paul Palmer	.10
176	*Brian Blades*	1.00
177	Brent Fullwood	.10
178	*Anthony Miller*	1.00
179	Brian Sochia	.10
180	*Stephen Baker*	.20
181	Jesse Solomon	.10
182	John Grimsley	.10
183	Timmy Newsome	.10
184	*Steve Sewell*	.10
185	Dean Biasucci	.10
186	Alonzo Highsmith	.10
187	Randy Grimes	.10
188	*Mark Carrier ERR* (back shows Bruce Hill)	1.50
188a	Mark Carrier COR (corrected)	1.50
189	Vann McElroy	.10
190	Greg Bell	.10
191	*Quinn Early*	2.00
192	Lawrence Taylor	.50
193	Albert Bentley	.10
194	Ernest Givins	.20
195	Jackie Slater	.10
196	Jim Sweeney	.10
197	Freddie Joe Nunn	.10
198	Keith Byars	.10
199	*Hardy Nickerson*	1.50
200	*Steve Beuerlein*	5.00
201	*Bruce Armstrong*	.20
202	Lionel Manuel	.10
203	J.T. Smith	.10
204	*Mark Ingram*	1.00
205	Fred Smerlas	.10
206	*Bryan Hinkle*	.10
207	Steve McMichael	.10
208	Nick Lowery	.10
209	Jack Trudeau	.10
210	Lorenzo Hampton	.10
211	*Thurman Thomas*	5.00
212	Steve Young	2.00
213	James Lofton	.10
214	Jim Covert	.10
215	Ronnie Lott	.20
216	Stephone Paige	.10
217	Mark Duper	.10
218	Willie Gault ERR (shows Greg Townsend)	.25
218a	Willie Gault COR (corrected)	.50
219	*Ken Ruettgers*	.10
220	*Kevin Ross*	.10
221	Jerry Rice	3.00
222	Billy Ray Smith	.10
223	Jim Kelly	1.00
224	Vinny Testaverde	.40
225	Steve Largent	.75
226	*Warren Williams*	.10
227	Morten Andersen	.10
228	Bill Brooks	.10
229	*Reggie Langhorne*	.20
230	Pepper Johnson	.10
231	Pat Leahy	.10
232	Fred Marion	.10
233	Gary Zimmerman	.10
234	Marcus Allen	.50
235	*Gaston Green*	.20
236	*John Stephens*	.20
237	Terry Kinard	.10
238	*John Taylor*	1.50
239	Brian Bosworth	.10
240	Anthony Toney	.10
241	Ken O'Brien	.10
242	Howie Long	.10
243	Doug Flutie	2.00
244	Jim Everett	.30
245	*Broderick Thomas*	.20
246	*Deion Sanders*	10.00
247	*Donnell Woolford*	1.00
248	*Wayne Martin*	.75
249	*David Williams*	.10
250	Bill Hawkins	.10
251	*Eric Hill*	.10
252	*Burt Grossman*	.20
253	Tracy Rocker	.10
254	*Steve Wisniewski*	.20
255	*Jessie Small*	.10
256	David Braxton	.10
257	*Barry Sanders*	40.00
258	*Derrick Thomas*	5.00
259	*Eric Metcalf*	2.00
260	*Keith DeLong*	.20
261	Hart Lee Dykes	.10
262	*Sammie Smith*	.20
263	*Steve Atwater*	1.00
264	*Eric Ball*	.20
265	*Don Beebe*	1.00
266	Brian Williams	.10
267	*Jeff Lageman*	.30
268	*Tim Worley*	.20
269	Tony Mandarich	.10
270	*Troy Aikman*	30.00
271	*Andy Heck*	.20
272	*Andre Rison*	5.00
273	AFC Championship Game	.20
274	Joe Montana NFC Championship	1.00
275	Joe Montana, Jerry Rice	3.00
276	Rodney Carter	.10
277	Mark Jackson, Vance Johnson, Ricky Nattiel	.10
278	John Williams, Curt Warner	.10
279	Joe Montana, Jerry Rice	3.00
280	Roy Green, Neil Lomax	.10
281	Randall Cunningham, Keith Jackson	.20
282	Chris Doleman, Keith Millard	.10
283	Mark Duper, Mark Clayton	.10
284	Allen, Jackson	.50
285	Frank Minnifield (AP)	.10
286	Bruce Matthews (AP)	.10
287	Joey Browner (AP)	.10
288	Jay Hilgenberg (AP)	.10
289	*Carl Lee* (AP)	.10
290	Scott Norwood (AP)	.10
291	John Taylor (AP)	.50
292	Jerry Rice (AP)	1.00
293	Keith Jackson ERR (AP) (incorrect number)	.50
293a	Keith Jackson COR (AP)(corrected)	.50
294	Gary Zimmerman (AP)	.10
295	Lawrence Taylor (AP)	.20
296	Reggie White (AP)	.20
297	Roger Craig (AP)	.10
298	Boomer Esiason (AP)	.10
299	Cornelius Bennett (AP)	.10
300	Mike Horan (AP)	.10
301	Deron Cherry (AP)	.10
302	Tom Newberry (AP)	.10
303	Mike Singletary (AP)	.10
304	Shane Conlan (AP)	.10
305	Tim Brown ERR (AP) (shows James Lofton)	2.00
305a	Tim Brown COR (AP)(corrected)	2.00
306	Henry Ellard (AP)	.10
307	Bruce Smith (AP)	.10
308	Tim Krumrie (AP)	.10
309	Anthony Munoz (AP)	.10
310	Darrell Green (SB)	.10
311	Anthony Miller (SB)	.50
312	Wesley Walker (SB)	.10
313	Ron Brown (SB)	.10
314	Bo Jackson (SB)	.40
315	Philip Epps (SB)	.10
316	*Eric Thomas ERR* (SB) (wrong number)	.25
316a	*Eric Thomas COR* (SB)(corrected)	.50
317	Herschel Walker (SB)	.20
318	Jacob Green (PD)	.10
319	Andre Tippett	.10
320	Freddie Joe Nunn (PD)	.10
321	Reggie White (PD)	.20
322	Lawrence Taylor (PD)	.20
323	Greg Townsend (PD)	.10
324	Tim Harris (PD)	.10
325	Bruce Smith (PD)	.10
326	Tony Dorsett (RB)	.30
327	Steve Largent (RB)	.50
328	Tim Brown (RB)	2.00
329	Joe Montana (RB)	1.50
330	Tom Landry (Tribute)	1.00

1989 Score Supplemental

These 110 cards continue with numbers where the 1989 Score regular set left off at - 330. The cards are numbered using an "S" prefix, however. The design is similar to the regular issue's, but the supplemental cards have purple borders. The cards were distributed as a complete, boxed set only.

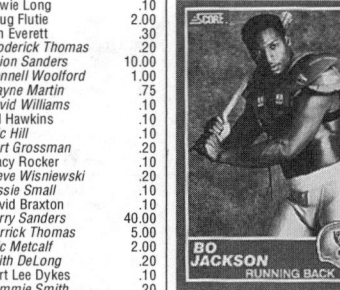

		NM/M
Complete Set (110):		15.00
Common Player:		.05
Minor Stars:		.10
331	Herschel Walker	.10
332	*Allen Pinkett*	.05
333	*Sterling Sharpe*	3.00
334	*Alvin Walton*	.05
335	*Frank Reich*	.50
336	*Jim Thornton*	.05
337	David Fulcher	.05
338	Raul Allegre	.05
339	John Elway	2.00
340	Michael Cofer	.05
341	Jim Skow	.05
342	Steve DeBerg	.05
343	Mervyn Fernandez	.05
344	Mike Lansford	.05
345	Reggie Roby	.05
346	Raymond Clayborn	.05
347	Lonzell Hill	.05
348	Ottis Anderson	.05
349	*Erik McMillan*	.05
350	*Al Harris*	.05
351	*Jack Del Rio*	1.00
352	Gary Anderson	.10
353	Jim McMahon	.10
354	Keena Turner	.05
355	*Tony Woods*	.05
356	Donald Igwebuike	.05
357	Gerald Riggs	.05
358	Eddie Murray	.05
359	Dino Hackett	.05
360	*Brad Muster*	.05
361	Paul Palmer	.05
362	Jerry Robinson	.05
363	*Simon Fletcher*	.50
364	Tommy Kramer	.05
365	Jim C. Jensen	.05
366	*Lorenzo White*	.50
367	Fredd Young	.05
368	Ron Jaworski	.05
369	Mel Owens	.05
370	Dave Waymer	.05
371	Sean Landeta	.05
372	Sam Mills	.05
373	Todd Blackledge	.05
374	JoJo Townsell	.05
375	Ron Wolfley	.05
376	Ralf Mojsiejenko	.05
377	Eric Wright	.05
378	Newsby Glasgow	.05
379	Darryl Talley	.05
380	*Eric Allen*	.40
381	Dennis Smith	.05
382	John Tice	.05
383	Jesse Solomon	.05
384	Bo Jackson	1.50
385	Mike Merriweather	.05
386	Maurice Carthon	.05
387	Dave Grayson	.05
388	Wilber Marshall	.05
389	David Wyman	.05
390	*Thomas Everett*	.05
391	Alex Gordon	.05
392	D.J. Dozier	.05
393	*Scott Radecic*	.05
394	Eric Thomas	.05
395	Mike Gann	.05
396	William Perry	.05
397	Carl Hariston	.05
398	Billy Ard	.05
399	Donnell Thompson	.05
400	Mike Webster	.05
401	Scott Davis	.05
402	Sean Farrell	.05
403	*Mike Golic*	.05
404	Mike Kenn	.05
405	*Keith Van Horne*	.05
406	Bob Golic	.05
407	*Neil Smith*	1.00
408	*Dermontti Dawson*	.05
409	Leslie O'Neal	.10
410	Matt Bahr	.05
411	*Guy McIntyre*	.10
412	Bryan Millard	.05
413	Joe Jacoby	.05
414	*Rob Taylor*	.05
415	Tony Zendejas	.05
416	Vai Sikahema	.05
417	Gary Reasons	.05
418	*Shawn Collins*	.05
419	*Mark Green*	.05
420	*Courtney Hall*	.05
421	*Bobby Humphrey*	.05
422	*Myron Guyton*	.05
423	Darryl Ingram	.05
424	*Chris Jacke*	.10
425	Keith Jones	.05
426	*Robert Massey*	.05
427	*Bubba McDowell*	.05
428	*Dave Meggett*	1.00
429	*Louis Oliver*	.05
430	Danny Peebles	.05
431	*Rodney Peete*	1.00
432	*Jeff Query*	.10
433	*Timm Rosenbach*	.05
434	*Frank Stams*	.05
435	*Lawyer Tillman*	.05
436	*Billy Joe Tolliver*	.10
437	*Floyd Turner*	.30
438	*Steve Walsh*	.75
439	*Joe Wolf*	.05
440	*Trace Armstrong*	.05

1989 Score Franco Harris

This card, which has two versions, was given to those who received Franco Harris' autograph at the Super Bowl show in New Orleans. The unnumbered standard-size cards have identical fronts and are similar in design to Score's 1989 regular set. The difference on the card backs is in the text which describes Harris' status as a potential Hall of Famer. Earlier versions say Harris was a "sure-shot" to be elected to the Hall of Fame. He was elected during the show, so the text was changed to say "Hall of Famer." The "sure-shot" cards are scarcer.

		NM/M
Complete Set (2):		100.00
Common Player:		40.00
1A	Franco Harris (Sure-shot)	60.00
1B	Franco Harris (Hall of Famer)	40.00

1990 Score Promos

These cards were sent to dealers along with order forms for Score's 1990 regular set. The design is similar to the regular issue, except the photos are cropped tighter. They also use a registered symbol on them, not the trademark symbol which is used on the regular cards.

		NM/M
Complete Set (3):		8.00
Common Player:		1.00
20	Barry Sanders	7.00
184	Robert Delpino	1.00
256	Cornelius Bennett	2.00

1990 Score

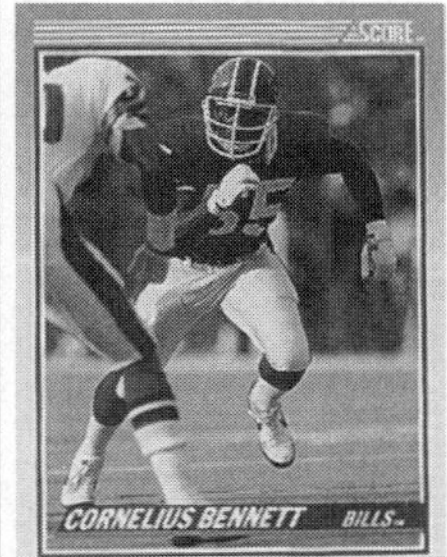

Variations in the set include #134, Kevin Butler (uncorrected photo on back shows him wearing a helmet; corrected photo shows him without helmet), #136, Vai Sikahema (uncorrected photo on back shows him wearing a helmet; corrected photo shows him without a helmet), #147, Joey Browner (uncorrected back shows him looking into the sun; corrected back show more of a profile); #208, Ralf Mojsiejenko (uncorrected stats read "Chargers"; corrected stats read "Redskins."); and #600, Buck Buchanan (uncorrected back says he was the first player selected in the '83 AFL draft; it was corrected to read the '63 draft). Note: Rookie cards in the first series contained no information on which NFL team the player was drafted by; thus they are considered first cards, not rookie cards. (Key: HG - Hot Gun; GF - Ground Force; DP - draft pick)

		NM/M
Complete Set (660):		8.00
Complete Series 1 (1-330):		4.00
Complete Series 2 (331-660):		4.00
Common Player:		.04
Series 1 Pack (16):		.50
Series 1 Wax Box (36):		9.00
Series 2 Pack (6):		.50
Series 2 Wax Box (36):		9.00
1	Joe Montana	1.00
2	Christian Okoye	.04
3	Mike Singletary	.04
4	Jim Everett	.04
5	Phil Simms	.10
6	Brent Fullwood	.04
7	Bill Fralic	.04
8	Leslie O'Neal	.04
9	John Taylor	.20
10	Bo Jackson	.40
11	John Stephens	.04
12	Art Monk	.04
13	Dan Marino	1.50

14 John Settle .04
15 Don Majkowski .04
16 Bruce Smith .04
17 Brad Muster .04
18 Jason Buck .04
19 James Brooks .04
20 Barry Sanders 1.25
21 Troy Aikman 1.00
22 Allen Pinkett .04
23 Duane Bickett .04
24 Kevin Ross .04
25 John Elway .40
26 Jeff Query .04
27 Eddie Murray .04
28 Richard Dent .04
29 Lorenzo White .15
30 Eric Metcalf .10
31 *Jeff Dellenbach* .10
32 Leon White .04
33 Jim Jeffcoat .04
34 Herschel Walker .04
35 Mike Johnson .04
36 Joe Phillips .04
37 Willie Gault .04
38 Keith Millard .04
39 Fred Marion .04
40 Boomer Esiason .20
41 Dermontti Dawson .04
42 Dino Hackett .04
43 Reggie Roby .04
44 Roger Vick .04
45 Bobby Hebert .15
46 Don Beebe .15
47 Neal Anderson .10
48 Johnny Holland .04
49 Bobby Humphery .04
50 Lawrence Taylor .10
51 Billy Ray Smith .04
52 Robert Perryman .04
53 Gary Anderson .04
54 Raul Allegre .04
55 Pat Swilling .04
56 Chris Doleman .04
57 Andre Reed .20
58 Seth Joyner .04
59 Bart Oates .04
60 Bernie Kosar .04
61 Dave Krieg .04
62 Lars Tate .04
63 Scott Norwood .04
64 Kyle Clifton .04
65 Alan Veingrad .04
66 Gerald Riggs .04
67 Tim Worley .04
68 Rodney Holman .04
69 Tony Zendejas .04
70 Chris Miller .10
71 Wilber Marshall .04
72 *Skip McClendon* .10
73 Jim Covert .04
74 Sam Mills .04
75 Chris Hinton .04
76 Irv Eatman .04
77 Bubba Paris .04
78 John Elliott .04
79 Thomas Everett .04
80 Steve Smith .04
81 Jackie Slater .04
82 *Kelvin Martin* .25
83 JoJo Townsell .04
84 Jim Jensen .04
85 Bobby Humphrey .04
86 Mike Dyal .04
87 Andre Rison .25
88 Brian Sochia .04
89 Greg Bell .04
90 Dalton Hilliard .04
91 Carl Banks .04
92 Dennis Smith .04
93 Bruce Matthews .04
94 Charles Haley .04
95 Deion Sanders .35
96 Stephone Paige .04
97 Marion Butts .10
98 Howie Long .04
99 Donald Igwebuike .04
100 Roger Craig .04
101 Charles Mann .04
102 Fredd Young .04
103 Chris Jacke .04
104 Scott Case .04
105 Warren Moon .25
106 Clyde Simmons .04
107 Steve Atwater .04
108 Morten Andersen .04
109 Eugene Marve .04
110 Thurman Thomas .40
111 Carnell Lake .04
112 Jim Kelly .30
113 Stanford Jennings .04
114 Jacob Green .04
115 Karl Mecklenberg .04
116 Ray Childress .04
117 Erik McMillan .04
118 Harry Newsome .04
119 James Dixon .04
120 Hassan Jones .04
121 Eric Allen .04
122 Felix Wright .04
123 Merril Hoge .04
124 Eric Ball .04
125 Willie Anderson .10
126 James Jefferson .04
127 Tim McDonald .04
128 Larry Kinnebrew .04
129 Mark Collins .04
130 Ickey Woods .04
131 Jeff Donaldson .04
132 Rich Camarillo .04
133 Melvin Bratton .04
134 Kevin Butler (helmet) .05
134a Kevin Butler (without helmet) .05
135 Albert Bentley .04
136 Vai Sikahema (helmet on back) .08
136a Vai Sikahema (without helmet) .08
137 *Todd McNair* .10
138 Alonzo Highsmith .04
139 Brian Blades .10
140 Jeff Lageman .04
141 Eric Thomas .04
142 Derek Hill .04
143 Rick Fenney .04
144 Herman Heard .04
145 Steve Young 1.00
146 Kent Hull .04
147 Joey Browner .04
148 Frank Minnifield .04
149 Robert Massey .04
150 Dave Meggett .10
151 Bubba McDowell .04
152 *Rickey Dixon* .10
153 Ray Donaldson .04
154 Alvin Walton .04
155 Mike Cofer .04
156 Darryl Talley .04
157 A.J. Johnson .04
158 Jerry Gray .04
159 Keith Byars .04
160 Andy Heck .04
161 Mike Munchak .04
162 Dennis Gentry .04
163 Timm Rosenbach .04
164 Randall McDaniel .04
165 Pat Leahy .04
166 Bubby Brister .04
167 Aundray Bruce .04
168 Bill Brooks .04
169 *Eddie Anderson* .10
170 Ronnie Lott .10
171 Jay Hilgenberg .04
172 Joe Nash .04
173 Simon Fletcher .04
174 Shane Conlan .04
175 Sean Landeta .04
176 *John Alt* .10
177 Clay Matthews .04
178 Anthony Munoz .04
179 Pete Holohan .04
180 Robert Awalt .04
181 Rohn Stark .04
182 Vance Johnson .04
184 Robert Delpino .04
185 Drew Hill .04
186 Reggie Langhorne .04
187 Lonzell Hill .04
188 Tom Rathman .04
189 *Greg Montgomery* .10
190 Leonard Smith .04
191 Chris Spielman .04
192 Tom Newberry .04
193 Cris Carter .35
194 Kevin Porter .04
195 Donnell Thompson .04
196 Vaughan Johnson .04
197 Steve McMichael .04
198 Jim Sweeney .04
199 Rich Karlis .04
200 Jerry Rice 1.00
201 Dan Hampton .04
202 Jim Lachey .04
203 Reggie White .15
204 Jerry Ball .04
205 Russ Grimm .04
206 *Tim Green* .08
207 Shawn Collins .04
208 Ralf Mojsiejenko (Chargers on back) .05
208a Ralf Mojsiejenko (Redskins on back) .05
209 Trace Armstrong .04
210 Keith Jackson .25
211 Jamie Holland .04
212 Mark Clayton .04
213 Jeff Cross .04
214 Bob Gagliano .04
215 Louis Oliver .04
216 Jim Arnold .04
217 *Robert Clark* .08
218 Gill Byrd .04
219 Rodney Peete .08
220 Anthony Miller .30
221 Steve Grogan .04
222 Vince Newsome .04
223 Tom Benson .04
224 Kevin Murphy .04
225 Henry Ellard .04
226 Richard Johnson .04
227 Jim Skow .04
228 Keith Jones .04
229 Dave Brown .04
230 Marcus Allen .04
231 Steve Walsh .04
232 Jim Harbaugh .10
233 Mel Gray .04
234 David Treadwell .04
235 John Offerdahl .04
236 Gary Reasons .04
237 Tim Krumrie .04
238 Dave Duerson .04
239 Gary Clark .10
240 Mark Jackson .04
241 Mark Murphy .04
242 Jerry Holmes .04
243 Tim McGee .04
244 Mike Tomczak .04
245 Sterling Sharpe .10
246 Bennie Blades .04
247 *Ken Harvey* .10
248 Ron Heller .04
249 Louis Lipps .04
250 Wade Wilson .04
251 Freddie Joe Nunn .04
252 Jerome Brown .04
253 Myron Guyton .04
254 *Nate Odomes* .25
255 Rod Woodson .25
256 Cornelius Bennett .04
257 Keith Woodside .04
258 Jeff Uhlenhake .04
259 Harry Hamilton .04
260 Mark Bavaro .04
261 Vinny Testaverde .10
262 Steve DeBerg .04
263 Steve Wisniewski .04
264 Pete Mandley .04
265 Tim Harris .04
266 Jack Trudeau .04
267 Mark Kelso .04
268 Brian Noble .04
269 *Jessie Tuggle* .20
270 Ken O'Brien .04
271 David Little .04
272 Pete Stoyanovich .04
273 *Odessa Turner* .10
274 Anthony Toney .04
275 Tunch Ilkin .04
276 Carl Lee .04
277 Hart Lee Dykes .04
278 Al Noga .04
279 Greg Lloyd .04
280 Billy Joe Tolliver .04
281 Kirk Lowdermilk .04
282 Earl Ferrell .04
283 Eric Sievers .04
284 Steve Jordan .04
285 Burt Grossman .04
286 Johnny Rembert .04
287 *Jeff Jaeger* .10
288 James Hasty .04
289 Tony Mandarich .04
290 *Chris Singleton* (DP) .10
291 Lynn James (DP)(FC) .04
292 *Andre Ware* (DP) .20
293 *Ray Agnew* (DP) .10
294 *Joel Smeenge* (DP) .10
295 *Marc Spindler* (DP) .10
296 *Renaldo Turnbull* (DP) .40
297 Reggie Rembert (DP) .04
298 Jeff Alm (DP) .04
299 *Cortez Kennedy* (DP) .30
300 *Blair Thomas* (DP) .10
301 *Pat Terrell* (DP) .10
302 *Junior Seau* (DP) 1.00
303 Mohammed Elewonibi (DP) .04
304 *Tony Bennett* (DP) .35
305 *Percy Snow* (DP) .08
306 *Richmond Webb* (DP) .15
307 *Rodney Hampton* (DP) 1.00
308 *Barry Foster* (DP) .10
309 *John Friesz* (DP) .25
310 *Ben Smith* (DP) .08
311 Joe Montana (HG) .50
312 Jim Everett (HG) .04
313 Mark Rypien (HG) .08
314 Phil Simms (HG) .08
315 Don Majkowski (HG) .04
316 Boomer Esiason (HG) .10
317 Warren Moon (HG) .10
318 Jim Kelly (HG) .10
319 Bernie Kosar (HG) .04
320 Dan Marino (HG) .40
321 Christian Okoye (GF) .04
322 Thurman Thomas (GF) .20
323 James Brooks (GF) .04
324 Bobby Humphrey (GF) .04
325 Barry Sanders (GF) .75
326 Neal Anderson (GF) .04
327 Dalton Hilliard (GF) .04
328 Greg Bell (GF) .04
329 Roger Craig (GF) .04
330 Bo Jackson (GF) .20
331 Don Warren .04
332 Rufus Porter .04
333 Sammie Smith .04
334 Lewis Tillman .20
335 Michael Walter .04
336 Marc Logan .04
337 *Ron Hallstrom* .08
338 Stanley Morgan .04
339 Mark Robinson .04
340 Frank Reich .20
341 Chip Lohmiller .10
342 Steve Beuerlein .25
343 John L. Williams .04
344 Irving Fryar .04
345 Anthony Carter .04
346 Al Toon .04
347 J.T. Smith .04
348 *Pierce Holt* .10
349 Ferrell Edmunds .04
350 Mark Rypien .15
351 Paul Gruber .04
352 Ernest Givins .04
353 Ervin Randle .04
354 Guy McIntyre .04
355 Webster Slaughter .04
356 Reuben Davis .04
357 Rickey Jackson .04
358 Earnest Byner .04
359 Eddie Brown .04
360 Troy Stradford .04
361 Pepper Johnson .04
362 Ravin Caldwell .04
363 *Chris Mohr* .08
364 Jeff Bryant .04
365 Bruce Collie .04
366 Courtney Hall .04
367 Jerry Olsavsky .04
368 David Galloway .04
369 Wes Hopkins .04
370 Johnny Hector .04
371 Clarence Verdin .04
372 Nick Lowery .04
373 Tim Brown .45
374 Kevin Greene .04
375 Leonard Marshall .04
376 Roland James .04
377 Scott Studwell .04
378 Jarvis Williams .04
379 Mike Saxon .04
380 Kevin Mack .04
381 Joe Kelly .04
382 *Tom Thayer* .10
383 Roy Green .04
384 *Michael Brooks* .20
385 Michael Cofer .04
386 Ken Ruettgers .04
387 Dean Steinkuhler .04
388 Maurice Carthon .04
389 Ricky Sanders .04
390 *Winton Moss* .10
391 Tony Woods .04
392 Keith DeLong .04
393 David Wyman .04
394 Vencie Glenn .04
395 Harris Barton .04
396 Bryan Hinkle .04
397 Derek Kennard .04
398 *Heath Sherman* .20
399 Troy Benson .04
400 Gary Zimmerman .04
401 Mark Duper .04
402 Eugene Lockhart .04
403 Tim Manoa .04
404 Reggie Williams .04
405 *Mark Bortz* .10
406 Mike Kenn .04
407 John Grimsley .04
408 *Bill Romanowski* .10
409 Perry Kemp .04
410 Norm Johnson .04
411 Broderick Thomas .04
412 Joe Wolf .04
413 Andre Waters .04
414 Jason Staurovsky .04
415 Eric Martin .04
416 Joe Prokop .04
417 Steve Sewell .04
418 Cedric Jones .04
419 Alphonso Carreker .04
420 Keith Willis .04
421 Bobby Butler .04
422 John Roper .04
423 Tim Spencer .04
424 *Jesse Sapolu* .08
425 Ron Wolfley .04
426 Doug Smith .04
427 William Howard .04
428 Keith Van Horne .04
429 Tony Jordan .04
430 Mervyn Fernandez .04
431 *Shaun Gayle* .10
432 Ricky Nattiel .04
433 Albert Lewis .04
434 *Fred Banks* .10
435 Henry Thomas .04
436 Chet Brooks .04
437 Mark Ingram .04
438 Jeff Gossett .04
439 Mike Wilcher .04
440 Deron Cherry .04
441 Mike Rozier .04
442 Jon Hand .04
443 Ozzie Newsome .10
444 Sammy Martin .04
445 Luis Sharpe .04
446 Lee Williams .04
447 *Chris Martin* .10
448 Kevin Fagan .04
449 Gene Lang .04
450 Greg Townsend .04
451 Robert Lyles .04
452 Eric Hill .04
453 John Teltschik .04
454 Vestee Jackson .04
455 Bruce Reimers .04
456 *Butch Rolle* .10
457 Lawyer Tillman .04
458 Andre Tippett .04
459 James Thornton .04
460 Randy Grimes .04
461 Larry Roberts .04
462 Ron Holmes .04
463 Mike Wise .04
464 *Danny Copeland* .10
465 *Bruce Wilkerson* .10
466 Mike Quick .04
467 Mickey Shuler .04
468 Mike Prior .04
469 Ron Rivera .04
470 Dean Biasucci .04
471 Perry Williams .04
472 Darren Comeaux .04
473 Freeman McNeil .04
474 Tyrone Braxton .04
475 Jay Schroeder .04
476 Naz Worthen .04
477 Lionel Washington .04
478 Carl Zander .04
479 Al Baker .04
480 Mike Merriweather .04
481 Mike Gann .04
482 Brent Williams .04
483 Eugene Robinson .04
484 Ray Horton .04
485 Bruce Armstrong .04
486 John Fourcade .04
487 Lewis Billups .04
489 Ken Sims .04
490 Chris Chandler .04
491 Mark Lee .04
492 Johnny Meads .04
493 Tim Irwin .04
494 E.J. Junior .04
495 Hardy Nickerson .04
496 Rob McGovern .04
497 *Fred Strickland* .10
498 *Reggie Rutland* .10
499 Mel Owens .04
500 Derrick Thomas .25
501 Jerrol Williams .04
502 *Maurice Hurst* .10
503 *Larry Kelm* .10
504 Herman Fontenot .04
505 Pat Beach .04
506 *Haywood Jeffires* .85
507 Neil Smith .25
508 Cleveland Gary .10
509 William Perry .04
510 Michael Carter .04
511 Walker Lee Ashley .04
512 Bob Golic .04
513 *Danny Villa* .08
514 Matt Millen .04
515 Don Griffin .04
516 Jonathan Hayes .04
517 *Gerald Williams* .08
518 Scott Fulhage .04
519 Irv Pankey .04
520 *Randy Dixon* .08
521 Terry McDaniel .04
522 Dan Saleaumua .04
523 Darrin Nelson .04
524 Leonard Griffin .04
525 Michael Ball .04
526 *Ernie Jones* .25
527 Tony Eason .04
528 Ed Reynolds .04
529 Gary Hogeboom .04
530 Don Mosebar .04
531 Ottis Anderson .04
532 Bucky Scribner .04
533 Aaron Cox .04
534 Sean Jones .04
535 Doug Flutie .75
536 Leo Lewis .04
537 Art Still .04
538 Matt Bahr .04
539 Keena Turner .04
540 Sammy Winder .04
541 Mike Webster .04
542 *Doug Riesenberg* .10
543 Dan Fike .04
544 Clarence Kay .04
545 Jim Burt .04
546 Mike Horan .04
547 Al Harris .04
548 Maury Buford .04
549 Jerry Robinson .04
550 Tracy Rocker .04
551 Karl Mecklenburg (CC) .04
552 Lawrence Taylor (CC) .08
553 Derrick Thomas (CC) .20
554 Mike Singletary (CC) .04
555 Tim Harris (CC) .04
556 Jerry Rice (RM) .40
557 Art Monk (RM) .04
558 Mark Carrier (RM) .04
559 Andre Reed (RM) .08
560 Sterling Sharpe (RM) .30
561 Herschel Walker (GF) .04
562 Ottis Anderson (GF) .04
563 Randall Cunningham (HG) .08
564 John Elway (HG) .20
565 David Fulcher (AP) .04
566 Ronnie Lott (AP) .04
567 Jerry Gray (AP) .04
568 Albert Lewis (AP) .04
569 Karl Mecklenburg (AP) .04
570 Mike Singletary (AP) .04
571 Lawrence Taylor (AP) .08
572 Tim Harris (AP) .04
573 Keith Millard (AP) .04
574 Reggie White (AP) .04
575 Chris Doleman (AP) .04
576 Dave Meggett (AP) .04
577 Rod Woodson (AP) .04
578 Sean Landeta (AP) .04
579 Eddie Murray (AP) .04
580 Barry Sanders (AP) .75
581 Christian Okoye (AP) .04
582 Joe Montana (AP) .50
583 Jay Hilgenberg (AP) .04
584 Bruce Matthews (AP) .04
585 Tom Newberry (AP) .04
586 Gary Zimmerman (AP) .04
587 Anthony Munoz (AP) .04
588 Keith Jackson (AP) .08
589 Sterling Sharpe (AP) .30
590 Jerry Rice (AP) .40
591 Bo Jackson (RB) .15
592 Steve Largent (RB) .10
593 Flipper Anderson (RB) .04
594 Joe Montana (RB) .50
595 Franco Harris (HOF) .08
596 Bob St. Clair (HOF) .04
597 Tom Landry (HOF) .08
598 Jack Lambert (HOF) .04
599 Ted Hendricks (HOF) .04
600 Buck Buchanan (HOF) ("drafted '83") .05
600a Buck Buchanan (HOF) ("drafted '63") .05
601 Bob Griese (HOF) .04
602 Super Bowl .04
603 Vince Lombardi .04
604 Mark Carrier .04
605 Randall Cunningham .10
606 Percy Snow (C90) .04
607 Andre Ware (C90) .10
608 Blair Thomas (C90) .04
609 Eric Green (C90) .10
610 Reggie Rembert (C90) .04
611 Richmond Webb (C90) .10
612 Bern Brostek (C90) .04
613 James Williams (C90) .04
614 Mark Carrier (C90) .04
615 Renaldo Turnbull (C90) .20
616 Cortez Kennedy (C90) .40
617 Keith McCants (C90) .04
618 *Anthony Thompson* (DP) .10
619 *LeRoy Butler* (DP) .20
620 *Aaron Wallace* (DP) .10
621 *Alexander Wright* (DP) .15
622 *Keith McCants* (DP) .10
623 *Jimmie Jones* (DP) .10
624 *Anthony Johnson* (DP) .20
625 Fred Washington (DP) .04
626 Mike Bellamy (DP) .04
627 *Mark Carrier* (DP) .20
628 *Harold Green* (DP) .25
629 *Eric Green* (DP) .40
630 *Andre Collins* (DP) .10
631 *Lamar Lathon* (DP) .10
632 *Terry Wooden* (DP) .10
633 Jesse Anderson (DP) .04
634 *Jeff George* (DP) 1.25
635 *Carwell Gardner* (DP) .10
636 *Darrell Thompson* (DP) .25
637 Vince Buck (DP) .10
638 Mike Jones (DP) .04
639 *Charles Arbuckle* (DP) .10
640 *Dennis Brown* (DP) .10
641 *James Williams* (DP) .10
642 *Bern Brostek* (DP) .10
643 *Darion Conner* (DP) .08
644 *Mike Fox* (DP) .08
645 *Cary Conklin* (DP) .40
646 *Tim Grunhard* (DP) .08
647 *Ron Cox* (DP) .08
648 *Keith Sims* (DP) .08
649 *Alton Montgomery* (DP) .10
650 *Greg McMurtry* (DP) .10
651 *Scott Mitchell* (DP) .75
652 Tim Ryan (DP) .04
653 Jeff Mills (DP) .04
654 *Ricky Proehl* (DP) .50
655 *Steve Broussard* (DP) .08
656 *Peter Tom Willis* (DP) .15
657 *Dexter Carter* (DP) .15
658 Tony Casillas .04
659 Joe Morris .04
660 Greg Kragen .04

1990 Score Hot Card

Score test-marketed a 100-card football blister pack subset in August 1990, available only at select retail accounts. Blister packs featuring 100 assorted cards from Series I and Series II. As an incentive to buy the blister packs, one "Hot Card" was included in each blister pack.

NM/M
Complete Set (10): 12.00
Common Player: .50
1 Joe Montana 3.00
2 Bo Jackson 1.00
3 Barry Sanders 2.00
4 Jerry Rice 2.00
5 Eric Metcalf .50
6 Don Majkowski .50
7 Christian Okoye .50
8 Bobby Humphrey .50
9 Dan Marino 3.00
10 Sterling Sharpe 1.00

1990 Score Update

These cards were sold in sets only to hobby stores and included traded players as well as rookies in team uniforms.

NM/M
Complete Set (110): 120.00
Common Player: .10
Minor Stars: .20
1 Marcus Dupree .10
2 Jerry Kauric .10
3 Everson Walls .10
4 Elliott Smith .10
5 *Donald Evans* .10
6 Jerry Holmes .10
7 *Dan Stryzinski* .10
8 Gerald McNeil .10
9 *Rick Tuten* .10
10 Mickey Shuler .10
11 Jay Novacek 1.00
12 *Eric Williams* .20
13 Stanley Morgan .10
14 *Wayne Haddix* .20
15 Gary Anderson .20
16 *Stan Humphries* 1.00
17 Raymond Clayborn .10
18 *Mark Boyer* .10
19 Dave Waymer .10
20 Andre Rison .50
21 Daniel Stubbs .10
22 Mike Rozier .10
23 Damian Johnson .10
24 Don Smith .10
25 Max Montoya .10
26 *Terry Kinard* .10
27 Herb Welch .10
28 Cliff Odom .10
29 John Kidd .10
30 *Barry Word* .20
31 Rich Karlis .10
32 Mike Baab .10
33 Ronnie Harmon .10
34 Jeff Donaldson .10

35 Riki Ellison .10
36 Steve Walsh .20
37 *Bill Lewis* .10
38 Tim McKyer .10
39 James Wilder .10
40 Tony Paige .10
41 *Derrick Fenner* .20
42 Thane Gash .10
43 Dave Duerson .10
44 Clarence Weathers .10
45 Matt Bahr .10
46 Alonzo Highsmith .10
47 Joe Kelly .10
48 Chris Hinton .10
49 Bobby Humphery .10
50 Greg Bell .10
51 Fred Smerlas .10
52 Dennis McKinnon .10
53 Jim Skow .10
54 Renaldo Turnbull .20
55 Bern Brostek .10
56 *Charles Wilson* .10
57 Keith McCants .10
58 Alexander Wright .20
59 *Ian Beckles* .10
60 *Eric Davis* .20
61 Chris Singleton .10
62 *Rob Moore* 10.00
63 Darion Conner .10
64 Tim Gunhard .10
65 Junior Seau 5.00
66 Tony Stargell .10
67 Anthony Thompson .20
68 Cortez Kennedy .50
69 Darrell Thompson .10
70 *Calvin Williams* .20
71 Rodney Hampton 1.50
72 Terry Wooden .10
73 Leo Goeas .10
74 Ken Willis .10
75 Ricky Proehl .75
76 *Steve Christie* .50
77 Andre Ware .20
78 Jeff George 3.00
79 Walter Wilson .10
80 *Johnny Bailey* .20
81 *Harold Green* .20
82 Mark Carrier .50
83 Frank Cornish .10
84 James Williams .10
85 *James Francis* .20
86 Percy Snow .10
87 Anthony Johnson 1.00
88 Tim Ryan .10
89 *Dan Owens* .20
90 Aaron Wallace .10
91 Steve Broussard .20
92 Eric Green .50
93 Blair Thomas .20
94 *Robert Blackmon* .20
95 *Alan Grant* .10
96 Andre Collins .10
97 Dexter Carter .20
98 *Reggie Cobb* .20
99 Dennis Brown .10
100 *Kenny Davidson* .10
101 *Emmitt Smith* 110.00
102 Jeff Alm .10
103 Alton Montgomery .10
104 Tony Bennett .20
105 *Johnny Johnson* .50
106 *Leroy Hoard* 1.50
107 Ray Agnew .10
108 Richmond Webb .20
109 Keith Sims .10
110 Barry Foster .20

1990 Score 100 Hottest

These cards featuring 100 top NFL players, have the same photos on them as the regular issue 1990 Score cards, but they are numbered differently. Publications International published a magazine to accompany the set; the magazine offered additional information about the players.

NM/M
Complete Set (100): 15.00
Common Player: .10
1 Bo Jackson .25
2 Joe Montana 2.00
3 Deion Sanders .50
4 Dan Marino 1.25
5 Barry Sanders 1.00
6 Neal Anderson .15
7 Phil Simms .20
8 Bobby Humphrey .10
9 Roger Craig .20
10 John Elway .60
11 James Brooks .15
12 Ken O'Brien .10
13 Thurman Thomas .50
14 Troy Aikman 2.00
15 Karl Mecklenburg .10
16 Dave Krieg .10
17 Chris Spielman .10
18 Tim Harris .15
19 Tim Worley .10
20 Clay Matthews .15
21 Lars Tate .10
22 Hart Lee Dykes .10
23 Cornelius Bennett .15
24 Anthony Miller .15
25 Lawrence Taylor .30
26 Jay Hilgenberg .10
27 Tom Rathman .15
28 Brian Blades .25
29 David Fulcher .10
30 Cris Carter .40
31 Marcus Allen .30
32 Eric Metcalf .15
33 Bruce Smith .15
34 Jim Kelly .60
35 Wade Wilson .15
36 Rich Camarillo .10
37 Boomer Esiason .20
38 John Offerdahl .10
39 Vance Johnson .10
40 Ronnie Lott .20
41 Kevin Ross .15
42 Greg Bell .10
43 Erik McMillan .10
44 Mike Singletary .20
45 Roger Vick .10
46 Keith Jackson .30
47 Henry Ellard .15
48 Gary Anderson .15
49 Art Monk .30
50 Jim Everett .15
51 Anthony Munoz .15
52 Ray Childress .15
53 Howie Long .20
54 Chris Hinton .10
55 John Stephens .20
56 Reggie White .25
57 Rodney Peete .15
58 Don Majkowski .10
59 Michael Cofer .10
60 Bubby Brister .10
61 Jerry Gray .10
62 Rodney Holman .10
63 Vinny Testaverde .20
64 Sterling Sharpe .65
65 Keith Millard .10
66 Jim Lachey .10
67 Dave Meggett .15
68 Brent Fullwood .10
69 Bobby Hebert .15
70 Joey Browner .10
71 Flipper Anderson .15
72 Tim McGee .10
73 Eric Allen .10
74 Charles Haley .25
75 Christian Okoye .15
76 Herschel Walker .20
77 Kelvin Martin .15
78 Bill Fralic .10
79 Leslie O'Neal .15
80 Bernie Kosar .20
81 Eric Sievers .10
82 Timm Rosenbach .10
83 Steve DeBerg .15
84 Duane Bickett .10
85 Chris Doleman .15
86 Carl Banks .15
87 Vaughan Johnson .10
88 Dennis Smith .10
89 Billy Joe Tolliver .15
90 Dalton Hilliard .10
91 John Taylor .20
92 Mark Rypien .20
93 Chris Miller .30
94 Mark Clayton .15
95 Andre Reed .25
96 Warren Moon .50
97 Bruce Matthews .10
98 Rod Woodson .25
99 Pat Swilling .15
100 Jerry Rice 1.25

1990 Score Young Superstars

This 40-card glossy set was a 1990 Score mail-in offer featuring some of the top young players in the NFL. Each card front has an action photo framed by black borders. Each back has a full color close-up photo, plus statistics, a card number, team logo and career summary.

NM/M
Complete Set (40): 8.00
Common Player: .10
1 Barry Sanders 1.50
2 Bobby Humphrey .40
3 Ickey Woods .20
4 Shawn Collins .10
5 Dave Meggett .25
6 Keith Jackson .25
7 Sterling Sharpe .25
8 Troy Aikman .75
9 Tim McDonald .10
10 Tim Brown .25
11 Trace Armstrong .10
12 Eric Metcalf (Led Bears in rushing, should be Browns) .20
13 Derrick Thomas .35
14 Eric Hill .10
15 Deion Sanders .50
16 Steve Atwater .15
17 Carnell Lake .10
18 Andre Reed .30
19 Chris Spielman .15
20 Eric Allen .10
21 Erik McMillan .15
22 Louis Oliver .10
23 Robert Massey .10
24 John Roper .10
25 Burt Grossman .15
26 Chris Jacke .10
27 Steve Wisniewski .10
28 Alonzo Highsmith .15
29 Mark Carrier .20
30 Bruce Armstrong .10
31 Jerome Brown .10
32 Cornelius Bennett .20
33 Flipper Anderson .15
34 Brian Blades .25
35 Anthony Miller .20
36 Thurman Thomas .90
37 Chris Miller .35
38 Aundray Bruce .15
39 Robert Clark .15
40 Robert Delpino .15

1990 Score Final Five

These five cards were inserted in 1990 Score Football factory sets and feature the last five picks in the 1990 NFL Draft. The "Final Five" logo is on each card front, along with a color photo of the player selected. The back has his name, position and summary of his collegiate accomplishments. Cards are numbered with a "B" prefix.

NM/M
Complete Set (5): .50
Common Player: .05
1 Judd Garrett .05
2 Matt Stover .15
3 Ken McMichael .05
4 Demetrius Davis .05
5 Elliott Searcy .05

1990 Score Franco Harris

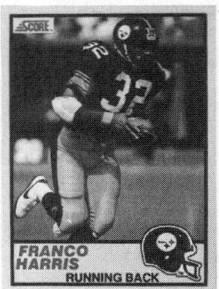

This card was given away to collectors who acquired Franco Harris' autograph at the Super Bowl Card Show in Tampa. The card is unnumbered and features a Leroy Nieman painting of Harris on the front with a picture of him celebrating a Super Bowl win on the back. Production of this card was estimated between 1,500 and 5,000.

NM/M
Complete Set (1): 50.00
1 Franco Harris 50.00

1991 Score Promos

These six cards were designed to preview Score's 1991 regular set. The card numbers, which are on the card back, are identical to those in the regular set, except for Lawrence Taylor, who is #529 in the regular set. The prototype cards can be distinguished from the regular cards by several differences, including: the statistics on the back are in blue-green, not green; the promo cards omit the tiny trademark symbol next to the Team NFL logo; and cards 1, 5 and 7 are cropped slightly different.

NM/M
Complete Set (6): 10.00
Common Player: 1.00
1 Joe Montana 5.00
4 Lawrence Taylor 1.25
5 Derrick Thomas 1.50
6 Mike Singletary 1.00
7 Boomer Esiason 1.25
12 Randall Cunningham 1.50

1991 Score

Score's 1991 first series was released in May 1991. The size increased by 15 cards over the previous year's Series I. Carried over from Score baseball was the "Dream Team" subset - this time featuring card-size profile shots with a smaller action insert. Artist Chris Greco worked on the MVP and Top Leader cards. Because Draft Pick cards carry no NFL team designation, they technically are not considered true rookie cards. (Key: DP - Draft Pick, 90 - 90-Plus Club, TL - Top Leader, DT - Dream Team)

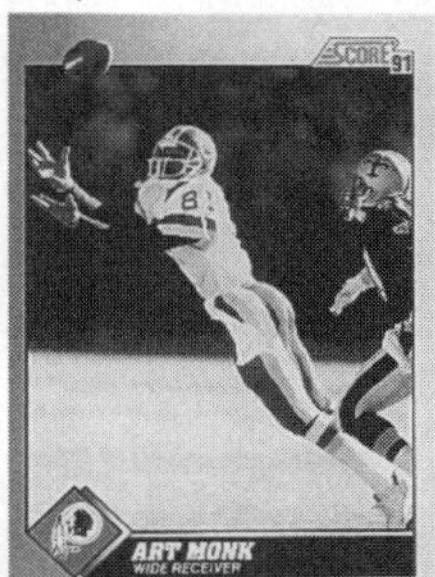

NM/M
Complete Set (686): 9.00
Factory Set (690): 9.00
Complete Series 1 (345): 4.50
Complete Series 2 (341): 4.50
Common Player: .04
Pack (16): .40
Wax Box (36): 9.00
1 Joe Montana 1.00
2 Eric Allen .04
3 Rohn Stark .04
4 Frank Reich .04
5 Derrick Thomas .25
6 Mike Singletary .04
7 Boomer Esiason .10
8 Matt Millen .04
9 Chris Spielman .04
10 Gerald McNeil .04
11 Nick Lowery .04
12 Randall Cunningham .10
13 Marion Butts .04
14 Tim Brown .25
15 Emmitt Smith 1.75
16 Rich Camarillo .04
17 Mike Merriweather .04
18 Derrick Fenner .10
19 Clay Matthews .04
20 Barry Sanders 1.75
21 James Brooks .04
22 Alton Montgomery .04
23 Steve Atwater .04
24 Ron Morris .04
25 Brad Muster .04
26 Andre Rison .25
27 Brian Brennan .04
28 Leonard Smith .04
29 Kevin Butler .04
30 Tim Harris .04
31 Jay Novacek .15
32 Eddie Murray .04
33 Keith Woodside .04
34 *Ray Crockett* .10
35 Eugene Lockhart .04
36 Bill Romanowski .04
37 Eddie Brown .04
38 Eugene Daniel .04
39 Scott Fulhage .04
40 Harold Green .10
41 Mark Jackson .04
42 Sterling Sharpe .10
43 Mel Gray .04
44 Jerry Holmes .04
45 Allen Pinkett .04
46 Warren Powers .04
47 Rodney Peete .04
48 Lorenzo White .10
49 Dan Owens .04
50 James Francis .04
51 Ken Norton .04
52 Ed West .04
53 Andre Reed .10
54 John Grimsley .04
55 Michael Cofer .04
56 Chris Doleman .04
57 Pat Swilling .04
58 Jessie Tuggle .04
59 Mike Johnson .04
60 Steve Walsh .04
61 Sam Mills .04
62 Don Mosebar .04
63 Jay Hilgenberg .04
64 Cleveland Gary .04
65 Andre Tippett .04
66 Tom Newberry .04
67 Maurice Hurst .04
68 Louis Oliver .04
69 Fred Marion .04
70 Christian Okoye .04
71 Marv Cook .04
72 Darryl Talley .04
73 Rick Fenney .04
74 Kelvin Martin .04
75 Howie Long .04
76 Steve Wisniewski .04
77 Karl Mecklenburg .04
78 Dan Saleaumua .04
79 Ray Childress .04
80 Henry Ellard .04
81 Ernest Givins .04
82 Ferrell Edmunds .04
83 Steve Jordan .04
84 Tony Mandarich .04
85 Eric Martin .04
86 Rich Gannon .10
87 Irving Fryar .04
88 Tom Rathman .04
89 Dan Hampton .04
90 Barry Word .10
91 Kevin Greene .04
92 Sean Landeta .04
93 Trace Armstrong .04
94 Dennis Byrd .04
95 Timm Rosenbach .04
96 Anthony Toney .04
97 Tim Krumrie .04
98 Jerry Ball .04
99 Tim Green .04
100 Bo Jackson .35
101 Myron Guyton .04
102 Mike Mularkey .04
103 Jerry Gray .04
104 Scott Stephen .04
106 Lomas Brown .04
107 David Little .04
108 Brad Baxter .10
109 Freddie Joe Nunn .04
110 Dave Meggett .04
111 Mark Rypien .10
112 Warren Williams .04
113 Ron Rivera .04
114 Terance Mathis .10
115 Anthony Munoz .04
116 Jeff Bryant .04
117 Issaic Holt .04
118 Steve Sewell .04
119 Tim Newton .04
120 Emile Harry .04
121 Gary Anderson (Pitt.) .04
122 Mark Lee .04
123 Alfred Anderson .04
124 Tony Blaylock .04
125 Ernest Byner .04
126 Bill Maas .04
127 Keith Taylor .04
128 Cliff Odom .04
129 Bob Golic .04
130 Bart Oates .04
131 Jim Arnold .04
132 Jerr Herrod .04
133 Bruce Armstrong .04
134 Craig Heyward .06
135 Joey Browner .04
136 Darren Comeaux .04
137 Pat Beach .04
138 Dalton Hilliard .06
139 David Treadwell .04
140 Gary Anderson (T.B.) .04
141 Eugene Robinson .04
142 Scott Case .04
143 Paul Farren .04
144 Gill Fenerty .04
145 Tim Irwin .04
146 Norm Johnson .04
147 Willie Gault .06
148 Clarence Verdin .04
149 Jeff Uhlenhake .04
150 Erik McMillan .04
151 Kevin Ross .04
152 Pepper Johnson .04
153 Bryan Hinkle .04
154 Gary Clark .08
155 Robert Delpino .04
156 Doug Smith .04
157 Chris Martin .04
158 Ray Berry .04
159 Steve Christie .04
160 Don Smith .04
161 Greg McMurtry .04
162 Jack Del Rio .04
163 Floyd Dixon .04
164 Buford McGee .04
165 Brett Maxie .04
166 Morten Andersen .06
167 Kent Hull .04
168 Skip McClendon .04
169 Keith Sims .04
170 Leonard Marshall .04
171 Tony Woods .04
172 Byron Evans .04
173 *Rob Burnett* .15
174 Tory Epps .04
175 *Toi Cook* .10
176 John Elliott .04
177 Tommie Agee .04
178 Keith Van Horne .04
179 Dennis Smith .04
180 James Lofton .04
181 Art Monk .04
182 Anthony Carter .04
183 Louis Lipps .04
184 Bruce Hill .04
185 Mike Young .04
186 Eric Green .10
187 *Barney Bussey* .10
188 Curtis Duncan .04
189 Robert Awalt .04
190 Johnny Johnson .20
191 Jeff Cross .04
192 Keith McKeller .04
193 Robert Brown .04
194 Vincent Brown .04
195 Calvin Williams .20
196 Sean Jones .04
197 Willie Drewrey .04
198 Bubba McDowell .04
199 Al Noga .04
200 Ronnie Lott .10
201 Warren Moon .20
202 Chris Hinton .04
203 Jim Sweeney .04
204 Wayne Haddix .04
205 *Tim Jorden* .10
206 Marvin Allen .04
207 *Jim Morrissey* .10
208 Ben Smith .04
209 William White .04
210 Jim Jensen .04
211 Doug Reed .04
212 Ethan Horton .04
213 Chris Jacke .04
214 Johnny Hector .04
215 Drew Hill .04
216 Roy Green .04
217 Dean Steinhuhler .04
218 Cedric Mack .04
219 Chris Miller .04
220 Keith Byars .04
221 Lewis Billups .04
222 Roger Craig .04
223 Shaun Gayle .04
224 Mike Rozier .04
225 Troy Aikman 1.00
226 Bobby Humphrey .04
227 Eugene Marve .04
228 Michael Carter .04
229 Richard Johnson .04
230 Billy Joe Tolliver .08
231 Mark Murphy .04
232 John L. Williams .04
233 Ronnie Harmon .08
234 Thurman Thomas .40
235 Martin Mayhew .04
236 Richmond Webb .04
237 Gerald Riggs .04
238 Mike Prior .04
239 Mike Gann .04
240 Alvin Walton .04
241 Tim McGee .04
242 Bruce Matthews .04
243 Johnny Holland .04
244 Martin Bayless .04
245 Eric Metcalf .04
246 John Alt .04
247 Max Montoya .04
248 Rod Bernstine .04
249 Paul Gruber .04
250 Charles Haley .04
251 Scott Norwood .04
252 Michael Haddix .04
253 Ricky Sanders .06
254 Ervin Randle .04
255 Duane Bickett .04
256 Mike Munchak .04
257 Keith Jones .04
258 Riki Ellison .04
259 Vince Newsome .04
260 Lee Williams .04
261 Steve Smith .04
262 Sam Clancy .04
263 Pierce Holt .04
264 Jim Harbaugh .08
265 Dino Hackett .04
266 Andy Heck .04
267 Leo Goeas .04
268 Russ Grimm .04
269 Gill Byrd .04
270 Neal Anderson .08
271 Jackie Slater .04
272 Joe Nash .04
273 Todd Bowles .04
274 D.J. Dozier .04
275 Kevin Fagan .04
276 Don Warren .04
277 Jim Jeffcoat .04
278 Bruce Smith .08
279 Cortez Kennedy .25
280 Thane Gash .04
281 Perry Kemp .04
282 John Taylor .10
283 Stephone Paige .04
284 Paul Skansi .04
285 Shawn Collins .04
286 Mervyn Fernandez .04
287 Daniel Stubbs .04
288 Chip Lohmiller .04
289 Brian Blades .04
290 Mark Carrier .04
291 Carl Zander .04
292 David Wyman .04
293 Jeff Bostic .04
294 Irv Pankey .04
295 Keith Millard .04
296 Jamie Mueller .04
297 Bill Fralic .04
298 Wendell Davis .08
299 Ken Clarke .04
300 Wymon Henderson .04
301 Jeff Campbell .04
302 *Cody Carlson* .35
303 *Matt Brock* .10
304 Maurice Carthon .04
305 *Scott Mersereau* .10
306 Steve Wright .04
307 J.B. Brown .04
308 Ricky Reynolds .04
309 Darryl Pollard .04
310 Donald Evans .04
311 *Nick Bell* (DP) .20
312 *Pat Harlow* (DP) .10
313 *Dan McGwire* (DP) .10
314 Mike Dumas (DP) .04
315 *Mike Croel* (DP) .20
316 Chris Smith (DP) .04
317 *Kenny Walker* (DP) .10
318 *Todd Lyght* (DP) .10
319 Mike Stonebreaker (DP) .04
320 Randall Cunningham (90) .08
321 Terance Mathis (90) .04
322 Gaston Green (90) .04
323 Johnny Bailey (90) .04
324 Donnie Elder (90) .04
325 Dwight Stone (90) .04
326 *J.J. Birden* (90) .35
327 Alex Wright (90) .04
328 Eric Metcalf (90) .04
329 Andre Rison (TL) .15
330 Warren Moon (TL) .10
331 Steve Tasker, Reyna Thompson (DT) .04
332 Mel Gray (DT) .04
333 Nick Lowery (DT) .04
334 Sean Landeta (DT) .04
335 David Fulcher (DT) .04
336 Joey Browner (DT) .04
337 Albert Lewis (DT) .04
338 Rod Woodson (DT) .06
339 Shane Conlan (DT) .04
340 Pepper Johnson (DT) .04
341 Chris Spielman (DT) .06
342 Derrick Thomas (DT) .08
343 Ray Childress (DT) .04
344 Reggie White (DT) .08
345 Bruce Smith (DT) .06
346 Darrell Green .04
347 Ray Bentley .04
348 Herschel Walker .06
349 Rodney Holman .04
350 Al Toon .04
351 Harry Hamilton .04

#	Player	Price
352	Albert Lewis	.04
353	Renaldo Turnbull	.04
354	Junior Seau	.25
355	Merril Hoge	.04
356	Shane Conlan	.04
357	Jay Schroeder	.04
358	Steve Broussard	.04
359	Mark Bavaro	.04
360	Jim Lachey	.04
361	Greg Townsend	.04
362	Dave Krieg	.04
363	Jessie Hester	.04
364	Steve Tasker	.04
365	Ron Hall	.04
366	Pat Leahy	.04
367	Jim Everett	.06
368	Felix Wright	.04
369	Ricky Proehl	.04
370	Anthony Miller	.05
371	Keith Jackson	.08
372	Pete Stoyanovich	.04
373	Tommy Kane	.04
374	Richard Johnson	.04
375	Randall McDaniel	.04
376	John Stephens	.04
377	Haywood Jeffires	.15
378	Rodney Hampton	.50
379	Tim Grunhard	.04
380	Jerry Rice	1.00
381	Ken Harvey	.04
382	Vaughan Johnson	.04
383	J.T. Smith	.04
384	Carnell Lake	.04
385	Dan Marino	1.75
386	Kyle Clifton	.04
387	Wilber Marshall	.04
388	Pete Holohan	.04
389	Gary Plummer	.04
390	William Perry	.04
391	Mark Robinson	.04
392	Nate Odomes	.06
393	Ickey Woods	.04
394	Reyna Thompson	.04
395	Deion Sanders	.40
396	Harris Barton	.04
397	Sammie Smith	.04
398	Vinny Testaverde	.04
399	Ray Donaldson	.04
400	Tim McKyer	.04
401	Nesby Glasgow	.04
402	Brent Williams	.04
403	Rob Moore	.10
404	Bubby Brister	.05
405	David Fulcher	.04
406	Reggie Cobb	.20
407	Jerome Brown	.04
408	Erik Howard	.04
409	Tony Paige	.04
410	John Elway	.35
411	Charles Mann	.04
412	Luis Sharpe	.04
413	Hassan Jones	.04
414	Frank Minnifield	.04
415	Steve DeBerg	.04
416	Mark Carrier	.04
417	Brian Jordan	.04
418	Reggie Langhorne	.04
419	Don Majkowski	.04
420	Marcus Allen	.05
421	Michael Brooks	.04
422	Vai Sikahema	.04
423	Dermontti Dawson	.04
424	Jacob Green	.04
425	Flipper Anderson	.04
426	Bill Brooks	.04
427	Keith McCants	.04
428	Ken O'Brien	.04
429	Fred Barnett	.10
430	Mark Duper	.04
431	Mark Kelso	.04
432	Leslie O'Neal	.04
433	Ottis Anderson	.05
434	Jesse Sapolu	.04
435	Gary Zimmerman	.04
436	Kevin Porter	.04
437	Anthony Thompson	.04
438	Robert Clark	.04
439	Chris Warren	.20
440	Gerald Williams	.04
441	Jim Skow	.04
442	Rick Donnelly	.04
443	Guy McIntyre	.04
444	Jeff Lageman	.04
445	John Offerdahl	.04
446	Clyde Simmons	.04
447	John Kidd	.04
448	Chip Banks	.04
449	Johnny Meads	.04
450	Rickey Jackson	.04
451	Lee Johnson	.04
452	Michael Irvin	.25
453	Leon Seals	.04
454	Darrell Thompson	.20
455	Everson Walls	.04
456	LeRoy Butler	.06
457	Marcus Dupree	.04
458	Kirk Lowdermilk	.04
459	Chris Singleton	.04
460	Seth Joyner	.04
461	Rueben Mayes (Hayes in bio should be Heyward)	.04
462	Ernie Jones	.04
463	Greg Kragen	.04
464	Bennie Blades	.04
465	Mark Bortz	.04
466	Tony Stargell	.04
467	Mike Cofer	.05
468	Randy Grimes	.04
469	Tim Worley	.04
470	Kevin Mack	.04
471	Wes Hopkins	.04
472	Will Wolford	.04
473	Sam Seale	.04
474	Jim Ritcher	.04
475	Jeff Hostetler	.20
476	Mitchell Price	.04
477	Ken Lanier	.04
478	Naz Worthen	.04
479	Ed Reynolds	.04
480	Mark Clayton	.05
481	Matt Bahr	.04
482	Gary Reasons	.04
483	Dave Szott	.04
484	Barry Foster	.45
485	Bruce Reimers	.04
486	Dean Biasucci	.04
487	Cris Carter	.05
488	Albert Bentley	.04
489	Robert Massey	.04
490	Al Smith	.04
491	Greg Lloyd	.08
492	Steve McMichael (Photo on back actually Dan Hampton)	.05
493	*Jeff Wright*	.08
494	Scott Davis	.04
495	Freeman McNeil	.04
496	Simon Fletcher	.04
497	Terry McDaniel	.04
498	Heath Sherman	.04
499	Jeff Jaeger	.04
500	Mark Collins	.04
501	Tim Goad	.04
502	Jeff George	.25
503	Jimmie Jones	.05
504	Henry Thomas	.04
505	Steve Young	.60
506	William Roberts	.04
507	Neil Smith	.04
508	Mike Saxon	.04
509	Johnny Bailey	.04
510	Broderick Thomas	.04
511	Wade Wilson	.04
512	Hart Lee Dykes	.04
513	Hardy Nickerson	.04
514	Tim McDonald	.05
515	Frank Cornish	.04
516	Jarvis Williams	.04
517	Carl Lee	.04
518	Carl Banks	.04
519	Mike Golic	.04
520	Brian Noble	.04
521	James Hasty	.04
522	Bubba Paris	.04
523	*Kevin Walker*	.08
524	William Fuller	.04
525	Eddie Anderson	.04
526	Roger Ruzek	.04
527	Robert Blackmon	.04
528	Vince Buck	.04
529	Lawrence Taylor	.10
530	Reggie Roby	.04
531	Doug Riesenberg	.04
532	Joe Jacoby	.04
533	Kirby Jackson	.04
534	Robb Thomas	.04
535	Don Griffin	.04
536	Andre Waters	.05
537	Marc Logan	.04
538	James Thornton	.04
539	Ray Agnew	.04
540	Frank Stams	.04
541	Brett Perriman	.05
542	Andre Ware	.10
543	Kevin Haverdink	.04
544	*Greg Jackson*	.08
545	Tunch Ilkin	.04
546	Dexter Carter	.04
547	Rod Woodson	.06
548	Donnell Woolford	.04
549	Mark Boyer	.04
550	Jeff Query	.04
551	Burt Grossman	.04
552	Mike Kenn	.04
553	Richard Dent	.04
554	Gaston Green	.04
555	Phil Simms	.10
556	Brent Jones	.05
557	Ronnie Lippett	.04
558	Mike Horan	.04
559	Danny Noonan	.04
560	Reggie White	.15
561	Rufus Porter	.04
562	Aaron Wallace	.04
563	Vance Johnson	.04
564	Aaron Craver (No copyright line on back)	.04
565A	*Russell Maryland* (No copyright line on back)	.40
565B	*Russell Maryland*	.40
566	Paul Justin	.04
567	Walter Dean	.04
568	*Herman Moore*	3.00
569	*Bill Musgrave*	.10
570	*Rob Carpenter*	.10
571	*Greg Lewis*	.10
572	*Ed King*	.10
573	*Ernie Mills*	.08
574	*Jake Reed*	1.00
575	*Ricky Watters*	2.00
576	*Derek Russell*	.25
577	*Shawn Moore*	.15
578	*Eric Bieniemy*	.15
579	*Chris Zorich*	.30
580	Scott Miller	.05
581	*Jarrod Bunch*	.10
582	*Ricky Ervins*	.20
583	*Browning Nagle*	.20
584	*Eric Turner*	.20
585	*William Thomas*	.08
586	*Stanley Richard*	.30
587	*Adrian Cooper*	.15
588	*Harvey Williams*	.10
589	*Alvin Harper*	.10
590	John Carney	.04
591	Mark Vander Poel	.04
592	*Mike Pritchard*	.35
593	*Eric Moten*	.08
594	*Moe Gardner*	.10
595	*Wesley Carroll*	.10
596	*Eric Swann*	.10
597	Joe Kelly	.05
598	*Steve Jackson*	.10
599	*Kelvin Pritchett*	.15
600	*Jesse Campbell*	.08
601	*Darryll Lewis* (Misspelled Darryl on card)	.08
602	Howard Griffith	.04
603	Blaise Bryant	.04
604	*Vinnie Clark*	.08
605	*Mel Agee*	.08
606	*Bobby Wilson*	.08
607	Kevin Donnalley	.04
608	*Randal Hill*	.35
609	Stan Thomas	.04
610	Mike Heldt	.04
611	*Brett Favre*	4.00
612	*Lawrence Dawsey*	.25
613	Dennis Gibson	.04
614	Dean Dingman	.04
615	*Bruce Pickens*	.08
616	*Todd Marinovich*	.08
617	Gene Atkins	.04
618	Marcus Dupree (Comeback Player)	.04
619	Warren Moon (Man of the Year)	.10
620	Joe Montana (MVP)	.50
621	Neal Anderson (Team MVP)	.05
622	James Brooks (Team MVP)	.05
623	Thurman Thomas (Team MVP)	.20
624	Bobby Humphrey (Team MVP)	.04
625	Kevin Mack (Team MVP)	.04
626	Mark Carrier (Team MVP)	.04
627	Johnny Johnson (Team MVP)	.08
628	Marion Butts (Team MVP)	.05
629	Steve DeBerg (Team MVP)	.05
630	Jeff George (Team MVP)	.10
631	Troy Aikman (MVP)	.50
632	Dan Marino (MVP)	.25
633	Randall Cunningham (Team MVP)	.08
634	Andre Rison (Team MVP)	.08
635	Pepper Johnson (Team MVP)	.04
636	Pat Leahy (Team MVP)	.04
637	Barry Sanders (MVP)	.50
638	Warren Moon (Team MVP)	.08
639	Sterling Sharpe (MVP)	.25
640	Bruce Armstrong (Team MVP)	.04
641	Bo Jackson (Team MVP)	.10
642	Henry Ellard (Team MVP)	.05
643	Earnest Byner (Team MVP)	.04
644	Pat Swilling (Team MVP)	.04
645	John L. Williams (Team MVP)	.04
646	Rod Woodson (Team MVP)	.06
647	Chris Doleman (Team MVP)	.04
648	Joey Browner (Crunch Crew)	.04
649	Erik McMillan (Crunch Crew)	.04
650	David Fulcher (Crunch Crew)	.04
651A	Ronnie Lott (Front 47, back 42)	.08
651B	Ronnie Lott (Front 47, back 42 is now blacked out)	.05
652	Louis Oliver (Crunch Crew)	.04
653	Mark Robinson (Crunch Crew)	.04
654	Dennis Smith (Crunch Crew)	.04
655	Reggie White (Sack Attack)	.08
656	Charles Haley (Sack Attack)	.04
657	Leslie O'Neal (Sack Attack)	.04
658	Kevin Greene (Sack Attack)	.04
659	Dennis Byrd (Sack Attack)	.04
660	Bruce Smith (Sack Attack)	.08
661	Derrick Thomas (Sack Attack)	.10
662	Steve DeBerg (Top Leader)	.04
663	Barry Sanders (TL)	.50
664	Thurman Thomas (TL)	.20
665	Jerry Rice (TL)	.40
666	Derrick Thomas (Top Leader)	.10
667	Bruce Smith (Top Leader)	.08
668	Mark Carrier (Top Leader)	.04
669	Richard Johnson (Top Leader)	.04
670	Jan Stenerud (Hall of Fame)	.05
671	Stan Jones (Hall of Fame)	.05
672	John Hannah (Hall of Fame)	.05
673	Tex Schramm (Hall of Fame)	.05
674	Earl Campbell (Hall of Fame)	.10
675	Mark Carrier, Emmitt Smith (ROY ROY)	.25
676	Warren Moon (DT)	.10
677	Barry Sanders (DT)	.50
678	Thurman Thomas (DT)	.20
679	Andre Reed (DT)	.06
680	Andre Rison (DT)	.15
681	Keith Jackson (DT)	.05
682	Bruce Armstrong (DT)	.05
683	Jim Lachey (DT)	.04
684	Bruce Matthews (DT)	.04
685	Mike Munchak (DT)	.04
686	Don Mosebar (DT)	.04

1991 Score Dream Team Autographs

The 11-card, standard-size set was inserted every 5,000 packs of Series II packs. Each player autographed approximately 500 cards.

		NM/M
	Common Player:	10.00
676	Warren Moon	60.00
677	Barry Sanders	250.00
678	Thurman Thomas	65.00
679	Andre Reed	55.00
680	Andre Rison	50.00
681	Keith Jackson	50.00
682	Bruce Armstrong	10.00
683	Jim Lachey	10.00
684	Bruce Matthews	10.00
685	Mike Munchak	10.00
686	Don Mosebar	10.00

1991 Score Hot Rookie

1991 Score blister packs contained these random inserts which have card fronts showing action shots of the players in their collegiate uniforms against a hot pink/yellow background. The fronts are bordered in black. Each card back is numbered and includes a close-up shot of the player, plus a brief career summary.

		NM/M
	Complete Set (10):	3.00
	Common Player:	.40
1	Dan McGwire	.50
2	Todd Lyght	.50
3	Mike Dumas	.40
4	Pat Harlow	.40
5	Nick Bell	1.00
6	Chris Smith	.40
7	Mike Stonebreaker	.40
8	Mike Croel	.50
9	Kenny Walker	.50
10	Rob Carpenter	.40

1991 Score Supplemental

Rookies and players who were traded during the regular season are featured in this 110-card update set. The fronts have the same design as the regular cards do, except the borders shade from blue-green to white. The backs have a mug shot and player information in a horizontal format framed by a gold border. Card numbering is done on the back with a "T" suffix.

		NM/M
	Complete Set (110):	8.00
	Common Player:	.04
1	Ronnie Oliver	.10
2	Matt Millen	.04
3	Tim McKyer	.04
4	Vince Newsome	.04
5	Gaston Green	.04
6	Brett Perriman	.08
7	Roger Craig	.06
8	Pete Holohan	.04
9	Tony Zendejas	.04
10	Lee Williams	.04
11	Mike Stonebreaker	.04
12	Felix Wright	.04
13	Lonnie Young	.04
14	*Hugh Millen*	.10
15	Roy Green	.04
16	*Greg Davis*	.10
17	Dexter Manley	.04
18	*Ted Washington*	.10
19	Norm Johnson	.04
20	Joe Morris	.04
21	Robert Perryman	.04
22	Mike Iaquaniello	.04
23	*Gerald Perry*	.10
24	Zeke Mowatt	.04
25	*Rich Miano*	.10
26	Nick Bell	.10
27	*Terry Orr*	.15
28	*Matt Stover*	.15
29	Bubba Paris	.04
30	Ron Brown	.04
31	Don Davey	.04
32	Lee Rouson	.04
33	Terry Hoage	.04
34	Tony Covington	.04
35	John Rienstra	.04
36	*Charles Dimry*	.08
37	Todd Marinovich	.08
38	Winston Moss	.04
39	Vestee Jackson	.04
40	Brian Hansen	.04
41	Irv Eatman	.04
42	Jarrod Bunch	.08
43	*Kanavis McGhee*	.10
44	Vai Sikahema	.04
45	*Charles McRae*	.10
46	Quinn Early	.04
47	*Jeff Faulkner*	.10
48	*William Frizzell*	.10
49	John Booty	.04
50	Tim Harris	.04
51	Derek Russell	.10
52	*John Flannery*	.10
53	*Tim Barnett*	.15
54	*Alfred Williams*	.15
55	Dan McGwire	.04
56	Ernie Mills	.10
57	Stanley Richard	.04
58	Huey Richardson	.04
59	*Jerome Henderson*	.10
60	*Bryan Cox*	.40
61	Russell Maryland	.25
62	*Reggie Jones*	.15
63	*Mo Lewis*	.10
64	Moe Gardner	.04
65	Wesley Carroll	.10
66	*Michael Jackson*	.25
67	*Shawn Jefferson*	.10
68	Chris Zorich	.10
69	Kenny Walker	.04
70	*Erric Pegram*	.10
71	Alvin Harper	.10
72	*Harry Colon*	.10
73	Scott Miller	.04
74	Lawrence Dawsey	.10
75	*Phil Hansen*	.15
76	*Roman Phifer*	.15
77	Greg Lewis	.04
78	*Merton Hanks*	.15
79	*James Jones*	.10
80	Vinnie Clark	.04
81	R.J. Kors	.04
82	Mike Pritchard	.25
83	Stan Thomas	.04
84	Lamar Rogers	.04
85	*Eric Williams*	.25
86	*Keith Traylor*	.10
87	Mike Dumas	.04
88	Mel Agee	.04
89	Harvey Williams	.25
90	Todd Lyght	.04
91	Jake Reed	.50
92	Pat Harlow	.04
93	*Antone Davis*	.10
94	*Aeneas Williams*	.10
95	Eric Bieniemy	.04
96	*John Kasay*	.10
97	Robert Wilson	.04
98	Ricky Ervins	.15
99	Mike Croel	.10
100	*David Lang*	.15
101	*Esera Tuaolo*	.10
102	Randal Hill	.20
103	*Jon Vaughn*	.25
104	Dave McCloughan	.04
105	David Daniels	.04
106	Eric Moten	.04
107	*Anthony Morgan*	.15
108	Ed King	.04
109	*Leonard Russell*	.10
110	Aaron Craver	.08

1991 Score National 10

These 10 cards were distributed at the 12th National Sports Collectors Covention in a cello wrapper. A panel on the card back indicates the cards were created for the convention. A mug shot, card number, biographical information and career summary are also provided on the back. The front has a color action photo of the player, with a player/football pattern above and below the photo.

		NM/M
	Complete Set (10):	10.00
	Common Player:	.75
1	Emmitt Smith	8.00
2	Mark Carrier	1.00
3	Steve Broussard	1.00
4	Johnny Johnson	2.00
5	Steve Christie	1.00
6	Richmond Webb	.75
7	James Francis	.75
8	Jeff George	2.00
9	Rodney Hampton	3.00
10	Calvin Williams	1.00

1991 Score Young Superstars

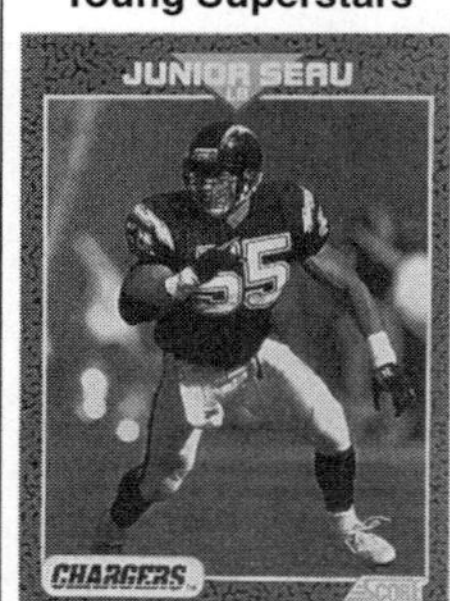

These cards, available in October 1990 via a mail-in offer found on Score wax packs, featured up-and-coming stars of the game. Each front has game-day photography surrounded by black borders and team colors. The card back shows a head shot, a player profile and a scouting report quote.

		NM/M
	Complete Set (40):	7.00
	Common Player:	.10
1	Johnny Bailey	.15
2	Johnny Johnson	.20
3	Fred Barnett	.15
4	Keith McCants	.10
5	Brad Baxter	.10
6	Dan Owens	.10
7	Steve Broussard	.15
8	Ricky Proehl	.15
9	Marion Butts	.20
10	Reggie Cobb	.10
11	Dennis Byrd	.10
12	Emmitt Smith	3.00
13	Mark Carrier	.15
14	Keith Sims	.10
15	Dexter Carter	.15
16	Chris Singleton	.10
17	Steve Christie	.10
18	Frank Cornish	.10
19	Timm Rosenbach	.10
20	Sammie Smith	.10
21	Calvin Williams	.15
22	Merril Hoge	.10
23	Hart Lee Dykes	.10
24	Darrell Thompson	.10
25	James Francis	.10
26	John Elliott	.10
27	Jeff George	.25
28	Broderick Thomas	.15
29	Eric Green	.15
30	Steve Walsh	.10
31	Harold Green	.15
32	Andre Ware	.10
33	Richmond Webb	.15
34	Junior Seau	.40
35	Tim Grunhard	.10
36	Tim Worley	.10
37	Haywood Jeffires	.20
38	Rod Woodson	.20
39	Rodney Hampton	.20
40	Dave Szott	.10

1992 Score

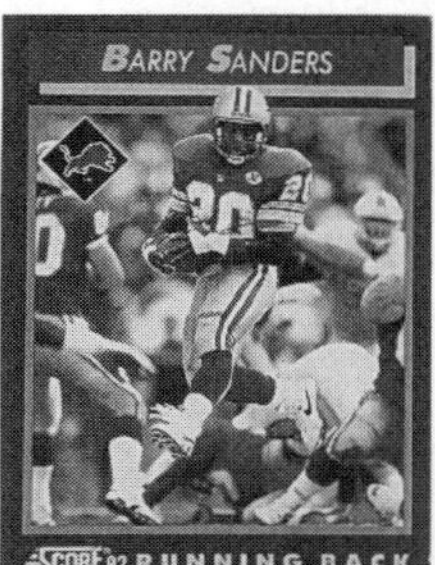

This 550-card set features color action photos surrounded by a solid colored border. The player's position is at the bottom in a dark blue band; his name is at the top in a green band. The back has a mug shot, biography, statistics and profile. Subsets include Draft Picks, Crunch Crew, Rookie of the Year, Little Big Men, Sack Attack, Hall of Famers, and the 90 Plus Club. Two insert sets were also made - Dream Team (25 cards, in foil packs), and Gridiron Stars (45 cards), which were in jumbo packs.

		NM/M
	Complete Set (550):	25.00
	Common Player:	.05
	Minor Stars:	.10
	Pack (17):	.30
	Wax Box (36):	8.00
1	Barry Sanders	2.00
2	Pat Swilling	.05
3	Moe Gardner	.05
4	Steve Young	1.50
5	Chris Spielman	.05
6	Richard Dent	.05
7	Anthony Munoz	.05
8	Martin Mayhew	.05
9	Terry McDaniel	.05
10	Thurman Thomas	.40
11	Ricky Sanders	.05
12	Steve Atwater	.05
13	Tony Tolbert	.05
14	Vince Workman	.05
15	Haywood Jeffires	.05
16	Duane Bickett	.05
17	Jeff Uhlenhake	.05
18	Tim McDonald	.05
19	Cris Carter	.10
20	Derrick Thomas	.10
21	Hugh Millen	.05
22	Bart Oates	.05
23	Eugene Robinson	.05
24	Jerrol Williams	.05
25	Reggie White	.10
26	Marion Butts	.05
27	Jim Sweeney	.05
28	Tom Newberry	.05
29	Pete Stoyanovich	.05
30	Ronnie Lott	.05
31	Simon Fletcher	.05
32	Dino Hackett	.05

#	Player	NM/M
33	Morten Andersen	.05
34	Clyde Simmons	.05
35	Mark Rypien	.05
36	Greg Montgomery	.05
37	Nate Lewis	.05
38	Henry Ellard	.05
39	Luis Sharpe	.05
40	Michael Irvin	.30
41	Louis Lipps	.05
42	John L. Williams	.05
43	Broderick Thomas	.05
44	Michael Haynes	.05
45	Don Majkowski	.05
46	William Perry	.05
47	David Fulcher	.05
48	Tony Bennett	.05
49	Clay Matthews	.05
50	Warren Moon	.10
51	Bruce Armstrong	.05
52	Harry Newsome	.05
53	Bill Brooks	.05
54	Greg Townsend	.05
55	Tom Rathman	.05
56	Sean Landeta	.05
57	Kyle Clifton	.05
58	Steve Broussard	.05
59	Mark Carrier	.05
60	Mel Gray	.05
61	Tim Krumrie	.05
62	Rufus Porter	.05
63	Kevin Mack	.05
64	Todd Bowles	.05
65	Emmitt Smith	3.00
66	Mike Croel	.05
67	Brian Mitchell	.05
68	Bennie Blades	.05
69	Carnell Lake	.05
70	Cornelius Bennett	.05
71	Darrell Thompson	.05
72	Wes Hopkins	.05
73	Jessie Hester	.05
74	Irv Eatman	.05
75	Marv Cook	.05
76	Tim Brown	.10
77	Pepper Johnson	.05
78	Mark Duper	.05
79	Robert Delpino	.05
80	Charles Mann	.05
81	Brian Jordan	.10
82	Wendell Davis	.05
83	Lee Johnson	.05
84	Ricky Reynolds	.05
85	Vaughan Johnson	.05
86	Brian Seale	.05
87	Sam Seale	.05
88	Ed King	.05
89	Gaston Green	.05
90	Christian Okoye	.05
91	Chris Jacke	.05
92	Rohn Stark	.05
93	Kevin Greene	.05
94	Jay Novacek	.10
95	Chip Lohmiller	.05
96	Cris Dishman	.05
97	Ethan Horton	.05
98	Pat Harlow	.05
99	Mark Ingram	.05
100	Mark Carrier	.05
101	Deron Cherry	.05
102	Sam Mills	.05
103	Mark Higgs	.05
104	Keith Jackson	.05
105	Steve Tasker	.05
106	Ken Harvey	.05
107	Bryan Hinkle	.05
108	Anthony Carter	.05
109	Johnny Hector	.05
110	Randall McDaniel	.05
111	Johnny Johnson	.05
112	Shane Conlan	.05
113	Ray Horton	.05
114	Sterling Sharpe	.10
115	Guy McIntyre	.05
116	Tom Waddle	.05
117	Albert Lewis	.05
118	Riki Ellison	.05
119	Chris Doleman	.05
120	Andre Rison	.05
121	Bobby Hebert	.05
122	Dan Owens	.05
123	Rodney Hampton	.10
124	Ron Holmes	.05
125	Ernie Jones	.05
126	Michael Carter	.05
127	Reggie Cobb	.05
128	Esera Tuaolo	.05
129	Wilber Marshall	.05
130	Mike Munchak	.05
131	Cortez Kennedy	.05
132	Lamar Lathon	.05
133	Todd Lyght	.05
134	Jeff Feagles	.05
135	Burt Grossman	.05
136	Mike Cofer	.05
137	Frank Warren	.05
138	Jarvis Williams	.05
139	Eddie Brown	.05
140	John Elliott	.05
141	Jim Everett	.05
142	Hardy Nickerson	.05
143	Eddie Murray	.05
144	Andre Tippett	.05
145	Heath Sherman	.05
146	Ronnie Harmon	.05
147	Eric Metcalf	.05
148	Tony Martin	.25
149	Chris Burkett	.05
150	Andre Waters	.05
151	Ray Donaldson	.05
152	Paul Gruber	.05
153	Chris Singleton	.05
154	Clarence Kay	.05
155	Ernest Givins	.05
156	Eric Hill	.05
157	Jesse Sapolu	.05
158	Jack Del Rio	.05
159	Erric Pegram	.10
160	Joey Browner	.05
161	Marcus Allen	.10
162	Eric Moten	.05
163	Donnell Thompson	.05
164	Chuck Cecil	.05
165	Matt Millen	.05
166	Barry Foster	.05
167	Kent Hull	.05
168	Tony Jones	.05
169	Mike Prior	.05
170	Neal Anderson	.05
171	Roger Craig	.05
172	Felix Wright	.05
173	James Francis	.05
174	Eugene Lockhart	.05
175	Dalton Hilliard	.05
176	Nick Lowery	.05
177	Tim McKyer	.05
178	Lorenzo White	.05
179	Jeff Hostetler	.10
180	*Jackie Harris*	.25
181	Ken Norton	.05
182	Flipper Anderson	.05
183	Don Warren	.05
184	Brad Baxter	.05
185	John Taylor	.05
186	Harold Green	.05
187	James Washington	.05
188	Aaron Craver	.05
189	Mike Merriweather	.05
190	Gary Clark	.05
191	Vince Buck	.05
192	Cleveland Gary	.05
193	Dan Saleaumua	.05
194	Gary Zimmerman	.05
195	Richmond Webb	.05
196	Gary Plummer	.05
197	Willie Green	.05
198	Chris Warren	.30
199	Mike Pritchard	.05
200	Art Monk	.05
201	Matt Stover	.05
202	Tim Grunhard	.05
203	Mervyn Fernandez	.05
204	Mark Jackson	.05
205	Freddie Joe Nunn	.05
206	Stan Thomas	.05
207	Keith McKeller	.05
208	Jeff Lageman	.05
209	Kenny Walker	.05
210	Dave Krieg	.05
211	Dean Clasucci	.05
212	Herman Moore	1.00
213	Jon Vaughn	.05
214	Howard Cross	.05
215	Greg Davis	.05
216	Bubby Brister	.05
217	John Kasay	.05
218	Ron Hall	.05
219	Mo Lewis	.05
220	Eric Green	.05
221	Scott Case	.05
222	Sean Jones	.05
223	Winston Moss	.05
224	Reggie Langhorne	.05
225	Greg Lewis	.05
226	Todd McNair	.05
227	Rod Bernstine	.05
228	Joe Jacoby	.05
229	Brad Muster	.05
230	Nick Bell	.05
231	Terry Allen	.40
232	Cliff Odom	.05
233	Brian Hansen	.05
234	William Fuller	.05
235	Issiac Holt	.05
236	Dexter Carter	.05
237	Gene Atkins	.05
238	Pat Beach	.05
239	Tim McGhee	.05
240	Dermontti Dawson	.05
241	Dan Fike	.05
242	Don Beebe	.05
243	Jeff Bostic	.05
244	Mark Collins	.05
245	Steve Sewell	.05
246	Steve Walsh	.05
247	Erik Kramer	.10
248	Scott Norwood	.05
249	Jesse Solomon	.05
250	Jerry Ball	.05
251	Eugene Daniel	.05
252	Michael Stewart	.05
253	Fred Barnett	.05
254	Rodney Holman	.05
255	Stephen Baker	.05
256	Don Griffin	.05
257	Will Wolford	.05
258	Perry Kemp	.05
259	Leonard Russell	.05
260	Jeff Gossett	.05
261	Dwayne Harper	.05
262	Vinny Testaverde	.05
263	Maurice Hurst	.05
264	Tony Casillas	.05
265	Louis Oliver	.05
266	Jim Morrissey	.05
267	Kenneth Davis	.05
268	John Alt	.05
269	*Michael Zordick*	.05
270	Brian Brennan	.05
271	Greg Kragen	.05
272	Andre Collins	.05
273	Dave Meggett	.05
274	Scott Fulhage	.05
275	Tony Zendejas	.05
276	Herschel Walker	.05
277	Keith Henderson	.05
278	Johnny Bailey	.05
279	Vince Newsome	.05
280	Chris Hinton	.05
281	Robert Blackmon	.05
282	James Hasty	.05
283	John Offerdahl	.05
284	Wesley Carroll	.05
285	Lomas Brown	.05
286	Neil O'Donnell	.25
287	Kevin Porter	.05
289	Carlton Bailey	.05
290	Leonard Marshall	.05
291	John Carney	.05
292	Bubba McDowell	.05
293	Nate Newton	.05
294	Dave Waymer	.05
295	Rob Moore	.05
296	Earnest Byner	.05
297	Jason Staurovsky	.05
298	Keith McCants	.05
299	Floyd Turner	.05
300	Steve Jordan	.05
301	Nate Odomes	.05
302	Gerald Riggs	.05
303	Marvin Washington	.05
304	Anthony Thompson	.05
305	Steve DeBerg	.05
306	Jim Harbaugh	.10
307	Larry Brown	.05
308	Roger Ruzek	.05
309	Jessie Tuggle	.05
310	Al Smith	.05
311	Mark Kelso	.05
312	Lawrence Dawsey	.05
313	*Steve Bono*	1.00
314	Greg Lloyd	.10
315	Steve Wisniewski	.05
316	Gill Fenerty	.05
317	Mark Stepnoski	.05
318	Derek Russell	.05
319	Chris Martin	.05
320	Shaun Gayle	.05
321	Bob Golic	.05
322	Larry Kelm	.05
323	*Mike Brim*	.05
324	Tommy Kane	.05
325	*Mark Schlereth*	.05
326	Ray Childress	.05
327	*Richard Brown*	.05
328	Vincent Brown	.05
329	Mike Farr	.05
330	Eric Swann	.05
331	Bill Fralic	.05
332	Rodney Peete	.10
333	Jerry Gray	.05
334	Ray Berry	.05
335	Dennis Smith	.05
336	Jeff Herrod	.05
337	Tony Mandarich	.05
338	Matt Bahr	.05
339	Mike Saxon	.05
340	Bruce Matthews	.05
341	Rickey Jackson	.05
342	Eric Allen	.05
343	Lonnie Young	.05
344	Steve McMichael	.05
345	Willie Gault	.05
346	Barry Word	.05
347	Rich Camarillo	.05
348	Bill Romanowski	.05
349	Jim Lachey	.05
350	Jim Ritcher	.05
351	Irving Fryar	.05
352	Gary Anderson	.05
353	Henry Rolling	.05
354	Mark Bortz	.05
355	Mark Clayton	.05
356	Keith Woodside	.05
357	Jonathan Hayes	.05
358	Derrick Fenner	.05
359	Keith Byars	.05
360	Drew Hill	.05
361	Harris Barton	.05
362	John Kidd	.05
363	Aeneas Williams	.05
364	Brian Washington	.05
365	John Stephens	.05
366	Norm Johnson	.05
367	Darryl Henley	.05
368	William White	.05
369	Mark Murphy	.05
370	Myron Guyton	.05
371	Leon Seals	.05
372	Rich Gannon	.05
373	Toi Cook	.05
374	Anthony Johnson	.05
375	Rod Woodson	.05
376	Alexander Wright	.05
377	Kevin Butler	.05
378	Neil Smith	.05
379	Gary Anderson	.05
380	Reggie Roby	.05
381	Jeff Bryant	.05
382	Ray Crockett	.05
383	Richard Johnson	.05
384	Hassan Jones	.05
385	Karl Mecklenburg	.05
386	Jeff Jaeger	.05
387	Keith Wills	.05
388	Phil Simms	.05
389	Kevin Ross	.05
390	Chris Miller	.05
391	Brian Noble	.05
392	*Jamie Dukes*	.05
393	George Jamison	.05
394	Rickey Dixon	.05
395	Carl Lee	.05
396	Jon Hand	.05
397	Kirby Jackson	.05
398	Pat Terrell	.05
399	Howie Long	.05
400	Mike Young	.05
401	Keith Sims	.05
402	Tommy Barnhardt	.05
403	Greg McMurty	.05
404	Keith Van Horne	.05
405	Seth Joyner	.05
406	Jim Jeffcoat	.05
407	Courtney Hall	.05
408	Tony Covington	.05
409	Jacob Green	.05
410	Charles Haley	.05
411	Darryl Talley	.05
412	Jeff Cross	.05
413	John Elway	.40
414	Donald Evans	.05
415	Jackie Slater	.05
416	John Friesz	.05
417	Anthony Smith	.05
418	Gill Byrd	.05
419	Willie Drewrey	.05
420	Jay Hilgenberg	.05
421	David Treadwell	.05
422	Curtis Duncan	.05
423	Sammie Smith	.05
424	Henry Thomas	.05
425	James Lofton	.05
426	Fred Marion	.05
427	Bryce Paup	.40
428	*Eric Andolsek*	.05
429	Reyna Thompson	.05
430	Mike Kenn	.05
431	Bill Maas	.05
432	Quinn Early	.05
433	Everson Walls	.05
434	Jimmie Jones	.05
435	Dwight Stone	.05
436	Harry Colon	.05
437	Don Mosebar	.05
438	Calvin Williams	.05
439	Tom Tupa	.05
440	Darrell Green	.05
441	Eric Thomas	.05
442	Terry Wooden	.05
443	Brett Perriman	.10
444	Todd Marinovich	.05
445	Jim Breech	.05
446	Eddie Anderson	.05
447	Jay Schroeder	.05
448	William Roberts	.05
449	Brad Edwards	.05
450	Tunch Ilkin	.05
451	Joe Ivy	.05
452	Robert Clark	.05
453	Tim Barnett	.05
454	Jarrod Bunch	.05
455	Tim Harris	.05
456	James Brooks	.05
457	Trace Armstrong	.05
458	Michael Brooks	.05
459	Andy Heck	.05
460	Greg Jackson	.05
461	Vance Johnson	.05
462	Kirk Lowdermilk	.05
463	Erik McMillan	.05
464	Scott Mersereau	.05
465	Jeff Wright	.05
466	Mike Tomczak	.05
467	David Alexander	.05
468	Bryan Millard	.05
469	John Randle	.05
470	Joel Hilgenberg	.05
471	*Bennie Thompson*	.05
472	Freeman McNeil	.05
473	Terry Orr	.05
474	Mike Horan	.05
475	Leroy Hoard	.05
476	*Patrick Rowe* (DP)	.05
477	*Siran Stacy* (DP)	.05
478	*Amp Lee* (DP)	.20
479	*Eddie Blake* (DP)	.05
480	*Joe Bowden* (DP)	.05
481	*Roderick Milstead* (DP)	.05
482	*Keith Hamilton* (DP)	.05
483	*Darryl Williams* (DP)	.05
484	*Robert Porcher* (DP)	.10
485	*Ed Cunningham* (DP)	.05
486	*Chris Mims* (DP)	.10
487	*Chris Hakel* (DP)	.05
488	*Jimmy Smith* (DP)	3.50
489	*Todd Harrison* (DP)	.05
490	*Edgar Bennett* (DP)	.75
491	*Dexter McNabb* (DP)	.05
492	*Leon Searcy* (DP)	.05
493	*Tommy Vardell* (DP)	.10
494	*Terrell Buckley* (DP)	.10
495	*Kevin Turner* (DP)	.05
496	*Russ Campbell* (DP)	.05
497	*Torrance Small* (DP)	.30
498	*Nate Turner* (DP)	.05
499	*Cornelius Benton* (DP)	.05
500	*Matt Elliott* (DP)	.05
501	*Robert Stewart* (DP)	.05
502	*Muhammad Shamsid-Deen* (DP)	.05
503	*George Williams* (DP)	.05
504	*Pumpy Tudors* (DP)	.05
505	*Matt LaBounty* (DP)	.05
506	*Darryl Hardy* (DP)	.05
507	*Derrick Moore* (DP)	.50
508	*Willie Clay* (DP)	.05
509	*Bob Whitfield* (DP)	.05
510	*Ricardo McDonald* (DP)	.05
511	*Carlos Huerta* (DP)	.05
512	*Selwyn Jones* (DP)	.05
513	*Steve Gordon* (DP)	.05
514	*Bob Meeks* (DP)	.05
515	Bennie Blades (CC)	.05
516	Andre Waters (CC)	.05
517	Bubba McDowell (CC)	.05
518	Kevin Porter (CC)	.05
519	Carnell Lake (CC)	.05
520	Leonard Russell (ROY)	.05
521	Mike Croel (ROY)	.05
522	Lawrence Dawsey (ROY)	.05
523	Moe Gardner (ROY)	.05
524	Steve Broussard (LBM)	.05
525	Dave Meggett (LBM)	.05
526	Darrell Green (LBM)	.05
527	Tony Jones (LBM)	.05
528	Barry Sanders (LBM)	1.00
529	Pat Swilling (SA)	.05
530	Reggie White (SA)	.05
531	William Fuller (SA)	.05
532	Simon Fletcher (SA)	.05
533	Derrick Thomas (SA)	.05
534	Mark Rypien (MOY)	.05
535	John Mackey (HOF)	.05
536	John Riggins (HOF)	.05
537	Lem Barney (HOF)	.05
538	Shawn McCarthy (90)	.05
539	Al Edwards (90)	.05
540	Alexander Wright (90)	.05
541	Ray Crockett (90)	.05
542	Steve Young (90)	.40
543	Nate Lewis (90)	.05
544	Dexter Carter (90)	.05
545	Reggie Rutland (90)	.05
546	Jon Vaughn (90)	.05
547	Chris Martin (90)	.05
548	Warren Moon (HL)	.05
549	Super Bowl logo	.05
550	Robb Thomas	.05

1992 Score NFL Follies

This three-card set was available exclusively through the purchase of NFL Football Card Follies, a tape produced by NFL Films and distributed by Polygram Video. It featured three of the game's wacky and wildest plays. The video was available in video stores nationwide for a suggested retail price of $19.95.

		NM/M
Complete Set (3):		20.00
Common Player:		4.00
1	Franco Harris	12.00
2	Garo Yepremian	4.00
3	Jim Marshall	4.00

1992 Score Dream Team

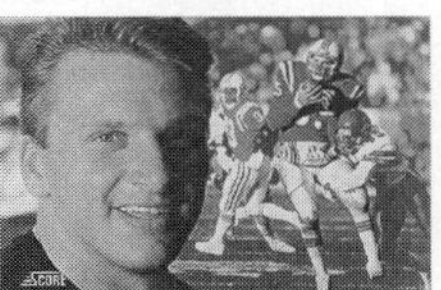

These cards have horizontal fronts which feature a full-bleed color action photo. The team logo is in a diamond in the lower left corner, intersected by color-coded stripes which have the player's name and position (bottom) and set name (left side) in them. The set name is in gold foil. The card back has a portrait shot, team logo, player profile, statistics, biography and card number. Cards were randomly inserted in 1992 Score jumbo packs.

		NM/M
Complete Set (25):		25.00
Common Player:		.50
Minor Stars:		1.00
1	Michael Irvin	1.00
2	Haywood Jeffires	.50
3	Emmitt Smith	10.00
4	Barry Sanders	8.00
5	Marv Cook	.50
6	Bart Oates	.50
7	Steve Wisniewski	.50
8	Randall McDaniel	.50
9	Jim Lachey	.50
10	Lomas Brown	.50
11	Reggie White	2.00
12	Clyde Simmons	.50
13	Derrick Thomas	1.00
14	Seth Joyner	.50
15	Darryl Talley	.50
16	Karl Mecklenburg	.50
17	Sam Mills	.50
18	Darrell Green	.50
19	Steve Atwater	.50
20	Mark Carrier	.50
21	Jeff Gossett	.50
22	Chip Lohmiller	.50
23	Mel Gray	.50
24	Steve Tasker	.50
25	Mark Rypien	.50

1992 Score Gridiron Stars

Each 1992 Score jumbo pack contained three of these cards, which are devoted to "Gridiron Stars." This is gold foil-stamped along the left side of the card front, which has an action photo of the player, plus his name, position and logo. The numbered card back includes a player profile shot, statistics and a career summary.

		NM/M
Complete Set (45):		12.00
Common Player:		.25
Minor Stars:		.50
1	Barry Sanders	3.00
2	Mike Croel	.25
3	Thurman Thomas	.50
4	Lawrence Dawsey	.25
5	Brad Baxter	.25
6	Moe Gardner	.25
7	Emmitt Smith	3.00
8	Sammie Smith	.25
9	Rodney Hampton	.50
10	Mark Carrier	.25
11	Mo Lewis	.25
12	Andre Rison	.50
13	Eric Green	.50
14	Richmond Webb	.25
15	Johnny Bailey	.25
16	Mike Pritchard	.25
17	John Friesz	.50
18	Leonard Russell	.25
19	Derrick Thomas	.50
20	Ken Harvey	.25
21	Fred Barnett	.25
22	Aeneas Williams	.25
23	Marion Butts	.25
24	Harold Green	.25
25	Michael Irvin	.50
26	Dan Owens	.25
27	Curtis Duncan	.25
28	Rodney Peete	.25
29	Brian Blades	.25
30	Marv Cook	.25
31	Burt Grossman	.25
32	Michael Haynes	.25
33	Bennie Blades	.25
34	Cornelius Bennett	.25
35	Louis Oliver	.25
36	Rod Woodson	.25
37	Steve Wisniewski	.25
38	Neil Smith	.25
39	Gaston Green	.25
40	Jeff Lageman	.25
41	Chip Lohmiller	.25
42	Tim McDonald	.25
43	John Elliott	.25
44	Steve Atwater	.25
45	Flipper Anderson	.25

1992 Score Young Superstars

Promising stars of the NFL are featured in this 40-card boxed set from Score. Each card front has a glossy, color action photo, framed by two borders - a green one and a purple outer border with black specks inside. The Score logo, player's name and team name also appear on the card front. The back is numbered and includes a mug shot of the player, plus statistics, biographical information, a career summary and a scouting report analyzing the player's skills.

		NM/M
Complete Set (40):		5.00
Common Player:		.10
1	Michael Irvin	1.00
2	Cortez Kennedy	.30
3	Ken Harvey	.10
4	Bubba McDowell	.10
5	Mark Higgs	.35
6	Andre Rison	.50
7	Lamar Lathon	.10
8	Bennie Blades	.15
9	Anthony Johnson	.10
10	Vince Buck	.10
11	Pat Harlow	.10
12	Mike Croel	.10
13	Myron Guyton	.10
14	Curtis Duncan	.15
15	Michael Haynes	.25
16	Alexander Wright	.10
17	Greg Lewis	.10
18	Chip Lohmiller	.10
19	Nate Lewis	.10
20	Rodney Peete	.15
21	Marv Cook	.15
22	Lawrence Dawsey	.15
23	Pat Terrell	.10
24	John Friesz	.20
25	Tony Bennett	.10
26	Gaston Green	.10
27	Kevin Porter	.10
28	Mike Pritchard	.20
29	Keith Henderson	.10
30	Mo Lewis	.10
31	John Randle	.10
32	Aeneas Williams	.10
33	Floyd Turner	.10
34	Neil Smith	.15
35	Tom Waddle	.10
36	Jeff Lageman	.10
37	Cris Carter	.20
38	Leonard Russell	.25
39	Terry McDaniel	.10
40	Moe Gardner	.10

1993 Score Samples

The six-card, regular-size set was issued to preview the base 1993 set. The six cards are virtually identical to the first six cards in the base set, except for a "Promo" stamp on the lower right corner of the card backs.

		NM/M
Complete Set (6):		5.00
Common Player:		.50
1	Barry Sanders	3.00
2	Moe Gardner	.50
3	Ricky Watters	1.25
4	Todd Lyght	.50
5	Rodney Hampton	.75
6	Curtis Duncan	.50

1993 Score

Score's 440-card 1993 set features subsets for Rookies, Super Bowl Highlights, Double Trouble, Rookie of the Year, 90 Plus Club, Highlights, and Hall of Famers. The card fronts have action photos with a white border. The player's team name is in a panel along the side in the appropriate colors, as is the player's name, which is at the bottom of the card. Backs have a profile, mug shot, statistics, biographical information and team logo. Insert sets include Dream Team (26 cards), Franchise (28 cards, one per team), and Men of Autumn (55) - a Score Pinnacle "Men Of Autumn" card which was not included in regular Pinnacle packs.

		NM/M
Complete Set (440):		15.00
Common Player:		.05
Minor Stars:		.10
Autograph Butkus:		25.00
Pack (15):		1.00
Wax Box (36):		20.00
1	Barry Sanders	1.25
2	Moe Gardner	.05
3	Ricky Watters	.25
4	Todd Lyght	.05
5	Rodney Hampton	.10
6	Curtis Duncan	.05
7	Barry Word	.05
8	Reggie Cobb	.05
9	Mike Kenn	.05
10	Michael Irvin	.30
11	Bryan Cox	.05
12	Chris Doleman	.05
13	Rod Woodson	.10
14	Emmitt Smith	2.00
15	Pete Stoyanovich	.05
16	Steve Young	.75
17	Randall McDaniel	.05
18	Cortez Kennedy	.10
19	Mel Gray	.05
20	Barry Foster	.10
21	Tim Brown	.10
22	Todd McNair	.05
23	Anthony Johnson	.05
24	Nate Odomes	.05
25	Brett Favre	4.00
26	Jack Del Rio	.05
27	Terry McDaniel	.05
28	Haywood Jeffires	.05
29	Jay Novacek	.05
30	Wilber Marshall	.05
31	Richmond Webb	.05
32	Steve Atwater	.05
33	James Lofton	.05
34	Harold Green	.05
35	Eric Metcalf	.05
36	Bruce Matthews	.05
37	Albert Lewis	.05
38	Jeff Herrod	.05
39	Vince Workman	.05
40	John Elway	.50
41	Brett Perriman	.05
42	Jon Vaughn	.05
43	Terry Allen	.05
44	Clyde Simmons	.05
45	Bennie Thompson	.05
46	Wendall Davis	.05
47	Bobby Hebert	.05
48	John Offerdahl	.05
49	Jeff Graham	.05
50	Steve Wisniewski	.05
51	Louis Oliver	.05
52	Rohn Stark	.05
53	Cleveland Gary	.05
54	John Randle	.05
55	Jim Everett	.05
56	Donnell Woolford	.05
57	Pepper Johnson	.05
58	Irving Fryar	.05
59	Greg Townsend	.05
60	Chris Burkett	.05
61	Johnny Johnson	.05
62	Ronnie Harmon	.05
63	Don Griffin	.05
64	Wayne Martin	.05
65	John L. Williams	.05
66	Brad Edwards	.05
67	Toi Cook	.05
68	Lawrence Dawsey	.05
69	Johnny Bailey	.05
70	Mike Brim	.05
71	Andre Rison	.10
72	Cornelius Bennett	.05
73	Brad Muster	.05
74	Broderick Thomas	.05
75	Tom Waddle	.05
76	Paul Gruber	.05
77	Jackie Harris	.05
78	Kenneth Davis	.05
79	Norm Johnson	.05
80	Jim Jeffcoat	.05
81	Chris Warren	.10
82	Greg Kragen	.05
83	Ricky Reynolds	.05
84	Hardy Nickerson	.05
85	Brian Mitchell	.05
86	Rufus Porter	.05
87	Greg Jackson	.05
88	Seth Joyner	.05
89	Tim Grunhard	.05
90	Tim Harris	.05
91	Sterling Sharpe	.10
92	Daniel Stubbs	.05
93	Rob Burnett	.05
94	Rich Camarillo	.05
95	Al Smith	.05
96	Thurman Thomas	.10
97	Morten Andersen	.05
98	Reggie White	.10
99	Gill Byrd	.05
100	Pierce Holt	.05
101	Tim McGee	.05
102	Rickey Jackson	.05
103	Vince Newsome	.05
104	Chris Spielman	.05
105	Tim McDonald	.05
106	James Francis	.05
107	Andre Tippett	.05
108	Sam Mills	.05
109	Hugh Millen	.05
110	Brad Baxter	.05
111	Ricky Sanders	.05
112	Marion Butts	.05
113	Fred Barnett	.05
114	Wade Wilson	.05
115	Dave Meggett	.05
116	Kevin Greene	.05
117	Reggie Langhorne	.05
118	Simon Fletcher	.05
119	Tommy Vardell	.05
120	Darion Conner	.05
121	Darren Lewis	.05
122	Charles Mann	.05
123	David Fulcher	.05
124	Tommy Kane	.05
125	Richard Brown	.05
126	Nate Lewis	.05
127	Tony Tolbert	.05
128	Greg Lloyd	.05
129	Herman Moore	.50
130	Robert Massey	.05
131	Chris Jacke	.05
132	Keith Byars	.05
133	William Fuller	.05
134	Rob Moore	.05
135	Duane Bickett	.05
136	Jarrod Bunch	.05
137	Ethan Horton	.05
138	Leonard Russell	.05
139	Darryl Henley	.05
140	Tony Bennett	.05
141	Harry Newsome	.05
142	Kelvin Martin	.05
143	Audray McMillian	.05
144	Chip Lohmiller	.05
145	Henry Jones	.05
146	Rod Bernstine	.05
147	Darryl Talley	.05
148	Clarence Verdin	.05
149	Derrick Thomas	.10
150	Raleigh McKenzie	.05
151	Phil Hansen	.05
152	*Lin Elliott*	.05
153	Chip Banks	.05
154	Shannon Sharpe	.10
155	David Williams	.05
156	Gaston Green	.05
157	Trace Armstrong	.05
158	Todd Scott	.05
159	Stan Humphries	.10
160	Christian Okoye	.05
161	Dennis Smith	.05
162	Derek Kennard	.05
163	Melvin Jenkins	.05
164	Tommy Barnhardt	.05
165	Eugene Robinson	.05
166	Tom Rathman	.05
167	Chris Chandler	.05
168	Steve Broussard	.05
169	Wymon Henderson	.05
170	Bryce Paup	.05
171	Kent Hull	.05
172	Willie Davis	.05
173	Richard Dent	.05
174	Rodney Peete	.05
175	Clay Matthews	.05
176	Eric Williams	.05
177	Mike Cofer	.05
178	Mark Kelso	.05
179	Kurt Gouveia	.05
180	Keith McCants	.05
181	Jim Arnold	.05
182	Sean Jones	.05
183	Chuck Cecil	.05
184	Mark Rypien	.05
185	William Perry	.05
186	Mark Jackson	.05
187	Jim Dombrowski	.05
188	Heath Sherman	.05
189	Bubba McDowell	.05
190	Fuad Reveiz	.05
191	Darren Perry	.05
192	Karl Mecklenburg	.05
193	Frank Reich	.05
194	Tony Casillas	.05
195	Jerry Ball	.05
196	Jessie Hester	.05
197	David Lang	.05
198	Sean Landeta	.05
199	Jerry Gray	.05
200	Mark Higgs	.05
201	Bruce Armstrong	.05
202	Vaughan Johnson	.05
203	Calvin Williams	.05
204	Leonard Marshall	.05
205	Mike Munchak	.05
206	Kevin Ross	.05
207	Daryl Johnston	.05
208	Jay Schroeder	.05
209	Mo Lewis	.05
210	Carlton Haselrig	.05
211	Cris Carter	.10
212	Marv Cook	.05
213	Mark Duper	.05
214	Jackie Slater	.05
215	Mike Prior	.05
216	Warren Moon	.10
217	Mike Saxon	.05
218	Derrick Fenner	.05
219	Brian Washington	.05
220	Jessie Tuggle	.05
221	Jeff Hostetler	.10
222	Deion Sanders	.50
223	Neal Anderson	.05
224	Kevin Mack	.05
225	Tommy Maddox	.05
226	Neil Smith	.05
227	Ronnie Lott	.05
228	Willie Anderson	.05
229	Keith Jackson	.05
230	Pat Swilling	.05
231	Carl Banks	.05
232	Eric Allen	.05
233	Randal Hill	.05
234	Burt Grossman	.05
235	Jerry Rice	.75
236	Santana Dotson	.05
237	Andre Reed	.10
238	Troy Aikman	.75
239	Ray Childress	.05
240	Phil Simms	.05
241	Steve McMichael	.05
242	Browning Nagle	.05
243	Anthony Miller	.05
244	Earnest Byner	.05
245	Jay Hilgenberg	.05
246	Jeff George	.10
247	Marco Coleman	.05
248	Herschel Walker	.05
249	Howie Long	.05
250	Ed McCaffrey	.05
251	Jim Kelly	.10
252	Henry Ellard	.05
253	Joe Montana	1.25
254	Dale Carter	.05
255	John Elliott	.05
256	Gary Clark	.05
257	Carl Pickens	.75
258	Dave Krieg	.05
259	Russell Maryland	.05
260	Randall Cunningham	.10
261	Leslie O'Neal	.05
262	Vinny Testaverde	.05
263	Ricky Ervins	.05
264	Chris Mims	.05
265	Dan Marino	2.00
266	Eric Martin	.05
267	Bruce Smith	.05
268	Jim Harbaugh	.05
269	Steve Emtman	.05
270	Ricky Proehl	.05
271	Vaughn Dunbar	.05
272	Junior Seau	.10
273	Sean Gilbert	.05
274	Jim Lachey	.05
275	Dalton Hilliard	.05
276	David Klingler	.05
277	Robert Jones	.05
278	David Treadwell	.05
279	Tracy Scroggins	.05
280	Terrell Buckley	.05
281	Quentin Coryatt	.05
282	Jason Hanson	.05
283	Desmond Howard	.05
284	Guy McIntyre	.05
285	Gary Zimmerman	.05
286	Marty Carter	.05
287	Jim Sweeney	.05
288	*Arthur Marshall*	.10
289	Eugene Chung	.05
290	Mike Pritchard	.05
291	Jim Ritcher	.05
292	Todd Marinovich	.05
293	Courtney Hall	.05
294	Mark Collins	.05
295	Troy Auzenne	.05
296	Aeneas Williams	.05
297	Andy Heck	.05
298	Shaun Gayle	.05
299	Kevin Fagan	.05
300	Carnell Lake	.05
301	Antone Davis	.05
302	Maurice Hurst	.05
303	Mike Merriweather	.05
304	Reggie Roby	.05
305	Darryl Williams	.05
306	*Jerome Bettis*	1.50
307	*Curtis Conway*	1.00
308	*Drew Bledsoe*	3.00
309	*John Copeland*	.10
310	*Eric Curry*	.10
311	*Lincoln Kennedy*	.10
312	*Dan Williams*	.10
313	*Patrick Bates*	.10
314	*Tom Carter*	.10
315	*Garrison Hearst*	1.50
316	*Joel Hilgenberg*	.05
317	Harris Barton	.05
318	Jeff Lageman	.05
319	*Charles Mincy*	.10
320	Ricardo McDonald	.05
321	Lorenzo White	.05
322	Troy Vincent	.05
323	Bennie Blades	.05
324	Dana Hall	.05
325	Ken Norton	.05
326	Will Wolford	.05
327	Neil O'Donnell	.10
328	Tracy Simien	.05
329	Darrell Green	.05
330	Kyle Clifton	.05
331	*Elbert Shelley*	.05
332	Jeff Wright	.05
333	Mike Johnson	.05
334	John Gesek	.05
335	Michael Brooks	.05
336	George Jamison	.05
337	Johnny Holland	.05
338	Lamar Lathon	.05
339	Bern Brostek	.05
340	Steve Jordan	.05
341	Gene Atkins	.05
342	Aaron Wallace	.05
343	Adrian Cooper	.05
344	Amp Lee	.05
345	Vincent Brown	.05
346	James Hasty	.05
347	Ron Hall	.05
348	Matt Elliott	.05
349	Tim Krumrie	.05
350	Mark Stepnoski	.05
351	Mat Stover	.05
352	James Washington	.05
353	Marc Spindler	.05
354	Frank Warren	.05
355	Vai Sikahema	.05
356	Dan Saleaumua	.05
357	Mark Clayton	.05
358	Brent Jones	.05
359	*Andy Harmon*	.05
360	Anthony Parker	.05
361	Chris Hinton	.05
362	Greg Montgomery	.05
363	Greg McMurtry	.05
364	Craig Heyward	.05
365	David Johnson	.05
366	Bill Romanowski	.05
367	Steve Christie	.05
368	Art Monk	.05
369	Howard Ballard	.05
370	Andre Collins	.05
371	Alvin Harper	.10
372	*Blaise Winter*	.05
373	Al Del Greco	.05
374	Eric Green	.05
375	Chris Mohr	.05
376	Tom Newberry	.05
377	Cris Dishman	.05
378	James Geathers	.05
379	Don Mosebar	.05
380	Andre Ware	.05
381	Marvin Washington	.05
382	Bobby Humphrey	.05
383	Marc Logan	.05
384	Lomas Brown	.05
385	Steve Tasker	.05
386	Chris Miller	.05
387	Tony Paige	.05
388	Charles Haley	.05
389	Rich Moran	.05
390	Mike Sherrard	.05
391	Nick Lowery	.05
392	Henry Thomas	.05
393	Keith Sims	.05
394	Thomas Everett	.05
395	Steve Wallace	.05
396	John Carney	.05
397	Tim Johnson	.05
398	Jeff Gossett	.05
399	Anthony Smith	.05
400	Kelvin Pritchett	.05
401	Dermontti Dawson	.05
402	Alfred Williams	.05
403	Michael Haynes	.05
404	Bart Oates	.05
405	Ken Lanier	.05
406	Vencie Glenn	.05
407	John Taylor	.05
408	Nate Newton	.05
409	Mark Carrier	.05
410	Ken Harvey	.05
411	Troy Aikman (SB)	.40
412	Charles Haley (SB)	.05
413	Warren Moon, Haywood Jeffires (DT)	.05
414	Henry Jones, Mark Kelso (DT)	.05
415	Rickey Jackson, Sam Mills (DT)	.05
416	Clyde Simmons, Reggie White (DT)	.05
417	Dale Carter (RY)	.05
418	Carl Pickens (RY)	.05
419	Vaughn Dunbar (RY)	.05
420	Santana Dotson (RY)	.05
421	Steve Emtman (90-plus)	.05
422	Louis Oliver (90-plus)	.05
423	Carl Pickens (90-plus)	.05
424	Eddie Anderson (90-plus)	.05
425	Deion Sanders(90-plus)	.20
426	Jon Vaughn (90-plus)	.05
427	Darren Lewis (90-plus)	.05
428	Kevin Ross (90-plus)	.05
429	David Brandon (90-plus)	.05
430	Dave Meggett (90-plus)	.05
431	Jerry Rice (H)	.35
432	Sterling Sharpe (H)	.10
433	Art Monk (H)	.05
434	James Lofton (H)	.05
435	Lawrence Taylor	.10
436	Bill Walsh (HF)	.05
437	Chuck Noll (HF)	.05
438	Dan Fouts (HF)	.05
439	Larry Little (HF)	.05
440	Steve Young (MY)	.30

1993 Score Dream Team

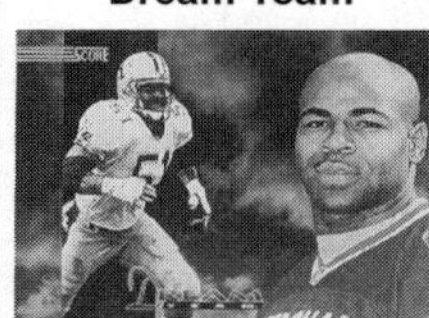

The best 13 offensive and 13 defensive players by position are represented in this 1993 Score insert set. Cards were randomly inserted in 1993 Score 35-card packs and were selections made by Score. The horizontal card front has a close-up shot of the player on the right side and an action shot of him on the left against a black panel. The card background is a cloudy sky tinted in brown. The card back has a photo identical to the action photo on the front, except it's bigger and fuzzier. A player profile appears at the bottom in a black panel. The back is numbered and also features a team logo.

		NM/M
Complete Set (26):		14.00
Common Player:		.50
Minor Stars:		1.00
1	Steve Young	2.00
2	Emmitt Smith	6.00
3	Barry Foster	1.00
4	Sterling Sharpe	1.00
5	Jerry Rice	5.00
6	Keith Jackson	.50
7	Steve Wallace	.50
8	Richmond Webb	.50
9	Guy McIntyre	.50
10	Carlton Haselrig	.50
11	Bruce Matthews	.50
12	Morten Andersen	.50
13	Rich Camarillo	.50
14	Deion Sanders	1.00
15	Steve Tasker	.50
16	Clyde Simmons	.50
17	Reggie White	1.00
18	Cortez Kennedy	.75
19	Rod Woodson	1.00
20	Terry McDaniel	.50
21	Chuck Cecil	.50
22	Steve Atwater	.50
23	Bryan Cox	.50
24	Derrick Thomas	1.00
25	Wilber Marshall	.50
26	Sam Mills	.50

1993 Score Franchise

A top player from each of the 28 NFL teams has been selected for this insert set. Cards were random inserts in 1993 Score foil packs at a rate of about one every 24 packs. The front has a color action photo and the set's logo; the numbered backs have a close-up shot of the player, plus a profile.

		NM/M
Complete Set (28):		40.00
Common Player:		.50
Minor Stars:		2.00
1	Andre Rison	.50
2	Thurman Thomas	1.00
3	Richard Dent	.50
4	Harold Green	.50
5	Eric Metcalf	.50
6	Emmitt Smith	12.00
7	John Elway	10.00
8	Barry Sanders	12.00
9	Sterling Sharpe	2.00
10	Warren Moon	2.00
11	Jeff Herrod	.50
12	Derrick Thomas	2.00
13	Steve Wisniewski	.50
14	Cleveland Gary	.50
15	Dan Marino	12.00
16	Chris Doleman	.50
17	Marv Cook	.50
18	Rickey Jackson	.50
19	Rodney Hampton	.50
20	Jeff Lageman	.50
21	Clyde Simmons	.50
22	Rich Camarillo	.50
23	Rod Woodson	1.00
24	Ronnie Harmon	.50
25	Steve Young	6.00
26	Cortez Kennedy	.50
27	Reggie Cobb	.50
28	Mark Rypien	.50

1993 Score Ore-Ida QB Club

The 18-card, standard-size set was issued with specially marked Ore-Ida Bagel Bites, Twice Baked and Topped Baked Potatoes. Purchasers had to send in six proof-of-purchase seals and $1.50 for two nine-card packs. The cards are indentical in design to cards in the base 1993 set, except for different numbering. Esiason (Jets) and Hostetler (Raiders) are pictured in their new uniforms.

		NM/M
Complete Set (18):		25.00
Common Player:		.75
1	John Elway	2.00
2	Steve Young	2.00
3	Warren Moon	1.25
4	Randall Cunningham	.75
5	Jeff Hostetler	.75
6	Phil Simms	1.00
7	Jim Everett	.75
8	David Klingler	.75
9	Brett Favre	6.00
10	Troy Aikman	3.50
11	Dan Marino	6.00
12	Mark Rypien	.75
13	Jim Kelly	1.25
14	Jim Harbaugh	1.00
15	Bernie Kosar	.75
16	Boomer Esiason	.75
17	Chris Miller	.75
18	Neil O'Donnell	.75

1994 Score Samples

The nine-card, standard-size set was issued to preview the 1994 base set and are identical in design to cards in the regular-issued set. The Glyn Milburn card is an example of the Gold Zone insert set.

		NM/M
Complete Set (9):		3.00
Common Player:		.25
21	Jerome Bettis	1.00
25	Steve Jordan	.25
50	Shannon Sharpe	.40
112	Glyn Milburn (FOIL)	.40
161	Ronnie Lott	.40
257	Derrick Thomas	.50
0	Generic Rookie Card	.25
NNO	Sample Redemption Card	.25
NNO	Score Ad Card	.25

1994 Score

Score's 330-card 1994 set includes Rookie Redemption, Dream Team and Sophomore Showcase insert cards, plus a Gold Zone parallel set. The Gold Zone cards are identical to the regular cards, except they are printed on gold foil; they are inserted one per pack. The card front has a full-color action photo with ragged, torn borders at the top and bottom of the card. The Score logo, player's name and position, and a team helmet are also on the front. Each card back has a mug shot, biographical information, player profile, and statistics. Subsets within the main set are devoted to checklists and 1994 rookies. Nine sample cards, each marked on the back as being a sample, were also made to preview the regular set.

	NM/M
Complete Set (330):	20.00
Common Player:	.05
Gold Cards:	2X-4X
Pack (12):	.75
Wax Box (36):	20.00

1 Barry Sanders 1.00
2 Troy Aikman .75
3 Sterling Sharpe .35
4 Deion Sanders .15
5 Bruce Smith .10
6 Eric Metcalf .08
7 John Elway .50
8 Bruce Matthews .05
9 Rickey Jackson .05
10 Cortez Kennedy .08
11 Jerry Rice .75
12 Stanley Richard .05
13 Rod Woodson .10
14 Eric Swann .10
15 Eric Allen .10
16 Richard Dent .06
17 Carl Pickens .08
18 Rohn Stark .05
19 Marcus Allen .10
20 Steve Wisniewski .08
21 Jerome Bettis .15
22 Darrell Green .05
23 Lawrence Dawsey .05
24 Larry Centers .10
25 Steve Jordan .08
26 Johnny Johnson .08
27 Phil Simms .10
28 Bruce Armstrong .05
29 Willis Roaf .08
30 Andre Rison .10
31 Henry Jones .05
32 Warren Moon .10
33 Sean Gilbert .08
34 Ben Coates .05
35 Seth Joyner .05
36 Ronnie Harmon .08
37 Quentin Coryatt .08
38 Ricky Sanders .05
39 Gerald Williams .05
40 Emmitt Smith 2.00
41 Jason Hanson .05
42 Kevin Smith .05
43 Irving Fryar .10
44 Boomer Esiason .08
45 Darryl Talley .05
46 Paul Gruber .05
47 Anthony Smith .05
48 John Copeland .05
49 Michael Jackson .08
50 Shannon Sharpe .15
51 Reggie White .15
52 Andre Collins .05
53 Jack Del Rio .05
54 John Elliott .05
55 Kevin Greene .08
56 Steve Young .75
57 Erric Pegram .20
58 Donnell Woolford .05
59 Darryl Williams .05
60 Michael Irvin .35
61 Mel Gray .05
62 Greg Montgomery .05
63 Neil Smith .10
64 Andy Harmon .05
65 Dan Marino 2.00
66 Leonard Russell .10
67 Joe Montana .75
68 John Taylor .10
69 Cris Dishman .08
70 Cornelius Bennett .10
71 Harold Green .08
72 Anthony Pleasant .05
73 Dennis Smith .05
74 Bryce Paup .05
75 Jeff George .08
76 Henry Ellard .05
77 Randall McDaniel .05
78 Derek Brown .35
79 Johnny Mitchell .10
80 Leroy Thompson .05
81 Junior Seau .08
82 Kelvin Martin .08
83 Guy McIntyre .05
84 Elbert Shelley .05
85 Louis Oliver .05
86 Tommy Vardell .05
87 Jeff Harrod .05
88 Edgar Bennett .05
89 Reggie Langhorne .05
90 Terry Kirby .20
91 Marcus Robertson .05
92 Mark Collins .05
93 Calvin Williams .08
94 Barry Foster .15
95 Brent Jones .05
96 Reggie Cobb .08
97 Ray Childress .05
98 Chris Miller .10
99 John Carney .05
100 Ricky Proehl .05
101 Renaldo Turnbull .08
102 John Randle .05
103 Willie Anderson .05
104 *Scottie Graham* .50
105 Webster Slaughter .08
106 Tyrone Hughes .05
107 Ken Norton .05
108 Jim Kelly .25
109 Michael Haynes .15
110 Mark Carrier .05
111 Eddie Murray .05
112 Glyn Milburn .25
113 Jackie Harris .15
114 Dean Biasucci .05
115 Tim Brown .15
116 Mark Higgs .05
117 Steve Emtman .05
118 Clay Matthews .05
119 Clyde Simmons .05
120 Howard Ballard .05
121 Ricky Watters .20
122 William Fuller .05
123 Robert Brooks .05
124 Brian Blades .05
125 Leslie O'Neal .05
126 Gary Clark .08
127 Jim Sweeney .05
128 Vaughan Johnson .05
129 Gary Brown .15
130 Todd Lyght .05
131 Nick Lowery .05
132 Ernest Givins .05
133 Lomas Brown .05
134 Craig Erickson .05
135 James Francis .05
136 Andre Reed .08
137 Jim Everett .08
138 Nate Odomes .05
139 Tom Waddle .05
140 Stevon Moore .05
141 Rod Bernstine .05
142 Brett Favre 2.00
143 Roosevelt Potts .05
144 Chester McGlockton .05
145 LeRoy Butler .05
146 Charles Haley .05
147 Rodney Hampton .30
148 George Teague .08
149 Gary Anderson .05
150 Mark Stepnoski .05
151 Courtney Hawkins .05
152 Tim Grunhard .05
153 David Klingler .15
154 Eric Williams .05
155 Herman Moore .15
156 Daryl Johnston .05
157 Chris Zorich .05
158 Shane Conlan .05
159 Santana Dotson .05
160 Sam Mills .08
161 Ronnie Lott .08
162 Jesse Sapolu .05
163 Marion Butts .05
164 Eugene Robinson .05
165 Mark Schlereth .05
166 John L. Williams .05
167 Anthony Miller .15
168 Rich Camarillo .05
169 Jeff Lageman .05
170 Michael Brooks .05
171 Scott Mitchell .30
172 Duane Bickett .05
173 Willie Davis .05
174 Maurice Hurst .05
175 Brett Perriman .05
176 Jay Novacek .05
177 Terry Allen .08
178 Pete Metzelaars .05
179 Erik Kramer .10
180 Neal Anderson .05
181 Ethan Horton .05
182 Tony Bennett .05
183 Gary Zimmerman .05
184 Jeff Hostetler .06
185 Jeff Cross .05
186 Vincent Brown .05
187 Herschel Walker .05
188 Courtney Hall .05
189 Norm Johnson .05
190 Hardy Nickerson .05
191 Greg Townsend .05
192 Mike Munchak .05
193 Dante Jones .05
194 Vinny Testaverde .08
195 Vance Johnson .05
196 Chris Jacke .05
197 Will Wolford .05
198 Terry McDaniel .05
199 Bryan Cox .05
200 Nate Newton .05
201 Keith Byars .05
202 Neil O'Donnell .15
203 Harris Barton .05
204 Thurman Thomas .25
205 Jeff Query .05
206 Russell Maryland .08
207 Pat Swilling .05
208 Haywood Jeffires .05
209 John Alt .05
210 O.J. McDuffie .30
211 Keith Sims .05
212 Eric Martin .05
213 Kyle Clifton .05
214 Luis Sharpe .05
215 Thomas Everett .05
216 Chris Warren .05
217 Chris Doleman .05
218 Tony Jones .05
219 Karl Mecklenburg .05
220 Rob Moore .10
221 Jessie Hester .05
222 Jeff Jaeger .05
223 Keith Jackson .08
224 Mo Lewis .05
225 Mike Horan .05
226 Eric Green .05
227 Jim Ritcher .05
228 Eric Curry .05
229 Stan Humphries .05
230 Mike Johnson .05
231 Alvin Harper .10
232 Bennie Blades .05
233 Cris Carter .05
234 Morten Anderson .05
235 Brian Washington .05
236 Eric Hill .05
237 Natrone Means .40
238 Carlton Bailey .05
239 Anthony Carter .05
240 Jessie Tuggle .05
241 Tim Irwin .05
242 Mark Currier .05
243 Steve Atwater .05
244 Sean Jones .05
245 Bernie Kosar .05
246 Richmond Webb .05
247 Dave Meggett .05
248 Vincent Brisby .35
249 Fred Barnett .05
250 Greg Lloyd .05
251 Tim McDonald .05
252 Mike Pirtchard .08
253 Greg Robinson .10
254 Tony McGee .05
255 Chris Spielman .05
256 Keith Loneker .10
257 Derrick Thomas .15
258 Wayne Martin .05
259 Art Monk .05
260 Andy Heck .05
261 Chip Lohmiller .05
262 Simon Fletcher .05
263 Ricky Reynolds .05
264 Chris Hinton .05
265 Ron Moore .35
266 Raghib Ismail .15
267 Pete Styanovich .05
268 Mark Jackson .05
269 Randall Cunningham .10
270 Dermontti Dawson .05
271 Bill Romanowski .05
272 Tim Johnson .05
273 Steve Tasker .05
274 Keith Hamilton .05
275 Pierce Holt .05
276 *Heath Shuler* .25
277 *Marshall Faulk* 4.00
278 *Charles Johnson* .50
279 *Sam Adams* .30
280 *Trev Alberts* .50
281 *Derrick Alexander* .25
282 *Bryant Young* .25
283 *Greg Hill* .50
284 *Darnay Scott* .75
285 *Willie McGinest* .50
286 *Thomas Randolph* .15
287 *Errict Rhett* .75
288 *Lamar Smith* 1.00
289 *William Floyd* .40
290 *Johnnie Morton* .60
291 *Jamir Miller* .30
292 *David Palmer* .50
293 *Dan Wilkinson* .60
294 *Trent Dilfer* 2.00
295 *Antonio Langham* .30
296 *Chuck Levy* .50
297 *John Thierry* .25
298 *Kevin Lee* .35
299 *Aaron Glenn* .25
300 *Charlie Garner* 2.50
301 *Lonnie Johnson* .15
302 *LeShon Johnson* .45
303 *Thomas Lewis* .50
304 *Ryan Yarborough* .40
305 *Mario Bates* .20
306 Bills/Cardinals Checklist .05
307 Bengals/Falcons Checklist .05
308 Browns/Bears Checklist .05
309 Broncos/Cowboys Checklist .05
310 Oilers/Lions Checklist .05
311 Colts/Packers Checklist .05
312 Chiefs/Rams Checklist .05
313 Raiders/Vikings Checklist .05
314 Dolphins/Saints Checklist .05
315 Patriots/Giants Checklist .05
316 Jets/Eagles Checklist .05
317 Steelers/49ers Checklist .05
318 Chargers/Bucs Checklist .05
319 Seahawks/Redskins Checklist .05
320 Garrison Hearst .20
321 Drew Bledsoe .75
322 Tyrone Hughes .05
323 James Jett .25
324 Tom Carter .05
325 Reggie Brooks .25
326 Dana Stubblefield .25
327 Jerome Bettis .15
328 Chris Slade .15
329 Rick Mirer .15
330 Emmitt Smith MVP 1.00

1994 Score Gold Zone

The 330-card, standard-size set is a parallel set with the card fronts having a metallic gold sheen.

NM/M
Common Player: .30
Veteran Stars: 3X-6X
Young Stars: 2X-4X
RCs: 1.5X-3X

1994 Score Dream Team

These cards were randomly inserted in 1994 Score packs at a rate of one every 72 packs. The cards have an animating hologram on the front, and feature 18 of the NFL's elite players. The hologram has an action shot and closeup photo of the player on the front, along with his name, Score logo, set logo and his team's name running across the card several times. The backs are numbered with a "DT" prefix and have a Score Football Fifth Anniversary logo, along with the player's 1989 Score card.

NM/M
Complete Set (18): 40.00
Common Player: .50
Minor Stars: 2.00
1 Troy Aikman 12.00
2 Steve Atwater .50
3 Cornelius Bennett .50
4 Tim Brown 2.00
5 Michael Irvin 2.00
6 Bruce Matthews .50
7 Eric Metcalf .50
8 Anthony Miller .50
9 Jerry Rice 12.00
10 Andre Rison 2.00
11 Barry Sanders 15.00
12 Deion Sanders 3.00
13 Sterling Sharpe 2.00
14 Neil Smith .50
15 Derrick Thomas 2.00
16 Thurman Thomas 2.00
17 Rod Woodson .50
18 Steve Young 10.00

1994 Score Rookie Redemption

The 10-card, regular-sized set was inserted every 72 packs as a redemption card. The card fronts have metallic imaging while the backs have a player headshot and season highlights.

NM/M
Complete Set (10): 75.00
Common Player: 1.00
Minor Stars: 2.00
1 Heath Shuler 2.00
2 Trent Dilfer 4.00
3 Marshall Faulk 50.00
4 Charlie Garner 6.00
5 LeShon Johnson 1.00
6 Charles Johnson 1.00
7 Errict Rhett 5.00
8 Lake Dawson 1.50
9 Bert Emanuel 2.00
10 Greg Hill 2.00

1994 Score Sophomore Showcase

Eighteen of the NFL's top second-year players are featured on these cards, which were random inserts in one out of every four Score jumbo packs. The card front has a full-bleed color photo and the Score logo. The player's name and set logo are stamped in gold foil at the bottom. The card back has the player's name running in a marble-like panel along the left side. There's a closeup shot of the player, along with the set's logo, plus a brief career summary on the other side. Cards are numbered with an "SS" prefix.

NM/M
Complete Set (18): 25.00
Common Player: .50
1 Jerome Bettis 2.00
2 Rick Mirer 1.00
3 Reggie Brooks .50
4 Drew Bledsoe 6.00
5 Ron Moore .50
6 Derek Brown .50
7 Roosevelt Potts .50
8 Terry Kirby 1.00
9 James Jett .50
10 Vincent Brisby 1.00
11 Tyrone Hughes .50
12 Rocket Ismail 3.00
13 Tony McGee .50
14 Garrison Hearst 4.00
15 Eric Curry .50
16 Dana Stubblefield 1.00
17 Tom Carter .50
18 Chris Slade .50

1995 Score Promos

The six-card, regular-size set was distributed in four-card packs as a preview for the 1995 base set. The card fronts have "Promo" stamps.

NM/M
Complete Set (6): 10.00
Common Player: .50
42 Drew Bledsoe 2.50
47 Barry Foster .50
58 Steve Broussard .50
211 Jerry Rice Star Struck Card 2.50
DT2 Troy Aikman Dream Team Card 5.00
NNO Title Card .50

1995 Score

Score's 1995 275-card football set includes two subsets (26 Draft Pick cards and 30 Star Struck cards), plus two parallel sets (Red Siege and Artist's Proofs). The regular cards have a color action photo on the front, with the player's name along the left side and his team's logo in the lower right corner. The card back has another color photo, plus a brief career summary and statistics. Red Siege cards (one in three packs) are the same, except they have a red-foil background and have "Red Siege" written on the back. The Artist's Proofs cards (one in 36) have an exclusive stamp on the Red Siege cards. Insert sets include Dream Team, Offense Inc., Pass Time and Reflextions.

NM/M
Complete Set (275): 15.00
Common Player: .05
Comp. Red Siege Set (275):
Common Red Siege: .30
Red Siege Cards: 2X-4X
Comp. RS Art. Proof Set (275):
Common RS Art. Proof: 3.00
RS Art. Proof Cards: 5X-10X
Hobby Pack (12): 1.50
Hobby Wax Box (36): 35.00
Retail Pack (12): 1.00
Retail Wax Box (36): 25.00
1 Steve Young .50
2 Barry Sanders 1.00
3 Jerry Rice .75
4 Marshall Faulk .75
5 Terance Mathis .05
6 Rod Woodson .10
7 Seth Joyner .05
8 Michael Timpson .05
9 Deion Sanders .30
10 Emmitt Smith 1.50
11 Cris Carter .10
12 Jake Reed .05
13 Reggie White .10
14 Shannon Sharpe .10
15 Troy Aikman .75
16 Andre Reed .10
17 Tyrone Hughes .05
18 Sterling Sharpe .10
19 Jerome Bettis .30
20 Irving Fryar .05
21 Warren Moon .10
22 Ben Coates .05
23 Frank Reich .05
24 Henry Ellard .05
25 Steve Atwater .05
26 Willie Davis .05
27 Michael Irvin .10
28 Harvey Williams .05
29 Aeneas Williams .05
30 Errict Rhett .15
31 Lorenzo White .05
32 John Elway .25
33 Rodney Hampton .10
34 Webster Slaughter .05
35 Eric Turner .05
36 Dan Marino 1.50
37 Daryl Johnston .05
38 Bruce Smith .05
39 Ron Moore .05
40 Larry Centers .05
41 Curtis Conway .05
42 Drew Bledsoe .75
43 Quinn Early .05
44 Marcus Allen .10
45 Andre Rison .10
46 *Jeff Blake* .50
47 Barry Foster .10
48 Antonio Langham .05
49 Herman Moore .10
50 Willie Anderson .05
51 Rick Mirer .30
52 Jay Novacek .05
53 Tim Bowens .05
54 Carl Pickens .10
55 Lewis Tillman .05
56 Lawrence Dawsey .05
57 Leroy Hoard .05
58 Steve Broussard .05
59 Dave Krieg .05
60 John Taylor .05
61 Johnny Mitchell .05
62 Jessie Hester .05
63 Johnny Bailey .05
64 Brett Favre 1.50
65 Bryce Paup .05
66 J.J. Birden .05
67 Steve Tasker .05
68 Edgar Bennett .05
69 Ray Buchanan .05
70 Brent Jones .05
71 Dave Meggett .05
72 Jeff Graham .05
73 Michael Brooks .05
74 Ricky Ervins .05
75 Chris Warren .05
76 Natrone Means .30
77 Tim Brown .10
78 Jim Everett .05
79 Chris Calloway .05
80 John L. Williams .05
81 Chris Chandler .05
82 Tim McDonald .05
83 Calvin Williams .05
84 Tony McGee .05
85 Erik Kramer .05
86 Eric Green .05
87 Nate Newton .05
88 Leonard Russell .05
89 Jeff George .10
90 Raymont Harris .10
91 Darnay Scott .40
92 Brian Mitchell .05
93 Craig Erickson .05
94 Cortez Kennedy .10
95 Derrick Alexander .10
96 Charles Haley .05
97 Randall Cunningham .10
98 Haywood Jeffires .05
99 Ronnie Harmon .05
100 Dale Carter .05
101 Dave Brown .05
102 Michael Haynes .05
103 Johnny Johnson .05
104 William Floyd .10
105 Jeff Hostetler .05
106 Bernie Parmalee .10
107 Mo Lewis .05
108 Bam Morris .10
109 Vincent Brisby .05
110 John Randle .05
111 Steve Walsh .05
112 Terry Allen .05
113 Greg Lloyd .05
114 Merton Hanks .05
115 Mel Gray .05
116 Jim Kelly .10
117 Don Beebe .05
118 Floyd Turner .05
119 Neil Smith .05
120 Keith Byars .05
121 Rocket Ismail .05
122 Leslie O'Neal .05
123 Mike Sherrard .05
124 Marion Butts .05
125 Andre Coleman .05
126 Charles Johnson .10
127 Derrick Fenner .05
128 Vinny Testaverde .05
129 Chris Spielman .05
130 Bert Emanuel .25
131 Craig Heyward .05
132 Anthony Miller .05
133 Rob Moore .05
134 Gary Brown .05
135 David Klingler .05
136 Sean Dawkins .10
137 Terry McDaniel .05
138 Fred Barnett .05
139 Bryan Cox .05
140 Andrew Jordan .05
141 Leroy Thompson .05
142 Richmond Webb .05
143 Kimble Anders .05
144 Mario Bates .25
145 Irv Smith .05
146 Carnell Lake .05
147 Mark Seay .05
148 Dana Stubblefield .05
149 Kelvin Martin .05
150 Pete Metzelaars .05
151 Roosevelt Potts .05
152 Bubby Brister .05
153 Trent Dilfer .40
154 Ricky Proehl .05
155 Aaron Glenn .05
156 Eric Metcalf .05
157 Kevin Williams .05
158 Charlie Garner .05
159 Glyn Milburn .05
160 Fuad Reveiz .05
161 Brett Perriman .05
162 Neil O'Donnell .05
163 Tony Martin .05
164 Sam Adams .05
165 John Friesz .05
166 Bryant Young .05
167 Junior Seau .10
168 Ken Harvey .05
169 Bill Brooks .05
170 Eugene Robinson .05
171 Ricky Sanders .05
172 Rodney Peete .05
173 Boomer Esiason .05
174 Reggie Roby .05

175 Michael Jackson .05
176 Gus Frerotte .10
177 Terry Kirby .05
178 Jessie Tuggle .05
179 Courtney Hawkins .05
180 Heath Shuler .20
181 Jack Del Rio .05
182 O.J. McDuffie .05
183 Ricky Watters .10
184 Willie Roaf .05
185 Glenn Foley .05
186 Blair Thomas .05
187 Darren Woodson .05
188 Kevin Greene .05
189 Jeff Burris .05
190 Jay Schroeder .05
191 Stan Humphries .10
192 Irving Spikes .10
193 Jim Harbaugh .05
194 Robert Brooks .05
195 Greg Hill .10
196 Herschel Walker .05
197 Brian Blades .05
198 Mark Ingram .05
199 Kevin Turner .05
200 Lake Dawson .10
201 Alvin Harper .05
202 Derek Brown .05
203 Qadry Ismail .05
204 Reggie Brooks .05
205 Steve Young (Starstruck) .25
206 Emmitt Smith (Starstruck) .50
207 Stan Humphries (Starstruck) .10
208 Barry Sanders (Starstruck) .50
209 Marshall Faulk (Starstruck) .50
210 Drew Bledsoe (Starstruck) .50
211 Jerry Rice (Starstruck) .50
212 Tim Brown (Starstruck) .10
213 Cris Carter (Starstruck) .10
214 Dan Marino (Starstruck) .75
215 Troy Aikman (Starstruck) .30
216 Jerome Bettis (Starstruck) .10
217 Deion Sanders (Starstruck) .10
218 Junior Seau (Starstruck) .10
219 John Elway (Starstruck) .10
220 Warren Moon (Starstruck) .10
221 Sterling Sharpe Starstruck) .10
222 Marcus Allen (Starstruck) .10
223 Michael Irvin (Starstruck) .10
224 Brett Favre (Starstruck) .40
225 Rodney Hampton (Starstruck) .10
226 Dave Brown (Starstruck) .05
227 Ben Coates (Starstruck) .05
228 Jim Kelly (Starstruck) .10
229 Heath Shuler (Starstruck) .40
230 Herman Moore (Starstruck) .10
231 Jeff Hostetler (Starstruck) .05
232 Rick Mirer (Starstruck) .10
233 Bam Morris (Starstruck) .10
234 Terance Mathis (Starstruck) .05
235 Checklist .05
236 Troy Aikman CL .20
237 Jerry Rice CL .20
238 Emmitt Smith CL .40
239 Steve Young CL .20
240 Drew Bledsoe CL .25
241 Marshall Faulk CL .25
242 Dan Marino CL .50
243 Junior Seau CL .05
244 *Ray Zellars* .10
245 *Rob Johnson* 1.00
246 *Tony Boselli* .10
247 *Kevin Carter* .10
248 *Steve McNair* 3.00
249 *Tyrone Wheatley* .50
250 *Steve Stenstrom* .10
251 *Stoney Case* .10
252 *Rodney Thomas* .10
253 *Michael Westbrook* 1.00
254 *Derrick Alexander* .10
255 *Kyle Brady* .10
256 *Kerry Collins* .10
257 *Rashaan Salaam* .50
258 *Frank Sanders* .25
259 *John Walsh* .10
260 *Sherman Williams* .10
261 *Ki-Jana Carter* .30
262 *Jack Jackson* .10
263 *J.J. Stokes* .75
264 *Kordell Stewart* 1.00
265 *Dave Barr* .10
266 *Eddie Goines* .10
267 *Warren Sapp* .50
268 *James Stewart* 1.50
269 *Joey Galloway* 1.50
270 *Tyrone Davis* .10
271 *Napoleon Kaufman* 1.00
272 *Mark Bruener* .30
273 *Todd Collins* .10
274 *Billy Williams* .10
275 *James Stewart* .10

1995 Score Red Siege

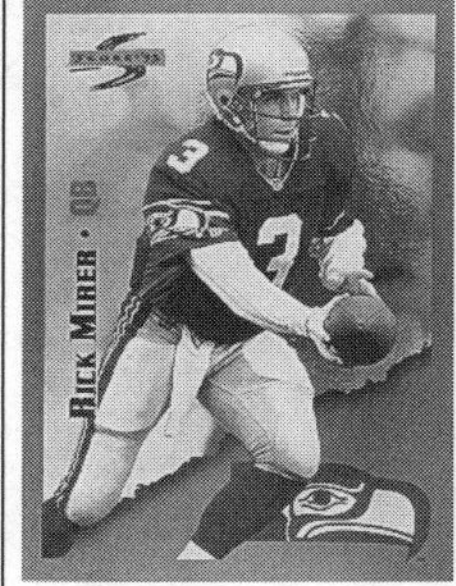

The 275-card, regular-size parallel set, inserted every three packs, have a silver-foil background instead of a white background. A Red Siege logo is printed on the card backs.

	NM/M
Common Player:	.30
Veteran Stars:	2X-4X
Young Stars:	2X-4X
RCs:	1.5X-2X

1995 Score Red Siege Artist's Proof

The 275-card, regular-size set, inserted every 36 packs, parallels the Red Siege set with an Artist's Proof stamp on the card front.

	NM/M
Common Player:	5.00
Veteran Stars:	5X-10X
Young Stars:	5X-10X
RCs:	2X-5X

1995 Score Dream Team

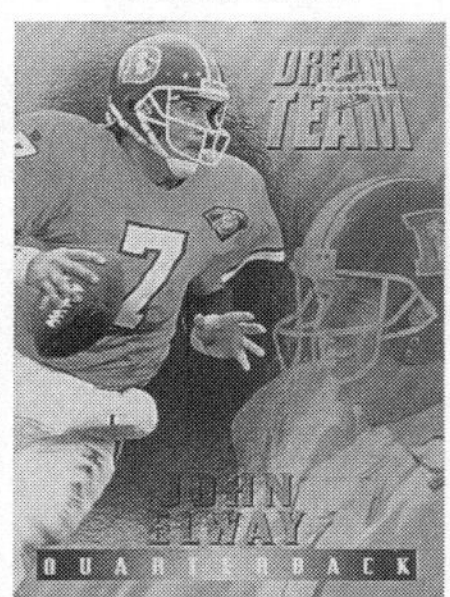

These 1995 Score football inserts were included one per 72 packs, making them the most elusive set. Ten of the league's elite players are featured on gold-foiled cards which have the set logo in the upper right corner. A color action photo and a ghosted image appear on the front. The horizontally-designed back, numbered using a "DT" prefix, has a photo on the top half, with a brief player profile underneath.

		NM/M
Complete Set (10):		25.00
Common Player:		2.00
1	Steve Young	4.00
2	Troy Aikman	4.00
3	Dan Marino	6.00
4	Drew Bledsoe	4.00
5	Emmitt Smith	5.00
6	Barry Sanders	5.00
7	Jerry Rice	5.00
8	Marshall Faulk	2.00
9	Deion Sanders	2.00
10	John Elway	2.00

1995 Score Offense Inc.

These 1995 Score football insert cards could be found one per 16 packs. The cards feature 30 of the NFL's top offensive players. The card front has a large and small photo of the player, with a foiled set logo shield in the lower right corner. The card back, numbered using an "OF" prefix, reuses the shield, plus a mug shot, a season recap and key statistics from the 1994 season.

		NM/M
Complete Set (30):		40.00
Common Player:		.50
1	Steve Young	3.00
2	Emmitt Smith	5.00
3	Dan Marino	6.00
4	Barry Sanders	5.00
5	Jeff Blake	.50
6	Jerry Rice	4.00
7	Troy Aikman	4.00
8	Brett Favre	6.00
9	Marshall Faulk	2.00
10	Drew Bledsoe	3.00
11	Natrone Means	.50
12	John Elway	4.00
13	Chris Warren	.50
14	Michael Irvin	1.00
15	Mario Bates	.50
16	Warren Moon	.50
17	Jerome Bettis	1.00
18	Herman Moore	.50
19	Barry Foster	.50
20	Jeff George	.50
21	Cris Carter	.50
22	Sterling Sharpe	.50
23	Jim Kelly	.50
24	Heath Shuler	.50
25	Marcus Allen	.50
26	Dave Brown	.50
27	Rick Mirer	.50
28	Rodney Hampton	.50
29	Errict Rhett	.50
30	Ben Coates	.50

1995 Score Pass Time

These horizontally-formated insert cards were included one per 18 1995 Score football jumbo packs. Each card front uses gold foil as a background and for the player's name and insert set logo. A larger head-and-shoulders shot and a smaller action photo are the main features. The player's position appears along the left side of the card, with his team logo included within the letters. The card back, numbered using a "PT" prefix, also has two photos, the set logo and a brief career summary.

		NM/M
Complete Set (18):		75.00
Common Player:		1.00
1	Steve Young	10.00
2	Dan Marino	15.00
3	Drew Bledsoe	10.00
4	Troy Aikman	10.00
5	Glenn Foley	1.00
6	John Elway	12.00
7	Brett Favre	15.00
8	Heath Shuler	1.00
9	Warren Moon	1.00
10	Rick Mirer	1.00
11	Stan Humphries	1.00
12	Jeff Hostetler	1.00
13	Jim Kelly	1.00
14	Randall Cunningham	1.00
15	Jeff Blake	1.00
16	Trent Dilfer	3.00
17	Jeff George	1.00
18	Dave Brown	1.00

1995 Score Reflextions

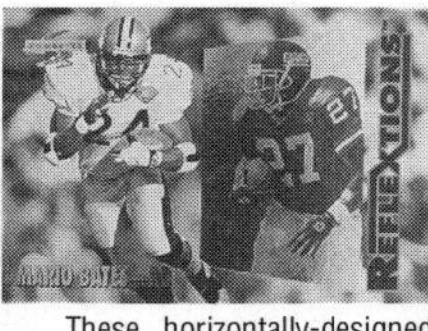

These horizontally-designed insert cards feature two players per card; each is his team's featured player at his position. Only one player's name is listed on the front; his photo is on the left; a photo of his idol is on the right, in a square next to "Reflextions," which is written along the right side. The card back, numbered using an "RF" prefix, has two photos of the players, plus a paragraph which indicates who the second player is. The set logo appears at the top, with the player's team name in a branching extension of the letter X. Cards were randomly included one per 36 hobby packs.

		NM/M
Complete Set (8):		40.00
Common Player:		1.00
1	Drew Bledsoe, Dan Marino	12.00
2	Charlie Garner, Barry Sanders	10.00
3	Rick Mirer, Warren Moon	1.00
4	Heath Shuler, Steve Young	6.00
5	Marshall Faulk, Emmitt Smith	12.00
6	Derrick Alexander, Jerry Rice	8.00
7	Barry Foster, Bam Morris	1.00
8	Natrone Means, Chris Warren	1.00

1995 Score Pin-Cards

The 40-card, regular-size set features a player from each team and three cards each for the expansion teams (Carolina, Jacksonville) and the new St. Louis Rams. Card No. 40 is a Super Bowl XXX card. Arizona, Atlanta, Carolina, Chicago, Cleveland, Houston, Indianapolis, Jacksonville, Kansas City and Tampa Bay are represented with a team-helmet card with a pin.

		NM/M
Complete Set (40):		15.00
Common Helmet Card:		.25
Common Player:		.50
1	Jacksonville Jaguars - History	.50
2	Jacksonville Jaguars - Stadium	.50
3	Jacksonville Jaguars - Logo Lore	.50
4	Carolina Panthers - History	.50
5	Carolina Panthers - Stadium	.50
6	Carolina Panthers - Logo Lore	.50
7	St. Louis Rams - History	.50
8	St. Louis Rams - Stadium	.50
9	St. Louis Rams - Logo Lore	.50
10	Drew Bledsoe	2.50
11	Dave Brown	.50
12	Randall Cunningham	.50
13	John Elway	1.25
14	Jim Everett	.50
15	Boomer Esiason	.50
16	Brett Favre	5.00
17	Jeff Hostetler	.50
18	Jim Kelly	1.00
19	David Klingler	.50
20	Dan Marino	5.00
21	Chris Miller	.50
22	Rick Mirer	1.00
23	Warren Moon	1.00
24	Neil O'Donnell	1.00
25	Jerry Rice	2.50
26	Barry Sanders	2.50
27	Junior Seau	1.00
28	Heath Shuler	1.50
29	Emmitt Smith	5.00
30	Arizona Cardinals	.25
31	Atlanta Falcons	.25
32	Carolina Panthers	.50
33	Chicago Bears	.25
34	Cleveland Browns	.50
35	Houston Oilers	.25
36	Indianapolis Colts	.25
37	Jacksonville Jaguars	.50
38	Kansas City Chiefs	.25
39	Tampa Bay Buccaneers	.25
40	Super Bowl XXX Logo	.25

1995 Score Young Stars

These cards were available at the 1995 NFL Experience Super Bowl Card Show. Pinnacle exchanged the cards for three or five Pinnacle wrappers. The four cards have Gold Zone (limited to 2,000) and Platinum versions (limited to 1,000). The cards are numbered with the "YSG" prefix.

		NM/M
Complete Set (4):		12.00
Common Player:		2.00
Platinum Cards:		2X
1	Marshall Faulk	4.00
2	Jeff Blake	2.00
3	Drew Bledsoe	6.00
4	Natrone Means	2.00

1995 Summit

Score's 1995 super-premium effort, Summitt, has 200 cards printed on 24-point stock, making them thicker than normal cards. Each card front has an action photo cutout against a white background. The player's name is stamped in gold foil in a banner at the bottom, alongside his team helmet, also stamped in gold. The horizontally-designed card back has a photo of the player on the left side, with a chart of his 1994 statistics on the right. A parallel set, Ground Zero, was also produced; all cards are reprinted on a prismatic foil. Three insert sets - Rookie Summit, Team Summit and Backfield Stars - were also produced.

		NM/M
Complete Set (200):		20.00
Common Player:		.05
Minor Stars:		.20
Ground Zero Cards:		3X-5X
Pack (7):		1.00
Wax Box (24):		20.00
1	Neil O'Donnell	.20
2	Jim Everett	.05
3	Craig Heyward	.05
4	*Jeff Blake*	.50
5	Alvin Harper	.20
6	Heath Shuler	1.00
7	Rodney Hampton	.20
8	Dave Krieg	.05
9	Mark Brunell	1.50
10	Rob Moore	.05
11	Daryl Johnston	.05
12	Marcus Allen	.20
13	Terance Mathis	.05
14	Frank Reich	.05
15	Gus Frerotte	.50
16	John Elway	.50
17	Amp Lee	.05
18	Chris Miller	.05
19	Leroy Hoard	.05
20	Stan Humphries	.20
21	Charlie Garner	.05
22	Jim Kelly	.20
23	Gary Brown	.05
24	Bam Morris	.20
25	Edgar Bennett	.05
26	Erik Kramer	.05
27	Dan Marino	3.00
28	Michael Haynes	.05
29	Lake Dawson	.25
30	Ben Coates	.05
31	Michael Jackson	.05
32	Brett Favre	3.00
33	Calvin Williams	.05
34	Steve Young	1.50
35	Troy Aikman	1.50
36	Greg Hill	.25
37	Leonard Russell	.05
38	Jeff George	.20
39	Herschel Walker	.05
40	Eric Green	.05
41	Haywood Jeffires	.05
42	Terry Kirby	.05
43	Darnay Scott	.50
44	Tim Brown	.20
45	Brian Mitchell	.05
46	Desmond Howard	.05
47	Warren Moon	.20
48	Andre Reed	.05
49	Ricky Proehl	.05
50	Marshall Faulk	.75
51	Lewis Tillman	.05
52	Don Beebe	.05
53	Jerome Bettis	.50
54	Brett Perriman	.20
55	Mario Bates	.30
56	Ronnie Harmon	.05
57	Isaac Bruce	1.00
58	Jackie Harris	.05
59	Dexter Carter	.05
60	Charles Johnson	.25
61	Herman Moore	.40
62	Craig Erickson	.05
63	Kenneth Davis	.05
64	Emmitt Smith	3.00
65	Brent Jones	.05
66	Ricky Watters	.20
67	Henry Ellard	.05
68	Vinny Testaverde	.05
69	Mark Pike	.05
70	Curtis Conway	.30
71	Michael Irvin	.40
72	Jay Novacek	.05
73	Howard Cross	.05
74	Drew Bledsoe	1.50
75	Steve Beuerlein	.05
76	Andre Rison	.20
77	Morten Andersen	.05
78	Trent Dilfer	.40
79	Cris Carter	.20
80	Natrone Means	.75
81	Bernie Parmalee	.30
82	Randall Cunningham	.05
83	Eric Metcalf	.05
84	Rick Mirer	.50
85	Mark Ingram	.05
86	David Klingler	.05
87	Kevin Williams	.05
88	Erric Pegram	.05
89	Keith Byars	.05
90	Sean Dawkins	.20
91	Chris Warren	.25
92	William Floyd	.40
93	Jeff Hostetler	.20
94	Carl Pickens	.20
95	Flipper Anderson	.05
96	Johnny Mitchell	.05
97	Larry Centers	.05
98	Shannon Sharpe	.05
99	Errict Rhett	.30
100	Fred Barnett	.05
101	Harold Green	.05
102	Scott Mitchell	.20
103	Jerry Rice	1.50
104	Shawn Jefferson	.05
105	Glyn Milburn	.05
106	Garrison Hearst	.20
107	John Taylor	.05
108	Keith Cash	.05
109	Robert Brooks	.20
110	Barry Sanders	2.00
111	Ernest Givins	.05
112	Steve Tasker	.05
113	Jeff Graham	.05
114	Chris Chandler	.05
115	Lorenzo Neal	.05
116	Bert Emanuel	.40
117	Mike Sherrard	.05
118	Harvey Williams	.05
119	Reggie Brooks	.05
120	Steve Walsh	.05
121	Leroy Thompson	.05
122	Dave Brown	.05
123	Lorenzo White	.05
124	Steve Bono	.25
125	Irving Fryar	.05
126	Jake Reed	.05
127	Boomer Esiason	.05
128	Rocket Ismail	.05
129	Vincent Brisby	.05
130	Robert Smith	.05
131	Anthony Miller	.05
132	Roosevelt Potts	.05
133	Dave Meggett	.05
134	Junior Seau	.05
135	Neil Smith	.05
136	Charles Haley	.05
137	Rod Woodson	.05
138	Deion Sanders	.75
139	Reggie White	.20
140	John Randle	.05
141	Greg Lloyd	.20
142	Cortez Kennedy	.05
143	Bruce Smith	.05
144	*J.J. Stokes*	1.50
145	*Kyle Brady*	.20
146	*Frank Sanders*	1.00
147	*Michael Westbrook*	1.50
148	*Rob Johnson*	1.00
149	*Tyrone Poole*	.20
150	*Lovell Pinkney*	.20
151	*Tyrone Wheatley*	1.00
152	*Steve McNair*	5.00
153	*Napoleon Kaufman*	1.00
154	*Tamarick Vanover*	1.00
155	*Todd Collins*	.20
156	*Kevin Carter*	.20
157	*Rodney Thomas*	.30
158	*Stoney Case*	.20
159	*Kordell Stewart*	3.00
160	*Tony Boselli*	.20

161	*Sherman Williams*	.20
162	*Christian Fauria*	.20
163	*Ray Zellars*	.20
164	*Ki-Jana Carter*	1.00
165	*Terrell Fletcher*	.20
166	*Curtis Martin*	6.00
167	*Eric Zeier*	.30
168	*Joey Galloway*	3.00
169	*Warren Sapp*	.75
170	*Kerry Collins*	3.00
171	*Mark Bruener*	.30
172	*Chris Sanders*	1.25
173	*Rashaan Salaam*	.50
174	Jerry Rice	.50
175	Marshall Faulk	.75
176	Drew Bledsoe	.75
177	Emmitt Smith	1.25
178	Tim Brown	.20
179	Steve Young	.50
180	Barry Sanders	1.00
181	Michael Irvin	.25
182	Dan Marino	1.25
183	Jeff George	.20
184	Chris Warren	.20
185	Herman Moore	.20
186	Andre Rison	.20
187	Bam Morris	.20
188	Troy Aikman	.50
189	Jim Kelly	.20
190	John Elway	.25
191	Cris Carter	.20
192	Shannon Sharpe	.05
193	Brett Favre	.50
194	Drew Bledsoe	.40
195	John Elway	.20
196	Dan Marino	.50
197	Brett Favre	.30
198	Troy Aikman	.30
199	Steve Young	.30
200	Randall Cunningham, Rick Mirer	.20

1995 Summit Ground Zero

Ground Zero was a 200-card parallel set to the 1995 Score Summit set, and was inserted one per seven packs. Card fronts featured a prismatic silver foil, while card backs contained the words "Ground Zero."

Ground Zero Cards:	3X-5X

1995 Summit Backfield Stars

The 1995 Score Summit inserts were included one per 37 packs. They feature 20 of the best running backs on a holographic silver foil printing that gives each runner a dimensional background effect. "Backfield Stars" is written along the left side of the card; the player's name is in the lower right corner. The numbered card back is horizontal and has a player photo on the left, with a brief career summary on the right. The player's name is at the top between two stars.

		NM/M
Complete Set (20):		35.00
Common Player:		1.00
1	Emmitt Smith	10.00
2	Marshall Faulk	5.00
3	Barry Sanders	8.00
4	Ricky Watters	1.00
5	Rodney Hampton	1.00
6	Chris Warren	1.00
7	Garrison Hearst	1.00
8	Tyrone Wheatley	1.00
9	Rashaan Salaam	1.00
10	Natrone Means	1.00
11	Bam Morris	1.00
12	Jerome Bettis	1.00
13	Errict Rhett	1.00
14	William Floyd	1.00
15	Edgar Bennett	1.00
16	Marcus Allen	1.00
17	Mario Bates	1.00
18	Lorenzo White	1.00
19	Gary Brown	1.00
20	Craig Heyward	1.00

1995 Summit Rookie Summit

These 1995 Score Summit inserts could be found one per 23 packs. The cards feature exclusive photography taken at Pinnacle's Rookie Photo Shoot before the season began. Each rookie is shown, in his team's NFL uniform, airborne against a goalpost background. Gold Rush foil is used on both sides. The numbered card back has a posed shot of the player in his NFL uniform, with a line describing one of his more recent accomplishments. The "Rookie Summit" logo appears on both sides.

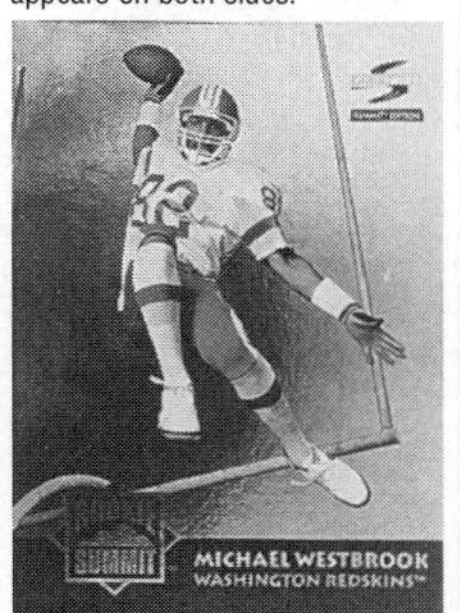

		NM/M
Complete Set (18):		35.00
Common Player:		.50
1	Kevin Carter	.50
2	Sherman Williams	.50
3	Kordell Stewart	4.00
4	Christian Fauria	.50
5	J.J. Stokes	3.00
6	Joey Galloway	6.00
7	Michael Westbrook	3.00
8	James Stewart	5.00
9	Stoney Case	.50
10	Kyle Brady	.50
11	Terrell Fletcher	.50
12	Todd Collins	.50
13	Jimmy Oliver	.50
14	Napoleon Kaufman	1.00
15	John Walsh	.50
16	Kerry Collins	5.00
17	Ki-Jana Carter	2.00
18	Terrell Davis	15.00

1995 Summit Team Summit

These cards feature 12 of the league's top players, utilizing spectroetching on a holographic foil card. Cards were randomly included in every 91 packs of 1995 Score Summit football and are numbered.

		NM/M
Complete Set (12):		60.00
Common Player:		1.00
Minor Stars:		2.00
Inserted 1:91		
1	Dan Marino	10.00
2	Emmitt Smith	6.00
3	Drew Bledsoe	5.00
4	Troy Aikman	5.00
5	Bam Morris	1.00
6	Steve Young	5.00
7	Randall Cunningham	2.00
8	Natrone Means	2.00
9	Barry Sanders	8.00
10	Brett Favre	10.00
11	Errict Rhett	1.00
12	Jerry Rice	6.00

1996 Score

Score's regular 1996 football issue has 275 cards and two parallel sets - Field Force and Artist's Proofs. Each regular card has a color action photo on the front, trimmed to look like a baseball diamond. The player's name and position are in white letters at the bottom in a black bar. The Score logo is in an upper corner. The horizontal back has a mug shot on one side, with the team name under it and a card number in the upper corner. Additional information on the back includes biographical and statistical data and a recap of the player's accomplishments. Field Force cards, found in every sixth pack, are printed on a matte finish. Artist's Proof cards, seeded one per 36 packs, have a gold stamp on a regular issue card. Insert sets include Dream Team, Footsteps, In the Zone, Numbers Game and Settle the Score.

		NM/M
Complete Set (275):		15.00
Common Player:		.05
Minor Stars:		.10
Field Force Cards:		2X-4X
Artist's Proof Cards:		5X-10X
Pack (10):		.75
Wax Box (36):		20.00
1	Emmitt Smith	1.50
2	Flipper Anderson	.05
3	Kordell Stewart	1.00
4	Bruce Smith	.05
5	Marshall Faulk	.75
6	William Floyd	.05
7	Darren Woodson	.05
8	Lake Dawson	.05
9	Terry Allen	.05
10	Ki-Jana Carter	.25
11	Tony Boselli	.05
12	Christian Fauria	.05
13	Jeff George	.05
14	Dan Marino	1.50
15	Rodney Thomas	.30
16	Anthony Miller	.05
17	Chris Sanders	.30
18	Natrone Means	.10
19	Curtis Conway	.05
20	Ben Coates	.05
21	Alvin Harper	.05
22	Frank Sanders	.05
23	Boomer Esiason	.05
24	Lovell Pinkney	.05
25	Troy Aikman	.75
26	Quinn Early	.05
27	Adrian Murrell	.05
28	Chris Spielman	.05
29	Tyrone Wheatley	.05
30	Tim Brown	.05
31	Erik Kramer	.05
32	Warren Moon	.05
33	Jimmy Oliver	.05
34	Herman Moore	.20
35	Quentin Coryatt	.05
36	Heath Shuler	.25
37	Jim Kelly	.05
38	Chris Miller	.05
39	Harvey Williams	.05
40	Vinny Testaverde	.05
41	Steve McNair	.75
42	Jerry Rice	.75
43	Darick Holmes	.05
44	Kyle Brady	.05
45	Greg Lloyd	.05
46	Kerry Collins	.25
47	Willie McGinest	.05
48	Isaac Bruce	.40
49	Carnell Lake	.05
50	Charles Haley	.05
51	Troy Vincent	.05
52	Randall Cunningham	.05
53	Rashaan Salaam	.50
54	Willie Jackson	.05
55	Chris Warren	.15
56	Michael Irvin	.10
57	Mario Bates	.05
58	Warren Sapp	.05
59	John Elway	.25
60	Shannon Sharpe	.05
61	Bam Morris	.05
62	Robert Brooks	.05
63	Rodney Hampton	.05
64	Ken Norton Jr.	.05
65	Bryce Paup	.05
66	Eric Swann	.05
67	Rodney Peete	.05
68	Larry Centers	.05
69	Lamont Warren	.05
70	Jay Novacek	.05
71	Cris Carter	.05
72	Terrell Fletcher	.05
73	Andre Rison	.05
74	Ricky Watters	.05
75	Napoleon Kaufman	.30
76	Reggie White	.05
77	Yancey Thigpen	.40
78	Terry Kirby	.05
79	Deion Sanders	.50
80	Irving Fryar	.05
81	Marcus Allen	.05
82	Carl Pickens	.05
83	Drew Bledsoe	.75
84	Eric Metcalf	.05
85	Robert Smith	.05
86	Tamarick Vanover	.50
87	Henry Ellard	.05
88	Kevin Greene	.05
89	Mark Brunell	.50
90	Terrell Davis	.75
91	Brian Mitchell	.05
92	Aaron Bailey	.05
93	Rocket Ismail	.05
94	Dave Brown	.05
95	Rod Woodson	.05
96	Sean Gilbert	.05
97	Mark Seay	.05
98	Zack Crockett	.05
99	Scott Mitchell	.05
100	Erric Pegram	.05
101	David Palmer	.05
102	Vincent Brisby	.05
103	Brett Perriman	.05
104	Jim Everett	.05
105	Tony Martin	.05
106	Desmond Howard	.05
107	Stan Humphries	.05
108	Bill Brooks	.05
109	Neil Smith	.05
110	Michael Westbrook	.10
111	Herschel Walker	.05
112	Andre Coleman	.05
113	Derrick Alexander	.05
114	Jeff Blake	.60
115	Sherman Williams	.05
116	James Stewart	.05
117	Hardy Nickerson	.05
118	Elvis Grbac	.05
119	Brett Favre	1.50
120	Mike Sherrard	.05
121	Edgar Bennett	.05
122	Calvin Williams	.05
123	Brian Blades	.05
124	Jeff Graham	.05
125	Gary Brown	.05
126	Bernie Parmalee	.05
127	Kimble Anders	.05
128	Hugh Douglas	.05
129	James Stewart	.05
130	Eric Bjornson	.05
131	Ken Dilger	.05
132	Jerome Bettis	.05
133	Cortez Kennedy	.05
134	Bryan Cox	.05
135	Darnay Scott	.05
136	Bert Emanuel	.05
137	Steve Bono	.05
138	Charles Johnson	.05
139	Glyn Milburn	.05
140	Derrick Alexander	.05
141	Dave Meggett	.05
142	Trent Dilfer	.05
143	Eric Zeier	.05
144	Jim Harbaugh	.05
145	Antonio Freeman	.05
146	Orlanda Thomas	.05
147	Russell Maryland	.05
148	Chad May	.05
149	Craig Heyward	.05
150	Aeneas Williams	.05
151	Kevin Williams	.05
152	Charlie Garner	.05
153	J.J. Stokes	.10
154	Stoney Case	.05
155	Mark Chmura	.20
156	Mark Bruener	.05
157	Derek Loville	.05
158	Justin Armour	.05
159	Brent Jones	.05
160	Aaron Craver	.05
161	Terance Mathis	.05
162	Chris Zorich	.05
163	Glenn Foley	.05
164	Johnny Mitchell	.05
165	Junior Seau	.05
166	Willie Davis	.05
167	Rick Mirer	.05
168	Leroy Hoard	.05
169	Greg Hill	.05
170	Steve Tasker	.05
171	Tony Bennett	.05
172	Jeff Hostetler	.05
173	Dave Krieg	.05
174	Mark Carrier	.05
175	Michael Haynes	.05
176	Chris Chandler	.05
177	Ernie Mills	.05
178	Jake Reed	.05
179	Errict Rhett	.50
180	Garrison Hearst	.10
181	Derrick Thomas	.05
182	*Aaron Hayden*	.30
183	Jackie Harris	.05
184	Curtis Martin	1.50
185	Neil O'Donnell	.05
186	Derrick Moore	.05
187	Steve Young	.75
188	Pat Swilling	.05
189	Amp Lee	.05
190	Rob Johnson	.05
191	Todd Collins	.05
192	J.J. Birden	.05
193	O.J. McDuffie	.05
194	Shawn Jefferson	.05
195	Sean Dawkins	.05
196	Fred Barnett	.05
197	Roosevelt Potts	.05
198	Rob Moore	.05
199	Qadry Ismail	.05
200	Barry Sanders	1.00
201	Floyd Turner	.05
202	Wayne Chrebet	.05
203	Andre Reed	.05
204	Tyrone Hughes	.05
205	Keenan McCardell	.05
206	Gus Frerotte	.05
207	Daryl Johnston	.05
208	Haywood Jeffires	.05
209	Steve Atwater	.05
210	Michael Jackson	.05
211	Andre Hastings	.05
212	Joey Galloway	.75
213	Robert Green	.05
214	*Keyshawn Johnson*	2.00
215	*Tony Brackens*	.05
216	*Stepfret Williams*	.05
217	*Mike Alstott*	1.00
218	*Terry Glenn*	1.50
219	*Tim Biakabutuka*	.75
220	*Eric Moulds*	1.50
221	*Jeff Lewis*	.50
222	*Bobby Engram*	.50
223	*Cedric Jones*	.05
224	*Stanley Pritchett*	.05
225	*Kevin Hardy*	.20
226	*Alex Van Dyke*	.30
227	*Willie Anderson*	.05
228	*Regan Upshaw*	.05
229	*Leeland McElroy*	.20
230	*Marvin Harrison*	4.00
231	*Eddie George*	3.00
232	*Lawrence Phillips*	.50
233	Daryl Gardener	.05
234	Alex Molden	.05
235	*Derrick Mayes*	.75
236	John Mobley	.05
237	Isreal Ifeanyi	.05
238	Pete Kendall	.05
239	*Danny Kanell*	.50
240	Jonathan Ogden	.05
241	Reggie Brown	.05
242	Marcus Jones	.05
243	Jon Stark	.05
244	Barry Sanders	.50
245	Brett Favre	.30
246	John Elway	.15
247	Dan Marino	.75
248	Drew Bledsoe	.30
249	Michael Irvin	.05
250	Troy Aikman	.30
251	Emmitt Smith	.75
252	Steve Young	.30
253	Jerry Rice	.30
254	Jeff Blake	.25
255	Tim Brown	.05
256	Bam Morris	.05
257	Rodney Hampton	.05
258	Scott Mitchell	.05
259	Garrison Hearst	.05
260	Larry Centers	.05
261	Neil O'Donnell	.05
262	Orlanda Thomas	.05
263	Hugh Douglas	.05
264	Bill Brooks	.05
265	Harvey Williams	.05
266	Charles Haley	.05
267	Greg Lloyd	.05
268	Daryl Johnston	.05
269	Dan Marino	.30
270	Jeff Blake	.10
271	John Elway	.05
272	Emmitt Smith	.30
273	Brett Favre	.30
274	Jerry Rice	.30
275	Dan Marino, Jeff Blake, John Elway, Emmitt Smith, Brett Favre, Jerry Rice	.50

1996 Score Field Force

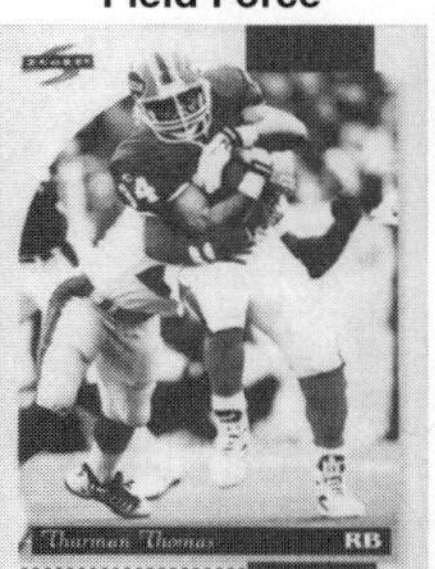

The 275-card, standard-size parallel set, features a matte finish instead of the gloss card-front finish of the base cards. The set was inserted every six packs; 1:3 for jumbo.

	NM/M
Complete Set (275):	300.00
Common Player:	.40
Veteran Stars:	2X-4X
Young Stars:	2X-4X
RCs:	1X-3X

1996 Score Artist's Proofs

The 275-card, regular-sized parallel set, inserted every 36 packs, features an Artist's Proof logo on the card front. The set is inserted every 18 jumbo packs.

		NM/M
Common Player:		.50
Semistars:		1.00
Veteran Stars:		5X-10X
Young Stars:		5X-10X
RCs:		2X-5X
1	Emmitt Smith	75.00
3	Kordell Stewart	30.00
5	Marshall Faulk	30.00
14	Dan Marino	75.00
25	Troy Aikman	35.00
41	Steve McNair	20.00
42	Jerry Rice	35.00
46	Kerry Collins	30.00
59	John Elway	20.00
79	Deion Sanders	25.00
83	Drew Bledsoe	30.00
90	Terrell Davis	20.00
119	Brett Favre	35.00
184	Curtis Martin	60.00
187	Steve Young	30.00
200	Barry Sanders	50.00
212	Joey Galloway	20.00
214	Keyshawn Johnson	50.00
218	Terry Glenn	35.00
231	Eddie George	50.00
232	Lawrence Phillips	35.00
244	Barry Sanders (SE)	20.00
245	Brett Favre (SE)	20.00
247	Dan Marino (SE)	40.00
248	Drew Bledsoe (SE)	15.00
250	Troy Aikman (SE)	20.00
251	Emmitt Smith (SE)	40.00
252	Steve Young (SE)	15.00
253	Jerry Rice (SE)	20.00
269	Dan Marino (CL)	20.00
273	Brett Favre (CL)	15.00
274	Jerry Rice (CL)	15.00

1996 Score Dream Team

These 1996 Score football inserts feature 10 players who an NFL coach would love to build a team around. The cards were random inserts, one per 72 packs; they are the most exclusive card in 1996 Score.

		NM/M
Complete Set (10):		30.00
Common Player:		1.00
1	Troy Aikman	5.00
2	Michael Irvin	1.00
3	Emmitt Smith	7.00
4	John Elway	1.00
5	Barry Sanders	7.00
6	Brett Favre	8.00
7	Dan Marino	8.00
8	Drew Bledsoe	4.00
9	Jerry Rice	5.00
10	Steve Young	5.00

1996 Score Footsteps

These 1996 Score football inserts were seeded one per 35 hobby packs. A top rookie from the 1995 season is paired with a top veteran he most wants to emulate. The 15 dual-player cards are printed with rainbow holographic highlights.

		NM/M
Complete Set (15):		50.00
Common Player:		1.00
1	Darick Holmes, Errict Rhett	4.00
2	Rashaan Salaam, Natrone Means	1.00
3	Ki-Jana Carter, Barry Sanders	8.00
4	Terrell Davis, Marshall Faulk	6.00
5	Rodney Thomas, Chris Warren	1.00
6	Curtis Martin, Emmitt Smith	8.00
7	Kerry Collins, Troy Aikman	6.00
8	Eric Zeier, Drew Bledsoe	6.00
9	Steve McNair, Brett Favre	8.00
10	Steve Young, Kordell Stewart	5.00
11	J.J. Stokes, Jerry Rice	6.00
12	Joey Galloway, Michael Irvin	2.00
13	Michael Westbrook, Cris Carter	2.00
14	Tamarick Vanover, Isaac Bruce	2.00
15	Orlanda Thomas, Deion Sanders	2.00

1996 Score Numbers Game

These 25 cards were randomly inserted into every 17 packs of 1996 Score football. The card front has a color action photo on it, with a smaller photo on the right in four pieces. The player's name and position are stamped in gold under this photo. Gold foil stamping is also used for the set icon in the lower left corner. The player's team name is in black letters in the foil band at the bottom. The card back has a color photo of the player, with the rest of the full-bleed photo in black-and-white. The card number is in the upper left corner in a white rectangle; the player's name, position and team name run horizontally down the left side. Four rectangles on the right side each have a tidbit of statistical information.

		NM/M
	Complete Set (25):	40.00
	Common Player:	1.00
1	Barry Sanders	5.00
2	Drew Bledsoe	4.00
3	Brett Favre	6.00
4	John Elway	4.00
5	Dan Marino	6.00
6	Michael Irvin	1.00
7	Troy Aikman	4.00
8	Emmitt Smith	5.00
9	Steve Young	4.00
10	Jerry Rice	5.00
11	Chris Sanders	1.00
12	Herman Moore	3.00
13	Frank Sanders	1.00
14	Kordell Stewart	2.00
15	Jeff Blake	1.00
16	Robert Brooks	1.00
17	Marshall Faulk	3.00
18	Carl Pickens	1.00
19	Greg Lloyd	1.00
20	Curtis Conway	1.00
21	Chris Warren	1.00
22	Natrone Means	1.00
23	Deion Sanders	2.00
24	Neil O'Donnell	1.00
25	Ricky Watters	1.00

1996 Score In the Zone

This set features 20 offensive players who excel in getting into the end zone. Cards were exclusive to 1996 Score retail packs, every 33rd pack. The front has a color action photo, with red foil highlights for the set name along the right side and for the stadium background. The player's name is in the lower left corner; the Score logo is in the upper left corner. The numbered back has a color photo, with the player's name, a player profile and a set icon below the card number.

		NM/M
	Complete Set (20):	70.00
	Common Player:	1.00
1	Brett Favre	20.00
2	Warren Moon	3.00
3	Erik Kramer	1.00
4	Scott Mitchell	1.00
5	Jeff Blake	1.00
6	Steve Bono	1.00
7	Dan Marino	20.00
8	Troy Aikman	12.00
9	Emmitt Smith	15.00
10	Curtis Martin	10.00
11	Errict Rhett	2.00
12	Terrell Davis	10.00
13	Derek Loville	1.00
14	Rodney Hampton	1.00
15	Cris Carter	3.00
16	Herman Moore	2.00
17	Jerry Rice	10.00
18	Ben Coates	1.00
19	Michael Irvin	1.00
20	Carl Pickens	1.00

1996 Score Settle the Score

These cards were random inserts in 1996 Score football, one every 36 jumbo packs. Each card features two players on it.

		NM/M
	Complete Set (30):	150.00
	Common Player:	1.00
1	Frank Sanders, Charlie Garner	1.00
2	Drew Bledsoe, Neil O'Donnell	4.00
3	Jerry Rice, Craig Heyward	8.00
4	Emmitt Smith, Rod Woodson	10.00
5	Darick Holmes, Dan Marino	12.00
6	Kerry Collins, Steve Young	8.00
7	Rashaan Salaam, Brett Favre	12.00
8	Curtis Conway, Barry Sanders	8.00
9	Troy Aikman, Dan Marino	12.00
10	Dan Marino, Neil O'Donnell	12.00
11	Eric Zeier, Steve McNair	5.00
12	Jeff Blake, Kordell Stewart	4.00
13	Troy Aikman, Heath Shuler	6.00
14	Michael Irvin, Jerry Rice	8.00
15	Emmitt Smith, Ricky Watters	10.00
16	John Elway, Steve Bono	6.00
17	John Elway, Rick Mirer	6.00
18	John Elway, Tim Brown	6.00
19	Barry Sanders, Brett Favre	15.00
20	Barry Sanders, Warren Moon	10.00
21	Brett Favre, Trent Dilfer	12.00
22	Rodney Thomas, James Stewart	1.00
23	Jim Harbaugh, Drew Bledsoe	6.00
24	Marcus Allen, Harvey Williams	1.00
25	Tamarick Vanover, Joey Galloway	8.00
26	Dan Marino, Drew Bledsoe	12.00
27	Mario Bates, Jerry Rice	8.00
28	Tyrone Wheatley, Michael Westbrook	1.00
29	Napoleon Kaufman, Junior Seau	1.00
30	J.J. Stokes, Isaac Bruce	2.00

1996 Summit

The 200-card, regular-sized set came in seven-card packs and included three subsets: Rookies (35), Quarterhorses (15) and Checklists (4). The card fronts feature the player's name and team helmet in gold foil. The card backs include a headshot of the player with three statistical categories and the card number in the upper left corner. A parallel insert set, Ground Zero, is inserted every six packs and features prismatic foil renditions of the base set. Artist's Proofs, another 200-card parallel set, adds special holographic foil stamps to the base set and are inserted every 35 packs. Other insert sets in Summit are Turf Team, Inspirations, 3rd & Long and its parallel insert set - 3rd & Long Mirage.

		NM/M
	Complete Set (200):	30.00
	Common Player:	.05
	Minor Stars:	.20
	Ground Zero Cards:	2X-4X
	Artist's Proof Cards:	5X-10X
	Hobby Pack (7):	2.00
	Hobby Wax Box (18):	35.00
1	Troy Aikman	1.25
2	Marshall Faulk	.50
3	Bruce Smith	.05
4	Jerome Bettis	.20
5	Bryan Cox	.05
6	Robert Brooks	.20
7	Dan Marino	2.50
8	Irving Fryar	.05
9	Jerry Rice	1.25
10	Ki-Jana Carter	.20
11	Herman Moore	.30
12	Derrick Thomas	.05
13	Curtis Martin	1.75
14	Jeff Hostetler	.05
15	Errict Rhett	.30
16	Emmitt Smith	2.50
17	Aaron Craver	.05
18	Kyle Brady	.05
19	Tony Martin	.05
20	Vinny Testaverde	.05
21	Charles Haley	.05
22	Rodney Thomas	.05
23	Jim Everett	.05
24	Brian Blades	.05
25	Frank Sanders	.05
26	Bryce Paup	.05
27	Anthony Miller	.05
28	Ken Dilger	.05
29	Orlando Thomas	.05
30	Rodney Hampton	.05
31	Ken Norton Jr.	.05
32	Darren Woodson	.05
33	Antonio Freeman	.05
34	Steve Bono	.05
35	Ben Coates	.05
36	Jeff George	.05
37	Curtis Conway	.05
38	Steve Atwater	.05
39	Fred Barnett	.05
40	Joey Galloway	1.25
41	Jim Kelly	.20
42	Michael Irvin	.20
43	Steve Tasker	.05
44	Warren Moon	.05
45	Hugh Douglas	.05
46	Steve Walsh	.05
47	Kerry Collins	.30
48	Barry Sanders	1.75
49	Steve Young	.75
50	Jim Harbaugh	.05
51	Tyrone Wheatley	.05
52	Boomer Esiason	.05
53	Deion Sanders	.75
54	Steve McNair	1.00
55	Willie McGinest	.05
56	Adrian Murrell	.05
57	Thurman Thomas	.20
58	John Elway	.75
59	William Floyd	.05
60	Eric Zeier	.05
61	Dave Krieg	.05
62	Eric Bjornson	.05
63	Brett Favre	2.50
64	Derrick Alexander	.05
65	Charlie Garner	.05
66	Stan Humphries	.05
67	Bert Emanuel	.05
68	Scott Mitchell	.05
69	Quentin Coryatt	.05
70	Eric Green	.05
71	Jeff Graham	.05
72	Ernie Mills	.05
73	Trent Dilfer	.20
74	Sherman Williams	.05
75	Tamarick Vanover	.50
76	Drew Bledsoe	1.25
77	Jay Novacek	.05
78	Edgar Bennett	.05
79	Tim Brown	.05
80	Greg Lloyd	.05
81	Darick Holmes	.05
82	Carl Pickens	.05
83	Flipper Anderson	.05
84	Bernie Kosar	.05
85	Dave Brown	.05
86	Calvin Williams	.05
87	Michael Westbrook	.20
88	Kevin Williams	.05
89	Chris Sanders	.05
90	Robert Smith	.05
91	Cris Carter	.05
92	Gus Frerotte	.05
93	Larry Centers	.05
94	Eric Metcalf	.05
95	Isaac Bruce	.50
96	Kordell Stewart	1.50
97	Ricky Watters	.20
98	Terrell Fletcher	.05
99	Bernie Parmalee	.05
100	Harvey Williams	.05
101	Hardy Nickerson	.05
102	Jeff Blake	.50
103	Terry Allen	.05
104	Yancey Thigpen	.30
105	Greg Hill	.05
106	Chris Warren	.20
107	Terrell Davis	1.50
108	Mark Brunell	1.00
109	Alvin Harper	.05
110	Marcus Allen	.20
111	Garrison Hearst	.05
112	Derek Loville	.05
113	Craig Heyward	.05
114	Kimble Anders	.05
115	O.J. McDuffie	.05
116	Junior Seau	.20
117	Terry Kirby	.05
118	Erric Pegram	.05
119	Rick Mirer	.05
120	Erik Kramer	.05
121	Brett Perriman	.05
122	Shawn Jefferson	.05
123	J.J. Stokes	.20
124	Kevin Greene	.05
125	Daryl Johnston	.05
126	Mark Chmura	.05
127	James Stewart	.05
128	Mario Bates	.05
129	Rodney Peete	.05
130	Quinn Early	.05
131	Shannon Sharpe	.05
132	Neil Smith	.05
133	Herschel Walker	.05
134	Aaron Bailey	.05
135	Rashaan Salaam	.40
136	Kevin Smith	.05
137	Sean Dawkins	.05
138	Jake Reed	.05
139	Neil O'Donnell	.05
140	Reggie White	.20
141	Vincent Brisby	.05
142	Napoleon Kaufman	.05
143	Brent Jones	.05
144	Mark Seay	.05
145	Heath Shuler	.05
146	Wayne Chrebet	.05
147	*Leeland McElroy*	.30
148	*Tim Biakabutuka*	1.00
149	*John Mobley*	.05
150	*Tony Brackens*	.20
151	*Danny Kanell*	.75
152	*Eddie Kennison*	.40
153	*Jonathan Ogden*	.20
154	*Bobby Engram*	.30
155	*Chris Darkins*	.05
156	*Daryl Gardener*	.05
157	*Keyshawn Johnson*	3.00
158	*Mike Alstott*	1.75
159	*Simeon Rice*	.20
160	*Eric Moulds*	2.50
161	*Stepfret Williams*	.05
162	*Eddie George*	4.00
163	*Duane Clemons*	.05
164	*Amani Toomer*	.20
165	*Rickey Dudley*	.30
166	*Bobby Hoying*	1.00
167	*Lawrence Phillips*	.50
168	*Willie Anderson*	.05
169	*Derrick Mayes*	1.00
170	*Kevin Hardy*	.20
171	*Terry Glenn*	1.75
172	*Stephen Davis*	3.00
173	*Walt Harris*	.20
174	*Marvin Harrison*	3.00
175	*Karim Abdul-Jabbar*	.75
176	*Alex Molden*	.05
177	*Regan Upshaw*	.05
178	*Jerald Moore*	.05
179	*Alex Van Dyke*	.20
180	*Jeff Lewis*	.75
181	*Cedric Jones*	.05
182	Jim Kelly	.05
183	Troy Aikman	.50
184	Jim Harbaugh	.05
185	Neil O'Donnell	.05
186	Steve Young	.30
187	Kerry Collins	.30
188	Scott Mitchell	.05
189	Drew Bledsoe	.50
190	Kordell Stewart	.75
191	Erik Kramer	.05
192	Brett Favre	1.00
193	Warren Moon	.05
194	Jeff Blake	.25
195	Mark Brunell	.50
196	John Elway	.25
197	Emmitt Smith Checklist	.30
198	Dan Marino Checklist	.30
199	Brett Favre Checklist	.30
200	Jim Harbaugh Checklist	.05

1996 Summit Ground Zero

Ground Zero is a 200-card prismatic foil rendition of the regular-issue set. These parallel cards are inserted every six packs.

Ground Zero Cards:	2X-4X

1996 Summit Artist's Proofs

Artist's Proofs add a holographic Artist's Proof stamp to all 200 cards in the regular-issue set. These parallel cards are inserted at a rate of one per 35 packs.

Artist's Proof Cards:	5X-10X

1996 Summit Premium Stock

Premium Stock was available in hobby stores and was an upgraded version of Summit Football. In 13-card packs of Premium Stock, the regular-issue set was reprinted in a rainbow holographic foil version. In addition, Turf Team inserts also received special prismatic foil treatment. Other inserts were the same as the regular-issue product.

Premium Stock Cards:	1.5X

1996 Summit Inspirations

The 18-card, regular-sized set was inserted in every 17 packs of Summit football. The cards feature foil printing and the production run was limited to 8,000.

		NM/M
	Complete Set (18):	40.00
	Common Player:	1.00
1	Jim Harbaugh	1.00
2	Alex Van Dyke	1.00
3	Mike Alstott	2.00
4	Jonathan Ogden	1.00
5	Brett Favre	6.00
6	Tony Brackens	1.00
7	Drew Bledsoe	4.00
8	Danny Kanell	1.00
9	Eric Moulds	3.00
10	John Elway	5.00
11	Eddie George	4.00
12	Karim Abdul-Jabbar	1.00
13	Tim Biakabutuka	1.00
14	Jeff Lewis	1.00
15	Terry Glenn	3.00
16	Jeff Blake	1.00
17	Kevin Hardy	1.00
18	Bobby Engram	2.00

1996 Summit Turf Team

The 16-card, regular-sized set, inserted in hobby packs of Summit football, features spot-embossed technology and is limited to a production run of 4,000.

		NM/M
	Complete Set (16):	100.00
	Common Player:	1.00
1	Emmitt Smith	8.00
2	Brett Favre	10.00
3	Curtis Martin	6.00
4	Steve Young	6.00
5	Kerry Collins	3.00
6	Barry Sanders	8.00
7	Dan Marino	10.00
8	Isaac Bruce	3.00
9	Troy Aikman	6.00
10	Marshall Faulk	5.00
11	Joey Galloway	3.00
12	Jeff Blake	1.00
13	Drew Bledsoe	6.00
14	John Elway	6.00
15	Jerry Rice	8.00
16	Michael Irvin	1.00

1996 Summit Third and Long

The 18-card, regular-sized set was inserted in hobby, retail and magazine packs and was limited to a production run of 2,000. The cards are printed on rainbow holographic foil with sequential numbering. An 18-card parallel insert set, Mirage, features a floating football hologram behind the player's image. Mirage is limited to 600 sets.

		NM/M
	Complete Set (18):	150.00
	Common Player:	1.00
	Minor Stars: Production 2,000 Sets	3.00
	Mirage Prize Cards: Production 600 Sets	2X
1	Michael Irvin	3.00
2	Dan Marino	10.00
3	Keyshawn Johnson	3.00
4	Chris Warren	1.00
5	Rashaan Salaam	1.00
6	Brett Favre	10.00
7	Terry Glenn	3.00
8	Steve Young	6.00
9	Kerry Collins	3.00
10	Emmitt Smith	8.00
11	Marvin Harrison	3.00
12	Jerry Rice	7.00
13	John Elway	6.00
14	Drew Bledsoe	6.00
15	Eddie Kennison	1.00
16	Troy Aikman	6.00
17	Barry Sanders	8.00
18	Terrell Davis	6.00

1996 Summit Hit The Hole

The 16-card, regular-sized set, limited to a production run of 1,000, was randomly inserted in five-card retail packs of 1996 Pinnacle Summit. The set features 16 top offensive players on all-foil printing.

		NM/M
	Complete Set (16):	100.00
	Common Player:	1.00
1	Rashaan Salaam	1.00
2	Marshall Faulk	10.00
3	Ricky Watters	1.00
4	Leeland McElroy	1.00
5	Emmitt Smith	14.00
6	Eddie George	6.00
7	Curtis Martin	12.00
8	Lawrence Phillips	1.00
9	Darick Holmes	1.00
10	Barry Sanders	12.00
11	Karim Abdul-Jabbar	2.00
12	Errict Rhett	2.00
13	Terrell Davis	8.00
14	Chris Warren	1.00
15	Rodney Thomas	1.00
16	Tim Biakabutuka	2.00

1997 Score

The 330-card set features a player photo in the center on the front, with the team and the player's position printed at the top. The Score logo is in the upper left of the photo, while goalposts appear on the center of each side of the photo. The player's name is printed at the bottom. The base set is paralleled by a Showcase Series and Artist's Proof version.

		NM/M
	Complete Set (330):	15.00
	Common Player:	.05
	Minor Stars:	.10
	Showcase Series:	2X-4X
	Artist's Proofs:	5X-10X
	Retail Pack (10):	1.25
	Retail Wax Box (36):	30.00
	Hobby Pack (15):	1.50
	Hobby Wax Box (20):	20.00
1	John Elway	.50
2	Drew Bledsoe	.75
3	Brett Favre	1.75
4	Emmitt Smith	1.50
5	Kerry Collins	.25
6	Jerry Rice	.75
7	Kordell Stewart	.75
8	Barry Sanders	1.25
9	Dan Marino	1.50
10	Steve Young	.50
11	Erik Kramer	.05
12	Warren Moon	.10
13	Chris Calloway	.05
14	Doug Evans	.05
15	Darren Woodson	.05
16	Alonzo Spellman	.05
17	Greg Hill	.05
18	Aaron Craver	.05
19	Jeff Hostetler	.05
20	William Thomas	.05
21	Marco Coleman	.05
22	Wayne Simmons	.05
23	Donnell Woolford	.05
24	Vinny Testaverde	.10
25	Ed McCaffrey	.05
26	Jim Everett	.05
27	Gilbert Brown	.05
28	Jason Dunn	.05
29	Stanley Pritchett	.05
30	Joey Galloway	.15
31	Amani Toomer	.05
32	Chris Penn	.05

33 Aeneas Williams .05
34 Bobby Taylor .05
35 Bryan Still .05
36 Ty Law .05
37 Shannon Sharpe .05
38 Marty Carter .05
39 Sam Mills .05
40 William Floyd .05
41 Brad Johnson .05
42 Sean Dawkins .05
43 Michael Irvin .10
44 Jeff George .10
45 Brent Jones .05
46 Mark Brunell .75
47 Rob Moore .05
48 Hardy Nickerson .05
49 Chris Chandler .05
50 Willie Anderson .05
51 Isaac Bruce .15
52 Natrone Means .10
53 Tony Banks .15
54 Marshall Faulk .15
55 Michael Westbrook .05
56 Bruce Smith .05
57 Jamal Anderson .15
58 Jackie Harris .05
59 Sean Gilbert .05
60 Ki-Jana Carter .05
61 Eric Moulds .10
62 James Stewart .05
63 Jeff Blake .10
64 O.J. McDuffie .05
65 Neil Smith .05
66 Kevin Smith .05
67 Terry Allen .05
68 Sean LaChapelle .05
69 Rashaan Salaam .10
70 Jeff Graham .05
71 Mark Carrier .05
72 Allen Aldridge .05
73 Keenan McCardell .05
74 Willie McGinest .05
75 Napoleon Kaufman .10
76 Jerris McPhail .05
77 Eric Swann .05
78 Kimble Anders .05
79 Charles Johnson .05
80 Bryan Cox .05
81 Johnnie Morton .05
82 Andre Rison .05
83 Corey Miller .05
84 Troy Drayton .05
85 Jim Harbaugh .05
86 Wesley Walls .05
87 Bryce Paup .05
88 Curtis Martin 1.00
89 Michael Sinclair .05
90 Chris T. Jones .05
91 Jake Reed .05
92 LeRoy Butler .05
93 Reggie Tongue .05
94 Bert Emanual .05
95 Stan Humphries .05
96 Neil O'Donnell .05
97 Troy Vincent .05
98 Mike Alstott .15
99 Chad Cota .05
100 Marvin Harrison .30
101 Terrell Owens .30
102 Dave Brown .05
103 Harvey Williams .05
104 Desmond Howard .05
105 Carl Pickens .05
106 Kent Graham .05
107 Michael Bates .05
108 Terrell Davis 1.00
109 Marcus Allen .10
110 Ray Zellars .05
111 Chris Warren .05
112 Phillippi Sparks .05
113 Craig Erickson .05
114 Eddie George 1.00
115 Daryl Johnston .05
116 Ricky Watters .10
117 Tedy Bruschi .05
118 Mike Mamula .05
119 Ken Harvey .05
120 John Randle .05
121 Mark Chmura .05
122 Sam Gash .05
123 John Kasay .05
124 Barry Minter .05
125 Raymont Harris .05
126 Derrick Thomas .05
127 Trent Dilfer .10
128 Carnell Lake .05
129 Brian Dawkins .05
130 Tyronne Drakeford .05
131 Daryl Gardener .05
132 Fred Strickland .05
133 Kevin Hardy .05
134 Winslow Oliver .05
135 Herman Moore .15
136 Keith Byars .05
137 Harold Green .05
138 Ty Detmer .05
139 Lamar Thomas .05
140 Elvis Grbac .05
141 Edgar Bennett .05
142 Cornelius Bennett .05
143 Tony Tolbert .05
144 James Hasty .05
145 Ben Coates .05
146 Errict Rhett .10
147 Jason Seahorn .05
148 Michael Jackson .05
149 John Mobley .05
150 Walt Harris .05
151 Terry Kirby .05
152 Devin Wyman .05
153 Ray Crockett .05
154 Quinn Early .05
155 Rodney Thomas .05
156 Mark Seay .05
157 Derrick Alexander .05
158 Lamar Lathon .05
159 Anthony Miller .05
160 Shawn Wooden .05
161 Antonio Freeman .15
162 Cortez Kennedy .05
163 Rickey Dudley .10
164 Tony Carter .05
165 Kevin Williams .05
166 Reggie White .10
167 Tim Bowens .05
168 Roy Barker .05
169 Adrian Murrell .05
170 Anthony Johnson .05
171 Terry Glenn .25
172 Jeff Lewis .05
173 Dorsey Levens .10
174 Willie Jackson .05
175 Willie Clay .05
176 Richmond Webb .05
177 Shawn Lee .05
178 Joe Aska .05
179 Rod Woodson .05
180 Jim Schwantz .05
181 Alfred Williams .05
182 Ferric Collons .05
183 Ken Norton Jr. .05
184 Rick Mirer .10
185 Leeland McElroy .05
186 Rodney Hampton .05
187 Ted Popson .05
188 Fred Barnett .05
189 Junior Seau .10
190 Micheal Barrow .05
191 Corey Widmer .05
192 Rodney Peete .05
193 Rod Smith .05
194 Muhsin Muhammad .15
195 Keith Jackson .05
196 Jimmy Smith .05
197 Dave Meggett .05
198 Lawrence Phillips .10
199 Chad Brown .05
200 Darrin Smith .05
201 Larry Centers .05
202 Kevin Greene .05
203 Sherman Williams .05
204 Chris Sanders .05
205 Shawn Jefferson .05
206 Thurman Thomas .10
207 Keyshawn Johnson .30
208 Bryant Young .05
209 Tim Biakabutuka .15
210 Troy Aikman .75
211 Quentin Coryatt .05
212 Karim Abdul-Jabbar .50
213 Brian Blades .05
214 Ray Farmer .05
215 Simeon Rice .05
216 Tyrone Braxton .05
217 Jerome Woods .05
218 Charles Way .05
219 Garrison Hearst .05
220 Bobby Engram .10
221 Billy Davis .05
222 Ken Dilger .05
223 Robert Smith .05
224 John Friesz .05
225 Charlie Garner .05
226 Jerome Bettis .10
227 Darnay Scott .05
228 Terance Mathis .05
229 Brian Williams .05
230 Cris Carter .05
231 Michael Haynes .05
232 Cedric Jones .05
233 Danny Kanell .05
234 Deion Sanders .30
235 Steve Atwater .05
236 Jonathan Ogden .05
237 Lake Dawson .05
238 Eric Allen .05
239 Eddie Kennison .30
240 Irving Fryar .05
241 Michael Strahan .05
242 Steve McNair .40
243 Terrell Buckley .05
244 Merton Hanks .05
245 Jessie Armstead .05
246 Dana Stubblefield .05
247 Brett Perriman .05
248 Mark Collins .05
249 Willie Roaf .05
250 Gus Frerotte .05
251 William Fuller .05
252 Tamarick Vanover .10
253 Scott Mitchell .05
254 Eric Metcalf .05
255 Herschel Walker .05
256 Robert Brooks .05
257 Zach Thomas .15
258 Alvin Harper .05
259 Wayne Chrebet .05
260 Bill Romanowski .05
261 Willie Green .05
262 Dale Carter .05
263 Chris Slade .05
264 J.J. Stokes .05
265 Tim Brown .05
266 Eric Davis .05
267 Mark Carrier .05
268 Tony Martin .05
269 Tyrone Wheatley .05
270 Eugene Robinson .05
271 Curtis Conway .05
272 Michael Timpson .05
273 *Orlando Pace* .50
274 *Tiki Barber* 2.00
275 *Byron Hanspard* .25
276 *Warrick Dunn* 1.25
277 *Rae Carruth* .50
278 *Bryant Westbrook* .30
279 *Antowain Smith* 1.25
280 *Peter Boulware* .05
281 *Reidel Anthony* 1.00
282 *Troy Davis* .20
283 *Jake Plummer* 1.00
284 *Chris Canty* .05
285 *Dwayne Rudd* .05
286 *Ike Hilliard* 1.00
287 *Reinard Wilson* .05
288 *Corey Dillon* 3.00
289 *Tony Gonzalez* .50
290 *Darnell Autry* .50
291 *Kevin Lockett* .20
292 *Darrell Russell* .05
293 *Jim Druckenmiller* .40
294 *Scott Mitchell* .05
295 *Joey Kent* .30
296 *Shawn Springs* .50
297 *James Farrior* .05
298 *Sedrick Shaw* .50
299 *Marcus Harris* .05
300 *Danny Wuerffel* .50
301 *Marc Edwards* .20
302 *Michael Booker* .05
303 *David LaFleur* .50
304 *Mike Adams* .05
305 *Pat Barnes* .20
306 *George Jones* .05
307 *Yatil Green* .30
308 Drew Bledsoe .30
309 Troy Aikman .30
310 Terrell Davis .40
311 Jim Everett .05
312 John Elway .20
313 Barry Sanders .50
314 Jim Harbaugh .05
315 Steve Young .20
316 Dan Marino .75
317 Michael Irvin .05
318 Emmitt Smith .75
319 Jeff Hostetler .05
320 Mark Brunell .30
321 Jeff Blake .05
322 Scott Mitchell .05
323 Boomer Esiason .05
324 Jerome Bettis .05
325 Warren Moon .05
326 Neil O'Donnell .05
327 Jim Kelly .05
328 Dan Marino Checklist .75
329 John Elway Checklist .20
330 Drew Bledsoe Checklist .30

1997 Score Franchise

This 16-card set includes the Franchise players from various NFL teams, including Emmitt Smith and Barry Sanders.

NM/M
Complete Set (16): 50.00
Common Player: 1.00
1 Emmitt Smith 10.00
2 Barry Sanders 10.00
3 Brett Favre 12.00
4 Drew Bledsoe 6.00
5 Jerry Rice 8.00
6 Troy Aikman 8.00
7 Dan Marino 12.00
8 John Elway 6.00
9 Steve Young 6.00
10 Eddie George 4.00
11 Keyshawn Johnson 1.00
12 Terrell Davis 6.00
13 Marshall Faulk 1.00
14 Kerry Collins 2.00
15 Deion Sanders 2.00
16 Joey Galloway 1.00

1997 Score New Breed

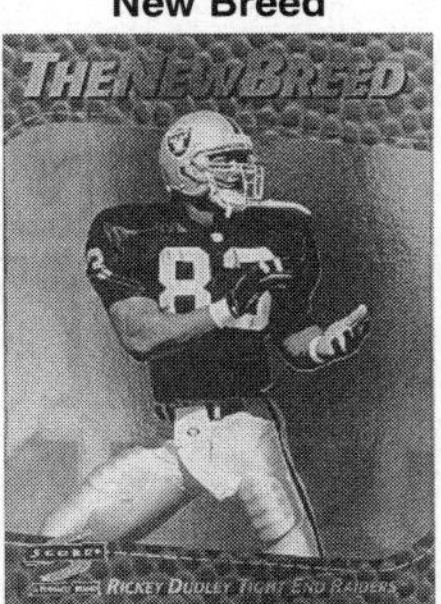

This 18-card set features a player photo superimposed over a holographic background on the card front. "The New Breed" is printed at the top. A football's brown pebble grain is on the top and bottom border of the front. The Score logo is in the lower left, while his name, position and team are printed to the right of the logo. The backs are numbered in the upper left corner.

NM/M
Complete Set (18): 40.00
Common Player: .50
1 Eddie George 4.00
2 Terrell Davis 4.00
3 Curtis Martin 3.00
4 Tony Banks .50
5 Lawrence Phillips .50
6 Terry Glenn 1.00
7 Jerome Bettis .50
8 Karim Abdul-Jabbar 1.00
9 Napoleon Kaufman .50
10 Isaac Bruce .50
11 Keyshawn Johnson .50
12 Rickey Dudley .50
13 Eddie Kennison 2.00
14 Marvin Harrison 5.00
15 Emmitt Smith 5.00
16 Barry Sanders 5.00
17 Kerry Collins 1.50
18 Brett Favre 6.00

1997 Score The Specialist

The 18-card chase set features a holographic front, with the player over a background which repeats "The Specialist" many times. The player's name is printed in red at the bottom center. The cards are numbered on the back.

NM/M
Complete Set (18): 40.00
Common Player: .50
1 Brett Favre 6.00
2 Drew Bledsoe 4.00
3 Mark Brunell 3.00
4 Kerry Collins 1.50
5 John Elway 4.00
6 Barry Sanders 5.00
7 Troy Aikman 4.00
8 Jerry Rice 4.00
9 Dan Marino 6.00
10 Neil O'Donnell .50
11 Scott Mitchell .50
12 Jim Harbaugh .50
13 Emmitt Smith 5.00
14 Steve Young 4.00
15 Dave Brown .50
16 Jeff Blake 2.00
17 Jim Everett .50
18 Kordell Stewart 2.00

1998 Score

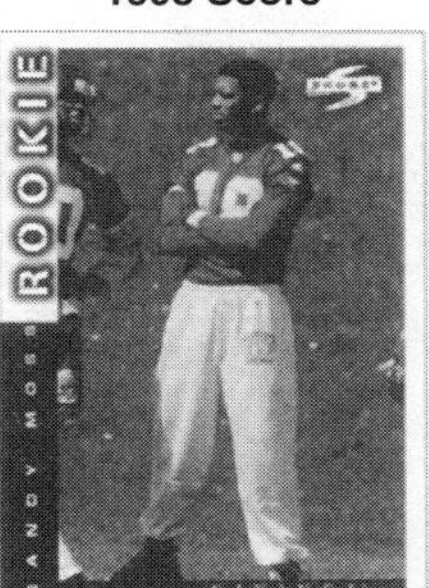

The 270-card base set is made up of 15 Off Season cards, 3 checklists, 20 rookies and 232 veterans. Three parallel sets that include Showcase, Artist's Proofs and One on One. The Showcase set includes only the top 110 players and were inserted 1:7 packs. The Artist's Proof set is made up of the best 50 players in the set and were found 1:35 packs. The last parallel set is the One on One set in which there is only one of each card in the 160-card set. A special hobby exclusive Ryan Leaf autographed card was added with only 200 signed.

NM/M
Complete Set (270): 35.00
Common Player: .10
Minor Stars: .20
Common Rookie: 1.00
Showcase Cards: 2X-4X
Showcase Rookies: 2X
Inserted 1:7
AP Cards: 3X-5X
Inserted 1:35
Pack: 2.50
Wax Box (24): 40.00
1 John Elway 1.00
2 Kordell Stewart .75
3 Warrick Dunn .75
4 Brad Johnson .30
5 Kerry Collins .20
6 Danny Kanell .10
7 Emmitt Smith 1.50
8 Jamal Anderson .50
9 Jim Harbaugh .20
10 Tony Martin .20
11 Rod Smith .30
12 Dorsey Levens .30
13 Steve McNair .40
14 Derrick Thomas .10
15 Rob Moore .20
16 Peter Boulware .10
17 Terry Allen .20
18 Joey Galloway .30
19 Jerome Bettis .30
20 Carl Pickens .20
21 Napoleon Kaufman .30
22 Troy Aikman 1.00
23 Curtis Conway .20
24 Adrian Murrell .20
25 Elvis Grbac .20
26 Garrison Hearst .30
27 Chris Sanders .10
28 Scott Mitchell .20
29 Junior Seau .20
30 Chris Chandler .20
31 Kevin Hardy .10
32 Terrell Davis 1.00
33 Keyshawn Johnson .30
34 Natrone Means .20
35 Antowain Smith .30
36 Jake Plummer .75
37 Isaac Bruce .20
38 Tony Banks .20
39 Reidel Anthony .20
40 Darren Woodson .10
41 Corey Dillon .50
42 Antonio Freeman .30
43 Eddie George .75
44 Yancey Thigpen .20
45 Tim Brown .20
46 Wayne Chrebet .30
47 Andre Rison .20
48 Michael Strahan .10
49 Deion Sanders .30
50 Eric Moulds .30
51 Mark Brunell .75
52 Rae Carruth .10
53 Warren Sapp .10
54 Mark Chmura .20
55 Darrell Green .10
56 Quinn Early .10
57 Barry Sanders 1.50
58 Neil O'Donnell .20
59 Tony Brackens .10
60 Willie Davis .10
61 Shannon Sharpe .30
62 Shawn Springs .10
63 Tony Gonzalez .10
64 Rodney Thomas .10
65 Terance Mathis .10
66 Brett Favre 2.00
67 Eric Swann .10
68 Kevin Turner .10
69 Tyrone Wheatley .10
70 Trent Dilfer .20
71 Bryan Cox .10
72 Lake Dawson .10
73 Will Blackwell .10
74 Fred Lane .20
75 Ty Detmer .10
76 Eddie Kennison .20
77 Jimmy Smith .30
78 Chris Calloway .10
79 Shawn Jefferson .10
80 Dan Marino 1.50
81 LeRoy Butler .10
82 William Roaf .10
83 Rick Mirer .10
84 Dermontti Dawson .10
85 Errict Rhett .10
86 Lamar Thomas .10
87 Lamar Lathon .10
88 John Randle .10
89 Darryl Williams .10
90 Keenan McCardell .20
91 Erik Kramer .10
92 Ken Dilger .10
93 Dave Meggett .10
94 Jeff Blake .20
95 Ed McCaffrey .20
96 Charles Johnson .20
97 Irving Spikes .10
98 Mike Alstott .30
99 Vincent Brisby .10
100 Michael Westbrook .10
101 Rickey Dudley .10
102 Bert Emanuel .10
103 Daryl Johnston .10
104 Lawrence Phillips .10
105 Eric Bieniemy .10
106 Bryant Westbrook .10
107 Rob Johnson .20
108 Ray Zellars .10
109 Anthony Johnson .10
110 Reggie White .30
111 Wesley Walls .10
112 Amani Toomer .10
113 Gary Brown .10
114 Brian Blades .10
115 Alex Van Dyke .10
116 Michael Haynes .10
117 Jessie Armstead .10
118 James Jett .10
119 Troy Drayton .10
120 Craig Heyward .10
121 Steve Atwater .10
122 Tiki Barber .10
123 Karim Abdul .20
124 Kimble Anders .10
125 Frank Sanders .10
126 David Sloan .10
127 Andre Hastings .10
128 Vinny Testaverde .20
129 Robert Smith .20
130 Horace Copeland .10
131 Larry Centers .10
132 J.J. Stokes .20
133 Ike Hilliard .10
134 Muhsin Muhammad .10
135 Sean Dawkins .10
136 Raymont Harris .10
137 Lamar Smith .10
138 David Palmer .10
139 Steve Young .75
140 Bryan Still .10
141 Keith Byars .10
142 Cris Carter .30
143 Charlie Garner .10
144 Drew Bledsoe 1.00
145 Simeon Rice .10
146 Merton Hanks .10
147 Aeneas Williams .10
148 Rodney Hampton .10
149 Zach Thomas .20
150 Mark Bruener .10
151 Jason Dunn .10
152 Danny Wuerffel .10
153 Jim Druckenmiller .20
154 Greg Hill .10
155 Earnest Byner .10
156 Greg Lloyd .10
157 John Mobley .10
158 Tim Biakabutuka .20
159 Terrell Owens .50
160 O.J. McDuffie .20
161 Glenn Foley .20
162 Derrick Brooks .10
163 Dave Brown .10
164 Ki-Jana Carter .10
165 Bobby Hoying .20
166 Randal Hill .10
167 Michael Irvin .20
168 Bruce Smith .10
169 Troy Davis .10
170 Derrick Mayes .10
171 Henry Ellard .10
172 Dana Stubblefield .10
173 Willie McGinest .10
174 Leeland McElroy .10
175 Edgar Bennett .10
176 Robert Porcher .10
177 Randall Cunningham .30
178 Jim Everett .10
179 Jake Reed .10
180 Quentin Coryatt .10
181 William Floyd .10
182 Jason Sehorn .10
183 Carnell Lake .10
184 Dexter Coakley .10
185 Derrick Alexander .10
186 Johnnie Morton .10
187 Irving Fryar .10
188 Warren Moon .20
189 Todd Collins .10
190 Ken Norton Jr. .10
191 Terry Glenn .20
192 Rashaan Salaam .20
193 Jerry Rice 1.00
194 James Stewart .10
195 David LaFleur .10
196 Eric Green .10
197 Gus Frerotte .20
198 Willie Green .10
199 Marshall Faulk .30
200 Brett Perriman .10
201 Darnay Scott .10
202 Marvin Harrison .20
203 Joe Aska .10
204 Darrien Gordon .10
205 Herman Moore .20
206 Curtis Martin .30
207 Derek Loville .10
208 Dale Carter .10
209 Heath Shuler .10
210 Jonathan Ogden .10
211 Leslie Shepherd .10
212 Tony Boselli .10
213 Eric Metcalf .10
214 Neil Smith .10
215 Anthony Miller .10
216 Jeff George .20
217 Charles Way .10
218 Mario Bates .10
219 Ben Coates .20
220 Michael Jackson .10
221 Thurman Thomas .20
222 Kyle Brady .10
223 Marcus Allen .20
224 Robert Brooks .10
225 Yatil Green .20
226 Byron Hanspard .10
227 Andre Reed .20
228 Chris Warren .10
229 Jackie Harris .10
230 Ricky Watters .20
231 Bobby Engram .10
232 Tamarick Vanover .10
233 *Peyton Manning* 8.00
234 *Curtis Enis* 1.50
235 *Randy Moss* 6.00
236 *Charles Woodson* 2.00
237 *Robert Edwards* 1.00
238 *Jacquez Green* 1.50
239 *Keith Brooking* .50
240 *Jerome Pathon* .50
241 *Kevin Dyson* 1.50
242 *Fred Taylor* 3.00
243 *Tavian Banks* .50
244 *Marcus Nash* .50
245 *Brian Griese* 3.00
246 *Andre Wadsworth* .50
247 *Ahman Green* 6.00
248 *Joe Jurevicius* .50
249 *Germane Crowell* 1.50
250 *Skip Hicks* .75
251 *Ryan Leaf* 1.50
252 *Hines Ward* 3.00
253 John Elway .50
254 Mark Brunell .30
255 Brett Favre 2.00
256 Troy Aikman .50
257 Warrick Dunn .30
258 Barry Sanders 1.00
259 Eddie George .30
260 Kordell Stewart .30
261 Emmitt Smith .75
262 Steve Young .25
263 Terrell Davis .75
264 Dorsey Levens .10
265 Dan Marino .75
266 Jerry Rice .50
267 Drew Bledsoe .30
268 Brett Favre 1.00
269 Barry Sanders 1.00
270 Terrell Davis .75

1998 Score Complete Players

Only 10 of the NFL's all-around athletes are included in this set that has three different cards highlighting three specific attributes on special cards with holographic foil stamping. Singles were inserted 1:11 packs.

NM/M
Complete Set (30): 60.00
Common Player: 1.00
Inserted 1:11
1a Brett Favre 6.00
1b Brett Favre 6.00
1c Brett Favre 6.00
2a John Elway 5.00
2b John Elway 5.00
2c John Elway 5.00
3a Emmitt Smith 5.00
3b Emmitt Smith 5.00
3c Emmitt Smith 5.00
4a Kordell Stewart 1.00
4b Kordell Stewart 1.00
4c Kordell Stewart 1.00
5a Dan Marino 6.00
5b Dan Marino 6.00
5c Dan Marino 6.00
6a Mark Brunell 3.00
6b Mark Brunell 3.00
6c Mark Brunell 3.00
7a Terrell Davis 4.00
7b Terrell Davis 4.00
7c Terrell Davis 4.00
8a Barry Sanders 5.00
8b Barry Sanders 5.00
8c Barry Sanders 5.00
9a Warrick Dunn 1.00
9b Warrick Dunn 1.00
9c Warrick Dunn 1.00
10a Jerry Rice 4.00
10b Jerry Rice 4.00
10c Jerry Rice 4.00

1998 Score Rookie Autographs

The 33-card set includes all of the top rookies from 1998. Each is hand signed and limited to 500.

NM/M
Common Player: 10.00
Minor Stars: 40.00
Production 500 Sets
Stephen Alexander 40.00
Tavian Banks 10.00
Charlie Batch 35.00
Keith Brooking 10.00
Thad Busby 10.00
John Dutton 10.00
Tim Dwight 40.00
Kevin Dyson 40.00
Robert Edwards 40.00
Greg Ellis 10.00
Curtis Enis 10.00
Chris Fuamatu-Ma'afala 30.00
Ahman Green 50.00
Jacquez Green 25.00
Brian Griese 50.00
Skip Hicks 25.00
Robert Holcombe 25.00
Tebucky Jones 10.00
Joe Jurevicius 30.00
Ryan Leaf 10.00
Leonard Little 10.00
Alonzo Mayes 10.00
Michael Myers 10.00
Randy Moss 125.00
Marcus Nash 25.00
Jerome Pathon 25.00
Jason Peter 10.00
Anthony Simmons 10.00
Tony Simmons 10.00
Takeo Spikes 25.00
Duane Starks 10.00
Fred Taylor 75.00
Hines Ward 40.00

1998 Score Star Salute

This set highlights the top 20 players in the NFL and puts each of them on a foil board with micro-etching. Singles were issued 1:35 packs.

NM/M
Complete Set (20): 60.00
Common Player: 1.00
Inserted 1:35
1 Terrell Davis 5.00
2 Barry Sanders 8.00
3 Steve Young 6.00
4 Drew Bledsoe 6.00
5 Kordell Stewart 2.00
6 Emmitt Smith 8.00
7 Dorsey Levens 1.00
8 Corey Dillon 3.00
9 Jerome Bettis 1.00
10 Herman Moore 1.00
11 Brett Favre 10.00
12 Antonio Freeman 5.00
13 Mark Brunell 4.00
14 John Elway 6.00
15 Terry Glenn 1.00
16 Warrick Dunn 3.00
17 Eddie George 3.00
18 Troy Aikman 6.00
19 Deion Sanders 1.00
20 Jerry Rice 6.00

1998 Score Rookie Preview

The 160-card Rookie Preview set was released before the 270-card Score set. The singles are identical to the Score set and included rookie cards of Ryan Leaf and Peyton Manning.

NM/M
Complete Set (160): 20.00
Common Player: .10
Minor Stars: .20
1 John Elway 1.00
2 Kordell Stewart .75
3 Warrick Dunn .75
7 Emmitt Smith 1.50
11 Rod Smith .20
12 Dorsey Levens .20
13 Steve McNair .50
16 Peter Boulware .10
18 Joey Galloway .30
19 Jerome Bettis .20
20 Carl Pickens .20
21 Napoleon Kaufman .30
22 Troy Aikman 1.00
24 Adrian Murrell .10
25 Elvis Grbac .10
27 Chris Sanders .10
28 Scott Mitchell .10
29 Junior Seau .20
30 Chris Chandler .10
31 Kevin Hardy .10
32 Terrell Davis 1.50
35 Antowain Smith .30
36 Jake Plummer .75
37 Isaac Bruce .20
38 Tony Banks .20
40 Darren Woodson .10
41 Corey Dillon .50
42 Antonio Freeman .30
43 Eddie George .75
48 Michael Strahan .10
51 Mark Brunell .75
56 Quinn Early .10
57 Barry Sanders 2.00
58 Neil O'Donnell .10
59 Tony Brackens .10
60 Willie Davis .10
61 Shannon Sharpe .20
62 Shawn Springs .10
63 Tony Gonzalez .10
64 Rodney Thomas .10
65 Terance Mathis .10
66 Brett Favre 2.00
68 Kevin Turner .10
69 Tyrone Wheatley .10
70 Trent Dilfer .20
71 Bryan Cox .10
72 Lake Dawson .10
74 Fred Lane .10
75 Ty Detmer .10
76 Eddie Kennison .10
78 Chris Calloway .10
79 Shawn Jefferson .10
80 Dan Marino 1.50
81 LeRoy Butler .10
82 William Roaf .10
83 Rick Mirer .10
84 Dermontti Dawson .10
86 Lamar Thomas .10
87 Lamar Lathon .10
88 John Randle .10
89 Darryl Williams .10
91 Erik Kramer .10
92 Ken Dilger .10
93 Dave Meggett .10
94 Jeff Blake .20
97 Irving Spikes .10
98 Mike Alstott .30
99 Vincent Brisby .10
101 Rickey Dudley .10
102 Bert Emanuel .10
105 Eric Bieniemy .10
106 Bryant Westbrook .10
108 Ray Zellars .10
110 Reggie White .20
111 Wesley Walls .10
113 Gary Brown .10
114 Brian Blades .10
115 Alex Van Dyke .10
116 Michael Haynes .10
117 Jessie Armstead .10
118 James Jett .10
119 Troy Drayton .10
120 Craig Heyward .10
121 Steve Atwater .10
123 Karim Abdul .20
125 Frank Sanders .10
126 David Sloan .10
127 Andre Hastings .10
130 Horace Copeland .10
135 Sean Dawkins .10
137 Lamar Smith .10
138 David Palmer .10
139 Steve Young .75
140 Bryan Still .10
141 Keith Byars .10
142 Cris Carter .30
144 Drew Bledsoe 1.00
145 Simeon Rice .10
146 Merton Hanks .10
147 Aeneas Williams .10
148 Rodney Hampton .10
149 Zach Thomas .10
150 Mark Bruener .10
151 Jason Dunn .10
155 Earnest Byner .10
156 Greg Lloyd .10
157 John Mobley .10
160 O.J. McDuffie .20
161 Glenn Foley .20
162 Derrick Brooks .10
163 Dave Brown .10
166 Randal Hill .10
167 Michael Irvin .20
168 Bruce Smith .10
170 Derrick Mayes .10
171 Henry Ellard .10
172 Dana Stubblefield .10
173 Willie McGinest .10
175 Edgar Bennett .10
176 Robert Porcher .10
177 Randall Cunningham .30
178 Jim Everett .10
180 Quentin Coryatt .10
181 William Floyd .10
182 Jason Sehorn .10
183 Carnell Lake .10
184 Dexter Coakley .10
185 Derrick Alexander .10
186 Johnnie Morton .10
188 Warren Moon .20
189 Todd Collins .10
190 Ken Norton Jr. .10
191 Terry Glenn .30
193 Jerry Rice 1.00
194 James Stewart .10
196 Eric Green .10
198 Willie Green .10
200 Brett Perriman .10
201 Darnay Scott .10
203 Joe Aska .10
204 Darrien Gordon .10
205 Herman Moore .20
206 Curtis Martin .50
207 Derek Loville .10
208 Dale Carter .10
209 Heath Shuler .20
210 Jonathan Ogden .10
211 Leslie Shepherd .10
212 Tony Boselli .10
213 Eric Metcalf .10
214 Neil Smith .10
215 Anthony Miller .10
216 Jeff George .20
217 Charles Way .10
218 Mario Bates .10
222 Kyle Brady .10
228 Chris Warren .10
229 Jackie Harris .10
233 *Peyton Manning* 8.00
251 *Ryan Leaf* 1.00

1998 Score Rookie Preview Star Salute

Singles from this set were printed on silver foil stock and inserted 1:35 packs.

NM/M
Complete Set (20): 50.00
Common Player: 1.00
1 Terrell Davis 5.00
2 Barry Sanders 8.00
3 Steve Young 5.00
4 Drew Bledsoe 5.00
5 Kordell Stewart 3.00
6 Emmitt Smith 8.00
7 Dorsey Levens 1.00
8 Corey Dillon 1.00
9 Jerome Bettis 1.00
10 Herman Moore 1.00
11 Brett Favre 10.00
12 Antonio Freeman 1.00
13 Mark Brunell 4.00
14 John Elway 6.00
15 Terry Glenn 1.00
16 Warrick Dunn 3.00
17 Eddie George 3.00
18 Troy Aikman 6.00
19 Deion Sanders 1.00
20 Jerry Rice 6.00

1999 Score

This is a 275-card set that had 55 short-printed cards found 1:3 hobby packs and 1:9 retail packs. The short-prints were of 40 Rookies, 10 All-Pros and 5 Great Combos. The base set is divided into three colors like the first set was in 1989. Red, blue and green borders with the short- prints in green. Inserts include: Showcase, Artist's Proofs, Reprints, Reprint Autographs, Complete Players, Franchise, Future Franchise, Millenium Men, Numbers Game, Rookie Preview Autographs, Scoring Core and Settle the Score.

NM/M
Complete Set (275): 75.00
Common Player: .10
Minor Stars: .20
Common Rookie (221-260): 1.00
Common All-Pros (261-270): 1.00
Inserted 1:3
Hobby Pack (10): 1.00
Hobby Wax Box (36): 25.00
Retail Pack (10): 1.00
Retail Wax Box (36): 25.00
1 Randy Moss 2.50
2 Randall Cunningham .50
3 Cris Carter .50
4 Robert Smith .20
5 Jake Reed .10
6 Leroy Hoard .10
7 John Randle .10
8 Brett Favre 2.00
9 Antonio Freeman .50
10 Dorsey Levens .20
11 Robert Brooks .20
12 Derrick Mayes .10
13 Mark Chmura .20
14 Darick Holmes .10
15 Vonnie Holliday .20
16 Mike Alstott .50
17 Warrick Dunn .75
18 Trent Dilfer .20
19 Jacquez Green .20
20 Reidel Anthony .20
21 Warren Sapp .10
22 Bert Emanuel .10
23 Curtis Enis .50
24 Curtis Conway .20
25 Bobby Engram .10
26 Erik Kramer .10
27 Moses Moreno .10
28 Edgar Bennett .10
29 Barry Sanders 2.00
30 Charlie Batch .75
31 Herman Moore .50
32 Johnnie Morton .10
33 Germane Crowell .20
34 Terry Fair .10
35 Gary Brown .10
36 Kent Graham .10
37 Kerry Collins .20
38 Charles Way .10
39 Tiki Barber .20
40 Ike Hilliard .10
41 Joe Jurevicius .20
42 Michael Strahan .10
43 Jason Sehorn .10
44 Brad Johnson .50
45 Terry Allen .20
46 Skip Hicks .50
47 Michael Westbrook .20
48 Leslie Shepherd .10
49 Stephen Alexander .10
50 Albert Connell .10
51 Darrell Green .10
52 Jake Plummer 1.00
53 Adrian Murrell .20
54 Frank Sanders .20
55 Rob Moore .20
56 Larry Centers .10
57 Simeon Rice .10
58 Andre Wadsworth .20
59 Duce Staley .10
60 Charles Johnson .10
61 Charlie Garner .10
62 Bobby Hoying .20
63 Darryl Johnston .10
64 Emmitt Smith 1.50
65 Troy Aikman 1.00
66 Michael Irvin .20
67 Deion Sanders .50
68 Chris Warren .20
69 Darren Woodson .10
70 Rod Woodson .10
71 Travis Jervey .10
72 Jerry Rice 1.00
73 Terrell Owens .50
74 Steve Young .75
75 Garrison Hearst .20
76 J.J. Stokes .20
77 Ken Norton .10
78 R.W. McQuarters .10
79 Bryant Young .10
80 Jamal Anderson .50
81 Chris Chandler .20
82 Terrance Mathis .10
83 Tim Dwight .50
84 O.J. Santiago .10
85 Chris Calloway .10
86 Keith Brooking .10
87 Eddie Kennison .10
88 Willie Roaf .10
89 Cameron Cleeland .20
90 Lamar Smith .10
91 Sean Dawkins .10
92 Tim Biakabutuka .20
93 Muhsin Muhammad .10
94 Steve Beuerlein .10
95 Rae Carruth .10
96 Wesley Walls .10
97 Kevin Greene .10
98 Trent Green .50
99 Tony Banks .20
100 Greg Hill .10
101 Robert Holcombe .20
102 Isaac Bruce .30
103 Amp Lee .10
104 Az-Zahir Hakim .20
105 Warren Moon .20
106 Jeff George .20
107 Raghib Ismail .10
108 Kordell Stewart .75
109 Jerome Bettis .20
110 Courtney Hawkins .10
111 Chris Fuamatu-Ma'afala .20
112 Levon Kirkland .10
113 Hines Ward .20
114 Will Blackwell .10
115 Corey Dillon .50
116 Carl Pickens .20
117 Neil O'Donnell .20
118 Jeff Blake .20
119 Darnay Scott .20
120 Takeo Spikes .10
121 Steve McNair .75
122 Frank Wycheck .10
123 Eddie George .75
124 Chris Sanders .10
125 Yancy Thigpen .20
126 Kevin Dyson .20
127 Blaine Bishop .10
128 Fred Taylor .50
129 Mark Brunell .75
130 Jimmy Smith .20
131 Keenan McCardell .10
132 Kyle Brady .10
133 Tavian Banks .20
134 James Stewart .10
135 Kevin Hardy .10
136 Jonathan Quinn .10
137 Jermaine Lewis .20
138 Priest Holmes .50
139 Scott Mitchell .20
140 Eric Zeier .10
141 Patrick Johnson .20
142 Ray Lewis .10
143 Terry Kirby .10
144 Ty Detmer .10
145 Irv Smith .10
146 Chris Spielman .10
147 Antonio Langham .10
148 Dan Marino 1.50
149 O.J. McDuffie .20
150 Oronde Gadsden .20
151 Karim Abdul .30
152 Yatil Green .10
153 Zach Thomas .20
154 John Avery .20
155 Lamar Thomas .10
156 Drew Bledsoe .75
157 Terry Glenn .30
158 Ben Coates .20
159 Shawn Jefferson .10
160 Cedric Shaw .10
161 Tony Simmons .20
162 Ty Law .10
163 Robert Edwards .30
164 Curtis Martin .50
165 Keyshawn Johnson .50
166 Vinny Testaverde .20
167 Aaron Glenn .10
168 Wayne Chrebet .30
169 Dedric Ward .10
170 Peyton Manning 1.50
171 Marshall Faulk .50
172 Marvin Harrison .20
173 Jerome Pathon .20
174 Ken Dilger .10
175 E.G. Green .20
176 Doug Flutie .75
177 Thurman Thomas .20
178 Andre Reed .20
179 Eric Moulds .50
180 Antowain Smith .30
181 Bruce Smith .10
182 Rob Johnson .20
183 Terrell Davis 1.50
184 John Elway 1.50
185 Ed McCaffrey .20
186 Rod Smith .20
187 Shannon Sharpe .20
188 Marcus Nash .20
189 Brian Griese .50
190 Neil Smith .10
191 Bubby Brister .20
192 Ryan Leaf .50
193 Natrone Means .50
194 Mikhael Ricks .20
195 Junior Seau .20
196 Jim Harbaugh .20
197 Bryan Still .10
198 Freddie Jones .10
199 Andre Rison .20
200 Elvis Grbac .20
201 Bam Morris .20
202 Rashaan Shehee .10
203 Kimble Anders .10
204 Donnell Bennett .10
205 Tony Gonzalez .20
206 Derrick Alexander .10
207 Jon Kitna .50
208 Ricky Watters .20
209 Joey Galloway .50
210 Ahman Green .20
211 Shawn Springs .10
212 Michael Sinclair .10
213 Napoleon Kaufman .50
214 Tim Brown .20
215 Charles Woodson .50
216 Harvey Williams .10
217 Jon Ritchie .10
218 Rich Gannon .10
219 Rickey Dudley .20
220 James Jett .10
221 *Tim Couch* 5.00
222 *Ricky Williams* 5.00
223 *Donovan McNabb* 10.00
224 *Edgerrin James* 10.00
225 *Torry Holt* 5.00
226 *Daunte Culpepper* 10.00
227 *Akili Smith* 2.00
228 *Champ Bailey* 3.00
229 *Chris Claiborne* 2.50
230 *Chris McAlister* 2.00
231 *Troy Edwards* 3.00
232 *Jevon Kearse* 3.00
233 *Shaun King* 3.00
234 *David Boston* 5.00
235 *Peerless Price* 4.00
236 *Cecil Collins* 3.00
237 *Rob Konrad* 2.00
238 *Cade McNown* 3.00
239 *Shawn Bryson* 1.00
240 *Kevin Faulk* 3.00
241 *Scott Covington* 2.00
242 *James Johnson* 3.00
243 *Mike Cloud* 2.00
244 *Aaron Brooks* 7.00
245 *Sedrick Irvin* 3.00
246 *Amos Zereoue* 4.00
247 *Jermaine Fazande* 1.00
248 *Joe Germaine* 3.00
249 *Brock Huard* 3.00
250 *Craig Yeast* 1.00
251 *Travis McGriff* 2.00
252 *D'Wayne Bates* 2.00
253 *Na Brown* 1.00
254 *Tai Streets* 2.00
255 *Andy Katzenmoyer* 2.00
256 *Kevin Johnson* 3.00
257 *Joe Montgomery* 2.00
258 *Karsten Bailey* 2.00
259 *De'Mond Parker* 2.00
260 *Reg Kelly* 1.00
261 Eddie George 2.00
262 Jamal Anderson 1.00
263 Barry Sanders 3.00
264 Fred Taylor 1.00
265 Keyshawn Johnson 1.00
266 Jerry Rice 3.50
267 Doug Flutie 2.50
268 Deion Sanders 1.00
269 Randall Cunningham 1.00
270 Steve Young 2.50
271 Terrell Davis, John Elway 5.00
272 Marshall Faulk, Peyton Manning 4.00
273 Brett Favre, Antonio Freeman 5.00
274 Troy Aikman, Emmitt Smith 4.00
275 Cris Carter, Randy Moss 5.00

1999 Score Anniversary Showcase

This is a parallel to the base with each card the same except for a gold foil border around the photo and a gold foil stamp on the front. The backs are sequentially numbered to 1989 and say Anniversary Showcase next to it.

NM/M
Showcase Cards: 3X-6X
Showcase Rookies: 1.5X
Showcase AP/GC: 2X
Production 1,989 Sets
1 Randy Moss 15.00
2 Randall Cunningham .10
3 Cris Carter .10
4 Robert Smith .10
5 Jake Reed .10
6 Leroy Hoard .10
7 John Randle .10
8 Brett Favre .10
9 Antonio Freeman .10
10 Dorsey Levens .10
11 Robert Brooks .10
12 Derrick Mayes .10
13 Mark Chmura .10
14 Darick Holmes .10
15 Vonnie Holliday .10
16 Mike Alstott .10
17 Warrick Dunn .10
18 Trent Dilfer .10
19 Jacquez Green .10
20 Reidel Anthony .10
21 Warren Sapp .10
22 Bert Emanuel .10
23 Curtis Enis .10
24 Curtis Conway .10
25 Bobby Engram .10
26 Erik Kramer .10
27 Moses Moreno .10
28 Edgar Bennett .10
29 Barry Sanders .10
30 Charlie Batch .10
31 Herman Moore .10
32 Johnnie Morton .10
33 Germane Crowell .10
34 Terry Fair .10
35 Gary Brown .10
36 Kent Graham .10
37 Kerry Collins .10
38 Charles Way .10

39 Tiki Barber .10
40 Ike Hilliard .10
41 Joe Jurevicius .10
42 Michael Strahan .10
43 Jason Sehorn .10
44 Brad Johnson .10
45 Terry Allen .10
46 Skip Hicks .10
47 Michael Westbrook .10
48 Leslie Shepherd .10
49 Stephen Alexander .10
50 Albert Connell .10
51 Darrell Green .10
52 Jake Plummer .10
53 Adrian Murrell .10
54 Frank Sanders .10
55 Rob Moore .10
56 Larry Centers .10
57 Simeon Rice .10
58 Andre Wadsworth .10
59 Duce Staley .10
60 Charles Johnson .10
61 Charlie Garner .10
62 Bobby Hoying .10
63 Darryl Johnston .10
64 Emmitt Smith .10
65 Troy Aikman .10
66 Michael Irvin .10
67 Deion Sanders .10
68 Chris Warren .10
69 Darren Woodson .10
70 Rod Woodson .10
71 Travis Jervey .10
72 Jerry Rice .10
73 Terrell Owens .10
74 Steve Young .10
75 Garrison Hearst .10
76 J.J. Stokes .10
77 Ken Norton .10
78 R.W. McQuarters .10
79 Bryant Young .10
80 Jamal Anderson .10
81 Chris Chandler .10
82 Terrance Mathis .10
83 Tim Dwight .10
84 O.J. Santiago .10
85 Chris Calloway .10
86 Keith Brooking .10
87 Eddie Kennison .10
88 Willie Roaf .10
89 Cameron Cleeland .10
90 Lamar Smith .10
91 Sean Dawkins .10
92 Tim Biakabutuka .10
93 Muhsin Muhammad .10
94 Steve Beuerlein .10
95 Rae Carruth .10
96 Wesley Walls .10
97 Kevin Greene .10
98 Trent Green .10
99 Tony Banks .10
100 Greg Hill .10
101 Robert Holcombe .10
102 Isaac Bruce .10
103 Amp Lee .10
104 Az-Zahir Hakim .10
105 Warren Moon .10
106 Jeff George .10
107 Raghib Ismail .10
108 Kordell Stewart .10
109 Jerome Bettis .10
110 Courtney Hawkins .10
111 Chris Fuamatu-Ma'afala .10
112 Levon Kirkland .10
113 Hines Ward .10
114 Will Blackwell .10
115 Corey Dillon .10
116 Carl Pickens .10
117 Neil O'Donnell .10
118 Jeff Blake .10
119 Darnay Scott .10
120 Takeo Spikes .10
121 Steve McNair .10
122 Frank Wycheck .10
123 Eddie George .10
124 Chris Sanders .10
125 Yancy Thigpen .10
126 Kevin Dyson .10
127 Blaine Bishop .10
128 Fred Taylor .10
129 Mark Brunell .10
130 Jimmy Smith .10
131 Keenan McCardell .10
132 Kyle Brady .10
133 Tavian Banks .10
134 James Stewart .10
135 Kevin Hardy .10
136 Jonathan Quinn .10
137 Jermaine Lewis .10
138 Priest Holmes .10
139 Scott Mitchell .10
140 Eric Zeier .10
141 Patrick Johnson .10
142 Ray Lewis .10
143 Terry Kirby .10
144 Ty Detmer .10
145 Irv Smith .10
146 Chris Spielman .10
147 Antonio Langham .10
148 Dan Marino .10
149 O.J. McDuffie .10
150 Oronde Gadsden .10
151 Karim Abdul .10
152 Yatil Green .10
153 Zach Thomas .10
154 John Avery .10
155 Lamar Thomas .10
156 Drew Bledsoe .10
157 Terry Glenn .10
158 Ben Coates .10
159 Shawn Jefferson .10
160 Cedric Shaw .10
161 Tony Simmons .10
162 Ty Law .10
163 Robert Edwards .10
164 Curtis Martin .10
165 Keyshawn Johnson .10
166 Vinny Testaverde .10
167 Aaron Glenn .10
168 Wayne Chrebet .10
169 Dedric Ward .10
170 Peyton Manning 10.00
171 Marshall Faulk .10
172 Marvin Harrison .10
173 Jerome Pathon .10
174 Ken Dilger .10
175 E.G. Green .10
176 Doug Flutie .10
177 Thurman Thomas .10
178 Andre Reed .10
179 Eric Moulds .10
180 Antowain Smith .10
181 Bruce Smith .10
182 Rob Johnson .10
183 Terrell Davis .10
184 John Elway .10
185 Ed McCaffrey .10
186 Rod Smith .10
187 Shannon Sharpe .10
188 Marcus Nash .10
189 Brian Griese .10
190 Neil Smith .10
191 Bubby Brister .10
192 Ryan Leaf .10
193 Natrone Means .10
194 Mikhael Ricks .10
195 Junior Seau .10
196 Jim Harbaugh .10
197 Bryan Still .10
198 Freddie Jones .10
199 Andre Rison .10
200 Elvis Grbac .10
201 Bam Morris .10
202 Rashaan Shehee .10
203 Kimble Anders .10
204 Donnell Bennett .10
205 Tony Gonzalez .10
206 Derrick Alexander .10
207 Jon Kitna .10
208 Ricky Watters .10
209 Joey Galloway .10
210 Ahman Green .10
211 Shawn Springs .10
212 Michael Sinclair .10
213 Napoleon Kaufman .10
214 Tim Brown .10
215 Charles Woodson .10
216 Harvey Williams .10
217 Jon Ritchie .10
218 Rich Gannon .10
219 Rickey Dudley .10
220 James Jett .10
221 *Tim Couch* .10
222 *Ricky Williams* .10
223 *Donovan McNabb* .10
224 *Edgerrin James* .10
225 *Torry Holt* .10
226 *Daunte Culpepper* .10
227 *Akili Smith* .10
228 *Champ Bailey* .10
229 *Chris Claiborne* .10
230 *Chris McAlister* .10
231 *Troy Edwards* .10
232 *Jevon Kearse* .10
233 *Shaun King* .10
234 *David Boston* .10
235 *Peerless Price* .10
236 *Cecil Collins* .10
237 *Rob Konrad* .10
238 *Cade McNown* .10
239 *Shawn Bryson* .10
240 *Kevin Faulk* .10
241 *Scott Covington* .10
242 *James Johnson* .10
243 *Mike Cloud* .10
244 *Aaron Brooks* .10
245 *Sedrick Irvin* .10
246 *Amos Zereoue* .10
247 *Jermaine Fazande* .10
248 *Joe Germaine* .10
249 *Brock Huard* .10
250 *Craig Yeast* .10
251 *Travis McGriff* .10
252 *D'Wayne Bates* .10
253 *Na Brown* .10
254 *Tai Streets* .10
255 *Marty Booker* .10
256 *Kevin Johnson* .10
257 *Joe Montgomery* .10
258 *Karsten Bailey* .10
259 *De'Mond Parker* .10
260 *Reg Kelly* .10
261 Eddie George .10
262 Jamal Anderson .10
263 Barry Sanders .10
264 Fred Taylor .10
265 Keyshawn Johnson .10
266 Jerry Rice .10
267 Doug Flutie .10
268 Deion Sanders .10
269 Randall Cunningham .10
270 Steve Young .10
271 Terrell Davis, John Elway .10
272 Marshall Faulk, Peyton Manning 25.00
273 Brett Favre, Antonio Freeman .10
274 Troy Aikman, Emmitt Smith .10
275 Cris Carter, Randy Moss 20.00

1999 Score Anniversary Artist Proof

This is a parallel to the base and each card is sequentially numbered to 10.

Production 10 Sets

A card number in parenthese ( ) indicates the set is unnumbered.

1999 Score 1989 Score Reprints

This was a 20-card reprint of the 1989 Score cards that included all of the top rookies and stars from the premiere release. These were only found in hobby product and were sequentially numbered to 1989. The first 150 of each card were autographed.

		NM/M
Complete Set (20):		45.00
Common Player:		1.00
Production 1,989 Sets		
1	Barry Sanders	8.00
2	Troy Aikman	6.00
3	John Elway	6.00
4	Cris Carter	4.00
5	Tim Brown	4.00
6	Doug Flutie	2.00
7	Chris Chandler	1.00
8	Thurman Thomas	1.00
9	Steve Young	6.00
10	Dan Marino	10.00
11	Derrick Thomas	1.00
12	Bubby Brister	1.00
13	Jerry Rice	6.00
14	Andre Rison	1.00
15	Randall Cunningham	2.00
16	Vinny Testaverde	1.00
17	Michael Irvin	1.00
18	Rod Woodson	1.00
19	Neil Smith	1.00
20	Deion Sanders	3.00

1999 Score 1989 Score Reprints Autographs

These are the same cards as the Reprint set except for each is autographed and has the words "Authentic Signature" down the side of the fronts of the cards. Only 150 of each were signed.

		NM/M
Common Player:		30.00
Production 150 Sets		
1	Barry Sanders	275.00
2	Troy Aikman	200.00
3	John Elway	225.00
4	Cris Carter	50.00
5	Tim Brown	50.00
6	Doug Flutie	40.00
7	Chris Chandler	30.00
8	Thurman Thomas	40.00
9	Steve Young	85.00
10	Dan Marino	225.00
11	Derrick Thomas	30.00
12	Bubby Brister	30.00
13	Jerry Rice	175.00
14	Andre Rison	30.00
15	Randall Cunningham	40.00
16	Vinny Testaverde	30.00
17	Michael Irvin	40.00
18	Rod Woodson	30.00
19	Neil Smith	30.00
20	Deion Sanders	60.00

1999 Score Complete Players

These singles were found in both hobby (1:17) and retail (1:35) product. Each of the 30 cards are printed on foil board with foil stamping and have one large color photo of the player on the front along with four smaller shots in black and white on the side.

		NM/M
Complete Set (30):		50.00
Common Player:		1.00
Minor Stars:		2.00
Inserted 1:17		
1	Antonio Freeman	1.00
2	Troy Aikman	3.00
3	Jerry Rice	4.00
4	Brett Favre	5.00
5	Cris Carter	1.00
6	Jamal Anderson	1.00
7	John Elway	4.00
8	Mark Brunell	2.00
9	Steve McNair	2.00
10	Kordell Stewart	2.00
11	Drew Bledsoe	3.00
12	Tim Couch	5.00
13	Dan Marino	5.00
14	Akili Smith	2.00
15	Peyton Manning	4.00
16	Jake Plummer	2.00
17	Jerome Bettis	1.00
18	Randy Moss	4.00
19	Keyshawn Johnson	1.00
20	Barry Sanders	5.00
21	Ricky Williams	5.00
22	Emmitt Smith	4.00
23	Corey Dillon	1.00
24	Dorsey Levens	1.00
25	Donovan McNabb	4.00
26	Curtis Martin	1.00
27	Eddie George	2.00
28	Fred Taylor	2.00
29	Steve Young	3.00
30	Terrell Davis	3.00

1999 Score Franchise

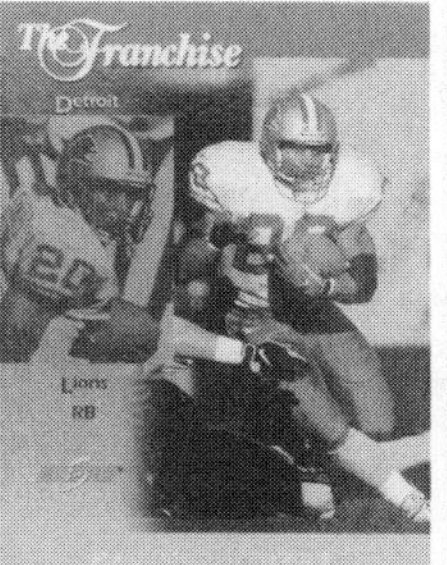

This 31-card set was a retail exclusive (1:35) and picked a star player from each team. Each card is printed on holographic foil board and has a large color photo of the player on the front along with a smaller black and white next to it.

		NM/M
Complete Set (31):		65.00
Common Player:		1.00
Minor Stars:		2.00
Inserted 1:35		
1	Brett Favre	6.00
2	Randy Moss	5.00
3	Mike Alstott	2.00
4	Barry Sanders	5.00
5	Curtis Enis	1.00
6	Ike Hilliard	1.00
7	Emmitt Smith	5.00
8	Jake Plummer	2.00
9	Brad Johnson	1.00
10	Duce Staley	1.00
11	Jamal Anderson	2.00
12	Steve Young	4.00
13	Eddie Kennison	1.00
14	Isaac Bruce	2.00
15	Muhsin Muhammad	1.00
16	Dan Marino	6.00
17	Drew Bledsoe	4.00
18	Curtis Martin	2.00
19	Doug Flutie	2.00
20	Peyton Manning	5.00
21	Kordell Stewart	2.00
22	Ty Detmer	1.00
23	Corey Dillon	2.00
24	Mark Brunell	2.00
25	Priest Holmes	2.00
26	Eddie George	2.00
27	John Elway	4.00
28	Natrone Means	1.00
29	Tim Brown	2.00
30	Andre Rison	1.00
31	Joey Galloway	2.00

1999 Score Future Franchise

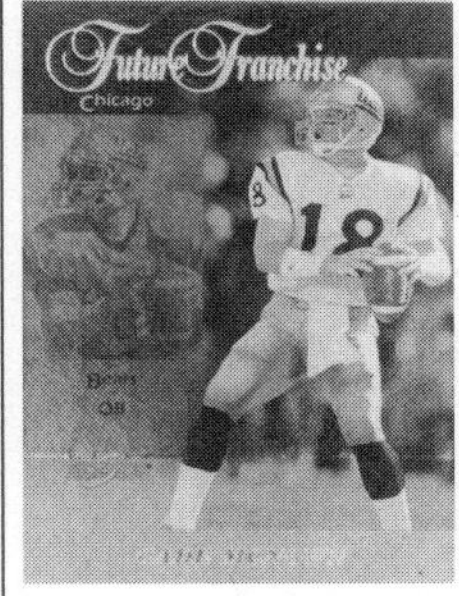

This 31-card set was a hobby exclusive and included a rookie on one side and a star player on the other from the same team. Singles were found 1:35 packs and each were printed on holographic foil board.

		NM/M
Complete Set (31):		80.00
Common Player:		1.00
Minor Stars:		2.00
Inserted 1:35		
1	Aaron Brooks, Brett Favre	6.00
2	Daunte Culpepper, Randy Moss	6.00
3	Shaun King, Mike Alstott	1.00
4	Sedrick Irvin, Barry Sanders	5.00
5	Cade McNown, Curtis Enis	1.00
6	Joe Montgomery, Ike Hilliard	1.00
7	Wayne McGarity, Emmitt Smith	5.00
8	David Boston, Jake Plummer	2.00
9	Champ Bailey, Brad Johnson	2.00
10	Donovan McNabb, Duce Staley	3.00
11	Reg Kelly, Jamal Anderson	1.00
12	Tai Streets, Steve Young	4.00
13	Ricky Williams, Eddie Kennison	6.00
14	Torry Holt, Isaac Bruce	3.00
15	Mike Rucker, Muhsin Muhammad	1.00
16	James Johnson, Dan Marino	6.00
17	Kevin Faulk, Drew Bledsoe	4.00
18	Randy Thomas, Curtis Martin	2.00
19	Peerless Price, Doug Flutie	4.00
20	Edgerrin James, Peyton Manning	6.00
21	Troy Edwards, Kordell Stewart	3.00
22	Tim Couch, Ty Detmer	6.00
23	Akili Smith, Corey Dillon	3.00
24	Fernando Bryant, Mark Brunell	3.00
25	Chris McAlister, Priest Holmes	3.00
26	Jevon Kearse, Eddie George	3.00
27	Travis McGriff, John Elway	5.00
28	Jermaine Fazande, Natrone Means	1.00
29	Dameane Douglas, Tim Brown	3.00
30	Mike Cloud, Andre Rison	1.00
31	Brock Huard, Joey Galloway	2.00

1999 Score Millenium Men

The Millennium Men set has Barry Sanders, representing ten years of NFL excellence with Ricky Williams, representing the outstanding future generation of running backs. Each player has an individual card and a back-to-back single in this 3-card set. Each is sequentially numbered to 1,000 and the first 100 of each are autographed. These were only found in retail product.

		NM/M
Complete Set (3):		40.00
Common Player:		15.00
Production 1,000 Sets		
1	Barry Sanders	20.00
2	Ricky Williams	15.00
3	Barry Sanders, Ricky Williams	20.00
1AU	Barry Sanders AUTO	275.00
2AU	Ricky Williams AUTO	275.00
3AU	Barry Sanders, Ricky Williams AUTO	400.00

1999 Score Numbers Game

This was a 30-card set that was printed on holographic foil board with gold foil stamping. Each card is sequentially numbered to the player's specific stat.

		NM/M
Complete Set (30):		55.00
Common Player:		1.00
Numbered to Stat		
1	Brett Favre 4212	5.00
2	Steve Young 4170	3.00
3	Jake Plummer 3737	2.00
4	Drew Bledsoe 3633	3.00
5	Dan Marino 3497	5.00
6	Peyton Manning 3739	4.00
7	Randall Cunningham 3704	1.00
8	John Elway 2806	4.00
9	Doug Flutie 2711	1.00
10	Mark Brunell 2601	2.00
11	Troy Aikman 2330	4.00
12	Terrell Davis 2008	4.00
13	Jamal Anderson 1846	1.00
14	Garrison Hearst 1570	1.00
15	Barry Sanders 1491	4.00
16	Emmitt Smith 1332	4.00
17	Marshall Faulk 1319	3.00
18	Eddie George 1294	2.00
19	Curtis Martin 1287	3.00
20	Fred Taylor 1223	2.00
21	Corey Dillon 1130	2.00
22	Antonio Freeman 1424	1.00
23	Eric Moulds 1368	2.00
24	Randy Moss 1313	4.00
25	Rod Smith 1222	1.00
26	Jerry Rice 1157	4.00
27	Keyshawn Johnson 1131	2.00
28	Terrell Owens 1097	3.00
29	Tim Brown 1012	1.00
30	Cris Carter 1011	2.00

1999 Score Rookie Preview Autographs

Each of these singles were randomly inserted into hobby packs with each player signing a total of 600 cards. Each card is printed on foil board with the signature on the bottom of the card.

	NM/M
Common Player:	10.00
Minor Stars:	20.00
Production 600 Sets	
Ricky Williams	50.00
Donovan McNabb	50.00
Edgerrin James	60.00
Torry Holt	40.00
Daunte Culpepper	50.00
Akili Smith	25.00
Champ Bailey	20.00
Chris Claiborne	10.00
Chris McAlister	10.00
Troy Edwards	20.00
Jevon Kearse	25.00
David Boston	40.00
Peerless Price	40.00
Cecil Collins	20.00
Rob Konrad	10.00
Cade McNown	20.00
Shawn Bryson	10.00
Kevin Faulk	20.00
Corby Jones	10.00
James Johnson	10.00
Mike Cloud	10.00
Autrey Denson	10.00
Sedrick Irvin	30.00
Michael Bishop	10.00

	Joe Germaine	10.00
	De'Mond Parker	20.00
	Shaun King	20.00
	D'Wayne Bates	20.00
	Na Brown	10.00
	Tai Streets	25.00
	Kevin Johnson	30.00
	Jim Kleinsasser	20.00
	Darnell McDonald	10.00
	Travis McGriff	10.00

1999 Score Scoring Core

Scoring Core's holographic foil design highlights 30 players who find their way into the end zone. Singles were found 1:17 hobby packs and 1:35 retail.

		NM/M
Complete Set (30):		50.00
Common Player:		1.00
Minor Stars:		2.00
Inserted 1:17		
1	Antonio Freeman	1.00
2	Troy Aikman	4.00
3	Jerry Rice	4.00
4	Brett Favre	5.00
5	Cris Carter	1.00
6	Jamal Anderson	1.00
7	John Elway	4.00
8	Tim Brown	2.00
9	Mark Brunell	2.00
10	Terrell Owens	3.00
11	Drew Bledsoe	3.00
12	Tim Couch	4.00
13	Dan Marino	5.00
14	Marshall Faulk	2.00
15	Peyton Manning	4.00
16	Jake Plummer	2.00
17	Jerome Bettis	2.00
18	Randy Moss	4.00
19	Charlie Batch	1.00
20	Barry Sanders	4.00
21	Ricky Williams	5.00
22	Emmitt Smith	4.00
23	Joey Galloway	1.00
24	Herman Moore	1.00
25	Natrone Means	1.00
26	Mike Alstott	1.00
27	Eddie George	2.00
28	Fred Taylor	2.00
29	Steve Young	4.00
30	Terrell Davis	4.00

1999 Score Settle the Score

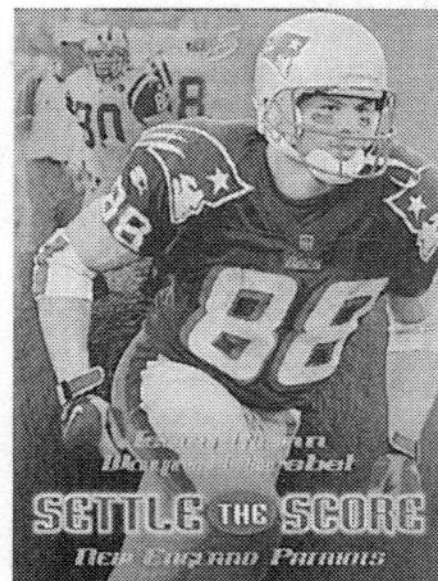

This retail exclusive insert is a dual-sided foil set that matches two players who need to settle the score between each other. Singles were inserted 1:17 packs.

		NM/M
Complete Set (30):		50.00
Common Player:		1.00
Minor Stars:		2.00
Inserted 1:17 Retail		
1	Randall Cunningham, Brett Favre	5.00
2	Doug Flutie, Dan Marino	5.00
3	Terry Allen, Emmitt Smith	4.00
4	Warrick Dunn, Barry Sanders	4.00
5	Corey Dillon, Eddie George	2.00
6	Drew Bledsoe, Vinny Testaverde	3.00
7	Troy Aikman, Jake Plummer	3.00
8	Jamal Anderson, Terrell Davis	3.00
9	Chris Chandler, John Elway	4.00
10	Mark Brunell, Steve Young	3.00
11	Cris Carter, Herman Moore	1.00
12	Steve McNair, Kordell Stewart	2.00
13	Napoleon Kaufman, Natrone Means	1.00
14	Marshall Faulk, Curtis Martin	3.00
15	Antonio Freeman, Terrell Owens	2.00
16	Wayne Chrebet, Terry Glenn	1.00
17	Garrison Hearst, Dorsey Levens	1.00
18	Jon Kitna, Ryan Leaf	1.00
19	Mike Alstott, Robert Smith	1.00
20	Randy Moss, Jerry Rice	5.00
21	Charlie Batch, Peyton Manning	4.00
22	Jerome Bettis, Fred Taylor	2.00
23	Keyshawn Johnson, Eric Moulds	2.00
24	Tim Couch, Ricky Williams	6.00
25	Isaac Bruce, Carl Pickens	1.00
26	Deion Sanders, Charles Woodson	1.00
27	Tim Brown, Rod Smith	2.00
28	Daunte Culpepper, Donovan McNabb	4.00
29	Joey Galloway, Ed McCaffrey	1.00
30	Karim Abdul, Antowain Smith	1.00

1999 Score Supplemental

This was a 110-card set that could only be found in factory set form. The set included 24 Mid-Season Updates, 20 Star Salutes and 66 new Rookies. Each set included two insert cards. Inserts included Behind the Numbers, Inscriptions, Quantum Leaf Previews and Zenith Z-Team. SRP was $24.99 per factory set.

		NM/M
Complete Set (110):		30.00
Common Player:		.10
Minor Stars:		.20
Common Rookie:		.50
1	*Chris Griesen*	2.00
2	*Sherdrick Bonner*	1.00
3	*Joel Makovicka*	2.00
4	*Andy McCullough*	1.00
5	*Jeff Paulk*	1.50
6	*Brandon Stokley*	1.50
7	*Sheldon Jackson*	1.00
8	*Bobby Collins*	2.00
9	*Kamil Loud*	1.00
10	*Antoine Winfield*	1.50
11	*Jerry Azumah*	1.00
12	*James Allen*	1.50
13	*Nick Williams*	1.00
14	*Michael Basnight*	1.00
15	*Damon Griffin*	1.50
16	*Ronnie Powell*	1.00
17	*Darrin Chiaverini*	2.00
18	*Mark Campbell*	1.00
19	*Mike Lucky*	1.00
20	*Wane McGarity*	2.00
21	*Jason Tucker*	1.50
22	*Ebenezer Ekuban*	1.50
23	*Robert Thomas*	1.00
24	*Dat Nguyen*	1.50
25	*Olandis Gary*	3.00
26	*Desmond Clark*	1.00
27	*Andre Cooper*	1.00
28	*Chris Watson*	1.25
29	*Al Wilson*	1.50
30	*Cory Sauter*	1.00
31	*Brock Olivo*	.50
32	*Basil Mitchell*	1.50
33	*Matt Snider*	.50
34	*Antwan Edwards*	1.50
35	*Mike McKenzie*	1.50
36	*Terrence Wilkins*	2.00
37	*Fernando Bryant*	1.00
38	*Larry Parker*	1.00
39	*Autry Denson*	2.00
40	*Jim Kleinsasser*	2.00
41	*Michael Bishop*	2.00
42	*Andy Katzenmoyer*	1.50
43	*Brett Bech*	1.00
44	*Sean Bennett*	1.50
45	*Dan Campbell*	.50
46	*Ray Lucas*	2.00
47	*Scott Dreisbach*	1.50
48	*Cecil Martin*	1.50
49	*Dameane Douglas*	1.00
50	*Jed Weaver*	.50
51	*Jerame Tuman*	1.00
52	*Steve Heiden*	.50
53	*Jeff Garcia*	5.00
54	*Terry Jackson*	1.50
55	*Charlie Rogers*	1.00
56	*Lamar King*	.50
57	*Kurt Warner*	6.00
58	*Dre' Bly*	1.00
59	*Justin Watson*	1.00
60	*Rabih Abdullah*	.50
61	*Martin Gramatica*	1.00
62	*Darnell McDonald*	2.00
63	*Anthony McFarland*	1.00
64	*Larry Brown*	.50
65	*Kevin Daft*	1.50
66	*Mike Sellers*	.50
67	Ken Oxendine	.20
68	Errict Rhett	.20
69	Stoney Case	.10
70	Jonathon Linton	.20
71	Marcus Robinson	1.50
72	Shane Matthews	.20
73	Cade McNown	2.00
74	Akili Smith	2.00
75	Karim Abdul	.20
76	Tim Couch	2.00
77	Kevin Johnson	2.00
78	Ron Rivers	.10
79	Bill Schroeder	.10
80	Edgerrin James	3.00
81	Cecil Collins	2.00
82	Matthew Hatchette	.20
83	Daunte Culpepper	3.00
84	Ricky Williams	3.00
85	Tyrone Wheatley	.20
86	Donovan McNabb	3.00
87	Marshall Faulk	.50
88	Torry Holt	2.00
89	Stephen Davis	.50
90	Brad Johnson	.50
91	Jake Plummer	.50
92	Emmitt Smith	1.00
93	Troy Aikman	1.00
94	John Elway	1.00
95	Terrell Davis	1.00
96	Barry Sanders	1.50
97	Brett Favre	1.50
98	Antonio Freeman	.50
99	Peyton Manning	1.50
100	Fred Taylor	1.00
101	Mark Brunell	.50
102	Dan Marino	1.00
103	Randy Moss	1.50
104	Cris Carter	.50
105	Drew Bledsoe	.75
106	Terry Glenn	.40
107	Keyshawn Johnson	.40
108	Jerry Rice	1.00
109	Steve Young	.75
110	Eddie George	.50

1999 Score Supplemental Behind The Numbers

This 30-card insert included both veterans and rookies. Each single was printed on holographic foil board with foil stamping. Singles were sequentially numbered to 1,000. A parallel Gold version was also issued with each card numbered to the player's jersey number.

		NM/M
Complete Set (30):		90.00
Common Player:		1.00
Production 1,000 Sets		
Gold Version (too limited to price)		
Production to players jersey number		
1	Kurt Warner	6.00
2	Tim Couch	4.00
3	Randy Moss	5.00
4	Brett Favre	6.00
5	Marvin Harrison	2.00
6	Terry Glenn	1.00
7	John Elway	5.00
8	Troy Aikman	5.00
9	Steve McNair	2.00
10	Kordell Stewart	1.00
11	Drew Bledsoe	4.00
12	Jon Kitna	1.00
13	Dan Marino	6.00
14	Jerry Rice	4.00
15	Edgerrin James	6.00
16	Jake Plummer	2.00
17	Antonio Freeman	1.00
18	Peyton Manning	5.00
19	Keyshawn Johnson	2.00
20	Barry Sanders	5.00
21	Cris Carter	1.00
22	Emmitt Smith	5.00
23	Steve Young	4.00
24	Ricky Williams	6.00
25	Doug Flutie	2.00
26	Mark Brunell	2.00
27	Eddie George	2.00
28	Fred Taylor	3.00
29	Donovan McNabb	4.00
30	Terrell Davis	4.00

1999 Score Supplemental Inscriptions

This 30-card insert included autographs of both past and present players. The never-released 1997 Inscriptions of Barry Sanders was randomly inserted into this product. The rest of the singles were found at one in three boxes.

		NM/M
Common Player:		10.00
Minor Stars:		20.00
1	Eric Moulds	20.00
2	Chris Chandler	10.00
3	Thurman Thomas	20.00
4	Tim Brown	30.00
5	Priest Holmes	40.00
6	Wesley Walls	10.00
7	Corey Dillon	25.00
8	Duce Staley	20.00
9	Natrone Means	20.00
10	Isaac Bruce	20.00
11	Joey Galloway	20.00
12	Skip Hicks	20.00
13	Terrell Owens	20.00
14	Eric Moss	10.00
15	Kurt Warner	60.00
16	Johnny Unitas	125.00
17	Bart Starr	125.00
18	Earl Campbell	50.00
19	Jim Brown	100.00
20	Vinny Testaverde	20.00
21	Kordell Stewart	40.00
22	Steve McNair	40.00
23	Stephen Davis	20.00
24	Ricky Williams	125.00
25	Marvin Harrison	40.00
26	Brad Johnson	20.00
27	Dorsey Levens	20.00
28	Jon Kitna	10.00
29	Brian Griese	40.00
30	Tim Biakabutuka	10.00

1999 Score Supplemental Quantum Leaf Previews

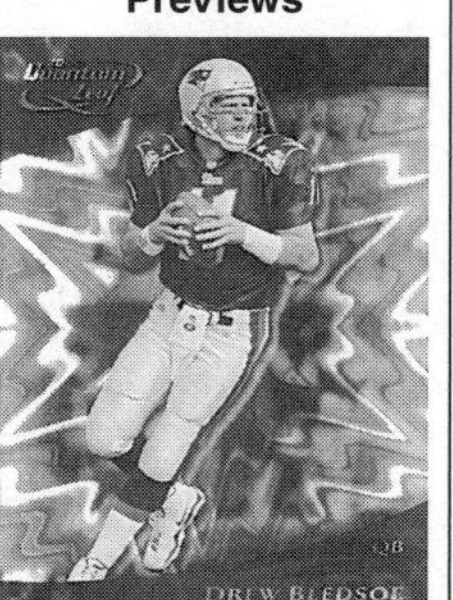

This 18-card insert gave collectors a look at the first 2000 release. Each player was pictured on dot matrix hologram foil and randomly inserted.

		NM/M
Complete Set (18):		75.00
Common Player:		1.00
1	Barry Sanders	5.00
2	Ricky Williams	5.00
3	Terrell Davis	4.00
4	John Elway	4.00
5	Edgerrin James	5.00
6	Tim Couch	3.00
7	Peyton Manning	4.00
8	Kurt Warner	5.00
9	Randy Moss	4.00
10	Dan Marino	6.00
11	Brett Favre	6.00
12	Eddie George	1.00
13	Marvin Harrison	2.00
14	Jerry Rice	4.00
15	Emmitt Smith	5.00
16	Keyshawn Johnson	1.00
17	Drew Bledsoe	4.00
18	Marshall Faulk	3.00

1999 Score Supplemental Zenith Z-Team

This 20-card insert included the cream of the crop in the NFL. Each was pictured on clear plastic with holographic foil stamping and were sequentially numbered to 100.

		NM/M
Common Player:		5.00
Production 100 Sets		
1	Steve Young	12.00
2	Barry Sanders	20.00
3	Fred Taylor	8.00
4	Marshall Faulk	12.00
5	Emmitt Smith	20.00
6	Brett Favre	25.00
7	Troy Aikman	15.00
8	Terrell Davis	15.00
9	Edgerrin James	20.00
10	Drew Bledsoe	12.00
11	Dan Marino	25.00
12	Randy Moss	20.00
13	Ricky Williams	20.00
14	Mark Brunell	10.00
15	Jake Plummer	8.00
16	Jerry Rice	20.00
17	Peyton Manning	20.00
18	Tim Couch	15.00
19	Eddie George	5.00
20	John Elway	15.00

2000 Score

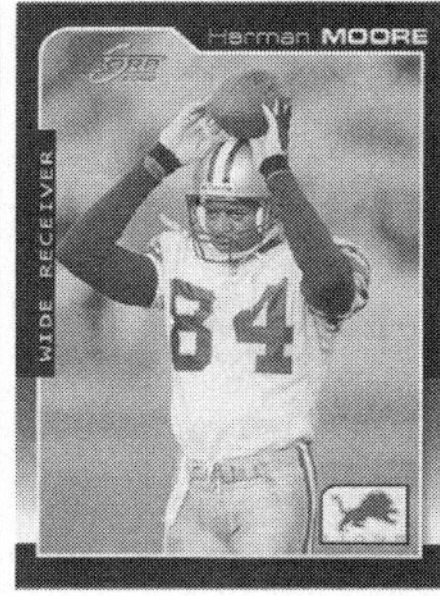

		NM/M
Common Player:		.10
Minor Stars:		.20
Common Player (#221-275):		.20
Inserted 1:2		
Common Rookie:		1.50
Inserted 1:4		
Pack (10):		1.75
Wax Box (36):		45.00
1	Michael Pittman	.10
2	Jake Plummer	.50
3	Rob Moore	.20
4	David Boston	.50
5	Frank Sanders	.20
6	Jamal Anderson	.50
7	Chris Chandler	.20
8	Tim Dwight	.50
9	Terance Mathis	.10
10	Shawn Jefferson	.10
11	Ashley Ambrose	.10
12	Peter Boulware	.10
13	Priest Holmes	.50
14	Tony Banks	.30
15	Qadry Ismail	.10
16	Shannon Sharpe	.20
17	Rod Woodson	.10
18	Matt Stover	.10
19	Michael McCrary	.10
20	Doug Flutie	.50
21	Rob Johnson	.30
22	Eric Moulds	.50
23	Peerless Price	.50
24	Jonathon Linton	.20
25	Antowain Smith	.50
26	Jay Riemersma	.10
27	Muhsin Muhammad	.20
28	Tim Biakabutuka	.20
29	Patrick Jeffers	.50
30	Wesley Walls	.20
31	Steve Beuerlein	.30
32	John Kasay	.10
33	Curtis Enis	.50
34	Cade McNown	.75
35	Marcus Robinson	.50
36	Bobby Engram	.10
37	Eddie Kennison	.10
38	Akili Smith	.50
39	Carl Pickens	.20
40	Corey Dillon	.50
41	Darnay Scott	.20
42	Errict Rhett	.20
43	Karim Abdul	.20
44	Tim Couch	1.25
45	Kevin Johnson	.50
46	Darrin Chiaverini	.10
47	Terry Kirby	.10
48	Jason Tucker	.20
49	Raghib Ismail	.10
50	Joey Galloway	.50
51	Michael Irvin	.20
52	Troy Aikman	1.00
53	Emmitt Smith	1.50
54	David LaFleur	.10
55	Trevor Pryce	.10
56	Brian Griese	.50
57	Olandis Gary	.50
58	Terrell Davis	1.00
59	Rod Smith	.30
60	Ed McCaffrey	.30
61	Gus Frerotte	.20
62	Jason Elam	.10
63	Kavika Pittman	.10
64	James Stewart	.30
65	Charlie Batch	.50
66	Johnnie Morton	.20
67	Herman Moore	.30
68	Germane Crowell	.20
69	Barry Sanders	2.00
70	Chris Claiborne	.10
71	Brett Favre	2.00
72	Antonio Freeman	.50
73	Dorsey Levens	.50
74	De'Mond Parker	.20
75	Corey Bradford	.20
76	Basil Mitchell	.10
77	Bill Schroeder	.10
78	Peyton Manning	1.50
79	Marvin Harrison	.50
80	Terrence Wilkins	.10
81	Edgerrin James	2.00
82	E.G. Green	.10
83	Chad Bratzke	.10
84	Mark Brunell	.75
85	Fred Taylor	.75
86	Jimmy Smith	.30
87	Keenan McCardell	.20
88	Kevin Hardy	.10
89	Aaron Beasley	.10
90	Elvis Grbac	.20
91	Derrick Alexander	.10
92	Tony Gonzalez	.20
93	Donnell Bennett	.10
94	Warren Moon	.20
95	Andre Rison	.20
96	James Hasty	.10
97	Dan Marino	1.50
98	Thurman Thomas	.20
99	James Johnson	.10
100	O.J. McDuffie	.20
101	Tony Martin	.10
102	Oronde Gadsden	.20
103	Zach Thomas	.20
104	Sam Madison	.10
105	Jay Fiedler	.20
106	Damon Huard	.50
107	Robert Smith	.50
108	Leroy Hoard	.10
109	Randy Moss	1.75
110	Cris Carter	.50
111	Daunte Culpepper	.75
112	John Randle	.10
113	Randall Cunningham	.50
114	Gary Anderson	.10
115	Drew Bledsoe	.75
116	Terry Glenn	.50
117	Kevin Faulk	.30
118	Terry Allen SP	15.00
119	Adam Vinatieri	.10
120	Ty Law	.10
121	Lawyer Milloy	.10
122	Troy Brown	.10
123	Ben Coates	.20
124	Cameron Cleeland	.20
125	Jeff Blake	.20
126	Ricky Williams	1.00
127	Jake Reed	.20
128	*Jake Delhomme*	2.00
129	Andrew Glover	.10
130	Keith Poole	.10
131	Joe Horn	.10
132	Kerry Collins	.20
133	Joe Montgomery	.10
134	Sean Bennett	.10
135	Amani Toomer	.20
136	Ike Hilliard	.20
137	Joe Jurevicius	.10
138	Tiki Barber	.20
139	Victor Green	.10
140	Ray Lucas	.50
141	Vinny Testaverde	.30
142	Curtis Martin	.50
143	Wayne Chrebet	.30
144	Tyrone Wheatley	.20
145	Rich Gannon	.20
146	Napoleon Kaufman	.20
147	Tim Brown	.30
148	Rickey Dudley	.20
149	Charles Woodson	.50
150	James Jett	.10
151	Duce Staley	.50
152	Charles Johnson	.10
153	Donovan McNabb	.75
154	Troy Vincent	.10
155	Troy Edwards	.50
156	Jerome Bettis	.50
157	Kordell Stewart	.50
158	Richard Huntley	.20
159	Hines Ward	.20
160	Levon Kirkland	.10
161	Ryan Leaf	.30
162	Jim Harbaugh	.20
163	Jermaine Fazande	.20
164	Natrone Means	.20
165	Junior Seau	.20
166	Curtis Conway	.20
167	Freddie Jones	.20
168	Jeff Graham	.10
169	Terrell Owens	.50
170	Jeff Garcia	.50
171	Jerry Rice	1.00
172	Steve Young	.75
173	Garrison Hearst	.30
174	Charlie Garner	.20
175	Fred Beasley	.10
176	Bryant Young	.10
177	Derrick Mayes	.20
178	Sean Dawkins	.10
179	Jon Kitna	.50
180	Ricky Watters	.30
181	Charlie Rogers	.10
182	Kurt Warner	2.00
183	Marshall Faulk	.50
184	Isaac Bruce	.50
185	Az-Zahir Hakim	.20
186	Trent Green	.20
187	Jeff Wilkins	.10
188	Torry Holt	.50
189	London Fletcher	.10
190	Robert Holcombe	.10
191	Todd Lyght	.10
192	Keyshawn Johnson	.50
193	Derrick Brooks	.10
194	Warren Sapp	.20
195	Shaun King	.75
196	Warrick Dunn	.50
197	Mike Alstott	.50
198	Jacquez Green	.20
199	Reidel Anthony	.20
200	Martin Gramatica	.10
201	Donnie Abraham	.10
202	Steve McNair	.60
203	Eddie George	.60
204	Jevon Kearse	.60
205	Frank Wycheck	.10
206	Kevin Dyson	.20
207	Yancey Thigpen	.20
208	Al Del Greco	.10
209	Jeff George	.30
210	Adrian Murrell	.20
211	Brad Johnson	.50
212	Stephen Davis	.50
213	Stephen Alexander	.10
214	Michael Westbrook	.30
215	Darrell Green	.10
216	Champ Bailey	.30
217	Albert Connell	.20
218	Larry Centers	.10
219	Bruce Smith	.10
220	Deion Sanders	.50
221	Ricky Williams	1.00
222	Edgerrin James	2.00
223	Tim Couch	1.00

224	Cade McNown	.75
225	Olandis Gary	.50
226	Torry Holt	.50
227	Donovan McNabb	.75
228	Shaun King	.75
229	Kevin Johnson	.50
230	Kurt Warner	3.00
231	Tony Gonzalez	.20
232	Frank Wycheck	.20
233	Eddie George	.75
234	Mark Brunell	1.00
235	Corey Dillon	.50
236	Peyton Manning	2.00
237	Keyshawn Johnson	.50
238	Rich Gannon	.20
239	Terry Glenn	.50
240	Tony Brackens	.20
241	Edgerrin James	2.00
242	Tim Brown	.30
243	Michael Strahan	.20
244	Kurt Warner	3.00
245	Brad Johnson	.50
246	Aeneas Williams	.20
247	Marshall Faulk	.50
248	Dexter Coakley	.20
249	Warren Sapp	.20
250	Mike Alstott	.50
251	David Sloan	.20
252	Cris Carter	.50
253	Muhsin Muhammad	.30
254	Isaac Bruce	.50
255	Wesley Walls	.20
256	Steve Beuerlein	.30
257	Kurt Warner	3.00
258	Peyton Manning	2.00
259	Brad Johnson	.50
260	Edgerrin James	2.00
261	Curtis Martin	.50
262	Stephen Davis	.50
263	Emmitt Smith	1.50
264	Marvin Harrison	.50
265	Jimmy Smith	.30
266	Randy Moss	2.00
267	Marcus Robinson	.50
268	Kevin Carter	.20
269	Simeon Rice	.20
270	Robert Porcher	.20
271	Jevon Kearse	.60
272	Mike Vanderjagt	.20
273	Olindo Mare	.20
274	Todd Peterson	.20
275	Mike Hollis	.20
276	*Mike Anderson 500*	25.00
277	*Peter Warrick*	4.00
278	*Courtney Brown*	2.00
279	*Plaxico Burress*	5.00
280	*Corey Simon*	2.00
281	*Thomas Jones*	3.00
282	*Travis Taylor*	3.00
283	*Shaun Alexander*	6.00
284	*Patrick Pass 500*	10.00
285	*Chris Redman*	3.00
286	*Chad Pennington*	10.00
287	*Jamal Lewis*	6.00
288	*Brian Urlacher*	5.00
289	*Bubba Franks*	3.00
290	*Dez White*	3.00
291	*Frank Moreau 500*	10.00
292	*Ron Dayne*	2.00
293	*Sylvester Morris*	2.00
294	*R. Jay Soward*	2.00
295	*Deon Dyer*	1.50
296	*Spregon Wynn 500*	10.00
297	*Rondell Mealey*	2.00
298	*Travis Prentice*	2.50
299	*Darrell Jackson*	4.00
300	*Giovanni Carmazzi*	2.00
301	*Anthony Lucas*	1.50
302	*Danny Farmer*	2.00
303	*Dennis Northcutt*	2.00
304	*Troy Walters*	1.50
305	*Laveranues Coles*	4.00
306	*Kwame Cavil*	1.50
307	*Tee Martin*	2.00
308	*J.R. Redmond*	2.00
309	*Tim Rattay*	3.00
310	*Jerry Porter*	4.00
311	*Michael Wiley*	2.00
312	*Reuben Droughns*	3.00
313	*Trung Canidate*	3.00
314	*Shyrone Stith*	1.50
315	*Marc Bulger*	5.00
316	*Tom Brady*	12.00
317	*Doug Johnson*	2.00
318	*Todd Husak*	2.00
319	*Gari Scott*	1.50
320	*Windrell Hayes 500*	10.00
321	*Chris Cole*	1.50
322	*Sammy Morris*	2.00
323	*Trevor Gaylor*	2.00
324	*Jarious Jackson*	2.00
325	*Doug Chapman 500*	10.00
326	*Ron Dugans*	2.00
327	*Ron Dixon 500*	10.00
328	*Joe Hamilton*	2.00
329	*Todd Pinkston*	3.00
330	*Chad Morton*	2.00

2000 Score Final Score

	NM/M
Cards #'d 25-35:	20X-40X
Subsets #'d 25-35:	5X-15X
Rookies #'d 25-35:	4X-8X
Cards #'d 40-54:	10X-20X
Subsets #'d 40-54:	5X-15X
Rookies #'d 40-54:	2X-5X
Cards #'d to 66:	8X-15X
Subsets #'d to 66:	4X-8X
Rookies #'d to 66:	2X-4X

Card #118 Never Issued
Production #'d To A 1999 Stat

		NM/M
1	Michael Pittman	.10
2	Jake Plummer	.50
3	Rob Moore	.20
4	David Boston	.50
5	Frank Sanders	.20
6	Jamal Anderson	.50
7	Chris Chandler	.20
8	Tim Dwight	.50
9	Terance Mathis	.10
10	Shawn Jefferson	.10
11	Ashley Ambrose	.10
12	Peter Boulware	.10
13	Priest Holmes	10.00
14	Tony Banks	.30
15	Qadry Ismail	.50
16	Shannon Sharpe	.20
17	Rod Woodson	.50
18	Matt Stover	.10
19	Michael McCrary	.10
20	Doug Flutie	.50
21	Rob Johnson	.30
22	Eric Moulds	.50
23	Peerless Price	.50
24	Jonathon Linton	.20
25	Antowain Smith	.50
26	Jay Riemersma	.10
27	Muhsin Muhammad	.20
28	Tim Biakabutuka	.20
29	Patrick Jeffers	.50
30	Wesley Walls	.20
31	Steve Beuerlein	.30
32	John Kasay	.10
33	Curtis Enis	.50
34	Cade McNown	.75
35	Marcus Robinson	.50
36	Bobby Engram	.10
37	Eddie Kennison	.10
38	Akili Smith	.50
39	Carl Pickens	.20
40	Corey Dillon	.50
41	Darnay Scott	.20
42	Errict Rhett	.20
43	Karim Abdul	.20
44	Tim Couch	1.25
45	Kevin Johnson	.50
46	Darrin Chiaverini	.10
47	Terry Kirby	.10
48	Jason Tucker	.20
49	Raghib Ismail	.10
50	Joey Galloway	.50
51	Michael Irvin	.20
52	Troy Aikman	1.00
53	Emmitt Smith	1.50
54	David LaFleur	.10
55	Trevor Pryce	.10
56	Brian Griese	.50
57	Olandis Gary	.50
58	Terrell Davis	1.50
59	Rod Smith	.30
60	Ed McCaffrey	.30
61	Gus Frerotte	.20
62	Jason Elam	.10
63	Kavika Pittman	.10
64	James Stewart	.30
65	Charlie Batch	.50
66	Johnnie Morton	.20
67	Herman Moore	.30
68	Germane Crowell	.20
69	Barry Sanders	2.00
70	Chris Claiborne	.10
71	Brett Favre	2.00
72	Antonio Freeman	.50
73	Dorsey Levens	.50
74	De'Mond Parker	.20
75	Corey Bradford	.20
76	Basil Mitchell	.10
77	Bill Schroeder	.10
78	Peyton Manning	1.50
79	Marvin Harrison	.50
80	Terrence Wilkins	.20
81	Edgerrin James	2.00
82	E.G. Green	.10
83	Chad Bratzke	.10
84	Mark Brunell	.75
85	Fred Taylor	.75
86	Jimmy Smith	.30
87	Keenan McCardell	.20
88	Kevin Hardy	.10
89	Aaron Beasley	.10
90	Elvis Grbac	.20
91	Derrick Alexander	.10
92	Tony Gonzalez	.20
93	Donnell Bennett	.10
94	Warren Moon	.20
95	Andre Rison	.20
96	James Hasty	.10
97	Dan Marino	1.50
98	Thurman Thomas	.20
99	James Johnson	.10
100	O.J. McDuffie	.20
101	Tony Martin	.10
102	Oronde Gadsden	.20
103	Zach Thomas	.20
104	Sam Madison	.10
105	Jay Fiedler	.20
106	Damon Huard	.50
107	Robert Smith	.50
108	Leroy Hoard	.10
109	Randy Moss	1.75
110	Cris Carter	.50
111	Daunte Culpepper	.75
112	John Randle	.10
113	Randall Cunningham	.50
114	Gary Anderson	.10
115	Drew Bledsoe	.75
116	Terry Glenn	.50
117	Kevin Faulk	.30
119	Adam Vinatieri	.10
120	Ty Law	.10
121	Lawyer Milloy	.10
122	Troy Brown	.10
123	Ben Coates	.20
124	Cameron Cleeland	.20
125	Jeff Blake	.20
126	Ricky Williams	1.25
127	Jake Reed	.20
128	*Jake Delhomme*	2.00
129	Andrew Glover	.10
130	Keith Poole	.10
131	Joe Horn	.10
132	Kerry Collins	.20
133	Joe Montgomery	.10
134	Sean Bennett	.10
135	Amani Toomer	.20
136	Ike Hilliard	.20
137	Joe Jurevicius	.10
138	Tiki Barber	.20
139	Victor Green	.10
140	Ray Lucas	.50
141	Vinny Testaverde	.30
142	Curtis Martin	.50
143	Wayne Chrebet	.30
144	Tyrone Wheatley	.20
145	Rich Gannon	.20
146	Napoleon Kaufman	.50
147	Tim Brown	.30
148	Rickey Dudley	.20
149	Charles Woodson	.50
150	James Jett	.10
151	Duce Staley	.50
152	Charles Johnson	.10
153	Donovan McNabb	.75
154	Troy Vincent	.10
155	Troy Edwards	.50
156	Jerome Bettis	.50
157	Kordell Stewart	.50
158	Richard Huntley	.20
159	Hines Ward	.10
160	Levon Kirkland	.10
161	Ryan Leaf	.30
162	Jim Harbaugh	.20
163	Jermaine Fazande	.20
164	Natrone Means	.50
165	Junior Seau	.20
166	Curtis Conway	.20
167	Freddie Jones	.20
168	Jeff Graham	.20
169	Terrell Owens	.50
170	Jeff Garcia	.50
171	Jerry Rice	1.00
172	Steve Young	.75
173	Garrison Hearst	.30
174	Charlie Garner	.20
175	Fred Beasley	.10
176	Bryant Young	.10
177	Derrick Mayes	.20
178	Sean Dawkins	.20
179	Jon Kitna	.50
180	Ricky Watters	.30
181	Charlie Rogers	.10
182	Kurt Warner	2.50
183	Marshall Faulk	.50
184	Isaac Bruce	.50
185	Az-Zahir Hakim	.20
186	Trent Green	.20
187	Jeff Wilkins	.10
188	Torry Holt	.50
189	London Fletcher	.10
190	Robert Holcombe	.10
191	Todd Lyght	.10
192	Keyshawn Johnson	.50
193	Derrick Brooks	.10
194	Warren Sapp	.20
195	Shaun King	.75
196	Warrick Dunn	.50
197	Mike Alstott	.50
198	Jacquez Green	.20
199	Reidel Anthony	.20
200	Martin Gramatica	.10
201	Donnie Abraham	.10
202	Steve McNair	.60
203	Eddie George	.60
204	Jevon Kearse	.60
205	Frank Wycheck	.10
206	Kevin Dyson	.20
207	Yancey Thigpen	.20
208	Al Del Greco	.10
209	Jeff George	.30
210	Adrian Murrell	.20
211	Brad Johnson	.50
212	Stephen Davis	.50
213	Stephen Alexander	.10
214	Michael Westbrook	.30
215	Darrell Green	.10
216	Champ Bailey	.30
217	Albert Connell	.20
218	Larry Centers	.10
219	Bruce Smith	.10
220	Deion Sanders	.50
221	Ricky Williams	1.00
222	Edgerrin James	2.00
223	Tim Couch	1.00
224	Cade McNown	.75
225	Olandis Gary	.50
226	Torry Holt	.50
227	Donovan McNabb	.75
228	Shaun King	.75
229	Kevin Johnson	.50
230	Kurt Warner	3.00
231	Tony Gonzalez	.20
232	Frank Wycheck	.20
233	Eddie George	.75
234	Mark Brunell	1.00
235	Corey Dillon	.50
236	Peyton Manning	2.00
237	Keyshawn Johnson	.50
238	Rich Gannon	.20
239	Terry Glenn	.50
240	Tony Brackens	.20
241	Edgerrin James	2.00
242	Tim Brown	.30
243	Michael Strahan	.20
244	Kurt Warner	3.00
245	Brad Johnson	.50
246	Aeneas Williams	.20
247	Marshall Faulk	.50
248	Dexter Coakley	.20
249	Warren Sapp	.20
250	Mike Alstott	.50
251	David Sloan	.20
252	Cris Carter	.50
253	Muhsin Muhammad	.30
254	Isaac Bruce	.50
255	Wesley Walls	.20
256	Steve Beuerlein	.30
257	Kurt Warner	3.00
258	Peyton Manning	2.00
259	Brad Johnson	.50
260	Edgerrin James	2.00
261	Curtis Martin	.50
262	Stephen Davis	.50
263	Emmitt Smith	1.50
264	Marvin Harrison	.50
265	Jimmy Smith	.30
266	Randy Moss	2.00
267	Marcus Robinson	.50
268	Kevin Carter	.20
269	Simeon Rice	.20
270	Robert Porcher	.20
271	Jevon Kearse	.60
272	Mike Vanderjagt	.20
273	Olindo Mare	.20
274	Todd Peterson	.20
275	Mike Hollis	.20
276	Redemption	10.00
277	*Peter Warrick*	15.00
278	*Courtney Brown*	4.00
279	*Plaxico Burress*	10.00
280	*Corey Simon*	1.50
281	*Thomas Jones*	8.00
282	*Travis Taylor*	5.00
283	*Shaun Alexander*	6.00
284	Redemption	3.00
285	*Chris Redman*	4.00
286	*Chad Pennington*	10.00
287	*Jamal Lewis*	8.00
288	*Brian Urlacher*	3.00
289	*Bubba Franks*	3.00
290	*Dez White*	3.00
291	*Frank Moreau*	3.00
292	*Ron Dayne*	15.00
293	*Sylvester Morris*	4.00
294	*R. Jay Soward*	3.50
295	*Deon Dyer*	1.50
296	Redemption	4.00
297	*Rondell Mealey*	2.50
298	*Travis Prentice*	4.00
299	*Darrell Jackson*	1.50
300	*Giovanni Carmazzi*	6.00
301	*Anthony Lucas*	1.50
302	*Danny Farmer*	2.50
303	*Dennis Northcutt*	3.00
304	*Troy Walters*	1.50
305	*Laveranues Coles*	2.50
306	*Kwame Cavil*	1.50
307	*Tee Martin*	4.00
308	*J.R. Redmond*	4.00
309	*Tim Rattay*	3.50
310	*Jerry Porter*	3.50
311	*Michael Wiley*	3.00
312	*Reuben Droughns*	3.00
313	*Trung Canidate*	2.50
314	*Shyrone Stith*	1.50
315	*Marc Bulger*	2.00
316	*Tom Brady*	20.00
317	*Doug Johnson*	1.50
318	*Todd Husak*	2.50
319	*Gari Scott*	1.50
320	Redemption	4.00
321	*Chris Cole*	1.50
322	*Sammy Morris*	1.50
323	*Trevor Gaylor*	1.50
324	*Jarious Jackson*	2.50
325	*Doug Chapman*	2.50
326	*Ron Dugans*	2.50
327	*Ron Dixon*	4.00
328	*Joe Hamilton*	3.00
329	*Todd Pinkston*	2.50
330	*Chad Morton*	1.50

2000 Score Scorecard

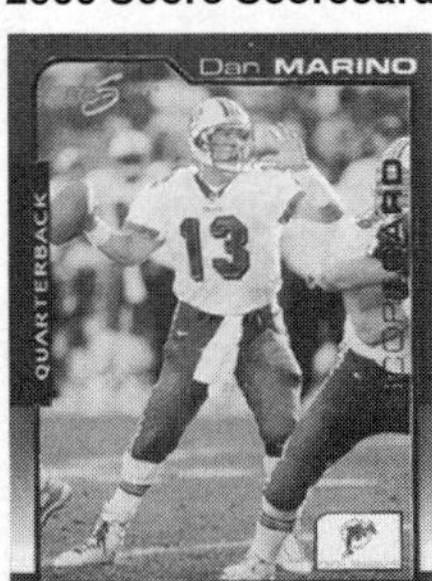

	NM/M
Scorecard Cards:	3X-6X
Scorecard Subsets:	2X
Scorecard Rookies:	2X

Card #118 Never Issued
Production 2,000 Sets

2000 Score Air Mail

	NM/M
Complete Set (30):	75.00
Common Player:	1.00
Minor Stars:	2.00
Inserted 1:70	
First Class Cards:	3X-6X
Production 50 Sets	

		NM/M
AM1	Isaac Bruce	2.00
AM2	Cris Carter	2.00
AM3	Tim Dwight	2.00
AM4	Joey Galloway	2.00
AM5	Marvin Harrison	4.00
AM6	Keyshawn Johnson	2.00
AM7	Jon Kitna	2.00
AM8	Steve McNair	2.00
AM9	Eric Moulds	2.00
AM10	Drew Bledsoe	4.00
AM11	John Elway	6.00
AM12	Brett Favre	7.00
AM13	Antonio Freeman	2.00
AM14	Peyton Manning	5.00
AM15	Randy Moss	5.00
AM16	Steve Young	5.00
AM17	Jake Plummer	2.00
AM18	Troy Aikman	5.00
AM19	Mark Brunell	3.00
AM20	Tim Couch	4.00
AM21	Dan Marino	7.00
AM22	Jerry Rice	5.00
AM23	Kevin Johnson	2.00
AM24	Michael Westbrook	1.00
AM25	Kurt Warner	5.00
AM26	Doug Flutie	2.00
AM27	Jimmy Smith	1.00
AM28	Germane Crowell	1.00
AM29	Cade McNown	2.00
AM30	Muhsin Muhammad	1.00

2000 Score Building Blocks

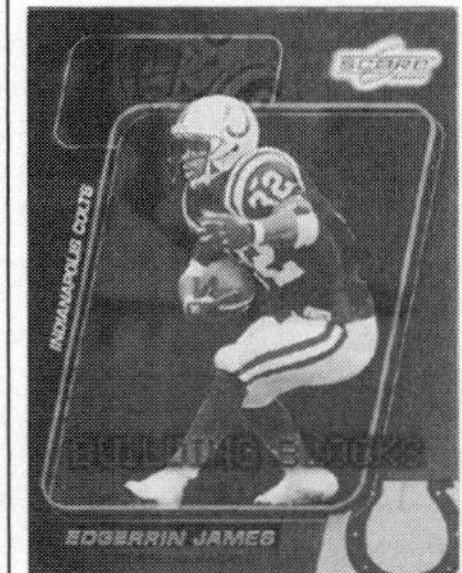

		NM/M
Complete Set (30):		40.00
Common Player:		.75
Minor Stars:		1.50
Inserted 1:17		
BB1	Cade McNown	1.00
BB2	Peerless Price	2.00
BB3	Akili Smith	1.00
BB4	Randy Moss	3.00
BB5	Edgerrin James	4.00
BB6	Kurt Warner	3.00
BB7	Ray Lucas	.75
BB8	Jevon Kearse	1.00
BB9	Torry Holt	1.50
BB10	Ricky Williams	4.00
BB11	Daunte Culpepper	2.00
BB12	Fred Taylor	2.00
BB13	Brian Griese	1.50
BB14	Marcus Robinson	1.50
BB15	David Boston	.75
BB16	James Johnson	.75
BB17	Charlie Batch	.75
BB18	Jake Plummer	1.50
BB19	Duce Staley	1.50
BB20	Germane Crowell	.75
BB21	Curtis Enis	.75
BB22	Donovan McNabb	3.00
BB23	Tim Couch	2.00
BB24	Stephen Davis	1.50
BB25	Jon Kitna	.75
BB26	Shaun King	.75
BB27	Kevin Johnson	1.00
BB28	Peyton Manning	3.00
BB29	Olandis Gary	1.00
BB30	Muhsin Muhammad	.75

2000 Score Complete Players

		NM/M
Complete Set (40):		60.00
Common Player:		.75
Minor Stars:		1.50
Inserted 1:17		
Green Cards:		2X-5X
Inserted 1:359		
Blue Cards:		3X-6X
Inserted 1:718		
CP1	Eric Moulds	1.50
CP2	Tim Couch	2.50
CP3	Marvin Harrison	2.00

		NM/M
CP4	Brett Favre	5.00
CP5	Steve Young	2.00
CP6	Brad Johnson	1.50
CP7	Randy Moss	4.00
CP8	Mark Brunell	2.00
CP9	Steve McNair	1.50
CP10	Donovan McNabb	1.75
CP11	Drew Bledsoe	2.00
CP12	Kurt Warner	4.00
CP13	Dan Marino	4.00
CP14	Muhsin Muhammad	.75
CP15	Jimmy Smith	.75
CP16	Fred Taylor	2.00
CP17	Corey Dillon	1.50
CP18	Peyton Manning	4.00
CP19	Keyshawn Johnson	1.50
CP20	Barry Sanders	4.00
CP21	Brian Griese	1.50
CP22	Emmitt Smith	4.00
CP23	Jerry Rice	3.00
CP24	Joey Galloway	1.50
CP25	Cris Carter	1.50
CP26	Robert Smith	.75
CP27	Eddie George	1.75
CP28	Marshall Faulk	1.50
CP29	Tim Brown	.75
CP30	Terrell Davis	3.00
CP31	Jamal Anderson	1.50
CP32	Edgerrin James	3.00
CP33	Antowain Smith	1.50
CP34	Antonio Freeman	1.50
CP35	Isaac Bruce	1.50
CP36	Stephen Davis	1.50
CP37	Troy Aikman	3.00
CP38	Kevin Johnson	1.50
CP39	Ricky Watters	.75
CP40	Mike Alstott	1.50

2000 Score Franchise

		NM/M
Complete Set (31):		45.00
Common Player:		.50
Minor Stars:		1.00
Inserted 1:35 Retail		
F1	Emmitt Smith	4.00
F2	Amani Toomer	.50
F3	Jake Plummer	1.00
F4	Brad Johnson	1.00
F5	Donovan McNabb	2.50
F6	Jerry Rice	4.00
F7	Jamal Anderson	1.00
F8	Marshall Faulk	2.00
F9	Steve Beuerlein	.50
F10	Ricky Williams	4.00
F11	Brett Favre	5.00
F12	Barry Sanders	4.00
F13	Randy Moss	4.00
F14	Shaun King	1.00
F15	Cade McNown	1.00
F16	Dan Marino	5.00
F17	Drew Bledsoe	3.00
F18	Curtis Martin	3.00
F19	Peyton Manning	4.00
F20	Eric Moulds	1.00
F21	Mark Brunell	2.00
F22	Akili Smith	1.00
F23	Tim Couch	3.00
F24	Jerome Bettis	1.00
F25	Qadry Ismail	.50
F26	Eddie George	2.00
F27	Jim Harbaugh	.50
F28	Terrell Davis	4.00
F29	Elvis Grbac	.50
F30	Tim Brown	2.00
F31	Jon Kitna	1.00

2000 Score Future Franchise

		NM/M
Complete Set (30):		70.00
Common Player:		.50
Minor Stars:		1.00
Inserted 1:35 Hobby		
FF1	Michael Wiley, Emmitt Smith	4.00

FF2 Ron Dayne, Amani Toomer 2.00
FF3 Thomas Jones, Jake Plummer 2.00
FF4 Redemption .50
FF5 Todd Pinkston, Donovan McNabb 3.00
FF6 Giovanni Carmazzi, Jerry Rice 3.00
7 Mareno Philyaw, Jamal Anderson 1.00
8 Trung Canidate, Marshall Faulk 2.00
9 Deon Grant, Steve Beuerlein .50
10 Marc Bulger, Ricky Williams 4.00
11 Bubba Franks, Brett Favre 5.00
12 Reuben Droughns, Barry Sanders 4.00
13 Doug Chapman, Randy Moss 5.00
14 Joe Hamilton, Shaun King 1.00
15 Dez White, Cade McNown 1.00
16 Ben Kelly, Dan Marino 5.00
17 J.R. Redmond, Drew Bledsoe 3.00
18 Chad Pennington, Curtis Martin 6.00
19 Rob Morris, Peyton Manning 4.00
20 Avion Black, Eric Moulds 1.00
21 R. Jay Soward, Mark Brunell 2.00
22 Peter Warrick, Akili Smith 2.00
23 Courtney Brown, Tim Couch 4.00
24 Plaxico Burress, Jerome Bettis 4.00
25 Jamal Lewis, Qadry Ismail 3.00
26 Keith Bulluck, Eddie George 1.00
27 Trevor Gaylor, Jim Harbaugh .50
28 Chris Cole, Terrell Davis 4.00
29 Sylvester Morris, Elvis Grbac 2.50
30 Jerry Porter, Tim Brown 1.00
31 Shaun Alexander, Jon Kitna 3.00

2000 Score Numbers Game

NM/M
Complete Set (50): 100.00
Common Player: 1.00
Minor Stars: 2.00
Production #'d To Season Stat
1A Kurt Warner 4353 3.00
1B Kurt Warner 325 6.00
2A Steve Beuerlein 4436 1.00
2B Steve Beuerlein 343 2.00
3A Peyton Manning 4135 3.00
3B Peyton Manning 331 6.00
4A Brad Johnson 4005 1.00
4B Brad Johnson 316 3.00
5A Steve McNair 2179 2.00
5B Steve McNair 187 4.00
6A Mark Brunell 3060 2.00
6B Mark Brunell 259 4.00
7A Marvin Harrison 1663 2.00
7B Marvin Harrison 115 4.00
8A Isaac Bruce 1165 2.50
8B Isaac Bruce 77 4.00
9A Cris Carter 1241 2.00
9B Cris Carter 90 4.00
10A Randy Moss 1413 3.00
10B Randy Moss 80 8.00
11A Marcus Robinson 1444 2.00
11B Marcus Robinson 84 4.00
12A Terry Glenn 1147 2.00
12B Terry Glenn 69 4.00
13A Edgerrin James 1553 3.00
13B Edgerrin James 369 6.00
14A Curtis Martin 1464 2.00
14B Curtis Martin 367 4.00
15A Stephen Davis 1405 1.00
15B Stephen Davis 290 3.00
16A Emmitt Smith 1397 3.00
16B Emmitt Smith 329 6.00
17A Marshall Faulk 1381 2.00
17B Marshall Faulk 253 4.00
18A Eddie George 1304 2.00
18B Eddie George 320 4.00
19A Olandis Gary 1159 1.00
19B Olandis Gary 276 3.00
20A Dorsey Levens 1034 1.00
20B Dorsey Levens 279 3.00
21A Robert Smith 1015 1.00
21B Robert Smith 221 3.00
22A Jerome Bettis 1091 1.00
22B Jerome Bettis 299 3.00
23A Corey Dillon 1200 2.00
23B Corey Dillon 263 4.00
24A Drew Bledsoe 3985 2.00
24B Drew Bledsoe 305 4.00
25A Fred Taylor 732 2.00
25B Fred Taylor 159 5.00

2000 Score Rookie Preview Autographs

NM/M
Common Player: 10.00
Inserted 1:70 Hobby
Production 300 to 700 Sets
Roll Call Cards: 2X
Production 50 Sets
SR1 Ahmed Plummer 10.00
SR2 Peter Warrick 30.00
SR4 Plaxico Burress 35.00
SR5 Corey Simon 10.00
SR6 Thomas Jones 30.00
SR7 Travis Taylor 25.00
SR8 Shaun Alexander 40.00
SR9 Deon Grant 10.00
SR10 Chris Redman 30.00
SR11 Chad Pennington 75.00
SR12 Jamal Lewis 40.00
SR15 Dez White 15.00
SR16 Ron Dayne 30.00
SR17 Sylvester Morris 30.00
SR18 R. Jay Soward 20.00
SR19 Sherrod Gideon 10.00
SR20 Travis Prentice 25.00
SR21 Darrell Jackson 20.00
SR22 Giovanni Carmazzi 10.00
SR23 Anthony Lucas 10.00
SR24 Danny Farmer 15.00
SR25 Dennis Northcutt 10.00
SR26 Troy Walters 10.00
SR27 Laveranues Coles 20.00
SR28 Kwame Cavil 10.00
SR29 Tee Martin 20.00
SR30 J.R. Redmond 25.00
SR31 Tim Rattay 25.00
SR32 Jerry Porter 15.00
SR33 Michael Wiley 15.00
SR34 Reuben Droughns 10.00
SR35 Trung Canidate 15.00
SR36 Shyrone Stith 10.00
SR37 Marc Bulger 35.00
SR38 Tom Brady 60.00
SR39 Doug Johnson 15.00
SR40 Todd Husak 15.00
SR41 Gari Scott 10.00
SR42 Chafie Fields 10.00
SR43 Sammy Morris 20.00
SR44 Trevor Gaylor 10.00
SR45 Ron Dugans 15.00
SR46 Chris Daniels 10.00
SR47 Joe Hamilton 15.00
SR48 Todd Pinkston 15.00

2000 Score Team 2000

NM/M
Complete Set (20): 40.00
Common Player: 1.00
Minor Stars: 2.00
Blue Production 1,500 Sets
1:Hobby Box
Gold Cards: 1X
Production #'d To Player's Rookie Year
Randomly Inserted In Retail
Green Cards: 2X-4X
Production 200 Sets
Red Cards: 2X
Production 500 Sets
TM1 Barry Sanders 4.00
TM2 Troy Aikman 3.00
TM3 Cris Carter 2.00
TM4 Emmitt Smith 5.00
TM5 Brett Favre 6.00
TM6 Jimmy Smith 1.00
TM7 Drew Bledsoe 2.50
TM8 Marshall Faulk 2.00
TM9 Steve McNair 2.00
TM10 Marvin Harrison 2.00
TM11 Eddie George 2.25
TM12 Eric Moulds 2.00
TM13 Jake Plummer 2.00
TM14 Antowain Smith 2.00
TM15 Fred Taylor 2.00
TM16 Randy Moss 4.00
TM17 Peyton Manning 4.00
TM18 Ricky Williams 3.00
TM19 Edgerrin James 4.00
TM20 Kurt Warner 4.00

2000 Score Team 2000 Autographs

NM/M
Common Player: 35.00
Randomly Inserted In Hobby
Production 50 Sets
TM1 Barry Sanders 250.00
TM2 Troy Aikman 150.00
TM3 Cris Carter 70.00
TM4 Emmitt Smith 200.00
TM5 Brett Favre 250.00
TM6 Jimmy Smith 35.00
TM7 Drew Bledsoe 100.00
TM8 Marshall Faulk 70.00
TM9 Steve McNair 70.00
TM10 Marvin Harrison 70.00
TM11 Eddie George 85.00
TM12 Eric Moulds 35.00
TM13 Jake Plummer 70.00
TM14 Antowain Smith 35.00
TM15 Fred Taylor 85.00
TM16 Randy Moss 200.00
TM17 Peyton Manning 200.00
TM18 Ricky Williams 150.00
TM19 Edgerrin James 225.00
TM20 Kurt Warner 200.00

2001 Score

NM/M
Common Player: .10
Minor Star: .40
Common Rookie: .50
Scorecard 2X-8X
1 David Boston .40
2 Frank Sanders .10
3 Jake Plummer .30
4 Michael Pittman .10
5 Rob Moore .10
6 Thomas Jones .10
7 Chris Chandler .10
8 Doug Johnson .10
9 Jamal Anderson .40
10 Tim Dwight .10
11 Brandon Stokley .10
12 Chris Redman .10
13 Jamal Lewis .75
14 Qadry Ismail .10
15 Ray Lewis .10
16 Rod Woodson .40
17 Shannon Sharpe .40
18 Travis Taylor .40
19 Trent Dilfer .40
20 Elvis Grbac .10
21 Eric Moulds .75
22 Jay Riemersma .10
23 Peerless Price 1.00
24 Rob Johnson .10
25 Sam Cowart .10
26 Sammy Morris .10
27 Shawn Bryson .10
28 Donald Hayes .10
29 Muhsin Muhammad .75
30 Patrick Jeffers .10
31 Reggie White .50
32 Steve Beuerlein .10
33 Tim Biakabutuka .10
34 Wesley Walls .10
35 Brian Urlacher 2.00
36 Cade McNown .40
37 Dez White .10
38 James Allen .10
39 Marcus Robinson .40
40 Marty Booker .40
41 Akili Smith .10
42 Corey Dillon 1.00
43 Danny Farmer .10
44 Peter Warrick .40
45 Ron Dugans .10
46 Takeo Spikes .40
47 Courtney Brown .10
48 Dennis Northcutt .10
49 JaJuan Dawson .40
50 Kevin Johnson .10
51 Tim Couch 1.00
52 Travis Prentice .50
53 Anthony Wright .10
54 Emmitt Smith 3.00
55 James McKnight .10
56 Joey Galloway .50
57 Raghib Ismail .10
58 Randall Cunningham .10
59 Troy Aikman 2.00
60 Brian Griese 1.00
61 Ed McCaffrey 1.00
62 Gus Frerotte .10
63 John Elway 3.00
64 Mike Anderson 1.00
65 Olandis Gary .50
66 Rod Smith .50
67 Terrell Davis 1.00
68 Barry Sanders 3.00
69 Charlie Batch .10
70 Germane Crowell .10
71 Herman Moore .50
72 James Stewart .50
73 Johnnie Morton .50
74 Robert Porcher .10
75 Jim Harbaugh .10
76 Ahman Green 1.00
77 Antonio Freeman .40
78 Bill Schroeder .10
79 Brett Favre 4.00
80 Bubba Franks .10
81 Dorsey Levens .40
82 E.G. Green .10
83 Edgerrin James 2.00
84 Jerome Pathon .10
85 Ken Dilger .50
86 Marcus Pollard .10
87 Marvin Harrison 1.00
88 Peyton Manning 3.00
89 Terrence Wilkins .10
90 Fred Taylor .50
91 Hardy Nickerson .10
92 Jimmy Smith .10
93 Keenan McCardell .10
94 Kyle Brady .10
95 Mark Brunell .75
96 Tony Brackens .10
97 Derrick Alexander .10
98 Sylvester Morris .50
99 Tony Gonzalez .40
100 Tony Richardson .10
101 Kimble Anders .10
102 Warren Moon .10
103 Dan Marino 3.00
104 Jay Fiedler .10
105 Lamar Smith .40
106 O.J. McDuffie .40
107 Oronde Gadsden .10
108 Sam Madison .10
109 Thurman Thomas .75
110 Tony Martin .10
111 Zach Thomas .40
112 Cris Carter .75
113 Daunte Culpepper 1.50
114 Matthew Hatchette .10
115 Randy Moss 4.00
116 Robert Smith .40
117 Drew Bledsoe 3.00
118 J.R. Redmond .10
119 Kevin Faulk .10
120 Michael Bishop .10
121 Terry Glenn .50
122 Troy Brown .10
123 Ty Law .10
124 Aaron Brooks 1.00
125 Darren Howard .10
126 Jake Reed .30
127 Jeff Blake .50
128 Joe Horn .10
129 La'Roi Glover .10
130 Ricky Williams 2.00
131 Willie Jackson .10
132 Albert Connell .10
133 Amani Toomer .50
134 Ike Hilliard .40
135 Jason Sehorn .10
136 Jessie Armstead .10
137 Kerry Collins .75
138 Michael Strahan .40
139 Ron Dayne .40
140 Ron Dixon .10
141 Tiki Barber .60
142 Anthony Becht .10
143 Chad Pennington 3.00
144 Curtis Martin 1.00
145 Dedric Ward .10
146 Laveranues Coles 1.00
147 Vinny Testaverde .40
148 Wayne Chrebet .30
149 Andre Rison .30
150 Charles Woodson .30
151 Darrell Russell .10
152 Napoleon Kaufman .10
153 Rich Gannon .40
154 Tim Brown 1.00
155 Tyrone Wheatley .10
156 Chad Lewis .10
157 Charles Johnson .10
158 Donovan McNabb 1.00
159 Duce Staley .10
160 Hugh Douglas .10
161 Na Brown .10
162 Todd Pinkston .40
163 James Thrash .10
164 Bobby Shaw .10
165 Hines Ward 1.00
166 Jerome Bettis 1.00
167 Kordell Stewart 1.00
168 Levon Kirkland .10
169 Plaxico Burress 1.50
170 Richard Huntley .10
171 Troy Edwards .50
172 Jeff Graham .10
173 Junior Seau .75
174 Doug Flutie .40
175 Charlie Garner .50
176 Jeff Garcia 1.00
177 Jerry Rice 3.00
178 Steve Young 1.00
179 Terrell Owens 1.00
180 Brock Huard .10
181 Darrell Jackson .10
182 Derrick Mayes .10
183 Ricky Watters .60
184 Shaun Alexander 1.00
185 Matt Hasselbeck .50
186 John Randle .10
187 Az-Zahir Hakim .75
188 Isaac Bruce .75
189 Kurt Warner 3.00
190 Marshall Faulk 2.00
191 Torry Holt .50
192 Trent Green 1.00
193 Derrick Brooks .40
194 Jacquez Green .10
195 John Lynch .10
196 Keyshawn Johnson 1.00
197 Mike Alstott .50
198 Reidel Anthony .10
199 Shaun King .40
200 Warren Sapp .40
201 Warrick Dunn .75
202 Ryan Leaf .10
203 Carl Pickens .40
204 Derrick Mason 1.00
205 Eddie George 1.00
206 Frank Wycheck .10
207 Jevon Kearse .40
208 Neil O'Donnell .40
209 Steve McNair 1.00
210 Yancey Thigpen .10
211 Andre Reed .10
212 Brad Johnson .50
213 Bruce Smith .50
214 Champ Bailey .50
215 Darrell Green .50
216 Deion Sanders 1.00
217 Irving Fryar .40
218 Jeff George .10
219 Michael Westbrook .40
220 Stephen Davis 1.00
221 Terrell Owens 1.00
222 Peyton Manning 3.00
223 Stephen Davis 1.00
224 Marvin Harrison 1.00
225 Donovan McNabb 1.00
226 Edgerrin James 2.00
227 Eric Moulds 1.00
228 Daunte Culpepper 2.00
229 Eddie George 1.00
230 Cris Carter 1.00
231 Rich Gannon 1.00
232 Jeff Garcia 1.00
233 Jimmy Smith .50
234 Tony Gonzalez .50
235 Torry Holt .50
236 Jevon Kearse .50
237 Ray Lewis .50
238 Warren Sapp .50
239 Brian Urlacher 2.00
240 Champ Bailey .50
241 Peyton Manning 2.00
242 Jeff Garcia 1.00
243 Elvis Grbac .40
244 Daunte Culpepper 1.00
245 Brett Favre 3.00
246 Edgerrin James 1.50
247 Robert Smith .50
248 Eddie George 1.00
249 Mike Anderson .50
250 Corey Dillon .75
251 Torry Holt .40
252 Rod Smith .40
253 Isaac Bruce .60
254 Terrell Owens 1.00
255 Randy Moss 2.00
256 La'Roi Glover .40
257 Trace Armstrong .40
258 Warren Sapp .40
259 Hugh Douglas .40
260 Jason Taylor .40
261 Mike Anderson .60
262 Jamal Lewis .60
263 Sylvester Morris .40
264 Darrell Jackson .40
265 Peter Warrick .40
266 Ron Dayne .40
267 *Shaun Alexander* 1.00
268 *Plaxico Burress* 1.00
269 *Brian Urlacher* 2.00
270 *Courtney Brown* .50
271 *Michael Vick* 12.00
272 *Drew Brees* 5.00
273 *Chris Weinke* 1.00
274 *Quincy Carter* 1.00
275 *Sage Rosenfels* 1.00
276 *Josh Heupel* .50
277 *David Rivers* .50
278 *Ben Leard* .50
279 *Marques Tuiasosopo* 1.00
280 *Mike McMahon* 1.00
281 *Deuce McAllister* 5.00
282 *LaMont Jordan* 1.00
283 *LaDainian Tomlinson* 6.00
284 *James Jackson* 1.00
285 *Anthony Thomas* 2.00
286 *Travis Henry* 2.00
287 *Travis Minor* 1.00
288 *Rudi Johnson* .50
289 *Michael Bennett* 5.00
290 *Kevan Barlow* 3.00
291 *Reggie White* 1.00
292 *Moran Norris* .50
293 *Ja'Mar Toombs* .50
294 *Heath Evans* .50
295 *David Terrell* 1.00
296 *Santana Moss* 1.00
297 *Rod Gardner* 2.00
298 *Quincy Morgan* 2.00
299 *Freddie Mitchell* 4.00
300 *Eddie "Boo" Williams* .50
301 *Reggie Wayne* 1.00
302 *Ronney Daniels* .50
303 *Bobby Newcombe* .50
304 *Vinny Sutherland* .50
305 *Cedrick Wilson* .50
306 *Robert Ferguson* 1.00
307 *Ken-Yon Rambo* 1.00
308 *Alex Bannister* .50
309 *Koren Robinson* 1.00
310 *Chad Johnson* 1.00
311 *Chris Chambers* 4.00
312 *Javon Green* .50
313 *Marvin "Snoop" Minnis* 1.00
314 *Scotty Anderson* .50
315 *Todd Heap* 1.00
316 *Alge Crumpler* 1.00
317 *Marcellus Rivers* .50
318 *Rashon Burns* .50
319 *Jamal Reynolds* .50
320 *Andre Carter* .50
321 *Justin Smith* .50
322 *Gerard Warren* .50
323 *Tommy Polley* .50
324 *Dan Morgan* 1.00
325 *Torrance Marshall* .50
326 *Correll Buckhalter* 1.00
327 *Derrick Gibson* .50
328 *Adam Archuleta* 1.00
329 *Jamar Fletcher* .50
330 *Nate Clements* .50

2001 Score Behind the Numbers

NM/M
Complete Set (40): 45.00
Common Player: .75
1 Brett Favre 4.00
2 Marshall Faulk 2.00
3 Michael Vick 5.00
4 Peyton Manning 3.00
5 David Terrell .75
6 Randy Moss 3.00
7 Kurt Warner 2.00
8 Edgerrin James 2.00
9 Drew Brees 2.00
10 Daunte Culpepper .75
11 Jeff Garcia .75
12 Mike Anderson .75
13 Jamal Lewis .75
14 Eddie George .75
15 Michael Bennett 2.00
16 Emmitt Smith 3.00
17 Chris Weinke .75
18 Timmy Brown 2.00
19 Eric Moulds .75
20 Marvin Harrison .75
21 Deuce McAllister 3.00
22 Donovan McNabb 2.00
23 Fred Taylor .75
24 Santana Moss .75
25 Cris Carter .75
26 Robert Smith .75
27 LaDainian Tomlinson 3.00
28 Isaac Bruce .75
29 Terrell Owens .75
30 Torry Holt .75
31 Ricky Williams .75
32 Curtis Martin .75
33 Stephen Davis .75
34 Corey Dillon .75
35 Ed McCaffrey .75
36 Steve McNair .75
37 Rudi Johnson .75
38 Antonio Freeman .75
39 Jerry Rice 3.00
40 Aaron Brooks .75

2001 Score Complete Players

NM/M
Complete Set (30): 50.00
Common Player: 1.00
1 Edgerrin James 2.00
2 Marshall Faulk 2.00
3 Kurt Warner 2.00
4 Daunte Culpepper 2.00
5 Donovan McNabb 2.00
6 Koren Robinson 1.00
7 Peyton Manning 3.00
8 Eddie George 1.00
9 Fred Taylor 1.00
10 Drew Brees 3.00
11 Randy Moss 3.00
12 Cris Carter 1.00
13 Steve Young 1.00
14 Marvin Harrison 1.00
15 Isaac Bruce 1.00
16 Terrell Owens 1.00
17 Mike Anderson 1.00
18 Jamal Lewis 1.00
19 Curtis Martin 1.00
20 Ricky Williams 2.00
21 Jerry Rice 3.00
22 Steve McNair 1.00
23 Michael Vick 5.00
24 Brett Favre 5.00
25 John Elway 4.00
26 Dan Marino 5.00
27 Barry Sanders 4.00
28 Michael Bennett 1.00
29 David Terrell 1.00
30 Emmitt Smith 4.00

2001 Score Franchise Fabrics

NM/M
Common Player: 10.00
1 Daunte Culpepper 25.00
2 Stephen Davis 10.00
3 Kurt Warner 25.00
4 Ricky Williams 30.00
5 Terrell Owens 15.00
6 Ricky Watters 10.00
7 Rich Gannon 10.00
8 Mike Anderson 10.00
9 Tony Gonzalez 10.00
10 Jerome Bettis 10.00
11 Peter Warrick 10.00
12 Tim Couch 15.00
13 Mark Brunell 12.00
14 Edgerrin James 20.00
15 Curtis Martin 15.00
16 Brett Favre 35.00
17 Donovan McNabb 15.00
18 Drew Bledsoe 15.00
19 Jake Plummer 10.00
20 Eric Moulds 10.00
21 Lamar Smith 10.00
22 Junior Seau 12.00
23 Wesley Walls 10.00
24 Jamal Anderson 10.00
25 Warren Sapp 10.00
26 Ron Dayne 10.00
27 Jamal Lewis 10.00
28 Cade McNown 10.00
29 Charlie Batch 10.00
30 Eddie George 12.00
31 Troy Aikman 25.00

2001 Score Millennium Men

NM/M
Complete Set (40): 50.00
Common Player: 1.00
1 Michael Vick 3.00
2 Marvin Harrison 1.00
3 Curtis Martin 1.00
4 Eric Moulds 1.00
5 Dan Marino 4.00
6 Edgerrin James 2.00
7 Drew Bledsoe 2.00
8 Drew Brees 2.00
9 Jamal Lewis 1.00
10 Marshall Faulk 2.00
11 Eddie George 1.00
12 Koren Robinson 1.00
13 Peter Warrick 1.00
14 Jerome Bettis 1.00
15 Warren Sapp 1.00
16 Mark Brunell 1.00
17 David Terrell 1.00
18 Steve Young 2.00
19 Ron Dayne 1.00
20 Michael Bennett 2.00
21 Brian Griese 1.00
22 Deuce McAllister 2.00
23 Kurt Warner 2.00
24 Mike Anderson 1.00
25 Rudi Johnson 1.00
26 John Elway 3.00
27 Terrell Owens 1.00
28 Ricky Williams 2.00
29 Jerry Rice 3.00
30 Jeff Garcia 1.00
31 Isaac Bruce 1.00
32 Aaron Brooks 1.00
33 Brett Favre 4.00
34 Daunte Culpepper 2.00
35 Ricky Watters 1.00
36 Tony Gonzalez 1.00
37 Stephen Davis 1.00
38 Santana Moss 1.00
39 Cris Carter 1.00
40 Donovan McNabb 2.00

A card number in parenthese ( ) indicates the set is unnumbered.

2001 Score Numbers Game

		NM/M
Complete Set (40):		50.00
Common Player:		.50
Minor Star:		1.00
1	Brett Favre	4.00
2	Marshall Faulk	2.00
3	Michael Vick	4.00
4	Peyton Manning	2.00
5	David Terrell	.50
6	Randy Moss	3.00
7	Kurt Warner	2.00
8	Edgerrin James	2.00
9	Drew Brees	1.00
10	Daunte Culpepper	2.00
11	Jeff Garcia	1.00
12	Mike Anderson	.50
13	Jamal Lewis	1.00
14	Eddie George	.50
15	Michael Bennett	2.00
16	Emmitt Smith	4.00
17	Chris Weinke	.50
18	Tim Brown	1.00
19	Eric Moulds	.50
20	Marvin Harrison	1.00
21	Deuce McAllister	1.00
22	Donovan McNabb	2.00
23	Fred Taylor	1.00
24	Santana Moss	.50
25	Cris Carter	.50
26	Robert Smith	.50
27	LaDainian Tomlinson	2.00
28	Isaac Bruce	.50
29	Terrell Owens	1.00
30	Torry Holt	.50
31	Ricky Williams	2.00
32	Curtis Martin	1.00
33	Stephen Davis	.50
34	Corey Dillon	.50
35	Ed McCaffrey	.50
36	Steve McNair	1.00
37	Rudi Johnson	.50
38	Antonio Freeman	.50
39	Jerry Rice	4.00
40	Aaron Brooks	.50

2001 Score Rookie Preview

		NM/M
Complete Set (60):		50.00
Common Player:		.50
1	Michael Vick	4.00
2	Drew Brees	1.00
3	Chris Weinke	.50
4	Quincy Carter	.50
5	Josh Heupel	.50
6	David Terrell	.50
7	Santana Moss	.50
8	Freddie Mitchell	1.00
9	Reggie Wayne	.50
10	Rod Gardner	1.00
11	Chris Chambers	2.00
12	Chad Johnson	.50
13	Ken-Yon Rambo	.50
14	Deuce McAllister	2.00
15	LaDainian Tomlinson	2.50
16	Travis Henry	1.00
17	Anthony Thomas	1.00
18	Michael Bennett	2.00
19	LaMont Jordan	.50
20	Kevan Barlow	.50
21	Reggie White	.50
22	Sage Rosenfels	.50
23	David Rivers	.50
24	Mike McMahon	1.00
25	Quincy Morgan	1.00
26	Eddie "Boo" Williams	.50
27	Vinny Sutherland	.50
28	Alex Bannister	.50
29	Marvin "Snoop" Minnis	.50
30	Cedrick Wilson	.50
31	Torrance Marshall	.50
32	Bobby Newcombe	.50
33	Ja'Mar Toombs	.50
34	Correll Buckhalter	.50
35	Andre Carter	.50
36	Jamal Reynolds	.50
37	Richard Seymour	.50
38	Tommy Polley	.50
39	Jamar Fletcher	.50
40	Fred Smoot	.50
41	Dan Morgan	1.00
42	James Jackson	.50
43	Rudi Johnson	.50
44	Scotty Anderson	.50
45	Travis Minor	.50
46	Robert Ferguson	.50
47	Ronney Daniels	.50
48	Heath Evans	.50
49	Justin Smith	.50
50	Gerard Warren	.50
51	Koren Robinson	.50
52	T.J. Houshmandzadeh	.50
53	Todd Heap	1.00
54	Javon Green	.50
55	Alge Crumpler	1.00
56	Derrick Gibson	.50
57	Marcellus Rivers	.50
58	Ken Lucas	.50
59	Nate Clements	.50
60	Will Allen	.50

2001 Score Settle the Score

		NM/M
Complete Set (30):		45.00
Common Player:		1.00
1	Kurt Warner, Steve McNair	2.00
2	Isaac Bruce, Randy Moss	3.00
3	Emmitt Smith, Stephen Davis	3.00
4	Marshall Faulk, Robert Smith	2.00
5	Eddie George, Ray Lewis	1.00
6	Fred Taylor, Jerome Bettis	1.00
7	Drew Bledsoe, Peyton Manning	3.00
8	Aaron Brooks, Daunte Culpepper	1.00
9	Eric Moulds, Marvin Harrison	1.00
10	Cris Carter, Jerry Rice	3.00
11	Curtis Martin, Edgerrin James	2.00
12	Donovan McNabb, Ron Dayne	2.00
13	Brett Favre, Warren Sapp	3.00
14	Shannon Sharpe, Tony Gonzalez	1.00
15	Keyshawn Johnson, Wayne Chrebet	1.00
16	Cade McNown, Tim Couch	1.00
17	Jamal Anderson, Terrell Davis	2.00
18	Jamal Lewis, Mike Anderson	1.00
19	Antonio Freeman, Terrell Owens	1.00
20	Brian Griese, Rich Gannon	2.00
21	Charlie Garner, Ricky Watters	1.00
22	Muhsin Muhammad, Ricky Williams	2.00
23	Elvis Grbac, Jeff Garcia	1.00
24	Jimmy Smith, Rod Smith	1.00
25	Ahman Green, Brian Urlacher	2.00
26	Darrell Jackson, Sylvester Morris	1.00
27	Peter Warrick, Travis Taylor	1.00
28	Dan Marino, John Elway	4.00
29	Mark Brunell, Steve Young	2.00
30	Jake Plummer, Troy Aikman	2.00

2001 Score The Franchise

		NM/M
Complete Set (31):		50.00
Common Player:		1.00
1	Tim Couch	2.00
2	Peter Warrick	1.00
3	Jerome Bettis	1.00
4	Fred Taylor	1.00
5	Eddie George	2.00
6	Jamal Lewis	1.50
7	Peyton Manning	4.00
8	Drew Bledsoe	2.00
9	Curtis Martin	2.00
10	Eric Moulds	1.00
11	Lamar Smith	1.00
12	Tony Gonzalez	1.00
13	Rich Gannon	1.00
14	Ricky Watters	1.00
15	Junior Seau	1.00
16	Brian Griese	1.00
17	Terrell Owens	2.00
18	Ricky Williams	2.00
19	Kurt Warner	3.00
20	Muhsin Muhammad	1.00
21	Jamal Anderson	1.00
22	Brett Favre	5.00
23	Randy Moss	4.00
24	Marcus Robinson	1.00
25	Warrick Dunn	1.00
26	James Stewart	1.00
27	Jake Plummer	1.00
28	Kerry Collins	1.00
29	Emmitt Smith	4.00
30	Stephen Davis	1.00
31	Donovan McNabb	2.00

2001 Score The Future Franchise

		NM/M
Complete Set (31):		60.00
Common Player:		1.00
1	James Jackson, Tim Couch	2.00
2	Justin Smith, Peter Warrick	1.00
3	Casey Hampton, Jerome Bettis	1.00
4	Fred Taylor, Marcus Stroud	1.00
5	Dan Alexander, Eddie George	2.00
6	Jamal Lewis, Todd Heap	1.00
7	Peyton Manning, Reggie Wayne	4.00
8	Drew Bledsoe, Jabari Holloway	3.00
9	Curtis Martin, Santana Moss	2.00
10	Eric Moulds, Travis Henry	1.00
11	Chris Chambers, Lamar Smith	2.00
12	Marvin "Snoop" Minnis, Tony Gonzalez	1.00
13	Marques Tuiasosopo, Rich Gannon	2.00
14	Koren Robinson, Ricky Watters	1.00
15	Junior Seau, LaDainian Tomlinson	3.00
16	Brian Griese, Kevin Kasper	1.00
17	Kevan Barlow, Terrell Owens	2.00
18	Deuce McAllister, Ricky Williams	3.00
19	Damione Lewis, Kurt Warner	2.00
20	Chris Weinke, Muhsin Muhammad	1.00
21	Jamal Anderson, Michael Vick	4.00
22	Brett Favre, Robert Ferguson	4.00
23	Michael Bennett, Randy Moss	3.00
24	David Terrell, Marcus Robinson	1.00
25	Kenyatta Walker, Warrick Dunn	1.00
26	James Stewart, Mike McMahon	1.00
27	Bobby Newcombe, Jake Plummer	1.00
28	Jesse Palmer, Kerry Collins	1.00
29	Emmitt Smith, Quincy Carter	3.00
30	Rod Gardner, Stephen Davis	1.00
31	Donovan McNabb, Freddie Mitchell	2.00

2001 Score Zenith Z-Team

		NM/M
Complete Set (38):		65.00
Common Player:		1.00
1	Michael Vick	4.00
2	Donovan McNabb	2.00
3	Daunte Culpepper	2.00
4	Kurt Warner	2.00
5	Peyton Manning	3.00
6	Brett Favre	4.00
7	Dan Marino	4.00
8	John Elway	3.00
9	Steve Young	2.00
10	Troy Aikman	2.00
11	Chad Pennington	2.00
12	Brian Griese	1.00
13	Drew Brees	1.00
14	David Terrell	1.00
15	Eric Moulds	1.00
16	Marvin Harrison	1.00
17	Randy Moss	3.00
18	Reggie Wayne	1.00
19	Terrell Owens	1.00
20	Jerry Rice	3.00
21	Cris Carter	1.00
22	Isaac Bruce	1.00
23	Peter Warrick	1.00
24	Deuce McAllister	1.00
25	Edgerrin James	2.00
26	Robert Smith	1.00
27	Marshall Faulk	2.00
28	Ricky Williams	2.00
29	Michael Bennett	2.00
30	Emmitt Smith	3.00
31	Eddie George	1.00
32	Jamal Lewis	1.00
33	Ron Dayne	1.00
34	Mike Anderson	1.00
35	Barry Sanders	3.00
36	Stephen Davis	1.00
37	Koren Robinson	1.00
38	LaDainian Tomlinson	2.00

2001 Score Select

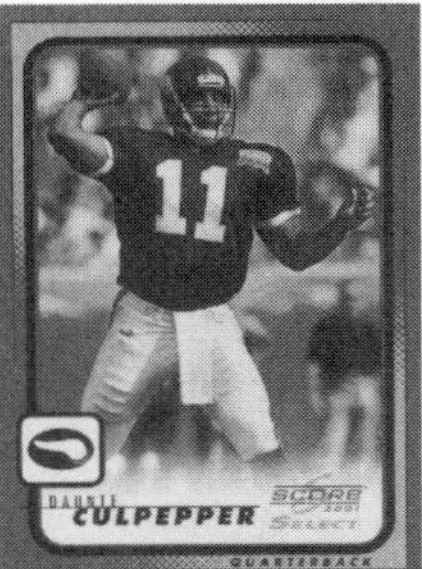

		NM/M
Complete Set (330):		1,000
Common Player:		.15
Minor Stars:		.30
Common SP (221-270):		.50
Production 325 Sets		
Common Rookie:		5.00
Production 275 Sets		
Pack (5):		5.00
Wax Box (20):		85.00
1	David Boston	.50
2	Frank Sanders	.15
3	Jake Plummer	.50
4	Michael Pittman	.15
5	Rob Moore	.15
6	Thomas Jones	.15
7	Chris Chandler	.15
8	Doug Johnson	.15
9	Jamal Anderson	.50
10	Tim Dwight	.50
11	Brandon Stokley	.15
12	Chris Redman	.50
13	Jamal Lewis	2.00
14	Qadry Ismail	.15
15	Ray Lewis	.15
16	Rod Woodson	.15
17	Shannon Sharpe	.15
18	Travis Taylor	.15
19	Trent Dilfer	.15
20	Elvis Grbac	.15
21	Eric Moulds	.15
22	Jay Riemersma	.15
23	Peerless Price	.15
24	Rob Johnson	.15
25	Sam Cowart	.15
26	Sammy Morris	.15
27	Shawn Bryson	.15
28	Donald Hayes	.15
29	Muhsin Muhammad	.15
30	Patrick Jeffers	.15
31	Reggie White	.50
32	Steve Beuerlein	.15
33	Tim Biakabutuka	.15
34	Wesley Walls	.15
35	Brian Urlacher	1.25
36	Cade McNown	.50
37	Dez White	.15
38	James Allen	.15
39	Marcus Robinson	.50
40	Marty Booker	.15
41	Akili Smith	.50
42	Corey Dillon	.50
43	Danny Farmer	.15
44	Peter Warrick	1.25
45	Ron Dugans	.15
46	Takeo Spikes	.15
47	Courtney Brown	.15
48	Dennis Northcutt	.15
49	JaJuan Dawson	.15
50	Kevin Johnson	.30
51	Tim Couch	.75
52	Travis Prentice	.15
53	Anthony Wright	.15
54	Emmitt Smith	1.75
55	James McKnight	.15
56	Joey Galloway	.50
57	Raghib Ismail	.15
58	Randall Cunningham	.50
59	Troy Aikman	1.25
60	Brian Griese	1.00
61	Ed McCaffrey	.50
62	Gus Frerotte	.15
63	John Elway	2.00
64	Mike Anderson	1.50
65	Olandis Gary	.15
66	Rod Smith	.15
67	Terrell Davis	1.25
68	Barry Sanders	2.00
69	Charlie Batch	.50
70	Germane Crowell	.15
71	Herman Moore	.15
72	James Stewart	.15
73	Johnnie Morton	.15
74	Robert Porcher	.15
75	Jim Harbaugh	.15
76	Ahman Green	.15
77	Antonio Freeman	.50
78	Bill Schroeder	.15
79	Brett Favre	2.50
80	Bubba Franks	.15
81	Dorsey Levens	.15
82	E.G. Green	.15
83	Edgerrin James	2.00
84	Jerome Pathon	.15
85	Ken Dilger	.15
86	Marcus Pollard	.15
87	Marvin Harrison	.50
88	Peyton Manning	2.00
89	Terrence Wilkins	.15
90	Fred Taylor	.75
91	Hardy Nickerson	.15
92	Jimmy Smith	.15
93	Keenan McCardell	.15
94	Kyle Brady	.15
95	Mark Brunell	.75
96	Tony Brackens	.15
97	Derrick Alexander	.15
98	Sylvester Morris	.15
99	Tony Gonzalez	.15
100	Tony Richardson	.15
101	Kimble Anders	.15
102	Warren Moon	.50
103	Dan Marino	2.00
104	Jay Fiedler	.50
105	Lamar Smith	.15
106	O.J. McDuffie	.15
107	Oronde Gadsden	.15
108	Sam Madison	.15
109	Thurman Thomas	.15
110	Tony Martin	.15
111	Zach Thomas	.15
112	Cris Carter	.50
113	Daunte Culpepper	1.25
114	Matthew Hatchette	.15
115	Randy Moss	2.00
116	Robert Smith	.50
117	Drew Bledsoe	.75
118	J.R. Redmond	.15
119	Kevin Faulk	.15
120	Michael Bishop	.15
121	Terry Glenn	.15
122	Troy Brown	.15
123	Ty Law	.15
124	Aaron Brooks	.75
125	Darren Howard	.15
126	Jake Reed	.15
127	Jeff Blake	.15
128	Joe Horn	.15
129	La'Roi Glover	.15
130	Ricky Williams	1.00
131	Willie Jackson	.15
132	Albert Connell	.15
133	Amani Toomer	.15
134	Ike Hilliard	.15
135	Jason Sehorn	.15
136	Jessie Armstead	.15
137	Kerry Collins	.15
138	Michael Strahan	.15
139	Ron Dayne	1.25
140	Ron Dixon	.15
141	Tiki Barber	.15
142	Anthony Becht	.15
143	Chad Pennington	1.25
144	Curtis Martin	.50
145	Dedric Ward	.15
146	Laveranues Coles	.50
147	Vinny Testaverde	.15
148	Wayne Chrebet	.15
149	Andre Rison	.15
150	Charles Woodson	.15
151	Darrell Russell	.15
152	Napoleon Kaufman	.15
153	Rich Gannon	.15
154	Tim Brown	.50
155	Tyrone Wheatley	.15
156	Chad Lewis	.15
157	Charles Johnson	.15
158	Donovan McNabb	1.00
159	Duce Staley	.50
160	Hugh Douglas	.15
161	Na Brown	.15
162	Todd Pinkston	.15
163	James Thrash	.15
164	Bobby Shaw	.15
165	Hines Ward	.15
166	Jerome Bettis	.50
167	Kordell Stewart	.50
168	Levon Kirkland	.15
169	Plaxico Burress	.50
170	Richard Huntley	.15
171	Troy Edwards	.15
172	Jeff Graham	.15
173	Junior Seau	.15
174	Doug Flutie	.60
175	Charlie Garner	.15
176	Jeff Garcia	.50
177	Jerry Rice	1.50
178	Steve Young	.75
179	Terrell Owens	.15
180	Brock Huard	.15
181	Darrell Jackson	.50
182	Derrick Mayes	.15
183	Ricky Watters	.15
184	Shaun Alexander	.75
185	Matt Hasselbeck	.15
186	John Randle	.15
187	Az-Zahir Hakim	.15
188	Isaac Bruce	.50
189	Kurt Warner	2.00
190	Marshall Faulk	.75
191	Torry Holt	.50
192	Trent Green	.15
193	Derrick Brooks	.15
194	Jacquez Green	.15
195	John Lynch	.15
196	Keyshawn Johnson	.50
197	Mike Alstott	.50
198	Reidel Anthony	.15
199	Shaun King	.50
200	Warren Sapp	.15
201	Warrick Dunn	.50
202	Ryan Leaf	.50
203	Carl Pickens	.15
204	Derrick Mason	.15
205	Eddie George	.75
206	Frank Wycheck	.15
207	Jevon Kearse	.50
208	Neil O'Donnell	.15
209	Steve McNair	.50
210	Yancey Thigpen	.15
211	Andre Reed	.15
212	Brad Johnson	.50
213	Bruce Smith	.15
214	Champ Bailey	.50
215	Darrell Green	.15
216	Deion Sanders	.50
217	Irving Fryar	.15
218	Jeff George	.15
219	Michael Westbrook	.15
220	Stephen Davis	.50
221	Terrell Owens AP	2.00
222	Peyton Manning AP	7.00
223	Stephen Davis AP	2.00
224	Marvin Harrison AP	2.00
225	Donovan McNabb AP	3.00
226	Edgerrin James AP	6.00
227	Eric Moulds AP	.15
228	Daunte Culpepper AP	4.00
229	Eddie George AP	2.50
230	Cris Carter AP	2.00
231	Rich Gannon AP	.15
232	Jeff Garcia AP	2.00
233	Jimmy Smith AP	.15
234	Tony Gonzalez AP	.15
235	Torry Holt AP	2.00
236	Jevon Kearse AP	2.00
237	Ray Lewis AP	.15
238	Warren Sapp AP	.15
239	Brian Urlacher AP	4.00
240	Champ Bailey AP	.15
241	Peyton Manning LL	7.00
242	Jeff Garcia LL	2.00
243	Elvis Grbac LL	.15
244	Daunte Culpepper LL	4.00
245	Brett Favre LL	8.00
246	Edgerrin James LL	6.00
247	Robert Smith LL	.15
248	Eddie George LL	2.50
249	Mike Anderson LL	4.00
250	Corey Dillon LL	2.00
251	Torry Holt LL	2.00
252	Rod Smith LL	.15
253	Isaac Bruce LL	2.00
254	Terrell Owens LL	2.00
255	Randy Moss LL	7.00
256	La'Roi Glover LL	.15
257	Trace Armstrong LL	.15
258	Warren Sapp LL	.15
259	Hugh Douglas LL	.15
260	Jason Taylor LL	.15
261	Mike Anderson SS	4.00
262	Jamal Lewis SS	5.00
263	Sylvester Morris SS	.15
264	Darrell Jackson SS	2.00
265	Peter Warrick SS	3.00
266	Ron Dayne SS	3.00
267	Shaun Alexander SS	2.00
268	Plaxico Burress SS	2.00
269	Brian Urlacher SS	2.00
270	Courtney Brown SS	.15
271	*Michael Vick*	100.00
272	*Drew Brees*	30.00
273	*Chris Weinke*	40.00
274	*Quincy Carter*	20.00
275	*Sage Rosenfels*	15.00
276	*Josh Heupel*	15.00
277	*David Rivers*	5.00
278	*Ben Leard*	10.00
279	*MarquesTuiasosopo*	15.00
280	*Mike McMahon*	15.00
281	*Deuce McAllister*	50.00
282	*LaMont Jordan*	15.00
283	*LaDainian Tomlinson*	60.00
284	*James Jackson*	15.00
285	*Anthony Thomas*	15.00
286	*Travis Henry*	20.00
287	*Travis Minor*	10.00
288	*Rudi Johnson*	15.00
289	*Michael Bennett*	30.00
290	*Kevan Barlow*	15.00
291	*Reggie White*	10.00
292	*Moran Norris*	5.00
293	*Ja'Mar Toombs*	10.00
294	*Heath Evans*	5.00
295	*David Terrell*	15.00
296	*Santana Moss*	25.00
297	*Rod Gardner*	20.00
298	*Quincy Morgan*	15.00
299	*Freddie Mitchell*	10.00
300	*Boo Williams*	5.00
301	*Reggie Wayne*	15.00
302	*Ronney Daniels*	10.00
303	*Bobby Newcombe*	10.00
304	*Vinny Sutherland*	12.00
305	*Cedrick Wilson*	10.00
306	*Robert Ferguson*	10.00
307	*Ken-Yon Rambo*	10.00
308	*Alex Bannister*	10.00
309	*Koren Robinson*	15.00
310	*Chad Johnson*	20.00
311	*Chris Chambers*	20.00
312	*Javon Green*	10.00
313	*Marvin "Snoop" Minnis*	10.00
314	*Scotty Anderson*	10.00
315	*Todd Heap*	12.00
316	*Alge Crumpler*	12.00
317	*Marcellus Rivers*	10.00
318	*Rashon Burns*	5.00
319	*Jamal Reynolds*	5.00
320	*Andre Carter*	12.00
321	*Justin Smith*	12.00
322	*Gerard Warren*	10.00
323	*Tommy Polley*	10.00
324	*Dan Morgan*	15.00
325	*Torrance Marshall*	5.00
326	*Correll Buckhalter*	15.00
327	*Derrick Gibson*	5.00
328	*Adam Archuleta*	12.00
329	*Jamar Fletcher*	8.00
330	*Nate Clements*	8.00
NNO	Supplemental Set Exch	50.00

2001 Score Select Behind The Numbers

		NM/M
Common Player:		3.00
Numbered to Season Stat		
BN1	Brett Favre/338	10.00
BN2	Marshall Faulk/253	7.00
BN3	Michael Vick/87	35.00
BN4	Peyton Manning/357	8.00
BN5	David Terrell/63	6.00
BN6	Randy Moss/77	10.00
BN7	Kurt Warner/235	6.00
BN8	Edgerrin James/387	8.00
BN9	Drew Brees/309	8.00
BN10	Daunte Culpepper/297	6.00
BN11	Jeff Garcia/355	3.00
BN12	Mike Anderson/297	6.00
BN13	Jamal Lewis/309	8.00
BN14	Eddie George/403	7.00
BN15	Michael Bennett/310	8.00
BN16	Emmitt Smith/294	8.00
BN17	Chris Weinke/266	2.00
BN18	Tim Brown/76	6.00
BN19	Eric Moulds/94	3.00
BN20	Marvin Harrison/102	8.00
BN21	Deuce McAllister/105	12.00
BN22	Donovan McNabb/330	8.00
BN23	Fred Taylor/292	4.00
BN24	Santana Moss/45	10.00
BN25	Cris Carter/96	8.00
BN26	Robert Smith/295	4.00
BN27	LaDainian Tomlinson/369	8.00
BN28	Isaac Bruce/87	6.00
BN29	Terrell Owens/97	6.00
BN30	Torry Holt/82	6.00
BN31	Ricky Williams/248	8.00
BN32	Curtis Martin/312	3.00
BN33	Stephen Davis/332	3.00
BN34	Corey Dillon/315	3.00
BN35	Ed McCaffrey/101	3.00
BN36	Steve McNair/248	3.00
BN37	Rudi Johnson/324	3.00
BN38	Antonio Freeman/62	6.00
BN39	Jerry Rice/75	8.00
BN40	Aaron Brooks/113	6.00

2001 Score Select Complete Players

		NM/M
Complete Set (30):		90.00
Common Player:		1.00
Production 550 Sets		
CP1	Edgerrin James	6.00
CP2	Marshall Faulk	3.00
CP3	Kurt Warner	5.00
CP4	Daunte Culpepper	4.00
CP5	Donovan McNabb	3.00
CP6	Koren Robinson	1.00

		NM/M
CP7	Peyton Manning	5.00
CP8	Eddie George	2.00
CP9	Fred Taylor	1.00
CP10	Drew Brees	4.00
CP11	Randy Moss	5.00
CP12	Cris Carter	1.00
CP13	Steve Young	3.00
CP14	Marvin Harrison	2.00
CP15	Isaac Bruce	1.00
CP16	Terrell Owens	1.00
CP17	Mike Anderson	1.00
CP18	Jamal Lewis	1.00
CP19	Curtis Martin	3.00
CP20	Ricky Williams	5.00
CP21	Jerry Rice	5.00
CP22	Steve McNair	1.00
CP23	Michael Vick	8.00
CP24	Brett Favre	8.00
CP25	John Elway	6.00
CP26	Dan Marino	6.00
CP27	Barry Sanders	6.00
CP28	Michael Bennett	5.00
CP29	David Terrell	2.00
CP30	Emmitt Smith	6.00

2001 Score Select Franchise Fabrics/Tags

		NM/M
Common Player:		50.00
Production 50 Sets		
FT1	Daunte Culpepper	125.00
FT2	Stephen Davis	60.00
FT3	Kurt Warner	150.00
FT4	Ricky Williams	150.00
FT5	Terrell Owens	60.00
FT6	Ricky Watters	50.00
FT7	Rich Gannon	50.00
FT8	Mike Anderson	125.00
FT9	Tony Gonzalez	60.00
FT10	Jerome Bettis	60.00
FT11	Peter Warrick	100.00
FT12	Tim Couch	100.00
FT13	Mark Brunell	100.00
FT14	Edgerrin James	180.00
FT15	Curtis Martin	60.00
FT16	Brett Favre	250.00
FT17	Donovan McNabb	125.00
FT18	Drew Bledsoe	100.00
FT19	Jake Plummer	60.00
FT20	Eric Moulds	60.00
FT21	Lamar Smith	60.00
FT22	Junior Seau	50.00
FT23	Wesley Walls	50.00
FT24	Jamal Anderson	60.00
FT25	Warren Sapp	60.00
FT26	Ron Dayne	125.00
FT27	Jamal Lewis	150.00
FT28	Cade McNown	60.00
FT29	Charlie Batch	60.00
FT30	Eddie George	85.00
FT31	Troy Aikman	175.00

2001 Score Select The Future Franchise

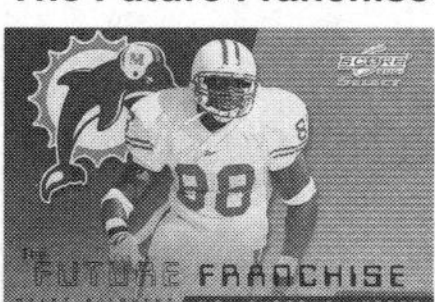

		NM/M
Complete Set (31):		90.00
Common Player:		1.00
Minor Stars:		2.00
Production 550 Sets		
FF1	Tim Couch, James Jackson	3.00
FF2	Peter Warrick, Justin Smith	1.00
FF3	Jerome Bettis, Casey Hampton	1.00
FF4	Fred Taylor, Marcus Stroud	2.00
FF5	Eddie George, Dan Alexander	3.00
FF6	Jamal Lewis, Todd Heap	3.00
FF7	Peyton Manning, Reggie Wayne	5.00
FF8	Drew Bledsoe, Jabari Holloway	4.00
FF9	Curtis Martin, Santana Moss	3.00
FF10	Eric Moulds, Travis Henry	3.00
FF11	Lamar Smith, Chris Chambers	3.00
FF12	Tony Gonzalez, Marvin "Snoop" Minnis	2.00
FF13	Rich Gannon, Marques Tuiasosopo	3.00
FF14	Ricky Watters, Koren Robinson	2.00
FF15	Junior Seau, LaDainian Tomlinson	5.00
FF16	Brian Griese, Kevin Kasper	2.00
FF17	Terrell Owens, Kevan Barlow	2.00
FF18	Ricky Williams, Deuce McAllister	5.00
FF19	Kurt Warner, Damione Lewis	4.00
FF20	Muhsin Muhammad, Chris Weinke	2.00
FF21	Jamal Anderson, Michael Vick	10.00
FF22	Brett Favre, Robert Ferguson	8.00
FF23	Randy Moss, Michael Bennett	6.00
FF24	Marcus Robinson, David Terrell	2.00
FF25	Warrick Dunn, Kenyatta Walker	2.00
FF26	James Stewart, Mike McMahon	1.00
FF27	Jake Plummer, Bobby Newcombe	2.00
FF28	Kerry Collins, Jesse Palmer	1.00
FF29	Emmitt Smith, Quincy Carter	6.00
FF30	Stephen Davis, Rod Gardner	2.00
FF31	Donovan McNabb, Freddie Mitchell	4.00

2001 Score Select Rookie Preview

		NM/M
Common Player:		7.00
RP1	Michael Vick/150	150.00
RP2	Drew Brees/150	70.00
RP3	Chris Weinke/250	30.00
RP4	Quincy Carter	7.00
RP5	Josh Heupel/450	15.00
RP6	David Terrell/150	40.00
RP7	Santana Moss/250	30.00
RP8	Freddie Mitchell/350	20.00
RP9	Reggie Wayne/250	20.00
RP10	Rod Gardner/50	45.00
RP11	Chris Chambers/450	12.00
RP12	Chad Johnson/450	10.00
RP13	Ken-Yon Rambo/550	10.00
RP14	Deuce McAllister/150	35.00
RP15	LaDainian Tomlinson/250	45.00
RP16	Travis Henry/450	15.00
RP17	Anthony Thomas/250	20.00
RP18	Michael Bennett/250	35.00
RP19	LaMont Jordan/350	12.00
RP20	Kevan Barlow/450	10.00
RP21	Reggie White/550	12.00
RP22	Sage Rosenfels/50	20.00
RP23	David Rivers	7.00
RP24	Mike McMahon/450	10.00
RP25	Quincy Morgan/450	12.00
RP26	Boo Williams	7.00
RP27	Vinny Sutherland	7.00
RP28	Alex Bannister/450	10.00
RP29	Marvin "Snoop" Minnis/450	12.00
RP30	Cedrick Wilson/450	7.00
RP31	Torrance Marshall	7.00
RP32	Bobby Newcombe	7.00
RP33	Ja'Mar Toombs	7.00
RP34	Correll Buckhalter/550	12.00
RP35	Andre Carter	7.00
RP36	Jamal Reynolds/350	8.00
RP37	Richard Seymour/350	8.00
RP38	Tommy Polley	7.00
RP39	Jamar Fletcher	7.00
RP40	Fred Smoot	7.00
RP41	Dan Morgan	7.00
RP42	James Jackson/350	12.00
RP43	Rudi Johnson/350	10.00
RP44	Scotty Anderson	7.00
RP45	Travis Minor/750	12.00
RP46	Robert Ferguson/350	12.00
RP47	Ronney Daniels	7.00
RP48	Heath Evans	7.00
RP49	Justin Smith/350	10.00
RP50	Gerard Warren/350	10.00
RP51	Koren Robinson/50	45.00
RP52	T.J. Houshmandzadeh/450	8.00
RP53	Todd Heap/750	7.00
RP54	Javon Green	7.00
RP55	Alge Crumpler/750	7.00
RP56	Derrick Gibson	7.00
RP57	Marcellus Rivers	7.00
RP58	Ken Lucas	7.00
RP59	Nate Clements	7.00
RP60	Will Allen/750	7.00

2001 Score Select Rookie Roll Call Autographs

		NM/M
Common Player:		15.00
Production 50 Sets		
RP1	Michael Vick	200.00
RP2	Drew Brees	75.00
RP3	Chris Weinke	35.00
RP5	Josh Heupel	35.00
RP6	David Terrell	20.00
RP7	Santana Moss	40.00
RP8	Freddie Mitchell	40.00
RP9	Reggie Wayne	35.00
RP101	Rod Gardner	35.00
RP11	Chris Chambers	40.00
RP12	Chad Johnson	25.00
RP13	Ken-Yon Rambo	20.00
RP14	Deuce McAllister	65.00
RP15	LaDainian Tomlinson	100.00
RP16	Travis Henry	40.00
RP17	Anthony Thomas	25.00
RP18	Michael Bennett	75.00
RP19	LaMont Jordan	25.00
RP20	Kevan Barlow	25.00
RP21	Reggie White	20.00
RP22	Sage Rosenfels	25.00
RP24	Mike McMahon	25.00
RP25	Quincy Morgan	25.00
RP28	Alex Bannister	25.00
RP29	Marvin "Snoop" Minnis	30.00
RP30	Cedrick Wilson	20.00
RP34	Correll Buckhalter	25.00
RP36	Jamal Reynolds	20.00
RP37	Richard Seymour	15.00
RP42	James Jackson	25.00
RP43	Rudi Johnson	20.00
RP45	Travis Minor	30.00
RP46	Robert Ferguson	30.00
RP49	Justin Smith	25.00
RP50	Gerard Warren	25.00
RP51	Koren Robinson	50.00
RP52	T.J. Houshmandzadeh	15.00
RP53	Todd Heap	20.00
RP55	Alge Crumpler	20.00
RP60	Will Allen	15.00

2001 Score Select Settle The Score

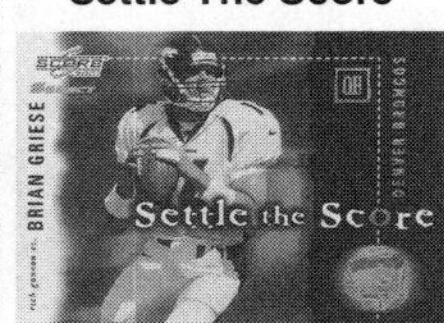

		NM/M
Complete Set (30):		75.00
Common Player:		1.00
Minor Stars:		2.00
Production 550 Sets		
SS1	Kurt Warner, Steve McNair	5.00
SS2	Randy Moss, Isaac Bruce	5.00
SS3	Emmitt Smith, Stephen Davis	5.00
SS4	Marshall Faulk, Robert Smith	3.00
SS5	Eddie George, Ray Lewis	2.00
SS6	Fred Taylor, Jerome Bettis	2.00
SS7	Peyton Manning, Drew Bledsoe	4.00
SS8	Daunte Culpepper, Aaron Brooks	3.00
SS9	Marvin Harrison, Eric Moulds	2.00
SS10	Jerry Rice, Cris Carter	4.00
SS11	Curtis Martin, Edgerrin James	4.00
SS12	Donovan McNabb, Ron Dayne	3.00
SS13	Brett Favre, Warren Sapp	6.00
SS14	Tony Gonzalez, Shannon Sharpe	1.00
SS15	Wayne Chrebet, Keyshawn Johnson	1.00
SS16	Tim Couch, Cade McNown	3.00
SS17	Terrell Davis, Jamal Anderson	3.00
SS18	Mike Anderson, Jamal Lewis	3.00
SS19	Terrell Owens, Antonio Freeman	2.00
SS20	Brian Griese, Rich Gannon	3.00
SS21	Ricky Watters, Charlie Garner	1.00
SS22	Muhsin Muhammad, Ricky Williams	4.00
SS23	Jeff Garcia, Elvis Grbac	2.00
SS24	Rod Smith, Jimmy Smith	1.00
SS25	Brian Urlacher, Ahman Green	3.00
SS26	Darrell Jackson, Sylvester Morris	1.00
SS27	Peter Warrick, Travis Taylor	2.00
SS28	Dan Marino, John Elway	6.00
SS29	Steve Young, Mark Brunell	4.00
SS30	Troy Aikman, Jake Plummer	4.00

2001 Score Select Zenith Z-Team

		NM/M
Complete Set (38):		300.00
Common Player:		2.00
Minor Stars:		5.00
Production 100 Sets		
ZT1	Michael Vick	50.00
ZT2	Donovan McNabb	12.00
ZT3	Daunte Culpepper	12.00
ZT4	Kurt Warner	12.00
ZT5	Peyton Manning	15.00
ZT6	Brett Favre	20.00
ZT7	Dan Marino	15.00
ZT8	John Elway	15.00
ZT9	Steve Young	12.00
ZT10	Troy Aikman	12.00
ZT11	Chad Pennington	15.00
ZT12	Brian Griese	8.00
ZT13	Drew Brees	15.00
ZT14	David Terrell	10.00
ZT15	Eric Moulds	2.00
ZT16	Marvin Harrison	5.00
ZT17	Randy Moss	12.00
ZT18	Reggie Wayne	6.00
ZT19	Terrell Owens	5.00
ZT20	Jerry Rice	12.00
ZT21	Cris Carter	5.00
ZT22	Isaac Bruce	5.00
ZT23	Peter Warrick	2.00
ZT24	Deuce McAllister	12.00
ZT25	Edgerrin James	10.00
ZT26	Robert Smith	2.00
ZT27	Marshall Faulk	8.00
ZT28	Ricky Williams	15.00
ZT29	Michael Bennett	15.00
ZT30	Emmitt Smith	15.00
ZT31	Eddie George	10.00
ZT32	Jamal Lewis	10.00
ZT33	Ron Dayne	6.00
ZT34	Mike Anderson	6.00
ZT35	Barry Sanders	15.00
ZT36	Stephen Davis	5.00
ZT37	Koren Robinson	5.00
ZT38	LaDainian Tomlinson	20.00

2002 Score

		NM/M
Complete Set (330):		50.00
Common Player:		.15
Unlisted Stars:		.60
Minor Stars:		.40
Common Rookie (251-330):		.75
Minor Rookie Star:		1.00
Pack (7):		1.25
Wax Box (36):		40.00
1	David Boston	.40
2	Arnold Jackson	.15
3	MarTay Jenkins	.15
4	Thomas Jones	.15
5	Kwamie Lassiter	.15
6	Michael Pittman	.15
7	Jake Plummer	.15
8	Chris Chandler	.15
9	Alge Crumpler	.15
10	Terance Mathis	.15
11	Maurice Smith	.15
12	Ray Buchanan	.15
13	Jamal Anderson	.25
14	Keith Brooking	.15
15	Michael Vick	2.00
16	Obafemi Ayanbadejo	.15
17	Jason Brookins	.15
18	Randall Cunningham	.15
19	Elvis Grbac	.15
20	Todd Heap	.15
21	Qadry Ismail	.15
22	Shannon Sharpe	.25
23	Travis Taylor	.25
24	Ray Lewis	.25
25	Jamal Lewis	.75
26	Larry Centers	.15
27	Rob Johnson	.15
28	Shawn Bryson	.15
29	Eric Moulds	.15
30	Peerless Price	.25
31	Nate Clements	.15
32	Travis Henry	.40
33	Isaac Byrd	.15
34	Nick Goings	.15
35	Donald Hayes	.15
36	Richard Huntley	.15
37	Muhsin Muhammad	.15
38	Steve Smith	.15
39	Wesley Walls	.15
40	Chris Weinke	.60
41	James Allen	.15
42	Marty Booker	.15
43	Jim Miller	.15
44	David Terrell	.60
45	Dez White	.15
46	Brian Urlacher	1.50
47	Mike Brown	.15
48	Anthony Thomas	1.50
49	T.J. Houshmandzadeh	.15
50	Chad Johnson	.15
51	Darnay Scott	.25
52	Peter Warrick	.50
53	Akili Smith	.50
54	Jon Kitna	.15
55	Justin Smith	.15
56	Corey Dillon	.40
57	Benjamin Gay	.15
58	Kevin Johnson	.15
59	Quincy Morgan	.40
60	James Jackson	.40
61	Anthony Henry	.25
62	Gerard Warren	.15
63	Jamir Miller	.15
64	Tim Couch	.40
65	Quincy Carter	1.25
66	Joey Galloway	.25
67	Troy Hambrick	.15
68	Raghib Ismail	.15
69	Dexter Coakley	.15
70	Darren Woodson	.15
71	Emmitt Smith	2.00
72	Mike Anderson	.75
73	Terrell Davis	.75
74	Kevin Kasper	.15
75	Rod Smith	.40
76	Ed McCaffrey	.25
77	Olandis Gary	.15
78	Dwayne Carswell	.15
79	Deltha O'Neal	.15
80	Brian Griese	.40
81	Scotty Anderson	.15
82	Johnnie Morton	.15
83	Cory Schlesinger	.15
84	James Stewart	.50
85	Shaun Rogers	.15
86	Mike McMahon	.60
87	Charlie Batch	.15
88	Robert Porcher	.15
89	Bubba Franks	.15
90	Robert Ferguson	.15
91	Antonio Freeman	.15
92	Ahman Green	.60
93	Bill Schroeder	.15
94	Kabeer Gbaja-Biamila	.25
95	Jamal Reynolds	.25
96	Darren Sharper	.15
97	Brett Favre	3.00
98	Marvin Harrison	.25
99	Dominic Rhodes	.15
100	Edgerrin James	1.50
101	Reggie Wayne	.25
102	Terrence Wilkins	.25
103	Ken Dilger	.15
104	Peyton Manning	2.00
105	Elvis Joseph	.15
106	Stacey Mack	.15
107	Fred Taylor	.60
108	Keenan McCardell	.15
109	Jimmy Smith	.15
110	Mark Brunell	.50
111	Derrick Alexander	.15
112	Tony Gonzalez	.40
113	Trent Green	.25
114	Marvin "Snoop" Minnis	.50
115	Priest Holmes	.40
116	Chris Chambers	.60
117	Jay Fiedler	.15
118	Oronde Gadsden	.15
119	Travis Minor	.40
120	Lamar Smith	.50
121	Zach Thomas	.25
122	Michael Bennett	.60
123	Todd Bouman	.15
124	Cris Carter	.25
125	Byron Chamberlain	.15
126	Randy Moss	2.00
127	Jake Reed	.15
128	Daunte Culpepper	1.25
129	Drew Bledsoe	1.25
130	Troy Brown	.15
131	David Patten	.15
132	J.R. Redmond	.40
133	Antowain Smith	.40
134	Ty Law	.15
135	Richard Seymour	.15
136	Adam Vinatieri	.15
137	Tom Brady	2.00
138	Joe Horn	.15
139	Willie Jackson	.25
140	Deuce McAllister	.75
141	Eddie "Boo" Williams	.15
142	Ricky Williams	1.25
143	La'Roi Glover	.15
144	Sammy Knight	.75
145	Aaron Brooks	.75
146	Tiki Barber	.15
147	Ron Dayne	.40
148	Ike Hilliard	.15
149	Amani Toomer	.15
150	Will Allen	.15
151	Michael Strahan	.40
152	Jason Sehorn	.15
153	Kerry Collins	.15
154	Anthony Becht	.15
155	Wayne Chrebet	.15
156	Laveranues Coles	.15
157	LaMont Jordan	.15
158	Santana Moss	.40
159	Chad Pennington	.40
160	John Abraham	.15
161	Vinny Testaverde	.15
162	Curtis Martin	.50
163	Tim Brown	.50
164	Rich Gannon	.40
165	Charlie Garner	.25
166	Jerry Porter	.15
167	Marques Tuiasosopo	.40
168	Tyrone Wheatley	.40
169	Charles Woodson	.40
170	Jerry Rice	2.00
171	Correll Buckhalter	.15
172	Chad Lewis	.15
173	Brian Mitchell	.15
174	Freddie Mitchell	.60
175	Todd Pinkston	.15
176	Duce Staley	.40
177	Tony Stewart	.15
178	James Thrash	.15
179	Hugh Douglas	.15
180	Donovan McNabb	1.25
181	Plaxico Burress	.60
182	Chris Fuamatu-Ma'afala	.15
183	Kordell Stewart	.40
184	Hines Ward	.25
185	Amos Zereoue	.15
186	Kendrell Bell	.15
187	Casey Hampton	.15
188	Jerome Bettis	.40
189	Drew Brees	1.50
190	Curtis Conway	.15
191	Tim Dwight	.15
192	Doug Flutie	.50
193	Junior Seau	.25
194	Marcellus Wiley	.15
195	Ryan McNeil	.15
196	Jeff Graham	.15
197	LaDainian Tomlinson	1.50
198	Kevan Barlow	.15
199	Garrison Hearst	.25
200	Eric Johnson	.15
201	Terrell Owens	.40
202	J.J. Stokes	.15
203	Andre Carter	.15
204	Jeff Garcia	.40
205	Trent Dilfer	.40
206	Matt Hasselbeck	.15
207	Darrell Jackson	.15
208	Koren Robinson	.40
209	Ricky Watters	.25
210	John Randle	.15
211	Shaun Alexander	.50
212	Isaac Bruce	.40
213	Trung Canidate	.15
214	Marshall Faulk	1.25
215	Az-Zahir Hakim	.15
216	Torry Holt	.25
217	Yo Murphy	.15
218	Ricky Proehl	.15
219	Adam Archuleta	.15
220	Dre' Bly	.15
221	London Fletcher	.15
222	Tommy Polley	.15
223	Aeneas Williams	.25
224	Kurt Warner	2.00
225	Mike Alstott	.25
226	Warrick Dunn	.25
227	Jacquez Green	.15
228	Derrick Brooks	.15
229	John Lynch	.15
230	Warren Sapp	.25
231	Ronde Barber	.15
232	Brad Johnson	.40
233	Keyshawn Johnson	.25
234	Drew Bennett	.15
235	Kevin Dyson	.15
236	Eddie George	.40
237	Derrick Mason	.15
238	Justin McCareins	.15
239	Frank Wycheck	.15
240	Jevon Kearse	.25
241	Samari Rolle	.15
242	Steve McNair	.40
243	Tony Banks	.25
244	Stephen Davis	.50
245	Michael Westbrook	.15
246	Champ Bailey	.25
247	Darrell Green	.25
248	Bruce Smith	.25
249	Fred Smoot	.15
250	Rod Gardner	.75
251	*David Carr*	8.00
252	*Joey Harrington*	8.00
253	*Patrick Ramsey*	2.00
254	*Kurt Kittner*	1.50
255	*Eric Crouch*	2.00
256	*Travis Stephens*	.75
257	*David Garrard*	.75
258	*Rohan Davey*	2.00
259	*Ronald Curry*	1.00
260	*Chad Hutchinson*	.75
261	*William Green*	3.00
262	*T.J. Duckett*	4.00
263	*Clinton Portis*	8.00
264	*DeShaun Foster*	2.00
265	*Luke Staley*	1.50
266	*Wes Pate*	.75
267	*Travis Stephens*	.75
268	*Adrian Peterson*	.75
269	*Zak Kustok*	.75
270	*Maurice Morris*	1.00
271	*Lamar Gordon*	.75
272	*Chester Taylor*	.75
273	*Najeh Davenport*	.75
274	*Ladell Betts*	1.00
275	*Ashley Lelie*	4.00
276	*Josh Reed*	2.00
277	*Cliff Russell*	.75
278	*Javon Walker*	3.00
279	*Ron Johnson*	1.00
280	*Antwann Randle El*	3.00
281	*Andre Davis*	2.00
282	*Marquise Walker*	1.50
283	*Kelly Campbell*	1.00
284	*Tavon Mason*	.75
285	*Antonio Bryant*	3.00
286	*Jabar Gaffney*	2.00
287	*Donte Stallworth*	4.00
288	*Tim Carter*	.75
289	*Donald Reche Caldwell*	1.50
290	*Freddie Milons*	.75
291	*Brian Poli-Dixon*	.75
292	*Brian Westbrook*	1.00
293	*Josh Scobey*	.75
294	*Jeremy Shockey*	5.00
295	*Daniel Graham*	1.50
296	*Deion Branch*	1.00
297	*Julius Peppers*	3.00
298	*Kalimba Edwards*	.75
299	*Dwight Freeney*	.75
300	*Terry Charles*	.75

301 *Alex Brown* .75
302 *Jason McAddley* .75
303 *Michael Lewis* .75
304 *Dennis Johnson* .75
305 *Albert Haynesworth* 1.00
306 *Ryan Sims* 1.00
307 *Larry Tripplett* .75
308 *Anthony Weaver* .75
309 *Wendell Bryant* .75
310 *John Henderson* 1.00
311 *Alan Harper* .75
312 *Napoleon Harris* .75
313 *Bryan Thomas* .75
314 *Andra Davis* .75
315 *Levar Fisher* .75
n16 *Woody Dantzler* .75
317 *Robert Thomas* .75
318 *Quentin Jammer* 1.50
319 *Lito Sheppard* 1.00
320 *Travis Fisher* 1.00
321 *Roy Williams* 3.00
322 *Phillip Buchanon* 1.50
323 *Joseph Jefferson* .75
324 *Edward Reed* .75
325 *Lamont Thompson* .75
326 *Raonell Smith* .75
327 *Mike Rumph* .75
328 *Rocky Calmus* .75
329 *Bryant McKinnie* 1.00
330 *Mike Williams* .75

2002 Score Changing Stripes

NM/M
Common Player: 25.00
Production 150 sets
1 Curtis Martin 40.00
2 Doug Flutie 40.00
3 John Riggins 75.00
4 Jerome Bettis 60.00
5 Jerry Rice 100.00
7 Eric Dickerson 30.00
8 Kerry Collins 25.00
9 Keyshawn Johnson 25.00
10 Marcus Allen 50.00
11 Mark Brunell 25.00
12 Priest Holmes 30.00
13 Ricky Watters 25.00
14 Thurman Thomas 40.00
15 Warren Moon 30.00

2002 Score Franchise Fabrics

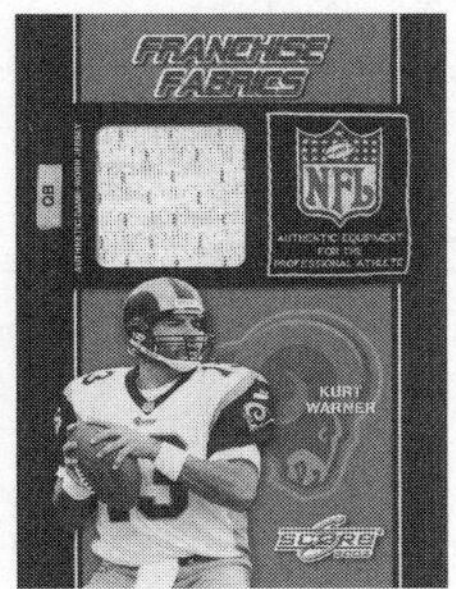

NM/M
Common Player: 10.00
1 Ahman Green 25.00
2 Amani Toomer 10.00
3 Brad Johnson 10.00
4 Charles Woodson 20.00
5 Corey Dillon 10.00
6 Cris Carter 15.00
7 David Boston 25.00
8 Derrick Mason 10.00
9 Donovan McNabb 25.00
10 Emmitt Smith 50.00
11 Hines Ward 10.00
12 John Elway 50.00
13 Junior Seau 20.00
14 Kevin Johnson 10.00
15 Kurt Warner 40.00
16 LaDainian Tomlinson 30.00
17 Marvin Harrison 10.00
18 Michael Strahan 10.00
19 Mike Alstott 10.00
20 Ricky Williams 10.00
21 Rob Johnson 10.00
22 Rod Smith 10.00
23 Stephen Davis 10.00
24 Troy Aikman 40.00
25 Zach Thomas 20.00

2002 Score In The Zone

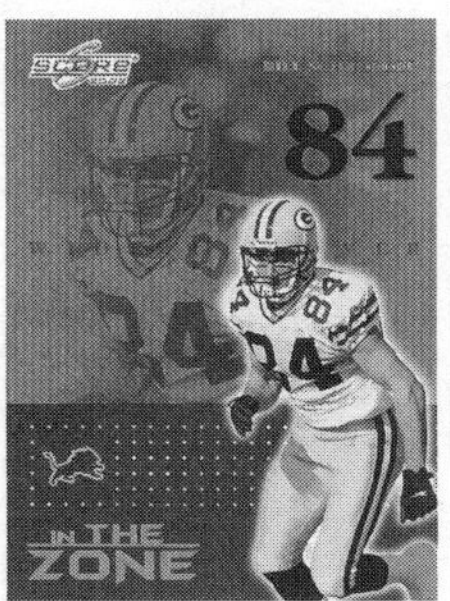

NM/M
Common Player: 1.00
Inserted 1:25
1 Marshall Faulk 2.00
2 Terrell Owens 1.00
3 Shaun Alexander 2.00
4 Marvin Harrison 1.00
5 Antowain Smith 1.00
6 Corey Dillon 1.00
7 Mike Alstott 1.00
8 Rod Smith 2.00
9 Ahman Green 1.00
10 Derrick Mason 1.00
11 Tim Brown 2.00
12 Curtis Martin 1.00
13 Priest Holmes 1.00
14 Stacey Mack 1.00
15 LaDainian Tomlinson 3.00
16 Dominic Rhodes 1.00
17 Randy Moss 4.00
18 Bill Schroeder 1.00
19 Joe Horn 1.00
20 Jerry Rice 3.00

2002 Score Inscriptions

NM/M
Common Player: 25.00
Inserted 1:347
Personalized Production 25 Sets
1 Anthony Thomas 25.00
2 Brian Griese/50 40.00
3 Brian Urlacher 50.00
4 Chad Johnson 20.00
5 Chad Pennington/100 40.00
6 Chris Weinke 20.00
7 Corey Dillon/75 20.00
8 Correll Buckhalter 15.00
9 Cris Carter/25 50.00
10 Daunte Culpepper/75 40.00
11 David Terrell/100 25.00
12 Deuce McAllister/125 40.00
13 Eric Moulds 20.00
14 Jamal Lewis/100 30.00
15 James Jackson 15.00
16 Jimmy Smith 15.00
17 Kurt Warner/50 40.00
18 Marshall Faulk/50 60.00
19 Snoop Minnis/ 100 No Auto 10.00
20 Mike McMahon 15.00
21 Terrell Owens 30.00
22 Travis Henry/ 100 No Auto 10.00
23 Aaron Brooks/100 25.00
24 Junior Seau 30.00
25 Troy Aikman/50 75.00
26 Antwann Randle El 30.00
27 Jeremy Shockey 40.00
28 Jabar Gaffney 25.00
29 Rocky Calmus 20.00
30 Donte Stallworth 30.00
31 Ashley Lelie 30.00
32 Marquise Walker 15.00
33 Javon Walker/No Auto 20.00
34 Donald Reche Caldwell 15.00
35 Daniel Graham 15.00
36 T.J. Duckett 30.00
37 Antonio Bryant 25.00
38 William Green 30.00
39 David Carr/150 125.00
40 Ron Johnson 15.00

2002 Score Monday Matchup

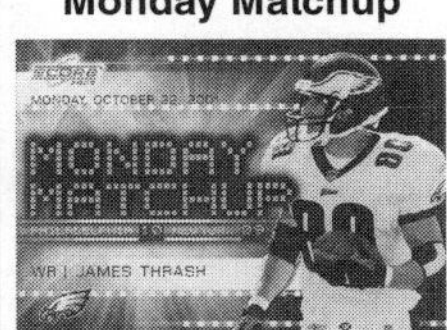

NM/M
Common Player: 1.00
Inserted 1:35
1 Brian Griese 1.00
2 Ahman Green 1.00
3 Garrison Hearst 1.00
4 Kurt Warner 4.00
5 Emmitt Smith 3.00
6 James Thrash 1.00
7 Plaxico Burress 2.00
8 Tim Brown 1.00
9 Qadry Ismail 1.00
10 Randy Moss 4.00
11 Mike Alstott 1.00
12 Brett Favre 6.00
13 Jay Fiedler 1.00
14 Kurt Warner 4.00
15 Derrick Mason 1.00
16 Mike Alstott 1.00
17 Terry Allen 1.00

2002 Score Numbers Game

NM/M
Common Player: 1.00
Production to 2001 season statistics
1 Kurt Warner/4830 4.00
2 Rich Gannon/3828 1.00
3 Trent Green/3783 1.00
4 Kerry Collins/3764 1.00
5 Jake Plummer/3653 1.00
6 Steve McNair/3350 1.00
7 Kordell Stewart/3109 1.00
8 Tim Couch/3040 2.00
9 Chris Weinke/2931 2.00
10 Tom Brady/2843 5.00
11 Priest Holmes/1555 1.00
12 Curtis Martin/1513 1.00
13 Ahman Green/1387 1.00
14 Marshall Faulk/1382 2.00

1,524
YARDS RECEIVING
WR
NUMBERS GAME
MARVIN HARRISON

NM/M
15 Shaun Alexander/1318 1.00
16 LaDainian Tomlinson/1236 1.00
17 Garrison Hearst/1206 1.00
18 Anthony Thomas/1183 4.00
19 Emmitt Smith/1021 3.00
20 Travis Henry/729 1.50
21 David Boston/1598 1.50
22 Marvin Harrison/1524 1.00
23 Terrell Owens/1412 1.00
24 Torry Holt/1363 1.00
25 Randy Moss/1224 4.00
26 Troy Brown/1199 1.00
27 Tim Brown/1165 2.00
28 Marty Booker/1071 1.00
29 Plaxico Burress/1008 2.00
30 Chris Chambers/883 3.00

2002 Score The Franchise

NM/M
Common Player: 1.00
Inserted 1:35
1 David Boston 1.00
2 Michael Vick 4.00
3 Ray Lewis 1.00
4 Travis Henry 1.00
5 Chris Weinke 2.00
6 Anthony Thomas 4.00
7 Corey Dillon 1.00
8 Tim Couch 2.00
9 Emmitt Smith 3.00
10 Rod Smith 1.00
11 Mike McMahon 2.00
12 Ahman Green 1.00
13 Peyton Manning 4.00
14 Jimmy Smith 1.00
15 Priest Holmes 1.00
16 Chris Chambers 2.00
17 Randy Moss 4.00
18 Tom Brady 5.00
19 Aaron Brooks 1.00
20 Kerry Collins 1.00
21 Curtis Martin 1.00
22 Tim Brown 1.00
23 Donovan McNabb 1.00
24 Jerome Bettis 1.00
25 LaDainian Tomlinson 2.00
26 Jeff Garcia 1.00
27 Shaun Alexander 1.00
28 Marshall Faulk 1.50
29 Keyshawn Johnson 1.00
30 Steve McNair 1.00
31 Stephen Davis 1.00

2002 Score QBC

NM/M
Common Player: 12.00
1 Donovan McNabb/ 2001 Jersey 20.00
2 Jake Plummer/ 2001 Jersey 12.00
3 Jeff Garcia/ 2001 Jersey 15.00
4 Peyton Manning/ 2001 Jersey 25.00
5 Rob Johnson/ 2001 Jersey 12.00
6 Trent Dilfer/ 2001 Jersey 12.00
7 Bernie Kosar/ 2001 Jersey 12.00
8 Boomer Esiason/ 2001 Jersey 12.00
9 Jim Everett/ 2001 Jersey 12.00
10 Jim Kelly/ 2001 Jersey 15.00
11 Steve Young/ 2001 Jersey 20.00
12 Warren Moon/ 2001 Jersey 12.00
13 Donovan McNabb/ 2001 Football 20.00
14 Jeff Garcia/ 2001 Football 15.00
15 Peyton Manning/ 2001 Football 20.00
16 Boomer Esiason/ 2001 Football 12.00
17 Jim Kelly/ 2001 Football 15.00
18 Steve Young/ 2001 Football 20.00
19 Warren Moon/ 2001 Football 12.00
20 Peyton Manning/ 2002 Jersey 25.00
21 Doug Flutie/ 2002 Jersey 15.00
22 Jeff Garcia/ 2002 Jersey 15.00
23 Jake Plummer/ 2002 Jersey 12.00
24 Aaron Brooks/ 2002 Jersey 20.00
25 John Elway/ 2002 Jersey 30.00
26 Boomer Esiason/ 2001 Jersey 12.00
27 Warren Moon/ 2002 Jersey 12.00
28 Jim Everett/ 2002 Jersey 12.00
29 John Elway/ 2002 Football 30.00
30 Warren Moon/ 2002 Football 12.00
31 Jake Plummer/ 2002 Football 12.00
32 Peyton Manning/ 2002 Football 20.00
33 Jeff Garcia/ 2002 Football 15.00
34 Aaron Brooks/ 2002 Football 15.00
35 Doug Flutie/ 2002 Football 12.00
36 Boomer Esiason/ 2002 Football 12.00
37 Ken O'Brien/ 2002 Jersey 15.00

2003 Score

NM/M
Common Player: .10
Unlisted Star: .60
Minor Star: .40
Unlisted Rookie Star: 1.00
Minor Rookie Star: .75
Scorecard 1X-3X
Production 500 sets
Final Score
Production to player's team win total
Pack(18): 2.25
Wax Box(20): 30.00
Cards 292,323 & 328 not produced
1 Jeff Blake .10
2 Todd Heap .30
3 Ron Johnson .10
4 Jamal Lewis .60
5 Ray Lewis .40
6 Chris Redman .40
7 Ed Reed .10
8 Travis Taylor .40
9 Anthony Weaver .10
10 Drew Bledsoe 1.00
11 Larry Centers .10
12 Nate Clements .10
13 Travis Henry .40
14 Eric Moulds .40
15 Peerless Price .60
16 Josh Reed .40
17 Coy Wire .10
18 Corey Dillon .60
19 T.J. Houshmandzadeh .10
20 Chad Johnson .10
21 Jon Kitna .10
22 Lorenzo Neal .10
23 Peter Warrick .10
24 Nick Luchey .10
25 Tim Couch 1.00
26 Andre Davis .40
27 William Green .60
28 Kevin Johnson .40
29 Quincy Morgan .40
30 Dennis Northcutt .10
31 Jamel White .10
32 Mike Anderson .40
33 Steve Beuerlein .10
34 Jason Elam .10
35 Olandis Gary .40
36 Brian Griese .60
37 Ashley Lelie .75
38 Ed McCaffrey .40
39 Clinton Portis 1.50
40 Shannon Sharpe .40
41 Rod Smith .40
42 James Allen .10
43 Corey Bradford .10
44 David Carr 1.25
45 JaJuan Dawson .10
46 Jabar Gaffney .40
47 Aaron Glenn .10
48 Billy Miller .10
49 Jonathan Wells .40
50 Dwight Freeney .10
51 Marvin Harrison .60
52 Qadry Ismail .10
53 Edgerrin James 1.25
54 Peyton Manning 1.50
55 James Mungro .10
56 Marcus Pollard .10
57 Reggie Wayne .40
58 Kyle Brady .10
59 Mark Brunell .60
60 David Garrard .40
61 John Henderson .10
62 Stacey Mack .10
63 Jimmy Smith .10
64 Fred Taylor .60
65 Marc Boerigter .50
66 Tony Gonzalez .40
67 Trent Green .40
68 Priest Holmes .75
69 Eddie Kennison .40
70 Marvin "Snoop" Minnis .40
71 Johnnie Morton .40
72 Cris Carter .40
73 Chris Chambers .60
74 Robert Edwards .10
75 Jay Fiedler .40
76 Ray Lucas .10
77 Randy McMichael .10
78 Travis Minor .10
79 Zach Thomas .10
80 Ricky Williams 1.00
81 Tom Brady 1.50
82 Deion Branch .40
83 Troy Brown .40
84 Tedy Bruschi .10
85 Kevin Faulk .10
86 Daniel Graham .10
87 David Patten .40
88 Antowain Smith .40
89 Adam Vinatieri .10
90 Donnie Abraham .10
91 Anthony Becht .10
92 Wayne Chrebet .10
93 Laveranues Coles .60
94 LaMont Jordan .10
95 Curtis Martin .60
96 Chad Morton .10
97 Santana Moss .40
98 Chad Pennington .75
99 Vinny Testaverde .40
100 Tim Brown .60
101 Phillip Buchanon .50
102 Rich Gannon .60
103 Charlie Garner .40
104 Doug Jolley .10
105 Jerry Porter .40
106 Jerry Rice 1.50
107 Marques Tuiasosopo .40
108 Charles Woodson .40
109 Rod Woodson .40
110 Kendrell Bell .10
111 Jerome Bettis .40
112 Plaxico Burress .60
113 Tommy Maddox .60
114 Joey Porter .40
115 Antwann Randle El 1.00
116 Kordell Stewart .40
117 Hines Ward .40
118 Amos Zereoue .10
119 Drew Brees 1.25
120 Donald Reche Caldwell .40
121 Curtis Conway .40
122 Tim Dwight .10
123 Doug Flutie .40
124 Quentin Jammer .40
125 Ben Leber .10
126 Josh Norman .10
127 Junior Seau .40
128 LaDainian Tomlinson 1.25
129 Keith Bulluck .10
130 Rocky Calmus .40
131 Kevin Carter .40
132 Kevin Dyson .10
133 Eddie George .60
134 Albert Haynesworth .10
135 Jevon Kearse .40
136 Derrick Mason .40
137 Justin McCareins .10
138 Steve McNair .60
139 Frank Wycheck .10
140 David Boston .60
141 MarTay Jenkins .10
142 Freddie Jones .10
143 Thomas Jones .40
144 Jason McAddley .10
145 Josh McCown .40
146 Jake Plummer .60
147 Marcel Shipp .10
148 Alge Crumpler .10
149 T.J. Duckett .60
150 Warrick Dunn .40
151 Brian Finneran .10
152 Trevor Gaylor .10
153 Shawn Jefferson .10
154 Michael Vick 1.75
155 Randy Fasani .10
156 DeShaun Foster .40
157 Muhsin Muhammad .40
158 Rodney Peete .10
159 Julius Peppers .60
160 Lamar Smith .40
161 Steve Smith .10
162 Chris Weinke .10
163 Wesley Walls .10
164 Marty Booker .40
165 Mike Brown .40
166 Chris Chandler .10
167 Jim Miller .10
168 Marcus Robinson .30
169 David Terrell .40
170 Anthony Thomas .60
171 Brian Urlacher 1.25
172 Dez White .40
173 Antonio Bryant .60
174 Quincy Carter .60
175 Dexter Coakley .10
176 Joey Galloway .40
177 La'Roi Glover .10
178 Troy Hambrick .10
179 Chad Hutchinson .60
180 Raghib Ismail .10
181 Emmitt Smith 1.50
182 Roy Williams .60
183 Scotty Anderson .10
184 Germane Crowell .10
185 Az-Zahir Hakim .60
186 Joey Harrington 1.25
187 Cory Schlesinger .10
188 Bill Schroeder .10
189 James Stewart .40
190 Marques Anderson .10
191 Najeh Davenport .40
192 Donald Driver .40
193 Brett Favre 2.00
194 Bubba Franks .10
195 Terry Glenn .10
196 Ahman Green .60
197 Darren Sharper .10
198 Javon Walker .40
199 D'Wayne Bates .10
200 Michael Bennett .60
201 Todd Bouman .10
202 Byron Chamberlain .10
203 Daunte Culpepper 1.00
204 Randy Moss 1.50
205 Kelly Campbell .10
206 Aaron Brooks .75
207 Charles Grant .10
208 Joe Horn .10
209 Michael Lewis .10
210 Deuce McAllister .75
211 Jerome Pathon .10
212 Donte Stallworth .75
213 Eddie "Boo" Williams .10
214 Tiki Barber .40
215 Tim Carter .40
216 Kerry Collins .40
217 Ron Dayne .40
218 Jesse Palmer .10
219 Will Peterson .10
220 Jason Sehorn .10
221 Jeremy Shockey 1.25
222 Michael Strahan .40
223 Amani Toomer .40
224 Koy Detmer .10
225 Antonio Freeman .10
226 Dorsey Levens .10
227 Chad Lewis .40
228 Donovan McNabb 1.00
229 Freddie Mitchell .40
230 Duce Staley .40
231 James Thrash .10
232 Brian Westbrook .40
233 Kevan Barlow .10
234 Andre Carter .10
235 Jeff Garcia .60
236 Garrison Hearst .40
237 Eric Johnson .10
238 Terrell Owens .60
239 Jamal Robertson .10
240 Tai Streets .10
241 Shaun Alexander .60
242 Trent Dilfer .40
243 Bobby Engram .10
244 Matt Hasselbeck .10
245 Darrell Jackson .10
246 Maurice Morris .10
247 Koren Robinson .40
248 Jerramy Stevens .10
249 Isaac Bruce .60
250 Marc Bulger .60
251 Marshall Faulk 1.00
252 Lamar Gordon .40
253 Torry Holt .40
254 Ricky Proehl .10
255 Kurt Warner 1.25
256 Aeneas Williams .10
257 Mike Alstott .40
258 Ken Dilger .10
259 Brad Johnson .40
260 Keyshawn Johnson .60
261 Rob Johnson .10
262 John Lynch .10
263 Keenan McCardell .10
264 Michael Pittman .10
265 Warren Sapp .40
266 Marquise Walker .40
267 Champ Bailey .10
268 Stephen Davis .40
269 Rod Gardner .40
270 Darren Green .10
271 Shane Matthews .10
272 Darnerian McCants .10
273 Patrick Ramsey .60
274 Bruce Smith .10
275 Kenny Watson .10
276 *Carson Palmer* 3.00
277 *Byron Leftwich* 4.00
278 *Kyle Boller* 2.25
279 *Chris Simms* 1.50
280 *Dave Ragone* 1.00
281 *Rex Grossman* 2.00
282 *Brian St. Pierre* .75
283 *Larry Johnson* 1.50
284 *Lee Suggs* 2.00
285 *Justin Fargas* .75
286 *Onterrio Smith* 2.00
287 *Willis McGahee* 3.00
288 *Chris Brown* 2.00
289 *Musa Smith* .75
290 *Artose Pinner* .75
291 *Cecil Sapp* .50
292 No Card
293 *LaBrandon Toefield* .50
294 *Charles Rogers* 2.25
295 *Andre Johnson* 2.25
296 *Taylor Jacobs* 1.00
297 *Bryant Johnson* 1.50

298	*Kelley Washington*	1.00
299	*Brandon Lloyd*	1.50
300	*Justin Gage*	.75
301	*Tyrone Calico*	1.50
302	*Kevin Curtis*	.75
303	*Sam Aiken*	.75
304	*Doug Gabriel*	.60
305	*Talman Gardner*	.75
306	*Jason Witten*	1.50
307	*Mike Pinkard*	.60
308	*Teyo Johnson*	.75
309	*Bennie Joppru*	1.00
310	*Dallas Clark*	1.50
311	*Terrell Suggs*	1.50
312	*Chris Kelsay*	.50
313	*Jerome McDougal*	.75
314	*Andrew Williams*	.10
315	*Michael Haynes*	.75
316	*Jimmy Kennedy*	.75
317	*Kevin Williams*	.50
318	*Ken Dorsey*	1.50
319	*William Joseph*	.75
320	*Kenny Peterson*	.50
321	*Rien Long*	.60
322	*Boss Bailey*	1.00
324	*Terence Newman*	1.50
325	*Marcus Trufant*	.75
326	*Andre Woolfolk*	.75
327	*Dennis Weathersby*	.75
328	No Card	
329	*Mike Doss*	.75
330	*Rashean Mathis*	.75

2003 Score Changing Stripes

		NM/M
Common Player:		8.00
Production 250 sets		
1	Drew Bledsoe	35.00
2	Ricky Williams	35.00
3	Terry Glenn	8.00
4	Rich Gannon	20.00
5	Brad Johnson	8.00
6	James Stewart	
7	Trent Green	12.00
8	Joe Montana	125.00
9	Art Monk	20.00
10	Warrick Dunn	15.00

2003 Score Franchise Fabrics

		NM/M
Common Player:		6.00
Production 250 sets		
1	Ahman Green	15.00
2	Corey Dillon	8.00
3	Curtis Martin	8.00
4	Darrell Green	15.00
5	Emmitt Smith	25.00
6	Garrison Hearst	6.00
7	Jake Plummer	6.00
8	Jimmy Smith	6.00
9	Junior Seau	15.00
10	Kevin Johnson	8.00
11	Michael Strahan	6.00
12	Mike Alstott	12.00
13	Plaxico Burress	15.00
14	Ray Lewis	20.00
15	Rod Smith	15.00
16	Stephen Davis	6.00
17	Steve McNair	8.00
18	Tim Brown	10.00
19	Tony Gonzalez	10.00
20	Warren Sapp	8.00

2003 Score Inscriptions

		NM/M
Common Player:		8.00
Inserted 1:65		
Personalized		2X-3X
Production 25 sets		
1	Joe Montana	175.00
2	Kurt Warner	60.00
3	Jeff Garcia	30.00
4	Donald Driver	30.00
5	Shaun Alexander	
6	Peerless Price	20.00
7	Derrick Mason	18.00
8	Artose Pinner	15.00
9	Boss Bailey	15.00
10	Chris Simms	30.00
11	Jason Witten	15.00
12	Jimmy Kennedy	15.00
13	Justin Fargas	15.00
14	Justin Gage	8.00
15	Kevin Curtis	10.00
16	Marcus Trufant/Redem	15.00
17	Mike Pinkard	8.00
18	Rex Grossman	35.00
19	Rien Long	10.00
20	Sam Aiken	10.00
21	Tyrone Calico	
22	Willis McGahee	

2003 Score Material Reflextions

		NM/M
Common Player:		8.00
Production 250 sets		
1	Terrell Owens, David Boston	8.00
2	Eddie George, Anthony Thomas	10.00
3	Emmitt Smith, LaDainian Tomlinson	
4	Marshall Faulk, Priest Holmes	12.00
5	Randy Moss, Plaxico Burress	20.00
6	Brett Favre, Kurt Warner	30.00
7	Zach Thomas, Brian Urlacher	22.00
8	Fred Taylor, Michael Bennett	15.00
9	Jerome Bettis, T.J. Duckett	12.00
10	Peyton Manning, Joey Harrington	
11	Torry Holt, Donte Stallworth	8.00
12	Jerry Rice, Marvin Harrison	35.00
13	Keyshawn Johnson, Rod Gardner	8.00
14	Daunte Culpepper, Aaron Brooks	15.00
15	Rich Gannon, Jeff Garcia	12.00
16	Steve McNair, Donovan McNabb	18.00
17	Edgerrin James, Deuce McAllister	12.00
18	Eric Moulds, Chris Chambers	12.00
19	Isaac Bruce, Joe Horn	10.00
20	Jevon Kearse, Julius Peppers	15.00

2003 Score Monday Night Heroes

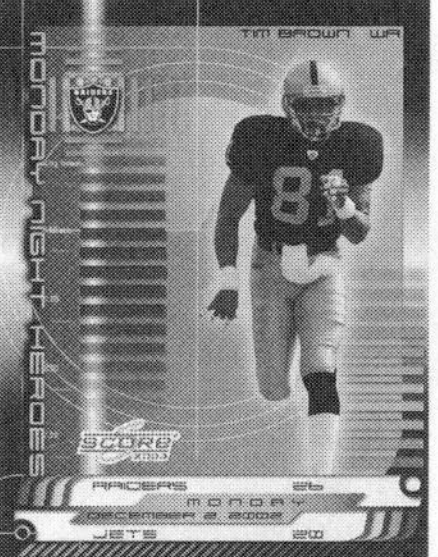

		NM/M
Complete Set (17):		25.00
Common Player:		1.00
Inserted 1:9		
1	Tom Brady	2.50
2	Donovan McNabb	2.00
3	Derrick Brooks	1.00
4	Todd Heap	1.00
5	Brett Favre	4.00
6	Terrell Owens	2.00
7	Hines Ward	2.00
8	Donovan McNabb	2.00
9	Ahman Green	2.00
10	Rich Gannon	2.00
11	Marc Bulger	2.00
12	Koy Detmer	1.00
13	Tim Brown	2.00
14	Ricky Williams	2.00
15	Steve McNair	1.50
16	Plaxico Burress	1.50
17	Dre' Bly	1.00

2003 Score Numbers Game

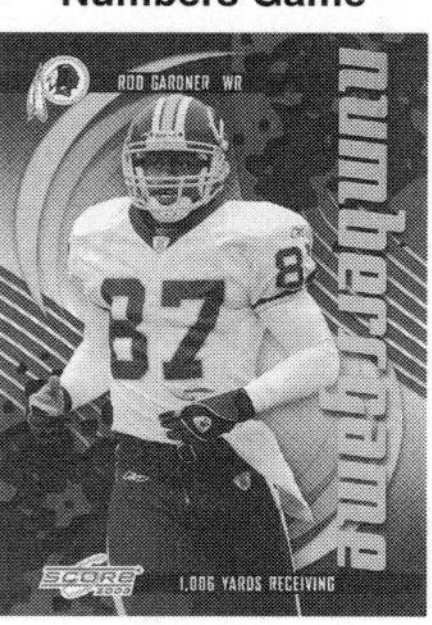

		NM/M
Common Player:		1.00
Production to player's 2002 stat		
1	Rich Gannon/4689	3.00
2	Drew Bledsoe/4359	3.00
3	Peyton Manning/4200	4.00
4	Tom Brady/3764	3.00
5	Joey Harrington/2294	4.00
6	Brett Favre/3658	5.00
7	Aaron Brooks/3572	3.00
8	Michael Vick/2936	4.00
9	Steve McNair/3387	2.00
10	David Carr/2592	3.00
11	Priest Holmes/1615	2.00
12	LaDainian Tomlinson/1683	2.00
13	Ricky Williams/1853	3.00
14	Travis Henry/1438	1.00
15	Deuce McAllister/1388	2.00
16	Clinton Portis/1508	4.00
17	William Green/887	2.00
18	Jamal Lewis/1327	1.00
19	Michael Bennett/1269	2.00
20	Ahman Green/1240	3.00
21	Eddie George/1329	2.00
22	Marvin Harrison/1722	2.00
23	Hines Ward/1329	2.00
24	Rod Gardner/1006	1.00
25	Jerry Rice/1211	4.00
26	Jeremy Shockey/894	4.00
27	Peerless Price/1252	2.00
28	Eric Moulds/1287	1.00
29	Chad Johnson/1166	1.00
30	Donald Driver/1064	2.00
31	Koren Robinson/1240	1.00

2003 Score Personalized Inscriptions

Production 25 sets	
1	Joe Montana
2	Kurt Warner
3	Jeff Garcia
4	Donald Driver
5	Shaun Alexander
6	Peerless Price
7	Derrick Mason
8	Artose Pinner
9	Boss Bailey
10	Chris Simms
11	Jason Witten
12	Jimmy Kennedy
13	Justin Fargas
14	Justin Gage
15	Kevin Curtis
16	Marcus Trufant
17	Mike Pinkard
18	Rex Grossman
19	Rien Long
20	Sam Aiken
21	Tyrone Calico
22	Willis McGahee

2003 Score Reflextions

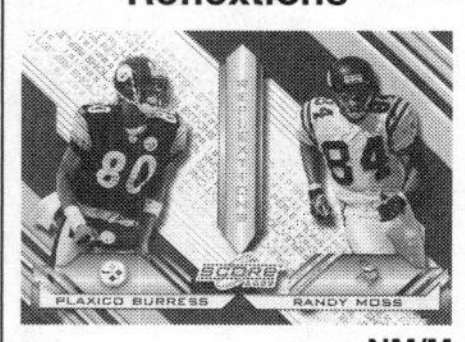

		NM/M
Common Player:		.50
Inserted 1:9		
1	Terrell Owens, David Boston	.50
2	Eddie George, Anthony Thomas	1.00
3	Emmitt Smith, LaDainian Tomlinson	3.00
4	Marshall Faulk, Priest Holmes	2.00
5	Randy Moss, Plaxico Burress	2.00
6	Brett Favre, Kurt Warner	4.00
7	Zach Thomas, Brian Urlacher	2.00
8	Fred Taylor, Michael Bennett	1.00
9	Jerome Bettis, T.J. Duckett	1.00
10	Peyton Manning, Joey Harrington	3.00
11	Torry Holt, Donte Stallworth	.50
12	Jerry Rice, Marvin Harrison	2.00
13	Keyshawn Johnson, Rod Gardner	.50
14	Daunte Culpepper, Aaron Brooks	1.00
15	Rich Gannon, Jeff Garcia	1.00
16	Steve McNair, Donovan McNabb	1.00
17	Edgerrin James, Deuce McAllister	1.00
18	Eric Moulds, Chris Chambers	.50
19	Isaac Bruce, Joe Horn	.50
20	Jevon Kearse, Julius Peppers	.50

2003 Score The Franchise

		NM/M
Common Player:		.50
Inserted 1:9		
1	David Boston	.50
2	Michael Vick	3.00
3	Jamal Lewis	.50
4	Drew Bledsoe	1.50
5	Julius Peppers	.50
6	Anthony Thomas	.50
7	Chad Johnson	.50
8	William Green	1.00
9	Emmitt Smith	3.00
10	Clinton Portis	2.00
11	Joey Harrington	2.00
12	Brett Favre	3.50
13	David Carr	2.00
14	Edgerrin James	1.00
15	Fred Taylor	.50
16	Priest Holmes	1.00
17	Ricky Williams	1.00
18	Michael Bennett	.50
19	Tom Brady	1.50
20	Deuce McAllister	.50
21	Tiki Barber	.50
22	Chad Pennington	1.50
23	Jerry Rice	2.00
24	Donovan McNabb	1.50
25	Tommy Maddox	1.00
26	Drew Brees	1.00
27	Terrell Owens	.50
28	Shaun Alexander	.50
29	Marshall Faulk	1.00
30	Warren Sapp	.50
31	Eddie George	.75
32	Patrick Ramsey	.75

2004 Score

		NM/M
Common Player (1-370):		.15
Minor Stars (1-370):		.25
Unlisted Stars (1-370):		.50
Common Rookie (271-440):		.50
Pack (7):		1.25
Box (36):		50.00
1	Emmitt Smith	1.50
2	Anquan Boldin	.50
3	Bryant Johnson	1.50
4	Marcel Shipp	.15
5	Josh McCown	.15
6	Dexter Jackson	.15
7	Bert Berry	.15
8	Freddie Jones	.15
9	Duane Starks	.15
10	Michael Vick	1.50
11	T.J. Duckett	.25
12	Warrick Dunn	.15
13	Peerless Price	.25
14	Alge Crumpler	.15
15	Brian Finneran	.15
16	Jason Webster	.15
17	Dez White	.15
18	Keith Brooking	.15
19	Rod Coleman	.15
20	Jamal Lewis	.50
21	Kyle Boller	.50
22	Todd Heap	.25
23	Jonathan Ogden	.15
24	Travis Taylor	.15
25	Ray Lewis	.25
26	Peter Boulware	.15
27	Terrell Suggs	.15
28	Chris McAlister	.15
29	Ed Reed	.15
30	Drew Bledsoe	.50
31	Travis Henry	.15
32	Eric Moulds	.15
33	Josh Reed	.15
34	Willis McGahee	.50
35	Takeo Spikes	.15
36	Lawyer Milloy	.15
37	Troy Vincent	.15
38	Sam Adams	.15
39	Nate Clements	.15
40	Jake Delhomme	.50
41	Stephen Davis	.25
42	DeShaun Foster	.15
43	Muhsin Muhammad	.25
44	Steve Smith	.15
45	Ricky Proehl	.15
46	Julius Peppers	.15
47	Kris Jenkins	.15
48	Dan Morgan	.15
49	Ricky Manning	.15
50	Brad Hoover	.15
51	Carson Palmer	.75
52	Rudi Johnson	.25
53	Corey Dillon	.25
54	Chad Johnson	.25
55	Peter Warrick	.25
56	Kelley Washington	.15
57	Kevin Hardy	.15
58	Tory James	.15
59	Ickey Woods	.25
60	Anthony Thomas	.25
61	Thomas Jones	.25
62	Rex Grossman	.50
63	Marty Booker	.15
64	Justin Gage	.15
65	David Terrell	.15
66	Brian Urlacher	.50
67	Mike Brown	.15
68	Charles Tillman	.15
69	Jeff Garcia	.50
70	Lee Suggs	.25
71	William Green	.25
72	Kelly Holcomb	.15
73	Quincy Morgan	.15
74	Andre Davis	.15
75	Dennis Northcutt	.15
76	Gerard Warren	.15
77	Courtney Brown	.15
78	Joey Harrington	.50
79	Shawn Bryson	.15
80	Charles Rogers	.15
81	Mikhael Ricks	.15
82	Artose Pinner	.15
83	Az-Zahir Hakim	.15
84	Dre' Bly	.15
85	Fernando Bryant	.15
86	Boss Bailey	.15
87	Tai Streets	.15
88	Jake Plummer	.25
89	Quentin Griffin	.15
90	Mike Anderson	.15
91	Garrison Hearst	.15
92	Rod Smith	.15
93	Ashley Lelie	.15
94	Shannon Sharpe	.25
95	Al Wilson	.15
96	Champ Bailey	.15
97	Jason Elam	.15
98	John Lynch	.15
99	Quincy Carter	.50
100	Antonio Bryant	.15
101	Terry Glenn	.15
102	Keyshawn Johnson	.25
103	Jason Witten	.15
104	La'Roi Glover	.15
105	Dat Nguyen	.15
106	Dexter Coakley	.15
107	Terence Newman	.15
108	Darren Woodson	.15
109	Roy Williams	.25
110	Brett Favre	2.00
111	Ahman Green	.50
112	Najeh Davenport	.15
113	Donald Driver	.15
114	Robert Ferguson	.15
115	Javon Walker	.25
116	Bubba Franks	.15
117	Kabeer Gbaja-Biamila	.15
118	Darren Sharper	.15
119	Mike McKenzie	.15
120	Nick Barnett	.15
121	David Carr	.75
122	Domanick Davis	.50
123	Andre Johnson	.50
124	Corey Bradford	.15
125	Jabar Gaffney	.15
126	Billy Miller	.15
127	Gary Walker	.15
128	Jamie Sharper	.15
129	Aaron Glenn	.15
130	Robaire Smith	.15
131	Peyton Manning	1.00
132	Edgerrin James	.75
133	Dominic Rhodes	.15
134	Marvin Harrison	.50
135	Reggie Wayne	.15
136	Brandon Stokley	.15
137	Marcus Pollard	.15
138	Dallas Clark	.15
139	Mike Vanderjagt	.15
140	Dwight Freeney	.15
141	Mike Doss	.15
142	Byron Leftwich	1.00
143	Fred Taylor	.50
144	LaBrandon Toefield	.15
145	Jimmy Smith	.15
146	Kevin Johnson	.15
147	Marcus Stroud	.15
148	John Henderson	.15
149	Donovin Darius	.15
150	Deon Grant	.15
151	Rashean Mathis	.15
152	Trent Green	.15
153	Priest Holmes	.75
154	Johnnie Morton	.15
155	Eddie Kennison	.15
156	Marc Boerigter	.15
157	Tony Gonzalez	.25
158	Dante Hall	.15
159	Tony Richardson	.15
160	Gary Stills	.15
161	Daunte Culpepper	.50
162	Michael Bennett	.15
163	Moe Williams	.15
164	Onterrio Smith	.15
165	Jim Kleinsasser	.15
166	Antoine Winfield	.15
167	Nate Burleson	.15
168	Randy Moss	1.00
169	Marcus Robinson	.15
170	Chris Hovan	.15
171	*Brian Russell*	.15
172	A.J. Feeley	.15
173	Jay Fiedler	.15
174	Ricky Williams	.50
175	Chris Chambers	.50
176	David Boston	.25
177	Randy McMichael	.15
178	Jason Taylor	.15
179	Adewale Ogunleye	.15
180	Zach Thomas	.15
181	Junior Seau	.15
182	Patrick Surtain	.15
183	Tom Brady	1.00
184	Kevin Faulk	.15
185	Troy Brown	.15
186	Deion Branch	.15
187	David Givens	.15
188	Bethel Johnson	.15
189	Richard Seymour	.15
190	Tedy Bruschi	.15
191	Ty Law	.15
192	Rodney Harrison	.15
193	Willie McGinest	.15
194	Adam Vinatieri	.15
195	Aaron Brooks	.50
196	Deuce McAllister	.15
197	Joe Horn	.15
198	Donte Stallworth	.25
199	Jerome Pathon	.15
200	Eddie "Boo" Williams	.15
201	Charles Grant	.15
202	Darren Howard	.15
203	Michael Lewis	.15
204	Johnathan Sullivan	.15
205	LeCharles Bentley	.15
206	Kerry Collins	.15
207	Tiki Barber	.15
208	Amani Toomer	.25
209	Ike Hilliard	.15
210	Tim Carter	.15
211	Jeremy Shockey	.50
212	Michael Strahan	.15
213	Will Allen	.15
214	Will Peterson	.15
215	William Joseph	.15
216	Chad Pennington	.75
217	Curtis Martin	.50
218	LaMont Jordan	.15
219	Santana Moss	.15
220	Justin McCareins	.15
221	Wayne Chrebet	.15
222	Anthony Becht	.15
223	Shaun Ellis	.15
224	John Abraham	.15
225	Dewayne Robertson	.15
226	Rich Gannon	.25
227	Justin Fargas	.15
228	Tyrone Wheatley	.15
229	Jerry Rice	1.50
230	Tim Brown	.50
231	Jerry Porter	.15
232	Teyo Johnson	.15
233	Charles Woodson	.15
234	Phillip Buchanon	.15
235	Rod Woodson	.15
236	Warren Sapp	.15
237	Donovan McNabb	.75
238	Brian Westbrook	.15
239	Correll Buckhalter	.15
240	Chad Lewis	.15
241	L.J. Smith	.15
242	Terrell Owens	.50
243	Todd Pinkston	.15
244	Freddie Mitchell	.15
245	Jevon Kearse	.15
246	Brian Dawkins	.15
247	Corey Simon	.15
248	Tommy Maddox	.50
249	Duce Staley	.15
250	Jerome Bettis	.25
251	Hines Ward	.25
252	Plaxico Burress	.15
253	Antwann Randle El	.15
254	Kendrell Bell	.15
255	Joey Porter	.15
256	Alan Faneca	.15
257	Casey Hampton	.15
258	Drew Brees	.25
259	Doug Flutie	.15
260	LaDainian Tomlinson	.75
261	Reche Caldwell	.15
262	Tim Dwight	.15
263	Eric Parker	.15
264	Kevin Dyson	.15
265	Antonio Gates	.15
266	Quentin Jammer	.15
267	Zeke Moreno	.15
268	Tim Rattay	.25
269	Kevan Barlow	.15
270	Cedrick Wilson	.15
271	Brandon Lloyd	.15
272	Fred Beasley	.15
273	Andre Carter	.15
274	Julian Peterson	.15
275	Ahmed Plummer	.15
276	Tony Parrish	.15
277	Bryant Young	.15
278	Matt Hasselbeck	.25
279	Shaun Alexander	.50
280	Maurice Morris	.15
281	Koren Robinson	.15
282	Darrell Jackson	.15
283	Bobby Engram	.15
284	Grant Wistrom	.15
285	Chad Brown	.15
286	Marcus Trufant	.15
287	Bobby Taylor	.15
288	Marc Bulger	.25
289	Kurt Warner	.50
290	Marshall Faulk	.75
291	Lamar Gordon	.15
292	Torry Holt	.50
293	Isaac Bruce	.25
294	Leonard Little	.15
295	Aeneas Williams	.15
296	Orlando Pace	.15
297	Tommy Polley	.15
298	Pisa Tinoisamoa	.15
299	Brad Johnson	.15
300	Michael Pittman	.15
301	Charlie Garner	.15
302	Mike Alstott	.15
303	Keenan McCardell	.15
304	Joey Galloway	.15
305	Joe Jurevicius	.15
306	Anthony McFarland	.15
307	Derrick Brooks	.15
308	Ronde Barber	.15
309	Shelton Quarles	.15
310	Steve McNair	.50
311	Eddie George	.50
312	Chris Brown	.25
313	Derrick Mason	.15
314	Tyrone Calico	.15
315	Drew Bennett	.15
316	Kevin Carter	.15
317	Keith Bulluck	.15
318	Samari Rolle	.15
319	Albert Haynesworth	.15
320	Erron Kinney	.15
321	Mark Brunell	.25

322	Patrick Ramsey	.25
323	Laveranues Coles	.25
324	Rod Gardner	.15
325	Darnerian McCants	.15
326	Clinton Portis	1.00
327	LaVar Arrington	.50
328	Shawn Springs	.15
329	Fred Smoot	.15
330	James Thrash	.15
331	Marvin Harrison	.50
332	Steve McNair	.50
333	Ray Lewis	.25
334	Trent Green	.15
335	Peyton Manning	1.00
336	Priest Holmes	.75
337	Clinton Portis	1.00
338	Torry Holt	.50
339	Anquan Boldin	.50
340	Daunte Culpepper	.50
341	Ahman Green	.50
342	Brian Urlacher	.50
343	Donovan McNabb	.75
344	Marc Bulger	.25
345	Shaun Alexander	.50
346	Peyton Manning	1.00
347	Daunte Culpepper	.50
348	Brett Favre	2.00
349	Steve McNair	.50
350	Tom Brady	1.00
351	Jamal Lewis	.50
352	Deuce McAllister	.50
353	Clinton Portis	1.00
354	Ahman Green	.50
355	LaDainian Tomlinson	.75
356	Torry Holt	.50
357	Anquan Boldin	.50
358	Randy Moss	1.00
359	Chad Johnson	.25
360	Marvin Harrison	.50
361	Peyton Manning	1.00
362	Jamal Lewis	.50
363	Ray Lewis	.25
364	Anquan Boldin	.50
365	Terrell Suggs	.25
366	Jamal Lewis	.50
367	Priest Holmes	.75
368	Tom Brady	1.00
369	Marc Bulger	.25
370	Steve McNair	.50
371	*Eli Manning*	5.00
372	*Robert Gallery*	1.25
373	*Larry Fitzgerald*	3.00
374	*Philip Rivers*	4.00
375	*Sean Taylor*	2.00
376	*Kellen Winslow Jr.*	2.50
377	*Roy Williams*	3.00
378	*DeAngelo Hall*	1.50
379	*Reggie Williams*	2.00
380	*Dunta Robinson*	1.00
381	*Ben Roethlisberger*	6.00
382	*Jonathan Vilma*	1.25
383	*Lee Evans*	2.00
384	*Tommie Harris*	1.25
385	*Michael Clayton*	2.00
386	*D.J. Williams*	1.25
387	*Will Smith*	1.00
388	*Kenechi Udeze*	.75
389	*Vince Wilfork*	.75
390	*J.P. Losman*	2.00
391	*Marcus Tubbs*	.75
392	*Steven Jackson*	2.50
393	*Ahmad Carroll*	.75
394	*Chris Perry*	1.50
395	*Jason Babin*	.75
396	*Chris Gamble*	.75
397	*Michael Jenkins*	1.50
398	*Kevin Jones*	2.50
399	*Rashaun Woods*	2.00
400	*Ben Watson*	.75
401	*Karlos Dansby*	.50
402	*Igor Olshansky*	.50
403	*Junior Siavii*	.50
404	*Teddy Lehman*	1.00
405	*Ricardo Colclough*	.50
406	*Daryl Smith*	.50
407	*Ben Troupe*	.75
408	*Tatum Bell*	.75
409	*Travis LaBoy*	.50
410	*Julius Jones*	2.50
411	*Mewelde Moore*	.75
412	*Drew Henson*	2.00
413	*Dontarrious Thomas*	.50
414	*Keiwan Ratliff*	.50
415	*Devery Henderson*	1.00
416	Dwan Edwards	.50
417	*Michael Boulware*	.50
418	*Darius Watts*	1.00
419	*Greg Jones*	1.25
420	*Madieu Williams*	.50
421	*Antwan Odom*	.75
422	*Shawntae Spencer*	.50
423	*Sean Jones*	.50
424	*Courtney Watson*	.50
425	*Kris Wilson*	.75
426	*Keary Colbert*	.75
427	*Marquise Hill*	.50
428	*Darnell Dockett*	.50
429	*Stuart Schweigert*	.50
430	*Ben Hartsock*	.50
431	*Joey Thomas*	.50
432	*Randy Starks*	.50
433	*Keith Smith*	.50
434	*Derrick Hamilton*	.75
435	*Bernard Berrian*	1.00
436	*Chris Cooley*	.75
437	*Devard Darling*	1.00
438	*Matt Schaub*	1.00
439	*Luke McCown*	1.00
440	*Cedric Cobbs*	1.00

2004 Score Glossy

Stars (1-370):	1X-3X
Rookies (371-440):	.75X-1.5X
Inserted 1:1	

2004 Score Final Score

No Pricing
Numbered to team win total

2004 Score Inscriptions

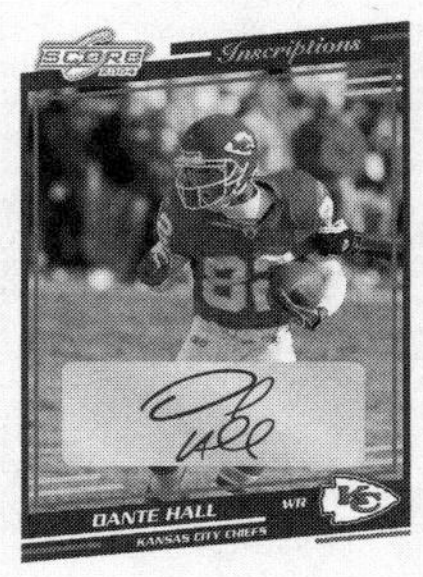

		NM/M
Common Player:		10.00
6	Dexter Jackson	15.00
7	Bert Berry	10.00
38	Sam Adams	15.00
59	Ickey Woods	15.00
147	Marcus Stroud	10.00
170	Chris Hovan	10.00
205	LeCharles Bentley	
265	Antonio Gates	30.00
267	Zeke Moreno	15.00
320	Erron Kinney	10.00

2004 Score Scorecard

Stars (1-370):	3X-5X
Rookies (371-440):	1.5X-3X
Production 625 Sets	

1997 Score Board NFL Experience

The 100-card, regular-sized set was sold in six-card packs. The card fronts feature a color action photo with the player's name and position printed on the bottom edge. The team's logo appears in the lower left corner. The card backs include another photo, a short highlight and a trivia question with answer. The base cards are printed on vintage-style cards. Inserts include Foundations, Teams Of The 90's and NFL Vintage cards.

		NM/M
Complete Set (100):		12.00
Common Player:		.05
Minor Stars:		.10
Pack (6):		1.50
Wax Box (36):		15.00
1	Emmitt Smith	1.50
2	Kordell Stewart	.75
3	Antonio Freeman	.05
4	William Thomas	.05
5	Simeon Rice	.05
6	Drew Bledsoe	.75
7	Elvis Grbac	.05
8	Ken Dilger	.05
9	John Elway	.50
10	Curtis Conway	.05
11	Adrian Murrell	.05
12	Karim Abdul-Jabbar	.25
13	Terry Allen	.05
14	Lawrence Phillips	.50
15	Barry Sanders	1.25
16	Shannon Sharpe	.05
17	Troy Aikman	.75
18	Kevin Greene	.05
19	Cris Carter	.05
20	Jim Kelly	.05
21	Eric Metcalf	.05
22	Joey Galloway	.50
23	Eddie George	1.00
24	Scott Mitchell	.05
25	Neil O'Donnell	.05
26	Ben Coates	.05
27	Andre Reed	.05
28	Michael Jackson	.05
29	Keith Jackson	.05
30	J.J. Stokes	.20
31	Rickey Dudley	.25
32	Ricky Watters	.10
33	Marcus Allen	.10
34	Brett Favre	1.25
35	Kevin Hardy	.05
36	Jim Everett	.05
37	Zach Thomas	.25
38	Lamar Lathon	.05
39	LeShon Johnson	.05
40	Bruce Smith	.05
41	Junior Seau	.05
42	Tony Banks	.50
43	Brian Mitchell	.05
44	Chris T. Jones	.05
45	Ty Detmer	.05
46	Robert Brooks	.05
47	Derrick Thomas	.05
48	Dan Wilkinson	.05
49	Michael Sinclair	.05
50	Dave Brown	.05
51	Carl Pickens	.05
52	Jim Harbaugh	.05
53	Wayne Chrebet	.05
54	Warren Moon	.05
55	Steve Young	.50
56	Sean Gilbert	.05
57	Jerome Bettis	.10
58	Dan Marino	1.50
59	Terrell Davis	.75
60	Mark Brunell	.20
61	Kent Graham	.05
62	Rashaan Salaam	.25
63	Tony Martin	.05
64	Robert Smith	.05
65	Thurman Thomas	.10
66	Marshall Faulk	.40
67	Dale Carter	.05
68	Stan Humphries	.05
69	Isaac Bruce	.40
70	Warren Sapp	.05
71	Kerry Collins	.25
72	Jamal Anderson	.40
73	Chris Chandler	.05
74	Herman Moore	.20
75	Rodney Hampton	.05
76	Tim Brown	.05
77	Keenan McCardell	.05
78	Anthony Miller	.05
79	Jake Reed	.05
80	Earnest Byner	.05
81	Chris Warren	.05
82	Deion Sanders	.50
83	Mike Tomczak	.05
84	Curtis Martin	1.00
85	John Friesz	.05
86	Gus Frerotte	.05
87	Vinny Testaverde	.05
88	Jason Dunn	.05
89	James Stewart	.05
90	Steve Bono	.05
91	Levon Kirkland	.05
92	Merton Hanks	.05
93	Marvin Harrison	.60
94	Reggie Brooks	.05
95	Reggie White	.10
96	Jeff Blake	.30
97	Terry Glenn	.25
98	Jerry Rice	.75
99	Keyshawn Johnson	.75
100	Checklist	.05

1997 Score Board NFL Rookies

The 100-card set features the player's name at the top, while the logo of the teams that drafted him is included in a black stripe in the upper left corner. The '97 Rookies Score Board logo is in the lower center. The team's name is printed inside a black half oval at the bottom. The black stripe that runs along the left side of the back includes the various logos, player's name, bio and card number. To the right of the stripe is the player's photo, highlights and stats. The set was paralleled by the Dean's List, which was inserted 1:5 packs. Vintage rookie cards and autographed rookie cards of current and ex-NFL players were also randomly inserted.

		NM/M
Complete Set (100):		10.00
Common Player:		.05
Minor Stars:		.10
Dean's List:		2X-3X
1	Jake Plummer	2.00
2	Tony Gonzalez	.20
3	Trevor Pryce	.05
4	Greg Jones	.05
5	Koy Detmer	1.25
6	Rae Carruth	.75
7	Peter Boulware	.05
8	Warrick Dunn	2.00
9	Antowain Smith	.30
10	Troy Davis	1.00
11	David LaFleur	.30
12	Yatil Green	1.00
13	Michael Booker	.05
14	Shawn Springs	.30
15	Bryant Westbrook	.30
16	Byron Hanspard	.50
17	Darrell Russell	.05
18	Corey Dillon	1.00
19	Tyrus McCloud	.05
20	Reinard Wilson	.05
21	Adam Meadows	.05
22	Tremain Mack	.05
23	Ricky Parker	.05
24	George Jones	.05
25	Terry Battle	.05
26	Will Blackwell	.05
27	Jerald Sowell	.05
28	Isaac Byrd	.05
29	Chris Naeole	.05
30	Kevin Lockett	.05
31	Freddie Jones	.05
32	Pat Barnes	.05
33	Torrian Gray	.05
34	Brian Manning	.05
35	Dedric Ward	.05
36	Pete Monty	.05
37	Sam Madison	.05
38	Sedrick Shaw	.05
39	Mike Logan	.05
40	Albert Connell	.05
41	Canute Curtis	.05
42	Ronde Barber	.05
43	Orlando Pace	.75
44	Edward Perry	.05
45	Tiki Barber	.50
46	Kevin Jackson	.05
47	Jerry Wunsch	.05
48	Michael Hamilton	.05
49	Darnell Autry	.50
50	Jim Druckenmiller	.50
51	James Farrior	.05
52	Derrick Mason	.25
53	Ty Howard	.05
54	Jason Taylor	.05
55	Reidel Anthony	1.00
56	Bert Berry	.05
57	Marc Edwards	.05
58	James Hamilton	.05
59	Ike Hilliard	1.00
60	Tommy Knight	.05
61	Walter Jones	.05
62	Chad Levitt	.05
63	Pratt Lyons	.05
64	Greg Clark	.05
65	Ryan Phillips	.05
66	Jason Martin	.05
67	Scott Sanderson	.05
68	Alshermond Singleton	.05
69	Duce Staley	.50
70	Jared Tomich	.05
71	Ross Verba	.05
72	Derrick Rodgers	.05
73	Mike Vrabel	.05
74	John Allred	.05
75	Bob Sapp	.05
76	Brad Otton	.05
77	Tarik Glenn	.05
78	Chad Scott	.05
79	Nathan Davis	.05
80	Henri Crockett	.05
81	Tarik Saleh	.05
82	Seth Payne	.05
83	Pete Chryplewicz	.05
84	Reidel Anthony	.50
85	Reinard Wilson	.05
86	Byron Hanspard	.20
87	Shawn Springs	.20
88	David LaFleur	.20
89	Troy Davis	.50
90	Warrick Dunn	1.00
91	Peter Boulware	.05
92	Rae Carruth	.20
93	Tony Gonzalez	.10
94	Jake Plummer	.25
95	Orlando Pace	.25
96	Ike Hilliard	.50
97	Kevin Jackson	.05
98	Jim Druckenmiller	.60
99	Shawn Springs	.20
100	Warrick Dunn	1.00

1997 Score Board NFL Rookies Dean's List

Dean's List is a parallel set of the NFL Rookies base cards. Dean's List cards were inserted one per five packs.

Dean's List Cards:	2X-3X

1997 Score Board NFL Rookies NFL War Room

The 20-card set was inserted 1:100 packs. It includes comments from NFL insiders on players that were selected on draft day. The cards carry a "W" prefix.

		NM/M
Complete Set (20):		60.00
Common Player:		1.00
Minor Stars:		5.00
1	Yatil Green	5.00
2	Antowain Smith	8.00
3	Tony Gonzalez	8.00
4	Corey Dillon	12.00
5	Jake Plummer	12.00
6	Peter Boulware	1.00
7	Orlando Pace	5.00
8	Darrell Russell	1.00
9	Reinard Wilson	1.00
10	Shawn Springs	5.00
11	Bryant Westbrook	5.00
12	Rae Carruth	1.00
13	Warrick Dunn	15.00
14	David LaFleur	5.00
15	Byron Hanspard	5.00
16	Michael Booker	1.00
17	Reidel Anthony	5.00
18	Troy Davis	5.00
19	Chris Naeole	1.00
20	Jim Druckenmiller	5.00

1997 Score Board NFL Rookies Varsity Club

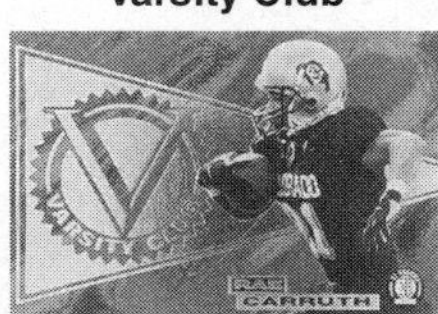

Inserted 1:36 packs, the 30-card set features the school pennant and team logo of the player's college or university. The cards are numbered and carry a "V" prefix.

		NM/M
Complete Set (30):		40.00
Common Player:		.50
Minor Stars:		1.00
1	Tiki Barber	5.00
2	Sedrick Shaw	.50
3	Kevin Lockett	.50
4	Byron Hanspard	1.00
5	David LaFleur	1.00
6	Warrick Dunn	10.00
7	Yatil Green	2.00
8	Corey Dillon	6.00
9	Orlando Pace	2.00
10	Tony Gonzalez	4.00
11	Darrell Russell	.50
12	Jake Plummer	6.00
13	Peter Boulware	.50
14	Shawn Springs	1.00
15	Bryant Westbrook	3.00
16	Rae Carruth	1.00
17	Antowain Smith	6.00
18	Reidel Anthony	2.00
19	Michael Booker	.50
20	Freddie Jones	.50
21	Pat Barnes	.50
22	Troy Davis	2.00
23	Walter Jones	.50
24	Reinard Wilson	.50
25	George Jones	.50
26	Terry Battle	.50
27	Tommy Knight	.50
28	Tremain Mack	.50
29	Jim Druckenmiller	2.00
30	Ike Hilliard	5.00

1997 Score Board Playbook

		NM/M
Complete Set (100):		8.00
Common Player:		.10
1	Warren Moon	.10
2	Troy Aikman	.50
3	Jeff George	.10
4	Brett Favre	1.00
5	Jim Harbaugh	.10
6	Jeff Blake	.10
7	John Elway	.50
8	Mark Brunell	.10
9	Steve McNair	.10
10	Kordell Stewart	.10
11	Drew Bledsoe	.50
12	Kerry Collins	.10
13	Dan Marino	1.00
14	Jim Druckenmiller	.10
15	Todd Collins	.10
16	Jake Plummer	.10
17	Pat Barnes	.10
18	Vinny Testaverde	.10
19	Scott Mitchell	.10
20	Rob Johnson	.10
21	Elvis Grbac	.10
22	Danny Wuerffel	.10
23	Neil O'Donnell	.10
24	Tony Banks	.10
25	Stan Humpheries	.10
26	Brad Johnson	.10
27	Trent Dilfer	.10
28	Ty Detmer	.10
29	Steve Young	.50
30	Gus Frerotte	.10
31	Leeland McElroy	.10
32	Byron Hanspard	.10
33	Jamal Anderson	.10
34	Thurman Thomas	.25
35	Antowain Smith	.25
36	Tim Biakabutuka	.10
37	Raymont Harris	.10
38	Corey Dillon	.50
39	Emmitt Smith	1.00
40	Terrell Davis	.75
41	Barry Sanders	1.00
42	Dorsey Levens	.10
43	Marshall Faulk	.50
44	Natrone Means	.10
45	Marcus Allen	.50
46	Karim Abdul-Jabbar	.10
47	Robert Smith	.10
48	Curtis Martin	.50
49	Troy Davis	.10
50	Tiki Barber	.25
51	Adrian Murrell	.10
52	Napoleon Kaufman	.10
53	Ricky Watters	.10
54	Jerome Bettis	.25
55	Lawrence Phillips	.10
56	Garrison Hearst	.10
57	Warrick Dunn	.10
58	Eddie George	.50
59	Terry Allen	.10
60	Michael Jackson	.10
61	Rae Carruth	.10
62	Carl Pickens	.10
63	Michael Irvin	.50
64	Shannon Sharpe	.25
65	Herman Moore	.10
66	Robert Brooks	.10
67	Antonio Freeman	.25
68	Marvin Harrison	.50
69	Keenan McCardell	.10
70	Jimmy Smith	.10
71	Tim Brown	.50
72	Ben Coates	.10
73	Terry Glenn	.10
74	Ike Hilliard	.10
75	Keyshawn Johnson	.50
76	Eddie Kennison	.10
77	Tim Brown	.50
78	Irving Fryar	.10
79	Jake Reed	.10
80	Isaac Bruce	.50
81	Tony Martin	.10
82	Jerry Rice	.75
83	Joey Galloway	.10
84	Reidel Anthony	.10
85	Yatil Green	.10
86	Tony Gonzalez	.10
87	Simeon Rice	.25
88	Peter Boulware	.10
89	Bruce Smith	.10
90	Reinard Wilson	.10
91	Deion Sanders	.25
92	Bryant Westbrook	.10
93	Reggie White	.25
94	Dwayne Rudd	.10
95	Darrell Russell	.10
96	Greg Lloyd	.10
97	Junior Seau	.50
98	Shawn Springs	.10
99	Cortez Kennedy	.10
100	Kordell Stewart	
	Checklist	.25

1997 Score Board Playbook By The Numbers

Playbook By The Numbers consists of a 50-card base set. The base set is divided into five subsets: quarterbacks, running backs, wide receivers, defensive players and rookies. The base cards are numbered within their subset. Silver Magnified (sequentially numbered to 2,000; inserted one per two packs) and Gold Magnified (numbered to 200; 1:21) parallel versions were also produced. Three insert sets were included in this product: Standout Numbers, Red Zone Stats and Master Signings.

NM/M

Complete Set (50): 30.00
Common Player: .10
Minor Stars: .20
Gold Magnified Cards: 3X-5X
Silver Magnified Cards: 2X
Wax Box: 35.00

1 Troy Aikman (Quarterback) 1.00
2 Mark Brunell (Quarterback) 1.00
3 Dan Marino (Quarterback) 2.00
4 Brett Favre (Quarterback) 2.50
5 Kordell Stewart (Quarterback) 1.00
6 Drew Bledsoe (Quarterback) 1.00
7 John Elway (Quarterback) .75
8 Kerry Collins (Quarterback) .30
9 Steve Young (Quarterback) .75
10 Jeff Blake (Quarterback) .20
1 Emmitt Smith (Running Back) 2.00
2 Terrell Davis (Running Back) 1.00
3 Barry Sanders (Running Back) 1.00
4 Marshall Faulk (Running Back) .20
5 Robert Smith (Running Back) .10
6 Curtis Martin (Running Back) 1.00
7 Jerome Bettis (Running Back) .20
8 Eddie George (Running Back) 1.50
9 Terry Allen (Running Back) .10
10 Ricky Watters (Running Back) .20
1 Carl Pickens (Wide Receiver) .10
2 Michael Irvin (Wide Receiver) .20
3 Herman Moore (Wide Receiver) .20
4 Robert Brooks (Wide Receiver) .10
5 Cris Carter (Wide Receiver) .10
6 Terry Glenn (Wide Receiver) .75
7 Tim Brown (Wide Receiver) .10
8 Jerry Rice (Wide Receiver) 1.00
9 Keyshawn Johnson (Wide Receiver) .30
10 Isaac Bruce (Wide Receiver) .20
1 Simeon Rice (Defense) .10
2 Peter Boulware (Defense) .10
3 Bruce Smith (Defense) .10
4 Deion Sanders (Defense) .50
5 Reggie White (Defense) .20
6 Darrell Russell (Defense) .10
7 Greg Lloyd (Defense) .10
8 Junior Seau (Defense) .10
9 Shawn Springs (Defense) .20
10 Cortez Kennedy (Defense) .10
1 Tony Gonzalez (Rookie) .30
2 Rae Carruth (Rookie) .50
3 Warrick Dunn (Rookie) 4.00
4 Tiki Barber (Rookie) .40
5 Antowain Smith (Rookie) 2.00
6 Corey Dillon (Rookie) 2.00
7 Troy Davis (Rookie) .40
8 Danny Wuerffel (Rookie) .60
9 Jim Druckenmiller (Rookie) 2.50
10 Pat Barnes (Rookie) .30

1997 Score Board Playbook Franchise Player

NM/M

Complete Set (30): 30.00
Common Player: .50

1 Simeon Rice .50
2 Jamal Anderson .50
3 Peter Boulware .50
4 Bruce Smith .50
5 Kerry Collins .50
6 Rashaan Salaam .50
7 Jeff Blake .50
8 Emmitt Smith 3.00
9 Terrell Davis 2.00
10 Barry Sanders 3.00
11 Brett Favre 4.00
12 Marshall Faulk 2.00
13 Mark Brunell .50
14 Derrick Thomas .50
15 Dan Marino 3.00
16 Brad Johnson .50
17 Drew Bledsoe 2.00
18 Troy Davis .50
19 Ike Hilliard .50
20 Keyshawn Johnson .50
21 Tim Brown .50
22 Ricky Watters .50
23 Jerome Bettis .50
24 Isaac Bruce .50
25 Junior Seau .50
26 Jerry Rice 3.00
27 Joey Galloway .50
28 Warrick Dunn .50
29 Eddie George 1.00
30 Gus Frerotte .50

A card number in parenthese ( ) indicates the set is unnumbered.

1997 Score Board Playbook Master Signing

Master Signing is a 30-card insert. Each of the 30 players in the set has a total of four cards, all of which are autographed.

Troy Aikman
Marcus Allen
Mike Alstott
Peter Boulware
Rae Carruth
Kerry Collins
Terrell Davis
Jim Druckenmiller
Warrick Dunn
Brett Favre
Gus Frerotte
Eddie George
Terry Glenn
Tony Gonzalez
Kevin Hardy
Ike Hilliard
Keyshawn Johnson
Curtis Martin
Keenan McCardell
Steve McNair
Orlando Pace
Darrell Russell
Antowain Smith
Emmitt Smith
Jimmy Smith
Kordell Stewart
Bryant Westbrook
Reinard Wilson
Danny Wuerffel
Steve Young

1997 Score Board Playbook Mirror Image

NM/M

Complete Set (20): 50.00
Common Player: 1.00

1 Brett Favre 10.00
2 Warrick Dunn 1.00
3 Emmitt Smith 8.00
4 Steve Young 5.00
5 Terrell Davis 1.00
6 Kordell Stewart 1.00
7 Kerry Collins 1.00
8 John Elway 5.00
9 Barry Sanders 7.00
10 Drew Bledsoe 5.00
11 Troy Aikman 5.00
12 Curtis Martin 3.00
13 Mark Brunell 2.00
14 Terry Glenn 1.00
15 Antowain Smith 1.00
16 Reggie White 1.00
17 Jeff Blake 1.00
18 Darrell Russell 1.00
19 Terry Allen 1.00
20 Keyshawn Johnson 1.00

1997 Score Board Playbook Mirror Image Autographs

NM/M

Complete Set (7):
Common Player: 15.00

1 Brett Favre 100.00
2 Warrick Dunn 35.00
3 Emmitt Smith 75.00
4 Steve Young 50.00
5 Terrell Davis 40.00
6 Kordell Stewart 25.00
7 Kerry Collins 25.00

1997 Score Board Playbook Red Zone Stats

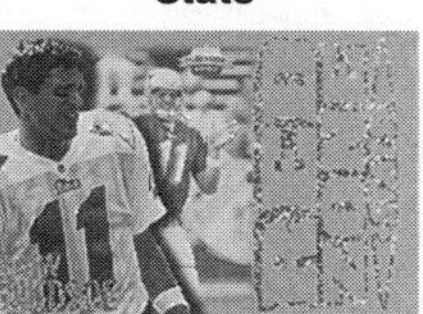

Red Zone Stats is a 10-card insert, seeded one per 20 packs. This insert has Silver Magnified (numbered to 1,000; inserted one per 21 packs) and Gold Magnified (numbered to 100; 1:210) parallel versions. They have a "RZ" prefix.

NM/M

Complete Set (10): 15.00
Common Player: .50
Minor Stars: 1.00
Magnified Gold Cards: 2X-4X
Magnified Silver Cards: 1X

1 Emmitt Smith 5.00
2 Terry Allen .50
3 Troy Aikman 3.00
4 Brett Favre 5.00
5 John Elway 3.00
6 Drew Bledsoe 3.00
7 Terrell Davis 3.00
8 Karim Abdul-Jabbar 1.00
9 Curtis Martin 2.00
10 Warrick Dunn 2.00

1997 Score Board Playbook Standout Numbers

Standout Numbers is a 30-card insert which was inserted one per four packs. Standout Numbers also has Silver Magnified (numbered to 2,700, inserted one per three packs) and Gold Magnified (numbered to 270; 1:26) parallel versions. The cards are numbered with a "SN" prefix.

NM/M

Complete Set (30): 40.00
Common Player: .50
Minor Stars: 1.00
Magnified Golds: 2X-4X
Magnified Silvers: 1X

1 Drew Bledsoe 3.00
2 Emmitt Smith 5.00
3 Cris Carter .50
4 Brett Favre 5.00
5 Jerome Bettis 1.00
6 Mark Brunell 2.00
7 John Elway 3.00
8 Troy Aikman 3.00
9 Steve Young 3.00
10 Kordell Stewart 2.00
11 Reggie White 1.00
12 Isaac Bruce 1.00
13 Dan Marino 5.00
14 Kevin Greene .50
15 Tim Brown 2.00
16 Terry Glenn 1.00
17 Ricky Watters 1.00
18 Carl Pickens .50
19 Keyshawn Johnson 1.00
20 Barry Sanders 4.00
21 Marshall Faulk 1.00
22 James Stewart .50
23 Jerry Rice 4.00
24 Curtis Martin 2.00
25 Herman Moore 1.00
26 Terry Allen .50
27 Eddie George 2.00
28 Warrick Dunn 2.00
29 Marcus Allen 1.00
30 Terrell Davis 3.00

1997 Score Board Playbook Title Quest

NM/M

Complete Set (12): 25.00
Common Player: .50

1 Brett Favre 5.00
2 Terrell Davis 3.00
3 Emmitt Smith 4.00
4 Drew Bledsoe 3.00
5 Mark Brunell 1.00
6 Warrick Dunn 1.00
7 Jim Druckenmiller .50
8 Derrick Thomas .50
9 Rae Carruth .50
10 Jerome Bettis 1.00
11 Dan Marino 4.00
12 Barry Sanders 4.00

1977 Seahawks Fred Meyer

The 13-card, 7-1/4" x 6" set, distributed by Fred Meyer Department Stores, feature a color action shot with a headshot inset in a lower corner (cards 3, 5, 12, and 13a have no insets). Seahawks quarterback Jim Zorn is represented on two No. 13 cards, one having no inset. All card backs are blank.

NM/M

Complete Set (14): 75.00
Common Player: 5.00

1 Steve August 5.00
2 Autry Beamon 5.00
3 Terry Beeson 5.00
4 Dennis Boyd 5.00
5 Norm Evans 5.00
6 Sammy Green 5.00
7 Ron Howard 5.00
8 Steve Largent 20.00
9 Steve Myer 5.00
10 Steve Niehaus 5.00
11 Sherman Smith 5.00
12 Don Testerman 5.00
13A Jim Zorn (No inset photo) 12.00
13B Jim Zorn (With inset photo) 12.00

1977 Seahawks Team Issue

The 10-card, 5" x 7" set features black and white headshots of Seattle players with blank backs. A facsimile autograph also appears on each card front.

NM/M

Complete Set (10): 75.00
Common Player: 5.00

1 Ron Howard 5.00
2 Steve Largent 25.00
3 John Leypoldt 5.00
4 Bob Lurtsema 5.00
5 Steve Myer 5.00
6 Steve Niehaus 5.00
7 Jack Patera (CO) 6.00
8 Sherman Smith 5.00
9 Don Testerman 5.00
10 Jim Zorn 12.00

1978-80 Seahawks Nalley's

The 24-card, 10-3/4" x 9" set was available on the box backs of eight-ounce Nally's potato chip products. The color posed fronts feature a facsimile autograph with Seattle's schedule and player stats on the box sides. Prices are for complete boxes.

NM/M

Complete Set (24): 750.00
Common Player (1-8): 25.00
Common Player (9-16): 20.00
Common Player (17-24): 15.00

1 Steve Largent 300.00
2 Autry Beamon 25.00
3 Jim Zorn 65.00
4 Sherman Smith 40.00
5 Ron Coder 25.00
6 Terry Beeson 25.00
7 Steve Niehaus 30.00
8 Ron Howard 25.00
9 Steve Myer 20.00
10 Tom Lynch 20.00
11 David Sims 20.00
12 John Yarno 20.00
13 Bill Gregory 25.00
14 Steve Raible 25.00
15 Dennis Boyd 20.00
16 Steve August 20.00
17 Keith Simpson 15.00
18 Michael Jackson 15.00
19 Manu Tuiasosopo 20.00
20 Sam McCullum 20.00
21 Keith Butler 15.00
22 Sam Akins 15.00
23 Dan Doornink 20.00
24 Dave Brown 20.00

1979 Seahawks Police

The 16-card, 2-5/8" x 4-1/8" set, sponsored by Coca-Cola, Kiwanis, the Washington State Crime Prevention Association and local law enforcement, contain "Tips from the Seahawks" on the card backs.

NM/M

Complete Set (16): 12.00
Common Player: .75

1 Steve August .75
2 Autry Beamon .75
3 Terry Beeson .75
4 Dennis Boyd .75
5 Dave Brown .75
6 Efren Herrera .75
7 Steve Largent 8.00
8 Tom Lynch .75
9 Bob Newton .75
10 Jack Patera (CO) 1.00
11 Keri Truscan Sea Gal .75
12 Seahawk (Mascot) .75
13 David Sims .75
14 Sherman Smith .75
15 John Yarno .75
16 Jim Zorn 3.00

1980 Seahawks Police

The 16-card, 2-5/8" x 4-1/8" set, sponsored by local law enforcement, Coca-Cola, Kiwanis, the Washington State Crime Prevention Association and Ernst Home Centers, features "tips from the Seahawks" on the card backs.

NM/M

Complete Set (16): 10.00
Common Player: .60

1 Sam McCullum .60
2 Dan Doornink .60
3 Sherman Smith .60
4 Efren Herrera .60
5 Bill Gregory .60
6 Keith Simpson .60
7 Manu Tuiasosopo .60
8 Michael Jackson .60
9 Steve Raible .60
10 Steve Largent 6.00
11 Jim Zorn 2.00
12 Nick Bebout .60
13 The Seahawk (mascot) .60
14 Jack Patera (CO) .75
15 Robert Hardy .60
16 Keith Butler .60

1980 Seahawks 7-Up

The 10-card, 2-3/8" x 3-1/4" set features a player closeup on the card fronts with player bio information on the card backs. Quarterback Jim Zorn and receiver Steve Largent do not appear due to their sponsorships with Darigold Dairy.

NM/M

Complete Set (10): 125.00
Common Player: 12.00

1 Steve August 12.00
2 Terry Beeson 12.00
3 Dan Doornink 12.00
4 Michael Jackson 12.00
5 Tom Lynch 12.00
6 Steve Myer 12.00
7 Steve Raible 20.00
8 Sherman Smith 20.00
9 Manu Tuiasosopo 12.00
10 John Yarno 12.00

1981 Seahawks 7-Up

The 30-card, 3-1/2" x 5-1/2" set features color action shots and facsimile autographs on the card fronts. The card backs contain a brief player bio. As with the 1980 set, Zorn and Largent do not appear because of conflicting sponsorships.

NM/M

Complete Set (30): 64.00
Common Player: 2.25

1 Sam Adkins 2.25
2 Steve August 2.25
3 Terry Beeson 2.25
4 Dennis Boyd 2.25
5 Dave Brown 3.00
6 Louis Bullard 2.25
7 Keith Butler 2.25
8 Peter Cronan 2.25
9 Dan Doornink 3.00
10 Jacob Green 4.50
11 Bill Gregory 2.25
12 Robert Hardy 2.25
13 Efren Herrera 2.25
14 Michael Jackson 2.25
15 Art Kuehn 2.25
16 Steve Largent 15.00
17 Tom Lynch 2.25
18 Sam McCullum 3.00
19 Steve Myer 2.25
20 Jack Patera (CO) 3.00
21 Steve Raible 2.25
22 The Sea Gals 2.25
23 The Seahawk Mascot 2.25
24 Keith Simpson 2.25
25 Sherman Smith 2.25
26 Manu Tuiasosopo 2.25
27 Herman Weaver 2.25
28 Cornell Webster 2.25
29 John Yarno 2.25
30 Jim Zorn 6.00

1982 Seahawks Police

The 16-card, 2-5/8" x 4-1/8" set, issued by the Washington State Crime Prevention Association, Kiwanis, Coca-Cola, local law enforcement and Ernst Home Centers, includes "Tips from the Seahawks" on the card backs and the set contains the card of team mascot Sea Gal (No. 4). Also, the cards of Sam McCullum and Jack Patera were distributed in lesser quantities.

NM/M

Complete Set (16): 12.00
Common Player: .40

1 Sam McCullum (SP) 2.00
2 Manu Tuiasosopo .50
3 Sherman Smith .60
4 Karen Godwin (Sea Gal) .40
5 Dave Brown .60
6 Keith Simpson .40
7 Steve Largent 5.00
8 Michael Jackson .40
9 Kenny Easley .75
10 Dan Doornink .40
11 Jim Zorn 2.00
12 Jack Patera (CO SP) 2.00
13 Jacob Green .60
14 Dave Krieg 3.00
15 Steve August .40
16 Keith Butler .40

1982 Seahawks 7-Up

The 15-card, 3-1/2" x 5-1/2" set features color action shots on the card fronts with "Seahawks Fan Mail Courtesy" printed, as well as a facsimile autograph. The card backs include "Tips from the Seahawks" and the cards of Zorn and Largent are included with Darigold logo on the backs.

NM/M

Complete Set (15): 75.00
Common Player: 3.00

1 Edwin Bailey 3.00
2 Dave Brown 3.00
3 Kenny Easley 5.00
4 Ron Essink 3.00
5 Jacob Green (No facsimile autograph) 5.00
6 Robert Hardy 3.00
7 John Harris 3.00
8 David Hughes 3.00
9 Paul Johns (HOR) 3.00
10 Kerry Justin 3.00
11 Dave Krieg 12.00
12 Steve Largent (Darigold logo or Gold-n-Soft) 20.00
13 Keith Simpson 3.00
14 Manu Tuiasosopo 3.00
15 Jim Zorn (HOR) (Darigold logo or Gold-n-Soft) 8.00

1984 Seahawks GTE

The 12-card, 3-1/2" x 5-1/2" set features a color shot with a headshot inset in a corner, along with a facsimile autograph on the card front. The card backs have a brief player bio.

NM/M

Complete Set (12): 40.00
Common Player: 2.00

1 Kenny Easley 3.00
2 Jacob Green 3.00
3 John Harris 2.00
4 Norm Johnson 4.00
5 Chuck Knox (CO) 2.00
6 Dave Krieg 7.00
7 Steve Largent 16.00
8 Joe Nash 2.00
9 Keith Simpson 2.00
10 Mike Tice 2.00
11 Curt Warner 7.00
12 Charley Young 3.00

1984 Seahawks Nalley's

The four-card, 10-3/4" x 9" set was available on the box backs of Nalley's potato chips. The box sides contain Seattle's schedule and player bio information. Prices are for complete boxes.

NM/M

Complete Set (4): 50.00
Common Player: 10.00

1 Kenny Easley 10.00
2 Dave Krieg 15.00
3 Steve Largent 25.00
4 Curt Warner 15.00

1985 Seahawks Police

The 16-card, 2-5/8" x 4-1/8" set was sponsored by Kiwanis, Coca-Cola, KOMO-TV4, McDonald's, the Washington State Crime Prevention Association and local law enforcement. The card backs contain "Tips from the Seahawks."

NM/M

Complete Set (16): 8.00
Common Player: .40

1 Dave Brown .50
2 Jeff Bryant .50
3 Blair Bush .50
4 Keith Butler .40
5 Dan Doornink .40
6 Kenny Easley 1.00
7 Jacob Green .60
8 John Harris .40
9 Norm Johnson 1.00
10 Chuck Knox (CO) 1.00
11 Dave Krieg 1.50
12 Steve Largent 3.00
13 Joe Nash .50
14 Bruce Scholtz .40
15 Curt Warner 1.25
16 Fredd Young .60

1986 Seahawks Police

The 16-card, 2-5/8" x 4-1/8" set, sponsored by local law enforcement, contain "Tips from the Seahawks" on the card backs.

NM/M

Complete Set (16): 8.00
Common Player: .40

1 Edwin Bailey .40
2 Dave Brown .50
3 Jeff Bryant .50
4 Blair Bush .50
5 Keith Butler .40
6 Kenny Easley .60
7 Jacob Green .60
8 Michael Jackson .40
9 Chuck Knox (CO) .60
10 Dave Krieg 1.50
11 Steve Largent 3.00
12 Joe Nash .50
13 Bruce Scholtz .40
14 Terry Taylor .40
15 Curt Warner .75
16 Fredd Young .60

1987 Seahawks GTE

The 24-card, 3-5/8" x 5-1/2" set features color fronts with a facsimile player signature. The card backs have a career summary and a greeting from the player with another autograph.

NM/M

Complete Set (24): 60.00
Common Player: 1.50

1 Edwin Bailey 1.50
2 Brian Bosworth 2.50
3 Dave Brown 2.00
4 Jeff Bryant 2.00
5 Bobby Joe Edmonds 3.00
6 Jacob Green 3.00
7 Michael Jackson 1.50
8 Norm Johnson 3.00
9 Jeff Kemp 2.50
10 Chuck Knox (CO) 3.00
11 Dave Krieg 5.00
12 Steve Largent 10.00
13 Ron Mattes 1.50
14 Bryan Millard 1.50
15 Paul Moyer 1.50
16 Eugene Robinson 2.00
17 Paul Skansi 1.50
18 Kelly Stouffer 2.00
19 Terry Taylor 1.50
20 Mike Tice 1.50
21 Daryl Turner 2.00
22 Curt Warner 4.00
23 John L. Williams 4.00
24 Fredd Young 2.00

1987 Seahawks Police

The 16-card, 2-5/8" x 4-1/8" set features a silver border with a blue/green Seahawks logo. The card backs contain a safety tip.

		NM/M
Complete Set (16):		5.00
Common Player:		.35
1	Jeff Bryant	.35
2	Kenny Easley	.60
3	Bobby Joe Edmonds	.35
4	Jacob Green	.60
5	Chuck Knox (CO)	.60
6	Dave Krieg	1.50
7	Steve Largent	2.50
8	Ron Mattes	.35
9	Bryan Millard	.35
10	Eugene Robinson	.60
11	Bruce Scholtz	.35
12	Paul Skansi	.35
13	Curt Warner	.75
14	John L. Williams	1.00
15	Mike Wilson	.35
16	Fredd Young	.35

1987 Seahawks Snyder's/Franz

The 12-card, standard-size set was distributed in the Spokane area (Snyder bread) and Portland area (Franz bread). The card fronts contain a color photo with blue borders while the backs feature a player career summary.

		NM/M
Complete Set (12):		60.00
Common Player:		5.00
1	Jeff Bryant	5.00
2	Keith Butler	5.00
3	Randy Edwards	5.00
4	Byron Franklin	5.00
5	Jacob Green	7.00
6	Dave Krieg	10.00
7	Bryan Millard	5.00
8	Paul Moyer	5.00
9	Eugene Robinson	7.00
10	Mike Tice	5.00
11	Daryl Turner	6.00
12	Curt Warner	8.00

1988 Seahawks Domino's

The 50-card, 2-1/2" x 8-1/2" set was distributed in panel strips with coupons for each Domino's pizza ordered. The first panel contained nine-cards and included a 12-1/2" x 8-1/2" team photo. Cards 10-13, 14-17, 18-21, 22-25, 26-29, 30-33, 34-38, 39-42, 43-46 and 47-50 were issued on a weekly basis.

		NM/M
Complete Set (51):		45.00
Common Player:		.60
1	Steve Largent	10.00
2	Kelly Stouffer	.75
3	Bobby Joe Edmonds	1.00
4	Patrick Hunter	.75
5	Ventrella/Valle/Gellos	.60
6	Edwin Bailey	.60
7	Alonzo Mitz	.60
8	Tommy Kane	1.00
9	Chuck Knox (CO)	1.00
10	Curt Warner	2.00
11	Alvin Powell	.60
12	Joe Nash	.60
13	Brian Blades	3.00
14	Blair Bush	.75
15	Melvin Jenkins	.60
16	Ruben Rodriguez	.60
17	Tommie Agee	.60
18	Eugene Robinson	.75
19	Dwayne Harper	.60
20	Raymond Butler	.60
21	Jeff Kemp	1.00
22	Norm Johnson	.75
23	Bryan Millard	.60
24	Tony Woods	1.00
25	Paul Skansi	.60
26	Jacob Green	1.00
27	Randall Morris	.60
28	Mike Tice	.60
29	Kevin Harmon	.60
30	Dave Krieg	2.50
31	Nesby Glasgow	.75
32	Bruce Scholtz	.60
33	John Spagnola	.60
34	Jeff Bryant	.75
35	Stan Eisenhooth	.60
36	Dave Wyman	.60
37	Greg Gaines	.60
38	Charlie Jones (NBC ANN)	.60
39	Terry Taylor	.60
40	Vernon Dean	.60
41	Mike Wilson	.60
42	Darrin Miller	.60
43	John L. Williams	2.50
44	Grant Feasel	.60
45	M.L. Johnson	.60
46	Ken Clarke	.75
47	Brian Bosworth	.75
48	Ron Mattes	.60
49	Paul Moyer	.60
50	Rufus Porter	1.00
NNO	Team Photo (Large size)	7.00

A player's name in *italic* type indicates a rookie card.

1988 Seahawks Police

The 16-card, 2-5/8" x 4-1/8" set features color photos with gray borders and the backs include safety tips. Terry Taylor's card was pulled from distribution after he was suspended from the team.

		NM/M
Complete Set (16):		10.00
Common Player:		.50
1	Brian Bosworth	1.00
2	Jeff Bryant	.60
3	Raymond Butler	.50
4	Jacob Green	1.00
5	Patrick Hunter	.60
6	Norm Johnson	.75
7	Chuck Knox (CO)	.75
8	Dave Krieg	1.50
9	Steve Largent	2.50
10	Ron Mattes	.50
11	Bryan Millard	.50
12	Paul Moyer	.50
13	Terry Taylor (SP)	2.50
14	Curt Warner	1.00
15	John L. Williams	1.25
16	Fredd Young (SP)	4.50

1988 Seahawks Snyder's/Franz

The 12-card, standard-size set was issued in the Spokane area in Snyder's bread and in the Portland area in Franz bread. The card fronts have a color photo with blue borders.

		NM/M
Complete Set (10):		125.00
Common Player:		12.00
1	Steve August	12.00
2	Terry Beeson	12.00
3	Dan Doornink	15.00
4	Michael Jackson	12.00
5	Tom Lynch	12.00
6	Steve Myer	12.00
7	Steve Raible	20.00
8	Sherman Smith	20.00
9	Manu Tuiasosopo	15.00
10	John Yarno	12.00

1989 Seahawks Oroweat

The 20-card, standard-size set was produced for Oroweat by Pacific and features silver borders. The horizontal backs contain player bio and stat information with career highlights. Each card was available in Oroweat's Oatnut Bread with a total distribution of 1.5 million.

		NM/M
Complete Set (20):		25.00
Common Player:		.60
1	Paul Moyer	.60
2	Dave Wyman	.60
3	Tony Woods	1.00
4	Kelly Stouffer	1.00
5	Brian Blades	3.00
6	Norm Johnson	1.50
7	Curt Warner	2.00
8	John L. Williams	2.00
9	Edwin Bailey	.60
10	Jacob Green	1.00
11	Paul Skansi	.60
12	Jeff Bryant	.75
13	Bruce Scholtz	.60
14	Dave Krieg	3.00
15	Steve Largent	8.00
16	Joe Nash	.75
17	Mike Wilson	.60
18	Ron Mattes	.60
19	Grant Feasel	.60
20	Bryan Millard	.60

1989 Seahawks Police

The 16-card, 2-5/8" x 4-1/8" set feature light blue borders with color action shots. The card backs contain safety tips, except for Largent's card, which lists his NFL records.

		NM/M
Complete Set (16):		5.00
Common Player:		.40
1	Brian Blades	1.00
2	Brian Bosworth	.50
3	Jeff Bryant	.50
4	Jacob Green	.60
5	Chuck Knox (CO)	.60
6	Dave Krieg	1.25
7	Steve Largent	2.00
8	Bryan Millard	.40
9	Rufus Porter	.50
10	Paul Moyer	.40
11	Eugene Robinson	.50
12	Ruben Rodriguez	.40
13	Kelly Stouffer	.50
14	Curt Warner	1.00
15	John L. Williams	1.00
16	Tony Woods	.60

1990 Seahawks Oroweat

The 50-card, regular-size set, produced by Pacific, was available in loaves of Oroweat's Oat Nut, Health Nut and Twelve Grain breads. The first 20 cards of the set were issued before the season with the remaining cards issued during the season. No card No. 25 was produced.

		NM/M
Complete Set (50):		30.00
Common Player (1-20):		.35
Common Player (21-50):		.50
1	Dave Krieg	1.50
2	Rick Donnelly	.35
3	Brian Blades	1.50
4	Cortez Kennedy	1.75
5	John L. Williams	1.50
6	Jeff Chadwick	.35
7	Thom Kaumeyer	.35
8	Bryan Millard	.35
9	Eugene Robinson	.50
10	Jacob Green	.50
11	Willie Bouyer	.35
12	Jeff Bryant	.50
13	Chris Warren	3.00
14	Derrick Fenner	.75
15	Paul Skansi	.35
16	Joe Cain	.35
17	Tommy Kane	.60
18	Tom Flores (GM)	.60
19	Terry Wooden	.60
20	Tony Woods	.60
21	Ricky Andrews	.50
22	Joe Tofflemire	.50
23	Ned Bolcar	.50
24A	Kelly Stouffer	1.00
24B	Melvin Jenkins	.50
26	Norm Johnson	.75
27	Eric Hayes	.50
28	Mike Morris	.50
29	Edwin Bailey	.50
30	Ron Heller	.50
31	Darren Comeaux	.60
32	Andy Heck	.60
33	Ronnie Lee	.60
34	Robert Blackmon	.60
35	Joe Nash	.60
36	Patrick Hunter	.60
37	Darrick Brilz	.50
38	Ron Mattes	.50
39	Nesby Glasgow	.60
40	Dwayne Harper	.50
41	Chuck Knox (CO)	.75
42	Travis McNeal	.60
43	Derek Loville	1.50
44	Dave Wyman	.50
45	Louis Clark	.50
46	Grant Feasel	.50
47	James Jones	.60
48	Rufus Porter	1.00
49	Jeff Kemp	1.00
50	James Jefferson	.60
NNO	Title Card	3.00

1990 Seahawks Police

The 16-card, 2-5/8" x 4-1/8" set has green borders around a color action shot with safety tips appearing on the backs.

		NM/M
Complete Set (16):		5.00
Common Player:		.35
1	Brian Blades	.75
2	Grant Feasel	.35
3	Jacob Green	.75
4	Andy Heck	.50
5	James Jefferson	.50
6	Norm Johnson	.75
7	Cortez Kennedy	1.00
8	Chuck Knox (CO)	.75
9	Dave Krieg	1.00
10	Travis McNeal	.35
11	Bryan Millard	.35
12	Rufus Porter	.50
13	Paul Skansi	.35
14	John L. Williams	.75
15	Tony Woods	.50
16	David Wyman	.35

1991 Seahawks Oroweat

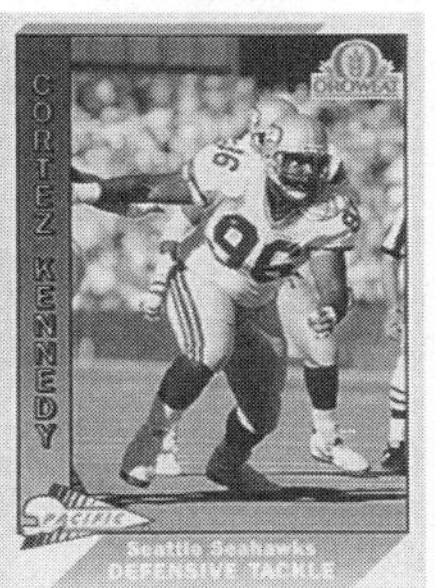

The 50-card, standard-size set, produced by Pacific, was distributed in loaves of Oroweat bread and in five-card packs at a Seattle home game. The cards are very similar to Pacific's 1991 inaugural NFL set, except for the Oroweat logo in the upper right corner of the card front.

		NM/M
Complete Set (50):		30.00
Common Player:		.50
1	Tommy Kane	.75
2	Norm Johnson	.75
3	Robert Blackmon	.50
4	Mike Tice	.50
5	Cortez Kennedy	1.50
6	Bryan Millard	.50
7	Tony Woods	.50
8	Paul Skansi	.50
9	John L. Williams	1.50
10	Terry Wooden	.75
11	Brian Blades	1.25
12	Jacob Green	.75
13	Joe Nash	.75
14	Eugene Robinson	.75
15	Rufus Porter	.75
16	Andy Heck	.50
17	Derrick Fenner	1.00
18	Nesby Glasgow	.50
19	Chris Warren	3.00
20	Dave Krieg	1.50
21	Vann McElroy	.50
22	Jeff Bryant	.50
23	Warren Wheat	.50
24	Marcus Cotton	.50
25	David Wyman	.50
26	Joe Cain	.50
27	Darrick Brilz	.50
28	Eric Hayes	.50
29	Ronnie Lee	.50
30	Louis Clark	.50
31	James Jones	.50
32	Dwayne Harper	.50
33	Grant Feasel	.50
34	Trey Junkin	.50
35	James Jefferson	.50
36	Edwin Bailey	.50
37	Derrick Loville	1.50
38	Travis McNeal	.50
39	Rick Donnelly	.50
40	Rod Stephens	.50
41	Darren Comeaux	.50
42	Brian Davis	.50
43	Bill Hitchcock	.50
44	Jeff Chadwick	.75
45	Patrick Hunter	.75
46	David Daniels	.50
47	Doug Thomas	.50
48	Dan McGwire	.75
49	John Kasay	.75
50	Jeff Kemp	.75
NNO	Title Card	2.50

1992 Seahawks Oroweat

The 50-card, regular-size set, produced by Pacific, was delivered in various loaves of Oroweat bread. The card design is very similar to the base 1992 Pacific set, except for the Oroweat and KIRO Newsradio logos.

		NM/M
Complete Set (51):		25.00
Common Player:		.50
1	Brian Blades	1.00
2	Patrick Hunter	.75
3	Jeff Bryant	.75
4	Robert Blackmon	.50
5	Joe Cain	.50
6	Grant Feasel	.50
7	Dan McGwire	.75
8	David Wyman	.50
9	Jacob Green	.75
10	Theo Adams	.50
11	Brian Davis	.50
12	Andy Heck	.50
13	Bill Hitchcock	.50
14	Joe Nash	.50
15	Rod Stephens	.50
16	John Hunter	.50
17	Paul Green	.50
18	James Jones	.50
19	Robb Thomas	.75
20	Tony Woods	.50
21	Dedrick Dodge	.50
22	Tracy Johnson	.50
23	Darrick Brilz	.50
24	Joe Tofflemire	.50
25	Louis Clark	.50
26	Rueben Mayes	.75
27	Natu Tuatagaloa	.50
28	Terry Wooden	.75
29	Tommy Kane	.50
30	Stan Gelbaugh	.75
31	Nesby Glasgow	.50
32	Kelly Stouffer	.50
33	Ray Roberts	.50
34	Doug Thomas	.50
35	David Daniels	.50
36	John Kasay	.75
37	Cortez Kennedy	.75
38	Tyrone Rodgers	.50
39	Bryan Millard	.50
40	Eugene Robinson	.75
41	Malcolm Frank	.50
42	Dwayne Harper	.50
43	Ron Heller	.50
44	Rick Tuten	.50
45	Trey Junkin	.50
46	Bob Spitulski	.50
47	Chris Warren	2.00
48	John L. Williams	.75
49	Ronnie Lee	.50
50	Rufus Porter	.75
NNO	Title/Ad Card	1.00

1993 Seahawks Oroweat

The 50-card, standard size set, sponsored by Oroweat and KIRO Newsradio, was produced by Pacific. The cards' design is very similar to Pacific's 1993 base set and were included in various loaves of Oroweat bread.

		NM/M
Complete Set (50):		25.00
Common Player:		.50
1	Cortez Kennedy	1.00
2	Robb Thomas	.75
3	Rueben Mayes	.75
4	Rick Tuten	.50
5	Tracy Johnson	.50
6	Michael Bates	.50
7	Andy Heck	.50
8	Stan Gelbaugh	.75
9	Dan McGwire	.75
10	Mike Keim	.50
11	Grant Feasel	.50
12	Brian Blades	1.00
13	Tyrone Rodgers	.50
14	Paul Green	.50
15	Rafael Robinson	.50
16	John Kasay	.75
17	Chris Warren	2.00
18	Michael Sinclair	.50
19	John L. Williams	.75
20	Bob Spitulski	.50
21	Eugene Robinson	.75
22	Patrick Hunter	.75
23	Kevin Murphy	.50
24	Dave McCloughan	.50
25	Rick Mirer	5.00
26	Ray Donaldson	.75
27	E.J. Junior	.50
28	Jeff Bryant	.75
29	Ferrell Edmunds	.50
30	Tommy Kane	.75
31	Terry Wooden	.75
32	Doug Thomas	.50
33	Carlton Gray	.50
34	Kelvin Martin	.75
35	Rod Stephens	.50
36	Darrick Brilz	.50
37	Joe Tofflemire	.50
38	James Jefferson	.50
39	Rufus Porter	.50
40	Jeff Blackshear	.50
41	Dwayne Harper	.50
42	Ray Roberts	.50
43	Robert Blackmon	.50
44	Joe Nash	.50
45	Michael McCrary	.50
46	Trey Junkin	.50
47	Natu Tuatagaloa	.50
48	Bill Hitchcock	.50
49	Jon Vaughn	.75
50	Dean Wells	.50

1994 Seahawks Oroweat

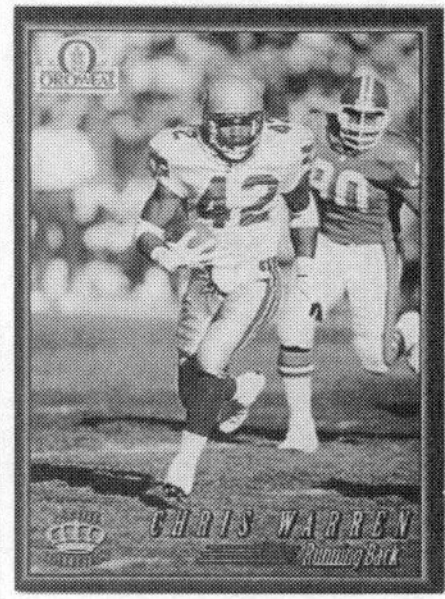

The 50-card, standard-size set, produced by Pacific, was issued in various loaves of Oroweat bread in the Northwest area. The cards are almost identical in design to Pacific's 1994 football set, except for the Oroweat logo in the upper right corner of the card front.

		NM/M
Complete Set (50):		25.00
Common Player:		.50
1	Brian Blades	.75
2	Terrence Warren	.50
3	Carlton Gray	.50
4	Bob Spitulski	.50
5	Dean Wells	.50
6	Lamar Smith	.50
7	Michael Bates	.50
8	Duane Bickett	.60
9	Cortez Kennedy	1.00
10	Dave McCloughan	.50
11	Tracy Johnson	.50
12	Eugene Robinson	.60
13	Jeff Blackshear	.50
14	Tyrone Rodgers	.50
15	Trey Junkin	.50
16	Ferrell Edmunds	.50
17	Tony Brown	.50
18	Orlando Watters	.50
19	John Kasay	.60
20	Rafael Robinson	.50
21	Kelvin Martin	.60
22	Stan Gelbaugh	.60
23	Steve Smith	.50
24	Ray Donaldson	.60
25	Rufus Porter	.50
26	Patrick Hunter	.60
27	Terry Wooden	.60
28	Sam Adams	.60
29	Mack Strong	.60
30	Chris Warren	1.25
31	Bill Hitchcock	.50
32	David Brandon	.50
33	Michael McCrary	.50
34	Jon Vaughn	.60
35	Paul Green	.50
36	Mike Keim	.50
37	Joe Tofflemire	.50
38	Rick Tuten	.50
39	Rick Mirer	3.00
40	Rod Stephens	.50
41	Robert Blackmon	.50
42	Howard Ballard	.50
43	Michael Sinclair	.50
44	Kevin Mawae	.50
45	Brent Williams	.50
46	Ray Roberts	.50
47	Robb Thomas	.60
48	Antonio Edwards	.50
49	Dan McGwire	.50
50	Joe Nash	.50

1982 Sears-Roebuck

The 12-card, 5" x 7" set, issued by 37 different Sears district stores, closely resembles the Marketcom posters. The card backs contain bio and career highlight information with the Sears Roebuck logo on the card back bottom. Because of the football strike in 1982, many of the cards were not distributed and were either destroyed or thrown out.

		NM/M
Complete Set (12):		265.00
Common Player:		8.00
1	Ken Anderson	15.00
2	Terry Bradshaw	25.00
3	Earl Campbell	25.00
4	Dwight Clark	8.00
5	Cris Collinsworth	8.00
6	Tony Dorsett	20.00
7	Dan Fouts	18.00
8	Franco Harris	20.00
9	Joe Montana	75.00
10	Walter Payton	40.00
11	Randy White	15.00
12	Kellen Winslow	15.00

1993 Select

Score's 1993 Select set includes 200 cards which are framed on two sides by green. A 10-card insert set, Gridiron Skills, was also produced; cards were randomly inserted in packs.

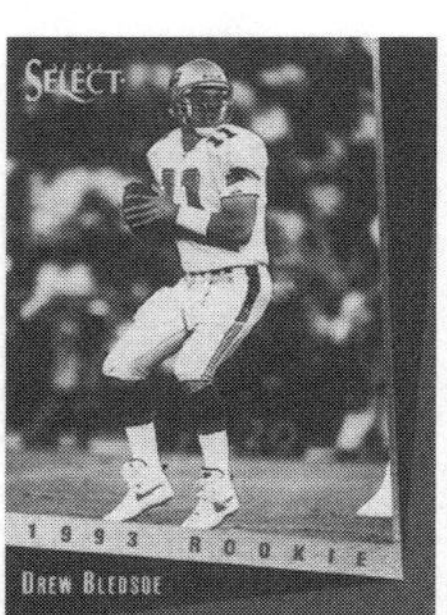

		NM/M
Complete Set (200):		20.00
Common Player:		.10
Minor Stars:		.50
Pack (15):		1.50
Wax Box (36):		40.00
1	Steve Young	3.00
2	Andre Reed	.50
3	Deion Sanders	2.00
4	Harold Green	.10
5	Wendell Davis	.10
6	Mike Johnson	.10
7	Troy Aikman	3.00
8	Johnny Mitchell	.10
9	Dale Carter	.10
10	Bruce Matthews	.10
11	Terrell Buckley	.10
12	Steve Emtman	.10
13	Neil Smith	.10
14	Tim Brown	.50
15	Chris Doleman	.10
16	Dan Marino	4.00
17	Terry McDaniel	.10
18	Neal Anderson	.10
19	Phil Simms	.10
20	Jeff Lageman	.10
21	Jerry Rice	3.00
22	Dermontti Dawson	.10
23	Reggie Cobb	.10
24	Junior Seau	.50
25	Darrell Green	.10
26	Chris Warren	.50
27	Randall Cunningham	.50
28	Bruce Smith	.10
29	Bryan Cox	.10
30	David Klingler	.10
31	Chip Lohmiller	.10
32	Eric Metcalf	.10
33	Ken Norton	.10
34	John Elway	3.00
35	Harris Barton	.10
36	Tim Barnett	.10
37	Rodney Hampton	.50
38	Desmond Howard	.10
39	Tom Rathman	.10
40	Derrick Thomas	.50
41	Randal Hill	.10
42	Steve Wisniewski	.10
43	Brett Favre	4.00
44	Darryl Talley	.10
45	Shane Conlan	.10
46	Anthony Miller	.50
47	Randall McDaniel	.10
48	Rod Woodson	.10
49	Eric Martin	.10
50	Ronnie Lott	.10
51	Chris Spielman	.10
52	Vincent Brown	.10
53	Donnell Woolford	.10
54	Richmond Webb	.10
55	Emmitt Smith	4.00
56	Haywood Jeffires	.10
57	Jim Kelly	.50
58	James Francis	.10
59	Steve Wallace	.10
60	Jarrod Bunch	.10
61	Lawrence Dawsey	.10
62	Steve Atwater	.10
63	Art Monk	.50
64	Eric Green	.10
65	Lawrence Taylor	.50
66	Ronnie Harmon	.10
67	Fred Barnett	.10
68	Cortez Kennedy	.10
69	Mark Collins	.10
70	Howie Long	.50
71	Jackie Harris	.10
72	Irving Fryar	.10
73	Jim Everett	.10
74	Troy Vincent	.10
75	Cris Carter	.50
76	Boomer Esiason	.10
77	Sam Mills	.10
78	Lorenzo White	.10
79	Andre Rison	.50
80	Quentin Coryatt	.10
81	Steve McMichael	.10
82	Nick Lowery	.10
83	Michael Irvin	.50
84	Thurman Thomas	.50
85	Bill Romanowski	.10
86	Carl Pickens	2.00
87	Tim McDonald	.10
88	Bernie Kosar	.10
89	Greg Lloyd	.10
90	Barry Sanders	4.00
91	Shannon Sharpe	.50
92	Henry Thomas	.10
93	Barry Foster	.10
94	Antone Davis	.10
95	Stan Humphries	.50
96	Eric Swann	.10
97	Mike Pritchard	.10
98	Reggie White	.50
99	Jeff Hostetler	.10
100	Willie Anderson	.10
101	Gary Clark	.10
102	Morten Andersen	.10
103	Leonard Russell	.10
104	Chris Hinton	.10
105	John Stephens	.10
106	Byron Evans	.10
107	Warren Moon	.50
108	Marv Cook	.10
109	*Carlton Gray*	.10
110	Jay Novacek	.10
111	Gary Anderson	.10
112	Andre Tippett	.10
113	Cornelius Bennett	.10
114	Clyde Simmons	.10
115	Jeff George	.50
116	Audray McMillian	.10
117	Mark Carrier	.10
118	Vaughan Johnson	.10
119	Kevin Greene	.10
120	John Taylor	.10
121	Jerry Ball	.10
122	Pat Swilling	.10
123	*George Teague*	.50
124	Ricky Reynolds	.10
125	Marcus Allen	.50
126	Henry Jones	.10
127	Ricky Watters	.50
128	Leon Searcy	.10
129	Chris Miller	.10
130	Jim Harbaugh	.50
131	Luis Sharpe	.10
132	Simon Fletcher	.10
133	Eric Allen	.10
134	Carlton Haselrig	.10
135	Harvey Williams	.10
136	Leslie O'Neal	.10
137	Sterling Sharpe	.50
138	Tim Harris	.10
139	Mark Rypien	.10
140	Harry Galbreath	.10
141	Sean Gilbert	.10
142	Keith Jackson	.10
143	Mark Clayton	.10
144	Guy McIntyre	.10
145	Jessie Tuggle	.10
146	Leonard Marshall	.10
147	Willie Davis	.10
148	Herman Moore	2.00
149	Charles Haley	.10
150	Amp Lee	.10
151	Gary Zimmerman	.10
152	Bennie Blades	.10
153	Pierce Holt	.10
154	Edgar Bennett	.50
155	Joe Montana	4.00
156	Ted Washington	.10
157	Hardy Nickerson	.10
158	Rohn Stark	.10
159	Brent Jones	.10
160	Eugene Robinson	.10
161	Pepper Johnson	.10
162	Dan Saleaumua	.10
163	Seth Joyner	.10
165	Mike Munchak	.10
166	*Drew Bledsoe*	15.00
167	*Curtis Conway*	3.00
168	*Lincoln Kennedy*	.50
169	*Dana Stubblefield*	1.00
170	*Wayne Simmons*	.50
171	*Garrison Hearst*	5.00
172	*Jerome Bettis*	8.00
173	*Eric Curry*	.50
174	*Natrone Means*	5.00
175	*Glyn Milburn*	.50
176	*Marvin Jones*	.50
177	*O.J. McDuffie*	3.00
178	*Dan Williams*	.50
179	*Rick Mirer*	.75
180	*John Copeland*	.50
181	*Willie Roaf*	.50
182	*Patrick Bates*	.50
183	*Troy Drayton*	.75
184	*Vincent Brisby*	.50
185	*Irv Smith*	.50
186	Marion Butts	.10
187	Wayne Martin	.10
188	Brian Blades	.10
189	Mel Gray	.10
190	Mark Stepnoski	.10
191	Ernest Givins	.10
192	Steve Tasker	.10
193	Tim Grunhard	.10
194	Stanley Richard	.10
195	Jeff Wright	.10
196	Rodney Peete	.10
197	Tunch Ilkin	.10
198	Rich Camarillo	.10
199	Eric Williams	.10
200	Pete Stoyanovich	.10

1993 Select Gridiron Skills

These cards were random inserts in 1993 Score Select foil packs at a rate of about one every 72 packs. Five top wide receivers and five top quarterbacks are represented. The card front has a player action photo against a shiny, metallic-like background. The player's name and position are at the bottom in a red stripe, along with the set logo. The back has a player photo and a description of the skills he brings to the football field. Each card is numbered.

		NM/M
Complete Set (10):		40.00
Common Player:		1.00
Minor Stars:		2.00
1	Warren Moon	2.00
2	Steve Young	4.00
3	Dan Marino	6.00
4	John Elway	4.00
5	Troy Aikman	4.00
6	Sterling Sharpe	2.00
7	Jerry Rice	4.00
8	Andre Rison	2.00
9	Haywood Jeffires	1.00
10	Michael Irvin	2.00

1993 Select Young Stars

These metallic-like cards, sold as a set in a black box, use FX printing technology. Each card front has a color action photo against a tombstone-like background. The player's name and "Young Stars" are written at the top of the card, above the arch. The Select logo is in the lower left corner. The front and back use team colors in the design. The back has a team helmet in the center, above a player profile. Cards are numbered. There were 5,900 sets produced; each includes a certificate of authenticity which indicates the set's serial number.

		NM/M
Complete Set (38):		20.00
Common Player:		.25
1	Brett Favre	4.00
2	Anthony Miller	.25
3	Rodney Hampton	1.00
4	Cortez Kennedy	.25
5	Junior Seau	1.00
6	Ricky Watters	1.00
7	Terry Allen	.50
8	Drew Bledsoe	2.00
9	Rick Mirer	.25
10	Jeff Graham	.25
11	Barry Foster	.25
12	Eric Green	.25
13	Troy Aikman	3.00
14	Michael Haynes	.25
15	Johnny Mitchell	.25
16	Lawrence Dawsey	.25
17	Mo Lewis	.25
18	Andre Ware	.25
19	Neil O'Donnell	.50
20	Broderick Thomas	.25
21	Tim Barnett	.25
22	Fred Barnett	.25
23	Carl Pickens	1.00
24	Santana Dotson	.25
25	Sean Gilbert	.25
26	Quentin Coryatt	.25
27	Arthur Marshall	.25
28	Dale Carter	.25
29	Henry Jones	.25
30	Terrell Buckley	.25
31	Tommy Vardell	.25
32	Russell Maryland	.25
33	Steve Emtman	.25
34	Jarrod Bunch	.25
35	Alfred Williams	.25
36	Brian Mitchell	.25
37	Chris Warren	.50
38	Deion Sanders	1.00

1994 Select Samples

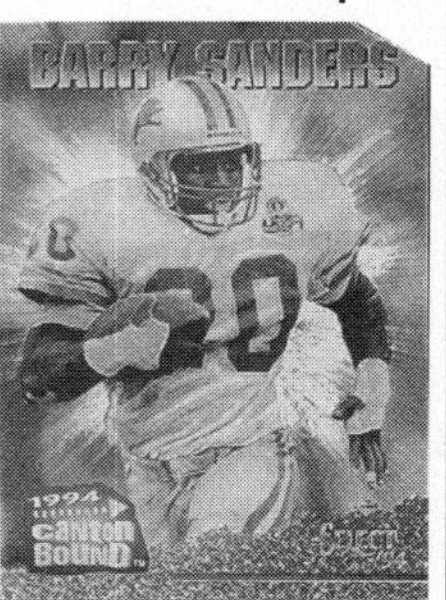

The seven-card, regular-sized set was issued to preview the 1994 Select set. The cards are virtually identical to the base set and include a Canton Bound and Future Force insert sample. The card numbers are the same as the base card counterparts.

		NM/M
Complete Set (7):		10.00
Common Player:		1.00
5	Rod Woodson	1.00
19	Junior Seau	1.50
33	Mark Carrier (DB)	1.00
218	Charlie Garner	1.00
CB4	Barry Sanders	4.00
FF2	Drew Bledsoe	4.00
NNO	Title Card	1.00

1994 Select

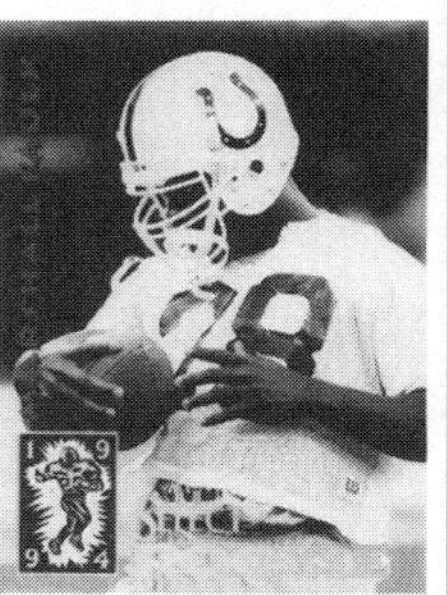

Select consists of a 225-card base set. The cards feature a full-bleed photo and a small, oval-shaped, black and white photo with a gold-foil border on the front. A 25-card rookie subset is included in the base series. Insert sets in Select include Canton Bound (12 cards, 1:48) and Future Force (12 cards, 1:48).

		NM/M
Complete Set (225):		15.00
Common Player:		.10
Minor Stars:		.30
Pack (12):		1.50
Wax Box (24):		25.00
1	Emmitt Smith	3.00
2	Bruce Smith	.10
3	Randall McDaniel	.10
4	Drew Bledsoe	2.50
5	Rod Woodson	.10
6	Richard Dent	.10
7	Norm Johnson	.10
8	Jim Everett	.10
9	Harold Green	.10
10	John Elway	3.00
11	Barry Sanders	4.00
12	Sterling Sharpe	.30
13	Marcus Robertson	.10
14	Steve Wisniewski	.10
15	Irving Fryar	.10
16	Tyrone Hughes	.10
17	Garrison Hearst	1.00
18	Randall Cunningham	.30
19	Junior Seau	.30
20	Rick Mirer	.10
21	Jerry Rice	2.00
22	Eric Metcalf	.10
23	Roosevelt Potts	.10
24	Neil Smith	.10
25	Jerome Bettis	1.00
26	Keith Hamilton	.10
27	Hardy Nickerson	.10
28	Steve Tasker	.10
29	Johnny Johnson	.10
30	Tom Carter	.10
31	Andre Rison	.30
32	Cortez Kennedy	.30
33	Mark Carrier	.10
34	Shannon Sharpe	.30
35	Eric Swann	.10
36	Steve Young	1.50
37	Johnny Maryland	.10
38	Dermontti Dawson	.10
39	Mike Johnson	.10
40	Troy Aikman	2.00
41	Pierce Holt	.10
42	Derrick Thomas	.30
43	Reggie Cobb	.10
44	Michael Jackson	.10
45	Lomas Brown	.10
46	Jeff Hostetler	.10
47	Pete Stoyanovich	.10
48	Reggie White	.50
49	Quentin Coryatt	.10
50	Cris Carter	.75
51	Sean Gilbert	.10
52	Chris Slade	.10
53	Ronnie Harmon	.10
54	Renaldo Turnbull	.10
55	Fred Barnett	.10
56	John Elliott	.10
57	Deion Sanders	1.00
58	John Carney	.10
59	Louis Oliver	.10
60	Greg Lloyd	.10
61	Chris Hinton	.10
62	Ron Moore	.10
63	Vincent Brown	.10
64	Tony McGee	.10
65	Eric Williams	.10
66	Thurman Thomas	.30
67	Neil O'Donnell	.30
68	Scott Mitchell	.30
69	Keith Byars	.10
70	Henry Ellard	.10
71	Chris Spielman	.10
72	LeRoy Butler	.10
73	Tim Brown	.30
74	Darrell Green	.10
75	Bruce Matthews	.10
76	Stan Humphries	.30
77	Will Wolford	.10
78	John Taylor	.10
79	Joe Montana	3.00
80	Chris Warren	.30
81	Michael Brooks	.10
82	Vance Johnson	.10
83	Rob Moore	.30
84	Herschel Walker	.10
85	Alvin Harper	.10
86	Wayne Martin	.10
87	Leslie O'Neal	.10
88	Willie Anderson	.10
89	Tommy Vardell	.10
90	Mike Sherrard	.10
91	Chris Jacke	.10
92	Jim Kelly	.30
93	Jeff Graham, Thomas Everett	.10
94	Bryan Cox	.10
95	Michael Irvin	.30
96	Jeff Lageman	.10
97	Webster Slaughter	.10
98	Eugene Robinson	.10
99	Vencie Glenn	.10
100	Sean Jones	.10
101	Calvin Williams	.10
102	Jim Harbaugh	.30
103	Eric Curry	.10
104	Terry Allen	.30
105	Darryl Williams	.10
106	Gary Clark	.10
107	Marcus Allen	.50
108	Chip Lohmiller	.10
109	Vaughan Johnson	.10
110	Herman Moore	.75
111	Barry Foster	.10
112	Rocket Ismail	.10
113	Erric Pegram	.10
114	Anthony Miller	.10
115	Shane Conlan	.10
116	David Klingler	.10
117	Mark Collins	.10
118	Tony Bennett	.10
119	Donnell Woolford	.10
120	Reggie Brooks	.10
121	Sam Mills	.10
122	Greg Montgomery	.10
123	Kevin Greene	.10
124	Terry McDaniel	.10
125	Henry Jones	.10
126	Ricky Watters	.30
127	Dan Marino	3.00
128	Steve Atwater	.10
129	Ricky Proehl	.10
130	Ernest Givins	.10
131	John L. Williams	.10
132	John Randle	.10
133	Jay Novacek	.10
134	Boomer Esiason	.30
135	Jessie Hester	.10
136	Courtney Hawkins	.10
137	Ben Coates	.30
138	Stevon Moore	.10
139	Eric Allen	.10
140	Jessie Tuggle	.10
141	Marion Butts	.10
142	Brett Favre	4.00
143	Andre Reed	.30
144	Rodney Hampton	.30
145	Keith Sims	.10
146	Derek Brown	.10
147	Eric Green	.10
148	Greg Robinson	.10
149	Nate Newton	.10
150	Mark Higgs	.10
151	Nick Lowery	.10
152	Craig Erickson	.10
153	Anthony Carter	.10
154	Simon Fletcher	.10
155	Ronnie Lott	.30
156	Gary Brown	.10
157	Brent Jones	.10
158	Jim Sweeney	.10
159	Robert Brooks	.10
160	Keith Jackson	.10
161	Daryl Johnston	.10
162	Tom Waddle	.10
163	Eric Martin	.10
164	Cornelius Bennett	.10
165	Tim McDonald	.10
166	Chris Doleman	.10
167	Gary Zimmerman	.10
168	Al Smith	.10
169	Mark Carrier	.10
170	Harris Barton	.10
171	Ray Childress	.10
172	Darryl Talley	.10
173	James Jett	.10
174	Mark Stepnoski	.10
175	Jeff Query	.10
176	Charles Haley	.10
177	Rod Bernstine	.10
178	Richmond Webb	.10
179	Rich Camarillo	.10
180	Pat Swilling	.10
181	Chris Miller	.10
182	Mike Pritchard	.10
183	Checklist	.10
184	Natrone Means	.75
185	Erik Kramer	.10
186	Clyde Simmons	.10
187	Checklist	.10
188	Warren Moon	.30
189	Michael Haynes	.10
190	Terry Kirby	.30
191	Brian Blades	.10
192	Haywood Jeffires	.10
194	Morten Andersen	.10
195	Dana Stubblefield	.10
196	Ken Norton	.10
197	Art Monk	.10
198	Seth Joyner	.10
199	*Heath Shuler*	.40
200	*Marshall Faulk*	6.00
201	*Charles Johnson*	.40
202	*Derrick Alexander*	.40
203	*Greg Hill*	.50
204	*Darnay Scott*	.75
205	*Willie McGinest*	.50
206	*Thomas Randolph*	.25
207	*Errict Rhett*	.75
208	*William Floyd*	.50
209	*Johnnie Morton*	1.00
210	*David Palmer*	1.00
211	*Dan Wilkinson*	.50
212	*Trent Dilfer*	2.50
213	*Antonio Langham*	.50
214	*Chuck Levy*	.25
215	*John Thierry*	.25
216	*Kevin Lee*	.25
217	*Aaron Glenn*	.25
218	*Charlie Garner*	1.75
219	*Jeff Burris*	.25
220	*LeShon Johnson*	.25
221	*Thomas Lewis*	.25
222	*Ryan Yarborough*	.25
223	*Mario Bates*	.50
224	Checklist	.10
225	Checklist	.10
SR1	Marshall Faulk SR	40.00
SR2	Dan Wilkinson SR	10.00

1994 Select Canton Bound

Canton Bound is a 12-card insert featuring Dufex technology. The set features players destined for the Hall of Fame and was inserted 1:48.

		NM/M
Complete Set (12):		55.00
Common Player:		1.00
Minor Stars:		2.00
Inserted 1:48		
1	Emmitt Smith	8.00
2	Sterling Sharpe	2.00
3	Joe Montana	8.00
4	Barry Sanders	8.00
5	Jerry Rice	6.00
6	Ronnie Lott	2.00
7	Reggie White	1.00
8	Steve Young	6.00
9	Jerome Bettis	2.00
10	Bruce Smith	1.00
11	Troy Aikman	6.00
12	Thurman Thomas	2.00

1994 Select Future Force

Future Force is a 12-card insert which was seeded 1:48. The cards feature Dufex technology.

		NM/M
Complete Set (12):		15.00
Common Player:		.50
Minor Stars:		1.00
Inserted 1:48		
1	Rick Mirer	.50
2	Drew Bledsoe	5.00
3	Jerome Bettis	2.00
4	Reggie Brooks	.50
5	Natrone Means	1.00
6	James Jett	.50
7	Terry Kirby	1.00
8	Vincent Brisby	.50
9	Gary Brown	.50
10	Tyrone Hughes	.50
11	Dana Stubblefield	1.00
12	Garrison Hearst	3.00

1994 Select Franco Harris

The standard-size Harris card was given away at Pinnacle's party at the 15th National Sports Card Convention. The card front features a metallic Harris image with his signature on the card's back. The card is numbered as "x of 5,000."

		NM/M
Complete Set (1):		25.00
Common Player:		25.00
1	Franco Harris	25.00

1995 Select Certified Promos

This three-card promo set was issued to give collectors and dealers a look at the designs for 1995 Select Certified. It included two base cards and one Gold Team insert.

		NM/M
Complete Set (3):		20.00
Common Player:		5.00
10	Steve Young	5.00
44	Troy Aikman	5.00
7	Dan Marino (Gold Team)	15.00

1995 Select Certified

These 1995 Select cards feature 24-point stock and double lamination for each card. The 135-card set includes 29 rookies. Gold foil printing is used for the player's name and the brand logo on the front, which has a full-bleed action photo on it. Each card is also reprinted using a gold mirror mylar foil technology to form a parallel set. These cards were randomly inserted into every fifth pack. Insert sets include Certified Future, Certified Gold Team and The Select Few.

		NM/M
Complete Set (135):		40.00
Common Player:		.10
Minor Stars:		.50
Comp. Checklist Set (7):		3.00
Pack (6):		7.00
Wax Box (20):		100.00
1	Marshall Faulk	3.00
2	Heath Shuler	1.00
3	Garrison Hearst	.50
4	Errict Rhett	1.00
5	Jeff George	.50
6	Jerome Bettis	2.00
7	Jim Kelly	.50
8	Rick Mirer	.50
9	Willie Davis	.10
10	Steve Young	3.00
11	Erik Kramer	.10
12	Natrone Means	1.00
13	*Jeff Blake*	1.50
14	Neil O'Donnell	.50
15	Andre Rison	.10
16	Randall Cunningham	.10
17	Emmitt Smith	4.00
18	Tim Brown	.50
19	Shannon Sharpe	.10
20	Boomer Esiason	.10
21	Barry Sanders	4.00
22	Rodney Hampton	.50
23	Robert Brooks	1.00
24	Jim Everett	.10
25	Gary Brown	.10
26	Drew Bledsoe	4.00
27	Desmond Howard	.10
28	Cris Carter	.50
29	Marcus Allen	.50
30	Dan Marino	5.00
31	Warren Moon	.50
32	Dave Krieg	.10
33	Ben Coates	.10
34	Terance Mathis	.10
35	Mario Bates	1.00
36	Andre Reed	.10
37	Dave Brown	.10
38	Jeff Graham	.10
39	Johnny Mitchell	.10
40	Carl Pickens	1.00
41	Jeff Hostetler	.10
42	Vinny Testaverde	.10
43	Ricky Watters	.50
44	Troy Aikman	4.00
45	Bam Morris	1.00
46	John Elway	3.00
47	Junior Seau	.50
48	Scott Mitchell	.50
49	Jerry Rice	4.00
50	Brett Favre	5.00
51	Chris Warren	.50
52	Chris Chandler	.10
53	Lorenzo White	.10
54	Craig Erickson	.10
55	Alvin Harper	.10
56	Steve Beuerlein	.10
57	Edgar Bennett	.10
58	Steve Bono	.50
59	Eric Green	.10
60	Jake Reed	.10
61	Terry Kirby	.10
62	Vincent Brisby	.10
63	Lake Dawson	.50
64	Torrance Small	.10
65	Mark Brunell	2.00
66	Haywood Jeffires	.10
67	Flipper Anderson	.10
68	Ron Moore	.10
69	LeShon Johnson	.10
70	Rocket Ismail	.10
71	Herman Moore	2.00
72	Charlie Garner	.10
73	Anthony Miller	.10
74	Greg Lloyd	.10
75	Michael Irvin	1.00
76	Stan Humphries	.50
77	Leroy Hoard	.10
78	Deion Sanders	2.00
79	Darnay Scott	1.50
80	Chris Miller	.10
81	Curtis Conway	.50
82	Trent Dilfer	1.00
83	Bruce Smith	.10
84	Reggie Brooks	.10
85	Frank Reich	.10
86	Henry Ellard	.10
87	Eric Metcalf	.10
88	Sean Gilbert	.10
89	Larry Centers	.10
90	Ricky Ervins	.10
91	Craig Heyward	.10
92	Rod Woodson	.10
93	Steve Walsh	.10
94	Fred Barnett	.10
95	William Floyd	1.00
96	Harvey Williams	.10
97	Greg Hill	.50
98	Irving Fryar	.10
99	Kevin Williams	.10
100	Herschel Walker	.10
101	Sean Dawkins	.10
102	Michael Haynes	.10
103	Reggie White	.50
104	Robert Smith	.10
105	*Todd Collins*	.50
106	*Michael Westbrook*	4.00
107	*Frank Sanders*	5.00
108	*Christian Fauria*	.50
109	*Stoney Case*	1.50
110	*Jimmy Oliver*	.50
111	*Mark Bruener*	1.00
112	*Rodney Thomas*	.50
113	*Chris Jones*	2.00
114	*James Stewart*	.50
115	*Kevin Carter*	1.00
116	*Eric Zeier*	1.00
117	*Curtis Martin*	15.00
118	*James Stewart*	10.00
119	*Joe Aska*	.50
120	*Ken Dilger*	1.00
121	*Tyrone Wheatley*	2.00
122	*Ray Zellars*	.50
123	*Kyle Brady*	1.50
124	*Chad May*	.50
125	*Napoleon Kaufman*	1.00
126	*Terrell Davis*	10.00
127	*Warren Sapp*	3.00
128	*Sherman Williams*	.50
129	*Kordell Stewart*	3.00
130	*Ki-Jana Carter*	1.50
131	*Terrell Fletcher*	.50
132	*Rashaan Salaam*	1.00
133	*J.J. Stokes*	2.00
134	*Kerry Collins*	10.00
135	*Joey Galloway*	3.00

1995 Select Certified Mirror Golds

These cards are a parallel set to Select Certified's main set, except they use gold mirror mylar foil technology. Cards were seeded one per five packs.

	NM/M
Complete Set (135):	1,200
Common Player:	2.00
Minor Stars:	4.00
Mirror Gold Cards:	2X-4X

1995 Select Certified Checklists

The seven-card, standard-size set was issued one per pack of Select Certified and features members of the Quarterback Club.

		NM/M
Complete Set (7):		3.00
Common Player:		.25
1	Drew Bledsoe	.75
2	John Elway	.40
3	Dan Marino	1.50
4	Brett Favre	1.50
5	Troy Aikman	.75
6	Steve Young	.60
7	Rick Mirer (UER), Randall Cunningham (Gold Team list incorrect)	.25

1995 Select Certified Future

These cards pay tribute to the 10 best rookies in the 1995 season. Each card is done in gold foil background. Cards were random inserts, one per 19 packs of 1995 Score Select Certified product.

		NM/M
Complete Set (10):		40.00
Common Player:		1.00
1	Ki-Jana Carter	1.00
2	Steve McNair	10.00
3	Kerry Collins	6.00
4	Michael Westbrook	2.00
5	Joey Galloway	4.00
6	J.J. Stokes	3.00
7	Rashaan Salaam	1.00
8	Tyrone Wheatley	1.00
9	Todd Collins	1.00
10	Curtis Martin	15.00

1995 Select Certified Gold Team

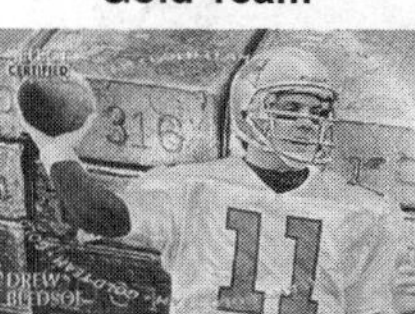

Ten of the NFL's biggest stars are featured on these 1995 Select Certified inserts. The cards use gold Dufex, with textured gold foil highlights on both sides of the card. Gold Team inserts were seeded one per 41 packs.

		NM/M
Complete Set (10):		75.00
Common Player:		5.00
1	Jerry Rice	12.00
2	Emmitt Smith	15.00
3	Drew Bledsoe	10.00
4	Marshall Faulk	5.00
5	Troy Aikman	12.00
6	Barry Sanders	15.00
7	Dan Marino	20.00
8	Errict Rhett	5.00
9	Brett Favre	20.00
10	Steve McNair	12.00

1995 Select Certified Select Few

These cards, which appear one per 32 packs of 1995 Select Certified product, showcase 20 top talents. Another version of Select Few appears in a plastic holder and is inserted on the inside of sealed boxes.

		NM/M
Complete Set (20):		100.00
Common Player:		1.00
Cards are numbered of 2250		
Comp. 1028 Numb. Set (20):		1,200
1028 Numb. Cards:		1X-2X
1	Dan Marino	15.00
2	Emmitt Smith	12.00
3	Marshall Faulk	4.00
4	Barry Sanders	12.00
5	Drew Bledsoe	10.00
6	Brett Favre	15.00
7	Troy Aikman	10.00
8	Jerry Rice	12.00
9	Steve Young	8.00
10	Natrone Means	2.00
11	Bam Morris	1.00
12	Errict Rhett	1.00
13	John Elway	10.00
14	Heath Shuler	2.00
15	Ki-Jana Carter	2.00
16	Kerry Collins	4.00
17	Steve McNair	8.00
18	Rashaan Salaam	1.00
19	Tyrone Wheatley	1.00
20	J.J. Stokes	2.00

1996 Select Promos

The three-card, standard-size set was issued to preview the 1996 Select card set. Aikman's and Favre's cards are base cards while the Marino card previews the Prime Cut insert.

		NM/M
Complete Set (3):		8.00
Common Player:		1.50
1	Troy Aikman	1.50
10	Dan Marino Prime Cut card	5.00
19	Brett Favre	4.00

Post-1980 cards in Near Mint condition will generally sell for about 75% of the quoted Mint value. Excellent-condition cards bring no more than 40%.

1996 Select

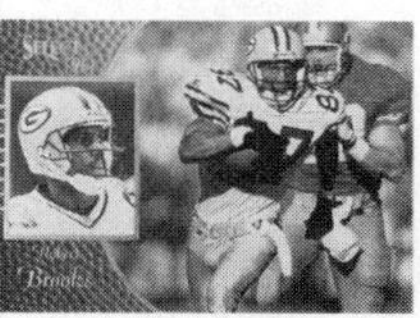

Only hobby shops were able to carry Select football. The 200-card set has five checklists, 30 top rookies, and 15 Fluid and Fleet cards. Each regular card is also featured in a parallel Artist's Proof set, seeded one card per 23 packs. Each regular card front is horizontal, with a gold-foil framed box with a mug shot on the left side, against a pigskin football background. The Select logo above the picture and the player's name below are also in gold foil. The right side of the card has a full-bleed color action photo. The back also uses a football motif for the background, along with a checkerboard pattern with a photo inside it. The Select logo is in one square, as is a team logo. A card number is in the upper right corner in a white square, with a player photo underneath. Statistics run along the bottom of the card. Insert sets are: Building Blocks, Four-midable and Prime Cut.

		NM/M
Complete Set (200):		20.00
Common Player:		.10
Minor Stars:		.20
Artist's Proof Cards:		3X-10X
Pack (10):		1.25
Wax Box (24):		20.00
1	Troy Aikman	1.50
2	Marshall Faulk	1.00
3	Kordell Stewart	1.50
4	Larry Centers	.10
5	Tamarick Vanover	1.00
6	Ken Norton Jr.	.10
7	Steve Tasker	.10
8	Dan Marino	3.00
9	Heath Shuler	.50
10	Anthony Miller	.10
11	Mario Bates	.10
12	Natrone Means	.20
13	Darren Woodson	.10
14	Chris Sanders	.50
15	Chris Warren	.20
16	Eric Metcalf	.10
17	Quentin Coryatt	.10
18	Jeff Hostetler	.10
19	Brett Favre	3.00
20	Curtis Martin	2.50
21	Floyd Turner	.10
22	Curtis Conway	.10
23	Orlando Thomas	.10
24	Lee Woodall	.10
25	Darick Holmes	.10
26	Marcus Allen	.10
27	Ricky Watters	.10
28	Herman Moore	.30
29	Rodney Hampton	.10
30	Alvin Harper	.10
31	Jeff Blake	1.00
32	Wayne Chrebet	.10
33	Jerry Rice	1.50
34	Dave Krieg	.10
35	Mark Brunell	.75
36	Terry Allen	.10
37	Emmitt Smith	3.00
38	Bryan Cox	.10
39	Tony Martin	.10
40	John Elway	.50
41	Warren Moon	.10
42	Yancey Thigpen	1.00
43	Jeff George	.20
44	Rodney Thomas	.50
45	Joey Galloway	1.25
46	Jim Kelly	.10
47	Drew Bledsoe	1.50
48	Greg Lloyd	.10
49	Michael Irvin	.20
50	Quinn Early	.10
51	Brent Jones	.10
52	Rashaan Salaam	1.00
53	James Stewart	.10
54	Gus Frerotte	.10
55	Edgar Bennett	.10
56	Lamont Warren	.10
57	Napoleon Kaufman	.20
58	Kevin Williams	.10
59	Irving Fryar	.10
60	Trent Dilfer	.10
61	Eric Zeier	.10
62	Tyrone Wheatley	.10
63	Isaac Bruce	.75
64	Terrell Davis	1.00
65	Lake Dawson	.10
66	Carnell Lake	.10
67	Kerry Collins	.30
68	Kyle Brady	.10
69	Rodney Peete	.10
70	Carl Pickens	.20
71	Robert Smith	.10
72	Rod Woodson	.10
73	Deion Sanders	.75
74	Sean Dawkins	.10
75	William Floyd	.10
76	Barry Sanders	1.50
77	Ben Coates	.10
78	Neil O'Donnell	.10
79	Bill Brooks	.10
80	Steve Bono	.10
81	Jay Novacek	.10
82	Bernie Parmalee	.10
83	Derek Loville	.10
84	Frank Sanders	.20
85	Robert Brooks	.10
86	Jim Harbaugh	.10
87	Rick Mirer	.10
88	Craig Heyward	.10
89	Greg Hill	.10
90	Andre Coleman	.10
91	Shannon Sharpe	.10
92	Hugh Douglas	.10
93	Andre Hastings	.10
94	Bryce Paup	.10
95	Jim Everett	.10
96	Brian Mitchell	.10
97	Jeff Graham	.10
98	Steve McNair	1.00
99	Charlie Garner	.10
100	Willie McGinest	.10
101	Harvey Williams	.10
102	Daryl Johnston	.10
103	Cris Carter	.10
104	J.J. Stokes	.20
105	Garrison Hearst	.20
106	Mark Chmura	.50
107	Derrick Thomas	.10
108	Errict Rhett	.75
109	Terance Mathis	.10
110	Dave Brown	.10
111	Erric Pegram	.10
112	Scott Mitchell	.10
113	Aaron Bailey	.10
114	Stan Humphries	.10
115	Bruce Smith	.10
116	Rob Johnson	.10
117	O.J. McDuffie	.10
118	Brian Blades	.10
119	Steve Atwater	.10
120	Tyrone Hughes	.10
121	Michael Westbrook	.20
122	Ki-Jana Carter	.50
123	Adrian Murrell	.40
124	Steve Young	1.50
125	Charles Haley	.10
126	Vincent Brisby	.10
127	Jerome Bettis	.10
128	Erik Kramer	.10
129	Roosevelt Potts	.10
130	Tim Brown	.10
131	Reggie White	.10
132	Jake Reed	.10
133	Junior Seau	.10
134	Stoney Case	.10
135	Kimble Anders	.10
136	Brett Perriman	.10
137	Todd Collins	.10
138	Sherman Williams	.10
139	Hardy Nickerson	.10
140	Ernie Mills	.10
141	Glyn Milburn	.10
142	Terry Kirby	.10
143	Bert Emanuel	.10
144	Aeneas Williams	.10
145	Aaron Craver	.10
146	Jackie Harris	.10
147	Amp Lee	.10
148	*Aaron Hayden*	.50
149	Antonio Freeman	.10
150	Kevin Greene	.10
151	*Kevin Hardy*	.40
152	*Eric Moulds*	2.00
153	*Tim Biakabutuka*	1.00
154	*Keyshawn Johnson*	2.50
155	*Jeff Lewis*	.50
156	*Stepfret Williams*	.10
157	*Tony Brackens*	.20
158	*Mike Alstott*	1.50
159	*Willie Anderson*	.10
160	*Marvin Harrison*	5.00
161	*Regan Upshaw*	.10
162	*Bobby Engram*	.50
163	*Leeland McElroy*	.20
164	*Alex Van Dyke*	.20
165	*Stanley Pritchett*	.10
166	*Cedric Jones*	.10
167	*Terry Glenn*	1.75
168	*Eddie George*	4.00
169	*Lawrence Phillips*	.50
170	*Jonathan Ogden*	.10
171	*Danny Kanell*	.50
172	*Alex Molden*	.10
173	*Daryl Gardener*	.10
174	*Derrick Mayes*	1.00
175	*Marco Battaglia*	.10
176	*Jon Stark*	.10
177	*Karim Abdul-Jabbar*	.75
178	*Stephen Davis*	4.00
179	*Rickey Dudley*	.30
180	*Eddie Kennison*	.30
181	Barry Sanders	.75
182	Brett Favre	.50
183	John Elway	.30
184	Steve Young	.50
185	Michael Irvin	.10
186	Jerry Rice	.50
187	Emmitt Smith	1.00
188	Isaac Bruce	.20
189	Chris Warren	.10
190	Errict Rhett	.40
191	Herman Moore	.10
192	Carl Pickens	.10
193	Cris Carter	.10
194	Terrell Davis	.75
195	Rodney Thomas	.10
196	Dan Marino	.50
197	Drew Bledsoe	.20
198	Emmitt Smith	.50
199	Jerry Rice	.30
200	John Elway, Barry Sanders	.30

1996 Select Artist's Proofs

The 200-card, standard-size set parallels the base set, inserted every 23 packs, with Artist's Proof printed in gold foil.

		NM/M
Veteran Stars:		3X-10X
Young Stars:		2X-10X
RCs:		2X-5X
1	Troy Aikman	70.00
2	Marshall Faulk	40.00
3	Kordell Stewart	60.00
8	Dan Marino	125.00
10	Brett Favre	70.00
20	Curtis Martin	90.00
33	Jerry Rice	60.00
37	Emmitt Smith	125.00
40	John Elway	30.00
45	Joey Galloway	50.00
47	Drew Bledsoe	50.00
64	Terrell Davis	50.00
67	Kerry Collins	60.00
73	Deion Sanders	35.00
76	Barry Sanders	60.00
98	Steve McNair	50.00
124	Steve Young	50.00
154	Keyshawn Johnson	60.00
167	Terry Glenn	50.00
168	Eddie George	75.00
169	Lawrence Phillips	50.00
181	Barry Sanders (FF)	30.00
182	Brett Favre (FF)	35.00
184	Steve Young (FF)	25.00
186	Jerry Rice (FF)	30.00
187	Emmitt Smith (FF)	60.00
196	Dan Marino (CL)	35.00
197	Drew Bledsoe (CL)	15.00
198	Emmitt Smith (CL)	35.00
199	Jerry Rice (CL)	20.00
200	Barry Sanders (CL), John Elway	20.00

1996 Select Building Blocks

This 1996 Score Select insert set features first- and second-year players who appear to be headed to stardom. The cards, seeded one per 48 packs, use all-foil Dufex print technology. The card front has a color action photo, with a background similar to a television display room; the "screens" have a smaller mug shot taken from the larger action photo. The player's name and "Building Blocks" are written in silver foil in the lower left corner. The vertical back has a color action photo on one half, with a card number in a black rectangle above. The other side has the brand logo, player's name, set name, position and team, and brief player profile.

		NM/M
Complete Set (20):		40.00
Common Player:		1.00
1	Curtis Martin	5.00
2	Terrell Davis	6.00
3	Darick Holmes	1.00
4	Rashaan Salaam	1.00
5	Ki-Jana Carter	1.00
6	Rodney Thomas	1.00
7	Kerry Collins	3.00
8	Eric Zeier	1.00
9	Steve McNair	5.00
10	Kordell Stewart	3.00
11	J.J. Stokes	2.00
12	Joey Galloway	2.00
13	Michael Westbrook	2.00
14	Mike Alstott	2.00
15	Tony Brackens	1.00
16	Terry Glenn	3.00
17	Kevin Hardy	1.00
18	Leeland McElroy	1.00
19	Tim Biakabutuka	1.00
20	Keyshawn Johnson	4.00

1996 Select Four-midable

These 1996 Score Select inserts were seeded one per 18 packs. Each card front has a full-motion hologram which features crashing AFC and NFC helmets, as well as a color photo of a player who appeared in the championship games. The hologram is at the bottom; the color photo is in a conference color-coordinated panel at the top. Blue is used for the NFC; red is used for the AFC. The logos are included in the background. The brand name and set name are written in silver foil, as is the player's team name, which is repeated above the hologram. The horizontal back has a color action photo incorporated into a black-and-white stadium scene, plus a black rectangle which recaps the player's championship game performance. A card number is also given.

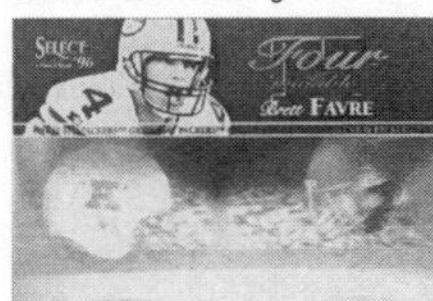

		NM/M
Complete Set (16):		20.00
Common Player:		.50
1	Troy Aikman	4.00
2	Michael Irvin	1.00
3	Emmitt Smith	5.00
4	Deion Sanders	2.00
5	Brett Favre	5.00
6	Robert Brooks	.50
7	Edgar Bennett	.50
8	Reggie White	1.00
9	Kordell Stewart	1.00
10	Yancey Thigpen	.50
11	Neil O'Donnell	.50
12	Greg Lloyd	.50
13	Jim Harbaugh	.50
14	Sean Dawkins	.50
15	Marshall Faulk	3.00
16	Quentin Coryatt	.50

1996 Select Prime Cut

These cards are the highlight inserts in Score's 1996 Select football product. The cards are die-cut and feature 18 of the NFL's most elite players. The top of the card is die-cut around a football which has a facsimile autograph of the player. Below is a larger color action photo, flanked by two smaller ones. The player's name is in a bar at the bottom, along with "Prime Cut" and a team logo in the center. Cards were limited to 1,996 each and were inserted in every 80th pack.

		NM/M
Complete Set (18):		125.00
Common Player:		1.00
1	Emmitt Smith	12.00
2	Troy Aikman	10.00
3	Michael Irvin	2.00
4	Steve Young	10.00
5	Jerry Rice	10.00
6	Drew Bledsoe	8.00
7	Brett Favre	15.00
8	John Elway	10.00
9	Barry Sanders	12.00
10	Dan Marino	15.00
11	Isaac Bruce	5.00
12	Marshall Faulk	5.00
13	Errict Rhett	1.00
14	Chris Warren	1.00
15	Herman Moore	1.00
16	Deion Sanders	4.00
17	Joey Galloway	3.00
18	Curtis Martin	8.00

1996 Select Certified

The 125-card, regular-sized set was available in six-card packs. The card fronts feature a full mirror background with the color player action shot. The player's name is printed down the right border with in-depth statistics printed on the horizontal card back. Parallel versions of the base set are available in Certified Red (1:5) and Certified Blue (1:50). Mirror Red (1:100), Mirror Blue (1:200) and Mirror Gold (1:300) parallel inserts were also issued. Artist's Proof (1:18), Gold Team (1:38) and Thumbs Up (1:41) were the other inserts and each card was also available in Premium Stock, nine-card packs.

		NM/M
Complete Set (125):		40.00
Common Player:		.10
Minor Stars:		.40
Artist's Proof Stars:		2X-5X
Artist's Proof Rookies:		2X-4X
Certified Blue Stars:		4X-10X
Certified Blue Rookies:		2X-5X
Mirror Blue Stars:		10X-30X
Mirror Blue Rookies:		4X-10X
Certified Red Stars:		2X-4X
Certified Red Rookies:		1X-3X
Mirror Red Stars:		10X-20X
Mirror Red Rookies:		5X-10X
Mirror Gold Stars:		15X-40X
Mirror Gold Rookies:		10X-25X
Pack (6):		7.00
Wax Box (20):		100.00
1	Isaac Bruce	1.00
2	Rick Mirer	.10
3	Jake Reed	.10
4	Reggie White	.40
5	Harvey Williams	.10
6	Jim Everett	.10
7	Tony Martin	.10
8	Craig Heyward	.10
9	Tamarick Vanover	1.25
10	Hugh Douglas	.10
11	Erik Kramer	.10
12	Charlie Garner	.10
13	Erric Pegram	.10
14	Scott Mitchell	.10
15	Michael Westbrook	.75
16	Robert Smith	.10
17	Kerry Collins	.75
18	Derek Loville	.10
19	Jeff Blake	.40
20	Terry Kirby	.10
21	Bruce Smith	.10
22	Stan Humphries	.10
23	Rodney Thomas	.10
24	Wayne Chrebet	.10
25	Napoleon Kaufman	.10
26	Marshall Faulk	1.00
27	Emmitt Smith	4.00
28	Natrone Means	.10
29	Neil O'Donnell	.10
30	Warren Moon	.40
31	Junior Seau	.40
32	Chris Sanders	.10
33	Barry Sanders	3.00
34	Jeff Graham	.10
35	Kordell Stewart	2.50
36	Jim Harbaugh	.10
37	Chris Warren	.10
38	Cris Carter	.10
39	J.J. Stokes	.75
40	Tyrone Wheatley	.40
41	Terrell Davis	4.00
42	Mark Brunell	1.50
43	Steve Young	2.00
44	Rodney Hampton	.10
45	Drew Bledsoe	2.00
46	Larry Centers	.10
47	Ken Norton Jr.	.10
48	Deion Sanders	2.00
49	Alvin Harper	.10
50	Trent Dilfer	.40
51	Steve McNair	2.00
52	Robert Brooks	.10
53	Edgar Bennett	.10
54	Troy Aikman	2.50
55	Dan Marino	5.00
56	Steve Bono	.10
57	Marcus Allen	.40
58	Rodney Peete	.10
59	Ben Coates	.10
60	Yancey Thigpen	.40
61	Tim Brown	.10
62	Jerry Rice	2.50
63	Quinn Early	.10
64	Ricky Watters	.40
65	Thurman Thomas	.40
66	Greg Lloyd	.10
67	Eric Metcalf	.10
68	Jeff George	.10
69	John Elway	2.00
70	Frank Sanders	.10
71	Curtis Conway	.10
72	Greg Hill	.10
73	Darick Holmes	.10
74	Herman Moore	.40
75	Carl Pickens	.10
76	Eric Zeier	.10
77	Curtis Martin	3.50
78	Rashaan Salaam	1.00
79	Joey Galloway	1.50
80	Jeff Hostetler	.10
81	Jim Kelly	.40
82	Dave Brown	.10
83	Errict Rhett	.75
84	Michael Irvin	.40
85	Brett Favre	5.00
86	Cedric Jones	.10
87	*Jeff Lewis*	2.00
88	*Alex Van Dyke*	.40
89	*Regan Upshaw*	.10
90	*Karim Abdul-Jabbar*	2.50
91	*Marvin Harrison*	12.00
92	*Stephen Davis*	5.00
93	*Terry Glenn*	3.00
94	*Kevin Hardy*	.40
95	*Stanley Pritchett*	.40
96	*Willie Anderson*	.10
97	*Lawrence Phillips*	.50
98	*Bobby Hoying*	1.00
99	*Amani Toomer*	.40
100	*Eddie George*	10.00
101	*Stepfret Williams*	.10
102	*Eric Moulds*	6.00
103	*Simeon Rice*	.40
104	*John Mobley*	.40
105	*Keyshawn Johnson*	8.00
106	*Daryl Gardener*	.10
107	*Tony Banks*	4.00
108	*Bobby Engram*	.75
109	*Jonathan Ogden*	.40
110	*Eddie Kennison*	.75
111	*Danny Kanell*	1.00
112	*Tony Brackens*	.40
113	*Tim Biakabutuka*	1.00
114	*Leeland McElroy*	1.00
115	*Rickey Dudley*	1.00
116	Troy Aikman	1.00
117	Brett Favre	5.00
118	Drew Bledsoe	1.00
119	Steve Young	1.00
120	Kerry Collins	1.00
121	John Elway	1.00
122	Dan Marino	2.50
123	Kordell Stewart	1.25
124	Jeff Blake	.40
125	Jim Harbaugh	.10

1996 Select Certified Red

Certified Red parallel cards were a parallel set to the 125-card Select Certified set in 1996. They were inserted every five packs and feature a full red background.

	NM/M
Complete Set (125):	300.00
Certified Red Cards:	2X-4X

1996 Select Certified Blue

This 125-card set paralleled the 1996 Select Certified set, but pictured each card on a full blue background. Certified Blue inserts were seeded every 50 packs.

	NM/M
Complete Set (125):	2,500
Certified Blue Cards:	10X-30X

1996 Select Certified Artist's Proofs

This 125-card set paralleled the 1996 Select Certified set, but includes a holographic Artist's Proof stamp on the front of the card. Artist's Proofs were seeded every 18 packs.

	NM/M
Complete Set (125):	1,200
Artist's Proof Cards:	2X-5X

1996 Select Certified Mirror Red

Mirror Red included all 125 cards in 1996 Select Certified, but featured roughly three-fourths of the background in red, with the remaining portion unchanged from regular-issue cards. The entire front then has a mirror effect. Mirror Red inserts were seeded every 100 packs.

Mirror Red Cards:	10X-20X

1996 Select Certified Mirror Blue

This 125-card set featured a mostly blue background, with the rest still having the regular-issue background color, then a mirror background over the entire front. Mirror Blues parallel the regular-issue set and are seeded every 200 packs.

Mirror Blue Cards:	10X-30X

1996 Select Certified Mirror Gold

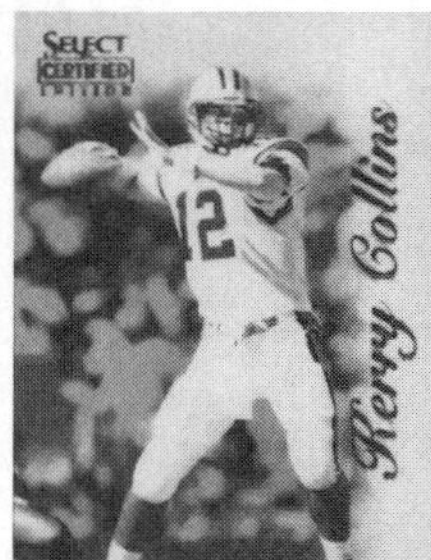

Mirror Golds parallel the 125-card base set and feature most of the background in gold, with the remaining portion in regular-issue card color. The entire front is put through a mirror process that gives it a holographic appearance. Mirror Gold inserts are found every 300 packs.

Mirror Gold Cards:	15X-40X

1996 Select Certified Gold Team

The Gold Team is an 18-card, regular-sized insert set that was found every 38 packs of 1996 Select Certified. The card fronts feature a full gold action shot while the backs, also in complete gold, are individually numbered.

		NM/M
Complete Set (18):		100.00
Common Player:		1.00
1	Emmitt Smith	12.00
2	Barry Sanders	12.00
3	Dan Marino	15.00
4	Steve Young	8.00
5	Troy Aikman	8.00
6	Jerry Rice	10.00
7	Rashaan Salaam	1.00
8	Marshall Faulk	5.00
9	Drew Bledsoe	8.00
10	Steve McNair	5.00
11	Brett Favre	15.00
12	Terrell Davis	8.00
13	Kordell Stewart	4.00
14	Keyshawn Johnson	4.00
15	Kerry Collins	4.00
16	Curtis Martin	12.00
17	Isaac Bruce	5.00
18	Terry Glenn	3.00

1996 Select Certified Thumbs Up

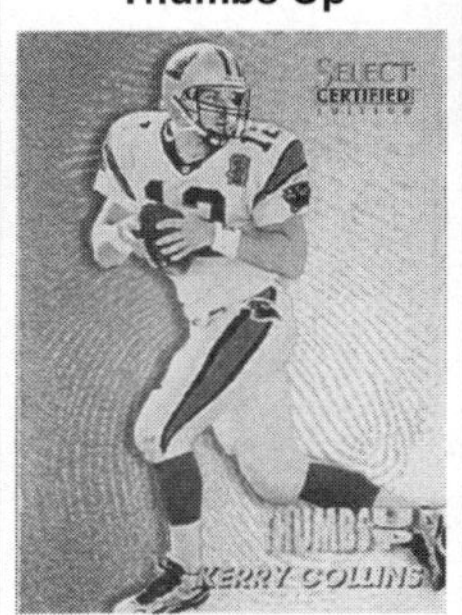

The 24-card, regular-sized set was inserted every 41 packs of Select Certified. The silver card fronts feature an actual thumbprint of the Quarterback Club member pictured. The card backs include another photo and the player's "Thumbs Up Moment" and are individually numbered.

		NM/M
Complete Set (24):		125.00
Common Player:		1.00
1	Steve Young	8.00
2	Jeff Blake	2.00
3	Dan Marino	14.00
4	Kerry Collins	4.00
5	John Elway	10.00
6	Neil O'Donnell	1.00
7	Brett Favre	14.00
8	Scott Mitchell	1.00
9	Troy Aikman	10.00
10	Jim Harbaugh	1.00
11	Drew Bledsoe	8.00
12	Jeff Hostetler	1.00
13	Marvin Harrison	5.00
14	Tim Biakabutuka	1.00
15	Eddie George	6.00
16	Tony Brackens	1.00
17	Karim Abdul-Jabbar	1.00
18	Daryl Gardener	1.00
19	Alex Van Dyke	1.00
20	Terry Glenn	3.00
21	Eric Moulds	5.00
22	Eddie Kennison	3.00
23	Regan Upshaw	1.00
24	Mike Alstott	5.00

1996 Select Certified Premium Stock

Premium Stock was an enhanced version of Select Certified that was available to the hobby only in jumbo nine-card packs. Premium Stock treated the base cards and the Mirror Red inserts with a micro-etching process, while all other inserts are the same. Packs of Premium Stock contained all of the inserts, but at easier insertion rates than regular packs. The odds in Premium Stock were: Certified Red (1:3), Certified Blue (1:33), Mirror Red (1:66), Mirror Blue (1:133), Mirror Gold (1:199), Artist's Proof (1:12), Gold Team (1:25) and Thumbs Up (1:27).

Premium Stock Cards:	2X

1996 Select Certified Premium Stock Etched Mirror Red

Premium Stock Etched Mirror Red inserts paralleled the 125-card Select Certified set, but were available only in Premium Stock packs at a rate of one per 66 packs. This was the only insert that was changed in Premium Stock versus the regular-issue packs. The fronts of these cards have etched foil similar to the base set for Premium Stock.

Etched Mirror Red Cards:	25X-60X

1996 Sentry Foods Packers-Bears Rivalry

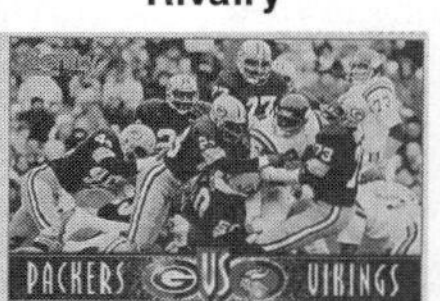

This six-card set was issued through Sentry Foods stores in Wisconsin commemorating the past 23 years of the Green Bay Packers and Chicago Bears rivalry. The set was issued as a perforated sheet with color action photos and both team's helmets at the bottom along with a Sentry Foods logo in the lower left of the horizontal card. The card backs are unnumbered and include the date of the game, highlights and the box score. A full sheet also included coupons below the six cards.

		NM/M
Complete Set (6):		4.00
Common Player:		.50
1	Dec. 16, 1973 (John Brockington)	.50
2	Sep. 7, 1980 (Chester Marcol)	.50
3	Nov. 5, 1989 (Sterling Sharpe and many Packers celebrating)	.50
4	Oct. 31, 1994 (Edgar Bennett)	.50
5	Nov. 12, 1995 (Brett Favre handing off to Edgar Bennett)	2.00
6	Oct. 6, 1996 (Packers defense)	.50

1997 Sentry Foods Packers-Vikings

This set was issued as a 10-card perforated sheet and included highlights from the past 30 years of the Green Bay Packers and Minnesota Vikings rivalry. Fronts feature a horizontal game action photo with the Sentry Foods logo in the upper left corner and "Packers vs. Vikings" across the bottom in a strip along with both team's logos. The black-and-white backs have the game's date, Sentry logo, highlights and a box score with a large Packers logo in the background. Cards are unnumbered with the bottom right card in an uncut sheet being an entry form for children to join the Junior Power Pack Club. The sheet was available at participating Sentry stores in Wisconsin.

		NM/M
Complete Set (9):		6.00
Common Player:		.50
1	Dec. 3, 1967 (Don Chandler kicks)	.50
2	Dec. 10, 1972 (Packer offense)	.50
3	Nov. 26, 1978 (Packer defense stops Chuck Foreman)	.50
4	Nov. 11, 1979 (Packer defense)	.50
5	Oct. 26, 1980 (Lynn Dickey)	.50
6	Nov. 13, 1983 (Packer offense)	.50
7	Dec. 13, 1987 (Paul Ott Carruth)	.50
8	Nov. 26, 1989 (Don Majkowski)	.50
9	Sep. 4, 1994 (Brett Favre handing off to Edgar Bennett)	2.00

1972 7-11 Slurpee Cups

Each of these 60 white plastic cups measures 5-1/4" tall, 3-1/4" in diameter at the mouth and 2" in diameter at the base. The fronts feature a color player portrait with his name and team name. Most of the cups feature a facsimile autograph between the portrait and the player's name. The backs include biographical information, the player's team helmet and the 7-Eleven logo. Another set of 80 cups was released in 1973. The cups are similar except the 1972 cups have a smaller typeface for the player's name (1/16") and do not have "Made in USA" printed on the sides.

		NM/M
Complete Set (60):		250.00
Common Player:		4.00
1	Donny Anderson	4.00
2	Elvin Bethea	4.00
3	Fred Biletnikoff	8.00
4	Bill Bradley	4.00
5	Terry Bradshaw	25.00
6	Larry Brown	4.00
7	Willie Brown	5.00
8	Norm Bulaich	4.00
9	Dick Butkus	15.00
10	Ray Chester	4.00
11	Bill Curry	4.00
12	Len Dawson	8.00
13	Willie Ellison	4.00
14	Ed Flanagan	4.00
15	Gary Garrison	4.00
16	Gale Gillingham	4.00
17	Joe Greene	8.00
18	Cedrick Hardman	4.00
19	Jim Hart	5.00
20	Ted Hendricks	5.00
21	Winston Hill	4.00
22	Ken Houston	5.00
23	Chuck Howley	4.00
24	Claude Humphrey	4.00
25	Roy Jefferson	4.00
26	Sonny Jurgensen	6.00
27	Leroy Kelly	5.00
28	Paul Krause	4.00
29	George Kunz	4.00
30	Jake Kupp	4.00
31	Ted Kwalick	4.00
32	Willie Lanier	5.00
33	Bob Lilly	6.00
34	Floyd Little	4.00
35	Larry Little	5.00
36	Tom Mack	4.00
37	Milt Morin	4.00
38	Mercury Morris	5.00
39	John Niland	4.00
40	Jim Otto	5.00
41	Steve Owens	4.00
42	Alan Page	5.00
43	Jim Plunkett	5.00
44	Mike Reid	5.00
45	Mel Renfro	5.00
46	Isiah Robertson	4.00
47	Andy Russell	4.00
48	Charlie Sanders	4.00
49	O.J. Simpson	15.00
50	Bubba Smith	5.00
51	Bill Stanfill	4.00
52	Jan Stenerud	5.00
53	Walt Sweeney	4.00
54	Bob Tucker	4.00
55	Jim Tyrer	4.00
56	Rick Volk	4.00
57	Gene Washington	4.00
58	Dave Wilcox	4.00
59	Del Williams	4.00
60	Ron Yary	4.00

1973 7-11 Slurpee Cups

This 80-cup series is similar to the 1972 series except the player's name is printed in larger type (1/8") and the words "Made in USA" are printed down the sides.

		NM/M
Complete Set (80):		450.00
Common Player:		5.00
1	Dan Abramowicz	6.00
2	Ken Anderson	10.00
3	Jim Beirne	5.00
4	Ed Bell	5.00
5	Bob Berry	5.00
6	Jim Bertelsen	5.00
7	Marlin Briscoe	5.00
8	John Brockington	5.00
9	Larry Brown	6.00
10	Buck Buchanan	7.50
11	Dick Butkus	25.00
12	Larry Carwell	5.00
13	Rich Caster	5.00
14	Bobby Douglass	5.00
15	Pete Duranko	5.00
16	Cid Edwards	5.00
17	Mel Farr	5.00
18	Pat Fischer	5.00
19	Mike Garrett	5.00
20	Walt Garrison	6.00
21	George Goeddeke	5.00
22	Bob Gresham	5.00
23	Jack Ham	10.00
24	Chris Hanburger	5.00
25	Franco Harris	20.00
26	Calvin Hill	6.00
27	J.D. Hill	5.00
28	Marv Hubbard	5.00
29	Scott Hunter	5.00
30	Harold Jackson	6.00
31	Randy Jackson	5.00
32	Bob Johnson	5.00
33	Jim Johnson	7.50
34	Ron Johnson	5.00
35	Leroy Keyes	5.00
36	Greg Landry	6.00
37	Gary Larsen	5.00
38	Frank Lewis	5.00
39	Bob Lilly	10.00
40	Dale Lindsey	5.00
41	Larry Little	7.50
42	Carl (Spider) Lockhart	5.00
43	Mike Lucci	5.00
44	Jim Lynch	5.00
45	Art Malone	5.00
46	Ed Marinaro	6.00
47	Jim Marshall	7.50
48	Ray May	5.00
49	Don Maynard	10.00
50	Don McCauley	5.00
51	Mike McCoy	5.00
52	Tom Mitchell	5.00
53	Tommy Nobis	7.50
54	Dan Pastorini	6.00
55	Mac Percival	5.00
56	Mike Phipps	6.00
57	Ed Podolak	5.00
58	John Reaves	5.00
59	Tim Rossovich	5.00
60	Bo Scott	5.00
61	Ron Sellers	5.00
62	Dennis Shaw	5.00
63	Mike Siani	5.00
64	O.J. Simpson	25.00
65	Bubba Smith	7.50
66	Larry Smith	5.00
67	Jackie Smith	7.50
68	Norm Snead	6.00
69	Jack Snow	5.00
70	Steve Spurrier	20.00
71	Doug Swift	5.00
72	Jack Tatum	7.50
73	Bruce Taylor	5.00
74	Otis Taylor	6.00
75	Bob Trumpy	6.00
76	Jim Turner	5.00
77	Phil Villapiano	5.00
78	Roger Wehrli	5.00
79	Ken Willard	5.00
80	Jack Youngblood	7.50

1983 7-11 Discs

These discs were available at participating 7-Eleven stores in 1983. Each disc, which is numbered on the back as "x of Fifteen," has a portrait and an action picture on the front. The player's team name is at the top of the disc, while his name is at the bottom. His jersey number is on each side. The disc back has the player's career totals, pro honors, a Slurpee logo and the year, 1983.

		NM/M
Complete Set (15):		30.00
Common Player:		1.00
1	Franco Harris	5.00
2	Dan Fouts	3.00
3	Lee Roy Selmon	1.25
4	Nolan Cromwell	1.25
5	Marcus Allen	5.00
6	Joe Montana	10.00
7	Kellen Winslow	2.00
8	Hugh Green	1.00
9	Ted Hendricks	2.00
10	Danny White	1.50
11	Wes Chandler	1.00
12	Jimmie Giles	1.00
13	Jack Youngblood	2.00
14	Lester Hayes	1.00
15	Vince Ferragamo	1.00

1984 7-11 Discs

These discs, available at participating 7-Eleven stores, were available in two regions, East and West, as indicated by the card number prefix. The disc has a diameter of 1-3/4" and is designed like the previous year's issue, except the year on the back is 1984.

		NM/M
Complete Set (40):		60.00
Common Player:		.75
1E	Franco Harris	3.00
2E	Lawrence Taylor	2.00
3E	Mark Gastineau	.75
4E	Lee Roy Selmon	1.00
5E	Ken Anderson	1.50
6E	Walter Payton	4.00
7E	Ken Stabler	1.50
8E	Marcus Allen	2.00
9E	Fred Smerlas	.75
10E	Ozzie Newsome	1.25
11E	Steve Bartkowski	1.00
12E	Tony Dorsett	2.00
13E	John Riggins	1.50
14E	Billy Sims	.75
15E	Dan Marino	9.00
16E	Tony Collins	.75
17E	Curtis Dickey	.75
18E	Ron Jaworski	.75
19E	William Andrews	.75
20E	Joe Theismann	1.50
1W	Franco Harris	2.00
2W	Joe Montana	10.00
3W	Matt Blair	.75
4W	Warren Moon	6.00
5W	Marcus Allen	2.00
6W	John Riggins	1.50
7W	Walter Payton	4.00
8W	Vince Ferragamo	.75
9W	Billy Sims	.75
10W	Ken Anderson	1.25
11W	Lynn Dickey	.75
12W	Tony Dorsett	2.00
13W	Bill Kenney	.75
14W	Ottis Anderson	1.00
15W	Dan Fouts	1.50
16W	Eric Dickerson	3.00
17W	John Elway	6.00
18W	Ozzie Newsome	1.25
19W	Curt Warner	1.00
20W	Joe Theismann	1.50

1981 Shell Posters

The works of three different artists are featured on these 10-7/8" x 13-7/8" posters available at participating Shell Oil stations across the country in 1981. Each poster has a black-and-white drawing of the featured player, as rendered by either K. Atkins, Nick Galloway or Tanenbawm (these signatures are on the corresponding poster fronts). There are, however, some posters which were not signed by the artist (#s 7, 11, 12 and 93). The posters are listed alphabetically by teams, then alphabetically by players. Team sets consist of six posters. A national set of six posters was also made (Payton, Griffin, Logan, Pearson, Campbell and O. Anderson) and was available in markets where a pro team did not exist.

		NM/M
Complete Set (96):		300.00
Common Player:		3.00
(1)	William Andrews	3.75
(2)	Steve Bartkowski	5.25
(3)	Buddy Curry	2.75
(4)	Wallace Francis	3.75
(5)	Mike Kenn	3.75
(6)	Jeff Van Note	3.75
(7)	Mike Barnes	3.00
(8)	Roger Carr	3.00
(9)	Curtis Dickey	3.75
(10)	Bert Jones	5.25
(11)	Bruce Laird	3.00
(12)	Randy McMillan	3.75
(13)	Brian Baschnagel	3.00
(14)	Vince Evans	3.75
(15)	Gary Fencik	3.75
(16)	Roland Harper	3.00
(17)	Alan Page	6.75
(18)	Walter Payton	7.50
(19)	Ken Anderson	6.00
(20)	Ross Browner	3.75
(21)	Archie Griffin	3.00
(22)	Pat McInally	3.75
(23)	Anthony Munoz	6.00
(24)	Reggie Williams	3.75
(25)	Lyle Alzado	4.50
(26)	Joe DeLamielleure	3.00
(27)	Doug Dieken	3.00
(28)	Dave Logan	3.00
(29)	Reggie Rucker	3.75
(30)	Brian Sipe	3.75
(31)	Benny Barnes	3.00
(32)	Bob Breunig	3.00
(33)	D.D. Lewis	3.00
(34)	Harvey Martin	4.50
(35)	Drew Pearson	3.00
(36)	Rafael Septien	3.00
(37)	Al (Bubba) Baker	3.75
(38)	Dexter Bussey	3.00
(39)	Gary Danielson	3.75
(40)	Freddie Scott	3.00
(41)	Billy Sims	4.50
(42)	Tom Skladany	3.00
(43)	Robert Brazile	4.50
(44)	Ken Burrough	4.50
(45)	Earl Campbell	6.75
(46)	Leon Gray	3.75
(47)	Carl Mauck	3.75
(48)	Ken Stabler	6.00
(49)	Bob Baumhower	3.75
(50)	Jimmy Cefalo	3.75
(51)	A.J. Duhe	3.75
(52)	Nat Moore	4.50
(53)	Ed Newman	3.00
(54)	Uwe Von Schamann	3.00
(55)	Steve Grogan	5.25
(56)	John Hannah	3.50
(57)	Don Hasselbeck	3.00
(58)	Mike Haynes	4.50
(59)	Harold Jackson	3.75
(60)	Steve Nelson	3.00
(61)	Elois Grooms	3.75
(62)	Rickey Jackson	5.75
(63)	Archie Manning	6.00
(64)	Tommy Myers	3.75
(65)	Benny Ricardo	3.75
(66)	George Rogers	4.50
(67)	Harry Carson	5.25
(68)	Dave Jennings	3.00
(69)	Gary Jeter	3.00
(70)	Phil Simms	6.00
(71)	Lawrence Taylor	9.00
(72)	Brad Van Pelt	3.75
(73)	Greg Buttle	3.75
(74)	Bruce Harper	3.00
(75)	Joe Klecko	3.75
(76)	Randy Rasmussen	3.00
(77)	Richard Todd	3.75
(78)	Wesley Walker	4.50
(79)	Ottis Anderson	3.00
(80)	Dan Dierdorf	6.75
(81)	Mel Gray	3.75
(82)	Jim Hart	4.50
(83)	E.J. Junior	3.75
(84)	Pat Tilley	3.75
(85)	Jimmie Giles	3.75
(86)	Charley Hannah	3.00
(87)	Bill Kollar	3.00
(88)	David Lewis	3.00
(89)	Lee Roy Selmon	4.50
(90)	Doug Williams	3.75
(91)	Joe Lavender	3.00
(92)	Mark Moseley	3.75
(93)	Mark Murphy	3.00
(94)	Lemar Parrish	3.75
(95)	John Riggins	6.75
(96)	Joe Washington	3.75

1994 Signature Rookies

The 60-card, standard-size set featured top NFL prospects in their collegiate uniforms. The player's name and position appear on the bottom edge and the cards are numbered as "x of 45,000" or "Authentic Signature" along the left edge in gold foil. Production was limited to 12,500 boxes. Inserts included Hottest Prospect, Gale Sayers, Charlie Ward and Tony Dorsett.

		NM/M
Complete Set (60):		8.00
Common Player:		.05
1	Sam Adams	.05
2	Trev Alberts	.05
3	Derrick Alexander	.25
4	Aubrey Beavers	.05
5	Lou Benfatti	.05
6	James Bostic	.05
7	Tim Bowens	.25
8	Rich Braham	.05
9	Isaac Bruce	1.50
10	Vaughn Bryant	.05
11	Brentson Buckner	.05
12	Jeff Burris	.10
13	Carlester Crumpler	.05
14	Lake Dawson	.30
15	Tyronne Drakeford	.05
16	Dan Eichloff	.05
17	Rob Fredrickson	.20
18	Gus Frerotte	.75
19	William Gaines	.05
20	Wayne Gandy	.05
21	Jason Gildon	.05
22	Lemanski Hall	.05
23	Shelby Hill	.05
24	LeShon Johnson	.15
25	Alan Kline	.05
26	Antonio Langham	.10
27	Keith Lyle	.05
28	Van Malone	.05
29	Jamir Miller	.10
30	Byron "Bam" Morris	.50
31	Jeremy Nunley	.05
32	Brad Ottis	.05
33	Joe Panos	.05
34	John Reece	.05
35	Tony Richardson	.05
36	Tim Ruddy	.05
37	Corey Sawyer	.05
38	Malcolm Seabron	.05
39	John Thierry	.05
40	Jason Seahorn	.05
41	Eric Zomalt	.05
42	Toby Wright	.05
43	Willie Jackson	.05
44	Tre Johnson	.05
45	Darren Krein	.05
46	Corey Louchiey	.05
47	Eric Mahlum	.05
48	Chris Maumalanga	.05
49	Jim Miller	.05
50	Aaron Mundy	.05
51	Turhon O'Brannon	.05
52	David Palmer	.10
53	Jim Pyne	.05
54	Errict Rhett	1.25
55	Sam Rogers	.05
56	Jason Winrow	.05
57	Ronnie Woolfork	.05
58	Rob Waldrop	.05
59	Ryan Yarborough	.05
60	Checklist	.05

1994 Signature Rookies Signatures

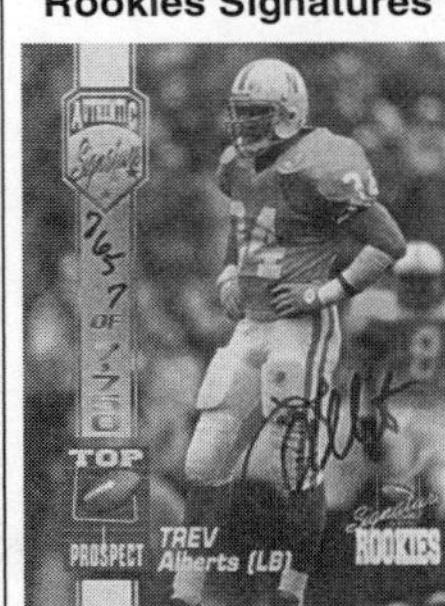

The 59-card, standard-size set was inserted in each six-card pack of Signature Rookies. Each card was numbered as "x of 7,750." Reportedly, 700 Errict Rhett cards are not actually signed by the running back, but that he had an aquaintance autograph the cards for him. Autographed Rhett cards could be sent in to Signature Rookies for verification.

		NM/M
Complete Set (59):		225.00
Common Autograph:		4.00
1	Sam Adams	4.00
2	Trev Alberts	4.00
3	Derrick Alexander (WR)	6.00
4	Larry Allen	4.00
5	Aubrey Beavers	4.00
6	Lou Benfatti	4.00
7	James Bostic	4.00
8	Tim Bowens	4.00
9	Rich Braham	4.00
10	Isaac Bruce	20.00
11	Vaughn Bryant	4.00
12	Brentson Buckner	4.00
13	Jeff Burris	4.00
14	Carlester Crumpler	6.00
15	Lake Dawson	6.00
16	Tyronne Drakeford	4.00
17	Dan Eichloff	4.00
18	Rob Fredrickson	4.00
19	Gus Frerotte	10.00
20	William Gaines	4.00
21	Wayne Gandy	4.00
22	Jason Gildon	4.00
23	Lemanski Hall	4.00
24	Shelby Hill	4.00
25	Willie Jackson	4.00
26	LeShon Johnson	6.00
27	Tre Johnson	4.00
28	Alan Kline	4.00
29	Darren Krein	4.00
30	Antonio Langham	6.00
31	Corey Louchiey	4.00
32	Keith Lyle	4.00
33	Eric Mahlum	4.00
34	Van Malone	4.00
35	Chris Maumalanga	4.00
36	Jamir Miller	4.00
37	Jim Miller	6.00
38	Byron "Bam" Morris	6.00
39	Aaron Mundy	4.00
40	Jeremy Nunley	4.00
41	Turhonn O'Bannon	4.00
42	Brad Ottis	4.00
43	David Palmer	5.00
44	Joe Panos	4.00
45	Jim Pyne	4.00
46	John Reece	4.00
47	Errict Rhett	10.00
48	Tony Richardson	4.00
49	Sam Rogers	4.00
50	Tim Ruddy	4.00
51	Corey Sawyer	4.00
52	Malcolm Seabron	4.00
53	Jason Sehorn	12.00
54	John Thierry	4.00
55	Jason Winrow	4.00
56	Ronnie Woolford	4.00
57	Toby Wright	4.00
58	Ryan Yarborough	4.00
59	Eric Zomalt	4.00

1994 Signature Rookies Bonus Signatures

The 15-card, standard-size set was hand-numbered out of 7,750 and the player's signature appeared on the bottom edge. Cards were randomly inserted in 1994 Tetrad packs.

		NM/M
Complete Set (15):		35.00
Common Signature:		3.00
Coupons Replace Some Cards		
1	Jamal Anderson	10.00
2	Myron Bell	3.00
3	Mitch Berger	3.00
4	Jocelyn Borgella	3.00
5	Chris Brantley	3.00
6	Ron Edwards	3.00
7	Rob Holmberg	3.00
8	Fred Lester	3.00
9	Joseph Patton	3.00
10	Eric Ravotti	3.00
11	Jim Reid	3.00
12	Jerry Reynolds	3.00
13	Bracey Walker	3.00
14	Gabe Wilkins	3.00
15	Brant Boyer	3.00

1994 Signature Rookies Tony Dorsett

The two-card, standard-size set, limited to 5,000, are numbered as out of 5,000 autographed 1,000 cards. Dallas Cowboys Hall of Fame running back.

	NM/M
Complete Set (2):	6.00
Common Player:	3.00
Complete Signature Set (2):	125.00
Tony Dorsett AU/1000	60.00

1994 Signature Rookies Hottest Prospects

The five-card, standard-size set was numbered out of 15,000 and featured the players in their collegiate uniforms. The cards are numbered and carry an "A" prefix.

		NM/M
Complete Set (5):		3.00
Common Player:		.50
1	Willie McGinest	1.00
2	Bryant Young	1.00
3	DeWayne Washington	.50
4	Aaron Taylor	.50
5	Charles Johnson	.50

1994 Signature Rookies Gale Sayers

The two-card, standard-size set was randomly inserted into packs and was limited to 5,000 of each card. The former Chicago Bears star autographed 1,000 of the cards.

	NM/M
Complete Set (2):	8.00
Common Sayers:	4.00
Comp. Signature Set (2):	100.00
Gale Sayers AU/1000	50.00

1994 Signature Rookies Charlie Ward

The five-card, standard-size set highlights Florida State's 1993 Heisman winner and 5,000 of each card was produced. Ward autographed 525 of his cards. The cards are numbered with a "C" prefix.

		NM/M
Complete Set (5):		4.00
Common Ward:		1.00
Complete Signed Set (5):		75.00
Charlie Ward AU/25		15.00
1	Charlie Ward (In throwing motion)	1.00
2	Charlie Ward (Ready to hand-off)	1.00
3	Charlie Ward (Posed football shot)	1.00
4	Charlie Ward (Holding basketball at waist)	1.00
5	Charlie Ward (holding basketball overhead)	1.00

A player's name in *italic* type indicates a rookie card.

1995 SR Auto-Phonex

The 40-card, standard-size set features card fronts with triple images of the key player in his collegiate uniform. The player's name appears in gold foil along the bottom edge with "1 of 19,000" printed on the bottom. Each case of Auto-Phonex features Hot Packs, which include an autographed phone card plus five additional autographed cards. J.J. Stokes was featured on the $5 card (1:287) while the $25 card (Kevin Carter) is inserted every 1,437. Ten Warren Sapp $100 cards (1:14,371) and eight $1,000 (Rashaan Salaam and Ki-Jana Carter) were included every 35,928 packs.

		NM/M
Complete Set (40):		10.00
Common Player:		.10
1	Warren Sapp	.30
2	Kevin Carter	.20
3	Ki-Jana Carter	.75
4	J.J. Stokes	1.00
5	Derrick Alexander	.20
6	Rashaan Salaam	1.25
7	Jamal Willis	.10
8	Frank Sanders	.60
9	Rob Johnson	.10
10	Derrick Brooks	.20
11	Sherman Williams	.30
12	Dave Barr	.10
13	Christian Fauria	.20
14	Stoney Case	.10
15	Rodney Thomas	.60
16	James A. Stewart	.20
17	Ray Zellars	.30
18	Jack Jackson	.10
19	Terrell Davis	1.25
20	Kyle Brady	.20
21	Ruben Brown	.20
22	Brent Moss	.10
23	John Sacca	.10
24	David Dunn	.20
25	Eddie Goines	.10
26	Curtis Martin	1.50
27	Billy Williams	.10
28	Steve Stenstrom	.10
29	Mark Bruener	.30
30	Kelvin Anderson	.10
31	Ellis Johnson	.20
32	Steve Ingram	.10
33	Larry Jones	.10
34	Bobby Taylor	.30
35	Joe Aska	.10
36	Jerrott Willard	.10
37	Chris T. Jones	.30
38	Mark Birchmeier	.10
39	Jimmy Hitchcock	.10
40	Tyrone Davis	.10
NNO	Ki-Jana Carter (CL)	.30

1995 SR Auto-Phonex Phone Card Signatures

The 40-card, 2-3/8" x 3-1/8" phone card set was inserted in each pack of SR Auto-Phonex. The cards have rounded corners and the common card has $2 of calling time. $5 cards of J.J. Stokes (1:287), $25 cards of Kevin Carter (1:1,437) and $100 cards of Warren Sapp (1:14,371) were also inserted, as were eight $1,000 cards of Ki-Jana Carter and Rashaan Salaam (1:35,928).

		NM/M
Complete Set (40):		75.00
Common Player:		1.00
1	Warren Sapp	3.00
2	Kevin Carter	1.00
3	Ki-Jana Carter	1.00
4	J.J. Stokes	4.00
5	Derrick Alexander	1.00
6	Rashaan Salaam	1.00
7	Jamal Willis	1.00
8	Frank Sanders	6.00
9	Eric Zeier	1.00
10	Derrick Brooks	2.00
11	Sherman Williams	1.00
12	Dave Barr	1.00
13	Christian Fauria	1.00
14	Stoney Case	1.00
15	Rodney Thomas	2.00
16	James A. Stewart	2.00
17	Ray Zellars	1.00
18	Jack Jackson	1.00
19	Terrell Davis	25.00
20	Kyle Brady	2.00
21	Ruben Brown	1.00
22	Brent Moss	1.00
23	John Sacca	1.00
24	David Dunn	1.00
25	Eddie Goines	1.00
26	Curtis Martin	20.00
27	Billy Williams	1.00
28	Steve Stenstrom	1.00
29	Mark Bruener	1.00
30	Kelvin Anderson	1.00
31	Ellis Johnson	1.00
32	Steve Ingram	1.00
33	Larry Jones	1.00
34	Bobby Taylor	3.00
35	Joe Aska	1.00
36	Jerrott Willard	1.00
37	Chris T. Jones	1.00
38	Mark Birchmeier	1.00
39	Jimmy Hitchcock	1.00
40	Tyrone Davis	2.00
NNO	J.J. Stokes $5 Card	2.00
NNO	Kevin Carter $25 Card	10.00

1995 SR Auto-Phonex Signatures

The 10-card, standard-size set was randomly inserted in Hot Packs and was also available through a mail-in redemption offer. The cards are identical in design to the regular-issue cards, except for the signatures.

		NM/M
Common Player:		10.00
3A	Ki-Jana Carter	20.00
6A	Rashaan Salaam	20.00
8A	Frank Sanders	35.00
11A	Sherman Williams	10.00
12A	Dave Barr	10.00
14A	Stoney Case	10.00
16A	James A. Stewart	15.00
17A	Ray Zellars	10.00
20A	Kyle Brady	10.00
23A	John Sacca	10.00

1995 SR Draft Preview

The 80-card, standard-size set was issued in six-card packs for $5, and included an autographed card. Each player signed 7,750 of his own cards, and 39,000 of each card was produced. An international version was also produced, limited to a production total of 13,500, 2,750 of which were signed.

		NM/M
Complete Set (80):		15.00
Common Player:		.10
International:		1X-2X
1	Derrick Alexander	.15
2	Kelvin Anderson	.10
3	Antonio Armstrong	.10
4	Jamie Asher	.10
5	Joe Aska	.10
6	Dave Barr	.10
7	Brandon Bennett	.10
8	Tony Berti	.10
9	Mark Birchmeier	.10
10	Tony Boselli	.15
11	Derrick Brooks	.15
12	Anthony Brown	.10
13	Ruben Brown	.15
14	Mark Bruener	.30
15	Ontiwaun Carter	.10
16	Stoney Case	.10
17	Byron Chamberlain	.10
18	Shannon Clavelle	.10
19	Jamal Cox	.10
20	Zack Crockett	.15
21	Terrell Davis	1.50
22	Tyrone Davis	.10
23	Lee DeRamus	.10
24	Ken Dilger	.40
25	Hugh Douglas	.50
26	David Dunn	.15
27	Chad Eaton	.10
28	Hicham El-Mashtoub	.10
29	Christian Fauria	.15
30	Terrell Fletcher	.30
31	Antonio Freeman	.10
32	Eddie Goines	.10
33	Roger Graham	.10
34	Carl Greenwood	.10
35	Ed Hervey	.10
36	Jimmy Hitchcock	.10
37	Darius Holland	.10
38	Torey Hunter	.10
39	Steve Ingram	.10
40	Jack Jackson	.10
41	Trezelle Jenkins	.10
42	Ellis Johnson	.15
43	Eric Johnson	.10
44	Rob Johnson	.10
45	Chris T. Jones	.25
46	Larry Jones	.10
47	Shawn King	.10
48	Scotty Lewis	.10
49	Curtis Martin	2.00
50	Oscar McBride	.10
51	Kez McCorvey	.10
52	Bronzell Miller	.10
53	Pete Mitchell	.25
54	Brent Moss	.10
55	Craig Newsome	.15
56	Herman O'Berry	.10
57	Matt O'Dwyer	.10
58	Tyrone Poole	.15
59	Brian Pruitt	.10
60	Cory Raymer	.10
61	John Sacca	.10
62	Frank Sanders	.75
63	J.J. Smith	.10
64	Brendan Stai	.10
65	Steve Stenstrom	.10
66	James O. Stewart	.40
67	Kordell Stewart	1.50
68	Ben Talley	.10
69	Bobby Taylor	.25
70	Johnny Thomas	.10
71	Orlando Thomas	.15
72	Rodney Thomas	.75
73	Zach Wiegert	.15
74	Jerrott Willard	.10
75	Billy Williams	.10
76	Sherman Williams	.25
77	Jamal Willis	.10
78	Dave Wohlabaugh	.10
79	Eric Zeier	.75
80	Checklist	.10

1995 SR Draft Preview Signatures

The 79-card, standard-size parallel set (minus the checklist), was included in each pack of SR Draft Preview. Each player signed 7,750 cards out of the 39,000 produced, and 2,750 out of the 13,500 produced for the international set.

		NM/M
Common Player:		2.50
International:		1X-2X
1	Derrick Alexander	3.00
2	Kelvin Anderson	2.50
3	Antonio Armstrong	2.50
4	Jamie Asher	2.50
5	Joe Aska	2.50
6	Dave Barr	2.50
7	Brandon Bennett	2.50
8	Tony Berti	2.50
9	Mark Birchmeier	2.50
10	Tony Boselli	3.00
11	Derrick Brooks	3.00
12	Anthony Brown	2.50
13	Ruben Brown	3.00
14	Mark Bruener	4.00
15	Ontiwaun Carter	2.50
16	Stoney Case	2.50
17	Byron Chamberlain	2.50
18	Shannon Clavelle	2.50
19	Jamal Cox	2.50
20	Zack Crockett	3.00
21	Terrell Davis	30.00
22	Tyrone Davis	2.50
23	Lee DeRamus	2.50
24	Ken Dilger	5.00
25	Hugh Douglas	5.00
26	David Dunn	3.00
27	Chad Eaton	2.50
28	Hicham El-Mashtoub	2.50
29	Christian Fauria	3.00
30	Terrell Fletcher	4.00
31	Antonio Freeman	20.00
32	Eddie Goines	2.50
33	Roger Graham	2.50
34	Carl Greenwood	2.50
35	Ed Hervey	2.50
36	Jimmy Hitchcock	2.50
37	Darius Holland	2.50
38	Torey Hunter	2.50
39	Steve Ingram	2.50
40	Jack Jackson	2.50
41	Trezelle Jenkins	2.50
42	Ellis Johnson	3.00
43	Eric Johnson	3.00
44	Rob Johnson	2.50
45	Chris T. Jones	8.00
46	Larry Jones	2.50
47	Shawn King	2.50
48	Scotty Lewis	2.50
49	Curtis Martin	20.00
50	Oscar McBride	2.50
51	Kez McCorvey	2.50
52	Bronzell Miller	2.50
53	Pete Mitchell	4.00
54	Brent Moss	2.50
55	Craig Newsome	3.00
56	Herman O'Berry	2.50
57	Matt O'Dwyer	2.50
58	Tyrone Poole	3.00
59	Brian Pruitt	2.50
60	Cory Raymer	2.50
61	John Sacca	2.50
62	Frank Sanders	8.00
63	J.J. Smith	2.50
64	Brendan Stai	2.50
65	Steve Stenstrom	2.50
66	James O. Stewart	10.00
67	Kordell Stewart	20.00
68	Ben Talley	2.50
69	Bobby Taylor	4.00
70	Johnny Thomas	2.50
71	Orlando Thomas	3.00
72	Rodney Thomas	5.00
73	Zach Wiegert	3.00
74	Jerrott Willard	2.50
75	Billy Williams	2.50
76	Sherman Williams	4.00
77	Jamal Willis	2.50
78	Dave Wohlabaugh	2.50
79	Eric Zeier	5.00

1995 SR Draft Preview Franchise Rookies

The 10-card, standard-size set was inserted every eight packs of SR Draft Preview. Production was limited to 10,000 sets with each player signing 2,500 of his own card. The cards are numbered with a "R" prefix.

		NM/M
Complete Set (10):		4.00
Common Player:		.25
1	Kyle Brady	.25
2	Kevin Carter	.25
3	Ki-Jana Carter	1.00
4	Luther Ellis	.25
5	Rashaan Salaam	1.00
6	Warren Sapp	1.50
7	James A. Stewart	.25
8	J.J. Stokes	1.00
9	Michael Westbrook	2.00
10	Ray Zellars	.75

1995 SR Draft Preview Franchise Rookies Signatures

The 10-card, standard-size set was limited to 2,500 of each card and is identical in design to the Franchise Rookies insert set with the exception of the player's autograph on the card front. The cards carry a "R" prefix.

		NM/M
Common Player:		4.00
1	Kyle Brady	5.00
2	Kevin Carter	4.00
3	Ki-Jana Carter	6.00
4	Luther Ellis	4.00
5	Rashaan Salaam	10.00
6	Warren Sapp (1125)	8.00
7	James A. Stewart	4.00
8	J.J. Stokes	12.00
9	Michael Westbrook	15.00
10	Ray Zellars	4.00

1995 SR Draft Preview International Franchise Duo

The 10-card, regular-size set was inserted every 10 packs and features one draft choice on each side of the card. "International" appears in the silver triangle and the player's name is divided (first and last) on the left and right sides.

		NM/M
Complete Set (10):		20.00
Common Player:		1.50
1	Ki-Jana Carter, Kevin Carter	3.00
2	Warren Sapp, Derrick Alexander	2.00
3	James A. Stewart, James O. Stewart	2.00
4	Michael Westbrook, J.J. Stokes	2.50
5	Kyle Brady, Kerry Collins	3.00
6	Steve McNair, Kerry Collins	5.00
7	Eric Zeier, Kordell Stewart	5.00
8	Rob Johnson, Stoney Case	1.50
9	Rashaan Salaam, Ki-Jana Carter	3.00
10	Ray Zellars, Sherman Williams	2.00

1995 SR Draft Preview Int'l Franchise Duo Signatures

The 16-card, standard-size set features one draft choice on each side of the card and is a parallel set in design with the International Franchise Duo insert set. Warren Sapp and James A. Stewart, included in the regular-issue set, did not sign and the set skips No. 12.

		NM/M
Common Player:		15.00
1	Derrick Alexander (AU/200)	15.00
2	Kyle Brady (AU/242)	20.00
3	Kevin Carter (AU/315)	15.00
4	Ki-Jana Carter (AU/400)	15.00
5	Stoney Case (AU/200)	15.00
6	Kerry Collins (AU/600)	40.00
7	Rob Johnson (AU/309)	15.00
8	Steve McNair (AU/600)	60.00
9	Rashaan Salaam (AU/299)	25.00
10	Kordell Stewart (AU/309)	50.00
11	James O. Stewart (AU/200)	30.00
13	J.J. Stokes (AU/284)	30.00
14	Michael Westbrook (AU/282)	30.00
15	Sherman Williams (AU/312)	10.00
16	Eric Zeier (AU/314)	10.00
17	Ray Zellars (AU/310)	10.00

1995 SR Draft Preview Masters of the Mic

The five-card, standard-size set features some of the top announcers. Each announcer autographed 1,000 of his cards with 30,000 total sets produced. The card backs contain a brief announcer profile. An international version was also produced with the only difference being the silver-foil "International" stamp.

		NM/M
Complete Set (5):		10.00
Common Player:		2.00
International:		1X-2X

1995 SR Draft Preview Masters of the Mic Signatures

This five-card insert consists of autographed versions of the Masters of the Mic set. Each announcer signed 1,000 cards, which were inserted 1:4. The cards are numbered with a "M" prefix.

		NM/M
Complete Set (5):		75.00
Common Player:		15.00
1	Todd Christensen	15.00
2	Jerry Glanville	15.00
3	Howie Long	15.00
4	Dick Stockton	15.00
5	Joe Theismann UER	15.00

1995 SR Draft Preview Peripheral Vision

Peripheral Vision was a five-card insert that featured Rashaan Salaam and Ki-Jana Carter, each with two cards of their own as well as sharing the double sided card No. 5. These inserts are numbered "1 of 5,000," and carry a V1-V5 card number. Autographed versions of each card are also available and limited to 100 of each.

		NM/M
Complete Set (5):		3.00
Common Player:		.30
Signature Stars:		5X-10X
1	Rashaan Salaam	.50
2	Rashaan Salaam	.50
3	Ki-Jana Carter	.30
4	Ki-Jana Carter	.30
5	Ki-Jana Carter, Rashaan Salaam	.60

1995 SR Draft Preview Peripheral Vision Signatures

This five-card autographed set was inserted one per 24 packs.

		NM/M
Common Player:		80.00
1/2	Rashaan Salaam	20.00
3/4	Ki-Jana Carter	20.00
5/6	Ki-Jana Carter, Rashaan Salaam	30.00
V2	Rashaan Salaam	20.00
V4	Ki-Jana Carter	20.00

1995 SR Draft Preview Old Judge Previews

Inserted 1:24, the cards in this five-card set measure 2" x 3". They are designed to look like the old tobacco cards. The card fronts feature a color photo on a solid background with the words "Old Judge, T-95 Test Issue" printed across the top. The backs contain basic player information.

		NM/M
Complete Set (5):		8.00
Common Player:		.50
Signatures:		10X
1	Blake Brockemeyer	.50
2	Kerry Collins	4.00
3	Steve McNair	5.00
4	J.J. O'Laughlin	.50
5	John Walsh	.50

1995 SR Draft Preview Old Judge Previews Signatures

An autographed version of Old Judge Previews, these cards were inserted 1:24. Each player signed 515 cards for this insert.

		NM/M
Common Player:		5.00
1	Blake Brockemeyer	5.00
2	Kerry Collins	25.00
3	Steve McNair	35.00
4	J.J. O'Laughlin	5.00
5	John Walsh	5.00

1995 SR Signature Prime Previews

This five-card set was randomly inserted in packs of Basketball Autobilia. The cards are borderless and feature a color photo on both sides. The backs feature biographical information and college stats.

		NM/M
Complete Set (5):		3.00
Common Player:		.50
1	Ki-Jana Carter	.50
2	Kyle Brady	.50
3	J.J. Stokes	1.00
4	Rashaan Salaam	.50
5	Steve McNair	3.00

1995 SR Signature Prime

SR Signature Prime consists of a 50-card base set with one parallel and one insert. The base cards feature a borderless color photo on the front. The player's name is printed in gold in a red stripe on the left side of the card. The card backs contain another color photo, biographical information and college stats. The only insert is TD Club (1:1). Both the base set and TD Club have autographed versions as well.

		NM/M
Complete Set (50):		10.00
Common Player:		.05
Checklist (NNO)		.10
1	Justin Armour	.05
2	Joe Aska	.05
3	Henry Bailey	.05
4	Jay Barker	.05
5	Dave Barr	.05
6	Kevin Bouie	.05
7	Mark Bruener	.40
8	Stoney Case	.05
9	Curtis Ceaser	.05
10	Todd Collins	.75
11	Jerry Colquitt	.05
12	Terrell Davis	4.00
13	David Dunn	.40
14	O'Mar Ellison	.05
15	Christian Fauria	.40
16	Antonio Freeman	3.00
17	Eddie Goines	.05
18	Aaron Hayden	.40
19	William Henderson	.05
20	Kevin Hickman	.05

21	Jack Jackson	.05
22	Travis Jervey	.05
23	Rob Johnson	.40
24	Chris T. Jones	.75
25	Larry Jones	.05
26	Curtis Marsh	.05
27	Curtis Martin	4.00
28	Fred McCrary	.05
29	Mike Miller	.05
30	Shannon Myers	.05
31	Jimmy Oliver	.05
32	Dino Philyaw	.05
33	Lovell Pinkney	.05
34	Michael Roan	.05
35	Chris Sanders	.75
36	Frank Sanders	.75
37	Cory Schlesinger	.40
38	Charlie Simmons	.05
39	David Sloan	.40
40	Steve Stenstrom	.05
41	James A. Stewart	.05
42	Rodney Thomas	.40
43	A.C. Tellison	.05
44	Tamarick Vanover	.75
45	John Walsh	.05
46	Kendell Watkins	.05
47	Charles Way	.40
48	Craig Whelihan	.05
49	Eric Zeier	.40
50	Ray Zellars	.40

1995 SR Signature Prime Signatures

This set consists of autographed versions of the Signature Prime base set. The cards were inserted one per pack and sealed in a protective holder. Each player signed 3,000 of his cards which are numbered in the bottom right corner.

		NM/M
Common Player:		4.00
1	Justin Armour	4.00
2	Joe Aska	4.00
3	Henry Bailey	4.00
4	Jay Barker	4.00
5	Dave Barr	4.00
6	Kevin Bouie	4.00
7	Mark Bruener	8.00
8	Stoney Case	4.00
9	Curtis Ceaser	4.00
10	Todd Collins	8.00
11	Jerry Colquitt	4.00
12	Terrell Davis	30.00
13	David Dunn	8.00
14	O'Mar Ellison	4.00
15	Christian Fauria	8.00
16	Antonio Freeman	12.00
17	Eddie Goines	4.00
18	Aaron Hayden	8.00
19	William Henderson	4.00
20	Kevin Hickman	4.00
21	Jack Jackson	4.00
22	Travis Jervey	4.00
23	Rob Johnson	4.00
24	Chris T. Jones	4.00
25	Larry Jones	4.00
26	Curtis Marsh	4.00
27	Curtis Martin	25.00
28	Fred McCrary	4.00
29	Mike Miller	4.00
30	Shannon Myers	4.00
31	Jimmy Oliver	4.00
32	Dino Philyaw	4.00
33	Lovell Pinkney	4.00
34	Michael Roan	4.00
35	Chris Sanders	12.00
36	Frank Sanders	12.00
37	Cory Schlesinger	8.00
38	Charlie Simmons	4.00
39	David Sloan	8.00
40	Steve Stenstrom	4.00
41	James A. Stewart	4.00
42	Rodney Thomas	8.00
43	A.C. Tellison	4.00
44	Tamarick Vanover	10.00
45	John Walsh	4.00
46	Kendell Watkins	4.00
47	Charles Way	8.00
48	Craig Whelihan	4.00
49	Eric Zeier	8.00
50	Ray Zellars	4.00

1995 SR Signature Prime TD Club

TD Club is a 10-card insert, limited to 15,000 cards per player. The fronts feature a player photo against a silver foil background and a "T" prefix.

		NM/M
Complete Set (10):		6.00
Common Player:		.50
1	Kyle Brady	.50
2	Ki-Jana Carter	.50
3	Kerry Collins	3.00
4	Joey Galloway	2.00
5	Steve McNair	3.00
6	Rashaan Salaam	.50
7	James O. Stewart	.75
8	J.J. Stokes	1.00
9	Michael Westbrook	1.00
10	Sherman Williams	.50

1995 SR Signature Prime TD Club Signatures

Each player in the TD Club insert signed 1,000 of their cards for this parallel set. The cards are sequentially numbered carrying a "T" prefix and are sealed in a protective holder.

		NM/M
Common Player:		5.00
1	Kyle Brady	5.00
2	Ki-Jana Carter	12.00
3	Kerry Collins	35.00
4	Joey Galloway	20.00
5	Steve McNair	45.00
6	Rashaan Salaam	5.00
7	James O. Stewart	10.00
8	J.J. Stokes	12.00
9	Michael Westbrook	12.00
10	Sherman Williams	5.00

1996 SR Autobilia

SR Autobilia consists of a 55-card base set featuring rookies from the 1995 and 1996 seasons. Instant win cards were randomly inserted in packs. The cards were redeemable for autographs and memorabilia.

		NM/M
Complete Set (55):		15.00
Common Player:		.10
1	Ruben Brown	.10
2	Kevin Carter	.10
3	Ki-Jana Carter	.25
4	Stoney Case	.10
5	Kerry Collins	.75
6	Terrell Davis	3.00
7	Antonio Freeman	.50
8	Joey Galloway	.75
9	Darick Holmes	.25
10	Jack Jackson	.10
11	Curtis Martin	1.00
12	O.J. McDuffie	.25
13	Steve McNair	.30
14	Byron "Bam" Morris	.50
15	Craig Newsome	.10
16	Errict Rhett	.50
17	Rashaan Salaam	.75
18	Frank Sanders	.25
19	James O. Stewart	.25
20	Kordell Stewart	.75
21	J.J. Stokes	.50
22	Rodney Thomas	.25
23	Tamarick Vanover	.50
24	Michael Westbrook	.50
25	Sherman Williams	.10
26	Eric Zeier	.40
27	Karim Abdul-Jabbar	.50
28	Mike Alstott	1.00
29	Willie Anderson	.10
30	Tony Banks	.50
31	Marco Battaglia	.40
32	Tim Biakabutuka	.50
33	Stephen Davis	.60
34	Chris Doering	.10
35	Daryl Gardener	.10
36	Eddie George	2.00
37	Terry Glenn	1.00
38	Randall Godfrey	.10
39	Marvin Harrison	1.00
40	Aaron Hayden	.25
41	Mercury Hayes	.40
42	Dietrich Jells	.10
43	Cedric Jones	.10
44	Jeff Lewis	.30
45	Derrick Mayes	.75
46	Leland McElroy	.50
47	Jerald Moore	.40
48	Eric Moulds	.75
49	Kendrick Nord	.10
50	Stanley Pritchett	.25
51	Jon Stark	.10
52	Steve Taneyhill	.10
53	Amani Toomer	.75
54	Stepfret Williams	.50
55	Checklist	.10

1992 SkyBox Impel Impact Prime Time Promos

These unnumbered promotional cards were distributed as a set in January 1992 during the Super Bowl XXVI show. The Earnest Byner card shows him in action on the front, with his name and number above the photo in maroon. A maroon bar along the right side of the card contains his team's name, in white letters. A Prime Time logo appears in the lower left corner. The card back, as does the one for Jim Kelly, says the card is a limited-edition commemorative card and includes an advertisement for Impel's Impact and Prime Time products. The Kelly card front shows him ready to pass. Because the cards were produced before Impel changed its name to SkyBox, subtle card front design changes can be detected on the later-released base brands.

		NM/M
Complete Set (2):		4.00
Common Player:		1.00
----	Jim Kelly Impact	3.00
----	Earnest Byner PrimeTime	1.00

1992 SkyBox Impact Promos

These three cards, available together in a promotional pack, preview the 1992 SkyBox Impact set. The cards' design is similar to the regular issue, except the numbers, which are on the card back. They use 001, 002 and 003.

		NM/M
Complete Set (3):		4.00
Common Player:		1.00
1	Jim Kelly	3.00
2	Michael Dean Perry	1.00
3	Reggie Roby	1.00

1992 SkyBox Impact

This 350-card set features full-bleed action photos with the players' names printed in block letters across the top. The back has an action photo, career highlights, stats, a biography and the player's position, as diagramed with Xs and Os. Subsets include Team Checklists, High Impact League Leaders, Sudden Impact Hardest Hitters, and Instant Impact Rookies. Insert sets include Major Impact (20 cards featuring top players) and Holograms (two feature Jim Kelly and Lawrence Taylor; the rest are mail-in offers).

		NM/M
Complete Set (350):		14.00
Common Player:		.05
Pack (12):		.50
Wax Box (36):		14.00
1	Jim Kelly	.25
2	Andre Rison	.25
3	Michael Dean Perry	.05
4	Herman Moore	.50
5	*Fred McAfee*	.15
6	Ricky Proehl	.05
7	Jim Everett	.05
8	Mark Carrier	.05
9	Eric Martin	.05
10	John Elway	1.00
11	Michael Irvin	.25
12	Keith McCants	.05
13	Greg Lloyd	.05
14	Lawrence Taylor	.10
15	Mike Tomczak	.05
16	Cortez Kennedy	.10
17	William Fuller	.05
18	James Lofton	.05
19	Kevin Fagan	.05
20	Bill Brooks	.05
21	Roger Craig	.05
22	Jay Novacek	.10
23	Steve Sewell	.05
24	William Perry	.05
25	Jerry Rice	1.00
26	James Joseph	.05
27	Timm Rosenbach	.05
28	Pat Terrell	.05
29	Jon Vaughn	.08
30	Steve Walsh	.05
31	James Hasty	.05
32	Dwight Stone	.05
33	Derrick Fenner	.05
34	Mark Bortz	.05
35	Dan Saleaumua	.05
36	Sammie Smith	.05
37	Antone Davis	.05
38	Steve Young	1.00
39	Mike Baab	.05
40	Rick Fenney	.05
41	Chris Hinton	.05
42	Bart Oates	.05
43	Bryan Hinkle	.05
44	James Francis	.05
45	Ray Crockett	.05
46	Eric Dickerson	.05
47	Hart Lee Dykes	.05
48	Percy Snow	.05
49	Ron Hall	.05
50	Warren Moon	.25
51	Ed West	.05
52	Clarence Verdin	.05
53	Eugene Lockhart	.05
54	Andre Reed	.15
55	Kevin Ross	.05
56	Al Noga	.05
57	Wes Hopkins	.05
58	Rufus Porter	.05
59	Brian Mitchell	.05
60	Reggie Roby	.05
61	Rodney Peete	.05
62	Jeff Herrod	.05
63	Anthony Smith	.05
64	Brad Muster	.05
65	Jessie Tuggle	.05
66	Al Smith	.05
67	Jeff Hostetler	.20
68	John L. Williams	.05
69	Paul Gruber	.05
70	Cornelius Bennett	.05
71	William White	.05
72	Tom Rathman	.05
73	Boomer Esiason	.10
74	Neil Smith	.05
75	Sterling Sharpe	.10
76	James Jones	.05
77	David Treadwell	.05
78	Flipper Anderson	.05
79	Eric Allen	.05
80	Joe Jacoby	.05
81	Keith Sims	.05
82	Bubba McDowell	.05
83	Ronnie Lippett	.05
84	Cris Carter	.05
85	Chris Burkett	.05
86	Issiac Holt	.05
87	Duane Bickett	.05
88	Leslie O'Neal	.05
89	Gill Fenerty	.05
90	Pierce Holt	.05
91	Willie Drewrey	.05
92	Brian Blades	.05
93	Tony Martin	.05
94	Jessie Hester	.05
95	John Stephens	.05
96	Keith Willis	.05
97	Vai Sikahema	.05
98	Mark Higgs	.15
99	Steve McMichael	.05
100	Deion Sanders	.15
101	Marvin Washington	.05
102	Ken Norton	.05
103	Barry Word	.10
104	Sean Jones	.05
105	Ronnie Harmon	.05
106	Donnell Woolford	.05
107	Ray Agnew	.05
108	Lemuel Stinson	.05
109	Dennis Smith	.05
110	Lorenzo White	.05
111	Craig Heyward	.05
112	Jeff Query	.05
113	Gary Plummer	.05
114	John Taylor	.08
115	Rohn Stark	.05
116	Tom Waddle	.08
117	Jeff Cross	.05
118	Tim Green	.05
119	Anthony Munoz	.05
120	Mel Gray	.05
121	Ray Donaldson	.05
122	Dennis Byrd	.05
123	Carnell Lake	.05
124	Broderick Thomas	.05
125	Charles Mann	.05
126	Darion Conner	.05
127	John Roper	.05
128	Jack Del Rio	.05
129	Rickey Dixon	.05
130	Eddie Anderson	.05
131	Steve Broussard	.05
132	Michael Young	.05
133	Lamar Lathon	.05
134	Rickey Jackson	.05
135	Billy Ray Smith	.05
136	Tony Casillas	.05
137	Ickey Woods	.05
138	Ray Childress	.05
139	Vance Johnson	.05
140	Brett Perriman	.05
141	Calvin Williams	.10
142	Dino Hackett	.05
143	Jacob Green	.05
144	Robert Delpino	.05
145	Marv Cook	.05
146	Dwayne Harper	.05
147	Ricky Ervins	.08
148	Kelvin Martin	.08
149	Leroy Hoard	.05
150	Dan Marino	1.25
151	Richard Johnson	.05
152	Henry Ellard	.05
153	Al Toon	.05
154	Dermontti Dawson	.05
155	Robert Blackmon	.05
156	Howie Long	.05
157	David Fulcher	.05
158	Mike Merriweather	.05
159	Gary Anderson	.05
160	John Friesz	.05
161	Eugene Robinson	.05
162	Brad Baxter	.05
163	Bennie Blades	.05
164	Harold Green	.05
165	Ernest Givins	.05
166	Deron Cherry	.05
167	Carl Banks	.05
168	Keith Jackson	.10
169	Pat Leahy	.05
170	Alvin Harper	.10
171	David Little	.05
172	Anthony Carter	.05
173	Willie Gault	.05
174	Bruce Armstrong	.05
175	Junior Seau	.15
176	Eric Metcalf	.05
177	Tony Mandarich	.05
178	Ernie Jones	.05
179	Albert Bentley	.05
180	Mike Pritchard	.15
181	Bubby Brister	.05
182	Vaughan Johnson	.05
183	Robert Clark	.05
184	Lawrence Dawsey	.05
185	Eric Green	.05
186	Jay Schroeder	.05
187	Andre Tippett	.05
188	Vinny Testaverde	.05
189	Wendell Davis	.05
190	Russell Maryland	.15
191	Chris Singleton	.05
192	Ken O'Brien	.05
193	Merril Hoge	.05
194	*Steve Bono*	.50
195	Earnest Byner	.05
196	Mike Singletary	.05
197	Gaston Green	.05
198	Mark Carrier	.05
199	Harvey Williams	.10
200	Randall Cunningham	.15
201	Cris Dishman	.05
202	Greg Townsend	.05
203	Christian Okoye	.05
204	Sam Mills	.05
205	Kyle Clifton	.05
206	Jim Harbaugh	.08
207	Anthony Thompson	.05
208	Rob Moore	.08
209	Irving Fryar	.05
210	Derrick Thomas	.15
211	Chris Miller	.05
212	Doug Smith	.05
213	Michael Haynes	.20
214	Phil Simms	.10
215	Charles Haley	.05
216	Burt Grossman	.05
217	Rod Bernstine	.05
218	Louis Lipps	.05
219	Dan McGwire	.05
220	Ethan Horton	.05
221	Michael Carter	.05
222	Neil O'Donnell	.10
223	Anthony Miller	.05
224	Eric Swann	.05
225	Thurman Thomas	.40
226	Jeff George	.25
227	Joe Montana	1.00
228	Leonard Marshall	.05
229	Haywood Jeffires	.10
230	Mark Clayton	.05
231	Chris Doleman	.05
232	Troy Aikman	1.50
233	Gary Anderson	.05
234	Pat Swilling	.05
235	Ronnie Lott	.07
236	Brian Jordan	.05
237	Bruce Smith	.07
238	Tony Jones	.05
239	Tim McKyer	.05
240	Gary Clark	.05
241	Mitchell Price	.05
242	John Kasay	.05
243	Stephone Paige	.05
244	Jeff Wright	.05
245	Shannon Sharpe	.15
246	Keith Byars	.05
247	Charles Dimry	.05
248	Steve Smith	.05
249	Erric Pegram	.15
250	Bernie Kosar	.05
251	Peter Tom Willis	.05
252	Mark Ingram	.05
253	Keith McKeller	.05
254	Lewis Billups	.05
255	Alton Montgomery	.05
256	Jimmie Jones	.05
257	Brent Williams	.05
258	Gene Atkins	.05
259	Reggie Rutland	.05
260	Sam Seale	.05
261	Andre Ware	.07
262	Fred Barnett	.10
263	Randal Hill	.10
264	Patrick Hunter	.05
265	Johnny Rembert	.05
266	Monte Coleman	.05
267	Aaron Wallace	.05
268	Ferrell Edmunds	.05
269	Stan Thomas	.05
270	Robb Thomas	.05
271	Martin Bayless	.05
272	Dean Biasucci	.05
273	Keith Henderson	.05
274	Vinnie Clark	.05
275	Emmitt Smith	2.00
276	Mark Rypien	.10
277	Atlanta Falcons Wing and a Prayer	.10
278	Buffalo Bills Machine Gun	.10
279	Chicago Bears Grizzly	.05
280	Cincinnati Bengals Price is Right	.05
281	Cleveland Browns Coasting	.05
282	Dallas Cowboys Gunned Down	.15
283	Denver Broncos The Drive II	.15
284	Detroit Lions Lions Roar	.05
285	Green Bay Packers Razor Sharpe	.15
286	Houston Oilers Oil's Well	.10
287	Indianapolis Colts Whew	.10
288	Kansas City Chiefs Ambush	.10
289	Los Angeles Raiders Lott of Defense	.05
290	Los Angeles Rams Ram It	.05
291	Miami Dolphins Miami Ice	.15
292	Minnesota Vikings Purple Blaze	.05
293	New England Patriots Surprise Attack	.05
294	New Orlean Saints Marching In	.05
295	New York Giants Almost Perfect	.05
296	New York Jets Playoff Bound	.05
297	Philadelphia Eagles Flying High	.05
298	Phoenix Cardinals	.05
299	Pittsburgh Steelers Steel Curtain	.05
300	San Diego Chargers Lightning	.05
301	San Francisco 49ers Instant Rice	.15
302	Seattle Seahawks Defense Never Rests	.05
303	Tampa Bay Buccaneers Stunned	.05
304	Washington Redskins Super	.05
305	Jim Kelly (LL)	.10
306	Steve Young (LL)	.15
307	Thurman Thomas (LL)	.20
308	Emmitt Smith (LL)	1.00
309	Haywood Jeffires (LL)	.05
310	Michael Irvin (LL)	.30
311	William Fuller (LL)	.05
312	Pat Swilling (LL)	.05
313	Ronnie Lott (LL)	.07
314	Deion Sanders (LL)	.07
315	Cornelius Bennett	.05
316	David Fulcher	.05
317	Ronnie Lott	.05
318	Pat Swilling	.05
319	Lawrence Taylor	.07
320	Derrick Thomas	.07
321	*Steve Emtman*	.15
322	*Carl Pickens*	1.50
323	*David Klingler*	.25
324	*Dale Carter*	.25
325	*Mike Gaddis*	.08
326	*Quentin Coryatt*	.35
327	*Darryl Williams*	.15
328	*Jeremy Lincoln*	.15
329	*Robert Jones*	.15
330	*Bucky Richardson*	.30
331	*Tony Brooks*	.10
332	*Alonzo Spellman*	.20
333	*Robert Brooks*	1.00
334	*Marco Coleman*	.20
335	*Siran Stacy*	.15
336	*Tommy Maddox*	.25
337	*Steve Israel*	.15
338	*Vaughn Dunbar*	.15
339	*Shane Collins*	.15
340	*Kevin Smith*	.25
341	*Chris Mims*	.25
342	*Chester McGlockton*	.25
343	*Tracy Scroggins*	.25
344	*Howard Dinkins*	.10
345	*Levon Kirkland*	.10
346	*Terrell Buckley*	.30
347	*Marquez Pope*	.10
348	*Phillippi Sparks*	.10
349	*Joe Bowden*	.10
350	*Edgar Bennett*	.75

1992 SkyBox Impact Holograms

These holograms were included as random inserts in foil packs (#s H1 and H2) or offered to those who responded to the mail-in offer which made them available (#s H3-H6). The card front has a full-bleed hologram photo, plus the player's last name. The back has a color photo and a career summary.

		NM/M
Complete Set (6):		7.00
Common Player:		1.00
1	Jim Kelly	3.00
2	Lawrence Taylor	2.50
3	Christian Okoye	1.00
4	Mark Rypien	1.00
5	Pat Swilling	1.00
6	Ricky Ervins	1.00

1992 SkyBox Impact Major Impact

These cards feature 20 players who have a tremendous impact on NFL games. Each borderless card front has a full-bleed color photo and the player's last name stamped in silver-foil block letters across the top. The back has an action shot and career summary. A blue stripe separates these items on the cards for NFC players (11-20), while a red stripe is used for AFC cards (1-10). Cards are numbered with an "M" prefix and were randomly inserted in 1992 SkyBox Impact jumbo packs.

		NM/M
Complete Set (20):		6.00
Common Player:		.25
Minor Stars:		.50
1	Cornelius Bennett	.25
2	David Fulcher	.25
3	Haywood Jeffires	.25
4	Ronnie Lott	.25
5	Dan Marino	3.00
6	Warren Moon	.50
7	Christian Okoye	.25
8	Andre Reed	.25
9	Derrick Thomas	.50
10	Thurman Thomas	.50
11	Troy Aikman	2.00
12	Randall Cunningham	.25
13	Michael Irvin	.50
14	Jerry Rice	2.00
15	Joe Montana	2.50
16	Mark Rypien	.25
17	Deion Sanders	1.50
18	Emmitt Smith	3.00
19	Pat Swilling	.25
20	Lawrence Taylor	.50

1992 SkyBox Primetime Previews

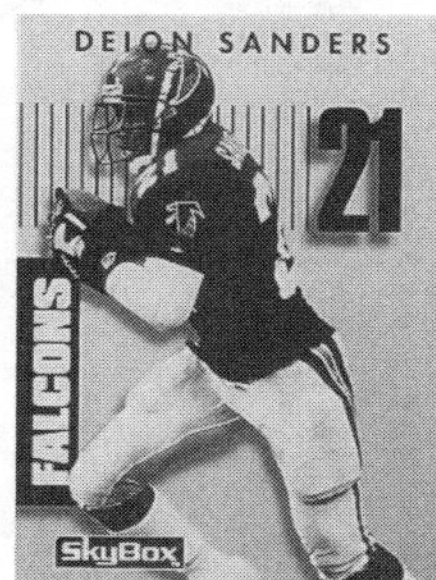

This five-card set allowed collectors to see what the Primetime sets would look like and are exact replicas of the regular-issue cards, except for being numbered A-D, plus a title card. Five-card sets were originally packaged in cello packs.

		NM/M
Complete Set (5):		6.00
Common Player:		1.00
A	Jerry Rice	3.00
B	Deion Sanders	1.00
C	John Elway	2.00
D	Vaughn Dunbar	1.00
NNO	Title Card (Advertisement)	1.00

1992 SkyBox Primetime

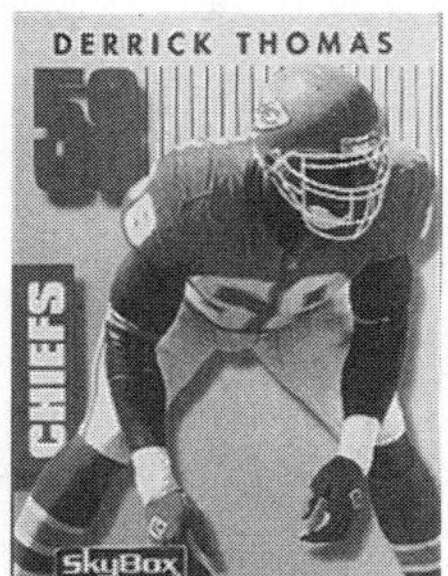

This 360-card set features cards which use cut-out action photos superimposed against a grey background with thin black lines. The player's name is at the top, while his jersey number is included at the bottom in his team's colors. His team name is in a color-coded bar on the left. Half of the card back features an action photo; the rest has stats, a biography and career summary. A team color-coded band with the player's name separates the photo and the remaining information. A 28-card subset, Team MVP, was also made. Insert cards feature Costacos Brothers poster art (15 silver foil cards); a poster checklist; a Kelly hologram; and a Steve Emtman Horse-Power card. Five promo cards were also made and were available in cello packs.

		NM/M
Complete Set (360):		20.00
Common Player:		.05
Minor Stars:		.20
Pack (12):		.75
Wax Box (36):		25.00
1	Deion Sanders	1.25
2	*Shane Collins*	.20
3	*James Patton*	.05
4	Reggie Roby	.05
5	Merril Hoge	.05
6	Vinny Testaverde	.05
7	Boomer Esiason	.05
8	Troy Aikman	2.50
9	*Tommy Jeter*	.05
10	Brent Williams	.05
11	Mark Rypien	.05
12	Jim Kelly	.25
13	Dan Marino	4.00
14	Bill Cowher	.05
15	Leslie O'Neal	.05
16	Joe Montana	2.50
17	William Fuller	.05
18	Paul Gruber	.05
19	Bernie Kosar	.05
20	Rickey Jackson	.05
21	Earnest Byner	.05
22	Emmitt Smith	5.00
23	Neal Anderson	.05
24	Greg Lloyd	.20
25	Ronnie Harmon	.05
26	Ray Donaldson	.05
27	Kevin Ross	.05
28	Irving Fryar	.05
29	John Williams	.05
30	Chris Hinton	.05
31	*Tracy Scroggins*	.20
32	Rohn Stark	.05
33	David Fulcher	.05
34	Thurman Thomas	.50
35	Christian Okoye	.05
36	*Vaughn Dunbar*	.20
37	*Joel Steed*	.05
38	James Francis (card number on back is actually 354)	.05
39	Dermontti Dawson	.05
40	Mark Higgs	.05
41	Flipper Anderson	.05
42	Ronnie Lott	.05
43	Jim Everett	.05
44	Burt Grossman	.05
45	Charles Haley	.05
46	Ricky Proehl	.05
47	*Marquez Pope*	.05
48	David Treadwell	.05
49	William White	.05
50	John Elway	1.00
51	Mark Carrier	.05
52	Brian Blades	.05
53	Keith McKeller	.05
54	Art Monk	.20
55	Lamar Lathon	.05
56	Pat Swilling	.05
57	Steve Broussard	.05
58	Derrick Thomas	.20
59	Keith Jackson	.20
60	Leonard Marshall	.05
61	Eric Metcalf (card number on back is actually 350)	.05
62	Andy Heck	.05
63	Mark Carrier	.05
64	Neil O'Donnell	.05
65	Broderick Thomas	.05
66	Erik Kramer	.05
67	Joe Montana	1.25
68	Robert Delpino	.05
69	*Steve Israel*	.05
70	Herman Moore	1.25
71	Jacob Green	.05
72	Lorenzo White	.05
73	Nick Lowery	.05
74	Eugene Robinson	.05
75	Carl Banks	.05
76	Bruce Smith	.05
77	Mark Rypien	.05
78	Anthony Munoz	.05
79	*Clayton Holmes*	.05
80	Jerry Rice	2.50
81	Henry Ellard	.05
82	Tim McGee	.05
83	Al Toon	.05
84	Haywood Jeffires	.05
85	Mike Singletary	.05
86	Thurman Thomas	.25
87	Jessie Hester	.05
88	Michael Irvin	.50
89	Jack Del Rio	.05
90	Seth Joyner (No player photo)	.05
91	Jeff Herrod	.05
92	Michael Dean Perry	.05
93	Louis Oliver	.05
94	Dan McGwire	.05
95	Cris Carter	.20
96	*Dale Carter*	.50
97	Cornelius Bennett	.05
98	*Edgar Bennett*	.50
99	Steve Young	2.50
100	Warren Moon	.20
101	Deion Sanders	.50
102	Mel Gray	.05
103	Mark Murphy	.05
104	Jeff George	.50
105	Anthony Miller	.05
106	Tom Rathman	.05
107	*Fred McAfee*	.05
108	*Paul Siever*	.05
109	Lemuel Stinson	.05
110	Vance Johnson	.05
111	Jay Schroeder	.05
112	Calvin Williams	.05
113	Cortez Kennedy	.05
114	*Quentin Coryatt*	.30
115	Ronnie Lippett	.05
116	Brad Baxter	.05
117	Bubba McDowell	.05
118	Cris Carter	.20
119	John Stephens	.05
120	James Hasty	.05
121	Bubby Brister	.05
122	*Robert Jones*	.20
123	Sterling Sharpe	.20
124	*Jason Hanson*	.20
125	Sam Mills	.05
126	Ernie Jones	.05
127	*Chester McGlockton*	.50
128	*Troy Vincent*	.20
129	*Chuck Smith*	.05
130	Tim McKyer	.05
131	Tom Newberry	.05
132	*Leonard Wheeler*	.05
133	*Patrick Rowe*	.05
134	Eric Swann	.05
135	*Jeremy Lincoln*	.05
136	Brian Noble	.05
137	Allen Pinkett	.05
138	*Carl Pickens*	1.50
139	Eric Green	.05
140	Louis Lipps	.05
141	Chris Singleton	.05
142	Gary Clark	.05
143	Tim Green	.05
144	*Dennis Green*	.05
145	Gary Anderson	.05
146	Miami Dolphins	.05
147	Kelvin Martin	.05
148	*Mike Holmgren*	.05
149	Gaston Green	.05
150	*Terrell Buckley*	.05
151	*Robert Brooks*	1.50
152	Anthony Smith	.05
153	Jay Novacek	.05
154	Webster Slaughter	.05
155	John Roper	.05
156	*Steve Emtman*	.20
157	Tony Sacca	.05
158	Ray Crockett	.05
159	Jerry Rice	1.00
160	*Alonzo Spellman*	.20
161	Deion Sanders	.50
162	Robert Clark	.05
163	Mark Ingram	.05
164	*Ricardo McDonald*	.05
165	Emmitt Smith	3.00
166	*Tommy Maddox*	.20
167	*Tom Myslinski*	.05
168	Tony Bennett (No player photo on card)	.05
169	Ernest Givins	.05
170	Eugene Robinson	.05
171	Roger Craig	.05
172	Irving Fryar	.05
173	Jeff Herrod	.05
174	*Chris Mims*	.20
175	Bart Oates	.05
176	Michael Irvin	.50
177	Lawrence Dawsey	.05
178	Warren Moon	.05
179	Timm Rosenbach	.05
180	Bobby Ross	.05
181	Chris Burkett	.05
182	*Tony Brooks*	.05
183	Clarence Verdin	.05
184	Bernie Kosar	.05
185	Eric Martin	.05
186	Jeff Bryant	.05
187	Carnell Lake	.05
188	*Darren Woodson*	.40
189	Dwayne Harper	.05
190	Bernie Kosar	.05
191	Keith Sims	.05
192	Rich Gannon	.05
193	Broderick Thomas	.05
194	Michael Young	.05
195	Cris Dishman	.05
196	Wes Hopkins	.05
197	Christian Okoye	.05
198	David Little	.05
199	*Chris Crooms*	.05
200	Lawrence Taylor	.20
201	*Marc Boutte*	.05
202	Mark Carrier	.05
203	Keith McCants	.05
204	*Dwayne Sabb*	.05
205	Brian Mitchell	.05
206	Keith Byars	.05
207	Jeff Hostetler	.20
208	Percy Snow	.05
209	Lawrence Taylor	.05
210	*Troy Auzenne*	.05
211	Warren Moon	.05
212	Mike Pritchard	.05
213	Eric Dickerson	.05
214	Harvey Williams	.05
215	Phil Simms (Misspelled Sims on card front)	.05
216	*Sean Lumpkin* (Card number on back is actually 002)	.05
217	*Marco Coleman*	.05
218	*Phillippi Sparks*	.05
219	*Gerald Dixon*	.05
220	Steve Walsh	.05
221	Russell Maryland	.05
222	Eddie Anderson	.05
223	*Shane Dronett*	.05
224	*Todd Collins*	.20
225	*Leon Searcy*	.05
226	Andre Rison	.05
227	James Lofton	.05
228	Ken O'Brien	.05
229	Jeff George	.05
230	Nick Bell	.05
231	Ben Smith	.05
232	Wendell Davis	.05
233	*Craig Thompson*	.05
234	*Dana Hall*	.05
235	*Larry Webster*	.05
236	Jerry Rice	1.00
237	Rod Bernstine	.05
238	*David Klingler*	.20
239	*Greg Skrepenak*	.05
240	*Mark Wheeler*	.05
241	*Kevin Smith*	.20
242	Charles Mann	.05
243	Barry Sanders	.20
244	*Curtis Whitley*	.05
245	Ronnie Harmon	.05
246	Brent Jones	.05
247	*Robert Harris*	.05
248	Ted Marchibroda	.05
249	Willie Gault	.05
250	*Siran Stacy*	.05
251	Dennis Byrd	.05
252	*Corey Harris*	.05
253	Al Noga	.05
254	*David Shula*	.05
255	Rob Moore	.05
256	Marv Cook	.05
257	John Elway	.30
258	Harold Green	.05
259	Tom Flores	.05
260	Andre Reed	.05
261	Anthony Thompson	.05
262	Issiac Holt	.05
263	*Mike Evans*	.05
264	*Jimmy Smith*	3.50
265	Anthony Carter	.05
266	*Ashley Ambrose*	.05
267	*John Fina* (Card number on back is actually 357)	.05
268	*Sean Gilbert*	.40
269	Ken Norton Jr.	.05
270	Barry Word	.05
271	Pat Swilling	.05
272	Dan Marino	1.50
273	David Fulcher	.05
274	William Perry	.05
275	Ed West	.05
276	Gene Atkins	.05
277	Neal Anderson	.05
278	Dino Hackett	.05
279	Greg Townsend	.05
280	Andre Tippett	.05
281	*Darryl Williams*	.05
282	*Kurt Barber*	.05
283	Pat Terrell	.05
284	Derrick Thomas	.05
285	*Eddie Robinson*	.05
286	Howie Long	.05
287	Tim McDonald (No player photo)	.05
288	Thurman Thomas	.05
289	Wendell Davis	.05
290	Jeff Cross	.05
291	Duane Bickett	.05
292	*Tony Smith*	.05
293	Jerry Ball	.05
294	Jessie Tuggle	.05
295	Chris Burkett	.05
296	*Eugene Chung*	.05
297	Chris Miller	.05
298	Albert Bentley	.05
299	Richard Johnson	.05
300	Randall Cunningham	.05
301	*Courtney Hawkins*	.05
302	Ray Childress	.05
303	Rodney Peete	.05
304	Kevin Fagan	.05
305	Ronnie Lott	.05
306	Michael Carter	.05
307	Derrick Thomas	.05
308	Jarvis Williams	.05
309	Greg Lloyd	.05
310	Ethan Horton	.05
311	Ricky Ervins	.05
312	Bennie Blades	.05
313	Troy Aikman	1.00
314	Bruce Armstrong	.05
315	Leroy Hoard	.05
316	Gary Anderson	.05
317	Steve McMichael	.05
318	Junior Seau	.50
319	*Mark Thomas*	.05
320	Fred Barnett	.05
321	Mike Merriweather	.05
322	Keith Willis	.05
323	Brett Perriman	.05
324	Michael Haynes	.05
325	Jim Harbaugh	.05
326	Sammie Smith	.05
327	Robert Delpino	.05
328	Tony Mandarich	.05
329	Mark Bortz	.05
330	*Ray Etheridge*	.05
331	Jarvis Williams	.05
332	Dan Marino	1.50
333	Dwight Stone	.05
334	Billy Ray Smith	.05
335	Darion Connor	.05
336	*Howard Dinkins*	.05
337	*Robert Porcher*	.50
338	Chris Doleman	.05
339	Alvin Harper	.20
340	John Taylor	.05
341	Ray Agnew	.05
342	Jon Vaughn	.05
343	*James Brown*	.05
344	Michael Irvin	.50
345	Neil Smith	.05
346	Vaughn Johnson	.05
347	Checklist	.05
348	Checklist	.05
349	Checklist	.05
350	Checklist (See also number 61)	.05
351	Checklist	.05
352	Checklist	.05
353	Checklist	.05
354	Checklist (See also number 38)	.05
355	Checklist	.05
356	Checklist	.05
357	Checklist (See also number 267)	.05
358	Checklist (See also number 138)	.05
359	Checklist	.05
360	Checklist	.05

A player's name in *italic* type indicates a rookie card.

1992 SkyBox Primetime Poster Cards

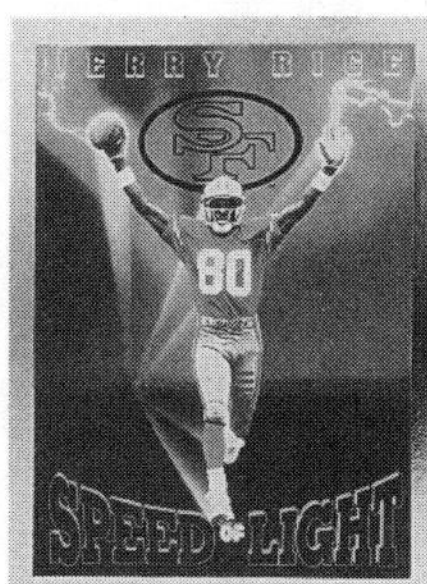

These insert cards feature photos used on posters made by Costacos to capture the essence of the player's nickname, image or city he plays in. The cards, randomly inserted in 1992 SkyBox Primetime foil packs, are identical to their counterparts in SkyBox's regular 1992 Primetime set, except the inserts have silver foil-stamped borders on the front. The cards were estimated to be two per 36-pack box of cards and were found in the 10,000 numbered cases distributed to the hobby only. Card backs have the Primetime logo in the upper left, along with a card number, which uses an "M" prefix, in the upper right. A photo, career summary and team logo also appear.

		NM/M
Complete Set (16):		15.00
Common Player:		.50
1	Bernie Kosar	.50
2	Mark Carrier	.50
3	Neal Anderson	.50
4	Thurman Thomas	2.00
5	Deion Sanders	2.00
6	Joe Montana	4.00
7	Jerry Rice	3.00
8	Jarvis Williams	.50
9	Dan Marino	4.00
10	Derrick Thomas	1.00
11	Christian Okoye	.50
12	Warren Moon	1.00
13	Michael Irvin	1.00
14	Troy Aikman	2.00
15	Emmitt Smith	4.00
16	Checklist	.50

1993 SkyBox Premium

SkyBox Premium's 270-card set features silhouetted action photos highlighted by the contrast of the team color, two-tone background. Team logos, the player's name and a foil-stamped SkyBox Premium logo is also on the front. The back has a color action photo, a biography, four-year statistics, and career totals. Cards are UV-coated. Insert sets include Costacos Brothers posters (10 cards), Chris Mortensen's PrimeTime Rookies (10 cards) and Thunder and Lightning (nine dual teammate cards).

		NM/M
Complete Set (270):		25.00
Common Player:		.10
Minor Stars:		.20
Comp. Poster Card Set (10):		5.00
Pack (12):		1.25
Wax Box (36):		30.00
1	Eric Martin	.10
2	Earnest Byner	.10
3	Ricky Proehl	.10
4	Mark Carrier	.10
5	Shannon Sharpe	.20
6	Anthony Thompson	.10
7	*Drew Bledsoe*	7.00
8	*Tom Carter*	.40
9	*Ryan McNeil*	.20
10	Troy Aikman	2.00
11	Robert Jones	.10
12	Rodney Peete	.10
13	Wendell Davis	.10
14	Thurman Thomas	.50
15	John Stephens	.10
16	Rodney Hampton	.25
17	Eric Bieniemy	.10
18	Santana Dotson	.10
19	Jeff George	.20
20	John L. Williams	.10
21	Barry Wood	.10
22	Chris Miller	.10
23	Jeff Hostetler	.20
24	Dwight Stone	.10
25	Brad Baxter	.10
26	Randall Cunningham	.20
27	Mark Higgs	.10
28	Vaughn Dunbar	.10
29	Ricky Ervins	.10
30	Johnny Bailey	.10
31	Michael Jackson	.10
32	Mike Croel	.10
33	Steve Young	2.00
34	*Deon Figures*	.20
35	*Robert Smith*	3.00
36	*Irv Smith*	.20
37	Charles Haley	.10
38	Cris Dishman	.10
39	Barry Sanders	3.00
40	Jim Harbaugh	.10
41	Darryl Talley	.10
42	Jackie Harris	.10
43	Phil Simms	.10
44	Marion Butts	.10
45	Anthony Munoz	.10
46	Steve Emtman	.10
47	Kelvin Martin	.10
48	Joe Montana	3.00
49	Andre Rison	.25
50	Ethan Horton	.10
51	Kevin Greene	.10
52	Browning Nagle	.10
53	Tim Harris	.10
54	Keith Byars	.10
55	Terry Allen	.10
56	Chip Lohmiller	.10
57	Robert Massey	.10
58	Michael Dean Perry	.10
59	Tommy Maddox	.10
60	Jerry Rice	2.00
61	*Lincoln Kennedy*	.10
62	*Jerome Bettis*	2.50
63	*Coleman Rudolph*	.10
64	Emmitt Smith	4.00
65	Curtis Duncan	.10
66	Andre Ware	.10
67	Neal Anderson	.10
68	Jim Kelly	.25
69	Reggie White	.25
70	Dave Meggett	.10
71	Junior Seau	.40
72	Courtney Hawkins	.10
73	Clarence Verdin	.10
74	Tommy Kane	.10
75	Dale Carter	.10
76	Michael Haynes	.10
77	Willie Gault	.10
78	Eric Green	.10
79	Ronnie Lott	.10
80	Vai Sikahema	.10
81	Mark Ingram	.10
82	Anthony Carter	.10
83	Mark Rypien	.10
84	Gary Clark	.10
85	Bernie Kosar	.10
86	Cleveland Gary	.10
87	Tom Rathman	.10
88	*Tony McGee*	.40
89	*Rick Mirer*	.50
90	*John Copeland*	.50
91	Michael Irvin	.20
92	Wilber Marshall	.10
93	Mel Gray	.10
94	Craig Heyward	.10
95	Don Beebe	.10
96	Andre Tippett	.10
97	Derek Brown	.10
98	Ronnie Harmon	.10
99	Derrick Fenner	.10
100	Rodney Culver	.10
101	Cortez Kennedy	.20
102	Marcus Allen	.20
103	Steve Broussard	.10
104	Tim Brown	.25
105	Merril Hoge	.10
106	Chris Burkett	.10
107	Fred Barnett	.10
108	Dan Marino	4.00
109	Chris Doleman	.10
110	Art Monk	.10
111	Ernie Jones	.10
112	Jay Hilgenberg	.10
113	Jim Everett	.10
114	John Taylor	.10
115	*Steve Everett*	.25
116	*Carlton Gray*	.20
117	*Eric Curry*	.50
118	Ken Norton	.10
119	Lorenzo White	.10
120	Pat Swilling	.10
121	William Perry	.10
122	Brett Favre	4.00
123	Jon Vaughn	.10
124	Mark Jackson	.10
125	Stan Humphries	.20
126	Harold Green	.10
127	Anthony Jackson	.10
128	Brian Blades	.10
129	Willie Davis	.10
130	Bobby Hebert	.10
131	Terry McDaniel	.10
132	Jeff Graham	.10
133	Jeff Lageman	.10
134	Andre Waters	.10
135	Steve Walsh	.10
136	Cris Carter	.20
137	Tim McGee	.10
138	Chuck Cecil	.10
139	John Elway	1.00
140	Todd Lyght	.10
141	Brent Jones	.10
142	*Patrick Bates*	.25
143	*Darrien Gordon*	.50
144	*Michael Strahan*	.10
145	Jay Novacek	.10
146	Warren Moon	.25
147	Rodney Holman	.10
148	Anthony Morgan	.10
149	Sterling Sharpe	.20
150	Leonard Russell	.10
151	Lawrence Taylor	.20
152	Leslie O'Neal	.10
153	Carl Pickens	1.00
154	Aaron Cox	.10
155	Ferrell Edmunds	.10
156	Neil O'Donnell	.20

157 Tony Smith .10
158 James Lofton .10
159 *George Teague* .50
160 Boomer Esiason .20
161 Eric Allen .10
162 Floyd Turner .10
163 Esera Tuaolo .10
164 Darrell Green .10
165 Steve Beuerlein .10
166 Vance Johnson .10
167 Willie Anderson .10
168 Ricky Watters .20
169 *Marvin Jones* .20
170 *Dana Stubblefield* .75
171 *Willie Roaf* .25
172 Russell Maryland .10
173 Ernest Givins .10
174 Willie Green .10
175 Bruce Smith .10
176 Terrell Buckley .10
177 Scott Zolak .10
178 Mike Sherrard .10
179 Lawrence Dawsey .10
180 Jay Schroeder .10
181 Quentin Coryatt .10
182 Harvey Williams .10
183 *Natrone Means* 3.00
184 Eric Dickerson .20
185 Gaston Green .10
186 *Thomas Smith* .25
187 Johnny Johnson .10
188 Marco Coleman .10
189 Wade Wilson .10
190 Rich Gannon .10
191 Brian Mitchell .10
192 Eric Metcalf .10
193 Robert Delpino .10
194 Shane Conlan .10
195 Dexter Carter .10
196 *Garrison Hearst* 3.00
197 *Chris Slade* .20
198 *Troy Drayton* .30
199 *Lin Elliot* .10
200 Haywood Jeffires .10
201 Herman Moore 1.00
202 Cornelius Bennett .10
203 Mark Clayton .10
204 Marv Cook .10
205 Stephen Baker .10
206 Gary Anderson .10
207 Eddie Brown .10
208 Will Wolford .10
209 Derrick Thomas .20
210 Seth Joyner .10
211 Mike Pritchard .10
212 Rod Woodson .20
213 *Todd Kelly* .20
214 Rob Moore .10
215 Keith Jackson .10
216 Wesley Carroll .10
217 Steve Jordan .10
218 Ricky Sanders .10
219 Tommy Vardell .10
220 Rod Bernstine .10
221 Henry Ellard .10
222 Amp Lee .10
223 *O.J. McDuffie* 2.00
224 *Carl Simpson* .20
225 *Dan Williams* .20
226 Thomas Everett .10
227 Webster Slaughter .10
228 Trace Armstrong .10
229 Kenneth Davis .10
230 Tony Bennett .10
231 Reyna Thompson .10
232 Anthony Miller .10
233 Reggie Cobb .10
234 Mark Duper .10
235 Chris Warren .30
236 Christian Okoye .10
237 Irving Fryar .10
238 Deion Sanders 1.00
239 Barry Foster .10
240 *Ernest Dye* .10
241 Calvin Williams .10
242 Louis Oliver .10
243 Dalton Hilliard .10
244 Roger Craig .10
245 Randall Hill .10
246 Vinny Testaverde .10
247 Steve Atwater .10
248 Jim Price .10
249 *Martin Harrison* .20
250 *Curtis Conway* 2.00
251 *Demetrius DuBose* .20
252 *Leonard Renfro* .10
253 Alvin Harper .40
254 Leonard Harris .10
255 Tom Waddle .10
256 Andre Reed .20
257 Sanjay Beach .10
258 Michael Timpson .10
259 Nate Lewis .10
260 Steve DeBerg .10
261 David Klingler .10
262 Dan McGwire .10
263 Dave Krieg .10
264 Brad Muster .10
265 Nick Bell .10
266 Checklist 1 .10
267 Checklist 2 .10
268 Checklist 3 .10
269 Checklist 4 .10
270 Checklist 5 .10

1993 SkyBox Poster Art Cards

These cards were randomly inserted in SkyBox's 1993 packs. The front of each card pictures a sports poster created by the Costacos Brothers. Each reproduction is framed by a black border. The back has a photo at the top half, with a gold stripe underneath containing the player's name. A team logo and brief career summary are at the bottom against a white background. The cards are numbered with a "CB" prefix.

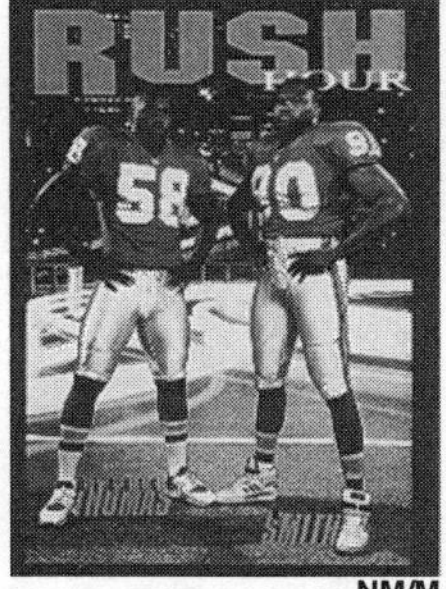

NM/M
Complete Set (10): 3.00
Common Player: .25
1 Cowboys Defense .25
2 Cowboys Champs 1.00
3 Barry Foster .25
4 Art Monk .25
5 Jerry Rice 1.00
6 Barry Sanders 1.00
7 Deion Sanders .75
8 Junior Seau .75
9 Derrick Thomas, Neil Smith .75
10 Steve Young .50

1993 SkyBox Premium Rookies

These 10 rookies were selected for this set by Chris Mortensen, of ESPN and The Sporting News. He predicted the players would be "prime timers" in 1993. The card front, which has a gold-and-black metallic background, shows the player in his collegiate uniform. A black stripe at the left contains the player's name, set title and Mortensen's facsimile signature. Mortensen is pictured on the bottom half of the card back, along with his player evaluation and the player's position. The top half has a photo of the player, plus his name, in a gold stripe, and a card number, which uses a "PR" prefix.

NM/M
Complete Set (10): 25.00
Common Player: 1.00
1 Patrick Bates 1.00
2 Drew Bledsoe 15.00
3 Darrien Gordon 1.00
4 Garrison Hearst 6.00
5 Marvin Jones 1.00
6 Terry Kirby 2.00
7 Natrone Means 1.00
8 Rick Mirer 1.00
9 Willie Roaf 1.00
10 Dan Williams 1.00

1993 SkyBox Premium Thunder and Lightning

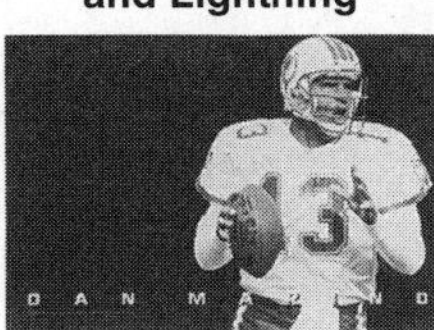

These cards are in a horizontal format and feature two teammates per card, one on each side. The player on the Thunder side is featured against a metallic black-and-gold background. Those on the Lightning side are featured against a black-and-silver metallic background with lightning bolts running through it. The player's name is in white lettering across the bottom. A TL prefix is used to number the cards; the number is on the Lightning side of the card. Cards were random inserts in every ninth 1993 SkyBox Premium 12-card foil pack.

NM/M
Complete Set (9): 12.00
Common Player: 1.00
1 Jim Kelly, Thurman Thomas 1.00
2 Brett Favre, Sterling Sharpe 3.00
3 Dan Marino, Keith Jackson 3.00
4 Sam Mills, Vaughan Johnson 1.00
5 Warren Moon, Haywood Jeffires 1.00
6 Troy Aikman, Michael Irvin 3.00
7 Randall Cunningham, Fred Barnett 1.00
8 Steve Young, Jerry Rice 3.00
9 Dennis Smith, Steve Atwater 1.00

1993 SkyBox Celebrity Cycle Protypes

This four-card set includes three actual celebrities and one mystery card, which pictures a Harley-Davidson motorcycle against an American flag background. Backs are blank except for a large red stamp that reads "UNFINISHED SKYBOX PROTOTYPE."

NM/M
Complete Set (4): 3.00
Common Player: .50
1 Mitch Frerotte .50
2 Jerry Glanville (CO) .50
3 Kenny Lofton (Cleveland Indians) 2.00
4 Mystery Celebrity Cycle Card 1.00

1993 SkyBox Impact Promos

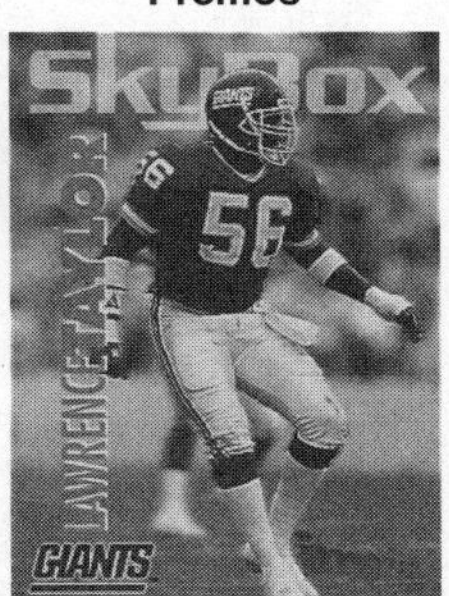

This two-card promotional set was mailed to dealers to promote the 1993 Impact set, and was numbered IP1 and IP2. Cards contain the same design as the regular-issue product. Another version of the Jim Kelly card was distributed at the 1993 Chicago National, but is differentiated by a blue foil stamp commemorating the event.

NM/M
Complete Set (2): 3.00
Common Player: 1.00
1 Jim Kelly 2.00
2 Lawrence Taylor 1.00

1993 SkyBox Impact

SkyBox's 1993 Impact set has 400 cards featuring full-bleed color action photos; the backgrounds are not in focus, so the player appears to stand out. The player's name and logo are at the bottom; SkyBox is written at the top. The back has a color photo, four-year statistics, a biography and career totals. Subsets include Class of '83, checklists, Rookies First Round and Rookies Second Round. Insert cards include redemption cards for a set of draft picks (29 cards) and a dual-sport card of Magic Johnson/Jim Kelley. SkyBox color foil cards were also created for each player in the 400-card set. Four different foil colors were used; each player is done in one color only. They can be collected to form a 400-card set. Two promo cards, using the same design as the regular 1993 SkyBox Impact set, were also produced.

NM/M
Complete Set (400): 15.00
Common Player: .03
Color Cards: 2X-4X
Pack (12): .50
Wax Box (36): 14.00
1 Steve Broussard .03
2 Michael Haynes .10
3 Tony Smith .03
4 Tory Epps .03
5 Chris Hinton .03
6 Bobby Hebert .03
7 Tim McKyer .03
8 Chris Miller .03
9 Bruce Pickens .03
10 Mike Pritchard .05
11 Andre Rison .20
12 Deion Sanders .10
13 Pierce Holt .03
14 Jessie Tuggle .03
15 Don Beebe .03
16 Cornelius Bennett .03
17 Kenneth Davis .03
18 Kent Hull .03
19 Jim Kelly .25
20 Mark Kelso .03
21 Keith McKellar .03
22 Andre Reed .10
23 Jim Richter .03
24 Bruce Smith .04
25 Thurman Thomas .10
26 Steve Christie .03
27 Darryl Talley .03
28 Pete Metzelaars .03
29 Steve Tasker .03
30 Henry Jones .03
31 Neal Anderson .05
32 Trace Armstrong .03
33 Mark Bortz .03
34 Mark Carrier .03
35 Wendell Davis .03
36 Richard Dent .03
37 Jim Harbaugh .05
38 Steve McMichael .03
39 Craig Heyward .03
40 William Perry .03
41 Donnell Woolford .03
42 Tom Waddle .05
43 Anthony Morgan .03
44 Jim Breech .03
45 David Klingler .15
46 Derrick Fenner .03
47 David Fulcher .03
48 James Francis .03
49 Harold Green .03
50 Carl Pickens .15
51 Jay Schroeder .03
52 Alex Gordon .03
53 Eric Ball .03
54 Eddie Brown .03
55 Jay Hilgenberg .03
56 Michael Jackson .05
57 Bernie Kosar .05
58 Kevin Mack .03
59 Eric Metcalf .05
60 Michael Dean Perry .03
61 Tommy Vardell .05
62 Leroy Hoard .03
63 Clay Matthews .03
64 Vinny Testaverde .05
65 Mark Carrier .03
66 Troy Aikman 1.00
67 *Lin Elliot* .08
68 Thomas Everett .03
69 Alvin Harper .25
70 Ray Horton .03
71 Michael Irvin .10
72 Russell Maryland .05
73 Jay Novacek .03
74 Emmitt Smith 2.00
75 Tony Casillas .03
76 Robert Jones .03
77 Ken Norton .03
78 Daryl Johnston .03
79 Charles Haley .03
80 *Leon Lett* .25
81 Steve Atwater .03
82 Mike Croel .05
83 John Elway 1.00
84 Simon Fletcher .03
85 Vance Johnson .03
86 Shannon Sharpe .08
87 Rod Bernstine .03
88 Robert Delpino .03
89 Karl Mecklenburg .03
90 Steve Sewell .03
91 Tommy Maddox .15
92 *Arthur Marshall* .25
93 Dennis Smith .03
94 Derek Russell .03
95 Bernie Blades .03
96 Michael Cofer .03
97 Willie Green .08
98 Herman Moore .40
99 Rodney Peete .05
100 Andre Ware .03
101 Barry Sanders 1.25
102 Chris Spielman .03
103 Jason Hanson .03
104 Mel Gray .03
105 Pat Swilling .03
106 Bill Fralic .03
107 Rodney Herman .03
108 Brett Favre 2.00
109 Sterling Sharpe .10
110 Reggie White .10
111 Terrell Buckley .15
112 Sanjay Beach .03
113 Tony Bennett .03
114 Jackie Harris .15
115 Bryce Paup .03
116 Shawn Patterson .03
117 John Stephens .03
118 Cris Dishman .03
119 Ernest Givins .03
120 Haywood Jeffires .10
121 Lamar Lathon .03
122 Warren Moon .15
123 Lorenzo White .03
124 Curtis Duncan .03
125 Webster Slaughter .03
126 Cody Carlson .03
127 Leonard Harris .03
128 Bruce Matthews .03
129 Ray Childress .03
130 Al Smith .03
131 Jeff George .15
132 Anthony Johnson .03
133 Steve Emtman .08
134 Quentin Coryatt .08
135 Rodney Culver .03
136 Jessie Hester .03
137 Aaron Cox .03
138 Clarence Verdin .03
139 Joe Montana 1.25
140 Dave Krieg .03
141 Harvey Williams .03
142 Derrick Thomas .15
143 Barry Word .05
144 Christian Okoye .03
145 Nick Lowery .03
146 Dale Carter .03
147 Willie Davis .10
148 Tim Barnett .03
149 Neal Smith .10
150 Marcus Allen .06
151 Nick Bell .04
152 Tim Brown .35
153 Eric Dickerson .03
154 Willie Gault .03
155 Howie Long .03
156 Gaston Green .03
157 Chester McGlockton .03
158 Eddie Anderson .03
159 Ethan Horton .03
160 James Lofton .03
161 Jeff Hostetler .10
162 Terry McDaniel .03
163 Flipper Anderson .03
164 Shane Conlan .03
165 Jim Everett .05
166 Henry Ellard .03
167 Cleveland Gary .03
168 Todd Lyght .03
169 Sean Gilbert .03
170 Jim Price .03
171 Bill Hawkins .03
172 Mark Clayton .03
173 Mark Higgs .10
174 Dan Marino 2.00
175 Louis Oliver .03
176 Reggie Roby .03
177 Bobby Humphrey .03
178 Troy Vincent .10
179 Marco Coleman .05
180 Aaron Craver .05
181 Keith Jackson .10
182 Mark Duper .03
183 Pete Stoyanovich .03
184 Irving Fryar .03
185 Brian Cox .03
186 Terry Allen .06
187 Anthony Carter .03
188 Cris Carter .03
189 Chris Doleman .03
190 Rich Gannon .06
191 Sean Salisbury .03
192 Hassan Jones .03
193 Steve Jordan .03
194 Roger Craig .05
195 Todd Scott .03
196 Esera Tualo .03
197 Ray Agnew .03
198 Marv Cook .03
199 Tom Hodson .03
200 Chris Singleton .03
201 Michael Timpson .03
202 Jon Vaughn .03
203 Leonard Russell .10
204 Scott Zolak .03
205 Renya Thompson .03
206 Andre Tippett .03
207 Morten Andersen .03
208 Wesley Carroll .03
209 Vince Buck .03
210 Rickey Jackson .03
211 Vaughn Johnson .03
212 Eric Martin .03
213 Sam Mills .03
214 Steve Walsh .05
215 Wade Wilson .05
216 Vaughn Dunbar .05
217 Brad Muster .03
218 Dalton Hilliard .03
219 Floyd Turner .03
220 Stephen Baker .03
221 Mark Jackson .03
222 Jarrod Bunch .05
223 Mark Collins .03
224 Rodney Hampton .25
225 Phil Simms .10
226 Pepper Johnson .03
227 Dave Meggett .03
228 Derek Brown .03
229 Mike Sherrard .03
230 Lawrence Taylor .10
231 Leonard Marshall .03
232 Brad Baxter .03
233 Dennis Byrd .03
234 Ronnie Lott .05
235 Boomer Esiason .10
236 Browning Nagle .05
237 Rob Moore .05
238 Jeff Lageman .03
239 Johnny Mitchell .25
240 Chris Burkett .03
241 Eric Thomas .03
242 Johnny Johnson .10
243 Eric Allen .05
244 Fred Barnett .05
245 Keith Byars .03
246 Randall Cunningham .10
247 Heath Sherman .03
248 Calvin Williams .05
249 Erik McMillan .03
250 Byron Evans .03
251 Seth Joyner .03
252 Vai Sikahema .03
253 Andre Waters .03
254 Tim Harris .03
255 Mark Bavaro .03
256 Clyde Simmons .03
257 Steve Beuerlein .10
258 Randal Hill .05
259 Ernie Jones .03
260 Robert Massey .03
261 Ricky Proehl .05
262 Aeneas Williams .03
263 Johnny Bailey .03
264 Cris Chandler .03
265 Anthony Thompson .03
266 Gary Clark .05
267 Chuck Cecil .03
268 Rich Camarillo .03
269 Neil O'Donnell .25
270 Gerald Williams .03
271 Greg Lloyd .03
272 Eric Green .03
273 Merril Hoge .03
274 Ernie Mills .03
275 Rod Woodson .05
276 Gary Anderson .03
277 Barry Foster .10
278 Jeff Graham .03
279 Dwight Stone .03
280 Kevin Greene .03
281 Eric Bieniemy .03
282 Marion Butts .05
283 Gill Byrd .03
284 Stan Humphries .03
285 Anthony Miller .05
286 Leslie O'Neal .03
287 Junior Seau .15
288 Ronnie Harmon .03
289 Nate Lewis .03
290 John Kidd .03
291 Steve Young 1.00
292 John Taylor .06
293 Jerry Rice .75
294 Tim McDonald .03
295 Brent Jones .03
296 Tom Rathman .03
297 Dexter Carter .03
298 Mike Cofer .03
299 Ricky Watters .40
300 Mervyn Fernandez .03
301 Amp Lee .08
302 Kevin Fagan .03
303 Roy Foster .03
304 Bill Romanowski .03
305 Brian Blades .03
306 John L. Williams .03
307 Tommy Kane .03
308 John Kasay .03
309 Chris Warren .10
310 Rufus Porter .03
311 Cortez Kennedy .10
312 Dan McGwire .05
313 Stan Gelbaugh .03
314 Kelvin Martin .03
315 Ferrell Edmunds .03
316 Eugene Robinson .03
317 Gary Anderson .03
318 Reggie Cobb .05
319 Lawrence Dawsey .03
320 Courtney Hawkins .03
321 Santana Dotson .03
322 Ron Hall .03
323 Keith McCants .03
324 Martin Mayhew .03
325 Anthony Munoz .03
326 Steve DeBerg .03
327 Vince Workman .03
328 Earnest Byner .03
329 Ricky Ervins .05
330 Jim Lachey .03
331 Chip Lohmiller .03
332 Ricky Sanders .03
333 Brad Edwards .03
334 Tim McGee .03
335 Darrell Green .05
336 Charles Mann .03
337 Wilber Marshall .03
338 Brian Mitchell .05
339 Art Monk .05
340 Mark Rypien .08
341 John Elway (C83) .10
342 Jim Kelly (C83) .10
343 Dan Marino (C83) .20
344 Eric Dickerson (C83) .08
345 Willie Gault (C83) .05
346 Ken O'Brien (C83) .05
347 Darrell Green (C83) .05
348 Richard Dent (C83) .05
349 Karl Mecklenburg (C83) .03
350 Henry Ellard (C83) .03
351 Roger Craig (C83) .05
352 Charles Mann (C83) .03
353 Checklist A .03
354 Checklist B .03
355 Checklist C .03
356 Checklist D .03
357 Checklist E .03
358 Checklist F .03
359 Checklist G .03
360 Checklist (rookies) .03

361 *Drew Bledsoe* 2.50
362 *Rick Mirer* .25
363 *Garrison Hearst* 1.00
364 *Marvin Jones* .15
365 *John Copeland* .25
366 *Eric Curry* .25
367 *Curtis Conway* 1.00
368 *Willie Roaf* .15
369 *Lincoln Kennedy* .20
370 *Jerome Bettis* 1.00
371 *Dan Williams* .10
372 *Patrick Bates* .10
373 *Brad Hopkins* .10
374 *Steve Everett* .10
375 *Wayne Simmons* .10
376 *Tom Carter* .15
377 *Ernest Dye* .10
378 *Lester Holmes* .10
379 *Irv Smith* .25
380 *Robert Smith* 1.00
381 *Darrien Gordon* .20
382 *Deon Figures* .20
383 *O.J. McDuffie* .75
384 *Dana Stubblefield* .50
385 *Todd Kelly* .10
386 *Thomas Smith* .10
387 *George Teague* .25
388 *Carlton Gray* .10
389 *Chris Slade* .25
390 *Ben Coleman* .10
391 *Ryan McNeil* .10
392 *Demetrius DuBose* .20
393 *Carl Simpson* .10
394 *Coleman Rudolph* .10
395 *Tony McGee* .15
396 *Roger Harper* .15
397 *Troy Drayton* .25
398 *Michael Strahan* .10
399 *Natrone Means* 1.00
400 *Glyn Milburn* .60

1993 SkyBox Impact Colors

Colors was a 392-card set (400 minus the eight checklists) that came one per pack and were designated by UV coating and a foil Impact logo on the front in one of four colors - gold, silver, blue and red.

NM/M

Colors 2X-4X
1 Patrick Bates 3.00
2 Drew Bledsoe 25.00
3 Darrien Gordon 3.00
4 Garrison Hearst 16.00
5 Marvin Jones 3.00
6 Terry Kirby 5.00
7 Natrone Means 12.00
8 Rick Mirer 14.00
9 Willie Roaf 5.00
10 Dan Williams 3.00

1993 SkyBox Impact Kelly/Magic

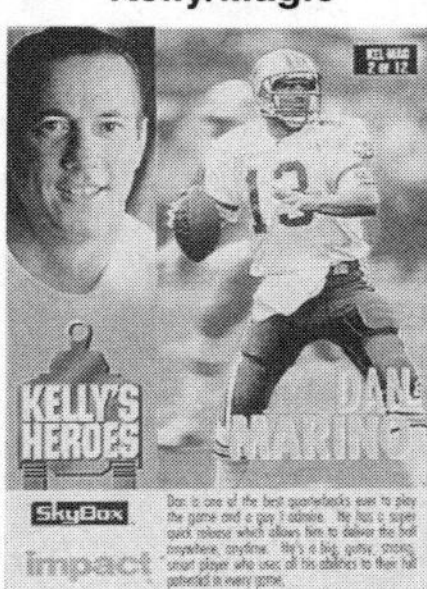

SkyBox spokesmen Jim Kelly and Magic Johnson selected a team of their favorite players for this insert set. The cards are foil stamped and indicate which player selected them by either a Kelly's Heroes logo or Magic's Kingdom logo on it, in a small panel along the left which has a player portrait shot. An action photo and the player's name are on the right. Each card has selection by both players on opposite sides. The cards were random inserts in foil packs. The two spokesmen also autographed 500 cards which were offered to those who found individually numbered redemption certificates randomly included among packs. Those who obtained cards 12 and 32, the uniform numbers of Kelly and Johnson, were to receive the autographed cards personally from the players.

NM/M

Complete Set (12): 10.00
Common Player: .50
Minor Stars: 1.00
Inserted 1:12
1 Title card .50
2 Dan Marino, Jim Kelly 3.00
3 Jay Novacek, Keith Jackson .50
4 Thurman Thomas, Barry Sanders 3.00
5 Barry Sanders, Emmitt Smith 3.00
6 Jerry Rice, Sterling Sharpe 2.00
7 Andre Reed, Jerry Rice 2.00
8 Thurman Thomas, Patrick Swilling 1.00
9 Darryl Talley, Lawrence Taylor 1.00
10 Rod Woodson, Darrell Green .50
11 Steve Tasker, Elvis Patterson .50
12 Morten Andersen, Chip Lowery .50

1993 SkyBox Impact Update

This 20-card set could be obtained by sending five Impact wrappers plus $3.99 for postage and handling. The set focuses on players who switched teams through free agency and pictures the player in his new uniform in front of the player in his old uniform. Cards are numbered and have a "U" prefix.

NM/M

Complete Set (20): 10.00
Common Player: .25
Minor Stars: .50
1 Pierce Holt .25
2 Vinny Testaverde .50
3 Rod Bernstine .25
4 Reggie White .50
5 Mark Clayton .25
6 Joe Montana 5.00
7 Marcus Allen .50
8 Jeff Hostetler .25
9 Shane Conlan .25
10 Brad Muster .25
11 Mike Sherrard .25
12 Ronnie Lott .50
13 Steve Beuerlein .25
14 Gary Clark .25
15 Kevin Greene .25
16 Tim McDonald .25
17 Wilber Marshall .25
18 Keith Byars .25
19 Pat Swilling .25
20 Boomer Esiason .25

1993 SkyBox Impact Rookie Redemption

This 29-card set features all of the first round picks from the 1993 NFL Draft, excluding Sean Dawkins (16th), who signed an exclusive contract with Courtside. The set could be obtained either by pulling a redemption card (seeded one per 180 packs) or by a second chance drawing. Cards picture the players in their pro uniforms, with the name running up the left side and the draft position in the lower right corner. Cards are numbered with a "R" prefix.

NM/M

Complete Set (29): 10.00
Common Player: .50
Minor Stars: 1.00
1 Drew Bledsoe Title Card/Checklist 1.00
2 Drew Bledsoe 3.00
3 Rick Mirer .50
4 Garrison Hearst 1.00
5 Marvin Jones .50
6 John Copeland .50
7 Eric Curry (UER) (Card front states he was selected in sixth round instead of sixth pick) .50
8 Curtis Conway .50
9 Willie Roaf .50
10 Lincoln Kennedy .50
11 Jerome Bettis 1.00
12 Dan Williams .50
13 Patrick Bates .50
14 Brad Hopkins .50
15 Steve Everitt .50
16 Wayne Simmons .50
17 Tom Carter .50
18 Ernest Dye .50
19 Lester Holmes .50
20 Irv Smith .50
21 Robert Smith 1.00
22 Darrien Gordon .50
23 Deon Figures .50
24 Leonard Renfro .50
25 O.J. McDuffie .50
26 Dana Stubblefield .50
27 Todd Kelly .50
28 Thomas Smith .50
29 George Teague .50
NNO Rookie Redemption Card Expired .50

1994 SkyBox Promos

Six different players and a commemorative card were issued for this set, which promotes the 1994 SkyBox Premium set. The cards are numbered S1-S6, with the commemorative card having no number.

NM/M

Complete Set (7): 4.00
Common Player: .50
1 Tom Carter .50
2 Gary Clark .50
3 James Jett .50
4 Jim Kelly 1.00
5 Ronnie Lott 1.50
6 John Taylor .50
NNO Sample Commemorative Game Card .50

1994 SkyBox Premium

SkyBox released its 1994 premium football set in a single-series, 200-card issue. Cards have a borderless design on the front and show a player against an action background, highlighted with team colors. The flip side presents an up-close photo, biographical information, 1993 season and NFL career stats and a scouting report written by Chris Mortensen. The regular-issue set contains several subsets, including 23 Prime Movers and 40 rookies. SkyBox also had various randomly inserted sets, autographed cards and a sweepstakes game card. Insert sets were entitled SkyTech Stars, SkyBox Revolution and Prime Time Rookies.

NM/M

Complete Set (200): 25.00
Common Player: .05
Minor Stars: .20
Pack (10): 1.00
Wax Box (36): 25.00
1 Steve Beuerlein .05
2 Gary Clark .05
3 Garrison Hearst 1.00
4 Ron Moore .05
5 Eric Swann .05
6 Chuck Cecil .05
7 Seth Joyner .05
8 Clyde Simmons .05
9 Andre Rison .20
10 Deion Sanders 1.00
11 Erric Pegram .05
12 Steve Broussard .05
13 Chris Doleman .05
14 Jeff George .30
15 Cornelius Bennett .05
16 Jim Kelly .20
17 Andre Reed .05
18 Bruce Smith .05
19 Darryl Talley .05
20 Thurman Thomas .30
21 Mark Carrier .05
22 Dante Jones .05
23 Curtis Conway .30
24 Tim Worley .05
25 Erik Kramer .05
26 John Copeland .05
27 David Klingler .05
28 Derrick Fenner .05
29 Harold Green .05
30 Carl Pickens .50
31 Tony McGee .05
32 Steve Everitt .05
33 Michael Jackson .05
34 Eric Metcalf .05
35 Vinny Testaverde .20
36 Michael Dean Perry .05
37 Troy Aikman 2.00
38 Alvin Harper .20
39 Michael Irvin .60
40 Jay Novacek .05
41 Emmitt Smith 4.00
42 Charles Haley .05
43 Daryl Johnston .05
44 Kevin Williams .30
45 Rodney Peete .05
46 John Elway 1.00
47 Shannon Sharpe .20
48 Rod Bernstine .05
49 Glyn Milburn .20
50 Mike Pritchard .05
51 Anthony Miller .05
52 Herman Moore 1.50
53 Barry Sanders 3.50
54 Scott Mitchell .20
55 Pat Swilling .05
56 Willie Green .05
57 Edgar Bennett .05
58 Brett Favre 4.00
59 Sterling Sharpe .20
60 Reggie White .20
61 Sean Jones .05
62 Reggie Cobb .05
63 Haywood Jeffires .05
64 Lorenzo White .05
65 Webster Slaughter .05
66 Gary Brown .05
67 Steve Emtman .05
68 Quentin Coryatt .05
69 *Sean Dawkins* .30
70 Jim Harbaugh .05
71 Tony Bennett .05
72 Marcus Allen .20
73 Steve Bono .20
74 Dale Carter .05
75 Joe Montana 3.00
76 Neil Smith .05
77 Derrick Thomas .20
78 Keith Cash .05
79 Tim Brown .20
80 Raghib Ismail .05
81 Jeff Hostetler .20
82 Patrick Bates .05
83 James Jett .05
84 Jerome Bettis 1.00
85 Chris Miller .05
86 Marc Boutte .05
87 Sean Gilbert .20
88 Keith Jackson .05
89 Terry Kirby .20
90 Dan Marino 4.00
91 Brian Cox .05
92 Bernie Kosar .05
93 Qadry Ismail .20
94 Robert Smith .25
95 Terry Allen .05
96 Scottie Graham .30
97 Warren Moon .20
98 Drew Bledsoe 3.00
99 Ben Coates .40
100 Leonard Russell .05
101 Vincent Brisby .40
102 Marion Butts .05
103 Morten Andersen .05
104 Derek Brown .05
105 Michael Haynes .05
106 Sam Mills .05
107 Lorenzo Neal .05
108 Willie Roaf .05
109 Jim Everett .05
110 Michael Brooks .05
111 Rodney Hampton .20
112 Dave Brown .20
113 Dave Meggett .05
114 Ronnie Lott .05
115 Boomer Esiason .05
116 Rob Moore .05
117 Johnny Johnson .05
118 Marvin Jones .05
119 Johnny Mitchell .05
120 Fred Barnett .05
121 Randall Cunningham .20
122 Herschel Walker .05
123 Calvin Williams .05
124 Neil O'Donnell .20
125 Eric Green .05
126 Leroy Thompson .05
127 Rod Woodson .20
128 Barry Foster .20
129 Deon Figures .05
130 John L. Williams .05
131 Chris Mims .05
132 Darrien Gordon .05
133 Stan Humphries .30
134 Natrone Means .75
135 Junior Seau .30
136 Brent Jones .05
137 Jerry Rice 3.00
138 Dana Stubblefield .20
139 John Taylor .05
140 Ricky Watters .20
141 Steve Young 3.00
142 Ken Norton .05
143 Brian Blades .05
144 Cortez Kennedy .20
145 Kelvin Martin .05
146 Rick Mirer .20
147 Chris Warren .20
148 Eric Curry .05
149 Santana Dotson .05
150 Craig Erickson .05
151 Hardy Nickerson .05
152 Paul Gruber .05
153 Reggie Brooks .20
154 Tom Carter .05
155 Desmond Howard .05
156 Ken Harvey .05
157 *Dan Wilkinson* .40
158 *Marshall Faulk* 4.00
159 *Heath Shuler* .50
160 *Willie McGinest* .50
161 *Trev Alberts* .20
162 *Trent Dilfer* 2.00
163 *Bryant Young* .50
164 *Sam Adams* .20
165 *Antonio Langham* .20
166 *Jamir Miller* .20
167 *John Thierry* .20
168 *Aaron Glenn* .20
169 *Joe Johnson* .20
170 *Bernard Williams* .20
171 *Wayne Gandy* .20
172 *Aaron Taylor* .20
173 *Charles Johnson* .50
174 *DeWayne Washington* .20
175 *Todd Steussie* .20
176 *Tim Bowens* .20
177 *Johnnie Morton* 1.00
178 *Rob Fredrickson* .20
179 *Shante Carver* .20
180 *Thomas Lewis* .20
181 *Greg Hill* .75
182 *Henry Ford* .20
183 *Jeff Burris* .20
184 *William Floyd* .50
185 *Derrick Alexander* .50
186 *Glenn Foley* 1.50
187 *Charlie Garner* 2.50
188 *Errict Rhett* .75
189 *Chuck Levy* .20
190 *Bam Morris* 1.00
191 *Donnell Bennett* .75
192 *LeShon Johnson* .20
193 *Mario Bates* .50
194 *David Palmer* .50
195 *Darnay Scott* 1.00
196 *Lake Dawson* .50
197 Checklist .05
198 Checklist .05
199 Checklist .05
200 Checklist for Insert Cards .05

1994 SkyBox Premium Inside the Numbers

Inside the Numbers is a 20-card set that features a borderless design on gold foil. The set was inserted at a rate of one per retail pack.

NM/M

Complete Set (20): 10.00
Common Player: .40
1 Jim Kelly .75
2 Ronnie Lott .75
3 Morten Andersen .40
4 Reggie White .75
5 Terry Kirby .60
6 Marcus Allen 1.00
7 Thurman Thomas 1.00
8 Joe Montana 4.00
9 Tom Carter .40
10 Jerome Bettis 1.00
11 Sterling Sharpe .75
12 Andre Rison .75
13 Reggie Brooks .40
14 Hardy Nickerson .60
15 Ricky Watters 1.00
16 Gary Brown .40
17 Natrone Means .50
18 LeShon Johnson .60
19 Errict Rhett .75
20 Trent Dilfer 1.00

1994 SkyBox QB Autograph Exchange Set

SkyBox randomly inserted 500 SkyBox QB Autograph Exchange Cards in its packs, giving collectors a chance to receive a limited, three-card autographed set of Ken Stabler, Jim Kelly and Trent Dilfer. Each set was presented in an individually numbered lucite card holder. Cards were numbered with a "QB" prefix.

NM/M

1 Ken Stabler 30.00
2 Jim Kelly 30.00
3 Trent Dilfer 20.00

1994 SkyBox Premium Revolution

This insert set provides an up-close look at 15 of the NFL's premium players. Each card front is printed with portrait photography on a pewter foil background. Revolution cards are numbered on the back with an "R" prefix and were inserted one every 20th pack of SkyBox Premium cards. The card back uses the player's team colors for a background, and includes a team logo and a player biography.

NM/M

Complete Set (15): 25.00
Common Player: 1.00
Minor Stars: 2.00
1 Jim Kelly 2.00
2 Thurman Thomas 2.00
3 Troy Aikman 5.00
4 Michael Irvin 2.00
5 Emmitt Smith 6.00
6 John Elway 4.00
7 Barry Sanders 5.00
8 Sterling Sharpe 2.00
9 Joe Montana 5.00
10 Jerome Bettis 2.00
11 Dan Marino 5.00
12 Drew Bledsoe 3.00
13 Jerry Rice 3.00
14 Steve Young 3.00
15 Rick Mirer 1.00

1994 SkyBox Premium Rookies

Prime Time Rookies consists of 10 Chris Mortensen-selected rookies who were expected to make the biggest impact in the 1994 season. Cards from this set were randomly inserted at a rate of one every 96th pack of SkyBox Premium cards. Card backs are numbered with a "PT" prefix.

NM/M

Complete Set (10): 50.00
Common Player: 2.00
1 Trent Dilfer 4.00
2 Heath Shuler 2.00
3 Marshall Faulk 20.00
4 Charlie Garner 5.00
5 Errict Rhett 4.00
6 Greg Hill 2.00
7 William Floyd 2.00
8 Charles Johnson 2.00
9 Derrick Alexander 2.00
10 David Palmer 2.00

1994 SkyBox Premium SkyTech Stars

SkyTech Stars were found in one of every six packs of SkyBox Premium cards. The set features 30 selected players printed over a foil background; cards are the same as they appear in the regular set except for the foil printing. Cards are numbered on the back with an "ST" prefix and include a photo, team logo, biography and statistics.

NM/M

Complete Set (30): 25.00
Common Player: .50

Minor Stars:		1.00
1	Troy Aikman	3.00
2	Emmitt Smith	4.00
3	Michael Irvin	1.00
4	John Elway	3.00
5	Sterling Sharpe	1.00
6	Joe Montana	4.00
7	Drew Bledsoe	3.00
8	Rick Mirer	1.00
9	Junior Seau	1.00
10	Jerome Bettis	1.00
11	Rod Woodson	.50
12	Tim Brown	1.00
13	Jeff George	1.00
14	Brett Favre	4.00
15	Reggie White	1.00
16	Cortez Kennedy	.50
17	Ricky Watters	1.00
18	Shannon Sharpe	.50
19	Reggie Brooks	.50
20	Heath Shuler	1.00
21	Marshall Faulk	4.00
22	Thurman Thomas	1.00
23	Barry Foster	.50
24	Sean Gilbert	.50
25	Jerry Rice	3.00
26	Andre Rison	1.00
27	Barry Sanders	4.00
28	Jim Kelly	1.00
29	Steve Young	3.00
30	Dan Marino	4.00

1994 SkyBox Impact Promos

This six-card set was issued to preview the SkyBox Impact set and carried the same card designs as the regular-issue cards. The cards are numbered with an "S" prefix on the back. In addition, the cards were also issued as a 7-1/2" x 8-1/2" unperforated sheet at the 1994 National Sports Collectors Convention.

		NM/M
Complete Set (6):		4.00
Common Player:		.50
1	Marcus Allen	1.00
2	Chris Doleman	.50
3	Craig Erickson	.50
4	Jim Kelly	2.00
5	Reggie Roby	.50
6	Rod Woodson	1.00

1994 SkyBox Impact

These cards feature a borderless design which shows a player highlighted against a ghosted action background. The set's name is in one of the bottom corners; the player's name is in a top corner. The card back has an oversized action photo, biographical information, stats, a card number and a player profile. There are 30 rookies and five checklists in the set. Insert cards included with the set are: Instant Impact Rookies (one in 30 packs); Ultimate Impact Players (one in 15 packs); and the SkyBox Impact NFL Rookie Exchange Card, found one in every 350 packs. This "IOU" card is redeemable for a limited-edition set of NFL first-round draft choice selections pictured in their NFL uniforms. There were also six promo cards created to preview the regular set. They have the same basic design, except they are numbered with an "S" prefix.

		NM/M
Complete Set (300):		15.00
Common Player:		.05
Minor Stars:		.10
Pack (12):		.75
Wax Box (36):		25.00
1	Johnny Bailey	.05
2	Steve Beuerlein	.05
3	Gary Clark	.05
4	Garrison Hearst	.50
5	Ron Moore	.05
6	Ricky Proehl	.05
7	Eric Swann	.05
8	Aeneas Williams	.05
9	Robert Massey	.05
10	Chuck Cecil	.05
11	Ken Harvey	.05
12	Michael Haynes	.05
13	Tony Smith	.05
14	Bobby Hebert	.05
15	Mike Pritchard	.05
16	Andre Rison	.10
17	Deion Sanders	.50
18	Pierce Holt	.05
19	Erric Pegram	.10
20	Jessie Tuggle	.05
21	Steve Broussard	.05
22	Don Beebe	.05
23	Cornelius Bennett	.05
24	Kenneth Davis	.05
25	Bill Brooks	.05
26	Jim Kelly	.10
27	Andre Reed	.05
28	Bruce Smith	.05
29	Darryl Talley	.05
30	Thurman Thomas	.10
31	Steve Tasker	.05
32	Neal Anderson	.05
33	Mark Carrier	.05
34	Richard Dent	.05
35	Jim Harbaugh	.10
36	Chris Gedney	.05
37	Tom Waddle	.05
38	Curtis Conway	.50
39	Dante Jones	.05
40	Donnell Woolford	.05
41	Tim Worley	.05
42	John Copeland	.05
43	David Klingler	.05
44	Derrick Fenner	.05
45	Harold Green	.05
46	Carl Pickens	.50
47	Tony McGee	.05
48	Darryl Williams	.05
49	Steve Everitt	.05
50	Michael Jackson	.05
51	Eric Metcalf	.05
52	Tommy Vardell	.05
53	Vinny Testaverde	.05
54	Mark Carrier	.05
55	Michael Dean Perry	.05
56	Eric Turner	.05
57	Troy Aikman	1.00
58	Alvin Harper	.10
59	Michael Irvin	.10
60	Leon Lett	.05
61	Russell Maryland	.05
62	Jay Novacek	.05
63	Emmitt Smith	2.00
64	Ken Norton Jr.	.05
65	Charles Haley	.05
66	Daryl Johnston	.05
67	Kevin Smith	.05
68	James Washington	.05
69	Kevin Williams	.30
70	Bernie Kosar	.05
71	Mike Croel	.05
72	John Elway	.50
73	Shannon Sharpe	.05
74	Rod Bernstine	.05
75	Simon Fletcher	.05
76	Arthur Marshall	.05
77	Glyn Milburn	.05
78	Dennis Smith	.05
79	Herman Moore	.50
80	Rodney Peete	.10
81	Barry Sanders	1.25
82	Mel Gray	.05
83	Erik Kramer	.10
84	Pat Swilling	.05
85	Willie Green	.05
86	Chris Spielman	.05
87	Robert Porcher	.05
88	Derrick Moore	.05
89	Edgar Bennett	.05
90	Tony Bennett	.05
91	LeRoy Butler	.05
92	Brett Favre	2.00
93	Jackie Harris	.05
94	Sterling Sharpe	.10
95	Darrell Thompson	.05
96	Reggie White	.10
97	Terrell Buckley	.05
98	Cris Dishman	.05
99	Ernest Givins	.05
100	Haywood Jeffires	.05
101	Warren Moon	.10
102	Lorenzo White	.05
103	Webster Slaughter	.05
104	Ray Childress	.05
105	Wilbur Marshall	.05
106	Gary Brown	.05
107	Mariusu Robertson	.05
108	Sean Jones	.05
109	Jeff George	.10
110	Steve Emtman	.05
111	Quentin Coryatt	.05
112	*Sean Dawkins*	.40
113	Jeff Herrod	.05
114	Roosevelt Potts	.05
115	Marcus Allen	.10
116	Kimble Anders	.05
117	Tim Barnett	.05
118	J.J. Birden	.05
119	Dale Carter	.05
120	Willie Davis	.05
121	Nick Lowery	.05
122	Joe Montana	1.00
123	Kevin Ross	.05
124	Neil Smith	.05
125	Derrick Thomas	.05
126	Keith Cash	.05
127	Tim Brown	.10
128	Raghib Ismail	.05
129	Ethan Horton	.05
130	Jeff Hostetler	.10
131	Patrick Bates	.05
132	Terry McDaniel	.05
133	Anthony Smith	.05
134	Greg Robinson	.05
135	James Jett	.05
136	Alexander Wright	.05
137	Willie Anderson	.05
138	Shane Conlan	.05
139	Jim Everett	.05
140	Henry Ellard	.05
141	Jerome Bettis	.25
142	Troy Drayton	.05
143	Sean Gilbert	.05
144	Chris Miller	.05
145	Keith Byars	.05
146	Marco Coleman	.05
147	Bryan Cox	.05
148	Irving Fryar	.05
149	Mark Ingram	.05
150	Keith Jackson	.05
151	Terry Kirby	.05
152	Dan Marino	2.00
153	O.J. McDuffie	.20
154	Scott Mitchell	.10
155	Anthony Carter	.05
156	Cris Carter	.10
157	Chris Doleman	.05
158	Steve Jordan	.05
159	Qadry Ismail	.05
160	Randall McDaniel	.05
161	John Randle	.05
162	Robert Smith	.20
163	Henry Thomas	.05
164	Terry Allen	.05
165	*Scottie Graham*	.10
166	Drew Bledsoe	1.00
167	Vincent Brown	.05
168	Ben Coates	.05
169	Leonard Russell	.05
170	Andre Tippett	.05
171	Vincent Brisby	.05
172	Michael Timpson	.05
173	Bruce Armstrong	.05
174	Morten Andersen	.05
175	Derek Brown	.05
176	Quinn Early	.05
177	Rickey Jackson	.05
178	Vaughan Johnson	.05
179	Lorenzo Neal	.05
180	Sam Mills	.05
181	Irv Smith	.05
182	Renaldo Turnbull	.05
183	Wade Wilson	.05
184	Willie Roaf	.05
185	Michael Brooks	.05
186	Mark Jackson	.05
187	Rodney Hampton	.10
188	Phil Simms	.05
189	Dave Meggett	.05
190	Mike Sherrard	.05
191	Chris Calloway	.05
192	Brad Baxter	.05
193	Ronnie Lott	.05
194	Boomer Esiason	.05
195	Rob Moore	.05
196	Johnny Johnson	.05
197	Marvin Jones	.10
198	Mo Lewis	.05
199	Johnny Mitchell	.05
200	Brian Washington	.05
201	Eric Allen	.05
202	Fred Barnett	.05
203	Mark Bavaro	.05
204	Randall Cunningham	.10
205	Vaughn Hebron	.05
206	Seth Joyner	.05
207	Clyde Simmons	.05
208	Herschel Walker	.05
209	Calvin Williams	.05
210	Neil O'Donnell	.10
211	Eric Green	.05
212	Leroy Thompson	.05
213	Rod Woodson	.05
214	Barry Foster	.05
215	Jeff Graham	.05
216	Kevin Greene	.05
217	Deon Figures	.05
218	Greg Lloyd	.10
219	Marion Butts	.05
220	Chris Mims	.05
221	Darrien Gordon	.05
222	Ronnie Harmon	.05
223	Stan Humphries	.10
224	Nate Lewis	.05
225	Natrone Means	.40
226	Anthony Miller	.05
227	Leslie O'Neal	.05
228	Junior Seau	.10
229	Brent Jones	.05
230	Tim McDonald	.05
231	Tom Rathman	.05
232	Jerry Rice	1.00
233	Dana Stubblefield	.10
234	John Taylor	.05
235	Ricky Watters	.10
236	Steve Young	1.00
237	Amp Lee	.05
238	Robert Blackmon	.05
239	Brian Blades	.05
240	Cortez Kennedy	.05
241	Kelvin Martin	.05
242	Rick Mirer	.25
243	Eugene Robinson	.05
244	Chris Warren	.10
245	John L. Williams	.05
246	Jon Vaughn	.05
247	Reggie Cobb	.05
248	Horace Copeland	.05
249	*Derrick Alexander*	.25
250	Santana Dotson	.05
251	Craig Erickson	.05
252	Courtney Hawkins	.05
253	Hardy Nickerson	.05
254	Vince Workman	.05
255	Paul Gruber	.05
256	Reggie Brooks	.05
257	Tom Carter	.05
258	Andre Collins	.05
259	Darrell Green	.05
260	Desmond Howard	.05
261	Tim McGee	.05
262	Brian Mitchell	.05
263	Art Monk	.05
264	John Friesz	.05
265	Ricky Sanders	.05
266	Checklist A	.05
267	Checklist B	.05
268	Checklist C	.05
269	Checklist D	.05
270	Checklist E	.05
271	Carolina Panthers	.20
272	Jacksonville Jaguars	.20
273	*Dan Wilkinson*	.10
274	*Marshall Faulk*	4.00
275	*Heath Shuler*	.25
276	*Willie McGinest*	.25
277	*Trev Alberts*	.10
278	*Trent Dilfer*	.50
279	*Bryant Young*	.40
280	*Sam Adams*	.10
281	*Antonio Langham*	.10
282	*Jamir Miller*	.10
283	*John Thierry*	.10
284	*Aaron Glenn*	.10
285	*Joe Johnson*	.10
286	*Bernard Williams*	.10
287	*Wayne Gandy*	.10
288	*Aaron Taylor*	.10
289	*Charles Johnson*	.50
290	*DeWayne Washington*	.10
291	*Todd Steussie*	.10
292	*Tim Bowens*	.10
293	*Johnnie Morton*	.50
294	*Rob Fredrickson*	.10
295	*Shante Carver*	.10
296	*Thomas Lewis*	.10
297	*Greg Hill*	.50
298	*Henry Ford*	.10
299	*Jeff Burris*	.10
300	*William Floyd*	.50
NNO	Carolina Panthers	10.00

1994 SkyBox Impact Instant Impact

Each of these card fronts features a full-bleed color photo against a faded background. The Instant Impact logo is stamped in gold foil in the lower right corner, while the player's name is in the upper left corner in team color-coded boxes. The backs are horizontal and have another action photo, plus a brief player profile. The player's name and team logo are in a color stripe at the top of the card, next to "Instant Impact," which is written in a black box. Cards, numbered with an "R" prefix, were randomly inserted one out of every 30th SkyBox Impact pack.

		NM/M
Complete Set (12):		20.00
Common Player:		1.00
1	Rick Mirer	1.00
2	Jerome Bettis	3.00
3	Reggie Brooks	1.00
4	Terry Kirby	1.00
5	Vincent Brisby	1.00
6	James Jett	1.00
7	Drew Bledsoe	6.00
8	Dana Stubblefield	1.00
9	Natrone Means	1.00
10	Curtis Conway	2.00
11	O.J. McDuffie	2.00
12	Garrison Hearst	2.00

1994 SkyBox Impact Quarterback Update

This 10-card set contains traded and rookie quarterbacks in their new uniforms and are identical to the Impact base card design. The set was available through a redemption offer, as well as a one per pack retail exclusive insert.

		NM/M
Complete Set (11):		5.00
Common Player:		.40
1	Warren Moon	.60
2	Trent Dilfer	.75
3	Jeff George	.60
4	Heath Shuler	.75
5	Jim Harbaugh	.60
6	Rodney Peete	.40
7	Chris Miller	.40
8	Jim Everett	.40
9	Scott Mitchell	.60
10	Erik Kramer	.40
NNO	Checklist	.40

1994 SkyBox Impact Rookie Redemption

This redemption set included the first 29 players chosen in the 1994 NFL Draft. The redemption card was randomly inserted into packs of 1994 SkyBox Impact.

		NM/M
Complete Set (30):		10.00
Common Player:		.25
Minor Stars:		.50
1	Dan Wilkinson	.50
2	Marshall Faulk	5.00
3	Heath Shuler	1.00
4	Willie McGinest	.50
5	Trev Alberts	.25
6	Trent Dilfer	3.00
7	Bryant Young	.50
8	Sam Adams	.25
9	Antonio Langham	.25
10	Jamir Miller	.25
11	John Thierry	.25
12	Aaron Glenn	.50
13	Joe Johnson	.25
14	Bernard Williams	.25
15	Wayne Gandy	.25
16	Aaron Taylor	.25
17	Charles Johnson	1.00
18	DeWayne Washington	.50
19	Todd Steussie	.50
20	Tim Bowens	.25
21	Johnnie Morton	1.00
22	Rob Fredrickson	.25
23	Shante Carver	.25
24	Thomas Lewis	.25
25	Greg Hill	1.00
26	Henry Ford	.25
27	Jeff Burris	.25
28	William Floyd	1.00
29	Derrick Alexander (WR)	1.00
NNO	Rookie Redemption Exp.	.50

1994 SkyBox Impact Ultimate Impact

These cards, randomly inserted in every 15th pack of 1994 SkyBox Impact cards, feature 15 top NFL players. Each card front has a color action photo against a borderless background. The player's name is spelled out in boxes at the top. The Ultimate logo is stamped in silver foil in the lower right corner. Each card back is numbered with a "U" prefix and is in a horizontal format. A color action shot takes up more than half of the card. A player profile fills the rest.

		NM/M
Complete Set (15):		40.00
Common Player:		1.00
Minor Stars:		2.00
1	Troy Aikman	4.00
2	Emmitt Smith	5.00
3	Michael Irvin	1.00
4	Joe Montana	5.00
5	Jerry Rice	4.00
6	Sterling Sharpe	1.00
7	Steve Young	4.00
8	Ricky Watters	1.00
9	Barry Sanders	5.00
10	John Elway	4.00
11	Reggie White	1.00
12	Jim Kelly	2.00
13	Thurman Thomas	1.00
14	Dan Marino	5.00
15	Brett Favre	5.00

1995 SkyBox

SkyBox Premium football for 1995 includes 200 cards, comprised of 120 veteran players, 40 rookies, 10 Style Points, 10 Mirror Images and four each for the Jacksonville and Carolina expansion teams. Each card has a color action photo of the player on the left, with his team name and position along the right side in a sandpaper-colored panel. The player's name is in the lower left corner, with a gold foil SkyBox logo sandwiched in between. The back has a mug shot, biographical information, 1994 and career stats, and a player profile, all against a background of his team's primary color. Insert sets include Paydirt, QuickStrike, The Promise and Prime Time Rookies. Also, Premium Moments merchandise cards, offering collectors a chance to purchase autographed memorabilia, were included one per hobby pack. In every sixth retail pack, the cards are replaced by a decoder game card called Great Men Make Great Moments Make Great Cards, which could be decoded at special displays at participating hobby shops.

		NM/M
Complete Set (200):		20.00
Common Player:		.05
Minor Stars:		.20
Pack (10):		1.00
Wax Box (36):		20.00
1	Garrison Hearst	.20
2	Dave Krieg	.05
3	Rob Moore	.05
4	Eric Swann	.05
5	Larry Centers	.05
6	Jeff George	.20
7	Craig Heyward	.05
8	Terance Mathis	.05
9	Eric Metcalf	.05
10	Jim Kelly	.20
11	Andre Reed	.05
12	Bruce Smith	.05
13	Thurman Thomas	.20
14	Randy Baldwin	.05
15	Don Beebe	.05
16	Barry Foster	.05
17	Lamar Lathon	.05
18	Frank Reich	.05
19	Jeff Graham	.05
20	Raymont Harris	.05
21	Lewis Tillman	.05
22	Michael Timpson	.05
23	*Jeff Blake*	.50
24	Carl Pickens	.20
25	Darnay Scott	.50
26	Dan Wilkinson	.05
27	Derrick Alexander	.25
28	Leroy Hoard	.05
29	Antonio Langham	.05
30	Andre Rison	.20
31	Eric Turner	.05
32	Troy Aikman	1.00
33	Michael Irvin	.30
34	Darryl Johnston	.05
35	Emmitt Smith	2.00
36	John Elway	.40
37	Glyn Milburn	.05
38	Anthony Miller	.05
39	Shannon Sharpe	.05
40	Scott Mitchell	.05
41	Herman Moore	.20
42	Barry Sanders	2.00
43	Chris Spielman	.05
44	Edgar Bennett	.05
45	Robert Brooks	.05
46	Brett Favre	2.00
47	Reggie White	.20
48	Mel Gray	.05
49	Haywood Jeffires	.05
50	Webster Slaughter	.05
51	Craig Erickson	.05
52	Quentin Coryatt	.05
53	Sean Dawkins	.05
54	Marshall Faulk	1.00
55	Steve Beuerlein	.05
56	Reggie Cobb	.05
57	Desmond Howard	.05
58	Ernest Givins	.05
59	Jeff Lageman	.05
60	Marcus Allen	.20
61	Steve Bono	.25
62	Greg Hill	.25
63	Derrick Thomas	.20
64	Tim Bowens	.05
65	Irving Fryar	.05
66	Eric Green	.05
67	Terry Kirby	.05
68	Dan Marino	2.00
69	O.J. McDuffie	.05
70	Bernie Parmalee	.25
71	Terry Allen	.05
72	Cris Carter	.20
73	Qadry Ismail	.05
74	Warren Moon	.20
75	Jake Reed	.05
76	Drew Bledsoe	1.00
77	Vincent Brisby	.05
78	Ben Coates	.05
79	Dave Meggett	.05
80	Mario Bates	.30
81	Jim Everett	.05
82	Michael Haynes	.05
83	Tyrone Hughes	.05
84	Dave Brown	.05
85	Rodney Hampton	.05
86	Thomas Lewis	.05
87	Herschel Walker	.05
88	Mike Sherrard	.05
89	Boomer Esiason	.05
90	Aaron Glenn	.05
91	Johnny Johnson	.05
92	Johnny Mitchell	.05
93	Ron Moore	.05
94	Tim Brown	.20
95	Raghib Ismail	.05
96	Jeff Hostetler	.20
97	Chester McGlockton	.05
98	Fred Barnett	.05
99	Randall Cunningham	.05
100	Charlie Garner	.05
101	Ricky Watters	.20
102	Calvin Williams	.05
103	Charles Johnson	.30
104	Bam Morris	.05
105	Neil O'Donnell	.05
106	Rod Woodson	.05
107	Jerome Bettis	.30
108	Troy Drayton	.05
109	Sean Gilbert	.05
110	Chris Miller	.05
111	Leonard Russell	.05
112	Ronnie Harmon	.05
113	Stan Humphries	.20
114	Shawn Jefferson	.05

115	Natrone Means	.20
116	Junior Seau	.20
117	William Floyd	.40
118	Brent Jones	.05
119	Jerry Rice	1.00
120	Deion Sanders	1.00
121	Dana Stubblefield	.05
122	Bryant Young	.05
123	Steve Young	1.00
124	Brian Blades	.05
125	Cortez Kennedy	.05
126	Rick Mirer	.40
127	Ricky Proehl	.05
128	Chris Warren	.20
129	Horace Copeland	.05
130	Trent Dilfer	.50
131	Alvin Harper	.20
132	Jackie Harris	.05
133	Hardy Nickerson	.05
134	Errict Rhett	.20
135	Henry Ellard	.05
136	Brian Mitchell	.05
137	Heath Shuler	.75
138	Tydus Winans	.05
139	Drew Bledsoe, Brett Favre	1.00
140	Marshall Faulk, William Floyd	1.00
141	Brett Favre, Trent Dilfer	.50
142	Dan Marino, Brett Favre	1.00
143	Errict Rhett, Trent Dilfer	.50
144	Jerry Rice, Eric Turner	.50
145	Andre Rison, Eric Turner	.05
146	Barry Sanders, Dave Meggett	.50
147	Emmitt Smith, Daryl Johnston	.75
148	Steve Young, Brett Favre	1.00
149	Emmitt Smith, Errict Rhett	.75
150	Barry Sanders, Marshall Faulk	1.00
151	Jerry Rice, Darnay Scott	.50
152	Daryl Johnston, William Floyd	.25
153	Dan Marino, Trent Dilfer	1.00
154	John Elway, Heath Shuler	.40
155	Natrone Means, Bam Morris	.30
156	Dan Wilkinson, Reggie White	.05
157	Rodney Hampton, Mario Bates	.05
158	Marvin Jones, Junior Seau	.05
159	*Ki-Jana Carter*	.50
160	*Tony Boselli*	.20
161	*Steve McNair*	4.00
162	*Michael Westbrook*	1.50
163	*Kerry Collins*	2.00
164	*Kevin Carter*	.20
165	*Mike Mamula*	.20
166	*Joey Galloway*	2.00
167	*Kyle Brady*	.20
168	*J.J. Stokes*	1.50
169	*Warren Sapp*	.75
170	*Rob Johnson*	1.00
171	*Tyrone Wheatley*	.75
172	*Napoleon Kaufman*	1.50
173	*James Stewart*	3.00
174	*Joe Aska*	.25
175	*Rashaan Salaam*	.40
176	*Tyrone Poole*	.20
177	*Ty Law*	.20
178	*Dino Philyaw*	.20
179	*Mark Bruener*	.20
180	*Derrick Brooks*	.20
181	*Jack Jackson*	.20
182	*Ray Zellars*	.20
183	*Eddie Goines*	.20
184	*Chris Sanders*	.40
185	*Charlie Simmons*	.20
186	*Lee DeRamus*	.20
187	*Frank Sanders*	.30
188	*Rodney Thomas*	.20
189	*Steve Stenstrom*	.20
190	*Stoney Case*	.25
191	*Tyrone Davis*	.20
192	*Kordell Stewart*	2.00
193	*Christian Fauria*	.25
194	*Todd Collins*	.20
195	*Sherman Williams*	.20
196	*Lovell Pinckney*	.20
197	*Eric Zeier*	.20
198	*Zack Crockett*	.20
199	Checklist A	.05
200	Checklist B	.05

1995 SkyBox Inside the Numbers

Inside the Numbers featured 20 players on a design that was very similar to the regular-issue set. These were seeded at a rate of one per retail pack.

		NM/M
Complete Set (20):		15.00
Common Player:		.40
1	William Floyd	.75
2	Marshall Faulk	1.50
3	Warren Moon	.75
4	Cris Carter	.75
5	Deion Sanders	1.50
6	Drew Bledsoe	2.50
7	Natrone Means	1.00
8	Herschel Walker	.40
9	Ben Coates	.75
10	Mel Gray	.40
11	Barry Sanders	3.00
12	Steve Young	2.00
13	Rashaan Salaam	2.00
14	Andre Reed	.40
15	Tyrone Hughes	.40
16	Eric Turner	.40
17	Ki-Jana Carter	.50
18	Dan Marino	5.00
19	Errict Rhett	1.50
20	Jerry Rice	2.50

1995 SkyBox Paydirt

These 1995 SkyBox Premium football inserts feature 30 of the top NFL players who can put the ball in the end zone. Each card front has a color action photo, with the player's name at the bottom in gold foil. Gold foil yard markers run along the left side of the card, which has a prismatic background which alternates between saying SkyBox and Paydirt. The card back is numbered with a "PD" prefix and features a square in the upper right corner with a photo inside, plus a brief description of the player's talents below. "Paydirt" is written along the left side of the card. Cards were random inserts, one every four packs.

		NM/M
Complete Set (30):		25.00
Common Gold Player:		.40
Minor Gold Stars:		1.00
Colors Cards:		2X-4X
1	Troy Aikman	2.00
2	J.J. Stokes	1.00
3	Ki-Jana Carter	1.00
4	Steve McNair	2.00
5	Jerome Bettis	.40
6	Tim Brown	.40
7	Cris Carter	.40
8	John Elway	3.00
9	Marshall Faulk	1.00
10	Brett Favre	4.00
11	Michael Westbrook	1.00
12	Rodney Hampton	.40
13	Michael Irvin	1.00
14	Dan Marino	4.00
15	Natrone Means	.50
16	David Meggett	.40
17	Joey Galloway	1.00
18	Herman Moore	1.00
19	Bam Morris	.40
20	Carl Pickens	.50
21	Errict Rhett	.50
22	Kerry Collins	1.00
23	Barry Sanders	3.00
24	Deion Sanders	1.00
25	Emmitt Smith	3.00
26	Thurman Thomas	1.00
27	Ricky Watters	.40
28	Rod Woodson	.40
29	Chris Warren	.40
30	Steve Young	2.00

1995 SkyBox The Promise

This 1995 SkyBox Premium insert set features 18 young stars. The cards, included one per 24 packs, have a color action photo on the front, with a large ghosted head shot as the background. The card has a gold metallic effect, and uses gold foil for the insert set name. The back is horizontal and includes a small photo and a brief summary of the player's accomplishments. Cards are numbered with a "P" prefix in the upper right corner.

		NM/M
Complete Set (14):		15.00
Common Player:		.50
Minor Stars:		1.00
1	Derrick Alexander	1.00
2	Mario Bates	1.00
3	Trent Dilfer	1.00
4	Marshall Faulk	4.00
5	William Floyd	1.00
6	Aaron Glenn	1.00
7	Raymont Harris	1.00
8	Greg Hill	1.00
9	Charles Johnson	1.00
10	Bam Morris	1.00
11	Errict Rhett	.50
12	Darnay Scott	.50
13	Heath Shuler	.50
14	Dan Wilkinson	1.00

1995 SkyBox Quick Strike

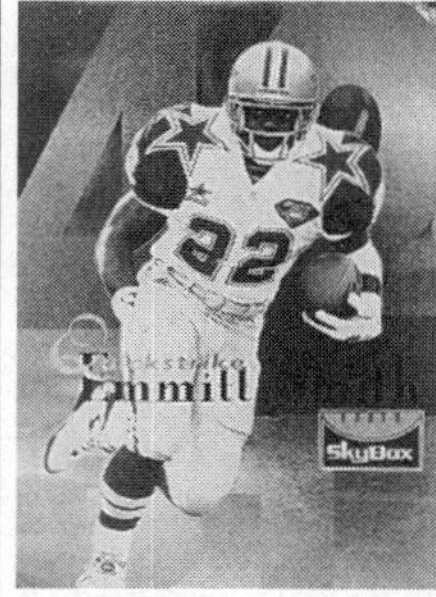

These 1995 SkyBox Premium inserts feature 10 of the NFL's most potent scoring threats. The cards were random inserts, one per 12 packs. The card front has an action photo of the player, against a metallic-like background which has the score of one of his team's wins in which he played a prominent role. The insert set and SkyBox logos are stamped in gold foil. The horizontal back has a photo and a brief summary of the game. Cards are numbered with a "Q" prefix.

		NM/M
Complete Set (10):		15.00
Common Player:		1.00
1	Chris Warren	1.00
2	Marshall Faulk	3.00
3	William Floyd	1.00
4	Jerry Rice	3.00
5	Eric Turner	1.00
6	Tim Brown	1.00
7	Deion Sanders	2.00
8	Emmitt Smith	4.00
9	Rod Woodson	1.00
10	Steve Young	3.00

1995 SkyBox Rookie Receivers

This eight-card set was inserted as a complete set in every retail box. The cards are identical in design to the rookies in the regular-issue set, except for the numbering which is "X" of 8.

		NM/M
Complete Set (8):		5.00
Common Player:		.50
1	Michael Westbrook	1.00
2	Joey Galloway	1.50
3	J.J. Stokes	1.00
4	Frank Sanders	.75
5	Chris Sanders	.75
6	Tyrone Davis	.50
7	Jimmy Oliver	.50
NNO	Cover/Checklist Card	.50

1995 SkyBox Prime Time Rookies

These 1995 SkyBox Premium inserts feature 10 rookies who might be destined for greatness in the NFL. These cards were included one per 96 packs and are numbered using a "PT" prefix. The card front has a photo of the player superimposed against a clockface. Gold foil stamping is used for the player's name and insert set name, which appears at the bottom of the card in script. The horizontal back has a photo on one side, and biographical and collegiate information on the other, all against a background of cogs.

		NM/M
Complete Set (10):		60.00
Common Player:		2.00
1	Ki-Jana Carter	2.00
2	Kerry Collins	10.00
3	Joey Galloway	8.00
4	Steve McNair	15.00
5	Rashaan Salaam	2.00
6	James Stewart	5.00
7	J.J. Stokes	5.00
8	Rodney Thomas	2.00
9	Michael Westbrook	5.00
10	Tyrone Wheatley	2.00

1995 SkyBox Impact

SkyBox Impact's 1995 NFL football set has 200 cards, including 30 top rookies, five cards each for the expansion Jacksonville Jaguars and Carolina Panthers, and subsets such as Specialists and Super Sophs. Each UV-coated front has a full-bleed color action photo, with the player's name and position at the bottom, flanked by a SkyBox logo. The player's first name is stamped in gold foil. The card back is horizontal, with a photo on the right with career stats printed over it. All 49ers cards have a Super Bowl Champion logo on them. The card number is in a black circle in the upper right corner. The left side of the card has the player's name at the top in team color-coded bars. Below follows a team logo and biographical information, then a brief player profile. Insert sets include the hobby-only Future Hall of Famers, Impact Power, Fox More Attitude, and Countdown to Impact. Included in each pack is a SkyBox/NFL on Fox Play Action Match & Win instant win game card, which gave collectors a chance to win tickets and a VIP trip to the 1995-96 NFC Championship Game, NFL on Fox varsity jackets, T-shirts, caps and 1995 SkyBox Premium NFL packs. In addition, there is a redemption for a SkyMotion card, which captures three seconds of actual game action. There are two cards, both of Brett Favre (one running, one passing). One is available through the redemption card (one per 360 packs), the other through an on-wrapper offer.

		NM/M
Complete Set (200):		15.00
Common Player:		.05
Minor Stars:		.10
Hobby Pack (12):		1.00
Hobby Wax Box (36):		30.00
Retail Pack (12):		.50
Retail Wax Box (36):		20.00
1	Garrison Hearst	.10
2	Ron Moore	.05
3	Eric Swann	.05
4	Aeneas Williams	.05
5	Jeff George	.05
6	Craig Heyward	.05
7	Terrance Mathis	.05
8	Andre Rison	.10
9	Cornelius Bennett	.05
10	Jim Kelly	.10
11	Andre Reed	.05
12	Bruce Smith	.05
13	Thurman Thomas	.15
14	Frank Reich	.05
15	Lamar Lathon	.05
16	Darrien Connor	.05
17	Randy Baldwin	.05
18	Don Beebe	.05
19	Mark Carrier	.05
20	Jeff Graham	.05
21	Raymont Harris	.15
22	Alonzo Spellman	.05
23	Lewis Tillman	.05
24	Steve Walsh	.05
25	*Jeff Blake*	.50
26	Carl Pickens	.05
27	Darnay Scott	.40
28	Dan Wilkinson	.05
29	Derrick Alexander	.20
30	Leroy Hoard	.05
31	Antonio Langham	.05
32	Vinny Testaverde	.05
33	Eric Turner	.05
34	Troy Aikman	.75
35	Charles Haley	.05
36	Alvin Harper	.05
37	Michael Irvin	.20
38	Daryl Johnston	.05
39	Jay Novacek	.05
40	Leon Lett	.05
41	Emmitt Smith	1.50
42	John Elway	.25
43	Glyn Milburn	.05
44	Anthony Miller	.05
45	Leonard Russell	.05
46	Shannon Sharpe	.10
47	Scott Mitchell	.05
48	Herman Moore	.10
49	Barry Sanders	1.00
50	Chris Spielman	.05
51	Edgar Bennett	.05
52	Robert Brooks	.05
53	Brett Favre	1.50
54	Bryce Paup	.05
55	Sterling Sharpe	.10
56	Reggie White	.10
57	Ray Childress	.05
58	Haywood Jeffires	.05
59	Webster Slaughter	.05
60	Lorenzo White	.05
61	Trev Alberts	.05
62	Quentin Coryatt	.05
63	Sean Dawkins	.15
64	Marshall Faulk	.50
65	Jeff Lageman	.05
66	Steve Beuerlein	.05
67	Desmond Howard	.05
68	Kelvin Martin	.05
69	Reggie Cobb	.05
70	Marcus Allen	.10
71	Greg Hill	.20
72	Joe Montana	.75
73	Neil Smith	.05
74	Derrick Thomas	.10
75	Tim Brown	.10
76	Rocket Ismail	.05
77	Jeff Hostetler	.05
78	Chester McGlockton	.05
79	Harvey Williams	.05
80	Tim Bowens	.05
81	Irving Fryar	.05
82	Keith Jackson	.05
83	Terry Kirby	.05
84	Dan Marino	1.50
85	O.J. McDuffie	.05
86	Bernie Parmalee	.15
87	Terry Allen	.05
88	Cris Carter	.10
89	Qadry Ismail	.05
90	Warren Moon	.10
91	Jake Reed	.05
92	Drew Bledsoe	1.00
93	Vincent Brisby	.05
94	Ben Coates	.05
95	Michael Timpson	.05
96	Jim Everett	.05
97	Michael Haynes	.05
98	Willie Roaf	.05
99	Michael Brooks	.05
100	Dave Brown	.05
101	Rodney Hampton	.05
102	Thomas Lewis	.05
103	Dave Meggett	.05
104	Boomer Esiason	.05
105	Johnny Johnson	.05
106	Johnny Mitchell	.05
107	Rob Moore	.05
108	Fred Barnett	.05
109	Randall Cunningham	.10
110	Charlie Garner	.05
111	Herschel Walker	.05
112	Barry Foster	.05
113	Eric Green	.05
114	Charles Johnson	.20
115	Greg Lloyd	.05
116	Bam Morris	.35
117	Neil O'Donnell	.10
118	Rod Woodson	.10
119	Willie Anderson	.05
120	Jerome Bettis	.25
121	Troy Drayton	.05
122	Sean Gilbert	.05
123	Ronnie Harmon	.05
124	Stan Humphries	.10
125	Shawn Jefferson	.05
126	Natrone Means	.30
127	Leslie O'Neal	.05
128	Junior Seau	.10
129	William Floyd	.25
130	Brent Jones	.05
131	Jerry Rice	.50
132	Deion Sanders	.40
133	Dana Stubblefield	.05
134	Ricky Watters	.10
135	Bryant Young	.05
136	Steve Young	.50
137	Brian Blades	.05
138	Cortez Kennedy	.10
139	Rick Mirer	.30
140	Chris Warren	.05
141	Horace Copeland	.05
142	Trent Dilfer	.30
143	Hardy Nickerson	.05
144	Errict Rhett	.10
145	Henry Ellard	.05
146	Brian Mitchell	.05
147	Heath Shuler	.25
148	Tydus Winans	.05
149	Steve Tasker	.05
150	Jeff Burris	.05
151	Tyrone Hughes	.05
152	Mel Gray	.05
153	Kevin Williams	.05
154	Andre Coleman	.05
155	Corey Sawyer	.05
156	Darrien Gordon	.05
157	Aaron Glenn	.05
158	Eric Metcalf	.05
159	Errict Rhett	.40
160	Marshall Faulk	.75
161	Darnay Scott	.05
162	William Floyd	.10
163	Charlie Garner	.05
164	Heath Shuler	.40
165	Trent Dilfer	.20
166	Willie McGinest	.05
167	Bam Morris	.20
168	Mario Bates	.05
169	*Ki-Jana Carter*	.50
170	*Tony Boseli*	.10
171	*Steve McNair*	2.50
172	*Michael Westbrook*	.75
173	*Kerry Collins*	1.00
174	*Kevin Carter*	.10
175	*Mike Mamula*	.10
176	*Joseph Galloway*	1.50
177	*Kyle Brady*	.10
178	*J.J. Stokes*	.75
179	*Warren Sapp*	.50
180	*Rob Johnson*	1.00
181	*Tyrone Wheatley*	.50
182	*Napoleon Kaufman*	.50
183	*James Stewart*	1.00
184	*Dino Philyaw*	.10
185	*Rashaan Salaam*	.40
186	*Tyrone Poole*	.10
187	*Ty Law*	.10
188	*Joe Aska*	.10
189	*Mark Bruener*	.10
190	*Derrick Brooks*	.10
191	*Jack Jackson*	.10
192	*Ray Zellars*	.10
193	*Eddie Goines*	.10
194	*Chris Sanders*	.30
195	*Charlie Simmons*	.10
196	*Lee DeRamus*	.10
197	*Frank Sanders*	.30
198	*Rodney Thomas*	.30
199	Checklist A	.05
200	Checklist B	.05
M1	Brett Favre SKY (SkyMotion)	25.00

1995 SkyBox Impact Countdown

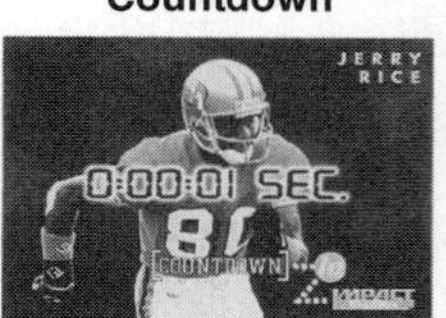

These 10 cards address some of the more unique stats of the NFL's best players in a whole new way. For example, how many minutes did it actually take for Barry Sanders to run for a league-leading 1,883 yards? His insert card, like the rest, will provide the foiled answer on the front. The cards are horizontal, with the set logo and brand logo toward the bottom of the card. The player's name is in the upper right corner. The card back has a photo on one side, and a brief explanation of the unique stat which is being featured. A card number, using a "C" prefix, is in a red circle in the upper right corner.

		NM/M
Complete Set (10):		25.00
Common Player:		1.00
1	Barry Sanders	5.00
2	Jerry Rice	4.00
3	Steve Young	4.00
4	Troy Aikman	4.00
5	Dan Marino	6.00
6	Emmitt Smith	5.00
7	Junior Seau	1.00
8	Drew Bledsoe	3.00
9	Brett Favre	6.00
10	Deion Sanders	2.00

1995 SkyBox Impact Future Hall of Famers

This 1995 SkyBox Impact insert set presents eight solid candidates who are on their way to the Pro Football Hall of Fame. The cards were random inserts in hobby packs only, one per 60 packs. Cards are numbered using an "HF" prefix; fronts have "Hall of Fame" written on them.

		NM/M
Complete Set (7):		45.00
Common Player:		8.00
#2 was never made.		
1	Jerry Rice	8.00
3	Steve Young	8.00

4	John Elway	8.00
5	Dan Marino	12.00
6	Emmitt Smith	10.00
7	Barry Sanders	10.00
8	Troy Aikman	8.00

1995 SkyBox Impact Fox More Attitude

These 15 cards include seven young NFL veterans and eight 1995 first-round draft picks who represent a fresh new attitude of SkyBox and the NFL on Fox. Cards were seeded one per nine packs of 1995 SkyBox Impact product. The card front has a color action photo of the player with a football field for a background. "Same Game" and "More Attitude," in foil, are written along the left side of the card, as is the player's name, which is also stamped in foil. The "NFL on Fox" logo is stamped in foil in the lower right corner. The card back has a parallelogram in the center which contains a color photo towards the top, with a summary of the player's attitude underneath. There's biographical information along the left side of the card; a card number in the upper right in a black circle, and the player's name are along the right side. The card number uses an "F" prefix.

		NM/M
Complete Set (15):		15.00
Common Player:		.50
1	Ki-Jana Carter	.50
2	Steve McNair	4.00
3	Michael Westbrook	1.00
4	Kerry Collins	2.00
5	Joseph Galloway	2.00
6	J.J. Stokes	.50
7	Tyrone Wheatley	.50
8	Rashaan Salaam	.50
9	Trent Dilfer	3.00
10	William Floyd	1.00
11	Marshall Faulk	4.00
12	Errict Rhett	1.00
13	Heath Shuler	1.00
14	Drew Bledsoe	4.00
15	Ben Coates	1.00

1995 SkyBox Impact Power

Thirty of the NFL's impact players are featured on these two insert sets. Cards IP1-IP10, DE-Terminators, are devoted to 10 defensive players who make big hits. Cards IP11-IP30, Stars of the Ozone, are devoted to 20 offensive stars who make big plays. There was, however, no card made for IP25. Cards were seeded one per three packs of 1995 SkyBox Impact product. The card fronts for each set are similar; both have foil backgrounds, have the set icon in the upper left corner and have the player's name in foil along the right side of the card. The backs are similar, too. There's a smaller color photo in a box in the upper right corner; a card number, using an "IP" prefix, is in a black circle in the opposite corner. The player's name and "Impact Power" are written along the left side. An assessment of the player's skills is below the photo.

		NM/M
Complete Set (30):		15.00
Common Player:		.25
Minor Stars:		.50
IP25 was never made.		
1	Junior Seau	.50
2	Reggie White	.50
3	Eric Swann	.25
4	Bruce Smith	.25
5	Rod Woodson	.25
6	Derrick Thomas	.50
7	Chester McGlockton	.25
8	Cortez Kennedy	.25
9	Deion Sanders	1.50
10	Bryan Cox	.25
11	Jerry Rice	3.00
12	Sterling Sharpe	.50
13	Tim Brown	.50
14	Marshall Faulk	.50
15	Brett Favre	5.00
16	Chris Warren	.25
17	Herman Moore	.25
18	Steve Young	3.00
19	Andre Rison	.50
20	Thurman Thomas	.50
21	Marcus Allen	.50
22	Michael Irvin	.50
23	Emmitt Smith	5.00
24	John Elway	2.00
26	Barry Sanders	4.00
27	Troy Aikman	3.00
28	Natrone Means	.50
29	Ben Coates	.25
30	Errict Rhett	.50

1995 SkyBox Impact Rookie Running Backs

Rookie Running Backs was available as a set and inserted into each retail box. It included eight different rookies, with designs very similar to the rookies in the base set, except for the numbering (1-8), and one unnumbered header card.

		NM/M
Complete Set (9):		4.00
Common Player:		.50
1	Ki-Jana Carter	.50
2	Tyrone Wheatley	.50
3	Napoleon Kaufman	.75
4	James O. Stewart	1.00
5	Rashaan Salaam	.50
6	Ray Zellars	.50
7	Rodney Thomas	.75
8	Curtis Martin	3.00
NNO	Cover/Checklist Card	.30

1995 SkyBox Impact Fox Announcers

This seven-card set featured FOX's NFL Sunday announcers and was done to promote SyBox's ties to the network. Fronts pictured teams of announcers, while the back contained information about them. There was also an unnumbered header card included.

		NM/M
Complete Set (8):		10.00
Common Player:		1.00
1	Pat Summerall, John Madden	3.00
2	James Brown, Jimmy Johnson, Terry Bradshaw, Howie Long	3.00
3	Dick Stockton, Matt Millen	1.00
4	Kevin Harlan, Jerry Glanville	1.00
5	Joe Buck, Tim Green	1.00
6	Kenny Albert, Anthony Munoz	1.50
7	Thom Brennaman, Ron Pitts	1.00
NNO	Cover Card	1.00

1996 SkyBox

SkyBox Premium was a 250-card set that marked the fifth anniversary of the product. The regular-issue set includes 178 regular player cards, 50 rookies (179-228), 10 Prime Time Rookie Retrospectives (229-238), which are quad cards, 10 Panorama (239-248) and two checklists (249-250). SkyBox Premium was issued in 10-card packs and contains the Brett Favre MVP Series (cards 1, 2, 3 were in Impact), side B of the Favre Lenticular Exchange card, six SkyBox spokesperson autographs and a Rubies parallel set. Inserts include: V, Next Big Thing, Thunder and Lightning, Close-Ups and Prime Time Rookies.

		NM/M
Complete Set (250):		25.00
Common Player:		.05
Minor Stars:		.20
Rubie Stars:		8X-20X
Rubie Rookies:		5X-10X
Pack (10):		1.25
Wax Box (24):		20.00
1	Larry Centers	.05
2	Boomer Esiason	.05
3	Garrison Hearst	.05
4	Rob Moore	.05
5	Frank Sanders	.20
6	Eric Swann	.05
7	Bert Emanuel	.05
8	Jeff George	.05
9	Craig Heyward	.05
10	Terance Mathis	.05
11	Eric Metcalf	.05
12	Derrick Alexander	.05
13	Leroy Hoard	.05
14	Michael Jackson	.05
15	Vinny Testaverde	.05
16	Eric Turner	.05
17	Darick Holmes	.40
18	Jim Kelly	.20
19	Bryce Paup	.05
20	Andre Reed	.05
21	Bruce Smith	.05
22	Thurman Thomas	.20
23	Tim Tindale	.05
24	Mark Carrier	.05
25	Kerry Collins	.50
26	Willie Green	.05
27	Lamar Lathon	.05
28	Tyrone Poole	.05
29	Curtis Conway	.05
30	Bryan Cox	.05
31	Erik Kramer	.05
32	Nate Lewis	.05
33	Rashaan Salaam	.75
34	Alonzo Spellman	.05
35	Michael Timpson	.05
36	Jeff Blake	.75
37	Ki-Jana Carter	.20
38	David Dunn	.05
39	Carl Pickens	.05
40	Darnay Scott	.05
41	Troy Aikman	1.50
42	Charles Haley	.05
43	Michael Irvin	.05
44	Daryl Johnston	.05
45	Jay Novacek	.05
46	Deion Sanders	1.00
47	Emmitt Smith	2.50
48	Kevin Williams	.05
49	Steve Atwater	.05
50	Terrell Davis	1.25
51	John Elway	.75
52	Anthony Miller	.05
53	Shannon Sharpe	.05
54	Mike Sherrard	.05
55	Scott Mitchell	.05
56	Herman Moore	.50
57	Johnnie Morton	.05
58	Brett Perriman	.05
59	Barry Sanders	1.75
60	Edgar Bennett	.05
61	Robert Brooks	.05
62	Mark Chmura	.25
63	Brett Favre	2.50
64	Antonio Freeman	.05
65	Keith Jackson	.05
66	Reggie White	.20
67	Chris Chandler	.05
68	Mel Gray	.05
69	Steve McNair	1.00
70	Chris Sanders	.40
71	Rodney Thomas	.30
72	Quentin Coryatt	.05
73	Sean Dawkins	.05
74	Ken Dilger	.05
75	Marshall Faulk	.75
76	Jim Harbaugh	.05
77	Lamont Warren	.05
78	Tony Boselli	.05
79	Mark Brunell	1.00
80	Willie Jackson	.05
81	Natrone Means	.05
82	James Stewart	.05
83	Marcus Allen	.05
84	Kimble Anders	.05
85	Steve Bono	.05
86	Lake Dawson	.05
87	Neil Smith	.05
88	Derrick Thomas	.05
89	Tamarick Vanover	.75
90	Fred Barnett	.05
91	Terry Kirby	.05
92	Dan Marino	2.50
93	O.J. McDuffie	.05
94	Bernie Parmalee	.05
95	Richmond Webb	.05
96	Cris Carter	.05
97	Qadry Ismail	.05
98	Scottie Graham	.05
99	Warren Moon	.05
100	Jake Reed	.05
101	Robert Smith	.05
102	Drew Bledsoe	1.25
103	Vincent Brisby	.05
104	Ben Coates	.05
105	Curtis Martin	2.00
106	David Meggett	.05
107	Chris Slade	.05
108	Mario Bates	.05
109	Jim Everett	.05
110	Michael Haynes	.05
111	Tyrone Hughes	.05
112	Renaldo Turnbull	.05
113	Dave Brown	.05
114	Chris Calloway	.05
115	Rodney Hampton	.05
116	Thomas Lewis	.05
117	Tyrone Wheatley	.05
118	Kyle Brady	.05
119	Hugh Douglas	.05
120	Aaron Glenn	.05
121	Jeff Graham	.05
122	Adrian Murrell	.05
123	Neil O'Donnell	.05
124	Tim Brown	.05
125	Nolan Harrison	.05
126	Billy Joe Hobert	.05
127	Jeff Hostetler	.05
128	Napoleon Kaufman	.30
129	Chester McGlockton	.05
130	Harvey Williams	.05
131	Charlie Garner	.05
132	Andy Harmon	.05
133	Chris T. Jones	.05
134	Mike Mamula	.05
135	Rodney Peete	.05
136	Bobby Taylor	.05
137	Ricky Watters	.05
138	Jerome Bettis	.20
139	Greg Lloyd	.05
140	Jim Miller	.05
141	Ernie Mills	.05
142	Kordell Stewart	1.25
143	Yancey Thigpen	.30
144	Rod Woodson	.05
145	Andre Coleman	.05
146	Terrell Fletcher	.05
147	*Aaron Hayden*	.30
148	Stan Humphries	.05
149	Junior Seau	.05
150	Isaac Bruce	.75
151	Kevin Carter	.05
152	Todd Kinchen	.05
153	Leslie O'Neal	.05
154	Mark Rypien	.05
155	William Floyd	.05
156	Merton Hanks	.05
157	Brent Jones	.05
158	Derek Loville	.05
159	Ken Norton	.05
160	Jerry Rice	1.50
161	J.J. Stokes	.75
162	Steve Young	1.00
163	Brian Blades	.05
164	Christian Fauria	.05
165	Joey Galloway	1.00
166	Rick Mirer	.05
167	Chris Warren	.20
168	Trent Dilfer	.05
169	Alvin Harper	.05
170	Jackie Harris	.05
171	Hardy Nickerson	.05
172	Errict Rhett	.50
173	Terry Allen	.05
174	Henry Ellard	.05
175	Gus Frerotte	.05
176	Brian Mitchell	.05
177	Heath Shuler	.05
178	Michael Westbrook	.75
179	*Karim Abdul-Jabbar*	.75
180	*Mike Alstott*	1.50
181	*Willie Anderson*	.05
182	*Marco Battaglia*	.05
183	*Tim Biakabutuka*	1.00
184	*Tony Brackens*	.05
185	*Duane Clemons*	.05
186	*Marcus Coleman*	.05
187	*Ernie Conwell*	.05
188	*Chris Darkins*	.05
189	*Stephen Davis*	4.00
190	*Brian Dawkins*	.05
191	*Rickey Dudley*	.30
192	*Jason Dunn*	.20
193	*Bobby Engram*	.30
194	*Daryl Gardener*	.05
195	*Eddie George*	4.00
196	*Terry Glenn*	2.00
197	*Kevin Hardy*	.30
198	*Walt Harris*	.20
199	*Marvin Harrison*	4.00
200	*Bobby Hoying*	1.00
201	*Isreal Ifeanyi*	.05
202	*DeRon Jenkins*	.05
203	*Keyshawn Johnson*	2.50
204	*Lance Johnstone*	.05
205	*Cedric Jones*	.30
206	*Marcus Jones*	.05
207	*Eddie Kennison*	.50
208	*Jevon Langford*	.05
209	*Dedric Mathis*	.05
210	*Jermaine Mayberry*	.05
211	*Leeland McElroy*	.30
212	*Johnny McWilliams*	.05
213	*Ray Mickens*	.05
214	*John Mobley*	.25
215	*Jerald Moore*	.25
216	*Eric Moulds*	2.00
217	*Mushin Muhammad*	1.00
218	*Jonathan Ogden*	.20
219	*Lawrence Phillips*	.75
220	*Kavika Pittman*	.05
221	*Stanley Pritchett*	.50
222	*Simeon Rice*	.30
223	*Detron Smith*	.05
224	*Bryan Still*	.50
225	*Amani Toomer*	.50
226	*Regan Upshaw*	.05
227	*Alex Van Dyke*	.20
228	*Stepfret Williams*	.05
229	Quentin Coryatt, Chester McGlockton, Carl Pickens, Robert Brooks Retrospective	.20
230	Dale Carter, Edgar Bennett, Drew Bledsoe, Garrison Hearst Retrospective	.40
231	Natrone Means, Rick Mirer, Jerome Bettis, Robert Smith Retrospective	.20
232	O.J. McDuffie, Curtis Conway, Marshall Faulk, Greg Hill Retrospective	.20
233	Heath Shuler, Trent Dilfer, William Floyd, Charles Johnson Retrospective	.20
234	Errict Rhett, Sean Dawkins, Mario Bates, Ki-Jana Carter Retrospective	.20
235	Kerry Collins, Steve McNair, Joey Galloway, Rashaan Salaam Retrospective	.40
236	J.J. Stokes, Michael Westbrook, Kyle Brady, Kordell Stewart Retrospective	.40
237	Keyshawn Johnson, Eddie George, Leeland McElroy, Lawrence Phillips Retrospective	.20
238	Bobby Engram, Rickey Dudley, Eric Moulds, Tim Biakabutuka Retrospective	.20
239	Kordell Stewart, Quentin Coryatt Panorama Jan. 14, 1996	.40
240	Robert Brooks Panorama Nov. 26, 1995	.20
241	Henry Jones, Terance Mathis Panorama Nov. 12, 1995	.05
242	Mark Seay, Alfred Pupunu Panorama Dec. 9, 1995	.05
243	Robert Brooks, Willie Beamon Panorama Sept. 17, 1995	.20
244	Panorama Oct. 29, 1995 - 49ers Halloween	.05
245	Panorama Oct. 15, 1995	.05
246	Zack Crockett, Junior Seau Panorama Dec. 31, 1995	.20
247	Kevin Williams, Doug Evans Panorama Jan. 14, 1996	.05
248	Tim Jacobs, Antonio Freeman Panorama Nov. 19, 1995	.20
249	Checklist (1-141)	.05
250	Checklist (141-250)	.05

1996 SkyBox Rubies

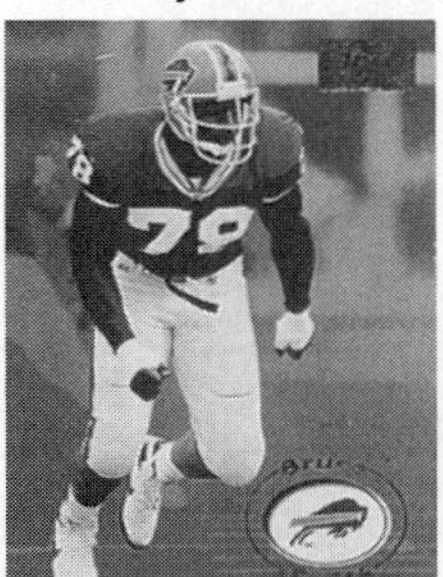

Rubies was a 248-card parallel set (250 minus checklists) that were inserted into hobby boxes under the packs. Rubies awarded collectors that purchased sealed boxes since the person who opened the box would pull a Rubies insert. Rubies are distinguished by ruby foil in place of the gold foil found on common cards.

	NM/M
Complete Set (228):	1,800
Rubies:	8X-20X

1996 SkyBox V

Ten players who changed the game over the last five years are featured in V, which was seeded every 18 packs. This insert celebrates SkyBox's fifth anniversary with die-cut, V-shaped designs.

		NM/M
Complete Set (10):		20.00
Common Player:		1.00
1	Ki-Jana Carter	1.00
2	Kerry Collins	3.00
3	Trent Dilfer	1.00
4	Joey Galloway	3.00
5	Herman Moore	2.00
6	Errict Rhett	2.00
7	Rashaan Salaam	1.00
8	Deion Sanders	2.00
9	Thurman Thomas	2.00
10	Reggie White	1.00

1996 SkyBox Next Big Thing

Next Big Thing showcases 15 young players that are expected to produce big things through their careers. Inserted at a one per 40 rate, these inserts feature a multi-colored foil background with the words "Next Big Thing" in bold.

		NM/M
Complete Set (15):		40.00
Common Player:		1.00
1	Mark Brunell	4.00
2	Rickey Dudley	1.00
3	Bobby Engram	1.00
4	Antonio Freeman	1.00
5	Eddie George	8.00
6	Terry Glenn	5.00
7	Marvin Harrison	8.00
8	Keyshawn Johnson	4.00
9	Napoleon Kaufman	1.00
10	Steve McNair	10.00
11	Alex Molden	1.00
12	Frank Sanders	4.00
13	Kordell Stewart	5.00
14	Amani Toomer	1.00
15	Alex Van Dyke	1.00

1996 SkyBox Thunder and Lightning

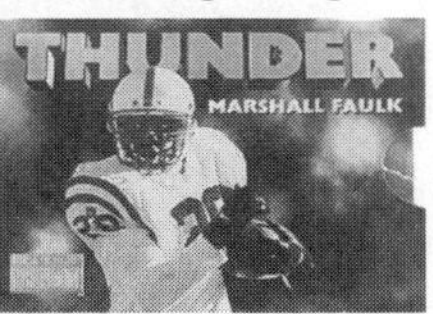

Thunder and Lightning was made up of 20 players featured on 10 different cards (numbered 1-10 a & b) who make lethal 1-2 combinations. Each card is actually a card- within-a-card where the "lightning" player is inserted into the "thunder" card. Thunder and Lightning inserts were found every 72 packs.

		NM/M
Complete Set (10):		75.00
Common Player:		2.00
1	Emmitt Smith, Troy Aikman	12.00
2	Barry Sanders, Scott Mitchell	10.00
3	Marshall Faulk, Jim Harbaugh	6.00
4	Dan Marino, O.J. McDuffie	10.00
5	Jerry Rice, Steve Young	10.00
6	Jeff Blake, Carl Pickens	2.00
7	Brett Favre, Edgar Bennett	12.00
8	Curtis Martin, Drew Bledsoe	8.00
9	Errict Rhett, Trent Dilfer	2.00
10	Rick Mirer, Chris Warren	2.00

A card number in parenthese ( ) indicates the set is unnumbered.

1996 SkyBox Prime-Time Rookies

Prime Time Rookies returned to Premium as a hobby-only insert that showcased the top rookies from the 1996 NFL Draft. These inserts were found every 96 packs.

		NM/M
Complete Set (10):		75.00
Common Player:		2.00
1	Tim Biakabutuka	2.00
2	Rickey Dudley	2.00
3	Bobby Engram	4.00
4	Eddie George	20.00
5	Terry Glenn	10.00
6	Marvin Harrison	15.00
7	Keyshawn Johnson	12.00
8	Leeland McElroy	2.00
9	Eric Moulds	5.00
10	Lawrence Phillips	1.00

1996 SkyBox Close-Ups

Ten NFL stars are featured in close-up shots in this retail exclusive insert, which was found every 30 packs.

		NM/M
Complete Set (10):		60.00
Common Player:		1.00
1	Troy Aikman	12.00
2	Drew Bledsoe	12.00
3	Isaac Bruce	6.00
4	Terrell Davis	10.00
5	John Elway	12.00
6	Barry Sanders	14.00
7	Emmitt Smith	15.00
8	Kordell Stewart	5.00
9	Tamarick Vanover	1.00
10	Ricky Watters	3.00

1996 SkyBox Autographs

The six spokesman for Fleer/SkyBox signed cards to be inserted into packs of Premium at a rate of one per 450. Highlighted by Brett Favre, the set also includes Trent Dilfer, Daryl Johnston, Eric Turner, Dave Meggett and William Floyd.

	NM/M
Common Player:	10.00
Trent Dilfer	20.00
Brett Favre	200.00
William Floyd	10.00
Daryl Johnston	15.00
Dave Meggett	10.00
Eric Turner	10.00

1996 SkyBox Brett Favre MVP

Brett Favre MVP Series was a five-card insert devoted to SkyBox spokesman and NFL MVP Brett Favre. Cards 1-3A were found in Impact, with a one per 480 insert rate, while cards 3B-5 were in packs of Premium, with a one per 240 insertion rate. Each card showed off a different technology, with No. 1 printed on foil, No. 2 printed on acrylic, No. 3 utilizing lenticular technology, No. 4 was die-cut and No. 5 was printed on leather. Card No. 3 required collectors to obtain sides A and B, from Impact and Premium, respectively, to redeem it for the actual lenticular card.

		NM/M
Common Player:		1.00
1	Brett Favre Foil	12.00
2	Brett Favre Acrylic	12.00
3a	Brett Favre Exch.A	1.00
3b	Brett Favre Exch.B	1.00
3c	Brett Favre Prize	20.00
4	Brett Favre Die-Cut	12.00
5	Brett Favre Leather	12.00

1996 SkyBox Impact

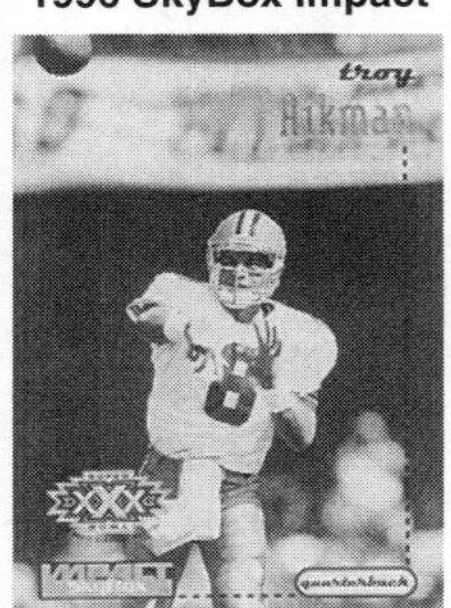

Impact Football was a 200-card set that featured borderless action shots and commentary on card backs by Fox analyst Matt Millen. The set includes 148 veterans, 40 rookies (149-188), five Inspirations (189-193), five Brett Favre Highlights and two checklists. There were five different inserts sets - NFL on Fox, Excelerators, Intimidators, No Surrender and VersaTeam - and three Brett Favre MVP Series cards and a Favre SkyMint Exchange card.

		NM/M
Complete Set (200):		18.00
Common Player:		.05
Minor Stars:		.10
Pack (10):		1.00
Wax Box (24):		20.00
1	Garrison Hearst	.05
2	Rob Moore	.05
3	Frank Sanders	.05
4	Eric Swann	.05
5	Aeneas Williams	.05
6	Bert Emanuel	.05
7	Jeff George	.05
8	Craig Heyward	.05
9	Terance Mathis	.05
10	Eric Metcalf	.05
11	Leroy Hoard	.05
12	Michael Jackson	.05
13	Andre Rison	.05
14	Vinny Testaverde	.05
15	Eric Turner	.05
16	Darrick Holmes	.05
17	Jim Kelly	.05
18	Bryce Paup	.05
19	Bruce Smith	.05
20	Thurman Thomas	.05
21	Mark Carrier	.05
22	Kerry Collins	.25
23	Derrick Moore	.05
24	Tyrone Poole	.05
25	Curtis Conway	.05
26	Jeff Graham (Jets)	.05
27	Erik Kramer	.05
28	Rashaan Salaam	.50
29	Jeff Blake	.60
30	Ki-Jana Carter	.25
31	Carl Pickens	.05
32	Darnay Scott	.05
33	Troy Aikman	.75
34	Charles Haley	.05
35	Michael Irvin	.10
36	Daryl Johnston	.05
37	Jay Novacek	.05
38	Deion Sanders	.50
39	Emmitt Smith	1.50
40	Steve Atwater	.05
41	Terrell Davis	.75
42	John Elway	.25
43	Anthony Miller	.05
44	Shannon Sharpe	.05
45	Scott Mitchell	.05
46	Herman Moore	.20
47	Brett Perriman	.05
48	Barry Sanders	1.00
49	Edgar Bennett	.05
50	Robert Brooks	.05
51	Mark Chmura	.20
52	Brett Favre	1.50
53	Reggie White	.10
54	Mel Gray	.05
55	Steve McNair	.75
56	Chris Sanders	.25
57	Rodney Thomas	.30
58	Quentin Coryatt	.05
59	Sean Dawkins	.05
60	Ken Dilger	.05
61	Marshall Faulk	.75
62	Jim Harbaugh	.05
63	Tony Boselli	.05
64	Mark Brunell	.50
65	Keenan McCardell	.05
66	James Stewart	.05
67	Marcus Allen	.05
68	Steve Bono	.05
69	Neil Smith	.05
70	Derrick Thomas	.05
71	Tamarick Vanover	.50
72	Bryan Cox (Bears)	.05
73	Irving Fryar (Eagles)	.05
74	Eric Green	.05
75	Dan Marino	1.50
76	O.J. McDuffie	.05
77	Bernie Parmalee	.05
78	Cris Carter	.05
79	Qadry Ismail	.05
80	Warren Moon	.05
81	Jake Reed	.05
82	Robert Smith	.05
83	Drew Bledsoe	.75
84	Ben Coates	.05
85	Curtis Martin	1.25
86	Willie McGinnest	.05
87	David Meggett	.05
88	Mario Bates	.05
89	Quinn Early (Bills)	.05
90	Jim Everett	.05
91	Michael Haynes	.05
92	Renaldo Turnbull	.05
93	Dave Brown	.05
94	Rodney Hampton	.05
95	Thomas Lewis	.05
96	Phillippi Sparks	.05
97	Tyrone Wheatley	.05
98	Kyle Brady	.05
99	Hugh Douglas	.05
100	Mo Lewis	.05
101	Adrian Murrell	.05
102	Tim Brown	.05
103	Jeff Hostetler	.05
104	Raghib Ismail	.05
105	Chester McGlockton	.05
106	Harvey Williams	.05
107	Fred Barnett (Dolphins)	.05
108	William Fuller	.05
109	Charlie Garner	.05
110	Rodney Peete	.05
111	Ricky Watters	.05
112	Calvin Williams	.05
113	Bam Morris	.05
114	Neil O'Donnell (Jets)	.05
115	Erric Pegram	.05
116	Kordell Stewart	1.00
117	Yancey Thigpen	.30
118	Rod Woodson	.05
119	Jerome Bettis (Steelers)	.05
120	Isaac Bruce	.40
121	Troy Drayton	.05
122	Leslie O'Neal	.05
123	*Aaron Hayden*	.30
124	Stan Humphries	.05
125	Natrone Means (Jaguars)	.10
126	Junior Seau	.05
127	William Floyd	.05
128	Brent Jones	.05
129	Derek Loville	.05
130	Ken Norton	.05
131	Jerry Rice	.75
132	J.J. Stokes	.10
133	Steve Young	.75
134	Brian Blades	.05
135	Joey Galloway	.75
136	Cortez Kennedy	.05
137	Rick Mirer	.10
138	Chris Warren	.15
139	Trent Dilfer	.05
140	Alvin Harper	.05
141	Jackie Harris	.05
142	Hardy Nickerson	.05
143	Errict Rhett	.50
144	Terry Allen	.05
145	Henry Ellard	.05
146	Brian Mitchell	.05
147	Heath Shuler	.25
148	Michael Westbrook	.10
149	*Karim Abdul-Jabbar*	.50
150	*Mike Alstott*	1.50
151	*Marco Battaglia*	.05
152	*Tim Biakabutuka*	.75
153	*Sean Boyd*	.05
154	*Tony Brackens*	.05
155	*Duane Clemons*	.05
156	*Marcus Coleman*	.05
157	*Chris Darkins*	.30
158	*Rickey Dudley*	.30
159	*Jason Dunn*	.20
160	*Bobby Engram*	.10
161	*Daryl Gardener*	.05
162	*Eddie George*	3.00
163	*Terry Glenn*	1.50
164	*Kevin Hardy*	.20
165	*Marvin Harrison*	3.00
166	*Dietrich Jells*	.05
167	*DeRon Jenkins*	.05
168	*Darrius Johnson*	.05
169	*Keyshawn Johnson*	2.00
170	*Lance Johnstone*	.05
171	*Cedric Jones*	.05
172	*Marcus Jones*	.05
173	*Danny Kanell*	.50
174	*Eddie Kennison*	.30
175	*Jevon Langford*	.05
176	*Markco Maddox*	.05
177	*Derrick Mayes*	.75
178	*Leeland McElroy*	.20
179	*Del McGee*	.05
180	*Johnny McWilliams*	.05
181	*Alex Molden*	.05
182	*Eric Moulds*	1.50
183	*Jonathan Ogden*	.05
184	*Lawrence Phillips*	.50
185	*Simeon Rice*	.20
186	*Amani Toomer*	.30
187	*Regan Upshaw*	.05
188	*Jerome Woods*	.05
189	Darrell Green (Inspirations)	.05
190	Daryl Johnston (Inspirations)	.05
191	Sam Mills (Inspirations)	.05
192	Earnest Byner (Inspirations)	.05
193	Herschel Walker (Inspirations)	.05
194	Brett Favre (Highlights)	.25
195	Brett Favre (Highlights)	.25
196	Brett Favre (Highlights)	.25
197	Brett Favre (Highlights)	.25
198	Brett Favre (Highlights)	.25
199	Checklist	.05
200	Checklist	.05

1996 SkyBox Impact Excelerators

Excelerators included 15 players who have breakaway speed. The word "Excelerators" is written across the top in foil, with the player's name across the bottom, with his last name in large letters, with flames rising up. These inserts were seeded every 12 packs.

		NM/M
Complete Set (15):		20.00
Common Player:		1.00
1	Robert Brooks	1.00
2	Isaac Bruce	2.00
3	William Floyd	1.00
4	Joey Galloway	2.00
5	Michael Irvin	1.00
6	Napoleon Kaufman	1.00
7	Anthony Miller	1.00
8	Herman Moore	2.00
9	Barry Sanders	4.00
10	Chris Sanders	1.00
11	Kordell Stewart	2.00
12	Rodney Thomas	1.00
13	Tamarick Vanover	1.00
14	Ricky Watters	1.00
15	Michael Westbrook	1.00

1996 SkyBox Impact Intimidators

Intimidators was a 10-card insert that displayed the NFL's toughest players against a shattered-looking background. The word "Intimidators' runs down the right side and gets smaller toward the bottom. Intimidators inserts were seeded every 20 packs of Impact.

		NM/M
Complete Set (10):		20.00
Common Player:		1.00
1	Terrell Davis	3.00
2	Hugh Douglas	1.00
3	Dan Marino	5.00
4	Curtis Martin	3.00
5	Carl Pickens	1.00
6	Errict Rhett	1.00
7	Jerry Rice	4.00
8	Emmitt Smith	4.00
9	Eric Swann	1.00
10	Chris Warren	1.00

A card number in parenthese ( ) indicates the set is unnumbered.

1996 SkyBox Impact More Attitude

More Attitide was the easiest insert to get in Impact, with an insertion rate of one per three packs. The insert displayed 20 rookies from 1996 in their college uniforms with silver foil backgrounds.

		NM/M
Complete Set (20):		15.00
Common Player:		.50
1	Karim Abdul-Jabbar	1.00
2	Tim Biakabutuka	.50
3	Bobby Engram	1.00
4	Daryl Gardener	.50
5	Eddie George	3.00
6	Terry Glenn	2.00
7	Kevin Hardy	.50
8	Marvin Harrison	2.50
9	DeRon Jenkins	.50
10	Keyshawn Johnson	2.00
11	Cedric Jones	.50
12	Eddie Kennison	1.50
13	Jevon Langford	.50
14	Leeland McElroy	.50
15	Johnny McWilliams	.50
16	Eric Moulds	2.00
17	Lawrence Phillips	.50
18	Jonathan Ogden	.50
19	Simeon Rice	.50
20	Amani Toomer	1.00

1996 SkyBox Impact No Surrender

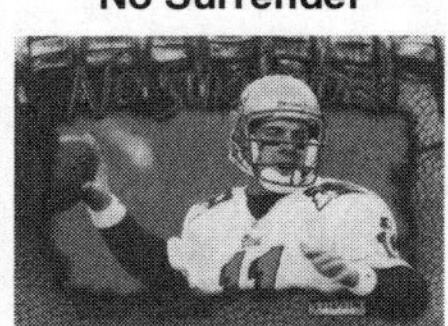

No Surrender featured 20 top players in a horizontal format with the player's image embossed against a football background. The words "No Surrender" are written across the top of the card in red foil. This insert is seeded in every 40 hobby packs.

		NM/M
Complete Set (20):		50.00
Common Player:		1.00
1	Marcus Allen	3.00
2	Jeff Blake	1.00
3	Drew Bledsoe	5.00
4	Ben Coates	1.00
5	Brett Favre	7.00
6	Terry Glenn	3.00
7	Jim Harbaugh	1.00
8	Kevin Hardy	1.00
9	Keyshawn Johnson	4.00
10	Dan Marino	7.00
11	Leeland McElroy	1.00
12	Steve McNair	5.00
13	Herman Moore	3.00
14	Lawrence Phillips	1.00
15	Errict Rhett	2.00
16	Jerry Rice	6.00
17	Simeon Rice	1.00
18	Barry Sanders	6.00
19	Rodney Thomas	1.00
20	Tyrone Wheatley	1.00

1996 SkyBox Impact Versateam

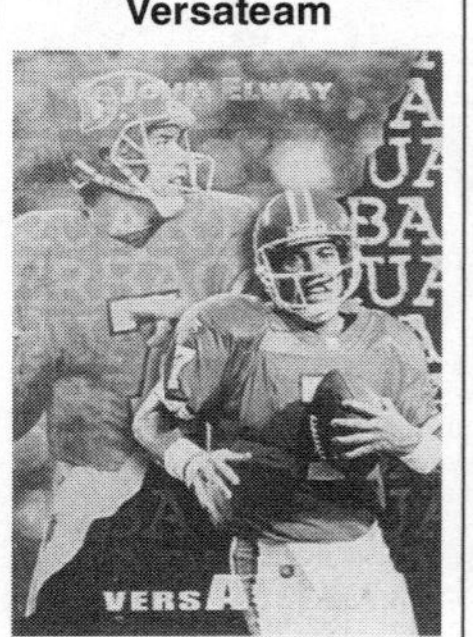

This 10-card insert featured NFL stars that excel at multiple things. The cards, which are found every 120 packs, feature a color action shot of the player over a green tinted background. The background is split diagonally, with half containing the player's position and half with another shot of the player.

		NM/M
Complete Set (10):		50.00
Common Player:		1.00
1	Tim Brown	4.00
2	Terrell Davis	6.00
3	John Elway	6.00
4	Marshall Faulk	5.00
5	Joey Galloway	4.00
6	Curtis Martin	5.00
7	Deion Sanders	3.00
8	Kordell Stewart	4.00
9	Chris Warren	1.00
10	Steve Young	5.00

1996 SkyBox Impact Rookies

Although released in early 1997, Impact Rookies is generally considered a 1996 product due to its focus on 1996 rookies. The set consists of 150 cards, including 70 1996 rookies, 50 All-Time Impact Rookies, 20 Rookie Sleepers and 10 Rookie Record Holders. Ten-card packs had the following inserts: 1996 All-Rookie Team, Draft Board, Rookie Rewind, 1997 NFL Draft Exchange and 1996 Rookies. In addition, autographed versions of Karim Abdul-Jabbar, Rickey Dudley, Marvin Harrison, Lawrence Phillips, Eddie Kennison and Amani Toomer 1996 Rookies inserts were available through a case topper redemption offer. One redemption card was included in six-box cases, with two per 12-box case and three per 20-box case.

		NM/M
Complete Set (150):		12.00
Common Player:		.05
Minor Stars:		.10
Pack (10):		1.25
Wax Box (36):		35.00
1	Leeland McElroy	.10
2	Johnny McWilliams	.05
3	Simeon Rice	.10
4	DeRon Jenkins	.05
5	*Jermaine Lewis*	1.00
6	Ray Lewis	.75
7	Jonathan Ogden	.10
8	*Eric Moulds*	1.50
9	*Tim Biakabutuka*	.50
10	*Muhsin Muhammad*	.50
11	Winslow Oliver	.05
12	Bobby Engram	.20
13	Walt Harris	.10
14	Willie Anderson	.05
15	Marco Battaglia	.05
16	Jevon Langford	.05
17	Kavika Pittman	.05
18	Stepfret Williams	.05
19	Tory James	.05
20	*Jeff Lewis*	.50
21	John Mobley	.05
22	Detron Smith	.05
23	*Derrick Mayes*	.75
24	*Eddie George*	2.50
25	*Marvin Harrison*	3.00
26	Dedric Mathis	.05
27	Tony Brackens	.05
28	Kevin Hardy	.10
29	Jerome Woods	.05
30	*Karim Abdul-Jabbar*	.50
31	Daryl Gardener	.05
32	Jerris McPhail	.05
33	Stanley Pritchett	.05
34	*Zach Thomas*	.50
35	Duane Clemons	.05
36	Moe Williams	.05
37	Tedy Bruschi	.05
38	*Terry Glenn*	1.25
39	Alex Molden	.05
40	Ricky Whittle	.05
41	Cedric Jones	.05
42	*Danny Kanell*	.50
43	Amani Toomer	.10
44	Marcus Coleman	.05
45	*Keyshawn Johnson*	1.50
46	Ray Mickens	.05
47	Alex Van Dyke	.10

48 *Rickey Dudley* .20
49 Lance Johnstone .05
50 Brian Dawkins .05
51 Jason Dunn .05
52 Ray Farmer .05
53 *Bobby Hoying* .50
54 Jermaine Mayberry .05
55 Bryan Still .05
56 *Tony Banks* .50
57 Ernie Conwell .05
58 *Eddie Kennison* .20
59 Jerald Moore .10
60 *Lawrence Phillips* .50
61 Isreal Ifeanyi .10
62 *Terrell Owens* 3.00
63 Iheanyi Uwaezuoke .10
64 *Mike Alstott* 1.25
65 Marcus Jones .05
66 Nilo Silvan .05
67 Regan Upshaw .05
68 *Stephen Davis* 2.00
69 Troy Aikman .50
70 Terry Allen .05
71 Edgar Bennett .05
72 Jerome Bettis .10
73 Drew Bledsoe .50
74 Tim Brown .10
75 Mark Brunell .50
76 Cris Carter .10
77 Kerry Collins .10
78 Terrell Davis 1.00
79 John Elway .50
80 Marshall Faulk .10
81 Brett Favre 1.00
82 Joey Galloway .10
83 Rodney Hampton .05
84 Jim Harbaugh .05
85 Michael Irvin .10
86 Chris T. Jones .05
87 Napoleon Kaufman .20
88 Jim Kelly .10
89 Dan Marino .75
90 Curtis Martin .30
91 Terance Mathis .05
92 Steve McNair .30
93 Anthony Miller .05
94 Scott Mitchell .05
95 Herman Moore .10
96 Brett Perriman .05
97 Carl Pickens .10
98 Jerry Rice .50
99 Andre Rison .05
100 Rashaan Salaam .05
101 Barry Sanders 1.00
102 Chris Sanders .05
103 Deion Sanders .20
104 Frank Sanders .05
105 Bruce Smith .05
106 Emmitt Smith .75
107 Robert Smith .10
108 Kordell Stewart .75
109 J.J. Stokes .05
110 Yancey Thigpen .05
111 Thurman Thomas .05
112 Eric Turner .05
113 Tamarick Vanover .05
114 Chris Warren .05
115 Ricky Watters .10
116 Michael Westbrook .05
117 Reggie White .10
118 Steve Young .30
119 Jeff Blake .05
120 Robert Brooks .05
121 Isaac Bruce .10
122 Mark Chmura .05
123 Wayne Chrebet .10
124 Ben Coates .05
125 Ken Dilger .05
126 Bert Emanuel .05
127 Gus Frerotte .05
128 Kevin Greene .05
129 Erik Kramer .05
130 Greg Lloyd .05
131 Tony Martin .05
132 Brian Mitchell .05
133 Bryce Paup .05
134 Jake Reed .05
135 Errict Rhett .05
136 Yancey Thigpen .05
137 Tamarick Vanover .05
138 Chris Warren .05
139 Marcus Allen .10
140 Jerome Bettis .10
141 Tim Brown .10
142 Mark Carrier .05
143 Marshall Faulk .10
144 Tyrone Hughes .05
145 Dan Marino .75
146 Curtis Martin .30
147 Barry Sanders 1.00
148 Orlando Thomas .10
149 Checklist (1-107) .05
150 Checklist (108-150/inserts) .05
NNO Draft Exchange Card (Expired 7/22/97) 1.00

1996 SkyBox Impact Rookies All-Rookie Team

This 10-card insert includes some of the top rookies from the 1996 season. The fronts feature an embossed image of the player on a matte finish, with the words All-Rookie Team and the names of different members of the team printed in the background in white, embossed letters. All-Rookie Team inserts are numbered and inserted every six packs.

NM/M
Complete Set (10): 12.00
Common Player: 1.00
1 Karim Abdul-Jabbar 1.0

NM/M
2 Tim Biakabutuka 1.00
3 Eddie George 3.00
4 Marvin Harrison 3.00
5 Keyshawn Johnson 2.00
6 Eddie Kennison 1.00
7 Lawrence Phillips 1.00
8 Zach Thomas 2.00
9 Amani Toomer 2.00
10 Simeon Rice 1.00

1996 SkyBox Impact Rookies Draft Board

Draft Board has 20 cards that feature multiple players on the front in a horizontal format against a maroon background. The back explains the tie between the players - whether they were all late round picks or attended the same college - and are numbered. Draft Board inserts are found every 24 packs.

NM/M
Complete Set (20): 75.00
Common Player: 1.00
1 Terry Glenn, Rickey Dudley, Bobby Hoying 3.00
2 Simeon Rice, Kevin Hardy 1.00
3 Emmitt Smith, Errict Rhett 6.00
4 Deion Sanders, Corey Sawyer, Derrick Brooks 3.00
5 Terry Allen, Marcus Allen 2.00
6 John Mobley, Andre Reed 1.00
7 Drew Bledsoe, Rick Mirer, Mark Brunell 5.00
8 John Elway, Jim Kelly, Dan Marino 10.00
9 Carl Pickens, Anthony Miller 1.00
10 Antonio Freeman, Robert Brooks, Chris T. Jones 1.00
11 Jerome Bettis, Ricky Watters, Tim Brown 3.00
12 Jerry Rice, Herman Moore, Michael Irvin 6.00
13 Terrell Davis, Rodney Hampton, Garrison Hearst 4.00
14 Kerry Collins, Ki-Jana Carter, Kyle Brady 3.00
15 Barry Sanders, Thurman Thomas 6.00
16 Jermaine Lewis, Jeff Lewis, Ray Lewis 2.00
17 Steve Young, Troy Aikman 5.00
18 Curtis Martin, Chris Warren, Jamal Anderson 5.00
19 Kordell Stewart, Rashaan Salaam, Michael Westbrook 2.00
20 Tony Banks, Muhsin Muhammad 2.00

1996 SkyBox Impact Rookies Rookie Rewind

Rookie Rewind looks back on past drafts to reflect their rise to stardom. Ten different players are featured over a swirl background with the words "Rookie Rewind" in gold foil across the bottom. Rookie Rewind inserts were found only in hobby packs and carried an insertion rate of one per 120.

NM/M
Complete Set (10): 20.00
Common Player: 1.00
1 Jamal Anderson 1.00
2 Jeff Blake 1.00
3 Robert Brooks 1.00
4 Mark Brunell 3.00

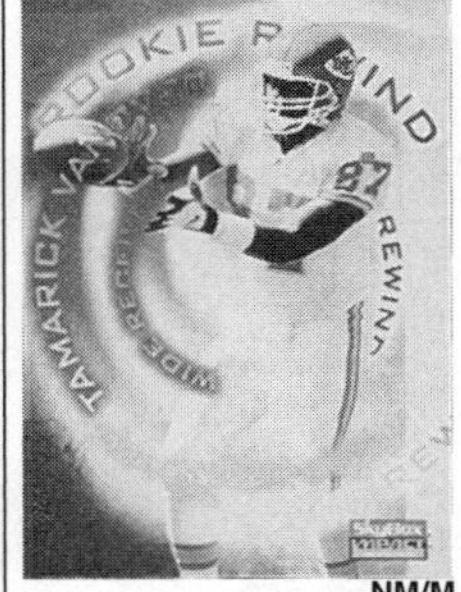

NM/M
5 Brett Favre 6.00
6 Aaron Hayden 1.00
7 Derek Loville 1.00
8 Emmitt Smith 5.00
9 Robert Smith 1.00
10 Tamarick Vanover 2.00

1996 SkyBox Impact Rookies 1996 Rookies

This insert showcased the top rookies of 1996 on cards that were individually numbered to 1,996. The 10 offensive stars included in this insert are found every 144 packs. Autographed versions of Abdul-Jabbar, Dudley, Harrison, Phillips, Kennison and Toomer were available as case toppers.

NM/M
Complete Set (10): 55.00
Common Player: 1.00
1 Karim Abdul-Jabbar 2.00
2 Tim Biakabutuka 1.00
3 Rickey Dudley 1.00
4 Eddie George 18.00
5 Terry Glenn 6.00
6 Marvin Harrison 15.00
7 Keyshawn Johnson 10.00
8 Eddie Kennison 5.00
9 Lawrence Phillips 1.00
10 Amani Toomer 5.00

1996 SkyBox SkyMotion

SkyBox's 1996 SkyMotion set features the video work of NFL films to reproduce 3.5 seconds of game action on each card. No special lights or glasses are needed to get the full effect of the card; all it takes is a flick of the wrist. The cards provide the whole picture of how the play unfolds. The cards are laminated onto paper, enabling SkyBox to print stats and other information on the back for the first time. (Previous cards were plastic, printed on one side only). In addition, there's a Replay parallel set of all 60 cards; these cards feature rounded edges with special foil stamping on the card back. One Replay card is included in each box. Two other insert sets were also made - Big Bang and Team Galaxy.

NM/M
Complete Set (60): 25.00
Common Player: .20
Minor Stars: .50
Gold Cards: 2X-4X
Pack (2): 4.00
Wax Box (24): 20.00
1 Troy Aikman 3.00
2 Marcus Allen .50
3 Jeff Blake 1.00
4 Drew Bledsoe 3.00
5 Tim Brown .20
6 Isaac Bruce 1.00
7 Mark Brunell 2.00
8 Cris Carter .20
9 Kerry Collins 1.00
10 Ben Coates .20
11 Curtis Conway .20
12 Terrell Davis 2.00
13 Trent Dilfer .20
14 Hugh Douglas .20
15 John Elway 3.00
16 Marshall Faulk 3.00
17 Brett Favre 5.00
18 William Floyd .20
19 Joey Galloway 1.00
20 Jeff George .20
21 Rodney Hampton .20
22 Jim Harbaugh .20
23 *Aaron Hayden* .50
24 Jeff Hostetler .20
25 Tyrone Hughes .20
26 Michael Irvin .50
27 Daryl Johnston .20
28 Jim Kelly .20
29 Greg Lloyd .20
30 Dan Marino 5.00
31 Curtis Martin 3.00
32 Chester McGlockton .20
33 Steve McNair 3.00
34 Eric Metcalf .20
35 Scott Mitchell .20
36 Herman Moore 1.00
37 Bryce Paup .20
38 Carl Pickens .20
39 Errict Rhett 1.00
40 Jerry Rice 4.00
41 Rashaan Salaam .50
42 Barry Sanders 4.00
43 Chris Sanders .20
44 Deion Sanders 1.00
45 Junior Seau .20
46 Heath Shuler .20
47 Bruce Smith .20
48 Emmitt Smith 4.00
49 Kordell Stewart 1.00
50 Eric Swann .20
51 Derrick Thomas .20
52 Thurman Thomas .20
53 Eric Turner .20
54 Tamarick Vanover .50
55 Chris Warren .50
56 Ricky Watters .20
57 Michael Westbrook .50
58 Reggie White .50
59 Rod Woodson .20
60 Steve Young 3.00

1996 SkyBox SkyMotion Gold

Actually called Replay, but referred to in the hobby as Golds, this 60-card parallel set featured rounded edges and special foil stamping on the card back to differentiate it from regular-issue cards. Gold parallels were inserted as a box topper into every other hobby box as a reward to box purchasers.

Gold Cards: 2X-4X

1996 SkyBox SkyMotion Big Bang

These 1996 SkyBox SkyMotion inserts have 10 top rookies against a background of exploding fireworks. The cards, using lenticular printing, were seeded one per every packs.

NM/M
Complete Set (10): 20.00
Common Player: 1.00
Tim Biakabutuka 1.00
Rickey Dudley 1.00
Eddie George 5.00
Terry Glenn 3.00
Kevin Hardy 1.00
Marvin Harrison 5.00
Keyshawn Johnson 4.00
Leeland McElroy 1.00
Lawrence Phillips 1.00
Simeon Rice 2.00

1996 SkyBox SkyMotion Team Galaxy

These 1996 SkyBox SkyMotion inserts showcase five of the NFL's top stars against a backdrop of planets and footballs. The cards, printed using lenticular printing, were seeded one per 35 packs.

NM/M
Complete Set (5): 40.00
Common Player: 2.00
1 Karim Abdul-Jabbar 2.00
2 Brett Favre 12.00
3 Curtis Martin 8.00
4 Jerry Rice 10.00
5 Emmitt Smith 10.00

1997 SkyBox

This 250-card base set features 208 veterans, 40 rookies and two checklists. The base cards have a holographic foil design on 20 pt. card stock. The inserts for the set include Rookie Preview, Close Ups, PrimeTime Rookies, Premium Players, Larger Than Life, Autographics and Star Rubies.

NM/M
Complete Set (250): 35.00
Common Player: .10
Minor Stars: .20
Ruby Cards: 20X-50X
Ruby Rookies: 10X-20X
Pack (8): 2.00
Wax Box (24): 40.00
1 Brett Favre 3.00
2 Michael Bates .10
3 Jeff Graham .10
4 Terry Glenn .30
5 Stephen Davis .10
6 Wesley Walls .10
7 Barry Sanders 1.50
8 Chris Sanders .10
9 O.J. McDuffie .10
10 Ken Dilger .10
11 Kimble Anders .10
12 Keenan McCardell .10
13 Ki-Jana Carter .10
14 Gary Brown .10
15 Andre Rison .10
16 Edgar Bennett .10
17 Jerome Bettis .20
18 Ted Johnson .10
19 John Friez .10
20 Tony Brackens .10
21 Bryan Cox .10
22 Eric Moulds .10
23 Johnnie Morton .10
24 Brad Johnson .10
25 Bam Morris .10
26 Anthony Johnson .10
27 Jim Harbaugh .10
28 Keyshawn Johnson .20
29 Cary Blanchard .10
30 Curtis Conway .10
31 Herschel Walker .10
32 Thurman Thomas .20
33 Frank Sanders .10
34 Lawrence Phillips .20
35 Scottie Graham .10
36 Jim Everett .10
37 Dale Carter .10
38 Ashley Ambrose .10
39 Mark Chmura .20
40 James Stewart .10
41 John Mobley .10
42 Terrell Davis 1.25
43 Ben Coates .10
44 Jeff George .10
45 Ty Detmer .10
46 Isaac Bruce .20
47 Chris Warren .10
48 Steve Walsh .10
49 Bruce Smith .10
50 Cris Carter .10
51 Jamal Anderson .10
52 Tim Biakabutuka .10
53 Steve Young .75
54 Eric Turner .10
55 Jessie Tuggle .10
56 Chris T. Jones .10
57 Daryl Johnston .10
58 Randall Cunningham .10
59 Trent Dilfer .20
60 Mark Brunell 1.25
61 Warren Moon .10
62 Terry Kirby .10
63 Eddie George 1.75
64 Neil Smith .10
65 Gilbert Brown .10
66 Emmitt Smith 2.50
67 Chad Brown .10
68 Jamie Asher .10
69 Willie McGinest .10
70 Tim Brown .10
71 Quentin Coryatt .10
72 Mario Bates .10
73 Fred Barnett .10
74 Hugh Douglas .10
75 Eric Swann .10
76 Chris Chandler .10
77 Larry Centers .10
78 Vinny Testaverde .10
79 Jermaine Lewis .10
80 Junior Seau .10
81 Kevin Greene .10
82 Ricky Watters .20
83 Anthony Miller .10
84 Michael Westbrook .10
85 Charles Way .10
86 Andre Reed .10
87 Darrell Green .10
88 Troy Aikman 1.25
89 Jim Pyne .10
90 Dan Marino 2.50
91 Elvis Grbac .10
92 Mel Gray .10
93 Marcus Allen .20
94 Terry Allen .10
95 Karim Abdul-Jabbar .30
96 Rick Mirer .10
97 Bert Emanuel .10
98 John Elway .75
99 Tony Martin .10
100 Zach Thomas .20
101 Harvey Williams .10
102 Jason Sehorn .10
103 Lawyer Milloy .10
104 Thomas Lewis .10
105 Michael Irvin .20
106 James Hundon .10
107 Willie Green .10
108 Bobby Engram .10
109 Mike Alstott .20
110 Greg Lloyd .10
111 Shannon Sharpe .10
112 Desmond Howard .10
113 Jason Elam .10
114 Qadry Ismail .10
115 William Thomas .10
116 Marshall Faulk .20
117 Tyrone Wheatley .10
118 Tommy Vardell .10
119 Rashaan Salaam .20
120 Brian Mitchell .10
121 Terance Mathis .10
122 Dorsey Levens .20
123 Todd Collins .20
124 Derrick Alexander .10
125 Stan Humphries .10
126 Kordell Stewart 1.25
127 Kent Graham .10
128 Yancey Thigpen .10
129 Bryan Still .10
130 Carl Pickens .10
131 Ray Lewis .10
132 Curtis Martin 1.25
133 Kerry Collins .30
134 Ed McCaffrey .10
135 Darick Holmes .10
136 Glyn Milburn .10
137 Rickey Dudley .10
138 Terrell Owens .75
139 Kevin Williams .10
140 Reggie White .20
141 Darnay Scott .10
142 Brett Perriman .10
143 Neil O'Donnell .10
144 Natrone Means .20
145 Jerris McPhail .10
146 Lamar Lathon .10
147 Michael Jackson .10
148 Simeon Rice .10
149 Greg Hill .10
150 Erik Kramer .10
151 Quinn Early .10
152 Tamarick Vanover .10
153 Derrick Thomas .10
154 Nilo Silvan .10
155 Deion Sanders .50
156 Lorenzo Neal .10
157 Steve McNair 1.00
158 Levon Kirkland .10
159 Bobby Hebert .10
160 William Floyd .20
161 Leeland McElroy .10
162 Chester McGlockton .10
163 Michael Haynes .10
164 Aeneas Williams .10
165 Hardy Nickerson .10
166 Rodney Woodson .10
167 Iheanyi Uwaezuoke .10
168 Chris Slade .10
169 Herman Moore .20
170 Rob Moore .10
171 Andre Hastings .10
172 Antonio Freeman .40
173 Tony Boselli .10
174 Drew Bledsoe 1.25
175 Sam Mills .10
176 Robert Smith .10
177 Jimmy Smith .10
178 Alex Molden .10
179 Joey Galloway .20
180 Irving Fryar .10
181 Wayne Chrebet .10
182 Dave Brown .10
183 Robert Brooks .20
184 Tony Banks .30
185 Eric Metcalf .10
186 Napoleon Kaufman .20
187 Frank Wycheck .10
188 Donnell Woolford .10
189 Kevin Turner .10
190 Eddie Kennison .40
191 Cortez Kennedy .10
192 Raymont Harris .10
193 Ronnie Harmon .10
194 Kevin Hardy .10
195 Gus Frerotte .10
196 Marvin Harrison .40
197 Jeff Blake .20
198 Mike Tomczak .10
199 William Roaf .10
200 Jerry Rice 1.25
201 Jake Reed .10
202 Ken Norton .10
203 Errict Rhett .20
204 Adrian Murrell .20
205 Rodney Hampton .10
206 Scott Mitchell .10
207 Jason Dunn .10
208 Ray Zellars .10
209 *Michael Adams* .10
210 *John Allred* .10
211 *Reidel Anthony* 1.50
212 *Darnell Autry* .30
213 *Tiki Barber* 3.00
214 *Will Blackwell* .20
215 *Peter Boulware* .10
216 *Macey Brooks* .10
217 *Rae Carruth* 1.50
218 *Troy Davis* .30
219 *Corey Dillon* 4.00
220 *Jim Druckenmiller* 2.50
221 *Warrick Dunn* 2.00
222 *Marc Edwards* .10
223 *James Farrior* .10
224 *Tony Gonzalez* .75
225 *Jay Graham* .50
226 *Yatil Green* .30
227 *Byron Hanspard* .50
228 *Ike Hilliard* 1.25
229 *Leon Johnson* .10
230 *Damon Jones* .10
231 *Freddie Jones* .50
232 *Joey Kent* .50
233 *David LaFleur* .75
234 *Kevin Lockett* .10
235 *Sam Madison* .10
236 *Brian Manning* .10
237 *Ronnie McAda* .10
238 *Orlando Pace* .50
239 *Jake Plummer* 1.00
240 *Keith Poole* .10
241 *Darrell Russell* .10
242 *Sedrick Shaw* .30
243 *Antowain Smith* 1.50
244 *Shawn Springs* .50
245 *Duce Staley* 6.00
246 *Dedric Ward* .50
247 *Bryant Westbrook* .20
248 *Danny Wuerffel* .75
249 Checklist .10
250 Checklist .10

1997 SkyBox Rubies

Rubies paralleled all 250 cards in SkyBox, but contained Ruby colored foil on the front. Rubies were sequentially numbered to 50 sets on the back.

Ruby Cards:	50X-100X
Ruby Rookies:	25X-50X
Production 50 Sets	

1997 SkyBox Autographics

Inserted 1:240 packs, the cards featured signed fronts. In addition, an Autographics Century Marks parallel set was also randomly seeded.

	NM/M
Common Player:	5.00
Minor Stars:	10.00
Century Marks:	2X
Karim Abdul-Jabbar	15.00
Larry Allen	5.00
Terry Allen	15.00
Mike Alstott	20.00
Darnell Autry	15.00
Tony Banks	15.00
Pat Barnes	5.00
Jeff Blake	10.00
Michael Booker	5.00
Reuben Brown	5.00
Rae Carruth	5.00
Cris Carter	30.00
Ben Coates	30.00
Ernie Conwell	5.00
Terrell Davis	50.00
Ty Detmer	15.00
Ken Dilger	15.00
Corey Dillon	80.00
Jim Druckenmiller	10.00
Rick Dudley	15.00
Brett Favre CM	400.00
Antonio Freeman	30.00
Daryl Gardner	15.00
Chris Gedney	15.00
Eddie George	100.00
Hunter Goodwin	15.00
Marvin Harrison	60.00
Garrison Hearst	30.00
William Henderson	30.00
Michael Jackson	30.00
Tory James	5.00
Rob Johnson	30.00
Chris T. Jones	5.00
Pete Kendall	5.00
Eddie Kennison	10.00
David LaFleur	5.00
Jeff Lewis	5.00
Thomas Lewis	5.00
Keith Lockett	5.00
Brian Manning	5.00
Dan Marino	300.00
Ed McCaffrey	15.00
Keenan McCardell	30.00
Glyn Milburn	15.00
Alex Molden	5.00
Johnnie Morton	25.00
Winslow Oliver	15.00
Jerry Rice	250.00
Rashaan Salaam	15.00
Frank Sanders	25.00
Shannon Sharpe	30.00
Sedrick Shaw	5.00
Alex Smith	5.00
Antowain Smith	80.00
Emmitt Smith	250.00
Jimmy Smith	15.00
Shawn Springs	5.00
James Stewart	15.00
Kordell Stewart	25.00
Rodney Thomas	5.00
Amani Toomer	25.00
Floyd Turner	5.00
Alex Van Dyke	5.00
Mike Vrabel	5.00
Chris Warren	5.00
Charles Way	5.00
Reggie White (Century)	60.00
Rickey Whittle	5.00
Sherman Williams	5.00
John Wittman	5.00

1997 SkyBox Close Ups

This 10-card insert features head shots of young NFL players. Four more pictures are included on the card. Close Ups were inserted 1:18.

		NM/M
Complete Set (10):		30.00
Common Player:		1.00
1	Terrell Davis	5.00
2	Troy Aikman	5.00
3	Drew Bledsoe	5.00
4	Steve McNair	5.00

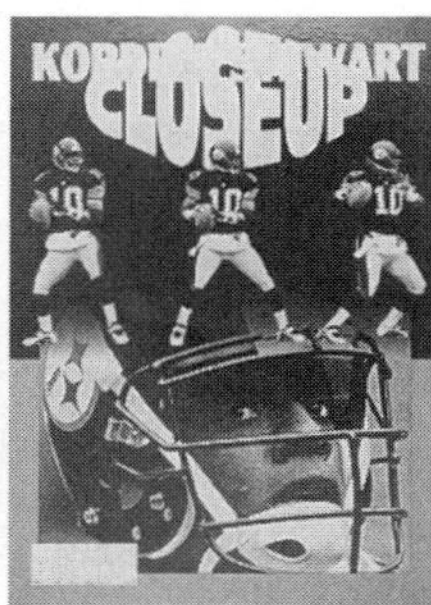

		NM/M
5	Jerry Rice	6.00
6	Kordell Stewart	3.00
7	Kerry Collins	3.00
8	John Elway	6.00
9	Deion Sanders	2.00
10	Joey Galloway	1.00

1997 SkyBox Larger Than Life

Larger Than Life is a 10-card insert featuring the legends of today. Larger Than Life cards were inserted one per 360 packs.

		NM/M
Complete Set (10):		100.00
Common Player:		3.00
1	Emmitt Smith	15.00
2	Barry Sanders	15.00
3	Curtis Martin	10.00
4	Dan Marino	18.00
5	Keyshawn Johnson	5.00
6	Marvin Harrison	5.00
7	Terry Glenn	3.00
8	Eddie George	8.00
9	Brett Favre	20.00
10	Karim Abdul-Jabbar	3.00

1997 SkyBox Premium Players

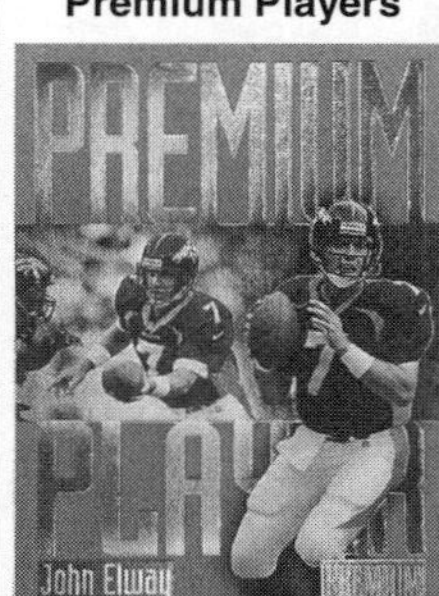

Premium Players is a 15-card insert set which was seeded one per 192 packs.

		NM/M
Complete Set (15):		150.00
Common Player:		2.00
1	Eddie George	15.00
2	Terry Glenn	5.00
3	Karim Abdul-Jabbar	2.00
4	Emmitt Smith	20.00
5	Dan Marino	25.00
6	Brett Favre	25.00
7	Keyshawn Johnson	5.00
8	Curtis Martin	15.00
9	Marvin Harrison	8.00
10	Barry Sanders	20.00
11	Jerry Rice	15.00
12	Terrell Davis	15.00
13	Troy Aikman	15.00
14	Drew Bledsoe	15.00
15	John Elway	15.00

1997 SkyBox PrimeTime Rookies

PrimeTime Rookies is a 10-card insert featuring the top rookies of 1997. This set was inserted one per 96 packs.

		NM/M
Complete Set (10):		25.00
Common Player:		1.00
1	Jim Druckenmiller	1.00
2	Antowain Smith	3.00
3	Rae Carruth	1.00
4	Yatil Green	2.00
5	Ike Hilliard	3.00
6	Reidel Anthony	2.00
7	Orlando Pace	2.00
8	Peter Boulware	1.00
9	Warrick Dunn	10.00
10	Troy Davis	5.00

1997 SkyBox Reebok Bronze

The Reebok Value Added set came in bronze, silver, gold, ruby and emerald versions. The overall insertion rate for the Reebok Value Added set was one per pack.

		NM/M
Complete Set (15):		4.00
Common Player:		.10
Gold:		3X
Green:		5X-10X
Red:		3X-8X
Silver:		2X
12	Keenan McCardell	.10
37	Dale Carter	.10
38	Ashley Ambrose	.10
43	Ben Coates	.10
66	Emmitt Smith	1.50
95	Karim Abdul-Jabbar	.50
98	John Elway	1.50
110	Greg Lloyd	.10
123	Todd Collins	.10
161	Leeland McElroy	.10
169	Herman Moore	.10
175	Sam Mills	.10
180	Irving Fryar	.10
202	Ken Norton	.10
205	Rodney Hampton	.10

1997 SkyBox Rookie Preview

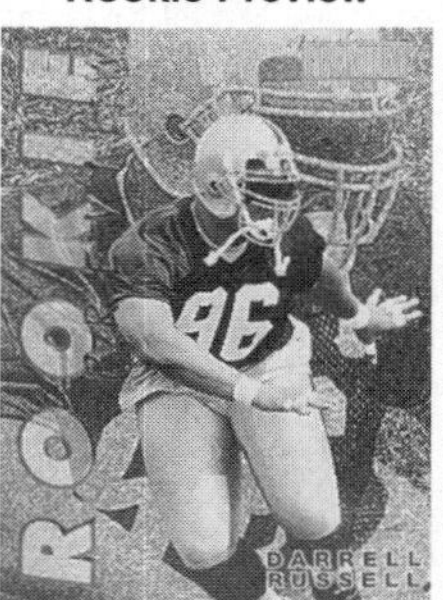

These 15 embossed insert cards feature some of the top rookies of 1997. Rookie Preview cards were inserted 1:6.

		NM/M
Complete Set (15):		12.00
Common Player:		.50
1	Reidel Anthony	.50
2	Tiki Barber	3.00
3	Peter Boulware	.50
4	Rae Carruth	.50
5	Jim Druckenmiller	.50
6	Warrick Dunn	4.00
7	James Farrior	.50
8	Yatil Green	1.00
9	Byron Hanspard	.50
10	Ike Hilliard	2.50
11	Orlando Pace	1.50
12	Darrell Russell	.50
13	Antowain Smith	3.00
14	Shawn Springs	1.00
15	Bryant Westbrook	.50

1997 SkyBox Impact

The 250-card set contains 207 player cards, three checklists and 40 rookies. The cards feature the player's photo superimposed over a jagged background, with the player's name printed in 3-D block letters at the top. The player's first and last name and team are printed at the bottom right in gold foil, while the Impact logo is in the lower left. The backs include the player's name, position, quote, Impact stats, bio, stats, photo and team helmet over a team-colored football background. A Rave parallel set was randomly seeded. SkyBox produced less than 150 Rave sets.

		NM/M
Complete Set (250):		20.00
Common Player:		.05
Minor Stars:		.10
Circa Rave Stars:		10X-25X
Circa Rave Rookies:		3X-8X
Pack (8):		1.00
Wax Box (36):		35.00
1	Carl Pickens	.05
2	Ray Lewis	.05
3	Darrell Green	.05
4	Brett Favre	1.75
5	Todd Collins	.05
6	Errict Rhett	.10
7	John Elway	.50
8	Troy Aikman	.75
9	Steve McNair	.75
10	Kordell Stewart	.75
11	Drew Bledsoe	.75
12	Kerry Collins	.25
13	Dan Marino	1.50
14	Ricky Watters	.10
15	Marvin Harrison	.30
16	Simeon Rice	.05
17	Qadry Ismail	.05
18	Andre Coleman	.05
19	Keyshawn Johnson	.30
20	Barry Sanders	1.25
21	Rickey Dudley	.10
22	Emmitt Smith	1.50
23	Erik Kramer	.05
24	Tony Boselli	.05
25	Steve Young	.50
26	Rod Woodson	.05
27	Eddie George	1.00
28	Curtis Martin	1.00
29	Amani Toomer	.05
30	Terrell Davis	1.00
31	Jim Everett	.05
32	Marcus Allen	.10
33	Karim Abdul-Jabbar	.50
34	Thurman Thomas	.10
35	Cortez Kennedy	.05
36	Jerome Bettis	.10
37	Kevin Carter	.05
38	Gilbert Brown	.05
39	Bert Emanuel	.05
40	Kyle Brady	.05
41	Trent Dilfer	.10
42	Garrison Hearst	.05
43	Kevin Greene	.05
44	Bryan Cox	.05
45	Desmond Howard	.05
46	Larry Centers	.05
47	Quentin Coryatt	.05
48	Michael Jackson	.05
49	John Randle	.05
50	Mark Brunell	.75
51	William Thomas	.05
52	Glyn Milburn	.05
53	Mike Alstott	.10
54	Chris Spielman	.05
55	Junior Seau	.10
56	Brian Blades	.05
57	Lamar Lathon	.05
58	Derrick Thomas	.05
59	Dave Brown	.05
60	Frank Wycheck	.05
61	Chris Slade	.05
62	Neil Smith	.05
63	Ashley Ambrose	.05
64	Alex Molden	.05
65	Edgar Bennett	.05
66	Alvin Harper	.05
67	Jamal Anderson	.15
68	Eddie Kennison	.30
69	Ken Norton	.05
70	Zach Thomas	.20
71	Leeland McElroy	.10
72	Terry Allen	.05
73	Raymont Harris	.05
74	Ken Dilger	.05
75	Jason Dunn	.05
76	Robert Smith	.05
77	William Roaf	.05
78	Bruce Smith	.05
79	Vinny Testaverde	.05
80	Jerry Rice	.75
81	Tim Brown	.05
82	James Stewart	.05
83	Andre Reed	.05
84	Herman Moore	.15
85	Stan Humphries	.05
86	Chris Warren	.05
87	Tyrone Wheatley	.05
88	Michael Irvin	.10
89	Dan Wilkinson	.05
90	Tony Banks	.20
91	Chester McGlockton	.05
92	Reggie White	.10
93	Elvis Grbac	.05
94	Willie Davis	.05
95	Greg Lloyd	.05
96	Ben Coates	.05
97	Rashaan Salaam	.10
98	Eric Swann	.05
99	Hugh Douglas	.05
100	Henry Ellard	.05
101	Rod Smith	.05
102	Tim Biakabutuka	.10
103	Chad Brown	.05
104	Kevin Hardy	.05
105	Chris T. Jones	.05
106	Antonio Freeman	.20
107	Lamont Warren	.05
108	Derrick Alexander	.05
109	Brett Perriman	.05
110	Antonio Langham	.05
111	Eric Moulds	.05
112	O.J. McDuffie	.05
113	Eric Metcalf	.05
114	Ray Zellars	.05
115	Marco Coleman	.05
116	Terry Kirby	.05
117	Darren Woodson	.05
118	Charles Johnson	.05
119	Sam Mills	.05
120	Rodney Hampton	.05
121	Rick Mirer	.10
122	Derrick Brooks	.05
123	Greg Hill	.05
124	John Mobley	.05
125	Chris Sanders	.05
126	Kent Graham	.05
127	Michael Westbrook	.05
128	Harvey Williams	.05
129	Keenan McCardell	.05
130	Neil O'Donnell	.05
131	LeRoy Butler	.05
132	Willie McGinest	.05
133	Ki-Jana Carter	.05
134	Robert Jones	.05
135	Jim Harbaugh	.05
136	Wesley Walls	.05
137	Jackie Harris	.05
138	Jermaine Lewis	.05
139	Jake Reed	.05
140	John Friesz	.05
141	Jerris McPhail	.05
142	Charlie Garner	.05
143	Bryce Paup	.05
144	Tony Martin	.05
145	Shannon Sharpe	.05
146	Terrell Owens	.50
147	Curtis Conway	.10
148	Jamie Asher	.05
149	Lawrence Phillips	.10
150	Deion Sanders	.30
151	Frank Sanders	.05
152	Joey Galloway	.20
153	Mel Gray	.05
154	Robert Brooks	.10
155	Jeff George	.05
156	Michael Haynes	.05
157	Chris Chandler	.05
158	Adrian Murrell	.05
159	Tamarick Vanover	.05
160	Marshall Faulk	.10
161	Thomas Lewis	.05
162	Ty Detmer	.05
163	Darnay Scott	.05
164	Bam Morris	.05
165	Scott Mitchell	.05
166	Brad Johnson	.05
167	Dave Meggett	.05
168	Bobby Engram	.05
169	Natrone Means	.10
170	Erric Pegram	.05
171	Leonard Russell	.05
172	Muhsin Muhammad	.05
173	Aeneas Williams	.05
174	Fred Barnett	.05
175	William Floyd	.05
176	Kimble Anders	.05
177	Darick Holmes	.05
178	Willie Green	.05
179	Rodney Thomas	.05
180	Derrick Alexander	.05
181	Sean Dawkins	.05
182	Dorsey Levens	.10
183	Napoleon Kaufman	.05
184	Mario Bates	.05
185	Yancey Thigpen	.05
186	Johnnie Morton	.05
187	Gus Frerotte	.05
188	Terance Mathis	.05
189	Tyrone Hughes	.05
190	Wayne Chrebet	.05
191	Tony Brackens	.05
192	Hardy Nickerson	.05
193	Daryl Johnston	.05
194	Irving Fryar	.05
195	Jeff Blake	.15
196	Charles Way	.05
197	Brian Mitchell	.05
198	Brent Jones	.05
199	Mark Chmura	.05
200	Terry Glenn	.30
201	Cris Carter	.05
202	Steve Atwater	.05
203	Rob Moore	.05
204	Anthony Johnson	.05
205	Warren Moon	.10
206	Darrien Gordon	.05
207	Isaac Bruce	.15
208	*Reidel Anthony*	1.00
209	*Darnell Autry*	.50
210	*Tiki Barber*	1.50
211	*Pat Barnes*	.30
212	*Terry Battle*	.10
213	*Michael Booker*	.10
214	*Peter Boulware*	.20
215	*Chris Canty*	.10
216	*Rae Carruth*	1.00
217	*Troy Davis*	.30
218	*Corey Dillon*	3.00
219	*Jim Druckenmiller*	.50
220	*Warrick Dunn*	1.25
221	*James Farrior*	.10
222	*Tarik Glenn*	.10
223	*Tony Gonzalez*	.50
224	*Yatil Green*	.30
225	*Byron Hanspard*	.30
226	*Ike Hilliard*	1.00
227	*Kenny Holmes*	.10
228	*Walter Jones*	.10
229	*Tom Knight*	.10
230	*David LaFleur*	.40
231	*Kenard Lang*	.10
232	*Kevin Lockett*	.10
233	*Tremain Mack*	.10
234	*Sam Madison*	.10
235	*Chris Naeole*	.10
236	*Orlando Pace*	.40
237	*Jake Plummer*	2.50
238	*Dwayne Rudd*	.10
239	*Darrell Russell*	.25
240	*Jamie Sharper*	.10
241	*Sedrick Shaw*	.50
242	*Antowain Smith*	1.25
243	*Shawn Springs*	.50
244	*Bryant Westbrook*	.20
245	*Reinard Wilson*	.10
246	*Danny Wuerffel*	.50
247	*Renaldo Wynn*	.10
248	Checklist	.05
249	Checklist	.05
250	Checklist	.05

1997 SkyBox Impact Raves

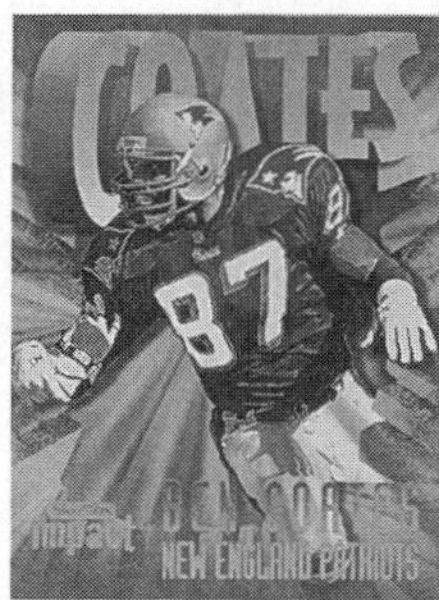

Rave is a parallel of the SkyBox Impact base set. The Rave set parallels 247 cards (not the checklists) and was limited to 150 sets.

Rave Stars:	10X-25X
Rave Rookies:	3X-8X

1997 SkyBox Impact Boss

Inserted 1:6 packs, the 20-card set features the player's photo, name and team name embossed on the front. The backs have the player's name, team, position and highlights on the left side, while the Boss logo runs vertically along the right border. The cards are numbered "of 20" in the upper right corner. The Super Boss parallel set was inserted 1:36 packs. The cards are identical to the base Boss, except the cards are printed on foil. The Super Boss logo appears in the lower left of the card front. The Super Boss cards also have an "SB" suffix with the card numbers on the back.

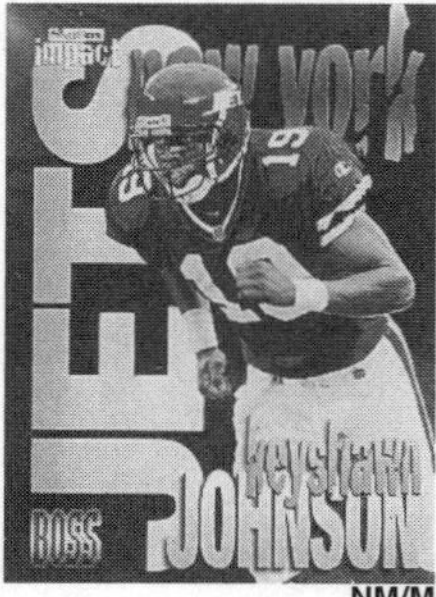

		NM/M
Complete Set (20):		20.00
Common Player:		.50
Super Boss Cards:		2X-4X
1	Karim Abdul-Jabbar	.50
2	Troy Aikman	3.00
3	Tim Biakabutuka	.50
4	Mark Brunell	2.00
5	Rae Carruth	.50
6	Kerry Collins	1.00
7	Corey Dillon	2.00
8	Jim Druckenmiller	.50
9	Warrick Dunn	2.00
10	Brett Favre	4.00
11	Eddie George	2.00
12	Marvin Harrison	1.50
13	Keyshawn Johnson	1.50
14	Eddie Kennison	1.50
15	Dan Marino	4.00
16	Curtis Martin	2.00
17	Steve McNair	2.00
18	Orlando Pace	.50
19	Barry Sanders	3.00
20	Steve Young	2.00

1997 SkyBox Impact Excelerators

The 12-card set was inserted 1:48 packs. The die-cut cards have the player's photo superimposed over a black and silver background, with a shield in the center. Excelerators is printed in red in the center of the background, while the player's name is printed in silver over the center of the player photo. The SkyBox logo is at the bottom center of the front. The backs have a player photo in the center, with his name and highlights printed inside the shield. The card numbers are printed "of 12."

		NM/M
Complete Set (12):		35.00
Common Player:		1.00
1	Mark Brunell	3.00
2	Rae Carruth	1.00
3	Terrell Davis	6.00
4	Joey Galloway	1.00
5	Marvin Harrison	4.00
6	Keyshawn Johnson	2.00
7	Eddie Kennison	2.00
8	Steve McNair	5.00
9	Jerry Rice	6.00
10	Emmitt Smith	6.00
11	Shawn Springs	1.00
12	Kordell Stewart	3.00

1997 SkyBox Impact Instant Impact

The 15-card set was inserted 1:24 packs. The player's last name is printed in black at the top inside a white stripe. The Impact logo is printed in silver in the lower right of the photo. A black stripe at the bottom includes "Instant Impact," player's name and team in silver foil. The team's helmet is located in the bottom center. The backs have the card number "of 15" printed at the top, while his highlights are printed in the center of the card. The black stripe on the bottom repeats the information from the front, without the silver foil.

		NM/M
Complete Set (15):		25.00
Common Player:		1.00
1	Reidel Anthony	1.00
2	Darnell Autry	1.00
3	Tiki Barber	3.00
4	Peter Boulware	1.00
5	Troy Davis	1.00
6	Jim Druckenmiller	1.00
7	Warrick Dunn	5.00
8	Yatil Green	2.00
9	Ike Hilliard	3.00
10	Orlando Pace	2.00
11	Darrell Russell	1.00
12	Sedrick Shaw	1.00
13	Shawn Springs	1.00
14	Bryant Westbrook	1.00
15	Danny Wuerffel	2.00

1997 SkyBox Impact Rave Reviews

Inserted 1:288 packs, the 12-card set includes a player photo superimposed over a holofoil background of numbers. The Rave Reviews logo is printed above the player's name in the lower left corner. "Rave Review" is printed in holofoil vertically along the right border. The backs have the player's name at the top, with a quote from Ronnie Lott along the left border. The player's photo is on the right. Lott's photo and description, along with the card number "of 12" are printed in the lower left.

		NM/M
Complete Set (12):		125.00
Common Player:		5.00
Inserted 1:288		
1	Terrell Davis	15.00
2	John Elway	15.00
3	Brett Favre	20.00
4	Joey Galloway	5.00
5	Eddie George	10.00
6	Terry Glenn	5.00
7	Dan Marino	20.00
8	Curtis Martin	10.00
9	Jerry Rice	15.00
10	Barry Sanders	15.00
11	Deion Sanders	5.00
12	Emmitt Smith	15.00

1997 SkyBox Impact Total Impact

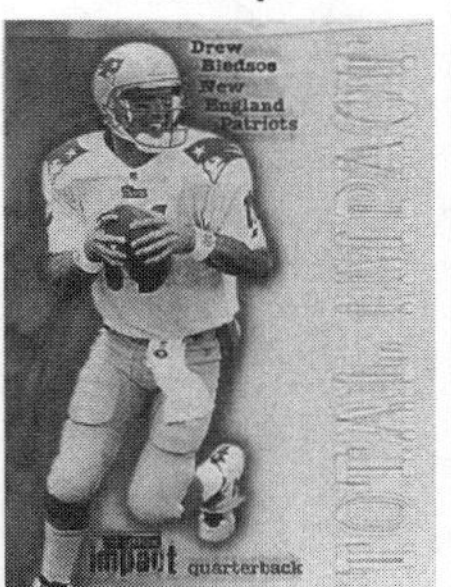

Inserted 1:36 retail packs, the 10-card set is printed on plastic over a white background.

		NM/M
Complete Set (10):		20.00
Common Player:		1.00
1	Karim Abdul-Jabbar	1.00
2	Troy Aikman	4.00
3	Drew Bledsoe	4.00
4	Isaac Bruce	2.00
5	Kerry Collins	2.00
6	John Elway	4.00
7	Terry Glenn	2.00
8	Lawrence Phillips	1.00
9	Deion Sanders	2.00
10	Kordell Stewart	4.00

1998 SkyBox

This 250-card included 195 veteran stars, 15 One for the Ages subset cards and 40 rookies seeded one per four packs. Each card featured a borderless design on the front, with the player's name, team, position and SkyBox logo printed in a prismatic gold foil. Backs contain a closeup of the player over a black background. Each card was paralleled in a Star Rubies parallel which was numbered to 50 sets. Insert sets include: Autographics, D'Stroyers, Intimidation Nation, Prime Time Rookies, Rap Show and Soul of the Game.

		NM/M
Complete Set (250):		75.00
Common Player:		.10
Minor Stars:		.20
Common Rookie (211-250):		1.50
Inserted 1:4		
Star Ruby Cards:		25X-60X
Star Ruby Rookies:		4X-8X
Production 50 Sets		
Pack (8):		3.00
Wax Box (24):		50.00
1	John Elway	1.25
2	Drew Bledsoe	1.25
3	Antonio Freeman	.50
4	Merton Hanks	.10
5	James Jett	.10
6	Ricky Proehl	.10
7	Deion Sanders	.50
8	Frank Sanders	.10
9	Bruce Smith	.10
10	Tiki Barber	.20
11	Isaac Bruce	.20
12	Mark Brunell	1.00
13	Quinn Early	.10
14	Terry Glenn	.20
15	Darrien Gordon	.10
16	Keith Byars	.10
17	Terrell Davis	1.00
18	Charlie Garner	.10
19	Eddie Kennison	.20
20	Keenan McCardell	.10
21	Eric Moulds	.10
22	Jimmy Smith	.20
23	Reidel Anthony	.20
24	Rae Carruth	.10
25	Michael Irvin	.50
26	Dorsey Levens	.20
27	Derrick Mayes	.10
28	Adrian Murrell	.20
29	Dwayne Rudd	.10
30	Leslie Shepherd	.10
31	Jamal Anderson	.20
32	Robert Brooks	.10
33	Sean Dawkins	.10
34	Cris Dishman	.10
35	Rickey Dudley	.10
36	Bobby Engram	.10
37	Chester McGlockton	.10
38	Terrell Owens	.20
39	Wayne Chrebet	.10
40	Dexter Coakley	.10
41	Kerry Collins	.20
42	Trent Dilfer	.20
43	Bobby Hoying	.10
44	Glyn Milburn	.10
45	Rob Moore	.10
46	Jake Reed	.10
47	Dana Stubblefield	.10
48	Reggie White	.20
49	Natrone Means	.20
50	Troy Aikman	1.25
51	Aaron Bailey	.10
52	William Floyd	.10
53	Eric Metcalf	.10
54	Warrick Dunn	1.00
55	Chad Lewis	.10
56	Curtis Martin	.75
57	Tony Martin	.10
58	John Randle	.10
59	Jeff Burris	.10
60	Larry Centers	.10
61	Bert Emanuel	.10
62	Sean Gilbert	.10
63	David Palmer	.10
64	Eric Bieniemy	.10
65	Peter Boulware	.10
66	Charles Johnson	.10
67	Jerris McPhail	.10
68	Scott Mitchell	.10
69	Chris Sanders	.10
70	Ken Dilger	.10
71	Brad Johnson	.20
72	Danny Kanell	.10
73	Fred Lane	.20
74	Warren Sapp	.10
75	Carl Pickens	.20
76	Cris Carter	.20
77	Marshall Faulk	.20
78	Keyshawn Johnson	.20
79	Tony McGee	.10
80	Muhsin Muhammad	.10
81	Kordell Stewart	1.00
82	Karl Williams	.10
83	Willie Davis	.10
84	David Dunn	.10
85	Marvin Harrison	.20
86	Michael Jackson	.10
87	John Mobley	.10
88	Shawn Springs	.10
89	Wesley Walls	.10
90	Jermaine Lewis	.10
91	Ed McCaffrey	.10
92	Chris Calloway	.10
93	Lamont Warren	.10
94	Ricky Watters	.20
95	Tony Banks	.20
96	Tony Brackens	.10
97	Gary Brown	.10
98	Howard Griffith	.10
99	Ray Lewis	.10
100	Jeff Blake	.20
101	Charlie Jones	.10
102	Glenn Foley	.20
103	Jay Graham	.10
104	James McKnight	.10
105	Steve McNair	.75
106	Chad Scott	.10
107	Rod Smith	.20
108	Jason Taylor	.10
109	Corey Dillon	1.00
110	Eddie George	1.00
111	Jim Harbaugh	.20
112	Warren Moon	.20
113	Shannon Sharpe	.20
114	Darnell Autry	.10
115	Brett Favre	2.50
116	Jeff George	.20
117	Tony Gonzalez	.10
118	Garrison Hearst	.20
119	Randal Hill	.10
120	Eric Swann	.10
121	Jamie Asher	.10
122	Tim Brown	.20
123	Stephen Davis	.10
124	Chris Chandler	.10
125	Jerry Rice	1.25
126	Troy Davis	.10
127	Ronnie Harmon	.10
128	Andre Rison	.10
129	Duce Staley	.10
130	Charles Way	.10
131	Bryant Westbrook	.10
132	Mike Alstott	.50
133	Gus Frerotte	.10
134	Travis Jervey	.10
135	Daryl Johnston	.10
136	Jake Plummer	1.00
137	Junior Seau	.20
138	Robert Smith	.20
139	Thurman Thomas	.20
140	Karim Abdul-Jabbar	.20
141	Jerome Bettis	.20
142	Byron Hanspard	.10
143	Raymont Harris	.10
144	Willie McGinest	.10
145	Barry Sanders	2.00
146	Irv Smith	.10
147	Michael Strahan	.10
148	Frank Wycheck	.10
149	Steve Broussard	.10
150	Joey Galloway	.50
151	Courtney Hawkins	.10
152	O.J. McDuffie	.10
153	Herman Moore	.20
154	Chris Penn	.10
155	O.J. Santiago	.10
156	Yancey Thigpen	.10
157	Jason Sehorn	.10
158	Ben Coates	.10
159	Ernie Conwell	.10
160	Dale Carter	.10
161	Jeff Graham	.10
162	Rob Johnson	.20
163	Damon Jones	.10
164	Mark Chmura	.20
165	Curtis Conway	.20
166	Elvis Grbac	.10
167	Andre Hastings	.10
168	Terry Kirby	.10
169	Aeneas Williams	.10
170	Derrick Alexander	.10
171	Troy Brown	.10
172	Irving Fryar	.10
173	Jerald Moore	.10
174	Andre Reed	.10
175	James Stewart	.20
176	Chris Warren	.10
177	Will Blackwell	.10
178	Erik Kramer	.10
179	Dan Marino	2.00
180	Terance Mathis	.10
181	Johnnie Morton	.10
182	J.J. Stokes	.20
183	Rodney Thomas	.10
184	Steve Young	.75
185	Kimble Anders	.10
186	Napoleon Kaufman	.50
187	Orlando Pace	.10
188	Antowain Smith	.75
189	Emmitt Smith	2.00
190	Terry Allen	.10
191	Mark Bruener	.10
191	Mark Bruener	.10
192	Rodney Harrison	.10
193	Billy Joe Hobert	.10
194	Leon Johnson	.10
195	Freddie Jones	.10
196	Super Bowl	.10
197	Super Bowl	.10
198	Super Bowl	.10
199	Super Bowl	.10
200	Super Bowl	.10
201	Super Bowl	.10
202	Super Bowl	.10
203	Super Bowl	.10
204	Super Bowl	.10
205	Super Bowl	.10
206	Super Bowl	.10
207	Super Bowl	.10
208	Super Bowl	.10
209	Super Bowl	.10
210	Super Bowl	.10
211	*Robert Edwards*	3.00
212	*Roland Williams*	1.50
213	*Joe Jurevicius*	3.00
214	*Wilmont Perry*	1.50
215	*Robert Holcombe*	4.00
216	*Larry Shannon*	1.50
217	*Skip Hicks*	3.00
218	*Patrick Johnson*	1.50
219	*Pat Palmer*	1.50
220	*John Dutton*	1.50
221	*Az-Zahir Hakim*	4.00
222	*Mikhael Ricks*	3.00
223	*Rashaan Shehee*	3.00
224	*Ryan Leaf*	3.00
225	*Alvis Whitted*	1.50
226	*Marcus Nash*	2.00
227	*Fred Taylor*	8.00
228	*Hines Ward*	8.00
229	*Chris Fuamatu-Ma'afala*	4.00
230	*Jerome Pathon*	3.00
231	*Peyton Manning*	25.00
232	*Charles Woodson*	5.00
233	*Jon Ritchie*	1.50
234	*Scott Frost*	1.50
235	*John Avery*	4.00
236	*Jonathon Linton*	3.00
237	*Jacquez Green*	3.00
238	*Andre Wadsworth*	3.00
239	*Cam Quayle*	1.50
240	*Randy Moss*	20.00
241	*Raymond Priester*	1.50
242	*Donald Hayes*	1.50
243	*Brian Griese*	8.00
244	*Brian Alford*	1.50
245	*Kevin Dyson*	3.00
246	*Jammi German*	1.50
247	*Cameron Cleeland*	4.00
248	*Curtis Enis*	3.00
249	*Terry Hardy*	1.50
250	*Tony Simmons*	4.00

1998 SkyBox Star Rubies

Star Rubies paralleled all 250 cards in SkyBox. The gold foil stamps of the regular cards were replaced by red foil and backs were numbered to 50.

Star Ruby Cards:	25X-60X
Star Ruby Rookies:	4X-8X

1998 SkyBox Autographics

A total of 73 different NFL players signed cards for Autographics in 1998. The program ran through Thunder, Metal Universe, SkyBox and E-X2001 products. Regular versions are signed in black ink, while Blue versions are individually numbered to 50. Cards were inserted 1:112 in Thunder, 1:68 in Metal Universe and Premium and 1:48 packs of E-X2001.

	NM/M
Common Player:	10.00
Minor Stars:	20.00
Inserted 1:48 E-X2001	
Inserted 1:68 Metal Universe	
Inserted 1:68 SkyBox Premium	
Inserted 1:112 Thunder	
Blue Signatures:	2X-4X
Production 50 Sets	
Kevin Abrams	10.00
Mike Alstott	25.00
Jamie Asher	10.00
Jon Avery	10.00
Tavian Banks	10.00
Pat Barnes	10.00
Jerome Bettis	30.00
Eric Bjornson	10.00
Peter Boulware	10.00
Troy Brown	10.00
Mark Breunner	10.00
Mark Brunell	25.00
Rae Carruth	10.00
Ray Crockett	10.00
Germane Crowell	10.00
Stephen Davis	20.00
Troy Davis	10.00
Sean Dawkins	10.00
Trent Dilfer	30.00
Corey Dillon	35.00
Jim Druckenmiller	10.00
Kevin Dyson	35.00
Marc Edwards	10.00
Robert Edwards	25.00
Bobby Engram	10.00
Curtis Enis	15.00
William Floyd	20.00
Glenn Foley	10.00
Chris Fuamatu-Ma'afala	30.00
Joey Galloway	25.00
Jeff George	10.00
Ahman Green	40.00
Jacquez Green	25.00
Yatil Green	10.00
Byron Hanspard	10.00
Marvin Harrison	30.00
Skip Hicks	10.00
Robert Holcombe	25.00
Bobby Hoying	10.00
Travis Jervey	10.00
Rob Johnson	30.00
Freddie Jones	10.00
Eddie Kennison	20.00
Fred Lane	10.00
Ryan Leaf	15.00
Dorsey Levens	15.00
Jeff Lewis	10.00
Jermaine Lewis	10.00
Dan Marino	125.00
Curtis Martin	60.00
Steve Matthews	10.00
Alonzo Mayes	10.00
Keenan McCardell	20.00
Willie McGinnest	10.00
James McKnight	10.00
Glyn Milburn	10.00
Warren Moon	35.00
Randy Moss	125.00
Marcus Nash	15.00
Terrell Owens	40.00
Jason Peter	20.00
Jake Plummer	40.00
John Randle	20.00
Shannon Sharpe	40.00
Jimmy Smith	20.00
Lamar Smith	10.00
Robert Smith	20.00
Duce Staley	20.00
Kordell Stewart	25.00
Fred Taylor	45.00
Rodney Thomas	10.00
Kevin Turner	10.00
Hines Ward	40.00
Charles Way	10.00
Frank Wycheck	10.00

1998 SkyBox D'stroyers

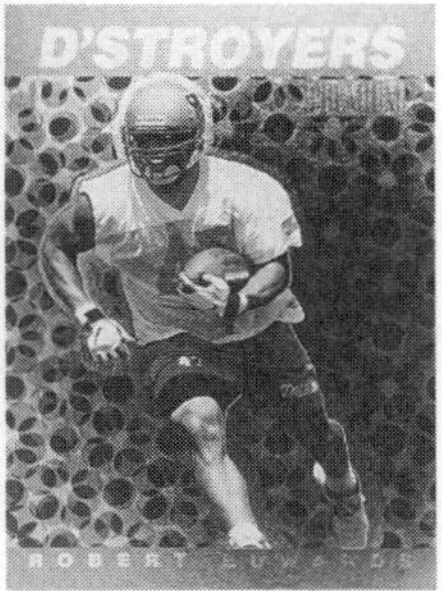

D'Stroyers was a 15-card insert that highlighted top young players in the league. The players were featured over a prismatic foil background and inserted one per six packs.

		NM/M
Complete Set (15):		15.00
Common Player:		.25
Minor Stars:		1.00
Inserted 1:6		
1	Antowain Smith	1.00
2	Corey Dillon	2.00
3	Charles Woodson	2.00
4	Randy Moss	5.00
5	Deion Sanders	1.00
6	Robert Edwards	1.00
7	Herman Moore	1.00
8	Mark Brunell	2.00
9	Dorsey Levens	.25
10	Curtis Enis	.25
11	Drew Bledsoe	4.00
12	Steve McNair	2.00
13	Keyshawn Johnson	1.00
14	Bobby Hoying	.25
15	Trent Dilfer	1.00

1998 SkyBox Intimidation Nation

Intimidation Nation captured 15 of the top players in the league over a flaming background. This insert was the toughest to find in SkyBox and inserted one per 360 packs.

		NM/M
Complete Set (15):		160.00
Common Player:		5.00
Inserted 1:360		
1	Terrell Davis	20.00
2	Emmitt Smith	25.00
3	Barry Sanders	25.00
4	Brett Favre	25.00
5	Eddie George	15.00
6	Jerry Rice	20.00
7	John Elway	15.00
8	Mark Brunell	5.00
9	Troy Aikman	12.00
10	Peyton Manning	20.00
11	Ryan Leaf	5.00
12	Curtis Martin	10.00
13	Dan Marino	20.00
14	Warrick Dunn	5.00
15	Jake Plummer	5.00

1998 SkyBox Prime Time Rookies

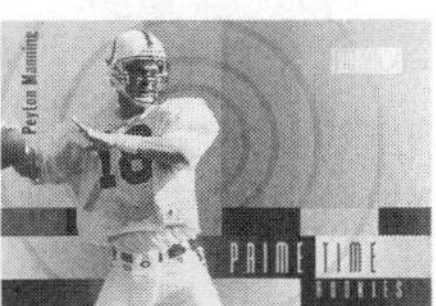

Ten rookies were featured on this horizontal, multi-colored background insert set. The cards featured the rookie on the left side with a bullseye over the background. Prime Time Rookies were seeded one per 96 packs.

		NM/M
Complete Set (10):		50.00
Common Player:		3.00
Inserted 1:96		
1	Curtis Enis	3.00
2	Robert Edwards	3.00
3	Fred Taylor	10.00
4	Robert Holcombe	3.00
5	Ryan Leaf	3.00
6	Peyton Manning	20.00
7	Randy Moss	20.00
8	Charles Woodson	5.00
9	Andre Wadsworth	3.00
10	Kevin Dyson	3.00

1998 SkyBox Rap Show

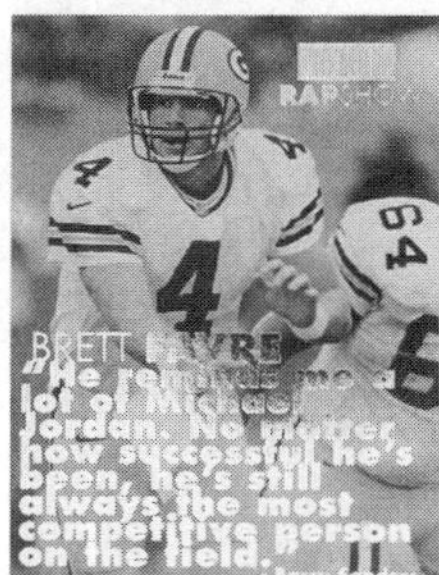

This 15-card insert featured an action shot of the player with a silver foil-stamped quote from one of his peers on the front. Rap Show inserts were seeded per 36 packs.

		NM/M
Complete Set (15):		50.00
Common Player:		3.00
Minor Stars:		5.00
Inserted 1:36		
1	John Elway	6.00
2	Drew Bledsoe	6.00
3	Corey Dillon	3.00
4	Brett Favre	8.00
5	Barry Sanders	6.00
6	Eddie George	3.00
7	Emmitt Smith	6.00
8	Jake Plummer	3.00
9	Joey Galloway	2.00
10	Ricky Watters	3.00
11	Mike Alstott	3.00
12	Kordell Stewart	4.00
13	Antonio Freeman	3.00
14	Terrell Davis	5.00
15	Warrick Dunn	3.00

1998 SkyBox Soul of the Game

Soul of the Game were horizontal inserts that resembled a record sleeve with the album half out. The cards were one solid piece of plastic and inserted one per 18 packs.

		NM/M
Complete Set (15):		40.00
Common Player:		1.00
Minor Stars:		2.00
Inserted 1:18		
1	Troy Aikman	5.00
2	Dorsey Levens	1.00
3	Deion Sanders	2.00
4	Antonio Freeman	2.00
5	Dan Marino	6.00
6	Keyshawn Johnson	2.00
7	Terry Glenn	2.00
8	Tim Brown	3.00
9	Curtis Martin	5.00
10	Bobby Hoying	1.00
11	Kordell Stewart	4.00
12	Jerry Rice	6.00
13	Steve McNair	4.00
14	Joey Galloway	2.00
15	Steve Young	4.00

1998 SkyBox Double Vision

Each single in this 32-card set measures 5-1/2" x 7" and has an interactive team color-coded slide on the front. So when you pull the tab the player goes from black and white to color. Along with another color picture of that player with his name, team and position.

		NM/M
Complete Set (32):		50.00
Common Player:		1.00
Production 5,000 Sets		
1	Dan Marino	6.00
2	John Elway	4.00
3	Troy Aikman	4.00
4	Steve Young	4.00
5	Terrell Davis	4.00
6	Barry Sanders	5.00
7	Jerry Rice	5.00
8	Kordell Stewart	2.00
9	Jake Plummer	2.00
10	Brett Favre	6.00
11	Drew Bledsoe	3.00
12	Tony Banks	1.00
13	Kerry Collins	1.00
14	Steve McNair	2.00
15	Warren Moon	1.00
16	Ryan Leaf	1.00
17	Peyton Manning	4.00
18	Elvis Grbac	1.00
19	Jeff Blake	1.00
20	Brad Johnson	1.00
21	Trent Dilfer	1.00
22	Scott Mitchell	1.00
23	Dan Marino	5.00
24	John Elway	3.00
25	Troy Aikman	3.00
26	Steve Young	2.00
27	Terrell Davis	3.00
28	Barry Sanders	4.00
29	Jerry Rice	3.00
30	Kordell Stewart	2.00
31	Jake Plummer	1.00
32	Brett Favre	16.00

1998 SkyBox Thunder

This 250-card set replaced Thunder in 1998 and arrived with 225 veterans and 25 rookies. Thunder was tiered, with 1-100 seeded 4:1 packs, 101-200 seeded 3:1 and 201-250 seeded 1:1. Cards featured a borderless artsy design with the color image of the player over it. The player's last name was foil stamped in large letters down either side. Each card was reprinted in both Rave and Super Rave parallel sets. Thunder also included five insert sets: Boss, Destination: End Zone, Number Crushers, Quick Strike, Autographics and Star-Burst.

		NM/M
Complete Set (250):		40.00
Common Player (1-200):		.10
Minor Stars (1-200):		.20
Common Player (201-250):		.20
Minor Stars (201-250):		.40
Rave Cards (1-200):		25X-40X
Rave Stars (201-250):		10X-20X
Rave Rookies (201-250):		5X-10X
Pack (8):		1.50
Wax Box (36):		50.00
1	Reggie White	.20
2	Elvis Grbac	.10
3	Ed McCaffrey	.10
4	O.J. McDuffie	.10
5	Scott Mitchell	.10
6	Byron Hanspard	.20
7	John Randle	.10
8	Shawn Jefferson	.10
9	Peter Boulware	.10
10	Karl Williams	.10
11	Napoleon Kaufman	.50
12	Barry Minter	.10
13	Cris Dishman	.10
14	James Stewart	.10
15	Marcus Robertson	.10
16	Rodney Harrison	.10
17	Micheal Barrow	.10
18	Michael Sinclair	.10
19	DeWayne Washington	.10
20	Phillippi Sparks	.10
21	Ernie Conwell	.10
22	Ken Dilger	.10
23	Johnnie Morton	.10
24	Eric Swann	.10
25	Curtis Conway	.20
26	Duce Staley	.10
27	Darrell Green	.10
28	Quinn Early	.10
29	LeRoy Butler	.10
30	Winfred Tubbs	.10
31	Darren Woodson	.10
32	Marcus Allen	.20
33	Glenn Foley	.10
34	Tom Knight	.10
35	Sam Shade	.10
36	James McKnight	.10
37	Leeland McElroy	.10
38	Earl Holmes	.10
39	Ryan McNeil	.10
40	Cris Carter	.20
41	Jessie Armstead	.10
42	Bryce Paup	.10
43	Chris Slade	.10
44	Eric Metcalf	.10
45	Jim Harbaugh	.20
46	Terry Kirby	.10
47	Donnie Edwards	.10
48	Darryl Williams	.10
49	Neil Smith	.10
50	Warren Sapp	.10
51	Jason Taylor	.10
52	Irving Fryar	.10
53	Jeff George	.20
54	Yancey Thigpen	.10
55	Ricky Proehl	.10
56	Kevin Greene	.10
57	Joel Steed	.10
58	Larry Allen	.10
59	Thurman Thomas	.20
60	Aaron Glenn	.10
61	Natrone Means	.20
62	Chris Calloway	.10
63	Chuck Smith	.10
64	Chidi Ahanotu	.10
65	Mario Bates	.10
66	Jonathan Ogden	.10
67	Drew Bledsoe	1.00
68	John Mobley	.10
69	Antowain Smith	.60
70	Aeneas Williams	.10
71	Brian Williams	.10
72	Derrick Thomas	.10
73	Ted Johnson	.10
74	Troy Drayton	.10
75	Mike Pritchard	.10
76	Darnay Scott	.10
77	James Jett	.10
78	Dwayne Rudd	.10
79	Marvin Harrison	.20
80	Dermontti Dawson	.10
81	Keith Lyle	.10
82	Steve Atwater	.10
83	Tyrone Wheatley	.10
84	Tony Brackens	.10
85	Dale Carter	.10
86	Robert Porcher	.10
87	Merton Hanks	.10
88	Leon Johnson	.10
89	Simeon Rice	.10
90	Robert Brooks	.10
91	William Thomas	.10
92	Wesley Walls	.10
93	Chester McGlockton	.10
94	Chris Chandler	.10
95	Michael Strahan	.10
96	Ray Zellars	.10
97	Dexter Coakley	.10
98	Rob Johnson	.20
99	Eric Green	.10
100	Darrien Gordon	.10
101	Gary Brown	.10
102	Reidel Anthony	.20
103	Keenan McCardell	.10
104	Leslie O'Neal	.10
105	Bryant Westbrook	.10
106	Derrick Alexander	.10
107	Jeff Blake	.20
108	Ben Coates	.10
109	Shawn Springs	.10
110	Robert Smith	.20
111	Karim Abdul-Jabbar	.20
112	Willie Davis	.10
113	Mark Chmura	.20
114	Terry Allen	.10
115	Will Blackwell	.10
116	Jamal Anderson	.10
117	Dana Stubblefield	.10
118	Trent Dilfer	.20
119	Jermaine Lewis	.10
120	Chad Brown	.10
121	Tamarick Vanover	.10
122	Tony Martin	.10
123	Larry Centers	.10
124	J.J. Stokes	.10
125	Danny Kanell	.10
126	Wayne Chrebet	.10
127	Kerry Collins	.20
128	Tony Banks	.30
129	Randal Hill	.10
130	Jimmy Smith	.10
131	Tim Brown	.20
132	Zach Thomas	.10
133	Rod Smith	.20
134	Frank Wycheck	.10
135	Garrison Hearst	.20
136	Bruce Smith	.10
137	Hardy Nickerson	.10
138	Sean Dawkins	.10
139	Willie McGinest	.10
140	Kimble Anders	.10
141	Michael Westbrook	.10
142	Chris Doleman	.10
143	Ricky Watters	.20
144	Levon Kirkland	.10
145	Rob Moore	.20
146	Eddie Kennison	.20
147	Rickey Dudley	.10
148	Jay Graham	.10
149	Brad Johnson	.30
150	Bobby Hoying	.10
151	Sherman Williams	.10
152	Charles Way	.10
153	Adrian Murrell	.20
154	Chris Sanders	.10
155	Greg Hill	.10
156	Rae Carruth	.20
157	Mike Alstott	.50
158	Terance Mathis	.10
159	Antonio Freeman	.30
160	Junior Seau	.20
161	Chris Warren	.10
162	Shannon Sharpe	.20
163	Derrick Rodgers	.10
164	Charles Johnson	.10
165	Marshall Faulk	.20
166	Jamie Asher	.10
167	Michael Jackson	.10
168	Terrell Owens	.30
169	Jason Sehorn	.10
170	Raymont Harris	.10
171	Jake Reed	.10
172	Kevin Hardy	.10
173	Jerald Moore	.10
174	Michael Irvin	.20
175	Freddie Jones	.10
176	Steve McNair	.50
177	Carnell Lake	.10
178	Troy Brown	.10
179	Hugh Douglas	.10
180	Andre Rison	.20
181	Leslie Shepherd	.10
182	Andre Hastings	.10
183	Fred Lane	.20
184	Andre Reed	.10
185	Darrell Russell	.10
186	Frank Sanders	.10
187	Derrick Brooks	.10
188	Charlie Garner	.10
189	Bert Emanuel	.10
190	Terrell Buckley	.10
191	Carl Pickens	.20
192	Tiki Barber	.30
193	Pete Mitchell	.10
194	Gilbert Brown	.10
195	Isaac Bruce	.30
196	Ray Lewis	.10
197	Warren Moon	.20
198	Tony Gonzalez	.20
199	John Mobley	.10
200	Gus Frerotte	.10
201	Brett Favre	4.00
202	Terrell Davis	1.00
203	Dan Marino	3.50
204	Barry Sanders	3.00
205	Steve Young	1.00
206	Deion Sanders	1.00
207	Kordell Stewart	2.00
208	Eddie George	2.50
209	Jake Plummer	2.00
210	Warrick Dunn	2.00
211	John Elway	2.00
212	Terry Glenn	.40
213	Mark Brunell	2.00
214	Corey Dillon	1.50
215	Joey Galloway	.40
216	Dorsey Levens	.40
217	Troy Aikman	2.00
218	Keyshawn Johnson	.40
219	Jerome Bettis	.40
220	Curtis Martin	1.25
221	Herman Moore	.40
222	Emmitt Smith	3.50
223	Jerry Rice	2.00
224	Drew Bledsoe	2.00
225	Antowain Smith	1.25
226	*Stephen Alexander*	.20
227	*John Avery*	.50
228	*Kevin Dyson*	2.00
229	*Robert Edwards*	.75
230	*Greg Ellis*	.20
231	*Curtis Enis*	3.00
232	*Chris Fuamatu-Ma'afala*	.75
233	*Ahman Green*	8.00
234	*Jacquez Green*	2.00
235	*Az-Zahir Hakim*	.75
236	*Skip Hicks*	.75
237	*Joe Jurevicius*	.50
238	*Ryan Leaf*	2.00
239	*Peyton Manning*	10.00
240	*Alonzo Mayes*	.50
241	*R.W. McQuarters*	.20
242	*Randy Moss*	8.00
243	*Marcus Nash*	.50
244	*Jerome Pathon*	.50
245	*Jason Peter*	.50
246	*Brian Simmons*	.50
247	*Takeo Spikes*	.50
248	*Fred Taylor*	4.00
249	*Andre Wadsworth*	.50
250	*Charles Woodson*	3.00

1998 SkyBox Thunder Rave

Rave was a 250-card parallel set to Thunder, and featured prismatic silver foil on the front to distinguish them from the base cards. Rave parallels were sequentially numbered to 150 on the back in silver foil and were found only in hobby packs.

Rave Cards (1-200):	25X-40X
Rave Stars (201-250):	10X-20X
Rave Rookies (201-250):	5X-10X

1998 SkyBox Thunder Super Rave

Super Rave was a 250-card parallel set that was found only in hobby packs. Cards were sequentially numbered to 25 sets.

Super Rave Cards (1-200):	50X-80X
Super Rave Stars (201-250):	30X-50X
Super Rave Rookies (201-250):	10X-20X

1998 SkyBox Thunder Boss

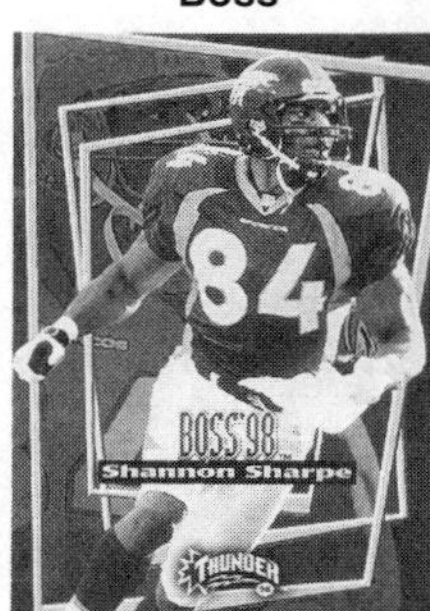

This insert featured 20 players on an embossed design. Backgrounds on the front were done in team colors with several quardrilaterals added. Boss cards were inserted one per eight packs and numbered with a "B" suffix.

		NM/M
Complete Set (20):		20.00
Common Player:		.25
Minor Stars:		.50
1	Troy Aikman	3.00
2	Drew Bledsoe	3.00
3	Tim Brown	1.00
4	Antonio Freeman	.50
5	Joey Galloway	.50
6	Terry Glenn	.50
7	Bobby Hoying	.25
8	Michael Irvin	.50
9	Keyshawn Johnson	1.00
10	Dorsey Levens	.50
11	Curtis Martin	3.00
12	John Mobley	.25
13	Jake Plummer	1.00
14	John Randle	.25
15	Deion Sanders	1.00
16	Junior Seau	.25
17	Shannon Sharpe	.25
18	Bruce Smith	.25
19	Robert Smith	.25
20	Dana Stubblefield	.25

1998 SkyBox Thunder Destination End Zone

This 15-card insert captured top scorers in the league on a green background. A small image of the player is placed in a bottom corner with his name in silver letters, and the insert name in red foil. These were inserted one per 96 packs and numbered with a "DE" suffix.

		NM/M
Complete Set (15):		45.00
Common Player:		1.00
1	Jerome Bettis	2.00
2	Mark Brunell	3.00
3	Terrell Davis	5.00
4	Corey Dillon	3.00
5	Warrick Dunn	2.00
6	John Elway	5.00
7	Brett Favre	7.00
8	Eddie George	3.00
9	Dorsey Levens	1.00
10	Curtis Martin	3.00
11	Herman Moore	1.00
12	Barry Sanders	6.00
13	Emmitt Smith	6.00
14	Kordell Stewart	2.00
15	Steve Young	4.00

1998 SkyBox Thunder Number Crushers

Number Crushers was a 10-card insert that featured the player on the front over a gridlike background. Backs were numbered with a "NC" suffix and included a Q&A section with a pull-out card that contained the answers. These were inserted one per 16 packs.

		NM/M
Complete Set (10):		15.00
Common Player:		1.00
Minor Stars:		4.00
1	Troy Aikman	3.00
2	Jerome Bettis	1.00
3	Tim Brown	1.00
4	Mark Brunell	1.00
5	Dan Marino	4.00
6	Herman Moore	1.00
7	Rob Moore	1.00
8	Jerry Rice	3.00
9	Shannon Sharpe	1.00
10	Emmitt Smith	5.00

1998 SkyBox Thunder Quick Strike

This 12-card, matchbook-like insert featured players over an olive background, with a black strip across the bottom resembling a match strike area. The card opened up to reveal another card of the player, while the back of the matchbook contained only the insert logo. Cards were inserted one per 300 packs and numbered with a "QS" suffix.

		NM/M
Complete Set (12):		75.00
Common Player:		3.00
1	Terrell Davis	6.00
2	John Elway	6.00
3	Brett Favre	10.00
4	Joey Galloway	3.00
5	Eddie George	3.00
6	Keyshawn Johnson	3.00
7	Dan Marino	10.00
8	Jerry Rice	8.00
9	Barry Sanders	8.00
10	Deion Sanders	3.00
11	Kordell Stewart	3.00
12	Steve Young	6.00

1998 SkyBox Thunder Star Burst

StarBurst was a 10-card insert featuring the player over a gold holofoil background that "bursts" against a regular background tinted in team colors. These were inserted one per 32 packs and numbered with a "SB" suffix.

		NM/M
Complete Set (10):		22.00
Common Player:		1.00

1	Tiki Barber	1.00
2	Corey Dillon	2.00
3	Warrick Dunn	2.00
4	Curtis Enis	1.00
5	Ryan Leaf	1.00
6	Peyton Manning	6.00
7	Randy Moss	6.00
8	Jake Plummer	2.00
9	Antowain Smith	2.00
10	Charles Woodson	4.00

1999 SkyBox Premium

This was a 290-card set that included 40 rookies with two different cards. One version wasn't seeded while the other was found 1:8 packs. The seeded version pictured the rookies in an action photo, while the other version was posed. Insert sets included: Star Rubies, 2000 Men, Autographics, Box Tops, Deja Vu, Genuine Coverage, Prime Time Rookies and Year 2. SRP was $2.69 for eight-card packs.

		NM/M
Complete Set (290):		325.00
Common Player:		.10
Minor Stars:		.30
Common Rookie:		.50
Common SP:		1.50
SP in Action Photos		
Inserted 1:8		
Hobby Pack (8):		2.75
Hobby Wax Box (24):		45.00
1	Randy Moss	2.50
2	Jamie Asher	.10
3	Joey Galloway	.50
4	Kent Graham	.10
5	Leslie Shepherd	.10
6	Levon Kirkland	.10
7	Marcus Pollard	.10
8	O.J. McDuffie	.10
9	Bill Romanowski	.10
10	Priest Holmes	.50
11	Tim Biakabutuka	.30
12	Duce Staley	.30
13	Isaac Bruce	.50
14	Jay Riemersma	.10
15	Karim Abdul	.30
16	Kevin Dyson	.30
17	Rickey Dudley	.30
18	Rocket Ismail	.10
19	Billy Davis	.10
20	James Jett	.10
21	Jerome Bettis	.50
22	Michael McCrary	.10
23	Michael Westbrook	.30
24	Oronde Gadsden	.30
25	Brad Johnson	.50
26	Shawn Springs	.10
27	Cris Carter	.50
28	Ed McCaffrey	.30
29	Gary Brown	.10
30	Hines Ward	.30
31	Hugh Douglas	.10
32	Jamir Miller	.10
33	Michael Bates	.10
34	Peyton Manning	2.00
35	Tony Banks	.30
36	Charles Way	.10
37	Charlie Batch	1.00
38	Jake Reed	.10
39	Mark Brunell	1.00
40	Skip Hicks	.30
41	Steve Young	.75
42	Wesley Walls	.10
43	Antonio Langham	.10
44	Antowain Smith	.50
45	Brian Griese	1.00
46	Jessie Armstead	.10
47	Thurman Thomas	.30
48	Jeff George	.50
49	Jessie Tuggle	.10
50	Jim Harbaugh	.30
51	Marvin Harrison	.50
52	Randall Cunningham	.50
53	Stephen Alexander	.10
54	Tiki Barber	.30
55	Billy Joe Tolliver	.10
56	Bruce Smith	.30
57	Eddie George	.75
58	Eugene Robinson	.10
59	John Elway	2.00
60	Ken Dilger	.10
61	Rodney Harrison	.10
62	Ty Detmer	.10
63	Andre Reed	.10
64	Dorsey Levens	.50
65	Eddie Kennison	.10
66	Freddie Jones	.10
67	Jacquez Green	.30
68	Jason Elam	.10
69	Marc Edwards	.10
70	Terance Mathis	.10
71	Alonzo Mayes	.10
72	Andre Wadsworth	.10
73	Barry Sanders	2.50
74	Derrick Alexander	.10
75	Garrison Hearst	.30
76	Leon Johnson	.10
77	Mike Alstott	.50
78	Shawn Jefferson	.10
79	Andre Hastings	.10
80	Eric Moulds	.50
81	Ryan Leaf	.50
82	Takeo Spikes	.10
83	Terrell Davis	1.00
84	Tim Dwight	.50
85	Trent Dilfer	.30
86	Vonnie Holliday	.10
87	Antonio Freeman	.50
88	Carl Pickens	.30
89	Chris Chandler	.30
90	Dale Carter	.10
91	La'Roi Glover	.10
92	Natrone Means	.30
93	Reidel Anthony	.30
94	Brett Favre	2.50
95	Bubby Brister	.30
96	Cameron Cleeland	.30
97	Chris Calloway	.10
98	Corey Dillon	.30
99	Greg Hill	.10
100	Vinny Testaverde	.30
101	Trent Green	.30
102	Sam Gash	.10
103	Mikhael Ricks	.10
104	Emmitt Smith	2.00
105	Doug Flutie	.75
106	Deion Sanders	.50
107	Charles Johnson	.10
108	Bam Morris	.10
109	Andre Rison	.30
110	Doug Pederson	.10
111	Marshall Faulk	.50
112	Tim Brown	.30
113	Warren Sapp	.10
114	Bryan Still	.10
115	Chris Penn	.10
116	Jamal Anderson	.50
117	Keyshawn Johnson	.50
118	Ricky Proehl	.10
119	Robert Brooks	.10
120	Tony Gonzalez	.30
121	Ty Law	.10
122	Elvis Grbac	.30
123	Jeff Blake	.30
124	Mark Chmura	.30
125	Junior Seau	.30
126	Mo Lewis	.10
127	Ray Buchanan	.10
128	Robert Holcombe	.30
129	Tony Simmons	.30
130	David Palmer	.10
131	Ike Hilliard	.10
132	Mike Vanderjagt	.10
133	Rae Carruth	.10
134	Sean Dawkins	.10
135	Shannon Sharpe	.30
136	Curtis Conway	.30
137	Darrell Green	.10
138	Germane Crowell	.30
139	J.J. Stokes	.30
140	Kevin Hardy	.10
141	Rob Moore	.30
142	Robert Smith	.50
143	Wayne Chrebet	.30
144	Yancey Thigpen	.30
145	Jerome Pathon	.10
146	John Mobley	.10
147	Kerry Collins	.30
148	Peter Boulware	.10
149	Matthew Hatchette	.10
150	Kordell Stewart	.50
151	Koy Detmer	.10
152	Sedrick Shaw	.10
153	Steve Beuerlein	.30
154	Zach Thomas	.30
155	Adrian Murrell	.30
156	Bobby Engram	.10
157	Bryan Cox	.10
158	Drew Bledsoe	1.00
159	Jerry Rice	1.25
160	Keenan McCardell	.30
161	Steve McNair	.50
162	Terry Fair	.10
163	Derrick Brooks	.10
164	Eric Green	.10
165	Erik Kramer	.10
166	Frank Sanders	.10
167	Fred Taylor	1.25
168	Johnnie Morton	.10
169	R.W. McQuarters	.10
170	Terry Glenn	.50
171	Frank Wycheck	.10
172	John Avery	.30
173	Kevin Turner	.10
174	Larry Centers	.10
175	Michael Irvin	.30
176	Rich Gannon	.30
177	Ricky Watters	.30
178	Rodney Thomas	.10
179	Scott Mitchell	.10
180	Chad Brown	.10
181	John Randle	.10
182	Michael Strahan	.10
183	Muhsin Muhammad	.30
184	Reggie Barlow	.10
185	Rod Smith	.30
186	Dan Marino	2.00
187	Dexter Coakley	.10
188	Jermaine Lewis	.30
189	Jon Kitna	.75
190	Napoleon Kaufman	.50
191	Will Blackwell	.10
192	Aaron Glenn	.10
193	Ben Coates	.30
194	Curtis Enis	.50
195	Herman Moore	.50
196	Jake Plummer	1.25
197	Jimmy Smith	.50
198	Terrell Owens	.50
199	Warrick Dunn	.50
200	Charles Woodson	.50
201	Ahman Green	.30
202	Mark Bruener	.10
203	Ray Lewis	.10
204	Tony Martin	.10
205	Troy Aikman	1.25
206	Curtis Martin	.50
207	Darnay Scott	.30
208	Derrick Mayes	.30
209	Keith Poole	.10
210	Warren Moon	.30
211	*Chris Claiborne*	1.00
211	Chris Claiborne SP	3.00
212	*Ricky Williams*	6.00
212	Ricky Williams SP	18.00
213	*Tim Couch*	2.00
213	Tim Couch SP	7.00
214	*Champ Bailey*	1.50
214	Champ Bailey SP	4.00
215	*Torry Holt*	3.00
215	Torry Holt SP	10.00
216	*Donovan McNabb*	6.00
216	Donovan McNabb SP	18.00
217	*David Boston*	3.00
217	David Boston SP	10.00
218	*Chris McAllister*	1.00
218	Chris McAllister SP	3.00
219	*Michael Bishop*	1.75
219	Michael Bishop SP	4.00
220	*Daunte Culpepper*	6.00
220	Daunte Culpepper SP	18.00
221	*Joe Germaine*	1.50
221	Joe Germaine SP	3.00
222	*Edgerrin James*	6.00
222	Edgerrin James SP	18.00
223	*Jevon Kearse*	2.50
223	Jevon Kearse SP	5.00
224	*Ebenezer Ekuban*	1.00
224	Ebenezer Ekuban SP	3.00
225	*Scott Covington*	.50
225	Scott Covington SP	1.50
226	*Aaron Brooks*	6.00
226	Aaron Brooks SP	18.00
227	*Cecil Collins*	2.00
227	Cecil Collins SP	6.00
228	*Akili Smith*	2.00
228	Akili Smith SP	5.00
229	*Shaun King*	2.00
229	Shaun King SP	5.00
230	*Chad Plummer*	.50
230	Chad Plummer SP	1.50
231	*Peerless Price*	2.50
231	Peerless Price SP	8.00
232	*Antoine Winfield*	1.00
232	Antoine Winfield SP	3.00
233	*Antwan Edwards*	1.00
233	Antwan Edwards SP	3.00
234	*Rob Konrad*	1.00
234	Rob Konrad SP	3.00
235	*Troy Edwards*	2.50
235	Troy Edwards SP	6.00
236	*Terry Jackson*	.50
236	Terry Jackson SP	1.50
237	*Jimmy Kleinsasser*	1.00
237	Jim Kleinsasser SP	5.00
238	*Joe Montgomery*	1.50
238	Joe Montgomery SP	3.00
239	*Desmond Clark*	.50
239	Desmond Clark SP	1.50
240	*Lamar King*	.50
240	Lamar King SP	1.50
241	*Dameane Douglas*	.50
241	Dameane Douglas SP	1.50
242	*Martin Gramatica*	1.25
242	Martin Gramatica SP	3.00
243	*James Finn*	.50
243	James Finn SP	1.50
244	*Andy Katzenmoyer*	1.25
244	Andy Katzenmoyer SP	5.00
245	*Dee Miller*	.50
245	Dee Miller SP	1.50
246	*D'Wayne Bates*	1.00
246	D'Wayne Bates SP	3.00
247	*Amos Zereoue*	2.00
247	Amos Zereoue SP	5.00
248	*Karsten Bailey*	1.00
248	Karsten Bailey SP	3.00
249	*Kevin Johnson*	2.00
249	Kevin Johnson SP	5.00
250	*Cade McNown*	2.00
250	Cade McNown SP	5.00

1999 SkyBox Premium Shining Star Rubies

This was a 290-card parallel to the base set. Each of the singles was sequentially numbered to 30 except for the seeded rookie cards which were numbered to 15.

	NM/M
Ruby Cards:	25X-75X
Ruby Rookies:	5X-20X
Production 30 Sets	
Ruby SP's:	
Production 15 Sets	

1999 SkyBox Premium Autographics

This was a 79-card insert that was found in several SkyBox products. Singles were issued in Dominion, E-X Century, Molten Metal, Metal Universe and SkyBox Premium at 1:68 hobby packs and 1:90 retail packs. Each single had the autograph on the front of the card and each also had a parallel Red version that was sequentially numbered to 50.

	NM/M
Common Player:	10.00
Minor Stars:	20.00
Inserted 1:68	
Foil Cards:	2X
Production 50 Sets	
Stephen Alexander	20.00
Mike Alstott	20.00
Champ Bailey	10.00
Karsten Bailey	10.00
Charlie Batch	10.00
D'Wayne Bates	10.00
Michael Bishop	15.00
Dre' Bly	10.00
David Boston	35.00
Gary Brown	10.00
Na Brown	10.00
Tim Brown	30.00
Troy Brown	10.00
Mark Bruener	10.00
Mark Brunell	35.00
Shawn Bryson	10.00
Wayne Chrebet	15.00
Chris Claiborne	10.00
Cam Cleeland	10.00
Cecil Collins	15.00
Daunte Culpepper	60.00
Randall Cunningham	25.00
Terrell Davis	65.00
Ty Detmer	10.00
Jared DeVries	10.00
Troy Edwards	15.00
Kevin Faulk	15.00
Marshall Faulk	40.00
Doug Flutie	25.00
Oronde Gadsden	10.00
Joey Galloway	15.00
Eddie George	25.00
Martin Gramatica	10.00
Anthony Gray	10.00
Ahman Green	35.00
Brian Griese	45.00
Howard Griffith	10.00
Marvin Harrison	35.00
Courtney Hawkins	10.00
Vonnie Holliday	10.00
Torry Holt	25.00
Sedrick Irvin	10.00
Edgerrin James	75.00
Patrick Jeffers	10.00
James Johnson	10.00
Kevin Johnson	15.00
Freddie Jones	10.00
Jevon Kearse	25.00
Shaun King	15.00
Jon Kitna	15.00
Rob Konrad	10.00
Dorsey Levens	10.00
Peyton Manning	100.00
Darnell McDonald	10.00
Donovan McNabb	75.00
Cade McNown	15.00
Eric Moss	10.00
Randy Moss	100.00
Eric Moulds	30.00
Marcus Nash	10.00
Terrell Owens	35.00
Jerome Pathon	20.00
Jake Plummer	35.00
Peerless Price	35.00
Mikhael Ricks	10.00
Frank Sanders	20.00
Tony Simmons	10.00
Akili Smith	15.00
Antowain Smith	35.00
L.C. Stevens	10.00
Michael Strahan	10.00
Tai Streets	10.00
Lamar Thomas	10.00
Jerame Tuman	10.00
Kevin Turner	10.00
Tyrone Wheatley	20.00
Ricky Williams	100.00
Frank Wycheck	10.00
Amos Zereoue	25.00

1999 SkyBox Premium Autographics Foil

This was a 79-card parallel to the Autographics insert set. Each of these singles was printed with red foil and sequentially numbered to 50.

Foil Cards:	2X
Production 50 Sets	

1999 SkyBox Premium Box Tops

This 15-card insert set included veterans from the NFL. Singles were inserted 1:12 packs.

		NM/M
Complete Set (15):		25.00
Common Player:		1.00
Inserted 1:12		
1	Terrell Davis	4.00
2	Troy Aikman	4.00
3	Peyton Manning	4.00
4	Mark Brunell	2.00
5	Eddie George	2.00
6	Corey Dillon	1.00
7	Dan Marino	5.00
8	Brett Favre	5.00
9	Barry Sanders	4.00
10	Emmitt Smith	5.00
11	Fred Taylor	2.00
12	Jerry Rice	4.00
13	Jamal Anderson	1.00
14	Joey Galloway	1.00
15	Randy Moss	4.00

1999 SkyBox Premium Deja Vu

This 15-card insert set included a draft pick paired with a veteran who was the same number pick in a previous draft. Singles were inserted 1:36 picks. A parallel die-cut version was also issued with each of those singles sequentially numbered to 99.

		NM/M
Complete Set (15):		35.00
Common Player:		1.00
Inserted 1:36		
1	Akili Smith, Barry Sanders	5.00
2	Cade McNown, Warrick Dunn	2.00
3	Cecil Collins, Jerris McPhail	1.00
4	Champ Bailey, Curtis Conway	2.00
5	Daunte Culpepper, Michael Irvin	4.00
6	David Boston, Tim Biakabutuka	2.00
7	Donovan McNabb, Marshall Faulk	4.00
8	Edgerrin James, Michael Westbrook	5.00
9	Kevin Faulk, Joey Kent	1.00
10	Kevin Johnson, Jerome Pathon	2.00
11	Ricky Williams, Deion Sanders	5.00
12	Shaun King, Germane Crowell	1.00
13	Tim Couch, Troy Aikman	4.00
14	Torry Holt, Tim Brown	3.00
15	Troy Edwards, Eric Metcalf	1.00

1999 SkyBox Premium Genuine Coverage

This was a six-card insert set that included a piece of a game-worn jersey. Each card had a different amount issued and was randomly inserted.

	NM/M
Common Player:	30.00
Drew Bledsoe	50.00
Mark Brunell	35.00
Randall Cunningham	35.00
Brett Favre	125.00
Herman Moore	30.00
Randy Moss	75.00

1999 SkyBox Premium Prime Time Rookies

This 15-card insert set included the best rookies from 1999. Singles were found 1:96 packs. A parallel Autograph version was also issued with each of those singles sequentially numbered to 25.

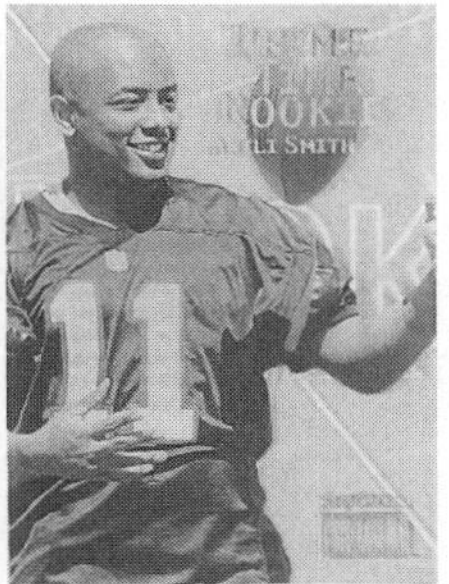

		NM/M
Common Player:		2.00
Inserted 1:96		
1	Ricky Williams	15.00
2	Tim Couch	10.00
3	Edgerrin James	13.00
4	Daunte Culpepper	12.00
5	David Boston	6.00
6	Akili Smith	4.00
7	Cecil Collins	3.00
8	Cade McNown	3.00
9	Torry Holt	5.00
10	Donovan McNabb	12.00
11	Kevin Johnson	5.00
12	Shaun King	3.00
13	Champ Bailey	2.00
14	Troy Edwards	3.00
15	Kevin Faulk	3.00

1999 SkyBox Premium Prime Time Rookies Autographs

This was a 15-card parallel to the Prime Time Rookie insert set. Each of these singles was autographed and sequentially numbered to 25.

		NM/M
Common Player:		50.00
Production 25 Sets		
1	Ricky Williams	225.00
2	Tim Couch	100.00
3	Edgerrin James	200.00
4	Daunte Culpepper	150.00
5	David Boston	75.00
6	Akili Smith	50.00
7	Cecil Collins	50.00
8	Cade McNown	50.00
9	Torry Holt	75.00
10	Donovan McNabb	150.00
11	Kevin Johnson	75.00
12	Shaun King	50.00
13	Champ Bailey	50.00
14	Troy Edwards	75.00
15	Kevin Faulk	50.00

1999 SkyBox Premium 2000 Men

This 15-card insert set included players who looked to be the stars for the next millennium. Each single was sequentially numbered to 100.

		NM/M
Common Player:		10.00
Production 100 Sets		
1	Warrick Dunn	10.00
2	Tim Couch	30.00
3	Fred Taylor	25.00
4	Jake Plummer	20.00
5	Jerry Rice	40.00
6	Edgerrin James	40.00
7	Mark Brunell	15.00
8	Peyton Manning	35.00
9	Randy Moss	40.00
10	Terrell Davis	30.00
11	Charlie Batch	10.00
12	Dan Marino	45.00
13	Emmitt Smith	40.00
14	Brett Favre	45.00
15	Barry Sanders	40.00

1999 SkyBox Premium Year 2

This 15-card insert set included players who were in their second year as a pro. Singles were found 1:6 packs.

		NM/M
Complete Set (15):		7.00
Common Player:		.50
Minor Stars:		1.00
Inserted 1:6		
1	Ahman Green	2.00
2	Terry Fair	.50
3	Charlie Batch	.50

4	Ryan Leaf	.50
5	Skip Hicks	.50
6	John Avery	.50
7	Charles Woodson	1.00
8	Jacquez Green	.50
9	Kevin Dyson	1.00
10	Marcus Nash	.50
11	Robert Holcombe	.50
12	Germane Crowell	.50
13	Curtis Enis	.50
14	Tim Dwight	1.00
15	Brian Griese	2.00

1999 SkyBox Dominion

This was a 250-card set that included 50 unseeded rookie cards. Each base card included game-action photography with the player's name and team in silver foil. Insert sets included: Atlantattitude, Generation Next, Goal 2 Go, Hats Off and Hats Off Autographs. SRP was $1.89 for nine-card packs.

		NM/M
Complete Set (250):		35.00
Common Player:		.10
Minor Stars:		.30
Common Rookie:		.50
Pack (9):		2.00
Wax Box (36):		55.00
1	Randy Moss	2.00
2	James Jett	.10
3	Lawyer Milloy	.10
4	Mike Alstott	.50
5	Courtney Hawkins	.10
6	Carl Pickens	.30
7	Marvin Harrison	.50
8	Robert Smith	.50
9	Fred Taylor	1.00
10	Barry Sanders	2.00
11	Tony Gonzalez	.10
12	Leroy Hoard	.10
13	Drew Bledsoe	.75
14	Cam Cleeland	.30
15	Steve Atwater	.10
16	Eric Moulds	.50
17	Herman Moore	.50
18	Rickey Dudley	.10
19	Jeff Blake	.30
20	Eddie George	.50
21	Antonio Freeman	.50
22	Stephen Alexander	.10
23	Larry Centers	.10
24	Chris Chandler	.30
25	James Stewart	.30
26	Randall Cunningham	.50
27	Mark Brunell	.75
28	David Palmer	.10
29	Eric Green	.10
30	Terry Glenn	.50
31	Jerry Rice	1.00
32	Ricky Proehl	.10
33	Tony Banks	.30
34	John Elway	1.50
35	Johnnie Morton	.10
36	Tony Simmons	.30
37	Jon Kitna	.50
38	Trent Green	.30
39	Peyton Manning	1.50
40	Emmitt Smith	1.50
41	Warrick Dunn	.50
42	Jerome Bettis	.50
43	Ricky Watters	.30
44	Raghib Ismail	.10
45	Ryan Leaf	.30
46	Jackie Harris	.10
47	Robert Holcombe	.10
48	Dorsey Levens	.50
49	Duce Staley	.30
50	Brett Favre	2.00
51	Andre Rison	.10
52	Curtis Conway	.30
53	Mark Chmura	.30
54	Doug Flutie	.75
55	Ernie Mills	.10
56	Jeff George	.30
57	Chris Warren	.10
58	Alonzo Mayes	.10
59	Freddie Jones	.10
60	Shannon Sharpe	.30
61	O.J. Santiago	.10
62	Shawn Springs	.10
63	Kent Graham	.10
64	Muhsin Muhammad	.10
65	Keith Poole	.10
66	Chris Spielman	.10
67	Curtis Enis	.30
68	Lamar Smith	.10
69	Charles Johnson	.10
70	Kerry Collins	.30
71	Charlie Batch	.75
72	Keenan McCardell	.30
73	Ty Detmer	.30
74	Mark Bruener	.10
75	Lamar Thomas	.10
76	Kwamie Lassiter	.10
77	Bam Morris	.10
78	Michael Sinclair	.10
79	Darnay Scott	.30
80	Napoleon Kaufman	.50
81	Ed McCaffery	.30
82	Reidel Anthony	.30
83	Kevin Greene	.10
84	Michael Irvin	.30
85	Charles Way	.10
86	Tim Brown	.30
87	Johnny McWilliams	.10
88	Brad Johnson	.50
89	Antonio Langham	.10
90	Bruce Smith	.10
91	Reggie Barlow	.10
92	Ty Law	.10
93	Bobby Engram	.10
94	Kimble Anders	.10
95	Dale Carter	.10
96	Jimmy Smith	.30
97	Marc Edwards	.10
98	Ken Dilger	.10
99	Adrian Murrell	.30
100	Terance Mathis	.10
101	Gary Anderson	.10
102	Garrison Hearst	.30
103	Ahman Green	.30
104	Daryl Johnston	.10
105	O.J. McDuffie	.30
106	Matthew Hatchette	.10
107	Chris Doleman	.10
108	Steve McNair	.50
109	Leon Johnson	.10
110	Terrell Davis	1.50
111	Rob Moore	.30
112	Troy Aikman	1.00
113	John Avery	.30
114	Frank Wycheck	.10
115	Curtis Martin	.50
116	Jim Harbaugh	.30
117	Sean Dawkins	.10
118	Glenn Foley	.30
119	Warren Sapp	.10
120	R.W. McQuarters	.10
121	Yancey Thigpen	.30
122	Frank Sanders	.30
123	Tim Dwight	.50
124	Pete Mitchell	.10
125	Steve Beuerlein	.30
126	Tyrone Davis	.10
127	Jamie Asher	.10
128	Corey Dillon	.50
129	Doug Pederson	.10
130	Deion Sanders	.50
131	J.J. Stokes	.30
132	Jermaine Lewis	.30
133	Gary Brown	.10
134	Derrick Alexander	.10
135	Tony McGee	.10
136	Kyle Brady	.10
137	Mikhael Ricks	.10
138	Germane Crowell	.30
139	Skip Hicks	.30
140	Ben Coates	.30
141	Will Blackwell	.10
142	Al Del Greco	.10
143	Jake Plummer	1.00
144	Marshall Faulk	.50
145	Antowain Smith	.50
146	Corey Fuller	.10
147	Keyshawn Johnson	.50
148	John Randle	.10
149	Terrell Buckley	.10
150	Terry Kirby	.10
151	Robert Brooks	.10
152	Karim Abdul	.30
153	Jason Seahorn	.10
154	Elvis Grbac	.30
155	Andre Reed	.10
156	Ike Hilliard	.10
157	Jamal Anderson	.50
158	Jake Reed	.10
159	Rich Gannon	.10
160	Michael Jackson	.10
161	Bert Emanuel	.10
162	Charles Woodson	.50
163	Ray Lewis	.10
164	Trent Dilfer	.30
165	Oronde Gadsden	.30
166	Wesley Walls	.30
167	Joey Galloway	.50
168	Mo Lewis	.10
169	Darren Woodson	.10
170	Cris Carter	.50
171	Brian Mitchell	.10
172	Tim Biakabutuka	.30
173	Michael Westbrook	.30
174	Dan Marino	1.50
175	Greg Hill	.10
176	Priest Holmes	.50
177	Fred Lane	.10
178	Isaac Bruce	.30
179	Erik Kramer	.10
180	Steve Young	.75
181	Terry Fair	.10
182	Brian Griese	.75
183	Leslie Shepherd	.10
184	Kordell Stewart	.75
185	Charlie Jones	.10
186	Chris Calloway	.10
187	Wayne Chrebet	.30
188	Natrone Means	.30
189	David LaFleur	.10
190	Rod Smith	.30
191	Kevin Dyson	.30
192	Scott Mitchell	.10
193	Andre Wadsworth	.10
194	Vinny Testaverde	.30
195	Az-Zahir Hakim	.30
196	Joe Jurevicius	.10
197	Junior Seau	.30
198	Jason Elam	.10
199	Terrell Owens	.50
200	Jacquez Green	.10
201	*Tim Couch*	3.00
202	*Donovan McNabb*	5.00
203	*Cade McNown*	2.00
204	*Akili Smith*	2.00
205	*Kevin Faulk*	2.00
206	*Sedrick Irvin*	1.50
207	*Edgerrin James*	5.00
208	*Ricky Williams*	5.00
209	*D'Wayne Bates*	1.00
210	*David Boston*	3.00
211	*Torry Holt*	3.00
212	*Peerless Price*	2.50
213	*Daunte Culpepper*	5.00
214	*Troy Edwards*	2.00
215	*Rob Konrad*	1.00
216	*Joe Germaine*	1.00
217	*James Johnson*	1.50
218	*Brock Huard*	1.50
219	*Cecil Collins*	1.50
220	*Jeff Paulk, Eugene Baker*	.50
221	*Marty Booker, Jim Finn*	.50
222	*Scott Covington, Nick Williams*	.50
223	*Kevin Johnson, Darrin Chiaverini*	2.00
224	*Ebenezer Ekuban, Dat Nguyen*	.75
225	*Al Wilson, Chad Plummer*	.50
226	*Chris Claiborne, Aaron Gibson*	.75
227	*Aaron Brooks, De'Mond Parker*	5.00
228	*John Tait, Michael Cloud*	.75
229	*Andy Katzenmoyer, Michael Bishop*	1.50
230	*Joe Montgomery, Dan Campbell*	.75
231	*Na Brown, C ecil Martin*	.50
232	*Amos Zereoue, Jerame Tuman*	1.50
233	*Jermaine Fazande, Steve Heiden*	.50
234	*Karsten Bailey, Charlie Rogers*	.50
235	*Shaun King, Martin Gramatica*	1.00
236	*Jevon Kearse, Kevin Daft*	1.50
237	*Champ Bailey, Tim Alexander*	1.50
238	*Karsten Bailey, Darnell McDonald*	1.00
239	*Lamarr Glenn, Terry Jackson*	.50
240	*Troy Smith, Malcolm Johnson*	.50
241	*Rondel Menendez, Craig Yeast*	.50
242	*Jed Weaver, James Dearth*	.50
243	*Joel Makovicka, Shawn Bryson*	.50
244	*Desmond Clark, Jim Kleinsasser*	.75
245	*Sean Bennett, Autry Denson*	1.00
246	*Billy Miller, Wane McGarity*	.75
247	*Mike Lucky, Justin Swift*	.50
248	*Travis McGriff, Mar Tay Jenkins*	.75
249	*Donald Driver, Larry Parker*	.75
250	*Antoine Winfield, Dre' Bly*	.75

1999 SkyBox Dominion Atlantattitude

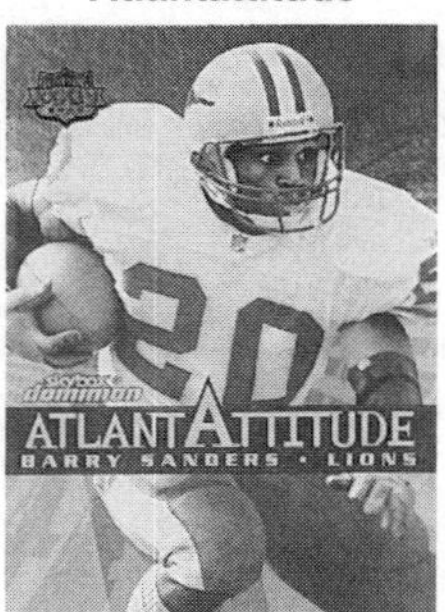

This 15-card insert set included players who had the chance to lead their team to Super Bowl XXXIV in Atlanta. Singles were inserted 1:24 packs. Parallel Plus sets (1:240) and Warp Tek (numbered to player's uniform number) were also issued.

		NM/M
Complete Set (15):		40.00
Common Player:		1.00
Minor Stars:		2.00
Inserted 1:24		
Plus Cards:		3X
Inserted 1:240		
Warp Tek Cards:		
Production to player's uniform number		
1	Charlie Batch	1.00
2	Mark Brunell	3.00
3	Tim Couch	6.00
4	Terrell Davis	5.00
5	Warrick Dunn	2.00
6	Brett Favre	7.00
7	Peyton Manning	5.00
8	Dan Marino	7.00
9	Randy Moss	6.00
10	Jake Plummer	3.00
11	Barry Sanders	6.00
12	Akili Smith	1.00
13	Emmitt Smith	6.00
14	Fred Taylor	3.00
15	Ricky Williams	5.00

1999 SkyBox Dominion Atlantattitude Warp Tek

This was a 15-card insert set that paralleled the Atlantattitude insert. Each single in this set was sequentially numbered to the player's jersey number.

		NM/M
Production to player's uniform number		
Most too uncommon to price		
1	Charlie Batch 10	135.00
2	Mark Brunell 8	150.00
3	Tim Couch 2	500.00
4	Terrell Davis 30	140.00
5	Warrick Dunn 28	50.00
6	Brett Favre 4	400.00
7	Peyton Manning 18	225.00
8	Dan Marino 13	275.00
9	Randy Moss 84	100.00
10	Jake Plummer 16	150.00
11	Barry Sanders 20	275.00
12	Akili Smith 11	135.00
13	Emmitt Smith 22	175.00
14	Fred Taylor 28	125.00
15	Ricky Williams 34	200.00

1999 SkyBox Dominion Generation Next

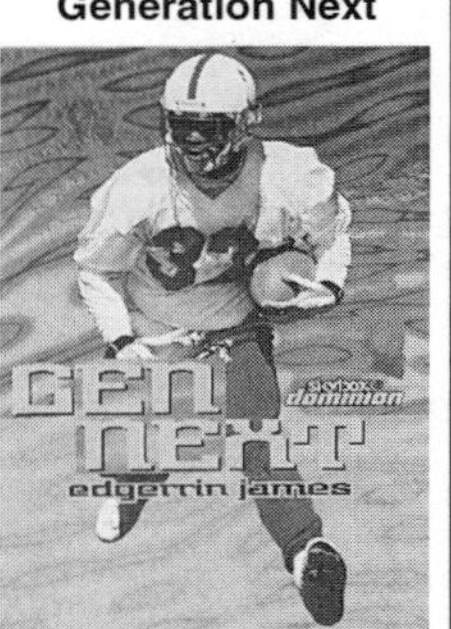

This 20-card insert set included the hottest rookies from the 1999 season. Singles were inserted 1:3 packs. Two parallel sets were issued: Plus (1:30) and Warp Tek (1:300).

		NM/M
Complete Set (20):		12.00
Common Player:		.25
Minor Stars:		.50
Inserted 1:3		
Plus Cards:		2X
Inserted 1:30		
Warp Tek Cards:		2X-3X
Inserted 1:300		
1	D'Wayne Bates	.25
2	David Boston	1.50
3	Cecil Collins	1.00
4	Tim Couch	3.00
5	Daunte Culpepper	2.50
6	Troy Edwards	1.50
7	Kevin Faulk	1.25
8	Joe Germaine	.50
9	Torry Holt	1.50
10	Brock Huard	.50
11	Sedrick Irvin	.50
12	Edgerrin James	4.00
13	James Johnson	.50
14	Kevin Johnson	1.50
15	Shaun King	.50
16	Donovan McNabb	2.50
17	Cade McNown	.50
18	Akili Smith	.50
19	Ricky Williams	5.00
20	Amos Zereoue	1.00

1999 SkyBox Dominion Generation Next Plus

This was a 20-card insert set that paralleled the Generation Next insert. These singles were found 1:30 packs.

		NM/M
Plus Cards:		2X
Inserted 1:30		
1	D'Wayne Bates	.50
2	David Boston	1.50
3	Cecil Collins	2.50
4	Tim Couch	5.00
5	Daunte Culpepper	2.50
6	Troy Edwards	1.50
7	Kevin Faulk	1.25

		NM/M
8	Joe Germaine	1.00
9	Torry Holt	1.50
10	Brock Huard	1.00
11	Sedrick Irvin	1.00
12	Edgerrin James	4.00
13	James Johnson	1.25
14	Kevin Johnson	1.50
15	Shaun King	1.25
16	Donovan McNabb	2.50
17	Cade McNown	2.50
18	Akili Smith	2.50
19	Ricky Williams	5.00
20	Amos Zereoue	1.25

1999 SkyBox Dominion Generation Next Warp Tek

This was a 20-card insert set that paralleled the Generation Next insert. These singles were found 1:300 packs.

		NM/M
Warp Tek Cards:		2X-3X
Inserted 1:300		
1	D'Wayne Bates	6.00
2	David Boston	10.00
3	Cecil Collins	8.00
4	Tim Couch	35.00
5	Daunte Culpepper	20.00
6	Troy Edwards	10.00
7	Kevin Faulk	8.00
8	Joe Germaine	6.00
9	Torry Holt	12.00
10	Brock Huard	6.00
11	Sedrick Irvin	8.00
12	Edgerrin James	50.00
13	James Johnson	8.00
14	Kevin Johnson	15.00
15	Shaun King	20.00
16	Donovan McNabb	20.00
17	Cade McNown	20.00
18	Akili Smith	15.00
19	Ricky Williams	35.00
20	Amos Zereoue	8.00

1999 SkyBox Dominion Goal 2 Go

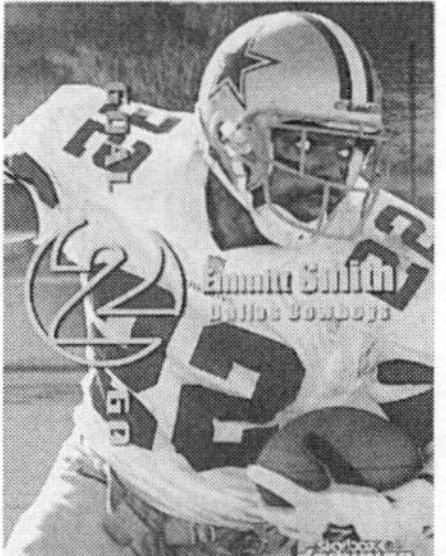

This was a 10-card insert set that pictured two players on the same card with one on each side. Singles were inserted 1:9 packs. A Plus parallel (1:90) and Warp Tek parallel (1:900) were also issued.

		NM/M
Complete Set (10):		12.00
Common Player:		1.00
Inserted 1:9		
Plus Cards:		2X
Inserted 1:90		
Warp Tek Cards:		3X-5X
Inserted 1:900		
1	Terrell Davis, Jamal Anderson	1.00
2	Brett Favre, Jake Plummer	2.00
3	Randy Moss, Jerry Rice	2.00
4	Warrick Dunn, Barry Sanders	1.50
5	Eddie George, Fred Taylor	1.00
6	Emmitt Smith, Marshall Faulk	2.00
7	Keyshawn Johnson, Terrell Owens	1.00
8	Peyton Manning, Ryan Leaf	1.50
9	Dan Marino, John Elway	2.00
10	Cade McNown, Charlie Batch	1.00

1999 SkyBox Dominion Goal 2 Go Plus

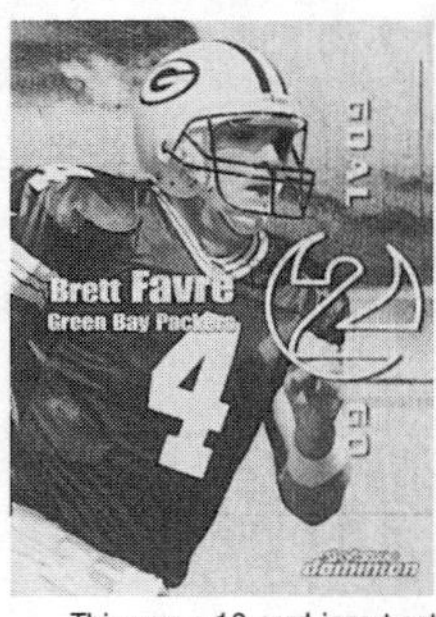

This was a 10-card insert set that paralleled the Goal 2 Go insert. Singles were found 1:90 packs.

		NM/M
Plus Cards:		2X
Inserted 1:90		
1	Terrell Davis, Jamal Anderson	4.00
2	Brett Favre, Jake Plummer	5.00
3	Randy Moss, Jerry Rice	5.00
4	Warrick Dunn, Barry Sanders	5.00
5	Eddie George, Fred Taylor	1.50
6	Emmitt Smith, Marshall Faulk	4.00
7	Keyshawn Johnson, Terrell Owens	1.50
8	Peyton Manning, Ryan Leaf	4.00
9	Dan Marino, John Elway	4.00
10	Cade McNown, Charlie Batch	3.00

1999 SkyBox Dominion Goal 2 Go Warp Tek

This was a 10-card insert set that paralleled the Goal 2 Go insert. Singles were inserted 1:900 packs.

		NM/M
Warp Tek Cards:		3X-5X
Inserted 1:900		
1	Terrell Davis, Jamal Anderson	25.00
2	Brett Favre, Jake Plummer	40.00
3	Randy Moss, Jerry Rice	35.00
4	Warrick Dunn, Barry Sanders	35.00
5	Eddie George, Fred Taylor	20.00
6	Emmitt Smith, Marshall Faulk	25.00
7	Keyshawn Johnson, Terrell Owens	15.00
8	Peyton Manning, Ryan Leaf	35.00
9	Dan Marino, John Elway	35.00
10	Cade McNown, Charlie Batch	35.00

1999 SkyBox Dominion Hats Off

This six-card insert set included swatches of caps worn at the 1999 NFL Draft on April 10, 1999 in New York City by six NFL rookies. Each card has a different amount produced and singles were randomly inserted.

		NM/M
Common Player:		35.00
1	Tim Couch 135	60.00
2	Donovan McNabb 130	75.00
3	Akili Smith 85	35.00
4	Ricky Williams 130	90.00
5	Daunte Culpepper 100	75.00
6	Cade McNown 120	35.00

1999 SkyBox Dominion Hats Off Autographs

This is a five-card insert set that parallels the Hats Off insert. Each of these singles was autographed. Tim Couch did not sign in this insert. Each player signed a total of 20 cards.

	NM/M
Common Player:	100.00
Production 20 Sets	
Couch did not sign	
Donovan McNabb	400.00
Akili Smith	100.00
Ricky Williams	500.00
Daunte Culpepper	400.00
Cade McNown	100.00

1999 SkyBox Molten Metal

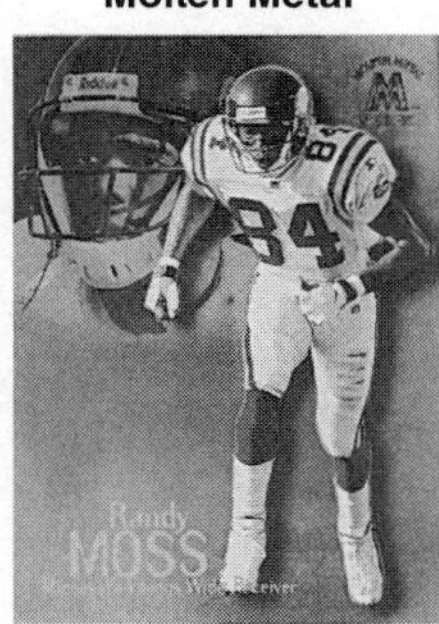

This 151-card set had a 26-card rookie subset that was inserted 1:5 packs. Each of the rookie cards had rounded corners and was printed on actual metal. Insert sets included: Autographics, Gridiron Gods, Patchworks, Perfect Fit and Top Notch. SRP was $2.99 for five-card packs.

		NM/M
Complete Set (151):		75.00
Common Player:		.15
Minor Stars:		.50
Common Rookie:		1.00
Inserted 1:5		
Pack (5):		4.50
Wax Box (24):		75.00
1	Terrell Davis	3.00
2	Chris Chandler	.50
3	Terry Glenn	1.00
4	Jon Kitna	1.25
5	Bubby Brister	.50
6	Jermaine Lewis	.15
7	Doug Flutie	2.00
8	Napoleon Kaufman	1.00
9	Yancey Thigpen	.50
10	Bobby Engram	.15
11	Barry Sanders	5.00
12	Ben Coates	.50
13	Joey Galloway	1.00
14	Charlie Batch	2.00
15	Jerome Bettis	1.00
16	Brad Johnson	1.00
17	Brian Griese	2.50
18	Jeff Lewis	.15
19	Jake Plummer	2.50
20	Mark Brunell	2.50
21	Robert Smith	1.00
22	Steve Young	2.00
23	Derrick Mayes	.50
24	Wayne Chrebet	.75
25	Rich Gannon	.50
26	Steve McNair	1.25
27	Charles Johnson	.15
28	Stephen Alexander	.15
29	Jeff Blake	.50
30	Tony Gonzalez	.50
31	Eddie Kennison	.15
32	Hines Ward	.50
33	Isaac Bruce	1.00
34	Peyton Manning	4.50
35	Doug Pederson	.15
36	Stephen Davis	1.00
37	Terance Mathis	.15
38	Herman Moore	1.00
39	Fred Taylor	1.00
40	Courtney Hawkins	.15
41	Michael Westbrook	.50
42	Vinny Testaverde	.50
43	Jacquez Green	.50
44	Rocket Ismail	.15
45	Curtis Martin	1.00
46	Tim Brown	.50
47	Kevin Dyson	.50
48	Steve Beuerlein	.50
49	Adrian Murrell	.50
50	Randall Cunningham	1.00
51	Jerry Rice	3.00
52	Tim Biakabutuka	.50
53	Muhsin Muhammad	.50
54	Antonio Freeman	1.00
55	Cris Carter	1.00
56	Lawrence Phillips	.50
57	Michael Irvin	.50
58	Terrell Owens	1.00
59	Warrick Dunn	1.00
60	Leslie Shepherd	.15
61	O.J. McDuffie	.50
62	Byron Hanspard	.15
63	Trent Dilfer	.50
64	Eric Moulds	1.00
65	Scott Mitchell	.15
66	Marc Edwards	.15
67	Dorsey Levens	1.00
68	Dan Marino	4.50
69	Jason Sehorn	.15
70	Junior Seau	.50
71	Reidel Anthony	.50
72	Rob Moore	.50
73	Deion Sanders	1.00
74	Rickey Dudley	.50
75	Keyshawn Johnson	1.00
76	Eddie George	1.25
77	E.G. Green	.50
78	Terry Kirby	.15
79	John Avery	.50
80	Pete Mitchell	.15
81	Natrone Means	.75
82	Mike Alstott	1.00
83	Carl Pickens	.50
84	Karim Abdul	.50
85	Kerry Collins	.50
86	Erik Kramer	.15
87	Robert Holcombe	.50
88	Willie Jackson	.15
89	Marcus Pollard	.15
90	Bam Morris	.15
91	Gary Brown	.15
92	Freddie Jones	.15
93	*Kurt Warner*	8.00
94	Priest Holmes	1.00
95	Duce Staley	1.00
96	Skip Hicks	.50
97	Frank Sanders	.50
98	Corey Dillon	1.00
99	Shannon Sharpe	.75
100	Randy Moss	5.00
101	Sean Dawkins	.15
102	Marshall Faulk	1.00
103	Mark Chmura	.50
104	Keenan McCardell	.50
105	Jimmy Smith	1.00
106	Jim Harbaugh	.50
107	Jamal Anderson	1.00
108	Elvis Grbac	.50
109	Ed McCaffrey	.75
110	Drew Bledsoe	2.50
111	Curtis Conway	.50
112	Billy Joe Tolliver	.15
113	J.J. Stokes	.50
114	Curtis Enis	1.00
115	Antowain Smith	1.00
116	Troy Aikman	3.00
117	Ricky Watters	.50
118	Kordell Stewart	1.00
119	Derrick Alexander	.15
120	Emmitt Smith	4.50
121	Billy Joe Hobert	.15
122	Johnnie Morton	.15
123	Rod Smith	.75
124	Marvin Harrison	1.00
125	Brett Favre	6.00
126	*Craig Yeast*	1.00
127	*Ricky Williams*	10.00
128	*Brandon Stokley*	2.00
129	*Akili Smith*	3.00
130	*Peerless Price*	4.00
131	*Joe Montgomery*	1.00
132	*Cade McNown*	2.00
133	*Donovan McNabb*	10.00
134	*Shaun King*	2.00
135	*J.J. Johnson*	3.00
136	*Kevin Johnson*	3.00
137	*Edgerrin James*	10.00
138	*Terry Jackson*	1.00
139	*Sedrick Irvin*	1.00
140	*Brock Huard*	1.00
141	*Torry Holt*	5.00
142	*Amos Zereoue*	2.00
143	*Kevin Faulk*	3.00
144	*Troy Edwards*	3.00
145	*Donald Driver*	2.00
146	*Daunte Culpepper*	10.00
147	*Tim Couch*	3.00
148	*Cecil Collins*	3.00
149	*David Boston*	5.00
150	*Champ Bailey*	3.00
151	*Olandis Gary*	2.00

1999 SkyBox Molten Metal Gridiron Gods

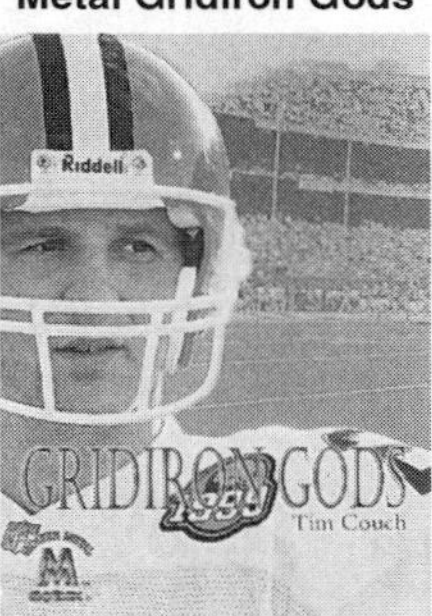

This 20-card insert set included the top players in the NFL. Singles were inserted 1:6 packs. Parallel Silver (1:24), Gold (1:72) and Blue (numbered to 99) sets were also released.

		NM/M
Complete Set (20):		35.00
Common Player:		1.00
Inserted 1:6		
Silver Cards:		1X
Inserted 1:24		
Gold Cards:		2X
Inserted 1:72		
Blue Cards:		3X-6X
Production 99 Sets		
1	Randy Moss	4.00
2	Keyshawn Johnson	1.00
3	Mike Alstott	1.00
4	Brian Griese	2.00
5	Tim Couch	4.00
6	Troy Aikman	4.00
7	Warrick Dunn	1.00
8	Mark Brunell	2.00
9	Jerry Rice	4.00
10	Dorsey Levens	1.00
11	Fred Taylor	2.00
12	Emmitt Smith	5.00
13	Edgerrin James	5.00
14	Eddie George	2.50
15	Drew Bledsoe	3.00
16	Deion Sanders	1.00
17	Charlie Batch	1.00
18	Kordell Stewart	1.00
19	Brad Johnson	1.00
20	Akili Smith	1.00

1999 SkyBox Molten Metal Gridiron Gods Blue

This was a 20-card parallel to the Gridiron God insert set. Each of these singles was sequentially numbered to 99.

		NM/M
Blue Cards:		3X-6X
Production 99 Sets		
1	Randy Moss	6.00
2	Keyshawn Johnson	2.00
3	Mike Alstott	2.00
4	Brian Griese	3.00
5	Tim Couch	8.00
6	Troy Aikman	4.00
7	Warrick Dunn	2.00
8	Mark Brunell	3.00
9	Jerry Rice	4.00
10	Dorsey Levens	2.00
11	Fred Taylor	4.00
12	Emmitt Smith	5.00
13	Edgerrin James	12.00
14	Eddie George	2.50
15	Drew Bledsoe	3.00
16	Deion Sanders	2.00
17	Charlie Batch	2.50
18	Kordell Stewart	2.00
19	Brad Johnson	2.00
20	Akili Smith	3.50

1999 SkyBox Molten Metal Gridiron Gods Gold

This was a 20-card parallel to the Gridiron Gods insert set. These singles were found 1:72 packs.

		NM/M
Gold Cards:		2X
Inserted 1:72		
1	Randy Moss	6.00
2	Keyshawn Johnson	2.00
3	Mike Alstott	2.00
4	Brian Griese	3.00
5	Tim Couch	8.00
6	Troy Aikman	4.00
7	Warrick Dunn	2.00
8	Mark Brunell	3.00
9	Jerry Rice	4.00
10	Dorsey Levens	2.00
11	Fred Taylor	4.00
12	Emmitt Smith	5.00
13	Edgerrin James	12.00
14	Eddie George	2.50
15	Drew Bledsoe	3.00
16	Deion Sanders	2.00
17	Charlie Batch	2.50
18	Kordell Stewart	2.00
19	Brad Johnson	2.00
20	Akili Smith	3.50

1999 SkyBox Molten Metal Gridiron Gods Silver

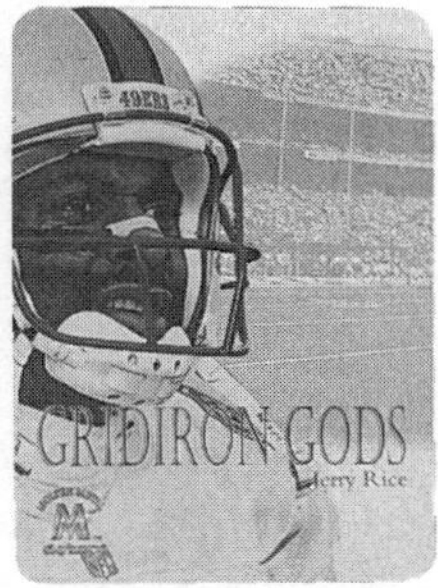

This was a 20-card parallel to the Gridiron Gods insert set. These singles were found 1:24 packs.

		NM/M
Silver Cards:		1.5X
Inserted 1:24		
1	Randy Moss	6.00
2	Keyshawn Johnson	2.00
3	Mike Alstott	2.00
4	Brian Griese	3.00
5	Tim Couch	8.00
6	Troy Aikman	4.00
7	Warrick Dunn	2.00
8	Mark Brunell	3.00
9	Jerry Rice	4.00
10	Dorsey Levens	2.00
11	Fred Taylor	4.00
12	Emmitt Smith	5.00
13	Edgerrin James	12.00
14	Eddie George	2.50
15	Drew Bledsoe	3.00
16	Deion Sanders	2.00
17	Charlie Batch	2.50
18	Kordell Stewart	2.00
19	Brad Johnson	2.00
20	Akili Smith	3.50

1999 SkyBox Molten Metal Patchworks

This nine-card insert set included pieces of numbers, names or patches from player-worn jerseys. Singles were inserted 1:360 packs.

		NM/M
Common Player:		50.00
Inserted 1:360		
1	Drew Bledsoe	65.00
2	Terrell Davis	65.00
3	Brett Favre	100.00
4	Peyton Manning	75.00
5	Dan Marino	100.00
6	Herman Moore	50.00
7	Randy Moss	75.00
8	Jerry Rice	65.00
9	Steve Young	65.00

1999 SkyBox Molten Metal Perfect Fit

This 10-card insert set included players who make their teams complete. Singles were inserted 1:24 packs. Parallel Silver (1:72), Gold (1:216) and Red (numbered to 25) versions were also released.

		NM/M
Complete Set (10):		45.00
Common Player:		1.00
Inserted 1:24		
Silver Cards:		1.5X
Inserted 1:72		
Gold Cards:		2X
Inserted 1:216		
Red Cards:		8X-16X
Production 25 Sets		
1	Barry Sanders	5.00
2	Brett Favre	6.00
3	Dan Marino	6.00
4	Edgerrin James	5.00
5	Emmitt Smith	5.00
6	Fred Taylor	1.00
7	Randy Moss	4.00
8	Terrell Davis	3.00
9	Tim Couch	4.00
10	Peyton Manning	5.00

1999 SkyBox Molten Metal Perfect Fit Gold

This was a ten-card parallel to the Perfect Fit insert. Singles were found 1:216 packs.

		NM/M
Gold Cards:		2X
Inserted 1:216		
1	Barry Sanders	12.00
2	Brett Favre	12.00
3	Dan Marino	10.00
4	Edgerrin James	20.00
5	Emmitt Smith	10.00
6	Fred Taylor	5.00
7	Randy Moss	12.00
8	Terrell Davis	10.00
9	Tim Couch	12.00
10	Peyton Manning	10.00

1999 SkyBox Molten Metal Perfect Fit Red

This was a ten-card parallel to the Perfect Fit insert set. Each single was sequentially numbered to 25.

		NM/M
Red Cards:		8X-16X
Production 25 Sets		
1	Barry Sanders	12.00
2	Brett Favre	12.00
3	Dan Marino	10.00
4	Edgerrin James	20.00
5	Emmitt Smith	10.00
6	Fred Taylor	5.00
7	Randy Moss	12.00
8	Terrell Davis	10.00
9	Tim Couch	12.00
10	Peyton Manning	10.00

1999 SkyBox Molten Metal Perfect Fit Silver

This was a ten-card parallel to the Perfect Fit insert set. Singles were inserted 1:72 packs.

		NM/M
Silver Cards:		1.5X
Inserted 1:72		
1	Barry Sanders	12.00
2	Brett Favre	12.00
3	Dan Marino	10.00
4	Edgerrin James	20.00
5	Emmitt Smith	10.00
6	Fred Taylor	5.00
7	Randy Moss	12.00
8	Terrell Davis	10.00
9	Tim Couch	12.00
10	Peyton Manning	10.00

1999 SkyBox Molten Metal Player's Party

	NM/M
Complete Set (125):	50.00
Common Player:	.40
Singles:	.5X to 1.2X

1999 SkyBox Molten Metal Top Notch

This 15-card insert set included the top players in the NFL. Singles were found 1:12 packs. Parallel Silver (1:36), Gold (1:108) and Green (numbered to 75) versions were also produced.

		NM/M
Complete Set (15):		35.00
Common Player:		1.00
Inserted 1:12		
Silver Cards:		1.5X
Inserted 1:36		
Gold Cards:		2X
Inserted 1:108		
Green Cards:		3X-5X
Production 75 Sets		
1	Jake Plummer	2.00
2	Cade McNown	2.00
3	Tim Couch	4.00
4	Emmitt Smith	5.00
5	Charlie Batch	1.00
6	Donovan McNabb	4.00
7	Steve Young	4.00
8	Brian Griese	2.00
9	Doug Flutie	2.00
10	Edgerrin James	5.00
11	Fred Taylor	2.00
12	Keyshawn Johnson	1.00
13	Mark Brunell	2.00
14	Randy Moss	5.00
15	Ricky Williams	5.00

1999 SkyBox Molten Metal Top Notch Gold

This was a 15-card parallel to the Top Notch insert set. Each of these singles was inserted 1:108 packs.

		NM/M
Gold Cards:		2X
Inserted 1:108		
1	Jake Plummer	5.00
2	Cade McNown	6.00
3	Tim Couch	10.00
4	Emmitt Smith	7.00
5	Charlie Batch	4.00
6	Donovan McNabb	6.00
7	Steve Young	4.00
8	Brian Griese	4.00
9	Doug Flutie	4.00
10	Edgerrin James	15.00
11	Fred Taylor	5.00
12	Keyshawn Johnson	2.00
13	Mark Brunell	4.00
14	Randy Moss	10.00
15	Ricky Williams	10.00

1999 SkyBox Molten Metal Top Notch Green

This was a 15-card parallel to the Top Notch insert set. Singles were sequentially numbered to 75.

		NM/M
Green Cards:		3X-5X
Production 75 Sets		
1	Jake Plummer	5.00
2	Cade McNown	6.00
3	Tim Couch	10.00
4	Emmitt Smith	7.00
5	Charlie Batch	4.00
6	Donovan McNabb	6.00
7	Steve Young	4.00
8	Brian Griese	4.00
9	Doug Flutie	4.00
10	Edgerrin James	15.00
11	Fred Taylor	5.00
12	Keyshawn Johnson	2.00
13	Mark Brunell	4.00
14	Randy Moss	10.00
15	Ricky Williams	10.00

1999 SkyBox Molten Metal Top Notch Silver

This was a 15-card parallel to the Top Notch insert set. Singles were found 1:36 packs.

		NM/M
Silver Cards:		1.5X
Inserted 1:36		
1	Jake Plummer	5.00
2	Cade McNown	6.00
3	Tim Couch	10.00
4	Emmitt Smith	7.00
5	Charlie Batch	4.00
6	Donovan McNabb	6.00
7	Steve Young	4.00
8	Brian Griese	4.00
9	Doug Flutie	4.00
10	Edgerrin James	15.00
11	Fred Taylor	5.00
12	Keyshawn Johnson	2.00
13	Mark Brunell	4.00
14	Randy Moss	10.00
15	Ricky Williams	10.00

2000 SkyBox

		NM/M
Complete Set (300):		375.00
Common Player:		.15
Minor Stars:		.30
Common Rookie:		.50
Common SP:		5.00
SP Cards Horizontal Photo		
Production 2,000 Sets		
Pack (10):		1.75
Wax Box (24):		30.00
1	Tim Couch	1.00
2	Edgerrin James	1.50
3	Wesley Walls	.30
4	Brian Griese	.60
5	Herman Moore	.30
6	Mark Brunell	.75
7	John Randle	.15
8	Victor Green	.15
9	Michael Sinclair	.15
10	Jevon Kearse	.60
11	Peter Boulware	.15
12	Kevin Johnson	.50
13	Vonnie Holliday	.15
14	Jason Taylor	.15
15	Cameron Cleeland	.30
16	Jeff Graham	.15
17	Jacquez Green	.30
18	Chris McAlister	.15
19	Takeo Spikes	.15
20	Marvin Harrison	.50
21	Jay Fiedler	.50
22	Jake Reed	.15
23	Jerry Rice	1.00
24	Shaun King	.75
25	Donovan McNabb	.75
26	David Boston	.50
27	Curtis Enis	.50
28	Olandis Gary	.60
29	James Stewart	.50
30	Jimmy Smith	.50
31	Randy Moss	1.75
32	Keyshawn Johnson	.50
33	Kevin Carter	.15
34	Stephen Davis	.50
35	Jay Riemersma	.30
36	Emmitt Smith	1.25
37	E.G. Green	.15
38	Dwayne Rudd	.15
39	Michael Strahan	.15
40	Troy Edwards	.50
41	Derrick Mayes	.30
42	Eddie George	.60
43	Bruce Smith	.15
44	Andre Wadsworth	.15
45	Bobby Engram	.15
46	Byron Chamberlain	.15
47	Antonio Freeman	.50
48	Hardy Nickerson	.15
49	Terry Glenn	.50
50	Wayne Chrebet	.30
51	London Fletcher	.15
52	Michael Westbrook	.30
53	Rob Moore	.30
54	Eddie Kennison	.15
55	Ed McCaffrey	.30

56 Dorsey Levens .50
57 Andre Rison .30
58 Willie McGinest .15
59 Tyrone Wheatley .30
60 Kurt Warner 2.00
61 Stephen Alexander .15
62 Jessie Tuggle .15
63 Jim Miller .15
64 Luther Elliss .15
65 Bill Schroeder .30
66 Elvis Grbac .30
67 Ty Law .15
68 Tim Brown .30
69 Marshall Faulk .50
70 Champ Bailey .30
71 Charlie Batch .50
72 Steve Beuerlein .30
73 Raghib Ismail .15
74 Kevin Hardy .15
75 Zach Thomas .30
76 Aaron Glenn .15
77 Jerome Bettis .50
78 Chris Chandler .30
79 Marcus Robinson .50
80 Derrick Alexander .15
81 Drew Bledsoe .75
82 Charles Woodson .30
83 Isaac Bruce .50
84 Darrell Green .15
85 Tim Dwight .50
86 Darnay Scott .30
87 Chris Claiborne .15
88 Tony Gonzalez .30
89 Tony Simmons .15
90 Rich Gannon .30
91 Torry Holt .50
92 Jamal Anderson .50
93 Akili Smith .60
94 Germane Crowell .50
95 Lawyer Milloy .15
96 Napoleon Kaufman .50
97 Grant Wistrom .15
98 Terance Mathis .15
99 Karim Abdul .15
100 Kerry Collins .30
101 Troy Vincent .15
102 Jermaine Fazande .15
103 Warren Sapp .30
104 Tony Banks .30
105 Darrin Chiaverini .15
106 Corey Bradford .15
107 Tony Martin .15
108 Jeff Blake .30
109 Torrance Small .15
110 Freddie Jones .15
111 Warrick Dunn .50
112 Tim Biakabutuka .30
113 Rod Smith .50
114 Kyle Brady .15
115 Oronde Gadsden .15
116 Dedric Ward .15
117 Mikhael Ricks .15
118 Bryant Young .15
119 Michael Bates .15
120 Junior Seau .30
121 Bill Romanowski .15
122 Reggie Barlow .15
123 Jeff Garcia .30
124 Peerless Price .50
125 Jeff George .30
126 Cornelius Bennett .15
127 Amani Toomer .30
128 Charles Johnson .15
129 Cortez Kennedy .15
130 Samari Rolle .15
131 Eric Moulds .50
132 Joey Galloway .50
133 Peyton Manning 1.50
134 Robert Smith .30
135 Jessie Armstead .15
136 Will Blackwell .15
137 Jon Kitna .50
138 Kevin Dyson .30
139 Jake Plummer .50
140 Cade McNown .75
141 Terrell Davis 1.00
142 Johnnie Morton .15
143 Fred Taylor .75
144 Ed McDaniel .15
145 Vinny Testaverde .50
146 Az-Zahir Hakim .30
147 Brad Johnson .50
148 Antowain Smith .30
149 Rob Konrad .15
150 Sam Cowart .15
151 Cris Carter .50
152 Jason Sehorn .15
153 Levon Kirkland .15
154 Shawn Springs .15
155 Frank Wycheck .15
156 Troy Aikman 1.00
157 Keenan McCardell .30
158 Sam Madison .15
159 Curtis Martin .50
160 Hines Ward .15
161 Steve Young .75
162 Blaine Bishop .15
163 Shannon Sharpe .30
164 Michael Pittman .15
165 Brett Favre 1.75
166 Damon Huard .30
167 Keith Poole .15
168 Curtis Conway .30
169 Derrick Brooks .15
170 Duce Staley .50
171 Rob Johnson .30
172 Pete Gonzalez .15
173 Ken Dilger .15
174 Ike Hilliard .30
175 Bobby Taylor .15
176 Ricky Watters .30
177 Steve McNair .60
178 Patrick Johnson .15
179 Carl Pickens .30
180 Terrence Wilkins .30
181 Rashaan Shehee .15
182 Ricky Williams 1.00
183 James Jett .15
184 Terrell Owens .50
185 John Lynch .15
186 Muhsin Muhammad .30
187 Ryan McNeil .15
188 Jerome Pathon .15
189 Daunte Culpepper .75
190 Joe Jurevicius .15
191 Kordell Stewart .50
192 Christian Fauria .15
193 Yancey Thigpen .15
194 Patrick Jeffers .50
195 Corey Dillon .50
196 Tamarick Vanover .15
197 Doug Flutie .60
198 Rickey Dudley .15
199 Charlie Garner .30
200 Mike Alstott .50
201 *Courtney Brown* .60
201S Courtney Brown SP 3.00
202 *Peter Warrick* 1.25
202S Peter Warrick SP 6.00
203 *Thomas Jones* 1.00
203S Thomas Jones SP 5.00
204 *Sylvester Morris* .50
204S Sylvester Morris SP 3.00
205 *Chad Pennington* 3.00
205S Chad Pennington SP 15.00
206 *Ron Dayne* 1.00
206S Ron Dayne SP 5.00
207 *Todd Pinkston* 1.00
207S Todd Pinkston SP 5.00
208 *Todd Husak* .50
208S Todd Husak SP 3.00
209 *Chris Redman* 1.00
209S Chris Redman SP 5.00
210 *Jerry Porter* 1.25
210S Jerry Porter SP 6.00
211 *Michael Wiley* .60
211S Michael Wiley SP 3.00
212 *J.R. Redmond* .60
212S J.R. Redmond SP 3.00
213 *Dennis Northcutt* 1.00
213S Dennis Northcutt SP 5.00
214 *Gari Scott* .50
214S Gari Scott SP 3.00
215 *Bashir Yamini* .50
215S Bashir Yamini SP 3.00
216 *Danny Farmer* .60
216S Danny Farmer SP 3.00
217 *Corey Simon* .60
217S Corey Simon SP 3.00
218 *Plaxico Burress* 1.50
218S Plaxico Burress SP 8.00
219 *Chad Morton* .60
219S Chad Morton SP 3.00
220 *Bubba Franks* .60
220S Bubba Franks SP 3.00
221 *Shaun Alexander* 2.00
221S Shaun Alexander SP 10.00
222 *Dez White* 1.00
222S Dez White SP 3.00
223 *Mareno Philyaw* .50
223S Mareno Philyaw SP 3.00
224 *Travis Taylor* 1.00
224S Travis Taylor SP 5.00
225 *Brian Urlacher* 1.50
225S Brian Urlacher SP 8.00
226 *Jamal Lewis* 2.00
226S Jamal Lewis SP 10.00
227 *Sherrod Gideon* .50
227S Sherrod Gideon SP 3.00
228 *Shyrone Stith* .50
228S Shyrone Stith SP 3.00
229 *Chris Cole* .50
229S Chris Cole SP 3.00
230 *Darrell Jackson* 1.25
230S Darrell Jackson SP 6.00
231 *Quinton Spotwood* .50
231S Quinton Spotwood SP 3.00
232 *Tee Martin* .60
232S Tee Martin SP 3.00
233 *Tim Rattay* 1.00
233S Tim Rattay SP 5.00
234 *Marc Bulger* 1.50
234S Marc Bulger SP 8.00
235 *Doug Johnson* 1.00
235S Doug Johnson SP 5.00
236 *Joe Hamilton* .60
236S Joe Hamilton SP 3.00
237 *Trevor Gaylor* .60
237S Trevor Gaylor SP 3.00
238 *Travis Prentice* 1.00
238S Travis Prentice SP 5.00
239 *R. Jay Soward* .60
239S R. Jay Soward SP 3.00
240 *Trung Canidate* 1.00
240S Trung Canidate SP 5.00
241 *Giovanni Carmazzi* .60
241S Giovanni Carmazzi SP 3.00
242 *Reuben Droughns* 1.00
242S Reuben Droughns SP 5.00
243 *Curtis Keaton* .50
243S Curtis Keaton SP 3.00
244 *Laveranues Coles* 1.25
244S Laveranues Coles SP 6.00
245 *Ron Dugans* .60
245S Ron Dugans SP 3.00
246 *Mike Anderson* 1.00
246S Mike Anderson SP 6.00
247 *Anthony Becht* .60
247S Anthony Becht SP 3.00
248 *Raynoch Thompson* .50
248S Raynoch Thompson SP 3.00
249 *Rob Morris* .50
249S Rob Morris SP 3.00
250 *Chafie Fields* .50
250S Chafie Fields SP 3.00

2000 SkyBox Star Rubies

NM/M
Ruby Cards: 3X-6X
Ruby Rookies: 2X-4X
Inserted 1:12

A player's name in *italic* type indicates a rookie card.

2000 SkyBox Star Rubies Extreme

NM/M
Extreme Cards: 10X-25X
Extreme Rookies: 5X-12X
Production 50 Sets

2000 SkyBox Autographics

NM/M
Common Player: 5.00
Minor Stars: 20.00
Inserted 1:72
Silver Cards: 1.2X
Production 250 Sets
Kimble Anders 5.00
Champ Bailey 12.00
Charlie Batch 12.00
Donnell Bennett 5.00
David Boston 25.00
Peter Boulware 5.00
Mark Brunell 35.00
Wayne Chrebet 20.00
Stephen Davis 25.00
Jake Delhomme 12.00
Corey Dillon 20.00
Reuben Droughns 15.00
Deon Dyer 5.00
Danny Farmer 5.00
Kevin Faulk 10.00
Sherrod Gideon 5.00
Damon Griffith 5.00
Priest Holmes 35.00
Raghib Ismail 5.00
Patrick Jeffers 20.00
Rob Johnson 5.00
Terry Kirby 5.00
Shane Matthews 5.00
Ed McCaffrey 20.00
Cade McNown 12.00
Rondell Mealey 5.00
Johnnie Morton 5.00
Terrell Owens 20.00
Chad Pennington 65.00
John Randle 5.00
Jake Reed 5.00
Marcus Robinson 10.00
Akili Smith 12.00
Jimmy Smith 12.00
R. Jay Soward 10.00
Kordell Stewart 12.00
Shyrone Stith 5.00
Amani Toomer 5.00
Dedric Ward 5.00
Dez White 10.00
Frank Wycheck 5.00

2000 SkyBox Genuine Coverage Common

NM/M
Common Player: 10.00
Inserted 1:288
David Boston 25.00
Corey Dillon 25.00
Tim Dwight 25.00
Terry Kirby 10.00
Shane Matthews 10.00
Rob Moore 10.00
Johnnie Morton 10.00
Frank Sanders 10.00

2000 SkyBox Genuine Coverage Hobby

NM/M
Common Player: 10.00
Inserted 1:144
Shaun Alexander 75.00
Courtney Brown 35.00
Ron Dayne 45.00
Reuben Droughns 10.00
Bubba Franks 30.00
Sylvester Morris 20.00
Chad Pennington 100.00
Jerry Porter 25.00
Travis Prentice 25.00
J.R. Redmond 25.00
Peter Warrick 35.00

2000 SkyBox Patchworks

NM/M
Common Player: 20.00
Troy Aikman 60.00
Jamal Anderson 20.00
Drew Bledsoe 45.00
Mark Brunell 25.00
Tim Couch 45.00
Brett Favre 75.00
Eddie George 25.00
Marvin Harrison 25.00
Edgerrin James 60.00
Cade McNown 20.00
Jake Plummer 20.00
Jerry Rice 55.00
Junior Seau 35.00
Emmitt Smith 60.00
Fred Taylor 25.00
Kurt Warner 50.00

2000 SkyBox Preemptive Strike

NM/M
Complete Set (15): 10.00
Common Player: .50
Minor Stars: 1.00
Inserted 1:4
Star Ruby Cards: 2X-5X
Production 100 Sets
1 Tim Couch 1.75
2 Edgerrin James 3.00
3 Jake Plummer 1.00
4 Akili Smith 1.00
5 Cade McNown 1.00
6 Isaac Bruce 1.00

NM/M
7 Marvin Harrison 1.00
8 Troy Aikman 2.00
9 Germane Crowell 1.00
10 Cris Carter 1.00
11 Keyshawn Johnson 1.00
12 Donovan McNabb 1.25
13 Charlie Batch 1.00
14 Muhsin Muhammad .50
15 Marcus Robinson 1.00

2000 SkyBox SkyLines

NM/M
Complete Set (10): 12.00
Common Player: .50
Inserted 1:11
Star Ruby Cards: 3X-6X
Production 50 Sets
1 Tim Couch 2.00
2 Edgerrin James 3.00
3 Terrell Davis 2.00
4 Jamal Anderson .50
5 Kurt Warner 2.00
6 Charlie Batch .50
7 Emmitt Smith 3.00
8 Peyton Manning 3.00
9 Cade McNown 1.00
10 Mark Brunell 1.00

2000 SkyBox Sole Train

NM/M
Complete Set (10): 10.00
Common Player: 1.00
Inserted 1:8
Star Ruby Cards: 2X-5X
Production 100 Sets
1 Edgerrin James 2.00
2 Eddie George 1.50
3 Marshall Faulk 1.00
4 Emmitt Smith 2.50
5 Fred Taylor 1.75
6 Stephen Davis 1.00
7 Ricky Williams 2.00
8 Jamal Anderson 1.00
9 Warrick Dunn 1.00
10 Jerome Bettis 1.00

2000 SkyBox Sunday's Best

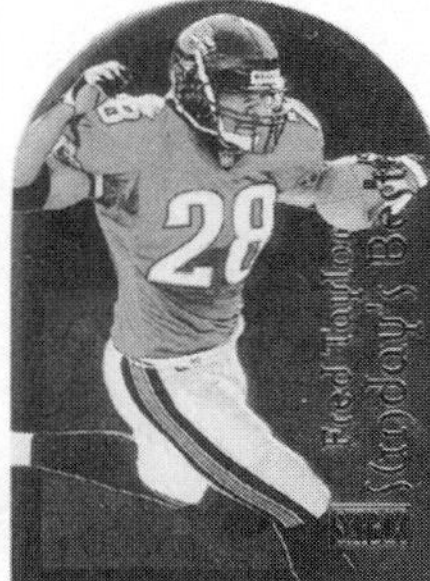

NM/M
Complete Set (10): 25.00
Common Player: 1.00
Inserted 1:24
Star Ruby Cards: 3X-6X
Production 50 Sets
1 Tim Couch 3.00
2 Edgerrin James 4.00
3 Terrell Davis 3.00
4 Peyton Manning 4.00
5 Marshall Faulk 1.00
6 Brett Favre 5.00
7 Emmitt Smith 4.00
8 Randy Moss 4.00
9 Fred Taylor 2.00
10 Ricky Williams 3.00

2000 SkyBox Superlatives

NM/M
Complete Set (15): 15.00
Common Player: .50
Minor Stars: 1.00
Inserted 1:11
Star Ruby Cards: 3X-6X
Production 50 Sets
1 Tim Couch 2.00
2 Edgerrin James 3.00
3 Randy Moss 3.00
4 Marshall Faulk 2.00
5 Fred Taylor 1.00
6 Jake Plummer 1.00
7 Vinny Testaverde .50
8 Troy Aikman 2.50
9 Drew Bledsoe 2.00
10 Stephen Davis 1.00
11 Marvin Harrison 1.00
12 Steve Young 2.00
13 Jimmy Smith 1.00
14 Ricky Williams 2.50
15 Kurt Warner 2.00

2000 SkyBox The Bomb

NM/M
Complete Set (10): 20.00
Common Player: 1.00
Inserted 1:24
Star Ruby Cards: 3X-6X
Production 50 Sets
1 Tim Couch 3.00
2 Kurt Warner 3.00
3 Edgerrin James 4.00
4 Randy Moss 4.00
5 Keyshawn Johnson 1.00
6 Brett Favre 5.00
7 Peyton Manning 3.00
8 Eddie George 2.00
9 Isaac Bruce 1.00
10 Marvin Harrison 1.00

2000 Impact

NM/M
Complete Set (199): 20.00
Common Player: .10
Minor Stars: .20
Common Rookie: .30
Card #137 Never Issued
Pack (10): 1.00
Wax Box (36): 20.00
1 Kurt Warner 2.00
2 Dan Marino 1.50
3 Sedrick Irvin .20
4 *Chris Redman* 1.00
5 Robert Smith .30
6 Amani Toomer .20
7 Richard Huntley .10
8 Ahman Green .20
9 Fred Lane .10
10 Eddie George .50
11 Raghib Ismail .10
12 Shannon Sharpe .20
13 Shawn Jefferson .10
14 *Michael Wiley* .75
15 Jeff Graham .10
16 Steve Beuerlein .20
17 Tim Biakabutuka .20
18 Chris Watson .10
19 Kevin Faulk .20
20 Emmitt Smith 1.50
21 *Plaxico Burress* 1.00
22 Hines Ward .20
23 Jacquez Green .20
24 Doug Flutie .50
25 Leslie Shepherd .10
26 Johnnie Morton .10
27 *Tom Brady* 2.00
28 Jeff George .20
29 Derrick Mason .10
30 Marshall Faulk .50
31 Derrick Mayes .20
32 Jerome Bettis .30
33 Adrian Murrell .20
34 Curtis Enis .30
35 Kimble Anders .10
36 *Travis Prentice* .75
37 Curtis Martin .30
38 *Ronnie Powell* .30
39 Steve Christie .10
40 Brett Favre 1.75
41 Michael Bates .10
42 *Rondell Mealey* .50
43 Randall Cunningham .30
44 Kerry Collins .20
45 William Thomas .10
46 Ricky Watters .30
47 Marvin Harrison .50
48 Corey Bradford .20
49 Terry Kirby .10
50 Troy Aikman 1.25
51 Cris Carter .50
52 *Jamal Lewis* 1.50
53 Duce Staley .30
54 Isaac Bruce .50
55 Yancey Thigpen .20
56 *R. Jay Soward* 1.00
57 Jermaine Lewis .20
58 Zach Thomas .20
59 *Sylvester Morris* .75
60 Steve McNair .50
61 Tiki Barber .20
62 Torrance Small .10
63 Champ Bailey .20
64 Tim Dwight .30
65 Willie Jackson .10
66 Edgerrin James 1.75
67 *Ron Dayne* 1.00
68 Rich Gannon .20
69 Junior Seau .20
70 Warren Sapp .20
71 Rob Johnson .20
72 Antonio Freeman .50
73 O.J. McDuffie .10
74 Tamarick Vanover .10
75 *Courtney Brown* .60
76 Donovan McNabb .75
77 Az-Zahir Hakim .20
78 Albert Connell .20
79 Qadry Ismail .10
80 Terrell Davis 1.50
81 Dorsey Levens .50
82 Tony Martin .10
83 *Laveranues Coles* .50
84 Karim Abdul .20
85 Charles Johnson .10
86 Torry Holt .50
87 Stephen Davis .50
88 Tony Banks .20
89 Akili Smith .50
90 Tim Couch 1.00
91 Bill Schroeder .10
92 Andre Hastings .10
93 Eddie Kennison .10
94 Randy Moss 1.75
95 Tony Horne .10
96 *Sherrod Gideon* .30
97 Wesley Walls .20
98 Brian Griese .50
99 *Jake Delhomme* 1.00
100 Peyton Manning 1.50
101 Brad Johnson .50
102 *Trung Canidate* .50
103 Freddie Jones .10
104 Muhsin Muhammad .20
105 Eric Moulds .50
106 Ed McCaffrey .30
107 Joe Montgomery .10
108 Olandis Gary .50
109 J.J. Stokes .20
110 Ricky Williams 1.00
111 Jim Harbaugh .20
112 Mike Alstott .50
113 Errict Rhett .20
114 Terance Mathis .10
115 Kevin Johnson .50
116 Tremain Mack .10
117 *Peter Warrick* 1.00
118 Lamont Warren .10
119 Damon Huard .30
120 Cade McNown .75
121 Natrone Means .20
122 Ken Oxendine .10
123 *J.R. Redmond* 1.00
124 Ken Dilger .10
125 J.J. Johnson .20
126 Napoleon Kaufman .30
127 Ryan Leaf .30
128 Michael Westbrook .20
129 Mario Bates .10
130 Jake Plummer .75
131 James Jett .10
132 Darnay Scott .20
133 Curtis Conway .20
134 Fred Taylor .75
135 Wayne Chrebet .30
136 Sean Dawkins .10
137 Keenan McCardell .20
138 Donnell Bennett .10
139 Jerry Rice 1.25
140 Vinny Testaverde .30
141 *Chad Pennington* 2.00
142 Jonathon Linton .10
143 Herman Moore .30
144 David Patten .10
145 Troy Edwards .50
146 Jon Kitna .50
147 Jimmy Smith .30
148 *Tee Martin* 1.00
149 Jevon Kearse .50
150 Frank Sanders .20
151 Marcus Robinson .50
152 Mike Hollis .10
153 Frank Wycheck .20
154 *Tim Rattay* .75
155 Dedric Ward .10
156 Terrell Owens .50
157 Chris Chandler .20
158 Damon Griffin .10

160 Mike Vanderjagt .10
161 Elvis Grbac .20
162 Rickey Dudley .20
163 Jeff Garcia .20
164 *Thomas Jones* .75
165 Tyrone Wheatley .20
166 Rod Smith .30
167 *Bubba Franks* .75
168 Chris Warren .20
169 *Anthony Lucas* .50
170 Terry Glenn .50
171 John Carney .10
172 Warrick Dunn .50
173 *Shaun Alexander* 1.50
174 David Boston .50
175 Bobby Engram .10
176 *Travis Taylor* .50
177 Derrick Alexander .10
178 Keyshawn Johnson .50
179 Steve Young .75
180 Deion Sanders .50
181 Charlie Batch .50
182 Drew Bledsoe .75
183 *Reuben Droughns* 1.50
184 Ray Lucas .50
185 Shaun King .75
186 Jamal Anderson .50
187 Corey Dillon .50
188 *Joe Hamilton* .75
189 Terrence Wilkins .20
190 Mark Brunell .75
191 Tony Gonzalez .20
192 Tim Brown .30
193 Charlie Garner .20
194 Antowain Smith .50
195 David LaFleur .10
196 Germane Crowell .20
197 Terry Allen .20
198 Marc Bulger .10
199 Kevin Dyson .20
200 Kordell Stewart .50

2000 Impact Autographics

NM/M

Complete Set (47):
Common Player:
1 Karim Abdul
2 Troy Aikman
3 Kimble Anders
4 Jamal Anderson
5 Tim Biakabutuka
6 David Boston
7 Tom Brady
8 Isaac Bruce
9 Mark Brunell
10 Germane Crowell
11 Terrell Davis
12 Ron Dayne
13 Corey Dillon
14 Deon Dyer
15 Troy Edwards
16 Christian Fauria
17 Jermaine Fazande
18 Rich Gannon
19 Charlie Garner
20 Olandis Gary
21 Sherrod Gideon
22 Damon Griffin
23 Marvin Harrison
24 Torry Holt
25 Tony Horne
26 Damon Huard
27 Darrell Jackson
28 Edgerrin James
29 Jon Kitna
30 Shane Matthews
31 Cade McNown
32 Joe Montgomery
33 Muhsin Muhammad
34 Chad Pennington
35 Jake Plummer
36 Travis Prentice
37 Tim Rattay
38 Jake Reed
39 Marcus Robinson
40 Bill Schroeder
41 Shannon Sharpe
42 Antowain Smith
43 R. Jay Soward
44 Kordell Stewart
45 Dedric Ward
46 Kurt Warner
47 Chris Watson

2000 Impact Hat's Off

NM/M

Common Player: 25.00
Inserted 1:720
1 Karim Abdul 25.00
2 Jamal Anderson 35.00
3 David Boston 35.00
4 Isaac Bruce 35.00
5 Chris Chandler 25.00
6 Curtis Conway 25.00
7 Tim Couch 35.00
8 Tim Dwight 35.00
9 Curtis Enis 35.00
10 Marshall Faulk 40.00
11 Az-Zahir Hakim 25.00
12 Torry Holt 25.00
13 Kevin Johnson 25.00
14 Terry Kirby 25.00
15 Terance Mathis 25.00
16 Shane Matthews 25.00
17 Cade McNown 25.00
18 Rob Moore 25.00
19 Jake Plummer 25.00
20 Marcus Robinson 25.00
21 Frank Sanders 25.00

2000 Impact Point of Impact

NM/M

Complete Set (10): 25.00
Common Player: 1.50
Inserted 1:30
PI1 Peyton Manning 6.00
PI2 Edgerrin James 5.00
PI3 Brett Favre 8.00
PI4 Marshall Faulk 1.50
PI5 Fred Taylor 3.00
PI6 Tim Couch 4.00
PI7 Emmitt Smith 6.00
PI8 Eddie George 3.00
PI9 Randy Moss 5.00
PI10 Terrell Davis 3.00

2000 Impact Rewind '99

NM/M

Complete Set (40): 15.00
Common Player: .15
Minor Stars: .30
Inserted 1:1
1 Jake Plummer .50
2 Tim Dwight .30
3 Tony Banks .15
4 Doug Flutie .50
5 Tim Biakabutuka .15
6 Marcus Robinson .50
7 Corey Dillon .50
8 Tim Couch 1.00
9 Troy Aikman 1.25
10 Olandis Gary .50
11 Germane Crowell .15
12 Brett Favre 2.00
13 Peyton Manning 1.50
14 Mark Brunell .75
15 Tony Gonzalez .30
16 Dan Marino 1.50
17 Randy Moss 2.00
18 Drew Bledsoe .75
19 Ricky Williams 1.00
20 Amani Toomer .15
21 Keyshawn Johnson .50
22 Rich Gannon .15
23 Duce Staley .30
24 Jerome Bettis .30
25 Kenny Bynum .15
26 Charlie Garner .30
27 Jon Kitna .50
28 Kurt Warner 1.00
29 Mike Alstott .50
30 Eddie George .50
31 Stephen Davis .50
32 Kurt Warner 1.00
33 Edgerrin James 1.50
34 Jevon Kearse .50
35 Marshall Faulk .50
36 Edgerrin James 1.50
37 Marvin Harrison .50
38 Jimmy Smith .30
39 Steve Beuerlein .15
40 Kurt Warner 1.00

2000 Impact Tattoos

NM/M

Complete Set (31): 15.00
Common Tattoo: .50
Inserted 1:4

2003 SkyBox LE

NM/M

Common Player (1-60): .20
Minor Stars: .40
Unlisted Stars: .60
Common Rookie (61-160): 12.00
Minor Rookies: 15.00
Unlisted Rookies: 20.00
Production 99 Sets
Pack (3): 4.00
Box (18): 70.00
1 Emmitt Smith 1.50
2 Eric Moulds .40
3 William Green .60
4 Clinton Portis 1.50
5 Tony Gonzalez .40
6 Aaron Brooks .60
7 Chad Pennington .75
8 Jerry Rice 1.50
9 LaDainian Tomlinson .75
10 Torry Holt .60
11 Warren Sapp .40
12 Steve McNair .60
13 Marc Bulger .60
14 Patrick Ramsey .60
15 Peerless Price .40
16 Jamal Lewis .60
17 Rich Gannon .40
18 Plaxico Burress .60
19 Drew Brees .60
20 Eddie George .60
21 Ray Lewis .40
22 Drew Bledsoe .75
23 Antonio Bryant .40
24 David Carr 1.25
25 Priest Holmes .60
26 Ricky Williams 1.00
27 Peyton Manning 1.00
28 Daunte Culpepper .60
29 Jeremy Shockey 1.25
30 Tiki Barber .40
31 Koren Robinson .40
32 Keyshawn Johnson .40
33 Laveranues Coles .40
34 Brian Urlacher 1.00
35 Jake Plummer .40
36 Edgerrin James .75
37 Marvin Harrison .60
38 Tom Brady 1.00
39 Curtis Martin .60
40 Donovan McNabb .60
41 Hines Ward .40
42 Charlie Garner .40
43 Tommy Maddox .60
44 Terrell Owens .60
45 Shaun Alexander .60
46 Ahman Green .60
47 Fred Taylor .60
48 Randy Moss 1.00
49 Deuce McAllister .60
50 Quincy Carter .40
51 Jeff Garcia .40
52 Marshall Faulk .75
53 Dante Hall .60
54 Michael Vick 2.00
55 Stephen Davis .40
56 Corey Dillon .60
57 Travis Henry .40
58 Chad Johnson .40
59 Joey Harrington 1.00
60 Brett Favre 2.00
61 *Bryant Johnson* 15.00
62 *Terence Newman* 40.00
63 *LaBrandon Toefield* 15.00
64 *Visanthe Shiancoe* 12.00
65 *Josh Brown* 12.00
66 *Andre Woolfolk* 20.00
67 *Jeremi Johnson* 12.00
68 *Mike Doss* 15.00
69 *Talman Gardner* 20.00
70 *Arnaz Battle* 20.00
71 *Troy Polamalu* 20.00
72 *Brock Forsey* 25.00
73 *Domanick Davis* 50.00
74 *Onterrio Smith* 30.00
75 *Kassim Osgood* 20.00
76 *Asante Samuel* 20.00
77 *Terrell Suggs* 30.00
78 *Boss Bailey* 25.00
79 *Larry Johnson* 40.00
80 *Teyo Johnson* 25.00
81 *Chris Simms* 40.00
82 *Walter Young* 15.00
83 *Dave Ragone* 20.00
84 *E.J. Henderson* 15.00
85 *Billy McMullen* 12.00
86 *Taylor Jacobs* 15.00
87 *Sam Aiken* 12.00
88 *Avon Cobourne* 20.00
89 *J.R. Tolver* 15.00
90 *Doug Gabriel* 15.00
91 *Chris Brown* 40.00
92 *Musa Smith* 20.00
93 *Charles Rogers* 40.00
94 *Seth Marler* 12.00
95 *Dewayne Robertson* 15.00
96 *Shaun McDonald* 15.00
97 *Reno Mahe* 15.00
98 *Carson Palmer* 100.00
99 *Dallas Clark* 20.00
100 *Jonathon Sullivan* 12.00
101 *Brandon Lloyd* 25.00
102 *Ken Dorsey* 30.00
103 *Kelley Washington* 20.00
104 *Tony Hollings* 15.00
105 *Bethel Johnson* 30.00
106 *Antonio Gates* 25.00
107 *Tyler Brayton* 15.00
108 *Michael Haynes* 15.00
109 *Andre Johnson* 60.00
110 *Nate Burleson* 30.00
111 *Sammy Davis* 15.00
112 *Nick Barnett* 30.00
113 *Willis McGahee* 60.00
114 *Casey Fitzsimmons* 15.00
115 *Donald Lee* 12.00
116 *L.J. Smith* 15.00
117 *Tyrone Calico* 30.00
118 *Anquan Boldin* 50.00
119 *Jason Witten* 30.00
120 *George Wrighster* 12.00
121 *William Joseph* 15.00
122 *Kevin Curtis* 12.00
123 *Anthony Adams* 12.00
124 *Kyle Boller* 50.00
125 *Artose Pinner* 20.00
126 *Rashean Mathis* 12.00
127 *Justin Fargas* 30.00
128 *Pisa Tinoisamoa* 20.00
129 *Justin Griffith* 12.00
130 *Quentin Griffin* 50.00
131 *Cortez Hankton* 12.00
132 *B.J. Askew* 20.00
133 *Arlen Harris* 20.00
134 *Dan Klecko* 20.00
135 *Lee Suggs* 50.00
136 *Byron Leftwich* 100.00
137 *David Tyree* 12.00
138 *Aaron Walker* 12.00
139 *Marcus Trufant* 15.00
140 *Rex Grossman* 60.00
141 *Bennie Joppru* 12.00
142 *Kevin Williams* 12.00
143 *Jerome McDougle* 12.00
144 *Ken Hamlin* 15.00
145 *Zuriel Smith* 15.00
146 *Brooks Bollinger* 20.00
147 *Ivan Taylor* 12.00
148 *Brad Pyatt* 12.00
149 *DeJuan Groce* 12.00
150 *Keenan Howry* 20.00
151 *Seneca Wallace* 15.00
152 *Richard Angulo* 12.00
153 *Jimmy Kennedy* 15.00
154 *Ty Warren* 15.00
155 *Nnamdi Asomugha* 12.00
156 *Chris Kelsay* 12.00
157 *Terry Pierce* 12.00
158 *Victor Hobson* 15.00
159 *Brian St. Pierre* 20.00
160 *Dewayne White* 12.00

2003 SkyBox LE Artist's Proofs

Stars: 10X-20X
Production 50 Sets

2003 SkyBox LE Executive Proofs

Production 1 Set

2003 SkyBox LE Gold Proofs

Stars: 3X-6X
Production 150 Sets

2003 SkyBox LE Photographers Proofs

Stars: 15X-30X
Production 25 Sets

2003 SkyBox LE History of the Draft Jerseys

NM/M

Common Player: 10.00
Silver: 1X-1.5X
Production 50 Sets
Gold Production 10 Sets
HD-MA Mike Alstott 10.00
HD-TB Tiki Barber 12.00
HD-DB Drew Bledsoe 20.00
HD-DB Derrick Brooks 10.00
HD-IB Isaac Bruce 15.00
HD-KC Kerry Collins 10.00
HD-TC Tim Couch 10.00
HD-DC Daunte Culpepper 15.00
HD-SD Stephen Davis 10.00
HD-CD Corey Dillon 10.00
HD-MF Marshall Faulk 20.00
HD-BF Brett Favre 50.00
HD-JG Joey Galloway 10.00
HD-CG Charlie Garner 10.00
HD-EG Eddie George 15.00
HD-TG Tony Gonzalez 12.00
HD-AG Ahman Green 15.00
HD-MH Marvin Harrison 15.00
HD-TH Torry Holt 15.00
HD-EJ Edgerrin James 20.00
HD-KJ Keyshawn Johnson 12.00
HD-JK Jevon Kearse 10.00
HD-RL Ray Lewis 15.00
HD-PM Peyton Manning 25.00
HD-CM Curtis Martin 12.00
HD-DM Donovan McNabb 20.00
HD-SM Steve McNair 15.00
HD-RM Randy Moss 25.00
HD-EM Eric Moulds 10.00
HD-TO Terrell Owens 15.00
HD-JP Jake Plummer 10.00
HD-SR Simeon Rice 10.00
HD-WS Warren Sapp 10.00
HD-ES Emmitt Smith 40.00
HD-FT Fred Taylor 15.00
HD-ZT Zach Thomas 10.00
HD-AT Amani Toomer 10.00
HD-HW Hines Ward 12.00
HD-RW Ricky Williams 20.00
HD-CW Charles Woodson 10.00

2003 SkyBox LE Jersey Proofs

NM/M

Common Player: 6.00
Production 175 Sets
Gold Production 10 Sets
1 Emmitt Smith 25.00
2 Eric Moulds 6.00
4 Clinton Portis 15.00
5 Tony Gonzalez 8.00
7 Chad Pennington 12.00
8 Jerry Rice 20.00
9 LaDainian Tomlinson 12.00
10 Torry Holt 10.00
11 Warren Sapp 6.00
12 Steve McNair 10.00
21 Ray Lewis 10.00
22 Drew Bledsoe 10.00
24 David Carr 12.00
25 Priest Holmes 12.00
26 Ricky Williams 10.00
27 Peyton Manning 15.00
28 Daunte Culpepper 10.00
29 Jeremy Shockey 10.00
30 Tiki Barber 6.00
32 Keyshawn Johnson 6.00
34 Brian Urlacher 12.00
35 Jake Plummer 6.00
36 Edgerrin James 12.00
37 Marvin Harrison 10.00
39 Curtis Martin 8.00
40 Donovan McNabb 10.00
41 Hines Ward 8.00
42 Charlie Garner 6.00
44 Terrell Owens 8.00
45 Shaun Alexander 8.00
46 Ahman Green 10.00
47 Fred Taylor 8.00
48 Randy Moss 12.00
49 Deuce McAllister 10.00
52 Marshall Faulk 10.00
54 Michael Vick 25.00
55 Stephen Davis 6.00
56 Corey Dillon 6.00
59 Joey Harrington 10.00
60 Brett Favre 30.00

2003 SkyBox LE League Leaders

NM/M

Common Player: 2.00
Inserted 1:18
1LL Ricky Williams 4.00
2LL Marvin Harrison 2.00
3LL Chad Pennington 3.00
4LL Terrell Owens 2.00
5LL Brian Urlacher 4.00
6LL Shaun Alexander 2.00
7LL Marshall Faulk 3.00
8LL Ray Lewis 2.00
9LL Randy Moss 4.00
10LL Peyton Manning 4.00

2003 SkyBox LE League Leaders Jerseys

NM/M

Common Player: 15.00
Production 75 Sets
Silver: 1X-1.5X
Production 50 Sets
Gold Production 10 Sets
LL-SA Shaun Alexander 15.00
LL-MF Marshall Faulk 20.00
LL-MH Marvin Harrison 15.00
LL-RL Ray Lewis 15.00
LL-PM Peyton Manning 25.00
LL-RM Randy Moss 25.00
LL-TO Terrell Owens 15.00
LL-CP Chad Pennington 20.00
LL-BU Brian Urlacher 20.00
LL-RW Ricky Williams 15.00

2003 SkyBox LE Rare Form

NM/M

Common Player: 12.00
Inserted 1:288
1RF Brett Favre 20.00
2RF Emmitt Smith 20.00
3RF Michael Vick 20.00
4RF Clinton Portis 12.00
5RF Jeremy Shockey 12.00
6RF Jerry Rice 15.00
7RF David Carr 12.00
8RF Peyton Manning 12.00
9RF Randy Moss 12.00
10RF Brian Urlacher 12.00

2003 SkyBox LE Rare Form Jerseys

NM/M

Common Player: 20.00
RF-DC David Carr/8
RF-BF Brett Favre/4
RF-PM Peyton Manning/18
RF-PM Randy Moss/84 30.00
RF-CP Clinton Portis/26 40.00
RF-JR Jerry Rice/80 40.00
RF-JS Jeremy Shockey/80 20.00
RF-ES Emmitt Smith/22
RF-BU Brian Urlacher/54 20.00
RF-MV Michael Vick/7

2003 SkyBox LE Rare Form Jerseys Silver

NM/M

Common Player: 25.00
Production 50 Sets
Gold Production 10 Sets
RF-DC David Carr 30.00
RF-BF Brett Favre 50.00
RF-PM Peyton Manning 30.00
RF-PM Randy Moss 30.00
RF-CP Clinton Portis 30.00
RF-JR Jerry Rice 40.00
RF-JS Jeremy Shockey 25.00
RF-ES Emmitt Smith 50.00
RF-BU Brian Urlacher 30.00
RF-MV Michael Vick 50.00

2003 SkyBox LE Sky's the Limit

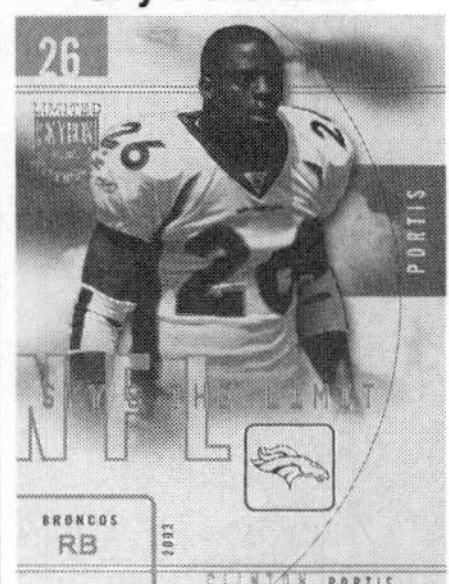

NM/M

Common Player: 2.00
Inserted 1:6
1SL Donovan McNabb 2.00
2SL Jeremy Shockey 3.00
3SL Michael Vick 6.00
4SL Peyton Manning 4.00
5SL Randy Moss 4.00
6SL Clinton Portis 4.00
7SL Joey Harrington 3.00
8SL Ricky Williams 3.00
9SL Deuce McAllister 2.00
10SL LaDainian Tomlinson 2.00
11SL Priest Holmes 2.00
12SL Carson Palmer 5.00
13SL Byron Leftwich 6.00
14SL Andre Johnson 4.00
15SL Larry Johnson 3.00
16SL Rex Grossman 4.00
17SL Terence Newman 3.00
18SL David Carr 4.00
19SL Daunte Culpepper 2.00
20SL Brian Urlacher 3.00

A player's name in *italic* type indicates a rookie card.

2003 SkyBox LE Sky's the Limit Jerseys

NM/M
Common Player: 15.00
Production 99 Sets
Silver: 1X-1.5X
Production 50 Sets
Gold Production 10 Sets
SL-DC David Carr 25.00
SL-DC Daunte Culpepper 15.00
SL-RG Rex Grossman 20.00
SL-JH Joey Harrington 20.00
SL-PH Priest Holmes 20.00
SL-AJ Andre Johnson 20.00
SL-LJ Larry Johnson 15.00
SL-BL Byron Leftwich 30.00
SL-PM Peyton Manning 25.00
SL-DM Deuce McAllister 15.00
SL-DM Donovan McNabb 15.00
SL-RM Randy Moss 25.00
SL-TN Terence Newman 15.00
SL-CP Carson Palmer 25.00
SL-CP Clinton Portis 25.00
SL-JS Jeremy Shockey 20.00
SL-LT LaDainian Tomlinson 15.00
SL-BU Brian Urlacher 20.00
SL-MV Michael Vick 30.00
SL-RW Ricky Williams 20.00

2004 SkyBox LE

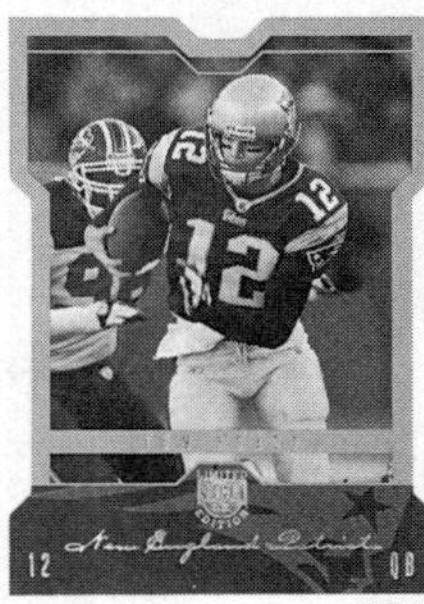

NM/M
Common Player (1-60): .25
Minor Stars (1-60): .50
Unlisted Stars (1-60): .75
Common Rookie (61-160): 10.00
Minor Rookie (61-160): 15.00
Production 99 Sets
Pack (3): 6.75
Box (16): 75.00
1 Anquan Boldin .75
2 Quincy Carter .75
3 Chad Pennington 1.00
4 Brett Favre 2.50
5 Marc Bulger .50
6 David Carr 1.00
7 Byron Leftwich 1.50
8 Hines Ward .50
9 Drew Bledsoe .75
10 Domanick Davis .75
11 Plaxico Burress .75
12 Mark Brunell .50
13 Terrell Owens .75
14 Peyton Manning 1.50
15 Matt Hasselbeck .50
16 Willis McGahee .75
17 Fred Taylor .75
18 Torry Holt .75
19 Priest Holmes 1.00
20 Charlie Garner .25
21 Brian Urlacher .75
22 Corey Dillon .50
23 Daunte Culpepper .75
24 Clinton Portis 1.50
25 Chad Johnson .50
26 Tom Brady 1.50
27 Deuce McAllister .75
28 Randy Moss 1.50
29 A.J. Feeley .25
30 Steve McNair .75
31 Aaron Brooks .75
32 Carson Palmer 1.00
33 Jeremy Shockey .75
34 Emmitt Smith 2.00
35 Jeff Garcia .75
36 Kurt Warner .75
37 Andre Johnson .75
38 LaDainian Tomlinson 1.00
39 Ray Lewis .50
40 Charles Rogers .75
41 Rich Gannon .50
42 Jake Delhomme .75
43 Marvin Harrison .75
44 Shaun Alexander .75
45 Ricky Williams .75
46 Eddie George .75
47 Edgerrin James 1.00
48 Chris Chambers .75
49 Jamal Lewis .75
50 Joey Harrington .75
51 Jerry Rice 2.00
52 Kyle Boller .75
53 Ahman Green .75
54 Donovan McNabb 1.00
55 Stephen Davis .50
56 Tony Gonzalez .50
57 Marshall Faulk 1.00
58 Michael Vick 2.00
59 Jake Plummer .50
60 Curtis Martin .75
61 *Eli Manning* 80.00
62 *Robert Gallery* 20.00
63 *Larry Fitzgerald* 50.00
64 *Philip Rivers* 50.00
65 *Sean Taylor* 25.00
66 *Kellen Winslow Jr.* 30.00
67 *Roy Williams* 50.00
68 *DeAngelo Hall* 25.00
69 *Reggie Williams* 25.00
70 *Dunta Robinson* 15.00
71 *Ben Roethlisberger* 100.00
72 *Jonathan Vilma* 20.00
73 *Lee Evans* 25.00
74 *Tommie Harris* 20.00
75 *Michael Clayton* 25.00
76 *D.J. Williams* 20.00
77 *Tim Euhus* 10.00
78 *Kenechi Udeze* 10.00
79 *Vince Wilfork* 20.00
80 *J.P. Losman* 30.00
81 *Jared Lorenzen* 10.00
82 *Steven Jackson* 40.00
83 *Ricky Ray* 10.00
84 *Chris Perry* 25.00
85 *Jason Babin* 10.00
86 *Chris Gamble* 10.00
87 *Michael Jenkins* 25.00
88 *Kevin Jones* 40.00
89 *Rashaun Woods* 30.00
90 *Ben Watson* 10.00
91 *Karlos Dansby* 10.00
92 *Teddy Lehman* 15.00
93 *Ben Troupe* 10.00
94 *Tatum Bell* 25.00
95 *Julius Jones* 40.00
96 *Devery Henderson* 15.00
97 *Drew Henson* 30.00
98 *Darius Watts* 15.00
99 *Greg Jones* 20.00
100 *Luke McCown* 15.00
101 *Keary Colbert* 20.00
102 *Mewelde Moore* 15.00
103 *Ben Hartsock* 10.00
104 *Derrick Hamilton* 10.00
105 *Bernard Berrian* 15.00
106 *Chris Cooley* 10.00
107 *Devard Darling* 15.00
108 *Matt Schaub* 15.00
109 *Carlos Francis* 10.00
110 *Will Poole* 10.00
111 *Samie Parker* 10.00
112 *Derrick Knight* 10.00
113 *Jericho Cotchery* 10.00
114 *Rod Rutherford* 10.00
115 *Ernest Wilford* 10.00
116 *Cedric Cobbs* 15.00
117 *Johnnie Morant* 10.00
118 *Craig Krenzel* 15.00
119 *Maurice Mann* 10.00
120 *Michael Turner* 10.00
121 *Ryan Dinwiddie* 10.00
122 *Drew Carter* 10.00
123 *P.K. Sam* 20.00
124 *Jamaar Taylor* 10.00
125 *Ryan Krause* 10.00
126 *Triandos Luke* 10.00
127 *Andy Hall* 10.00
128 *Josh Harris* 10.00
129 *Jim Sorgi* 10.00
130 *Jason Fife* 10.00
131 *Clarence Moore* 10.00
132 *Jeff Smoker* 20.00
133 *John Navarre* 20.00
134 *Justin Jenkins* 10.00
135 *Adimchinobe Echemandu* 10.00
136 *Jammal Lord* 10.00
137 *Erik Jensen* 10.00
138 *Cody Pickett* 15.00
139 *Casey Bramlet* 10.00
140 *Quincy Wilson* 20.00
141 *Thomas Tapeh* 10.00
142 *Matt Brandt* 10.00
143 *Bruce Perry* 10.00
144 *Mark Jones* 10.00
145 *Keith Smith* 10.00
146 *B.J. Symons* 10.00
147 *Patrick Crayton* 10.00
148 *Daryl Smith* 10.00
149 *Demorrio Williams* 10.00
150 *Casey Clausen* 15.00
151 *Jarrett Payton* 25.00
152 *Kris Wilson* 10.00
153 *Renaldo Works* 10.00
154 *Shawn Andrews* 10.00
155 *Ricardo Colclough* 10.00
156 *Travis LaBoy* 10.00
157 *Bob Sanders* 10.00
158 *Chad Lavalais* 10.00
159 *Derrick Strait* 15.00
160 *Darnell Dockett* 10.00

2004 SkyBox LE Gold Proof

Current (1-60): 2X-5X
Rookies (61-160): .5X-1X
Production 150 Sets

A player's name in *italic* type indicates a rookie card.

2004 SkyBox LE Artist Proof

Current (1-60): 5X-10X
Rookies (61-160): .75X-1.25X
Production 50 Sets

2004 SkyBox LE Photographer Proof

Current (1-60): 8X-15X
Rookies (61-160): .75X-1.5X
Production 35 Sets

2004 SkyBox LE Executive Proof

No Pricing
Production 1 Set

2004 SkyBox LE Future Legends

NM/M
Common Player: 2.00
Inserted 1:16
Executive Proof: No Pricing
Production 1 Set
1FL Tatum Bell 5.00
2FL Bernard Berrian 2.00
3FL Michael Clayton 6.00
4FL Lee Evans 6.00
5FL Devery Henderson 2.00
6FL Michael Jenkins 5.00
7FL Greg Jones 3.00
8FL Julius Jones 6.00
9FL Kevin Jones 8.00
10FL J.P. Losman 6.00
11FL Eli Manning 12.00
12FL Chris Perry 5.00
13FL Ben Troupe 2.00
14FL Philip Rivers 10.00
15FL Ben Roethlisberger 15.00
16FL Matt Schaub 2.00
17FL Sean Taylor 6.00
18FL Roy Williams-Lions 10.00
19FL Kellen Winslow Jr. 8.00
20FL Rashaun Woods 6.00
21FL Reggie Williams 6.00
22FL Steven Jackson 8.00
23FL Larry Fitzgerald 10.00
24FL Drew Henson 8.00
25FL Luke McCown 2.00

2004 SkyBox LE Future Legends Autographed Patch

No Pricing
Production 25 Sets
TB Tatum Bell
BB Bernard Berrian
MC Michael Clayton
LE Lee Evans
DH Devery Henderson
MJ Michael Jenkins
GJ Greg Jones
JJ Julius Jones
KJ Kevin Jones
JL J.P. Losman
EM Eli Manning
CP Chris Perry
WP Will Poole
PR Philip Rivers
BR Ben Roethlisberger
MS Matt Schaub
RW3 Reggie Williams
RW Roy Williams-Lions
KW Kellen Winslow Jr.
RW2 Rashaun Woods

2004 SkyBox LE Future Legends Autographed Patches

No Pricing
Production 1 Set
BBDH Bernard Berrian, Devery Henderson
BRLM Ben Roethlisberger, Julius Jones
EMPR Eli Manning, Philip Rivers
GJCP Greg Jones, Chris Perry
KWMC Kellen Winslow Jr., Reggie Williams
LEJL Lee Evans, J.P. Losman
MJMS Michael Jenkins, Matt Schaub
RWKJ Roy Williams-Lions, Kevin Jones
TBRW Tatum Bell, Rashaun Woods
WPMC Will Poole, Michael Clayton

2004 SkyBox LE Future Legends Jerseys Silver

NM/M
Common Player: 6.00
Production 75 Sets
Copper Proof: .75X-1.5X
Production 50 Sets
Gold Proof: 1X-3X
Production 25 Sets
FLTB Tatum Bell 10.00
FLBB Bernard Berrian 6.00
FLMC Michael Clayton 12.00
FLLE Lee Evans 12.00
FLLF Larry Fitzgerald 20.00
FLDH Devery Henderson 6.00
FLDH Drew Henson 12.00
FLSJ Steven Jackson 15.00
FLMJ Michael Jenkins 10.00
FLGJ Greg Jones 8.00
FLJJ Julius Jones 20.00
FLKJ Kevin Jones 15.00
FLJL J.P. Losman 15.00
FLEM Eli Manning 30.00
FLLM Luke McCown 6.00
FLCP Chris Perry 10.00
FLPR Philip Rivers 20.00
FLBR Ben Roethlisberger 50.00
FLMS Matt Schaub 6.00
FLST Sean Taylor 12.00
FLBT Ben Troupe 6.00
FLRW2 Reggie Williams 12.00
FLRW3 Roy Williams-Lions 20.00
FLKW Kellen Winslow Jr. 12.00
FLRW Rashaun Woods 12.00

2004 SkyBox LE Future Legends Platinum Dual Patch

No Pricing
Production 10 Sets
Executive Proof No Pricing
Production 1 Set
BBDH Bernard Berrian, Devery Henderson
BRLM Ben Roethlisberger, Luke McCown
DHJJ Drew Henson, Julius Jones
EMPR Eli Manning, Philip Rivers
GJRW Greg Jones, Reggie Williams
KWBT Kellen Winslow Jr., Ben Troupe
LEJL Lee Evans, J.P. Losman
LFMC Larry Fitzgerald, Michael Clayton
MJMS Michael Jenkins, Matt Schaub
RWKJ Roy Williams-Lions, Kevin Jones
SJCP Steven Jackson, Chris Perry
TBRW Tatum Bell, Rashaun Woods

2004 SkyBox LE Jersey Proof Silver

NM/M
Common Player: 6.00
Production 250 Sets
Copper Proof: .75X-2X
Production 99 Sets
Gold Proof: 1X-3X
Production 50 Sets
Platinum Proof: No Pricing
Production 15 Sets
Executive Proof: No Pricing
Production 1 Set
1 Anquan Boldin 8.00
2 Quincy Carter 8.00
3 Chad Pennington 10.00
4 Brett Favre 25.00
5 Marc Bulger 6.00
6 David Carr 10.00
7 Byron Leftwich 12.00
8 Hines Ward 6.00
9 Drew Bledsoe 8.00
10 Domanick Davis 8.00
11 Plaxico Burress 8.00
12 Mark Brunell 6.00
13 Terrell Owens 8.00
14 Peyton Manning 12.00
15 Matt Hasselbeck 6.00
16 Willis McGahee 8.00
17 Fred Taylor 8.00
18 Torry Holt 8.00
19 Priest Holmes 10.00
20 Charlie Garner 6.00
21 Brian Urlacher 8.00
22 Corey Dillon 6.00
23 Daunte Culpepper 8.00
24 Clinton Portis 12.00
25 Chad Johnson 6.00
26 Tom Brady 12.00
27 Deuce McAllister 8.00
28 Randy Moss 12.00
29 A.J. Feeley 6.00
30 Steve McNair 8.00
31 Aaron Brooks 6.00
32 Carson Palmer 10.00
33 Jeremy Shockey 8.00
34 Emmitt Smith 15.00
35 Jeff Garcia 8.00
36 Kurt Warner 8.00
37 Andre Johnson 8.00
38 LaDainian Tomlinson 10.00
39 Ray Lewis 6.00
40 Charles Rogers 8.00
41 Rich Gannon 6.00
42 Jake Delhomme 8.00
43 Marvin Harrison 8.00
44 Shaun Alexander 8.00
45 Ricky Williams 8.00
46 Eddie George 8.00
47 Edgerrin James 10.00
48 Chris Chambers 8.00
49 Jamal Lewis 8.00
50 Joey Harrington 8.00
51 Jerry Rice 15.00
52 Kyle Boller 8.00
53 Ahman Green 8.00
54 Donovan McNabb 10.00
55 Stephen Davis 6.00
56 Tony Gonzalez 6.00
57 Marshall Faulk 10.00
58 Michael Vick 15.00
59 Jake Plummer 6.00
60 Curtis Martin 8.00

2004 SkyBox LE LEgends of the Draft Autographed Patch

No Pricing
Production 25 Sets
ABO Anquan Boldin
KB Kyle Boller
TB Tom Brady
TC Tyrone Calico
DC David Carr
CC Chris Chambers
DD Domanick Davis
BF Brett Favre
AF A.J. Feeley
DF DeShaun Foster
AJ Andre Johnson
CJ Chad Johnson
RJ Rudi Johnson
BL Byron Leftwich
JL Jamal Lewis
PM Peyton Manning
WM Willis McGahee
DM Donovan McNabb
RM Randy Moss
SMO Santana Moss
LT LaDainian Tomlinson
MV Michael Vick
BW Brian Westbrook

2004 SkyBox LE LEgends of the Draft Dual Auto. Patch

No Pricing
Production 1 Set
ABTC Anquan Boldin, Tyrone Calico
BFPM Brett Favre, Peyton Manning
BLRM Byron Leftwich, Randy Moss
CCAF Chris Chambers, A.J. Feeley
CJRJ Chad Johnson, Rudi Johnson
DCDD David Carr, Domanick Davis
DFLT DeShaun Foster, LaDainian Tomlinson
DMBW Donovan McNabb, Brian Westbrook
KBJL Kyle Boller, Jamal Lewis
SMAJ Santana Moss, Andre Johnson
TBMV Tom Brady, Michael Vick

2004 SkyBox LE LEgends of the Draft Silver Jersey

NM/M
Common Player: 8.00
Numbered to year drafted
Copper: .75X-1.5X
Production 50 Sets
Gold: 1X-3X
Production 25 Sets
LDTA Troy Aikman/89 20.00
LDLA LaVar Arrington/100 10.00
LDAB Anquan Boldin/103 10.00
LDKB Kyle Boller/103 10.00
LDTB Tom Brady/100 15.00
LDTC Tyrone Calico/103 8.00
LDDC David Carr/102 12.00
LDCC Chris Chambers/101 10.00
LDDD Domanick Davis/103 10.00
LDJE John Elway/83 40.00
LDBF Brett Favre/91 25.00
LDAF A.J. Feeley/101 8.00
LDDF DeShaun Foster/102 8.00
LDJH Joey Harrington/100 10.00
LDCP Bo Jackson/87 25.00
LDAJ Andre Johnson/103 10.00
LDCJ Chad Johnson/101 8.00
LDRJ Rudi Johnson/101 8.00
LDBL Byron Leftwich/103 15.00
LDJL Jamal Lewis/100 10.00
LDPM Peyton Manning/98 12.00
LDDM Dan Marino/83 50.00
LDDM2 Deuce McAllister/100 10.00
LDWM Willis McGahee/100 10.00
LDDM Donovan McNabb/99 12.00
LDJM Joe Montana/86 50.00
LDRM Randy Moss/98 15.00
LDSM Santana Moss/101 8.00
LDCP Clinton Portis/102 15.00
LDJR Jerry Rice/85 20.00
LDBS Barry Sanders/89 40.00
LDDS Deion Sanders/89 15.00
LDJS Jeremy Shockey/102 10.00
LDES Emmitt Smith/90 20.00
LDLT Lawrence Taylor/81 20.00
LDLT2 LaDainian Tomlinson/101 12.00
LDBU Brian Urlacher/100 10.00
LDMV Michael Vick/101 20.00
LDBW Brian Westbrook/102 8.00
LDSY Steve Young/84 30.00

2004 SkyBox LE LEgends of the Draft Platinum Dual Patch

No Pricing
Production 10 Sets
Executive Proof: No Pricing
Production 1 Set
ABTC Anquan Boldin, Tyrone Calico
AJSM Andre Johnson, Santana Moss
BFPM Brett Favre, Peyton Manning
BJLT Bo Jackson, LaDainian Tomlinson
BLRM Byron Leftwich, Randy Moss
CCAF Chris Chambers, A.J. Feeley
CJRJ Chad Johnson, Rudi Johnson
DCDD David Carr, Domanick Davis
DFBU DeShaun Foster, Brian Urlacher
DMBW Donovan McNabb, Brian Westbrook
DMWM Deuce McAllister, Willis McGahee
ESTA Emmitt Smith, Troy Aikman
JEDM John Elway, Dan Marino
JHBS Joey Harrington, Barry Sanders
JRSY Jerry Rice, Steve Young
JSLT Jeremy Shockey, Lawrence Taylor
KBJL Kyle Boller, Jamal Lewis
LACP LaVar Arrington, Clinton Portis
MVDS Michael Vick, Deion Sanders
TBJM Tom Brady, Joe Montana

2004 SkyBox LE Rare Form

NM/M
Common Player: 5.00
Inserted 1:256
Executive Proof: No Pricing
Production 1 Set
1RF Randy Moss 10.00
2RF Donovan McNabb 8.00
3RF Chad Pennington 8.00
4RF Tom Brady 10.00
5RF Brett Favre 15.00
6RF Priest Holmes 8.00
7RF Ricky Williams 5.00
8RF Byron Leftwich 10.00
9RF Carson Palmer 8.00
10RF Michael Vick 12.00

2004 SkyBox LE Rare Form Jersey Copper

NM/M
Common Card: 10.00
Production 50 Sets
Silver:
84: .5X-1X
31-34: .75X-1.25X
13: No Pricing
Numbered to player's jersey number
Gold: 1X-2X
Production 25 Sets
RFTB Tom Brady 20.00
RFBF Brett Favre 30.00
RFPH Priest Holmes 15.00
RFBL Byron Leftwich 20.00
RFDM Donovan McNabb 15.00
RFRM Randy Moss 20.00
RFCP2 Carson Palmer 15.00
RFCP Chad Pennington 15.00
RFMV Michael Vick 25.00
RFRW Ricky Williams 10.00

2004 SkyBox LE Rare Form Platinum Dual Patch

No Pricing
Production 10 Sets
Executive Proof: No Pricing
Production 1 Set
BFTB Brett Favre, Tom Brady
CPBL Carson Palmer, Byron Leftwich
DMMV Donovan McNabb, Michael Vick
RMCP Randy Moss, Chad Pennington
RWPH Ricky Williams, Priest Holmes

2004 SkyBox LE Sky's the Limit

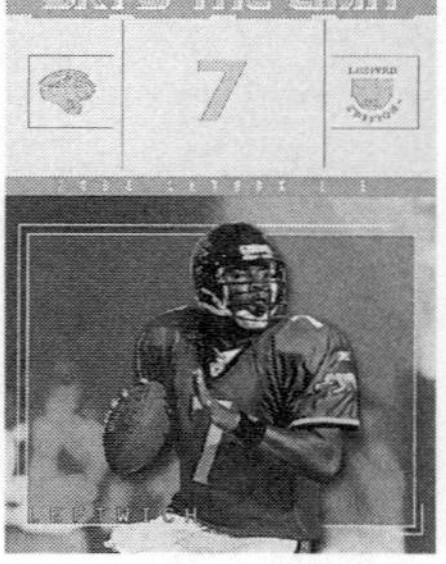

NM/M
Common Player: 1.50
Inserted 1:4
Executive Proof: No Pricing
Production 1 Set
1SL Eli Manning 6.00
2SL Peyton Manning 3.00
3SL Philip Rivers 4.00
4SL LaDainian Tomlinson 2.00
5SL Steven Jackson 3.00
6SL Marshall Faulk 2.00
7SL Ben Roethlisberger 12.00
8SL Hines Ward 1.50
9SL Reggie Williams 2.00
10SL Byron Leftwich 3.00
11SL Kevin Jones 3.00
12SL Joey Harrington 1.50
13SL Larry Fitzgerald 4.00
14SL Anquan Boldin 1.50
15SL Roy Williams-Cowboys 1.50
16SL Charles Rogers 1.50
17SL Julius Jones 2.00
18SL Emmitt Smith 4.00
19SL Tatum Bell 1.50
20SL Clinton Portis 3.00

2004 SkyBox LE Sky's the Limit Jersey Silver

NM/M
Common Player: 8.00
Production 99 Sets
Copper Proof: .75X-1.5X
Production 50 Sets
Gold Proof: .75X-2X
Production 25 Sets
SLTB Tatum Bell 12.00
SLAB Anquan Boldin 8.00
SLMF Marshall Faulk 10.00
SLLF Larry Fitzgerald 20.00
SLJH Joey Harrington 8.00
SLSJ Steven Jackson 15.00
SLJJ Julius Jones 20.00
SLKJ Kevin Jones 15.00
SLBL Byron Leftwich 12.00
SLEM Eli Manning 40.00
SLPM Peyton Manning 15.00
SLCP Clinton Portis 12.00
SLPR Philip Rivers 20.00
SLBR Ben Roethlisberger 60.00
SLCR Charles Rogers 8.00
SLES Emmitt Smith 20.00
SLLT LaDainian Tomlinson 10.00
SLHW Hines Ward 12.00
SLRW Reggie Williams 12.00
SLRW2 Roy Williams-Lions 20.00

2004 SkyBox LE Sky's the Limit Platinum Dual Patch

No Pricing
Production 10 Sets
Executive Proof: No Pricing
Production 1 Set
BRHW Ben Roethlisberger, Hines Ward
EMPM Eli Manning, Peyton Manning
JJES Julius Jones, Emmitt Smith
KJJH Kevin Jones, Joey Harrington
LFAB Larry Fitzgerald, Anquan Boldin
PRLT Philip Rivers, LaDainian Tomlinson
RWBL Reggie Williams, Byron Leftwich
RWCR Roy Williams-Lions, Charles Rogers
SJMF Steven Jackson, Marshall Faulk
TBCP Tatum Bell, Clinton Portis

1992 Slam Thurman Thomas

Thurman Thomas was featured in this 11-card (10 cards, plus one promo) set. Slam reported the production run to be 25,000 total sets and included an autographed (limited to 1,000) edition card for every 25 sets ordered.

NM/M
Complete Set (11): 10.00
Common Player: 1.00
1 Thurman Thomas (RB-Willowridge HS) 1.00
2 Thurman Thomas (HS-All American) 1.00
3 Thurman Thomas (Gator Bowl MVP) 1.00
4 Thurman Thomas (RB-Oklahoma State) 1.00
5 Thurman Thomas (All Big 8) 1.00
6 Thurman Thomas (1st Team All-American) 1.00
7 Thurman Thomas (RB-Buffalo) 1.00
8 Thurman Thomas (AFC All-Pro) 1.00
9 Thurman Thomas (AFC Rushing Champion) 1.00
10 Thurman Thomas (NFL Leader-Total Yards) 1.00
P1 Thurman Thomas (Promo 1) 1.00
AU Thurman Thomas (Autographed) 80.00

1993 Slam Jerome Bettis

Jerome Bettis is featured in this six-card set (five cards, plus a promo) by Slam. Sets arrived with one autographed card, 4 regular issue cards, plus the promo card. There is also a certificate of authenticity that lists the production number out of a total of 5,000 produced.

NM/M
Complete Set (6): 12.00
Common Player: 2.00
1 Jerome Bettis (High School All-American) 2.00
2 Jerome Bettis (Freshman Notre Dame) 2.00
3 Jerome Bettis (1991 Notre Dame Co-MVP) 2.00
4 Jerome Bettis (All-American) 2.00
5 Jerome Bettis (10th Pick Overall) 2.00
P1 Jerome Bettis (Promo 1) (FB Notre Dame) 2.00
1AU Jerome Bettis (High School All-American) 15.00
2AU Jerome Bettis (Freshman Notre Dame) 15.00
3AU Jerome Bettis (1991 Notre Dame Co-MVP) 15.00
4AU Jerome Bettis (All-American) 20.00
5AU Jerome Bettis (10th Pick Overall) 20.00

1978 Slim Jim

Specially-marked Slim Jim products in 1978 contained a 3" x 5-3/4" panel featuring two football player discs. The discs, featuring a player mug shot, biographical data, an NFLPA logo and "Slim Jim Collection" on the front, were issued by Michael Schechter Associates. MSA is also on the disc front. Each disc has a diameter of 2-3/8" and is perforated so it can be cut out from the panel. The same two players were always on the same panel. They are listed according to the pairs on the panel, starting with 1A and 1B and ending 69-70. Note: The prices for each disc are actually the value of the panel. So, 1A and 1B would be $20, not $40.

NM/M
Complete Set (70): 350.00
Common Player: 8.00
1A Lyle Alzado 20.00
1B Archie Manning 20.00
2A Bill Bergey 20.00
2B John Riggins 20.00
3A Fred Biletnikoff 20.00
3B Dan Dierdorf 20.00
4A John Cappelletti 8.00
4B Bob Chandler 8.00
5A Tommy Casanova 8.00
5B Darryl Stingley 8.00
6A Billy Joe Dupree 8.00
6B Nat Moore 8.00
7A John Dutton 8.00
7B Paul Krause 8.00
8A Leon Gray 8.00
8B Richard Caster 8.00
9A Mel Gray 8.00
9B Claude Humphrey 8.00
10A Joe Greene 12.00
10B Dexter Bussey 12.00
11A Jack Gregory 8.00
11B Billy Johnson 8.00
12A Steve Grogan 8.00
12B Jerome Barkum 8.00
13A John Hannah 10.00
13B Isaac Curtis 10.00
14A Jim Hart 9.00
14B Otis Sistrunk 9.00
15A Tommy Hart 8.00
15B Ron Howard 8.00
16A Wilbur Jackson 8.50
16B Riley Odoms 8.50
17A Ron Jaworski 10.00
17B Mike Thomas 10.00
18A Larry Little 12.00
18B Isiah Robertson 12.00
19A Ron McDole 8.00
19B Willie Buchanon 8.00
20A Lydell Mitchell 8.50
20B Glen Edwards 8.50
21A Robert Newhouse 8.00
21B Glenn Doughty 8.00
22A Alan Page 10.00
22B Fred Carr 10.00
23A Walter Payton 55.00
23B Larry Csonka 55.00
24A Greg Pruitt 8.00
24B Doug Buffone 8.00
25A Ahmad Rashad 12.00
25B Jeff Van Note 12.00
26A Golden Richards 10.00
26B Rocky Bleier 10.00
27A Clarence Scott 8.00
27B Joe DeLamielleure 8.00
28A Lee Roy Selmon 10.00
28B Charlie Sanders 10.00
29A Bruce Taylor 8.50
29B Otis Armstrong 8.50
30A Emmitt Thomas 8.00
30B Elvin Bethea 8.00
31A Brad Van Pelt 8.00
31B Ted Washington 8.00
32A Gene Washington 15.00
32B Charlie Joiner 15.00
33A Clarence Williams 8.00
33B Lemar Parrish 8.00
34A Roger Wehrli 12.00
34B Gene Upshaw 12.00
35A Don Woods 8.00
35B Ron Jessie 8.00

1993 SP

These cards, sold only through hobby dealers, feature gold foil logos, a Premier Prospects subset printing using Light F/X and Electric printing processes, and full-bleed color photos. The borders are team color-coded, too. Gold foil is used for the player's name and set logo. The back has a photo, player stats, biographical information, a card number and a gold-foil Upper Deck hologram. Random foil packs had a card from the 15-card All-Pro insert set. Upper Deck also created a promo card to preview the design for its new set. The card features Kansas City Chiefs quarterback Joe Montana, but it is not identified as a promo card. However, the promo card's number, 19, is different from the number he is assigned in the regular set (#122). The promo card is worth $4.

NM/M
Complete Set (270): 80.00
Common Player: .10
Minor Stars: .50
Foil Prospects: 1.00
Pack (12): 7.00
Wax Box (24): 140.00
1 *Curtis Conway* 5.00
2 *John Copeland* 1.00
3 *Kevin Williams* 1.00
4 *Dan Williams* 1.00
5 *Patrick Bates* 1.00
6 *Jerome Bettis* 20.00
7 *O.J. McDuffie* 5.00
8 *Robert Smith* 10.00
9 *Drew Bledsoe* 40.00
10 *Irv Smith* 2.00
11 *Marvin Jones* 1.00
12 *Victor Bailey* 1.00
13 *Garrison Hearst* 5.00
14 *Natrone Means* 2.00
15 Todd Kelly 1.00
16 *Rick Mirer* 1.00
17 *Eric Curry* 1.00
18 *Reggie Brooks* 1.00
19 Eric Dickerson .50
20 *Roger Harper* .10
21 Michael Haynes .10
22 Bobby Hebert .10
23 *Lincoln Kennedy* .50
24 Chris Miller .10
25 Mike Pritchard .10
26 Andre Rison .75
27 Deion Sanders 1.00
28 Cornelius Bennett .10
29 Kenneth Davis .10
30 Henry Jones .10
31 Jim Kelly 1.00
32 *John Parrella* .10
33 Andre Reed .50
34 Bruce Smith .50
35 *Thomas Smith* .10
36 Thurman Thomas 1.00
37 Neal Anderson .10
38 *Myron Baker* .10
39 Mark Carrier .10
40 Richard Dent .50
41 *Chris Gedney* .10
42 Jim Harbaugh .50
43 Craig Heyward .10
44 *Carl Simpson* .10
45 Alonzo Spellman .10
46 Derrick Fenner .10
47 Harold Green .10
48 David Klingler .10
49 Ricardo McDonald .10
50 *Tony McGee* .50
51 Carl Pickens 1.50
52 *Steve Tovar* .10
53 Alfred Williams .10
54 Darryl Williams .10
55 Jerry Ball .10
56 *Michael Caldwell* .10
57 Mark Carrier .10
58 *Steve Everitt* .10
59 *Dan Footman* .10
60 Pepper Johnson .10
61 Bernie Kosar .50
62 Eric Metcalf .50
63 Michael Dean Perry .50
64 Troy Aikman 3.00
65 Charles Haley .50
66 Michael Irvin 1.00
67 Robert Jones .10
68 *Derrick Lassic* .50
69 Russell Maryland .50
70 Ken Norton .10
71 *Darrin Smith* .50
72 Emmitt Smith 6.00
73 Steve Atwater .10
74 Rod Bernstine .10
75 *Jason Elam* 1.00
76 John Elway 3.00
77 Simon Fletcher .10
78 Tommy Maddox .75
79 *Glyn Milburn* 1.00
80 Derek Russell .10
81 Shannon Sharpe .50
82 Bennie Blades .10
83 Willie Green .10
84 *Antonio London* .10
85 *Ryan McNeil* .10
86 Herman Moore 1.50
87 Rodney Peete .50
88 Barry Sanders 6.00
89 Chris Spielman .10
90 Pat Swilling .10
91 *Mark Brunell* 10.00
92 Terrell Buckley .10
93 Brett Favre 6.00
94 Jackie Harris .10
95 Sterling Sharpe 1.00
96 John Stephens .10
97 Reggie White 1.00
98 *Wayne Simmons* .50
99 *George Teague* .50
100 *Micheal Barrow* .10
101 Cody Carson .10
102 Ray Childress .10
103 *Brad Hopkins* .10
104 Haywood Jeffires .10
105 Wilber Marshall .10
106 Warren Moon 1.00
107 Webster Slaughter .10
108 Lorenzo White .10
109 John Baylor .10
110 Duane Bickett .10
111 Quentin Coryatt .10
112 Steve Emtman .10
113 Jeff George 1.00
114 Jessie Hester .10
115 Anthony Johnson .10
116 Reggie Langhorne .10
117 *Roosevelt Potts* .10
118 Marcus Allen 1.00
119 J.J. Birden .10
120 Willie Davis .10
121 *Jaime Fields* .10
122 Joe Montana 4.00
123 *Will Shields* .10
124 Neil Smith .10
125 Derrick Thomas .50
126 Harvey Williams .50
127 Tim Brown 1.00
128 *Billy Joe Hobert* 1.00
129 Jeff Hostetler .50
130 Ethan Horton .10
131 Raghib Ismail .10
132 Howie Long .10
133 Terry McDaniel .10
134 *Greg Robinson* .10
135 Anthony Smith .10
136 Willie Anderson .10
137 Marc Boutte .10
138 Shane Conlan .10
139 *Troy Drayton* .75
140 Henry Ellard .10
141 Jim Everett .50
142 Cleveland Gary .10
143 Sean Gilbert .10
144 David Lang .10
145 Marco Coleman .10
146 Bryan Cox .10
147 Irving Fryar .50
148 Keith Jackson .10
149 *Terry Kirby* 1.50
150 Dan Marino 6.00
151 Scott Mitchell .50
152 Troy Vincent .10
153 Richmond Webb .10
154 Anthony Carter .10
155 Cris Carter 1.50
156 Roger Craig .50
157 Chris Doleman .10
158 *Qadry Ismail* 2.00
159 Steve Jordan .10
160 Audray McMillian .10
161 Gino Torretta .10
162 Barry Word .10
163 Vincent Brown .10
164 Marv Cook .10
165 *Sam Gash* .50
166 Pat Harlow .10
167 Greg McMurtry .10
168 *Todd Rucci* .10
169 Leonard Russell .10
170 *Scott Sisson* .10
171 *Chris Slade* .50
172 Morten Andersen .10
173 *Derek Brown* .50
174 *Reggie Freeman* .10
175 Rickey Jackson .10
176 Eric Martin .10
177 Wayne Martin .10
178 Brad Muster .10
179 *Willie Roaf* .50
180 Renaldo Turnbull .10
181 Derek Brown .10
182 *Marcus Buckley* .10
183 Jarrod Bunch .10
184 Rodney Hampton .50
185 Ed McCaffrey 1.00
186 Kanavis McGhee .10
187 Phil Simms .50
188 *Michael Strahan* .10
189 Lawrence Taylor 1.00
190 Kurt Barber .10
191 Boomer Esiason .50
192 Johnny Johnson .10
193 Ronnie Lott .50
194 Johnny Mitchell .10
195 Rob Moore .50
196 *Adrian Murrell* 1.00
197 Coleman Rudolph .10
198 Marvin Washington .10
199 Eric Allen .10
200 Fred Barnett .10
201 Randall Cunningham 1.00
202 Byron Evans .10
203 Lester Holmes .10
204 Seth Joyner .10
205 *Leonard Renfro* .10
206 Heath Sherman .10
207 Clyde Simmons .10
208 Johnny Bailey .10
209 Steve Beuerlein .10
210 Chuck Cecil .10
211 *Larry Centers* 1.50
212 Ben Coleman .10
213 *Ernest Dye* .10
214 Ken Harvey .10
215 Randal Hill .10
216 Ricky Proehl .10
217 *Deon Figures* .50
218 Barry Foster .10
219 Eric Green .10
220 Kevin Greene .50
221 Carlton Haselrig .10
222 *Andre Hasting* 1.00
223 Greg Lloyd .10
224 Neil O'Donnell .50
225 Rod Woodson .50
226 Marion Butts .10
227 *Darren Carrington* .50
228 *Darrien Gordon* .50
229 Ronnie Harmon .10
230 Stan Humphries .50
231 Anthony Miller .10
232 Chris Mims .10
233 Leslie O'Neal .10
234 Junior Seau .75
235 Dana Hall .10
236 *Adrian Hardy* .10
237 Brent Jones .10
238 Tim McDonald .10
239 Tom Rathman .10
240 Jerry Rice 3.00
241 *Dana Stubblefield* 1.00
242 Ricky Watters 1.00
243 Steve Young 2.50
244 Brian Blades .10
245 Ferrell Edmunds .10
246 *Carlton Gray* .10
247 Cortez Kennedy .10
248 Kelvin Martin .10
249 Dan McGwire .10
250 Jon Vaughn .10
251 Chris Warren .50
252 John L. Williams .10
253 Reggie Cobb .50
254 *Horace Copeland* .50
255 Lawrence Dawsey .10
256 *Demetrius DuBose* .10
257 Craig Erickson .50
258 Courtney Hawkins .10
259 *John Lynch* 3.00
260 Hardy Nickerson .10
261 *Lamar Thomas* .50
262 Carl Banks .10
263 *Tom Carter* .50
264 Brad Edwards .10
265 Kurt Gouveia .10
266 Darrell Green .10
267 Charles Mann .10
268 Art Monk .50
269 Mark Rypien .10
270 Ricky Sanders .10

1993 SP All-Pros

These cards, using a die-cut technique, feature 15 All-Pros, as indicated by the "All-Pro" logo stamped in gold foil on the card front. The front has a color action photo against a black background, plus a statistical category which the player led the league in. His name is in the gold-foil arc at the top of the card. The back has another photo, along with the player's name and team, which run along the left side. Season highlights and a card number, using an "AP" prefix, are also given on the back. The cards were randomly included in 1993 Upper Deck SP packs.

NM/M
Complete Set (15): 30.00
Common Player: .50
Minor Stars: 1.00
Inserted 1:15
1 Steve Young 4.00
2 Warren Moon 1.00
3 Troy Aikman 4.00
4 Dan Marino 6.00
5 Barry Sanders 5.00
6 Barry Foster .50
7 Emmitt Smith 5.00
8 Thurman Thomas 1.00
9 Jerry Rice 4.00
10 Sterling Sharpe 1.00
11 Anthony Miller .50
12 Haywood Jeffires .50
13 Junior Seau 1.00
14 Reggie White 1.00
15 Derrick Thomas .50

1994 SP

This set has reduced in size from the 270 cards in 1993 to 200 in 1994, and also has a smaller print run. The set includes more than 40 rookies in it, too. Each card in the set has a 1994 game-action photograph, including players in their throwback uniforms. A strip down the right side contains the SP logo, fading from dark to light, with an Upper Deck hologram about two-thirds of the way up. The player's name and position is also in this strip. His team name is in the lower right corner. The back has a photo of the player in the top half, with statistics and a biography in the bottom half. A card number and Upper Deck are in the upper corners. The player's name and position are under the photo. Every card in the set is also reprinted using a die-cut design to form a parallel set. One die-cut card was included in each pack. These cards have a silver-foil hologram on the back, rather than a gold-foil hologram, which appears on the regular cards. A 40-card insert set, All-Pro/Future All-Pro, was also produced; cards were randomly included in every fifth pack. These cards were also produced in a die-cut version; they were randomly included in every 75th pack. Two commemorative record-breaker cards, honoring accomplishments by Dan Marino and Jerry Rice, were also produced. One of each card was included in every case made.

NM/M
Complete Set (200): 65.00
Common Player: .20
Minor Stars: .40
Foil Prospects: .75
Die Cut Cards: 1X-3X
Pack (8): 2.75
Wax Box (32): 60.00
1 *Dan Wilkinson* 1.00
2 *Heath Shuler* 1.00
3 *Marshall Faulk* 30.00
4 *Willie McGinest* 1.00
5 *Trent Dilfer* 6.00
6 *Bryant Young* 1.00
7 *Antonio Langham* .75
8 *John Thierry* .75
9 *Aaron Glenn* .75
10 *Charles Johnson* 1.50
11 *DeWayne Washington* .75
12 *Johnnie Morton* 2.00
13 *Greg Hill* 1.50
14 *William Floyd* 1.25
15 *Derrick Alexander* 1.50
16 *Darnay Scott* 1.00
17 *Errict Rhett* 2.00
18 *Charlie Garner* 6.00
19 *Thomas Lewis* .75
20 *David Palmer* .75
21 Andre Reed .40
22 Thurman Thomas .50
23 Bruce Smith .20
24 Jim Kelly .50
25 Cornelius Bennett .20
26 *Bucky Brooks* .40
27 *Jeff Burris* .75
28 Jim Harbaugh .40
29 Tony Bennett .20
30 Quentin Coryatt .20
31 Floyd Turner .20
32 Roosevelt Potts .20
33 Jeff Herrod .20
34 Irving Fryar .20
35 Bryan Cox .20
36 Dan Marino 5.00

37	Terry Kirby	.20
38	Michael Stewart	.20
39	Bernie Kosar	.20
40	*Aubrey Beavers*	.40
41	Vincent Brisby	.75
42	Ben Coates	.50
43	Drew Bledsoe	3.00
44	Marion Butts	.20
45	Chris Slade	.20
46	Michael Timpson	.20
47	Ray Crittenden	.40
48	Rob Moore	.20
49	Johnny Mitchell	.20
50	Art Monk	.40
51	Boomer Esiason	.20
52	Ronnie Lott	.20
53	*Ryan Yarborough*	.75
54	Carl Pickens	.75
55	David Klingler	.20
56	Harold Green	.20
57	John Copeland	.20
58	Louis Oliver	.20
59	*Corey Sawyer*	.20
60	Michael Jackson	.20
61	Mark Rypien	.20
62	Vinny Testaverde	.20
63	Eric Metcalf	.20
64	Eric Turner	.20
65	Haywood Jeffires	.20
66	Micheal Barrow	.20
67	Cody Carlson	.20
68	Gary Brown	.20
69	Bucky Richardson	.20
70	Al Smith	.20
71	Eric Green	.20
72	Neil O'Donnell	.40
73	Barry Foster	.20
74	Greg Lloyd	.20
75	Rod Woodson	.40
76	*Bam Morris*	1.00
77	John L. Williams	.20
78	Anthony Miller	.20
79	Mike Pritchard	.20
80	John Elway	2.00
81	Shannon Sharpe	.40
82	Steve Atwater	.20
83	Simon Fletcher	.20
84	Glyn Milburn	.20
85	Mark Collins	.20
86	Keith Cash	.20
87	Willie Davis	.20
88	Joe Montana	3.00
89	Marcus Allen	.40
90	Neil Smith	.20
91	Derrick Thomas	.40
92	Tim Brown	.40
93	Jeff Hostetler	.40
94	Terry McDaniel	.20
95	Raghib Ismail	.20
96	*Rob Fredrickson*	.75
97	Harvey Williams	.20
98	Steve Wisniewski	.20
99	Stan Humphries	.50
100	Natrone Means	.50
101	Leslie O'Neal	.20
102	Junior Seau	.50
103	Ronnie Harmon	.20
104	Shawn Jefferson	.20
105	Howard Ballard	.20
106	Rick Mirer	.50
107	Cortez Kennedy	.20
108	Chris Warren	.40
109	Brian Blades	.20
110	*Sam Adams*	.50
111	Gary Clark	.20
112	Steve Beuerlein	.20
113	Ron Moore	.20
114	Eric Swann	.20
115	Clyde Simmons	.20
116	Seth Joyner	.20
117	Troy Aikman	3.00
118	Charles Haley	.20
119	Alvin Harper	.20
120	Michael Irvin	1.00
121	Daryl Johnston	.20
122	Emmitt Smith	5.00
123	*Shante Carver*	.40
124	Dave Brown	.20
125	Rodney Hampton	.40
126	Dave Meggett	.20
127	Chris Calloway	.20
128	Mike Sherrard	.20
129	Carlton Bailey	.20
130	Randall Cunningham	.40
131	William Fuller	.20
132	Eric Allen	.20
133	*Calvin Williams*	.40
134	Herschel Walker	.20
135	*Bernard Williams*	.20
136	Henry Ellard	.20
137	Ethan Horton	.20
138	Desmond Howard	.20
139	Reggie Brooks	.20
140	John Friesz	.20
141	Tom Carter	.20
142	Terry Allen	.20
143	Adrian Cooper	.20
144	Qadry Ismail	.20
145	Warren Moon	.40
146	Henry Thomas	.20
147	*Todd Steussie*	.40
148	Cris Carter	.40
149	Andy Heck	.20
150	Curtis Conway	1.50
151	Erik Kramer	.40
152	Lewis Tillman	.20
153	Dante Jones	.20
154	Alonzo Spellman	.20
155	Herman Moore	1.00
156	Broderick Thomas	.20
157	Scott Mitchell	.40
158	Barry Sanders	4.00
159	Chris Speilman	.20
160	Pat Swilling	.20
161	Bennie Blades	.20
162	Sterling Sharpe	.40
163	Brett Favre	5.00
164	Reggie Cobb	.20
165	Reggie White	.40
166	Sean Jones	.20
167	George Teague	.20
168	LeShon Johnson	.20
169	Courtney Hawkins	.20
170	Jackie Harris	.20
171	Craig Erickson	.20
172	Santana Dotson	.20
173	Eric Curry	.20
174	Hardy Nickerson	.20
175	Derek Brown	.20
176	Jim Everett	.20
177	Michael Haynes	.20
178	Tyrone Hughes	.20
179	Wayne Martin	.20
180	Willie Roaf	.20
181	Irv Smith	.20
182	Jeff George	.50
183	Andre Rison	.40
184	Erric Pegram	.20
185	*Bert Emanuel*	1.00
186	Chris Doleman	.20
187	Ron George	.20
188	Chris Miller	.20
189	Troy Drayton	.20
190	Chris Chandler	.20
191	Jerome Bettis	2.00
192	Jimmie Jones	.20
193	Sean Gilbert	.20
194	Jerry Rice	3.00
195	Brent Jones	.20
196	Deion Sanders	2.50
197	Steve Young	3.00
198	Ricky Watters	.40
199	Dana Stubblefield	.20
200	Ken Norton	.20
RB1	Dan Marino 300 TDs	30.00
RB2	Jerry Rice 127 TDs	25.00

1994 Sp Die-Cuts

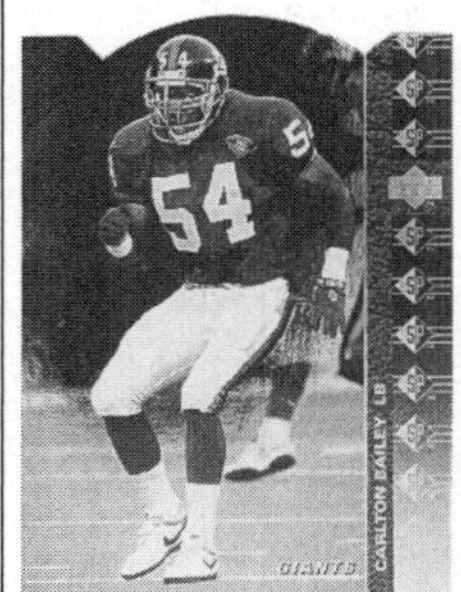

This set has reduced in size from the 270 cards in 1993 to 200 in 1994, and also has a smaller print run. The set includes more than 40 rookies in it, too. Each card in the set has a 1994 game-action photograph, including players in their throwback uniforms. A strip down the right side contains the SP logo, fading from dark to light, with an Upper Deck hologram about two-thirds of the way up. The player's name and position is also in this strip. His team name is in the lower right corner. The back has a photo of the player in the top half, with statistics and a biography in the bottom half. A card number and Upper Deck are in the upper corners. The player's name and position are under the photo. Every card in the set is also reprinted using a die-cut design to form a parallel set. One die-cut card was included in each pack. These cards have a silver-foil hologram on the back, rather than a gold-foil hologram, which appears on the regular cards. A 40-card insert set, All-Pro/Future All-Pro, was also produced; cards were randomly included in every fifth pack. These cards were also produced in a die-cut version; they were randomly included in every 75th pack. Two commemorative record-breaker cards, honoring accomplishments by Dan Marino and Jerry Rice, were also produced. One of each card was included in every case made.

	NM/M
Complete Set (200):	200.00
Common Player:	.50
Minor Stars:	1X-3X
Unlisted Stars:	1X-3X

1994 SP All-Pro Holoviews

This 40-card Upper Deck SP insert set, titled All-Pro and Future All-Pro, uses Upper Deck's new Holoview technology. To create these holograms, each player was videotaped on a rotating turntable. The individual frames were then synthesized to produce a three-dimensional picture of the player. These cards were inserted into every fifth pack. These insert cards were also reprinted in a version using a die-cut design and rainbow foil. These cards were inserted into packs at a rate of one per every 75 packs.

		NM/M
Complete Set (40):		60.00
Common Player:		1.00
Minor Stars:		2.00
Inserted 1:5		
Die-Cut Cards:		2X-4X
Inserted 1:75		
1	Jamir Miller	1.00
2	Andre Rison	2.00
3	Bucky Brooks	1.00
4	Thurman Thomas	2.00
5	John Thierry	1.00
6	Dan Wilkinson	1.00
7	Darnay Scott	2.00
8	Antonio Langham	1.00
9	Troy Aikman	6.00
10	Emmitt Smith	10.00
11	John Elway	8.00
12	Barry Sanders	10.00
13	Johnnie Morton	1.00
14	Reggie White	2.00
15	Brett Favre	10.00
16	LeShon Johnson	1.00
17	Joe Montana	6.00
18	Greg Hill	1.00
19	Calvin Jones	1.00
20	Tim Brown	2.00
21	Isaac Bruce	4.00
22	Jerome Bettis	2.00
23	Dan Marino	10.00
24	O.J. McDuffie	2.00
25	Willie McGinest	1.00
26	Mario Bates	1.00
27	Rodney Hampton	1.00
28	Thomas Lewis	1.00
29	Aaron Glenn	1.00
30	Barry Foster	1.00
31	Charles Johnson	2.00
32	Steve Young	5.00
33	Jerry Rice	6.00
34	Bryant Young	1.00
35	William Floyd	1.00
36	Sam Adams	1.00
37	Rick Mirer	2.00
38	Errict Rhett	1.00
39	Reggie Brooks	1.00
40	Heath Shuler	2.00

1994 Sp All-Pro Holoview Die-Cuts

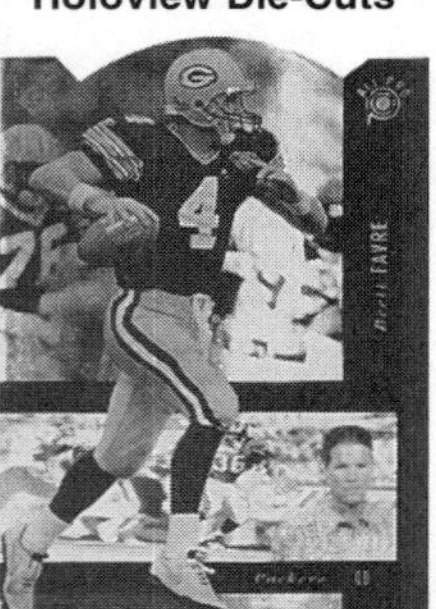

This 40-card Upper Deck SP insert set, titled All-Pro and Future All-Pro, uses Upper Deck's new Holoview technology. To create these holograms, each player was videotaped on a rotating turntable. The individual frames were then synthesized to produce a three-dimensional picture of the player. These cards were inserted into every fifth pack. These insert cards were also reprinted in a version using a die-cut design and rainbow foil. These cards were inserted into packs at a rate of one per every 75 packs.

	NM/M
Complete Set (40):	1,600
Common Player:	15.00
Minor Stars:	2X

1995 Sp

Upper Deck's 1995 SP football contains 200 cards - 180 regular players and 20 Premier Prospects. Each regular card front has a full-bleed color photo on it, with the player's name stamped in copper foil on the right side. Copper foil is also used along the right side for the brand logo and a border between the photo and the logo. A second color photo appears on the card back, which includes biographical information, a career achievement and statistics. "Premier Prospects" are labeled on the fronts as being such. Insert cards in the set include: All-Pros, Holoview F/X and Special FX, and Joe Montana Trilogy (MT17-MT20). A special Dan Marino Record Breaker (DM1) insert and a Montana Tribute card were also produced.

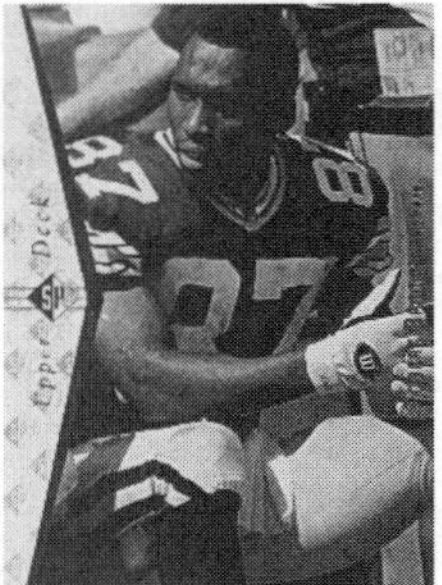

		NM/M
Complete Set (200):		60.00
Common Player:		.20
Minor Stars:		.40
Pack (8):		3.00
Wax Box (32):		60.00
1	*Ki-Jana Carter*	1.00
2	*Eric Zeier*	2.00
3	*Steve McNair*	10.00
4	*Michael Westbrook*	5.00
5	*Kerry Collins*	6.00
6	*Joey Galloway*	4.00
7	*Kevin Carter*	1.00
8	*Mike Mamula*	.40
9	*Kyle Brady*	1.00
10	*J.J. Stokes*	1.50
11	*Tyrone Poole*	.40
12	*Rashaan Salaam*	.75
13	*Sherman Williams*	.50
14	*Luther Elliss*	.40
15	*James Stewart*	2.00
16	*Tamarick Vanover*	1.00
17	*Napoleon Kaufman*	2.00
18	*Curtis Martin*	8.00
19	*Tyrone Wheatley*	2.00
20	*Frank Sanders*	2.00
21	*Devin Bush*	.40
22	Terance Mathis	.20
23	Bert Emanual	.75
24	Eric Metcalf	.20
25	Craig Heyward	.20
26	Jeff George	.40
27	Mark Carrier	.20
28	Pete Metzelaars	.20
29	Frank Reich	.20
30	Sam Mills	.20
31	John Kasay	.20
32	Willie Green	.20
33	Jeff Graham	.20
34	Curtis Conway	.75
35	Steve Walsh	.20
36	Erik Kramer	.40
37	Michael Timpson	.20
38	Mark Carrier	.20
39	Troy Aikman	3.00
40	Michael Irvin	.40
41	Charles Haley	.20
42	Deion Sanders	2.50
43	Jay Novacek	.20
44	Emmitt Smith	4.00
45	Herman Moore	1.00
46	Scott Mitchell	.40
47	Bennie Blades	.20
48	Johnnie Morton	.20
49	Chris Spielman	.20
50	Barry Sanders	3.00
51	Edgar Bennett	.20
52	Reggie White	.40
53	Sean Jones	.20
54	Mark Ingram	.20
55	Robert Brooks	.40
56	Brett Favre	4.00
57	Lovell Pinkney	.20
58	Chris Miller	.20
59	Isaac Bruce	.50
60	Roman Phifer	.20
61	Sean Gilbert	.20
62	Jerome Bettis	1.00
63	Derrick Alexander	.20
64	Cris Carter	.40
65	Jake Reed	.20
66	Robert Smith	.20
67	David Palmer	.20
68	Warren Moon	.40
69	*Ray Zellars*	.40
70	Jim Everett	.20
71	Michael Haynes	.20
72	Quinn Early	.20
73	Willie Roaf	.20
74	Mario Bates	1.00
75	Mike Sherrard	.20
76	Chris Calloway	.20
77	Dave Brown	.20
78	Thomas Lewis	.20
79	Herschel Walker	.20
80	Rodney Hampton	.40
81	Fred Barnett	.20
82	Calvin Williams	.20
83	Randall Cunningham	.20
84	Charlie Garner	.20
85	Bobby Taylor	.20
86	Ricky Watters	.40
87	Dave Kreig	.20
88	Rob Moore	.20
89	Eric Swann	.20
90	Clyde Simmons	.20
91	Seth Joyner	.20
92	Garrison Hearst	.40
93	Jerry Rice	3.00
94	Bryant Young	.20
95	Brent Jones	.20
96	Ken Norton	.20
97	William Floyd	1.50
98	Steve Young	2.00
99	*Warren Sapp*	4.00
100	Trent Dilfer	1.00
101	Alvin Harper	.40
102	Hardy Nickerson	.20
103	Derrick Brooks	3.00
104	Errict Rhett	.40
105	Henry Ellard	.20
106	Ken Harvey	.20
107	Gus Frerotte	1.00
108	Brian Mitchell	.20
109	Terry Allen	.20
110	Heath Shuler	1.50
111	Jim Kelly	.40
112	Andre Reed	.20
113	Bruce Smith	.20
114	*Darick Holmes*	1.50
115	Bryce Paup	.20
116	Cornelius Bennett	.20
117	Carl Pickens	.50
118	Darnay Scott	1.25
119	*Jeff Blake*	2.00
120	Steve Tovar	.20
121	Tony McGee	.20
122	Dan Wilkinson	.20
123	Craig Powell	.20
124	Vinny Testaverde	.20
125	Eric Turner	.20
126	Leroy Hoard	.20
127	Lorenzo White	.20
128	Andre Rison	.40
129	Shannon Sharpe	.20
130	*Terrell Davis*	8.00
131	Anthony Miller	.20
132	Mike Pritchard	.20
133	Steve Atwater	.20
134	John Elway	3.00
135	Haywood Jeffires	.20
136	Gary Brown	.20
137	Al Smith	.20
138	*Rodney Thomas*	.50
139	Ray Childress	.20
140	Mel Gray	.20
141	Craig Erickson	.20
142	Sean Dawkins	.20
143	*Ken Dilger*	1.25
144	Ellis Johnson	.20
145	Quentin Coryatt	.20
146	Marshall Faulk	1.50
147	*Tony Boselli*	.40
148	*Rob Johnson*	3.00
149	Desmond Howard	.20
150	Steve Beuerlein	.20
151	Reggie Cobb	.20
152	Jeff Lageman	.20
153	Willie Davis	.20
154	Marcus Allen	.40
155	Neil Smith	.20
156	Greg Hill	.75
157	Steve Bono	.50
158	Derrick Thomas	.40
159	Jeff Hostetler	.40
160	Harvey Williams	.20
161	Raghib Ismail	.20
162	Chester McGlockton	.20
163	Terry McDaniel	.20
164	Tim Brown	.40
165	Terry Kirby	.20
166	Irving Fryar	.20
167	O.J. McDuffie	.20
168	Bryan Cox	.20
169	Eric Green	.20
170	Dan Marino	4.00
171	Ben Coates	.20
172	Vincent Brisby	.20
173	Chris Slade	.20
174	Ty Law	.20
175	Vincent Brown	.20
176	Drew Bledsoe	3.00
177	Johnny Mitchell	.20
178	Boomer Esiason	.20
179	*Wayne Chrebet*	5.00
180	Hugh Douglas	.20
181	Ron Moore	.20
182	Aaron Glenn	.20
183	*Mark Bruener*	1.00
184	Neil O'Donnell	.40
185	Charles Johnson	.75
186	Greg Lloyd	.40
187	Rod Woodson	.40
188	Bam Morris	1.50
189	*Terrell Fletcher*	1.00
190	Terrance Shaw	.20
191	Stan Humphries	.40
192	Junior Seau	.40
193	Leslie O'Neal	.20
194	Natrone Means	1.00
195	*Christian Fauria*	.40
196	Rick Mirer	1.00
197	Sam Adams	.20
198	Cortez Kennedy	.20
199	Eugene Robinson	.20
200	Chris Warren	.40
NNO	Dan Marino Tribute	25.00
NNO	Joe Montana Salute	25.00

A player's name in *italic* type indicates a rookie card.

1995 Sp All-Pros

These All-Pro die-cut cards came in two versions - silver, which was randomly inserted one per every five packs, and gold, which was found one per every 62 packs. The top and bottom of the card are die-cut, with either silver or gold foil; the player's name is at the top, while his team name is at the bottom. All-Pro is written in foil on the left side of the card; the player's position is in foil on the right, along with the brand logo. Card backs, numbered with an "AP" prefix, have a close-up shot of the player, plus a brief summary of the player's achievements.

		NM/M
Complete Set (20):		30.00
Common Player:		1.00
Gold Cards:		2X-4X
1	Marshall Faulk	3.00
2	Natrone Means	1.00
3	Emmitt Smith	4.00
4	Brett Favre	4.00
5	Michael Westbrook	1.00
6	Jerry Rice	3.00
7	John Elway	3.00
8	Troy Aikman	3.00
9	Rashaan Salaam	1.00
10	Jerome Bettis	1.00
11	Drew Bledsoe	2.00
12	Kerry Collins	1.00
13	Dan Marino	4.00
14	Tyrone Wheatley	1.00
15	Steve McNair	2.00
16	Steve Young	3.00
17	Eric Zeier	1.00
18	Errict Rhett	1.00
19	Michael Irvin	1.00
20	Barry Sanders	4.00

1995 Sp Holoviews

Some of the NFL's top stars and promising rookies are showcased in this 40-card insert set. Cards were randomly included in 1995 Upper Deck football, one per every five packs. The horizontal card front features a glossy color photo on the right side, along with a rectangle which says "Holoview." A hologram of the player up close, plus his name, team name and position, are on the left side. The back is also horizontal and includes an action photo on the left, plus a summary of the player's accomplishments on the right. Cards are numbered using a fraction format - 13/40, etc. Each Holoview was also made in a die-cut version, seeded one per every 75 packs.

		NM/M
Complete Set (40):		45.00
Common Player:		.50
Minor Stars:		1.00
Inserted 1:5		
Die-Cut Cards:		2X-3X
Inserted 1:75		
1	Joe Montana	4.00
2	Dan Marino	4.00
3	Drew Bledsoe	3.00
4	Ben Coates	.50
5	Curtis Martin	3.00
6	Kyle Brady	.50
7	Marshall Faulk	2.00
8	Ki-Jana Carter	1.00
9	Leroy Hoard	.50
10	James O. Stewart	.50
11	Mark Bruener	.50
12	Charles Johnson	.50
13	Rod Woodson	.50
14	John Elway	3.00
15	Tim Brown	.50
16	Napoleon Kaufman	1.00

17 Natrone Means 1.00
18 Jimmy Oliver .50
19 Christian Fauria .50
20 Joey Galloway 1.00
21 Chris Warren .50
22 Kerry Collins 1.00
23 Mario Bates .50
24 Jerome Bettis 1.00
25 William Floyd .50
26 Jerry Rice 3.00
27 J.J. Stokes 1.00
28 Steve Young 2.00
29 Troy Aikman 3.00
30 Michael Irvin 1.00
31 Emmitt Smith 4.00
32 Rodney Hampton .50
33 Heath Shuler 1.00
34 Michael Westbrook 1.00
35 Barry Sanders 4.00
36 Brett Favre 5.00
37 Cris Carter 1.00
38 Warren Moon 1.00
39 James A. Stewart .50
40 Errict Rhett .50

1995 Sp Championship

Upper Deck's debut SP Championship series has 225 cards, including 45 Future Champions subset cards. The Championship series of cards is the retail-only spinoff of Upper Deck's hobby-only SP product. All cards, inserts, wrappers and box designs are completely different in the retail and hobby versions. Each card front has a full-bleed color photo on it, plus a brand logo stamped in gold foil. The player's name and position are at the bottom, along with the team name, which is in an oval. Each card in the regular-issue set is also paralleled in a die-cut version that appears one per pack. One per every 15 packs holds a Showcase of the Playoffs insert card. This is a 20-card set of top NFL stars who could make an impact in the playoffs. This insert is also featured in a die-cut version that is seeded one card per every 40 packs.

NM/M
Complete Set (225): 55.00
Common Player: .15
Minor Stars: .30
Die-Cut Cards: 3X
Die-Cut Rookies: 2X
Inserted 1:1
Pack (6): 1.75
Wax Box (44): 50.00
1 *Frank Sanders* 1.50
2 *Stoney Case* .75
3 *Lorenzo Styles* .30
4 *Todd Collins* .30
5 *Darick Holmes* .60
6 *Brian DeMarco* .30
7 *Tyrone Poole* .30
8 *Kerry Collins* 3.00
9 *Rashaan Salaam* .50
10 *Steve Stenstrom* .30
11 *Ki-Jana Carter* .50
12 *Eric Zeier* .75
13 *Sherman Williams* .30
14 *Terrell Davis* 6.00
15 *David Dunn* .30
16 *Luther Elliss* .30
17 *Craig Newsome* .30
18 *Antonio Freeman* 2.00
19 *Steve McNair* 6.00
20 *Anthony Cook* .30
21 *Rodney Thomas* .30
22 *Ellis Johnson* .30
23 *Ken Dilger* .50
24 *James O. Stewart* 2.00
25 *Pete Mitchell* .30
26 *Tamarick Vanover* .60
27 *Orlanda Thomas* .30
28 *Corey Fuller* .30
29 *Curtis Martin* 5.00
30 *Ty Law* .75
31 *Roell Preston* .75
32 *Mark Fields* .30
33 *Tyrone Wheatley* 2.50
34 *Kyle Brady* .50
35 *Napoleon Kaufman* 2.00
36 *Kordell Stewart* 3.00
37 *Mark Bruener* .75
38 *Terrance Shaw* .30
39 *Terrell Fletcher* .50
40 *J.J. Stokes* 1.00
41 *Christian Fauria* .30
42 *Joey Galloway* 2.00
43 *Kevin Carter* .50
44 *Warren Sapp* 1.00
45 *Michael Westbrook* 2.00
46 Clyde Simmons .15
47 Rob Moore .15
48 Seth Joyner .15
49 Dave Kreig .15
50 Garrison Hearst .40
51 Aeneas Williams .15
52 Terance Mathis .15
53 Bert Emanual .50
54 Chris Doleman .15
55 Craig Heyward .15
56 Jeff George .15
57 Eric Metcalf .15
58 Jim Kelly .30
59 Andre Reed .15
60 Russell Copeland .15
61 Bruce Smith .15
62 Cornelius Bennett .15
63 Jeff Burris .15
64 Mark Carrier .15
65 Pete Metzelaars .15
66 Frank Reich .15
67 Sam Mills .15
68 John Kasay .15
69 Willie Green .15
70 Curtis Conway .15
71 Erik Kramer .15
72 Donnell Woolford .15
73 Mark Carrier .15
74 Jeff Graham .15
75 Raymont Harris .15
76 Carl Pickens .30
77 Darnay Scott .30
78 *Jeff Blake* 1.00
79 Dan Wilkinson .15
80 Tony McGee .15
81 Eric Bienemy .15
82 Vinny Testaverde .15
83 Eric Turner .15
84 Leroy Hoard .15
85 Lorenzo White .15
86 Antonio Langham .15
87 Andre Rison .15
88 Troy Aikman 1.50
89 Michael Irvin .50
90 Charles Haley .15
91 Daryl Johnston .15
92 Jay Novacek .15
93 Emmitt Smith 3.00
94 Shannon Sharpe .15
95 Anthony Miller .15
96 Mike Pritchard .15
97 Glyn Milburn .15
98 Simon Fletcher .15
99 John Elway .75
100 Henry Thomas .15
101 Herman Moore .50
102 Scott Mitchell .15
103 Bennie Blades .15
104 Chris Spielman .15
105 Barry Sanders 2.00
106 Mark Ingram .15
107 Edgar Bennett .15
108 Reggie White .30
109 Sean Jones .15
110 Robert Brooks .30
111 Brett Favre 3.00
112 Chris Chandler .15
113 Haywood Jeffires .15
114 Gary Brown .15
115 Al Smith .15
116 Ray Childress .15
117 Mel Gray .15
118 Jim Harbaugh .15
119 Sean Dawkins .15
120 Roosevelt Potts .15
121 Marshall Faulk 1.00
122 Tony Bennett .15
123 Quentin Coryatt .15
124 Desmond Howard .15
125 Tony Boselli .15
126 Steve Beuerlein .15
127 Jeff Lageman .15
128 *Rob Johnson* 2.00
129 Ernest Givins .15
130 Willie Davis .15
131 Marcus Allen .30
132 Neil Smith .15
133 Greg Hill .50
134 Steve Bono .30
135 Lake Dawson .50
136 Dan Marino 3.00
137 Terry Kirby .15
138 Irvin Fryar .15
139 O.J. McDuffie .15
140 Bryan Cox .15
141 Eric Green .15
142 Cris Carter .15
143 Robert Smith .15
144 John Randle .15
145 Jake Reed .15
146 DeWayne Washington .15
147 Warren Moon .30
148 Dave Meggett .15
149 Ben Coates .15
150 Vincent Brisby .15
151 Willie McGinest .15
152 Chris Slade .15
153 Drew Bledsoe 2.00
154 Eric Allen .15
155 Mario Bates .50
156 Jim Everett .15
157 Renaldo Turnbull .15
158 Tyrone Hughes .15
159 Michael Haynes .15
160 Mike Sherrard .15
161 Dave Brown .15
162 Chris Calloway .15
163 Keith Hamilton .15
164 Rodney Hampton .15
165 Herschel Walker .15
166 Adrian Murrell .50
167 Johnny Mitchell .15
168 Boomer Esiason .15
169 Mo Lewis .15
170 Brad Baxter .15
171 Aaron Glenn .15
172 Jeff Hostetler .15
173 Harvey Williams .15
174 Tim Brown .30
175 Terry McDaniel .15
176 Pat Swilling .15
177 Raghib Ismail .15
178 Randall Cunningham .15
179 Calvin Williams .15
180 Ricky Watters .30
181 Charlie Garner .15
182 Fred Barnett .15
183 Rodney Peete .15
184 Neil O'Donnell .30
185 Charles Johnson .40
186 Rod Woodson .15
187 Bam Morris .75
188 Kevin Greene .15
189 Greg Lloyd .15
190 Chris Miller .15
191 Isaac Bruce 1.50
192 Roman Phifer .15
193 Jerome Bettis .30
194 Carlos Jenkins .15
195 Troy Drayton .15
196 Andre Coleman .15
197 Natrone Means .75
198 Leslie O'Neal .15
199 Junior Seau .30
200 Tony Martin .15
201 Stan Humphries .15
202 Steve Young 2.00
203 Jerry Rice 2.00
204 Brent Jones .15
205 Dana Stubblefield .15
206 Lee Woodall .15
207 Merton Hanks .15
208 Rick Mirer .30
209 Brian Blades .15
210 Chris Warren .30
211 Sam Adams .15
212 Cortez Kennedy .15
213 Eugene Robinson .15
214 Alvin Harper .15
215 Trent Dilfer .50
216 Hardy Nickerson .15
217 Errict Rhett .30
218 Eric Curry .15
219 Jackie Harris .15
220 Henry Ellard .15
221 Terry Allen .15
222 Brian Mitchell .15
223 Ken Harvey .15
224 Gus Frerotte .75
225 Heath Shuler 1.25

1995 Sp Championship Die-Cuts

The 225-card, regular-size set was a parallel set to the SP Championship issue, inserted every pack. The cards are essentially identical, except for the die-cut card tops.

NM/M
Common Player (1-225): .50
Die-Cut Cards: 2X-4X

1995 Sp Championship Playoff Showcase

These cards feature a color action photo of a player in a box in the center. The set name is in foil at the bottom, along with the player's name and position. A gold-foiled brand logo is above the photo. Card backs are numbered using a "PS" prefix. Cards were randomly included in every 15th pack of 1995 Upper Deck SP Championship product. The inserts were also created in a die-cut version; these cards are seeded one per every 40 packs.

NM/M
Complete Set (20): 40.00
Common Player: .50
Minor Stars: 1.00
Inserted 1:15 275.00
Die-Cut Cards: 2X
Inserted 1:20
1 Troy Aikman 3.00
2 Jerry Rice 4.00
3 Isaac Bruce 1.00
4 Rodney Peete .50
5 Rashaan Salaam 1.00
6 Brett Favre 5.00
7 Alvin Harper .50
8 Cris Carter 1.00
9 Michael Westbrook 1.00
10 Jeff George 1.00
11 Natrone Means 1.00
12 Dan Marino 5.00
13 Steve Bono 1.00
14 Greg Lloyd .50
15 Jim Kelly 1.00
16 Jeff Hostetler .50
17 Marshall Faulk 3.00
18 John Elway 3.00
19 Jeff Blake 1.00
20 Andre Rison .50

1996 Sp

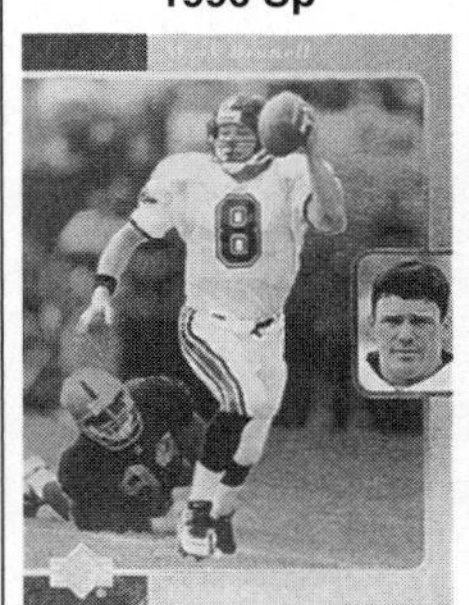

The 188-card, regular-sized set was issued in eight-card packs and included the subset, Premiere Prospects. The release included a five-card SPX Force preview along with an autographed parallel version. Other inserts were: Focus On The Future, Explosive, Holoview and F/X Holoview. The base set cards include an action shot with a player headshot inset along the right border. The player's name appears on the top border with team nickname and position along the bottom.

NM/M
Complete Set (188): 110.00
Common Player: .20
Minor Stars: .40
Pack (8): 8.00
Wax Box (30): 165.00
1 *Keyshawn Johnson* 12.00
2 *Kevin Hardy* .75
3 *Simeon Rice* 2.00
4 *Jonathan Ogden* .20
5 *Eddie George* 15.00
6 *Terry Glenn* 6.00
7 *Terrell Owens* 18.00
8 *Tim Biakabutuka* 1.00
9 *Lawrence Phillips* .50
10 *Alex Molden* .20
11 *Regan Upshaw* .20
12 *Rickey Dudley* 1.75
13 *Duane Clemons* .20
14 *John Mobley* .20
15 *Eddie Kennison* 1.00
16 *Karim Abdul-Jabbar* .75
17 *Eric Moulds* 12.00
18 *Marvin Harrison* 18.00
19 *Stepfret Williams* .20
20 *Stephen Davis* 10.00
21 Deion Sanders 1.50
22 Emmitt Smith 3.00
23 Troy Aikman 2.00
24 Michael Irvin .40
25 Herschel Walker .20
26 Kavika Pittman .20
27 Andre Hastings .20
28 Jerome Bettis .40
29 Mike Tomczak .20
30 Kordell Stewart 1.00
31 Charles Johnson .20
32 Greg Lloyd .20
33 Brett Favre 4.00
34 Mark Chmura .20
35 Edgar Bennett .20
36 Robert Brooks .20
37 Craig Newsome .20
38 Reggie White .40
39 Marshall Faulk 1.50
40 Jim Harbaugh .20
41 Sean Dawkins .20
42 Quentin Coryatt .20
43 Ray Buchanan .20
44 Ken Dilger .20
45 Jerry Rice 2.50
46 J.J. Stokes .40
47 Steve Young 2.00
48 Derek Loville .20
49 Terry Kirby .20
50 Ken Norton .20
51 Tamarick Vanover 1.00
52 Steve Bono .20
53 Marcus Allen .40
54 Neil Smith .20
55 Derrick Thomas .20
56 Dale Carter .20
57 Terance Mathis .20
58 Eric Metcalf .20
59 *Jamal Anderson* 5.00
60 Bert Emanuel .20
61 Craig Heyward .20
62 Cornelius Bennett .20
63 Tony Martin .20
64 Stan Humphries .20
65 Andre Coleman .20
66 Junior Seau .20
67 Terrell Fletcher .20
68 John Carney .20
69 Charlie Jones .20
70 Ricky Watters .40
71 Charlie Garner .20
72 *Bobby Hoying* .75
73 Jason Dunn .20
74 Bobby Taylor .20
75 Irving Fryar .20
76 Jim Kelly .20
77 Thurman Thomas .40
78 Darick Holmes .20
79 Bryce Paup .20
80 Bruce Smith .20
81 Andre Reed .20
82 Glyn Milburn .20
83 Brett Perriman .20
84 Herman Moore .75
85 Scott Mitchell .20
86 Barry Sanders 3.00
87 Johnnie Morton .20
88 Dan Marino 4.00
89 O.J. McDuffie .20
90 Stanley Pritchett .20
91 *Zach Thomas* 2.50
92 Daryl Gardner .20
93 Rashaan Salaam .75
94 Erik Kramer .20
95 Curtis Conway .20
96 *Bobby Engram* .75
97 Walt Harris .20
98 Bryan Cox .20
99 John Elway 2.00
100 Terrell Davis 2.00
101 Anthony Miller .20
102 Shannon Sharpe .20
103 Steve Atwater .20
104 *Jeff Lewis* .50
105 Joey Galloway 1.50
106 Chris Warren .20
107 Rick Mirer .20
108 Cortez Kennedy .20
109 Michael Sinclair .20
110 John Friesz .20
111 Warren Moon .20
112 Cris Carter .20
113 Jake Reed .20
114 Robert Smith .20
115 John Randle .20
116 Orlanda Thomas .20
117 Jeff Hostetler .20
118 Tim Brown .20
119 Joe Aska .20
120 Napoleon Kaufman .20
121 Terry McDaniel .20
122 Harvey Williams .20
123 Trent Dilfer .20
124 Reggie Brooks .20
125 Alvin Harper .20
126 *Mike Alstott* 8.00
127 Hardy Nickerson .20
128 Mario Bates .20
129 Jim Everett .20
130 Tyrone Hughes .20
131 Michael Haynes .20
132 Eric Allen .20
133 Isaac Bruce 1.50
134 Kevin Carter .20
135 Leslie O'Neal .20
136 *Tony Banks* 3.00
137 Chris Chandler .20
138 Steve McNair 2.00
139 Chris Sanders .20
140 Ronnie Harmon .20
141 Willie Davis .20
142 Michael Westbrook .40
143 Terry Allen .20
144 Brian Mitchell .20
145 Henry Ellard .20
146 Gus Frerotte .20
147 Kerry Collins .50
148 Sam Mills .20
149 Wesley Walls .20
150 Kevin Greene .20
151 *Mushin Muhammad* 5.00
152 Winslow Oliver .20
153 Jeff Blake .50
154 Carl Pickens .20
155 Darnay Scott .20
156 Garrison Hearst .20
157 Marco Battaglia .20
158 Drew Bledsoe 2.00
159 Curtis Martin 4.00
160 Shawn Jefferson .20
161 Ben Coates .20
162 Lawyer Milloy .20
163 Tyrone Wheatley .20
164 Rodney Hampton .20
165 Chris Calloway .20
166 Dave Brown .20
167 *Amani Toomer* 4.00
168 Vinny Testaverde .20
169 Michael Jackson .20
170 Eric Turner .20
171 DeRon Jenkins .20
172 *Jermaine Lewis* 2.00
173 Frank Sanders .20
174 Rob Moore .20
175 Kent Graham .50
176 *Leeland McElroy* .50
177 Larry Centers .20
178 Eric Swann .20
179 Mark Brunell 1.50
180 Willie Jackson .20
181 James O. Stewart .20
182 Natrone Means .20
183 *Tony Brackens* .75
184 Adrian Murrell .20
185 Neil O'Donnell .20
186 Hugh Douglas .20
187 Jeff Graham .20
188 *Alex Van Dyke* .40

1996 Sp Explosive

The 20-card, regular-sized, die-cut set was inserted every 360 packs of 1996 Upper Deck SP football. The die-cut cards are in the shape of an "X" and feature a circular headshot of the player over a black-and-white background. The player's first name appears in the lower left corner in lowercase letters with the last name in the right corner, also in lowercase. The card backs are numbered with the "X" prefix.

NM/M
Common Player: 5.00
1 Emmitt Smith 75.00
2 Jerry Rice 75.00
3 Rashaan Salaam 5.00
4 Brett Favre 100.00
5 Tim Brown 15.00
6 Tim Biakabutuka 5.00
7 John Elway 60.00
8 Steve Young 60.00
9 Napoleon Kaufman 5.00
10 Troy Aikman 60.00
11 Drew Bledsoe 60.00
12 Carl Pickens 5.00
13 Dan Marino 75.00
14 Eddie George 35.00
15 Joey Galloway 35.00
16 Deion Sanders 25.00
17 Curtis Martin 35.00
18 Marshall Faulk 45.00
19 Keyshawn Johnson 35.00
20 Barry Sanders 75.00

1996 Sp Focus on the Future

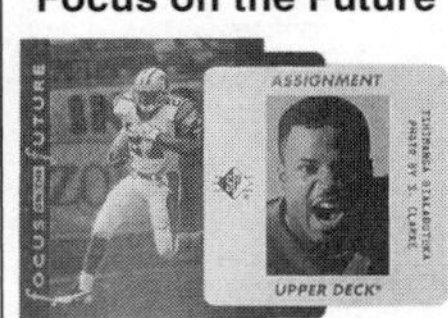

The 30-card, regular-sized, die-cut set was inserted every 30 packs of SP football. The card fronts feature a color player shot over a gold background with a slide film-type addition on the right side. The cel contains a color headshot of the player with the photographer listed along the right border. The card backs are numbered with the "F" prefix.

NM/M
Complete Set (30): 75.00
Common Player: 1.00
1 Leeland McElroy 1.00
2 Frank Sanders 2.00
3 Darick Holmes 1.00
4 Eric Moulds 1.00
5 Kerry Collins 1.00
6 Tim Biakabutuka 1.00
7 Ki-Jana Carter 3.00
8 Jeff Blake 2.00
9 John Mobley 1.00
10 Johnnie Morton 4.00
11 Eddie George 10.00
12 Steve McNair 10.00
13 Marshall Faulk 12.00
14 Kevin Hardy 1.00
15 Greg Hill 1.00
16 Tamarick Vanover 1.00
17 Karim Abdul-Jabbar 2.00
18 Drew Bledsoe 12.00
19 Curtis Martin 12.00
20 Danny Kanell 1.00
21 Keyshawn Johnson 8.00

22 Napoleon Kaufman 1.00
23 Rickey Dudley 3.00
24 Kordell Stewart 4.00
25 Lawrence Phillips 1.00
26 Isaac Bruce 10.00
27 J.J. Stokes 4.00
28 Joey Galloway 5.00
29 Errict Rhett 2.00
30 Mike Alstott 5.00

1996 Sp Holoview

The 48-card, regular-sized set was inserted every seven packs of SP football. The card fronts feature a color player shot over a Holoview image headshot and multiple team logo. The player's name, position and team nickname appears in the upper right quadrant. A 48-card, die-cut parallel version was inserted every 75 packs. The cards also feature the same Holoview image but have a gold top border instead of a team-color top border.

NM/M
Complete Set (48): 60.00
Common Player: .50
Die-Cut Cards: 2X-4X
1 Jerry Rice 4.00
2 Herman Moore .50
3 Kerry Collins 1.00
4 Brett Favre 5.00
5 Junior Seau .50
6 Troy Aikman 4.00
7 John Elway 4.00
8 Steve Young 4.00
9 Reggie White .50
10 Kordell Stewart .50
11 Drew Bledsoe 3.00
12 Jeff Blake .50
13 Dan Marino 5.00
14 Curtis Martin 3.00
15 Marshall Faulk 3.00
16 Greg Lloyd .50
17 Cris Carter .50
18 Isaac Bruce 2.00
19 Joey Galloway 2.00
20 Barry Sanders 4.00
21 Emmitt Smith 5.00
22 Edgar Bennett .50
23 Rashaan Salaam .50
24 Steve McNair 3.00
25 Tamarick Vanover .50
26 Deion Sanders 1.00
27 Keyshawn Johnson 2.00
28 Kevin Hardy .50
29 Simeon Rice .50
30 Lawrence Phillips .50
31 Tim Biakabutuka .50
32 Terry Glenn .50
33 Rickey Dudley 1.00
34 Regan Upshaw .50
35 Eddie George 2.00
36 John Mobley .50
37 Eddie Kennison .50
38 Marvin Harrison 3.00
39 Leeland McElroy .50
40 Eric Moulds 2.00
41 Alex Van Dyke .50
42 Mike Alstott 2.00
43 Jeff Lewis .50
44 Bobby Engram .50
45 Derrick Mayes .50
46 Karim Abdul-Jabbar .50
47 Stepfret Williams .50
48 Stephen Davis 1.00

1996 Sp Holoview Die-Cuts

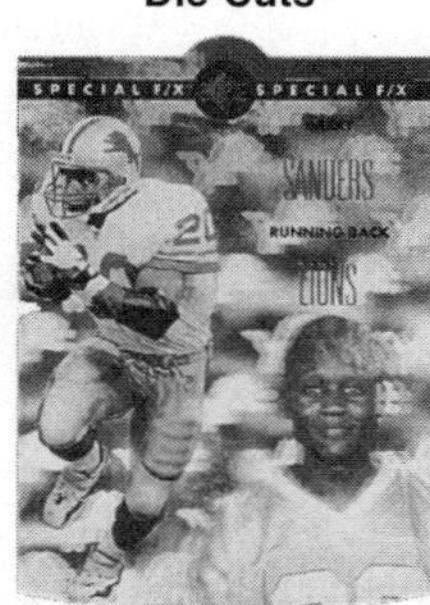

Holoview Die-Cuts are a parallel set to the Holoview Collection, and seeded one per 74 packs. The 48 regular Holoviews are double die-cut on the top and bottom and have gold foil added to them.

Complete Set (48):
Holoview Die-Cuts: 2X-4X

1996 Sp Spx Force

The five-card, regular-size die-cut set was inserted every 950 packs of 1996 SP football. Each card contained four Holoview images of top players at quarterback, running back, wide receiver and rookies. The fifth card features Holoviews of the top four at each position (and rookies) and will have an autographed parallel version (1:8,820).

NM/M
Complete Set (4): 45.00
Common Player: 5.00
Set price does not include Autographs.
1 Keyshawn Johnson, Lawrence Phillips, Terry Glenn, Tim Biakabutuka 5.00
2 Barry Sanders, Emmitt Smith, Marshall Faulk, Curtis Martin 25.00
3 Dan Marino, Brett Favre, Drew Bledsoe, Troy Aikman 25.00
4 Jerry Rice, Herman Moore, Carl Pickens, Isaac Bruce 10.00
5A Keyshawn Johnson AUTO 75.00
5B Dan Marino AUTO 200.00
5C Jerry Rice AUTO 175.00
5D Barry Sanders AUTO 200.00

1996 Spx

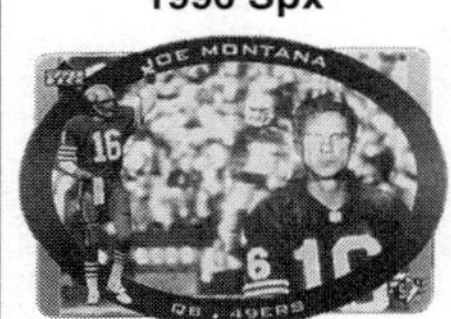

This 50-card die-cut Upper Deck set utilizes Holoview technology on 32-point stock. It combines the top stars of the NFL with the top rookies of the 1995 season. To make a Holoview card, each athlete is videotaped while on a turntable. More than seven seconds - or 200 frames - of videotape are then synthesized to produce a 50-degree, 3D picture. A mug shot also appears in the card, which has an oval (using the team's primary color) that has the player's name at the top and his position and team name below. A small color photo is also on the card front. The card back has a rectangle that includes a color photo, biographical and statistical information, and a recap of his accomplishments. Each card in the regular issue is also reprinted in a Gold parallel set; they are inserted one per every seven packs. Insert cards include a Joe Montana Tribute card (one in 95), a Dan Marino Record Breaker card (one in 81), autographed versions of the Marino and Montana cards (one in 433), and HoloFame Collection.

NM/M
Complete Set (50): 75.00
Common Player: 1.50
Minor Stars: 3.00
Gold Cards: 1X-2X
Marino Auto: 300.00
Montana Auto: 225.00
Pack (1): 3.00
Wax Box (36): 100.00
1 Frank Sanders 1.00
2 Terance Mathis 1.00
3 Todd Collins 1.00
4 Kerry Collins 4.00
5 Carl Pickens 3.00
6 Darnay Scott 1.00
7 Ki-Jana Carter 1.00
8 Eric Zeier 1.00
9 Andre Rison 1.50
10 Sherman Williams 1.00
11 Troy Aikman 5.00
12 Michael Irvin 2.00
13 Emmitt Smith 8.00
14 Shannon Sharpe 1.50
15 John Elway 5.00
16 Barry Sanders 8.00
17 Brett Favre 8.00
18 Rodney Thomas 1.00
19 Marshall Faulk 5.00
20 James O. Stewart 1.00
21 Greg Hill 1.50
22 Tamarick Vanover 1.00
23 Dan Marino 8.00
24 Cris Carter 1.50
25 Warren Moon 1.50
26 Drew Bledsoe 6.00
27 Ben Coates 1.50
28 Curtis Martin 6.00
29 Mario Bates 1.00
30 Tyrone Wheatley 1.00
31 Rodney Hampton 1.50
32 Kyle Brady 1.50
33 Jeff Hostetler 1.50
34 Napoleon Kaufman 1.00
35 Tim Brown 1.50
36 Charles Johnson 1.00
37 Rod Woodson 1.50
38 Natrone Means 1.00
39 J.J. Stokes 2.00
40 Steve Young 5.00
41 Brent Jones 1.50
42 Jerry Rice 6.00
43 Joe Montana 6.00
44 Rick Mirer 1.00
45 Chris Warren 1.00
46 Joey Galloway 2.00
47 Isaac Bruce 3.00
48 Jerome Bettis 3.00
49 Errict Rhett 1.00
50 Michael Westbrook 1.00
UDT-13 Dan Marino R.B. 12.00
UDT-19 Joe Montana Tr. 12.00

1996 Spx Gold

The 50-card, regular-size set was the parallel gold version of the SPx set.

NM/M
Common Player: 4.00
Gold Cards: 2X

1996 Spx Holofame

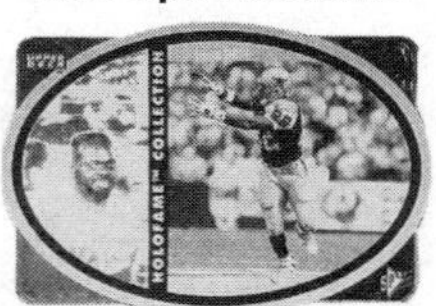

These 1996 Upper Deck SPx insert cards were seeded one per every 24 packs. They showcase players who are likely to be enshrined in the Hall of Fame someday. Cards are numbered using an "Hx" prefix.

NM/M
Complete Set (10): 40.00
Common Player: 1.00
1 Troy Aikman 4.00
2 Emmitt Smith 5.00
3 Barry Sanders 5.00
4 Steve Young 4.00
5 Jerry Rice 4.00
6 John Elway 4.00
7 Marshall Faulk 3.00
8 Dan Marino 5.00
9 Drew Bledsoe 3.00
10 Natrone Means 1.00

1997 Spx ProMotion Autographs

This insert included autographed versions of each of the six ProMotion inserts. Cards were autographed on the front and sequentially numbered to 100 on the back.

NM/M
Common Player: 100.00
1 Dan Marino 250.00
2 Joe Montana 250.00
3 Troy Aikman 100.00
4 Barry Sanders 200.00
5 Karim Abdul-Jabbar 50.00
6 Eddie George 75.00

1997 SP Authentic

SP Authentic Football is a 198-card set featuring 168 veterans and a subset called Future Watch which contains 30 of the year's top rookies. The front of the cards features an action shot with the player's name in the bottom right corner and team name in the upper left. The card backs feature another action shot and career stats. The inserts include Aikman PowerDeck Audio Cards, ProFiles, Sign of the TImes, Mark of a Legend, Tradition, SP Authentics, and SP Authentics Collection.

NM/M
Complete Set (198): 150.00
Common Player: .30
Minor Stars: .60
Pack (5): 7.00
Wax Box (24): 125.00
1 *Orlando Pace* 1.00
2 *Darrell Russell* .75
3 *Shawn Springs* .75
4 *Peter Boulware* 1.00
5 *Bryant Westbrook* 1.00
6 *Walter Jones* .75
7 *Ike Hilliard* 5.00
8 *James Farrior* .75
9 *Tom Knight* .75
10 *Warrick Dunn* 12.00
11 *Tony Gonzalez* 20.00
12 *Reinard Wilson* .75
13 *Yatil Green* 1.00
14 *Reidel Anthony* 2.00
15 *Kenny Holmes* .75
16 *Dwayne Rudd* .75
17 *Renaldo Wynn* .75
18 *David LaFleur* .75
19 *Antowain Smith* 10.00
20 *Jim Druckenmiller* 2.00
21 *Rae Carruth* .75
22 *Byron Hanspard* .75
23 *Jake Plummer* 12.00
24 *Joey Kent* 1.00
25 *Corey Dillon* 20.00
26 *Danny Wuerffel* 2.00
27 *Will Blackwell* .75
28 *Troy Davis* .75
29 *Darnell Autry* .75
30 *Pat Barnes* .75
31 Kent Graham .30
32 Simeon Rice .30
33 Frank Sanders .30
34 Rob Moore .30
35 Eric Swann .30
36 Chris Chandler .30
37 Jamal Anderson .60
38 Terance Mathis .30
39 Bert Emanuel .30
40 Michael Booker .30
41 Vinny Testaverde .30
42 Bam Morris .30
43 Michael Jackson .30
44 Derrick Alexander .30
45 Jamie Sharper .30
46 Kim Herring .30
47 Todd Collins .30
48 Thurman Thomas .60
49 Andre Reed .30
50 Quinn Early .30
51 Bryce Paup .30
52 Marcellus Wiley .30
53 Kerry Collins .75
54 Anthony Johnson .30
55 Tshimanga Biakabutuka .30
56 Muhsin Muhammad .30
57 Sam Mills .30
58 Wesley Walls .30
59 Rick Mirer .30
60 Raymont Harris .30
61 Curtis Conway .60
62 Bobby Engram .30
63 Bryan Cox .30
64 John Allred .30
65 Jeff Blake .60
66 Ki-Jana Carter .30
67 Darnay Scott .30
68 Carl Pickens .30
69 Dan Wilkerson .30
70 Troy Aikman 3.00
71 Emmitt Smith 5.00
72 Michael Irvin .60
73 Deion Sanders 1.50
74 Anthony Miller .30
75 Antonio Anderson .30
76 John Elway 1.75
77 Terrell Davis 2.00
78 Rod Smith .30
79 Shannon Sharpe .30
80 Neil Smith .30
81 Trevor Pryce .30
82 Scott Mitchell .30
83 Barry Sanders 3.00
84 Herman Moore .60
85 Johnnie Morton .30
86 Matt Russell .30
87 Brett Favre 6.00
88 Edgar Bennett .30
89 Robert Brooks .30
90 Antonio Freeman .60
91 Reggie White .60
92 Craig Newsome .30
93 Jim Harbaugh .30
94 Marshall Faulk 1.25
95 Sean Dawkins .30
96 Marvin Harrison 1.00
97 Quentin Coryatt .30
98 Tarik Glenn .30
99 Mark Brunell 2.00
100 Natrone Means .30
101 Keenan McCardell .30
102 Jimmy Smith .30
103 Tony Brackens .30
104 Kevin Hardy .30
105 Elvis Grbac .30
106 Marcus Allen .60
107 Greg Hill .30
108 Derrick Thomas .30
109 Dale Carter .30
110 Dan Marino 5.00
111 Karim Abdul-Jabbar .75
112 Brian Manning .30
113 Qadry Ismail .30
114 Troy Drayton .30
115 Zach Thomas .60
116 Jason Taylor .30
117 Brad Johnson .60
118 Robert Smith .30
119 John Randle .30
120 Cris Carter .30
121 Jake Reed .30
122 Randall Cunningham .30
123 Drew Bledsoe 2.00
124 Curtis Martin 2.00
125 Terry Glenn 1.00
126 Willie McGinest .30
127 Chris Canty .30
128 Sedrick Shaw .30
129 Heath Shuler .30
130 Mario Bates .30
131 Ray Zellars .30
132 Andre Hastings .30
133 Dave Brown .30
134 Tyrone Wheatley .30
135 Rodney Hampton .30
136 Chris Calloway .30
137 *Tiki Barber* 20.00
138 Neil O'Donnell .30
139 Adrian Murrell .60
140 Wayne Chrebet .30
141 Keyshawn Johnson .60
142 Hugh Douglas .30
143 Jeff George .30
144 Napoleon Kaufman .60
145 Tim Brown .30
146 Desmond Howard .30
147 Rickey Dudley .30
148 Terry McDaniel .30
149 Ty Detmer .30
150 Ricky Watters .60
151 Chris T. Jones .30
152 Irving Fryar .30
153 Mike Mamula .30
154 Jon Harris .30
155 Kordell Stewart 1.00
156 Jerome Bettis .60
157 Charles Johnson .30
158 Greg Lloyd .30
159 George Jones .30
160 Terrell Fletcher .30
161 Stan Humphries .30
162 Tony Martin .30
163 Eric Metcalf .30
164 Junior Seau .30
165 Rod Woodson .30
166 Steve Young 1.75
167 Terry Kirby .30
168 Garrison Hearst .30
169 Jerry Rice 3.00
170 Ken Norton .30
171 Kevin Greene .30
172 Lamar Smith .30
173 Warren Moon .30
174 Chris Warren .30
175 Cortez Kennedy .30
176 Joey Galloway .60
177 Tony Banks .75
178 Isaac Bruce .60
179 Eddie Kennison .60
180 Kevin Carter .30
181 Craig Heyward .30
182 Trent Dilfer .60
183 Errict Rhett .30
184 Mike Alstott .60
185 Hardy Nickerson .30
186 Ronde Barber .30
187 Steve McNair 2.00
188 Eddie George 2.00
189 Chris Sanders .30
190 Blaine Bishop .30
191 *Derrick Mason* 10.00
192 Gus Frerotte .30
193 Terry Allen .30
194 Brian Mitchell .30
195 Alvin Harper .30
196 Jeff Hostetler .30
197 Lesley Sheppard .30
198 Stephen Davis .30
A1 Aikman Audio Blue 5.00
A2 Aikman Audio Pro Bowl 10.00
A3 Aikman Audio White/500 25.00

1997 SP Authentic Aikman PowerDeck

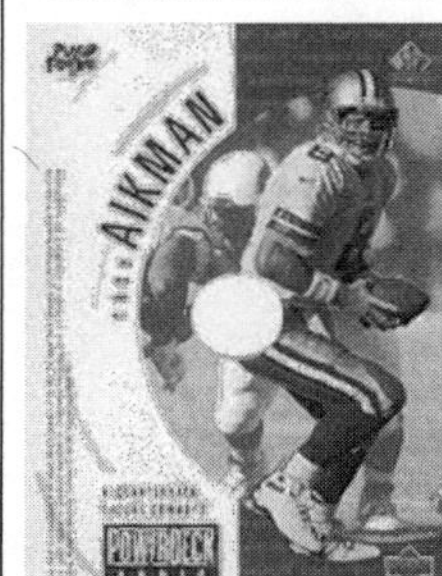

Aikman PowerDeck was a three-card insert that contained a mini-compact disc within a trading card. Regular Blue versions were seeded every 22 packs, Pro Bowl versions were seeded every 130 and White versions were numbered to 500.

NM/M
Common Player: 5.00
A1 Aikman Audio Blue 5.00
A2 Aikman Audio Pro Bowl 15.00
A3 Aikman Audio White/500 50.00

1997 SP Authentic Authentics

This 30-card insert was found in packs of SP Authentic. It allowed the collector to redeem the card for the specific piece of autographed memorabilia noted. Cards SPA1-SPA10 were for Dan Marino autograhped memorabilia, SPA11-SPA20 were for Joe Montana autographed memorabilia and SPA21-SPA26 were for Troy Aikman autographed memorabilia. SPC27 was for a two-card Dan Marino set. The final three cards were numbered with a "SPC" prefix and entitled the collector to get either a Marino, Montana or Aikman collection of autographed memorabilia.

SPA1 Dan Marino (Signed Helmet)
SPA2 Dan Marino (Signed Jersey)
SPA3 Dan Marino (Signed NFL Football)
SPA4 Dan Marino (Replica Signed Helmet)
SPA5 Dan Marino (Collector's Choice Football)
SPA6 Dan Marino (Signed Mini Football)
SPA7 Dan Marino (Signed Sports Illustrated Cover)
SPA8 Dan Marino (Signed Mini Helmet)
SPA9 Dan Marino (Signed Photo)(8X10)
SPA10 Dan Marino (C-Card)
SPA11 Joe Montana (Signed Jersey)
SPA12 Joe Montana (Signed NFL Football)
SPA13 Joe Montana (Collector's Choice Football)
SPA14 Joe Montana (Signed Sports Illustrated Cover)
SPA15 Joe Montana (Signed Mini Helmet)
SPA16 Joe Montana (Signed Photo)(8X10)
SPA17 Joe Montana (C-Card)
SPA18 Joe Montana (Signed Helmet)
SPA19 Joe Montana (Collector's Choice Helmet)
SPA20 Joe Montana (Signed Two-Card Set)
SPA21 Troy Aikman (Signed NFL Football)
SPA22 Troy Aikman (Signed Mini Football)
SPA23 Troy Aikman (Signed Sports Illustrated Cover)
SPA25 Troy Aikman (Signed Photo)(8X10)
SPA26 Troy Aikman (Signed Two-Card Set)
SPA27 Dan Marino (Signed Two-Card Set)

1997 SP Authentic Mark of a Legend

This seven-card collection features autographs from some of the NFL's greatest players. The inserts were seeded 1:168 packs. They have a "ML" prefix.

NM/M
Complete Set (7): 600.00

Common Player:		50.00
1	Bob Griese	30.00
2	Roger Staubach	75.00
3	Joe Montana	100.00
4	Franco Harris	50.00
5	Gale Sayers	75.00
6	Steve Largent	50.00
7	Tony Dorsett	50.00

1997 SP Authentic ProFiles

ProFiles is a three-tiered, 40-card insert. The first tier has an action shot of the player with the NFL logo in the background and is inserted 1:5. The second tier card is a die-cut version of tier one and is inserted 1:12. Tier three cards are sequentially numbered to 100.

		NM/M
Complete Set (40):		55.00
Common Player:		.50
Die-Cut Cards:		2X
Inserted 1:12		
Die-Cut 100's:		7X-14X
Production 100 Sets		
1	Dan Marino	5.00
2	Kordell Stewart	2.00
3	Emmitt Smith	4.00
4	Brett Favre	5.00
5	Marcus Allen	1.00
6	Jerry Rice	3.00
7	Jeff George	.50
8	Mark Brunell	1.00
9	Eddie George	1.00
10	Cris Carter	.50
11	Tshimanga Biakabutuka	.50
12	Ike Hilliard	1.00
13	Darrell Russell	.50
14	Jim Druckenmiller	.50
15	Rae Carruth	.50
16	Warrick Dunn	1.00
17	Herman Moore	.50
18	Deion Sanders	2.00
19	Drew Bledsoe	3.00
20	Jeff Blake	.50
21	Keyshawn Johnson	.50
22	Curtis Martin	2.00
23	Michael Irvin	.50
24	Barry Sanders	4.00
25	Carl Pickens	.50
26	Steve McNair	2.00
27	Terry Allen	.50
28	Terrell Davis	3.00
29	Lawrence Phillips	.50
30	Marshall Faulk	.50
31	Karim Abdul-Jabbar	1.00
32	Steve Young	3.00
33	Tim Brown	.50
34	Antowain Smith	1.00
35	Kerry Collins	1.00
36	Reggie White	.50
37	John Elway	3.00
38	Jerome Bettis	.50
39	Troy Aikman	3.00
40	Junior Seau	.50

1997 SP Authentic Sign of the Times

This 30-card insert consists of cards autographed by current NFL players. They were inserted once in 24 packs.

		NM/M
Complete Set (28):		2,000
Common Player:		20.00
	Jeff Blake	15.00
	Kerry Collins	20.00
	Warrick Dunn	40.00
	Rae Carruth	10.00
	Karim Abdul-Jabbar	10.00
	Reidel Anthony	10.00
	Terrell Davis	50.00
	Joey Galloway	40.00
	Marshall Faulk	40.00
	Robert Brooks	20.00
	Will Blackwell	10.00
	Emmitt Smith	275.00
	Herman Moore	15.00
	Napoleon Kaufman	15.00
	Antowain Smith	25.00
	Terry Allen	20.00
	Tim Brown	30.00
	Jerome Bettis	30.00
	Rashaan Salaam	10.00
	Jim Druckenmiller	10.00
	George Jones	20.00
	Isaac Bruce	30.00
	Tony Gonzalez	20.00
	Troy Aikman	75.00
	Dan Marino	100.00
	Jerry Rice	150.00
	Curtis Martin	60.00
	Eddie George	40.00

1997 SP Authentic Traditions

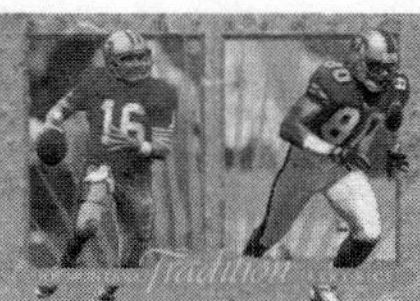

Tradition is a six-card insert. The cards feature two autographs, one from an NFL legend and the other from a proven superstar, both from the same team. Tradition was inserted once per 1,440 packs. The cards carry a "TD" prefix.

		NM/M
Complete Set (6):		2,800
Common Player:		150.00
1	Dan Marino, Bob Griese	425.00
2	Troy Aikman, Roger Staubach	250.00
3	Jerry Rice, Joe Montana	750.00
4	Jerome Bettis, Franco Harris	150.00
5	Emmitt Smith, Tony Dorsett	350.00
6	Joey Galloway, Steve Largent	175.00

1997 Spx

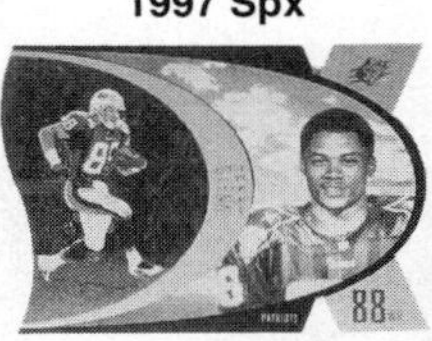

The 50-card, regular-sized, die-cut set was available in one-card packs. The card fronts a hologram panorama-type headshot on the right half of the horizontal card with a color action shot on the left half. The cards are die-cut in the shape of an "X" on the right side.

		NM/M
Complete Set (50):		60.00
Common Player:		1.00
Minor Stars:		2.00
Gold Cards:		3X
Pack (1):		1.75
Wax Box (36):		45.00
1	Jerry Rice	5.00
2	Steve Young	2.00
3	Karim Abdul-Jabbar	.50
4	Dan Marino	6.00
5	Bobby Engram	.50
6	Rashaan Salaam	.50
7	Marvin Harrison	4.00
8	Jim Harbaugh	.50
9	Marshall Faulk	4.00
10	Eric Moulds	2.00
11	Thurman Thomas	2.00
12	Tamarick Vanover	.50
13	Steve Bono	.50
14	Warren Moon	1.00
15	Cris Carter	1.00
16	Carl Pickens	1.00
17	Ki-Jana Carter	1.00
18	Jeff Blake	1.00
19	Tim Biakabutuka	.50
20	Kerry Collins	2.00
21	Leeland McElroy	.50
22	Simeon Rice	1.00
23	John Elway	6.00
24	Terrell Davis	4.00
25	Jeff Lewis	.50
26	Terry Glenn	1.00
27	Curtis Martin	4.00
28	Drew Bledsoe	4.00
29	Lawrence Phillips	.50
30	Isaac Bruce	3.00
31	Eddie Kennison	.50
32	Keyshawn Johnson	3.00
33	Stepfret Williams	.50
34	Emmitt Smith	6.00
35	Troy Aikman	5.00
36	Deion Sanders	2.00
37	Joey Galloway	1.00
38	Rick Mirer	.50
39	Rickey Dudley	1.00
40	Jeff Hostetler	1.00
41	Junior Seau	1.00
42	Derrick Mayes	.50
43	Brett Favre	6.00
44	Edgar Bennett	1.00
45	Barry Sanders	6.00
46	Herman Moore	2.00
47	Kordell Stewart	2.00
48	Jerome Bettis	2.00
49	Eddie George	4.00
50	Steve McNair	4.00

1997 Spx Gold

This 50-card set featured the same die-cut design as the base set, but instead of the border being printed in team colors it was printed in gold. Gold parallels were inserted every nine packs.

Gold Cards: 3X

1997 Spx Holofame

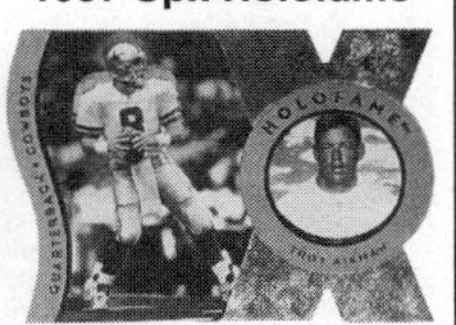

The 10-card, regular-sized set was inserted every 75 packs of Upper Deck's 1997 SPx football. The cards are numbered and carry the "HF" prefix.

		NM/M
Complete Set (20):		100.00
Common Player:		3.00
1	Jerry Rice	8.00
2	Emmitt Smith	10.00
3	Karim Abdul-Jabbar	3.00
4	Brett Favre	12.00
5	Curtis Martin	6.00
6	Eddie Kennison	3.00
7	Troy Aikman	8.00
8	Steve Young	8.00
9	Tim Biakabutuka	3.00
10	Reggie White	5.00
11	Terry Glenn	5.00
12	Lawrence Phillips	3.00
13	Dan Marino	12.00
14	Deion Sanders	15.00
15	Terrell Davis	8.00
16	Marvin Harrison	6.00
17	Eddie George	6.00
18	Marshall Faulk	6.00
19	Keyshawn Johnson	5.00
20	Barry Sanders	10.00

1997 Spx ProMotion

The six-card, regular-sized set was inserted every 433 packs of Upper Deck's 1997 SPx football. They are numbered with a "P" prefix.

		NM/M
Complete Set (6):		75.00
Common Player:		5.00
1	Dan Marino	25.00
2	Joe Montana	20.00
3	Troy Aikman	15.00
4	Barry Sanders	20.00
5	Karim Abdul-Jabbar	5.00
6	Eddie George	12.00

1998 SP Authentic

The 126-card regular set features top-notch photography of the league's best players, along with subsets Future Watch and Time Warp. The 30-card Future Watch set is made up of the top rookies from 1998 and each player is sequentially numbered to 2,000. The 12-card Time Warp set pictures today's top stars shown in action during their respective rookie campaigns. This set is also numbered to 2,000. Each single in this set has a parallel Die-Cut card that is numbered to 500.

		NM/M
Common Player:		.25
Minor Stars:		.50
Die-Cut Cards:		2X-5X
Production 500 Sets		
Common Rookie (1-30):		3.00
Production 2,000 Sets		
Die-Cut Rookies:		1X
Production 500 Sets		
Common Time Warp (31-42):		1.00
Production 2,000 Sets		
Die-Cut Time Warps:		2X
Pack (5):		30.00
Wax Box (24):		575.00
1	*Andre Wadsworth*	3.00
2	*Corey Chavous*	3.00
3	*Keith Brooking*	3.00
4	*Duane Starks*	3.00
5	*Patrick Johnson*	3.00
6	*Jason Peter*	3.00
7	*Curtis Enis*	10.00
8	*Takeo Spikes*	10.00
9	*Greg Ellis*	3.00
10	*Marcus Nash*	3.00
11	*Brian Griese*	100.00
12	*Germane Crowell*	12.00
13	*Vonnie Holliday*	10.00
14	*Peyton Manning*	400.00
15	*Jerome Pathon*	15.00
16	*Fred Taylor*	75.00
17	*John Avery*	10.00
18	*Randy Moss*	250.00
19	*Robert Edwards*	12.00
20	*Tony Simmons*	3.00
21	*Shaun Williams*	3.00
22	*Joe Jurevicius*	10.00
23	*Charles Woodson*	40.00
24	*Tre Thomas*	3.00
25	*Grant Wistrom*	3.00
26	*Ryan Leaf*	5.00
27	*Ahman Green*	150.00
28	*Jacquez Green*	10.00
29	*Kevin Dyson*	12.00
30	*Stephen Alexander*	10.00
31	John Elway	3.00
32	Jerry Rice	3.00
33	Emmitt Smith	20.00
34	Steve Young	10.00
35	Jerome Bettis	7.00
36	Deion Sanders	7.00
37	Andre Rison	5.00
38	Warren Moon	7.00
39	Mark Brunell	5.00
40	Ricky Watters	7.00
41	Dan Marino	20.00
42	Brett Favre	25.00
43	Jake Plummer	.50
44	Adrian Murrell	.25
45	Eric Swann	.25
46	Jamal Anderson	.75
47	Chris Chandler	.50
48	Jim Harbaugh	.25
49	Michael Jackson	.25
50	Jermaine Lewis	.25
51	Rob Johnson	.50
52	Antowain Smith	.75
53	Thurman Thomas	.50
54	Kerry Collins	.50
55	Fred Lane	.25
56	Rae Carruth	.25
57	Erik Kramer	.25
58	Curtis Conway	.25
59	Corey Dillon	1.00
60	Neil O'Donnell	.25
61	Carl Pickens	.50
62	Troy Aikman	2.00
63	Emmitt Smith	3.00
64	Deion Sanders	.75
65	Terrell Davis	1.50
66	John Elway	2.00
67	Rod Smith	.50
68	Scott Mitchell	.25
69	Barry Sanders	3.00
70	Herman Moore	.50
71	Brett Favre	4.00
72	Dorsey Levens	.50
73	Antonio Freeman	.75
74	Marshall Faulk	.75
75	Marvin Harrison	.75
76	Mark Brunell	1.00
77	Keenan McCardell	.25
78	Jimmy Smith	.50
79	Andre Rison	.25
80	Elvis Grbac	.25
81	Derrick Alexander	.25
82	Dan Marino	3.00
83	Kareem Abdul-Jabbar	.50
84	O.J. McDuffie	.25
85	Brad Johnson	.75
86	Cris Carter	.75
87	Robert Smith	.50
88	Drew Bledsoe	1.50
89	Terry Glenn	.50
90	Ben Coates	.25
91	Lamar Smith	.25
92	Danny Wuerffel	.25
93	Tiki Barber	.50
94	Danny Kanell	.25
95	Ike Hilliard	.25
96	Curtis Martin	.75
97	Keyshawn Johnson	.75
98	Glenn Foley	.25
99	Jeff George	.50
100	Tim Brown	.50
101	Napoleon Kaufman	.75
102	Bobby Hoying	.25
103	Charlie Garner	.25
104	Irving Fryar	.25
105	Kordell Stewart	.75
106	Jerome Bettis	.50
107	Charles Johnson	.25
108	Tony Banks	.50
109	Isaac Bruce	.50
110	Natrone Means	.50
111	Junior Seau	.50
112	Steve Young	1.00
113	Jerry Rice	3.00
114	Garrison Hearst	.50
115	Ricky Watters	.50
116	Warren Moon	.50
117	Joey Galloway	.75
118	Trent Dilfer	.50
119	Warrick Dunn	1.00
120	Mike Alstott	.75
121	Steve McNair	1.00
122	Eddie George	1.00
123	Yancey Thigpen	.25
124	Gus Frerotte	.25
125	Terry Allen	.50
126	Michael Westbrook	.25

1998 SP Authentic Maximum Impact

This set was made up of the 30 players who provide the greatest contribution to their team's overall success. Singles were inserted 1:4 packs.

		NM/M
Complete Set (30):		45.00
Common Player:		.50
Minor Stars:		1.00
Inserted 1:4		
MI1	Brett Favre	3.00
MI2	Warrick Dunn	1.00
MI3	Junior Seau	.50
MI4	Steve Young	1.50
MI5	Herman Moore	.50
MI6	Antowain Smith	1.00
MI7	John Elway	2.00
MI8	Troy Aikman	2.00
MI9	Dorsey Levens	.50
MI10	Kordell Stewart	.50
MI11	Peyton Manning	2.00
MI12	Eddie George	1.00
MI13	Dan Marino	3.00
MI14	Joey Galloway	.50
MI15	Mark Brunell	.50
MI16	Jake Plummer	.50
MI17	Curtis Enis	.50
MI18	Corey Dillon	1.00
MI19	Rob Johnson	.50
MI20	Barry Sanders	3.00
MI21	Deion Sanders	1.00
MI22	Napoleon Kaufman	.50
MI23	Ryan Leaf	.50
MI24	Jerry Rice	3.00
MI25	Drew Bledsoe	2.00
MI26	Jerome Bettis	1.00
MI27	Emmitt Smith	3.00
MI28	Tim Brown	1.00
MI29	Curtis Martin	1.00
MI30	Terrell Davis	2.00

1998 SP Authentic Memorabilia

Each card appears in different quanities and could be redeemed for a special piece of autographed memorabilia from the NFL's top rookies.

		NM/M
Common Player:		20.00
Inserted 1:864		
M1	Curtis Enis Ball (signed NFL game football)	20.00
M2	Ryan Leaf Ball (signed NFL game football)	45.00
M3	Randy Moss Ball (signed NFL game football)	300.00
M4	Takeo Spikes Ball (signed NFL game football)	20.00
M5	Andre Wadsworth Ball (signed NFL game football)	20.00
M6	Marcus Nash Ball (signed NFL game football)	20.00
M7	Curtis Enis Mini FB (signed mini football)	30.00
M8	Ryan Leaf Mini FB (signed mini football)	30.00
M9	Randy Moss Mini FB (signed mini football)	200.00
M10	Takeo Spikes Mini FB (signed mini football)	20.00
M11	Andre Wadsworth Mini FB (signed mini football)	20.00
M12	Marcus Nash Mini FB (signed mini football)	20.00
M13	Curtis Enis Helmet (signed NFL helmet)	60.00
M14	Ryan Leaf Helmet (signed NFL helmet)	75.00
M15	Randy Moss Helmet (signed NFL helmet)	400.00
M16	Takeo Spikes Helmet (signed NFL helmet)	85.00
M17	Andre Wadsworth Helmet (signed NFL helmet)	85.00
M18	Marcus Nash Helmet (signed NFL helmet)	100.00
M19	Curtis Enis Mini Helmet (signed mini helmet)	40.00
M20	Ryan Leaf Mini Helmet (signed mini helmet)	20.00
M21	Randy Moss Mini Helmet (signed mini helmet)	200.00
M22	Takeo Spikes Mini Helmet (signed mini helmet)	20.00
M23	Andre Wadsworth Mini Helmet (signed mini helmet)	20.00
M24	Marcus Nash Mini Helmet (signed mini helmet)	20.00
M25	"Players Ink" Autograph Collection	20.00
M26	Brett Favre (game-worn authentics ("1-of-1's"))	20.00
M27	Terrell Davis (game-worn authentics ("1-of-1's"))	20.00
M28	Dan Marino (game-worn authentics ("1-of-1's"))	20.00
M29	Jerry Rice (game-worn authentics ("1-of-1's"))	20.00
M30	Mark Brunell (game-worn authentics ("1-of-1's"))	20.00

1998 SP Authentic Player's Ink

This autographed insert comes in three versions. The base set has the green background, aren't numbered and were inserted 1:23 packs. The first parallel are the Silver cards and each single was sequentially numbered to 100. The last parallel was the Gold version in which each single was numbered to the players jersey number. Some singles were through redemption cards only.

		NM/M
Common Player:		10.00
Inserted 1:23		
Silver Cards:		2X
Production 100 Sets		
TA	Troy Aikman	80.00
BF	Brett Favre	200.00
RL	Ryan Leaf	15.00
DM	Dan Marino	200.00
JR	Jerry Rice	120.00
KS	Kordell Stewart	35.00
JP	Jake Plummer	40.00
KJ	Keyshawn Johnson	35.00
SS	Shannon Sharpe	35.00
MA	Mike Alstott	40.00
BH	Bobby Hoying	10.00
RM	Randy Moss	200.00
KM	Keenan McCardell	10.00
JM	Johnnie Morton	10.00
JA	Jamal Anderson	50.00
OE	Curtis Enis	10.00
MJ	Michael Jackson	10.00
AW	Andre Wadsworth	10.00
GC	Germane Crowell	10.00
BG	Brian Griese	50.00
SH	Skip Hicks	10.00
MN	Marcus Nash	10.00
JP	Jerome Pathon	25.00
TS	Takeo Spikes	25.00
FT	Fred Taylor	40.00
CD	Corey Dillon	30.00
RE	Robert Edwards	45.00
EG	Eddie George	60.00
DL	Dorsey Levens	30.00
TV	Tamarick Vanover	10.00

1998 SP Authentic Special Forces

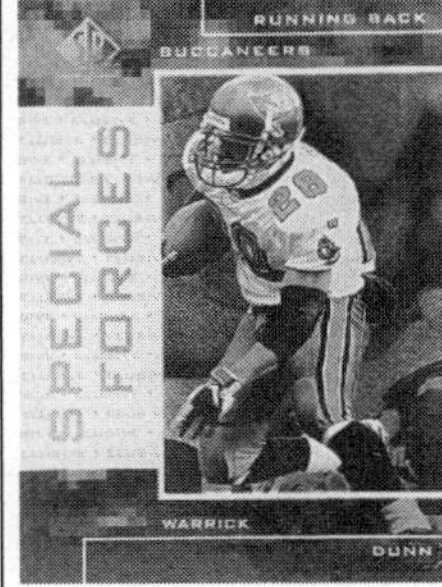

The top specialists in the NFL were showcased in this premium collection set. Each single was sequentially numbered to 1,000.

		NM/M
Complete Set (30):		60.00
Common Player:		.50
Minor Stars:		1.00
Production 1,000 Sets		
S1	Kordell Stewart	1.00
S2	Charles Woodson	3.00
S3	Terrell Davis	4.00
S4	Brett Favre	6.00
S5	Joey Galloway	2.00
S6	Warrick Dunn	1.00
S7	Ryan Leaf	.50
S8	Drew Bledsoe	2.00
S9	Takeo Spikes	1.00
S10	Barry Sanders	5.00
S11	Troy Aikman	4.00
S12	John Elway	4.00
S13	Jerome Bettis	1.00
S14	Karim Abdul-Jabbar	.50
S15	Tony Gonzalez	.50
S16	Steve Young	3.00
S17	Napoleon Kaufman	.50
S18	Andre Wadsworth	.50
S19	Herman Moore	.50
S20	Fred Taylor	1.00
S21	Deion Sanders	1.00
S22	Peyton Manning	4.00
S23	Jerry Rice	4.00
S24	Dan Marino	5.00
S25	Antonio Freeman	1.00
S26	Curtis Enis	.50
S27	Jake Plummer	1.00
S28	Steve McNair	1.00
S29	Mark Brunell	1.00
S30	Robert Edwards	1.00

1998 SPx

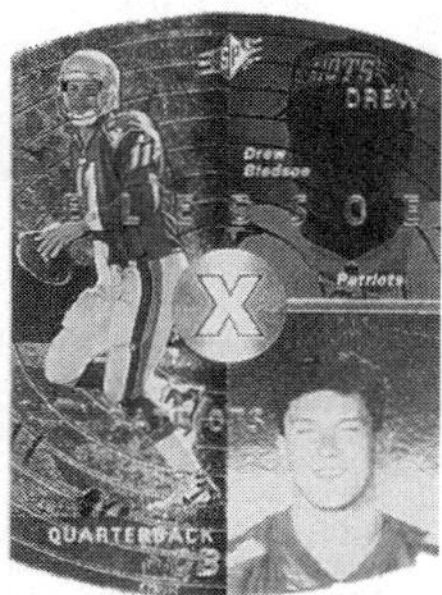

SPx Football features Holoview cards. The 50-card base set utilizes decorative foil and Light F/X on 32-point card stock. Each card features three player photos on the front. SPx Football also has five parallel sets and three inserts. The parallels are Steel Parallel Universe (1:1), Bronze Parallel Universe (1:3), Silver Parallel Universe (1:6), Gold Parallel Universe (1:17) and Grand Finale Parallel Universe (50 total sets). The insert sets are HoloFame (1:54), ProMotion (1:252) and Piece of History (500 total cards). Piece of History cards could be redeemed for a framed, un-cut, numbered HoloFame Holoview sheet.

		NM/M
Complete Set (50):		70.00
Common Player:		.50
Minor Stars:		1.00
Steel Cards:		1.5X
Bronze Cards:		2X
Silver Cards:		2X-4X
Gold Cards:		4X-8X
Pack (3):		4.25
Wax Box (18):		55.00
1	Jake Plummer	1.00
2	Byron Hanspard	1.00
3	Vinny Testaverde	.50
4	Antowain Smith	2.50
5	Kerry Collins	2.00
6	Rae Carruth	1.00
7	Darnell Autry	.50
8	Rick Mirer	.50
9	Jeff Blake	1.00
10	Carl Pickens	.50
11	Troy Aikman	3.50
12	Emmitt Smith	4.00
13	Deion Sanders	1.50
14	John Elway	3.00
15	Terrell Davis	2.00
16	Herman Moore	1.00
17	Barry Sanders	4.00
18	Brett Favre	5.00
19	Reggie White	1.00
20	Marshall Faulk	1.00
21	Mark Brunell	2.50
22	Elvis Grbac	.50
23	Marcus Allen	1.00
24	Karim Abdul-Jabbar	1.00
25	Dan Marino	4.00
26	Cris Carter	.50
27	Drew Bledsoe	3.00
28	Curtis Martin	2.50
29	Heath Shuler	.50
30	Ike Hilliard	1.00
31	Keyshawn Johnson	1.00
32	Jeff George	.50
33	Napoleon Kaufman	1.00
34	Darrell Russell	.50
35	Ricky Watters	1.00
36	Kordell Stewart	1.50
37	Jerome Bettis	1.00
38	Junior Seau	.50
39	Steve Young	2.00
40	Jerry Rice	4.00
41	Joey Galloway	1.00
42	Chris Warren	.50
43	Orlando Pace	1.00
44	Isaac Bruce	1.00
45	Tony Banks	1.00
46	Trent Dilfer	1.00
47	Warrick Dunn	2.00
48	Steve McNair	2.50
49	Eddie George	2.50
50	Terry Allen	.50

1998 SPx Bronze/Gold/Silver/Steel

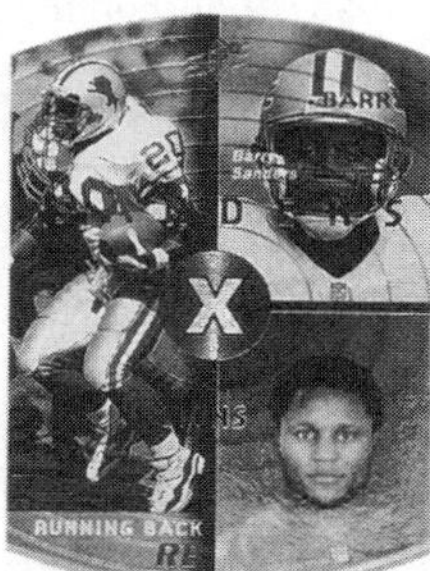

The SPx base set had five parallels, including Steel (1:1), Bronze (1:3), Silver (1:6) and Gold (1:17).

Bronze Cards:	2X
Gold Cards:	4X-8X
Silver Cards:	2X-4X
Steel Cards:	1.5X

1998 SPx Grand Finale

Grand Finale parallels the SPx base set. The all-gold Holoview cards commemorate the final SPx Holoview set. Only 50 sets were produced.

		NM/M
Common Player:		5.00
Minor Stars:		10.00
1	Jake Plummer	25.00
2	Byron Hanspard	10.00
3	Vinny Testaverde	5.00
4	Antowain Smith	25.00
5	Kerry Collins	175.00
6	Rae Carruth	5.00
7	Darnell Autry	5.00
8	Rick Mirer	5.00
9	Jeff Blake	5.00
10	Carl Pickens	5.00
11	Troy Aikman	45.00
12	Emmitt Smith	60.00
13	Deion Sanders	20.00
14	John Elway	45.00
15	Terrell Davis	45.00
16	Herman Moore	10.00
17	Barry Sanders	50.00
18	Brett Favre	60.00
19	Reggie White	10.00
20	Marshall Faulk	35.00
21	Mark Brunell	25.00
22	Elvis Grbac	5.00
23	Marcus Allen	10.00
24	Karim Abdul-Jabbar	10.00
25	Dan Marino	60.00
26	Cris Carter	5.00
27	Drew Bledsoe	35.00
28	Curtis Martin	35.00
29	Heath Shuler	5.00
30	Ike Hilliard	10.00
31	Keyshawn Johnson	10.00
32	Jeff George	5.00
33	Napoleon Kaufman	5.00
34	Darrell Russell	5.00
35	Ricky Watters	10.00
36	Kordell Stewart	15.00
37	Jerome Bettis	10.00
38	Junior Seau	25.00
39	Steve Young	45.00
40	Jerry Rice	50.00
41	Joey Galloway	10.00
42	Chris Warren	5.00
43	Orlando Pace	5.00
44	Isaac Bruce	10.00
45	Tony Banks	10.00
46	Trent Dilfer	10.00
47	Warrick Dunn	35.00
48	Steve McNair	35.00
49	Eddie George	35.00
50	Terry Allen	5.00

1998 SPx HoloFame

HoloFame is a 20-card insert, seeded one per 54 packs. The cards feature top players embossed on Holoview cards with silver decorative foil. Cards are numbered with a "HF" prefix.

		NM/M
Complete Set (20):		110.00
Common Player:		2.00
1	Troy Aikman	6.00
2	Emmitt Smith	8.00
3	John Elway	6.00
4	Terrell Davis	6.00
5	Herman Moore	2.00
6	Reggie White	2.00
7	Brett Favre	10.00
8	Napoleon Kaufman	2.00
9	Dan Marino	10.00
10	Karim Abdul-Jabbar	2.00
11	Cris Carter	2.00
12	Drew Bledsoe	6.00
13	Curtis Martin	6.00
14	Kordell Stewart	4.00
15	Junior Seau	2.00
16	Steve Young	6.00
17	Jerry Rice	8.00
18	Marshall Faulk	2.00
19	Eddie George	4.00
20	Terry Allen	2.00

1998 SPx ProMotion

ProMotion is a 10-card insert (1:252) produced on copper and silver Holoview cards. Cards are numbered with a "P" prefix.

		NM/M
Complete Set (10):		150.00
Common Player:		5.00
1	Troy Aikman	15.00
2	Emmitt Smith	20.00
3	Terrell Davis	15.00
4	Brett Favre	25.00
5	Marcus Allen	10.00
6	Dan Marino	25.00
7	Drew Bledsoe	15.00
8	Ike Hilliard	5.00
9	Warrick Dunn	5.00
10	Eddie George	15.00

1998 SPx Finite

SPx Finite Series One consists of a 190-card base set built from five subsets. The base cards feature silver foil. The set consists of 90 regular cards (numbered to 7,600), 30 Playmakers (5,500), 30 Youth Movement (3,000), 20 Pure Energy (2,500) and 10 Heroes of the Game (1,250). Ten rookie cards were also added to SPx Finite, numbered to 1,998.

		NM/M
Common Player (1-90):		1.00
Minor Stars (1-90):		1.00
Production 7,600 Sets		
Common Player (91-120):		.50
Minor Stars (91-120):		1.00
Production 5,500 Sets		
Common Player (121-150):		.50
Minor Stars (121-150):		1.00
Production 3,000 Sets		
Common Player (151-170):		.50
Minor Stars (151-170):		1.00
Production 2,500 Sets		
Common Player (171-180):		.50
Production 1,250 Sets		
Common Player (181-190):		5.00
Production 1,998 Sets		
Common Player (191-280):		.50
Minor Stars (191-280):		1.00
Common Rookie (191-280):		1.00
Production 10,100 Sets		
Production 1,998 for #218,221,239		
Common Player (281-310):		.50
Minor Stars (281-310):		1.50
Production 7,200 Sets		
Common Player (311-340):		.50
Minor Stars (311-340):		3.00
Production 4,000 Sets		
Production 1,700 for #321,338,339		
Common Player (341-360):		.50
Minor Stars (341-360):		3.00
Production 2,700 Sets		
Common Player (361-370):		2.00
Production 1,620 Sets		
Pack (3):		6.00
Wax Box Series 1 (18):		150.00
Wax Box Series 2 (18):		100.00
1	Jake Plummer	1.00
2	Eric Swann	1.00
3	Rob Moore	1.00
4	Jamal Anderson	2.00
5	Byron Hanspard	1.00
6	Cornelius Bennett	1.00
7	Michael Jackson	1.00
8	Peter Boulware	1.00
9	Jermaine Lewis	1.00
10	Antowain Smith	3.00
11	Bruce Smith	1.00
12	Bryce Paup	1.00
13	Rae Carruth	1.00
14	Michael Bates	1.00
15	Fred Lane	1.00
16	Darnell Autry	1.00
17	Curtis Conway	2.00
18	Erik Kramer	1.00
19	Corey Dillon	3.50
20	Darnay Scott	1.00
21	Reinard Wilson	1.00
22	Troy Aikman	5.00
23	David LaFleur	1.00
24	Emmitt Smith	8.00
25	John Elway	5.00
26	John Mobley	1.00
27	Terrell Davis	3.00
28	Rod Smith	2.00
29	Bryant Westbrook	1.00
30	Scott Mitchell	1.00
31	Barry Sanders	8.00
32	Dorsey Levens	2.00
33	Antonio Freeman	2.00
34	Reggie White	2.00
35	Marshall Faulk	3.00
36	Marvin Harrison	2.00
37	Ken Dilger	1.00
38	Mark Brunell	2.00
39	Keenan McCardell	1.00
40	Renaldo Wynn	1.00
41	Marcus Allen	2.00
42	Elvis Grbac	1.00
43	Andre Rison	1.00
44	Yatil Green	1.00
45	Zach Thomas	1.00
46	Karim Abdul-Jabbar	2.00
47	John Randle	1.00
48	Brad Johnson	2.00
49	Jake Reed	1.00
50	Danny Wuerffel	1.00
51	Andre Hastings	1.00
52	Drew Bledsoe	3.00
53	Terry Glenn	2.00
54	Ty Law	1.00
55	Danny Kanell	1.00
56	Tiki Barber	2.00
57	Jesse Armstead	1.00
58	Glenn Foley	1.00
59	James Farrior	1.00
60	Wayne Chrebet	2.00
61	Tim Brown	2.00
62	Napoleon Kaufman	1.00
63	Darrell Russell	1.00
64	Bobby Hoying	1.00
65	Irving Fryar	1.00
66	Charlie Garner	1.00
67	Will Blackwell	1.00
68	Kordell Stewart	2.00
69	Levon Kirkland	1.00
70	Tony Banks	1.00
71	Ryan McNeil	1.00
72	Isaac Bruce	2.00
73	Tony Martin	1.00
74	Junior Seau	2.00
75	Natrone Means	2.00
76	Jerry Rice	5.00
77	Garrison Hearst	2.00
78	Terrell Owens	2.00
79	Warren Moon	2.00
80	Joey Galloway	2.00
81	Chad Brown	1.00
82	Warrick Dunn	2.00
83	Mike Alstott	2.00
84	Hardy Nickerson	1.00
85	Steve McNair	3.00
86	Chris Sanders	1.00
87	Darryll Lewis	1.00
88	Gus Frerotte	1.00
89	Terry Allen	1.00
90	Chris Dishman	1.00
91	Kordell Stewart	3.00
92	Jerry Rice	8.00
93	Michael Irvin	3.00
94	Brett Favre	15.00
95	Jeff George	3.00
96	Joey Galloway	3.00
97	John Elway	8.00
98	Troy Aikman	8.00
99	Steve Young	5.00
100	Andre Rison	1.50
101	Ben Coates	1.50
102	Robert Brooks	1.50
103	Dan Marino	10.00
104	Isaac Bruce	3.00
105	Junior Seau	3.00
106	Jake Plummer	2.00
107	Curtis Conway	3.00
108	Jeff Blake	2.00
109	Rod Smith	3.00
110	Barry Sanders	10.00
111	Deion Sanders	4.00
112	Drew Bledsoe	7.00
113	Emmitt Smith	10.00
114	Herman Moore	3.00
115	Dorsey Levens	3.00
116	Jimmy Smith	3.00
117	Tony Martin	1.50
118	Carl Pickens	1.50
119	Keyshawn Johnson	3.00
120	Cris Carter	3.00
121	Warrick Dunn	4.00
122	Marshall Faulk	4.00
123	Trent Dilfer	4.00
124	Napoleon Kaufman	3.00
125	Corey Dillon	5.00
126	Darrell Russell	2.00
127	Danny Kanell	2.00
128	Reidel Anthony	2.00
129	Steve McNair	6.00
130	Ike Hilliard	2.00
131	Tony Banks	3.00
132	Yatil Green	2.00
133	J.J. Stokes	2.00
134	Fred Lane	2.00
135	Bryant Westbrook	2.00
136	Jake Plummer	3.00
137	Byron Hanspard	2.00
138	Rae Carruth	2.00
139	Keyshawn Johnson	4.00
140	Jim Druckenmiller	2.00
141	Amani Toomer	2.00
142	Troy Davis	2.00
143	Antowain Smith	4.00
144	Shawn Springs	2.00
145	Rickey Dudley	2.00
146	Terry Glenn	3.00
147	Johnnie Morton	2.00
148	David LaFleur	2.00
149	Eddie Kennison	2.00
150	Bobby Hoying	2.00
151	Junior Seau	4.00
152	Shannon Sharpe	4.00
153	Bruce Smith	2.50
154	Brett Favre	22.00
155	Emmitt Smith	15.00
156	Keenan McCardell	2.50
157	Kordell Stewart	6.00
158	Troy Aikman	12.00
159	Steve Young	8.00
160	Tim Brown	5.00
161	Eddie George	6.00
162	Herman Moore	3.00
163	Dan Marino	12.00
164	Dorsey Levens	5.00
165	Jerry Rice	12.00
166	Warren Sapp	2.50
167	Robert Smith	3.00
168	Mark Brunell	3.00
169	Terrell Davis	6.00
170	Jerome Bettis	3.00
171	Dan Marino	30.00
172	Barry Sanders	30.00
173	Marcus Allen	6.00
174	Brett Favre	35.00
175	Warrick Dunn	10.00
176	Eddie George	12.00
177	John Elway	20.00
178	Troy Aikman	20.00
179	Cris Carter	6.00
180	Terrell Davis	15.00
181	*Peyton Manning*	120.00
182	*Ryan Leaf*	15.00
183	*Andre Wadsworth*	15.00
184	*Charles Woodson*	35.00
185	*Curtis Enis*	20.00
186	*Grant Wistrom*	12.00
187	*Fred Taylor*	40.00
188	*Takeo Spikes*	20.00
189	*Kevin Dyson*	20.00
190	*Robert Edwards*	20.00
191	Adrian Murrell	1.00
192	Simeon Rice	.50
193	Frank Sanders	.50
194	Chris Chandler	1.00
195	Terrance Mathis	.50
196	*Keith Brooking*	1.50
197	Jim Harbaugh	1.00
198	Errict Rhett	.50
199	*Patrick Johnson*	1.00
200	Rob Johnson	1.00
201	Andre Reed	1.00
202	Thurman Thomas	1.00
203	Kerry Collins	1.00
204	William Floyd	.50
205	Sean Gilbert	.50
206	Bobby Engram	.50
207	Edgar Bennett	.50
208	Walt Harris	.50
209	Carl Pickens	1.00
210	Neil O'Donnell	1.00
211	Tony McGee	.50
212	Deion Sanders	1.50
213	Michael Irvin	1.00
214	*Greg Ellis*	1.00
215	Shannon Sharpe	1.00
216	Neil Smith	.50
217	*Marcus Nash*	4.00
218	*Brian Griese*	40.00
219	Johnnie Morton	.50
220	Herman Moore	1.00
221	*Charlie Batch*	4.00
222	Robert Brooks	.50
223	Mark Chmura	1.00
224	Brett Favre	6.00
225	*Jerome Pathon*	2.00
226	Zack Crockett	.50
227	Dan Footman	.50
228	Jimmy Smith	1.00
229	Bryce Paup	.50
230	James Stewart	.50
231	Derrick Thomas	.50
232	Derrick Alexander	.50
233	Tony Gonzalez	.50
234	Dan Marino	5.00
235	O.J. McDuffie	.50
236	Troy Drayton	.50
237	Cris Carter	1.00
238	Robert Smith	1.00
239	*Randy Moss*	75.00
240	Lamar Smith	.50
241	Sean Dawkins	.50
242	Alex Molden	.50
243	Ben Coates	1.00
244	Ted Johnson	.50
245	Sedrick Shaw	.50
246	Ike Hilliard	.50
247	Jason Sehorn	.50
248	Michael Strahan	.50
249	Keyshawn Johnson	1.00
250	Curtis Martin	1.50
251	Jeff George	.50
252	Rickey Dudley	.50
253	James Jett	.50
254	Bobby Taylor	.50
255	Rodney Peete	.50
256	William Thomas	.50
257	Jerome Bettis	1.00
258	Charles Johnson	.50
259	*Chris Fuamatu-Ma'afala*	2.50
260	Eddie Kennison	.50
261	*Az-Zahir Hakim*	7.00
262	*Robert Holcombe*	3.00
263	Bryan Still	.50
264	*Mikhael Ricks*	1.00
265	Charlie Jones	.50
266	J.J. Stokes	1.00
267	Marc Edwards	.50
268	Steve Young	2.00
269	Ricky Watters	1.00
270	Cortez Kennedy	.50
271	Shawn Springs	.50
272	Trent Dilfer	1.00
273	Warren Sapp	.50
274	Reidel Anthony	1.00
275	Yancey Thigpen	.50
276	Chris Sanders	.50
277	Eddie George	2.50
278	Leslie Shepherd	.50
279	*Skip Hicks*	2.00
280	Dana Stubblefield	.50
281	John Elway	5.00
282	Brett Favre	8.00
283	Junior Seau	1.50
284	Barry Sanders	8.00
285	Jerry Rice	5.00
286	Antonio Freeman	1.50
287	Peyton Manning	20.00
288	Warrick Dunn	3.00
289	Steve Young	2.00
290	Dan Marino	6.00
291	Jerome Bettis	1.50
292	Ryan Leaf	2.00
293	Deion Sanders	1.50
294	Eddie George	3.00
295	Joey Galloway	1.50
296	Troy Aikman	4.00
297	Andre Wadsworth	1.50
298	Terrell Davis	3.00
299	Steve McNair	2.00
300	Jake Plummer	3.00
301	Emmitt Smith	6.00
302	Isaac Bruce	1.50
303	Kordell Stewart	3.00
304	Dorsey Levens	1.50
305	Antowain Smith	1.75
306	Drew Bledsoe	3.00
307	Marshall Faulk	1.50
308	Herman Moore	1.50
309	Mark Brunell	3.00
310	Charles Woodson	6.00
311	Peyton Manning	30.00
312	Curtis Enis	10.00
313	*Terry Fair*	3.00
314	Andre Wadsworth	5.00
315	*Anthony Simmons*	3.00
316	*Jacquez Green*	12.00
317	Takeo Spikes	4.00
318	*Vonnie Holliday*	3.00
319	*Kyle Turley*	2.00
320	Keith Brooking	4.00
321	Randy Moss	30.00
322	*Shaun Williams*	2.00
323	Greg Ellis	2.00
324	Mikhael Ricks	2.00
325	Charles Woodson	10.00
326	*Corey Chavous*	2.00
327	*Stephen Alexander*	7.00
328	Marcus Nash	3.00
329	*Tre Thomas*	2.00
330	*Duane Starks*	3.00
331	*John Avery*	3.00
332	Kevin Dyson	7.00
333	Fred Taylor	10.00
334	Grant Wistrom	2.00
335	Ryan Leaf	3.00
336	Robert Edwards	5.00
337	*Jason Peter*	2.00
338	Brian Griese	15.00
339	Charlie Batch	5.00
340	Patrick Johnson	4.00
341	John Elway	10.00
342	Curtis Enis	3.00
343	Antonio Freeman	2.00
344	Mark Brunell	3.00
345	Robert Edwards	4.00
346	Ryan Leaf	3.00
347	Steve Young	5.00
348	Jerome Bettis	3.00
349	Antowain Smith	3.00
350	Tim Brown	4.00
351	Peyton Manning	30.00
352	Troy Aikman	8.00
353	Natrone Means	3.00
354	Dan Marino	15.00
355	Junior Seau	1.50
356	Brad Johnson	3.00
357	Jerry Rice	8.00
358	Drew Bledsoe	6.00
359	Fred Taylor	6.00
360	Emmitt Smith	12.00
361	Terrell Davis	10.00
362	Kordell Stewart	4.00
363	Barry Sanders	15.00
364	Jake Plummer	3.00
365	Brett Favre	20.00
366	Curtis Enis	3.00
367	Eddie George	10.00
368	Napoleon Kaufman	5.00
369	Randy Moss	40.00
370	Warrick Dunn	5.00

1998 SPx Finite Radiance

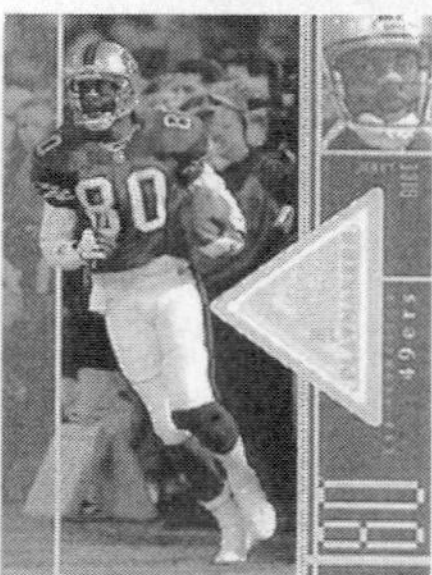

Radiance is a gold-foil parallel of the SPx Finite base set. Regular cards are numbered to 3,800, Playmakers to 2,750, Youth Movement to 1,500, Pure Energy to 1,000 and Heroes of the Game to 100. The ten rookie cards are numbered to 50 in this set.

	NM/M
Cards (1-90):	2X
Production 3,800 Sets	
Cards (91-120):	2X
Production 2,750 Sets	
Cards (121-150):	2X
Production 1,500 Sets	
Cards (151-170):	2X
Production 1,000 Sets	
Cards (171-180):	5X
Production 100 Sets	
Cards (181-190):	4X
Production 50 Sets	
Cards (191-280):	2X
Production 5,050 Sets	
Production 500 for #218,221,239	
Cards (281-310):	2X
Production 3,600 Sets	
Cards (311-340):	2X
Production 1,885 Sets	
Production 350 for #321,338,339	
Cards (341-360):	2X
Production 900 Sets	
Cards (361-370):	2X
Production 540 Sets	

1998 SPx Finite Spectrum

Spectrum is a rainbow foil version of the SPx Finite base set. Regular cards are numbered to 1,900, Playmakers to 1,375, Youth Movement to 750, Pure Energy to 50 and Heroes of the Game is a 1-of-1 set. The ten rookie cards are also 1-of-1 in this parallel.

Cards (1-90):	3X
Production 1,900 Sets	
Cards (91-120):	3X
Production 1,375 Sets	
Cards (121-150):	4X
Production 750 Sets	
Cards (151-170):	5X-10X
Production 50 Sets	
Cards (171-190):	
Production 1 Set	
Cards (191-280):	4X-8X
Rookies (191-280):	1.5X-3X
Production 325 Sets	
Cards (281-310):	5X-10X
Rookies (281-310):	1.5X-3X
Production 150 Sets	
Cards (311-340):	4X-8X
#321,338,339:	2X-4X
Production 50 Sets	
Cards (341-360):	8X-20X
Rookies(341-360):	3X-5X
Production 25 Sets	
Cards (361-370):	
Production 1 Set	

1998 SPx Finite UD Authentics Autographs

	NM/M
Complete Set (4):	500.00
Common Player:	75.00
Troy Aikman(1992)	75.00
Dan Marino(400)	225.00
Joe Montana (1995)	135.00
Roger Staubach (463)	100.00

1999 SP Authentic

This 145-card set included 55 rookies that were sequentially numbered to 1,999. Parallel sets included Excitement and Excitement Gold. Other insert sets include: Authentic Athletic, Buy Back Autographs, Maximum Impact, New Classics, NFL Headquarters, Player's Ink, Rookie Blitz and Supremacy. SRP was $4.99 for five-card packs.

		NM/M
Common Player:		.25
Minor Stars:		.50
Common Rookie:		8.00
Production 1,999 Sets		
Pack (5):		7.00
Wax Box (24):		150.00
1	Jake Plummer	.75
2	Adrian Murrell	.25
3	Frank Sanders	.50
4	Jamal Anderson	.75
5	Chris Chandler	.50
6	Terance Mathis	.25
7	Priest Holmes	1.50
8	Jermaine Lewis	.25
9	Antowain Smith	.75
10	Doug Flutie	.75
11	Eric Moulds	.75
12	Muhsin Muhammad	.75
13	Tim Biakabutuka	.50
14	Wesley Walls	.50
15	Curtis Enis	.75
16	Bobby Engram	.25
17	Corey Dillon	.75
18	Darnay Scott	.50
19	Terry Kirby	.25
20	Ty Detmer	.25
21	Troy Aikman	2.00
22	Michael Irvin	.50
23	Emmitt Smith	3.00
24	Terrell Davis	1.50
25	Brian Griese	1.00
26	Rod Smith	.75
27	Shannon Sharpe	.75
28	Barry Sanders	3.00
29	Charlie Batch	.75
30	Herman Moore	.75
31	Johnnie Morton	.25
32	Brett Favre	4.00
33	Antonio Freeman	.75
34	Dorsey Levens	.75
35	Mark Chmura	.50
36	Peyton Manning	3.00
37	Marvin Harrison	.75
38	Mark Brunell	1.25
39	Fred Taylor	1.00
40	Jimmy Smith	.75
41	Elvis Grbac	.50
42	Andre Rison	.50
43	Dan Marino	3.00
44	O.J. McDuffie	.25
45	Yatil Green	.25
46	Randall Cunningham	.75
47	Randy Moss	3.00
48	Robert Smith	.75
49	Cris Carter	.75
50	Drew Bledsoe	1.25
51	Ben Coates	.50
52	Terry Glenn	.75
53	Eddie Kennison	.25
54	Cam Cleeland	.50
55	Ike Hilliard	.50
56	Gary Brown	.25
57	Kerry Collins	.50
58	Vinny Testaverde	.50
59	Keyshawn Johnson	.75
60	Wayne Chrebet	.75
61	Curtis Martin	.75
62	Tim Brown	.50
63	Napoleon Kaufman	.75
64	Charles Woodson	.75
65	Duce Staley	.75
66	Charles Johnson	.25
67	Kordell Stewart	.75
68	Jerome Bettis	.75
69	Marshall Faulk	.75
70	Isaac Bruce	.75
71	Trent Green	.75
72	Jim Harbaugh	.50
73	Junior Seau	.50
74	Natrone Means	.50
75	Steve Young	1.25
76	Jerry Rice	3.00
77	Terrell Owens	.75
78	Lawrence Phillips	.25
79	Joey Galloway	.75
80	Ricky Watters	.50
81	Jon Kitna	.75
82	Warrick Dunn	.75
83	Trent Dilfer	.50
84	Mike Alstott	.75
85	Eddie George	1.00
86	Steve McNair	1.00
87	Yancey Thigpen	.25
88	Brad Johnson	.75
89	Skip Hicks	.50
90	Michael Westbrook	.50
91	*Ricky Williams*	150.00
92	*Tim Couch*	60.00
93	*Akili Smith*	20.00
94	*Edgerrin James*	150.00
95	*Donovan McNabb*	140.00
96	*Torry Holt*	75.00
97	*Cade McNown*	25.00
98	*Shaun King*	25.00
99	*Daunte Culpepper*	100.00
100	*Brock Huard*	25.00
101	*Chris Claiborne*	15.00
102	*James Johnson*	25.00
103	*Rob Konrad*	20.00
104	*Peerless Price*	50.00
105	*Kevin Faulk*	20.00
106	*Andy Katzenmoyer*	20.00
107	*Troy Edwards*	20.00
108	*Kevin Johnson*	20.00
109	*Mike Cloud*	20.00
110	*David Boston*	50.00
111	*Champ Bailey*	25.00
112	*D'Wayne Bates*	20.00
113	*Joe Germaine*	20.00
114	*Antoine Winfield*	20.00
115	*Fernando Bryant*	15.00
116	*Jevon Kearse*	40.00
117	*Chris McAlister*	20.00
118	*Brandon Stokley*	15.00
119	*Karsten Bailey*	20.00
120	*Daylon McCutcheon*	15.00
121	*Jermaine Fazande*	20.00
122	*Joel Makovicka*	15.00
123	*Ebenezer Ekuban*	20.00
124	*Joe Montgomery*	20.00
125	*Sean Bennett*	20.00
126	*Na Brown*	15.00
127	*De'Mond Parker*	15.00
128	*Sedrick Irvin*	15.00
129	*Terry Jackson*	15.00
130	*Jeff Paulk*	15.00
131	*Cecil Collins*	20.00
132	*Bobby Collins*	15.00
133	*Amos Zereoue*	30.00
134	*Travis McGriff*	15.00
135	*Larry Parker*	15.00
136	*Wane McGarity*	15.00
137	*Cecil Martin*	15.00
138	*Al Wilson*	15.00
139	*Jim Kleinsasser*	25.00
140	*Dat Nguyen*	20.00
141	*Marty Booker*	40.00
142	*Reggie Kelly*	15.00
143	*Scott Covington*	20.00
144	*Antwan Edwards*	20.00
145	*Craig Yeast*	20.00

1999 SP Authentic Athletic

This 10-card insert set included the most exciting and athletic players in the NFL. Singles were inserted 1:10 packs.

		NM/M
Complete Set (10):		20.00
Common Player:		1.00
Inserted 1:10		
1	Randy Moss	4.00
2	Steve McNair	1.00
3	Jamal Anderson	1.00
4	Curtis Martin	1.00
5	Kordell Stewart	1.00
6	Barry Sanders	4.00
7	Fred Taylor	1.00
8	Doug Flutie	1.00
9	Emmitt Smith	4.00
10	Steve Young	3.00

1999 SP Authentic Buy-Back Autographs

Troy Aikman
Jerome Bettis
Drew Bledsoe
Tim Brown
Mark Brunell
Wayne Chrebet
Terrell Davis
Warrick Dunn
Marshall Faulk
Joey Galloway
Eddie George
Brad Johnson
Peyton Manning
Dan Marino
Natrone Means
Herman Moore
Randy Moss
Terrell Owens
Jake Plummer
Jerry Rice

1999 SP Authentic Excitement

This was a 145-card parallel to the base set. Each single was sequentially numbered to 250 and printed on the front of the cards.

	NM/M
Excitement Cards:	3X-5X
Excitement Rookies:	1.5X
Production 250 Sets	

1999 SP Authentic Excitement Gold

This was a 145-card parallel to the base set. Each single was sequentially numbered to 25 and printed on the front of the singles.

	NM/M
Excitement Cards:	20X-50X
Excitement Rookies:	3X
Production 25 Sets	

1999 SP Authentic Maximum Impact

This 10-card insert set included players who provide the greatest contribution to their team's overall success. Singles were inserted 1:4 packs.

		NM/M
Complete Set (10):		12.00
Common Player:		1.00
Inserted 1:4		
1	Jerry Rice	3.00
2	Eddie George	1.50
3	Marshall Faulk	1.00
4	Keyshawn Johnson	1.00
5	Terrell Davis	2.00
6	Warrick Dunn	1.00
7	Jerome Bettis	1.00
8	Drew Bledsoe	2.00
9	Curtis Martin	1.00
10	Brett Favre	6.00

1999 SP Authentic New Classics

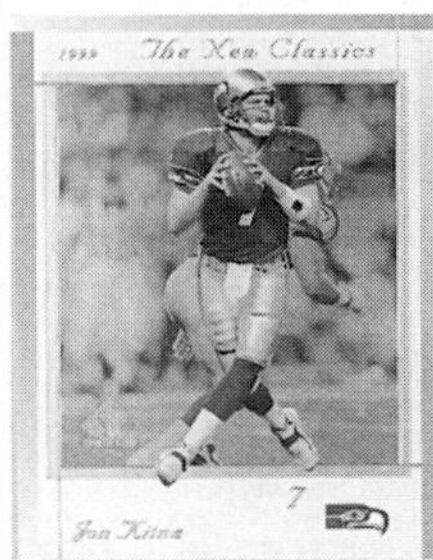

This 10-card insert set included players to watch for the future. Singles were inserted 1:23 packs.

		NM/M
Complete Set (10):		25.00
Common Player:		1.00
Inserted 1:23		
1	Steve McNair	1.00
2	Jon Kitna	1.00
3	Curtis Enis	1.00
4	Peyton Manning	4.00
5	Fred Taylor	1.00
6	Randy Moss	4.00
7	Donovan McNabb	3.00
8	Terrell Owens	1.00
9	Keyshawn Johnson	1.00
10	Ricky Williams	5.00

1999 SP Authentic NFL Headquarters

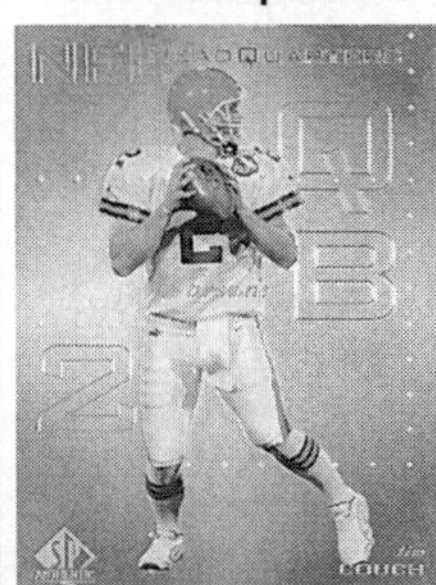

This 10-card insert set included the game's hottest quarterbacks. Singles were inserted 1:10 packs.

		NM/M
Complete Set (10):		20.00
Common Player:		1.00
Inserted 1:10		
1	Brett Favre	5.00
2	Jake Plummer	1.00
3	Charlie Batch	1.00
4	Akili Smith	1.00
5	Troy Aikman	3.00
6	Drew Bledsoe	3.00
7	Dan Marino	5.00
8	Jon Kitna	1.00
9	Mark Brunell	2.00
10	Tim Couch	3.00

1999 SP Authentic Player's Ink

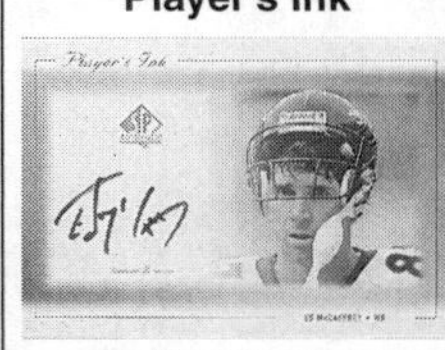

This 40-card insert set included autographs of the top players in the NFL. Many of the rookies were included and singles were inserted 1:23 packs. A parallel Level 2 version was also released and each was sequentially numbered to 100.

		NM/M
Common Player:		10.00
Inserted 1:23		
Version 2 Cards:		2X
Production 100 Cards		
TA	Troy Aikman	125.00
JA	Jamal Anderson	10.00
CB	Champ Bailey	10.00
CH	Charlie Batch	10.00
JB	Jerome Bettis	10.00
MB	Michael Bishop	10.00
DR	Drew Bledsoe	75.00
DB	David Boston	45.00
BR	Mark Brunell	45.00
WC	Wayne Chrebet	10.00
CL	Michael Cloud	10.00
TC	Tim Couch	50.00
DC	Daunte Culpepper	60.00
TD	Terrell Davis	75.00
CD	Corey Dillon	35.00
TE	Troy Edwards	15.00
KF	Kevin Faulk	10.00
MF	Marshall Faulk	50.00
DF	Doug Flutie	15.00
AF	Antonio Freeman	10.00
JG	Joey Galloway	10.00
EG	Eddie George	25.00
TH	Torry Holt	25.00
BH	Brock Huard	10.00
EJ	Edgerrin James	75.00
BJ	Brad Johnson	30.00
SK	Shaun King	15.00
PM	Peyton Manning	125.00
DM	Dan Marino	225.00
ED	Ed McCaffrey	10.00
CM	Cade McNown	10.00
NM	Natrone Means	10.00
HM	Herman Moore	10.00
RM	Randy Moss	125.00
EM	Eric Moulds	10.00
TO	Terrell Owens	10.00
JP	Jake Plummer	35.00
JR	Jerry Rice	125.00
SS	Shannon Sharpe	10.00
AS	Akili Smith	10.00

1999 SP Authentic Rookie Blitz

This 19-card insert set included the top rookies from the 1999 season. Singles were inserted 1:11 packs.

		NM/M
Complete Set (19):		45.00
Common Player:		1.00
Inserted 1:11		
1	Edgerrin James	5.00
2	Tim Couch	3.00
3	Daunte Culpepper	4.00
4	Champ Bailey	1.00
5	Donovan McNabb	4.00
6	Kevin Johnson	2.00
7	Shaun King	1.00
8	Peerless Price	3.00
9	David Boston	3.00
10	Ricky Williams	6.00
11	Akili Smith	1.00
12	Kevin Faulk	1.00
13	D'Wayne Bates	1.00
14	Brock Huard	1.00
15	Rob Konrad	1.00
16	Torry Holt	3.00
17	Troy Edwards	2.00
18	Cade McNown	2.00
19	Cecil Collins	1.00

1999 SP Authentic Supremacy

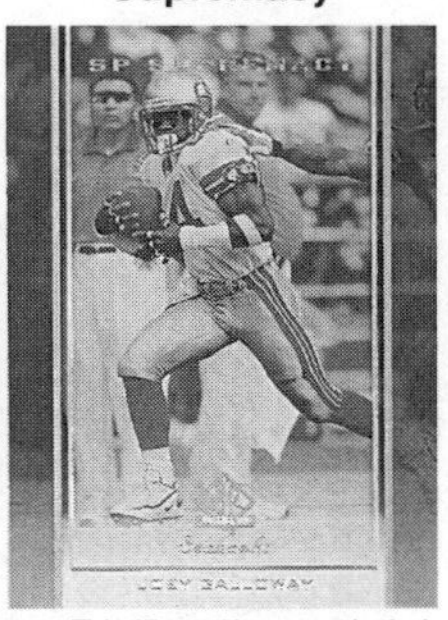

This 12-card insert set included the premier performers in the NFL. Singles were inserted 1:23 packs.

		NM/M
Complete Set (12):		40.00
Common Player:		1.00
Inserted 1:23		
1	Terrell Davis	4.00
2	Joey Galloway	1.00
3	Dan Marino	6.00
4	Brett Favre	6.00
5	Emmitt Smith	5.00
6	Barry Sanders	5.00
7	Curtis Martin	2.00
8	Jamal Anderson	1.00
9	Jake Plummer	1.00
10	Randy Moss	4.00
11	Tim Couch	3.00
12	Peyton Manning	4.00

1999 SP Authentic Walter Payton

A total of 100 Payton autographed cards were released along with 34 Payton Game-Jersey autographed cards. Each card was randomly inserted.

		NM/M
WPA	Walter Payton AUTO/100	350.00
WPSP	Walter Payton JER/AUTO 34	3,000

1999 SP Signature

This 180-card release from Upper Deck includes both past and present stars from the NFL. The last 10 cards in the set never made it into the product and were later released to dealers from the manufacture. Inserts include: Autographs and Montana Great Performances.

		NM/M
Complete Set (180):		475.00
Common Player:		.50
Minor Stars:		1.00
Pack (2):		45.00
Wax Box (12):		400.00
Rookie Pack (2):		30.00
1	Jake Plummer	1.00
2	Mario Bates	.50
3	Adrian Murrell	.50
4	Jamal Anderson	1.00
5	Chris Chandler	.50
6	Bob Christian	.50
7	O.J. Santiago	.50
8	Jim Harbaugh	.50
9	Priest Holmes	1.50
10	Ray Lewis	.50
11	Michael Jackson	.50
12	Tony Siragusa	.50
13	Doug Flutie	1.00
14	Antowain Smith	1.00
15	Eric Moulds	1.00
16	William Floyd	.50
17	Fred Lane	.50
18	Muhsin Muhammad	.50
19	Bobby Engram	.50
20	Curtis Enis	.50
21	Curtis Conway	1.00
22	Corey Dillon	1.50
23	Carl Pickens	.50
24	Ashley Ambrose	.50

25	Darnay Scott	.50
26	Troy Aikman	3.00
27	Jason Garrett	.50
28	Emmitt Smith	4.50
29	Deion Sanders	1.25
30	John Elway	4.50
31	Terrell Davis	2.00
32	Ed McCaffrey	1.00
33	John Mobley	.50
34	Maa Tanuvasa	.50
35	Ray Crockett	.50
36	Barry Sanders	4.00
37	Herman Moore	.50
38	Charlie Batch	.50
39	Robert Porcher	.50
40	Tommy Vardell	.50
41	Brett Favre	6.00
42	Antonio Freeman	1.00
43	Darick Holmes	.50
44	Robert Brooks	.50
45	Peyton Manning	4.00
46	Marshall Faulk	2.50
47	Torrance Small	.50
48	Lamont Warren	.50
49	Zack Crockett	.50
50	Mark Brunell	1.00
51	Pete Mitchell	.50
52	Fred Taylor	1.00
53	Jimmy Smith	1.00
54	Andre Rison	1.00
55	Rich Gannon	.50
56	Donnell Bennett	.50
57	Dan Marino	4.50
58	Karim Abdul	.50
59	Troy Drayton	.50
60	Jason Taylor	.50
61	Cris Carter	1.25
62	Randy Moss	4.00
63	Robert Smith	1.00
64	Leroy Hoard	.50
65	Randall Cunningham	1.25
66	Derrick Alexander	.50
67	Drew Bledsoe	2.00
68	Robert Edwards	.50
69	Willie McGinest	.50
70	Chris Slade	.50
71	Terry Glenn	.75
72	Ty Law	.50
73	Kerry Collins	.50
74	Sean Dawkins	.50
75	Cameron Cleeland	.50
76	Sammy Knight	.50
77	Danny Kanell	.50
78	Gary Brown	.50
79	Chris Calloway	.50
80	Curtis Martin	1.25
81	Keyshawn Johnson	1.25
82	Vinny Testaverde	1.00
83	Leon Johnson	.50
84	Kyle Brady	.50
85	Tim Brown	1.00
86	Jeff George	.50
87	Rickey Dudley	.50
88	Napoleon Kaufman	.50
89	James Jett	.50
90	Harvey Williams	.50
91	Koy Detmer	.50
92	Duce Staley	.50
93	Charlie Garner	.50
94	Jerome Bettis	1.00
95	Kordell Stewart	1.00
96	Courtney Hawkins	.50
97	Hines Ward	1.00
98	Isaac Bruce	1.00
99	Tony Banks	.50
100	Greg Hill	.50
101	Keith Lyle	.50
102	Ryan Leaf	.50
103	Craig Whelihan	.50
104	Charlie Jones	.50
105	Junior Seau	1.00
106	Natrone Means	.50
107	Rodney Harrison	.50
108	Steve Young	2.00
109	Garrison Hearst	1.00
110	Jerry Rice	4.00
111	Chris Doleman	.50
112	Roy Barker	.50
113	Ricky Watters	1.00
114	Jon Kitna	.50
115	Joey Galloway	.75
116	Chad Brown	.50
117	Michael Sinclair	.50
118	Warrick Dunn	1.00
119	Mike Alstott	1.25
120	Bert Emanuel	.50
121	Hardy Nickerson	.50
122	Eddie George	1.50
123	Steve McNair	1.50
124	Yancey Thigpen	.50
125	Frank Wycheck	.50
126	Jackie Harris	.50
127	Terry Allen	.50
128	Trent Green	1.00
129	Jamie Asher	.50
130	Brian Mitchell	.50
131	Lance Alworth	1.00
132	Fred Biletnikoff	1.25
133	Mel Blount	.50
134	Cliff Branch	.50
135	Harold Carmichael	.50
136	Larry Csonka	1.25
137	Eric Dickerson	1.00
138	Randy Gradishar	.50
139	Joe Greene	1.00
140	Jack Ham	.50
141	Ted Hendricks	.50
142	Charlie Joiner	1.00
143	Ed Jones	.50
144	Billy Kilmer	.50
145	Paul Krause	.50
146	James Lofton	.50
147	Archie Manning	1.00
148	Don Maynard	1.00
149	Ozzie Newsome	.50
150	Jim Otto	.50
151	Lee Roy Selmon	.50
152	Billy Sims	1.00
153	Mike Singletary	1.00
154	Ken Stabler	1.50
155	John Stallworth	1.00
156	Roger Staubach	2.00
157	Charley Taylor	.50
158	Paul Warfield	1.25
159	Kellen Winslow	1.00
160	Jack Youngblood	.50
161	Bill Bergey	.50
162	Raymond Berry	.50
163	Chuck Howley	.50
164	Rocky Bleier	.50
165	Russ Francis	.50
166	Drew Pearson	.50
167	Mercury Morris	.50
168	Dick Anderson	.50
169	Earl Morrall	.50
170	Jim Hart	.50
171	*Ricky Williams*	30.00
172	*Cade McNown*	6.00
173	*Tim Couch*	10.00
174	*Daunte Culpepper*	30.00
175	*Akili Smith*	6.00
176	*Brock Huard*	5.00
177	*Donovan McNabb*	30.00
178	*Michael Bishop*	5.00
179	*Shaun King*	6.00
180	*Tory Holt*	15.00

1999 SP Signature Autographs

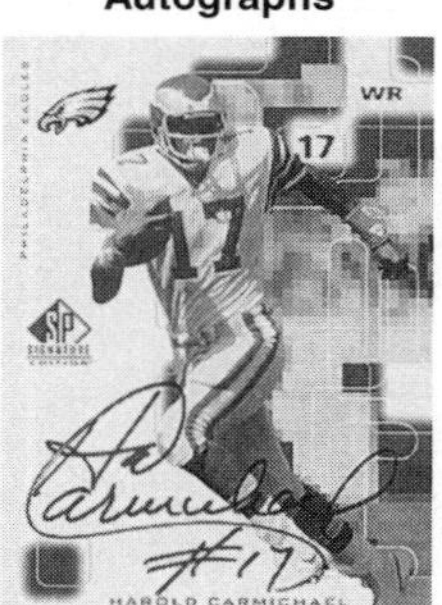

Cards in this insert are the same as the base except for the signature on the front. The backs are different then the regular base card. Singles were inserted one-per-pack. A Gold parallel was produced and inserted 1:59 packs.

		NM/M
Common Player:		10.00
Minor Stars:		20.00
Inserted 1:1		
Gold Cards:		2X
Inserted 1:59		
KA	Karim Abdul	20.00
TA	Troy Aikman	125.00
DA	Derrick Alexander	10.00
MA	Mike Alstott	50.00
AA	Ashley Ambrose	10.00
AN	Dick Anderson	10.00
TE	Jamie Asher	10.00
DE	Roy Barker	10.00
CB	Charlie Batch	20.00
MB	Mario Bates	10.00
DB	Donnell Bennett	10.00
BB	Bill Bergey	10.00
RY	Raymond Berry	25.00
MI	Michael Bishop	50.00
ML	Mel Blount	20.00
KB	Kyle Brady	10.00
RB	Robert Brooks	20.00
LB	Chad Brown	10.00
GB	Gary Brown	10.00
TB	Tim Brown	100.00
IB	Isaac Bruce	40.00
MK	Mark Brunell	75.00
CY	Chris Calloway	10.00
HC	Harold Carmichael	20.00
CC	Chris Chandler	30.00
BC	Bob Christian	10.00
CL	Cameron Cleeland	20.00
CW	Curtis Conway	20.00
TC	Tim Couch	300.00
CK	Ray Crockett	10.00
ZC	Zack Crockett	10.00
DC	Daunte Culpepper	325.00
NO	Sean Dawkins	10.00
KD	Koy Detmer	10.00
CD	Corey Dillon	35.00
TR	Troy Drayton	10.00
RD	Rickey Dudley	10.00
RE	Robert Edwards	25.00
JE	John Elway	300.00
BT	Bert Emanuel	20.00
BE	Bobby Engram	10.00
CE	Curtis Enis	30.00
MF	Marshall Faulk	75.00
BF	Brett Favre	300.00
WF	William Floyd	10.00
RF	Russ Francis	10.00
AF	Antonio Freeman	75.00
GA	Joey Galloway	70.00
CG	Charlie Garner	20.00
JG	Jason Garrett	10.00
EG	Eddie George	85.00
GE	Jeff George	20.00
GR	Randy Gradishar	10.00
GN	Trent Green	25.00
JH	Jack Ham	20.00
JK	Jackie Harris	10.00
RH	Rodney Harrison	10.00
HT	Jim Hart	20.00
GH	Garrison Hearst	25.00
TH	Ted Hendricks	20.00
HL	Greg Hill	10.00
LH	Leroy Hoard	10.00
DH	Darick Holmes	10.00
PH	Priest Holmes	70.00
WP	Torry Holt	140.00
HY	Chuck Howley	20.00
BH	Brock Huard	50.00
MJ	Michael Jackson	20.00
JJ	James Jett	20.00
KJ	Keyshawn Johnson	50.00
LJ	Leon Johnson	10.00
CJ	Charlie Joiner	20.00
SD	Charlie Jones	20.00
EJ	Ed Jones	20.00
NK	Napoleon Kaufman	30.00
SH	Shaun King	75.00
KI	Jon Kitna	30.00
SK	Sammy Knight	20.00
PK	Paul Krause	20.00
FL	Fred Lane	20.00
TL	Ty Law	10.00
RL	Ray Lewis	10.00
JL	James Lofton	20.00
KL	Keith Lyle	10.00
MG	Archie Manning	30.00
DM	Dan Marino	325.00
NY	Don Maynard	20.00
WM	Willie McGinest	10.00
MN	Donovan McNabb	200.00
QB	Cade McNown	75.00
NM	Natrone Means	30.00
KR	Brian Mitchell	10.00
PT	Pete Mitchell	10.00
JM	John Mobley	10.00
HM	Herman Moore	35.00
MO	Earl Morrall	20.00
MY	Mercury Morris	20.00
RM	Randy Moss	275.00
EM	Eric Moulds	40.00
MM	Muhsin Muhammad	10.00
AM	Adrian Murrell	20.00
HN	Hardy Nickerson	10.00
OZ	Ozzie Newsome	25.00
DP	Drew Pearson	25.00
JP	Jake Plummer	60.00
RP	Robert Porcher	10.00
OJ	O.J. Santiago	10.00
JR	Junior Seau	25.00
LS	Lee Roy Selmon	20.00
MS	Michael Sinclair	10.00
SY	Mike Singletary	25.00
TS	Tony Siragusa	10.00
CS	Chris Slade	10.00
TO	Torrance Small	10.00
AK	Akili Smith	50.00
AS	Antowain Smith	25.00
ES	Emmitt Smith	250.00
JS	Jimmy Smith	30.00
KS	Ken Stabler	40.00
ST	Duce Staley	30.00
SW	John Stallworth	25.00
MT	Maa Tanuvasa	10.00
CT	Charley Taylor	20.00
FT	Fred Taylor	50.00
JT	Jason Taylor	10.00
TV	Tommy Vardell	10.00
HW	Hines Ward	20.00
PW	Paul Warfield	25.00
LW	Lamont Warren	10.00
ND	Ricky Watters	40.00
WH	Craig Whelihan	10.00
HV	Harvey Williams	10.00
RW	Ricky Williams	375.00
KW	Kellen Winslow	25.00
FW	Frank Wycheck	10.00
JY	Jack Youngblood	20.00

1999 SP Signature Legendary Cuts

VL1	Vince Lombardi
VL2	Vince Lombardi
VL3	Vince Lombardi
VL4	Vince Lombardi
VL5	Vince Lombardi
BN1	Bronko Nagurski
BN2	Bronko Nagurski
BN3	Bronko Nagurski
BN4	Bronko Nagurski
RG1	Harold "Red" Grange

1999 SP Signature Montana Great Performances

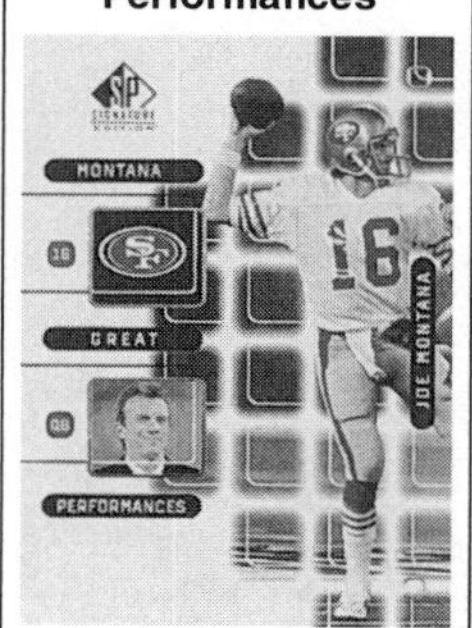

This was a 10-card set that highlights the career of Montana. Singles were randomly inserted. A parallel Autographed version was also produced and found 1:47 packs and a Gold Autographed parallel was made and found 1:880 packs.

		NM/M
Complete Set (10):		70.00
Common Player:		7.00
Randomly Inserted		
Montana Autographs:		125.00
Inserted 1:47		
Montana Gold Autographs:		600.00
Inserted 1:880		
1	Joe Montana	7.00
2	Joe Montana	7.00
3	Joe Montana	7.00
4	Joe Montana	7.00
5	Joe Montana	7.00
6	Joe Montana	7.00
7	Joe Montana	7.00
8	Joe Montana	7.00
9	Joe Montana	7.00
10	Joe Montana	7.00

1999 SPx

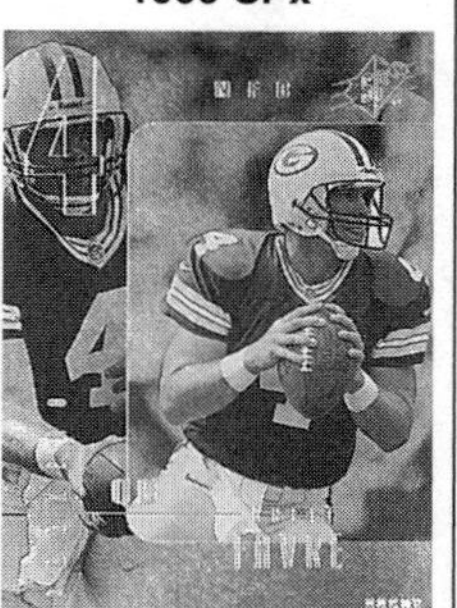

This was a 135-card set that included 45 sequentially numbered rookie cards. A total of 21 of the rookies were numbered to 1,999 and were autographed, 19 rookies were unsigned and numbered to 1,999 and only five were autographed and numbered to 500. Each single had a parallel Radiance and Spectrum single. Other inserts included: Highlight Heroes, Masters, Prolifics, SPxcitement, SPxtreme, Starscape and Winning Materials. SRP was $5.99 for three-card packs.

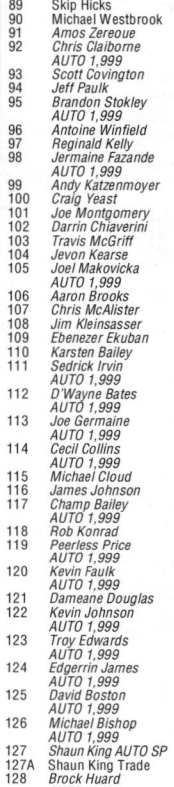

		NM/M
Complete Set (135):		3,000
Common Player:		.25
Minor Stars:		.50
Common Rookie:		6.00
Production 1,999 Sets		
Pack (3):		10.00
Wax Box (18):		150.00
1	Jake Plummer	2.00
2	Adrian Murrell	.50
3	Frank Sanders	.50
4	Jamal Anderson	1.00
5	Chris Chandler	.50
6	Terance Mathis	.25
7	Tony Banks	.50
8	Priest Holmes	1.50
9	Jermaine Lewis	.50
10	Antowain Smith	.75
11	Doug Flutie	.75
12	Eric Moulds	1.00
13	Tshimanga Biakabutuka	.50
14	Steve Beuerlein	.50
15	Muhsin Muhammad	.25
16	Bobby Engram	.25
17	Curtis Conway	.50
18	Curtis Enis	.50
19	Corey Dillon	1.00
20	Jeff Blake	.50
21	Carl Pickens	.50
22	Ty Detmer	.25
23	Terry Kirby	.25
24	Leslie Shepherd	.25
25	Troy Aikman	2.50
26	Emmitt Smith	3.50
27	Deion Sanders	1.00
28	Terrell Davis	2.00
29	Rod Smith	.50
30	Bubby Brister	.50
31	Barry Sanders	4.00
32	Herman Moore	.50
33	Charlie Batch	.50
34	Brett Favre	5.00
35	Antonio Freeman	.75
36	Dorsey Levens	.75
37	Peyton Manning	3.50
38	Marvin Harrison	1.00
39	Jerome Pathon	.25
40	Mark Brunell	1.00
41	Jimmy Smith	.50
42	Fred Taylor	1.00
43	Elvis Grbac	.50
44	Andre Rison	.25
45	Warren Moon	.50
46	Dan Marino	3.50
47	Karim Abdul	.75
48	O.J. McDuffie	.50
49	Randall Cunningham	.50
50	Robert Smith	.50
51	Randy Moss	4.00
52	Drew Bledsoe	2.00
53	Terry Glenn	1.00
54	Tony Simmons	.50
55	Danny Wuerffel	.50
56	Cameron Cleeland	.50
57	Kerry Collins	.50
58	Gary Brown	.25
59	Ike Hilliard	.25
60	Vinny Testaverde	.50
61	Curtis Martin	1.00
62	Keyshawn Johnson	1.00
63	Rich Gannon	.25
64	Napoleon Kaufman	.50
65	Tim Brown	.50
66	Duce Staley	.50
67	Doug Pederson	.25
68	Charles Johnson	.25
69	Kordell Stewart	.75
70	Jerome Bettis	.75
71	Trent Green	.75
72	Marshall Faulk	1.50
73	Ryan Leaf	.50
74	Natrone Means	.50
75	Jim Harbaugh	.50
76	Steve Young	1.75
77	Garrison Hearst	.50
78	Jerry Rice	4.00
79	Terrell Owens	1.00
80	Ricky Watters	.75
81	Joey Galloway	.75
82	Jon Kitna	.50
83	Warrick Dunn	.75
84	Trent Dilfer	.50
85	Mike Alstott	1.00
86	Steve McNair	1.25
87	Eddie George	1.00
88	Yancey Thigpen	.50
89	Skip Hicks	.75
90	Michael Westbrook	.75
91	*Amos Zereoue*	25.00
92	*Chris Claiborne AUTO 1,999*	10.00
93	*Scott Covington*	8.00
94	*Jeff Paulk*	6.00
95	*Brandon Stokley AUTO 1,999*	15.00
96	*Antoine Winfield*	6.00
97	*Reginald Kelly*	6.00
98	*Jermaine Fazande AUTO 1,999*	15.00
99	*Andy Katzenmoyer*	10.00
100	*Craig Yeast*	6.00
101	*Joe Montgomery*	6.00
102	*Darrin Chiaverini*	6.00
103	*Travis McGriff*	8.00
104	*Jevon Kearse*	30.00
105	*Joel Makovicka AUTO 1,999*	15.00
106	*Aaron Brooks*	50.00
107	*Chris McAlister*	6.00
108	*Jim Kleinsasser*	10.00
109	*Ebenezer Ekuban*	6.00
110	*Karsten Bailey*	6.00
111	*Sedrick Irvin AUTO 1,999*	15.00
112	*D'Wayne Bates AUTO 1,999*	20.00
113	*Joe Germaine AUTO 1,999*	15.00
114	*Cecil Collins AUTO 1,999*	15.00
115	*Michael Cloud*	10.00
116	*James Johnson*	10.00
117	*Champ Bailey AUTO 1,999*	35.00
118	*Rob Konrad*	10.00
119	*Peerless Price AUTO 1,999*	50.00
120	*Kevin Faulk AUTO 1,999*	25.00
121	*Dameane Douglas*	6.00
122	*Kevin Johnson AUTO 1,999*	20.00
123	*Troy Edwards AUTO 1,999*	30.00
124	*Edgerrin James AUTO 1,999*	120.00
125	*David Boston AUTO 1,999*	50.00
126	*Michael Bishop AUTO 1,999*	20.00
127	*Shaun King AUTO SP*	60.00
127A	Shaun King Trade	10.00
128	*Brock Huard AUTO 1,999*	20.00
129	*Torry Holt AUTO 1,999*	60.00
130	*Cade McNown AUTO 500*	50.00
131	*Tim Couch AUTO 500*	175.00
132	*Donovan McNabb AUTO 1,999*	150.00
133	*Akili Smith AUTO 500*	50.00
134	*Daunte Culpepper AUTO 500*	300.00
135	*Ricky Williams AUTO 500*	200.00

1999 SPx Radiance

This was a 135-card parallel to the base set including unsigned versions of the autographed rookie cards. Each single was printed with a holographic green-foil treatment and was sequentially numbered to 100.

Radiance Cards (1-90):	5X-15X
Radiance Rookies (1,999):	3X
Radiance Rookies (Auto.):	2X
Radiance Rookies (Auto. 500):	1X
Production 100 Sets	

1999 SPx Spectrum

This was a 135-card parallel to the base set and each was printed with a holographic red-foil treatment and numbered one-of-one.

NM/M

Production 1 Set

1999 SPx Highlight Heroes

This was a 10-card insert set that included mostly quarterbacks. Singles were inserted 1:9 packs.

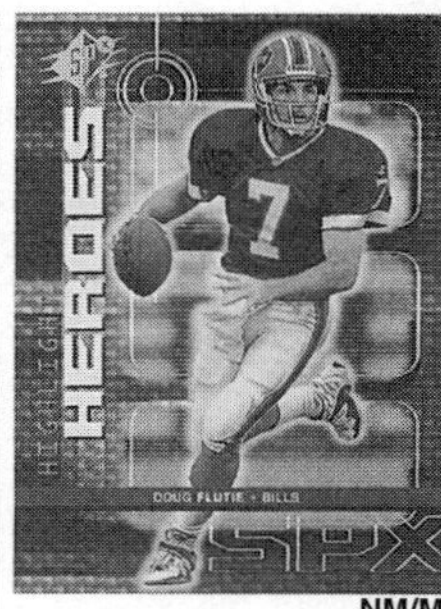

		NM/M
Complete Set (10):		20.00
Common Player:		2.00
Inserted 1:9		
1	Jake Plummer	2.00
2	Doug Flutie	2.00
3	Garrison Hearst	2.00
4	Fred Taylor	2.00
5	Dorsey Levens	2.00
6	Kordell Stewart	2.00
7	Marshall Faulk	2.00
8	Steve Young	4.00
9	Troy Aikman	6.00
10	Jerome Bettis	2.00

1999 SPx Masters

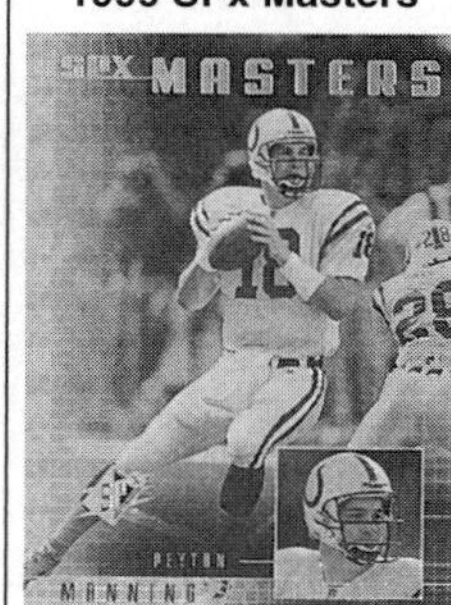

This was a 15-card insert set that included the best players at their respective positions. Singles were inserted 1:17 packs.

		NM/M
Complete Set (15):		30.00
Common Player:		1.00
Inserted 1:17		
1	Dan Marino	6.00
2	Barry Sanders	5.00
3	Peyton Manning	4.00
4	Joey Galloway	1.00
5	Steve Young	4.00
6	Warrick Dunn	1.00
7	Deion Sanders	1.00
8	Fred Taylor	2.00
9	Charlie Batch	1.00
10	Jamal Anderson	1.00
11	Jake Plummer	2.00
12	Terrell Davis	3.00
13	Eddie George	2.00
14	Mark Brunell	1.00
15	Randy Moss	5.00

1999 SPx Prolifics

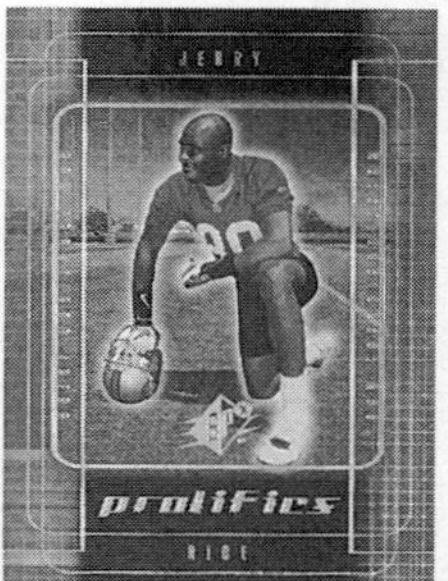

This was a 15-card insert set that included stars who had the ability to score points, yards and wins. Singles were inserted 1:17 packs.

		NM/M
Complete Set (15):		30.00
Common Player:		1.00
Inserted 1:17		
1	John Elway	4.00
2	Barry Sanders	5.00
3	Jamal Anderson	1.00
4	Terrell Owens	3.00
5	Marshall Faulk	3.00
6	Napoleon Kaufman	1.00
7	Antonio Freeman	1.00
8	Doug Flutie	1.00
9	Vinny Testaverde	1.00
10	Jerry Rice	5.00
11	Eric Moulds	1.00

12	Emmitt Smith	5.00
13	Brett Favre	6.00
14	Randall Cunningham	1.00
15	Keyshawn Johnson	1.00

1999 SPx SPxcitement

This was a 20-card insert set who featured players who provide non-stop thrills. Singles were inserted 1:3 packs.

		NM/M
Complete Set (20):		20.00
Common Player:		.50
Inserted 1:3		
1	Troy Aikman	3.00
2	Edgerrin James	3.00
3	Jerry Rice	4.00
4	Daunte Culpepper	3.00
5	Antowain Smith	.50
6	Kevin Faulk	.50
7	Steve McNair	2.00
8	Antonio Freeman	.50
9	Torry Holt	1.00
10	Napoleon Kaufman	.50
11	Curtis Martin	.50
12	Randall Cunningham	.50
13	Eric Moulds	.50
14	Priest Holmes	2.00
15	David Boston	2.00
16	Herman Moore	.50
17	Champ Bailey	1.50
18	Vinny Testaverde	.50
19	Garrison Hearst	.50
20	Jon Kitna	.50

1999 SPx SPxtreme

This 20-card insert set highlighted the most collectible stars and saluted their extreme talents to the game. Singles were inserted 1:6 packs.

		NM/M
Complete Set (20):		30.00
Common Player:		1.00
Inserted 1:6		
1	Emmitt Smith	5.00
2	Brock Huard	1.00
3	David Boston	2.00
4	Edgerrin James	4.00
5	Kevin Faulk	1.00
6	Daunte Culpepper	3.00
7	Charlie Batch	1.00
8	Torry Holt	1.00
9	Andre Rison	1.00
10	Karim Abdul	1.00
11	Kordell Stewart	2.00
12	Curtis Enis	1.00
13	Terrell Owens	2.00
14	Curtis Martin	2.00
15	Ricky Watters	1.00
16	Corey Dillon	1.00
17	Tim Brown	1.00
18	Warrick Dunn	1.00
19	Drew Bledsoe	3.00
20	Eddie George	2.00

1999 SPx Starscape

This was a 10-card insert set that featured ten superstars and highlighted their spectacular achievement to date. Singles were inserted 1:9 packs.

		NM/M
Complete Set (10):		20.00
Common Player:		1.00
Inserted 1:9		
1	Randy Moss	4.00
2	Keyshawn Johnson	1.00
3	Curtis Enis	1.00
4	Jerome Bettis	2.00

		NM/M
5	Mark Brunell	2.00
6	Antowain Smith	2.00
7	Joey Galloway	2.00
8	Drew Bledsoe	3.00
9	Corey Dillon	2.00
10	Steve McNair	2.00

1999 SPx Winning Materials

This 10-card insert set featured two pieces of game-used memorabilia (jersey swatch and football) of the featured player. Singles were inserted 1:252 packs.

		NM/M
Common Player:		40.00
Inserted 1:252		
DB	David Boston	50.00
TC	Tim Couch	75.00
DC	Daunte Culpepper	75.00
BF	Brett Favre	150.00
TH	Torry Holt	50.00
DM	Dan Marino	125.00
MC	Donovan McNabb	75.00
CM	Cade McNown	40.00
JR	Jerry Rice	100.00
RW	Ricky Williams	100.00

1999 SPx Winning Materials (Autographed)

		NM/M
TC	Tim Couch	
JR	Jerry Rice	350.00

2000 SP Authentic

		NM/M
Common Player:		.15
Minor Stars:		.30
Common Rookie:		8.00
Production 1,250 Sets		
Pack (5):		13.25
Wax Box (24):		225.00
Common Rookie (151-171):		8.00
Production 1,250 Sets		
1	Jake Plummer	.50
2	David Boston	.50
3	Frank Sanders	.30
4	Chris Chandler	.30
5	Jamal Anderson	.50
6	Shawn Jefferson	.15
7	Tony Banks	.30
8	Shannon Sharpe	.30
9	Rob Johnson	.30
10	Antowain Smith	.30
11	Muhsin Muhammad	.30
12	Steve Beuerlein	.30
13	Cade McNown	.75
14	Curtis Enis	.30
15	Marcus Robinson	.50
16	Akili Smith	.50
17	Corey Dillon	.50
18	Tim Couch	1.25
19	Kevin Johnson	.30
20	Errict Rhett	.30
21	Troy Aikman	1.50
22	Emmitt Smith	2.00
23	Raghib Ismail	.15
24	Joey Galloway	.50
25	Terrell Davis	1.25
26	Olandis Gary	.50
27	Ed McCaffrey	.30
28	Brian Griese	.75
29	Charlie Batch	.50
30	Germane Crowell	.50
31	James O. Stewart	.30
32	Brett Favre	2.50
33	Antonio Freeman	.50
34	Dorsey Levens	.50
35	Peyton Manning	2.50
36	Edgerrin James	1.75
37	Marvin Harrison	.50
38	Mark Brunell	.50
39	Fred Taylor	.50
40	Jimmy Smith	.50
41	Elvis Grbac	.30
42	Tony Gonzalez	.30
43	James Johnson	.15
44	Oronde Gadsden	.30
45	Damon Huard	.50
46	Randy Moss	2.00
47	Cris Carter	.50
48	Daunte Culpepper	1.25
49	Drew Bledsoe	1.00
50	Terry Glenn	.50
51	Ricky Williams	1.00
52	Jeff Blake	.30
53	Keith Poole	.15
54	Kerry Collins	.30
55	Amani Toomer	.15
56	Ike Hilliard	.15
57	Wayne Chrebet	.50
58	Curtis Martin	.50
59	Vinny Testaverde	.30
60	Tim Brown	.50
61	Rich Gannon	.30
62	Tyrone Wheatley	.30
63	Duce Staley	.50
64	Donovan McNabb	1.00
65	Troy Edwards	.50
66	Jerome Bettis	.50
67	Kordell Stewart	.60
68	Marshall Faulk	1.00
69	Kurt Warner	2.00
70	Isaac Bruce	.50
71	Torry Holt	.50
72	Ryan Leaf	.50
73	Jim Harbaugh	.30
74	Jermaine Fazande	.15
75	Jerry Rice	2.00
76	Terrell Owens	.50
77	Jeff Garcia	.50
78	Ricky Watters	.30
79	Jon Kitna	.50
80	Derrick Mayes	.30
81	Shaun King	.50
82	Mike Alstott	.50
83	Keyshawn Johnson	.50
84	Warrick Dunn	.50
85	Eddie George	.75
86	Steve McNair	.75
87	Jevon Kearse	.50
88	Brad Johnson	.50
89	Stephen Davis	.50
90	Michael Westbrook	.30
91	*Anthony Lucas*	8.00
92	*Avion Black*	8.00
93	*Dante Hall*	50.00
94	*Darrell Jackson*	30.00
95	*Deltha O'Neal*	8.00
96	*Erron Kinney*	8.00
97	*Doug Chapman*	8.00
98	*Frank Murphy*	8.00
99	*Gari Scott*	8.00
100	*Giovanni Carmazzi*	8.00
101	*JaJuan Dawson*	8.00
102	*Jarious Jackson*	12.00
103	*Rashard Anderson*	8.00
104	*Michael Wiley*	8.00
105	*Spergon Wynn*	8.00
106	*Muneer Moore*	8.00
107	*Ahmed Plummer*	8.00
108	*Chad Morton*	8.00
109	*Rob Morris*	8.00
110	*Ron Dixon*	8.00
111	*Rondell Mealey*	8.00
112	*Sebastian Janikowski*	10.00
113	*Shaun Ellis*	8.00
114	*Rogers Beckett*	8.00
115	*Shyrone Stith*	8.00
116	*Tim Rattay*	40.00
117	*Todd Husak*	12.00
118	*Tom Brady*	825.00
119	*Trevor Gaylor*	8.00
120	*Windrell Hayes*	8.00
121	*Anthony Becht*	12.00
122	*Brian Urlacher*	100.00
123	*Bubba Franks*	20.00
124	*Chad Pennington*	250.00
125	*Chris Redman*	20.00
126	*Corey Simon*	10.00
127	*Curtis Keaton*	10.00
128	*Danny Farmer*	12.00
129	*Dennis Northcutt*	20.00
130	*Dez White*	20.00
131	*J.R. Redmond*	10.00
132	*Jamal Lewis*	100.00
133	*Jerry Porter*	50.00
134	*Joe Hamilton*	15.00
135	*Laveranues Coles*	40.00
136	*R. Jay Soward*	8.00
137	*Reuben Droughns*	40.00
138	*Ron Dayne*	25.00
139	*Ron Dugans*	12.00
140	*Shaun Alexander*	100.00
141	*Sylvester Morris*	8.00
142	*Tee Martin*	8.00
143	*Thomas Jones*	40.00
144	*Todd Pinkston*	25.00
145	*Travis Prentice*	12.00
146	*Travis Taylor*	25.00
147	*Trung Canidate*	35.00
148	*Courtney Brown*	15.00
149	*Plaxico Burress*	60.00
150	*Peter Warrick*	40.00
151	*Billy Volek*	15.00
152	*Bobby Shaw*	8.00
153	*Brad Hoover*	8.00
154	*Brian Finneran*	8.00
155	*Charles Lee*	8.00
156	*Chris Cole*	8.00
157	*Clint Stoerner*	8.00
158	*Doug Johnson*	20.00
159	*Frank Moreau*	8.00
160	*Jake Delhomme*	50.00
161	*KaRon Coleman*	8.00
162	*Kevin McDougal*	8.00
163	*Larry Foster*	8.00
164	*Mike Anderson*	30.00
165	*Patrick Pass*	8.00
166	*Reggie Jones*	8.00
167	*Sammy Morris*	8.00
168	*Shockmain Davis*	8.00
169	*Terrelle Smith*	8.00
170	*Ronney Jenkins*	8.00
171	*Troy Walters*	8.00

2000 SP Authentic Game-Jersey Greats

		NM/M
Production 175 Sets		300.00
JN	Joe Namath 175	300.00

2000 SP Authentic New Classics

		NM/M
Complete Set (10):		15.00
Common Player:		1.50
Inserted 1:11		
NC1	Peter Warrick	1.00
NC2	Courtney Brown	1.75
NC3	Trung Canidate	1.50
NC4	Dennis Northcutt	1.75
NC5	J.R. Redmond	2.00
NC6	Daunte Culpepper	2.50
NC7	Edgerrin James	5.00
NC8	Marcus Robinson	1.50
NC9	Shaun King	1.00
NC10	Ricky Williams	4.00

2000 SP Authentic Rookie Fusion

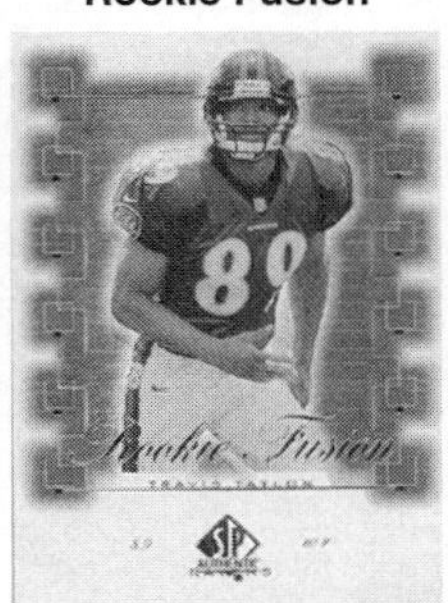

		NM/M
Complete Set (7):		18.00
Common Player:		1.00
Inserted 1:18		
RF1	Plaxico Burress	4.00
RF2	Chad Pennington	5.00
RF3	Travis Taylor	3.00
RF4	Ron Dayne	2.00
RF5	Thomas Jones	2.00
RF6	Jamal Lewis	4.00
RF7	Sylvester Morris	1.00

2000 SP Authentic SP Athletic

		NM/M
Complete Set (10):		7.00
Common Player:		.50
Inserted 1:11		
A1	Marshall Faulk	1.50
A2	Kevin Johnson	1.00
A3	Olandis Gary	.50
A4	Jeff Garcia	1.50
A5	Akili Smith	.50
A6	Donovan McNabb	2.00
A7	Rob Johnson	.50
A8	Marcus Robinson	1.00
A9	Shaun King	.50
A10	Troy Edwards	.50

2000 SP Authentic Sign of the Times

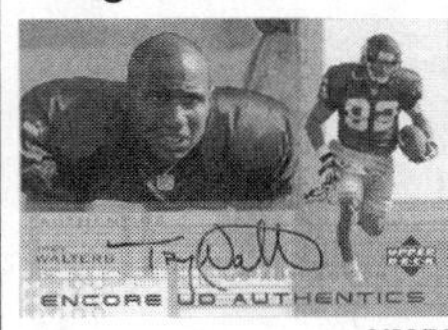

		NM/M
Common Player:		5.00
Minor Stars:		10.00
Inserted 1:23		
SA	Shaun Alexander	50.00
FB	Mike Alstott	10.00
JA	Jamal Anderson	10.00
CH	Champ Bailey	10.00
CB	Charlie Batch	10.00
BL	Drew Bledsoe	35.00
DB	David Boston	10.00
CO	Courtney Brown	25.00
IB	Isaac Bruce	10.00
MB	Mark Brunell	35.00
PB	Plaxico Burress	25.00
CA	Trung Canidate	5.00
GC	Giovanni Carmazzi	5.00
CC	Cris Carter	25.00
KC	Kwame Cavil	5.00
CR	Chris Chandler	10.00
WC	Wayne Chrebet	10.00
DL	Chris Claiborne	5.00
CL	Chris Coleman	5.00
LC	Laveranues Coles	25.00
KE	Kerry Collins	10.00
TC	Tim Couch	40.00
DC	Daunte Culpepper	60.00
SD	Stephen Davis	10.00
JD	JaJuan Dawson	10.00
RD	Ron Dayne	50.00
TD	Trent Dilfer	10.00
DR	Reuben Droughns	15.00
DU	Ron Dugans	5.00
TE	Troy Edwards	5.00
DF	Danny Farmer	5.00
KF	Kevin Faulk	5.00
MF	Marshall Faulk	25.00
FL	Doug Flutie	25.00
BF	Bubba Franks	10.00
AF	Antonio Freeman	10.00
GF	Gus Frerotte	5.00
JG	Joey Galloway	10.00
OG	Olandis Gary	10.00
TG	Trevor Gaylor	10.00
EG	Eddie George	35.00
SG	Sherrod Gideon	5.00
GO	Tony Gonzalez	10.00
BG	Brian Griese	35.00
JH	Joe Hamilton	10.00
MH	Marvin Harrison	10.00
WH	Windrell Hayes	5.00
TH	Torry Holt	10.00
QI	Qadry Ismail	5.00
DJ	Darrell Jackson	10.00
EJ	Edgerrin James	75.00
BJ	Brad Johnson	10.00
JO	Kevin Johnson	5.00
KJ	Keyshawn Johnson	10.00
RB	Rob Johnson	10.00
TJ	Thomas Jones	25.00
CK	Curtis Keaton	5.00
JK	Jon Kitna	10.00
JL	Jamal Lewis	75.00
AL	Anthony Lucas	5.00
RL	Ray Lucas	10.00
PM	Peyton Manning	100.00
DM	Dan Marino	85.00
TM	Tee Martin	10.00
CM	Cade McNown	25.00
MO	Corey Moore	5.00
HM	Herman Moore	10.00
SM	Sylvester Morris	40.00
RM	Randy Moss	100.00
EM	Eric Moulds	10.00
JN	Joe Namath	125.00
DN	Dennis Northcutt	10.00
TO	Terrell Owens	10.00
CP	Chad Pennington	100.00
JP	Jake Plummer	10.00
PO	Jerry Porter	10.00
TP	Travis Prentice	25.00
TR	Tim Rattay	25.00
RE	Chris Redman	30.00
JR	J.R. Redmond	10.00
SS	Shannon Sharpe	10.00
CS	Corey Simon	10.00
AS	Akili Smith	10.00
RJ	R. Jay Soward	10.00
KS	Kordell Stewart	10.00
JJ	J.J. Stokes	5.00
TT	Travis Taylor	25.00
BU	Brian Urlacher	60.00
TW	Troy Walters	5.00
KW	Kurt Warner	100.00
PW	Peter Warrick	40.00
WA	Ricky Watters	10.00
DW	Dez White	10.00
MW	Michael Wiley	10.00
SY	Steve Young	45.00

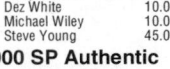

2000 SP Authentic Supremacy

		NM/M
Complete Set (15):		25.00
Common Player:		1.50
Inserted 1:8		
S1	Mark Brunell	2.00
S2	Terrell Davis	2.00
S3	Jamal Anderson	1.50
S4	Jerry Rice	3.50
S5	Emmitt Smith	3.50
S6	Troy Aikman	2.50
S7	Randy Moss	3.50
S8	Brad Johnson	1.50
S9	Brett Favre	5.00
S10	Keyshawn Johnson	1.50
S11	Fred Taylor	2.00
S12	Kurt Warner	3.50
S13	Tim Couch	2.50
S14	Eddie George	1.75
S15	Drew Bledsoe	2.00

2000 SPx

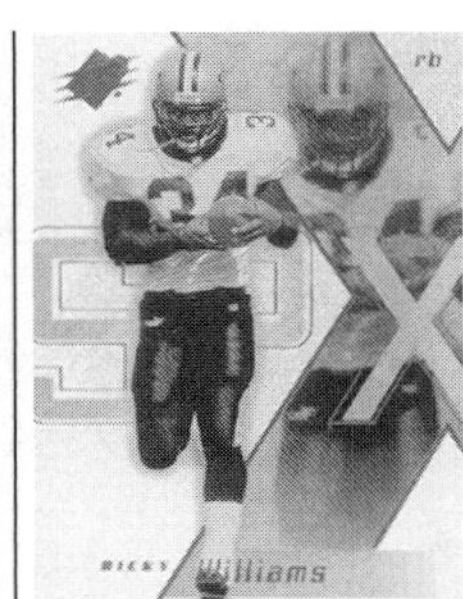

		NM/M
Common Player:		.25
Minor Stars:		.50
Common Rookie:		7.00
Production 1,350 Sets		
Common Rookie Jersey:		20.00
Production 2,000 Sets		
Pack (4):		11.25
Wax Box (18):		145.00
1	Jake Plummer	.75
2	David Boston	.75
3	Frank Sanders	.50
4	Chris Chandler	.50
5	Jamal Anderson	.75
6	Shawn Jefferson	.25
7	Qadry Ismail	.25
8	Tony Banks	.50
9	Shannon Sharpe	.50
10	Rob Johnson	.50
11	Eric Moulds	.75
12	Muhsin Muhammad	.50
13	Steve Beuerlein	.50
14	Cade McNown	.50
15	Marcus Robinson	.75
16	Akili Smith	.50
17	Corey Dillon	.75
18	Darnay Scott	.50
19	Tim Couch	1.50
20	Kevin Johnson	.75
21	Errict Rhett	.50
22	Troy Aikman	1.50
23	Emmitt Smith	3.00
24	Joey Galloway	.75
25	Terrell Davis	1.00
26	Olandis Gary	.50
27	Brian Griese	1.00
28	Charlie Batch	.50
29	Germane Crowell	.75
30	James O. Stewart	.50
31	Brett Favre	4.00
32	Antonio Freeman	.75
33	Dorsey Levens	.50
34	Peyton Manning	3.00
35	Edgerrin James	2.50
36	Marvin Harrison	.75
37	Mark Brunell	.75
38	Fred Taylor	.75
39	Jimmy Smith	.50
40	Keenan McCardell	.50
41	Elvis Grbac	.50
42	Tony Gonzalez	.50
43	Tony Martin	.25
44	Jay Fiedler	.50
45	Damon Huard	.50
46	Randy Moss	3.00
47	Robert Smith	.75
48	Cris Carter	.75
49	Daunte Culpepper	1.50
50	Drew Bledsoe	1.25
51	Terry Glenn	.75
52	Ricky Williams	1.00
53	Jeff Blake	.50
54	Keith Poole	.25
55	Kerry Collins	.50
56	Amani Toomer	.50
57	Ike Hilliard	.50
58	Ray Lucas	.75
59	Curtis Martin	.75
60	Vinny Testaverde	.75
61	Tim Brown	.75
62	Rich Gannon	.50
63	Tyrone Wheatley	.50
64	Napoleon Kaufman	.75
65	Duce Staley	.75
66	Donovan McNabb	1.25
67	Troy Edwards	.50
68	Jerome Bettis	.75
69	Kordell Stewart	.75
70	Marshall Faulk	2.00
71	Kurt Warner	3.00
72	Isaac Bruce	.75
73	Torry Holt	.75
74	Ryan Leaf	.75
75	Jim Harbaugh	.50
76	Jerry Rice	3.00
77	Terrell Owens	.75
78	Jeff Garcia	.75
79	Ricky Watters	.50
80	Jon Kitna	.75
81	Derrick Mayes	.50
82	Shaun King	.50
83	Mike Alstott	.75
84	Keyshawn Johnson	.75
85	Eddie George	1.00
86	Steve McNair	.75
87	Jevon Kearse	.75
88	Brad Johnson	.75
89	Stephen Davis	.75
90	Michael Westbrook	.50
91	*Anthony Lucas*	7.00
92	*Avion Black*	7.00
93	*Corey Moore*	7.00
94	*Chris Cole*	7.00
95	*Chris Hovan*	10.00
96	*Dante Hall*	40.00
97	*Darrell Jackson*	25.00
98	*Deltha O'Neal*	7.00
99	*Doug Chapman*	7.00
100	*Doug Johnson*	15.00
101	*Erron Kinney*	7.00
102	*Frank Moreau*	7.00
103	*Patrick Pass*	7.00
104	*Gari Scott*	7.00
105	*Giovanni Carmazzi*	7.00
106	*JaJuan Dawson*	7.00
107	*James Williams*	7.00
108	*Jarious Jackson*	12.00

109 *John Abraham* 7.00
110 *Keith Bulluck* 7.00
111 *Jonas Lewis* 7.00
112 *Mike Green* 7.00
113 *Ronney Jenkins* 7.00
114 *Michael Wiley* 7.00
115 *Mike Anderson* 15.00
116 *Mareno Philyaw* 7.00
117 *Muneer Moore* 7.00
118 *Paul Smith* 7.00
119 *Raynoch Thompson* 7.00
120 *Rob Morris* 7.00
121 *Ron Dixon* 7.00
122 *Rondell Mealey* 7.00
124 *Shaun Ellis* 7.00
125 *Charles Lee* 7.00
126 *Shyrone Stith* 7.00
127 *Thomas Hamner* 7.00
128 *Tim Rattay* 20.00
129 *Todd Husak* 10.00
130 *Tom Brady* 175.00
131 *Trevor Gaylor* 7.00
132 *Windrell Hayes* 7.00
133 *Anthony Becht* 12.00
134 *Brian Urlacher* 100.00
135 *Bubba Franks* 40.00
136 *Chad Pennington* 150.00
137 *Chris Redman* 30.00
138 *Corey Simon* 15.00
139 *Curtis Keaton* 15.00
140 *Danny Farmer* 15.00
141 *Dennis Northcutt* 20.00
142 *Dez White* 25.00
143 *J.R. Redmond* 20.00
144 *Jamal Lewis* 75.00
145 *Jerry Porter* 50.00
146 *Joe Hamilton* 20.00
147 *Laveranues Coles* 50.00
148 *R. Jay Soward* 15.00
149 *Reuben Droughns* 50.00
150 *Ron Dayne* 30.00
151 *Ron Dugans* 20.00
152 *Shaun Alexander* 75.00
153 *Sylvester Morris* 20.00
154 *Tee Martin* 25.00
155 *Thomas Jones* 12.00
156 *Todd Pinkston* 30.00
157 *Travis Prentice* 20.00
158 *Travis Taylor* 40.00
159 *Trung Canidate* 30.00
160 *Courtney Brown 500* 40.00
162 *Plaxico Burress 500* 125.00
161 *Peter Warrick 500* 60.00

2000 SPx Spectrum

Spectrum Cards: 15X-30X
Spectrum Rookies: 1X
Spectrum Rookie Jersey: 1X
Production 25 Sets

2000 SPx Game Jersey Greats

NM/M
Production 400 Sets
JU Johnny Unitas 400 300.00

2000 SPx Highlight Heroes

NM/M
Complete Set (12): 15.00
Common Player: 1.00
Inserted 1:8
HH1 Fred Taylor 1.00
HH2 Eddie George 1.50
HH3 Marshall Faulk 1.00
HH4 Shaun King 1.00
HH5 Cris Carter 1.00
HH6 Emmitt Smith 3.00
HH7 Jerry Rice 3.00
HH8 Tim Couch 2.00
HH9 Keyshawn Johnson 1.00
HH10 Troy Aikman 3.00
HH11 Terrell Davis 2.00
HH12 Ricky Williams 2.50

2000 SPx Powerhouse

NM/M
Complete Set (10): 7.00
Common Player: .75
Minor Stars: 1.50
Inserted 1:9
PH1 Akili Smith 1.00
PH2 Kevin Johnson 1.00
PH3 Olandis Gary 1.00
PH4 Jeff Garcia 1.50
PH5 Germane Crowell .75
PH6 Donovan McNabb 2.00
PH7 Rob Johnson .75
PH8 Marcus Robinson 1.50
PH9 Shaun King 1.00
PH10 Troy Edwards .75

2000 SPx Prolifics

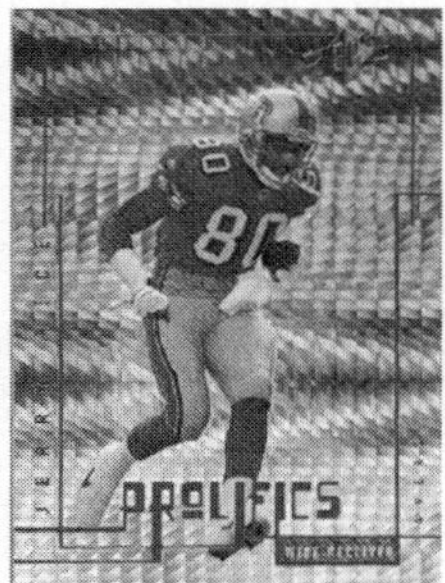

NM/M
Complete Set (12): 25.00
Common Player: 1.00
Inserted 1:18
P1 Stephen Davis 1.00
P2 Terrell Davis 3.00
P3 Jamal Anderson 1.00
P4 Jerry Rice 4.00
P5 Emmitt Smith 5.00
P6 Troy Aikman 4.00
P7 Cris Carter 1.00
P8 Brett Favre 6.00
P9 Mark Brunell 3.00
P10 Tim Couch 2.00
P11 Eddie George 2.00
P12 Marshall Faulk 2.00

2000 SPx SPXcitement

NM/M
Complete Set (10): 8.00
Common Player: .50
Inserted 1:5
XC1 Plaxico Burress 2.00
XC2 Peter Warrick 1.00
XC3 Todd Pinkston .50
XC4 Ron Dayne 1.00
XC5 Reuben Droughns .50
XC6 Danny Farmer .50
XC7 Bubba Franks 1.00
XC8 Laveranues Coles 1.00
XC9 Chad Pennington 3.00
XC10 J.R. Redmond .50

2000 SPx SPXtreme

NM/M
Complete Set (18): 25.00
Common Player: 1.00
Inserted 1:12
X1 Isaac Bruce 1.00
X2 Cade McNown 1.00
X3 Daunte Culpepper 3.50
X4 Donovan McNabb 2.50
X5 Brett Favre 5.00
X6 Peyton Manning 4.00
X7 Edgerrin James 4.00
X8 Jon Kitna 1.00
X9 Mark Brunell 1.00
X10 Brad Johnson 1.00
X11 Jevon Kearse 1.00
X12 Curtis Martin 1.00
X13 Steve McNair 1.00
X14 Ricky Williams 4.00
X15 Stephen Davis 1.00
X16 Kurt Warner 3.00
X17 Marvin Harrison 1.00
X18 Randy Moss 4.00

A player's name in *italic* type indicates a rookie card.

2000 SPx Starscape

NM/M
Complete Set (12): 25.00
Common Player: 1.00
Inserted 1:18
RS1 Thomas Jones 1.00
RS2 Courtney Brown 1.00
RS3 Peter Warrick 1.00
RS4 Jamal Lewis 4.00
RS5 Sylvester Morris 3.00
RS6 Plaxico Burress 4.50
RS7 Travis Taylor 1.00
RS8 Chad Pennington 10.00
RS9 Ron Dayne 4.00
RS10 Shaun Alexander 6.00
RS11 Giovanni Carmazzi 1.00
RS12 Ron Dugans 1.00

2000 SPx Winning Materials

NM/M
Common Player: 10.00
Inserted 1:83
Autographed Cards: 2X-4X
Production 225 Cards:
WMSA Shaun Alexander 40.00
WMCB Courtney Brown 20.00
WMPB Plaxico Burress 35.00
WMTC Trung Canidate 20.00
WMTD Terrell Davis 30.00
WMRD Ron Dayne 30.00
WMDR Reuben Droughns 20.00
WMWD Warrick Dunn 20.00
WMMF Marshall Faulk 30.00
WMBF Brett Favre 60.00
WMDF Bubba Franks 20.00
WMEG Eddie George 25.00
WMBG Brian Griese 25.00
WMTH Torry Holt 20.00
WMEJ Edgerrin James 40.00
WMKJ Keyshawn Johnson 25.00
WMTJ Thomas Jones 25.00
WMSK Shaun King 20.00
WMJL Jamal Lewis 30.00
WMPM Peyton Manning 40.00
WMTM Tee Martin 20.00
WMMC Steve McNair 20.00
WMCM Cade McNown 15.00
WMSM Sylvester Morris 15.00
WMRM Randy Moss 40.00
WMTO Terrell Owens 20.00
WMCP Chad Pennington 50.00
WMJP Jerry Porter 20.00
WMCR Chris Redman 20.00
WMNE J.R. Redmond 20.00
WMJR Jerry Rice 45.00
WMRJ R. Jay Soward 20.00
WMJJ J.J. Stokes 20.00
WMKW Kurt Warner 40.00
WMPW Peter Warrick 20.00
WMDW Dez White 20.00

2000 SPx Autograph Winning Materials

NM/M
Common Player: 40.00
SA Shaun Alexander 100.00
CB Courtney Brown
TC Tim Couch 100.00
TD Terrell Davis 75.00
RD Ron Dayne 50.00
EG Eddie George 75.00
BG Brian Griese
EJ Edgerrin James 100.00
KJ Keyshawn Johnson 50.00
TJ Thomas Jones 40.00
JL Jamal Lewis 75.00
PM Peyton Manning 150.00
TM Tee Martin 40.00
RM Randy Moss 150.00
CP Chad Pennington 150.00
TT Travis Taylor 40.00
KW Kurt Warner 100.00
PW Peter Warrick 40.00

2001 SP Authentic

NM/M
Common Player: .15
Minor Stars: .30
Pack (5): 18.00
Wax Box (24): 310.00
1 Jake Plummer .50
2 Thomas Jones .30
3 Frank Sanders .15
4 Jamal Anderson .50
5 Chris Chandler .30
6 Tony Martin .15
7 Jamal Lewis 1.50
8 Elvis Grbac .30
9 Travis Taylor .50
10 Peerless Price .30
11 Rob Johnson .30
12 Eric Moulds .50
13 Muhsin Muhammad .30
14 Isaac Byrd .15
15 Wesley Walls .30
16 James Allen .30
17 Marcus Robinson .50
18 Brian Urlacher 1.25
19 Jon Kitna .30
20 Peter Warrick .60
21 Corey Dillon .50
22 Kevin Johnson .30
23 JaJuan Dawson .15
24 Tim Couch .75
25 Raghib Ismail .15
26 Emmitt Smith 1.50
27 Joey Galloway .50
28 Terrell Davis 1.25
29 Mike Anderson 1.00
30 Brian Griese .60
31 Ed McCaffrey .50
32 Charlie Batch .50
33 James O. Stewart .30
34 Johnnie Morton .30
35 Brett Favre 2.50
36 Antonio Freeman .50
37 Bill Schroeder .30
38 Ahman Green .50
39 Peyton Manning 2.00
40 Edgerrin James 1.75
41 Marvin Harrison .50
42 Mark Brunell .60
43 Fred Taylor .60
44 Jimmy Smith .50
45 Tony Gonzalez .30
46 Trent Green .30
47 Oronde Gadsden .15
48 Jay Fiedler .50
49 Lamar Smith .30
50 Randy Moss 2.00
51 Cris Carter .50
52 Daunte Culpepper 1.25
53 Drew Bledsoe .60
54 Terry Glenn .30
55 Antowain Smith .30
56 Ricky Williams 1.00
57 Joe Horn .30
58 Aaron Brooks .50
59 Kerry Collins .30
60 Tiki Barber .50
61 Ron Dayne 1.25
62 Vinny Testaverde .30
63 Wayne Chrebet .30
64 Curtis Martin .50
65 Tim Brown .50
66 Rich Gannon .30
67 Jerry Rice 1.25
68 Duce Staley .50
69 Donovan McNabb 1.00
70 Kordell Stewart .50
71 Jerome Bettis .50
72 Marshall Faulk .75
73 Kurt Warner 2.00
74 Isaac Bruce .50
75 Doug Flutie .30
76 Junior Seau .30
77 Jeff Garcia .50
78 Garrison Hearst .30
79 Terrell Owens .50
80 Ricky Watters .30
81 Matt Hasselbeck .40
82 Brad Johnson .30
83 Warrick Dunn .50
84 Mike Alstott .50
85 Kevin Dyson .30
86 Eddie George .75
87 Steve McNair .50
88 Champ Bailey .30
89 Michael Westbrook .30
90 Stephen Davis .50
91 *Michael Vick 250* 1,500
92 *Rod Gardner 250* 200.00
93 *Freddie Mitchell 250* 100.00
94 *Koren Robinson 500* 50.00
95 *David Terrell 500* 50.00
96 *Michael Bennett 800* 60.00
97 *Robert Ferguson 800* 30.00
98 *Deuce McAllister 800* 100.00
99 *Travis Henry 800* 50.00
100 *Andre Carter 800* 20.00
101 *Drew Brees 800* 60.00
102 *Santana Moss 500* 80.00
103 *Chris Weinke 390* 40.00
104 *Chad Johnson 160* 350.00
105 *Reggie Wayne 800* 60.00
106 *Kevan Barlow 500* 100.00
107 *Chris Chambers 500* 100.00
108 *Todd Heap 500* 50.00
109 *Anthony Thomas 500* 80.00
110 *James Jackson 500* 30.00
111 *Rudi Johnson 500* 100.00
112 *Mike McMahon 800* 40.00
113 *Josh Heupel 800* 25.00
114 *Travis Minor 500* 50.00
115 *Quincy Morgan 500* 40.00
116 *Dan Morgan 500* 25.00
117 *Jesse Palmer 500* 40.00
118 *Sage Rosenfels 300* 50.00
119 *Marques Tuiasosopo 800* 30.00
120 *LaDainian Tomlinson 500* 250.00
121 *Adam Archuleta 550* 20.00
122 *Alex Bannister 550* 15.00
123 *Alge Crumpler 550* 20.00
124 *Arnold Jackson 550* 15.00
125 *Bobby Newcombe 550* 15.00
126 *Brandon Manumaleuna 550* 12.00
127 *Cedrick Wilson 550* 20.00
128 *Brian Allen 550* 12.00
129 *Dadrian Dee Brown 550* 12.00
130 *Darnerian McCants 550* 12.00
131 *Dave Dickenson 550* 15.00
132 *Derrick Blaylock 550* 20.00
133 *Eddie Berlin 550* 20.00
134 *Francis St. Paul 550* 12.00
135 *Jamar Fletcher 550* 15.00
136 *Josh Booty 550* 15.00
137 *Scotty Anderson 550* 12.00
138 *Ken-Yon Rambo 550* 15.00
139 *Kenyatta Walker 550* 12.00
140 *Kevin Kasper 550* 20.00
141 *Marvin "Snoop" Minnis 550* 20.00
142 *T.J. Houshmandzadeh 550* 20.00
143 *Quincy Carter 550* 60.00
144 *Ronney Daniels 550* 12.00
145 *Sedrick Hodge 550* 15.00
146 *Steve Smith 550* 60.00
147 *Tim Hasselbeck 550* 15.00
148 *Vinny Sutherland 550* 15.00
149 *Richard Seymour 550* 20.00
150 *Jamie Winborn 550* 15.00
151 *Gerard Warren 800* 12.00
152 *Justin Smith 800* 12.00
153 *David Martin 800* 10.00
154 *Jamal Reynolds 800* 12.00
155 *Dominic Rhodes 800* 30.00
156 *Nate Clements 800* 10.00
157 *Michael Lewis 800* 10.00
158 *Andre King 800* 10.00
159 *Benjamin Gay 800* 12.00
160 *Correll Buckhalter 800* 25.00
161 *Roderick Robinson 800* 10.00
162 *Moran Norris 800* 10.00
163 *Onome Ojo 800* 10.00
164 *Will Allen 800* 10.00
165 *Jonathan Carter 800* 10.00
166 *LaMont Jordan 800* 20.00
167 *DeLawrence Grant 800* 10.00
168 *Derrick Gibson 800* 10.00
169 *A.J. Feeley 800* 30.00
170 *Tim Baker 800* 10.00
171 *Kendrell Bell 800* 30.00
172 *Zeke Moreno 800* 10.00
173 *Carlos Polk 800* 10.00
174 *Ken Lucas 800* 10.00
175 *Heath Evans 800* 10.00
176 *Elvis Joseph 800* 10.00
177 *Damione Lewis 800* 10.00
178 *Tommy Polley 800* 10.00
179 *Fred Smoot 800* 12.00
180 *Jason Brookins 800* 15.00
181 *Nick Goings 800* 15.00
182 *Drew Bennett 800* 20.00
183 *Justin McCareins 800* 25.00
184 *Kabeer Gbaja-Biamila 800* 20.00
185 *Edgerton Hartwell 800* 10.00
186 *Robert Carswell 800* 10.00
187 *Aaron Schobel 800* 10.00
188 *Dan Alexander 800* 12.00
189 *Jamie Winborn 800* 10.00
190 *Kenny Riley 800* 10.00

2001 SP Authentic Sign of the Times

NM/M
Common Player: 12.00
Inserted 1:47
MA Marcus Allen 20.00
TBa Tiki Barber 12.00
CB Charlie Batch 15.00
JBl Jeff Blake 12.00
DB Drew Bledsoe 25.00
TB Terry Bradshaw 50.00
DBr Drew Brees 50.00
JBr Jim Brown 60.00
TBr Tim Brown 15.00
WC Wayne Chrebet 12.00
DC Daunte Culpepper 40.00
SD Stephen Davis 15.00
TDa Terrell Davis 40.00
TDi Trent Dilfer 12.00
DF Doug Flutie 18.00
JoG Joey Galloway 12.00
JGa Jeff Garcia 30.00
JGe Jeff George 12.00
AG Ahman Green 15.00
TH Torry Holt 15.00
PH Paul Hornung 25.00
BJ Brad Johnson 18.00
EJ Ed "Too Tall" Jones 25.00
JJ Joe Jurivicius 12.00
JK Jim Kelly 25.00
HL Howie Long 35.00
JL John Lynch 15.00
PM Peyton Manning 45.00
DM Dan Marino 75.00
CM Cade McNown 12.00
JM Joe Montana 100.00
JMo Johnnie Morton 12.00
RM Randy Moss 85.00
JN Joe Namath 60.00
TO Terrell Owens 20.00
JPl Jake Plummer 15.00
JP Jim Plunkett 18.00
JR John Riggins 40.00
JS Junior Seau 15.00
JSe Jason Sehorn 12.00
AS Akili Smith 12.00
RS Roger Staubach 45.00
KS Kordell Stewart 18.00
CT Charley Taylor 12.00
VT Vinny Testaverde 12.00
AT Amani Toomer 12.00
JU Johnny Unitas 50.00
BU Brian Urlacher 30.00
KW Kurt Warner 50.00
PW Peter Warrick 18.00
RW Ricky Williams 30.00
CW Charles Woodson 12.00
SY Steve Young 45.00
JY Jack Youngblood 12.00

2001 SP Authentic Stat Jerseys

NM/M
Common Player: 8.00
Inserted 1:23
SP-TA Troy Aikman 23 65.00
SP-TA Troy Aikman 165 30.00
SP-MA Mike Alstott 1219 10.00
SP-JA Jesse Armstead 529 8.00
SP-MB Michael Bennett 55 40.00
SP-MB Michael Bennett 1681 15.00
SP-DB Drew Brees 194 45.00
SP-DB Drew Brees 349 25.00
SP-IB Isaac Bruce 1471 12.00
SP-MBr Mark Brunell 236 15.00
SP-TC Tim Couch 1483 15.00
SP-DC Daunte Culpepper 40 50.00
SP-DC Daunte Culpepper 470 20.00
SP-SD Stephen Davis 1318 8.00
SP-RD Ron Dayne 770 15.00
SP-WD Warrick Dunn 422 10.00
SP-WD Warrick Dunn 1133 8.00
SP-JE John Elway 300 45.00
SP-BF Brett Favre 255 45.00
SP-BF Brett Favre 260 45.00
SP-MF Marshall Faulk 26 150.00
SP-MF Marshall Faulk 1359 15.00
SP-JF Jay Fiedler 225 15.00
SP-DF Doug Flutie 129 25.00
SP-AF Antonio Freeman 1424 8.00
SP-BG Brian Griese 102 30.00
SP-BG Brian Griese 327 20.00
SP-IH Ike Hilliard 787 8.00
SP-JK Jim Kelly 237 30.00
SP-JK Jim Kelly 403 20.00
SP-RL Ray Lewis 137 25.00
SP-PM Peyton Manning 33 85.00
SP-PM Peyton Manning 87 45.00
SP-PM Peyton Manning 94 45.00
SP-PM Peyton Manning 231 30.00
SP-PM Peyton Manning 440 25.00
SP-DM Dan Marino 48 100.00
SP-DM Dan Marino 420 45.00
SP-CM Curtis Martin 1204 10.00
SP-RM Randy Moss 43 85.00
SP-RM Randy Moss 226 35.00
SP-JR Jerry Rice 1281 20.00
SP-BS Barry Sanders 99 70.00
SP-BS Barry Sanders 1000 25.00
SP-WS Warren Sapp 58 30.00
SP-JS Junior Seau 1058 8.00
SP-SE Jason Sehorn 260 12.00
SP-ES Emmitt Smith 156 70.00
SP-FT Fred Taylor 1399 12.00
SP-LT LaDainian Tomlinson 113 60.00
SP-LT LaDainian Tomlinson 196 50.00
SP-AT Amani Toomer 1094 8.00
SP-MV Michael Vick 32 150.00
SP-MV Michael Vick 1234 40.00
SP-CW Chris Weinke 16 75.00
SP-CW Chris Weinke 223 25.00

2001 SP Game-Used Edition

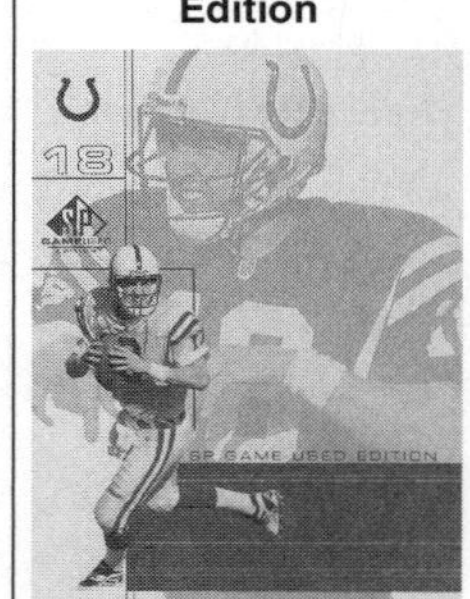

NM/M
Common Player: .50
Minor Stars: 1.00
Common Rookie Jersey: 25.00
Common Rookie: 10.00
Production 500 Sets
Pack (3): 31.50
Wax Box (6): 135.00
1 Jake Plummer 2.00
2 David Boston 2.00
3 Frank Sanders .50
4 Jamal Anderson 2.00
5 Doug Johnson .50
6 Shawn Jefferson .50
7 Jamal Lewis 5.00
8 Shannon Sharpe .50
9 Qadry Ismail .50
10 Shawn Bryson .50
11 Rob Johnson .50
12 Eric Moulds .50
13 Muhsin Muhammad .50
14 Brad Hoover 2.00
15 Tim Biakabutuka .50
16 Cade McNown 2.00
17 Marcus Robinson 2.00
18 Brian Urlacher 4.00
19 Akili Smith 2.00
20 Peter Warrick 4.00
21 Corey Dillon 2.00
22 Kevin Johnson 2.00
23 Rickey Dudley .50
24 Tim Couch 3.00
25 Tony Banks .50
26 Emmitt Smith 6.00
27 Carl Pickens .50
28 Terrell Davis 5.00
29 Mike Anderson 6.00
30 Brian Griese 2.50
31 Ed McCaffrey 2.00
32 Charlie Batch 2.00
33 Germane Crowell .50
34 James O. Stewart .50
35 Brett Favre 10.00
36 Antonio Freeman 2.00
37 Ahman Green .50
38 Peyton Manning 8.00
39 Edgerrin James 7.00
40 Marvin Harrison 2.00
41 Mark Brunell 2.50
42 Fred Taylor 3.00

43 Jimmy Smith .50
44 Tony Gonzalez .50
45 Derrick Alexander .50
46 Oronde Gadsden .50
47 Ray Lucas .50
48 Lamar Smith .50
49 Randy Moss 8.00
50 Cris Carter 2.00
51 Daunte Culpepper 4.00
52 Drew Bledsoe 2.50
53 Terry Glenn .50
54 Ricky Williams 3.00
55 Jeff Blake .50
56 Joe Horn .50
57 Aaron Brooks 2.00
58 Kerry Collins .50
59 Tiki Barber .50
60 Ron Dayne 4.00
61 Vinny Testaverde .50
62 Wayne Chrebet .50
63 Curtis Martin 2.00
64 Tim Brown 2.00
65 Rich Gannon .50
66 Tyrone Wheatley .50
67 Duce Staley 2.00
68 Donovan McNabb 3.00
69 Kordell Stewart 2.00
70 Jerome Bettis 2.00
71 Marshall Faulk 2.50
72 Kurt Warner 8.00
73 Isaac Bruce 2.00
74 Doug Flutie 2.50
75 Curtis Conway .50
76 Jeff Garcia 2.00
77 Jerry Rice 5.00
78 Charlie Garner .50
79 Terrell Owens 2.00
80 Ricky Watters .50
81 Matt Hasselbeck .50
82 Levon Kirkland .50
83 Keyshawn Johnson 2.00
84 Brad Johnson 2.00
85 Mike Alstott 2.00
86 Eddie George 2.50
87 Steve McNair 2.00
88 Jeff George .50
89 Michael Westbrook 2.00
90 Stephen Davis 2.00
91 *Michael Vick* 100.00
92 *Chris Weinke* 12.00
93 *Drew Brees* 30.00
94 *Deuce McAllister* 40.00
95 *Michael Bennett* 30.00
96 *LaDainian Tomlinson* 40.00
97 *Kevan Barlow* 25.00
98 *Travis Minor* 15.00
99 *Rudi Johnson* 25.00
100 *Todd Heap* 15.00
101 *Freddie Mitchell* 12.00
102 *Santana Moss* 25.00
103 *Reggie Wayne* 25.00
104 *Koren Robinson* 15.00
105 *Josh Heupel* 12.00
106 *Rod Gardner* 25.00
107 *Quincy Morgan* 20.00
108 *Chad Johnson* 30.00
109 *Dan Morgan* 15.00
110 *Gerard Warren* 12.00
111 *Chris Chambers* 30.00
112 *James Jackson* 15.00
113 *Jesse Palmer* 15.00
114 *Sage Rosenfels* 15.00
115 *Mike McMahon* 15.00
116 *Marques Tuiasosopo* 20.00
117 *Robert Ferguson* 20.00
118 *Travis Henry* 20.00
119 *Richard Seymour* 15.00
120 *Andre Carter* 15.00
121 *LaMont Jordan* 15.00
122 *Vinny Sutherland* 10.00
123 *Nate Clements* 10.00
124 *David Terrell* 15.00
125 *A.J. Freely* 15.00
126 *David Rivers* 8.00
127 *Marvin "Snoop" Minnis* 8.00
128 *Josh Booty* 10.00
129 *Correll Buckhalter* 12.00
130 *Will Allen* 10.00
131 *Dan Alexander* 10.00
132 *Leonard Davis* 8.00
133 *Anthony Thomas* 15.00
134 *Alge Crumpler* 12.00
135 *Jamal Reynolds* 8.00
136 *Ken-Yon Rambo* 8.00
137 *Bobby Newcombe* 8.00
138 *Alex Bannister* 10.00
139 *Jabari Holloway* 12.00
140 *Jamar Fletcher* 10.00
141 *Adam Archuleta* 12.00
142 *Heath Evans* 8.00
143 *Scotty Anderson* 8.00
144 *Moran Norris* 10.00
145 *Justin Smith* 8.00
146 *Quincy Carter* 12.00
147 *Ronney Daniels* 8.00
148 *Ben Leard* 8.00
149 *Fred Smoot* 10.00
150 *Milton Wynn* 8.00

2001 SP Game-Used Edition Fabric Jersey

NM/M
Common Player: 8.00
Inserted 1:1
Gold Cards: 2X-4X
Production 25 Sets
Multi-Colored Swatches: 1.5X
TA Troy Aikman 45.00
MA Marcus Allen 20.00
AL Mike Alstott 12.00
JA Jamal Anderson 8.00
CB Champ Bailey 12.00
BA Tiki Barber 12.00
JB Jerome Bettis 12.00
DB Drew Bledsoe 20.00
BO David Boston 12.00
TB Terry Bradshaw 65.00
BR Drew Brees 70.00

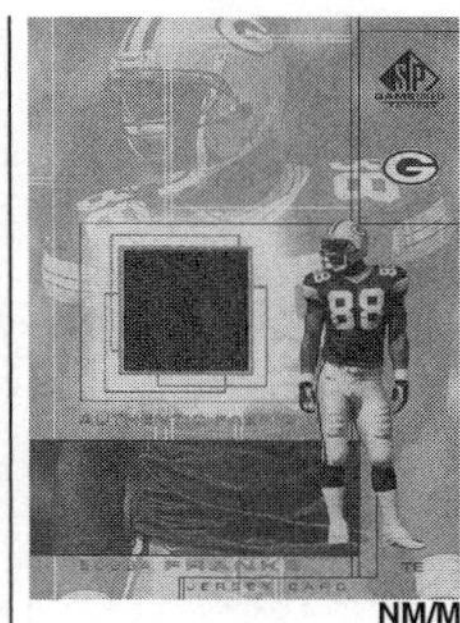

NM/M
IB Isaac Bruce 12.00
MB Mark Brunell 20.00
PB Plaxico Burress 12.00
CC Chris Chambers 15.00
CH Chris Chandler 8.00
KC Kerry Collins 8.00
CO Curtis Conway 8.00
TC Tim Couch 20.00
DC Daunte Culpepper 50.00
SD Stephen Davis 12.00
TD Terrell Davis 25.00
RD Ron Dayne 15.00
CD Corey Dillon 12.00
WD Warrick Dunn 12.00
JE John Elway 60.00
MF Marshall Faulk 20.00
BF Brett Favre 50.00
DF Bubba Franks 8.00
AF Antonio Freeman 12.00
JG Jeff Garcia 20.00
TG Terry Glenn 12.00
AG Ahman Green 12.00
BG Brian Griese 20.00
AZ Az-Zahir Hakim 8.00
IH Ike Hilliard 8.00
TH Torry Holt 12.00
EJ Edgerrin James 60.00
BJ Brad Johnson 12.00
TJ Thomas Jones 12.00
SK Shaun King 12.00
DL Dorsey Levens 12.00
JL Jamal Lewis 30.00
RL Ray Lewis 12.00
PM Peyton Manning 45.00
MC Ed McCaffrey 12.00
DM Deuce McCallister 45.00
FM Freddie Mitchell 25.00
JM Joe Montana 85.00
RM Randy Moss 60.00
EM Eric Moulds 12.00
TO Terrell Owens 12.00
WP Walter Payton 100.00
MP Michael Pittman 8.00
JP Jake Plummer 8.00
JR Jerry Rice 30.00
FS Frank Sanders 8.00
WS Warren Sapp 8.00
JS Junior Seau 8.00
SE Jason Sehorn 8.00
AS Akili Smith 12.00
JS Justin Smith 8.00
RS Rod Smith 12.00
BS Bart Starr 75.00
KS Kordell Stewart 12.00
JJ J.J. Stokes 8.00
FT Fran Tarkenton 45.00
FTa Fred Taylor 20.00
LT LaDainian Tomlinson 70.00
AT Amani Toomer 8.00
MT Marques Tuiasosopo 25.00
JU Johnny Unitas 60.00
KW Kurt Warner 40.00
PW Peter Warrick 15.00
WE Chris Weinke 40.00
MW Michael Westbrook 8.00
CW Charles Woodson 12.00

2001 SP Game-Used Edition Fabric Combo Jersey

NM/M
Common Player: 50.00
Production 50 Sets
2C-JS Keyshawn Johnson, Warren Sapp 50.00
2C-MJ Peyton Manning, Edgerrin James 175.00
2C-WH Kurt Warner, Torry Holt 175.00
2C-FF Brett Favre, Antonio Freeman 175.00
2C-DC Ron Dayne, Kerry Collins 50.00
2C-BM Mark Brunell, Keenan McCardell 50.00
2C-AS Troy Aikman, Emmitt Smith 75.00
2C-WD Peter Warrick, Corey Dillon 50.00
2C-SB Kordell Stewart, Jerome Bettis 50.00
2C-BS Frank Sanders, David Boston 50.00
2C-WB Charles Woodson, Tim Brown 50.00
2C-OG Terrell Owens, Jeff Garcia 50.00
2C-AD Mike Alstott, Warrick Dunn 50.00
2C-CM Cris Carter, Randy Moss 175.00
2C-CS Doug Chapman, Robert Smith 50.00

2001 SP Game-Used Edition Fabric Triple Jersey

NM/M
Common Player: 85.00
Production 25 Sets
3C-FWM Brett Favre, Kurt Warner, Peyton Manning 300.00
3C-DGJ Terrell Davis, Eddie George, Edgerrin James 200.00
3C-HHB Torry Holt, Az-Zahir Hakim, Isaac Bruce 85.00
3C-CMC Cris Carter, Randy Moss, Daunte Culpepper 250.00
3C-DCB Ron Dayne, Kerry Collins, Tiki Barber 125.00
3C-LLD Jamal Lewis, Ray Lewis, Trent Dilfer 125.00

2001 SPx

NM/M
Common Player: .20
Minor Stars: .40
Common Rookie: 4.00
Pack (4): 12.00
Box (18): 150.00
1 Jake Plummer .60
2 David Boston .60
3 Jamal Anderson .40
4 Chris Chandler .40
5 Tony Martin .40
6 Elvis Grbac .50
7 Qadry Ismail .20
8 Ray Lewis .50
9 Rob Johnson .50
10 Shawn Bryson .20
11 Eric Moulds .60
12 Tim Biakabutuka .20
13 Jeff Lewis .40
14 Muhsin Muhammad .20
15 Shane Matthews .40
16 Marcus Robinson .60
17 Brian Urlacher 1.50
18 Jon Kitna .40
19 Peter Warrick .60
20 Corey Dillon .60
21 Tim Couch 1.00
22 Travis Prentice .20
23 Kevin Johnson .75
24 Raghib Ismail .20
25 Emmitt Smith 2.00
26 Joey Galloway .50
27 Terrell Davis 1.50
28 Brian Griese 1.00
29 Rod Smith .60
30 Ed McCaffrey .60
31 Charlie Batch .40
32 Germane Crowell .20
33 James O. Stewart .40
34 Brett Favre 3.00
35 Antonio Freeman .60
36 Ahman Green .75
37 Peyton Manning 2.50
38 Edgerrin James 2.00
39 Marvin Harrison .75
40 Mark Brunell 1.00
41 Fred Taylor 1.00
42 Jimmy Smith .50
43 Tony Gonzalez .50
44 Trent Green .50
45 Priest Holmes .40
46 Lamar Smith .40
47 Jay Fiedler .50
48 Oronde Gadsden .20
49 Daunte Culpepper 1.50
50 Randy Moss 2.50
51 Cris Carter .75
52 Drew Bledsoe 1.00
53 Troy Brown .40
54 Ricky Williams 1.25
55 Joe Horn .40
56 Aaron Brooks 1.00
57 Albert Connell .20
58 Kerry Collins .75
59 Tiki Barber .40
60 Ron Dayne .40
61 Vinny Testaverde .60
62 Wayne Chrebet .50
63 Curtis Martin .75
64 Tim Brown .75
65 Jerry Rice 2.00
66 Rich Gannon .60
67 Duce Staley .40
68 Donovan McNabb 1.50
69 Kordell Stewart .75
70 Jerome Bettis .50
71 Marshall Faulk 1.00
72 Kurt Warner 2.50
73 Isaac Bruce .75
74 Torry Holt .75
75 Doug Flutie 1.00
76 Junior Seau .50
77 Jeff Garcia 1.00
78 Garrison Hearst .40
79 Terrell Owens .60
80 Ricky Watters .40
81 Matt Hasselbeck .50
82 Brad Johnson .60
83 Keyshawn Johnson .75
84 Warrick Dunn .40
85 Mike Alstott .40
86 Kevin Dyson .40
87 Eddie George 1.00
88 Steve McNair .75
89 Michael Westbrook .50
90 Stephen Davis .60
91 *Deuce McAllister* 200.00
92 *Freddie Mitchell* 30.00
93 *Koren Robinson* 12.00
94 *David Terrell* 10.00
95 *Michael Vick* 500.00
96 *Michael Bennett* 60.00
97 *Robert Ferguson* 10.00
98 *Rod Gardner* 15.00
99 *Travis Henry* 40.00
100 *Chad Johnson* 50.00
101 *Drew Brees* 75.00
102 *Santana Moss* 40.00
103 *Chris Weinke* 30.00
104 *Richard Seymour* 20.00
105 *Reggie Wayne* 12.00
106 *Kevan Barlow* 50.00
107 *Chris Chambers* 50.00
108 *Todd Heap* 30.00
109 *Anthony Thomas* 40.00
110 *James Jackson* 20.00
111 *Rudi Johnson* 40.00
112 *Mike McMahon* 25.00
113 *Josh Heupel* 20.00
114 *Travis Minor* 20.00
115 *Quincy Morgan* 10.00
116 *Dan Morgan* 15.00
117 *Jesse Palmer* 25.00
118 *Sage Rosenfels* 15.00
119 *Marques Tuiasosopo* 25.00
120 *Darnerian McCants* 6.00
121 *Marvin "Snoop" Minnis* 10.00
122 *LaDainian Tomlinson* 100.00
123 *Quincy Carter* 15.00
124 *Arnold Jackson* 4.00
125 *Justin McCareins* 10.00
126 *Eddie Berlin* 6.00
127 *Quentin McCord* 4.00
128 *Vinny Sutherland* 6.00
129 *Willie Middlebrooks* 6.00
130 *Dan Alexander* 6.00
131 *Dadrian "Dee" Brown* 6.00
132 *Andre Carter* 6.00
133 *Justin Smith* 6.00
134 *T.J. Houshmandzadeh* 6.00
135 *Andre King* 6.00
136 *Nick Goings* 8.00
137 *Scotty Anderson* 6.00
138 *David Martin* 6.00
139 *Derrick Blaylock* 8.00
140 *Onome Ojo* 4.00
141 *Jonathan Carter* 4.00
142 *Lamont Jordon* 10.00
143 *Dominic Rhodes* 12.00
145 *A.J. Feeley* 15.00
146 *Correll Buckhalter* 10.00
147 *Steve Smith* 10.00
148 *Dave Dickenson* 8.00
149 *Cedrick Wilson* 6.00
150 *Jamie Winborn* 4.00
151 *Alex Bannister* 6.00
152 *Heath Evans* 4.00
153 *Josh Booty* 8.00
154 *Adam Archuleta* 8.00
155 *Francis St. Paul* 4.00
156 *Andre Dyson* 6.00

2001 SPx "Winning Materials"

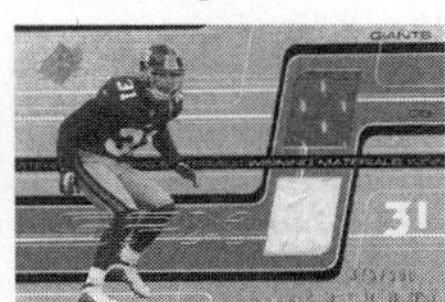

"Prices are for most common version."

NM/M
Common Player: 10.00
WM-TA Troy Aikman 25.00
WM-MA Mike Alstott 10.00
WM-TB Tiki Barber 10.00
WM-KB Kevan Barlow 10.00
WM-BE Michael Bennett 25.00
WM-BO David Boston 15.00
WM-DB Drew Brees 20.00
WM-DB2 Drew Brees 20.00
WM-MB Mark Brunell 15.00
WM-AC Andre Carter 10.00
WM-CH Chris Chambers 25.00
WM-TC Tim Couch 20.00
WM-DC Daunte Culpepper 20.00
WM-RD Ron Dayne 15.00
WM-MF Marshall Faulk 20.00
WM-BF Brett Favre 40.00
WM-BF2 Brett Favre 40.00
WM-RF Robert Ferguson 20.00
WM-JF Jay Fiedler 10.00
WM-DF Doug Flutie 15.00
WM-AF Antonio Freeman 10.00
WM-RG Rich Gannon 10.00
WM-JG Jeff Garcia 15.00
WM-GA Rod Gardner 10.00
WM-CG Charlie Garner 10.00
WM-EG Elvis Grbac 10.00
WM-BG Brian Griese 15.00
WM-HE Travis Henry 10.00
WM-JJ James Jackson 10.00
WM-EJ Edgerrin James 30.00
WM-TJ Thomas Jones 10.00
WM-PM Peyton Manning 40.00
WM-DU Deuce McAllister 10.00
WM-FM Freddie Mitchell 10.00
WM-MO Dan Morgan 10.00
WM-QM Quincy Morgan 10.00
WM-RM Randy Moss 20.00
WM-RM2 Randy Moss 20.00
WM-SM Santana Moss 10.00
WM-TO Terrell Owen 10.00
WM-PA Jesse Palmer 10.00
WM-JP Jake Plummer 10.00
WM-JR Jerry Rice 25.00
WM-KR Koren Robinson 10.00
WM-JS Junior Seau 15.00
WM-SE Jason Sehorn 10.00
WM-AS Akili Smith 10.00
WM-FT Fred Taylor 10.00
WM-DT David Terrell 10.00
WM-AT Anthony Thomas 40.00
WM-LT LaDainian Tomlinson 30.00
WM-LT2 LaDainian Tomlinson 30.00
WM-MT Marques Tuiasosopo 15.00
WM-MV Michael Vick 75.00
WM-KW Kurt Warner 20.00
WM-PW Peter Warrick 10.00
WM-MA Reggie Wayne 10.00
WM-CW Chris Weinke 20.00

2002 SP Authentic

NM/M
Common Player: .25
Unlisted Star: .75
Minor Star: .50
Cards 91-94 Autographed
Cards 95-124 Production 2000 sets
Cards 125-154 Production 1150 sets
Cards 155-214 Rookies Production 1150
Cards 215-234 JERSEY 350 or 850 sets
Cards 235-244 AUTO/JERSEY 250 sets
Unlisted Rookie Star: 8.00
Minor Rookie Star: 4.00
Pack (5): 8.00
Wax Box (24): 130.00
1 Tom Brady 2.50
2 Antowain Smith .25
3 Troy Brown .50
4 Kurt Warner 2.50
5 Marshall Faulk 1.50
6 Isaac Bruce .75
7 Kordell Stewart .50
8 Jerome Bettis .50
9 Plaxico Burress .75
10 Hines Ward .50
11 Donovan McNabb 1.50
12 Duce Staley .50
13 Dorsey Levens .25
14 Antonio Freeman .25
15 Jerry Rice 2.50
16 Rich Gannon .75
17 Tim Brown .75
18 Jim Miller .25
19 Marty Booker .50
20 Brian Urlacher 2.00
21 Jamal Lewis 1.25
22 Chris Redman .50
23 Ray Lewis .50
24 Brett Favre 3.00
25 Ahman Green .75
26 Terry Glenn .50
27 Keyshawn Johnson .75
28 Keenan McCardell .50
29 Michael Pittman .25
30 Curtis Martin .75
31 Vinny Testaverde .25
32 Chad Pennington 1.25
33 Wayne Chrebet .50
34 Terrell Owens .75
35 Garrison Hearst .50
36 Jay Fiedler .50
37 Ricky Williams 1.50
38 Chris Chambers .75
39 Shaun Alexander .75
40 Darrell Jackson .25
41 Drew Bledsoe 1.50
42 Travis Henry .50
43 Eric Moulds .50
44 Stephen Davis .50
45 Rod Gardner .50
46 Brian Griese .75
47 Olandis Gary .25
48 Shannon Sharpe .50
49 Tim Couch 1.25
50 Kevin Johnson .25
51 Steve McNair .75
52 Eddie George .75
53 Aaron Brooks 1.25
54 Deuce McAllister 1.25
55 Joe Horn .50
56 Michael Vick 2.50
57 Warrick Dunn .50
58 Kerry Collins .50
59 Tiki Barber .50
60 Amani Toomer .50
61 Jake Plummer .50
62 David Boston .75
63 Thomas Jones .25
64 Edgerrin James 2.00
65 Marvin Harrison .75
66 Mark Brunell .75
67 Jimmy Smith .25
68 Fred Taylor .75
69 Corey Dillon .75
70 Jon Kitna .25
71 Michael Westbrook .50
72 Trent Green .50
73 Priest Holmes 1.25
74 Tony Gonzalez .50
75 Daunte Culpepper 1.50
76 Michael Bennett .75
77 Randy Moss 2.50
78 Drew Brees 2.00
79 Curtis Conway .50
80 Junior Seau .50
81 Quincy Carter 1.25
82 Emmitt Smith 2.50
83 Joey Galloway .50
84 Cory Schlesinger .25
85 James Stewart .25
86 Az-Zahir Hakim .50
87 Rodney Peete .25
88 Lamar Smith .25
89 Corey Bradford .25
90 Jermaine Lewis .25
91 Peyton Manning Auto 60.00
92 Anthony Thomas Auto 25.00
93 LaDainian Tomlinson Auto 30.00
94 Jeff Garcia Auto 20.00
95 Kurt Warner 3.00
96 Brett Favre 3.50
97 Michael Vick 3.00
98 Donovan McNabb 2.00
99 Daunte Culpepper 2.00
100 Tom Brady 3.00
101 Drew Brees 1.75
102 Kordell Stewart 1.25
103 Steve McNair 1.25
104 Peyton Manning 3.00
105 Mark Brunell 1.25
106 Jeff Garcia 1.25
107 Aaron Brooks 1.75
108 Rich Gannon 1.25
109 Tim Couch 1.75
110 Jake Plummer 1.25
111 Drew Bledsoe 2.00
112 Brian Griese 1.25
113 Quincy Carter 1.75
114 Vinny Testaverde 1.00
115 Chad Pennington 1.75
116 Brad Johnson 1.00
117 Trent Dilfer 1.00
118 Jim Miller 1.00
119 Tommy Maddox 1.00
120 Trent Green 1.25
121 Rodney Peete 1.00
122 Jay Fiedler 1.00
123 Kerry Collins 1.00
124 Chris Redman 1.00
125 Marshall Faulk 2.50
126 Donovan McNabb 2.50
127 Michael Vick 3.50
128 Brett Favre 4.00
129 Peyton Manning 3.50
130 Kurt Warner 3.50
131 Curtis Martin 1.75
132 Randy Moss 3.50
133 Edgerrin James 3.00
134 Jerome Bettis 1.50
135 Emmitt Smith 3.50
136 LaDainian Tomlinson 3.00
137 Jeff Garcia 1.75
138 Kordell Stewart 1.50
139 Anthony Thomas 2.25
140 Tom Brady 3.50
141 Daunte Culpepper 2.50
142 Drew Bledsoe 2.50
143 Ricky Williams 2.50
144 Warrick Dunn 1.50
145 Steve McNair 1.75
146 Rich Gannon 1.75
147 Jake Plummer 1.75
148 Jerry Rice 3.50
149 Mark Brunell 1.75
150 Brian Griese 1.75
151 Eddie George 1.75
152 Tim Couch 2.25
153 Keyshawn Johnson 1.75
154 Shannon Sharpe 1.50
155 *Phillip Buchanon* 8.00
156 *Brian Allen* 5.00
157 *Brian Westbrook* 30.00
158 *Lito Sheppard* 5.00
159 *Daryl Jones* 5.00
160 *Javin Hunter* 5.00
161 *Derrick Lewis* 5.00
162 *Javon Walker* 30.00
163 *Tank Williams* 5.00
164 *Shaun Hill* 5.00
165 *Napoleon Harris* 6.00
166 *Herb Haygood* 5.00
167 *Jake Schifino* 5.00
168 *Quentin Jammer* 10.00
169 *Jason McAddley* 5.00
170 *Jerramy Stevens* 6.00
171 *Jesse Chatman* 10.00
172 *Larry Ned* 5.00
173 *Najeh Davenport* 8.00
174 *Lamont Thompson* 5.00
175 *Darrell Hill* 5.00
176 *Ryan Sims* 5.00
177 *Ryan Denney* 5.00
178 *Jamin Elliott* 5.00
179 *Sam Simmons* 5.00
180 *Seth Burford* 5.00
181 *Tellis Redmon* 5.00
182 *Ben Leber* 5.00
183 *Kendall Newson* 5.00
184 *Marques Anderson* 5.00
185 *Adrian Peterson* 8.00
186 *Albert Haynesworth* 6.00
187 *Antwoine Womack* 5.00
188 *Brandon Doman* 5.00
189 *Craig Nall* 8.00
190 *Chad Hutchinson* 12.00
191 *Chester Taylor* 8.00
192 *Damien Anderson* 6.00
193 *Deion Branch* 35.00
194 *Dusty Bonner* 5.00
195 *Ed Reed* 30.00
196 *Eric McCoo* 5.00
197 *J.T. O'Sullivan* 5.00
198 *Kalimba Edwards* 5.00
199 *Jonathan Wells* 8.00
200 *Josh Scobey* 6.00
201 *Kelly Campbell* 8.00
202 *Kurt Kittner* 8.00
203 *Lamar Gordon* 8.00
204 *Lee Mays* 5.00

205 Leonard Henry 5.00
206 Luke Staley 6.00
207 Justin Peelle 5.00
208 Randy Fasani 6.00
209 Ricky Williams 8.00
210 Ronald Curry 25.00
211 Travis Stephens 8.00
212 Wendell Bryant 5.00
213 Woodrow Dantzler III 8.00
214 Kahlil Hill 5.00
215 Donte Stallworth 50.00
216 Joey Harrington 300.00
217 Cliff Russell 20.00
218 Clinton Portis 175.00
219 Daniel Graham 25.00
220 David Garrard 30.00
221 DeShaun Foster 60.00
222 Julius Peppers 40.00
223 Jeremy Shockey 80.00
224 Patrick Ramsey 60.00
225 Josh Reed 30.00
226 Ladell Betts 30.00
227 Mike Williams/350 30.00
228 Reche Caldwell 50.00
229 Rohan Davey 50.00
230 Ron Johnson 20.00
231 Roy Williams/350 100.00
232 T.J. Duckett 60.00
233 Tim Carter 25.00
234 William Green 60.00
235 Antwann Randle El Auto/JSY 100.00
236 Ashley Lelie Auto/JSY 200.00
237 David Carr Auto/JSY 400.00
238 Andre Davis Auto/JSY 100.00
239 Eric Crouch Auto/JSY 75.00
240 Antonio Bryant Auto/JSY 125.00
241 Jabar Gaffney Auto/JSY 75.00
242 Marquise Walker Auto/JSY 60.00
243 Maurice Morris Auto/JSY 75.00
244 Josh McCown Auto/JSY 125.00
AP1 Walter Payton Auto/34 300.00
SW1 Walter Payton Jsy/150 100.00
SW1 Walter Payton Gold Jsy/34 200.00
SCPS Walter Payton, Emmitt Smith Jsy/250 125.00
SCPS Walter Payton, Emmitt Smith Gold Jsy/34 300.00

2002 SP Authentic Gold

1-90 Stars: 10X-20X
Production 50 Sets

2002 SP Authentic Sign of the Times

NM/M
Common Player: 15.00
Inserted 1:96
Gold Production 25 Sets
ST-DB Drew Bledsoe 30.00
ST-MB Marty Booker 15.00
ST-BR Drew Brees 15.00
ST-AB Aaron Brooks 15.00
ST-BT Antonio Bryant 35.00
ST-CA David Carr 75.00
ST-RC Rosevelt Colvin 20.00
ST-TC Tim Couch 20.00
ST-DC Daunte Culpepper 30.00
ST-JG Jabar Gaffney 15.00
ST-RG Rich Gannon 50.00
ST-DG David Garrard 20.00
ST-TG Tony Gonzalez 25.00
ST-AG Ahman Green 25.00
ST-CH Chad Hutchinson 40.00
ST-BJ Brad Johnson 20.00
ST-AL Ashley Lelie 40.00
ST-PM Peyton Manning 40.00
ST-FM Freddie Mitchell 15.00
ST-MM Maurice Morris 20.00
ST-PE Julius Peppers 35.00
ST-JP Jake Plummer 15.00
ST-EL Antwann Randle El 40.00
ST-JR John Riggins 35.00
ST-AS Antowain Smith 15.00
ST-ES Emmitt Smith/22 200.00
ST-LT LaDainian Tomlinson 30.00
ST-MV Michael Vick 75.00

2002 SP Authentic Threads Single

NM/M
Common Player: 10.00
Inserted 1:52
Gold Production 25 Sets
AT1-AB Antonio Bryant 15.00
AT1-DC David Carr 20.00
AT1-EC Eric Crouch 10.00
AT1-DF DeShaun Foster 12.00
AT1-JH Joey Harrington 20.00
AT1-AL Ashley Lelie 15.00
AT1-MM Maurice Morris 10.00
AT1-JP Julius Peppers 12.00
AT1-PR Patrick Ramsey 12.00
AT1-DS Donte Stallworth 15.00
AT1-JW Javon Walker 12.00
AT1-MW Marquise Walker 10.00

2002 SP Authentic Threads Double

NM/M
Common Player: 10.00
Inserted 1:70
Gold Production 25 Sets
AT2-CB Reche Caldwell, Drew Brees 10.00
AT2-CC David Carr, Tim Couch 25.00
AT2-CW David Carr, Kurt Warner 30.00
AT2-HC Joey Harrington, Daunte Culpepper 25.00
AT2-HM Joey Harrington, Donovan McNabb 25.00
AT2-MF Maurice Morris, Marshall Faulk 15.00
AT2-RB Patrick Ramsey, Tom Brady 15.00
AT2-SM Donte Stallworth, Peyton Manning 15.00

2002 SP Authentic Threads Triple

NM/M
Common Player: 20.00
Production 250 sets
Gold Production 10 Sets
AT3-BP Drew Bledsoe, Peerless Price, Josh Reed 25.00
AT3-CC David Carr, Tim Couch, Peyton Manning 35.00
AT3-CD Eric Crouch, Ron Dayne, Ricky Williams 20.00
AT3-CH David Carr, Joey Harrington, Patrick Ramsey 50.00
AT3-CM Daunte Culpepper, Donovan McNabb, Michael Vick 50.00
AT3-CW Eric Crouch, Kurt Warner, Marshall Faulk 25.00
AT3-FMDeShaun Foster, Freddie Mitchell, J.J. Stokes 20.00
AT3-FW Brett Favre, Kurt Warner, Peyton Manning 50.00
AT3-PB Jake Plummer, David Boston, Josh McCown 20.00
AT3-PL Clinton Portis, Ray Lewis, Santana Moss 40.00
AT3-SS Donte Stallworth, Travis Stephens, Peyton Manning 35.00
AT3-WG Marquise Walker, Brian Griese, Desmond Howard 20.00

2002 SP Authentic Threads Quads

NM/M
Common Player: 25.00
Production 100 sets
Gold Production 25 Sets
AT4-CBEric Crouch, Tim Brown, Eddie George, Charles Woodson 25.00
AT4-CHDavid Carr, Joey Harrington, Patrick Ramsey, Rohan Davey 50.00
AT4-CWEric Crouch, Kurt Warner, Marshall Faulk, Isaac Bruce 40.00
AT4-SLJeremy Shockey, Ray Lewis, Santana Moss, Warren Sapp
AT4-SSDonte Stallworth, Travis Stephens, Peyton Manning, Jamal Lewis 45.00
AT4-WGKurt Warner, Brian Griese, Rich Gannon, Quincy Carter 40.00

2002 SP Auth. Sign of the Times Hawaii Trade Conference

JR John Riggins/500 60.00

2002 SP Legendary Cuts

NM/M
Common Player: .25
Unlisted Star: .75
Minor Star: .50
Cards 91-100 Production 2500 sets
Cards 101-110 Production 1500 sets
Cards 111-120 Production 800 sets
Cards 121-150 Production 500 sets
Cards 151-210 Production 1100 sets
Unlisted Rookie Star: 4.00
Minor Rookie Star: 3.00
Pack (4): 8.00
Wax Box (12): 65.00
1 Tom Brady 2.50
2 Antowain Smith .25
3 Troy Brown .50
4 Drew Bledsoe 1.50
5 Travis Henry .50
6 Eric Moulds .50
7 Ricky Williams 1.50
8 Jay Fiedler .50
9 Chris Chambers .75
10 Curtis Martin .75
11 Chad Pennington 1.25
12 Wayne Chrebet .50
13 Jerome Bettis .50
14 Tommy Maddox .50
15 Hines Ward .50
16 Tim Couch 1.25
17 Kevin Johnson .25
18 Jamal Lewis 1.25
19 Chris Redman .50
20 Corey Dillon .75
21 Michael Westbrook .50
22 Peyton Manning 2.50
23 Edgerrin James 2.00
24 Marvin Harrison .75
25 Qadry Ismail .25
26 Mark Brunell .75
27 Jimmy Smith .50
28 Stacey Mack .25
29 Fred Taylor .50
30 Steve McNair .75
31 Eddie George .75
32 Kevin Dyson .50
33 James Allen .25
34 Corey Bradford .25
35 Shannon Sharpe .50
36 Brian Griese .75
37 Ed McCaffrey .50
38 Jerry Rice 2.50
39 Rich Gannon .75
40 Tim Brown .75
41 Trent Green .50
42 Priest Holmes 1.25
43 Tony Gonzalez .50
44 LaDainian Tomlinson 2.00
45 Drew Brees 2.00
46 Curtis Conway .50
47 Donovan McNabb 1.50
48 Duce Staley .50
49 Antonio Freeman .25
50 James Thrash .25
51 Kerry Collins .25
52 Tiki Barber .50
53 Amani Toomer .25
54 Emmitt Smith 2.50
55 Quincy Carter 1.25
56 Joey Galloway .50
57 Stephen Davis .50
58 Champ Bailey .25
59 Anthony Thomas 1.25
60 Jim Miller .50
61 Brian Urlacher 2.00
62 Brett Favre 3.00
63 Ahman Green .75
64 Robert Ferguson .25
65 Randy Moss 2.50
66 Daunte Culpepper 1.50
67 Moe Williams .25
68 James Stewart .50
69 Az-Zahir Hakim .50
70 Keyshawn Johnson .75
71 Brad Johnson .50
72 Mike Alstott .50
73 Michael Vick 2.50
74 Warrick Dunn .75
75 Shawn Jefferson .25
76 Aaron Brooks 1.25
77 Deuce McAllister 1.25
78 Joe Horn .50
79 Rodney Peete .25
80 Steve Smith .25
81 Terrell Owens .75
82 Jeff Garcia .75
83 Garrison Hearst .50
84 Kurt Warner 2.50
85 Marshall Faulk 1.50
86 Torry Holt .75
87 Jake Plummer .50
88 David Boston .75
89 Shaun Alexander .75
90 Trent Dilfer .50
91 Tom Brady 3.00
92 Michael Vick 3.00
93 LaDainian Tomlinson 2.50
94 Rich Gannon 1.25
95 Randy Moss 3.00
96 Aaron Brooks 1.75
97 Mark Brunell 1.25
98 Jeff Garcia 1.25
99 Ahman Green 1.25
100 Shaun Alexander 1.25
101 Ricky Williams 2.50
102 Bruce Smith 1.00
103 Curtis Martin 1.75
104 Brian Urlacher 3.00
105 Jerome Bettis 1.50
106 Ray Lewis 1.50
107 Edgerrin James 3.00
108 Junior Seau 1.50
109 Priest Holmes 2.25
110 Warren Sapp 1.50
111 Emmitt Smith 4.50
112 Jerry Rice 4.50
113 Brett Favre 5.00
114 Marshall Faulk 3.50
115 Drew Bledsoe 3.50
116 Tim Brown 2.75
117 Donovan McNabb 3.50
118 Peyton Manning 4.50
119 Kurt Warner 4.50
120 Shannon Sharpe 2.75
121 *Andre Davis* 10.00
122 *Antonio Bryant* 12.00
123 *Antwann Randle El* 10.00
124 *Ashley Lelie* 12.00
125 *Ben Leber* 8.00
126 *Chad Hutchinson* 10.00
127 *Clinton Portis* 30.00
128 *David Carr* 30.00
129 *Deion Branch* 12.00
130 *DeShaun Foster* 12.00
131 *Donte Stallworth* 12.00
132 *Jabar Gaffney* 8.00
133 *Javon Walker* 15.00
134 *Jeremy Shockey* 20.00
135 *Joey Harrington* 25.00
136 *Josh McCown* 12.00
137 *Josh Reed* 10.00
138 *Julius Peppers* 10.00
139 *Marquise Walker* 6.00
140 *Maurice Morris* 8.00
141 *Patrick Ramsey* 12.00
142 *Quentin Jammer* 6.00
143 *Randy Fasani* 4.00
144 *Reche Caldwell* 8.00
145 *Rohan Davey* 8.00
146 *Ron Johnson* 6.00
147 *Roy Williams* 15.00
148 *T.J. Duckett* 12.00
149 *Travis Stephens* 6.00
150 *William Green* 12.00
151 *Albert Haynesworth* 3.00
152 *Alex Brown* 2.00
153 *Andra Davis* 2.00
154 *Andre Gurode* 2.00
155 *Anthony Weaver* 2.00
156 *Brandon Doman* 2.00
157 *Brian Westbrook* 12.00
158 *Brian Williams* 2.00
159 *Lamont Brightful* 2.00
160 *Charles Grant* 2.00
161 *Chester Taylor* 2.00
162 *Cliff Russell* 3.00
163 *Daniel Graham* 6.00
164 *David Garrard* 4.00
165 *James Mungro* 2.00
166 *Dennis Johnson* 2.00
167 *Derek Ross* 2.00
168 *Dwight Freeney* 8.00
169 *Ed Reed* 2.00
170 *Carlos Hall* 2.00
171 *Jarrod Baxter* 2.00
172 *Jason McAddley* 2.00
173 *Jerramy Stevens* 3.00
174 *Jesse Chatman* 2.00
175 *John Henderson* 3.00
176 *Jon McGraw* 2.00
177 *Jonathan Wells* 6.00
178 *Justin Peelle* 2.00
179 *Kalimba Edwards* 2.00
180 *Keyuo Craver* 2.00
181 *Kurt Kittner* 4.00
182 *Ladell Betts* 4.00
183 *Lamar Gordon* 4.00
184 *Lamont Thompson* 2.00
185 *Larry Tripplett* 2.00
186 *Randy McMichael* 3.00
187 *Lito Sheppard* 3.00
188 *Marques Anderson* 3.00
189 *Michael Lewis* 2.00
190 *Mike Pearson* 2.00
191 *Mike Rumph* 3.00
192 *Najeh Davenport* 8.00
193 *Napoleon Harris* 3.00
194 *Phillip Buchanon* 4.00
195 *Quinn Gray* 2.00
196 *Raonall Smith* 2.00
197 *Ricky Williams* 3.00
198 *Robert Thomas* 2.00
199 *Rocky Calmus* 4.00
200 *Ryan Denney* 2.00
201 *Ryan Sims* 3.00
202 *Jamal Robertson* 2.00
203 *Shaun Hill* 2.00
204 *Tank Williams* 2.00
205 *Tellis Redmon* 3.00
206 *Tim Carter* 3.00
207 *Tony Fisher* 4.00
208 *Travis Fisher* 2.00
209 *Verron Haynes* 2.00
210 *Wendell Bryant* 3.00

2002 SP Legendary Cuts Autographs

NM/M
Production Quantities Listed Below
LC-RB Morris "Red" Badgro/57 125.00
LC-BU Buck Buchanon/8
LC-CN Jack Christiansen/3
LC-TE Turk Edwards/12
LC-TF Tom Fears/9
LC-RF Ray Flaherty/25
LC-LF Len Ford/4
LC-DF Dan Fortmann/30 200.00
LC-BG Bill George/8
LC-RG Harold "Red" Grange/9
LC-LG Lou Groza/20
LC-AH Arnie Herber/25 150.00
LC-TL Tom Landry/20
LC-BL Bobby Layne/4
LC-VL Vince Lombardi/240 300.00
LC-SL Sid Luckman/22
LC-LL Link Lyman/11
LC-MM Mike Michalske/7
LC-MO Marion Motley/12
LC-BN Bronko Nagurski/75 275.00
LC-RN Ray Nitschke/115 200.00
LC-SO Steve Owen/5
LC-WP Walter Payton/65 400.00
LC-KS Ken Strong/120 200.00
LC-JU Johnny Unitas/29 300.00
LC-VB Norm Van Brocklin/3
LC-PW Pop Warner/1
LC-BW Bob Waterfield/12
LC-AW Alex Wojciechowicz/28 200.00

2002 SP Legendary Cuts Rookie Recruits

NM/M
Common Player: 8.00
Production 850 sets
Gold: 1X-2X
Production 75 sets
RR-LB Ladell Betts 10.00
RR-AB Antonio Bryant 15.00
RR-RC Reche Caldwell 8.00
RR-DC David Carr 25.00
RR-TC Tim Carter 8.00
RR-EC Eric Crouch 10.00
RR-RD Rohan Davey 10.00
RR-AD Andre Davis 10.00
RR-TJ T.J. Duckett 15.00
RR-FO DeShaun Foster 12.00
RR-JG Jabar Gaffney 8.00
RR-DG Daniel Graham 8.00
RR-WG William Green 15.00
RR-JH Joey Harrington 25.00
RR-RJ Ron Johnson 8.00
RR-AL Ashley Lelie 15.00
RR-JM Josh McCown 12.00
RR-MM Maurice Morris 10.00
RR-JP Julius Peppers 12.00
RR-CP Clinton Portis 20.00
RR-PR Patrick Ramsey 12.00
RR-EL Antwann Randle El 15.00
RR-JR Josh Reed 12.00
RR-CR Cliff Russell 8.00
RR-JS Jeremy Shockey 20.00
RR-DS Donte Stallworth 15.00
RR-TS Travis Stephens 10.00
RR-JW Javon Walker 12.00
RR-WA Marquise Walker 8.00
RR-RO Roy Williams 15.00

2002 SP Legendary Cuts SP Classic Threads

NM/M
Common Player: 8.00
Production 350 sets
Gold: 1X-2X
Production 75 sets
CC-MA Marcus Allen 15.00
CC-JB Jerome Bettis 10.00
CC-DB Drew Bledsoe 15.00
CC-BO David Boston 8.00
CC-BY Tom Brady 15.00
CC-BR Drew Brees 12.00
CC-AB Aaron Brooks 10.00
CC-TB Tim Brown 15.00
CC-KC Kerry Collins 8.00
CC-TC Tim Couch 12.00
CC-DC Daunte Culpepper 12.00
CC-CD Corey Dillon 8.00
CC-JE John Elway 40.00
CC-MF Marshall Faulk 12.00
CC-BF Brett Favre 35.00
CC-RG Rich Gannon 12.00
CC-JG Jeff Garcia 12.00
CC-EG Eddie George 12.00
CC-AG Ahman Green 12.00
CC-BG Brian Griese 12.00
CC-MH Marvin Harrison 10.00
CC-GH Garrison Hearst 8.00
CC-PH Priest Holmes 15.00
CC-EJ Edgerrin James 15.00
CC-KJ Keyshawn Johnson 8.00
CC-JK Jim Kelly 25.00
CC-JL Jamal Lewis 8.00
CC-PM Peyton Manning 20.00
CC-DM Dan Marino 45.00
CC-CM Curtis Martin 8.00
CC-MC Donovan McNabb 15.00
CC-SM Steve McNair 8.00
CC-RM Randy Moss 20.00
CC-WP Walter Payton 50.00
CC-JR Jerry Rice 30.00
CC-ES Emmitt Smith 30.00
CC-AT Anthony Thomas 8.00
CC-LT LaDainian Tomlinson 15.00
CC-MV Michael Vick 30.00
CC-KW Kurt Warner 15.00
CC-CW Chris Weinke 8.00
CC-RW Ricky Williams 15.00

2002 SPx

NM/M
Common Player: .25
Unlisted Star: .75
Minor Star: .50
Cards 91-150 Production 1500 sets
Cards 151-175 Production 999 sets
Cards 176-78 Production 250 or 650 sets
Unlisted Rookie Star: 3.00
Minor Rookie Star: 2.00
Pack (4): 6.00
Wax Box (18): 75.00
1 Drew Bledsoe 1.50
2 Peerless Price .50
3 Travis Henry .50
4 Ricky Williams 1.50
5 Jay Fiedler .50
6 Tom Brady 2.50
7 Troy Brown .50
8 Antowain Smith .50
9 Santana Moss .25
10 Curtis Martin .75
11 Vinny Testaverde .25
12 Jamal Lewis 1.25
13 Chris Redman .50
14 Travis Taylor .50
15 Corey Dillon .75
16 T.J. Houshmandzadeh .25
17 Peter Warrick .25
18 Courtney Brown .25
19 Kevin Johnson .25
20 Tim Couch 1.25
21 Hines Ward .50
22 Jerome Bettis .50
23 Kordell Stewart .50
24 Corey Bradford .25
25 Jermaine Lewis .25
26 Edgerrin James 2.00
27 Marvin Harrison .75
28 Peyton Manning 2.50
29 Jimmy Smith .25
30 Mark Brunell .75
31 Fred Taylor .50
32 Eddie George .75
33 Steve McNair .75
34 Brian Griese .75
35 Shannon Sharpe .50
36 Rod Smith .50
37 Trent Green .50
38 Johnnie Morton .25
39 Priest Holmes 1.25
40 Jerry Rice .25
41 Rich Gannon .75
42 Tim Brown .75
43 Drew Brees 2.00
44 Junior Seau .50
45 LaDainian Tomlinson 2.00
46 Emmitt Smith 2.50
47 Quincy Carter 1.25
48 Raghib Ismail .25
49 Amani Toomer .50
50 Kerry Collins .50
51 Ron Dayne .50
52 Donovan McNabb 1.50
53 Duce Staley .50
54 Antonio Freeman .25
55 Rod Gardner .50
56 Stephen Davis .50
57 Brian Urlacher 2.00
58 Anthony Thomas 1.50
59 Jim Miller .25
60 Marty Booker .50
61 Az-Zahir Hakim .50
62 James Stewart .25
63 Ahman Green .75
64 Brett Favre 3.00
65 Robert Ferguson .25
66 Terry Glenn .50
67 Randy Moss 2.50
68 Daunte Culpepper 1.50
69 Michael Bennett .75
70 Michael Vick 2.50
71 Warrick Dunn .50
72 Rodney Peete .25
73 Muhsin Muhammad .50
74 Aaron Brooks 1.25
75 Deuce McAllister 1.25
76 Keyshawn Johnson .75
77 Michael Pittman .25
78 Brad Johnson .50
79 Thomas Jones .25
80 David Boston .75
81 Jake Plummer .50
82 Terrell Owens .75
83 Garrison Hearst .50
84 Jeff Garcia .75
85 Darrell Jackson .25
86 Shaun Alexander .75
87 Trent Dilfer .50
88 Isaac Bruce .50
89 Kurt Warner 2.50
90 Marshall Faulk 1.50
91 *Saleem Rasheed* 2.00
92 *Jason McAddley* 2.00
93 *Brandon Doman* 2.00
94 *Mike Rumph* 3.00
95 *Wendell Bryant* 2.00
96 *Bryan Thomas* 2.00
97 *Anthony Weaver* 2.00
98 *Chester Taylor* 4.00
99 *Ed Reed* 10.00
100 *Lamar Gordon* 4.00
101 *Tellis Redmon* 2.00
102 *Ben Leber* 2.00
103 *Javin Hunter* 2.00
104 *Javon Walker* 15.00
105 *Shaun Hill* 2.00
106 *Raonall Smith* 2.00
107 *Darrell Hill* 2.00
108 *Kalimba Edwards* 2.00
109 *Robert Thomas* 2.00
110 *Craig Nall* 8.00
111 *Marques Anderson* 3.00
112 *Najeh Davenport* 6.00
113 *Jonathan Wells* 5.00
114 *Dwight Freeney* 8.00
115 *Larry Tripplett* 2.00
116 *T.J. Duckett* 12.00
117 *John Henderson* 3.00
118 *Albert Haynesworth* 3.00
119 *Tank Williams* 2.00
120 *Ryan Sims* 3.00
121 *Leonard Henry* 2.00
122 *Clinton Portis* 75.00
123 *Josh Reed* 6.00
124 *Chad Hutchinson* 6.00
125 *Deion Branch* 15.00
126 *Rocky Calmus* 4.00
127 *Donte Stallworth* 12.00
128 *Daryl Jones* 2.00
129 *Joey Harrington* 40.00
130 *Napoleon Harris* 3.00
131 *Phillip Buchanon* 6.00
132 *Patrick Ramsey* 12.00
133 *Brian Westbrook* 12.00
134 *Freddie Milons* 3.00
135 *Lito Sheppard* 5.00
136 *Michael Lewis* 2.00
137 *Jamin Elliott* 2.00
138 *Lee Mays* 2.00
139 *Verron Haynes* 2.00
140 *Jesse Chatman* 8.00
141 *Quentin Jammer* 6.00
142 *Seth Burford* 2.00
143 *Julius Peppers* 12.00
144 *William Green* 10.00
145 *DeShaun Foster* 10.00
146 *Daniel Graham* 8.00
147 *David Garrard* 8.00
148 *Reche Caldwell* 8.00
149 *Randy Fasani* 3.00
150 *J.T. O'Sullivan* 2.00
151 *Josh McCown* 40.00
152 *Kurt Kittner* 25.00
153 *Kahlil Hill* 12.00
154 *Ladell Betts* 20.00
155 *Ron Johnson* 12.00
156 *Maurice Morris* 20.00
157 *Andre Davis* 25.00
158 *Antonio Bryant* 25.00
159 *Roy Williams* 50.00
160 *Lamont Thompson* 15.00
161 *Cliff Russell* 15.00
162 *Woodrow Dantzler III* 15.00
163 *Travis Stephens* 15.00
164 *Tony Fisher* 25.00
165 *Eric McCoo* 15.00
166 *Eric Crouch* 30.00
167 *Rohan Davey* 25.00
168 *Marquise Walker* 15.00
169 *Jeremy Shockey* 75.00
170 *Tim Carter* 20.00
171 *Atrews Bell* 12.00
172 *Antwann Randle El* 40.00
173 *Ricky Williams* 25.00
174 *Mike Williams* 15.00
175 *Adrian Peterson* 25.00
176 *Jabar Gaffney/650* 30.00
177 *Ashley Lelie/250* 75.00
178 *David Carr/250* 250.00

2002 SPx Supreme Signatures

NM/M
Common Player: 10.00
Inserted 1:36
SS-KB Kevan Barlow
SS-MBe Michael Bennett 25.00
SS-MBo Marty Booker
SS-BO David Boston 15.00
SS-DB Drew Brees 25.00
SS-JB Jim Brown 75.00
SS-CC Chris Chambers 15.00
SS-TC Tim Couch 20.00
SS-DC Daunte Culpepper
SS-JE John Elway 260.00
SS-JF Jay Fiedler
SS-JG Jeff Garcia 20.00
SS-RG Rod Gardner
SS-AG Ahman Green 25.00
SS-TH Travis Henry
SS-PH Priest Holmes 30.00
SS-BJ Brad Johnson 15.00
SS-KJ Kevin Johnson 10.00
SS-JL Jamal Lewis 15.00
SS-AM Archie Manning 25.00
SS-PM Peyton Manning 35.00
SS-MM Mike McMahon 10.00
SS-JM Jim Miller
SS-FM Freddie Mitchell 10.00
SS-MO Dan Morgan 15.00
SS-QM Quincy Morgan 10.00
SS-RM Randy Moss
SS-SM Santana Moss 15.00
SS-JP Jesse Palmer
SS-PL Jake Plummer
SS-JR John Riggins 35.00
SS-SR Sage Rosenfels 10.00
SS-KS Kordell Stewart 20.00
SS-AT Anthony Thomas 15.00
SS-LT LaDainian Tomlinson
SS-MT Marques Tuiasosopo 12.00
SS-BU Brian Urlacher
SS-MV Michael Vick 100.00
SS-CW Chris Weinke 10.00

2002 SPx Winning Materials

NM/M
Common Player: 8.00
Inserted 1:28
Gold: 1X-1.2X
Production 250 sets
NFL Logo Production 5 Sets
WM-MA Mike Anderson 8.00
WM-JB Jerome Bettis 10.00
WM-DB Drew Bledsoe 15.00
WM-BO David Boston 8.00
WM-BR Tom Brady 20.00
WM-DW Drew Brees 12.00
WM-BL Mark Brunell 8.00
WM-KC Kerry Collins 8.00
WM-MF Marshall Faulk 12.00
WM-BF Brett Favre 35.00
WM-JG Jeff Garcia 10.00
WM-EJ Edgerrin James 12.00
WM-PM Peyton Manning 25.00
WM-DM Donovan McNabb 15.00
WM-SM Steve McNair 10.00
WM-RM Randy Moss 25.00
WM-TO Terrell Owens 12.00
WM-JR Jerry Rice 25.00
WM-ES Emmitt Smith 35.00
WM-DT David Terrell 8.00
WM-VT Vinny Testaverde 8.00
WM-AT Anthony Thomas 12.00
WM-LT LaDainian Tomlinson 15.00
WM-MV Michael Vick 30.00
WM-KW Kurt Warner 15.00
WM-CW Chris Weinke 8.00
WM-RW Ricky Williams 15.00

2002 SPx Winning Materials Rookies

NM/M
Common Player: 10.00
Inserted 1:85
Gold: 1X-2X
Production 50 sets
NFL Logo Production 5 Sets
WMR-AB Antonio Bryant 15.00
WMR-DC David Carr 30.00
WMR-DF DeShaun Foster 10.00
WMR-JG Jabar Gaffney 10.00
WMR-WG William Green 20.00
WMR-JH Joey Harrington 30.00
WMR-AL Ashley Lelie 20.00
WMR-JM Josh McCown 10.00
WMR-JP Julius Peppers 15.00
WMR-CP Clinton Portis 25.00
WMR-PR Patrick Ramsey 12.00
WMR-JR Josh Reed 10.00
WMR-DS Donte Stallworth 20.00
WMR-MW Marquise Walker 10.00

2003 SP Authentic

NM/M
Common Player (1-90): .30
Minor Stars: .60
Unlisted Stars: .75
Common Rookie (91-120): 2.00
Production 2,200 Sets
Common Star Status (121-150): 2.00
Production 1,200 Sets
Common Rookie (151-211): 3.00
Production 1,200 Sets
Common Rookie AU 213-240): 8.00
Production 1,200 Sets
Common Rookie Patch (241-270): 20.00
Production 850 Sets
Pack (5): 5.00
Box (24): 95.00
1 Donovan McNabb 1.00
2 Tim Couch .75
3 Joey Harrington 1.50
4 Brett Favre 3.00
5 Jeff Garcia .60
6 Kerry Collins .60
7 Michael Vick 3.00
8 David Carr 2.00
9 Steve McNair .75
10 Chad Pennington 1.00
11 Patrick Ramsey .75
12 Rich Gannon .60
13 Kurt Warner 1.00
14 Brad Johnson .60
15 Jay Fiedler .30
16 Jake Plummer .60
17 Mark Brunell .60
18 Peyton Manning 1.50
19 Brian Griese .75
20 Kordell Stewart .75
21 Kelly Holcomb .30
22 Josh McCown .60
23 Matt Hasselbeck .75
24 Marc Bulger .75
25 Chris Redman .60
26 Rodney Peete .30
27 Jake Delhomme .60
28 Jon Kitna .60
29 Trent Green .60
30 Quincy Carter .75
31 Chad Hutchinson .60
32 Edgerrin James 1.00
33 Deuce McAllister .75
34 Ricky Williams 1.50
35 Priest Holmes .75
36 Curtis Martin .75
37 Shaun Alexander .75
38 Eddie George .60
39 Marshall Faulk 1.00
40 Garrison Hearst .60
41 Ahman Green .75
42 Corey Dillon .75
43 Jamal Lewis .75
44 William Green .75
45 Travis Henry .60
46 Mike Alstott .60
47 Amos Zereoue .60
48 Stephen Davis .60
49 Duce Staley .60
50 Fred Taylor .75
51 Anthony Thomas .60
52 Charlie Garner .60
53 Kevan Barlow .60
54 Brian Urlacher 1.50
55 Junior Seau .60
56 Zach Thomas .30
57 Ray Lewis .60
58 Jerry Porter .60
59 Marty Booker .60
60 Javon Walker .60
61 Donald Driver .60
62 Amani Toomer .60
63 Peerless Price .60
64 Santana Moss .60
65 Laveranues Coles .60
66 Troy Brown .60
67 Chris Chambers .75
68 Rod Smith .60
69 Ashley Lelie .60
70 Plaxico Burress .75
71 Keyshawn Johnson .60
72 Isaac Bruce .60
73 Torry Holt .75
74 Koren Robinson .60
75 Derrick Mason .60
76 Kevin Johnson .60
77 Andre Davis .60
78 Antonio Bryant .60
79 Eric Moulds .60
80 Jerry Rice 2.50
81 Tim Brown .60
82 Antwann Randle El .60
83 Donte Stallworth .30
84 Randy Moss 1.50
85 Chad Johnson .60
86 Hines Ward .60
87 Rod Gardner .60
88 Marvin Harrison .75
89 David Boston .75
90 Julius Peppers .60
91 *Dewayne White* 3.00
92 *Casey Fitzsimmons* 4.00
93 *Aaron Moorehead* 4.00
94 *Jimmy Farris* 3.00
95 *Eric Parker* 3.00
96 *Michael Haynes* 4.00
97 *J.J. Moses* 3.00
98 *Ken Hamlin* 4.00
99 *William Joseph* 4.00
100 *Alonzo Jackson* 3.00
101 *Tyler Brayton* 3.00
102 *Eddie Moore* 3.00
103 *Cleo Lemon* 3.00
104 *Arlen Harris* 6.00
105 *Cortez Hankton* 3.00
106 *Angelo Crowell* 3.00
107 *Johnathan Sullivan* 3.00
108 *Pisa Tinoisamoa* 6.00
109 *Boss Bailey* 5.00
110 *Tommy Jones* 3.00
111 *E.J. Henderson* 4.00
112 *Jimmy Kennedy* 4.00
113 *Nnamdi Asomugha* 2.00
114 *Hanik Milligan* 3.00
115 *Sammy Davis* 4.00
116 *Drayton Florence* 2.00
117 *Andre Woolfolk* 4.00
118 *Dennis Weathersby* 2.00
119 *Mike Doss* 5.00
120 *Troy Polamalu* 5.00
121 Clinton Portis 4.00
122 Daunte Culpepper 2.00
123 Jeremy Shockey 3.00
124 Drew Brees 2.00
125 Marshall Faulk 2.50
126 Emmitt Smith 5.00
127 Terrell Owens 2.00
128 Ricky Williams 3.00
129 Deuce McAllister 2.00
130 Ahman Green 2.00
131 Chad Pennington 2.50
132 Plaxico Burress 2.00
133 Steve McNair 2.00
134 Keyshawn Johnson 2.00
135 Jeff Garcia 2.00
136 Drew Bledsoe 2.00
137 Jerry Rice 5.00
138 Randy Moss 3.00
139 David Carr 4.00
140 Joey Harrington 3.00
141 Michael Vick 6.00
142 Tom Brady 3.00
143 Brian Urlacher 3.00
144 Brett Favre 6.00
145 Kurt Warner 2.00
146 LaDainian Tomlinson 2.00
147 Aaron Brooks 2.00
148 Edgerrin James 2.50
149 Peyton Manning 3.00
150 Donovan McNabb 2.50
151 *Jason Gesser* 6.00
152 *Ken Dorsey* 15.00
153 *Jason Johnson* 5.00
154 *Avon Cobourne* 8.00
155 *Andrew Pinnock* 5.00
156 *Kirk Farmer* 3.00
157 *Reno Mahe* 5.00
158 *Lon Sheriff* 5.00
159 *Marquel Blackwell* 3.00
160 *Quentin Griffin* 50.00
161 *Rashean Mathis* 5.00
162 *Lee Suggs* 30.00
163 *Jeremi Johnson* 5.00
164 *Ovie Mughelli* 3.00
165 *Nick Barnett* 15.00
166 *Brock Forsey* 12.00
167 *Malaefou MacKenzie* 3.00
168 *Ahmaad Galloway* 3.00
169 *Cecil Sapp* 8.00
170 *Kerry Carter* 5.00
171 *Dahrran Diedrick* 5.00
172 *Joffrey Reynolds* 5.00
173 *Sultan McCullough* 6.00
174 *Brandon Drumm* 3.00
175 *Casey Moore* 3.00
176 *Gerald Hayes* 3.00
177 *Terrence Edwards* 6.00
178 *Jamal Burke* 3.00
179 *Antonio Chatman* 12.00
180 *Reggie Newhouse* 5.00
181 *Chris Horn* 5.00
182 *Denero Marriott* 3.00
183 *DeAndrew Rubin* 3.00
184 *Taco Wallace* 5.00
185 *Doug Gabriel* 5.00
186 *Willie Ponder* 3.00
187 *David Tyree* 5.00
188 *Kevin Walter* 5.00
189 *Zuriel Smith* 6.00
190 *Keenan Howry* 8.00
191 *C.J. Jones* 5.00
192 *Arnaz Battle* 5.00
193 *Walter Young* 6.00
194 *Anthony Adams* 5.00
195 *Jerome McDougle* 6.00
196 *Will Heller* 5.00
197 *Cecil Moore* 3.00
198 *Mike Seidman* 3.00
199 *Jason Witten* 12.00
200 *L.J. Smith* 8.00
201 *Bennie Joppru* 6.00
202 *Donald Lee* 5.00
203 *Aaron Walker* 5.00
204 *Antonio Brown* 6.00
205 *George Wrighster* 3.00
206 *Danny Curley* 3.00
207 *Mike Banks* 3.00
208 *Mike Pinkard* 5.00
209 *Ryan Hoag* 5.00
210 *Brad Pyatt* 5.00
211 *Charles Rogers* 30.00
212 *Chris Simms Auto/250* 200.00
213 *Nate Hybl Auto/1200* 15.00
214 *Brandon Lloyd Auto/1200* 40.00
215 *Rashard Lee Auto/1200* 10.00
216 *Dwone Hicks Auto/1200* 10.00
217 *Tony Romo Auto/1200* 15.00
218 *Brett Engemann Auto/1200* 8.00
219 *Nick Maddox Auto/1200* 8.00
220 *James MacPherson Auto/1200* 8.00
221 *Juston Wood Auto/1200* 10.00
222 *Adrian Madise Auto/1200* 10.00
223 *Shaun McDonald Auto/1200* 10.00
224 *Carl Ford Auto/1200* 15.00
225 *Visanthe Shiancoe Auto/1200* 8.00
226 *Gibran Hamden Auto/1200* 10.00
227 *Brooks Bollinger Auto/1200* 12.00
228 *B.J. Askew Auto/1200* 12.00
229 *Domanick Davis Auto/1200* 60.00
230 *LaBrandon Toefield Auto/1200* 20.00
231 *Bobby Wade Auto/1200* 15.00
232 *Justin Gage Auto/1200* 20.00
233 *Billy McMullen Auto/1200* 20.00
234 *David Kircus Auto/1200* 15.00
235 *J.R. Tolver Auto/1200* 15.00
236 *Sam Aiken Auto/1200* 10.00
237 *LaTarence Dunbar Auto/1200* 10.00
238 *Kassim Osgood Auto/1200* 10.00
239 *Tony Hollings Auto/1200* 12.00
240 *Justin Griffith Auto/1200* 10.00
241 *Brian St. Pierre* 30.00
242 *Kevin Curtis* 20.00
243 *Dallas Clark* 30.00
244 *Willis McGahee* 80.00
245 *Terence Newman* 50.00
246 *Justin Fargas Auto/250* 160.00
247 *Artose Pinner* 40.00
248 *Kelley Washington* 40.00
249 *Dewayne Robertson* 20.00
250 *Nate Burleson* 30.00
251 *Kliff Kingsbury* 30.00
252 *Bethel Johnson* 40.00
253 *Anquan Boldin* 80.00
254 *Bryant Johnson Auto/250* 100.00
255 *Terrell Suggs Auto/250* 120.00
256 *Musa Smith* 30.00
257 *Chris Brown* 40.00
258 *Marcus Trufant* 20.00
259 *Teyo Johnson* 30.00
260 *Tyrone Calico* 50.00
261 *Dave Ragone Auto/250* 120.00
262 *Kyle Boller Auto/250* 200.00
263 *Onterrio Smith Auto/250* 175.00
264 *Rex Grossman* 125.00
265 *Larry Johnson* 50.00
266 *Seneca Wallace Auto/250* 80.00
268 *Taylor Jacobs Auto/250* 100.00
269 *Byron Leftwich Auto/250* 500.00
270 *Carson Palmer Auto/250* 350.00

2003 SP Authentic Buyback Autographs

TA Troy Aikman/3
MA Marcus Allen/4
TB Tim Brown/4
JE John Elway/3
TM Tommy Maddox/8
JM Joe Montana/4
JR Jerry Rice/4
BS Barry Sanders/7
SY Steve Young/7

2003 SP Authentic Sign of the Times

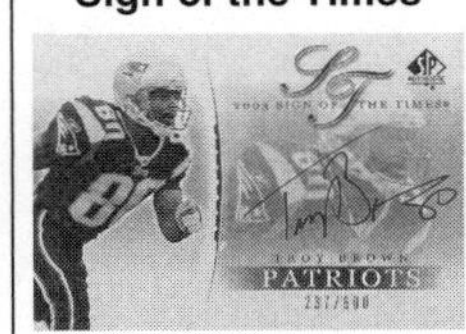

NM/M
Common Player: 10.00
TA Troy Aikman/97 100.00
SA Shaun Alexander/250 25.00
MA Marcus Allen/21
AL Mike Alstott/275 15.00
DR Drew Bledsoe/250 30.00
DA David Boston/250 15.00
DB Drew Brees/250 15.00
AB Aaron Brooks/250 15.00
JB Jim Brown/75 80.00
TB Tim Brown/246 20.00
BR Troy Brown/600 12.00
TC Tyrone Calico/200 25.00
DC David Carr/250 30.00
EL John Elway/12
JF Justin Fargas EX
JG Jeff Garcia/50 40.00
RG Rod Gardner/215 10.00
TG Trent Green/200 20.00
MH Matt Hasselbeck EX 80.00
KH Kelly Holcomb/475 10.00
PH Priest Holmes/75 100.00
BJ Bryant Johnson/475 12.00
TE Teyo Johnson/250 12.00
BL Byron Leftwich/75 150.00
JL Jamal Lewis/400 25.00
RL Ray Lewis EX 40.00
TM Tommy Maddox/592 12.00
PM Peyton Manning/900 50.00
DM Deuce McAllister/250 20.00
DO Donovan McNabb/75 80.00
JM Joe Montana EX
JN Joe Namath/35 150.00
TO Terrell Owens EX 25.00
CP Chad Pennington/141 40.00
JE Jerry Porter/600 15.00
PO Clinton Portis/520 40.00
PP Peerless Price/350 12.00
JR Jerry Rice/16
RI John Riggins/105 60.00
KR Koren Robinson/530 10.00
BA Barry Sanders/43 200.00
BS Bart Starr/120 125.00
SU Lee Suggs EX 40.00
TS Terrell Suggs EX 15.00
LS Lynn Swann/125 125.00
ZT Zach Thomas EX 20.00
BU Brian Urlacher/250 50.00
JW Javon Walker/600 15.00
RW Ricky Williams/50 100.00

2003 SP Authentic Threads

NM/M
Common Player: 6.00
JC-AB Anquan Boldin 12.00
JC-KB Kyle Boller 10.00
JC-TB Tom Brady 15.00
JC-NB Nate Burleson 6.00
JC-TC Tyrone Calico 8.00
JC-DC David Carr 12.00
JC-CL Dallas Clark 6.00
JC-CU Daunte Culpepper 8.00
JC-KC Kevin Curtis 6.00
JC-BF Brett Favre 20.00
JC-RG Rich Gannon 6.00
JC-AG Ahman Green 10.00
JC-MH Marvin Harrison 8.00
JC-TH Travis Henry 6.00
JC-PH Priest Holmes 12.00
JC-HO Torry Holt 8.00
JC-EJ Edgerrin James 10.00
JC-AJ Andre Johnson 12.00
JC-BJ Bethel Johnson 8.00
JC-BR Bryant Johnson 8.00
JC-LJ Larry Johnson 8.00
JC-TJ Teyo Johnson 6.00
JC-KK Kliff Kingsbury 6.00
JC-PM Peyton Manning 12.00
JC-WM Willis McGahee 12.00
JC-MC Donovan McNabb 10.00
JC-TC Steve McNair 8.00
JC-SM Santana Moss 8.00
JC-PA Carson Palmer 15.00
JC-CP Chad Pennington 10.00
JC-JP Jake Plummer 6.00
JC-PO Clinton Portis 12.00
JC-PP Peerless Price 6.00
JC-DR Dave Ragone 6.00
JC-JR Jerry Rice 15.00
JC-ES Emmitt Smith 20.00
JC-MS Musa Smith 6.00
JC-OS Onterrio Smith 10.00
JC-RS Rod Smith 6.00
JC-MV Michael Vick 20.00
JC-KW Kurt Warner 6.00
JC-KE Kelley Washington 6.00

2003 SP Authentic Threads Dual

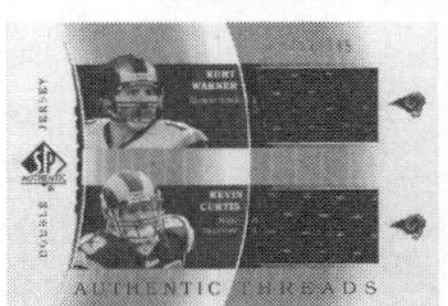

NM/M
Common Player: 10.00
DC/AJ David Carr, Andre Johnson 15.00
DC/NB Daunte Culpepper, Nate Burleson 10.00
TH/WM Travis Henry, Willis McGahee 12.00
TB/BJ Tom Brady, Bethel Johnson 15.00
TB/KK Tom Brady, Kliff Kingsbury 12.00
KK/BJ Kliff Kingsbury, Bethel Johnson 10.00
CP/SM Chad Pennington, Santana Moss 15.00
ES/CP Emmitt Smith, Clinton Portis 20.00
AB/BJ Anquan Boldin, Bryant Johnson 15.00
JP/CP Jake Plummer, Clinton Portis 15.00
JP/RS Jake Plummer, Rod Smith 10.00
JR/RG Jerry Rice, Rich Gannon 15.00
RG/TJ Rich Gannon, Teyo Johnson 10.00
PM/MH Peyton Manning, Marvin Harrison 20.00
PM/DC Peyton Manning, Dallas Clark 15.00
EJ/CP Edgerrin James, Clinton Portis 15.00
MV/PP Michael Vick, Peerless Price 20.00
KW/TH Kurt Warner, Torry Holt 12.00
KW/KC Kurt Warner, Kevin Curtis 10.00
LJ/PH Larry Johnson, Priest Holmes 15.00
CP/KW Carson Palmer, Kelley Washington 15.00
KB/MS Kyle Boller, Musa Smith 12.00
SM/TC Steve McNair, Tyrone Calico 10.00
PM/CP Peyton Manning, Carson Palmer 25.00
DM/MV Donovan McNabb, Michael Vick 25.00
JF/TJ Justin Fargas, Teyo Johnson 10.00
OS/NB Onterrio Smith, Nate Burleson 10.00
DC/OS Daunte Culpepper, Onterrio Smith 15.00
DC/DR David Carr, Dave Ragone 12.00
BF/AG Brett Favre, Ahman Green 40.00

2003 SP Authentic Threads Triple

NM/M
Common Player: 15.00
Production 175 Sets
TJC-VCP Michael Vick, David Carr, Carson Palmer 40.00
TJC-HWC Torry Holt, Kurt Warner, Kevin Curtis 15.00
TJC-RGJ Jerry Rice, Rich Gannon, Teyo Johnson 20.00
TJC-MCB Randy Moss, Daunte Culpepper, Nate Burleson 30.00
TJC-JCR Andre Johnson, David Carr, Dave Ragone 20.00
TJC-JBK Bethel Johnson, Tom Brady, Kliff Kingsbury 30.00
TJC-PPS Clinton Portis, Jake Plummer, Rod Smith 25.00
TJC-MPM Santana Moss, Chad Pennington, Curtis Martin 25.00
TJC-MPJ Willis McGahee, Clinton Portis, Edgerrin James 30.00
TJC-HMJ Marvin Harrison, Peyton Manning, Edgerrin James 30.00

2003 SP Game-Used

NM/M
Common Player: .40
Unlisted Star: .50
Unlisted Rookie Star: 8.00
Minor Rookie Star: 6.00
Gold 2X-5X
Production 50 sets
Cards 91-135 & 177-181 numbered to 600
Cards 136-176 Base Jersey some #'d to 99
Pack (3): 23.00
Wax Box (6): 100.00
1 Chad Hutchinson .50
2 Quincy Carter .50
3 Joey Galloway .75
4 Kerry Collins .75
5 Jeremy Shockey 3.00
6 Amani Toomer .40
7 A.J. Feeley .40
8 Duce Staley .40
9 Dorsey Levens .40
10 Ladell Betts .40
11 Patrick Ramsey 1.00
12 Anthony Thomas .60
13 Marty Booker .40
14 Brian Urlacher 2.00
15 Joey Harrington 3.00
16 James Stewart .40
17 Az-Zahir Hakim .75
18 Donald Driver .75
19 Javon Walker .75
20 Kordell Stewart 1.00
21 Randy Moss 3.00
22 Shaun Hill .40
23 Brian Finneran .40
24 T.J. Duckett .75
25 Warrick Dunn .60
26 Rodney Peete .40
27 Stephen Davis .40
28 Muhsin Muhammad .50
29 Aaron Brooks 1.00
30 Deuce McAllister 2.00
31 Joe Horn .40
32 Keyshawn Johnson .75
33 Brad Johnson .50
34 Keenan McCardell .40
35 Jake Plummer .75
36 Josh McCown .40
37 Thomas Jones .40
38 Tai Streets .40
39 Kevan Barlow .40
40 Garrison Hearst .50

41	Maurice Morris	.40
42	Matt Hasselbeck	.40
43	Koren Robinson	.40
44	Marc Bulger	1.00
45	Trung Canidate	.40
46	Emmitt Smith	3.00
47	Alex Van Pelt	.40
48	Travis Henry	.75
49	Eric Moulds	.60
50	Jason Taylor	.40
51	Jay Fiedler	.60
52	Randy McMichael	.40
53	Tom Brady	1.50
54	Antowain Smith	.40
55	Troy Brown	.40
56	Curtis Martin	1.00
57	Vinny Testaverde	.40
58	Santana Moss	.40
59	Jamal Lewis	.40
60	Chris Redman	.40
61	Ray Lewis	.40
62	Jon Kitna	.40
63	Peter Warrick	.40
64	Kelly Holcomb	.40
65	William Green	1.50
66	Kevin Johnson	.40
67	Amos Zereoue	.40
68	Tommy Maddox	1.00
69	Hines Ward	.75
70	Corey Bradford	.50
71	Jonathan Wells	.75
72	Jabar Gaffney	.40
73	Edgerrin James	2.00
74	David Garrard	.40
75	Mark Brunell	1.00
76	Jimmy Smith	.40
77	Steve McNair	1.00
78	Kevin Dyson	.40
79	Terrell Davis	1.00
80	Shannon Sharpe	.40
81	Rod Smith	.40
82	Trent Green	.40
83	Priest Holmes	1.00
84	Tony Gonzalez	.60
85	Jerry Rice	3.00
86	Charlie Garner	.40
87	Jerry Porter	.75
88	Reche Caldwell	.40
89	Tim Dwight	.40
90	Junior Seau	.60
91	*Carson Palmer*	50.00
92	*Byron Leftwich*	60.00
93	*Dave Ragone*	10.00
94	*Kyle Boller*	30.00
95	*Rex Grossman*	50.00
96	*Chris Simms*	20.00
97	*Kliff Kingsbury*	10.00
98	*Jason Gesser*	8.00
99	*Brad Banks*	10.00
100	*Ken Dorsey*	15.00
101	*Juston Wood*	6.00
102	*Brian St. Pierre*	8.00
103	*Domanick Davis*	15.00
104	*Quentin Griffin*	20.00
105	*B.J. Askew*	6.00
106	*Onterrio Smith*	12.00
107	*Seneca Wallace*	12.00
108	*Artose Pinner*	10.00
109	*Justin Fargas*	10.00
110	*Chris Brown*	10.00
111	*Willis McGahee*	30.00
112	*Larry Johnson*	30.00
113	*Lee Suggs*	20.00
114	*Billy McMullen*	6.00
115	*Sultan McCullough*	6.00
116	*Musa Smith*	10.00
117	*Earnest Graham*	8.00
118	*Antwone Savage*	5.00
119	*Kirk Farmer*	8.00
120	*Kareem Kelly*	6.00
121	*J.R. Tolver*	6.00
122	*Tyrone Calico*	8.00
123	*Kevin Curtis*	6.00
124	*Bobby Wade*	.40
125	*Justin Gage*	6.00
126	*Bryant Johnson*	15.00
127	*Doug Gabriel*	6.00
128	*Teyo Johnson*	8.00
129	*Brandon Lloyd*	8.00
130	*Kelley Washington*	12.00
131	*Talman Gardner*	6.00
132	*Anquan Boldin*	10.00
133	*Taylor Jacobs*	10.00
134	*Andre Johnson*	25.00
135	*Charles Rogers*	30.00
136	Antonio Bryant	6.00
137	Donovan McNabb/99	20.00
138	Rod Gardner	4.00
139	Ahman Green	10.00
140	Brett Favre/99	35.00
141	Daunte Culpepper	10.00
142	Michael Bennett	8.00
143	Michael Vick/99	55.00
144	Jeff Garcia	6.00
145	Terrell Owens	6.00
146	Shaun Alexander	5.00
147	Torry Holt	5.00
148	Isaac Bruce	5.00
149	Marshall Faulk/99	20.00
150	Kurt Warner/99	15.00
151	Drew Bledsoe	10.00
152	Josh Reed	5.00
153	Peerless Price	10.00
154	David Boston	6.00
155	Ricky Williams/99	20.00
156	Chris Chambers	6.00
157	Wayne Chrebet	5.00
158	Chad Pennington/99	20.00
159	Laveranues Coles	6.00
160	Corey Dillon	6.00
161	Tim Couch	8.00
162	Jerome Bettis	6.00
163	Plaxico Burress	8.00
164	Antwann Randle El	10.00
165	David Carr/99	20.00
166	Marvin Harrison	8.00
167	Peyton Manning	15.00
168	Fred Taylor	6.00
169	Eddie George	6.00
170	Clinton Portis/99	20.00
171	Ashley Lelie	6.00
172	Rich Gannon	10.00
173	Phillip Buchanon	6.00
174	Tim Brown	10.00
175	LaDainian Tomlinson	10.00
176	Drew Brees/99	12.00
177	*Jason Johnson*	5.00
178	*Sam Aiken*	5.00
179	*Nate Burleson*	5.00
180	*Tony Romo*	12.00
181	*Arnaz Battle*	8.00

2003 SP Game-Used Field Fabrics

		NM/M
Common Player:		5.00
Gold		1X-2X
Production 75 sets		
FF1-BF	Brett Favre	15.00
FF1-TG	Tony Gonzalez	5.00
FF1-BJ	Brad Johnson	5.00
FF1-KJ	Keyshawn Johnson	5.00
FF1-JL	Jamal Lewis	5.00
FF1-PM	Peyton Manning	8.00
FF1-DM	Deuce McAllister	5.00
FF1-RM	Randy Moss	12.00
FF1-EM	Eric Moulds	5.00
FF1-TO	Terrell Owens	5.00
FF1-PP	Peerless Price	5.00
FF1-JR	Jerry Rice	12.00
FF1-ES	Emmitt Smith	12.00
FF1-BU	Brian Urlacher	10.00
FF1-RW	Ricky Williams	10.00

2003 UD SP Game-Used SP Field Fabrics Signatures

Production 99 sets	
FFS-RG	Rod Gardner
FFS-TG	Tony Gonzalez
FFS-TH	Travis Henry
FFS-PM	Peyton Manning
FFS-DM	Deuce McAllister

2003 SP Game-Used Formations

		NM/M
Common Player:		5.00
Production as low as 99 sets		
Gold		1X-3X
Production from 25-50 sets		
F1-DB	Drew Bledsoe/99	15.00
F1-DB	Drew Brees	8.00
F1-DC	David Carr	12.00
F1-MF	Marshall Faulk/99	10.00
F1-JG	Jeff Garcia/99	10.00
F1-TG	Trent Green	5.00
F1-JH	Joey Harrington	15.00
F1-GH	Garrison Hearst	5.00
F1-TH	Travis Henry	5.00
F1-PH	Priest Holmes/99	15.00
F1-KJ	Keyshawn Johnson	8.00
F1-JL	Jamal Lewis	5.00
F1-PM	Peyton Manning/99	15.00
F1-CM	Curtis Martin	10.00
F1-DM	Donovan McNabb/99	18.00
F1-RM	Randy Moss/99	18.00
F1-SM	Santana Moss	8.00
F1-TO	Terrell Owens/99	12.00
F1-CP	Chad Pennington/99	12.00
F1-CP	Clinton Portis	12.00
F1-JR	Jerry Rice/99	18.00
F1-ES	Emmitt Smith/99	20.00
F1-AT	Anthony Thomas	5.00
F1-LT	LaDainian Tomlinson/99	8.00
F1-BU	Brian Urlacher	12.00
F1-MV	Michael Vick	15.00
F1-KW	Kurt Warner	8.00

2003 SP Game-Used Formations Duals

		NM/M
Common Player:		15.00
Production 50 sets TWINS		
Gold		1X-2X
Production 25 sets		
F2-CM	Daunte Culpepper, Randy Moss	35.00
F2-WH	Kurt Warner, Torry Holt	15.00
F2-MH	Peyton Manning, Marvin Harrison	20.00
F2-PM	Chad Pennington, Santana Moss	15.00
F2-FS	Marshall Faulk, Emmitt Smith	40.00
F2-BT	Drew Brees, LaDainian Tomlinson	15.00
F2-VM	Michael Vick, Donovan McNabb	45.00
F2-GO	Jeff Garcia, Terrell Owens	
F2-FG	Brett Favre, Ahman Green	45.00
F2-BM	Drew Bledsoe, Eric Moulds	25.00

2003 SP Game-Used Formations Triples

		NM/M
Common Player:		20.00
Production 35 sets		
Gold		2X-3X
Production 15 sets		
F3-WCG	Kurt Warner, Tim Couch, Rich Gannon	35.00
F3-RHO	Jerry Rice, Marvin Harrison, Terrell Owens	75.00
F3-BHM	Drew Bledsoe, Travis Henry, Eric Moulds	35.00
F3-PCH	Chad Pennington, David Carr, Joey Harrington	95.00
F3-CVM	Daunte Culpepper, Michael Vick, Donovan McNabb	95.00
F3-FBV	Brett Favre, Drew Bledsoe, Michael Vick	
F3-GRB	Rich Gannon, Jerry Rice, Tim Brown	50.00
F3-FSG	Marshall Faulk, Emmitt Smith, Ahman Green	
F3-MJH	Peyton Manning, Edgerrin James, Marvin Harrison	
F3-OHG	Terrell Owens, Garrison Hearst, Jeff Garcia	30.00

2003 SP Game-Used Formations Quads

		NM/M
Productions 25 sets		
Gold		2X-3X
Production 10 sets		
F4-JETS	Chad Pennington, Curtis Martin, Santana Moss, Wayne Chrebet	
F4-WGAB	Ricky Williams, Ahman Green, Shaun Alexander, Jerome Bettis	85.00
F4-MFCH	Donovan McNabb, Brett Favre, Daunte Culpepper, Joey Harrington	160.00
F4-FPSM	Marshall Faulk, Clinton Portis, Emmitt Smith, Deuce McAllister	125.00
F4-RHOJ	Jerry Rice, Marvin Harrison, Terrell Owens, Keyshawn Johnson	
F4-MCCV	Peyton Manning, Tim Couch, David Carr, Michael Vick	110.00
F4-FBBH	Brett Favre, Mark Brunell, Aaron Brooks, Matt Hasselbeck	
F4-GRBG	Rich Gannon, Jerry Rice, Tim Brown, Charlie Garner	
F4-WFBH	Kurt Warner, Marshall Faulk, Isaac Bruce, Torry Holt	

2003 SP Game-Used Patch Cards

		NM/M
Common Player:		10.00
Production 99 sets		
Multi-Color		2X-4X
PC1-SA	Shaun Alexander	20.00
PC1-JB	Jerome Bettis	15.00
PC1-DB	Drew Bledsoe	25.00
PC1-BO	David Boston	10.00
PC1-TB	Tom Brady	20.00
PC1-BR	Drew Brees	15.00
PC1-DC	David Carr	30.00
PC1-TC	Tim Couch	15.00
PC1-DC	Daunte Culpepper	15.00
PC1-CD	Corey Dillon	12.00
PC1-MF	Marshall Faulk	25.00
PC1-BF	Brett Favre	40.00
PC1-JG	Jeff Garcia	20.00
PC1-EG	Eddie George	20.00
PC1-AG	Ahman Green	20.00
PC1-TG	Trent Green	15.00
PC1-GH	Garrison Hearst	15.00
PC1-PH	Priest Holmes	25.00
PC1-TH	Torry Holt	10.00
PC1-EJ	Edgerrin James	15.00
PC1-KJ	Keyshawn Johnson	10.00
PC1-PM	Peyton Manning	30.00
PC1-DM	Deuce McAllister	20.00
PC1-DN	Donovan McNabb	30.00
PC1-SM	Steve McNair	20.00
PC1-RM	Randy Moss	30.00
PC1-TO	Terrell Owens	20.00
PC1-CP	Chad Pennington	18.00
PC1-CP	Clinton Portis	30.00
PC1-AR	Antwann Randle El	25.00
PC1-JR	Jerry Rice	30.00
PC1-ES	Emmitt Smith	40.00
PC1-FT	Fred Taylor	15.00
PC1-AT	Anthony Thomas	15.00
PC1-LT	LaDainian Tomlinson	18.00
PC1-BU	Brian Urlacher	30.00
PC1-MV	Michael Vick	50.00
PC1-KW	Kurt Warner	15.00
PC1-RW	Ricky Williams	25.00

2003 SP Game-Used Patch Cards Doubles

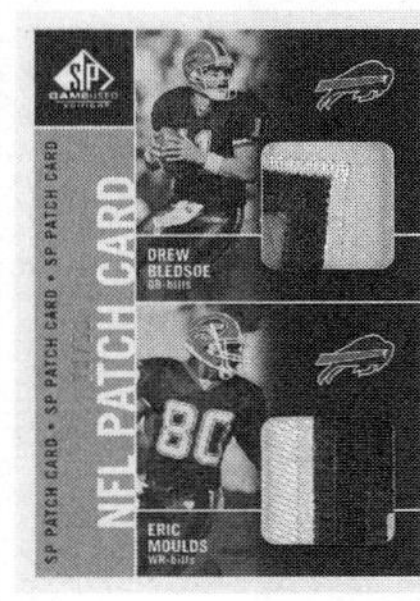

		NM/M
Common Player:		25.00
Production 50 sets		
Multi-Color		2X-3X
PC2-WF	Kurt Warner, Marshall Faulk	45.00
PC2-DT	Corey Dillon, Anthony Thomas	
PC2-BF	Drew Brees, LaDainian Tomlinson	35.00
PC2-MG	Steve McNair, Eddie George	
PC2-FG	Brett Favre, Ahman Green	65.00
PC2-MP	Curtis Martin, Chad Pennington	
PC2-DM	Daunte Culpepper, Randy Moss	55.00
PC2-GO	Jeff Garcia, Terrell Owens	25.00
PC2-MH	Peyton Manning, Marvin Harrison	
PC2-RB	Jerry Rice, Tim Brown	
PC2-BT	Mark Brunell, Fred Taylor	25.00
PC2-GD	Clinton Portis, Ashley Lelie	55.00
PC2-BE	Drew Bledsoe, Eric Moulds	40.00
PC2-RG	Jerry Rice, Rich Gannon	45.00
PC2-JW	Edgerrin James, Ricky Williams	45.00
PC2-GH	Trent Green, Priest Holmes	40.00
PC2-BP	Tom Brady, Chad Pennington	45.00
PC2-BR	Plaxico Burress, Antwaan Randle El	40.00
PC2-JP	Edgerrin James, Clinton Portis	40.00
PC2-WM	Ricky Williams, Deuce McAllister	50.00
PC2-JM	Keyshawn Johnson, Randy Moss	45.00
PC2-VM	Michael Vick, Donovan McNabb	55.00
PC2-MC	Michael Vick, Donovan McNabb	35.00
PC2-CM	Tim Couch, Peyton Manning	45.00

2003 SP Game-Used Signed Patch Cards

		NM/M
Common Player:		25.00
Production from 25 to 75 sets		
PCA-SA	Shaun Alexander/50	40.00
PCA-MB	Michael Bennett/75	55.00
PCA-DB	Drew Brees/50	75.00
PCA-AB	Aaron Brooks/50	65.00
PCA-BR	Mark Brunell/40	50.00
PCA-TC	Tim Couch/40	25.00
PCA-JF	Jay Fiedler/40	
PCA-JG	Jeff Garcia/25	80.00
PCA-RG	Rod Gardner/50	50.00
PCA-TG	Trent Green/50	25.00
PCA-TR	Travis Henry/50	30.00
PCA-PM	Peyton Manning/75	100.00
PCA-SC	Carson Palmer/25	475.00
PCA-CP	Chad Pennington/25	200.00
PCA-LT	LaDainian Tomlinson/25	140.00

2003 SP Game-Used Patch Cards Triples

		NM/M
Production 25 sets		
Multi-Color		2X-3X
PC3-WFB	Kurt Warner, Brett Favre, Tom Brady	
PC3-GMC	Jeff Garcia, Peyton Manning, Tim Couch	
PC3-BPM	Drew Bledsoe, Chad Pennington, Peyton Manning	
PC3-GBC	Jeff Garcia, Drew Brees, David Carr	
PC3-CVM	Daunte Culpepper, Michael Vick, Donovan McNabb	
PC3-BFB	Aaron Brooks, Brett Favre, Mark Brunell	
PC3-MVD	Steve McNair, Michael Vick, Aaron Brooks	
PC3-CCV	David Carr, Tim Couch, Michael Vick	
PC3-MMP	Santana Moss, Curtis Martin, Chad Pennington	
PC3-OHG	Terrell Owens, Garrison Hearst, Jeff Garcia	55.00
PC3-AMC	Aaron Brooks, Donovan McNabb, Daunte Culpepper	
PC3-CCW	Kurt Warner, David Carr, Brett Favre	200.00
PC3-FTB	Doug Flutie, LaDainian Tomlinson, Drew Brees	
PC3-MJR	Randy Moss, Keyshawn Johnson, Jerry Rice	85.00

2003 SP Game-Used Significant Signatures

		NM/M
Common Player:		18.00
Production from 25 to 99 sets		
SS2-SA	Shaun Alexander/40	35.00
SS-BB	Brad Banks/99	35.00
SS-BE	Michael Bennett/99	25.00
SS2-DB	Drew Brees/50	30.00
SS-AB	Aaron Brooks/99	18.00
SS-CB	Chris Brown/99	30.00
SS-MB	Mark Brunell/99	20.00
SS2-DC	David Carr/25	
SS2-TC	Tim Couch/40	25.00
SS-KD	Ken Dorsey/99	30.00
SS-JF	Justin Fargas/99	18.00
SS2-BF	Brett Favre/25	
SS-JF	Jay Fiedler/99	25.00
SS2-JG	Jeff Garcia/25	35.00
SS-RG	Rod Gardner/99	20.00
SS-EG	Earnest Graham/99	18.00
SS-GR	Trent Green/99	18.00
SS-QG	Quentin Griffin/99	30.00
SS-TJ	Taylor Jacobs/99	35.00
SS-LJ	Larry Johnson/99	55.00
SS-KK	Kareem Kelly/99	20.00
SS-KK	Kliff Kingsbury/99	35.00
SS2-BL	Byron Leftwich/25	225.00
SS-PM	Peyton Manning/99	75.00
SS2-PM	Peyton Manning/50	50.00
SS2-DE	Deuce McAllister/25	45.00
SS2-WM	Willis McGahee/50	145.00
SS2-SC	Carson Palmer/25	230.00
SS2-CP	Chad Pennington/50	40.00
SS2-JR	Jerry Rice/25	200.00
SS-CS	Chris Simms/99	75.00
SS-TS	Terrell Suggs/99	50.00
SS-AT	Anthony Thomas/99	18.00
SS2-LT	LaDainian Tomlinson/25	35.00
SS-SW	Seneca Wallace/99	25.00
SS-KW	Kelley Washington/99	25.00

2003 UD SP Game-Used Significant Signatures Duals

		NM/M
Production 10 sets		
DS-PP	Chad Pennington, Carson Palmer	
DS-TB	LaDainian Tomlinson, Drew Brees	
DS-MC	Peyton Manning, Tim Couch	
DS-JG	Taylor Jacobs, Earnest Graham	
DS-PL	Chad Pennington, Byron Leftwich	375.00
DS-PK	Carson Palmer, Kareem Kelly	
DS-BS	Mark Brunell, Chris Simms	
DS-BB	Aaron Brooks, Brad Banks	
DS-DM	Ken Dorsey, Willis McGahee	200.00
DS-MW	Peyton Manning, Kelley Washington	

A card number in parenthese ( ) indicates the set is unnumbered.

2003 SP Signature

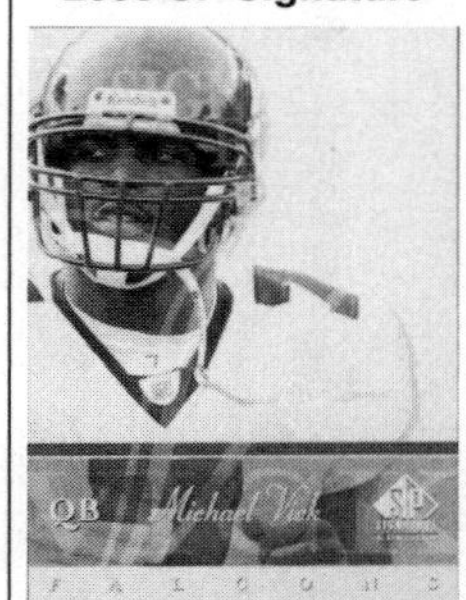

		NM/M
Common Player (1-100):		2.00
Minor Stars:		3.00
Unlisted Stars:		4.00
Common Rookie (101-170):		3.00
Minor Rookies:		4.00
Unlisted Rookies:		5.00
Production 750 Sets		
Common Rookie (171-200):		4.00
Production 250 Sets		
Pack (3):		30.00
Box (5):		110.00
1	Michael Vick	10.00
2	Aaron Brooks	2.00
3	Jim Brown	8.00
4	Steve Young	5.00
5	Jeff Garcia	2.00
6	Warren Moon	3.00
7	John Elway	10.00
8	Troy Aikman	6.00
9	Drew Brees	2.00
10	Chad Pennington	5.00
11	Fran Tarkenton	4.00
12	Joe Namath	8.00
13	Dan Marino	10.00
14	Terry Bradshaw	8.00
15	Edgerrin James	5.00
16	Joe Montana	12.00
17	Ken Stabler	6.00
18	Peyton Manning	6.00
19	Johnny Unitas	10.00
20	Barry Sanders	8.00
21	Jim Kelly	6.00
22	Michael Bennett	3.00
23	Phil Simms	5.00
24	David Carr	8.00
25	Deuce McAllister	4.00
26	Clinton Portis	8.00
27	Brad Johnson	2.00
28	Tim Couch	2.00
29	Archie Manning	3.00
30	Ahman Green	4.00
31	Priest Holmes	6.00
32	Marcus Allen	6.00
33	Ricky Williams	6.00
34	Walter Payton	15.00
35	Anthony Thomas	2.00
36	Eddie George	3.00
37	Shaun Alexander	3.00
38	Rich Gannon	2.00
39	Jay Fiedler	2.00
40	Travis Henry	2.00
41	Chad Johnson	2.00
42	Eric Moulds	2.00
43	Julius Peppers	2.00
44	John Riggins	5.00
45	Antonio Bryant	2.00
46	Laveranues Coles	2.00
47	Josh McCown	2.00
48	Matt Hasselbeck	3.00
49	William Green	3.00
50	Peerless Price	2.00
51	Kerry Collins	2.00
52	Zach Thomas	2.00
53	Frank "Bruiser" Kinard	3.00
54	Brian Urlacher	5.00
55	Junior Seau	2.00
56	Jamal Lewis	4.00
57	Duce Staley	6.00
58	Chris Redman	5.00
59	Kordell Stewart	2.00
60	Chad Hutchinson	2.00
61	Kevan Barlow	2.00
62	Charlie Garner	2.00
63	Fred Taylor	3.00
64	Jerome Bettis	2.00
65	Donte Stallworth	2.00
66	Rod Smith	2.00
67	Antwann Randle El	2.00
68	Brian Griese	2.00
69	Corey Dillon	3.00
70	Chris Chambers	3.00
71	Steve McNair	3.00
72	Jake Plummer	2.00
73	Keyshawn Johnson	2.00
74	Marvin Harrison	3.00
75	Plaxico Burress	3.00
76	Tim Brown	2.00
77	Mark Brunell	2.00
78	Curtis Martin	3.00
79	Robert "Cal" Hubbard	2.00
80	Isaac Bruce	2.00
81	Terrell Owens	3.00
82	Santana Moss	2.00
83	Tommy Maddox	3.00
84	Randy Moss	6.00
85	Drew Bledsoe	5.00
86	Az-Zahir Hakim	2.00
87	Rod Gardner	2.00
88	Tom Brady	6.00
89	David Boston	2.00
90	Trent Green	2.00
91	Jeremy Shockey	5.00

92 Daunte Culpepper 3.00
93 Emmitt Smith 8.00
94 Jerry Rice 8.00
95 LaDainian Tomlinson 4.00
96 Marshall Faulk 5.00
97 Kurt Warner 3.00
98 Brett Favre 10.00
99 Doak Walker 6.00
100 Donovan McNabb 6.00
101 *Ken Dorsey* 10.00
102 *Kirk Farmer* 3.00
103 *Nate Hybl* 4.00
104 *Marquel Blackwell* 3.00
105 *Brett Engemann* 3.00
106 *Tony Romo* 5.00
107 *Derick Armstrong* 3.00
108 *Lon Sheriff* 4.00
109 *Casey Moore* 3.00
110 *Jason Gesser* 4.00
111 *Brock Forsey* 8.00
112 *Willis McGahee* 15.00
113 *Nick Maddox* 4.00
114 *LaBrandon Toefield* 5.00
115 *Kareem Kelly* 4.00
116 *Malaefou MacKenzie* 3.00
117 *Troy Polamalu* 6.00
118 *Terence Newman* 10.00
119 *Marcus Trufant* 4.00
120 *Terrell Suggs* 8.00
121 *Dewayne Robertson* 3.00
122 *Justin Griffith* 3.00
123 *Lee Suggs* 8.00
124 *Bryant Johnson* 6.00
125 *Andre Woolfolk* 3.00
126 *Cedric Henry* 3.00
127 *Billy McMullen* 4.00
128 *Charles Rogers* 12.00
129 *David Kircus* 4.00
130 *Jerome McDougle* 3.00
131 *Ryan Hoag* 3.00
132 *Mike Pinkard* 3.00
133 *Shaun McDonald* 4.00
134 *Bobby Wade* 4.00
135 *Kassim Osgood* 3.00
136 *Ovie Mughelli* 3.00
137 *Doug Gabriel* 4.00
138 *Aaron Walker* 3.00
139 *Brandon Lloyd* 6.00
140 *Donald Lee* 3.00
141 *George Wrighster* 3.00
142 *Antwone Savage* 4.00
143 *Keenan Howry* 4.00
144 *Kevin Walter* 4.00
145 *Gerald Hayes* 3.00
146 *Walter Young* 4.00
147 *Casey Fitzsimmons* 4.00
148 *Visanthe Shiancoe* 3.00
149 *Lance Briggs* 4.00
150 *Zuriel Smith* 4.00
151 *Terrence Edwards* 4.00
152 *Arnaz Battle* 4.00
153 *DeAndrew Rubin* 3.00
154 *Pisa Tinoisamoa* 5.00
155 *David Tyree* 4.00
156 *Bradie James* 3.00
157 *Anquan Boldin* 15.00
158 *Kevin Curtis* 4.00
159 *Taylor Jacobs* 4.00
160 *Cato June* 3.00
161 *Jason Witten* 8.00
162 *Mike Seidman* 3.00
163 *Dallas Clark* 4.00
164 *Gibran Hamdan* 3.00
165 *Kliff Kingsbury* 4.00
166 *Brooks Bollinger* 4.00
167 *Nick Barnett* 8.00
168 *Rex Grossman* 20.00
169 *Byron Leftwich* 30.00
170 *Kyle Boller* 10.00
171 *Chris Brown* 10.00
172 *Carl Ford* 6.00
173 *Kelley Washington* 10.00
174 *Charles Tillman* 12.00
175 *Ken Hamlin* 4.00
176 *Bennie Joppru* 4.00
177 *Nate Burleson* 8.00
178 *Boss Bailey* 6.00
179 *LaTarence Dunbar* 6.00
180 *Adrian Madise* 4.00
181 *J.R. Tolver* 6.00
182 *Tyrone Calico* 12.00
183 *Justin Gage* 10.00
184 *Teyo Johnson* 8.00
185 *B.J. Askew* 6.00
186 *Sam Aiken* 4.00
187 *Andre Johnson* 20.00
188 *Bethel Johnson* 12.00
189 *Artose Pinner* 8.00
190 *Quentin Griffin* 15.00
191 *Musa Smith* 6.00
192 *Larry Johnson* 15.00
193 *Onterrio Smith* 12.00
194 *Justin Fargas* 12.00
195 *Dwone Hicks* 4.00
196 *Brian St. Pierre* 6.00
197 *Dave Ragone* 6.00
198 *Seneca Wallace* 6.00
199 *Chris Simms* 15.00
200 *Carson Palmer* 30.00

2003 SP Signature Autographs Black Ink

NM/M
Common Player: 8.00
SA Shaun Alexander 15.00
BB Brad Banks 10.00
AR Arnaz Battle 8.00
MB Michael Bennett 12.00
AB Anquan Boldin 40.00
KB Kyle Boller 30.00
BO Brooks Bollinger 12.00
DA David Boston/25 40.00
AA Aaron Brooks 10.00
CB Chris Brown 12.00
DB Drew Brees/20 80.00
IB Isaac Bruce 12.00
NB Nate Burleson 12.00
CA Tyrone Calico 20.00
DC David Carr 40.00
TC Tim Couch 10.00
KC Kevin Curtis 10.00
KD Ken Dorsey 20.00
FA Justin Fargas 20.00
JF Jay Fiedler 10.00
RG Rod Gardner 8.00
EG Earnest Graham 12.00
QG Quentin Griffin 30.00
RE Rex Grossman 50.00
AH Az-Zahir Hakim 8.00
PH Priest Holmes/25 100.00
TJ Taylor Jacobs 15.00
AJ Andre Johnson 50.00
BJ Brad Johnson SP 20.00
BR Bryant Johnson 15.00
LJ Larry Johnson 25.00
JO Teyo Johnson 15.00
KA Kareem Kelly 8.00
KK Kliff Kingsbury 12.00
BY Byron Leftwich 80.00
BL Brandon Lloyd 15.00
MM Malaefou MacKenzie 8.00
TM Tommy Maddox/25 40.00
AM Archie Manning 30.00
PM Peyton Manning 50.00
DM Dan Marino SP 200.00
MC Deuce McAllister 20.00
JM Joe Montana 150.00
SM Santana Moss 15.00
JN Joe Namath SP 150.00
TN Terence Newman 25.00
SC Carson Palmer 60.00
CP Chad Pennington 40.00
AP Artose Pinner 12.00
RA Dave Ragone 12.00
DR Dewayne Robertson 8.00
SP Brian St. Pierre 15.00
CS Chris Simms 30.00
MS Musa Smith 15.00
OS Onterrio Smith 25.00
KS Ken Stabler SP 40.00
LS Lee Suggs 20.00
TS Terrell Suggs 15.00
FT Fran Tarkenton SP 40.00
AT Anthony Thomas 12.00
MT Marcus Trufant 10.00
SW Seneca Wallace 15.00
KW Kelley Washington 15.00

2003 SP Signature Autographs Blue Ink

NM/M
Common Player: 8.00
Autos Inserted 1:1
SA Shaun Alexander 15.00
BB Brad Banks 10.00
AR Arnaz Battle 8.00
MB Michael Bennett 12.00
AB Anquan Boldin 40.00
KB Kyle Boller 30.00
BO Brooks Bollinger 12.00
DB Drew Brees SP 20.00
AA Aaron Brooks 10.00
CB Chris Brown 12.00
JB Jim Brown SP 100.00
IB Isaac Bruce 12.00
NB Nate Burleson 12.00
CA Tyrone Calico 20.00
DC David Carr 40.00
TC Tim Couch 10.00
KC Kevin Curtis 10.00
KD Ken Dorsey 20.00
FA Justin Fargas 20.00
JF Jay Fiedler 10.00
JG Jeff Garcia/24 40.00
RG Rod Gardner 8.00
EG Earnest Graham 12.00
QG Quentin Griffin 40.00
RE Rex Grossman 40.00
AH Az-Zahir Hakim 8.00
TJ Taylor Jacobs 15.00
AJ Andre Johnson 50.00
BJ Brad Johnson/25 30.00
BR Bryant Johnson 15.00
LJ Larry Johnson 25.00
JO Teyo Johnson 15.00
KA Kareem Kelly 8.00
KK Kliff Kingsbury 12.00
BY Byron Leftwich 80.00
BL Brandon Lloyd 15.00
MM Malaefou MacKenzie 8.00
AM Archie Manning/25 50.00
PM Peyton Manning 50.00
WM Willis McGahee/SP 100.00
DO Donovan McNabb/19
MO Warren Moon 30.00
RM Randy Moss/10
SM Santana Moss 15.00
TN Terence Newman 25.00
SC Carson Palmer 60.00
CP Chad Pennington SP 40.00
AP Artose Pinner 12.00
PO Clinton Portis/25
RA Dave Ragone 12.00
DR Dewayne Robertson 8.00
CS Chris Simms SP 50.00
OS Onterrio Smith 25.00
MS Musa Smith 15.00
SP Brian St. Pierre 15.00
LS Lee Suggs 20.00
TS Terrell Suggs 15.00
AT Anthony Thomas 12.00
MT Marcus Trufant 10.00
SW Seneca Wallace 15.00
KW Kelley Washington 15.00
RW Ricky Williams/25

2003 UD SP Signature Autographs Blue Ink Numbered

Prices same as Red Autos
BF Brett Favre/7

2003 SP Signature Autographs Red Ink

NM/M
Common Player: 12.00
Production 100 Sets
Green Autos: 1X-1.5X
Production 50 Sets
SA Shaun Alexander 20.00
MA Marcus Allen 40.00
BB Brad Banks 12.00
AR Arnaz Battle 12.00
MB Michael Bennett 15.00
AB Anquan Boldin 60.00
KB Kyle Boller 40.00
BO Brooks Bollinger 20.00
DA David Boston 20.00
TB Terry Bradshaw 80.00
DB Drew Brees 20.00
AA Aaron Brooks 15.00
CB Chris Brown 25.00
JB Jim Brown 100.00
IB Isaac Bruce 15.00
NB Nate Burleson 25.00
CA Tyrone Calico 30.00
DC David Carr 50.00
TC Tim Couch 12.00
KC Kevin Curtis 15.00
KD Ken Dorsey 25.00
JE John Elway 100.00
FA Justin Fargas 30.00
JF Jay Fiedler 12.00
RG Rod Gardner 10.00
EG Earnest Graham 15.00
TG Trent Green 20.00
QG Quentin Griffin 50.00
RE Rex Grossman 50.00
AH Az-Zahir Hakim 10.00
PH Priest Holmes 60.00
TJ Taylor Jacobs 25.00
AJ Andre Johnson 60.00
BJ Brad Johnson 20.00
BR Bryant Johnson 20.00
LJ Larry Johnson 40.00
JO Teyo Johnson 25.00
JK Jim Kelly 60.00
KA Kareem Kelly 10.00
KK Kliff Kingsbury 20.00
BY Byron Leftwich 100.00
BL Brandon Lloyd 20.00
MM Malaefou MacKenzie 10.00
TM Tommy Maddox 25.00
AM Archie Manning 40.00
PM Peyton Manning 50.00
MC Deuce McAllister 25.00
WM Willis McGahee 100.00
JM Joe Montana 150.00
MO Warren Moon 40.00
SM Santana Moss 20.00
JN Joe Namath 120.00
TN Terence Newman 30.00
TO Terrell Owens 60.00
SC Carson Palmer 80.00
CP Chad Pennington 50.00
AP Artose Pinner 15.00
RA Dave Ragone 15.00
JR John Riggins 40.00
DR Dewayne Robertson 15.00
SP Brian St. Pierre 20.00
BA Barry Sanders 100.00
CS Chris Simms 40.00
MS Musa Smith 20.00
OS Onterrio Smith 40.00
KS Ken Stabler 40.00
LS Lee Suggs 30.00
TS Terrell Suggs 30.00
FT Fran Tarkenton 40.00
AT Anthony Thomas 15.00
MT Marcus Trufant 15.00
SW Seneca Wallace 25.00
KW Kelley Washington 25.00
SY Steve Young 60.00

2003 SP Signature Dual Signatures

NM/M
Common Player: 20.00
Production 75 Sets
JN/CP Joe Namath, Chad Pennington 200.00
CP/KW Carson Palmer, Kelley Washington 100.00
PM/AM Peyton Manning, Archie Manning 125.00
AB/KK Aaron Brooks, Kareem Kelly 20.00
DB/DB Drew Brees, David Boston 25.00
CP/SM Chad Pennington, Santana Moss 60.00
TM/BS Tommy Maddox, Brian St. Pierre 40.00
MB/OS Michael Bennett, Onterrio Smith 50.00
DC/AJ David Carr, Andre Johnson 100.00
PH/LJ Priest Holmes, Larry Johnson 60.00
JM/KD Joe Montana, Ken Dorsey 200.00
RG/AT Rex Grossman, Anthony Thomas 60.00
PS/CS Phil Simms, Chris Simms 60.00
BJ/AB Bryant Johnson, Anquan Boldin 80.00
KD/TO Ken Dorsey, Terrell Owens 60.00
CP/VT Chad Pennington, Vinny Testaverde 50.00

2003 SP Signature SP Legendary Cuts

LC-CH Robert "Cal" Hubbard
LC-BK Frank "Bruiser" Kinard
LC-WP Walter Payton
LC-JU Johnny Unitas
LC-DW Doak Walker

2003 SPx

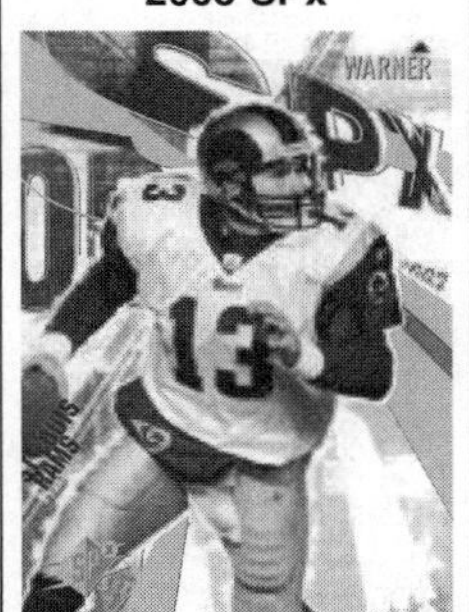

NM/M
Common Player (1-110): .30
Minor Stars: .60
Unlisted Stars: .75
71-80 Production 500 Sets
Common Rookie (111-220): 4.00
Minor Rookies: 5.00
Unlisted Rookies: 6.00
111-190 Production 1500 Sets
Cards 209, 214 Do Not Exist
Pack (5): 6.00
Box (18): 80.00
1 Peyton Manning 1.50
2 Aaron Brooks .75
3 Joey Harrington 2.00
4 Tim Couch .75
5 Jeff Garcia .75
6 Jay Fiedler .60
7 Chad Hutchinson .60
8 Tommy Maddox .75
9 Drew Brees 1.00
10 Trent Green .75
11 Patrick Ramsey 1.00
12 Daunte Culpepper .75
13 Kurt Warner 1.50
14 Brad Johnson .60
15 Rich Gannon .60
16 Jake Plummer .60
17 Steve McNair .75
18 Mark Brunell .60
19 Drew Bledsoe 1.00
20 Kordell Stewart .60
21 Kelly Holcomb .60
22 Josh McCown .60
23 Matt Hasselbeck .60
24 Marc Bulger .75
25 Chris Redman .60
26 Rodney Peete .60
27 Jake Delhomme .60
28 Jon Kitna .60
29 Kerry Collins .60
30 Quincy Carter .75
31 Ricky Williams 1.50
32 Clinton Portis 2.50
33 Deuce McAllister .75
34 Ahman Green .75
35 Priest Holmes .75
36 Curtis Martin .75
37 Michael Bennett .75
38 Eddie George .75
39 Marshall Faulk 1.00
40 Garrison Hearst .60
41 Shaun Alexander .75
42 Corey Dillon .75
43 Jamal Lewis .75
44 William Green .75
45 Travis Henry .60
46 Randy Moss 1.50
47 Terrell Owens .75
48 Peerless Price .60
49 David Boston .75
50 Eric Moulds .60
51 Marvin Harrison .75
52 Laveranues Coles .60
53 Santana Moss .60
54 Troy Brown .60
55 Chris Chambers .60
56 Tim Brown .60
57 Rod Smith .60
58 Hines Ward .60
59 Keyshawn Johnson .60
60 Isaac Bruce .60
61 Torry Holt .75
62 Koren Robinson .60
63 Chad Johnson .60
64 Derrick Mason .60
65 Antonio Bryant .60
66 Kevin Johnson .60
67 Todd Heap .30
68 Tony Gonzalez .60
69 Jeremy Shockey 2.00
70 Brian Urlacher 1.50
71 Emmitt Smith 12.00
72 Edgerrin James 3.00
73 LaDainian Tomlinson 4.00
74 Brett Favre 10.00
75 Donovan McNabb 3.00
76 Tom Brady 4.00
77 Michael Vick 10.00
78 David Carr 6.00
79 Jerry Rice 8.00
80 Chad Pennington 4.00
81 Joey Harrington 2.00
82 Clinton Portis 2.50
83 Jeremy Shockey 1.50
84 David Boston 1.00
85 Marshall Faulk 1.25
86 Emmitt Smith 2.50
87 Terrell Owens 1.00
88 Randy Moss 1.50
89 Deuce McAllister 1.00
90 Ahman Green 1.00
91 Peerless Price 1.00
92 Plaxico Burress 1.00
93 Marvin Harrison 1.00
94 Keyshawn Johnson 1.00
95 Laveranues Coles 1.00
96 Drew Bledsoe 1.25
97 Eric Moulds 1.00
98 Chad Pennington 1.25
99 Jerry Rice 2.50
100 David Carr 2.00
101 Michael Vick 3.00
102 Tom Brady 1.25
103 Donovan McNabb 1.25
104 Brett Favre 3.00
105 Kurt Warner 1.25
106 LaDainian Tomlinson 1.25
107 Drew Brees 1.00
108 Edgerrin James 1.25
109 Peyton Manning 1.50
110 Ricky Williams 1.25
111 Brooks Bollinger 8.00
112 Gibran Hamdan 6.00
113 Jason Johnson 5.00
114 Tony Romo 8.00
115 Juston Wood 5.00
116 Kirk Farmer 4.00
117 Kliff Kingsbury 8.00
118 Jason Gesser 8.00
119 Brad Banks 8.00
120 Rob Adamson 6.00
121 Ken Dorsey 10.00
122 Curt Anes 6.00
123 George Wrighster 5.00
124 Brett Engemann 5.00
125 Aaron Walker 5.00
126 Nate Hybl 6.00
127 Chris Simms 12.00
128 Marquel Blackwell 4.00
129 *Domanick Davis* 20.00
130 Quentin Griffin 15.00
131 B.J. Askew 6.00
132 Earnest Graham 6.00
133 Sultan McCullough 5.00
134 Dahrran Diedrick 6.00
135 Cecil Sapp 6.00
136 LaBrandon Toefield 8.00
137 Reshard Lee 6.00
138 Dwone Hicks 5.00
139 Brock Forsey 6.00
140 Bethel Johnson 6.00
141 Andrew Pinnock 5.00
142 Ahmaad Galloway 5.00
143 J.T. Wall 5.00
144 Tom Lopienski 5.00
145 Justin Griffith 5.00
146 Lee Suggs 8.00
147 Nick Maddox 5.00
148 Jeremi Johnson 5.00
149 Doug Gabriel 6.00
150 Bobby Wade 6.00
151 Justin Gage 6.00
152 Arnaz Battle 5.00
153 Brandon Lloyd 8.00
154 Talman Gardner 6.00
155 Kareem Kelly 6.00
156 Billy McMullen 5.00
157 Antwone Savage 5.00
158 J.R. Tolver 5.00
159 Kassim Osgood 5.00
160 Shaun McDonald 5.00
161 Sam Aiken 5.00
162 Adrian Madise 5.00
163 Charles Rogers 20.00
164 David Kircus 5.00
165 Zuriel Smith 5.00
166 LaTarence Dunbar 5.00
167 Willie Ponder 5.00
168 David Tyree 4.00
169 Kevin Walter 5.00
170 Keenan Howry 6.00
171 Walter Young 5.00
172 DeAndrew Rubin 5.00
173 Carl Ford 6.00
174 Taco Wallace 5.00
175 Travis Anglin 4.00
176 Ryan Hoag 5.00
177 Ronald Bellamy 6.00
178 Terrence Edwards 6.00
179 Jerel Myers 4.00
180 Mike Bush 5.00
181 Dan Curley 4.00
182 Carl Morris 4.00
183 Reggie Newhouse 5.00
184 Troy Polamalu 8.00
185 Cecil Moore 4.00
186 Bennie Joppru 5.00
187 Donald Lee 5.00
188 Jason Witten 6.00
189 Mike Seidman 4.00
190 Visanthe Shiancoe 4.00
191 Anquan Boldin/1000 AU 60.00
192 Kyle Boller/450 AU 100.00
193 Chris Brown/1100 AU 50.00
194 Nate Burleson/1100 AU 25.00
195 Tyrone Calico/450 AU 50.00
196 Dallas Clark/1100 AU 30.00
197 Kevin Curtis/1100 AU 15.00
198 Kliff Kingsbury/1100 AU 20.00
199 Justin Fargas/1100 AU 40.00
200 Rex Grossman/450 AU 150.00
201 Taylor Jacobs/1100 AU 30.00
202 Andre Johnson/250 AU 150.00
203 Malaefou MacKenzie/1100 AU 10.00
204 Bryant Johnson/1100 AU 30.00
205 Larry Johnson/1100 AU 40.00
206 Teyo Johnson/450 AU 50.00
207 Byron Leftwich/250 AU 300.00
208 Willis McGahee/450 AU 120.00
210 Carson Palmer/250 AU 250.00
211 Artose Pinner/1100 AU 20.00
212 Dave Ragone/1100 AU 30.00
213 Terrell Suggs/1100 AU 30.00
215 Onterrio Smith/1100 AU 40.00
216 Musa Smith/1100 AU 20.00
217 Brian St. Pierre/1100 AU 20.00
218 Marcus Trufant/1100 AU 20.00
219 Seneca Wallace/1100 AU 25.00
220 Kelley Washington/1100 AU 25.00

2003 SPx Spectrum

Cards 1-70, 81-110: 6X-12X
Cards 71-80: 2X
Rookies 111-190: 2X-3X
Production 50 Sets
Cards 209, 214 Do Not Exist

2003 SPx Winning Materials

NM/M
Common Player: 8.00
Production 350 Sets
NFL-AN Anquan Boldin 15.00
NFL-TB Tom Brady 12.00
NFL-AB Aaron Brooks 8.00
NFL-BR Tim Brown 10.00
NFL-MB Mark Brunell 8.00
NFL-DC David Carr 15.00
NFL-CC Chris Chambers/300 10.00
NFL-KC Kevin Curtis 8.00
NFL-CD Corey Dillon/266 10.00
NFL-MF Marshall Faulk 12.00
NFL-WG William Green 10.00
NFL-JH Joey Harrington 15.00
NFL-MH Marvin Harrison/278 10.00
NFL-PR Priest Holmes 20.00
NFL-TJ Taylor Jacobs 8.00
NFL-EJ Edgerrin James 12.00
NFL-AJ Andre Johnson 20.00
NFL-BJ Bryant Johnson 10.00
NFL-CJ Chad Johnson/200 10.00
NFL-JK Keyshawn Johnson 10.00
NFL-LJ Larry Johnson 15.00
NFL-BL Byron Leftwich 30.00
NFL-PM Peyton Manning 15.00
NFL-CM Curtis Martin 10.00
NFL-WM Willis McGahee 20.00
NFL-DM Donovan McNabb 12.00
NFL-EM Eric Moulds/264 10.00
NFL-TN Terence Newman 15.00
NFL-SC Carson Palmer 30.00
NFL-PO Clinton Portis 15.00
NFL-CP Chad Pennington 12.00
NFL-JP Julius Peppers 8.00
NFL-AP Artose Pinner 8.00
NFL-JR Jerry Rice/300 20.00
NFL-SH Jeremy Shockey 12.00
NFL-ES Emmitt Smith 25.00
NFL-RS Rod Smith/300 8.00
NFL-MT Marcus Trufant 8.00
NFL-SW Seneca Wallace 10.00
NFL-KW Kurt Warner 10.00
NFL-RW Ricky Williams 15.00

2003 SPx Supreme Signatures

NM/M
Common Player: 12.00
Inserted 1:43
Spectrum Cards:
Production 50 Sets
SS-BB Brad Banks 12.00
SS-KB Kevan Barlow 12.00
SS-MI Michael Bennett 20.00
SS-KB Kyle Boller 40.00
SS-TB Tom Brady 120.00
SS-AB Aaron Brooks 15.00
SS-IB Isaac Bruce 15.00
SS-MB Mark Brunell 15.00
SS-DC David Carr 50.00
SS-TC Tim Couch 15.00
SS-JG Jeff Garcia 15.00
SS-RG Rod Gardner 15.00
SS-EG Earnest Graham 12.00
SS-TG Trent Green 20.00
SS-QG Quentin Griffin 20.00
SS-AH Az-Zahir Hakim 12.00
SS-MH Matt Hasselbeck
SS-TH Travis Henry 15.00
SS-TJ Taylor Jacobs 12.00
SS-BR Brad Johnson 15.00
SS-BJ Bryant Johnson 15.00
SS-JK Jim Kelly
SS-KK Kareem Kelly 12.00
SS-KL Kliff Kingsbury 15.00
SS-BL Byron Leftwich 100.00
SS-AM Archie Manning 20.00

SS-PM Peyton Manning 40.00
SS-CP Carson Palmer 80.00
SS-CH Chad Pennington 40.00
SS-PO Clinton Portis 60.00
SS-DR Dave Ragone 15.00
SS-BS Brian St. Pierre 12.00
SS-CS Chris Simms 30.00
SS-OS Onterrio Smith 30.00
SS-RS Rod Smith 30.00
SS-LS Lee Suggs 20.00
SS-TS Terrell Suggs 15.00
SS-MV Michael Vick 80.00
SS-KW Kelley Washington 15.00

2003 SPx Winning Materials Patches

NM/M
Common Player: 20.00
Production 75 Sets
WMP-DB Drew Brees/17 50.00
WMP-DC David Carr 50.00
WMP-TC Tim Couch 30.00
WMP-BF Brett Favre 100.00
WMP-JG Jeff Garcia/15 60.00
WMP-BJ Bryant Johnson 20.00
WMP-PM Peyton Manning 40.00
WMP-DM Donovan McNabb 40.00
WMP-RM Randy Moss 50.00
WMP-SM Santana Moss/47 30.00
WMP-CP Chad Pennington 40.00
WMP-PO Clinton Portis 50.00
WMP-JR Jerry Rice 50.00
WMP-LT LaDainian Tomlinson 40.00
WMP-MV Michael Vick 100.00
WMP-SW Seneca Wallace 25.00
WMP-RW Ricky Williams 30.00

2003 SPx Winning Materials Team Logos

NM/M
Common Player: 8.00
Production 250 Sets
Spectrum: 1X-2X
Production 50 Sets
AN Anquan Boldin/250 15.00
TB Tom Brady/250 12.00
AB Aaron Brooks/250 8.00
BR Tim Brown/250 10.00
MB Mark Brunell/203 8.00
DC David Carr/99 20.00
CC Chris Chambers/50 15.00
KC Kevin Curtis/250 8.00
CD Corey Dillon/53 15.00
MF Marshall Faulk/99 15.00
WG William Green/250 10.00
JH Joey Harrington/250 15.00
PR Priest Holmes/250 20.00
TJ Taylor Jacobs/250 8.00
EJ Edgerrin James/99 15.00
AJ Andre Johnson/250 20.00
BJ Bryant Johnson/250 10.00
KJ Keyshawn Johnson/53 15.00
LJ Larry Johnson/250 15.00
BL Byron Leftwich/250 30.00
PM Peyton Manning/250 15.00
CM Curtis Martin/250 10.00
WM Willis McGahee/250 20.00
DM Donovan McNabb/250 12.00
EM Eric Moulds/192 10.00
TN Terence Newman/250 15.00
CP Chad Pennington/150 15.00
JP Julius Peppers/250 8.00
AP Artose Pinner/147 8.00
PO Clinton Portis/219 20.00
SH Jeremy Shockey/250 12.00
ES Emmitt Smith/200 25.00
RS Rod Smith/94 15.00
MT Marcus Trufant/250 8.00
MV Michael Vick/150 40.00
SW Seneca Wallace/250 10.00
KW Kurt Warner/250 10.00
RW Ricky Williams/250 15.00

2003 SPx Winning Materials Patches Autograph

NM/M
Common Player: 60.00
SA Shaun Alexander/50 75.00
DB Drew Brees/50 60.00
TC Tim Couch/50 75.00
JG Jeff Garcia/50 60.00
BL Byron Leftwich/25
PM Peyton Manning/50 150.00
RM Randy Moss/50 150.00
TO Terrell Owens RED
SC Carson Palmer/25
CP Chad Pennington/50 125.00
JR Jerry Rice/25
LTO LaDainian Tomlinson/50 100.00
MV Michael Vick RED/25

2004 SP Authentic

NM/M
Common Player (1-90): .30
Minor Stars: .60
Unlisted Stars: 1.00
Common Rookie (91-150): 3.00
91-150 Production 1,199 Sets
Common Rookie Auto (151-185): 10.00
151-185 Production 990 Sets
Common Rookie Jsy/Auto (186-216): 40.00
186-200 Production 799 Sets
201-206 Production 499 Sets
207-216 Production 299 Sets
Pack (5): 10.50
Box (24): 225.00
1 Josh McCown .60
2 Anquan Boldin 1.00
3 Michael Vick 2.50
4 Peerless Price .60
5 Todd Heap .60
6 Kyle Boller .60
7 Jamal Lewis 1.00
8 Drew Bledsoe 1.00
9 Travis Henry .60
10 Eric Moulds .60
11 Steve Smith .30
12 Stephen Davis .60
13 Jake Delhomme 1.00
14 Rex Grossman 1.00
15 Brian Urlacher 1.00
16 Thomas Jones .60
17 Chad Johnson .60
18 Rudi Johnson .60
19 Carson Palmer 1.50
20 William Green .60
21 Andre Davis .60
22 Jeff Garcia .60
23 Roy Williams 1.00
24 Eddie George .60
25 Keyshawn Johnson .60
26 Ashley Lelie .60
27 Jake Plummer .60
28 Champ Bailey .60
29 Charles Rogers 1.00
30 Joey Harrington 1.00
31 Ahman Green 1.00
32 Brett Favre 3.00
33 Javon Walker 1.00
34 David Carr 1.50
35 Domanick Davis .60
36 Andre Johnson 1.00
37 Marvin Harrison 1.00
38 Edgerrin James 1.50
39 Peyton Manning 2.00
40 Byron Leftwich 2.00
41 Fred Taylor 1.00
42 Trent Green .60
43 Tony Gonzalez .60
44 Priest Holmes 1.50
45 Ricky Williams 1.00
46 Chris Chambers 1.00
47 Jay Fiedler .60
48 Daunte Culpepper 1.00
49 Randy Moss 2.00
50 Onterrio Smith .60
51 Tom Brady 2.00
52 Troy Brown .60
53 Corey Dillon 1.00
54 Deuce McAllister 1.00
55 Aaron Brooks 1.00
56 Joe Horn .60
57 Amani Toomer .60
58 Kurt Warner .60
59 Jeremy Shockey 1.00
60 Chad Pennington 1.50
61 Santana Moss .60
62 Curtis Martin 1.00
63 Rich Gannon .60
64 Jerry Rice 2.50
65 Jerry Porter .60
66 Terrell Owens 1.00
67 Jevon Kearse .60
68 Donovan McNabb 1.50
69 Hines Ward .60
70 Plaxico Burress .60
71 Tommy Maddox .60
72 Drew Brees 1.00
73 LaDainian Tomlinson 1.50
74 Tim Rattay .60
75 Brandon Lloyd .60
76 Kevan Barlow .60
77 Shaun Alexander 1.00
78 Koren Robinson .60
79 Matt Hasselbeck .60
80 Marshall Faulk 1.50
81 Torry Holt 1.00
82 Marc Bulger 1.00
83 Brad Johnson .60
84 Joey Galloway .60
85 Steve McNair 1.00
86 Derrick Mason .60
87 Chris Brown .60
88 Mark Brunell .60
89 Laveranues Coles .60
90 Clinton Portis 1.50
91 *Triandos Luke* 5.00
92 *Keith Smith* 4.00
93 *Shaun Phillips* 4.00
94 *D.J. Williams* 8.00
95 *Keiwan Ratliff* 5.00
96 *Madieu Williams* 4.00
97 *Chris Cooley* 6.00
98 *Stuart Schweigert* 5.00
99 *Sloan Thomas* 4.00
100 *Chad Lavalais* 4.00
101 *Jared Allen* 4.00
102 *Brian Jones* 4.00
103 *Matt Ware* 6.00
104 *Daryl Smith* 5.00
105 *J.R. Reed* 5.00
106 *D.J. Hackett* 5.00
107 *Jeris McIntyre* 5.00
108 *Dexter Reid* 4.00
109 *Courtney Anderson* 4.00
110 *Courtney Watson* 6.00
111 *Larry Croom* 4.00
112 *Jonathan Smith* 4.00
113 *Vernon Carey* 3.00
114 *Michael Gaines* 4.00
115 *Chris Snee* 3.00
116 *Nathan Vasher* 6.00
117 *Teddy Lehman* 6.00
118 *Marcus Tubbs* 5.00
119 *Ben Utecht* 3.00
120 *Maurice Mann* 4.00
121 *Thomas Tapeh* 3.00
122 *Will Allen* 6.00
123 *Demorrio Williams* 5.00
124 *Ran Carthon* 5.00
125 *Tim Euhus* 4.00
126 *Bradlee Van Pelt* 6.00
127 *Patrick Crayton* 5.00
128 *Ryan Krause* 4.00
129 *Joey Thomas* 5.00
130 *Antwan Odom* 6.00
131 *Karlos Dansby* 6.00
132 *Junior Siavii* 5.00
133 *Jamaar Taylor* 5.00
134 *Kendrick Starling* 3.00
135 *Wes Welker* 4.00
136 *Igor Olshansky* 6.00
137 *Mark Jones* 3.00
138 *Bruce Thornton* 3.00
139 *Michael Boulware* 6.00
140 *Matt Mauck* 6.00
141 *Clarence Moore* 5.00
142 *Derrick Strait* 6.00
143 *Jarrett Payton* 6.00
144 *Dontarrious Thomas* 4.00
145 *Shawntae Spencer* 5.00
146 *Bob Sanders* 6.00
147 *Darnell Dockett* 5.00
148 *Sean Taylor* 10.00
149 *Jason Babin* 8.00
150 *Ricardo Colclough* 6.00
151 *Brandon Chillar Auto* 10.00
152 *Clarence Farmer Auto* 10.00
153 *B.J. Symons Auto* 15.00
154 *John Navarre Auto* 15.00
155 *P.K. Sam Auto* 15.00
156 *Casey Clausen Auto* 15.00
157 *Drew Henson Auto* 40.00
158 *Kris Wilson Auto* 12.00
159 *Vince Wilfork Auto* 15.00
160 *Michael Turner Auto* 10.00
161 *Jonathan Vilma Auto* 20.00
162 *Samie Parker Auto* 15.00
163 *B.J. Sams Auto* 12.00
164 *Adimchinobe Echemandu Auto* 10.00
165 *Ernest Wilford Auto* 15.00
166 *Troy Fleming Auto* 10.00
167 *Tommie Harris Auto* 15.00
168 *Jammal Lord Auto* 12.00
169 *Kenechi Udeze Auto* 12.00
170 *Chris Gamble Auto* 15.00
171 *Carlos Francis Auto* 12.00
172 *Mewelde Moore Auto* 30.00
173 *Jared Lorenzen Auto* 10.00
174 *Jeff Smoker Auto* 15.00
175 *Ben Hartsock Auto* 12.00
176 *Jerricho Cotchery Auto* 15.00
177 *Josh Harris Auto* 12.00
178 *Cody Pickett Auto* 15.00
179 *Quincy Wilson Auto* 12.00
180 *Will Smith Auto* 12.00
181 *Ahmad Carroll Auto* 15.00
182 *B.J. Johnson Auto* 12.00
183 *Dunta Robinson Auto* 15.00
184 *Craig Krenzel Auto* 15.00
185 *Johnnie Morant Auto* 12.00
186 *Cedric Cobbs Jsy/Auto* 40.00
187 *Matt Schaub Jsy/Auto* 60.00
188 *Bernard Berrian Jsy/Auto* 40.00
189 *Devard Darling Jsy/Auto* 40.00
190 *Ben Watson Jsy/Auto* 40.00
191 *Darius Watts Jsy/Auto* 50.00
192 *DeAngelo Hall Jsy/Auto* 50.00
193 *Ben Troupe Jsy/Auto* 40.00
194 *Michael Jenkins Jsy/Auto* 50.00
195 *Keary Colbert Jsy/Auto* 60.00
196 *Robert Gallery Jsy/Auto* 40.00
197 *Greg Jones Jsy/Auto* 50.00
198 *Michael Clayton Jsy/Auto* 100.00
199 *Luke McCown Jsy/Auto* 50.00
200 *Derrick Hamilton Jsy/Auto* 40.00
201 *Rashaun Woods Jsy/Auto* 60.00
202 *Chris Perry Jsy/Auto* 100.00
203 *Devery Henderson Jsy/Auto* 50.00
204 *Tatum Bell Jsy/Auto* 200.00
205 *Lee Evans Jsy/Auto* 100.00
206 *J.P. Losman Jsy/Auto* 150.00
207 *Kellen Winslow Jr.* 125.00
208 *Reggie Williams* 100.00
209 *Julius Jones Jsy/Auto* 400.00
210 *Steven Jackson Jsy/Auto* 300.00
211 *Kevin Jones Jsy/Auto* 300.00
212 *Roy Williams Jsy/Auto* 300.00
213 *Ben Roethlisberger Jsy/Auto* 900.00
214 *Philip Rivers Jsy/Auto* 400.00
215 *Larry Fitzgerald Jsy/Auto* 250.00
216 *Eli Manning Jsy/Auto* 500.00

2004 SP Authentic Gold

1-150 Production 50 Sets
Rookies (186-200): 1.5X-3X
Rookies (201-206): 1X-2X
Rookies (207-216): 1X-1.5X
186-216 Production 25 Sets
Black Production 10 Sets
151-185 Do Not Exist

2004 SP Authentic Authentic Artifacts

NM/M
Common Player: 10.00
Production 75 Sets
AA-TB Tatum Bell 20.00
AA-DB Drew Bledsoe 10.00
AA-TO Tom Brady 30.00
AA-DC David Carr 15.00
AA-MC Michael Clayton 20.00
AA-KC Keary Colbert 12.00
AA-LE Lee Evans 20.00
AA-MF Marshall Faulk 12.00
AA-BF Brett Favre 40.00
AA-LF Larry Fitzgerald 25.00
AA-RG Robert Gallery 12.00
AA-DH Devery Henderson 10.00
AA-PH Priest Holmes 15.00
AA-SJ Steven Jackson 25.00
AA-EJ Edgerrin James 12.00
AA-MJ Michael Jenkins 12.00
AA-GJ Greg Jones 12.00
AA-JJ Julius Jones 25.00
AA-KJ Kevin Jones 25.00
AA-BL Byron Leftwich 15.00
AA-JP J.P. Losman 15.00
AA-EM Eli Manning 50.00
AA-PM Peyton Manning 25.00
AA-DE Deuce McAllister 10.00
AA-DM Donovan McNabb 15.00
AA-SM Steve McNair 12.00
AA-RM Randy Moss 15.00
AA-CH Chad Pennington 15.00
AA-CP Chris Perry 15.00
AA-CL Clinton Portis 12.00
AA-JR Jerry Rice 25.00
AA-PR Philip Rivers 25.00
AA-BR Ben Roethlisberger 100.00
AA-JS Jeremy Shockey 10.00
AA-LT LaDainian Tomlinson 12.00
AA-MV Michael Vick 30.00
AA-KU Kurt Warner 10.00
AA-RE Reggie Williams 12.00
AA-RI Ricky Williams 12.00
AA-RO Roy Williams 25.00
AA-KW Kellen Winslow Jr. 20.00
AA-RW Rashaun Woods 12.00

2004 SP Authentic Scripts for Success

NM/M
Common Player: 8.00
Inserted 1:24
SS-DB Drew Bledsoe SP 20.00
SS-KC Keary Colbert 15.00
SS-JC Jerricho Cotchery 10.00
SS-LE Lee Evans 25.00
SS-BF Brett Favre SP 200.00
SS-CA Carlos Francis 8.00
SS-CG Chris Gamble 12.00
SS-TG Tony Gonzalez 15.00
SS-AG Ahman Green SP 25.00
SS-DA Dante Hall 15.00
SS-DH Derrick Hamilton 8.00
SS-TH Tommie Harris 12.00
SS-BH Ben Hartsock 8.00
SS-HE Todd Heap 10.00
SS-DV Devery Henderson 10.00
SS-TR Travis Henry 10.00
SS-HO Joe Horn 12.00
SS-MJ Michael Jenkins 10.00
SS-CJ Chad Johnson 15.00
SS-RJ Rudi Johnson 15.00
SS-DM Derrick Mason 15.00
SS-JO Josh McCown 10.00
SS-LM Luke McCown 10.00
SS-MM Mewelde Moore 15.00
SS-JM Johnnie Morant 8.00
SS-JN John Navarre 10.00
SS-JP Jesse Palmer 10.00
SS-SP Samie Parker 12.00
SS-CP Cody Pickett 12.00
SS-AR Antwann Randle El 12.00
SS-DR Dunta Robinson 12.00
SS-PK P.K. Sam 10.00
SS-BJ B.J. Sams 8.00
SS-MS Matt Schaub 15.00
SS-WS Will Smith 10.00
SS-JS Jeff Smoker 12.00
SS-BS B.J. Symons 8.00
SS-ZT Zach Thomas 12.00
SS-BT Ben Troupe 10.00
SS-MT Michael Turner 8.00
SS-KU Kenechi Udeze 10.00
SS-MV Michael Vick 80.00
SS-JV Jonathan Vilma 15.00
SS-BW Ben Watson 10.00
SS-DW Darius Watts 12.00
SS-EW Ernest Wilford 10.00
SS-VW Vince Wilfork 10.00
SS-RW Roy Williams 20.00
SS-RA Rashaun Woods 10.00

2004 SP Authentic Sign of the Times

NM/M
Common Player: 12.00
Inserted 1:72
Gold Autos: 1X-2X
Gold SP Autos: 1X-1.5X
Gold Production 25 Sets
SOT-TA Troy Aikman 100.00
SOT-BE Tatum Bell 30.00
SOT-KB Kyle Boller 12.00
SOT-TB Tom Brady
SOT-MB Mark Brunell 12.00
SOT-DA David Carr 25.00
SOT-DC Daunte Culpepper 30.00
SOT-JE John Elway SP 150.00
SOT-BF Brett Favre SP 200.00
SOT-JF John Fox 12.00
SOT-RO Robert Gallery 15.00
SOT-TG Tony Gonzalez 15.00
SOT-RG Rex Grossman 15.00
SOT-JG Jon Gruden 20.00
SOT-DH Dante Hall 12.00
SOT-TH Travis Henry 12.00
SOT-HD Drew Henson 30.00
SOT-SJ Steven Jackson 50.00
SOT-CJ Chad Johnson 12.00
SOT-GJ Greg Jones 12.00
SOT-JJ Julius Jones 60.00
SOT-KJ Kevin Jones 50.00
SOT-BL Byron Leftwich 25.00
SOT-HL Howie Long 40.00
SOT-JP J.P. Losman 25.00
SOT-AM Archie Manning 25.00
SOT-EM Eli Manning 120.00
SOT-PM Peyton Manning 80.00
SOT-MA Derrick Mason 12.00
SOT-DE Deuce McAllister 20.00
SOT-JM Josh McCown 12.00
SOT-DM Donovan McNabb SP 60.00
SOT-SM Steve McNair SP 40.00
SOT-JO Joe Montana SP 200.00
SOT-BP Bill Parcells 40.00
SOT-CP Chad Pennington 40.00
SOT-CH Chris Perry 12.00
SOT-AR Andy Reid 20.00
SOT-PR Philip Rivers 60.00
SOT-BR Ben Roethlisberger 250.00
SOT-BS Barry Sanders SP 125.00
SOT-RS Roger Staubach SP
SOT-LT LaDainian Tomlinson SP 40.00
SOT-MV Michael Vick SP 80.00
SOT-RE Reggie Williams 12.00
SOT-RW Roy Williams 30.00
SOT-WI Roy Williams 40.00
SOT-KE Kellen Winslow Jr. 40.00
SOT-KW Kellen Winslow Sr. 20.00

2004 SP Authentic Sign of the Times Dual

NM/M
Common Player: 50.00
Production 50 Sets
SOT2-AE Archie Manning, Eli Manning
SOT2-MM Eli Manning, Peyton Manning 400.00
SOT2-WW Kellen Winslow Sr., Kellen Winslow Jr. 50.00
SOT2-SJ Barry Sanders, Kevin Jones 200.00
SOT2-LG Howie Long, Robert Gallery 80.00
SOT2-PR Bill Parcells, Andy Reid 50.00
SOT2-JG Jimmy Johnson, Jon Gruden 50.00
SOT2-PJ Chris Perry, Steven Jackson 100.00
SOT2-LE J.P. Losman, Lee Evans 80.00
SOT2-RR Philip Rivers, Ben Roethlisberger 400.00

2004 SP Authentic Sign of the Times Triple

Production 10 Sets
SOT3MMM Archie Manning, Peyton Manning, Eli Manning
SOT3RRM Philip Rivers, Ben Roethlisberger, Eli Manning
SOT3JPJ Steven Jackson, Chris Perry, Kevin Jones
SOT3WWF Roy Williams, Reggie Williams, Larry Fitzgerald
SOT3ENM John Elway, Joe Namath, Joe Namath
SOT3ASH Troy Aikman, Roger Staubach, Drew Henson
SOT3SJW Barry Sanders, Kevin Jones, Roy Williams
SOT3VPB Michael Vick, Chad Pennington, Tom Brady
SOT3JPG Jimmy Johnson, Bill Parcells, John Gruden
SOT3FMM Brett Favre, Donovan McNabb, Steve McNair

2004 SP Game-Used

NM/M
Common Player (1-100): .60
Minor Stars: 1.00
Unlisted Stars: 2.00
Common Rookie (101-200): 5.00
Minor Rookies: 6.00

NM/M
Unlisted Rookies: 8.00
Production 425 Sets
Pack (3): 35.00
Box (6): 150.00
1 Anquan Boldin 2.00
2 Marcel Shipp .60
3 Josh McCown 1.00
4 Michael Vick 5.00
5 T.J. Duckett 1.00
6 Peerless Price 1.00
7 Jamal Lewis 2.00
8 Todd Heap .60
9 Kyle Boller 2.00
10 Drew Bledsoe 2.00
11 Travis Henry 1.00
12 Eric Moulds 1.00
13 Jake Delhomme 2.00
14 Stephen Davis 2.00
15 Julius Peppers 1.00
16 Anthony Thomas 1.00
17 Rex Grossman 2.00
18 Brian Urlacher 2.00
19 Carson Palmer 3.00
20 Chad Johnson 2.00
21 Rudi Johnson 1.00
22 Jeff Garcia 2.00
23 Dennis Northcutt .60
24 Andre Davis 1.00
25 Quincy Carter 1.00
26 Roy Williams 1.00
27 Keyshawn Johnson 1.00
28 Quentin Griffin 1.00
29 Jake Plummer 1.00
30 Ashley Lelie 1.00
31 Shannon Sharpe 1.00
32 Joey Harrington 2.00
33 Charles Rogers 2.00
34 Az-Zahir Hakim 1.00
35 Brett Favre 6.00
36 Javon Walker 1.00
37 Ahman Green 2.00
38 Andre Johnson 2.00
39 David Carr 3.00
40 Domanick Davis 1.00
41 Peyton Manning 4.00
42 Edgerrin James 3.00
43 Marvin Harrison 2.00
44 Byron Leftwich 4.00
45 Fred Taylor 2.00
46 Jimmy Smith 1.00
47 Priest Holmes 2.00
48 Trent Green 1.00
49 Dante Hall 1.00
50 Tony Gonzalez 1.00
51 Ricky Williams 3.00
52 Jay Fiedler 1.00
53 Chris Chambers 2.00
54 Randy Moss 4.00
55 Daunte Culpepper 2.00
56 Moe Williams .60
57 Tom Brady 4.00
58 Deion Branch 1.00
59 Corey Dillon 1.00
60 Deuce McAllister 2.00
61 Aaron Brooks 2.00
62 Joe Horn 1.00
63 Jeremy Shockey 2.00
64 Amani Toomer 1.00
65 Michael Strahan 1.00
66 Curtis Martin 2.00
67 Chad Pennington 3.00
68 Santana Moss 2.00
69 Jerry Rice 5.00
70 Tim Brown 2.00
71 Jerry Porter 1.00
72 Donovan McNabb 3.00
73 Brian Westbrook 1.00
74 Terrell Owens 2.00
75 Hines Ward 2.00
76 Plaxico Burress 2.00
77 Duce Staley 1.00
78 LaDainian Tomlinson 3.00
79 Quentin Jammer 1.00
80 Drew Brees 2.00
81 Brandon Lloyd 1.00
82 Kevan Barlow 1.00
83 Tim Rattay 1.00
84 Matt Hasselbeck 1.00
85 Shaun Alexander 2.00
86 Darrell Jackson 1.00
87 Marc Bulger 2.00
88 Torry Holt 2.00
89 Marshall Faulk 3.00
90 Isaac Bruce 1.00
91 Brad Johnson 1.00
92 Derrick Brooks 1.00
93 Warren Sapp 1.00
94 Steve McNair 2.00
95 Derrick Mason 1.00
96 Eddie George 1.00
97 Clinton Portis 4.00
98 Mark Brunell 1.00
99 Laveranues Coles 1.00
100 LaVar Arrington 2.00
101 *Ben Troupe* 6.00

102 *Chris Gamble* 10.00
103 *DeAngelo Hall* 15.00
104 *Dunta Robinson* 8.00
105 *Jason Shivers* 5.00
106 *Keary Colbert* 8.00
107 *Craig Krenzel* 8.00
108 *Philip Rivers* 40.00
109 *Roy Williams* 50.00
110 *Will Allen* 8.00
111 *Bob Sanders* 8.00
112 *Kris Wilson* 6.00
113 *D.J. Williams* 10.00
114 *Devery Henderson* 8.00
115 *Carlos Francis* 8.00
116 *Jonathan Vilma* 10.00
117 *Luke McCown* 10.00
118 *Michael Turner* 10.00
119 *Richard Seigler* 6.00
120 *Jared Lorenzen* 8.00
121 *P.K. Sam* 8.00
122 *Justin Smiley* 8.00
123 *Marquise Hill* 6.00
124 *Ernest Wilford* 8.00
125 *Jerricho Cotchery* 8.00
126 *Kevin Jones* 40.00
127 *Michael Boulware* 8.00
128 *Jarrett Payton* 15.00
129 *Sean Taylor* 30.00
130 *Will Smith* 8.00
131 *Bernard Berrian* 8.00
132 *Ahmad Carroll* 8.00
133 *Derrick Hamilton* 6.00
134 *Dwan Edwards* 5.00
135 *Jeff Smoker* 15.00
136 *Kenechi Udeze* 12.00
137 *Mewelde Moore* 6.00
138 *Joey Thomas* 8.00
139 *Sean Jones* 8.00
140 *Will Poole* 8.00
141 *Casey Clausen* 12.00
142 *Stuart Schweigert* 6.00
143 *Cody Pickett* 8.00
144 *Derrick Strait* 8.00
145 *Greg Jones* 12.00
146 *John Navarre* 10.00
147 *Larry Fitzgerald* 50.00
148 *Michael Clayton* 20.00
149 *Rashaun Woods* 30.00
150 *Shawn Andrews* 6.00
151 *B.J. Symons* 8.00
152 *Cedric Cobbs* 10.00
153 *Darius Watts* 8.00
154 *B.J. Johnson* 8.00
155 *Max Starks* 5.00
156 *Josh Harris* 6.00
157 *Kendrick Starling* 5.00
158 *Brandon Miree* 6.00
159 *Robert Gallery* 15.00
160 *Tatum Bell* 30.00
161 *Ben Hartsock* 6.00
162 *Derek Abney* 8.00
163 *Ricardo Colclough* 8.00
164 *Justin Jenkins* 6.00
165 *Chris Cooley* 6.00
166 *Julius Jones* 40.00
167 *Matt Mauck* 12.00
168 *Vernon Carey* 6.00
169 *John Standeford* 8.00
170 *Teddy Lehman* 8.00
171 *Ben Roethlisberger* 150.00
172 *Ben Utecht* 5.00
173 *D.J. Hackett* 6.00
174 *Drew Henson* 30.00
175 *Rich Gardner* 6.00
176 *Karlos Dansby* 8.00
177 *Matt Schaub* 8.00
178 *Darrion Scott* 6.00
179 *Keyaron Fox* 6.00
180 *Tommie Harris* 10.00
181 *Ben Watson* 6.00
182 *Chris Perry* 25.00
183 *Travelle Wharton* 5.00
184 *Eli Manning* 100.00
185 *Demorrio Williams* 6.00
186 *Kellen Winslow Jr.* 30.00
187 *Jason Babin* 10.00
188 *Quincy Wilson* 8.00
189 *Samie Parker* 6.00
190 *Vince Wilfork* 8.00
191 *Antwan Odom* 8.00
192 *Josh Davis* 6.00
193 *Courtney Watson* 8.00
194 *Devard Darling* 8.00
195 *J.P. Losman* 10.00
196 *Johnnie Morant* 15.00
197 *Lee Evans* 20.00
198 *Michael Jenkins* 15.00
199 *Reggie Williams* 15.00
200 *Steven Jackson* 40.00

2004 SP Game-Used Gold

Stars: 1.5X-3X
Production 100 Sets
Rookies: 1X-2X
Production 50 Sets

2004 SP Game-Used All-Pro Fabrics

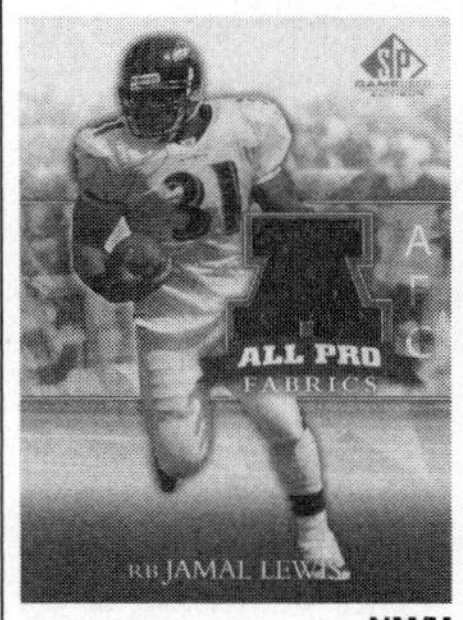

NM/M
Common Player: 8.00
APF-DC Daunte Culpepper 8.00
APF-SD Stephen Davis 6.00
APF-BF Brett Favre 20.00
APF-AG Ahman Green 8.00
APF-PH Priest Holmes 10.00
APF-CJ Chad Johnson 6.00
APF-JL Jamal Lewis 8.00
APF-PM Peyton Manning 12.00
APF-DM Donovan McNabb 10.00
APF-SM Steve McNair 8.00
APF-RM Randy Moss 10.00
APF-CP Clinton Portis 10.00

2004 SP Game-Used Authentic Fabrics

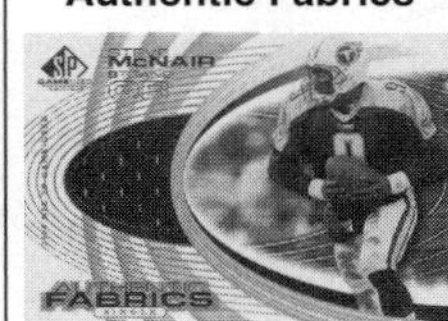

NM/M
Common Player: 5.00
Inserted 1:1
Golds: 1X-2X
Gold Production 100 Sets
AF-SA Shaun Alexander 6.00
AF-LA LaVar Arrington 10.00
AF-JB Jerome Bettis 6.00
AF-DR Drew Bledsoe 6.00
AF-AB Anquan Boldin 8.00
AF-KB Kyle Boller 6.00
AF-TB Tom Brady 10.00
AF-BR Aaron Brooks 6.00
AF-DB Derrick Brooks 5.00
AF-TY Troy Brown 5.00
AF-IB Isaac Bruce 6.00
AF-MA Mark Brunell 5.00
AF-MB Marc Bulger 6.00
AF-DA David Carr 10.00
AF-LC Laveranues Coles 6.00
AF-DC Daunte Culpepper 8.00
AF-DD Domanick Davis 6.00
AF-SD Stephen Davis 6.00
AF-CD Corey Dillon 6.00
AF-MF Marshall Faulk 8.00
AF-BF Brett Favre 15.00
AF-TG Tony Gonzalez 6.00
AF-AG Ahman Green 8.00
AF-TR Trent Green 6.00
AF-RG Rex Grossman 6.00
AF-DH Dante Hall 6.00
AF-MH Marvin Harrison 8.00
AF-HA Matt Hasselbeck 6.00
AF-PH Priest Holmes 8.00
AF-TH Torry Holt 6.00
AF-EJ Edgerrin James 8.00
AF-AJ Andre Johnson 6.00
AF-CJ Chad Johnson 6.00
AF-TJ Thomas Jones 5.00
AF-JK Jevon Kearse 5.00
AF-TL Ty Law 5.00
AF-BL Byron Leftwich 10.00
AF-JL Jamal Lewis 8.00
AF-RL Ray Lewis 8.00
AF-LY John Lynch 5.00
AF-PM Peyton Manning 10.00
AF-DK Derrick Mason 6.00
AF-DE Deuce McAllister 6.00
AF-KM Keenan McCardell 5.00
AF-WM Willis McGahee 6.00
AF-DM Donovan McNabb 8.00
AF-SM Steve McNair 6.00
AF-RM Randy Moss 10.00
AF-EM Eric Moulds 5.00
AF-TO Terrell Owens 6.00
AF-CA Carson Palmer 8.00
AF-CP Chad Pennington 10.00
AF-CL Clinton Portis 10.00
AF-JP Jake Plummer SP 6.00
AF-PP Peerless Price 5.00
AF-JR Jerry Rice 12.00
AF-CR Charles Rogers 8.00
AF-WS Warren Sapp 6.00
AF-JU Junior Seau 6.00
AF-SS Shannon Sharpe SP 6.00
AF-JS Jeremy Shockey 8.00
AF-ES Emmitt Smith 12.00
AF-DS Duce Staley 5.00
AF-MS Michael Strahan 6.00
AF-TS Terrell Suggs 5.00
AF-FT Fred Taylor 6.00
AF-LT LaDainian Tomlinson 8.00
AF-BU Brian Urlacher 10.00
AF-MV Michael Vick 15.00
AF-HW Hines Ward 6.00
AF-KW Kurt Warner 6.00
AF-RW Ricky Williams 8.00
AF-RO Roy Williams 8.00

2004 SP Game-Used Authentic Fabrics Dual

NM/M
Common Player: 10.00
Production 100 Sets
AF2-VP Michael Vick, Peerless Price 20.00
AF2-FG Brett Favre, Ahman Green 40.00
AF2-PM Chad Pennington, Santana Moss 15.00
AF2-MH Peyton Manning, Marvin Harrison 25.00
AF2-MM Steve McNair, Peyton Manning 20.00
AF2-WC Ricky Williams, Chris Chambers 15.00
AF2-CB Laveranues Coles, Mark Brunell 10.00
AF2-CM Daunte Culpepper, Randy Moss 25.00
AF2-MW Donovan McNabb, Brian Westbrook 15.00
AF2-HH Priest Holmes, Daniel Hall 12.00
AF2-BP Mark Brunell, Clinton Portis 20.00
AF2-JJ Chad Johnson, Rudi Johnson 10.00
AF2-CD Davis Carr, Domanick Davis 15.00
AF2-BH Isaac Bruce, Torry Holt 12.00
AF2-BF Marc Bulger, Marshall Faulk 15.00
AF2-WN Roy Williams, Terence Newman 20.00
AF2-GG Trent Green, Tony Gonzalez 15.00
AF2-HA Matt Hasselbeck, Shaun Alexander 12.00
AF2-SB Emmitt Smith, Anquan Boldin 25.00
AF2-BW Jerome Bettis, Hines Ward 15.00
AF2-DD Jake Delhomme, Stephen Davis 15.00
AF2-LS Byron Leftwich, Jimmy Smith 15.00
AF2-LL Jamal Lewis, Ray Lewis 20.00
AF2-BM Aaron Brooks, Deuce McAllister 12.00
AF2-BL Tom Brady, Ty Law 20.00
AF2-GU Rex Grossman, Brian Urlacher 20.00
AF2-MB Willis McGahee, Drew Bledsoe 15.00
AF2-BA Derrick Brooks, LaVar Arrington 25.00
AF2-RJ Jerry Rice, Keyshawn Johnson 20.00
AF2-LP Byron Leftwich, Chad Pennington 25.00
AF2-DF Donovan McNabb, Freddie Mitchell 20.00
AF2-MG Steve McNair, Eddie George 15.00
AF2-FM Brett Favre, Peyton Manning 50.00
AF2-HP Priest Holmes, Clinton Portis 20.00
AF2-HP Priest Holmes, Clinton Portis 20.00

2004 SP Game-Used Authentic Fabris Triple

NM/M
Common Player: 30.00
Production 25 Sets
AF3-CMS Daunte Culpepper, Randy Moss, Onterrio Smith 50.00
AF3-GHH Trent Green, Priest Holmes, Dante Hall 40.00
AF3-MHJ Peyton Manning, Marvin Harrison, Edgerrin James 60.00
AF3-VPD Michael Vick, Peerless Price, Warrick Dunn 50.00
AF3-PBL Jake Plummer, Champ Bailey, Ashley Lelie 30.00
AF3-PMM Chad Pennington, Curtis Martin, Santana Moss 40.00
AF3-BHF Marc Bulger, Torry Holt, Marshall Faulk 40.00
AF3-MWM Donovan McNabb, Brian Westbrook, Freddie Mitchell 40.00
AF3-FGW Brett Favre, Ahman Green, Javon Walker 80.00
AF3-CDJ David Carr, Domanick Davis, Andre Johnson 40.00

2004 SP Game-Used Authentic Fabrics Quad

Production 10 Sets
AF4MMMF Peyton Manning, Steve McNair, Donovan McNabb, Brett Favre
AF4GHPL Ahman Green, Priest Holmes, Clinton Portis, Jamal Lewis
AF4MHHJ Randy Moss, Torry Holt, Marvin Harrison, Chad Johnson
AF4VWTC Michael Vick, Ricky Williams, LaDainian Tomlinson, Daunte Culpepper
AF4SULT Michael Strahan, Brian Urlacher, Ray Lewis, Zach Thomas
AF4LPGB Byron Leftwich, Carson Palmer, Rex Grossman, Kyle Boller

2004 SP Game-Used Authentic Fabrics Autos

NM/M
Common Player: 20.00
Production 100 Sets
AAF-TA Troy Aikman 120.00
AAF-DB Drew Bledsoe 50.00
AAF-KB Kyle Boller 30.00
AAF-TB Tom Brady 125.00
AAF-MA Mark Brunell 30.00
AAF-DA David Carr 50.00
AAF-DC Daunte Culpepper 40.00
AAF-DD Domanick Davis 30.00
AAF-BF Brett Favre 250.00
AAF-TG Tony Gonzalez 30.00
AAF-AG Ahman Green 60.00
AAF-DH Dante Hall 40.00
AAF-JH Joe Horn 20.00
AAF-CJ Chad Johnson 30.00
AAF-BL Byron Leftwich 60.00
AAF-PM Peyton Manning 100.00
AAF-DE Deuce McAllister 40.00
AAF-WM Willis McGahee 40.00
AAF-DM Donovan McNabb 60.00
AAF-SM Steve McNair 60.00
AAF-JP Jesse Palmer 20.00
AAF-CP Chad Pennington 50.00
AAF-KS Ken Stabler 80.00
AAF-ZT Zach Thomas 30.00
AAF-LT LaDainian Tomlinson 50.00
AAF-RW Ricky Williams 50.00

2004 SP Game-Used Authentic Fabrics Autographs Dual

NM/M
Common Player: 50.00
Production 50 Sets
AAF2-BB Mark Brunell, Drew Bledsoe 60.00
AAF2-ML Steve McNair, Byron Leftwich 100.00
AAF2-TK Tom Brady, Kyle Boller 120.00
AAF2-CD David Carr, Domanick Davis 80.00
AAF2-TB Joe Theismann, Mark Brunell 60.00
AAF2-LC Byron Leftwich, Daunte Culpepper 100.00
AAF2-DS Daunte Culpepper, Steve McNair 80.00
AAF2-MB Willis McGahee, Drew Bledsoe 60.00
AAF2-GH Tony Gonzalez, Dante Hall 50.00
AAF2-DK Drew Bledsoe, Kyle Boller 60.00
AAF2-JJ Chad Johnson, Rudi Johnson 50.00
AAF2-LP Byron Leftwich, Chad Pennington 120.00
AAF2-PK Peyton Manning, Kyle Boller 100.00
AAF2-MH Deuce McAllister, Joe Horn 50.00
AAF2-PD Peyton Manning, Drew Bledsoe 120.00
AAF2-ST Ken Stabler, Fran Tarkenton 100.00
AAF2-MW Donovan McNabb, Michael Westbrook 80.00
AAF2-RZ Ricky Williams, Zach Thomas 80.00
AAF2-DT Drew Bledsoe, Tom Brady 120.00
AAF2-HM Travis Henry, Willis McGahee 50.00
AAF2-WT Ricky Williams, LaDainian Tomlinson 100.00
AAF2-BP Tom Brady, Chad Pennington
AAF2-PT Peyton Manning, Tom Brady
AAF2-FG Brett Favre, Ahman Green
AAF2-EF John Elway, Brett Favre

2004 SP Game-Used Authentic Patches

NM/M
Common Player: 10.00
Production 100 Sets
AP-AB Anquan Boldin 12.00
AP-TB Tom Brady 30.00
AP-MA Mark Brunell 12.00
AP-LC Laveranues Coles 12.00
AP-DD Domanick Davis 12.00
AP-GO Tony Gonzalez 12.00
AP-TG Trent Green 12.00
AP-RG Rex Grossman 12.00
AP-DH Dante Hall 12.00
AP-JH Joey Harrington 12.00
AP-PH Priest Holmes 15.00
AP-TH Torry Holt 12.00
AP-JO Joe Horn 10.00
AP-EJ Edgerrin James 12.00
AP-CJ Chad Johnson 10.00
AP-PM Peyton Manning 20.00
AP-DN Donovan McNabb 15.00
AP-JN Joe Namath 40.00
AP-CP Chad Pennington 15.00
AP-JP Jake Plummer 12.00
AP-JS Jeremy Shockey 12.00
AP-LT LaDainian Tomlinson 15.00
AP-MV Michael Vick 25.00
AP-RW Roy Williams 12.00

2004 SP Game-Used Authentic Patches Dual

NM/M
Common Player: 40.00
Production 25 Sets
AP2-BP Tom Brady, Chad Pennington 60.00
AP2-MV Donovan McNabb, Michael Vick 80.00
AP2-FC Brett Favre, David Carr 100.00
AP2-MM Peyton Manning, Steve McNair 60.00
AP2-MH Randy Moss, Marvin Harrison 60.00
AP2-PJ Clinton Portis, Edgerrin James 40.00
AP2-BD Brett Favre, Daunte Culpepper 100.00

2004 SP Game-Used Authentic Patches Triple

Production 10 Sets
AP3-BMF Tom Brady, Peyton Manning, Brett Favre
AP3-MVC Donovan McNabb, Michael Vick, Daunte Culpepper
AP3-UTS Brian Urlacher, Zach Thomas, Junior Seau
AP3-HTP Priest Holmes, LaDainian Tomlinson, Clinton Portis
AP3-MHR Randy Moss, Marvin Harrison, Jerry Rice
AP3-SHG Jeremy Shockey, Todd Heap, Tony Gonzalez

2004 SP Game-Used Authentic Patches Autos

Production 25 Sets
AAP-DB Drew Bledsoe
AAP-KB Kyle Boller
AAP-TB Tom Brady
AAP-IB Isaac Bruce
AAP-MA Mark Brunell
AAP-DD Domanick Davis
AAP-TG Tony Gonzalez
AAP-AG Ahman Green
AAP-DH Dante Hall
AAP-TH Todd Heap
AAP-JO Joe Horn
AAP-CJ Chad Johnson
AAP-BL Byron Leftwich
AAP-PM Peyton Manning
AAP-WM Willis McGahee
AAP-DN Donovan McNabb
AAP-SM Steve McNair
AAP-JN Joe Namath
AAP-CP Chad Pennington
AAP-ZT Zach Thomas
AAP-LT LaDainian Tomlinson
AAP-RW Roy Williams

2004 SP Game-Used Authentic Patches Autos Dual

Production 5 Sets
AAP2-ST Barry Sanders, LaDainian Tomlinson
AAP2-TC Fran Tarkenton, Daunte Culpepper
AAP2-EF John Elway, Brett Favre
AAP2-MB Joe Montana, Tom Brady
AAP2-NP Joe Namath, Chad Pennington
AAP2-TB Joe Theismann, Mark Brunell
AAP2-EB John Elway, Tom Brady
AAP2-LT Howie Long, Zach Thomas
AAP2-SB Roger Staubach, Kyle Boller
AAP2-AM Troy Aikman, Peyton Manning
AAP2-SC Ken Stabler, David Carr
AAP2-MM Archie Manning, Peyton Manning

2004 SP Game-Used Awesome Authentics

NM/M
Common Player: 10.00
Production 100 Sets
AA-AB Anquan Boldin 12.00
AA-TB Tom Brady 20.00
AA-MA Mark Brunell 10.00
AA-MB Marc Bulger 12.00
AA-DA David Carr 20.00
AA-LC Laveranues Coles 12.00
AA-DC Daunte Culpepper 15.00
AA-MF Marshall Faulk 15.00
AA-BF Brett Favre 40.00
AA-AG Ahman Green 15.00
AA-DH Dante Hall 12.00
AA-JH Joey Harrington 12.00
AA-MH Marvin Harrison 12.00
AA-HE Todd Heap 10.00
AA-PH Priest Holmes 15.00
AA-TH Torry Holt 12.00
AA-EJ Edgerrin James 15.00
AA-CJ Chad Johnson 10.00
AA-BL Byron Leftwich 20.00
AA-JL Jamal Lewis 12.00
AA-PM Peyton Manning 20.00
AA-DE Deuce McAllister 12.00
AA-DM Donovan McNabb 15.00
AA-SM Steve McNair 15.00
AA-RM Randy Moss 15.00
AA-CH Chad Pennington 20.00
AA-CP Clinton Portis 20.00
AA-JS Jeremy Shockey 12.00
AA-LT LaDainian Tomlinson 15.00
AA-MV Michael Vick 30.00
AA-RW Ricky Williams 15.00
AA-RO Roy Williams 12.00

2004 SP Game-Used Legendary Fabrics Autos

NM/M
Common Player: 50.00
Production 50 Sets
ALF-TA Troy Aikman 120.00
ALF-JE John Elway 200.00
ALF-HL Howie Long 120.00
ALF-AM Archie Manning 50.00
ALF-JM Joe Montana 300.00
ALF-JN Joe Namath 150.00
ALF-BS Barry Sanders 200.00
ALF-KS Ken Stabler 80.00
ALF-RS Roger Staubach 120.00
ALF-FT Fran Tarkenton 80.00
ALF-JT Joe Theismann 60.00
ALF-KW Kellen Winslow Jr. 80.00

2004 SP Game-Used Rookie Exclusives Autos

NM/M
Common Player: 25.00
Production 100 Sets
RE-BB Bernard Berrian 40.00
RE-BC Brandon Chillar 25.00
RE-MC Michael Clayton 60.00
RE-CC Cedric Cobbs 40.00
RE-KC Keary Colbert 60.00
RE-JC Jerricho Cotchery 40.00
RE-DD Devard Darling 40.00
RE-LE Lee Evans 80.00
RE-LF Larry Fitzgerald 200.00
RE-RG Robert Gallery 100.00
RE-DH DeAngelo Hall 60.00
RE-TH Tommie Harris 40.00
RE-DR Drew Henson 120.00
RE-SJ Steven Jackson 150.00
RE-MJ Michael Jenkins 60.00
RE-GJ Greg Jones 60.00
RE-KJ Kevin Jones 150.00
RE-JP J.P. Losman 120.00
RE-EM Eli Manning 500.00
RE-LM Luke McCown 40.00
RE-JM Johnnie Morant 40.00
RE-JN John Navarre 60.00
RE-SP Samie Parker 40.00
RE-CH Chris Perry 80.00
RE-CP Cody Pickett 40.00
RE-PR Philip Rivers 200.00
RE-BR Ben Roethlisberger 800.00
RE-MS Matt Schaub 120.00
RE-WS Will Smith 30.00
RE-BJ B.J. Symons 40.00
RE-ST Sean Taylor 150.00
RE-BT Ben Troupe 30.00
RE-KU Kenechi Udeze 50.00
RE-JV Jonathan Vilma 60.00
RE-BW Ben Watson 40.00
RE-EW Ernest Wilford 40.00
RE-VW Vince Wilfork 50.00
RE-RE Reggie Williams 80.00
RE-RW Roy Williams 150.00
RE-KW Kellen Winslow Jr. 150.00
RE-RA Rashaun Woods 100.00

2004 SP Game-Used SIGnificance

NM/M
Common Player: 12.00
Production 100 Sets
Gold Production 10 Sets
SIG-KB Kyle Boller 20.00
SIG-MA Mark Brunell 20.00
SIG-DC Daunte Culpepper 30.00
SIG-DD Domanick Davis 25.00
SIG-JF John Fox 20.00
SIG-JO Joey Galloway 12.00
SIG-GO Tony Gonzalez 25.00
SIG-AG Ahman Green 50.00
SIG-GR John Gruden 40.00

SIG-DH Dante Hall 25.00
SIG-HE Todd Heap 20.00
SIG-TH Travis Henry 15.00
SIG-JH Joe Horn 12.00
SIG-CJ Chad Johnson 20.00
SIG-JJ Jimmy Johnson 50.00
SIG-BY Byron Leftwich 50.00
SIG-BL Brandon Lloyd 12.00
SIG-HL Howie Long 100.00
SIG-AM Archie Manning 25.00
SIG-DM Derrick Mason 12.00
SIG-DE Deuce McAllister 20.00
SIG-WM Willis McGahee 20.00
SIG-JP Jesse Palmer 12.00
SIG-BP Bill Parcells 60.00
SIG-RE Andy Reid 20.00
SIG-TS Tony Siragusa 12.00
SIG-KS Ken Stabler 40.00
SIG-JT Joe Theismann 30.00

2004 SP Game-Used SIGnificance Extra

Production 25 Sets
Gold Production 5 Sets
XSIG-LS Howie Long, Ken Stabler
XSIG-BT Mark Brunell, Joe Theismann
XSIG-TS Fran Tarkenton, Ken Stabler
XSIG-PF Chad Pennington, Brett Favre
XSIG-MM Archie Manning, Peyton Manning
XSIG-SA Roger Staubach, Troy Aikman
XSIG-JA Jimmy Johnson, Troy Aikman
XSIG-MB Joe Montana, Tom Brady
XSIG-ME Joe Montana, John Elway
XSIG-ST Barry Sanders, LaDainian Tomlinson

2004 SP Game-Used SIGnificant Numbers

SN-TA Troy Aikman/8
SN-TB Tom Brady/12
SN-DC David Carr/8
SN-JE John Elway/7
SN-BF Brett Favre/4
SN-PM Peyton Manning/18
SN-DM Donovan McNabb/5
SN-SM Steve McNair/9
SN-JM Joe Montana/16
SN-JN Joe Namath/12
SN-CP Chad Pennington/10
SN-MV Michael Vick/7

2004 SPx

NM/M
Common Player (1-100): .30
Minor Stars: .60
Unlisted Stars: 1.00
Common Rookie (101-165): 3.00
101-165 Production 1,650 Sets
Common Rookie (166-190): 6.00
166-190 Production 799 Sets
Common Rookie (191-221): 15.00
191-221 Production 1,499 Sets
Pack (4): 13.25
Box (18): 170.00
1 Anquan Boldin 1.00
2 Marcel Shipp .30
3 Josh McCown .30
4 Peerless Price .60
5 Michael Vick 2.50
6 T.J. Duckett .60
7 Kyle Boller .60
8 Todd Heap .60
9 Jamal Lewis 1.00
10 Travis Henry .60
11 Drew Bledsoe 1.00
12 Eric Moulds .60
13 Jake Delhomme 1.00
14 Steve Smith .60
15 Stephen Davis .60
16 Brian Urlacher 1.00
17 Rex Grossman 1.00
18 Thomas Jones .60
19 Chad Johnson .60
20 Carson Palmer 1.00
21 Rudi Johnson .60
22 William Green .60
23 Jeff Garcia .60
24 Andre Davis .60
25 Roy Williams 1.00
26 Eddie George .60
27 Keyshawn Johnson .60
28 Jake Plummer .60
29 Ashley Lelie .60
30 Quentin Griffin .60
31 Charles Rogers 1.00
32 Olandis Gary .60
33 Joey Harrington 1.00
34 Brett Favre 3.00
35 Javon Walker 1.00
36 Ahman Green 1.00
37 Andre Johnson 1.00
38 Domanick Davis .60
39 David Carr 1.50
40 Peyton Manning 2.00
41 Edgerrin James 1.50
42 Marvin Harrison 1.00
43 Byron Leftwich 2.00
44 Jimmy Smith .60
45 Fred Taylor 1.00
46 Trent Green .60
47 Priest Holmes 1.50
48 Dante Hall .60
49 Tony Gonzalez .60
50 A.J. Feeley .60
51 Marty Booker .30
52 Chris Chambers 1.00
53 Zach Thomas .60
54 Randy Moss 2.00
55 Daunte Culpepper 1.00
56 Onterrio Smith .60
57 Troy Brown .60
58 Corey Dillon 1.00
59 Tom Brady 2.00
60 Deuce McAllister 1.00
61 Joe Horn .60
62 Aaron Brooks 1.00
63 Jeremy Shockey 1.00
64 Kurt Warner .60
65 Tiki Barber .60
66 Chad Pennington 1.50
67 Curtis Martin 1.00
68 Santana Moss .60
69 Rich Gannon .60
70 Jerry Rice 2.50
71 Warren Sapp .60
72 Donovan McNabb 1.50
73 Terrell Owens 1.00
74 Jevon Kearse .60
75 Brian Westbrook .60
76 Hines Ward .60
77 Duce Staley .60
78 Tommy Maddox .60
79 LaDainian Tomlinson 1.50
80 Drew Brees 1.00
81 Tim Rattay .60
82 Kevan Barlow .60
83 Brandon Lloyd .60
84 Shaun Alexander 1.00
85 Matt Hasselbeck .60
86 Koren Robinson .60
87 Marc Bulger 1.00
88 Marshall Faulk 1.50
89 Torry Holt 1.00
90 Isaac Bruce .60
91 Brad Johnson .60
92 Keenan McCardell .30
93 Derrick Brooks .30
94 Steve McNair 1.00
95 Chris Brown .60
96 Derrick Mason .60
97 Clinton Portis 2.00
98 Mark Brunell .60
99 Laveranues Coles .60
100 LaVar Arrington 1.00
101 *B.J. Johnson* 3.00
102 *Craig Krenzel* 5.00
103 *Will Smith* 5.00
104 *Jamaar Taylor* 4.00
105 *Tommie Harris* 8.00
106 *Shawn Andrews* 3.00
107 *Kendrick Starling* 3.00
108 *Jeris McIntyre* 3.00
109 *Jason Babin* 8.00
110 *Marcus Tubbs* 4.00
111 *Triandos Luke* 3.00
112 *Karlos Dansby* 4.00
113 *Vernon Carey* 3.00
114 *Ryan Krause* 3.00
115 *Daryl Smith* 3.00
116 *Ricardo Colclough* .30
117 *Michael Boulware* 4.00
118 *Chris Cooley* 4.00
119 *Terry Johnson* 3.00
120 *Marquise Hill* 4.00
121 *Teddy Lehman* 6.00
122 *Antwan Odom* 4.00
123 *Sean Jones* 3.00
124 *Junior Siavii* 3.00
125 *Joey Thomas* 3.00
126 *Shawntae Spencer* 3.00
127 *Dontarrious Thomas* 3.00
128 *Travis LaBoy* 3.00
129 *Justin Jenkins* 3.00
130 *Dwan Edwards* 3.00
131 *Derrick Strait* 6.00
132 *Matt Ware* 4.00
133 *Jared Lorenzen* 4.00
134 *Demorrio Williams* 3.00
135 *Bob Sanders* 4.00
136 *Justin Smiley* 3.00
137 *Casey Bramlet* 3.00
138 *Jake Grove* 3.00
139 *Thomas Tapeh* 3.00
140 *Igor Olshansky* 3.00
141 *Stuart Schweigert* 3.00
142 *Cody Pickett* 4.00
143 *Derrick Ward* 3.00
144 *Gilbert Gardner* 3.00
145 *D.J. Hackett* 3.00
146 *Marquis Cooper* 3.00
147 *Courtney Watson* 3.00
148 *Jim Sorgi* 5.00
149 *Caleb Miller* 3.00
150 Casey Clausen 8.00
151 *Jammal Lord* 4.00
152 *Sloan Thomas* 3.00
153 *Keyaron Fox* 3.00
154 *Joe Echemandu* 3.00
155 *Ryan Dinwiddie* 3.00
156 *Kris Wilson* 3.00
157 *D.J. Williams* 8.00
158 *Tim Euhus* 3.00
159 *Bradlee Van Pelt* 8.00
160 *Keiwan Ratliff* 4.00
161 *Darnell Dockett* 5.00
162 *Troy Fleming* 3.00
163 *Tramon Douglas* 3.00
164 *Andrew LeSueur* 3.00
165 *Matt Mauck* 5.00
166 *Sean Taylor* 20.00
167 *B.J. Symons* 6.00
168 *Quincy Wilson* 6.00
169 *Ernest Wilford* 6.00
170 *Jerricho Cotchery* 6.00
171 *Michael Turner* 6.00
172 *Samie Parker* 6.00
173 *Andrew Hall* 6.00
174 *Keith Smith* 6.00
175 *Josh Harris* 6.00
176 *Maurice Mann* 6.00
177 *Jonathan Vilma* 12.00
178 *Jeff Smoker* 12.00
179 *Ben Hartsock* 6.00
180 *Chris Gamble* 10.00
181 *Derrick Hamilton* 6.00
182 *John Navarre* 8.00
183 *P.K. Sam* 8.00
184 *Kenechi Udeze* 10.00
185 *Mewelde Moore* 10.00
186 *Carlos Francis* 6.00
187 *Dunta Robinson* 8.00
188 *Johnnie Morant* 6.00
189 *Ahmad Carroll* 10.00
190 *Vince Wilfork* 10.00
191 *Tatum Bell Jsy Auto/1499* 40.00
192 *Cedric Cobbs Jsy Auto/1499* 15.00
193 *Darius Watts Jsy Auto/1499* 20.00
194 *Julius Jones Jsy Auto/375* 200.00
195 *Robert Gallery Jsy Auto/1499* 20.00
196 *DeAngelo Hall Jsy Auto/1499* 20.00
197 *Ben Watson Jsy Auto/1499* 15.00
198 *Ben Troupe Jsy Auto/1499* 15.00
199 *Matt Schaub Jsy Auto/1499* 25.00
200 *Michael Jenkins Jsy Auto/1499* 20.00
201 *Luke McCown Jsy Auto/1499* 20.00
202 *Devery Henderson Jsy Auto/1499* 15.00
203 *Bernard Berrian Jsy Auto/1499* 15.00
204 *Keary Colbert Jsy Auto/1499* 30.00
205 *Devard Darling Jsy Auto/1499* 15.00
206 *Lee Evans Jsy Auto/1499* 40.00
207 *Greg Jones Jsy Auto/1499* 20.00
208 *Michael Clayton Jsy Auto/1499* 50.00
209 *Reggie Williams Jsy Auto/1499* 20.00
210 *Chris Perry Jsy Auto/799* 40.00
211 *Rashaun Woods Jsy Auto/1499* 25.00
212 *J.P. Losman Jsy Auto/1499* 40.00
213 *Kevin Jones Jsy Auto/1499* 80.00
214 *Kellen Winslow Jr. Jsy Auto/375* 60.00
215 *Steven Jackson Jsy Auto/375* 200.00
216 *Derrick Hamilton Jsy Auto/1499* 15.00
217 *Roy Williams Jsy Auto/375* 200.00
218 *Philip Rivers Jsy Auto/375* 120.00
219 *Larry Fitzgerald Jsy Auto/100* 300.00
220 *Ben Roethlisberger Jsy Auto/375* 600.00
221 *Eli Manning Jsy Auto/375* 300.00

2004 SPx Spectrum

NM/M
Stars: 6X-12X
Rookies (101-165): 1.5X-3X
Rookies (166-190): 1X-2X
Rookies Auto/1499 (191-221): 2X-4X
Production 25 Sets
194 Julius Jones Jsy Auto 400.00
210 Chris Perry Jsy Auto 100.00
214 Kellen Winslow Jr. Jsy Auto 150.00
215 Steven Jackson Jsy Auto 300.00
217 Roy Williams Jsy Auto 300.00
218 Philip Rivers Jsy Auto 250.00
219 Larry Fitzgerald Jsy Auto 300.00
220 Ben Roethlisberger Jsy Auto 1,500
221 Eli Manning Jsy Auto 800.00

A player's name in *italic* type indicates a rookie card.

2004 SPx Rookie Swatch Supremacy

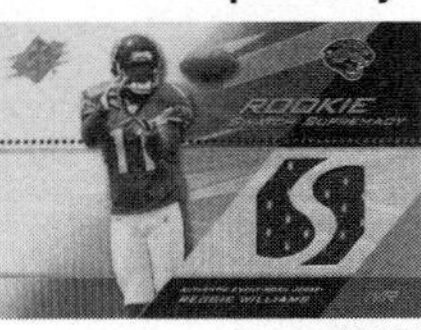

NM/M
Common Player: 5.00
Inserted 1:18
SWR-TB Tatum Bell 10.00
SWR-BB Bernard Berrian 5.00
SWR-MC Michael Clayton 10.00
SWR-CC Cedric Cobbs 5.00
SWR-KC Keary Colbert 6.00
SWR-DD Devard Darling 5.00
SWR-LE Lee Evans 10.00
SWR-LF Larry Fitzgerald 12.00
SWR-RG Robert Gallery 6.00
SWR-DH DeAngelo Hall 8.00
SWR-HA Derrick Hamilton 5.00
SWR-DE Devery Henderson 5.00
SWR-SJ Steven Jackson 12.00
SWR-MJ Michael Jenkins 6.00
SWR-GJ Greg Jones 6.00
SWR-JJ Julius Jones 12.00
SWR-KJ Kevin Jones 12.00
SWR-JP J.P. Losman 8.00
SWR-EM Eli Manning 20.00
SWR-LM Luke McCown 5.00
SWR-CP Chris Perry 8.00
SWR-PR Philip Rivers 12.00
SWR-BR Ben Roethlisberger 60.00
SWR-BT Ben Troupe 5.00
SWR-BW Ben Watson 5.00
SWR-DW Darius Watts 6.00
SWR-RW Reggie Williams 6.00
SWR-RO Roy Williams 12.00
SWR-KW Kellen Winslow Jr. 10.00
SWR-RA Rashaun Woods 6.00

2004 SPx Rookie Winning Materials

NM/M
Common Player: 8.00
Inserted 1:8
WMR-TB Tatum Bell 15.00
WMR-BB Bernard Berrian 8.00
WMR-MC Michael Clayton 12.00
WMR-CC Cedric Cobbs 8.00
WMR-KC Keary Colbert 8.00
WMR-DD Devard Darling 8.00
WMR-LE Lee Evans 10.00
WMR-LF Larry Fitzgerald 25.00
WMR-RG Robert Gallery 8.00
WMR-DH DeAngelo Hall 10.00
WMR-HA Derrick Hamilton 8.00
WMR-DE Devery Henderson 8.00
WMR-SJ Steven Jackson 20.00
WMR-MJ Michael Jenkins 8.00
WMR-GJ Greg Jones 8.00
WMR-JJ Julius Jones 20.00
WMR-KJ Kevin Jones 20.00
WMR-JP J.P. Losman 10.00
WMR-EM Eli Manning 40.00
WMR-LM Luke McCown 8.00
WMR-CP Chris Perry 10.00
WMR-PR Philip Rivers 20.00
WMR-BR Ben Roethlisberger 100.00
WMR-BT Ben Troupe 8.00
WMR-BW Ben Watson 8.00
WMR-DW Darius Watts 8.00
WMR-RW Reggie Williams 8.00
WMR-RO Roy Williams 25.00
WMR-KW Kellen Winslow Jr. 12.00
WMR-RA Rashaun Woods 8.00

2004 SPx Super Scripts Autos

NM/M
Common Player: 10.00
Inserted 1:54
SS-DB Drew Bledsoe 15.00
SS-KB Kyle Boller 15.00
SS-TB Tom Brady SP 100.00
SS-MB Mark Brunell 12.00
SS-DC David Carr 25.00
SS-CC Chris Chambers 15.00
SS-BC Brandon Chillar 10.00
SS-DD Domanick Davis 15.00
SS-KD Ken Dorsey 10.00
SS-JF Justin Fargas 12.00
SS-CF Clarence Farmer 10.00
SS-BF Brett Favre SP 150.00
SS-JO Joey Galloway 10.00
SS-TG Tony Gonzalez 15.00
SS-AG Ahman Green 25.00
SS-RG Rex Grossman 15.00
SS-JG Jon Gruden 15.00
SS-DH Dante Hall 15.00
SS-BH Ben Hartsock 10.00
SS-HE Todd Heap 12.00
SS-TH Travis Henry 10.00
SS-JH Joe Horn 10.00
SS-CJ Chad Johnson 15.00
SS-JJ Jimmy Johnson 20.00
SS-RJ Rudi Johnson 15.00
SS-BY Byron Leftwich 30.00
SS-BL Brandon Lloyd 10.00
SS-PM Peyton Manning 80.00
SS-DM Derrick Mason 10.00
SS-DE Deuce McAllister 15.00
SS-WM Willis McGahee 25.00
SS-DO Donovan McNabb SP 10.00
SS-SM Steve McNair 20.00
SS-JP Jesse Palmer 10.00
SS-CP Chad Pennington 30.00
SS-EL Antwann Randle El 10.00
SS-AR Andy Reid 15.00
SS-ZT Zach Thomas 15.00
SS-LT LaDainian Tomlinson 25.00
SS-MV Michael Vick SP 80.00
SS-JW Javon Walker 20.00
SS-KW Kelley Washington 10.00
SS-BW Brian Westbrook 12.00
SS-RW Roy Williams 20.00

2004 SPx Super Scripts Triple Autos

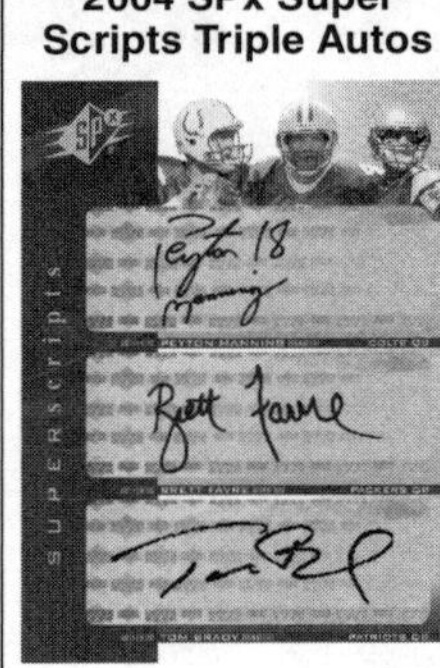

NM/M
Production 25 Sets
SS3-GBL Rex Grossman, Kyle Boller, Byron Leftwich 200.00
SS3-GSL Robert Gallery, Ken Stabler, Howie Long 200.00
SS3-JGR Jimmy Johnson, Jon Gruden, Andy Reid 150.00
SS3-JJJ Steven Jackson, Julius Jones, Kevin Jones 400.00
SS3-MBM Steve McNair, Chris Brown, Derrick Mason 125.00
SS3-RRM Philip Rivers, Ben Roethlisberger, Eli Manning 1,000
SS3-TMG LaDainian Tomlinson, Deuce McAllister, Ahman Green 200.00
SS3-TST Joe Theismann, Ken Stabler, Fran Tarkenton 250.00
SS3-SEA Barry Sanders, John Elway, Troy Aikman 600.00
SS3-WWE Roy Williams, Reggie Williams, Lee Evans 200.00
SS3-BFM Tom Brady, Brett Favre, Peyton Manning/10
SS3-EMN John Elway, Joe Montana, Joe Namath/10
SS3-MVM Donovan McNabb, Michael Vick, Steve McNair/10
SS3-MMM Archie Manning, Peyton Manning, Eli Manning/10
SS3-SAH Roger Staubach, Troy Aikman, Drew Henson/10

2004 SPx Swatch Supremacy

NM/M
Common Player: 5.00
Inserted 1:18
SW-KB Kyle Boller 6.00
SW-TB Tom Brady 12.00
SW-CB Chris Brown 6.00
SW-MB Mark Brunell 5.00
SW-CC Chris Chambers 6.00
SW-DC Daunte Culpepper 8.00
SW-DD Domanick Davis 6.00
SW-JG Joey Galloway 5.00
SW-TG Tony Gonzalez 6.00
SW-AG Ahman Green 8.00
SW-RG Rex Grossman 6.00
SW-DH Dante Hall 6.00
SW-HE Todd Heap 5.00
SW-TH Travis Henry 5.00
SW-JH Joe Horn 5.00
SW-CJ Chad Johnson 6.00
SW-RJ Rudi Johnson 6.00
SW-BL Byron Leftwich 10.00
SW-PM Peyton Manning 12.00
SW-DE Derrick Mason 5.00
SW-DM Deuce McAllister 6.00
SW-DO Donovan McNabb 10.00
SW-CP Chad Pennington 10.00
SW-AR Antwann Randle El 5.00
SW-ZT Zach Thomas 5.00
SW-LT LaDainian Tomlinson 8.00
SW-MV Michael Vick 15.00
SW-JW Javon Walker 8.00
SW-BW Brian Westbrook 5.00
SW-RW Roy Williams 8.00

2004 SPx Swatch Supremacy Autos

NM/M
Common Player: 20.00
Production 100 Sets
SWA-KB Kyle Boller 25.00
SWA-TB Tom Brady 120.00
SWA-CB Chris Brown 40.00
SWA-MB Mark Brunell 25.00
SWA-CC Chris Chambers 25.00
SWA-DC Daunte Culpepper 50.00
SWA-DD Domanick Davis 25.00
SWA-JG Joey Galloway 20.00
SWA-TG Tony Gonzalez 25.00
SWA-AG Ahman Green 50.00
SWA-RG Rex Grossman 25.00
SWA-DH Dante Hall 25.00
SWA-HE Todd Heap 20.00
SWA-TH Travis Henry 20.00
SWA-JH Joe Horn 20.00
SWA-CJ Chad Johnson 25.00
SWA-RJ Rudi Johnson 25.00
SWA-BL Byron Leftwich 40.00
SWA-PM Peyton Manning 100.00
SWA-DE Derrick Mason 25.00
SWA-DM Deuce McAllister 30.00
SWA-DO Donovan McNabb 60.00
SWA-CP Chad Pennington 60.00
SWA-AR Antwann Randle El 25.00
SWA-ZT Zach Thomas 25.00
SWA-LT LaDainian Tomlinson 40.00
SWA-MV Michael Vick 100.00
SWA-JW Javon Walker 40.00
SWA-BW Brian Westbrook 25.00
SWA-RW Roy Williams 30.00

2004 SPx Winning Materials

NM/M
Common Player: 8.00
Inserted 1:72
WM-AC LaVar Arrington, Laveranues Coles 10.00
WM-BD Tom Brady, Corey Dillon 15.00
WM-BM Aaron Brooks, Deuce McAllister 10.00
WM-BP Mark Brunell, Clinton Portis 10.00
WM-CJ David Carr, Andre Johnson 12.00
WM-CM Daunte Culpepper, Randy Moss 15.00
WM-DF Stephen Davis, DeShaun Foster 8.00
WM-DT Drew Bledsoe, Travis Henry 10.00
WM-FG Brett Favre, Ahman Green 25.00
WM-FH Marshall Faulk, Torry Holt 12.00
WM-FM Brett Favre, Donovan McNabb 25.00
WM-HA Matt Hasselbeck, Shaun Alexander 8.00
WM-GG Trent Green, Tony Gonzalez 8.00
WM-HR Joey Harrington, Charles Rogers 8.00
WM-HW Priest Holmes, Ricky Williams 12.00
WM-MJ Peyton Manning, Edgerrin James 20.00
WM-MM Curtis Martin, Santana Moss 12.00
WM-MO Donovan McNabb, Terrell Owens 15.00
WM-MR Randy Moss, Jerry Rice 20.00
WM-MV Steve McNair, Michael Vick 15.00
WM-PG Jake Plummer, Quentin Griffin 8.00
WM-PJ Carson Palmer, Rudi Johnson 10.00
WM-PL Chad Pennington, Byron Leftwich 15.00
WM-PS Peyton Manning, Steve McNair 15.00
WM-RG Jerry Rice, Rich Gannon 15.00
WM-SK Michael Strahan, Jevon Kearse 8.00
WM-SU Junior Seau, Brian Urlacher 10.00
WM-SW Jeremy Shockey, Kurt Warner 10.00
WM-TH LaDainian Tomlinson, Priest Holmes 12.00
WM-VB Michael Vick, Tom Brady 25.00

2004 SPx Winning Materials Autos

NM/M
Production 25 Sets
WMA-BF Tom Brady, Brett Favre 500.00
WMA-BH Larry Fitzgerald, Reggie Williams 200.00
WMA-SA Roger Staubach, Troy Aikman 250.00
WMA-JJ Kevin Jones, Steven Jackson 300.00
WMA-MG Deuce McAllister, Ahman Green 100.00
WMA-MM Peyton Manning, Steve McNair 150.00
WMA-PE Peyton Manning, Eli Manning 500.00
WMA-PL Chad Pennington, Byron Leftwich 125.00
WMA-RR Philip Rivers, Ben Roethlisberger 750.00
WMA-TB Joe Theismann, Mark Brunell 80.00
WMA-TC Fran Tarkenton, Daunte Culpepper 125.00
WMA-TM LaDainian Tomlinson, Deuce McAllister 100.00

WMA-VM Michael Vick, Donovan McNabb 300.00
WMA-WJ Roy Williams, Kevin Jones 250.00
WMA-WW Kellen Winslow Jr., Kellen Winslow Sr. 125.00

1993 Spectrum QB Club Tribute Sheet Promos

The two-sheet, 8-1/2" x 11" set, featuring Aikman and Marino, was issued as a preview for the 1993 Spectrum Quarterback Club Tribute Sheets. Production was limited to 5,000 sheets each.

NM/M
Complete Set (2): 10.00
Common Player: 4.00
1 Troy Aikman 4.00
2 Dan Marino 6.00

1993 Spectrum QB Club Tribute Sheets

The 12-sheet, 8-1/2" x 11" set featured 12 top quarterbacks with color photos over a black marble background with the player's signature in 24 kt. gold foil. As with the promos, the backs are blank and are limited to a production of 5,000.

NM/M
Complete Set (12): 30.00
Common Player: 1.50
1 Troy Aikman 4.00
2 Randall Cunningham 1.50
3 John Elway 3.00
4 Boomer Esiason 1.50
5 Brett Favre 8.00
6 Jim Kelly 2.00
7 Dan Marino 8.00
8 Warren Moon 2.00
9 Phil Simms 1.50
10 Steve Young 3.00
11 Jeff Hostetler, Bernie Kosar, Neil O'Donnell AFC Stars 1.50
12 Jim Everett, Chris Miller, Mark Rypien NFC Stars 1.50

1993 Spectrum/Front Row Promos

The five-card, standard-size set was issued as a preview of Spectrum Holdings Group and its purchase of the Front Row trademark. The fronts feature action color shots with the backs containing bio and stat information inset over another player shot. An oval with "For Promotional Use Only" printed inside was featured on the card backs.

NM/M
Complete Set (5): 8.00
Common Player: 1.50
1 Eric Curry 1.50
2 Andre Hastings 1.50
3 Qadry Ismail 2.00
4 Lincoln Kennedy 1.50
5 O.J. McDuffie 2.50

1993 Spectrum/Front Row Tribute Sheet

The 8-1/2" x 11" sheet was issued to promote Spectrum Holdings Group and its purchase of the Front Row trademark. A gold-foil bar edged in purple contains "Outstanding Players of the 1993 Draft" over a black granite-like background. Production run was 5,000 and the backs were blank.

NM/M
Complete Set (1): 2.00
1 Qadry Ismail, Lincoln Kennedy, O.J. McDuffie, Andre Hastings, Eric Curry 2.00

1992 Sport Decks Promo Aces

These four playing card Aces were produced by Junior Card and Toy Inc. to promote the premier edition of Sport Decks NFL playing cards. One standard-size card was given away during each of the four days of the National Sports Collectors Convention in Atlanta. The front has a color action photo on it against a full-bleed metallic-sheen background. The card number and suit are in the upper left corner; a Team NFL logo is in the upper right corner. These are situated on a metallic bar running across the top. A similar bar runs along the bottom. It contains a team helmet, the player's name and position, and a Sport Decks logo. There were reportedly 6,000 silver-barred cards and 1,000 gold-barred cards made (three times more valuable than the values listed below for silver ones). The card backs are white, with pink and black lettering which provides advertisements, logos and the players who will be featured in the suit corresponding to the pictured player.

NM/M
Complete Set (4): 12.00
Common Player: 1.00
AC Emmitt Smith 6.00
AD Thurman Thomas 2.00
AH Dan Marino 5.00
AS Mark Rypien 1.00

1992 Sport Decks

This 55-card deck of playing cards was produced after Sport Decks debuted the set at the 1992 National Sports Collectors Convention in Atlanta. Each card front has rounded corners and features a full-bleed color action shot. A stripe at the top contains a card number and suit in the upper left corner, with a Team NFL logo in the upper right corner. The bottom stripe contains a team helmet, player's name and position and card number and suit. The back has a white-bordered blue-green football field which has an "Official 1992 Season Football Star Cards" logo in the middle of a goal post.

NM/M
Complete Set (55): 5.00
Common Player: .05
AC Troy Aikman .75
2C Rodney Peete .07
3C Cris Carter .10
4C Randal Hill .07
5C Jeff Hostetler .07
6C Flipper Anderson .05
7C Chris Miller .10
8C Anthony Carter .07
9C Timm Rosenbach .05
10C Sterling Sharpe .25
JC Ricky Ervins .05
QC Jerry Rice .50
KC Emmitt Smith 1.00
AD Jim Kelly .25
2D John Friesz .10
3D Gaston Green .05
4D Hugh Millen .05
5D Dan McGwire .05
6D Eric Green .05
7D Christian Okoye .07
8D Ronnie Lott .10
9D Rob Moore .07
10D Mark Clayton .05
JD Thurman Thomas .25
QD John Elway .45
KD Warren Moon .30
AH Dan Marino .75
2H Anthony Munoz .10
3H Nick Bell .05
4H Michael Dean Perry .05
5H Haywood Jeffires .05
6H Bubby Brister .05
7H Andre Reed .10
8H Anthony Miller .07
9H Ken O'Brien .07
10H Bernie Kosar .10
JH Derrick Thomas .15
QH Jeff George .10
KH Boomer Esiason .15
AS Mark Rypien .10
2S Phil Simms .15
3S Pat Swilling .07
4S Jim Harbaugh .15
5S Mike Singletary .10
6S Lawrence Taylor .15
7S John Taylor .10
8S Keith Jackson .10
9S Vinny Testaverde .10
10S Andre Rison .10
JS Michael Irvin .25
QS Earnest Byner .05
KS Randall Cunningham .10
JK Eric Dickerson .10
JK Jim Everett .10
xx Title Card .05

1994 Sportflics Samples

The seven-card, regular-sized set was issued as a preview for the 1994 Sportflics base set. The upper right corners of the cards are cut off indicating it as a sample. The set is virtually identical in design to the regular-issue set.

NM/M
Complete Set (7): 8.00
Common Player: .50
3 Flipper Anderson (yellow "Anderson" name on back missing shadow) .50
50 Reggie Brooks (yellow "Brooks" name on back missing shadow) .50
70 Herman Moore (name on front 1/4" away from year logo) 1.50
145 Chuck Levy (back photo black and white) .50
180 Jerome Bettis ("TM" by Starflics logo on front) 2.00
HH1 Barry Jones (Head-to-Head production number box on back missing) 2.50
NNO Sportflics Ad Card (corners intact) .50

1994 Sportflics

Pinnacle revealed its premier edition of Sportflics 2000 Football in a 184-card set. Each card contains two different shots of the player on the same card. One shot is visible instantly, the second is apparent with a slight turn. Sportflics contained five insert sets. Random cards from Sack Attack, Head to Head, Artist's Proof, Find the Football and Rookie Rivalry were inserted in the five-card packs. Within the primary set itself, there were two subsets, entitled Starflics and The Rookies.

NM/M
Complete Set (184): 30.00
Common Player: .15
Minor Stars: .30
Comp. Artist Proof (184): 850.00
Artist Proof Cards: 4X-10X
Pack (5): 2.00
Wax Box (36): 50.00
1 Deion Sanders 1.25
2 Leslie O'Neal .15
3 Willie Anderson .15
4 Anthony Carter .15
5 Thurman Thomas, Vincent Brisby .15
6 Johnny Mitchell .15
7 Jeff Hostetler .15
8 Renaldo Turnbull .15
9 Chris Warren .40
10 Darrell Green .15
11 Randall Cunningham .15
12 Barry Sanders 2.00
13 Jeff Cross .15
14 Glyn Milburn .15
15 Willie Davis .15
16 Tony McGee .15
17 Gary Clark .15
18 Michael Jackson .15
19 Alvin Harper .15
20 Tim Worley .15
21 Quentin Coryatt .15
22 Michael Brooks .15
23 Boomer Esiason .15
24 Ricky Watters .30
25 Craig Erickson .15
26 Willie Green .15
27 Brett Favre 3.00
28 John Elway 1.00
29 Steve Beuerlein .15
30 Emmitt Smith 4.00
31 Troy Aikman 2.00
32 Cody Carlson .15
33 Brian Mitchell .15
34 Herschel Walker .15
35 Bruce Smith .15
36 Harold Green .15
37 Erric Pegram .15
38 Ronnie Harmon .15
39 Brian Blades .15
40 Sterling Sharpe .30
41 Leonard Russell .15
42 Cleveland Gary .15
43 Tom Waddle, Lamar Smith .15
44 Lawrence Dawsey .15
45 Jerry Rice 2.00
46 Terry Allen .15
47 Reggie Langhorne .15
48 Derek Brown .15
49 Terry Kirby, Lake Dawson .15
50 Reggie Brooks .15
51 Calvin Williams .15
52 Cornelius Bennett .15
53 Russell Maryland .15
54 Rob Moore .15
55 Dana Stubblefield .15
56 Rod Woodson .15
57 Rodney Hampton .30
58 Neil Smith .15
59 Anthony Smith .15
60 Neal Anderson .15
61 Drew Bledsoe 2.00
62 John Copeland .15
63 David Klingler .15
64 Phil Simms .15
65 Vincent Brisby .15
66 Richard Dent .15
67 Eric Metcalf .15
68 Eric Curry .15
69 Victor Bailey .15
70 Herman Moore 1.00
71 Steve Jordan .15
72 Jerome Bettis .50
73 Natrone Means .75
74 Webster Slaughter .15
75 Jackie Harris .15
76 Michael Irvin .30
77 Steve Emtman .15
78 Eugene Robinson .15
79 Tim Brown .30
80 Derrick Thomas .15
81 Vinny Testaverde .15
82 Mark Jackson .15
83 Ricky Proehl .15
84 Stan Humphries .15
85 Garrison Hearst 1.00
86 Jim Kelly .30
87 Brent Jones .15
88 Eric Martin .15
89 Wilber Marshall .15
90 Chris Spielman .15
91 Eric Green .15
92 Andre Rison .15
93 Andre Reed .15
94 Carl Pickens .75
95 Junior Seau .30
96 Dwight Stone .15
97 Mike Sherrard .15
98 Vincent Brown .15
99 Cris Carter .15
100 Mark Higgs .15
101 Steve Young 2.00
102 Mark Carrier .15
103 Barry Foster .15
104 Tommy Vardell .15
105 Shannon Sharpe .15
106 Reggie White .30
107 Ernest Givins .15
108 Marcus Allen .30
109 James Jett .15
110 Keith Jackson .15
111 Irving Fryar .15
112 Ronnie Lott .15
113 Cortez Kennedy .15
114 Ron Moore .15
115 Rick Mirer .75
116 Neil O'Donnell .30
117 Courtney Hawkins .15
118 Johnny Johnson .15
119 Ben Coates .30
120 Dan Marino 4.00
121 Sean Gilbert .15
122 Rocket Ismail .15
123 Joe Montana 2.00
124 Roosevelt Potts .15
125 Gary Brown .15
126 Reggie Cobb .15
127 Marion Butts .15
128 Scott Mitchell .15
129 John L. Williams .15
130 Jeff George .30
131 Bobby Hebert .15
132 John Friesz .15
133 Anthony Miller .15
134 Jim Harbaugh .15
135 Erik Kramer .15
136 Jim Everett .15
137 Michael Haynes .15
138 Rod Bernstine .15
139 Chris Miller .15
140 Henry Ellard .15
141 William Fuller .15
142 Warren Moon .30
143 *Lamar Smith* .15
144 *Charlie Garner* 1.50
145 *Chuck Levy* .15
146 *Dan Wilkinson* .30
147 *Perry Klein* .15
148 *William Floyd* 1.00
149 *Lake Dawson* 1.00
150 *David Palmer* .50
151 *James Bostic* .15
152 *Marshall Faulk* 6.00
153 *Greg Hill* 1.00
154 *Heath Shuler* 1.00
155 *Erric Rhett* 2.00
156 *Sam Adams* .15
157 *Charles Johnson* .75
158 *Ryan Yarborough* .15
159 *Thomas Lewis* .15
160 *Willie McGinest* .50
161 *Jamir Miller* .15
162 *Calvin Jones* .15
163 *Donnell Bennett* .15
164 *Trev Alberts* .15
165 *LeShon Johnson* .15
166 *Johnnie Morton* 1.00
167 *Derrick Alexander* .50
168 *Jeff Cothran* .15
169 *Bucky Brooks* .30
170 *Bert Emanuel* .75
171 *Darnay Scott* .75
172 *Kevin Lee* .15
173 *Mario Bates* 1.00
174 *Bryant Young* .75
175 *Trent Dilfer* 2.00
176 Joe Montana 1.00
177 Emmitt Smith 2.00
178 Troy Aikman 1.00
179 Steve Young 1.00
180 Jerome Bettis .40
181 John Elway .50
182 Dan Marino 2.00
183 Brett Favre 1.00
184 Barry Sanders 1.00

1994 Sportflics Artist's Proofs

The 184-card, standard-size set was issued as a parallel version to the base set. "Artist's Proof" is printed on the card fronts.

NM/M
Common Player: 2.00
Artist's Proof Cards: 4X-10X

1994 Sportflics Head-To-Head

Head-to-Head captured some of the game's fiercest rivalries. Cards show a close-up shot of both players with their helmets on, on opposing sides of the card. The second picture captures the player in action, with three photos to give the illusion of movement. The Sportflics logo is between the helmets on the one shot and, on the second shot it turns into a large Head to Head logo with both players' names. The back shows a close shot of the two, with their name and team name next to them.

NM/M
Complete Set (10): 30.00
Common Player: 1.00
1 Barry Sanders, Dante Jones 4.00
2 Emmitt Smith, Carlton Bailey 4.00
3 Rod Woodson, Dan Marino 5.00
4 Jerry Rice, Deion Sanders 4.00
5 Vaughan Johnson, Jerome Bettis 1.00
6 Reggie White, Troy Aikman 3.00
7 Steve Young, Renaldo Turnbull 3.00
8 Sterling Sharpe, Eric Allen 1.00
9 Joe Montana, Anthony Smith 5.00
10 John Elway, Neil Smith 4.00

1994 Sportflics Pride of Texas

The four-card, standard-size set was given away at the National Convention in Houston by Pinnacle. One Dallas Cowboys (Harper), one Houston Oilers (Brown) and two Dallas Stars (Modano, Hatcher). Production was limited to 2,500 of each card. Each card has an "N" prefix.

NM/M
Complete Set (4): 3.00
Common Player: .50
1 Alvin Harper 1.00
2 Gary Brown .50
3 Mike Modano 3.00
4 Derian Hatcher .50

1994 Sportflics Rookie Rivalry

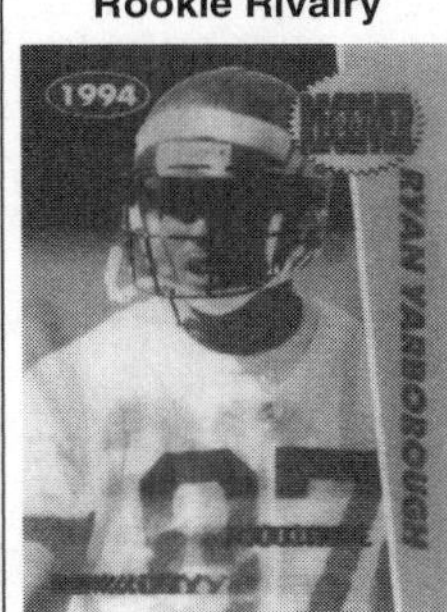

Rookie Rivalry pits two of the league's top prospects against each other. This 12-card insert had an insertion ratio of one per 24 packs and was in hobby packs only.

NM/M
Complete Set (10): 10.00
Common Player: .50
Minor Stars: 1.00
1 William Floyd, Marshall Faulk 4.00
2 Dan Wilkinson, Sam Adams .50
3 Trent Dilfer, Heath Shuler 1.00
4 Jamir Miller, Trev Alberts .50
5 Johnnie Morton, Charles Johnson 1.00
6 Chuck Levy, Charles Garner .50
7 Thomas Lewis, Derrick Alexander .50
8 Darnay Scott, Isaac Bruce 4.00
9 David Palmer, Ryan Yarborough .50
10 LeShon Johnson, Donnell Bennett .50

1995 Sportflix

This set marked Pinnacle's debut for Sportflix Football cards. The 175-card set includes more than 30 top rookies, plus a 20-card Game Winners subset. Cards were issued in packs of five, which could also contain one of five different insert cards - Artist's Proof (175-card parallel set, one per every 36 packs), Rolling Thunder, Rookie Lightning, ProMotion and Man 2 Man, which could be found in jumbo packs only. The regular cards feature two different pictures on the front, each visible through the concept of "magic motion" when the card is tilted. The player's name appears along the right side, with the letters increasing in size as the card is tilted. His position and the Sportflix logo are also along the side. The horizontal card back has a photo of the player on one side, flanked by key career statistical totals in the middle and a brief career summary on the opposite side. The player's name is in the upper left corner; the Sportflix logo is in the lower right corner.

NM/M
Complete Set (175): 30.00
Common Player: .10
Minor Stars: .20
Artist Proof Cards: 4X-10X
Artist Proof Rookies: 3X-5X
Inserted 1:36 Hobby
Pack (5): 1.50
Wax Box (36): 40.00
1 Troy Aikman 1.00
2 Rodney Hampton .10
3 Jerry Rice 1.00
4 Reggie White .30
5 Mark Ingram .10
6 Chris Spielman .10
7 Curtis Conway .20
8 Erik Kramer .20
9 Emmitt Smith 1.50
10 Alvin Harper .10
11 Junior Seau .20
12 Mike Pritchard .10
13 Ricky Ervins .10
14 Jim Harbaugh .20
15 Dan Marino 1.50
16 Marshall Faulk .50
17 Lorenzo White .10
18 Cortez Kennedy .10
19 Rocket Ismail .10
20 Eric Metcalf .10
21 Chris Chandler .20
22 John Elway 1.00
23 Boomer Esiason .20
24 Herman Moore .20
25 Deion Sanders .50
26 Charles Johnson .20
27 Daryl Johnston .10
28 Dave Krieg .10
29 Jim Kelly .20
30 Warren Moon .20
31 Lewis Tillman .10
32 Bruce Smith .10
33 Jake Reed .20
34 Craig Heyward .10
35 Frank Reich .10
36 Stan Humphries .10
37 Charles Haley .10
38 Andre Rison .20
39 James Jett .10
40 Jay Novacek .10
41 Gary Brown .10

42 Steve Bono .20
43 Cris Carter .30
44 Steve Atwater .10
45 Andre Reed .20
46 Greg Lloyd .10
47 Mark Seay .10
48 Dave Meggett .10
49 Steve Beuerlein .10
50 Jeff Graham .10
51 Barry Sanders 2.00
52 Willie Davis .10
53 Robert Smith .30
54 Steve Walsh .10
55 Michael Irvin .20
56 Natrone Means .30
57 Chris Warren .10
58 Tim Brown .20
59 Steve Young .75
60 Jerome Bettis .30
61 Shannon Sharpe .20
62 Errict Rhett .20
63 Scott Mitchell .20
64 Leroy Hoard .20
65 Garrison Hearst .30
66 Terance Mathis .20
67 Sean Gilbert .10
68 Fred Barnett .10
69 Hardy Nickerson .10
70 Jim Everett .10
71 Randall Cunningham .30
72 Carl Pickens .20
73 Jeff Hostetler .10
74 Marcus Allen .30
75 Jeff George .20
76 Brett Favre 2.00
77 Chris Miller .10
78 Craig Erickson .10
79 Herschel Walker .20
80 Bert Emanuel .20
81 Leonard Russell .10
82 Ricky Watters .20
83 Robert Brooks .20
84 Dave Brown .10
85 Henry Ellard .10
86 Barry Foster .10
87 Johnny Mitchell .10
88 Eric Allen .10
89 Darnay Scott .20
90 Harvey Williams .10
91 Neil O'Donnell .20
92 Drew Bledsoe 1.00
93 Ken Harvey .10
94 Irving Fryar .20
95 Rod Woodson .10
96 Anthony Miller .10
97 Mario Bates .20
98 *Jeff Blake* .50
99 Rick Mirer .20
100 William Floyd .20
101 Michael Haynes .10
102 Flipper Anderson .10
103 Greg Hill .20
104 Mark Brunell 1.00
105 Vinny Testaverde .30
106 Heath Shuler .20
107 Ron Moore .10
108 Ernest Givins .10
109 Mike Sherrard .10
110 Charlie Garner .20
111 Trent Dilfer .30
112 Bam Morris .20
113 Lake Dawson .10
114 Brian Blades .10
115 Brent Jones .10
116 Ronnie Harmon .10
117 Eric Green .10
118 Ben Coates .20
119 *Ki-Jana Carter* .30
120 *Steve McNair* 3.00
121 *Michael Westbrook* 1.25
122 *Kerry Collins* 2.00
123 *Joey Galloway* 2.50
124 *Kyle Brady* .30
125 *J.J. Stokes* 1.50
126 *Tyrone Wheatley* .30
127 *Rashaan Salaam* .30
128 *Napoleon Kaufman* 1.00
129 *Frank Sanders* .50
130 *Stoney Case* .20
131 *Todd Collins* .20
132 *Lovell Pinkney* .10
133 *Sherman Williams* .20
134 *Rob Johnson* 1.00
135 *Mark Bruener* .30
136 *Lee DeRamus* .10
137 *Chad May* .20
138 *James Stewart* .30
139 *Ray Zellars* .20
140 *Dave Barr* .20
141 *Kordell Stewart* 2.00
142 *Jimmy Oliver* .10
143 *Terrell Fletcher* .30
144 *James Stewart* 2.50
145 *Terrell Davis* 8.00
146 *Joe Aska* .10
147 *John Walsh* .20
148 *Tyrone Davis* .10
149 Emmitt Smith .75
150 Barry Sanders 1.00
151 Jerry Rice .50
152 Steve Young .40
153 Dan Marino .75
154 Troy Aikman .50
155 Drew Bledsoe .50
156 John Elway .50
157 Brett Favre 1.00
158 Michael Irvin .10
159 Heath Shuler .10
160 Warren Moon .10
161 Jim Kelly .10
162 Randall Cunningham .15
163 Jeff Hostetler .10
164 Dave Brown .10
165 Neil O'Donnell .10
166 Rick Mirer .10
167 Jim Everett .10
168 Boomer Esiason .10
169 Dan Marino .75
170 Drew Bledsoe .50
171 John Elway .50
172 Emmitt Smith .75
173 Steve Young .40
174 Barry Sanders 1.00
175 Jerry Rice .50

1995 Sportflix Artist's Proofs

The 175-card, standard-size set was a parallel version of the base set and was inserted every 36 packs. The Artist's Proof logo in gold and black appears on the card front.

NM/M
Complete Set (175): 1,400
Common Player: 2.50
Artist's Proof Cards: 4X-10X
Artist's Proof Rookies: 3X-5X

1995 Sportflix Man 2 Man

These 1995 Pinnacle Sportflix cards were randomly included one per every eight jumbo packs of the base product. Each card front features two players, so 24 are represented in the 12-card set. The cards do not use the "magic motion" concept, but do feature the players superimposed against a football game scene. The player's names are on the front, along with the Sportflix and insert set logos. The card back is numbered 1 of 12, etc., and includes a color photo of each player superimposed against a black-and-white photo of the same shot. Two small paragraphs between the photos offer brief descriptions of the players' skills.

NM/M
Complete Set (12): 20.00
Common Player: 1.00
1 Troy Aikman, Dan Marino 5.00
2 Emmitt Smith, Marshall Faulk 4.00
3 Kerry Collins, Drew Bledsoe 2.00
4 Steve Young, Steve McNair 3.00
5 Barry Sanders, Ki-Jana Carter 3.00
6 Heath Shuler, John Elway 3.00
7 Rashaan Salaam, Bam Morris 1.00
8 Ricky Watters, Natrone Means 1.00
9 Jerry Rice, J.J. Stokes 3.00
10 Kordell Stewart, Warren Moon 2.00
11 Brett Favre, Jeff Blake 4.00
12 Michael Westbrook, Joey Galloway 1.00

1995 Sportflix ProMotion

These 1995 Pinnacle Sportflix insert cards showcase the company's unique morphing technology, in which a player turns into, or morphs into, his team logo through 36 frames of action. The Sportflix logo is in the upper right corner; the player's last name appears above a football, which says "Pro" inside and is located alongside the word "Motion." The horizontal card back uses this same design at the bottom; a player photo and brief player profile are also included on the back. Cards are numbered using a "PM" prefix. Cards were randomly included one per every 48 packs.

NM/M
Complete Set (12): 40.00
Common Player: 1.00
1 Steve Young 4.00
2 Troy Aikman 4.00
3 Dan Marino 6.00
4 Drew Bledsoe 4.00
5 John Elway 4.00
6 Jim Kelly 3.00
7 Jerry Rice 4.00
8 Michael Irvin 2.00
9 Emmitt Smith 5.00
10 Marshall Faulk 3.00
11 Natrone Means 1.00
12 Ki-Jana Carter 1.00

1995 Sportflix Rolling Thunder

These Rolling Thunder insert cards feature 12 running backs each against a spinning pinwheel background on the front. "Rolling Thunder" is written along the left side of the card; the player's name, which increases in size as the card is tilted, is in the lower left corner. A Sportflix logo is in the upper right corner. The card back, numbered 1 of 12, etc., has a full color photo of the player in the upper portion of the card; the bottom portion contains the bottom half of the photo in a ghosted format, with the insert set name and a brief player profile superimposed over it. A team helmet is also in the upper right corner. Cards were random inserts, one every 12 packs of 1995 Pinnacle Sportflix.

NM/M
Complete Set (12): 15.00
Common Player: .50
1 Emmitt Smith 4.00
2 Barry Sanders 4.00
3 Marshall Faulk 2.00
4 Ki-Jana Carter 1.00
5 Rashaan Salaam .50
6 Tyrone Wheatley .50
7 Natrone Means .50
8 Jerome Bettis 2.00
9 Errict Rhett 1.00
10 Bam Morris .50
11 William Floyd .50
12 Mario Bates .50

1995 Sportflix Rookie Lightning

These insert cards feature 12 of the top rookies entering the NFL in 1995. Cards were random inserts, one per every 36 packs of 1995 Pinnacle Sportflix. The card front uses the "magic motion" concept to create two different photos when the card is tilted. "Rookie" and "Lightning" alternate along the right side when the card is tilted, while the player's name at the bottom increases in size. The Sportflix logo and the player's position are in the upper left corner. The card back has the set logo and number (1 of 12, etc.) in the upper right corner. The outline of one of the photos from the front is also on the back.

NM/M
Complete Set (11): 20.00
Common Player: 1.00
1 Ki-Jana Carter 1.00
2 Steve McNair 4.00
3 Michael Westbrook 2.00
4 Kerry Collins 3.00
5 Joey Galloway 2.00
6 J.J. Stokes 2.00
7 Tyrone Wheatley 1.00
8 Rashaan Salaam 1.00
9 Napoleon Kaufman 1.00
10 Kordell Stewart 3.00
11 James Stewart 2.00

1999 Sports Illustrated

This was a 150-card release that included 90 stars of yesterday and today, 30 Fresh Faces (impact rookies of 1998) and 30 Super Bowl MVP's. Top inserts include: Autographs, Canton Calling and SI Covers.

NM/M
Complete Set (150): 40.00
Common Player: .10
Minor Stars: .30
Common Rookie: 1.00
Pack (7): 10.00
Wax Box (12): 100.00
1 Bart Starr .50
2 Bart Starr .50
3 Joe Namath .50
4 Len Dawson .30
5 Chuck Howley .10
6 Roger Staubach .50
7 Jake Scott .10
8 Larry Csonka .30
9 Franco Harris .30
10 Fred Biletnikoff .10
11 Harvey Martin, Randy White .10
12 Terry Bradshaw .50
13 Terry Bradshaw .50
14 Jim Plunkett .30
15 Joe Montana 1.00
16 Marcus Allen .50
17 Joe Montana 1.00
18 Richard Dent .10
19 Phil Simms .30
20 Doug Williams .10
21 Jerry Rice 1.00
22 Joe Montana 1.00
23 Ottis Anderson .30
24 Mark Rypien .10
25 Troy Aikman 1.00
26 Emmitt Smith 1.50
27 Steve Young .50
28 Larry Brown .10
29 Desmond Howard .10
30 Terrell Davis 1.00
31 Y.A. Tittle .30
32 Paul Hornung .50
33 Gale Sayers .50
34 Garo Yepremian .10
35 Bert Jones .30
36 Joe Washington .10
37 Joe Theismann .30
38 Roger Craig .30
39 Mike Singletary .30
40 Bobby Bell .10
41 Ken Houston .10
42 Lenny Moore .10
43 Mark Moseley .10
44 Chuck Bednarik .10
45 Ted Hendricks .10
46 Steve Largent .50
47 Bob Lilly .10
48 Don Maynard .50
49 John Mackey .10
50 Anthony Munoz .10
51 Bobby Mitchell .10
52 Jim Brown .50
53 Otto Graham .50
54 Earl Morrall .10
55 Danny White .30
56 Karim Abdul-Jabbar .50
57 Charlie Garner .10
58 Jeff Blake .30
59 Reggie White .50
60 Derrick Thomas .10
61 Duce Staley .10
62 Tim Brown .30
63 Elvis Grbac .30
64 Tony Banks .30
65 Rob Johnson .30
66 Danny Kanell .10
67 Marshall Faulk .50
68 Warrick Dunn 1.25
69 Dan Marino 3.00
70 Jimmy Smith .50
71 John Elway 2.50
72 Charles Way .10
73 Ricky Watters .30
74 Terry Glenn .30
75 Bobby Hoying .30
76 Curtis Martin .50
77 Trent Dilfer .30
78 Emmitt Smith 3.00
79 Irving Fryar .10
80 Troy Aikman 2.00
81 Barry Sanders 3.00
82 Brett Favre 4.00
83 Robert Smith .50
84 Dorsey Levens .50
85 Cris Carter .50
86 Jeff George .30
87 Jerome Bettis .30
88 Warren Moon .30
89 Steve Young .75
90 Fred Lane .30
91 Jerry Rice 2.00
92 Natrone Means .50
93 Mike Alstott .50
94 Kordell Stewart 1.50
95 Jake Plummer 1.75
96 Jamal Anderson .75
97 Corey Dillon 1.00
98 Deion Sanders .50
99 Mark Brunell 1.50
100 Garrison Hearst .50
101 Andre Rison .10
102 Antowain Smith .75
103 Drew Bledsoe 1.50
104 Eddie George 1.50
105 Keyshawn Johnson .50
106 Isaac Bruce .30
107 Rob Moore .30
108 Steve McNair .75
109 Terrell Davis 2.00
110 Carl Pickens .30
111 Wayne Chrebet .50
112 Kerry Collins .30
113 Eric Metcalf .10
114 Joey Galloway .50
115 Shannon Sharpe .30
116 Robert Brooks .10
117 Glenn Foley .30
118 Yancey Thigpen .30
119 Frank Sanders .30
120 Herman Moore .50
121 Antonio Freeman .75
122 Michael Irvin .30
123 Brad Johnson .50
124 James Stewart .10
125 Jim Harbaugh .30
126 Peyton Manning 8.00
127 Ryan Leaf 6.00
128 Curtis Enis 4.00
129 Fred Taylor 4.00
130 Randy Moss 8.00
131 John Avery 3.00
132 Charles Woodson 5.00
133 Robert Edwards 3.50
134 Charlie Batch 8.00
135 Brian Griese 5.00
136 Skip Hicks 3.00
137 Jacquez Green 3.00
138 Robert Holcombe 2.00
139 Kevin Dyson 3.00
140 Rodney Williams 1.00
141 Ahman Green 2.00
142 Tavian Banks 2.00
143 Donald Hayes 1.00
144 Tony Simmons 3.00
145 Patrick Johnson 2.00
146 Marcus Nash 3.00
147 Germane Crowell 3.00
148 R.W. McQuarters 2.00
149 Jonathan Quinn 2.00
150 Andre Wadsworth 2.00

1999 Sports Illustrated Autographs

A total of 35 players from the past signed cards in this insert with numbers unknown. Singles were found one-per-pack.

NM/M
Complete Set (35): 3,000
Common Player: 10.00
Minor Stars: 20.00
Inserted 1:1
Ottis Anderson 20.00
Chuck Bednarik 10.00
Bobby Bell 10.00
Terry Bradshaw 400.00
Jim Brown 250.00
Roger Craig 25.00
Len Dawson 175.00
Otto Graham 30.00
Franco Harris 175.00
Ted Hendricks 10.00
Paul Hornung 185.00
Ken Houston 10.00
Bert Jones 10.00
Steve Largent 35.00
Bob Lilly 10.00
John Mackey 10.00
Don Maynard 20.00
Bobby Mitchell 10.00
Joe Montana 425.00
Lenny Moore 10.00
Earl Morrall 10.00
Mark Moseley 10.00
Anthony Munoz 20.00
Joe Namath 450.00
Jim Plunkett 20.00
Gale Sayers 35.00
Mike Singletary 100.00
Bart Starr 400.00
Roger Staubach 200.00
Joe Theismann 85.00
Y.A. Tittle 100.00
Joe Washington 10.00
Danny White 10.00
Doug Williams 100.00
Garo Yepremian 10.00

1999 Sports Illustrated Canton Calling

This was an 8-card set that included players who are on their way to the Hall of Fame. Singles were inserted 1:12 packs and a parallel Gold insert was also produced and found 1:120 packs.

NM/M
Complete Set (8): 25.00
Common Player: 1.00
Inserted 1:12
Gold Cards: 2X-4X
Inserted 1:120
1 Warren Moon 1.00
2 Emmitt Smith 4.00
3 Jerry Rice 3.00
4 Brett Favre 5.00
5 Barry Sanders 4.00
6 Dan Marino 5.00
7 John Elway 4.00
8 Troy Aikman 4.00

1999 Sports Illustrated Covers

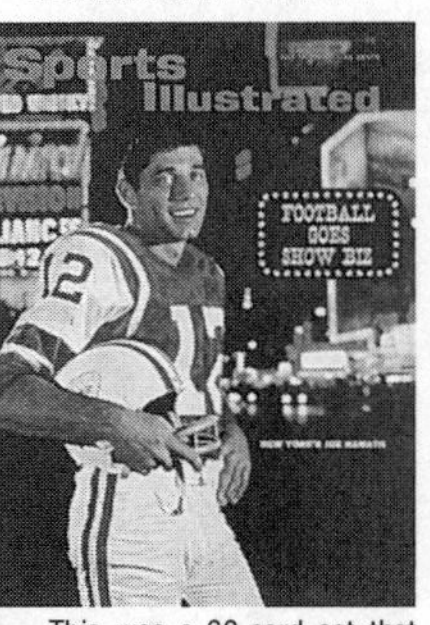

This was a 60-card set that took the best covers from the past and reproduced them on a card. Singles were found one-per-pack.

NM/M
Complete Set (60): 30.00
Common Player: .25
Minor Stars: .50
Inserted 1:1
1 Jim Brown .50
2 Y.A. Tittle .25
3 Dallas Cowboys .25
4 Joe Namath .75
5 Bart Starr .50
6 Earl Morrall .25
7 Minnesota Vikings .25
8 Kansas City Chiefs .25
9 Len Dawson .25
10 Monday Night Football .25
11 Jim Plunkett .25
12 Garo Yepremian .25
13 Larry Csonka .25
14 Terry Bradshaw .50
15 Franco Harris .25
16 Bert Jones .25
17 Harvey Martin, Randy White .25
18 Roger Staubach .50
19 Marcus Allen .50
20 Joe Washington .25
21 Dan Marino 2.50
22 Joe Theismann .25
23 Roger Craig .25
24 Mike Singletary .25
25 Chicago Bears .25
26 Phil Simms .25
27 Vinny Testaverde .25
28 Doug Williams .25
29 Jerry Rice 1.50
30 Herschel Walker .25
31 Joe Montana 1.75
32 Ottis Anderson .25
33 Rocket Ismail .25
34 Bruce Smith .25
35 Thurman Thomas .25
36 Mark Rypien .25
37 Jim Harbaugh .25
38 Randall Cunningham .50
39 Troy Aikman 1.50
40 Reggie White .50
41 Junior Seau .25
42 Emmitt Smith 2.50
43 Natrone Means .25
44 Ricky Watters .25
45 Pittsburgh Steelers .25
46 Steve Young, Troy Aikman 1.00
47 Steve Young 1.00
48 Deion Sanders .50
49 Elvis Grbac .25
50 Green Bay Packers .25
51 Brett Favre 3.00
52 Mark Brunell, Kerry Collins 1.00
53 Antonio Freeman .75
54 Desmond Howard .25
55 AFC Central Quarterbacks .25
56 Warrick Dunn .50
57 Jerome Bettis .25
58 John Elway 2.00
59 Brent Jones .25
60 Terrell Davis 3.00

1976 Sportstix

The 10-sticker, 3-1/2" in diameter set was numbered as a continuation of non-sport issues. The helmet logos on the stickers have been erased and two major errors exist: Drew Pearson's card actually has Gloster Richardson on the card while Fred Biletnikoff's last name is spelled wrong on card No. 32.

NM/M
Complete Set (11): 200.00
Common Player: 10.00
31 Carl Eller 20.00

32 Fred Biletnikoff (UER) (Misspelled Belitnikoff) 30.00
33 Terry Metcalf 15.00
34 Gary Huff 10.00
35 Steve Bartkowski 20.00
36 Dan Pastorini 15.00
37 Drew Pearson (UER) (photo is of Gloster Richardson) 20.00
38 Bert Jones 15.00
39 Otis Armstrong 15.00
40 Don Woods 10.00
C Dick Butkus 60.00

1991 Stadium Club

Topps made its premiere edition debut with its 1991 Stadium Club set of 500 cards. The glossy cards feature full-bleed action photos on the front. The player's name is at the bottom in an aqua stripe that is bordered in gold. The back uses a horizontal format with a football field and stadium for a background. A biography, Sporting News Football Analysis Report and miniature replica of the player's Topps rookie card are also included on the back.

NM/M

Complete Set (500): 100.00
Common Player: .20
Minor Stars: .40
Pack (12): 3.00
Wax Box (36): 70.00
1 Pepper Johnson .20
2 Emmitt Smith 10.00
3 Deion Sanders 3.00
4 Andre Collins .20
5 Eric Metcalf .30
6 Richard Dent .30
7 Eric Martin .20
8 Marcus Allen .50
9 Gary Anderson .20
10 Joey Browner .20
11 Lorenzo White .20
12 Bruce Smith .20
13 Mark Boyer .20
14 Mike Piel .20
15 Albert Bentley .20
16 Bennie Blades .20
17 Jason Staurovsky .20
18 Anthony Toney .20
19 Dave Krieg .20
20 *Harvey Williams* 2.00
21 Bubba Paris .20
22 Tim McGee .20
23 Brian Noble .20
24 Vinny Testaverde .30
25 Doug Widell .20
26 John Jackson .20
27 Marion Butts .20
28 Deron Cherry .20
29 Don Warren .20
30 Rod Woodson .75
31 Mike Baab .20
32 Greg Jackson .20
33 Jerry Robinson .20
34 Dalton Hilliard .20
35 Brian Jordan .20
36 James Thornton (Misspelled Thorton on cards back) .20
37 Michael Irvin 1.00
38 Billy Joe Tolliver .20
39 Jeff Herrod .20
40 Scott Norwood .20
41 Ferrell Edmunds .20
42 Andre Waters .20
43 Kevin Glover .20
44 Ray Berry .20
45 Timm Rosenbach .20
46 Reuben Davis .20
47 Charles Wilson .20
48 *Todd Marinovich* .20
49 Harris Barton .20
50 Jim Breech .20
51 Ron Holmes .20
52 Chris Singleton .20
53 Pat Leahy .20
54 Tom Newberry .20
55 Greg Montgomery .20
56 Robert Blackmon .20
57 Jay Hilgenberg .20
58 Rodney Hampton 1.00
59 Brett Perriman .75
60 *Ricky Watters* 7.00
61 Howie Long .20
62 Frank Cornish .20
63 Chris Miller .20
64 Keith Taylor .20
65 Tony Paige .20
66 Gary Zimmerman .20
67 Mark Royals .20
68 Ernie Jones .20
69 David Grant .20
70 Shane Conlan .20
71 Jerry Rice 5.00
72 Christian Okoye .20
73 Eddie Murray .20
74 Reggie White .75
75 *Jeff Graham* 2.00
76 Mark Jackson .20
77 David Grayson .20
78 Dan Stryzinski .20
79 Sterling Sharpe .75
80 Cleveland Gary .20
81 Johnny Meads .20
82 Howard Cross .20
83 Ken O'Brien .20
84 Brian Blades .20
85 Ethan Horton .20
86 Bruce Armstrong .20
87 *James Washington* .40
88 Eugene Daniel .20
89 James Lofton .20
90 Louis Oliver .20
91 Boomer Esiason .30
92 Seth Joyner .20
93 Mark Carrier .20
94 *Brett Favre* (Favre misspelled as Farve) 80.00
95 Lee Williams .20
96 Neal Anderson .20
97 Brent Jones .20
98 John Alt .20
99 Rodney Peete .20
100 Steve Broussard .20
101 Cedric Mack .20
102 Pat Swilling .20
103 Stan Humphries 2.00
104 Darrell Thompson .20
105 Reggie Langhorne .20
106 Kenny Davidson .20
107 Jim Everett .30
108 Keith Millard .20
109 Garry Lewis .20
110 Jeff Hostetler 1.00
111 Lamar Lathon .20
112 Johnny Bailey .20
113 Cornelius Bennett .20
114 Travis McNeal .20
115 Jeff Lageman .20
116 *Nick Bell* .20
117 Calvin Williams .50
118 Shawn Lee .20
119 Anthony Munoz .20
120 Jay Novacek .40
121 Kevin Fagan .20
122 Leo Goeas .20
123 Vance Johnson .20
124 Brent Williams .20
125 Clarence Verdin .20
126 Luis Sharpe .20
127 Darrell Green .20
128 Barry Word .20
129 Steve Walsh .40
130 Bryan Hinkle .20
131 Ed West .20
132 Jeff Campbell .20
133 Dennis Byrd .20
134 Nate Odomes .20
135 Trace Armstrong .20
136 Jarvis Williams .20
137 Warren Moon 1.00
138 *Eric Moten* .20
139 Tony Woods .20
140 Phil Simms .20
141 Ricky Reynolds .20
142 Frank Stams .20
143 Kevin Mack .20
144 Wade Wilson .20
145 Shawn Collins .20
146 Roger Craig .20
147 Jeff Feagles .20
148 Norm Johnson .20
149 Terrance Mathis 2.00
150 Reggie Cobb .20
151 Chip Banks .20
152 Darryl Pollard .20
153 Karl Mecklenburg .20
154 Ricky Proehl .20
155 Pete Stoyanovich .20
156 John Stephens .20
157 Ron Morris .20
158 Steve DeBerg .20
159 Mike Munchak .20
160 Brett Maxie .20
161 Don Beebe .20
162 Martin Mayhew .20
163 Merril Hoge .20
164 Kelvin Pritchett .20
165 Jim Jeffcoat .20
166 Myron Guyton .20
167 Ickey Woods .20
168 Andre Ware .20
169 Gary Plummer .20
170 Henry Ellard .20
171 Scott Davis .20
172 Randall McDaniel .20
173 *Randal Hill* 1.00
174 Anthony Bell .20
175 Gary Anderson .20
176 Byron Evans .20
177 Tony Mandarich .20
178 Jeff George 2.00
179 Art Monk .40
180 Mike Kenn .20
181 Sean Landeta .20
182 Shaun Gayle .20
183 Michael Carter .20
184 Robb Thomas .20
185 Richmond Webb .20
186 Carnell Lake .20
187 Rueben Mayes .20
188 Issiac Holt .20
189 Leon Seals .20
190 Al Smith .20
191 Steve Atwater .20
192 Greg McMurtry .20
193 Al Toon .20
194 Cortez Kennedy .40
195 Gill Byrd .20
196 Carl Zander .20
197 Robert Brown .20
198 Buford McGee .20
199 Mervyn Fernandez .20
200 Mike Dumas .20
201 *Rob Burnett* .40
202 Brian Mitchell .20
203 Randall Cunningham .50
204 Sammie Smith .20
205 Ken Clarke .20
206 Floyd Dixon .20
207 Ken Norton .20
208 Tony Siragusa .20
209 Louis Lipps .20
210 Chris Martin .20
211 Jamie Mueller .20
212 Dave Waymer .20
213 Donnell Woolford .20
214 Paul Gruber .20
215 Ken Harvey .20
216 *Henry Jones* .40
217 Tommy Barnhardt .20
218 Arthur Cox .20
219 Pat Terrell .20
220 Curtis Duncan .20
221 Jeff Jaeger .20
222 Scott Stephen .20
223 Rob Moore .20
224 Chris Hinton .20
225 Marv Cook .20
226 Patrick Hunter .20
227 Earnest Byner .20
228 Troy Aikman 4.00
229 Kevin Walker .20
230 Keith Jackson .20
231 *Russell Maryland* .75
232 Charles Haley .20
233 Nick Lowery .20
234 Erik Howard .20
235 Leonard Smith .20
236 Tim Irwin .20
237 Simon Fletcher .20
238 Thomas Everett .20
240 Leroy Hoard .20
241 Wayne Haddix .20
242 Gary Clark .20
243 Eric Andolsek .20
244 Jim Wahler .20
245 Vaughan Johnson .20
246 Kevin Butler .20
247 Steve Tasker .20
248 LeRoy Butler .20
250 *Eric Turner* 1.00
251 Kevin Ross .20
252 Stephen Baker .20
253 Harold Green .20
254 Rohn Stark .20
255 Joe Nash .20
256 Jesse Sapolu .20
257 Willie Gault .20
258 Jerome Brown .20
259 Ken Willis .20
260 Courtney Hall .20
261 Hart Lee Dykes .20
262 William Fuller .20
263 Stan Thomas .20
264 Dan Marino 6.00
265 Ron Cox .20
266 Eric Green .50
267 Anthony Carter .20
268 Jerry Ball .20
269 Ron Hall .20
270 Dennis Smith .20
271 Eric Hill .20
272 *Dan McGwire* .20
273 Lewis Billups .20
274 Rickey Jackson .20
275 Jim Sweeney .20
276 Pat Beach .20
277 Kevin Porter .20
278 Mike Sherrard .20
279 Andy Heck .20
280 Ron Brown .20
281 Lawrence Taylor .50
282 Anthony Pleasant .20
283 Wes Hopkins .20
284 Jim Lachey .20
285 Tim Harris .20
286 Tony Epps .20
287 Wendell Davis .20
288 Bubba McDowell .20
289 Reggie Roby, Bubby Brister .20
290 *Chris Zorich* 1.00
291 Mike Merriweather .20
292 Burt Grossman .20
293 Eric McMillan .20
294 John Elway 2.00
295 Toi Cook .20
297 Matt Bahr .20
298 Chris Spielman .20
299 Freddie Joe Nunn (Troy Aikman and Emmitt Smith shown in background) .30
300 Jim C. Jenson .20
301 David Fulcher (Rookie card should be '88, not '89) .20
302 Tommy Hodson .20
303 Stephone Page .20
304 Greg Townsend .20
305 Dean Biasucci .20
306 Jimmie Jones .20
307 Eugene Marve .20
308 Flipper Anderson .20
309 Darryl Talley .20
310 *Mike Croel* .40
311 Thane Gash .20
312 Perry Kemp .20
313 Heath Sherman .20
314 Mike Singletary .20
315 Chip Lohmiller .20
316 Tunch Ilkin .20
317 Junior Seau 2.00
318 Mike Gann .20
319 Tim McDonald .20
320 Kyle Clifton .20
321 Dan Owens .20
322 Tim Grunhard .20
323 Stan Brock .20
324 Rodney Holman .20
325 Mark Ingram .20
326 *Browning Nagle* .40
327 Joe Montana 5.00
328 Carl Lee .20
329 John L. Williams .20
330 David Griggs .20
331 Clarence Kay .20
332 Irving Fryar .20
333 Doug Smith .20
334 Kent Hull .20
335 Mike Wilcher .20
336 Ray Donaldson .20
337 Mark Carrier (Rookie card should be '90, not '89) .20
338 Kelvin Martin .20
339 Keith Byars .20
340 Wilber Marshall .20
341 Ronnie Lott .20
342 Blair Thomas .20
343 Ronnie Harmon .20
344 Brian Brennan .20
345 *Charles McRae* .20
346 Michael Cofer .20
347 Keith Willis .20
348 Bruce Kozerski .20
349 Dave Meggett .20
350 John Taylor .20
351 Johnny Holland .20
352 Steve Christie .20
353 *Ricky Ervins* 1.00
354 Robert Massey .20
355 Derrick Thomas .50
356 Tommy Kane .20
357 Melvin Bratton .20
358 Bruce Matthews .20
359 Mark Duper .20
360 Jeff Wright .20
361 Barry Sanders 6.00
362 Chuck Webb .20
363 Darryl Grant .20
364 William Roberts .20
365 Reggie Rutland .20
366 Clay Matthews .20
367 Anthony Miller .20
368 Mike Prior .20
369 Jessie Tuggle .20
370 Brad Muster .20
371 Jay Schroeder .20
372 Greg Lloyd .20
373 Mike Cofer .20
374 James Brooks .20
375 Danny Noonan (Misspelled Noonen on card back) .20
376 Latin Berry .20
377 Brad Baxter .20
378 Godfrey Myles .20
379 Morten Andersen .20
380 Keith Woodside .20
381 Bobby Humphrey .20
382 Mike Golic .20
383 Keith McCants .20
384 Anthony Thompson .20
385 Mark Clayton .20
386 Neil Smith .20
387 Bryan Millard .20
388 Mel Gray (Wrong Mel Gray pictured on card back) .20
389 Ernest Givins .20
390 Reyna Thompson .20
391 *Eric Bieniemy* .40
392 Jon Hand .20
393 Mark Rypien .20
394 Bill Romanowski .20
395 Thurman Thomas 1.50
396 Jim Harbaugh .20
397 Don Mosebar .20
398 Andre Rison .50
399 Mike Johnson .20
400 Dermontti Dawson .20
401 Herschel Walker .30
402 Joe Prokop .20
403 Eddie Brown .20
404 Nate Newton .20
405 Damone Johnson .20
406 Jessie Hester .20
407 Jim Arnold .20
408 Ray Agnew .20
409 Michael Brooks .20
410 Keith Sims .20
411 Carl Banks .20
412 Jonathan Hayes .20
413 Richard Johnson .20
414 *Darryll Lewis* .20
415 Jeff Bryant .20
416 Leslie O'Neal .20
417 Andre Reed .30
418 Charles Mann .20
419 Keith DeLong .20
420 Bruce Hill .20
421 Matt Brock .20
422 Johnny Johnson .30
423 Mark Bortz .20
424 Ben Smith .20
425 Jeff Cross .20
426 Irv Pankey .20
427 Hassan Jones .20
428 Andre Tippett .20
429 Tim Worley .20
430 Daniel Stubbs .20
431 Max Montoya .20
432 Jumbo Elliott .20
433 Duane Bickett .20
434 *Nate Lewis* .50
435 *Leonard Russell* 1.00
436 Hoby Brenner .20
437 Ricky Sanders .20
438 Pierce Holt .20
439 Derrick Fenner .20
440 Drew Hill .20
441 Will Wolford .20
442 Albert Lewis .20
443 James Francis .20
444 Chris Jackie (Jacke) .20
445 Mike Farr .20
446 Stephen Braggs .20
447 Michael Haynes 1.00
448 Freeman McNeil (2008 pounds, sic) .20
449 Kevin Donnalley .20
450 John Offerdahl .20
451 Eric Allen .20
452 Keith McKeller .20
453 Kevin Greene .20
454 Ronnie Lippett .20
455 Ray Childress .20
456 Mike Saxon .20
457 Mark Robinson .20
458 Greg Kragen .20
459 Steve Jordan .20
460 John Johnson .20
461 Sam Mills .20
462 Bo Jackson .40
463 Mark Collins .20
464 Percy Snow .20
465 Jeff Bostic .20
466 Jacob Green .20
467 Dexter Carter .20
468 Rich Camarillo .20
469 Bill Brooks .20
470 John Carney .20
471 Don Majkowski .20
472 Ralph Tamm .20
473 Fred Barnett 1.00
474 Jim Covert .20
475 Kenneth Davis .20
476 Jerry Gray .20
477 Broderick Thomas .20
478 Chris Doleman .20
479 Haywood Jeffires .40
480 Craig Heyward .20
481 Markus Koch .20
482 Tim Krumrie .20
483 Robert Clark .20
484 Mike Rozier .20
485 Danny Villa .20
486 Gerald Williams .20
487 Steve Wisniewski .20
488 J.B. Brown .20
489 Eugene Robinson .20
490 Ottis Anderson .20
491 Tony Stargell .20
492 Jack Del Rio .20
493 Lamar Rogers .20
494 Ricky Nattiel .20
495 Dan Saleaumua .20
496 Checklist Card .20
497 Checklist Card .20
498 Checklist Card .20
499 Checklist Card .20
500 Checklist Card .20

1992 Stadium Club Promo Sheet

This nine-card promotional sheet was distributed at the 13th National Sports Collector's Convention in 1992. The sheet pictures the cards in a larger-than-the-finished- product format, but has a gold foil line framing the card that reveals the standard sized card. Sheet backs have a large logo promoting the event.

NM/M

Complete Set (1): 10.00
NNO Barry Sanders, Gene Atkins, Louis Oliver, Paul Gruber, Emmitt Smith, Steve Jordan, Warren Moon, Seth Joyner, Ronnie Lott Promo Sheet 10.00

1992 Stadium Club

This three-card series contains 700 cards. Each glossy card has a full-bleed color photo on the front, with a Stadium Club logo and player's name at the bottom. The team name is between two gold foil stripes. The back is done horizontally and includes a career summary, Sporting News Skills Rating System report and a miniature version of the player's Topps rookie card. The set has 30 Members Choice cards (#s 291-310 and 601-610), which are labeled on the card fronts.

NM/M

Complete Set (700): 150.00
Complete Series 1 (300): 15.00
Complete Series 2 (300): 15.00
Complete Hi Series (100): 125.00
Common Player: .10
Common Player (601-700): .30
Series 1 Pack (12): .75
Series 1 Wax Box (36): 15.00
Series 2 Pack (12): .50
Series 2 Wax Box (36): 10.00
Series 3 Pack (12): 20.00
Series 3 Wax Box (36): 500.00
1 Mark Rypien .10
2 *Carlton Bailey* .15
3 Kevin Glover .10
4 Vance Johnson .10
5 Jim Jeffcoat .10
6 Dan Saleaumua .10
7 Darion Conner .10
8 Don Maggs .10
9 Richard Dent .15
10 Mark Murphy .10
11 Wesley Carroll .10
12 Chris Burkett .10
13 Steve Wallace .10
14 Jacob Green .10
15 Roger Ruzek .10
16 J.B. Brown .10
17 Dave Meggett .10
18 David Johnson .10
19 Rich Gannon .10
20 Kevin Mack .10
21 Reggie Cobb .10
22 Nate Lewis .10
23 Doug Smith .10
24 Irving Fryar .10
25 Anthony Thompson .10
26 Duane Bickett .10
27 Don Majkowski .10
28 Mark Schlereth .10
29 Melvin Jenkins .10
30 Michael Haynes .15
31 Greg Lewis .10
32 Kenneth Davis .10
33 Derrick Thomas .20
34 David Williams .10
35 Neal Anderson .10
36 Andre Collins .10
37 Jesse Solomon .10
38 Barry Sanders 3.00
39 Jeff Gossett .10
40 Rickey Jackson .10
41 Ray Berry .10
42 Leroy Hoard .10
43 Eric Thomas .10
44 Brian Washington .10
45 Pat Terrell .10
46 Eugene Robinson .10
47 Luis Sharpe .10
48 Jerome Brown .10
49 Mark Collins .10
50 Johnny Holland .10
51 Tony Paige .10
52 Willie Green .10
53 Steve Atwater .10
54 Brad Muster .10
55 Cris Dishman .10
56 Eddie Anderson Sam .10
57 Sam Mills .10
58 Donald Evans .10
59 Jon Vaughn .10
60 Marion Butts .10
61 Rodney Holman .10
62 *Dwayne White* .10
63 Martin Mayhew .10
64 Jonathan Hayes .10
65 Andre Rison .15
66 Calvin Williams .10
67 James Washington .10
68 Tim Harris .10
69 Jim Richter .10
70 Johnny Johnson .10
71 John Offerdahl .10
72 Herschel Walker .10
73 Perry Kemp .10
74 Erik Howard .10
75 Lamar Lathon .10
76 Greg Kragen .10
77 Jay Schroeder .10
78 Jim Arnold .10
79 Chris Miller .10
80 Deron Cherry .10
81 Jim Harbaugh .20
82 Gill Fenerty .10
83 Fred Stokes .10
84 Roman Phifer .10
85 Clyde Simmons .10
86 Vince Newsome .10
87 Lawrence Dawsey .10
88 Eddie Brown .10
89 Greg Montgomery .10
90 Jeff Lageman .10
91 Terry Wooden .10
92 Nate Newton .10
93 David Richards .10
94 Derek Russell .10
95 Steve Jordan .10
96 Hugh Millen .10
97 Mark Duper .10
98 Sean Landeta .10
99 James Thornton .10
100 Darrell Green .10
101 Harris Barton .10
102 John Alt .10
103 Mike Farr .10
104 Bob Golic .10
105 Gene Atkins .10
106 Gary Anderson .10
107 Norm Johnson .10
108 Eugene Daniel .10
109 Kent Hull .10
110 John Elway 1.00
111 Rich Camarillo .10
112 Charles Wilson .10
113 Matt Bahr .10
114 Mark Carrier .10
115 Richmond Webb .10
116 Charles Mann .10
117 Tim McGee .10
118 Wes Hopkins .10
119 Mo Lewis .10
120 Warren Moon .25

121 Damone Johnson .10
122 Kevin Gogan .10
123 Joey Browner .10
124 Tommy Kane .10
125 Vincent Brown .10
126 Barry Word .10
127 Michael Brooks .10
128 Jumbo Elliot .10
129 Marcus Allen .25
130 Tom Waddle .10
131 Jim Dombrowski .10
132 Aeneas Williams .10
133 Clay Matthews .10
134 Thurman Thomas .50
135 Dean Biasucci .10
136 Moe Gardner .10
137 James Campen .10
138 Tim Johnson .10
139 Erik Kramer .15
140 Keith McCants .10
141 John Carney .10
142 Tunch Ilkin .10
143 Louis Oliver .10
144 Bill Maas .10
145 Wendell Davis .10
146 Pepper Johnson .10
147 Howie Long .10
148 Brett Maxie .10
149 Tony Casillas .10
150 Michael Carter .10
151 Byron Evans .10
152 Lorenzo White .10
153 Larry Kelm .10
154 Andy Heck .10
155 Harry Newsome .10
156 Chris Singleton .10
157 Mike Kenn .10
158 Jeff Faulkner .10
159 Ken Lanier .10
160 Darryl Talley .10
161 *Louie Aguiar* .10
162 Danny Copeland .10
163 Kevin Porter .10
164 Trace Armstrong .10
165 Dermontti Dawson .10
166 *Fred McAfee* .10
167 Ronnie Lott .10
168 Tony Mandarich .10
169 Howard Cross .10
170 Vestee Jackson .10
171 Jeff Herrod .10
172 *Randy Hilliard* .10
173 Robert Wilson .10
174 *Joe Walter* .10
175 Chris Spielman .10
176 Darryl Henley .10
177 Jay Hilgenberg .10
178 John Kidd .10
179 Doug Widell .10
180 Seth Joyner .10
181 Nick Bell .10
182 Don Griffin .10
183 Johnny Meads .10
184 Jeff Bostic .10
185 Johnny Hector .10
186 Jessie Tuggle .10
187 Robb Thomas .10
188 Shane Conlan .10
189 *Michael Zordich* .10
190 Emmitt Smith 5.00
191 Robert Blackmon .10
192 Carl Lee .10
193 Harry Galbreath .10
194 Ed King .10
195 Stan Thomas .10
196 Andre Waters .10
197 Pat Harlow .10
198 Zefross Moss .10
199 Bobby Hebert .10
200 Doug Riesenberg .10
201 Mike Croel .10
202 Jeff Jaeger .10
203 Gary Plummer .10
204 Chris Jacke .10
205 Neil O'Donnell .50
206 Mark Bortz .10
207 Tim Barnett .10
208 Jerry Ball .10
209 Chip Lohmiller .10
210 Jim Everett .10
211 Tim McKyer .10
212 Aaron Craver .10
213 John L. Williams .10
214 Simon Fletcher .10
215 Walter Reeves .10
216 Terance Mathis .10
217 Mike Pitts .10
218 Bruce Matthews .10
219 Howard Ballard .10
220 Leonard Russell .10
221 Michael Stewart .10
222 Mike Merriweather .10
223 Ricky Sanders .10
224 Ray Horton .10
225 Michael Jackson .10
226 Bill Romanowski .10
227 Steve McMichael .10
228 Chris Martin .10
229 Tim Green .10
230 Karl Mecklenburg .10
231 Felix Wright .10
232 Charles McRae .10
233 Pete Stoyanovich .10
234 Stephen Baker .10
235 Herman Moore 1.50
236 Terry McDaniel .10
237 Dalton Hilliard .10
238 Gill Byrd .10
239 Leron Seals .10
240 Rod Woodson .15
241 Curtis Duncan .10
242 Keith Jackson .10
243 Mark Stepnoski .10
244 Art Monk .15
245 Matt Stover .10
246 John Roper .10
247 Rodney Hampton .40
248 Steve Wisniewski .10
249 Bryan Millard .10
250 Todd Lyght .10
251 Marvin Washington .10
252 Eric Swann .10
253 Bruce Kozerski .10
254 Jon Hand .10
255 Scott Fulhage .10
256 Chuck Cecil .10
257 Eric Martin .10
258 Eric Metcalf .10
259 T.J. Turner .10
260 Kirk Lowdermilk .10
261 Keith McKeller .10
262 Wymon Henderson .10
263 David Alexander .10
264 George Jamison .10
265 Ken Norton .10
266 Jim Lachey .10
267 *Bo Orlando* .10
268 Nick Lowery .10
269 Keith Van Horne .10
270 Dwight Stone .10
271 Kerith DeLong .10
272 James Francis .10
273 Greg McMurtry .10
274 Ethan Horton .10
275 Stan Brock .10
276 Ken Harvey .10
277 Ronnie Harmon .10
278 Mike Pritchard .10
279 Kyle Clifton .10
280 Anthony Johnson .10
281 Esera Tuaolo .10
282 Vernon Turner .10
283 David Griggs .10
284 Dino Hackett .10
285 Carwell Gardner .10
286 Ron Hall .10
287 Reggie White .20
288 S.C. Checklist 1-100 .10
289 S.C. Checklist 101-200 .10
290 S.C. Checklist 201-300 .10
291 Mark Clayton .10
292 Pat Swilling .10
293 Ernest Givins .10
294 Broderick Thomas .10
295 John Friesz .10
296 Cornelius Bennett .10
297 Anthony Carter .10
298 Earnest Byner .10
299 Michael Irvin .50
300 Cortez Kennedy .10
301 Barry Sanders 2.00
302 Mike Croel .10
303 Emmitt Smith 3.00
304 Leonard Russell .10
305 Neal Anderson .10
306 Derrick Thomas .15
307 Mark Rypien .10
308 Reggie White .20
309 Rod Woodson .15
310 Rodney Hampton .20
311 Carnell Lake .10
312 Robert Delpino .10
313 Brian Blades .10
314 Marc Spindler .10
315 Scott Norwood .10
316 Frank Warren .10
317 David Treadwell .10
318 Steve Broussard .10
319 Lorenzo Lynch .10
320 Ray Agnew .10
321 Derrick Walker .10
322 *Vinson Smith* .10
323 Gary Clark .10
324 Charles Haley .10
325 Keith Byars .10
326 Winston Moss .10
327 *Paul McJulien* .10
328 Tony Covington .10
329 Mark Carrier .10
330 Mark Tuinei .10
331 *Tracy Simien* .10
332 Jeff Wright .10
333 Bryan Cox .10
334 Lonnie Young .10
335 Clarence Verdin .10
336 Dan Fike .10
337 Steve Sewell .10
338 Gary Zimmerman .10
339 Barney Bussey .10
340 William Perry .10
341 Jeff Hostetler .15
342 Doug Smith .10
343 Cleveland Gary .10
344 Todd Marinovich .10
345 Rich Moran .10
346 Tony Woods .10
347 Vaughan Johnson .10
348 Marv Cook .10
349 Pierce Holt .10
350 Gerald Williams .10
351 Kevin Butler .10
352 William White .10
353 Henry Rolling .10
354 James Joseph .10
355 Vinny Testaverde .10
356 Scott Radecic .10
357 Lee Johnson .10
358 Steve Tasker .10
359 David Lutz .10
360 Audrey McMillan .10
361 Brad Baxter .10
362 Mark Dennis .10
363 Erric Pegram .15
364 Sean Jones .10
365 William Roberts .10
366 Steve Young 1.75
367 Joe Jacoby .10
368 *Richard Brown* .10
369 Keith Kartz .10
370 Freddie Joe Nunn .10
371 Darren Comeaux .10
372 Larry Brown .10
373 Haywood Jeffires .10
374 Tom Newberry .10
375 *Steve Bono* 1.25
376 Kevin Ross .10
377 Kelvin Pritchett .10
378 Jessie Hester .10
379 Mitchell Price .10
380 Barry Foster .10
381 Reyna Thompson .10
382 Cris Carter .20
383 Lemuel Stinson .10
384 Rod Bernstine .10
385 James Lofton .10
386 Kevin Murphy .10
387 Greg Townsend .10
388 *Edgar Bennett* .75
389 Rob Moore .10
390 Eugene Lockhart .10
391 Bern Brostek .10
392 Craig Heyward .10
393 Ferrell Edmunds .10
394 John Kasay .10
395 Jesse Sapolu .10
396 Jim Breech .10
397 Neil Smith .10
398 Bryce Paup .40
399 Tony Tolbert .10
400 Bubby Brister .10
401 Dennis Smith .10
402 Dan Owens .10
403 Steve Beuerlein .10
404 Rick Tuten .10
405 Eric Allen .10
406 Eric Hill .10
407 Don Warren .10
408 Greg Jackson .10
409 Chris Doleman .10
410 Anthony Munoz .10
411 Michael Young .10
412 Cornelius Bennett .10
413 Ray Childress .10
414 Kevin Call .10
415 Burt Grossman .10
416 Scott Miller .10
417 Tim Newton .10
418 Robert Young .10
419 *Tommy Vardell* .15
420 Michael Walter .10
421 *Chris Port* .10
422 *Carlton Haselrig* .10
423 Rodney Peete .10
424 Scott Stephen .10
425 Chris Warren 1.00
426 *Scott Galbraith* .10
427 Fuad Reveiz .10
428 Irv Eatman .10
429 David Szott .10
430 Brent Williams .10
431 Mike Horan .10
432 Brent Jones .10
433 Paul Gruber .10
434 Carlos Huerta .10
435 Scott Case .10
436 Greg Davis .10
437 Ken Clarke .10
438 Alfred Williams .10
439 Jim Jensen .10
440 Louis Lipps .10
441 Larry Roberts .10
442 James Jones .10
443 Don Mosebar .10
444 Quinn Early .10
445 Robert Brown .10
446 Tom Thayer .10
447 Michael Irvin .40
448 Jarrod Bunch .10
449 Riki Ellison .10
450 Joe Phillips .10
451 Ernest Givins .10
452 Glenn Parker .10
453 Brett Perriman .25
454 *Jayice Pearson* .10
455 Mark Jackson .10
456 *Siran Stacy* .10
457 Rufus Porter .10
458 Michael Ball .10
459 Craig Taylor .10
460 *George Thomas* .10
461 Alvin Wright .10
462 Ron Hallstrom .10
463 *Mike Mooney* .10
464 Dexter Carter .10
465 *Marty Carter* .10
466 Pat Swilling .10
467 Mike Golic .10
468 Reggie Roby .10
469 Randall McDaniel .10
470 John Stephens .10
471 *Ricardo McDonald* .10
472 Wilber Marshall .10
473 Jim Sweeney .10
474 Ernie Jones .10
475 Bennie Blades .10
476 Don Beebe .10
477 Grant Feasel .10
478 Ernie Mills .10
479 Tony Jones .10
480 Jeff Uhlenhake .10
481 Gaston Green .10
482 John Taylor .10
483 Anthony Smith .10
484 Tony Bennett .10
485 *David Brandon* .10
486 Shawn Jefferson .10
487 Christian Okoye .10
488 Leonard Marshall .10
489 Jay Novacek .10
490 Harold Green .10
491 Bubba McDowell .10
492 Gary Anderson .10
493 *Terrell Buckley* .20
494 *Jamie Dukes* .10
495 Morten Andersen .10
496 Henry Thomas .10
497 Bill Lewis .10
498 Jeff Cross .10
499 Hardy Nickerson .10
500 Henry Ellard .10
501 *Joe Bowden* .10
502 Brian Noble .10
503 Mike Cofer .10
504 Jeff Bryant .10
505 Lomas Brown .10
506 Chip Banks .10
507 Keith Taylor .10
508 Mark Kelso .10
509 *Dexter McNabb* .10
510 *Gene Chilton* .10
511 George Thornton .10
512 Jeff Criswell .10
513 Brad Edwards .10
514 Ron Heller .10
515 Tim Brown .20
516 *Keith Hamilton* .10
517 Mark Higgs .10
518 Tommy Barnhardt .10
519 Brian Jordan .10
520 Ray Crockett .10
521 Karl Wilson .10
522 Ricky Reynolds .10
523 Max Montoya .10
524 David Little .10
525 *Alonzo Mitz* .10
526 Darryll Lewis .10
527 Keith Henderson .10
528 Leroy Butler .10
529 Rob Burnett .10
530 Chris Chandler .10
531 Maury Buford .10
532 Mark Ingram .10
533 Mike Saxon .10
534 Bill Fralic .10
535 *Craig Patterson* .10
536 John Randle .10
537 Dwayne Harper .10
538 *Chris Hakel* .10
539 Maurice Hurst .10
540 Warren Powers .10
541 Will Wolford .10
542 Dennis Gibson .10
543 Jackie Slater .10
544 Floyd Turner .10
545 Guy McIntyre .10
546 Eric Green .10
547 Rohn Stark .10
548 William Fuller .10
549 Alvin Harper .20
550 Mark Clayton .10
551 *Natu Tuatagaloa* .10
552 Fred Barnett .10
553 *Bob Whitfield* .10
554 Courtney Hall .10
555 Brian Mitchell .10
556 Patrick Hunter .10
557 Rick Bryan .10
558 Anthony Carter .10
559 Jim Wahler .10
560 Joe Morris .10
561 Tony Zendejas .10
562 Mervyn Fernandez .10
563 Jamie Williams .10
564 Darrell Thompson .10
565 Adrian Cooper .10
566 Chris Goode .10
567 *Jeff Davidson* .10
568 James Hasty .10
569 *Chris Mims* .50
570 *Ray Seals* .15
571 Myron Guyton .10
572 Todd McNair .10
573 Andre Tippett .10
574 Kirby Jackson .10
575 Mel Gray .10
576 Stephone Paige .10
577 Scott Davis .10
578 John Gesek .10
579 Earnest Byner .10
580 John Friesz .10
581 Al Smith .10
582 Flipper Anderson .10
583 *Amp Lee* .25
584 Greg Lloyd .15
585 Cortez Kennedy .10
586 Keith Sims .10
587 Terry Allen .50
588 David Fulcher .10
589 Chris Hinton .10
590 Tim McDonald .10
591 Bruce Armstrong .10
592 Sterling Sharpe .20
593 Tom Rathman .10
594 Bill Brooks .10
595 Broderick Thomas .10
596 Jim Wilks .10
597 Tyrone Braxton .10
598 Checklist 301-400 .10
599 Checklist 401-500 .10
600 Checklist 501-600 .10
601 Andre Reed (MC) .50
602 Troy Aikman (MC) 3.00
603 Dan Marino (MC) 6.00
604 Randall Cunningham (MC) .50
605 Jim Kelly (MC) 1.00
606 Deion Sanders (MC) 2.00
607 Junior Seau (MC) 1.00
608 Jerry Rice (MC) 3.00
609 Bruce Smith (MC) .50
610 Lawrence Taylor (MC) .50
611 *Todd Collins* .50
612 *Ty Detmer* 2.00
613 Browning Nagle .30
614 Tony Sacca .30
615 Boomer Esiason .30
616 Billy Joe Tolliver .30
617 Leslie O'Neal .30
618 *Mark Wheeler* .30
619 Eric Dickerson .50
620 Phil Simms .30
621 *Troy Vincent* 1.00
622 *Jason Hanson* .50
623 Andre Reed .50
624 Russell Maryland .50
625 *Steve Emtman* 1.00
626 *Sean Gilbert* 1.50
627 *Dana Hall* 1.00
628 Dan McGwire .30
629 Lewis Billups .30
630 *Darryl Williams* .50
631 *Dwayne Sabb* .50
632 Mark Royals .30
633 Cary Conklin .30
634 Al Toon .30
635 Junior Seau 1.50
636 *Greg Skrepenak* .30
637 Deion Sanders 3.00
638 Steve DeOssie .30
639 Randall Cunningham .50
640 Jim Kelly 1.00
641 *Michael Brandon* .30
642 *Clayton Holmes* .30
643 Webster Slaughter .30
644 Ricky Proehl .30
645 Jerry Rice 5.00
646 Carl Banks .30
647 J.J. Birden .30
648 *Tracy Scroggins* 1.00
649 *Alonzo Spellman* 1.00
650 Joe Montana 5.00
651 *Courtney Hawkins* 1.00
652 *Corey Widmer* .30
653 *Robert Brooks* 7.00
654 *Darren Woodson* 1.00
655 Derrick Bengals .30
656 Steve Christie .30
657 *Chester McGlockton* 3.00
658 *Steve Israel* .30
659 *Robert Harris* .30
660 Dan Marino 10.00
661 Ed McCaffrey 2.50
662 *Johnny Mitchell* 1.00
663 Timm Rosenbach .30
664 Anthony Miller .30
665 Merril Hoge .30
666 *Eugene Chung* .30
667 Rueben Mayes .30
668 Martin Bayless .30
669 *Ashley Ambrose* .30
670 Michael Cofer .30
671 *Shane Dronett* .30
672 Bernie Kosar .50
673 Mike Singletary .50
674 *Mike Lodish* .30
675 *Phillippi Sparks* .50
676 Joel Steed .30
677 Kevin Fagan .30
678 Randal Hill .30
679 Ken O'Brien .30
680 Lawrence Taylor .50
681 Harvey Williams .50
682 *Quentin Coryatt* 1.00
683 Brett Favre 100.00
684 *Robert Jones* 1.00
685 Michael Dean Perry .50
686 Bruce Smith .50
687 *Troy Auzenne* .30
688 *Thomas McLemore* .30
689 *Dale Carter* 1.50
690 *Marc Boutte* .30
691 Jeff George 2.00
692 *Dion Lambert* .30
693 *Vaughn Dunbar* .30
694 *Derek Brown* .30
695 Troy Aikman 5.00
696 *John Fina* .30
697 *Kevin Smith* 1.00
698 *Corey Miller* .30
699 *Lance Olberding* .30
700 Checklist 601-700 .50

1992 Stadium Club No.1 Draft Picks

This four-card insert set features three former #1 draft picks, plus Rocket Ismail. Cards were randomly inserted in 1992 Topps Stadium Club Series II packs, and are numbered on the back. Each card front has a full-bleed photo, along with the player's name, Stadium Club logo and #1 symbol at the bottom. A football in the top upper right has the year the player was selected in it. The card back has a closeup shot of the player, a player biography and set logo.

		NM/M
Complete Set (4):		30.00
Common Player:		7.00
1	Jeff George	10.00
2	Russell Maryland	7.00
3	Steve Emtman	7.00
4	Raghib Ismail	7.00

1992 Stadium Club QB Legends

These cards, featuring six Hall of Fame quarterbacks, were random inserts in 1992 Topps Stadium Club Series II packs, one per every 72 packs. The card front has a color action photo, along with the player's name and Stadium Club logo at the bottom. The set's name is given in a blue bar at the bottom, too, adjacent to a gold foil football helmet on the left. A lime green football appears in the upper right corner, with the year the player was inducted into the Hall of Fame inside it. The football is edged in gold foil and has three gold-foil stripes running down from it. The horizontal backs have a green and black background which includes a player photo, career statistics, a mini version of the player's first Topps card, and the player's facsimile autograph stamped in gold foil. Each card back is also numbered.

		NM/M
Complete Set (6):		15.00
Common Player:		3.00
1	Y.A. Tittle	3.00
2	Bart Starr	4.00
3	John Unitas	4.00
4	George Blanda	3.00
5	Roger Staubach	5.00
6	Terry Bradshaw	5.00

1993 Stadium Club Promo Sheet

This nine-card promo sheet was distributed at the 1993 National Sports Collectors Convention in Chicago. Similar to the 1992 sheet, the photos are shown larger than normal and contain a gold line that reveals the true standard size card. Sheet backs contain a large logo celebrating the event.

		NM/M
Complete Set (1):		8.00
NNO	Johnny Bailey, Vai Sikahema, Richard Dent, Sterling Sharpe, Tommy Barnhardt, Cris Carter, Cortez Kennedy, Christian Okoye, Reggie Cobb Promo Sheet	8.00

1993 Stadium Club

1993 Stadium Club football cards were issued in two 250-card series. Each card front has a full-bleed color photo and the player's name is foil stamped in gold at the bottom in a green stripe. The backs have statistics, a Football News Skills Rating Systems review and a miniature version of the player's Topps rookie card. A high-number series (#s 501-550) was also issued and includes Members Choice cards, Draft Picks, 1st-Year Players and Key Acquisitions. Super Team cards were randomly inserted into packs, one per every 24 packs. If the team pictured on a Super Team card wins a division title, conference championship or the Super Bowl, the card can be redeemed for special prizes. Other insert cards include First Day Production (silver foil) and Master Photo winner cards, which can be redeemed for a group of three Stadium Club Master Photos.

		NM/M
Complete Set (550):		40.00
Complete Series 1 (250):		25.00
Complete Series 2 (250):		15.00
Complete High Series (50):		10.00
Common Player:		.10
Minor Stars:		.20
First Day Cards:		3X-8X
First Day Rookies:		2X-4X
Series 1 Pack (15):		1.25
Series 1 Wax Box (24):		20.00
Series 2 or 3 Pack (15):		1.25
Series 2 or 3 Wax Box (24):		20.00
1	Sterling Sharpe	.50
2	Chris Burkett	.10
3	Santana Dotson	.10
4	Michael Jackson	.10
5	Neal Anderson	.10
6	Bryan Cox	.10

7 Dennis Gibson .10
8 Jeff Graham .10
9 Roger Ruzek .10
10 Duane Bickett .10
11 Charles Mann .10
12 Tommy Maddox .15
13 Vaughn Dunbar .10
14 Gary Plummer .10
15 Chris Miller .10
16 Chris Warren .75
17 Alvin Harper .20
18 Eric Dickerson .10
19 Mike Jones .10
20 Ernest Givins .10
21 *Natrone Means* 2.00
22 Doug Riesenberg .10
23 Barry Word .10
24 Sean Salisbury .10
25 Derrick Fenner .10
26 David Howard .10
27 Mark Kelso .10
28 Todd Lyght .10
29 Dana Hall .10
30 Eric Metcalf .10
31 Jason Hanson .10
32 Dwight Stone .10
33 Johnny Mitchell .20
34 Reggie Roby .10
35 Terrell Buckley .15
36 Steve McMichael .10
37 Marty Carter .10
38 Seth Joyner .10
39 Rohn Stark .10
40 *Eric Curry* .50
41 Tommy Barnhardt .10
42 Karl Mecklenburg .10
43 Darion Conner .10
44 Ronnie Harmon .10
45 Cortez Kennedy .20
46 Tim Brown .10
47 Bill Lewis .10
48 Randall McDaniel .10
49 Curtis Duncan .10
50 Troy Aikman 3.00
51 David Klingler .20
52 Brent Jones .10
53 Dave Krieg .10
54 Bruce Smith .10
55 Vincent Brown .10
56 *O.J. McDuffie* 2.25
57 Cleveland Gary .10
58 *Larry Centers* .75
59 Pepper Johnson .10
60 Dan Marino 4.00
61 Robert Porcher .10
62 Jim Harbaugh .10
63 Sam Mills .10
64 Gary Anderson .10
65 Neil O'Donnell .50
66 Keith Byars .10
67 Jeff Herrod .10
68 Marion Butts .10
69 Terry McDaniel .10
70 John Elway 1.00
71 Steve Broussard .10
72 Kelvin Martin .10
73 *Tom Carter* .20
74 Bryce Paup .10
75 Jim Kelly .50
76 Bill Romanowski .10
77 Andre Collins .10
78 Mike Farr .10
79 Henry Ellard .10
80 Dale Carter .10
81 Johnny Bailey .10
82 *Garrison Hearst* 2.50
83 Brent Williams .10
84 Richard McDonald .10
85 Emmitt Smith 4.00
86 Vai Sikahema .10
87 Jackie Harris .20
88 Alonzo Spellman .10
89 Mark Wheeler .10
90 Dalton Hilliard .10
91 Mark Higgs .20
92 Aaron Wallace .10
93 Earnest Byner .10
94 Stanley Richard .10
95 Cris Carter .10
96 *Bobby Houston* .20
97 Craig Heyward .10
98 Bernie Kosar .10
99 Mike Croel .10
100 Deion Sanders 1.00
101 Warren Moon .20
102 Christian Okoye .10
103 Ricky Watters .50
104 Eric Swann .10
105 Rodney Hampton .20
106 Daryl Johnston .10
107 Andre Reed .20
108 *Jerome Bettis* 2.50
109 Eugene Daniel .10
110 Leonard Russell .15
111 Darryl Williams .10
112 Rod Woodson .10
113 Boomer Esiason .20
114 James Hasty .10
115 Marc Boutte .10
116 Tom Waddle .10
117 Lawrence Dawsey .10
118 Mark Collins .10
119 Willie Gault .10
120 Barry Sanders 2.50
121 Leroy Hoard .10
122 Anthony Munoz .10
123 Jesse Sapolu .10
124 Art Monk .10
125 Randal Hill .10
126 John Offerdahl .10
127 Carlos Jenkins .10
128 Al Smith .10
129 Michael Irvin .50
130 Kenneth Davis .10
131 *Curtis Conway* 2.00
132 Steve Atwater .10
133 Neil Smith .10
134 *Steve Everitt* .20
135 Chris Mims .10
136 Rickey Jackson .10
137 Edgar Bennett .60
138 Mike Pritchard .10
139 Richard Dent .10
140 Barry Foster .10
141 Eugene Robinson .10
142 Jackie Slater .10
143 Paul Gruber .10
144 Rob Moore .20
145 *Robert Smith* 3.00
146 Lorenzo White .10
147 Tommy Vardell .10
148 Dave Meggett .10
149 Vince Workman .10
150 Terry Allen .15
151 Howie Long .10
152 Charles Haley .10
153 Pete Metzelaars .10
154 *John Copeland* .50
155 Aeneas Williams .10
156 Ricky Sanders .10
157 Andre Ware .10
158 Tony Paige .10
159 Jerome Henderson .10
160 Harold Green .10
161 Wymon Henderson .10
162 Andre Rison .20
163 Donald Evans .10
164 Todd Scott .10
165 Steve Emtman .20
166 William Fuller .10
167 Michael Dean Perry .10
168 Randall Cunningham .20
169 Toi Cook .10
170 Browning Nagle .10
171 Darryl Henley .10
172 *George Teague* .40
173 Derrick Thomas .20
174 Jay Novacek .10
175 Mark Carrier .10
176 Kevin Fagan .10
177 Nate Lewis .10
178 Courtney Hawkins .20
179 Robert Blackmon .10
180 *Rick Mirer* .50
181 Mike Lodish .10
182 Jarrod Bunch .10
183 Anthony Smith .10
184 Brian Noble .10
185 Eric Bieniemy .10
186 Keith Jackson .20
187 Eric Martin .10
188 Vance Johnson .10
189 Kevin Mack .10
190 Rich Camarillo .10
191 Ashley Ambrose .10
192 Ray Childress .10
193 Jim Arnold .10
194 Ricky Ervins .10
195 Gary Anderson .10
196 Eric Allen .10
197 Roger Craig .10
198 Jon Vaughn .10
199 Tim McDonald .10
200 Broderick Thomas .10
201 Jessie Tuggle .10
202 Alonzo Mitz .10
203 Harvey Williams .10
204 Russell Maryland .10
205 Marvin Washington .10
206 Jim Everett .10
207 Trace Armstrong .10
208 Steve Young 2.00
209 Tony Woods .10
210 Brett Favre 4.00
211 Nate Odomes .10
212 Ricky Proehl .10
213 Jim Dombrowski .10
214 Anthony Carter .10
215 Tracy Simien .10
216 Clay Matthews .10
217 *Patrick Bates* .35
218 Jeff George .25
219 David Fulcher .10
220 Phil Simms .15
221 Eugene Chung .10
222 Reggie Cobb .10
223 Jim Sweeney .10
224 Greg Lloyd .10
225 Sean Jones .10
226 *Marvin Jones* .40
227 Bill Brooks .10
228 Moe Gardner .10
229 Louis Oliver .10
230 Flipper Anderson .10
231 Marc Spindler .10
232 Jerry Rice 2.00
233 Chip Lohmiller .10
234 Nolan Harrison .10
235 Heath Sherman .10
236 Reyna Thompson .10
237 Derrick Walker .10
238 Rufus Porter .10
239 Checklist 1-125 .10
240 Checklist 126-250 .10
241 John Elway .40
242 Troy Aikman 1.25
243 Steve Emtman .15
244 Ricky Watters .50
245 Barry Foster .20
246 Dan Marino 1.50
247 Reggie White .15
248 Thurman Thomas .60
249 Broderick Thomas .10
250 Joe Montana 2.00
251 Tim Goad .10
252 Joe Nash .10
253 Anthony Johnson .10
254 Carl Pickens 1.00
255 Steve Beuerlein .15
256 *Anthony Newman* .10
257 Corey Miller .10
258 Steve DeBerg .10
259 Johnny Holland .10
260 Jerry Ball .10
261 *Siupeli Malamala* .15
262 Steve Wisniewski .10
263 Kelvin Pritchett .10
264 Chris Gardocki .10
265 Henry Thomas .10
266 *Arthur Marshall* .40
267 Quinn Early .10
268 Jonathan Hayes .10
269 Erric Pegram .40
270 Clyde Simmons .10
271 Eric Moten .10
272 Brian Mitchell .10
273 Adrian Cooper .10
274 Gaston Green .10
275 John Taylor .10
276 Jeff Uhlenhake .10
277 Phil Hansen .10
278 *Kevin Williams* .50
279 Robert Massey .10
280a *Drew Bledsoe* 6.00
280b *Drew Bledsoe Err.* 12.00
281 Walter Reeves .10
282 *Carlton Gray* .20
283 Derek Brown .10
284 Martin Mayhew .10
285 Sean Gilbert .10
286 Jessie Hester .10
287 Mark Clayton .10
288 Blair Thomas .10
289 J.J. Birden .10
290 Shannon Sharpe .20
291 *Richard Fain* .15
292 Gene Atkins .10
293 Burt Grossman .10
294 Chris Doleman .10
295 Pat Swilling .10
296 Mike Kenn .10
297 Merril Hoge .10
298 Don Mosebar .10
299 Kevin Smith .10
300 Darrell Green .10
301 *Dan Footman* .20
302 Vestee Jackson .10
303 Carwell Gardner .10
304 Amp Lee .10
305 Bruce Matthews .10
306 Antone Davis .10
307 Dean Biasucci .10
308 Maurice Hurst .10
309 John Kasay .10
310 Lawrence Taylor .15
311 Ken Harvey .10
312 Willie Davis .15
313 Tony Bennett .15
314 Jay Schroeder .10
315 Darren Perry .10
316 *Troy Drayton* 1.00
317 *Dan Williams* .20
318 Michael Haynes .15
319 Renaldo Turnbull .10
320 Junior Seau .15
321 Ray Crockett .10
322 Will Furrer .10
323 Byron Evans .10
324 Jim McMahon .10
325 Robert Jones .10
326 Eric Davis .10
327 Jeff Cross .10
328 Kyle Clifton .10
329 Haywood Jeffires .15
330 Jeff Hostetler .15
331 Darryl Talley .10
332 Keith McCants .10
333 Mo Lewis .10
334 Matt Stover .10
335 Ferrell Edmunds .10
336 Matt Brock .10
337 Ernie Mills .10
338 Shane Dronett .10
339 Brad Muster .10
340 Jesse Solomon .10
341 John Randle .10
342 Chris Spielman .10
343 David Whitmore .10
344 Glenn Parker .10
345 Marco Coleman .10
346 Kenneth Gant .10
347 Cris Dishman .10
348 Kenny Walker .10
349 *Roosevelt Potts* .45
350 Reggie White .30
351 Gerald Robinson .10
352 Mark Rypien .15
353 Stan Humphries .15
354 Chris Singleton .10
355 Herschel Walker .10
356 Ron Hall .10
357 Ethan Horton .10
358 Anthony Pleasant .10
359 *Thomas Smith* .20
360 Audray McMillian .10
361 D.J. Johnson .10
362 Ron Heller .10
363 Bern Brostek .10
364 Ronnie Lott .10
365 Reggie Johnson .10
366 *Lin Elliott* .15
367 Lemuel Stinson .10
368 William White .10
369 Ernie Jones .10
370 Tom Rathman .10
371 Tommy Kane .10
372 David Brandon .10
373 Lee Johnson .10
374 Wade Wilson .10
375 Nick Lowery .10
376 Bubba McDowell .10
377 *Wayne Simmons* .15
378 Calvin Williams .10
379 Courtney Hall .10
380 Troy Vincent .10
381 Tim McGee .10
382 *Russell Freeman* .15
383 Steve Tasker .10
384 *Michael Strahan* .15
385 Greg Skrepenak .15
386 Jake Reed .10
387 Pete Stoyanovich .10
388 *Levon Kirkland* .15
389 Mel Gray .10
390 Brian Washington .10
391 Don Griffin .10
392 Desmond Howard .50
393 Luis Sharpe .10
394 Mike Johnson .10
395 Andre Tippett .10
396 Donnell Woolford .10
397 *Demetrius DuBose* .20
398 Pat Terrell .10
399 Todd McNair .10
400 Ken Norton .10
401 Keith Hamilton .10
402 Andy Heck .10
403 Jeff Gossett .10
404 Dexter McNabb .10
405 Richmond Webb .10
406 Irving Fryar .10
407 Brian Hansen .10
408 David Little .10
409 *Glyn Milburn* .25
410 Doug Dawson .10
411 Scott Mersereau .10
412 Don Beebe .10
413 Vaughan Johnson .10
414 Jack Del Rio .10
415 *Darrien Gordon* .20
416 Mark Schlereth .10
417 Lomas Brown .10
418 William Thomas .10
419 James Francis .10
420 Quentin Coryatt .15
421 Tyji Armstrong .10
422 Hugh Millen .10
423 *Adrian White* .15
424 Eddie Anderson .10
425 Mark Ingram .10
426 Ken O'Brien .10
427 Simon Fletcher .10
428 Tim McKyer .10
429 Leonard Marshall .10
430 Eric Green .10
431 Leonard Harris .10
432 *Darin Jordan* .15
433 Erik Howard .10
434 David Lang .10
435 Eric Turner .10
436 Michael Cofer .10
437 Jeff Bryant .10
438 Charles McRae .10
439 Henry Jones .10
440 Joe Montana 3.00
441 Morten Andersen .10
442 Jeff Jaeger .10
443 Leslie O'Neal .10
444 Leroy Butler .10
445 Steve Jordan .10
446 Brad Edwards .10
447 J.B. Brown .10
448 Kerry Cash .10
449 Mark Tuinei .10
450 Rodney Peete .10
451 Sheldon White .10
452 Wesley Carroll .10
453 Brad Baxter .10
454 Mike Pitts .10
455 Greg Montgomery .10
456 Kenny Davidson .10
457 Scott Fulhage .10
458 Greg Townsend .10
459 Rod Bernstine .10
460 Gary Clark .10
461 Hardy Nickerson .10
462 Sean Landeta .10
463 Rob Burnett .10
464 Fred Barnett .15
465 John L. Williams .10
466 Anthony Miller .15
467 Roman Phifer .10
468 Rich Moran .10
469 *Willie Roaf* .50
470 William Perry .10
471 Marcus Allen .15
472 Carl Lee .10
473 Kurt Gouveia .10
474 Jarvis Williams .10
475 Alfred Williams .10
476 Mark Stepnoski .10
477 Steve Wallace .10
478 Pat Harlow .10
479 Chip Banks .10
480 Cornelius Bennett .10
481 *Ryan McNeil* .20
482 Norm Johnson .10
483 Dermontti Dawson .10
484 Dwayne White .10
485 Derek Russell .10
486 Lionel Washington .10
487 Eric Hill .10
488 *Micheal Barrow* .15
489 Checklist 251-375 .10
490 Checklist 376-500 .10
491 Emmitt Smith (MC) 2.00
492 Derrick Thomas (MC) .15
493 Deion Sanders (MC) .50
494 Randall Cunningham (MC) .15
495 Sterling Sharpe (MC) .20
496 Barry Sanders (MC) 1.25
497 Thurman Thomas .50
498 Brett Favre (MC) 1.50
499 Vaughan Johnson (MC) .10
500 Steve Young (MC) 1.00
501 Marvin Jones .20
502 *Reggie Brooks* .20
503 Eric Curry .10
504 Drew Bledsoe 2.00
505 Glyn Milburn .15
506 Jerome Bettis 1.00
507 Robert Smith .75
508 Dana Stubblefield .50
509 Tom Carter .10
510 Rick Mirer .50
511 Russell Copeland 1.00
512 *Deon Figures* .30
513 *Tony McGee* .50
514 *Derrick Lassic* .30
515 Everett Lindsay .10
516 *Derek Brown* 1.00
517 Harold Alexander .10
518 Tom Scott .10
519 *Elvis Grbac* 4.00
520 *Terry Kirby* 1.00
521 Doug Pelfrey .10
522 *Horace Copeland* .75
523 *Irv Smith* .20
524 *Lincoln Kennedy* .40
525 Jason Elam .10
526 *Qadry Ismail* .75
527 Artie Smith .10
528 *Tyrone Hughes* 1.00
529 Lance Gunn .10
530 *Vincent Brisby* 1.00
531 Patrick Robinson .10
532 Raghib Ismail .50
533 Willie Beamon .10
534 *Vaughn Hebron* .25
535 Darren Drozdov .10
536 *James Jett* .75
537 *Michael Bates* .50
538 Tom Rouen .10
539 Michael Husted .10
540 *Greg Robinson* .50
541 Carl Banks .10
542 Kevin Greene .10
543 Scott Mitchell .50
544 Michael Brooks .10
545 Shane Conlan .10
546 Vinny Testaverde .10
547 Robert Delpino .10
548 Bill Fralic .10
549 Carlton Bailey .10
550 Johnny Johnson .10
NNO Jerry Rice 15.00

1993 Stadium Club First Day Cards

1993 Stadium Club football cards were issued in two 250-card series. Each card front has a full-bleed color photo and the player's name is foil stamped in gold at the bottom in a green stripe. The backs have statistics, a Football News Skills Rating Systems review and a miniature version of the player's Topps rookie card. A high-number series (#s 501-550) was also issued and includes Members Choice cards, Draft Picks, 1st-Year Players and Key Acquisitions. Super Team cards were randomly inserted into packs, one per every 24 packs. If the team pictured on a Super Team card wins a division title, conference championship or the Super Bowl, the card can be redeemed for special prizes. Other insert cards include First Day Production (silver foil) and Master Photo winner cards, which can be redeemed for a group of three Stadium Club Master Photos.

NM/M

Complete Set (550): 2,000
Complete Series 1 (250): 1,100
Complete Series 2 (250): 600.00
Complete Hi Series (50): 300.00
Common Player: 2.00
Minor Stars: 5.00
Unlisted Stars: 2X-8X
1 Sterling Sharpe 10.00
2 Chris Burkett 2.00
3 Santana Dotson 2.00
4 Michael Jackson 2.00
5 Neal Anderson 2.00
6 Bryan Cox 2.00
7 Dennis Gibson 2.00
8 Jeff Graham 2.00
9 Roger Ruzek 2.00
10 Duane Bickett 2.00
11 Charles Mann 2.00
12 Tommy Maddox 2.00
13 Vaughn Dunbar 2.00
14 Gary Plummer 2.00
15 Chris Miller 2.00
16 Chris Warren 10.00
17 Alvin Harper 10.00
18 Eric Dickerson 5.00
19 Mike Jones 2.00
20 Ernest Givins 2.00
21 *Natrone Means* 15.00
22 Doug Riesenberg 2.00
23 Barry Word 2.00
24 Sean Salisbury 2.00
25 Derrick Fenner 2.00
26 David Howard 2.00
27 Mark Kelso 2.00
28 Todd Lyght 2.00
29 Dana Hall 2.00
30 Eric Metcalf 5.00
31 Jason Hanson 2.00
32 Dwight Stone 2.00
33 Johnny Mitchell 5.00
34 Reggie Roby 2.00
35 Terrell Buckley 2.00
36 Steve McMichael 2.00
37 Marty Carter 2.00
38 Seth Joyner 2.00
39 Rohn Stark 2.00
40 *Eric Curry* 8.00
41 Tommy Barnhardt 2.00
42 Karl Mecklenburg 2.00
43 Darion Conner 2.00
44 Ronnie Harmon 2.00
45 Cortez Kennedy 5.00
46 Tim Brown 5.00
47 Bill Lewis 2.00
48 Randall McDaniel 2.00
49 Curtis Duncan 2.00
50 Troy Aikman 90.00
51 David Klingler 5.00
52 Brent Jones 2.00
53 Dave Krieg 2.00
54 Bruce Smith 2.00
55 Vincent Brown 2.00
56 *O.J. McDuffie* 40.00
57 Cleveland Gary 2.00
58 *Larry Centers* 8.00
59 Pepper Johnson 2.00
60 Dan Marino 125.00
61 Robert Porcher 2.00
62 Jim Harbaugh 2.00
63 Sam Mills 2.00
64 Gary Anderson 2.00
65 Neil O'Donnell 8.00
66 Keith Byars 2.00
67 Jeff Herrod 2.00
68 Marion Butts 2.00
69 Terry McDaniel 2.00
70 John Elway 25.00
71 Steve Broussard 2.00
72 Kelvin Martin 2.00
73 *Tom Carter* 6.00
74 Bryce Paup 2.00
75 Jim Kelly 10.00
76 Bill Romanowski 2.00
77 Andre Collins 2.00
78 Mike Farr 2.00
79 Henry Ellard 2.00
80 Dale Carter 2.00
81 Johnny Bailey 2.00
82 *Garrison Hearst* 30.00
83 Brent Williams 2.00
84 Richard McDonald 2.00
85 Emmitt Smith 125.00
86 Vai Sikahema 2.00
87 Jackie Harris 2.00
88 Alonzo Spellman 2.00
89 Mark Wheeler 2.00
90 Dalton Hilliard 2.00
91 Mark Higgs 2.00
92 Aaron Wallace 2.00
93 Earnest Byner 2.00
94 Stanley Richard 2.00
95 Cris Carter 5.00
96 *Bobby Houston* 2.00
97 Craig Heyward 2.00
98 Bernie Kosar 5.00
99 Mike Croel 2.00
100 Deion Sanders 20.00
101 Warren Moon 10.00
102 Christian Okoye 2.00
103 Ricky Watters 10.00
104 Eric Swann 2.00
105 Rodney Hampton 10.00
106 Daryl Johnston 2.00
107 Andre Reed 5.00
108 *Jerome Bettis* 60.00
109 Eugene Daniel 2.00
110 Leonard Russell 2.00
111 Darryl Williams 2.00
112 Rod Woodson 5.00
113 Boomer Esiason 5.00
114 James Hasty 2.00
115 Marc Boutte 2.00
116 Tom Waddle 2.00
117 Lawrence Dawsey 2.00
118 Mark Collins 2.00
119 Willie Gault 2.00
120 Barry Sanders 80.00
121 Leroy Hoard 2.00
122 Anthony Munoz 2.00
123 Jesse Sapolu 2.00
124 Art Monk 5.00
125 Randal Hill 5.00
126 John Offerdahl 2.00
127 Carlos Jenkins 2.00
128 Al Smith 2.00
129 Michael Irvin 30.00
130 Kenneth Davis 2.00
131 *Curtis Conway* 15.00
132 Steve Atwater 2.00
133 Neil Smith 2.00
134 *Steve Everitt* 5.00
135 Chris Mims 2.00
136 Rickey Jackson 2.00
137 Edgar Bennett 2.00
138 Mike Pritchard 2.00
139 Richard Dent 2.00
140 Barry Foster 10.00
141 Eugene Robinson 2.00
142 Jackie Slater 2.00
143 Paul Gruber 2.00
144 Rob Moore 5.00
145 *Robert Smith* 40.00
146 Lorenzo White 2.00
147 Tommy Vardell 2.00
148 Dave Meggett 5.00
149 Vince Workman 2.00
150 Terry Allen 2.00
151 Howie Long 2.00
152 Charles Haley 2.00
153 Pete Metzelaars 2.00
154 *John Copeland* 5.00
155 Aeneas Williams 2.00
156 Ricky Sanders 2.00
157 Andre Ware 2.00
158 Tony Paige 2.00

159 Jerome Henderson 2.00
160 Harold Green 2.00
161 Wymon Henderson 2.00
162 Andre Rison 5.00
163 Donald Evans 2.00
164 Todd Scott 2.00
165 Steve Emtman 2.00
166 William Fuller 2.00
167 Michael Dean Perry 2.00
168 Randall Cunningham 10.00
169 Toi Cook 2.00
170 Browning Nagle 2.00
171 Darryl Henley 2.00
172 *George Teague* 6.00
173 Derrick Thomas 10.00
174 Jay Novacek 2.00
175 Mark Carrier 2.00
176 Kevin Fagan 2.00
177 Nate Lewis 2.00
178 Courtney Hawkins 2.00
179 Robert Blackmon 2.00
180 *Rick Mirer* 6.00
181 Mike Lodish 2.00
182 Jarrod Bunch 2.00
183 Anthony Smith 2.00
184 Brian Noble 2.00
185 Eric Bieniemy 2.00
186 Keith Jackson 2.00
187 Eric Martin 2.00
188 Vance Johnson 2.00
189 Kevin Mack 2.00
190 Rich Camarillo 2.00
191 Ashley Ambrose 2.00
192 Ray Childress 2.00
193 Jim Arnold 2.00
194 Ricky Ervins 2.00
195 Gary Anderson 2.00
196 Eric Allen 2.00
197 Roger Craig 2.00
198 Jon Vaughn 2.00
199 Tim McDonald 2.00
200 Broderick Thomas 2.00
201 Jessie Tuggle 2.00
202 Alonzo Mitz 2.00
203 Harvey Williams 2.00
204 Russell Maryland 2.00
205 Marvin Washington 2.00
206 Jim Everett 2.00
207 Trace Armstrong 2.00
208 Steve Young 50.00
209 Tony Woods 2.00
210 Brett Favre 125.00
211 Nate Odomes 2.00
212 Ricky Proehl 2.00
213 Jim Dombrowski 2.00
214 Anthony Carter 2.00
215 Tracy Simien 2.00
216 Clay Matthews 2.00
217 *Patrick Bates* 5.00
218 Jeff George 8.00
219 David Fulcher 2.00
220 Phil Simms 5.00
221 Eugene Chung 2.00
222 Reggie Cobb 2.00
223 Jim Sweeney 2.00
224 Greg Lloyd 2.00
225 Sean Jones 2.00
226 *Marvin Jones* 5.00
227 Bill Brooks 2.00
228 Moe Gardner 2.00
229 Louis Oliver 2.00
230 Flipper Anderson 2.00
231 Marc Spindler 2.00
232 Jerry Rice 100.00
233 Chip Lohmiller 2.00
234 Nolan Harrison 2.00
235 Heath Sherman 2.00
236 Reyna Thompson 2.00
237 Derrick Walker 2.00
238 Rufus Porter 2.00
239 Checklist 1-125 2.00
240 Checklist 126-250 2.00
241 John Elway 10.00
242 Troy Aikman 35.00
243 Steve Emtman 2.00
244 Ricky Watters 7.00
245 Barry Foster 5.00
246 Dan Marino 90.00
247 Reggie White 5.00
248 Thurman Thomas 8.00
249 Broderick Thomas 2.00
250 Joe Montana 70.00
251 Tim Goad 2.00
252 Joe Nash 2.00
253 Anthony Johnson 2.00
254 Carl Pickens 2.00
255 Steve Beuerlein 2.00
256 *Anthony Newman* 2.00
257 Corey Miller 2.00
258 Steve DeBerg 2.00
259 Johnny Holland 2.00
260 Jerry Ball 2.00
261 *Siupeli Malamala* 2.00
262 Steve Wisniewski 2.00
263 Kelvin Pritchett 2.00
264 Chris Gardocki 2.00
265 Henry Thomas 2.00
266 *Arthur Marshall* 5.00
267 Quinn Early 2.00
268 Jonathan Hayes 2.00
269 Eric Pegram 2.00
270 Clyde Simmons 2.00
271 Eric Moten 2.00
272 Brian Mitchell 2.00
273 Adrian Cooper 2.00
274 Gaston Green 2.00
275 John Taylor 5.00
276 Jeff Uhlenhake 2.00
277 Phil Hansen 2.00
278 *Kevin Williams* 20.00
279 Robert Massey 2.00
280 *Drew Bledsoe* 150.00
281 Walter Reeves 2.00
282 *Carlton Gray* 5.00
283 Derek Brown 2.00
284 Martin Mayhew 2.00
285 Sean Gilbert 2.00
286 Jessie Hester 2.00
287 Mark Clayton 2.00
288 Blair Thomas 2.00
289 J.J. Birden 2.00
290 Shannon Sharpe 6.00
291 *Richard Fain* 2.00
292 Gene Atkins 2.00
293 Burt Grossman 2.00
294 Chris Doleman 2.00
295 Pat Swilling 2.00
296 Mike Kenn 2.00
297 Merril Hoge 2.00
298 Don Mosebar 2.00
299 Kevin Smith 2.00
300 Darrell Green 2.00
301 *Dan Footman* 2.00
302 Vestee Jackson 2.00
303 Carwell Gardner 2.00
304 Amp Lee 2.00
305 Bruce Matthews 2.00
306 Antone Davis 2.00
307 Dean Biasucci 2.00
308 Maurice Hurst 2.00
309 John Kasay 2.00
310 Lawrence Taylor 5.00
311 Ken Harvey 2.00
312 Willie Davis 2.00
313 Tony Bennett 2.00
314 Jay Schroeder 2.00
315 Darren Perry 2.00
316 *Troy Drayton* 10.00
317 *Dan Williams* 5.00
318 Michael Haynes 2.00
319 Renaldo Turnbull 2.00
320 Junior Seau 8.00
321 Ray Crockett 2.00
322 Will Furrer 2.00
323 Byron Evans 2.00
324 Jim McMahon 2.00
325 Robert Jones 2.00
326 Eric Davis 2.00
327 Jeff Cross 2.00
328 Kyle Clifton 2.00
329 Haywood Jeffires 5.00
330 Jeff Hostetler 5.00
331 Darryl Talley 2.00
332 Keith McCants 2.00
333 Mo Lewis 2.00
334 Matt Stover 2.00
335 Ferrell Edmunds 2.00
336 Matt Brock 2.00
337 Ernie Mills 2.00
338 Shane Dronett 2.00
339 Brad Muster 2.00
340 Jesse Solomon 2.00
341 John Randle 2.00
342 Chris Spielman 2.00
343 David Whitmore 2.00
344 Glenn Parker 2.00
345 Marco Coleman 2.00
346 Kenneth Gant 2.00
347 Cris Dishman 2.00
348 Kenny Walker 2.00
349 *Roosevelt Potts* 5.00
350 Reggie White 5.00
351 Gerald Robinson 2.00
352 Mark Rypien 2.00
353 Stan Humphries 5.00
354 Chris Singleton 2.00
355 Herschel Walker 5.00
356 Ron Hall 2.00
357 Ethan Horton 2.00
358 Anthony Pleasant 2.00
359 *Thomas Smith* 5.00
360 Audray McMillian 2.00
361 D.J. Johnson 2.00
362 Ron Heller 2.00
363 Bern Brostek 2.00
364 Ronnie Lott 5.00
365 Reggie Johnson 2.00
366 *Lin Elliott* 2.00
367 Lemuel Stinson 2.00
368 William White 2.00
369 Ernie Jones 2.00
370 Tom Rathman 2.00
371 Tommy Kane 2.00
372 David Brandon 2.00
373 Lee Johnson 2.00
374 Wade Wilson 2.00
375 Nick Lowery 2.00
376 Bubba McDowell 2.00
377 *Wayne Simmons* 2.00
378 Calvin Williams 2.00
379 Courtney Hall 2.00
380 Troy Vincent 2.00
381 Tim McGee 2.00
382 *Russell Freeman* 2.00
383 Steve Tasker 2.00
384 *Michael Strahan* 2.00
385 Greg Skrepenak 2.00
386 Jake Reed 2.00
387 Pete Stoyanovich 2.00
388 *Levon Kirkland* 2.00
389 Mel Gray 2.00
390 Brian Washington 2.00
391 Don Griffin 2.00
392 Desmond Howard 5.00
393 Luis Sharpe 2.00
394 Mike Johnson 2.00
395 Andre Tippett 2.00
396 Donnell Woolford 2.00
397 *Demetrius DuBose* 5.00
398 Pat Terrell 2.00
399 Todd McNair 2.00
400 Ken Norton 2.00
401 Keith Hamilton 2.00
402 Andy Heck 2.00
403 Jeff Gossett 2.00
404 Dexter McNabb 2.00
405 Richmond Webb 2.00
406 Irving Fryar 2.00
407 Brian Hansen 2.00
408 David Little 2.00
409 *Glyn Milburn* 10.00
410 Doug Dawson 2.00
411 Scott Mersereau 2.00
412 Don Beebe 2.00
413 Vaughan Johnson 2.00
414 Jack Del Rio 2.00
415 *Darrien Gordon* 5.00
416 Mark Schlereth 2.00
417 Lomas Brown 2.00
418 William Thomas 2.00
419 James Francis 2.00
420 Quentin Coryatt 2.00
421 Tyji Armstrong 2.00
422 Hugh Millen 2.00
423 *Adrian White* 2.00
424 Eddie Anderson 2.00
425 Mark Ingram 2.00
426 Ken O'Brien 2.00
427 Simon Fletcher 2.00
428 Tim McKyer 2.00
429 Leonard Marshall 2.00
430 Eric Green 2.00
431 Leonard Harris 2.00
432 *Darin Jordan* 2.00
433 Erik Howard 2.00
434 David Lang 2.00
435 Eric Turner 2.00
436 Michael Cofer 2.00
437 Jeff Bryant 2.00
438 Charles McRae 2.00
439 Henry Jones 2.00
440 Joe Montana 100.00
441 Morten Andersen 2.00
442 Jeff Jaeger 2.00
443 Leslie O'Neal 2.00
444 Leroy Butler 2.00
445 Steve Jordan 2.00
446 Brad Edwards 2.00
447 J.B. Brown 2.00
448 Kerry Cash 2.00
449 Mark Tuinei 2.00
450 Rodney Peete 2.00
451 Sheldon White 2.00
452 Wesley Carroll 2.00
453 Brad Baxter 2.00
454 Mike Pitts 2.00
455 Greg Montgomery 2.00
456 Kenny Davidson 2.00
457 Scott Fulhage 2.00
458 Greg Townsend 2.00
459 Rod Bernstine 2.00
460 Gary Clark 2.00
461 Hardy Nickerson 2.00
462 Sean Landeta 2.00
463 Rob Burnett 2.00
464 Fred Barnett 2.00
465 John L. Williams 2.00
466 Anthony Miller 5.00
467 Roman Phifer 2.00
468 Rich Moran 2.00
469 *Willie Roaf* 5.00
470 William Perry 2.00
471 Marcus Allen 10.00
472 Carl Lee 2.00
473 Kurt Gouveia 2.00
474 Jarvis Williams 2.00
475 Alfred Williams 2.00
476 Mark Stepnoski 2.00
477 Steve Wallace 2.00
478 Pat Harlow 2.00
479 Chip Banks 2.00
480 Cornelius Bennett 5.00
481 *Ryan McNeil* 2.00
482 Norm Johnson 2.00
483 Dermontti Dawson 2.00
484 Dwayne White 2.00
485 Derek Russell 2.00
486 Lionel Washington 2.00
487 Eric Hill 2.00
488 *Micheal Barrow* 2.00
489 Checklist 251-375 2.00
490 Checklist 376-500 2.00
491 Emmitt Smith (MC) 75.00
492 Derrick Thomas (MC) 5.00
493 Deion Sanders (MC) 10.00
494 Randall Cunningham (MC) 5.00
495 Sterling Sharpe (MC) 5.00
496 Barry Sanders (MC) 40.00
497 Thurman Thomas (MC) 10.00
498 Brett Favre (MC) 14.00
499 Vaughan Johnson (MC) 2.00
500 Steve Young (MC) 15.00
501 Marvin Jones 2.00
502 *Reggie Brooks* 6.00
503 Eric Curry 2.00
504 Drew Bledsoe 75.00
505 Glyn Milburn 5.00
506 Jerome Bettis 15.00
507 Robert Smith 5.00
508 Dana Stubblefield 10.00
509 Tom Carter 2.00
510 Rick Mirer 20.00
511 Russell Copeland 2.00
512 *Deon Figures* 8.00
513 *Tony McGee* 5.00
514 *Derrick Lassic* 2.00
515 Everett Lindsay 2.00
516 *Derek Brown* 10.00
517 Harold Alexander 2.00
518 Tom Scott 2.00
519 *Elvis Grbac* 10.00
520 *Terry Kirby* 10.00
521 Doug Pelfrey 2.00
522 *Horace Copeland* 6.00
523 *Irv Smith* 6.00
524 *Lincoln Kennedy* 5.00
525 Jason Elam 2.00
526 *Qadry Ismail* 20.00
527 Artie Smith 2.00
528 *Tyrone Hughes* 20.00
529 Lance Gunn 2.00
530 *Vincent Brisby* 30.00
531 Patrick Robinson 2.00
532 Raghib Ismail 5.00
533 Willie Beamon 2.00
534 *Vaughn Hebron* 5.00
535 Darren Drozdov 2.00
536 *James Jett* 7.00
537 *Michael Bates* 5.00
538 Tom Rouen 2.00
539 Michael Husted 2.00
540 *Greg Robinson* 2.00
541 Carl Banks 2.00
542 Kevin Greene 2.00
543 Scott Mitchell 5.00
544 Michael Brooks 2.00
545 Shane Conlan 2.00
546 Vinny Testaverde 2.00
547 Robert Delpino 2.00
548 Bill Fralic 2.00
549 Carlton Bailey 2.00
550 Johnny Johnson 2.00

1993 Stadium Club Master Photos I

Master Photos were available through redemption cards inserted every 24 packs of Stadium Club. The redemption cards offered three Master Photos, with the entire set containing 12 players. The fronts were larger than the normal cards, but contained a gold border to reveal a standard sized card. Backs were full of text and statistics, with the player's name printed in a strip down the middle.

NM/M
Complete Set (12): 15.00
Common Player: .75
Minor Stars: 1.50
1 Barry Foster .75
2 Barry Sanders 6.00
3 Reggie Cobb .75
4 Cortez Kennedy .75
5 Steve Young 3.00
6 Ricky Watters 1.50
7 Rob Moore 1.50
8 Derrick Thomas 1.50
9 Jeff George 1.50
10 Sterling Sharpe 1.50
11 Bruce Smith .75
12 Deion Sanders 2.00

1993 Stadium Club Master Photos II

Similar to the Series I Master Photos, every 24 packs of Series II also had redemption cards that could be redeemed for three Master Photos. There were also redemption cards for complete sets. This 12-card set was 5" x 7" and contained larger than normal cards that contain gold borders to reveal the standard sized cards.

NM/M
Complete Set (12): 10.00
Common Player: .75
Minor Stars: 1.50
1 Morten Andersen .75
2 Ken Norton Jr .75
3 Clyde Simmons .75
4 Roman Phifer .75
5 Greg Townsend .75
6 Darryl Talley .75
7 Herschel Walker .75
8 Reggie White 1.50
9 Jesse Solomon .75
10 Joe Montana 5.00
11 John Taylor .75
12 Cornelius Bennett .75

1993 Stadium Club Super Teams

Twenty-eight different NFL teams had Super Team cards that were inserted into Stadium Club Series II Football. Team cards featuring division winners (Cowboys, 49ers, Lions, Bills, Oilers, Chiefs), conference championship teams (Cowboys, Bills) or Super Bowl XXVII winner (Cowboys) were redeemable for prizes. Division winners could get embossed, gold foil Stadium Club cards of that team with a division winner logo. Conference Champion cards were redeemable for 12 special embossed gold Master Photos of that team. Super Bowl cards were redeemable for a 500-card complete set of Stadium Club cards with a Super Bowl logo.

NM/M
Complete Set (28): 40.00
Common Player: 1.00
Minor Stars: 2.00
Inserted 1:24
1 Jim Harbaugh 2.00
2 David Klingler 1.00
3 Jim Kelly 2.00
4 John Elway 4.00
5 Bernie Kosar 1.00
6 Reggie Cobb 1.00
7 Eric Swann 1.00
8 Stan Humphries 1.00
9 Derrick Thomas 2.00
10 Steve Emtman 1.00
11 Emmitt Smith 5.00
12 Dan Marino 5.00
13 Randall Cunningham 2.00
14 Deion Sanders 2.00
15 Steve Young 4.00
16 Lawrence Taylor 2.00
17 Brad Baxter 1.00
18 Barry Sanders 5.00
19 Warren Moon 2.00
20 Brett Favre 5.00
21 Brent Williams 1.00
22 Howie Long 1.00
23 Cleveland Gary 1.00
24 Mark Rypien 1.00
25 Sam Mills 1.00
26 Cortez Kennedy 1.00
27 Barry Foster 1.00
28 Terry Allen 1.00

1993 Stadium Club Super Teams Division Winners

Super Team Division Winners were available to those collectors who had the Cowboys, 49ers, Lions, Bills, Oilers and Chiefs team cards and redeemed them for the team set. The cards are similar to the base cards, but contain a logo reading "Division Winner" on the front.

NM/M
Complete Bag Bills (13): 8.00
Complete Bag Chiefs (13): 10.00
Complete Bag Cowboys (13): 15.00
Complete Bag 49ers (13): 12.00
Complete Bag Lions (13): 8.00
Complete Bag Oilers (13): 8.00
Common Player: .50
B27 Mark Kelso .50
B54 Bruce Smith 1.00
B75 Jim Kelly 1.25
B107 Andre Reed 1.00
B153 Pete Metzelaars .50
B211 Nate Odomes .50
B227 Bill Brooks .50
B331 Darryl Talley .50
B383 Steve Tasker .50
B412 Don Beebe .50
B439 Henry Jones .50
B480 Cornelius Bennett .75
F29 Dana Hall .50
F52 Brent Jones .75
F76 Bill Romanowski .50
F103 Ricky Watters 1.25
F176 Kevin Fagan .50
F199 Tim McDonald .50
F208 Steve Young 3.00
F232 Jerry Rice 3.00
F275 John Taylor .75
F326 Eric Davis .50
F370 Tom Rathman .50
L7 Dennis Gibson .50
L31 Jason Hanson .50
L61 Robert Porcher .50
L120 Barry Sanders 3.00
L231 Marc Spindler .50
L263 Kelvin Pritchett .50
L295 Pat Swilling .75
L321 Ray Crockett .50
L342 Chris Spielman .50
L368 William White .50
L389 Mel Gray .75
L450 Rodney Peete .75
O20 Ernest Givins .75
O101 Warren Moon 1.25
O128 Al Smith .50
O146 Lorenzo White .75
O166 William Fuller .50
O192 Ray Childress .75
O225 Sean Jones .50
O305 Bruce Mathews .50
O329 Haywood Jeffires .75
O347 Cris Dishman .50
O376 Bubba McDowell .50
O455 Greg Montgomery .50
CH80 Dale Carter .75
CH133 Neil Smith .75
CH173 Derrick Thomas 1.00
CH203 Harvey Williams .75
CH215 Tracy Simien .50
CH268 Jonathan Hayes .50
CH289 J.J. Birden .75
CH312 Willie Davis .75
CH375 Nick Lowery .50
CH399 Todd McNair .50
CH440 Joe Montana 3.00
CH471 Marcus Allen .75
CO17 Alvin Harper .75
CO50 Troy Aikman 3.00
CO85 Emmitt Smith 5.00
CO106 Daryl Johnston .75
CO129 Michael Irvin 1.50
CO152 Charles Haley .75
CO174 Jay Novacek .75
CO204 Russell Maryland .50
CO278 Kevin Williams (WR) 1.00
CO299 Kevin Smith .50
CO325 Robert Jones .50
CO400 Ken Norton Jr .50
DW3 Jim Kelly Bills Super Team DW 1.00
DW9 Derrick Thomas Chiefs Super Team DW 1.00
DW11 Emmitt Smith Cowboys Super Team DW 3.00
DW15 Steve Young 49ers Super Team DW 1.75
DW18 Barry Sanders Lions Super Team DW 1.75
DW19 Warren Moon Oilers Super Team DW 1.00

1993 Stadium Club Super Teams Conference Winners

Super Team Division Winners were available to those collectors who redeemed their 1993 Super Team cards of Cowboys or Bills. Collectors received a 12-card set stamped with a gold foil conference logo, as well as a Master Photo set of the team. The cards are similar to base cards in Stadium Club, except for the conference champions logo on the front.

NM/M
Complete Bag Bills (13): 7.00
Complete Bag Cowboys (13): 15.00
Common Player: .50
B27 Mark Kelso .50
B54 Bruce Smith 1.00
B75 Jim Kelly 1.25
B107 Andre Reed 1.00
B153 Pete Metzelaars .50
B211 Nate Odomes .50
B227 Bill Brooks .50
B331 Darryl Talley .50
B383 Steve Tasker .50
B412 Don Beebe .50
B439 Henry Jones .50
B480 Cornelius Bennett .75
CO17 Alvin Harper .75
CO50 Troy Aikman 3.00
CO85 Emmitt Smith 5.00
CO106 Daryl Johnston .75
CO129 Michael Irvin 1.50
CO152 Charles Haley .75
CO174 Jay Novacek .75
CO204 Russell Maryland .50
CO278 Kevin Williams (WR) 1.50
CO299 Kevin Smith .50
CO325 Robert Jones .50
CO400 Ken Norton Jr. .50
CW3 Emmitt Smith Cowboys Super Team CW 3.00
CW11 Jim Kelly Bills Super Team CW 1.00

1993 Stadium Club Super Team Master Photos

Super Team Master Photos were available to those collectors with either a Bills or Cowboys Super Team card. Along with a specially stamped team set, collectors also received these 5" x 7", uncropped Master Photos. The sets arrived in a bag and had blank backs and either a gold foil "N" for NFC or "A" for AFC edged by stars beneath the player photo.

NM/M
Complete Bag Bills (12): 10.00
Complete Bag Cowboys (12): 20.00
Common Player: .75
B1 Don Beebe .75
B2 Cornelius Bennett 1.00
B3 Bill Brooks .75
B4 Henry Jones .75
B5 Jim Kelly 1.50
B6 Mark Kelso .75
B7 Pete Metzelaars .75
B8 Nate Odomes .75
B9 Andre Reed 1.25
B10 Bruce Smith 1.25
B11 Darryl Talley .75
B12 Steve Tasker .75
CO1 Troy Aikman 4.00
CO2 Charles Haley 1.00
CO3 Alvin Harper 1.00
CO4 Michael Irvin 2.00
CO5 Daryl Johnston 1.00
CO6 Robert Jones .75
CO7 Russell Maryland .75
CO8 Ken Norton Jr .75
CO9 Jay Novacek 1.00
CO10 Emmitt Smith 7.50
CO11 Kevin Smith .75
CO12 Kevin Williams (WR) 2.00

1993 Stadium Club Super Teams Super Bowl

Collectors holding the Cowboys Super Team card from 1993 Stadium Club could redeem that card for a 500-card Stadium Club set stamped with a gold foil Super Bowl XXVIII logo stamped on the front. The set arrived with the redeemed Super Team Cowboys card that also has a Super Bowl logo.

NM/M
Complete Set (501): 75.00
Common Player: .15
Semistars: .30
SB3 Emmitt Smith Cowboys Super Team SB 4.00

1993 Stadium Club Members Only

Only Stadium Club members could purchase this 579-card set from Topps that included the entire 550-card Stadium Club set, along with 28 Super Teams and a signed Jerry Rice Record Breaker card. Production was limited to 10,000 factory sets, with each costing $199. The cards are identical to the regular-issue cards, except for a gold-foil "Members Only" logo.

	NM/M
Complete Set (579):	200.00
Common Player (1-550):	.20
Semistars:	.40
NNO Jerry Rice (RB Auto) (signed card)	50.00

1994 Stadium Club

Stadium Club Football Series I contains 270 cards, including several new subsets, like Chalk Talk, Chain Gang, Great Expectations and Topps Best cards. Chalk Talk (221-229) offers players that frequently move the chains. Chalk Talk cards (71-74) display photographs on the fronts and illustrations on the backs. Great Expectations (182-190) highlight the best rookies of 1993, while Topps Best utilizes Topps Finest technology to showcase the top players at each position. Topps Stadium Club Football also has a three-card insert set called Dynasty and Destiny, as well as 1st Day Production and Super Team cards. Stadium Club cards have a borderless, high-gloss look on the front with the players name centered on the bottom. The backs feature a shot of the player and statistics. Series II also had 270 cards (#s 271-540) and three insert sets. 1st Day Production cards were once again offered in Series II packs. Two new insert sets - Ring Leaders and Frequent Scorers - were also produced. A 90-card High series was also issued, featuring rookies and veterans in their NFL 75th anniversary throwback uniforms. Each card is also available in a parallel 1st Day Issue set, seeded one per every 12 packs. Three insert sets were also made, utilizing Finest's chromium technology. The sets are Bowman's Best Black (veteran stars), Bowman's Best Blue (Rookies) and Bowman's Best Mirror Images (veteran and a rookie on the same card). These three insert types were each seeded at a rate of one per every three packs. A parallel Bowman's Refractors set of the 45 cards was also made; they were seeded one per every 12 packs. In addition, each 24th pack contained one of six Expansion Team Redemption cards - offense, defense or special teams - for the Carolina Panthers and Jacksonville Jaguars. The cards entitled the finders to a 22-card Topps Finest set of the players for the team depicted on the redemption card, or both teams.

	NM/M
Complete Set (630):	50.00
Complete Series 1 (270):	30.00
Complete Series 2 (270):	25.00
Complete High Series (90):	15.00
Common Player:	.10
Minor Stars:	.20
First Day Cards:	3X-5X
First Day Rookies:	2X-4X
Inserted 1:24	
Series 1 Pack(12):	1.25
Series 1 Wax Box (24):	20.00
Series 2 Pack (12):	1.00
Series 2 Wax Box (24):	15.00
Series 3 Pack (10):	1.00
Series 3 Wax Box (24):	15.00

No.	Player	Price
1	*Dan Wilkinson*	.20
2	Chip Lohmiller	.10
3	Roosevelt Potts	.10
4	Martin Mayhew	.10
5	Shane Conlan	.10
6	*Sam Adams*	.20
7	Mike Kenn	.10
8	Tim Goad	.10
9	Tony Jones	.10
10	Ron Moore	.25
11	Mark Bortz	.10
12	Darren Carrington	.10
13	Eric Martin	.10
14	Eric Allen	.10
15	*Aaron Glenn*	.25
16	Bryan Cox	.10
17	Levon Kirkland	.10
18	Qadry Ismail	.20
19	Shane Dronett	.10
20	Chris Spielman	.10
21	*Rob Fredrickson*	.20
22	Wayne Simmons	.10
23	*Glenn Montgomery*	.20
24	*Jason Sehorn*	.20
25	Nick Lowery	.10
26	Dennis Brown	.10
27	Kenneth Davis	.10
28	*Shante Carver*	.25
29	*Ryan Yarborough*	.20
30	Cortez Kennedy	.20
31	Anthony Pleasant	.10
32	Jessie Tuggle	.10
33	Herschel Walker	.20
34	Andre Collins	.10
35	*William Floyd*	.50
36	Harold Green	.10
37	Courtney Hawkins	.10
38	Curtis Conway	.20
39	Ben Coates	.20
40	Natrone Means	.50
41	Eric Hill	.10
42	Keith Kartz	.10
43	Alexander Wright	.10
44	William Roaf	.10
45	Vencie Glenn	.10
46	Ronnie Lott, David Lutz	.10
47	George Koonce, Kelvin Martin	.10
48	Rod Woodson	.20
49	Tim Grunhard	.10
50	Cody Carlson	.10
51	*Bryant Young*	.75
52	Jay Novacek	.10
53	Darryl Talley	.10
54	Gary Anderson, Harry Colon	.10
55	David Meggett	.10
56	*Aubrey Beavers*	.25
57	James Folston	.10
58	Willie Davis	.10
59	Jason Elam	.10
60	Eric Metcalf	.10
61	Bruce Armstrong	.10
62	Ron Heller	.10
63	LeRoy Butler	.10
64	Terry Obee	.10
65	Kurt Gouveia	.10
66	Pierce Holt	.10
67	David Alexander	.10
68	*Deral Boykin*	.20
69	Carl Pickens	.10
70	Broderick Thomas	.10
71	Barry Sanders	1.25
72	Qadry Ismail	.20
73	Thurman Thomas	.25
74	Junior Seau, Bob Dahl	.10
75	Vinny Testaverde	.10
76	Tyrone Hughes	.10
77	Nate Newton	.10
78	Eric Swann	.10
79	Brad Baxter	.10
80	Dana Stubblefield	.10
81	John Elliott	.10
82	Steve Wisniewski	.10
83	Eddie Robinson	.10
84	*Isaac Davis*	.20
85	Cris Carter	.20
86	Mel Gray	.10
87	Cornelius Bennett	.10
88	Neil O'Donnell	.20
89	Jon Hand	.10
90	John Elway	.75
91	Bill Hitchcock	.10
92	Neil Smith	.10
93	*Joe Johnson*	.20
94	Edgar Bennett	.10
95	Vincent Brown	.10
96	Tommy Vardell	.10
97	Donnell Woolford	.10
98	Lincoln Kennedy	.10
99	O.J. McDuffie	.50
100	*Heath Shuler*	.50
101	Jerry Rice	1.00
102	Eric Williams	.10
103	Randall McDaniel	.10
104	Dermontti Dawson	.10
105	Nate Newton	.10
106	Harris Barton	.10
107	Shannon Sharpe	.20
108	Sterling Sharpe	.20
109	Steve Young	1.00
110	Emmitt Smith	2.00
111	Thurman Thomas	.20
112	Kyle Clifton	.10
113	Desmond Howard	.20
114	Quinn Early	.10
115	David Klingler	.10
116	Bern Brostek	.10
117	Gary Clark	.10
118	Courtney Hall	.10
119	*Joe King*	.10
120	Quentin Coryatt	.10
121	*Johnnie Morton*	.50
122	Andre Reed	.20
123	Eric Davis	.10
124	Jack Del Rio	.10
125	Greg Lloyd	.10
126	Bubba McDowell	.10
127	Mark Jackson	.10
128	Jeff Jaeger	.10
129	Chris Warren	.20
130	Tom Waddle	.10
131	Tony Smith	.10
132	Todd Collins	.10
133	Mark Bavaro	.10
134	Joe Phillips	.10
135	Chris Jacke	.10
136	Glyn Milburn	.20
137	Keith Jackson	.10
138	Steve Tovar	.10
139	Tim Johnson	.10
140	Brian Washington	.10
141	Troy Drayton	.10
142	*DeWayne Washington*	.25
143	Eric Williams	.10
144	Eric Turner	.10
145	John Taylor	.20
146	Richard Cooper	.10
147	*Van Malone*	.10
148	*Tim Ruddy*	.20
149	Henry Jones	.10
150	Tim Brown	.20
151	Stan Humphries	.20
152	Harry Newsome	.10
153	Craig Erickson	.20
154	Gary Anderson	.10
155	Ray Childress	.10
156	Howard Cross	.10
157	Heath Sherman	.10
158	Terrell Buckley	.10
159	J.B. Brown	.10
160	Joe Montana	2.50
161	David Wyman	.10
162	Norm Johnson	.10
163	Rod Stephens	.10
164	*Willie McGinest*	.50
165	Barry Sanders	2.50
166	Marc Logan	.10
167	Anthony Newman	.10
168	Russell Maryland	.10
169	Luis Sharpe	.10
170	Jim Kelly	.25
171	*Tre' Johnson*	.10
172	Johnny Mitchell	.10
173	*David Palmer*	.50
174	Bob Dahl	.10
175	Aaron Wallace	.10
176	Chris Gardocki	.10
177	Hardy Nickerson	.10
178	Jeff Query	.10
179	Leslie O'Neal	.10
180	Kevin Greene	.10
181	Alonzo Spellman	.10
182	Reggie Brooks	.10
183	Dana Stubblefield	.10
184	Tyrone Hughes	.10
185	Drew Bledsoe	1.00
186	Ron Moore	.20
187	Jason Elam	.10
188	Rick Mirer	.50
189	William Roaf	.10
190	Jerome Bettis	.50
191	Brad Hopkins	.10
192	Derek Brown	.10
193	Nolan Harrison	.10
194	Jon Randle	.10
195	Carlton Bailey	.10
196	Kevin Williams	.25
197	*Greg Hill*	1.00
198	Mark McMillian	.10
199	Brad Edwards	.10
200	Dan Marino	4.00
201	Ricky Watters	.20
202	George Teague	.10
203	Steve Beuerlein	.10
204	*Jeff Burris*	.20
205	Steve Atwater	.10
206	*John Thierry*	.50
207	Patrick Hunter	.10
208	*Wayne Gandy*	.10
209	Derrick Moore	.10
210	Phil Simms	.10
211	Kirk Lowdermilk	.10
212	Patrick Robinson	.10
213	Kevin Mitchell	.10
214	Jonathan Hayes	.10
215	Michael Dean Perry	.10
216	John Fina	.10
217	Anthony Smith	.10
218	Paul Gruber	.10
219	Carnell Lake	.10
220	Carl Lee	.10
221	Steve Christie	.10
222	Greg Montgomery	.10
223	Reggie Brooks	.10
224	Derrick Thomas	.20
225	Eric Metcalf	.10
226	Michael Haynes	.10
227	Bobby Hebert	.10
228	Tyrone Hughes	.10
229	Donald Frank	.10
230	Vaughan Johnson	.10
231	Eric Thomas	.10
232	Ernest Givins	.10
233	Charles Haley	.10
234	Darrell Green	.10
235	Harold Alexander	.10
236	Dwayne Sabb	.10
237	Harris Barton	.10
238	Randall Cunningham	.20
239	Ray Buchanan	.10
240	Sterling Sharpe	.20
241	Chris Mims	.10
242	Mark Carrier	.10
243	Ricky Proehl	.10
244	Michael Brooks	.10
245	Sean Gilbert	.10
246	David Lutz	.10
247	Kelvin Martin	.10
248	*Scottie Graham*	.50
249	Irving Fryar	.10
250	Ricardo McDonald	.10
251	Marvcus Patton	.10
252	*Errict Rhett*	1.00
253	Winston Moss	.10
254	Rod Vernstine	.10
255	Terry Wooden	.10
256	*Antonio Langham*	.50
257	Tommy Barnhardt	.10
258	Marvin Washington	.10
259	Bo Orlando	.10
260	Marcus Allen	.20
261	*Mario Bates*	.25
262	Marco Coleman	.10
263	Doug Riesenberg	.10
264	Jesse Sapolu	.10
265	Dermontti Dawson	.10
266	*Fernando Smith*	.20
267	David Szott	.10
268	Steve Christie	.10
269	Bruce Matthews	.10
270	Michael Irvin	.50
271	Seth Joyner	.10
272	Santana Dotson	.10
273	Vincent Brisby	.50
274	Rohn Stark	.10
275	John Copeland	.10
276	Toby Wright	.10
277	David Griggs	.10
278	*Aaron Taylor*	.20
279	Chris Doleman	.10
280	Reggie Brooks	.10
281	Willie Anderson	.10
282	Alvin Harper	.20
283	Chris Hinton	.10
284	Kelvin Pritchett	.10
285	Russell Copeland	.10
286	Dwight Stone	.10
287	Jeff Gossett	.10
288	Larry Allen	.10
289	Kevin Mawae	.10
290	Mark Collins	.10
291	Chris Zorich	.10
292	Vince Buck	.10
293	Gene Atkins	.10
294	Webster Slaughter	.10
295	Steve Young	1.50
296	Dan Williams	.10
297	Jesse Armstead	.10
298	Victor Bailey	.10
299	John Carney	.10
300	Emmitt Smith	4.00
301	*Bucky Brooks*	.50
302	Mo Lewis	.10
303	Eugene Daniel	.10
304	Tyji Armstrong	.10
305	Eugene Chung	.10
306	Raghib Ismail	.20
307	Sean Jones	.10
308	Rick Cunningham	.10
309	Ken Harvey	.10
310	Jeff George	.20
311	Jon Vaughn	.10
312	Roy Barker	.10
313	Micheal Barrow	.10
314	Ryan McNeil	.10
315	Pete Stoyanovich	.10
316	Darryl Williams	.10
317	Renaldo Turnbull	.10
318	Eric Green	.10
319	Nate Lewis	.10
320	Mike Flores	.10
321	Derek Russell	.10
322	Marcus Spears	.10
323	Corey Miller	.10
324	Derrick Thomas	.20
325	Steve Everitt	.10
326	Brent Jones	.10
327	*Marshall Faulk*	8.00
328	Don Beebe	.10
329	Harry Swayne	.10
330	Boomer Esiason	.10
331	Don Mosebar	.10
332	*Isaac Bruce*	5.00
333	Rickey Jackson	.10
334	Daryl Johnston	.10
335	Lorenzo Lynch	.10
336	Brian Blades	.10
337	Michael Timpson	.10
338	Reggie Cobb	.10
339	Joe Walter	.10
340	Barry Foster	.20
341	Richmond Webb	.10
342	Pat Swilling	.10
343	Shaun Gayle	.10
344	Reggie Roby	.10
345	Chris Calloway	.10
346	Doug Dawson	.10
347	Rob Burnett	.10
348	Dana Hall	.10
349	Horace Copeland	.10
350	Shannon Sharpe	.20
351	Rich Miano	.10
352	Henry Thomas	.10
353	Dan Saleaumua	.10
354	Kevin Ross	.10
355	Morten Andersen	.10
356	Anthony Blaylock	.10
357	Stanley Richard	.10
358	Albert Lewis	.10
359	Darren Woodson	.10
360	Drew Bledsoe	2.00
361	Eric Mahlum	.10
362	*Trent Dilfer*	3.00
363	William Roberts	.10
364	Robert Brooks	.10
365	Jason Hanson	.10
366	Troy Vincent	.10
367	William Thomas	.10
368	Lonnie Johnson	.10
369	*Jamir Miller*	.20
370	Michael Jackson	.10
371	*Charlie Ward*	1.25
372	Shannon Sharpe	.20
373	Jackie Slater	.10
374	Steve Young	.20
375	Bobby Wilson	.10
376	Paul Frase	.10
377	Dale Carter	.10
378	Robert Delpino	.10
379	*Bert Emanuel*	1.00
380	Rick Mirer	.50
381	Carlos Jenkins	.10
382	Gary Brown	.10
383	Doug Pelfrey	.10
384	Dexter Carter	.10
385	Chris Miller	.10
386	*Charles Johnson*	1.00
387	James Joseph	.10
388	Darrin Smith	.10
389	James Jett	.10
390	Junior Seau	.20
391	Chris Slade	.10
392	Jim Harbaugh	.10
393	Herman Moore	.75
394	Thomas Randolph	.10
395	Lamar Thomas	.10
396	Reggie Rivers	.10
397	Larry Centers	.10
398	Chad Brown	.10
399	Terry Kirby	.20
400	Bruce Smith	.10
401	*Keenan McCardell*	2.00
402	Tim McDonald	.10
403	Robert Smith	.10
404	Matt Brock	.10
405	Tony McGee	.10
406	Ethan Horton	.10
407	Michael Haynes	.10
408	Steve Jackson	.10
409	Erik Kramer	.10
410	Jerome Bettis	1.00
411	D.J. Johnson	.10
412	John Alt	.10
413	Jeff Lageman	.10
414	Rick Tuten	.10
415	Jeff Robinson	.10
416	*Kevin Lee*	.20
417	*Thomas Lewis*	.20
418	Kerry Cash	.10
419	*Chuck Levy*	.20
420	Mark Ingram	.10
421	Dennis Gibson	.10
422	Tyronne Drakeford	.10
423	James Washington	.10
424	Dante Jones	.10
425	Eugene Robinson	.10
426	Johnny Johnson	.10
427	Brian Mitchell	.10
428	Charles Mincy	.10
429	Mark Carrier	.10
430	Vince Workman	.10
431	James Francis	.10
432	Clay Matthews	.10
433	Randall McDaniel	.10
434	Brad Ottis	.10
435	Bruce Smith	.10
436	Cortez Kennedy	.20
437	John Randle	.10
438	Neil Smith	.10
439	Cornelius Bennett	.10
440	Junior Seau	.20
441	Derrick Thomas	.20
442	Rod Woodson	.20
443	Terry McDaniel	.10
444	Tim McDonald	.10
445	Mark Carrier	.10
446	Irv Smith	.10
447	Steve Wallace	.10
448	Cris Dishman	.10
449	Bill Brooks	.10
450	Jeff Hostetler	.10
451	Brentson Buckner	.10
452	Ken Ruettgers	.10
453	Marc Boutte	.10
454	John Offerdahl	.10
455	Allen Aldridge	.10
456	Steve Emtman	.10
457	Andre Rison	.20
458	Shawn Jefferson	.10
459	*Todd Steussie*	.20
460	Scott Mitchell	.20
461	Tom Carter	.10
462	*Donnell Bennett*	.20
463	James Jones	.10
464	Antone Davis	.10
465	Jim Everett	.10
466	Tony Tolbert	.10
467	Merril Hoge	.10
468	Michael Bates	.10
469	Phil Hansen	.10
470	Rodney Hampton	.20
471	Aeneas Williams	.10
472	Al Del Greco	.10
473	Todd Lyght	.10
474	Joel Steed	.10
475	Merton Hanks	.10
476	Tony Stargell	.10
477	Greg Robinson	.10
478	Roger Duffy	.10
479	Simon Fletcher	.10
480	Reggie White	.20
481	Lee Johnson	.10
482	Wayne Martin	.10
483	Thurman Thomas	.20
484	Warren Moon	.20
485	Sam Rogers	.10
486	Erric Pegram	.10
487	Will Wolford	.10
488	Duane Young	.10
489	Keith Hamilton	.10
490	Haywood Jeffires	.10
491	Trace Armstrong	.10
492	J.J. Birden	.10
493	Ricky Ervins	.10
494	Robert Blackmon	.10
495	William Perry	.10
496	Robert Massey	.10
497	Jim Jeffcoat	.10
498	Pat Harlow	.10
499	Jeff Cross	.10
500	Jerry Rice	1.25
501	*Darnay Scott*	1.00
502	Clyde Simmons	.10
503	Henry Rolling	.10
504	James Hasty	.10
505	Leroy Thompson	.10
506	Darrell Thompson	.10
507	Tim Bowens	.10
508	Gerald Perry	.10
509	Mike Croel	.10
510	Sam Mills	.10
511	Steve Young	.50
512	Hardy Nickerson	.10
513	Cris Carter	.20
514	Boomer Esiason	.10
515	Bruce Smith	.10
516	Emmitt Smith	2.00
517	Eugene Robinson	.10
518	Gary Brown	.10
519	Jerry Rice	.75
520	Troy Aikman	1.00
521	Marcus Allen	.20
522	Junior Seau	.20
523	Sterling Sharpe	.20
524	Dana Stubblefield	.10
525	Tom Carter	.10
526	Pete Metzelaars	.10
527	Russell Freeman	.10
528	Keith Cash	.10
529	Willie Drewrey	.10
530	Randal Hill	.10
531	Pepper Johnson	.10
532	Rob Moore	.20
533	Todd Kelly	.10
534	Keith Byars	.10
535	Mike Fox	.10
536	Brett Favre	4.00
537	Terry McDaniel	.10
538	Darren Perry	.10
539	Maurice Hurst	.10
540	Troy Aikman	2.00
541	Junior Seau	.20
542	Steve Broussard	.10
543	Lorenzo White	.10
544	Terry McDaniel	.10
545	Henry Thomas	.10
546	Tyrone Hughes	.10
547	Mark Collins	.10
548	Gary Anderson	.10
549	Darrell Green	.10
550	Jerry Rice	1.50
551	Cornelius Bennett	.10
552	Aeneas Williams	.10
553	Eric Metcalf	.10
554	John Elliott	.10
555	Mo Lewis	.10
556	Darren Carrington	.10
557	Kevin Greene	.10
558	John Elway	.50
559	Eugene Robinson	.10
560	Drew Bledsoe	2.00
561	Fred Barnett	.10
562	*Bernie Parmalee*	1.00
563	Bryce Paup	.10
564	Donnell Woolford	.10
565	Terance Mathis	.20
566	Santana Dotson	.10
567	Randall McDaniel	.10
568	Stanley Richard	.10
569	Brian Blades	.10
570	Jerome Bettis	1.00
571	Neil Smith	.10
572	Andre Reed	.20
573	Michael Bankston	.10
574	Dana Stubblefield	.10
575	Rod Woodson	.20
576	Ken Harvey	.10
577	Andre Rison	.20
578	Darion Conner	.10
579	Michael Strahan	.10
580	Barry Sanders	2.00
581	Pepper Johnson	.10
582	Lewis Tillman	.10
583	Jeff George	.20
584	Michael Haynes	.10
585	Herschel Walker	.20
586	Tim Brown	.20
587	Jim Kelly	.20
588	Ricky Watters	.20
589	Randall Cunningham	.20
590	Troy Aikman	2.00
591	Ken Norton	.10
592	Cortez Kennedy	.20
593	Ricky Ervins	.10
594	Cris Carter	.20
595	Sterling Sharpe	.20
596	John Randle	.10
597	Shannon Sharpe	.20
598	*Ray Crittenden*	.20
599	Barry Foster	.25
600	Deion Sanders	1.00
601	Seth Joyner	.10
602	Chris Warren	.20
603	Tom Rathman	.10
604	Brett Favre	3.00
605	Marshall Faulk	2.00
606	Terry Allen	.10
607	Ben Coates	.50
608	Brian Washington	.10
609	Henry Ellard	.10
610	David Meggett	.10
611	Stan Humphries	.20
612	Warren Moon	.20
613	Marcus Allen	.20
614	Ed McDaniel	.10
615	Joe Montana	2.00
616	Jeff Hostetler	.10
617	Johnny Johnson	.10
618	Andre Coleman	.10
619	Willie Davis	.10
620	Rick Mirer	.50
621	Dan Marino	3.00
622	Rob Moore	.20
623	*Byron Morris*	.50
624	Natrone Means	.50
625	Steve Young	1.00
626	Jim Everett	.10
627	Michael Brooks	.10
628	Dermontti Dawson	.10
629	Reggie White	.20
630	Emmitt Smith	2.50

A card number in parenthese ( ) indicates the set is unnumbered.

1994 Stadium Club First Day Cards

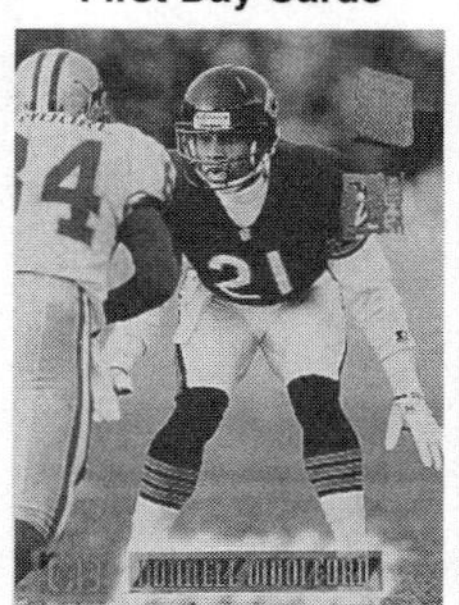

First Day Issues parallel cards were inserted one per 12 packs, and parallel the 630-card base set. The cards are distinguished by a gold foil "First Day" stamp on front.

	NM/M
Complete Set (630):	3,000
Complete Series 1 (270):	1,200
Complete Series 2 (270):	1,200
Complete High Series (90):	600.00
Common Player:	2.00
Minor Stars:	5.00
Unlisted Stars:	12X-25X

#	Player	Price
1	*Dan Wilkinson*	10.00
2	Chip Lohmiller	2.00
3	Roosevelt Potts	2.00
4	Martin Mayhew	2.00
5	Shane Conlan	2.00
6	*Sam Adams*	8.00
7	Mike Kenn	2.00
8	Tim Goad	2.00
9	Tony Jones	2.00
10	Ron Moore	8.00
11	Mark Bortz	2.00
12	Darren Carrington	2.00
13	Eric Martin	2.00
14	Eric Allen	2.00
15	*Aaron Glenn*	6.00
16	Bryan Cox	2.00
17	Levon Kirkland	2.00
18	Qadry Ismail	5.00
19	Shane Dronett	2.00
20	Chris Spielman	2.00
21	*Rob Fredrickson*	8.00
22	Wayne Simmons	2.00
23	*Glenn Montgomery*	5.00
24	*Jason Sehorn*	5.00
25	Nick Lowery	2.00
26	Dennis Brown	2.00
27	Kenneth Davis	2.00
28	*Shante Carver*	5.00
29	*Ryan Yarborough*	7.00
30	Cortez Kennedy	5.00
31	Anthony Pleasant	2.00
32	Jessie Tuggle	2.00
33	Herschel Walker	5.00
34	Andre Collins	2.00
35	*William Floyd*	40.00
36	Harold Green	2.00
37	Courtney Hawkins	2.00
38	Curtis Conway	5.00
39	Ben Coates	5.00
40	Natrone Means	45.00
41	Eric Hill	2.00
42	Keith Kartz	2.00
43	Alexander Wright	2.00
44	William Roaf	2.00
45	Vencie Glenn	2.00
46	Ronnie Lott, David Lutz	2.00
47	George Koonce, Kelvin Martin	2.00
48	Rod Woodson	5.00
49	Tim Grunhard	2.00
50	Cody Carlson	2.00
51	*Bryant Young*	18.00
52	Jay Novacek	2.00
53	Darryl Talley	2.00
54	Gary Anderson, Harry Colon	2.00
55	David Meggett	2.00
56	*Aubrey Beavers*	5.00
57	James Folston	2.00
58	Willie Davis	2.00
59	Jason Elam	2.00
60	Eric Metcalf	2.00
61	Bruce Armstrong	2.00
62	Ron Heller	2.00
63	LeRoy Butler	2.00
64	Terry Obee	2.00
65	Kurt Gouveia	2.00
66	Pierce Holt	2.00
67	David Alexander	2.00
68	*Deral Boykin*	2.00
69	Carl Pickens	2.00
70	Broderick Thomas	2.00
71	Barry Sanders	25.00
72	Qadry Ismail	5.00
73	Thurman Thomas	8.00
74	Junior Seau, Bob Dahl	2.00
75	Vinny Testaverde	2.00
76	Tyrone Hughes	2.00
77	Nate Newton	2.00
78	Eric Swann	2.00
79	Brad Baxter	2.00
80	Dana Stubblefield	2.00
81	John Elliott	2.00
82	Steve Wisniewski	2.00
83	Eddie Robinson	2.00
84	*Isaac Davis*	5.00
85	Cris Carter	5.00
86	Mel Gray	2.00
87	Cornelius Bennett	2.00
88	Neil O'Donnell	5.00
89	Jon Hand	2.00
90	John Elway	20.00
91	Bill Hitchcock	2.00
92	Neil Smith	2.00
93	*Joe Johnson*	2.00
94	Edgar Bennett	2.00
95	Vincent Brown	5.00
96	Tommy Vardell	2.00
97	Donnell Woolford	2.00
98	Lincoln Kennedy	2.00
99	O.J. McDuffie	10.00
100	*Heath Shuler*	12.00
101	Jerry Rice	25.00
102	Eric Williams	2.00
103	Randall McDaniel	2.00
104	Dermontti Dawson	2.00
105	Nate Newton	2.00
106	Harris Barton	2.00
107	Shannon Sharpe	5.00
108	Sterling Sharpe	5.00
109	Steve Young	25.00
110	Emmitt Smith	45.00
111	Thurman Thomas	7.00
112	Kyle Clifton	2.00
113	Desmond Howard	2.00
114	Quinn Early	2.00
115	David Klingler	2.00
116	Bern Brostek	2.00
117	Gary Clark	2.00
118	Courtney Hall	2.00
119	*Joe King*	2.00
120	Quentin Coryatt	2.00
121	*Johnnie Morton*	6.00
122	Andre Reed	5.00
123	Eric Davis	2.00
124	Jack Del Rio	2.00
125	Greg Lloyd	2.00
126	Bubba McDowell	2.00
127	Mark Jackson	2.00
128	Jeff Jaeger	2.00
129	Chris Warren	5.00
130	Tom Waddle	2.00
131	Tony Smith	2.00
132	Todd Collins	2.00
133	Mark Bavaro	2.00
134	Joe Phillips	2.00
135	Chris Jacke	2.00
136	Glyn Milburn	5.00
137	Keith Jackson	2.00
138	Steve Tovar	2.00
139	Tim Johnson	2.00
140	Brian Washington	2.00
141	Troy Drayton	2.00
142	*DeWayne Washington*	5.00
143	Eric Williams	2.00
144	Eric Turner	2.00
145	John Taylor	5.00
146	Richard Cooper	2.00
147	*Van Malone*	2.00
148	*Tim Ruddy*	2.00
149	Henry Jones	2.00
150	Tim Brown	5.00
151	Stan Humphries	5.00
152	Harry Newsome	2.00
153	Craig Erickson	5.00
154	Gary Anderson	2.00
155	Ray Childress	2.00
156	Howard Cross	2.00
157	Heath Sherman	2.00
158	Terrell Buckley	2.00
159	J.B. Brown	2.00
160	Joe Montana	60.00
161	David Wyman	2.00
162	Norm Johnson	2.00
163	Rod Stephens	2.00
164	*Willie McGinest*	5.00
165	Barry Sanders	50.00
166	Marc Logan	2.00
167	Anthony Newman	2.00
168	Russell Maryland	2.00
169	Luis Sharpe	2.00
170	Jim Kelly	8.00
171	*Tre' Johnson*	2.00
172	Johnny Mitchell	2.00
173	*David Palmer*	6.00
174	Bob Dahl	2.00
175	Aaron Wallace	2.00
176	Chris Gardocki	2.00
177	Hardy Nickerson	2.00
178	Jeff Query	2.00
179	Leslie O'Neal	2.00
180	Kevin Greene	2.00
181	Alonzo Spellman	2.00
182	Reggie Brooks	2.00
183	Dana Stubblefield	2.00
184	Tyrone Hughes	2.00
185	Drew Bledsoe	35.00
186	Ron Moore	5.00
187	Jason Elam	2.00
188	Rick Mirer	15.00
189	William Roaf	2.00
190	Jerome Bettis	15.00
191	Brad Hopkins	2.00
192	Derek Brown	2.00
193	Nolan Harrison	2.00
194	Jon Randle	2.00
195	Carlton Bailey	2.00
196	Kevin Williams	5.00
197	*Greg Hill*	25.00
198	Mark McMillian	2.00
199	Brad Edwards	2.00
200	Dan Marino	90.00
201	Ricky Watters	5.00
202	George Teague	2.00
203	Steve Beuerlein	2.00
204	*Jeff Burris*	8.00
205	Steve Atwater	2.00
206	*John Thierry*	5.00
207	Patrick Hunter	2.00
208	*Wayne Gandy*	2.00
209	Derrick Moore	2.00
210	Phil Simms	2.00
211	Kirk Lowdermilk	2.00
212	Patrick Robinson	2.00
213	Kevin Mitchell	2.00
214	Jonathan Hayes	2.00
215	Michael Dean Perry	2.00
216	John Fina	2.00
217	Anthony Smith	2.00
218	Paul Gruber	2.00
219	Carnell Lake	2.00
220	Carl Lee	2.00
221	Steve Christie	2.00
222	Greg Montgomery	2.00
223	Reggie Brooks	2.00
224	Derrick Thomas	5.00
225	Eric Metcalf	2.00
226	Michael Haynes	2.00
227	Bobby Hebert	2.00
228	Tyrone Hughes	2.00
229	Donald Frank	2.00
230	Vaughan Johnson	2.00
231	Eric Thomas	2.00
232	Ernest Givins	2.00
233	Charles Haley	2.00
234	Darrell Green	2.00
235	Harold Alexander	2.00
236	Dwayne Sabb	2.00
237	Harris Barton	2.00
238	Randall Cunningham	6.00
239	Ray Buchanan	2.00
240	Sterling Sharpe	10.00
241	Chris Mims	2.00
242	Mark Carrier	2.00
243	Ricky Proehl	2.00
244	Michael Brooks	2.00
245	Sean Gilbert	2.00
246	David Lutz	2.00
247	Kelvin Martin	2.00
248	*Scottie Graham*	5.00
249	Irving Fryar	2.00
250	Ricardo McDonald	2.00
251	Marvcus Patton	2.00
252	*Errict Rhett*	40.00
253	Winston Moss	2.00
254	Rod Vernstine	2.00
255	Terry Wooden	2.00
256	*Antonio Langham*	10.00
257	Tommy Barnhardt	2.00
258	Marvin Washington	2.00
259	Bo Orlando	2.00
260	Marcus Allen	5.00
261	*Mario Bates*	30.00
262	Marco Coleman	2.00
263	Doug Riesenberg	2.00
264	Jesse Sapolu	2.00
265	Dermontti Dawson	2.00
266	*Fernando Smith*	2.00
267	David Szott	2.00
268	Steve Christie	2.00
269	Bruce Matthews	2.00
270	Michael Irvin	20.00
271	Seth Joyner	2.00
272	Santana Dotson	2.00
273	Vincent Brisby	10.00
274	Rohn Stark	2.00
275	John Copeland	2.00
276	Toby Wright	2.00
277	David Griggs	2.00
278	*Aaron Taylor*	2.00
279	Chris Doleman	2.00
280	Reggie Brooks	2.00
281	Willie Anderson	2.00
282	Alvin Harper	5.00
283	Chris Hinton	2.00
284	Kelvin Pritchett	2.00
285	Russell Copeland	2.00
286	Dwight Stone	2.00
287	Jeff Gossett	2.00
288	Larry Allen	2.00
289	Kevin Mawae	2.00
290	Mark Collins	2.00
291	Chris Zorich	2.00
292	Vince Buck	2.00
293	Gene Atkins	2.00
294	Webster Slaughter	2.00
295	Steve Young	35.00
296	Dan Williams	2.00
297	Jesse Armstead	2.00
298	Victor Bailey	2.00
299	John Carney	2.00
300	Emmitt Smith	90.00
301	*Bucky Brooks*	5.00
302	Mo Lewis	2.00
303	Eugene Daniel	2.00
304	Tyji Armstrong	2.00
305	Eugene Chung	2.00
306	Raghib Ismail	5.00
307	Sean Jones	2.00
308	Rick Cunningham	2.00
309	Ken Harvey	2.00
310	Jeff George	5.00
311	Jon Vaughn	2.00
312	Roy Barker	2.00
313	Micheal Barrow	2.00
314	Ryan McNeil	2.00
315	Pete Stoyanovich	2.00
316	Darryl Williams	2.00
317	Renaldo Turnbull	2.00
318	Eric Green	2.00
319	Nate Lewis	2.00
320	Mike Flores	2.00
321	Derek Russell	2.00
322	Marcus Spears	2.00
323	Corey Miller	2.00
324	Derrick Thomas	5.00
325	Steve Everitt	2.00
326	Brent Jones	2.00
327	*Marshall Faulk*	100.00
328	Don Beebe	2.00
329	Harry Swayne	2.00
330	Boomer Esiason	2.00
331	Don Mosebar	2.00
332	*Isaac Bruce*	60.00
333	Rickey Jackson	2.00
334	Daryl Johnston	2.00
335	Lorenzo Lynch	2.00
336	Brian Blades	2.00
337	Michael Timpson	2.00
338	Reggie Cobb	2.00
339	Joe Walter	2.00
340	Barry Foster	7.00
341	Richmond Webb	2.00
342	Pat Swilling	2.00
343	Shaun Gayle	2.00
344	Reggie Roby	2.00
345	Chris Calloway	2.00
346	Doug Dawson	2.00
347	Rob Burnett	2.00
348	Dana Hall	2.00
349	Horace Copeland	2.00
350	Shannon Sharpe	5.00
351	Rich Miano	2.00
352	Henry Thomas	2.00
353	Dan Saleaumua	2.00
354	Kevin Ross	2.00
355	Morten Andersen	2.00
356	Anthony Blaylock	2.00
357	Stanley Richard	2.00
358	Albert Lewis	2.00
359	Darren Woodson	2.00
360	Drew Bledsoe	60.00
361	Eric Mahlum	2.00
362	*Trent Dilfer*	35.00
363	William Roberts	2.00
364	Robert Brooks	2.00
365	Jason Hanson	2.00
366	Troy Vincent	2.00
367	William Thomas	2.00
368	Lonnie Johnson	2.00
369	*Jamir Miller*	5.00
370	Michael Jackson	2.00
371	*Charlie Ward*	20.00
372	Shannon Sharpe	5.00
373	Jackie Slater	2.00
374	Steve Young	5.00
375	Bobby Wilson	2.00
376	Paul Frase	2.00
377	Dale Carter	2.00
378	Robert Delpino	2.00
379	*Bert Emanuel*	25.00
380	Rick Mirer	20.00
381	Carlos Jenkins	2.00
382	Gary Brown	2.00
383	Doug Pelfrey	2.00
384	Dexter Carter	2.00
385	Chris Miller	2.00
386	*Charles Johnson*	25.00
387	James Joseph	2.00
388	Darrin Smith	2.00
389	James Jett	2.00
390	Junior Seau	5.00
391	Chris Slade	2.00
392	Jim Harbaugh	2.00
393	Herman Moore	15.00
394	Thomas Randolph	2.00
395	Lamar Thomas	2.00
396	Reggie Rivers	2.00
397	Larry Centers	2.00
398	Chad Brown	2.00
399	Terry Kirby	5.00
400	Bruce Smith	2.00
401	Keenan McCardell	25.00
402	Tim McDonald	2.00
403	Robert Smith	2.00
404	Matt Brock	2.00
405	Tony McGee	2.00
406	Ethan Horton	2.00
407	Michael Haynes	2.00
408	Steve Jackson	2.00
409	Erik Kramer	2.00
410	Jerome Bettis	20.00
411	D.J. Johnson	2.00
412	John Alt	2.00
413	Jeff Lageman	2.00
414	Rick Tuten	2.00
415	Jeff Robinson	2.00
416	*Kevin Lee*	5.00
417	*Thomas Lewis*	8.00
418	Kerry Cash	2.00
419	*Chuck Levy*	2.00
420	Mark Ingram	2.00
421	Dennis Gibson	2.00
422	Tyronne Drakeford	2.00
423	James Washington	2.00
424	Dante Jones	2.00
425	Eugene Robinson	2.00
426	Johnny Johnson	2.00
427	Brian Mitchell	2.00
428	Charles Mincy	2.00
429	Mark Carrier	2.00
430	Vince Workman	2.00
431	James Francis	2.00
432	Clay Matthews	2.00
433	Randall McDaniel	2.00
434	Brad Ottis	2.00
435	Bruce Smith	2.00
436	Cortez Kennedy	5.00
437	John Randle	2.00
438	Neil Smith	2.00
439	Cornelius Bennett	2.00
440	Junior Seau	5.00
441	Derrick Thomas	5.00
442	Rod Woodson	5.00
443	Terry McDaniel	2.00
444	Tim McDonald	2.00
445	Mark Carrier	2.00
446	Irv Smith	2.00
447	Steve Wallace	2.00
448	Cris Dishman	2.00
449	Bill Brooks	2.00
450	Jeff Hostetler	2.00
451	Brentson Buckner	2.00
452	Ken Ruettgers	2.00
453	Marc Boutte	2.00
454	John Offerdahl	2.00
455	Allen Aldridge	2.00
456	Steve Emtman	2.00
457	Andre Rison	5.00
458	Shawn Jefferson	2.00
459	*Todd Steussie*	2.00
460	Scott Mitchell	5.00
461	Tom Carter	2.00
462	*Donnell Bennett*	5.00
463	James Jones	2.00
464	Antone Davis	2.00
465	Jim Everett	2.00
466	Tony Tolbert	2.00
467	Merril Hoge	2.00
468	Michael Bates	2.00
469	Phil Hansen	2.00
470	Rodney Hampton	5.00
471	Aeneas Williams	2.00
472	Al Del Greco	2.00
473	Todd Lyght	2.00
474	Joel Steed	2.00
475	Merton Hanks	2.00
476	Tony Stargell	2.00
477	Greg Robinson	2.00
478	Roger Duffy	2.00
479	Simon Fletcher	2.00
480	Reggie White	5.00
481	Lee Johnson	2.00
482	Wayne Martin	2.00
483	Thurman Thomas	8.00
484	Warren Moon	6.00
485	Sam Rogers	2.00
486	Erric Pegram	2.00
487	Will Wolford	2.00
488	Duane Young	2.00
489	Keith Hamilton	2.00
490	Haywood Jeffires	2.00
491	Trace Armstrong	2.00
492	J.J. Birden	2.00
493	Ricky Ervins	2.00
494	Robert Blackmon	2.00
495	William Perry	2.00
496	Robert Massey	2.00
497	Jim Jeffcoat	2.00
498	Pat Harlow	2.00
499	Jeff Cross	2.00
500	Jerry Rice	45.00
501	*Darnay Scott*	40.00
502	Clyde Simmons	2.00
503	Henry Rolling	2.00
504	James Hasty	2.00
505	Leroy Thompson	2.00
506	Darrell Thompson	2.00
507	Tim Bowens	2.00
508	Gerald Perry	2.00
509	Mike Croel	2.00
510	Sam Mills	2.00
511	Steve Young	20.00
512	Hardy Nickerson	2.00
513	Cris Carter	5.00
514	Boomer Esiason	2.00
515	Bruce Smith	2.00
516	Emmitt Smith	50.00
517	Eugene Robinson	2.00
518	Gary Brown	2.00
519	Jerry Rice	20.00
520	Troy Aikman	20.00
521	Marcus Allen	5.00
522	Junior Seau	5.00
523	Sterling Sharpe	5.00
524	Dana Stubblefield	2.00
525	Tom Carter	2.00
526	Pete Metzelaars	2.00
527	Russell Freeman	2.00
528	Keith Cash	2.00
529	Willie Drewrey	2.00
530	Randal Hill	2.00
531	Pepper Johnson	2.00
532	Rob Moore	5.00
533	Todd Kelly	2.00
534	Keith Byars	2.00
535	Mike Fox	2.00
536	Brett Favre	90.00
537	Terry McDaniel	2.00
538	Darren Perry	2.00
539	Maurice Hurst	2.00
540	Troy Aikman	45.00
541	Junior Seau	7.00
542	Steve Broussard	2.00
543	Lorenzo White	2.00
544	Terry McDaniel	2.00
545	Henry Thomas	2.00
546	Tyrone Hughes	2.00
547	Mark Collins	2.00
548	Gary Anderson	2.00
549	Darrell Green	2.00
550	Jerry Rice	45.00
551	Cornelius Bennett	2.00
552	Aeneas Williams	2.00
553	Eric Metcalf	2.00
554	John Elliott	2.00
555	Mo Lewis	2.00
556	Darren Carrington	2.00
557	Kevin Greene	2.00
558	John Elway	20.00
559	Eugene Robinson	2.00
560	Drew Bledsoe	45.00
561	Fred Barnett	2.00
562	*Bernie Parmalee*	30.00
563	Bryce Paup	2.00
564	Donnell Woolford	2.00
565	Terance Mathis	2.00
566	Santana Dotson	2.00
567	Randall McDaniel	2.00
568	Stanley Richard	2.00
569	Brian Blades	2.00
570	Jerome Bettis	20.00
571	Neil Smith	2.00
572	Andre Reed	5.00
573	Michael Bankston	2.00
574	Dana Stubblefield	2.00
575	Rod Woodson	5.00
576	Ken Harvey	2.00
577	Andre Rison	5.00
578	Darion Conner	2.00
579	Michael Strahan	2.00
580	Barry Sanders	35.00
581	Pepper Johnson	2.00
582	Lewis Tillman	2.00
583	Jeff George	6.00
584	Michael Haynes	2.00
585	Herschel Walker	5.00
586	Tim Brown	5.00
587	Jim Kelly	6.00
588	Ricky Watters	5.00
589	Randall Cunningham	5.00
590	Troy Aikman	45.00
591	Ken Norton	2.00
592	Cortez Kennedy	5.00
593	Ricky Ervins	2.00
594	Cris Carter	5.00
595	Sterling Sharpe	10.00
596	John Randle	2.00
597	Shannon Sharpe	5.00
598	*Ray Crittenden*	5.00
599	Barry Foster	6.00
600	Deion Sanders	35.00
601	Seth Joyner	2.00
602	Chris Warren	5.00
603	Tom Rathman	2.00
604	Brett Favre	25.00
605	Marshall Faulk	45.00
606	Terry Allen	2.00
607	Ben Coates	10.00
608	Brian Washington	2.00
609	Henry Ellard	2.00
610	David Meggett	2.00
611	Stan Humphries	5.00
612	Warren Moon	5.00
613	Marcus Allen	5.00
614	Ed McDaniel	2.00
615	Joe Montana	60.00
616	Jeff Hostetler	2.00
617	Johnny Johnson	2.00
618	Andre Coleman	2.00
619	Willie Davis	2.00
620	Rick Mirer	20.00
621	Dan Marino	90.00
622	Rob Moore	2.00
623	*Byron Morris*	40.00
624	Natrone Means	40.00
625	Steve Young	30.00
626	Jim Everett	2.00
627	Michael Brooks	2.00
628	Dermontti Dawson	2.00
629	Reggie White	5.00
630	Emmitt Smith	75.00

1994 Stadium Club Bowman Black

These 17 insert cards, featuring NFL veterans, were included in 1994-95 Stadium Club Football High series packs, one per every three packs. The cards utilize Finest chromium technology and have a black tint to them. "Bowman's Best" is written on the front. The back has a card number, close-up shot and summaries of the player's stats and skills. Refractor versions were also made for each Blue card; they were seeded one per every 12 packs.

	NM/M
Complete Set (17):	30.00
Common Player:	1.00
Refractor Cards:	1X-3X

#	Player	Price
1	Jerry Rice	4.00
2	Deion Sanders	2.00
3	Reggie White	1.00
4	Dan Marino	5.00
5	Natrone Means	1.00
6	Rick Mirer	1.00
7	Michael Irvin	2.00
8	John Elway	4.00
9	Junior Seau	1.00
10	Drew Bledsoe	3.00
11	Sterling Sharpe	1.00
12	Brett Favre	5.00
13	Troy Aikman	3.00
14	Barry Sanders	4.00
15	Steve Young	3.00
16	Emmitt Smith	5.00
17	Joe Montana	5.00

1994 Stadium Club Bowman Blue

These 1994-95 Topps Stadium Club High Series inserts feature 17 of the NFL's most promising rookies. Cards, which use the Finest chromium technology, were seeded one per three packs. The cards are similar in design to the Bowman Black inserts, except these have a blue tint to them. There were also Refractors made for each Blue card; they are seeded one per every 12 packs.

	NM/M
Complete Set (17):	20.00
Common Player:	1.00
Refractor Cards:	1X-3X

#	Player	Price
1	Marshall Faulk	3.00
2	Derrick Alexander	1.00
3	Darnay Scott	1.00
4	Gus Frerotte	1.00
5	Jeff Blake	1.00
6	Charles Johnson	1.00
7	Thomas Lewis	1.00
8	Charlie Garner	1.00

9 Aaron Glenn 1.00
10 William Floyd 2.00
11 Antonio Langham 1.00
12 Errict Rhett 2.00
13 Heath Shuler 1.00
14 Jeff Burris 1.00
15 Dan Wilkinson 1.00
16 Rob Fredrickson 1.00
17 Tim Bowens 1.00

1994 Stadium Club Bowman Mirror Images

These cards match a top NFL veteran with a promising rookie. The horizontal front, using Finest chromium technology, shows both players, with their names underneath. The cards were random inserts in 1994-95 Topps Stadium High Series packs, one per every three packs. Refractor versions were also made; they could be found one per every 12 packs.

NM/M
Complete Set (11): 20.00
Common Player: 1.00
Refractor Cards: 1X-3X
18 Deion Sanders, Aaron Glenn 1.00
19 Barry Sanders, Marshall Faulk 4.00
20 Darryl Johnston, William Floyd 1.00
21 Reggie White, Tim Bowens 1.00
22 Troy Aikman, Heath Shuler 3.00
23 Donnell Woolford, Antonio Langham 1.00
24 Rodney Hampton, Errict Rhett 1.00
25 Tyrone Hughes, Jeff Burris 1.00
26 Henry Thomas, Dan Wilkinson 1.00
27 Jerry Rice, Derrick Alexander 3.00
28 Emmitt Smith, Bam Morris 4.00

1994 Stadium Club Dynasty and Destiny

Dynasty and Destiny is a Stadium Club insert set which compares former NFL players who are or will be Hall of Fame members with current players. Three cards appeared in Series I and three more followed in Series II. Each card front shows both players, with their names, the set name and Stadium Club logo stamped in gold foil. Destiny and Dynasty are also written on the card front. The back, numbered 1 of 6, etc., compares statistics for both players from their first year in the league and their career totals. Mug shots are also given.

NM/M
Complete Set (6): 10.00
Common Player: 1.00
1 Walter Payton, Emmitt Smith 5.00
2 Steve Largent, Tom Waddle 1.00
3 Randy White, Cortez Kennedy 1.00
4 Dan Fouts, Troy Aikman 3.00
5 Mike Singletary, Junior Seau 1.00
6 Ozzie Newsome, Shannon Sharpe 1.00

1994 Stadium Club Expansion Team Redemption

This 44-card Finest set was available through redemption cards in Stadium Club Series III, seeded one per 24 packs. The set introduced the two new expansion teams - Jacksonville Jaguars and Carolina Panthers - with three redemption cards per franchise, labeled offense, defense and special teams, which could be redeemed for that group of players in their new uniforms. There was also a complete set redemption card found every 336 packs. The deadline for redemptions was February 20, 1996.

NM/M
Jaguars Prize Set (22): 10.00
Panthers Prize Set (22): 10.00
Common Jaguar (J1-J22): .25
Common Panther (P1-P22): .25
Comp. Trade Card Set (6): 1.00
J1 James O. Stewart 2.00
J2 Kelvin Pritchett .25
J3 Mike Dumas .25
J4 Brian DeMarco .25
J5 James Williams .25
J6 Ernest Givins .25
J7 Harry Colon .25
J8 Derek Brown .25
J9 Santo Stephens .25
J10 Jeff Lageman .25
J11 Bryan Barker .25
J12 Dave Widell .25
J13 Willie Jackson 1.00
J14 Vinnie Clark .25
J15 Mickey Washington .25
J16 Le'Shai Maston .25
J17 Darren Carrington .25
J18 Steve Beuerlein .25
J19 Mark Williams .25
J20 Keith Goganious .25
J21 Shawn Bouwens .25
J22 Chris Hudson .25
P1 Kerry Collins 8.00
P2 Rod Smith .25
P3 Willie Green .25
P4 Greg Kragen .25
P5 Blake Brockermeyer .25
P6 Bob Christian .25
P7 Carlton Bailey .25
P8 Bubba McDowell .25
P9 Matt Elliott .25
P10 Tyrone Poole 1.00
P11 John Kasay .25
P12 Gerald Williams .25
P13 Derrick Moore .25
P14 Don Beebe .25
P15 Sam Mills .25
P16 Darion Conner .25
P17 Eric Guliford .25
P18 Mike Fox .25
P19 Pete Metzelaars .25
P20 Frank Reich 1.00
P21 Mark Carrier .25
P22 Vince Workman .25
NNO Card .50
NNO Card .50
NNO Redemption Card .50
NNO Card .50
NNO Card .50
NNO Redemption Card .50
NNO Redemption .50

1994 Stadium Club Frequent Scorers

These Stadium Club Series II inserts feature 10 different players, each having five different point cards, worth six points each. Collectors can receive a Finest quality upgrade set of the player by sending in 30 Frequent Scorer point cards of him. The point cards were included one per every three packs.

NM/M
Complete Set (10): 20.00
Common Player: 1.00
1 Chris Warren 1.00
2 Marshall Faulk 5.00
3 Drew Bledsoe 3.00
4 Dan Marino 5.00
5 Vinny Testaverde 1.00
6 Jeff George 1.00
7 Steve Young 3.00
8 Dave Meggett 1.00
9 Stan Humphries 1.00
10 Rick Mirer 1.00

1994 Stadium Club Ring Leaders

These Stadium Club Series II inserts feature active players who have played in a Pro Bowl and have led the league in a statistical category. Topps used a "Power Matrix" technology that "makes the cards shine beyond belief." These cards were randomly included in every 24th pack.

NM/M
Complete Set (12): 20.00
Common Player: 1.00
1 Emmitt Smith 4.00
2 Steve Young 3.00
3 Deion Sanders 1.00
4 Warren Moon 1.00
5 Thurman Thomas 1.00
6 Jerry Rice 4.00
7 Sterling Sharpe 1.00
8 Barry Sanders 4.00
9 Reggie White 1.00
10 Michael Irvin 1.00
11 Ronnie Lott 1.00
12 Herschel Walker 1.00

1994 Stadium Club Super Teams

Stadium Club Football also inserted Super Team cards into one of every 24 packs. The cards feature a wide-angle action shot of the team. If the team pictured won the Super Bowl, conference title or division championship, the Super Team card could be redeemed for additional cards that formed a parallel set but had either Super Bowl logo, conference championship logo or division winner logo, respectively.

NM/M
Complete Set (28): 20.00
Common Player: .50
1 Cardinals .50
2 Falcons .50
3 Bills .50
4 Bears .50
5 Bengals .50
6 Browns .50
7 Cowboys 5.00
8 Broncos 3.00
9 Lions 1.00
10 Packers 4.00
11 Oilers .50
12 Colts .50
13 Chiefs 2.00
14 Raiders .50
15 Rams .50
16 Dolphins 2.00
17 Vikings 2.00
18 Patriots 2.00
19 Saints .50
20 Giants .50
21 Jets .50
22 Eagles .50
23 Steelers 1.00
24 Chargers 1.00
25 49ers 3.00
26 Seahawks 1.00
27 Buccaneers .50
28 Redskins .50

1994 Stadium Club Super Teams Division Winners

Collectors who had Super Team cards of the Cowboys, 49ers, Vikings, Chargers, Steelers and Dolphins could redeem the cards for a 10-card team bag set via mail. The cards were essentially the same as regular-issue cards, except for a division winner gold foil logo.

NM/M
Complete Bag Chargers (11): 3.00
Complete Bag Cowboys (11): 6.00
Complete Bag Dolphins (11): 6.00
Complete Bag 49ers (11): 6.00
Complete Bag Vikings (11): 3.00
Complete Bag Steelers (11): 3.00
Common Player: .20
7DW Emmitt Smith, Troy Aikman Cowboys Super Team DW 2.50
16DW Irving Fryar Dolphins Super Team DW .75
17DW Cris Carter DW Vikings Super Team DW .75
23DW Neil O'Donnell Steelers Super Team DW .75
24DW Natrone Means Chargers Super Team DW .75
25DW Jerry Rice, Steve Young, Ricky Watters 49ers Super Team DW 1.50
D16 Bryan Cox .20
D56 Aubrey Beavers .20
D99 O.J. McDuffie 1.00
D200 Dan Marino 4.00
D249 Irving Fryar .60
D262 Marco Coleman .20
D341 Richmond Webb .20
D399 Terry Kirby .60
D507 Tim Bowens .60
D562 Bernie Parmalee 1.50
F35 William Floyd 2.00
F51 Bryant Young 1.25
F80 Dana Stubblefield 1.00
F201 Ricky Watters .60
F295 Steve Young 2.50
F326 Brent Jones .60
F402 Tim McDonald .20
F475 Merton Hanks .20
F500 Jerry Rice 2.50
F600 Deion Sanders 1.50
V18 Qadry Ismail 1.00
V85 Cris Carter .60
V124 Jack Del Rio .20
V142 DeWayne Washington .60
V173 David Palmer .60
V194 John Randle .20
V352 Henry Thomas .20
V433 Randall McDaniel .20
V459 Todd Steussie .60
V484 Warren Moon 1.00
CH12 Darren Carrington .20
CH40 Natrone Means .75
CH84 Isaac Davis .20
CH151 Stan Humphries 1.00
CH179 Leslie O'Neal .60
CH299 John Carney .20
CH357 Stanley Richard .20
CH390 Junior Seau 1.00
CH421 Dennis Gibson .20
CH458 Shawn Jefferson .60
CO52 Jay Novacek .60
CO168 Russell Maryland .20
CO233 Charles Haley .60
CO270 Michael Irvin 1.00
CO282 Alvin Harper .60
CO300 Emmitt Smith 4.00
CO334 Daryl Johnston .60
CO359 Darren Woodson .20
CO423 James Washington .20
CO540 Troy Aikman 2.50

1994 Stadium Club Super Teams Master Photos

Super Team cards of the AFC and NFC Champions - the Chargers and 49ers - were redeemable for this 10-card team bag set of Master Photos of that respective team. The Master Photos were essentially the same as the base cards, but were printed on an oversized card, with a white border around the photo, and they have a conference winner gold foil logo.

NM/M
Complete Bag Chargers (11): 7.50
Complete Bag 49ers (11): 15.00
Common Player: .50
24CW Natrone Means Chargers Super Team CW .75
25CW Jerry Rice, Steve Young, Ricky Watters 49ers Super Team CW 1.50
F35 William Floyd 2.50
F51 Bryant Young 1.50
F80 Dana Stubblefield 1.25
F201 Ricky Watters .75
F295 Steve Young 3.00
F326 Brent Jones .75
F402 Tim McDonald .75
F475 Merton Hanks .50
F500 Jerry Rice 3.00
F600 Deion Sanders 1.75
CH12 Darren Carrington .50
CH40 Natrone Means 1.00
CH84 Isaac Davis .50
CH151 Stan Humphries 1.25
CH179 Leslie O'Neal .75
CH299 John Carney .50
CH357 Stanley Richard .50
CH390 Junior Seau 1.25
CH421 Dennis Gibson .50
CH458 Shawn Jefferson .75

1994 Stadium Club Super Teams Super Bowl

Super Team cards of the Super Bowl XXIX Champion 49ers could be redeemed for a 540-card parallel set to the regular-issue Stadium Club set. The cards are essentially the same as regular-issue cards, except for a "Super Bowl XXIX" logo on the front. The sets also came with a 49ers Super Team card that also had a "Super Bowl XXIX" logo on the front.

NM/M
Complete Set (541): 60.00
Common Player: .10
SB25 Jerry Rice, Steve Young, Ricky Watters 49ers Super Team SB 2.00

1994 Stadium Club Members Only

Stadium Club Members Only parallel sets were only available directly from Topps to Stadium Club members. The sets include all base cards and inserts, and are essentially the same as regular-issue cards, except for a special "Members Only" logo on the front.

NM/M
Complete Fact. Set (722): 150.00
Common Player (1-630): .25
Common Player (DD1-DD6): .25
Common Player (RL1-RL12): .50
Common Player (ST1-ST28): .25
DD1 Emmitt Smith, Walter Payton 8.00
DD2 Steve Largent, Tom Waddle .25
DD3 Randy White, Cortez Kennedy .40
DD4 Troy Aikman, Dan Fouts 5.00
DD5 Junior Seau, Mike Singletary .40
DD6 Shannon Sharpe, Ozzie Newsome .25
RL1 Emmitt Smith 12.00
RL2 Steve Young 6.00
RL3 Deion Sanders 4.00
RL4 Warren Moon .75
RL5 Thurman Thomas .75
RL6 Jerry Rice 8.00
RL7 Sterling Sharpe .75
RL8 Barry Sanders 8.00
RL9 Reggie White .75
RL10 Michael Irvin .75
RL11 Ronnie Lott .50
RL12 Herschel Walker .50
ST1 Steve Beuerlein .25
ST2 Drew Hill .25
ST3 Jim Kelly .40
ST4 Joe Cain .25
ST5 Derrick Fenner .25
ST6 Tommy Vardell .25
ST7 Emmitt Smith 12.00
ST8 John Elway 4.00
ST9 Barry Sanders 8.00
ST10 Brent Favre 8.00
ST11 Gary Brown .25
ST12 Zefross Moss .25
ST13 Joe Montana 8.00
ST14 Howie Long .40
ST15 Jerome Bettis 2.50
ST16 Irving Fryar .40
ST17 Cris Carter .40
ST18 Drew Bledsoe 6.00
ST19 Rickey Jackson .25
ST20 Phil Simms .40
ST21 Boomer Esiason .40
ST22 Herschel Walker .40
ST23 Neil O'Donnell 1.00
ST24 Natrone Means 2.50
ST25 Jerry Rice, Steve Young 8.00
ST26 Rick Mirer 2.50
ST27 Craig Erickson .25
ST28 Reggie Brooks .25

1994 Stadium Club Members Only 50

This 50-card set was exclusively available to Stadium Club members and contained 45 regular Stadium Club cards and five Finest cards. The words "Topps Stadium Club Members Only" appear in gold foil in one of the top corners.

NM/M
Complete Set (50): 10.00
Common Player: .25
1 Jerry Rice 3.00
2 Eric Williams .25
3 Nate Newton .25
4 Jesse Sapolu .25
5 Randall McDaniel .25
6 Harris Barton .25
7 Jay Novacek .40
8 Michael Irvin .75
9 Steve Young 2.50
10 Jerome Bettis 1.50
11 Daryl Johnston .40
12 Neil Smith .40
13 Cortez Kennedy .40
14 Ray Childress .25
15 Leslie O'Neal .40
16 Derrick Thomas .40
17 Junior Seau .75
18 Greg Lloyd .40
19 Rod Woodson .40
20 Nate Odomes .25
21 Dennis Smith .25
22 Steve Atwater .25
23 Reggie White .75
24 John Randle .25
25 Sean Gilbert .25
26 Richard Dent .40
27 Rickey Jackson .25
28 Hardy Nickerson .25
29 Renaldo Turnbull .25
30 Deion Sanders 2.00
31 Eric Allen .25
32 Tim McDonald .25
33 Mark Carrier (DB) .25
34 Tim Brown .75
35 Richmond Webb .25
36 Keith Sims .25
37 Bruce Matthews .25
38 Steve Wisniewski .25
39 Howard Ballard .25
40 Shannon Sharpe .40
41 Anthony Miller .40
42 John Elway 2.50
43 Thurman Thomas .75
44 Marcus Allen .60
45 Andre Rison .40
46 Drew Bledsoe .25
47 Willie Roaf .25
48 Reggie Brooks .40
49 Dana Stubblefield .40
50 Rick Mirer .40

1995 Stadium Club

Topps released its 1995 Stadium Club issue in two 225-card series. Series I has 180 regular cards of the top NFL players, plus 15 Draft Picks and 30 Extreme Corps subset cards. Series II has two subsets also - Xpansion Team and Draft Pixs. Each regular card front has full-bleed photography and is stamped with textured foil. Regular cards are stamped with gold; subset cards are emblazoned with rainbow and silver foil. Card backs have a second full-bleed photo, biographical data, 1994 and career stats, Skills Ratings and Trench Talk, an assessment of the player's strengths and career highlights. In addition, hobbyists can see the winners of Stadium Club's Extreme Fans contest from 1994. Four different fans can be found on the back of each regular card holding up one of the Skills Ratings cards. Series I inserts include Power Surge, Metalists, Nemeses, and Nightmares (hobby only). Series II inserts include MVPs, Power Surge, Ground Attack and Nightmares II (hobby only.) Also, as a special to Series II jumbo and rack packs, parallel sets have been created for the Draft Pix and Extreme Corps cards. These double foil-stamped (green and gold vs. the regular rainbow and silver) theme cards use diffraction foil and are in every jumbo and rack pack.

NM/M
Complete Set (450): 70.00
Comp. Series 1 (225): 40.00
Comp. Series 2 (225): 35.00
Common Player: .10
Minor Stars: .20
Ser. 1 Hobby Pack (12): 1.25
Ser. 1 Hobby Wax Box (24): 20.00
Ser. 2 Hobby Pack (12): 1.50
Ser. 2 Hobby Wax Box (24): 25.00
Ser. 1 or 2 Ret. Pack (12): 1.25
Ser. 1 or 2 Ret. Wax Box (24): 20.00
1 Steve Young 1.00
2 Stan Humphries .25
3 Chris Boniol .20
4 Darren Perry .10
5 Vinny Testaverde .10
6 Aubrey Beavers .10
7 DeWayne Washington .10
8 Marion Butts .10
9 George Koonce .10
10 Joe Cain .10
11 Mike Johnson .10
12 Dale Carter .10
13 Greg Biekert .10
14 Aaron Pierce .10
15 Aeneas Williams .10
16 Steve Grant .20
17 Henry Jones .10
18 James Williams .10
19 Andy Harmon .10
20 Anthony Miller .10
21 Kevin Ross .10
22 Erik Howard .10
23 Brian Blades .10
24 Trent Dilfer .50
25 Roman Phifer .10
26 Bruce Kozerski .10
27 Henry Ellard .10
28 Rich Camarillo .10
29 Richmond Webb .10
30 George Teague .10
31 Antonio Langham .10
32 Barry Foster .10
33 Bruce Armstrong .10
34 Tim McDonald .10
35 James Harris .10
36 Lomas Brown .10
37 Jay Novacek .10
38 John Thierry .10
39 John Elliott .10
40 Terry McDaniel .10
41 Shawn Lee .10
42 Shane Dronett .10
43 Cornelius Bennett .10

No.	Player	Price
44	Steve Bono	.20
45	Byron Evans	.10
46	Eugene Robinson	.10
47	Tony Bennett	.10
48	Michael Bankston	.10
49	William Roaf	.10
50	Bobby Houston	.10
51	Ken Harvey	.10
52	Bruce Matthews	.10
53	Lincoln Kennedy	.10
54	Todd Lyght	.10
55	Paul Gruber	.10
56	Corey Sawyer	.10
57	Myron Guyton	.10
58	John Jackson	.10
59	Sean Jones	.10
60	Pepper Johnson	.10
61	Steve Walsh	.10
62	Corey Miller	.10
63	Fuad Reveiz	.10
64	Rickey Jackson	.10
65	Scott Mitchell	.10
66	Michael Irvin	.30
67	Andre Reed	.10
68	Mark Seay	.10
69	Keith Byars	.10
70	Marcus Allen	.20
71	Shannon Sharpe	.20
72	Eric Hill	.10
73	James Washington	.10
74	Greg Jackson	.10
75	Chris Warren	.20
76	Will Wolford	.10
77	Anthony Smith	.10
78	Cris Dishman	.10
79	Carl Pickens	.10
80	Tyrone Hughes	.10
81	Chris Miller	.10
82	Clay Matthews	.10
83	Lonnie Marts	.10
84	Jerome Henderson	.10
85	Ben Coates	.10
86	Deon Figures	.10
87	Anthony Pleasant	.10
88	Guy McIntyre	.10
89	Jake Reed	.10
90	Rodney Hampton	.10
91	Santana Dotson	.10
92	Jeff Blackshear	.10
93	Willie Clay	.10
94	Nate Newton	.10
95	Bucky Brooks	.10
96	Lamar Lathon	.10
97	Tim Grunhard	.10
98	Harris Barton	.10
99	Brian Mitchell	.10
100	Natrone Means	.75
101	Sean Dawkins	.10
102	Chris Slade	.10
103	Tom Rathman	.10
104	Fred Barnett	.10
105	Gary Brown	.10
106	Leonard Russell	.10
107	Alfred Williams	.10
108	Kelvin Martin	.10
109	Alexander Wright	.10
110	O.J. McDuffie	.10
111	Mario Bates	.40
112	Tony Casillas	.10
113	Michael Timpson	.10
114	Robert Brooks	.10
115	Rob Burnett	.10
116	Mark Collins	.10
117	Chris Calloway	.10
118	Courtney Hawkins	.10
119	Marvcus Patton	.10
120	Greg Lloyd	.10
121	Ryan McNeil	.10
122	Gary Plummer	.10
123	Dwayne Sabb	.10
124	Jessie Hester	.10
125	Terance Mathis	.10
126	Steve Atwater	.10
127	Lorenzo Lynch	.10
128	James Francis	.10
129	John Fina	.10
130	Emmitt Smith	3.00
131	Bryan Cox	.10
132	Robert Blackmon	.10
133	Kenny Davidson	.10
134	Eugene Daniel	.10
135	Vince Buck	.10
136	Leslie O'Neal	.10
137	James Jett	.10
138	Johnny Johnson	.10
139	Michael Zordich	.10
140	Warren Moon	.25
141	William White	.10
142	Carl Banks	.10
143	Marty Carter	.10
144	Keith Hamilton	.10
145	Alvin Harper	.20
146	Corey Harris	.10
147	Elijah Alexander	.25
148	Darrell Green	.10
149	*Yancey Thigpen*	1.50
150	Deion Sanders	.75
151	Burt Grossman	.10
152	J.B. Brown	.10
153	Johnny Bailey	.10
154	Harvey Williams	.10
155	*Jeff Blake*	.50
156	Al Smith	.10
157	Chris Doleman	.10
158	Garrison Hearst	.20
159	Bryce Paup	.10
160	Herman Moore	.20
161	Cortez Kennedy	.10
162	Marquez Pope	.10
163	Quinn Early	.10
164	Broderick Thomas	.10
165	Jeff Herrod	.10
166	Robert Jones	.10
167	Mo Lewis	.10
168	Ray Crittenden	.10
169	Raymont Harris	.20
170	Bruce Smith	.10
171	Dana Stubblefield	.10
172	Charles Haley	.10
173	Charles Johnson	.40
174	Shawn Jefferson	.10
175	Leroy Hoard	.10
176	Bernie Parmalee	.30
177	Scottie Graham	.10
178	Edgar Bennett	.10
179	Aubrey Matthews	.10
180	Don Beebe	.10
181	Eric Swann (Extreme Corps)	.10
182	Jeff George (Extreme Corps)	.20
183	Jim Kelly (Extreme Corps)	.20
184	Sam Mills (Extreme Corps)	.10
185	Mark Carrier (Extreme Corps)	.10
186	Dan Wilkinson (Extreme Corps)	.10
187	Eric Turner (Extreme Corps)	.10
188	Troy Aikman (Extreme Corps)	2.50
189	John Elway (Extreme Corps)	1.00
190	Barry Sanders (Extreme Corps)	2.50
191	Brett Favre (Extreme Corps)	4.00
192	Micheal Barrow (Extreme Corps)	.10
193	Marshall Faulk (Extreme Corps)	1.00
194	Steve Beuerlein (Extreme Corps)	.10
195	Neil Smith (Extreme Corps)	.10
196	Jeff Hostetler (Extreme Corps)	.20
197	Jerome Bettis (Extreme Corps)	.75
198	Dan Marino (Extreme Corps)	4.00
199	Cris Carter (Extreme Corps)	.20
200	Drew Bledsoe (Extreme Corps)	2.50
201	Jim Everett (Extreme Corps)	.20
202	Dave Brown (Extreme Corps)	.10
203	Boomer Esiason (Extreme Corps)	.10
204	Randall Cunningham (Extreme Corps)	.20
205	Rod Woodson (Extreme Corps)	.10
206	Junior Seau (Extreme Corps)	.20
207	Jerry Rice (Extreme Corps)	2.50
208	Rick Mirer (Extreme Corps)	1.00
209	Errict Rhett (Extreme Corps)	.30
210	Heath Shuler (Extreme Corps)	.50
211	*Bobby Taylor* (Draft Picks)	.20
212	*Jesse James* (Draft Picks)	.20
213	*Devin Bush* (Draft Picks)	.20
214	*Luther Elliss* (Draft Picks)	.20
215	*Kerry Collins* (Draft Picks)	2.00
216	*Derrick Alexander* (Draft Picks)	.20
217	*Rashaan Salaam* (Draft Picks)	.50
218	*J.J. Stokes* (Draft Picks)	2.00
219	*Todd Collins* (Draft Picks)	.20
220	*Ki-Jana Carter* (Draft Picks)	.50
221	*Kyle Brady* (Draft Picks)	1.00
222	*Kevin Carter* (Draft Picks)	.20
223	*Tony Boselli* (Draft Picks)	.20
224	*Scott Gragg* (Draft Picks)	.20
225	*Warren Sapp* (Draft Picks)	1.50
226	Ricky Reynolds	.10
227	Roosevelt Potts	.10
228	Jessie Tuggle	.10
229	Anthony Newman	.10
230	Randall Cunningham	.10
231	Jason Elam	.10
232	Darnay Scott	.50
233	Tom Carter	.10
234	Micheal Barrow	.10
235	Steve Tasker	.10
236	Howard Cross	.10
237	Charles Wilson	.10
238	Rob Fredrickson	.10
239	Russell Maryland	.10
240	Dan Marino	3.00
241	Rafael Robinson	.10
242	Ed McDaniel	.10
243	Brett Perriman	.20
244	Chuck Levy	.10
245	Errict Rhett	1.50
246	Tracy Simien	.10
247	Steve Everitt	.10
248	John Jurkovic	.10
249	Johnny Mitchell	.10
250	Mark Carrier	.10
251	Merton Hanks	.10
252	Joe Johnson	.10
253	Andre Coleman	.10
254	Ray Buchanan	.10
255	Jeff George	.20
256	Shane Conlan	.10
257	Gus Frerotte	.50
258	Doug Pelfrey	.10
259	Glenn Montgomery	.10
260	John Elway	.50
261	Larry Centers	.10
262	Calvin Williams	.10
263	Gene Atkins	.10
264	Tim Brown	.20
265	Leon Lett	.10
266	Martin Mayhew	.10
267	Arthur Marshall	.10
268	Maurice Hurst	.10
269	Greg Hill	.40
270	Junior Seau	.20
271	Rick Mirer	.40
272	Jack Del Rio	.10
273	Lewis Tillman	.10
274	Renaldo Turnbull	.10
275	Dan Footman	.10
276	John Taylor	.10
277	Russell Copeland	.10
278	Tracy Scroggins	.10
279	Lou Benfatti	.10
280	Rod Woodson	.10
281	Troy Drayton	.10
282	Quentin Coryatt	.10
283	Craig Heyward	.10
284	Jeff Cross	.10
285	Hardy Nickerson	.10
286	Dorsey Levens	.75
287	Derek Russell	.10
288	Seth Joyner	.10
289	Kimble Anders	.10
290	Drew Bledsoe	1.00
291	Bryant Young	.10
292	Chris Zorich	.10
293	Michael Strahan	.10
294	Kevin Greene	.10
295	Aaron Glenn	.10
296	Jimmy Spencer	.10
297	Eric Turner	.10
298	William Thomas	.10
299	Dan Wilkinson	.10
300	Troy Aikman	1.00
301	Terry Wooden	.10
302	Heath Shuler	1.00
303	Jeff Burris	.10
304	Mark Stepnoski	.10
305	Chris Mims	.10
306	Todd Steussie	.10
307	Johnnie Morton	.10
308	Darryl Talley	.10
309	Nolan Harrison	.10
310	Dave Brown	.10
311	Brent Jones	.10
312	Curtis Conway	.10
313	Ronald Humphrey	.10
314	Richie Anderson	.10
315	Jim Everett	.10
316	Willie Davis	.10
317	Ed Cunningham	.10
318	Willie McGinest	.10
319	Sean Gilbert	.10
320	Brett Favre	4.00
321	Bennie Thompson	.10
322	Neil O'Donnell	.20
323	Vince Workman	.10
324	Terry Kirby	.10
325	Simon Fletcher	.10
326	Ricardo McDonald	.10
327	Duane Young	.10
328	Jim Harbaugh	.10
329	D.J. Johnson	.10
330	Boomer Esiason	.10
331	Donnell Woolford	.10
332	Mike Sherrard	.10
333	Tyrone Legette	.10
334	Larry Brown	.10
335	William Floyd	.40
336	Reggie Brooks	.10
337	Patrick Bates	.10
338	Jim Jeffcoat	.10
339	Ray Childress	.10
340	Cris Carter	.20
341	Charlie Garner	.10
342	Bill Hitchcock	.10
343	Levon Kirkland	.10
344	Robert Porcher	.10
345	Darryl Williams	.10
346	Vincent Brisby	.10
347	Kenyon Rasheed	.10
348	Floyd Turner	.10
349	Bob Whitfield	.10
350	Jerome Bettis	.40
351	Brad Baxter	.10
352	Darrin Smith	.10
353	Lamar Thomas	.10
354	Lorenzo Neal	.10
355	Erik Kramer	.10
356	Dwayne Harper	.10
357	Doug Evans	.10
358	Jeff Feagles	.10
359	Ray Crockett	.10
360	Neil Smith	.10
361	Troy Vincent	.10
362	Don Griffin	.10
363	Michael Brooks	.10
364	Carlton Gray	.10
365	Thomas Smith	.10
366	Ken Norton	.10
367	Tony McGee	.10
368	Eric Metcalf	.10
369	Mel Gray	.10
370	Barry Sanders	2.50
371	Raghib Ismail	.10
372	Chad Brown	.20
373	Qadry Ismail	.10
374	Anthony Prior	.10
375	Kevin Lee	.10
376	Robert Young	.10
377	Kevin Williams	.10
378	Tydus Winans	.10
379	Ricky Watters	.20
380	Jim Kelly	.20
381	Eric Swann	.10
382	Mike Pritchard	.10
383	Derek Brown	.10
384	Dennis Gibson	.10
385	Byron Morris	.10
386	Reggie White	.20
387	Jeff Graham	.10
388	Marshall Faulk	1.00
389	Joe Phillips	.10
390	Jeff Hostetler	.10
391	Irving Fryar	.10
392	Stevon Moore	.10
393	Bert Emanuel	.40
394	Leon Searcy	.10
395	Robert Smith	.10
396	Michael Bates	.10
397	Thomas Lewis	.10
398	Joe Bowden	.10
399	Steve Tovar	.10
400	Jerry Rice	1.25
401	Toby Wright	.10
402	Daryl Johnston	.10
403	Vincent Brown	.10
404	Marvin Washington	.10
405	Chris Spielman	.10
406	Willie Jackson	.10
407	Harry Boatswain	.10
408	Kelvin Pritchett	.10
409	Dave Widell	.10
410	Frank Reich	.10
411	Corey Mayfield	.10
413	Keith Goganious	.10
414	John Kasay	.10
415	Ernest Givins	.10
416	Randy Baldwin	.10
417	Shawn Bouwens	.10
418	Mike Fox	.10
419	Mark Carrier	.10
420	Steve Beuerlein	.10
421	Steve Lofton	.10
422	Jeff Lageman	.10
423	Paul Butcher	.10
424	Mark Brunell	3.00
425	Vernon Turner	.10
426	Tim McKyer	.10
427	James Williams	.10
428	Tommy Barnhardt	.10
429	Rogerick Green	.10
430	Desmond Howard	.10
431	Darion Conner	.10
432	Reggie Clark	.10
433	Eric Guliford	.10
434	*Rob Johnson*	3.00
435	Sam Mills	.10
436	*Kordell Stewart*	3.00
437	*James Stewart*	2.00
438	*Zach Wiegert*	.10
439	*Ellis Johnson*	.10
440	*Matt O'Dwyer*	.10
441	*Anthony Cook*	.10
442	*Ron Davis*	.10
443	*Chris Hudson*	.10
444	*Hugh Douglas*	.20
445	*Tyrone Poole*	.10
446	*Korey Stringer*	.10
447	*Ruben Brown*	.10
448	*Brian DeMarco*	.10
449	*Michael Westbrook*	1.50
450	*Steve McNair*	5.00

1995 Stadium Club Ground Attack

These 1995 Topps Stadium Club Series II inserts feature 10 of the NFL's best backfield combinations together on one card. Etched foil is used on both sides. Cards were random inserts, one per every 14 retail and one per every 18 hobby packs.

		NM/M
Complete Set (15):		20.00
Common Player:		.50
Minor Stars:		1.00
Inserted 1:18 Hobby		
1	Emmitt Smith, Daryl Johnston	4.00
2	Edgar Bennett, Brett Favre	4.00
3	Bernie Parmalee, Irving Spikes	.50
4	John Elway, Glyn Milburn	3.00
5	Chris Warren, Rick Mirer	.50
6	Marcus Allen, Greg Hill	1.00
7	Errict Rhett, Vince Workman	1.00
8	Byron Morris, Eric Pegram	.50
9	Mario Bates, Derek Brown	.50
10	William Floyd, Steve Young	3.00
11	Charlie Garner, Randall Cunningham	1.00
12	Lewis Tillman, Raymont Harris	.50
13	Harvey Williams, Jeff Hostetler	.50
14	Larry Centers, Garrison Hearst	1.00
15	Marshall Faulk, Roosevelt Potts	1.00

1995 Stadium Club Metalists

These cards, Topps' first ever laser-cut cards, feature eight players who have won multiple awards in their distinguished careers. The laser process allows for more precise and detailed cutting on the inside of the cards, giving them a unique look which is patterned after the color photo on the front. "Metalists" is written at the top of the card; the player's name is written along the bottom. The brand logo is also on the card front. The back, numbered using an "M" prefix, has the laser-cut image on one side, flanked by a brief recap of the awards the player won. Cards were seeded one per every 18 retail packs and one per every 24 hobby packs of 1995 Topps Stadium Club Series I product.

		NM/M
Complete Set (8):		20.00
Common Player:		1.00
1	Jerry Rice	4.00
2	Barry Sanders	5.00
3	John Elway	4.00
4	Dana Stubblefield	1.00
5	Emmitt Smith	5.00
6	Deion Sanders	2.00
7	Marshall Faulk	3.00
8	Steve Young	4.00

1995 Stadium Club MVPs

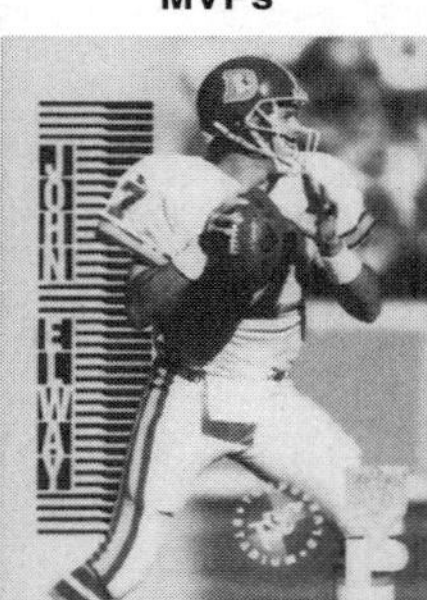

These eight cards celebrate the achievements of several players who have become the best of the best in the NFL while on their way to the Hall of Fame. The cards, seeded one per every 18 retail and one per every 24 hobby packs of 1995 Topps Stadium Club Series II product, are laser cut and highlight gold foil stamping on chromium stock. The player's name is laser cut along the left side of the card. Foil stamping is used for the MVP logo at the bottom of the card.

		NM/M
Complete Set (8):		10.00
Common Player:		1.00
1	Jerry Rice	3.00
2	Boomer Esiason	1.00
3	Randall Cunningham	1.00
4	Marcus Allen	1.00
5	John Elway	3.00
6	Dan Marino	5.00
7	Emmitt Smith	4.00
8	Steve Young	3.00

1995 Stadium Club Nemeses

Fifteen cards highlighting football's top rivalries make up this 1995 Topps Stadium Club Series I insert set. Complete with etched foil on both sides, the cards match up two players who are known for their classic confrontations, one on each side. Nemeses is written at the top of the card; the player's name, position and team helmet are at the bottom. The cards were seeded one per every 24th pack.

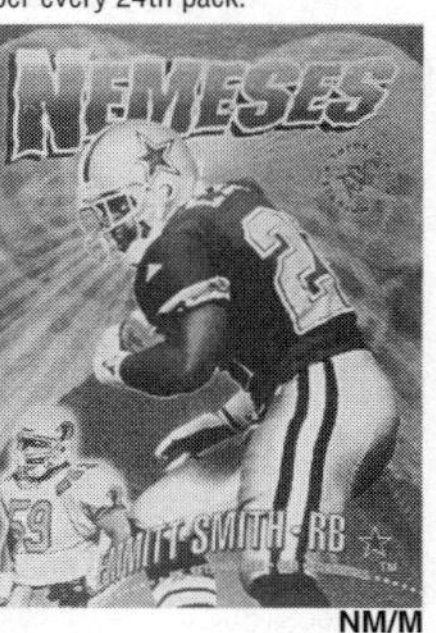

		NM/M
Complete Set (15):		40.00
Common Player:		1.00
1	Barry Sanders, Jack Del Rio	5.00
2	Reggie White, Lomas Brown	1.00
3	Terry McDaniel, Anthony Miller	1.00
4	Brett Favre, Chris Spielman	6.00
5	Junior Seau, Chris Warren	1.00
6	Cortez Kennedy, Steve Wisniewski	1.00
7	Rod Woodson, Tim Brown	1.00
8	Troy Aikman, Michael Brooks	4.00
9	Bruce Smith, Bruce Armstrong	1.00
10	Jerry Rice, Donnell Woolford	4.00
11	Emmitt Smith, Seth Joyner	5.00
12	Dan Marino, Cornelius Bennett	5.00
13	Marshall Faulk, Bryan Cox	3.00
14	Stan Humphries, Greg Lloyd	1.00
15	Michael Irvin, Deion Sanders	1.00

1995 Stadium Club Nightmares

This 30-card series was released as two 15-card insert sets; cards 1-15 were in 1995 Topps Stadium Club Series I hobby packs only (1 in 24), while 16-30 were in Series II hobby packs (1 in 18). "Biting" commentary on each player is provided by Vampirella, Topps' original "bad girl" comic character, who describes how the player terrorizes his opponents. The Series II Nightmare cards, which premiere artwork from the "Vampirella Gallery" release, feature a new etched foil design.

		NM/M
Complete Set (30):		75.00
Comp. Series 1 (15):		45.00
Comp. Series 2 (15):		30.00
Common Player:		1.00
1	Drew Bledsoe	4.00
2	Barry Sanders	6.00
3	Reggie White	1.00
4	Michael Irvin	1.00
5	Jerry Rice	5.00
6	Jerome Bettis	1.00
7	Dan Marino	6.00
8	Bruce Smith	1.00
9	Steve Young	4.00
10	Junior Seau	1.00
11	Emmitt Smith	6.00
12	Deion Sanders	3.00
13	Rod Woodson	1.00
14	Marshall Faulk	3.00
15	Troy Aikman	4.00

16 Stan Humphries 1.00
17 Chris Warren 1.00
18 Jack Del Rio 1.00
19 Randall Cunningham 1.00
20 Natrone Means 1.00
21 Dana Stubblefield 1.00
22 Jim Kelly 1.00
23 Cris Carter 1.00
24 Cornelius Bennett 1.00
25 Errict Rhett 1.00
26 Terry McDaniel 1.00
27 Rodney Hampton 1.00
28 Brett Favre 6.00
29 Bryan Cox 1.00
30 John Elway 4.00

1995 Stadium Club Power Surge

These 12 cards feature Topps' foil technology called Power Matrix. The cards, random inserts in 1995 Topps Stadium Club Series I packs, showcase the NFL's best players when the game is on the line. Cards were inserted one per every 18 packs.

NM/M
Complete Set (24): 50.00
Comp. Series 1 (12): 30.00
Comp. Series 2 (12): 20.00
Common Player: 1.00
P1 Steve Young 4.00
P2 Natrone Means 1.00
P3 Cris Carter 1.00
P4 Junior Seau 2.00
P5 Barry Sanders 5.00
P6 Michael Irvin 2.00
P7 John Elway 4.00
P8 Emmitt Smith 5.00
P9 Greg Lloyd 1.00
P10 Jerry Rice 5.00
P11 Marshall Faulk 3.00
P12 Drew Bledsoe 3.00
PS1 Dan Marino 6.00
PS2 Ken Harvey 1.00
PS3 Chris Warren 1.00
PS4 Henry Ellard 1.00
PS5 Marshall Faulk 4.00
PS6 Irving Fryar 1.00
PS7 Kevin Ross 1.00
PS8 Vince Workman 1.00
PS9 Ray Buchanan 1.00
PS10 Tony Martin 1.00
PS11 D.J. Johnson 1.00
PS12 Steve Young 4.00

1995 Stadium Club Members Only

The 550-card, standard-size set was a parallel issue to the base 1995 Stadium Club issue and was released in two, 275-card series, available only through the Members Only Club. Just 2,000 sets were produced and were available for $99.95 for each series in a factory box that also included parallels of each insert. The cards are differentiated with the base cards by a gold-foil Members Only stamp. Each complete set order also came with three-pin set and a replica game ticket of the 1995 Pro Football Hall of Fame game between Jacksonville and Carolina.

NM/M
Complete Set (550): 150.00
Common Player (1-450): .20
Common Player (GA1-GA15): .35
Common Player (ME1-ME8): 35.00
Common Player (MV1-MV8): .35
Common Player (NE1-NE15): .35
Common Player (NM1-NM30): .35
Common Player (P1-P12/PS1-PS12): .35
P1 Steve Young 3.00
P2 Natrone Means .50
P3 Cris Carter .50
P4 Junior Seau .50
P5 Barry Sanders 4.00
P6 Michael Irvin 1.00
P7 John Elway 2.50
P8 Emmitt Smith 8.00
P9 Greg Lloyd .35
P10 Jerry Rice 4.00
P11 Marshall Faulk 3.00
P12 Drew Bledsoe 3.00
GA1 Emmitt Smith 8.00
GA2 Brett Favre 4.00
GA4 John Elway 2.50
GA5 Rick Mirer .50
GA6 Greg Hill .50
GA7 Errict Rhett 3.00
GA8 Byron "Bam" Morris .35
GA9 Derek Brown (RB) .35
GA10 Steve Young 3.00
GA11 Charlie Garner .35
GA12 Lewis Tillman .35
GA13 Harvey Williams .35
GA14 Garrison Hearst .75
GA15 Marshall Faulk 3.00
ME1 Jerry Rice 4.00
ME2 Barry Sanders 4.00
ME3 John Elway 2.50
ME4 Dana Stubblefield .35
ME5 Emmitt Smith 8.00
ME6 Deion Sanders 2.50
ME7 Marshall Faulk 3.00
ME8 Steve Young 3.00
MV1 Jerry Rice 4.00
MV2 Boomer Esiason .35
MV3 Randall Cunningham .35
MV4 Marcus Allen .50
MV5 John Elway 2.50
MV6 Dan Marino 8.00
MV7 Emmitt Smith 8.00
MV8 Steve Young 3.00
NE1 Barry Sanders, Jack Del Rio 4.00
NE2 Reggie White, Lomas Brown .50
NE3 Terry McDaniel, Anthony Miller .35
NE4 Brett Favre, Chris Spielman 4.00
NE5 Junior Seau, Chris Warren .50
NE6 Cortez Kennedy, Steve Wisniewski .35
NE7 Rod Woodson, Tim Brown .50
NE8 Troy Aikman, Michael Brooks 4.00
NE9 Bruce Smith, Bruce Armstrong .50
NE10 Jerry Rice, Donnell Woolford 4.00
NE11 Emmitt Smith, Seth Joyner 8.00
NE12 Dan Marino, Cornelius Bennett 8.00
NE13 Marshall Faulk, Bryan Cox 3.00
NE14 Stan Humphries, Greg Lloyd .50
NE15 Michael Irvin, Deion Sanders .75
NM1 Drew Bledsoe 3.00
NM2 Barry Sanders 4.00
NM3 Reggie White .50
NM4 Michael Irvin 1.00
NM5 Jerry Rice 4.00
NM6 Jerome Bettis .50
NM7 Dan Marino 8.00
NM8 Bruce Smith .35
NM9 Steve Young 3.00
NM10 Junior Seau .50
NM11 Emmitt Smith 8.00
NM12 Deion Sanders 2.50
NM13 Rod Woodson .50
NM14 Marshall Faulk 3.00
NM15 Troy Aikman 4.00
NM16 Stan Humphries .50
NM17 Chris Warren .50
NM18 Jack Del Rio .35
NM19 Randall Cunningham .35
NM20 Natrone Means .50
NM21 Dana Stubblefield .35
NM22 Jim Kelly .50
NM23 Cris Carter .50
NM24 Cornelius Bennett .35
NM25 Errict Rhett 3.00
NM26 Terry McDaniel .35
NM27 Rodney Hampton .50
NM28 Brett Favre 4.00
NM29 Bryan Cox .35
NM30 John Elway 2.50
PS1 Dan Marino 8.00
PS2 Ken Harvey .35
PS3 Chris Warren .50
PS4 Henry Ellard .35
PS5 Marshall Faulk 3.00
PS6 Irving Fryar .35
PS7 Kevin Ross .35
PS8 Vince Workman .35
PS9 Ray Buchanan .35
PS10 Tony Martin .50
PS11 D.J. Johnson .35
PS12 Steve Young 3.00

1995 Stadium Club Members Only 50

The 50-card, standard-size boxed set featured the 44 starting players from the 1995 Pro Bowl and five Finest cards of the top rookies from the 1994 class. The remaining card was of Jerry Rice and Emmitt Smith who were elected to start in the Pro Bowl, but missed it due to injuries. The set was available to Members Only club members.

NM/M
Complete Set (50): 10.00
Common Player: .25
1 Tim Brown .40
2 Richmond Webb .25
3 Keith Sims .25
4 Dermontti Dawson .25
5 Duval Love .25
6 Bruce Armstrong .25
7 Ben Coates .40
8 Andre Reed .40
9 John Elway .25
10 Marshall Faulk .25
11 Natrone Means .40
12 Charles Haley .25
13 John Randle .25
14 Leon Lett .25
15 William Fuller .25
16 Ken Harvey .25
17 Chris Spielman .25
18 Bryce Paup .40
19 Deion Sanders 1.50
20 Aeneas Williams .25
21 Darren Woodson .25
22 Merton Hanks .25
23 Michael Irvin .75
24 William Roaf .25
25 Nate Newton .25
26 Mark Stepnoski .25
27 Randall McDaniel .25
28 Lomas Brown .25
29 Brent Jones .40
30 Cris Carter .40
31 Steve Young 2.00
32 Barry Sanders 4.00
33 Jerome Bettis .75
34 Bruce Smith .40
35 Michael Dean Perry .25
36 Cortez Kennedy .40
37 Leslie O'Neal .40
38 Derrick Thomas .40
39 Junior Seau .75
40 Greg Lloyd .40
41 Rod Woodson .40
42 Terry McDaniel .25
43 Eric Turner .25
44 Carnell Lake .25
45 Jerry Rice, Emmitt Smith 6.00
46 William Floyd 1.00
47 Tim Bowens .40
48 Heath Shuler 1.50
49 Bryant Young .75
50 Marshall Faulk 2.50

1996 Stadium Club

Topps' 1996 Stadium Club football has 180 cards in its initial series. Insert sets include Contact Prints, Dot Matrix Parallel, Pro Bowl Embossed, Laser Sites, Cut Backs, and three versions of Extreme Player cards (bronze, silver and gold). Series II also has 180 cards in it, featuring 45 of the league's top rookies and traded players in their new uniforms. All regular cards in both series have etched gold foil and are UV coated. Series II inserts include Photo Gallery, New Age, TSC Matrix Parallel, NFL Playoff Box, Fusion Laser Cut (hobby exclusive) and Brace Yourself (retail only). Interactive game cards (Sunday Night Box, in Series I, and NFL Playoff Box, in Series II) were seeded in packs (one in 12 and 1 in 24 packs, respectively). Those who find the cards were eligible to win prizes based on the final scores of selected games.

NM/M
Complete Set (360): 70.00
Complete Series 1 (180): 40.00
Complete Series 2 (180): 40.00
Common Player: .10
Minor Stars: .20
Dot Matrix: 3X
Match Proofs: 10X-15X
Ser. 1 Pack (10): 1.50
Ser. 1 Wax Box (24): 25.00
Ser. 2 Pack (10): 1.50
Ser. 2 Wax Box (24): 25.00
1 Kyle Brady (TSC Matrix Parallel Set) .10
2 Mickey Washington .10
3 Seth Joyner .10
4 Vinny Testaverde .10
5 Thomas Randolph .10
6 Heath Shuler (TSC Matrix Parallel Set) .20
7 Ty Law .10
8 Blake Brockermeyer .10
9 Darryll Lewis .10
10 Jeff Blake (TSC Matrix Parallel Set) .75
11 Tyrone Hughes (TSC Matrix Parallel Set) .10
12 Horace Copeland .10
13 Roman Phifer .10
14 Eugene Robinson .10
15 Anthony Miller (TSC Matrix Parallel Set) .10
16 Robert Smith .10
17 Chester McGlockton .10
18 Marty Carter .10
19 Scott Mitchell (TSC Matrix Parallel Set) .10
20 O.J. McDuffie .10
21 Stan Humphries (TSC Matrix Parallel Set) .10
22 Eugene Daniel .10
23 Devin Bush .10
24 Darick Holmes .10
25 Ricky Watters (TSC Matrix Parallel Set) .10
26 J.J. Stokes (TSC Matrix Parallel Set) .20
27 George Koonce .10
28 Tamarick Vanover (TSC Matrix Parallel Set) .75
29 Yancey Thigpen (TSC Matrix Parallel Set) .50
30 Troy Aikman (TSC Matrix Parallel Set) 1.25
31 Rashaan Salaam (TSC Matrix Parallel Set) .50
32 Anthony Cook .10
33 Tim McKyer .10
34 Dale Carter .10
35 Marvin Washington .10
36 Terry Allen .10
37 Keith Goganious .10
38 Pepper Johnson .10
39 Dave Brown .10
40 Levon Kirkland .10
41 Ken Dilger .10
42 Harvey Williams (TSC Matrix Parallel Set) .10
43 Robert Blackmon .10
44 Kevin Carter .10
45 Warren Moon (TSC Matrix Parallel Set) .10
46 Allen Aldridge .10
47 Terance Mathis (TSC Matrix Parallel Set) .10
48 Junior Seau (TSC Matrix Parallel Set) .10
49 William Fuller .10
50 Lee Woodall (TSC Matrix Parallel Set) .10
51 Aeneas Williams (TSC Matrix Parallel Set) .10
52 Thomas Smith .10
53 Chris Slade .10
54 Eric Allen (TSC Matrix Parallel Set) .10
55 David Sloan .10
56 Hardy Nickerson .10
57 Michael Irvin (TSC Matrix Parallel Set) .20
58 Corey Sawyer .10
59 Eric Green .10
60 Reggie White (TSC Matrix Parallel Set) .10
61 Isaac Bruce (TSC Matrix Parallel Set) .75
62 Darrell Green .10
63 Aaron Glenn .10
64 Mark Brunell (TSC Matrix Parallel Set) 1.00
65 Mark Carrier .10
66 Mel Gray .10
67 Phillippi Sparks .10
68 Ernie Mills .10
69 Rick Mirer (TSC Matrix Parallel Set) .10
70 Neil Smith (TSC Matrix Parallel Set) .10
71 Terry McDaniel .10
72 Terrell Davis (TSC Matrix Parallel Set) 2.00
73 Alonzo Spellman .10
74 Jessie Tuggle .10
75 Terry Kirby .10
76 David Palmer .10
77 Calvin Williams .10
78 Shaun Gayle .10
79 Bryant Young .10
80 Jim Harbaugh (TSC Matrix Parallel Set) .10
81 Michael Jackson (TSC Matrix Parallel Set) .10
82 David Meggett (TSC Matrix Parallel Set) .10
83 Henry Thomas .10
84 Jim Kelly (TSC Matrix Parallel Set) .10
85 Frank Sanders (TSC Matrix Parallel Set) .10
86 Daryl Johnston .10
87 Alvin Harper .10
88 John Copeland .10
89 Mark Chmura (TSC Matrix Parallel Set) .25
90 Jim Everett (TSC Matrix Parallel Set) .10
91 Bobby Houston .10
92 Willie Jackson .10
93 Carlton Bailey .10
94 Todd Lyght .10
95 Ken Harvey .10
96 Erric Pegram .10
97 Anthony Smith .10
98 Kimble Anders .10
99 Steve McNair (TSC Matrix Parallel Set) .75
100 Jeff George (TSC Matrix Parallel Set) .20
101 Michael Timpson .10
102 Brent Jones .10
103 Mike Mamula .10
104 Jeff Cross .10
105 Craig Newsome .10
106 Howard Cross .10
107 Terry Wooden .10
108 Randall McDaniel .10
109 Andre Reed .10
110 Steve Atwater .10
111 Larry Centers .10
112 Tony Bennett .10
113 Drew Bledsoe (TSC Matrix Parallel Set) 1.25
114 Terrell Fletcher .10
115 Warren Sapp .10
116 Deion Sanders (TSC Matrix Parallel Set) .75
117 Bryce Paup (TSC Matrix Parallel Set) .10
118 Mario Bates .10
119 Steve Tovar .10
120 Barry Sanders (TSC Matrix Parallel Set) 2.00
121 Tony Boselli .10
122 Micheal Barrow .10
123 Sam Mills (TSC Matrix Parallel Set) .10
124 Tim Brown (TSC Matrix Parallel Set) .10
125 Darren Perry .10
126 Brian Blades .10
127 Tyrone Wheatley .10
128 Derrick Thomas (TSC Matrix Parallel Set) .10
129 Edgar Bennett .10
130 Cris Carter (TSC Matrix Parallel Set) .10
131 Steve Grant .10
132 Kevin Williams .10
133 Darnay Scott .20
134 Rod Stephens .10
135 Ken Norton (TSC Matrix Parallel Set) .10
136 *Tim Biakabutuka* (Draft Pick) 1.00
137 *Willie Anderson* (Draft Pick) .10
138 *Lawrence Phillips* (Draft Pick) .75
139 *Jonathan Ogden* (Draft Pick) .10
140 *Simeon Rice* (Draft Pick) .25
141 *Alex Van Dyke* (Draft Pick) .20
142 *Jerome Woods* (Draft Pick) .10
143 *Eric Moulds* (Draft Pick) 2.00
144 *Mike Alstott* (Draft Pick) 1.50
145 *Marvin Harrison* (Draft Pick) 5.00
146 *Duane Clemons* (Draft Pick) .10
147 *Regan Upshaw* (Draft Pick) .10
148 *Eddie Kennison* (Draft Pick) .50
149 *John Mobley* (Draft Pick) .10
150 *Keyshawn Johnson* (Draft Pick) 2.50
151 *Marco Battaglia* (Draft Pick) .10
152 *Rickey Dudley* (Draft Pick) .50
153 *Kevin Hardy* (Draft Pick) .20
154 Curtis Martin (Shining Moments) 2.00
155 Dan Marino (Shining Moments) 2.00
156 Rashaan Salaam (Shining Moments) .50
157 Joey Galloway (Shining Moments) .75
158 John Elway (Shining Moments) .40
159 Marshall Faulk (Shining Moments) .50
160 Jerry Rice (Shining Moments) 1.00
161 Darren Bennett (Shining Moments) .10
162 Tamarick Vanover (Shining Moments) .50
163 Orlando Thomas (Shining Moments) .10
164 Jim Kelly (Shining Moments) .10
165 Larry Brown (Shining Moments) .10
166 Errict Rhett (Shining Moments) .40
167 Warren Moon (Shining Moments) .10
168 Hugh Douglas (Shining Moments) .10
169 Jim Everett (Shining Moments) .10
170 AFC Championship Game (Shining Moments) .10
171 Larry Centers (Shining Moments) .10
172 Marcus Allen (Golden Moments) .10
173 Morten Andersen (Golden Moments) .10
174 Brett Favre (Golden Moments) 2.00
175 Jerry Rice (Golden Moments) .75
176 Glyn Milburn (Golden Moments) .10
177 Thurman Thomas (Golden Moments) .10
178 Michael Irvin (Golden Moments) .10
179 Barry Sanders (Golden Moments) 2.00
180 Dan Marino (Golden Moments) 2.00
181 Joey Galloway 1.00
182 Dwayne Harper .10
183 Antonio Langham .10
184 Chris Zorich .10
185 Willie McGinest .10
186 Wayne Chrebet .10
187 Dermontti Dawson .10
188 Charlie Garner .10
189 Quentin Coryatt .10
190 Rodney Hampton .10
191 Kelvin Pritchett .10
192 Willie Green .10
193 Garrison Hearst .10
194 Tracy Scroggins .10
195 Raghib Ismail .10
196 Michael Westbrook .30
197 Troy Drayton .10
198 Rob Fredrickson .10
199 Sean Lumpkin .10
200 John Elway .75
201 Bernie Parmalee .10
202 Chris Chandler .10
203 Lake Dawson .10
204 Orlando Thomas .10
205 Carl Pickens .20
206 Kurt Schulz .10
207 Clay Matthews .10
208 Winston Moss .10
209 Sean Dawkins .10
210 Emmitt Smith 2.50
211 Mark Carrier .10
212 Clyde Simmons .10
213 Derrick Brooks .10
214 William Floyd .20
215 Aaron Hayden .10
216 Brian DeMarco .10
217 Ben Coates .10
218 Renaldo Turnbull .10
219 Adrian Murrell .10
220 Marcus Allen .20
221 Brett Maxie .10
222 Trev Alberts .10
223 Darren Woodson .10
224 Brian Mitchell .10
225 Michael Haynes .10
226 Sean Jones .10
227 Eric Zeier .10
228 Herman Moore .30
229 Shane Conlan .10
230 Chris Warren .20
231 Dana Stubblefield .10
232 Andre Coleman .10
233 Kordell Stewart 1.25
234 Ray Crockett .10
235 Craig Heyward .10
236 Mike Fox .10
237 Derek Brown .10
238 Thomas Lewis .10
239 Hugh Douglas .10
240 Tom Carter .10
241 Toby Wright .10
242 Jason Belser .10
243 Rodney Peete .10
244 Napoleon Kaufman .10
245 Merton Hanks .10
246 Harry Colon .10
247 Greg Hill .10
248 Vincent Brisby .10
249 Eric Hill .10
250 Brett Favre 2.50
251 Leroy Hoard .10
252 Eric Guliford .10
253 Stanley Richard .10
254 Carlos Jenkins .10
255 D'Marco Farr .10
256 Carlton Gray .10
257 Derek Loville .10
258 Ray Buchanan .10
259 Jake Reed .10
260 Dan Marino 2.50
261 Brad Baxter .10
262 Pat Swilling .10
263 Andy Harmon .10
264 Harold Green .10
265 Shannon Sharpe .10
266 Erik Kramer .10
267 Lamar Lathon .10
268 Stevon Moore .10
269 Tony Martin .10
270 Bruce Smith .10
271 James Washington .10
272 Tyrone Poole .10
273 Eric Swann .10
274 Dexter Carter .10
275 Greg Lloyd .10
276 Michael Zordich .10
277 Steve Wisniewski .10
278 Chris Calloway .10
279 Irv Smith .10
280 Steve Young 1.00
281 James Stewart .10
282 Blaine Bishop .10
283 Rob Moore .10
284 Eric Metcalf .10
285 Kerry Collins .30
286 Dan Wilkinson .10
287 Curtis Conway .10
288 Jay Novacek .10
289 Henry Ellard .10
290 Curtis Martin 2.00
291 Brett Perriman .10
292 Jeff Lageman .10
293 Trent Dilfer .10
294 Cortez Kennedy .10
295 Jeff Hostetler .10
296 Mark Fields .10
297 Qadry Ismail .10
298 Steve Bono .10
299 Tony Tolbert .10
300 Jerry Rice 1.25
301 Marvcus Patton .10
302 Robert Brooks .20
303 Terry Ray .10
304 John Thierry .10
305 Errict Rhett .30
306 Ricardo McDonald .10
307 Antonio London .10
308 Lonnie Johnson .10
309 Mark Collins .10
310 Marshall Faulk .50
311 Anthony Pleasant .10
312 Howard Griffith .10
313 Roosevelt Potts .10
314 Jim Flanigan .10

315	'Omar Ellison	.10
316	Boomer Esiason	.10
317	Leslie O'Neal	.10
318	Jerome Bettis	.20
319	Larry Brown	.10
320	Neil O'Donnell	.10
321	Andre Rison	.10
322	Cornelius Bennett	.10
323	Quinn Early	.10
324	Bryan Cox	.10
325	Irving Fryar	.10
326	Eddie Robinson	.10
327	Chris Doleman	.10
328	Sean Gilbert	.10
329	Steve Walsh	.10
330	Kevin Greene	.10
331	Chris Spielman	.10
332	Jeff Graham	.10
333	*Anthony Dorsett Jr.*	.20
334	*Amani Toomer*	.50
335	*Walt Harris*	.20
336	*Ray Mickens*	.10
337	*Danny Kanell*	.50
338	*Daryl Gardener*	.10
339	*Jonathan Ogden*	.50
340	*Eddie George*	5.00
341	*Jeff Lewis*	.75
342	*Terrell Owens*	4.00
343	*Brian Dawkins*	.10
344	Tim Biakabutuka	.50
345	Marvin Harrison	1.50
346	*Lawyer Milloy*	.10
347	Eric Moulds	1.00
348	Alex Van Dyke	.20
349	*John Mobley*	.10
350	*Kevin Hardy*	.10
351	*Ray Lewis*	2.00
352	Lawrence Phillips	.30
353	*Stepfret Williams*	.10
354	*Bobby Engram*	.50
355	*Leeland McElroy*	.30
356	*Marco Battaglia*	.10
357	*Rickey Dudley*	.20
358	*Bobby Hoying*	.75
359	*Cedric Jones*	.10
360	Keyshawn Johnson	1.00

1996 Stadium Club Dot Matrix

Ninety of the cards from Topps' 1996 Stadium Club set have been duplicated for a parallel insert set. Forty-five cards from Series I have been selected, using dot matrix foil for the design. There were also 45 Series II cards chosen; these cards also have holographic foil in the design. Cards were seeded one per every 12 packs in the corresponding series. The TSC logo is on the card front.

		NM/M
Complete Set (90):		85.00
Common Player:		1.00
1	Kyle Brady	1.00
6	Heath Shuler	1.00
10	Jeff Blake	6.00
11	Tyrone Hughes	1.00
15	Anthony Miller	1.00
19	Scott Mitchell	1.00
21	Stan Humphries	1.00
25	Ricky Watters	1.00
26	J.J. Stokes	6.00
28	Tamarick Vanover	7.00
29	Yancey Thigpen	5.00
30	Troy Aikman	12.00
31	Rashaan Salaam	5.00
42	Harvey Williams	1.00
45	Warren Moon	1.00
47	Terance Mathis	1.00
48	Junior Seau	1.00
50	Lee Woodall	1.00
51	Aeneas Williams	1.00
54	Eric Allen	1.00
57	Michael Irvin	2.00
60	Reggie White	3.00
61	Isaac Bruce	5.00
64	Mark Brunell	5.00
69	Rick Mirer	2.00
70	Neil Smith	1.00
72	Terrell Davis	15.00
80	Jim Harbaugh	1.00
81	Michael Jackson	1.00
82	David Meggett	1.00
84	Jim Kelly	2.00
85	Frank Sanders	1.00
89	Mark Chmura	1.00
90	Jim Everett	1.00
99	Steve McNair	10.00
100	Jeff George	1.00
113	Drew Bledsoe	10.00
116	Deion Sanders	10.00
117	Bryce Paup	1.00
120	Barry Sanders	20.00
123	Sam Mills	1.00
124	Tim Brown	1.00
128	Derrick Thomas	1.00
130	Cris Carter	1.00
135	Ken Norton	1.00
181	Joey Galloway	10.00
182	Chris Zorich	1.00
185	Willie McGinest	1.00
186	Wayne Chrebet	1.00
190	Rodney Hampton	1.00
196	Michael Westbrook	5.00
200	John Elway	10.00
204	Orlando Thomas	1.00
205	Carl Pickens	2.00
210	Emmitt Smith	25.00
213	Derrick Brooks	1.00
217	Ben Coates	1.00
220	Marcus Allen	2.00
224	Brian Mitchell	1.00
227	Eric Zeier	1.00
228	Herman Moore	4.00
230	Chris Warren	2.00
233	Kordell Stewart	12.00
235	Craig Heyward	1.00
239	Hugh Douglas	1.00
240	Tom Carter	1.00
243	Rodney Peete	1.00
244	Napoleon Kaufman	1.00
250	Brett Favre	25.00
260	Dan Marino	25.00
265	Shannon Sharpe	1.00
266	Erik Kramer	1.00
267	Lamar Lathon	1.00
270	Bruce Smith	1.00
275	Greg Lloyd	1.00
280	Steve Young	10.00
282	Blaine Bishop	1.00
284	Eric Metcalf	1.00
285	Kerry Collins	15.00
286	Dan Wilkinson	1.00
287	Curtis Conway	1.00
288	Jay Novacek	1.00
290	Curtis Martin	20.00
293	Trent Dilfer	1.00
295	Jeff Hostetler	1.00
298	Steve Bono	1.00
300	Jerry Rice	12.00
302	Robert Brooks	2.00
305	Errict Rhett	3.00
310	Marshall Faulk	5.00

1996 Stadium Club Match Proofs

Match Proofs are a parallel set that runs through all 270 cards from Series I and II. This parallel set features identical fronts, but has different backs than regular-issue cards. Production of Match Proofs was limited to only 100 sets.

Proof Cards: 10X-15X

1996 Stadium Club Brace Yourself

These cards are Stadium Club's retail-only inserts in Series II. Each card features a gridiron great on an embossed, holographic foil card. The front has a photo in the middle, with a bull's-eye as the background. The TSC logo is in the upper right corner; the player's name is in the lower left corner. "Brace Yourself" is written along the right side. The card back repeats the bull's-eye pattern as the background, with the player's name, team name, position and card number (using a "BY" prefix) toward the top. The middle of the card comments about the player's talents. Cards were seeded one per every 24 packs.

		NM/M
Complete Set (10):		30.00
Common Player:		1.00
1	Dan Marino	6.00
2	Marshall Faulk	3.00
3	Greg Lloyd	1.00
4	Steve Young	4.00
5	Emmitt Smith	5.00
6	Junior Seau	2.00
7	Chris Warren	1.00
8	Jerry Rice	4.00
9	Troy Aikman	4.00
10	Barry Sanders	5.00

A player's name in *italic* type indicates a rookie card.

1996 Stadium Club Contact Prints

These 10 cards were included in 1996 Topps Stadium Club Series I packs, one per every 12 packs. The cards feature a bone-jarring hit on the front in color, against a contact sheet which shows several smaller black-and-white prints of cards from the set as the background. "Contact Print" is in red foil along the left side of the card; "Takedown" is in blue foil along the bottom. The TSC logo is stamped in the upper right corner of the horizontally-designed front. The horizontal back has a closeup photo of one of the players featured on the front, along with an extended cutline on the right side about the photo on the front. The name of the featured player is in white letters at the top; the name of the player being hit is in smaller white letters next to it. "Takedown" is written along the bottom of the card, with a card number (using a "CP" prefix) next to it.

		NM/M
Complete Set (10):		4.00
Common Player:		.50
1	Ken Norton	.50
2	Chris Zorich	.50
3	Corey Harris	.50
4	Sam Mills	.50
5	Bryce Paup	.50
6	Rob Fredrickson	.50
7	Darnell Walker	.50
8	Derrick Thomas	.50
9	Hardy Nickerson	.50
10	Reggie White	1.00

1996 Stadium Club Cut Backs

These eight cards were randomly included in 1996 Topps Stadium Club Series I hobby packs only, one per every 36 packs. Speedster running backs such as Curtis Martin and Barry Sanders are featured on these precisely-cut laser designed cards.

		NM/M
Complete Set (8):		20.00
Common Player:		1.00
1	Emmitt Smith	6.00
2	Barry Sanders	6.00
3	Curtis Martin	4.00
4	Chris Warren	1.00
5	Errict Rhett	1.00
6	Rodney Hampton	1.00
7	Ricky Watters	1.00
8	Terry Allen	1.00

1996 Stadium Club Fusion

These cards were found exclusively in 1996 Topps Stadium Club Series II packs, one per every 24 packs. Cards, which are laser cut along one side, are intended to be "fused" together to match up a pair of teammates, forming a larger image. Eight different dynamic duos are spotlighted in this set.

		NM/M
Complete Set (16):		40.00
Common Player:		1.00
1A	Steve Young	4.00
1B	Jerry Rice	4.00
2A	Drew Bledsoe	4.00
2B	Curtis Martin	5.00
3A	Trent Dilfer	1.00
3B	Errict Rhett	1.00
4A	Jeff Hostetler	1.00
4B	Tim Brown	3.00
5A	Brett Favre	6.00
5B	Robert Brooks	1.00
6A	Jim Harbaugh	1.00
6B	Marshall Faulk	4.00
7A	Erik Kramer	1.00
7B	Rashaan Salaam	1.00
8A	Scott Mitchell	1.00
8B	Barry Sanders	5.00

1996 Stadium Club Laser Sites

These eight cards were inserted one per every 36 hobby packs of 1996 Topps Stadium Club Series I football. Each card has an intricate laser cut design, polished off with diffraction foil stamping. Eight top quarterbacks were selected for the set.

		NM/M
Complete Set (8):		20.00
Common Player:		1.00
1	Brett Favre	5.00
2	Dan Marino	5.00
3	Steve Young	3.00
4	Troy Aikman	3.00
5	Jim Harbaugh	1.00
6	Scott Mitchell	1.00
7	Erik Kramer	1.00
8	Warren Moon	1.00

1996 Stadium Club Namath Finest

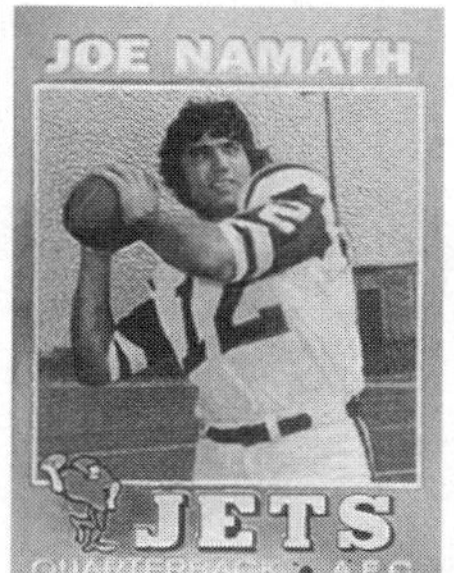

Following on the heels of the Joe Namath reprints in 1996 Topps packs, Finest and Finest Refractor versions of these 10 cards were included in 1996 Topps Stadium Club Series I packs. Finest cards were seeded one per every 24 packs; Refractor versions were one per every 96 packs. Cards are labeled on the back as being part of a reprint set, with a number (1 of 10, etc.) also included. The Refractors are also labeled on the back as being such.

		NM/M
Complete Set (10):		50.00
Common Player:		5.00
Refractors:		3X
1	1965	15.00
2	1966	5.00
3	1967	5.00
4	1968	5.00
5	1969	5.00
6	1970	5.00
7	1971	5.00
8	1972	5.00
9	1972	5.00
10	1973	5.00

1996 Stadium Club Namath Finest Refractors

This 10-card insert is a parallel to the Finest Namath Reprints, with Refractor versions seeded every 96 packs. Namath Reprints first appeared in Topps Football and were then reprinted in Finest technology for Stadium Club Series I packs. The insert showcases some of Namath's top cards throughout his career.

Refractors: 3X

1996 Stadium Club New Age

These cards were seeded one per every 24 packs of 1996 Topps Stadium Club Series II product. Twenty 1996 NFL draft picks and first-year rookies are spotlighted on the cards, which use etched dot matrix technology for the front. The front also has a color photo in the middle with a frame around it. A team logo is in the upper left corner of the frame. A TSC logo is at the top of the card; the player's name is along the bottom. The card back has a rectangle in the middle which has the player's name, team name and position toward the top, just below a card number (which uses an "NA" prefix). Inside the rectangle is a recap of the player's collegiate accomplishments. "New Age" is at the top of the card.

		NM/M
Complete Set (20):		40.00
Common Player:		1.00
1	Alex Van Dyke	1.00
2	Lawrence Phillips	1.00
3	Tim Biakabutuka	1.00
4	Reggie Brown	1.00
5	Duane Clemons	1.00
6	Marco Battaglia	1.00
7	Cedric Jones	1.00
8	Jerome Woods	1.00
9	Eric Moulds	5.00
10	Kevin Hardy	1.00
11	Rickey Dudley	3.00
12	Regan Upshaw	1.00
13	Eddie Kennison	4.00
14	Jonathan Ogden	1.00
15	John Mobley	1.00
16	Mike Alstott	5.00
17	Alex Molden	1.00
18	Marvin Harrison	10.00
19	Simeon Rice	1.00
20	Keyshawn Johnson	6.00

1996 Stadium Club Photo Gallery

These cards were seeded one per every 18 packs of 1996 Topps Stadium Club Series II product. Each card features a customized design that complements the outstanding photography, and is printed on smooth cast-coated stock with an exclusive Topps high gloss laminate. The Photo Gallery logo, player's name, opponent, and game date from when the picture was taken are stamped in red, blue or silver foil on the front. The card back has the player's team name and position listed at the top, with the player's name below. The date of the game is under his name, with a recap of the game below, on one side. A color photo is on the other side. The card number, using a "PG" prefix, is in the lower left corner.

		NM/M
Complete Set (21):		75.00
Common Player:		1.00
1	Emmitt Smith	6.00
2	Jeff Blake	1.00
3	Junior Seau	1.00
4	Robert Brooks	1.00
5	Barry Sanders	5.00
6	Drew Bledsoe	4.00
7	Joey Galloway	2.00
8	Marshall Faulk	4.00
9	Mark Brunell	3.00
10	Jerry Rice	5.00
11	Rashaan Salaam	1.00
12	Troy Aikman	4.00
13	Steve Young	4.00
14	Tim Brown	1.00
15	Brett Favre	6.00
16	Kerry Collins	2.00
17	John Elway	4.00
18	Curtis Martin	4.00
19	Deion Sanders	2.00
20	Dan Marino	5.00
21	Chris Warren	1.00

1996 Stadium Club Pro Bowl

These 20 embossed cards were seeded one per every 24 retail packs of 1996 Topps Stadium Club Series I product. The cards used etched Power Matrix technology. Twenty participants in the 1996 Pro Bowl game are featured in the set.

		NM/M
Complete Set (20):		40.00
Common Player:		1.00
Minor Stars:		2.00
Inserted 1:24 Retail		
1	Brett Favre	6.00
2	Bruce Smith	1.00
3	Ricky Watters	2.00
4	Yancey Thigpen	1.00
5	Barry Sanders	5.00
6	Jim Harbaugh	1.00
7	Michael Irvin	2.00
8	Chris Warren	1.00
9	Dana Stubblefield	1.00
10	Jeff Blake	1.00
11	Emmitt Smith	6.00
12	Bryce Paup	1.00
13	Steve Young	4.00
14	Kevin Greene	1.00
15	Jerry Rice	5.00
16	Curtis Martin	4.00
17	Reggie White	2.00
18	Derrick Thomas	1.00
19	Cris Carter	2.00
20	Greg Lloyd	1.00

1996 Stadium Club Members Only

This set is a complete parallel of the 1996 Stadium Club set. It was sold through Topps' Members Only Club. This issue was available in factory set form and included all the base set and insert cards. Club members could purchase the entire set or an individual series. Each card featured a special Members Only stamp.

	NM/M
Complete Set (476):	150.00
Common Player (1-360):	.20
Common Player (C1-C8):	.35
Common Player (F1A-F8B):	.35
Common Player (N1-N10):	1.00
Common Player (BY1-BY10):	.35
Common Player (CP1-CP10):	.35
Common Player (NA1-NA20):	.35
Common Player (PB1-PB20):	.35

Common Player (PG1-PG20): .50
Semistars Inserts: .50
Stars Inserts: .75
Stars: 2X to4X
*RCs: 2X
C1 Emmitt Smith 8.00
C2 Barry Sanders 5.00
C3 Curtis Martin 4.00
C4 Chris Warren .50
C5 Errict Rhett .50
C6 Rodney Hampton .35
C7 Ricky Watters .50
C8 Terry Allen .50
F1A Steve Young 3.00
F1B Jerry Rice 4.00
F2A Drew Bledsoe 4.00
F2B Curtis Martin 4.00
F3A Trent Dilfer .50
F3B Errict Rhett .50
F4A Jeff Hostetler .35
F4B Tim Brown .50
F5A Brett Favre 10.00
F5B Robert Brooks .75
F6A Jim Harbaugh .50
F6B Marshall Faulk .75
F7A Rashaan Salaam .75
F7B Erik Kramer .35
F8A Scott Mitchell .35
F8B Barry Sanders 5.00
N1 Joe Namath 1965 1.00
N2 Joe Namath 1966 1.00
N3 Joe Namath 1967 1.00
N4 Joe Namath 1968 1.00
N5 Joe Namath 1969 1.00
N6 Joe Namath 1970 1.00
N7 Joe Namath 1971 1.00
N8 Joe Namath 1972 1.00
N9 Joe Namath 1972 1.00
N10 Joe Namath 1973 1.00
BY1 Dan Marino 8.00
BY2 Marshall Faulk .75
BY3 Greg Lloyd .35
BY4 Steve Young 3.00
BY5 Emmitt Smith 8.00
BY6 Junior Seau .50
BY7 Chris Warren .50
BY8 Jerry Rice 4.00
BY9 Troy Aikman 4.00
BY10 Barry Sanders 5.00
CP1 Ken Norton, Drew Bledsoe 3.00
CP2 Chris Zorich, Barry Sanders 3.00
CP3 Corey Harris, Harvey Williams .35
CP4 Sam Mills, Thurman Thomas .75
CP5 Bryce Paup, Derrick Moore .35
CP6 Rob Fredrickson, Chris Warren .50
CP7 Darnell Walker, Bernie Parmalee .35
CP8 Derrick Thomas, Gus Frerotte .50
CP9 Hardy Nickerson, Robert Smith .35
CP10 Reggie White, Dave Brown .75
NA1 Alex Van Dyke .50
NA2 Lawrence Phillips 1.00
NA3 Tim Biakabutuka 1.00
NA4 Reggie Brown .35
NA5 Duane Clemons .35
NA6 Marco Battaglia .35
NA7 Cedric Jones .35
NA8 Jerome Woods .35
NA9 Eric Moulds 1.00
NA10 Kevin Hardy .35
NA11 Rickey Dudley .50
NA12 Regan Upshaw .35
NA13 Eddie Kennison 2.50
NA14 Jonathan Ogden .35
NA15 John Mobley .35
NA16 Mike Alstott 1.50
NA17 Alex Molden .35
NA18 Marvin Harrison 2.50
NA19 Simeon Rice .35
NA20 Keyshawn Johnson 2.50
PB1 Brett Favre 10.00
PB2 Bruce Smith .50
PB3 Ricky Watters .50
PB4 Yancey Thigpen .50
PB5 Barry Sanders 5.00
PB6 Jim Harbaugh .50
PB7 Michael Irvin .75
PB8 Chris Warren .50
PB9 Dana Stubblefield .35
PB10 Jeff Blake .50
PB11 Emmitt Smith 8.00
PB12 Bryce Paup .35
PB13 Steve Young 3.00
PB14 Kevin Greene .35
PB15 Jerry Rice 4.00
PB16 Curtis Martin 4.00
PB17 Reggie White .75
PB18 Derrick Thomas .50
PB19 Cris Carter .50
PB20 Greg Lloyd .35
PG1 Emmitt Smith 8.00
PG2 Jeff Blake .50
PG3 Junior Seau .50
PG4 Robert Brooks .75
PG5 Barry Sanders 5.00
PG6 Drew Bledsoe 4.00
PG7 Joey Galloway .75
PG8 Marshall Faulk .75
PG9 Mark Brunell 4.00
PG10 Jerry Rice 4.00
PG11 Rashaan Salaam .75
PG12 Troy Aikman 4.00
PG13 Steve Young 3.00
PG14 Tim Brown .50
PG15 Brett Favre 10.00
PG16 Kerry Collins 3.00
PG17 John Elway 3.00
PG18 Curtis Martin 4.00
PG19 Deion Sanders 2.00
PG20 Dan Marino 8.00
PG21 Chris Warren .50

1996 Stadium Club Sunday Night Redemption

Sunday Night Redemption cards were inserted in Stadium Club Series One packs (1:24 hobby and retail; 1:20 jumbo). The cards were designated for a certain week of the NFL season and if the score of that week's Sunday night game matched the two numbers on the card, collectors could mail the card in and receive two jumbo Finest cards featuring players in that week's game.

NM/M
Complete Set (32): 150.00
Common Player: 5.00
1A Rodney Hampton 5.00
1B Jim Kelly 8.00
2A Dan Marino 25.00
2B Frank Sanders 5.00
3A Trent Dilfer 7.00
3B John Elway 12.00
4A Eric Metcalf 5.00
4B Ricky Watters 6.00
5A Terry Allen 6.00
5B Keyshawn Johnson 8.00
6A Jeff Blake 8.00
6B Steve McNair 10.00
7A Marshall Faulk 8.00
7B Eric Zeier 5.00
9A Drew Bledsoe 15.00
9B Bruce Smith 5.00
10A Jim Everett 5.00
10B Steve Young 12.00
11A Dave Brown 5.00
11B Kerry Collins 12.00
12A Tim Brown 6.00
12B Cris Carter 6.00
13A Isaac Bruce 8.00
13B Brett Favre 30.00
14A Curtis Martin 15.00
14B Junior Seau 6.00
15A Warren Moon 6.00
15B Barry Sanders 18.00
16A Mark Brunell 15.00
16B Chris Warren 5.00
17A Terrell Davis 15.00
17B Stan Humphries 5.00

1997 Stadium Club

The 170-card Series I set included a full-bleed photo on the front, with the Stadium Club logo at the top and a "wave" on the bottom that included the player's name and position. The backs included an action shot, with the player's name, bio and highlights on the left side in a "ripped out" area. The stats appear in a box in the lower right, along with one highlight. There are three parallel sets. Printing Plates (cyan, yellow, magenta and black plates of each card for a total of 640 cards) were inserted in Home Team Advantage packs. One-of-a-Kind parallel cards were seeded 1:48 packs, while First Day Issue parallel cards were found 1:24 retail packs. Series II also had 170 cards and the base set did include a 20-card Transaction subset, featuring important off-season moves.

NM/M
Complete Set (340): 60.00
Complete Series 1 (170): 30.00
Complete Series 2 (170): 30.00
Common Player: .10
Minor Stars: .20
First Day Stars: 8X-20X
First Day Rookies: 4X-10X
One of a Kind Stars: 10X-25X
One of a Kind Rookies: 5X-12X
Hobby Ser 1/2 Pack (9): 1.75
Hobby Ser 1/2 Wax Box (24): 30.00
Retail Set 1/2 Pack (6): 2.00
Retail Set 1/2 Wax Box (36): 65.00
1 Junior Seau .20
2 Michael Irvin .20
3 Marcus Allen .20
4 Dale Carter .10
5 *Darnell Autry* .40
6 Isaac Bruce .20
7 Darrell Green .10
8 Joey Galloway .30
9 Steve Atwater .10
10 Kordell Stewart 1.50
11 Tony Brackens .10
12 Gus Frerotte .10
13 Henry Ellard .10
14 Charles Way .10
15 *Jim Druckenmiller* 2.00
16 Orlando Thomas .10
17 Terrell Davis 1.25
18 Jim Schwantz .10
19 Derrick Thomas .10
20 Curtis Martin 1.50
21 Deion Sanders .50
22 Bruce Smith .10
23 Jake Reed .10
24 Leeland McElroy .10
25 Jerome Bettis .20
26 Neil Smith .10
27 Terry Allen .10
28 Gilbert Brown .10
29 Steve McNair .75
30 Kerry Collins .30
31 Thurman Thomas .20
32 Kenny Holmes .10
33 Karim Abdul-Jabbar .30
34 Steve Young 1.00
35 Jerry Rice 1.25
36 Jeff George .10
37 Errict Rhett .20
38 Mike Alstott .20
39 Tim Brown .10
40 Keyshawn Johnson .20
41 Jim Harbaugh .10
42 Kevin Hardy .10
43 Kevin Greene .10
44 Eric Metcalf .10
45 Troy Aikman 1.25
46 Marshall Faulk .20
47 Shannon Sharpe .10
48 Warren Moon .10
49 Mark Brunell 1.25
50 Dan Marino 3.00
51 *Byron Hanspard* 1.00
52 Chris Chandler .10
53 Wayne Chrebet .10
54 Antonio Langham .10
55 Barry Sanders 2.00
56 Curtis Conway .10
57 Ricky Watters .20
58 William Thomas .10
59 Chris Warren .10
60 Terry Glenn .30
61 *Peter Boulware* .10
62 Chad Cota .10
63 Eddie Kennison .50
64 Lamar Smith .10
65 Brett Favre 3.00
66 Michael Westbrook .10
67 Larry Centers .10
68 Trent Dilfer .20
69 Stevon Moore .10
70 John Elway 1.00
71 Bryce Paup .10
72 Quentin Coryatt .10
73 Rashaan Salaam .20
74 Thomas Lewis .10
75 Drew Bledsoe 1.25
76 Cris Carter .10
77 Joe Bowden .10
78 Allen Aldridge .10
79 Zach Thomas .30
80 Emmitt Smith 3.00
81 Daryl Johnston .10
82 Vinny Testaverde .10
83 James Stewart .10
84 Edgar Bennett .10
85 *Shawn Springs* .30
86 Elvis Grbac .10
87 Levon Kirkland .10
88 Jeff Graham .10
89 Terrell Fletcher .10
90 Eddie George 2.00
91 Jessie Tuggle .10
92 Terrell Owens .75
93 Wayne Martin .10
94 Dwayne Harper .10
95 Mark Collins .10
96 Marvcus Patton .10
97 Napoleon Kaufman .10
98 Keenan McCardell .10
99 Ty Detmer .10
100 Reggie White .20
101 William Floyd .10
102 Scott Mitchell .10
103 Robert Blackmon .10
104 Dan Wilkinson .10
105 Warren Sapp .10
106 Raymont Harris .10
107 Brian Mitchell .10
108 Tyrone Poole .10
109 Derrick Alexander .10
110 David Palmer .10
111 James Farrior .10
112 Daryl Gardener .10
113 Marty Carter .10
114 Lawrence Phillips .20
115 Wesley Walls .10
116 John Friesz .10
117 Roman Phifer .10
118 Jason Sehorn .10
119 Henry Thomas .10
120 Natrone Means .20
121 Ty Law .10
122 *Tony Gonzalez* 1.00
123 Kevin Williams .10
124 Regan Upshaw .10
125 Antonio Freeman .30
126 Jessie Armstead .10
127 *Pat Barnes* .30
128 Charlie Garner .10
129 Irving Fryar .10
130 Rickey Dudley .10
131 Rodney Harrison .10
132 Brent Jones .10
133 Neil O'Donnell .10
134 Darryll Lewis .10
135 Jason Belser .10
136 Mark Chmura .10
137 Seth Joyner .10
138 Herschel Walker .10
139 Santana Dotson .10
140 Carl Pickens .10
141 Terance Mathis .10
142 Walt Harris .10
143 John Mobley .10
144 Gabe Northern .10
145 Herman Moore .20
146 Michael Jackson .10
147 Chris Sanders .10
148 LeShon Johnson .10
149 Darrell Russell .10
150 Winslow Oliver .10
151 Tamarick Vanover .10
152 Tony Martin .10
153 Lamar Lathon .10
154 Stanley Richard .10
155 Derrick Brooks .10
156 *Warrick Dunn* 2.50
157 Tim McDonald .10
158 Keith Lyle .10
159 Terry McDaniel .10
160 Andre Hastings .10
161 Phillippi Sparks .10
162 Tedy Bruschi .10
163 *Bryant Westbrook* .20
164 Victor Green .10
165 Jimmy Smith .10
166 Greg Biekert .10
167 Frank Sanders .10
168 Chris Doleman .10
169 Phil Hansen .10
170 Walter Jones .10
171 Mark Carrier .10
172 Greg Hill .10
173 Erik Kramer .10
174 Chris Spielman .10
175 Tom Knight .10
176 Sam Mills .10
177 Robert Smith .10
178 Dorsey Levens .20
179 Chris Slade .10
180 Troy Vincent .10
181 Mario Bates .10
182 Ed McCaffrey .10
183 Mike Mamula .10
184 Chad Hennings .10
185 Stan Humphries .10
186 Reinard Wilson .10
187 Kevin Carter .10
188 Qadry Ismail .10
189 Cortez Kennedy .10
190 Eric Swann .10
191 *Corey Dillon* 5.00
192 Renaldo Wynn .10
193 Bobby Hebert .10
194 Fred Barnett .10
195 Ray Lewis .10
196 Robert Jones .10
197 Brian Williams .10
198 Willie McGinest .10
199 *Jake Plummer* 2.00
200 Aeneas Williams .10
201 Ashley Ambrose .10
202 Cornelius Bennett .10
203 Mo Lewis .10
204 James Hasty .10
205 Carnell Lake .10
206 Heath Shuler .10
207 Dana Stubblefield .10
208 Corey Miller .10
209 *Ike Hilliard* 1.50
210 Bryant Young .10
211 Hardy Nickerson .10
212 Blaine Bishop .10
213 Marcus Robertson .10
214 Tony Bennett .10
215 Kent Graham .10
216 Steve Bono .10
217 *Will Blackwell* .50
218 Tyrone Braxton .10
219 Eric Moulds .20
220 Rod Woodson .10
221 Anthony Johnson .10
222 Willie Davis .10
223 Darrin Smith .10
224 Rick Mirer .10
225 Marvin Harrison .50
226 Dixon Edwards .10
227 Joe Aska .10
228 *Yatil Green* .50
229 William Fuller .10
230 Eddie Robinson .10
231 Brian Blades .10
232 Michael Sinclair .10
233 Ken Harvey .10
234 Harvey Williams .10
235 Simeon Rice .10
236 Chris T. Jones .10
237 Bert Emanuel .10
238 Corey Sawyer .10
239 Chris Calloway .10
240 Jeff Blake .20
241 Alonzo Spellman .10
242 Bryan Cox .10
243 *Antowain Smith* 2.50
244 Tim Biakabutuka .20
245 Ray Crockett .10
246 Dwayne Rudd .10
247 Glyn Milburn .10
248 Gary Plummer .10
249 O.J. McDuffie .10
250 Willie Clay .10
251 Jim Everett .10
252 Eugene Daniel .10
253 Jessie Armstead .10
254 Mel Gray .10
255 Ken Norton .10
256 Johnnie Morton .10
257 Courtney Hawkins .10
258 Ricardo McDonald .10
259 Todd Lyght .10
260 Micheal Barrow .10
261 Aaron Glenn .10
262 Clay Matthews .10
263 *Troy Davis* .30
264 Eric Hill .10
265 Darrien Gordon .10
266 Lake Dawson .10
267 John Randle .10
268 Lamar Thomas .10
269 Mickey Washington .10
270 Amani Toomer .10
271 Steve Grant .10
272 Adrian Murrell .20
273 Derrick Witherspoon .10
274 Michael Zordich .10
275 Ben Coates .10
276 *Reidel Anthony* 1.50
277 Jim Schwantz .10
278 Aaron Hayden .10
279 Ryan McNeil .10
280 LeRoy Butler .10
281 Craig Newsome .10
282 Bill Romanowski .10
283 Michael Bankston .10
284 Kevin Smith .10
285 Byron Morris .10
286 Darnay Scott .10
287 *David LaFleur* .50
288 Randall Cunningham .20
289 Eric Davis .10
290 Todd Collins .10
291 Steve Tovar .10
292 Jermaine Lewis .10
293 Alfred Williams .10
294 Brad Johnson .20
295 Charles Johnson .10
296 Ted Johnson .10
297 Merton Hanks .10
298 Andre Coleman .10
299 Keith Jackson .10
300 Terry Kirby .10
301 Tony Banks .30
302 Terrance Shaw .10
303 Bobby Engram .10
304 Hugh Douglas .10
305 Lawyer Milloy .10
306 James Jett .10
307 *Joey Kent* .50
308 Rodney Hampton .10
309 DeWayne Washington .10
310 Kevin Lockett .10
311 Ki-Jana Carter .10
312 Jeff Lageman .10
313 Don Beebe .10
314 Willie Williams .10
315 Tyrone Wheatley .10
316 Leslie O'Neal .10
317 Quinn Early .10
318 Sean Gilbert .10
319 Tim Bowens .10
320 Sean Dawkins .10
321 Ken Dilger .10
322 George Koonce .10
323 Jevon Langford .10
324 Mike Caldwell .10
325 *Orlando Pace* .50
326 Garrison Hearst .10
327 Mike Tomczak .10
328 Rob Moore .10
329 Andre Reed .10
330 Kimble Anders .10
331 Qadry Ismail .10
332 Eric Allen .10
333 Dave Brown .10
334 Bennie Blades .10
335 Jamal Anderson .20
336 John Lynch .10
337 Tyrone Hughes .10
338 Ronnie Harmon .10
339 *Rae Carruth* 1.25
340 Robert Brooks .10

1997 Stadium Club First Day

First Day Issue is a retail-only parallel of the Stadium Club Series base set which was inserted one per 24 packs. Each card was marked with a gold foil logo with the parallel name on the front of the card.

First Day Stars: 8X-20X
First Day Rookies: 4X-10X

1997 Stadium Club One of a Kind

One of a Kind is a hobby-only parallel which was seeded one per 48 packs. Each card is marked with a special security stamp. All 340 cards from Series I and II are paralleled.

One of a Kind Stars: 10X-25X
One of a Kind Rookies: 5X-12X

1997 Stadium Club Aerial Assault

The 10-card set was inserted 1:12 packs. A player photo is superimposed over a holographic background of the United States, with the team's city targeted. "Aerial Assault" is printed at the top left, while the Stadium Club logo and the player's name are in the lower right. The backs, which are numbered with an "AA" prefix, has the player photo on the left, with the player's name, team and 1996 passing stats all to the right.

NM/M
Complete Set (10): 20.00
Common Player: 1.00
1 Dan Marino 4.00
2 Mark Brunell 2.00
3 Troy Aikman 3.00
4 Ty Detmer 1.00
5 John Elway 3.00
6 Drew Bledsoe 3.00
7 Steve Young 3.00
8 Vinny Testaverde 1.00
9 Kerry Collins 1.00
10 Brett Favre 4.00

1997 Stadium Club Bowman's Best Previews

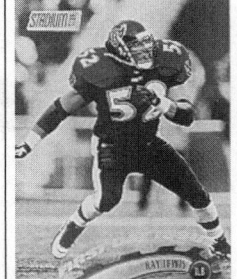

The 15-card set was a sneak peek at the 1997 set. The cards were inserted at a 1:24 rate. The foil cards have a Bowman's Best logo in the upper left, with the player's name and team logo in the lower right. The backs, which are numbered with a "BBP" prefix, have the player photo on the left, with his name, bio, stats and highlights on the right. A Refractor parallel version was seeded 1:96 packs, while an Atomic Refractor version was found 1:192 packs.

NM/M
Complete Set (15): 30.00
Common Player: 1.00
Refractors: 2X-3X
Atomic Refractors: 2X-4X
1 Dan Marino 6.00
2 Terry Allen 1.00
3 Jerome Bettis 1.00
4 Kevin Greene 1.00
5 Junior Seau 1.00
6 Brett Favre 6.00
7 Isaac Bruce 2.00
8 Michael Irvin 1.00
9 Kerry Collins 2.00
10 Karim Abdul-Jabbar 1.00
11 Keenan McCardell 1.00
12 Ricky Watters 1.00

13	Mark Brunell	2.00
14	Jerry Rice	4.00
15	Drew Bledsoe	3.00

1997 Stadium Club Bowman's Best Rookie Preview

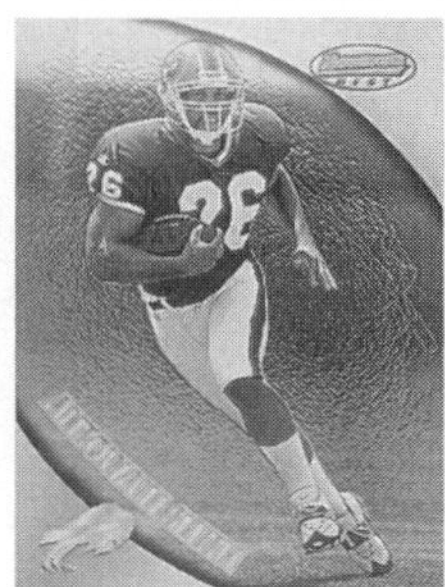

These 15 chromium cards feature top rookies from 1997. The cards were inserted 1:24, with Refractor (1:96) and Atomic Refractor (1:192) versions also available. Cards are numbered with a "BBP" prefix.

		NM/M
Complete Set (15):		20.00
Common Player:		1.00
Refractors:		2X-3X
Atomic Refractors:		3X-6X
1	Orlando Pace	1.00
2	David LaFleur	1.00
3	James Farrior	1.00
4	Tony Gonzalez	4.00
5	Ike Hilliard	4.00
6	Antowain Smith	5.00
7	Tom Knight	1.00
8	Troy Davis	1.00
9	Yatil Green	1.00
10	Jim Druckenmiller	1.00
11	Bryant Westbrook	2.00
12	Darrell Russell	1.00
13	Rae Carruth	1.00
14	Shawn Springs	1.00
15	Peter Boulware	1.00

1997 Stadium Club Co-Signers

Seventy-two NFL players autographed these two-sided cards. There are 108 Co-Signers matchups. Co-Signers were found one per 63 Series I packs and one per 68 Series II packs.

		NM/M
Common Player (1-36):		15.00
Common Player (37-72):		15.00
Common Player (73-108):		5.00
1	Karim Abdul-Jabbar, Eddie George	125.00
2	Trace Armstrong, Alonzo Spellman	15.00
3	Steve Atwater, Kevin Hardy	15.00
4	Fred Barnett, Lake Dawson	15.00
5	Blaine Bishop, Darrell Green	15.00
6	Jeff Blake, Gus Frerotte	35.00
7	Steve Bono, Cris Carter	65.00
8	Tim Brown, Isaac Bruce	75.00
9	Wayne Chrebet, Mickey Washington	15.00
10	Curtis Conway, Eddie Kennison	45.00
11	Eric Davis, Jason Sehorn	15.00
12	Terrell Davis, Thurman Thomas	75.00
13	Ken Dilger, Kent Graham	15.00
14	Stephen Grant, Marvcus Patton	15.00
15	Keith Hamilton, Mike Tomczak	15.00
16	Rodney Hampton, David Meggett	15.00
17	Merton Hanks, Aeneas Williams	15.00
18	No Card	
19	Brent Jones, Wesley Walls	15.00
20	Carnell Lake, Tim McDonald	15.00
21	Thomas Lewis, Keith Lyle	15.00
22	Leeland McElroy, Jeff Lageman	15.00
23	Ray Mickens, Willie Davis	15.00
24	Herman Moore, Desmond Howard	45.00
25	Stevon Moore, William Thomas	15.00
26	Adrian Murrell, Levon Kirkland	20.00
27	Simeon Rice, Winslow Oliver	15.00
28	Bill Romanowski, Gary Plummer	15.00
29	Junior Seau, Chris Spielman	15.00
30	Chris Slade, Kevin Greene	15.00
31	Derrick Thomas, Chris T. Jones	15.00
32	Orlando Thomas, Bobby Engram	15.00
33	Amani Toomer, Thomas Randolph	15.00
34	Steve Tovar, Ellis Johnson	15.00
35	Herschel Walker, Anthony Johnson	15.00
36	Darren Woodson, Aaron Glenn	15.00
37	Karim Abdul-Jabbar, Thurman Thomas	50.00
38	Blaine Bishop, Tim McDonald	15.00
39	Jeff Blake, Derrick Thomas	25.00
40	No Card	15.00
41	Cris Carter, Marvin Harrison	45.00
42	Curtis Conway, Wesley Walls	15.00
43	Willie Davis, Amani Toomer	15.00
44	Lake Dawson, Ray Mickens	15.00
45	Ken Dilger, Ellis Johnson	15.00
46	Bobby Engram, Thomas Lewis	15.00
47	Gus Frerotte, Chris T. Jones	15.00
48	Eddie George, Terrell Davis	125.00
49	Aaron Glenn, Eric Davis	15.00
50	Kent Graham, Steve Tovar	15.00
51	Darrell Green, Carnell Lake	15.00
52	Kevin Greene, Steve Atwater	15.00
53	Rodney Hampton, Anthony Johnson	15.00
54	Kevin Hardy, Merton Hanks	15.00
55	Desmond Howard, Tim Brown	45.00
56	Eddie Kennison, Brent Jones	15.00
57	Levon Kirkland, Simeon Rice	15.00
58	Jeff Lageman, Adrian Murrell	15.00
59	Keith Lyle, Wayne Chrebet	15.00
60	David Meggett, Herschel Walker	15.00
61	Herman Moore, Isaac Bruce	45.00
62	Winslow Oliver, Leeland McElroy	15.00
63	Marvcus Patton, Keith Hamilton	15.00
64	Gary Plummer, Junior Seau	20.00
65	Thomas Randolph, Fred Barnett	15.00
66	Alonzo Spellman, Stephen Grant	15.00
67	Chris Spielman, Stevon Moore	15.00
68	William Thomas, Bill Romanowski	15.00
69	Mike Tomczak, Trace Armstrong	15.00
70	Mickey Washington, Orlando Thomas	15.00
71	Aeneas Williams, Chris Slade	15.00
72	Darren Woodson, Jason Sehorn	15.00
73	Trace Armstrong, Keith Hamilton	5.00
74	Isaac Bruce, Desmond Howard	15.00
75	Terrell Davis, Karim Abdul-Jabbar	75.00
76	Tim Brown, Herman Moore	45.00
77	Derrick Thomas, Gus Frerotte	40.00
78	Thurman Thomas, Eddie George	100.00
79	Steve Atwater, Chris Slade	5.00
80	Merton Hanks, Kevin Greene	5.00
81	Marvin Harrison, Steve Bono	15.00
82	Anthony Johnson, David Meggett	5.00
83	Stephen Grant, Mike Tomczak	5.00
84	Herschel Walker, Rodney Hampton	5.00
85	Aeneas Williams, Kevin Hardy	5.00
86	Anthony Johnson, David Meggett	5.00
87	Brent Jones, Curtis Conway	5.00
88	Carnell Lake, Blaine Bishop	5.00
89	Tim McDonald, Darrell Green	5.00
90	Trace Armstrong, Keith Hamilton	5.00
91	Winslow Oliver, Levon Kirkland	5.00
92	Simeon Rice, Jeff Lageman	5.00
93	Wesley Walls, Eddie Kennison	40.00
94	Adrian Murrell, Leeland McElroy	40.00
95	Winslow Oliver, Levon Kirkland	5.00
96	Marvcus Patton, Alonzo Spellman	5.00
97	No Card	15.00
98	Ray Mickens, Thomas Randolph	5.00
99	Junior Seau, Bill Romanowski	25.00
100	Marvcus Patton, Alonzo Spellman	5.00
101	Derrick Thomas, Gus Frerotte	15.00
102	Orlando Thomas, Keith Lyle	5.00
103	Thurman Thomas, Eddie George	125.00
104	Wayne Chrebet, Thomas Lewis	5.00
105	Steve Tovar, Ken Dilger	5.00
106	Ellis Johnson, Kent Graham	5.00
107	Wesley Walls, Eddie Kennison	40.00
108	Aeneas Williams, Kevin Hardy	5.00

1997 Stadium Club Grid Kids

Inserted 1:36 packs, 20 1997 NFL Draft picks are showcased in their game uniforms in the set. The cards are numbered with a "GK" prefix.

		NM/M
Complete Set (20):		40.00
Common Player:		1.00
Minor Stars:		2.00
1	Orlando Pace	1.00
2	Darrell Russell	1.00
3	Shawn Springs	1.00
4	Peter Boulware	1.00
5	Bryant Westbrook	2.00
6	Darnell Autry	2.00
7	Ike Hilliard	4.00
8	James Farrior	1.00
9	Jake Plummer	5.00
10	Tony Gonzalez	4.00
11	Yatil Green	2.00
12	Corey Dillon	5.00
13	Dwayne Rudd	1.00
14	Renaldo Wynn	1.00
15	David LaFleur	1.00
16	Antowain Smith	4.00
17	Jim Druckenmiller	1.00
18	Rae Carruth	1.00
19	Tom Knight	1.00
20	Byron Hanspard	1.00

1997 Stadium Club Never Compromise

This 40-card insert features 10 veterans and 30 rookies. The cards could be found every 12 packs. They are numbered with a "NC" prefix.

		NM/M
Complete Set (40):		60.00
Common Player:		.60
Minor Stars:		1.00
1	Orlando Pace	.50
2	Corey Dillon	4.00
3	Tony Gonzalez	2.00
4	Tom Knight	.50
5	Deion Sanders	3.00
6	Dwayne Rudd	.50
7	Warrick Dunn	4.00
8	Kenny Holmes	.50
9	Will Blackwell	.50
10	Shawn Springs	.50
11	Rae Carruth	.50
12	Edgar Bennett	1.50
13	Walter Jones	.50
14	Reidel Anthony	1.00
15	Troy Davis	.50
16	Mark Brunell	3.00
17	Pat Barnes	1.00
18	Reggie White	1.00
19	Darrell Russell	.50
20	Ike Hilliard	1.00
21	Emmitt Smith	5.00
22	David LaFleur	.50
23	Yatil Green	1.00
24	Barry Sanders	5.00
25	Bryant Westbrook	1.50
26	Lawrence Phillips	.50
27	Peter Boulware	1.00
28	Joey Kent	.50
29	Kevin Lockett	.50
30	Derrick Thomas	.50
31	Antowain Smith	3.00
32	James Farrior	.50
33	Kordell Stewart	3.00
34	Byron Hanspard	.50
35	Jim Druckenmiller	.50
36	Reinard Wilson	.50
37	Darnell Autry	.50
38	Steve Young	4.00
39	Renaldo Wynn	.50
40	Jake Plummer	2.00

1997 Stadium Club Offensive Strikes

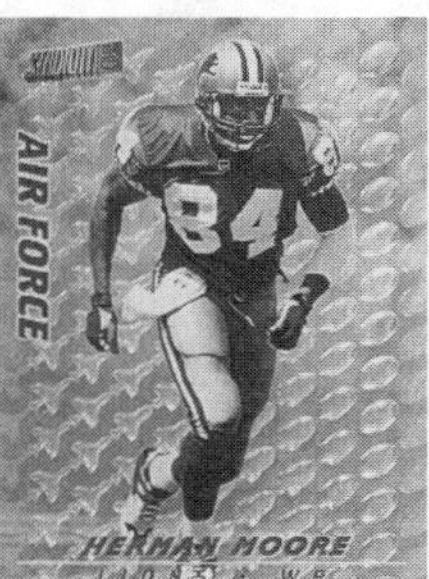

Inserted 1:12 packs, the top five running backs and wide receivers from 1996 are featured in this set. The cards are borderless foil-board.

		NM/M
Complete Set (10):		20.00
Common Player:		1.00
AF1	Jerry Rice (Air Force)	3.00
AF2	Carl Pickens (Air Force)	1.00
AF3	Shannon Sharpe (Air Force)	1.00
AF4	Herman Moore (Air Force)	1.00
AF5	Terry Glenn (Air Force)	1.00
GC1	Barry Sanders (Ground Control)	4.00
GC2	Curtis Martin (Ground Control)	3.00
GC3	Emmitt Smith (Ground Control)	4.00
GC4	Terrell Davis (Ground Control)	3.00
GC5	Eddie George (Ground Control)	3.00

1997 Stadium Club Triumvirate

Exclusive to retail packs, the laser-cut cards featured a trio of leading NFL offensive teammates fused together. There are six different complete cards made up of three players per, each player card is seeded at a 1:36 pack ratio. Refractor versions were found 1:96, while Atomic Refractor versions were seeded 1:192.

		NM/M
Complete Set (18):		50.00
Common Player:		1.00
Refractors:		2X-4X
Atomic Refractors:		3X-6X
T1A	Emmitt Smith	5.00
T1B	Troy Aikman	4.00
T1C	Michael Irvin	1.00
T2A	Curtis Martin	3.00
T2B	Drew Bledsoe	3.00
T2C	Terry Glenn	2.00
T3A	Barry Sanders	5.00
T3B	Scott Mitchell	1.00
T3C	Herman Moore	1.00
T4A	William Floyd	1.00
T4B	Steve Young	4.00
T4C	Jerry Rice	4.00
T5A	Terrell Davis	4.00
T5B	John Elway	4.00
T5C	Shannon Sharpe	1.00
T6A	Edgar Bennett	1.00
T6B	Brett Favre	6.00
T6C	Antonio Freeman	1.00

1997 Stadium Club Triumvirate II

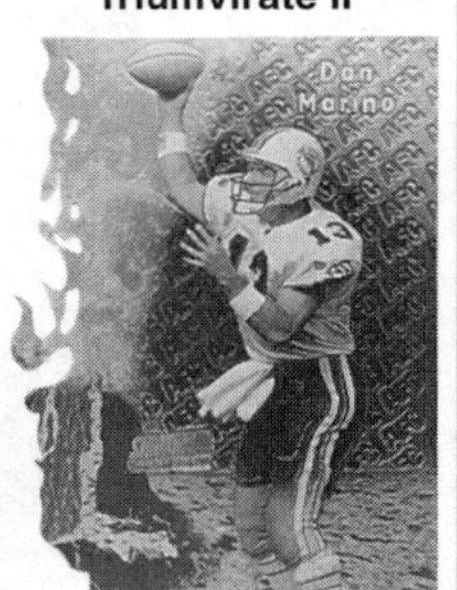

This 18-card, laser-cut insert consists of six trios of players, whose cards can be fit together. Triumvirate was seeded 1:36, with Refractor (1:144) and Atomic Refractor (1:288) also created.

		NM/M
Complete Set (18):		50.00
Common Player:		1.00
Refractors:		2X-3X
Atomic Refractors:		3X-6X
T1A	John Elway	4.00
T1B	Drew Bledsoe	3.00
T1C	Dan Marino	6.00
T2A	Troy Aikman	4.00
T2B	Brett Favre	6.00
T2C	Steve Young	4.00
T3A	Terrell Davis	4.00
T3B	Eddie George	3.00
T3C	Curtis Martin	3.00
T4A	Emmitt Smith	5.00
T4B	Ricky Watters	1.00
T4C	Barry Sanders	5.00
T5A	Shannon Sharpe	1.00
T5B	Terry Glenn	1.00
T5C	Carl Pickens	1.00
T6A	Jake Plummer	2.00
T6B	Orlando Pace	1.00
T6C	Jim Druckenmiller	1.00

1998 Stadium Club

Stadium Club was issued in a single-series, 195-card set in 1998, with a 30-card Star Rookies subset seeded one per two packs (1:1 jumbo pack). Cards featured a borderless design with embossed, holographic foil on 20-point stock. Stadium Club was paralleled in three different sets, with each exclusive to specific packs: First Day Issue (retail), One of a Kind (hobby) and Printing Plates (Home Team Advantage). Inserts include: Chrome, Chrome Refractors, Co-Signers (hobby), Double Threat, Leading Legends (retail), Prime Rookies, Triumvirates (hobby) and SuperChrome Oversized cards.

		NM/M
Complete Set (195):		60.00
Common Player:		.15
Minor Stars:		.30
Common Rookie (166-195):		.50
Inserted 1:2		
One Of A Kind Cards:		8X-20X
One Of A Kind Rookies:		3X-6X
Inserted 1:32 Hobby		
Production 150 Sets		
First Day Issue Cards:		6X-15X
First Day Issue Rookies:		2X-4X
Inserted 1:47 Retail		
Production 200 Sets		
Pack (9):		3.50
Wax Box (24):		60.00
1	Barry Sanders	2.00
2	Tony Martin	.15
3	Fred Lane	.30
4	Darren Woodson	.15
5	Andre Reed	.30
6	Blaine Bishop	.15
7	Robert Brooks	.30
8	Tony Banks	.30
9	Charles Way	.15
10	Mark Brunell	1.25
11	Darrell Green	.15
12	Aeneas Williams	.15
13	Rob Johnson	.30
14	Deion Sanders	.50
15	Marshall Faulk	.30
16	Stephen Boyd	.15
17	Adrian Murrell	.30
18	Wayne Chrebet	.30
19	Michael Sinclair	.15
20	Dan Marino	2.00
21	Willie Davis	.15
22	Chris Warren	.30
23	John Mobley	.15
24	Shannon Sharpe	.30
25	Thurman Thomas	.30
26	Corey Dillon	1.00
27	Zach Thomas	.30
28	James Jett	.15
29	Eric Metcalf	.15
30	Drew Bledsoe	1.25
31	Scott Greene	.15
32	Simeon Rice	.15
33	Robert Smith	.30
34	Keenan McCardell	.15
35	Jessie Armstead	.15
36	Jerry Rice	.50
37	Eric Green	.15
38	Terrell Owens	.50
39	Tim Brown	.30
40	Vinny Testaverde	.15
41	Brian Stablein	.15
42	Bert Emanuel	.15
43	Terry Glenn	.30
44	Chad Cota	.15
45	Jermaine Lewis	.15
46	Derrick Thomas	.15
47	O.J. McDuffie	.15
48	Frank Wycheck	.15
49	Steve Broussard	.15
50	Terrell Davis	1.00
51	Eric Allen	.15
52	Napoleon Kaufman	.50
53	Dan Wilkinson	.15
54	Kerry Collins	.30
55	Frank Sanders	.15
56	Jeff Burris	.15
57	Michael Westbrook	.15
58	Michael McCrary	.15
59	Bobby Hoying	.15
60	Jerome Bettis	.30
61	Amp Lee	.15
62	Levon Kirkland	.15
63	Dana Stubblefield	.15
64	Terance Mathis	.15
65	Mark Chmura	.30
66	Bryant Westbrook	.15
67	Rod Smith	.30
68	Derrick Alexander	.15
69	Jason Taylor	.15
70	Eddie George	1.25
71	Elvis Grbac	.15
72	Junior Seau	.30
73	Marvin Harrison	.30
74	Neil O'Donnell	.15
75	Johnnie Morton	.15
76	John Randle	.15
77	Danny Kanell	.15
78	Charlie Garner	.15
79	J.J. Stokes	.30
80	Troy Aikman	.50
81	Gus Frerotte	.15
82	Jake Plummer	1.25
83	Andre Hastings	.15
84	Steve Atwater	.15
85	Larry Centers	.15
86	Kevin Hardy	.15
87	Willie McGinest	.15
88	Joey Galloway	.30
89	Charles Johnson	.15
90	Warrick Dunn	1.25
91	Derrick Rodgers	.15
92	Aaron Glenn	.15
93	Shawn Jefferson	.15
94	Antonio Freeman	.30
95	Jake Reed	.15
96	Reidel Anthony	.30
97	Cris Dishman	.15
98	Jason Sehorn	.15
99	Herman Moore	.30
100	John Elway	.50
101	Brad Johnson	.30
102	Jeff George	.30
103	Emmitt Smith	2.00
104	Steve McNair	.75
105	Ed McCaffrey	.15
106	Errict Rhett	.15
107	Dorsey Levens	.30
108	Michael Jackson	.15
109	Carl Pickens	.15
110	James Stewart	.30
111	Karim Abdul-Jabbar	.30
112	Jim Harbaugh	.15
113	Yancey Thigpen	.15
114	Chad Brown	.15
115	Chris Sanders	.15
116	Cris Carter	.30
117	Glenn Foley	.30
118	Ben Coates	.15
119	Jamal Anderson	.30

120 Steve Young .75
121 Scott Mitchell .15
122 Rob Moore .15
123 Bobby Engram .15
124 Rod Woodson .15
125 Terry Allen .15
126 Warren Sapp .15
127 Irving Fryar .15
128 Isaac Bruce .30
129 Rae Carruth .15
130 Sean Dawkins .15
131 Andre Rison .15
132 Kevin Greene .15
133 Warren Moon .30
134 Keyshawn Johnson .30
135 Jay Graham .15
136 Mike Alstott .50
137 Peter Boulware .15
138 Doug Evans .15
139 Jimmy Smith .30
140 Kordell Stewart 1.25
141 Tamarick Vanover .15
142 Chris Slade .15
143 Freddie Jones .15
144 Erik Kramer .15
145 Ricky Watters .30
146 Chris Chandler .15
147 Garrison Hearst .30
148 Trent Dilfer .30
149 Bruce Smith .15
150 Brett Favre 3.00
151 Will Blackwell .15
152 Rickey Dudley .15
153 Natrone Means .30
154 Curtis Conway .30
155 Tony Gonzalez .15
156 Jeff Blake .30
157 Michael Irvin .30
158 Curtis Martin .75
159 Tim McDonald .15
160 Wesley Walls .15
161 Michael Strahan .15
162 Reggie White .30
163 Jeff Graham .15
164 Ray Lewis .15
165 Antowain Smith .75
166 *Ryan Leaf* 2.00
167 *Jerome Pathon* .50
168 *Duane Starks* .50
169 *Brian Simmons* .50
170 *Patrick Johnson* .50
171 *Keith Brooking* .50
172 *Kevin Dyson* 3.00
173 *Robert Edwards* 3.00
174 *Grant Wistrom* .50
175 *Curtis Enis* 1.00
176 *John Avery* 1.00
177 *Jason Peter* .50
178 *Brian Griese* 6.00
179 *Tavian Banks* .50
180 *Andre Wadsworth* .50
181 *Skip Hicks* .50
182 *Hines Ward* 6.00
183 *Greg Ellis* .50
184 *Robert Holcombe* 2.00
185 *Joe Jurevicius* 2.00
186 *Takeo Spikes* 2.00
187 *Ahman Green* 10.00
188 *Jacquez Green* 2.00
189 *Randy Moss* 15.00
190 *Charles Woodson* 4.00
191 *Fred Taylor* 6.00
192 *Marcus Nash* 2.00
193 *Germane Crowell* 2.00
194 *Tim Dwight* 3.00
195 *Peyton Manning* 12.00

1998 Stadium Club First Day Issue

First Day Issue cards parallel the 195-card regular-issue set, but are distinguished by a gold foil "First Day Issue" stamp on the front. These parallels were exclusive to retail packs, are numbered to 200 in gold foil on the back and inserted one per 47 packs.

First Day Issue Cards: 6X-15X
First Day Issue Rookies: 2X-4X

1998 Stadium Club One of a Kind

One of a Kind cards paralleled the 195-card base set in Stadium Club, but added a darkened, foil finish the the front, with the insert name below the Stadium Club logo in the lower left corner. These parallel cards were exclusive to hobby packs, numbered on the back to 150 in gold foil and inserted one per 32 packs.

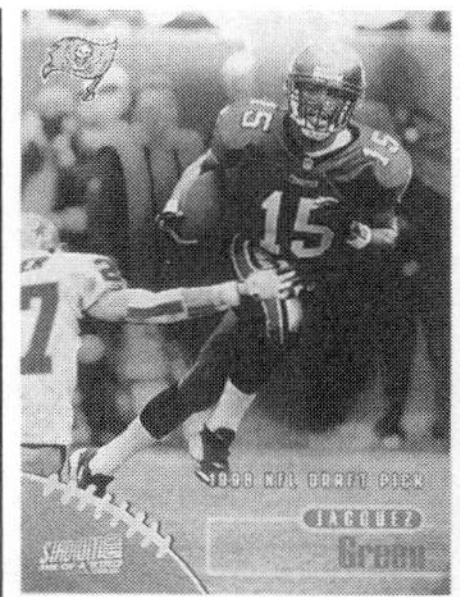

One of a Kind Cards: 8X-20X
One of a Kind Rookies: 3X-6X

1998 Stadium Club Chrome

This 20-card insert was seeded one per 12 packs of Stadium Club. Cards previewed the upcoming Chrome set, however with a different design. While normal Chrome cards were patterned after Topps cards, these inserts were chromium versions of the Stadium Club base cards. Chrome inserts were numbered with a "SCC" prefix and also had Refractor versions seeded one per 48 packs.

NM/M
Complete Set (20): 50.00
Common Player: 1.00
Minor Stars: 2.00
Inserted 1:12
Refractors: 2X
Inserted 1:48
1 John Elway 4.00
2 Mark Brunell 3.00
3 Jerome Bettis 2.00
4 Steve Young 4.00
5 Herman Moore 2.00
6 Emmitt Smith 5.00
7 Warrick Dunn 2.00
8 Dan Marino 5.00
9 Kordell Stewart 2.00
10 Barry Sanders 5.00
11 Tim Brown 2.00
12 Dorsey Levens 1.00
13 Eddie George 3.00
14 Jerry Rice 4.00
15 Terrell Davis 4.00
16 Napoleon Kaufman 1.00
17 Troy Aikman 3.00
18 Drew Bledsoe 3.00
19 Antonio Freeman 1.00
20 Brett Favre 5.00

1998 Stadium Club Co-Signers

This 12-card hobby exclusive insert featured eight total players with both autographs on the same side of the card. Each arrived with a gold foil Topps "Certified Autograph Issue" stamp. Cards 1-4 were inserted 1:9,400 hobby and 1:5,640 jumbos, 5-8 were inserted 1:3,133 hobby and 1:1,880 jumbos and 9-12 were inserted one per 261 hobby and 1:141 jumbo packs. Co-Signers were numbered with a "CO" prefix.

NM/M
Common Player: 50.00
CO1 Peyton Manning, Ryan Leaf 425.00
CO2 Dan Marino, Kordell Stewart 400.00
CO3 Eddie George, Corey Dillon 200.00
CO4 Dorsey Levens, Mike Alstott 150.00
CO5 Ryan Leaf, Dan Marino 400.00
CO6 Peyton Manning, Kordell Stewart 350.00
CO7 Eddie George, Mike Alstott 150.00
CO8 Dorsey Levens, Corey Dillon 125.00
CO9 Peyton Manning, Dan Marino 200.00
CO10 Ryan Leaf, Kordell Stewart 100.00
CO11 Eddie George, Dorsey Levens 70.00
CO12 Mike Alstott, Corey Dillon 50.00

1998 Stadium Club Double Threat

This 10-card insert features two top tandems from 10 different NFL teams. Each player takes up half the card and contains the insert name printed repeatedely across the background along with the team logo. Double Threat inserts are seeded one per eight packs and are numbered with a "DT" prefix.

NM/M
Complete Set (10): 20.00
Common Player: 1.00
Inserted 1:8
1 Marshall Faulk, Peyton Manning 5.00
2 Curtis Conway, Curtis Enis 2.00
3 Drew Bledsoe, Robert Edwards 3.00
4 Warrick Dunn, Jacquez Green 2.00
5 John Elway, Marcus Nash 3.00
6 Mark Brunell, Fred Taylor 3.00
7 Eddie George, Kevin Dyson 3.00
8 Michael Jackson, Patrick Johnson 1.00
9 Terry Glenn, Tony Simmons 1.00
10 Natrone Means, Ryan Leaf 1.00

1998 Stadium Club Leading Legends

Leading Legends was a retail-exclusive insert that displayed the NFL's current record-holders among quarterbacks, wide receivers and running backs. The cards are printed on plastic with a gold foil background and card back. These were inserted one per 12 packs and unnumbered.

NM/M
Complete Set (10): 20.00
Common Player: 1.00
Inserted 1:12 Retail
1 Jerry Rice 4.00
2 Bruce Smith 1.00
3 Reggie White 1.00
4 Warren Moon 1.00
5 Dan Marino 4.00
6 John Elway 3.00
7 Emmitt Smith 4.00
8 Brett Favre 5.00
9 Steve Young 3.00
10 Barry Sanders 4.00

1998 Stadium Club Prime Rookies

This 10-card insert displayed the top draft picks in 1998 on a silver foil finish, with the insert name running up the right side. Prime Rookies were inserted one per eight packs and numbered with a "PR" prefix.

NM/M
Complete Set (10): 25.00
Common Player: 1.00
Inserted 1:8
1 Ryan Leaf 1.00
2 Andre Wadsworth 1.00
3 Fred Taylor 4.00
4 Kevin Dyson 3.00
5 Charles Woodson 3.00
6 Robert Edwards 2.00
7 Grant Wistrom 1.00
8 Curtis Enis 1.00
9 Randy Moss 5.00
10 Peyton Manning 5.00

1998 Stadium Club Super Chrome

SuperChrome featured 3-1/4" x 4-9/16" versions of the 20-card Chrome insert. These were inserted one per hobby box, with Refractor versions every 12 Home Team Advantage/ Hobby Collector Pack boxes.

NM/M
Complete Set (20): 50.00
Common Player: 1.00
Minor Stars: 4.00
Refractors: 2X
1 John Elway 3.00
2 Mark Brunell 3.00
3 Jerome Bettis 3.00
4 Steve Young 4.00
5 Herman Moore 1.00
6 Emmitt Smith 5.00
7 Warrick Dunn 2.00
8 Dan Marino 5.00
9 Kordell Stewart 2.00
10 Barry Sanders 4.00
11 Tim Brown 1.00
12 Dorsey Levens 4.00
13 Eddie George 2.00
14 Jerry Rice 4.00
15 Terrell Davis 3.00
16 Napoleon Kaufman 1.00
17 Troy Aikman 3.00
18 Drew Bledsoe 3.00
19 Antonio Freeman 1.00
20 Brett Favre 5.00

1998 Stadium Club Triumvirate Luminous

Triumvirate was a 15-card, hobby-only insert in 1998. It featured three teammates on die-cut, fit-together cards numbered with a "T" prefix and either an A, B or C suffix. Regular, Luminous versions were seeded one per 24 packs, Luminescent versions were one per 96 and Illuminators were one per 192 packs.

NM/M
Complete Set (15): 40.00
Common Player: 1.00
Minor Stars: 6.00
Inserted 1:24 Hobby
Luminescent Cards: 2X
Inserted 1:96 Hobby
Illuminator Cards: 5X
Inserted 1:192 Hobby
T1A Terrell Davis 3.00
T1B John Elway 3.00
T1C Shannon Sharpe 1.00
T2A Barry Sanders 4.00
T2B Scott Mitchell 1.00
T2C Herman Moore 1.00
T3A Dorsey Levens 1.00
T3B Brett Favre 5.00
T3C Antonio Freeman 1.00
T4A Emmitt Smith 5.00
T4B Troy Aikman 4.00
T4C Michael Irvin 1.00
T5A Napoleon Kaufman 1.00
T5B Jeff George 1.00
T5C Tim Brown 2.00

1999 Stadium Club

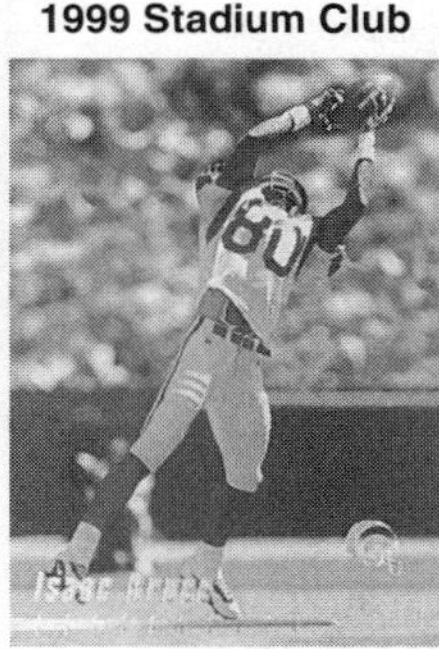

This was a 200-card set that included two subsets consisting of 25 Transactions and 25 Draft Picks found 1:3 packs. Each card was embossed and printed full-bleed on 20-point stock with a holographic foil logo. Two parallel sets were issued: First Day and One of a Kind. Other inserts included: Chrome Previews, Co-Signers, Emperors of the Zone, Lone Star Autographs, 3x3 Luminous and Never Compromise. SRP was $2.00 for six-card packs.

NM/M
Complete Set (200): 60.00
Common Player: .10
Minor Stars: .30
Common Rookie: 1.00
Inserted 1:3
Pack (6): 2.25
Wax Box (24): 35.00
1 Dan Marino 2.00
2 Andre Reed .10
3 Michael Westbrook .30
4 Isaac Bruce .50
5 Curtis Martin .50
6 Courtney Hawkins .10
7 Charles Way .10
8 Terrell Owens .50
9 Warrick Dunn .50
10 Jake Plummer .50
11 Chad Brown .10
12 Yancey Thigpen .30
13 Lamar Thomas .10
14 Keenan McCardell .30
15 Shannon Sharpe .30
16 Robert Brooks .10
17 Cameron Cleeland .30
18 Derrick Thomas .10
19 Mark Brunell .75
20 Jamal Anderson .50
21 Germane Crowell .30
22 Rod Smith .30
23 Ty Law .10
24 Cris Carter .50
25 Terrell Davis 1.00
26 Takeo Spikes .10
27 Tim Biakabutuka .30
28 Jermaine Lewis .30
29 Adrian Murrell .30
30 Doug Flutie .75
31 Curtis Enis .50
32 Skip Hicks .30
33 Steve McNair .75
34 Charles Woodson .50
35 Jessie Armstead .10
36 Shawn Springs .10
37 Levon Kirkland .10
38 Freddie Jones .30
39 Warren Sapp .10
40 Emmitt Smith 2.00
41 Reidel Anthony .30
42 Tony Simmons .30
43 Andre Hastings .10
44 Byron Morris .10
45 Jimmy Smith .30
46 Antonio Freeman .50
47 Herman Moore .50
48 Muhsin Muhammed .30
49 Chris Chandler .30
50 John Elway 2.00
51 Aeneas Williams .10
52 Bobby Engram .10
53 Billy Davis .10
54 Zach Thomas .30
55 Mike Alstott .50
56 Junior Seau .30
57 Aaron Glenn .10
58 Darrell Green .10
59 Thurman Thomas .30
60 Troy Aikman 1.50
61 Bill Romanowski .10
62 Wesley Walls .10
63 Andre Wadsworth .10
64 Robert Smith .50
65 Elvis Grbac .30
66 Terry Fair .10
67 Ben Coates .30
68 Bert Emanuel .10
69 Jacquez Green .30
70 Barry Sanders 2.00
71 James Jett .10
72 Gary Brown .10
73 Stephen Alexander .10
74 Wayne Chrebet .50
75 Drew Bledsoe 1.00
76 John Lynch .10
77 Jake Reed .30
78 Marvin Harrison .50
79 Johnnie Morton .10
80 Brett Favre 3.00
81 Charlie Batch 1.00
82 Antowain Smith .50
83 O.J. Santiago .10
84 Larry Centers .10
85 John Mobley .10
86 Ernie Mills .10
87 Jeff Blake .30
88 Curtis Conway .30
89 Bruce Smith .10
90 Peyton Manning 2.00
91 Ray Lewis .10
92 Ray Buchanan .10
93 Tim Dwight .50
94 O.J. McDuffie .30
95 Vonnie Holliday .30
96 Jon Kitna .75
97 Trent Dilfer .30
98 Jerome Bettis .50
99 Dedric Ward .10
100 Fred Taylor 1.50
101 Ike Hilliard .10
102 Frank Wycheck .10
103 Eric Moulds .50
104 Rob Moore .30
105 Ed McCaffrey .50
106 Carl Pickens .30
107 Priest Holmes .50
108 Kevin Hardy .10
109 Terry Glenn .50
110 Keyshawn Johnson .50
111 Karim Abdul .30
112 Stephen Boyd .10
113 Ahman Green .30
114 Duce Staley .50
115 Vinny Testaverde .30
116 Napoleon Kaufman .50
117 Frank Sanders .10
118 Peter Boulware .10
119 Kevin Greene .10
120 Steve Young .75
121 Darnay Scott .30
122 Deion Sanders .50
123 Corey Dillon .50
124 Randall Cunningham .50
125 Eddie George .75
126 Derrick Alexander .10
127 Mark Chmura .30
128 Michael Sinclair .10
129 Rickey Dudley .30
130 Joey Galloway .50
131 Michael Strahan .10
132 Ricky Proehl .10
133 Natrone Means .30
134 Dorsey Levens .50
135 Andre Rison .30
136 John Avery .30
137 John Randle .10
138 Terance Mathis .10
139 Erik Kramer .10
140 Jerry Rice 1.50
141 Michael Irvin .30
142 Oronde Gadsden .30
143 Jerome Pathon .10
144 Ricky Watters .50
145 J.J. Stokes .30
146 Kordell Stewart .75
147 Tim Brown .30
148 Garrison Hearst .50
149 Tony Gonzalez .30
150 Randy Moss 3.00
151 *Daunte Culpepper* 6.00
152 *Amos Zereoue* 2.00
153 *Champ Bailey* 2.00
154 *Peerless Price* 2.00
155 *Edgerrin James* 6.00
156 *Joe Germaine* 1.00
157 *David Boston* 3.00
158 *Kevin Faulk* 1.00
159 *Troy Edwards* 1.00
160 *Akili Smith* 1.00
161 *Kevin Johnson* 1.00
162 *Rob Konrad* 1.00
163 *Shaun King* 1.00
164 *James Johnson* 1.00
165 *Donovan McNabb* 6.00
166 *Torry Holt* 3.00
167 *Michael Cloud* 1.00
168 *Sedrick Irvin* 1.00
169 *Cade McNown* 2.00
170 *Ricky Williams* 6.00
171 *Karsten Bailey* 1.00
172 *Cecil Collins* 2.00
173 *Brock Huard* 1.00
174 *D'Wayne Bates* 1.00
175 *Tim Couch* 2.00
176 Torrance Small Transactions .10
177 Warren Moon Transactions .30
178 Raghib Ismail Transactions .10
179 Marshall Faulk Transactions .50
180 Trent Green Transactions .50
181 Sean Dawkins Transactions .10
182 Pete Mitchell Transactions .10
183 Jeff Graham Transactions .10
184 Eddie Kennison Transactions .10
185 Kerry Collins Transactions .30
186 Eric Green Transactions .10

187	Kyle Brady Transactions	.10
188	Tony Martin Transactions	.10
189	Jim Harbaugh Transactions	.30
190	Carnell Lake Transactions	.10
191	Steve Atwater Transactions	.10
192	Dale Carter Transactions	.10
193	Charles Johnson Transactions	.10
194	Tony Banks Transactions	.10
195	Jeff George Transactions	.30
196	Scott Mitchell Transactions	.10
197	Chris Calloway Transactions	.10
198	Rich Gannon Transactions	.10
199	Leslie Shepherd Transactions	.10
200	Brad Johnson Transactions	.50

1999 Stadium Club First Day Issue

This 200-card insert set was a parallel to the base set and was a retail exclusive. Each single had the "First Day Issue" foil stamp on the fronts. Singles were sequentially numbered to 150 and found 1:38 packs.

First Day Cards: 5X-10X
First Day Rookies: 2X-4X
Production 150 Sets
Inserted 1:38 Retail

1999 Stadium Club One of a Kind

This was a 200-card insert set that was a hobby exclusive and paralleled the base set. Singles were sequentially numbered to 150 and inserted 1:48 packs.

One of a Kind Cards: 5X-10X
One of a Kind Rookies: 2X-4X
Production 150 Sets
Inserted 1:48 Hobby

1999 Stadium Club Chrome Preview

This was a 20-card insert set that included the hottest players from the Stadium Club set and pictured them with chromium stock. Singles were inserted 1:24 packs. A parallel Refractor version was made and inserted 1:96 packs. A Jumbo version was issued and found one-per-box and a Jumbo Refractor version was issued one every twelve boxes.

		NM/M
Complete Set (20):		45.00
Common Player:		1.00
Inserted 1:24		
Refractors:		2X
Inserted 1:96		
Jumbos:		1X
Inserted 1:box		
Jumbo Refractors:		3X
Inserted 1:12 boxes		
1	Randy Moss	4.00
2	Terrell Davis	3.00
3	Peyton Manning	4.00
4	Fred Taylor	2.00
5	John Elway	3.00
6	Steve Young	3.00
7	Brett Favre	5.00
8	Jamal Anderson	1.00
9	Barry Sanders	4.00
10	Dan Marino	5.00
11	Jerry Rice	4.00
12	Emmitt Smith	4.00
13	Randall Cunningham	1.00
14	Troy Aikman	3.00
15	Akili Smith	1.00
16	Donovan McNabb	3.00
17	Edgerrin James	3.00
18	Torry Holt	2.00
19	Ricky Williams	4.00
20	Tim Couch	2.00

1999 Stadium Club Co-Signers

This six-card insert set was a hobby exclusive and showcased six different double-autographed cards. Both players and their autographs were pictured on the same side of the card. Each single included the gold foil Topps "Certified Autograph Issue" stamp. Cards #1 and #2 were inserted 1:2,854 packs and cards #3-#6 were issued 1:1,189.

		NM/M
Common Player:		150.00
Inserted 1:2,854 (1-3)		
Inserted 1:1,189 (4-6)		
1	Ricky Williams, Terrell Davis	200.00
2	Edgerrin James, Terrell Davis	200.00
3	Tim Couch, Dan Marino	250.00
4	Tim Couch, Peyton Manning	250.00
5	Randy Moss, Jerry Rice	300.00
6	Vinny Testaverde, Dan Marino	150.00

1999 Stadium Club Emperors of the Zone

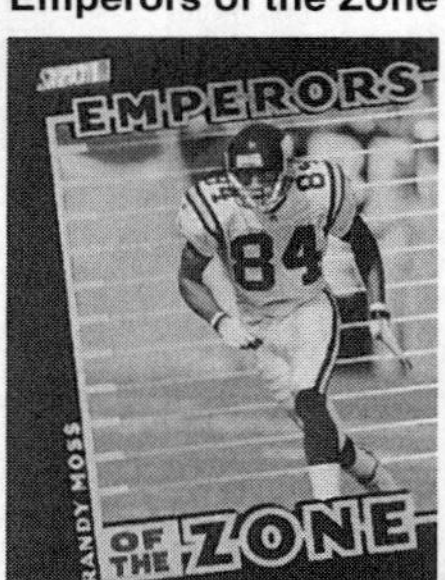

This 10-card insert set included the best touchdown producers in the NFL. Each was featured on a solid black styrene card with silver foil. Singles were inserted 1:12 packs.

		NM/M
Complete Set (10):		20.00
Common Player:		1.00
Inserted 1:12		
1	Ricky Williams	3.00
2	Brett Favre	4.00
3	Donovan McNabb	2.00
4	Peyton Manning	3.00
5	Terrell Davis	3.00
6	Jamal Anderson	1.00
7	Edgerrin James	2.00
8	Fred Taylor	1.00
9	Tim Couch	2.00
10	Randy Moss	3.00

1999 Stadium Club Lone Star Autographs

This 11-card insert set included autographs from some of the top players in the NFL. Each single included the Topps "Certified Autograph Issue" stamp. Singles were found 1:697 packs.

		NM/M
Common Player:		15.00
Inserted 1:697		
1	Randy Moss	125.00
2	Jerry Rice	150.00
3	Peyton Manning	150.00
4	Vinny Testaverde	30.00
5	Tim Couch	75.00
6	Dan Marino	175.00
7	Edgerrin James	100.00
8	Fred Taylor	45.00
9	Garrison Hearst	30.00
10	Antonio Freeman	15.00
11	Torry Holt	45.00

1999 Stadium Club 3 X 3 Luminous

This 15-card insert set featured three stars on three different technologies, Luminous, Luminescent and Illuminator, with each combination arranged by position and conference. Each single is featured on a laser-cut design where the collector could fuse three players together to form one oversized card. Luminous singles were found 1:36 packs. The Luminescent parallel singles were found 1:144 packs and the Illuminator cards were inserted 1:288 packs.

		NM/M
Complete Set (15):		40.00
Common Player:		1.00
Inserted 1:36		
Luminescent Cards:		3X
Inserted 1:144		
Illuminator Cards:		4X
Inserted 1:288		
1A	Brett Favre	5.00
1B	Troy Aikman	3.00
1C	Jake Plummer	2.00
2A	Jamal Anderson	1.00
2B	Emmitt Smith	4.00
2C	Barry Sanders	4.00
3A	Antonio Freeman	1.00
3B	Randy Moss	4.00
3C	Jerry Rice	4.00
4A	Peyton Manning	4.00
4B	John Elway	3.00
4C	Dan Marino	4.00
5A	Fred Taylor	2.00
5B	Terrell Davis	3.00
5C	Curtis Martin	1.00

1999 Stadium Club Never Compromise

This 30-card insert set was divided into three different subsets. The Rookies featured ten hot newcomers, The ten Stars included current NFL stars at the pinnacle of their success and the Legends featured ten Canton-bound season veterans whose play should enshrine them in the Hall of Fame. They were inserted 1:12 packs.

		NM/M
Complete Set (30):		35.00
Common Player:		.50
Minor Stars:		1.00
Inserted 1:12		
1	Tim Couch	1.00
2	David Boston	.50
3	Daunte Culpepper	2.00
4	Donovan McNabb	2.00
5	Ricky Williams	3.00
6	Troy Edwards	.50
7	Akili Smith	.50
8	Torry Holt	.50
9	Cade McNown	.50
10	Edgerrin James	3.00
11	Randy Moss	3.00
12	Peyton Manning	3.00
13	Eddie George	.50
14	Fred Taylor	.50
15	Jamal Anderson	.50
16	Joey Galloway	.50
17	Terrell Davis	2.00
18	Keyshawn Johnson	.50
19	Antonio Freeman	.50
20	Jake Plummer	1.00
21	Steve Young	2.00
22	Barry Sanders	3.00
23	Dan Marino	4.00
24	Emmitt Smith	3.00
25	Brett Favre	4.00
26	Randall Cunningham	.50
27	John Elway	2.00
28	Drew Bledsoe	2.00
29	Jerry Rice	3.00
30	Troy Aikman	3.00

1999 Stadium Club Chrome

This was a 150-card set that utilized Chrome technology and each single was printed on 23-point stock. Parallel sets included First Day Issues and Refractors. Other inserts included: Clear Shots, Eyes of the Game, Never Compromise and True Colors. SRP was $4.00 for five-card packs.

		NM/M
Complete Set (150):		60.00
Common Player:		.10
Minor Stars:		.50
Common Rookie:		2.00
Pack (5):		1.75
Wax Box (24):		30.00
1	Dan Marino	3.00
2	Andre Reed	.50
3	Michael Westbrook	.50
4	Isaac Bruce	1.00
5	Curtis Martin	1.00
6	Terrell Owens	1.00
7	Warrick Dunn	1.00
8	Jake Plummer	1.50
9	Chad Brown	.10
10	Yancey Thigpen	.50
11	Keenan McCardell	.50
12	Shannon Sharpe	.50
13	Cameron Cleeland	.50
14	Mark Brunell	1.50
15	Jamal Anderson	1.00
16	Germane Crowell	.50
17	Rod Smith	.75
18	Cris Carter	1.00
19	Terrell Davis	2.00
20	Tim Biakabutuka	.50
21	Jermaine Lewis	.10
22	Adrian Murrell	.50
23	Doug Flutie	1.25
24	Curtis Enis	1.00
25	Skip Hicks	.50
26	Steve McNair	1.25
27	Charles Woodson	1.00
28	Freddie Jones	.10
29	Warren Sapp	.10
30	Emmitt Smith	3.00
31	Reidel Anthony	.50
32	Tony Simmons	.50
33	Andre Hastings	.10
34	Byron Morris	.10
35	Jimmy Smith	1.00
36	Antonio Freeman	1.00
37	Herman Moore	1.00
38	Muhsin Muhammed	.50
39	Chris Chandler	.50
40	John Elway	3.00
41	Bobby Engram	.10
42	Keith Poole	.10
43	Mike Alstott	1.00
44	Junior Seau	.50
45	Thurman Thomas	.50
46	Troy Aikman	2.00
47	Wesley Walls	.50
48	Robert Smith	1.00
49	Elvis Grbac	.50
50	Ben Coates	.50
51	Bert Emanuel	.10
52	Jacquez Green	.50
53	Barry Sanders	3.00
54	James Jett	.10
55	Gary Brown	.10
56	Stephen Alexander	.10
57	Wayne Chrebet	1.00
58	Drew Bledsoe	1.50
59	Jake Reed	.50
60	Marvin Harrison	1.00
61	Johnnie Morton	.10
62	Brett Favre	4.00
63	Charlie Batch	1.25
64	Antowain Smith	1.00
65	Ernie Mills	.10
66	Jeff Blake	.50
67	Curtis Conway	.50
68	Bruce Smith	.10
69	Peyton Manning	3.00
70	Tim Dwight	1.00
71	O.J. McDuffie	.50
72	Jon Kitna	1.00
73	Trent Dilfer	.50
74	Jerome Bettis	1.00
75	Dedric Ward	.10
76	Fred Taylor	2.00
77	Ike Hilliard	.50
78	Frank Wycheck	.10
79	Eric Moulds	1.00
80	Rob Moore	.75
81	Ed McCaffrey	.75
82	Carl Pickens	.50
83	Priest Holmes	1.00
84	Terry Glenn	1.00
85	Keyshawn Johnson	1.00
86	Karim Abdul	.50
87	Ahman Green	.50
88	Duce Staley	1.00
89	Vinny Testaverde	.50
90	Napoleon Kaufman	1.00
91	Frank Sanders	.50
92	Steve Young	1.25
93	Darnay Scott	.50
94	Deion Sanders	1.00
95	Corey Dillon	1.00
96	Randall Cunningham	1.00
97	Eddie George	1.25
98	Derrick Alexander	.10
99	Mark Chmura	.50
100	Rickey Dudley	.50
101	Joey Galloway	1.00
102	Ricky Proehl	.10
103	Natrone Means	.75
104	Dorsey Levens	1.00
105	Andre Rison	.50
106	John Avery	.50
107	Terance Mathis	.10
108	Rae Carruth	.10
109	Jerry Rice	2.00
110	Michael Irvin	.50
111	Oronde Gadsden	.50
112	Jerome Pathon	.10
113	Ricky Watters	.50
114	J.J. Stokes	.50
115	Kordell Stewart	1.00
116	Tim Brown	1.00
117	Tony Gonzalez	.50
118	Randy Moss	4.00
119	*Daunte Culpepper*	8.00
120	*Amos Zereoue*	3.00
121	*Champ Bailey*	2.00
122	*Peerless Price*	3.00
123	*Edgerrin James*	8.00
124	*Joe Germaine*	1.00
125	*David Boston*	4.00
126	*Kevin Faulk*	1.00
127	*Troy Edwards*	1.00
128	*Akili Smith*	1.00
129	*Kevin Johnson*	1.00
130	*Rob Konrad*	1.00
131	*Shaun King*	1.00
132	*James Johnson*	1.00
133	*Donovan McNabb*	8.00
134	*Torry Holt*	4.00
135	*Michael Cloud*	1.00
136	*Sedrick Irvin*	1.00
137	*Cade McNown*	2.00
138	*Ricky Williams*	8.00
139	*Karsten Bailey*	1.00
140	*Cecil Collins*	2.00
141	*Brock Huard*	1.00
142	*D'Wayne Bates*	1.00
143	*Tim Couch*	2.00
144	Raghib Ismail	.10
145	Marshall Faulk	1.00
146	Trent Green	.50
147	Tony Martin	.10
148	Jim Harbaugh	.10
149	Rich Gannon	.10
150	Brad Johnson	.75

1999 Stadium Club Chrome First Day

This was a 150-card parallel to the base set. Each single included the "First Day Issue" stamp and was sequentially numbered to 100. They were inserted 1:59 packs. A parallel Refractor version was also released and each of those was sequentially numbered to 25 and inserted 1:235 packs.

First Day Cards: 5X-10X
First Day Rookies: 4X-8X
Inserted 1:59
Production 100 Sets

> Values quoted in this guide reflect the retail price of a card—the price a collector can expect to pay when buying a card from a dealer. The wholesale price—that which a collector can expect to receive from a dealer when selling cards—will be significantly lower, depending on desirability and condition.

1999 Stadium Club Chrome Refractors

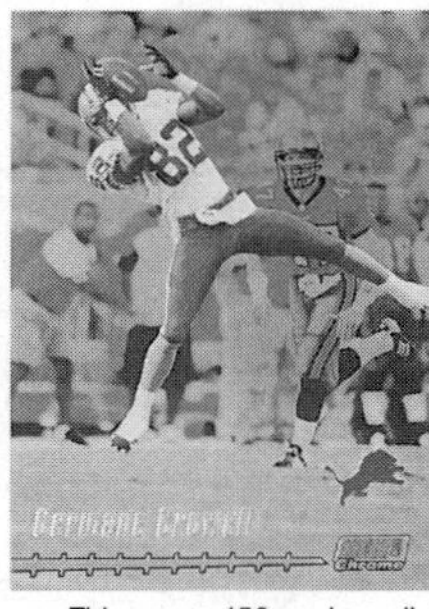

This was a 150-card parallel to the base set. Each single was printed with iridescent technology and inserted 1:12 packs.

Refractor Cards: 2X-4X
Refractor Rookies: 2X
Inserted 1:12

1999 Stadium Club Chrome Clear Shots

This nine-card insert set was an exclusive to the Stadium Club Chrome product. Each single was printed on a clear polycarbonate stock and was die cut. Singles were inserted 1:22 packs. A Refractor version was also released with each of those singles inserted 1:110 packs.

		NM/M
Complete Set (9):		20.00
Common Player:		1.00
Inserted 1:22		
Refractor Cards:		3X
Inserted 1:110		
1	David Boston	2.00
2	Edgerrin James	5.00
3	Chris Claiborne	1.00
4	Torry Holt	2.00
5	Tim Couch	3.00
6	Donovan McNabb	4.00
7	Akili Smith	1.00
8	Champ Bailey	1.00
9	Troy Edwards	1.00

1999 Stadium Club Chrome Eyes of the Game

This seven-card insert set was an exclusive insert to Stadium Club Chrome Football. A mix of rookies and veterans was included in this set. Singles were inserted 1:20 packs. A parallel Refractor version was also issued and found 1:100 packs.

		NM/M
Complete Set (7):		20.00
Common Player:		1.00
Inserted 1:20		
Refractor Cards:		3X
Inserted 1:100		
1	Tim Couch	3.00
2	Ricky Williams	5.00

3 Barry Sanders 4.00
4 Brett Favre 5.00
5 Terrell Davis 2.00
6 Peyton Manning 3.00
7 Randy Moss 3.00

1999 Stadium Club Chrome Never Compromise

This 40-card insert set included 20 rookies and 20 veterans. Singles were inserted 1:6 packs. A parallel Refractor version was issued and inserted 1:30 packs.

NM/M
Complete Set (40): 70.00
Common Player: .50
Minor Stars: 1.00
Inserted 1:6
Refractor Cards: 3X
Inserted 1:30
1 Tim Couch 3.00
2 David Boston 1.00
3 Daunte Culpepper 4.00
4 Donovan McNabb 4.00
5 Ricky Williams 5.00
6 Troy Edwards 1.00
7 Akili Smith 1.00
8 Torry Holt 2.00
9 Cade McNown 1.00
10 Edgerrin James 5.00
11 Cecil Collins 1.00
12 Peerless Price 3.00
13 Kevin Johnson 1.00
14 Champ Bailey 1.00
15 Kevin Faulk 1.00
16 D'Wayne Bates .50
17 Shaun King 1.00
18 Sedrick Irvin .50
19 James Johnson .50
20 Rob Konrad .50
21 Randy Moss 3.00
22 Peyton Manning 3.00
23 Eddie George 1.00
24 Fred Taylor 1.00
25 Jamal Anderson .50
26 Joey Galloway .50
27 Terrell Davis 3.00
28 Keyshawn Johnson 1.00
29 Antonio Freeman .50
30 Jake Plummer 1.00
31 Steve Young 3.00
32 Barry Sanders 4.00
33 Dan Marino 4.00
34 Emmitt Smith 4.00
35 Brett Favre 5.00
36 Randall Cunningham .50
37 John Elway 3.00
38 Drew Bledsoe 3.00
39 Jerry Rice 3.00
40 Troy Aikman 3.00

1999 Stadium Club Chrome True Colors

This was a 10-card insert set that was an exclusive to the Stadium Club Chrome product. Singles were inserted 1:24 packs. A parallel Refractor version was also released and found 1:120 packs.

NM/M
Complete Set (10): 65.00
Common Player: 5.00
Inserted 1:24
Refractor Cards: 3X
Inserted 1:120
1 Doug Flutie 5.00
2 Steve Young 5.00
3 Jake Plummer 7.00
4 Jerry Rice 8.00
5 Randy Moss 12.00
6 Fred Taylor 8.00
7 Peyton Manning 12.00
8 Dan Marino 10.00
9 Brett Favre 12.00
10 Terrell Davis 8.00

2000 Stadium Club Promos

NM/M
Complete Set (6): 3.00
Common Player: .50
PP1 Peyton Manning 2.00
PP2 Antonio Freeman .50
PP3 O.J. McDuffie .50
PP4 Junior Seau .50
PP5 Mark Brunell 1.00
PP6 Ed McCaffrey .50

2000 Stadium Club

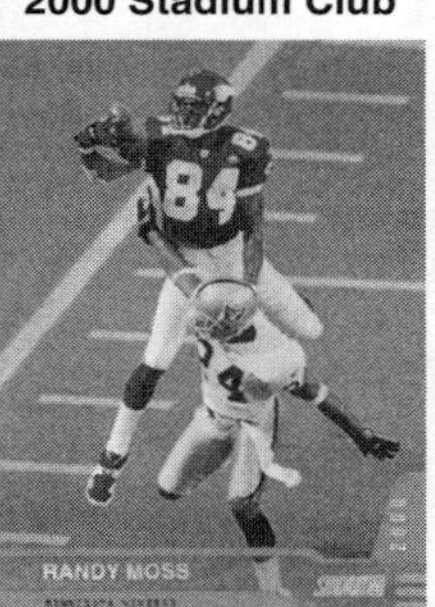

NM/M
Complete Set (175): 50.00
Common Player: .15
Minor Stars: .30
Common Rookie: 1.50
Inserted 1:4
Pack (7): 1.75
Wax Box (24): 30.00
1 Peyton Manning 1.75
2 Pete Mitchell .15
3 Napoleon Kaufman .50
4 Mikhael Ricks .15
5 Mike Alstott .50
6 Brad Johnson .50
7 Tony Gonzalez .30
8 Germane Crowell .30
9 Marcus Robinson .50
10 Stephen Davis .50
11 Terance Mathis .15
12 Jake Plummer .50
13 Qadry Ismail .15
14 Cade McNown .75
15 Zach Thomas .30
16 Curtis Martin .50
17 Torrance Small .15
18 Steve McNair .60
19 Jim Harbaugh .30
20 Keyshawn Johnson .50
21 Antonio Freeman .50
22 Ed McCaffrey .30
23 Elvis Grbac .30
24 Peerless Price .50
25 Jerome Bettis .50
26 Yancey Thigpen .30
27 *Jake Delhomme* 4.00
28 Keith Poole .15
29 Carl Pickens .30
30 Jerry Rice 1.00
31 Rob Moore .30
32 Reidel Anthony .30
33 Jimmy Smith .50
34 Ray Lucas .30
35 Troy Aikman 1.00
36 Steve Beuerlein .30
37 Charlie Batch .50
38 Derrick Mayes .30
39 Tim Brown .30
40 Eddie George .60
41 O.J. McDuffie .30
42 Ike Hilliard .30
43 Bill Schroeder .30
44 Jim Miller .15
45 Chris Chandler .30
46 Fred Taylor .75
47 Ricky Watters .30
48 Tyrone Wheatley .30
49 Bruce Smith .30
50 Marshall Faulk .50
51 Terry Kirby .15
52 Champ Bailey .30
53 Troy Edwards .50
54 Doug Flutie .60
55 Charles Johnson .15
56 Michael Westbrook .30
57 Frank Wycheck .15
58 Drew Bledsoe .75
59 Terrence Wilkins .30
60 Ricky Williams 1.25
61 Rod Smith .30
62 Errict Rhett .30
63 Vinny Testaverde .30
64 Jacquez Green .30
65 Curtis Conway .30
66 Wayne Chrebet .50
67 Albert Connell .30
68 Kordell Stewart .50
69 Bert Emanuel .15
70 Randy Moss 1.75
71 Akili Smith .60
72 Brian Griese .60
73 Frank Sanders .30
74 Wesley Walls .15
75 Michael Pittman .15
76 Steve Young .60
77 Jevon Kearse .60
78 Az-Zahir Hakim .30
79 James Stewart .30
80 Brett Favre 2.00
81 Dan Marino 1.50
82 Joe Horn .15
83 Mark Brunell .75
84 Eddie Kennison .15
85 Deion Sanders .50
86 Priest Holmes .50
87 Terry Glenn .50
88 Olandis Gary .60
89 Patrick Jeffers .50
90 Emmitt Smith 1.50
91 J.J. Stokes .15
92 Warrick Dunn .50
93 Damon Huard .50
94 Herman Moore .50
95 Corey Dillon .50
96 Joey Galloway .50
97 Jamal Anderson .50
98 Junior Seau .30
99 Robert Smith .50
100 Edgerrin James 2.00
101 Derrick Alexander .15
102 Johnnie Morton .15
103 Sean Dawkins .15
104 Derrick Brooks .15
105 Rickey Dudley .15
106 Keenan McCardell .30
107 Kerry Collins .30
108 Kevin Johnson .50
109 Eric Moulds .50
110 Terrell Davis 1.00
111 Shawn Jefferson .15
112 Donovan McNabb .75
113 Torry Holt .50
114 Marvin Harrison .50
115 Amani Toomer .30
116 Tony Martin .15
117 Curtis Enis .50
118 Tiki Barber .30
119 Freddie Jones .15
120 Muhsin Muhammad .30
121 Shaun King .75
122 Isaac Bruce .50
123 Duce Staley .60
124 Hardy Nickerson .15
125 Corey Bradford .30
126 Kevin Hardy .15
127 Hines Ward .30
128 Charlie Garner .30
129 Warren Sapp .30
130 Tim Couch 1.25
131 Kevin Dyson .30
132 Raghib Ismail .15
133 Tim Dwight .50
134 Darnay Scott .30
135 Jeff George .50
136 Dorsey Levens .50
137 Jeff Blake .30
138 Jon Kitna .50
139 Rich Gannon .30
140 Cris Carter .50
141 Jeff Graham .15
142 James Johnson .30
143 Tim Biakabutuka .30
144 Bobby Engram .15
145 Tony Banks .30
146 Shannon Sharpe .30
147 Antowain Smith .50
148 Terrell Owens .50
149 Rob Johnson .30
150 Kurt Warner 2.00
151 *Thomas Jones* 4.00
152 *Chad Pennington* 10.00
153 *Ron Dayne* 2.00
154 *Tee Martin* 3.00
155 *Reuben Droughns* 5.00
156 *Jerry Porter* 4.00
157 *R. Jay Soward* 2.00
158 *Sylvester Morris* 2.00
159 *Todd Pinkston* 1.50
160 *Courtney Brown* 2.00
161 *Travis Taylor* 3.00
162 *Ron Dugans* 3.00
163 *Laveranues Coles* 4.00
164 *Joe Hamilton* 3.00
165 *Curtis Keaton* 1.50
166 *Bubba Franks* 3.00
167 *Dennis Northcutt* 3.00
168 *Chris Redman* 3.00
169 *Travis Prentice* 3.00
170 *Shaun Alexander* 6.00
171 *Jamal Lewis* 6.00
172 *Peter Warrick* 4.00
173 *J.R. Redmond* 3.00
174 *Trung Canidate* 2.50
175 *Plaxico Burress* 5.00

2000 Stadium Club All-Pro Competition

NM/M
Common Player: 25.00
Production 50 Sets
HTA Only
APC1 Jevon Kearse, Warren Sapp 25.00
APC2 Marshall Faulk, Edgerrin James 50.00
APC3 Keyshawn Johnson, Randy Moss 50.00
APC4 Frank Wycheck, Wesley Walls 25.00
APC5 Stephen Davis, Eddie George 35.00
APC6 Cris Carter, Isaac Bruce 25.00

2000 Stadium Club All-Pro Relics

NM/M
Common Player: 25.00
Inserted 1:353
SB Steve Beuerlein 25.00
PB Peter Boulware 25.00
IB Isaac Bruce 40.00
CC Cris Carter 45.00
SD Stephen Davis 25.00
MF Marshall Faulk 50.00
EG Eddie George 45.00
KH Kevin Hardy 25.00
EJ Edgerrin James 55.00
KJ Keyshawn Johnson 25.00
JK Jevon Kearse 25.00
TL Todd Lyght 25.00
RM Randy Moss 60.00
MM Muhsin Muhammad 25.00
HN Hardy Nickerson 25.00
WS Warren Sapp 30.00
WW Wesley Walls 25.00
FW Frank Wycheck 25.00

2000 Stadium Club All-Pro Relics Autographs

NM/M
Common Player: 50.00
Inserted 1:5,474
Production 50 Sets
APA1 Eddie George 75.00
APA2 Edgerrin James 125.00
APA4 Stephen Davis 50.00
APA5 Isaac Bruce 50.00

2000 Stadium Club Beam Team

NM/M
Complete Set (30): 50.00
Common Player: 1.00
Minor Stars: 2.00
Inserted 1:171
Production 500 Sets
BT1 Brett Favre 5.00
BT2 Stephen Davis 1.00
BT3 Germane Crowell 1.00
BT4 Jevon Kearse 1.00
BT5 Edgerrin James 4.00
BT6 Randy Moss 4.00
BT7 Isaac Bruce 2.00
BT8 Charlie Garner 1.00
BT9 Eddie George 2.00
BT10 Kurt Warner 4.00
BT11 Raghib Ismail 1.00
BT12 Doug Flutie 1.00
BT13 Jimmy Smith 1.00
BT14 Eric Moulds 2.00
BT15 Marvin Harrison 2.00
BT16 Ricky Watters 1.00
BT17 Marcus Robinson 1.00
BT18 Mark Brunell 2.00
BT19 Tim Dwight 1.00
BT20 Peyton Manning 4.00
BT21 Patrick Jeffers 1.00
BT22 Az-Zahir Hakim 1.00
BT23 Fred Taylor 2.00
BT24 Tim Biakabutuka 1.00
BT25 Marshall Faulk 3.00
BT26 Shannon Sharpe 1.00
BT27 Tony Gonzalez 1.00
BT28 Steve McNair 2.00
BT29 Antonio Freeman 1.00
BT30 Keyshawn Johnson 2.00

2000 Stadium Club Capture the Action

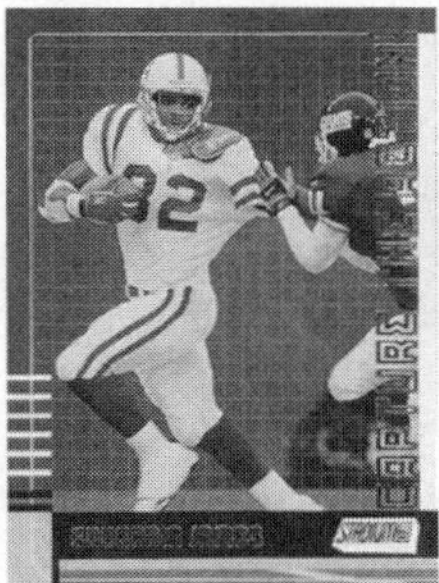

NM/M
Complete Set (30): 25.00
Common Player: .50
Minor Stars: 1.00
Inserted 1:8
Game View Cards: 2X-4X
Inserted 1:454
Production 100 Sets
CA1 Brett Favre 4.00
CA2 Drew Bledsoe 2.00
CA3 Dan Marino 4.00
CA4 Peyton Manning 3.00
CA5 Kurt Warner 3.00
CA6 Brad Johnson 1.00
CA7 Steve Beuerlein .50
CA8 Troy Aikman 3.00
CA9 Edgerrin James 3.00
CA10 Marshall Faulk 1.00
CA11 Stephen Davis 1.00
CA12 Eddie George 1.00
CA13 Emmitt Smith 3.00
CA14 Curtis Martin 1.00
CA15 Ricky Williams 2.00
CA16 Jimmy Smith .50
CA17 Marvin Harrison 1.00
CA18 Muhsin Muhammad .50
CA19 Keyshawn Johnson 1.00
CA20 Marcus Robinson .50
CA21 Antonio Freeman .50
CA22 Randy Moss 3.00
CA23 Tim Brown 1.00
CA24 Eric Moulds 1.00
CA25 Isaac Bruce 1.00
CA26 Zach Thomas .50
CA27 Warren Sapp .50
CA28 Jevon Kearse .50
CA29 Junior Seau .50
CA30 Kevin Carter .50

2000 Stadium Club Co-Signers

NM/M
Common Player: 60.00
Inserted 1:2,270
CS1 Peyton Manning, Kurt Warner 400.00
CS2 Edgerrin James, Marshall Faulk 200.00
CS3 Stephen Davis, Eddie George 100.00
CS4 Jimmy Smith, Cris Carter 60.00
CS5 Marvin Harrison, Isaac Bruce 60.00
CS6 Jon Kitna, Cade McNown 60.00

2000 Stadium Club Goal to Go

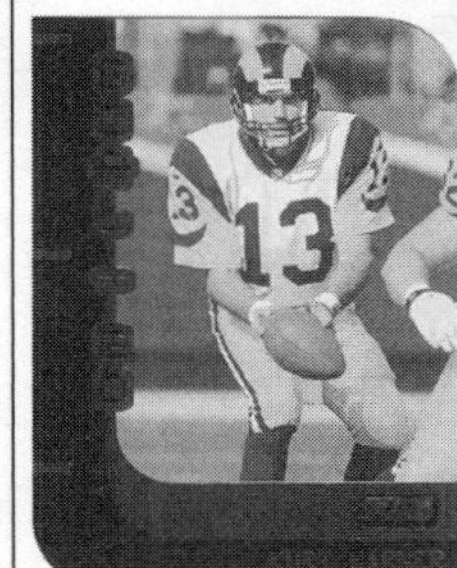

NM/M
Complete Set (16): 10.00
Common Player: .50
Minor Stars: 1.00
Inserted 1:8
G1 Cris Carter 1.00
G2 Stephen Davis 1.00
G3 Marvin Harrison 1.00
G4 Edgerrin James 2.50
G5 Zach Thomas .50
G6 Terrell Davis 2.00
G7 Leroy Hoard .50
G8 Kurt Warner 3.00
G9 Tony Gonzalez .50
G10 James Stewart .50
G11 Isaac Bruce 1.00
G12 Emmitt Smith 2.00
G13 Dorsey Levens 1.00
G14 Jevon Kearse 1.00
G15 Eddie George 1.50
G16 Warren Sapp .50

2000 Stadium Club Lone Star Autographs

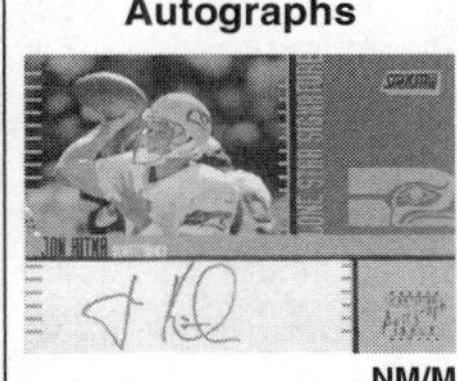

NM/M
Common Player: 10.00
Inserted 1:202
Card #17 Never Released
LS1 Edgerrin James 60.00
LS2 Stephen Davis 20.00
LS3 Marshall Faulk 25.00
LS4 Eddie George 45.00
LS5 Isaac Bruce 25.00
LS6 Jimmy Smith 10.00
LS7 Cris Carter 25.00
LS8 Kurt Warner 60.00
LS9 Marvin Harrison 25.00
LS10 Kevin Carter 10.00
LS11 Ron Dayne 35.00
LS12 Chad Pennington 60.00
LS13 Sylvester Morris 25.00
LS14 Thomas Jones 25.00
LS15 Shaun Alexander 45.00
LS16 Chris Redman 25.00
LS18 Peter Warrick 25.00
LS19 Jon Kitna 10.00
LS20 Cade McNown 15.00
LS21 Az-Zahir Hakim 10.00
LS22 Amani Toomer 10.00
LS23 Wesley Walls 10.00
LS24 Marcus Robinson 15.00
LS25 Zach Thomas 25.00
LS26 Tony Gonzalez 25.00
LS27 Muhsin Muhammad 25.00
LS28 Ed McCaffrey 25.00
LS29 Eric Moulds 25.00
LS30 Peyton Manning 100.00
LS31 Joe Montana 200.00

2000 Stadium Club Tunnel Vision

NM/M
Complete Set (8): 12.00
Common Player: 1.00
Inserted 1:Box
TV1 Edgerrin James 3.00
TV2 Brett Favre 3.00
TV3 Marshall Faulk 1.00
TV4 Emmitt Smith 2.00
TV5 Peyton Manning 3.00
TV6 Eddie George 1.50
TV7 Kurt Warner 4.00
TV8 Fred Taylor 1.75

2001 Stadium Club

NM/M
Complete Set (175): 80.00
Common Player: .15
Minor Stars: .30
Common Rookie: 1.00
Inserted 1:4
Pack (6): 2.75
Wax Box (24): 45.00
1 Peyton Manning 1.50
2 Akili Smith .50
3 Brian Griese .60
4 Wayne Chrebet .15
5 Oronde Gadsden .15
6 Marvin Harrison .50
7 Charles Johnson .15
8 Jay Fiedler .50
9 Kerry Collins .15
10 Troy Aikman 1.00
11 Donovan McNabb .75
12 Ike Hilliard .15
13 Warrick Dunn .50
14 Derrick Alexander .15
15 Jake Plummer .50
16 Corey Dillon .50
17 Ahman Green .15
18 Keenan McCardell .15
19 Derrick Mason .15
20 Jerry Rice 1.25
21 Emmitt Smith 1.50
22 Dedric Ward .15
23 Jamal Anderson .50
24 Charlie Garner .15
25 Vinny Testaverde .15
26 Shaun Alexander .60
27 Terry Glenn .15
28 Cade McNown .50
29 Germane Crowell .15
30 Jeff Graham .15
31 Rich Gannon .15
32 Jevon Kearse .50
33 Shannon Sharpe .15
34 Marcus Robinson .50
35 Rod Smith .15
36 Curtis Martin .50
37 Robert Smith .50
38 Marshall Faulk .60
39 Tony Richardson .15
40 Travis Prentice .15
41 Edgerrin James 1.50
42 Duce Staley .50
43 Keyshawn Johnson .50
44 Joe Horn .15
45 Shawn Bryson .15
46 Ray Lewis .15
47 Fred Taylor .75
48 Jeff George .15
49 Sean Dawkins .15
50 Daunte Culpepper 1.00
51 Chris Chandler .15
52 Tim Couch .75
53 Trent Dilfer .15
54 Steve McNair .50
55 Kordell Stewart .50
56 Aaron Brooks .50
57 Michael Pittman .15
58 Bill Schroeder .15
59 Junior Seau .15
60 Kurt Warner 1.50
61 Drew Bledsoe .60
62 Steve Beuerlein .15
63 Mike Anderson 1.25
64 Brad Johnson .50
65 Tim Brown .50
66 Qadry Ismail .15
67 Doug Flutie .60
68 Terrell Owens .50

69 Raghib Ismail .15
70 Charlie Batch .50
71 Jerome Pathon .15
72 Peter Warrick 1.00
73 Hines Ward .15
74 Ron Dayne 1.00
75 Lamar Smith .15
76 Amani Toomer .15
77 Joey Galloway .50
78 James Allen .15
79 Isaac Bruce .50
80 David Boston .50
81 James Thrash .15
82 Tony Gonzalez .15
83 Jason Taylor .15
84 Ricky Watters .15
85 Terance Mathis .15
86 Troy Brown .15
87 Mark Brunell .75
88 Rob Johnson .15
89 Freddie Jones .15
90 Eddie George .60
91 Tiki Barber .15
92 Donald Hayes .15
93 Muhsin Muhammad .15
94 Johnnie Morton .15
95 Warren Sapp .15
96 Bobby Shaw .15
97 Randy Moss 1.50
98 Jerome Bettis .50
99 Antonio Freeman .50
100 Jamal Lewis 1.25
101 Andre Rison .15
102 Kevin Faulk .15
103 Jon Kitna .50
104 Shawn Jefferson .15
105 Kevin Johnson .50
106 Torry Holt .50
107 Cris Carter .50
108 Chad Lewis .15
109 Stephen Davis .50
110 Jeff Blake .15
111 Elvis Grbac .15
112 Ed McCaffrey .50
113 Tim Biakabutuka .15
114 Trent Green .15
115 Jeff Garcia .50
116 Jacquez Green .15
117 Shaun King .50
118 Jimmy Smith .15
119 James Stewart .15
120 Brian Urlacher 1.00
121 Tyrone Wheatley .15
122 J.R. Redmond .15
123 Eric Moulds .15
124 Ricky Williams .75
125 Brett Favre 2.00
126 *Koren Robinson* 3.00
127 *Richard Seymour* 1.00
128 *Jamal Reynolds* 1.00
129 *Kevin Kasper* 1.00
130 *LaMont Jordan* 2.50
131 *Reggie Wayne* 4.00
132 *Travis Henry* 3.00
133 *Alge Crumpler* 2.00
134 *Quincy Carter* 3.00
135 *Michael Bennett* 5.00
136 *Jamie Winborn* 1.00
137 *Josh Heupel* 2.00
138 *Will Allen* 1.00
139 *Scotty Anderson* 1.00
140 *LaDainian Tomlinson* 10.00
141 *Freddie Mitchell* 3.00
142 *Gerard Warren* 1.00
143 *Chad Johnson* 5.00
144 *Todd Heap* 2.00
145 *Leonard Davis* 1.00
146 *Kevan Barlow* 4.00
147 *Correll Buckhalter* 1.00
148 *Fred Smoot* 2.00
149 *Steve Smith* 3.00
150 *David Terrell* 2.00
151 *Chris Chambers* 5.00
152 *Mike McMahon* 2.00
153 *Rudi Johnson* 4.00
154 *Marques Tuiasosopo* 3.00
155 *Deuce McAllister* 8.00
156 *Marcus Stroud* 1.00
157 *Bobby Newcombe* 2.00
158 *Rod Gardner* 5.00
159 *Drew Brees* 6.00
160 *Jesse Palmer* 2.00
161 *Derrick Gibson* 1.00
162 *James Jackson* 2.00
163 *Dan Morgan* 2.00
164 *Michael Vick* 15.00
165 *Marvin "Snoop" Minnis* 3.00
166 *Anthony Thomas* 4.00
167 *Andre Carter* 2.00
168 *Travis Minor* 3.00
169 *Quincy Morgan* 2.50
170 *Justin Smith* 1.00
171 *Tay Cody* 1.00
172 *Santana Moss* 4.00
173 *Sage Rosenfels* 2.50
174 *Robert Ferguson* 3.00
175 *Chris Weinke* 2.00

2001 Stadium Club All-Pro Autos

NM/M
Complete Set (6): 175.00
Common Player: 25.00
SPA-DC Daunte Culpepper 50.00
SPA-SD Stephen Davis 25.00
SPA-EG Eddie George 50.00
SPA-TG Tony Gonzalez 25.00
SPA-MH Marvin Harrison 25.00
SPA-EJ Edgerrin James 75.00

Post-1980 cards in Near Mint condition will generally sell for about 75% of the quoted Mint value. Excellent-condition cards bring no more than 40%.

2001 Stadium Club All-Pro Relics

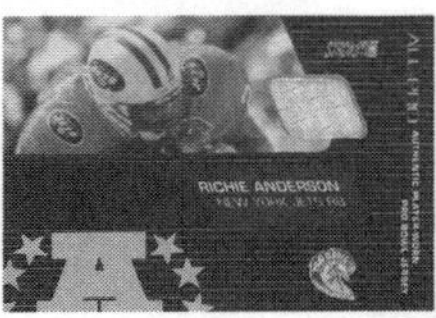

NM/M
Common Player: 8.00
SP-DA Donnie Abraham 8.00
SP-SA Stephen Alexander 10.00
SP-LA Larry Allen 8.00
SP-RA Richie Anderson 8.00
SP-JA Jessie Armstead 8.00
SP-TA Trace Armstrong 8.00
SP-CB Champ Bailey 15.00
SP-RB Ruben Brown 8.00
SP-CC Cris Carter 15.00
SP-JC Jeff Christy 8.00
SP-MC Marco Coleman 8.00
SP-DC Daunte Culpepper 25.00
SP-HD Hugh Douglas 8.00
SP-LE Luther Elliss 8.00
SP-ENG Eddie George 25.00
SP-LG La'Roi Glover 8.00
SP-TG Tony Gonzalez 10.00
SP-MG Martin Grammatica 8.00
SP-RG Robert Griffith 8.00
SP-MH Marvin Harrison 15.00
SP-DH Desmond Howard 8.00
SP-EJ Edgerrin James 30.00
SP-JK Jevon Kearse 10.00
SP-BM Brock Marion 8.00
SP-KM Keith Mitchell 8.00
SP-JO Jonathan Ogden 8.00
SP-TO Terrell Owens 15.00
SP-WS Warren Sapp 10.00
SP-JS Jimmy Smith 8.00
SP-RS Rod Smith 8.00
SP-JT Jeremiah Trotter 8.00
SP-TV Troy Vincent 8.00
SP-RW Rod Woodson 10.00

2001 Stadium Club Common Threads

NM/M
Complete Set (6): 100.00
Common Player: 20.00
CT-CR Daunte Culpepper, David Rivers 30.00
CT-GT Eddie George, LaDainian Tomlinson 30.00
CT-JB Edgerrin James, Kevan Barlow 40.00
CT-DM Corey Dillon, Travis Minor 20.00
CT-MJ Eric Moulds, Chad Johnson 20.00
CT-HW Marvin Harrison, Reggie Wayne 30.00

2001 Stadium Club Common Threads Autographs

NM/M
Complete Set (6): 275.00
Common Player: 30.00
CTA-CR Daunte Culpepper, David Rivers 75.00
CTA-GT Eddie George, LaDainian Tomlinson 75.00
CTA-JB Edgerrin James, Kevan Barlow 75.00
CTA-DM Corey Dillon, Travis Minor 40.00
CTA-MJ Eric Moulds, Chad Johnson 30.00
CTA-HW Marvin Harrison, Reggie Wayne 50.00

2001 Stadium Club Co-Signers

NM/M
Common Player: 60.00
CO-FJ Edgerrin James, Marshall Faulk 125.00
CO-MO Randy Moss, Terrell Owens 100.00
CO-FB Brett Favre, Aaron Brooks 200.00
CO-CG Daunte Culpepper, Jeff Garcia 60.00
CO-AL Mike Anderson, Jamal Lewis 60.00

2001 Stadium Club Highlight Reels

NM/M
Complete Set (5): 15.00
Common Player: 2.00
Inserted 1:8
HR-AA Alan Ameche 2.00
HR-JE John Elway 5.00
HR-BG Bob Griese 3.00
HR-JN Joe Namath 6.00
HR-BS Bart Starr 5.00

2001 Stadium Club In Focus

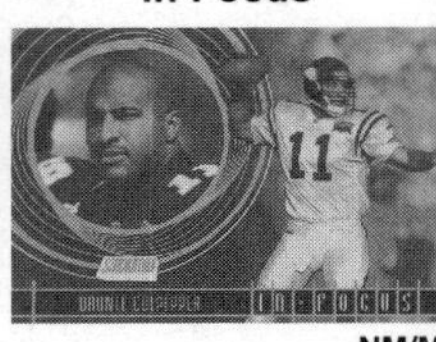

NM/M
Complete Set (15): 20.00
Common Player: 1.00
Inserted 1:8
IF1 Peyton Manning 5.00
IF2 Marshall Faulk 1.50
IF3 Torry Holt 1.00
IF4 Daunte Culpepper 2.50
IF5 Edgerrin James 4.00
IF6 Marvin Harrison 1.00
IF7 Jeff Garcia 1.00
IF8 Robert Smith 1.00
IF9 Randy Moss 5.00
IF10 Mike Anderson 2.50
IF11 Corey Dillon 1.00
IF12 Rod Smith 1.00
IF13 Brett Favre 6.00
IF14 Eddie George 1.50
IF15 Terrell Owens 1.00

2001 Stadium Club Jersey All-Pro

NM/M
Common Player: 10.00
Inserted 1:44
SP-DA Donnie Abraham 15.00
SP-SA Stephen Alexander 15.00
SP-LA Larry Allen 10.00
SP-RA Richie Anderson 10.00
SP-JA Jessie Armstead 12.00
SP-TA Trace Armstrong 12.00
SP-CB Champ Bailey 20.00
SP-RB Ruben Brown 10.00
SP-CC Cris Carter 30.00
SP-JC Jeff Christy 10.00
SP-MC Marco Coleman 12.00
SP-DC Daunte Culpepper 30.00
SP-HD Hugh Douglas 10.00
SP-LE Luther Ellis 12.00
SP-EGE Eddie George 30.00
SP-LG La'Roi Glover 12.00
SP-TG Tony Gonzalez 15.00
SP-MG Martin Gramatica 12.00
SP-RG Robert Griffith 10.00
SP-MH Marvin Harrison 20.00
SP-DH Desmond Howard 15.00
SP-EJ Edgerrin James 50.00
SP-JK Jevon Kearse 20.00
SP-BM Brock Marion 10.00
SP-KM Keith Mitchell 10.00
SP-JO Jonathan Ogden 10.00
SP-TO Terrell Owens 15.00
SP-WS Warren Sapp 15.00
SP-JS Jimmy Smith 12.00
SP-RS Rod Smith 12.00
SP-JT Jeremiah Trotter 10.00
SP-TV Troy Vincent 10.00
SP-RW Rod Woodson 15.00

2001 Stadium Club Lone Star Signatures

NM/M
Common Player: 10.00
Inserted 1:84
LS-DA Dan Alexander 25.00
LS-MA Mike Anderson 35.00
LS-KB Kevan Barlow 10.00
LS-JB Josh Booty 10.00
LS-DB Drew Brees 60.00
LS-DC Daunte Culpepper 40.00
LS-SD Stephen Davis 20.00
LS-MF Marshall Faulk 25.00
LS-EG Eddie George 25.00
LS-MH Marvin Harrison 20.00
LS-TH Travis Henry 25.00
LS-JH Joe Horn 10.00
LS-EJ Edgerrin James 50.00
LS-DM Deuce McAllister 40.00
LS-QM Quincy Morgan 20.00
LS-TO Terrell Owens 20.00
LS-JP Jesse Palmer 10.00
LS-DT David Terrell 40.00
LS-AT Anthony Thomas 35.00
LS-LT LaDainian Tomlinson 70.00
LS-MV Michael Vick 150.00
LS-KW Kenyatta Walker 10.00
LS-RW Reggie Wayne 30.00

2001 Stadium Club Stepping Up

NM/M
Complete Set (15): 35.00
Common Player: 1.00
SU1 David Terrell 2.00
SU2 LaDainian Tomlinson 7.00
SU3 Michael Vick 12.00
SU4 Koren Robinson 3.00
SU5 Michael Bennett 5.00
SU6 Chad Johnson 1.00
SU7 Drew Brees 7.00
SU8 Reggie Wayne 2.50
SU9 Freddie Mitchell 2.50
SU10 Chris Weinke 2.00
SU11 Rod Gardner 3.00
SU12 Chris Chambers 4.00
SU13 Deuce McAllister 4.00

NM/M
SU14 Santana Moss 3.00
SU15 Robert Ferguson 1.50

2002 Stadium Club

NM/M
Common Player: .15
Unlisted Stars: .60
Minor Stars: .40
Common Rookie (126-200): 1.00
Pack (15): 40.00
Wax Box (24): 250.00
1 Randy Moss 2.50
2 Kordell Stewart .50
3 Marvin Harrison .50
4 Chris Weinke .60
5 James Allen .15
6 Michael Pittman .15
7 Quincy Carter 1.50
8 Mike Anderson 1.00
9 Mike McMahon .60
10 Chris Chambers .60
11 Laveranues Coles .15
12 Curtis Conway .15
13 Brad Johnson .15
14 Shaun Alexander .60
15 Jerry Rice 2.50
16 Rod Gardner .15
17 Derrick Mason .15
18 Tom Brady 2.50
19 Jimmy Smith .50
20 Tim Couch 1.00
21 Jim Miller .15
22 Eric Moulds .15
23 Michael Vick 2.50
24 Jon Kitna .15
25 Johnnie Morton .15
26 Priest Holmes .50
27 Aaron Brooks 1.00
28 Duce Staley .50
29 LaDainian Tomlinson 2.00
30 Lamar Smith .50
31 Rod Smith .50
32 Richard Huntley .15
33 Antonio Freeman .15
34 Amani Toomer .40
35 Hines Ward .40
36 Marshall Faulk 1.50
37 Steve McNair .60
38 Tim Brown .60
39 Curtis Martin .50
40 Kevin Johnson .15
41 Rob Johnson .15
42 Qadry Ismail .15
43 Daunte Culpepper 1.50
44 Willie Jackson .15
45 Jeff Garcia .60
46 Matt Hasselbeck .15
47 Corey Bradford .50
48 Marvin "Snoop" Minnis .50
49 Ron Dayne .50
50 Peyton Manning 2.50
51 Drew Bledsoe 1.50
52 Terry Glenn .50
53 Warrick Dunn .50
54 Mark Brunell .60
55 James Stewart .15
56 Muhsin Muhammad .40
57 Jake Plummer .40
58 Terance Mathis .15
59 Raghib Ismail .15
60 Joe Horn .40
61 Wayne Chrebet .40
62 James Thrash .15
63 Stephen Davis .50
64 Isaac Bruce .50
65 Peter Warrick .50
66 Anthony Thomas 2.00
67 Maurice Smith .15
68 Tony Gonzalez .50
69 Michael Bennett .60
70 Ike Hilliard .15
71 Plaxico Burress .60
72 Darrell Jackson .15
73 Kevan Barlow .15
74 Ray Lewis .50
75 Emmitt Smith 2.50
76 Bill Schroeder .40
77 Az-Zahir Hakim .40
78 Troy Brown .60
79 Keyshawn Johnson .40
80 Tim Dwight .40
81 Peerless Price .40
82 Marty Booker .15
83 Terrell Davis 1.00
84 Dominic Rhodes .15
85 Jay Fiedler .40
86 Rich Gannon .50
87 Terrell Owens .60
88 Donald Hayes .15
89 Thomas Jones .15
90 Ricky Williams 1.50
91 Donovan McNabb 1.50
92 Eddie George .60
93 Germane Crowell .15
94 David Terrell .60
95 Alex Van Pelt .15
96 Antowain Smith .50
97 Jerome Bettis .50
98 Mike Alstott .50
99 Doug Flutie .60
100 Kurt Warner 2.50
101 Cris Carter .40
102 Oronde Gadsden .15
103 Ahman Green .60
104 Corey Dillon .60
105 Marcus Robinson .50
106 Shannon Sharpe .40
107 Kerry Collins .50
108 Garrison Hearst .40
109 David Boston .60
110 Travis Henry .50
111 James Jackson .50
112 Fred Taylor .50
113 Edgerrin James 2.00
114 Vinny Testaverde .15
115 Todd Pinkston .15
116 Koren Robinson .50
117 Torry Holt .15
118 Brian Griese .60
119 Trent Green .50
120 James McKnight .15
121 Charlie Garner .50
122 Tiki Barber .15
123 Joey Galloway .40
124 Quincy Morgan .50
125 Brett Favre 3.50
126 *Joey Harrington* 12.00
127 *Ashley Lelie* 8.00
128 *Terry Charles* 1.00
129 *Charles Grant* 1.00
130 *Levar Fisher* 1.00
131 *Larry Tripplett* 1.00
132 *Quentin Jammer* 4.00
133 *Ron Johnson* 3.00
134 *Maurice Morris* 6.00
135 *Roy Williams* 10.00
136 *Kurt Kittner* 4.00
137 *Dennis Johnson* 3.00
138 *Seth Burford* 1.00
139 *Michael Lewis* 1.00
140 *William Green* 8.00
141 *Rohan Davey* 6.00
142 *Rocky Calmus* 4.00
143 *Robert Thomas* 1.00
144 *Travis Stephens* 4.00
145 *Ladell Betts* 4.00
146 *Daniel Graham* 4.00
147 *Chester Taylor* 1.00
148 *Tim Carter* 1.00
149 *Lito Sheppard* 3.00
150 *David Carr* 15.00
151 *Alex Brown* 1.00
152 *John Henderson* 3.00
153 *Jamar Martin* 1.00
154 *Raonall Smith* 1.00
155 *Leonard Henry* 3.00
156 *T.J. Duckett* 8.00
157 *Patrick Ramsey* 8.00
158 *Antwann Randle El* 8.00
159 *Luke Staley* 4.00
160 *Jon McGraw* 1.00
161 *Phillip Buchanon* 4.00
162 *Dwight Freeney* 8.00
163 *Mike Rumph* 1.00
164 *Albert Haynesworth* 3.00
165 *Antonio Bryant* 8.00
166 *Josh Reed* 8.00
167 *Eric Crouch* 5.00
168 *Donald Reche Caldwell* 4.00
169 *Adrian Peterson* 4.00
170 *Jonathan Wells* 5.00
171 *Wendell Bryant* 2.00
172 *Tellis Redmon* 1.00
173 *Josh McCown* 4.00
174 *DeShaun Foster* 6.00
175 *Cliff Russell* 2.00
176 *David Garrard* 3.00
177 *Brian Westbrook* 4.00
178 *Anthony Weaver* 2.00
179 *Bryan Thomas* 2.00
180 *Kalimba Edwards* 2.00
181 *Javon Walker* 10.00
182 *Marquise Walker* 4.00
183 *Deion Branch* 10.00
184 *Lamar Gordon* 4.00
185 *Jeremy Shockey* 12.00
186 *Clinton Portis* 15.00
187 *Napoleon Harris* 3.00
188 *Freddie Milons* 3.00
189 *Julius Peppers* 8.00
190 *Andre Davis* 6.00
191 *Travis Fisher* 3.00
192 *Chad Hutchinson* 3.00
193 *Najeh Davenport* 6.00
194 *Edward Reed* 8.00
195 *Donte Stallworth* 8.00
196 *Brandon Doman* 3.00
197 *Zak Kustok* 3.00
198 *Randy Fasani* 3.00
199 *J.T. O'Sullivan* 3.00
200 *Jabar Gaffney* 6.00

2002 Stadium Club Photographer's Proofs

Stars: 5X-10X
Rookies: 2X-4X
Production 199 Sets

2002 Stadium Club Co-Signers

NM/M
Common Player: 100.00
Inserted 1:640
CS-CH David Carr, Joey Harrington 200.00
CS-WB Kurt Warner, Tom Brady 75.00
CS-OB Terrell Owens, David Boston 40.00
CS-FW Brett Favre, Kurt Warner 125.00
CS-CB Chris Chambers, Marty Booker 45.00
CS-GF Willie Green, DeShaun Foster 60.00

2002 Stadium Club Fabric of Champions

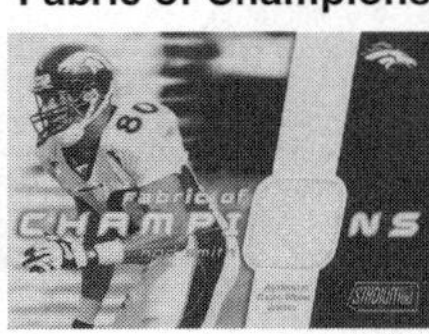

NM/M
Common Player: 20.00
Production 1499 sets
Gold Production 25 Sets
FC-TD Terrell Davis 8.00
FC-WD Warrick Dunn 8.00
FC-AF Antonio Freeman 8.00
FC-PH Priest Holmes 12.00
FC-JK Jevon Kearse 8.00
FC-RL Ray Lewis 10.00
FC-RS Rod Smith 12.00
FC-SY Steve Young 15.00

2002 Stadium Club Highlight Materials

NM/M
Common Player: 20.00
Inserted 1:31
Gold Production 25 Sets
HM-MA Mike Alstott 8.00
HM-JA Jessie Armstead 8.00
HM-DB David Boston 12.00
HM-TB Tim Brown 15.00
HM-HD Hugh Douglas 8.00
HM-RG Rich Gannon 10.00
HM-JG Jeff Garcia 10.00
HM-AG Ahman Green 12.00
HM-MH Marvin Harrison 10.00
HM-GH Garrison Hearst 8.00
HM-TO Terrell Owens 12.00
HM-JR John Randle 8.00
HM-JS Junior Seau 12.00
HM-SS Stan Smith 8.00
HM-KS Kordell Stewart 10.00
HM-MS Michael Strahan 8.00
HM-BU Brian Urlacher 15.00
HM-KW Kurt Warner 12.00

2002 Stadium Club Lone Star Signatures

NM/M
Common Player: 20.00
Inserted 1:92
LS-JA John Abraham 8.00
LS-MB Marty Booker 25.00
LS-DB David Boston 12.00
LS-TB Tom Brady 100.00
LS-DC David Carr 100.00
LS-CC Chris Chambers 20.00
LS-BF Brett Favre 100.00
LS-DF DeShaun Foster 25.00
LS-WG William Green 20.00
LS-JH Joey Harrington 75.00
LS-KK Kurt Kittner 20.00
LS-TO Terrell Owens 15.00
LS-MP Mike Pearson 8.00
LS-AP Adrian Peterson 10.00
LS-JR Josh Reed 15.00
LS-AS Antowain Smith 8.00
LS-JT James Thrash 8.00
LS-KW Kurt Warner 50.00
LW-RW Roy Williams 25.00

2002 Stadium Club Reel Time

NM/M
Common Player: 3.00
Inserted 1:12
RT1 Marshall Faulk 3.00
RT2 Peyton Manning 5.00
RT3 Randy Moss 5.00
RT4 Stephen Davis 3.00
RT5 Jeff Garcia 3.00

NM/M

RT6 Donovan McNabb 3.00
RT7 Edgerrin James 4.00
RT8 Trent Green 3.00
RT9 Eddie George 3.00
RT10 Ahman Green 3.00
RT11 Plaxico Burress 4.00
RT12 David Boston 3.00
RT13 Tom Brady 10.00
RT14 Marvin Harrison 3.00
RT15 Brett Favre 10.00
RT16 Ricky Williams 3.00
RT17 Kordell Stewart 3.00
RT18 Curtis Martin 3.00
RT19 Anthony Thomas 5.00
RT20 Shaun Alexander 4.00
RT21 LaDainian Tomlinson 5.00
RT22 Kurt Warner 6.00
RT23 Jerome Bettis 3.00
RT24 Priest Holmes 3.00
RT25 Terrell Owens 3.00

2002 Stadium Club Touchdown Treasures

NM/M

Common Player: 40.00
Inserted 1:686
Gold Production 25 Sets
TT-TB Tom Brady 100.00
TT-TL Ty Law 30.00
TT-DP David Patten 15.00
TT-RP Ricky Proehl 15.00
TT-KW Kurt Warner 75.00

1963 Stancraft Playing Cards

This 54-card set, titled "Official NFL All-Time Greats," commemorates the opening of the Pro Football Hall of Fame in Canton, Ohio. Each of the cards, designed as playing cards, features an artistic drawing of the player, with his name, position, team name and years played below the picture, which is done in brown ink. The Aces and Jokers, however, have NFL logos on them instead of artwork. Two styles were used for the card backs - an NFL logo in the center surrounded by the 14 NFL team logos in a checkerboard pattern, all against a red background, or a green background with the 14 team helmets contained within it. Cards, 2-1/4" x 3-1/2" with rounded corners, came in a plastic box.

NM/M

Complete Set (54): 125.00
Common Player: 1.50
AC NFL Logo 1.50
2C Johnny "Blood" McNally 2.00
3C Bobby Mitchell 3.00
4C Bill Howton 1.50
5C Wilbur Fats Henry 2.00
6C Tony Canedeo 2.00
7C Bulldog Turner 3.00
8C Charlie Trippi 2.00
9C Tommy Mason 1.50
10C Earl "Dutch" Clark 2.00
JC Y.A. Tittle 5.00
QC Lou Groza 5.00
KC Bobby Layne 6.00
AD NFL Logo 1.50
2D Frankie Albert 1.50
3D Del Shofner 1.50
4D Ollie Matson 4.00
5D Mike Ditka 8.00
6D Otto Graham 6.00
7D Chuck Bednarik 4.00
8D Jim Taylor 3.00
9D Mel Hein 2.00
10D Eddie Price 1.50
JD Sonny Randle 1.50
QD Joe Perry 4.00
KD Bob Waterfield 5.00
AH NFL Logo 1.50
2H Paul Hornung 5.00
3H Johnny Unitas 10.00
4H Doak Walker 5.00
5H Tom Fears 3.00
6H Jim Thorpe 10.00
7H Gino Marchetti 3.00
8H Claude Buddy Young 1.50
9H Jim Benton 2.00
10H Jim Brown 12.00
JH George Halas 1.50
QH Sammy Baugh 4.00
KH Bill Dudley 2.50
1S NFL Logo 1.50
2S Eddie LeBaron 2.00
3S Don Hutson 3.50
4S Clarke Hinkle 2.00
5S Charley Conerly 2.50
6S Earl (Curly) Lambeau 2.00
7S Sid Luckman 5.00
8S Pete Pihos 2.00
9S Dante Lavelli 2.00
10S Norm Van Brocklin 4.00
JS Cloyce Box 1.50
QS Joe Schmidt 3.00
KS Elroy Hirsch 3.00
xx Joker (NFL Logo) 2.00
xx Joker (NFL Logo) 2.00

1991 Star Pics Promos

Star Pics issued these cards to promote their 1991 set. They were distributed in two-card panels and inserted in an issue of Pro Football Weekly. The card fronts feature a color photo with a football border. The backs are green and include basic player information and a close-up photo.

NM/M

Complete Set (4): 4.00
Common Player: 1.00
1 Mark Carrier DB 1.00
2 Aaron Craver 1.00
3 Dan McGwire 1.00
4 Eric Turner 1.00

1991 Star Pics

The company's first set of college prospects was released in June 1991. The set features 44 out of 55 first- and second-round picks from the 1991 draft. All 91 players in the set -- the roster of which was set before the draft -- were selected. Subsets include the nine-card flashback issue (NFL players in college uniforms) and Top Pick Agents, featuring player representatives. At least one in 50 sets contained a randomly- inserted autograph. (Key: FL - flashback, A - agent). Two promo panels, each featuring two standard-size cards, were also produced to preview the regular 1991 set's design. The players paired together were 1) Mark Carrier, $1, and 2) Aaron Craver, $1, and 3) Dan McGwire, $1, and 4) Eric Turner, $1.

NM/M

Complete Set (112): 6.00
Common Player: .05
Common Autograph: 6.00
Autograph Cards: 20X-40X
NFL Autographs: 200X-400X
1 1991 NFL Draft Overview .05
2 Barry Sanders (FL) .10
3 Nick Bell .10
4 Kevin Pritchett .05
5 Huey Richardson .05
6 Mike Croel .10
7 Paul Justin .05
8 Ivory Lee Brown .05
9 Herman Moore 1.25
10 Derrick Thomas (FL) .15
11 Keith Taylor .05
12 Joe Johnson .05
13 Dan McGwire .10
14 Harvey Williams .50
15 Eric Moten .05
16 Steve Zucker .05
17 Randal Hill .20
18 Browning Nagle .20
19 Stan Thomas .05
20 Emmitt Smith (FL) .50
21 Ted Washington .05
22 Lamar Rogers .05
23 Kenny Walker .05
24 Howard Griffith .05
25 Reggie Johnson .05
26 Lawrence Dawsey .05
27 Joe Garten .05
28 Moe Gardner .05
29 Michael Stonebreaker .05
30 Jeff George (FL) .15
31 Leigh Steinberg (A) .05
32 John Flannery .05
33 Pat Harlow .05
34 Kanavis McGhee .05
35 Michael Dumas .05
36 Godfrey Myles .05
37 Shawn Moore .05
38 Jeff Graham .50
39 Ricky Watters 1.00
40 Andre Ware (FL) .05
41 Henry Jones .10
42 Eric Turner .30
43 Bob Wolf (A) .05
44 Randy Baldwin .05
45 Morris Lewis .05
46 Jerry Evans .05
47 Derek Russell .05
48 Merton Hanks .40
49 Kevin Donnalley .05
50 Troy Aikman (FL) .30
51 William Thomas .05
52 Chris Thome .05
53 Ricky Ervins .10
54 Jake Reed .25
55 Jerome Henderson .05
56 Mark Vander Poel .05
57 Bernard Ellison .05
58 Jack Mills (A) .05
59 Jarrod Bunch .05
60 Mark Carrier (FL) .05
61 Rocen Keeton .05
62 Louis Riddick .05
63 Bobby Wilson .05
64 Steve Jackson .05
65 Brett Favre 2.50
66 Ernie Mills .20
67 Joe Valerio .05
68 Chris Smith .05
69 Ralph Cindrich .05
70 Christian Okoye (FL) .05
71 Charles McRae .05
72 Jon Vaughn .05
73 Eric Swann .30
74 Bill Musgrave .05
75 Eric Bieniemy .20
76 Pat Tyrance .05
77 Vince Clark .05
78 Eugene Williams .05
79 Rob Carpenter .05
80 Deion Sanders (FL) .25
81 Roman Phifer .10
82 Greg Lewis .05
83 John Johnson .05
84 Richard Howell (A) .05
85 Jesse Campbell .05
86 Stanley Richard .05
87 Alfred Williams .05
88 Mike Pritchard .25
89 Mel Agee .05
90 Aaron Craver .05
91 Tim Barnett .05
92 Wesley Carroll .05
93 Kevin Scott .05
94 Darren Lewis .05
95 Tim Bruton .05
96 Tim James .05
97 Darryl Lewis .05
98 Shawn Jefferson .20
99 Mitch Donahue .05
100 Marvin Demoff (A) .05
101 Adrian Cooper .05
102 Bruce Pickens .05
103 Scott Zolak .05
104 Phil Hansen .05
105 Ed King .05
106 Mike Jones .05
107 Alvin Harper .50
108 Robert Young .05
109 Offensive Top Prospects .05
110 Defensive Top Prospects .05

1992 Star Pics

The top collegiate pro prospects are featured in this 100-card set from Star Pics. Each card front has a glossy color action photo on the front, with a white border. The player's name and position run vertically along the left side of the card. A Star Pics logo appears in the lower right corner. The card back has a mug shot of the player, and summarizes his collegiate accomplishments. A scouting report, which lists the player's strengths and weaknesses, is also given. A card number appears in the upper left corner. Cards were sold as a factory set, or in 10-card packs. Subsets in the main set included five Flashback cards (#s 10, 20, 30, 50 and 70) and 10 StarStat cards. Two StarStat cards (#s 1 and 65) were included in the factory sets. The eight others were random inserts in packs.

NM/M

Complete Set (100): 6.00
Common Player: .05
Common Autograph: 6.00
Autograph Cards: 20X-40X
NFL Autographs: 100X-200X
1 Steve Emtman .10
2 Chris Hakel .05
3 Phillippi Sparks .05
4 Howard Dinkins .05
5 Robert Brooks .75
6 Chris Pederson .05
7 Bucky Richardson .10
8 Keith Goganious .05
9 Robert Porcher .05
10 Andre Rison .20
11 Jason Hanson .30
12 Tommy Vardell .10
13 Kurt Barber .05
14 Bernard Dafney .05
15 Levon Kirkland .05
16 Corey Widmer .05
17 Santana Dotson .10
18 Chris Holder .05
19 Elbert Turner .05
20 Mike Croel .10
21 Darren Perry .05
22 Troy Vincent .10
23 Quentin Coyratt .40
24 John Brown III .05
25 John Ray .05
26 Vaughn Dunbar .10
27 Stacey Dillard .05
28 Alonzo Spellman .20
29 Darren Woodson .10
30 Pat Swilling .10
31 Eddie Robinson .05
32 Tyji Armstrong .05
33 Bill Johnson .05
34 Eugene Chung .05
35 Ricardo McDonald .05
36 Sean Lumpkin .05
37 Greg Skrepenak .05
38 Ashley Ambrose .05
39 Kevin Smith .05
40 Todd Collins .05
41 Shane Dronett .05
42 Ronnie West .05
43 Darryl Williams .05
44 Rodney Blackshear .05
45 Dion Lambert .05
46 Mike Saunders .05
47 Keo Coleman .05
48 Dana Hall .10
49 Arthur Marshall .05
50 Leonard Russell .05
51 Matt Rodgers .05
52 Shane Collins .05
53 Courtney Hawkins .10
54 Chuck Smith .05
55 Joe Bowden .05
56 Gene McGuire .05
57 Tracy Scroggins .10
58 Mark D'Onofrio .05
59 Jimmy Smith 1.00
60 Carl Pickens 1.50
61 Robert Harris .05
62 Erick Anderson .05
63 Doug Rigby .05
64 Keith Hamilton .05
65 Vaughn Dunbar .10
66 Willie Clay .05
67 Robert Jones .05
68 Leon Searcy Jr. .05
69 Elliot Pilton .05
70 Thurman Thomas .20
71 Mark Wheeler .05
72 Jeremy Lincoln .10
73 Tony McCoy .05
74 Charles Davenport .05
75 Patrick Rowe .05
76 Tommy Jeter .05
77 Rod Smith .05
78 Johnny Mitchell .25
79 Corey Barlow .05
80 Scottie Graham .15
81 Mark Bounds .05
82 Chester McGlockton .10
83 Ray Roberts .05
84 Dale Carter .10
85 James Patton .05
86 Tyrone Legette .05
87 Leodis Flowers .05
88 Rico Smith .05
89 Kevin Turner .10
90 Steve Emtman .10
91 Rodney Culver .10
92 Chris Mims .15
93 Carlos Snow .05
94 Corey Harris .10
95 Nate Williams .05
96 Timothy Roberts .05
97 Steve Israel .05
98 Tony Smith .05
99 Dwayne Sabb .05
100 Checklist .05

1992 Star Pics StarStat Bonus

Eight top collegiate NFL prospects are featured in this insert set. Cards were random inserts in 10-card foil StarPaks and compare the players' collegiate statistics to those of NFL greats. Fronts have the "StarStats" logo on them; backs have the card number. Two additional StarStat cards, for Steve Emtman and Vaughn Dunbar, were also made and were included in the 1992 Star Pics factory set.

NM/M

Complete Set (8): 8.00
Common Player: .50
1 Dale Carter 1.00
2 Carl Pickens 6.00
3 Alonzo Spellman 1.00
4 Jimmy Smith 1.25
5 Quentin Coryatt 2.00
6 Troy Vincent .50
7 Darryl Williams .50
8 Courtney Hawkins .50

1989 Star-Cal Decals

The 54-card, 3" x 4-1/2" sticker set featured players from six NFL teams, and was licensed by the NFL and the NFL Players' Association. The cards have rounded edges with a silver logo (First Edition 1989) in the upper left corner. Each decal also came with a pennant-shaped mini team banner decal in the player's team colors.

NM/M

Complete Set (54): 80.00
Common Player: 1.00
1 Raul Allegre 1.00
2 Carl Banks 1.00
3 Cornelius Bennett 1.50
4 Brian Blades 1.50
5 Kevin Butler 1.00
6 Harry Carson 1.00
7 Anthony Carter 1.00
8 Michael Carter 1.00
9 Shane Conlan 1.00
10 Roger Craig 1.50
11 Richard Dent 1.25
12 Chris Doleman 1.00
13 Tony Dorsett 4.00
14 Dave Duerson 1.00
15 Charles Haley 1.50
16 Dan Hampton 1.00
17 Al Harris 1.00
18 Mark Jackson 1.00
19 Vance Johnson 1.00
20 Steve Jordan 1.00
21 Clarence Kay 1.00
22 Jim Kelly 4.00
23 Tommy Kramer 1.00
24 Ronnie Lott 2.00
25 Lionel Manuel 1.00
26 Guy McIntyre 1.00
27 Steve McMichael 1.25
28 Karl Mecklenburg 1.25
29 Orson Mobley 1.00
30 Joe Montana 20.00
31 Joe Morris 1.00
32 Joe Nash 1.00
33 Ricky Nattiel 1.00
34 Chuck Nelson 1.00
35 Darrin Nelson 1.00
36 Karl Nelson 1.00
37 Scott Norwood 1.00
38 Bart Oates 1.00
39 Rufus Porter 1.00
40 Andre Reed 2.00
41 Phil Simms 2.00
42 Mike Singletary 1.50
43 Fred Smerlas 1.00
44 Bruce Smith 2.00
45 Kelly Stouffer 1.00
46 Scott Studwell 1.00
47 Matt Suhey 1.00
48 Steve Tasker 1.00
49 Keena Turner 1.00
50 John L. Williams 1.25
51 Wade Wilson 1.00
52 Sammy Winder 1.00
53 Tony Woods 1.00
54 Eric Wright 1.00

1990 Star-Cal Decals Prototypes

The four-card, 3" x 4-1/2" set was issued as a preview to the 1990 94-card decal set.

NM/M

Complete Set (4): 5.00
Common Player: 1.00
1 Jeff Hostetler 1.00
2 Mike Kenn 1.00
3 Freeman McNeil 1.00
4 Steve Young 3.00

1990 Star-Cal Decals

The 94-card, 3" x 4-1/2" decal set was similar to the 1989 release, complete with facsimile autographs. Six players each from 12 of the league's top teams are featured. Each player decal was issued with a pennant-shaped mini team banner (3-1/2" x 2"). The set is also known as the Grid-Star decal set.

NM/M

Complete Set (94): 160.00
Common Player: 1.00
1 Eric Allen 1.00
2 Marcus Allen 2.00
3 Flipper Anderson 1.00
4A Neal Anderson (printed name in black letters) 1.00
4B Neal Anderson (printed name in white letters) 1.00
5A Carl Banks (printed name in black letters) 1.00
5B Carl Banks (printed name in white letters) 1.00
6 Mark Bavaro 1.00
7 Cornelius Bennett 1.50
8 Brian Blades 1.00
9 Joey Browner 1.00
10 Keith Byars 1.00
11A Anthony Carter (printed name in black letters) 1.00
11B Anthony Carter (printed name in white letters) 1.00
12 Cris Carter 2.00
13 Michael Carter 1.00
14 Gary Clark 1.00
15 Mark Collins 1.00
16 Shane Conlan 1.00
17 Jim Covert 1.00
18A Roger Craig (printed name black letters) 1.50
18B Roger Craig (printed name white letters) 1.50
19 Richard Dent 1.25
20 Chris Doleman 1.00
21 Dave Duerson 1.00
22 Henry Ellard 1.50
23A John Elway (printed name in black letters) 6.00
23B John Elway (printed name in white letters) 8.00
24 Jim Everett 1.25
25 Mervyn Fernandez 1.00
26 Willie Gault 1.25
27 Bob Golic 1.00
28 Darrell Green 1.25
29 Kevin Greene 1.25
30 Charles Haley 1.25
31 Jay Hilgenberg 1.00
32 Pete Holohan 1.00
33 Kent Hull 1.00
34 Bobby Humphrey 1.00
35A Bo Jackson (printed name in black letters) 2.00
35B Bo Jackson (printed name in white letters) 2.00
36 Keith Jackson 1.25
37 Mark Jackson 1.25
38 Joe Jacoby 1.00
39 Vance Johnson 1.00
40 Jim Kelly 3.00
41 Bernie Kosar 1.25
42 Greg Kragen 1.00
43 Jeff Lageman 1.00
44 Pat Leahy 1.00
45 Howie Long 1.25
46A Ronnie Lott (serial numbered 11419) 1.50
46B Ronnie Lott (serial numbered 11414) 1.50
47 Kevin Mack 1.00
48 Charles Mann 1.00
49 Leonard Marshall 1.00
50 Clay Matthews 1.25
51 Eric McMillan 1.00
52 Karl Mecklenburg 1.25
53 Dave Meggett (UER) (name misspelled Megget) 1.25
54A Eric Metcalf (serial numbered 11414) 2.00
54B Eric Metcalf (serial numbered 11424) 1.50
55 Keith Millard 1.00
56 Frank Minnifield 1.00
57A Joe Montana (printed name in black letters autograph covers only left leg) 12.00
57B Joe Montana (printed name in black letters autograph covers both legs) 15.00
57C Joe Montana (printed name in white letters autograph covers only left leg) 20.00
58 Joe Nash 1.00
59 Ken O'Brien 1.25
60 Rufus Porter 1.00
61 Andre Reed 1.50
62 Mark Rypien 1.25
63 Gerald Riggs 1.00
64 Mickey Shuler 1.00
65 Clyde Simmons 1.25
66A Phil Simms (printed name in black letters) 1.50
66B Phil Simms (printed name in white letters) 1.50
67A Mike Singletary (printed name in black letters) 1.50
67B Mike Singletary (printed name in white letters) 1.50
68 Jackie Slater 1.00
69 Bruce Smith 1.50
70A Kelly Stouffer (serial numbered 11414) 1.00
70B Kelly Stouffer (serial numbered 11427) 1.00
71 John Taylor 1.25
72 Lawyer Tillman 1.00
73 Al Toon 1.25
74A Herschel Walker (printed name in black letters) 1.50
74B Herschel Walker (printed name in white letters) 1.50
75 Reggie White 2.00
76A John L. Williams (printed name in black letters autograph below knees) 1.00
76B John L. Williams (printed name in black letters autograph above knees) 1.00
76C John L. Williams (printed name in white letters autograph below knees) 1.00
77 Tony Woods 1.00
78 Gary Zimmerman 1.00

1988 Starline Prototypes

The four-card, regular-size set was never issued to the public and just 75 sets were produced. Each card in the set features a color photo with a blue border.

NM/M

Complete Set (4): 500.00
Common Player: 75.00
1 John Elway 150.00
2 Bernie Kosar 75.00
3 Joe Montana 275.00
4 Phil Simms 75.00

1961 Steelers Jay Publishing

The 12-card, 5" x 7" set features black and white photos with blank backs and were issued in 12-card packs for 25 cents.

		NM/M
Complete Set (12):		30.00
Common Player:		2.50
1	Preston Carpenter	2.50
2	Dean Derby	2.50
3	Buddy Dial	2.50
4	John Henry Johnson	2.50
5	Bobby Layne	2.50
6	Gene Lipscomb	2.50
7	Bill Mack	2.50
8	Fred Mautino	2.50
9	Lou Michaels	2.50
10	Buddy Parker (CO)	2.50
11	Myron Pottios	2.50
12	Tom Tracy	2.50

1963 Steelers IDL

The 26-card, 4" x 5" set features black and white photos with white borders and an IDL logo in the bottom left corner. The backs are blank.

		NM/M
Complete Set (26):		75.00
Common Player:		3.00
1	Frank Atkinson	3.00
2	Jim Bradshaw	3.00
3	Ed Brown	3.00
4	John Burrell	3.00
5	Preston Carpenter	3.00
6	Lou Cordileone	3.00
7	Buddy Dial	3.00
8	Bob Ferguson	3.00
9	Glenn Glass	3.00
10	Dick Haley	3.00
11	Dick Hoak	3.00
12	John Henry Johnson	3.00
13	Brady Keys	3.00
14	Joe Krupa	3.00
15	Ray Lemek	3.00
16	Bill Mack	3.00
17	Lou Michaels	3.00
18	Bill Nelsen	3.00
19	Buzz Nutter	3.00
20	Myron Pottios	3.00
21	John Reger	3.00
22	Mike Sandusky	3.00
23	Ernie Stautner	3.00
24	George Tarasovic	3.00
25	Clendon Thomas	3.00
26	Tom Tracy	3.00

1968 Steelers KDKA

The 15-card, 2-3/8" x 4-1/8" set featured multiple players on each horizontal card front by position.

		NM/M
Complete Set (15):		30.00
Common Player:		2.50
1	John Knight, Ray Mansfield Centers:	2.50
2	Bill Austin (Head), Fletcher, Torgeson, McLaughlin, Taylor, Heinrich, DePasqua, Berlin (trainer) Coaches:	2.50
3	Bob Hohn, Paul Martha, Marv Woodson Defensive Backs:	2.50
4	John Foruria, Clendon Thomas, Bob Morgan Defensive Backs:	2.50
5	Ben McGhee, Chuck Hinton, Dick Arndt, Ken Kortas, Lloyd Voss Defensive Linemen:	2.50
6	Roy Jefferson, Ken Hebert (End-Kicker) Flankers:	2.50
7	Earl Gros, Bill Asbury Fullbacks:	2.50
8	Larry Granger, Sam Davis, Bruce Van Dyke Guards:	2.50
9	Andy Russell, Bill Saul, John Campbell, Ray May Linebackers:	2.50
10	Dick Shiner, Kent Nix Quarterbacks:	2.50
11	Ken Hebert, Ernie Ruple, Mike Taylor Rookies:	2.50
12	Dick Hoak, Don Shy, Jim Butler Running Backs:	2.50
13	J.R. Wilburn, Dick Compton Split Ends:	2.50
14	Fran O'Brien, Mike Haggerty, John Brown Tackles:	2.50
15	John Hilton, Chet Anderson Tight Ends:	2.50

1972 Steelers Photo Sheets

The eight-card, 2" x 3" set was issued in 10" x 8" sheets. The card fronts feature a black and white photo with the Steelers helmet appearing in the lower left corner. The backs are blank.

		NM/M
Complete Set (8):		30.00
Common Player:		1.50
1	Ralph Anderson, Jim Clack, Bobby Maples, Henry Davis, Jon Kolb, Ray Mansfield, Sam Davis, Chuck Allen	1.50
2	Jim Brumfield, Chuck Beatty, Bobby Walden, Frank Lewis, Lee Calland, Warren Bankston, Mel Blount, John Rowser	1.50
3	Bud Carson (CO), Bob Fry (CO), Dick Hoak (CO), Babe Parilli (CO), George Perles (CO), Lou Riecke (CO), Charley Sumner (CO), Lionel Taylor (CO)	1.50
4	Jack Ham, Ben McGee, Brian Stenger, Lloyd Voss, Bruce Van Dyke, L.C. Greenwood, Gerry Mullins, John Brown	1.50
5	Joe Greene, Bert Askson (UER), Mel Holmes, Dwight White, Bob Adams, Larry Brown, Dave Smith, John McMakin (Misspelled Burt)	1.50
6	Chuck Noll (CO), Jon Staggers, Terry Hanratty, Roy Gerela, Terry Bradshaw, Bob Leahy, Joe Gilliam, Rocky Bleier	1.50
7	Dick Post, Franco Harris, Dennis Meyer, Lorenzo Brinkley, Steve Furness, Gordon Gravelle, Rick Sharp, Dave Kalina	1.50
8	Mike Wagner, Ron Shanklin, Preston Pearson, Glen Edwards, Al Young, John Fuqua, Andy Russell, Steve Davis	1.50

1978 Steelers Team Issue

This set consists of eight 8" x 10" sheets which feature eight black-and-white photos each. Each player photo measures 2" x 3". The sheets are blank-backed and unnumbered.

		NM/M
Complete Set (8):		80.00
Common Panel:		10.00
1	B. Carr, Reggie Harrison RB, Mel Blount, Doug Becker, Tom Brzoza, Loren Toews, Mike Webster, Dennis Winston	12.00
2	Jack Deloplaine, Wentford Gains, Sidney Thornton, Rick Moser, Randy Reutershan, Nat Terry, Frank Lewis, Brad Wagner	10.00
3	Willie Fry, Steve Furness, Tom Beasley, Ted Petersen, Gary Dunn, L.C. Greenwood, Fred Anderson, Lance Reynolds	12.00
4	Dave LaCrosse, Jon Kolb, Robin Cole, Sam Davis G, Jack Lambert, Jack Ham, Brad Cousina, John Hicks	12.00
5	Gerry Mullins, Dave Pureifory, Ray Pinney, Joe Greene, John Banaszak, Steve Courson, Dwight White, Larry Brown	12.00
6	Chuck Noll CO, Craig Colquitt, Roy Gerela, Terry Bradshaw, Mike Kruczek, Cliff Stoudt, Rocky Bleier, Tony Dungy	18.00
7	John Stallworth, Theo Bell, Randy Grossman, Andre Keys, Jim Smith, L. McCarthey, Lynn Swann, Bennie Cunningham	15.00
8	Mike Wagner, R. Scott, Glen Edwards, Alvin Maxson, Ron Johnson DB, Larry Anderson, Donnie Shell, Franco Harris	12.00

1981 Steelers Police

The 16-card, 2-5/8" x 4-1/8" set was sponsored by the Steelers, Kiwanis, Coca-Cola and local law enforcement. The card fronts feature an action shot with the player's name, postion, uniform number, height and weight. The card backs have "Steeler's Tips."

		NM/M
Complete Set (16):		18.50
Common Player:		.60
9	Matt Bahr	.90
12	Terry Bradshaw (Passing)	7.50
31	Donnie Shell (Referee back)	1.25
32	Franco Harris (Running with ball)	4.50
47	Mel Blount (Running without ball)	2.25
52	Mike Webster (Standing)	1.25
57	Sam Davis	.60
58	Jack Lambert (Facing left)	3.75
9	Jack Ham (Sportsmanship back)	2.25
64	Steve Furness	.60
68	L.C. Greenwood	1.50
75	Joe Greene	3.75
76	John Banaszak	.60
79	Larry Brown (Chin 7/16" from bottom)	.60
82	John Stallworth (Running with ball)	2.00
88	Lynn Swann (Double coverage back)	4.50

1982 Steelers Police

The 16-card, 2-5/8" x 4-1/8" set is virtually identical in design with the 1981 set. The cards are sponsored by Coca-Cola, local law enforcement, Kiwanis and the Steelers. The card backs contain "Steeler's Tips."

		NM/M
Complete Set (16):		12.00
Common Player:		.40
12	Terry Bradshaw (Portrait)	5.00
31	Donnie Shell (Double Coverage back)	.60
32	Franco Harris (Portrait)	2.50
44	Frank Pollard	.40
47	Mel Blount (Running with ball)	1.50
52	Mike Webster (Portrait)	.75
58	Jack Lambert (Facing forward)	2.50
59	Jack Ham (Teamwork back)	1.50
65	Tom Beasley	.40
67	Gary Dunn	.40
74	Ray Pinney	.40
79	Larry Brown (Chin 5/16" from bottom)	.40
82	John Stallworth (Posed shot)	1.25
88	Lynn Swann (Sportsmanship back)	3.00
89	Bennie Cunningham	.50
90	Bob Kohrs	.40

1983 Steelers Police

The 17-card, 2-5/8" x 4-1/8" set is similar to the Police sets from 1981 and 1982. Card No. 2 has two variations of the spelling of coach Chuck Noll's last name.

		NM/M
Complete Set (16):		8.00
Common Player:		.25
1	Walter Abercrombie	.35
2	Gary Anderson (K)	.50
3	Mel Blount	.75
4	Terry Bradshaw	3.00
5	Robin Cole	.25
6	Steve Courson	.25
7	Bennie Cunningham	.35
8	Franco Harris	2.00
9	Greg Hawthorne	.25
10	Jack Lambert	1.00
11A	Chuck Noll (CO ERRM) (Misspelled Knoll)	5.00
11B	Chuck Noll (CO COR)	1.00
12	Donnie Shell	.35
13	John Stallworth	1.00
14	Mike Webster	.75
15	Dwayne Woodruff	.25
16	Rick Woods	.25

1984 Steelers Police

The 16-card, 2-5/8" x 4-1/8" set, sponsored by McDonald's, Kiwanis, the Steelers and local law enforcement, features action shots with "Steeler Tips" on the card backs. The cards are similar to the previous Police sets, except for the McDonald's and Kiwanis logos on the card fronts.

		NM/M
Complete Set (16):		8.00
Common Player:		.40
1	Gary Anderson (K)	.60
16	Mark Malone	.60
19	David Woodley	.60
30	Frank Pollard	.40
32	Franco Harris	2.00
34	Walter Abercrombie	.50
49	Dwayne Woodruff	.40
52	Mike Webster	.75
57	Mike Merriweather	.60
58	Jack Lambert	1.50
67	Gary Dunn	.40
73	Craig Wolfley	.40
82	John Stallworth	1.50
83	Louis Lipps	1.00
92	Keith Gary	.40
92	Keith Willis	.50

1985 Steelers Police

The 16-card, 2-5/8" x 4-1/8" set was sponsored by local law enforcement, Giant Eagle, the Steelers and Kiwanis. The card backs have "Steeler Tips."

		NM/M
Complete Set (16):		5.00
Common Player:		.40
1	Gary Anderson K (Kickoff back)	.50
16	Mark Malone (Playbook back)	.50
21	Eric Williams	.40
30	Frank Pollard (Second Effort back)	.40
31	Donnie Shell (Zone back)	.50
34	Walter Abercrombie (Teamwork back)	.50
49	Dwayne Woodruff (Turnover back)	.40
50	David Little	.50
52	Mike Webster (Offside back)	.75
53	Bryan Hinkle (Blindside back)	.40
56	Robin Cole (Timeout back)	.40
57	Mike Merriweather (Blitz back)	.60
82	John Stallworth (Captains back)	1.50
83	Louis Lipps (Pride back)	.60
93	Keith Willis (QB Sack card)	.40
NNO	Chuck Noll CO (Coach back)	1.25

1986 Steelers Police

The 15-card, 2-5/8" x 4-1/8" set was issued by Kiwanis, Giant Eagle, local law enforcement and the Steelers. The card fronts are virtually identical to the 1985 set, with the Giant Eagle and Kiwanis logos found in the top corners and brief bio information located along the bottom edge. The card backs contain "Steeler Tips."

		NM/M
Complete Set (15):		5.00
Common Player:		.35
1	Gary Anderson (K) (Field Goal back)	.60
16	Mark Malone (Quarterback back)	.60
24	Rich Erenberg	.50
30	Frank Pollard (Running Back back)	.50
31	Donnie Shell (Interception back)	.60
34	Walter Abercrombie (Penalty back)	.50
49	Dwayne Woodruff	.35
52	Mike Webster (Possession back)	.75
53	Bryan Hinkle (Prevent back)	.35
56	Robin Cole (Equipmen back)	.35
57	Mike Merriweather (Linebacker back)	.50
62	Tunch Ilkin	.50
64	Edmund Nelson	.35
67	Gary Dunn (Defensive Holding back)	.35
82	John Stallworth (Victory back)	1.00
83	Louis Lipps (Receiver back)	.75

1987 Steelers Police

The 16-card, 2-5/8" x 4-1/8" set has basically the same design as the 1985 and 1986 sets, complete with Kiwanis and Giant Eagle logos and "Steeler Tips."

		NM/M
Complete Set (16):		5.00
Common Player:		.35
1	Walter Abercrombie (Option Pass back)	.50
2	Gary Anderson (K) (Extra Point back)	.60
3	Bubby Brister	.90
4	Gary Dunn (Neutral Zone back)	.35
5	Preston Gothard	.35
6	Bryan Hinkle (Outside Linebackers back)	.50
7	Earnest Jackson	.50
8	Louis Lipps (Corner Pattern back)	.75
9	Mark Malone (Adverse Conditions back)	.60
10	Mike Merriweather (Instant Replay back)	.50
11	Chuck Noll (CO) (Referee back)	.75
12	John Rienstra	.35
13	Donnie Shell (Defense back)	.60
14	John Stallworth (Crackback Block back)	1.00
15	Mike Webster (Sportsmanship back)	.75
16	Keith Willis (Down back)	.35

1988 Steelers Police

The 16-card, 2-5/8" x 4-1/8" set is similar in design to the previous mid-1980s Steelers Police set as it is sponsored by Giant Eagle and Kiwanis and features "Steeler Tips" on the card backs. The Steelers helmet on the card backs have three white diamonds as opposed to the previous three years' helmets which had two black diamonds.

		NM/M
Complete Set (16):		5.00
Common Player:		.35
1	Gary Anderson (K)	.60
2	Bubby Brister	.75
3	Thomas Everett	.60
4	Delton Hall	.35
5	Bryan Hinkle	.50
6	Tunch Ilkin	.35
7	Earnest Jackson	.50
8	Louis Lipps	.60
9	David Little	.35
10	Mike Merriweather	.50
11	Frank Pollard	.35
12	John Rienstra	.35
13	Mike Webster	.75
14	Keith Willis	.35
15	Craig Wolfley	.35
16	Rod Woodson	1.50

1989 Steelers Police

The 16-card, 2-5/8" x 4-1/8" set is virtually identical to previous Police sets with sponsorships by Kiwanis and Giant Eagle. The card backs contain "Steeler Tips '89."

		NM/M
Complete Set (16):		5.00
Common Player:		.40
1	Gary Anderson	.60
6	Bubby Brister	.60
18	Harry Newsome	.40
24	Rodney Carter	.40
26	Rod Woodson	1.00
27	Thomas Everett	.60
33	Merril Hoge	.40
53	Bryan Hinkle	.40
54	Hardy Nickerson	.75
62	Tunch Ilkin	.40
63	Dermontti Dawson	.60
74	Terry Long	.40
78	Tim Johnson	.40
83	Louis Lipps	.75
97	Aaron Jones	.40
98	Gerald Williams	.40

1990 Steelers Police

The 16-card, 2-5/8" x 4-1/8" set features identical front designs as previous Police sets, with the Kiwanis and Giant Eagle logos. The card backs have "Steelers '90 Tips."

		NM/M
Complete Set (16):		5.00
Common Player:		.35
1	Gary Anderson (K)	.35
2	Bubby Brister	.60
3	Thomas Everett	.35
4	Merril Hoge	.35
5	Tunch Ilkin	.35
6	Carnell Lake	.50
7	Louis Lipps	.75
8	David Little	.35
9	Greg Lloyd	.75
10	Mike Mularkey	.35
11	Hardy Nickerson	.75
12	Chuck Noll (CO)	.75
13	John Rienstra	.35
14	Keith Willis	.35
15	Rod Woodson	.90
16	Tim Worley	.50

1991 Steelers Police

The 16-card, 2-5/8" x 4-1/8" set features front and back designs which are similar to previous Police sets. The card backs contain "Steelers Tips '91" while the Giant Eagle and Kiwanis logos appear on both sides.

		NM/M
Complete Set (16):		5.00
Common Player:		.35
1	Gary Anderson (K)	.35
2	Bubby Brister	.60
3	Dermontti Dawson	.35
4	Eric Green	.75
5	Bryan Hinkle	.35
6	Merril Hoge	.50
7	John Jackson	.35
8	D.J. Johnson	.35
9	Carnell Lake	.50
10	Louis Lipps	.60
11	Greg Lloyd	1.00
12	Mike Mularkey	.35
13	Chuck Noll (CO)	.75
14	Dan Stryzinski	.35
15	Gerald Williams	.35
16	Rod Woodson	.90

1992 Steelers Police

The 16-card, 2-5/8" x 4-3/16" set was sponsored by Kiwanis and Giant Eagle and featured a color shot on the card front. The player's height, weight and position appear below his name with "Steelers Tips '92" and the Steelers' 60th anniversary logo featured on the card backs.

		NM/M
Complete Set (16):		5.00
Common Player:		.35
1	Gary Anderson (K)	.35
2	Bubby Brister	.50
3	Bill Cowher (CO)	.75
4	Dermontti Dawson	.35
5	Eric Green	.50
6	Carlton Haselrig	.35
7	Merril Hoge	.35
8	John Jackson	.35
9	Carnell Lake	.50
10	Louis Lipps	.60
11	Greg Lloyd	.75
12	Neil O'Donnell	1.00
13	Tom Ricketts	.35
14	Gerald Williams	.35
15	Jerrol Williams	.35
16	Rod Woodson	.75

1993 Steelers Police

The 16-card, 2-1/2" x 4" set, sponsored by Giant Eagle and Kiwanis, features a color action shot on the card front with "Steelers Tips '93" on the back. The Kiwanis and Giant Eagle logos appear on both the card front and back.

		NM/M
Complete Set (16):		5.00
Common Player:		.30
1	Gary Anderson (K)	.30
2	Adrian Cooper	.30
3	Bill Cowher (CO)	.50
4	Dermontti Dawson	.30
5	Donald Evans	.30
6	Eric Green	.50
7	Bryan Hinkle	.30
8	Merril Hoge	.30
9	Garry Howe	.30
10	Greg Lloyd	.75
11	Neil O'Donnell	1.00
12	Jerry Olsavsky	.30
13	Leon Searcy	.30
14	Dwight Stone	.30
15	Gerald Williams	.30
16	Rod Woodson	.75

1995 Steelers Eat'n Park

The four-strip card set was issued by Eat'n Park during a four-week window and each strip contained three peel-off player cards. The card fronts feature a color image over a silver background. Each strip was sold for 99 cents.

		NM/M
Complete Set (4):		5.00
Common Player:		1.00
1	Darren Perry, Rod Woodson, Greg Lloyd	1.50
2	Ray Seals, Carnell Lake, Kevin Greene	1.00
3	Dermontti Dawson, Erric Pegram, Mark Bruener	1.00
4	Kordell Stewart, Yancey Thigpen, Neil O'Donnell	2.50

1995 Steelers Giant Eagle Coins

The nine-coin set was distributed by Giant Eagle and was produced by Classic Pro Line. The coins were available in packs with cards for $1.89. The coins/cards were issued over a nine-week period beginning Sept. 3. The coin fronts have the player's face while the backs have the Pittsburgh team logo.

		NM/M
Complete Set (9):		10.00
Common Player:		1.00
1	Mel Blount	1.00
2	Bill Cowher (CO)	1.00
3	Joe Greene	1.50
4	Kevin Greene	1.00
5	Franco Harris	1.50

6 Jack Lambert 1.50
7 Greg Lloyd 1.50
8 Byron "Bam" Morris 1.00
9 Rod Woodson 1.50

1995 Steelers Giant Eagle ProLine

The nine-card, standard-size set, issued by Giant Eagle and produced by Classic Pro Line, was distributed in packs with the nine-coin set. The card fronts feature a color action shot with the Steelers logo appearing in the lower left corner. The card backs have a checklist of the nine players.

NM/M
Complete Set (9): 8.00
Common Player: .75
1 Kevin Greene .75
2 Franco Harris 1.00
3 Greg Lloyd 1.00
4 Joe Greene 1.00
5 Byron "Bam" Morris .75
6 Jack Lambert 1.00
7 Rod Woodson 1.00
8 Mel Blount .75
9 Bill Cowher (CO) .75

1996 Steelers Kids Club

The Steelers sponsored this four-card set. The cards feature color photography and black and yellow borders.

NM/M
Complete Set (4): 5.00
Common Player: 1.00
1 Bill Cowher CO 1.50
2 Greg Lloyd 1.00
3 Kordell Stewart 3.00
4 Rod Woodson 1.00

1979 Stop 'N' Go

These 18 3D cards were available at Stop 'N' Go markets in 1979. Each front has a 3D effect player photo on the front, along with his team's helmet at the top. His name and team name are in a panel at the bottom of the card; "NFL 3-D Football Stars" is written at the top. The back of the card is numbered 1 of 18, etc., and includes yearly stats, plus summaries of the player's professional and collegiate accomplishments. The Stop 'N' Go logo is also on the card back. The cards measure 2-1/8" x 3-1/4".

NM/M
Complete Set (18): 45.00
Common Player: 1.25
1 Gregg Bingham 1.25
2 Ken Burrough 1.50
3 Preston Pearson 1.50
4 Sam Cunningham 2.00
5 Robert Newhouse 2.00
6 Walter Payton 13.00
7 Robert Brazile 1.50
8 Rocky Bleier 2.50
9 Toni Fritsch 1.25
10 Jack Ham 3.00
11 Jay Saldi 1.25
12 Roger Staubach 15.00
13 Franco Harris 8.00
14 Otis Armstrong 2.00
15 Lyle Alzado 2.00
16 Billy Johnson 1.50
17 Elvin Bethea 1.50
18 Joe Greene 5.00

1980 Stop 'N' Go

These 3D cards were available with beverage purchases at participating Stop 'N' Go markets in 1980. The card design is similar to the previous year's design, except the card front has a star on each side of the panel at the bottom where the player's name is. The card back is somewhat different, however, with the main difference being the 1979 statistics and a 1980 copyright logo.

NM/M
Complete Set (48): 50.00
Common Player: .75
1 John Jefferson 1.00
2 Herbert Scott .75
3 Pat Donovan .75
4 William Andrews 1.25
5 Frank Corral .75
6 Fred Dryer 1.50
7 Franco Harris 5.00
8 Leon Gray .75
9 Gregg Bingham .75
10 Louis Kelcher .75
11 Robert Newhouse 1.25
12 Preston Pearson 1.00
13 Wallace Francis 1.00
14 Pat Haden 2.00
15 Jim Youngblood .75
16 Rocky Bleier 1.50
17 Gifford Nielsen .75
18 Elvin Bethea 1.00
19 Charlie Joiner 3.00
20 Tony Hill 1.00
21 Drew Pearson 1.25
22 Alfred Jenkins 1.00
23 Dave Elmendorf .75
24 Jack Reynolds 1.25
25 Joe Greene 3.00
26 Robert Brazile 1.00
27 Mike Reinfeldt .75
28 Bob Griese 4.50
29 Harold Carmichael 1.50
30 Ottis Anderson 4.00
31 Ahmad Rashad 3.50
32 Archie Manning 1.50
33 Ricky Bell 1.00
34 Jay Saldi .75
35 Ken Burrough 1.00
36 Don Woods .75
37 Henry Childs .75
38 Wilbur Jackson .75
39 Steve DeBerg 1.50
40 Ron Jessie .75
41 Mel Blount 2.50
42 Cliff Branch 1.50
43 Chuck Muncie 1.25
44 Ken MacAfee .75
45 Charley Young 1.00
46 Cody Jones .75
47 Jack Ham 2.00
48 Ray Guy 1.50

1976 Sunbeam NFL Die Cuts

The 28-card, standard-sized set is die-cut so that each card can stand up when perforated. The team's helmet, name and player drawing appear on the card fronts while the backs have a brief team history with the Sunbeam logo. The cards were printed on white or gray stock, with or without the Sunbeam logo.

NM/M
Complete Set (29): 200.00
Common Player: 8.00
1 Atlanta Falcons 8.00
2 Baltimore Colts 8.00
3 Buffalo Bills 8.00
4 Chicago Bears 8.00
5 Cincinnati Bengals 8.00
6 Cleveland Browns 8.00
7 Dallas Cowboys 10.00
8 Denver Broncos 8.00
9 Detroit Lions 8.00
10 Green Bay Packers 10.00
11 Houston Oilers 8.00
12 Kansas City Chiefs 8.00
13 Los Angeles Rams 8.00
14 Miami Dolphins 10.00
15 Minnesota Vikings 8.00
16 New England Patriots 8.00
17 New Orleans Saints 8.00
18 New York Giants 8.00
19 New York Jets 8.00
20 Oakland Raiders 10.00
21 Philadelphia Eagles 8.00
22 Pittsburgh Steelers 8.00
23 St. Louis Cardinals 8.00
24 San Diego Chargers 8.00
25 San Francisco 49ers 10.00
26 Seattle Seahawks 8.00
27 Tampa Bay Buccaneers 8.00
28 Washington Redskins 10.00
NNO NFL Logo (Blankbacked) 8.00

1976 Sunbeam SEC Die Cuts

The 20-card, standard-size set was die-cut so when each card was perforated, it could stand up. The set is similar in design to the NFL set of the same year, except with SEC teams. The card fronts feature the school's logo with the backs containing the school's 1976 schedule. The cards were distributed in Sunbeam bread packages.

NM/M
Complete Set (20): 125.00
Common Player: 5.00
1 Alabama Crimson Tide (Team Profile) 10.00
2 Alabama Crimson Tide (Schedule) 10.00
3 Auburn War Eagle (Team Profile) 6.00
4 Auburn War Eagle (Schedule) 6.00
5 Florida Gators (Team Profile) 7.00
6 Florida Gators (Schedule) 7.00
7 Georgia Bulldogs (Team Profile) 6.00
8 Georgia Bulldogs (Schedule) 6.00
9 Kentucky Wildcats (Team Profile) 6.00
10 Kentucky Wildcats (Schedule) 6.00
11 Louisiana St. Tigers (Team Profile) 6.00
12 Louisiana St. Tigers (Schedule) 6.00
13 Miss. St. Bulldogs (Team Profile) 5.00
14 Miss. St. Bulldogs (Schedule) 5.00
15 Ole Miss Rebels (Team Profile) 5.00
16 Ole Miss Rebels (Schedule) 5.00
17 Tennessee Volunteers (Team Profile) 7.00
18 Tennessee Volunteers (Schedule) 7.00
19 Vanderbilt Commodores (Team Profile) 5.00
20 Vanderbilt Commodores (Schedule) 5.00

1972 Sunoco Stamps

Each NFL team is represented by 24 players in this 624-stamp set - 12 offensive and 12 defensive players have been chosen. The stamps measure 1-5/8" x 2-3/8" and were given away in perforated sheets of nine at participating Sun Oil Co. gas stations. Each stamp, featuring an oval with a player photo inside against a corresponding team color-coded background, is unnumbered. Two albums were issued to hold the stamps - a 56-page "NFL Action '72" album and a 128-page album. The albums had specific spots for each sticker, as indicated by a square providing the player's name, uniform number, age, height, weight and college he attended. There were 16 additional perforated sheets inside the album, too. The stamps could be placed inside the album by using the tabs which were provided with the album, instead of licking them.

NM/M
Complete Set (624): 125.00
Common Player: .10
(1) Ken Burrow .15
(2) Bill Sandeman .10
(3) Andy Maurer .10
(4) Jeff Van Note .20
(5) Malcolm Snider .10
(6) George Kunz .25
(7) Jim Mitchell .10
(8) Wes Chesson .10
(9) Bob Berry .20
(10) Dick Shiner .10
(11) Jim Butler .10
(12) Art Malone .10
(13) Claude Humphrey .25
(14) John Small .10
(15) Glen Condren .10
(16) John Zook .20
(17) Don Hansen .10
(18) Tommy Nobis 1.25
(19) Greg Brezina .20
(20) Ken Reaves .10
(21) Tom Hayes .10
(22) Tom McCauley .10
(23) Bill Bell .15
(24) Bill Lothridge .20
(25) Ed Hinton .10
(26) Bob Vogel .10
(27) Glenn Ressler .10
(28) Bill Curry .30
(29) John Williams .10
(30) Dan Sullivan .10
(31) Tom Mitchell .10
(32) John Mackey 1.50
(33) Ray Perkins 2.00
(34) John Unitas 6.00
(35) Tom Matte .30
(36) Norm Bulaich .25
(37) Bubba Smith 1.00
(38) Bill Newsome .10
(39) Fred Miller .10
(40) Roy Hinton .10
(41) Ray May .10
(42) Ted Hendricks 1.50
(43) Charlie Stukes .10
(44) Rex Kern .30
(45) Jerry Logan .10
(46) Rick Volk .20
(47) David Lee .15
(48) Jim O'Brien .25
(49) J.D. Hill .20
(50) Willie Young .10
(51) Jim Reilly .10
(52) Bruce Jarvis .15
(53) Levert Carr .10
(54) Donnie Green .10
(55) Jan White .20
(56) Marlin Briscoe .40
(57) Dennis Shaw .15
(58) O.J. Simpson 12.00
(59) Wayne Patrick .10
(60) John Leypoldt .10
(61) Al Cowlings .75
(62) Jim Dunaway .20
(63) Bob Tatarek .10
(64) Cal Snowden .10
(65) Paul Guidry .10
(66) Edgar Chandler .20
(67) Al Andrews .10
(68) Robert James .10
(69) Alvin Wyatt .10
(70) John Pitts .10
(71) Pete Richardson .15
(72) Spike Jones .10
(73) Dick Gordon .20
(74) Randy Jackson .10
(75) Glen Holloway .10
(76) Rick Coady .10
(77) Jim Cadile .10
(78) Steve Wright .10
(79) Bob Wallace .10
(80) George Farmer .15
(81) Bobby Douglass .40
(82) Don Shy .10
(83) Cyril Pinder .10
(84) Mac Percival .10
(85) Willie Holman .10
(86) George Seals .15
(87) Bill Staley .10
(88) Ed O'Bradovich .20
(89) Doug Buffone .10
(90) Dick Butkus 3.00
(91) Ross Brupbacher .20
(92) Charlie Ford .10
(93) Joe Taylor .10
(94) Ron Smith .20
(95) Jerry Moore .10
(96) Bobby Joe Green .15
(97) Chip Myers .10
(98) Rufus Mayes .10
(99) Howard Fest .10
(100) Bob Johnson .30
(101) Pat Matson .10
(102) Vern Holland .10
(103) Bruce Coslet .75
(104) Bob Trumpy 1.00
(105) Virgil Carter .20
(106) Fred Willis .10
(107) Jess Phillips .10
(108) Horst Muhlmann .15
(109) Royce Berry .10
(110) Mike Reid .50
(111) Steve Chomyszak .10
(112) Ron Carpenter .10
(113) Al Beauchamp .15
(114) Bill Bergey .50
(115) Ken Avery .10
(116) Lemar Parrish .40
(117) Ken Riley .40
(118) Sandy Durko .10
(119) Dave Lewis .10
(120) Paul Robinson .20
(121) Fair Hooker .20
(122) Doug Dieken .10
(123) John Demarie .10
(124) Jim Copeland .10
(125) Gene Hickerson .10
(126) Bob McKay .10
(127) Milt Morin .20
(128) Frank Pitts .10
(129) Mike Phipps .50
(130) Leroy Kelly 1.50
(131) Bo Scott .20
(132) Don Cockroft .10
(133) Ron Snidow .10
(134) Walter Johnson .10
(135) Jerry Sherk .30
(136) Jack Gregory .10
(137) Jim Houston .10
(138) Dale Lindsey .10
(139) Bill Andrews .25
(140) Clarence Scott .20
(141) Ernie Kellerman .10
(142) Walt Sumner .10
(143) Mike Howell .10
(144) Reece Morrison .10
(145) Bob Hayes 1.00
(146) Ralph Neely .20
(147) John Niland .10
(148) Dave Manders .20
(149) Blaine Nye .10
(150) Rayfield Wright .20
(151) Billy Truax .10
(152) Lance Alworth 3.00
(153) Roger Staubach 10.00
(154) Duane Thomas .50
(155) Walt Garrison .30
(156) Mike Clark .10
(157) Larry Cole .10
(158) Jethro Pugh .20
(159) Bob Lilly 2.00
(160) George Andrie .20
(161) Dave Edwards .10
(162) Lee Roy Jordan .90
(163) Chuck Howley .30
(164) Herb Adderley 1.00
(165) Mel Renfro .75
(166) Cornell Green .30
(167) Cliff Harris .20
(168) Ron Widby .10
(169) Jerry Simmons .10
(170) Roger Shoals .10
(171) Larron Jackson .10
(172) George Goeddeke .10
(173) Mike Schnitker .10
(174) Mike Current .10
(175) Billy Masters .15
(176) Jack Gehrke .10
(177) Don Horn .20
(178) Floyd Little 1.00
(179) Bobby Anderson .30
(180) Jim Turner .20
(181) Rich Jackson .10
(182) Paul Smith .10
(183) Dave Costa .10
(184) Lyle Alzado 1.00
(185) Olen Underwood .10
(186) Fred Forsberg .10
(187) Chip Myrtle .10
(188) Leroy Mitchell .10
(189) Billy Thompson .20
(190) Charlie Greer .10
(191) George Saimes .20
(192) Billy Van Heusen .10
(193) Earl McCullouch .20
(194) Jim Yarbrough .10
(195) Chuck Walton .15
(196) Ed Flanagan .10
(197) Frank Gallagher .10
(198) Rockne Freitas .10
(199) Charlie Sanders .25
(200) Larry Walton .10
(201) Greg Landry .40
(202) Altie Taylor .20
(203) Steve Owens .40
(204) Errol Mann .10
(205) Joe Robb .10
(206) Dick Evey .10
(207) Jerry Rush .10
(208) Larry Hand .15
(209) Paul Naumoff .20
(210) Mike Lucci .20
(211) Wayne Walker .10
(212) Lem Barney 1.00
(213) Dick LeBeau .20
(214) Mike Weger .10
(215) Wayne Rasmussen .10
(216) Herman Weaver .10
(217) John Spilis .10
(218) Francis Peay .10
(219) Bill Lueck .10
(220) Ken Bowman .10
(221) Gale Gillingham .20
(222) Dick Himes .10
(223) Rich McGeorge .10
(224) Carroll Dale .20
(225) Bart Starr 3.50
(226) Scott Hunter .30
(227) John Brockington .30
(228) Dave Hampton .20
(229) Clarence Williams .10
(230) Mike McCoy .20
(231) Bob Brown .20
(232) Alden Roche .10
(233) Dave Robinson .25
(234) Jim Carter .20
(235) Fred Carr .20
(236) Ken Ellis .15
(237) Doug Hart .10
(238) Al Randolph .10
(239) Al Matthews .10
(240) Tim Webster .10
(241) Jim Beirne .10
(242) Bob Young .10
(243) Elbert Drungo .10
(244) Sam Walton .20
(245) Alvin Reed .10
(246) Charlie Joiner 1.50
(247) Dan Pastorini .30
(248) Charlie Johnson .30
(249) Lynn Dickey .40
(250) Woody Campbell .10
(251) Robert Holmes .20
(252) Mark Moseley .30
(253) Pat Holmes .10
(254) Mike Tilleman .10
(255) Leo Brooks .10
(256) Elvin Bethea .30
(257) George Webster .30
(258) Garland Boyette .10
(259) Ron Pritchard .15
(260) Zeke Moore .10
(261) Willie Alexander .10
(262) Ken Houston 1.00
(263) John Charles .10
(264) Linzy Cole .10
(265) Elmo Wright .25
(266) Jim Tyrer .20
(267) Ed Budde .20
(268) Jack Rudnay .10
(269) Mo Moorman .10
(270) Dave Hill .10
(271) Morris Stroud .10
(272) Otis Taylor .40
(273) Len Dawson 3.00
(274) Ed Podolak .30
(275) Wendell Hayes .10
(276) Jan Stenerud 1.25
(277) Marvin Upshaw .10
(278) Curley Culp .30
(279) Buck Buchanan 1.00
(280) Aaron Brown .10
(281) Bobby Bell 1.25
(282) Willie Lanier 1.50
(283) Jim Lynch .20
(284) Jim Marsalis .20
(285) Emmitt Thomas .20
(286) Jim Kearney .10
(287) Johnny Robinson .40
(288) Jerrel Wilson .10
(289) Jack Snow .35
(290) Charlie Cowan .10
(291) Tom Mack .50
(292) Ken Iman .10
(293) Joe Scibelli .10
(294) Harry Schuh .10
(295) Rob Klein .20
(296) Lance Rentzel .35
(297) Roman Gabriel .60
(298) Les Josephson .20
(299) Willie Ellison .20
(300) David Ray .10
(301) Jack Youngblood 1.25
(302) Merlin Olsen 1.75
(303) Phil Olsen .10
(304) Coy Bacon .10
(305) Jim Purnell .10
(306) Marlin McKeever .20
(307) Isiah Robertson .30
(308) Jim Nettles .10
(309) Gene Howard .10
(310) Kermit Alexander .20
(311) Dave Elmendorf .10
(312) Pat Studstill .20
(313) Paul Warfield 1.50
(314) Doug Crusan .10
(315) Bob Kuechenberg .50
(316) Bob DeMarco .20
(317) Larry Little 1.00
(318) Norm Evans .20
(319) Marv Fleming .20
(320) Howard Twilley .30
(321) Bob Griese 2.50
(322) Jim Klick .60
(323) Larry Csonka 2.00
(324) Garo Yepremian .30
(325) Jim Riley .10
(326) Manny Fernandez .30
(327) Bob Heinz .10
(328) Bill Stanfill .30
(329) Doug Swift .10
(330) Nick Buoniconti 1.00
(331) Mike Kolen .10
(332) Tim Foley .30
(333) Curtis Johnson .10
(334) Dick Anderson .40
(335) Jake Scott .50
(336) Larry Seiple .10
(337) Gene Washington .20
(338) Grady Alderman .10
(339) Ed White .25
(340) Mick Tingelhoff .20
(341) Milt Sunde .10
(342) Ron Yary .50
(343) John Beasley .10
(344) John Henderson .10
(345) Fran Tarkenton 4.00
(346) Clint Jones .20
(347) Dave Osborn .20
(348) Fred Cox .20
(349) Carl Eller .50
(350) Gary Larsen .10
(351) Alan Page 1.00
(352) Jim Marshall 1.00
(353) Roy Winston .20
(354) Lonnie Warwick .10
(355) Wally Hilgenberg .10
(356) Bobby Bryant .15
(357) Ed Sharockman .10
(358) Charlie West .10
(359) Paul Krause .60
(360) Bob Lee .20
(361) Randy Vataha .40
(362) Mike Montler .10
(363) Halvor Hagen .10
(364) Jon Morris .10
(365) Len St. Jean .10
(366) Tom Neville .10
(367) Tom Beer .15
(368) Ron Sellers .20
(369) Jim Plunkett 1.00
(370) Carl Garrett .20
(371) Jim Nance .30
(372) Charlie Gogolak .20
(373) Ike Lassiter .10
(374) Dave Rowe .10
(375) Julius Adams .20
(376) Dennis Wirgowski .10
(377) Ed Weisacosky .10
(378) Jim Cheyunski .10
(379) Steve Kiner .10
(380) Larry Carwell .10
(381) John Outlaw .10
(382) Rickie Harris .10
(383) Don Webb .10
(384) Tom Janik .10
(385) Al Dodd .20
(386) Don Morrison .10
(387) Jake Kupp .10
(388) John Didion .10
(389) Del Williams .10
(390) Glen Ray Hines .10
(391) Dave Parks .20
(392) Dan Abramowicz .40
(393) Archie Manning 2.00
(394) Bob Gresham .10
(395) Virgil Robinson .10
(396) Charlie Durkee .10
(397) Richard Neal .10
(398) Bob Pollard .10
(399) Dave Long .10
(400) Joe Owens .10
(401) Carl Cunningham .10
(402) Jim Flanigan .15
(403) Wayne Colman .10
(404) D'Artagnan Martin .10
(405) Delles Howell .10
(406) Hugo Hollas .10
(407) Doug Wyatt .10
(408) Julian Fagan .10
(409) Don Hermann .10
(410) Willie Young .10
(411) Bob Hyland .10
(412) Greg Larson .10
(413) Doug Van Horn .10
(414) Charlie Harper .10
(415) Bob Tucker .25
(416) Joe Morrison .20
(417) Randy Johnson .20
(418) Tucker Frederickson .30
(419) Ron Johnson .30
(420) Pete Gogolak .20
(421) Henry Reed .10
(422) Jim Kanicki .10
(423) Roland Lakes .10
(424) John Douglas .10
(425) Ron Hornsby .10
(426) Jim Files .10
(427) Willie Williams .10
(428) Otto Brown .10
(429) Scott Eaton .10
(430) Carl Lockhart .20
(431) Tom Blanchard .20
(432) Rocky Thompson .20
(433) Rich Caster .30
(434) Randy Rasmussen .10
(435) John Schmitt .10
(436) Dave Herman .20
(437) Winston Hill .20
(438) Pete Lammons .20
(439) Don Maynard 2.00
(440) Joe Namath 10.00
(441) Emerson Boozer .30
(442) John Riggins 4.00
(443) George Nock .10
(444) Bobby Howfield .10
(445) Gerry Philbin .10
(446) John Little .10
(447) Chuck Hinton .10

(448)	Mark Lomas	.10
(449)	Ralph Baker	.10
(450)	Al Atkinson	.10
(451)	Larry Grantham	.20
(452)	John Dockery	.10
(453)	Earlie Thomas	.10
(454)	Phil Wise	.10
(455)	W.K. Hicks	.10
(456)	Steve O'Neal	.15
(457)	Drew Buie	.10
(458)	Art Shell	2.00
(459)	Gene Upshaw	2.00
(460)	Jim Otto	.75
(461)	Geprge Buehler	.10
(462)	Bob Brown	.40
(463)	Ray Chester	.40
(464)	Fred Biletnikoff	2.00
(465)	Daryle Lamonica	.60
(466)	Marv Hubbard	.20
(467)	Clarence Davis	.20
(468)	George Blanda	2.00
(469)	Tony Cline	.10
(470)	Art Thoms	.10
(471)	Tom Keating	.20
(472)	Ben Davidson	1.00
(473)	Phil Villapiano	.40
(474)	Dan Conners	.10
(475)	Duane Benson	.10
(476)	Nemiah Wilson	.10
(477)	Willie Brown	1.00
(478)	George Atkinson	.20
(479)	Jack Tatum	.40
(480)	Jerry DePoyster	.10
(481)	Harold Jackson	.50
(482)	Wade Key	.10
(483)	Henry Allison	.10
(484)	Mike Evans	.10
(485)	Steve Smith	.20
(486)	Harold Carmichael	1.25
(487)	Ben Hawkins	.20
(488)	Pete Liske	.40
(489)	Rick Arrington	.10
(490)	Lee Bouggess	.10
(491)	Tom Woodeshick	.20
(492)	Tom Dempsey	.50
(493)	Richard Harris	.20
(494)	Don Hultz	.10
(495)	Ernie Calloway	.15
(496)	Mel Tom	.10
(497)	Steve Zabel	.20
(498)	Tim Rossovich	.20
(499)	Ron Porter	.10
(500)	Al Nelson	.10
(501)	Nate Ramsey	.10
(502)	Leroy Keyes	.40
(503)	Bill Bradley	.50
(504)	Tom McNeill	.10
(505)	Dave Smith	.10
(506)	Jon Kolb	.10
(507)	Gerry Mullins	.10
(508)	Ray Mansfield	.10
(509)	Bruce Van Dyke	.10
(510)	John Brown	.10
(511)	Ron Shanklin	.30
(512)	Terry Bradshaw	7.50
(513)	Terry Hanratty	.40
(514)	Preston Pearson	.40
(515)	John Fuqua	.20
(516)	Roy Gerela	.10
(517)	L.C. Greenwood	.75
(518)	Joe Greene	2.50
(519)	Lloyd Voss	.10
(520)	Dwight White	.20
(521)	Jack Ham	2.50
(522)	Chuck Allen	.10
(523)	Brian Stenger	.10
(524)	Andy Russell	.75
(525)	John Rowser	.10
(526)	Mel Blount	2.00
(527)	Mike Wagner	.20
(528)	Bobby Walden	.10
(529)	Mel Gray	.30
(530)	Bob Reynolds	.10
(531)	Dan Dierdorf	.60
(532)	Wayne Mulligan	.10
(533)	Clyde Williams	.10
(534)	Ernie McMillan	.10
(535)	Jackie Smith	1.00
(536)	John Gilliam	.20
(537)	Jim Hart	.50
(538)	Pete Beathard	.40
(539)	Johnny Roland	.30
(540)	Jim Bakken	.30
(541)	Ron Yankowski	.10
(542)	Fred Heron	.15
(543)	Bob Rowe	.10
(544)	Chuck Walker	.10
(545)	Larry Stallings	.20
(546)	Jamie Rivers	.10
(547)	Mike McGill	.10
(548)	Miller Farr	.10
(549)	Roger Wehrli	.30
(550)	Larry Willingham	.10
(551)	Larry Wilson	1.00
(552)	Chuck Latourette	.10
(553)	Billy Parks	.20
(554)	Terry Owens	.25
(555)	Doug Wilkerson	.10
(556)	Carl Mauck	.10
(557)	Walt Sweeney	.10
(558)	Russ Washington	.10
(559)	Pettis Norman	.20
(560)	Garry Garrison	.20
(561)	John Hadl	.60
(562)	Mike Montgomery	.10
(563)	Mike Garrett	.30
(564)	Dennis Partee	.10
(565)	Deacon Jones	1.00
(566)	Ron East	.10
(567)	Kevin Hardy	.10
(568)	Steve DeLong	.20
(569)	Rick Redman	.10
(570)	Bob Babich	.15
(571)	Pete Barnes	.10
(572)	Bob Howard	.10
(573)	Joe Beauchamp	.10
(574)	Bryant Salter	.10
(575)	Chris Fletcher	.10
(576)	Jerry LeVias	.20
(577)	Dick Witcher	.10
(578)	Len Rohde	.12
(579)	Randy Beisler	.10
(580)	Forrest Blue	.20
(581)	Woody Peoples	.10
(582)	Cas Banaszek	.10
(583)	Ted Kwalick	.40
(584)	Gene Washington	.50
(585)	John Brodie	1.25
(586)	Ken Willard	.40
(587)	Vic Washington	.20
(588)	Bruce Gossett	.10
(589)	Tommy Hart	.15
(590)	Charlie Krueger	.20
(591)	Earl Edwards	.10
(592)	Cedric Hardman	.20
(593)	Dave Wilcox	.25
(594)	Frank Nunley	.10
(595)	Skip Vanderbundt	.10
(596)	Jimmy Johnson	.60
(597)	Bruce Taylor	.30
(598)	Mel Phillips	.10
(599)	Rosey Taylor	.20
(600)	Steve Spurrier	2.50
(601)	Charley Taylor	1.50
(602)	Jim Snowden	.10
(603)	Ray Schoenke	.10
(604)	Len Hauss	.20
(605)	John Wilbur	.10
(606)	Walt Rock	.10
(607)	Jerry Smith	.20
(608)	Roy Jefferson	.20
(609)	Bill Kilmer	1.00
(610)	Larry Brown	1.00
(611)	Charlie Harraway	.20
(612)	Curt Knight	.10
(613)	Ron McDole	.10
(614)	Manuel Sistrunk	.10
(615)	Diron Talbert	.20
(616)	Verlon Biggs	.10
(617)	Jack Pardee	.75
(618)	Myron Pottios	.20
(619)	Chris Hanburger	.50
(620)	Pat Fischer	.20
(621)	Mike Bass	.10
(622)	Richie Petitbon	.20
(623)	Brig Owens	.10
(624)	Mike Bragg	.15

1972 Sunoco Stamps Update

These unnumbered 1-5/8" x 2-3/8" stamps are identical to the 1972 Sunoco stamps, but were not listed in the album which was produced to house the stamps. They were issued as team sheets later in the year.

		NM/M
Complete Set (82):		75.00
Common Player:		1.00
(1)	Clarence Ellis	1.00
(2)	Dave Hampton	1.50
(3)	Dennis Havig	1.00
(4)	John James	1.00
(5)	Joe Profit	1.00
(6)	Lonnie Hepburn	1.00
(7)	Dennis Nelson	1.00
(8)	Mike McBath	1.00
(9)	Walt Patulski	1.00
(10)	Bob Asher	1.00
(11)	Steve DeLong	1.00
(12)	Tony McGee	1.00
(13)	James Osborne	1.00
(14)	Jim Seymour	1.00
(15)	Tommy Casanova	1.50
(16)	Neil Craig	1.00
(17)	Essex Johnson	1.25
(18)	Sherman White	1.00
(19)	Bob Briggs	1.00
(20)	Thom Darden	1.25
(21)	Marv Bateman	1.00
(22)	Toni Fritsch	1.00
(23)	Calvin Hill	3.00
(24)	Pat Toomay	1.25
(25)	Pete Duranko	1.00
(26)	Marv Montgomery	1.00
(27)	Rod Sherman	1.00
(28)	Bob Kowalkowski	1.00
(29)	Jim Mitchell	1.00
(30)	Larry Woods	1.00
(31)	Willie Buchanon	1.50
(32)	Leland Glass	1.00
(33)	MacArthur Lane	1.50
(34)	Chester Marcol	1.00
(35)	Ron Widby	1.00
(36)	Ken Burrough	1.50
(37)	Calvin Hunt	1.00
(38)	Ron Saul	1.00
(39)	Greg Simpson	1.00
(40)	Mike Sensibaugh	1.00
(41)	Dave Chapple	1.00
(42)	Jim Langer	6.00
(43)	Mike Eischeid	1.00
(44)	John Gilliam	1.25
(45)	Ron Acks	1.00
(46)	Bob Gladieux	1.00
(47)	Honoe Jackson	1.00
(48)	Reggie Rucker	1.50
(49)	Pat Studstill	1.00
(50)	Bob Windsor	1.00
(51)	Joe Federspiel	1.00
(52)	Bob Newland	4.00
(53)	Pete Athas	1.00
(54)	Charlie Evans	1.00
(55)	Jack Gregory	1.00
(56)	John Mendenhall	1.00
(57)	Ed Bell	1.00
(58)	John Elliott	1.00
(59)	Chris Farasopoulos	1.00
(60)	Bob Svihus	1.00
(61)	Steve Tannen	1.00
(62)	Cliff Branch	3.00
(63)	Gus Otto	1.00
(64)	Otis Sistrunk	1.25
(65)	Charlie Smith	1.00
(66)	John Reaves	1.00
(67)	Larry Watkins	1.00
(68)	Henry Davis	1.00
(69)	Ben McGee	1.00
(70)	Donny Anderson	1.25
(71)	Walker Gillette	1.00
(72)	Martin Imhoff	1.00
(73)	Bobby Moore (aka Ahmad Rashad)	8.00
(74)	Norm Thompson	1.00
(75)	Lionel Aldridge	1.00
(76)	Dave Costa	1.00
(77)	Cid Edwards	1.00
(78)	Tim Rossovich	1.00
(79)	Dave Williams	1.00
(80)	Johnny Fuller	1.00
(81)	Terry Hermeling	1.00
(82)	Paul Laaveg	1.00

2001 Super Bowl XXXV Marino

		NM/M
Common Player:		8.00
1	Dan Marino/Topps	10.00
3	Dan Marino/Fleer	8.00
4	Dan Marino/Pacific	8.00
5	Dan Marino/Playoff	10.00
6	Dan Marino/ Upper Deck	10.00

2003 Super Bowl XXXVII Chargers

		NM/M
Common Player:		1.00
1	Drew Brees	3.00
2	LaDainian Tomlinson	4.00
3	Curtis Conway	1.00
4	Junior Seau	2.00
5	Quentin Jammer	1.50
6	Tim Dwight	1.00
7	Quentin Jammer	1.50
8	Drew Brees	4.00
9	Tim Dwight	1.00
10	Junior Seau	2.00
11	Curtis Conway	1.00
12	LaDainian Tomlinson	4.00

2004 Texans Super Bowl XXXVIII Promos

		NM/M
Common Player:		2.00
1	Aaron Glenn Topps	2.00
2	Corey Bradford Playoff	2.00
3	Billy Miller Fleer	2.00
4	Dave Ragone Upper Deck	2.00
5	Andre Johnson Upper Deck	4.00
6	Jabar Gaffney Fleer	2.00
7	Domanick Davis Playoff	4.00
8	David Carr Topps	5.00

1995 Superior Pix Promos

This four-card preview of the 1995 Superior Pix set was distributed through mail and at the 1995 National. The cards are identical to the Superior Pix set except that the promo cards have the National logo on the back.

		NM/M
Complete Set (4):		8.00
Common Player:		1.00
1	Steve McNair	3.00
2	Kerry Collins	2.00
3	Tyrone Wheatley	1.00
4	Joey Galloway	2.00

1995 Superior Pix

Superior Pix consists of a 110-card base set, an autographed variant and four insert sets. The base cards include the words "95 Draft" printed in gold foil on the front. The inserts include Deep Threat (five cards, 1:9), Instant Impact (five cards, 1:18), Open Field (five cards, 1:18) and Top Defender (five cards, 1:9).

		NM/M
Complete Set (110):		10.00
Common Player:		.05
1	Ki-Jana Carter	.25
2	Tony Boselli	.25
3	Steve McNair	1.50
4	Michael Westbrook	.50
5	Kerry Collins	1.50
6	Terrell Davis	2.00
7	Kevin Bouie	.05
8	Brian Williams	.05
9	Kez McCorvey	.05
10	Kyle Brady	.25
11	Rob Johnson	.50
12	Carl Greenwood	.05
13	Mark Fields	.05
14	Andrew Greene	.05
15	Orlando Thomas	.05
16	Don Sasa	.05
17	Brent Moss	.05
18	Jamal Willis	.05
19	Michael Hendricks	.05
20	Rashaan Salaam	.50
21	John Sacca	.05
22	Cory Raymer	.05
23	Kirby Dar Dar	.05
24	Lee DeRamus	.05
25	Joey Galloway	.75
26	Mike Frederick	.05
27	Todd Collins	.50
28	Stoney Case	.05
29	Devin Bush	.05
30	Chad May	.05
31	Darick Holmes	.25
32	Johnny Thomas	.05
33	Luther Ellis	.05
34	Tyrone Wheatley	.25
35	Terry Connealy	.05
36	Ruben Brown	.05
37	Kelvin Anderson	.05
38	Tony Berti	.05
39	Steve Ingram	.05
40	Kevin Carter	.25
41	Dave Wohlabaugh	.05
42	Mike Morton	.05
43	Steve Stenstrom	.05
44	Zach Wiegert	.05
45	Rodney Thomas	.10
46	Eddie Goines	.05
47	Kenny Gales	.05
48	Jamal Ellis	.05
49	Demetrius Edwards	.05
50	Justin Armour	.05
51	Billy Williams	.05
52	Ed Hervey	.05
53	Antonio Armstrong	.05
54	Oliver Gibson	.05
55	David Dunn	.10
56	Tyrone Davis	.05
57	Craig Newsome	.05
58	William Strong	.05
59	Sherman Williams	.05
60	James O. Stewart	.25
61	Bryan Schwartz	.05
62	Frank Sanders	.25
63	Barrett Robbins	.05
64	Bronzell Miller	.05
65	Curtis Martin	2.00
66	Chris T. Jones	.50
67	Dave Barr	.05
68	Anthony Brown	.05
69	Ken Dilger	.25
70	Warren Sapp	.25
71	James A. Stewart	.05
72	Corey Fuller	.05
73	Christian Fauria	.25
74	Brian DeMarco	.05
75	J.J. Stokes	.50
76	Hicham El-Mashtoub	.05
77	Anthony Cook	.05
78	Mark Bruener	.25
79	Blake Brockemeyer	.05
80	Derrick Brooks	.05
81	Joe Aska	.05
82	Lance Brown	.05
83	Pete Mitchell	.05
84	Kordell Stewart	2.00
85	Bobby Taylor	.25
86	Jimmy Hitchcock	.05
87	Jack Jackson	.05
88	Ray Zellars	.05
89	Darius Holland	.05
90	Derrick Alexander	.25
91	Torey Hunter	.05
92	Scotty Lewis	.05
93	Carl Reeves	.05
94	Terrell Fletcher	.05
95	Ontiwaun Carter	.05
96	Trezelle Jenkins	.05
97	Mark Birchmeier	.05
98	Len Raney	.05
99	Ronald Cherry	.05
100	Tyrone Wheatley	.25
101	John Jones	.05
102	Zack Crockett	.05
103	Larry Jones	.05
104	Michael McCoy	.05
105	Ellis Johnson	.05
106	Jerrott Willard	.05
107	Jason James	.05
108	J.J. Smith	.05
109	Mike Mamula	.05
110	Checklist	.05

1995 Superior Pix Autographs

This set is a parallel of the Superior Pix base set. Each player autographed a number of their cards. The card fronts have "authentic signature" printed on them and are individually numbered. They were inserted one per pack.

		NM/M
Complete Set (109):		300.00
Common Player:		2.00
1	Ki-Jana Carter/1000	20.00
2	Tony Boselli/4000	3.00
3	Steve McNair/3000	15.00
4	Michael Westbrook/ 4000	7.00
5	Kerry Collins/3000	15.00
6	Terrell Davis/5000	18.00
7	Kevin Bouie	2.00
8	Brian Williams	2.00
9	Kez McCorvey/6500	2.00
10	Kyle Brady/3500	3.00
11	Rob Johnson/3000	8.00
12	Carl Greenwood	2.00
13	Mark Fields/5000	2.00
14	Andrew Greene/5000	2.00
15	Orlando Thomas/6000	2.00
16	Don Sasa/6500	2.00
17	Brent Moss	2.00
18	Jamal Willis	2.00
19	Michael Hendricks	2.00
20	Rashaan Salaam/3500	7.00
21	John Sacca	2.00
22	Cory Raymer/6000	2.00
23	Kirby Dar Dar	2.00
24	Lee DeRamus/6500	2.00
25	Joey Galloway/4000	10.00
26	Mike Frederick/6000	2.00
27	Todd Collins/5000	3.00
28	Stoney Case/4000	2.00
29	Devin Bush/5000	2.00
30	Chad May/4000	2.00
31	Darrick Holmes/5500	8.00
32	Johnny Thomas/6500	2.00
33	Luther Ellis/5000	2.00
34	Tyrone Wheatley/5000	3.00
35	Terry Connealy/6500	2.00
36	Ruben Brown/3500	2.00
37	Kelvin Anderson	2.00
38	Tony Berti	2.00
39	Steve Ingram	2.00
40	Kevin Carter/4000	3.00
41	Dave Wohlabaugh/6500	2.00
42	Mike Morton/4000	2.00
43	Steve Stenstrom/5000	2.00
44	Zach Wiegert/5000	2.00
45	Rodney Thomas/5000	3.00
46	Eddie Goines	2.00
47	Kenny Gales/6500	2.00
48	Jamal Ellis/6500	2.00
49	Demetrius Edwards/6500	2.00
50	Justin Armour/5000	2.00
51	Billy Williams	2.00
52	Ed Hervey	2.00
53	Antonio Armstrong	2.00
54	Oliver Gibson	2.00
55	David Dunn/5000	3.00
56	Tyrone Davis	2.00
57	Craig Newsome/4000	2.00
58	William Strong	2.00
59	Sherman Williams/3500	2.00
60	James O. Stewart/4000	3.00
61	Bryan Schwartz/6000	2.00
62	Frank Sanders/5000	7.00
63	Barrett Robbins/6000	2.00
64	Bronzell Miller	2.00
65	Curtis Martin/4000	18.00
66	Chris T. Jones/4000	7.00
67	Dave Barr/5000	2.00
68	Anthony Brown/6500	2.00
69	Ken Dilger/6000	3.00
70	Warren Sapp/4000	3.00
71	James A. Stewart	2.00
72	Corey Fuller/5000	2.00
73	Christian Fauria/5000	3.00
74	Brian DeMarco/6000	2.00
75	J.J. Stokes/1000	16.00
76	Hicham El-Mashtoub	2.00
77	Anthony Cook/6000	2.00
78	Mark Bruener/4000	3.00
79	Blake Brockermeyer/4000	2.00
80	Derrick Brooks/4000	2.00
81	Joe Aska/4000	2.00
82	Lance Brown/6500	2.00
83	Pete Mitchell/6500	2.00
84	Kordell Stewart/6500	15.00
85	Bobby Taylor/4000	3.00
86	Jimmy Hitchcock	2.00
87	Jack Jackson/5000	2.00
88	Ray Zellars/4000	3.00
89	Darius Holland	2.00
90	Derrick Alexander/4000	3.00
91	Torey Hunter/6000	2.00
92	Scotty Lewis/6500	2.00
93	Carl Reeves	2.00
94	Terrell Fletcher/6000	3.00
95	Ontiwaun Carter/6500	2.00
96	Trezelle Jenkins/5000	2.00
97	Mark Birchmeier	2.00
98	Len Raney	2.00
99	Ronald Cherry/6500	2.00
100	Tyrone Wheatley/6500	3.00
101	John Jones	2.00
102	Zack Crockett/6000	2.00
103	Larry Jones/4000	2.00
104	Michael McCoy	2.00
105	Ellis Johnson/3500	2.00
106	Jerrott Willard/5000	2.00
107	Jason James	2.00
108	J.J. Smith	2.00
109	Mike Mamula/4000	2.00

1995 Superior Pix Deep Threat

This five-card insert (1:9) features the top wide receiver prospects from the 1995 Draft. The card fronts have a player photo on a prism background, with the words "1995 Draft Pix Series" at the top.

		NM/M
Complete Set (5):		8.00
Common Player:		1.00
1	Michael Westbrook	2.00
2	Joey Galloway	2.50
3	J.J. Stokes	2.00
4	Kyle Brady	1.00
5	Frank Sanders	2.00

A player's name in *italic* type indicates a rookie card.

1995 Superior Pix Instant Impact

Instant Impact is a five-card insert (1:18). The fronts have a split blue/silver/green foil background.

		NM/M
Complete Set (5):		8.00
Common Player:		.75
1	Steve McNair	3.00
2	Kerry Collins	3.00
3	Tyrone Wheatley	.75
4	Joey Galloway	1.50
5	Tony Boselli	.75

1995 Superior Pix Open Field

Open Field features the top running back prospects from the 1995 Draft on a split-color prism background. This five-card set was inserted 1:18.

		NM/M
Complete Set (5):		5.00
Common Player:		.75
1	Ki-Jana Carter	1.25
2	Tyrone Wheatley	.75
3	James O. Stewart	1.25
4	Rashaan Salaam	1.50
5	Ray Zellars	.75

1995 Superior Pix Top Defender

The top defensive linemen from the 1995 Draft are featured in this five-card set (1:9). The players are pictured on a blue and gold wood grain background.

		NM/M
Complete Set (5):		4.00
Common Player:		1.00
1	Kevin Carter	1.00
2	Derrick Alexander	1.00
3	Warren Sapp	1.00
4	Derrick Brooks	1.00
5	Mike Mamula	1.00

1991 Surge WLAF Police

The 39-card, 2-3/8" x 3-1/2" set, sponsored by American Airlines, features players from the WLAF Sacramento Surge team. The card fronts feature a color photo with an American Airlines logo appearing along the top border. The lower right corner contains a triangle with the Surge helmet. The card backs give bio information and a safety tip.

		NM/M
Complete Set (39):		20.00
Common Player:		.60
1	Mike Adams	.75
2	Sam Archer	.60
3	John Buddenberg	.60
4	Jon Burman	.60
5	Tony Burse	.75
6	Ricardo Cartwright	.60
7	Greg Coauette	.60
8	Paco Craig	.60
9	John Dominic	.60
10	Mike Elkins	1.00
11	Oliver Erhorn	.60
12	Mel Farr	1.00
13	Victor Floyd	.60
14	Byron Forsythe	.60
15	Paul Frazier	.60
16	Tom Gerhart	.60
17	Mike Hall	.60
18	Anthony Henton	.60
19	Nate Hill	.60
20	Kubanai Kalombo	.60
21	Shawn Knight	1.00
22	Sean Kugler	.60
23	Matti Lindholm	.60
24	Art Malone	.75
25	Robert McWright	.60
26	Tim Moore	.60
27	Pete Najarian	.60
28	Mark Nua	.60
29	Carl Parker	.60
30	Leon Perry	.60
31	Juha Salo	.60
32	Saute Sapolu	.60
33	Paul Soltis	.60
34	Richard Stephens	.60
35	Kay Stephenson (CO)	.75
36	Kendall Trainor	.75
37	Mike Wallace	.60
38	Curtis Wilson	.60
39	Rick Zumwalt	.60

1988 Swell Football Greats

Swell's first set picturing members of the Pro Football Hall of Fame featured 144 players, coaches and executives. The set was released in 10-card wax packs and in complete sets in August 1988. A separate checklist was included. The standard-size cards feature full-color photos or sepia-toned black-and-white photos (in the case of older players) enclosed in a blue border. A red Swell logo is seen in the upper left corner; the Hall of Fame's 25th Anniversary logo is in the lower left, and the player's name and position is in white type in a red box in the lower right corner. Card backs feature blue borders and the player's biographical notes and career statistics in a white rectangle. Cards are printed on white cardboard stock. There have been some reports of small nicks and notches along the tops of some of the cards in the factory-issued sets.

NM/M

Complete Set (144): 15.00
Common Player: .10
1 Pete Rozell .30
2 Joe Namath 1.50
3 Frank Gatski .10
4 O.J. Simpson 2.00
5 Roger Staubach 1.50
6 Herb Adderly .10
7 Lance Alworth .25
8 Doug Atkins .10
9 Red Badgro .10
10 Cliff Battles .10
11 Sammy Baugh .35
12 Raymond Berry .15
13 Charles Bidwell Sr. .10
14 Chuck Bednarik .15
15 Bert Bell .10
16 Bobby Bell .10
17 George Blanda .25
18 Jim Brown 1.00
19 Paul Brown .15
20 Roosevelt Brown .10
21 Ray Flaherty .10
22 Len Ford .15
23 Dan Fortmann .10
24 Bill George .10
25 Art Donovan .10
26 John (Paddy) Driscoll .10
27 Jimmy Conzelman .10
28 Willie Davis .10
29 Earl "Dutch" Clark .10
30 George Connor .10
31 Guy Chamberlain .10
32 Jack Christiansen .10
33 Tony Canadeo .15
34 Joe Carr .10
35 Willie Brown .10
36 Dick Butkus .35
37 Bill Dudley .10
38 Turk Edwards .10
39 Weeb Ewbank .20
40 Tom Fears .10
41 Otto Graham .40
42 Harold "Red" Grange .50
43 Frank Gifford .60
44 Sid Gillman .10
45 Forrest Gregg .10
46 Lou Groza .25
47 Joe Guyon .10
48 George Halas .20
49 Ed Healy .10
50 Mel Hein .10
51 Pete Henry .15
52 Arnie Herber .10
53 Bill Hewitt .10
54 Clark Hinkle .10
55 Elroy Hirsch .25
56 Robert Hubbard .10
57 Sam Huff .10
58 Lamar Hunt .15
59 Don Hutson .20
60 Deacon Jones .10
61 Sonny Jurgensen .15
62 Walt Kiesling .10
63 Frank Kinard .10
64 Curley Lambeau .10
65 Dick "Night Train" Lane .10
66 Yale Lary .10
67 Dante Lavelli .10
68 Bobby Lane .20
69 Alphonse Leemans .10
70 Bob Lilly .15
71 Vince Lombardi .35
72 Sid Luckman .20
73 William Roy Lyman .10
74 Tim Mara .10
75 Gino Marchetti .15
76 George Preston Marshall .10
77 Ollie Matson .15
78 George McAfee .10
79 Mike McCormack .10
80 Hugh McElhenny .15
81 John McNally .15
82 Mike Michalske .10
83 Wayne Millner .10
84 Bobby Mitchell .10
85 Ron Mix .15
86 Lenny Moore .15
87 Marion Motley .15
88 George Musso .10
89 Bronko Nagurski .35
90 Earle Neale .10
91 Ernie Nevers .20
92 Ray Nitschke .20
93 Leo Nomellini .10
94 Merlin Olsen .15
95 Jim Otto .10
96 Steve Owen .10
97 Clarence Parker .10
98 Jim Parker .10
99 Joe Perry .15
100 Pete Pihos .10
101 Hugh Ray .10
102 Dan Reeves .10
103 Jim Ringo .10
104 Andy Robustelli .10
105 Art Rooney .10
106 Gale Sayers .50
107 Joe Schmidt .10
108 Bart Starr .75
109 Ernie Stautner .15
110 Ken Strong .10
111 Joe Stydahar .15
112 Charley Taylor .15
113 Jim Taylor .15
114 Jim Thorpe .75
115 Y.A. Tittle .35
116 George Trafton .10
117 Charley Trippi .10
118 Emlen Tunnell .10
119 Clyde Turner .10
120 Johnny Unitas 1.75
121 Norm Van Brocklin .20
122 Steve Van Buren .10
123 Paul Warfield .10
124 Bob Waterfield .20
125 Arnie Weinmeister .10
126 Bill Willis .10
127 Larry Wilson .10
128 Alex Wojciechowicz .10
129 Doak Walker .25
130 Willie Lanier .10
131 Paul Hornung .25
132 Ken Houston .10
133 Fran Tarkenton .50
134 Don Maynard .15
135 Larry Csonka .30
136 Joe Greene .15
137 Len Dawson .15
138 Gene Upshaw .10
139 Jim Langer .10
140 John Henry Johnson .10
141 Fred Biletnikoff .15
142 Mike Ditka .50
143 Jack Ham .15
144 Alan Page .15

1989 Swell Football Greats

The 1989 edition of Swell Football Greats again included every member of the Pro Football Hall of Fame inducted through 1989. Swell had released its initial set of HOFers in 1988. The standard-size cards featured white borders with red striping. The Swell logo is in the upper left corner, and a blue flag carries the "Football Greats" slogan across the bottom of the card, just above the player's name and position. Most of the photos are in color. Those that feature early greats are sepia-toned. Backs are printed in two colors and contain biographical notes and career highlights as well as the year of Hall of Fame induction. Cards, which were released in late August 1989, were issued in wax packs of 10 cards each. Collector's Sets were also released by Swell, which is a division of the Philadelphia Chewing Gum Corp. One variation exists in the set: In the upper right corner of card #27, Sid Luckman. The scarcer error card shows "Sid" and the first part of "Chicago" printed in white. This was air-brushed out in later versions. The set has so little collector interest, however, that the error has no real additional value.

NM/M

Complete Set (150): 15.00
Common Player: .10
1 Terry Bradshaw 1.00
2 Bert Bell .10
3 Joe Carr .10
4 Earl "Dutch" Clark .10
5 Harold "Red" Grange .60
6 Wilbur "Pete" Henry .10
7 Mel Hein .10
8 Cal Hubbard .10
9 George Halas .30
10 Don Hutson .15
11 Curley Lambeau .10
12 Tim Mara .10
13 George Preston Marshall .10
14 John McNally .10
15 Bronko Nagurski .40
16 Ernie Nevers .15
17 Jim Thorpe .50
18 Ed Healy .10
19 Clarke Hinkle .10
20 Link Lyman .10
21 Mike Michalske .10
22 George Trafton .10
23 Guy Chamberlain .15
24 John "Paddy" Driscoll .10
25 Dan Fortmann .10
26 Otto Graham .40
27A Sid Luckman .35
27B Sid Luckman (corrected) 1.25
28 Steve Van Buren .15
29 Bob Waterfield .20
30 Bill Dudley .15
31 Joe Guyon .10
32 Arnie Herber .10
33 Walt Kiesling .10
34 Jimmy Conzelman .10
35 Art Rooney .10
36 Willie Wood .10
37 Art Shell .25
38 Sammy Baugh .45
39 Mel Blount .10
40 Lamar Hunt .15
41 Norm Van Brocklin .30
42 Y.A. Tittle .35
43 Andy Robustelli .10
44 Vince Lombardi .35
45 Frank Kinard .10
46 Bill Hewitt .10
47 Jim Brown 1.00
48 Pete Pihos .10
49 Hugh McElhenny .15
50 Tom Fears .15
51 Jack Christiansen .10
52 Ernie Stautner .15
53 Joe Perry .15
54 Leo Nomellini .15
55 Earl "Greasy" Neale .10
56 Turk Edwards .10
57 Alex Wojciechowicz .10
58 Charley Trippi .10
59 Marion Motley .20
60 Wayne Miller .10
61 Elroy Hirsch .15
62 Art Donovan .10
63 Cliff Battles .10
64 Emlen Tunnell .15
65 Joe Stydahar .10
66 Ken Strong .10
67 Dan Reeves .10
68 Bobby Layne .30
69 Paul Brown .20
70 Charles Bidwell Sr. .10
71 Chuck Bednarik .15
72 Bulldog Turner .10
73 Hugh "Shorty" Ray .10
74 Steve Owen .10
75 George McAfee .10
76 Forrest Gregg .15
77 Frank Gifford .50
78 Jim Taylor .15
79 Len Ford .10
80 Ray Flaherty .10
81 Lenny Moore .15
82 Dante Lavelli .10
83 George Connor .15
84 Roosevelt Grier .10
85 Dick "Night Train" Lane .10
86 Lou Groza .30
87 Bill George .10
88 Tony Canadeo .10
89 Joe Schmidt .10
90 Jim Parker .10
91 Wayne Millner .10
92 Raymond Berry .20
93 Ollie Matson .15
94 Gino Marchetti .10
95 Larry Wilson .10
96 Ray Nitschke .25
97 Tuffy Leemans .10
98 Weeb Ewbank .10
99 Lance Alworth .30
100 Bill Willis .10
101 Bart Starr .35
102 Gale Sayers .35
103 Herb Adderly .10
104 Johnny Unitas 1.00
105 Ron Mix .10
106 Yale Lary .10
107 Red Badgro .10
108 Jim Otto .10
109 Bob Lilly .15
110 Deacon Jones .15
111 Doug Atkins .10
112 Jim Ringo .10
113 Willie Davis .10
114 George Blanda .35
115 Bobby Bell .10
116 Merlin Olsen .15
117 George Musso .10
118 Sam Huff .15
119 Paul Warfield .25
120 Bobby Mitchell .10
121 Sonny Jurgensen .25
122 Sid Gilman .10
123 Arnie Weinmeister .10
124 Charley Taylor .10
125 Mike McCormack .10
126 Willie Brown .10
127 O.J. Simpson 1.50
128 Pete Rozelle .25
129 Joe Namath 1.25
130 Frank Gatski .10
131 Willie Lanier .10
132 Ken Houston .10
133 Paul Hornung .25
134 Roger Staubach 1.25
135 Len Dawson .15
136 Larry Csonka .30
137 Doak Walker .15
138 Fran Tarkenton .60
139 Don Maynard .15
140 Jim Langer .15
141 John Henry Johnson .10
142 Joe Greene .20
143 Jack Ham .10
144 Mike Ditka .75
145 Alan Page .10
146 Fred Biletnikoff .15
147 Gene Upshaw .10
148 Dick Butkus .50
149 Checklist 1 & 2 .10
150 Checklist 3 & 4 .10

1990 Swell Football Greats

Swell, which had released two straight sets of Pro Football Hall of Famers, returned with this 160-card set, also featuring HOFers. Produced by the Philadelphia Gum Co., the set includes 155 HOFers, two checklists, and three Hall of Fame cards. Cards are standard size, with a white border and blue and yellow lines. As in previous issues, some cards of the older players may have sepia-toned, rather than full-color, photos.

NM/M

Complete Set (160): 15.00
Common Player: .10
1 Terry Bradshaw 1.00
2 Bert Bell .10
3 Joe Carr .10
4 Dutch Clark .15
5 Harold "Red" Grange .40
6 Pete Henry .10
7 Mel Hein .10
8 Cal Hubbard .10
9 George Halas .25
10 Don Hutson .15
11 Curly Lambeau .15
12 Tim Mara .10
13 G. Preston Marshall .10
14 John McNally .10
15 Bronko Nagurski .35
16 Ernie Nevers .15
17 Jim Thorpe .75
18 Ed Healy .10
19 Clark Hinkle .10
20 Link Lyman .10
21 Mike Michalske .10
22 George Trafton .10
23 Guy Chamberlain .10
24 Paddy Driscoll .10
25 Dan Fortmann .10
26 Otto Graham .50
27 Sid Luckman .40
28 Steve Van Buren .15
29 Bob Waterfield .25
30 Bill Dudley .10
31 Joe Guyon .10
32 Arnie Herber .10
33 Walt Kiesling .10
34 Jimmy Conzelman .10
35 Art Rooney .15
36 Willie Wood .10
37 Art Shell .15
38 Sammy Baugh .40
39 Mel Blount .10
40 Lamar Hunt .15
41 Norm Van Brocklin .25
42 Y.A. Tittle .30
43 Andy Robustelli .10
44 Vince Lombardi .25
45 Bruiser Kinard .10
46 Bill Hewitt .10
47 Jim Brown 1.00
48 Pete Pihos .10
49 Hugh McElhenny .15
50 Tom Fears .15
51 Jack Christiansen .10
52 Ernie Stautner .15
53 Joe Perry .15
54 Leo Nomellini .15
55 Greasy Neale .10
56 Turk Edwards .10
57 Alex Wojciechowicz .20
58 Charlie Trippi .10
59 Marion Motley .15
60 Wayne Miller .10
61 Elroy Hirsch .20
62 Art Donovan .10
63 Cliff Battles .10
64 Emlen Tunnell .10
65 Joe Stydahar .10
66 Ken Strong .10
67 Dan Reeves .15
68 Bobby Layne .25
69 Paul Brown .20
70 Charles Bidwell Sr. .10
71 Chuck Bednarik .15
72 Bulldog Turner .10
73 Shorty Ray .10
74 Steve Owen .10
75 George McAfee .10
76 Forrest Gregg .10
77 Frank Gifford .40
78 Jim Taylor .15
79 Len Ford .10
80 Ray Flaherty .15
81 Lenny Moore .15
82 Dante Lavelli .10
83 George Connor .15
84 Roosevelt Brown .10
85 Dick "Night Train" Lane .10
86 Lou Groza .20
87 Bill George .10
88 Tony Canadeo .10
89 Joe Schmidt .15
90 Jim Parker .10
91 Raymond Berry .15
92 Ace Parker .10
93 Ollie Matson .15
94 Gino Marchetti .10
95 Larry Wilson .10
96 Ray Nitschke .15
97 Tuffy Leemans .10
98 Weeb Ewbank .15
99 Lance Alworth .20
100 Bill Willis .10
101 Bart Starr .30
102 Gale Sayers .30
103 Herb Adderly .10
104 Johnny Unitas 1.00
105 Ron Mix .10
106 Yale Lary .10
107 Red Badgro .10
108 Jim Otto .10
109 Bob Lilly .15
110 Deacon Jones .10
111 Doug Atkins .10
112 Jim Ringo .15
113 Willie Davis .10
114 George Blanda .35
115 Bobby Bell .10
116 Merlin Olsen .15
117 George Musso .10
118 Sam Huff .10
119 Paul Warfield .15
120 Bobby Mitchell .10
121 Sonny Jurgensen .15
122 Sid Gilman .10
123 Arnie Weinmeister .10
124 Charley Taylor .10
125 Mike McCormack .10
126 Willie Brown .10
127 O.J. Simpson 1.50
128 Pete Rozelle .25
129 Joe Namath 1.25
130 Frank Gatski .10
131 Willie Lanier .15
132 Ken Houston .10
133 Paul Hornung .25
134 Roger Staubach 1.00
135 Len Dawson .15
136 Larry Csonka .25
137 Doak Walker .15
138 Fran Tarkenton .40
139 Don Maynard .15
140 Jim Langer .10
141 John H. Johnson .10
142 Joe Greene .20
143 Jack Ham .10
144 Mike Ditka .50
145 Alan Page .10
146 Fred Biletnikoff .15
147 Gene Upshaw .10
148 Dick Butkus .30
149 Buck Buchanan .10
150 Franco Harris .30
151 Tom Landry .35
152 Ted Hendricks .10
153 Bob St. Clair .10
154 Jack Lambert .20
155 Bob Griese .20
156 Admission Coupon .10
157 Enshrinement Day .10
158 Hall of Fame .10
159 Checklist 1 & 2 .10
160 Checklist 3 & 4 .10

T

1962 Tang Team Photos

The 14-card, 8" x 10" set features a team photo with the players' names along the bottom border. The backs are blank. The set was available for 50 cents back in 1962 with a Tang seal. Reprints have been made in recent years.

NM/M

Complete Set (14): 100.00
Common Player: 8.00
1 Baltimore Colts 8.00
2 Chicago Bears 8.00
3 Cleveland Browns 8.00
4 Dallas Cowboys 15.00
5 Detroit Lions 8.00
6 Green Bay Packers 15.00
7 Los Angeles Rams 8.00
8 Minnesota Vikings 12.00
9 New York Giants 8.00
10 Philadelphia Eagles 8.00
11 Pittsburgh Steelers 12.00
12 St. Louis Cardinals 8.00
13 San Francisco 49ers 12.00
14 Washington Redskins 12.00

1981 TCMA Greats

These standard-size cards were issued by TCMA in 1981. Each card front has a color photo of a player from the 1950s or '60s, framed by a white border. The card back is white and uses black ink to provide a career summary, biographical information, a TCMA copyright and a card number. Some cards, however, went unnumbered and command values about 2 times more than their numbered counterparts.

NM/M

Complete Set (78): 18.50
Common Player: .20
1 Alex Karras .70
2 Fran Tarkenton 2.25
3 John Unitas 3.50
4 Bobby Layne 1.50
5 Roger Staubach 4.50
6 Joe Namath 4.50
7 1954 New York Giants .40
8 Jimmy Brown 4.50
9 Ray Wietecha .20
10 R.C. Owens .20
11 Alex Webster .25
12 Jim Otto .70
13 Jim Taylor .70
14 Kyle Rote .60
15 Roger Ellis .20
16 Nick Pietrosante .25
17 Milt Plum .25
18 Eddie LeBaron .40
19 Jimmy Patton .20
20 Yale Lary .70
21 Leo Nomellini .90
22 Johnny Olszewski .20
23 Ernie Koy .25
24 Bill Wade .25
25 Billy Wells .20
26 Ron Waller .20
27 Pat Summerall .45
28 Joe Schmidt .90
29 Bob St. Clair .60
30 Dick Lynch .25
31 Tommy McDonald .40
32 Earl Morrall .40
33 Jim Martin .20
34 Dick Modzelewski .25
35 Dick LeBeau .25
36 Dick Post .20
37 Les Richter .25
38 Andy Robustelli .60
39 Pete Retzlaff .25
40 Fred Biletnikoff 1.25
41 Timmy Brown .25
42 Babe Parilli .25
43 Lance Alworth 1.25
44 Sammy Baugh 1.25
45 Paul (Tank) Younger .25
46 Chuck Bednarik 1.25
47 Art Donovan .90
48 Len Dawson 1.50
49 Don Maynard .90
50 Joe Morrison .25
51 John Eliott .20
52 Jim Ringo .60
53 Max McGee .25
54 Art Powell .25
55 Galen Fiss .20
56 Jack Stroud .20
57 Bake Turner .25
58 Mike McCormack .60
59 L.G. Dupre .25
60 Bill McPeak .20
61 Art Spinney .20
62 Fran Rogel .20
63 Ollie Matson .90
64 Doak Walker .90
65 Lenny Moore .90
66 George Shaw, Bert Rechichar .20
67 Kyle Rote, Jim Lee Howell, Ray Krause .25
68 Andy Robustelli, Roosevelt Grier, Dick Modzelewski, Jim Katcavage .50
69 Tucker Frederickson, Ernie Koy .25
70 Gino Marchetti .70
71 Earl Morrall, Allie Sherman .40
72 Roosevelt Brown .60
73 Howard Cassady (Hopalong) .25
74 Don Chandler .25
75 Joe Childress .20
76 Rick Casares .25
77 Charley Conerly .70
78 Don Heinrich, Tom Dublinski, Charlie Conerly 1958 Giants QB's .40

1987 TCMA Update

This set, produced by TCMA's successor (CMC), is a reissue of TCMA's 1981 set, but 12 additional cards were added. The extra cards were numbered from were the first issue ended, at 79. The copyright on the card back is CMC 1987.

NM/M

Complete Set (12): 20.00
Common Player: .75

79 Fred Dryer 1.00
80 Ed Marinaro 1.00
81 O.J. Simpson 10.00
82 Joe Theismann 2.50
83 Roman Gabriel 1.00
84 Terry Metcalf .75
85 Lyle Alzado 1.50
86 Jake Scott .75
87 Cliff Branch 1.50
88 Rocky Bleier 1.00
89 Cliff Harris .75
90 Archie Manning 2.00

1960 Texans 7-Eleven

The standard-sized cards feature a black and white photo of the player with his name, position and team along the bottom edge. The horizontal card backs have player highlights in typewriter-style print. Even though there are 11 cards checklisted, there may have been more in the unnumbered set.

NM/M
Complete Set (11): 400.00
Common Player: 35.00
1 Max Boydston 35.00
2 Mel Branch 35.00
3 Chris Burford 35.00
4 Ray Collins (UER) (No team name on front) 35.00
5 Cotton Davidson 35.00
6 Abner Haynes 60.00
7 Sherrill Headrick 35.00
8 Bill Krisher 35.00
9 Paul Miller 35.00
10 Johnny Robinson 60.00
11 Jack Spikes 35.00

1992 Thunderbolts Arena

Area Temps sponsored this set featuring the Cleveland Thunderbolts of the Arena Football League. The 24 cards are printed on plain white card stock. The fronts feature a black and white player photo framed by a purple line. The backs contain basic player information. Both sides feature the Area Temps logo. The cards are unnumbered.

NM/M
Complete Set (24): 20.00
Common Player: .60
1 Eric Anderson .60
2 Robert Banks .60
3 Bobby Bounds .60
4 Marvin Bowman .60
5 George Cooper .60
6 Michael Denbrock ACO .60
7 Chris Drennan .60
8 Dennis Fitzgerald ACO .60
9 John Fletcher .60
10 Andre Giles .60
11 Chris Harkness .60
12 Major Harris 5.00
13 Luther Johnson .60
14 Marvin Mattox .60
15 Cedric McKinnon .60
16 Cleo Miller ACO .75
17 Tony Missick .60
18 Anthony Newsom .60
19 Phil Poirier .60
20 Alvin Powell .60
21 Ray Puryear .60
22 Dave Whinham CO .60
23 Brian Williams .60
24 Kennedy Wilson .60

1961 Titans Jay Publishing

The 12-card, 5" x 7" set features black and white photos of the New York Titans, an original AFL team that eventually became the New York Jets. The cards were originally packaged 12 to a pack and sold for 25 cents. The backs are blank.

NM/M
Complete Set (12): 75.00
Common Player: 5.00
1 Al Dorow 5.00
2 Larry Grantham 6.00
3 Mike Hagler 5.00
4 Mike Hudock 5.00
5 Bob Jewett 5.00
6 Jack Klotz 5.00
7 Don Maynard 20.00
8 John McMullan 5.00
9 Bob Mischak 5.00
10 Art Powell 10.00
11 Bob Reifsnyder 6.00
12 Sid Youngelman 6.00

1995 Tombstone Pizza

The 12-card, standard-size set was randomly inserted in specially marked Tombstone pizzas. The entire set was available for $1 and three Tombstone proof of purchase seals. The card fronts feature a color photo with the quarterback's last name along the top border in large print. The card backs include career statistics and a player quote.

NM/M
Complete Set (12): 20.00
Common Player: 1.00
1 Ken Anderson 1.00
2 Terry Bradshaw 4.00
3 Len Dawson 1.50
4 Dan Fouts 1.50
5 Bob Griese 2.00
6 Billy Kilmer 1.00
7 Joe Namath 6.00
8 Jim Plunkett 1.00
9 Ken Stabler 2.50
10 Bart Starr 2.00
11 Joe Theismann 1.00
12 Johnny Unitas 3.00

1995 Tombstone Pizza Autographs

The 12-card, standard-size set was a parallel to the base Classic Quarterback Series. Each quarterback signed 10,000 of his own cards.

NM/M
Complete Set (12): 300.00
Common Player: 15.00
1 Ken Anderson 15.00
2 Terry Bradshaw 45.00
3 Len Dawson 25.00
4 Dan Fouts 25.00
5 Bob Griese 25.00
6 Billy Kilmer 15.00
7 Joe Namath 60.00
8 Jim Plunkett 15.00
9 Ken Stabler 35.00
10 Bart Starr 35.00
11 Joe Theismann 15.00
12 Johnny Unitas 40.00

1996 Tombstone Pizza Quarterback Club Caps

The 14-card, 1-5/8" cap set was distributed by Tombstone Pizza and produced by Pinnacle. The caps were issued on a punch-out board (8-1/2" x 11"). A black plastic slammer was also included with the set.

NM/M
Complete Set (14): 15.00
Common Player: .50
1 Steve Young 1.00
2 Emmitt Smith 2.50
3 Junior Seau .50
4 Barry Sanders 1.25
5 Jerry Rice 1.25
6 Dan Marino 2.50
7 Jim Kelly .60
8 Michael Irvin .60
9 Brett Favre 1.25
10 Marshall Faulk 1.00
11 John Elway .75
12 Randall Cunningham .50
13 Drew Bledsoe 1.00
14 Troy Aikman 1.25

1950 Topps Felt Backs

These 7/8" x 1-7/16" cards feature several top collegiate players of the era on the front; a mug shot has the player's name, position and college under it. The card back is felt and includes his college's team pennant. Cards come with either brown or yellow backgrounds; yellow backgrounds are generally twice the listed values. The following cards come in both versions: 5, 6, 9, 13, 30, 35, 36, 39, 46, 51, 52, 54, 55, 57, 61, 66, 71, 75, 76, 78, 84, 86, 87, 92, and 100.

NM/M
Complete Set (100): 5,500
Common Player: 45.00
Lou Allen 65.00
Morris Bailey 65.00
George Bell 65.00
Lindy Berry 65.00
Mike Boldin 65.00
Bernie Botula 65.00
Bob Bowlby 65.00
Bob Bucher 65.00
Al Burnett 65.00
Don Burson 65.00
Paul Campbell 65.00
Herb Carey 65.00
Bimbo Cecconi 65.00
Bill Chauncey 65.00
Dick Clark 65.00
Tom Coleman 65.00
Billy Conn 65.00
John Cox 65.00
Lou Creekmur 65.00
Glen Davis 65.00
Warren Davis 65.00
Bob Deuber 65.00
Ray Dooney 65.00
Tom Dublinski 65.00
Jeff Fleischman 65.00
Jack Friedland 65.00
Bob Fuchs 65.00
Arnold Galiffa 65.00
Dick Gilman 65.00
Frank Gitschier 65.00
Gene Glick 65.00
Bill Gregus 65.00
Harold Hagan 65.00
Charles Hall 65.00
Leon Hart 85.00
Bob Hester 65.00
George Hughes 65.00
Levi Jackson 65.00
Jackie Jensen 125.00
Charlie Justice 100.00
Gary Kerkorian 65.00
Bernie Krueger 65.00
Bill Kuhn 65.00
Dean Laun 65.00
Chet Leach 65.00
Bobby Lee 65.00
Roger Lehew 65.00
Glenn Lippman 65.00
Melvin Lyle 65.00
Len Makowski 65.00
Al Malekoff 65.00
Jim Martin 80.00
Frank Mataya 65.00
Ray Matthews 45.00
Dick McKissack 65.00
Frank Miller 65.00
John Miller 65.00
Ed Modzelewski 65.00
Don Mouser 65.00
James Murphy 65.00
Ray Nagle 65.00
Leo Nomellini 140.00
James O'Day 65.00
Joe Paterno 375.00
Andy Pavich 65.00
Pete Perini 65.00
Jim Powers 65.00
Dave Rakestraw 65.00
Herb Rich 65.00
Fran Rogel 65.00
Darrell Royal 100.00
Steve Sawle 65.00
Nick Sebeck 65.00
Herb Seidell 65.00
Charles Shaw 65.00
Emil Sitko 65.00
Ed (Butch) Songin 65.00
Mariano Stalloni 65.00
Ernie Stautner 160.00
Don Stehley 65.00
Gil Stevenson 45.00
Bishop Strickland 65.00
Harry Szulborski 65.00
Wally Teninga Clayton 65.00
Tonnemaker 65.00
Deacon Dan Towler 80.00
Bert Turek 65.00
Harry Ulinski 65.00
Leon
Van Billingham 65.00
Langdon Viracola 65.00
Leo Wagner 65.00
Doak Walker 175.00
Jim Ward 65.00
Art Weiner 65.00
Dick Weiss 65.00
Froggie Williams 65.00
Robert (Red) Wilson 65.00
Roger (Red) Wilson 65.00
Carl Wren 65.00
Pete Zinaich 65.00

1951 Topps

Refered to as the 1951 Topps "Magic" set, this 1951 issue was Topps' first major football card set. The 75-card set featured the nation's top college players. The backs of the cards include a football trivia question with the answer concealed under a scratch-off area.

NM/M
Complete Set (75): 1,000
Common Player: 16.00
1 *Jimmy Monahan* 25.00
2 *Bill Wade* 45.00
3 Bill Reichardt 16.00
4 *Babe Parilli* 35.00
5 Billie Burkhalter 16.00
6 Ed Weber 16.00
7 Tom Scott 16.00
8 Frank Guthridge 16.00
9 John Karras 16.00
10 *Vic Janowicz* 100.00
11 Lloyd Hill 16.00
12 *Jim Weatherall* 20.00
13 Howard Hansen 16.00
14 Lou D'Achille 16.00
15 Johnny Turco 16.00
16 Jerrell Price 16.00
17 John Coatta 16.00
18 Bruce Patton 16.00
19 *Marion Campbell* 32.00
20 Blaine Earon 16.00
21 Dewey McConnell 16.00
22 Ray Beck 16.00
23 Jim Prewett 16.00
24 Bob Steele 16.00
25 Art Betts 16.00
26 Walt Trillhaase 16.00
27 Gil Bartosh 16.00
28 Bob Bestwick 16.00
29 Tom Rushing 16.00
30 *Bert Rechichar* 32.00
31 Bill Owens 16.00
32 Mike Goggins 16.00
33 John Petitbon 16.00
34 Byron Townsend 16.00
35 Ed Rotticci 16.00
36 Steve Wadiak 16.00
37 *Bobby Marlow* 17.00
38 Bill Fuchs 16.00
39 Ralph Staub 16.00
40 Bill Vesprini 16.00
41 Zack Jordan 16.00
42 Bob Smith 16.00
43 Charles Hanson 16.00
44 Glenn Smith 16.00
45 Armand Kitto 16.00
46 Vinnie Drake 16.00
47 Bill Putich 16.00
48 *George Young* 40.00
49 Don McRae 16.00
50 Frank Smith 16.00
51 Dick Hightower 16.00
52 Clyde Pickard 16.00
53 Bob Reynolds 16.00
54 Dick Gregory 16.00
55 Dale Samuels 16.00
56 Gale Galloway 16.00
57 Vic Pujo 16.00
58 Dave Waters 16.00
59 Joe Ernest 16.00
60 Elmer Costa 16.00
61 Nick Liotta 16.00
62 John Dottley 16.00
63 Hi Faubion 16.00
64 David Harr 16.00
65 Bill Matthews 16.00
66 Carroll McDonald 16.00
67 Dick Dewing 16.00
68 Joe Johnson 16.00
69 Arnold Burwitz 16.00
70 Ed Dobrowolski 16.00
71 Joe Dudeck 16.00
72 *John Bright* 20.00
73 Harold Loehlein 16.00
74 Lawrence Hairston 16.00
75 *Bob Carey* 20.00

1955 Topps All-American

This was the last Topps set to have college stars. The 100-card All-American set includes past and contemporary college stars. Cards measure 2-5/8" x 3-5/8" and feature a horizontal format. A number of the cards were short-printed in this set. Because the set featured many stars of the past, this set includes the only "regular issue" cards of several Hall of Famers (though technically these cards shouldn't qualify as "regular issue" cards since they weren't released during the player's career). Some of these rookie cards include Red Grange, Mel Hein, Jim Thorpe, Ernie Nevers, Bruiser Kinard, Ace parker, Don Hutson and Pete Henry. The only card issued of the Four Horsemen also appears in this set. The second (and last) "regular issue" cards of these players appear in this set: Knute Rockne, Ken Strong, Turk Edwards, and Alex Wojciechowicz. This set also includes the last cards of Bill Dudley, Otto Graham, Whizzer White (his second-year card, which actually should be his rookie card, since the 1954 Bowman card showed not Byron "Whizzer" White but Wilford White) and Sid Luckman. Two variations exist in the set. The backs on #14 Gaynell Tinsley and #21 Whizzer White were switched. The corrected versions are more plentiful than the errors. (Key: SP - short-printed)

NM/M
Complete Set (100): 3,500
Common Player: 25.00
SP Cards: 35.00
Glassine Pack (9): 2,000
Cello Pack (20): 3,200
1 *Herman Hickman* 225.00
2 John Kimbrough 25.00
3 Ed Weir 25.00
4 Ernie Pinckert 25.00
5 Bobby Grayson 25.00
6 *Niles Kinnick* 70.00
7 Andy Bershak 25.00
8 George Cafego 25.00
9 Tom Hamilton (SP) 35.00
10 Bill Dudley 30.00
11 Bobby Dodd (SP) 35.00
12 Otto Graham 175.00
13 Aaron Rosenberg 25.00
14 Gaynell "Gus" Tinsley (Whizzer White back) 25.00
14a Gaynell "Gus" Tinsley 25.00
15 Ed Kaw (SP) 35.00
16 Knute Rockne 325.00
17 Bob Reynolds 25.00
18 Pudge Heffelfinger (SP) 35.00
19 *Bruce A. Smith* 25.00
20 Sammy Baugh 200.00
21 *Whizzer White* (SP) (Gaynell Tinsley back) 70.00
21a Whizzer White (SP) 70.00
22 Brick Muller 25.00
23 *Dick Kazmaier* 20.00
24 Ken Strong 30.00
25 Casimir Myslinski (SP) 35.00
26 *Larry Kelley* (SP) 35.00
27 Harold "Red" Grange 350.00
28 *Mel Hein* (SP) 40.00
29 Leo Nomellini (SP) 50.00
30 Wes E. Fesler 25.00
31 *George Sauer Sr.* 20.00
32 Hank Foldberg 25.00
33 Bob Higgins 25.00
34 *Davey O'Brien* 25.00
35 *Tom Harmon* (SP) 50.00
36 Turk Edwards (SP) 40.00
37 Jim Thorpe 400.00
38 *Amos Alonzo Stagg* 60.00
39 Jerome Holland 25.00
40 Donn Moomaw 25.00
41 Joseph Alexander (SP) 35.00
42 J. Edward Tryon (SP) 35.00
43 George Savitsky 25.00
44 Ed Garbisch 25.00
45 Elmer Oliphant 25.00
46 Arnold Lassman 25.00
47 Bo McMillan 25.00
48 Ed Widseth 25.00
49 Don Zimmerman 25.00
50 Ken Kavanaugh 25.00
51 Duane Purvis (SP) 35.00
52 John Lujack 50.00
53 John F. Green 25.00
54 Edwin Dooley (SP) 35.00
55 Frank Merritt (SP) 35.00
56 *Ernie Nevers* 50.00
57 Vic Hanson (SP) 35.00
58 Ed Franco 25.00
59 *Doc Blanchard* 45.00
60 Dan Hill 25.00
61 Charles Brickley (SP) 35.00
62 Harry Newman 25.00
63 Charlie Justice 30.00
64 Benny Friedman 25.00
65 Joe Donchess (SP) 35.00
66 *Bruiser Kinard* 20.00
67 Frankie Albert 25.00
68 Four Horsemen (SP) 500.00
69 *Frank Sinkwich* 18.00
70 Bill Daddio 25.00
71 Bob Wilson 25.00
72 Chub Peabody 25.00
73 Hugh Governali 25.00
74 Gene McEver 25.00
75 Hugh Gallarneau 25.00
76 *Angelo Bertelli* 18.00
77 Bowden Wyatt (SP) 35.00
78 *Jay Berwanger* 20.00
79 Pug Lund 25.00
80 Bennie Oosterbaan 25.00
81 Cotton Warburton 25.00
82 Alex Wojciechowicz 25.00
83 Ted Coy (SP) 35.00
84 *Ace Parker* (SP) 40.00
85 Sid Luckman 85.00
86 Albie Booth (SP) 35.00
87 Adolph Schultz (SP) 35.00
88 Ralph G. Kercheval 25.00
89 Marshall Goldberg 25.00
90 Charlie O'Rourke 25.00
91 Bob Odell 25.00
92 Biggie Munn 25.00
93 Willie Heston (SP) 35.00
94 Joe Bernard (SP) 35.00
95 Red Cagle (SP) 35.00
96 Bill Hollenbeck (SP) 35.00
97 *Don Hutson* (SP) 250.00
98 *Beattie Feathers* (SP) 75.00
99 Don Witmire (SP) 35.00
100 *Wilbur "Fats" Henry* 225.00

1956 Topps

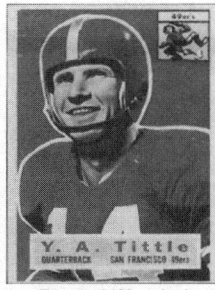

This set of 120 cards plus an unnumbered (and probably short-printed) checklist was oversized, measuring 2-5/8" x 3-5/8". This was Topps' first set to feature only professional football players. Most notable about this set was the inclusion of the first team cards by any company (cards of the Chicago Cardinals and Washington Redskins players, however, were short-printed). Rookies in this set include Hall of Famers Roosevelt Brown, Joe Schmidt, Bill George and Lenny Moore, plus Rosey Grier. Second-year cards in this set are those of Alan Ameche, Art Donovan and Mike McCormack.

NM/M
Complete Set (120): 1,500
Common Player: 5.00
SP Cards: 30.00
Team Cards: 17.00
Checklist: 400.00
Wax Pack Dark Gr. (6): 400.00
1 Jack Carson 75.00
2 Gordon Soltau 5.00
3 Frank Varrichione 5.00
4 Eddie Bell 5.00
5 *Alex Webster* 15.00
6 Norm Van Brocklin 30.00
7 Green Bay Packers 17.00
8 Lou Creekmur 5.00
9 Lou Groza 25.00
10 Tom Bienemann 30.00
11 George Blanda 50.00
12 Alan Ameche 10.00
13 Vic Janowicz 40.00
14 Dick Moegle 5.00
15 Fran Rogel 5.00
16 Harold Giancanelli 5.00
17 Emlen Tunnell 15.00
18 Tank Younger 5.00
19 Bill Howton 8.00
20 Jack Christiansen 15.00
21 Darrell Brewster 5.00
22 Chicago Cardinals 100.00
23 Ed Brown 5.00
24 Joe Campanella 5.00
25 Leon Heath 30.00
26 San Francisco 49ers 17.00
27 Dick Flanagan 5.00
28 Chuck Bednarik 25.00
29 Kyle Rote 15.00
30 Les Richter 5.00
31 Howard Ferguson 5.00
32 Dorne Dibble 5.00
33 Kenny Konz 5.00
34 Dave Mann 30.00
35 Rick Casares 5.00
36 Art Donovan 25.00
37 Chuck Drazenovich 30.00
38 Joe Arenas 5.00
39 Lynn Chandnois 5.00
40 Philadelphia Eagles 17.00
41 *Roosevelt Brown* 40.00
42 Tom Fears 15.00
43 Gary Knafelc 5.00
44 *Joe Schmidt* 45.00
45 Cleveland Browns 17.00
46 Len Teeuws 30.00
47 *Bill George* 35.00
48 Baltimore Colts 17.00
49 Eddie LeBaron 40.00
50 Hugh McElhenry 25.00
51 Ted Marchibroda 5.00
52 Adrian Burk 5.00
53 Frank Gifford 60.00
54 Charley Toogood 5.00
55 Tobin Rote 8.00
56 Bill Stits 5.00
57 Don Colo 5.00
58 Ollie Matson 75.00
59 Harlon Hill 5.00
60 *Lenny Moore* 85.00
61 Washington Redskins 85.00
62 Billy Wilson 5.00
63 Pittsburgh Steelers 17.00
64 Bob Pellegrini 5.00
65 Ken MacAfee 5.00
66 Willard Sherman 5.00
67 Roger Zatkoff 5.00
68 Dave Middleton 5.00
69 Ray Renfro 5.00
70 Don Stonesifer 30.00
71 *Stan Jones* 30.00
72 Jim Mutscheller 5.00
73 Volney Peters 30.00
74 Leo Nomellini 20.00
75 Ray Mathews 5.00
76 Dick Bielski 5.00
77 Charley Conerly 25.00

78 Elroy Hirsch 25.00
79 *Bill Forester* 8.00
80 Jim Doran 5.00
81 Fred Morrison 5.00
82 Jack Simmons 30.00
83 Bill McColl 5.00
84 Bert Rechichar 5.00
85 Joe Scudero 30.00
86 Y.A. Tittle 40.00
87 Ernie Stautner 20.00
88 Norm Willey 5.00
89 Bob Schnelker 5.00
90 Dan Towler 8.00
91 John Martinkovic 5.00
92 Detroit Lions 17.00
93 George Ratterman 5.00
94 Chuck Ulrich 30.00
95 Bobby Watkins 5.00
96 Buddy Young 5.00
97 Billy Wells 30.00
98 Bob Toneff 5.00
99 Bill McPeak 5.00
100 Bobby Thompason 5.00
101 *Roosevelt Grier* 30.00
102 Ron Waller 5.00
103 Bobby Dillon 5.00
104 Leon Hart 8.00
105 Mike McCormack 15.00
106 John Olszewski 30.00
107 Bill Wightkin 5.00
108 *George Shaw* 8.00
109 Dale Atkeson 30.00
110 Joe Perry 20.00
111 Dale Dodrill 5.00
112 Tom Scott 5.00
113 New York Giants 17.00
114 Los Angeles Rams 17.00
115 Al Carmichael 5.00
116 Bobby Layne 40.00
117 Ed Modzelewski 5.00
118 Lamar McHan 30.00
119 Chicago Bears 17.00
120 *Billy Vessels* 35.00

1957 Topps

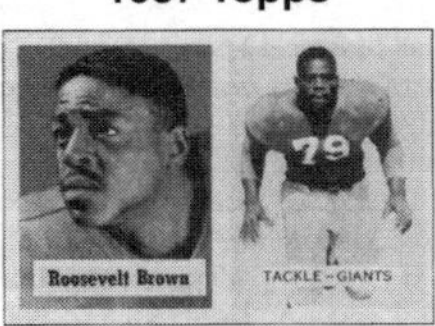

This 154-card set (not including the unnumbered checklist) has a horizontal format with two different pictures of the player on each side -- a head shot and a posed action shot. Issued in two series, the second series is more difficult to obtain than the first. Rookie cards in this set include Night Train Lane, Ray Berry, Earl Morrall, Bart Starr, John Unitas and Paul Hornung. Second-year cards include Roosevelt Brown, Pat Summerall, John Henry Johnson, Bob St. Clair, Lenny Moore and Len Ford (this is also his last regular-issued card). The final regular-issue card of Elroy Hirsch is also in this set. One variation does exist: The scarce card #58 of Willard Sherman has no team name on the front. The corrected version reads "Los Angeles Rams." It's believed that a number of the high series cards are short-printed, including Starr, Unitas and Hornung.

NM/M

Complete Set (155): 2,400
Common Player (1-88): 4.50
Common Player (89-154): 6.50
Checklist: 800.00
Series 1 Wax Pack (6): 400.00
Series 2 Wax Pack (6): 800.00
1 Eddie LeBaron 30.00
2 *Pete Retzlaff* 8.00
3 Mike McCormack 10.00
4 Lou Baldacci 4.50
5 Gino Marchetti 14.00
6 Leo Nomellini 13.00
7 Bobby Watkins 6.00
8 Dave Middleton 6.00
9 Bobby Dillon 6.00
10 Les Richter 6.00
11 Roosevelt Brown 13.00
12 *Lavern Torgeson* 6.00
13 Dick Bielski 4.50
14 Pat Summerall 13.00
15 *Jack Butler* 7.00
16 John Henry Johnson 13.00
17 Art Spinney 4.50
18 Bob St. Clair 10.00
19 Perry Jeter 4.50
20 Lou Creekmur 4.50
21 Dave Hanner 4.50
22 Norm Van Brocklin 25.00
23 *Don Chandler* 6.50
24 Al Dorow 4.50
25 Tom Scott 4.50
26 Ollie Matson 16.00
27 Fran Rogel 4.50
28 Lou Groza 20.00
29 Billy Vessels 4.50
30 Y.A. Tittle 32.50
31 George Blanda 45.00
32 Bobby Layne 30.00
33 Bill Howton 4.50
34 Bill Wade 4.50
35 Emlen Tunnell 12.00
36 Leo Elter 4.50
37 *Clarence Peaks* 6.00
38 Don Stonesifer 4.50
39 George Tarasovic 4.50
40 Darrell Brewster 4.50
41 Bert Rechichar 4.50
42 Billy Wilson 4.50
43 Ed Brown 4.50
44 Gene Gedman 4.50
45 Gary Knafelc 4.50
46 Elroy Hirsch 20.00
47 Don Heinrich 4.50
48 Gene Brito 4.50
49 Chuck Bednarik 15.00
50 Dave Mann 4.50
51 Bill McPeak 4.50
52 Kenny Konz 4.50
53 Alan Ameche 8.00
54 Gordon Soltau 4.50
55 Rick Casares 4.50
56 Charlie Ane 4.50
57 Al Carmichael 4.50
58A Willard Sherman ERR (no team name on front) 300.00
58B Willard Sherman COR (Rams) 5.00
59 Kyle Rote 8.00
60 Chuck Drazenovich 4.50
61 Bobby Walston 4.50
62 John Olszewski 4.50
63 Ray Mathews 4.50
64 Maurice Bassett 4.50
65 Art Donovan 20.00
66 Joe Arenas 4.50
67 Harlon Hill 4.50
68 Yale Lary 10.00
69 Bill Forester 4.50
70 Bob Boyd 4.50
71 Andy Robustelli 13.00
72 *Sam Baker* 7.00
73 Bob Pellegrini 4.50
74 Leo Sanford 4.50
75 Sid Watson 4.50
76 Ray Renfro 4.50
77 Carl Taseff 4.50
78 Clyde Conner 4.50
79 J.C. Caroline 4.50
80 *Howard Cassady* 10.00
81 Tobin Rote 6.00
82 Ron Waller 4.50
83 *Jim Patton* 7.00
84 Volney Peters 4.50
85 *Dick "Night Train" Lane* 40.00
86 Royce Womble 4.50
87 *Duane Putnam* 6.00
88 Frank Gifford 85.00
89 Steve Meilinger 6.50
90 Buck Lansford 6.50
91 Lindon Crow 6.50
92 Ernie Stautner 15.00
93 *Preston Carpenter* 10.00
94 *Raymond Berry* 125.00
95 Hugh McElhenny 25.00
96 Stan Jones 12.00
97 Dorne Dibble 6.50
98 Joe Scudero 6.50
99 Eddie Bell 6.50
100 Joe Childress 6.50
101 Elbert Nickel 6.50
102 Walt Michaels 6.50
103 Jim Mutscheller 6.50
104 *Earl Morrall* 50.00
105 Larry Strickland 6.50
106 Jack Christiansen 15.00
107 Fred Cone 6.50
108 *Bud McFadin* 10.00
109 Charley Conerly 25.00
110 Tom Runnels 6.50
111 Ken Keller 6.50
112 James Root 6.50
113 Ted Marchibroda 6.50
114 Don Paul 6.50
115 George Shaw 6.50
116 Dick Moegle 6.50
117 Don Bingham 6.50
118 Leon Hart 10.00
119 *Bart Starr* 450.00
120 Paul Miller 6.50
121 Alex Webster 10.00
122 Ray Wietecha 6.50
123 Johnny Carson 6.50
124 *Tommy McDonald* 14.00
125 *Jerry Tubbs* 10.00
126 Jack Scarbath 6.50
127 Ed Modzelewski 6.50
128 Lenny Moore 45.00
129 Joe Perry 25.00
130 Bill Wightkin 6.50
131 Jim Doran 6.50
132 Howard Ferguson 6.50
133 Tom Wilson 6.50
134 Dick James 6.50
135 Jimmy Harris 6.50
136 Chuck Ulrich 6.50
137 Lynn Chandnois 6.50
138 *Johnny Unitas* 450.00
139 Jim Ridlon 6.50
140 Zeke Bratkowski 10.00
141 Ray Krouse 6.50
142 John Martinkovic 6.50
143 Jim Cason 6.50
144 Ken MacAfee 6.50
145 *Sid Youngelman* 10.00
146 Paul Larson 6.50
147 Len Ford 15.00
148 Bob Toneff 6.50
149 Ronnie Knox 6.50
150 *Jim David* 10.00
151 *Paul Hornung* 450.00
152 Tank Younger 6.50
153 Bill Svoboda 6.50
154 Fred Morrison 40.00

1958 Topps

This 132-card set features an oval photo of the player on the front and a bright red background on the back. The card set also includes team cards, which had been missing from the previous year's set. Rookies here include Jim Brown and Sonny Jurgensen. Second-year cards are those of Bart Starr, Jim Ringo (his rookie was in '55), Bill George, and Ray Berry. This set also includes the last Topps card of Jack Christiansen.

NM/M

Complete Set (132): 1,300
Common Player: 2.00
Wax Pack (6): 475.00
1 *Gene Filipski* 14.00
2 Bobby Layne 25.00
3 Joe Schmidt 15.00
4 Bill Barnes 3.75
5 *Milt Plum* 8.00
6 Billie Howton 2.00
7 Howard Cassady 4.00
8 James Dooley 2.00
9 Cleveland Browns Team 6.50
10 Lenny Moore 15.00
11 Pete Brewster 3.75
12 Alan Ameche 5.00
13 Jim David 3.75
14 Jim Mutscheller 3.75
15 Andy Robustelli 9.00
16 Gino Marchetti 9.00
17 Ray Renfro 2.00
18 Yale Lary 8.50
19 Gary Glick 3.75
20 *Jon Arnett* 8.00
21 Bob Boyd 3.75
22 Johnny Unitas 115.00
23 Zeke Bratkowski 4.00
24 Sid Youngelman 3.75
25 Leo Elter 3.75
26 Ken Konz 3.75
27 Washington Redskins Team 7.00
28 C. Brettschneider 3.75
29 Chicago Bears Team 7.00
30 Alex Webster 4.00
31 Al Carmichael 3.75
32 Bobby Dillon 3.75
33 Steve Meilinger 3.75
34 Sam Baker 2.00
35 Chuck Bednarik 15.00
36 Vic Zucco 3.75
37 George Tarasovic 3.75
38 Bill Wade 3.75
39 Dick Stanfell 3.75
40 Jerry Norton 3.75
41 San Francisco 49ers Team 7.00
42 Emlen Tunnell 20.00
43 Jim Doran 3.75
44 Ted Marchibroda 3.75
45 Chet Hanulak 3.75
46 Dale Dodrill 3.75
47 John Carson 3.75
48 Dick Deschaine 3.75
49 Billy Wells 3.75
50 Larry Morris 3.75
51 Jack McClairen 3.75
52 Lou Groza 15.00
53 Rick Casares 3.75
54 Don Chandler 3.75
55 Duane Putnam 3.75
56 Gary Knafelc 3.75
57 Earl Morrall 10.00
58 *Ron Kramer* 4.00
59 Mike McCormack 8.00
60 Gern Nagler 3.75
61 New York Giants Team 7.00
62 *Jim Brown* 450.00
63 *Joe Marconi* 4.00
64 *R.C. Owens* 4.00
65 *Jimmy Carr* 4.00
66 Bart Starr 95.00
67 Tom Wilson 3.75
68 Lamar McHan 2.00
69 Chicago Cardinals Team 7.00
70 Jack Christiansen 8.00
71 *Don McElhenny* 4.00
72 Ron Waller 3.75
73 Frank Gifford 75.00
74 Bert Rechichar 3.75
75 John H. Johnson 10.00
76 Jack Butler 3.75
77 Frank Varrichione 3.75
78 Ray Mathews 3.75
79 Mary Matsuzak 3.75
80 Harlon Hill 3.75
81 Lou Creekmur 3.75
82 Woody Lewis 3.75
83 Don Heinrich 2.00
84 Charley Conerly 15.00
85 Los Angeles Rams Team 7.00
86 Y.A. Tittle 30.00
87 Bob Walston 3.75
88 Earl Putnam 3.75
89 Leo Nomellini 8.50
90 *Sonny Jurgensen* 100.00
91 Don Paul 3.75
92 Paige Cothren 3.75
93 Joe Perry 13.00
94 Tobin Rote 4.00
95 Billy Wilson 3.75
96 Green Bay Packers Team 7.00
97 Torgy Torgeson 3.75
98 Milt Davis 3.75
99 Larry Strickland 3.75
100 *Matt Hazeltine* 4.00
101 Walt Yowarski 3.75
102 Roosevelt Brown 8.00
103 Jim Ringo 8.00
104 Joe Krupa 3.75
105 Les Richter 3.75
106 Art Donovan 15.00
107 John Olszewski 3.75
108 Ken Keller 3.75
109 Philadelphia Eagles Team 5.50
110 Baltimore Colts Team 7.00
111 Dick Bielski 3.75
112 Eddie LeBaron 4.00
113 Gene Brito 3.75
114 *William Galimore* 12.00
115 Detroit Lions Team 7.00
116 Pittsburgh Steelers Team 7.00
117 L.G. Dupre 3.75
118 Babe Parilli 4.00
119 Bill George 8.00
120 Raymond Berry 30.00
121 Jim Podoley 3.75
122 Hugh McElhenny 15.00
123 Ed Brown 3.75
124 Dicky Moegle 3.75
125 Tom Scott 3.75
126 Tom McDonald 4.00
127 Ollie Matson 15.00
128 Preston Carpenter 3.75
129 George Blanda 35.00
130 Gordy Soltau 3.75
131 *Dick Nolan* 4.00
132 *Don Bosseler* 16.00

1959 Topps

This 176-card set, featuring alternating blue and red letters for player names, was issued in two series, with the first being more valuable than the second. Team cards also included checklists on the back of each, and pennant cards were included and numbered as part of the set. This set showcases the rookie cards of Max McGee, Sam Huff, Alex Karras, John David Crow, Jerry Kramer, Jim Parker, Bobby Mitchell, and Jim Taylor (actually not the HOFer; see below). Second-year cards in the set are those of Paul Hornung and Jim Brown. Card #155, Jim Taylor, does not show the HOF running back for the Packers, as the card reads; instead, it shows Chicago Cardinal linebacker Jim Taylor. This mistake was repeated the following year, meaning a card actually depicting Taylor did not appear until 1961.

NM/M

Complete Set (176): 1,000
Common Player (1-88): 2.50
Common Player (89-176): 2.00
Team Cards: 5.00
Series 1 Wax Pack (6): 350.00
Series 2 Wax Pack (6): 300.00
1 Johnny Unitas 100.00
2 Gene Brito 2.50
3 Detroit Lions Team Card 5.00
4 *Max McGee* 20.00
5 Hugh McElhenny 12.00
6 Joe Schmidt 8.00
7 Kyle Rote 5.00
8 Clarence Peaks 2.50
9 Pittsburgh Steelers Pennant Card 5.00
10 Jim Brown 140.00
11 Ray Mathews 2.50
12 Bobby Dillon 2.50
13 Joe Childress 2.50
14 Terry Barr 2.50
15 *Del Shofner* 4.50
16 Bob Pellegrini 2.50
17 Baltimore Colts Team Card 5.00
18 Preston Carpenter 2.50
19 Leo Nomellini 7.00
20 Frank Gifford 30.00
21 Charlie Ane 2.50
22 Jack Butler 2.50
23 Bart Starr 55.00
24 Chicago Cardinals Pennant Card 2.50
25 Bill Barnes 2.50
26 Walt Michaels 2.00
27 Clyde Conner 2.50
28 Paige Cothren 2.50
29 Roosevelt Grier 5.00
30 Alan Ameche 5.00
31 Philadelphia Eagles Team Card 5.00
32 Dick Nolan 2.00
33 R.C. Owens 2.50
34 Dale Dodrill 2.50
35 Gene Gedman 2.50
36 *Gene Lipscomb* 8.00
37 Ray Renfro 2.50
38 Cleveland Brown Pennant Card 2.50
39 Bill Forester 2.50
40 Bobby Layne 25.00
41 Pat Summerall 8.50
42 Jerry Mertens 2.50
43 Steve Myhra 2.50
44 John Henry Johnson 7.00
45 Woody Lewis 2.50
46 Green Bay Packers Team Card 5.00
47 Don Owens 2.50
48 Ed Beatty 2.50
49 Don Chandler 2.00
50 Ollie Matson 12.00
51 *Sam Huff* 40.00
52 Tom Miner 2.50
53 New York Giants Pennant Card 2.50
54 Kenny Konz 2.50
55 Raymond Berry 15.00
56 Howard Ferguson 2.50
57 Chuck Ulrich 2.50
58 Bob St. Clair 5.00
59 *Don Burroughs* 3.00
60 Lou Groza 15.00
61 San Francisco 49ers Team Card 5.00
62 Andy Nelson 2.50
63 Hal Bradley 2.50
64 Dave Hanner 2.50
65 Chuck Connerly 11.00
66 Gene Cronin 2.50
67 Duane Putnam 2.50
68 Baltimore Colts Pennant Card 2.50
69 Ernie Stautner 8.00
70 Jon Arnett 3.00
71 Ken Panfil 2.50
72 Matt Hazeltine 2.50
73 Harley Sewell 2.50
74 Mike McCormack 5.00
75 Jim Ringo 5.00
76 Los Angeles Rams Team Card 5.00
77 *Bob Gain* 3.00
78 Buzz Nutter 2.50
79 Jerry Norton 2.50
80 Joe Perry 12.00
81 Carl Brettschneider 2.50
82 Paul Hornung 60.00
83 Philadelphia Eagles Pennant Card 2.50
84 Les Richter 2.00
85 Howard Cassady 2.00
86 Art Donovan 8.00
87 Jim Patton 2.50
88 Pete Retzlaff 3.50
89 Jim Mutscheller 2.00
90 Zeke Bratkowski 3.00
91 Washington Redskins Team Card 5.00
92 Art Hunter 2.00
93 Gern Nagler 2.00
94 Chuck Weber 2.00
95 *Lew Carpenter* 2.50
96 Stan Jones 5.00
97 Ralph Guglielmi 2.00
98 Green Bay Packer Pennant Card 2.50
99 Ray Wietecha 2.00
100 Lenny Moore 10.00
101 *Jim Ray Smith* 3.00
102 *Abe Woodson* 5.00
103 *Alex Karras* 40.00
104 Chicago Bears Team Card 5.00
105 *Johnny Crow* 10.00
106 *Joe Fortunato* 5.00
107 Babe Parilli 3.00
108 Proverb Jacobs 2.00
109 Gino Marchetti 8.00
110 Bill Wade 2.00
111 San Francisco 49ers Pennant Card 2.50
112 Karl Rubke 2.00
113 Dave Middleton 2.00
114 Roosevelt Brown 5.00
115 John Olszewski 2.00
116 *Jerry Kramer* 25.00
117 *King Hill* 3.50
118 Chicago Cardinals Team Card 5.00
119 Frank Varrichione 2.00
120 Rick Casares 2.00
121 George Strugar 2.00
122 *Bill Glass* 2.50
123 Don Bosseler 2.50
124 John Reger 2.50
125 *Jim Ninowski* 3.00
126 Los Angeles Rams Pennant Card 2.50
127 Willard Sherman 2.00
128 Bob Schnelker 2.00
129 Ollie Spencer 2.00
130 Y.A. Tittle 25.00
131 Yale Lary 6.00
132 *Jim Parker* 20.00
133 New York Giants Team Card 5.00
134 Jim Schrader 2.00
135 M.C. Reynolds 2.00
136 Mike Sandusky 2.00
137 Ed Brown 2.00
138 Al Barry 2.00
139 Detroit Lions Pennant Card 2.50
140 *Bobby Mitchell* 35.00
141 Larry Morris 2.00
142 *Jim Phillips* 3.00
143 Jim David 2.00
144 Joe Krupa 2.00
145 Willie Galimore 3.00
146 Pittsburgh Steelers Team Card 5.00
147 Andy Robustelli 7.50
148 Bill Wilson 2.00
149 Leo Sanford 2.00
150 Eddie LeBaron 5.00
151 Bill McColl 2.00
152 Buck Lansford 2.00
153 Chicago Bears Pennant Card 2.50
154 Leo Sugar 2.00
155 *Jim Taylor* 18.00
156 Lindon Crow 2.00
157 Jack McClairen 2.00
158 *Vince Costello* 2.50
159 Stan Wallace 2.00
160 *Mel Triplett* 3.00
161 Cleveland Browns Team Card 5.00
162 Dan Currie 2.00
163 L.G. Dupre 2.00
164 John Morrow 2.00
165 Jim Podoley 2.00
166 *Bruce Bosley* 2.50
167 Harlon Hill 2.00
168 Washington Redskins Pennant Card 2.50
169 Junior Wren 2.00
170 Tobin Rote 2.50
171 Art Spinney 2.00
172 Chuck Drazenovich 2.00
173 *Bobby Joe Conrad* 5.00
174 Jesse Richardson 2.00
175 Sam Baker 2.00
176 *Tom Tracy* 8.00

1960 Topps

This 132-card set by Topps, featuring NFL players only (Fleer picked up teams from the AFL in its 1960 set), showcased the inclusion of the expansion Dallas Cowboys. Cards are again numbered alphabetically according to city name. Card backs had a "Football Funnies" quiz which revealed the answer underneath a scratch-off area. This set marks the rookie cards of HOFer Forrest Gregg, future announcer Tom Brookshier, and former Jets coach Joe Walton. Second-year cards in the set include Jim Parker, Doug Atkins (his rookie card was six years prior to his second-year card), Bobby Mitchell, and Sam Huff. There are three errors in the set. Card #52, Jim Taylor, shows not the HOF running back of the Packers, as advertised; it again shows Cardinals linebacker Jim Taylor. This mistake was made in the 1959 set as well. The other errors are reversed negatives; on the card of #97, Frank Varrichione, and on card #20, Doug Atkins.

NM/M

Complete Set (132): 625.00
Common Player: 1.75
Team Cards: 5.00
Wax Pack (6): 400.00
1 Johnny Unitas 80.00
2 Alan Ameche 5.00
3 Lenny Moore 7.00
4 Raymond Berry 7.00
5 Jim Parker 7.00
6 George Preas 1.75
7 Art Spinney 1.75
8 *Bill Pellington* 2.50
9 *Johnny Sample* 2.50
10 Gene Lipscomb 3.50
11 Baltimore Colts Team Card (Checklist 67-132) 5.00
12 Ed Brown 1.75
13 Rick Casares 1.75
14 Willie Galimore 1.75
15 Jim Dooley 1.75
16 Harlon Hill 1.75
17 Stan Jones 4.50
18 Bill George 4.50
19 *Erich Barnes* 3.00
20 Doug Atkins 5.50
21 Chicago Bears Team Card (Checklist 1-66) 5.00
22 Milt Plum 2.50
23 Jim Brown 100.00
24 Sam Baker 1.75
25 Bobby Mitchell 10.00
26 Ray Renfro 1.75
27 Billy Howton 1.75
28 Jim Ray Smith 1.75
29 *Jim Shofner* 3.50
30 Bob Gain 1.75
31 Cleveland Browns Team Card (Checklist 1-66) 5.00

32 Don Heinrich 1.75
33 Ed Modzelewski 1.75
34 Fred Cone 1.75
35 L.G. Dupre 1.75
36 Dick Bielski 1.75
37 Charlie Ane 1.75
38 Jerry Tubbs 1.75
39 Doyle Nix 1.75
40 Ray Krouse 1.75
41 Earl Morrall 5.00
42 Hopalong Cassady 1.75
43 Dave Middleton 1.75
44 *Jim Gibbons* 2.50
45 Darris McCord 1.75
46 Joe Schmidt 5.50
47 Terry Barr 1.75
48 Yale Lary 5.00
49 Gil Mains 1.75
50 Detroit Lions Team Card (Checklist 1-66) 5.00
51 Bart Starr 40.00
52 Jim Taylor 8.00
53 Lew Carpenter 1.75
54 Paul Hornung 35.00
55 Max McGee 3.00
56 *Forrest Gregg* 28.00
57 Jim Ringo 5.50
58 Bill Forester 1.75
59 Dave Hanner 1.75
60 Green Bay Packers Team Card (Checklist 67-132) 5.00
61 Bill Wade 1.75
62 *Frank Ryan* 8.00
63 Ollie Matson 8.00
64 Jon Arnett 1.75
65 Del Shofner 1.75
66 Jim Phillips 1.75
67 Art Hunter 1.75
68 Les Richter 1.75
69 *Lou Michaels* 3.00
70 John Baker 1.75
71 Los Angeles Rams Team Card (Checklist 1-66) 5.00
72 Charley Conerly 10.00
73 Mel Triplett 1.75
74 Frank Gifford 45.00
75 Alex Webster 1.75
76 Bob Schnelker 1.75
77 Pat Summerall 7.00
78 Roosevelt Brown 5.50
79 Jimmy Patton 1.75
80 Sam Huff 15.00
81 Andy Robustelli 6.00
82 New York Giants Team Card (Checklist 1-66) 5.00
83 Clarence Peaks 1.75
84 Bill Barnes 1.75
85 Pete Retzlaff 1.75
86 Bobby Walston 1.75
87 Chuck Bednarik 7.00
88 Bob Pellagrini 1.75
89 *Tom Brookshier* 6.00
90 Marion Campbell 1.75
91 Jesse Richardson 1.75
92 Philadelphia Eagles Team Card (Checklist 1-66) 5.00
93 Bobby Layne 23.00
94 John Henry Johnson 5.50
95 Tom Tracy 1.75
96 Preston Carpenter 1.75
97 Frank Varrichione 1.75
98 John Nisby 1.75
99 Dean Derby 1.75
100 George Tarasovic 1.75
101 Ernie Stautner 6.00
102 Pittsburgh Steelers Team Card (Checklist 67-132) 5.00
103 King Hill 1.75
104 Mal Hammack 1.75
105 John Crow 3.50
106 Bobby Joe Conrad 1.75
107 Woodley Lewis 1.75
108 Don Gillis 1.75
109 Carl Brettschneider 1.75
110 Leo Sugar 1.75
111 Frank Fuller 1.75
112 St. Louis Cardinals Team Card (Checklist 67-132) 5.00
113 Y.A. Tittle 22.00
114 Joe Perry 7.00
115 *J.D. Smith* 3.00
116 Hugh McElhenny 4.00
117 Billy Wilson 1.75
118 Bob St. Clair 3.50
119 Matt Hazeltine 1.75
120 Abe Woodson 1.75
121 Leo Nomellini 5.00
122 San Francisco 49ers Team Card (Checklist 67-132) 5.00
123 Ralph Gugliemi 1.75
124 Don Bosseler 1.75
125 Johnny Olszewski 1.75
126 Bill Anderson 1.75
127 *Joe Walton* 3.50
128 Jim Schrader 1.75
129 Ralph Felton 1.75
130 Gary Glick 1.75
131 Bob Toneff 1.75
132 Washington Redskins 25.00

1960 Topps Team Emblem Stickers

One of each of these 33 metallic inserts was included in a wax pack of 1960 Topps football cards. The team emblem stickers are unnumbered and included NFL teams (1-13) and college teams (14-33). This was Topps' first football insert set. Future Topps inserts in the early '60s would also include college teams. These sticker fronts are bordered in black and show either a blue, silver or gold background. The stickers measure about 2" x 3".

NM/M
Complete Set (33): 175.00
Common Pro Team: 6.00
Common College Team: 4.50
(1) Baltimore Colts 6.00
(2) Chicago Bears 6.00
(3) Cleveland Browns 6.00
(4) Dallas Cowboys 8.00
(5) Detroit Lions 8.00
(6) Green Bay Packers 6.00
(7) Los Angeles Rams 6.00
(8) New York Giants 6.00
(9) Philadelphia Eagles 6.00
(10) Pittsburgh Steelers 6.00
(11) St. Louis Cardinals 6.00
(12) San Francisco 49ers 6.00
(13) Washington Redskins 8.00
(14) Air Force 4.50
(15) Army 4.50
(16) California 4.50
(17) Dartmouth 4.50
(18) Duke 4.50
(19) LSU 4.50
(20) Michigan 4.50
(21) Mississippi 4.50
(22) Navy 4.50
(23) Notre Dame 15.00
(24) SMU 4.50
(25) USC 4.50
(26) Syracuse 4.50
(27) Tennessee 4.50
(28) Texas 4.50
(29) UCLA 4.50
(30) Minnesota 4.50
(31) Washington 4.50
(32) Wisconsin 4.50
(33) Yale 4.50

1961 Topps

This set of 198 cards was the last full Topps set to include both AFL players and NFL players. The AFL segment of the set (133-197) does not include team checklists. Cards are similar to the 1961 Topps baseball issue and feature a ruboff game on the back. The set is once again numbered in order of teams - alphabetically by city. Rookies in this set include John Brodie, Don Maynard, Jim Otto and Tom Flores. Second-year cards include Alex Karras, Henry Jordan, Sonny Jurgensen (three years after his rookie card debuted), Abner Haynes, Jack Kemp and Ron Mix. This set included the last regular-issue cards of Alan Ameche, Charley Conerly, Kyle Rote, Chuck Bednarik and Tom Brookshier. Card #41 could actually be considered Packer running back Jim Taylor's rookie card. His rookie and second- year cards Topps printed in 1959 and 1960 actually depicted Cardinal linebacker Jim Taylor instead of HOFer Jim Taylor.

NM/M
Complete Set (198): 1,100
Common Player: 2.00
Series 1 Wax Pack (5): 410.00
Series 2 Wax Pack (5): 425.00
1 Johnny Unitas 90.00
2 Lenny Moore 7.00
3 Alan Ameche 4.00
4 Raymond Berry 7.00
5 Jim Mutscheller 2.00
6 Jim Parker 4.50
7 Gino Marchetti 5.50
8 Gene Lipscomb 3.00
9 Baltimore Colts 4.00
10 Bill Wade 2.00
11 *Johnny Morris* 6.00
12 Rick Casares 2.00
13 Harlon Hill 2.00
14 Stan Jones 4.50
15 Doug Atkins 5.00
16 Bill George 4.50
17 J.C. Caroline 2.00
18 Chicago Bears 4.00
19 Eddie LeBaron Big Time Football comes to Texas 3.25
20 Eddie LeBaron 3.00
21 Don McElhenny 2.00
22 L.G. Dupre 2.00
23 Jim Doran 2.00
24 Billy Howton 2.00
25 Buzz Guy 2.00
26 *Jack Patera* 2.00
27 Tom Frankauser 2.00
28 Dallas Cowboys 10.00
29 Jim Ninowski 2.00
30 *Dan Lewis* 2.00
31 *Nick Pietrosante* 3.00
32 *Gail Cogdill* 2.00
33 Jim Gibbons 2.00
34 Jim Martin 2.00
35 Alex Karras 20.00
36 Joe Schmidt 5.00
37 Detroit Lions 4.00
38 Paul Hornung Set Scoring Record 10.00
39 Bart Starr 40.00
40 Paul Hornung 28.00
41 Jim Taylor 24.00
42 Max McGee 2.00
43 *Boyd Dowler* 5.00
44 Jim Ringo 4.25
45 *Henry Jordan* 15.00
46 Bill Forester 2.00
47 Green Bay Packers 4.00
48 Frank Ryan 2.00
49 Jon Arnett 2.00
50 Ollie Matson 6.50
51 Jim Phillips 2.00
52 Del Shofner 2.00
53 Art Hunter 2.00
54 Gene Brito 2.00
55 Lindon Crow 2.00
56 Los Angeles Rams 4.00
57 Johnny Unitas 25-TD Passes 15.00
58 Y.A. Tittle 22.00
59 *John Brodie* 40.00
60 J.D. Smith 2.00
61 R.C. Owens 2.00
62 Clyde Conner 2.00
63 Bob St. Clair 4.00
64 Leo Nomellini 5.00
65 Abe Woodson 2.00
66 San Francisco 49ers 4.00
67 Checklist 50.00
68 Milt Plum 2.00
69 Ray Renfro 2.00
70 Bobby Mitchell 7.00
71 Jim Brown 100.00
72 Mike McCormack 4.00
73 Jim Ray Smith 2.00
74 Sam Baker 2.00
75 Walt Michaels 2.00
76 Cleveland Browns 4.00
77 Jim Brown IA 35.00
78 George Shaw 2.00
79 Hugh McElhenny 6.00
80 Clancy Osborne 2.00
81 Dave Middleton 2.00
82 Frank Youso 2.00
83 Don Joyce 2.00
84 Ed Culpepper 2.00
85 Charley Conerly 8.00
86 Mel Triplett 2.00
87 Kyle Rote 4.00
88 Roosevelt Brown 4.50
89 Ray Wietecha 2.00
90 Andy Robustelli 6.00
91 Sam Huff 7.50
92 Jim Patton 2.00
93 New York Giants 4.00
94 Chas Conerly Leads Giants for 13th Year 5.00
95 Sonny Jurgensen 20.00
96 Tommy McDonald 2.00
97 Billy Barnes 2.00
98 Bobby Waltson 2.00
99 Pete Retzlaff 2.00
100 Jim McCusker 2.00
101 Chuck Bednarik 7.00
102 Tom Brookshier 3.00
103 Philadelphia Eagles 4.00
104 Bobby Layne 20.00
105 John Henry Johnson 5.00
106 Tom Tracy 2.00
107 *Buddy Dial* 3.00
108 *Jim Orr* 3.50
109 Mike Sandusky 2.00
110 John Reger 2.00
111 Junior Wren 2.00
112 Pittsburgh Steelers 4.00
113 Bobby Layne Sets New Passing Record 7.00
114 John Roach 2.00
115 *Sam Etcheverry* 2.00
116 John David Crow 3.00
117 Mal Hammack 2.00
118 *Sonny Randle* 2.00
119 Leo Sugar 2.00
120 Jerry Norton 2.00
121 St. Louis Cardinals 4.00
122 Checklist 35.00
123 Ralph Guglielmi 2.00
124 Dick James 2.00
125 Don Bosseler 2.00
126 Joe Walton 2.00
127 Bill Anderson 2.00
128 *Vince Promuto* 2.25
129 Bob Toneff 2.00
130 John Paluck 2.00
131 Washington Redskins 4.00
132 Milt Plum Wins NFL Passing Title 3.00
133 Abner Haynes 3.50
134 Mel Branch 2.00
135 Jerry Cornelison 2.00
136 Bill Krisher 2.00
137 Paul Miller 2.00
138 Jack Spikes 2.00
139 *Johnny Robinson* 6.00
140 *Cotton Davidson* 4.00
141 Dave Smith 2.00
142 Bill Groman 2.00
143 Rich Michael 2.00
144 Mike Dukes 2.00
145 George Blanda 26.00
146 Billy Cannon 4.00
147 Dennit Morris 2.00
148 Jacky Lee 2.00
149 Al Dorrow 2.00
150 *Don Maynard* 50.00
151 *Art Powell* 6.00
152 Sid Youngelman 2.00
153 Bob Mischak 2.00
154 Larry Grantham 2.00
155 Tom Saidock 2.00
156 Roger Donnahoo 2.00
157 Lavern Torczon 2.00
158 *Archie Matsos* 2.00
159 Elbert Dubenion 3.00
160 *Wray Carlton* 2.00
161 Rich McCabe 2.00
162 Ken Rice 2.00
163 Art Baker 2.00
164 Tom Rychiec 2.00
165 Mack Yoho 2.00
166 Jack Kemp 150.00
167 Paul Lowe 3.25
168 Ron Mix 9.00
169 Paul Maguire 3.00
170 Volney Peters 2.00
171 Ernie Wright 2.00
172 Ron Nery 2.00
173 *Dave Kocourek* 2.00
174 Jim Colclough 2.00
175 Babe Parilli 3.25
176 Billy Lott 2.00
177 Fred Bruney 2.00
178 Ross O'Hanley 2.00
179 Walt Cudzik 2.00
180 Charles Leo 2.00
181 Bob Dee 2.00
182 *Jim Otto* 40.00
183 Eddie Macon 2.00
184 Dick Christy 2.00
185 Alan Miller 2.00
186 *Tom Flores* 25.00
187 Joe Cannavino 2.00
188 Don Manoukian 2.00
189 Bob Coolbaugh 2.00
190 *Lionel Taylor* 7.00
191 Bud McFadin 2.00
192 Goose Gonsoulin 2.00
193 Frank Tripucka 2.75
194 *Gene Mingo* 3.00
195 Eldon Danenhauer 2.00
196 Bob McNamara 2.00
197 Dave Rolle 2.00
198 Checklist 80.00

1961 Topps Stickers

This set of 48 stickers was included one per pack in the 1961 Topps football set. Stickers are unnumbered and are grouped according to NFL (1-15), AFL (16-24), and colleges (25-48). The stickers were issued with tabs that could be peeled off. For the sticker to be considered Mint, tabs would have to be intact.

NM/M
Complete Set (48): 175.00
Common Pro Team: 6.00
Common College Team: 3.50
(1) NFL Emblem 6.00
(2) Baltimore Colts 6.00
(3) Chicago Bears 6.00
(4) Cleveland Browns 6.00
(5) Dallas Cowboys 8.00
(6) Detroit Lions 6.00
(7) Green Bay Packers 8.00
(8) Los Angeles Rams 6.00
(9) Minnesota Vikings 6.00
(10) New York Giants 6.00
(11) Philadelphia Eagles 6.00
(12) Pittsburgh Steelers 6.00
(13) San Francisco 49ers 6.00
(14) St. Louis Cardinals 6.00
(15) Washington Redskins 8.00
(16) AFL Emblem 8.00
(17) Boston Patriots 6.00
(18) Buffalo Bills 8.00
(19) Dallas Texans 8.00
(20) Denver Broncos 6.00
(21) Houston Oilers 6.00
(22) Oakland Raiders 8.00
(23) San Diego Chargers 6.00
(24) Titans of New York 6.00
(25) Air Force 3.50
(26) Alabama 6.00
(27) Arkansas 3.50
(28) Army 5.00
(29) Baylor 3.50
(30) California 3.50
(31) Georgia Tech 3.50
(32) Illinois 3.50
(33) Kansas 3.50
(34) Kentucky 3.50
(35) Miami 3.50
(36) Michigan 6.00
(37) Missouri 3.50
(38) Navy 5.00
(39) Oregon 3.50
(40) Penn State 6.00
(41) Pittsburgh 3.50
(42) Purdue 3.50
(43) USC 6.00
(44) Stanford 3.50
(45) TCU 3.50
(46) Virginia 3.50
(47) Washington 3.50
(48) Washington State 3.50

1962 Topps

This 176-card set is one of the decade's toughest to complete in mint condition because of the easily-scuffed black borders. Like many of the Topps sets of this era, a good number of the cards in the set are short-printed, probably because the number of cards in the set didn't exactly match the amount that would fit onto printing sheets. Cards are again grouped by teams, which are listed in alphabetical order by city. This was the first time in five years Topps tried a horizontal format; Topps would try it again in 1966. Rookies in this set include Mike Ditka, Ernie Davis (his only regular-issue card), Roman Gabriel, Fran Tarkenton, Bill Kilmer and Norm Snead. Second-year cards in the set include Don Meredith (his first Topps card) and John Brodie. Last-year cards in the set include Max McGee and Hall of Famers Joe Perry, Ollie Matson and Bobby Layne. The last Topps cards of Frank Gifford and Andy Robustelli are also included. (Key: SP - short printed)

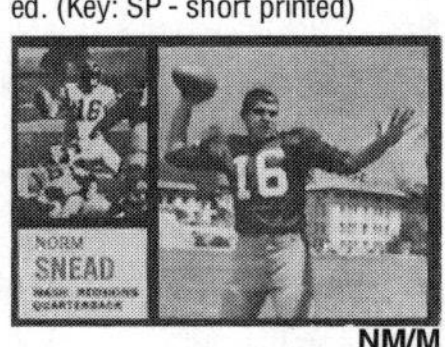

NM/M
Complete Set (176): 1,700
Common Player: 3.50
SP Cards: 8.00
Wax Pack (FB Bucks): 360.00
Wax Pack (Pro Stars): 385.00
1 Johnny Unitas 125.00
2 Lenny Moore 9.00
3 *Alex Hawkins* (SP) 8.00
4 Joe Perry 9.00
5 Raymond Berry (SP) 20.00
6 Steve Myhra 3.50
7 Tom Gilburg (SP) 7.50
8 Gino Marchetti 7.50
9 Bill Pellington 3.50
10 Andy Nelson 3.50
11 Wendell Harris (SP) 7.50
12 Baltimore Colts Team 3.50
13 Billy Wade (SP) 7.50
14 Willie Galimore 3.50
15 Johnny Morris (SP) 7.50
16 Rick Casares 3.50
17 *Mike Ditka* 225.00
18 Stan Jones 4.50
19 Roger LeClerc 3.50
20 Angelo Coia 3.50
21 Doug Atkins 7.50
22 Bill George 5.00
23 *Richie Petitbon* 5.00
24 Ron Bull (SP) 8.00
25 Chicago Bears Team 3.50
26 Howard Cassady 3.50
27 Ray Renfro (SP) 7.50
28 Jim Brown 150.00
29 Rick Kreitling 3.50
30 Jim Ray Smith 3.50
31 John Morrow 3.50
32 Lou Groza 12.00
33 Bob Gain 3.50
34 Bernie Parrish 3.50
35 Jim Shofner 3.50
36 *Ernie Davis* (SP) 110.00
37 Cleveland Browns Team 3.50
38 Eddie LeBaron 3.50
39 Don Meredith (SP) 90.00
40 J.W. Lockett (SP) 7.50
41 *Don Perkins* 7.50
42 Billy Howton 3.50
43 Dick Bielski 3.50
44 *Mike Connelly* 3.00
45 Jerry Tubbs (SP) 7.50
46 Don Bishop (SP) 7.50
47 Dick Moegle 3.50
48 Bobby Plummer (SP) 7.50
49 Dallas Cowboys Team 10.00
50 Milt Plum 3.50
51 Dan Lewis 3.50
52 Nick Pietrosante (SP) 7.50
53 Gail Cogdill 3.50
54 Jim Gibbons 3.50
55 Jim Martin 3.50
56 Yale Lary 7.50
57 Darris McCord 3.50
58 Alex Karras 15.00
59 Joe Schmidt 7.50
60 Dick "Night Train" Lane 6.00
61 John Lomakoski (SP) 7.50
62 Detroit Lions Team (SP) 15.00
63 Bart Starr (SP) 70.00
64 Paul Hornung (SP) 50.00
65 Tom Moore (SP) 7.50
66 Jim Taylor (SP) 30.00
67 Max McGee (SP) 7.50
68 Jim Ringo (SP) 15.00
69 *Fuzzy Thurston* (SP) 15.00
70 Forrest Gregg 7.50
71 Boyd Dowler 3.50
72 Henry Jordan (SP) 6.50
73 Bill Forester (SP) 7.50
74 Earl Gros (SP) 7.50
75 Green Bay Packers (SP) 20.00
76 Checklist (SP) 80.00
77 Zeke Bratkowski (SP) 7.50
78 Jon Arnett (SP) 7.50
79 Ollie Matson (SP) 20.00
80 Dick Bass (SP) 7.50
81 Jim Phillips 3.50
82 *Carroll Dale* 4.00
83 Frank Varrichione 3.50
84 Art Hunter 3.50
85 *Danny Villanueva* 3.00
86 Les Richter (SP) 7.50
87 Lindon Crow 3.50
88 *Roman Gabriel* (SP) 50.00
89 Los Angeles Rams (SP) 15.00
90 *Fran Tarkenton* (SP) 200.00
91 Jerry Reichow (SP) 7.50
92 Hugh McElhenny (SP) 20.00
93 Mel Triplett (SP) 7.50
94 *Tommy Mason* (SP) 7.00
95 Dave Middleton (SP) 7.50
96 Frank Youso (SP) 7.50
97 Mike Mercer (SP) 7.50
98 Rip Hawkins (SP) 7.50
99 Cliff Livingston (SP) 7.50
100 *Roy Winston* (SP) 7.00
101 Minnesota Vikings Team (SP) 20.00
102 Y.A. Tittle 30.00
103 Joe Walton 3.50
104 Frank Gifford 40.00
105 Alex Webster 3.50
106 Del Shofner 3.50
107 Don Chandler 3.50
108 Andy Robustelli 7.50
109 Jim Katcavage 3.50
110 Sam Huff (SP) 20.00
111 Erich Barnes 3.50
112 Jimmy Patton 3.50
113 Jerry Hillebrand (SP) 7.50
114 New York Giants Team 3.50
115 Sonny Jurgensen 20.00
116 Tommy McDonald 3.50
117 Ted Dean (SP) 7.50
118 Clarence Peaks 3.50
119 Bobby Walston 3.50
120 Pete Retzlaff (SP) 7.50
121 Jim Schrader (SP) 7.50
122 J.D. Smith 3.50
123 King Hill 3.50
124 Maxie Baughan 3.50
125 Pete Case (SP) 7.50
126 Philadelphia Eagles Team 3.50
127 Bobby Layne 25.00
128 Tom Tracy 3.50
129 John Henry Johnson 7.00
130 Buddy Dial (SP) 7.50
131 Preston Carpenter 3.50
132 Lou Michaels (SP) 7.50
133 Gene Lipscomb (SP) 8.00
134 Ernie Stautner (SP) 15.00
135 John Reger (SP) 7.50
136 Myron Pottios 3.50
137 Bob Ferguson (SP) 7.50
138 Pittsburgh Steelers Team 3.50
139 Sam Etcheverry 3.50
140 John David Crow (SP) 7.50
141 Bobby Joe Conrad (SP) 7.50
142 *Prentice Gautt* (SP) 8.00
143 Frank Mestnik 3.50
144 Sonny Randle 3.50
145 Gerry Perry 3.50
146 Jerry Norton 3.50
147 Jimmy Hill 3.50
148 Bill Stacy 3.50
149 Fate Echols (SP) 7.50
150 St. Louis Cardinals Team 3.50
151 *Bill Kilmer* 25.00
152 John Brodie 15.00
153 J.D. Smith 3.50
154 C.R. Roberts (SP) 7.50
155 Monty Stickles 3.50
156 Clyde Conner 3.50
157 Bob St. Clair 7.50
158 *Tommy Davis* 3.50
159 Leo Nomellini 5.50
160 Matt Hazeltine 3.50
161 Abe Woodson 3.50
162 Dave Baker 3.50
163 San Francisco 49ers Team 3.50
164 *Norm Snead* (SP) 30.00
165 Dick James 3.50
166 Bobby Mitchell 8.00
167 Sam Horner 3.50
168 Bill Barnes 3.50
169 Bill Anderson 3.50
170 Fred Dugan 3.50
171 John Aveni (SP) 7.50
172 Bob Toneff 3.50
173 Jim Kerr 3.50
174 Leroy Jackson (SP) 7.50
175 Washington Redskins Team 3.50
176 Checklist 125.00

1962 Topps Bucks

This 48-card set was issued one per wax pack in the 1962 Topps football issue. The 1-1/4" x 4-1/4" "cards" have a dollar bill motif with the player's head in the middle and his name underneath. Backs show the same motif, with the NFL and team logo encircled. The Topps Bucks were printed on white paper.

NM/M
Complete Set (48): 400.00
Common Player: 4.50
1 J.D. Smith 4.50
2 Bart Starr 25.00
3 Dick James 4.50
4 Alex Webster 6.00
5 Paul Hornung 18.00
6 John David Crow 6.00

7 Jimmy Brown 60.00
8 Don Perkins 4.50
9 Bobby Walston 4.50
10 Jim Phillips 4.50
11 Y.A. Tittle 20.00
12 Sonny Randle 4.50
13 Jerry Reichow 4.50
14 Yale Lary 7.00
15 Buddy Dial 4.50
16 Ray Renfro 4.50
17 Norm Snead 4.50
18 Leo Nemellini 6.00
19 Hugh McElhenny 8.00
20 Eddie LeBaron 4.50
21 Bill Howton 4.50
22 Bobby Mitchell 9.00
23 Nick Pietrosante 4.50
24 John Unitas 30.00
25 Raymond Berry 9.00
26 Billy Kilmer 7.00
27 Lenny Moore 8.00
28 Tommy McDonald 4.50
29 Del Shofner 4.50
30 Jim Taylor 12.00
31 Joe Schmidt 7.00
32 Bill George 6.00
33 Fran Tarkenton 65.00
34 Willie Galimore 4.50
35 Bobby Layne 17.00
36 Max McGee 4.50
37 Jon Arnett 4.50
38 Lou Groza 10.00
39 Frank Varrichione 4.50
40 Milt Plum 4.50
41 Prentice Gault 4.50
42 Billy Wade 6.00
43 Gino Marchetti 7.00
44 John Brodie 10.00
45 Sonny Jurgensen 10.00
46 Clarence Peaks 4.50
47 Mike Ditka 20.00
48 John Henry Johnson 7.00

1963 Topps

Topps' 170-card set of NFL players features teams grouped in alphabetical order by city name. As with many Topps sets in this era, numerous cards were short-printed because the number of cards didn't match the size of Topps' printing sheets, meaning some were produced in more quantities than others. Rookies in this set include Hall of Famers Deacon Jones, Bob Lilly, Willie Wood, and Ray Nitschke. Other important rookie cards include Jim Marshall and Charlie Johnson. The set also features the second-year cards of Roman Gabriel, Mike Ditka, Fran Tarkenton and Bill Kilmer. Last-year cards here include Eddie LeBaron, Fuzzy Thurston, Hugh McElhenny, Ernie Stautner and Leo Nomellini. The final Topps cards of such players as Night Train Lane, Yale Lary, Joe Schmidt, Y.A. Tittle, Rosey Grier, Sam Huff, John Henry Johnson and Bob St. Clair are also in this set. (Key: SP - short printed)

NM/M

Complete Set (170): 1,300
Common Player: 2.00
SP Commons
Wax Pack (5): 375.00
1 Johnny Unitas 100.00
2 Lenny Moore 7.00
3 Jimmy Orr 2.00
4 Raymond Berry 7.00
5 Jim Parker 5.00
6 Alex Sandusky 2.00
7 Dick Szymanski 2.00
8 Gino Marchetti 5.00
9 *Billy Ray Smith* 3.00
10 Bill Pellington 2.00
11 *Bob Boyd* 2.00
12 Baltimore Colts Team (SP) 8.50
13 Frank Ryan (SP) 6.00
14 Jim Brown (SP) 200.00
15 Ray Renfro (SP) 4.50
16 Rich Kreitling (SP) 4.50
17 Mike McCormack (SP) 9.00
18 Jim Ray Smith (SP) 4.50
19 Lou Groza (SP) 17.00
20 Bill Glass (SP) 4.50
21 Galen Fiss (SP) 4.50
22 *Don Fleming* (SP) 6.00
23 Bob Gain (SP) 4.50
24 Cleveland Browns (SP) 8.50
25 Milt Plum 2.00
26 Dan Lewis 2.00
27 Nick Pietrosante 2.00
28 Gail Cogdill 2.00
29 Harley Sewell 2.00
30 Jim Gibbons 2.00
31 Carl Brettschneider 2.00
32 Dick "Night Train" Lane 3.50
33 Yale Lary 4.00
34 *Roger Brown* 3.00
35 Joe Schmidt 4.75
36 Detroit Lions Team (SP) 8.50
37 Roman Gabriel 7.00
38 Zeke Bratkowski 2.00
39 Dick Bass 2.00
40 Jon Arnett 2.00
41 Jim Phillips 2.00
42 Frank Varrichione 2.00
43 Danny Villanueva 2.00
44 *Deacon Jones* 50.00
45 Lindon Crow 2.00
46 Marlin McKeever 2.00
47 *Ed Meador* 2.50
48 Los Angeles Rams Team 4.00
49 Y.A. Tittle (SP) 40.00
50 Del Shofner (SP) 3.50
51 Alex Webster (SP) 6.00
52 Phil King (SP) 4.50
53 Jack Stroud (SP) 4.50
54 Darrell Dess (SP) 4.50
55 Jim Katcavage (SP) 4.50
56 Roosevelt Grier (SP) 8.00
57 Erich Barnes (SP) 4.50
58 Jim Patton (SP) 4.50
59 Sam Huff (SP) 14.00
60 New York Giants Team 4.00
61 Bill Wade 2.00
62 Mike Ditka 60.00
63 Johnny Morris 2.00
64 Roger LeClerc 2.00
65 Roger Davis 2.00
66 Joe Marconi 2.00
67 Herman Lee 2.00
68 Doug Atkins 5.00
69 Joe Fortunato 2.00
70 Bill George 4.75
71 Richie Petitbon 5.00
72 Chicago Bears Team (SP) 8.50
73 Eddie LeBaron (SP) 6.00
74 Don Meredith (SP) 50.00
75 Don Perkins (SP) 6.00
76 Amos Marsh (SP) 4.50
77 Bill Howton (SP) 4.50
78 Andy Cverko (SP) 4.50
79 Sam Baker (SP) 4.50
80 Jerry Tubbs (SP) 4.50
81 Don Bishop (SP) 4.50
82 *Bob Lilly* 200.00
83 Jerry Norton (SP) 4.50
84 Dallas Cowboys 16.00
85 Checklist 25.00
86 Bart Starr 40.00
87 Jim Taylor 16.00
88 Boyd Dowler 2.00
89 Forrest Gregg 5.25
90 Fuzzy Thurston 3.00
91 Jim Ringo 4.75
92 Ron Kramer 2.00
93 Hank Jordan 2.00
94 Bill Forester 2.00
95 *Willie Wood* 27.00
96 *Ray Nitschke* 80.00
97 Green Bay Packers Team 4.00
98 Fran Tarkenton 50.00
99 Tommy Mason 2.00
100 Mel Triplett 2.00
101 Jerry Reichow 2.00
102 Frank Youso 2.00
103 Hugh McElhenny 7.00
104 Gerry Huth 2.00
105 Ed Sharockman 2.00
106 Rip Hawkins 2.00
107 *Jim Marshall* 25.00
108 Jim Prestel 2.00
109 Minnesota Vikings Team 4.00
110 Sonny Jurgensen (SP) 22.00
111 *Timmy Brown* (SP) 8.00
112 Tommy McDonald (SP) 4.50
113 Clarence Peaks (SP) 4.50
114 Pete Retzlaff (SP) 4.50
115 Jim Schrader (SP) 4.50
116 Jim McCusker (SP) 4.50
117 Don Burroughs (SP) 4.50
118 Maxie Buaghan (SP) 4.50
119 Riley Gunnels (SP) 4.50
120 Jimmy Carr (SP) 4.50
121 Philadelphia Eagles (SP) 8.50
122 Ed Brown (SP) 4.50
123 John Henry Johnson 12.00
124 Buddy Dial (SP) 4.50
125 Red Mack (SP) 4.50
126 Preston Carpenter (SP) 4.50
127 Ray Lemek (SP) 4.50
128 Buzz Nutter (SP) 4.50
129 Ernie Stautner (SP) 12.00
130 Lou Michaels (SP) 4.50
131 *Clendon Thomas* (SP) 6.00
132 Tom Bettis (SP) 4.50
133 Pittsburgh Steelers (SP) 8.50
134 John Brodie 10.00
135 J.D. Smith 2.00
136 Bill Kilmer 5.00
137 *Bernie Casey* 4.50
138 Tommy Davis 2.00
139 Ted Connolly 2.00
140 Bob St. Clair 5.00
141 Abe Woodson 2.00
142 Matt Hazeltine 2.00
143 Leo Nomellini 5.50
144 Dan Colchico 2.00
145 San Francisco 49ers (SP) 8.50
146 *Charlie Johnson* 8.00
147 John David Crow 2.00
148 Bobby Joe Conrad 2.00
149 Sonny Randle 2.00
150 Prentice Gault 2.00
151 Taz Anderson 2.00
152 *Ernie McMillan* 2.00
153 Jimmy Hill 2.00
154 Bill Koman 2.00
155 *Larry Wilson* 25.00
156 Don Owens 2.00
157 St. Louis Cardinals (SP) 8.50
158 Norm Snead (SP) 8.00
159 *Bobby Mitchell* (SP) 14.00
160 Billy Barnes (SP) 4.50
161 Fred Dugan (SP) 4.50
162 Don Bosseler (SP) 4.50
163 John Nisby (SP) 4.50
164 Riley Mattson (SP) 4.50
165 Bob Toneff (SP) 4.50
166 Rod Breedlove (SP) 4.50
167 Dick James (SP) 4.50
168 Claud Crabb (SP) 4.50
169 Washington Redskins Team (SP) 8.50
170 Checklist 90.00

1964 Topps

Considered to be one of the toughest sets of the decade, this 176-card set was Topps' first to feature only American Football League players. Because of the awkward size of the set and the inability to print the cards on two sheets, some of the cards in the set are short-printed. Cards are numbered by city and by player. This set contains the rookie cards of Daryle Lamonica, Buck Buchanan, John Hadl, and Hall of Famers Bobby Bell and Matt Snell. Second-year cards in the set include Nick Buoniconti, Len Dawson and Lance Alworth. An interesting error exists in the set: Bo Roberson, #151, has a helmet with the Raiders logo at the bottom of the card. Helmets were not part of the card design, and logos were always airbrushed. (Key: SP - short printed)

NM/M

Complete Set (176): 1,500
Common Player: 3.00
SP Cards: 7.50
Wax Pack (5): 420.00
Wax Pack (8): 550.00
1 Tommy Addison (SP) 30.00
2 *Houston Antwine* 4.00
3 Nick Buoniconti 12.00
4 Ron Burton (SP) 6.00
5 Gino Cappelletti 6.00
6 Jim Colclough (SP) 6.00
7 Bob Dee (SP) 6.00
8 Larry Eisenhauer 3.00
9 Dick Felt (SP) 6.00
10 Larry Garron 3.00
11 Art Graham 3.00
12 Ron Hall 3.00
13 Charles Long 3.00
14 Don McKinnon 3.00
15 Don Oakes (SP) 6.00
16 Ross O'Hanley (SP) 6.00
17 Babe Parilli (SP) 6.00
18 Jesse Richardson (SP) 6.00
19 Jack Rudolph (SP) 6.00
20 *Don Webb* 4.00
21 Boston Patriots Team 4.50
22 Ray Abbruzzese 3.00
23 *Stew Barber* 4.00
24 Dave Behrman 3.00
25 Al Bemiller 3.00
26 Elbert Dubenion (SP) 6.00
27 *Jim Dunaway* (SP) 10.00
28 Booker Edgerson (SP) 6.00
29 Cookie Gilchrist (SP) 15.00
30 Jack Kemp (SP) 200.00
31 *Daryle Lamonica* 60.00
32 Bill Miller 3.00
33 *Herb Paterra* 4.00
34 Ken Rice (SP) 6.00
35 Ed Rutkowski 3.00
36 *George Saimes* 4.00
37 Tom Sestak 3.00
38 Billy Shaw (SP) 6.00
39 Mike Stratton 3.00
40 Gene Sykes 3.00
41 John Tracey (SP) 6.00
42 Sid Youngelman (SP) 6.00
43 Buffalo Bills Team 4.50
44 Eldon Danenhauer (SP) 6.00
45 Jim Fraser (SP) 6.00
46 Chuck Gavin (SP) 6.00
47 Goose Gonsoulin (SP) 6.00
48 *Ernie Barnes* 4.00
49 Tom Janik 3.00
50 *Billy Joe* 4.00
51 *Ike Lassiter* 4.00
52 John McCormick (SP) 6.00
53 Lewis Bud McFadin (SP) 3.00
54 Gene Mingo (SP) 3.00
55 Charlie Mitchell 3.00
56 John Nocera (SP) 6.00
57 Tom Nomina 3.00
58 Harold Olson (SP) 6.00
59 Bob Scarpitto 3.00
60 John Sklopan 3.00
61 Mickey Slaughter 3.00
62 Don Stone 3.00
63 Jerry Sturm 3.00
64 Lionel Taylor (SP) 12.00
65 Denver Broncos Team (SP) 17.00
66 *Scott Appleton* 4.00
67 Tony Banfield (SP) 6.00
68 George Blanda (SP) 60.00
69 Billy Cannon 4.50
70 Doug Cline (SP) 6.00
71 Gary Cutsinger (SP) 6.00
72 Willard Dewveall (SP) 6.00
73 Don Floyd (SP) 6.00
74 Freddy Gick (SP) 6.00
75 Charlie Hennigan (SP) 10.00
76 Ed Husmann (SP) 6.00
77 Bobby Jancik (SP) 6.00
78 Jacky Lee (SP) 6.00
79 Bob McLeod (SP) 6.00
80 Rich Michael (SP) 6.00
81 *Larry Onesti* 4.00
82 Checklist 50.00
83 Bob Schmidt (SP) 6.00
84 Walt Suggs (SP) 6.00
85 Bob Talamini (SP) 6.00
86 Charley Tolar (SP) 6.00
87 *Don Trull* 5.00
88 Houston Oilers Team 4.50
89 Fred Arbanas 3.00
90 *Bobby Bell* 35.00
91 Mel Branch (SP) 6.00
92 *Buck Buchanan* 35.00
93 *Ed Budde* 6.00
94 Chris Burford (SP) 6.00
95 *Walt Corey* 6.00
96 Len Dawson (SP) 75.00
97 *Dave Grayson* 4.00
98 Abner Haynes 4.00
99 Sherrill Headrick (SP) 6.00
100 E.J. Holub 3.00
101 Bobby Hunt 3.00
102 Frank Jackson (SP) 6.00
103 Curtis McClinton 3.00
104 Jerry Mays (SP) 3.00
105 Johnny Robinson (SP) 6.75
106 Jack Spikes (SP) 6.00
107 Smokey Stover (SP) 6.00
108 *Jim Tyrer* 6.00
109 Duane Wood (SP) 6.00
110 Kansas City Chiefs Team 4.50
111 Dick Christy (SP) 6.00
112 Dan Ficca (SP) 6.00
113 Larry Grantham 3.00
114 Curley Johnson (SP) 7.00
115 Gene Heeter 3.00
116 Jack Klotz 3.00
117 *Pete Liske* 4.00
118 Bob McAdam 3.00
119 Dee Mackey (SP) 6.00
120 Bill Mathis (SP) 6.00
121 Don Maynard 30.00
122 Dainard Paulson (SP) 6.00
123 *Gerry Philbin* 4.00
124 Mark Smolinski (SP) 6.00
125 *Matt Snell* 15.00
126 Mike Taliaferro 3.00
127 *Bake Turner* (SP) 12.00
128 Jeff Ware 3.00
129 Clyde Washington 3.00
130 *Dick Wood* 4.00
131 New York Jets Team 4.50
132 Dalva Allen (SP) 6.00
133 Dan Birdwell 3.00
134 *Dave Costa* 4.00
135 Dobiue Craig 3.00
136 Clem Daniels 3.00
137 Cotton Davidson (SP) 6.00
138 Claude Gibson 3.00
139 Tom Flores 15.00
140 Wayne Hawkins (SP) 6.00
141 Ken Herock 3.00
142 Jon Jelacic (SP) 6.00
143 Joe Krakoski 3.00
144 Archie Matsos (SP) 6.00
145 Mike Mercer 3.00
146 Alan Miller (SP) 6.00
147 Bob Mischak (SP) 6.00
148 Jim Otto (SP) 25.00
149 Clancy Osborne (SP) 6.00
150 Art Powell (SP) 9.00
151 Bo Roberson 3.00
152 Fred Williamson (SP) 10.00
153 Oakland Raiders Team 4.50
154 *Chuck Allen* (SP) 10.00
155 Lance Alworth 40.00
156 George Blair 3.00
157 Earl Faison 3.00
158 Sam Gruniesen 3.00
159 *John Hadl* 35.00
160 Dick Harris (SP) 6.00
161 Emil Karas (SP) 6.00
162 Dave Kocourek (SP) 6.00
163 Ernie Ladd 6.00
164 Keith Lincoln 6.00
165 Paul Lowe (SP) 10.00
166 Charles McNeil 3.00
167 Jacque MacKinnon (SP) 6.00
168 Ron Mix (SP) 15.00
169 Don Norton (SP) 6.00
170 Don Rogers (SP) 6.00
171 Tobin Rote (SP) 10.00
172 Henry Schmidt (SP) 6.00
173 Bud Whitehead 3.00
174 Ernie Wright (SP) 6.00
175 San Diego Chargers Team 4.50
176 Checklist (SP) 150.00

1964 Topps Pennant Stickers

These 24 peel-off stickers (they measure about 2" x 4-1/2") were inserted one per wax pack of the 1964 Topps football cards. The unnumbered pennants covered AFL teams and major college teams. Since stickers were folded to fit into the backs, all of them are found with a crease.

NM/M

Complete Set (24): 240.00
AFL Team: 12.00
College Team: 7.00
(1) Boston Patriots 12.00
(2) Buffalo Bills 12.00
(3) Denver Broncos 12.00
(4) Houston Oilers 12.00
(5) K.C. Chiefs 12.00
(6) New York Jets 12.00
(7) Oakland Raiders 12.00
(8) San Diego Chargers 12.00
(9) Air Force 7.00
(10) Army 7.00
(11) Dartmouth 7.00
(12) Duke 7.00
(13) Michigan 7.00
(14) Minnesota 7.00
(15) Mississippi 7.00
(16) Navy 7.00
(17) Notre Dame 15.00
(18) SMU 7.00
(19) USC 7.00
(20) Syracuse 7.00
(21) Texas 7.00
(22) Washington 7.00
(23) Wisconsin 7.00
(24) Yale 7.00

1965 Topps

Topps' second set featuring only AFL players is easily the most valued set of the decade for several reasons - the oversized (about 2-1/2" x 5") cards are attractive; it includes Joe Namath's rookie card; and Topps' unorthodox printing method created an abundance of certain cards, but a scarcity of others - all throughout the 176-card set, too, not just in one sequentially-numbered series. There may be a variation on Namath's rookie card as well. There's a report of a card showing Broadway Joe with a butterfly tattoo on his arm; on other cards, this tattoo is airbrushed off. It's uncertain how many, or even if, this variation exists. Besides Namath, other rookies in this set include Fred Biletnikoff, Willie Brown, and Ben Davidson. Second-year cards include those of Daryle Lamonica, Bobby Bell, Buck Buchanon, Matt Snell and John Hadl. (Key: SP - short printed)

NM/M

Complete Set (176): 3,800
Common Player: 6.50
SP Cards: 12.00
Wax Pack (5): 675.00
1 Tommy Addison (SP) 35.00
2 Houston Antwine (SP) 11.50
3 Nick Buoniconti (SP) 24.00
4 Ron Burton (SP) 11.50
5 Gino Cappelletti (SP) 20.00
6 Jim Colclough 6.50
7 Bob Dee (SP) 11.50
8 Larry Eisenhauer 6.50
9 J.D. Garrett 6.50
10 Larry Garron 6.50
11 Art Graham (SP) 11.50
12 Ron Hall 6.50
13 Charles Long 6.50
14 *Jon Morris* 10.00
15 Bill Neighbors (SP) 11.50
16 Ross O'Hanley 6.50
17 Babe Parilli (SP) 11.50
18 Tony Romeo (SP) 11.50
19 Jack Rudolph (SP) 11.50
20 Bob Schmidt 6.50
21 Don Webb (SP) 11.50
22 Jim Whalen (SP) 11.50
23 Stew Barber 6.50
24 Glenn Bass (SP) 11.50
25 Al Bemiller (SP) 11.50
26 Wray Carlton (SP) 11.50
27 Tom Day 6.50
28 Elbert Dubenion (SP) 11.50
29 Jim Dunaway 6.50
30 *Pete Gogolak* (SP) 19.00
31 Dick Hudson (SP) 11.50
32 Harry Jacobs (SP) 11.50
33 Billy Joe (SP) 11.50
34 *Tom Keating* (SP) 17.00
35 Jack Kemp (SP) 200.00
36 Daryle Lamonica (SP) 40.00
37 Paul Maguire (SP) 20.00
38 *Ron McDole* (SP) 15.00
39 George Saimes (SP) 11.50
40 Tom Sestak (SP) 11.50
41 Billy Shaw (SP) 11.50
42 Mike Stratton (SP) 11.50
43 John Tracey (SP) 11.50
44 Ernie Warlick 6.50
45 Odell Barry 6.50
46 *Willie Brown* (SP) 65.00
47 Gerry Bussell (SP) 11.50
48 Eldon Danehauer (SP) 11.50
49 Al Denson (SP) 11.50
50 *Hewritt Dixon* (SP) 19.00
51 Cookie Gilchrist (SP) 25.00
52 Goose Gonsoulin (SP) 11.50
53 Abner Haynes (SP) 18.00
54 Jerry Hopkins (SP) 11.50
55 Ray Jacobs (SP) 11.50
56 Jacky Lee (SP) 11.50
57 John McCormick 6.50
58 Bob McCullough (SP) 11.50
59 John McGeever 6.50
60 Charlie Mitchell (SP) 11.50
61 Jim Perkins (SP) 11.50
62 Bob Scarpitto (SP) 11.50
63 Mickey Slaughter (SP) 11.50
64 Jerry Sturm (SP) 11.50
65 Lionel Taylor (SP) 20.00
66 Scott Appleton (SP) 11.50
67 Johnny Baker (SP) 11.50
68 Sonny Bishop (SP) 11.50
69 George Blanda (SP) 90.00
70 Sid Blanks (SP) 11.50
71 Ode Burrell (SP) 11.50
72 Doug Cline (SP) 11.50
73 Willard Dewveall 6.50
74 *Larry Elkins* 10.00
75 Don Floyd (SP) 11.50
76 Freddy Glick 6.50
77 Tom Goode (SP) 11.50
78 Charlie Hennigan (SP) 18.00
79 Ed Husmann 6.50
80 Bobby Jancik (SP) 11.50
81 Bud McFadin (SP) 11.50
82 Bob McLeod (SP) 11.50
83 Jim Norton (SP) 11.50
84 Walt Suggs 6.50
85 Bob Talamini 6.50
86 Charley Tolar (SP) 11.50
87 Checklist 1-88 (SP) 150.00
88 Don Trull (SP) 11.50
89 Fred Arbanas (SP) 11.50
90 *Pete Beathard* (SP) 22.00
91 Bobby Bell (SP) 25.00
92 Mel Branch (SP) 11.50
93 Tommy Brooker (SP) 11.50
94 Buck Buchanan (SP) 25.00
95 Ed Budde (SP) 11.50
96 Chris Burford (SP) 11.50
97 Walt Corey 6.50
98 Jerry Cornelison 6.50
99 Len Dawson (SP) 80.00
100 Jon Gilliam (SP) 11.50
101 Sherrill Headrick (SP) 11.50
102 Dave Hill (SP) 11.50
103 E.J. Holub (SP) 11.50
104 Bobby Hunt (SP) 11.50
105 Frank Jackson (SP) 11.50
106 Jerry Mays 6.50
107 Curtis McClinton (SP) 11.50
108 Bobby Ply (SP) 11.50
109 Johnny Robinson(SP) 11.50
110 Jim Tyrer (SP) 11.50
111 Bill Baird (SP) 11.50
112 *Ralph Baker* (SP) 15.00
113 Sam DeLuca (SP) 11.50
114 Larry Grantham (SP) 11.50
115 Gene Heeter (SP) 11.50
116 *Winston Hill* (SP) 20.00
117 *John Huarte* (SP) 30.00
118 Cosmo Iacavazzi (SP) 11.50
119 Curley Johnson (SP) 11.50
120 Dee Mackey 6.50
121 Don Maynard 35.00
122 *Joe Namath* (SP) 1,800
123 Dainard Paulson 6.50
124 Gerry Philbin (SP) 11.50
125 *Sherman Plunkett* 19.00
126 Mark Smolinski 6.50
127 Matt Snell (SP) 25.00
128 Mike Taliaferro (SP) 11.50
129 Bake Turner (SP) 15.00
130 Clyde Washington (SP) 11.50
131 *Verlon Biggs* (SP) 15.00
132 Dalva Allen 6.50
133 *Fred Biletnikoff* (SP) 200.00
134 Billy Cannon (SP) 20.00
135 Dave Costa (SP) 11.50
136 Clem Daniels (SP) 11.50
137 *Ben Davidson* (SP) 50.00
138 Cotton Davidson (SP) 11.50
139 Tom Flores (SP) 27.00
140 Claude Gibson 6.50
141 Wayne Hawkins 6.50
142 Archie Matsos (SP) 11.50
143 Mike Mercer (SP) 11.50

144	Bob Mischak (SP)	11.50
145	Jim Otto	25.00
146	Art Powell (SP)	13.00
147	Warren Powers (SP)	11.50
148	Ken Rice (SP)	11.50
149	Bo Roberson (SP)	11.50
150	*Harry Schuh*	12.00
151	Larry Todd (SP)	11.50
152	Fred Williamson (SP)	20.00
153	J.R. Williamson	6.50
154	Chuck Allen	6.50
155	Lance Alworth	65.00
156	Frank Buncom	6.50
157	*Steve DeLong* (SP)	17.00
158	Earl Faison (SP)	11.50
159	Kenny Graham (SP)	11.50
160	George Gross (SP)	11.50
161	John Hadl (SP)	28.00
162	Emil Karas (SP)	11.50
163	Dave Kocourek (SP)	11.50
164	Ernie Ladd (SP)	20.00
165	Keith Lincoln (SP)	20.00
166	Paul Lowe (SP)	20.00
167	Jacque MacKinnon	6.50
168	Ron Mix	20.00
169	Don Norton (SP)	11.50
170	Bob Petrich	6.50
171	Rick Redman (SP)	11.50
172	Pat Shea	6.50
173	*Walt Sweeney* (SP)	15.00
174	*Dick Westmoreland*	12.00
175	Ernie Wright (SP)	11.50
176	Checklist 89-176 (SP)	225.00

1965 Topps Rub-Offs

This 36-card, unnumbered set was included one per pack in wax packs of 1965 Topps football. The set, which measures two by three inches, includes the eight American Football League teams plus 28 college team emblems. Similar in design to the 1961 Topps baseball rub-offs, the fronts carried a team logo and team name in reverse type, while the backs carried instructions on how to use the rub-offs.

		NM/M
Complete Set (36):		400.00
Common AFL Team:		15.00
Common College Team:		10.00
(1)	Boston Patriots	15.00
(2)	Buffalo Bills	20.00
(3)	Denver Broncos	25.00
(4)	Houston Oilers	20.00
(5)	Kansas City Chiefs	15.00
(6)	New York Jets	20.00
(7)	Oakland Raiders	35.00
(8)	San Diego Chargers	15.00
(9)	Alabama	15.00
(10)	Air Force Academy	10.00
(11)	Arkansas	15.00
(12)	Army	15.00
(13)	Boston College	10.00
(14)	Duke	15.00
(15)	Illinois	10.00
(16)	Kansas	15.00
(17)	Kentucky	10.00
(18)	Maryland	10.00
(19)	Miami	15.00
(20)	Minnesota	15.00
(21)	Mississippi	10.00
(22)	Navy	15.00
(23)	Nebraska	15.00
(24)	Notre Dame	35.00
(25)	Penn State	15.00
(26)	Purdue	10.00
(27)	Southern California	10.00
(28)	Southern Methodist	15.00
(29)	Stanford	10.00
(30)	Syracuse	10.00
(31)	Texas	10.00
(32)	Texas Christian	15.00
(33)	Virginia	10.00
(34)	Washington	15.00
(35)	Wisconsin	10.00
(36)	Yale	10.00

1966 Topps

This set, which shows AFL players only (Topps' third straight) is quite popular with collectors. It uses a TV motif. Cards were once again grouped in alphabetical order by city name, then by the player's last name. Joe Namath's second-year card is the set's biggest selling player card, but "card" #15, the Funny Ring checklist, is a very difficult find and is easily the most expensive card in the set. Other key cards include rookie cards of Otis Taylor, Jim Turner and George Sauer Jr., second-year cards of Fred Biletnikoff and Ben Davidson, and cards showing Hall of Famers George Blanda, Bobby Bell, Len Dawson, Don Maynard, Ron Mix, Jim Otto and Lance Alworth. A Jack Kemp card is the set's third most expensive card; other high-priced cards are checklists, which are hard to find in mint.

		NM/M
Complete Set (132):		1,300
Common Player:		4.00
Wax Pack (5+1):		325.00
1	Tom Addison	20.00
2	Houston Antwine	4.00
3	Nick Buoniconti	9.00
4	Gino Cappelletti	6.00
5	Bob Dee	4.00
6	Larry Garron	4.00
7	Art Graham	4.00
8	Ron Hall	4.00
9	Charles Long	4.00
10	Jon Morris	4.00
11	Don Oakes	4.00
12	Babe Parilli	4.00
13	Don Webb	4.00
14	Jim Whalen	4.00
15	Funny Ring CL	275.00
16	Stew Barber	4.00
17	Glenn Bass	4.00
18	Dave Behrman	4.00
19	Al Bemiller	4.00
20	*Butch Byrd*	5.00
21	Wray Carlton	4.00
22	Tom Day	4.00
23	Elbert Dubenion	4.00
24	Jim Dunaway	4.00
25	Dick Hudson	4.00
26	Jack Kemp	170.00
27	Daryle Lamonica	10.00
28	Tom Sestak	4.00
29	Billy Shaw	4.00
30	Mike Stratton	4.00
31	Eldon Danenhauer	4.00
32	Cookie Gilchrist	7.00
33	Goose Gonsoulin	4.00
34	*Wendell Hayes*	8.00
35	Abner Haynes	4.00
36	Jerry Hopkins	4.00
37	Ray Jacobs	4.00
38	Charlie Janerette	4.00
39	Ray Kubala	4.00
40	John McCormick	4.00
41	Leroy Moore	4.00
42	Bob Scarpitto	4.00
43	Mickey Slaughter	4.00
44	Jerry Sturm	4.00
45	Lionel Taylor	6.50
46	Scott Appleton	4.00
47	Johnny Baker	4.00
48	George Blanda	40.00
49	Sid Blanks	4.00
50	Danny Brabham	4.00
51	Ode Burrell	4.00
52	Gary Cutsinger	4.00
53	Larry Elkins	4.00
54	Don Floyd	4.00
55	*Willie Frazier*	6.00
56	Freddy Glick	4.00
57	Charles Henningan	5.00
58	Bobby Jancik	4.00
59	Rich Michael	4.00
60	Don Trull	4.00
61	Checklist	40.00
62	Fred Arbanas	4.00
63	Pete Beathard	5.00
64	Bobby Bell	8.00
65	Ed Budde	4.00
66	Chris Burford	4.00
67	Len Dawson	35.00
68	Jon Gilliam	4.00
69	Sherrill Headrick	4.00
70	E.J. Holub	4.00
71	Bobby Hunt	4.00
72	Curtis McClinton	4.00
73	Jerry Mays	5.00
74	Johnny Robinson	5.00
75	*Otis Taylor*	17.00
76	Tom Erlandson	4.00
77	*Norman Evans*	8.00
78	Tom Goode	4.00
79	Mike Hudock	4.00
80	Frank Jackson	4.00
81	Billy Joe	4.00
82	Dave Kocourek	4.00
83	Bo Roberson	4.00
84	Jack Spikes	4.00
85	*Jim Warren*	8.00
86	*Willie West*	5.00
87	Dick Westmoreland	4.00
88	Eddie Wilson	4.00
89	Dick Wood	4.00
90	Verlon Biggs	4.00
91	Sam DeLuca	4.00
92	Winston Hill	4.00
93	Dee Mackey	4.00
94	Bill Mathis	4.00
95	Don Maynard	25.00
96	Joe Namath	340.00
97	Dainard Paulson	4.00
98	Gerry Philbin	4.00
99	Sherman Plunkett	4.00
100	Paul Rochester	4.00
101	*George Sauer Jr.*	12.00
102	Matt Snell	7.00
103	*Jim Turner*	6.00
104	Fred Biletnikoff	50.00
105	Bill Budness	4.00
106	Billy Cannon	6.00
107	Clem Daniels	4.00
108	Ben Davidson	10.00
109	Cotton Davidson	4.00
110	Claude Gibson	4.00
111	Wayne Hawkins	4.00
112	Ken Herock	4.00
113	Bob Mischak	4.00
114	Gus Otto	4.00
115	Jim Otto	15.00
116	Art Powell	6.00
117	Harry Schuh	4.00
118	Chuck Allen	4.00
119	Lance Alworth	30.00
120	Frank Buncom	4.00
121	Steve DeLong	4.50
122	John Farris	4.00
123	Ken Graham	4.00
124	Sam Gruneisen	4.00
125	John Hadl	8.00
126	Walt Sweeney	4.00
127	Keith Lincoln	4.00
128	Ron Mix	9.00
129	Don Norton	4.00
130	Pat Shea	4.00
131	Ernie Wright	4.00
132	Checklist	90.00

1966 Topps Funny Rings

The 24-card, 1-1/4" x 3" set was issued in each pack of 1966 Topps Football. The card fronts feature a ring that can be punched out and folded to make a ring. The backs are blank.

		NM/M
Complete Set (24):		500.00
Common Player:		25.00
1	Funny Ring - Kiss Me	25.00
2	Funny Ring - Bloodshot Eye	25.00
3	Funny Ring - Big Mouth	25.00
4	Funny Ring - Tooth-ache	25.00
5	Funny Ring - Fish eats Fish	25.00
6	Funny Ring - Mrs. Skull	25.00
7	Funny Ring - Hot Dog	25.00
8	Funny Ring - Head with Nail	25.00
9	Funny Ring - Ah	25.00
10	Funny Ring - Apple with Worm	25.00
11	Funny Ring - Snake	25.00
12	Funny Ring - Yicch	25.00
13	Funny Ring - If You Can Read This	25.00
14	Funny Ring - Nuts to You	25.00
15	Funny Ring - Get Lost	25.00
16	Funny Ring - You Fink	25.00
17	Funny Ring - Hole in Shoe	25.00
18	Funny Ring - Head with One Eye	25.00
19	Funny Ring - Mr. Ugly	25.00
20	Funny Ring - Mr. Fang	25.00
21	Funny Ring - Mr. Fright	25.00
22	Funny Ring - Mr. Boo	25.00
23	Funny Ring - Mr. Glug	25.00
24	Funny Ring - Mr. Blech	25.00

1967 Topps

This 132-card set is the last AFL-only set issued by Topps. Best-known for the inclusion of Joe-Namath's second-year card, the set also features another Jack Kemp card. Wahoo McDaniels' only card is also in this set. Cards are grouped according to each of the nine AFL teams. It's very difficult to find an unmarked checklist; consequently, prices are pretty high on those two cards.

		NM/M
Complete Set (132):		650.00
Common Player:		2.50
Wax Pack (5):		255.00
1	John Huarte	10.00
2	Babe Parilli	2.50
3	Gino Cappelletti	3.00
4	Larry Garron	2.50
5	Tom Addison	2.50
6	Jon Morris	2.50
7	Houston Antwine	2.50
8	Don Oakes	2.50
9	Larry Eisenhauer	2.50
10	Jim Hunt	2.50
11	Jim Whalen	2.50
12	Art Graham	2.50
13	Nick Buoniconti	6.00
14	Bob Dee	2.50
15	Keith Lincoln	4.00
16	Tom Flores	5.50
17	Art Powell	3.00
18	Stew Barber	2.50
19	Wray Carlton	2.50
20	Elbert Dubenion	2.50
21	Jim Dunanaway	2.50
22	Dick Hudson	2.50
23	Harry Jacobs	2.50
24	Jack Kemp	100.00
25	Ron McDole	2.50
26	George Saimes	2.50
27	Tom Sestak	2.50
28	Billy Shaw	2.50
29	Mike Stratton	2.50
30	*Nemiah Wilson*	3.00
31	John McCormick	2.50
32	Rex Mirich	2.50
33	Dave Costa	2.50
34	Goose Gonsoulin	2.50
35	Abner Haynes	3.50
36	Wendell Hayes	2.50
37	Archie Matsos	2.50
38	John Bramlett	2.50
39	Jerry Sturm	2.50
40	Max Leetzow	2.50
41	Bob Scarpitto	2.50
42	Lionel Taylor	3.50
43	Al Denson	2.50
44	*Miller Farr*	3.50
45	Don Trull	1.50
46	Jacky Lee	2.50
47	Bobby Jancik	2.50
48	Ode Burrell	2.50
49	Larry Elkins	2.50
50	W.K. Hicks	2.50
51	Sid Blanks	2.50
52	Jim Norton	2.50
53	*Bobby Maples*	3.00
54	Bob Talamini	2.50
55	Walter Suggs	2.50
56	Gary Cutsinger	2.50
57	Danny Brabham	2.50
58	Ernie Ladd	4.00
59	Checklist	40.00
60	Pete Beathard	2.50
61	Len Dawson	20.00
62	Bobby Hunt	2.50
63	Bert Coan	2.50
64	Curtis McClinton	2.50
65	Johnny Robinson	2.50
66	E.J. Holub	2.50
67	Jerry Mays	2.50
68	Jim Tyrer	2.50
69	Bobby Bell	5.50
70	Fred Arbanas	2.50
71	Buck Buchanan	5.50
72	Chris Burford	2.50
73	Otis Taylor	4.00
74	Cookie Gilchrist	5.00
75	Earl Faison	2.50
76	George Wilson Jr.	2.50
77	Rick Norton	2.50
78	Frank Jackson	2.50
79	Joe Auer	2.50
80	Willie West	2.50
81	Jim Warren	2.50
82	*Wahoo McDaniel*	30.00
83	Ernie Park	2.50
84	Bill Neighbors	2.50
85	Norm Evans	2.50
86	Tom Nomina	2.50
87	Rich Zecher	2.50
88	Dave Kocourek	2.50
89	Bill Baird	2.50
90	Ralph Baker	2.50
91	Verlon Biggs	2.50
92	Sam DeLuca	2.50
93	Larry Grantham	2.50
94	Jim Harris	2.50
95	Winston Hill	2.50
96	Bill Mathis	2.50
97	Don Maynard	20.00
98	Joe Namath	185.00
99	Gerry Philbin	2.50
100	Paul Rochester	2.50
101	George Sauer	3.50
102	Matt Snell	3.50
103	Daryle Lamonica	6.00
104	Glenn Bass	2.50
105	Jim Otto	6.00
106	Fred Biletnikoff	30.00
107	Cotton Davidson	2.50
108	Larry Todd	2.50
109	Billy Cannon	3.00
110	Clem Daniels	2.50
111	Dave Grayson	2.50
112	*Kent McCloughan*	2.50
113	Bob Svihus	2.50
114	Isaac Lassiter	2.50
115	Harry Schuh	2.50
116	Ben Davidson	6.00
117	Tom Day	2.50
118	Scott Appleton	2.50
119	*Steve Tensi*	3.00
120	John Hadl	5.00
121	Paul Lowe	3.00
122	Jim Allison	2.50
123	Lance Alworth	25.00
124	Jacque MacKinnon	2.50
125	Ron Mix	5.50
126	Bob Petrich	2.50
127	Howard Kingdig	2.50
128	Steve DeLong	2.50
129	Chuck Allen	2.50
130	Frank Buncom	2.50
131	*Speedy Duncan*	5.00
132	Checklist	60.00

1967 Topps Comic Pennants

The 31-card, standard-size sticker set was issued in packs of 1967 Topps and is considered to be scarce - the set was probably discontinued before the end of the shipping. The cards contain juvenile humor (Denver girls look like Broncos). The cards are numbered in the upper right corner.

		NM/M
Complete Set (31):		600.00
Common Player:		20.00
1	Navel Academy	20.00
2	City College of Useless Knowledge	20.00
3	Notre Dame (Hunchback of)	40.00
4	Psychedelic State	20.00
5	Minneapolis Mini-skirts	20.00
6	School of Art - Go, Van Gogh	20.00
7	Washington Is Dead	25.00
8	School of Hard Knocks	20.00
9	Alaska (If I See Her ...)	20.00
10	Confused State	20.00
11	Yale Locks Are Tough to Pick	20.00
12	University of Transylvania	20.00
13	Down With Teachers	20.00
14	Cornell Caught Me Cheating	20.00
15	Houston Oilers (You're a Fink)	25.00
16	Harvard (Flunked Out)	25.00
17	Diskotech	20.00
18	Dropout U	20.00
19	Air Force (Gas Masks)	20.00
20	Nutstu U	20.00
21	Michigan State Pen	20.00
22	Denver Broncos (Girls Look Like)	25.00
23	Buffalo Bills (Without Paying My)	25.00
24	Army of Dropouts	20.00
25	Miami Dolphins (Bitten by Two)	30.00
26	Too Many) Chiefs	20.00
27	Boston Patriots (Banned In)	20.00
28	Icebox) Raiders	30.00
29	The Right Direction)	20.00
30	New York Jets (Skies Are Crowded With)	25.00
31	San Diego Chargers (Police Will Press)	20.00

1968 Topps

Topps' first set to clear 200 cards in number was also its first set in five years to feature NFL players as well as AFL players. Released in two series, the second series is a little tougher to find. First-series cards show blue printing on the backs, while second series issues have green. The 219-card set features a special design for cards of players from the Super Bowl teams, the Oakland Raiders and Green Bay Packers. Cards of players from these teams show players in a horizontal format set against a stylized football backdrop. Remaining cards are in a vertical format. Each carries a player photo inside a white frame with the players name, position and team in an oval at the card bottom. A number of second-series card backs can be pieced together to show a picture of Bart Starr or Len Dawson (10 cards per player). Puzzle-piece card backs are found on cards 141, 145, 146, 148, 151-53, 155, 163, 168, 170, 172, 186, 195 and 197. One error in the set is on #12, Kent McCloughan. The back spells his name "McCloughlan." Another mix-up occurs on card #70, Dick Van Raaphorst's card. The back lists his name as "Van Raap Horst." Also, there are two different checklist cards; the back of one is blue, the back of the other is green. Rookies in this set include Bob Griese, Jim Hart, Craig Morton, Joe Kapp, Jim Grabowski, Jack Snow, and Donny Anderson. Other valuable cards include Bart Starr, Don Meredith, Joe Namath, Gale Sayers, Johnny Unitas, Dick Butkis, George Blanda, Jack Kemp, and Fran Tarkenton. This set featured the final regular-issue cards of Hall of Famers Mike Ditka and Jim Taylor.

		NM/M
Complete Set (219):		575.00
Common Player (1-131):		.80
Common Player (132-219):		1.50
Series 1 Wax Pack (5+1):		220.00
Series 1 Wax Box (24):		4600.00
Series 2 Wax Pack (5+1):		300.00
Series 2 Wax Box (24):		6375.00
1	Bart Starr	35.00
2	Dick Bass	.80
3	Grady Alderman	1.25
4	Obert Logan	1.25
5	*Ernie Koy*	1.50
6	Don Hultz	1.25
7	Earl Gros	1.25
8	Jim Bakken	.80
9	George Mira	.80
10	Carl Kammerer	1.25
11	Willie Frazier	.80
12	Kent McCloughan	1.25
13	George Sauer	1.50
14	Jack Clancy	.80
15	Jim Tyrer	.80
16	Bobby Maples	1.25
17	Bo Hickey	1.25
18	Frank Buncom	1.25
19	Keith Lincoln	1.50
20	Jim Whalen	.80
21	Junior Coffey	1.25
22	Billy Ray Smith	1.25
23	Johnny Morris	1.50
24	Ernie Green	1.25
25	Don Meredith	21.00
26	Wayne Walker	.80
27	Carroll Dale	.80
28	Bernie Casey	.80
29	*Dave Osborn*	1.50
30	Ray Poage	1.25
31	Homer Jones	.80
32	Sam Baker	.80
33	Bill Saul	1.25
34	Ken Willard	.80
35	Bobby Mitchell	4.00
36	Gary Garrison	1.50
37	Billy Cannon	1.50
38	Ralph Baker	1.25
39	*Howard Twilley*	3.50
40	Wendell Hayes	.80
41	Jim Norton	1.25
42	Tom Beer	1.25
43	Chris Burford	1.25
44	Stew Barber	1.25
45	Leroy Mitchell	1.25
46	Dan Grimm	1.25
47	Jerry Logan	1.25
48	Andy Livingston	1.25
49	Paul Warfield	10.00
50	Don Perkins	1.25
51	Ron Kramer	.80
52	Bob Jeter	1.50
53	*Les Josephson*	1.50
54	Bobby Walden	1.25
55	Checklist	15.00
56	Walter Roberts	1.25
57	Henry Carr	.80
58	Gary Ballman	.80
59	J.R. Wilburn	1.25
60	*Jim Hart*	8.00
61	Jimmy Johnson	.80
62	Chris Hanburger	1.50
63	John Hadl	3.00
64	Hewritt Dixon	1.25
65	Joe Namath	80.00
66	Jim Warren	1.25
67	Curtis McClinton	.80
68	Bob Talamini	.80
69	Steve Tensi	1.25
70	Dick Van Raaphorst	1.25
71	Art Powell	1.50
72	*Jim Nance*	3.50
73	Bob Riggle	1.25
74	John Mackey	3.50
75	Gale Sayers	50.00
76	Gene Hickerson	1.25
77	Dan Reeves	10.00
78	Tom Nowatzke	1.25
79	Elijah Pitts	.80
80	Lamar Lundy	1.25
81	Paul Flatley	1.25
82	Dave Whitsell	1.25
83	Spider Lockhart	.80
84	Dave Lloyd	1.25
85	Roy Jefferson	.80
86	Jackie Smith	5.00
87	John David Crow	1.50
88	Sonny Jurgensen	6.50
89	Ron Mix	3.50
90	Clem Daniels	.80
91	Cornell Gordon	1.25
92	Tom Goode	1.25
93	Bobby Bell	3.50
94	Walt Suggs	1.25
95	Eric Crabtree	1.25
96	Sherrill Headrick	.80
97	Wray Carlton	.80
98	Gino Cappelletti	1.50
99	Tommy McDonald	.80
100	Johnny Unitas	25.00
101	Richie Petitbon	1.50
102	Erich Barnes	.80
103	Bob Hayes	3.00
104	Milt Plum	1.50
105	Boyd Dowler	.80
106	Ed Meador	.80
107	Fred Cox	.80
108	*Steve Stonebreaker*	1.50
109	Aaron Thomas	1.25
110	Norm Snead	1.50

111	*Paul Martha*	1.50
112	Jerry Stovall	.80
113	Kay McFarland	1.25
114	Pat Richter	1.25
115	Rick Redman	1.25
116	Tom Keating	1.25
117	Matt Snell	2.50
118	Dick Westmoreland	1.25
119	Jerry Mays	.80
120	Sid Blanks	1.25
121	Al Denson	1.25
122	Bobby Hunt	1.25
123	Mike Mercer	1.25
124	Nick Buoniconti	3.00
125	*Ron Vanderkelen*	.80
126	Ordell Braase	1.25
127	Dick Butkus	36.00
128	Gary Collins	.80
129	Mel Renfro	1.50
130	Alex Karras	6.00
131	Herb Adderley	3.00
132	Roman Gabriel	3.50
133	Bill Brown	1.50
134	Kent Kramer	1.50
135	Tucker Frederickson	1.50
136	Nate Ramsey	1.50
137	Marv Woodson	1.50
138	Ken Gray	1.50
139	John Brodie	7.00
140	Jerry Smith	1.50
141	Brad Hubbert	1.50
142	George Blanda	23.00
143	*Pete Lammons*	1.50
144	Doug Moreau	1.50
145	E.J. Holub	1.50
146	Ode Burrell	1.50
147	Bob Scarpitto	1.50
148	Andre White	1.50
149	Jack Kemp	60.00
150	Art Graham	1.50
151	Tommy Nobis	4.00
152	*Willie Richardson*	1.50
153	Jack Concannon	1.50
154	Bill Glass	1.50
155	*Craig Morton*	12.00
156	Pat Studstill	1.50
157	Ray Nitschke	5.00
158	Roger Brown	1.50
159	Joe Kapp	5.00
160	Jim Taylor	10.00
161	Fran Tarkenton	20.00
162	Mike Ditka	25.00
163	*Andy Russell*	5.00
164	Larry Wilson	4.00
165	Tommy Davis	1.50
166	Paul Krause	1.35
167	Leslie Duncan	1.50
168	Fred Biletnikoff	11.00
169	Don Maynard	10.00
170	Frank Emanuel	1.50
171	Len Dawson	13.00
172	Miller Farr	1.50
173	*Floyd Little*	20.00
174	Lonnie Wright	1.50
175	Paul Costa	1.50
176	Don Trull	1.50
177	Jerry Simmons	1.50
178	Tom Matte	1.50
179	Bennie McRae	1.50
180	Jim Kanicki	1.50
181	Bob Lilly	7.00
182	Tom Watkins	1.50
183	*Jim Grabowski*	2.00
184	*Jack Snow*	4.50
185	*Gary Cuzzo*	1.50
186	Billy Kilmer	4.00
187	Jim Katcavage	1.50
188	Floyd Peters	1.50
189	Bill Nelsen	1.50
190	Bobby J. Conrad	1.50
191	Kermit Alexander	1.50
192	Charley Taylor	6.00
193	Lance Alworth	13.00
194	Daryle Lamonica	5.00
195	Al Atkinson	1.50
196	*Bob Griese*	85.00
197	Buck Buchanan	4.00
198	Pete Beathard	1.50
199	Nemiah Wilson	1.50
200	Ernie Wright	1.50
201	George Saimes	1.50
202	John Charles	1.50
203	Randy Johnson	1.50
204	Tony Lorick	1.50
205	Dick Evey	1.50
206	Leroy Kelly	7.50
207	Lee Roy Jordan	5.00
208	Jim Gibbons	1.50
209	*Donny Anderson*	4.00
210	Maxie Baughan	1.50
211	Joe Morrison	1.50
212	Jim Snowden	1.50
213	Lenny Lyles	1.50
214	Bobby Joe Green	1.50
215	Frank Ryan	1.35
216	Cornell Green	1.50
217	Karl Sweetan	1.50
218	Dave Williams	1.50
219	Checklist (blue)	20.00

1968 Topps Posters

Sixteen players from both the AFL and NFL are included in this set. Posters, printed on paper, measure about 5" x 7" and were issued in gum packs, similar to the Topps baseball posters of the same year. A full-color posed action shot is on the front, with the players, name, team and position shown in an oval at the bottom of the front. Backs are blank.

		NM/M
Complete Set (16):		50.00
Common Player:		1.50
1	Johnny Unitas	9.00
2	Leroy Kelly	1.50
3	Bob Hayes	1.50
4	Bart Starr	5.00
5	Charley Taylor	1.50
6	Fran Tarkenton	4.50
7	Jim Bakken	1.50
8	Gale Sayers	6.00
9	Gary Cuozzo	1.50
10	Les Josephson	1.50
11	Jim Nance	1.50
12	Brad Hubbert	1.50
13	Keith Lincoln	1.50
14	Don Maynard	2.00
15	Len Dawson	3.00
16	Jack Clancy	1.50

1968 Topps Stand-Ups

These 22 unnumbered card-size (2-1/2" x 3-1/2") issues were meant to be punched and folded in order to make them stand. Cards lose much of their value if they're not complete; obviously, not too many complete sets have been found. Cards show a head shot of the player, with his name beneath the photo. Backs are blank. Cards are listed below in alphabetical order.

		NM/M
Complete Set (22):		225.00
Common Player:		5.00
(1)	Sid Blanks	5.00
(2)	John Brodie	12.00
(3)	Jack Concannon	5.00
(4)	Roman Gabriel	7.00
(5)	Art Graham	5.00
(6)	Jim Grabowski	5.00
(7)	John Hadl	7.00
(8)	Jim Hart	7.00
(9)	Homer Jones	5.00
(10)	Sonny Jurgensen	15.00
(11)	Alex Karras	9.00
(12)	Billy Kilmer	7.00
(13)	Daryle Lamonica	5.00
(14)	Floyd Little	5.00
(15)	Curtis McClinton	5.00
(16)	Don Meredith	35.00
(17)	Joe Namath	85.00
(18)	Bill Nelsen	5.00
(19)	Dave Osborn	5.00
(20)	Willie Richardson	5.00
(21)	Frank Ryan	5.00
(22)	Norm Snead	5.00

1968 Topps Test Teams

These were printed in an extremely limited number by Topps. Cards are a bit oversize -- about 2-1/2" x 4-5/8" -- and show a posed shot of the entire team on the front. A nameplate is beneath the picture, and a "frame" features footballs in each of the corners. The back is a guide to the photo, complete with little footballs to indicate each row. Cards were issued in alphabetical order by city name, and are numbered on the back.

		NM/M
Complete Set (25):		2,700
Common Team:		100.00
1	Atlanta Falcons	100.00
2	Baltimore Colts	100.00
3	Buffalo Bills	100.00
4	Chicago Bears	135.00
5	Cleveland Browns	100.00
6	Dallas Cowboys	135.00
7	Denver Broncos	135.00
8	Detroit Lions	100.00
9	Green Bay Packers	135.00
10	Houston Oilers	100.00
11	Kansas City Chiefs	100.00
12	Los Angeles Rams	100.00
13	Miami Dolphins	135.00
14	Minnesota Vikings	100.00
15	New England Patriots	100.00
16	New Orleans Saints	100.00
17	New York Giants	135.00
18	New York Jets	135.00
19	Oakland Raiders	135.00
20	Philadelphia Eagles	100.00
21	Pittsburgh Steelers	135.00
22	St. Louis Cardinals	100.00
23	San Diego Chargers	100.00
24	San Francisco 49ers	135.00
25	Washington Redskins	100.00

1968 Topps Team Patch/Stickers

These patches, inserted into packs of Topps test team cards, feature team logos for each NFL team. One test team card and a sticker were in each pack; the stickers were supposed to be the main item inside, according to the wrapper. The stickers measure 2-1/2" x 3-1/2".

		NM/M
Complete Set (44):		1,600
Common Sticker:		10.00
1	1 and 2	15.00
2	3 and 4	10.00
3	5 and 6	12.00
4	7 and 8	10.00
5	9 and 0	10.00
6	A and B	12.00
7	C and D	10.00
8	E and F	10.00
9	G and H	12.00
10	I and W	10.00
11	J and X	10.00
12	Atlanta Falcons	60.00
13	Baltimore Colts	65.00
14	Chicago Bears	80.00
15	Cleveland Browns	60.00
16	Dallas Cowboys	140.00
17	Detroit Lions	60.00
18	Green Bay Packers	80.00
19	Los Angeles Rams	60.00
20	Minnesota Vikings	65.00
21	New Orleans Saints	60.00
22	New York Giants	75.00
23	K and L	10.00
24	M and O	12.00
25	N and P	10.00
26	Q and R	10.00
27	S and T	12.00
28	U and V	10.00
29	Y and Z	10.00
30	Philadelphia Eagles	60.00
31	Pittsburgh Steelers	80.00
32	St. Louis Cardinals	60.00
33	San Francisco 49ers	75.00
34	Washington Redskins	120.00
35	Boston Patriots	60.00
36	Buffalo Bills	75.00
37	Denver Broncos	120.00
38	Houston Oilers	75.00
39	Kansas City Chiefs	60.00
40	Miami Dolphins	110.00
41	New York Jets	75.00
42	Oakland Raiders	140.00
43	San Diego Chargers	60.00
44	Cincinnati Bengals	70.00

1969 Topps

This 263-card set was printed in two series and in two different styles. The first series cards (1-132) have no borders, while the second series has white borders. In the borderless version, a player photo is set against a brightly colored background. A large team logo is in the lower right hand corner, and a player name and position and team name are in a white box at the card bottom. Second-series cards are of identical design, except for a white border around the player photo. This development is not pleasing for collectors searching for the first series in mint condition, since the lack of borders makes it tough to find any in superb condition. The variation in the set is the checklist card, #132, which is found with and without borders, depending on the series in which it was printed. Another variation in the set involved card #18, Tom Beer. In some versions of the card, the "B" in his last name is slightly raised above the rest of the name on the card front. Versions of each have been reported. The key card in this set is Brian Piccolo's rookie card; this and his Four In One issue are the only cards on which he appears. Other rookies in this set include Larry Csonka, Lance Rentzel, and Mike Curtis. Hall of Famers Doug Atkins and Bobby Mitchell were featured on their final regular-issue cards.

		NM/M
Complete Set (263):		550.00
Common Player (1-132):		1.00
Common Player (133-263):		1.15
Series 1 Wax Pack (12+1):		340.00
Series 1 Wax Box (24):		7175.00
Series 2 Wax Pack (12+2):		300.00
Series 2 Wax Box (24):		6300.00
1	LeRoy Kelly	12.00
2	Paul Flatley	1.00
3	Jim Cadile	1.00
4	Erich Barnes	1.00
5	Willie Richardson	1.00
6	Bob Hayes	3.00
7	Bob Jeter	1.00
8	Jim Colclough	1.00
9	Sherrill Headrick	1.00
10	Jim Dunaway	1.00
11	Bill Munson	1.00
12	Jack Pardee	1.75
13	Jim Lindsey	1.00
14	Dave Whitsell	1.00
15	Tucker Frederickson	1.00
16	Alvin Haymond	1.00
17	Andy Russell	1.00
18	Tom Beer	1.00
19	Bobby Maples	1.00
20	Len Dawson	8.00
21	Willis Crenshaw	1.00
22	Tommy Davis	1.00
23	Rickie Harris	1.00
24	Jerry Simmons	1.00
25	Johnny Unitas	25.00
26	*Brian Piccolo*	75.00
27	Bob Matheson	1.00
28	Howard Twilley	1.00
29	Jim Turner	1.00
30	*Pete Banaszak*	1.50
31	*Lance Rentzel*	1.50
32	Bill Triplett	1.00
33	Boyd Dowler	1.00
34	Merlin Olsen	5.00
35	Joe Kapp	1.50
36	*Dan Abramowicz*	3.00
37	Spider Lockhart	1.00
38	Tom Day	1.00
39	Art Graham	1.00
40	Bob Cappadona	1.00
41	Gary Ballman	1.00
42	Clendon Thomas	1.00
43	Jackie Smith	3.00
44	Dave Wilcox	1.00
45	Jerry Smith	1.00
46	Dan Grimm	1.00
47	Tom Matte	1.00
48	John Stofa	1.00
49	Rex Mirich	1.00
50	Miller Farr	1.00
51	Gale Sayers	50.00
52	Bill Nelsen	1.00
53	Bob Lilly	6.00
54	Wayne Walker	1.00
55	Ray Nitschke	5.00
56	Ed Meador	1.00
57	Lonnie Warwick	1.00
58	Wendell Hayes	1.00
59	*Dick Anderson*	3.00
60	Don Maynard	6.00
61	Tony Lorick	1.00
62	Pete Gogolak	1.00
63	Nate Ramsey	1.00
64	Dick Shiner	1.00
65	Larry Wilson	3.25
66	Ken Willard	1.00
67	Charley Taylor	5.50
68	Billy Cannon	1.50
69	Lance Alworth	8.00
70	Jim Nance	1.00
71	Nick Rassas	1.00
72	Lenny Lyles	1.00
73	Bennie McRae	1.00
74	Bill Glass	1.00
75	Don Meredith	20.00
76	Dick LeBeau	1.00
77	Carroll Dale	1.00
78	Ron McDole	1.00
79	Charley King	1.00
80	Checklist 1-132	14.00
81	Dick Bass	1.00
82	Roy Winston	1.00
83	Don McCall	1.00
84	Jim Katcavage	1.00
85	Norm Snead	3.00
86	Earl Gros	1.00
87	Don Brumm	1.00
88	Sonny Bishop	1.00
89	Fred Arbanas	1.00
90	Karl Noonan	1.00
91	Dick Witcher	1.00
92	Vince Promuto	1.00
93	Tommy Nobis	3.00
94	Jerry Hill	1.00
95	*Ed O'Bradovich*	1.75
96	Ernie Kellerman	1.00
97	Chuck Howley	1.00
98	Hewritt Dixon	1.00
99	Ron Mix	3.25
100	Joe Namath	80.00
101	Billy Gambrell	1.00
102	Elijah Pitts	1.00
103	Billy Truax	1.00
104	Ed Sharockman	1.00
105	Doug Atkins	3.25
106	Greg Larson	1.00
107	Israel Lang	1.00
108	Houston Antwine	1.00
109	Paul Guidry	1.00
110	Al Denson	1.00
111	Roy Jefferson	1.00
112	Chuck LaTourette	1.00
113	Jimmy Johnson	1.00
114	Bobby Mitchell	4.00
115	Randy Johnson	1.00
116	Lou Michaels	1.00
117	Rudy Kuechenberg	1.00
118	Walt Suggs	1.00
119	Goldie Sellers	1.00
120	*Larry Csonka*	80.00
121	Jim Houston	1.00
122	Craig Baynham	1.00
123	Alex Karras	6.00
124	Jim Grabowski	1.25
125	Roman Gabriel	3.00
126	Larry Bowie	1.00
127	Dave Parks	1.00
128	Ben Davidson	2.00
129	Steve DeLong	1.00
130	Fred Hill	1.00
131	Ernie Koy	1.00
132	Checklist 133-263	15.00
133	Dick Hoak	1.15
134	*Larry Stallings*	1.50
135	*Clifton McNeil*	1.50
136	Walter Rock	1.15
137	Billy Lothridge	1.15
138	Bob Vogel	1.15
139	Dick Butkus	25.00
140	Frank Ryan	1.50
141	Larry Garron	1.15
142	George Saimes	1.15
143	Frank Buncom	1.15
144	Don Perkins	1.50
145	Johnny Robinson	1.15
146	Lee Roy Caffey	1.15
147	Bernie Casey	1.15
148	Billy Martin	1.15
149	Gene Howard	1.15
150	Fran Tarkenton	20.00
151	Eric Crabtree	1.15
152	W.K. Hicks	1.15
153	Bobby Bell	4.00
154	Sam Baker	1.15
155	Marv Woodson	1.15
156	Dave Williams	1.15
157	Bruce Bosley	1.15
158	Carl Kammerer	1.15
159	Jim Burson	1.15
160	Roy Hilton	1.15
161	Bob Griese	30.00
162	Bob Talamini	1.15
163	Jim Otto	3.75
164	Ron Bull	1.15
165	Walter Johnson	1.50
166	Lee Roy Jordan	3.50
167	Mike Lucci	1.15
168	Willie Wood	3.50
169	Maxie Baughan	1.15
170	Bill Brown	1.15
171	John Hadl	3.00
172	Gino Cappelletti	1.75
173	George Byrd	1.15
174	Steve Stonebreaker	1.15
175	Joe Morrison	1.15
176	Joe Scarpati	1.15
177	Bobby Walden	1.15
178	Roy Shivers	1.15
179	Kermit Alexander	1.15
180	Pat Richter	1.15
181	Pete Perreault	1.15
182	Pete Duranko	1.15
183	Leroy Mitchell	1.15
184	Jim Simon	1.15
185	Billy Ray Smith	1.15
186	Jack Concannon	1.15
187	Ben Davis	1.15
188	Mike Clark	1.15
189	Jim Gibbons	1.15
190	Dave Robinson	1.15
191	Otis Taylor	2.00
192	Nick Buoniconti	2.75
193	Matt Snell	2.00
194	Bruce Gossett	1.15
195	Mick Tingelhoff	1.50
196	Earl Leggett	1.15
197	Pete Case	1.15
198	*Tom Woodeshick*	1.50
199	Ken Kortas	1.15
200	Jim Hart	3.00
201	Fred Biletnikoff	10.00
202	Jacque MacKinnon	1.15
203	Jim Whalen	1.15
204	Matt Hazeltine	1.15
205	Charlie Gogolak	1.15
206	Ray Ogden	1.15
207	John Mackey	3.75
208	Rosey Taylor	1.15
209	Gene Hickerson	1.15
210	*Dave Edwards*	1.50
211	Tom Sestak	1.15
212	Ernie Wright	1.15
213	Dave Costa	1.15
214	Tom Vaughn	1.15
215	Bart Starr	25.00
216	Les Josephson	1.15
217	Fred Cox	1.15
218	Mike Tilleman	1.15
219	Darrell Dess	1.15
220	Dave Lloyd	1.15
221	Pete Beathard	1.15
222	Buck Buchanan	3.50
223	Frank Emanuel	1.15
224	Paul Martha	1.15
225	Johnny Roland	1.15
226	Gary Lewis	1.15
227	Sonny Jurgensen	7.00
228	Jim Butler	1.15
229	*Mike Curtis*	4.00
230	Richie Petitbon	1.50
231	George Sauer Jr.	1.15
232	George Blanda	20.00
233	Gary Garrison	1.15
234	Gary Collins	1.15
235	Craig Morton	4.00
236	Tom Nowatzke	1.15
237	Donny Anderson	1.15
238	Deacon Jones	4.00
239	Grady Alderman	1.15
240	Bill Kilmer	3.00
241	Mike Taliaferro	1.15
242	Stew Barber	1.15
243	Bobby Hunt	1.15
244	Homer Jones	1.15
245	Bob Brown	1.15
246	Bill Asbury	1.15
247	Charley Johnson	1.75
248	Chris Hanburger	1.15
249	John Brodie	8.00
250	Earl Morrall	2.00
251	Floyd Little	5.00
252	*Jerrell Wilson*	1.50
253	Jim Keyes	1.15
254	Mel Renfro	1.50
255	Herb Adderley	4.00
256	Jack Snow	1.15
257	Charlie Durkee	1.15
258	Charlie Harper	1.15
259	J.R. Wilburn	1.15
260	Charlie Krueger	1.15
261	Pete Jacquess	1.15
262	Gerry Philbin	1.15
263	Daryle Lamonica	12.00

A player's name in *italic* type indicates a rookie card.

1969 Topps Four In Ones

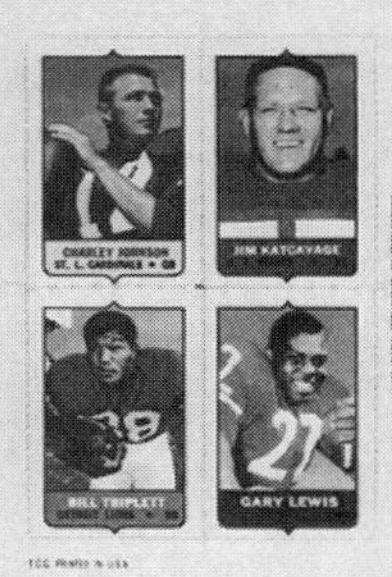

Issued one per pack in the 1969 Topps football wax packs, each "card" contained four perforated cards of NFL players which could be punched out and inserted into each team's mini-album. The cards are unnumbered, but appear here in alphabetical order according to the last name of the player who appears in the upper left corner of the card. One variation does exist: Cards #27 and 28 show the same four players, but Charlie Johnson on #27 has a red logo while #28 gives him a white one. Bill Triplett on #27 has a white logo, while #28 is red. Both seem to have been issued in equal quantities. Most of the cards in this set are of the key players, including Brian Piccolo and Larry Csonka rookies. A few of the lesser-known NFL players appeared in this set only and not the regular 1969 set (and vice versa). An important note: the entire card is priced here. The small, individual cards have very little value when separated from the rest of the card, as is the case with Topps' 1980-81 basketball issue.

		NM/M
Complete Set (66):		185.00
Common Card:		1.00
(1)	Grady Alderman, Jerry Smith, Gale Sayers, Dick LeBeau	6.00
(2)	Jim Allison, Frank Buncom, Frank Emanuel, George Sauer Jr.	1.00
(3)	Lance Alworth, Don Maynard, Ron McDole, Billy Cannon	3.00
(4)	Dick Anderson, Mike Taliaferro, Fred Biletnikoff, Otis Taylor	2.25
(5)	Ralph Baker, Les Duncan, Eric Crabtree, Bobby Bell	1.00
(6)	Gary Ballman, Jerry Hill, Roy Jefferson, Boyd Dowler	1.00
(7)	Tom Beer, Miller Farr, Jim Colclough, Steve DeLong	1.00
(8)	Sonny Bishop, Pete Banaszak, Paul Guidry, Tom Day	1.00
(9)	Bruce Bosley, J.R. Wilburn, Tom Nowatzke, Jim Simon	1.00
(10)	Larry Bowie, Willis Crenshaw, Tommy Davis, Paul Flatley	1.00
(11)	Nick Buoniconti, George Saimes, Jacque MacKinnon, Pete Duranko	1.00
(12)	Jim Burson, Dan Abramowicz, Ed O'Bradovich, Dick Witcher	1.00
(13)	Reg Carolan, Larry Garron, W.K. Hicks, Pete Jacques	1.00
(14)	Bert Coan, John Hadl, Dan Birdwell, Sam Brunelli	1.00
(15)	Hewritt Dixon, Goldie Sellers, Joe Namath, Howard Twilley	20.00
(16)	Charlie Durkee, Clinton McNeil, Maxie Baughan, Fran Tarkenton	6.00
(17)	Pete Gogolak, Ron Bull, Chuck LaTourette, Willie Richardson	1.00
(18)	Bob Griese, Jim Lemoine, Dave Grayson, Walt Sweeney	4.00
(19)	Jim Hart, Darrell Dess, Kermit Alexander, Mick Tingelhoff	1.00
(20)	Alvin Haymond, Elijah Pitts, Billy Ray Smith, Ken Willard	1.00
(21)	Gene Hickerson, Donny Anderson, Dick Butkus, Mike Lucci	4.00

(22)	Fred Hill, Ernie Koy, Tommy Nobis, Bennie McRae	1.00
(23)	Dick Hoak, Roman Gabriel, Ed Sharockman, Dave Williams	1.00
(24)	Jim Houston, Roy Shivers, Carroll Dale, Bill Asbury	1.00
(25)	Gene Howard, Joe Morrison, Billy Martin, Ben Davis	1.00
(26)	Chuck Howley, Brian Piccolo, Chris Hanburger, Erich Barnes	14.00
(27)	Charlie Johnson, Jim Katcavage, Gary Lewis, Bill Triplett (red white)	4.00
(28)	Charlie Johnson, Jim Katcavage, Gary Lewis, Bill Triplett (white red)	4.00
(29)	Walter Johnson, Tucker Frederickson, Dave Lloyd, Bobby Walden	1.00
(30)	Sonny Jurgensen, Dick Bass, Paul Martha, Dave Parks	3.00
(31)	Leroy Kelly, Ed Meador, Bart Starr, Ray Ogden	6.00
(32)	Charlie King, Bob Cappadona, Fred Arbanas, Ben Davidson	1.00
(33)	Daryle Lamonica, Carl Cunningham, Bobby Hunt, Stew Barber	1.00
(34)	Israel Lang, Bob Lilly, Jim Butler, John Brodie	4.00
(35)	Jim Lindsey, Ray Nitschke, Rickie Harris, Bob Vogel	1.00
(36)	Billy Lothridge, Herb Adderly, Charlie Gogolak, John Mackey	2.00
(37)	Bobby Maples, Karl Noonan, Houston Antwine, Wendell Hayes	1.00
(38)	Don Meredith, Gary Collins, Homer Jones, Marv Woodson	6.00
(39)	Rex Mirich, Art Graham, Jim Turner, John Stofa	1.00
(40)	Leroy Mitchell, Sid Blanks, Paul Rochester, Pete Perreault	1.00
(41)	Jim Nance, Jim Dunaway, Larry Csonka, Ron Mix	2.00
(42)	Bill Nelsen, Bill Munson, Nate Ramsey, Mike Curtis	1.00
(43)	Jim Otto, Dave herman, Dave Costa, Dennis Randall	1.00
(44)	Jack Pardee, Norm Snead, Craig Baynham	1.00
(45)	Richie Petitbon, John Robinson, Mike Clark, Jack Snow	1.00
(46)	Nick Rassas, Tom Matte, Lance Rentzel, Bobby Mitchell	1.00
(47)	Pat Richter, Dave Whitsell, Joe Kapp, Bill Glass	1.00
(48)	Johnny Roland, Craig Morton, Bill Brown, Sam Baker	1.00
(49)	Andy Russell, Randy Johnson, Bob Matheson, Alex Karras	2.00
(50)	Joe Scarpati, Walter Rock, Jack Concannon, Bernie Casey	1.00
(51)	Tom Sestak, Ernie Wright, Doug Moreau, Matt Snell	1.00
(52)	Jerry Simmons, Bob Hayes, Doug Atkins, Spider Lockhart	1.00
(53)	Jackie Smith, Jim Grabowski, Jim Johnson, Charley Taylor	2.00
(54)	Larry Stallings, Roosevelt Taylor, Jim Gibbons, Bob Brown	1.00
(55)	Mike Stratton, Marion Rushing, Soloman Brannan, Jim Keyes	1.00
(56)	Walt Suggs, Len Dawson, Sherrill Headrick, Al Denson	2.00
(57)	Bob Talamini, George Blanda, Jim Whalen, Jack Kemp	22.00
(58)	Clendon Thomas, Don McCall, Earl Morrall, Lonnie Warwick	1.00
(59)	Don Trull, Gerry Philbin, Gary Garrison, Buck Buchanan	1.00
(60)	John Unitas, Les Josephson, Fred Cox, Mel Renfro	9.00
(61)	Wayne Walker, Tony Lorick, Dave Wilcox, Merlin Olsen	2.00
(62)	Willie West, Ken Herock, George Byrd, Gino Cappelletti	1.00
(63)	Jerrel Wilson, John Bramlett, Pete Beathard, Floyd Little	1.00
(64)	Larry Wilson, Lou Michaels, Billy Gambrell, Earl Gros	1.00
(65)	Willie Wood, Steve Stonebreaker, Vince Promuto, Jim Cadie	1.00
(66)	Tom Woodeshick, Greg Larson, Billy Kilmer, Don Perkins	1.50

1969 Topps mini-albums

The 26 team booklets were intended as stamp books for the 1969 Topps Four In Ones. You punched out the four players on the card and stuck them into this 2-1/2" x 3-1/2" book, right over the picture of the player. The booklets are numbered on the back and arranged in alphabetical order by city name. Aside from its condition, in order for a book to be considered mint, there must be no stamps in it.

		NM/M
Complete Set (26):		50.00
Common Booklet:		2.00
1	Atlanta Falcons	2.00
2	Baltimore Colts	2.00
3	Chicago Bears	4.00
4	Cleveland Browns	2.00
5	Dallas Cowboys	5.00
6	Detroit Lions	2.00
7	Green Bay Packers	5.00
8	Los Angeles Rams	2.00
9	Minnesota Vikings	2.00
10	New Orleans Saints	2.00
11	New York Giants	4.00
12	Philadelphia Eagles	2.00
13	Pittsburgh Steelers	4.00
14	St. Louis Cardinals	2.00
15	San Francisco 49ers	4.00
16	Washington Redskins	4.00
17	Boston Patriots	2.00
18	Buffalo Bills	4.00
19	Cincinnati Bengals	2.00
20	Denver Broncos	5.00
21	Houston Oilers	4.00
22	Kansas City Chiefs	2.00
23	Miami Dolphins	4.00
24	New York Jets	4.00
25	Oakland Raiders	5.00
26	San Diego Chargers	2.00

1970 Topps

The 1970 Topps set, which included 263 cards, was printed in two series. The second series is a little tougher to find than the first, since it was printed in lesser quantities. One variation that appears in the set is #113, Lance Rentzel. His name appears in red on the "common" card; on the hard-to-find variation, his name appears in black. Card #132, the second-series checklist card, was double-printed, a common practice for Topps during its multi-series production days. The set is best known for its inclusion of the O.J. Simpson rookie card, but other rookies in the set are Leroy Brown, Jan Stenerud, Alan Page, Bob Trumpy, Bubba Smith, Bill Bergey, Calvin Hill and Fred Dryer.

		NM/M
Complete Set (263):		450.00
Common Player (1-132):		.50
Common Player (133-263):		.75
Series 1 Wax Pack (10+1):		175.00
Series 1 Wax Box (24):		3,650
Series 2 Wax Pack (10+1):		182.50
Series 2 Wax Box (24):		3,725
1	Len Dawson	15.00
2	Doug Hart	.50
3	Verlon Biggs	.50
4	*Ralph Neely*	.75
5	Harmon Wages	.50
6	Dan Conners	.50
7	Gino Cappelletti	1.00
8	Erich Barnes	.75
9	Checklist 1-132	7.50
10	Bob Griese	15.00
11	Ed Flanagan	.50
12	George Seals	.50
13	Harry Jacobs	.50
14	Mike Haffner	.50
15	Bob Vogel	.50
16	Bill Peterson	.50
17	Spider Lockhart	.50
18	Billy Truax	.50
19	Jim Beirne	.50
20	Leroy Kelly	4.00
21	Dave Lloyd	.50
22	Mike Tilleman	.50
23	Gary Garrison	.50
24	*Larry Brown*	7.00
25	*Jan Stenerud*	12.00
26	Rolf Krueger	.50
27	Roland Lakes	.50
28	Dick Hoak	.50
29	*Gene Washington* (Vikings)	.75
30	Bart Starr	20.00
31	Dave Grayson	.50
32	Jerry Rush	.50
33	Len St. Jean	.50
34	Randy Edmunds	.50
35	Matt Snell	1.50
36	Paul Costa	.50
37	Mike Pyle	.50
38	Roy Hilton	.50
39	Steve Tensi	.50
40	Tommy Nobis	2.00
41	Pete Case	.50
42	Andy Rice	.50
43	*Elvin Bethea*	3.50
44	Jack Snow	.50
45	Mel Renfro	1.00
46	Andy Livingston	.50
47	Gary Ballman	.50
48	Bob DeMarco	.50
49	Steve DeLong	.50
50	Daryle Lamonica	3.50
51	*Jim Lynch*	.75
52	*Mel Farr*	.75
53	Bob Long	.50
54	John Elliott	.50
55	Ray Nitschke	4.00
56	Jim Shorter	.50
57	Dave Wilcox	.50
58	Eric Crabtree	.50
59	*Alan Page*	40.00
60	Jim Nance	.50
61	Glen Ray Hines	.50
62	John Mackey	3.00
63	Ron McDole	.50
64	Tom Beier	.50
65	Bill Nelsen	.65
66	Paul Flatley	.50
67	Sam Brunelli	.50
68	Jack Pardee	1.50
69	Brig Owens	.50
70	Gale Sayers	35.00
71	Lee Roy Jordan	2.00
72	*Harold Jackson*	8.00
73	John Hadl	2.50
74	Dave Parks	.50
75	*Lem Barney*	15.00
76	Johnny Roland	.50
77	Ed Budde	.50
78	Ben McGee	.50
79	Ken Bowman	.50
80	Fran Tarkenton	20.00
81	*Gene Washington*	4.00
82	Larry Grantham	.50
83	Bill Brown	.50
84	John Charles	.50
85	Fred Biletnikoff	7.00
86	Royce Berry	.50
87	Bob Lilly	4.50
88	Earl Morrall	2.00
89	Jerry LeVias	.50
90	*O.J. Simpson*	80.00
91	Mike Howell	.50
92	Ken Gray	.50
93	Chris Hanburger	.50
94	*Larry Seiple*	.75
95	*Rich Jackson*	.75
96	Rockne Freitas	.50
97	*Dick Post*	.75
98	Ben Hawkins	.50
99	Ken Reaves	.50
100	Roman Gabriel	2.50
101	Dave Rowe	.50
102	Dave Robinson	.50
103	Otis Taylor	1.50
104	Jim Turner	.50
105	Joe Morrison	.50
106	Dick Evey	.50
107	Ray Mansfield	.50
108	Grady Alderman	.50
109	Bruce Gossett	.50
110	*Bob Trumpy*	5.00
111	Jim Hunt	.50
112	Larry Stallings	.50
113	Lance Rentzel (red)	1.50
113a	Lance Rentzel (black)	1.50
114	*Bubba Smith*	25.00
115	Norm Snead	.75
116	Jim Otto	2.50
117	*Bo Scott*	.75
118	Rick Redman	.50
119	George Byrd	.50
120	*George Webster*	2.00
121	Chuck Walton	.50
122	Dave Costa	.50
123	Al Dodd	.50
124	Len Hauss	.50
125	Deacon Jones	3.50
126	Randy Johnson	.50
127	Ralph Heck	.50
128	*Emerson Boozer*	2.50
129	Johnny Robinson	.65
130	John Brodie	6.00
131	*Gale Gillingham*	1.00
132	Checklist 133-263 (DP)	8.00
133	Chuck Walker	.75
134	Bennie McRae	.75
135	Paul Warfield	6.00
136	Dan Darragh	.75
137	*Paul Robinson*	1.00
138	Ed Philpott	.75
139	Craig Morton	2.00
140	*Tom Dempsey*	5.00
141	Al Nelson	.75
142	Tom Matte	.75
143	Dick Schafrath	.75
144	Willie Brown	4.00
145	Charley Taylor	4.50
146	John Huard	.75
147	Dave Osborn	.75
148	Gene Mingo	.75
149	Larry Hand	.75
150	Joe Namath	60.00
151	*Tom Mack*	7.00
152	Kenny Graham	.75
153	Don Herrmann	.75
154	Bobby Bell	3.75
155	Hoyle Granger	.75
156	*Claude Humphrey*	1.25
157	Clifton McNeil	.75
158	Mick Tingelhoff	1.00
159	*Don Horn*	1.00
160	Larry Wilson	3.00
161	Tom Neville	.75
162	Larry Csonka	25.00
163	*Doug Buffone*	.75
164	Cornell Green	.75
165	*Haven Moses*	2.50
166	Bill Kilmer	2.50
167	*Tim Rossovich*	.75
168	*Bill Bergey*	5.00
169	Gary Collins	.75
170	Floyd Little	3.00
171	Tom Keating	.75
172	Pat Fischer	.75
173	Walt Sweeney	.75
174	Greg Larson	.75
175	Carl Eller	3.00
176	George Sauer	.75
177	Jim Hart	2.00
178	Bob Brown	.75
179	*Mike Garrett*	4.00
180	Johnny Unitas	30.00
181	Tom Regner	.75
182	Bob Jeter	.75
183	Gail Cogdill	.75
184	Earl Gros	.75
185	Dennis Partee	.75
186	Charlie Krueger	.75
187	Martin Baccaglio	.75
188	Charlie Long	.75
189	Bob Hayes	3.00
190	Dick Butkus	13.00
191	Al Bemiller	.75
192	Dick Westmoreland	.75
193	Joe Scarpati	.75
194	Ron Snidow	.75
195	*Earl McCullough*	1.00
196	Jake Kupp	.75
197	Bob Lurtsema	.75
198	Mike Current	.75
199	Charlie Smith	.75
200	Sonny Jurgensen	6.50
201	Mike Curtis	.75
202	Aaron Brown	.75
203	Richie Petitbon	1.00
204	Walt Suggs	.75
205	Roy Jefferson	.75
206	*Russ Washington*	1.00
207	*Woody Peoples*	1.00
208	Dave Williams	.75
209	*John Zook*	1.00
210	Tom Woodeshick	.75
211	Howard Fest	.75
212	Jack Concannon	.75
213	Jim Marshall	2.75
214	Jon Morris	.75
215	Dan Abramowicz	.75
216	Paul Martha	.75
217	Ken Willard	.75
218	Walter Rock	.75
219	Garland Boyette	.75
220	Buck Buchanan	3.75
221	Bill Munson	.75
222	*David Lee*	1.00
223	Karl Noonan	.75
224	Harry Schuh	.75
225	Jackie Smith	1.25
226	Gerry Philbin	.75
227	Ernie Koy	.75
228	Chuck Howley	.75
229	Billy Shaw	.75
230	Jerry Hillebrand	.75
231	*Bill Thompson*	1.50
232	Carroll Dale	.75
233	Gene Hickerson	.75
234	Jim Butler	.75
235	*Greg Cook*	1.50
236	Lee Roy Caffey	.75
237	Merlin Olsen	4.50
238	Fred Cox	.75
239	Nate Ramsey	.75
240	Lance Alworth	6.00
241	Chuck Hinton	.75
242	Jerry Smith	.75
243	Tony Baker	.75
244	Nick Buoniconti	2.50
245	Jim Johnson	.75
246	Willie Richardson	.75
247	*Fred Dryer*	15.00
248	Bobby Maples	.75
249	Alex Karras	5.50
250	Joe Kapp	2.00
251	Ben Davidson	2.50
252	Mike Stratton	.75
253	Les Josephson	.75
254	Don Maynard	6.00
255	Houston Antwine	.75
256	*Mac Percival*	1.00
257	George Goeddeke	.75
258	Homer Jones	.75
259	Bob Berry	.75
260	*Calvin Hill*	10.00
261	Willie Wood	3.00
262	Ed Weisacosky	.75
263	Jim Tyrer	3.00

1970 Topps Super Glossy

A collector favorite, this 33-card set is among the decade's most expensive subsets. These were found in the second series of 1970 Topps football wax packs and had full-color action-pose glossy fronts, heavy white cardboard stock, and rounded corners. The only information on the white backs is the player's name, team, position and card number.

		NM/M
Complete Set (33):		300.00
Common Player:		3.00
1	Tommy Nobis	3.00
2	John Unitas	27.50
3	Tom Matte	3.00
4	Mac Percival	3.00
5	Leroy Kelly	3.00
6	Mel Renfro	3.00
7	Bob Hayes	3.00
8	Earl McCullouch	3.00
9	Bart Starr	22.00
10	Willie Wood	7.00
11	Jack Snow	3.00
12	Joe Kapp	5.00
13	Dave Osborn	3.00
14	Dan Abramowicz	3.00
15	Fran Tarkenton	22.00
16	Tom Woodeshick	3.00
17	Roy Jefferson	3.00
18	Jackie Smith	3.00
19	Jim Johnson	3.00
20	Sonny Jurgensen	12.00
21	Houston Antwine	3.00
22	O.J. Simpson	60.00
23	Greg Cook	3.00
24	Floyd Little	4.00
25	Rich Jackson	3.00
26	George Webster	3.00
27	Len Dawson	9.00
28	Bob Griese	14.00
29	Joe Namath	70.00
30	Matt Snell	3.00
31	Daryle Lamonica	4.00
32	Fred Biletnikoff	7.00
33	Dick Post	3.00

1970 Topps posters

This 24-poster set was included one per pack in the first series of 1970 Topps football wax packs. The posters, which measure about 8" x 10", were folded several times; it's very difficult to find any in top condition.

		NM/M
Complete Set (24):		50.00
Common Player:		1.00
1	Gale Sayers	4.50
2	Bobby Bell	3.00
3	Roman Gabriel	3.25
4	Jim Tyrer	1.00
5	Willie Brown	3.00
6	Carl Eller	3.00
7	Tom Mack	1.50
8	Deacon Jones	3.00
9	Johnny Robinson	1.00
10	Jan Stenerud	2.00
11	Dick Butkus	5.00
12	Lem Barney	1.00
13	David Lee	1.00
14	Larry Wilson	2.00
15	Gene Hickerson	1.00
16	Lance Alworth	3.00
17	Merlin Olsen	3.00
18	Bob Trumpy	2.00
19	Bob Lilly	3.00
20	Mick Tingelhoff	1.50
21	Calvin Hill	2.00
22	Paul Warfield	2.00
23	Chuck Howley	1.00
24	Bob Brown	1.00

1970 Topps Supers

A 35-card set issued three per pack with a stick of gum, the cards featured an action pose of an NFL star with a facsimile autograph. No other identification is on the front. Card backs show the reverse of the player's regular 1970 card. These were printed on heavy white cardboard stock and measure about 3-1/8" x 5-1/4". The final seven in the set were apparently short-printed (possibly added late) and are much harder to find than the first 28 cards.

		NM/M
Complete Set (35):		300.00
Common Player:		2.75
1	Fran Tarkenton	16.00
2	Floyd Little	3.00
3	Bart Starr	16.00
4	Len Dawson	8.50
5	Dick Post	2.75
6	Sonny Jurgensen	8.50
7	Deacon Jones	5.00
8	Leroy Kelly	2.75
9	Larry Wilson	2.75
10	Greg Cook	2.75
11	Carl Eller	4.50
12	Lem Barney	2.75
13	Lance Alworth	7.00
14	Dick Butkus	12.00
15	John Unitas	25.00
16	Roy Jefferson	2.75
17	Bobby Bell	5.00
18	John Brodie	9.00
19	Dan Abramowicz	2.75
20	Matt Snell	2.75
21	Tom Matte	2.75
22	Gale Sayers	20.00
23	Tom Woodeshick	2.75
24	O.J. Simpson	50.00
25	Roman Gabriel	5.00
26	Jim Nance	2.75
27	Joe Morrison	2.75
28	Calvin Hill	2.75
29	Tommy Nobis	6.50
30	Bob Hayes	6.50
31	Joe Kapp	6.50
32	Daryle Lamonica	6.50
33	Joe Namath	65.00
34	George Webster	6.50
35	Bob Griese	15.00

1971 Topps

This 263-card set was released in two series, with the first containing cards #1-132 and the second with cards #133-263. The second-series checklist (card #106) is double-printed. There aren't any subsets in the 1971 issue, but the NFC players are designated by red borders and AFC players have blue borders. All-stars have blue borders. This, incidentally, is the last Topps set that would not contain some type of subset. Hall of Famers with rookie cards in this set include Terry Bradshaw, Joe Greene, Willie Lanier, and Ken Houston. Other rookies include Duane Thomas, Ron Johnson, Mercury Morris, Garo Yepremian, Mark Mosley, and Charlie Sanders.

		NM/M
Complete Set (263):		500.00
Common Player (1-132):		.50
Common Player (133-263):		.75
Series 1 Wax Pack (8+2):		250.00
Series 1 Wax Box (24):		5,300
Series 2 Wax Pack (8+2):		300.00
Series 2 Wax Box (24):		6,375
1	Johnny Unitas	40.00
2	Jim Butler	.50
3	*Marty Schottenheimer*	20.00
4	Joe O'Donnell	.50
5	Tom Dempsey	1.00
6	Chuck Allen	.50
7	Ernie Kellerman	.50
8	*Walt Garrison*	2.50
9	Bill Van Heusen	.50
10	Lance Alworth	5.00
11	*Greg Landry*	5.00
12	Larry Krause	.50
13	Buck Buchanan	2.50
14	*Roy Gerela*	1.00
15	Clifton McNeil	.50
16	Bob Brown	.50
17	Lloyd Mumphord	.50
18	Gary Cuozzo	.50
19	Don Maynard	5.00
20	Larry Wilson	2.50
21	Charlie Smith	.50
22	Ken Avery	.50
23	Billy Walik	.50
24	Jim Johnson	2.00
25	Dick Butkus	20.00
26	Charley Taylor	4.25
27	Checklist 1-132	8.00
28	*Lionel Aldridge*	1.00
29	Billy Lothridge	.50
30	*Terry Hanratty*	1.25
31	Lee Roy Jordan	2.00
32	*Rick Volk*	.75
33	Howard Kindig	.50
34	*Carl Garrett*	1.00
35	Bobby Bell	2.50
36	Gene Hickerson	.50
37	Dave Parks	.50
38	Paul Martha	.50
39	George Blanda	15.00
40	Tom Woodeshick	.50
41	Alex Karras	4.00
42	Rick Redman	.50
43	Zeke Moore	.50
44	Jack Snow	.50
45	Larry Csonka	12.00
46	Karl Kassulke	.50

#	Player	NM/M
47	Jim Hart	2.00
48	Al Atkinson	.50
49	*Horst Muhlmann*	.75
50	Sonny Jurgensen	6.00
51	*Ron Johnson*	2.50
52	Cas Banaszek	.50
53	Bubba Smith	8.00
54	*Bobby Douglass*	1.50
55	Willie Wood	2.50
56	Bake Turner	.50
57	Mike Morgan	.50
58	George Byrd	.50
59	Don Horn	.50
60	Tommy Nobis	2.00
61	Jan Stenerud	3.00
62	*Altie Taylor*	.75
63	Gary Pettigrew	.50
64	Spike Jones	.50
65	*Duane Thomas*	2.50
66	*Marty Domres*	.75
67	Dick Anderson	.50
68	Ken Iman	.50
69	Miller Farr	.50
70	Daryle Lamonica	2.50
71	Alan Page	8.00
72	Pat Matson	.50
73	Emerson Boozer	1.00
74	Pat Fischer	.50
75	Gary Collins	.50
76	*John Fuqua*	1.00
77	Bruce Gossett	.50
78	Ed O'Bradovich	.50
79	*Bob Tucker*	1.50
80	Mike Curtis	.50
81	Rich Jackson	.50
82	Tom Janik	.50
83	Gale Gillingham	.50
84	Jim Mitchell	.50
85	Charlie Johnson	1.00
86	Edgar Chandler	.50
87	Cyril Pinder	.50
88	Johnny Robinson	.50
89	Ralph Neely	.50
90	Dan Abramowicz	.50
91	*Mercury Morris*	6.00
92	Steve DeLong	.50
93	Larry Stallings	.50
94	Tom Mack	2.50
95	Hewritt Dixon	.50
96	Fred Cox	.50
97	Chris Hanburger	.50
98	Gerry Philbin	.50
99	Ernie Wright	.50
100	John Brodie	5.00
101	Tucker Frederickson	.50
102	Bobby Walden	.50
103	Dick Gordon	.50
104	Walter Johnson	.50
105	Mike Lucci	.50
106	Checklist 133-263	6.00
107	Ron Berger	.50
108	Dan Sullivan	.50
109	*George Kunz*	2.00
110	Floyd Little	2.50
111	Zeke Bratkowski	.50
112	Haven Moses	.50
113	*Ken Houston*	20.00
114	*Willie Lanier*	20.00
115	Larry Brown	2.00
116	Tim Rossovich	.50
117	Errol Linden	.50
118	Mel Renfro	1.25
119	Mike Garrett	1.00
120	Fran Tarkenton	20.00
121	*Garo Yepremian*	3.00
122	Glen Condren	.50
123	Johnny Roland	.50
124	Dave Herman	.50
125	Merlin Olsen	4.00
126	Doug Buffone	.50
127	Earl McCullouch	.50
128	Spider Lockhart	.50
129	Ken Willard	.50
130	Gene Washington (MN)	.50
131	*Mike Phipps*	1.75
132	Andy Russell	.50
133	Ray Nitschke	4.50
134	Jerry Logan	.75
135	*MacArthur Lane*	2.00
136	Jim Turner	.75
137	Kent McCloughan	.75
138	Paul Guidry	.75
139	Otis Taylor	1.50
140	*Virgil Carter*	1.00
141	Joe Dawkins	.75
142	Steve Preece	.75
143	*Mike Bragg*	.75
144	Bob Lilly	4.50
145	Joe Kapp	1.25
146	Al Dodd	.75
147	Nick Buoniconti	2.50
148	Speedy Duncan	.75
149	*Cedrick Hardman*	1.00
150	Gale Sayers	30.00
151	Jim Otto	3.00
152	Billy Truax	.75
153	John Elliott	.75
154	Dick LeBeau	.75
155	Bill Bergey	1.75
156	*Terry Bradshaw*	175.00
157	Leroy Kelly	4.50
158	Paul Krause	2.00
159	Ted Vactor	.75
160	Bob Griese	12.00
161	Ernie McMillan	.75
162	Donny Anderson	.75
163	John Pitts	.75
164	Dave Costa	.75
165	Gene Washington (SF)	1.50
166	John Zook	.55
167	Pete Gogolak	.75
168	Erich Barnes	.55
169	Alvin Reed	.75
170	Jim Nance	.75
171	Craig Morton	2.00
172	Gary Garrison	.75
173	Joe Scarpati	.75
174	Adrian Young	.75
175	John Mackey	2.50
176	Mac Percival	.75
177	*Preston Pearson*	4.00
178	Fred Biletnikoff	6.00
179	*Mike Battle*	1.00
180	Len Dawson	7.00
181	Les Josephson	.75
182	Royce Berry	.75
183	Herman Weaver	.75
184	Norm Snead	1.25
185	Sam Brunelli	.75
186	*Jim Kiick*	4.00
187	Austin Denney	.75
188	*Roger Wehrli*	3.00
189	Dave Wilcox	.75
190	Bob Hayes	2.00
191	Joe Morrison	.75
192	Manny Sistrunk	.75
193	*Don Cockroft*	1.50
194	Lee Bouggess	.75
195	Bob Berry	.75
196	Ron Sellers	.75
197	George Webster	.75
198	Hoyle Granger	.75
199	Bob Vogel	.75
200	Bart Starr	25.00
201	Mike Mercer	.75
202	Dave Smith	.75
203	Lee Roy Caffey	.75
204	Mick Tingelhoff	.75
205	Matt Snell	1.50
206	Jim Tyrer	.75
207	Willie Brown	3.50
208	*Bob Johnson*	1.50
209	Deacon Jones	3.00
210	*Charlie Sanders*	4.50
211	*Jake Scott*	5.00
212	*Bob Anderson*	2.00
213	Charlie Krueger	.75
214	Jim Bakken	.75
215	Harold Jackson	2.50
216	Bill Brundige	.75
217	Calvin Hill	2.00
218	Claude Humphrey	.75
219	Glen Ray Hines	.75
220	Bill Nelsen	.75
221	Roy Hilton	.75
222	Don Herrmann	.75
223	John Bramlett	.75
224	Ken Ellis	.75
225	Dave Osborn	.75
226	*Edd Hargett*	.75
227	Gene Mingo	.75
228	Larry Grantham	.75
229	Dick Post	.75
230	Roman Gabriel	3.00
231	Mike Eischeid	.75
232	Jim Lynch	.75
233	*Lemar Parrish*	3.00
234	Cecil Turner	.75
235	*Dennis Shaw*	1.00
236	Mel Farr	.75
237	Curt Knight	.75
238	Chuck Howley	.75
239	*Bruce Taylor*	1.00
240	Jerry LeVias	.75
241	Bob Lurtsema	.75
242	Earl Morrall	2.00
243	Kermit Alexander	.75
244	Jackie Smith	1.00
245	*Joe Greene*	60.00
246	Harmon Wages	.75
247	Errol Mann	.75
248	Mike McCoy	.75
249	*Milt Morin*	1.00
250	Joe Namath	50.00
251	Jackie Burkett	.75
252	Steve Chomyszak	.75
253	Ed Sharockman	.75
254	*Robert Holmes*	1.00
255	John Hadl	2.00
256	Cornell Gordon	.75
257	*Mark Moseley*	5.00
258	Gus Otto	.75
259	Mike Taliaferro	.75
260	O.J. Simpson	25.00
261	Paul Warfield	7.00
262	Jack Concannon	.75
263	Tom Matte	3.00

1971 Topps Game Cards

The 53 cards in this set came one per pack inside wax packs of 1971 Topps football cards. Intended for use in a card game, these cards are similar to playing cards and carry a head "Action" shot of the player, his name and team in a diagonal stripe across the front, and a play (such as "Interception," "Touchdown" and "Fumble") on the top and bottom. Card backs are light blue and show the Topps logo inside a football helmet surrounding a football. The set has 52 "playing cards" plus a "first down/field marker" for use with the game. Six of the cards in the series were double-printed: Dick Butkus, Bob Berry, Joe Namath, Andy Russell, Tom Woodeshick, and Bart Starr. (Key: DP -- double-printed)

		NM/M
	Complete Set (53):	125.00
	Common Player:	.50
1	Dick Butkus (DP)	4.00
2	Bob Berry (DP)	.50
3	Joe Namath (DP)	17.00
4	Mike Curtis	.50
5	Jim Nance	.50
6	Ron Berger	.50
7	O.J. Simpson	20.00
8	Haven Moses	.50
9	Tommy Nobis	.50
10	Gale Sayers	9.00
11	Virgil Carter	.50
12	Andy Russell (DP)	.50
13	Bill Nelsen	.50
14	Gary Collins	.50
15	Duane Thomas	.50
16	Bob Hayes	.80
17	Floyd Little	.80
18	Sam Brunelli	.50
19	Charlie Sanders	.50
20	Mike Lucci	.50
21	Gene Washington (SF)	.80
22	Willie Wood	3.00
23	Jerry LeVias	.50
24	Charlie Johnson	.80
25	Len Dawson	3.00
26	Bobby Bell	2.00
27	Merlin Olsen	3.00
28	Roman Gabriel	2.00
29	Bob Griese	4.00
30	Larry Csonka	4.00
31	Dave Osborn	.50
32	Gene Washington (MN)	.50
33	Dan Abramowicz	.50
34	Tom Dempsey	.50
35	Fran Tarkenton	9.00
36	Clifton McNeil	.50
37	Johnny Unitas	12.00
38	Matt Snell	.50
39	Daryle Lamonica	.80
40	Hewritt Dixon	.50
41	Tom Woodeshick (DP)	.50
42	Harold Jackson	.50
43	Terry Bradshaw	20.00
44	Ken Avery	.50
45	MacArthur Lane	.50
46	Larry Wilson	2.00
47	John Hadl	1.00
48	Lance Alworth	2.00
49	John Brodie	4.00
50	Bart Starr (DP)	6.00
51	Sonny Jurgensen	6.00
52	Larry Brown	.50
53	Field Marker	.50

1971 Topps Pin-Ups

These mini-posters (about 5" x 7") were folded twice and inserted into wax packs. The front features a head shot of the player, with his name in bold capitals above the photo and his team in smaller type at the bottom. Backs showed a football field with side markers, as well as the accompanying instructions. Because these posters were folded, it's very difficult, if not impossible, to find any in Mint condition.

		NM/M
	Complete Set (32):	40.00
	Common Player:	.65
1	Gene Washington	.75
2	Andy Russell	.65
3	Harold Jackson	.65
4	Joe Namath	12.00
5	Fran Tarkenton	5.00
6	Dave Osborn	.65
7	Bob Griese	2.50
8	Roman Gabriel	1.00
9	Jerry LeVias	.65
10	Bart Starr	5.00
11	Bob Hayes	1.00
12	Gale Sayers	5.50
13	O.J. Simpson	7.50
14	Sam Brunelli	.65
15	Jim Nance	.65
16	Bill Nelsen	.65
17	Sonny Jurgensen	2.50
18	John Brodie	2.50
19	Lance Alworth	1.50
20	Larry Wilson	1.00
21	Daryle Lamonica	.75
22	Dan Abramowicz	.65
23	Gene Washington (Minn)	.65
24	Bobby Bell	1.50
25	Merlin Olsen	2.00
26	Charlie Sanders	.65
27	Virgil Carter	.65
28	Dick Butkus	2.50
29	Johnny Unitas	7.00
30	Tommy Nobis	.75
31	Floyd Little	.65
32	Larry Brown	.65

1972 Topps

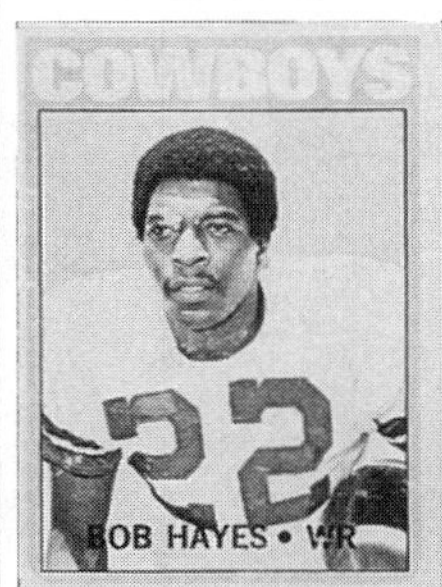

The 1972 set, a 351-card edition, was Topps' last to be issued in series form. The first series includes cards #1-132; the second - somewhat harder to find than the first - includes cards #133-263; and the final series - the difficult series - shows cards #264-351. Because of the difficulty in acquiring a complete set, this is easily the most expensive Topps set of the 1970s. Subsets in this issue include statistical leaders, playoffs, All-Pros and In Action cards. Rookies in the set include John Riggins, Archie Manning, Jim Plunkett, John Brockington, Ted Hendricks, L.C. Greenwood, Lyle Alzado, Dan Pastorini, Gene Upshaw, Roger Staubach, Charlie Joiner and Steve Spurrier. (Key: IA - in action, AP - All Pro)

		NM/M
	Complete Set (351):	2,300
	Common Player (1-132):	.50
	Common Player (133-263):	.75
	Comm Player (264-351):	20.00
	Series 1 Wax Pack (10):	75.00
	Series 1 Wax Box (24):	1,525
	Series 2 Wax Pack (10):	110.00
	Series 2 Wax Box (24):	2,250
	Series 3 Wax Pack (10):	310.00
	Series 3 Wax Box (24):	6,325
1	Floyd Little, Larry Csonka AFC rushing leaders	3.50
2	John Brockington, Steve Owens, Willie Ellison NFC rushing leaders	1.00
3	Bob Griese, Len Dawson AFC passing leaders	2.00
4	Roger Staubach, Bill Kilmer NFC passing leaders	4.00
5	Fred Biletnikoff, Otis Taylor, Randy Vataha AFC receiving leaders	1.00
6	Bob Tucker, Ted Kwalick, Harold Jackson, Roy Jefferson NFC receiving leaders	1.00
7	Garo Yepremian, Jan Stenerud AFC scoring leaders	1.50
8	Curt Knight, Errol Mann, Bruce Gossett NFC scoring leaders	1.00
9	Jim Kiick	1.25
10	Otis Taylor	1.25
11	Bobby Joe Green	.50
12	Ken Ellis	.50
13	*John Riggins*	25.00
14	Dave Parks	.50
15	John Hadl	1.50
16	Ron Hornsby	.50
17	Chip Myers	.50
18	Bill Kilmer	1.50
19	Fred Hoaglin	.50
20	Carl Eller	1.50
21	Steve Zabel	.50
22	*Vic Washington*	.50
23	Len St. Jean	.50
24	Bill Thompson	.50
25	*Steve Owens*	2.50
26	*Ken Burrough*	1.50
27	Mike Clark	.50
28	Willie Brown	3.00
29	Checklist 1-132	6.00
30	Marlin Briscoe	.50
31	Jerry Logan	.50
32	Donny Anderson	.50
33	Rich McGeorge	.50
34	Charlie Durkee	.50
35	Willie Lanier	4.00
36	Chris Farasopoulos	.50
37	Ronnie Shanklin	.50
38	*Forrest Blue*	1.25
39	Ken Reaves	.50
40	Roman Gabriel	2.00
41	Mac Percival	.50
42	Lem Barney	3.00
43	Nick Buoniconti	1.75
44	Charlie Gogolak	.50
45	*Bill Bradley*	2.00
46	Joe Jones	.50
47	Dave Williams	.50
48	Pete Athas	.50
49	Virgil Carter	.50
50	Floyd Little	2.00
51	Curt Knight	.50
52	Bobby Maples	.50
53	Charlie West	.50
54	*Marv Hubbard*	1.25
55	*Archie Manning*	20.00
56	*Jim O'Brien*	1.00
57	Wayne Patrick	.50
58	Ken Bowman	.50
59	Roger Wehrli	.50
60	Charlie Sanders	1.00
61	Jan Stenerud	2.00
62	Willie Ellison	.50
63	Walt Sweeney	.50
64	Ron Smith	.50
65	*Jim Plunkett*	20.00
66	Herb Adderly	2.50
67	*Mike Reid*	4.00
68	*Richard Caster*	1.50
69	Dave Wilcox	.50
70	Leroy Kelly	2.50
71	*Bob Lee*	1.00
72	Verlon Biggs	.50
73	Henry Allison	.50
74	Steve Ramsey	.50
75	Claude Humphrey	.50
76	*Bob Grim*	1.00
77	John Fuqua	.50
78	Ken Houston	4.00
79	Checklist 133-263	4.50
80	Bob Griese	8.00
81	Lance Rentzel	.50
82	*Ed Podolak*	1.75
83	Ike Hill	.50
84	George Farmer	.50
85	*John Brockington*	4.00
86	Jim Otto	2.00
87	Richard Neal	.50
88	Jim Hart	1.50
89	Bob Babich	.50
90	Gene Washington (S.F.)	.75
91	John Zook	.50
92	Bobby Duhon	.50
93	*Ted Hendricks*	20.00
94	Rockne Freitas	.50
95	Larry Brown	1.50
96	Mike Phipps	1.00
97	Julius Adams	.50
98	Dick Anderson	.50
99	Fred Willis	.50
100	Joe Namath	40.00
101	*L.C. Greenwood*	20.00
102	Mark Nordquist	.50
103	Robert Holmes	.50
104	*Ron Yary*	3.50
105	Bob Hayes	1.75
106	*Lyle Alzado*	14.00
107	Bob Berry	.50
108	*Phil Villapiano*	2.00
109	Dave Elmendorf	.50
110	Gale Sayers	22.00
111	Jim Tyrer	.50
112	*Mel Gray*	4.00
113	Gerry Philbin	.50
114	Bob James	.50
115	Garo Yepremian	1.00
116	Dave Robinson	.50
117	Jeff Queen	.50
118	Norm Snead	.50
119	Jim Nance (IA)	.50
120	Terry Bradshaw (IA)	15.00
121	Jim Kiick (IA)	.50
122	Roger Staubach (IA)	20.00
123	Bo Scott (IA)	.50
124	John Brodie (IA)	2.00
125	Rick Volk (IA)	.50
126	John Riggins (IA)	8.00
127	Bubba Smith (IA)	1.75
128	Roman Gabriel (IA)	1.00
129	Calvin Hill (IA)	.50
130	Bill Nelsen (IA)	.50
131	Tom Matte (IA)	.50
132	Bob Griese (IA)	3.50
133	AFC semi-final	1.50
134	Duane Thomas NFC semi-final	1.50
135	Don Nottingham AFC semi-final	1.50
136	NFC semi-final	1.50
137	AFC Championship	2.50
138	NFC Championship	2.50
139	Super Bowl	5.00
140	Larry Csonka	7.00
141	Rick Volk	.75
142	Roy Jefferson	.75
143	*Raymond Chester*	1.50
144	Bobby Douglass	.75
145	Bob Lilly	4.00
146	Harold Jackson	2.00
147	Pete Gogolak	.75
148	Art Malone	.75
149	Ed Flanagan	.75
150	Terry Bradshaw	45.00
151	MacArthur Lane	.75
152	Jack Snow	.75
153	Al Beauchamp	.75
154	Bob Anderson	.75
155	*Ted Kwalick*	1.75
156	*Dan Pastorini*	2.00
157	*Emmitt Thomas*	1.50
158	*Randy Vataha*	1.25
159	Al Atkinson	.75
160	O.J. Simpson	15.00
161	Jackie Smith	1.00
162	Ernie Kellerman	.75
163	Dennis Partee	.75
164	Jake Kupp	.75
165	Johnny Unitas	25.00
166	Clint Jones	.75
167	Paul Warfield	6.00
168	Roland McDole	.75
169	Daryle Lamonica	2.25
170	Dick Butkus	10.00
171	Jim Butler	.75
172	Mike McCoy	.75
173	Dave Smith	.75
174	Greg Landry	1.50
175	Tom Dempsey	.75
176	John Charles	.75
177	Bobby Bell	2.50
178	Don Horn	.75
179	Bob Trumpy	2.00
180	Duane Thomas	1.25
181	Merlin Olsen	3.50
182	Dave Herman	.75
183	Jim Nance	.75
184	Pete Beathard	.75
185	Bob Tucker	.75
186	*Gene Upshaw*	14.00
187	Bo Scott	.75
188	*J.D. Hill*	1.25
189	Bruce Gossett	.75
190	Bubba Smith	3.50
191	Edd Hargett	1.00
192	Gary Garrison	.75
193	Jake Scott	1.25
194	Fred Cox	.75
195	Sonny Jurgensen	4.50
196	*Greg Brezina*	1.00
197	Ed O'Bradovich	.75
198	John Rowser	.75
199	Altie Taylor	.75
200	*Roger Staubach*	175.00
201	*Leroy Keyes*	1.50
202	Garland Boyette	.75
203	Tom Beer	.75
204	Buck Buchanan	2.50
205	Larry Wilson	2.50
206	*Scott Hunter*	1.00
207	Ron Johnson	.75
208	Sam Brunelli	.75
209	Deacon Jones	2.50
210	Fred Biletnikoff	5.00
211	Bill Nelson	.75
212	George Nock	.75
213	Dan Abramowicz	.75
214	Irv Goode	.75
215	*Isiah Robertson*	2.00
216	Tom Matte	.75
217	Pat Fischer	.75
218	Gene Washington	.75
219	Paul Robinson	.75
220	John Brodie	4.00
221	*Manny Fernandez*	2.00
222	Errol Mann	.75
223	Dick Gordon	.75
224	Calvin Hill	1.75
225	Fran Tarkenton	16.00
226	Jim Turner	.75
227	Jim Mitchell	.75
228	Pete Liske	.75
229	Carl Garrett	.75
230	Joe Greene	20.00
231	Gale Gillingham	.75
232	*Norm Bulaich*	1.25
233	Spider Lockhart	.75
234	Ken Willard	.75
235	George Blanda	11.00
236	Wayne Mulligan	.75
237	Dave Lewis	.75
238	Dennis Shaw	.75
239	Fair Hooker	.75
240	*Larry Little*	17.00
241	Mike Garrett	1.00
242	Glen Ray Hines	.75
243	Myron Pottios	.75
244	*Charlie Joiner*	25.00
245	Len Dawson	6.50
246	W.K. Hicks	.75
247	Les Josephson	.75
248	Lance Alworth	6.00
249	Frank Nunley	.75
250	Mel Farr (IA)	.75
251	Johnny Unitas (IA)	8.00
252	George Farmer (IA)	.75
253	Duane Thomas (IA)	.75
254	John Hadl (IA)	1.00
255	Vic Washington (IA)	.75
256	Don Horn (IA)	.75
257	L.C. Greenwood (IA)	3.00
258	Bob Lee (IA)	.75
259	Larry Csonka (IA)	3.50
260	Mike McCoy (IA)	.75
261	Greg Landry (IA)	.75
262	Ray May (IA)	.75
263	Bobby Douglass (IA)	.75
264	Charlie Sanders (AP)	22.00
265	Ron Yary (AP)	27.50
266	Rayfield Wright (AP)	20.00
267	Larry Little (AP)	40.00
268	John Niland (AP)	20.00
269	Forrest Blue (AP)	20.00
270	Otis Taylor (AP)	20.00
271	Paul Warfield (AP)	60.00
272	Bob Griese (AP)	75.00
273	John Brockington (AP)	20.00
274	Floyd Little (AP)	27.00
275	Garo Yepremian (AP)	30.00
276	Jerrel Wilson (AP)	20.00
277	Carl Eller (AP)	30.00
278	Bubba Smith (AP)	40.00
279	Alan Page (AP)	40.00
280	Bob Lilly (AP)	50.00
281	Ted Hendricks (AP)	45.00
282	Dave Wilcox (AP)	20.00
283	Willie Lanier (AP)	30.00
284	Jim Johnson (AP)	20.00
285	Willie Brown (AP)	30.00
286	Bill Bradley (AP)	20.00
287	Ken Houston (AP)	30.00
288	Mel Farr	20.00
289	Kermit Alexander	20.00
290	*John Gilliam*	25.00
291	*Steve Spurrier*	60.00
292	Walter Johnson	20.00

No.	Player	NM/M
293	Jack Pardee	20.00
294	Checklist 264-351	100.00
295	Winston Hill	20.00
296	Hugo Hollas	20.00
297	*Ray May*	25.00
298	Jim Bakken	20.00
299	Larry Carwell	20.00
300	Alan Page	50.00
301	Walt Garrison	25.00
302	Mike Lucci	20.00
303	Nemiah Wilson	20.00
304	Carroll Dale	20.00
305	Jim Kanicki	20.00
306	Preston Pearson	25.00
307	Lemar Parrish	20.00
308	Earl Morrall	22.00
309	Tommy Nobis	25.00
310	Rich Jackson	20.00
311	Doug Cunningham	20.00
312	Jim Marsalis	20.00
313	Jim Beirne	20.00
314	Tom McNeill	20.00
315	Milt Morin	20.00
316	*Rayfield Wright*	24.00
317	Jerry LeVias	20.00
318	*Travis Williams*	27.50
319	Edgar Chandler	20.00
320	Bob Wallace	20.00
321	Delles Howell	20.00
322	Emerson Boozer	20.00
323	*George Atkinson*	22.00
324	Mike Montler	20.00
325	Randy Johnson	20.00
326	Mike Curtis	20.00
327	Miller Farr	20.00
328	Horst Muhlmann	20.00
329	*John Niland*	25.00
330	Andy Russell	20.00
331	Mercury Morris	35.00
332	Jim Johnson	20.00
333	Jerrel Wilson	20.00
334	Charley Taylor	40.00
335	Dick LeBeau	20.00
336	Jim Marshall	25.00
337	Tom Mack	25.00
338	Steve Spurrier (IA)	40.00
339	Floyd Little (IA)	25.00
340	Len Dawson (IA)	40.00
341	Dick Butkus (IA)	70.00
342	Larry Brown (IA)	27.50
343	Joe Namath (IA)	250.00
344	Jim Turner (IA)	20.00
345	Doug Cunningham (IA)	20.00
346	Edd Hargett (IA)	20.00
347	Steve Owens (IA)	21.00
348	George Blanda (IA)	45.00
349	Ed Podolak (IA)	20.00
350	Rich Jackson (IA)	20.00
351	Ken Willard (IA)	40.00

1973 Topps

This issue might have been Topps' most important of the decade for a number of reasons. The 1973 set was Topps' first of 10 consecutive football sets at 528 cards, and its first major set that was issued all at once instead of in a series. This coincides with its cutback in baseball cards (787 to 660) and emphasis on football and basketball; it also signaled the end of Topps' high-series release. Subsets in the 1973 release include the usual statistical leaders and playoffs, plus three cards depicting childhood photos of NFL stars. Rookies in this set include Ken Anderson, Lydell Mitchell, Franco Harris, Jack Ham, Art Shell, Ken Riley, Jack Tatum, Dan Dierdorf, Jim Langer, Jack Youngblood and Ken Stabler. Though he went on to play several more years with the Rams and Jets, Joe Namath's final regular-issue card appears in this set. Like Earl Campbell several years later, he apparently was unable to reach a contract agreement after this season. One other item of note: this set has a few of the most unique player names of any football issue: Chip Glass, Happy Feller, and the immortal Remi Prudhomme.

	NM/M
Complete Set (528):	425.00
Common Player:	.40
Wax Pack (10+1):	88.50
Wax Box (24):	1,850
Wax Pack (15):	115.00
Wax Box (24):	2,450

No.	Player	NM/M
1	Larry Brown, O.J. Simpson Rushing Leaders	6.00
2	Norm Snead, Earl Morrall Passing Leaders	.75
3	Harold Jackson, Fred Biletnikoff Receiving Leaders	1.00
4	Chester Marcol, Bobby Howfield Scoring Leaders	.75
5	Bill Bradley, Mike Sensibaugh Interception Leaders	.75
6	Dave Chapple, Jerrell Wilson Punting Leaders	.75
7	Bob Trumpy	1.25
8	Mel Tom	.40
9	Clarence Ellis	.40
10	John Niland	.40
11	Randy Jackson	.40
12	Greg Landry	1.00
13	Cid Edwards	.40
14	Phil Olsen	.40
15	Terry Bradshaw	25.00
16	*Al Cowlings*	2.00
17	Walker Gillette	.40
18	Bob Atkins	.40
19	*Diron Talbert*	1.00
20	*Jim Johnson*	1.00
21	Howard Twilley	.40
22	Dick Enderle	.40
23	Wayne Colman	.40
24	John Schmitt	.40
25	George Blanda	7.50
26	Milt Morin	.40
27	Mike Current	.40
28	*Rex Kern*	.60
29	MacArthur Lane	.40
30	Alan Page	3.00
31	Randy Vataha	.40
32	Jim Kearney	.40
33	Steve Smith	.40
34	*Ken Anderson*	20.00
35	Calvin Hill	1.00
36	Andy Maurer	.40
37	Joe Taylor	.40
38	Deacon Jones	2.50
39	Mike Weger	.40
40	Roy Gerela	.40
41	Les Josephson	.40
42	Dave Washington	.40
43	*Bill Curry*	1.00
44	Fred Heron	.40
45	John Brodie	4.00
46	Roy Winston	.40
47	Mike Bragg	.40
48	Mercury Morris	1.25
49	Jim Files	.40
50	Gene Upshaw	3.50
51	Hugo Hollas	.40
52	Rod Sherman	.40
53	Ron Snidow	.40
54	Steve Tannen	.40
55	Jim Carter	.40
56	*Lydell Mitchell*	3.00
57	*Jack Rudnay*	.60
58	Halvor Hagen	.40
59	Tom Dempsey	.40
60	Fran Tarkenton	15.00
61	Lance Alworth	3.50
62	Vern Holland	.40
63	Steve DeLong	.40
64	Art Malone	.40
65	Isiah Robertson	.40
66	Jerry Rush	.40
67	Bryant Salter	.40
68	Checklist 1-132	4.00
69	J.D. Hill	.40
70	Forrest Blue	.40
71	Myron Pottios	.40
72	*Norm Thompson*	.60
73	Paul Robinson	.40
74	Larry Grantham	.40
75	Manny Fernandez	.40
76	Kent Nix	.40
77	*Art Shell*	17.00
78	George Saimes	.40
79	Don Cockroft	.40
80	Bob Tucker	.40
81	*Don McCauley*	1.00
82	Bob Brown	.40
83	Larry Carwell	.40
84	Mo Moorman	.40
85	John Gilliam	.40
86	Wade Key	.40
87	Ross Brupbacher	.40
88	Dave Lewis	.40
89	*Franco Harris*	50.00
90	Tom Mack	.40
91	Mike Tilleman	.40
92	Carl Mauck	.40
93	Larry Hand	.40
94	Dave Foley	.40
95	Frank Nunley	.40
96	John Charles	.40
97	Jim Bakken	.40
98	Pat Fischer	.40
99	Randy Rasmussen	.40
100	Larry Csonka	5.00
101	*Mike Siani*	.75
102	Tom Roussel	.40
103	*Clarence Scott*	.75
104	Charlie Johnson	.60
105	Rick Volk	.40
106	Willie Young	.40
107	Emmitt Thomas	.40
108	Jon Morris	.40
109	Clarence Williams	.40
110	Rayfield Wright	.40
111	Norm Bulaich	.40
112	Mike Eischeid	.40
113	Speedy Thomas	.40
114	Glen Holloway	.40
115	*Jack Ham*	25.00
116	Jim Nettles	.40
117	Errol Mann	.40
118	John Mackey	2.00
119	George Kunz	.40
120	Bob James	.40
121	Garland Boyette	.40
122	Mel Phillips	.40
123	Johnny Roland	.40
124	Doug Swift	.40
125	Archie Manning	2.50
126	Dave Herman	.40
127	Carleton Oats	.40
128	Bill Van Heusen	.40
129	Rich Jackson	.40
130	Len Hauss	.40
131	*Billy Parks*	.75
132	Ray May	.40
133	Roger Staubach NFC Semi-Final	3.00
134	AFC Semi-Final	1.50
135	NFC Semi-Final	.75
136	Bob Griese, Larry Csonka AFC Semi-Final	2.00
137	Bill Kilmer, Larry Brown NFC Championship	1.50
138	AFC Championship	.75
139	Super Bowl	1.50
140	*Dwight White*	2.00
141	Jim Marsalis	.40
142	Doug Van Horn	.40
143	Al Matthews	.40
144	Bob Windsor	.40
145	*Dave Hampton*	.75
146	Horst Muhlmann	.40
147	*Wally Hilgenberg*	1.00
148	Ron Smith	.40
149	*Coy Bacon*	1.50
150	Winston Hill	.40
151	*Ron Jessie*	1.25
152	Ken Iman	.40
153	Ron Saul	.40
154	*Jim Braxton*	.75
155	Bubba Smith	3.00
156	Gary Cuozzo	.40
157	Charlie Krueger	.40
158	*Tim Foley*	.75
159	Lee Roy Jordan	2.00
160	Bob Brown	.40
161	Margene Adkins	.40
162	Ron Widby	.40
163	Jim Houston	.40
164	Joe Dawkins	.40
165	L.C. Greenwood	3.50
166	Richmond Flowers	.40
167	*Curley Culp*	2.00
168	Len St. Jean	.40
169	Walter Rock	.40
170	Bill Bradley	.40
171	*Ken Riley*	2.50
172	Rich Coady	.40
173	Don Hansen	.40
174	Lionel Aldridge	.40
175	Don Maynard	3.00
176	Dave Osborn	.40
177	Jim Bailey	.40
178	John Pitts	.40
179	Dave Parks	.40
180	*Chester Marcol*	.75
181	Len Rohde	.40
182	Jeff Staggs	.40
183	Gene Hickerson	.40
184	Charlie Evans	.40
185	Mel Renfro	1.00
186	Marvin Upshaw	.40
187	George Atkinson	.40
188	Norm Evans	.40
189	Steve Ramsey	.40
190	Dave Chapple	.40
191	Gerry Mullins	.40
192	John Didion	.40
193	Bob Gladieux	.40
194	Don Hultz	.40
195	Mike Lucci	.40
196	John Wilbur	.40
197	George Farmer	.40
198	*Tommy Casanova*	1.25
199	Russ Washington	.40
200	Claude Humphrey	.40
201	Pat Hughes	.40
202	Zeke Moore	.40
203	Chip Glass	.40
204	Glenn Ressler	.40
205	Willie Ellison	.40
206	John Leypoldt	.40
207	Johnny Fuller	.40
208	Bill Hayhoe	.40
209	Ed Bell	.40
210	Willie Brown	2.00
211	Carl Eller	1.50
212	Mark Nordquist	.40
213	Larry Willingham	.40
214	Nick Buoniconti	1.75
215	John Hadl	1.25
216	*Jethro Pugh*	1.50
217	Leroy Mitchell	.40
218	Billy Newsome	.40
219	John McMakin	.40
220	Larry Brown	1.25
221	Clarence Scott	.40
222	Paul Naumoff	.40
223	Ted Fritsch	.40
224	Checklist 133-264	4.00
225	Dan Pastorini	1.00
226	Joe Beauchamp	.40
227	Pat Matson	.40
228	Tony McGee	.40
229	Mike Phipps	.40
230	Harold Jackson	1.25
231	Willie Williams	.40
232	Spike Jones	.40
233	Jim Tyrer	.40
234	Roy Hilton	.40
235	Phil Villapiano	.40
236	Charley Taylor	4.00
237	Malcolm Snider	.40
238	Vic Washington	.40
239	Grady Alderman	.40
240	Dick Anderson	.40
241	Ron Yankowski	.40
242	Billy Masters	.40
243	Herb Adderly	2.25
244	David Ray	.40
245	John Riggins	9.00
246	*Mike Wagner*	2.00
247	Don Morrison	.40
248	Earl McCullouch	.40
249	Dennis Wirgowksi	.40
250	Chris Hanburger	.40
251	*Pat Sullivan*	2.00
252	Walt Sweeney	.40
253	Willie Alexander	.40
254	Doug Dressler	.40
255	Walter Johnson	.40
256	Ron Hornsby	.40
257	Ben Hawkins	.40
258	Donnie Green	.40
259	Fred Hoaglin	.40
260	Jerrill Wilson	.40
261	Horace Jones	.40
262	Woody Peoples	.40
263	Jim Hill	.40
264	John Fuqua	.40
265	Donny Anderson Childhood Photo:	.50
266	Roman Gabriel Childhood Photo:	1.00
267	Mike Garrett Childhood Photo:	.50
268	Rufus Mayes	.60
269	Chip Myrtle	.40
270	*Bill Stanfill*	1.00
271	Clint Jones	.40
272	Miller Farr	.40
273	Harry Schuh	.40
274	Bob Hayes	1.25
275	Bobby Douglass	.40
276	Gus Hollomon	.40
277	Del Williams	.40
278	Julius Adams	.40
279	Herman Weaver	.40
280	Joe Greene	6.00
281	Wes Chesson	.40
282	Charlie Harraway	.40
283	Paul Guidry	.40
284	Terry Owens	.40
285	Jan Stenerud	1.50
286	Pete Athas	.40
287	Dale Lindsey	.40
288	*Jack Tatum*	7.00
289	Floyd Little	1.50
290	Bob Johnson	.40
291	Tommy Hart	.40
292	Tom Mitchell	.40
293	*Walt Patulski*	.90
294	Jim Skaggs	.40
295	Bob Griese	7.00
296	Mike McCoy	.40
297	Mel Gray	1.00
298	Bobby Bryant	.40
299	*Blaine Nye*	.60
300	Dick Butkus	6.00
301	Charlie Cowan	.40
302	Mark Lomas	.40
303	Josh Ashton	.40
304	Happy Feller	.40
305	Ronnie Shanklin	.40
306	Wayne Rasmussen	.40
307	Jerry Smith	.40
308	Ken Reaves	.40
309	Ron East	.40
310	Otis Taylor	1.00
311	John Garlington	.40
312	Lyle Alzado	3.50
313	Remi Prudhomme	.40
314	Cornelius Johnson	.40
315	Lemar Parrish	.40
316	Jim Kiick	.40
317	Steve Zabel	.40
318	Alden Roche	.40
319	Tom Blanchard	.40
320	Fred Biletnikoff	4.00
321	Ralph Neely	.40
322	*Dan Dierdorf*	20.00
323	Richard Caster	.40
324	Gene Howard	.40
325	Elvin Bethea	.40
326	Carl Garrett	.40
327	Ron Billingsley	.40
328	Charlie West	.40
329	Tom Neville	.40
330	Ted Kwalick	.40
331	Rudy Redmond	.40
332	Henry Davis	.40
333	John Zook	.40
334	Jim Turner	.40
335	Len Dawson	3.50
336	*Bob Chandler*	1.25
337	Al Beauchamp	.40
338	Tom Matte	.40
339	Paul Laaveg	.40
340	Ken Ellis	.40
341	*Jim Langer*	13.00
342	Ron Porter	.40
343	*Jack Youngblood*	15.00
344	Cornell Green	.40
345	Marv Hubbard	.40
346	Bruce Taylor	.40
347	Sam Havrilak	.40
348	Walt Sumner	.40
349	Steve O'Neal	.40
350	Ron Johnson	.40
351	Rockne Freitas	.40
352	Larry Stallings	.40
353	Jim Cadile	.40
354	Ken Burrough	.40
355	Jim Plunkett	4.00
356	Dave Long	.40
357	Ralph Anderson	.40
358	Checklist 265-396	4.00
359	Gene Washington	.40
360	Dave Wilcox	.40
361	Paul Smith	.40
362	Alvin Wyatt	.40
363	Charlie Smith	.40
364	Royce Berry	.40
365	Dave Elmendorf	.40
366	Scott Hunter	.40
367	*Bob Kuechenberg*	3.00
368	Pete Gogolak	.40
369	Dave Edwards	.40
370	Lem Barney	2.50
371	Verlon Biggs	.40
372	*John Reaves*	.60
373	Ed Podolak	.40
374	Chris Farasopoulos	.40
375	Gary Garrison	.40
376	Tom Funchess	.40
377	Bobby Joe Green	.40
378	Don Brumm	.40
379	Jim O'Brien	.40
380	Paul Krause	1.25
381	Leroy Kelly	2.00
382	Ray Mansfield	.40
383	Dan Abramowicz	.40
384	*John Outlaw*	.60
385	Tommy Nobis	1.50
386	Tom Domres	.40
387	Ken Willard	.40
388	Mike Stratton	.40
389	Fred Dryer	3.00
390	Jake Scott	.40
391	Rich Houston	.40
392	Virgil Carter	.40
393	Tody Smith	.40
394	Ernie Calloway	.40
395	Charlie Sanders	.40
396	Fred Willis	.40
397	Curt Knight	.40
398	Nemiah Wilson	.40
399	Carroll Dale	.40
400	Joe Namath	30.00
401	Wayne Mulligan	.40
402	Jim Harrison	.40
403	Tim Rossovich	.40
404	David Lee	.40
405	Frank Pitts	.40
406	Jim Marshall	1.50
407	Bob Brown	.40
408	John Rowser	.40
409	Mike Montler	.40
410	Willie Lanier	2.00
411	Bill Bell	.40
412	Cedrick Hardman	.40
413	Bob Anderson	.40
414	*Earl Morrall*	1.25
415	Ken Houston	1.75
416	Jack Snow	.40
417	Dick Cunningham	.40
418	Greg Larson	.40
419	Mike Bass	.40
420	Mike Reid	2.00
421	Walt Garrison	.40
422	Pete Liske	.40
423	Jim Yarbrough	.40
424	Rich McGeorge	.40
425	Bobby Howfield	.40
426	Pete Banaszak	.40
427	Willie Holman	.40
428	Dale Hackbart	.40
429	Fair Hooker	.40
430	Ted Hendricks	4.00
431	Mike Garrett	.40
432	Glen Ray Hines	.40
433	Fred Cox	.40
434	Bobby Walden	.40
435	Bobby Bell	2.00
436	David Rowe	.40
437	Bob Berry	.40
438	Bill Thompson	.40
439	Jim Beirne	.40
440	Larry Little	3.00
441	Rocky Thompson	.40
442	Brig Owens	.40
443	Richard Neal	.40
444	Al Nelson	.40
445	Chip Myers	.40
446	Ken Bowman	.40
447	Jim Purnell	.40
448	Altie Taylor	.40
449	Linzy Cole	.40
450	Bob Lilly	4.00
451	Charlie Ford	.40
452	Milt Sunde	.40
453	Doug Wyatt	.40
454	*Don Nottingham*	.75
455	Johnny Unitas	25.00
456	*Frank Lewis*	1.50
457	Roger Wehrli	.40
458	Jim Cheyunski	.40
459	*Jerry Sherk*	1.00
460	Gene Washington	.40
461	Jim Otto	2.25
462	Ed Budde	.40
463	Jim Mitchell	.40
464	Emerson Boozer	.40
465	Garo Yepremian	.40
466	Pete Duranko	.40
467	Charlie Joiner	6.00
468	Spider Lockhart	.40
469	Marty Domres	.40
470	John Brockington	1.00
471	Ed Flanagan	.40
472	Roy Jefferson	.40
473	Julian Fagan	.40
474	Bill Brown	.40
475	Roger Staubach	40.00
476	Jan White	.40
477	Pat Holmes	.40
478	Bob DeMarco	.40
479	Merlin Olsen	3.50
480	Andy Russell	.40
481	Steve Spurrier	8.00
482	Nate Ramsey	.40
483	Dennis Partee	.40
484	Jerry Simmons	.40
485	Donny Anderson	.40
486	Ralph Baker	.40
487	*Ken Stabler*	60.00
488	Ernie McMillan	.40
489	Ken Burrow	.40
490	*Jack Gregory*	.60
491	Larry Seiple	.40
492	Mick Tingelhoff	.40
493	Craig Morton	1.50
494	Cecil Turner	.40
495	Steve Owens	.50
496	Richie Harris	.40
497	Buck Buchanan	2.00
498	Checklist 397-528	4.00
499	Bill Kilmer	1.50
500	O.J. Simpson	15.00
501	Bruce Gossett	.40
502	Art Thoms	.40
503	Larry Kaminski	.40
504	Larry Smith	.40
505	Bruce Van Dyke	.40
506	Alvin Reed	.40
507	Delles Howell	.40
508	Leroy Keyes	.40
509	Bo Scott	.40
510	Ron Yary	1.00
511	Paul Warfield	5.00
512	Mac Percival	.40
513	Essex Johnson	.40
514	Jackie Smith	1.00
515	Norm Snead	.40
516	Charlie Stukes	.40
517	*Reggie Rucker*	1.50
518	Bill Sandeman	.40
519	Mel Farr	.40
520	Raymond Chester	.40
521	*Fred Carr*	1.00
522	Jerry LeVias	.40
523	Jim Strong	.40
524	Roland McDole	.40
525	Dennis Shaw	.40
526	Dave Manders	.40
527	Skip Vanderbundt	.40
528	*Mike Sensibaugh*	1.25

1973 Topps Team Checklists

This was the first time Topps issued separate team checklists in its 528-card sets, a practice that would end with the 1974 set. The cards showed an anonymous action shot at the top of the card, with a Topps logo in a football helmet facing the team name. The checklist was beneath all that, and showed the card number, name, uniform number and position (as it would in 1974). Card backs carried pieces to a puzzle of either Larry Brown or Joe Namath; or they carried a message that read, "Collect all 26 Team Checklists and complete your Joe Namath & Larry Brown Puzzles."

		NM/M
	Complete Set (26):	35.00
	Common Team:	1.50
1	Atlanta Falcons	1.50
2	Baltimore Colts	1.50
3	Buffalo Bills	1.50
4	Chicago Bears	1.50
5	Cincinnati Bengals	1.50
6	Cleveland Browns	1.50
7	Dallas Cowboys	1.50
8	Denver Broncos	1.50
9	Detroit Lions	1.50
10	Green Bay Packers	1.50
11	Houston Oilers	1.50
12	Kansas City Chiefs	1.50
13	Los Angeles Rams	1.50
14	Miami Dolphins	1.50
15	Minnesota Vikings	1.50
16	New England Patriots	1.50
17	New Orleans Saints	1.50
18	New York Giants	1.50
19	New York Jets	1.50
20	Oakland Raiders	1.50
21	Philadelphia Eagles	1.50
22	Pittsburgh Steelers	1.50
23	St. Louis Cardinals	1.50
24	San Diego Chargers	1.50
25	San Francisco 49ers	1.50
26	Washington Redskins	1.50

1974 Topps

This was Topps' second 528-card set, and marked the second and last time team checklists would be issued unnumbered and separate from the set. Rookies in this set include Ahmad Rashad, Greg Pruitt, Chuck Foreman, Harold Carmichael, Ray Guy, John Matuszak, Conrad Dobler, Ed Marinaro, Darryl Stingley, Lynn Dickey, Billy Joe DuPree, D.D. Lewis, John Hannah, Terry Metcalf, Joe Ferguson and Bert Jones. In addition, this set features the last regularly-issued card of Johnny Unitas. All Pro cards showing individual players are found on cards 121-144. Other subsets include statistical leader and playoff cards. There is one error in the set, on card #265, Bob Lee. The back of the card lists his team as the Atlanta Hawks instead of the Falcons.

	NM/M
Complete Set (528):	350.00
Common Player:	.35
Wax Pack (10-ALL 528):	41.00
Wax Box (24):	865.00
Wax Pack (10+1 - B.T.C.):	42.00
Wax Box (36):	1,300

No.	Player	NM/M
1	O.J. Simpson	20.00
2	Blaine Nye	.35
3	Don Hansen	.35
4	Ken Bowman	.35
5	Carl Eller	1.00
6	Jerry Smith	.35
7	Ed Podolak	.35
8	Mel Gray	.35
9	Pat Matson	.35
10	Floyd Little	1.25
11	Frank Pitts	.35
12	*Vern Den Herder*	.75
13	John Fuqua	.35
14	Jack Tatum	1.50
15	Winston Hill	.35
16	John Beasley	.35
17	David Lee	.35
18	Rich Coady	.35
19	Ken Willard	.35
20	Coy Bacon	.35
21	Ben Hawkins	.35
22	Paul Guidry	.35
23	Norm Snead	.75
24	Jim Yarbrough	.35
25	*Jack Reynolds*	2.25
26	Josh Ashton	.35
27	Donnie Green	.35
28	Bob Hayes	1.00
29	John Zook	.35
30	Bobby Bryant	.35
31	Scott Hunter	.35
32	Dan Dierdorf	5.00
33	Curt Knight	.35
34	*Elmo Wright*	.60
35	Essex Johnson	.35
36	Walt Sumner	.35
37	Marv Montgomery	.35
38	Tim Foley	.35
39	Mike Siani	.35
40	Joe Greene	6.00
41	Bobby Howfield	.35
42	Del Williams	.35
43	Don McCauley	.35
44	Randy Jackson	.35
45	Ron Smith	.35
46	Gene Washington	.50
47	Po James	.35
48	Soloman Freelon	.35
49	Bob Windsor	.35
50	John Hadl	1.00
51	Greg Larson	.35
52	Steve Owens	.35
53	Jim Cheyunski	.35
54	Rayfield Wright	.35
55	Dave Hampton	.35
56	Ron Widby	.35
57	Milt Sunde	.35
58	Bill Kilmer	1.25
59	Bobby Bell	1.50
60	Jim Bakken	.50
61	Rufus Mayes	.35
62	Vic Washington	.35
63	Gene Washington	.35
64	Clarence Scott	.35
65	Gene Upshaw	2.00
66	Larry Seiple	.35
67	John McMakin	.35
68	Ralph Baker	.35
69	Lydell Mitchell	1.00
70	Archie Manning	1.75
71	George Farmer	.35
72	Ron East	.35
73	Al Nelson	.35
74	Pat Hughes	.35
75	Fred Willis	.35
76	Larry Walton	.35
77	Tom Neville	.35
78	Ted Kwalick	.35
79	Walt Patulski	.35
80	John Niland	.35
81	Ted Fritsch	.35
82	Paul Krause	1.00
83	Jack Snow	.35
84	Mike Bass	.35
85	Jim Tyrer	.35
86	Ron Yankowski	.35
87	Mike Phipps	.35
88	Al Beauchamp	.35
89	*Riley Odoms*	2.00
90	MacArthur Lane	.35
91	Art Thoms	.35
92	Marlin Briscoe	.35
93	Bruce Van Dyke	.35
94	Tom Myers	.35
95	Calvin Hill	.75
96	Bruce Laird	.35
97	Tony McGee	.35
98	Len Rohde	.35
99	Tom McNeill	.35
100	Delles Howell	.35
101	Gary Garrison	.35
102	Dan Goich	.35
103	Len St. Jean	.35
104	Zeke Moore	.35
105	*Ahmad Rashad*	15.00
106	Mel Renfro	1.00
107	Jim Mitchell	.35
108	Ed Budde	.35
109	Harry Schuh	.35
110	*Greg Pruitt*	4.00
111	Ed Flanagan	.35
112	Larry Stallings	.35
113	*Chuck Foreman*	4.00
114	Royce Berry	.35
115	Gale Gillingham	.35
116	Charlie Johnson	.75
117	Checklist 1-132	2.50
118	Bill Butler	.35
119	Roy Jefferson	.35
120	Bobby Douglass	.35
121	*Harold Carmichael*	15.00
122	George Kuntz (AP)	.35
123	Larry Little (AP)	1.50
124	Forrest Blue (AP)	.35
125	Ron Yary (AP)	.75
126	Tom Mack (AP)	.35
127	Bob Tucker (AP)	.35
128	Paul Warfield (AP)	4.00
129	Fran Tarkenton (AP)	10.00
130	O.J. Simpson (AP)	15.00
131	Larry Csonka (AP)	3.50
132	Bruce Gossett (AP)	.35
133	Bill Stanfill (AP)	.35
134	Alan Page (AP)	2.25
135	Paul Smith (AP)	.35
136	Claude Humphrey (AP)	.35
137	Jack Ham (AP)	7.00
138	Lee Roy Jordan (AP)	1.50
139	Phil Villapiano (AP)	.35
140	Ken Ellis (AP)	.35
141	Willie Brown (AP)	1.25
142	Dick Anderson (AP)	.35
143	Bill Bradley (AP)	.35
144	Jerrel Wilson (AP)	.35
145	Reggie Rucker	.60
146	Marty Domres	.35
147	Bob Kowalkowski	.35
148	*John Matuszak*	4.00
149	*Mike Adamle*	.75
150	Johnny Unitas	20.00
151	Charlie Ford	.35
152	*Bob Klein*	.60
153	Jim Merlo	.35
154	Willie Young	.35
155	Donny Anderson	.35
156	Brig Owens	.35
157	Bruce Jarvis	.35
158	Ron Carpenter	.35
159	Don Cockroft	.35
160	Tommy Nobis	1.25
161	Craig Morton	1.25
162	Jon Staggers	.35
163	Mike Eischeid	.35
164	*Jerry Sisemore*	.60
165	Cedric Hardman	.35
166	Bill Thompson	.35
167	Jim Lynch	.35
168	Bob Moore	.35
169	Glen Edwards	.35
170	Mercury Morris	1.00
171	Julius Adams	.35
172	Cotton Speyrer	.35
173	Bill Munson	.35
174	Benny Johnson	.35
175	*Burgess Owens*	.60
176	Cid Edwards	.35
177	Doug Buffone	.35
178	Charlie Cowan	.35
179	Bob Newland	.35
180	Ron Johnson	.35
181	Bob Rowe	.35
182	Len Hauss	.35
183	*Joe DeLamielleure*	2.00
184	*Sherman White*	.75
185	Fair Hooker	.35
186	Nick Mike-Mayer	.35
187	Ralph Neely	.35
188	Rich McGeorge	.35
189	*Ed Marinaro*	4.50
190	Dave Wilcox	.35
191	Joe Owens	.35
192	Bill Van Heusen	.35
193	Jim Kearney	.35
194	*Otis Sistrunk*	3.00
195	Ronnie Shanklin	.35
196	Bill Lenkaitis	.35
197	Tom Drougas	.35
198	Larry Hand	.35
199	Mack Alston	.35
200	Bob Griese	5.00
201	Earlie Thomas	.35
202	Carl Gersbach	.35
203	Jim Harrison	.35
204	Jake Kupp	.35
205	Merlin Olsen	3.50
206	Spider Lockhart	.35
207	Walter Gillette	.35
208	Verlon Biggs	.35
209	Bob James	.35
210	Bob Trumpy	1.00
211	Jerry Sherk	.35
212	Andy Maurer	.35
213	Fred Carr	.35
214	Mick Tingelhoff	.35
215	Steve Spurrier	7.00
216	Richard Harris	.35
217	Charlie Greer	.35
218	Buck Buchanan	2.00
219	*Ray Guy*	10.00
220	Franco Harris	20.00
221	*Darryl Stingley*	2.50
222	Rex Kern	.35
223	Toni Fritsch	.35
224	Levi Johnson	.35
225	Bob Kuechenberg	.60
226	Elvin Bethea	.35
227	*Al Woodall*	.50
228	Terry Owens	.35
229	Bivian Lee	.35
230	Dick Butkus	6.00
231	*Jim Bertelsen*	.50
232	*John Mendenhall*	.50
233	*Conrad Dobler*	2.50
234	J.D. Hill	.35
235	Ken Houston	1.50
236	Dave Lewis	.35
237	John Garlington	.35
238	Bill Sandeman	.35
239	Alden Roche	.35
240	John Gilliam	.35
241	Bruce Taylor	.35
242	Vern Winfield	.35
243	Bobby Maples	.35
244	Wendell Hayes	.35
245	George Blanda	7.00
246	Dwight White	.35
247	Sandy Durko	.35
248	Tom Mitchell	.35
249	Chuck Walton	.35
250	Bob Lilly	4.00
251	Doug Swift	.35
252	*Lynn Dickey*	3.00
253	*Jerome Barkum*	1.50
254	Clint Jones	.35
255	Billy Newsome	.35
256	Bob Asher	.35
257	Joe Scibelli	.35
258	Tom Blanchard	.35
259	Norm Thompson	.35
260	Larry Brown	1.00
261	Paul Seymour	.35
262	Checklist 133-264	2.50
263	*Doug Dieken*	.75
264	Lemar Parrish	.35
265	Bob Lee	.35
266	Bob Brown	.35
267	Roy Winston	.35
268	Randy Beisler	.35
269	Joe Dawkins	.35
270	Tom Dempsey	.35
271	Jack Rudnay	.35
272	Art Shell	6.00
273	Mike Wagner	.75
274	Rick Cash	.35
275	Greg Landry	1.00
276	Glenn Ressler	.35
277	*Billy Joe DuPree*	4.00
278	Norm Evans	.35
279	Billy Parks	.35
280	John Riggins	6.00
281	Lionel Aldridge	.35
282	Steve O'Neal	.35
283	Craig Clemons	.35
284	Willie Williams	.35
285	Isiah Robertson	.35
286	Dennis Shaw	.35
287	Bill Brundige	.35
288	John Leypoldt	.35
289	John DeMarie	.35
290	Mike Reid	1.25
291	Greg Brezina	.35
292	*Willie Buchanon*	1.00
293	Dave Osborn	.35
294	Mel Phillips	.35
295	Haven Moses	.35
296	Wade Key	.35
297	Marvin Upshaw	.35
298	Ray Mansfield	.35
299	Edgar Chandler	.35
300	Marv Hubbard	.35
301	Herman Weaver	.35
302	Jim Bailey	.35
303	*D.D. Lewis*	1.50
304	Ken Burrough	.35
305	Jake Scott	.35
306	Randy Rasmussen	.35
307	Pettis Norman	.35
308	Carl Johnson	.35
309	Joe Taylor	.35
310	Pete Gogolak	.35
311	Tony Baker	.35
312	John Richardson	.35
313	Dave Robinson	.35
314	*Reggie McKenzie*	2.50
315	*Isaac Curtis*	3.00
316	Tom Darden	.35
317	Ken Reaves	.35
318	Malcolm Snider	.35
319	*Jeff Siemon*	1.50
320	Dan Abramowicz	.35
321	Lyle Alzado	2.50
322	John Reaves	.35
323	Morris Stroud	.35
324	Bobby Walden	.35
325	Randy Vataha	.35
326	Nemiah Wilson	.35
327	Paul Naumoff	.35
328	O.J. Simpson, John Brockington Rushing Leaders	5.00
329	Ken Stabler, Roger Staubach Passing Leaders	4.00
330	Fred Willis, Harold Carmichael Receiving Leaders	1.25
331	Scoring Leaders (Roy Gerela, David Ray)	.60
332	Interception Leaders (Dick Anderson, Mike Wagner, Bobby Bryan t)	.60
333	Punting Leaders (Jerrell Wilson, Tom Wittum)	.60
334	Dennis Nelson	.35
335	Walt Garrison	.35
336	Tody Smith	.35
337	Ed Bell	.35
338	Bryant Salter	.35
339	Wayne Colman	.35
340	Garo Yepremian	.35
341	Bob Newton	.35
342	*Vince Clements*	.50
343	Ken Iman	.35
344	Jim Tolbert	.35
345	Chris Hanburger	.35
346	Dave Foley	.35
347	Tommy Casanova	.60
348	John James	.35
349	Clarence Williams	.35
350	Leroy Kelly	1.00
351	*Stu Voigt*	.75
352	Skip Vanderbundt	.35
353	Pete Duranko	.35
354	John Outlaw	.35
355	Jan Stenerud	1.25
356	Barry Pearson	.35
357	Brian Dowling	.50
358	Dan Conners	.35
359	Bob Bell	.35
360	Rick Volk	.35
361	Pat Toomay	.35
362	Bob Gresham	.35
363	John Schmitt	.35
364	Mel Rogers	.35
365	Manny Fernandez	.35
366	Ernie Jackson	.35
367	*Gary Huff*	1.00
368	Bob Grim	.35
369	Ernie McMillan	.35
370	Dave Elmendorf	.35
371	Mike Bragg	.35
372	John Skorupan	.35
373	Howard Fest	.35
374	*Jerry Tagge*	1.00
375	Art Malone	.35
376	Bob Babich	.35
377	Jim Marshall	1.25
378	Bob Hoskins	.35
379	Dan Zimmerman	.35
380	Ray May	.35
381	Emmitt Thomas	.35
382	Terry Hanratty	.35
383	*John Hannah*	15.00
384	George Atkinson	.35
385	Ted Hendricks	3.00
386	Jim O'Brien	.35
387	Jethro Pugh	.35
388	Elbert Drungo	.35
389	Richard Caster	.35
390	Deacon Jones	2.25
391	Checklist 265-396	2.50
392	Jess Phillips	.35
393	Gary Lyle	.35
394	Jim Files	.35
395	Jim Hart	1.50
396	Dave Chapple	.35
397	Jim Langer	2.50
398	John Wilbur	.35
399	Dwight Harrison	.35
400	John Brockington	.60
401	Ken Anderson	6.50
402	Mike Tilleman	.35
403	Charlie Hall	.35
404	Tommy Hart	.35
405	Norm Bulaich	.35
406	Jim Turner	.35
407	Mo Moorman	.35
408	Ralph Anderson	.35
409	Jim Otto	2.00
410	Andy Russell	.35
411	Glenn Doughty	.35
412	Altie Taylor	.35
413	Marv Bateman	.35
414	Willie Alexander	.35
415	Bill Zapalac	.35
416	Russ Washington	.35
417	Joe Federspiel	.35
418	Craig Cotton	.35
419	Randy Johnson	.35
420	Harold Jackson	1.00
421	Roger Wehrli	.35
422	Charlie Harraway	.35
423	Spike Jones	.35
424	Bob Johnson	.35
425	Mike McCoy	.35
426	Dennis Havig	.35
427	Bob McKay	.35
428	Steve Zabel	.35
429	Horace Jones	.35
430	Jim Johnson	1.00
431	Roy Gerela	.35
432	Tom Graham	.35
433	Curley Culp	.35
434	Ken Mendenhall	.35
435	Jim Plunkett	3.00
436	Julian Fagan	.35
437	Mike Garrett	.35
438	Bobby Joe Green	.35
439	Jack Gregory	.35
440	Charlie Sanders	.35
441	Bill Curry	.35
442	Bob Pollard	.35
443	David Ray	.35
444	*Terry Metcalf*	4.50
445	Pat Fischer	.35
446	Bob Chandler	.35
447	Bill Bergey	1.00
448	Walter Johnson	.35
449	*Charlie Young*	1.50
450	Chester Marcol	.35
451	Ken Stabler	20.00
452	Preston Pearson	.75
453	Mike Current	.35
454	Ron Bolton	.35
455	Mark Lomas	.35
456	Raymond Chester	.35
457	Jerry LeVias	.35
458	Skip Butler	.35
459	*Mike Livingston*	.75
460	AFC Semi-finals	.75
461	Roger Staubach NFC Semi-finals	3.00
462	Ken Stabler, Fran Tarkenton Playoff Championship	2.50
463	Super Bowl	2.00
464	Wayne Mulligan	.35
465	Horst Muhlmann	.35
466	Milt Morin	.35
467	Don Parish	.35
468	Richard Neal	.35
469	Ron Jessie	.35
470	Terry Bradshaw	20.00
471	Fred Dryer	2.50
472	Jim Carter	.35
473	Ken Burrow	.35
474	*Wally Chambers*	1.00
475	Dan Pastorini	.75
476	Don Morrison	.35
477	Carl Mauck	.35
478	*Larry Cole*	.75
479	Jim Kiick	.35
480	Willie Lanier	1.50
481	Don Herrmann	.35
482	George Hunt	.35
483	Bob Howard	.35
484	Myron Pottios	.35
485	Jackie Smith	1.00
486	Vern Holland	.35
487	Jim Braxton	.35
488	Joe Reed	.35
489	Wally Hilgenberg	.35
490	Fred Biletnikoff	3.50
491	Bob DeMarco	.35
492	Mark Nordquist	.35
493	Larry Brooks	.35
494	Pete Athas	.35
495	Emerson Boozer	.35
496	L.C. Greenwood	1.50
497	Rockne Freitas	.35
498	Checklist 397-528	2.50
499	Joe Schmiesing	.35
500	Roger Staubach	28.00
501	Al Cowlings	1.00
502	*Sam Cunningham*	2.00
503	Dennis Partee	.35
504	John Didion	.35
505	Nick Buoniconti	1.25
506	Carl Garrett	.35
507	Doug Van Horn	.35
508	Jamie Rivers	.35
509	Jack Youngblood	3.50
510	Charley Taylor	2.50
511	Ken Riley	.60
512	*Joe Ferguson*	2.50
513	Bill Lueck	.35
514	Ray Brown	.35
515	Fred Cox	.35
516	Joe Jones	.35
517	Larry Schreiber	.35
518	Dennis Wirgowski	.35
519	Leroy Mitchell	.35
520	Otis Taylor	.75
521	Henry Davis	.35
522	Bruce Barnes	.35
523	Charlie Smith	.35
524	*Bert Jones*	5.00
525	Lem Barney	2.00
526	*John Fitzgerald*	.50
527	Tom Funchess	.35
528	Steve Tannen	.60

1974 Topps Team Checklists

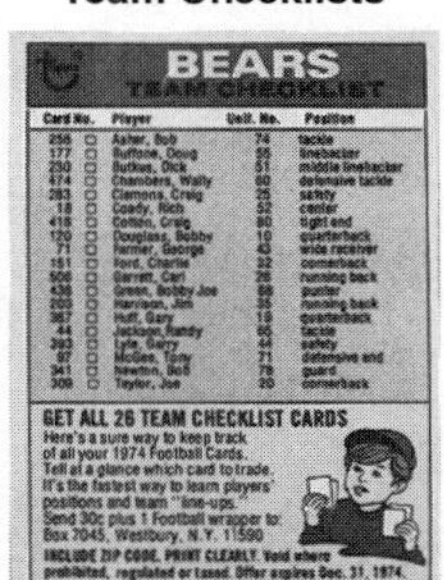

These unnumbered checklists were issued in wax packs of 1974 Topps cards. At the bottom of the card was an ad for a sendaway offer where collectors could buy the entire run of checklists through Topps. The back of the card carried instructions for a game that could be played with football cards. This was the last time Topps would issue team checklists separate from the rest of the set.

		NM/M
Complete Set (26):		35.00
Common Team:		1.50
(1)	Atlanta Falcons	1.50
(2)	Baltimore Colts	1.50
(3)	Buffalo Bills	1.50
(4)	Chicago Bears	1.50
(5)	Cincinnati Bengals	1.50
(6)	Cleveland Browns	1.50
(7)	Dallas Cowboys	1.50
(8)	Denver Broncos	1.50
(9)	Detroit Lions	1.50
(10)	Green Bay Packers	1.50
(11)	Houston Oilers	1.50
(12)	Kansas City Chiefs	1.50
(13)	Los Angeles Rams	1.50
(14)	Miami Dolphins	1.50
(15)	Minnesota Vikings	1.50
(16)	New England Patriots	1.50
(17)	New Orleans Saints	1.50
(18)	New York Giants	1.50
(19)	New York Jets	1.50
(20)	Oakland Raiders	1.50
(21)	Philadelphia Eagles	1.50
(22)	Pittsburgh Steelers	1.50
(23)	St. Louis Cardinals	1.50
(24)	San Diego Chargers	1.50
(25)	San Francisco 49ers	1.50
(26)	Washington Redskins	1.50

1975 Topps

The 528-card 1975 issue was arguably Topps' most attractive offering of the decade. Its clean design and white borders leaves room for the photo, player's name, a pennant with the team name, and the player's position in a green helmet. Most notable for the inclusion of the Dan Fouts rookie card, other rookies in this set are Mel Blount, Rocky Bleier, Drew Pearson, Lynn Swann, James Harris, Otis Armstrong, Lawrence McCutcheon and Joe Theismann. One feature of this set is the larger number of separate All-Pro cards, numbered 201-225. Each shows two star players. Other subsets include Statistical Leaders, Record Breakers, Highlights and Playoff Action. George Blanda has two "honorary" cards in this set, numbers 7 and 8. The first shows him in a black jersey and lists his career highlights on the back; the second shows him in a white Oakland jersey and documents his career statistics. No team checklists were issued for this set.

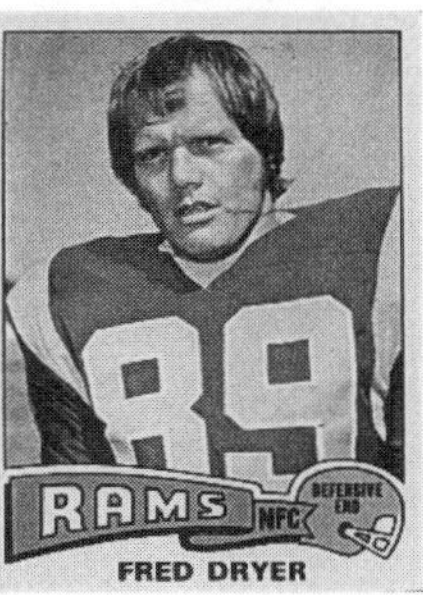

	NM/M
Complete Set (528):	300.00
Common Player:	.30
Wax Pack (10):	50.00
Wax Box (36):	275.00

No.	Player	NM/M
1	Lawrence McCutcheon, Otis Armstrong Rushing Leaders	1.75
2	Sonny Jurgensen, Ken Anderson Passing Leaders	1.50
3	Charley Young, Lydell Mitchell Receiving Leaders	.60
4	Chester Marcol, Roy Gerela Scoring Leaders	.60
5	Ray Brown, Emmitt Thomas Interception Leaders	.60
6	Tom Blanchard, Ray Guy Punting Leaders	.60
7	George Blanda (highlights, black jersey)	5.00
8	George Blanda (career, white jersey)	5.00
9	Ralph Baker	.30
10	Don Woods	.30
11	Bob Asher	.30
12	*Mel Blount*	25.00
13	Sam Cunningham	.60
14	Jackie Smith	.30
15	Greg Landry	.75
16	Buck Buchanan	1.50
17	Haven Moses	.30
18	Clarence Ellis	.30
19	Jim Carter	.30
20	Charley Taylor	2.25
21	Jess Phillips	.30
22	Larry Seiple	.30
23	Doug Dieken	.30
24	Ron Saul	.30
25	Isaac Curtis	.75
26	*Gary Larsen*	.75
27	Bruce Jarvis	.30
28	Steve Zabel	.30
29	John Mendenhall	.30
30	Rick Volk	.30
31	Checklist 1-132	2.50
32	Dan Abramowicz	.30
33	Bubba Smith	2.00
34	David Ray	.30
35	Dan Dierdorf	2.00
36	Randy Rasmussen	.30
37	Bob Howard	.30
38	Gary Huff	.30
39	*Rocky Bleier*	15.00
40	Mel Gray	.30
41	Tony McGee	.30
42	Larry Hand	.30
43	Wendell Hayes	.30
44	*Doug Wilkerson*	.50
45	Paul Smith	.30
46	Dave Robinson	.30
47	Bivian Lee	.30
48	*Jim Mandich*	.50
49	Greg Pruitt	1.00
50	Dan Pastorini	.60
51	Ron Pritchard	.30
52	Dan Conners	.30
53	Fred Cox	.30
54	Tony Greene	.30
55	Craig Morton	1.00
56	Jerry Sisemore	.30
57	Glenn Doughty	.30
58	Larry Schreiber	.30
59	*Charlie Waters*	4.00
60	Jack Youngblood	1.50
61	Bill Lenkaitis	.30
62	Greg Brezina	.30
63	Bob Pollard	.30
64	Mack Alston	.30
65	*Drew Pearson*	15.00
66	Charlie Stukes	.30
67	Emerson Boozer	.30
68	Dennis Partee	.30
69	Bob Newton	.30
70	Jack Tatum	.30
71	Frank Lewis	.30
72	Bob Young	.30
73	Julius Adams	.30

74	Paul Naumoff	.30
75	Otis Taylor	.60
76	Dave Hampton	.30
77	Mike Current	.30
78	Brig Owens	.30
79	Bobby Scott	.30
80	Harold Carmichael	4.00
81	Bill Stanfill	.30
82	Bob Babich	.30
83	Vic Washington	.30
84	Mick Tingelhoff	.30
85	Bob Trumpy	1.00
86	Earl Edwards	.30
87	Ron Hornsby	.30
88	Don McCauley	.30
89	Jimmy Johnson	.30
90	Andy Russell	.30
91	Cornell Green	.30
92	Charlie Cowan	.30
93	Jon Staggers	.30
94	Billy Newsome	.30
95	Willie Brown	1.25
96	Carl Mauck	.30
97	Doug Buffone	.30
98	Preston Pearson	.60
99	Jim Bakken	.30
100	Bob Griese	5.00
101	Bob Windsor	.30
102	Rockne Freitas	.30
103	Jim Marsalis	.30
104	Bill Thompson	.30
105	Ken Burrow	.30
106	Diron Talbert	.30
107	Joe Federspiel	.30
108	Norm Bulaich	.30
109	Bob DeMarco	.30
110	Tom Wittum	.30
111	Larry Hefner	.30
112	Tody Smith	.30
113	Stu Voigt	.30
114	Horst Muhlmann	.30
115	Ahmad Rashad	5.00
116	Joe Dawkins	.30
117	George Kunz	.30
118	D.D. Lewis	.30
119	Levi Johnson	.30
120	Len Dawson	3.50
121	Jim Bertelsen	.30
122	Ed Bell	.30
123	Art Thoms	.30
124	Joe Beauchamp	.30
125	Jack Ham	5.00
126	Carl Garrett	.30
127	Roger Finnie	.30
128	Howard Twilley	.30
129	Bruce Barnes	.30
130	Nate Wright	.30
131	Jerry Tagge	.30
132	Floyd Little	1.25
133	John Zook	.30
134	Len Hauss	.30
135	Archie Manning	1.50
136	Po James	.30
137	Walt Sumner	.30
138	Randy Beisler	.30
139	Willie Alexander	.30
140	Garo Yepremian	.30
141	Chip Myers	.30
142	Jim Braxton	.30
143	Doug Van Horn	.30
144	Stan White	.30
145	Roger Staubach	25.00
146	Herman Weaver	.30
147	Marvin Upshaw	.30
148	Bob Klein	.30
149	Earlie Thomas	.30
150	John Brockington	.30
151	Mike Siani	.30
152	Sam Davis	.30
153	Mike Wagner	.30
154	Larry Stallings	.30
155	Wally Chambers	.30
156	Randy Vataha	.30
157	Jim Marshall	1.00
158	Jim Turner	.30
159	Walt Sweeney	.30
160	Ken Anderson	3.50
161	Ray Brown	.30
162	John Didion	.30
163	Tom Dempsey	.30
164	Clarence Scott	.30
165	Gene Washington	.30
166	Willie Rodgers	.30
167	Doug Swift	.30
168	Rufus Mayes	.30
169	Marv Bateman	.30
170	Lydell Mitchell	.30
171	Ron Smith	.30
172	Bill Munson	.30
173	Bob Grim	.30
174	Ed Budde	.30
175	Bob Lilly	3.50
176	*Jim Youngblood*	2.00
177	Steve Tannen	.30
178	Rich McGeorge	.30
179	Jim Tyrer	.30
180	Forrest Blue	.30
181	Jerry LeVias	.30
182	*Joe Gilliam*	.60
183	*Jim Otis*	1.25
184	Mel Tom	.30
185	Paul Seymour	.30
186	George Webster	.30
187	Pete Duranko	.30
188	Essex Johnson	.30
189	Bob Lee	.30
190	Gene Upshaw	1.50
191	Tom Myers	.30
192	Don Zimmerman	.30
193	John Garlington	.30
194	Skip Butler	.30
195	Tom Mitchell	.30
196	Jim Langer	1.50
197	Ron Carpenter	.30
198	Dave Foley	.30
199	Bert Jones	1.50
200	Larry Brown	.75
201	Charley Taylor, Fred Biletnikoff All Pro Receivers	2.00
202	Russ Washington, Rayfield Wright All Pro Tackles	.50
203	Tom Mack, Larry Little All Pro Guards	1.00
204	Jeff Van Note, Jack Rudnay All Pro Centers	.50
205	Gale Gillingham, John Hannah All Pro Guards	1.00
206	Winston Hill, Dan Dierdorf All Pro Tackles	.50
207	Riley Odoms, Charley Young All Pro Tight Ends	.50
208	Fran Tarkenton, Ken Stabler All Pro Quarterbacks	3.00
209	Lawrence McCutcheon, O.J. Simpson All Pro Backs	5.00
210	Otis Armstrong, Terry Metcalf All Pro Backs	.50
211	Isaac Curtis, Mel Gray All Pro Receivers	.50
212	Roy Gerela, Chester Marcol All Pro Kickers	.50
213	Elvin Bethea, Jack Youngblood All Pro Ends	.50
214	Otis Sistrunk, Alan Page All Pro Tackles	.50
215	Merlin Olsen, Mike Reid All Pro Tackles	1.25
216	Carl Eller, Lyle Alzado All Pro Ends	1.00
217	Ted Hendricks, Phil Villapiano All Pro Linebackers	1.00
218	Willie Lanier, Lee Roy Jordan All Pro Linebackers	1.00
219	Andy Russell, Isiah Robertson All Pro Linebackers	.50
220	Emmitt Thomas, Nate Wright All Pro Cornerbacks	.50
221	Lemar Parrish, Willie Buchanon All Pro Cornerbacks	.50
222	Ken Houston, Dick Anderson All Pro Safeties	1.00
223	Cliff Harris, Jack Tatum All Pro Safeties	1.00
224	Tom Wittum, Ray Guy All Pro Punters	.50
225	Greg Pruitt, Terry Metcalf All Pro Returners	.50
226	Ted Kwalick	.30
227	Spider Lockhart	.30
228	Mike Livingston	.30
229	Larry Cole	.30
230	Gary Garrison	.30
231	Larry Brooks	.30
232	Bobby Howfield	.30
233	Fred Carr	.30
234	Norm Evans	.30
235	Dwight White	.30
236	Conrad Dobler	.30
237	Garry Lyle	.30
238	Darryl Stingley	1.00
239	Tom Graham	.30
240	Chuck Foreman	1.00
241	Ken Riley	.30
242	Don Morrison	.30
243	Lynn Dickey	.75
244	Don Cockroft	.30
245	Claude Humphrey	.30
246	John Skorupan	.30
247	Raymond Chester	.30
248	Cas Banaszek	.30
249	Art Malone	.30
250	Ed Flanagan	.30
251	Checklist 133-264	2.50
252	Nemiah Wilson	.30
253	Ron Jessie	.30
254	Jim Lynch	.30
255	Bob Tucker	.30
256	Terry Owens	.30
257	John Fitzgerald	.30
258	Jack Snow	.30
259	Garry Puetz	.30
260	Mike Phipps	.30
261	Al Matthews	.30
262	Bob Kuechenberg	.30
263	Ron Yankowski	.30
264	Ron Shanklin	.30
265	Bobby Douglass	.30
266	Josh Ashton	.30
267	Bill Van Heusen	.30
268	Jeff Siemon	.30
269	Bob Newland	.30
270	Gale Gillingham	.30
271	Zeke Moore	.30
272	Mike Tilleman	.30
273	John Leypoldt	.30
274	Ken Mendenhall	.30
275	Norm Snead	.30
276	Bill Bradley	.30
277	Jerry Smith	.30
278	Clarence Davis	.30
279	Jim Yarbrough	.30
280	Lemar Parrish	.30
281	Bobby Bell	1.50
282	*Lynn Swann*	45.00
283	John Hicks	.30
284	Coy Bacon	.30
285	Lee Roy Jordan	1.25
286	Willie Buchanon	.30
287	Al Woodall	.30
288	Reggie Rucker	.30
289	John Schmitt	.30
290	Carl Eller	1.00
291	Jake Scott	.30
292	Donny Anderson	.30
293	Charley Wade	.30
294	John Tanner	.30
295	Charley Johnson	.30
296	Tom Blanchard	.30
297	Curley Culp	.30
298	*Jeff Van Note*	1.25
299	Bob James	.30
300	Franco Harris	12.00
301	Tim Berra	.30
302	Bruce Gossett	.30
303	Berlon Biggs	.30
304	Bob Kowalkowski	.30
305	Marv Hubbard	.30
306	Ken Avery	.30
307	Mike Adamle	.30
308	Don Herrmann	.30
309	Chris Fletcher	.30
310	Roman Gabriel	1.25
311	Billy Joe DuPree	1.00
312	Fred Dryer	2.00
313	John Riggins	5.00
314	Bob McKay	.30
315	Ted Hendricks	1.50
316	Bobby Bryant	.30
317	Don Nottingham	.30
318	John Hannah	4.00
319	Rich Coady	.30
320	Phil Villapiano	.30
321	Jim Plunkett	2.00
322	Lyle Alzado	1.25
323	Ernie Jackson	.30
324	Billy Parks	.30
325	Willie Lanier	1.50
326	John James	.30
327	Joe Ferguson	1.00
328	*Ernie Holmes*	1.00
329	Bruce Laird	.30
330	Chester Marcol	.30
331	Dave Wilcox	.30
332	Pat Fischer	.30
333	Steve Owens	.30
334	Royce Berry	.30
335	Russ Washington	.30
336	Walker Gillette	.30
337	Mark Nordquist	.30
338	*James Harris*	1.00
339	Warren Koegel	.30
340	Emmitt Thomas	.30
341	Walt Garrison	.30
342	Thom Darden	.30
343	Mike Eischeid	.30
344	Ernie McMillan	.30
345	Nick Buoniconti	1.00
346	George Farmer	.30
347	Sam Adams	.30
348	Larry Cipa	.30
349	Bob Moore	.30
350	*Otis Armstrong*	4.00
351	George Blanda (RH)	2.50
352	Fred Cox (RH)	.60
353	Tom Dempsey (RH)	.60
354	Ken Houston (RH)	.60
355	O.J. Simpson (RH)	7.00
356	Ron Smith (RH)	.60
357	Bob Atkins	.30
358	Pat Sullivan	.30
359	Joe DeLamielleure	.60
360	*L. McCutcheon*	2.50
361	David Lee	.30
362	Mike McCoy	.30
363	Skip Vanderbundt	.30
364	Mark Moseley	.75
365	Lem Barney	1.50
366	Doug Dressler	.30
367	*Dan Fouts*	50.00
368	Bob Hyland	.30
369	John Outlaw	.30
370	Roy Gerela	.30
371	Isiah Robertson	.30
372	Jerome Barkum	.30
373	Ed Podolak	.30
374	Milt Morin	.30
375	John Niland	.30
376	Checklist 265-396	2.50
377	Ken Iman	.30
378	Manny Fernandez	.30
379	Dave Gallagher	.30
380	Ken Stabler	14.00
381	Mack Herron	.30
382	Bill McClard	.30
383	Ray May	.30
384	Don Hansen	.30
385	Elvin Bethea	.30
386	Joe Scibelli	.30
387	Neal Craig	.30
388	Marty Domres	.30
389	Ken Ellis	.30
390	Charley Young	.30
391	Tommy Hart	.30
392	Moses Denson	.30
393	Larry Walton	.30
394	Dave Green	.30
395	Ron Johnson	.30
396	Ed Bradley	.30
397	J.T. Thomas	.30
398	Jim Bailey	.30
399	Barry Pearson	.30
400	Fran Tarkenton	8.50
401	Jack Rudnay	.30
402	Rayfield Wright	.30
403	Roger Wehrli	.30
404	Vern Den Herder	.30
405	Fred Biletnikoff	3.00
406	Ken Grandberry	.30
407	Bob Adams	.30
408	Jim Merlo	.30
409	John Pitts	.30
410	Dave Osborn	.30
411	Dennis Havig	.30
412	Bob Johnson	.30
413	Ken Burrow	.30
414	Jim Cheyunski	.30
415	MacArthur Lane	.30
416	*Joe Theismann*	25.00
417	*Mike Boryla*	.50
418	Bruce Taylor	.30
419	Chris Hanburger	.30
420	Tom Mack	.30
421	Errol Mann	.30
422	Jack Gregory	.30
423	Harrison Davis	.30
424	Burgess Owens	.30
425	Joe Greene	4.00
426	Morris Stroud	.30
427	John DeMarie	.30
428	Mel Renfro	.75
429	Cid Edwards	.30
430	Mike Reid	1.00
431	Jack Mildren	.30
432	Jerry Simmons	.30
433	Ron Yary	.30
434	Howard Stevens	.30
435	Ray Guy	1.75
436	Tommy Nobis	1.00
437	Solomon Freelon	.30
438	J.D. Hill	.30
439	Toni Linhart	.30
440	Dick Anderson	.30
441	Guy Morriss	.30
442	Bob Hoskins	.30
443	John Hadl	1.00
444	Roy Jefferson	.30
445	Charlie Sanders	.30
446	Pat Curran	.30
447	David Knight	.30
448	Bob Brown	.30
449	Pete Gogolak	.30
450	Terry Metcalf	1.00
451	Bill Bergey	.75
452	Dan Abramowicz (HL)	.60
453	Otis Armstrong (HL)	1.00
454	Cliff Branch (HL)	1.50
455	John James (HL)	.60
456	Lydell Mitchell (HL)	.60
457	Lemar Parrish (HL)	.60
458	Ken Stabler (HL)	4.00
459	Lynn Swann (HL)	7.00
460	Emmitt Thomas (HL)	.60
461	Terry Bradshaw	15.00
462	Jerrel Wilson	.30
463	Walter Johnson	.30
464	Golden Richards	.30
465	Tommy Casanova	.30
466	Randy Jackson	.30
467	Ron Bolton	.30
468	Joe Owens	.30
469	Wally Hilgenberg	.30
470	Riley Odoms	.50
471	Otis Sistrunk	.30
472	Eddie Ray	.30
473	Reggie McKenzie	.75
474	Elbert Drungo	.30
475	Mercury Morris	.75
476	Dan Dickel	.30
477	Merritt Kersey	.30
478	Mike Holmes	.30
479	Clarence Williams	.30
480	Bill Kilmer	.50
481	Altie Taylor	.30
482	Dave Elmendorf	.30
483	Bob Rowe	.30
484	Pete Athas	.30
485	Winston Hill	.30
486	Bo Mathews	.30
487	Earl Thomas	.30
488	Jan Stenerud	1.25
489	Steve Holden	.30
490	*Cliff Harris*	4.00
491	*Boobie Clark*	.50
492	Joe Taylor	.30
493	Tom Neville	.30
494	Wayne Colman	.30
495	Jim Mitchell	.30
496	Paul Krause	.75
497	Jim Otto	2.00
498	John Rowser	.30
499	Larry Little	1.00
500	O.J. Simpson	12.00
501	*John Dutton*	1.50
502	Pat Hughes	.30
503	Malcolm Snider	.30
504	Fred Willis	.30
505	Harold Jackson	.90
506	Mike Bragg	.30
507	Jerry Sherk	.30
508	Mirro Roder	.30
509	Tom Sullivan	.30
510	Jim Hart	1.00
511	Cedrick Hardman	.30
512	Blaine Nye	.30
513	Elmo Wright	.30
514	Herb Orvis	.30
515	Richard Caster	.30
516	*Doug Kotar*	.30
517	Checklist 397-528	2.50
518	Jesse Freitas	.30
519	Ken Houston	1.25
520	Alan Page	1.75
521	Tim Foley	.30
522	Bill Olds	.30
523	Bobby Maples	.30
524	*Cliff Branch*	10.00
525	Merlin Olsen	3.00
526	Terry Bradshaw, Franco Harris AFC Champions	2.50
527	Chuck Foreman NFC Champions	1.00
528	Terry Bradshaw Super Bowl	4.00

1975 Topps Team Checklists

Each of the 26 NFL teams is represented in this set, which was available as a mail-in offer from Topps as an uncut sheet. Each card is standard size, and shows the team's 1975 schedule on the front. The card back is unnumbered and contains a checklist for the players in the team set.

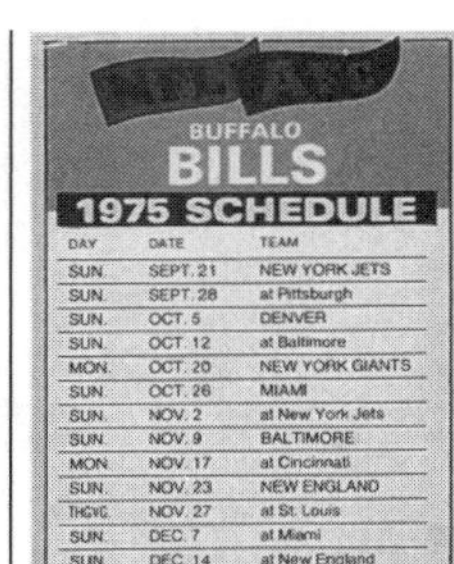

		NM/M
Complete Set (26):		195.00
Common Player:		8.00
(1)	Atlanta Falcons	8.50
(2)	Baltimore Colts	8.00
(3)	Buffalo Bills	8.00
(4)	Chicago Bears	9.00
(5)	Cincinnati Bengals	8.00
(6)	Cleveland Browns	9.00
(7)	Dallas Cowboys	10.00
(8)	Denver Broncos	10.00
(9)	Detroit Lions	8.00
(10)	Green Bay Packers	8.00
(11)	Houston Oilers	8.00
(12)	Kansas City Chiefs	8.00
(13)	Los Angeles Rams	8.00
(14)	Miami Dolphins	10.00
(15)	Minnesota Vikings	9.00
(16)	New England Patriots	8.00
(17)	New York Giants	9.00
(18)	New York Jets	9.00
(19)	New Orleans Saints	8.00
(20)	Oakland Raiders	10.00
(21)	Philadelphia Eagles	8.00
(22)	Pittsburgh Steelers	9.00
(23)	St. Louis Cardinals	9.00
(24)	San Diego Chargers	8.00
(25)	San Francisco 49ers	9.00
(26)	Washington Redskins	10.00

1976 Topps

This is the most valuable of the 528-card sets issued by Topps, primarily because of the inclusion of Walter Payton's rookie card. Other rookies in this set include Steve Bartkowski, Harvey Martin, Russ Francis, Randy White, Jack Lambert, Randy Gradishar, Steve Grogan, and Ron Jaworski. The set also features the second-year card of Dan Fouts. Hall of Famers (and future Hall of Famers) showing up in the 1976 Topps issue include Payton, Fouts, Martin, White, Lambert, Willie Lanier, Fred Biletnikoff, Ray Guy, Alan Page, Bob Griese, Franco Harris, O.J. Simpson, John Riggins, Len Dawson, Paul Warfield, George Blanda, Roger Staubach, Ken Stabler, Larry Csonka, Charley Taylor and Fran Tarkenton. (Key: AP - All Pro)

		NM/M
Complete Set (528):		350.00
Common Player:		.25
Team Cards:		1.25
Wax Pack (10):		70.00
Wax Box (36):		1,800
1	George Blanda	5.00
2	Neil Colzie	.50
3	Chuck Foreman	.50
4	Jim Marshall	.50
5	Terry Metcalf	.50
6	O.J. Simpson	3.00
7	Fran Tarkenton	3.00
8	Charley Taylor	1.00
9	Ernie Holmes	.25
10	Ken Anderson (AP)	2.00
11	Bobby Bryant	.25
12	Jerry Smith	.25
13	David Lee	.25
14	*Robert Newhouse*	1.25
15	Vern Den Herder	.25
16	John Hannah	2.00
17	J.D. Hill	.25
18	James Harris	.25
19	Willie Buchanon	.25
20	Charley Young (AP)	.25
21	Jim Yarbrough	.25
22	Ronnie Coleman	.25
23	Don Cockroft	.25
24	Willie Lanier	1.00
25	Fred Biletnikoff	3.00
26	Ron Yankowski	.25
27	Spider Lockhart	.25
28	Bob Johnson	.25
29	J.T. Thomas	.25
30	Ron Yary (AP)	.25
31	*Brad Dusek*	.50
32	Raymond Chester	.25
33	Larry Little	.75
34	*Pat Leahy*	1.00
35	*Steve Bartkowski*	4.00
36	Tom Myers	.25
37	Bill Van Heusen	.25
38	Russ Washington	.25
39	Tom Sullivan	.25
40	Curley Culp (AP)	.25
41	Johnnie Gray	.25
42	Bob Klein	.25
43	Lem Barney	1.00
44	*Harvey Martin*	4.00
45	Reggie Rucker	.25
46	Neil Clabo	.25
47	Ray Hamilton	.25
48	Joe Ferguson	.75
49	Ed Podolak	.25
50	Ray Guy (AP)	1.50
51	Glen Edwards	.25
52	Jim LeClair	.25
53	Mike Barnes	.25
54	*Nat Moore*	4.00
55	Bill Kilmer	.75
56	Larry Stallings	.25
57	Jack Gregory	.25
58	Steve Mike-Mayer	.25
59	Virgil Livers	.25
60	Jerry Sherk (AP)	.25
61	Guy Morriss	.25
62	Barty Smith	.25
63	Jerome Barkum	.25
64	Ira Gordon	.25
65	Paul Krause	.60
66	John McMakin	.25
67	Checklist 1-132	2.00
68	Charley Johnson	.25
69	Tommy Nobis	.75
70	Lydell Mitchell	.25
71	Vern Holland	.25
72	Tim Foley	.25
73	Golden Richards	.25
74	Bryant Salter	.25
75	Terry Bradshaw	14.00
76	Ted Hendricks	1.25
77	*Rich Saul*	.35
78	John Smith	.25
79	Altie Taylor	.25
80	Cedrick Hardman (AP)	.25
81	Ken Payne	.25
82	Zeke Moore	.25
83	Alvin Maxson	.25
84	Wally Hilgenberg	.25
85	John Niland	.25
86	Mike Sensibaugh	.25
87	Ron Johnson	.25
88	Winston Hill	.25
89	Charlie Joiner	2.00
90	Roger Wehrli (AP)	.75
91	Mike Bragg	.25
92	Dan Dickel	.25
93	Earl Morrall	.75
94	Pat Toomay	.25
95	Gary Garrison	.25
96	Ken Geddes	.25
97	Mike Current	.25
98	Bob Avellini	.35
99	Dave Pureifory	.25
100	Franco Harris (AP)	7.00
101	Randy Logan	.25
102	John Fitzgerald	.25
103	*Gregg Bingham*	.40
104	Jim Plunkett	1.50
105	Carl Eller	.75
106	Larry Walton	.25
107	Clarence Scott	.25
108	Skip Vanderbundt	.25
109	Boobie Clark	.25
110	Tom Mack (AP)	.25
111	Bruce Laird	.25
112	*Dave Dalby*	.60
113	John Leypoldt	.25
114	Barry Pearson	.25
115	Larry Brown	.60
116	Jackie Smith	.25
117	Pat Hughes	.25
118	Al Woodall	.25
119	John Zook	.25
120	Jake Scott (AP)	.25
121	Rich Glover	.25
122	Ernie Jackson	.25
123	Otis Armstrong	1.00
124	Bob Grim	.25
125	Jeff Siemon	.25
126	Harold Hart	.25
127	John DeMarie	.25
128	Dan Fouts	10.00
129	Jim Kearney	.25
130	John Dutton (AP)	.40
131	Calvin Hill	.50
132	Toni Fritsch	.25
133	Ron Jessie	.25
134	Don Nottingham	.25
135	Lemar Parrish	.25
136	*Russ Francis*	4.00
137	Joe Reed	.25
138	C.L. Whittington	.25
139	Otis Sistrunk	.25
140	Lynn Swann (AP)	15.00
141	Jim Carter	.25
142	Mike Montler	.25
143	Walter Johnson	.25
144	Doug Kotar	.25
145	Roman Gabriel	1.00
146	Billy Newsome	.25
147	Ed Bradley	.25
148	*Walter Payton*	250.00
149	Johnny Fuller	.25
150	Alan Page (AP)	1.50
151	Frank Grant	.25
152	Dave Green	.25
153	Nelson Munsey	.25
154	Jim Mandich	.25
155	Lawrence McCutcheon	.75

No.	Player	Price
156	Steve Ramsey	.25
157	Ed Flanagan	.25
158	*Randy White*	25.00
159	Gerry Mullins	.25
160	Jan Stenerud (AP)	.75
161	Steve Odom	.25
162	Roger Finnie	.25
163	Norm Snead	.25
164	Jeff Van Note	.40
165	Bill Bergey	.60
166	Allen Carter	.25
167	Steve Holden	.25
168	Sherman White	.25
169	Bob Berry	.25
170	Ken Houston (AP)	1.00
171	Bill Olds	.25
172	Larry Seiple	.25
173	Cliff Branch	3.00
174	Reggie McKenzie	.25
175	Dan Pastorini	.50
176	Paul Naumoff	.25
177	Checklist 133-265	2.00
178	Durwood Keeton	.25
179	Earl Thomas	.25
180	L.C. Greenwood (AP)	.85
181	John Outlaw	.25
182	Frank Nunley	.25
183	*Dave Jennings*	1.00
184	McArthur Lane	.25
185	Chester Marcol	.25
186	J.J. Jones	.25
187	Tom DeLeone	.25
188	Steve Zabel	.25
189	Ken Johnson	.25
190	Rayfield Wright (AP)	.25
191	Brent McClanahan	.25
192	Pat Fischer	.25
193	*Roger Carr*	1.00
194	Manny Fernandez	.25
195	Roy Gerela	.25
196	Dave Elmendorf	.25
197	Bob Kowalkowski	.25
198	Phil Villapiano	.25
199	Will Wynn	.25
200	*Terry Metcalf*	.50
201	Ken Anderson, Fran Tarkenton Passing Leaders:	2.00
202	Reggie Rucker, Lydell Mitchell, Chuck Foreman Receiving Leaders:	.50
203	O.J. Simpson, Jim Otis Rushing Leaders:	3.00
204	O.J. Simpson, Chuck Foreman Scoring Leaders:	3.00
205	Mel Blount, Paul Krause Interception Leaders:	.75
206	Ray Guy, Herman Weaver Punting Leaders:	.50
207	Ken Ellis	.25
208	Ron Saul	.25
209	Toni Linhart	.25
210	Jim Langer (AP)	1.25
211	Jeff Wright	.25
212	Moses Denson	.25
213	Earl Edwards	.25
214	Walker Gillette	.25
215	Bob Trumpy	.50
216	Emmitt Thomas	.25
217	Lyle Alzado	1.25
218	Carl Garrett	.25
219	Van Green	.25
220	*Jack Lambert* (AP)	30.00
221	Spike Jones	.25
222	John Hadl	.75
223	*Billy Johnson*	2.50
224	Tony McGee	.25
225	Preston Pearson	.50
226	Isiah Robertson	.25
227	Errol Mann	.25
228	Paul Seal	.25
229	*Roland Harper*	.75
230	*Ed White*	.75
231	Joe Theismann	6.50
232	Jim Cheyunski	.25
233	Bill Stanfill	.25
234	Marv Hubbard	.25
235	Tommy Casanova	.25
236	Bob Hyland	.25
237	Jesse Freitas	.25
238	Norm Thompson	.25
239	Charlie Smith	.25
240	John James (AP)	.25
241	Alden Roche	.25
242	Gordon Jolley	.25
243	Larry Ely	.25
244	Richard Caster	.25
245	Joe Greene	3.25
246	Larry Schreiber	.25
247	Terry Schmidt	.25
248	Jerrel Wilson	.25
249	Marty Domres	.25
250	Isaac Curtis (AP)	.25
251	Harold McClinton	.25
252	Fred Dryer	2.00
253	Bill Lenkaitis	.25
254	Don Hardeman	.25
255	Bob Griese	4.00
256	*Oscar Roan*	.40
257	*Randy Gradishar*	3.00
258	*Bob Thomas*	.50
259	Joe Owens	.25
260	Cliff Harris (AP)	1.00
261	Frank Lewis	.25
262	Mike McCoy	.25
263	*Rickey Young*	.60
264	*Brian Kelley*	.40
265	Charlie Sanders	.25
266	Jim Hart	1.00
267	Gregg Gantt	.25
268	John Ward	.25
269	Al Beauchamp	.25
270	Jack Tatum (AP)	.25
271	Jim Lash	.25
272	Diron Talbert	.25
273	Checklist 265-396	2.00
274	Steve Spurrier	4.00
275	Greg Pruitt	.60
276	Jim Mitchell	.25
277	Jack Rudnay	.25
278	*Freddie Solomon*	1.00
279	Frank LeMaster	.25
280	Wally Chambers (AP)	.25
281	Mike Collier	.25
282	Clarence Williams	.25
283	Mitch Hoopes	.25
284	Ron Bolton	.25
285	Harold Jackson	.75
286	Greg Landry	.60
287	Tony Greene	.25
288	Howard Stevens	.25
289	Roy Jefferson	.25
290	Jim Bakken (AP)	.25
291	Doug Sutherland	.25
292	Marvin Cobb	.25
293	Mack Alston	.25
294	Rod McNeil	.25
295	Gene Upshaw	1.00
296	Dave Gallagher	.25
297	Larry Ball	.25
298	Ron Howard	.25
299	*Don Strock*	1.50
300	O.J. Simpson (AP)	10.00
301	Ray Mansfield	.25
302	Larry Marshall	.25
303	Dick Himes	.25
304	*Ray Wersching*	.40
305	John Riggins	4.00
306	Bob Parsons	.25
307	Ray Brown	.25
308	Len Dawson	3.00
309	Andy Maurer	.25
310	Jack Youngblood (AP)	1.00
311	Essex Johnson	.25
312	Stan White	.25
313	Drew Pearson	4.00
314	Rockne Freitas	.25
315	Mercury Morris	.60
316	Willie Alexander	.25
317	Paul Warfield	3.00
318	Bob Chandler	.25
319	Bobby Walden	.25
320	Riley Odoms (AP)	.25
321	Mike Boryla	.25
322	Bruce Van Dyke	.25
323	Pete Banaszak	.25
324	Darryl Stingley	.50
325	John Mendenhall	.25
326	Dan Dierdorf	1.50
327	Bruce Taylor	.25
328	Don McCauley	.25
329	John Reaves	.25
330	Chris Hanburger (AP)	.25
331	Roger Staubach NFC Champions	3.00
332	Franco Harris AFC Champions	2.00
333	Terry Bradshaw Super Bowl X	2.25
334	Godwin Turk	.25
335	Dick Anderson	.25
336	Woody Green	.25
337	Pat Curran	.25
338	Council Rudolph	.25
339	Joe Lavender	.25
340	John Gilliam (AP)	.25
341	*Steve Furness*	.75
342	D.D. Lewis	.25
343	Duane Carrell	.25
344	Jon Morris	.25
345	John Brockington	.25
346	Mike Phipps	.25
347	*Lyle Blackwood*	.60
348	Julius Adams	.25
349	Terry Hermeling	.25
350	*Rolland Lawrence* (AP)	.50
351	Glenn Doughty	.25
352	Doug Swift	.25
353	Mike Strachan	.25
354	Craig Morton	.50
355	George Blanda	5.00
356	Garry Puetz	.25
357	Carl Mauck	.25
358	Walt Patulski	.25
359	Stu Voigt	.25
360	Fred Carr (AP)	.25
361	Po James	.25
362	Otis Taylor	.50
363	Jeff West	.25
364	Gary Huff	.25
365	Dwight White	.25
366	Dan Ryczek	.25
367	*Jon Keyworth*	.50
368	Mel Renfro	.60
369	*Bruce Coslet*	1.00
370	Len Hauss (AP)	.25
371	Rick Volk	.25
372	Howard Twilley	.25
373	*Cullen Bryant*	.60
374	Bob Babich	.25
375	Herman Weaver	.25
376	*Steve Grogan*	8.00
377	Bubba Smith	1.50
378	Burgess Owens	.25
379	Alvin Matthews	.25
380	Art Shell	2.00
381	Larry Brown	.25
382	Horst Muhlmann	.25
383	Ahmad Rashad	2.50
384	Bobby Maples	.25
385	Jim Marshall	.90
386	Joe Dawkins	.25
387	Dennis Partee	.25
388	Eddie McMillan	.25
389	Randy Johnson	.25
390	Bob Kuechenberg (AP)	.25
391	Rufus Mayes	.25
392	Lloyd Mumphord	.25
393	Ike Harris	.25
394	Dave Hampton	.25
395	Roger Staubach	15.00
396	Doug Buffone	.25
397	Howard Fest	.25
398	Wayne Mulligan	.25
399	Bill Bradley	.25
400	Chuck Foreman (AP)	.60
401	Jack Snow	.25
402	Bob Howard	.25
403	John Matuszak	1.00
404	Bill Munson	.25
405	Andy Russell	.25
406	Skip Butler	.25
407	Hugh McKinnis	.25
408	Bob Penchion	.25
409	Mike Bass	.25
410	George Kunz (AP)	.25
411	Ron Pritchard	.25
412	Barry Smith	.25
413	Norm Bulaich	.25
414	Marv Bateman	.25
415	Ken Stabler	8.00
416	Conrad Dobler	.25
417	Bob Tucker	.25
418	Gene Washington	.25
419	Ed Marinaro	1.00
420	Jack Ham (AP)	3.25
421	Jim Turner	.25
422	Chris Fletcher	.25
423	Carl Barzilauskas	.25
424	*Robert Brazile*	2.50
425	Harold Carmichael	1.50
426	*Ron Jaworski*	4.00
427	*Ed "Too Tall" Jones*	20.00
428	Larry McCarren	.25
429	*Mike Thomas*	.50
430	Joe DeLamielleure (AP)	.25
431	Tom Blanchard	.25
432	Ron Carpenter	.25
433	Levi Johnson	.25
434	Sam Cunningham	.25
435	Garo Yepremian	.25
436	Mike Livingston	.25
437	Larry Csonka	3.00
438	Doug Dieken	.25
439	Bill Lueck	.25
440	Tom MacLeod (AP)	.25
441	Mick Tingelhoff	.25
442	Terry Hanratty	.25
443	Mike Siani	.25
444	Dwight Harrison	.25
445	Jim Otis	.25
446	Jack Reynolds	.25
447	*Jean Fugett*	.40
448	Dave Beverly	.25
449	*Bernard Jackson*	1.00
450	Charley Taylor	2.00
451	Atlanta Falcons Team	1.50
452	Baltimore Colts Team	1.50
453	Buffalo Bills Team	1.50
454	Chicago Bears Team	1.50
455	Cincinnati Bengals Team	1.50
456	Cleveland Browns Team	1.50
457	Dallas Cowboys Team	1.50
458	Denver Broncos Team	1.50
459	Detroit Lions Team	1.50
460	Green Bay Packers Team	1.50
461	Houston Oilers Team	1.50
462	Kansas City Chiefs Team	1.50
463	Los Angeles Rams Team	1.50
464	Miami Dolphins Team	1.50
465	Minnesota Vikings Team	1.50
466	New England Patriots Team	1.50
467	New Orleans Saints Team	1.50
468	New York Giants Team	1.50
469	New York Jets Team	1.50
470	Oakland Raiders Team	1.50
471	Philadelphia Eagles Team	1.50
472	Pittsburgh Steelers Team	1.50
473	St. Louis Cardinals Team	1.50
474	San Diego Chargers Team	1.50
475	San Francisco 49ers Team	1.50
476	Seattle Seahawks Team	1.50
477	Tampa Bay Bucaneers Team	1.50
478	Washington Redskins Team	1.50
479	Fred Cox	.25
480	Mel Blount (AP)	5.00
481	John Bunting	.25
482	Ken Mendenhall	.25
483	Will Harrell	.25
484	Marlin Briscoe	.25
485	Archie Manning	1.00
486	Tody Smith	.25
487	George Hunt	.25
488	Roscoe Word	.25
489	Paul Seymour	.25
490	Lee Roy Jordan (AP)	1.00
491	Chip Myers	.25
492	Norm Evans	.25
493	Jim Bertelsen	.25
494	Mark Moseley	.50
495	George Buehler	.25
496	Charlie Hall	.25
497	Marvin Upshaw	.25
498	*Tom Banks*	.50
499	Randy Vataha	.25
500	Fran Tarkenton (AP)	7.00
501	Mike Wagner	.25
502	Art Malone	.25
503	Fred Cook	.25
504	Rich McGeorge	.25
505	Ken Burrough	.25
506	Nick Mike-Mayer	.25
507	Checklist 397-528	2.00
508	Steve Owens	.25
509	*Brad Van Pelt*	.75
510	Ken Riley (AP)	.25
511	Art Thoms	.25
512	Ed Bell	.25
513	Tom Wittum	.25
514	Jim Braxton	.25
515	Nick Buoniconti	.60
516	*Brian Sipe*	2.00
517	Jim Lynch	.25
518	Prentice McCray	.25
519	Tom Dempsey	.25
520	Mel Gray (AP)	.25
521	Nate Wright	.25
522	Rocky Bleier	3.00
523	Dennis Johnson	.25
524	Jerry Sisemore	.25
525	Bert Jones	1.00
526	Perry Smith	.25
527	Blaine Nye	.25
528	Bob Moore	.50

1976 Topps Team Checklists

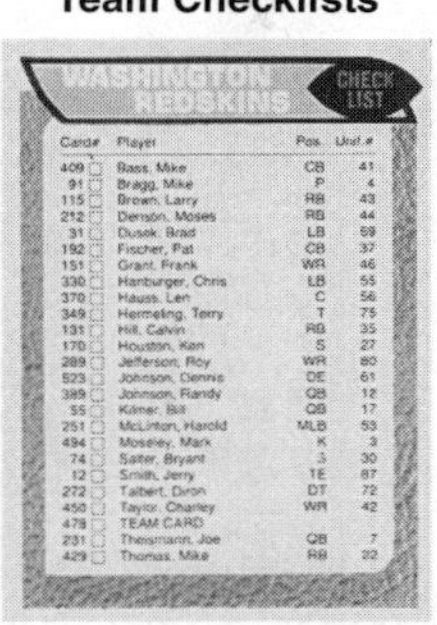

The 30-card, standard-size set includes team checklist for each of the 28 NFL teams and two checklists. The set was available in uncut sheets from Topps and was unnumbered. The cards parallel the team checklists in the base sets (451-478), but come in thinner stock.

		NM/M
	Complete Set (30):	130.00
	Common Player:	5.00
1	Atlanta Falcons	5.00
2	Baltimore Colts	5.00
3	Buffalo Bills	5.00
4	Chicago Bears	7.50
5	Cincinnati Bengals	5.00
6	Cleveland Browns	5.00
7	Dallas Cowboys	10.00
8	Denver Broncos	5.00
9	Detroit Lions	5.00
10	Green Bay Packers	5.00
11	Houston Oilers	5.00
12	Kansas City Chiefs	5.00
13	Los Angeles Rams	5.00
14	Miami Dolphins	7.50
15	Minnesota Vikings	5.00
16	New England Patriots	5.00
17	New York Giants	5.00
18	New York Jets	5.00
19	New Orleans Saints	5.00
20	Oakland Raiders	7.50
21	Philadelphia Eagles	5.00
22	Pittsburgh Steelers	7.50
23	St. Louis Cardinals	5.00
24	San Diego Chargers	5.00
25	San Francisco 49ers	7.50
26	Seattke Seahawks	5.00
27	Tampa Bay Buccaneers	5.00
28	Washington Redskins	7.50
29	Checklist 1-132	5.00
30	Checklist 133-264	5.00

1977 Topps

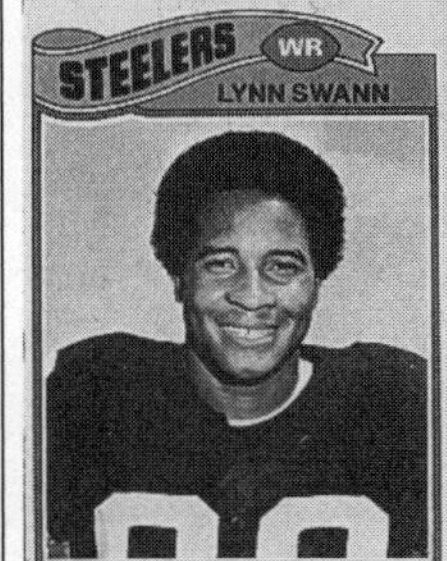

Known primarily for containing Steve Largent's rookie issue, this set of 528 cards also has the second-year card of Walter Payton. Other rookie cards included in the set are Pat Haden, Jim Zorn, John Cappeletti, Richard Todd, Harry Carson, Chuck Muncie, Archie Griffin and Dave Casper. All-Pro designations were once again placed on the regular-issued card. Of the subsets, the "Record" run appears in the middle of the set; AFC/NFC championship and the Super Bowl card are the last three in the set; and the statistical leader cards are the first six. This was the last year in which team checklists were issued; future cards would show team leaders with the checklists.

		NM/M
	Complete Set (528):	230.00
	Common Player:	.20
	Wax Pack (10):	21.00
	Wax Box (36):	640.00
	Wax Pack (14):	25.00
	Wax Box (36):	600.00
1	James Harris, Ken Stabler Passing Leaders:	1.75
2	Drew Pearson, MacArthur Lane Receiving Leaders:	.50
3	Walter Payton, O.J. Simpson Rushing Leaders:	10.00
4	Mark Moseley, Toni Linhart Scoring Leaders:	.35
5	Monte Jackson, Ken Riley Interception Leaders:	.35
6	John James, Marv Bateman Punting Leaders:	.35
7	Mike Phipps	.20
8	Rick Volk	.20
9	Steve Furness	.20
10	Isaac Curtis	.20
11	Nate Wright	.20
12	Jean Fugett	.20
13	Ken Mendenhall	.20
14	Sam Adams	.20
15	Charlie Waters	1.00
16	Bill Stanfill	.20
17	John Holland	.20
18	*Pat Haden*	3.00
19	Bob Young	.20
20	Wally Chambers (AP)	.20
21	Lawrence Gaines	.20
22	Larry McCarren	.20
23	Horst Muhlmann	.20
24	Phil Villapiano	.20
25	Greg Pruitt	.40
26	Ron Howard	.20
27	Craig Morton	.75
28	Rufus Mayes	.20
29	*Lee Roy Selmon*	9.00
30	Ed White (AP)	.20
31	Harold McClinton	.20
32	Glenn Doughty	.20
33	Bob Kuechenberg	.20
34	Duane Carrell	.20
35	Riley Odoms	.20
36	Bobby Scott	.20
37	Nick Mike-Mayer	.20
38	Bill Lenkaitis	.20
39	Roland Harper	.20
40	Tommy Hart (AP)	.20
41	Mike Sensibaugh	.20
42	Rusty Jackson	.20
43	Levi Johnson	.20
44	Mike McCoy	.20
45	Roger Staubach	10.00
46	Fred Cox	.20
47	Bob Babich	.20
48	Reggie McKenzie	.20
49	Dave Jennings	.20
50	*Mike Haynes* (AP)	5.00
51	Larry Brown	.20
52	Marvin Cobb	.20
53	Fred Cook	.20
54	Freddie Solomon	.30
55	John Riggins	2.50
56	John Bunting	.20
57	Ray Wersching	.20
58	Mike Livingston	.20
59	Billy Johnson	.50
60	Mike Wagner (AP)	.20
61	Waymond Bryant	.20
62	Jim Otis	.20
63	Ed Galigher	.20
64	Randy Vataha	.20
65	*Jim Zorn*	4.00
66	Jon Keyworth	.20
67	Checklist 1-132	1.50
68	Henry Childs	.20
69	Thom Darden	.20
70	George Kunz (AP)	.20
71	Lenvil Elliott	.20
72	Curtis Johnson	.20
73	Doug Van Horn	.20
74	Joe Theismann	4.00
75	Dwight White	.20
76	Scott Laidlaw	.20
77	Monte Johnson	.20
78	Dave Beverly	.20
79	Jim Mitchell	.20
80	Jack Youngblood (AP)	.75
81	Mel Gray	.20
82	Dwight Harrison	.20
83	John Hadl	.50
84	*Matt Blair*	2.00
85	Charlie Sanders	.20
86	Noah Jackson	.20
87	Ed Marinaro	.40
88	Bob Howard	.20
89	John McDaniel	.20
90	Dan Dierdorf (AP)	1.25
91	Mark Moseley	.35
92	Cleo Miller	.20
93	Andre Tillman	.20
94	Bruce Taylor	.20
95	Bert Jones	1.00
96	*Anthony Davis*	1.00
97	Don Goode	.20
98	*Ray Rhodes*	5.00
99	*Mike Webster*	8.00
100	O.J. Simpson (AP)	5.00
101	*Doug Plank*	.75
102	Efren Herrera	.20
103	Charlie Smith	.20
104	Carlos Brown	.20
105	Jim Marshall	.70
106	Paul Naumoff	.20
107	Walter White	.20
108	*John Cappelletti*	2.50
109	Chip Myers	.20
110	Ken Stabler (AP)	8.00
111	Joe Ehrmann	.20
112	Rick Engles	.20
113	Jack Dolbin	.20
114	Ron Bolton	.20
115	Mike Thomas	.20
116	Mike Fuller	.20
117	John Hill	.20
118	*Richard Todd*	1.00
119	*Duriel Harris*	.50
120	John James (AP)	.20
121	Lionel Antoine	.20
122	John Skorupan	.20
123	Skip Butler	.20
124	Bob Tucker	.20
125	Paul Krause	.50
126	Dave Hampton	.20
127	Tom Wittum	.20
128	Gary Huff	.20
129	Emmitt Thomas	.20
130	Drew Pearson (AP)	2.00
131	Ron Saul	.20
132	Steve Niehaus	.20
133	Fred Carr	.20
134	Norm Bulaich	.20
135	Bob Trumpy	.40
136	Greg Landry	.30
137	George Buehler	.20
138	Reggie Rucker	.20
139	Julius Adams	.20
140	Jack Ham (AP)	2.50
141	Wayne Morris	.20
142	Marv Bateman	.20
143	Bobby Maples	.20
144	Harold Carmichael	1.00
145	Bob Avellini	.20
146	*Harry Carson*	7.00
147	Lawrence Pillers	.20
148	Ed Williams	.20
149	Dan Pastorini	.40
150	Ron Yary (AP)	.20
151	Joe Lavender	.20
152	Pat McInally	.75
153	Lloyd Mumphord	.20
154	Cullen Bryant	.20
155	Willie Lanier	.75
156	Gene Washington	.30
157	Scott Hunter	.20
158	Jim Merlo	.20
159	Randy Grossman	.20
160	Blaine Nye (AP)	.20
161	Ike Harris	.20
162	Doug Dieken	.20
163	Guy Morriss	.20
164	Bob Parsons	.20
165	Steve Grogan	2.00
166	John Brockington	.20
167	Charlie Joiner	1.50
168	Ron Carpenter	.20
169	Jeff Wright	.20
170	Chris Hanburger (AP)	.20
171	*Roosevelt Leaks*	.40
172	Larry Little	.60
173	John Matuszak	.30
174	Joe Ferguson	.50
175	Brad Van Pelt	.20
176	*Dexter Bussey*	.30
177	*Steve Largent*	50.00
178	Dewey Selmon	.20
179	Randy Gradishar	1.00
180	Mel Blount (AP)	3.00
181	Dan Neal	.20
182	Rich Szaro	.20
183	Mike Boryla	.20
184	Steve Jones	.20
185	Paul Warfield	2.00
186	*Greg Buttle*	.40
187	Rich McGeorge	.20
188	*Leon Gray*	.50
189	John Shinners	.20
190	Toni Linhart (AP)	.20
191	Robert Miller	.20
192	Jake Scott	.20
193	Jon Morris	.20
194	Randy Crowder	.20
195	Lynn Swann	10.00
196	Marsh White	.20
197	*Rod Perry*	.30
198	Willie Hall	.20
199	Mike Hartenstine	.20
200	Jim Bakken (AP)	.20
201	Atlanta Falcons Team	1.00
202	Baltimore Colts Team	1.00
203	Buffalo Bills Team	1.00
204	Chicago Bears Team	1.00
205	Cincinnati Bengals Team	1.00
206	Cleveland Browns Team	1.00
207	Dallas Cowboys Team	1.00
208	Denver Broncos Team	1.00
209	Detroit Lions Team	1.00
210	Green Bay Packers Team	1.00
211	Houston Oilers Team	1.00
212	Kansas City Chiefs Team	1.00
213	Los Angeles Rams Team	1.00
214	Miami Dolphins Team	1.00
215	Minnesota Vikings Team	1.00
216	New England Patriots Team	1.00
217	New Orleans Saints Team	1.00
218	New York Giants Team	1.00
219	New York Jets Team	1.00
220	Oakland Raiders Team	1.00
221	Philadelphia Eagles Team	1.00
222	Pittsburgh Steelers Team	1.00
223	St. Louis Cardinals Team	1.00
224	San Diego ChargersTeam	1.00
225	San Francisco 49ers Team	1.00
226	Seattle Seahawks Team	1.00
227	Tampa Bay Bucaneers Team	1.00
228	Washington Redskins Team	1.00
229	Sam Cunningham	.20
230	Alan Page (AP)	1.25
231	Eddie Brown	.20
232	Stan White	.20
233	Vern Den Herder	.20
234	Clarence Davis	.20
235	Ken Anderson	1.75
236	Karl Chandler	.20
237	Will Harrell	.20
238	Clarence Scott	.20
239	Bo Rather	.20
240	Robert Brazile (AP)	.40
241	Bob Bell	.20
242	Rolland Lawrence	.20

243 Tom Sullivan .20
244 Larry Brunson .20
245 Terry Bradshaw 7.00
246 Rich Saul .20
247 Cleveland Elam .20
248 Don Woods .20
249 Bruce Laird .20
250 Coy Bacon (AP) .20
251 Russ Francis .60
252 Jim Braxton .20
253 Perry Smith .20
254 Jerome Barkum .20
255 Garo Yepremian .20
256 Checklist 133-264 1.50
257 *Tony Galbreath* .50
258 Troy Archer .20
259 Brian Sipe 1.00
260 Billy Joe DuPree (AP) .50
261 Bobby Walden .20
262 Larry Marshall .20
263 Ted Fritsch .20
264 Larry Hand .20
265 Tom Mack .30
266 Ed Bradley .20
267 Pat Leahy .75
268 Louis Carter .20
269 *Archie Griffin* 5.00
270 Art Shell (AP) 1.50
271 Stu Voigt .20
272 Prentice McCray .20
273 MacArthur Lane .20
274 Dan Fouts 5.00
275 Charley Young .20
276 *Wilbur Jackson* .50
277 John Hicks .20
278 Nat Moore .60
279 Virgil Livers .20
280 Curley Culp (AP) .20
281 Rocky Bleier 1.00
282 John Zook .20
283 Tom DeLeone .20
284 *Danny White* 5.00
285 Otis Armstrong .40
286 Larry Walton .20
287 Jim Carter .20
288 Don McCauley .20
289 Frank Grant .20
290 Roger Wehrli (AP) .20
291 Mick Tinglehoff .20
292 Bernard Jackson .20
293 *Tom Owen* .30
294 Mike Esposito .20
295 Fred Biletnikoff 2.00
296 *Revie Sorey* .30
297 John McMakin .20
298 Dan Ryczek .20
299 Wayne Moore .20
300 Franco Harris (AP) 4.00
301 *Rick Upchurch* 2.00
302 Jim Stienke .20
303 Charlie Davis .20
304 Don Cockroft .20
305 Ken Burrough .20
306 Clark Gaines .20
307 Bobby Douglass .20
308 Ralph Perretta .20
309 Wally Hilgenberg .20
310 *Monte Jackson* (AP) .40
311 *Chris Bahr* .50
312 Jim Cheyunski .20
313 Mike Patrick .20
314 Ed "Too Tall" Jones 5.00
315 Bill Bradley .20
316 Benny Malone .20
317 Paul Seymour .20
318 Jim Laslavic .20
319 Frank Lewis .20
320 Ray Guy (AP) .75
321 Allen Ellis .20
322 Conrad Dobler .30
323 Chester Marcol .20
324 Doug Kotar .20
325 Lemar Parrish .20
326 Steve Holden .20
327 Jeff Van Note .20
328 Howard Stevens .20
329 Brad Dusek .20
330 Joe DeLamielleure (AP) .20
331 Jim Plunkett 1.00
332 Checklist 265-396 1.50
333 Lou Piccone .20
334 Ray Hamilton .20
335 Jan Stenerud .60
336 Jeris White .20
337 *Sherman Smith* .35
338 Dave Green .20
339 Terry Schmidt .20
340 *Sammie White* (AP) 1.25
341 *Jon Kolb* .30
342 Randy White 7.00
343 Bob Klein .20
344 Bob Kowalkowski .20
345 Terry Metcalf .30
346 Joe Danelo .20
347 Ken Payne .20
348 Neal Craig .20
349 Dennis Johnson .20
350 Bill Bergey (AP) .50
351 Raymond Chester .20
352 Bob Matheson .20
353 Mike Kadish .20
354 *Mark Van Eeghen* .75
355 L.C. Greenwood .60
356 Sam Hunt .50
357 Darrell Austin .20
358 Jim Turner .20
359 Ahmad Rashad 2.00
360 Walter Payton (AP) 40.00
361 Mark Arneson .20
362 Jerrel Wilson .20
363 Steve Bartkowski 1.00
364 John Watson .20
365 Ken Riley .20
366 Gregg Bingham .20
367 Golden Richards .20
368 Clyde Powers .20
369 Diron Talbert .20
370 Lydell Mitchell .30
371 Bob Jackson .20
372 Jim Mandich .20
373 Frank LeMaster .20
374 Benny Ricardo .20
375 Lawrence McCutcheon .30
376 Lynn Dickey .50
377 Phil Wise .20
378 Tony McGee .20
379 Norm Thompson .20
380 *Dave Casper* (AP) 5.00
381 Glen Edwards .20
382 Bob Thomas .20
383 Bob Chandler .20
384 Rickey Young .20
385 Carl Eller .60
386 Lyle Alzado 1.00
387 John Leypoldt .20
388 Gordon Bell .20
389 Mike Bragg .20
390 Jim Langer (AP) 1.00
391 Vern Holland .20
392 Nelson Munsey .20
393 Mack Mitchell .20
394 Tony Adams .20
395 Preston Pearson .35
396 Emanuel Zanders .20
397 Vince Papale .20
398 *Joe Fields* .30
399 Craig Clemons .20
400 Fran Tarkenton (AP) 6.00
401 Andy Johnson .20
402 Willie Buchanon .20
403 Pat Curran .20
404 Ray Jarvis .20
405 Joe Greene 2.00
406 Bill Simpson .20
407 Ronnie Coleman .20
408 J.K. McKay .20
409 Pat Fischer .20
410 John Dutton (AP) .20
411 Boobie Clark .20
412 *Pat Tilley* 1.00
413 Don Strock .30
414 Brian Kelley .20
415 Gene Upshaw 1.00
416 Mike Montler .20
417 Checklist 397-528 1.50
418 John Gilliam .20
419 Brent McClanahan .20
420 Jerry Sherk (AP) .20
421 Roy Gerela .20
422 Tim Fox .20
423 John Ebersole .20
424 James Scott .20
425 *Delvin Williams* .75
426 Spike Jones .20
427 Harvey Martin 1.25
428 Don Herrmann .20
429 Calvin Hill .40
430 Isiah Robertson (AP) .20
431 Tony Greene .20
432 Bob Johnson .20
433 Lem Barney .90
434 Eric Torkelson .20
435 John Mendenhall .20
436 Larry Seiple .20
437 Art Kuehn .20
438 John Vella .20
439 Greg Latta .20
440 Roger Carr (AP) .20
441 Doug Sutherland .20
442 Mike Kruczek .20
443 Steve Zabel .20
444 *Mike Pruitt* 1.00
445 Harold Jackson .60
446 George Jakowenko .20
447 John Fitzgerald .20
448 Terry Joyce .20
449 Jim LeClair .20
450 Ken Houston (AP) .75
451 Steve Grogan Record: .40
452 Jim Marshall Record: .40
453 O.J. Simpson Record: 5.00
454 Tarkenton Record: 3.00
455 Jim Zorn Record: .40
456 Robert Pratt .20
457 Walker Gillette .20
458 Charlie Hall .20
459 Robert Newhouse .30
460 John Hannah (AP) 1.25
461 Ken Reaves .20
462 Herman Weaver .20
463 James Harris .20
464 Howard Twilley .20
465 Jeff Siemon .20
466 John Outlaw .20
467 *Chuck Muncie* 1.50
468 Bob Moore .20
469 Robert Woods .20
470 Cliff Branch (AP) 1.50
471 Johnnie Gray .20
472 Don Hardeman .20
473 Steve Ramsey .20
474 Steve Mike-Mayer .20
475 Gary Garrison .20
476 Walter Johnson .20
477 Neil Clabo .20
478 Len Hauss .20
479 Darryl Stingley .40
480 Jack Lambert (AP) 7.00
481 Mike Adamle .20
482 David Lee .20
483 Tom Mullen .20
484 Claude Humphrey .20
485 Jim Hart .60
486 Bobby Thompson .20
487 Jack Rudnay .20
488 Rich Sowells .20
489 Reuben Gant .20
490 Cliff Harris (AP) .75
491 Bob Brown .20
492 Don Nottingham .20
493 Ron Jessie .20
494 Otis Sistrunk .30
495 Bill Kilmer .60
496 Oscar Roan .20
497 Bill Van Heusen .20
498 Randy Logan .20
499 John Smith .20
500 Chuck Foreman (AP) .50
501 J.T. Thomas .20
502 Steve Schubert .20
503 Mike Barnes .20
504 J.V. Cain .20
505 Larry Csonka 2.00
506 Elvin Bethea .20
507 Ray Easterling .20
508 Joe Reed .20
509 Steve Odom .20
510 Tommy Casanova (AP) .20
511 Dave Dalby .20
512 Richard Caster .20
513 Fred Dryer 1.50
514 Jeff Kinney .20
515 Bob Griese 4.00
516 *Butch Johnson* .75
517 Gerald Irons .20
518 Don Calhoun .20
519 Jack Gregory .20
520 Tom Banks (AP) .20
521 Bobby Bryant .20
522 Reggie Harrison .20
523 Terry Hermeling .20
524 David Taylor .20
525 *Brian Baschnagel* .50
526 Ken Stabler AFC Championship: .40
527 NFC Championship .40
528 Super Bowl XI 1.50

1977 Topps Holsum Packers/Vikings

The 22-card, standard-size set featuring 11 Green Bay players (1-11) and 11 Minnesota players (12-22) was issued in Holsum Bread packages. For an unapparent reason, Holsum did not print its name or logo anywhere on the cards.

		NM/M
Complete Set (22):		45.00
Common Player:		1.00
1	Lynn Dickey	3.00
2	John Brockington	2.00
3	Will Harrell	1.00
4	Ken Payne	1.00
5	Rich McGeorge	1.00
6	Steve Odom	1.00
7	Jim Carter	1.00
8	Fred Carr	1.00
9	Willie Buchanon	2.00
10	Mike McCoy	1.00
11	Chester Marcol	1.00
12	Chuck Foreman	4.00
13	Ahmad Rashad	7.00
14	Sammie White	3.00
15	Stu Voigt	1.00
16	Fred Cox	1.00
17	Carl Eller	4.00
18	Alan Page	6.00
19	Jeff Siemon	1.00
20	Bobby Bryant	1.00
21	Paul Krause	3.00
22	Ron Yary	2.00

1977 Topps Mexican

The 528-card, standard-size set is the Spanish parallel set to the standard 1977 Topps set. All text on the card fronts and backs is in Spanish. The wrappers are also deemed collectible as they depict various NFL stars.

		NM/M
Complete Set (528):		6,000
Common Player:		8.00
Common Checklist:		12.00
Semistars:		10.00
1	James Harris, Ken Stabler Passing Leaders	100.00
2	Drew Pearson, MacArthur Lane Receiving Leaders	15.00
3	Walter Payton, O.J. Simpson Rushing Leaders	180.00
4	Mark Moseley, Toni Linhart Scoring Leaders	25.00
18	Pat Haden	30.00
29	Lee Roy Selmon (UER) (Misspelled Leroy)	75.00
45	Roger Staubach	100.00
50	Mike Haynes (AP)	25.00
55	John Riggins	30.00
65	Jim Zorn	30.00
74	Joe Theismann	40.00
80	Jack Youngblood (AP)	15.00
90	Dan Dierdorf (AP)	20.00
95	Bert Jones	15.00
96	Anthony Davis	20.00
98	Ray Rhodes	25.00
99	Mike Webster	50.00
100	O.J. Simpson (AP)	100.00
108	John Cappelletti	20.00
110	Ken Stabler (AP)	100.00
130	Drew Pearson (AP)	25.00
140	Jack Ham (AP)	30.00
144	Harold Carmichael	15.00
146	Harry Carson	40.00
165	Steve Grogan	20.00
167	Charlie Joiner	20.00
173	John Matuszak	20.00
177	Steve Largent	550.00
179	Randy Gradishar	15.00
180	Mel Blount (AP)	30.00
185	Paul Warfield	30.00
195	Lynn Swann	100.00
230	Alan Page (AP)	20.00
235	Ken Anderson	20.00
245	Terry Bradshaw	100.00
259	Brian Sipe	15.00
269	Archie Griffin	50.00
270	Art Shell (AP)	15.00
274	Dan Fouts	60.00
281	Rocky Bleier	30.00
284	Danny White	50.00
295	Fred Biletnikoff	30.00
300	Franco Harris (AP)	50.00
314	Ed "Too Tall" Jones	75.00
320	Ray Guy (AP)	15.00
331	Jim Plunkett	15.00
342	Randy White	60.00
359	Ahmad Rashad	20.00
360	Walter Payton (AP)	400.00
380	Dave Casper (AP)	40.00
386	Lyle Alzado	15.00
400	Fran Tarkenton (AP)	60.00
405	Joe Greene	30.00
412	Pat Tilley	20.00
415	Gene Upshaw	20.00
427	Harvey Martin	20.00
433	Lem Barney	15.00
444	Mike Pruitt	20.00
450	Ken Houston (AP)	20.00
453	O.J. Simpson (RB)	70.00
454	Fran Tarkenton Most Yardage, Passing,Lifetime (RB)	35.00
455	Jim Zorn Most Passing Yards Season, Rookie (RB)	25.00
460	John Hannah (AP)	15.00
467	Chuck Muncie	15.00
470	Cliff Branch (AP)	30.00
480	Jack Lambert (AP)	60.00
505	Larry Csonka	45.00
515	Bob Griese	45.00
526	Ken Stabler AFC Championship	75.00
527	NFC Championship	75.00
528	Super Bowl XI	200.00

1977 Topps Team Checklists

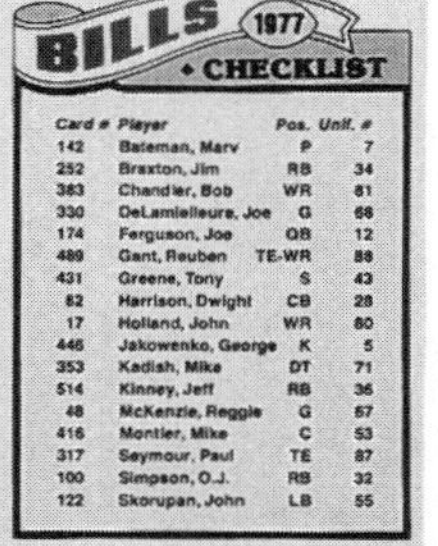

The 30-card, standard-size set contains a 28 team checklist and two checklist cards and was available through Topps as an uncut sheet. The cards are identical to the checklists in the base set, except for the thinner stock.

		NM/M
Complete Set (30):		120.00
Common Player:		5.00
1	Atlanta Falcons	5.00
2	Baltimore Colts	5.00
3	Buffalo Bills	5.00
4	Chicago Bears	8.00
5	Cincinnati Bengals	5.00
6	Cleveland Browns	5.00
7	Dallas Cowboys	10.00
8	Denver Broncos	5.00
9	Detroit Lions	5.00
10	Green Bay Packers	8.00
11	Houston Oilers	5.00
12	Kansas City Chiefs	5.00
13	Los Angeles Rams	5.00
14	Miami Dolphins	8.00
15	Minnesota Vikings	5.00
16	New England Patriots	5.00
17	New York Giants	5.00
18	New York Jets	5.00
19	New Orleans Saints	5.00
20	Oakland Raiders	8.00
21	Philadelphia Eagles	5.00
22	Pittsburgh Steelers	8.00
23	St. Louis Cardinals	5.00
24	San Diego Chargers	5.00
25	San Francisco 49ers	8.00
26	Seattle Seahawks	5.00
27	Tampa Bay Buccaneers	5.00
28	Washington Redskins	8.00
NN01	Checklist 1-132	5.00
NN02	Checklist 133-264	5.00

1978 Topps

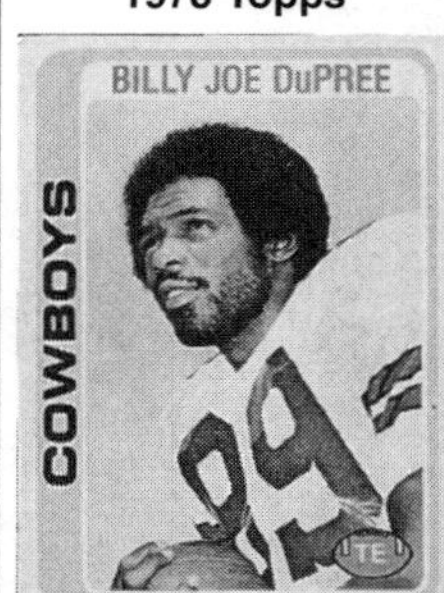

Topps' fourth 528-card set featured a colorful design, with the team name in white inside a solid border of color down the left side of the card. The subsets in the 1978 set include highlights, conference leader cards, and team leader cards (the last cards in the set; the team leader cards are arranged alphabetically by city name). This is the first time Topps pictured the actual team leaders on its team cards. The set is most notable for the inclusion of the Dorsett rookie card, the Largent second-year card, and the Payton third-year card. Other rookies in the set include Johnny Rodgers, Joe Klecko, John Stallworth, Wesley Walker, Stanley Morgan and Pete Johnson. (Key: AP - All Pro)

		NM/M
Complete Set (528):		150.00
Common Player:		.15
Wax Pack (14):		11.50
Wax Box (36):		345.00
1	Gary Huff (HL)	.25
2	Craig Morton (HL)	.25
3	Walter Payton (HL)	6.00
4	O.J. Simpson (HL)	3.00
5	Fran Tarkenton (HL)	2.00
6	Bob Thomas (HL)	.25
7	Joe Pisarcik	.15
8	Skip Thomas	.15
9	Roosevelt Leaks	.15
10	Ken Houston (AP)	.75
11	Tom Blanchard	.15
12	Jim Turner	.15
13	Tom DeLeone	.15
14	Jim LeClair	.15
15	Bob Avellini	.15
16	Tony McGee	.15
17	James Harris	.15
18	Terry Nelson	.15
19	Rocky Bleier	.75
20	Joe DeLamielleure (AP)	.15
21	Richard Caster	.15
22	*A.J. Duhe*	1.00
23	John Outlaw	.15
24	Danny White	1.50
25	Larry Csonka	1.50
26	David Hill	.15
27	Mark Arneson	.15
28	Jack Tatum	.15
29	Norm Thompson	.15
30	Sammie White	.30
31	Dennis Johnson	.15
32	Robin Earl	.15
33	Don Cockroft	.15
34	Bob Johnson	.15
35	John Hannah	.75
36	Scott Hunter	.15
37	Ken Burrough	.15
38	Wilbur Jackson	.15
39	Rich McGeorge	.15
40	Lyle Alzado (AP)	.75
41	John Ebersole	.15
42	*Gary Green*	.15
43	Art Kuehn	.15
44	Glen Edwards	.15
45	Lawrence McCutcheon	.15
46	Duriel Harris	.15
47	Rich Szaro	.15
48	Mike Washington	.15
49	Stan White	.15
50	Dave Casper (AP)	1.00
51	Len Hauss	.15
52	James Scott	.15
53	Brian Sipe	.60
54	Gary Shirk	.15
55	Archie Griffin	.60
56	Mike Patrick	.15
57	Mario Clark	.15
58	Jeff Siemon	.15
59	Steve Mike-Mayer	.15
60	Randy White (AP)	2.50
61	Darrell Austin	.15
62	Tom Sullivan	.15
63	*Johnny Rodgers*	1.75
64	Ken Reaves	.15
65	Terry Bradshaw	10.00
66	Fred Steinfort	.15
67	Curley Culp	.15
68	Ted Hendricks	.75
69	Raymond Chester	.15
70	Jim Langer (AP)	.75
71	Calvin Hill	.30
72	Mike Hartenstine	.15
73	Gerald Irons	.15
74	Billy Brooks	.15
75	John Mendenhall	.15
76	Andy Johnson	.15
77	Tom Wittum	.15
78	Lynn Dickey	.25
79	Carl Eller	.40
80	Tom Mack	.15
81	Clark Gaines	.15
82	Lem Barney	.75
83	Mike Montler	.15
84	Jon Kolb	.15
85	Bob Chandler	.15
86	Robert Newhouse	.15
87	Frank LeMaster	.15
88	Jeff West	.15
89	Lyle Blackwood	.15
90	Gene Upshaw (AP)	.15
91	Frank Grant	.50
92	Tom Hicks	.15
93	Mike Pruitt	.35
94	Chris Bahr	.15
95	Russ Francis	.35
96	Norris Thomas	.15
97	*Gary Barbaro*	.40
98	Jim Merlo	.15
99	Karl Chandler	.15
100	Fran Tarkenton	4.00
101	Abdul Salaam	.15
102	Marv Kellum	.15
103	Herman Weaver	.15
104	Roy Gerela	.15
105	Harold Jackson	.50
106	Dewey Selmon	.15
107	Checklist 1-132	1.00
108	Clarence Davis	.15
109	Robert Pratt	.15
110	Harvey Martin (AP)	.60
111	Brad Dusek	.15
112	Greg Latta	.15
113	Tony Peters	.15
114	Jim Braxton	.15
115	Ken Riley	.15
116	Steve Nelson	.15
117	Rick Upchurch	.35
118	Spike Jones	.15
119	Doug Kotar	.15
120	Bob Griese (AP)	3.00
121	Burgess Owens	.15
122	Rolf Benirschke	.60
123	Haskel Stanback	.15
124	J.T. Thomas	.15
125	Ahmad Rashad	1.25
126	Rick Kane	.15
127	Elvin Bethea	.15
128	Dave Dalby	.15
129	Mike Barnes	.15
130	Isiah Robertson	.15
131	Jim Plunkett	.75
132	Allan Ellis	.15
133	Mike Bragg	.15
134	Bob Jackson	.15
135	Coy Bacon	.15
136	John Smith	.15
137	Chuck Muncie	.35
138	Johnnie Gray	.15
139	Jimmy Robinson	.15
140	Tom Banks	.15
141	*Marvin Powell*	.40
142	Jerrell Wilson	.15
143	Ron Howard	.15
144	*Rob Lytle*	.35
145	L.C. Greenwood	.50
146	Morris Owens	.15
147	Joe Reed	.15
148	Mike Kadish	.15
149	Phil Villapiano	.15
150	Lydell Mitchell	.15
151	Randy Logan	.15
152	Mike Williams	.15
153	Jeff Van Note	.15
154	Steve Schubert	.15
155	Bill Kilmer	.50
156	Boobie Clark	.15
157	Charlie Hall	.15
158	*Raymond Clayborn*	.60
159	Jack Gregory	.15
160	Cliff Harris (AP)	.50
161	Joe Fields	.15
162	Don Nottingham	.15
163	Ed White	.15
164	Toni Fritsch	.15
165	Jack Lambert	3.00
166	Roger Staubach NFC Champions	1.50
167	Rob Lytle AFC Champions:	.30
168	Tony Dorsett Super Bowl XII	2.50
169	*Neal Colzie*	.20
170	Cleveland Elam (AP)	.15
171	David Lee	.15
172	Jim Otis	.15
173	Archie Manning	.75
174	Jim Carter	.15
175	Jean Fugett	.15
176	Willie Parker	.15
177	Haven Moses	.15
178	Horace King	.15
179	Bob Thomas	.15
180	Monte Jackson	.15

181 Steve Zabel .15
182 John Fitzgerald .15
183 Mike Livingston .15
184 Larry Poole .15
185 Isaac Curtis .15
186 Chuck Ramsey .15
187 Bob Klein .15
188 Ray Rhodes .15
189 Otis Sistrunk .15
190 Bill Bergey .30
191 Sherman Smith .15
192 Dave Green .15
193 Carl Mauck .15
194 Reggie Harrison .15
195 Roger Carr .15
196 Steve Bartkowski .75
197 Ray Wersching .15
198 Willie Buchanon .15
199 Neil Clabo .15
200 Walter Payton (AP) 20.00
201 Sam Adams .15
202 Larry Gordon .15
203 Pat Tilley .15
204 Mack Mitchell .15
205 Ken Anderson 1.25
206 Scott Dierking .15
207 Jack Rudnay .15
208 Jim Stienke .15
209 Bill Simpson .15
210 Errol Mann .15
211 Bucky Dilts .15
212 Reuben Gant .15
213 *Thomas Henderson* .50
214 Steve Furness .15
215 John Riggins 2.00
216 *Keith Krepfle* .35
217 *Fred Dean* 1.25
218 Emanuel Zanders .15
219 Don Testerman .15
220 George Kunz .15
221 Darryl Stingley .25
222 Ken Sanders .15
223 Gary Huff .15
224 Gregg Bingham .15
225 Jerry Sherk .15
226 Doug Plank .15
227 Ed Taylor .15
228 Emery Moorehead .15
229 *Reggie Williams* 2.50
230 Claude Humphrey .15
231 *Randy Cross* 2.50
232 Jim Hart .50
233 Bobby Bryant .15
234 Larry Brown .15
235 Mark Van Eeghen .15
236 Terry Hermeling .15
237 Steve Odom .15
238 Jan Stenerud .50
239 Andre Tillman .15
240 *Tom Jackson* (AP) 4.00
241 Ken Mendenhall .15
242 Tim Fox .15
243 Don Herrmann .15
244 Eddie McMillan .15
245 Greg Pruitt .30
246 J.K. McKay .15
247 Larry Keller .15
248 Dave Jennings .15
249 Bo Harris .15
250 Revie Sorey .15
251 Tony Greene .15
252 Butch Johnson .35
253 Paul Naumoff .15
254 Rickey Young .15
255 Dwight White .15
256 Joe Lavender .15
257 Checklist 133-264 1.00
258 Ronnie Coleman .15
259 Charlie Smith .15
260 Ray Guy (AP) .50
261 David Taylor .15
262 Bill Lenkaitis .15
263 Jim Mitchell .15
264 Delvin Williams .15
265 Jack Youngblood .60
266 Chuck Crist .15
267 Richard Todd .30
268 *Dave Logan* .35
269 Rufus Mayes .15
270 Brad Van Pelt .15
271 Chester Marcol .15
272 J.V. Cain .15
273 Larry Seiple .15
274 Brent McClanahan .15
275 Mike Wagner .15
276 Diron Talbert .15
277 Brian Baschnagel .15
278 Ed Podolak .15
279 Don Goode .15
280 John Dutton .15
281 Don Calhoun .15
282 Monte Johnson .15
283 Ron Jessie .15
284 Jon Morris .15
285 Riley Odoms .15
286 Marv Bateman .15
287 *Joe Klecko* 2.00
288 Oliver Davis .15
289 John McDaniel .15
290 Roger Staubach 10.00
291 Brian Kelley .15
292 Mike Hogan .15
293 John Leypoldt .15
294 Jack Novak .15
295 Joe Greene 1.50
296 John Hill .15
297 Danny Buggs .15
298 Ted Albrecht .15
299 Nelson Munsey .15
300 Chuck Foreman .40
301 Dan Pastorini .30
302 Tommy Hart .15
303 Dave Beverly .15
304 *Tony Reed* .30
305 Cliff Branch 1.00
306 Clarence Duren .15
307 Randy Rasmussen .15
308 Oscar Roan .15
309 Lenvil Elliott .15
310 Dan Dierdorf (AP) 1.00
311 Johnny Perkins .15
312 *Rafael Septien* .30
313 Terry Beeson .15
314 Lee Roy Selmon .50
315 *Tony Dorsett* 40.00
316 Greg Landry .30
317 Jake Scott .15
318 Dan Peiffer .15
319 John Bunting .15
320 *John Stallworth* 20.00
321 Bob Howard .15
322 Larry Little .50
323 Reggie McKenzie .15
324 Duane Carrell .15
325 Ed Simonini .15
326 John Vella .15
327 *Wesley Walker* 3.50
328 Jon Keyworth .15
329 Ron Bolton .15
330 Tommy Casanova .15
331 Bob Griese, Roger Staubach Passing Leaders: 3.50
332 Lydell Mitchell, Ahmad Rashad Receiving Leaders: .25
333 Mark Van Eeghen, Walter Payton Rushing Leaders: 2.25
334 Errol Mann, Walter Payton Scoring Leaders: 2.25
335 Lyle Blackwood, Rolland Lawrence Interception Leaders: .25
336 Ray Guy, Tom Blanchard Punting Leaders: .25
337 Robert Brazile .15
338 Charlie Joiner 1.00
339 Joe Ferguson .30
340 Bill Thompson .15
341 Sam Cunningham .15
342 Curtis Johnson .15
343 Jim Marshall .50
344 Charlie Sanders .15
345 Willie Hall .15
346 Pat Haden .75
347 Jim Bakken .15
348 Bruce Taylor .15
349 Barty Smith .15
350 Drew Pearson 1.00
351 Mike Webster 2.00
352 Bobby Hammond .15
353 Dave Mays .15
354 Pat McInally .15
355 Toni Linhart .15
356 Larry Hand .15
357 Ted Fritsch .15
358 Larry Marshall .15
359 Waymond Bryant .15
360 *Louie Kelcher* .35
361 *Stanley Morgan* 4.00
362 *Bruce Harper* .30
363 Bernard Jackson .15
364 Walter White .15
365 Ken Stabler 6.00
366 Fred Dryer 1.00
367 Ike Harris .15
368 Norm Bulaich .15
369 Merv Krakau .15
370 John James .15
371 *Bennie Cunningham* .30
372 Doug Van Horn .15
373 Thom Darden .15
374 *Eddie Edwards* .15
375 Mike Thomas .15
376 Fred Cook .15
377 Mike Phipps .15
378 Paul Krause .15
379 Harold Carmichael .75
380 Mike Haynes (AP) 1.00
381 Wayne Morris .15
382 Greg Buttle .15
383 Jim Zorn .50
384 Jack Dolbin .15
385 Charlie Waters .50
386 Dan Ryczek .15
387 *Joe Washington* 1.00
388 Checklist 265-396 1.00
389 James Hunter .15
390 Billy Johnson .15
391 Jim Allen .15
392 George Buehler .15
393 Harry Carson 1.25
394 Cleo Miller .15
395 Gary Burley .15
396 Mark Moseley .25
397 Virgil Livers .15
398 Joe Ehrmann .15
399 Freddie Solomon .15
400 O.J. Simpson 5.00
401 Julius Adams .15
402 Artimus Parker(.15
403 Gene Washington .15
404 Herman Edwards .15
405 Craig Morton .50
406 Alan Page .75
407 Larry McCarren .15
408 Tony Galbreath .15
409 Roman Gabriel .60
410 Efren Herrera (AP) .15
411 *Jim Smith* .60
412 Bill Bryant .15
413 Doug Dieken .15
414 Marvin Cobb .15
415 Fred Biletnikoff 1.50
416 Joe Theismann 2.50
417 Roland Harper .15
418 Derrel Luce .15
419 Ralph Perretta .15
420 *Louis Wright* 1.00
421 Prentice McCray .15
422 Garry Puetz .15
423 *Alfred Jenkins* .50
424 Paul Seymour .15
425 Garo Yepremian .15
426 Emmitt Thomas .15
427 Dexter Bussey .15
428 John Sanders .15
429 Ed "Too Tall" Jones 2.00
430 Frank Lewis .15
431 Frank Lewis .15
432 Jerry Golsteyn .15
433 Clarence Scott .15
434 *Pete Johnson* .50
435 Charley Young .15
436 Harold McLinton .15
437 Noah Jackson .15
438 Bruce Laird .15
439 John Matuszak .15
440 Nat Moore (AP) .35
441 Leon Gray .15
442 Jerome Barkum .15
443 Steve Largent 15.00
444 John Zook .15
445 Preston Pearson .30
446 Conrad Dobler .15
447 Wilbur Summers .15
448 Lou Piccone .15
449 Ron Jaworski .60
450 Jack Ham (AP) 1.50
451 Mick Tingelhoff .15
452 Clyde Powers .15
453 John Cappelletti .50
454 Dick Ambrose .15
455 Lemar Parrish .15
456 Ron Saul .15
457 Bob Parsons .15
458 Glenn Doughty .15
459 Don Woods .15
460 Art Shell (AP) 1.00
461 Sam Hunt .15
462 Lawrence Pillers .15
463 Henry Childs .15
464 Roger Wehrli .15
465 Otis Armstrong .30
466 *Bob Baumhower* .75
467 Ray Jarvis .15
468 Guy Morriss .15
469 Matt Blair .35
470 Bill Joe DuPree .35
471 Roland Hooks .15
472 Joe Danelo .15
473 Reggie Rucker .15
474 Vern Holland .15
475 Mel Blount 1.25
476 Eddie Brown .15
477 Bo Rather .15
478 Don McCauley .15
479 Glen Walker .15
480 Randy Gradishar (AP) .90
481 Dave Rowe .15
482 Pat Leahy .40
483 Mike Fuller .15
484 David Lewis .15
485 Steve Grogan .75
486 Mel Gray .15
487 *Eddie Payton* .30
488 Checklist 397-528 1.00
489 Stu Voigt .15
490 Rolland Lawrence (AP) .15
491 Nick Mike-Mayer .15
492 Troy Archer .15
493 Benny Malone .15
494 Golden Richards .15
495 Chris Hanburger .15
496 Dwight Harrison .15
497 *Gary Fencik* .75
498 Rich Saul .15
499 Dan Fouts 5.00
500 Franco Harris (AP) 2.50
501 Haskel Stanback, Alfred Jenkins, Claude Humphrey, Jeff Merrow, Rolland Lawrence Atlanta Falcons Team: .50
502 Lydell Mitchell, Lyle Blackwood, Fred Cook Baltimore Colts Team: .50
503 Bob Chandler, O.J. Simpson, Tony Greene, Sherman White Buffalo Bills Team: 2.00
504 James Scott, Allan Ellis, Ron Rydalch, Walter Payton Chicago Bears Team: 1.75
505 Billy Brooks, Lemar Parrish, Reggie Williams, Gary Burley, Pete Johnson Cincinnati Bengals Team: .75
506 Reggie Rucker, Thom Darden, Mack Mitchell, Greg Pruitt Cleveland Browns Team: .50
507 Drew Pearson, Cliff Harris, Harvey Martin, Tony Dorsett Dallas Cowboys Team: 2.00
508 Otis Armstrong, Haven Moses, Bill Thompson, Rick Upchurch Denver Broncos Team: .50
509 Horace King, David Hill, James Hunter, Ken Sanders Detroit Lions Team: .50
510 Barty Smith, Steve Odom, Steve Luke, M.C. McCoy, Dave Pureifory, Dave Roller Green Bay Packers Team: .50
511 Ronnie Coleman, Ken Burrough, Mike Reinfeldt, James Young Houston Oilers Team: .50
512 Ed Podolak, Walter White, Gary Barbaro, Wilbur Young Kansas City Chiefs Team: .50
513 Lawrence McCutcheon, Harold Jackson, Bill Simpson, Jack Youngblood Los Angeles Rams Team: .50
514 Benny Malone, Nat Moore, Curtis Johnson, A.J. Duhe Miami Dolphins Team: .50
515 Chuck Foreman, Sammie White, Bobby Bryant, Carl Eller Minnesota Vikings Team: .50
516 Sam Cunningham, Darryl Stingley, Mike Haynes, Tony McGee New England Patriots Team: .50
517 Chuck Muncie, Don Herrmann, Chuck Crist, Elois Grooms New Orleans Saints Team: .50
518 Bobby Hammond, Jimmy Robinson, Bill Bryant, John Mendenhall New York Giants Team: .50
519 Clark Gaines, Wesley Walker, Burgess Owens, Joe Klecko New York Jets Team: .75
520 Mark Van Eeghen, Dave Casper, Jack Tatum, Neal Colzie Oakland Raiders Team: .50
521 Mike Hogan, Harold Carmichael, Herman Edwards, John Sanders, Lem Burnham Philadelphia Eagles Team: .50
522 Jim Smith, Mel Blount, Steve Furness, Franco Harris Pittsburgh Steelers Team: 1.00
523 Terry Metcalf, Mel Gray, Roger Wehrli, Mike Dawson St. Louis Cardinals Team: .50
524 Rickey Young, Charlie Joiner, Mike Fuller, Gary Johnson San Diego Chargers Team: .50
525 Delvin Williams, G. Washington, Mel Phillips, Dave Washington, Cleveland Elam San Francisco 49ers Team: .50
526 Steve Largent, Autry Beamon, Walter Packer, Sherman Smith Seattle Seahawks Team: 1.50
527 Morris Owens, Isaac Hagins, Mike Washington, Lee Roy Selmon Tampa Bay Buccaneers Team: .50
528 Jean Fugett, Ken Houston, Dennis Johnson, Mike Thomas Washington Redskins Team: 1.00

1978 Topps Holsum

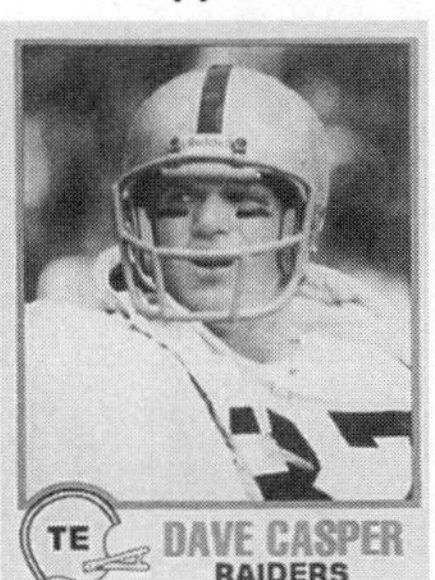

The 33-card, standard-size set was produced by Topps and distributed with loaves of Holsum Bread. For whatever reason, the cards do not have the Holsum name or logo printed anywhere on the card. As with the 1977 Packers/Vikings Holsum set, an uncut sheet was offered by Topps at an archives auction in 1989.

		NM/M
Complete Set (33):		250.00
Common Player:		3.00
1	Rolland Lawrence	3.00
2	Walter Payton	80.00
3	Lydell Mitchell	4.00
4	Joe DeLamielleure	3.00
5	Ken Anderson	10.00
6	Greg Pruitt	4.00
7	Harvey Martin	5.00
8	Tom Jackson	5.00
9	Chester Marcol	3.00
10	Jim Carter	3.00
11	Will Harrell	3.00
12	Greg Landry	4.00
13	Billy Johnson	4.00
14	Jan Stenerud	5.00
15	Lawrence McCutcheon	4.00
16	Bob Griese	20.00
17	Chuck Foreman	4.00
18	Sammie White	4.00
19	Jeff Siemon	3.00
20	Mike Haynes	4.00
21	Archie Manning	6.00
22	Brad Van Pelt	3.00
23	Richard Todd	4.00
24	Dave Casper	4.00
25	Bill Bergey	4.00
26	Franco Harris	20.00
27	Mel Gray	4.00
28	Louie Kelcher	3.00
29	O.J. Simpson	30.00
30	Jim Zorn	4.00
31	Lee Roy Selmon	6.00
32	Ken Houston	6.00
33	Checklist Card	8.00

1979 Topps

Topps' fifth 528-card set was similar in design to its 1973 set, which also showed a small flag. This set, though, showed only the lower half of the flag in solid color, and showed the player's position in a football superimposed over the flag. The team name appeared in any one of a number of colors in capital letters above the photo. Subsets in this year's issue include conference leaders and playoff results. This set is notable for the inclusion of the only four cards Topps issued depicting running back Earl Campbell. Topps was apparently unable to reach a contract agreement with Campbell after this season - possibly similar to the Joe Namath situation after 1973. In addition to Campbell, other rookie cards in this set include Doug Williams, Steve DeBerg, Wilbert Montgomery, Tony Hill, James Jefferson, Ozzie Newsome, and James Lofton. This set also contains the second-year card of Tony Dorsett. (Key: AP - All Pro)

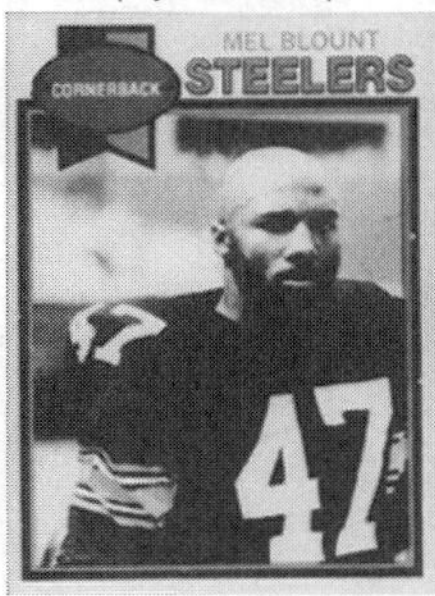

		NM/M
Complete Set (528):		140.00
Common Player:		.15
Wax Pack (12):		12.00
Wax Box (36):		325.00

1 Roger Staubach, Terry Bradshaw Passing Leaders 8.00
2 Rickey Young, Steve Largent Receiving Leaders .75
3 Walter Payton, Earl Campbell Rushing Leaders 8.00
4 Frank Corral, Pat Leahy Scoring Leaders .25
5 Willie Buchanon, Ken Stone, Thom Darden Interception Leaders .25
6 Tom Skladany, Pat McInally Punting Leaders .25
7 Johnny Perkins .15
8 Charles Phillips .15
9 Derrel Luce .15
10 John Riggins 1.50
11 Chester Marcol .15
12 Bernard Jackson .15
13 Dave Logan .15
14 Bo Harris .15
15 Alan Page .75
16 John Smith .15
17 Dwight McDonald .15
18 John Cappelletti .25
19 Franco Harris, Larry Anderson, Tim Dungy, L.C. Greenwood Pittsburgh Steelers Team .75
20 Bill Bergey (AP) .25
21 Jerome Barkum .15
22 Larry Csonka 1.25
23 Joe Ferguson .25
24 Ed "Too Tall" Jones 1.00
25 Dave Jennings .15
26 Horace King .15
27 Steve Little .15
28 Morris Bradshaw .15
29 Joe Ehrmann .15
30 Ahmad Rashad (AP) .75
31 Joe Lavender .15
32 Dan Neal .15
33 Johnny Evans .15
34 Pete Johnson .15
35 Mike Haynes (AP) .40
36 Tim Mazzetti .15
37 *Mike Barber* .20
38 O.J. Simpson, Freddie Solomon, Chuck Crist, Cedrick Hardman San Francisco 49ers Team 1.75
39 Bill Gregory .15
40 Randy Gradishar (AP) .50
41 Richard Todd .25
42 Henry Marshall .15
43 John Hill .15
44 Sidney Thornton .15
45 Ron Jessie .15
46 Bob Baumhower .15
47 Johnnie Gray .15
48 *Doug Williams* 5.00
49 Don McCauley .15
50 Ray Guy (AP) .30
51 Bob Klein .15
52 Golden Richards .15
53 Mark Miller .15
54 John Sanders .15
55 Gary Burley .15
56 Steve Nelson .15
57 Miller, Frank Lewis, Mario Clark, Lucius Sanford Buffalo Bills Team .50
58 Bobby Bryant .15
59 Rick Kane .15
60 Larry Little .35
61 Ted Fritsch .15
62 Larry Mallory .15
63 Marvin Powell .15
64 Jim Hart .30
65 Joe Greene (AP) 1.25
66 Walter White .15
67 Gregg Bingham .15
68 Errol Mann .15
69 Bruce Laird .15
70 Drew Pearson .75
71 Steve Bartkowski .60
72 Ted Albrecht .15
73 Charlie Hall .15
74 Pat McInally .15
75 *Al Baker* (AP) 1.00
76 Sam Cunningham, Stanley Morgan, Mike Haynes, Tony McGee New England Patriots Team .50
77 *Steve DeBerg* 4.00
78 John Yarno .15
79 Stu Voight .15
80 Frank Corral (AP) .15
81 Troy Archer .15
82 Bruce Harper .15
83 Tom Jackson .75
84 Larry Brown .15
85 *Wilbert Montgomery* 1.00
86 Butch Johnson .15
87 Mike Kadish .15
88 Ralph Perretta .15
89 David Lee .15
90 Mark Van Eeghen .15
91 John McDaniel .15
92 Gary Fencik .15
93 Mack Mitchell .15
94 Pete Johnson, Isaac Curtis, Dick Jauron, Ross Browner Cincinnati Bengals Team .50
95 Steve Grogan .50
96 Garo Yepremian .15
97 Barty Smith .15
98 Frank Reed .15
99 Jim Clark .15
100 Chuck Foreman .30
101 Joe Klecko .75
102 Pat Tilley .15
103 Conrad Dobler .15
104 Craig Colquitt .15
105 Dan Pastorini .20
106 Rod Perry (AP) .15
107 Nick Mike-Mayer .15
108 John Matuszak .15
109 David Taylor .15
110 Billy Joe DuPree (AP) .15
111 Harold McLinton .15
112 Virgil Livers .15
113 Greg Pruitt, Reggie Rucker, Thom Darden, Mack Mitchell Cleveland Browns Team .50
114 Checklist 1-132 1.00
115 Ken Anderson 1.25
116 Bill Lenkaitis .15
117 Bucky Dilts .15
118 Tony Greene .15
119 Bobby Hammond .15
120 Nat Moore .15
121 Pat Leahy (AP) .30
122 James Harris .15
123 Lee Roy Selmon .25
124 Bennie Cunningham .15
125 Matt Blair (AP) .15
126 Jim Allen .15
127 Alfred Jenkins .15
128 Arthur Whittington .15
129 Norm Thompson .15
130 Pat Haden .40
131 Freddie Solomon .15
132 Walter Payton, James Scott, Gary Fencik, Alan Page Chicago Bears Team 2.00
133 Mark Moseley .15
134 Cleo Miller .15
135 *Ross Browner* .30
136 Don Calhoun .15
137 David Whitehurst .15
138 Terry Beeson .15
139 Ken Stone .15
140 Brad Van Pelt AP .15
141 Wesley Walker (AP) .75
142 Jan Stenerud .50
143 Henry Childs .15
144 Otis Armstrong .25
145 Dwight White .15
146 Steve Wilson .15
147 Tom Skladany (AP) .15
148 Lou Piccone .15
149 Monte Johnson .15
150 Joe Washington .20
151 Wilbert Montgomery, Harold Carmichael, Herman Edwards, Dennis Harrison Philadelphia Eagles Team .60
152 Fred Dean .25
153 Rolland Lawrence .15
154 Brian Baschnagel .15
155 Joe Theismann 1.50
156 Marvin Cobb .15
157 Dick Ambrose .15
158 Mike Patrick .15
159 Gary Shirk .15
160 Tony Dorsett 10.00
161 Greg Buttle .15
162 A.J. Duhe .15
163 Mick Tingelhoff .15
164 Ken Burrough .15
165 Mike Wagner .15
166 Franco Harris AFC Championship 1.00
167 NFC Championship .30
168 Franco Harris Super Bowl XII 1.25

169 Mark Van Eeghen, Dave Casper, Charles Phillips, Ted Hendricks Oakland Raiders Team .60
170 O.J. Simpson 4.00
171 Doug Nettles .15
172 Dan Dierdorf (AP) .75
173 Dave Beverly .15
174 Jim Zorn .35
175 Mike Thomas .15
176 John Outlaw .15
177 Jim Turner .15
178 Freddie Scott .15
179 Mike Phipps .15
180 Jack Youngblood (AP) .50
181 Sam Hunt .15
182 *Tony Hill* 1.00
183 Gary Barbaro .15
184 Archie Griffin .40
185 Jerry Sherk .15
186 Bobby Jackson .15
187 Don Woods .15
188 Doug Kotar, Jimmy Robinson, Terry Jackson, George Martin New York Giants Team .15
189 Raymond Chester .15
190 Joe DeLamielleure (AP) .15
191 Tony Galbreath .15
192 Robert Brazile (AP) .15
193 Neil O'Donoghue .15
194 Mike Webster .75
195 Ed Simonini .15
196 Denny Malone .15
197 Tom Wittum .15
198 Steve Largent (AP) 8.00
199 Tommy Hart .15
200 Fran Tarkenton 4.00
201 Leon Gray (AP) .15
202 Leroy Harris .15
203 Eric Williams .15
204 Thom Darden (AP) .15
205 Ken Riley .15
206 Clark Gaines .15
207 Tony Reed, Tim Gray, Art Still Kansas CityChiefs Team .50
208 Joe Danelo .15
209 Glen Walker .15
210 Art Shell 1.00
211 Jon Keyworth .15
212 Herman Edwards .15
213 John Fitzgerald .15
214 Jim Smith .15
215 Coy Bacon .15
216 Dennis Johnson .15
217 *John Jefferson* 4.00
218 Gary Weaver .15
219 Tom Blanchard .15
220 Bert Jones .50
221 Stanley Morgan 1.50
222 James Hunter .15
223 Jim O'Bradovich .15
224 Carl Mauck .15
225 Chris Bahr .15
226 Kevin Long, Wesley Walker, Bobby Jackson, Burgess Owens, Joe Klecko New York Jets Team .60
227 Roland Harper .15
228 Randy Dean .15
229 Bob Jackson .15
230 Sammie White .25
231 Mike Dawson .15
232 Checklist 133-264 1.00
233 Ken MacAfee .15
234 Jon Kolb (AP) .15
235 Willie Hall .15
236 Ron Saul (AP) .15
237 Haskel Stanback .15
238 Zenon Andrusyshyn .15
239 Norris Thomas .15
240 Rick Upchurch .30
241 Robert Pratt .15
242 Julius Adams .15
243 Rich McGeorge .15
244 Sherman Smith, Steve Largent, Cornell Webster, Bill Gregory Seattle Seahawks Team 1.00
245 Blair Bush .15
246 Billy Johnson .15
247 Randy Rasmussen .15
248 Brian Kelley .15
249 Mike Pruitt .15
250 Harold Carmichael (AP) .60
251 Mike Hartenstine .15
252 Robert Newhouse .15
253 Gary Danielson .30
254 Mike Fuller .15
255 L.C. Greenwood (AP) .40
256 Lemar Parrish .15
257 Ike Harris .15
258 *Ricky Bell* 1.00
259 Willie Parker .15
260 Gene Upshaw .50
261 Glenn Doughty .15
262 Steve Zabel .15
263 Bubba Bean, Wallace Francis, Rolland Lawrence, Greg Brezina Atlanta Falcons Team 1.00
264 Ray Wersching .15
265 Lawrence McCutcheon .15
266 Willie Buchanon (AP) .15
267 Matt Robinson .15
268 Reggie Rucker .15
269 Doug Van Horn .15
270 Lydell Mitchell .15
271 Vern Holland .15
272 Eason Ramson .15
273 Steve Towle .15
274 Jim Marshall .40
275 Mel Blount 1.00
276 Bob Kuziel .15
277 James Scott .15
278 Tony Reed .15
279 Dave Green .15
280 Toni Linhart .15
281 Andy Johnson .15
282 Cullen Bryant, Willie Miller, Rod Perry, Pat Thomas, Larry Brooks Los Angeles Rams Team 1.00
283 Phil Villapiano .15
284 Dexter Bussey .15
285 Craig Morton .50
286 Guy Morriss .15
287 Lawrence Pillers .15
288 Gerald Irons .15
289 Scott Perry .15
290 Randy White 2.00
291 Jack Gregory .15
292 Bob Chandler .15
293 Rich Szaro .15
294 Sherman Smith .15
295 Tom Banks (AP) .15
296 Revie Sorey (AP) .15
297 Ricky Thompson .15
298 Ron Yary .15
299 Lyle Blackwood .15
300 Franco Harris 2.00
301 Earl Campbell, Ken Burrough, Willie Alexander, Elvin Bethea Houston Oilers Team 3.00
302 Scott Bull .15
303 Dewey Selmon .15
304 Jack Rudnay .15
305 Fred Biletnikoff 1.25
306 Jeff West .15
307 Shafer Suggs .15
308 *Ozzie Newsome* 15.00
309 Boobie Clark .15
310 *James Lofton* 15.00
311 Joe Pisarcik .15
312 Bill Simpson (AP) .15
313 Haven Moses .15
314 Jim Merlo .15
315 Preston Pearson .15
316 Larry Tearry .15
317 Tom Dempsey .15
318 Greg Latta .15
319 John Riggins, John McDaniel, Jake Scott, Coy Bacon Washington Redskins Team .75
320 Jack Ham (AP) 1.25
321 Harold Jackson .30
322 George Roberts .15
323 Ron Jaworski .40
324 Jim Otis .15
325 Roger Carr .15
326 Jack Tatum .15
327 Derrick Gaffney .15
328 Reggie Williams .50
329 Doug Dieken .15
330 Efren Herrea .15
331 Campbell Record: 6.00
332 Tony Galbreath Record: .25
333 Bruce Harper Record: .25
334 John James Record: .25
335 Walter Payton Record: 3.00
336 Rickey Young Record: .15
337 Jeff Van Note .15
338 Lydell Mitchell, John Jefferson, Mike Fuller, Fred Dean San Diego Chargers Team .60
339 *Stan Walters* (AP) .20
340 Louis Wright (AP) .15
341 Horace Ivory .15
342 Andre Tillman .15
343 Greg Coleman .15
344 *Doug English* (AP) .60
345 Ted Hendricks .50
346 Rich Saul .15
347 Mel Gray .15
348 Toni Fritsch .15
349 Cornell Webster .15
350 Ken Houston .50
351 Ron Johnson .15
352 Doug Kotar .15
353 Brian Sipe .40
354 Billy Brooks .15
355 John Dutton .15
356 Don Goode .15
357 Dexter Bussey, David Hill, Jim Allen, Al Baker Detroit Lions Team 1.00
358 Reuben Gant .15
359 Bob Parsons .15
360 Cliff Harris (AP) .35
361 Raymond Clayborn .20
362 Scott Dierking .15
363 Bill Bryan .15
364 Mike Livingston .15
365 Otis Sistrunk .15
366 Charley Young .15
367 Keith Wortman .15
368 Checklist 265-396 1.00
369 Mike Michel .15
370 Delvin Williams .15
371 Steve Furness .15
372 Emery Moorehead .15
373 Clarence Scott .15
374 Rufus Mayes .15
375 Chris Hanberger .15
376 Joe Washington, Roger Carr, Norm Thompson, John Dutton Baltimore Colts Team .50
377 Bob Avellini .15
378 Jeff Siemon .15
379 Roland Hooks .15
380 Russ Francis .15
381 Roger Wehrli .15
382 Joe Fields .15
383 Archie Manning .50
384 Rob Lytle .15
385 Thomas Henderson .15
386 Morris Owens .15
387 Dan Fouts 4.00
388 Chuck Crist .15
389 Ed O'Neil .15
390 *Earl Campbell* (AP) 30.00
391 Randy Grossman .15
392 Monte Jackson .15
393 John Mendenhall .15
394 Delvin Williams, Duriel Harris, Tim Foley, Vern Den Herder Miami Dolphins Team .50
395 Isaac Curtis .15
396 Mike Bragg .15
397 Doug Plank .15
398 Mike Barnes .15
399 Calvin Hill .20
400 Roger Staubach (AP) 8.00
401 Doug Beaudoin .15
402 Chuck Ramsey .15
403 Mike Hogan .15
404 Mario Clark .15
405 Riley Odoms .15
406 Carl Eller .30
407 Terdell Middleton, James Lofton, Willie Buchanon, Ezra Johnson Green Bay Packers Team 2.75
408 Mark Arenson .15
409 *Vince Ferragamo* .60
410 Cleveland Elam .15
411 *Donnie Shell* 3.00
412 Ray Rhodes .15
413 Don Cockroft .15
414 Don Bass .15
415 Cliff Branch .75
416 Diron Talbert .15
417 Tom Hicks .15
418 Roosevelt Leaks .15
419 Charlie Joiner .75
420 Lyle Alzado (AP) .75
421 Sam Cunningham .15
422 Larry Keller .15
423 Jim Mitchell .15
424 Randy Logan .15
425 Jim Langer .40
426 Gary Green .15
427 Luther Blue .15
428 Dennis Johnson .15
429 Danny White .75
430 Roy Gerela .15
431 Jimmy Robinson .15
432 Chuck Foreman, Ahmad Rashad, Bobby Bryant, Mark Mullaney Minnesota Vikings Team .50
433 Oliver Davis .15
434 Lenvill Elliott .15
435 Willie Miller .15
436 Brad Dusek .15
437 Bob Thomas .15
438 Ken Mendenhall .15
439 Clarence Davis .15
440 Bob Griese 2.00
441 Tony McGee .15
442 Ed Taylor .15
443 Ron Howard .15
444 Wayne Morris .15
445 Charlie Waters .35
446 Rick Danmeier .15
447 Paul Naumoff .15
448 Keith Krepfle .15
449 Rusty Jackson .15
450 John Stallworth 3.00
451 Tony Galbreath, Henry Childs, Tom Myers, Elex Price New Orleans Saints Team .50
452 Ron Mikolajczyk .15
453 Fred Dryer .75
454 Jim LeClair .15
455 Greg Pruitt .25
456 Jake Scott .15
457 Steve Schubert .15
458 George Kunz .15
459 Mike Williams .15
460 Dave Casper (AP) .15
461 Sam Adams .15
462 Abdul Salaam .15
463 Terdell Middleton .15
464 Mike Wood .15
465 Bill Thompson (AP) .15
466 Larry Gordon .15
467 Benny Ricardo .15
468 Reggie McKenzie .15
469 Tony Dorsett, Tony Hill, Benny Barnes, Harvey Martin, Randy White Dallas Cowboys Team 1.00
470 Rickey Young .15
471 Charlie Smith .15
472 Al Dixon .15
473 Tom DeLeone .15
474 Louis Breeden .15
475 Jack Lambert 2.00
476 Terry Hermeling .15
477 J.K. McKay .15
478 Stan White .15
479 Terry Nelson .15
480 Walter Payton (AP) 22.00
481 Dave Dalby .15
482 Burgess Owens .15
483 Rolf Benirschke .15
484 Jack Dolbin .15
485 John Hannah (AP) .60
486 Checklist 397-528 1.00
487 Greg Landry .20
488 Jim Otis, Pat Tilley, Ken Stone, Mike Dawson St. Louis Cardinals Team .50
489 Paul Krause .15
490 John James .15
491 Merv Krakau .15
492 Dan Doornink .15
493 Curtis Johnson .15
494 Rafael Septien .15
495 Jean Fugett .15
496 Frank LeMaster .15
497 Allan Ellis .15
498 *Billy Waddy* .20
499 Hank Bauer .15
500 Terry Bradshaw (AP) 10.00
501 Larry McCarren .15
502 Fred Cook .15
503 Chuck Muncie .20
504 Herman Weaver .15
505 Eddie Edwards .15
506 Tony Peters .15
507 Lonnie Perrin, Riley Odoms, Steve Foley, Bernard Jackson, Lyle Alzado Denver Broncos Team .50
508 Jimbo Elrod .15
509 David Hill .15
510 Harvey Martin .35
511 Terry Miller .15
512 *June Jones* 1.00
513 Randy Cross .30
514 Duriel Harris .15
515 Harry Carson .75
516 Tim Fox .15
517 John Zook .15
518 Bob Tucker .15
519 Kevin Long .15
520 Ken Stabler 4.00
521 John Bunting .15
522 Rocky Bleier .75
523 Noah Jackson .15
524 Cliff Parsley .15
525 Louie Kelcher (AP) .15
526 Ricky Bell, Morris Owens, Cedric Brown, Lee Roy Selmon Tampa Bay Bucaneers .60
527 Bob Brudzinski .15
528 Danny Buggs .15

1980 Topps

The cards in this set feature a football at the bottom of the card with the team name and position on either side of the player's name. The 528-card set has subsets featuring, as usual, record breakers and the previous year's playoff decisions. Rookies in this set include Ottis Anderson, Tommy Kramer, Phil Simms and Wes Chandler. (Key: AP - All Pro)

	NM/M
Complete Set (528):	65.00
Common Player:	.08
Wax Pack (12):	4.00
Wax Box (36):	100.00

1 O. Anderson Record: 1.00
2 Harold Carmichael Record: .15
3 Dan Fouts Record: 1.00
4 Paul Krause Record: .15
5 Rick Upchurch Record: .15
6 Garo Yepremian Record: .15
7 Harold Jackson .25
8 Mike Williams .08
9 Calvin Hill .15
10 Jack Ham 1.00
11 Dan Melville .08
12 Matt Robinson .08
13 Billy Campfield .08
14 Phil Tabor .08
15 Randy Hughes .08
16 Andre Tillman .08
17 Isaac Curtis .08
18 Charley Hannah .08
19 John Riggins, Danny Buggs, Joe Lavender, Coy Bacon Washington Redskins Team .50
20 Jim Zorn .30
21 Brian Baschnagel .08
22 Jon Keyworth .08
23 Phil Villapiano .08
24 Richard Osborne .08
25 Rich Saul (AP) .08
26 Doug Beaudoin .08
27 Cleveland Elam .08
28 Charlie Joiner .65
29 Dick Ambrose .08
30 *Mike Reinfeldt* (AP) .11
31 *Matt Bahr* 1.75
32 Keith Krepfle .08
33 Herbert Scott .08
34 Doug Kotar .08
35 Bob Griese 1.75
36 *Jerry Butler* .40
37 Rolland Lawrence .08
38 Gary Weaver .08
39 Ted McKnight, J.T. Smith, Gary Barbaro, Art Still Kansas City Chiefs Team .40
40 Chuck Muncie .08
41 Mike Hartenstine .08
42 Sammie White .20
43 Ken Clark .08
44 Clarence Harmon .08
45 Bert Jones .30
46 Mike Washington .08
47 Joe Fields .08
48 Mike Wood .08
49 Oliver Davis .08
50 Stan Walters (AP) .08
51 Riley Odoms .08
52 Steve Pisarkiewicz .08
53 Tony Hill .40
54 Scott Perry .08
55 *George Martin* .40
56 George Roberts .08
57 Sherman Smith, Steve Largent, Dave Brown, Manu Tuiasosopo Seattle Seahawks Team .75
58 Billy Johnson .08
59 Reuben Johnson .08
60 *Dennis Harrah* (AP) .20
61 Rocky Bleier .35
62 Sam Hunt .08
63 Allan Ellis .08
64 Ricky Thompson .08
65 Ken Stabler 1.50
66 Dexter Bussey .08
67 Ken Mendenhall .08
68 Woodrow Lowe .08
69 Thom Darden .08
70 Randy White (AP) 1.50
71 Ken MacAfee .08
72 Ron Jaworski .30
73 *William Andrews* 1.00
74 Jimmy Robinson .08
75 Roger Wehrli (AP) .08
76 Larry Csonka, Nat Moore, Neal Colzie, Gerald Small, Vern Den Herder Miami Dolphins Team .50
77 Jack Rudnay .08
78 James Lofton 4.00
79 Robert Brazile .08
80 Russ Francis .08
81 Ricky Bell .30
82 Bob Avellini .08
83 Bobby Jackson .08
84 Mike Bragg .08
85 Cliff Branch .30
86 Blair Bush .08
87 Sherman Smith .08
88 Glen Edwards .08
89 Don Cockroft .08
90 Louis Wright (AP) .15
91 Randy Grossman .08
92 *Carl Hariston* .75
93 Archie Manning .40
94 Billy Taylor, Earnest Gray, George Martin New York Giants Team .30
95 Preston Pearson .08
96 Rusty Chambers .08
97 Greg Coleman .08
98 Charley Young .08
99 *Matt Cavanaugh* .30
100 Jesse Baker .08
101 Doug Plank .08
102 Checklist 1-132 .65
103 *Luther Bradley* .11
104 Bob Kuziel .08
105 Craig Morton .35
106 Sherman White .08
107 *Jim Breech* .75
108 Hank Bauer .08
109 Tom Blanchard .08
110 Ozzie Newsome (AP) 4.00
111 Steve Furness .08
112 Frank LeMaster .08
113 Tony Dorsett, Tony Hill, Harvey Martin Dallas Cowboys Team .75
114 Doug Van Horn .08
115 Delvin Williams .08
116 Lyle Blackwood .08
117 Derrick Gaffney .08
118 Cornell Webster .08
119 Sam Cunningham .08
120 Jim Youngblood (AP) .08
121 Bob Thomas .08
122 *Jack Thompson* .15
123 Randy Cross .08
124 Karl Lorch .08
125 Mel Gray .08
126 John James .08
127 Terdell Middleton .08
128 Leroy Jones .08
129 Tom DeLeone .08
130 John Stallworth (AP) 1.00
131 *Jimmie Giles* .30
132 Wilbert Montgomery, Harold Carmichael, Brenard Wilson, Carl Hairston Philadelphia Eagles Team .30
133 Gary Green .08
134 John Dutton .08
135 Harry Carson (AP) .50
136 Bob Kuechenberg .08
137 Ike Harris .08
138 *Tommy Kramer* 1.00
139 Sam Adams .08
140 Doug English (AP) .15
141 Steve Schubert .08
142 Rusty Jackson .08
143 Reese McCall .08
144 Scott Dierking .08
145 Ken Houston (AP) .50
146 Bob Martin .08
147 Sam McCullum .08
148 Tom Banks .08
149 Willie Buchanon .08
150 Greg Pruitt .20
151 Otis Armstrong, Rick Upchurch, Steve Foley, Brison Manor Denver Broncos Team .30
152 Don Smith .08
153 Pete Johnson .08
154 Charlie Smith .08
155 Mel Blount .75
156 John Mendenhall .08
157 Danny White .50
158 *Jimmy Cefalo* .30
159 Richard Bishop (AP) .08
160 Walter Payton (AP) 15.00
161 Dave Dalby .08
162 Preston Dennard .08
163 Johnnie Gray .08
164 Russell Erxleben .08
165 Toni Fritsch (AP) .08
166 Terry Hermeling .08
167 Roland Hooks .08
168 Roger Carr .08
169 Clarence Williams, John Jefferson, Woodrow Lowe, Ray Preston, Wilbur Young San Diego Chargers Team .30
170 *Ottis Anderson* (AP) 5.00
171 Brian Sipe .30
172 Leonard Thompson .08
173 Tony Reed .08
174 Bob Tucker .08
175 Joe Greene 1.00
176 Jack Dolbin .08
177 Chuck Ramsey .08
178 Paul Hofer .08
179 Randy Logan .08
180 David Lewis (AP) .08
181 Duriel Harris .08
182 June Jones .50
183 Larry McCarren .08
184 Ken Johnson .08
185 Charlie Waters .30
186 Noah Jackson .08
187 Reggie Williams .25
188 Sam Cunningham, Harold Jackson, Raymond Clayborn, Tony McGee New England Patriots Team .30
189 Carl Eller .35
190 Ed White (AP) .08
191 Mario Clark .08
192 Roosevelt Leaks .08
193 Ted McKnight .08
194 Danny Buggs .08
195 *Lester Hayes* 1.50
196 Clarence Scott .08
197 Chuck Muncie, Wes Chandler, Tom Myers, Elois Grooms, Don Reese New Orleans Saints Team .30
198 Richard Caster .08
199 Louie Giammona .08
200 Terry Bradshaw 2.75
201 Ed Newman .08
202 Fred Dryer .50
203 Dennis Franks .08
204 *Bob Breunig* .40
205 Alan Page .50
206 Earnest Gray .15
207 Rickey Young, Ahmad Rashad, Tommy Hannon, Nate Wright, Mark Mullaney Minnesota Vikings Team .40
208 Horace Ivory .08
209 Isaac Hagins .08
210 Gary Johnson (Chargers)(AP) .08
211 Kevin Long .08
212 Bill Thompson .08
213 Don Bass .08
214 *George Starke* .20
215 Efren Herrera .08
216 Theo Bell .08
217 Monte Jackson .08
218 Reggie McKenzie .08
219 Bucky Dilts .08
220 Lyle Alzado .50
221 Tim Foley .08
222 Mark Arneson .08
223 Fred Quillan .08
224 Benny Ricardo .08
225 *Phil Simms* 12.00
226 Walter Payton, Brian Baschnagel, Gary Fencik, Terry Schmidt, Jon Osborne Chicago Bears Team 1.00
227 Max Runager .08
228 Barty Smith .08
229 Jay Saldi .08
230 John Hannah (AP) .50
231 Tim Wilson .08
232 Jeff Van Note .08
233 Henry Marshall .08
234 Diron Talbert .08
235 Garo Yepremian .08
236 Larry Brown .08
237 Clarence Williams .08
238 Burgess Owens .08
239 Vince Ferragamo .25
240 Rickey Young .08
241 Dave Logan .08
242 Larry Gordon .08
243 Terry Miller .08
244 Joe Washington, Fred Cook Baltimore Colts Team .30
245 Steve DeBerg 1.75
246 Checklist 133-264 .65
247 Greg Latta .08
248 Raymond Clayborn .08
249 Jim Clack .08
250 Drew Pearson .50
251 John Bunting .08
252 Rob Lytle .08
253 Jim Hart .25
254 John McDaniel .08
255 Dave Pear (AP) .08
256 Donnie Shell .50
257 Dan Doornink .08
258 *Wallace Francis* .35
259 Dave Beverly .08
260 Lee Roy Selmon (AP) .25
261 Doug Dieken .08
262 Gary David .08
263 Bob Rush .08
264 Curtis Brown, Frank Lewis, Keith Moody, Sherman White Buffalo Bills Team .30

265 Greg Landry .20
266 Jan Stenerud .40
267 Tom Hicks .08
268 Pat McInally .08
269 Tim Fox .08
270 Harvey Martin .30
271 Dan Lloyd .08
272 Mike Barber .08
273 *Wendell Tyler* .60
274 Jeff Komlo .08
275 *Wes Chandler* 2.50
276 Brad Dusek .08
277 Charlie Johnson .08
278 Dennis Swilley .08
279 Johnny Evans .08
280 Jack Lambert (AP) 1.25
281 Vern Den Herder .08
282 Ricky Bell, Isaac Hagins, Lee Roy Selmon Tampa Bay Bucaneers Team .30
283 Bob Klein .08
284 Jim Turner .08
285 Marvin Powell (AP) .08
286 Aaron Kyle .08
287 Dan Neal .08
288 Wayne Morris .08
289 Steve Bartkowski .35
290 Dave Jennings .08
291 John Smith .08
292 Bill Gregory .08
293 Frank Lewis .08
294 Fred Cook .08
295 David Hill (AP) .08
296 Wade Key .08
297 Sidney Thornton .08
298 Charlie Hall .08
299 Joe Lavender .08
300 *Tom Rafferty* .15
301 *Mike Renfro* .15
302 Wilbur Jackson .08
303 Terdell Middleton, James Lofton, Johnnie Gray, Robert Barber, Ezra Johnson Green Bay Packers Team 1.00
304 Henry Childs .08
305 Russ Washington (AP) .08
306 Jim LeClair .08
307 Tommy Hart .08
308 Gary Barbaro .08
309 Billy Taylor .08
310 Ray Guy .25
311 Don Hasselbeck .08
312 Doug Williams .75
313 Nick Mike-Mayer .08
314 Don McCauley .08
315 Wesley Walker .40
316 Dan Dierdorf .50
317 *Dave Brown* .30
318 Leroy Harris .08
319 Franco Harris, John Stallworth, Jack Lambert, Steve Furness, L.C. Greenwood Pittsburgh Steelers Team .75
320 Mark Moseley (AP) .08
321 Mark Dennard .08
322 Terry Nelson .08
323 Tom Jackson .50
324 Rick Kane .08
325 Jerry Sherk .08
326 Ray Preston .08
327 Golden Richards .08
328 Randy Dean .08
329 Rick Danmeier .08
330 Tony Dorsett 4.50
331 Dan Fouts, Roger Staubach Passing Leaders 2.00
332 Joe Washington, Ahmad Rashad Receiving Leaders .15
333 Jesse Baker, Al Baker, Jack Youngblood Sack Leaders .15
334 John Smith, Jack Moseley Scoring Leaders .15
335 Mike Reinfeldt, Lemar Parrish Interception Leaders .15
336 Bob Grupp, Dave Jennings Punting Leaders .15
337 Freddie Solomon .08
338 Pete Johnson, Don Bass, Dick Jauron, Gary Burley Cincinnati Bengals Team .30
339 Ken Stone .08
340 Greg Buttle (AP) .08
341 Bob Baumhower .08
342 Billy Waddy .08
343 Cliff Parsley .08
344 Walter White .08
345 Mike Thomas .08
346 Neil O'Donoghue .08
347 Freddie Scott .08
348 Joe Ferguson .20
349 Doug Nettles .08
350 Mike Webster (AP) .50
351 Ron Saul .08
352 Julius Adams .08
353 Rafael Septien .08
354 Cleo Miller .08
355 Keith Simpson (AP) .08
356 Johnny Perkins .08
357 Jerry Sisemore .08
358 Arthur Wittington .08
359 Ottis Anderson, Pat Tilley, Ken Stone, Bob Pollard St. Louis Cardinals Team .60
360 Rick Upchurch .08
361 Kim Bokamper .20
362 Roland Harper .08
363 Pat Leahy .08
364 Louis Breeden .08
365 John Jefferson .75
366 Jerry Eckwood .08
367 David Whitehurst .08
368 Willie Parker .08
369 Ed Simonini .08
370 Jack Youngblood (AP) .40
371 *Don Warren* 1.50
372 Andy Johnson .08
373 D.D. Lewis .08
374 *Beasley Reece* .30
375 L.C. Greenwood .30
376 Mike Pruitt, Dave Logan, Thom Darden, Jerry Sherk Cleveland Browns Team .30
377 Herman Edwards .08
378 *Rob Carpenter* .25
379 Herman Weaver .08
380 Gary Fencik (AP) .11
381 Don Strock .08
382 Art Shell .50
383 Tim Mazzetti .08
384 Bruce Harper .08
385 Al Baker .08
386 Conrad Dobler .08
387 Stu Voight .08
388 Ken Anderson .75
389 Pat Tilley .08
390 John Riggins 1.25
391 Checklist 265-396 .65
392 Fred Dean (AP) .15
393 *Benny Barnes* .15
394 Wendell Tyler, Preston Dennard, Nolan Cromwell, Jim Youngblood Los Angeles Rams Team .30
395 Brad Van Pelt .08
396 Eddie Hare .08
397 John Sciarra .15
398 Bob Jackson .08
399 John Yarno .08
400 Franco Harris (AP) 1.75
401 Ray Wersching .08
402 Virgil Livers .08
403 Raymond Chester .08
404 Leon Gray .08
405 Richard Todd .20
406 Larry Little .25
407 Ted Fritsch .08
408 Larry Mucker .08
409 Jim Allen .08
410 Randy Grandishar .40
411 William Andrews, Wallace Francis, Rolland Lawrence, Don Smith Atlanta Falcons Team .30
412 Louie Kelcher .08
413 Robert Newhouse .08
414 Gary Shirk .08
415 Mike Haynes (AP) .25
416 Craig Colquitt .08
417 Lou Piccone .08
418 *Clay Matthews* 3.00
419 Marvin Cobb .08
420 Harold Carmichael (AP) .50
421 Uwe Von Schamann .08
422 Mike Phipps .08
423 *Nolan Cromwell* 1.00
424 Glenn Doughty .08
425 Bob Young (AP) .08
426 Tony Galbreath .08
427 Luke Prestridge .08
428 Terry Beeson .08
429 Jack Tatum .08
430 Lemar Parrish (AP) .08
431 Chester Marcol .08
432 Dan Pastorini, Ken Burrough, Mike Reinfeldt, Jesse Baker Houston Oilers Team .30
433 John Fitzgerald .08
434 Gary Jeter .40
435 Steve Grogan .40
436 Jon Kolb .08
437 Jim O'Bradovich .08
438 Gerald Irons .08
439 Jeff West .08
440 Wilbert Montgomery .30
441 Norris Thomas .08
442 James Scott .08
443 Curtis Brown .08
444 Ken Fantetti .08
445 Pat Haden .30
446 Carl Mauck .08
447 Bruce Laird .08
448 Otis Armstrong .20
449 Gene Upshaw .30
450 Steve Largent (AP) 4.50
451 Benny Malone .08
452 Steve Nelson .08
453 Mark Cotney .08
454 Joe Danelo .08
455 Billy Joe DuPree .15
456 Ron Johnson .08
457 Archie Griffin .25
458 Reggie Rucker .08
459 Claude Humphrey .08
460 Lydell Mitchell .08
461 Steve Towle .08
462 Revie Sorey .08
463 Tom Skladany .08
464 Clark Gaines .08
465 Frank Corral .08
466 *Steve Fuller* .25
467 Ahmad Rashad (AP) .75
468 Mark Van Eeghen, Cliff Branch, Lester Hayes, Willie Jones Oakland Raiders Team .30
469 Brian Peets .08
470 *Pat Donovan* (AP) .20
471 Ken Burrough .08
472 Don Calhoun .08
473 Bill Bryan .08
474 Terry Jackson .08
475 Joe Theismann 1.50
476 Jim Smith .08
477 Joe DeLamielleure .08
478 Mike Pruitt (AP) .08
479 Steve Mike-Mayer .08
480 Bill Bergey .15
481 Mike Fuller .08
482 Bob Parsons .08
483 Billy Brooks .08
484 Jerome Barkum .08
485 Larry Csonka 1.00
486 John Hill .08
487 Mike Dawson .08
488 Dexter Bussey, Freddie Scott, Jim Allen, Luther Bradley, Al Baker Detroit Lions Team .30
489 Ted Hendricks .50
490 Dan Pastorini .15
491 Stanley Morgan .75
492 Rocky Bleier AFC Championship .20
493 Vince Ferragamo NFC Championship .20
494 Super Bowl XIV .50
495 Dwight White .08
496 Haven Moses .08
497 Guy Morriss .08
498 Dewey Selmon .08
499 *Dave Butz* 1.50
500 Chuck Foreman .20
501 Chris Bahr .08
502 Mark Miller .08
503 Tony Greene .08
504 Brian Kelley .08
505 Joe Washington .15
506 Butch Johnson .08
507 Clark Gaines, Wesley Walker, Burgess Owens, Joe Klecko New York Jets Team .30
508 Steve Little .08
509 Checklist 397-528 .65
510 Mark Van Eeghen .08
511 Gary Danielson .08
512 Manu Tuiasosopo .08
513 *Paul Coffman* .40
514 Cullen Bryant .08
515 Nat Moore .08
516 Bill Lenkaitis .08
517 *Lynn Cain* .25
518 Gregg Bingham .08
519 Ted Albrecht .08
520 Dan Fouts (AP) 2.00
521 Bernard Jackson .08
522 Coy Bacon .08
523 *Tony Franklin* .25
524 Bo Harris .08
525 Bob Grupp (AP) .08
526 Paul Hofer, Freddie Solomon, James Owens, Dwaine Board San Francisco 49ers Team .30
527 Steve Wilson .08
528 Bernie Cunningham .08

1980 Topps Super

Printed on heavy white cardboard stock, these oversize (around 5" x 7") cards featured 30 NFL stars. The front displays a color photo of the player and his name appears in a gold plaque atop the card; the back lists his name, position and team with the Topps logo in the center of the card. This is a set similar to the 1980 Topps Superstar Photo Baseball set.

NM/M

Complete Set (30): 15.00
Common Player: .30
1 Franco Harris 1.00
2 Bob Griese 1.00
3 Archie Manning .30
4 Harold Carmichael .30
5 Wesley Walker .30
6 Richard Todd .30
7 Dan Fouts .90
8 Ken Stabler .60
9 Jack Youngblood .30
10 Jim Zorn .30
11 Tony Dorsett 1.50
12 Lee Roy Selmon .30
13 Russ Francis .30
14 John Stallworth .30
15 Terry Bradshaw 1.50
16 Joe Theismann 1.00
17 Ottis Anderson .30
18 John Jefferson .30
19 Jack Ham .30
20 Joe Greene .30
21 Chuck Muncie .30
22 Ron Jaworski .30
23 John Hannah .30
24 Randy Gradishar .30
25 Jack Lambert .30
26 Ricky Bell .30
27 Drew Pearson .30
28 Rick Upchurch .30
29 Brad Van Pelt .30
30 Walter Payton 3.50

1981 Topps

Just one phrase describes this set: Joe Montana rookie. Other rookie cards in this set include Mark Gastineau, Art Monk, Billy Sims, Kellen Winslow, Joe Cribbs, Dwight Clark, Curtis Dickey and Charles White. The 528-card set is bordered in white. Around the photos is black piping which leads to a colored scroll at the bottom of the card showing the team and player. Super Action cards in this set - included along with the player's regular card - show the major stars in action. (Key: SA - Super Action, AP - All Pro)

NM/M

Complete Set (528): 185.00
Common Player: .06
Wax Pack (12 - '79 WR): 12.25
Wax Box (36): 350.00
Wax Pack (15): 15.00
Wax Box (36): 400.00
1 Passing Leaders .08
2 Receiving Leaders .40
3 Sack Leaders .08
4 Scoring Leaders .08
5 Interception Leaders .08
6 Punting Leaders .08
7 Don Calhoun .06
8 Jack Tatum .06
9 Reggie Rucker .06
10 Mike Webster (AP) .20
11 *Vince Evans* .70
12 Ottis Anderson .60
13 Leroy Harris .06
14 Gordon King .06
15 Harvey Martin .11
16 Johnny Lam Jones .11
17 Ken Greene .06
18 Frank Lewis .06
19 Seattle Seahawks Team .50
20 Lester Hayes (AP) .20
21 Uwe Von Schamann .06
22 Joe Washington .06
23 Louie Kelcher .06
24 Willie Miller .06
25 Steve Grogan .20
26 John Hill .06
27 Stan White .06
28 William Andrews (SA) .06
29 Clarence Scott .06
30 Leon Gray (AP) .06
31 Craig Colquitt .06
32 Doug Williams .20
33 Bob Breunig .06
34 Billy Taylor .06
35 Harold Carmichael .40
36 Ray Wersching .06
37 Dennis Johnson .06
38 Archie Griffin .11
39 Cullen Bryant, Billy Waddy, Nolan Cromwell, Jack Youngblood Los Angeles Rams Team .06
40 Gary Fencik (AP) .06
41 Lynn Dickey .11
42 Steve Bartkowski (SA) .06
43 Art Shell .40
44 Wilbur Jackson .06
45 Frank Corral .06
46 Ted McKnight .06
47 Joe Klecko .11
48 Dan Doornink .06
49 Doug Dieken .06
50 *Jerry Robinson* (AP) .40
51 Wallace Francis .06
52 Dave Preston .06
53 Jay Saldi .06
54 Rush Brown .06
55 Phil Simms 3.75
56 Nick Mike-Mayer .06
57 Washington Redskins Team 1.50
58 Mike Renfro .06
59 Ted Brown (SA) .06
60 Steve Nelson (AP) .06
61 Sidney Thornton .06
62 Kent Hill .06
63 Don Bessillieu .08
64 Fred Cook .06
65 Raymond Chester .06
66 Rick Kane .06
67 Mike Fuller .06
68 Dewey Selmon .08
69 *Charles White* .70
70 Jeff Van Note (AP) .06
71 Robert Newhouse .06
72 *Roynell Young* .15
73 Lynn Cain (SA) .06
74 Mike Friede .06
75 Earl Cooper .06
76 New Orleans Saints Team .11
77 Rick Danmeier .06
78 Darrol Ray .06
79 Gregg Bingham .06
80 John Hannah (AP) .30
81 Jack Thompson .06
82 Rick Upchurch .06
83 Mike Butler .06
84 Don Warren .20
85 Mark Van Eeghen .06
86 *J.T. Smith* .70
87 Herman Weaver .06
88 Terry Bradshaw (SA) .70
89 Charlie Hall .06
90 Donnie Shell .25
91 Ike Harris .06
92 Charlie Johnson .06
93 Rickey Watts .06
94 New England Patriots Team .11
95 Drew Pearson .45
96 Neil O'Donoghue .06
97 Conrad Dobler .06
98 Jewerl Thomas .06
99 Mike Barber .06
100 *Billy Sims* (AP) 1.25
101 Vern Den Herder .06
102 Greg Landry .11
103 Joe Cribbs (SA) .11
104 *Mark Murphy* .15
105 Chuck Muncie .06
106 Alfred Jackson .06
107 Chris Bahr .06
108 Gordon Jones .06
109 *Willie Harper* .08
110 Dave Jennings (AP) .06
111 Bennie Cunningham .06
112 Jerry Sisemore .06
113 Cleveland Browns Team .15
114 Rickey Young .06
115 Ken Anderson .60
116 Randy Gradishar .15
117 *Eddie Lee Ivery* .15
118 Wesley Walker .15
119 Chuck Foreman .15
120 Nolan Cromwell (AP) .15
121 Curtis Dickey (SA) .06
122 Wayne Morris .06
123 Greg Stemrick .06
124 Coy Bacon .06
125 Jim Zorn .15
126 Henry Childs .06
127 Checklist 1-132 .20
128 Len Walterscheid .06
129 Johnny Evans .06
130 Gary Barbaro (AP) .06
131 Jim Smith .06
132 New York Jets Team .11
133 Curtis Brown .06
134 D.D Lewis .06
135 Jim Plunkett .40
136 Nat Moore .06
137 Don McCauley .06
138 Tony Dorsett (SA) .60
139 Julius Adams .06
140 Ahmad Rashad (AP) .40
141 Rich Saul .06
142 Ken Fantetti .06
143 Kenny Johnson .06
144 Clark Gaines .06
145 Mark Moseley .06
146 *Vernon Perry* .11
147 Jerry Sherk .06
148 Freddie Solomon .06
149 Jerry Sherk .06
150 *Kellen Winslow* (AP) 7.50
151 Green Bay Packers Team .20
152 Ross Browner .06
153 Dan Fouts (SA) .45
154 Woody Peoples .06
155 Jack Lambert .70
156 Mike Dennis .06
157 Rafael Septien .06
158 Archie Manning .15
159 Don Hasselbeck .06
160 Alan Page (AP) .40
161 Arthur Whittington .06
162 Billy Waddy .06
163 Horace Belton .06
164 Luke Prestridge .06
165 Joe Theismann .60
166 Morris Towns .06
167 Dave Brown .06
168 Ezra Johnson .06
169 Tampa Bay Bucaneers Team .08
170 Joe DeLamielleure (AP) .06
171 Earnest Gray (SA) .06
172 Mike Thomas .06
173 Jim Haslett .06
174 *David Woodley* .08
175 Al Bubba Baker .15
176 *Nesby Glasgow* .15
178 Ton Brahaney .06
179 Herman Edwards .06
180 *Junior Miller* (AP) .15
181 Richard Wood .06
182 Lenvil Elliott .06
183 Sammie White .15
184 Russell Erxleben .06
185 Ed "Too Tall" Jones .60
186 Ray Guy (SA) .06
187 Haven Moses .06
188 New York Giants Team .15
189 David Whitehurst .06
190 John Jefferson (AP) .15
191 Terry Beeson .06
192 *Dan Ross* .20
193 Dave Williams .06
194 *Art Monk* 9.00
195 Roger Wehrli .06
196 Rickey Feacher .06
197 Tony Nathan, Gerald Small, Kim Bokamper, A.J. Duhe Miami Dolphins Team .06
198 Carl Roaches .06
199 Cilly Campfield .06
200 Ted Hendricks (AP) .11
201 *Fred Smerlas* .60
202 Walter Payton (SA) 1.50
203 Luther Bradley .06
204 Herbert Scott .06
205 Jack Youngblood .20
206 Danny Pittman .06
207 Carl Roaches, Mike Barber, Jack Tatum, Jesse Baker, Robert Brazile Houston Oilers Team .06
208 Vagas Ferguson .06
209 Mark Dennard .06
210 Lemar Parrish (AP) .06
211 Bruce Harper .06
212 Ed Simonini .06
213 *Nick Lowery* .70
214 *Kevin House* .15
215 *Mike Kenn* 1.25
216 *Joe Montana* 160.00
217 Joe Senser .06
218 Lester Hayes (SA) .06
219 Gene Upshaw .15
220 Franco Harris 1.25
221 Ron Bolton .06
222 Charles Alexander .06
223 Matt Robinson .06
224 Ray Oldham .06
225 George Martin .06
226 Buffalo Bills Team .15
227 Tony Franklin .06
228 George Cumby .06
229 Butch Johnson .06
230 Mike Haynes (AP) .06
231 Rob Carpenter .06
232 Steve Fuller .06
233 John Sawyer .06
234 Kenny King (SA) .06
235 Jack Ham .45
236 Jimmy Rogers .06
237 Bob Parsons .06
238 *Marty Lyons* .40
239 Pat Tilley .06
240 Dennis Harrah (AP) .06
241 Thom Darden .06
242 Rolf Benirschke .06
243 Gerald Small .06
244 Atlanta Falcons Team .11
245 Roger Carr .06
246 Sherman White .06
247 Ted Brown .06
248 Matt Cavanaugh .06
249 John Dutton .06
250 Bill Bergey (AP) .11
251 Jim Allen .06
252 Mike Nelms (SA) .06
253 Tom Blanchard .06
254 Ricky Thompson .06
255 John Matuszak .06
256 Randy Grossman .06
257 Ray Griffin .06
258 Lynn Cain .06
259 Checklist 133-164 .20
260 Mike Pruitt (AP) .06
261 Chris Ward .06
262 Fred Steinfort .06
263 James Owens .06
264 Chicago Bears Team 1.25
265 Dan Fouts 1.25
266 Arnold Morgado .06
267 John Jefferson (SA) .06
268 Bill Lenkaitis .06
269 James Jones .06
270 Brad Van Pelt .06
271 Steve Largent 1.25
272 Elvin Bethea .06
273 Cullen Bryant .06
274 Gary Danielson .06
275 Tony Galbreath .06
276 Dave Butz .15
277 Steve Mike-Mayer .06
278 Ron Johnson .06
279 Tom DeLeone .06
280 Ron Jaworski .15
281 Mel Gray .06
282 San Diego Chargers Team .11
283 Mark Brammer .06
284 Alfred Jenkins (SA) .06
285 Greg Buttle .06
286 Randy Hughes .06
287 Delvin Williams .06
288 Brian Baschnagel .06
289 Gary Jeter .06
290 Stanley Morgan (AP) .40
291 Gerry Ellis .06
292 Al Richardson .06
293 Jimmie Giles .06
294 Dave Jennings (SA) .06
295 Wilbert Montgomery .11
296 Dave Pureifory .06
297 Greg Hawthorne .06
298 Dick Ambrose .06
299 Terry Hermeling .06
300 Danny White .30
301 Ken Burrough .06
302 Paul Hofer .06
303 Denver Broncos Team .11
304 Eddie Payton .06
305 Isaac Curtis .06
306 Benny Ricardo .06
307 Riley Odoms .06
308 Bob Chandler .06
309 Larry Heater .06
310 *Art Still* (AP) .40
311 Harold Jackson .15
312 Charlie Joiner (SA) .20
313 Jeff Nixon .06
314 Aundra Thompson .06
315 Richard Todd .08
316 *Dan Hampton* 3.00
317 Doug Marsh .06
318 Louie Giammona .06
319 San Francisco 49ers Team .40
320 Manu Tuiasosopo .06
321 Rich Milot .06
322 Mike Guman .06
323 Bob Kuechenberg .06
324 Tom Skladany .06
325 Dave Logan .06
326 Bruce Laird .06
327 James Jones (SA) .06
328 Joe Danelo .06
329 *Kenny King* .15
330 Pat Donovan (Ap) .06
331 Earl Cooper Record: .08
332 John Jefferson Record: .08
333 Kenny King Record: .08
334 Rod Martin Record: .08
335 Jim Plunkett Record: .08
336 Bill Thompson Record: .08
337 John Cappelletti .08
338 Detroit Lions Team .15
339 Don Smith .06
340 Rod Perry (AP) .06
341 David Lewis .06
342 *Mark Gastineau* .60
343 Steve Largent (SA) .60
344 Charley Young .06
345 Toni Fritsch .06
346 Matt Blair .06
347 Don Bass .06
348 Jim Jensen .15
349 Karl Lorch .06
350 Brian Sipe (AP) .15
351 Theo Bell .06

352 Sam Adams .06
353 Paul Coffman .06
354 Eric Harris .06
355 Tony Hill .15
356 J.T. Turner .06
357 Frank LeMaster .06
358 Jim Jodat .06
359 Oakland Raiders Team .20
360 *Joe Cribbs* (AP) .70
361 James Lofton (SA) .70
362 Dexter Bussey .06
363 Bobby Jackson .06
364 Steve DeBerg .70
365 Ottis Anderson 1.25
366 Tom Myers .06
367 John James .06
368 Reese McCall .06
369 Jack Reynolds .06
370 Gary Jonson (AP) .06
371 Jimmy Cefalo .06
372 Horace Ivory .06
373 Garo Yepremian .06
374 Brian Kelley .06
375 Terry Bradshaw 2.00
376 Dallas Cowboys Team .40
377 Randy Logan .06
378 Tim Wilson .06
379 Archie Manning (SA) .06
380 Revie Sorey (AP) .06
381 Randy Holloway .06
382 Henry Lawrence .06
383 Pat McInally .06
384 Kevin Long .06
385 Louis Wright .06
386 Leonard Thompson .06
387 Jan Stenerud .15
388 *Raymond Butler* .15
389 Checklist 265-396 .06
390 Steve Bartkowski (Ap) .15
391 Clarence Harmon .06
392 Wilbert Montgomery (SA) .06
393 Billy Joe DuPree .15
394 Ted McKnight, Henry Marshall, Gary Barbaro, Art Still Kansas City Chiefs Team .06
395 Earnest Gray .06
396 Ray Hamilton .06
397 Brenard Wilson .06
398 Calvin Hill .08
399 Robin Cole .06
400 Walter Payton (AP) 7.50
401 Jim Hart .15
402 Ron Yary .06
403 Cliff Branch .30
404 Roland Hooks .06
405 Ken Stabler .70
406 Chuck Ramsey .06
407 Mike Nelms .06
408 Ron Jaworski (SA) .06
409 James Hunter .06
410 Lee Roy Selmon .15
411 Curtis Dickey, Roger Carr, Bruce Laird, Mike Barnes Baltimore Colts Team .06
412 Henry Marshall .06
413 Preston Pearson .06
414 Richard Bishop .06
415 Greg Pruitt .06
416 Matt Bahr .15
417 Tony Mullady .06
418 Glen Edwards .06
419 Sam McCullum .06
420 Stan Walters (AP) .06
421 George Roberts .06
422 *Dwight Clark* 3.00
423 *Pat Thomas* .08
424 Bruce Harper (SA) .06
425 Craig Morton .15
426 Derrick Gaffney .06
427 Pete Johnson .06
428 Wes Chandler .40
429 Burgess Owens .06
430 James Lofton (AP) 2.75
431 Tony Reed .06
432 Minnesota Vikings Team .30
433 *Ron Springs* .08
434 Tim Fox .06
435 Ozzie Newsome 2.25
436 Steve Furness .06
437 Will Lewis .06
438 Mike Hartenstine .06
439 John Bunting .06
440 *Eddie Murray* 1.50
441 Mike Pruitt (SA) .06
442 Larry Swider .06
443 Steve Freeman .06
444 Bruce Hardy .06
445 Pat Haden .15
446 *Curtis Dickey* .15
447 Doug Wilkerson .06
448 Alfred Jenkins .06
449 Dave Dalby .06
450 Robert Brazile (AP) .06
451 Bobby Hammond .06
452 Raymond Clayborn .06
453 Jim Miller .06
454 Roy Simmons .06
455 Charlie Waters .15
456 Ricky Bell .06
457 Ahmad Rashad (SA) .20
458 Don Cockroft .06
459 Keith Krepfle .06
460 Marvin Powell (AP) .06
461 Tommy Kramer .20
462 Jim LeClair .06
463 Freddie Scott .06
464 Rob Lytle .06
465 Johnnie Gray .06
466 *Doug France* .11
467 *Carlos Carson* .15
468 St. Louis Cardinals Team .15
469 Efren Herrera .06
470 Randy White (AP) .60
471 Richard Caster .06
472 Andy Johnson .06
473 Billy Sims (SA) .20
474 Joe Lavender .06
475 Harry Carson .30
476 John Stallworth .60
477 Bob Thomas .06
478 Keith Wright .06
479 Ken Stone .06
480 Carl Hariston (AP) .06
481 Reggie McKenzie .06
482 Bob Griese .70
483 Mike Bragg .06
484 Scott Dierking .06
485 David Hill .06
486 Brian Sipe (SA) .06
487 Rod Martin .20
488 Pete Johnson, Dan Ross, Louis Breeden, Eddie Edwards Cincinnati Bengals Team .06
489 Preston Dennard .06
490 John Smith (AP) .06
491 Mike Reinfeldt .06
492 Ron Jaworski NFC Championship .06
493 Jim Plunkett AFC Championship .06
494 Jim Plunkett, King Super Bowl XV .30
495 Joe Greene .70
496 Charlie Joiner .45
497 Rolland Lawrence .06
498 Bubba Baker (SA) .06
499 Brad Dusek .06
500 Tony Dorsett 2.00
501 Robin Earl .06
502 Theotis Brown .06
503 Joe Ferguson .11
504 Bealsey Reece .06
505 Lyle Alzado .15
506 *Tony Nathan* .30
507 Wilbert Montgomery, Charlie Smith, Brenard Wilson, Claude Humphrey Philadelphia Eagles Team .06
508 Herb Orvis .06
509 Clarence Williams .06
510 Ray Guy (AP) .20
511 Jeff Komlo .06
512 Freddie Solomon (SA) .06
513 Tim Mazzetti .06
514 Elvis Peacock .06
515 Russ Francis .06
516 Roland Harper .06
517 Checklist 397-528 .20
518 Billy Johnson .06
519 Dan Dierdorf .30
520 Fred Dean (AP) .06
521 Jerry Butler .06
522 Ron Saul .06
523 Charlie Smith .06
524 Kellen Winslow (SA) 2.25
525 Bert Jones .15
526 Pittsburgh Steelers Team .60
527 Duriel Harris .06
528 William Andrews .20

1981 Topps Red Border Stickers

These stickers came in their own little containers and measure 1-15/16" x 2-9/16". Each of the 28 NFL teams is represented in the set, which features red borders on the front, framing a color photo. The player's name and position are also listed. The sticker back has the sticker number, player name, position and team, biographical information and instructions on how to apply the sticker.

NM/M

Complete Set (28): 15.00
Common Player: .30
1 Steve Bartkowski .70
2 Bert Jones .70
3 Joe Cribbs .45
4 Walter Payton 3.75
5 Ross Browner .30
6 Brian Sipe .60
7 Tony Dorsett 2.00
8 Randy Gradishar .45
9 Billy Sims .70
10 James Lofton 1.25
11 Mike Barber .30
12 Art Still .30
13 Jack Youngblood .60
14 Dave Woodley .40
15 Ahmad Rashad .90
16 Russ Francis .40
17 Archie Manning .60
18 Dave Jennings .30
19 Richard Todd .40
20 Lester Hayes .45
21 Ron Jaworski .40
22 Franco Harris 1.50
23 Ottis Anderson .70
24 John Jefferson .40
25 Freddie Solomon .30
26 Steve Largent 2.75
27 Lee Roy Selmon .60
28 Art Monk 6.00

1981 Topps Stickers

These stickers, which measure 1-15/16" x 2-9/16", are numbered alphabetically by teams within divisions. The front has a color photo with a white frame, plus the sticker number. That number is also on the back, along with the player's name, position, team and instructions on how to apply the sticker. A sticker album was also made available as a mail-in offer. The album cover features a Buffalo Bills player.

NM/M

Complete Set (262): 18.50
Common Player: .04
1 Brian Sipe AFC Passing Leader .08
2 Dan Fouts AFC Passing Yardage Leader .40
3 John Jefferson AFC Receiving Yardage Leader .06
4 Bruce Harper AFC Kickoff Return Yardage Leader .04
5 J.T. Smith AFC Punt Return Yardage Leader .04
6 Luke Prestidge AFC Punting Leader .04
7 Lester Hayes AFC Interceptions Leader .04
8 Gary Johnson AFC Sacks Leader .04
9 Bert Jones .11
10 Fred Cook .04
11 Roger Carr .08
12 Greg Landry .06
13 Raymond Butler .06
14 Bruce Laird .04
15 Ed Simonini .04
16 Curtis Dickey .08
17 Joe Cribbs .08
18 Joe Ferguson .11
19 Ben Williams .04
20 Jerry Butler .06
21 Roland Hooks .04
22 Fred Smerlas .06
23 Frank Lewis .04
24 Mark Brammer .04
25 Dave Woodley .06
26 Nat Moore .08
27 Uwe Von Schamann .04
28 Vern Den Herder .04
29 Tony Nathan .08
30 Duriel Harris .06
31 Don McNeal .04
32 Delvin Williams .04
33 Stanley Morgan .11
34 John Hannah .11
35 Horace Ivory .04
36 Steve Nelson .04
37 Steve Grogan .11
38 Vagas Ferguson .08
39 John Smith .04
40 Mike Haynes .09
41 Mark Gastineau .11
42 Wesley Walker .11
43 Joe Klecko .08
44 Chris Ward .04
45 Johnny Lam Jones .06
46 Marvin Powell .06
47 Richard Todd .11
48 Greg Buttle .06
49 Eddie Edwards .04
50 Dan Ross .06
51 Ken Anderson .40
52 Ross Browner .06
53 Don Bass .06
54 Jim LeClair .04
55 Pete Johnson .06
56 Anthony Munoz .90
57 Brian Sipe .09
58 Mike Pruitt .08
59 Greg Pruitt .11
60 Thom Darden .04
61 Ozzie Newsome .30
62 Dave Logan .04
63 Lyle Alzado .11
64 Reggie Rucker .06
65 Robert Brazile .06
66 Mike Barber .06
67 Carl Roaches .08
68 Ken Stabler .25
69 Gregg Bingham .06
70 Mike Renfro .06
71 Leon Gray .04
72 Rob Carpenter .08
73 Franco Harris .40
74 Jack Lambert .25
75 Jim Smith .04
76 Mike Webster .11
77 Sidney Thornton .04
78 Joe Greene .30
79 John Stallworth .15
80 Tyrone McGriff .04
81 Randy Gradishar .09
82 Haven Moses .06
83 Riley Odoms .08
84 Matt Robinson .06
85 Craig Morton .09
86 Rulon Jones .06
87 Rick Upchurch .08
88 Jim Jensen .04
89 Art Still .09
90 J.T. Smith .09
91 Steve Fuller .04
92 Gary Barbaro .04
93 Ted McKnight .04
94 Bob Grupp .04
95 Henry Marshall .04
96 Mike Williams .04
97 Jim Plunkett .20
98 Lester Hayes .09
99 Cliff Branch .15
100 John Matuszak .08
101 Matt Millen .08
102 Kenny King .04
103 Ray Guy .11
104 Ted Hendricks .15
105 John Jefferson .09
106 Fred Dean .09
107 Dan Fouts .25
108 Charlie Joiner .20
109 Kellen Winslow .90
110 Gary Johnson .06
111 Mike Thomas .04
112 Louie Kelcher .09
113 Jim Zorn .09
114 Terry Beeson .04
115 Jacob Green .25
116 Steve Largent .90
117 Dan Doornink .04
118 Manu Tuiasosopo .04
119 John Sawyer .04
120 Jim Jodat .04
121 Walter Payton (All-Pro) 1.50
122 Brian Sipe (All-Pro) .20
123 Joe Cribbs (All-Pro) .20
124 James Lofton (All-Pro) .45
125 John Jefferson (All-Pro) .20
126 Leon Gray (All-Pro) .11
127 Joe DeLamielleure (All-Pro) .15
128 Mike Webster (All-Pro) .25
129 John Hannah (All-Pro) .25
130 Mike Kenn (All-Pro) .15
131 Kellen Winslow (All-Pro) 1.25
132 Lee Roy Selmon (All-Pro) .25
133 Randy White (All-Pro) .25
134 Gary Johnson (All-Pro) .11
135 Art Still (All-Pro) .15
136 Robert Brazile (All-Pro) .15
137 Nolan Cromwell (All-Pro) .15
138 Ted Hendricks (All-Pro) .40
139 Lester Hayes (All-Pro) .20
140 Randy Gradishar (All-Pro) .25
141 Lemar Parrish (All-Pro) .15
142 Donnie Shell (All-Pro) .15
143 Ron Jaworski NFC Passing Leader .09
144 Archie Manning NFC Passing Leader .15
145 Walter Payton NFC Rushing Yardage Leader .60
146 Billy Sims NFC Rushing Touchdowns Leader .20
147 James Lofton NFC Receiving Yardage Leader .20
148 Dave Jennings NFC Punting Leader .04
149 Nolan Cromwell NFC Interceptions Leader .06
150 Al (Bubba) Baker NFC Sacks Leader .06
151 Tony Dorsett .40
152 Harvey Martin .11
153 Danny White .20
154 Pat Donovan .04
155 Drew Pearson .11
156 Robert Newhouse .08
157 Randy White .30
158 Butch Johnson .08
159 Dave Jennings .04
160 Brad Van Pelt .04
161 Phil Simms .30
162 Mike Friede .04
163 Billy Taylor .06
164 Gary Jeter .06
165 George Martin .04
166 Earnest Gray .04
167 Ron Jaworski .11
168 Bill Bergey .08
169 Wilbert Montgomery .06
170 Charlie Smith .04
171 Jerry Robinson .06
172 Herman Edwards .04
173 Harold Carmichael .11
174 Claude Humphrey .08
175 Ottis Anderson .25
176 Jim Hart .11
177 Pat Tilley .06
178 Rush Brown .04
179 Tom Brahaney .04
180 Dan Dierdorf .20
181 Wayne Morris .04
182 Doug Marsh .04
183 Art Monk 2.25
184 Clarence Harmon .04
185 Lemar Parrish .09
186 Joe Theismann .25
187 Joe Lavender .04
188 Wilbur Jackson .04
189 Dave Butz .04
190 Coy Bacon .04
191 Walter Payton 1.25
192 Alan Page .11
193 Vince Evans .15
194 Roland Harper .06
195 Dan Hampton .60
196 Gary Fencik .06
197 Mike Hartenstine .04
198 Robin Earl .04
199 Billy Sims .20
200 Leonard Thompson .04
201 Jeff Komlo .06
202 Al (Bubba) Baker .08
203 Ed Murray .11
204 Dexter Bussey .04
205 Tom Ginn .04
206 Freddie Scott .06
207 James Lofton .40
208 Mike Butler .04
209 Lynn Dickey .09
210 Gerry Ellis .04
211 Edd Lee Ivery .08
212 Ezra Johnson .04
213 Paul Coffman .06
214 Aundra Thompson .04
215 Ahmad Rashad .20
216 Tommy Kramer .06
217 Matt Blair .06
218 Sammie White .06
219 Ted Brown .06
220 Joe Senser .06
221 Rickey Young .06
222 Randy Holloway .04
223 Lee Roy Selmon .11
224 Doug Williams .08
225 Ricky Bell .08
226 David Lewis .04
227 Gordon Jones .06
228 Dewey Selmon .06
229 Jimmie Giles .08
230 Mike Washington .04
231 William Andrews .11
232 Jeff Van Note .06
233 Steve Bartkowski .11
234 Junior Miller .06
235 Lynn Cain .06
236 Joel Williams .04
237 Alfred Jenkins .06
238 Kenny Johnson .04
239 Jack Youngblood .15
240 Elvis Peacock .06
241 Cullen Bryant .08
242 Dennis Harrah .04
243 Billy Waddy .04
244 Nolan Cromwell .08
245 Doug France .04
246 Johnnie Johnson .06
247 Archie Manning .20
248 Tony Galbreath .08
249 Wes Chandler .11
250 Stan Brock .04
251 Ike Harris .04
252 Russell Erxleben .04
253 Jimmy Rogers .04
254 Tom Myers .04
255 Dwight Clark .60
256 Earl Cooper .04
257 Steve DeBerg .20
258 Randy Cross .08
259 Freddie Solomon .06
260 Jim Miller .04
261 Charley Young .06
262 Bobby Leopold .04

1982 Topps

Topps' last 528-card set was issued in 1982, and the design was nearly a duplicate of the 1975 football set. Football helmets featuring the team's helmet design appeared on these cards for the first time. Also included in this set were in-action cards of top stars and a subset featuring NFL brother tandems. Cards are numbered alphabetically by team and by the last name of the player. Notable rookies in this set include Cris Collinsworth, Anthony Munoz, Freeman McNeil, George Rogers, Ronnie Lott, Lawrence Taylor and Neil Lomax. (Key: AP - All Pro, IA - In Action)

NM/M

Complete Set (528): 90.00
Common Player: .05
Wax Pack (15): 4.00
Wax Box (36): 120.00
1 Ken Anderson (RB) .50
2 Dan Fouts (RB) .50
3 LeRoy Irvin (RB) .10
4 Stump Mitchell (RB) .10
5 George Rogers (RB) .15
6 Dan Ross (RB) .10
7 Ken Anderson, Pete Johnson AFC Championship .15
8 Earl Cooper NFC Championship .15
9 Anthony Munoz Super Bowl XVI .75
10 Baltimore Colts Team .15
11 Raymond Butler .05
12 Roger Carr .05
13 Curtis Dickey .05
14 Zachary Dixon .05
15 Nesby Glasgow .05
16 Bert Jones .10
17 Bruce Laird .05
18 Reese McCall .05
19 Randy McMillan .05
20 Ed Simonini .05
21 Buffalo Bills Team .15
22 Mark Brammer .05
23 Curtis Brown .05
24 Jerry Butler .05
25 Mario Clark .05
26 Joe Cribbs .15
27 Joe Cribbs (IA) .05
28 Joe Ferguson .15
29 Jim Haslett .05
30 Frank Lewis (AP) .05
31 Frank Lewis (IA) .05
32 Shane Nelson .05
33 Charles Romes .05
34 Bill Simpson .05
35 Fred Smerlas .05
36 Cincinnati Bengals Team .15
37 Charles Alexander .05
38 Ken Anderson (AP) .50
39 Ken Anderson (IA) .20
40 Jim Breech .05
41 Jim Breech (IA) .05
42 Louis Breeden .05
43 Ross Browner .05
44 *Cris Collinsworth* 1.00
45 Cris Collinsworth (IA) .50
46 Isaac Curtis .05
47 Pete Johnson .05
48 Pete Johnson (IA) .05
49 Steve Kreider .05
50 Pat McInnaly (AP) .05
51 *Anthony Munoz* (AP) 7.00
52 Dan Ross .05
53 David Verser .05
54 Reggie Williams .05
55 Cleveland Browns Team .20
56 Lyle Alzado .20
57 Dick Ambrose .05
58 Ron Bolton .05
59 Steve Cox .05
60 Joe DeLamielleure .05
61 Tom DeLeone .05
62 Doug Dieken .05
63 Ricky Feacher .05
64 Don Goode .05
65 Robert L. Jackson .05
66 Dave Logan .05
67 Ozzie Newsome 1.50
68 Ozzie Newsome (IA) .75
69 Greg Pruitt .10
70 Mike Pruitt .05
71 Mike Pruitt (IA) .05
72 Reggie Rucker .05
73 Clarence Scott .05
74 Brian Sipe .10
75 Charles White .10
76 Denver Broncos Team .15
77 Rubin Carter .05
78 Steve Foley .05
79 Randy Gradishar .25
80 Tom Jackson .25
81 Craig Morton .25
82 Craig Morton (IA) .10
83 Riley Odoms .05
84 Rick Parros .05
85 Dave Preston .05
86 Tony Reed .05
87 Bob Swenson .05
88 Bill Thompson .05
89 Rick Upchurch .05
90 *Steve Watson* (AP) .25
91 Steve Watson (IA) .10
92 Houston Oilers Team .15
93 Mike Barber .05
94 Elvin Bethea .05
95 Gregg Bingham .05
96 Robert Brazile (AP) .05
97 Ken Burrough .05
98 Toni Fritsch .05
99 Leon Gray .05
100 *Gifford Nielsen* .15
101 Vernon Perry .05
102 Mike Reinfeldt .05
103 Mike Renfro .05
104 Carl Roaches (AP) .05
105 Ken Stabler 1.00
106 Greg Stemrick .05
107 J.C. Wilson .05
108 Tim Wilson .05
109 Kansas City Chiefs Team .15
110 Gary Barbaro (AP) .05
111 Brad Budde (AP) .05
112 *Joe Delaney* (AP) .25
113 Joe Delaney (IA) .10
114 Steve Fuller .05
115 Gary Green .05
116 James Hadnot .05
117 Eric Harris .05
118 Billy Jackson .05
119 Bill Kenney .05
120 Nick Lowery (AP) 1.50
121 Nick Lowery (IA) .60
122 Henry Marshall .05
123 J.T. Smith .25
124 Art Still .05
125 Miami Dolphins Team .15
126 Bob Baumhower (AP) .05
127 Glenn Blackwood .05
128 Jimmy Cefalo .05
129 A.J. Duhe .05
130 Andra Franklin .10
131 Duriel Harris .05
132 Nat Moore .05
133 Tony Nathan .05
134 Ed Newman .05
135 Earnie Rhone .05
136 Don Strock .05
137 Tommy Vigorito .05
138 Uwe Von Schamann .05
139 Uwe Von Schamann (IA) .05
140 David Woodley .05
141 New England Patriots Team .10
142 Julius Adams .05
143 Richard Bishop .05
144 Matt Cavanaugh .05
145 Raymond Clayborn .05
146 *Tony Collins* .20
147 Vagas Ferguson .05
148 Tim Fox .05
149 Steve Grogan .25
150 John Hannah (AP) .25
151 John Hannah (IA) .10
152 Don Hasselbeck .05
153 Mike Haynes .05
154 Harold Jackson .10
155 Andy Johnson .05
156 Stanley Morgan .10
157 Stanley Morgan (IA) .10
158 Steve Nelson .05
159 Rod Shoate .05
160 New York Jets Team .25
161 Dan Alexander .05
162 Mike Augustyniak .05
163 Jerome Barkum .05
164 Greg Buttle .05
165 Scott Dierking .05
166 Joe Fields .05
167 Mark Gastineau (AP) .20
168 Mark Gastineau (IA) .10
169 Bruce Harper .05
170 Johnny Lam Jones .05
171 Joe Klecko (AP) .10
172 Joe Klecko (IA) .05
173 Pat Leahy .05
174 Pat Leahy (IA) .05
175 Marty Lyons .10

176 *Freeman McNeil* 1.00
177 Marvin Powell AP .05
178 Chuck Ramsey .05
179 Darrol Ray .05
180 Abdul Salaam .05
181 Richard Todd .10
182 Richard Todd (IA) .05
183 Wesley Walker .20
184 Chris Ward .05
185 Oakland Raiders Team .15
186 Cliff Branch .25
187 Bob Chandler .05
188 Ray Guy .25
189 Lester Hayes (AP) .05
190 Ted Hendricks (AP) .05
191 Monte Jackson .05
192 Derrick Jensen .05
193 Kenny King .05
194 Rod Martin .05
195 John Matuszak .05
196 *Matt Millen* 1.25
197 Derrick Ramsey .05
198 Art Shell .40
199 Mark Van Eeghen .05
200 Arthur Whittington .05
201 *Marc Wilson* .20
202 Pittsburgh Steelers Team .50
203 Mel Blount (AP) .75
204 Terry Bradshaw 1.50
205 Terry Bradshaw (IA) .75
206 Craig Colquitt .05
207 Bennie Cunningham .05
208 Russell Davis .05
209 Gary Dunn .05
210 Jack Ham .75
211 Franco Harris .75
212 Franco Harris (IA) .50
213 Jack Lambert (AP) .75
214 Jack Lambert (IA) .50
215 *Mark Malone* .20
218 Jim Smith .05
219 John Stallworth .60
220 John Stallworth (IA) .30
221 David Trout .05
222 Mike Webster (AP) .20
223 San Diego Chargers Team .15
224 Rolf Bernirschke .05
225 Rolf Benirschke (IA) .05
226 *James Brooks* 1.00
227 Willie Buchanon .05
228 Wes Chandler .15
229 Wes Chandler (IA) .10
230 Dan Fouts 1.00
231 Dan Fouts (IA) .50
232 Gary Johnson (AP) .05
233 Charlie Joiner .40
234 Charlie Joiner (IA) .20
235 Louie Kelcher .05
236 Chuck Muncie (AP) .05
237 Chuck Muncie (IA) .05
238 George Roberts .05
239 Ed White .05
240 Doug Wilkerson (AP) .05
241 Kellen Winslow (AP) 2.00
242 Kellen Winslow IA (IA) 1.00
243 Seattle Seahawks Team .20
244 Theotis Brown .05
245 Don Doornink .05
246 John Harris .05
247 Efren Herrera .05
248 David Hughes .05
249 Steve Largent 1.75
250 Steve Largent (IA) .90
251 Sam McCullum .05
252 Sherman Smith .05
253 Manu Tuiasosopo .05
254 John Yarno .05
255 Jim Zorn .10
256 Jim Zorn (IA) .05
257 Joe Montana, Ken Anderson 2.00
258 Kellen Winslow, Dwight Clark Receiving Leaders .50
259 Joe Klecko, Curtis Greer Sack Leaders .10
260 Jim Breech, Nick Lowery, Ed Murray, Rafael Septien Scoring Leaders .10
261 John Harris, Everson Walls Interception Leaders .20
262 Pat McInally, Tom Skladany Punting Leaders .10
263 Chris Bahr, Matt Bahr Brothers: .10
264 Lyle Blackwood, Glenn Blackwood Brothers: .10
265 Pete Brock, Stan Brock Brothers: .10
266 Archie Griffin, Ray Griffin Brothers: .10
267 John Hannah, Charley Hannah Brothers: .20
268 Monte Jackson, Terry Jackson Brothers: .10
269 Eddie Payton, Walter Payton Brothers: 1.00
270 Dewey Selmon, Lee Roy Selmon Brothers: .10
271 Atlanta Falcons Team .15
272 Williams Andrews .05
273 William Anderws (IA) .05
274 Steve Bartkowski .25
275 Steve Bartkowski .05
276 Bobby Butler .05
277 Lynn Cain .05
278 Wallace Francis .05
279 Alfred Jackson .05
280 John James .05
281 Alfred Jenkins (AP) .05
282 Alfred Jenkins (IA) .05
283 Kenny Johnson .05
284 Mike Kenn (AP) .25
285 Fulton Kuykendall .05
286 Mike Luckhurst .05
287 Mick Luckhurst (IA) .05
288 Junior Miller .05
289 Al Richardson .05
290 R.C. Thielemann .05
291 Jeff Van Note .05
292 Chicago Bears Team .75
293 Brian Baschnagel .05
294 Robin Earl .05
295 Vince Evans .20
296 Gary Fencik (AP) .05
297 Dan Hampton 1.00
298 Noah Jackson .05
299 Ken Margerum .05
300 Jim Osborne .05
301 Bob Parsons .05
302 Walter Payton 7.00
303 Walter Payton IA (IA) 6.00
304 Revie Sorey .05
305 *Matt Suhey* .25
306 Rickey Watts .05
307 Dallas Cowboys Team .60
308 Bob Breunig .05
309 *Doug Cosbie* .25
310 Pat Donovan (AP) .05
311 Tony Dorsett (AP) 1.00
312 Tony Dorsett (IA) .60
313 Michael Downs .05
314 Billy Joe DuPree .15
315 John Dutton .05
316 Tony Hill .05
317 Butch Johnson .05
318 Ed "Too Tall" Jones (AP) .60
319 James Jones .05
320 Harvey Martin .15
321 Drew Pearson .40
322 Herbert Scott (AP) .05
323 Rafael Septien (AP) .05
324 Rafael Septien (IA) .05
325 Ron Springs .05
326 *Dennis Thurman* .10
327 *Everson Walls* .50
328 Everson Walls (IA) .25
329 Danny White .25
330 Danny White (IA) .10
331 Randy White (AP) .60
332 Randy White (IA) .25
333 Detroit Lions Team .15
334 Jim Allen .05
335 Al Bubba Baker .05
336 Dexter Bussey .05
337 Doug English (AP) .05
338 Ken Fantetti .05
339 William Gay .05
340 David Hill .05
341 *Eric Hipple* .10
342 Rick Kane .05
343 Ed Murray .40
344 Ed Murray (IA) .20
345 Ray Oldham .05
346 Dave Pureifory .05
347 Freddie Scott .05
348 Freddie Scott (IA) .05
349 Billy Sims (AP) .30
350 Billy Sims (IA) .15
351 Tom Skladany (AP) .05
352 Leonard Thompson .05
353 Stan White .05
354 Green Bay Packers Team .40
355 Paul Coffman .05
356 George Cumby .05
357 Lynn Dickey .10
358 Lynn Dickey (IA) .05
359 Gerry Ellis .05
360 Maurice Harvey .05
361 Harlan Huckleby .05
362 John Jefferson .20
363 Mark Lee .05
364 James Lofton (AP) 1.75
365 James Lofton (IA) .75
366 Jan Stenerud .25
367 Jan Stenerud (IA) .10
368 Rich Wingo .05
369 Los Angeles Rams Team .20
370 Frank Corral .05
371 Nolan Cromwell (AP) .25
372 Nolan Cromwell (IA) .10
373 Preston Dennard .05
374 Mike Fanning .05
375 Doug France .05
376 Mike Guman .05
377 Pat Haden .25
378 Dennis Harrah .05
379 *Drew Hill* 2.00
380 *LeRoy Irvin* .40
381 Cody Jones .05
382 Rod Perry .05
383 Rich Saul (AP) .05
384 Pat Thomas .05
385 Wendell Tyler .08
386 Wendell Tyler (IA) .05
387 Billy Waddy .05
388 Jack Youngblood .25
389 Minnesota Vikings Team .15
390 Matt Blair (AP) .05
391 Ted Brown .08
392 Ted Brown (IA) .05
393 Rick Danmeier .05
394 Tommy Kramer .25
395 Mark Mullaney .05
396 Eddie Payton .05
397 Ahmad Rashad .40
398 Joe Senser .08
399 Joe Senser (IA) .05
400 Sammy White .05
401 Sammy White (IA) .05
402 Ron Yary .05
403 Rickey Young .05
404 New Orleans Saints Team .50
405 Russell Erxleben .05
406 Elois Grooms .05
407 Jack Holmes .05
408 Archie Manning .25
409 Derland Moore .05
410 *George Rogers* 1.00
411 George Rogers (IA) .40
412 Toussaint Tyler .05
413 *Dave Waymer* .20
414 Wayne Wilson .05
415 New York Giants Team .15
416 *Scott Brunner* .10
417 Rob Carpenter .05
418 Harry Carson (AP) .25
419 Bill Currier .05
420 Joe Danelo .05
421 Joe Danelo (IA) .05
422 *Mark Haynes* .35
423 Terry Jackson .05
424 Dave Jennings .05
425 Gary Jeter .05
426 Brian Kelley .07
427 George Martin .05
428 Curtis McGriff .05
429 Bill Neill .05
430 Johnny Perkins .05
431 Beasley Reece .07
432 Gary Shirk .05
433 Phil Simms 1.50
434 *Lawrence Taylor* (AP) 30.00
435 Lawrence Taylor (IA) 10.00
436 Brad Van Pelt .05
437 Philadelphia Eagles Team .15
438 John Bunting .05
439 Billy Campfield .05
440 Harold Carmichael .25
441 Harold Carmichael (IA) .10
442 Herman Edwards .05
443 Tony Franklin .05
444 Tony Franklin (IA) .05
445 Carl Hariston .05
446 Dennis Harrison .05
447 Ron Jaworski .15
448 Charlie Johnson .05
449 Keith Krepfle .05
450 Frank LeMaster .05
451 Randy Logan .05
452 Wilbert Montgomery .07
453 Wilbert Montgomery (IA) .05
454 Hubert Oliver .05
455 Jerry Robinson .05
456 Jerry Robinson (IA) .05
457 Jerry Sisemore .05
458 Charlie Smith .05
459 Stan Walters .05
460 Brenard Wilson .05
461 Roynell Young (AP) .05
462 St. Louis Cardinals Team .25
463 Ottis Anderson 1.00
464 Ottis Anderson (IA) .60
465 Carl Birdsong .05
466 Rush Brown .05
467 Mel Gray .05
468 Ken Greene .05
469 Jim Hart .15
470 *E.J. Junior* .60
471 *Neil Lomax* .75
472 *Stump Mitchell* .40
473 Wayne Morris .05
474 Neil O'Donoghue .05
475 Pat Tilley .05
476 Pat Tilley (IA) .05
477 San Francisco 49ers Team .40
478 Dwight Clark 1.00
479 Dwight Clark (IA) .40
480 Earl Cooper .05
481 Randy Cross (AP) .05
482 Johnny Davis .05
483 Fred Dean .05
484 Fred Dean (IA) .05
485 *Dwight Hicks* .25
486 *Ronnie Lott* (AP) 15.00
487 Ronnie Lott IA (IA) 6.00
488 Joe Montana (AP) 35.00
489 Joe Montana IA (IA) 15.00
490 Ricky Patton .05
491 Jack Reynolds .05
492 Freddie Solomon .05
493 Ray Wersching .05
494 Charley Young .05
495 Tampa Bay Bucaneers Team .15
496 Cedric Brown .05
497 Neal Colzie .05
498 Jerry Eckwood .05
499 Jimmy Giles (AP) .05
500 *Hugh Green* .60
501 Kevin House .05
502 Kevin House (IA) .05
503 Cecil Johnson .05
504 James Owens .05
505 Lee Roy Selmon (AP) .15
506 Mike Washington .05
507 *James Wilder* .65
508 Doug Williams .25
509 Washington Redskins Team .75
510 Perry Brooks .05
511 Dave Butz .05
512 Wilbur Jackson .05
513 Joe Lavender .05
514 Terry Metcalf .15
515 Art Monk 4.00
516 Frank Pollard, Mark Moseley .05
517 Donnie Shell, Mark Murphy (AP) .05
518 Mike Neims (AP) .05
519 Lemar Parrish .05
520 John Riggins 1.00
521 Joe Theismann 1.00
522 Ricky Thompson .05
523 Don Warren .15
524 Joe Washington .05
525 Checklist 1-132 .25
526 Checklist 133-264 .25
527 Checklist 265-396 .25
528 Checklist 397-528 .25

1982 Topps "Coming Soon" Stickers

These stickers were inserted in 1982 Topps football card packs. They are 1-15/16" x 2-9/16", making them the same size as Topps' regular 1982 stickers. They also share the same card numbers, which is why the set is skip-numbered. The card number is on the back, along with the words "Coming Soon!" The fronts of the stickers are gold-bordered foil stickers.

NM/M

Complete Set (16): 5.00
Common Player: .10
5 Joe Montana MVP Super Bowl XVI 2.00
6 NFC Championship .10
9 Joe Montana Super Bowl XVI 1.50
71 Tommy Kramer .30
73 George Rogers .30
75 Tom Skladany .10
139 Nolan Cromwell .30
143 Jack Lambert .50
144 Lawrence Taylor 1.75
150 Billy Sims .40
154 Ken Anderson .50
159 John Hannah .40
160 Anthony Munoz .75
220 Ken Anderson .50
221 Dan Fouts .50
222 Frank Lewis .10

1982 Topps Stickers

These stickers follow the same format as the 1981 stickers, complete with an album featuring Joe Montana on the cover. However, these stickers have yellow borders and a 1982 copyright date on the back. Foil stickers were also produced again (#s 1-10, 70-77, 139-160, 220-227). Stickers 1 and 2 combine as a puzzle to form a picture of the San Francisco 49ers; 3 and 4 show Super Bowl theme art.

NM/M

Complete Set (288): 30.00
Common Player: .05
1 Super Bowl XVI (49er Team) .35
2 Super Bowl XVI (49er Team) .15
3 Super Bowl XVI (Theme Art Trophy) .15
4 Super Bowl XVI (Theme Art Trophy) .15
5 Joe Montana MVP Super Bowl XVI 3.50
6 1981 NFC Champions 49ers .15
7 Ken Anderson 1981 AFC Champions .25
8 Ken Anderson Super Bowl XVI .25
9 Joe Montana Super Bowl XVI 3.00
10 Super Bowl XVI (line blocking) .15
11 Steve Bartkowski .15
12 William Andrews .10
13 Lynn Cain .08
14 Wallace Francis .08
15 Alfred Jackson .08
16 Alfred Jenkins .10
17 Mike Kenn .08
18 Junior Miller .10
19 Vince Evans .10
20 Walter Payton 1.25
21 Dave Williams .05
22 Brian Baschnagel .05
23 Rickey Watts .05
24 Ken Margerum .08
25 Revie Sorey .05
26 Gary Fencik .05
27 Matt Suhey .08
28 Danny White .20
29 Tony Dorsett .50
30 Drew Pearson .25
31 Rafael Septien .08
32 Pat Donovan .05
33 Herbert Scott .05
34 Ed "Too Tall" Jones .20
35 Randy White .25
36 Tony Hill .08
37 Eric Hipple .08
38 Billy Sims .25
39 Dexter Bussey .05
40 Freddie Scott .08
41 David Hill .05
42 Ed Murray .10
43 Tom Skladany .05
44 Doug English .08
45 Al (Bubba) Baker .12
46 Lynn Dickey .12
47 Gerry Ellis .05
48 Harlan Huckleby .05
49 James Lofton .40
50 John Jefferson .08
51 Paul Coffman .05
52 Jan Stenerud .20
53 Rich Wingo .05
54 Wendell Tyler .10
55 Preston Dennard .05
56 Billy Waddy .05
57 Frank Corral .05
58 Jack Youngblood .15
59 Pat Thomas .05
60 Rod Perry .08
61 Nolan Cromwell .10
62 Tommy Kramer .10
63 Rickey Young .08
64 Ted Brown .05
65 Ahmad Rashad .25
66 Sammie White .08
67 Joe Senser .05
68 Ron Yary .08
69 Matt Blair .08
70 Joe Montana NFC Passing Leader 3.50
71 Tommy Kramer NFC Passing Yardage Leader .20
72 Alfred Jenkins NFC Receiving Yardage Leader .15
73 George Rogers NFC Rushing Yardage Leader .25
74 Wendell Tyler NFC Rushing Touchdowns Leader .30
75 Tom Skladany NFC Punting Leader .15
76 Everson Walls NFC Interceptions Leader .35
77 Curtis Greer MFC Sacks Leader .15
78 Archie Manning .25
79 Dave Waymer .05
80 George Rogers .20
81 Jack Holmes .05
82 Toussaint Tyler .05
83 Wayne Wilson .05
84 Russell Erxleben .05
85 Elois Grooms .05
86 Phil Simms .20
87 Scott Brunner .10
88 Rob Carpenter .08
89 Johnny Perkins .05
90 Dave Jennings .05
91 Harry Carson .12
92 Lawrence Taylor 2.50
93 Beasley Reece .05
94 Mark Haynes .05
95 Ron Jaworski .12
96 Wilbert Montgomery .08
97 Hubert Oliver .05
98 Harold Carmichael .10
99 Jerry Robinson .08
100 Stan Walters .05
101 Charlie Johnson .05
102 Roynell Young .05
103 Tony Franklin .05
104 Neil Lomax .15
105 Jim Hart .15
106 Ottis Anderson .20
107 Stump Mitchell .12
108 Pat Tilley .08
109 Rush Brown .05
110 E.J. Junior .05
111 Ken Greene .05
112 Mel Gray .08
113 Joe Montana 2.50
114 Ricky Patton .05
115 Earl Cooper .05
116 Dwight Clark .25
117 Freddie Solomon .08
118 Randy Cross .10
119 Fred Dean .08
120 Ronnie Lott 1.75
121 Dwight Hicks .08
122 Doug Williams .15
123 Jerry Eckwood .08
124 James Owens .08
125 Kevin House .08
126 Jimmie Giles .05
127 Charley Hannah .05
128 Lee Roy Selmon .15
129 Hugh Green .12
130 Joe Theismann .30
131 Joe Washington .08
132 John Riggins .25
133 Art Monk .50
134 Ricky Thompson .05
135 Don Warren .08
136 Perry Brooks .05
137 Mike Nelms .05
138 Mark Moseley .05
139 Nolan Cromwell (All-Pro) .20
140 Dwight Hicks (All-Pro) .15
141 Ronnie Lott (All-Pro) 2.00
142 Harry Carson (All-Pro) .20
143 Jack Lambert (All-Pro) .40
144 Lawrence Taylor (All-Pro) 2.50
145 Mel Blount (All-Pro) .30
146 Joe Klecko (All-Pro) .15
147 Randy White (All-Pro) .35
148 Doug English (All-Pro) .10
149 Fred Dean (All-Pro) .20
150 Billy Sims (All-Pro) .25
151 Tony Dorsett (All-Pro) .75
152 James Lofton (All-Pro) .75
153 Alfred Jenkins (All-Pro) .20
154 Ken Anderson (All-Pro) .35
155 Kellen Winslow (All-Pro) .50
156 Marvin Powell (All-Pro) .10
157 Randy Cross (All-Pro) .20
158 Mike Webster (All-Pro) .30
159 John Hannah (All-Pro) .30
160 Anthony Munoz (All-Pro) 1.25
161 Curtis Dickey .08
162 Randy McMillan .08
163 Roger Carr .08
164 Raymond Butler .05
165 Reese McCall .05
166 Ed Simonini .05
167 Herb Oliver .05
168 Nesby Glasgow .05
169 Joe Ferguson .08
170 Joe Cribbs .08
171 Jerry Butler .08
172 Frank Lewis .08
173 Mark Brammer .05
174 Fred Smerlas .10
175 Jim Haslett .05
176 Charles Alexander .05
177 Bill Simpson .05
178 Ken Anderson .20
179 Charles Alexander .05
180 Pete Johnson .05
181 Isaac Curtis .05
182 Cris Collinsworth .50
183 Pat McInally .08
184 Anthony Munoz .50
185 Louis Breeden .05
186 Jim Breech .10
187 Brian Sipe .10
188 Charles White .10
189 Mike Pruitt .08
190 Reggie Rucker .12
191 Dave Logan .05
192 Ozzie Newsome .30
193 Dick Ambrose .05
194 Joe DeLamielleure .05
195 Ricky Feacher .05
196 Craig Morton .12
197 Dave Preston .05
198 Rick Parros .05
199 Rick Upchurch .08
200 Steve Watson .10
201 Riley Odoms .08
202 Randy Gradishar .10
203 Steve Foley .05
204 Ken Stabler .30
205 Gifford Nielsen .08
206 Tim Wilson .05
207 Ken Burrough .10
208 Mike Renfro .10
209 Greg Stemrick .05
210 Robert Brazile .08
211 Gregg Bingham .08
212 Steve Fuller .08
213 Bill Kenney .08
214 Joe Delaney .20
215 Henry Marshall .05
216 Nick Lowery .10
217 Art Still .08
218 Gary Green .05
219 Gary Barbaro .05
220 Ken Anderson AFC PAssing Leader .35
221 Dan Fouts AFC PAssing Yardage Leader .50
222 Frank Lewis AFC Receiving Yardage Leader .20
223 James Brooks AFC Kickoff Return Yardage Leader .75
224 Chuck Muncie AFC Rushing Touchdowns Leader .20
225 Pat McInally AFC Punting Leader .20
226 John Harris AFC Interceptions Leader .20
227 Joe Klecko AFC Sacks Leader .20
228 Dave Woodley .08
229 Tony Nathan .08
230 Andra Franklin .05
231 Nat Moore .08
232 Duriel Harris .08
233 Uwe Von Schamann .05
234 Bob Baumhower .10
235 Glenn Blackwood .10
236 Tommy Vigorito .05
237 Steve Grogan .12
238 Matt Cavanaugh .08
239 Tony Collins .08
240 Vagas Ferguson .10
241 John Smith .05
242 Stanley Morgan .10
243 John Hannah .15
244 Steve Nelson .05
245 Don Hasselback .05
246 Richard Todd .12
247 Bruce Harper .05
248 Wesley Walker .12
249 Jerome Barkum .08
250 Marvin Powell .08
251 Mark Gastineau .15
252 Joe Klecko .08
253 Darrol Ray .05
254 Marty Lyons .08
255 Marc Wilson .10
256 Kenny King .08
257 Mark Van Eeghen .08
258 Cliff Branch .12
259 Bob Chandler .08
260 Ray Guy .15
261 Ted Hendricks .20
262 Lester Hayes .20
263 Terry Bradshaw .60
264 Franco Harris .35
265 John Stallworth .15
266 Jim Smith .05
267 Mike Webster .12
268 Jack Lambert .20
269 Mel Blount .15
270 Donnie Shell .12
271 Bennie Cunningham .08
272 Dan Fouts .40
273 Chuck Muncie .10
274 james Brooks .65
275 Charlie Joiner .20
276 Wes Chandler .12
277 Kellen Winslow .25
278 Doug Wilkerson .05
279 Gary Johnson .08
280 Rolf Benirschke .08
281 Jim Zorn .12
282 Theotis Brown .08
283 Dan Doornink .05
284 Steve Largent 1.25
285 Sam McCullum .08
286 Efren Herrera .05
287 Manu Tuiasosopo .05
288 John Harris .05

1983 Topps

Presumably adjusting for an increase in the size of its baseball card set, Topps cut the number of cards in its annual football card set in 1983 from 528 to 396. Because Topps still printed the cards on four sheets, one-third of the cards were double-printed - accounting for some of the apparent price discrepancies in the list below. Cards in the set are bordered in white and feature the team name in white block letters at the top of the card. The player's name and position are found in a white rectangle near the bottom. All-Pro designations are found above this box. This set is notable for several rookies: Gerald Riggs, Jim McMahon, Mike Singletary, Roy Green and Marcus Allen. It also features Lawrence Taylor's second-year card. Cards are again listed alphabetically by city name and by player name. (Key: PB - Pro Bowl)

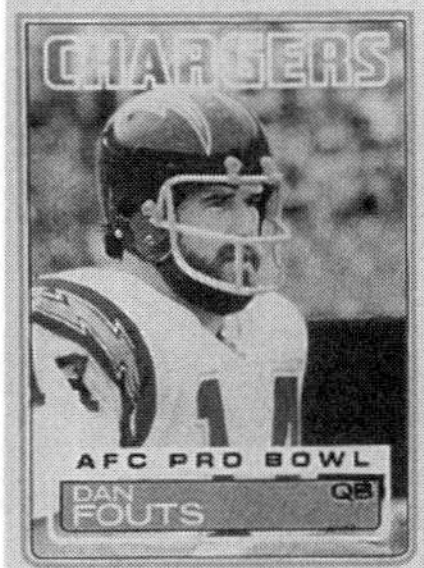

NM/M
Complete Set (396): 50.00
Common Player: .05
Wax Pack (13+1): 2.50
Wax Box (36): 65.00
1 Ken Anderson (RB) .25
2 Tony Dorsett (RB) .40
3 Dan Fouts (RB) .20
4 Joe Montana (RB) 4.00
5 Mark Moseley (RB) .10
6 Mike Nelms (RB) .10
7 Darrol Ray (RB) .10
8 John Riggins (RB) .25
9 Fulton Walker (RB) .10
10 John Riggins NFC Championship .10
11 AFC Championship .10
12 John Riggins Super Bowl XVII .25
13 William Andrews Atlanta Falcons Team .10
14 William Andrews (PB) .05
15 Steve Bartkowski .25
16 Bobby Butler .05
17 Buddy Curry .05
18 Alfred Jackson .05
19 Alfred Jenkins .05
20 Kenny Johnson .05
21 Mike Kenn (PB) .05
22 Mick Luckhurst .05
23 Junior Miller .05
24 Al Richardson .05
25 *Gerald Riggs* .75
26 R.C. Thielemann (PB) .05
27 Jeff Van Note (PB) .05
28 Walter Payton (TL) .75
29 Brian Baschnagel .05
30 Dan Hampton (PB) .50
31 Mike Hartenstine .05
32 Noah Jackson .05
33 *Jim McMahon* 4.00
34 Emery Moorehead .05
35 Bob Parsons .05
36 Walter Payton 7.00
37 Terry Schmidt .05
38 *Mike Singletary* 7.00
39 Matt Suhey .05
40 Rickey Watts .05
41 *Otis Wilson* .15
42 Tony Dorsett (TL) .25
43 Bob Breunig (PB) .05
44 Doug Cosbie .05
45 Pat Donovan (PB) .05
46 Tony Dorsett (PB) .75
47 Tony Hill .05
48 Butch Johnson .05
49 Ed "Too Tall" Jones (PB) .20
50 Harvey Martin .10
51 Drew Pearson .25
52 Rafael Septien .05
53 Ron Springs .05
54 Dennis Thurman .05
55 Everson Walls (PB) .40
56 Danny White (PB) .15
57 Randy White (PB) .60
58 Billy Sims Detroit Lions Team .05
59 Al "Bubba" Baker .05
60 Dexter Bussey .05
61 Gary Danielson .05
62 Keith Dorney (PB) .05
63 Doug English (PB) .05
64 Ken Fantetti .05
65 Alvin Hall .05
66 David Hill .05
67 Eric Hipple .05
68 Ed Murray .10
69 Freddie Scott .05
70 Billy Sims (PB) .10
71 Tom Skladany .05
72 Leonard Thompson .05
73 Bobby Watkins .05
74 Eddie Lee Ivery Green Bay Packers Team .10
75 John Anderson .05
76 Paul Coffman (PB) .05
77 Lynn Dickey .05
78 Mike Douglass .05
79 Eddie Lee Ivery .05
80 John Jefferson (PB) .10
81 Ezra Johnson .05
82 Mark Lee .05
83 James Lofton (PB) 1.00
84 Larry McCarren (PB) .05
85 Jan Stenerud .10
86 Wendell Tyler Los Angeles Rams Team .10
87 Bill Bain .05
88 Nolan Cromwell (PB) .05
89 Preston Dennard .05
90 Vince Ferragamo .05
91 Mike Guman .05
92 Kent Hill (PB) .05
93 Mike Lansford .05
94 Rod Perry .05
95 Pat Thomas .05
96 Jack Youngblood .15
97 Ted Brown Minnesota Vikings Team .10
98 Matt Blair (PB) .05
99 Ted Brown .05
100 Greg Coleman .05
101 Randy Holloway .05
102 Tommy Kramer .10
103 Doug Martin .05
104 Mark Mullaney .05
105 Joe Senser .05
106 Willie Teal .05
107 Sammy White .05
108 Rickey Young .05
109 George Rogers New Orleans Saints Team .10
110 *Stan Brock* .40
111 Bruce Clark .05
112 Russell Erxleben .05
113 Russell Gary .05
114 Jeff Groth .05
115 John Hill .05
116 Derland Moore .05
117 George Rogers (PB) .20
118 Ken Stabler .75
119 Wayne Wilson .05
120 Butch Woolfolk New York Giants Team .10
121 Scott Brunner .05
122 Rob Carpenter .05
123 Harry Carson (PB) .10
124 Joe Danelo .05
125 Earnest Gray .05
126 Mark Haynes (PB) .05
127 Terry Jackson .05
128 Dave Jennings (PB) .05
129 Brian Kelley .05
130 George Martin .05
131 Tom Mullady .05
132 Johnny Perkins .05
133 Lawrence Taylor (PB) 5.00
134 Brad Van Pelt .05
135 Butch Woolfolk .05
136 Wilbert Montgomery Philadelphia Eagles Team .10
137 Harold Carmichael .25
138 Herman Edwards .05
139 Tony Franklin .05
140 Carl Hairston .05
141 Dennis Harrison (PB) .05
142 Ron Jaworski .10
143 Frank LeMaster .05
144 Wilbert Montgomery .07
145 Guy Morriss .05
146 Jerry Robinson .05
147 Max Runager .05
148 Ron Smith .05
149 John Spagnola .05
150 Stan Walters .05
151 Roynell Young .05
152 Ottis Anderson St. Louis Cardinals Team .20
153 Ottis Anderson .40
154 Carl Birdsong .05
155 Dan Dierdorf .15
156 *Roy Green* .75
157 Elois Grooms .05
158 Neil Lomax .10
159 Wayne Morris .05
160 James Robbins .05
161 *Luis Sharpe* .20
162 Pat Tilley .05
163 Jeff Moore San Francisco 49ers Team .15
164 Dwight Clark (PB) .40
165 Randy Cross (PB) .05
166 Russ Francis .05
167 Dwight Hicks (PB) .05
168 Ronnie Lott (PB) 3.00
169 Joe Montana 9.00
170 Jeff Moore .05
171 *Renaldo Nehemiah* .10
172 Freddie Solomon .05
173 Ray Wersching .05
174 James Wilder Tampa Bay Buccaneers Team .10
175 Cedric Brown .05
176 Bill Capece .05
177 Neal Colzie .05
178 Jimmie Giles (PB) .07
179 Hugh Green (PB) .07
180 Kevin House .05
181 James Owens .05
182 Lee Roy Selmon (PB) .07
183 Mike Washington .05
184 James Wilder .10
185 Doug Williams .10
186 John Riggins Washington Redskins Team .25
187 Jeff Bostic .05
188 Charlie Brown (PB) .05
189 Vernon Dean .05
190 *Joe Jacoby* .75
191 *Dexter Manley* .25
192 Rich Milot .05
193 Art Monk 1.00
194 Mark Mosely (PB) .05
195 Mike Nelms (PB) .05
196 Neal Olkewicz .05
197 Tony Peters (PB) .05
198 John Riggins .60
199 Joe Theismann (PB) .60
200 Don Warren .05
201 Jeris White .05
202 Joe Theismann, Ken Anderson Passing Leaders .20
203 Dwight Clark, Kellen Winslow Receiving Leaders .10
204 Tony Dorsett, Freeman McNeil Rushing Leaders .40
205 Marcus Allen, Wendell Tyler Scoring Leaders .80
206 Everson Walls Interception Leaders .10
207 Carl Birdsong, Luke Prestridge Punting Leaders .10
208 Randy McMillan Baltimore Colts Team .10
209 Matt Bouza .05
210 Johnnie Cooks .05
211 Curtis Dickey .05
212 Nesby Glasgow .05
213 Derrick Hatchett .05
214 Randy McMillan .05
215 *Mike Pagel* .10
216 *Rohn Stark* .20
217 Donnell Thompson .05
218 Leo Wisniewski .05
219 Joe Cribbs Buffalo Bills Team .10
220 Curtis Brown .05
221 Jerry Butler .05
222 Greg Cater .05
223 Joe Cribbs .10
224 Joe Ferguson .10
225 Roosevelt Leaks .05
226 Frank Lewis .05
227 Eugene Marve .05
228 Fred Smerlas (PB) .08
229 Ben Williams (PB) .05
230 Pete Johnson Cincinnati Bengals Team .10
231 Charles Alexander .05
232 Ken Anderson (PB) .25
233 Jim Breech .05
234 Ross Browner .05
235 Cris Collinsworth (PB) .25
236 Isaac Curtis .05
237 Pete Johnson .05
238 Steve Kreider .05
239 Max Montoya .05
240 Anthony Munoz (PB) 1.50
241 Ken Riley .05
242 Dan Ross (PB) .07
243 Reggie Williams .05
244 Mike Pruitt Cleveland Browns Team .10
245 *Chip Banks* (PB) .25
246 Tom Cousineau .05
247 Joe DeLamielleure .05
248 Doug Dieken .05
249 *Hanford Dixon* .15
250 Ricky Feacher .05
251 Lawrence Johnson .05
252 Dave Logan .05
253 Paul McDonald .05
254 Ozzie Newsome .60
255 Mike Pruitt .05
256 Clarence Scott .05
257 Brian Sipe .10
258 Dwight Walker .05
259 Charles White .05
260 Gerald Wilhite Denver Broncos Team .10
261 Steve DeBerg .50
262 Randy Gradishar (PB) .07
263 Rulon Jones .05
264 Rick Karlis .05
265 Don Latimer .05
266 Rick Parros .05
267 Luke Prestridge (PB) .07
268 Rick Upchurch (PB) .07
269 Steve Watson .05
270 Gerald Wilhite .05
271 Gifford Nielson Houston Oilers Team .10
272 Harold Bailey .05
273 Jesse Baker .05
274 Gregg Bingham .05
275 Robert Brazile (PB) .07
276 Donnie Craft .05
277 Daryl Hunt .05
278 Archie Manning .10
279 Gifford Nielsen .05
280 Mike Renfro .05
281 Carl Roaches .05
282 Joe Delaney Kansas City Chiefs Team .10
283 Gary Barbaro (PB) .07
284 Joe Delaney .05
285 *Jeff Gossett* .60
286 Gary Green (PB) .05
287 Eric Harris .05
288 Billy Jackson .05
289 Bill Kenney .05
290 Nick Lowery .60
291 Henry Marshall .05
292 Art Still (PB) .05
293 Marcus Allen (TL) 2.00
294 *Marcus Allen* (PB) 18.00
295 Lyle Alzado .25
296 Chris Bahr .05
297 Cliff Branch .25
298 *Todd Christensen* 2.00
299 Ray Guy .10
300 Frank Hawkins .05
301 Lester Hayes (PB) .05
302 Ted Hendricks (PB) .15
303 Kenny King .05
304 Rod Martin .05
305 Matt Millen .15
306 Burgess Owens .05
307 Jim Plunkett .25
308 Andra Franklin Miami Dolphins Team .10
309 Bob Baumhower (PB) .07
310 Glenn Blackwood .05
311 Lyle Blackwood .05
312 A.J. Duhe .05
313 Andra Franklin (PB) .07
314 Duriel Harris .05
315 Bob Kuechenberg (PB) .07
316 Don McNeal .05
317 Tony Nathan .05
318 Ed Newman (PB) .05
319 Earnie Rhone .05
320 Joe Rose .05
321 Don Strock .07
322 Uwe Von Schamann .05
323 David Woodley .05
324 Tony Collins New England Patriots Team .10
325 Julius Adams .05
326 Pete Brock .05
327 *Rich Camarillo* .25
328 Tony Collins .05
329 Steve Grogan .25
330 John Hannah (PB) .25
331 Don Hasselbeck .05
332 Mike Haynes (PB) .05
333 Roland James .05
334 Stanley Morgan .75
335 Steve Nelson .05
336 Kenneth Sims .05
337 Mark Van Eeghen .05
338 Freeman McNeil New York Jets Team .10
339 Greg Buttle .05
340 Joe Fields (PB) .05
341 Mark Gastineau (PB) .08
342 Bruce Harper .05
343 Bobby Jackson .05
344 Bobby Jones .05
345 Johnny "Lam" Jones .07
346 Joe Klecko .10
347 Marty Lyons .05
348 Freeman McNeil (PB) .60
349 Lance Mehl .05
350 Marvin Powell (PB) .05
351 Darrol Ray .05
352 Abdul Salaam .05
353 Richard Todd .10
354 Wesley Walker (PB) .25
355 Franco Harris Pittsburgh Steelers Team .25
356 *Gary Anderson* .75
357 Mel Blount .25
358 Terry Bradshaw .75
359 Larry Brown (PB) .05
360 Bennie Cunningham .05
361 Gary Dunn .05
362 Franco Harris .75
363 Jack Lambert (PB) .60
364 Frank Pollard .05
365 Donnie Shell (PB) .08
366 John Stallworth (PB) .25
367 Loren Toews .05
368 Mike Webster (PB) .10
369 *Dwayne Woodruff* .10
370 Chuck Muncie San Diego Chargers Team .10
371 Rolf Benirschke (PB) .05
372 James Brooks .75
373 Wes Chandler (PB) .05
374 Dan Fouts (PB) .75
375 Tim Fox .05
376 Gary Johnson (PB) .05
377 Charlie Joiner .25
378 Louie Kelcher .05
379 Chuck Muncie (PB) .07
380 Cliff Thrift .05
381 Doug Wilkerson (PB) .05
382 Kellen Winslow (PB) .75
383 Sherman Smith Seattle Seahawks Team .10
384 *Kenny Easley* (PB) .40
385 *Jacob Green* .50
386 John Harris .05
387 Mike Jackson .05
388 *Norm Johnson* .50
389 Steve Largent .85
390 Keith Simpson .05
391 Sherman Smith .05
392 Jeff West .05
393 Jim Zorn .05
394 Checklist 1-132 .25
395 Checklist 133-264 .25
396 Checklist 265-396 .25

1983 Topps Sticker Inserts

These 33 different inserts, which came in each wax pack of 1983 Topps football cards, pictured an NFL star on the front and a piece to one of three different puzzles on the backs. A gold plaque at the bottom of the card identifies the player.

NM/M
Complete Set (33): 20.00
Common Player: .35
1 Marcus Allen 5.00
2 Ken Anderson .50
3 Ottis Anderson .35
4 William Andrews .35
5 Terry Bradshaw 1.25
6 Wes Chandler .35
7 Dwight Clark .50
8 Cris Collinsworth .35
9 Joe Cribbs .35
10 Nolan Cromwell .35
11 Tony Dorsett 1.50
12 Dan Fouts 1.00
13 Mark Gastineau .35
14 Jimmie Giles .35
15 Franco Harris 1.00
16 Ted Hendricks .60
17 Tony Hill .35
18 John Jefferson .35
19 James Lofton 1.00
20 Freeman McNeil .50
21 Joe Montana 6.00
22 Mark Moseley .35
23 Ozzie Newsome 1.00
24 Walter Payton 3.00
25 John Riggins 1.00
26 Billy Sims .35
27 John Stallworth .50
28 Lawrence Taylor 3.00
29 Joe Theismann 1.25
30 Richard Todd .35
31 Wesley Walker .35
32 Danny White .35
33 Kellen Winslow .50

1983 Topps Stickers

These stickers are similar to those issued in previous years, but can be identified by the rounded frame around the picture on the front and the reference on the back to the 1983 sticker album which was produced. Once again, Topps included foil stickers in the set (#s 1-4, 73-80, 143-152 and 264-271. Foil stickers 1-2 are right and left sides of Franco Harris; 3 and 4 portray Walter Payton.

NM/M
Complete Set (330): 30.00
Common Player: .05
1 Franco Harris .50
2 Franco Harris .50
3 Walter Payton 1.25
4 Walter Payton 1.25
5 John Riggins .35
6 Tony Dorsett .40
7 Mark Van Eeghen .05
8 Chuck Muncie .08
9 Wilbert Montgomery .08
10 Greg Pruitt .08
11 Sam Cunningham .10
12 Ottis Anderson .20
13 Mike Pruitt .08
14 Dexter Bussey .05
15 Mike Pagel .05
16 Curtis Dickey .08
17 Randy McMillan .08
18 Raymond Butler .05
19 Nesby Glasgow .05
20 Zachary Dixon .05
21 Matt Bouza .05
22 Johnie Cooks .05
23 Curtis Brown .05
24 Joe Cribbs .10
25 Roosevelt Leaks .08
26 Jerry Butler .08
27 Frank Lewis .08
28 Fred Smerlas .05
29 Ben Williams .05
30 Joe Ferguson .15
31 Isaac Curtis .08
32 Cris Collinsworth .15
33 Anthony Munoz .20
34 Max Montoya .05
35 Ross Browner .08
36 Reggie Williams .10
37 Ken Riley .10
38 Pete Johnson .08
39 Ken Anderson .20
40 Charles White .10
41 Dave Logan .05
42 Doug Dieken .05
43 Ozzie Newsome .20
44 Tom Cousineau .05
45 Bob Golic .08
46 Brian Sipe .10
47 Paul McDonald .05
48 Mike Pruitt .10
49 Luke Prestridge .05
50 Randy Gradishar .10
51 Rulon Jones .05
52 Rick Parros .05
53 Steve DeBerg .15
54 Tom Jackson .10
55 Rick Upchurch .08
56 Steve Watson .08
57 Robert Brazile .10
58 Willie Tullis .05
59 Archie Manning .15
60 Gifford Nielsen .08
61 Harold Bailey .05
62 Carl Roaches .08
63 Gregg Bingham .05
64 Daryl Hunt .05
65 Gary Green .05
66 Gary Barbaro .08
67 Bill Kenney .08
68 Joe Delaney .10
69 Henry Marshall .05
70 Nick Lowery .10
71 Jeff Gossett .05
72 Art Still .10
73 Ken Anderson AFC Passing Leader .40
74 Dan Fouts AFC PAssing Yardage Leader .50
75 Wes Chandler AFC Receiving Yardage Leader .25
76 James Brooks AFC Kickoff Return Yardage Leader .40
77 Rick Upchurch AFC Punt Return Yardage Leader .30
78 Luke Prestridge AFC Punting Leader .15
79 Jesse Baker AFC Sacks Leader .15
80 Freeman McNeil AFC Rushing Leader .30
81 Ray Guy .15
82 Jim Plunkett .15
83 Lester Hayes .08
84 Kenny King .05
85 Cliff Branch .12
86 Todd Christensen .12
87 Lyle Alzado .15
88 Ted Hendricks .20
89 Rod Martin .10
90 Dave Woodley .10
91 Ed Newman .05
92 Earnie Rhone .05
93 Don McNeal .05
94 Glenn Blackwood .08
95 Andra Franklin .08
96 Nat Moore .12
97 Lyle Blackwood .08
98 A.J. Duhe .10
99 Tony Collins .08
100 Stanley Morgan .10
101 Pete Brock .05
102 Steve Nelson .05
103 Steve Grogan .15
104 Mark Van Eeghen .08
105 Don Hasselbeck .05
106 John Hannah .15
107 Mike Haynes .15
108 Wesley Walker .10
109 Marvin Powell .05
110 Joe Klecko .08
111 Bobby Jackson .05
112 Richard Todd .10
113 Lance Mehl .08
114 Johnny Lam Jones .10
115 Mark Gastineau .10
116 Freeman McNeil .15
117 Franco Harris .30
118 Mike Webster .15
119 Mel Blount .15
120 Donnie Shell .10
121 Terry Bradshaw .75
122 John Stallworth .12
123 Jack Lambert .25
124 Dwayne Woodruff .05
125 Bennie Cunningham .05
126 Charlie Joiner .20
127 Kellen Winslow .20
128 Rolf Benirschke .05
129 Louis Kelcher .08
130 Chuck Muncie .08
131 Wes Chandler .10
132 Gary Johnson .08
133 James Brooks .15
134 Dan Fouts .35
135 Jacob Green .10
136 Michael Jackson .05
137 Jim Zorn .12
138 Sherman Smith .08
139 Keith Simpson .05
140 Steve Largent 1.25
141 John Harris .08
142 Jeff West .08
143 Ken Anderson (top) .45
144 Ken Anderson (bottom) .45
145 Tony Dorsett (top) .40
146 Tony Dorsett (bottom) .40
147 Dan Fouts (top) .40
148 Dan Fouts (bottom) .40
149 Joe Montana (top) 2.00
150 Joe Montana (bottom) 2.00
151 Mark Moseley (top) .15
152 Mark Moseley (bottom) .15
153 Richard Todd .10
154 Butch Johnson .10
155 Bill (Gary) Hogeboom .08
156 A.J. Duhe .08
157 Kurt Sohn .05
158 Drew Pearson .10
159 John Riggins .35
160 Pat Donovan .05
161 John Hannah .15
162 Jeff Van Note .10

163 Randy Cross .10
164 Marvin Powell .08
165 Kellen Winslow .25
166 Dwight Clark .20
167 Wes Chandler .08
168 Tony Dorsett .40
169 Freeman McNeil .12
170 Ken Anderson .25
171 Mark Moseley .05
172 Mark Gastineau .08
173 Gary Johnson .05
174 Randy White .30
175 Ed "Too Tall" Jones .12
176 Hugh Green .08
177 Harry Carson .10
178 Lawrence Taylor .30
179 Lester Hayes .08
180 Mark Haynes .05
181 Dave Jennings .05
182 Nolan Cromwell .08
183 Tony Peters .05
184 Jimmy Cefalo .05
185 A.J. Duhe .08
186 John Riggins .35
187 Charlie Brown .05
188 Mike Nelms .05
189 Mark Murphy .05
190 Fulton Walker .05
191 Marcus Allen 2.50
192 Chip Banks .08
193 Charlie Brown .05
194 Bob Crable .05
195 Vernon Dean .05
196 Jim McMahon .75
197 James Robbins .08
198 Luis Sharpe .08
199 Rohn Stark .05
200 Lester Williams .05
201 Leo Wisniewski .05
202 Butch Woolfolk .10
203 Mike Kenn .10
204 R.C. Thielemann .05
205 Buddy Curry .05
206 Steve Bartkowski .12
207 Alfred Jenkins .08
208 Don Smith .05
209 Alfred Jenkins .08
210 Fulton Kuykendall .05
211 William Andrews .10
212 Gary Fencik .08
213 Walter Payton 1.50
214 Mike Singletary 1.50
215 Otis Wilson .08
216 Matt Suhey .05
217 Dan Hampton .20
218 Emery Moorehead .05
219 Mike Hartenstine .05
220 Danny White .20
221 Drew Pearson .10
222 Rafael Septien .05
223 Ed "Too Tall" Jones .15
224 Everson Walls .10
225 Randy White .20
226 Harvey Martin .10
227 Tony Hill .08
228 John Jefferson .30
229 Billy Sims .20
230 Leonard Thompson .05
231 Ed Murray .05
232 Doug English .05
233 Ken Fantetti .05
234 Tom Skladany .05
235 Freddie Scott .05
236 Eric Hipple .08
237 David Hill .05
238 John Jefferson .08
239 Paul Coffman .05
240 Ezra Johnson .05
241 Mike Douglass .05
242 Mark Lee .08
243 John Anderson .10
244 Jan Stenerud .15
245 Lynn Dickey .10
246 James Lofton .30
247 Vince Ferragamo .12
248 Preston Dennard .05
249 Jack Youngblood .15
250 Mike Guman .05
251 LeRoy Irvin .08
252 Mike Lansford .05
253 Kent Hill .05
254 Nolan Cromwell .05
255 Doug Martin .05
256 Greg Coleman .05
257 Ted Brown .05
258 Mark Mullaney .05
259 Joe Senser .08
260 Randy Holloway .05
261 Matt Blair .08
262 Sammie White .10
263 Tommy Kramer .10
264 Joe Theismann NFC Passing Leader .40
265 Joe Montana NFC Passing Yardage Leader 1.50
266 Dwight Clark NFC Receiving Yardage Leader .25
267 Mike Nelms NFC Kickoff Return Yardage Leader .10
268 Carl Birdsong NFC Punting Leader .10
269 Everson Walls NFC Interceptions Leader .20
270 Doug Martin NFC Sacks Leader .15
271 Tony Dorsett NFC Rushing Yardage Leader .40
272 Russell Erxleben .05
273 Stan Brock .05
274 Jeff Groth .05
275 Bruce Clark .05
276 Ken Stabler .30
277 George Rogers .10
278 Derland Moore .08
279 Wayne Wilson .05
280 Lawrence Taylor .35
281 Harry Carson .10
282 Brian Kelley .05
283 Brad Van Pit .05
284 Earnest Gray .05
285 Dave Jennings .05
286 Rob Carpenter .05
287 Scott Brunner .05
288 Ron Jaworski .15
289 Jerry Robinson .08
290 Frank LeMaster .05
291 Wilbert Montgomery .08
292 Tony Franklin .05
293 Harold Carmichael .15
294 John Spagnola .05
295 Herman Edwards .05
296 Ottis Anderson .15
297 Carl Birdsong .05
298 Doug Marsh .05
299 Neil Lomax .12
300 Rush Brown .05
301 Pat Tilley .08
302 Wayne Morris .08
303 Dan Dierdorf .20
304 Roy Green .30
305 Joe Montana 1.75
306 Randy Cross .10
307 Freddie Solomon .08
308 Jack Reynolds .10
309 Ronnie Lott .50
310 Renaldo Nehemiah .15
311 Russ Francis .08
312 Dwight Clark .20
313 Doug Williams .12
314 Bill Capece .05
315 Mike Washington .05
316 Hugh Green .10
317 Kevin House .08
318 Lee Roy Selmon .12
319 Neal Colzie .10
320 Jimmie Giles .08
321 Cedric Brown .05
322 Tony Peters .05
323 Neal Olkewicz .05
324 Dexter Manley .05
325 Joe Theismann .30
326 Rich Milot .05
327 Mark Moseley .08
328 Art Monk .40
329 Mike Nelms .08
330 John Riggins .35

1983 Topps Sticker Boxes

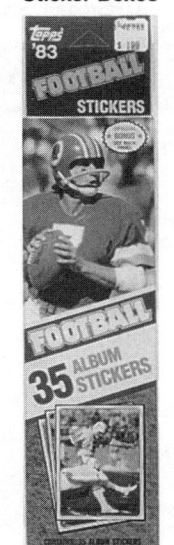

These boxes contained 35 stickers inside, but also had two 2-1/2" x 3-1/2" on them; an offensive player was on each box. The cards are not numbered, and there was no issue for #10, but the box is numbered with a tab. The prices below are for an uncut box.

NM/M
Complete Set (12): 15.00
Common Player: .75
1 Pat Donovan, Mark Gastineau .75
2 Wes Chandler, Nolan Cromwell 1.25
3 Marvin Powell, Ed "Too Tall" Jones 1.25
4 Ken Anderson, Tony Peters 1.25
5 Freeman McNeil, Lawrence Taylor 2.00
6 Mark Moseley, Dave Jennings .75
7 Dwight Clark, Mark Haynes 1.50
8 Jeff Van Note, Harry Carson .75
9 Tony Dorsett, Hugh Green 2.00
11 Randy Cross, Gary Johnson 1.00
12 Kellen Winslow, Lester Hayes 1.25
13 John Hannah, Randy White 2.00

1984 Topps

Topps' most sought-after NFL set of the decade is notable for its excellent array of rookies: Dickerson, Elway, Marino, Curt Warner, Mark Duper, Willie Gault and Roger Craig are among them. This is one of the better-designed sets of the decade as well. The 396-card set is numbered alphabetically by city and by player name; AFC teams are listed first, while NFC teams are listed after the NFL leaders. Team leader cards, which had for years shown team leaders in several categories, this year showed just one leader. Card fronts show an angled photo in a yellow stripe. The team logo and name appear at the bottom also at an angle. The Pro Bowl designation appears above the team name. Instant Replay cards issued in this set in addition to the player's regular card featured NFL stars in action poses. The score on the Super Bowl card (#9) is incorrect: instead of 28-9, it should read 38-9. (Key: PB - Pro Bowl, IR - Instant Replay)

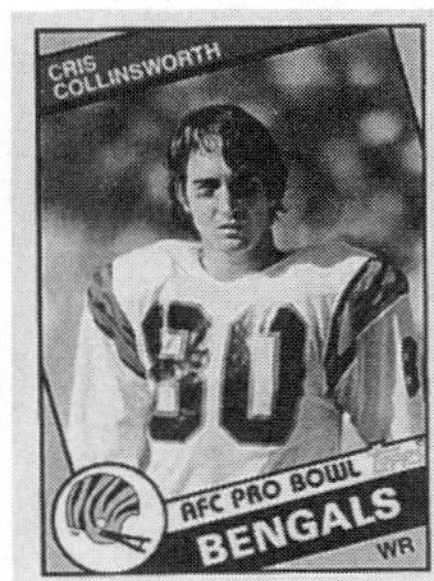

NM/M
Complete Set (396): 230.00
Common Player: .05
Wax Pack (15): 16.00
Wax Box (36): 425.00
1 Eric Dickerson (RB) .75
2 Ali Haji-Sheikh (RB) .10
3 Franco Harris (RB) .25
4 Mark Moseley (RB) .15
5 John Riggins (RB) .25
6 Jan Stenerud (RB) .10
7 AFC Championship .10
8 NFC Championship .10
9 Super Bowl XVIII .25
10 Curtis Dickey Indianapolis Colts Team: .10
11 *Raul Allegre* .10
12 Curtis Dickey .05
13 *Ray Donaldson* .10
14 Nesby Glasgow .05
15 *Chris Hinton* (PB) 1.50
16 *Vernon Maxwell* .15
17 Randy McMillan .05
18 Mike Pagel .05
19 Rohn Stark .05
20 Leo Wisniewski .05
21 Joe Cribbs Buffalo Bills Team: .10
22 Jerry Butler .05
23 Joe Danelo .05
24 Joe Ferguson .10
25 Steve Freeman .05
26 Roosevelt Leaks .05
27 Frank Lewis .05
28 Eugene Marve .05
29 Booker Moore .05
30 Fred Smerlas (PB) .07
31 Ben Williams .05
32 Cris Collinsworth Cincinnati Bengals Team: .10
33 Charles Alexander .05
34 Ken Anderson .25
35 Ken Anderson (IR) .10
36 Jim Breech .05
37 Cris Collinsworth (PB) .10
38 Cris Collinsworth (IR) .06
39 Isaac Curtis .05
40 Eddie Edwards .05
41 *Ray Horton* .20
42 Pete Johnson .05
43 Steve Kreider .05
44 Max Montoya .05
45 Anthony Munoz (PB) .75
46 Reggie Williams .05
47 Mike Pruitt Cleveland Browns Team: .10
48 Matt Bahr .05
49 Chip Banks (PB) .15
50 Tom Cousineau .05
51 Joe DeLamielleure .05
52 Doug Dieken .05
53 *Bob Golic* .50
54 Bobby Jones .05
55 Dave Logan .05
56 Clay Matthews 1.00
57 Paul McDonald .05
58 Ozzie Newsome .50
59 Ozzie Newsome (IR) .20
60 Mike Pruitt .05
61 Steve Watson .05
62 *Barney Chavous* .20
63 *John Elway* 100.00
64 Steve Foley .05
65 Tom Jackson .15
66 Rick Karlis .05
67 Luke Prestridge .05
68 Zack Thomas .05
69 Rick Upchurch .05
70 Steve Watson .05
71 *Sammy Winder* .25
72 Louis Wright (PB) .05
73 Tim Smith Houston Oilers Team: .10
74 Jesse Baker .05
75 Gregg Bingham .05
76 Robert Brazile .07
77 Steve Brown .05
78 Chris Dressel .05
79 Doug France .05
80 Florian Kempf .05
81 Carl Roaches .05
82 *Tim Smith* .15
83 Willie Tullis .05
84 Carlos Carson Kansas City Chiefs Team: .10
85 Mike Bell .05
86 Theotis Brown .05
87 Carlos Carson (PB) .10
88 Carlos Carson (IR) .06
89 *Deron Cherry* (PB) .75
90 Gary Green (PB) .05
91 Billy Jackson .05
92 Bill Kenney .05
93 Bill Kenney (IR) .05
94 Nick Lowery .25
95 Henry Marshall .05
96 Art Still .07
97 Todd Christensen Los Angeles Raiders Team: .10
98 Marcus Allen 4.00
99 Marcus Allen IR (IR) 2.00
100 Lyle Alzado .20
101 Lyle Alzado (IR) .08
102 Chris Bahr .05
103 Malcolm Barnwell .05
104 Cliff Branch .25
105 Todd Christensen (PB) .50
106 Todd Christensen (IR) .20
107 Ray Guy .20
108 Frank Hawkins .05
109 Lester Hayes (PB) .07
110 Ted Hendricks (PB) .20
111 *Howie Long* (PB) 8.00
112 Rod Martin (PB) .05
113 *Vann McElroy* (PB) .15
114 Jim Plunkett .15
115 Greg Pruitt (PB) .10
116 Mark Duper Miami Dolphins Team: .10
117 Bob Baumhower (PB) .05
118 *Doug Betters* (PB) .10
119 A.J. Duhe .05
120 *Mark Duper* (PB) 1.50
121 Andre Franklin (Andra) .05
122 William Judson .05
123 *Dan Marino* (PB) 110.00
124 Dan Marino IR (IR) 15.00
125 Nat Moore .05
126 Ed Newman (PB) .05
127 *Reggie Roby* .60
128 Gerald Small .05
129 *Dwight Stephenson* .75
130 Uwe Von Schamann .05
131 Tony Collins New England Patriots Team: .10
132 Rich Camarillo (PB) .05
133 Tony Collins (PB) .05
134 Tony Collins (IR) .05
135 Bob Cryder .05
136 Steve Grogan .10
137 John Hannah (PB) .15
138 *Brian Holloway* (PB) .15
139 Roland James .05
140 Stanley Morgan .25
141 Rick Sanford .05
142 Mosi Tatupu .05
143 *Andre Tippett* 1.00
144 Wesley Walker New York Jets Team: .10
145 Jerome Barkum .05
146 Mark Gastineau (PB) .07
147 Mark Gastineau (IR) .05
148 Bruce Harper .05
149 Johnny "Lam" Jones .05
150 Joe Klecko (PB) .07
151 Pat Leahy .05
152 Freeman McNeil .20
153 Lance Mehl .05
154 Marvin Powell (PB) .07
155 Darrol Ray .05
156 Pat Ryan .05
157 Kirk Springs .05
158 Wesley Walker .15
159 Franco Harris Pittsburgh Steelers Team: .25
160 *Walter Abercrombie* .15
161 Gary Anderson (PB) .05
162 Terry Bradshaw 1.00
163 Craig Colquitt .05
164 Bennie Cunningham .05
165 Franco Harris .75
166 Franco Harris (IR) .30
167 Jack Lambert (PB) .60
168 Jack Lambert (IR) .25
169 Frank Pollard .05
170 Donnie Shell .05
171 Mike Webster (PB) .25
172 Keith Willis .15
173 Rick Woods .05
174 Kellen Winslow San Diego Chargers Team: .20
175 Rolf Benirschke .05
176 James Brooks .20
177 Maury Buford .05
178 Wes Chandler (PB) .05
179 Dan Fouts (PB) .75
180 Dan Fouts (IR) .50
181 Charlie Joiner .25
182 Linden King .05
183 Chuck Muncie .05
184 *Billy Ray Smith* .25
185 Danny Walters .05
186 Kellen Winslow (PB) .60
187 Kellen Winslow (IR) .25
188 Curt Warner Seattle Seahawks Team: .10
189 Steve August .05
190 Dave Brown .05
191 Zachary Dixon .05
192 Kenny Easley .10
193 Jacob Green .15
194 Norm Johnson .05
195 *Dave Krieg* 3.50
196 Steve Largent .80
197 Steve Largent (IR) .60
198 *Curt Warner* (PB) .50
199 Curt Warner (IR) .20
200 Jeff West .05
201 Charley Young .05
202 Dan Marino, Steve Bartkowski Passing Leaders: (LL) 4.00
203 Todd Christensen, Charlie Brown, Earnest Gray, Roy Green Receiving Leaders: .10
204 Curt Warner, Eric Dickerson Rushing Leaders: .40
205 Gary Anderson, Mark Moseley Scoring Leaders: .10
206 Vann McElroy, Ken Riley, Mark Murphy Interception Leaders: .10
207 Rich Camarillo, Greg Coleman Punting Leaders: .10
208 William Andrews Atlanta Falcons Team: .10
209 William Andrews (PB) .05
210 William Andrews (IR) .05
211 *Stacey Bailey* .15
212 Steve Bartkowski .15
213 Steve Barkowski (IR) .05
214 Ralph Giacomarro .05
215 Billy Johnson (PB) .07
216 Mike Kenn (PB) .05
217 Mick Luckhurst .05
218 Gerald Riggs .10
219 R.C. Thielemann (PB) .05
220 Jeff Van Note .05
221 Walter Payton (TL) .75
222 *Jim Covert* .75
223 Leslie Frazier .05
224 *Willie Gault* .50
225 Mike Hartenstine .05
226 Noah Jackson .05
227 Jim McMahon 1.50
228 Walter Payton (PB) 4.00
229 Walter Payton IR (IR) 1.00
230 *Mike Richardson* .10
231 Terry Schmidt .05
232 Mike Singletary (PB) 1.75
233 Matt Suhey .05
234 Bob Thomas .05
235 Tony Dorsett Dallas Cowboys Team: .25
236 Bob Breunig .05
237 Doug Cosbie (PB) .05
238 Tony Dorsett (PB) .60
239 Tony Dorsett (IR) .25
240 John Dutton .05
241 Tony Hill .05
242 Ed "Too Tall" Jones (PB) .20
243 Drew Pearson .20
244 Rafael Septien .05
245 Ron Springs .05
246 Dennis Thurman .05
247 Everson Walls (PB) .15
248 Danny White .25
249 Randy White (PB) .60
250 Billy Sims Detroit Lions Team: .10
251 *Jeff Chadwick* .25
252 Garry Cobb .05
253 Doug English (PB) .05
254 William Gay .05
255 Eric Hipple .05
256 *James Jones* .25
257 Bruce McNorton .05
258 Ed Murray .05
259 Ulysses Norris .05
260 Billy Sims .15
261 Billy Sims (IR) .08
262 Leonard Thompson .05
263 James Lofton Green Bay Packers Team: .25
264 John Anderson .05
265 Paul Coffman (PB) .05
266 Lynn Dickey .07
267 Gerry Ellis .05
268 John Jefferson .07
269 John Jefferson (IR) .05
270 Ezra Johnson .05
271 Tim Lewis .05
272 James Lofton (PB) 1.50
273 James Lofton (IR) .75
274 Larry McCarren (PB) .05
275 Jan Stenerud .25
276 Eric Dickerson (TL) .75
277 Mike Barber .05
278 Jim Collins .05
279 Nolan Cromwell (PB) .05
280 *Eric Dickerson* (PB) 8.00
281 Eric Dickerson (IR) 2.00
282 George Farmer .05
283 Vince Ferragamo .10
284 Kent Hill (PB) .05
285 John Misko .05
286 *Jackie Slater* (PB) 2.00
287 Jack Youngblood .20
288 Darrin Nelson Minnesota Vikings Team: .10
289 Ted Brown .05
290 Greg Coleman .05
291 Steve Dils .05
292 Tony Galbreath .05
293 Tommy Kramer .10
294 Doug Martin .05
295 *Darrin Nelson* .25
296 Benny Ricardo .05
297 John Swain .05
298 John Turner .05
299 George Rogers New Orleans Saints Team: .10
300 *Morten Andersen* 3.00
301 Russell Erxleben .05
302 Jeff Groth .05
303 *Rickey Jackson* (PB) 3.00
304 Johnnie Poe .05
305 George Rogers .10
306 Richard Todd .10
307 Jim Wilks .05
308 Dave Wilson .05
309 Wayne Wilson .05
310 Earnest Gray New York Giants Team: .10
311 Leon Bright .05
312 Scott Brunner .05
313 Rob Carpenter .05
314 Harry Carson (PB) .20
315 Earnest Gray .05
316 Ali Haji-Sheikh (PB) .05
317 Mark Haynes (PB) .08
318 Dave Jennings .05
319 Brian Kelley .05
320 Phil Simms 1.00
321 Lawrence Taylor (PB) 3.00
322 Lawrence Taylor (IR) 2.00
323 Brad Van Pelt .05
324 Butch Woolfolk .05
325 Mike Quick Philadelphia Eagles Team: .15
326 Harold Carmichael .20
327 Herman Edwards .05
328 Michael Haddix .10
329 Dennis Harrison .05
330 Ron Jaworski .10
331 Wilbert Montgomery .07
332 Hubert Oliver .05
333 *Mike Quick* (PB) .75
334 Jerry Robinson .05
335 Max Runager .05
336 Michael Williams .05
337 Ottis Anderson St. Louis Cardinals Team: .15
338 Ottis Anderson .50
339 Al "Bubba" Baker .05
340 Carl Birdsong (PB) .05
341 David Galloway .05
342 Roy Green (PB) .25
343 Roy Green (IR) .10
344 *Curtis Greer* .10
345 Neil Lomax .10
346 Doug Marsh .05
347 Stump Mitchell .05
348 *Lionel Washington* .50
349 Dwight Clark San Francisco 49ers Team: .15
350 Dwaine Board .05
351 Dwight Clark .25
352 Dwight Clark (IR) .10
353 *Roger Craig* 5.00
354 Fred Dean .05
355 Fred Dean (IR) .10
356 Dwight Hicks (PB) .05
357 Ronnie Lott (PB) 1.50
358 Joe Montana (PB) 10.00
359 Joe Montana IR (IR) 5.00
360 Freddie Solomon .05
361 Wendell Tyler .05
362 Ray Wersching .05
363 *Eric Wright* .15
364 Kevin House Tampa Bay Buccaneers Team: .10
365 Gerald Carter .05
366 Hugh Green (PB) .07
367 Kevin House .05
368 Michael Morton .05
369 James Owens .05
370 Booker Reese .05
371 Lee Roy Selmon (PB) .07
372 Jack Thompson .05
373 James Wilder .10
374 Steve Wilson .05
375 John Riggins Washington Redskins Team: .20
376 Jeff Bostic (PB) .05
377 Charlie Brown (PB) .05
378 Charlie Brown (IR) .05
379 Dave Butz (PB) .05
380 *Darrell Green* 2.00
381 *Russ Grimm* (PB) .50
382 Joe Jacoby (PB) .05
383 Dexter Manley .05
384 Art Monk 1.00
385 Mark Moseley .05
386 Mark Murphy (PB) .05
387 Mike Nelms .05
388 John Riggins .60
389 John Riggins (IR) .25
390 Joe Theismann (PB) .50
391 Joe Theismann (IR) .25
392 Don Warren .05
393 Joe Washington .05
394 Checklist 1-132 .25
395 Checklist 133-264 .25
396 Checklist 265-396 .25

1984 Topps NFL Stars

This 11-card set was included, one per pack, in the 1984 Topps football card wax packs. Styled almost exactly as the 1985 NFL Stars set a year later, the glossy cards included an action photo of the player bordered in blue, plus the NFL logo and the player name at the bottom of the card. Cards were printed on heavy white cardboard stock.

NM/M
Complete Set (11): 6.00
Common Player: .25
1 Curt Warner .40

2	Eric Dickerson	2.50
3	Dan Marino	2.00
4	Steve Bartkowski	.25
5	Todd Christensen	.25
6	Roy Green	.25
7	Charlie Brown	.25
8	Earnest Gray	.25
9	Mark Gastineau	.25
10	Fred Dean	.25
11	Lawrence Taylor	.40

1984 Topps Play Cards

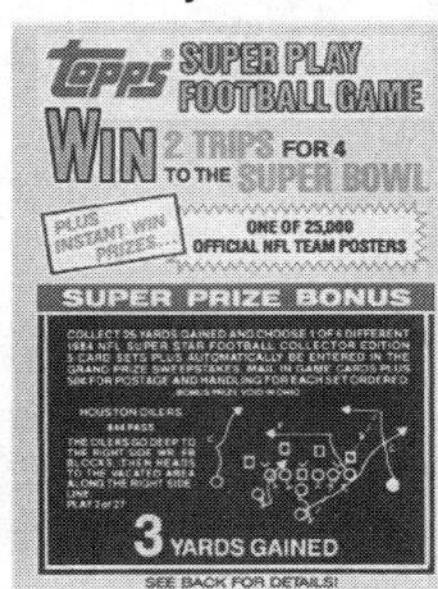

The 27-card, standard-size set was inserted in each pack of 1984 Topps Football. The card fronts describe prizes for the collectors and game rules, as well as the number of yards gained. Collectors had to collect at least 25 yards for five 1984 Glossy inserts. The card backs of the Play Cards contain game rules.

		NM/M
Complete Set (27):		15.00
Common Player:		.60
1	Houston Oilers (2 yards gained)	.60
2	Houston Oilers (3 yards gained)	.60
3	Cleveland Browns (4 yards gained)	.60
4	Cleveland Browns (5 yards gained)	.60
5	Cincinnati Bengals (6 yards gained)	.60
6	Pittsburgh Steelers (7 yards gained)	.75
7	New Orleans Saints (8 yards gained)	.75
8	New York Giants (2 yards gained)	.60
9	Washington Redskins (3 yards gained)	.75
10	Green Bay Packers (4 yards gained)	.60
11	Atlanta Falcons (5 yards gained)	.60
12	Detroit Lions (6 yards gained)	.60
13	New England Patriots (7 yards gained)	.60
14	New York Jets (8 yards gained)	.75
15	Buffalo Bills (2 yards gained)	.60
16	Kansas City Chiefs (3 yards gained)	.60
17	Miami Dolphins (4 yards gained)	.75
18	San Diego Chargers (5 yards gained)	.60
19	Seattle Seahawks (6 yards gained)	.60
20	Seattle Seahawks (7 yards gained)	.60
21	Dallas Cowboys (8 yards gained)	1.00
22	St. Louis Cardinals (2 yards gained)	.60
23	Chicago Bears (3 yards gained)	.60
24	San Francisco 49ers (4 yards gained)	1.00
25	Philadelphia Eagles (5 yards gained)	.60
26	Minnesota Vikings (6 yards gained)	.60
27	Los Angeles Rams (7 yards gained)	.75

1984 Topps Glossy Send-In

This 30-card set was available only through a mail-in offer. Cards show an action pose of the player on the front with a blackboard diagram as a background. His name, team and position are at the bottom. Backs identify the player, set and card number.

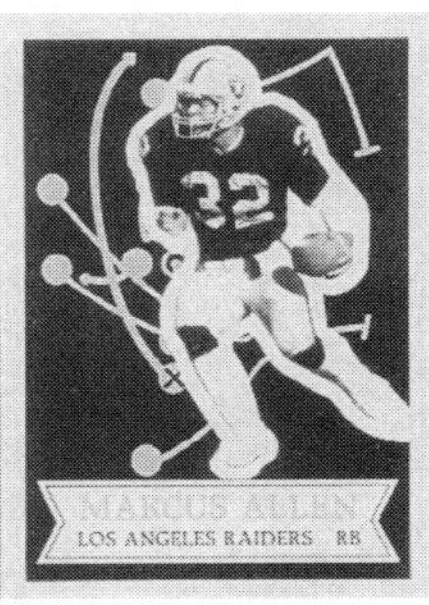

		NM/M
Complete Set (30):		14.00
Common Player:		.25
1	Marcus Allen	1.25
2	John Riggins	.40
3	Walter Payton	2.00
4	Tony Dorsett	1.00
5	Franco Harris	.75
6	Curt Warner	.40
7	Eric Dickerson	2.50
8	Mike Pruitt	.25
9	Ken Anderson	.25
10	Dan Fouts	.50
11	Terry Bradshaw	.75
12	Joe Theismann	.40
13	Joe Montana	2.00
14	Danny White	.25
15	Kellen Winslow	.25
16	Wesley Walker	.25
17	Drew Pearson	.25
18	James Lofton	.25
19	Cris Collinsworth	.25
20	Dwight Clark	.25
21	Mark Gastineau	.25
22	Lawrence Taylor	.40
23	Randy White	.25
24	Ed "Too Tall" Jones	.25
25	Jack Lambert	.25
26	Fred Dean	.25
27	Jan Stenerud	.40
28	Bruce Harper	.25
29	Todd Christensen	.25
30	Greg Pruitt	.25

1984 Topps Stickers

Topps has followed its same format for these stickers, except some of the stickers come in pairs, which are listed in parentheses. Those without are full stickers, comprising the entire card. An album, featuring Charlie Joiner on the front and Dan Fouts on the back, was also issued, as were foil stickers.

		NM/M
Complete Set (283):		35.00
Common Player:		.05
1	Super Bowl XVIII (Plunkett/Allen)	.35
2	Super Bowl XVIII (Plunkett/Allen)	.15
3	Super Bowl XVIII (Plunkett/Allen)	.15
4	Super Bowl XVIII (Plunkett/Allen)	.15
5	Marcus Allen (Super Bowl MVP)	.75
6	Walter Payton	1.00
7	Mike Richardson (157)	.03
8	Jim McMahon (158)	.10
9	Mike Hartenstine (159)	.05
10	Mike Singletary	.20
11	Willie Gault	.10
12	Terry Schmidt (162)	.05
13	Emery Moorehead (163)	.05
14	Leslie Frazier (164)	.06
15	Jack Thompson (165)	.05
16	Booker Reese (166)	.05
17	James Wilder (166)	.05
18	Lee Roy Selmon (167)	.08
19	Hugh Green	.06
20	Gerald Carter (170)	.05
21	Steve Wilson (171)	.05
22	Michael Morton (172)	.05
23	Kevin House	.05
24	Ottis Anderson	.12
25	Lionel Washington (175)	.08
26	Pat Tilley (176)	.05
27	Curtis Greer (177)	.05
28	Roy Green	.08
29	Carl Bridsong	.05
30	Neil Lomax (180)	.06
31	Lee Nelson (181)	.05
32	Stump Mitchell (182)	.04
33	Tony Hill (183)	.05
34	Everson Walls (184)	.05
35	Danny White (185)	.08
36	Tony Dorsett	.40
37	Ed "Too Tall" Jones	.12
38	Rafael Septien (188)	.05
39	Doug Crosbie (189)	.05
40	Drew Pearson (190)	.06
41	Randy White	.20
42	Ron Jaworski	.10
43	Anthony Griggs (193)	.05
44	Hubert Oliver (194)	.05
45	Wilbert Montgomery (195)	.05
46	Dennis Harrison	.05
47	Mike Quick	.08
48	Jerry Robinson (198)	.04
49	Michael Williams (199)	.05
50	Herman Edwards (200)	.05
51	Steve Bartkowski (201)	.06
52	Mick Luckhurst (202)	.05
53	Mike Pitts (203)	.05
54	William Andrews	.10
55	R.C. Thielemann	.05
56	Buddy Curry (206)	.05
57	Billy Johnson (207)	.04
58	Ralph Giacomaro (208)	.05
59	Mike Kenn	.08
60	Joe Montana	1.75
61	Fred Dean (211)	.05
62	Dwight Clark (212)	.10
63	Wendell Tyler (213)	.05
64	Dwight Hicks	.05
65	Ronnie Lott	.25
66	Roger Craig (216)	.40
67	Fred Solomon (217)	.05
68	Ray Wersching (218)	.05
69	Brad Van Pelt (219)	.05
70	Butch Woolfolk (220)	.05
71	Terry Kinard (221)	.05
72	Lawrence Taylor	.35
73	Aji Haji-Sheikh	.05
74	Mark Haynes (224)	.05
75	Rob Carpenter (225)	.05
76	Earnest Gray (226)	.05
77	Harry Carson	.10
78	Billy Sims	.15
79	Ed Murray (229)	.05
80	William Gay (230)	.05
81	Leonard Thompson (231)	.05
82	Doug English	.08
83	Eric Hipple	.08
84	Ken Fantetti (234)	.05
85	Bruce McNorton (235)	.05
86	James Jones (236)	.05
87	Lynn Dickey (237)	.06
88	Ezra Johnson (238)	.05
89	Jan Stenerud (239)	.08
90	James Lofton	.20
91	Larry McCarren	.05
92	John Jefferson (242)	.05
93	Mike Douglass (243)	.05
94	Gerry Ellis (244)	.05
95	Paul Coffman	.05
96	Eric Dickerson	1.00
97	Jackie Slater (247)	.20
98	Carl Ekern (248)	.05
99	Vince Ferragamo (249)	.06
100	Kent Hill	.05
101	Nolan Cromwell	.08
102	Jack Youngblood (252)	.10
103	John Misko (253)	.05
104	Mike Barber (254)	.07
105	Jeff Bostic (255)	.05
106	Mark Murphy (256)	.05
107	Joe Jacoby (257)	.05
108	John Riggins	.25
109	Joe Theismann	.30
110	Russ Grimm (260)	.05
111	Neal Olkewicz (261)	.07
112	Charlie Brown (262)	.05
113	Dave Butz	.08
114	George Rogers	.10
115	Jim Kovach (265)	.05
116	Dave Wilson (266)	.05
117	Johnnie Poe (267)	.05
118	Russell Erxleben	.05
119	Rickey Jackson	.50
120	Jeff Groth (270)	.05
121	Richard Todd (271)	.06
122	Wayne Wilson (272)	.05
123	Steve Dils (273)	.05
124	Benny Ricardo (274)	.05
125	John Turner (275)	.05
126	Ted Brown	.05
127	Greg Coleman	.05
128	Darrin Nelson (278)	.05
129	Scott Studwell (279)	.06
130	Tommy Kramer (280)	.06
131	Doug Martin	.05
132	Nolan Cromwell (144, All-Pro)	7.50
133	Carl Birdsong (145, All-Pro)	.10
134	Deron Cherry (146, All-Pro)	.20
135	Ronnie Lott (147, All-Pro)	.30
136	Lester Hayes (148, All-Pro)	.10
137	Lawrence Taylor (149, All-Pro)	.30
138	Jack Lambert (150, All-Pro)	.20
139	Chip Banks (151, All-Pro)	.10
140	Lee Roy Selmon (152, All-Pro)	.15
141	Fred Smerlas (153, All-Pro)	.10
142	Doug English (154, All-Pro)	.10
143	Doug Betters (155, All-Pro)	.10
144	Dan Marino (132, All-Pro)	3.00
145	Ali Haji-Sheikh (133, All-Pro)	.10
146	Eric Dickerson (134, All-Pro)	.65
147	Curt Warner (135, All-Pro)	.15
148	James Lofton (136, All-Pro)	.25
149	Todd Christensen (All-Pro)	.15
150	Cris Collinsworth (All-Pro)	.20
151	Mike Kenn (139, All-Pro)	.10
152	Russ Grimm (140, All-Pro)	.10
153	Jeff Bostic (141, All-Pro)	.10
154	John Hannah (142, All-Pro)	.15
155	Anthony Munoz (143, All-Pro)	.20
156	Ken Anderson	.35
157	Pete Johnson (7)	.05
158	Reggie Williams (8)	.06
159	Isaac Curtis (9)	.05
160	Anthony Munoz	.20
161	Cris Collinsworth	.15
162	Charles Alexander (12)	.05
163	Ray Horton (13)	.10
164	Steve Keider (14)	.05
165	Ben Williams (15)	.05
166	Frank Lewis (16)	.08
167	Roosevelt Leaks (17)	.05
168	Joe Ferguson	.08
169	Fred Smerlas	.08
170	Joe Danelo (20)	.05
171	Chris Keating (21)	.05
172	Jerry Butler (22)	.05
173	Eugene Marve	.05
174	Louis Wright	.08
175	Barney Chavous (25)	.10
176	Zack Thomas (26)	.05
177	Luke Prestridge (27)	.05
178	Steve Watson	.08
179	John Elway	5.00
180	Steve Foley (30)	.05
181	Sammy Winder (31)	.10
182	Rick Upchurch (32)	.05
183	Bobby Jones (33)	.08
184	Matt Bahr (34)	.05
185	Doug Dieken (35)	.05
186	Mike Pruitt	.08
187	Chip Banks	.10
188	Tom Cousineau (38)	.05
189	Paul McDonald (39)	.05
190	Clay Matthews (40)	.08
191	Ozzie Newsome	.20
192	Dan Fouts	.40
193	Chuck Muncie (43)	.05
194	Linden King (44)	.05
195	Charlie Joiner (45)	.08
196	Wes Chandler	.08
197	Kellen Winslow	.20
198	James Brooks (48)	.10
199	Mike Green (49)	.05
200	Rolf Benirschke (58)	.05
201	Henry Marshall (51)	.05
202	Nick Lowery (52)	.06
203	Jerry Blanton (53)	.05
204	Bill Kenney	.08
205	Carlos Carson	.08
206	Billy Jackson (56)	.05
207	Art Still (57)	.05
208	Theotis Brown (58)	.05
209	Deron Cherry	.25
210	Curtis Dickey	.08
211	Nesby Glasgow (61)	.05
212	Mike Pagel (62)	.05
213	Ray Donaldson (63)	.05
214	Raul Allegre	.05
215	Chris Hinton	.30
216	Rohn Stark (66)	.08
217	Randy McMillan (67)	.08
218	Vernon Maxwell (68)	.05
219	A.J. Duhe (69)	.10
220	Andra Franklin (70)	.05
221	Ed Newman (71)	.05
222	Dan Marino	7.50
223	Doug Betters	.08
224	Bob Baumhower (74)	.05
225	Reggie Roby (75)	.08
226	Dwight Stephenson (76)	.08
227	Mark Duper	.40
228	Mark Gastineau	.15
229	Freeman McNeil (79)	.08
230	Bruce Harper (80)	.05
231	Wesley Walker (81)	.06
232	Marvin Powell	.08
233	Joe Klecko	.08
234	Johnny Lam Jones (84)	.05
235	Lance Mehl (85)	.05
236	Pat Ryan (86)	.05
237	Florian Kempf (87)	.05
238	Carl Roaches (88)	.05
239	Gregg Bigham (89)	.05
240	Tim Smith	.05
241	Jesse Baker	.05
242	Doug France (92)	.08
243	Chris Dressel (93)	.05
244	Willie Tullis (94)	.05
245	Robert Brazile	.08
246	Tony Collins	.08
247	Brian Holloway (97)	.05
248	Stanley Morgan (98)	.06
249	Rick Sanford (99)	.05
250	John Hannah	.15
251	Rich Camarillo	.08
252	Andre Tippett (102)	.08
253	Steve Grogan (103)	.08
254	Clayton Weishuhn (104)	.05
255	Jim Plunkett (105)	.08
256	Rod Martin (106)	.08
257	Lester Hayes (107)	.05
258	Marcus Allen	.50
259	Todd Christensen	.10
260	Ted Hendricks (110)	.08
261	Greg Pruitt (111)	.05
262	Howie Long (112)	.50
263	Vann McElroy	.05
264	Curt Warner	.25
265	Jacob Green (115)	.06
266	Bruce Scholtz (116)	.05
267	Steve Largent (117)	.50
268	Kenny Easley	.08
269	Dave Krieg	.35
270	Dave Brown (120)	.05
271	Zachary Dixon (121)	.05
272	Norm Johnson (122)	.05
273	Terry Bradshaw (123)	.30
274	Keith Willis (124)	.05
275	Gary Anderson (125)	.05
276	Franco Harris	.35
277	Mike Webster	.15
278	Calvin Sweeney (128)	.05
279	Rick Woods (129)	.05
280	Bennie Cunningham(130)	.08
281	Jack Lambert	.15
282	Curt Warner (283)	.35
283	Todd Christensen (282)	.15

1984 Topps USFL

This 132-card set was Topps' first issue of United States Football League cards, and it's proven to be the most valuable set Topps issued in the 1980s. Several key rookie cards can be found in this set, including Jim Kelly, Herschel Walker, Reggie White, Anthony Carter, Bobby Hebert, Kelvin Bryant and Mike Rozier. Issued as a factory set, cards were printed on white cardboard stock. Bordered in red and blue piping over white space with the USFL logo and "Premier Edition" at the top of the card, a team helmet appears at lower left with the team name in red and the player name in black over a yellow background below the photo. Cards were numbered alphabetically by city name and by the player's last name.

		NM/M
Complete Set (132):		300.00
Common Player:		1.50
1	Luther Bradley	1.50
2	Frank Corral	1.50
3	Trumaine Johnson	1.50
4	Greg Landry	1.50
5	Kit Lathrop	1.50
6	Kevin Long	1.50
7	Tim Spencer	1.50
8	Stan White	1.50
9	Buddy Aydelette	1.50
10	Tom Banks	1.50
11	Fred Bohannon	1.50
12	Joe Cribbs	1.50
13	Joey Jones	1.50
14	Scott Norwood	1.50
15	Jim Smith	1.50
16	Cliff Stoudt	1.50
17	Vince Evans	2.00
18	Vagas Ferguson	1.50
19	John Gillen	1.50
20	Kris Haines	1.50
21	Glenn Hyde	1.50
22	Mark Keel	1.50
23	Garry Lewis	1.50
24	Doug Plank	1.50
25	Neil Balholm	1.50
26	David Dumars	1.50
27	David Martin	1.50
28	Craig Penrose	1.50
29	Dave Stalls	1.50
30	*Harry Sydney*	1.00
31	Vincent White	1.50
32	George Yarno	1.50
33	Kiki DeAyala	1.50
34	Sam Harrell	1.50
35	Mike Hawkins	1.50
36	*Jim Kelly*	80.00
37	Mark Rush	1.50
38	*Ricky Sanders*	10.00
39	Paul Bergmann	1.50
40	Tom Dinkel	1.50
41	Wyatt Henderson	1.50
42	*Vaughan Johnson*	5.00
43	Willie McClendon	1.50
44	Matt Robinson	1.50
45	George Achica	1.50
46	Mark Adickes	1.50
47	Howard Carson	1.50
48	Kevin Nelson	1.50
49	Jeff Partridge	1.50
50	JoJo Townsell	1.50
51	Eddie Weaver	1.50
52	*Steve Young*	250.00
53	Derrick Crawford	1.50
54	Walter Lewis	1.50
55	Phil McKinnely	1.50
56	Vic Minore	1.50
57	Gary Shirk	1.50
58	*Reggie White*	95.00
59	*Anthony Carter*	15.00
60	John Corker	1.50
61	David Greenwood	1.50
62	*Bobby Hebert*	10.00
63	Derek Holloway	1.50
64	Ken Lacy	1.50
65	Tyrone McGriff	1.50
66	Ray Pinney	1.50
67	Gary Barbaro	1.50
68	Sam Bowers	1.50
69	Clarence Collins	1.50
70	Willie Harper	1.50
71	Jim LeClair	1.50
72	Bob Leopold	1.50
73	Brian Sipe	2.00
74	*Herschel Walker*	18.00
75	Junior Ah You	1.50
76	*Marcus Dupree*	2.00
77	Marcus Marek	1.50
78	Tim Mazzetti	1.50
79	Mike Robinson	1.50
80	Dan Ross	1.50
81	Mark Schellen	1.50
82	Johnnie Walton	1.50
83	Gordon Banks	1.50
84	Fred Besana	1.50
85	Dave Browning	1.50
86	Eric Jordan	1.50
87	Frank Manumaleuga	1.50
88	*Gary Plummer*	4.00
89	Stan Talley	1.50
90	Arthur Whittington	1.50
91	Terry Beeson	1.50
92	*Mel Gray*	2.00
93	Mike Katolin	1.50
94	Dewey McClain	1.50
95	Sidney Thorton	1.50
96	Doug Williams	2.50
97	*Kelvin Bryant*	2.50
98	John Bunting	1.50
99	*Irv Eatman*	2.00
100	Scott Fitzkee	1.50
101	Chuck Fusina	1.50
102	*Sean Landeta*	3.00
103	David Trout	1.50
104	Scott Woerner	1.50
105	Glenn Carano	1.50
106	Ron Crosby	1.50
107	Jerry Holmes	1.50
108	Bruce Huther	1.50
109	*Mike Rozier*	4.00
110	Larry Swider	1.50
111	Danny Buggs	1.50
112	Putt Choate	1.50
113	Rich Garza	1.50
114	Joey Hackett	1.50
115	Rick Neuheisel	1.50
116	Mike St. Clair	1.50
117	*Gary Anderson*	4.00
118	Zenon Andrusyshyn	1.50
119	Doug Beaudoin	1.50
120	Mike Butler	1.50
121	Willie Gillespie	1.50
122	Fred Nordgren	1.50
123	John Reaves	1.50
124	Eric Truvillion	1.50
125	Reggie Collier	1.50
126	Mike Guess	1.50
127	Mike Hohensee	1.50
128	*Craig James*	4.00
129	Eric Robinson	1.50
130	Billy Taylor	1.50
131	Joey Walters	1.50
132	Checklist 1-132	1.50

1985 Topps

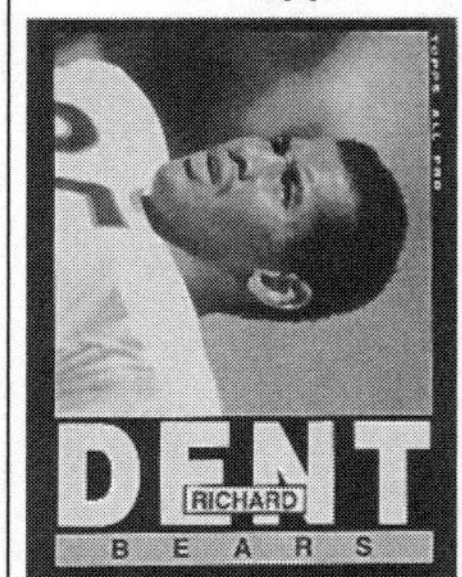

This was Topps' most radical card design in football cards in decades. Player photos were mounted horizontally in this 396-card set, with black borders surrounding the photo. The player's last name appeared in large white letters across the bottom of the card, with his first name in smaller letters in the middle of his last name. The team name appeared in smaller, darker type in the upper left corner. Cards in this issue were numbered alphabetically according to city name and conference, with NFC teams listed first and AFC teams listed after the league leader cards. This set includes rookie cards of Richard Dent, Henry Ellard, Joe Morris, Warren Moon, Mark Clayton, Tony Eason, Ken O'Brien and Louis Lipps. (Key: AP - All Pro)

		NM/M
Complete Set (396):		80.00
Common Player:		.05
Wax Pack (15):		4.00
Wax Box (36):		100.00
1	Mark Clayton Record:	.60
2	Eric Dickerson Record:	.50
3	Charlie Joiner Record:	.15
4	Dan Marino RB	8.00
5	Art Monk Record:	.30
6	Walter Payton RB	1.00

#	Player	Price
7	Matt Suhey NFC Championship:	.10
8	Bennett AFC Championship:	.10
9	Wendell Tyler Super Bowl XIX:	.15
10	Gerald Riggs Atlanta Falcons Team:	.10
11	William Andrews	.05
12	Stacey Bailey	.05
13	Steve Bartkowski	.15
14	*Rick Bryan*	.25
15	Alfred Jackson	.05
16	Kenny Johnson	.05
17	Mike Ken (AP)	.05
18	*Mike Pitts*	.25
19	Gerald Riggs	.05
20	Sylvester Stamps	.05
21	R.C. Theilemann	.05
22	Chicago Bears Team:	.75
23	*Todd Bell* (AP)	.12
24	*Richard Dent* (AP)	4.00
25	Gary Fencik	.05
26	Dave Finzer	.05
27	Leslie Frazier	.05
28	Steve Fuller	.05
29	Willie Gault	.40
30	Dan Hampton (AP)	.60
31	Jim McMahon	.60
32	*Steve McMichael*	1.00
33	Walter Payton (AP)	3.00
34	Mike Singletary	.75
35	Matt Suhey	.05
36	Bob Thomas	.05
37	Tony Dorsett Dallas Cowboys Team:	.25
38	*Bill Bates*	1.00
39	Doug Cosbie	.05
40	Tony Dorsett	.60
41	Michael Downs	.05
42	Mike Hegman	.05
43	Tony Hill	.05
44	*Gary Hogeboom*	.10
45	*Jim Jeffcoat*	.50
46	Ed "Too Tall" Jones	.25
47	Mike Renfro	.05
48	Rafael Septien	.05
49	Dennis Thurman	.05
50	Everson Walls	.05
51	Danny White	.20
52	Randy White	.40
53	Detroit Lions Team	.10
54	Jeff Chadwick	.05
55	*Mike Cofer*	.25
56	Gary Danielson	.05
57	Keith Dorney	.05
58	Doug English	.05
59	William Gay	.05
60	Ken Jenkins	.05
61	James Jones	.05
62	Ed Murray	.05
63	Billy Sims	.12
64	Leonard Thompson	.05
65	Bobby Watkins	.05
66	Lynn Dickey Green Bay Packers Team:	.10
67	Paul Coffman	.05
68	Lynn Dickey	.05
69	Mike Douglass	.05
70	Tom Flynn	.05
71	Eddie Lee Ivery	.05
72	Ezra Johnson	.05
73	Mark Lee	.05
74	Tim Lewis	.05
75	James Lofton	.50
76	Bucky Scribner	.05
77	Eric Dickerson Los Angeles Rams Team:	.40
78	Nolan Cromwell	.05
79	Eric Dickerson (AP)	1.00
80	*Henry Ellard*	5.00
81	Kent Hill	.05
82	LeRoy Irvin	.05
83	Jeff Kemp	.35
84	Mike Lansford	.05
85	Barry Redden	.05
86	Jackie Slater	.40
87	*Doug Smith*	.50
88	Jack Youngblood	.15
89	Minnesota Vikings Team	.10
90	Alfred Anderson	.15
91	Ted Brown	.05
92	Greg Coleman	.05
93	Tommy Hannon	.05
94	Tommy Kramer	.10
95	*Leo Lewis*	.20
96	Doug Martin	.05
97	Darrin Nelson	.05
98	Jan Stenerud (AP)	.20
99	Sammy White	.05
100	New Orleans Saints Team	.10
101	Morten Anderson	.75
102	*Hoby Brenner*	.15
103	Bruce Clark	.05
104	Hokie Gajan	.05
105	*Brian Hansen*	.15
106	Rickey Jackson	1.00
107	George Rogers	.15
108	Dave Wilson	.05
109	Tyrone Young	.05
110	New York Giants Team	.10
111	*Carl Banks*	1.00
112	*Jim Burt*	.40
113	Rob Carpenter	.05
114	Harry Carson	.15
115	Earnest Gray	.05
116	Ali Haji-Sheikh	.05
117	Mark Haynes (AP)	.05
118	Bobby Johnson	.05
119	*Lionel Manuel*	.12
120	*Joe Morris*	.75
121	*Zeke Mowatt*	.10
122	*Jeff Rutledge*	.20
123	Phil Simms	.60
124	Lawrence Taylor (AP)	1.25
125	Wilbert Montgomery Philadelphia Eagles Team:	.10
126	Greg Brown	.05
127	Ray Ellis	.05
128	Dennis Harrison	.05
129	Wes Hopkins, Marvin Harvey	.50
130	Mike Horan	.05
131	*Kenny Jackson*	.15
132	Ron Jaworski	.12
133	Paul McFadden	.05
134	Wilbert Montgomery	.05
135	Mike Quick	.12
136	John Spagnola	.05
137	St. Louis Cardinals Team	.10
138	Ottis Anderson	.30
139	Al "Bubba" Baker	.05
140	Roy Green	.15
141	Curtis Greer	.05
142	E.J. Junior (AP)	.05
143	Neil Lomax	.05
144	Stump Mitchell	.05
145	Neil O'Donoghue	.05
146	Pat Tilley	.05
147	Lionel Washington	.15
148	San Francisco 49ers	1.00
149	Dwaine Board	.05
150	Dwight Clark	.20
151	Roger Craig	1.25
152	Randy Cross (AP)	.05
153	Fred Dean	.05
154	Keith Fahnhorst	.05
155	Dwight Hicks	.05
156	Ronnie Lott	.50
157	Joe Montana	7.00
158	Renaldo Nehemiah	.05
159	Fred Quillan	.05
160	Jack Reynolds	.05
161	Freddie Solomon	.05
162	*Keena Turner*	.50
163	Wendell Tyler	.05
164	Ray Wersching	.05
165	Carlton Williamson	.05
166	Steve DeBerg Tampa Bay Buccaneers Team:	.10
167	Gerald Carter	.05
168	Mark Cotney	.05
169	Steve DeBerg	.40
170	Sean Farrell	.05
171	Hugh Green	.05
172	Kevin House	.05
173	David Logan	.05
174	Michael Morton	.05
175	Lee Roy Selmon	.05
176	James Wilder	.05
177	John Riggins Washington Redskins Team:	.20
178	Charlie Brown	.05
179	*Monte Coleman*	.75
180	Vernon Dean	.05
181	Darrell Green	.65
182	Russ Grimm	.15
183	Joe Jacoby	.05
184	Dexter Manley	.05
185	Art Monk	1.00
186	Mark Moseley	.05
187	Calvin Muhammad	.05
188	Mike Nelms	.05
189	John Riggins	.50
190	Joe Theismann	.50
191	Joe Washington	.05
192	Joe Montana, Dan Marino Passing Leaders:	15.00
193	Ozzie Newsome, Art Monk Receiving Leaders:	.35
194	Earnest Jackson, Eric Dickerson Rushing Leaders:	.40
195	Gary Anderson, Ray Wersching Scoring Leaders:	.10
196	Kenny Easley, Tom Flynn Interception Leaders:	.10
197	Jim Arnold, Brian Hansen Punting Leaders:	.10
198	Greg Bell Buffalo Bills Team:	.10
199	*Greg Bell*	.85
200	Preston Dennard	.05
201	Joe Ferguson	.05
202	Byron Franklin	.05
203	Steve Freeman	.05
204	Jim Haslett	.05
205	Charles Romes	.05
206	Fred Smerlas	.05
207	*Darryl Talley*	2.00
208	Van Williams	.05
209	Ken Anderson, Larry Kinnebrew Cincinnati Bengals Team:	.10
210	Ken Anderson	.20
211	Jim Breech	.05
212	Louis Breeden	.05
213	James Brooks	.25
214	Ross Browner	.05
215	Eddie Edwards	.05
216	M.L. Harris	.05
217	Bobby Kemp	.05
218	*Larry Kinnebrew*	.10
219	Anthony Munoz (AP)	.40
220	Reggie Williams	.05
221	Boyce Green Cleveland Browns Team:	.10
222	Matt Bahr	.05
223	Chip Banks	.05
224	Reggie Camp	.05
225	Tom Cousineau	.05
226	Joe DeLamielleure	.05
227	Ricky Feacher	.05
228	Boyce Green	.05
229	Al Gross	.05
230	Clay Matthews	.50
231	Paul McDonald	.05
232	Ozzie Newsome (AP)	.35
233	Mike Pruitt	.05
234	Don Rogers	.05
235	John Elway, Sammy Winder Denver Broncos	.70
236	Rubin Carter	.05
237	Barney Chavous	.40
238	John Elway	15.00
239	Steve Foley	.05
240	Mike Harden	.05
241	Tom Jackson	.15
242	Butch Johnson	.05
243	Rulon Jones	.05
244	Rick Karlis	.05
245	Steve Watson	.05
246	Gerald Wilhite	.05
247	Sammy Winder	.05
248	Larry Moriarty Houston Oilers Team:	.10
249	Jesse Baker	.05
250	Carter Hartwig	.05
251	*Warren Moon*	15.00
252	*Larry Moriarty*	.10
253	*Mike Munchak*	.50
254	Carl Roaches	.05
255	Tim Smith	.05
256	Willie Tullis	.05
257	Jamie Williams	.05
258	Art Schlichter Indianapolis Colts Team:	.10
259	Raymond Butler	.05
260	Johnie Cooks	.05
261	Eugene Daniel	.05
262	Curtis Dickey	.05
263	Chris Hinton	.20
264	Vernon Maxwell	.05
265	Randy McMillan	.05
266	Art Schlichter	.15
267	Rohn Stark	.05
268	Leo Wisniewski	.05
269	Bill Kenney Kansas City Chiefs Team:	.10
270	Jim Arnold	.05
271	Mike Bell	.05
272	Todd Blackledge	.15
273	Carlos Carson	.05
274	Deron Cherry	.25
275	*Herman Heard*	.10
276	Bill Kenney	.05
277	Nick Lowery	.30
278	*Bill Maas*	.30
279	Henry Marshall	.05
280	Art Still	.05
281	Marcus Allen Los Angeles Raiders Team:	.30
282	Marcus Allen	2.00
283	Lyle Alzado	.20
284	Chris Bahr	.05
285	Malcolm Barnwell	.05
286	Cliff Branch	.15
287	Todd Christensen	.05
288	Ray Guy	.15
289	Lester Hayes	.05
290	Mike Haynes (AP)	.05
291	Henry Lawrence	.05
292	Howie Long	2.00
293	Rod Martin (AP)	.05
294	Vann McElroy	.05
295	Matt Millen	.05
296	*Bill Pickel*	.15
297	Jim Plunkett	.20
298	*Dokie Williams*	.10
299	Marc Wilson	.05
300	Mark Duper Miami Dolphins Team:	.15
301	Bob Baumhower	.05
302	Doug Betters	.05
303	Glenn Blackwood	.05
304	Lyle Blackwood	.05
305	Kim Bokamper	.05
306	Charles Bowser	.05
307	Jimmy Cefalo	.05
308	*Mark Clayton* (AP)	1.00
309	A.J. Duhe	.05
310	Mark Duper	.50
311	Andra Franklin	.05
312	Bruce Hardy	.05
313	Pete Johnson	.05
314	Dan Marino (AP)	30.00
315	Tony Nathan	.05
316	Ed Newman	.05
317	Reggie Roby (AP)	.15
318	Dwight Stephenson (AP)	.05
319	Uwe Von Schamann	.05
320	Tony Collins New England Patriots Team:	.10
321	Raymond Clayborn	.05
322	Tony Collins	.05
323	*Tony Eason*	.30
324	Tony Franklin	.05
325	*Irving Fryar*	4.00
326	John Hannah (AP)	.20
327	Brian Holloway	.05
328	*Craig James*	.50
329	Stanley Morgan	.20
330	Steve Nelson (AP)	.05
331	Derrick Ramsey	.05
332	Stephen Starring	.05
333	Mosi Tatupu	.05
334	Andre Tippett	.50
335	Mark Gastineau, Ferguson New York Jets Team:	.10
336	Russell Carter	.05
337	Mark Gastineau (AP)	.05
338	Bruce Harper	.05
339	Bobby Humphery	.05
340	Johnny "Lam" Jones	.05
341	Joe Klecko	.05
342	Pat Leahy	.05
343	Marty Lyons	.05
344	Freeman McNeil	.20
345	Lance Mehl	.05
346	*Ken O'Brien*	.50
347	Marvin Powell	.05
348	Pat Ryan	.05
349	*Mickey Shuler*	.40
350	Wesley Walker	.15
351	Mark Malone Pittsburgh Steelers Team	.10
352	Walter Abercrombie	.05
353	Gary Anderson	.05
354	Robin Cole	.05
355	Bennie Cunningham	.05
356	Rich Erenberg	.05
357	Jack Lambert	.40
358	*Louis Lipps*	.50
359	Mark Malone	.05
360	*Mike Merriweather*	.60
361	Frank Pollard	.05
362	Donnie Shell	.05
363	John Stallworth	.15
364	Sam Washington	.05
365	Mike Webster	.20
366	Dwayne Woodruff	.05
367	San Diego Chargers Team	.10
368	Rolf Benirschke	.05
369	*Gill Byrd*	1.00
370	Wes Chandler	.05
371	Bobby Duckworth	.05
372	Dan Fouts	.60
373	Mike Green	.05
374	*Pete Holohan*	.60
375	Earnest Jackson	.20
376	Lionel James	.20
377	Charlie Joiner	.30
378	Billy Ray Smith	.05
379	Kellen Winslow	.30
380	Dave Krieg Seattle Seahawks Team	.10
381	Dave Brown	.05
382	Jeff Bryant	.05
383	Dan Doornink	.05
384	Kenny Easley (AP)	.05
385	Jacob Green	.05
386	David Hughes	.05
387	Norm Johnson	.05
388	Dave Krieg	.75
389	Steve Largent	.80
390	*Joe Nash*	.20
391	Daryl Turner	.05
392	Curt Warner	.15
393	*Fredd Young*	.20
394	Checklist 1-132	.15
395	Checklist 133-264	.15
396	Checklist 265-396	.15

1985 Topps Box Bottoms

The bottoms of 1985 Topps wax pack boxes featured these cards, which are numbered using a letter instead of a number. The design is the same as a regular 1985 Topps card, except the front border is red and "Topps Superstars" is printed at the top. The backs are identical to the regular cards' backs except for the letters used as card numbers.

		NM/M
Complete Set (16):		15.00
Common Player:		.30
A	Marcus Allen	1.50
B	Ottis Anderson	.30
C	Mark Clayton	1.00
D	Eric Dickerson	1.00
E	Tony Dorsett	.75
F	Dan Fouts	.75
G	Mark Gastineau	.30
H	Charlie Joiner	.50
I	James Lofton	.75
J	Neil Lomax	.30
K	Dan Marino	6.00
L	Art Monk	.75
M	Joe Montana	6.00
N	Walter Payton	2.50
O	John Stallworth	.30
P	Lawrence Taylor	.75

1985 Topps Star Set

This 11-card glossy set was a follow-up to the 1984 insert set. Cards were printed on heavy white cardboard stock, with red borders surrounding an action picture of each player. Cards were issued one per wax pack with the 1985 cards. Card backs were printed in blue and red and show pretty much the same design, front and back, as the 1984 insert set, but with smaller type indicating the year of issue on the back. This was the second and final year of Topps' production of United States Football League cards. The 132-card set was issued as a factory set. Cards were numbered alphabetically according to city and then according to the player's last name. Printed on white cardboard stock, fronts show a bright red border with a white and blue stripe across the middle; the USFL logo appears in the upper right corner. The team name appears in heavy red type at the bottom of the card, and the player's name and position is in a yellow football above the team name. Card backs show a goalpost design in blue and red. The set includes rookies Doug Flutie, Gary Clark and Gerald McNeill; plus Herschel Walker's second-year card.

		NM/M
Complete Set (11):		6.50
Common Player:		.25
1	Mark Clayton	.25
2	Eric Dickerson	1.75
3	John Elway	1.00
4	Mark Gastineau	.25
5	Ronnie Lott	.40
6	Dan Marino	1.25
7	Joe Montana	1.50
8	Walter Payton	1.50
9	John Riggins	.35
10	John Stallworth	.25
11	Lawrence Taylor	.35

1985 Topps "Coming Soon" Stickers

These stickers say "Coming Soon" on the backs and share identical card numbers with their counterparts in Topps' regular 1985 sticker set; thus, the checklist is skip-numbered. These stickers, which were random inserts in 1985 Topps football packs, measure 2-1/8" x 3" each but, unlike many of the regular stickers, feature only one player per sticker. The stickers have a colored photo on the front with a color frame and white border surrounding it.

		NM/M
Complete Set (30):		5.00
Common Player:		.08
6	Ken Anderson	.30
15	Greg Bell	.15
24	John Elway	.75
33	Ozzie Newsome	.25
42	Charlie Joiner	.25
51	Bill Kenney	.15
60	Randy McMillan	.08
69	Dan Marino	2.00
77	Mark Clayton	.50
78	Mark Gastineau	.08
87	Warren Moon	2.00
96	Tony Eason	.15
105	Marcus Allen	.50
114	Steve Largent	.60
123	John Stallworth	.20
156	Walter Payton	1.00
165	James Wilder	.12
174	Neil Lomax	.15
183	Tony Dorsett	.35
192	Mike Quick	.15
201	William Andrews	.10
210	Joe Montana	2.50
214	Dwight Clark	.35
219	Lawrence Taylor	.35
228	Billy Sims	.15
237	James Lofton	.30
246	Eric Dickerson	.50
255	John Riggins	.25
268	George Rogers	.12
281	Tommy Kramer	.08

1985 Topps Stickers

These stickers are different than those issued in previous years, because no foil stickers were produced. However, there were stickers issued in pairs on some cards; they are noted as being partners by the parenthesis which follows the player's name in the checklist. Charlie Joiner, Art Monk, Joe Montana, Dan Marino, Walter Payton and Eric Dickerson are all featured on the album cover; the 49ers team is on the back.

		NM/M
Complete Set (285):		20.00
Common Player:		.05
1	Super Bowl XIX	1.50
2	Super Bowl XIX	1.00
3	Super Bowl XIX	.10
4	Super Bowl XIX	.10
5	Super Bow XIX	.08
6	Ken Anderson	.30
7	M.L. Harris (157)	.05
8	Eddie Edwards (157)	.05
9	Louis Breeden (159)	.05
10	Larry Kinnebrew	.05
11	Isaac Curtis (161)	.06
12	James Brooks (162)	.12
13	Jim Breech (163)	.05
14	Boomer Esiason (164)	.75
15	Greg Bell	.10
16	Fred Smerlas (166)	.05
17	Joe Ferguson (167)	.06
18	Ken Johnson (168)	.05
19	Darryl Talley (169)	.25
20	Preston Dennard (170)	.05
21	Charles Romes (171)	.05
22	Jim Haslett (172)	.05
23	Byron Franklin	.05
24	John Elway	1.25
25	Rulon Jones (175)	.05
26	Butch Johnson (176)	.05
27	Rick Karlis (177)	.05
28	Sammy Winder	.05
29	Tom Jackson (179)	.10
30	Mike Harden (180)	.05
31	Steve Watson (181)	.05
32	Steve Foley (182)	.05
33	Ozzie Newsome	.25
34	Al Gross (184)	.05
35	Paul McDonald (185)	.05
36	Matt Bahr (186)	.07
37	Charles White (187)	.06
38	Don Rogers (188)	.05
39	Mike Pruitt (189)	.05
40	Reggie Camp (190)	.05
41	Boyce Green	.05
42	Charlie Joiner	.20
43	Dan Fouts (193)	.25
44	Keith Ferguson (194)	.05
45	Pete Holohan (195)	.05
46	Earnest Jackson	.08
47	Wes Chandler (197)	.06
48	Gill Byrd (198)	.15
49	Kellen Winslow (199)	.15
50	Billy Ray Smith (200)	.06
51	Bill Kenney	.08
52	Herman Heard (202)	.05
53	Art Still (203)	.05
54	Nick Lowery (204)	.05
55	Deron Cherry (205)	.08
56	Jenry Marshall (206)	.05
57	Mike Bell (207)	.05
58	Todd Blackledge (208)	.05
59	Carlos Carson	.08
60	Randy McMillan	.05
61	Donnell Thompson (211)	.05
62	Raymond Butler (212)	.05
63	Ray Donaldson (213)	.05
64	Art Schlichter	.15
65	Rohn Stark (215)	.05
66	Johnie Cooks (216)	.05
67	Mike Pagel (217)	.05
68	Eugene Daniel (218)	.05
69	Dan Marino	2.00
70	Pete Johnson (220)	.05
71	Tony Nathan (221)	.05
72	Glenn Blackwood (222)	.05
73	Woody Bennett (223)	.05
74	Dwight Stephenson (224)	.05
75	Mark Duper (225)	.10
76	Doug Betters (226)	.05
77	Mark Clayton	.50
78	Mark Gastineau	.08
79	Johnny Lam Jones (229)	.05
80	Mickey Shuler (230)	.05
81	Tony Paige (231)	.15
82	Freeman McNeil	.15
83	Russell Carter (233)	.06
84	Wesley Walker (234)	.06
85	Bruce Harper (235)	.15
86	Ken O'Brien (236)	1.75
87	Warren Moon	.05
88	Jesse Baker (238)	.05
89	Carl Roaches (239)	.05
90	Carter Hartwig (240)	.05
91	Larry Moriarty (241)	.05
92	Robert Brazile (242)	.05
93	Oliver Luck (243)	.05
94	Willie Tullis (244)	.05
95	Tim Smith	.05
96	Tony Eason	.12
97	Stanley Morgan (247)	.10
98	Mosi Tatupu (248)	.05
99	Raymond Clayborn (249)	.08
100	Andre Tippett	.10
101	Craig James (251)	.15
102	Derrick Ramsey (252)	.05
103	Tony Collins (253)	.05
104	Tony Franklin (254)	.05
105	Marcus Allen	.40
106	Chris Bahr (256)	.05
107	Marc Wilson (257)	.05
108	Howie Long (258)	.10
109	Bill Pickel (259)	.05
110	Mike Haynes (260)	.08
111	Malcolm Barnwell (261)	.05
112	Rod Martin (262)	.05
113	Todd Christensen	.10
114	Steve Largent	.75
115	Curt Warner (265)	.08
116	Kenny Easley (266)	.05
117	Jacob Green (267)	.05
118	Daryl Turner	.08
119	Norm Johnson (269)	.05
120	Dave Krieg (270)	.10
121	Eric Lane (271)	.05
122	Jeff Bryant (272)	.05
123	John Stallworth	.12
124	Donnie Shell (274)	.05
125	Gary Anderson (275)	.05
126	Mark Malone (276)	.05
127	Sam Washington (277)	.05
128	Frank Pollard (278)	.05
129	Mike Merriweather (279)	.10
130	Walter Abercrombie (280)	.05
131	Louis Lipps	.30
132	Mark Clayton (144)	.35
133	Randy Cross (145)	.06
134	Eric Dickerson (146)	.35
135	John Hannah (147)	.10
136	Mike Kenn (148)	.05
137	Dan Marino (149)	1.50

138 Art Monk (151) .15
139 Anthony Munoz (151) .10
140 Ozzie Newsome (152) .10
141 Walter Payton (153) .40
142 Jan Stenerud (154) .08
143 Dwight Stephenson (155) .05
144 Todd Bell (132) .05
145 Richard Dent (133) .50
146 Kenny Easley (134) .05
147 Mark Gastineau (135) .06
148 Dan Hampton (136) .10
149 Mark Haynes (137) .05
150 Mike Haynes (138) .06
151 E.J. Junior (139) .05
152 Rod Martin (140) .10
153 Steve Nelson (141) .05
154 Reggie Roby (142) .05
155 Lawrence Taylor (143) .15
156 Walter Payton .60
157 Dan Hampton (7) .08
158 Willie Gault (8) .06
159 Matt Suhey (9) .05
160 Richard Dent 1.00
161 Mike Singletary (11) .10
162 Gary Fencik (12) .05
163 Jim McMahon (13) .10
164 Bob Thomas (14) .05
165 James Wilder .08
166 Steve DeBerg (16) .08
167 Mark Cotney (17) .05
168 Adger Armstrong (18) .05
169 Gerald Carter (19) .05
170 David Logari (20) .05
171 Hugh Green (21) .05
172 Lee Roy Selmon (22) .06
173 Kevin House .10
174 Neil Lomax .12
175 Ottis Anderson (25) .10
176 Al (Bubba) Baker (26) .05
177 E.J. Junior (27) .08
178 Roy Green .10
179 Pat Tilley (29) .05
180 Stump Mitchell (30) .05
181 Lionel Washington (31) .05
182 Curtis Greer (32) .05
183 Tony Dorsett .25
184 Gary Hogeboom (34) .06
185 Jim Jeffcoat (35) .06
186 Danny White (36) .08
187 Michael Downs (37) .05
188 Doug Cosbie (38) .08
189 Tony Hill (39) .05
190 Rafael Septien (40) .05
191 Randy White .15
192 Mike Quick .08
193 Ray Ellis (43) .05
194 John Spagnola (44) .05
195 Dennis Harrison (45) .05
196 Wilbert Montgomery .08
197 Greg Brown (47) .05
198 Ron Jaworski (48) .08
199 Paul McFadden (49) .05
200 Wes Hopkins (50) .05
201 William Andrews .10
202 Mike Pitts (52) .05
203 Steve Bartkowski (53) .08
204 Gerald Riggs (54) .08
205 Alfred Jackson (55) .05
206 Don Smith (56) .05
207 Mike Kenn (57) .05
208 Kenny Johnson (58) .05
209 Stacey Bailey .05
210 Joe Montana 1.25
211 Wendell Tyler (61) .05
212 Keena Turner (62) .08
213 Ray Wersching (63) .05
214 Dwight Clark .15
215 Dwaine Board (65) .05
216 Roger Craig (66) .15
217 Ronnie Lott (67) .15
218 Freddie Solomon (68) .08
219 Lawrence Taylor .25
220 Zeke Mowatt (70) .05
221 Harry Carson (71) .06
222 Rob Carpenter (72) .05
223 Bobby Johnson (73) .05
224 Joe Morris (74) .07
225 Mark Haynes (75) .05
226 Lionel Manuel (76) .05
227 Phil Simms .15
228 Billy Simms .12
229 Leonard Thompson (79) .03
230 James Jones (80) .05
231 Ed Murray (81) .05
232 William Gay .05
233 Gary Danielson (83) .05
234 Curtis Green (84) .05
235 Bobby Watkins (85) .05
236 Doug English (86) .05
237 James Lofton .20
238 Eddie Lee Ivery (88) .06
239 Mike Douglas (89) .05
240 Gerry Ellis (90) .05
241 Tim Lewis (91) .08
242 Paul Coffman (92) .05
243 Tom Flynn (93) .05
244 Ezra Johnson (94) .05
245 Lynn Dickey .08
246 Eric Dickerson .60
247 Jack Youngblood (97) .08
248 Doug Smith (98) .05
249 Jeff Kemp (99) .05
250 Kent Hill .05
251 Mike Lansford (101) .05
252 Henry Ellard (102) .35
253 LeRoy Irvin (103) .06
254 Ron Brown (104) .20
255 John Riggins .06
256 Dexter Manley (106) .10
257 Darrell Green (107) .15
258 Joe Theismann (108) .05
259 Mark Moseley (109) .05
260 Clint Didier (110) .05
261 Vernon Dean (111) .05
262 Calvin Muhammad (112) .05
263 Art Monk .20
264 Bruce Clark .08
265 Hoby Brenner (115) .05
266 Dave Wilson (116) .06
267 Hokie Gajan (117) .05
268 George Rogers .10
269 Rickey Jackson (119) .08
270 Brian Hansen (120) .04
271 Dave Waymer (121) .05
272 Richard Todd (122) .05
273 Jan Stenerud .15
274 Ted Brown (124) .05
275 Leo Lewis (125) .05
276 Scott Studwell (126) .05
277 Alfred Anderson (127) .05
278 Rufus Bess (128) .05
279 Darrin Nelson (129) .05
280 Greg Coleman (130) .05
281 Tommy Kramer .08
282 Joe Montana (283) 1.25
283 Dan Marino (282) 1.00
284 Brian Hansen (285) .05
285 Jim Arnold (284) .05

1985 Topps USFL

This was the second and final year of Topps' production of United States Football League cards. The 132-card set was issued as a factory set. Cards were numbered alphabetically according to city and according to the player's last name. Printed on white cardboard stock, fronts show a bright red border with a white and blue stripe across the middle; the USFL logo appears in the upper right corner. The team name appears in heavy red type at the bottom of the card, and the player's name and position are in a yellow football above the team name. Card backs show a goalpost design in blue and red. The set includes rookies of Doug Flutie, Gary Clark and Gerald McNeil, plus Herschel Walker's second-year card.

NM/M
Complete Set (132): 100.00
Common Player: .35
1 Case DeBruijn .35
2 Mike Katolin .35
3 Bruce Laird .35
4 Kit Lathrop .35
5 Kevin Long .35
6 Karl Lorch .35
7 Dave Tipton .35
8 Doug Williams .40
9 Luis Zendejas .35
10 Kelvin Bryant .75
11 Willie Collier .35
12 Irv Eatman .50
13 Scott Fitzkee .35
14 *William Fuller* 6.00
15 Chuck Fusina .35
16 Pete Kugler .35
17 Garcia Lane .35
18 Mike Lush .35
19 *Sam Mills* 8.00
20 Buddy Aydelette .35
21 Joe Cribbs .50
22 David Dumars .35
23 Robin Earl .35
24 Joey Jones .35
25 Leon Perry .35
26 Dave Pureifory .35
27 Bill Roe .35
28 *Doug Smith* 2.00
29 Cliff Stoudt .35
30 Jeff Delaney .35
31 Vince Evans .50
32 *Leonard Harris* 2.00
33 Bill Johnson .35
34 Marc Lewis .35
35 David Martin .35
36 Bruce Thornton .35
37 Craig Walls .35
38 Vincent White .35
39 Luther Bradley .35
40 Pete Catan .35
41 Kiki DeAyala .35
42 Tony Fritsch .35
43 Sam Harrell .35
44 *Richard Johnson* 1.50
45 Jim Kelly 35.00
46 *Gerald McNeil* 1.50
47 *Clarence Verdin* 2.00
48 Dale Walters .35
49 *Gary Clark* 15.00
50 Tom Dinkel .35
51 Mike Edwards .35
52 Brian Franco .35
53 Bob Gruber .35
54 Robbie Mahfouz .35
55 Mike Rozier 1.75
56 Brian Sipe .50
57 J.T. Turner .35
58 Howard Carson .35
59 *Wymon Henderson* .60
60 Kevin Nelson .35
61 Jeff Partridge .35
62 Ben Rudolph .35
63 JoJo Townsell .35
64 Eddie Weaver .35
65 Steve Young 80.00
66 *Tony Zendejas* .75
67 Mossy Cade .35
68 *Leonard Coleman* .50
69 John Corker .35
70 Derrick Crawford .35
71 Art Kuehn .35
72 Walter Lewis .35
73 Tyrone McGriff .35
74 Tim Spencer .35
75 Reggie White 30.00
76 *Gizmo Williams* 2.00
77 Sam Bowers .35
78 *Maurice Carthon* 1.25
79 Clarence Collins .35
80 *Doug Flutie* 30.00
81 Freddie Gilbert .35
82 Kerry Justin .35
83 Dave Lapham .35
84 Rick Partridge .35
85 *Roger Ruzek* 1.00
86 Herschel Walker 6.00
87 Gordon Banks .35
88 Monte Bennett .35
89 *Albert Bentley* 3.00
90 Novo Bojovic .35
91 Dave Browning .35
92 Anthony Carter 4.00
93 Bobby Hebert 3.00
94 Ray Pinney .35
95 Stan Talley .35
96 Ruben Vaughan .35
97 Curtis Bledsoe .35
98 Reggie Collier .35
99 Jerry Doerger .35
100 Jerry Golsteyn .35
101 Bob Niziolek .35
102 Joel Patten .35
103 Ricky Simmons .35
104 Joey Walters .35
105 Marcus Dupree .35
106 Jeff Gossett .50
107 Frank Lockett .35
108 Marcus Marek .35
109 Kenny Neil .35
110 Robert Pennywell .35
111 Matt Robinson .35
112 Dan Ross .35
113 Doug Woodward .35
114 Danny Buggs .35
115 Putt Choate .35
116 Greg Fields .35
117 Ken Hartley .35
118 Nick Mike-Mayer .35
119 Rick Neuheisel .35
120 Peter Raeford .35
121 Gary Worthy .35
122 Gary Anderson 3.00
123 Zenon Andrusyshyn .35
124 Greg Boone .35
125 Mike Butler .35
126 Mike Clark .35
127 Willie Gillespie .35
128 James Harrell .35
130 John Reaves .35
131 Eric Truvillion .35
132 Checklist 1-132 .50

1985 Topps USFL New Jersey Generals

This nine-card sheet features members of the USFL's New Jersey Generals. The panel is 7-1/2" x 10-1/2"; individual cards would be the standard size if they were cut out of the panel. The card front has an action photo of the player, along with his name, team name and team logo. The back is numbered and includes biographical and statistical information, plus a brief player profile. The card stock is gray; the print is yellow and red on the back.

NM/M
Complete Set (9): 35.00
Common Player: 2.00
1 Walt Michaels 2.00
2 Sam Bowers 2.00
3 Clarence Collins 2.00
4 Doug Flutie 20.00
5 Gregory Johnson 2.00
6 Jim LeClair 3.00
7 Bobby Leopold 2.00
8 Herschel Walker 15.00
9 Membership card (schedule on back) 2.00

1986 Topps

Topps' 1986 offering was 396 cards for the fourth straight year. Cards showed a green background with diagonal white stripes; a photo of the player was enclosed in one of several colorful borders. The player's name is found at the bottom of the card; his team is at right. All-Pro cards show a small designation just above the player's name. Team cards show a yellow border. Cards were numbered according to the team's finish the previous season. Rookies in this set include William Perry, Al Toon, Jerry Rice, Keith Millard, Bernie Kosar, and Boomer Esiason. (Key: AP - All Pro)

NM/M
Complete Set (396): 180.00
Common Player: .05
Wax Pack (17+1): 15.00
Wax Box (36): 375.00
1 Marcus Allen .65
2 Eric Dickerson .30
3 Lionel James .10
4 Steve Largent .30
5 George Martin .10
6 Stephone Paige .10
7 Walter Payton .75
8 Super Bowl XX .20
9 Walter Payton Chicago Bears Team .75
10 Jim McMahon .30
11 Walter Payton (AP) 4.00
12 Matt Suhey .05
13 Willie Gault .10
14 *Dennis McKinnon* .25
15 Emery Moorhead .05
16 Jim Covert (AP) .10
17 *Jay Hilgenberg* (AP) .50
18 *Kevin Butler* 1.00
19 Richard Dent (AP) 1.00
20 *William Perry* .80
21 Steve McMichael .50
22 Dan Hampton .25
23 Otis Wilson .05
24 Mike Singletary .60
25 *Wilber Marshall* 1.00
26 Leslie Frazier .05
27 *Dave Duerson* .35
28 Gary Fencik .10
29 Craig James New England Patriots Team .10
30 Tony Eason .20
31 Steve Grogan .15
32 Craig James .10
33 Tony Collins .05
34 Irving Fryar 1.50
35 Brian Holloway (AP) .10
36 John Hannah (AP) .20
37 Tony Franklin .05
38 Garin Veris .10
39 Andre Tippett (AP) .20
40 Steve Nelson .05
41 Raymond Clayborn .05
42 *Fred Marion* .10
43 Rich Camarillo .05
44 Dan Marino Miami Dolphins Team 2.00
45 Dan Marino (AP) 12.00
46 Tony Nathan .10
47 Ron Davenport .10
48 Mark Duper .30
49 Mark Clayton .50
50 Nat Moore .05
51 Bruce Hardy .05
52 Roy Foster .05
53 Dwight Stephenson .05
54 *Fuad Reveiz* .20
55 Bob Baumhower .10
56 Mike Charles .05
57 Hugh Green .05
58 Glenn Blackwood .05
59 Reggie Roby .05
60 Marcus Allen Los Angeles Raiders Team .25
61 Marc Wilson .10
62 Marcus Allen (AP) 1.25
63 Dokie Williams .05
64 Todd Christensen .05
65 Chris Bahr .05
66 Fulton Walker .05
67 Howie Long .50
68 Bill Pickel .05
69 Ray Guy .15
70 *Greg Townsend* 1.00
71 Rod Martin .05
72 Matt Millen .05
73 Mike Haynes (AP) .10
74 Lester Hayes .05
75 Vann McElroy .05
76 Eric Dickerson Los Angeles Rams Team .15
77 Dieter Brock .10
78 Eric Dickerson 1.00
79 Henry Ellard 1.00
80 *Ron Brown* .30
81 Tony Hunter .10
82 Kent Hill (AP) .05
83 Doug Smith .05
84 Dennis Harrah .05
85 Jackie Slater .25
86 Mike Lansford .05
87 Gary Jeter .05
88 Mike Wilcher .05
89 Jim Collins .05
90 LeRoy Irvin .05
91 Gary Green .05
92 Nolan Cromwell .05
93 Dale Hatcher .05
94 Freeman McNeil New York Jets Team .10
95 Ken O'Brien .35
96 Freeman McNeil .20
97 *Tony Paige* .50
98 Johnny "Lam" Jones .05
99 Wesley Walker .10
100 Kurt Sohn .05
101 *Al Toon* 1.00
102 Mickey Shuler .05
103 Marvin Powell .10
104 Pat Leahy .05
105 Mark Gastineau .25
106 Joe Klecko (AP) .10
107 Marty Lyons .05
108 Lance Mehl .05
109 Bobby Jackson .05
110 Dave Jennings .05
111 Sammy Winder Denver Broncos Team .10
112 John Elway 10.00
113 Sammy Winder .10
114 Gerald Wilhite .10
115 Steve Watson .10
116 *Vance Johnson* .50
117 Rick Karlis .05
118 Rulon Jones .10
119 *Karl Mecklenburg* (AP) 2.50
120 Louis Wright .05
121 Mike Harden .05
122 *Dennis Smith* .50
123 Steve Foley .05
124 Tony Hill Dallas Cowboys Team .10
125 Danny White .20
126 Tony Dorsett .50
127 Timmy Newsome .05
128 Mike Renfro .05
129 Tony Hill .10
130 Doug Cosbie (AP) .10
131 Rafael Septien .10
132 Ed "Too Tall" Jones .25
133 Randy White .25
134 Jim Jeffcoat .20
135 Everson Walls (AP) .05
136 Dennis Thurman .05
137 Joe Morris New York Giants Team .10
138 Phil Simms .40
139 Joe Morris .20
140 *George Adams* .05
141 Lionel Manuel .05
142 Bobby Johnson .05
143 *Phil McConkey* .20
144 *Mark Bavaro* 1.00
145 Zeke Mowatt .05
146 Brad Benson .10
147 *Bart Oates* .60
148 *Leonard Marshall* (AP) .50
149 Jim Burt .05
150 George Martin .05
151 Lawrence Taylor (AP) .75
152 Harry Carson (AP) .15
153 Elvis Patterson .05
154 Sean Landeta .10
155 Roger Craig San Francisco 49ers Team .25
156 Joe Montana 10.00
157 Roger Craig .75
158 Wendell Tyler .10
159 Carl Monroe .05
160 Dwight Clark .25
161 *Jerry Rice* 150.00
162 Randy Cross .05
163 Keith Fahnhorst .05
164 Jeff Stover .05
165 *Michael Carter* .50
166 Dwaine Board .05
167 Eric Wright .05
168 Ronnie Lott .75
169 Carlton Williamson .05
170 Dave Butz Washington Redskins Team .10
171 Joe Theismann .40
172 *Jay Schroeder* .50
173 George Rogers .15
174 Ken Jenkins .05
175 Art Monk (AP) .75
176 *Gary Clark* 2.00
177 Joe Jacoby .05
178 Russ Grimm .05
179 Mark Moseley .10
180 Dexter Manely .15
181 *Charles Mann* 1.00
182 Vernon Dean .05
183 *Raphel Cherry* .15
184 Curtis Jordan .05
185 Bernie Kosar Cleveland Browns Team .40
186 Gary Danielson .05
187 *Bernie Kosar* 2.00
188 *Kevin Mack* .50
189 *Earnest Byner* 1.00
190 Glen Young .05
191 Ozzie Newsome .30
192 Mike Baab .05
193 Cody Risien .05
194 Bob Golic .10
195 Reggie Camp .05
196 Chip Banks .10
197 Tom Cousineau .10
198 *Frank Minnifield* .30
199 Al Gross .05
200 Curt Warner Seattle Seahawks Team .10
201 Dave Krieg .25
202 Curt Warner .15
203 Steve Largent (AP) .65
204 Norm Johnson .05
205 Daryl Turner .05
206 Jacob Green .05
207 Joe Nash .05
208 Jeff Bryant .05
209 Randy Edwards .05
210 Fredd Young .10
211 Kenny Easley .10
212 John Harris .05
213 Paul Coffman Green Bay Packers Team .10
214 Lynn Dickey .15
215 Gerry Ellis .05
216 Eddie Lee Ivery .05
217 Jessie Clark .05
218 James Lofton .60
219 Paul Coffman .05
220 Alphonso Carreker .05
221 Ezra Johnson .05
222 Mike Douglass .05
223 Tim Lewis .05
224 *Mark Murphy* .05
225 Joe Montana, Ken O'Brien Passing Leaders 1.00
226 Lionel James, Roger Craig Receiving Leaders .15
227 Marcus Allen, Gerald Riggs Rushing Leaders .25
228 Gary Anderson, Kevin Butler Scoring Leaders .05
229 Eugene Daniel, Albert Lewis, Everson Walls Interception Leaders .05
230 Dan Fouts San Diego Chargers Team .20
231 Dan Fouts .60
232 Lionel James .10
233 *Gary Anderson* 1.00
234 *Tim Spencer* .10
235 Wes Chandler .10
236 Charlie Joiner .25
237 Kellen Winslow .25
238 *Jim Lachey* .50
239 Bob Thomas .05
240 Jeffery Dale .05
241 Ralf Mojsiejenko .05
242 Eric Hipple Detroit Lions Team .10
243 Eric Hipple .05
244 Billy Sims .15
245 James Jones .05
246 *Pete Mandley* .15
247 Leonard Thompson .05
248 *Lomas Brown* .50
249 Ed Murray .05
250 Curtis Green .05
251 William Gay .05
252 Jimmy Williams .05
253 Bobby Watkins .05
254 Boomer Esiason Cincinnati Bengals Team .75
255 *Boomer Esiason* 4.00
256 James Brooks .35
257 Larry Kinnebrew .10
258 Cris Collinsworth .05
259 Mike Martin .05
260 *Eddie Brown* .50
261 Anthony Munoz .25
262 Jim Breech .05
263 Ross Browner .10
264 Carl Zander .05
265 James Griffin .05
266 Robert Jackson .05
267 Pat McInally .10
268 Ron Jaworski Philadelphia Eagles Team .10
269 Ron Jaworski .15
270 Earnest Jackson .05
271 Mike Quick .10
272 John Spagnola .05
273 Mark Dennard .05
274 Paul McFadden .05
275 *Reggie White* 12.00
276 Greg Brown .05
277 Herman Edwards .05
278 Roynell Young .10
279 Wes Hopkins (AP) .05
280 Walter Abercrombie Pittsburgh Steelers Team .10
281 Mark Malone .05
282 Frank Pollard .05
283 Walter Abercrombie .10
284 Louis Lipps .40
285 John Stallworth .15
286 Mike Webster .20
287 Gary Anderson (AP) .25
288 Keith Willis .05
289 Mike Merriweather .10
290 Dwayne Woodruff .05
291 Donnie Shell .10
292 Tommy Kramer Minnesota Vikings Team .10
293 Tommy Kramer .10
294 Darrin Nelson .05
295 Ted Brown .05
296 Buster Rhymes .15
297 *Anthony Carter* 2.00
298 *Steve Jordan* 1.00
299 *Keith Millard* .50
300 *Joey Browner* .75
301 John Turner .05
302 Greg Coleman .05
303 Todd Blackledge Kansas City Chiefs Team .10
304 Bill Kenney .05
305 Herman Heard .05
306 *Stephon Paige* .75
307 Carlos Carson .05
308 Nick Lowery .20
309 Mike Bell .05
310 Bill Maas .05
311 Art Still .10
312 *Albert Lewis* 1.25
313 Deron Cherry (AP) .20
314 Rohn Stark Indianapolis Colts Team .10
315 Mike Pagel .05
316 Randy McMillian .05
317 *Albert Bentley* .40
318 George Wonsley .10
319 Robbie Martin .05
320 Pat Beach .05
321 Chris Hinton .10
322 *Duane Bickett* .50
323 Eugene Daniel .05
324 *Cliff Odom* .15
325 Rohn Stark (AP) .05

326 Stump Mitchell St. Louis Cardinals Team .10
327 Neil Lomax .15
328 Stump Mitchell .05
329 Ottis Anderson .20
330 J.T. Smith .05
331 Pat Tilley .05
332 Roy Green .05
333 Lance Smith .05
334 Curtis Greer .05
335 *Freddie Joe Nunn* .35
336 E.J. Junior .05
337 *Lonnie Young* .20
338 Wayne Wilson New Orleans Saints Team .10
339 *Bobby Hebert* .75
340 Dave Wilson .05
341 Wayne Wilson .05
342 Hoby Brenner .05
343 Stan Brock .05
344 Morten Andersen .35
345 Bruce Clark .05
346 Rickey Jackson .60
347 Dave Waymer .05
348 Brian Hansen .05
349 Warren Moon Houston Oilers Team .60
350 Warren Moon 4.00
351 *Mike Rozier* .30
352 Butch Woolfolk .05
353 Drew Hill .30
354 *Willie Drewrey* .20
355 Tim Smith .05
356 Mike Munchak .30
357 *Ray Childress* 1.50
358 Frank Bush .05
359 Steve Brown .05
360 Gerald Riggs Atlanta Falcons Team .10
361 Dave Archer .05
362 Gerald Riggs .10
363 William Andrews .05
364 Billy Johnson .05
365 Arthur Cox .05
366 Mike Kenn .05
367 *Bill Fralic* .75
368 Mick Luckhurst .05
369 Rick Bryan .05
370 Bobby Butler .05
371 Rick Donnelly .05
372 James Wilder Tampa Bay Buccaneers Team .10
373 Steve DeBerg .25
374 *Steve Young* 30.00
375 James Wilder .05
376 Kevin House .05
377 Gerald Carter .05
379 Sean Farrell .05
380 Donald Igwebuike .05
381 David Logan .05
382 *Jeremiah Castille* .12
383 Greg Bell Buffalo Bills Team .10
384 *Bruce Mathison* .15
385 Joe Cribbs .05
386 Greg Bell .15
387 Jerry Butler .05
388 *Andre Reed* 5.00
389 *Bruce Smith* 6.00
390 Fred Smerlas .05
391 Darryl Talley .50
392 Jim Haslett .05
393 Charles Romes .05
394 Checklist 1-132 .15
395 Checklist 133-264 .15
396 Checklist 265-396 .15

1986 Topps Box Bottoms

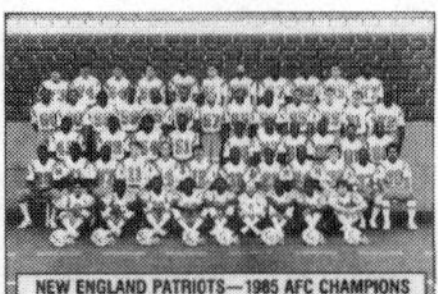

These four cards were featured on the sides of 1986 Topps wax pack boxes, one per box. The cards, which are standard size, feature the top four teams in the NFL in 1985 - the two Super Bowl participants and their opponents in the conference championship games. The team is pictured on the front; the back identifies those in the picture.

NM/M
Complete Set (4): 5.00
Common Player: 1.00
A Chicago Bears 2.50
B New England Patriots 1.00
C Los Angeles Rams 1.00
D Miami Dolphins 2.50

1986 Topps 1000 Yard Club

Issued one card per wax pack with the 1986 regular-issue cards, this 26-card set shows each player who gained 1,000 yards rushing or receiving the previous year. The card order was determined by the number of yards gained, with Marcus Allen, 1985's leading ground-gainer, ending up first. (San Francisco's Roger Craig gained 1,000 yards rushing and receiving the previous year, but only his rushing yardage is listed). Printed on heavy white cardboard stock, card fronts show an ornate arch design in light green. Backs are printed in red and orange.

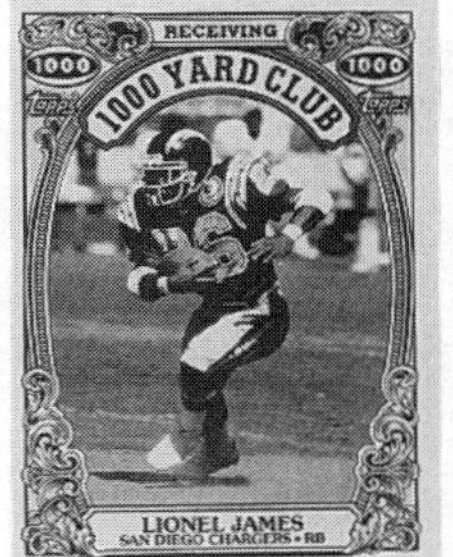

NM/M
Complete Set (26): 6.00
Common Player: .10
1 Marcus Allen .40
2 Gerald Riggs .20
3 Walter Payton 1.00
4 Joe Morris .30
5 Freeman McNeil .20
6 Tony Dorsett .50
7 James Wilder .10
8 Steve Largent 1.00
9 Mike Quick .10
10 Eric Dickerson 1.25
11 Craig James .10
12 Art Monk .20
13 Wes Chandler .10
14 Drew Hill .10
15 James Lofton .20
16 Louis Lipps .20
17 Cris Collinsworth .10
18 Tony Hill .10
19 Kevin Mack .10
20 Curt Warner .20
21 George Rogers .10
22 Roger Craig .40
23 Earnest Jackson .10
24 Lionel James .10
25 Stump Mitchell .10
26 Earnest Byner .10

1986 Topps Stickers

Topps included foil stickers in its sticker set again in 1986, and followed the format it used for previous issues. The stickers use a shadow box for the frame on the front, around a color photo. A card number appears on both sides. The back has its information printed in brown ink against a white background. Some stickers were issued in pairs, as indicated by the parenthesis after the player's name in the checklist. The All-Pro players are foil stickers (#s 132-143), as are #s 282-285. The Chicago Bears are featured on the covers of the corresponding album which was issued to hold the stickers; Walter Payton is on the front.

NM/M
Complete Set (285): 20.00
Common Player: .05
1 Walter Payton (left) .60
2 Walter Payton (right) .60
3 Richard Dent (left) .10
4 Richard Dent (right) .10
5 Richard Dent (Super Bowl MVP) .40
6 Walter Payton 1.00
7 William Perry .12
8 Jim McMahon (158) .10
9 Richard Dent (159) .10
10 Jim Covert (160) .05
11 Dan Hampton (161) .08
12 Mike Singletary (162) .08
13 Jay Hilgenberg (163) .06
14 Otis Wilson (164) .04
15 Jimmie Giles .05
16 Kevin House (166) .03
17 Jeremiah Castille (167) .03
18 James Wilder .05
19 Donald Igwebuike (169) .05
20 David Logan (170) .05
21 Jeff Davis (171) .05
22 Frank Garcia (172) .05
23 Steve Young (173) 1.00
24 Stump Mitchell .08
25 E.J. Junior .08
26 J.T. Smith (176) .05
27 Pat Tilley (177) .05
28 Neil Lomax (178) .06
29 Leonard Smith (179) .05
30 Ottis Anderson (180) .08
31 Curtis Greer (181) .05
32 Roy Green (182) .06
33 Tony Dorsett .30
34 Tony Hill (184) .05
35 Doug Cosbie (185) .06
36 Everson Walls .08
37 Randy White (187) .10
38 Rafael Septien (188) .05
39 Mike Renfro (189) .05
40 Danny White (190) .06
41 Ed "Too Tall" Jones (191) .10
42 Earnest Jackson .08
43 Mike Quick .08
44 Wes Hopkins (194) .05
45 Reggie White (195) .75
46 Greg Brown (196) .05
47 Paul McFadden (197) .05
48 John Spagnola (198) .05
49 Ron Jaworski (199) .05
50 Herman Hunter (200) .05
51 Gerald Riggs .10
52 Mike Pitts (202) .05
53 Buddy Curry (203) .05
54 Billy Johnson .12
55 Rick Donnelly (205) .05
56 Rick Bryan (206) .08
57 Bobby Butler (207) .05
58 Mike Luckhurst (208) .05
59 Mike Kenn (209) .05
60 Roger Craig .25
61 Joe Montana 1.75
62 Michael Carter (212) .10
63 Eric Wright (213) .05
64 Dwight Clark (214) .10
65 Ronnie Lott (215) .12
66 Carlton Williamson (216) .05
67 Wendell Tyler (217) .08
68 Dwaine Board (218) .05
69 Joe Morris .12
70 Leonard Marshall (220) .05
71 Lionel Manuel (221) .05
72 Harry Carson .10
73 Phil Simms (223) .10
74 Sean Landeta (224) .05
75 Lawrence Taylor (225) .15
76 Elvis Patterson (226) .05
77 George Adams (227) .05
78 James Jones .08
79 Leonard Thompson .05
80 William Graham (230) .05
81 Mark Nichols (231) .05
82 William Gay (232) .05
83 Jimmy Williams (233) .05
84 Billy Sims (234) .12
85 Bobby Watkins (235) .05
86 Ed Murray (236) .05
87 James Lofton .25
88 Jessie Clark (238) .05
89 Tim Lewis (239) .05
90 Eddie Lee Ivery .08
91 Phillip Epps (241) .05
92 Ezra Johnson (242) .05
93 Mike Douglass (243) .05
94 Paul Coffman (244) .05
95 Randy Scott (245) .03
96 Eric Dickerson .45
97 Dale Hatcher .05
98 Ron Brown (248) .06
99 LeRoy Irvin (249) .05
100 Ken Hill (250) .05
101 Dennis Harrah (251) .05
102 Jackie Slater (252) .08
103 Mike Wilcher (253) .05
104 Doug Smith (254) .05
105 Art Monk .25
106 Joe Jacoby (256) .05
107 Russ Grimm (257) .05
108 George Rogers .10
109 Dexter Manley (259) .05
110 Jay Schroeder (260) .12
111 Gary Calrk (261) .50
112 Curtis Jordan (262) .05
113 Charles Mann (263) .08
114 Morten Andersen .08
115 Rickey Jackson .10
116 Glen Redd (266) .05
117 Bobby Hebert (267) .20
118 Hoby Brenner (268) .05
119 Brian Hansen (269) .05
120 Dave Waymer (270) .05
121 Bruce Clark (271) .05
122 Wayne Wilson (272) .05
123 Joey Browner .25
124 Darrin Nelson (274) .08
125 Keith Millard (275) .15
126 Anthony Carter .35
127 Buster Rhymes (277) .04
128 Steve Jordan (278) .20
129 Greg Coleman (279) .05
130 Ted Brown (280) .05
131 John Turner (281) .05
132 Harry Carson (144, All-Pro) .20
133 Deron Cherry (145, All-Pro) .10
134 Richard Dent (146, All-Pro) .20
135 Mike Haynes (147, All-Pro) .12
136 Wes Hopkins (148, All-Pro) .10
137 Joe Klecko (149, All-Pro) .10
138 Leonard Marshall (150, All-Pro) .10
139 Karl Mecklenburg (151, All-Pro) .12
140 Rohn Stark (152, All-Pro) .10
141 Lawrence Taylor (153, All-Pro) .25
142 Andre Tippett (154, All-Pro) .12
143 Everson Walls (155, All-Pro) .12
144 Marcus Allen (132, All-Pro) .35
145 Gary Anderson (133, All-Pro) .10
146 Doug Cosbie (134, All-Pro) .15
147 Jim Covert (135, All-Pro) .15
148 John Hannah (136, All-Pro) .15
149 Jay Hilgenberg (137, All-Pro) .12
150 Ken Hil (138, All-Pro) .10
151 Brian Holloway (139, All-Pro) .10
152 Steve Largent (140, All-Pro) .75
153 Dan Marino (141, All-Pro) 1.50
154 Art Monk (142, All-Pro) .25
155 Walter Payton (143, All-Pro) .75
156 Anthony Munoz .15
157 Boomer Esiason .40
158 Cris Collinsworth (8) .06
159 Eddie Edwards (9) .05
160 James Griffin (10) .05
161 Jim Breech (11) .05
162 Eddie Brown (12) .05
163 Ross Browner (13) .05
164 James Brooks (14) .07
165 Greg Bell .08
166 Jerry Butler (16) .05
167 Don Wilson (17) .05
168 Andre Reed .75
169 Jim Haslett (19) .05
170 Bruce Mathison (20) .05
171 Bruce Smith (21) .40
172 Joe Cribbs (22) .05
173 Charles Romes (23) .05
174 Karl Mecklenburg .08
175 Rulon Jones .05
176 John Elway (26) .40
177 Sammy Winder (27) .10
178 Louis Wright (28) .05
179 Steve Watson (29) .05
180 Dennis Smith (30) .05
181 Mike Harden (31) .05
182 Vance Johnson (32) .10
183 Kevin Mack .10
184 Chip Banks (34) .05
185 Bob Golic (35) .05
186 Earnest Byner .35
187 Ozzie Newsome (37) .12
188 Bernie Kosar (38) .60
189 Don Rogers (39) .05
190 Al Gross (40) .05
191 Clarence Weathers (41) .08
192 Lionel James .08
193 Dan Fouts .40
194 Wes Chandler (44) .06
195 Kellen Winslow (45) .10
196 Gary Anderson (46) .07
197 Charlie Joiner (47) .08
198 Ralf Mojsiejenko (48) .05
199 Bob Thomas (49) .05
200 Tim Spencer (50) .05
201 Deron Cherry .10
202 Bill Maas (52) .05
203 Herman Heard (53) .05
204 Carlos Carson .08
205 Nick Lowery (55) .08
206 Bill Kenney (56) .05
207 Albert Lewis (57) .25
208 Art Still (58) .05
209 Stephone Paige (59) .25
210 Rohn Stark .05
211 Chris Hinton .10
212 Albert Bentley (62) .10
213 Eugene Daniel (63) .05
214 Pat Beach (64) .05
215 Cliff Odom (65) .05
216 Duane Bickett (66) .20
217 George Wonsley (67) .05
218 Randy McMillan (68) .05
219 Dan Marino 1.50
220 Dwight Stephenson (70) .08
221 Roy Foster (71) .05
222 Mark Clayton .20
223 Mark Duper (73) .10
224 Fuad Reveiz (74) .05
225 Reggie Roby (75) .05
226 Tony Nathan (76) .05
227 Ron Davenport (77) .05
228 Freeman McNeil .10
229 Joe Klecko .08
230 Mark Gastineau (80) .05
231 Ken O'Brien (81) .06
232 Lance Mehl (82) .05
233 Al Toon (83) .20
234 Mickey Shuler (84) .05
235 Pat Leahy (85) .05
236 Wesley Walker (86) .06
237 Drew Hill .10
238 Warren Moon (88) .40
239 Mike Rozier (89) .10
240 Mike Munchak .10
241 Tim Smith (91) .05
242 Butch Woolfolk (92) .05
243 Willie Drewrey (93) .05
244 Keith Bostic (94) .05
245 Jesse Baker (95) .05
246 Craig James .15
247 John Hannah .12
248 Tony Eason (98) .06
249 Andre Tippett (99) .06
250 Tony Collins (100) .05
251 Brian Holloway (101) .05
252 Irving Fryar (102) .10
253 Raymond Clayborn (103) .05
254 Steve Nelson (104) .05
255 Marcus Allen .25
256 Mike Haynes (106) .08
257 Todd Christensen (107) .06
258 Howie Long .12
259 Lester Hayes (109) .05
260 Rod Martin (110) .08
261 Dokie Williams (111) .08
262 Chris Bahr (112) .05
263 Bill Pickel (113) .05
264 Curt Warner .10
265 Steve Largent .60
266 Fredd Young (116) .06
267 Dave Krieg (117) .08
268 Daryl Turner (118) .05
269 John Harris (119) .05
270 Randy Edwards (120) .05
271 Kenny Easley (121) .05
272 Jacob Green (122) .05
273 Gary Anderson .05
274 Mike Webster (124) .07
275 Walter Abercombie (125) .08
276 Louis Lipps .10
277 Frank Pollard (127) .05
278 Mike Merriweather (128) .05
279 Mark Malone (129) .05
280 Donnie Shell (130) .08
281 John Stallworth (131) .06
282 Marcus Allen (284) .50
283 Ken O'Brien (285) .15
284 Kevin Butler (282) .15
285 Roger Craig (283) .35

1987 Topps

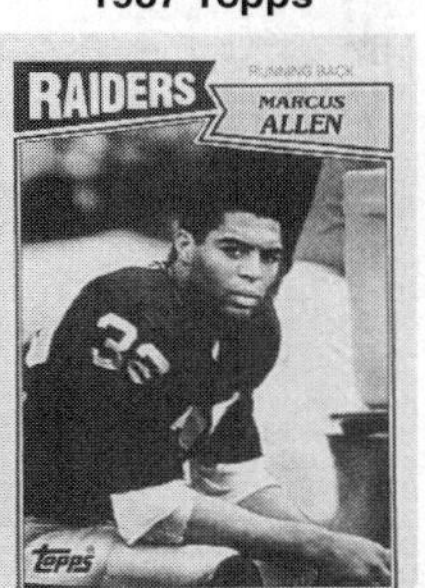

Topps' fifth straight 396-card set was bordered in white and carried two flags at the top of the card - one indicating the team, the other indicating the player name. His position was listed in the border above the name. Cards were numbered in order of the team's finish the previous year. This set, which seems to be one of the hottest sets since the '84 issue, includes such rookies as Randall Cunningham, Jim Everett, Reuben Mayes, John Offerdahl, Ernest Givins and Tim Harris. This set also features the last regular-issue card of all-time rushing leader Walter Payton. Three errors have been found in the set: On the back of card #274, Rueben Mayes, the statistical heading reads "Comp" for completions, when it should read "yards." The statistical heading was apparently intended for a quarterback instead of a running back. Also, the back of card #288, John Stallworth, is missing statistics from the years 1982-86. Finally, the reverse of Ross Browner's card (#263) contains a reference to the Bengals' 1982 Super Bowl win. The Bengals, however, lost to the 49ers that year. Not only that, the card also lists the Super Bowl date as 1-10-82 when it was actually played 1-24-82. (Key: AP - All Pro)

NM/M
Complete Set (396): 30.00
Common Player: .05
Wax Pack (15+1): 2.00
Wax Box (36): 50.00
1 Super Bowl XXI .15
2 Todd Christensen .05
3 Dave Jennings .05
4 Charlie Joiner .10
5 Steve Largent .25
6 Dan Marino 2.00
7 Donnie Shell .05
8 Phil Simms .15
9 Mark Bavaro Giants team .07
10 Phil Simms .35
11 Joe Morris (AP) .12
12 *Maurice Carthon* .15
13 Lee Rouson .05
14 Bobby Johnson .05
15 Lionel Manuel .05
16 Phil McConkey .05
17 Mark Bavaro (AP) .60
18 Zeke Mowatt .05
19 Raul Allegre .05
20 Sean Landeta .05
21 Brad Benson .05
22 Jim Burt .05
23 Leonard Marshall .40
24 Carl Banks .50
25 Harry Carson .12
26 Lawrence Taylor (AP) .50
27 *Terry Kinard* .20
28 *Pepper Johnson* 1.00
29 *Erik Howard* .15
30 Gerald Wilhite Broncos team .07
31 John Elway 4.00
32 Gerald Wilhite .05
33 Sammy Winder .05
34 Ken Bell .05
35 Steve Watson .05
36 Rick Karlis .05
37 Keith Bishop .05
38 Rulon Jones .05
39 Karl Mecklenburg (AP) .75
40 Louis Wright .05
41 Mike Harden .05
42 Dennis Smith .40
43 Walter Payton Bears team .50
44 Jim McMahon .25
45 *Doug Flutie* 5.00
46 Walter Payton 2.00
47 Matt Suhey .05
48 Willie Gault .15
49 *Dennis Gentry* .25
50 Kevin Butler .25
51 Jim Covert (AP) .05
52 Jay Hilgenberg .25
53 Dan Hampton .20
54 Steve McMichael .15
55 William Perry .15
56 Richard Dent .50
57 Otis Wilson .05
58 Mike Singletary (AP) .50
59 Wilber Marshall .50
60 Mike Richardson .05
61 Dave Duerson .15
62 Gary Fencik .05
63 George Rogers Redskins team .07
64 Jay Schroeder .35
65 George Rogers .05
66 *Kelvin Bryant* .25
67 Ken Jenkins .05
68 Gary Clark .50
69 Art Monk .50
70 *Clint Didier* .15
71 Steve Cox .05
72 Joe Jacoby .05
73 Russ Grimm .05
74 Charles Mann .30
75 Dave Butz .05
76 Dexter Manley (AP) .05
77 Darrell Green (AP) .30
78 Curtis Jordan .05
79 Browns team .07
80 Bernie Kosar .50
81 Curtis Dickey .05
82 Kevin Mack .20
83 Herman Fontenot .05
84 *Brian Brennan* .20
85 Ozzie Newsome .25
86 Jeff Gossett .05
87 Cody Risien (AP) .05
88 Reggie Camp .05
89 Bob Golic .05
90 Carl Hairston .05
91 Chip Banks .05
92 Frank Minnifield .05
93 Hanford Dixon (AP) .05
94 *Gerald McNeil* .20
95 Dave Puzzuoli .05
96 Andre Tippett Patriots team .07
97 Tony Eason .05
98 Craig James .05
99 Tony Collins .05
100 Mosi Tatupu .05
101 Stanley Morgan .15
102 Irving Fryar .65
103 Stephen Starring .05
104 Tony Franklin (AP) .05
105 Rich Camarillo .05
106 Garin Veris .05
107 Andre Tippett (AP) .12
108 Don Blackmon .05
109 *Ronnie Lippett* .30
110 Raymond Clayborn .05
111 Roger Craig 49ers team .12
112 Joe Montana 5.00
113 Roger Craig .30
114 Joe Cribbs .05
115 Jerry Rice (AP) 12.00
116 Dwight Clark .15
117 Ray Wersching .05
118 Max Runager .05
119 Jeff Stover .05
120 Dwaine Board .05
121 *Tim McKyer* .30
122 *Don Griffin* .40
123 Ronnie Lott (AP) .30
124 Tom Holmoe .05
125 *Charles Haley* 3.00
126 Mark Gastineau Jets team .05
127 Ken O'Brien .20
128 Pat Ryan .05
129 Freeman McNeil .15
130 *Johnny Hector* .30
131 Al Toon (AP) .50
132 Wesley Walker .12
133 Mickey Shuler .05
134 Pat Leahy .05
135 Mark Gastineau .05
136 Joe Klecko .05
137 Marty Lyons .05
138 Bob Crable .05
139 Lance Mehl .05
140 Dave Jennings .05
141 *Harry Hamilton* .15
142 Lester Lyles .05
143 Bobby Humphery .05
144 Eric Dickerson Rams team .15
145 *Jim Everett* 3.00
146 Eric Dickerson (AP) .50

147 Barry Redden .05
148 Ron Brown .15
149 Kevin House .05
150 Henry Ellard .60
151 Doug Smith .05
152 Dennis Harrah (AP) .05
153 Jackie Slater .15
154 Gary Jeter .05
155 Carl Ekern .05
156 Mike Wilcher .05
157 *Jerry Gray* .25
158 LeRoy Irvin .05
159 Nolan Cromwell .05
160 Todd Blackledge Chiefs team .07
161 Bill Kenney .05
162 Stephone Paige .25
163 Henry Marshall .05
164 Carlos Carson .05
165 Nick Lowery .15
166 *Irv Eatman* .10
167 Brad Budde .05
168 Art Still .05
169 Bill Maas (AP) .05
170 *Lloyd Burruss* .20
171 Deron Cherry (AP) .15
172 Curt Warner Seahawks team .07
173 Dave Krieg .20
174 Curt Warner .05
175 *John L. Williams* 1.00
176 *Bobby Joe Edmonds* .20
177 Steve Largent .60
178 Bruce Scholtz .05
179 Norm Johnson .05
180 Jacob Green .05
181 Fredd Young .05
182 Dave Brown .05
183 Kenny Easley .05
184 James Brooks Bengals team .07
185 Boomer Esiason .75
186 James Brooks .12
187 Larry Kinnebrew .05
188 Cris Collinsworth .05
189 Eddie Brown .35
190 *Tim McGee* 1.00
191 Jim Breech .05
192 Anthony Munoz .20
193 Max Montoya .05
194 Eddie Edwards .05
195 Ross Browner .05
196 Emanuel King .05
197 Louis Breeden .05
198 Darrin Nelson Vikings team .07
199 Tommy Kramer .05
200 Darrin Nelson .05
201 Allen Rice .05
202 Anthony Carter .30
203 Leo Lewis .05
204 Steve Jordan .40
205 Chuck Nelson .05
206 Greg Coleman .05
207 *Gary Zimmerman* .30
208 Doug Martin .05
209 Keith Millard .20
210 *Issiac Holt* .15
211 Joey Browner .20
212 Rufus Bess .05
213 Marcus Allen Raiders team .15
214 Jim Plunkett .15
215 Marcus Allen .90
216 *Napoleon McCallum* .12
217 Dokie Williams .05
218 Todd Christensen .05
219 Chris Bahr .05
220 Howie Long .25
221 Bill Pickel .05
222 *Sean Jones* 1.50
223 Lester Hayes .05
224 Mike Haynes .05
225 Vann McElroy .05
226 Fulton Walker .05
227 Tommy Kramer, Dan Marino Passing Leaders .50
228 Jerry Rice, Todd Christensen Receiving Leaders .50
229 Eric Dickerson, Curt Warner Rushing leaders .25
230 Kevin Butler, Tony Franklin Scoring leaders .07
231 Ronnie Lott, Deron Cherry Interception leaders .07
232 Reggie Roby Dolphins team .07
233 Dan Marino (AP) 8.00
234 *Lorenzo Hampton* .12
235 Tony Nathan .05
236 Mark Duper .12
237 Mark Clayton .50
238 Nat Moore .05
239 Bruce Hardy .05
240 Reggie Roby .05
241 Roy Foster .05
242 Dwight Stephenson (AP) .05
243 Hugh Green .05
244 *John Offerdahl* .50
245 Mark Brown .05
246 Doug Betters .05
247 Bob Baumhower .05
248 Gerald Riggs Falcons team .07
249 Dave Archer .15
250 Gerald Riggs .10
251 William Andrews .05
252 Charlie Brown .05
253 Arthur Cox .05
254 Rick Donnelly .05
255 Bill Fralic (AP) .30
256 *Mike Gann* .10
257 Rick Bryan .05
258 Bret Clark .05
259 Mike Pitts .05
260 Tony Dorsett Cowboys team .15
261 Danny White .15
262 *Steve Pelluer* .10
263 Tony Dorsett .40
264 *Herschel Walker* 2.50
265 Timmy Newsome .05
266 Tony Hill .05
267 *Mike Sherrard* .20
268 Jim Jeffcoat .05
269 Ron Fellows .05
270 Bill Bates .20
271 Michael Downs .05
272 Bobby Hebert Saints team .12
273 Dave Wilson .05
274 *Rueben Mayes* .30
275 Hoby Brenner .05
276 *Eric Martin* .75
277 Morten Andersen .35
278 Brian Hansen .05
279 Rickey Jackson .50
280 Dave Waymer .05
281 Bruce Clark .05
282 James Geathers .20
283 Walter Abercrombie Steelers team .07
284 Mark Malone .05
285 Earnest Jackson .05
286 Walter Abercrombie .05
287 Louis Lipps .15
288 John Stallworth .15
289 Gary Anderson .05
290 Keith Willis .05
291 Mike Merriweather .05
292 Lupe Sanchez .05
293 Donnie Shell .05
294 Keith Byars Eagles team .30
295 Mike Reichenbach .05
296 *Randall Cunningham* 4.00
297 *Keith Byars* 1.00
298 Mike Quick .05
299 Kenny Jackson .05
300 *John Teltschik* .10
301 Reggie White (AP) 3.00
302 Ken Clarke .05
303 Greg Brown .05
304 Roynell Young .05
305 *Andre Waters* .50
306 Warren Moon Oilers team .35
307 Warren Moon 2.25
308 Mike Rozier .10
309 Drew Hill .25
310 *Ernest Givins* 1.00
311 Lee Johnson .10
312 Kent Hill .05
313 *Dean Steinkuhler* .30
314 Ray Childress .60
315 *John Grimsley* .25
316 Jesse Baker .05
317 Eric Hipple Lions team .07
318 *Chuck Long* .12
319 James Jones .05
320 Garry James .05
321 Jeff Chadwick .05
322 Leonard Thompson .05
323 Pete Mandley .05
324 Jimmie Giles .05
325 Herman Hunter .05
326 Keith Ferguson .05
327 Devon Mitchell .05
328 Neil Lomax Cardinals team .07
329 Neil Lomax .05
330 Stump Mitchell .05
331 Earl Ferrell .05
332 *Vai Sikahema* .60
333 *Ron Wolfley* .15
334 J.T. Smith .05
335 Roy Green .05
336 Al Baker .05
337 Freddie Joe Nunn .05
338 Cedrick Mack .05
339 Gary Anderson Chargers team .07
340 Dan Fouts .50
341 Gary Anderson .25
342 Wes Chandler .05
343 Kellen Winslow .20
344 Ralf Mojsiejenko .05
345 Rolf Benirschke .05
346 *Lee Williams* .75
347 *Leslie O'Neal* 2.00
348 Billy Ray Smith .05
349 Gill Byrd .30
350 Paul Ott Caruth Packers team .05
351 Randy Wright .05
352 *Kenneth Davis* .75
353 Gerry Ellis .05
354 James Lofton .50
355 Phillip Epps .05
356 Walter Stanley .25
357 Eddie Lee Ivery .05
358 *Tim Harris* .50
359 Mark Lee .05
360 Mossy Cade .05
361 Jim Kelly Bills team 1.25
362 *Jim Kelly* 6.00
363 Robb Riddick .05
364 Greg Bell .10
365 Andre Reed 1.00
366 *Pete Metzelaars* .35
367 Sean McNanie .05
368 Fred Smerlas .05
369 Bruce Smith 1.00
370 Darryl Talley .25
371 Charles Romes .05
372 Rohn Stark Colts team .07
373 Jack Trudeau .25
374 Gary Hogeboom .05
375 Randy McMillan .05
376 Albert Bentley .10
377 Matt Bouza .05
378 *Bill Brooks* 2.00
379 Rohn Stark (AP) .05
380 Chris Hinton .05
381 Ray Donaldson .05
382 *Jon Hand* .25
383 James Wilder Buccaneers team .07
384 Steve Young 5.00
385 James Wilder .05
386 Frank Garcia .05
387 Gerald Carter .05
388 Phil Freeman .05
389 Calvin Magee .05
390 Donald Igwebuike .05
391 David Logan .05
392 Jeff Davis .05
393 Chris Washington .05
394 Checklist 1-132 .10
395 Checklist 133-264 .10
396 Checklist 265-396 .10

1987 Topps Box Bottoms

These cards can be distinguished from Topps' regular cards by the yellow borders around the photo on the front. Plus, the cards were on the bottom of 1987 Topps wax pack boxes, and would have to be cut out to measure the standard-size Topps cards. It's better to leave them intact. The cards also use a letter for numbering, instead of a number.

NM/M

Complete Set (16): 10.00
Common Player: .30
A Mark Bavaro .40
B Todd Christensen .50
C Eric Dickerson .65
D John Elway 1.50
E Rulon Jones .30
F Dan Marino 3.00
G Karl Mecklenburg .30
H Joe Montana 3.00
I Joe Morris .50
J Walter Payton 1.25
K Jerry Rice 3.50
L Phil Simms .50
M Lawrence Taylor .60
N Al Toon .30
O Curt Warner .40
P Reggie White 1.25

1987 Topps 1000 Yard Club

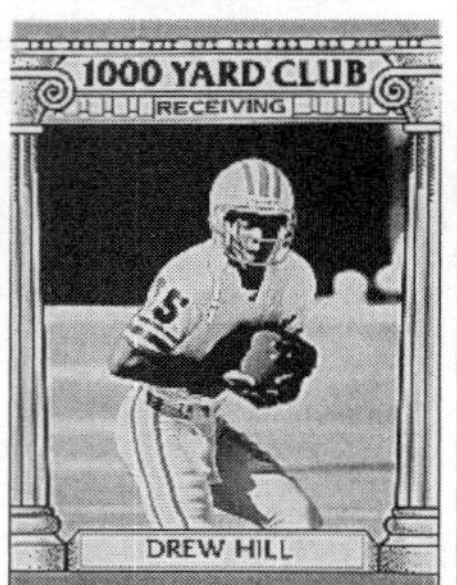

Printed on heavy white cardboard stock, 1,000 Yard Club cards were found inside wax packs of 1987 Topps football cards. Each card pictures a player who gained 1,000 or more yards rushing or receiving. Cards feature a parthenon design on the front in blue; backs are light blue and carry a game-by-game yardage summary for each player.

NM/M

Complete Set (24): 4.50
Common Player: .15
1 Eric Dickerson .75
2 Jerry Rice .75
3 Joe Morris .30
4 Stanley Morgan .15
5 Curt Warner .20
6 Reuben Mayes .25
7 Walter Payton 1.50
8 Gerald Riggs .20
9 Mark Duper .15
10 Gary Clark .15
11 George Rogers .15
12 Al Toon .25
13 Todd Christensen .15
14 Mark Clayton .15
15 Bill Brooks .25
16 Drew Hill .15
17 James Brooks .15
18 Steve Largent .60
19 Art Monk .15
20 Ernest Givins .20
21 Cris Collinsworth .20
22 Wesley Walker .15
23 J.T. Smith .15
24 Mark Bavaro .15

1987 Topps Stickers

Each of these stickers is 2-1/8" x 3" and features a new design element from previous years' issues - four footballs are included in the frame around the picture on the front, one for each corner. A sticker number appears on both sides. All-Pro foils were again produced, as were stickers in pairs; they are matched up as indicated by the number in parentheses. The backs have red ink on a white background. The album cover this time features artwork devoted to the New York Giants.

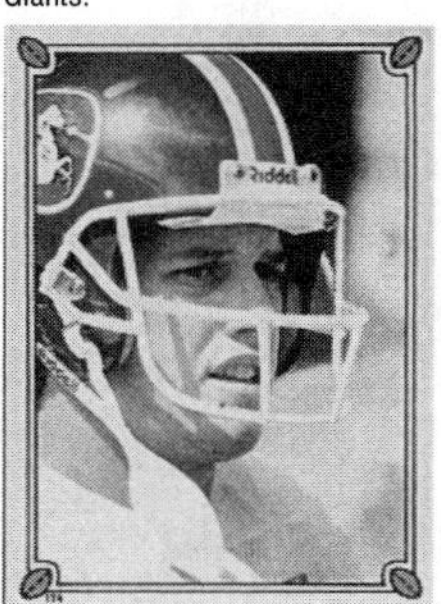

NM/M

Complete Set (285): 15.00
Common Player: .05
1 Phil Simms (Super Bowl MVP) .40
2 Super Bowl XXI (upper left) .15
3 Super Bowl XXI (upper right) .15
4 Super Bowl XXI (lower left) .15
5 Super Bowl XXI (lower right) .15
6 Mike Singletary .12
7 Jim Covert (156) .50
8 Willie Gault (157) .06
9 Jim McMahon (158) .08
10 Doug Flutie (159) 1.00
11 Richard Dent (160) .08
12 Kevin Butler (161) .05
13 Wilber Marshall (162) .08
14 Walter Payton .60
15 Calvin Magee .05
16 David Logan (165) .05
17 Jeff Davis (166) .05
18 Gerald Carter (167) .05
19 James Wilder .05
20 Chris Washington (168) .05
21 Phil Freeman (169) .05
22 Frank Garcia (170) .05
23 Donald Igwebuike (171) .05
24 Al (Bubba) Baker (175) .08
25 Vai Sikhema (176) .05
26 Leonard Smith (177) .05
27 Ron Wolgley (178) .05
28 J.T. Smith .08
29 Roy Green (179) .06
30 Cedric Mack (180) .05
31 Neil Lomax (181) .06
32 Stump Mitchell .08
33 Herschel Walker .50
34 Danny White (184) .06
35 Michael Downs (185) .05
36 Randy White (186) .08
37 Eugene Lockhart (188) .05
38 Mike Sherrard (189) .20
39 Jim Jeffcoat (190) .05
40 Tony Hill (191) .06
41 Tony Dorsett .35
42 Keith Byars (192) .30
43 Andre Waters (193) .06
44 Kenny Jackson (194) .05
45 John Teltschik (195) .05
46 Roynell Young (196) .05
47 Randall Cunningham (197) .60
48 Mike Reichenbach (198) .05
49 Reggie White .40
50 Mike Quick .08
51 Bill Fralic (201) .05
52 Sylvester Stamps (202) .05
53 Bret Clark (203) .05
54 William Andrews (204) .05
55 Buddy Curry (205) .05
56 Dave Archer (206) .10
57 Rick Bryan (207) .05
58 Gerald Riggs .12
59 Charlie Brown .05
60 Joe Montana 2.00
61 Jerry Rice 1.50
62 Carlton Williamson (212) .05
63 Roger Craig (213) .12
64 Ronnie Lott (214) .15
65 Dwight Clark (215) .15
66 Jeff Stover (216) .05
67 Charles Haley (217) .20
68 Ray Wersching (218) .05
69 Lawrence Taylor .30
70 Joe Morris .12
71 Carl Banks (221) .10
72 Mark Bavaro (222) .06
73 Harry Carson (223) .05
74 Phil Simms (224) .10
75 Jim Burt (225) .05
76 Brad Benson (226) .05
77 Leonard Marshall (227) .05
78 Jeff Chadwick .05
79 Devon Mitchell (228) .05
80 Chuck Long (229) .06
81 Demetrious Johnson (230) .05
82 Herman Hunter (231) .05
83 Kieth Ferguson (232) .05
84 Gary James (233) .05
85 Leonard Thompson (234) .05
86 James Jones .08
87 Kenneth Davis .35
88 Brian Noble (237) .07
89 Al Del Greco (238) .05
90 Mark Lee (239) .05
91 Randy Wright .05
92 Tim Harris (240) .25
93 Phillip Epps (241) .05
94 Walter Stanley (242) .10
95 Eddie Lee Ivery (243) .05
96 Doug Smith (247) .05
97 Jerry Gray (248) .05
98 Jim Everett (250) .05
99 Jim Everett (250) .60
100 Jackie Slater (251) .06
101 Vince Newsome (252) .10
102 LeRoy Irvin (253) .10
103 Henry Ellard .10
104 Eric Dickerson .60
105 George Rogers (256) .06
106 Darrell Green (257) .07
107 Art Monk (258) .10
108 Neal Olkewicz (260) .05
109 Russ Grimm (261) .05
110 Dexter Manley (262) .05
111 Kelvin Bryant (263) .05
112 Jay Schroeder .15
113 Gary Clark .15
114 Rickey Jackson .08
115 Eric Martin (264) .07
116 Dave Waymer (265) .05
117 Morten Andersen (266) .06
118 Bruce Clark (167) .08
119 Hoby Brenner (269) .07
120 Brian Hansen (270) .05
121 Dave Wilson (271) .05
122 Rueben Mayes .10
123 Tommy Kramer .08
124 Mark Malone (124) .05
125 Anthony Carter (275) .10
126 Keith Millard (276) .08
127 Steve Jordan .12
128 Chuck Nelson (277) .06
129 Issiac Holt (278) .05
130 Darrin Nelson (279) .05
131 Gary Zimmerman (280) .05
132 Mark Bavaro (146, All-Pro) .10
133 Jim Covert (147, All-Pro) .10
134 Eric Dickerson (148, All-Pro) .35
135 Bill Fralic (149, All-Pro) .10
136 Tony Franklin (150, All-Pro) .10
137 Dennis Harrah (151, All-Pro) .10
138 Dan Marino (152, All-Pro) 1.25
139 Joe Morris (153, All-Pro) .25
140 Jerry Rice (154, All-Pro) 1.00
141 Cody Risien (155, All-Pro) .10
142 Dwight Stephenson (282, All-Pro) .12
143 Al Toon (283, All-Pro) .20
144 Deron Cherry (284, All-Pro) .12
145 Hanford Dixon (285, All-Pro) .10
146 Darrell Green (132, All-Pro) .15
147 Ronnie Lott (133, All-Pro) .20
148 Bill Maas (134, All-Pro) .10
149 Dexter Manley (135, All-Pro) .10
150 Karl Mecklenburg (136, All-Pro) .12
151 Mike Singletary (137, All-Pro) .20
152 Rohn Stark (138, All-Pro) .10
153 Lawrence Taylor (139, All-Pro) .30
154 Andre Tippett (140, All-Pro) .12
155 Reggie White (141, All-Pro) .35
156 Boomer Esiason (7) .15
157 Anthony Munoz (8) .12
158 Tim McGee (9) .20
159 Max Montoya (10) .05
160 Jim Breech (11) .05
161 Tim Krumrie (12) .05
162 Eddie Brown (13) .06
163 James Brooks .10
164 Cris Collinsworth .12
165 Charles Romes (16) .05
166 Robb Riddick (17) .05
167 Eugene Marve (18) .05
168 Chris Burkett (20) .10
169 Bruce Smith (21) .12
170 Greg Bell (22) .05
171 Pete Metzelaars (23) .05
172 Jim Kelly 1.50
173 Andre Reed .30
174 John Elway .60
175 Mike Harden (24) .05
176 Gerald Willhite (25) .05
177 Rulon Jones (26) .05
178 Ricky Hunley (27) .05
179 Mark Jackson (29) .05
180 Rich Karlis (30) .05
181 Sammy Winder (31) .08
182 Karl Mecklenburg .08
183 Bernie Kosar .35
184 Kevin Mack (34) .05
185 Bob Golic (35) .08
186 Ozzie Newsome (36) .08
187 Brian Brennan .05
188 Gerald McNeil (37) .05
189 Hanford Dixon (38) .05
190 Cody Risien (39) .05
191 Chris Rockins (40) .05
192 Gill Byrd (42) .05
193 Kellen Winslow (43) .08
194 Billy Ray Smith (44) .05
195 Wes Chandler (45) .08
196 Leslie O'Neal (46) .25
197 Ralf Mojsiejenko (47) .05
198 Lee Williams (48) .20
199 Gary Anderson .08
200 Dan Fouts .30
201 Stephone Paige (51) .08
202 Irv Eatman (52) .05
203 Bill Kenney (53) .05
204 Dino Hackett (54) .08
205 Carlos Carson (55) .05
206 Art Still (56) .06
207 Lloyd Burruss (57) .05
208 Deron Cherry .08
209 Bill Maas .05
210 Gary Hogeboom .08
211 Rohn Stark .05
212 Cliff Odom (62) .05
213 Randy McMillan (63) .05
214 Chris Hinton (64) .05
215 Matt Bouza (65) .05
216 Ray Donaldson (66) .05
217 Bill Brooks (67) .08
218 Jack Trudeau (68) .06
219 Mark Duper .15
220 Dan Marino 1.50
221 Dwight Stephenson (71) .08
222 Mark Clayton (72) .10
223 Roy Foster (73) .05
224 John Offerdahl (74) .20
225 Lorenzo Hampton (75) .05
226 Reggie Roby (76) .05
227 Tony Nathan (77) .08
228 Johnny Hector (79) .08
229 Wesley Walker (80) .06
230 Mark Gastineau (81) .10
231 Ken O'Brien (82) .05
232 Dave Jennings (83) .05
233 Mickey Shuler (84) .05
234 Joe Klecko (85) .05
235 Freeman McNeil .10
236 Al Toon .08
237 Warren Moon (88) .35
238 Dean Steinkuhler (89) .08
239 Mike Rozier (90) .06
240 Ray Childress (92) .08
241 Tony Zendejas (93) .05
242 John Grimsley (94) .05
243 Jesse Baker (95) .05
244 Ernest Givins .50
245 Drew Hill .10
246 Tony Franklin .05
247 Steve Grogan (96) .06
248 Garin Veris (97) .05
249 Stanley Morgan (98) .06
250 Fred Morgan (98) .05
251 Raymond Clayborn (100) .07
252 Mosi Tatupu (101) .05
253 Tony Eason (102) .05
254 Andre Tippett .08
255 Todd Christensen .08
256 Howie Long (105) .06
257 Marcus Allen (106) .12
258 Vann McElroy (107) .05
259 Dokie Williams .05
260 Mike Haynes (108) .08
261 Sean Jones .10
262 Jim Plunkett (110) .07
263 Chris Bahr (111) .05
264 Dave Krieg (115) .08
265 Jacob Green (116) .05
266 Norm Johnson (117) .05
267 Fredd Young (118) .05
268 Steve Largent .50
269 Dave Brown (119) .05
270 Kenny Easley (120) .05
271 Bobby Joe Edmonds (121) .05
272 Curt Warner .15
273 Mike Merriweather .08
274 Mark Malone (124) .05
275 Bryan Hinkle (125) .05
276 Earnest Jackson (126) .05
277 Keith Willis (128) .05
278 Walter Abercrombie (129) .06
279 Donnie Shell (130) .08
280 John Stallworth (131) .06
281 Louis Lipps .10
282 Eric Dickerson (142) .30
283 Dan Marino (143) 1.00
284 Tony Franklin (144) .08
285 Todd Christensen .12

1987 Topps American/ United Kingdom

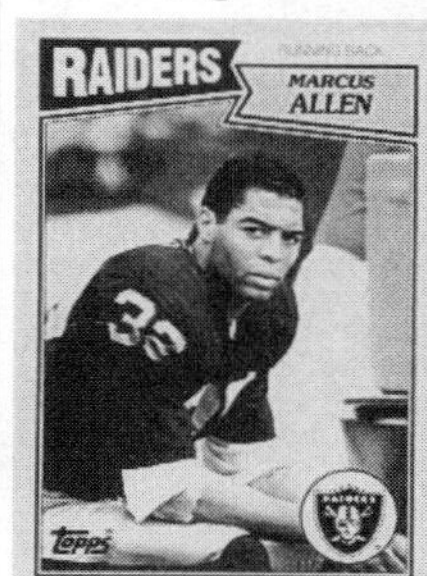

These cards are smaller in size than their regular set counterparts, measuring 2-1/8" x 3". The cards, which were made available in the United Kingdom, also have different photos. However, the basic design remains similar to Topps' 1986 regular issue. The back has a football term explained inside a football (Talking Football), plus a card number. A special collector's box was also produced to house the set. The box had a set checklist on its side. Cards 76-87 form a team action puzzle on one side and William Perry on the other.

NM/M
Complete Set (88): 40.00
Common Player: .10
1 Phil Simms .65
2 Joe Morris .35
3 Mark Bavaro .25
4 Sean Landeta .10
5 Lawrence Taylor 2.00
6 John Elway 4.00
7 Sammy Winder .10
8 Rulon Jones .10
9 Karl Mecklenburg .15
10 Walter Payton 4.00
11 Dennis Gentry .10
12 Kevin Butler .10
13 Jim Covert .10
14 Richard Dent .35
15 Mike Singletary .50
16 Jay Schroeder .50
17 George Rogers .25
18 Gary Clark .50
19 Art Monk .50
20 Dexter Manley .10
21 Darrell Green .35
22 Bernie Kosar 1.00
23 Cody Risien .10
24 Hanford Dixon .10
25 Tony Eason .25
26 Stanley Morgan .25
27 Tony Franklin .10
28 Andre Tippett .25
29 Joe Montana 8.00
30 Jerry Rice 8.00
31 Ronnie Lott .75
32 Ken O'Brien .25
33 Freeman McNeil .15
34 Al Toon .25
35 Wesley Walker .25
36 Eric Dickerson 1.50
37 Dennis Harrah .10
38 Bill Maas .10
39 Deron Cherry .25
40 Curt Warner .25
41 Bobby Joe Edmonds .25
42 Steve Largent 2.00
43 Boomer Esiason 2.00
44 James Brooks .25
45 Cris Collinsworth .25
46 Tim McGee .35
47 Tommy Kramer .25
48 Marcus Allen 1.00
49 Todd Christensen .35
50 Sean Jones .35
51 Dan Marino 8.00
52 Mark Duper .25
53 Mark Clayton .30
54 Dwight Stephenson .25
55 Gerald Riggs .25
56 Bill Fralic .25
57 Tony Dorsett 1.50
58 Herschel Walker 1.50
59 Rueben Mayes .25
60 Lupe Sanchez .10
61 Reggie White 2.50
62 Warren Moon 3.00
63 Ernest Givins 1.50
64 Drew Hill .25
65 Jeff Chadwick .25
66 Herman Hunter .10
67 Vai Sikhema .25
68 J.T. Smith .10
69 Dan Fouts 1.00
70 Lee Williams .50
71 Randy Wright .25
72 Jim Kelly 7.00
73 Bruce Smith .75
74 Bill Brooks .35
75 Rohn Stark .10
76 Team Action .10
77 Team Action .10
78 Team Action .10
79 Team Action .10
80 Team Action .10
81 Team Action .10
82 Team Action .10
83 Team Action .10
84 Team Action .10
85 Team Action .10
86 Team Action .10
87 Team Action .10
88 Checklist Card .10

1988 Topps

This set, issued in August 1988, was issued by teams in order of finish. These standard-size cards again showed the team helmets on front and All-Pro and Super Rookie designations (this was Topps' first year using Super Rookie labels). This set is noteworthy for the inclusion of Bo Jackson's rookie football card. (Key: AP - All Pro, SP - Super Rookie)

NM/M
Complete Set (396): 20.00
Common Player: .05
Wax Pack (15+1): .75
Wax Box (36): 15.00
1 Super Bowl XXII .10
2 Vencie Glenn .05
3 Steve Largent .15
4 Joe Montana .80
5 Walter Payton .30
6 Jerry Rice .70
7 Kelvin Bryant Redskins team .05
8 Doug Williams .05
9 George Rogers .05
10 Kelvin Bryant .05
11 Timmy Smith, Kent Hill (SR) .05
12 Art Monk, Ray Childress .25
13 Gary Clark .50
14 *Ricky Sanders* .50
15 Steve Cox .05
16 Joe Jacoby .05
17 Charles Mann .15
18 Dave Butz .05
19 Darrell Green (AP) .05
20 Dexter Manley .05
21 Barry Wilburn .05
22 Sammy Winder Broncos team .05
23 John Elway (AP) .75
24 Sammy Winder .05
25 Vance Johnson .20
26 *Mark Jackson* .70
27 *Ricky Nattiel* (SR) .12
28 Clarence Kay .05
29 Rich Karlis .05
30 Keith Bishop .05
31 Mike Horan .05
32 Rulon Jones .05
33 Karl Mecklenburg .12
34 Jim Ryan .05
35 Mark Haynes .05
36 Mike Harden .05
37 Roger Craig 49ers team .05
38 Joe Montana 2.00
39 Steve Young 1.00
40 Roger Craig .20
41 *Tom Rathman* .50
42 Joe Cribbs .35
43 Jerry Rice (AP) 2.00
44 Mike Wilson .05
45 *Ron Heller* .15
46 Ray Wersching .05
47 Michael Carter .05
48 Dwaine Board .05
49 Michael Walter .05
50 Don Griffin .05
51 Ronnie Lott .30
52 Charlie Haley .30
53 Dana McLemore .05
54 Bobby Hebert Saints Team .05
55 Bobby Hebert .30
56 Rueben Mayes .05
57 *Dalton Hilliard* .25
58 Eric Martin .30
59 John Tice .10
60 Brad Edelman .05
61 Morten Andersen (AP) .15
62 Brian Hansen .05
63 *Mel Gray* .60
64 Rickey Jackson .30
65 *Sam Mills* .50
66 *Pat Swilling* .50
67 Dave Waymer .05
68 Willie Gault Bears Team .05
69 Jim McMahon .15
70 *Mike Tomczak* .25
71 *Neal Anderson* .75
72 Willie Gault .10
73 Dennis Gentry .05
74 Dennis McKinnon .05
75 Kevin Butler .05
76 Jim Covert .05
77 Jay Hilgenberg .05
78 Steve McMichael .05
79 William Perry .05
80 Richard Dent .20
81 Ron Rivera .05
82 Mike Singletary (AP) .20
83 Dan Hampton .10
84 Dave Duerson .05
85 Bernie Kosar Browns team .05
86 Bernie Kosar .05
87 Earnest Byner .40
88 Kevin Mack .10
89 *Webster Slaughter* .75
90 Gerald McNeil .05
91 Brian Brennan .05
92 Ozzie Newsome .20
93 Cody Risien .05
94 Bob Golic .05
95 Carl Hairston .05
96 *Mike Johnson* .20
97 Clay Matthews .05
98 Frank Minnifield .05
99 Hanford Dixon (AP) .05
100 Dave Puzzuoli .05
101 *Felix Wright* .12
102 Warren Moon Oilers team .20
103 Warren Moon .75
104 Mike Rozier .05
105 *Alonzo Highsmith* (SR) .15
106 Drew Hill .20
107 Ernest Givins .40
108 *Curtis Duncan* .50
109 *Tony Zendejas* .12
110 Mike Munchak (AP) .12
113 *Al Smith* .35
114 Keith Bostic .05
115 Jeff Donaldson .05
116 Eric Dickerson Colts team .15
117 Jack Trudeau .05
118 Eric Dickerson (AP) .30
119 Albert Bentley .05
120 Matt Bouza .05
121 Bill Brooks .35
122 Dean Biasucci .12
123 Chris Hinton .05
124 Ray Donaldson .05
125 *Ron Solt* .10
126 Donnell Thompson .05
127 Barry Krauss .05
128 Duane Bickett .10
129 *Mike Prior* .15
130 Curt Warner Seahawks team .05
131 Dave Krieg .15
132 Curt Warner .05
133 John L. Williams .25
134 Bobby Joe Edmonds .05
135 Steve Largent .30
136 Raymond Butler .05
137 Norm Johnson .05
138 Ruben Rodriguez .05
139 Blair Bush .05
140 Jacob Green .05
141 Joe Nash .05
142 Jeff Bryant .05
143 Fredd Young (AP) .05
144 *Brian Bosworth* (SR) .15
145 Kenny Easley (AP) .05
146 Tommy Kramer Vikings team .05
147 *Wade Wilson* .50
148 Tommy Kramer .05
149 Darrin Nelson .05
150 *D.J. Dozier* (SR) .12
151 Anthony Carter .25
152 Leo Lewis .05
153 Steve Jordan .20
154 Gary Zimmerman .05
155 Chuck Nelson .05
156 *Henry Thomas* (SR) .50
157 *Chris Doleman* .60
158 *Scott Studwell* .12
159 *Jesse Solomon* .10
160 Joey Browner (AP) .15
161 Neal Guggemos .05
162 Louis Lipps Steelers team .05
163 Mark Malone .05
164 Walter Abercrombie .05
165 Earnest Jackson .05
166 Frank Pollard .05
167 *Dwight Stone* .30
168 Gary Anderson .05
169 *Harry Newsome* .10
170 Keith Willis .05
171 Keith Gray .05
172 *David Little* .12
173 Mike Merriweather .05
174 Dwayne Woodruff .05
175 Irving Fryar Patriots team .05
176 Steve Grogan .10
177 Tony Eason .05
178 Tony Collins .05
179 Mosi Tatupu .05
180 Stanley Morgan .05
181 Irving Fryar .30
182 Stephen Starring .05
183 Tony Franklin .05
184 Rich Camarillo .05
185 Garin Veris .05
186 Andre Tippett (AP) .05
187 Ronnie Lippett .05
188 Fred Marion .05
189 Dan Marino Dolphins team .50
190 Dan Marino 1.50
191 *Troy Stradford* (SR) .10
192 Lorenzo Hampton .05
193 Mark Duper .10
194 Mark Clayton .25
195 Reggie Roby .05
196 Dwight Stephenson (AP) .05
197 T.J. Turner .05
198 John Bosa (SR) .05
199 Jackie Shipp .05
200 John Offerdahl .05
201 Mark Brown .05
202 Paul Lankford .05
203 Kellen Winslow Chargers Team .05
204 Tim Spencer .05
205 Gary Anderson .10
206 Curtis Adams .05
207 Lionel James .05
208 Chip Banks .05
209 Kellen Winslow .15
210 Ralf Mojsiejenko .05
211 Jim Lachey .15
212 Lee Williams .15
213 Billy Ray Smith .05
214 *Vencie Glenn* .25
215 Bernie Kosar, Joe Montana NFL Passing Leaders .50
216 Al Toon, J.T. Smith NFL Receiving Leaders .05
217 Charles White, Eric Dickerson NFL Rushing Leaders .15
218 Jim Breech, Jerry Rice NFL Scoring Leaders .30
219 Keith Bostic, Mark Kelso, Mike Prior, Barry Wilburn NFL Interception Leaders .05
220 Jim Kelly Bills team .30
221 Jim Kelly 1.00
222 *Ronnie Harmon* .50
223 Robb Riddick .05
224 Andre Reed .50
225 *Chris Burkett* .50
226 Pete Metzelaars .05
227 Bruce Smith (AP) .50
228 Darryl Talley .12
229 Eugene Marve .05
230 *Cornelius Bennett* 1.00
231 *Mark Kelso* .20
232 *Shane Conlan* (SR) .50
233 Randall Cunningham Eagles team .25
234 Randall Cunningham .50
235 Keith Byars .50
236 Anthony Toney .05
237 Mike Quick .05
238 Kenny Jackson .05
239 John Spagnola .05
240 Paul McFadden .05
241 Reggie White (AP) .60
242 Ken Clarke .05
243 Mike Pitts .05
244 *Clyde Simmons* .50
245 *Seth Joyner* .85
246 Andre Waters .12
247 *Jerome Brown* (SR) .30
248 Stump Mitchell Cardinals team .05
249 Neil Lomax .05
250 Stump Mitchell .05
251 Earl Ferrell .05
252 Vai Sikahema .05
253 J.T. Smith (AP) .05
254 Roy Green .10
255 Robert Awalt (SR) .05
256 Freddie Joe Nunn .05
257 *Leonard Smith* .10
258 Travis Curtis .05
259 Herschel Walker Cowboys team .15
260 Danny White .10
261 Herschel Walker .25
262 Tony Dorsett .20
263 Doug Cosbie .05
264 *Roger Ruzek* .12
265 Darryl Clack .05
266 Ed "Too Tall" Jones .15
267 Jim Jeffcoat .05
268 Everson Walls .05
269 Bill Bates .05
270 Michael Downs .05
271 Mark Bavaro Giants team .05
272 Phil Simms .30
273 Joe Morris .05
274 Lee Rouson .05
275 George Adams .05
276 Lionel Manuel .05
277 Mark Bavaro (AP) .05
278 Raul Allegre .05
279 Sean Landeta .05
280 Erik Howard .05
281 Leonard Marshall .05
282 Carl Banks (AP) .15
283 Pepper Johnson .15
284 Harry Carson .10
285 Lawrence Taylor .25
286 Terry Kinard .05
287 Jim Everett Rams team .15
288 Jim Everett .40
289 Charles White (AP) .05
290 Ron Brown .05
291 Henry Ellard .25
292 Mike Lansford .05
293 Dale Hatcher .05
294 Doug Smith .05
295 Jackie Slater (AP) .05
296 Jim Collins .05
297 Jerry Gray .05
298 LeRoy Irvin .05
299 Nolan Cromwell .05
300 *Kevin Greene* 1.00
301 Ken O'Brien Jets team .05
302 Ken O'Brien .15
303 Freeman McNeil .05
304 Johnny Hector .05
305 Al Toon .20
306 JoJo Townsell .05
307 Mickey Shuler .05
308 Pat Leahy .05
309 Roger Vick .05
310 Alex Gordon .05
311 Troy Benson .05
312 Bob Crable .05
313 Harry Hamilton .05
314 Phil Epps Packers team .05
315 Randy Wright .05
316 Kenneth Davis .35
317 Phillip Epps .05
318 Walter Stanley .05
319 Frankie Neal .05
320 Don Bracken .05
321 *Brian Noble* .15
322 *Johnny Holland* (SR) .15
323 Tim Harris .35
324 Mark Murphy .05
325 Bo Jackson Raiders team .50
326 Marc Wilson .05
327 *Bo Jackson* (SR) 2.00
328 Marcus Allen .30
329 James Lofton .20
330 Todd Christensen .05
331 Chris Bahr .05
332 Stan Talley .05
333 Howie Long .10
334 Sean Jones .05
335 Matt Millen .05
336 Stacey Toran .05
337 Vann McElroy .05
338 Greg Townsend .15
339 Boomer Esiason Bengals team .15
340 Boomer Esiason .50
341 Larry Kinnebrew .05
342 Stanford Jennings .05
343 Eddie Brown .05
344 Jim Breech .05
345 Anthony Munoz (AP) .12
346 Scott Fulhage .05
347 *Tim Krumrie* .20
348 Reggie Williams .05
349 *David Fulcher* .30
350 James Wilder Buccaneers team .05
351 Frank Garcia .05
352 *Vinny Testaverde* (SR) 5.00
353 James Wilder .05
354 Jeff Smith .05
355 Gerald Carter .05
356 Calvin Magee .05
357 Donald Igwebuike .05
358 Ron Holmes .05
359 Chris Washington .05
360 Ervin Randle .05
361 Bill Kenney Chiefs team .05
362 Bill Kenney .05
363 *Christian Okoye* (SR) .25
364 Paul Palmer .05
365 Stephone Paige .12
366 Carlos Carson .05
367 Kelly Goodburn .05
368 Bill Maas (AP) .05
369 Mike Bell .05
370 *Dino Hackett* .15
371 Deron Cherry .05
372 James Jones Lions team .05
373 Chuck Long .05
374 Garry James .05
375 James Jones .05
376 Pete Mandley .05
377 Gary Lee (SR) .05
378 Ed Murray .05
379 Jim Arnold .05
380 Dennis Gibson (SR) .05
381 Mike Cofer .05
382 James Griffin .05
383 Gerald Riggs Falcons team .05
384 Scott Campbell .05
385 Gerald Riggs .05
386 Floyd Dixon .05
387 Rick Donnelly (AP) .05
388 Bill Fralic (AP) .05
389 Major Everett .05
390 Mike Gann .05
391 *Tony Casillas* .25
392 Rick Bryan .05
393 John Rade .05
394 Checklist 1-132 .05
395 Checklist 133-264 .05
396 Checklist 265-396 .05

1988 Topps Box Bottoms

The bottoms of 1988 Topps wax pack boxes had these cards, which honor award-winning achievements by professional players while they were in college. Two players are featured on each card. The cards are numbered on the back using a letter and include a summary of the player's collegiate accomplishment. The cards are standard size.

NM/M
Complete Set (16): 5.00
Common Player: .20
A Vinny Testaverde .50
B Dean Steinkuhler .20
C George Rogers .20
D Kenneth Sims .20
E Cornelius Bennett .50
F Bo Jackson 1.00
G Ross Browner .35
H Doug Flutie 1.00
I Herschel Walker .50
J Jim Plunkett .50
K Charles White .25
L Brad Budde .20
M Marcus Allen .20
N Mike Rozier .25
O Tony Dorsett .75
P Checklist .20

1988 Topps 1000 Yard Club

One card from this 28-card set was again issued in a wax pack of Topps football cards. The standard-size glossy cards on thick white cardboard stock feature "1000" in bold green border around a full-color action photo. Backs feature a game-by-game recap of the runner or receiver's yardage.

NM/M
Complete Set (28): 4.50
Common Player: .10
1 Charles White .10
2 Eric Dickerson .75
3 J.T. Smith .10
4 Jerry Rice .75
5 Gary Clark .10
6 Carlos Carson .10
7 Drew Hill .10
8 Curt Warner .10
9 Al Toon .10
10 Mike Rozier .10
11 Ernest Givins .10
12 Anthony Carter .10
13 Reuben Mayes .10
14 Steve Largent .75
15 Herschel Walker .75
16 James Lofton .10
17 Gerald Riggs .10
18 Mark Bavaro .10
19 Roger Craig .50
20 Webster Slaughter .10
21 Henry Ellard .10
22 Mike Quick .10
23 Stump Mitchell .10
24 Eric Martin .10
25 Mark Clayton .10
26 Chris Burkett .10
27 Marcus Allen .30
28 Andre Reed .10

1988 Topps Stickers

These stickers can be distinguished from Topps' previous efforts by the two frames used on the front to border the color photograph. An inner frame of yellow footballs is adjacent to an outer red frame of the picture. Each sticker measures 2-1/8" x 3" and is numbered on both sides. All-Pro stickers were produced as foil stickers again, and pairs of stickers were also made, as indicated by parentheses. Stickers 2-5 form a puzzle of Doug Williams featured in action during Super Bowl XXII. Williams is also featured on the back of the album cover which was produced to hold the stickers; the Redskins in action are featured on the front.

NM/M
Complete Set (285): 15.00
Common Player: .05
1 Doug Williams (Super Bowl XXII MVP) .20
2 Super Bowl XXII .08
3 Super Bowl XXII .08
4 Super Bowl XXII .08
5 Super Bowl XXII .08
6 Neal Anderson (234) .25
7 Willie Gault (224) .08
8 Dennis Gentry (219) .05
9 Dave Duerson (197) .05
10 Steve McMichael (266) .05
11 Dennis McKinnon (230) .05
12 Mike Singletary (209) .08
13 Jim McMahon .12
14 Richard Dent .10
15 Vinny Testaverde (167) .20
16 Gerald Carter (187) .05
17 Jeff Smith (185) .05
18 Chris Washington (212) .05
19 Bobby Futrell (231) .05
20 Calvin Magee (182) .05
21 Ron Holmes (169) .05
22 Ervin Randle .05
23 James Wilder .08
24 Neil Lomax .08
25 Robert Awalt (161) .05
26 Leonard Smith (177) .05
27 Stump Mitchell (178) .05
28 Vai Sikahema (280) .06
29 Freddie Joe Nunn (222) .05
30 Earl Ferrell (223) .05
31 Roy Green (157) .10
32 J.T. Smith .10
33 Michael Downs .05
34 Herschel Walker .30
35 Roger Ruzek (269) .05
36 Ed "Too Tall" Jones (245) .07
37 Everson Walls (252) .05
38 Bill Bates (213) .05
39 Doug Cosbie (179) .05
40 Eugene Lockhart (186) .05
41 Danny White (205) .07
42 Randall Cunningham .40
43 Reggie White .30
44 Anthony Toney (256) .05
45 Mike Quick (248) .08
46 John Spagnola (235) .05
47 Clyde Simmons (275) .20
48 Andre Waters (261) .05
49 Keith Byars (265) .08
50 Jerome Brown (240) .15
51 John Rade .05
52 Rick Donnelly .05
53 Scott Campbell (160) .05
54 Floyd Dixon (246) .05
55 Gerald Riggs (236) .06

56 Bill Fralic (267) .08
57 Mike Gann (165) .05
58 Tony Casillas (168) .15
59 Rick Bryan (257) .05
60 Jerry Rice 1.00
61 Ronnie Lott .25
62 Ray Wersching (220) .05
63 Charles Haley (281) .06
64 Joe Montana (190) .75
65 Joe Cribbs (221) .05
66 Mike Wilson (203) .05
67 Roger Craig (251) .12
68 Michael Walter (162) .05
69 Mark Bavaro .08
70 Carl Banks .10
71 George Adams (274) .03
72 Phil Simms (216) .15
73 Lawrence Taylor (181) .12
74 Joe Morris (198) .06
75 Lionel Manuel (204) .05
76 Sean Landeta (210) .05
77 Harry Carson (159) .05
78 Chuck Long (166) .05
79 James Jones (159) .08
80 Gary James (158) .05
81 Gary Lee (176) .05
82 Jim Arnold (260) .05
83 Dennis Gibson (232) .05
84 Mike Cofer (242) .05
85 Pete Mandley .05
86 James Griffin .05
87 Randy Wright (206) .05
88 Phillip Epps (191) .05
89 Brian Noble (249) .05
90 Johnny Holland (258) .10
91 Dave Brown (156) .05
92 Brent Fullwood (207) .05
93 Kenneth Davis (194) .08
94 Tim Harris .15
95 Walter Stanley .08
96 Charles White .15
97 Jackie Slater .08
98 Jim Everett (271) .12
99 Mike Lansford (200) .05
100 Henry Ellard (199) .06
101 Dale Hatcher (170) .05
102 Jim Collins (268) .05
103 Jerry Gray (214) .05
104 LeRoy Irvin (276) .05
105 Darrell Green .12
106 Doug Williams .10
107 Gary Clark (247) .10
108 Charles Mann (171) .10
109 Art Monk (270) .12
110 Barry Wilburn (196) .05
111 Alvin Walton (188) .05
112 Dexter Manley (233) .05
113 Kelvin Bryant (180) .04
114 Morten Andersen .10
115 Rueben Mayes (244) .06
116 Brian Hansen (279) .05
117 Dalton Hilliard (241) .10
118 Rickey Jackson (195) .06
119 Eric Martin (189) .06
120 Mel Gray (278) .05
121 Bobby Hebert (215) .08
122 Pat Swilling .40
123 Anthony Carter .12
124 Wade Wilson (225) .20
125 Darrin Nelson (250) .05
126 D.J. Dozier (239) .06
127 Chris Doleman .30
128 Henry Thomas (255) .05
129 Jesse Solomon (211) .05
130 Neal Guggemos (243) .05
131 Joey Browner (208) .06
132 Carl Banks (152, All-Pro) .10
133 Joey Browner (145, All-Pro) .10
134 Hanford Dixon (149, All-Pro) .10
135 Rick Donnelly (147, All-Pro) .10
136 Kenny Easley (155, All-Pro) .15
137 Darrell Green (151, All-Pro) .15
138 Bill Maas (148, All-Pro) .10
139 Mike Singletary (153, All-Pro) .15
140 Bruce Smith (154, All-Pro) .20
141 Andre Tippett (146, All-Pro) .10
142 Reggie White (150, All-Pro) .20
143 Fredd Young (144, All-Pro) .10
144 Morten Andersen (143, All-Pro) .10
145 Mark Bavaro (133, All-Pro) .10
146 Eric Dickerson (141, All-Pro) .30
147 John Elway (134, All-Pro) .75
148 Bill Fralic (138, All-Pro) .10
149 Mike Munchak (135, All-Pro) .10
150 Anthony Munoz (142, All-Pro) .15
151 Jerry Rice (137, All-Pro) 1.00
152 Jackie Slater (132, All-Pro) .12
153 J.T. Smith (139, All-Pro) .10
154 Dwight Stephenson (140, All-Pro) .12
155 Charles White (136, All-Pro) .12
156 Larry Kinnebrew (91) .05
157 Stanford Jennings (31) .05
158 Eddie Brown (80) .05
159 Scott Fulhage (77) .05
160 Boomer Esiason (53) .12
161 Tim Krumrie (25) .05
162 Anthony Munoz (68) .08
163 Jim Breech .05
164 Reggie Williams .08
165 Andre Reed (57) .20
166 Cornelius Bennett (78) .30
167 Ronnie Harmon (15) .15
168 Shane Conlan (58) .15
169 Chris Burkett (21) .06
170 Mark Kelso (101) .08
171 Robb Riddick (108) .05
172 Bruce Smith .15
173 Jim Kelly .60
174 Jim Ryan .05
175 John Elway .60
176 Sammy Winder (81) .05
177 Karl Mecklenburg (26) .05
178 Mark Haynes (27) .05
179 Rulon Jones (39) .05
180 Ricky Nattiel (113) .08
181 Vance Johnson (73) .05
182 Mike Harden (20) .05
183 Frank Minnifield .05
184 Bernie Kosar .25
185 Earnest Byner (17) .12
186 Webster Slaughter (40) .15
187 Brian Brennan (16) .05
188 Carl Hairston (111) .05
189 Mike Johnson (119) .05
190 Clay Matthews (64) .06
191 Kevin Mack (88) .06
192 Kellen Winslow .12
193 Billy Ray Smith .08
194 Gary Anderson (93) .06
195 Chip Banks (118) .05
196 Elvis Patterson (110) .05
197 Lee Williams (9) .07
198 Curtis Adams (74) .05
199 Vencie Glenn (100) .05
200 Ralf Mojsiejenko (99) .05
201 Carlos Carson .05
202 Bill Maas .05
203 Christian Okoye (66) .15
204 Deron Cherry (75) .08
205 Dino Hackett (41) .05
206 Mike Bell (87) .05
207 Stephone Paige (92) .06
208 Bill Kenney (131) .06
209 Paul Palmer (12) .05
210 Jack Trudeau (76) .06
211 Albert Bentley (129) .06
212 Bill Brooks (18) .06
213 Dean Biasucci (38) .05
214 Cliff Odom (103) .05
215 Barry Krauss (121) .05
216 Mike Prior (72) .06
217 Eric Dickerson .35
218 Duane Bickett .08
219 Dwight Stephenson (8) .08
220 John Offerdahl (62) .10
221 Troy Stradford (65) .06
222 John Bosa (29) .04
223 Jackie Shipp (30) .05
224 Paul Lankford (7) .05
225 Mark Duper (124) .08
226 Dan Marino 1.50
227 Mark Clayton .15
228 Bob Crable .05
229 Al Toon .08
230 Freeman McNeil (11) .06
231 Johnny Hector (19) .05
232 Pat Leahy (83) .05
233 Ken O'Brien (112) .05
234 Alex Gordon (6) .05
235 Harry Hamilton (46) .05
236 Mickey Shuler (55) .05
237 Mike Rozier .08
238 Al Smith .15
239 Ernest Givins (126) .15
240 Warren Moon (50) .25
241 Drew Hill (117) .10
242 Alonzo Highsmith (84) .15
243 Mike Munchak (130) .06
244 Keith Bostic (115) .05
245 Sean Jones (36) .08
246 Stanley Morgan (54) .06
247 Garin Veris (107) .05
248 Stephen Starring (45) .05
249 Steve Grogan (89) .06
250 Irving Fryar (125) .10
251 Rich Camarillo (67) .05
252 Ronnie Lippett (37) .05
253 Andre Tippett .08
254 Fred Marion .05
255 Howie Long (128) .10
256 James Lofton (44) .12
257 Vance Mueller (59) .05
258 Jerry Robinson (90) .05
259 Todd Christensen (79) .06
260 Vann McElroy (82) .05
261 Greg Townsend (48) .10
262 Bo Jackson .85
263 Marcus Allen .30
264 Curt Warner .08
265 Jacob Green (49) .06
266 Norm Johnson (10) .05
267 Brian Bosworth (56) .05
268 Bobby Joe Edmonds (102) .05
269 Dave Krieg (35) .07
270 Kenny Easley (109) .06
271 Steve Largent (98) .30
272 Fredd Young .05
273 David Little .05
274 Frank Pollard (71) .05
275 Dwight Stone (47) .08
276 Mike Merriweather (104) .06
277 Earnest Jackson .05
278 Delton Hall (120) .05
279 Gary Anderson (116) .05
280 Harry Newsome (28) .08
281 Dwayne Woodruff (63) .05
282 J.T. Smith (283) .05
283 Charles White (282) .05
284 Reggie White (285) .15
285 Morten Andersen (284) .10

1988 Topps Sticker Backs

These cards were left after collectors would remove the 1988 Topps stickers from their card. Each card measures 2-1/8" x 3" and features a prominent offensive player. The sticker has "Superstar" written at the top, above the color player photo. His name and card number appear at the bottom in a stat box, using 1 of 67, etc.

NM/M
Complete Set (67): 5.00
Common Player: .05
1 Doug Williams .10
2 Gary Clark .15
3 John Elway .50
4 Sammy Winder .05
5 Vance Johnson .07
6 Joe Montana 1.50
7 Roger Craig .15
8 Jerry Rice 1.00
9 Rueben Mayes .10
10 Eric Martin .10
11 Neal Anderson .30
12 Willie Gault .10
13 Bernie Kosar .25
14 Kevin Mack .05
15 Webster Slaughter .15
16 Warren Moon .40
17 Mike Rozier .10
18 Drew Hill .10
19 Eric Dickerson .30
20 Bill Brooks .05
21 Curt Warner .15
22 Steve Largent .40
23 Darrin Nelson .05
24 Anthony Carter .15
25 Earnest Jackson .05
26 Weegie Thompson .05
27 Stephen Starring .05
28 Stanley Morgan .10
29 Dan Marino 1.50
30 Troy Stradford .10
31 Mark Clayton .15
32 Curtis Adams .05
33 Kellen Winslow .15
34 Jim Kelly .60
35 Ronnie Harmon .25
36 Chris Burkett .05
37 Randall Cunningham .35
38 Anthony Toney .05
39 Mike Quick .10
40 Neil Lomax .10
41 Stump Mitchell .10
42 J.T. Smith .05
43 Herschel Walker .25
44 Herschel Walker .25
45 Joe Morris .12
46 Mark Bavaro .10
47 Charles White .15
48 Henry Ellard .10
49 Ken O'Brien .10
50 Freeman McNeil .10
51 Al Toon .12
52 Kenneth Davis .10
53 Walter Stanley .05
54 Marcus Allen .30
55 James Lofton .25
56 Boomer Esiason .20
57 Larry Kinnebrew .05
58 Eddie Brown .10
59 James Wilder .07
60 Gerald Carter .05
61 Christian Okoye .20
62 Carlos Carson .05
63 James Jones .05
64 Pete Mandley .05
65 Gerald Riggs .10
66 Floyd Dixon .05
67 Checklist Card .10

1989 Topps

Topps released its seventh straight 396-card set in late August 1989. Cards are standard size, with white borders and a multicolored stripe about three-quarters from the bottom. Player names and teams are at the bottom of the card in an opaque circle. Card backs feature a dark green on yellow design. There are a few errors in the set: Card #24, Eddie Brown, lists his birthday as 12/18 and it's actually 12/17; card #27, Boomer Esiason, has him a native of East Islip, when it should be West Islip; the front of card #56, Mark Kelso, reads "BILL" instead of "BILLS"; on Jay Hilgenberg's card, a "g" is missing from "Chicago" on the card front. The back of Mark Rypien's card (#253) lists 14 as his 1988 completion total, while it should read 114. Card #125, Robert Delpino, correctly shows his team designation as "Rams" on the front, but lists "Los Angeles Raiders" on the back; card #247, Karl Mecklenberg, lists him as being drafted in the second round when it should be the 12th. Rodney Holman's card also features a problem with the card front: there are six different variations of "BENGALS". One has a small space between the "B" and "E"; the second has the "B" a little above the rest of the line of type; the third has it just a little below; the fourth shows just the "B" with no other letters behind it; another shows the "B" partially superimposed over the "E"; another shows "CINCINNATI B" without the rest of "Bengals"; and the last one is the correct version. Rookies in this set include Sterling Sharpe, Don Majkowski, Ickey Woods, John Stephens, John Taylor, Erik McMillan, Keith Jackson and Tom Newberry. (Key: AP - All Pro, SR - Super Rookie)

NM/M
Complete Set (396): 15.00
Common Player: .05
Wax Pack (15+1): .50
Wax Box (36): 11.00
1 Super Bowl XXIII .50
2 Tim Brown .70
3 Eric Dickerson .12
4 Steve Largent .12
5 Dan Marino .60
6 Joe Montana 49ers Team .30
7 Jerry Rice (AP) 1.25
8 Roger Craig (AP) .05
9 Ronnie Lott .15
10 Michael Carter .05
11 Charles Haley .05
12 Joe Montana 2.00
13 *John Taylor* 1.00
14 Michael Walter .05
15 *Mike Cofer* .10
16 Tom Rathman .05
17 *Danny Stubbs* .12
18 Keena Turner .05
19 Tim McKyer .05
20 Larry Roberts .05
21 Jeff Fuller .05
22 Bubba Paris .05
23 Boomer Esiason Bengals Team .05
24 Eddie Brown (AP) .05
25 Boomer Esiason (AP) .30
26 Tim Krumrie (AP) .05
27 Ickey Woods (SR) .05
28 Anthony Munoz .05
29 Tim McGee .05
30 Max Montoya .05
31 David Grant .05
32 *Rodney Holman* .25
33 David Fulcher .05
34 Jim Skow .05
35 James Brooks .05
36 Reggie Williams .05
37 *Eric Thomas* .10
38 Stanford Jennings .05
39 Jim Breech .05
40 Jim Kelly Bills Team .15
41 Shane Conlan (AP) .15
42 Scott Norwood (AP) .05
43 Cornelius Bennett .30
44 Bruce Smith (AP) .15
45 *Thurman Thomas* (SR) 2.00
46 Jim Kelly .50
47 John Kidd .05
48 *Kent Hull* .15
49 Art Still .05
50 Fred Smerlas .05
51 Derrick Burroughs .05
52 Andre Reed .30
53 Robb Riddick .05
54 Chris Burkett .05
55 Ronnie Harmon .20
56 Mark Kelso .05
57 Thomas Sanders Bears Team .05
58 Mike Singletary (AP) .10
59 Jay Hilgenberg (AP) .05
60 Richard Dent .05
61 Ron Rivera .05
62 Jim McMahon .05
63 Mike Tomczak .12
64 Neal Anderson .30
65 Dennis Gentry .05
66 Dan Hampton .05
67 David Tate .05
68 *Thomas Sanders* .10
69 Steve McMichael .05
70 Dennis McKinnon .05
71 *Brad Muster* .20
72 *Vestee Jackson* .10
73 Dave Duerson .05
74 Keith Millard Vikings Team .05
75 Joey Browner (AP) .05
76 *Carl Lee* (AP) .10
77 Gary Zimmerman (AP) .05
78 *Hassan Jones* .10
79 Anthony Carter .05
80 Ray Berry .05
81 Steve Jordan .05
82 Issiac Holt .05
83 Wade Wilson .05
84 Chris Doleman .20
85 Alfred Anderson .05
86 Keith Millard .05
87 Darrin Nelson .05
88 D.J. Dozier .05
89 Scott Studwell .05
90 Tony Zendejas Oilers Team .05
91 *Bruce Matthews* (AP) .30
92 Curtis Duncan .20
93 Warren Moon .40
94 *Johnny Meads* .10
95 Drew Hill .05
96 Alonzo Highsmith .05
97 Mike Munchak .05
98 Mike Rozier .05
99 Tony Zendejas .05
100 Jeff Donaldson .05
101 Ray Childress .05
102 Sean Jones .05
103 Ernest Givins .20
104 *William Fuller* .40
105 *Allen Pinkett* .15
106 Randall Cunningham Eagles Team .10
107 *Keith Jackson* (AP) .50
108 Reggie White (AP) .25
109 Clyde Simmons .25
110 John Teltschik .05
111 Wes Hopkins .05
112 Keith Byars .05
113 Jerome Brown .05
114 Mike Quick .05
115 Randall Cunningham .40
116 Anthony Toney .05
117 Ron Johnson .05
118 Terry Hoage .05
119 Seth Joyner .25
120 *Eric Allen* .40
121 *Cris Carter* 2.00
122 Greg Bell Rams Team .05
123 *Tom Newberry* (AP) .15
124 Pete Holohan .05
125 *Robert Delpino* .35
126 Carl Ekern .05
127 Greg Bell .05
128 Mike Lansford .05
129 Jim Everett .15
130 Mike Wilcher .05
131 Jerry Gray .05
132 Dale Hatcher .05
133 Doug Smith .05
134 Kevin Greene .15
135 Jackie Slater .05
136 *Aaron Cox* .12
137 Henry Ellard .05
138 Bernie Kosar Browns Team .05
139 Frank Minnifield (AP) .05
140 Webster Slaughter .25
141 Bernie Kosar .20
142 Charles Buchanan .05
143 Clay Matthews .05
144 *Reggie Langhorne* .30
145 Hanford Dixon .05
146 Brian Brennan .05
147 Earnest Byner .05
148 *Michael Dean Perry* 1.00
149 Kevin Mack .05
150 Matt Bahr .05
151 Ozzie Newsome .20
152 Craig Heyward Saints Team .05
153 Morten Andersen .05
154 Pat Swilling .25
155 Sam Mills .05
156 Lonzell Hill .05
157 Dalton Hilliard .05
158 *Craig Heyward* .50
159 *Vaughan Johnson* .30
160 Reuben Mayes .05
161 *Gene Atkins* .10
162 Bobby Hebert .20
163 Rickey Jackson .05
164 Eric Martin .05
165 Joe Morris Giants Team .05
166 Lawrence Taylor (AP) .15
167 Bart Oates .05
168 Carl Banks .05
169 Eric Moore .05
170 *Sheldon White* .12
171 *Mark Collins* .12
172 Phil Simms .15
173 Jim Burt .05
174 *Stephen Baker* .25
175 Mark Bavaro .05
176 Pepper Johnson .05
177 Lionel Manuel .05
178 Joe Morris .05
179 *John Elliott* .15
180 Gary Reasons .05
181 Dave Krieg SeahawksTeam .05
182 *Brian Blades* (SR) .75
183 Steve Largent .25
184 *Rufus Porter* .15
185 Ruben Rodriguez .05
186 Curt Warner .05
187 Paul Moyer .05
188 Dave Krieg .05
189 Jacob Green .05
190 John L. Williams .05
191 *Eugene Robinson* .15
192 Brian Bosworth .05
193 Tony Eason Patriots Team .05
194 *John Stephens* (SR) .20
195 *Robert Perryman* .10
196 Andre Tippett .05
197 Fred Marion .05
198 Doug Flutie .75
199 Stanley Morgan .05
200 *Johnny Rembert* .10
201 Tony Eason .05
202 Marvin Allen .05
203 Raymond Clayborn .05
204 Irving Fryar .05
205 Chris Chandler Colts Team .05
206 Eric Dickerson (AP) .20
207 Chris Hinton (AP) .05
208 Duane Bickett .05
209 *Chris Chandler* 2.00
210 Jon Hand .05
211 Ray Donaldson .05
212 Dean Biasucci .05
213 Bill Brooks .05
214 *Chris Goode* .10
215 *Clarence Verdin* .20
216 Albert Bentley .05
217 Wade Wilson, Boomer Esiason Passing Leaders .05
218 Henry Ellard, Al Toon Receiving Leaders .05
219 Herschel Walker, Eric Dickerson Rushing Leaders .15
220 Mike Cofer, Scott Norwood Scoring Leaders .05
221 Scott Case, Erik McMillan Interception Leaders .05
222 Ken O'Brien Jets Team .05
223 Erik McMillan (SR) .10
224 *James Hasty* (SR) .12
225 Al Toon .05
226 *John Booty* .12
227 Johnny Hector .05
228 Ken O'Brien .05
229 Marty Lyons .05
230 Mickey Shuler .05
231 Robin Cole .05
232 Freeman McNeil .05
233 Marion Barber .05
234 JoJo Townsell .05
235 Wesley Walker .05
236 Roger Vick .05
237 Pat Leahy .05
238 John Elway Broncos Team .10
239 Mike Horan (AP) .05
240 Tony Dorsett .25
241 John Elway .50
242 Mark Jackson .05
243 Sammy Winder .05
244 Rich Karlis .05
245 Vance Johnson .05
246 *Steve Sewell* .10
247 Karl Mecklenburg .05
248 Rulon Jones .05
249 *Simon Fletcher* .30
250 Doug Williams Redskins Team .05
251 *Chip Lohmiller* (SR) .30
252 Jamie Morris (SR) .05
253 *Mark Rypien* (SR) .40
254 Barry Wilburn .05
255 Mark May .10
256 Wilbur Marshall .05
257 Charles Mann .05
258 Gary Clark .15
259 Doug Williams .05
260 Art Monk .15
261 Kelvin Bryant .05
262 Dexter Manley .05
263 Ricky Sanders .05
264 Marcus Allen Raiders Team .05
265 *Tim Brown* (AP) 2.00
266 Jay Schroeder .05
267 Marcus Allen .12
268 Mike Haynes .05
269 Bo Jackson .75
270 *Steve Beuerlein* 1.00
271 Vann McElroy .05
272 Willie Gault .05
273 Howie Long .05
274 Greg Townsend .05
275 Mike Wise .05
276 Neil Lomax Cardinals Team .05
277 Luis Sharpe .05
278 Scott Dill .05
279 Vai Sikahema .05
280 Ron Wolfley .05
281 David Galloway .05
282 *Jay Novacek* .75
283 Neil Lomax .05
284 Robert Awalt .05
285 Cedric Mack .05
286 Freddie Joe Nunn .05
287 J.T. Smith .05
288 Stump Mitchell .05
289 Roy Green .05
290 Dan Marino Dolphins Team .25
291 *Jarvis Williams* (SR) .10
292 Troy Stradford .05
293 Dan Marino 2.00
294 T.J. Turner .05
295 John Offerdahl .05
296 *Ferrell Edmunds* .15
297 Scott Schwedes .05
298 Lorenzo Hampton .05
299 Jim Jensen .05
300 Brian Sochia .05
301 Reggie Roby .05
302 Mark Clayton .05
303 Tim Spencer Chargers Team .05
304 Lee Williams .05
305 *Gary Plummer* .15
306 Gary Anderson .05
307 Gill Byrd .05
308 Jamie Holland .05
309 Billy Ray Smith .05
310 Lionel James .05
311 *Mark Vlasic* .20
312 Curtis Adams .05
313 *Anthony Miller* 1.00
314 Frank Pollard Steelers Team .05
315 *Bubby Brister* .50
316 David Little .05

317 Tunch Ilkin .05
318 Louis Lipps .05
319 *Warren Williams* .10
320 Dwight Stone .05
321 *Merril Hoge* .20
322 *Thomas Everett* .25
323 *Rod Woodson* .75
324 Gary Anderson .05
325 Ron Hall Buccaneer Team .05
326 Donnie Elder .05
327 Vinny Testaverde .15
328 Harry Hamilton .05
329 James Wilder .05
330 Lars Tate .05
331 *Mark Carrier* .65
332 Bruce Hill .05
333 *Paul Gruber* .12
334 Ricky Reynolds .05
335 Eugene Marve .05
336 J. Williams Falcons Team .05
337 *Aundray Bruce* (SR) .10
338 John Rade .05
339 *Scott Case* .10
340 Robert Moore .05
341 *Chris Miller* .60
342 Gerald Riggs .05
343 Gene Lang .05
344 Marcus Cotton .05
345 Rick Donnelly .05
346 *John Settle* .10
347 Bill Fralic .05
348 Dino Hackett Chiefs Team .05
349 Steve DeBerg .05
350 Mike Stensrud .05
351 Dino Hackett .05
352 Deron Cherry .05
353 Christian Okoye .12
354 Bill Maas .05
355 Carlos Carson .05
356 Albert Lewis .05
357 Paul Palmer .05
358 Nick Lowery .05
359 Stephone Paige .05
360 Chuck Long Lions Team .05
361 *Chris Spielman* (SR) .30
362 Jim Arnold .05
363 Devon Mitchell .05
364 Mike Cofer .05
365 *Bennie Blades* .15
366 James Jones .05
367 Garry James .05
368 Pete Mandley .05
369 Keith Ferguson .05
370 Dennis Gibson .05
371 Johnny Holland Packers Team .05
372 Brent Fullwood .05
373 Don Majkowski .20
374 Timothy Harris .05
375 *Keith Woodside* .10
376 Mark Murphy .05
377 Dave Brown .05
378 *Perry Kemp* .10
379 *Sterling Sharpe* 1.50
380 *Chuck Cecil* .25
381 Walter Stanley .05
382 Steve Pelleur Cowboys Team .05
383 *Michael Irvin* (SR) 1.50
384 Bill Bates .05
385 Herschel Walker .15
386 Darryl Clack .05
387 Danny Noonan .05
388 Eugene Lockhart .05
389 Ed "Too Tall" Jones .05
390 Steve Pelluer .05
391 Ray Alexander .05
392 *Nate Newton* .20
393 Garry Cobb .05
394 Checklist 1-132 .05
395 Checklist 133-264 .05
396 Checklist 265-396 .05

1989 Topps Box Bottoms

The 16-card, standard-size set featured the weekly offensive and defensive award winners for the 1988 season. The cards were included four to the bottom of each box of 1989 football. Two players (offensive and defensive) are on each card.

NM/M

Complete Set (16): 5.00
Common Player: .25
A Neal Anderson, Terry Hoage .25
B Boomer Esiason, Jacob Green .50
C Wesley Walker, Gary Jeter .25
D Jim Everett, Danny Noonan .25
E Neil Lomax, Dexter Manley .25
F Kelvin Bryant, Kevin Greene .25
G Roger Craig, Tim Harris .50
H Dan Marino, Carl Banks 2.00
I Drew Hill, Robin Cole .25
J Neil Lomax, Lawrence Taylor .50
K Roy Green, Tim Krumrie .25
L Bobby Hebert, Aundray Bruce .25
M Ickey Woods, Lawrence Taylor .50
N Louis Lipps, Greg Townsend .25
O Curt Warner, Tim Harris .25
P Dave Krieg, Kevin Greene .35

1989 Topps 1000 Yard Club

These standard-size cards, printed on heavy white cardboard stock and featuring a full-color action shot of each NFL player who gained more tha 1,000 yards rushing or receiving during the 1988 season, were included in wax packs of 1989 Topps football cards. Fronts feature a yellow-and-blue ribbon from the upper right corner, across the top and leading to a "1000 Yard Club" medal at lower left. The photo and medal are bordered in red, with the player's name in white and his position in black also in the border. Card backs are in orange, with an ornate "1000 Yard Club" medal and ribbon reaching from the card number at upper left to the bottom center of the card. Statistics mark the game-by-game progress of the runner-receiver's season.

NM/M

Complete Set (24): 4.00
Common Player: .10
1 Eric Dickerson .60
2 Herschel Walker .60
3 Roger Craig .40
4 Henry Ellard .10
5 Jerry Rice .60
6 Eddie Brown .10
7 Anthony Carter .10
8 Greg Bell .10
9 John Stephens .10
10 Ricky Sanders .10
11 Drew Hill .10
12 Mark Clayton .10
13 Gary Anderson .10
14 Neal Anderson .20
15 Roy Green .10
16 Eric Martin .10
17 Joe Morris .10
18 Al Toon .10
19 Ickey Woods .20
20 Bruce Hill .10
21 Lionel Manuel .10
22 Curt Warner .10
23 John Settle .10
24 Mike Rozier .10

1989 Topps Traded

This 132-card set was released in March of 1990. It was a boxed set through only hobby dealers, similar to the baseball "Traded" sets that Topps had been issuing since 1981. The set includes 1989 rookies, players not included in the regular '89 set and players that had been traded (now shown with their new team).

NM/M

Complete Set (132): 12.00
Common Player: .05
1 *Eric Ball* .10
2 Tony Mandarich .05
3 *Shawn Collins* .10
4 *Ray Bentley* .10
5 Tony Casillas .10
6 *Al Del Greco* .10
7 *Dan Saleaumua* .10
8 Keith Bishop .05
9 *Rodney Peete* .40
10 *Lorenzo White* .25
11 *Steve Smith* .25
12 Pete Mandley .05
13 Mervyn Fernandez .05
14 *Flipper Anderson* .30
15 *Louis Oliver* .15
16 Rick Fenney .05
17 Gary Jeter .05
18 Greg Cox .05
19 *Bubba McDowell* .15
20 Ron Heller .05
21 *Tim McDonald* .25
22 *Jerrol Williams* .10
23 *Marion Butts* .40
24 Steve Young 1.00
25 Mike Merriweather .05
26 Richard Johnson .05
27 Gerald Riggs .05
28 Dave Waymer .05
29 Isaac Holt .05
30 *Deion Sanders* 1.75
31 Todd Blackledge .05
32 *Jeff Cross* .30
33 *Steve Wisniewski* .20
34 Ron Brown .05
35 *Ron Bernstine* .35
36 *Jeff Uhlenhake* .08
37 *Donnell Woolford* .12
38 *Bob Gagliano* .12
39 Ezra Johnson .05
40 Ron Jaworski .05
41 *Lawyer Tillman* .10
42 *Lorenzo Lynch* .10
43 Mike Alexander .05
44 *Tim Worley* .15
45 Guy Bingham .05
46 *Cleveland Gary* .25
47 Danny Peebles .25
48 Clarence Weathers .05
49 *Jeff Lageman* .10
50 *Eric Metcalf* .65
51 *Myron Guyton* .10
52 *Steve Atwater* .20
53 John Fourcade .05
54 Randall McDaniel .12
55 *Al Noga* .15
56 *Sammie Smith* .10
57 Jesse Solomon .05
58 *Greg Kragen* .10
59 *Don Beebe* .50
60 Hart Lee Dykes .05
61 *Trace Armstrong* .15
62 Steve Pelluer .05
63 Barry Krauss .05
64 Kevin Murphy .05
65 *Steve Tasker* .30
66 *Jessie Small* .10
67 *Dave Meggett* .25
68 Dean Hamel .05
69 Jim Covert .05
70 *Troy Aikman* 3.00
71 Raul Allegre .05
72 *Chris Jacke* .15
73 Leslie O'Neal .25
74 *Keith Taylor* .10
75 *Steve Walsh* .50
76 Tracy Rocker .05
77 *Robert Massey* .12
78 Bryan Wagner .05
79 Steve DeOssie .05
80 *Carnell Lake* .12
81 *Frank Reich* .50
82 *Tyrone Braxton* .10
83 *Barry Sanders* 10.00
84 *Pete Stoyanovich* .20
85 Paul Palmer .05
86 *Billy Joe Tolliver* .10
87 *Eric Hill* .08
88 Gerald McNeil .05
89 Bill Hawkins .05
90 *Derrick Thomas* .75
91 *Jim Harbaugh* 1.00
92 Brian Williams .05
93 Jack Trudeau .05
94 Leonard Smith .05
95 Gary Hogeboom .05
96 *A.J. Johnson* .10
97 Jim McMahon .05
98 *David Williams* .12
99 Rohn Stark .05
100 Sean Landeta .05
101 *Tim Johnson* .08
102 *Andre Rison* .50
103 Earnest Byner .05
104 *Don McPherson* .08
105 *Zefross Moss* .08
106 *Frank Stams* .10
107 *Courtney Hall* .10
108 *Marc Logan* .15
109 James Lofton .15
110 *Lewis Tillman* .50
111 Irv Pankey .05
112 Ralf Mojsiejenko .05
113 *Bobby Humphrey* .08
114 Chris Burkett .05
115 *Greg Lloyd* .40
116 Matt Millen .05
117 Carl Zander .05
118 *Wayne Martin* .25
119 Mike Saxon .05
120 Herschel Walker .12
121 *Andy Heck* .08
122 Mark Robinson .05
123 *Keith Van Horne* .08
124 Ricky Hunley .05
125 *Timm Rosenbach* .15
126 Steve Grogan .05
127 *Stephen Braggs* .08
128 Terry Long .05
129 Evan Cooper .05
130 Robert Lyles .05
131 Mike Webster .05
132 Checklist .05

1989 Topps American/ United Kingdom

This boxed set of 33 cards was distributed in the United Kingdom using a design similar to Topps' regular 1989 set. However, the card stock for the back is not grey, like it is for the regular cards; these ones have white backs. The set's checklist is included on the box; card numbers do not match those in the regular set.

NM/M

Complete Set (33): 35.00
Common Player: 1.00
1 Anthony Carter 1.00
2 Jim Kelly 2.50
3 Bernie Kosar 1.50
4 John Elway 4.00
5 Andre Tippett 1.00
6 Henry Ellard 1.50
7 Eddie Brown 1.00
8 Gary Anderson 1.00
9 Eric Martin 1.00
10 Ickey Woods 1.00
11 Mike Singletary 1.00
12 Phil Simms 1.50
13 Brian Bosworth 1.00
14 Mark Clayton 1.25
15 Eric Dickerson 1.50
16 John Stephens 1.00
17 Neal Anderson 1.00
18 Al Toon 1.00
19 Lionel Manuel .75
20 Joe Montana 7.00
21 Reggie White 2.00
22 Randall Cunningham 1.75
23 Lawrence Taylor 1.50
24 Jim Everett 1.25
25 Neil Lomax 1.00
26 Herschel Walker 1.25
27 Roger Craig 1.25
28 Greg Bell 1.00
29 Ricky Sanders 1.00
30 Joe Morris 1.00
31 Curt Warner 1.00
32 Boomer Esiason 1.50
33 Dan Marino 7.00

1990 Topps

The 1990 Topps set, the largest since 1982, returned to 528 cards. A new addition to the Topps sets included 25 1990 draft pick cards; other subsets included four 1989 record breakers, four league leader cards and a Super Bowl card. Each wax pack included one of 31 glossy 1,000 Yard Club insert cards featuring players who gained 1,000 yards or more during the 1989 NFL season. Because NFL Properties denied Topps a license, cards have no free-standing team logos. A 196-card Bowman football set, also scheduled to be issued in 1990, was also scratched. Variations include cards #28, 193, 229 and 501-528 - all the Topps horizontal issues - which originally appeared without the small black vertical "hashmarks" running below the red border and underneath the Topps logo. These were corrected very early; no premium value has been put on them, but they should fetch 35-50 cents over the regular card price. Also, Topps issued "corrected" cards, presumably both in wax and in factory sets, that do not have the "unauthorized" tagline. These are thought to be scarcer than the unauthorized cards. (Key: RB - Record Breaker).

NM/M

Complete Set (528): 10.00
Common Player: .04
Wax Pack (15+1): .50
Wax Box (36): 8.50
1 Joe Montana (RB) .50
2 Flipper Anderson (RB) .04
3 Troy Aikman (RB) .50
4 Kevin Butler (RB) .04
5 Super Bowl XXIV .04
6 *Dexter Carter* .20
7 Matt Millen .04
8 Jerry Rice .75
9 Ronnie Lott .10
10 John Taylor .20
11 Guy McIntyre .04
12 Roger Craig .04
13 Joe Montana 1.00
14 *Brent Jones* .75
15 Tom Rathman .04
16 Harris Barton .04
17 Charles Haley .04
18 *Pierce Holt* .20
19 Michael Carter .04
20 Chet Brooks .04
21 Eric Wright .04
22 Mike Cofer .04
23 Jim Fahnhorst .04
24 Keena Turner .04
25 Don Griffin .04
26 *Kevin Fagan* .08
27 Bubba Paris .04
28 Rushing Leaders .15
29 Steve Atwater .04
30 Tyrone Braxton .04
31 Ron Holmes .04
32 Bobby Humphrey .04
33 Greg Kragen .04
34 David Treadwell .04
35 Karl Mecklenburg .04
36 Dennis Smith .04
37 John Elway .40
38 Vance Johnson .04
39 Simon Fletcher .04
40 Jim Juriga .04
41 Mark Jackson .04
42 Melvin Bratton .04
43 *Wymon Henderson* .10
44 Ken Ball .04
45 Sammy Winder .04
46 Alphonso Carreker .04
47 Orson Mobley .04
48 *Rodney Hampton* 1.00
49 Dave Meggett .12
50 Myron Guyton .04
51 Phil Simms .10
52 Lawrence Taylor .10
53 Carl Banks .04
54 Pepper Johnson .04
55 Leonard Marshall .04
56 Mark Collins .04
57 Erik Howard .04
58 *Eric Dorsey* .10
59 Ottis Anderson .04
60 Mark Bavaro .04
61 *Odessa Turner* .12
62 Gary Reasons .04
63 Maurice Carthon .04
64 Lionel Manuel .04
65 Sean Landeta .04
66 Perry Williams .04
67 *Pat Terrell* .12
68 Flipper Anderson .15
69 Jackie Slater .04
70 Tom Newberry .04
71 Jerry Gray .04
72 Henry Ellard .04
73 Doug Smith .04
74 Kevin Greene .04
75 Jim Everett .04
76 Mike Lansford .04
77 Greg Bell .04
78 Pete Holohan .04
79 Robert Delpino .04
80 Mike Wilcher .04
81 Mike Piel .04
82 Mel Owens .04
83 *Michael Stewart* .10
84 *Ben Smith* .10
85 Keith Jackson .25
86 Reggie White .15
87 Eric Allen .04
88 Jerome Brown .04
89 Robert Drummond .04
90 Anthony Toney .04
91 Keith Byars .04
92 Cris Carter .30
93 Randall Cunningham .20
94 Ron Johnson .04
95 Mike Quick .04
96 Clyde Simmons .04
97 Mike Pitts .04
98 Izel Jenkins .04
99 Seth Joyner .04
100 Mike Schad .04
101 Wes Hopkins .04
102 Kirk Lowdermilk .04
103 Rick Fenney .04
104 Randall McDaniel .04
105 Herschel Walker .04
106 Al Noga .04
107 Gary Zimmerman .04
108 Chris Doleman .04
109 Keith Millard .04
110 Carl Lee .04
111 Joey Browner .04
112 Steve Jordan .04
113 *Reggie Rutland* .10
114 Wade Wilson .04
115 Anthony Carter .04
116 Rich Karlis .04
117 Hassan Jones .04
118 Henry Thomas .04
119 Scott Studwell .04
120 Ralf Mojsiejenko .04
121 Earnest Byner .04
122 Gerald Riggs .04
123 Tracy Rocker .04
124 A.J. Johnson .04
125 Charles Mann .04
126 Art Monk .04
127 Rickey Sanders .04
128 Gary Clark .15
129 Jim Lachey .04
130 *Martin Mayhew* .15
131 Ravin Caldwell .04
132 Don Warren .04
133 Mark Rypien .25
134 *Ed Simmons* .10
135 Darryl Grant .04
136 Darryl Green .04
137 Chip Lommiller .04
138 *Tony Bennett* .35
139 Tony Mandarich .04
140 Sterling Sharpe .75
141 Tim Harris .04
142 Don Majkowski .04
143 Rich Moran .04
144 Jeff Query .04
145 Brent Fullwood .04
146 Chris Jacke .04
147 Keith Woodside .04
148 Perry Kemp .04
149 Herman Fontenot .04
150 Dave Brown .04
151 Brian Noble .04
152 Johnny Holland .04
153 Mark Murphy .04
154 Bob Nelson .04
155 *Darrell Thompson* .25
156 Lawyer Tillman .04
157 Eric Metcalf .12
158 Webster Slaughter .04
159 Frank Minnifield .04
160 Brian Brennan .04
161 Thane Gash .04
162 Robert Banks .04
163 Bernie Kosar .04
164 David Grayson .04
165 Kevin Mack .04
166 Mike Johnson .04
167 Tim Manoa .04
168 Ozzie Newsome .10
169 Felix Wright .04
170 Al Baker .04
171 Reggie Langhorne .04
172 Clay Matthews .04
173 Andrew Stewart .04
174 *Barry Foster* .10
175 Tim Worley .04
176 Tim Johnson .04
177 Carnell Lake .04
178 Greg Lloyd .04
179 Rod Woodson .15
180 Tunch Ilkin .04
181 Dermontti Dawson .04
182 Gary Anderson .04
183 Bubby Brister .10
184 Louis Lipps .04
185 Merril Hoge .04
186 Mike Mularkey .04
187 Derek Hill .04
188 Rodney Carter .04
189 Dwayne Carter .04
190 Keith Willis .04
191 Jerry Olsavsky .04
192 Mark Stock .04
193 Sacks Leaders .04
194 Leonard Smith .04
195 Darryl Talley .04
196 Mark Kelso .04
197 Kent Hull .04
198 *Nate Odomes* .30
199 Pete Metzelaars .04
200 Don Beebe .15
201 Ray Bentley .04
202 Steve Tasker .10
203 Scott Norwood .04
204 Andre Reed .20
205 Bruce Smith .04
206 Thurman Thomas .50
207 Jim Kelly .35
208 Cornelius Bennett .04
209 Shane Conlan .04
210 Larry Kinnebrew .04
211 *Jeff Alm* .10
212 Robert Lyles .04
213 Bubba McDowell .04
214 Mike Munchak .04
215 Bruce Matthews .04
216 Warren Moon .25
217 Drew Hill .04
218 Ray Childress .04
219 Steve Brown .04
220 Alonzo Highsmith .04
221 Allen Pinkett .04
222 Sean Jones .04
223 Johnny Meads .04
224 John Grimsley .04
225 *Haywood Jeffires* .50
226 Curtis Duncan .04
227 *Greg Montgomery* .10
228 Ernest Givins .04
229 Passing Leaders .20
230 Robert Massey .04
231 John Fourcade .04
232 Dalton Hilliard .04
233 Vaughan Johnson .04
234 Hoby Brenner .04
235 Pat Swilling .04
236 Kevin Haverdink .04
237 Bobby Hebert .15
238 Sam Mills .04
239 Eric Martin .04
240 Lonzell Hill .04
241 Steve Trapilo .04
242 Rickey Jackson .04
243 Craig Heyward .04
244 Rueben Mayes .04
245 Morten Anderson .04
246 *Percy Snow* .10
247 Pete Mandley .04
248 Derrick Thomas .30
249 Dan Saleaumua .04
250 *Todd McNair* .15
251 Leonard Griffin .04
252 Jonathan Hayes .04
253 Christian Okoye .04
254 Albert Lewis .04
255 Nick Lowery .04
256 Kevin Ross .04
257 Steve DeBerg .04
258 Stephone Paige .04
259 *James Saxon* .10
260 Herman Heard .04
261 Deron Cherry .04
262 Dino Hackett .04
263 Neil Smith .20
264 Steve Pelluer .04
265 Eric Thomas .04
266 Eric Ball .04
267 Leon White .04
268 Tim Krumrie .04
269 Jason Buck .04
270 Boomer Esiason .20
271 Carl Zander .04
272 Eddie Brown .04
273 David Fulcher .04
274 Tim McGee .04
275 James Brooks .04
276 *Rickey Dixon* .10
277 Ickey Woods .04
278 Anthony Munoz .04
279 Rodney Holman .04
280 Mike Alexander .04
281 Mervyn Fernandez .04
282 Steve Wisniewski .04
283 Steve Smith .04
284 Howie Long .04
285 Bo Jackson .45
286 Mike Dyal .04
287 Thomas Benson .04
288 Willie Gault .04
289 Marcus Allen .04
290 Greg Townsend .04
291 Steve Beurlein .30
292 Scott Davis .04
293 *Eddie Anderson* .10
294 Terry McDaniel .04
295 Tim Brown .45
296 Bob Golic .04
297 *Jeff Jaeger* .12
298 *Jeff George* 1.00
299 Chip Banks .04
300 Andre Rison .25
301 Rohn Stark .04
302 Keith Taylor .04
303 Jack Trudeau .04
304 Chris Hinton .04
305 Ray Donaldson .04
306 *Jeff Herrod* .10
307 Clarence Verdin .04
308 Jon Hand .04
309 Bill Brooks .04
310 Albert Bentley .04

No.	Player	Price
311	Mike Prior	.04
312	Pat Beach	.04
313	Eugene Daniel	.04
314	Duane Bickett	.04
315	Dean Biasucci	.04
316	*Richmond Webb*	.25
317	Jeff Cross	.04
318	Louis Oliver	.04
319	Sammie Smith	.04
320	Pete Stovanovich	.04
321	John Offerdahl	.04
322	Ferrell Edmunds	.04
323	Dan Marino	.75
324	Andre Brown	.04
325	Reggie Roby	.04
326	Jarvis Williams	.04
327	Roy Foster	.04
328	Mark Clayton	.04
329	Brian Sochia	.04
330	Mark Duper	.04
331	T.J. Turner	.04
332	Jeff Uhlenhake	.04
333	Jim Jensen	.04
334	*Cortez Kennedy*	.25
335	Andy Heck	.04
336	Rufus Porter	.04
337	Brian Blades	.15
338	Dave Krieg	.04
339	John L. Williams	.04
340	David Wyman	.04
341	*Paul Skansi*	.10
342	Eugene Robinson	.04
343	Joe Nash	.04
344	Jacob Green	.04
345	Jeff Bryant	.04
346	Ruben Rodriguez	.04
347	Norm Johnson	.04
348	Darren Comeaux	.04
349	*Andre Ware*	.20
350	Richard Johnson	.04
351	Rodney Peete	.10
352	Barry Sanders	1.25
353	Chris Spielman	.04
354	Eddie Murray	.04
355	Jerry Ball	.04
356	Mel Gray	.04
357	*Eric Williams*	.10
358	*Robert Clark*	.10
359	Jason Phillips	.04
360	*Terry Taylor*	.08
361	Bennie Blades	.04
362	Michael Cofer	.04
363	Jim Arnold	.04
364	*Marc Spindler*	.10
365	Jim Covert	.04
366	Jim Harbaugh	.20
367	Neal Anderson	.15
368	Mike Singletary	.04
369	John Roper	.04
370	Steve McMichael	.04
371	Dennis Gentry	.04
372	Brad Muster	.04
373	Ron Morris	.04
374	James Thornton	.04
375	Kevin Butler	.04
376	Richard Dent	.04
377	Dan Hampton	.04
378	Jay Hilgenberg	.04
379	Donnell Woolford	.04
380	Trace Armstrong	.04
381	*Junior Seau*	1.00
382	Rod Bernstine	.15
383	Marion Butts	.15
384	Burt Grossman	.04
385	Darrin Nelson	.04
386	Leslie O'Neal	.04
387	Billy Joe Tolliver	.04
388	Courtney Hall	.04
389	Lee Williams	.04
390	Anthony Miller	.30
391	Gill Byrd	.04
392	Wayne Walker	.04
393	Billy Ray Smith	.04
394	Vencie Glenn	.04
395	Tim Spencer	.04
396	Gary Plummer	.04
397	Arthur Cox	.04
398	Jamie Holland	.04
399	*Keith McCants*	.10
400	Kevin Murphy	.04
401	Danny Peebles	.04
402	Mark Robinson	.04
403	Broderick Thomas	.04
404	Ron Hall	.04
405	Mark Carrier	.04
406	Paul Gruber	.04
407	Vinny Testaverde	.10
408	Bruce Hill	.04
409	Lars Tate	.04
410	Harry Hamilton	.04
411	Ricky Reynolds	.04
412	Donald Igwebuike	.04
413	Reuben Davis	.04
414	William Howard	.04
415	*Winston Moss*	.10
416	*Chris Singleton*	.10
417	Hart Lee Dykes	.04
418	Steve Grogan	.04
419	Bruce Armstrong	.04
420	Robert Perryman	.04
421	Andre Tippett	.04
422	Sammy Martin	.04
423	Stanley Morgan	.04
424	Cedric Jones	.04
425	Sean Farrell	.04
426	Marc Wilson	.04
427	John Stephens	.04
428	Eric Sievers	.04
429	*Maurice Hurst*	.10
430	Johnny Rembert	.04
431	Receiving Leaders	.25
432	Eric Hill	.04
433	Gary Hogeboom	.04
434	Timm Rosenbach	.04
435	Tim McDonald	.04
436	Rich Camarillo	.04
437	Luis Sharpe	.04
438	J.T. Smith	.04
439	Roy Green	.04
440	*Ernie Jones*	.15
441	Robert Awalt	.04
442	Vai Sikahema	.04
443	Joe Wolf	.04
444	Stump Mitchell	.04
445	David Galloway	.04
446	Ron Wolfley	.04
447	Freddie Joe Nunn	.04
448	*Blair Thomas*	.15
449	Jeff Lageman	.04
450	Tony Eason	.04
451	Eric McMillan	.04
452	Jim Sweeney	.04
453	Ken O'Brien	.04
454	Johnny Hector	.04
455	JoJo Townsell	.04
456	Roger Vick	.04
457	Dennis Hasty	.04
458	*Dennis Byrd*	.25
459	Ron Stallworth	.04
460	Mickey Shuler	.04
461	Bobby Humphery	.04
462	Kyle Clifton	.04
463	Al Toon	.04
464	Freeman McNeil	.04
465	Pat Leahy	.04
466	Scott Case	.04
467	Shawn Collins	.04
468	Floyd Dixon	.04
469	Deion Sanders	.35
470	Tony Casillas	.04
471	*Michael Haynes*	.50
472	Chris Miller	.25
473	John Settle	.04
474	Aundray Bruce	.04
475	Gene Lang	.04
476	*Tim Gordon*	.10
477	Scott Fulhage	.04
478	Bill Fralic	.04
479	*Jessie Tuggle*	.25
480	Marcus Cotton	.04
481	Steve Walsh	.04
482	Troy Aikman	1.25
483	Ray Horton	.04
484	*Tony Tolbert*	.20
485	Steve Folsom	.04
486	*Ken Norton Jr.*	.50
487	*Kelvin Martin*	.25
488	Jack Del Rio	.04
489	*Daryl Johnston*	1.00
490	Bill Bates	.04
491	Jim Jeffcoat	.04
492	Vince Albritton	.04
493	Eugene Lockhart	.04
494	Mike Saxon	.04
495	James Dixon	.04
496	Willie Broughton	.04
497	Checklist 1-132	.04
498	Checklist 133-264	.04
499	Checklist 265-396	.04
500	Checklist 397-528	.04
501	Bears Team	.04
502	Bengals Team	.04
503	Bills Team	.04
504	Broncos Team	.04
505	Browns Team	.04
506	Buccaneers Team	.04
507	Cardinals Team	.04
508	Chargers Team	.04
509	Chiefs Team	.04
510	Colts Team	.04
511	Cowboys Team	.65
512	Dolphins Team	.04
513	Eagles Team	.04
514	Falcons Team	.04
515	49ers Team	.20
516	Giants Team	.04
517	Jets Team	.04
518	Lions Team	.04
519	Oilers Team	.10
520	Packers Team	.04
521	Patriots Team	.04
522	Raiders Team	.12
523	Rams Team	.04
524	Redskins Team	.04
525	Saints Team	.04
526	Seahawks Team	.04
527	Steelers Team	.04
528	Vikings Team	.04

1990 Topps Box Bottoms

These standard-size cards were included on the bottoms of 1990 Topps wax pack boxes. Each card has two photos on it; an offensive and defensive NFL Player of the Week from the 1989 season is featured. The back uses letters instead of card numbers and explains why the player was selected as the league's best performer for the week. The card design is similar to that which was used for Topps' regular 1990 set.

		NM/M
	Complete Set (16):	6.00
	Common Player:	.30
A	Jim Kelly, Dave Grayson	.50
B	Henry Ellard, Derrick Thomas	.50
C	Joe Montana, Vince Newsome	1.50
D	Bubby Brister, Tim Harris	.30
E	Christian Okoye, Keith Millard	.30
F	Warren Moon, Jerome Brown	.50
G	John Elway, Mike Merriweather	1.00
H	Webster Slaughter, Pat Swilling	.35
I	Rich Karlis, Lawrence Taylor	.35
J	Dan Marino, Greg Kragen	1.00
K	Boomer Esiason, Brent Williams	.35
L	Flipper Anderson, Pierce Holt	.30
M	Richard Johnson, David Fulcher	.30
N	John Taylor, Mike Prior	.50
O	Mark Rypien, Brett Faryniarz	.35
P	Greg Bell, Chris Doleman	.30

1990 Topps 1000 Yard Club

Players who gained more than 1,000 yards rushing or receiving during the 1989 NFL season are honored in this 30-card insert set. Cards were randomly included in 1990 Topps packs, one per pack. The front has a color picture, his and the set's name, plus the Topps' logo. Each back recaps each game from the 1989 season to show how the player reached the 1,000-yard milestone. The cards, numbered 1-30, are numbered according by yardage totals, with the leading yard gainer being #1, and so forth. The design for the card front is similar to the regular 1990 Topps football card design.

		NM/M
	Complete Set (30):	3.50
	Common Player:	.05
1	Jerry Rice	.50
2	Christian Okoye	.15
3	Barry Sanders	1.00
4	Sterling Sharpe	.40
5	Mark Carrier	.15
6	Henry Ellard	.05
7	Andre Reed	.25
8	Neal Anderson	.25
9	Dalton Hilliard	.05
10	Anthony Miller	.20
11	Thurman Thomas	.25
12	James Brooks	.15
13	Webster Slaughter	.05
14	Gary Clark	.05
15	Tim McGee	.05
16	Art Monk	.15
17	Bobby Humphrey	.25
18	Flipper Anderson	.05
19	Ricky Sanders	.05
20	Greg Bell	.05
21	Vance Johnson	.05
22	Richard Johnson	.05
23	Eric Martin	.05
24	John Taylor	.25
25	Mervyn Fernandez	.10
26	Anthony Carter	.10
27	Brian Blades	.10
28	Roger Craig	.20
29	Ottis Anderson	.20
30	Mark Clayton	.07

1990 Topps Traded

Like its predecessor, the Topps football update again pictured rookies and traded players on white cardboard stock. The issue was sold as a boxed set and was available only through hobby shops.

		NM/M
	Complete Set (132):	12.00
	Common Player:	.03
1	Gerald McNeil	.03
2	Andre Rison	.15
3	Steve Walsh	.10
4	Lorenzo White	.10
5	Max Montoya	.05
6	William Roberts	.03
7	Alonzo Highsmith	.10
8	Chris Hinton	.10
9	Stanley Morgan	.10
10	Mickey Shuler	.03
11	Bobby Humphrey	.03
12	Gary Anderson	.03
13	Mike Tomczak	.03
14	Anthony Pleasant	.03
15	Walter Stanley	.03
16	Greg Bell	.10
17	*Tony Martin*	2.00
18	Terry Kinard	.03
19	Cris Carter	.50
20	James Wilder	.03
21	Jerry Kauric	.03
22	Irving Fryer	.03
23	Ken Harvey	.03
24	James Williams	.15
25	Ron Cox	.03
26	Andre Ware	.50
27	*Emmitt Smith*	10.00
28	Junior Seau	.50
29	Mark Carrier	.50
30	Rodney Hampton	.50
31	*Rob Moore*	1.25
32	Bern Brostek	.10
33	Dexter Carter	.40
34	Blair Thomas	.65
35	Harold Green	.30
36	Darrell Thompson	.20
37	Eric Green	.25
38	Renaldo Turnbull	.20
39	*Leroy Hoard*	.50
40	Anthony Thompson	.25
41	Jeff George	.50
42	Alexander Wright	.15
43	Richmond Webb	.25
44	Cortez Kennedy	.75
45	Ray Agnew	.10
46	Percy Snow	.15
47	Chris Singleton	.10
48	James Francis	.20
49	Tony Bennett	.10
50	*Reggie Cobb*	.20
51	Barry Foster	.10
52	Ben Smith	.10
53	Anthony Smith	.10
54	Steve Christie	.10
55	Johnny Bailey	.20
56	Alan Grant	.03
57	Eric Floyd	.03
58	Robert Blackmon	.03
59	Brent Williams	.03
60	Raymond Clayborn	.03
61	Dave Duerson	.07
62	Derrick Fenner	.50
63	Ken Willis	.03
64	*Brad Baxter*	.25
65	Tony Paige	.03
66	Jay Schroeder	.15
67	Jim Breech	.03
68	Barry Word	.50
69	Anthony Dilweg	.10
70	*Rich Gannon*	2.00
71	*Stan Humphries*	.50
72	Jay Novacek	.50
73	Tommy Kane	.03
74	Everson Walls	.03
75	Mike Rozier	.10
76	Robb Thomas	.03
77	*Terance Mathis*	2.00
78	Leroy Irvin	.03
79	Jeff Donaldson	.03
80	Ethan Horton	.03
81	J.B. Brown	.03
82	Joe Kelly	.03
83	John Carney	.03
84	Dan Stryzinski	.03
85	John Kidd	.03
86	Al Smith	.03
87	Travis McNeal	.03
88	Reyna Thompson	.10
89	Rick Donnelly	.03
90	Marv Cook	.03
91	Mike Farr	.03
92	Daniel Stubbs	.03
93	Jeff Campbell	.20
94	Tim McKyer	.10
95	Ian Beckles	.03
96	Lemuel Stinson	.03
97	Frank Cornish	.03
98	Riki Ellison	.03
99	Jamie Mueller	.03
100	Brian Hansen	.03
101	Warren Powers	.03
102	Howard Cross	.03
103	Tim Grunhard	.03
104	*Johnny Johnson*	.20
105	*Calvin Williams*	.65
106	Keith McCants	.15
107	Lamar Lathon	.10
108	Steve Broussard	.35
109	Glenn Parker	.07
110	Alton Montgomery	.07
111	Jim McMahon	.07
112	Aaron Wallace	.25
113	Keith Sims	.07
114	Ervin Randle	.03
115	Walter Wilson	.03
116	Terry Wooden	.07
117	Bernard Cook	.03
118	Tony Stargell	.03
119	Jimmie Jones	.07
120	Andre Collins	.03
121	*Ricky Proehl*	.40
122	Darion Conner	.07
123	Jeff Rutledge	.03
124	Heath Sherman	.25
125	Tommie Agee	.03
126	Tory Epps	.03
127	Tom Hodson	.25
128	Jessie Hester	.03
129	Alfred Oglesby	.03
130	Chris Chandler	.03
131	*Fred Barnett*	.50
132	Checklist	.03

1991 Topps

Topps' largest-ever football set was issued in August 1991. The style of the cards is the same as in 1991 Topps baseball and hockey. Subsets include highlights, all-pros, draft picks and super rookies. (Key: HL - highlight, LL - league leader)

		NM/M
	Complete Set (660):	13.00
	Complete Factory Set (660):	17.00
	Common Player:	.04
	Pack (16):	.40
	Wax Box (36):	10.00
1	Super Bowl XXV	.08
2	Roger Craig (HL)	.04
3	Derrick Thomas (HL)	.12
4	Pete Stoyanovich (HL)	.04
5	Ottis Anderson (HL)	.04
6	Jerry Rice (HL)	.30
7	Warren Moon (HL)	.10
8	Warren Moon, Jim Everett (LL)	.10
9	Thurman Thomas, Barry Sanders (LL)	.50
10	Haywood Jeffires, Jerry Rice (LL)	.25
11	Richard Johnson, Mark Carrier (LL)	.04
12	Derrick Thomas, Charles Haley (LL)	.10
13	Jumbo Elliott	.04
14	Leonard Marshall	.04
15	William Roberts	.04
16	Lawrence Taylor	.10
17	Mark Ingram	.04
18	Rodney Hampton	.75
19	Carl Banks	.04
20	Ottis Anderson	.04
21	Mark Collins	.04
22	Pepper Johnson	.04
23	Dave Meggett	.04
24	Reyna Thompson	.04
26	Mike Fox	.04
27	Maurice Carthon	.04
28	Jeff Hostetler	.25
29	*Greg Jackson*	.10
30	Sean Landeta	.04
31	Bart Oates	.04
32	Phil Simms	.10
33	Erik Howard	.04
34	Myron Guyton	.04
35	Mark Bavaro	.04
36	Jarrod Bunch	.15
37	*Will Wolford*	.04
38	Ray Bentley	.04
39	Nate Odomes	.04
40	Scott Norwood	.04
41	Darryl Talley	.04
42	Carwell Gardner	.04
43	James Lofton	.04
44	Shane Conlan	.04
45	Steve Tasker	.04
46	James Williams	.04
47	Kent Hull	.04
48	Al Edwards	.04
49	Frank Reich	.04
50	Leon Seals	.04
51	Keith McKeller	.04
52	Thurman Thomas	.50
53	Leonard Smith	.04
54	Andre Reed	.15
55	Kenneth Davis	.04
56	*Jeff Wright*	.12
57	Jamie Mueller	.04
58	Jim Ritcher	.04
59	Bruce Smith	.04
60	*Ted Washington*	.10
61	Guy McIntyre	.04
62	Michael Carter	.04
63	Pierce Holt	.04
64	Darryl Pollard	.04
65	Mike Sherrard	.04
66	Dexter Carter	.04
67	Bubba Paris	.04
68	Harry Sydney	.04
69	Tom Rathman	.04
70	Jesse Sapolu	.04
71	Mike Cofer (S.F.)	.04
72	Keith DeLong	.04
73	Joe Montana	1.00
74	Bill Romanowski	.04
75	John Taylor	.15
76	Brent Jones	.04
77	Harris Barton	.04
78	Charles Haley	.04
79	Eric Davis	.04
80	Kevin Fagan	.04
81	Jerry Rice	1.00
82	Dave Waymer	.04
83	*Todd Marinovich*	.25
84	Steve Smith	.04
85	Tim Brown	.12
86	Ethan Horton	.04
87	Marcus Allen	.04
88	Terry McDaniel	.04
89	Thomas Benson	.04
90	Roger Craig	.04
91	Don Mosebar	.04
92	Aaron Wallace	.04
93	Eddie Anderson	.04
94	Willie Gault	.04
95	Howie Long	.04
96	Jay Schroeder	.04
97	Ronnie Lott	.10
98	Bob Golic	.04
99	Bo Jackson	.35
100	Max Montoya	.04
101	Scott Davis	.04
102	Greg Townsend	.04
103	Garry Lewis	.04
104	Mervyn Fernandez	.04
105	Steve Wisniewski	.04
106	Jeff Jaeger	.04
107	*Nick Bell*	.20
108	*Mark Dennis*	.08
109	Jarvis Williams	.04
110	Mark Clayton	.04
111	Harry Galbreah	.04
112	Dan Marino	2.00
113	Louis Oliver	.04
114	Pete Styoyanovich	.04
115	Ferrell Edmunds	.04
116	Jeff Cross	.04
117	Richmond Webb	.04
118	Jim Jensen	.04
119	Keith Sims	.04
120	Mark Duper	.04
121	*Shawn Lee*	.12
122	Reggie Roby	.04
123	Jeff Uhlenhake	.04
124	Sammie Smith	.04
125	John Offerdahl	.04
126	Hugh Green	.04
127	Tony Paige	.04
128	David Griggs	.04
129	J.B. Brown	.04
130	*Harvey Williams*	.50
131	John Alt	.04
132	Albert Lewis	.04
133	Robb Thomas	.04
134	Neil Smith	.04
135	Stephone Paige	.04
136	Nick Lowery	.04
137	Steve DeBerg	.04
138	*Rich Baldinger*	.10
139	Percy Snow	.04
140	Kevin Porter	.04
141	Chris Martin	.04
142	Deron Cherry	.04
143	Derrick Thomas	.30
144	Tim Grunhard	.04
145	Todd McNair	.04
146	David Szott	.04
147	Dan Saleaumua	.04
148	Jonathan Hayes	.04
149	Christian Okoye	.04
150	Dino Hackett	.04
151	*Bryan Barker*	.10
152	Kevin Ross	.04
153	Barry Word	.15
154	Stan Thomas	.04
155	Brad Muster	.04
156	Donnell Woolford	.04
157	Neal Anderson	.10
158	Jim Covert	.04
159	Jim Harbaugh	.10
160	Shaun Gayle	.04
161	William Perry	.04
162	Ron Morris	.04
163	Mark Bortz	.04
164	James Thornton	.04
165	Ron Rivera	.04
166	Kevin Butler	.04
167	Jay Hilgenberg	.04
168	Peter Tom Willis	.04
169	Johnny Bailey	.04
170	Ron Cox	.04
171	Keith Van Horne	.04
172	Mark Carrier	.04
173	Richard Dent	.04
174	Wendell Davis	.10
175	Trace Armstrong	.04
176	Mike Singletary	.04
177	*Chris Zorich*	.35
178	Gerald Riggs	.04
179	Jeff Bostic	.04
180	*Kurt Gouvela*	.15
181	Stan Humphries	.15
182	Chip Lohmiller	.04
183	*Raleigh McKenzie*	.10
184	Alvin Walton	.04
185	Ernest Byner	.04
186	Markus Koch	.04
187	Art Monk	.04
188	Ed Simmons	.04
189	*Bobby Wilson*	.10
190	Charles Mann	.04
191	Darrell Green	.04
192	Mark Rypien	.15
193	Ricky Sanders	.04
194	Jim Lachey	.04
195	Martin Mayhew	.04
196	Gary Clark	.15
197	Wilber Marshall	.04
198	Darryl Grant	.04
199	Don Warren	.04
200	*Ricky Ervins*	.20
201	Eric Allen	.04
202	Anthony Toney	.04
203	Ben Smith	.04
204	David Alexander	.04
205	Jerome Brown	.04
206	Mike Golic	.04
207	Roger Ruzek	.04
208	Andre Waters	.04
209	Fred Barnett	.15
210	Randall Cunningham	.15
211	Mike Schad	.04
212	Reggie White	.15
213	Mike Bellamy	.04
214	*Jeff Feagles*	.08
215	Wes Hopkins	.04
216	Clyde Simmons	.04
217	Keith Byars	.04
218	Seth Joyner	.04
219	Byron Evans	.04
220	Keith Jackson	.15
221	Calvin Williams	.15
222	Mike Dumas	.04
223	Ray Childress	.04
224	Ernest Givins	.04
225	Lamar Lathon	.04
226	Greg Montgomery	.04
227	Mike Munchak	.04
228	Al Smith	.04

229 Bubba McDowell .04
230 Haywood Jeffires .15
231 Drew Hill .04
233 Warren Moon .25
234 *Doug Smith* .10
235 *Cris Dishman* .15
236 Teddy Garcia .04
237 Richard Johnson .04
238 Bruce Matthews .04
239 Gerald McNeil .04
240 Johnny Meads .04
241 Curtis Duncan .04
242 Sean Jones .04
243 Lorenzo White .10
244 *Rob Carpenter* .12
245 Bruce Reimers .04
246 Ickey Woods .04
247 Lewis Billups .04
248 Boomer Esiason .15
249 Tim Krumrie .04
250 David Fulcher .04
251 Jim Breech .04
252 Mitchell Price .04
253 Carl Zander .04
254 *Barney Bussey* .10
255 Leon White .04
256 Eddie Brown .04
257 James Francis .04
258 Harold Green .15
259 Anthony Munoz .04
260 James Brooks .04
261 *Kevin Walker* .12
262 Bruce Kozerski .04
263 David Grant .04
264 Tim McGee .04
265 Rodney Holman .04
266 *Dan McGwire* .15
267 Andy Heck .04
268 Dave Krieg .04
269 David Wyman .04
270 Robert Blackmon .04
271 Grant Feasel .04
272 *Patrick Hunter* .12
273 Travis McNeal .04
274 John L. Williams .04
275 Tony Woods .04
276 Derrick Fenner .10
277 Jacob Green .04
278 Brian Blades .04
279 Eugene Robinson .04
280 Terry Wooden .04
281 Jeff Bryant .04
282 Norm Johnson .04
283 Joe Nash .04
284 Rick Donnelly .04
285 Chris Warren .75
286 Tommy Kane .04
287 Cortez Kennedy .30
288 *Ernie Mills* .15
289 Dermontti Dawson .04
290 Tunch Ilkin .04
291 Tim Worley .04
293 Gary Anderson (Pit.) .04
294 Chris Calloway .04
295 Carnell Lake .04
296 Dan Stryzinski .04
297 Rod Woodson .04
298 *John Jackson* .10
299 Bubby Brister .04
300 Thomas Everett .04
301 Merril Hoge .04
302 Eric Green .10
303 Greg Lloyd .04
304 Gerald Williams .04
305 Bryan Hinkle .04
306 Keith Willis .04
307 Louis Lipps .04
308 Donald Evans .04
309 David Johnson .04
310 *Wesley Carroll* .10
311 Eric Martin .04
312 Brett Maxie .04
313 Rickey Jackson .04
314 Robert Massey .04
315 Pat Swilling .04
316 Morten Andersen .04
317 *Toi Cook* .10
318 Sam Mills .04
319 Steve Walsh .04
320 *Tommy Barnhardt* .10
321 Vince Buck .04
322 Joel Hilgenberg .04
323 Rueben Mayes .04
325 Renaldo Turnbull .04
326 Vaughan Johnson .04
327 Gill Fenerty .04
328 Stan Brock .04
329 Dalton Hilliard .04
330 Hoby Brenner .04
331 Craig Heyward .04
332 Jon Hand .04
333 Duane Bickett .04
334 Jessie Hester .04
335 Rohn Stark .04
336 Zefross Moss .04
337 Bill Brooks .04
338 Clarence Verdin .04
339 Mike Prior .04
340 Chip Banks .04
341 Dean Biasucci .04
342 Ray Donaldson .04
343 Jeff Herrod .04
344 Donnell Thompson .04
345 Chris Goode .04
346 Eugene Daniel .04
347 Pat Beach .04
348 Keith Taylor .04
349 Jeff George .30
350 *Tony Siragusa* .10
351 Randy Dixon .04
352 Albert Bentley .04
353 *Russell Maryland* .50
354 Mike Saxon .04
355 Godfrey Myles .08
356 *Mark Stepnoski* .12
357 *James Washington* .12
358 Jay Novacek .25
359 Kelvin Martin .04
360 Emmitt Smith 2.00
361 Jim Jeffcoat .04
362 Alexander Wright .10
363 James Dixon .04
364 Daniel Stubbs .04
365 Jack Del Rio .04
366 Jack Del Rio .10
367 *Mark Tuinei* .10
368 Michael Irvin .25
369 *John Gesek* .10
370 Ken Willis .04
371 Troy Aikman 1.00
372 Jimmie Jones .04
373 Nate Newton .04
374 Issiac Holt .04
375 *Alvin Harper* .30
376 Todd Kalis .04
377 Wade Wilson .04
378 Joey Browner .04
379 Chris Doleman .04
380 Hassan Jones .04
381 Henry Thomas .04
382 Darrell Fullington .04
383 Steve Jordan .04
384 Gary Zimmerman .04
385 Ray Berry .04
386 Cris Carter .04
387 Mike Merriweather .04
388 Carl Lee .04
389 Keith Millard .04
390 Reggie Rutland .04
391 Anthony Carter .04
392 Mark Dusbabek .04
393 Kirk Lowerdermilk .04
394 Al Noga .04
395 Herschel Walker .04
396 Randall McDaniel .04
397 *Herman Moore* 2.00
398 John Jackson,
Eddie Murray .04
399 Lomas Brown .04
400 Marc Spindler .04
401 Bennie Blades .04
402 Kevin Glover .04
403 *Aubrey Matthews* .10
404 Michael Cofer (Det.) .04
405 Robert Clark .04
406 Eric Clark .04
407 William White .04
408 Rodney Peete .04
409 Mel Gray .04
410 Jim Arnold .04
411 Jeff Campbell .04
412 Chris Spielman .04
413 Jerry Ball .04
414 Dan Owens .04
415 Barry Sanders 1.25
416 Andre Ware .12
417 *Stanley Richard* .30
418 Gill Byrd .04
419 John Kidd .04
420 Sam Seale .04
421 Gary Plummer .04
422 Anthony Miller .04
423 Ronnie Harmon .04
424 Frank Cornish .04
425 Marion Butts .04
426 Leo Goeas .04
427 Junior Seau .30
428 Courtney Hall .04
429 Leslie O'Neal .04
430 Martin Bayless .04
431 John Carney .04
432 Lee Williams .04
433 Arthur Cox .04
434 Burt Grossman .04
435 *Nate Lewis* .25
436 Rod Bernstine .04
437 *Henry Rolling* .10
438 Billy Joe Tolliver .04
439 *Vince Clark* .10
440 Brian Noble .04
441 Charles Wilson .04
442 Don Majkowski .04
443 Tim Harris .04
444 Scott Stephen .04
445 Perry Kemp .04
446 Darrell Thompson .15
447 Chris Jacke .04
448 Mark Murphy .04
449 Ed West .04
450 LeRoy Butler .04
451 Keith Woodside .04
452 Tony Bennett .04
453 Mark Lee .04
454 *James Campen* .08
455 Robert Brown .04
456 Sterling Sharpe .10
457 Tony Mandarich .08
458 Johnny Holland .04
459 *Matt Brock* .12
460 Esera Tuaolo .08
461 Freeman McNeil .04
462 Terance Mathis .10
463 Rob Moore .20
464 Darrell Davis .04
465 Chris Burkett .04
466 Jeff Criswell .04
467 Tony Stargell .04
468 Ken O'Brien .04
469 Erik McMillan .04
470 Jeff Lageman .04
471 Pat Leahy .04
472 Dennis Byrd .04
473 Jim Sweeney .04
474 Brad Baxter .15
475 Joe Kelly .04
476 Al Toon .04
477 Joe Prokop .04
478 Mark Boyer .04
479 Kyle Clifton .04
480 James Hasty .04
481 *Browning Nagle* .25
482 Gary Anderson (T.B.) .04
483 Mark Carrier (T.B.) .04
484 Ricky Reynolds .04
485 Bruce Hill .04
486 Steve Christie .04
487 Paul Gruber .04
488 Jess Anderson .04
489 Reggie Cobb .30
490 Harry Hamilton .04
491 Vinny Testaverde .10
492 *Mark Royals* .08
493 Keith McCants .04
494 Ron Hall .04
495 Ian Beckles .04
496 Mark Robinson .04
497 Reuben Davis .04
498 Wayne Haddix .04
499 Kevin Murphy .04
500 Eugene Marve .04
501 Broderick Thomas .04
502 *Eric Swann* .20
503 Ernie Jones .04
504 Rich Camarillo .04
505 Tim McDonald .04
506 Freddie Joe Nunn .04
507 *Tim Jorden* .08
508 Johnny Johnson .30
509 Eric Hill .04
510 Derek Kennard .04
511 Ricky Proehl .12
512 Bill Lewis .04
513 Roy Green .04
514 Anthony Bell .04
515 Timm Rosenbach .04
516 *Jim Wahler* .10
517 Anthony Thompson .04
518 Ken Harvey .04
519 Luis Sharpe .04
520 Walter Reeves .04
521 Lonnie Young .04
522 Rod Saddler .04
523 *Todd Lyght* .15
524 Alvin Wright .04
525 Flipper Anderson .04
526 Jackie Slater .04
527 Damone Johnson .04
528 Cleveland Gary .04
529 Mike Piel .04
530 Buford McGee .04
531 Michael Stewart .04
532 Jim Everett .04
533 Mike Wilcher .04
534 Irv Pankey .04
535 Bern Brostek .04
536 Henry Ellard .04
537 Doug Smith .04
538 Larry Kelm .04
539 Pat Terrell .04
541 Jerry Gray .04
542 Kevin Greene .04
543 *Duval Love* .10
544 Frank Stams .04
545 *Mike Croel* .20
546 Mark Jackson .04
547 Greg Kragen .04
548 Karl Mecklenburg .04
549 Simon Fletcher .04
550 Bobby Humphrey .04
551 Ken Lanier .04
552 Vance Johnson .04
553 Ron Holmes .04
554 John Elway .40
555 Melvin Bratton .04
556 Dennis Smith .04
557 Ricky Nattiel .04
558 Clarence Kay .04
559 Michael Brooks .04
560 Mike Horan .04
561 Warren Powers .04
562 Keith Karts .04
563 Shannon Sharpe .10
564 Wymon Henderson .04
565 Steve Atwater .04
566 David Treadwell .04
567 *Bruce Pickens* .10
568 Jessie Tuggle .04
569 Chris Hinton .04
570 Keith Jones .04
571 Bill Fralic .04
572 Mike Rozier .04
573 Scott Fulhage .04
574 Floyd Dixon .04
575 Andre Rison .25
576 Darion Conner .04
577 Brian Jordan .15
578 Michael Haynes .35
579 Oliver Barnett .04
580 Shawn Collins .04
581 Tim Green .04
582 Deion Sanders .35
583 Mike Kenn .04
584 Mike Gann .04
585 Chris Miller .04
586 Tory Epps .04
587 Steve Broussard .04
588 Gary Wilkins .04
589 *Eric Turner* .30
590 Thane Gash .04
591 Clay Matthews .04
592 Mike Johnson .04
593 Raymond Clayborn .04
594 Leroy Hoard .10
595 Reggie Langhorne .04
596 Mike Baab .04
597 Anthony Pleasant .04
598 David Grayson .04
599 *Rob Burnett* .12
600 Frank Minnifield .04
601 Gregg Rakoczy .04
602 Eric Metcalf .04
603 Paul Farren .04
604 Brian Brennan .04
605 Tony Jones .04
606 Stephen Braggs .04
607 Kevin Mack .04
608 *Pat Harlow* .10
609 Marv Cook .04
610 John Stephens .04
611 Ed Reynolds .04
612 Tim Goad .04
613 Chris Singleton .04
614 Bruce Armstrong .04
615 Tom Hodson .04
616 Sammy Martin .04
617 Andre Tippett .04
618 Johnny Rembert .04
619 Maurice Hurst .04
620 Vincent Brown .04
621 Ray Agnew .04
622 Ronnie Lippett .04
623 Greg McMurtry .04
624 Brent Williams .04
625 Jason Staurovsky .04
626 Marvin Allen .04
627 Hart Lee Dykes .04
628 Falcons Team .04
629 Bills Team .04
630 Bears Team .04
631 Bengals Team .04
632 Browns Team .04
633 Cowboys Team .04
634 Broncos Team .04
635 Lions Team .04
636 Packers Team .04
637 Oilers Team .10
638 Colts Team .15
639 Chiefs Team .04
640 Tom Newberry
Raiders Team .04
641 Rams Team .04
642 Dolphins Team .04
643 Vikings Team .04
644 Patriots Team .04
645 Saints Team .04
646 Giants Team .04
647 Jets Team .04
648 Eagles Team .08
649 Cardinals Team .04
650 Steelers Team .04
651 Chargers Team .04
652 49ers Team .04
653 Seahawks Team .04
654 Buccaneers Team .04
655 Redskins Team .04
656 Checklist .04
657 Checklist .04
658 Checklist .04
659 Checklist .04
660 Checklist .04

1991 Topps 1000 Yard Club

The 18 players featured in this insert set were receivers and running backs who gained more than 1,000 yards during the 1990 NFL season. Each card front has a color action photo, with the "1000 Yard Club" logo at the top. The photo has a red border at the top, while the player's name is at the bottom in an orange stripe. There is no border at the bottom or on the right, but the left side of the card has a red and purple border. The card back gives the player's game-by-game totals in blue and pink against a white background. A card number is in the upper right corner.

NM/M

Complete Set (18): 6.00
Common Player: .25
1 Jerry Rice 1.50
2 Barry Sanders 1.75
3 Thurman Thomas .75
4 Henry Ellard .25
5 Marion Butts .75
6 Earnest Byner .25
7 Andre Rison .50
8 Bobby Humphrey .25
9 Gary Clark .35
10 Sterling Sharpe 1.25
11 Flipper Anderson .25
12 Neal Anderson .35
13 Haywood Jeffires .45
14 Stephone Paige .35
15 Drew Hill .25
16 Barry Word .35
17 Anthony Carter .30
18 James Brooks .25

1992 Topps

Topps issued its 759-card 1992 set in three series - 330, 330 and 99 cards. The fronts have action photos inside team color-coded frames bordered by white. The backs have a biography, statistics, a photo of the team's stadium and a player profile. Topps Gold cards were also produced for each card; these gold-foil versions were inserted one per foil pack.

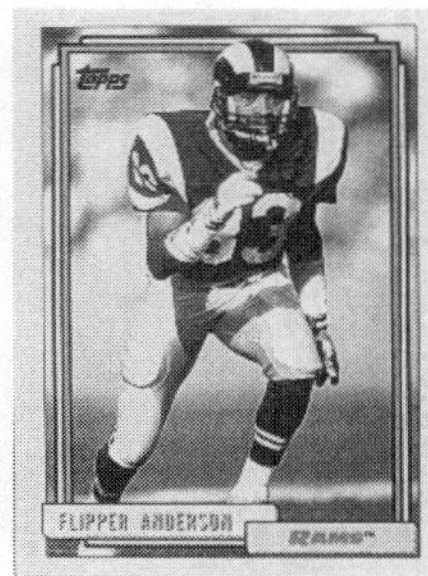

NM/M

Complete Set (759): 35.00
Complete Series 1 (330): 15.00
Complete Series 2 (330): 10.00
Complete Hi Series (99): 10.00
Common Player: .05
Minor Stars: .10
Complete Gold Set (759): 125.00
Complete Gold Series 1 (330): 55.00
Complete Gold Series 2 (330): 50.00
Complete Gold Hi Series (99): 20.00
Common Gold: .15
Unlisted Stars: 2X-4X
Series 1 or 2 Pack (15): .40
Series 1 or 2 Wax Box (36): 20.00
Series 3 Pack (15): .75
Series 3 Wax Box (36): 22.00
1 Tim McGee .05
2 Rich Camarillo .05
3 Anthony Johnson .05
4 Lary Kelm .05
5 Irving Fryar .05
6 Joey Browner .05
7 Michael Walter .05
8 Cortez Kennedy .15
9 Reyna Thompson .05
10 John Friesz .05
11 Leroy Hoard .05
12 Steve McMichael .05
13 Marvin Washington .05
14 Clyde Simmons .05
15 Stephone Paige .05
16 Mike Utley .20
17 Tunch Ilkin .05
18 Lawrence Dawsey .05
19 Vance Johnson .05
20 Bryce Paup .05
21 Jeff Wright .05
22 Gill Fenerty .05
23 Lamar Lathon .05
24 Danny Copeland .05
25 Marcus Allen .05
26 Tim Green .05
27 Pete Stoyanovich .05
28 Alvin Harper .10
29 Roy Foster .05
30 Eugene Daniel .05
31 Luis Sharpe .05
32 Terry Wooden .05
33 Jim Breech .05
34 *Randy Hilliard* .10
35 Roman Phifer .05
36 Erik Howard .05
37 Chris Singleton .05
38 Matt Stover .05
39 Tim Irwin .05
40 Karl Mecklenburg .05
41 Joe Phillips .05
42 Bill Jones .05
43 Mark Carrier .05
44 George Jamison .05
45 Rob Taylor .05
46 Jeff Jaeger .05
47 Don Majkowski .05
48 Al Edwards .05
49 Curtis Duncan .05
50 Sam Mills .05
51 Terance Mathis .05
52 Brian Mitchell .05
53 Mike Pritchard .20
54 Calvin Williams .12
55 Hardy Nickerson .05
56 Nate Newton .05
57 Steve Wallace .05
58 John Offerdahl .05
59 Aeneas Williams .05
60 Lee Johnson .05
61 Ricardo McDonald,
Jeff Feagles .12
62 David Richards .05
63 Paul Gruber .05
64 Greg McMurtry .05
65 Jay Hilgenberg .05
66 Tim Grunhard .05
67 *Dwayne White* .08
68 Don Beebe .05
69 Simon Fletcher .05
70 Warren Moon .20
71 Chris Jacke .05
72 Steve Wisniewski .05
73 Mike Coffer .05
74 Tim Johnson .05
75 T.J. Turner .05
76 Scott Case .05
77 Michael Jackson .10
78 Jon Hand .05
79 Stan Brock .05
80 Robert Blackmon .05
81 David Johnson .05
82 Damone Johnson .05
83 Marc Spindler .05
84 Larry Brown .05
85 Ray Berry .05
86 Andre Waters .05
87 Carlos Huerta .05
88 Brad Muster .05
89 Chuck Cecil .05
90 Nick Lowery .05
91 Cornelius Bennett .05
92 Jessie Tuggle .05
93 *Mark Schlereth* .10
94 Vestee Jackson .05
95 Eric Bieniemy .05
96 Jeff Hostetler .15
97 Ken Lanier .05
98 Wayne Haddix .05
99 Lorenzo White .05
100 Mervyn Fernandez .05
101 Brent Williams .05
102 Ian Beckles .05
103 Harris Barton .05
104 *Edgar Bennett* .50
105 Mike Pitts .05
106 Fuad Reveiz .05
107 Vernon Turner .05
108 *Tracy Hayworth* .10
109 Checklist 1-110 .05
110 Tom Waddle .15
111 Fred Stokes .05
112 Howard Ballard .05
113 David Szott .05
114 Tim McKyer .05
115 Kyle Clifton .05
116 Tony Bennett .05
117 Joel Hilgenberg .05
118 Dwayne Harper .05
119 Mike Baab .05
120 Mark Clayton .05
121 Eric Swann .05
122 Neil O'Donnell .10
123 Mike Munchak .05
124 Howie Long .05
125 John Elway .50
126 Joe Prokop .05
127 Pepper Johnson .05
128 Richard Dent .05
129 *Robert Porcher* .15
130 Earnest Byner .05
131 Kent Hull .05
132 Mike Merriweather .05
133 Scott Fulhage .05
134 Kevin Porter .05
135 Tony Casillas .05
136 Dean Biasucci .05
137 Ben Smith .05
138 Bruce Kozerski .05
139 Jeff Campbell .05
140 Kevin Greene .05
141 Gary Plummer .05
142 Vincent Brown .05
143 Ron Hall .05
144 *Louis Aguiar* .10
145 Mark Duper .05
146 Jesse Sapolu .05
147 Jeff Gossett .05
148 Brian Noble .05
149 Derek Russell .15
150 *Carlton Bailey* .15
151 Kelly Goodburn .05
152 Audrey McMillian .05
153 Neal Anderson .10
154 Bill Maas .05
155 Rickey Jackson .05
156 Chris Miller .05
157 Darren Comeaux .05
158 David Williams .05
159 Rich Gannon .10
160 Kevin Mack .05
161 Jim Arnold .05
162 Reggie White .15
163 Leonard Russell .25
164 Doug Smith .05
165 Tony Mandarich .05
166 Greg Lloyd .05
167 Jumbo Elliott .05
168 Jonathan Hayes .05
169 Jim Ritcher .05
170 Mike Kenn .05
171 James Washington .05
172 Tim Harris .05
173 James Thornton .05
174 *John Brandes* .10
175 *Fred McAfee* .15
176 Henry Rolling .05
177 Tony Paige .05
178 Jay Schroeder .05
179 Jeff Herrod .05
180 Emmitt Smith 2.50
181 Wymon Henderson .05
182 Rob Moore .05
183 Robert Wilson .05
184 *Michael Zordich* .10
185 Jim Harbaugh .05
186 Vince Workman .05
187 Ernest Givins .05
188 Herschel Walker .05
189 Dan Fike .05
190 Seth Joyner .05
191 Steve Young 1.00
192 Dennis Gibson .05
193 Darryl Talley .05
194 Emile Harry .05
195 Bill Fralic .05
196 Michael Stewart .05
197 James Francis .05
198 Jerome Henderson .05
199 John L. Williams .05
200 Rod Woodson .05
201 Mike Farr .05
202 Greg Montgomery .05
203 Andre Collins .05
204 Scott Miller .05
205 Clay Matthews .05
206 Ethan Horton .05
207 Rich Miano .05
208 *Chris Mims* .30
209 Anthony Morgan .05
210 Rodney Hampton .10
211 Chris Hinton .05
212 Esera Tuaolo .05
213 Shane Conlan .05
214 John Carney .05
215 Kenny Walker .05
216 Scott Radecic .05
217 Chris Martin .05

218 Checklist 111-220 .05
219 Weseley Carroll .05
220 Bill Romanowski .05
221 Reggie Cobb .15
222 Alfred Anderson .05
223 Cleveland Gary .05
224 *Eddie Blake* .10
225 Chris Spielman .05
226 John Roper .05
227 *George Thomas* .10
228 Jeff Faulkner .05
229 Chip Lohmiller .05
230 Hugh Millen .05
231 Ray Horton .05
232 James Campen .05
233 Howard Cross .05
234 Keith McKeller .05
235 Dino Hackett .05
236 Jerome Brown .05
237 Andy Heck .05
238 Jerome Brown .05
239 Bruce Matthews .05
240 Jeff Lageman .05
241 Bobby Hebert .05
242 Gary Anderson .05
243 Mark Bortz .05
244 Rich Moran .05
245 Jeff Uhlenhake .05
246 Ricky Sanders .05
247 Clarence Kay .05
248 Ed King .05
249 Eddie Anderson .05
250 *Amp Lee* .35
251 Norm Johnson .05
252 Michael Carter .05
253 Felix Wright .05
254 Leon Seals .05
255 Nate Lewis .05
256 Kevin Call .05
257 Darryl Henley .05
258 Jon Vaughn .10
259 Matt Bahr, David Alexander .05
260 Johnny Johnson .15
261 Ken Norton .05
262 Wendell Davis .05
263 Eugene Robinson .05
264 David Treadwell .05
265 Michael Haynes .25
266 Robb Thomas .05
267 Nate Odomes .05
268 Martin Mayhew .05
269 Perry Kemp .05
270 Jerry Ball .05
271 *Tommy Vardell* .20
272 Ernie Mills .05
273 Mo Lewis .05
274 Roger Ruzek .05
275 Steve Smith .05
276 *Bo Orlando* .10
277 Louis Oliver .05
278 Toi Cook .05
279 Eddie Brown .05
280 Keith McCants .05
281 Rob Burnett .05
282 Keith DeLong .05
283 Stan Thomas .05
284 Robert Brown .05
285 John Alt .05
286 Randy Dixon .05
287 Siran Stacy .20
288 Ray Agnew .05
289 Darion Conner .05
290 Kirk Lowdermilk .05
291 Greg Jackson .05
292 Ken Harvey .05
293 Jacob Green .05
294 Mark Tuinei .05
295 Mark Rypien .15
296 *Gerald Robinson* .08
297 Broderick Thompson .05
298 Doug Widell .05
299 Carwell Gardner .05
300 Barry Sanders 1.25
301 Eric Metcalf .05
302 Erick Thomas .05
303 *Terrell Buckley* .25
304 Byron Evans .05
305 Johnny Hector .05
306 Steve Broussard .05
307 Gene Atkins .05
308 Terry McDaniel .05
309 Charles McRae .05
310 Jim Lachey .05
311 Pat Harlow .05
312 Kevin Butler .05
313 Scott Stephen .05
314 Dermontti Dawson .05
315 Johnny Meads .05
316 Checklist 221-330 .05
317 Aaron Craver .05
318 Michael Brooks .05
319 Guy McIntyre .05
320 Thurman Thomas .25
321 Courtney Hall .05
322 Dan Saleaumua .05
323 *Vinson Smith* .10
324 Steven Jordan .05
325 Walter Reeves .05
326 Erik Kramer .05
327 Duane Bickett .05
328 Tom Newberry .05
329 John Kasay .05
330 Dave Meggett .05
331 Kevin Ross .05
332 *Keith Hamilton* .15
333 Dwight Stone .05
334 Mel Gray .05
335 Harry Galbreath .05
336 William Perry .05
337 Brian Blades .05
338 Randall McDaniel .05
339 *Pat Coleman* .12
340 Michael Irvin .25
341 Checklist 331-440 .05
342 Chris Mohr .05
343 Greg Davis .05
344 Dave Cadigan .05
345 Art Monk .05
346 Tim Goad .05
347 Vinnie Clark .05
348 David Fulcher .05
349 Craig Heward .05
350 Ronnie Lott .05
351 Dexter Carter .05
352 Mark Jackson .05
353 Brian Jordan .05
354 Ray Donaldson .05
355 Jim Price .05
356 Rod Bernstine .05
357 *Tony Mayberry* .10
358 *Richard Brown* .10
360 Haywood Jeffires .15
361 Henry Thomas .05
362 Jeff Graham .12
363 Don Warren .05
364 Scott Davis .05
365 Harlon Barnett .05
366 Mark Collins .05
367 Rick Tuten .05
368 *Lonnie Marts* .15
369 Dennis Smith .05
370 Steve Tasker .05
371 Robert Massey .05
372 Ricky Reynolds .05
373 Alvin Wright .05
374 Kelvin Martin .05
375 Vince Buck .05
376 John Kidd .05
378 Bryan Cox .05
379 *Jamie Dukes* .08
380 Anthony Munoz .05
381 *Mark Gunn* .10
382 Keith Henderson .05
383 Charles Wilson .05
384 *Shawn McCarthy* .10
385 Ernie Jones .05
386 Nick Bell .10
387 Derrick Walker .05
388 Mark Stepnoski .05
389 Broderick Thomas .05
390 Reggie Roby .05
391 Bubba McDowell .05
392 Eric Martin .05
393 *Toby Cashton* .10
394 Bern Brostek .05
395 Christian Okoye .05
396 Frank Minnifield .05
397 Mike Golic .05
398 Grant Feasel .05
399 Michael Ball .05
400 Mike Croel .05
401 Maury Buford .05
402 Jeff Bostic .05
403 Sean Landeta .05
404 Terry Allen .35
405 Donald Evans .05
406 Don Mosebar .05
407 D.J. Dozier .05
408 Bruce Pickens .05
409 Jim Dombrowski .05
410 Deron Cherry .05
411 Richard Johnson .05
412 Alexander Wright .05
413 Tom Rathman .05
414 Mark Dennis .05
415 Phil Hansen .05
416 Lonnie Young .05
417 Burt Grossman .05
418 Tony Covington .05
419 John Stephens .05
420 Jim Everett .05
421 Johnny Holland .05
422 *Mike Barber* .12
423 Carl Lee .05
424 *Craig Patterson* .10
425 Greg Townsend .05
426 Brett Perriman .05
427 Morten Andersen .05
428 John Gesek .05
429 Bryan Barker .05
430 John Taylor .05
431 Donnell Woolford .05
432 Ron Holmes .05
433 Lee Williams .05
434 Alfred Oglesby .05
435 Jarrod Bunch .05
436 *Carlton Haselrig* .10
437 Rufus Porter .05
438 Rohn Stark .05
439 Tony Jones .05
440 Andre Rison .25
441 Eric Hill .05
442 Jesse Solomon .05
443 Jackie Slater .05
444 Donnie Elder .05
445 Brett Maxie .05
446 Max Montoya .05
447 Will Wolford .05
448 Craig Taylor .05
449 Jimmie Jones .05
450 Anthony Carter .05
451 *Brian Bollinger* .08
452 Checklist 441-550 .05
453 Brad Edwards .05
454 *Gene Chilton* .08
455 Eric Allen .05
456 William Roberts .05
457 Eric Green .05
458 Irvin Eatman .05
459 Derrick Thomas .15
460 Tommy Kane .05
461 LeRoy Butler .05
462 Oliver Barnett .05
463 Anthony Smith .05
464 Chris Dishman .05
465 Pat Terrell .05
466 Greg Kragen .05
467 Rodney Peete .05
468 Willie Drewrey .05
469 Jim Wilks .05
470 Vince Newsome .05
471 Chris Gardocki .05
472 Chris Chandler .05
473 George Thornton .05
474 Albert Lewis .05
475 Kevin Glover .05
476 *Joe Bowden* .10
477 Harry Sydney .05
478 Bob Golic .05
479 Tony Zendejas .05
480 Brad Baxter .05
481 Steve Beuerlein .15
482 Mark Higgs .10
483 Drew Hill .05
484 Bryan Millard .05
485 Mark Kelso .05
486 David Grant .05
487 Gary Zimmerman .05
488 Leonard Marshall .05
489 Keith Jackson .15
490 Sterling Sharpe .10
491 Ferrell Edmunds .05
492 Wilber Marshall .05
493 Charles Haley .05
494 Riki Ellison .05
495 Bill Brooks .05
496 Bill Hawkins .05
497 Eric Williams .05
498 *Leon Searcy* .10
499 Mike Horan .05
500 Pat Swilling .05
501 Maurice Hurst .05
502 William Fuller .05
503 Tim Newton .05
504 Lorenzo Lynch .05
505 Tim Barnett .05
506 Tom Thayer .05
507 Chris Burkett .05
508 Ronnie Harmon .05
509 James Brooks .05
510 Bennie Blades .05
511 Roger Craig .05
512 Tony Woods .05
513 Greg Lewis .05
514 Eric Pegram .15
515 Elvis Patterson .05
516 Jeff Cross .05
517 Myron Guyton .05
518 Jay Novacek .15
519 *Leo Barker* .10
520 Keith Byars .05
521 Dalton Hilliard .05
522 Ted Washington .05
523 *Dexter McNabb* .10
524 Frank Reich .05
525 Henry Ellard .05
526 Barry Foster .05
527 Barry Word .15
528 Gary Anderson .05
529 Reggie Rutland .05
530 Stephen Baker .05
531 John Flannery .05
532 Steve Wright .05
533 Eric Sanders .05
534 *Bob Whitfield* .15
535 Gaston Green .05
536 Anthony Pleasant .05
537 Jeff Bryant .05
538 Jarvis Williams .05
539 Jim Morrissey .05
540 Andre Tippett .05
541 Gill Byrd .05
542 Raleigh McKenzie .05
543 Jim Sweeney .05
544 David Lutz .05
545 Wayne Martin .05
546 Karl Wilson .05
547 Pierce Holt .05
548 Doug Smith .05
549 *Nolan Harrison* .10
550 Freddie Joe Nunn .05
551 Eric Moore .05
552 Cris Carter .05
553 Kevin Gogan .05
554 Harold Green .05
555 Kenneth Davis .05
556 Travis McNeal .05
557 Jim Jensen .05
558 Willie Green .20
559 *Scott Galbraith* .12
560 Louis Lipps .05
561 Matt Brock .05
562 Mike Prior .05
563 Checklist 551-660 .05
564 Robert Delpino .05
565 Vinny Testaverde .05
566 Willie Gault .05
567 Quinn Early .05
568 Eric Moten .05
569 Lance Smith .05
570 Darrell Green .05
571 Moe Gardner .05
572 Steve Atwater .05
573 Ray Childress .05
574 Dave Krieg .05
575 Bruce Armstrong .05
576 Fred Barnett .15
577 Don Griffin .05
578 *David Brandon* .10
579 Robert Young .05
580 Keith Van Horne .05
581 Jeff Criswell .05
582 Lewis Tillman .05
583 Bubby Brister .05
584 Aaron Wallace .05
585 Chris Doleman .05
586 *Marty Carter* .15
587 Chris Warren .25
588 David Griggs .05
589 Darrell Thompson .05
590 Marion Butts .05
591 Scott Norwood .05
592 Lomas Brown .05
593 Daryl Johnston .05
594 *Alonzo Mitz* .10
595 Tommy Barnhardt .05
596 Tim Jorden .05
597 Neil Smith .05
598 Todd Marinovich .12
599 Sean Jones .05
600 Clarence Verdin .05
601 Trace Armstrong .05
602 *Steve Bono* .50
603 Mark Ingram .05
604 Flipper Anderson .05
605 James Jones .05
606 Al Noga .05
607 Rick Bryan .05
608 Eugene Lockhart .05
609 Charles Mann .05
610 James Hasty .05
612 Tim Brown .35
613 David Little .05
614 Keith Sims .05
615 Kevin Murphy .05
616 Ray Crockett .05
617 Jim Jeffcoat .05
618 Patrick Hunter .05
619 Keith Kartz .05
620 Peter Tom Willis .05
621 Vaughan Johnson .05
622 Shawn Jefferson .05
623 Anthony Thompson .05
624 John Rienstra .05
625 Don Maggs .05
626 Todd Lyght .05
627 Brent Jones .05
628 Todd McNair .05
629 Winston Moss .05
630 Mark Carrier .05
631 Dan Owens .05
632 Sammie Smith .05
633 James Lofton .05
634 *Paul McJulien* .10
635 Tony Tolbert .05
636 Carnell Lake .05
637 Gary Clark .05
638 Brian Washington .05
639 Jessie Hester .05
640 Doug Riesenberg .05
641 *Joe Walter* .10
642 John Rade .05
643 Wes Hopkins .05
644 Kelly Stouffer .05
645 Marv Cook .05
646 Ken Clarke .05
647 Bobby Humphrey .05
648 Tim McDonald .05
649 *Donald Frank* .12
650 Richmond Webb .05
651 Lemuel Stinson .05
652 Merton Hanks .05
653 Frank Warren .05
654 Thomas Benson .05
655 Al Smith .05
656 Steve DeBerg .05
657 *Jayice Pearson* .10
658 Joe Morris .05
659 Fred Strickland .05
660 Kelvin Pritchett .05
661 Lewis Billups .05
662 Todd Collins .05
663 Corey Miller .05
664 Levon Kirkland .05
665 Jerry Rice 1.00
666 Mike Lodish .05
667 Chuck Smith .05
668 Lance Olberding .05
669 *Kevin Smith* .30
670 *Dale Carter* .30
671 *Sean Gilbert* .30
672 Ken O'Brien .05
673 Ricky Proehl .05
674 Junior Seau .05
675 Courtney Hawkins .05
676 Eddie Robinson .05
677 Tom Jeter .05
678 Jeff George .05
679 Cary Conklin .05
680 Rueben Mayes .05
681 Sean Lumpkin .05
682 Dan Marino 1.50
683 *Ed McDaniel* .25
684 Greg Skrepenak .05
685 Tracy Scroggins .05
686 *Tommy Maddox* .30
687 Mike Singletary .05
688 Patrick Rowe .05
689 Phillipi Sparks .05
690 Joel Steed .05
691 Kevin Fagan .05
692 Deion Sanders .05
693 Bruce Smith .05
694 *David Klingler* .10
695 Clayton Holmes .05
696 Brett Favre 2.50
697 Marc Boutte .05
698 Dwayne Sabb .05
699 Ed McCaffrey .05
700 Randall Cunningham .05
701 *Quentin Coryatt* .30
702 Bernie Kosar .05
703 *Vaughn Dunbar* .15
704 Browning Nagle .05
705 Mark Wheeler .05
706 Paul Siever .05
707 Anthony Miller .05
708 Corey Widmer .05
709 Eric Dickerson .05
710 Martin Bayless .05
711 Jason Hanson .05
712 Michael Dean Perry .05
713 Billy Joe Toliver .05
714 Chad Hennings .05
715 *Bucky Richardson* .30
716 Steve Israel .05
717 Robert Harris .05
718 Timm Rosenbach .05
719 Joe Montana 1.00
720 *Derek Brown* .15
721 *Robert Brooks* 1.50
722 Boomer Esiason .05
723 Troy Auzenne .05
724 John Fina .05
725 Chris Crooms .05
726 Eugene Chung .05
727 Darren Woodson .05
728 Leslie O'Neal .05
729 Dan McGwire .05
730 Al Toon .05
731 Michael Brandon .05
732 Steve DeOssie .05
733 Jim Kelly .30
734 Webster Slaughter .05
735 Tony Smith .05
736 Shane Collins .05
737 Randal Hill .05
738 Chris Holder .05
739 Russell Maryland .05
740 *Carl Pickens* .75
741 Andre Reed .05
742 *Steve Emtman* .15
743 Carl Banks .05
744 Troy Aikman 1.00
745 Mark Royals .05
746 J.J. Birden .05
747 Michael Cofer .05
748 Darryl Ashmore .05
749 Dion Lambert .05
750 Phil Simms .05
751 Reggie E. White .05
752 Harvey Williams .05
753 Ty Detmer .05
754 Tony Brooks .05
755 Steve Christie .05
756 Lawrence Taylor .05
757 Merril Hoge .05
758 Robert Jones .05
759 Checklist 661-792 .05

1992 Topps Gold

The 759-card, standard-sized set was a parallel to the base set and was inserted once every pack; three every rack pack, and 20 per 660-card factory set. The cards listed below replaced the seven checklist cards. Ten gold cards were also included with each 99-card Hi Series.

		NM/M
Complete Set (759):		130.00
Complete Series 1 (330):		60.00
Complete Series 2 (330):		50.00
Complete Hi Series (99):		20.00
Common Player:		.20
Veteran Stars:		1.5X-3X
Young Stars:		2X
RCs:		1.25X-2.5X
109	Freeman McNeil	.40
218	David Daniels	.40
316	Chris Hakel	.40
341	Ottis Anderson	.40
452	Shawn Moore	.40
563	Mike Mooney	.40
759	Curtis Whitley	.40

1992 Topps No. 1 Draft Picks

The four-card, standard-size set features No. 1 draft picks from 1990, 1991 and 1992, as well as Notre Dame standout Raghib "Rocket" Ismail. The cards were randomly inserted in 1992 Hi Series packs and the entire set was included with the 99-card Hi Series factory set.

		NM/M
Complete Set (4):		4.00
Common Player:		1.00
1	Jeff George	1.50
2	Russell Maryland	1.00
3	Steve Emtman	1.00
4	Rocket Ismail	1.25

1992 Topps 1000 Yard Club

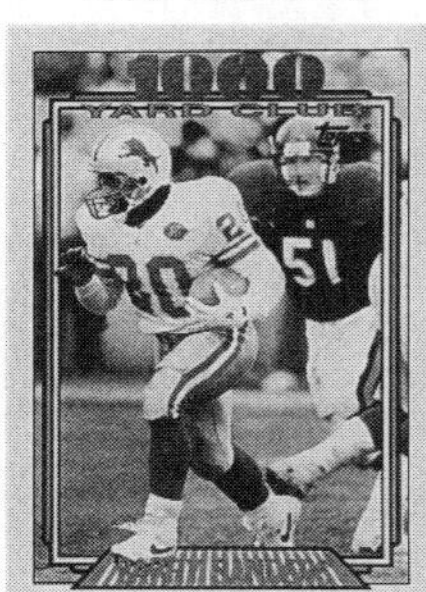

Receivers and running backs who gained more than 1,000 yards during the 1991 NFL season are featured in this 20-card insert set. The white-bordered card front has a color action photo, along with the set's name at the top. The player's name is at the bottom in a green-and-white striped bar. The player's name and 1000 on the front are in red foil. The back has a game-by-game summary in a lime green panel against a background designed like a football field. Each card back is also numbered.

		NM/M
Complete Set (20):		15.00
Common Player:		.50
1	Emmitt Smith	6.00
2	Barry Sanders	4.00
3	Michael Irvin	2.00
4	Thurman Thomas	2.00
5	Gary Clark	.75
6	Haywood Jeffires	.75
7	Michael Haynes	1.50
8	Drew Hill	.50
9	Mark Duper	.75
10	James Lofton	1.00
11	Rodney Hampton	2.50
12	Mark Clayton	.75
13	Erric Pegram	1.00
14	Art Monk	1.00
15	Earnest Byner	.50
16	Gaston Green	.50
17	Christian Okoye	.50
18	Irving Fryar	.65
19	John Taylor	.75
20	Brian Blades	.50

1993 Topps

Topps issued its 1993 set in two 330-card series. Subsets include Franchise Players (9 cards), Team Leaders (28), Record Breakers (2), League Leaders (5), Draft Picks (30) and Field Generals (10). The card front has a color action photo surrounded by white borders. The player's name and team are at the bottom between team color-coded diagonal bars. The back has a mug shot, statistics, career summary and biography against a team color-coded background. Each pack contains one Topps Gold card. Topps Black Gold cards were also made and inserted one per every 48 packs.

		NM/M
Complete Set (660):		25.00
Comp. Factory Set (673):		35.00
Complete Series 1 (330):		15.00
Complete Series 2 (330):		10.00
Common Player:		.05
Minor Stars:		.10
Complete Gold Set (660):		90.00
Complete Gold Series 1 (330):		50.00
Complete Gold Series 2 (330):		40.00
Common Gold:		.20
Minor Gold Stars:		.40
Unlisted Gold Stars:		2X-4X
Series 1 or 2 Pack (15):		.50
Series 1 or 2 Wax Box (36):		14.00
1	Art Monk	.05
2	Jerry Rice	.50
3	Stanley Richard	.05
4	Ron Hall	.05
5	Daryl Johnston	.10
6	Wendell Davis	.05
7	Vaughn Dunbar	.10
8	Mike Jones	.05
9	Anthony Johnson	.05
10	Chris Miller	.05
11	Kyle Clifton	.05
12	*Curtis Conway*	1.00
13	Lionel Washington	.05
14	Reggie Johnson	.05
15	David Little	.05
16	Nick Lowery	.05
17	Darryl Williams	.05
18	Brent Jones	.05
19	Bruce Matthews	.05
20	Heath Sherman, John Kasay	.05
22	*Troy Drayton*	.35
23	Eric Metcalf	.05
24	Andre Tippett	.05
25	Rodney Hampton	.35
26	Henry Jones	.05
27	Jim Everett	.05
28	Steve Jordan	.05
29	LeRoy Butler	.05
30	Troy Vincent	.15
31	Nate Lewis	.05

32 Rickey Jackson .05
33 Darion Conner .05
34 *Tom Carter* .25
35 Jeff George .20
36 *Larry Centers* .30
37 Reggie Cobb .15
38 Mike Saxon .05
39 Brad Baxter .05
40 Reggie White .12
41 Haywood Jeffires .15
42 Alfred Williams .05
43 Aaron Wallace .05
44 Tracy Simien .05
45 Pat Harlow .05
46 D.J. Johnson .05
47 Don Griffin .05
48 Flipper Anderson .05
49 Keith Kartz .05
50 Bernie Kosar .05
51 Kent Hull .05
52 Erik Howard .05
53 Pierce Holt .05
54 Dwayne Harper .05
55 Bennie Blades .05
56 Mark Duper .05
57 Brian Noble .05
58 Jeff Feagles .05
59 Michael Haynes .20
60 Junior Seau .15
61 Gary Anderson .05
62 Jon Hand .05
63 *Lin Elliott* .10
64 *Dana Stubblefield* .50
65 Vaughan Johnson .05
66 Mo Lewis .05
67 Aeneas Williams .05
68 David Fulcher .05
69 Chip Lohmiller .05
70 Greg Townsend .05
71 Simon Fletcher .05
72 Sean Salisbury .05
73 Christian Okoye .05
74 Jim Arnold .05
75 Bruce Smith .05
76 Fred Barnett .15
77 Bill Romanowski .05
78 Dermontti Dawson .05
79 Bern Brostek .05
80 Warren Moon .15
81 Bill Fralic .05
82 Lomas Brown .05
83 Duane Bickett .05
84 Neil Smith .05
85 Reggie White .05
86 Tim McDonald .05
87 Leslie O'Neal .05
88 Steve Young .50
89 Paul Gruber .05
90 Wilber Marshall .05
91 Trace Armstrong .05
92 *Bobby Houston* .10
93 George Thornton .05
94 Keith McCants .05
95 Ricky Sanders .05
96 Jackie Harris .20
97 Todd Marinovich .12
98 Henry Thomas .05
99 Jeff Wright .05
100 John Elway .50
101 *Garrison Hearst* 1.00
102 Roy Foster .05
103 David Lang .05
104 Matt Stover .05
105 Lawrence Taylor .10
106 Pete Stoyanovich .05
107 Jessie Tuggle .05
108 William White .05
109 *Andy Harmon* .12
110 John L. Williams .05
111 Jon Vaughn .05
112 John Alt .05
113 Chris Jacke .05
114 Jim Breech .05
115 Eric Martin .05
116 Derrick Walker .05
117 Ricky Ervins .12
118 Roger Craig .05
119 Jeff Gossett .05
120 Emmitt Smith 2.00
121 Bob Whitefield .05
122 Alonzo Spellman .05
123 David Klingler .15
124 Tommy Maddox .10
125 Robert Porcher .05
126 Edgar Bennett .15
127 Harvey Williams .15
128 *Dave Brown* 1.00
129 Johnny Mitchell .25
130 *Drew Bledsoe* 3.00
131 Zefross Moss .05
132 Nate Odomes .05
133 Rufus Porter .05
134 Jackie Slater .05
135 Steve Young .50
136 Chris Calloway .05
137 Steve Atwater .05
138 Mark Carrier .05
139 Marvin Washington .05
140 Barry Foster .05
141 Ricky Reynolds .05
142 Bubba McDowell .05
143 *Dan Footman* .15
144 Richmond Webb .05
145 Mike Pritchard .12
146 Chris Spielman .05
147 Dave Krieg .05
148 Nick Bell .15
149 Vincent Brown .05
150 Seth Joyner .05
151 Tommy Kane .05
152 *Carlton Gray* .25
153 Harry Newsome .05
154 Rohn Stark .05
155 Shannon Sharpe .05
156 Charles Haley .05
157 Cornelius Bennett .05
158 Doug Riesenberg .05
159 Amp Lee .10
160 Sterling Sharpe .40
161 Alonzo Mitz .05
162 Pat Terrill .05
163 Mark Schlereth .05
164 Gary Anderson .05
165 Quinn Early .05
166 *Jerome Bettis* 1.25
167 Lawrence Dawsey .05
168 Derrick Thomas .15
169 Rodney Peete .10
170 Jim Kelly .25
171 Deion Sanders .05
172 Richard Dent .05
173 Emmitt Smith .75
174 Barry Sanders .50
175 Sterling Sharpe .25
176 Cleveland Gary .05
177 Terry Allen .10
178 Vaughan Johnson .05
179 Rodney Hampton .10
180 Randall Cunningham .05
181 Ricky Proehl .05
182 Jerry Rice .20
183 Reggie Cobb .05
184 Earnest Byner .05
185 Jeff Lageman .05
186 Carlos Jenkins .05
187 Cardinals Draft Picks .50
188 Todd Lyght .05
189 *Carl Simpson* .12
190 Barry Sanders 1.25
191 Jim Harbaugh .10
192 Roger Ruzek .05
193 Brent Williams .05
194 Chip Banks .05
195 Mike Croel .05
196 Marion Butts .05
197 James Washington .05
198 John Offerdahl .05
199 Tom Rathman .05
200 Joe Montana 1.25
201 Pepper Johnson .05
202 Cris Dishman .05
203 *Adrian White* .10
204 *Reggie Brooks* .25
205 Cortez Kennedy .10
206 Robert Massey .05
207 Toi Cook .05
208 Harry Sydney .05
209 *Lincoln Kennedy* .15
210 Randall McDaniel .05
211 Eugene Daniel .05
212 Rob Burnett .05
213 Steve Broussard .05
214 Brian Washington .05
215 *Leonard Renfro* .12
216 Audray McMillian, Henry Jones .05
217 Sterling Sharpe, Anthony Miller .20
218 Clyde Simmons, Leslie O'Neal .05
219 Emmitt Smith, Barry Foster .50
220 Steve Young, Warren Moon .12
221 Mel Gray .05
222 Luis Sharpe .05
223 Eric Moten .05
224 Albert Lewis .05
225 Alvin Harper .30
226 Steve Wallace .05
227 Mark Higgs .15
228 Eugene Lockhart .05
229 Sean Jones .05
230 Buccaneers Draft Picks .15
231 Jimmy Williams .05
232 *Demetrius DuBose* .15
233 John Roper .05
234 Keith Hamilton .05
235 Donald Evans .05
236 Kenneth Davis .05
237 *John Copeland* .30
238 Leonard Russell .12
239 Ken Harvey .05
240 Dale Carter .10
241 Anthony Pleasant .05
242 Darrell Green .05
243 *Natrone Means* 1.00
244 Rob Moore .10
245 Chris Doleman .05
246 J.B. Brown .05
247 Ray Crockett .05
248 John Taylor .10
249 Russell Maryland .05
250 Brett Favre 2.00
251 Carl Pickens .50
252 Andy Heck .05
253 Jerome Henderson .05
254 Deion Sanders .15
255 Steve Emtman .10
256 Calvin Williams .05
257 Sean Gilbert .05
258 Don Beebe .05
259 *Robert Smith* 1.00
260 Rogert Blackmon .05
261 Jim Kelly .10
262 Harold Green .05
263 Clay Matthews .05
264 John Elway .10
265 Warren Moon .10
266 Jeff George .10
267 Derrick Thomas .05
268 Howie Long .05
269 Dan Marino .60
270 Jon Vaughn .05
271 Chris Burkett .05
272 Barry Foster .10
273 Marion Butts .05
274 Chris Warren .05
275 Giants Draft Picks .15
276 Tony Casillas .05
277 Jarrod Bunch .05
278 Eric Green .05
279 Stan Brock .05
280 Chester McGlockton .05
281 Ricky Watters .40
282 Dan Saleaumua .05
283 Rich Camarillo .05
284 Cris Carter .05
285 *Rick Mirer* .25
286 Matt Brock .05
287 Burt Grossman .05
288 Andre Collins .05
289 Mark Jackson .05
290 Dan Marino 2.00
291 Cornelius Bennett .05
292 Steve Atwater .05
293 Bryan Cox .05
294 Sam Mills .05
295 Pepper Johnson .05
296 Seth Joyner .05
297 Chris Spielman .05
298 Junior Seau .05
299 Cortez Kennedy .05
300 Broderick Thomas .05
301 Todd McNair .05
302 Nate Newton .05
303 Mike Waltr .05
304 Clyde Simmons .05
305 Ernie Mills .05
306 Steve Wisniewski .05
307 *Coleman Rudolph* .10
308 Thurman Thomas .50
309 Reggie Roby .05
310 Eric Swann .05
311 Mark Wheeler .05
312 Jeff Herrod .05
313 Leroy Hoard .05
314 *Patrick Bates* .10
315 Earnest Byner .05
316 Dave Meggett .05
317 *George Teague* .25
318 Ray Childress .05
319 Mike Kenn .05
320 Jason Hanson .05
321 Gary Clark .10
322 Chris Gardocki .05
323 Ken Norton .05
324 *Eric Curry* .30
325 Byron Evans .05
326 *O.J. McDuffie* 1.00
327 Dwight Stone .05
328 Tommy Barnhardt .05
329 Checklist 1-165 .05
330 Checklist 166-330 .05
331 Eric Williams .05
332 Phil Hansen .05
333 *Martin Harrison* .15
334 Mark Ingram .05
335 Mark Rypien .08
336 Anthony Miller .05
337 Antone Davis .05
338 Mike Munchak .05
339 Wayne Martin .05
340 Joe Montana 1.50
341 *Deon Figures* .15
342 Ed McDaniel .05
343 Chris Burkett .05
344 Tony Smith .05
345 James Lofton .05
346 Courtney Hawkins .05
347 Dennis Smith .05
348 Anthony Morgan .05
349 Chris Goode .05
350 Phil Simms .10
351 Patrick Hunter .05
352 Brett Perriman .07
353 Corey Miller .05
354 Harry Galbreath .05
355 Mark Carrier .05
356 Troy Drayton .05
357 Greg Davis .05
358 Tim Krumrie .05
359 Tim McDonald .05
360 Webster Slaughter .05
361 Steve Christie .05
362 Courtney Hall .05
363 Charles Mann .06
364 Vestee Jackson .05
365 Robert Jones .05
366 Rich Miano .06
367 Morten Andersen .06
368 Jeff Graham .05
369 Martin Mayhew .05
370 Anthony Carter .05
371 Greg Kragen .05
372 Ron Cox .05
373 Perry Williams .05
374 Willie Gault .05
375 Chris Warren .15
376 Reyna Thompson .05
377 Bennie Thompson .05
378 Kevin Mack .05
379 Clarence Verdin .05
380 Marc Boutte .05
381 *Marvin Jones* .15
382 Greg Jackson .05
383 Steve Bono .50
384 Terrell Buckley .10
385 Garrison Hearst .50
386 Mike Brim .05
387 Jesse Sapolu .05
388 Carl Lee .05
389 Jeff Cross .05
390 Karl Mecklenburg .05
391 Chad Hennings .05
392 Oliver Barnett .05
393 Dalton Hilliard .06
394 Broderick Thompson .05
395 Raghib Ismail .25
396 John Kidd .05
397 Eddie Anderson .05
398 Lamar Lathon .05
399 Darren Perry .05
400 Drew Bledsoe 2.00
401 Ferrell Edmunds .05
402 Lomas Brown .05
403 Drew Hill .05
404 David Whitmore .05
405 Mike Johnson .05
406 Paul Gruber .05
407 Kirk Lowdermilk .05
408 Curtis Conway .50
409 Bryce Paup .05
410 Boomer Esiason .08
411 Jay Schroeder .06
412 *Anthony Newman* .08
413 Ernie Jones .05
414 Carlton Bailey .05
415 Kenneth Gant .05
416 Todd Scott .05
417 Anthony Smith .05
418 Erik McMillan .05
419 Ronnie Harmon .06
420 Andre Reed .07
421 Wymon Henderson .05
422 Carnell Lake .05
423 Al Noga .05
424 Curtis Duncan .05
425 Mike Gann .05
426 Eugene Robinson .05
427 Scott Mersereau .05
428 Chris Singleton .05
429 Gerald Robinson .05
430 Pat Swilling .05
431 Ed McCaffrey .05
432 Neal Anderson .06
433 Joe Phillips .05
434 Jerry Ball .05
435 Tyrone Stowe .05
436 Dana Stubblefield .25
437 Eric Curry .10
438 Derrick Fenner .05
439 Mark Clayton .06
440 Quentin Coryatt .10
441 *Willie Roaf* .10
442 Earnest Dye .05
443 Jeff Jaeger .05
444 Stan Humphries .05
445 Johnny Johnson .07
446 Larry Brown .05
447 Kurt Gouveia .05
448 *Qadry Ismail* .25
449 Dan Footman .05
450 Tom Waddle .05
451 Kelvin Martin .05
452 Kanavis McGhee .05
453 Herman Moore .50
454 Jesse Solomon .05
455 Shane Conlan .05
456 Joel Steed .05
457 Charles Arbuckle .05
458 Shane Dronett .05
459 Steve Tasker .05
460 Herschel Walker .07
461 Willie Davis .10
462 Al Smith .05
463 O.J. McDuffie .50
464 Kevin Fagan .05
465 Hardy Nickerson .05
466 Leonard Marshall .05
467 John Baylor .05
468 Jay Novacek .06
469 *Wayne Simmons* .10
470 Tommy Vardell .06
471 Cleveland Gary .05
472 Mark Collins .05
473 Craig Heyward .05
474 John Copeland .08
475 Jeff Hostetler .08
476 Brian Mitchell .08
477 Natrone Means .75
478 Brad Muster .05
479 David Lutz .05
480 Andre Rison .30
481 Michael Zordich .05
482 Jim McMahon .06
483 Carlton Gray .05
484 Chris Mohr .05
485 Ernest Givins .05
486 Tony Tolbert .05
487 Vai Sikahema .05
488 Larry Webster .05
489 James Hasty .05
490 Reggie White .10
491 *Reggie Rivers* .25
492 Roman Phifer .05
493 Levon Kirkland .05
494 Demetrius DuBose .10
495 William Perry .06
496 Clay Matthews .05
497 Aaron Jones .05
498 Jack Trudeau .05
499 Michael Brooks .05
500 Jerry Rice .60
501 Lonnie Marts .05
502 Tim McGee .05
503 Kelvin Pritchett .05
504 Bobby Hebert .06
505 Audray McMillian .05
506 Chuck Cecil .05
507 Leonard Renfro .05
508 Ethan Horton .05
509 Kevin Smith .06
510 Louis Oliver .05
511 John Stephens .05
512 Browning Nagle .07
513 Ricardo McDonald .05
514 Leslie O'Neal .07
515 Lorenzo White .07
516 *Thomas Smith* .10
517 Tony Woods .05
518 Darryl Henley .05
519 Robert Delpino .05
520 Rod Woodson .07
521 Phillippi Sparks .05
522 Jessie Hester .05
523 Shaun Gayle .05
524 Brad Edwards .05
525 Randall Cunningham .10
526 Marv Cook .05
527 Dennis Gibson .05
528 Erric Pegram .25
529 Terry McDaniel .05
530 Troy Aikman 1.25
531 Irving Fryar .06
532 Blair Thomas .05
533 Jim Wilks .05
534 Michael Jackson .06
535 Eric Davis .05
536 James Campen .05
537 Steve Beuerlein .10
538 Robert Smith .15
539 J.J. Birden .05
540 Broderick Thomas .05
541 Darryl Talley .05
542 *Russell Freeman* .10
543 David Alexander .05
544 Chris Mims .07
545 Coleman Rudolph .05
546 Steve McMichael .05
547 David Williams .05
548 Chris Hinton .05
549 Jim Jeffcoat .05
550 Howie Long .05
551 *Roosevelt Potts* .25
552 Bryan Cox .05
553 David Richards .05
554 Reggie Brooks .40
555 Neil O'Donnell .25
556 Irv Smith .05
557 Henry Ellard .05
558 Steve DeBerg .05
559 Jim Sweeney .05
560 Harold Green .05
561 Darrell Thompson .05
562 Vinny Testaverde .08
563 Bubby Brister .06
564 Sean Landeta .05
565 Neil Smith .05
566 Craig Erickson .05
567 Jim Ritcher .05
568 Don Mosebar .05
569 John Gesek .05
570 Gary Plummer .05
571 Norm Johnson .05
572 Ron Heller .05
573 Carl Simpson .05
574 Greg Montgomery .05
575 Dana Hall .05
576 Vencie Glenn .05
577 Dean Biasucci .05
578 Rod Bernstine .05
579 Randal Hill .07
580 Sam Mills .05
581 Santana Dotson .05
582 Greg Lloyd .06
583 Eric Thomas .05
584 Henry Rolling .05
585 Tony Bennett .05
586 Sheldon White .05
587 Mark Kelso .05
588 Marc Spindler .05
589 Greg McMurtry .05
590 Art Monk .07
591 Marco Coleman .05
592 Tony Jones .05
593 Melvin Jenkins .05
594 Kevin Ross .05
595 William Fuller .05
596 James Joseph .05
597 *Lamar McGriggs* .15
598 Gill Byrd .05
599 Alexander Wright .05
600 Rick Mirer .10
601 Richard Dent .05
602 Thomas Everett .05
603 Jack Del Rio .05
604 Jerome Bettis .75
605 Ronnie Lott .06
606 Marty Carter .05
607 *Arthur Marshall* .30
608 Lee Johnson .05
609 Bruce Armstrong .05
610 Ricky Proehl .05
611 Will Wolford .05
612 Mike Prior .05
613 George Jamison .05
614 Gene Atkins .05
615 Merril Hoge .05
616 Desmond Howard .25
617 Jarvis Williams .05
618 Marcus Allen .07
619 Gary Brown .25
620 Bill Brooks .05
621 Eric Allen .05
622 *Todd Kelly* .10
623 Michael Dean Perry .05
624 David Braxton .05
625 Mike Sherrard .05
626 Jeff Bryant .05
627 Eric Bieniemy .06
628 Tim Brown .06
629 Troy Auzenne .05
630 Michael Irvin .35
631 Maurice Hurst .05
632 Duane Bickett .05
633 George Teague .08
634 Vince Workman .05
635 Renaldo Turnbull .05
636 Johnny Bailey .05
637 *Dan Williams* .15
638 James Thornton .05
639 Terry Allen .06
640 Kevin Greene .05
641 Tony Zendejas .05
642 *Scott Kowalkowski* .10
643 Jeff Query .05
644 Brian Blades .05
645 Keith Jackson .08
646 Monte Coleman .05
647 Guy McIntyre .05
648 Barry Word .05
649 *Steve Everitt* .10
650 Patrick Bates .10
651 Marcus Robertson .05
652 John Carney .05
653 Derek Brown .06
654 Carwell Gardner .05
655 Moe Gardner .05
656 Andre Ware .06
657 Keith Van Horne .05
658 Hugh Millen .05
659 Checklist 3 of 4 .05
660 Checklist 4 of 4 .05

A card number in parenthese ( ) indicates the set is unnumbered.

1993 Topps Gold

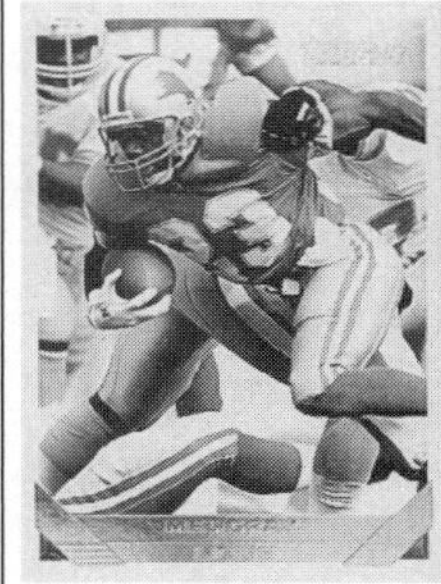

The 660-card, standard-size set was inserted in each pack (Three per rack pack, five per jumbo) and was a parallel to the 1993 base Topps set. The four checklist cards were replaced by the player cards listed below.

	NM/M
Complete Set (660):	90.00
Complete Series 1 (330):	50.00
Complete Series 2 (330):	40.00
Common Player:	.15
Veteran Stars:	1.5X-3X
Young Stars:	1.25X-2.5X
RCs:	1.25X-2.5X

329 Terance Mathis 1.00
330 Alex Wojchiechowicz .50
659 Pat Chaffey .50
660 Milton Mack .50

1993 Topps Black Gold

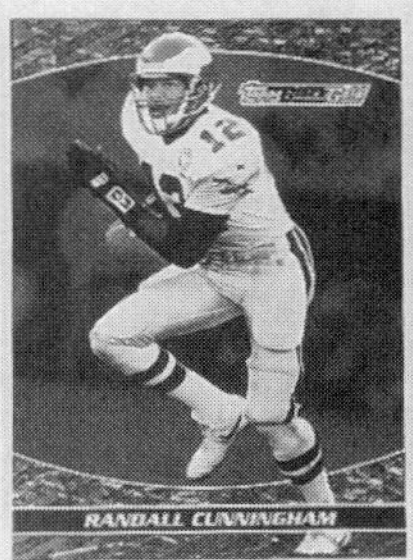

These cards feature an action photo against a curved, screened gold-foil background with white borders. The player's name is in a black stripe at the bottom; the set name is also on the card front. The numbered backs are in a horizontal format and include a player profile shot and a career summary against a blue-green background. Cards were randomly included in every 48th pack of 1993 Topps football; cards 1-22 were in Series I packs, while 23-44 were in Series II packs. "You Just Won" cards were also available in Series I packs, good for mail-in offers for cards 1-11, 12-22 and 1-22. Series II packs had offers for cards 23-33, 34-44, 23-44 and the entire set (1-44). Winners then became eligible to win one of 500 uncut sheets of the set.

	NM/M
Complete Set (44):	35.00
Complete Series 1 (22):	15.00
Complete Series 2 (22):	20.00
Common Player:	.50
Minor Stars:	1.00

1 Kelvin Martin .50
2 Audray McMillian .50
3 Terry Allen .50
4 Vai Sikahema .50
5 Clyde Simmons .50
6 Lorenzo White .50
7 Michael Irvin 2.00
8 Troy Aikman 5.00
9 Mark Kelso .50
10 Cleveland Gary .50
11 Greg Montgomery .50
12 Jerry Rice 5.00
13 Rod Woodson 1.00
14 Leslie O'Neal .50
15 Harold Green .50
16 Randall Cunningham 1.00
17 Ricky Watters 2.00
18 Andre Rison 1.00
19 Eugene Robinson .50
20 Wayne Martin .50
21 Chris Warren 1.00
22 Anthony Miller .50
23 Steve Young 3.00
24 Tim Harris .50
25 Emmitt Smith 8.00
26 Sterling Sharpe 1.00
27 Henry Jones .50

28 Warren Moon 1.00
29 Barry Foster .50
30 Dale Carter .50
31 Mel Gray .50
32 Barry Sanders 5.00
33 Dan Marino 8.00
34 Fred Barnett .50
35 Deion Sanders 3.00
36 Simon Fletcher .50
37 Donnell Woolford .50
38 Reggie Cobb .50
39 Brett Favre 8.00
40 Thurman Thomas 1.00
41 Rodney Hampton .50
42 Eric Martin .50
43 Pete Stoyanovich .50
44 Herschel Walker .50

1993 Topps FantaSports

The 200-card, 3" x 5" set is an interactive fantasy game in which the players are rated on a three-year basis. For $159, the collector could purchase the entire set which also included entry into the fantasy league, a stat book, worksheets and instructions. The collector who earned the best fantasy score over 18 games won four tickets to Super Bowl XXVIII. The game was test-marketed in four cities: Buffalo, Houston, Kansas City and Washington, D.C. "FantaSports" appears in gold foil on the top black border. The cards are arranged by position.

NM/M
Complete Set (200): 120.00
Common Player: .25
1 Chris Miller .50
2 Jim Kelly 1.00
3 Jim Harbaugh .75
4 David Klingler .25
5 Bernie Kosar .50
6 Troy Aikman 8.00
7 John Elway 5.00
8 Tommy Maddox .25
9 Rodney Peete .50
10 Andre Ware .50
11 Brett Favre 20.00
12 Warren Moon 1.00
13 Jeff George 1.00
14 Dave Krieg .50
15 Joe Montana 8.00
16 Todd Marinovich .25
17 Jim Everett .50
18 Dan Marino 20.00
19 Sean Salisbury .25
20 Drew Bledsoe 8.00
21 Dave Brown .75
22 Phil Simms .50
23 Boomer Esiason .50
24 Browning Nagle .25
25 Randall Cunningham .50
26 Neil O'Donnell .50
27 Stan Humphries 1.00
28 Steve Young 5.00
29 Rick Mirer 3.00
30 Mark Rypien .50
31 Kenneth Davis .25
32 Thurman Thomas 1.50
33 Steve Broussard .25
34 Neal Anderson .50
35 Craig Heyward .25
36 Derrick Fenner .25
37 Harold Green .25
38 Leroy Hoard .25
39 Kevin Mack .25
40 Eric Metcalf 1.00
41 Tommy Vardell .25
42 Daryl Johnston .75
43 Emmitt Smith 20.00
44 Barry Sanders 8.00
45 Edgar Bennett .75
46 Lorenzo White .50
47 Anthony Johnson .25
48 Todd McNair .25
49 Christian Okoye .25
50 Harvey Williams .75
51 Barry Word .25
52 Nick Bell .25
53 Eric Dickerson .75
54 Jerome Bettis 5.00
55 Cleveland Gary .25
56 Mark Higgs .25
57 Tony Paige .25
58 Terry Allen .75
59 Roger Craig .50
60 Robert Smith 1.25
61 Leonard Russell .50
62 Jon Vaughn .25
63 Vaughn Dunbar .25
64 Dalton Hilliard .25
65 Jarrod Bunch .25
66 Rodney Hampton .75
67 Dave Meggett .25
68 Brad Baxter .25
69 Heath Sherman .25
70 Vai Sikahema .25
71 Johnny Bailey .25
72 Larry Centers .75
73 Garrison Hearst 3.00
74 Barry Foster .25
75 Eric Bieniemy .25
76 Marion Butts .25
77 Ronnie Harmon .25
78 Natrone Means 4.00
79 Amp Lee .25
80 Tom Rathman .25
81 Ricky Watters 1.00
82 Chris Warren 1.00
83 John L. Williams .25
84 Gary Anderson (RB) .25
85 Reggie Cobb .25
86 Vince Workman .25
87 Reggie Brooks .75
88 Earnest Byner .25
89 Ricky Ervins .25
90 Michael Haynes .50
91 Mike Pritchard .75
92 Andre Rison .75
93 Don Beebe .50
94 Andre Reed .50
95 Curtis Conway 3.00
96 Wendell Davis .25
97 Tom Waddle .25
98 Carl Pickens 1.00
99 Michael Jackson .50
100 Alvin Harper .75
101 Michael Irvin 1.00
102 Vance Johnson .25
103 Mel Gray .50
104 Sterling Sharpe 1.00
105 Curtis Duncan .25
106 Ernest Givins .50
107 Haywood Jeffires .50
108 Tim Brown 1.00
109 Willie Gault .25
110 Flipper Anderson .25
111 Henry Ellard .75
112 Mark Duper .50
113 O.J. McDuffie 2.00
114 Anthony Carter .50
115 Cris Carter 1.00
116 Mike Farr .25
117 Quinn Early .50
118 Eric Martin .25
119 Chris Calloway .25
120 Mark Jackson .25
121 Rob Moore .50
122 Fred Barnett .50
123 Calvin Williams .50
124 Gary Clark .50
125 Randal Hill .25
126 Ricky Proehl .50
127 Jeff Graham .50
128 Ernie Mills .25
129 Dwight Stone .25
130 Nate Lewis .25
131 Jerry Rice 8.00
132 John Taylor .50
133 Tommy Kane .25
134 Kelvin Martin .25
135 Lawrence Dawsey .50
136 Courtney Hawkins .50
137 Art Monk .50
138 Pete Metzelaars .50
139 Jay Novacek .50
140 Reggie Johnson .25
141 Shannon Sharpe .75
142 Jackie Harris .50
143 Troy Drayton .50
144 Keith Jackson .50
145 Steve Jordan .50
146 Johnny Mitchell .50
147 Eric Green .50
148 Derrick Walker .25
149 Brent Jones .50
150 Ron Hall .25
151 Norm Johnson .25
152 Jim Breech .25
153 Matt Stover .25
154 Lin Elliott .25
155 Jason Hanson .25
156 Chris Jacke .25
157 Nick Lowery .25
158 Pete Stoyanovich .25
159 Roger Ruzek .25
160 Gary Anderson (K) .25
161 John Kasay .25
162 Chip Lohmiller .25
163 Chris Gardocki .25
164 Mike Saxon .25
165 Jim Arnold .25
166 Rohn Stark .25
167 Jeff Gossett .25
168 Reggie Roby .25
169 Harry Newsome .25
170 Tommy Barnhardt .25
171 Jeff Feagles .25
172 Rick Camarillo .25
173 Deion Sanders Falcons Defense 4.00
174 Cornelius Bennett Bills Defense .50
175 Mark Carrier Bears Defense (DB) .50
176 Darryl Williams Bengals Defense .25
177 Michael Dean Perry Browns Defense .50
178 Russell Maryland Cowboys Defense .50
179 Steve Atwater Broncos Defense .25
180 Bennie Blades Lions Defense .25
181 Reggie White Packers Defense 1.00
182 Cris Dishman Oilers Defense .25
183 Steve Emtman Colts Defense .25
184 Derrick Thomas Chiefs Defense 1.00
185 Howie Long Raiders Defense .50
186 Sean Gilbert Rams Defense .50
187 John Offerdahl Dolphins Defense .25
188 Chris Doleman Vikings Defense .25
189 Andre Tippett Patriots Defense .25
190 Sam Mills Saints Defense .25
191 Lawrence Taylor Giants Defense .75
192 James Hasty Jets Defense .25
193 Clyde Simmons Eagles Defense .50
194 Eric Swann Cardinals Defense .50
195 Greg Lloyd Steelers Defense .75
196 Junior Seau Chargers Defense 1.25
197 Kevin Fagan 49ers Defense .25
198 Cortez Kennedy Seahawks Defense .75
199 Broderick Thomas Buccaneers Defense .25
200 Darrell Green Redskins Defense .50

1994 Topps

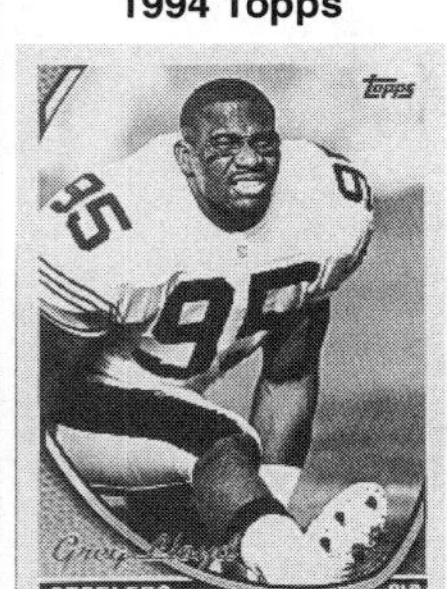

Topps issued its 1994 set in two 330-card series, along with its parallel Special Effects set. Two insert sets, Finest and Spectralight All-Pros, were also made. The regular cards have a front with a full-color action photo, bordered by a gold-foil border and white frame. The Topps logo appears on the front, too, along with the player's name, which is stamped in gold foil. The card back has a player photo, biographical and statistical information, a card number and a player profile. Subsets within the main set included Career Active Leaders, Draft Picks, Tools of the Game, and Measures of Greatness. Special Effects cards were issued one per pack.

NM/M
Complete Set (660): 45.00
Complete Series 1 (330): 22.00
Complete Series 2 (330): 22.00
Common Player: .05
Special Effects Set (660): 300.00
SE Cards: 3X-6X
Series 1 or 2 Pack (12): 1.25
Series 1 or 2 Wax Box (36): 30.00
1 Emmitt Smith 2.00
2 Russell Copeland .08
3 Jesse Sapolu .05
4 David Scott .05
5 Rodney Hampton .30
6 Bubba McDowell .05
7 Bryce Paup .05
8 Winston Moss .05
9 Brett Perriman .05
10 Rod Woodson .10
11 John Randle .05
12 David Wyman .05
13 Jeff Cross .05
14 Richard Cooper .05
15 Johnny Mitchell .10
16 David Alexander .05
17 Ronnie Harmon .07
18 Tyrone Stowe .05
19 Chris Zorich .05
20 Rob Burnett .05
21 Harold Alexander .05
22 Rod Stephens .05
23 Mark Wheeler .05
24 Dwayne Sabb .05
25 Troy Drayton .15
26 Kurt Gouveia .05
27 Warren Moon .15
28 Jeff Query .05
29 *Chuck Levy* .40
30 Bruce Smith .10
31 Doug Riesenberg .05
32 Willie Drewrey .05
33 Nate Newton .07
34 James Jett .20
35 George Teague .20
36 Marc Spindler .05
37 Jack Del Rio .05
38 Dale Carter .05
39 Steve Atwater .07
40 Herschel Walker .07
41 James Hasty .05
42 Seth Joyner .10
43 Keith Jackson .10
44 Tommy Vardell .05
45 Antonio Langham .05
46 Derek Brown .25
47 John Wojciechowski .05
48 Horace Copeland .15
49 Luis Sharpe .05
50 Pat Harlow .05
51 *David Palmer* .65
52 Tony Smith .05
53 Tim Johnson .05
54 Anthony Newman .05
55 Terry Wooden .05
56 Derrick Fenner .05
57 Mike Fox .05
58 Brad Hopkins .05
59 Daryl Johnson .08
60 Steve Young .75
61 *Scottie Graham* .35
62 Nolan Harrison .05
63 David Richards .05
64 Chris Mohr .05
65 Hardy Nickerson .05
66 Heath Sherman .05
67 Irving Fryar .10
68 Ray Buchanan .05
69 Jay Taylor .05
70 Shannon Sharpe .15
71 Vinny Testaverde .05
72 Renaldo Turnbull .05
73 Dwight Stone .05
74 *Willie McGinnest* .50
75 Darrell Green .07
76 Kyle Clifton .05
77 Leo Goeas .05
78 Ken Ruettgers .05
79 Craig Heyward .05
80 Andre Rison .20
81 Chris Mims .15
82 Gary Clark .07
83 Ricardo McDonald .05
84 Patrick Hunter .05
85 Bruce Matthews .05
86 Russell Maryland .06
87 Gary Anderson .05
88 Brad Edwards .05
89 Carlton Bailey .05
90 Qadry Ismail .50
91 Terry McDaniel .05
92 Willie Green .05
93 Cornelius Bennett .05
94 Paul Gruber .05
95 Pete Stoyanovich .08
96 Merton Hanks .05
97 Tre' Johnson .05
98 Jonathan Hayes .05
99 Jason Elam .15
100 Jerome Bettis .50
101 Ronnie Lott .08
102 Maurcie Hurst .05
103 Kirk Lowdermilk .05
104 Tony Jones .05
105 Steve Beuerlein .08
106 Isaac Davis .05
107 Vaughan Johnson .05
108 Terrell Buckley .05
109 Pierce Holt .05
110 Alonzo Spellman .05
111 Patrick Robinson .05
112 Cortez Kennedy .10
113 Kevin Williams .50
114 Danny Copeland .05
115 Chris Doleman .05
116 Jerry Rice .45
117 Neil Smith .08
118 Emmitt Smith .75
119 Eugene Robinson,
Nate Odomes .05
120 Steve Young .60
121 Carnell Lake .05
122 Ernest Givins .05
123 Henry Jones .05
124 Michael Brooks .05
125 Jason Hanson .07
126 Andy Harmon .05
127 *Errict Rhett* .75
128 Harris Barton .05
129 Greg Robinson .05
130 Derrick Thomas .10
131 Keith Kartz .05
132 Lincoln Kennedy .08
133 Leslie O'Neal .05
134 Tim Goad .05
135 Rohn Stark .05
136 O.J. McDuffie .40
137 Donnell Woolford .05
138 *Jamir Miller* .50
139 Eric Thomas .05
140 Willie Roaf .08
141 Wayne Gandy .05
142 Mike Brim .05
143 Kelvin Martin .08
144 Edgar Bennett .07
145 Michael Dean Perry .05
146 Shante Carver .05
147 Jesse Armstead .05
148 Mo Elewonibi .05
149 Dana Stubblefield .35
150 Cody Carlson .05
151 Vencie Glenn .05
152 Levon Kirkland .05
153 Derrick Moore .15
154 John Fina .05
155 Jeff Hostetler .15
156 Courtney Hawkins .20
157 Todd Collins .05
158 Neil Smith .05
159 Simon Fletcher .08
160 Dan Marino 2.00
161 *Sam Adams* .25
162 Marvin Washington .05
163 John Copeland .05
164 Eugene Robinson .05
165 Mark Carrier .05
166 Mike Kenn .05
167 Tyrone Hughes .05
168 Darren Carrington .05
169 Shane Conlan .05
170 Ricky Proehl .05
171 Jeff Herrod .05
172 Mark Carrier .05
173 George Koonce .05
174 Desmond Howard .08
175 David Meggett .05
176 Charles Haley .06
177 Steve Wisniewski .05
178 Dermontti Dawson .05
179 Tim McDonald .08
180 Broderick Thomas .05
181 Bernard Dafney .05
182 Bo Orlando .10
183 Andre Reed .10
184 Randall Cunningham .15
185 Chris Spielman .05
186 Keith Byars .05
187 Ben Coates .05
188 Tracy Simien .05
189 Carl Pickens .10
190 Reggie White .15
191 Norm Johnson .05
192 Brian Washington .05
193 Stan Humphries .05
194 Fred Stokes .05
195 Dan Williams .05
196 John Elway .40
197 Eric Allen .10
198 Hardy Nickerson .05
199 Jerome Bettis .25
200 Troy Aikman 1.00
201 Thurman Thomas .40
202 Cornelius Bennett .05
203 Michael Irvin .20
204 Jim Kelly .20
205 Junior Seau .10
206 *Heath Shuler* .25
207 Howard Cross .05
208 Pat Swilling .05
209 Pete Metzelaars .05
210 Tony McGee .05
211 Neil O'Donnell .08
212 Eugene Chung .05
213 J.B. Brown .05
214 Marcus Allen .15
215 Harry Newsome .05
216 *Greg Hill* .50
217 *Ryan Yarborough* .30
218 Marty Carter .05
219 Bern Brostek .05
220 Boomer Esiason .07
221 Vince Buck .05
222 Jim Jeffcoat .08
223 Bob Dahl .05
224 Marion Butts .06
225 Ron Moore .50
226 Robert Blackmon .05
227 Curtis Conway .30
228 Jon Hand .05
229 Shane Dronett .05
230 Eric Williams .05
231 Dennis Brown .05
232 Ray Childress .05
233 *Johnnie Morton* .50
234 Kent Hull .05
235 John Elliott .05
236 Ron Heller .05
237 J.J. Birden .05
238 Thomas Randolph .05
239 Chip Lohmiller .07
240 Tim Brown .10
241 Steve Tovar .05
242 Moe Gardner .05
243 Vincent Brown .05
244 Tony Zendejas .05
245 Eric Allen .08
246 *Joe King* .05
247 Mo Lewis .05
248 Rod Bernstine .07
249 Tom Waddle .05
250 Junior Seau .10
251 Eric Metcalf .05
252 Cris Carter .08
253 Bill Hitchcock .05
254 Zefross Moss .05
255 Morten Andersen .07
256 Keith Rucker .05
257 Chris Jacke .05
258 Richmond Webb .07
259 Herman Moore .10
260 Phil Simms .10
261 Mark Tuninei .05
262 Don Beebe .05
263 Marc Logan .05
264 Willie Davis .05
265 David Klingler .15
266 Martin Mayhew .05
267 Mark Bavaro .05
268 Greg Lloyd .05
269 Al Del Greco .05
270 Reggie Brooks .20
271 Greg Townsend .05
272 Rohn Stark .05
273 Marcus Allen .05
274 Ronnie Lott .05
275 Dan Marino .65
276 Sean Gilbert .07
277 LeRoy Butler .07
278 Troy Auzenne .05
279 Eric Swann .05
280 Quentin Coryatt .06
281 Anthony Pleasant .05
282 Brad Baxter .05
283 Carl Lee .05
284 Courtney Hall .08
285 Quinn Early .05
286 Eddie Robinson .05
287 Marco Coleman .05
288 Harold Green .05
289 Santana Dotson .05
290 Robert Porcher .05
291 Joe Phillips .05
292 Mark McMillian .05
293 Eric Davis .05
294 Mark Jackson .05
295 Darryl Talley .05
296 Curtis Duncan .05
297 Bruce Armstrong .05
298 Eric Hill .05
299 Andre Collins .05
300 Jay Novacek .08
301 Roosevelt Potts .15
302 Eric Martin .05
303 Chris Warren .05
304 Deral Boykin .05
305 Jessie Tuggle .05
306 Glyn Milburn .25
307 Terry Obee .05
308 Eric Turner .05
309 *DeWayne Washington* .25
310 Sterling Sharpe .35
311 Jeff Gossett .05
312 John Carney .05
313 *Aaron Glenn* .20
314 Nick Lowery .05
315 Thurman Thomas .15
316 Troy Aikman .65
317 Thurman Thomas .10
318 Michael Irvin .15
319 Steve Beuerlein .07
320 Jerry Rice .75
321 Alexander Wright .05
322 Michael Bates .05
323 Greg Davis .05
324 Mark Bortz .05
325 Kevin Greene .05
326 Wayne Simmons .05
327 Wayne Martin .05
328 Michael Irvin .30
329 Checklist 1 .05
330 Checklist 2 .05
331 Doug Pelfrey .05
332 Myron Quyton .05
333 Howard Ballard .05
334 Ricky Ervins .05
335 Steve Emtman .05
336 Eric Curry .05
337 *Bert Emanuel* .75
338 Darryl Ashmore .05
339 Stevon Moore .05
340 Garrison Hearst .50
341 Vance Johnson .05
342 Anthony Johnson .05
343 Merril Hoge .05
344 William Thomas .05
345 Scott Mitchell .15
346 Jim Everett .05
347 Ray Crockett .05
348 Bryan Cox .07
349 *Charles Johnson* .50
350 Randall McDaniel .05
351 Micheal Barrow .05
352 Darrell Thompson .05
353 Kevin Gogan .05
354 Brad Daluiso .05
355 Mark Collins .05
356 *Bryant Young* .30
357 Steve Christie .05
358 Derek Kennard .05
359 Jon Vaughn .05
360 Drew Bledsoe 1.00
361 Randy Baldwin .05
362 Kevin Ross .05
363 Reuben Davis .05
364 Chris Miller .05
365 Tim McGee .05
366 Tony Woods .05
367 Dean Biasucci .05
368 George Jamison .05
369 Lorenzo Lynch .05
370 Johnny Johnson .05
371 Greg Kragen .05
372 Vinson Smith .05
373 Vince Workman .05
374 *Allen Aldridge* .20
375 Terry Kirby .30
376 *Mario Bates* .20
377 Dixon Edwards .05
378 Leon Searcy .05
379 Eric Guliford .05
380 Gary Brown .05
381 Phil Hansen .05
382 Keith Hamilton .05
383 John Alt .05
384 John Taylor .05
385 Reggie Cobb .05
386 *Rob Fredrickson* .30
387 Pepper Johnson .05
388 *Kevin Lee* .35
389 Stanley Richard .05
390 Jackie Slater .05
391 Darrick Brilz .05
392 John Gesek .05
393 Kelvin Pritchett .05
394 Aeneas Williams .05
395 *Henry Ford* .25
396 *Eric Mahlum* .20
397 Tom Rouen .05
398 Vinnie Clark .05
399 Jim Sweeney .05
400 Troy Aikman 2.25
401 Toi Cook .05
402 Dan Saleauma .05
403 Andy Heck .05
404 Deon Figures .10
405 Henry Thomas .05
406 Glen Montgomery .05
407 *Trent Dilfer* 2.00
408 Eddie Murray .05
409 Gene Atkins .05
410 Mike Sherrard .05
411 Don Mosebar .05
412 Thomas Smith .05
413 Ken Norton .05
414 Robert Brooks .05

No.	Player	Price
415	Jeff Lageman	.05
416	Tony Siragusa	.05
417	Brian Blades	.05
418	Matt Stover	.05
419	Jesse Solomon	.05
420	Reggie Roby	.05
421	Shawn Jefferson	.05
422	Marc Boutte	.05
423	William White	.05
424	Clyde Simmons	.05
425	Anthony Miller	.08
426	Brent Jones	.05
427	Tim Grunhard	.05
428	Alfred Williams	.05
429	Roy Barker	.05
430	Dante Jones	.05
431	Leroy Thompson	.05
432	Marcus Robertson	.05
433	*Thomas Lewis*	.50
434	Sean Jones	.05
435	Michael Haynes	.05
436	Albert Lewis	.05
437	*Tim Bowens*	.30
438	Marvcus Patton	.05
439	Rich Miano	.05
440	Craig Erickson	.05
441	*Larry Allen*	.20
442	*Fernando Smith*	.20
443	D.J. Johnson	.05
444	Leonard Russell	.05
445	*Marshall Faulk*	5.00
446	Najee Mustafaa	.05
447	Brian Hansen	.05
448	*Isaac Bruce*	4.00
449	Kevin Scott	.05
450	Natrone Means	.40
451	Tracy Rogers	.05
452	Mike Croel	.05
453	Anthony Edwards	.05
454	*Brentson Buckner*	.20
455	Tom Carter	.05
456	Burt Grossman	.05
457	Jimmy Spencer	.05
458	Raghib Ismail	.20
459	Fred Strickland	.05
460	*Jeff Burris*	.30
461	Adrian Hardy	.05
462	Lamar McGriggs	.05
463	Webster Slaughter	.05
464	Demetrius DuBose	.05
465	Dave Brown	.20
466	Kenneth Gant	.05
467	Erik Kramer	.05
468	Mark Ingram	.05
469	Roman Phifer	.05
470	Steve Young	.12
471	Nick Lowery	.08
472	Irving Fryar	.08
473	Art Monk	.08
474	Mel Gray	.08
475	Reggie White	.08
476	Eric Ball	.05
477	Dwayne Harper	.05
478	Will Shields	.05
479	Roger Harper	.05
480	Rick Mirer	.50
481	Vincent Brisby	.20
482	John Jurkovic	.05
483	Michael Jackson	.05
484	Ed Cunningham	.05
485	*Brad Ottis*	.15
486	Sterling Palmer	.05
487	Tony Bennett	.05
488	Mike Pritchard	.05
489	*Bucky Brooks*	.35
490	Troy Vincent	.05
491	Eric Green	.05
492	*Van Malone*	.25
493	*Marcus Spears*	.25
494	Brian Williams	.05
495	Robert Smith	.15
496	Haywood Jeffires	.07
497	Darrin Smith	.05
498	Tommy Barnhardt	.05
499	Anthony Smith	.05
500	Ricky Watters	.05
501	Antone Davis	.05
502	David Braxton	.05
503	*Donnell Bennett*	.50
504	Donald Evans	.05
505	Lewis Tillman	.05
506	Lance Smith	.05
507	*Aaron Taylor*	.20
508	Ricky Sanders	.05
509	Dennis Smith	.05
510	Barry Foster	.30
511	Stan Brock	.05
512	Henry Rolling	.05
513	Walter Reeves	.05
514	John Booty	.05
515	Kenneth Davis	.05
516	Cris Dishman	.05
517	Bill Lewis	.05
518	Jeff Bryant	.05
519	Brian Mitchell	.05
520	Joe Montana	1.00
521	Keith Sims	.05
522	Harry Colon	.05
523	Leon Lett	.05
524	Carlos Jenkins	.05
525	Victor Bailey	.15
526	Harvey Williams	.05
527	Irv Smith	.10
528	*Jason Sehorn*	.20
529	*John Thierry*	.25
530	Brett Favre	2.00
531	*Sean Dawkins*	.30
532	Erric Pegram	.05
533	Jimmy Williams	.05
534	Michael Timpson	.05
535	Willie Anderson	.05
536	John Parrela	.05
537	Freddie Joe Nunn	.05
538	Doug Dawson	.05
539	Michael Stewart	.05
540	John Elway	.65
541	Ronnie Lott	.05
542	Barry Sanders	.50
543	Andre Reed	.08
544	Deion Sanders	.10
545	Dan Marino	.75
546	Carlton Bailey	.08
547	Emmitt Smith	1.00
548	Alvin Harper	.08
549	Eric Metcalf	.08
550	Jerry Rice	.50
551	Derrick Thomas	.08
552	Mark Collins	.08
553	Eric Turner	.08
554	Sterling Sharpe	.12
555	Steve Young	.20
556	*Darnay Scott*	.75
557	Joel Steed	.05
558	Dennis Gibson	.05
559	Charles Mincy	.05
560	Rickey Jackson	.05
561	Dave Cadigan	.05
562	Rick Tuten	.05
563	Mike Caldwell	.05
564	*Todd Steussie*	.30
565	Kevin Smith	.05
566	Arthur Marshall	.05
567	Aaron Wallace	.05
568	Calvin Williams	.05
569	Todd Kelly	.05
570	Barry Sanders	1.25
571	Shaun Gayle	.05
572	Will Wolford	.05
573	Ethan Norton	.05
574	Chris Slade	.15
575	Jeff Wright	.05
576	*Toby Wright*	.20
577	Lamar Thomas	.05
578	Chris Singleton	.05
579	Ed West	.05
580	Jeff George	.08
581	*Kevin Mitchell*	.15
582	Chad Brown	.05
583	Rich Camarillo	.05
584	Gary Zimmerman	.05
585	Randal Hill	.05
586	Keith Cash	.05
587	Sam Mills	.05
588	Shawn Lee	.05
589	Kent Graham	.12
590	Steve Everitt	.05
591	Rob Moore	.05
592	*Kevin Mawae*	.20
593	Jerry Ball	.05
594	Larry Brown	.05
595	Tim Krumrie	.05
596	*Aubrey Beavers*	.30
597	Chris Hinton	.05
598	Greg Montgomery	.05
599	Jimmie Jones	.05
600	Jim Kelly	.20
601	*Joe Johnson*	.25
602	Tim Irwin	.05
603	Steve Jackson	.05
604	James Williams	.05
605	Blair Thomas	.05
606	Daman Hughes	.05
607	Russell Freeman	.05
608	Andre Hastings	.10
609	Ken Harvey	.05
610	Jim Harbaugh	.05
611	Emmitt Smith	.80
612	Andre Rison	.10
613	Steve Young	.20
614	Anthony Miller	.10
615	Barry Sanders	.50
616	Bernie Kosar	.05
617	Chris Gardocki	.05
618	*William Floyd*	.30
619	Matt Brock	.05
620	*Dan Wilkinson*	.45
621	Tony Meola	.05
622	Tony Tolbert	.05
623	Mike Zandofsky	.05
624	William Fuller	.05
625	Steve Jordan	.05
626	Mike Johnson	.05
627	Ferrell Edmunds	.05
628	Gene Williams	.05
629	Willie Beamon	.05
630	Gerald Perry	.05
631	John Baylor	.05
632	Carwell Gardner	.05
633	Thomas Everett	.08
634	Lamar Lathon	.05
635	Michael Bankston	.05
636	Ray Crittenden	.05
637	Kimble Anders	.05
638	Robert Delpino	.05
639	Darren Perry	.05
640	Byron Evans	.05
641	Mark Higgs	.05
642	Lorenzo Neal	.05
643	Henry Ellard	.05
644	Trace Armstrong	.05
645	Greg McMurtry	.05
646	Steve McMichael	.05
647	Terance Mathis	.05
648	Eric Bieniemy	.05
649	Bobby Houston	.05
650	Alvin Harper	.05
651	*James Folston*	.15
652	Mel Gray	.05
653	Adrian Cooper	.05
654	Dexter Carter	.05
655	Don Griffin	.05
656	Corey Weimer	.05
657	Lee Johnson	.05
658	Nate Odomes	.05
659	Checklist 3	.05
660	Checklist 4	.05

1994 Topps Special Effects

The 660-card, regular-sized set was issued as a parallel to the 1994 base set. The cards were inserted every two packs (and rack packs) and feature a clear plastic prismatic coating with a holographic stripe.

	NM/M
Common Player:	.30
Veteran Stars:	2X-4X
Young Stars:	2X-4X
RCs:	2X-4X

1994 Topps All-Pro

These 1994 Topps football inserts were included at a rate of one per every 36 Series II packs. Topps introduces its new Spectralight foil process for these cards, which feature 25 of the NFL's top stars. Each card is printed on a foil-stamped, foil-backed card.

		NM/M
	Complete Set (25):	20.00
	Common Player:	.50
	Minor Stars:	1.00
1	Michael Irvin	1.00
2	Eric Williams	.50
3	Steve Wisniewski	.50
4	Dermontti Dawson	.50
5	Nate Newton	.50
6	Harris Barton	.50
7	Shannon Sharpe	1.00
8	Jerry Rice	4.00
9	Troy Aikman	4.00
10	Barry Sanders	4.00
11	Jerome Bettis	1.00
12	Jason Hanson	.50
13	Eric Metcalf	.50
14	Reggie White	1.00
15	Cortez Kennedy	.50
16	Michael Dean Perry	.50
17	Bruce Smith	.50
18	Darryl Talley	.50
19	Hardy Nickerson	.50
20	Derrick Thomas	1.00
21	Mark Collins	.50
22	Eric Allen	.50
23	Tim McDonald	.50
24	Marcus Robertson	.50
25	Greg Montgomery	.50

1994 Topps 1000/3000

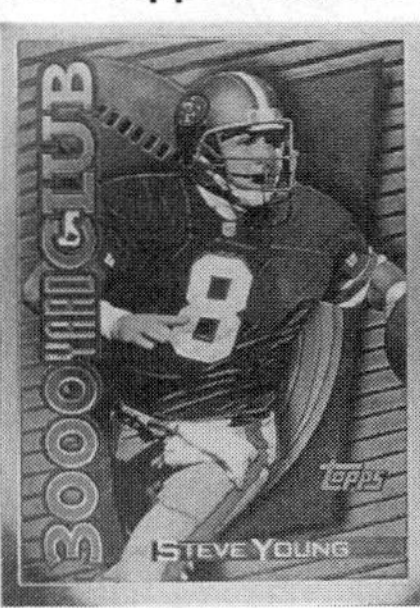

These cards were found one in every 32 packs of 1994 Topps football cards. They feature 20 receivers and running backs who gained 1,000 yards in 1993, plus 12 quarterbacks who threw for more than 3,000 yards. Each card front has the set name running along the left side of the card. The player's name and Topps' logo are in the bottom left corner. The back has an action photo and game-by-game recap of the player's 1993 season. Cards are numbered 1 of 32, etc.

		NM/M
	Complete Set (32):	40.00
	Common Player:	.50
	Minor Stars:	1.00
1	Jerry Rice	4.00
2	Chris Warren	1.00
3	Leonard Russell	.50
4	Gary Brown	.50
5	Tim Brown	1.00
6	Erric Pegram	.50
7	Irving Fryar	.50
8	Anthony Miller	.50
9	Reggie Langhorne	.50
10	Thurman Thomas	1.00
11	Reggie Brooks	.50
12	Andre Rison	1.00
13	Ron Moore	.50
14	Michael Irvin	1.00
15	Barry Sanders	4.00
16	Cris Carter	1.00
17	Rodney Hampton	1.00
18	Jerome Bettis	1.00
19	Sterling Sharpe	1.00
20	Emmitt Smith	5.00
21	John Elway	3.00
22	Brett Favre	5.00
23	Jim Kelly	1.00
24	Warren Moon	1.00
25	Phil Simms	.50
26	Craig Erickson	.50
27	Neil O'Donnell	.50
28	Steve Young	3.00
29	Steve Beuerlein	.50
30	Troy Aikman	3.00
31	Jeff Hostetler	.50
32	Boomer Esiason	.50

1994 Topps Archives 1956

The 120-card, standard-size set was a reprinted version of Topps' 1956 set (the checklist was not reprinted). The cards were sold in 12-card packs for $2 with whatever errors the originals had left in. The cards backs were printed in red and black on gray stock.

		NM/M
	Complete Set (120):	20.00
	Common Player:	.10
1	Johnny Carson	.10
2	Gordon Soltau	.10
3	Frank Varrichione	.10
4	Eddie Bell	.10
5	Alex Webster	.20
6	Norm Van Brocklin	2.00
7	Green Bay Packers Team Card	.30
8	Lou Creekmur	.20
9	Lou Groza	1.50
10	Tom Bienemann	.10
11	George Blanda	1.50
12	Alan Ameche	.40
13	Vic Janowicz	.40
14	Dick Moegle	.20
15	Fran Rogel	.10
16	Harold Giancanelli	.10
17	Emlen Tunnell	.60
18	Paul (Tank) Younger	.30
19	Bill Howton	.20
20	Jack Christiansen	.75
21	Darrell Brewster	.10
22	Chicago Cardinals Team Card	.30
23	Ed Brown	.20
24	Joe Campanella	.10
25	Leon Heath	.10
26	San Francisco 49ers Team Card	.30
27	Dick Flanagan	.10
28	Chuck Bednarik	1.00
29	Kyle Rote	.60
30	Les Richter	.20
31	Howard Ferguson	.10
32	Dorne Dibble	.10
33	Kenny Konz	.10
34	Dave Mann	.10
35	Rick Casares	.20
36	Art Donovan	1.00
37	Chuck Drazenovich	.10
38	Joe Arenas	.10
39	Lynn Chandnois	.10
40	Philadelphia Eagles Team Card	.30
41	Roosevelt Brown	.60
42	Tom Fears	.75
43	Gary Knafelc	.10
44	Joe Schmidt	1.00
45	Cleveland Browns Team Card (UER) (Card back does not credit the Browns with being Champs in 1955)	.60
46	Len Teeuws	.10
47	Bill George	.60
48	Baltimore Colts Team Card	.30
49	Eddie LeBaron	.40
50	Hugh McElhenny	1.25
51	Ted Marchibroda	.20
52	Adrian Burk	.10
53	Frank Gifford	3.50
54	Charley Toogood	.10
55	Tobin Rote	.20
56	Bill Stits	.10
57	Don Colo	.10
58	Ollie Matson	1.00
59	Harlon Hill	.10
60	Lenny Moore	2.00
61	Washington Redskins Team Card	.30
62	Billy Wilson	.20
63	Pittsburgh Steelers Team Card	.30
64	Bob Pellegrini	.10
65	Ken MacAfee	.20
66	Willard Sherman	.10
67	Roger Zatkoff	.10
68	Dave Middleton	.10
69	Ray Renfro	.20
70	Don Stonesifer	.10
71	Stan Jones	.60
72	Jim Mutscheller	.10
73	Volney Peters	.10
74	Leo Nomellini	.75
75	Ray Mathews	.10
76	Dick Bielski	.10
77	Charley Conerly	1.00
78	Elroy Hirsch	1.00
79	Bill Forester	.20
80	Jim Doran	.10
81	Fred Morrison	.10
82	Jack Simmons	.10
83	Bill McColl	.10
84	Bert Rechichar	.10
85	Joe Scudero	.10
86	Y.A. Tittle	3.00
87	Ernie Stautner	1.00
88	Norm Willey	.10
89	Bob Schnelker	.10
90	Dan Towler	.30
91	John Martinkovic	.10
92	Detroit Lions Team Card	.30
93	George Ratterman	.10
94	Chuck Ulrich	.10
95	Bobby Watkins	.10
96	Buddy Young	.30
97	Billy Wells	.10
98	Bob Toneff	.10
99	Bill McPeak	.10
100	Bobby Thomason	.10
101	Roosevelt Grier	.60
102	Ron Waller	.10
103	Bobby Dillon	.10
104	Leon Hart	.30
105	Mike McCormack	.60
106	John Olszewski	.10
107	Bill Wightkin	.10
108	George Shaw	.20
109	Dale Atkeson	.10
110	Joe Perry	1.00
111	Dale Dodrill	.10
112	Tom Scott	.10
113	New York Giants Team Card	.30
114	Los Angeles Rams Team Card (UER) (Back incorrect, Rams were not 1955 champs)	.30
115	Al Carmichael	.10
116	Bobby Layne	3.00
117	Ed Modzelewski	.20
118	Lamar McHan	.10
119	Chicago Bears Team Card	.30
120	Billy Vessels	.50

1994 Topps Archives 1956 Gold

The 120-card, standard-size set was issued as a gold parallel to the base 1956 reprint set and were randonly inserted into packs of 1956/57 packs.

	NM/M
Complete Set (120):	50.00
Common Player:	.25
Gold Cards:	1.25X-2.5X

1994 Topps Archives 1957

The 154-card, standard-size set was reprinted by Topps (except for the checklist) and was available in 12-card packs for $2. Any errors with the original 1957 set were not changed. The card backs were printed in red and black on gray card stock. Gold versions (3x) were also produced by Topps.

		NM/M
	Complete Set (154):	20.00
	Common Player:	.10
1	Eddie LeBaron	.30
2	Pete Retzlaff	.20
3	Mike McCormack	.50
4	Lou Baldacci	.10
5	Gino Marchetti	1.00
6	Leo Nomellini	.75
7	Bobby Watkins	.10
8	Dave Middleton	.10
9	Bobby Dillon	.10
10	Les Richter	.20
11	Roosevelt Brown	.50
12	Lavern Torgeson	.10
13	Dick Bielski	.10
14	Pat Summerall	1.00
15	Jack Butler	.10
16	John Henry Johnson	.75
17	Art Spinney	.10
18	Bob St. Clair	.50
19	Perry Jeter	.10
20	Lou Creekmur	.30
21	Dave Hanner	.10
22	Norm Van Brocklin	1.50
23	Don Chandler	.10
24	Al Dorow	.10
25	Tom Scott	.10
26	Ollie Matson	1.00
27	Fran Rogel	.10
28	Lou Groza	1.50
29	Billy Vessels	.20
30	Y.A. Tittle	2.00
31	George Blanda	1.50
32	Bobby Layne	2.00
33	Bill Howton	.20
34	Bill Wade	.20
35	Emlen Tunnell	.75
36	Leo Elter	.10
37	Clarence Peaks	.20
38	Don Stonesifer	.10
39	George Tarasovic	.10
40	Darrell Brewster	.10
41	Bert Rechichar	.10
42	Billy Wilson	.20
43	Ed Brown	.20
44	Gene Gedman	.10
45	Gary Knafelc	.10
46	Elroy Hirsch	1.00
47	Don Heinrich	.10
48	Gene Brito	.10
49	Chuck Bednarik	1.00
50	Dave Mann	.10
51	Bill McPeak	.10
52	Kenny Konz	.10
53	Alan Ameche	.40
54	Gordon Soltau	.10
55	Rick Casares	.30
56	Charlie Ane	.10
57	Al Carmichael	.10
58	Willard Sherman	.10
59	Kyle Rote	.50
60	Chuck Drazenovich	.10
61	Bobby Walston	.10
62	John Olszewski	.10
63	Ray Mathews	.10
64	Maurice Bassett	.10
65	Art Donovan	1.00
66	Joe Arenas	.10
67	Harlon Hill	.10
68	Yale Lary	.60
69	Bill Forester	.20
70	Bob Boyd	.10
71	Andy Robustelli	1.00
72	Sam Baker	.20
73	Bob Pellegrini	.10
74	Leo Sanford	.10
75	Sid Watson	.10
76	Ray Renfro	.20
77	Carl Taseff	.10
78	Clyde Conner	.10
79	J.C. Caroline	.10
80	Howard Cassady	.30
81	Tobin Rote	.20
82	Ron Waller	.10
83	Jim Patton	.20
84	Volney Peters	.10
85	Dick "Night Train" Lane	.60
86	Royce Womble	.10
87	Duane Putnam	.10
88	Frank Gifford	3.00
89	Steve Meilinger	.10
90	Buck Lansford	.10
91	Lindon Crow	.10
92	Ernie Stautner	.75
93	Preston Carpenter	.20
94	Raymond Berry	1.50
95	Hugh McElhenny	1.00
96	Stan Jones	.50
97	Dorne Dibble	.10
98	Joe Scudero	.10
99	Eddie Bell	.10
100	Joe Childress	.10
101	Elbert Nickel	.10
102	Walt Michaels	.20
103	Jim Mutscheller	.10
104	Earl Morrall	.40
105	Larry Strickland	.10
106	Jack Christiansen	.75

107 Fred Cone .10
108 Bud McFadin .10
109 Charley Conerly 1.00
110 Tom Runnels .10
111 Ken Keller .10
112 James Root .10
113 Ted Marchibroda .30
114 Don Paul .10
115 George Shaw .20
116 Dick Moegle .20
117 Don Bingham .10
118 Leon Hart .20
119 Bart Starr 4.00
120 Paul Miller .10
121 Alex Webster .20
122 Ray Wietecha .10
123 Johnny Carson .10
124 Tommy McDonald .30
125 Jerry Tubbs .10
126 Jack Scarbath .10
127 Ed Modzelewski .10
128 Lenny Moore 1.00
129 Joe Perry 1.00
130 Bill Wightkin .10
131 Jim Doran .10
132 Howard Ferguson (UER) (Name misspelled Furgeson on front) .10
133 Tom Wilson .10
134 Dick James .10
135 Jimmy Harris .10
136 Chuck Ulrich .10
137 Lynn Chandnois .10
138 Johnny Unitas 5.00
139 Jim Ridlon .10
140 Zeke Bratkowski .20
141 Ray Krouse .10
142 John Martinkovic .10
143 Jim Cason .10
144 Ken MacAfee .20
145 Sid Youngelman .10
146 Paul Larson .10
147 Len Ford 1.00
148 Bob Toneff .10
149 Ronnie Knox .10
150 Jim David .10
151 Paul Hornung 4.00
152 Paul (Tank) Younger .30
153 Bill Svoboda .10
154 Fred Morrison .30

1994 Topps Archives 1957 Gold

The 154-card, standard-size set was issued as a gold parallel to the base 1957 reprint issue. The cards were randomly inserted into 1956/57 packs.

NM/M
Complete Set (154): 50.00
Common Player: .25
Gold Cards: 1.25X-2.5X

1995 Topps

Topps released its 1995 football set in two series - 248 cards in Series I and 220 in Series II. Each card is UV-coated and gold-foil stamped. Top free agents, hot draft picks, expansion team players, and Steve Young tribute cards are among the subsets in the set. 1,000 and 3,000 Yard Club theme cards are also part of the main set. A new addition to the regular cards is that Topps spotlights the player's achievements; if he led the conference in a statistical category, the stat is printed in red on the back (with a diamond added if he tied). Also on the horizontal card back, which is team color coordinated, are a closeup shot, stats, biographical information and a brief player profile. Inserts in Series I are Topps Finest, Finest Refractors, Hit List, Sensational Sophomores, Power Boosters and Yesteryear. An Instant Winner card was also randomly inserted at a rate of one per every 1,980 packs; the card entitles the finder to a complete 27-card Finest set with Finest Protectors. Series II inserts include: Air Raid, Finest Refractors, ProFiles, Power Boosters, Finest, and All-Pro.

NM/M
Complete Set (468): 45.00
Comp. Series 1 (248): 25.00
Comp. Series 2 (220): 20.00
Common Player: .05
Minor Stars: .10
Ser. 1 or 2 Hob. Pack (12): 1.50
Ser. 1 or 2 Hob. Wax Box (36): 30.00
Ser. 1 or 2 Ret. Pack (12): 1.00
Ser. 1 or 2 Ret. Wax Box (36): 30.00
1 Barry Sanders (1,000 Yard Club) .50
2 Chris Warren (1,000 Yard Club) .05
3 Jerry Rice (1,000 Yard Club) .50
4 Emmitt Smith (1,000 Yard Club) 1.00
5 Henry Ellard (1,000 Yard Club) .05
6 Natrone Means (1,000 Yard Club) .25
7 Terance Mathis (1,000 Yard Club) .05
8 Tim Brown (1,000 Yard Club) .05
9 Andre Reed (1,000 Yard Club) .05
10 Marshall Faulk (1,000 Yard Club) .20
11 Irving Fryar (1,000 Yard Club) .05
12 Cris Carter (1,000 Yard Club) .05
13 Michael Irvin (1,000 Yard Club) .10
14 Jake Reed (1,000 Yard Club) .05
15 Ben Coates (1,000 Yard Club) .05
16 Herman Moore (1,000 Yard Club) .05
17 Carl Pickens (1,000 Yard Club) .05
18 Fred Barnett (1,000 Yard Club) .05
19 Sterling Sharpe (1,000 Yard Club) .05
20 Anthony Miller (1,000 Yard Club) .05
21 Thurman Thomas (1,000 Yard Club) .10
22 Andre Rison (1,000 Yard Club) .10
23 Brian Blades (1,000 Yard Club) .05
24 Rodney Hampton (1,000 Yard Club) .05
25 Terry Allen (1,000 Yard Club) .05
26 Jerome Bettis (1,000 Yard Club) .25
27 Errict Rhett (1,000 Yard Club) .40
28 Rob Moore (1,000 Yard Club) .05
29 Shannon Sharpe (1,000 Yard Club) .05
30 Drew Bledsoe (3,000 Yard Club) .50
31 Dan Marino (3,000 Yard Club) 1.00
32 Warren Moon (3,000 Yard Club) .10
33 Steve Young (3,000 Yard Club) .25
34 Brett Favre (3,000 Yard Club) 1.00
35 Jim Everett (3,000 Yard Club) .05
36 Jeff George (3,000 Yard Club) .05
37 John Elway (3,000 Yard Club) .25
38 Jeff Hostetler (3,000 Yard Club) .05
39 Randall Cunningham (3,000 Yard Club) .10
40 Stan Humphries (3,000 Yard Club) .05
41 Jim Kelly (3,000 Yard Club) .10
42 Tommy Barnhardt .05
43 Bob Whitfield .05
44 William Thomas .05
45 Glyn Milburn .05
46 Steve Christie .05
47 Kevin Mawae .05
48 Vencie Glenn .05
49 Eric Curry .05
50 Jeff Hostetler .05
51 Tyronne Stowe .05
52 Steve Jackson .05
53 Ben Coleman .05
54 Brad Baxter .05
55 Darryl Williams .05
56 Troy Drayton .05
57 George Teague .05
58 Calvin Williams .05
59 Jeff Cross .05
60 Leroy Hoard .05
61 John Carney .05
62 Daryl Johnston .05
63 Jim Jeffcoat .05
64 Matt Stover .05
65 Leroy Butler .05
66 Curtis Conway .05
67 O.J. McDuffie .05
68 Robert Massey .05
69 Ed McDaniel .05
70 William Floyd .25
71 Willie Davis .05
72 William Roberts .05
73 Chester McGlockton .05
74 D.J. Johnson .05
75 Rondell Jones .05
76 Morten Andersen .05
77 Glenn Parker .05
78 William Fuller .05
79 Ray Buchanan .05
80 Maurice Hurst .05
81 Wayne Gandy .05
82 Marcus Turner .05
83 Greg Davis .05
84 Terry Wooden .05
85 Thomas Everett .05
86 Steve Broussard .05
87 Tom Carter .05
88 Glenn Montgomery .05
89 Larry Allen .05
90 Donnell Woolford .05
91 John Alt .05
92 Phil Hansen .05
93 Seth Joyner .05
94 Michael Brooks .05
95 Randall McDaniel .05
96 Tydus Winans .05
97 Rob Fredrickson .05
98 Ray Crockett .05
99 Courtney Hall .05
100 Merton Hanks .05
101 Aaron Glenn .05
102 Roosevelt Potts .05
103 Leon Lett .05
104 Jessie Tuggle .05
105 Martin Mayhew .05
106 William Roaf .05
107 Todd Lyght .05
108 Ernest Givins .05
109 Tony McGee .05
110 Barry Sanders 1.25
111 Dermontti Dawson .05
112 Rick Tuten .05
113 Vincent Brisby .05
114 Charlie Garner .05
115 Irving Fryar .05
116 Stevon Moore .05
117 Matt Darby .05
118 Howard Cross .05
119 John Gesek .05
120 Jack Del Rio .05
121 Marcus Allen .10
122 Torrance Small .05
123 Chris Mims .05
124 Don Mosebar .05
125 Carl Pickens .05
126 Tom Rouen .05
127 Garrison Hearst .10
128 Charles Johnson .25
129 Derek Brown .05
130 Troy Aikman .75
131 Troy Vincent .05
132 Ken Ruettgers .05
133 Michael Jackson .05
134 Dennis Gibson .05
135 Brett Perriman .05
136 Jeff Graham .05
137 Chad Brown .05
138 Ken Norton .05
139 Chris Slade .05
140 Dave Brown .05
141 Bert Emanuel .25
142 Renaldo Turnbull .05
143 Jim Harbaugh .05
144 Micheal Barrow .05
145 Vincent Brown .05
146 Bryant Young .05
147 Boomer Esiason .05
148 Sean Gilbert .05
149 Greg Truitt .05
150 Rod Woodson .05
151 Robert Porcher .05
152 Joe Phillips .05
153 Gary Zimmerman .05
154 Bruce Smith .05
155 Randall Cunningham .10
156 Fred Strickland .05
157 Derrick Alexander .25
158 James Williams .05
159 Scott Dill .05
160 Tim Bowens .05
161 Floyd Turner .05
162 Ronnie Harmon .05
163 Wayne Martin .05
164 John Randle .05
165 Larry Centers .05
166 Larry Brown .05
167 Albert Lewis .05
168 Michael Strahan .05
169 Reggie Brooks .05
170 Craig Heyward .05
171 Pat Harlow .05
172 Eugene Robinson .05
173 Shane Conlan .05
174 Bennie Blades .05
175 Neil O'Donnell .05
176 Steve Tovar .05
177 Donald Evans .05
178 Brent Jones .05
179 Ray Childress .05
180 Reggie White .05
181 David Alexander .05
182 Greg Hill .25
183 Vinny Testaverde .05
184 Jeff Burris .05
185 Hardy Nickerson .05
186 Terry Kirby .05
187 Kirk Lowdermilk .05
188 Eric Swann .05
189 Chris Zorich .05
190 Simon Fletcher .05
191 Qadry Ismail .05
192 Heath Shuler .50
193 Michael Haynes .05
194 Mike Sherrard .05
195 Nolan Harrison .05
196 Marcus Robertson .05
197 Kevin Williams .05
198 Moe Gardner .05
199 Rick Mirer .40
200 Junior Seau .10
201 Byron Morris .10
202 Willie McGinest .05
203 Chris Spielman .05
204 Darnay Scott .40
205 Jesse Sapolu .05
206 Marvin Washington .05
207 Anthony Newman .05
208 Cortez Kennedy .10
209 Quentin Coryatt .05
210 Neil Smith .05
211 Keith Sims .05
212 Sean Jones .05
213 Tony Jones .05
214 Lewis Tillman .05
215 Darren Woodson .05
216 Jason Hanson .05
217 John Taylor .05
218 Shawn Lee .05
219 Kevin Greene .05
220 Jerry Rice .75
221 *Ki-Jana Carter* .30
222 *Tony Boselli* .10
223 *Michael Westbrook* 1.00
224 *Kerry Collins* 1.00
225 *Kevin Carter* .10
226 *Kyle Brady* .10
227 *J.J. Stokes* 1.00
228 *Derrick Alexander* .10
229 *Warren Sapp* .75
230 *Ruben Brown* .10
231 *Hugh Douglas* .10
232 *Luther Elliss* .10
233 *Rashaan Salaam* .30
234 *Tyrone Poole* .10
235 *Korey Stringer* .10
236 *Devin Bush* .10
237 *Cory Raymer* .10
238 *Zach Wiegert* .10
239 *Ron Davis* .10
240 *Todd Collins* .10
241 *Bobby Taylor* .10
242 *Patrick Riley* .10
243 *Scott Gragg* .10
244 *Marvcus Patton* .05
245 Alvin Harper .05
246 Ricky Watters .10
247 Checklist 1 of 2 .05
248 Checklist 2 of 2 .05
249 Terance Mathis .05
250 Mark Carrier .05
251 Elijah Alexander .05
252 George Koonce .05
253 Tony Bennett .05
254 Steve Wisniewski .05
255 Bernie Parmalee .20
256 Dwayne Sabb .05
257 Lorenzo Neal .05
258 Corey Miller .05
259 Fred Barnett .05
260 Greg Lloyd .05
261 Robert Blackmon .05
262 Ken Harvey .05
263 Eric Hill .05
264 Russell Copeland .05
265 *Jeff Blake* .30
266 Carl Banks .05
267 Jay Novacek .05
268 Mel Gray .05
269 Kimble Anders .05
270 Cris Carter .10
271 Johnny Mitchell .05
272 Shawn Jefferson .05
273 Doug Brien .05
274 Sean Landeta .05
275 Scott Mitchell .10
276 Charles Wilson .05
277 Anthony Smith .05
278 Anthony Miller .05
279 Steve Walsh .05
280 Drew Bledsoe .75
281 Jamir Miller .05
282 Robert Brooks .10
283 Sean Lumpkin .05
284 Bryan Cox .05
285 Byron Evans .05
286 Chris Doleman .05
287 Anthony Pleasant .05
288 Steve Grant .05
289 Doug Riesenberg .05
290 Natrone Means .40
291 Henry Thomas .05
292 Mike Pritchard .05
293 Courtney Hawkins .05
294 Bill Bates .05
295 Jerome Bettis .20
296 Russell Maryland .05
297 Stanley Richard .05
298 William White .05
299 Dan Wilkinson .05
300 Steve Young .75
301 Gary Brown .05
302 Jake Reed .05
303 Carlton Gray .05
304 Levon Kirkland .05
305 Shannon Sharpe .05
306 Luis Sharpe .05
307 Marshall Faulk .50
308 Stan Humphries .10
309 Chris Calloway .05
310 Tim Brown .10
311 Steve Everitt .05
312 Raymont Harris .05
313 Tim McDonald .05
314 Trent Dilfer .25
315 Jim Everett .05
316 Ray Crittenden .05
317 Jim Kelly .10
318 Andre Reed .05
319 Chris Miller .05
320 Bobby Houston .05
321 Charles Haley .05
322 James Francis .05
323 Bernard Williams .05
324 Michael Bates .05
325 Brian Mitchell .05
326 Mike Johnson .05
327 Eric Bieniemy .05
328 Aubrey Beavers .05
329 Dale Carter .05
330 Emmitt Smith 2.00
331 Darren Perry .05
332 Marquez Pope .05
333 Clyde Simmons .05
334 Corey Croom .05
335 Thomas Randolph .05
336 Harvey Williams .05
337 Michael Timpson .05
338 Eugene Daniel .05
339 Shane Dronett .05
340 Eric Turner .05
341 Eric Metcalf .05
342 Leslie O'Neal .05
343 Mark Wheeler .05
344 Mark Pike .05
345 Brett Favre 2.00
346 Johnny Bailey .05
347 Henry Ellard .05
348 Chris Gardocki .05
349 Henry Jones .05
350 Dan Marino 2.00
351 Lake Dawson .20
352 Mark McMillian .05
353 Deion Sanders .40
354 Antonio London .05
355 Cris Dishman .05
356 Ricardo McDonald .05
357 Dexter Carter .05
358 Kevin Smith .05
359 *Yancey Thigpen* .30
360 Chris Warren .10
361 Quinn Early .05
362 John Mangum .05
363 Santana Dotson .05
364 Raghib Ismail .05
365 Aeneas Williams .05
366 Dan Williams .05
367 Sean Dawkins .05
368 Pepper Johnson .05
369 Roman Phifer .05
370 Rodney Hampton .05
371 Darrell Green .05
372 Michael Zordich .05
373 Andre Coleman .05
374 Wayne Simmons .05
375 Michael Irvin .20
376 Clay Matthews .05
377 Dewayne Washington .05
378 Keith Byars .05
379 Todd Collins .25
380 Mark Collins .05
381 Joel Steed .05
382 Bart Oates .05
383 Al Smith .05
384 Rafael Robinson .05
385 Mo Lewis .05
386 Aubrey Matthews .05
387 Corey Sawyer .05
388 Bucky Brooks .05
389 Erik Kramer .05
390 Tyrone Hughes .05
391 Terry McDaniel .05
392 Craig Erickson .05
393 Mike Flores .05
394 Harry Swayne .05
395 Irving Spikes .05
396 Lorenzo Lynch .05
397 Antonio Langham .05
398 Edgar Bennett .05
399 Thomas Lewis .05
400 John Elway .30
401 Jeff George .10
402 Errict Rhett .75
403 Bill Romanowski .05
404 Alexander Wright .05
405 Warren Moon .10
406 Eddie Robinson .05
407 John Copeland .05
408 Robert Jones .05
409 Steve Bono .15
410 Cornelius Bennett .05
411 Ben Coates .05
412 Dana Stubblefield .05
413 Darryl Talley .05
414 Brian Blades .05
415 Herman Moore .20
416 Nick Lowery .05
417 Donnell Bennett .05
418 Van Malone .05
419 Pete Stoyanovich .05
420 Joe Montana 1.25
421 Steve Young (Steve Young Subset Cards) .30
422 Steve Young (Steve Young Subset Cards) .30
423 Steve Young (Steve Young Subset Cards) .30
424 Steve Young (Steve Young Subset Cards) .30
425 Steve Young (Steve Young Subset Cards) .30
426 Rod Stephens .05
427 *Ellis Johnson* (Draft Picks) .10
428 *Kordell Stewart* (Draft Picks) 2.00
429 *James Stewart* (Draft Picks) 1.50
430 *Steve McNair* (Draft Picks) 3.00
431 *Brian DeMarco* (Draft Picks) .10
432 *Matt O'Dwyer* (Draft Picks) .10
433 *Lorenzo Styles* (Draft Picks) .10
434 *Anthony Cook* (Draft Picks) .20
435 *Jesse James* (Draft Picks) .10
436 *Darryl Pounds* (Draft Picks) .10
437 Derrick Graham (Carolina Panther Team) .05
438 Vernon Turner (Carolina Panther Team) .05
439 Carlton Bailey (Carolina Panther Team) .05
440 Darion Conner (Carolina Panther Team) .05
441 Randy Baldwin (Carolina Panther Team) .05
442 Tim McKyer (Carolina Panther Team) .05
443 Sam Mills (Carolina Panther Team) .05
444 Bob Christian (Carolina Panther Team) .05
445 Steve Lofton (Carolina Panther Team) .05
446 Lamar Lathon (Carolina Panther Team) .05
447 Tony Smith (Carolina Panther Team) .05
448 Don Beebe (Carolina Panther Team) .05
449 Barry Foster (Carolina Panther Team) .05
450 Frank Reich (Carolina Panther Team) .05
451 Pete Metzelaars (Carolina Panther Team) .05
452 Reggie Cobb (Jacksonville Jaguar Expansion Team) .05
453 Jeff Lageman (Jacksonville Jaguar Expansion Team) .05
454 Derek Brown (Jacksonville Jaguar Expansion Team) .05
455 Desmond Howard (Jacksonville Jaguar Expansion Team) .05
456 Vinnie Clark (Jacksonville Jaguar Expansion Team) .05
457 Keith Goganious (Jacksonville Jaguar Expansion Team) .05
458 Shawn Bouwens (Jacksonville Jaguar Expansion Team) .05
459 *Rob Johnson* (Jacksonville Jaguar Expansion Team) 1.00
460 Steve Beuerlein (Jacksonville Jaguar Expansion Team) .05
461 Mark Brunell (Jacksonville Jaguar Expansion Team) 1.00
462 Harry Colon (Jacksonville Jaguar Expansion Team) .05
463 Chris Hudson (Jacksonville Jaguar Expansion Team) .05
464 Darren Carrington (Jacksonville Jaguar Expansion Team) .05
465 Ernest Givins (Jacksonville Jaguar Expansion Team) .05
466 Kelvin Pritchett (Jacksonville Jaguar Expansion Team) .05
467 Checklist 3 of 4 .05
468 Checklist 4 of 4 .05

1995 Topps Air Raid

These 10 1995-96 Topps football inserts utilize the dynamic Power Matrix technology to highlight the best NFL wide receiver/quarterback tandems. The cards were random inserts in every 24th pack of Series II product, retail packs only.

NM/M
Complete Set (10): 25.00
Common Player: 1.00
1 Steve Young, Jerry Rice 4.00
2 Warren Moon, Cris Carter 1.00
3 Jeff George, Terance Mathis 1.00
4 Dave Brown, Mike Sherrard 1.00
5 Drew Bledsoe, Ben Coates 3.00
6 John Elway, Shannon Sharpe 3.00
7 Jeff Blake, Carl Pickens 1.00
8 Dan Marino, Irving Fryar 4.00
9 Randall Cunningham, Fred Barnett 1.00
10 Troy Aikman, Michael Irvin 3.00

1995 Topps All-Pros

Twenty-two players who personify the best in the game are captured on these all-silver foil cards, exclusive inserts in 1995-96 Topps Seires II hobby packs. The cards are seeded one per every eight packs.

NM/M
Complete Set (22): 15.00
Common Player: .40
1 Jerry Rice 3.00
2 Lomas Brown .40
3 Nate Newton .40
4 Dermontti Dawson .40
5 Keith Sims .40

No.	Player	NM/M
6	Richmond Webb	.40
7	Shannon Sharpe	.40
8	Michael Irvin	.40
9	Steve Young	3.00
10	Barry Sanders	3.00
11	Marshall Faulk	2.00
12	Bruce Smith	.40
13	Dana Stubblefield	.40
14	John Randle	.40
15	Reggie White	.40
16	Greg Lloyd	.40
17	Junior Seau	.40
18	Cornelius Bennett	.40
19	Rod Woodson	.40
20	Deion Sanders	1.00
21	Darren Woodson	.40
22	Merton Hanks	.40

1995 Topps Expansion Team Boosters

The 20-card, standard-size set was randomly inserted every 36 Series II packs and is a parallel version of the expansion subset in Series II. The cards are printed on 28-point stock with diffraction foil.

No.	Player	NM/M
	Complete Set (30):	30.00
	Common Player:	.50
437	Derrick Graham	.50
438	Vernon Turner	.50
439	Carlton Bailey	.50
440	Darion Conner	.50
441	Randy Baldwin	.50
442	Tim McKyer	.50
443	Sam Mills	1.00
444	Bob Christian	.50
445	Steve Lofton	.50
446	Lamar Lathon	.50
447	Tony Smith (RB)	.50
448	Don Beebe	1.00
449	Barry Foster	.50
450	Frank Reich	1.00
451	Pete Metzelaars	.50
452	Reggie Cobb	.50
453	Jeff Lageman	.50
454	Derek Brown (TE)	.50
455	Desmond Howard	1.00
456	Vinnie Clark	.50
457	Keith Goganious	.50
458	Shawn Bowens	.50
459	Rob Johnson	1.00
460	Steve Beuerlein	.50
461	Mark Brunell	3.00
462	Harry Colon	.50
463	Chris Hudson	.50
464	Darren Carrington	1.00
465	Ernest Givins	1.00
466	Kelvin Pritchett	.50

1995 Topps Finest Inserts

Topps added a little mystery to its 1995-96 football set when it created its Series I Finest insert cards. The cards, seeded one per every 36 packs, have black opaque protectors over them instead of the clear protectors. This means that collectors have to peel off the protector to see what card they have. They will, however, be able to determine what position the player plays; three different card backs, which are visible, were made - for quarterbacks, wide receivers and running backs. The card could even be a Refractor version; this is a parallel set which has cards seeded one per every 36 hobby packs or 432 retail packs. In addition, an Instant Winner card was inserted at a rate of one per every 1,980 packs. The card entitles the finder to a complete 27-card set with clear Finest protectors.

	NM/M
Complete Set (27):	45.00
Common Player:	.50
Minor Stars:	1.00
Refractors:	1X-2X
Troy Aikman	3.00
Stan Humphries	.50
Dan Marino	5.00
Brett Favre	5.00
Steve Young	3.00
Jim Kelly	1.00
John Elway	3.00
Warren Moon	1.00
Drew Bledsoe	3.00
Barry Sanders	4.00
Natrone Means	1.00
Ricky Watters	1.00
Chris Warren	.50
Marshall Faulk	2.00
Jerome Bettis	.50
Rodney Hampton	.50
Errict Rhett	1.00
Emmitt Smith	4.00
Jerry Rice	4.00
Andre Reed	.50
Irving Fryar	.50
Herman Moore	.50
Tim Brown	.50
Terance Mathis	.50
Henry Ellard	.50
Michael Irvin	1.00
Cris Carter	.50

1995 Topps Finest Boosters

These cards were random inserts in 1995 Topps Series II packs. They are numbered B166-B187.

No.	Player	NM/M
	Complete Set (22):	40.00
	Common Player:	1.00
	Refractors:	1X-2X
166	Barry Sanders	4.00
167	Bryant Young	1.00
168	Boomer Esiason	1.00
169	Terance Mathis	1.00
170	Troy Aikman	3.00
171	Junior Seau	1.00
172	Rodney Hampton	1.00
173	Jim Everett	1.00
174	Dan Marino	5.00
175	Steve Young	3.00
176	Cris Carter	1.00
177	Eric Swann	1.00
178	Rick Mirer	1.00
179	Jerome Bettis	2.00
180	Emmitt Smith	4.00
181	Jim Kelly	1.00
182	John Elway	3.00
183	Dana Stubblefield	1.00
184	Drew Bledsoe	3.00
185	Jerry Rice	4.00
186	Michael Irvin	1.00
187	Bruce Smith	1.00

1995 Topps Florida Hot Bed

The 15-card standard-size set was inserted in each retail pack amd features top players who attended a Florida college. The card fronts depict a map outline of Florida with "Florida Hot Bed" printed in orange at the top. The player and team name are in gold foil near the card bottom. The card backs are numbered with the "FH" prefix and contain a player headshot with a commentary on his NFL career over a water background.

No.	Player	NM/M
	Complete Set (15):	10.00
	Common Player:	.40
1	Deion Sanders	1.00
2	Brian Blades	.40
3	Errict Rhett	.75
4	Kevin Williams	.40
5	Cortez Kennedy	.40
6	Corey Sawyer	.40
7	Russell Maryland	.40
8	Emmitt Smith	3.00
9	Vinny Testaverde	.40
10	William Floyd	.75
11	Brett Perriman	.40
12	Nate Newton	.40
13	Jim Kelly	1.50
14	LeRoy Butler	.40
15	Michael Irvin	1.00

1995 Topps Hit List

Hit List features 20 of the hardest most feared defenders in the league. Topps uses a stone-crushing design for the cards, which were inserts in 1995-96 Topps football Series I packs. They are seeded one per every four packs, making them the most common of the inserts.

No.	Player	NM/M
	Complete Set (20):	10.00
	Common Player:	.50
	Minor Stars:	1.00
1	Pepper Johnson	.50
2	Elijah Alexander	.50
3	Joe Cain	.50
4	Andre Collins	.50
5	Chris Spielman	.50
6	Bryan Cox	.50
7	Ed McDaniel	.50
8	Jack Del Rio	.50
9	Jeff Herrod	.50
10	Greg Lloyd	1.00
11	Reggie White	1.50
12	Robert Jones	.50
13	Eric Turner	.50
14	Vincent Brown	.50
15	Kevin Greene	.50
16	Bruce Smith	1.00
17	Hardy Nickerson	.50
18	Seth Joyner	.50
19	Darryl Talley	.50
20	Junior Seau	1.50

1995 Topps 1000/3000 Boosters

This Power Boosters set is a parallel set of the 1,000- and 3,000-Yard Club subset cards found in Topps 1995 Series I. Each card is "boosted" up to 28-point stock on a dynamic full foil board stock. A Power Boosters card replaces two regular cards in every 36th pack.

No.	Player	NM/M
	Complete Set (41):	45.00
	Common Player:	.50
1	Barry Sanders	4.00
2	Chris Warren	.50
3	Jerry Rice	3.00
4	Emmitt Smith	4.00
5	Henry Ellard	.50
6	Natrone Means	.50
7	Terance Mathis	.50
8	Tim Brown	1.00
9	Andre Reed	.50
10	Marshall Faulk	2.00
11	Irving Fryar	.50
12	Cris Carter	.50
13	Michael Irvin	.50
14	Jake Reed	.50
15	Ben Coates	.50
16	Herman Moore	.50
17	Carl Pickens	.50
18	Fred Barnett	.50
19	Sterling Sharpe	.50
20	Anthony Miller	.50
21	Thurman Thomas	.50
22	Andre Rison	.50
23	Brian Blades	.50
24	Rodney Hampton	.50
25	Terry Allen	.50
26	Jerome Bettis	.50
27	Errict Rhett	.50
28	Rob Moore	.50
29	Shannon Sharpe	.50
30	Drew Bledsoe	3.00
31	Dan Marino	5.00
32	Warren Moon	.50
33	Steve Young	3.00
34	Brett Favre	5.00
35	Jim Everett	.50
36	Jeff George	.50
37	John Elway	3.00
38	Jeff Hostetler	.50
39	Randall Cunningham	.50
40	Stan Humphries	.50
41	Jim Kelly	.50

A card number in parenthese ( ) indicates the set is unnumbered.

1995 Topps Profiles

Topps' spokesman, San Francisco 49ers quarterback Steve Young, lends his insights and unique observations of 15 key players for this 1995-96 Topps Series II insert set. These all-silver foil cards are inserted at a rate of one per every 12th pack.

No.	Player	NM/M
	Complete Set (15):	15.00
	Common Player:	.50
1	Emmitt Smith	3.00
2	Chris Spielman	.50
3	Rod Woodson	.50
4	Deion Sanders	1.00
5	Junior Seau	.50
6	Byron Evans	.50
7	Jerome Bettis	.50
8	Charles Haley	.50
9	Jerry Rice	3.00
10	Barry Sanders	3.00
11	Hardy Nickerson	.50
12	Natrone Means	.50
13	Darren Woodson	.50
14	Reggie White	.50
15	Troy Aikman	2.00

1995 Topps Sensational Sophomores

Ten of the hottest 1994 rookies, including Rookie of the Year Marshall Faulk, comprise this 1995-96 Topps Series I insert set. The cards, printed with Dot Matrix technology, are inserted at a rate of one per every 24 packs and are found exclusively in retail packs.

No.	Player	NM/M
	Complete Set (10):	5.00
	Common Player:	.50
1	Marshall Faulk	2.00
2	Heath Shuler	.50
3	Tim Bowens	.50
4	Bryant Young	.50
5	Dan Wilkinson	.50
6	Errict Rhett	.50
7	Andre Coleman	.50
8	Aaron Glenn	.50
9	Trent Dilfer	1.00
10	Byron Morris	.50

1995 Topps Yesteryear

The 15 players who make up this 1995-96 Topps football Series I insert set have not only survived the test but have risen to the top. Each card, printed using Finest technology, features past and present photos and compares the player's rookie season to the previous one. Cards were random inserts, one per every 72 hobby packs.

No.	Player	NM/M
	Complete Set (15):	25.00
	Common Player:	.50
1	Stan Humphries	.50
2	Dan Marino	5.00
3	Irving Fryar	.50
4	Warren Moon	.50
5	Steve Young	3.00
6	Kevin Greene	.50
7	Jeff Hostetler	.50
8	Jack Del Rio	.50
9	Reggie White	.50
10	Jerry Rice	4.00
11	Bruce Smith	.50
12	Rod Woodson	.50
13	Deion Sanders	1.00
14	Barry Sanders	4.00
15	Brett Favre	5.00

1995 Topps Factory Jaguars

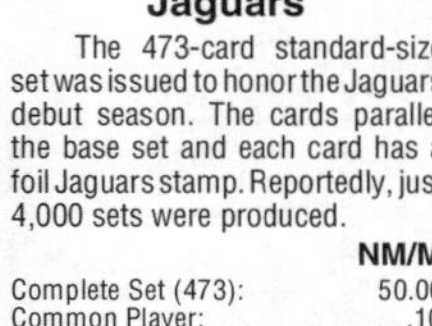

The 473-card standard-size set was issued to honor the Jaguars debut season. The cards parallel the base set and each card has a foil Jaguars stamp. Reportedly, just 4,000 sets were produced.

	NM/M
Complete Set (473):	50.00
Common Player:	.10
Veteran Stars:	.75X-1.5X
Young Stars:	.6X-1.25X

1995 Topps Factory Panthers

The 473-card standard-size set was issued to commemorate the Panthers debut season. The set parallels the base set with card having a foil Carolina stamp. Reportedly, there were just 4,000 sets produced.

	NM/M
Complete Set (473):	50.00
Common Player:	.10
Veteran Stars:	.75X-1.5X
Young Stars:	.6X-1.25X

1996 Topps Promos

This six-card promo set was sent to dealers and media to provide a sneak peak at the designs for 1996 Topps Football. It arrived in a clear, cello pack containing all six cards.

No.	Player	NM/M
	Complete Set (6):	8.00
	Common Player:	1.00
35	Quentin Coryatt	1.00
50	Kerry Collins	2.00
60	Mark Brunell	3.00
73	Mark Carrier	1.00
145	Mel Gray	1.00
405	Ben Coates	1.00

1996 Topps

Topps 1996 set marks the 40th year the company has been in football. To commemorate that milestone, Broadway Joe Namath, the New York Jets quarterback, who guaranteed a victory in the Super Bowl in 1969, guarantees this set is Topps best ever. As a tribute to Namath, Topps features him in a 10-card insert set which reprints his 10 Topps cards (1 in 18 packs). He also reviews 10 active NFL quarterbacks for his "Broadway's Reviews" insert set. A 40th Anniversary insert set features 40 of today's top stars pictured on original Topps card designs (one for every year). Other inserts include Turf Warriors, Hobby Masters, a Sweepstakes card (1 in 108 packs), which entitles the finder to one of the 40 sets made during the last 40 years, or all 40, if you're the grand prize winner). The regular 1996 Topps set has 440 cards in it. Each front has a color photo on it, with the player's name, position and team at the bottom between two parallel bars. Topps 40th Anniversary logo is also stamped on each card.

No.	Player	NM/M
	Complete Set (440):	35.00
	Common Player:	.05
	Minor Stars:	.10
	Pack (11):	2.25
	Wax Box (36):	55.00
1	Troy Aikman	1.00
2	Kevin Greene	.05
3	Robert Brooks	.05
4	Eugene Daniel	.05
5	Rodney Peete	.05
6	James Hasty	.05
7	Tim McDonald	.05
8	Darick Holmes	.05
9	Morten Andersen	.05
10	Junior Seau	.05
11	Brett Perriman	.05
12	Eric Green	.05
13	Jim Flanigan	.05
14	Cortez Kennedy	.05
15	Orlando Thomas	.05
16	Anthony Miller	.05
17	Sean Gilbert	.05
18	Rob Fredrickson	.05
19	Willie Green	.05
20	Jeff Blake	.50
21	Trent Dilfer	.05
22	Chris Chandler	.05
23	Renaldo Turnbull	.05
24	David Meggett	.05
25	Heath Shuler	.40
26	Michael Jackson	.05
27	Thomas Randolph	.05
28	Keith Goganious	.05
29	Seth Joyner	.05
30	Wayne Chrebet	.05
31	Craig Newsome	.05
32	William Fuller	.05
33	Merton Hanks	.05
34	Dale Carter	.05
35	Quentin Coryatt	.05
36	Robert Jones	.05
37	Eric Metcalf	.05
38	Byron Morris	.05
39	Bill Brooks	.05
40	Barry Sanders	2.00
41	Michael Haynes	.05
42	Joey Galloway	.50
43	Robert Smith	.05
44	John Thierry	.05
45	Bryan Cox	.05
46	Anthony Parker	.05
47	Harvey Williams	.05
48	Terrell Davis	3.00
49	Darnay Scott	.10
50	Kerry Collins	.25
51	Cris Dishman	.05
52	Dwayne Harper	.05
53	Warren Sapp	.05
54	Will Moore	.05
55	Earnest Byner	.05
56	Aaron Glenn	.05
57	Michael Westbrook	.50
58	Vencie Glenn	.05
59	Rob Moore	.05
60	Mark Brunell	.75
61	Craig Heyward	.05
62	Eric Allen	.05
63	Bill Romanowski	.05
64	Dana Stubblefield	.05
65	Steve Bono	.05
66	George Koonce	.05
67	Larry Brown	.05
68	Warren Moon	.05
69	Erric Pegram	.05
70	Jim Kelly	.05
71	Jason Belser	.05
72	Henry Thomas	.05
73	Mark Carrier	.05
74	Terry Wooden	.05
75	Terry McDaniel	.05
76	O.J. McDuffie	.05
77	Dan Wilkinson	.05
78	Blake Brockermeyer	.05
79	Micheal Barrow	.05
80	Dave Brown	.05
81	Todd Lyght	.05
82	Henry Ellard	.05
83	Jeff Lageman	.05
84	Anthony Pleasant	.05
85	Aeneas Williams	.05
86	Vincent Brisby	.05
87	Terrell Fletcher	.05
88	Brad Baxter	.05
89	Shannon Sharpe	.05
90	Errict Rhett	.20
91	Michael Zordich	.05
92	Dan Saleaumua	.05
93	Devin Bush	.05
94	Wayne Simmons	.05
95	Tyrone Hughes	.05
96	John Randle	.05
97	Tony Tolbert	.05
98	Yancey Thigpen	.40
99	J.J. Stokes	.50
100	Marshall Faulk	.40
101	Barry Minter	.05
102	Glenn Foley	.05
103	Chester McGlockton	.05
104	Carlton Gray	.05
105	Terry Kirby	.05
106	Darryll Lewis	.05
107	Thomas Smith	.05
108	Mike Fox	.05
109	Antonio Langham	.05
110	Drew Bledsoe	1.00
111	Troy Drayton	.05
112	Marcus Patton	.05
113	Tyrone Wheatley	.05
114	Desmond Howard	.05
115	Johnny Mitchell	.05
116	Dave Krieg	.05

#	Player	Price
117	Natrone Means	.15
118	Herman Moore	.20
119	Darren Woodson	.05
120	Ricky Watters	.05
121	Emmitt Smith (1,000 Yard Club)	1.00
122	Barry Sanders (1,000 Yard Club)	.50
123	Curtis Martin (1,000 Yard Club)	.75
124	Chris Warren (1,000 Yard Club)	.05
125	Terry Allen (1,000 Yard Club)	.05
126	Ricky Watters (1,000 Yard Club)	.05
127	Errict Rhett (1,000 Yard Club)	.40
128	Rodney Hampton (1,000 Yard Club)	.05
129	Terrell Davis (1,000 Yard Club)	.50
130	Harvey Williams (1,000 Yard Club)	.05
131	Craig Heyward (1,000 Yard Club)	.05
132	Marshall Faulk (1,000 Yard Club)	.40
133	Rashaan Salaam (1,000 Yard Club)	.25
134	Garrison Hearst (1,000 Yard Club)	.05
135	Edgar Bennett (1,000 Yard Club)	.05
136	Thurman Thomas (1,000 Yard Club)	.05
137	Brian Washington	.05
138	Derek Loville	.05
139	Curtis Conway	.05
140	Isaac Bruce	.25
141	Ricardo McDonald	.05
142	Bruce Armstrong	.05
143	Will Wolford	.05
144	Thurman Thomas	.10
145	Mel Gray	.05
146	Napoleon Kaufman	.20
147	Terry Allen	.05
148	Chris Calloway	.05
149	Harry Colon	.05
150	Pepper Johnson	.05
151	Marco Coleman	.05
152	Shawn Jefferson	.05
153	Larry Centers	.05
154	Lamar Lathon	.05
155	Mark Chmura	.20
156	Dermontti Dawson	.05
157	Alvin Harper	.05
158	Randall McDaniel	.05
159	Allen Aldridge	.05
160	Chris Warren	.10
161	Jessie Tuggle	.05
162	Sean Lumpkin	.05
163	Bobby Houston	.05
164	Dexter Carter	.05
165	Erik Kramer	.05
166	Brock Marion	.05
167	Toby Wright	.05
168	John Copeland	.05
169	Sean Dawkins	.05
170	Tim Brown	.05
171	Darion Conner	.05
172	Aaron Hayden	.05
173	Charlie Garner	.05
174	Anthony Cook	.05
175	Derrick Thomas	.05
176	Willie McGinest	.05
177	Thomas Lewis	.05
178	Sherman Williams	.05
179	Cornelius Bennett	.05
180	Frank Sanders	.05
181	Leroy Hoard	.05
182	Bernie Parmalee	.05
183	Sterling Palmer	.05
184	Kelvin Pritchett	.05
185	Kordell Stewart	1.00
186	Brent Jones	.05
187	Robert Blackmon	.05
188	Adrian Murrell	.05
189	Edgar Bennett	.05
190	Rashaan Salaam	.50
191	Ellis Johnson	.05
192	Andre Coleman	.05
193	Will Shields	.05
194	Derrick Brooks	.05
195	Carl Pickens	.10
196	Carlton Bailey	.05
197	Terance Mathis	.05
198	Carlos Jenkins	.05
199	Derrick Alexander	.05
200	Deion Sanders	.40
201	Glyn Milburn	.05
202	Chris Sanders	.25
203	Raghib Ismail	.05
204	Fred Barnett	.05
205	Quinn Early	.05
206	Henry Jones	.05
207	Herschel Walker	.05
208	James Washington	.05
209	Lee Woodall	.05
210	Neil Smith	.05
211	Tony Bennett	.05
212	Ernie Mills	.05
213	Clyde Simmons	.05
214	Chris Slade	.05
215	Tony Boselli	.05
216	Ryan McNeil	.05
217	Rob Burnett	.05
218	Stan Humphries	.05
219	Rick Mirer	.05
220	Troy Vincent	.05
221	Sean Jones	.05
222	Marty Carter	.05
223	Boomer Esiason	.05
224	Charles Haley	.05
225	Sam Mills	.05
226	Greg Biekert	.05
227	Bryant Young	.05
228	Ken Dilger	.05
229	Levon Kirkland	.05
230	Brian Mitchell	.05
231	Hardy Nickerson	.05
232	Elvis Grbac	.05
233	Kurt Schulz	.05
234	Chris Doleman	.05
235	Tamarick Vanover	.50
236	Jesse Campbell	.05
237	William Thomas	.05
238	Shane Conlan	.05
239	Jason Elam	.05
240	Steve McNair	.50
241	Jerry Rice (1,000 Yard Club)	.50
242	Isaac Bruce (1,000 Yard Club)	.30
243	Herman Moore (1,000 Yard Club)	.05
244	Michael Irvin (1,000 Yard Club)	.05
245	Robert Brooks (1,000 Yard Club)	.05
246	Brett Perriman (1,000 Yard Club)	.05
247	Cris Carter (1,000 Yard Club)	.05
248	Tim Brown (1,000 Yard Club)	.05
249	Yancey Thigpen (1,000 Yard Club)	.20
250	Jeff Graham (1,000 Yard Club)	.05
251	Carl Pickens (1,000 Yard Club)	.05
252	Tony Martin (1,000 Yard Club)	.05
253	Eric Metcalf (1,000 Yard Club)	.05
254	Jake Reed (1,000 Yard Club)	.05
255	Quinn Early (1,000 Yard Club)	.05
256	Anthony Miller (1,000 Yard Club)	.05
257	Joey Galloway (1,000 Yard Club)	.25
258	Bert Emanuel (1,000 Yard Club)	.05
259	Terance Mathis (1,000 Yard Club)	.05
260	Curtis Conway (1,000 Yard Club)	.05
261	Henry Ellard (1,000 Yard Club)	.05
262	Mark Carrier (1,000 Yard Club)	.05
263	Brian Blades (1,000 Yard Club)	.05
264	William Roaf	.05
265	Ed McDaniel	.05
266	Nate Newton	.05
267	Brett Maxie	.05
268	Anthony Smith	.05
269	Mickey Washington	.05
270	Jerry Rice	1.00
271	Shaun Gayle	.05
272	Gilbert Brown	.05
273	Mark Bruener	.05
274	Eugene Robinson	.05
275	Marvin Washington	.05
276	Keith Sims	.05
277	Ashley Ambrose	.05
278	Garrison Hearst	.05
279	Donnell Woolford	.05
280	Cris Carter	.05
281	Curtis Martin	1.50
282	Scott Mitchell	.05
283	Stevon Moore	.05
284	Roman Phifer	.05
285	Ken Harvey	.05
286	Rodney Hampton	.05
287	Willie Davis	.05
288	Yonel Jourdain	.05
289	Brian DeMarco	.05
290	Reggie White	.05
291	Kevin Williams	.05
292	Gary Plummer	.05
293	Terrance Shaw	.05
294	Calvin Williams	.05
295	Eddie Robinson	.05
296	Tony McGee	.05
297	Clay Matthews	.05
298	Joe Cain	.05
299	Tim McKyer	.05
300	Greg Lloyd	.05
301	Steve Wisniewski	.05
302	Ray Buchanan	.05
303	Lake Dawson	.05
304	Kevin Carter	.05
305	Phillippi Sparks	.05
306	Emmitt Smith	2.00
307	Ruben Brown	.05
308	Tom Carter	.05
309	William Floyd	.05
310	Jim Everett	.05
311	Vincent Brown	.05
312	Dennis Gibson	.05
313	Lorenzo Lynch	.05
314	Corey Harris	.05
315	James Stewart	.05
316	Kyle Brady	.05
317	Irving Fryar	.05
318	Jake Reed	.05
319	Vinny Testaverde	.05
320	John Elway	.30
321	Tracy Scroggins	.05
322	Chris Spielman	.05
323	Horace Copeland	.05
324	Chris Zorich	.05
325	Mike Mamula	.05
326	Henry Ford	.05
327	Steve Walsh	.05
328	Stanley Richard	.05
329	Mike Jones	.05
330	Jim Harbaugh	.05
331	Darren Perry	.05
332	Ken Norton	.05
333	Kimble Anders	.05
334	Harold Green	.05
335	Tyrone Poole	.05
336	Mark Fields	.05
337	Darren Bennett	.05
338	Mike Sherrard	.05
339	Terry Ray	.05
340	Bruce Smith	.05
341	Daryl Johnston	.05
342	Vinnie Clark	.05
343	Mike Caldwell	.05
344	Vinson Smith	.05
345	Mo Lewis	.05
346	Brian Blades	.05
347	Rod Stephens	.05
348	David Palmer	.05
349	Blaine Bishop	.05
350	Jeff George	.05
351	George Teague	.05
352	Jeff Hostetler	.05
353	Michael Strahan	.05
354	Eric Davis	.05
355	Jerome Bettis	.05
356	Irv Smith	.05
357	Jeff Herrod	.05
358	Jay Novacek	.05
359	Bryce Paup	.05
360	Neil O'Donnell	.05
361	Eric Swann	.05
362	Corey Sawyer	.05
363	Ty Law	.05
364	Bo Orlando	.05
365	Marcus Allen	.05
366	Mark McMillian	.05
367	Mark Carrier	.05
368	Jackie Harris	.05
369	Steve Atwater	.05
370	Steve Young	1.00
371	Brett Favre (3,000 Yard Club)	.75
372	Scott Mitchell (3,000 Yard Club)	.05
373	Warren Moon (3,000 Yard Club)	.05
374	Jeff George (3,000 Yard Club)	.05
375	Jim Everett (3,000 Yard Club)	.05
376	John Elway (3,000 Yard Club)	.15
377	Erik Kramer (3,000 Yard Club)	.05
378	Jeff Blake (3,000 Yard Club)	.25
379	Dan Marino (3,000 Yard Club)	1.00
380	Dave Krieg (3,000 Yard Club)	.05
381	Drew Bledsoe (3,000 Yard Club)	.50
382	Stan Humphries (3,000 Yard Club)	.05
383	Troy Aikman (3,000 Yard Club)	.50
384	Steve Young (3,000 Yard Club)	.50
385	Jim Kelly (3,000 Yard Club)	.05
386	Steve Bono (3,000 Yard Club)	.05
387	David Sloan	.05
388	Jeff Graham	.05
389	Hugh Douglas	.05
390	Dan Marino	1.50
391	Winston Moss	.05
392	Darrell Green	.05
393	Mark Stepnoski	.05
394	Bert Emanuel	.05
395	Eric Zeier	.05
396	Willie Jackson	.05
397	Qadry Ismail	.05
398	Michael Brooks	.05
399	D'Marco Farr	.05
400	Brett Favre	2.00
401	Carnell Lake	.05
402	Pat Swilling	.05
403	Steve Grant	.05
404	Steve Tasker	.05
405	Ben Coates	.05
406	Steve Tovar	.05
407	Tony Martin	.05
408	Grant Hill	.05
409	Eric Guliford	.05
410	Michael Irvin	.05
411	Eric Hill	.05
412	Mario Bates	.05
413	Brian Stablein	.05
414	*Marcus Jones*	.05
415	*Reggie Brown*	.05
416	*Lawrence Phillips*	.50
417	*Alex Van Dyke*	.10
418	*Daryl Gardener*	.05
419	*Mike Alstott*	1.50
420	*Kevin Hardy*	.10
421	*Rickey Dudley*	.20
422	*Jerome Woods*	.05
423	*Eric Moulds*	1.50
424	*Cedric Jones*	.05
425	*Simeon Rice*	.40
426	*Marvin Harrison*	4.00
427	*Tim Biakabutuka*	.75
428	*Duane Clemons*	.05
429	*Alex Molden*	.05
430	*Keyshawn Johnson*	2.00
431	*Willie Anderson*	.05
432	*John Mobley*	.05
433	*Leeland McElroy*	.20
434	*Regan Upshaw*	.05
435	*Eddie George*	3.00
436	*Jonathan Ogden*	.10
437	*Eddie Kennison*	.50
438	*Jermain Mayberry*	.05
439	Checklist	.05
440	Checklist	.05

A player's name in *italic* type indicates a rookie card.

1996 Topps Broadway's Reviews

These 1996 Topps football inserts feature 10 of today's top quarterbacks pictured with an archive photo of Joe Namath. The horizontally-designed card front is designed like a filmstrip. The card back has Namath's review of the player, written by the Hall of Famer himself. Cards were seeded one per every 12 packs.

		NM/M
	Complete Set (10):	20.00
	Common Player:	1.00
1	Kerry Collins	1.00
2	Drew Bledsoe	2.00
3	Jeff Blake	1.00
4	Brett Favre	4.00
5	Scott Mitchell	1.00
6	Troy Aikman	3.00
7	Steve Young	3.00
8	Jim Harbaugh	1.00
9	John Elway	3.00
10	Dan Marino	4.00

1996 Topps 40th Anniversary

Forty of today's top NFL stars are featured on these 1996 Topps football cards, which utilize Topps original designs from its first 40 years of producing cards. Each player in the set represents a different year, using a classic pose from that set. The cards, seeded one per every six packs, have Topps 40th Anniversary logo stamped in gold foil on the front.

		NM/M
	Complete Set (40):	40.00
	Common Player:	.50
	Minor Stars:	1.00
1	Jim Harbaugh '56	.50
2	Greg Lloyd '57	.50
3	Barry Sanders '58	3.00
4	Merton Hanks '59	.50
5	Herman Moore '60	1.00
6	Tim Brown '61	.50
7	Brett Favre '62	4.00
8	Cris Carter '63	.50
9	Curtis Martin '64	3.00
10	Bryce Paup '65	.50
11	Steve Bono '66	.50
12	Blaine Bishop '67	.50
13	Emmitt Smith '68	4.00
14	Carnell Lake '69	.50
15	Marshall Faulk '70	2.00
16	Mike Morris '71	.50
17	Shannon Sharpe '72	.50
18	Steve Young '73	3.00
19	Jeff George '74	1.00
20	Junior Seau '75	.50
21	Chris Warren '76	1.00
22	Heath Shuler '77	1.00
23	Jeff Blake '78	1.00
24	Reggie White '79	1.00
25	Jeff Hostetler '80	.50
26	Errict Rhett '81	1.00
27	Rodney Hampton '82	.50
28	Jerry Rice '83	3.00
29	Jim Everett '84	.50
30	Isaac Bruce '85	1.00
31	Dan Marino '86	4.00
32	Marcus Allen '87	1.00
33	Erik Kramer '88	.50
34	John Elway '89	1.00
35	Ricky Watters '90	.50
36	Troy Aikman '91	3.00
37	Drew Bledsoe '92	3.00
38	Scott Mitchell '93	.50
39	Rashaan Salaam '94	1.00
40	Kerry Collins '95	1.00

1996 Topps Hobby Masters

These 20 cards, a hobby only insert, feature the game's top 10 superstars, as chosen by hobbyists. The cards, seeded one per every 36 packs of 1996 Topps football hobby, use 28-point foil board. The card front has a color action photo in the middle, with a closeup shot as the background. "Hobby Masters" is written towards the bottom of the card, along with the player's name, position and a team logo. Topps 40th Anniversary logo is also on the front.

		NM/M
	Complete Set (20):	60.00
	Common Player:	1.00
	Minor Stars:	2.00
1	Brett Favre	8.00
2	Emmitt Smith	6.00
3	Drew Bledsoe	4.00
4	Marshall Faulk	4.00
5	Steve Young	4.00
6	Barry Sanders	6.00
7	Troy Aikman	4.00
8	Jerry Rice	5.00
9	Michael Irvin	2.00
10	Dan Marino	8.00
11	Chris Warren	1.00
12	Reggie White	1.00
13	Jeff Blake	1.00
14	Greg Lloyd	1.00
15	Curtis Martin	5.00
16	Junior Seau	1.00
17	Kerry Collins	1.00
18	Deion Sanders	2.00
19	Joey Galloway	2.00
20	John Elway	6.00

1996 Topps Namath Reprint

"Broadway Joe" Namath's 10 Topps cards are reprinted for this 1996 Topps football insert set, including his 1965 Topps rookie card, one of the most valuable modern-day football cards. The cards were seeded at a ratio of one per every 18 packs.

		NM/M
	Complete Set (10):	50.00
	Common Player:	5.00
1	1965	10.00
2	1966	5.00
3	1967	5.00
4	1968	5.00
5	1969	5.00
6	1970	5.00
7	1971	5.00
8	1972	5.00
9	1972	5.00
10	1973	5.00

1996 Topps Turf Warriors

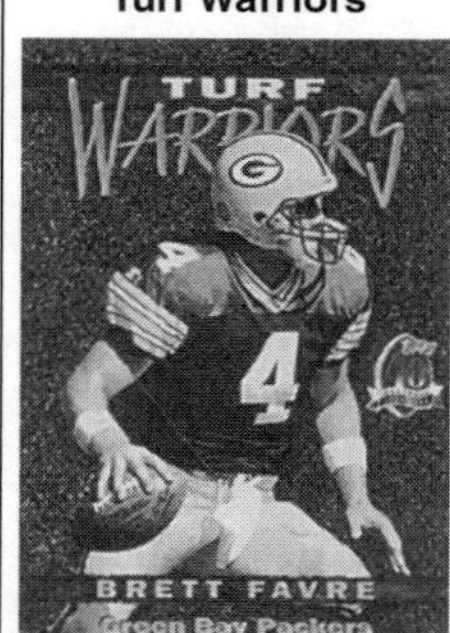

This insert features 22 players on coated cards with an astro-turf type surface. Turf Warriors are inserted every 36 packs of Topps Football.

		NM/M
	Complete Set (22):	45.00
	Common Player:	1.00
1	Bryce Paup	1.00
2	Ben Coates	1.00
3	Jim Harbaugh	1.00
4	Brian Mitchell	1.00
5	Brett Favre	6.00
6	Junior Seau	1.00
7	Michael Irvin	1.00
8	Steve Young	3.00
9	Terry McDaniel	1.00
10	Curtis Martin	4.00
11	Greg Lloyd	1.00
12	Cris Carter	1.00
13	Emmitt Smith	5.00
14	Reggie White	1.00
15	Marshall Faulk	3.00
16	Jerry Rice	4.00
17	Shannon Sharpe	1.00
18	Dan Marino	5.00
19	Ken Norton	1.00
20	Barry Sanders	5.00
21	Neil Smith	1.00
22	Troy Aikman	4.00

1996 Topps Chrome

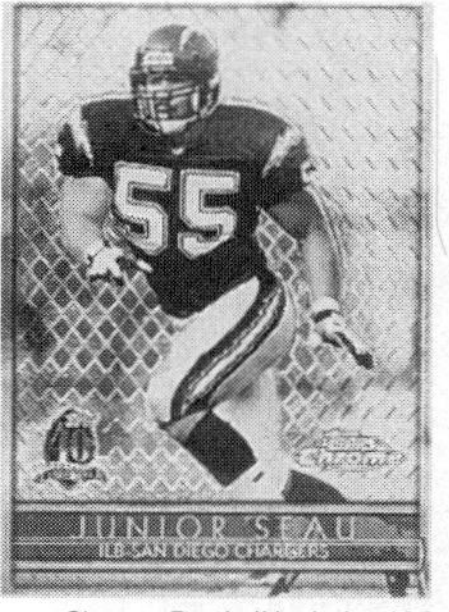

Chrome Football includes 165 of the best cards from Topps Football and adds its chromium finish. Among the cards in Chrome are Draft Picks, 1000 Yard Club and 3000 Yard Club subsets. Four-card packs included Tide Turners and 40th Anniversary inserts, as well as Refractor versions of the entire set and all inserts.

		NM/M
	Complete Set (165):	160.00
	Common Player:	.15
	Common Rookies (150-164):	1.00
	Minor Stars:	.50
	Pack (4):	6.00
	Wax Box (24):	100.00
1	Troy Aikman	3.00
2	Kevin Greene	.15
3	Robert Brooks	.15
4	Junior Seau	.50
5	Brett Perriman	.15
6	Cortez Kennedy	.15
7	Orlando Thomas	.15
8	Anthony Miller	.15
9	Jeff Blake	1.00
10	Trent Dilfer	1.00
11	Heath Shuler	.15
12	Michael Jackson	.15
13	Merton Hanks	.15
14	Dale Carter	.15
15	Eric Metcalf	.15
16	Barry Sanders	6.00
17	Joey Galloway	1.00
18	Bryan Cox	.15
19	Harvey Williams	.15
20	Terrell Davis	6.00
21	Darnay Scott	.15
22	Kerry Collins	.75
23	Warren Sapp	.15
24	Michael Westbrook	.15
25	Mark Brunell	3.00
26	Craig Heyward	.15
27	Eric Allen	.15
28	Dana Stubblefield	.15
29	Steve Bono	.15
30	Larry Brown	.15
31	Warren Moon	.50
32	Jim Kelly	.50
33	Terry McDaniel	.15
34	Dan Wilkinson	.15
35	Dave Brown	.15
36	Todd Lyght	.15
37	Aeneas Williams	.15
38	Shannon Sharpe	.50
39	Errict Rhett	.50
40	Yancey Thigpen	.50
41	J.J. Stokes	.15
42	Marshall Faulk	1.00
43	Chester McGlockton	.15
44	Darryll Lewis	.15
45	Drew Bledsoe	3.00
46	Tyrone Wheatley	.15
47	Herman Moore	1.00
48	Darren Woodson	.15
49	Ricky Watters	.50
50	Emmitt Smith TYC	2.50
51	Barry Sanders TYC	2.00
52	Curtis Martin TYC	1.50
53	Chris Warren TYC	.15
54	Errict Rhett TYC	.15
55	Rodney Hampton TYC	.15
56	Terrell Davis TYC	3.00
57	Marshall Faulk TYC	.50
58	Rashaan Salaam TYC	.15
59	Curtis Conway	.50
60	Isaac Bruce	1.00
61	Thurman Thomas	.50
62	Terry Allen	.15
63	Lamar Lathon	.15
64	Mark Chmura	.50
65	Chris Warren	.15
66	Jessie Tuggle	.15
67	Erik Kramer	.15
68	Tim Brown	.50
69	Derrick Thomas	.15
70	Willie McGinest	.15
71	Frank Sanders	.15
72	Bernie Parmalee	.15
73	Kordell Stewart	3.00
74	Brent Jones	.15
75	Edgar Bennett	.15
76	Rashaan Salaam	.50
77	Carl Pickens	.50
78	Terance Mathis	.15
79	Deion Sanders	1.50
80	Glyn Milburn	.15

81 Lee Woodall .15
82 Neil Smith .15
83 Stan Humphries .15
84 Rick Mirer .15
85 Troy Vincent .15
86 Sam Mills .15
87 Brian Mitchell .15
88 Hardy Nickerson .15
89 Tamarick Vanover .50
90 Steve McNair 3.00
91 Jerry Rice TYC 1.50
92 Isaac Bruce TYC .50
93 Herman Moore TYC .50
94 Cris Carter TYC .15
95 Tim Brown TYC .15
96 Carl Pickens TYC .15
97 Joey Galloway TYC .50
98 Jerry Rice 3.00
99 Cris Carter .50
100 Curtis Martin 3.00
101 Scott Mitchell .15
102 Ken Harvey .15
103 Rodney Hampton .15
104 Reggie White .50
105 Eddie Robinson .15
106 Greg Lloyd .15
107 Phillippi Sparks .15
108 Emmitt Smith 5.00
109 Tom Carter .15
110 Jim Everett .15
111 James Stewart .15
112 Kyle Brady .15
113 Irving Fryar .15
114 Vinny Testaverde .15
115 John Elway 3.00
116 Chris Spielman .15
117 Mike Mamula .15
118 Jim Harbaugh .50
119 Ken Norton .15
120 Bruce Smith .15
121 Daryl Johnston .15
122 Blaine Bishop .15
123 Jeff George .50
124 Jeff Hostetler .15
125 Jerome Bettis .50
126 Jay Novacek .15
127 Bryce Paup .15
128 Neil O'Donnell .15
129 Marcus Allen 1.00
130 Steve Young 2.00
131 Brett Favre TYC 3.00
132 Scott Mitchell TYC .15
133 John Elway TYC 2.00
134 Jeff Blake TYC .50
135 Dan Marino TYC 3.00
136 Drew Bledsoe TYC 1.50
137 Troy Aikman TYC 1.50
138 Steve Young TYC 1.00
139 Jim Kelly TYC .15
140 Jeff Graham .15
141 Hugh Douglas .15
142 Dan Marino 6.00
143 Darrell Green .15
144 Eric Zeier .15
145 Brett Favre 6.00
146 Carnell Lake .15
147 Ben Coates .15
148 Tony Martin .15
149 Michael Irvin .50
150 *Lawrence Phillips* 15.00
151 *Alex Van Dyke* 1.00
152 *Kevin Hardy* 1.00
153 *Rickey Dudley* 6.00
154 *Eric Moulds* 30.00
155 *Simeon Rice* 1.00
156 *Marvin Harrison* 40.00
157 *Tim Biakabutuka* 15.00
158 *Duane Clemons* 1.00
159 *Keyshawn Johnson* 30.00
160 *John Mobley* 1.00
161 *Leeland McElroy* 2.00
162 *Eddie George* 20.00
163 *Jonathan Ogden* 1.00
164 *Eddie Kennison* 5.00
165 Checklist .15

1996 Topps Chrome Refractors

Topps Chrome Refractors are a parallel of the Topps Chrome base set. Refractors were inserted one per 12 packs.

NM/M
Complete Set (165): 1,500
Common Player: 3.00
Common Rookies (150-164): 6.00
Minor Stars: 2X-4X

1996 Topps Chrome 40th Anniversary

Originally found in Topps, this 40-card insert was printed with a Chrome finish and inserted every eight packs. 40th Anniversary insert celebrated 40 years of Topps football with today's players in classic poses and original card designs from 1955 to 1995.

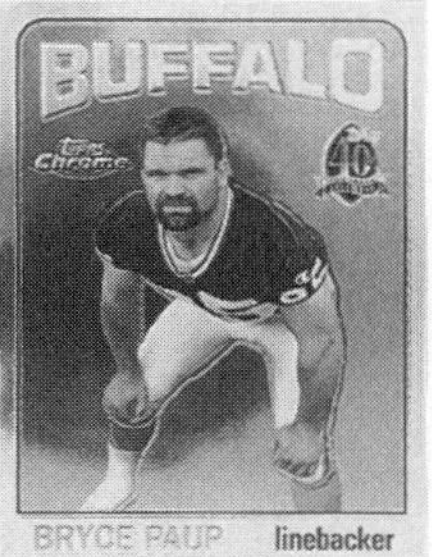

NM/M
Complete Set (40): 60.00
Common Player: .75
Refractors: 2X-3X
1 Jim Harbaugh (1956) .75
2 Greg Lloyd (1957) .75
3 Barry Sanders (1958) 6.00
4 Merton Hanks (1959) .75
5 Herman Moore (1960) .75
6 Tim Brown (1961) 2.00
7 Brett Favre (1962) 8.00
8 Cris Carter (1963) .75
9 Curtis Martin (1964) 4.00
10 Bryce Paup (1965) .75
11 Steve Bono (1966) .75
12 Blaine Bishop (1967) .75
13 Emmitt Smith (1968) 6.00
14 Carnell Lake (1969) .75
15 Marshall Faulk (1970) 4.00
16 Bam Morris (1971) .75
17 Shannon Sharpe (1972) .75
18 Steve Young (1973) 6.00
19 Jeff George (1974) .75
20 Junior Seau (1975) .75
21 Chris Warren (1976) .75
22 Heath Shuler (1977) .75
23 Jeff Blake (1978) 1.00
24 Reggie White (1979) .75
25 Jeff Hostetler (1980) .75
26 Errict Rhett (1981) .75
27 Rodney Hampton (1982) .75
28 Jerry Rice (1983) 6.00
29 Jim Everett (1984) .75
30 Isaac Bruce (1985) 5.00
31 Dan Marino (1986) 8.00
32 Marcus Allen (1987) .75
33 Erik Kramer (1988) .75
34 John Elway (1989) 6.00
35 Ricky Watters (1990) .75
36 Troy Aikman (1991) 6.00
37 Drew Bledsoe (1992) 6.00
38 Scott Mitchell (1993) .75
39 Rashaan Salaam (1994) .75
40 Kerry Collins (1995) 1.00

1996 Topps Chrome 40th Anniversary Refractors

Each card in Chrome's 40th Anniversary insert was also printed in a Refractor version. Refractors of this insert are found every 24 packs.

Refractors: 2X-3X

1996 Topps Chrome Tide Turners

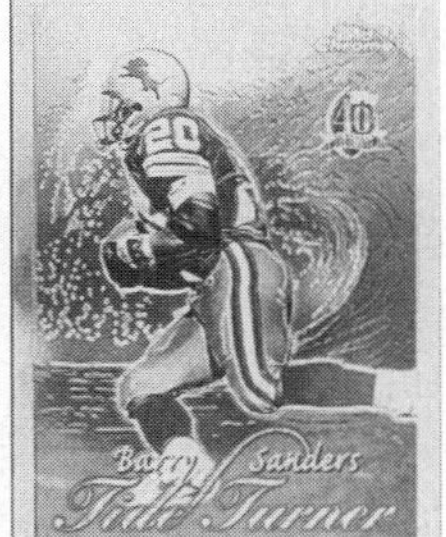

Tide Turners was a 10-card insert that was exclusively produced for Chrome. It featured top playmakers in the NFL and was inserted every 12 packs.

NM/M
Complete Set (15): 30.00
Common Player: 1.00
Refractors: 2X-3X
1 Rashaan Salaam 1.00
2 Warren Moon 1.00
3 Marshall Faulk 3.00
4 Jeff Blake 1.00
5 Curtis Martin 4.00
6 Eric Metcalf 1.00
7 Errict Rhett 1.00
8 Scott Mitchell 1.00
9 Ricky Watters 2.00
10 Jerry Rice 4.00
11 Emmitt Smith 5.00
12 Erik Kramer 1.00
13 Jim Harbaugh 1.00
14 Barry Sanders 5.00
15 John Elway 4.00

1996 Topps Chrome Tide Turners Refractors

This 10-card set is a parallel to the regular Tide Turners inserts. It includes Topps' popular Refractor finish and was inserted every 48 packs.

NM/M
Complete Set (15): 280.00
Refractors: 2X-3X

1996 Topps Gilt Edge

As part of its sponsorship of the first-ever NFL Pro Bowl Experience card show held in conjunction with the Pro Bowl Game in February 1996, Topps issued this 90-card hobby exclusive set. The cards feature 84 members from the Pro Bowl rosters, plus five players who had Pro Bowl-caliber seasons and a checklist. Each card utilizes Topps gilt edge technology, which places gold gilt edging around every card. A gilt edge logo replaces the Topps logo on each card front too, which has a color action photo and one of the set's icons on it. The card back has biographical and statistical information at the top, with a set icon in the background. A recap of the player's 1995 accomplishments, a team logo and a close-up shot round out the back's design. In addition, a parallel version of the set was created using platinum gilt edging. These cards were seeded one per pack, as were Gilt Edge Pro Bowl Skills insert cards.

NM/M
Complete Set (90): 20.00
Common Player: .05
Minor Stars: .30
Platinum Cards: 2X-4X
Pack (9): 1.25
Wax Box (20): 20.00
1 Brett Favre 4.00
2 Kevin Glover .05
3 Nate Newton .05
4 Randall McDaniel .05
5 William Roaf .05
6 Lomas Brown .05
7 Jay Novacek .05
8 Emmitt Smith 4.00
9 Barry Sanders 2.50
10 Jerry Rice 2.00
11 Herman Moore .50
12 Larry Centers .05
13 Chester McGlockton .05
14 Dan Saleaumua .05
15 Bruce Smith .05
16 Neil Smith .05
17 Junior Seau .30
18 Bryce Paup .05
19 Greg Lloyd .30
20 Terry McDaniel .05
21 Dale Carter .05
22 Carnell Lake .05
23 Steve Atwater .05
24 Elbert Shelley .05
25 Brian Mitchell .05
26 Jeff Feagles .05
27 Morten Andersen .05
28 Dan Marino 4.00
29 Dermontti Dawson .05
30 Steve Wisniewski .05
31 Bruce Matthews .05
32 Bruce Armstrong .05
33 Richmond Webb .05
34 Ben Coates .05
35 Marshall Faulk 1.50
36 Chris Warren .30
37 Carl Pickens .30
38 Tim Brown .05
39 Kimble Anders .05
40 John Randle .05
41 Eric Swann .05
42 Reggie White .30
43 Charles Haley .05
44 Ken Norton .05
45 Lee Woodall .05
46 Ken Harvey .05
47 Aeneas Williams .05
48 Eric Davis .05
49 Darren Woodson .05
50 Merton Hanks .05
51 Steve Tasker .05
52 Glyn Milburn .05
53 Jason Elam .05
54 Darren Bennett .05
55 Steve Young 2.00
56 Bart Oates .05
57 Larry Allen .05
58 Mark Tuinei .05
59 Mark Chmura .05
60 Michael Irvin .30
61 Ricky Watters .30
62 Cortez Kennedy .05
63 Leslie O'Neal .05
64 Bryan Cox .05
65 Derrick Thomas .05
66 Darryll Lewis .05
67 Blaine Bishop .05
68 Dana Stubblefield .05
69 William Fuller .05
70 Jessie Tuggle .05
71 William Thomas .05
72 Eric Allen .05
73 Tim McDonald .05
74 Jim Harbaugh .30
75 Mark Stepnoski .05
76 Keith Sims .05
77 Gary Zimmerman .05
78 Shannon Sharpe .05
79 Anthony Miller .05
80 Curtis Martin 3.00
81 Troy Aikman 2.00
82 Cris Carter .30
83 Jeff Blake 1.00
84 Yancey Thigpen 1.00
85 Isaac Bruce 1.00
86 Sam Mills .05
87 Terrell Davis 3.00
88 Larry Brown .05
89 Joey Galloway 2.00
90 Checklist .05

1996 Topps Gilt Edge Platinum

The 90-card, standard size parallel set was included in each pack. The card edges have a platinum "gilt edging" instead of gold.

NM/M
Common Player: .40
Veteran Stars: 1.5X-3X
Young Stars: 1.25X-2.5X

1996 Topps Gilt Edge Definitive Edge

This 15-card skills insert set features top players on cards using five different designs; each design is used to cover three themes - Fire, Volcano and Fury; Warrior, Chieftan and Guardian; Strength, Courage and Endurance; Hurricane, Speed and Lightning; and Illusion, Mischief and Tricks. Nine of the players chosen for the set were also chosen to play in the Pro Bowl Game. One skills card was inserted in every pack.

NM/M
Complete Set (15): 15.00
Common Player: .25
1 Bruce Smith (Strength) .25
2 Brett Favre (Courage) 5.00
3 Marcus Allen (Endurance) .25
4 Junior Seau (Hurricane) .25
5 Deion Sanders (Speed) 2.00
6 Jerry Rice (Lightning) 3.00
7 Steve Young (Fire) 3.00
8 Drew Bledsoe (Volcano) 2.00
9 Michael Irvin (Fury) .50
10 Reggie White (Warrior) .25
11 Dan Marino (Chieftan) 5.00
12 John Alt (Guardian) .25
13 Barry Sanders (Illusion) 4.00
14 Orlando Thomas (Mischief) .25
15 Kordell Stewart (Tricks) 1.00

1996 Topps Laser

After its debut in baseball, Topps Laser Football arrived in four-card packs with 128 cards in the regular issue set. Laser featured surgically precise cutting across the entire card surface, with silver stamped AFC cards and gold stamped NFC cards. Laser was released in a single series and included three insert sets, called Bright Spots, 1996 Draft Picks and Stadium Stars.

NM/M
Complete Set (128): 35.00
Common Player: .10
Minor Stars: .50
Pack (4): 2.00
Wax Box (24): 35.00
1 Marshall Faulk .50
2 Alonzo Spellman .10
3 Frank Sanders .10
4 Anthony Pleasant .10
5 Scott Mitchell .10
6 Robert Brooks .50
7 Robert Jones .10
8 Phillippi Sparks .10
9 Rodney Peete .10
10 Kordell Stewart 3.00
11 Ken Norton .10
12 Brian Mitchell .10
13 Ben Coates .10
14 Quinn Early .10
15 Emmitt Smith 4.00
16 Steve Bono .10
17 Anthony Miller .10
18 Mel Gray .10
19 Neil O'Donnell .10
20 Tim Brown .50
21 Terrell Fletcher .10
22 John Randle .10
23 Fred Barnett .10
24 Craig Heyward .10
25 Ki-Jana Carter .50
26 Eric Allen .10
27 Warren Sapp .10
28 Terry Wooden .10
29 Darion Conner .10
30 Mark Brunell 2.00
31 Vinny Testaverde .10
32 Chris Calloway .10
33 Steve Walsh .10
34 Ken Dilger .10
35 Bryan Cox .10
36 Rob Moore .10
37 Henry Thomas .10
38 Henry Ellard .10
39 Mark Chmura .10
40 Jerry Rice 3.00
41 Michael Irvin .50
42 Willie McGinest .10
43 Steve McNair 3.00
44 Tamarick Vanover 2.00
45 Cris Carter .10
46 Levon Kirkland .10
47 Terry McDaniel .10
48 Jessie Tuggle .10
49 O.J. McDuffie .10
50 Bruce Smith .10
51 Tyrone Hughes .10
52 Tony Martin .10
53 Hardy Nickerson .10
54 Garrison Hearst .10
55 Sam Mills .10
56 Mark Carrier .10
57 Quentin Coryatt .10
58 Neil Smith .10
59 Michael Westbrook 2.00
60 Greg Lloyd .10
61 Jeff Hostetler .10
62 Wayne Chrebet .10
63 Herschel Walker .10
64 Pepper Johnson .10
65 John Elway 3.00
66 Reggie White .50
67 James Stewart .10
68 Bernie Parmalee .10
69 Robert Smith .10
70 Drew Bledsoe 3.00
71 Marvcus Patton .10
72 Stan Humphries .10
73 Darnay Scott .50
74 Jim Kelly .50
75 Terance Mathis .10
76 Erik Kramer .10
77 Marcus Allen .50
78 Ernie Mills .10
79 Harvey Williams .10
80 Brett Favre 4.00
81 Seth Joyner .10
82 Tyrone Poole .10
83 Troy Aikman 3.00
84 Warren Moon .50
85 Isaac Bruce 1.00
86 Errict Rhett .50
87 Rick Mirer .10
88 Anthony Smith .10
89 Bert Emanuel .10
90 Junior Seau .50
91 Terry Allen .10
92 Brent Jones .10
93 Adrian Murrell .10
94 Dave Brown .10
95 Bryce Paup .10
96 Jim Everett .10
97 Brian Washington .10
98 Jim Harbaugh .10
99 Shannon Sharpe .10
100 Dan Marino 4.00
101 Curtis Martin 3.00
102 Ricky Watters .50
103 Yancey Thigpen .50
104 Trent Dilfer .50
105 Joey Galloway 3.00
106 Edgar Bennett .10
107 Willie Jackson .10
108 Mark Collins .10
109 Rashaan Salaam .50
110 Eric Metcalf .10
111 Terrell Davis 4.00
112 Darryll Lewis .10
113 Ken Harvey .10
114 Rob Fredrickson .10
115 Rodney Hampton .10
116 Chris Slade .10
117 Jeff George .10
118 Lamar Lathon .10
119 Curtis Conway .10
120 Barry Sanders 3.00
121 Eric Zeier .10
122 Jeff Blake 2.00
123 Derrick Thomas .10
124 Tyrone Wheatley .10
125 Steve Young 3.00
126 Napoleon Kaufman .10
127 David Meggett .10
128 Kerry Collins .75

1996 Topps Laser Bright Spots

Bright Spots included 16 top young players on full-bleed, double-diffraction foil-stamped cards. Bright Spots were seeded every 24 packs of Laser.

NM/M
Complete Set (16): 50.00
Common Player: 1.00
1 Curtis Martin 6.00
2 Tom Carter 1.00
3 Dave Brown 1.00
4 Wayne Chrebet 1.00
5 Rashaan Salaam 1.00
6 Mark Brunell 4.00
7 Elvis Grbac 1.00
8 Errict Rhett 1.00
9 Isaac Bruce 4.00
10 Kerry Collins 4.00
11 Mario Bates 1.00
12 Joey Galloway 5.00
13 Napoleon Kaufman 1.00
14 Tamarick Vanover 1.00
15 Marshall Faulk 8.00
16 Terrell Davis 12.00

1996 Topps Laser Draft Picks

Sixteen different 1996 draft picks can be found in this insert. Draft Picks inserts are laser cut with double-diffraction foil and inserted every 12 packs.

NM/M
Complete Set (16): 20.00
Common Player: 1.00
1 Keyshawn Johnson 5.00
2 Lawrence Phillips 1.00
3 Bobby Hoying 1.00
4 Marco Battaglia 1.00
5 Kevin Hardy 1.00
6 Jerome Woods 1.00
7 Ray Mickens 1.00
8 John Mobley 1.00
9 Marvin Harrison 7.00
10 Walt Harris 1.00
11 Duane Clemons 1.00
12 Regan Upshaw 1.00

No.	Player	Price
13	Brian Dawkins	1.00
14	Bobby Engram	2.00
15	Eddie Kennison	2.00
16	Jeff Lewis	1.00

1996 Topps Laser Stadium Stars

Stadium Stars included 16 of the top players in the NFL on cards that have a laser-sculpted cover that reveals a full-bleed card of the player underneath. These book-like inserts are seeded every 48 packs.

		NM/M
Complete Set (16):		90.00
Common Player:		1.00
1	Barry Sanders	12.00
2	Jim Harbaugh	1.00
3	Tim Brown	4.00
4	Jim Everett	3.00
5	Brett Favre	15.00
6	Junior Seau	3.00
7	Greg Lloyd	1.00
8	Cris Carter	1.00
9	Emmitt Smith	15.00
10	Dan Marino	15.00
11	Jeff Blake	1.00
12	Darrell Green	1.00
13	John Elway	10.00
14	Marcus Allen	3.00
15	Steve Young	10.00
16	Drew Bledsoe	10.00

1997 Topps

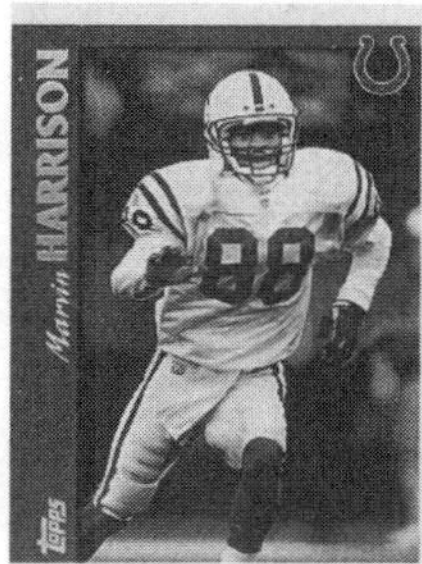

The 415-card set features a colored border on the left of the card front. In that border are the Topps' logo in gold foil in the lower left and the player's name in the upper left. The team's logo is in the upper right. A white border surrounds the three remaining sides. The backs have the player's name, team, position, bio, stats and highlights. A "Minted in Canton" parallel, which features a special gold foil stamp, was randomly seeded in packs.

		NM/M
Complete Set (415):		40.00
Common Player:		.05
Minor Stars:		.10
Minted Canton Cards:		5X-10X
Pack (11):		1.50
Wax Box (36):		40.00
1	Brett Favre	2.50
2	Lawyer Milloy	.05
3	Tim Biakabutuka	.10
4	Clyde Simmons	.05
5	Deion Sanders	.50
6	Anthony Miller	.05
7	Marquez Pope	.05
8	Mike Tomczak	.05
9	William Thomas	.05
10	Marshall Faulk	.20
11	John Randle	.05
12	Jim Kelly	.10
13	Steve Bono	.05
14	Rod Stephens	.05
15	Stan Humphries	.05
16	Terrell Buckley	.05
17	Ki-Jana Carter	.10
18	Marcus Robertson	.05
19	Corey Harris	.05
20	Rashaan Salaam	.10
21	Rickey Dudley	.05
22	Jamir Miller	.05
23	Martin Mayhew	.05
24	Jason Sehorn	.05
25	Isaac Bruce	.20
26	Johnnie Morton	.05
27	Antonio Langham	.05
28	Cornelius Bennett	.05
29	Joe Johnson	.05
30	Keyshawn Johnson	.40
31	Willie Green	.05
32	Craig Newsome	.05
33	Brock Marion	.05
34	Corey Fuller	.05
35	Ben Coates	.05
36	Ty Detmer	.05
37	Charles Johnson	.05
38	Willie Jackson	.05
39	Tyronne Drakeford	.05
40	Gus Frerotte	.05
41	Robert Blackmon	.05
42	Andre Coleman	.05
43	Mario Bates	.05
44	Chris Calloway	.05
45	Terry McDaniel	.05
46	Anthony Davis	.05
47	Stanley Pritchett	.05
48	Ray Buchanan	.05
49	Chris Chandler	.05
50	Ashley Ambrose	.05
51	Tyrone Braxton	.05
52	Pepper Johnson	.05
53	Frank Sanders	.05
54	Clay Matthews	.05
55	Bruce Smith	.05
56	Jermaine Lewis	.05
57	Mark Carrier	.05
58	Jeff Graham	.05
59	Keith Lyle	.05
60	Trent Dilfer	.10
61	Trace Armstrong	.05
62	Jeff Herrod	.05
63	Tyrone Wheatley	.05
64	Torrance Small	.05
65	Chris Warren	.05
66	Terry Kirby	.05
67	Erric Pegram	.05
68	Sean Gilbert	.05
69	Greg Biekert	.05
70	Ricky Watters	.10
71	Chris Hudson	.05
72	Tamarick Vanover	.10
73	Orlando Thomas	.05
74	Jimmy Spencer	.05
75	John Mobley	.05
76	Henry Thomas	.05
77	Santana Dotson	.05
78	Boomer Esiason	.05
79	Bobby Hebert	.05
80	Kerry Collins	.25
81	Bobby Engram	.05
82	Kevin Smith	.05
83	Rick Mirer	.10
84	Ted Johnson	.05
85	Derrick Alexander	.05
86	Hugh Douglas	.05
87	Rodney Harrison	.05
88	Roman Phifer	.05
89	Warren Moon	.10
90	Thurman Thomas	.10
91	Michael McCrary	.05
92	Dana Stubblefield	.05
93	Andre Hastings	.05
94	William Fuller	.05
95	Jeff Hostetler	.05
96	Danny Kanell	.05
97	Mark Fields	.05
98	Eddie Robinson	.05
99	Daryl Gardener	.05
100	Drew Bledsoe	1.00
101	Winslow Oliver	.05
102	Raymont Harris	.05
103	LeShon Johnson	.05
104	Byron Morris	.05
105	Herman Moore	.20
106	Keith Jackson	.05
107	Chris Penn	.05
108	Robert Griffith	.05
109	Jeff Burris	.05
110	Troy Aikman	1.00
111	Allen Aldridge	.05
112	Mel Gray	.05
113	Aaron Bailey	.05
114	Michael Strahan	.05
115	Adrian Murrell	.05
116	Chris Mims	.05
117	Robert Jones	.05
118	Derrick Brooks	.05
119	Tom Carter	.05
120	Carl Pickens	.05
121	Tony Brackens	.05
122	O.J. McDuffie	.05
123	Napoleon Kaufman	.05
124	Chris T. Jones	.05
125	Kordell Stewart	.75
126	Ray Zellars	.05
127	Jessie Tuggle	.05
128	Greg Kragen	.05
129	Brett Perriman	.05
130	Steve Young	.50
131	Willie Clay	.05
132	Kimble Anders	.05
133	Eugene Daniel	.05
134	Jevon Langford	.05
135	Shannon Sharpe	.05
136	Wayne Simmons	.05
137	Leeland McElroy	.05
138	Mike Caldwell	.05
139	Eric Moulds	.10
140	Eddie George	1.00
141	Jamal Anderson	.30
142	Michael Timpson	.05
143	Tony Tolbert	.05
144	Robert Smith	.05
145	Mike Alstott	.10
146	Gary Jones	.05
147	Terrance Shaw	.05
148	Carlton Gray	.05
149	Kevin Carter	.05
150	Darrell Green	.05
151	David Dunn	.05
152	Ken Norton	.05
153	Chad Brown	.05
154	Pat Swilling	.05
155	Irving Fryar	.05
156	Michael Haynes	.05
157	Shawn Jefferson	.05
158	Steve Grant	.05
159	James Stewart	.05
160	Derrick Thomas	.05
161	Tim Bowens	.05
162	Dixon Edwards	.05
163	Micheal Barrow	.05
164	Antonio Freeman	.10
165	Terrell Davis	1.25
166	Henry Ellard	.05
167	Daryl Johnston	.05
168	Bryan Cox	.05
169	Chad Cota	.05
170	Vinny Testaverde	.05
171	Andre Reed	.05
172	Larry Centers	.05
173	Craig Heyward	.05
174	Glyn Milburn	.05
175	Hardy Nickerson	.05
176	Corey Miller	.05
177	Bobby Houston	.05
178	Marco Coleman	.05
179	Winston Moss	.05
180	Tony Banks	.30
181	Jeff Lageman	.05
182	Jason Belser	.05
183	James Jett	.05
184	Wayne Martin	.05
185	David Meggett	.05
186	Terrell Owens	.50
187	Willie Williams	.05
188	Eric Turner	.05
189	Chuck Smith	.05
190	Simeon Rice	.05
191	Kevin Greene	.05
192	Lance Johnston	.05
193	Marty Carter	.05
194	Ricardo McDonald	.05
195	Michael Irvin	.10
196	George Koonce	.05
197	Robert Porcher	.05
198	Mark Collins	.05
199	Louis Oliver	.05
200	John Elway	.50
201	Jake Reed	.05
202	Rodney Hampton	.05
203	Aaron Glenn	.05
204	Mike Mamula	.05
205	Terry Allen	.05
206	John Lynch	.05
207	Todd Lyght	.05
208	Dean Wells	.05
209	Aaron Hayden	.05
210	Blaine Bishop	.05
211	Bert Emanuel	.05
212	Mark Carrier	.05
213	Dale Carter	.05
214	Jimmy Smith	.05
215	Jim Harbaugh	.05
216	Jeff George	.05
217	Anthony Newman	.05
218	Ty Law	.05
219	Brent Jones	.05
220	Emmitt Smith	2.00
221	Bennie Blades	.05
222	Alfred Williams	.05
223	Eugene Robinson	.05
224	Fred Barnett	.05
225	Errict Rhett	.20
226	Leslie O'Neal	.05
227	Michael Sinclair	.05
228	Marvcus Patton	.05
229	Darrien Gordon	.05
230	Jerome Bettis	.10
231	Troy Vincent	.05
232	Ray Mickens	.05
233	Lonnie Johnson	.05
234	Charles Way	.05
235	Chris Sanders	.05
236	Bracey Walker	.05
237	Dave Krieg	.05
238	Kent Graham	.05
239	Ray Lewis	.05
240	Cris Carter	.05
241	Elvis Grbac	.05
242	Eric Davis	.05
243	Harvey Williams	.05
244	Eric Allen	.05
245	Bryant Young	.05
246	Terrell Fletcher	.05
247	Darren Perry	.05
248	Ken Harvey	.05
249	Marvin Washington	.05
250	Marcus Allen	.10
251	Darrin Smith	.05
252	James Francis	.05
253	Michael Jackson	.05
254	Ryan McNeil	.05
255	Mark Chmura	.10
256	Keenan McCardell	.05
257	Tony Bennett	.05
258	Irving Spikes	.05
259	Jason Dunn	.05
260	Joey Galloway	.25
261	Eddie Kennison	.40
262	Lonnie Marts	.05
263	Thomas Lewis	.05
264	Tedy Bruschi	.05
265	Steve Atwater	.05
266	Dorsey Levens	.20
267	Kurt Schulz	.05
268	Rob Moore	.05
269	Walt Harris	.05
270	Steve McNair	.75
271	Bill Romanowski	.05
272	Sean Dawkins	.05
273	Don Beebe	.05
274	Fernando Smith	.05
275	Willie McGinest	.05
276	Levon Kirkland	.05
277	Tony Martin	.05
278	Warren Sapp	.05
279	Lamar Smith	.05
280	Mark Brunell	1.00
281	Jim Everett	.05
282	Victor Green	.05
283	Mike Jones	.05
284	Charlie Garner	.05
285	Karim Abdul-Jabbar	.75
286	Michael Westbrook	.10
287	Lawrence Phillips	.10
288	Amani Toomer	.05
289	Neil Smith	.05
290	Barry Sanders	1.25
291	Willie Davis	.05
292	Bo Orlando	.05
293	Alonzo Spellman	.05
294	Eric Hill	.05
295	Wesley Walls	.05
296	Todd Collins	.05
297	Stevon Moore	.05
298	Eric Metcalf	.05
299	Darren Woodson	.05
300	Jerry Rice	1.00
301	Scott Mitchell	.05
302	Ray Crockett	.05
303	Jim Schwantz	.05
304	Steve Tovar	.05
305	Terance Mathis	.05
306	Earnest Byner	.05
307	Chris Spielman	.05
308	Curtis Conway	.10
309	Chris Dishman	.05
310	Marvin Harrison	.40
311	Sam Mills	.05
312	Brent Alexander	.05
313	Shawn Wooden	.05
314	DeWayne Washington	.05
315	Terry Glenn	.25
316	Winfred Tubbs	.05
317	Dave Brown	.05
318	Neil O'Donnell	.05
319	Anthony Parker	.05
320	Junior Seau	.10
321	Brian Mitchell	.05
322	Regan Upshaw	.05
323	Darryl Williams	.05
324	Chris Doleman	.05
325	Rod Woodson	.05
326	Derrick Witherspoon	.05
327	Chester McGlockton	.05
328	Mickey Washington	.05
329	Greg Hill	.05
330	Reggie White	.10
331	John Copeland	.05
332	Doug Evans	.05
333	Lamar Lathon	.05
334	Mark Maddox	.05
335	Natrone Means	.10
336	Corey Widmer	.05
337	Terry Wooden	.05
338	Merton Hanks	.05
339	Cortez Kennedy	.05
340	Tyrone Hughes	.05
341	Tim Brown	.05
342	John Jurkovic	.05
343	Carnell Lake	.05
344	Stanley Richard	.05
345	Darryll Lewis	.05
346	Dan Wilkinson	.05
347	Broderick Thomas	.05
348	Brian Williams	.05
349	Eric Swann	.05
350	Dan Marino	2.00
351	Anthony Johnson	.05
352	Joe Cain	.05
353	Quinn Early	.05
354	Seth Joyner	.05
355	Garrison Hearst	.05
356	Edgar Bennett	.05
357	Brian Washington	.05
358	Kevin Hardy	.05
359	Quentin Coryatt	.05
360	Tim McDonald	.05
361	Brian Blades	.05
362	Courtney Hawkins	.05
363	Ray Farmer	.05
364	Jesse Armstead	.05
365	Curtis Martin	1.25
366	Zach Thomas	.30
367	Frank Wycheck	.05
368	Darnay Scott	.05
369	Percy Ellsworth	.05
370	Desmond Howard	.05
371	Aeneas Williams	.05
372	Bryce Paup	.05
373	Michael Bates	.05
374	Brad Johnson	.05
375	Jeff Blake	.25
376	Donnell Woolford	.05
377	Mo Lewis	.05
378	Phillippi Sparks	.05
379	Michael Bankston	.05
380	LeRoy Butler	.05
381	Tyrone Poole	.05
382	Wayne Chrebet	.05
383	Chris Slade	.05
384	Checklist 1 of 2	.05
385	Checklist 2 of 2	.05
386	*Will Blackwell*	.75
387	*Tom Knight*	.10
388	*Darnell Autry*	.30
389	*Bryant Westbrook*	.50
390	*David LaFleur*	1.50
391	*Antowain Smith*	3.00
392	*Kevin Lockett*	.75
393	*Rae Carruth*	2.00
394	*Renaldo Wynn*	.10
395	*Jim Druckenmiller*	4.00
396	*Kenny Holmes*	.10
397	*Shawn Springs*	.75
398	*Troy Davis*	.40
399	*Dwayne Rudd*	.10
400	*Orlando Pace*	.75
401	*Byron Hanspard*	.50
402	*Corey Dillon*	6.00
403	*Walter Jones*	.10
404	*Reidel Anthony*	3.00
405	*Peter Boulware*	.10
406	*Reinard Wilson*	.10
407	*Pat Barnes*	.30
408	*Yatil Green*	.40
409	*Joey Kent*	.75
410	*Ike Hilliard*	2.50
411	*Jake Plummer*	2.00
412	*Darrell Russell*	.10
413	*James Farrior*	.10
414	*Tony Gonzalez*	1.50
415	*Warrick Dunn*	3.00

1997 Topps Career Best

This chase set includes Dan Marino, two cards of Marcus Allen, Reggie White and Jerry Rice.

		NM/M
Complete Set (5):		20.00
Common Player:		2.00
1	Dan Marino	12.00
2	Marcus Allen	2.00
3	Marcus Allen	2.00
4	Reggie White	2.00
5	Jerry Rice	5.00

1997 Topps Hall of Fame Autograph

This four-card insert featured autographs from the four current Hall of Fame inductees and carried an "HF" prefix on the card back. The Haynes and Webster cards were inserted one per 436 hobby packs (1:120 jumbo), Mara was inserted one per 872 hobby packs (1:240 jumbo) and the Shula card was seeded one per 290 hobby packs (1:80 jumbo).

		NM/M
Complete Set (4):		200.00
Common Player:		25.00
1	Don Shula	80.00
2	Wellington Mara	75.00
3	Mike Webster	25.00
4	Mike Haynes	30.00

1997 Topps Hall Bound

This 15-card set was inserted 1:36 hobby packs. The embossed cards were produced on die-cut mirror board. Card are numbered with a "HB" prefix.

		NM/M
Complete Set (15):		40.00
Common Player:		1.00
1	Jerry Rice	4.00
2	Rod Woodson	1.00
3	Marcus Allen	1.00
4	Reggie White	1.00
5	Emmitt Smith	5.00
6	Junior Seau	1.00
7	Troy Aikman	4.00
8	Bruce Smith	1.00
9	John Elway	4.00
10	Brett Favre	6.00
11	Thurman Thomas	1.00
12	Deion Sanders	2.00
13	Dan Marino	6.00
14	Steve Young	4.00
15	Barry Sanders	5.00

1997 Topps High Octane

Inserted 1:36 packs, the 15-card chase set includes "High Octane" at the top front of the cards, with the player's photo superimposed over a unilustser back. The team's logo is in the lower left, with the player's name in the lower right. The backs, which are numbered with an "HO" prefix, have the player's bio on the upper left, with his photo in the upper right. Four bar graphs are included in the center, with his highlights in the lower left.

		NM/M
Complete Set (15):		40.00
Common Player:		1.00
1	Brett Favre	10.00
2	Jerome Bettis	1.00
3	Jerry Rice	6.00
4	Junior Seau	1.00
5	Emmitt Smith	8.00
6	Herman Moore	1.00
7	Shannon Sharpe	1.00
8	Curtis Martin	5.00
9	Eddie George	3.00
10	Barry Sanders	8.00
11	John Elway	6.00
12	Steve Young	6.00
13	Drew Bledsoe	6.00
14	Troy Aikman	6.00
15	Dan Marino	10.00

1997 Topps Mystery Finest

The Mystery Finest chase set features 20 Pro Bowl players pictured three different ways, in their team's away jersey (bronze card, 1:36 packs), the team's home uniform (silver card, 1:108) and their Pro Bowl jersey (gold card, 1:324). Bronze Refractor parallels are found 1:144, silver Refractors are located 1:432 and a Gold Refractor is seeded 1:1,296 packs. Cards are numbered with a "M" prefix.

		NM/M
Complete Set (20):		50.00
Common Player:		1.00
Bronze Refractors:		2X-3X
Silver Cards:		2X
Silver Refractors:		3X
Gold Cards:		3X
Gold Refractors:		4X-6X
1	Barry Sanders	6.00
2	Mark Brunell	3.00
3	Terrell Davis	4.00
4	Isaac Bruce	2.00
5	Jerry Rice	5.00
6	Drew Bledsoe	4.00
7	Carl Pickens	1.00
8	Steve Young	4.00
9	Cris Carter	1.00
10	John Elway	4.00
11	Junior Seau	1.00
12	Herman Moore	1.00
13	Vinny Testaverde	1.00
14	Jerome Bettis	1.00
15	Troy Aikman	4.00
16	Reggie White	1.00
17	Kerry Collins	1.00
18	Curtis Martin	3.00
19	Shannon Sharpe	1.00
20	Brett Favre	6.00

1997 Topps Season's Best

The 25-card chase set was seeded 1:16 packs. The set honors players in five different categories, rushing leaders (Thunder and Lightning), passing experts (Air Command), receiving specialists (Special Delivery), sack masters (Demolition Men) and all-purpose yardage gainers (Magicians).

		NM/M
Complete Set (25):		20.00
Common Player:		.25
Minor Stars:		1.50
1	Mark Brunell (Air Command)	1.00
2	Vinny Testaverde (Air Command)	.25
3	Drew Bledsoe (Air Command)	3.00
4	Brett Favre (Air Command)	5.00
5	Jeff Blake (Air Command)	1.50
6	Barry Sanders (Thunder & Lightning)	4.00
7	Terrell Davis (Thunder & Lightning)	3.00
8	Jerome Bettis (Thunder & Lightning)	1.50
9	Ricky Watters (Thunder & Lightning)	.25
10	Eddie George (Thunder & Lightning)	2.00
11	Brian Mitchell (Magicians)	.25
12	Tyrone Hughes (Magicians)	.25
13	Eric Metcalf (Magicians)	.25
14	Glyn Milburn (Magicians)	.25
15	Ricky Watters (Magicians)	.25
16	Kevin Greene (Demolition Men)	.25
17	Lamar Lathon (Demolition Men)	.25
18	Bruce Smith (Demolition Men)	.25
19	Michael Sinclair (Demolition Men)	.25
20	Derrick Thomas (Demolition Men)	.25
21	Jerry Rice (Special Delivery)	4.00
22	Herman Moore (Special Delivery)	.25
23	Carl Pickens (Special Delivery)	.25
24	Cris Carter (Special Delivery)	.25
25	Brett Perriman (Special Delivery)	.25

1997 Topps Underclassmen

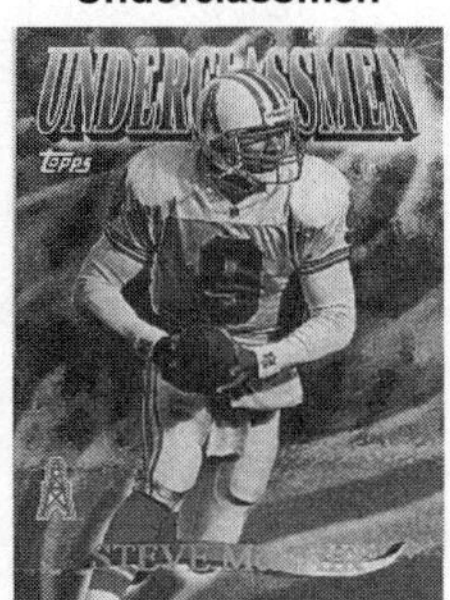

Inserted 1:24 retail packs, the 10-card set is comprised of first and second year players. The "Underclassmen" logo is at the top center, with the player's photo superimposed over a multicolored holographic background. The player's name is printed in holographic foil at the bottom center. The backs, which are numbered with an "U" prefix, have the player's photo, name, bio, highlights and stats.

		NM/M
Complete Set (10):		25.00
Common Player:		1.00
Minor Stars:		5.00
1	Kerry Collins	2.00
2	Karim Abdul-Jabbar	1.00
3	Simeon Rice	1.00
4	Keyshawn Johnson	3.00
5	Eddie George	5.00
6	Eddie Kennison	2.00
7	Terry Glenn	3.00
8	Kevin Hardy	1.00
9	Steve McNair	6.00
10	Kordell Stewart	3.00

1997 Topps Chrome

Chrome Football is a 165-card set created with Topps chromium technology and a Topps Chrome logo added to regular Topps cards. Chrome arrived with a full parallel set of Refractors and four inserts also from Topps: Draft Year, Underclassmen, Season's Best and Career Best.

		NM/M
Complete Set (165):		75.00
Common Player:		.15
Common Player (143-163):		1.00
Minor Stars:		.75
Pack (4):		3.50
Wax Box (24):		60.00

		NM/M
1	Brett Favre	6.00
2	Tim Biakabutuka	.15
3	Deion Sanders	1.50
4	Marshall Faulk	1.00
5	John Randle	.15
6	Stan Humphries	.15
7	Ki-Jana Carter	.75
8	Rashaan Salaam	.15
9	Rickey Dudley	.75
10	Isaac Bruce	1.00
11	Keyshawn Johnson	1.00
12	Ben Coates	.15
13	Ty Detmer	.15
14	Gus Frerotte	.15
15	Mario Bates	.15
16	Chris Calloway	.15
17	Frank Sanders	.15
18	Bruce Smith	.15
19	Jeff Graham	.15
20	Trent Dilfer	1.00
21	Tyrone Wheatley	.15
22	Chris Warren	.15
23	Terry Kirby	.15
24	*Tony Gonzalez*	6.00
25	Ricky Watters	.75
26	Tamarick Vanover	.15
27	Kerry Collins	2.00
28	Bobby Engram	.15
29	Derrick Alexander	.15
30	Hugh Douglas	.15
31	Thurman Thomas	.75
32	Drew Bledsoe	3.00
33	LeShon Johnson	.15
34	Byron Morris	.15
35	Herman Moore	1.00
36	Troy Aikman	3.00
37	Mel Gray	.15
38	Adrian Murrell	.75
39	Carl Pickens	.15
40	Tony Brackens	.15
41	O.J. McDuffie	.15
42	Napoleon Kaufman	1.00
43	Chris T. Jones	.15
44	Kordell Stewart	3.00
45	Steve Young	2.00
46	Shannon Sharpe	.15
47	Leeland McElroy	.15
48	Eric Moulds	.15
49	Eddie George	4.00
50	Jamal Anderson	.75
51	Robert Smith	.75
52	Mike Alstott	1.50
53	Darrell Green	.15
54	Irving Fryar	.15
55	Derrick Thomas	.15
56	Antonio Freeman	1.00
57	Terrell Davis	3.00
58	Henry Ellard	.15
59	Daryl Johnston	.15
60	Bryan Cox	.15
61	Vinny Testaverde	.15
62	Andre Reed	.15
63	Larry Centers	.15
64	Hardy Nickerson	.15
65	Tony Banks	1.50
66	David Meggett	.15
67	Simeon Rice	.15
68	*Warrick Dunn*	12.00
69	Michael Irvin	.75
70	John Elway	4.00
71	Jake Reed	.15
72	Rodney Hampton	.15
73	Aaron Glenn	.15
74	Terry Allen	.15
75	Blaine Bishop	.15
76	Bert Emanuel	.15
77	Mark Carrier	.15
78	Jimmy Smith	.15
79	Jim Harbaugh	.15
80	Brent Jones	.15
81	Emmitt Smith	5.00
82	Fred Barnett	.15
83	Errict Rhett	.15
84	Michael Sinclair	.15
85	Jerome Bettis	1.00
86	Chris Sanders	.15
87	Kent Graham	.15
88	Cris Carter	.15
89	Harvey Williams	.15
90	Eric Allen	.15
91	Bryant Young	.15
92	Marcus Allen	1.00
93	Michael Jackson	.15
94	Mark Chmura	.75
95	Keenan McCardell	.15
96	Joey Galloway	1.00
97	Eddie Kennison	1.00
98	Steve Atwater	.15
99	Dorsey Levens	1.00
100	Rob Moore	.15
101	Steve McNair	3.00
102	Sean Dawkins	.15
103	Don Beebe	.15
104	Willie McGinest	.15
105	Tony Martin	.15
106	Mark Brunell	3.00
107	Karim Abdul-Jabbar	1.00
108	Michael Westbrook	.15
109	Lawrence Phillips	.75
110	Barry Sanders	6.00
111	Willie Davis	.15
112	Wesley Walls	.15
113	Todd Collins	.15
114	Jerry Rice	3.00
115	Scott Mitchell	.15
116	Terance Mathis	.15
117	Chris Spielman	.15
118	Curtis Conway	.15
119	Marvin Harrison	1.00
120	Terry Glenn	2.00
121	Dave Brown	.15
122	Neil O'Donnell	.15
123	Junior Seau	.75
124	Reggie White	.75
125	Lamar Lathon	.15
126	Natrone Means	.75
127	Tim Brown	.15
128	Eric Swann	.15
129	Dan Marino	6.00
130	Anthony Johnson	.15
131	Edgar Bennett	.15
132	Kevin Hardy	.15
133	Brian Blades	.15
134	Curtis Martin	3.00
135	Zach Thomas	.75
136	Darnay Scott	.15
137	Desmond Howard	.15
138	Aeneas Williams	.15
139	Bryce Paup	.15
140	Brad Johnson	.75
141	Jeff Blake	1.00
142	Wayne Chrebet	.15
143	*Will Blackwell*	2.00
144	*Tom Knight*	1.00
145	*Darnell Autry*	2.00
146	*Bryant Westbrook*	2.00
147	*David LaFleur*	4.00
148	*Antowain Smith*	12.00
149	*Rae Carruth*	7.00
150	*Jim Druckenmiller*	8.00
151	*Shawn Springs*	1.00
152	*Troy Davis*	3.00
153	*Orlando Pace*	2.00
154	*Byron Hanspard*	7.00
155	*Corey Dillon*	10.00
156	*Reidel Anthony*	8.00
157	*Peter Boulware*	2.00
158	*Reinard Wilson*	1.00
159	*Pat Barnes*	1.25
160	*Joey Kent*	2.00
161	*Ike Hilliard*	8.00
162	*Jake Plummer*	5.00
163	*Darrell Russell*	1.00
164	Checklist 1	.15
165	Checklist 2	.15

1997 Topps Chrome Refractors

Refractors are a parallel of the Topps Chrome base set. They were inserted one per 12 packs.

	NM/M
Complete Set (165):	2,400
Common Player:	4.00
Common Player (143-163):	6.00
Minor Stars:	2X-6X

1997 Topps Chrome Draft Year

Draft Year is a 15-card insert highlighting two players from the last 15 draft classes. Each side features one of the best players to emerge from that particular draft. Draft Year was inserted 1:48. The Refractor versions were found once in every 144 packs.

		NM/M
Complete Set (15):		60.00
Common Player:		1.00
Minor Stars:		2.00
Refractors:		2X
DR1	Dan Marino, John Elway (1983)	10.00
DR2	Reggie White, Steve Young (1984)	6.00
DR3	Bruce Smith, Jerry Rice (1985)	6.00
DR4	Ronnie Harmon, Pat Swilling (1986)	1.00
DR5	Jim Harbaugh, Vinny Testaverde (1987)	1.00
DR6	Michael Irvin, Tim Brown (1988)	3.00
DR7	Troy Aikman, Barry Sanders (1989)	8.00
DR8	Emmitt Smith, Junior Seau (1990)	8.00
DR9	Brett Favre, Ricky Watters (1991)	8.00
DR10	Carl Pickens, Desmond Howard (1992)	1.00
DR11	Mark Brunell, Drew Bledsoe (1993)	6.00
DR12	Marshall Faulk, Isaac Bruce (1994)	2.00
DR13	Terrell Davis, Curtis Martin (1995)	6.00
DR14	Eddie George, Terry Glenn (1996)	6.00
DR15	Ike Hilliard, Shawn Springs (1997)	1.00

1997 Topps Chrome Season's Best

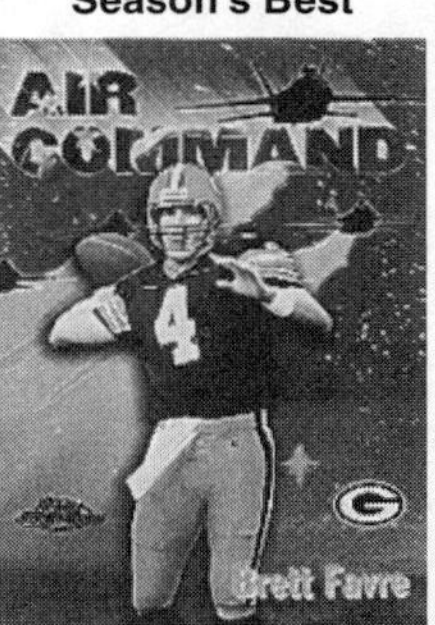

The 25-card Season's Best insert has five different subsets. Each of the five subsets consists of five cards featuring the season's top performers. Air Command features top quarterbacks, Thunder & Lightning has the top rushers, Magicians showcases the top total yardage gainers, Demolition Men highlights the top sack artists and Special Delivery has the top wide receivers. There are also five Career best cards for each category. Season's Best was inserted 1:12 with Refractors found 1:36.

		NM/M
Complete Set (25):		35.00
Common Player:		.50
Minor Stars:		1.00
Refractors:		2X-3X
1	Mark Brunell (Air Command)	2.00
2	Vinny Testaverde (Air Command)	.50
3	Drew Bledsoe (Air Command)	4.00
4	Brett Favre (Air Command)	6.00
5	Jeff Blake (Air Command)	1.00
6	Barry Sanders (Thunder & Lightning)	5.00
7	Terrell Davis (Thunder & Lightning)	4.00
8	Jerome Bettis (Thunder & Lightning)	1.00
9	Ricky Watters (Thunder & Lightning)	1.00
10	Eddie George (Thunder & Lightning)	3.00
11	Brian Mitchell (Magicians)	.50
12	Tyrone Hughes (Magicians)	.50
13	Eric Metcalf (Magicians)	.50
14	Glyn Milburn (Magicians)	.50
15	Ricky Watters (Magicians)	1.00
16	Kevin Greene (Demolition Men)	.50
17	Lamar Lathon (Demolition Men)	.50
18	Bruce Smith (Demolition Men)	.50
19	Michael Sinclair (Demolition Men)	.50
20	Derrick Thomas (Demolition Men)	.50
21	Jerry Rice (Special Delivery)	4.00
22	Herman Moore (Special Delivery)	1.00
23	Carl Pickens (Special Delivery)	.50
24	Cris Carter (Special Delivery)	.50
25	Brett Perriman (Special Delivery)	.50

1997 Topps Chrome Underclassmen

Underclassmen is a 10-card insert highlighting the top second and third year players. The set is inserted 1:8, with Refractor versions found 1:36. Cards are numbered with a "U" prefix.

		NM/M
Complete Set (10):		10.00
Common Player:		.50
Refractors:		2X-3X
1	Kerry Collins	1.00
2	Karim Abdul-Jabbar	.50
3	Simeon Rice	1.00
4	Keyshawn Johnson	2.00
5	Eddie George	4.00
6	Eddie Kennison	1.00
7	Terry Glenn	2.00
8	Kevin Hardy	.50
9	Steve McNair	4.00
10	Kordell Stewart	3.00

1997 Topps Gallery

This 135-card base set features top player photos framed by a foil design. The Players Private Issue parallel set includes foil stamping and was inserted 1:12. Insert sets included Photo Gallery, Gallery of Heroes, Critics Choice and Peter Max Serigraphs.

		NM/M
Complete Set (135):		20.00
Common Player:		.10
Minor Stars:		.40
Private Issue Cards:		8X-15X
Private Issue Rookies:		3X-5X
Pack (6):		2.00
Wax Box (24):		35.00
1	Orlando Pace	.50
2	Darrell Russell	.10
3	Shawn Springs	.50
4	Peter Boulware	.10
5	Bryant Westbrook	.40
6	Walter Jones	.10
7	*Ike Hilliard*	2.00
8	James Farrior	.10
9	Tom Knight	.10
10	*Warrick Dunn*	4.00
11	*Tony Gonzalez*	2.00
12	Reinard Wilson	.10
13	*Yatil Green*	.50
14	*Reidel Anthony*	3.00
15	Kenny Holmes	.10
16	Dwayne Rudd	.10
17	Renaldo Wynn	.10
18	*David LaFleur*	.75
19	*Antowain Smith*	3.00
20	*Jim Druckenmiller*	4.00
21	*Rae Carruth*	2.00
22	*Byron Hanspard*	.75
23	*Jake Plummer*	2.00
24	*Corey Dillon*	7.00
25	*Darnell Autry*	.50
26	*Kevin Lockett*	.10
27	*Troy Davis*	.75
28	Mike Alstott	.40
29	Napoleon Kaufman	.40
30	Terrell Davis	2.50
31	Byron Morris	.10
32	Dana Stubblefield	.10
33	Ki-Jana Carter	.40
34	Hugh Douglas	.10
35	Natrone Means	.40
36	Marshall Faulk	.40
37	Tyrone Wheatley	.10
38	Tony Banks	.50
39	Marvin Harrison	1.50
40	Eddie George	3.50
41	Eddie Kennison	.40
42	Ray Mickens	.10
43	Mike Mamula	.10
44	Tamarick Vanover	.10
45	Rashaan Salaam	.40
46	Trent Dilfer	.40
47	John Mobley	.10
48	Gus Frerotte	.10
49	Isaac Bruce	.50
50	Mark Brunell	2.50
51	Jamal Anderson	.40
52	Keyshawn Johnson	1.50
53	Curtis Conway	.10
54	Zach Thomas	.75
55	Simeon Rice	.10
56	Lawrence Phillips	.40
57	Ty Detmer	.10
58	Bobby Engram	.10
59	Joey Galloway	.75
60	Curtis Martin	2.50
61	Kevin Hardy	.10
62	Eric Moulds	.10
63	Michael Westbrook	.10
64	Robert Smith	.10
65	Karim Abdul-Jabbar	.50
66	Errict Rhett	.40
67	Ray Lewis	.10
68	Terry Glenn	.50
69	Leeland McElroy	.10
70	Kerry Collins	.50
71	Steve McNair	2.00
72	Kordell Stewart	2.00
73	Terry Allen	.10
74	Michael Irvin	.40
75	John Elway	1.50
76	Lamar Lathon	.10
77	Rob Moore	.10
78	Irving Fryar	.10
79	Jim Everett	.10
80	Steve Young	1.50
81	Bryan Cox	.10
82	Dale Carter	.10
83	Chris Warren	.10
84	Shannon Sharpe	.10
85	Reggie White	.40
86	Deion Sanders	1.00
87	Hardy Nickerson	.10
88	Edgar Bennett	.10
89	Kent Graham	.10
90	Dan Marino	4.00
91	Kevin Greene	.10
92	Derrick Thomas	.10
93	Carl Pickens	.10
94	Neil O'Donnell	.10
95	Drew Bledsoe	2.50
96	Michael Haynes	.10
97	Tony Martin	.10
98	Scott Mitchell	.10
99	Rodney Hampton	.10
100	Brett Favre	5.00
101	Darrell Green	.10
102	Rod Woodson	.10
103	Chris Spielman	.10
104	Jake Reed	.10
105	Jerry Rice	2.50
106	Jeff Hostetler	.10
107	Anthony Johnson	.10
108	Keenan McCardell	.10
109	Ben Coates	.10
110	Emmitt Smith	4.00
111	LeRoy Butler	.10
112	Steve Atwater	.10
113	Ricky Watters	.40
114	Jim Harbaugh	.10
115	Marcus Allen	.40
116	Levon Kirkland	.10
117	Jessie Tuggle	.10
118	Ken Norton	.10
119	Thurman Thomas	.40
120	Junior Seau	.40
121	Tim Brown	.10
122	Michael Jackson	.10
123	Eric Metcalf	.10
124	Herman Moore	.40
125	Bruce Smith	.10
126	Cris Carter	.10
127	Dave Brown	.10
128	Jeff Blake	.40
129	Robert Blackmon	.10
130	Barry Sanders	2.50
131	Blaine Bishop	.10
132	Jerome Bettis	.40
133	Stan Humphries	.10
134	Vinny Testaverde	.10
135	Troy Aikman	2.50

1997 Topps Gallery Critics Choice

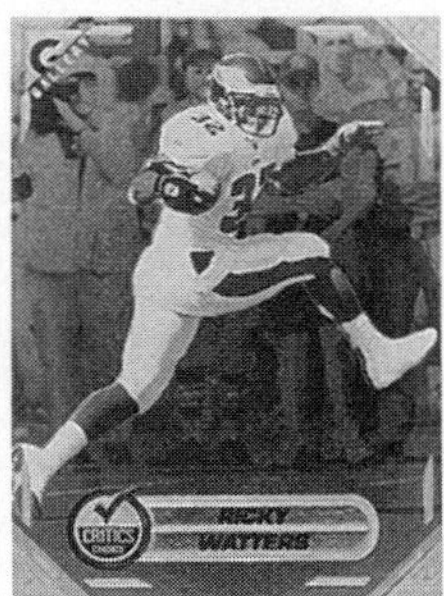

Critics Choice is a 20-card insert featuring player action shots. The cards were inserted 1:24. Cards are numbered and carry a "CC" prefix.

		NM/M
Complete Set (20):		50.00
Common Player:		1.00
Minor Stars:		2.00
Inserted 1:24		
1	Barry Sanders	8.00
2	Jeff Blake	1.00
3	Vinny Testaverde	2.00
4	Ricky Watters	2.00
5	John Elway	6.00
6	Drew Bledsoe	6.00
7	Kordell Stewart	3.00

8 Mark Brunell 3.00
9 Troy Aikman 6.00
10 Brett Favre 8.00
11 Kevin Hardy 1.00
12 Shannon Sharpe 1.00
13 Emmitt Smith 6.00
14 Rob Moore 1.00
15 Eddie George 4.00
16 Herman Moore 2.00
17 Terry Glenn 2.00
18 Jim Harbaugh 1.00
19 Terrell Davis 6.00
20 Junior Seau 1.00

1997 Topps Gallery Gallery of Heroes

This 15-card insert features a player shot on a transparent, luminous card that looks like a stained glass window. They were inserted 1:36. Cards are numbered with a "GH" prefix.

NM/M
Complete Set (15): 60.00
Common Player: 1.00
1 Desmond Howard 1.00
2 Marcus Allen 1.00
3 Kerry Collins 3.00
4 Troy Aikman 6.00
5 Jerry Rice 8.00
6 Drew Bledsoe 6.00
7 John Elway 6.00
8 Mark Brunell 4.00
9 Junior Seau 1.00
10 Brett Favre 8.00
11 Dan Marino 8.00
12 Barry Sanders 6.00
13 Reggie White 1.00
14 Emmitt Smith 6.00
15 Steve Young 5.00

1997 Topps Gallery Peter Max

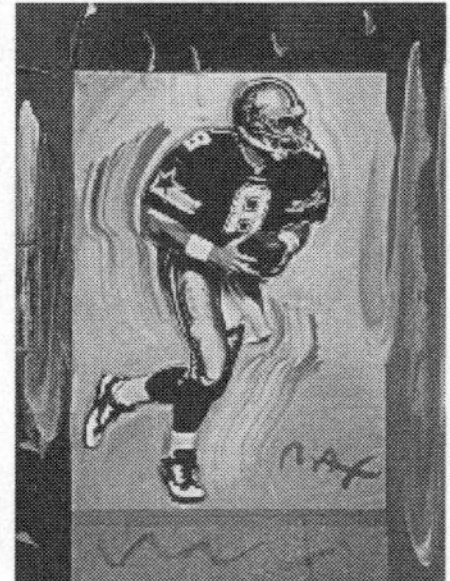

This 10-card insert combines player pictures with colorful art. This insert can be found 1:24. A limited number of the cards were autographed by the artist, Peter max. Cards are numbered and carry a "PM" prefix.

NM/M
Complete Set (10): 30.00
Common Player: 1.00
Autographs: 5X-15X
1 Brett Favre 6.00
2 Jerry Rice 4.00
3 Emmitt Smith 5.00
4 John Elway 4.00
5 Barry Sanders 5.00
6 Reggie White 1.00
7 Steve Young 4.00
8 Troy Aikman 4.00
9 Drew Bledsoe 3.00
10 Dan Marino 6.00

1997 Topps Gallery Photo Gallery

Photo Gallery features top players and double foil stamping. The 15-card set was inserted 1:24. Cards are numbered with a "PG" prefix.

NM/M
Complete Set (15): 50.00
Common Player: 1.00
1 Eddie George 4.00
2 Drew Bledsoe 5.00

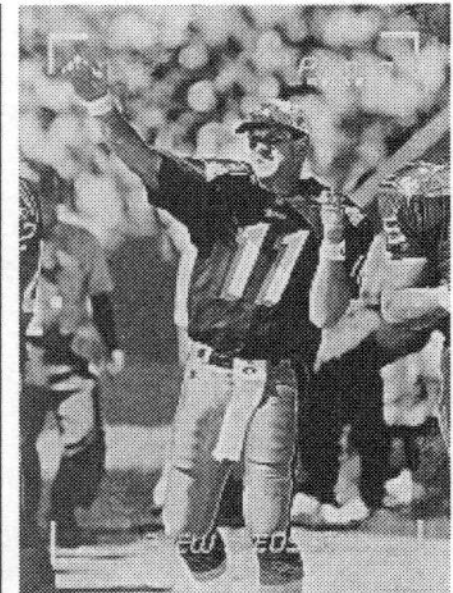

NM/M
3 Brett Favre 8.00
4 Emmitt Smith 6.00
5 Dan Marino 8.00
6 Terrell Davis 5.00
7 Kevin Greene 1.00
8 Troy Aikman 5.00
9 Curtis Martin 4.00
10 Barry Sanders 6.00
11 Junior Seau 1.00
12 Deion Sanders 2.00
13 Steve Young 5.00
14 Reggie White 1.00
15 Jerry Rice 5.00

1997 Topps Stars

The 125-card set includes 100 NFL stars and 25 1997 NFL draft picks. Each card features diffraction and matte gold foil stamping. The Always Mint parallel set was seeded 1:18 packs. Topps Stars was offered exclusively to Topps Home Team Advantage members.

NM/M
Complete Set (125): 30.00
Common Player: .10
Minor Stars: .20
Foil Stars: 6X-15X
Foil Rookies: 2X-6X
Pack (7): 1.75
Wax Box (24): 30.00
1 Brett Favre 4.00
2 Michael Jackson .10
3 Simeon Rice .10
4 Thurman Thomas .20
5 Karim Abdul-Jabbar .50
6 Marvin Harrison .20
7 John Elway 2.00
8 Carl Pickens .20
9 Rod Woodson .10
10 Kerry Collins .30
11 Cortez Kennedy .10
12 William Fuller .10
13 Michael Irvin .20
14 Tyrone Braxton .10
15 Steve Young 1.25
16 Keith Lyle .10
17 Blaine Bishop .10
18 Jeff Hostetler .10
19 Levon Kirkland .10
20 Barry Sanders 3.00
21 Deion Sanders 1.00
22 Jamal Anderson .20
23 Eric Davis .10
24 Hardy Nickerson .10
25 LeRoy Butler .10
26 Mark Brunell 1.75
27 Aeneas Williams .10
28 Curtis Martin 1.50
29 Wayne Chrebet .10
30 Jerry Rice 1.75
31 Jake Reed .10
32 Wayne Martin .10
33 Derrick Alexander .10
34 Isaac Bruce .20
35 Terrell Davis 2.00
36 Jerome Bettis .20
37 Keenan McCardell .10
38 Derrick Thomas .10
39 Jason Sehorn .10
40 Keyshawn Johnson .20
41 Jeff Blake .20
42 Terry Allen .10
43 Ben Coates .10
44 William Thomas .10
45 Bryce Paup .10
46 Bryant Young .10
47 Eric Swann .10
48 Tim Brown .20
49 Tony Martin .10
50 Eddie George 2.00
51 Sam Mills .10
52 Terry McDaniel .10
53 Darren Woodson .10
54 Ashley Ambrose .10
55 Drew Bledsoe 1.75
56 Larry Centers .10
57 Ty Detmer .20
58 Merton Hanks .10
59 Charles Johnson .10
60 Dan Marino 3.50
61 Joey Galloway .20
62 Junior Seau .20
63 Brett Perriman .10
64 Wesley Walls .10
65 Chad Brown .10
66 Henry Ellard .10
67 Keith Jackson .10
68 John Randle .10
69 Chester McGlockton .10
70 Emmitt Smith 3.50
71 Vinny Testaverde .20
72 Steve Atwater .10
73 Irving Fryar .10
74 Gus Frerotte .10
75 Terry Glenn .30
76 Anthony Johnson .10
77 Jimmy Smith .10
78 Terrell Buckley .10
79 Kimble Anders .10
80 Cris Carter .20
81 David Meggett .10
82 Shannon Sharpe .20
83 Adrian Murrell .20
84 Herman Moore .20
85 Bruce Smith .10
86 Lamar Lathon .10
87 Ken Harvey .10
88 Curtis Conway .20
89 Alfred Williams .10
90 Troy Aikman 1.75
91 Carnell Lake .10
92 Michael Sinclair .10
93 Ricky Watters .20
94 Kevin Greene .10
95 Reggie White .20
96 Tyrone Hughes .10
97 Dale Carter .10
98 Rob Moore .10
99 Tony Tolbert .10
100 Willie McGinest .10
101 *Orlando Pace* .20
102 *Yatil Green* .75
103 *Antowain Smith* 5.00
104 *David LaFleur* 1.50
105 *Jake Plummer* 2.00
106 *Will Blackwell* .50
107 *Dwayne Rudd* .20
108 *Corey Dillon* 8.00
109 *Pat Barnes* .50
110 *Peter Boulware* .20
111 *Tony Gonzalez* 2.00
112 *Renaldo Wynn* .20
113 *Darrell Russell* .20
114 *Bryant Westbrook* .20
115 *James Farrior* .20
116 *Joey Kent* .20
117 *Rae Carruth* 2.00
118 *Jim Druckenmiller* 3.00
119 *Byron Hanspard* .75
120 *Ike Hilliard* 2.00
121 *Kevin Lockett* .20
122 *Tom Knight* .20
123 *Shawn Springs* .20
124 *Troy Davis* .75
125 *Darnell Autry* .30

1997 Topps Stars Future Pro Bowlers

Inserted 1:12 packs, the 15-card set features a player photo superimposed over a backdrop of Pro Bowl 1997 logos. The Topps Stars logo is in the upper left, while the Future Pro Bowlers logo is in the lower left. The player's name is to the right of the logo. The cards are numbered on the back with a prefix of "FPB".

NM/M
Complete Set (15): 12.00
Common Player: .50
1 Ike Hilliard 2.00
2 Tom Knight .50
3 David LaFleur .50
4 Byron Hanspard .50
5 Kevin Lockett .50
6 Rae Carruth .50
7 Jim Druckenmiller 1.00
8 Darnell Autry 1.00
9 Joey Kent .50
10 Peter Boulware .50
11 Orlando Pace 2.00
12 Troy Davis .50
13 Antowain Smith 5.00
14 Bryant Westbrook 1.00
15 Yatil Green 1.00

1997 Topps Stars Hall of Fame Rookie Reprints

The 10-card set was inserted 1:64 packs, while autographed versions were found 1:128 packs.

NM/M
Complete Set (10): 15.00
Common Player: 1.00
Autographs: 5X-15X
1 George Blanda 1.00
2 Dick Butkus 3.00
3 Len Dawson 1.00
4 Jack Ham 1.00
5 Sam Huff 1.00
6 Deacon Jones 1.00
7 Ray Nitschke 2.00
8 Gale Sayers 3.00
9 Randy White 1.00
10 Kellen Winslow 1.00

1997 Topps Stars Pro Bowl Memories

The 10-card set was inserted 1:24 packs. The cards are laser cut through the middle with stars, which start small on the left and grow larger as the stars move to the right. The Pro Bowl logo is in the upper left, while "Pro Bowl Memories" and the player's name are printed vertically along the right border in the middle. The Topps Stars logo is in the lower right. The backs are numbered with a "PBM" prefix.

NM/M
Complete Set (10): 30.00
Common Player: 1.00
1 Barry Sanders 6.00
2 Jeff Blake 1.00
3 Ken Harvey 1.00
4 Brett Favre 7.00
5 Jerry Rice 5.00
6 John Elway 5.00
7 Marshall Faulk 2.00
8 Steve Young 4.00
9 Mark Brunell 2.00
10 Troy Aikman 5.00

1997 Topps Stars Pro Bowl Stars

The 30-card set was inserted 1:24 packs. The card fronts feature a player photo superimposed over a uniluster background of the Pro Bowl 1997 logo and the NFC or AFC logo. The Topps Stars logo is in the upper left, while the Pro Bowl logo is in the lower left, with the player's name and position to the right. The backs are numbered with a prefix of "PB".

NM/M
Complete Set (30): 30.00
Common Player: .50
Minor Stars: 1.00
Inserted 1:24
1 Brett Favre 8.00
2 Mark Brunell 3.00
3 Kerry Collins 1.00
4 Drew Bledsoe 4.00
5 Barry Sanders 6.00
6 Terrell Davis 4.00
7 Terry Allen .50
8 Jerome Bettis 1.00
9 Ricky Watters .50
10 Curtis Martin 4.00
11 Emmitt Smith 6.00
12 Kimble Anders .50
13 Jerry Rice 5.00
14 Carl Pickens .50
15 Herman Moore 1.00
16 Tony Martin .50
17 Isaac Bruce 1.00
18 Tim Brown 2.00
19 Wesley Walls .50
20 Shannon Sharpe .50
21 Dana Stubblefield .50
22 Reggie White 1.00
23 Bruce Smith .50
24 Bryant Young .50
25 Junior Seau 1.00
26 Kevin Greene .50
27 Derrick Thomas .50
28 Chad Brown .50
29 Deion Sanders 2.00
30 Rod Woodson .50

1998 Topps

Topps was issued in a single-series 360-card set in 1998. It contained a 30-card 1998 NFL Draft Picks subset that was seeded one per three packs. Cards utilize a gold border around the color shot of the player, with the Topps logo in the upper right, team logo in the lower left and the player's name and team printed up the right side. Backs are horizontal and add another shot of the player, along with statistics and bio information. Inserts in Topps include: Season's Best, Measures of Greatness, Myster Finest, Gridiron Gods (hobby), Hidden Gems (retail), Autographs (hobby) and Generation 2000.

NM/M
Complete Set (360): 50.00
Common Player: .10
Minor Stars: .20
Pack (11): 3.00
Wax Box (36): 70.00
1 Barry Sanders 1.50
2 Derrick Rodgers .10
3 Chris Calloway .10
4 Bruce Armstrong .10
5 Horace Copeland .10
6 Chad Brown .10
7 Ken Harvey .10
8 Levon Kirkland .10
9 Glenn Foley .10
10 Corey Dillon .50
11 Sean Dawkins .10
12 Curtis Conway .20
13 Chris Chandler .10
14 Kerry Collins .20
15 Jonathan Ogden .10
16 Sam Shade .10
17 Vaughn Hebron .10
18 Quentin Coryatt .10
19 Jerris McPhail .10
20 Warrick Dunn 1.00
21 Wayne Martin .10
22 Chad Lewis .10
23 Danny Kanell .10
24 Shawn Springs .10
25 Emmitt Smith 1.75
26 Todd Lyght .10
27 Donnie Edwards .10
28 Charlie Jones .10
29 Willie McGinest .10
30 Steve Young .75
31 Darrell Russell .10
32 Gary Anderson .10
33 Stanley Richard .10
34 Leslie O'Neal .10
35 Dermontti Dawson .10
36 Jeff Brady .10
37 Kimble Anders .10
38 Glyn Milburn .10
39 Greg Hill .10
40 Freddie Jones .10
41 Bobby Engram .10
42 Aeneas Williams .10
43 Antowain Smith .75
44 Reggie White .20
45 Rae Carruth .10
46 Leon Johnson .10
47 Bryant Young .10
48 Jamie Asher .10
49 Hardy Nickerson .10
50 Jerome Bettis .20
51 Michael Strahan .10
52 John Randle .10
53 Kevin Hardy .10
54 Eric Bjornson .10
55 Morten Andersen .10
56 Larry Centers .10
57 Bryce Paup .10
58 John Mobley .10
59 Michael Bates .10
60 Tim Brown .20
61 Doug Evans .10
62 Will Shields .10
63 Jeff Graham .10
64 Henry Jones .10
65 Steve Broussard .10
66 Blaine Bishop .10
67 Ernie Conwell .10
68 Heath Shuler .10
69 Eric Metcalf .10
70 Terry Glenn .20
71 James Hasty .10
72 Robert Porcher .10
73 Keenan McCardell .10
74 Tyrone Hughes .10
75 Troy Aikman 1.00
76 Peter Boulware .10
77 Rob Johnson .20
78 Erik Kramer .10
79 Kevin Smith .10
80 Andre Rison .10
81 Jim Harbaugh .20
82 Chris Hudson .10
83 Ray Zellars .10
84 Jeff George .20
85 Willie Davis .10
86 Jason Gildon .10
87 Robert Brooks .10
88 Chad Cota .10
89 Simeon Rice .10
90 Mark Brunell .75
91 Jay Graham .10
92 Scott Greene .10
93 Jeff Blake .20
94 Jason Belser .10
95 Derrick Alexander .10
96 Ty Law .10
97 Charles Johnson .10
98 James Jett .10
99 Darrell Green .10
100 Brett Favre 2.00
101 George Jones .10
102 Derrick Mason .10
103 Sam Adams .10
104 Lawrence Phillips .10
105 Randal Hill .10
106 John Mangum .10
107 Natrone Means .20
108 Bill Romanowski .10
109 Terance Mathis .10
110 Bruce Smith .10
111 Pete Mitchell .10
112 Duane Clemons .10
113 Willie Clay .10
114 Eric Allen .10
115 Troy Drayton .10
116 Derrick Thomas .10
117 Charles Way .10
118 Wayne Chrebet .10
119 Bobby Hoying .10
120 Michael Jackson .10
121 Gary Zimmerman .10
122 Yancey Thigpen .10
123 Dana Stubblefield .10
124 Keith Lyle .10
125 Marco Coleman .10
126 Karl Williams .10
127 Stephen Davis .10
128 Chris Sanders .10
129 Cris Dishman .10
130 Jake Plummer 1.00
131 Darryl Williams .10
132 Merton Hanks .10
133 Torrance Small .10
134 Aaron Glenn .10
135 Chester McGlockton .10
136 William Thomas .10
137 Kordell Stewart 1.00
138 Jason Taylor .10
139 Lake Dawson .10
140 Carl Pickens .10
141 Eugene Robinson .10
142 Ed McCaffrey .10
143 Lamar Lathon .10
144 Ray Buchanan .10
145 Thurman Thomas .20
146 Andre Reed .10
147 Wesley Walls .10
148 Rob Moore .10
149 Darren Woodson .10
150 Eddie George 1.00
151 Michael Irvin .20
152 Johnnie Morton .10
153 Ken Dilger .10
154 Tony Boselli .10
155 Randall McDaniel .10
156 Mark Fields .10
157 Phillippi Sparks .10
158 William Roaf .10

159	Troy Vincent	.10
160	Cris Carter	.10
161	Amp Lee	.10
162	Will Blackwell	.10
163	Chad Scott	.10
164	Henry Ellard	.10
165	Robert Jones	.10
166	Garrison Hearst	.10
167	James McKnight	.10
168	Rodney Harrison	.10
169	Adrian Murrell	.20
170	Rod Smith	.10
171	Desmond Howard	.10
172	Ben Coates	.10
173	David Palmer	.10
174	Zach Thomas	.10
175	Dale Carter	.10
176	Mark Chmura	.10
177	Elvis Grbac	.10
178	Jason Hanson	.10
179	Walt Harris	.10
180	Ricky Watters	.20
181	Ray Lewis	.10
182	Lonnie Johnson	.10
183	Marvin Harrison	.20
184	Dorsey Levens	.20
185	Tony Gonzalez	.10
186	Andre Hastings	.10
187	Kevin Turner	.10
188	Mo Lewis	.10
189	Jason Sehorn	.10
190	Drew Bledsoe	1.00
191	Michael Sinclair	.10
192	William Floyd	.10
193	Kenny Holmes	.10
194	Marvcus Patton	.10
195	Warren Sapp	.10
196	Junior Seau	.20
197	Ryan McNeil	.10
198	Tyrone Wheatley	.10
199	Robert Smith	.10
200	Terrell Davis	1.00
201	Brett Perriman	.10
202	Tamarick Vanover	.10
203	Stephen Boyd	.10
204	Zack Crockett	.10
205	Sherman Williams	.10
206	Neil Smith	.10
207	Jermaine Lewis	.10
208	Kevin Williams	.10
209	Byron Hanspard	.20
210	Warren Moon	.20
211	Tony McGee	.10
212	Raymont Harris	.10
213	Eric Davis	.10
214	Darrien Gordon	.10
215	James Stewart	.10
216	Derrick Mayes	.10
217	Brad Johnson	.10
218	Karim Abdul-Jabbar	.20
219	Hugh Douglas	.10
220	Terry Allen	.10
221	Rhett Hall	.10
222	Terrell Fletcher	.10
223	Carnell Lake	.10
224	Darryll Lewis	.10
225	Chris Slade	.10
226	Michael Westbrook	.10
227	Willie Williams	.10
228	Tony Banks	.20
229	Keyshawn Johnson	.20
230	Mike Alstott	.20
231	Tiki Barber	.20
232	Jake Reed	.10
233	Eric Swann	.10
234	Eric Moulds	.10
235	Vinny Testaverde	.10
236	Jessie Tuggle	.10
237	Ryan Wetnight	.10
238	Tyrone Poole	.10
239	Bryant Westbrook	.10
240	Steve McNair	.75
241	Jimmy Smith	.10
242	DeWayne Washington	.10
243	Robert Harris	.10
244	Rod Woodson	.10
245	Reidel Anthony	.20
246	Jessie Armstead	.10
247	O.J. McDuffie	.10
248	Carlton Gray	.10
249	LeRoy Butler	.10
250	Jerry Rice	1.00
251	Frank Sanders	.10
252	Todd Collins	.10
253	Fred Lane	.10
254	David Dunn	.10
255	Micheal Barrow	.10
256	Luther Ellis	.10
257	Scott Mitchell	.10
258	David Meggett	.10
259	Rickey Dudley	.10
260	Isaac Bruce	.20
261	Tony Martin	.10
262	Leslie Shepherd	.10
263	Derrick Thomas	.10
264	Greg Lloyd	.10
265	Terrell Buckley	.10
266	Antonio Freeman	.20
267	Tony Brackens	.10
268	Mark McMillian	.10
269	Dexter Coakley	.10
270	Dan Marino	1.75
271	Bryan Cox	.10
272	Leeland McElroy	.10
273	Jeff Burris	.10
274	Eric Green	.10
275	Darnay Scott	.10
276	Greg Clark	.10
277	Mario Bates	.10
278	Eric Turner	.10
279	Neil O'Donnell	.10
280	Herman Moore	.20
281	Gary Brown	.10
282	Terrell Owens	.20
283	Frank Wycheck	.10
284	Trent Dilfer	.20
285	Curtis Martin	.75
286	Ricky Proehl	.10
287	Steve Atwater	.10
288	Aaron Bailey	.10
289	William Henderson	.10
290	Marcus Allen	.20
291	Tom Knight	.10
292	Quinn Early	.10
293	Michael McCrary	.10
294	Bert Emanuel	.10
295	Tom Carter	.10
296	Kevin Glover	.10
297	Marshall Faulk	.20
298	Harvey Williams	.10
299	Chris Warren	.10
300	John Elway	.75
301	Eddie Kennison	.20
302	Gus Frerotte	.10
303	Regan Upshaw	.10
304	Kevin Gogan	.10
305	Napoleon Kaufman	.30
306	Charlie Garner	.10
307	Shawn Jefferson	.10
308	Tommy Vardell	.10
309	Mike Hollis	.10
310	Irving Fryar	.10
311	Shannon Sharpe	.10
312	Byron Morris	.10
313	Jamal Anderson	.10
314	Chris Gedney	.10
315	Chris Spielman	.10
316	Derrick Alexander	.10
317	O.J. Santiago	.10
318	Anthony Miller	.10
319	Ki-Jana Carter	.10
320	Deion Sanders	.40
321	Joey Galloway	.20
322	J.J. Stokes	.10
323	Rodney Thomas	.10
324	John Lynch	.10
325	Mike Pritchard	.10
326	Terrance Shaw	.10
327	Ted Johnson	.10
328	Ashley Ambrose	.10
329	Checklist	.10
330	Checklist	.10
331	*Jerome Pathon*	2.00
332	*Ryan Leaf*	2.00
333	*Duane Starks*	1.50
334	*Brian Simmons*	1.00
335	*Keith Brooking*	2.00
336	*Robert Edwards*	3.00
337	*Curtis Enis*	2.00
338	*John Avery*	2.00
339	*Fred Taylor*	6.00
340	*Germane Crowell*	2.00
341	*Hines Ward*	6.00
342	*Marcus Nash*	1.00
343	*Jacquez Green*	2.00
344	*Joe Jurevicius*	2.00
345	*Greg Ellis*	1.00
346	*Brian Griese*	6.00
347	*Tavian Banks*	2.00
348	*Robert Holcombe*	3.00
349	*Skip Hicks*	2.00
350	*Ahman Green*	4.00
351	*Takeo Spikes*	1.00
352	*Randy Moss*	12.00
353	*Andre Wadsworth*	1.00
354	*Jason Peter*	1.00
355	*Grant Wistrom*	1.00
356	*Charles Woodson*	3.00
357	*Kevin Dyson*	3.00
358	*Patrick Johnson*	1.00
359	*Tim Dwight*	3.00
360	*Peyton Manning*	20.00

1998 Topps Autographs

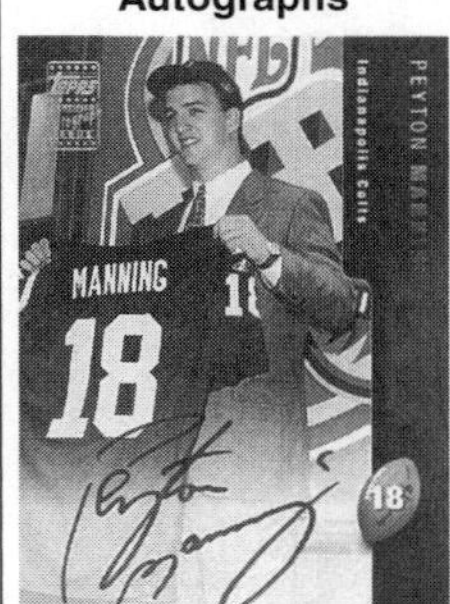

This hobby-only insert featured autographs from 15 top players, with eight veterans, two rookies and the five 1997 NFL Hall of Fame inductees. Each card has a gold foil "Topps Certified Autograph Issue" stamp and was inserted one per 260 hobby packs. Cards are numbered with a "A" prefix.

		NM/M
Complete Set (15):		650.00
Common Player:		30.00
1	Randy Moss	150.00
2	Mike Alstott	40.00
3	Jake Plummer	70.00
4	Corey Dillon	50.00
5	Kordell Stewart	70.00
6	Eddie George	60.00
7	Jason Sehorn	30.00
8	Joey Galloway	30.00
9	Ryan Leaf	25.00
10	Peyton Manning	150.00
11	Dwight Stephenson	30.00
12	Anthony Munoz	30.00
13	Mike Singletary	30.00
14	Tommy McDonald	30.00
15	Paul Krause	30.00

1998 Topps Generation 2000

Generation 2000 showcases 15 of football's top young players who should lead the game into the year 2000. The inserts have the word "Generation" across the top and "2000" printed in silver, embossed foil across the bottom. These were numbered with a "GE" prefix and inserted one per 18 packs.

		NM/M
Complete Set (15):		15.00
Common Player:		.50
Minor Stars:		1.00
1	Warrick Dunn	1.00
2	Tony Gonzalez	.50
3	Corey Dillon	1.00
4	Antowain Smith	1.00
5	Mike Alstott	1.00
6	Kordell Stewart	1.00
7	Peter Boulware	.50
8	Jake Plummer	2.00
9	Tiki Barber	1.00
10	Terrell Davis	4.00
11	Steve McNair	3.00
12	Curtis Martin	3.00
13	Napoleon Kaufman	1.00
14	Terrell Owens	.50
15	Eddie George	3.00

1998 Topps Gridiron Gods

This hobby exclusive insert captures 15 players on uniluster technology, which is a silver etched, holofoil looking background. Cards are numbered with a "G" prefix and inserted one per 36 packs.

		NM/M
Complete Set (15):		30.00
Common Player:		1.00
Minor Stars:		2.00
1	Barry Sanders	5.00
2	Jerry Rice	4.00
3	Herman Moore	1.00
4	Drew Bledsoe	3.00
5	Kordell Stewart	2.00
6	Tim Brown	2.00
7	Eddie George	3.00
8	Dorsey Levens	1.00
9	Warrick Dunn	2.00
10	Brett Favre	5.00
11	Terrell Davis	3.00
12	Steve Young	3.00
13	Jerome Bettis	1.00
14	Mark Brunell	1.00
15	John Elway	3.00

1998 Topps Hidden Gems

Hidden Gems were exclusive to retail packs and inserted one per 15. This 15-card set is printed on a plastic-like surface and numbered with a "HG" prefix.

		NM/M
Complete Set (15):		8.00
Common Player:		.25
1	Andre Reed	.25
2	Kevin Greene	.25
3	Tony Martin	.25
4	Shannon Sharpe	1.00
5	Terry Allen	1.00
6	Brett Favre	4.00
7	Ben Coates	1.00
8	Michael Sinclair	.25
9	Keenan McCardell	.25
10	Brad Johnson	1.00
11	Mark Brunell	1.00
12	Dorsey Levens	1.00
13	Terrell Davis	3.00
14	Curtis Martin	2.00
15	Derrick Rodgers	.25

1998 Topps Measures Of Greatness

Fifteen different players that are bound for the Hall of Fame are featured in this insert printed on micro dyna-etch technology. The silver foil fronts that feature markings of a football field includes the insert name up the left side, with the player's name in a banner below it. Cards are numbered with a "MG" prefix and inserted one per 36 packs.

		NM/M
Complete Set (15):		25.00
Common Player:		.50
Minor Stars:		1.00
1	John Elway	3.00
2	Marcus Allen	1.00
3	Jerry Rice	4.00
4	Tim Brown	1.00
5	Warren Moon	.50
6	Bruce Smith	.50
7	Troy Aikman	3.00
8	Reggie White	1.00
9	Irving Fryar	.50
10	Barry Sanders	4.00
11	Cris Carter	.50
12	Emmitt Smith	4.00
13	Dan Marino	5.00
14	Rod Woodson	.50
15	Brett Favre	5.00

1998 Topps Mystery Finest

This 20-card insert arrives with black opaque protectors over the front and four different players on the back. Collectors needed to peel the fronts in order to determine which of the four players it was. Mystery Finest cards are numbered with a "M" prefix and inserted one per 36 packs. Refractor versions were also available and seeded one per 144 packs.

		NM/M
Complete Set (20):		60.00
Common Player:		1.00
Minor Stars:		2.00
Refractors:		3X
1	Steve Young	3.00
2	Dan Marino	6.00
3	Brett Favre	6.00
4	Drew Bledsoe	3.00
5	Mark Brunell	2.00
6	Troy Aikman	4.00
7	Kordell Stewart	2.00
8	John Elway	4.00
9	Barry Sanders	5.00
10	Jerome Bettis	2.00
11	Eddie George	3.00
12	Emmitt Smith	5.00
13	Curtis Martin	3.00
14	Warrick Dunn	2.00
15	Dorsey Levens	2.00
16	Terrell Davis	4.00
17	Herman Moore	1.00
18	Jerry Rice	4.00
19	Tim Brown	3.00
20	Yancey Thigpen	1.00

1998 Topps Season's Best

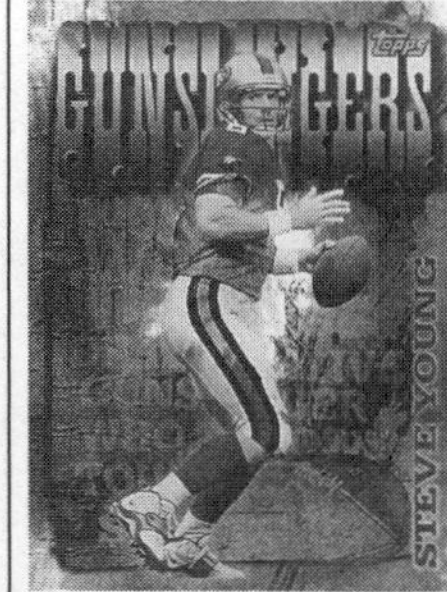

Season's Best includes 30 of the NFL's statistical leaders in six differerent categories on prismatic foilboard. Power & Speed are rushing leaders, Gunslingers are quarterbacks, Prime Targets are receiving leaders, Heavy Hitters are sack leaders, Quick Six are all-purpose yardage and Career Best are all-time leaders. These are numbered with a "SB" prefix and inserted one per 12 packs.

		NM/M
Complete Set (30):		25.00
Common Player:		.50
Minor Stars:		1.00
1	Terrell Davis	4.00
2	Barry Sanders	5.00
3	Jerome Bettis	1.00
4	Dorsey Levens	1.00
5	Eddie George	2.00
6	Brett Favre	5.00
7	Mark Brunell	2.00
8	Jeff George	.50
9	Steve Young	4.00
10	John Elway	4.00
11	Herman Moore	1.00
12	Rob Moore	.50
13	Yancey Thigpen	.50
14	Cris Carter	.50
15	Tim Brown	.50
16	Bruce Smith	.50
17	Michael Sinclair	.50
18	John Randle	.50
19	Dana Stubblefield	.50
20	Michael Strahan	.50
21	Tamarick Vanover	.50
22	Darrien Gordon	.50
23	Michael Bates	.50
24	David Meggett	.50
25	Jermaine Lewis	.50
26	Terrell Davis	3.00
27	Jerry Rice	4.00
28	Barry Sanders	5.00
29	John Randle	.50
30	John Elway	4.00

1998 Topps Action Flats

This was the debut issue of Action Flats with a checklist of eight of the NFL's most celebrated star and rookie players in dynamic action poses. Each figure came with an exclusive special edition foil-stamped trading card that was different than their card in the Topps set. SRP was $2.99 for this product.

	NM/M
Complete Set (8):	25.00
Common Player:	3.00
Troy Aikman	3.00
John Elway	3.00
Brett Favre	4.00
Ryan Leaf	3.00
Peyton Manning	5.00
Dan Marino	3.00
Jerry Rice	3.00
Barry Sanders	4.00

1998 Topps Chrome

Topps Chrome includes 165 cards from Topps reprinted with a chromium finish. The Topps logo is replaced on both the front and the back by a Topps Chrome logo. Cards are renumbered and reordered within the checklist for the mostpart. Each card was also available in a Refractor versions, while the three inserts - Hidden Gems, Measures of Greatness and Season's Best - are also reprinted from Topps and available in both regular and Refractor versions.

		NM/M
Complete Set (165):		175.00
Common Player:		.20
Common Rookie:		3.00
Minor Stars:		.75
Refractor Cards:		3X-5X
Refractor Rookies:		2X-4X
Pack (4):		8.00
Wax Box (24):		140.00
1	Barry Sanders	5.00
2	*Duane Starks*	3.00
3	J.J. Stokes	.20
4	Joey Galloway	.75
5	Deion Sanders	1.50
6	Anthony Miller	.20
7	Jamal Anderson	1.00
8	Shannon Sharpe	.20
9	Irving Fryar	.20
10	Curtis Martin	1.50
11	Shawn Jefferson	.20
12	Charlie Garner	.75
13	*Robert Edwards*	4.00
14	Napoleon Kaufman	1.50
15	Gus Frerotte	.20
16	John Elway	3.00
17	*Jerome Pathon*	3.00
18	Marshall Faulk	.75
19	Michael McCrary	.20
20	Marcus Allen	.75
21	Trent Dilfer	.75
22	Frank Wycheck	.20
23	Terrell Owens	.75
24	Herman Moore	.75
25	Neil O'Donnell	.20
26	Darnay Scott	.20
27	*Keith Brooking*	3.00
28	Eric Green	.20
29	Dan Marino	5.00
30	Antonio Freeman	.75
31	Tony Martin	.20
32	Isaac Bruce	.75
33	Rickey Dudley	.20
34	Scott Mitchell	.20
35	*Randy Moss*	25.00
36	Fred Lane	.75
37	Frank Sanders	.20
38	Jerry Rice	3.00
39	O.J. McDuffie	.20
40	Jessie Armstead	.20
41	Reidel Anthony	.20
42	Steve McNair	2.00
43	Jake Reed	.20
44	*Charles Woodson*	6.00
45	Tiki Barber	.20
46	Mike Alstott	.75
47	Keyshawn Johnson	.75
48	Tony Banks	.75
49	Michael Westbrook	.20
50	Chris Slade	.20
51	Terry Allen	.20
52	Karim Abdul-Jabbar	.75
53	Brad Johnson	.75
54	Tony McGee	.20
55	*Kevin Dyson*	5.00
56	Warren Moon	.75
57	Byron Hanspard	.20
58	Jermaine Lewis	.20
59	Neil Smith	.20
60	Tamarick Vanover	.20
61	Terrell Davis	2.00
62	Robert Smith	.75
63	Junior Seau	.75
64	Warren Sapp	.20
65	Michael Sinclair	.20
66	*Ryan Leaf*	5.00
67	Drew Bledsoe	3.00
68	Jason Sehorn	.20
69	Andre Hastings	.20
70	Tony Gonzalez	.75
71	Dorsey Levens	.75
72	Ray Lewis	.20
73	*Grant Wistrom*	3.00
74	Elvis Grbac	.20
75	Mark Chmura	.75
76	Zach Thomas	.20
77	Ben Coates	.20
78	Rod Smith	.20
79	*Andre Wadsworth*	6.00

80	Garrison Hearst	.20
81	Will Blackwell	.20
82	Cris Carter	.20
83	Mark Fields	.20
84	Ken Dilger	.20
85	Johnnie Morton	.20
86	Michael Irvin	.75
87	Eddie George	3.00
88	Rob Moore	.20
89	*Takeo Spikes*	3.00
90	Wesley Walls	.20
91	Andre Reed	.20
92	Thurman Thomas	.75
93	Ed McCaffrey	.20
94	Carl Pickens	.20
95	Jason Taylor	.20
96	Kordell Stewart	3.00
97	*Greg Ellis*	1.00
98	Aaron Glenn	.20
99	Jake Plummer	3.00
100	Checklist	.20
101	Chris Sanders	.20
102	Michael Jackson	.20
103	Bobby Hoying	.20
104	Wayne Chrebet	.20
105	Charles Way	.20
106	Derrick Thomas	.20
107	Troy Drayton	.20
108	*Robert Holcombe*	5.00
109	Pete Mitchell	.20
110	Bruce Smith	.20
111	Terance Mathis	.20
112	Lawrence Phillips	.20
113	Brett Favre	6.00
114	Darrell Green	.20
115	Charles Johnson	.20
116	Jeff Blake	.75
117	Mark Brunell	3.00
118	Simeon Rice	.20
119	Robert Brooks	.20
120	*Jacquez Green*	4.00
121	Willie Davis	.20
122	Jeff George	.75
123	Andre Rison	.20
124	Erik Kramer	.20
125	Peter Boulware	.20
126	*Marcus Nash*	4.00
127	Troy Aikman	3.00
128	Keenan McCardell	.20
129	Bryant Westbrook	.20
130	Terry Glenn	.75
131	Blaine Bishop	.20
132	Tim Brown	.75
133	*Brian Griese*	12.00
134	John Mobley	.20
135	Larry Centers	.20
136	Eric Bjornson	.20
137	Kevin Hardy	.20
138	John Randle	.20
139	Michael Strahan	.20
140	Jerome Bettis	.75
141	Rae Carruth	.20
142	Reggie White	.75
143	Antowain Smith	1.50
144	Aeneas Williams	.20
145	Bobby Engram	.20
146	*Germane Crowell*	4.00
147	Freddie Jones	.20
148	Kimble Anders	.20
149	Steve Young	2.00
150	Willie McGinest	.20
151	Emmitt Smith	5.00
152	*Fred Taylor*	10.00
153	Danny Kanell	.20
154	Warrick Dunn	3.00
155	Kerry Collins	.75
156	Chris Chandler	.20
157	Curtis Conway	.75
158	*Curtis Enis*	3.00
159	Corey Dillon	2.00
160	Glenn Foley	.75
161	Marvin Harrison	.75
162	Chad Brown	.20
163	Derrick Rodgers	.20
164	Levon Kirkland	.20
165	*Peyton Manning*	30.00

1998 Topps Chrome Refractors

All 165 cards in Topps Chrome were reprinted in Refractor versions and inserted one per 12 packs.

Refractor Cards:	3X-5X
Refractor Rookies:	2X-4X

1998 Topps Chrome Hidden Gems

This 15-card set was reprinted from Topps in a chromium version and inserted one per 12 packs. Cards are numbered with "HG" prefix, while Refractors are seeded one per 24 packs.

		NM/M
Complete Set (15):		25.00
Common Player:		1.00
Minor Stars:		2.00
Refractors:		2X
1	Andre Reed	1.00
2	Kevin Greene	1.00
3	Tony Martin	1.00
4	Shannon Sharpe	1.00
5	Terry Allen	1.00
6	Brett Favre	5.00
7	Ben Coates	1.00
8	Michael Sinclair	1.00
9	Keenan McCardell	1.00
10	Brad Johnson	2.00
11	Mark Brunell	2.00
12	Dorsey Levens	2.00
13	Terrell Davis	3.00
14	Curtis Martin	3.00
15	Derrick Rodgers	1.00

1998 Topps Chrome Measures of Greatness

This 15-card set is reprinted from Topps in a chromium version and seeded one per 12 packs. The cards are numbered with a "HG" prefix, while Refractor versions are seeded one per 48 packs.

		NM/M
Complete Set (15):		40.00
Common Player:		1.00
Minor Stars:		2.00
Refractors:		3X
1	John Elway	3.00
2	Marcus Allen	2.00
3	Jerry Rice	4.00
4	Tim Brown	1.00
5	Warren Moon	1.00
6	Bruce Smith	1.00
7	Troy Aikman	4.00
8	Reggie White	2.00
9	Irving Fryar	1.00
10	Barry Sanders	5.00
11	Cris Carter	1.00
12	Emmitt Smith	5.00
13	Dan Marino	6.00
14	Rod Woodson	1.00
15	Brett Favre	6.00

1998 Topps Chrome Season's Best

This 30-card insert was reprinted from Topps in a chromium version and inserted one per eight packs. The set is broken up with five cards in six different categories, including Power & Speed, Gunslingers, Prime Targets, Heavy Hitters, Quick Six and Career Best. Season's Best cards are numbered with a "SB" prefix and Refractor versions are seeded one per 24 packs.

		NM/M
Complete Set (30):		40.00
Common Player:		.25
Minor Stars:		.75
Refractors:		2X
1	Terrell Davis	3.00
2	Barry Sanders	4.00
3	Jerome Bettis	.75
4	Dorsey Levens	.75
5	Eddie George	2.00
6	Brett Favre	5.00
7	Mark Brunell	1.00
8	Jeff George	.75
9	Steve Young	3.00
10	John Elway	3.00
11	Herman Moore	.75
12	Rob Moore	.25
13	Yancey Thigpen	.25
14	Cris Carter	.75
15	Tim Brown	.75
16	Bruce Smith	.25
17	Michael Smith	.25
18	John Randle	.25
19	Dana Stubblefield	.25
20	Michael Strahan	.25
21	Tamarick Vanover	.25
22	Darrien Gordon	.25
23	Michael Bates	.25
24	David Meggett	.25
25	Jermaine Lewis	.25
26	Terrell Davis	3.00
27	Jerry Rice	4.00
28	Barry Sanders	4.00
29	John Randle	.25
30	John Elway	3.00

1998 Topps Gold Label

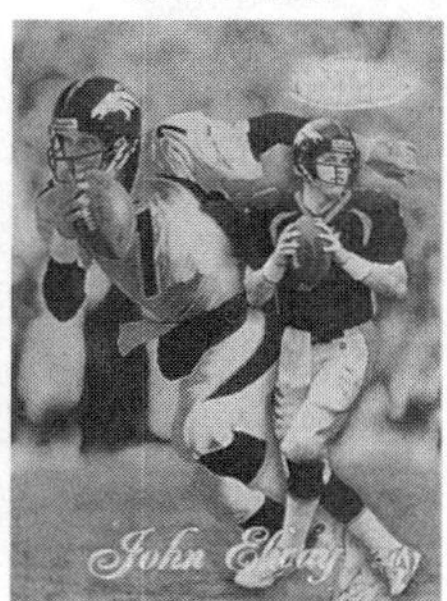

Each card in this set was printed on 35 point spectra-reflective rainbow stock and was gold foil-stamped with the player's name and the Gold Label logo. The backs of the cards reveal all relevant statistics, including career totals and career bests as well as insightful player commentary. Each card has a parallel Class 2 and a Class 3 card. The Class 2 cards have the name and logo in silver foil and were inserted 1:2 packs. The Class 3 singles were in prismatic gold foil and found 1:4 packs.

		NM/M
Complete Set (100):		70.00
Common Player:		.25
Minor Stars:		.50
Class 2 Cards:		2X
Class 2 Rookies:		1.5X
Name In Silver Foil		
Inserted 1:2		
Class 3 Cards:		3X
Class 3 Rookies:		2X
Name In Prismatic Gold Foil		
Inserted 1:4		
Hobby Pack (5):		3.00
Hobby Wax Box (24):		50.00
Retail Pack (3):		3.00
Retail Wax Box (36):		70.00
1	John Elway	4.00
2	Rob Moore	.25
3	Jamal Anderson	1.50
4	*Patrick Johnson*	1.50
5	Troy Aikman	4.00
6	Antowain Smith	1.50
7	Wesley Walls	.25
8	*Curtis Enis*	3.00
9	Jimmy Smith	.50
10	Terrell Davis	3.00
11	Marshall Faulk	1.00
12	*Germane Crowell*	2.00
13	*Marcus Nash*	2.00
14	Deion Sanders	1.00
15	Dorsey Levens	.50
16	Corey Dillon	1.50
17	*Fred Taylor*	8.00
18	Derrick Thomas	.25
19	*Kevin Dyson*	4.00
20	*Peyton Manning*	15.00
21	Warren Sapp	.25
22	*Robert Holcombe*	3.00
23	Joey Galloway	1.00
24	Garrison Hearst	.50
25	Brett Favre	8.00
26	Aeneas Williams	.25
27	Danny Kanell	.25
28	Robert Smith	.50
29	Brad Johnson	1.00
30	Dan Marino	6.00
31	Elvis Grbac	.50
32	Terry Allen	.25
33	Frank Sanders	.25
34	Peter Boulware	.25
35	Tim Brown	.50
36	Thurman Thomas	.50
37	Rae Carruth	.25
38	Michael Irvin	.50
39	*Brian Griese*	8.00
40	Kordell Stewart	3.00
41	Johnnie Morton	.25
42	Robert Brooks	.25
43	Keenan McCardell	.25
44	Ben Coates	.50
45	Jerry Rice	4.00
46	*Tony Simmons*	2.50
47	Irving Fryar	.25
48	*Jerome Pathon*	2.00
49	Steve McNair	1.50
50	Warrick Dunn	3.00
51	*Skip Hicks*	4.00
52	*Andre Wadsworth*	2.00
53	Chris Chandler	.50
54	Curtis Conway	.50
55	Eddie George	3.00
56	Jeff Blake	.50
57	*Greg Ellis*	1.50
58	Scott Mitchell	.25
59	Antonio Freeman	1.00
60	Drew Bledsoe	4.00
61	Mark Brunell	3.00
62	Andre Rison	.50
63	Cris Carter	1.00
64	Jake Reed	.25
65	Napoleon Kaufman	1.50
66	Terry Glenn	1.00
67	Jason Sehorn	.25
68	Rickey Dudley	.25
69	Junior Seau	.50
70	Jerome Bettis	1.00
71	J.J. Stokes	.50
72	Warren Moon	.50
73	Isaac Bruce	.50
74	Mike Alstott	1.00
75	Steve Young	2.50
76	*Jacquez Green*	4.00
77	Gus Frerotte	.25
78	Michael Jackson	.25
79	Carl Pickens	.50
80	Bruce Smith	.25
81	Shannon Sharpe	.50
82	Herman Moore	.50
83	Reggie White	1.00
84	Marvin Harrison	.75
85	Jake Plummer	3.00
86	Karim Abdul-Jabbar	.75
87	John Randle	.25
88	*Robert Edwards*	4.00
89	Jeff George	.50
90	Emmitt Smith	6.00
91	Terrell Owens	1.50
92	Trent Dilfer	1.00
93	Darrell Green	.25
94	Andre Reed	.25
95	*Ryan Leaf*	4.00
96	Rod Smith	.50
97	O.J. McDuffie	.25
98	*John Avery*	4.00
99	Charles Way	.25
100	Barry Sanders	6.00

1998 Topps Gold Label Black Label

Each of the three versions in this set are the same as in the base Gold Label set except for the logo is in black. Class 1 singles have the name in gold foil and are found 1:8 packs. Class 2 cards are in silver foil and inserted 1:16 packs. Class 3 singles are in prismatic gold foil and inserted 1:32 packs.

Class 1 Cards:	2X
Class 1 Rookies:	2X
Name In Gold Foil	
Inserted 1:8	
Class 2 Cards:	3X
Class 2 Rookies:	2X
Name In Silver Foil	
Inserted 1:16	
Class 3 Cards:	4X
Class 3 Rookies:	3X
Name In Prismatic Gold Foil	
Inserted 1:32	

1998 Topps Gold Label Red Label

Red Label cards are the same as the base Gold Label set except for the logo is in red foil and each card is sequentially numbered. Class 1 singles have the name in gold foil (1:94) and are numbered to 100. Class 2 singles are in silver foil (1:187) and numbered to 50. Class 3 cards are in prismatic gold foil (1:375) and numbered to 25.

	NM/M
Class 1 Cards:	10X-25X
Class 1 Rookies:	5X-10X
Name In Gold Foil	
Inserted 1:94	
Production 100 Sets	
Class 2 Cards:	12X-30X
Class 2 Rookies:	6X-12X
Name In Silver Foil	
Inserted 1:187	
Production 50 Sets	
Class 3 Cards:	15X-35X
Class 3 Rookies:	8X-15X
Name In Prismatic Gold Foil	
Inserted 1:375	
Production 25 Sets	

1998 Topps Season Opener

Topps Season Opener was a retail exclusive product comprised of 165 cards that paralleled Topps. While Topps cards were printed with a gold border, Season Opener cards used a silver border and a silver "Season Opener '98" stamp on a goal post to distinguish them. Packs contained seven cards and one Season Opener Sweepstakes card, with which collectors could win a trip to the Pro Bowl in Honolulu, Hawaii.

		NM/M
Complete Set (165):		100.00
Common Player:		.10
Minor Stars:		.20
Common Rookie:		2.50
Pack (8):		4.00
Wax Box (36):		100.00
1	*Peyton Manning*	25.00
2	*Jerome Pathon*	4.00
3	*Duane Starks*	2.50
4	*Brian Simmons*	2.50
5	*Keith Brooking*	2.50
6	*Robert Edwards*	4.00
7	*Curtis Enis*	2.00
8	*John Avery*	3.00
9	*Fred Taylor*	8.00
10	*Germane Crowell*	3.00
11	*Hines Ward*	8.00
12	*Marcus Nash*	2.50
13	*Jacquez Green*	4.00
14	*Joe Jurevicius*	2.50
15	*Greg Ellis*	2.50
16	*Brian Griese*	8.00
17	*Tavian Banks*	3.00
18	*Robert Holcombe*	3.00
19	*Skip Hicks*	4.00
20	*Ahman Green*	15.00
21	*Takeo Spikes*	2.50
22	*Randy Moss*	20.00
23	*Andre Wadsworth*	4.00
24	*Jason Peter*	2.50
25	*Grant Wistrom*	2.50
26	*Charles Woodson*	6.00
27	*Kevin Dyson*	4.00
28	*Patrick Johnson*	4.00
29	*Tim Dwight*	5.00
30	*Ryan Leaf*	4.00
31	Chad Brown	.10
32	Levon Kirkland	.10
33	Corey Dillon	.50
34	Curtis Conway	.20
35	Chris Chandler	.10
36	Warrick Dunn	.75
37	Danny Kanell	.10
38	Emmitt Smith	1.50
39	Steve Young	.75
40	Kimble Anders	.10
41	Freddie Jones	.10
42	Bobby Engram	.10
43	Aeneas Williams	.10
44	Antowain Smith	.40
45	Reggie White	.20
46	Rae Carruth	.10
47	Jamie Asher	.10
48	Hardy Nickerson	.10
49	Jerome Bettis	.20
50	Michael Strahan	.10
51	John Randle	.10
52	Larry Centers	.10
53	Tim Brown	.20
54	Terry Glenn	.20
55	Keenan McCardell	.10
56	Troy Aikman	1.00
57	Peter Boulware	.10
58	Erik Kramer	.10
59	Andre Rison	.10
60	Jeff George	.20
61	Robert Brooks	.10
62	Simeon Rice	.10
63	Mark Brunell	1.00
64	Jeff Blake	.20
65	Brett Favre	2.00
66	Lawrence Phillips	.10
67	Randal Hill	.10
68	Terance Mathis	.10
69	Bruce Smith	.10
70	Troy Drayton	.10
71	Derrick Thomas	.10
72	Charles Way	.10
73	Bobby Hoying	.10
74	Michael Jackson	.10
75	Chris Sanders	.10
76	Cris Dishman	.10
77	Jake Plummer	1.00
78	Kordell Stewart	.75
79	Carl Pickens	.20
80	Ed McCaffrey	.30
81	Ray Buchanan	.10
82	Thurman Thomas	.20
83	Andre Reed	.10
84	Wesley Walls	.10
85	Rob Moore	.20
86	Eddie George	.75
87	Michael Irvin	.20
88	Johnnie Morton	.10
89	Cris Carter	.30
90	Garrison Hearst	.20
91	Rod Smith	.20
92	Ben Coates	.10
93	Zach Thomas	.20
94	Dale Carter	.10
95	Mark Chmura	.20
96	Elvis Grbac	.10
97	Ray Lewis	.10
98	Lonnie Johnson	.10
99	Darrell Green	.10
100	Marvin Harrison	.20
101	Dorsey Levens	.20
102	Tony Gonzalez	.10
103	Andre Hastings	.10
104	Jason Sehorn	.10
105	Drew Bledsoe	1.00
106	Junior Seau	.20
107	Robert Smith	.20
108	Terrell Davis	1.50
109	Neil Smith	.10
110	Jermaine Lewis	.10
111	Warren Moon	.20
112	Brad Johnson	.20
113	Karim Abdul-Jabbar	.20
114	Terry Allen	.20
115	Chris Slade	.10
116	Michael Westbrook	.10
117	Tony Banks	.20
118	Mike Alstott	.20
119	Jake Reed	.10
120	Bryant Westbrook	.10
121	Steve McNair	.75
122	Jimmy Smith	.20
123	Reidel Anthony	.10
124	Jessie Armstead	.10
125	O.J. McDuffie	.10
126	Jerry Rice	1.00
127	Frank Sanders	.10
128	Fred Lane	.20
129	Scott Mitchell	.10
130	Rickey Dudley	.10
131	Isaac Bruce	.20
132	Tony Martin	.10
133	Leslie Shepherd	.10
134	Derrick Thomas	.10
135	Antonio Freeman	.20
136	Dan Marino	1.50
137	Eric Green	.10
138	Darnay Scott	.10
139	Herman Moore	.20
140	Terrell Owens	.30
141	Trent Dilfer	.20
142	Marshall Faulk	.20
143	John Elway	1.00
144	Gus Frerotte	.10
145	Napoleon Kaufman	.40
146	Charlie Garner	.10
147	Irving Fryar	.10
148	Shannon Sharpe	.20
149	Jamal Anderson	.30
150	Chris Spielman	.10
151	Deion Sanders	.40
152	Joey Galloway	.20
153	J.J. Stokes	.10
154	Quinn Early	.10
155	Michael McCrary	.10
156	Willie McGinest	.10
157	Kevin Hardy	.10
158	Micheal Barrow	.10
159	John Mobley	.10
160	Michael Sinclair	.10
161	Warren Sapp	.10
162	Michael Bates	.10
163	Pete Mitchell	.10
164	Barry Sanders	2.00
165	Checklist	.10

1998 Topps Stars

Each borderless card is printed on 20-point stock and uses luminous diffraction technology with matte gold-foil stamping. Every card in this product is sequentially numbered. The Red and Bronze set are both considered base sets and are each numbered to 8,799. Three parallel sets include Silver, Gold and Gold Rainbow. The Silver singles were numbered to 3,999, the Gold cards are to 1,999 and inserted 1:2 packs, and the Gold Rainbow cards were numbered to 99 and found 1:41 packs.

	NM/M
Complete Set (150):	75.00
Common Red Player:	.10
Minor Red Stars:	.40
Common Red Rookie:	1.00
Production 8,799 Sets	
Bronze Cards:	1X
Production 8,799 Sets	
Silver Cards:	1.5X
Production 3,999 Sets	
Gold Cards:	3X
Gold Rookies:	2X
Production 1,999 Sets	
Inserted 1:2	
Gold Rainbow Cards:	5X-10X
Gold Rainbow Rookies:	3X-5X
Production 99 Sets	
Inserted 1:41	
Pack (6):	3.00
Wax Box (24):	70.00

1	John Elway	2.50
2	*Duane Starks*	1.50
3	Bruce Smith	.10
4	Jeff Blake	.40
5	Carl Pickens	.40
6	Shannon Sharpe	.40
7	*Jerome Pathon*	2.00
8	Jimmy Smith	.40
9	Elvis Grbac	.10
10	Mark Brunell	2.00
11	Karim Abdul-Jabbar	.75
12	Terry Glenn	.75
13	Larry Centers	.10
14	Jeff George	.40
15	Terry Allen	.10
16	Charles Johnson	.10
17	Chris Spielman	.10
18	*Ahman Green*	10.00
19	*Kevin Dyson*	3.00
20	Dan Marino	4.00
21	*Andre Wadsworth*	1.50
22	Chris Chandler	.10
23	Kerry Collins	.40
24	Erik Kramer	.10
25	Warrick Dunn	2.00
26	Michael Irvin	.40
27	Herman Moore	.40
28	Dorsey Levens	.40
29	Cris Carter	.40
30	Drew Bledsoe	2.00
31	Kevin Greene	.10
32	Charles Way	.10
33	Bobby Hoying	.10
34	Tony Banks	.40
35	Steve Young	1.50
36	Trent Dilfer	.40
37	Warren Sapp	.10
38	*Skip Hicks*	2.00
39	Michael Jackson	.10
40	Curtis Martin	1.00
41	Thurman Thomas	.40
42	Corey Dillon	1.50
43	*Brian Griese*	6.00
44	Marshall Faulk	.75
45	Isaac Bruce	.40
46	*Fred Taylor*	6.00
47	Andre Rison	.10
48	O.J. McDuffie	.10
49	*John Avery*	1.00
50	Terrell Davis	2.00
51	*Robert Edwards*	1.00
52	Keyshawn Johnson	.40
53	Rickey Dudley	.10
54	*Hines Ward*	2.00
55	Irving Fryar	.10
56	Freddie Jones	.10
57	Michael Sinclair	.10
58	Darnay Scott	.10
59	*Tim Dwight*	3.00
60	Tim Brown	.40
61	Ray Lewis	.10
62	*Curtis Enis*	1.00
63	Emmitt Smith	4.00
64	Scott Mitchell	.10
65	Antonio Freeman	.75
66	*Randy Moss*	10.00
67	*Peyton Manning*	12.00
68	Danny Kanell	.10
69	Charlie Garner	.10
70	Mike Alstott	.75
71	*Grant Wistrom*	1.00
72	*Jacquez Green*	3.50
73	Gus Frerotte	.10
74	Peter Boulware	.10
75	Jerry Rice	2.50
76	Antowain Smith	1.00
77	*Brian Simmons*	1.00
78	Rod Smith	.40
79	Marvin Harrison	.40
80	*Ryan Leaf*	1.00
81	Keenan McCardell	.10
82	Derrick Thomas	.10
83	Zach Thomas	.40
84	Ben Coates	.10
85	Rob Moore	.10
86	Wayne Chrebet	.10
87	Napoleon Kaufman	.75
88	Levon Kirkland	.10
89	Junior Seau	.40
90	Eddie George	2.00
91	Warren Moon	.40
92	*Anthony Simmons*	1.00
93	Steve McNair	1.25
94	Frank Sanders	.10
95	Joey Galloway	.75
96	Jamal Anderson	.75
97	Rae Carruth	.10
98	Curtis Conway	.40
99	*Greg Ellis*	1.00
100	Kordell Stewart	2.00
101	*Germane Crowell*	2.00
102	Mark Chmura	.40
103	Robert Smith	.40
104	Andre Hastings	.10
105	Reggie White	.40
106	Jessie Armstead	.10
107	Kevin Hardy	.10
108	*Robert Holcombe*	2.00
109	Garrison Hearst	.40
110	Jerome Bettis	.40
111	Reidel Anthony	.40
112	Michael Westbrook	.10
113	*Patrick Johnson*	1.00
114	Andre Reed	.10
115	*Charles Woodson*	4.00
116	*Takeo Spikes*	1.50
117	*Marcus Nash*	2.00
118	*Tavian Banks*	2.00
119	Tony Gonzalez	.40
120	Jake Plummer	2.00
121	*Tony Simmons*	2.50
122	Aaron Glenn	.10
123	Ricky Watters	.40
124	Kimble Anders	.10
125	Barry Sanders	4.00
126	Terance Mathis	.10
127	Wesley Walls	.10
128	Bobby Engram	.10
129	Johnnie Morton	.10
130	Brett Favre	5.00
131	Brad Johnson	.40
132	John Randle	.10
133	Chris Sanders	.10
134	*Joe Jurevicius*	2.00
135	Deion Sanders	1.00
136	Terrell Owens	1.00
137	Darrell Green	.10
138	Jermaine Lewis	.10
139	James Stewart	.10
140	Troy Aikman	2.50
141	Hardy Nickerson	.10
142	Blaine Bishop	.10
143	*Keith Brooking*	2.00
144	*Jason Peter*	1.00
145	Jake Reed	.10
146	Jason Sehorn	.10
147	Robert Brooks	.10
148	J.J. Stokes	.40
149	Michael Strahan	.10
150	Glenn Foley	.40

1998 Topps Stars Galaxy

Each single in this set has the bronze foil, was sequentially numbered to 100 and inserted 1:611 packs. Silver foil cards were numbered to 75 and found 1:814 packs. Gold foil cards were numbered to 50 and inserted 1:1,222. Gold Rainbow singles were the toughest to find with only five printed and inserted 1:12,215.

		NM/M
Common Bronze Player:		10.00
Production 100 Sets		
Inserted 1:611		
Silver Cards:		1.5X
Production 75 Sets		
Inserted 1:814		
Gold Cards:		2X
Production 50 Sets		
Inserted 1:1,222		
G1	Brett Favre	40.00
G2	Barry Sanders	35.00
G3	Bruce Smith	15.00
G4	Herman Moore	10.00
G5	Tim Brown	20.00
G6	Steve Young	25.00
G7	Cris Carter	15.00
G8	John Elway	25.00
G9	Mark Brunell	15.00
G10	Terrell Davis	25.00

A card number in parenthese ( ) indicates the set is unnumbered.

1998 Topps Stars Luminaries

Each card in this set has bronze foil stamping and is sequentially numbered to 100. Singles were tough to pull from packs at 1:407. The Silver parallel set has the foil stamping in silver and is numbered to 75 and was inserted 1:543 packs. The Gold parallel was numbered to 50 and inserted 1:814 packs. The last parallel set was the Gold Rainbow that was limited to five of each and found 1:8,144.

		NM/M
Common Bronze Player:		10.00
Production 100 Sets		
Inserted 1:407		
Silver Cards:		1.5X
Production 75 Sets		
Inserted 1:543		
Gold Cards:		2X
Production 50 Sets		
Inserted 1:814		
L1	Brett Favre	30.00
L2	Steve Young	20.00
L3	John Elway	25.00
L4	Barry Sanders	30.00
L5	Terrell Davis	25.00
L6	Eddie George	15.00
L7	Herman Moore	10.00
L8	Tim Brown	10.00
L9	Jerry Rice	20.00
L10	Junior Seau	10.00
L11	Bruce Smith	10.00
L12	John Randle	10.00
L13	Peyton Manning	20.00
L14	Ryan Leaf	10.00
L15	Curtis Enis	10.00

1998 Topps Stars Rookie Reprints

Topps reprinted eight NFL Hall of Famers' rookie cards and inserted them 1:24 packs. Each card also has a parallel Autograph card with the odds at 1:153 packs.

		NM/M
Complete Set (8):		15.00
Common Player:		1.00
Inserted 1:24		
Autographs:		10X
Inserted 1:153		
1	Walter Payton	5.00
2	Don Maynard	2.00
3	Charlie Joiner	2.00
4	Fred Biletnikoff	1.00
5	Paul Hornung	3.00
6	Gale Sayers	3.00
7	John Hannah	1.00
8	Paul Warfield	2.00
9	Walter Payton/Auto	300.00

1998 Topps Stars Supernova

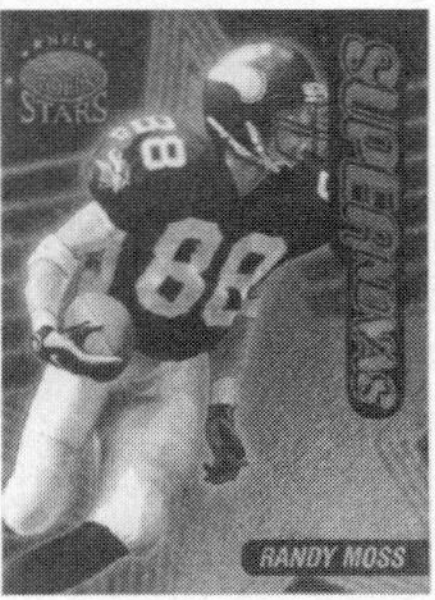

Each single in this set has the bronze foil, was sequentially numbered to 100 and inserted 1:611 packs. Silver foil cards were numbered to 75 and found 1:814 packs. Gold foil cards were numbered to 50 and inserted 1:1,222. Gold Rainbow singles were the toughest to find with only five printed and inserted 1:12,215.

		NM/M
Common Bronze Player:		10.00
Production 100 Sets		
Inserted 1:611		
Silver Cards:		1.5X
Production 75 Sets		
Inserted 1:814		
Gold Cards:		2X
Production 50 Sets		
Inserted 1:1,222		
S1	Ryan Leaf	10.00
S2	Curtis Enis	10.00
S3	Kevin Dyson	12.00
S4	Randy Moss	35.00
S5	Peyton Manning	35.00
S6	Duane Starks	10.00
S7	Grant Wistrom	10.00
S8	Charles Woodson	15.00
S9	Fred Taylor	15.00
S10	Andre Wadsworth	10.00

1999 Topps

Each card in this 357-card set was printed on 16-pt. stock, with green borders and gold foil stamping. Included are 27 rookies that were seeded 1:5 packs. Other subsets include 10 Season Highlights and five Cleveland Browns Expansion Draft cards. Top inserts include: MVP Promotion, All Matrix, Autographs, Hall of Fame Autographs, Mystery Chrome, Picture Perfect, Record Numbers and Season's Best.

	NM/M
Complete Set (357):	65.00
Common Player:	.10
Minor Stars:	.20
Common Rookie:	1.00
Inserted 1:5	
Pack (11):	1.25
Wax Box (36):	35.00
Jumbo Pack (40):	4.00
Jumbo Wax Box (12):	35.00
Season Opener Pack (7):	1.50
Season Opener Wax Box (24):	25.00

1	Terrell Davis	1.00
2	Adrian Murrell	.10
3	Ernie Mills	.10
4	Jimmy Hitchcock	.10
5	Charlie Garner	.10
6	Blaine Bishop	.10
7	Junior Seau	.20
8	Andre Rison	.20
9	Jake Reed	.10
10	Cris Carter	.40
11	Torrance Small	.10
12	Ronald McKinnon	.10
13	Tyrone Davis	.10
14	Warren Moon	.20
15	Joe Johnson	.10
16	Bert Emanuel	.10
17	Brad Culpepper	.10
18	Henry Jones	.10
19	Jonathan Ogden	.10
20	Terrell Owens	.40
21	Derrick Mason	.10
22	Jon Ritchie	.10
23	Eric Metcalf	.10
24	Kevin Carter	.10
25	Fred Taylor	1.00
26	DeWayne Washington	.10
27	William Thomas	.10
28	Raghib Ismail	.10
29	Jason Taylor	.10
30	Doug Flutie	.50
31	Michael Sinclair	.10
32	Yancey Thigpen	.10
33	Darnay Scott	.10
34	Amani Toomer	.10
35	Edgar Bennett	.10
36	LeRoy Butler	.10
37	Jessie Tuggle	.10
38	Andrew Glover	.10
39	Tim McDonald	.10
40	Marshall Faulk	.40
41	Ray Mickens	.10
42	Kimble Anders	.10
43	Trent Green	.40
44	Dermontti Dawson	.10
45	Greg Ellis	.10
46	Hugh Douglas	.10
47	Amp Lee	.10
48	Lamar Thomas	.10
49	Curtis Conway	.20
50	Emmitt Smith	1.50
51	Elvis Grbac	.10
52	Tony Simmons	.20
53	Darrin Smith	.10
54	Donovin Darius	.10
55	Corey Chavous	.10
56	Phillippi Sparks	.10
57	Luther Elliss	.10
58	Tim Dwight	.40
59	Andre Hastings	.10
60	Dan Marino	1.50
61	Micheal Barrow	.10
62	Corey Fuller	.10
63	Bill Romanowski	.10
64	Derrick Rodgers	.10
65	Natrone Means	.30
66	Peter Boulware	.10
67	Brian Mitchell	.10
68	Cornelius Bennett	.10
69	Dedric Ward	.10
70	Drew Bledsoe	.75
71	Freddie Jones	.10
72	Derrick Thomas	.10
73	Willie Davis	.10
74	Larry Centers	.10
75	Mark Brunell	.75
76	Chuck Smith	.10
77	Desmond Howard	.10
78	Sedrick Shaw	.10
79	Tiki Barber	.10
80	Curtis Martin	.40
81	Barry Minter	.10
82	Skip Hicks	.20
83	O.J. Santiago	.10
84	Ed McCaffrey	.30
85	Terrell Buckley	.10
86	Charlie Jones	.10
87	Pete Mitchell	.10
88	La'Roi Glover	.10
89	Eric Davis	.10
90	John Elway	1.50
91	Kavika Pittman	.10
92	Fred Lane	.10
93	Warren Sapp	.10
94	Lorenzo Bromell	.10
95	Lawyer Milloy	.10
96	Aeneas Williams	.10
97	Michael McCrary	.10
98	Rickey Dudley	.10
99	Bryce Paup	.10
100	Jamal Anderson	.50
101	D'Marco Farr	.10
102	Johnnie Morton	.10
103	Jeff Graham	.10
104	Sam Cowart	.10
105	Bryant Young	.10
106	Jermaine Lewis	.10
107	Chad Bratzke	.10
108	Jeff Burris	.10
109	Roell Preston	.10
110	Vinny Testaverde	.20
111	Ruben Brown	.10
112	Darryll Lewis	.10
113	Billy Davis	.10
114	Bryant Westbrook	.10
115	Stephen Alexander	.10
116	Terry Fletcher	.10
117	Terry Glenn	.30
118	Rod Smith	.20
119	Carl Pickens	.20
120	Tim Brown	.20
121	Mikhael Ricks	.10
122	Jason Gildon	.10
123	Charles Way	.10
124	Rob Moore	.20
125	Jerome Bettis	.30
126	Kerry Collins	.20
127	Bruce Smith	.10
128	James Hasty	.10
129	Ken Norton Jr.	.10
130	Charles Woodson	.40
131	Tony McGee	.10
132	Kevin Turner	.10
133	Jerome Pathon	.10
134	Garrison Hearst	.30
135	Craig Newsome	.10
136	Hardy Nickerson	.10
137	Ray Lewis	.10
138	Derrick Alexander	.10
139	Phil Hansen	.10
140	Joey Galloway	.50
141	Oronde Gadsden	.20
142	Herman Moore	.30
143	Bobby Taylor	.10
144	Mario Bates	.10
145	Kevin Dyson	.20
146	Aaron Glenn	.10
147	Ed McDaniel	.10
148	Terry Allen	.20
149	Ike Hilliard	.10
150	Steve Young	.50
151	Eugene Robinson	.10
152	John Mobley	.10
153	Kevin Hardy	.10
154	Lance Johnstone	.10
155	Willie McGinest	.10
156	Gary Anderson	.10
157	Dexter Coakley	.10
158	Mark Fields	.10
159	Steve McNair	.50
160	Corey Dillon	.50
161	Zach Thomas	.30
162	Kent Graham	.10
163	Tony Parrish	.10
164	Sam Gash	.10
165	Kyle Brady	.10
166	Donnell Bennett	.10
167	Tony Martin	.10
168	Michael Bates	.10
169	Bobby Engram	.10
170	Jimmy Smith	.20
171	Vonnie Holliday	.20
172	Simeon Rice	.10
173	Kevin Greene	.10
174	Mike Alstott	.40
175	Eddie George	.50
176	Michael Jackson	.10
177	Neil O'Donnell	.10
178	Sean Dawkins	.10
179	Courtney Hawkins	.10
180	Michael Irvin	.20
181	Thurman Thomas	.20
182	Cameron Cleeland	.20
183	Ellis Johnson	.10
184	Will Blackwell	.10
185	Ty Law	.10
186	Merton Hanks	.10
187	Dan Wilkinson	.10
188	Andre Wadsworth	.20
189	Troy Vincent	.10
190	Frank Sanders	.20
191	Stephen Boyd	.10
192	Jason Elam	.10
193	Kordell Stewart	.50
194	Ted Johnson	.10
195	Glyn Milburn	.10
196	Gary Brown	.10
197	Travis Hall	.10
198	John Randle	.10
199	Jay Riemersma	.10
200	Barry Sanders	2.00
201	Chris Spielman	.10
202	Rod Woodson	.10
203	Darrell Russell	.10
204	Tony Boselli	.10
205	Darren Woodson	.10
206	Muhsin Muhammad	.10
207	Jim Harbaugh	.20
208	Isaac Bruce	.30
209	Mo Lewis	.10
210	Dorsey Levens	.30
211	Frank Wycheck	.10
212	Napoleon Kaufman	.40
213	Walt Harris	.10
214	Leon Lett	.10
215	Karim Abdul	.20
216	Carnell Lake	.10
217	Byron Morris	.10
218	John Avery	.20
219	Chris Slade	.10
220	Robert Smith	.20
221	Mike Pritchard	.10
222	Ty Detmer	.10
223	Randall Cunningham	.40
224	Alonzo Mayes	.10
225	Jake Plummer	1.00
226	Derrick Mayes	.10
227	Jeff Brady	.10
228	John Lynch	.10
229	Steve Atwater	.10
230	Warrick Dunn	.50
231	Shawn Jefferson	.10
232	Erik Kramer	.10
233	Ken Dilger	.10
234	Ryan Leaf	.40
235	Ray Buchanan	.10
236	Kevin Williams	.10
237	Ricky Watters	.20
238	Dwayne Rudd	.10
239	Duce Staley	.10
240	Charlie Batch	.50
241	Tim Biakabutuka	.20
242	Tony Gonzalez	.20
243	Bryan Still	.10
244	Donnie Edwards	.10
245	Troy Aikman	1.00
246	Az-Zahir Hakim	.20
247	Curtis Enis	.40
248	Chris Chandler	.20
249	James Jett	.10
250	Brett Favre	2.00
251	Keith Poole	.10
252	Ricky Proehl	.10
253	Shannon Sharpe	.20
254	Robert Jones	.10
255	Chad Brown	.10
256	Ben Coates	.20
257	Jacquez Green	.20
258	Jessie Armstead	.10
259	Dale Carter	.10
260	Antowain Smith	.40
261	Mark Chmura	.20
262	Michael Westbrook	.20
263	Marvin Harrison	.20
264	Darrien Gordon	.10
265	Rodney Harrison	.10
266	Charles Johnson	.10
267	Roman Pfifer	.10
268	Reidel Anthony	.20
269	Jerry Rice	1.00
270	Eric Moulds	.50
271	Robert Porcher	.10
272	Deion Sanders	.40
273	Germane Crowell	.20
274	Randy Moss	2.00
275	Antonio Freeman	.40
276	Trent Dilfer	.30
277	Eric Turner	.10
278	Jeff George	.20
279	Levon Kirkland	.10
280	O.J. McDuffie	.10
281	Takeo Spikes	.10
282	Jim Flanigan	.10
283	Chris Warren	.10
284	J.J. Stokes	.20
285	Bryan Cox	.10
286	Sam Madison	.10
287	Priest Holmes	.40
288	Keenan McCardell	.10
289	Michael Strahan	.10
290	Robert Edwards	.30
291	Tommy Vardell	.10
292	Wayne Chrebet	.40
293	Chris Calloway	.10
294	Wesley Walls	.10
295	Derrick Brooks	.10
296	Trace Armstrong	.10
297	Brian Simmons	.10
298	Darrell Green	.10
299	Robert Brooks	.10
300	Peyton Manning	1.50
301	Dana Stubblefield	.10
302	Shawn Springs	.10
303	Leslie Shepherd	.10
304	Ken Harvey	.10
305	Jon Kitna	.50
306	Terance Mathis	.10
307	Andre Reed	.20
308	Jackie Harris	.10
309	Rich Gannon	.10
310	Keyshawn Johnson	.50
311	Victor Green	.10
312	Eric Allen	.10
313	Terry Fair	.10

314 Jason Elam Season Highlights .10
315 Garrison Hearst Season Highlights .10
316 Jake Plummer Season Highlights .50
317 Randall Cunningham Season Highlights .20
318 Randy Moss Season Highlights 1.00
319 Jamal Anderson Season Highlights .20
320 John Elway Season Highlights .75
321 Doug Flutie Season Highlights .20
322 Emmitt Smith Season Highlights .50
323 Terrell Davis Season Highlights .75
324 Jerris McPhail .10
325 Damon Gibson .10
326 Jim Pyne .10
327 Antonio Langham .10
328 Freddie Solomon .10
329 *Ricky Williams* 10.00
330 *Daunte Culpepper* 10.00
331 *Chris Claiborne* 1.75
332 *Amos Zereoue* 3.00
333 *Chris McAlister* 1.00
334 *Kevin Faulk* 3.00
335 *James Johnson* 2.50
336 *Mike Cloud* 1.75
337 *Jevon Kearse* 3.00
338 *Akili Smith* 2.00
339 *Edgerrin James* 10.00
340 *Cecil Collins* 2.00
341 *Donovan McNabb* 10.00
342 *Kevin Johnson* 3.00
343 *Torry Holt* 5.00
344 *Rob Konrad* 1.00
345 *Tim Couch* 3.00
346 *David Boston* 5.00
347 *Karsten Bailey* 1.75
348 *Troy Edwards* 3.00
349 *Sedrick Irvin* 1.75
350 *Shaun King* 3.00
351 *Peerless Price* 4.00
352 *Brock Huard* 2.50
353 *Cade McNown* 3.00
354 *Champ Bailey* 2.50
355 *D'Wayne Bates* 1.00
356 Checklist .10
357 Checklist .10

1999 Topps All Matrix

This 30-card insert is divided into three different subsets. 1200 Yard Club (10 running backs who rushed for 1200 yards or more), 3000 Yard Club (quarterbacks with rocket-arms) and '99 Rookie Rush (9 players from the 1999 NFL draft). Each is printed on dot matrix cards and were inserted 1:14 packs.

NM/M
Complete Set (30): 50.00
Common Player: 1.00
Minor Stars: 2.00
Inserted 1:14
1 Fred Taylor 1200 Yard Club 2.00
2 Ricky Watters 1200 Yard Club 2.00
3 Curtis Martin 1200 Yard Club 3.00
4 Eddie George 1200 Yard Club 2.00
5 Marshall Faulk 1200 Yard Club 2.00
6 Emmitt Smith 1200 Yard Club 4.00
7 Barry Sanders 1200 Yard Club 4.00
8 Garrison Hearst 1200 Yard Club 1.00
9 Jamal Anderson 1200 Yard Club 1.00
10 Terrell Davis 1200 Yard Club 3.00
11 Chris Chandler 3000 Yard Club 1.00
12 Steve McNair 3000 Yard Club 2.00
13 Vinny Testaverde 3000 Yard Club 1.00
14 Trent Green 3000 Yard Club 1.00
15 Dan Marino 3000 Yard Club 5.00
16 Drew Bledsoe 3000 Yard Club 3.00
17 Randall Cunningham 3000 Yard Club 1.00
18 Jake Plummer 3000 Yard Club 1.00
19 Peyton Manning 3000 Yard Club 4.00
20 Steve Young 3000 Yard Club 3.00
21 Brett Favre 3000 Yard Club 5.00
22 Tim Couch 99 Rookie Rush 3.00
23 Edgerrin James 99 Rookie Rush 4.00
24 David Boston 99 Rookie Rush 2.00
25 Akili Smith 99 Rookie Rush 1.00
26 Troy Edwards 99 Rookie Rush 1.00
27 Torry Holt 99 Rookie Rush 1.00
28 Donovan McNabb 99 Rookie Rush 3.00
29 Daunte Culpepper 99 Rookie Rush 3.00
30 Ricky Williams 99 Rookie Rush 5.00

1999 Topps Autographs

This 10-card set was a hobby exclusive that included 8 current stars and 2 top draft picks. Singles were found 1:509 packs except for the Ricky Williams single which was harder to find at 1:18,372.

NM/M
Common Player: 25.00
Inserted 1:509
#A5 Inserted 1:18,372
1 Randy Moss 100.00
2 Wayne Chrebet 35.00
3 Tim Couch 60.00
4 Joey Galloway 35.00
5 Ricky Williams 200.00
6 Doug Flutie 50.00
7 Terrell Owens 50.00
8 Marshall Faulk 35.00
9 Rod Smith 25.00
10 Dan Marino 150.00

1999 Topps Hall of Fame Autographs

The five inductees into the Hall of Fame for 1999 are included in this autographed set. Singles were inserted 1:1,832 packs.

NM/M
Complete Set (5): 185.00
Common Player: 25.00
Inserted 1:1,832
1 Eric Dickerson 50.00
2 Billy Shaw 25.00
3 Lawrence Taylor 80.00
4 Tom Mack 25.00
5 Ozzie Newsome 40.00

1999 Topps Mystery Chrome

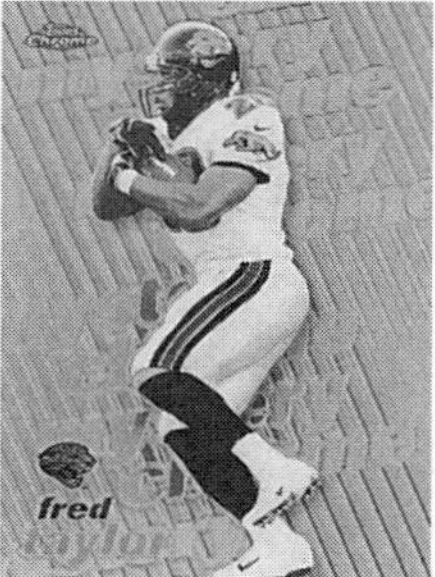

Each card in this 20-card set is printed on chrome technology and inserted 1:36 packs. A parallel Refractor version was also made and inserted 1:144 packs.

NM/M
Complete Set (20): 60.00
Common Player: 1.00
Inserted 1:36
Mystery Chrome Refractor: 3X
Inserted 1:144
1 Terrell Davis 4.00
2 Steve Young 3.00
3 Fred Taylor 2.00
4 Chris Claiborne 1.00
5 Terrell Davis 4.00
6 Randall Cunningham 1.00
7 Charlie Batch 1.00
8 Fred Taylor 2.00
9 Vinny Testaverde 1.00
10 Jamal Anderson 1.00
11 Randy Moss 5.00
12 Keyshawn Johnson 2.00
13 Vinny Testaverde 1.00
14 Chris Chandler 1.00
15 Fred Taylor 3.00
16 Ricky Williams 6.00
17 Chris Chandler 1.00
18 John Elway 4.00
19 Randy Moss 5.00
20 Troy Edwards 2.00

1999 Topps Picture Perfect

Each card in this 10-card set has an intentional error for collectors to find. A hint is printed on the back of each card and singles were inserted 1:14 packs.

NM/M
Complete Set (10): 20.00
Common Player: 1.00
Inserted 1:14
1 Steve Young 2.00
2 Brett Favre 4.00
3 Terrell Davis 2.00
4 Peyton Manning 3.00
5 Jake Plummer 1.00
6 Fred Taylor 2.00
7 Barry Sanders 4.00
8 Dan Marino 4.00
9 John Elway 3.00
10 Randy Moss 3.00

1999 Topps Record Numbers

This set features 10 NFL Record Holders on a white stock card with silver foil. Singles were inserted 1:18 packs.

NM/M
Complete Set (10): 20.00
Common Player: 1.00
Inserted 1:18
1 Randy Moss 4.00
2 Terrell Davis 3.00
3 Emmitt Smith 4.00
4 Barry Sanders 4.00
5 Dan Marino 5.00
6 Brett Favre 5.00
7 Doug Flutie 2.00
8 Jerry Rice 3.50
9 Peyton Manning 4.00
10 Jason Elam 1.00

1999 Topps Season's Best

Thirty dominate players show their mettle in six categories printed on metallic foilboard. The following categories are: Bull Rushers (Running Backs), Rocket Launchers (Quarterbacks), Deep Threats (Wide Receivers), Power Packed (Defensive stars), Strike Force (Special Teams) and Career Best (top players). Singles were found 1:18 packs.

NM/M
Complete Set (30): 60.00
Common Player: 1.00
Minor Stars: 2.00
Inserted 1:18
1 Terrell Davis Bull Rushers 4.00
2 Jamal Anderson Bull Rushers 2.00
3 Garrison Hearst Bull Rushers 2.00
4 Barry Sanders Bull Rushers 5.00
5 Emmitt Smith Bull Rushers 5.00
6 Randall Cunningham Rocket Launchers 2.00
7 Brett Favre Rocket Launchers 5.00
8 Steve Young Rocket Launchers 3.00
9 Jake Plummer Rocket Launchers 2.00
10 Peyton Manning Rocket Launchers 4.00
11 Antonio Freeman Deep Threats 2.00
12 Eric Moulds Deep Threats 2.00
13 Randy Moss Deep Threats 4.00
14 Rod Smith Deep Threats 1.00
15 Jimmy Smith Deep Threats 1.00
16 Michael Sinclair Power Packed 1.00
17 Kevin Greene Power Packed 1.00
18 Michael Strahan Power Packed 1.00
19 Michael McCrary Power Packed 1.00
20 Hugh Douglas Power Packed 1.00
21 Deion Sanders Strike Force 3.00
22 Terry Fair Strike Force 1.00
23 Jacquez Green Strike Force 2.00
24 Corey Harris Strike Force 1.00
25 Tim Dwight Strike Force 1.00
26 Dan Marino Career Best 5.00
27 Barry Sanders Career Best 5.00
28 Jerry Rice Career Best 3.00
29 Bruce Smith Career Best 1.00
30 Darrien Gordon Career Best 1.00

1999 Topps Chrome

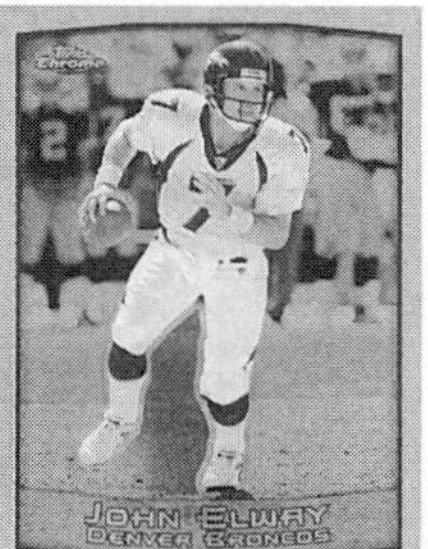

This 165-card set is the same as the regular Topps set except for each card is printed on a chromium card. For the first time in Topps Chrome the rookies were seeded 1:8 packs. Top inserts include: Refractors, All-Etch, Hall of Fame, Record Numbers and Season's Best. Each of the inserts also has a parallel Refractor version.

NM/M
Complete Set (165): 275.00
Common Player: .15
Minor Stars: .50
Common Rookie: 6.00
Inserted 1:8
Pack (4): 3.00
Wax Box (24): 55.00
1 Randy Moss 5.00
2 Keyshawn Johnson 1.00
3 Priest Holmes 1.25
4 Warren Moon .50
5 Joey Galloway 1.00
6 Zach Thomas .50
7 Cameron Cleeland .50
8 Jim Harbaugh .50
9 Napoleon Kaufman 1.00
10 Fred Taylor 2.50
11 Mark Brunell 2.00
12 Shannon Sharpe .50
13 Jacquez Green .50
14 Adrian Murrell .50
15 Cris Carter 1.00
16 Marshall Faulk 1.00
17 Drew Bledsoe 2.00
18 Curtis Martin 1.25
19 Johnnie Morton .15
20 Doug Flutie 1.50
21 Carl Pickens .50
22 Jerome Bettis 1.00
23 Derrick Alexander .15
24 Antowain Smith 1.00
25 Barry Sanders 4.00
26 Reidel Anthony .50
27 Wayne Chrebet 1.00
28 Terance Mathis .15
29 Shawn Springs .15
30 Emmitt Smith 3.50
31 Robert Smith 1.00
32 Charles Johnson .50
33 Mike Alstott 1.00
34 Ike Hilliard .15
35 Ricky Watters .75
36 Charles Woodson 1.00
37 Rod Smith .50
38 Pete Mitchell .15
39 Derrick Thomas .50
40 Dan Marino 3.50
41 Darnay Scott .50
42 Jake Reed .50
43 Chris Chandler .50
44 Dorsey Levens 1.00
45 Kordell Stewart 1.25
46 Eddie George 1.25
47 Corey Dillon 1.00
48 Rich Gannon .15
49 Chris Spielman .15
50 Jerry Rice 2.50
51 Trent Dilfer .75
52 Mark Chmura .50
53 Jimmy Smith .50
54 Isaac Bruce .50
55 Karim Abdul .75
56 Sedrick Shaw .15
57 Jake Plummer 2.50
58 Tony Gonzalez .50
59 Ben Coates .50
60 John Elway 3.50
61 Bruce Smith .15
62 Tim Brown .50
63 Tim Dwight 1.00
64 Yancey Thigpen .50
65 Terrell Owens 1.00
66 Kyle Brady .15
67 Tony Martin .15
68 Michael Strahan .15
69 Deion Sanders 1.00
70 Steve Young 1.50
71 Dale Carter .15
72 Ty Law .15
73 Frank Wycheck .15
74 Marshall Faulk 1.00
75 Vinny Testaverde .50
76 Chad Brown .15
77 Natrone Means .75
78 Bert Emanuel .15
79 Kerry Collins .50
80 Randall Cunningham 1.00
81 Garrison Hearst 1.00
82 Curtis Enis 1.00
83 Steve Atwater .15
84 Kevin Greene .15
85 Steve McNair 1.25
86 Andre Reed .50
87 J.J. Stokes .50
88 Eric Moulds 1.00
89 Marvin Harrison .75
90 Troy Aikman 2.50
91 Herman Moore .75
92 Michael Irvin .50
93 Frank Sanders .50
94 Duce Staley .50
95 James Jett .15
96 Ricky Proehl .15
97 Andre Rison .50
98 Leslie Shepherd .15
99 Trent Green .75
100 Terrell Davis 2.00
101 Freddie Jones .15
102 Skip Hicks 1.00
103 Jeff Graham .15
104 Rob Moore .50
105 Torrance Small .15
106 Antonio Freeman 1.00
107 Robert Brooks .15
108 Jon Kitna 1.25
109 Curtis Conway .50
110 Brett Favre 5.00
111 Warrick Dunn 1.25
112 Elvis Grbac .50
113 Corey Fuller .15
114 Rickey Dudley .15
115 Jamal Anderson 1.00
116 Terry Glenn .75
117 Raghib Ismail .15
118 John Randle .15
119 Chris Calloway .15
120 Peyton Manning 3.50
121 Keenan McCardell .15
122 O.J. McDuffie .50
123 Ed McCaffrey .50
124 Charlie Batch 1.25
125 Jason Elam (Season Highlights) .15
126 Randy Moss (Season Highlights) 2.50
127 John Elway (Season Highlights) 1.50
128 Emmitt Smith (Season Highlights) 1.50
129 Terrell Davis (Season Highlights) 1.50
130 Jerris McPhail .15
131 Damon Gibson .15
132 Jim Pyne .15
133 Antonio Langham .15
134 Freddie Solomon .15
135 *Ricky Williams* 12.00
136 *Daunte Culpepper* 25.00
137 *Chris Claiborne* 4.00
138 *Amos Zereoue* 8.00
139 *Chris McAlister* 4.00
140 *Kevin Faulk* 3.00
141 *James Johnson* 6.00
142 *Mike Cloud* 3.00
143 *Jevon Kearse* 8.00
144 *Akili Smith* 5.00
145 *Edgerrin James* 25.00
146 *Cecil Collins* 5.00
147 *Donovan McNabb* 25.00
148 *Kevin Johnson* 5.00
149 *Torry Holt* 12.00
150 *Rob Konrad* 5.00
151 *Tim Couch* 3.00
152 *David Boston* 12.00
153 *Karsten Bailey* 5.00
154 *Troy Edwards* 5.00
155 *Sedrick Irvin* 5.00
156 *Shaun King* 5.00
157 *Peerless Price* 10.00
158 *Brock Huard* 5.00
159 *Cade McNown* 5.00
160 *Champ Bailey* 5.00
161 *D'Wayne Bates* 5.00
162 *Joe Germaine* 5.00
163 *Andy Katzenmoyer* 5.00
164 *Antoine Winfield* 5.00
165 Checklist .15

1999 Topps Chrome Refractors

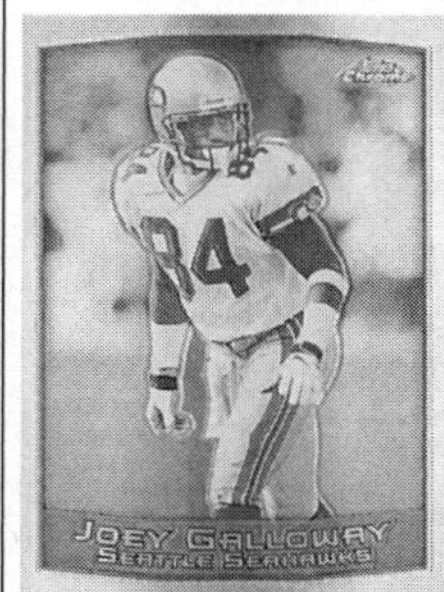

This is a parallel to the base with each single having a mirror shine to them. Singles were inserted 1:12 packs and rookies were found 1:32 packs.

NM/M
Complete Set (165): 1,800
Refractor Cards: 3X-5X
Inserted 1:12
Refractor Rookies: 2X
Inserted 1:32

1999 Topps Chrome All Etch

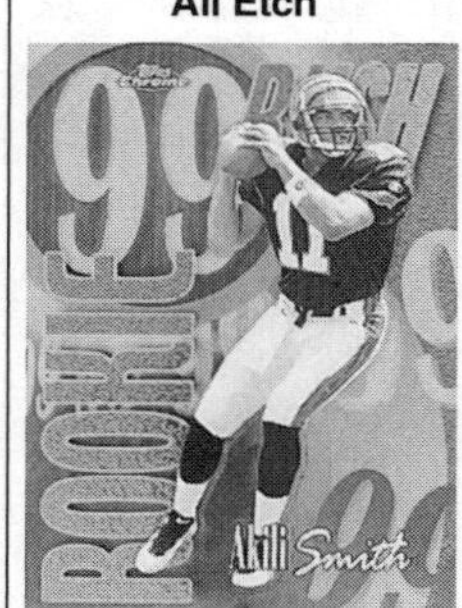

This 30-card insert is divided into three tiers with 1,200 Yard Club, 3,000 Yard Club and '99 Rookie Rush. Singles were inserted 1:24 packs and a Refractor version was also produced and found 1:120 packs.

NM/M
Complete Set (30): 80.00
Common Player: 1.00
Minor Stars: 2.00
Inserted 1:24
Refractors: 2X
Inserted 1:120
1 Fred Taylor (1200 Yard Club) 4.00
2 Ricky Watters (1200 Yard Club) 3.00
3 Curtis Martin (1200 Yard Club) 4.00
4 Eddie George (1200 Yard Club) 2.00
5 Marshall Faulk (1200 Yard Club) 4.00
6 Emmitt Smith (1200 Yard Club) 6.00
7 Barry Sanders (1200 Yard Club) 6.00
8 Garrison Hearst (1200 Yard Club) 2.00
9 Jamal Anderson (1200 Yard Club) 1.00
10 Terrell Davis (1200 Yard Club) 5.00
11 Chris Chandler (3000 Yard Club) 1.00
12 Steve McNair (3000 Yard Club) 2.00
13 Vinny Testaverde (3000 Yard Club) 1.00

14 Trent Green (3000 Yard Club) 1.00
15 Dan Marino (3000 Yard Club) 6.00
16 Drew Bledsoe (3000 Yard Club) 5.00
17 Randall Cunningham (3000 Yard Club) 2.00
18 Jake Plummer (3000 Yard Club) 3.00
19 Peyton Manning (3000 Yard Club) 5.00
20 Steve Young (3000 Yard Club) 4.00
21 Brett Favre (3000 Yard Club) 6.00
22 Tim Couch (99 Rookie Rushers) 3.00
23 Edgerrin James (99 Rookie Rushers) 4.00
24 David Boston (99 Rookie Rushers) 2.00
25 Akili Smith (99 Rookie Rushers) 2.00
26 Troy Edwards (99 Rookie Rushers) 2.00
27 Torry Holt (99 Rookie Rushers) 2.00
28 Donovan McNabb (99 Rookie Rushers) 3.00
29 Daunte Culpepper (99 Rookie Rushers) 3.00
30 Ricky Williams (99 Rookie Rushers) 5.00

1999 Topps Chrome Hall of Fame

This is a 30-card set of players that are gunning for a spot in Canton, Ohio. The set is divided into three categories (Hall Bound, Early Road to the Hall and Hall Hopefuls) each with a different card design. Hall Bound showcases veterans, Early Road to the Hall features young stars and Hall Hopefuls contains '99 draft picks. Singles were found 1:29 packs and Refractors were sequentially numbered to 100.

	NM/M
Complete Set (30):	80.00
Common Player:	1.00
Minor Stars:	2.00
Inserted 1:29	
Refractors:	4X
Inserted 1:485	
Production 100 Sets	

1 Akili Smith (Hall Hopefuls) 2.00
2 Troy Edwards (Hall Hopefuls) 2.00
3 Donovan McNabb (Hall Hopefuls) 3.00
4 Cade McNown (Hall Hopefuls) 2.00
5 Ricky Williams (Hall Hopefuls) 5.00
6 David Boston (Hall Hopefuls) 3.00
7 Daunte Culpepper (Hall Hopefuls) 3.00
8 Edgerrin James (Hall Hopefuls) 4.00
9 Torry Holt (Hall Hopefuls) 2.00
10 Tim Couch (Hall Hopefuls) 3.00
11 Terrell Davis (Early Road To) 4.00
12 Fred Taylor (Early Road To) 2.00
13 Antonio Freeman (Early Road To) 1.00
14 Jamal Anderson (Early Road To) 1.00
15 Randy Moss (Early Road To) 5.00
16 Joey Galloway (Early Road To) 2.00
17 Eddie George (Early Road To) 2.00
18 Jake Plummer (Early Road To) 2.00
19 Curtis Martin (Early Road To) 4.00
20 Peyton Manning (Early Road To) 5.00
21 Barry Sanders (Hall Bound) 6.00
22 Steve Young (Hall Bound) 4.00
23 Cris Carter (Hall Bound) 1.00
24 Emmitt Smith (Hall Bound) 6.00
25 John Elway (Hall Bound) 5.00
26 Drew Bledsoe (Hall Bound) 4.00
27 Troy Aikman (Hall Bound) 4.00
28 Brett Favre (Hall Bound) 6.00
29 Jerry Rice (Hall Bound) 5.00
30 Dan Marino (Hall Bound) 6.00

1999 Topps Chrome Record Numbers

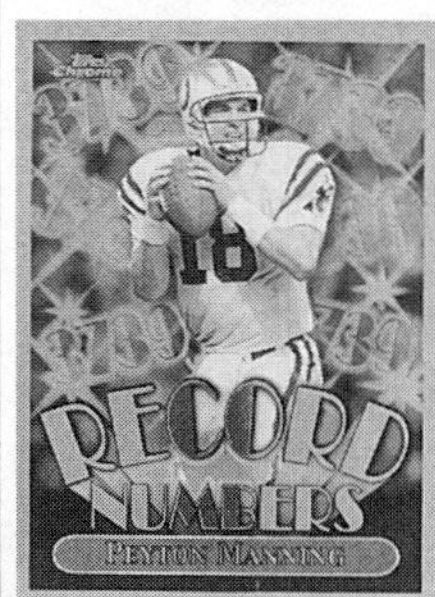

This was a 10-card insert set that included the top players in the game. Singles were inserted 1:72 packs. A parallel Refractor version was also released and found 1:360 packs.

	NM/M
Complete Set (10):	50.00
Common Player:	2.00
Inserted 1:72	
Refractors:	2X
Inserted 1:360	

1 Randy Moss 5.00
2 Terrell Davis 4.00
3 Emmitt Smith 5.00
4 Barry Sanders 5.00
5 Dan Marino 6.00
6 Brett Favre 6.00
7 Doug Flutie 2.00
8 Jerry Rice 5.00
9 Peyton Manning 5.00
10 Jason Elam 2.00

1999 Topps Chrome Season's Best

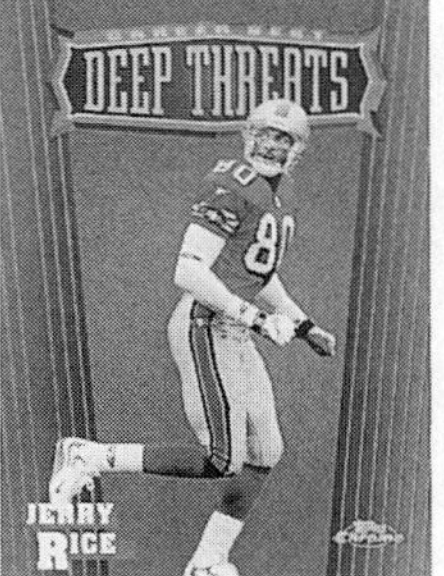

The 30-card set is divided into six categories. Bull Rushers, Rocket Launchers, Deep Threats, Power Packed, Strike Force and Career Best. Each has a different design and was inserted 1:24 packs. A Refractor version was also produced and inserted 1:120 packs.

	NM/M
Complete Set (30):	60.00
Common Player:	1.00
Minor Stars:	2.00
Inserted 1:24	
Refractors:	2X
Inserted 1:120	

1 Terrell Davis (Bull Rushers) 4.00
2 Jamal Anderson (Bull Rushers) 2.00
3 Garrison Hearst (Bull Rushers) 2.00
4 Barry Sanders (Bull Rushers) 5.00
5 Emmitt Smith (Bull Rushers) 5.00
6 Randall Cunningham (Rocket Launchers) 2.00
7 Brett Favre (Rocket Launchers) 6.00
8 Steve Young (Rocket Launchers) 4.00
9 Jake Plummer (Rocket Launchers) 2.00
10 Peyton Manning (Rocket Launchers) 5.00
11 Antonio Freeman (Deep Threats) 2.00
12 Eric Moulds (Deep Threats) 2.00
13 Randy Moss (Deep Threats) 5.00
14 Rod Smith (Deep Threats) 1.00
15 Jimmy Smith (Deep Threats) 1.00
16 Michael Sinclair (Power Packed) 1.00
17 Kevin Greene (Power Packed) 1.00
18 Michael Strahan (Power Packed) 1.00
19 Michael McCrary (Power Packed) 1.00
20 Hugh Douglas (Power Packed) 1.00
21 Deion Sanders (Strike Force) 2.00
22 Terry Fair (Strike Force) 1.00
23 Jacquez Green (Strike Force) 1.00
24 Corey Harris (Strike Force) 1.00
25 Tim Dwight (Stike Force) 2.00
26 Dan Marino (Career Best) 6.00
27 Barry Sanders (Career Best) 5.00
28 Jerry Rice (Career Best) 5.00
29 Bruce Smith (Career Best) 1.00
30 Darrien Gordon (Career Best) 1.00

1999 Topps Collection

This was a 357-card set that paralleled the regular Topps issue. Each single in this set included the "Topps Collection" gold foil stamp on the fronts of the cards. They were issued in factory set form and SRP was $29.00.

	NM/M
Complete Set (357):	40.00
Common Player:	.10
Minor Stars:	.20
Common Rookie:	2.00

1 Terrell Davis 1.50
2 Adrian Murrell .10
3 Ernie Mills .10
4 Jimmy Hitchcock .10
5 Charlie Garner .20
6 Blaine Bishop .10
7 Junior Seau .20
8 Andre Rison .20
9 Jake Reed .20
10 Cris Carter .50
11 Torrance Small .10
12 Ronald McKinnon .10
13 Tyrone Davis .10
14 Warren Moon .20
15 Joe Johnson .10
16 Bert Emanuel .20
17 Brad Culpepper .10
18 Henry Jones .10
19 Jonathan Ogden .10
20 Terrell Owens .50
21 Derrick Mason .10
22 Jon Ritchie .10
23 Eric Metcalf .10
24 Kevin Carter .10
25 Fred Taylor 1.00
26 DeWayne Washington .10
27 William Thomas .10
28 Raghib Ismail .10
29 Jason Taylor .10
30 Doug Flutie .50
31 Michael Sinclair .10
32 Yancey Thigpen .20
33 Darnay Scott .20
34 Amani Toomer .10
35 Edgar Bennett .10
36 LeRoy Butler .10
37 Jessie Tuggle .10
38 Andrew Glover .10
39 Tim McDonald .10
40 Marshall Faulk .50
41 Ray Mickens .10
42 Kimble Anders .10
43 Trent Green .20
44 Dermontti Dawson .10
45 Greg Ellis .10
46 Hugh Douglas .10
47 Amp Lee .10
48 Lamar Thomas .10
49 Curtis Conway .20
50 Emmitt Smith 1.50
51 Elvis Grbac .20
52 Tony Simmons .20
53 Darrin Smith .10
54 Donovin Darius .10
55 Corey Chavous .10
56 Phillippi Sparks .10
57 Luther Elliss .10
58 Tim Dwight .50
59 Andre Hastings .10
60 Dan Marino 1.50
61 Micheal Barrow .10
62 Corey Fuller .10
63 Bill Romanowski .10
64 Derrick Rodgers .10
65 Natrone Means .20
66 Peter Boulware .10
67 Brian Mitchell .10
68 Cornelius Bennett .10
69 Dedric Ward .10
70 Drew Bledsoe .75
71 Freddie Jones .10
72 Derrick Thomas .20
73 Willie Davis .10
74 Larry Centers .10
75 Mark Brunell .75
76 Chuck Smith .10
77 Desmond Howard .10
78 Sedrick Shaw .10
79 Tiki Barber .20
80 Curtis Martin .50
81 Barry Minter .10
82 Skip Hicks .20
83 O.J. Santiago .10
84 Ed McCaffrey .30
85 Terrell Buckley .10
86 Charlie Jones .10
87 Pete Mitchell .10
88 La'Roi Glover .10
89 Eric Davis .10
90 John Elway 1.50
91 Kavika Pittman .10
92 Fred Lane .20
93 Warren Sapp .20
94 Lorenzo Bromell .10
95 Lawyer Milloy .10
96 Aeneas Williams .10
97 Michael McCrary .10
98 Rickey Dudley .20
99 Bryce Paup .10
100 Jamal Anderson .50
101 D'Marco Farr .10
102 Johnnie Morton .10
103 Jeff Graham .10
104 Sam Cowart .10
105 Bryant Young .10
106 Jermaine Lewis .10
107 Chad Bratzke .10
108 Jeff Burris .10
109 Roell Preston .10
110 Vinny Testaverde .30
111 Ruben Brown .10
112 Darryll Lewis .10
113 Billy Davis .10
114 Bryant Westbrook .10
115 Stephen Alexander .10
116 Terrell Fletcher .10
117 Terry Glenn .50
118 Rod Smith .30
119 Carl Pickens .20
120 Tim Brown .30
121 Mikhael Ricks .10
122 Jason Gildon .10
123 Charles Way .10
124 Rob Moore .20
125 Jerome Bettis .50
126 Kerry Collins .20
127 Bruce Smith .20
128 James Hasty .10
129 Ken Norton Jr. .10
130 Charles Woodson .50
131 Tony McGee .10
132 Kevin Turner .10
133 Jerome Pathon .10
134 Garrison Hearst .30
135 Craig Newsome .10
136 Hardy Nickerson .10
137 Ray Lewis .10
138 Derrick Alexander .10
139 Phil Hansen .10
140 Joey Galloway .50
141 Oronde Gadsden .20
142 Herman Moore .30
143 Bobby Taylor .10
144 Mario Bates .10
145 Kevin Dyson .20
146 Aaron Glenn .10
147 Ed McDaniel .10
148 Terry Allen .20
149 Ike Hilliard .20
150 Steve Young .75
151 Eugene Robinson .10
152 John Mobley .10
153 Kevin Hardy .10
154 Lance Johnstone .10
155 Willie McGinest .10
156 Gary Anderson .10
157 Dexter Coakley .10
158 Mark Fields .10
159 Steve McNair .75
160 Corey Dillon .50
161 Zach Thomas .20
162 Kent Graham .10
163 Tony Parrish .10
164 Sam Gash .10
165 Kyle Brady .10
166 Donnell Bennett .10
167 Tony Martin .20
168 Michael Bates .10
169 Bobby Engram .10
170 Jimmy Smith .50
171 Vonnie Holliday .10
172 Simeon Rice .10
173 Kevin Greene .10
174 Mike Alstott .50
175 Eddie George .75
176 Michael Jackson .10
177 Neil O'Donnell .20
178 Sean Dawkins .10
179 Courtney Hawkins .10
180 Michael Irvin .20
181 Thurman Thomas .20
182 Cameron Cleeland .20
183 Ellis Johnson .10
184 Will Blackwell .10
185 Ty Law .10
186 Merton Hanks .10
187 Dan Wilkinson .10
188 Andre Wadsworth .10
189 Troy Vincent .10
190 Frank Sanders .20
191 Stephen Boyd .10
192 Jason Elam .10
193 Kordell Stewart .50
194 Ted Johnson .10
195 Glyn Milburn .10
196 Gary Brown .10
197 Travis Hall .10
198 John Randle .10
199 Jay Riemersma .10
200 Barry Sanders 2.00
201 Chris Spielman .10
202 Rod Woodson .10
203 Darrell Russell .10
204 Tony Boselli .10
205 Darren Woodson .10
206 Muhsin Muhammed .20
207 Jim Harbaugh .20
208 Isaac Bruce .50
209 Mo Lewis .10
210 Dorsey Levens .50
211 Frank Wycheck .10
212 Napoleon Kaufman .50
213 Walt Harris .10
214 Leon Lett .10
215 Karim Abdul .20
216 Carnell Lake .10
217 Byron Morris .10
218 John Avery .10
219 Chris Slade .10
220 Robert Smith .50
221 Mike Pritchard .10
222 Ty Detmer .10
223 Randall Cunningham .50
224 Alonzo Mayes .10
225 Jake Plummer .75
226 Derrick Mayes .20
227 Jeff Brady .10
228 John Lynch .10
229 Steve Atwater .10
230 Warrick Dunn .50
231 Shawn Jefferson .10
232 Erik Kramer .10
233 Ken Dilger .10
234 Ryan Leaf .50
235 Ray Buchanan .10
236 Kevin Williams .10
237 Ricky Watters .30
238 Dwayne Rudd .10
239 Duce Staley .50
240 Charlie Batch .75
241 Tim Biakabutuka .20
242 Tony Gonzalez .30
243 Bryan Still .10
244 Donnie Edwards .10
245 Troy Aikman 1.00
246 Az-Zahir Hakim .20
247 Curtis Enis .50
248 Chris Chandler .20
249 James Jett .10
250 Brett Favre 2.00
251 Kevin Poole .10
252 Ricky Proehl .10
253 Shannon Sharpe .20
254 Robert Jones .10
255 Chad Brown .10
256 Ben Coates .20
257 Jacquez Green .20
258 Jessie Armstead .10
259 Dale Carter .10
260 Antowain Smith .30
261 Mark Chmura .20
262 Michael Westbrook .20
263 Marvin Harrison .50
264 Darrien Gordon .10
265 Rodney Harrison .10
266 Charles Johnson .10
267 Roman Pfifer .10
268 Reidel Anthony .20
269 Jerry Rice 1.00
270 Eric Moulds .50
271 Robert Porcher .10
272 Deion Sanders .30
273 Germane Crowell .30
274 Randy Moss 2.00
275 Antonio Freeman .50
276 Trent Dilfer .20
277 Eric Turner .10
278 Jeff George .30
279 Levon Kirkland .10
280 O.J. McDuffie .20
281 Takeo Spikes .10
282 Jim Flanigan .10
283 Chris Warren .10
284 J.J. Stokes .20
285 Bryan Cox .10
286 Sam Madison .10
287 Priest Holmes .50
288 Keenan McCardell .20
289 Michael Strahan .10
290 Robert Edwards .30
291 Tommy Vardell .10
292 Wayne Chrebet .30
293 Chris Calloway .10
294 Wesley Walls .20
295 Derrick Brooks .10
296 Trace Armstrong .10
297 Brian Simmons .10
298 Darrell Green .10
299 Robert Brooks .10
300 Peyton Manning 1.75
301 Dana Stubblefield .10
302 Shawn Springs .10
303 Leslie Shepherd .10
304 Ken Harvey .10
305 Jon Kitna .50
306 Terance Mathis .10
307 Andre Reed .20
308 Jackie Harris .10
309 Rich Gannon .20
310 Keyshawn Johnson .50
311 Victor Green .10
312 Eric Allen .10
313 Terry Fair .10
314 Jason Elam .10
315 Garrison Hearst .10
316 Jake Plummer .30
317 Randall Cunningham .20
318 Randy Moss 1.00
319 Jamal Anderson .25
320 John Elway .75
321 Doug Flutie .30
322 Emmitt Smith .75
323 Terrell Davis .75
324 Jerris McPhail .10
325 Damon Gibson .10
326 Jim Pyne .10
327 Antonio Langham .10
328 Freddie Solomon .10
329 *Ricky Williams* 15.00
330 *Daunte Culpepper* 10.00
331 *Chris Claiborne* 2.00
332 *Amos Zereoue* 2.00
333 *Chris McAlister* 2.00
334 *Kevin Faulk* 3.00
335 *James Johnson* 3.00
336 *Mike Cloud* 2.00
337 *Jevon Kearse* 5.00
338 *Akili Smith* 6.00
339 *Edgerrin James* 12.00
340 *Cecil Collins* 3.00
341 *Donovan McNabb* 8.00
342 *Kevin Johnson* 6.00
343 *Torry Holt* 6.00
344 *Rob Konrad* 2.00
345 *Tim Couch* 8.00
346 *David Boston* 5.00
347 *Karsten Bailey* 2.00
348 *Troy Edwards* 5.00
349 *Sedrick Irvin* 2.00
350 *Shaun King* 2.00
351 *Peerless Price* 4.00
352 *Brock Huard* 3.00
353 *Cade McNown* 3.50
354 *Champ Bailey* 3.00
355 *D'Wayne Bates* 2.00
356 Checklist .10
357 Checklist .10

1999 Topps Gold Label

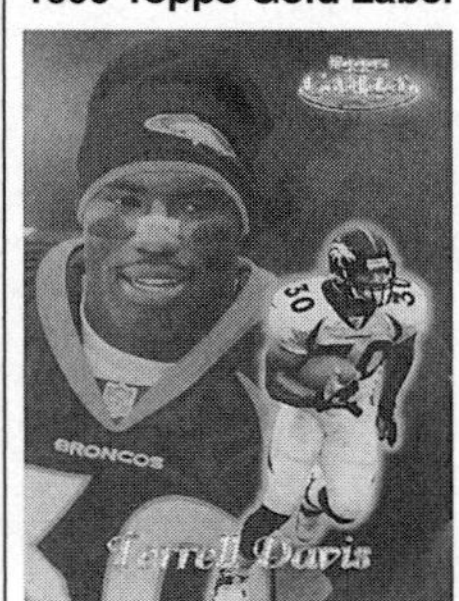

This was a 100-card set that featured each single on prismatic 35-pt. spectral-reflective rainbow stock with the player's name and the Gold Label logo in gold foil. Each player had two other singles with a different photo on the foreground of each card. Each of those cards then had a parallel Black and Red Class issue. The Race to Gold insert also has a Black and Red Class parallels. SRP was $3.99 for four- card packs.

	NM/M
Complete Set (100):	80.00
Common Player:	.15
Minor Stars:	.50
Common Rookie:	1.00
Class 2 Cards:	2X
Class 2 Rookies:	1X
Inserted 1:2	
Class 3 Cards:	3X
Class 3 Rookies:	1.5X
Inserted 1:4	
Pack (4):	3.00
Wax Box (24):	50.00

1 Terrell Davis 2.00
2 Jake Plummer 1.00
3 *Michael Cloud* 1.00
4 *D'Wayne Bates* 1.00
5 Jamal Anderson 1.00
6 *Cecil Collins* 1.00
7 Keyshawn Johnson 1.00
8 Jerome Bettis 1.00
9 Ricky Watters .50
10 Brett Favre 4.00
11 *Joe Germaine* 1.00
12 Eddie George 1.00
13 *Jevon Kearse* 2.00
14 Skip Hicks .50
15 *James Johnson* 2.00
16 Terry Glenn 1.00
17 *Troy Edwards* 2.00
18 *Karsten Bailey* 1.00
19 Trent Dilfer .50
20 Barry Sanders 3.00
21 Vinny Testaverde .50
22 Ed McCaffrey .75
23 Shannon Sharpe .50
24 Robert Smith 1.00
25 Emmitt Smith 3.00
26 Rob Moore .50
27 J.J. Stokes .50
28 *Champ Bailey* 2.00
29 Napoleon Kaufman .75
30 Fred Taylor 1.00
31 Corey Dillon 1.00
32 *Sedrick Irvin* 1.00
33 *Chris McAlister* 1.00
34 Warrick Dunn 1.00
35 Isaac Bruce 1.00
36 *Peerless Price* 2.50
37 Dorsey Levens 1.00
38 Wayne Chrebet .75
39 Randall Cunningham 1.00
40 Dan Marino 3.00
41 Chris Chandler .15
42 Mark Brunell 1.50
43 *Kevin Johnson* 2.00
44 Natrone Means .50
45 Jerome Pathon .15
46 *Daunte Culpepper* 6.00

47	*Akili Smith*	2.00
48	Keenan McCardell	.50
49	Steve McNair	1.00
50	Randy Moss	4.00
51	Terance Mathis	.15
52	Eric Moulds	1.00
53	Raghib Ismail	.15
54	*Cade McNown*	2.00
55	Kordell Stewart	1.25
56	*Rob Konrad*	2.00
57	Andre Rison	.50
58	Curtis Conway	.50
59	*Chris Claiborne*	2.00
60	Jerry Rice	2.00
61	Peyton Manning	3.00
62	Jimmy Smith	1.00
63	Doug Flutie	1.25
64	Frank Sanders	.50
65	Antowain Smith	.50
66	Curtis Enis	1.00
67	Charlie Batch	1.50
68	Marvin Harrison	1.00
69	Garrison Hearst	.75
70	*Ricky Williams*	5.00
71	*Torry Holt*	3.00
72	Mike Alstott	1.00
73	Drew Bledsoe	1.50
74	O.J. McDuffie	.50
75	*Donovan McNabb*	6.00
76	Curtis Martin	1.00
77	Priest Holmes	1.00
78	Antonio Freeman	1.00
79	Herman Moore	1.00
80	*Tim Couch*	2.00
81	Troy Aikman	2.00
82	*David Boston*	3.00
83	Tim Brown	.50
84	*Kevin Faulk*	1.50
85	Cris Carter	1.00
86	Marshall Faulk	1.00
87	*Shaun King*	3.00
88	Terrell Owens	1.00
89	Carl Pickens	.50
90	Steve Young	1.25
91	Rod Smith	.75
92	Michael Irvin	.50
93	Ike Hilliard	.15
94	Jon Kitna	1.25
95	*Brock Huard*	3.00
96	Joey Galloway	1.00
97	*Amos Zereoue*	3.00
98	Duce Staley	.75
99	John Elway	3.00
100	*Edgerrin James*	6.00

1999 Topps Gold Label Black Label

Each of the three Classes has a parallel Black Label card. The player's name and Topps Gold Label logo are in black foil. Class 1 singles were found 1:8 packs, Class 2 singles at 1:16 and Class 3 cards at 1:32.

Class 1 Cards:	4X
Class 1 Rookies:	1.5X
Inserted 1:8	
Class 2 Cards:	8X
Class 2 Rookies:	3X
Inserted 1:16	
Class 3 Cards:	12X
Class 3 Rookies:	5X
Inserted 1:32	

1999 Topps Gold Label Red Label

Each of the three Classes has a parallel Red Label card. The player's name and Topps Gold Label logo are in red foil. Class 1 singles were found 1:79 packs and were sequentially numbered to 100. Class 2 singles were inserted 1:157 and were numbered to 50. Class 3 singles were inserted 1:314 and numbered to 25.

Class 1 Cards:	10X-20X
Class 1 Rookies:	4X-8X
Inserted 1:79	
Production 100 Sets	
Class 2 Cards:	15X-30X
Class 2 Rookies:	6X-12X
Inserted 1:157	
Production 50 Sets	
Class 3 Cards:	25X-50X
Class 3 Rookies:	10X-20X
Inserted 1:314	
Production 25 Sets	

1999 Topps Gold Label Race to Gold

This 15-card insert set highlighted three players: Dan Marino, Walter Payton and Jerry Rice. Each player had five cards and was pictured with a current player who had the best chance of breaking a record that the original player owned. Singles were inserted 1:12 packs. Each single had a parallel Black Label version that was inserted 1:48 packs. Each also had a parallel Red Label version with #1-#5 inserted 1:11,867 and numbered to 13. Cards #6-#10 were found 1:4,638 and numbered to 34. Cards #11-#15 were found 1:1,968 and numbered to 80.

		NM/M
Complete Set (15):		40.00
Common Player:		1.00
Minor Stars:		2.00
Inserted 1:12		
Black Label Cards:		2X
Inserted 1:48		
Red Label Cards (1-5):		20X-40X
Inserted 1:11,867		
Red Label Cards (6-10):		12X-24X
Inserted 1:4,638		
Red Label Cards (11-15):		5X-10X
Inserted 1:1,968		
1	Brett Favre	6.00
2	Peyton Manning	5.00
3	Drew Bledsoe	4.00
4	Randall Cunningham	2.00
5	Jake Plummer	2.00
6	Emmitt Smith	5.00
7	Terrell Davis	4.00
8	Barry Sanders	5.00
9	Eddie George	3.00
10	Curtis Martin	3.00
11	Antonio Freeman	2.00
12	Eric Moulds	2.00
13	Joey Galloway	2.00
14	Rod Smith	2.00
15	Randy Moss	5.00

1999 Topps Season Opener

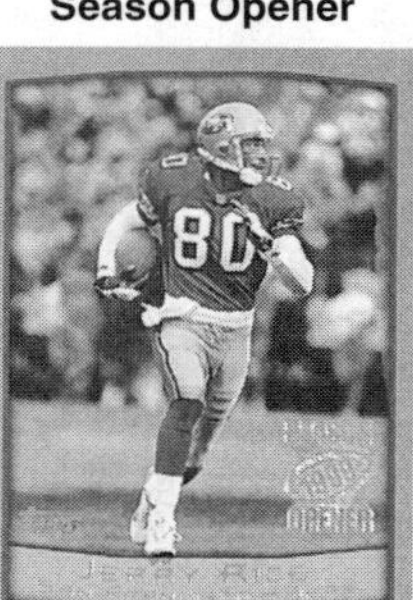

Topps Season Opener Football was a retail exclusive 165-card set that used the same photos as the regular Topps set but had blue borders and a Season Opener stamp in silver foil rather than green borders in the regular issue.

		NM/M
Complete Set (165):		30.00
Common Player:		.10
Minor Stars:		.20
Common Rookie:		1.50
Pack (6):		2.00
Wax Box (24):		50.00
1	Jerry Rice	1.00
2	Emmitt Smith	1.50
3	Curtis Martin	.30
4	Ed McCaffrey	.20
5	Oronde Gadsden	.20
6	Byron Morris	.20
7	Michael Irvin	.20
8	Shannon Sharpe	.20
9	Levon Kirkland	.10
10	Fred Taylor	1.00
11	Andre Reed	.20
12	Chad Brown	.10
13	Skip Hicks	.20
14	Tim Dwight	.30
15	Michael Sinclair	.10
16	Carl Pickens	.20
17	Derrick Alexander	.10
18	Kevin Green	.10
19	Duce Staley	.20
20	Dan Marino	1.50
21	Frank Sanders	.20
22	Ricky Proehl	.10
23	Frank Wycheck	.10
24	Andre Rison	.20
25	Natrone Means	.20
26	Steve McNair	.30
27	Vonnie Holliday	.20
28	Charles Woodson	.30
29	Rob Moore	.20
30	John Elway	1.50
31	Derrick Thomas	.20
32	Jake Plummer	.75
33	Mike Alstott	.30
34	Keenan McCardell	.20
35	Mark Chmura	.20
36	Keyshawn Johnson	.30
37	Priest Holmes	.30
38	Antonio Freeman	.30
39	Ty Law	.10
40	Jamal Anderson	.30
41	Courtney Hawkins	.10
42	James Jett	.10
43	Aaron Glenn	.10
44	Jimmy Smith	.20
45	Michael McCrary	.10
46	Junior Seau	.20
47	Bill Romanowski	.10
48	Mark Brunell	.75
49	Yancey Thigpen	.20
50	Steve Young	.75
51	Cris Carter	.30
52	Vinny Testaverde	.20
53	Zach Thomas	.20
54	Kordell Stewart	.50
55	Tim Biakabutuka	.10
56	J.J. Stokes	.10
57	Jon Kitna	.30
58	Jacquez Green	.20
59	Marvin Harrison	.20
60	Barry Sanders	2.00
61	Darrell Green	.10
62	Terance Mathis	.10
63	Ricky Watters	.20
64	Chris Chandler	.20
65	Cameron Cleeland	.20
66	Rod Smith	.20
67	Freddie Jones	.10
68	Adrian Murrell	.20
69	Terrell Owens	.30
70	Troy Aikman	1.00
71	John Mobley	.10
72	Corey Dillon	.30
73	Rickey Dudley	.10
74	Randall Cunningham	.30
75	Muhsin Muhammed	.10
76	Stephen Boyd	.10
77	Tony Gonzalez	.20
78	Deion Sanders	.30
79	Ben Coates	.20
80	Brett Favre	2.00
81	Shawn Springs	.10
82	Dorsey Levens	.30
83	Ray Buchanan	.10
84	Charlie Batch	.50
85	John Randle	.10
86	Eddie George	.50
87	Ray Lewis	.10
88	Johnnie Morton	.10
89	Kevin Hardy	.10
90	O.J. McDuffie	.20
91	Herman Moore	.30
92	Tim Brown	.30
93	Bert Emanuel	.10
94	Elvis Grbac	.20
95	Peter Boulware	.10
96	Curtis Conway	.20
97	Doug Flutie	.50
98	Jake Reed	.10
99	Ike Hilliard	.10
100	Randy Moss	2.00
101	Warren Sapp	.10
102	Bruce Smith	.10
103	Joey Galloway	.30
104	Napoleon Kaufman	.30
105	Warrick Dunn	.30
106	Wayne Chrebet	.30
107	Robert Brooks	.10
108	Antowain Smith	.30
109	Trent Dilfer	.20
110	Peyton Manning	1.50
111	Isaac Bruce	.20
112	John Lynch	.10
113	Terry Glenn	.30
114	Garrison Hearst	.30
115	Jerome Bettis	.30
116	Darnay Scott	.10
117	Lamar Thomas	.10
118	Chris Spielman	.10
119	Robert Smith	.20
120	Drew Bledsoe	.75
121	Reidel Anthony	.10
122	Wesley Walls	.10
123	Eric Moulds	.30
124	Terrell Davis	1.50
125	Dale Carter	.10
126	Charles Johnson	.10
127	Steve Atwater	.10
128	Jim Harbaugh	.20
129	Tony Martin	.10
130	Kerry Collins	.20
131	Trent Green	.30
132	Marshall Faulk	.30
133	Raghib Ismail	.10
134	Warren Moon	.30
135	Jerris McPhail	.10
136	Damon Gibson	.10
137	Jim Pyne	.10
138	Antonio Langham	.10
139	Freddie Solomon	.10
140	Randy Moss SH	1.00
141	John Elway SH	.75
142	Doug Flutie SH	.25
143	Emmitt Smith SH	.75
144	Terrell Davis SH	.75
145	*Troy Edwards*	2.00
146	*Torry Holt*	4.00
147	*Tim Couch*	4.00
148	*Sedrick Irvin*	2.00
149	*Ricky Williams*	8.00
150	*Peerless Price*	3.00
151	*Mike Cloud*	1.50
152	*Kevin Faulk*	2.00
153	*Kevin Johnson*	2.00
154	*James Johnson*	2.00
155	*Edgerrin James*	8.00
156	*D'Wayne Bates*	2.00
157	*Donovan McNabb*	8.00
158	*David Boston*	4.00
159	*Daunte Culpepper*	8.00
160	*Champ Bailey*	2.00
161	*Cecil Collins*	2.00
162	*Cade McNown*	2.00
163	*Brock Huard*	2.00
164	*Akili Smith*	2.00
165	Checklist	.10

1999 Topps Season Opener Autographs

Only two players signed in this insert and were inserted 1:7,126 packs.

		NM/M
Complete Set (2):		275.00
Common Player:		125.00
Inserted 1:7,126		
1	Tim Couch	125.00
2	Peyton Manning	150.00

1999 Topps Stars

Each card in this 140-card set was printed on 24-pt. stock with foil stamping, flood gloss and metallic ink. Each of the base cards had a star on the front. A parallel Two Star, Three Star and Four Star were released and each of the four issues had a parallel version. Insert sets include: Autographs, New Dawn, Pro Bowl Jersey Redemption, Rookie Relics, Rookie Reprints, Stars of the Game and Zone of Their Own. SRP was $3.00 for six-card packs.

		NM/M
Complete Set (140):		55.00
Common Player:		.10
Minor Stars:		.40
Common Rookie:		.75
Pack (6):		2.00
Wax Box (24):		45.00
1	*Champ Bailey*	1.50
2	*Akili Smith*	2.00
3	Randy Moss	3.00
4	*Cade McNown*	1.50
5	*Torry Holt*	2.50
6	*Troy Edwards*	1.50
7	*David Boston*	2.50
8	*Edgerrin James*	5.00
9	*Daunte Culpepper*	5.00
10	*Tim Couch*	2.50
11	*Ricky Williams*	5.00
12	Fred Taylor	1.00
13	Barry Sanders	2.00
14	Emmitt Smith	2.00
15	Jerry Rice	1.50
16	Jake Plummer	1.25
17	Terrell Owens	.75
18	Eric Moulds	.75
19	Dan Marino	2.00
20	Steve McNair	.75
21	*Donovan McNabb*	5.00
22	Curtis Martin	.75
23	Peyton Manning	2.00
24	Garrison Hearst	.40
25	Eddie George	.75
26	Antonio Freeman	.75
27	Doug Flutie	1.00
28	*Kevin Faulk*	1.50
29	Brett Favre	3.00
30	Randall Cunningham	.75
31	Mark Brunell	1.00
32	Keyshawn Johnson	.75
33	Terrell Davis	1.00
34	Drew Bledsoe	1.25
35	Jerome Bettis	.75
36	Charlie Batch	1.00
37	Steve Young	1.00
38	Jamal Anderson	.75
39	Troy Aikman	1.50
40	John Elway	2.00
41	*Amos Zereoue*	1.00
42	J.J. Stokes	.40
43	Antowain Smith	.75
44	Jimmy Smith	.75
45	*Shaun King*	2.00
46	*Jevon Kearse*	2.00
47	*Sedrick Irvin*	1.00
48	Rod Smith	.50
49	*Kevin Johnson*	1.50
50	Joey Galloway	.75
51	*Michael Cloud*	1.00
52	*D'Wayne Bates*	1.00
53	*Peerless Price*	2.00
54	Herman Moore	.50
55	*Rob Konrad*	1.00
56	*James Johnson*	1.00
57	*Cecil Collins*	1.50
58	Wayne Chrebet	.75
59	Cris Carter	.75
60	Tim Brown	.50
61	Frank Wycheck	.10
62	Charles Woodson	.75
63	*Antoine Winfield*	.75
64	Ryan Leaf	.50
65	Ricky Watters	.40
66	Yancey Thigpen	.10
67	Michael Westbrook	.40
68	Vinny Testaverde	.40
69	Kordell Stewart	.75
70	Duce Staley	.75
71	Shannon Sharpe	.40
72	Junior Seau	.40
73	Bruce Smith	.10
74	Frank Sanders	.10
75	Warren Sapp	.10
76	Robert Smith	.75
77	Andre Reed	.40
78	Darnay Scott	.40
79	Adrian Murrell	.40
80	Ricky Proehl	.10
81	Zach Thomas	.40
82	Deion Sanders	.75
83	Andre Rison	.40
84	Jake Reed	.40
85	Carl Pickens	.40
86	John Randle	.10
87	Jerome Pathon	.10
88	*Brock Huard*	1.50
89	Elvis Grbac	.40
90	Curtis Enis	.75
91	Rickey Dudley	.10
92	Amani Toomer	.10
93	Robert Brooks	.10
94	Derrick Alexander	.10
95	Reidel Anthony	.40
96	Mark Chmura	.40
97	Trent Dilfer	.40
98	*Ebenezer Ekuban*	.75
99	Tony Banks	.40
100	Terry Glenn	.75
101	Andre Hastings	.10
102	Ike Hilliard	.40
103	Michael Irvin	.40
104	Napoleon Kaufman	.75
105	Dorsey Levens	.75
106	Ed McCaffrey	.50
107	Natrone Means	.40
108	Skip Hicks	.40
109	James Jett	.10
110	Priest Holmes	.75
111	Tim Dwight	.75
112	Curtis Conway	.40
113	Jeff Blake	.40
114	Karim Abdul	.40
115	*Karsten Bailey*	1.25
116	Chris Chandler	.40
117	Germane Crowell	.40
118	Warrick Dunn	.75
119	Bert Emanuel	.10
120	*Jermaine Fazande*	1.25
121	*Joe Germaine*	1.25
122	Tony Gonzalez	.40
123	Jacquez Green	.40
124	Marvin Harrison	.75
125	Corey Dillon	.75
126	Ben Coates	.40
127	*Chris Claiborne*	1.00
128	Isaac Bruce	.75
129	Mike Alstott	.75
130	*Andy Katzenmoyer*	1.00
131	Jon Kitna	.75
132	Keenan McCardell	.40
133	Johnnie Morton	.10
134	O.J. McDuffie	.40
135	*Chris McAlister*	1.00
136	Terance Mathis	.10
137	Thurman Thomas	.40
138	Jermaine Lewis	.10
139	Rob Moore	.10
140	Brad Johnson	.75

1999 Topps Stars

This was a parallel to the base set. Each of the singles in this set were sequentially numbered to 299.

	NM/M
Parallel Cards:	2X-6X
Parallel Rookies:	2X-4X
Production 299 Sets	

1999 Topps Stars Two Star

This was a 60-card partial parallel to the base set. Each of the singles had two stars on the front and were inserted 1:1.5 packs.

	NM/M
Complete Set (60):	50.00
Two Star Cards:	1X

1999 Topps Stars Two Star

This was a parallel to the Two Star set. Singles from this insert were sequentially numbered to 249 and inserted 1:42 packs.

Two Star Cards:	3X-8X
Two Star Rookies:	2X-4X
Production 249 Sets	

1999 Topps Stars Three Star

This was a 40-card partial parallel to the base set. Each single had three stars on the front and was inserted one-per-pack.

Three Star Cards:	1X
Inserted 1:1	

1999 Topps Stars Three Star

This was a parallel to the Three Star insert. Each of the singles were sequentially numbered to 199 and inserted 1:79 packs.

Complete Set (40):	
Three Star Cards:	4X-10X
Three Star Rookies:	3X-6X
Production 199 Sets	

Post-1980 cards in Near Mint condition will generally sell for about 75% of the quoted Mint value. Excellent-condition cards bring no more than 40%.

1999 Topps Stars Four Star

This was a 10-card partial parallel to the base set. Each single had four stars across the front. Singles were inserted 1:4 packs.

NM/M
Complete Set (10): 25.00
Four Star Cards: 1X
Inserted 1:4

1999 Topps Stars Four Star

This was a parallel to the Four Star insert set. Each single was sequentially numbered to 99 and inserted 1:634 packs.

Complete Set (10):
Four Star Cards: 4X-12X
Four Star Rookies: 3X-6X
Production 99 Sets

1999 Topps Stars Autographs

This six-card insert set included autographs from the 1999 #1 overall draft pick Tim Couch and the 1998 Rookie of the Year Randy Moss. The first three cards in the set had a blue background and were inserted 1:419 packs. Cards #4 and #5 had a red background and were inserted 1:629. The last single had a gold background and was inserted 1:2,528 packs.

NM/M
Common Player: 25.00
Blue Inserted 1:419
Gold Inserted 1:2,528
Red Inserted 1:629
1 Tim Couch B 75.00
2 Torry Holt B 35.00
3 David Boston B 25.00
4 Fred Taylor R 60.00
5 Marshall Faulk R 50.00
6 Randy Moss G 100.00

1999 Topps Stars New Dawn

This 20-card insert set included rookies from the 1999 season. Each was printed on 24-pt. stock, with super-premium select metallization treatment and foil stamping. The cards were sequentially numbered to 1,000 and inserted 1:31 packs.

NM/M
Complete Set (20): 60.00
Common Player: 1.00
Minor Stars: 2.00
Inserted 1:31
Production 1,000 Sets
1 Tim Couch 5.00
2 Kevin Faulk 3.00
3 Troy Edwards 3.00
4 Champ Bailey 4.00
5 Peerless Price 4.00
6 Kevin Johnson 3.00
7 Edgerrin James 7.00
8 Daunte Culpepper 6.00
9 Torry Holt 4.00
10 Donovan McNabb 6.00
11 Shaun King 2.00
12 Michael Cloud 1.00
13 Cade McNown 2.00
14 David Boston 4.00
15 James Johnson 2.00
16 Karsten Bailey 1.00
17 Sedrick Irvin 1.00
18 Akili Smith 2.00
19 D'Wayne Bates 1.00
20 Ricky Williams 7.00

1999 Topps Stars Rookie Relics

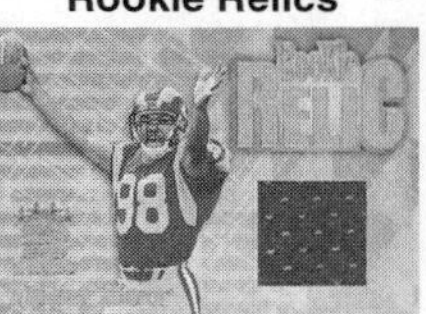

This three-card insert set included rookie Torry Holt and rookies Kurt Warner and Donovan McNabb through redemption cards. Each single included a piece of a game- worn jersey and singles were inserted 1:209 packs.

NM/M
Complete Set (3): 150.00
Common Player: 25.00
Inserted 1:209
1 Kurt Warner 100.00
2 Torry Holt 25.00
3 Donovan McNabb 50.00

1999 Topps Stars Rookie Reprints

This two-card set included reprints of Terry Bradshaw and Roger Staubach's rookie cards. Singles were inserted 1:16 packs. Autographed version were also released at 1:629 packs.

NM/M
Complete Set (2): 10.00
Common Player: 5.00
Inserted 1:16
Terry Bradshaw 5.00
Roger Staubach 5.00

1999 Topps Stars Stars of the Game

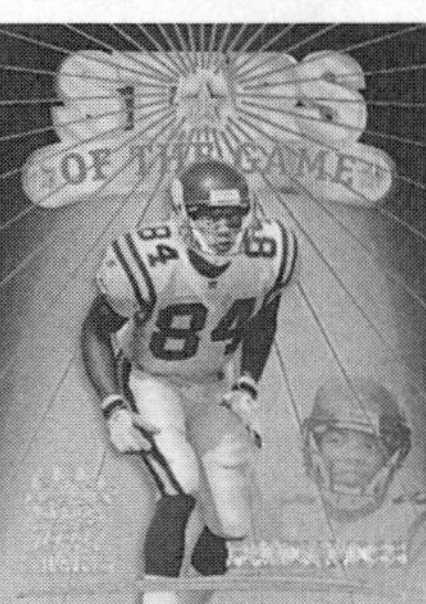

Each single in this 10-card insert set were printed on 24-pt. stock with foil stamping. Each was sequentially numbered to 1,999 and inserted 1:31 packs.

NM/M
Complete Set (10): 30.00
Common Player: 1.00
Inserted 1:31
Production 1,999 Sets
1 Jamal Anderson 1.00
2 Dan Marino 5.00
3 Barry Sanders 4.00
4 Brett Favre 5.00
5 Emmitt Smith 4.00
6 Fred Taylor 2.00
7 John Elway 4.00
8 Randy Moss 4.00
9 Peyton Manning 4.00
10 Terrell Davis 4.00

1999 Topps Stars Zone of Their Own

This 10-card insert set included stars who have won individual awards and team titles. Each was printed on 24 pt. stock, foil stamped and sequentially numbered to 1,999. Singles were found 1:31 packs.

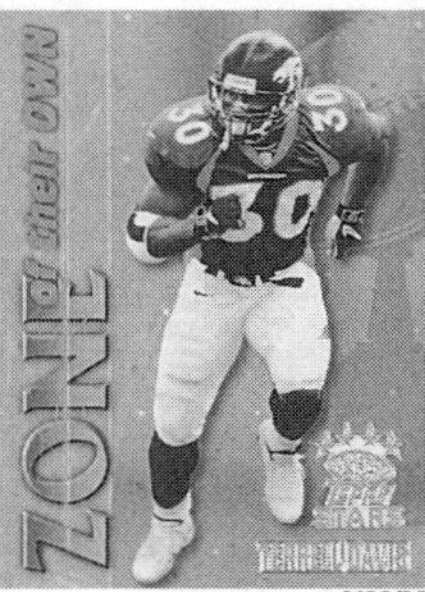

NM/M
Complete Set (10): 30.00
Common Player: 1.00
Inserted 1:31
Production 1,999 Sets
1 Randy Moss 4.00
2 Eddie George 2.00
3 Tim Brown 2.00
4 Curtis Martin 3.00
5 Brett Favre 6.00
6 Barry Sanders 5.00
7 Warrick Dunn 2.00
8 Terrell Davis 4.00
9 Ricky Williams 5.00
10 Doug Flutie 2.00

2000 Topps Promos

NM/M
Complete Set (6): 3.00
Common Player: .50
PP1 Peyton Manning 2.00
PP2 Zach Thomas .50
PP3 Eddie George 1.00
PP4 Raghib Ismail .50
PP5 Fred Taylor .50
PP6 Shaun King .50

2000 Topps

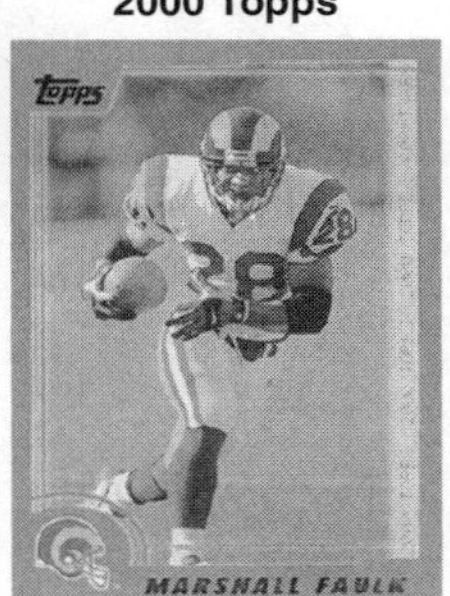

NM/M
Complete Set (400): 80.00
Common Player: .15
Minor Stars: .30
Common Rookie: 1.50
Inserted 1:5
Pack (10): 2.00
Wax Box (36): 50.00
1 Kurt Warner 2.50
2 Darrell Russell .15
3 Tai Streets .15
4 Bryant Young .15
5 Kent Graham .15
6 Shawn Jefferson .15
7 Wesley Walls .30
8 Jessie Armstead .15
9 Dedric Ward .15
10 Emmitt Smith 1.50
11 James Stewart .30
12 Frank Sanders .30
13 Ray Buchanan .15
14 Olindo Mare .30
15 Andre Reed .30
16 Curtis Conway .30
17 Patrick Jeffers .50
18 Greg Hill .15
19 Johnny Unitas .50
20 Brett Favre 2.00
21 Jerome Pathon .15
22 Jason Tucker .30
23 Charles Johnson .15
24 Brian Mitchell .15
25 Billy Miller .15
26 Jay Fiedler .15
27 Marcus Pollard .15
28 De'Mond Parker .15
29 Leslie Shepherd .15
30 Fred Taylor .75
31 Michael Pittman .15
32 Ricky Watters .30
33 Derrick Brooks .15
34 Junior Seau .30
35 Troy Vincent .15
36 Eric Allen .15
37 Pete Mitchell .15
38 Tony Simmons .15
39 Az-Zahir Hakim .30
40 Dan Marino 1.50
41 Mac Cody .15
42 Scott Dreisbach .15
43 Al Wilson .15
44 Luther Broughton .15
45 Wane McGarity .15
46 Stephen Boyd .15
47 Michael Strahan .15
48 Chris Chandler .30
49 Tony Martin .15
50 Edgerrin James 2.00
51 John Randle .15
52 Warrick Dunn .50
53 Elvis Grbac .30
54 Champ Bailey .30
55 Kyle Brady .15
56 John Lynch .15
57 Kevin Carter .15
58 Mike Pritchard .15
59 *Deon Mitchell* .30
60 Randy Moss 1.75
61 Jermaine Fazande .30
62 Donovan McNabb .75
63 Richard Huntley .30
64 Rich Gannon .30
65 Aaron Glenn .15
66 Amani Toomer .30
67 Andre Hastings .15
68 Ricky Williams 1.25
69 Sam Madison .15
70 Drew Bledsoe .75
71 Eric Moulds .50
72 Justin Armour .15
73 Jamal Anderson .50
74 Mario Bates .15
75 Sam Gash .15
76 Macey Brooks .15
77 Tremain Mack .15
78 David LaFleur .15
79 Dexter Coakley .15
80 Cris Carter .50
81 Byron Chamberlain .15
82 David Sloan .15
83 *Mike Devlin* .30
84 Jimmy Smith .30
85 Derrick Alexander .15
86 Damon Huard .50
87 Jake Reed .15
88 Darrell Green .15
89 Derrick Mason .15
90 Curtis Martin .50
91 Donnie Abraham .15
92 D'Marco Farr .15
93 Ahman Green .30
94 Shane Matthews .15
95 Torrance Small .15
96 Duce Staley .50
97 Jon Ritchie .15
98 Victor Green .15
99 Kerry Collins .30
100 Peyton Manning 1.50
101 Ben Coates .30
102 Thurman Thomas .30
103 Cornelius Bennett .15
104 Terance Mathis .15
105 Adrian Murrell .15
106 Donald Hayes .15
107 Terry Kirby .15
108 James Allen .15
109 Ty Law .15
110 Tim Brown .30
111 Chad Bratzke .15
112 Deion Sanders .50
113 James Johnson .30
114 Tony Richardson .15
115 Tony Brackens .15
116 Ken Dilger .15
117 Albert Connell .30
118 Neil O'Donnell .15
119 *Selucio Sanford* .30
120 Steve Young .75
121 Tony Horne .15
122 Charlie Rogers .15
123 J.J. Stokes .30
124 Kenny Bynum .15
125 Jeff Graham .15
126 Ike Hilliard .30
127 Ray Lucas .50
128 Terry Glenn .50
129 Rickey Dudley .30
130 Joey Galloway .50
131 Brian Dawkins .15
132 Rob Moore .30
133 Bob Christian .15
134 *Anthony Wright* 2.00
135 Antowain Smith .50
136 Kevin Johnson .50
137 Scott Covington .15
138 D'Wayne Bates .15
139 Sam Cowart .15
140 Isaac Bruce .50
141 Tony McGee .15
142 Dale Carter .15
143 Matt Hasselbeck .30
144 Torry Holt .50
145 Daunte Culpepper .75
146 Yatil Green .15
147 Chris Howard .15
148 Irving Fryar .15
149 Derrick Mayes .30
150 Warren Sapp .30
151 Ricky Proehl .15
152 Eric Kresser .15
153 Jeff Garcia .50
154 Freddie Jones .30
155 Michael Cloud .15
156 Wayne Chrebet .30
157 Joe Montgomery .15
158 Shannon Sharpe .30
159 Eddie Kennison .15
160 Eddie George .60
161 Jay Riemersma .15
162 Peter Boulware .15
163 Aeneas Williams .15
164 Jim Miller .15
165 Jamir Miller .15
166 Tim Biakabutuka .30
167 Kordell Stewart .50
168 Charlie Garner .30
169 Germane Crowell .30
170 Stephen Davis .50
171 Jeff George .30
172 Mark Brunell .75
173 Stephen Alexander .15
174 Mike Alstott .50
175 Terry Allen .30
176 Ed McCaffrey .30
177 Bobby Engram .15
178 Andre Cooper .15
179 Kevin Faulk .30
180 Errict Rhett .30
181 Jammi German .15
182 Oronde Gadsden .30
183 Jevon Kearse .50
184 Herman Moore .30
185 Terrence Wilkins .15
186 Raghib Ismail .15
187 Patrick Johnson .15
188 Simeon Rice .15
189 Mo Lewis .15
190 Qadry Ismail .15
191 Terry Jackson .15
192 Rashaan Shehee .15
193 Charles Woodson .50
194 Akili Smith .50
195 Yancey Thigpen .30
196 Michael Westbrook .30
197 Donnell Bennett .15
198 Sedrick Irvin .15
199 Keenan McCardell .30
200 Marshall Faulk .50
201 Jeff Blake .30
202 Rob Johnson .30
203 Vinny Testaverde .30
204 Andy Katzenmoyer .15
205 Michael Basnight .15
206 Lance Schulters .15
207 Shaun King .75
208 Bill Schroeder .15
209 Skip Hicks .15
210 Jake Plummer .50
211 Leroy Hoard .15
212 Reggie Barlow .15
213 E.G. Green .15
214 Fred Lane .15
215 Antonio Freeman .50
216 Grant Wistrom .15
217 Kevin Dyson .30
218 Mikhael Ricks .15
219 Rod Woodson .15
220 Tim Dwight .50
221 Darnay Scott .30
222 Curtis Enis .50
223 Sean Bennett .15
224 Napoleon Kaufman .50
225 Jonathon Linton .30
226 Jim Harbaugh .30
227 Hardy Nickerson .15
228 Todd Lyght .15
229 Dorsey Levens .50
230 Steve Beuerlein .30
231 Marty Booker .15
232 Andre Wadsworth .15
233 James Hasty .15
234 Shawn Bryson .15
235 Larry Centers .15
236 Charlie Batch .50
237 Steve McNair .60
238 Darrin Chiaverini .15
239 Jerome Bettis .50
240 Muhsin Muhammad .30
241 Terrell Fletcher .15
242 Jon Kitna .50
243 Frank Wycheck .15
244 Tony Gonzalez .30
245 Ron Rivers .15
246 Olandis Gary .50
247 Jermaine Lewis .15
248 Joe Jurevicius .15
249 Richie Anderson .15
250 Marcus Robinson .50
251 Shawn Springs .15
252 William Floyd .15
253 *Bobby Shaw* .30
254 Glyn Milburn .15
255 Brian Griese .50
256 Donnie Edwards .15
257 Joe Horn .15
258 Cameron Cleeland .30
259 Glenn Foley .15
260 Corey Dillon .50
261 Troy Brown .15
262 Stoney Case .15
263 Kevin Williams .15
264 London Fletcher .15
265 O.J. McDuffie .15
266 Jonathan Quinn .15
267 Trent Dilfer .30
268 Dameyune Craig .30
269 Terrell Owens .50
270 Tim Couch 1.25
271 Dameane Douglas .15
272 Moses Moreno .15
273 Bruce Smith .15
274 Peerless Price .50
275 Sam Garnes .15
276 Natrone Means .30
277 Na Brown .15
278 Dave Moore .15
279 Chris Sanders .15
280 Troy Aikman 1.00
281 Cecil Collins .30
282 Matthew Hatchette .15
283 Bill Romanowski .15
284 Basil Mitchell .15
285 Tony Banks .30
286 *Jake Delhomme* 3.00
287 Keyshawn Johnson .50
288 Dexter McLeon .15
289 Corey Bradford .30
290 Terrell Davis 1.00
291 Johnnie Morton .30
292 Kevin Lockett .15
293 Robert Smith .50
294 Jeff Lewis .15
295 Wali Rainer .15
296 Troy Edwards .50
297 Keith Poole .15
298 Priest Holmes .50
299 David Boston .50
300 Marvin Harrison .50
301 Levon Kirkland .15
302 Robert Holcombe .15
303 Autry Denson .15
304 Kevin Hardy .15
305 Rod Smith .30
306 Robert Porcher .15
307 Cade McNown .75
308 Craig Yeast .15
309 Doug Flutie .50
310 Jerry Rice 1.00
311 Brad Johnson .50
312 Tiki Barber .30
313 Will Blackwell .15
314 Sean Dawkins .15
315 Jacquez Green .30
316 Zach Thomas .30
317 Gus Frerotte .15
318 Chris Warren .15
319 Carl Pickens .30
320 Tyrone Wheatley .30
321 Kurt Warner 1.25
322 Dan Marino .75
323 Cris Carter .30
324 Brett Favre 1.00
325 Marshall Faulk .30
326 Jevon Kearse .30
327 Edgerrin James 1.00
328 Emmitt Smith .75
329 Andre Reed .15
330 Kevin Dyson, Frank Wycheck .15
331 Olindo Mare .15
332 Marcus Coleman .15
333 James Johnson .15
334 Ray Lucas .30
335 Dedric Ward .15
336 Richie Cunningham .15
337 James Hasty .15
338 Sedrick Shaw .15
339 Kurt Warner 1.25
340 Marshall Faulk .30
341 Brian Shay .50
342 L.C. Stevens .50
343 Corey Thomas .50
344 Scott Milanovich .50
345 Pat Barnes .50
346 Danny Wuerffel .50
347 Kevin Daft .50
348 *Ron Powlus* 1.50
349 Tony Graziani .50
350 *Norman Miller* .50
351 Cory Sauter .50
352 *Marcus Crandell* .50
353 *Sean Morey* .50
354 Jeff Ogden .50
355 Ted White .50
356 *Jim Kubiak* .50
357 *Aaron Stecker* .50
358 Ronnie Powell .50
359 *Matt Lytle* .50
360 *Kendrick Nord* .50
361 *Tim Rattay* 3.00
362 *Rob Morris* 1.50
363 *Chris Samuels* 2.00
364 *Todd Husak* 1.50
365 *Ahmed Plummer* 1.50
366 *Frank Murphy* 1.50
367 *Michael Wiley* 2.00
368 *Giovanni Carmazzi* 2.00
369 *Anthony Becht* 2.00
370 *John Abraham* 1.50
371 *Shaun Alexander* 6.00
372 *Thomas Jones* 4.00
373 *Courtney Brown* 2.00
374 *Curtis Keaton* 1.50
375 *Jerry Porter* 4.00
376 *Corey Simon* 2.00
377 *Dez White* 2.00
378 *Jamal Lewis* 6.00
379 *Ron Dayne* 2.00
380 *R. Jay Soward* 2.00
381 *Tee Martin* 2.00
382 *Shaun Ellis* 1.50
383 *Brian Urlacher* 5.00
384 *Reuben Droughns* 5.00
385 *Travis Taylor* 3.00
386 *Plaxico Burress* 5.00
387 *Chad Pennington* 10.00
388 *Sylvester Morris* 2.00
389 *Ron Dugans* 2.00
390 *Joe Hamilton* 2.00
391 *Chris Redman* 2.00
392 *Trung Canidate* 2.00
393 *J.R. Redmond* 2.50
394 *Danny Farmer* 2.00
395 *Todd Pinkston* 2.00
396 *Dennis Northcutt* 2.00
397 *Laveranues Coles* 4.00
398 *Bubba Franks* 2.00
399 *Travis Prentice* 2.00
400 *Peter Warrick* 4.00

2000 Topps MVP Promotion

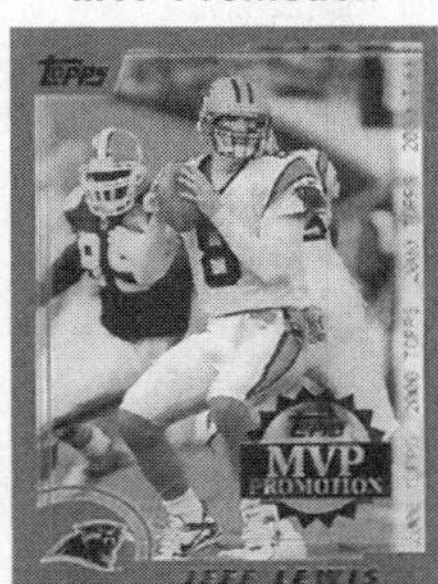

NM/M
MVP Cards: 15X-30X
MVP Rookies: 5X-10X
Inserted 1:234

2000 Topps Collection

NM/M
Complete Set (400): 50.00
Collection Cards: 1X
Collection Rookies: 1X

2000 Topps Autographs

NM/M
Common Player: 20.00
Minor Stars: 40.00
Inserted 1:1,015
Production 250-700
SA Shaun Alexander 50.00
SD Stephen Davis 40.00
RD Ron Dayne 50.00
MF Marshall Faulk 50.00
MH Marvin Harrison 40.00
EJ Edgerrin James 75.00
TJ Thomas Jones 60.00
JK Jon Kitna 20.00
PM Peyton Manning 125.00
SM Sylvester Morris 20.00
CP Chad Pennington 100.00
JS Jimmy Smith 20.00
ZT Zach Thomas 20.00
KW Kurt Warner 100.00
PW Peter Warrick 50.00

2000 Topps Chrome Previews

NM/M
Complete Set (20): 45.00
Common Player: 1.00
Minor Stars: 2.00
Inserted 1:18
CP1 Kurt Warner 4.00
CP2 Shaun King 2.50
CP3 Brad Johnson 2.00
CP4 Daunte Culpepper 2.50
CP5 Brett Favre 6.00
CP6 Eddie George 2.50
CP7 Dan Marino 5.00
CP8 Randy Moss 4.00
CP9 Troy Aikman 4.00
CP10 Peyton Manning 4.00
CP11 Fred Taylor 2.50
CP12 Ricky Williams 3.00
CP13 Jimmy Smith 1.00
CP14 Jerry Rice 4.00
CP15 Marshall Faulk 2.00
CP16 Marvin Harrison 2.00
CP17 Stephen Davis 2.00
CP18 Isaac Bruce 2.00
CP19 Emmitt Smith 5.00
CP20 Edgerrin James 4.00

2000 Topps Combos

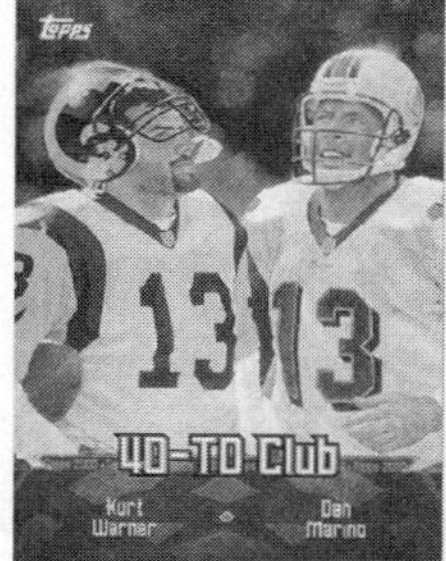

NM/M
Complete Set (10): 20.00
Common Player: 1.50
Inserted 1:12
TC1 Johnny Unitas, Peyton Manning 5.00
TC2 Cris Carter, Randy Moss 5.00
TC3 Ricky Williams, Edgerrin James 6.00
TC4 Marvin Harrison, Jimmy Smith 1.50
TC5 Isaac Bruce, Joey Galloway 1.50
TC6 Donovan McNabb, Tim Couch, Shaun King, Daunte Culpepper, Cade McNown, Akili Smith 4.00
TC7 Stephen Davis, Fred Taylor 2.50
TC8 Marshall Faulk, Eddie George 1.50
TC9 Emmitt Smith, Troy Aikman 4.00
TC10 Kurt Warner, Dan Marino 7.00

2000 Topps Hall of Fame Autographs

NM/M
Common Player: 50.00
Inserted 1:3,551
HOF1 Joe Montana 250.00
HOF2 Howie Long 80.00
HOF3 Ronnie Lott 60.00
HOF4 Dan Rooney 50.00
HOF5 Dave Wilcox 50.00

2000 Topps Johnny Unitas Reprints

NM/M
Complete Set (18): 75.00
Common Player: 5.00

NM/M
Inserted 1:19 Hobby
Chrome Cards: 2X
Inserted 1:72 Hobby
Autographs: 40X
Inserted 1:13,678 Hobby
R1 Johnny Unitas 5.00
R2 Johnny Unitas 5.00
R3 Johnny Unitas 5.00
R4 Johnny Unitas 5.00
R5 Johnny Unitas 5.00
R6 Johnny Unitas 5.00
R7 Johnny Unitas 5.00
R8 Johnny Unitas 5.00
R9 Johnny Unitas 5.00
R10 Johnny Unitas 5.00
R11 Johnny Unitas 5.00
R12 Johnny Unitas 5.00
R13 Johnny Unitas 5.00
R14 Johnny Unitas 5.00
R15 Johnny Unitas 5.00
R16 Johnny Unitas 5.00
R17 Johnny Unitas 5.00
R18 Johnny Unitas 5.00

2000 Topps Jumbos

NM/M
Complete Set (8): 20.00
Common Player: 1.50
1:Hobby Box
1 Peyton Manning 4.00
2 Marshall Faulk 1.50
3 Dan Marino 4.00
4 Randy Moss 4.00
5 Kurt Warner 3.00
6 Eddie George 2.00
7 Brett Favre 5.00
8 Edgerrin James 3.00

2000 Topps Own The Game

NM/M
Complete Set (30): 40.00
Common Player: 1.00
Minor Stars: 2.00
Inserted 1:12
OTG1 Steve Beuerlein 1.00
OTG2 Kurt Warner 3.00
OTG3 Peyton Manning 5.00
OTG4 Brett Favre 6.00
OTG5 Brad Johnson 2.00
OTG6 Edgerrin James 4.00
OTG7 Curtis Martin 2.00
OTG8 Stephen Davis 2.00
OTG9 Emmitt Smith 5.00
OTG10 Marshall Faulk 2.00
OTG11 Eddie George 2.50
OTG12 Duce Staley 2.00
OTG13 Charlie Garner 1.00
OTG14 Marvin Harrison 2.00
OTG15 Jimmy Smith 1.00
OTG16 Randy Moss 4.00
OTG17 Marcus Robinson 2.00
OTG18 Tim Brown 2.00
OTG19 Germane Crowell 1.00
OTG20 Muhsin Muhammad 1.00
OTG21 Cris Carter 2.00
OTG22 Michael Westbrook 1.00
OTG23 Amani Toomer 1.00
OTG24 Keyshawn Johnson 2.00
OTG25 Isaac Bruce 2.00
OTG26 Kurt Warner 3.00
OTG27 Stephen Davis 2.00
OTG28 Edgerrin James 4.00
OTG29 Cris Carter 2.00
OTG30 Marvin Harrison 2.00

2000 Topps Pro Bowl Jerseys

NM/M
Common Player: 10.00
Minor Stars: 20.00
Inserted 1:271
Mike Alstott 25.00
Jessie Armstead 10.00
Steve Beuerlein 20.00
Tony Brackens 10.00
Mark Brunell 35.00
Cris Carter 35.00
Kevin Carter 10.00
Corey Dillon 35.00
Rich Gannon 20.00
Eddie George 35.00
Tony Gonzalez 20.00
Kevin Hardy 10.00
Marvin Harrison 40.00
Keyshawn Johnson 30.00
Olindo Mare 10.00
Bruce Matthews 10.00
Muhsin Muhammad 20.00
Darrell Russell 10.00
Warren Sapp 20.00
Emmitt Smith 60.00
Michael Strahan 10.00
Zach Thomas 20.00
Kurt Warner 50.00
Rod Woodson 10.00

2000 Topps Rookie Photo Shoot Autographs

NM/M
Common Player: 25.00
Inserted 1:5,761
SA Shaun Alexander 250.00
AB Anthony Becht 25.00
CB Courtney Brown 60.00
PB Plaxico Burress 150.00
TC Trung Canidate 75.00
LC Laveranues Coles 125.00
RD Ron Dayne 75.00
RDR Reuben Droughns 200.00
RDU Ron Dugans 40.00
DF Danny Farmer 40.00
DFR Bubba Franks 50.00
JH Joe Hamilton 40.00
TJ Thomas Jones 125.00
CK Curtis Keaton 25.00
JL Jamal Lewis 250.00
TM Tee Martin 25.00
SM Sylvester Morris 75.00
DN Dennis Northcutt 25.00
CP Chad Pennington 300.00
TP Todd Pinkston 25.00
JP Jerry Porter 25.00
TPR Travis Prentice 75.00
CR Chris Redman 75.00
JR J.R. Redmond 75.00
CSA Chris Samuels 25.00
CS Corey Simon 25.00
TT Travis Taylor 100.00
BU Brian Urlacher 250.00
PW Peter Warrick 75.00
DW Dez White 25.00

2000 Topps Super Bowl MVP Autograph Relic

NM/M
Inserted 1:1,287
SB1 Kurt Warner 300.00

2000 Topps Chrome

NM/M
Complete Set (270): 750.00
Common Player: .15
Minor Stars: .50
Common Europe: 1.00
Common Rookie: 5.00
Production 1,650 Sets
Pack (4): 2.75
Wax Box (24): 45.00
1 Daunte Culpepper 1.50
2 Troy Edwards 1.00
3 Terrell Owens 1.00
4 Ricky Proehl .15
5 Shaun King 1.50
6 Jeff George .50
7 Champ Bailey .50
8 Amani Toomer .15
9 Stephen Boyd .15
10 Thurman Thomas .50
11 Patrick Jeffers .75
12 Jake Plummer 1.00
13 Peter Boulware .15
14 Darrin Chiaverini .15
15 Olandis Gary 1.25
16 Peyton Manning 3.00
17 Joe Horn .15
18 Wayne Chrebet .50
19 Freddie Jones .15
20 Kurt Warner 4.00
21 Mike Alstott 1.00
22 Stephen Davis 1.00
23 Tim Brown .75
24 Damon Huard .75
25 Terry Glenn 1.00
26 Ricky Williams 3.00
27 Tim Dwight 1.00
28 Jay Riemersma .15
29 Carl Pickens .50
30 Brett Favre 4.00
31 Oronde Gadsden .15
32 Steve McNair 1.00
33 Michael Pittman .15
34 Emmitt Smith 2.50
35 Mark Brunell 1.00
36 Ed McCaffrey .75
37 Tyrone Wheatley .15
38 Sean Dawkins .15
39 Jevon Kearse 1.00
40 Tai Streets .15
41 Keyshawn Johnson 1.00
42 Germane Crowell .75
43 Yatil Green .15
44 *Anthony Wright* 4.00
45 Jerry Rice 2.00
46 Az-Zahir Hakim .50
47 Stephen Alexander .15
48 Zach Thomas .50
49 Tony Simmons .15
50 Jessie Armstead .15
51 Kordell Stewart 1.00
52 Cade McNown 1.50
53 Tony Gonzalez .75
54 John Randle .15
55 Donovan McNabb 1.50
56 Warrick Dunn 1.00
57 Dorsey Levens 1.00
58 Errict Rhett .15
59 Priest Holmes .75
60 Terrell Davis 2.50
61 Natrone Means .50
62 Brad Johnson 1.00
63 Rickey Dudley .15
64 Billy Miller .15
65 Randy Moss 3.00
66 Joe Montgomery .15
67 Johnnie Morton .15
68 Peerless Price 1.00
69 Raghib Ismail .15
70 David Boston 1.00
71 Fred Taylor 1.00
72 Jermaine Fazande .50
73 Elvis Grbac .50
74 Derrick Mayes .15
75 Yancey Thigpen .15
76 Ike Hilliard .50
77 Muhsin Muhammad .50
78 Shawn Jefferson .15
79 Rod Smith .75
80 Darnay Scott .50
81 Cameron Cleeland .50
82 Steve Young 1.50
83 E.G. Green .15
84 Robert Smith 1.00
85 Jermaine Lewis .15
86 Tim Biakabutuka .50
87 Jerome Pathon .15
88 Kent Graham .15
89 Bruce Smith .15
90 Isaac Bruce 1.00
91 Curtis Enis 1.00
92 D'Marco Farr .15
93 Keith Poole .15
94 Troy Aikman 2.00
95 Rich Gannon .50
96 Michael Westbrook .50
97 Albert Connell .50
98 James Johnson .15
99 Jeff Blake .50
100 Joey Galloway 1.00
101 Rob Moore .50
102 Chris Chandler .50
103 Fred Lane .15
104 Eddie Kennison .15
105 Kevin Hardy .15
106 Napoleon Kaufman 1.00
107 Kevin Dyson .50
108 Keenan McCardell .50
109 Drew Bledsoe 1.50
110 Kevin Johnson .75
111 Terance Mathis .15
112 Gus Frerotte .15
113 Matthew Hatchette .15
114 Herman Moore .75
115 Curtis Martin 1.00
116 Jacquez Green .15
117 Jake Reed .15
118 Antonio Freeman 1.00
119 Jim Miller .15
120 Frank Sanders .15
121 Brian Griese 1.00
122 Troy Brown .15
123 Jeff Graham .15
124 Marshall Faulk 1.00
125 Vinny Testaverde .50
126 Frank Wycheck .15
127 Kerry Collins .50
128 Jay Fiedler 1.00
129 Cris Carter 1.00
130 Jason Tucker .15
131 Antowain Smith 1.00
132 Tony Banks .75
133 Terrence Wilkins .75
134 Tony Martin .15
135 Richard Huntley .15
136 J.J. Stokes .50
137 Ricky Watters .50
138 Pete Mitchell .15
139 Jimmy Smith 1.00
140 Doug Flutie 1.00
141 Corey Bradford .15
142 Curtis Conway .15
143 Moses Moreno .15
144 Torry Holt 1.00
145 Warren Sapp .15
146 Duce Staley 1.00
147 Mikhael Ricks .15
148 Edgerrin James 3.00
149 Charlie Batch 1.00
150 Rob Johnson .50
151 Jamal Anderson 1.00
152 Tim Couch 1.00
153 O.J. McDuffie .50
154 Charles Woodson .50
155 *Jake Delhomme* 2.50
156 Eddie George 1.25
157 Jim Harbaugh .15
158 Jon Kitna 1.00
159 Derrick Alexander .15
160 Marvin Harrison 1.00
161 James Stewart .50
162 Qadry Ismail .15
163 Wesley Walls .15
164 Steve Beuerlein .50
165 Marcus Robinson 1.00
166 Bill Schroeder .15
167 Charles Johnson .15
168 Charlie Garner .15
169 Eric Moulds 1.00
170 Jerome Bettis 1.00
171 Tai Streets .15
172 Akili Smith 1.25
173 Jonathon Linton .50
174 Corey Dillon 1.00
175 Junior Seau .50
176 Jonathan Quinn .15
177 Bobby Engram .15
178 Shannon Sharpe .50
179 Michael Basnight .15
180 Sedrick Irvin .15
181 *Sammy Morris* 12.00
182 *Ron Dixon* 12.00
183 *Trevor Gaylor* 12.00
184 *Chris Cole* 5.00
185 *Deltha O'Neal* 5.00
186 *Sebastian Janikowski* 12.00
187 *Kwame Cavil* 5.00
188 *Chad Morton* 12.00
189 *Terrelle Smith* 5.00
190 *Frank Moreau* 12.00
191 Kurt Warner 2.00
192 Dan Marino 1.50
193 Cris Carter .50
194 Brett Favre 1.75
195 Marshall Faulk .50
196 Jevon Kearse .50
197 Edgerrin James 1.75
198 Emmitt Smith 1.25
199 Andre Reed .15
200 Kevin Dyson, Frank Wycheck .15
201 Olindo Mare .15
202 Marcus Coleman .15
203 James Johnson .15
204 Ray Lucas .15
205 Dedric Ward .15
206 Richie Cunningham .15
207 James Hasty .15
208 Sedrick Shaw .15
209 Kurt Warner 2.00
210 Marshall Faulk .50
211 Brian Shay 1.00
212 L.C. Stevens 1.00
213 Corey Thomas 1.00
214 Scott Milanovich 1.00
215 Pat Barnes 1.00
216 Danny Wuerffel 1.00
217 Kevin Daft 1.00
218 *Ron Powlus* 2.50
219 Eric Kresser 1.00
220 Norman Miller 1.00
221 Cory Sauter 1.00
222 Marcus Crandell 1.00
223 Sean Morey 1.00
224 Jeff Ogden 1.00
225 Ted White 1.00
226 Jim Kubiak 1.00
227 Aaron Stecker 1.00
228 Ronnie Powell 1.00
229 Matt Lytle 1.00
230 Kendrick Nord 1.00
231 *Tim Rattay* 15.00
232 *Rob Morris* 5.00
233 *Chris Samuels* 5.00
234 *Todd Husak* 5.00
235 *Ahmed Plummer* 5.00
236 *Frank Murphy* 5.00
237 *Michael Wiley* 5.00
238 *Giovanni Carmazzi* 5.00
239 *Anthony Becht* 5.00
240 *John Abraham* 5.00
241 *Shaun Alexander* 40.00
242 *Thomas Jones* 20.00
243 *Courtney Brown* 12.00
244 *Curtis Keaton* 5.00
245 *Jerry Porter* 25.00
246 *Corey Simon* 5.00
247 *Dez White* 12.00
248 *Jamal Lewis* 40.00
249 *Ron Dayne* 12.00
250 *R. Jay Soward* 12.00
251 *Tee Martin* 12.00
252 *Shaun Ellis* 5.00
253 *Brian Urlacher* 40.00
254 *Reuben Droughns* 15.00
255 *Travis Taylor* 15.00
256 *Plaxico Burress* 30.00
257 *Chad Pennington* 60.00
258 *Sylvester Morris* 10.00
259 *Ron Dugans* 12.00
260 *Joe Hamilton* 12.00
261 *Chris Redman* 12.00
262 *Trung Canidate* 15.00
263 *J.R. Redmond* 12.00
264 *Danny Farmer* 12.00
265 *Todd Pinkston* 15.00
266 *Dennis Northcutt* 12.00
267 *Laveranues Coles* 25.00
268 *Bubba Franks* 15.00
269 *Travis Prentice* 12.00
270 *Peter Warrick* 25.00

Post-1980 cards in Near Mint condition will generally sell for about 75% of the quoted Mint value. Excellent-condition cards bring no more than 40%.

2000 Topps Chrome Refractors

Refractor Cards: 2X-4X
Inserted 1:12
Refractor Rookies: 2X
Production 150 Sets

2000 Topps Chrome Combos

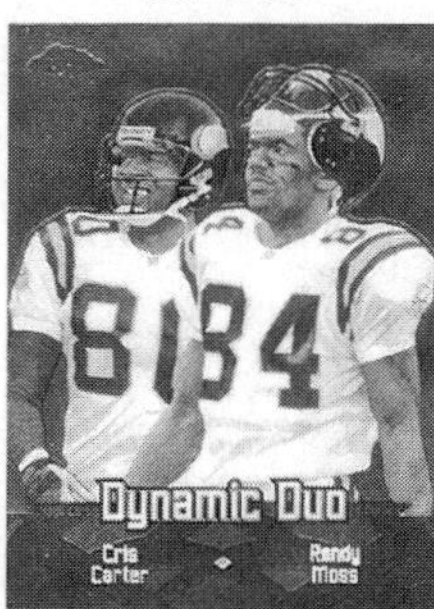

NM/M
Complete Set (10): 35.00
Common Player: 2.00
Inserted 1:20
Refractors: 4X
Inserted 1:200
TC1 Johnny Unitas, Peyton Manning 6.00
TC2 Cris Carter, Randy Moss 5.00
TC3 Ricky Williams, Edgerrin James 5.00
TC4 Marvin Harrison, Jimmy Smith 2.00
TC5 Isaac Bruce, Joey Galloway 2.00
TC6 Donovan McNabb, Tim Couch, Shaun King, Cade McNown, Daunte Culpepper, Akili Smith 4.00
TC7 Stephen Davis, Fred Taylor 3.00
TC8 Marshall Faulk, Eddie George 2.00
TC9 Emmitt Smith, Troy Aikman 4.00
TC10 Kurt Warner, Dan Marino 5.00

2000 Topps Chrome Own the Game

NM/M
Complete Set (30): 55.00
Common Player: 1.00
Minor Stars: 2.00
Inserted 1:12
Refractors: 4X
Inserted 1:120
OTG1 Steve Beuerlein 1.00
OTG2 Kurt Warner 4.00
OTG3 Peyton Manning 4.00
OTG4 Brett Favre 7.00
OTG5 Brad Johnson 2.00
OTG6 Edgerrin James 4.00
OTG7 Curtis Martin 2.00
OTG8 Stephen Davis 2.00
OTG9 Emmitt Smith 5.00
OTG10 Marshall Faulk 2.00
OTG11 Eddie George 2.50
OTG12 Duce Staley 2.00

OTG13 Charlie Garner 1.00
OTG14 Marvin Harrison 2.00
OTG15 Jimmy Smith 2.00
OTG16 Randy Moss 4.00
OTG17 Marcus Robinson 2.00
OTG18 Tim Brown 1.00
OTG19 Germane Crowell 1.00
OTG20 Muhsin Muhammad 1.00
OTG21 Cris Carter 2.00
OTG22 Michael Westbrook 1.00
OTG23 Amani Toomer 1.00
OTG24 Keyshawn Johnson 2.00
OTG25 Isaac Bruce 2.00
OTG26 Kurt Warner 4.00
OTG27 Stephen Davis 2.00
OTG28 Edgerrin James 4.00
OTG29 Cris Carter 2.00
OTG30 Marvin Harrison 2.00

2000 Topps Chrome Johnny Unitas Reprints

NM/M
Complete Set (18): 100.00
Common Player: 6.00
Inserted 1:14
R1 Johnny Unitas 10.00
R2 Johnny Unitas 6.00
R3 Johnny Unitas 6.00
R4 Johnny Unitas 6.00
R5 Johnny Unitas 6.00
R6 Johnny Unitas 6.00
R7 Johnny Unitas 6.00
R8 Johnny Unitas 6.00
R9 Johnny Unitas 6.00
R10 Johnny Unitas 6.00
R11 Johnny Unitas 6.00
R12 Johnny Unitas 6.00
R13 Johnny Unitas 6.00
R14 Johnny Unitas 6.00
R15 Johnny Unitas 6.00
R16 Johnny Unitas 6.00
R17 Johnny Unitas 6.00
R18 Johnny Unitas 6.00

2000 Topps Chrome Preseason Picks

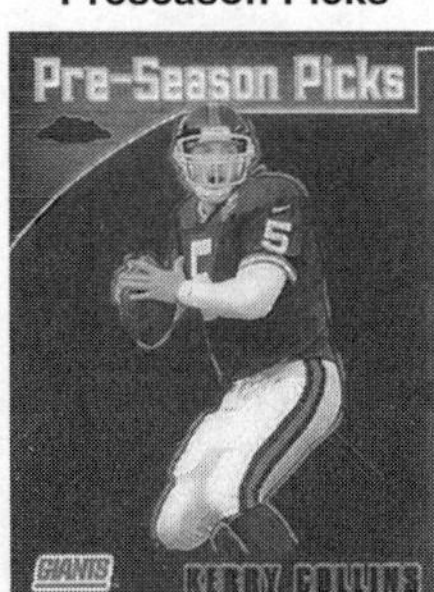

NM/M
Complete Set (31): 75.00
Common Player: 1.25
Minor Stars: 2.50
Inserted 1:22
Refractors: 4X
Inserted 1:220
P1 Jake Plummer 2.50
P2 Troy Aikman 5.00
P3 Kerry Collins 1.25
P4 Donovan McNabb 3.00
P5 Stephen Davis 2.50
P6 Cade McNown 3.00
P7 Charlie Batch 2.50
P8 Brett Favre 7.00
P9 Randy Moss 5.00
P10 Shaun King 2.00
P11 Tim Couch 3.00
P12 Jamal Anderson 2.50
P13 Steve Beuerlein 1.25
P14 Ricky Williams 5.00
P15 Kurt Warner 4.00
P16 Jerry Rice 5.00
P17 Eric Moulds 2.50
P18 Peyton Manning 4.00
P19 Zach Thomas 1.25
P20 Drew Bledsoe 4.00
P21 Curtis Martin 2.50
P22 Tony Banks 1.25
P23 Akili Smith 2.50
P24 Jimmy Smith 2.50
P25 Jerome Bettis 2.50
P26 Eddie George 3.00
P27 Terrell Davis 4.00
P28 Tony Gonzalez 1.25
P29 Tim Brown 1.25
P30 Junior Seau 1.25
P31 Jon Kitna 2.50

2000 Topps Gallery

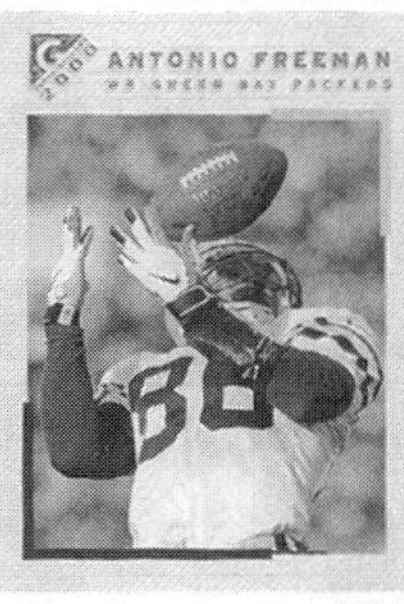

NM/M
Complete Set (175): 50.00
Common Player: .15
Minor Stars: .30
Common Subset (126-150): .75
Common Rookie: 1.00
Inserted 1:1
Pack (6): 2.00
Wax Box (24): 35.00
1 Marshall Faulk .50
2 Kordell Stewart .50
3 Priest Holmes .50
4 James Johnson .30
5 Charlie Garner .30
6 Jeff Blake .30
7 Joey Galloway .50
8 Terrell Davis 1.00
9 Jerome Bettis .50
10 Bobby Engram .15
11 Muhsin Muhammad .30
12 Marcus Robinson .50
13 Kerry Collins .30
14 Jake Plummer .50
15 J.J. Stokes .30
16 Tim Couch 1.50
17 Napoleon Kaufman .50
18 Az-Zahir Hakim .30
19 Jimmy Smith .50
20 Eddie George .75
21 Jacquez Green .30
22 Champ Bailey .30
23 Wesley Walls .30
24 Eric Moulds .50
25 Corey Dillon .50
26 Freddie Jones .15
27 Jevon Kearse .75
28 Ray Lucas .50
29 Germane Crowell .30
30 Randy Moss 2.00
31 Patrick Jeffers .50
32 Zach Thomas .30
33 Shannon Sharpe .30
34 Derrick Mayes .30
35 Antonio Freeman .50
36 Terance Mathis .15
37 Herman Moore .50
38 Tony Banks .30
39 Jerry Rice 1.50
40 Troy Aikman 1.50
41 Rickey Dudley .15
42 Troy Edwards .50
43 Curtis Martin .50
44 Eddie Kennison .15
45 Mark Brunell .50
46 Shaun King 1.00
47 Duce Staley .50
48 Darnay Scott .30
49 Sean Dawkins .15
50 Edgerrin James 2.50
51 Olandis Gary .75
52 Peerless Price .50
53 Akili Smith .75
54 Charlie Batch .50
55 Tim Biakabutuka .30
56 Rob Moore .30
57 Keenan McCardell .30
58 Dan Marino 2.00
59 Tony Gonzalez .30
60 Stephen Davis .50
61 Ricky Watters .30
62 Frank Wycheck .30
63 Kevin Johnson .50
64 Isaac Bruce .50
65 Andre Reed .15
66 Jamal Anderson .50
67 Dorsey Levens .50
68 Raghib Ismail .15
69 Albert Connell .30
70 Brett Favre 2.50
71 Wayne Chrebet .50
72 Jon Kitna .50
73 Brian Griese .60
74 Rob Johnson .30
75 Qadry Ismail .15
76 Derrick Alexander .15
77 Tim Dwight .50
78 Ike Hilliard .15
79 Frank Sanders .30
80 Fred Taylor 1.00
81 Robert Smith .50
82 Vinny Testaverde .50
83 Steve Young 1.00
84 Tyrone Wheatley .30
85 Mikhael Ricks .15
86 Tony Martin .15
87 Carl Pickens .30
88 Warrick Dunn .50
89 Emmitt Smith 2.00
90 Keyshawn Johnson .50
91 James Stewart .50
92 Doug Flutie .75
93 Torry Holt .50
94 Jeff Graham .15
95 Steve McNair .60
96 Errict Rhett .30
97 Terrell Owens .50
98 Terry Glenn .50
99 Steve Beuerlein .30
100 Kurt Warner 2.50
101 Jeff George .30
102 Deion Sanders .50
103 Johnnie Morton .15
104 Antowain Smith .50
105 O.J. McDuffie .30
106 Rod Smith .30
107 Jim Harbaugh .30
108 Marvin Harrison .50
109 Curtis Enis .50
110 Drew Bledsoe 1.00
111 Mike Alstott .50
112 Amani Toomer .30
113 Elvis Grbac .30
114 Tim Brown .30
115 Cris Carter .50
116 Donovan McNabb 2.00
117 Chris Chandler .30
118 Kevin Dyson .30
119 Rich Gannon .30
120 Ricky Williams 1.50
121 Brad Johnson .50
122 Cade McNown 1.00
123 Ed McCaffrey .30
124 Michael Westbrook .30
125 Peyton Manning 2.00
126 Brett Favre 4.00
127 Emmitt Smith 3.00
128 Tim Brown .75
129 Troy Aikman 2.50
130 Jimmy Smith .75
131 Dan Marino 3.00
132 Cris Carter 1.00
133 Jerry Rice 2.50
134 Steve Young 1.50
135 Marshall Faulk 1.00
136 Eddie George 1.25
137 Drew Bledsoe 1.50
138 Randy Moss 4.00
139 Germane Crowell .75
140 Akili Smith 1.25
141 Tim Couch 2.50
142 Marcus Robinson 1.00
143 Daunte Culpepper 1.50
144 Jevon Kearse 1.00
145 Edgerrin James 4.00
146 Tony Gonzalez .75
147 Cade McNown 1.50
148 Fred Taylor 1.50
149 Donovan McNabb 2.00
150 Ricky Williams 2.50
151 *Jamal Lewis* 6.00
152 *Tee Martin* 1.50
153 *Plaxico Burress* 5.00
154 *Chad Pennington* 10.00
155 *Curtis Keaton* 1.00
156 *Thomas Jones* 3.00
157 *Courtney Brown* 1.50
158 *Ron Dayne* 2.00
159 *Shaun Alexander* 6.00
160 *Travis Taylor* 2.00
161 *Sylvester Morris* 2.00
162 *Giovanni Carmazzi* 1.50
163 *Laveranues Coles* 4.00
164 *Chris Redman* 3.00
165 *Bubba Franks* 1.50
166 *R. Jay Soward* 1.50
167 *Reuben Droughns* 4.00
168 *Todd Pinkston* 1.50
169 *Trung Canidate* 1.50
170 *Danny Farmer* 1.00
171 *Ron Dugans* 1.50
172 *Dennis Northcutt* 1.50
173 *J.R. Redmond* 2.00
174 *Travis Prentice* 2.50
175 *Peter Warrick* 4.00

2000 Topps Gallery Player's Private Issue

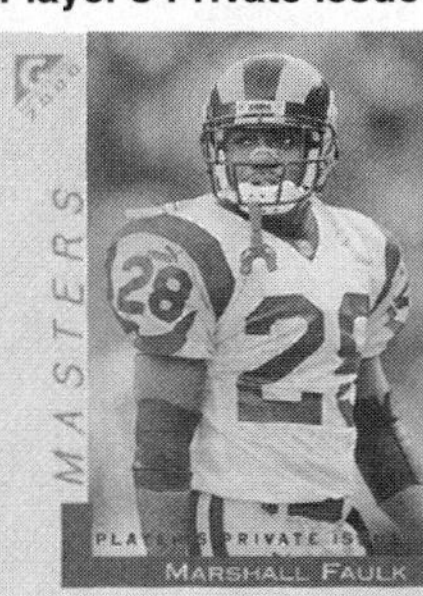

NM/M
Private Issue Cards: 3X-5X
Private Issue Subset: 3X
Private Issue Rookies: 2X-4X
Inserted 1:16
Production 250 Sets

> Values quoted in this guide reflect the retail price of a card—the price a collector can expect to pay when buying a card from a dealer. The wholesale price—that which a collector can expect to receive from a dealer when selling cards—will be significantly lower, depending on desirability and condition.

2000 Topps Gallery Autographs

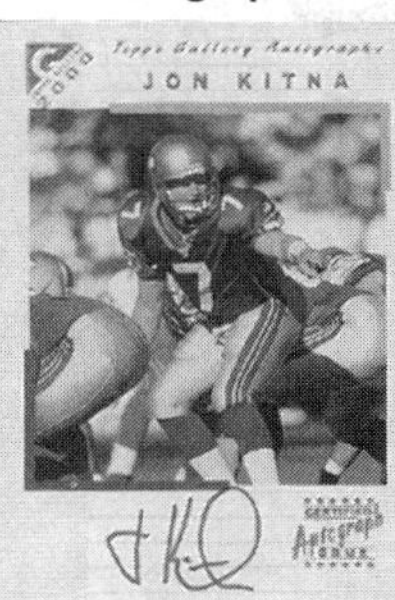

NM/M
Common Player: 20.00
Inserted 1:218
MF Marshall Faulk 45.00
TJ Thomas Jones 45.00
JK Jon Kitna 20.00
JL Jamal Lewis 45.00
SM Sylvester Morris 20.00
ZT Zach Thomas 20.00
PW Peter Warrick 25.00

2000 Topps Gallery Exhibitions

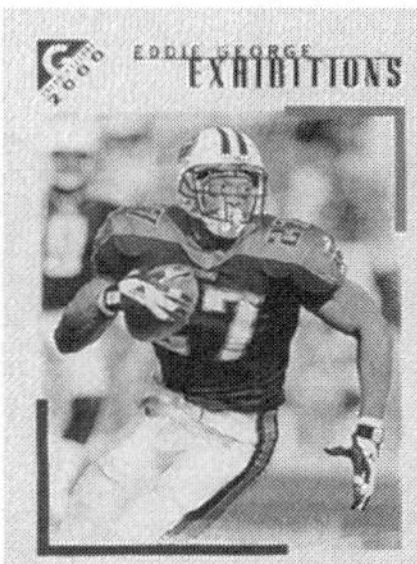

NM/M
Complete Set (15): 30.00
Common Player: 1.00
Inserted 1:32
GE1 Marshall Faulk 3.00
GE2 Muhsin Muhammad 1.00
GE3 Marvin Harrison 3.00
GE4 Stephen Davis 2.00
GE5 Eddie George 2.00
GE6 Antonio Freeman 1.00
GE7 Isaac Bruce 3.00
GE8 Jevon Kearse 2.00
GE9 Curtis Martin 3.00
GE10 Troy Aikman 5.00
GE11 Fred Taylor 3.00
GE12 Edgerrin James 4.00
GE13 Randy Moss 5.00
GE14 Steve Beuerlein 1.00
GE15 Kurt Warner 4.00

2000 Topps Gallery Gallery of Heroes

NM/M
Complete Set (10): 30.00
Common Player: 1.00
Inserted 1:24
GH1 Emmitt Smith 5.00
GH2 Troy Aikman 4.00
GH3 Brett Favre 6.00
GH4 Edgerrin James 4.00
GH5 Peyton Manning 4.00
GH6 Randy Moss 4.00
GH7 Marshall Faulk 2.00
GH8 Jerry Rice 4.00
GH9 Kurt Warner 3.00
GH10 Eddie George 3.00

2000 Topps Gallery Heritage

NM/M
Complete Set (10): 25.00
Common Player: 1.00
Inserted 1:12
Proof Cards: 2x
Inserted 1:48
H1 Marshall Faulk 2.00

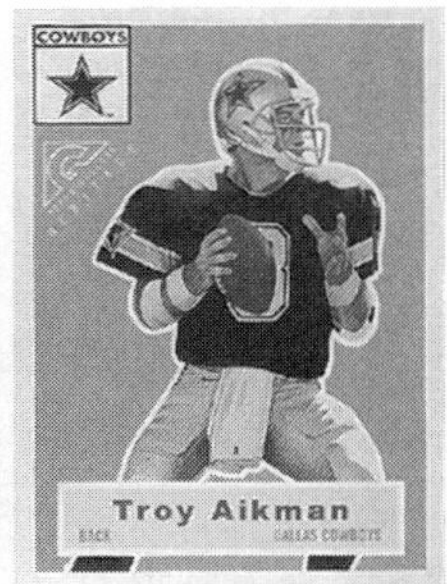

NM/M
H2 Troy Aikman 4.00
H3 Randy Moss 5.00
H4 Brett Favre 6.00
H5 Jerry Rice 4.00
H6 Dan Marino 5.00
H7 Peyton Manning 4.00
H8 Emmitt Smith 5.00
H9 Edgerrin James 4.00
H10 Kurt Warner 4.00

2000 Topps Gallery Proof Positive

NM/M
Complete Set (10): 30.00
Common Player: 1.00
Inserted 1:48
P1 Dan Marino, Kurt Warner 6.00
P2 Eddie George, Ricky Williams 4.00
P3 Jerry Rice, Keyshawn Johnson 4.00
P4 Bruce Smith, Jevon Kearse 1.00
P5 Marshall Faulk, Edgerrin James 4.00
P6 Marvin Harrison, Marcus Robinson 2.00
P7 Emmitt Smith, Stephen Davis 5.00
P8 Isaac Bruce, Randy Moss 4.00
P9 Steve Young, Mark Brunell 3.00
P10 Drew Bledsoe, Peyton Manning 5.00

2000 Topps Gold Label

NM/M
Complete Set (100): 45.00
Common Player: .15
Minor Stars: .30
Common Rookie: 1.00
Pack (5): 2.75
Wax Box (24): 45.00
1 Eric Moulds .50
2 Muhsin Muhammad .30
3 Patrick Jeffers .50
4 Joey Galloway .50
5 Edgerrin James 2.00
6 Germane Crowell .30
7 Ed McCaffrey .30
8 Dorsey Levens .50
9 Marcus Robinson .50
10 Tony Gonzalez .30
11 Robert Smith .50
12 Rich Gannon .30
13 Jerry Rice 1.25
14 Mike Alstott .50
15 Brad Johnson .30
16 Emmitt Smith 1.75
17 Marvin Harrison .50
18 Duce Staley .50
19 Terry Glenn .50
20 Terrell Owens .50
21 Antonio Freeman .30
22 Curtis Enis .30
23 Michael Westbrook .30
24 Cris Carter .50
25 Tim Brown .50
26 Terrell Davis 1.00
27 Fred Taylor .50
28 Amani Toomer .15
29 Donovan McNabb 1.00
30 Charlie Garner .30
31 Kurt Warner 2.00
32 Antowain Smith .30
33 Torry Holt .50
34 Jake Plummer .50
35 Steve Beuerlein .30
36 Raghib Ismail .15
37 Brett Favre 2.50
38 Mark Brunell .50
39 Qadry Ismail .15
40 Carl Pickens .30
41 James Stewart .50
42 Drew Bledsoe 1.00
43 Keenan McCardell .30
44 Jerome Bettis .50
45 Jon Kitna .50
46 Warrick Dunn .50
47 Jevon Kearse .50
48 Jamal Anderson .50
49 Shaun King .50
50 Ricky Williams 1.00
51 Elvis Grbac .30
52 Corey Dillon .50
53 Brian Griese .75
54 Steve Young 1.00
55 Tyrone Wheatley .50
56 Daunte Culpepper 1.25
57 Troy Aikman 1.25
58 Peyton Manning 2.00
59 Stephen Davis .50
60 Keyshawn Johnson .50
61 Doug Flutie .75
62 Ike Hilliard .15
63 Jeff Blake .30
64 Tony Banks .30
65 Tim Couch 1.25
66 Charlie Batch .50
67 Rob Johnson .30
68 Cade McNown .75
69 Steve McNair .50
70 Eddie George .75
71 Isaac Bruce .50
72 Ricky Watters .30
73 Kordell Stewart .60
74 Wayne Chrebet .50
75 Curtis Martin .50
76 Jimmy Smith .50
77 Randy Moss 2.00
78 Akili Smith .50
79 Marshall Faulk .50
80 Kerry Collins .30
81 *Ron Dayne* 2.00
82 *Chad Pennington* 5.00
83 *Sylvester Morris* 1.50
84 *Thomas Jones* 2.00
85 *Shaun Alexander* 3.00
86 *Chris Redman* 2.00
87 *Courtney Brown* 1.25
88 *Jerry Porter* 2.00
89 *Ron Dugans* 1.00
90 *Jamal Lewis* 3.00
91 *Travis Prentice* 1.50
92 *Travis Taylor* 1.50
93 *R. Jay Soward* 1.00
94 *Peter Warrick* 2.00
95 *Trung Canidate* 1.00
96 *Tee Martin* 1.25
97 *Bubba Franks* 1.25
98 *Plaxico Burress* 2.50
99 *J.R. Redmond* 1.25
100 *Dennis Northcutt* 1.00

2000 Topps Gold Label Class 2

Class 2 Cards: 1X

2000 Topps Gold Label Class 3

Class 3 Cards: 1X

2000 Topps Gold Label Premium

Premium Cards: 2X-4X
Premium Rookies: 2X
Production 1,000 Sets

2000 Topps Gold Label After Burners

NM/M
Complete Set (14): 25.00
Common Player: 1.00
Minor Stars: 2.00
Inserted 1:23
A1 Brett Favre 5.00
A2 Corey Dillon 2.00
A3 Drew Bledsoe 3.00
A4 Cris Carter 2.00
A5 Jimmy Smith 1.00
A6 Edgerrin James 4.00
A7 Fred Taylor 2.00
A8 Tim Brown 2.00
A9 Marshall Faulk 2.00

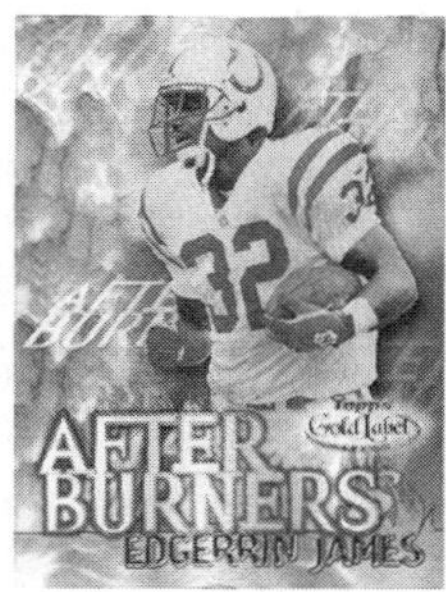

		NM/M
A10	Steve Beuerlein	1.00
A11	Antonio Freeman	1.00
A12	Peyton Manning	4.00
A13	Mike Alstott	2.00
A14	Mark Brunell	2.00

2000 Topps Gold Label Bullion

		NM/M
Complete Set (10):		25.00
Common Player:		1.00
Inserted 1:32		
B1	Daunte Culpepper, Randy Moss, Cris Carter	4.00
B2	Edgerrin James, Peyton Manning, Marvin Harrison	5.00
B3	Brad Johnson, Stephen Davis, Michael Westbrook	1.00
B4	Fred Taylor, Mark Brunell, Jimmy Smith	2.00
B5	Emmitt Smith, Troy Aikman, Joey Galloway	4.00
B6	Akili Smith, Corey Dillon, Peter Warrick	1.00
B7	Marshall Faulk, Kurt Warner, Isaac Bruce	4.00
B8	Steve McNair, Eddie George, Jevon Kearse	3.00
B9	Warren Sapp, Shaun King, Keyshawn Johnson	2.00
B10	Dorsey Levens, Brett Favre, Antonio Freeman	5.00

2000 Topps Gold Label Graceful Giants

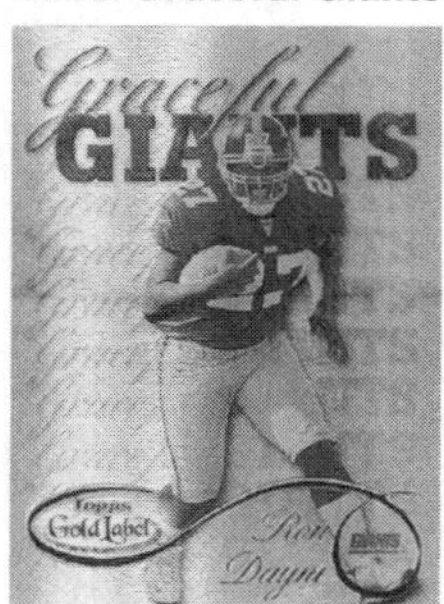

		NM/M
Complete Set (20):		25.00
Common Player:		.50
Minor Stars:		1.00
Inserted 1:16		
G1	Eddie George	1.00
G2	Randy Moss	4.00
G3	Keyshawn Johnson	1.00
G4	Warrick Dunn	1.00
G5	Jevon Kearse	1.00
G6	Sylvester Morris	1.00
G7	Ron Dayne	1.00
G8	Wayne Chrebet	.50
G9	Steve McNair	1.00
G10	Courtney Brown	.50
G11	Jacquez Green	.50
G12	Daunte Culpepper	3.00
G13	Tony Gonzalez	.50
G14	Mike Alstott	1.00
G15	Plaxico Burress	4.00
G16	Drew Bledsoe	3.00
G17	Travis Prentice	1.00
G18	Jerome Bettis	1.00
G19	Ricky Williams	4.00
G20	Jamal Lewis	5.00

2000 Topps Gold Label Holiday Match-Ups Fall

		NM/M
Complete Set (14):		35.00
Common Player:		1.00
Inserted 1:6		
T1	Randy Moss, Troy Aikman	4.00
T2	Drew Bledsoe, Germane Crowell	3.00
T3	Chris Chandler, Tim Brown	2.00
T4	Rob Johnson, Mike Alstott	1.00
T5	Cade McNown, Wayne Chrebet	1.00
T6	Courtney Brown, Jamal Lewis	2.00
T7	Terrell Davis, Jon Kitna	3.00
T8	Tony Gonzalez, Junior Seau	2.00
T9	Zach Thomas, Peyton Manning	4.00
T10	Ricky Williams, Marshall Faulk	3.50
T11	Duce Staley, Brad Johnson	1.00
T12	Jerome Bettis, Corey Dillon	1.00
T13	Steve McNair, Mark Brunell	2.00
T14	Ron Dayne, Thomas Jones	1.00

2000 Topps Gold Label Holiday Match-Ups Winter

		NM/M
Complete Set (14):		20.00
Common Player:		.50
Minor Stars:		1.00
Inserted 1:6		
C1	Jimmy Smith, Kerry Collins	1.00
C2	Charlie Garner, Ed McCaffrey	.50
C3	Antowain Smith, Shaun Alexander	1.00
C4	Jake Plummer, Michael Westbrook	1.00
C5	Steve Beuerlein, Rich Gannon	.50
C6	Curtis Enis, Charlie Batch	.50
C7	Akili Smith, Donovan McNabb	2.00
C8	Sylvester Morris, Jamal Anderson	2.00
C9	O.J. McDuffie, Terry Glenn	.50
C10	Cris Carter, Edgerrin James	4.00
C11	Curtis Martin, Travis Taylor	1.00
C12	Plaxico Burress, Jeff Graham	3.00
C13	Kurt Warner, Jeff Blake	3.00
C14	Shaun King, Brett Favre	5.00

2000 Topps Gold Label Rookie Autographs

		NM/M
Common Player:		15.00
Inserted 1:56		
SA	Shaun Alexander	40.00
CB	Courtney Brown	20.00
PB	Plaxico Burress	30.00
TC	Trung Canidate	15.00
RD	Ron Dayne	25.00
RDU	Ron Dugans	15.00
DF	Bubba Franks	15.00
TJ	Thomas Jones	25.00
JL	Jamal Lewis	50.00
TM	Tee Martin	20.00
SM	Sylvester Morris	30.00
DN	Dennis Northcutt	15.00
CP	Chad Pennington	50.00
JP	Jerry Porter	15.00
TP	Travis Prentice	25.00
CR	Chris Redman	30.00
JR	J.R. Redmond	25.00
RS	R. Jay Soward	15.00
TT	Travis Taylor	20.00
PW	Peter Warrick	25.00

2000 Topps Season Opener

		NM/M
Complete Set (220):		40.00
Common Player:		.10
Minor Stars:		.20
Common Rookie:		.50
Pack (7):		1.00
Wax Box (36):		25.00
1	Tyrone Wheatley	.20
2	Carl Pickens	.20
3	Zach Thomas	.10
4	Jacquez Green	.10
5	Sean Dawkins	.10
6	Brad Johnson	.30
7	Jerry Rice	.60
8	Doug Flutie	.30
9	Cade McNown	.50
10	Rod Smith	.10
11	Kevin Hardy	.10
12	Marvin Harrison	.30
13	David Boston	.30
14	Priest Holmes	.50
15	Keith Poole	.10
16	Troy Edwards	.30
17	Robert Smith	.30
18	Kevin Lockett	.10
19	Johnnie Morton	.10
20	Terrell Davis	.75
21	Corey Bradford	.10
22	Keyshawn Johnson	.30
23	Tony Banks	.20
24	Matthew Hatchette	.10
25	Troy Aikman	.60
26	Natrone Means	.10
27	Peerless Price	.30
28	Bruce Smith	.20
29	Tim Couch	.75
30	Terrell Owens	.30
31	O.J. McDuffie	.10
32	Troy Brown	.10
33	Corey Dillon	.30
34	Cameron Cleeland	.10
35	Brian Griese	.40
36	Shawn Springs	.10
37	Marcus Robinson	.30
38	Jermaine Lewis	.10
39	Olandis Gary	.40
40	Tony Gonzalez	.20
41	Frank Wycheck	.20
42	Jon Kitna	.30
43	Muhsin Muhammad	.20
44	Jerome Bettis	.30
45	Darrin Chiaverini	.10
46	Steve McNair	.30
47	Charlie Batch	.30
48	Steve Beuerlein	.20
49	Dorsey Levens	.30
50	Jim Harbaugh	.10
51	Jonathon Linton	.10
52	Napoleon Kaufman	.20
53	Curtis Enis	.30
54	Darnay Scott	.20
55	Tim Dwight	.30
56	Mikhael Ricks	.10
57	Kevin Dyson	.10
58	Antonio Freeman	.30
59	E.G. Green	.10
60	Jake Plummer	.30
61	Bill Schroeder	.10
62	Shaun King	.50
63	Michael Basnight	.10
64	Vinny Testaverde	.20
65	Rob Johnson	.20
66	Jeff Blake	.10
67	Marshall Faulk	.30
68	Keenan McCardell	.10
69	Michael Westbrook	.20
70	Yancey Thigpen	.10
71	Akili Smith	.40
72	Charles Woodson	.20
73	Qadry Ismail	.10
74	Patrick Johnson	.10
75	Raghib Ismail	.20
76	Terrence Wilkins	.10
77	Herman Moore	.20
78	Jevon Kearse	.30
79	Oronde Gadsden	.10
80	Errict Rhett	.10
81	Ed McCaffrey	.20
82	Mike Alstott	.30
83	Stephen Alexander	.10
84	Mark Brunell	.50
85	Jeff George	.10
86	Stephen Davis	.30
87	Germane Crowell	.10
88	Charlie Garner	.10
89	Kordell Stewart	.30
90	Tim Biakabutuka	.20
91	Jim Miller	.10
92	Eddie George	.40
93	Joe Montgomery	.10
94	Wayne Chrebet	.10
95	Freddie Jones	.10
96	Ricky Proehl	.10
97	Warren Sapp	.20
98	Derrick Mayes	.10
99	Daunte Culpepper	.50
100	Torry Holt	.30
101	Isaac Bruce	.30
102	Kevin Johnson	.30
103	Antowain Smith	.30
104	Rob Moore	.20
105	Joey Galloway	.30
106	Rickey Dudley	.20
107	Terry Glenn	.30
108	Ike Hilliard	.10
109	Jeff Graham	.10
110	J.J. Stokes	.10
111	Steve Young	.50
112	Albert Connell	.10
113	Tony Brackens	.10
114	James Johnson	.10
115	Tim Brown	.20
116	Terance Mathis	.10
117	Peyton Manning	1.00
118	Kerry Collins	.20
119	Duce Staley	.30
120	Torrance Small	.10
121	Curtis Martin	.30
122	Damon Huard	.20
123	Derrick Alexander	.10
124	Jimmy Smith	.20
125	Cris Carter	.30
126	Jamal Anderson	.30
127	Eric Moulds	.30
128	Drew Bledsoe	.50
129	Ricky Williams	.75
130	Andre Hastings	.10
131	Amani Toomer	.10
132	Rich Gannon	.10
133	Richard Huntley	.10
134	Donovan McNabb	.50
135	Jermaine Fazande	.10
136	Randy Moss	1.00
137	Champ Bailey	.20
138	Elvis Grbac	.10
139	Warrick Dunn	.30
140	John Randle	.10
141	Edgerrin James	1.25
142	Tony Martin	.10
143	Chris Chandler	.20
144	Stephen Boyd	.10
145	Az-Zahir Hakim	.10
146	Tony Simmons	.10
147	Pete Mitchell	.10
148	Junior Seau	.20
149	Ricky Watters	.20
150	Michael Pittman	.10
151	Fred Taylor	.50
152	Charles Johnson	.10
153	Jason Tucker	.10
154	Brett Favre	1.25
155	Patrick Jeffers	.30
156	Curtis Conway	.10
157	Frank Sanders	.10
158	James Stewart	.10
159	Emmitt Smith	.75
160	Jessie Armstead	.10
161	Wesley Walls	.20
162	Kent Graham	.10
163	Kurt Warner	1.50
164	Shawn Jefferson	.10
165	Jammi German	.10
166	Jay Riemersma	.10
167	Fred Lane	.10
168	Jamir Miller	.10
169	David LaFleur	.10
170	David Sloan	.10
171	Jerome Pathon	.10
172	Sam Madison	.10
173	Tiki Barber	.10
174	Yatil Green	.10
175	Checklist	.10
176	Kurt Warner	.75
177	Brett Favre	.50
178	Marshall Faulk	.20
179	Jevon Kearse	.20
180	Edgerrin James	.50
181	Troy Aikman	.30
182	Terrell Davis	.40
183	Steve Beuerlein	.10
184	Tim Brown	.10
185	Randy Moss	.50
186	Drew Bledsoe	.25
187	Curtis Martin	.10
188	Shannon Sharpe	.10
189	Brett Favre	.50
190	Brad Johnson	.10
191	Tony Gonzalez	.10
192	Jon Kitna	.10
193	Peyton Manning	.50
194	Mark Brunell	.25
195	Cade McNown	.25
196	Jim Harbaugh	.10
197	Shaun King	.25
198	Kurt Warner	.75
199	Eddie George	.20
200	Ricky Williams	.40
201	*Curtis Keaton*	.50
202	*Tee Martin*	1.25
203	*Thomas Jones*	2.00
204	*Giovanni Carmazzi*	1.50
205	*Courtney Brown*	1.75
206	*Shaun Alexander*	3.00
207	*Travis Taylor*	1.50
208	*Dennis Northcutt*	1.25
209	*Trung Canidate*	1.25
210	*Jamal Lewis*	3.00
211	*R. Jay Soward*	1.25
212	*Sylvester Morris*	1.75
213	*Ron Dugans*	1.25
214	*Chris Redman*	1.50
215	*Plaxico Burress*	2.50
216	*Peter Warrick*	2.00
217	*Travis Prentice*	1.75
218	*Ron Dayne*	2.00
219	*J.R. Redmond*	1.50
220	*Chad Pennington*	5.00

2000 Topps Season Opener Autograph Cards

		NM/M
1	Kurt Warner	100.00
2	Marvin Harrison	25.00
3	Stephen Davis	25.00
4	Joe Montana	150.00

2000 Topps Season Opener Auto. Super Bowl Memorabilia

		NM/M
1	Deacon Jones	25.00
2	Gale Sayers	75.00
3	Warren Moon	25.00
4	Fred Biletnikoff	25.00
5	Anthony Munoz	25.00

2000 Topps Season Opener Football Fever

		NM/M
Complete Set (55):		15.00
Common Player:		.15
Minor Stars:		.30
Three Cards Per Player For #F1-F5		
Four Cards Per Player For #F6-F15		
Inserted 1:1		
F1	Brett Favre	1.00
F2	Kurt Warner	1.25
F3	Brad Johnson	.30
F4	Peyton Manning	.75
F5	Drew Bledsoe	.40
F6	Terrell Davis	.60
F7	Edgerrin James	1.00
F8	Stephen Davis	.30
F9	Fred Taylor	.40
F10	Jamal Lewis	.75
F11	Marvin Harrison	.30
F12	Isaac Bruce	.30
F13	Jimmy Smith	.30
F14	Randy Moss	.75
F15	Peter Warrick	1.25

2000 Topps Stars Promos

		NM/M
Complete Set (6):		3.00
Common Player:		.50
PP1	Keyshawn Johnson	.50
PP2	Dorsey Levens	.50
PP3	Rich Gannon	1.00
PP4	Michael Westbrook	.50
PP5	Mike Alstott	.50
PP6	Edgerrin James	2.00

2000 Topps Stars

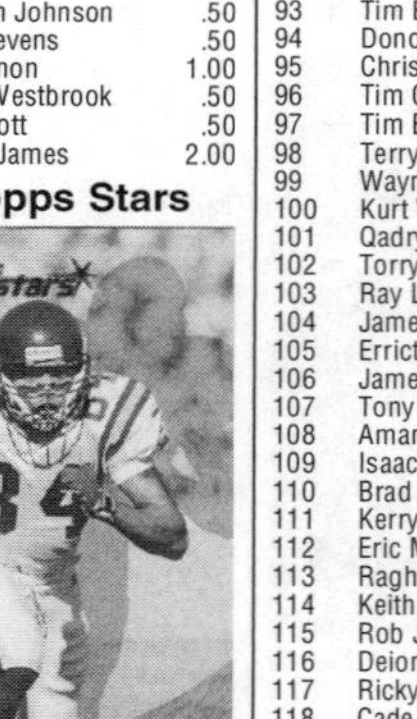

		NM/M
Complete Set (175):		50.00
Common Player:		.10
Minor Stars:		.30
Common Rookie:		.50
Pack (6):		1.75
Wax Box (24):		30.00
1	Keyshawn Johnson	.50
2	Marcus Robinson	.50
3	Antonio Freeman	.50
4	Jake Plummer	.50
5	Zach Thomas	.30
6	Kordell Stewart	.50
7	Mike Alstott	.50
8	Fred Taylor	1.00
9	J.J. Stokes	.30
10	Emmitt Smith	1.75
11	Derrick Mayes	.30
12	Stephen Davis	.50
13	Jamal Anderson	.50
14	Antowain Smith	.30
15	Steve Beuerlein	.30
16	Olandis Gary	.60
17	Rickey Dudley	.10
18	Sean Dawkins	.10
19	Mark Brunell	1.00
20	Brett Favre	2.50
21	Jim Harbaugh	.30
22	Darnay Scott	.30
23	Herman Moore	.50
24	Drew Bledsoe	1.00
25	Priest Holmes	.50
26	Albert Connell	.30
27	Ike Hilliard	.10
28	Charlie Garner	.30
29	Jimmy Smith	.50
30	Randy Moss	2.50
31	Peerless Price	.30
32	Terrell Davis	1.75
33	Troy Edwards	.50
34	Kevin Dyson	.30
35	O.J. McDuffie	.10
36	Troy Aikman	1.50
37	Frank Sanders	.30
38	Bobby Engram	.10
39	Tyrone Wheatley	.30
40	Ricky Williams	1.00
41	Warrick Dunn	.50
42	Elvis Grbac	.30
43	Dorsey Levens	.50
44	Curtis Conway	.30
45	Johnnie Morton	.30
46	Ed McCaffrey	.30
47	Kevin Johnson	.50
48	Muhsin Muhammad	.50
49	Terance Mathis	.10
50	Eddie George	.75
51	Daunte Culpepper	1.00
52	Jeff Graham	.10
53	Jon Kitna	.50
54	Marvin Harrison	.50
55	Steve McNair	.60
56	Jeff Blake	.30
57	Carl Pickens	.30
58	Germane Crowell	.50
59	Rob Moore	.30
60	Marshall Faulk	.50
61	Jerome Bettis	.50
62	Michael Westbrook	.30
63	Keenan McCardell	.30
64	Shannon Sharpe	.30
65	Rod Smith	.50
66	Curtis Enis	.50
67	Vinny Testaverde	.50
68	Freddie Jones	.30
69	Jevon Kearse	.60
70	Jerry Rice	1.50
71	Champ Bailey	.30
72	Peyton Manning	2.50
73	Rich Gannon	.30
74	Cris Carter	.50
75	Doug Flutie	.75
76	Corey Dillon	.50
77	Tony Gonzalez	.30
78	Shaun King	1.00
79	Terrell Owens	.50
80	Dan Marino	2.00
81	Curtis Martin	.50
82	Patrick Jeffers	.50
83	Brian Griese	.75
84	Akili Smith	.75
85	Charlie Batch	.50
86	Tim Dwight	.50
87	Robert Smith	.50
88	Duce Staley	.50
89	Jacquez Green	.30
90	Steve Young	1.00
91	Tony Martin	.10
92	Az-Zahir Hakim	.30
93	Tim Brown	.50
94	Donovan McNabb	1.00
95	Chris Chandler	.30
96	Tim Couch	1.50
97	Tim Biakabutuka	.30
98	Terry Glenn	.50
99	Wayne Chrebet	.30
100	Kurt Warner	2.50
101	Qadry Ismail	.10
102	Torry Holt	.50
103	Ray Lucas	.50
104	James Johnson	.30
105	Errict Rhett	.10
106	James Stewart	.50
107	Tony Banks	.30
108	Amani Toomer	.30
109	Isaac Bruce	.50
110	Brad Johnson	.50
111	Kerry Collins	.30
112	Eric Moulds	.50
113	Raghib Ismail	.10
114	Keith Poole	.10
115	Rob Johnson	.30
116	Deion Sanders	.50
117	Ricky Watters	.30
118	Cade McNown	1.00
119	Joey Galloway	.50
120	Edgerrin James	2.50
121	Jim Brown	1.00
122	Steve Largent	1.00
123	Joe Montana	3.00
124	Deacon Jones	.30
125	Ronnie Lott	.30
126	Mark Brunell	.50
127	Rich Gannon	.10
128	Tony Gonzalez	.10
129	Randy Moss	1.25
130	Kurt Warner	1.50
131	Marvin Harrison	.30
132	Jimmy Smith	.30
133	Edgerrin James	1.25
134	Corey Dillon	.30
135	Peyton Manning	1.25
136	Brad Johnson	.30
137	Steve Beuerlein	.10
138	Emmitt Smith	.75
139	Marshall Faulk	.30
140	Mike Alstott	.30
141	Deacon Jones	.10
142	Joe Montana	2.00
143	Jim Brown	.50
144	Steve Largent	.50
145	Ronnie Lott	.10
146	Chad Pennington	2.00
147	Peter Warrick	2.50
148	Plaxico Burress	2.00
149	Thomas Jones	1.75
150	Jamal Lewis	1.75
151	*Travis Taylor*	1.50
152	*Shaun Alexander*	3.00

153 *Dez White* 1.00
154 *Thomas Jones* 2.00
155 *Curtis Keaton* .50
156 *Courtney Brown* 1.25
157 *Danny Farmer* .50
158 *Trung Canidate* .75
159 *R. Jay Soward* 1.00
160 *Jamal Lewis* 3.00
161 *Todd Pinkston* 1.00
162 *Reuben Droughns* 2.50
163 *Ron Dugans* 1.00
164 *Ron Dayne* 1.00
165 *Laveranues Coles* 2.00
166 *Sylvester Morris* 1.75
167 *Peter Warrick* 2.00
168 *Dennis Northcutt* 1.00
169 *Tee Martin* 1.00
170 *Brian Urlacher* 2.50
171 *Chris Redman* 1.50
172 *Chad Pennington* 4.00
173 *J.R. Redmond* 1.25
174 *Travis Prentice* 1.25
175 *Plaxico Burress* 2.00

2000 Topps Stars Green

NM/M
Green Cards: 3X-5X
Production 299 Sets (1-125)
Green Cards: 5X-10X
Green Rookies: 3X-6X
Production 99 Sets (126-175)

2000 Topps Stars All-Pro Relics

NM/M
Common Player: 10.00
Inserted 1:85
MA Mike Alstott 15.00
MB Mitch Berger 10.00
SB Steve Beuerlein 10.00
PB Peter Boulware 10.00
SB Stephen Boyd 10.00
TB Tony Brackens 10.00
DB Derrick Brooks 10.00
CB Chad Brown 10.00
IS Isaac Bruce 25.00
MB Mark Brunell 25.00
CC Cris Carter 25.00
KC Kevin Carter 10.00
DC Dexter Coakley 10.00
SD Stephen Davis 25.00
BD Brian Dawkins 10.00
CD Corey Dillon 25.00
LE Luther Ellis 10.00
MF Marshall Faulk 35.00
RG Rich Gannon 25.00
SG Sam Gash 10.00
EG Eddie George 35.00
TG Tony Gonzalez 30.00
KH Kevin Hardy 10.00
MH Marvin Harrison 30.00
EJ Edgerrin James 55.00
BJ Brad Johnson 10.00
KJ Keyshawn Johnson 15.00
TJ Tre' Johnson 10.00
JK Jevon Kearse 15.00
CK Cortez Kennedy 10.00
CL Carnell Lake 10.00
TL Todd Lyght 10.00
TM Tremain Mack 10.00
SM Sam Madison 10.00
OM Olindo Mare 10.00
BM Bruce Matthews 10.00
KM Kevin Mawae 10.00
MM Michael McCrary 10.00
RM Randall McDaniel 10.00
GM Glyn Milburn 10.00
LM Lawyer Milloy 10.00
RM Randy Moss 55.00
MM Muhsin Muhammad 15.00
HN Hardy Nickerson 10.00
OP Orlando Pace 10.00
RP Robert Porcher 10.00
TP Trevor Pryce 10.00
WR William Roaf 10.00
DR Darrell Russell 10.00
WS Warren Sapp 15.00
LS Lance Schulters 10.00
LS Leon Searcy 10.00
DS David Sloan 10.00
DS Detron Smith 10.00
ES Emmitt Smith 45.00
JS Jimmy Smith 30.00
MS Michael Strahan 10.00
AZT Zach Thomas 15.00
TT Tom Tupa 10.00
WW Wesley Walls 10.00
KW Kurt Warner 40.00
CW Charles Woodson 15.00
RW Rod Woodson 10.00
FW Frank Wycheck 10.00

2000 Topps Stars Autographs

NM/M
Complete Set (12): 500.00
Common Player: 12.00
Inserted 1:411
CC Cris Carter 35.00
KC Kevin Carter 12.00
RD Ron Dayne 35.00
DG Darrell Green 12.00
FH Franco Harris 45.00
EJ Edgerrin James 65.00
DJ Deacon Jones 25.00
SL Steve Largent 45.00
RL Ronnie Lott 30.00
JM Joe Montana 180.00
CR Chris Redman 35.00
KW Kurt Warner 100.00

A card number in parenthese ( ) indicates the set is unnumbered.

2000 Topps Stars Pro-Bowl Powerhouse

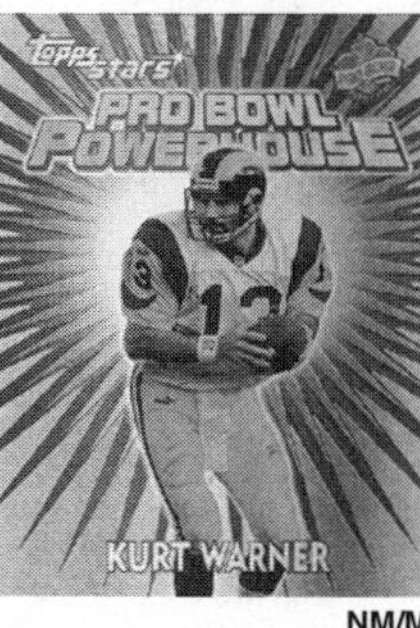

NM/M
Complete Set (15): 18.00
Common Player: .50
Inserted 1:12
PB1 Kurt Warner 3.00
PB2 Warren Sapp .50
PB3 Marvin Harrison 1.00
PB4 Kevin Carter .50
PB5 Jimmy Smith 1.00
PB6 Stephen Davis 1.00
PB7 Edgerrin James 4.00
PB8 Tony Gonzalez .50
PB9 Sam Madison .50
PB10 Mike Alstott 1.00
PB11 Marshall Faulk 1.00
PB12 Jevon Kearse 1.00
PB13 Kevin Hardy .50
PB14 Peyton Manning 4.00
PB15 Randy Moss 4.00

2000 Topps Stars Progression

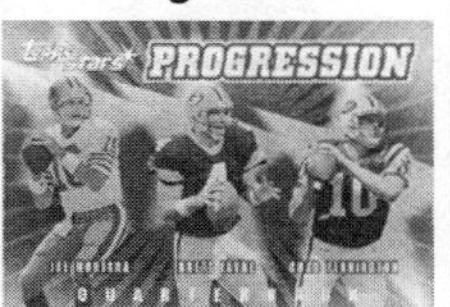

NM/M
Complete Set (5): 8.00
Common Player: 1.00
Inserted 1:15
P1 Joe Montana, Brett Favre, Chad Pennington 4.00
P2 Deacon Jones, Jevon Kearse, Courtney Brown 1.00
P3 Ronnie Lott, John Lynch, Deon Grant 1.00
P4 Steve Largent, Randy Moss, Peter Warrick 3.00
P5 Jim Brown, Edgerrin James, Thomas Jones 3.00

2000 Topps Stars Walk of Fame

NM/M
Complete Set (15): 15.00
Common Player: .50
Inserted 1:8
W1 Randy Moss 4.00
W2 Kurt Warner 3.00
W3 Jimmy Smith .50
W4 Cris Carter .50
W5 Brett Favre 4.00
W6 Ricky Williams 2.50
W7 Marvin Harrison .50
W8 Fred Taylor 1.50
W9 Eddie George 1.25
W10 Edgerrin James 3.00
W11 Jevon Kearse .50
W12 Emmitt Smith 3.00
W13 Marshall Faulk .50
W14 Terrell Davis 2.75
W15 Peyton Manning 3.00

2001 Topps Promos

NM/M
Complete Set (6): 3.00
Common Player: .50
PP1 Emmitt Smith 2.00
PP2 Warrick Dunn .50
PP3 Jeff Garcia 1.00
PP4 Wayne Chrebet .50
PP5 Jason Taylor .50
PP6 Tony Gonzalez .50

2001 Topps

NM/M
Complete Set (385): 60.00
Common Player: .10
Minor Stars: .30
Common Rookie: .50
Pack (10): 1.50
Wax Box (36): 50.00
1 Marshall Faulk .60
2 Lawyer Milloy .10
3 Rich Gannon .30
4 Rod Smith .30
5 David Boston .50
6 Jeremy McDaniel .10
7 Joey Galloway .50
8 Ron Dixon .10
9 Terrell Fletcher .10
10 Deion Sanders .50
11 Jevon Kearse .50
12 Charles Woodson .30
13 Brian Walker .10
14 Mike Peterson .10
15 Marcus Robinson .50
16 Duane Starks .10
17 KaRon Coleman .10
18 Randy Moss 1.50
19 Reggie Jones .30
20 Derrick Brooks .10
21 Eddie George .60
22 Wayne Chrebet .50
23 Kevin Hardy .10
24 Bill Schroeder .30
25 Doug Flutie .60
26 Tim Dwight .30
27 Eddie Kennison .10
28 Reggie Kelly .10
29 Ricky Watters .30
30 Stephen Alexander .10
31 Az-Zahir Hakim .30
32 Henri Crockett .10
33 Joe Horn .50
34 Danny Farmer .10
35 Shannon Sharpe .30
36 Brad Hoover .50
37 David Patten .10
38 Kevin Faulk .30
39 Freddie Jones .30
40 Michael Westbrook .30
41 Jacquez Green .10
42 Torrance Small .10
43 Terrence Wilkins .30
44 Brett Favre 2.00
45 Tony Banks .30
46 Johnnie Morton .30
47 Jimmy Smith .50
48 Jerry Rice 1.25
49 Jeff George .50
50 Ray Lewis .50
51 Joe Johnson .30
52 Raghib Ismail .10
53 Muhsin Muhammad .30
54 Ken Dilger .10
55 Ike Hilliard .30
56 Joey Porter .10
57 Shaun Alexander .50
58 Jeff Garcia .50
59 Jay Fiedler .30
60 Wane McGarity .10
61 Steve Beuerlein .30
62 Tywan Mitchell .10
63 Travis Prentice .50
64 Robert Griffith .10
65 Napoleon Kaufman .30
66 Randall Godfrey .10
67 Junior Seau .30
68 Willie Jackson .10
69 Larry Foster .10
70 Brandon Stokley .30
71 Hugh Douglas .10
72 James Thrash .30
73 Vinny Testaverde .30
74 Leslie Shepherd .10
75 Terrell Davis 1.50
76 Jake Plummer .50
77 Corey Dillon .50
78 Ron Dayne 1.00
79 Brock Huard .50
80 Todd Husak .30
81 Richard Huntley .30
82 Shaun Ellis .10
83 Kyle Brady .10
84 Corey Bradford .10
85 Eric Moulds .50
86 Brian Finneran .10
87 Antonio Freeman .50
88 Terry Glenn .50
89 Tai Streets .30
90 Chris Sanders .10
91 Sylvester Morris .50
92 Peter Warrick 1.00
93 Chris Greisen .10
94 Cade McNown .50
95 Jerome Pathon .10
96 John Randle .30
97 Curtis Conway .30
98 Keyshawn Johnson .50
99 Trent Green .50
100 Mike Anderson 1.50
101 Jeff Blake .30
102 Tee Martin .30
103 Darrell Jackson .30
104 Mark Brunell .60
105 Charlie Batch .50
106 Wesley Walls .10
107 Edgerrin James 1.25
108 Robert Wilson .10
109 Donovan McNabb .75
110 Champ Bailey .30
111 Isaac Bruce .50
112 Michael Strahan .10
113 Dennis Edwards .10
114 Randall Cunningham .30
115 Germane Crowell .50
116 Jermaine Jewis .10
117 Dennis McKinley .10
118 Ryan Leaf .50
119 Samari Rolle .10
120 Daunte Culpepper 1.00
121 Tim Couch .75
122 Greg Biekert .10
123 Warrick Dunn .50
124 Richie Anderson .10
125 Trace Armstrong .10
126 Bernardo Harris .10
127 Kwame Cavil .10
128 James Allen .50
129 Anthony Becht .10
130 Tiki Barber .30
131 Brad Johnson .30
132 Tyrone Wheatley .50
133 Kurt Warner 2.00
134 Desmond Howard .10
135 Thomas Jones .50
136 Peyton Manning 1.50
137 Tony Richardson .10
138 Chris Chandler .30
139 Plaxico Burress .50
140 J.R. Redmond .50
141 Fred Taylor .75
142 Akili Smith .50
143 Sammy Morris .50
144 Jessie Armstead .10
145 Charlie Garner .30
146 Steve McNair .50
147 Charles Johnson .10
148 Troy Aikman 1.00
149 Kevin Johnson .30
150 Brian Urlacher 1.00
151 Travis Taylor .50
152 Aaron Shea .10
153 Michael Cloud .10
154 Donald Driver .30
155 Chad Pennington 1.00
156 Troy Edwards .10
157 Reidel Anthony .10
158 Michael Bishop .30
159 Mo Lewis .10
160 Damon Huard .30
161 James McKnight .10
162 Craig Yeast .10
163 Michael Pittman .30
164 Robert Smith .30
165 Terrelle Smith .10
166 Jeremiah Trotter .10
167 Amani Toomer .30
168 JaJuan Dawson .30
169 Tim Biakabutuka .30
170 Oronde Gadsden .30
171 Ray Lucas .30
172 Jermaine Fazande .30
173 Todd Bouman .10
174 Frank Wycheck .30
175 Hines Ward .30
176 Ahman Green .30
177 Kaseem Sinceno .10
178 Jamal Anderson .50
179 Jay Riemersma .10
180 Jarious Jackson .10
181 Andre Rison .30
182 Jerome Bettis .50
183 Blaine Bishop .10
184 Dorsey Levens .50
185 James Stewart .50
186 Chad Lewis .30
187 Justin Watson .10
188 Warren Sapp .30
189 Rod Woodson .30
190 Ricky Williams .75
191 Marty Booker .10
192 MarTay Jenkins .10
193 Peerless Price .50
194 Tony Gonzalez .50
195 Jon Kitna .50
196 Stephen Davis .50
197 Curtis Martin .50
198 Matt Hasselbeck .50
199 Patrick Johnson .10
200 Emmitt Smith 1.50
201 Doug Johnson .50
202 Autry Denson .30
203 Troy Brown .10
204 Jeff Graham .10
205 Corey Simon .30
206 Jamel White .10
207 Jeff Lewis .30
208 Frank Sanders .30
209 Al Wilson .10
210 Jason Sehorn .10
211 Shaun King .50
212 Torry Holt .50
213 Kordell Stewart .50
214 Keenan McCardell .30
215 Dedric Ward .10
216 Michael Wiley .30
217 Rob Johnson .50
218 Jamal Lewis 1.50
219 Herman Moore .30
220 Ron Dugans .10
221 Jason Taylor .10
222 Charles Lee .10
223 J.J. Stokes .30
224 Albert Connell .30
225 Keith Poole .10
226 Elvis Grbac .30
227 Shawn Jefferson .10
228 Jackie Harris .10
229 Derrick Alexander .10
230 Darnell Autry .30
231 Bobby Shaw .10
232 Aaron Brooks .50
233 Cris Carter .50
234 Desmond Clark .10
235 Spergon Wynn .30
236 Qadry Ismail .10
237 Sam Cowart .10
238 Zach Thomas .30
239 Drew Bledsoe .60
240 Ronney Jenkins .10
241 Keith Mitchell .10
242 Laveranues Coles .50
243 Marcus Pollard .10
244 Darren Sharper .10
245 Donald Hayes .30
246 Brian Griese .60
247 Frank Moreau .10
248 Bruce Smith .10
249 Fred Beasley .10
250 Mike Alstott .50
251 Trent Dilfer .30
252 Terance Mathis .10
253 Shawn Bryson .10
254 Dennis Northcutt .30
255 Brandon Bennett .10
256 Stacey Mack .10
257 Tim Brown .30
258 Duce Staley .50
259 Sean Dawkins .10
260 Ricky Proehl .10
261 Chris Fuamatu-Ma'afala .10
262 La'Roi Glover .10
263 Bubba Franks .30
264 Kevin Lockett .10
265 Lamar Smith .50
266 Priest Holmes .30
267 Macey Brooks .10
268 Anthony Wright .50
269 Ed McCaffrey .30
270 Joe Jurevicius .30
271 Terrell Owens .50
272 Tony Simmons .10
273 Itula Mili .10
274 Chad Morton .10
275 Marvin Harrison .50
276 Jason Gildon .10
277 Derrick Mason .50
278 Greg Clark .10
279 Casey Crawford .10
280 Kerry Collins .30
281 Terrell Owens .30
282 Marshall Faulk .30
283 Mike Anderson .75
284 Cris Carter .30
285 Corey Dillon .30
286 Daunte Culpepper .50
287 Peyton Manning .75
288 Torry Holt .30
289 Marvin Harrison .30
290 Edgerrin James .75
291 Takeo Spikes .10
292 John Lynch .10
293 Sam Madison .10
294 Stephen Boyd .10
295 Tony Siragusa .10
296 Robert Porcher .10
297 Donnell Bennett .10
298 Hardy Nickerson .10
299 Jonathan Quinn .10
300 Rob Morris .10
301 E.G. Green .10
302 David Sloan .10
303 Jason Tucker .10
304 Darrin Chiaverini .10
305 Wali Rainer .10
306 Jerry Azumah .10
307 Jonathon Linton .10
308 Dameyune Craig .10
309 Courtney Brown .30
310 Jammi German .10
311 *Michael Vick* 6.00
312 *Jamar Fletcher* .75
313 *Will Allen* .50
314 *Jamal Reynolds* .50
315 *Quincy Morgan* 1.50
316 *Eric Kelly* .50
317 *Michael Stone* .50
318 *Rod Gardner* 2.50
319 *Ken-Yon Rambo* .75
320 *Eric Westmoreland* .50
321 *Steve Smith* .75
322 *George Layne* .50
323 *Justin McCareins* 1.50
324 *Adam Archuleta* .75
325 *Justin Smith* 1.25
326 *David Terrell* 1.50
327 *Correll Buckhelter* .75
328 *Drew Brees* 2.50
329 *Chris Barnes* .75
330 *Santana Moss* 2.00
331 *Josh Heupel* 2.00
332 *Cedrick Wilson* .75
333 *Gerard Warren* 1.50
334 *Jamie Henderson* .50
335 *Onomo Ojo* .75
336 *Marcus Stroud* .50
337 *Quincy Carter* 2.00
338 *Koren Robinson* 2.00
339 *Ryan Pickett* .50
340 *Chad Johnson* 2.50
341 *Nate Clements* .50
342 *Jesse Palmer* 1.00
343 *Marvin "Snoop" Minnis* 1.75
344 *Reggie Wayne* 2.50
345 *Kevin Kasper* .50
346 *Will Peterson* .50
347 *Marques Tuiasosopo* 2.00
348 *Sage Rosenfels* 1.50
349 *Dan Alexander* .75
350 *LaDainian Tomlinson* 4.00
351 *Dan Morgan* .50
352 *Scotty Anderson* .75
353 *Deuce McAllister* 3.00
354 *Todd Heap* .50
355 *Tony Dixon* .50
356 *Chris Chambers* 2.50
357 *Eddie Berlin* .75
358 *Anthony Thomas* 2.00
359 *James Jackson* 1.75
360 *Richard Seymour* .50
361 *Andre Carter* .50
362 *Bobby Newcombe* .75
363 *Robert Ferguson* 1.75
364 *Jonathan Carter* .75
365 *Damione Lewis* .50
366 *Darnerian McCants* .75
367 *Tim Hasselbeck* .75
368 *Derrick Gibson* .50
369 *Rudi Johnson* 2.00
370 *Alge Crumpler* .75
371 *Derrick Blaylock* 1.50
372 *Moran Norris* .75
373 *Travis Minor* 1.50
374 *LaMont Jordan* 1.50
375 *Kevan Barlow* 2.00
376 *Freddie Mitchell* 2.00
377 *Shaun Rogers* .50
378 *Tay Cody* .50
379 *Travis Henry* 2.00
380 *Chris Weinke* 1.50
381 *Willie Middlebrooks* .50
382 *Rashard Casey* .75
383 *Mike McMahon* 1.50
384 *Michael Bennett* 2.50
385 *Jabari Holloway* .75

2001 Topps Collection

NM/M
Complete Set (385): 40.00
Collection Cards: 1X

2001 Topps Own The Game Perfect Spiral

NM/M
Complete Set (7): 12.00
Common Player: 1.00
PS1 Brian Griese 1.50
PS2 Peyton Manning 4.00
PS3 Jeff Garcia 1.00
PS4 Daunte Culpepper 2.50
PS5 Brett Favre 5.00
PS6 Kurt Warner 3.00
PS7 Donovan McNabb 2.00

2001 Topps MVP Promotion

MVP Cards: 5X-12X
MVP Rookies: 3X-5X
Inserted 1:186

2001 Topps All-Pro Autograph Relics

NM/M
Common Player: 50.00
TPA-DC Daunte Culpepper 100.00
TPA-EJ Edgerrin James 125.00
TPA-RL Ray Lewis 75.00
TPA-DM Derrick Mason 50.00
TPA-JS Jimmy Smith 50.00

2001 Topps Autographs

NM/M
Common Player: 10.00
TA-KB Kevan Barlow 10.00
TA-JB Josh Booty 10.00
TA-DB Drew Brees 50.00
TA-CC Chris Chambers 50.00
TA-DC Daunte Culpepper 50.00
TA-MF Marshall Faulk 40.00
TA-DH Donald Hayes 10.00
TA-JH Joe Horn 10.00
TA-CJ Chad Johnson 10.00
TA-DM Derrick Mason 10.00
TA-DJM Deuce McAllister 100.00
TA-TM Travis Minor 10.00
TA-SM Santana Moss 25.00
TA-EM Eric Moulds 10.00
TA-JP Jesse Palmer 10.00
TA-ES Emmitt Smith 125.00
TA-JS Jimmy Smith 10.00
TA-JT James Thrash 10.00
TA-BU Brian Urlacher 75.00
TA-MV Michael Vick 125.00
TA-TW Terrence Wilkins 10.00

2001 Topps Combos

NM/M
Complete Set (19): 25.00
Common Player: 2.00
Inserted 1:8
TC1 Edgerrin James, Santana Moss 3.00
TC2 Torry Holt, Koren Robinson 2.50
TC3 Jamal Lewis, Travis Henry 2.00
TC4 Curtis Martin, Kevan Barlow 2.00
TC5 Cris Carter, Ken-Yon Rambo 2.00
TC6 Troy Aikman, Freddie Mitchell 3.00

TC7 Brian Griese, David Terrell 3.00
TC8 Tyrone Wheatley, Anthony Thomas 2.00
TC9 Warrick Dunn, Travis Minor 2.00
TC10 Peter Warrick, Marvin "Snoop" Minnis 2.00
TC11 Warren Sapp, Dan Morgan 2.00
TC12 Tony Gonzalez, Andre Carter 2.00
TC13 Antonio Freeman, Michael Vick 8.00
TC14 Ron Dayne, Michael Bennett 4.00
TC15 Mike Alstott, Drew Brees 5.00
TC16 Ahman Green, Correll Buckhelter 2.00
TC17 Brad Johnson, Chris Weinke 3.00
TC18 Eric Moulds, Fred Smoot 2.00
TC19 Ray Lewis, Reggie Wayne 2.00

2001 Topps Hall of Fame Autographs

NM/M
Common Player: 50.00
TA-DJ Deacon Jones 50.00
TA-ML Marv Levy 50.00
TA-MM Mike Munchak 50.00
TA-JS Jackie Slater 50.00
TA-RY Ron Yary 50.00
TA-JY Jack Youngblood 50.00

2001 Topps King Of Kings

NM/M
Common Player: 25.00
Inserted 1:580
K-CD Corey Dillon 40.00
K-DM Dan Marino 100.00
K-RM Randy Moss 100.00
K-TO Terrell Owens 25.00
K-WP Walter Payton 100.00
K-JR Jerry Rice 75.00
K-ES Emmitt Smith 100.00
K-FT Fred Taylor 50.00

2001 Topps Own The Game All the Way

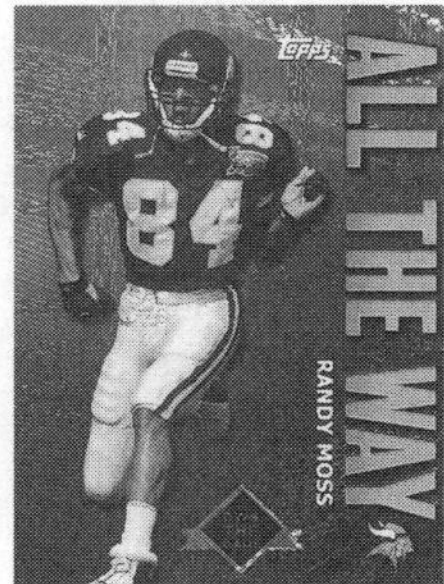

NM/M
Common Player: .50
AW1 Marvin Harrison 1.00
AW2 Muhsin Muhammad 1.00
AW3 Torry Holt 1.00
AW4 Rod Smith 1.00
AW5 Randy Moss 4.00
AW6 Cris Carter 1.00
AW7 Ed McCaffrey .50
AW8 Isaac Bruce 1.00
AW9 Terrell Owens 1.00
AW10 Tony Gonzalez .50

2001 Topps Own The Game Ground Warriors

NM/M
Common Player: .50
GW1 Edgerrin James 3.50
GW2 Robert Smith 1.00
GW3 Marshall Faulk 1.50
GW4 Mike Anderson 3.00
GW5 Eddie George 1.50
GW6 Corey Dillon 1.00
GW7 Fred Taylor 1.50

2001 Topps Own The Game Intimidators

NM/M
Common Player: .50
TI1 La'Roi Glover .50
TI2 Darren Sharper .50
TI3 Mike Peterson .50

2001 Topps Own The Game Showtime

NM/M
Common Player: .50
TS1 Derrick Mason 1.00
TS2 Az-Zahir Hakim 1.00
TS3 Jermaine Lewis .50

2001 Topps Originals

NM/M
Common Player: 75.00
Inserted 1:1,159
TO-DM Dan Marino 100.00
TO-WP Walter Payton 100.00
TO-JR Jerry Rice 75.00
TO-ES Emmitt Smith 100.00

2001 Topps Pro-Bowl Jerseys

NM/M
Common Player: 10.00
Inserted 1:425
TP-MA Mike Alstott 25.00
TP-RG Rich Gannon 20.00
TP-JG Jeff Garcia 30.00
TP-TH Torry Holt 25.00
TP-CL Chad Lewis 10.00
TP-RL Ray Lewis 25.00
TP-JL John Lynch 20.00
TP-DM Derrick Mason 20.00
TP-EM Eric Moulds 30.00
TP-JS Junior Seau 20.00
TP-JT Jason Taylor 10.00

2001 Topps Super Bowl Bunting

NM/M
Common Player: 12.00
Inserted 1:4,702
SBB1 Kerry Collins 12.00
SBB2 Trent Dilfer 12.00
SBB3 Ike Hilliard 12.00
SBB4 Shannon Sharpe 12.00
SBB5 Ron Dayne 12.00
SBB6 Jason Sehorn 12.00

2001 Topps Team Topps Legends Autographs

NM/M
TTR21 Billy Kilmer 20.00
TTR7 Art Donovan 30.00
TTF7 Art Donovan 30.00
TTF13 Joe Namath 75.00
TTR15 Mike Singletary 30.00
TTR12 Don Maynard 30.00
TTF12 Don Maynard 30.00
TTR20 Tom Dempsey 20.00
TTF20 Tom Dempsey 20.00

2001 Topps Walter Payton Reprints

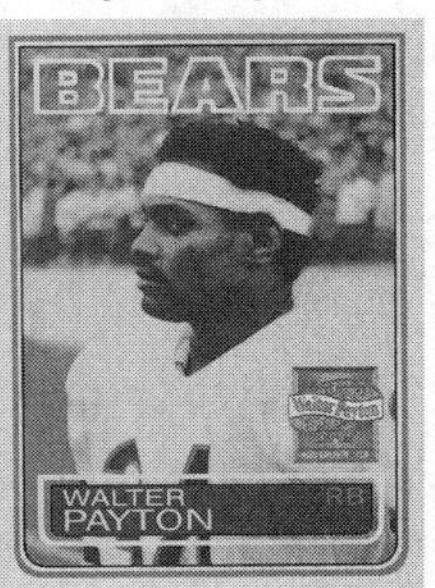

NM/M
Complete Set (12): 40.00
Common Player: 4.00
Inserted 1:12
WP1 Walter Payton 1976 10.00
WP2 Walter Payton 1977 4.00
WP3 Walter Payton 1978 4.00
WP4 Walter Payton 1979 4.00
WP5 Walter Payton 1980 4.00
WP6 Walter Payton 1981 4.00
WP7 Walter Payton 1982 4.00
WP8 Walter Payton 1983 4.00
WP9 Walter Payton 1984 4.00
WP10 Walter Payton 1985 4.00
WP11 Walter Payton 1986 4.00
WP12 Walter Payton 1987 4.00

2001 Topps Archives

NM/M
Complete Set (178): 50.00
Common Player: .50
Wax Box(20): 70.00
1 Warren Moon .50
2 Alan Ameche .50
3 Art Donovan .50
4 Jackie Slater .50
5 Bart Starr 3.00
6 Bill Howton .50
7 Jack Youngblood .50
8 Billy Kilmer 1.00
9 Billy Sims .50
10 Bo Jackson 1.00
11 Bob Griese 1.00
12 Boomer Esiason .50
13 Charley Conerly .50
14 Charlie Joiner .50
15 Christian Okoye .50
16 Chuck Bednarik .50
17 Cliff Branch .50
18 Dan Fouts .50
19 Dan Marino 1.00
20 Dave Casper .50
21 Deacon Jones .50
22 Dick "Night Train" Lane .50
23 Don Maynard .50
24 Doug Williams .50
25 Barry Sanders 2.00
26 Bubba Smith .50
27 Ed "Too Tall" Jones .50
28 Chuck Foreman .50
29 Elroy "Crazy Legs" Hirsch .50
30 Eric Dickerson 1.00
31 Harold Carmichael .50
32 Frank Gifford .50
33 Fred Biletnikoff .50
34 Gale Sayers 2.00
35 John Brodie .50
36 Henry Ellard .50
37 Jack Lambert .50
38 Jim Brown 3.00
39 James Lofton .50
40 Joe Montana 4.00
41 Joe Namath 3.00
42 Joe Theismann .50
43 Tommy McDonald .50
44 John Elway 3.00
45 John Riggins 2.00
46 Johnny Unitas 2.00
47 Kellen Winslow .50
48 Ken Anderson .50
49 Ken Stabler .50
50 Drew Pearson .50
51 Lawrence Taylor 1.00
52 Len Dawson .50
53 Lenny Moore .50
54 Lester Hayes .50
55 Troy Aikman 1.00
56 Mark Clayton .50
57 John Taylor .50
58 Norm Van Brocklin .50
59 Gene Upshaw .50
60 Otis Sistrunk .50
61 Ottis Anderson .50
62 Ozzie Newsome 1.00
63 Paul Hornung 2.00
64 Phil Simms 1.00
65 Raymond Berry .50
66 Roger Staubach 2.00
67 Ronnie Lott .50
68 Roosevelt Brown .50
69 Roosevelt Grier .50
70 Sonny Jurgensen 1.00
71 Marcus Allen 1.00
72 Steve Grogan .50
73 Roger Craig .50
74 Ted Hendricks .50
75 Jim Plunkett .50
76 Terry Metcalf .50
77 Tom Dempsey .50
78 Tom Fears .50
79 Tony Dorsett 1.00
80 Walter Payton 4.00
81 Y.A. Tittle .50
82 William Perry .50
83 Steve Young 1.00
84 Rodney Hampton .50
85 Jim Kelly 1.00
86 Gino Marchetti .50
87 Sid Luckman .50
88 Sammy Baugh 1.00
89 Harold "Red" Grange 3.00
90 Otto Graham .50
91 Knute Rockne 3.00
92 Jim Thorpe 3.00
93 Don Maynard .50
94 Barry Sanders 2.00
95 Joe Theismann 1.00
96 John Riggins 1.00
97 William Perry 1.00
98 Jim Brown 2.00
99 Chuck Bednarik .50
100 Warren Moon .50
101 Frank Gifford .50
102 Billy Sims 1.00
103 Doug Williams .50
104 Lester Hayes .50
105 Jim Plunkett .50
106 Dan Marino 2.00
107 Jack Youngblood .50
108 Tom Dempsey .50
109 Otis Sistrunk .50
110 Gale Sayers 2.00
111 Bill Howton .50
112 Chuck Foreman .50
113 Jim Kelly .50
114 Norm Van .50
115 Tommy McDonald .50
116 John Brodie .50
117 Art Donovan .50
118 Ted Hendricks .50
119 Henry Ellard .50
120 Bart Starr 2.00
121 Bo Jackson 1.00
122 Tom Fears .50
123 Drew Pearson .50
124 Ronnie Lott 1.00
125 Terry Metcalf .50
126 Lenny Moore .50
127 Raymond Berry .50
128 John Elway 3.00
129 Steve Grogan .50
130 Roger Craig .50
131 Bob Griese 1.00
132 Johnny Unitas 2.00
133 Cliff Branch .50
134 Billy Kilmer .50
135 Boomer Esiason .50
136 Fred Biletnikoff .50
137 Marcus Allen .50
138 Paul Hornung 1.00
139 Kellen Winslow .50
140 Joe Namath 2.00
141 Jackie Slater .50
142 John Taylor .50
143 Phil Simms .50
144 Ken Stabler .50
145 Dave Casper .50
146 Dan Fouts .50
147 Dick "Night Train" Lane 1.00
148 Alan Ameche 1.00
149 Sonny Jurgensen .50
150 Harold Carmichael .50
151 Ed "Too Tall" Jones .50
152 Lawrence Taylor 1.00
153 Ken Anderson .50
154 Deacon Jones 1.00
155 Ozzie Newsome .50
156 Steve Young 2.00
157 Charlie Joiner .50
158 Tony Dorsett 1.00
159 Christian Okoye .50
160 Charley Conerly .50
161 Elroy "Crazy Legs" Hirsch 1.00
162 Len Dawson .50
163 Jack Lambert .50
164 Mark Clayton .50
165 Y.A. Tittle 1.00
166 Troy Aikman 2.00
167 Roger Staubach 2.00
168 Roosevelt Grier .50
169 Gino Marchetti .50
170 Walter Payton 3.00
171 Rodney Hampton .50
172 Eric Dickerson 2.00
173 Ottis Anderson .50
174 James Lofton .50
175 Bubba Smith .50
176 Roosevelt Brown .50
177 Gene Upshaw .50
178 Joe Montana 3.00

2001 Topps Archives Rookie Reprint Autographs

NM/M
Common Player: 10.00
AA-MA Marcus Allen 35.00
AA-KA Ken Anderson 10.00
AA-OA Ottis Anderson 15.00
AA-CBE Chuck Bednarik 45.00
AA-RBE Raymond Berry 25.00
AA-JB Jim Brown 75.00
AA-RB Roosevelt Brown 10.00
AA-DB Dick Butkus 50.00
AA-DC Dave Casper 10.00
AA-MC Mark Clayton 10.00
AA-LD Len Dawson 10.00
AA-ED Eric Dickerson 25.00
AA-HE Henry Ellard 10.00
AA-DF Dan Fouts 25.00
AA-FG Frank Gifford 25.00
AA-RG Roosevelt Grier 10.00
AA-BG Bob Griese 50.00
AA-SG Steve Grogan 10.00
AA-RH Rodney Hampton 10.00
AA-LH Lester Hayes 10.00
AA-TH Ted Hendricks 10.00
AA-DJ Deacon Jones 10.00
AA-EJ Ed "Too Tall" Jones 10.00
AA-GM Gino Marchetti 10.00
AA-DMA Don Maynard 45.00
AA-JM Joe Montana 250.00
AA-JN Joe Namath 125.00
AA-ON Ozzie Newsome 10.00
AA-CO Christian Okoye 10.00
AA-WP William Perry 25.00
AA-JR John Riggins 50.00
AA-BS Barry Sanders 150.00
AA-GS Gale Sayers 50.00
AA-BSI Billy Sims 2.00
AA-BSM Bubba Smith 10.00
AA-JS John Stallworth 20.00
AA-RS Roger Staubach 100.00
AA-LT Lawrence Taylor
AA-YT Y.A. Tittle 35.00
AA-JU Johnny Unitas 100.00
AA-DW Doug Williams 10.00
AA-KW Kellen Winslow 10.00

2001 Topps Archives Rookie Reprint Jersey

NM/M
Common Player: 10.00
AS-MA Marcus Allen 15.00
AS-KA Ken Anderson 10.00
AS-SB Sammy Baugh 10.00
AS-CB Chuck Bednarik 10.00
AS-RB Raymond Berry 10.00
AS-JB Jim Brown 50.00
AS-LD Len Dawson 10.00
AS-ED Eric Dickerson 10.00
AS-FG Frank Gifford 15.00
AS-PH Paul Hornung 15.00
AS-SJ Sonny Jurgensen 10.00
AS-LM Lenny Moore 10.00
AS-CO Christian Okoye 10.00
AS-BS Bubba Smith 10.00
AS-BST Bart Starr 50.00
AS-JU Johnny Unitas 40.00

2001 Topps Archives Reserve

NM/M
Complete Set (94): 70.00
Common Player: 1.00
Minor Stars: 2.00
Box (10): 170.00
1 Warren Moon 3.00
2 Alan Ameche 1.00
3 Art Donovan 2.00
4 Jackie Slater 1.00
5 Bart Starr 8.00
6 Bill Howton 1.00
7 Jack Youngblood 1.00
8 Billy Kilmer 1.00
9 Billy Sims 2.00
10 Bo Jackson 5.00
11 Bob Griese 3.00
12 Boomer Esiason 2.00
13 Charley Conerly 1.00
14 Charlie Joiner 2.00
15 Christian Okoye 1.00
16 Chuck Bednarik 3.00
17 Cliff Branch 1.00
18 Dan Fouts 3.00
19 Dan Marino 10.00
20 Dave Casper 1.00
21 Deacon Jones 2.00
22 Dick "Night Train" Lane 2.00
23 Don Maynard 3.00
24 Doug Williams 1.00
25 Barry Sanders 6.00
26 Bubba Smith 1.00
27 Ed "Too Tall" Jones 2.00
28 Chuck Foreman 1.00
29 Elroy "Crazy Legs" Hirsch 3.00
30 Eric Dickerson 5.00
31 Harold Carmichael 1.00
32 Frank Gifford 3.00
33 Fred Biletnikoff 2.00
34 Gale Sayers 5.00
35 John Brodie 1.00
36 Henry Ellard 1.00
37 Jack Lambert 2.00
38 Jim Brown 6.00
39 James Lofton 1.00
40 Joe Montana 12.00
41 Joe Namath 8.00
42 Joe Theismann 4.00
43 Tommy McDonald 1.00
44 John Elway 10.00
45 John Riggins 3.00
46 Johnny Unitas 6.00
47 Kellen Winslow 3.00
48 Ken Anderson 1.00
49 Ken Stabler 5.00
50 Drew Pearson 1.00
51 Lawrence Taylor 3.00
52 Len Dawson 2.00
53 Lenny Moore 2.00
54 Lester Hayes 1.00
55 Troy Aikman 5.00
56 Mark Clayton 1.00
57 John Taylor 2.00
58 Norm Van Brocklin 2.00
59 Gene Upshaw 2.00
60 Otis Sistrunk 1.00
61 Ottis Anderson 2.00
62 Ozzie Newsome 3.00
63 Paul Hornung 4.00
64 Phil Simms 2.00
65 Raymond Berry 2.00
66 Roger Staubach 7.00
67 Ronnie Lott 3.00
68 Roosevelt Brown 2.00
69 Roosevelt Grier 2.00
70 Sonny Jurgensen 3.00
71 Marcus Allen 4.00
72 Steve Grogan 1.00
73 Roger Craig 2.00
74 Ted Hendricks 2.00
75 Jim Plunkett 3.00
76 Terry Metcalf 1.00
77 Tom Dempsey 2.00
78 Tom Fears 1.00
79 Tony Dorsett 4.00
80 Walter Payton 12.00
81 Y.A. Tittle 4.00
82 William Perry 1.00
83 Steve Young 5.00
84 Rodney Hampton 1.00
85 Jim Kelly 3.00
86 Gino Marchetti 1.00
87 Sid Luckman 2.00
88 Sammy Baugh 4.00
89 Harold "Red" Grange 5.00
90 Otto Graham 2.00
91 Mike Singletary 3.00
92 Dick Butkus 5.00
93 John Hannah 1.00
94 Derrick Thomas 3.00

2001 Topps Archives Reserve Autographed Mini-Helmets

NM/M
Common Player: 25.00
Marcus Allen 50.00
Ottis Anderson 25.00
Jim Brown 100.00
Dave Casper 25.00
Mark Clayton 25.00
Roger Craig 25.00
Eric Dickerson 40.00
John Elway 100.00
Roosevelt Grier 25.00
Rodney Hampton 25.00
Lester Hayes 25.00
Deacon Jones 25.00
Ed "Too Tall" Jones 25.00
Dan Marino 100.00
Don Maynard 25.00
Tommy McDonald 25.00
Terry Metcalf 25.00
Joe Montana 150.00
Joe Namath 100.00
Christian Okoye 25.00
Drew Pearson 25.00
Jim Plunkett 25.00
Gale Sayers 75.00
Mike Singletary 25.00
Otis Sistrunk 25.00
Lawrence Taylor 50.00
Doug Williams 25.00

2001 Topps Archives Reserve Autographed Rookie Reprints

NM/M
Complete Set (33):
Common Player: 15.00
ARA-MA Marcus Allen 25.00
ARA-RBE Raymond Berry 15.00
ARA-CB Cliff Branch 15.00
ARA-DB Dick Butkus 100.00
ARA-DC Dave Casper 15.00
ARA-MC Mark Clayton 15.00
ARA-LD Len Dawson 15.00
ARA-TD Tom Dempsey 15.00
ARA-ED Eric Dickerson 40.00
ARA-HE Henry Ellard 15.00
ARA-CF Chuck Foreman 15.00
ARA-FG Frank Gifford 50.00
ARA-RH Rodney Hampton 15.00
ARA-JH John Hannah 15.00
ARA-LH Lester Hayes 15.00
ARA-TH Ted Hendricks 15.00
ARA-CJ Charlie Joiner 15.00
ARA-DJ Deacon Jones 40.00
ARA-EJ Ed "Too Tall" Jones 15.00
ARA-BK Billy Kilmer 15.00
ARA-DMA Don Maynard 15.00
ARA-TMC Tommy McDonald 15.00
ARA-TM Terry Metcalf 15.00
ARA-JM Joe Montana 200.00
ARA-JN Joe Namath 175.00
ARA-ON Ozzie Newsome 25.00
ARA-WP William Perry 15.00
ARA-JR John Riggins 50.00
ARA-BS Barry Sanders 100.00
ARA-OS Otis Sistrunk 15.00
ARA-LT Lawrence Taylor 50.00
ARA-JU Johnny Unitas 75.00
ARA-DW Doug Williams 15.00

2001 Topps Archives Reserve Jersey Relics

NM/M
Common Player: 12.00
ARR-MA Marcus Allen 25.00
ARR-JE John Elway 50.00
ARR-BE Boomer Esiason 15.00
ARR-JK Jim Kelly 20.00
ARR-DM Dan Marino 60.00
ARR-JM Joe Montana 60.00
ARR-BS Barry Sanders 50.00
ARR-PS Phil Simms 15.00
ARR-LT Lawrence Taylor 25.00
ARR-DT Derrick Thomas 30.00
ARR-AT Al Toon 12.00
ARR-SY Steve Young 25.00

2001 Topps Chrome

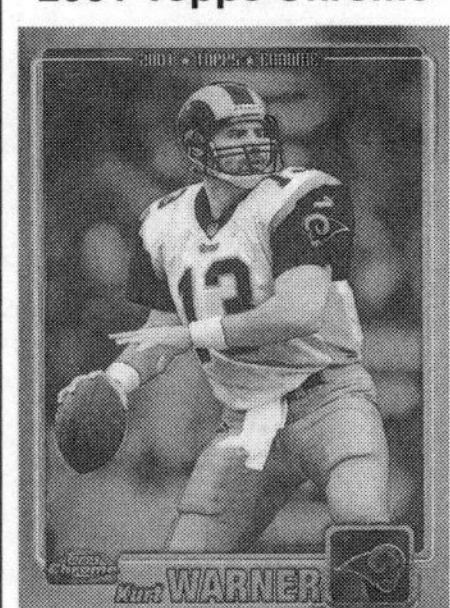

NM/M
Common Player: .25
Minor Stars: .50
Common Rookies: 7.00
Inserted 1:12
Production 999 Sets
Pack (4): 8.00
Wax Box (24): 140.00
1 Randy Moss 3.00
2 Desmond Howard .25
3 Shawn Bryson .25
4 Lamar Smith .75
5 Peter Warrick 2.00
6 Hines Ward .50
7 J.R. Redmond .50
8 Reidel Anthony .25
9 Rich Gannon .75
10 Ed McCaffrey 1.00
11 Jamel White .25
12 Michael Pittman .50
13 Rob Johnson .50
14 Tim Couch 1.25
15 Stephen Alexander .25
16 Ricky Watters .75
17 Kerry Collins .75
18 Ricky Williams 1.00
19 Joey Galloway 1.00
20 Chris Chandler .50
21 Marty Booker .25
22 Mark Brunell 1.25
23 Antonio Freeman .75
24 Richie Anderson .25
25 Amani Toomer .50
26 Trent Green .75
27 Terrell Fletcher .25
28 Kevin Lockett .25
29 Ron Dixon .50
30 Charlie Batch 1.00
31 Oronde Gadsden .50
32 Dorsey Levens .75
33 Jamal Lewis 2.50
34 Craig Yeast .25
35 Muhsin Muhammad .75
36 Willie Jackson .50
37 Isaac Bruce 1.00
38 Frank Wycheck .50
39 Troy Brown .25
40 Anthony Wright .75
41 Zach Thomas .75
42 Qadry Ismail .50
43 Jake Plummer 1.00
44 Keenan McCardell .50
45 Charles Johnson .25
46 Brett Favre 4.00
47 Jacquez Green .25
48 Matt Hasselbeck 1.00
49 Tiki Barber .75
50 Jeff Garcia 1.00
51 Shawn Jefferson .25
52 Kevin Johnson .75
53 Terrence Wilkins .50
54 Mike Anderson 2.50
55 Tim Brown 1.00
56 Champ Bailey .75
57 Jimmy Smith .75
58 Trent Dilfer .50
59 James Allen .50
60 David Boston 1.00
61 Jeremiah Trotter .25
62 Freddie Jones .50
63 Deion Sanders 1.00
64 Darrell Jackson .75

65	David Patten	.25
66	Jeremy McDaniel	.25
67	Jay Fiedler	1.00
68	Chad Lewis	.75
69	Raghib Ismail	.50
70	Cade McNown	1.00
71	Jevon Kearse	1.00
72	Jermaine Fazande	.50
73	Junior Seau	.75
74	Rod Smith	.75
75	Jermaine Lewis	.25
76	Dennis Northcutt	.75
77	Charlie Garner	.75
78	Charles Woodson	1.00
79	Wayne Chrebet	1.00
80	Ahman Green	.75
81	Donald Hayes	.50
82	Terance Mathis	.50
83	Warrick Dunn	1.00
84	Chris Sanders	.25
85	Albert Connell	.25
86	Robert Griffith	.25
87	Germane Crowell	.75
88	Tony Banks	.75
89	Travis Taylor	1.00
90	Akili Smith	1.00
91	Michael Westbrook	.75
92	Doug Flutie	1.25
93	Ike Hilliard	.50
94	Terry Glenn	.75
95	Leslie Shepherd	.25
96	Az-Zahir Hakim	.50
97	La'Roi Glover	.25
98	Peyton Manning	3.00
99	Jackie Harris	.25
100	Edgerrin James	2.50
101	Peerless Price	.75
102	Jamal Anderson	1.00
103	Keyshawn Johnson	1.00
104	Derrick Mason	.75
105	J.J. Stokes	.50
106	Kevin Faulk	.50
107	Tony Richardson	.25
108	James Stewart	.75
109	Tim Biakabutuka	.50
110	Jon Kitna	1.00
111	Thomas Jones	.75
112	Steve McNair	1.00
113	Sean Dawkins	.25
114	Jerome Bettis	1.00
115	Donovan McNabb	1.50
116	Bill Schroeder	.50
117	Rod Woodson	.25
118	James McKnight	.25
119	Daunte Culpepper	2.00
120	Todd Husak	.25
121	Shaun King	1.00
122	Tyrone Wheatley	.50
123	Curtis Martin	1.00
124	Terrell Davis	2.00
125	Steve Beuerlein	.50
126	Brad Johnson	.75
127	Joe Horn	.75
128	Fred Taylor	1.25
129	Brian Urlacher	2.00
130	Ray Lewis	1.00
131	Marshall Faulk	1.25
132	Curtis Conway	.25
133	Jason Sehorn	.25
134	Jerome Pathon	.25
135	Derrick Alexander	.50
136	Jerry Rice	2.00
137	Jeff George	.75
138	Johnnie Morton	.50
139	Eric Moulds	1.00
140	Duce Staley	1.00
141	Vinny Testaverde	.75
142	Eddie George	1.25
143	Shaun Alexander	1.25
144	Drew Bledsoe	1.25
145	Emmitt Smith	2.50
146	Marvin Harrison	1.00
147	Frank Sanders	.50
148	Aaron Shea	.25
149	Cris Carter	1.00
150	Tony Gonzalez	.75
151	Marcus Robinson	1.00
152	Danny Farmer	.50
153	Warren Sapp	.50
154	Kurt Warner	3.00
155	Jessie Armstead	.25
156	Lawyer Milloy	.25
157	Brian Griese	1.25
158	Jason Taylor	.50
159	Jeff Lewis	.25
160	Travis Prentice	.75
161	Tim Dwight	.75
162	Kyle Brady	.25
163	Bubba Franks	.50
164	James Thrash	.50
165	Bobby Shaw	.25
166	Ron Dayne	2.00
167	Mike Alstott	1.00
168	Bruce Smith	.50
169	Jeff Graham	.25
170	Jeff Blake	.75
171	Laveranues Coles	.75
172	Herman Moore	.75
173	Shannon Sharpe	.50
174	Corey Dillon	1.00
175	Ken Dilger	.25
176	Eddie Kennison	.50
177	Andre Rison	.50
178	Stephen Davis	1.00
179	Torry Holt	1.00
180	Samari Rolle	.25
181	Michael Strahan	.25
182	Plaxico Burress	1.00
183	Darnell Autry	.25
184	Wesley Walls	.50
185	Elvis Grbac	.75
186	Marcus Pollard	.25
187	Keith Poole	.25
188	Ryan Leaf	1.00
189	Terrell Owens	1.00
190	Dedric Ward	.25
191	Donald Driver	.25
192	Larry Foster	.25
193	Priest Holmes	.75
194	Sammy Morris	.75
195	Reggie Jones	.50
196	Kordell Stewart	1.00
197	Sylvester Morris	1.00
198	Aaron Brooks	1.00
199	Tai Streets	.50
200	Chad Pennington	2.00
201	Terrell Owens	.75
202	Marshall Faulk	.75
203	Mike Anderson	1.25
204	Cris Carter	.75
205	Corey Dillon	.75
206	Daunte Culpepper	.75
207	Peyton Manning	1.50
208	Torry Holt	.75
209	Marvin Harrison	.75
210	Edgerrin James	1.25
211	Sam Madison	.25
212	Jonathan Quinn	.25
213	Rob Morris	.25
214	E.G. Green	.25
215	David Sloan	.25
216	Jason Tucker	.25
217	Wali Rainer	.25
218	Jerry Azumah	.25
219	Dameyune Craig	.25
220	Jammi German	.25
221	*LaDainian Tomlinson*	100.00
222	*Quincy Morgan*	25.00
223	*Steve Smith*	25.00
224	*Santana Moss*	30.00
225	*Koren Robinson*	20.00
226	*Kevin Kasper*	15.00
227	*Jamie Henderson*	10.00
228	*Adam Archuleta*	15.00
229	*Drew Brees*	40.00
230	*Michael Stone*	7.00
231	*Jamar Fletcher*	12.00
232	*Eric Westmoreland*	10.00
233	*Chris Barnes*	12.00
234	*Gerard Warren*	20.00
235	*Marvin "Snoop" Minnis*	20.00
236	*Chris Chambers*	40.00
237	*Darnerian McCants*	10.00
238	*Kevan Barlow*	30.00
239	*Mike McMahon*	20.00
240	*Jabari Holloway*	10.00
241	*Travis Henry*	30.00
242	*Derrick Blaylock*	10.00
243	*Tim Hasselbeck*	15.00
244	*Andre Carter*	12.00
245	*Sage Rosenfels*	20.00
246	*Cedrick Wilson*	12.00
247	*Scotty Anderson*	10.00
248	*Ken-Yon Rambo*	15.00
249	*Marques Tuiasosopo*	25.00
250	*Reggie Wayne*	30.00
251	*Onomo Ojo*	12.00
252	*James Jackson*	25.00
253	*Moran Norris*	7.00
254	*Rashard Casey*	12.00
255	*Rudi Johnson*	30.00
256	*Willie Middlebrooks*	10.00
257	*Freddie Mitchell*	25.00
258	*Deuce McAllister*	60.00
259	*Chad Johnson*	40.00
260	*David Terrell*	25.00
261	*Jamal Reynolds*	15.00
262	*Michael Vick*	200.00
263	*Marcus Stroud*	12.00
264	*Dan Alexander*	15.00
265	*Jonathan Carter*	12.00
266	*Bobby Newcombe*	15.00
267	*Eddie Berlin*	12.00
268	*LaMont Jordan*	20.00
269	*Michael Bennett*	40.00
270	*Shaun Rogers*	7.00
271	*Travis Minor*	20.00
272	*Jesse Palmer*	15.00
273	*Derrick Gibson*	7.00
274	*Chris Weinke*	25.00
275	*Nate Clements*	10.00
276	*Eric Kelly*	7.00
277	*Justin Smith*	20.00
278	*Ryan Pickett*	7.00
279	*Anthony Thomas*	30.00
280	*Will Allen*	12.00
281	*Quincy Carter*	25.00
282	*Richard Seymour*	12.00
283	*Dan Morgan*	12.00
284	*Tay Cody*	7.00
285	*Alge Crumpler*	15.00
286	*Robert Ferguson*	20.00
287	*Will Peterson*	7.00
288	*Tony Dixon*	7.00
289	*Correll Buckhalter*	20.00
290	*Rod Gardner*	40.00
291	*Justin McCareins*	25.00
292	*Josh Heupel*	20.00
293	*Todd Heap*	15.00
294	*Damione Lewis*	12.00
295	*George Layne*	10.00
296	*Jamie Winborn*	10.00
297	*Billy Baber*	7.00
298	*T.J. Houshmandzadeh*	12.00
299	*Aaron Schobel*	7.00
300	*Gary Baxter*	7.00
301	*DeLawrence Grant*	7.00
302	*Morlon Greenwood*	10.00
303	*Shad Meier*	10.00
304	*Torrance Marshall*	15.00
305	*David Martin*	10.00
306	*Anthony Henry*	7.00
307	*Derrick Burgess*	7.00
308	*Andre Dyson*	7.00
309	*Ryan Helming*	7.00
310	*Fred Smoot*	15.00
311	*Arthur Love*	7.00
312	*John Capel*	15.00
313	*Brandon Spoon*	15.00
314	*Tony Stewart*	7.00
315	*Andre King*	10.00
316	*Quentin McCord*	10.00
317	*Zeke Moreno*	7.00
318	*Francis St. Paul*	10.00
319	*Richmond Flowers*	10.00
320	*Derek Combs*	12.00

2001 Topps Chrome Refractors

Refractor Cards: 3X-6X
Inserted 1:6
Rookie Cards: 3X
Inserted 1:125
Production 100 Sets

2001 Topps Chrome All the Way

		NM/M
Common Player:		3.00
AW1	Marvin Harrison	3.00
AW2	Muhsin Muhammad	3.00
AW3	Torry Holt	3.00
AW4	Rod Smith	3.00
AW5	Randy Moss	7.00
AW6	Cris Carter	3.00
AW7	Ed McCaffrey	3.00
AW8	Isaac Bruce	3.00
AW9	Terrell Owens	3.00
AW10	Tony Gonzalez	3.00

2001 Topps Chrome Combos

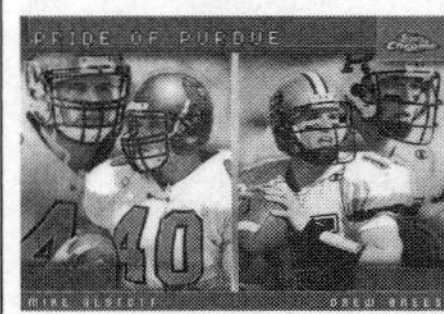

		NM/M
Complete Set (19):		45.00
Common Player:		2.00
Inserted 1:12		
TC1	Edgerrin James, Santana Moss	5.00
TC2	Torry Holt, Koren Robinson	3.00
TC3	Jamal Lewis,Travis Henry	5.00
TC4	Curtis Martin, Kevan Barlow	2.00
TC5	Cris Carter, Ken-Yon Rambo	2.00
TC6	Troy Aikman, Freddie Mitchell	6.00
TC7	Brian Griese, David Terrell	4.00
TC8	Tyrone Wheatley, Anthony Thomas	3.00
TC9	Warrick Dunn, Travis Minor	2.00
TC10	Peter Warrick, Marvin "Snoop" Minnis	4.00
TC11	Warren Sapp, Dan Morgan	2.00
TC12	Tony Gonzalez, Andre Carter	2.00
TC13	Antonio Freeman, Michael Vick	12.00
TC14	Ron Dayne, Michael Bennett	6.00
TC15	Mike Alstott, Drew Brees	7.00
TC16	Ahman Green, Correll Buckhalter	3.00
TC17	Brad Johnson, Chris Weinke	4.00
TC18	Eric Moulds, Fred Smoot	2.00
TC19	Ray Lewis, Reggie Wayne	3.00

2001 Topps Chrome Ground Warriors

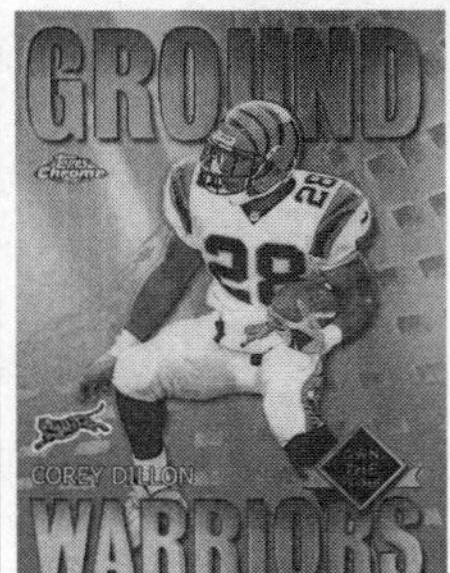

		NM/M
Complete Set (7):		20.00
Common Player:		2.00
GW1	Edgerrin James	5.00
GW2	Robert Smith	2.00
GW3	Marshall Faulk	5.00
GW4	Mike Anderson	3.00
GW5	Eddie George	3.00
GW6	Corey Dillon	3.00
GW7	Fred Taylor	3.00

2001 Topps Chrome Intimidators

		NM/M
Complete Set (2):		3.00
TI1	La'Roi Glover	1.00
TI2	Darren Sharper	2.00

2001 Topps Chrome King Of Kings

		NM/M
Common Player:		45.00
Inserted 1:734		
K-CD	Corey Dillon 375	45.00
K-DM	Dan Marino 125	150.00
K-RM	Randy Moss EX	125.00
K-TO	Terrell Owens 269	45.00
K-WP	Walter Payton 75	250.00
K-JR	Jerry Rice 125	100.00
K-ES	Emmitt Smith 150	125.00
K-FT	Fred Taylor 250	60.00

2001 Topps Chrome Own the Game

		NM/M
Complete Set (7):		20.00
Common Player:		1.00
PS1	Brian Griese	2.00
PS2	Peyton Manning	4.00
PS3	Jeff Garcia	1.00
PS4	Daunte Culpepper	3.00
PS5	Brett Favre	5.00
PS6	Kurt Warner	3.00
PS7	Donovan McNabb	3.00

2001 Topps Chrome Pro Bowl Jerseys

		NM/M
Common Player:		15.00
Inserted 1:299		
TP-MA	Mike Alstott 400	40.00
TP-RG	Rich Gannon 325	25.00
TP-JG	Jeff Garcia 250	50.00
TP-TH	Torry Holt 400	40.00
TP-CL	Chad Lewis 400	15.00
TP-RL	Ray Lewis 375	35.00
TP-JL	John Lynch 325	25.00
TP-DM	Derrick Mason 400	25.00
TP-EM	Eric Moulds 375	40.00
TP-JS	Junior Seau 375	35.00
TP-JT	Jason Taylor 400	20.00

2001 Topps Chrome Rookie Reprint Jerseys

		NM/M
Common Player:		150.00
Inserted 1:2,729		
TO-DM	Dan Marino 125	250.00
TO-WP	Walter Payton 75	300.00
TO-JR	Jerry Rice 100	150.00
TO-ES	Emmitt Smith 150	180.00

2001 Topps Chrome Showtime

		NM/M
Complete Set (3):		3.00
Common Player:		1.00
TS1	Derrick Mason	1.00
TS2	Az-Zahir Hakim	1.00
TS3	Jermaine Lewis	1.00

2001 Topps Chrome Walter Payton Reprints

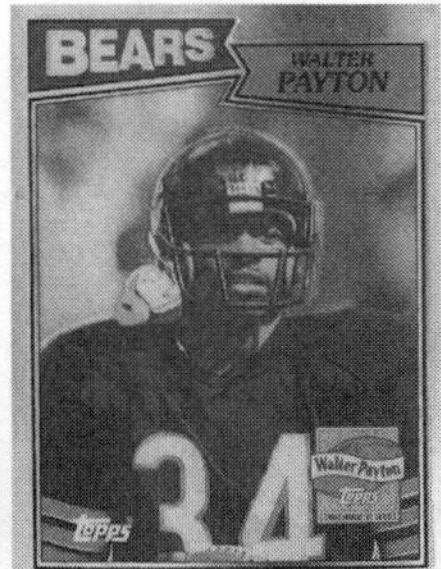

		NM/M
Complete Set (12):		70.00
Common Player:		8.00
Inserted 1:20		
WP1	Walter Payton 1976-#148	12.00
WP2	Walter Payton 1977-#360	8.00
WP3	Walter Payton 1978-#200	8.00
WP4	Walter Payton 1979-#480	8.00
WP5	Walter Payton 1980-#160	8.00
WP6	Walter Payton 1981-#400	8.00
WP7	Walter Payton 1982-#302	8.00
WP8	Walter Payton 1983-#36	8.00
WP9	Walter Payton 1984-#228	8.00
WP10	Walter Payton 1985-#33	8.00
WP11	Walter Payton 1986-#11	8.00
WP12	Walter Payton 1987-#46	8.00

2001 Topps Chrome Walter Payton Reprint Relic

		NM/M
Inserted 1:1,204		
WPR	Walter Payton Jersey	150.00

2001 Topps Debut

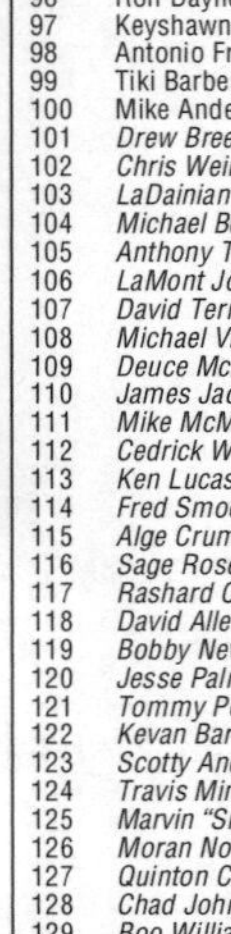

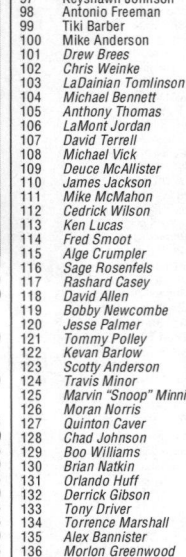

		NM/M
Common Player:		.25
Minor Stars:		.50
Common Rookie #101-110:		30.00
Inserted 1:183		
Production 499 Sets		
Common Rookie #111-150:		8.00
Inserted 1:23		
Production 999 Sets		
Common Rookie #151-175:		7.00
Inserted 1:25		
Production 1,499 Sets		
Pack (4):		2.25
Wax Box (24):		40.00
1	Marshall Faulk	.75
2	Ricky Watters	.50
3	Bill Schroeder	.25
4	Muhsin Muhammad	.50
5	Peter Warrick	1.25
6	Marvin Harrison	.75
7	Stephen Davis	.75
8	Cris Carter	.75
9	Charlie Batch	.50
10	David Boston	.50
11	Ike Hilliard	.25
12	Steve McNair	.50
13	Kordell Stewart	.50
14	Travis Prentice	.75
15	Sammy Morris	.75
16	Vinny Testaverde	.50
17	Tyrone Wheatley	.50
18	Jeff Garcia	.75
19	Brett Favre	2.25
20	Jake Plummer	.75
21	Cade McNown	.75
22	Rob Johnson	.50
23	Tim Couch	.75
24	Jerome Bettis	.50
25	Ricky Williams	1.00
26	Darrell Jackson	.50
27	Troy Brown	.25
28	Jamal Lewis	1.75
29	Isaac Bruce	.75
30	Lamar Smith	.50
31	Qadry Ismail	.25
32	Elvis Grbac	.50
33	Shaun Alexander	.75
34	Peyton Manning	1.75
35	Curtis Martin	.75
36	Jamal Anderson	.75
37	Mark Brunell	1.00
38	Emmitt Smith	1.50
39	Chad Lewis	.50
40	Randy Moss	1.75
41	Kurt Warner	1.50
42	Terrence Wilkins	.50
43	Corey Dillon	.75
44	Brian Griese	.75
45	Jon Kitna	.50
46	Eric Moulds	.75
47	Steve Beuerlein	.50
48	James Allen	.75
49	Amani Toomer	.50
50	Daunte Culpepper	1.25
51	Michael Pittman	.50
52	Warrick Dunn	.75
53	Terrell Owens	.75
54	Donald Hayes	.50
55	Keenan McCardell	.50
56	Tony Gonzalez	.50
57	Freddie Jones	.50
58	Charlie Garner	.50
59	Shawn Jefferson	.25
60	Brian Urlacher	1.25
61	Donovan McNabb	1.00
62	Az-Zahir Hakim	.50
63	James Thrash	.50
64	Hines Ward	.50
65	Shawn Bryson	.25
66	Wayne Chrebet	.50
67	Kevin Johnson	.50
68	Eddie George	.75
69	Derrick Alexander	.25
70	Tim Brown	.50
71	Jay Fiedler	.50
72	Aaron Brooks	.75
73	Torry Holt	.50
74	Edgerrin James	1.75
75	Shannon Sharpe	.50
76	Oronde Gadsden	.50
77	Rod Smith	.50
78	Rich Gannon	.50
79	Fred Taylor	1.00
80	Derrick Mason	.50
81	Joe Horn	.50
82	Robert Smith	.50
83	James Stewart	.50
84	Jeff George	.50
85	Troy Aikman	1.25
86	Charles Johnson	.25
87	Ahman Green	.50
88	Shaun King	.50
89	Ray Lewis	.50
90	Trent Dilfer	.50
91	Drew Bledsoe	1.00
92	Jimmy Smith	.50
93	Ed McCaffrey	.50
94	Kerry Collins	.50
95	Terry Glenn	.50
96	Ron Dayne	1.25
97	Keyshawn Johnson	.75
98	Antonio Freeman	.50
99	Tiki Barber	.50
100	Mike Anderson	1.75
101	*Drew Brees*	50.00
102	*Chris Weinke*	30.00
103	*LaDainian Tomlinson*	80.00
104	*Michael Bennett*	40.00
105	*Anthony Thomas*	40.00
106	*LaMont Jordan*	30.00
107	*David Terrell*	25.00
108	*Michael Vick*	250.00
109	*Deuce McAllister*	80.00
110	*James Jackson*	25.00
111	*Mike McMahon*	25.00
112	*Cedrick Wilson*	8.00
113	*Ken Lucas*	8.00
114	*Fred Smoot*	20.00
115	*Alge Crumpler*	10.00
116	*Sage Rosenfels*	25.00
117	*Rashard Casey*	10.00
118	*David Allen*	10.00
119	*Bobby Newcombe*	20.00
120	*Jesse Palmer*	25.00
121	*Tommy Polley*	8.00
122	*Kevan Barlow*	30.00
123	*Scotty Anderson*	8.00
124	*Travis Minor*	25.00
125	*Marvin "Snoop" Minnis*	25.00
126	*Moran Norris*	10.00
127	*Quinton Caver*	10.00
128	*Chad Johnson*	30.00
129	*Boo Williams*	8.00
130	*Brian Natkin*	8.00
131	*Orlando Huff*	8.00
132	*Derrick Gibson*	15.00
133	*Tony Driver*	20.00
134	*Torrence Marshall*	12.00
135	*Alex Bannister*	10.00
136	*Morlon Greenwood*	8.00
137	*Ennis Davis*	10.00
138	*Mike Cerimele*	10.00
139	*David Rivers*	8.00
140	*Dustin McClintock*	8.00
141	*Tay Cody*	10.00
142	*Arthur Love*	8.00
143	*Sly Johnson*	8.00
144	*Dan Alexander*	10.00
145	*Will Allen*	10.00
146	*Andre Dyson*	10.00
147	*Margin Hooks*	8.00
148	*Adam Archuleta*	20.00
149	*Sedrick Hodge*	8.00
150	*Kendrell Bell*	20.00
151	*Reggie Wayne*	12.00
152	*Rod Gardner*	12.00
153	*Chris Chambers*	12.00
154	*Jamal Reynolds*	7.00
155	*Ben Hamilton*	8.00
156	*Dan Morgan*	10.00
157	*Quincy Morgan*	6.00
158	*Travis Henry*	8.00
159	*Ken-Yon Rambo*	7.00
160	*Josh Heupel*	8.00
161	*Marcus Stroud*	8.00
162	*Marques Tuiasosopo*	10.00
163	*Reggie Germany*	8.00
164	*Freddie Milons*	8.00
165	*Jabari Holloway*	8.00
166	*Ben Leard*	7.00
167	*Bhawoh Jue*	7.00
168	*Freddie Mitchell*	8.00
169	*Vinny Sutherland*	7.00
170	*Jeff Backus*	7.00
171	*Correll Buckhelter*	10.00
172	*Mario Fatafehi*	7.00
173	*Jeff Chaney*	7.00
174	*Koren Robinson*	10.00
175	*Santana Moss*	10.00

2001 Topps Gallery

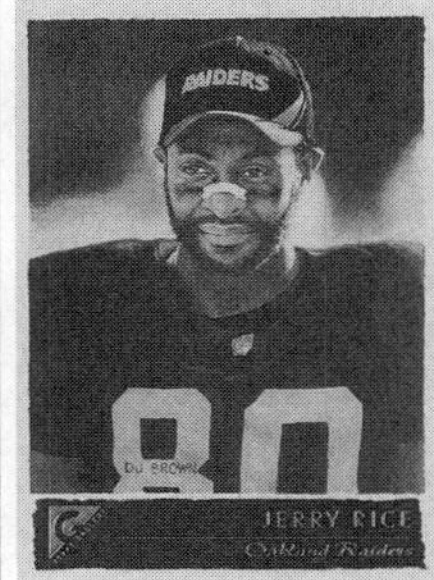

		NM/M
Complete Set (144):		85.00
Common Player:		.15
Minor Stars:		.30
Common Rookies:		.75
Inserted 1:1		
Pack (6):		3.00
Wax Box (24):		50.00
1	Donovan McNabb	1.00
2	Jamal Anderson	.50
3	Steve McNair	.50
4	Peyton Manning	2.00
5	Curtis Martin	.50
6	Joey Galloway	.50
7	Daunte Culpepper	1.25
8	Corey Dillon	.50
9	Brad Johnson	.30
10	Doug Flutie	.75
11	Jerome Bettis	.50
12	Elvis Grbac	.50
13	Aaron Brooks	.75
14	Ray Lewis	.50
15	Tim Dwight	.50

16 Robert Smith .30
17 Jake Plummer .50
18 Jay Fiedler .50
19 Fred Taylor .75
20 Jerry Rice 1.25
21 Shaun King .50
22 Cade McNown .50
23 Drew Bledsoe .75
24 Ricky Watters .30
25 Muhsin Muhammad .30
26 Shawn Jefferson .15
27 Tiki Barber .50
28 Derrick Alexander .30
29 Stephen Davis .50
30 James Stewart .30
31 Terrell Owens .50
32 Ed McCaffrey .50
33 Jeff Graham .15
34 Jamal Lewis 1.50
35 Edgerrin James 1.75
36 Tim Couch .75
37 Marshall Faulk .75
38 Ike Hilliard .30
39 Ahman Green .50
40 Tim Biakabutuka .30
41 Akili Smith .50
42 David Boston .50
43 Eddie George .75
44 Hines Ward .30
45 Chad Lewis .30
46 Brian Urlacher 1.25
47 Eric Moulds .50
48 Ricky Williams 1.00
49 Warrick Dunn .50
50 Kerry Collins .30
51 Isaac Bruce .50
52 Jimmy Smith .30
53 Emmitt Smith 1.50
54 Cris Carter .50
55 Jeff Garcia .50
56 Mike Anderson 1.50
57 Lamar Smith .50
58 Brett Favre 2.50
59 Steve Beuerlein .30
60 Terry Glenn .30
61 Tyrone Wheatley .30
62 Charlie Batch .30
63 Chris Chandler .30
64 Sylvester Morris .50
65 Joe Horn .30
66 Kevin Johnson .30
67 Rob Johnson .30
68 Jeff George .30
69 Keyshawn Johnson .50
70 Wayne Chrebet .30
71 Randy Moss 2.00
72 Marvin Harrison .50
73 Peter Warrick .50
74 Darrell Jackson .30
75 Derrick Mason .30
76 Oronde Gadsden .30
77 Charles Johnson .15
78 James Allen .30
79 Torry Holt .50
80 Troy Brown .15
81 Amani Toomer .30
82 Junior Seau .30
83 Troy Aikman 1.25
84 Mark Brunell .75
85 Brian Griese .60
86 Charlie Garner .30
87 Rich Gannon .30
88 Jeff Blake .30
89 Donald Hayes .15
90 Germane Crowell .50
91 Tony Gonzalez .30
92 Jon Kitna .30
93 Vinny Testaverde .30
94 Kordell Stewart .50
95 Keenan McCardell .30
96 Kurt Warner 2.00
97 Bill Schroeder .30
98 Rod Smith .50
99 Tim Brown .30
100 Trent Dilfer .30
101 *Michael Vick* 12.00
102 *Koren Robinson* 3.00
103 *LaDainian Tomlinson* 8.00
104 *Todd Heap* 1.25
105 *Correll Buckhelter* 1.50
106 *Freddie Mitchell* 2.00
107 *Josh Booty* .75
108 *Chris Chambers* 4.00
109 *Chris Weinke* 3.00
110 *Steve Smith* 3.00
111 *Travis Minor* 1.50
112 *Ken-Yon Rambo* 1.25
113 *Marques Tuiasosopo* 2.50
114 *Bobby Newcombe* 1.00
115 *Drew Brees* 4.00
116 *LaMont Jordan* 1.50
117 *Reggie Germany* 1.00
118 *Reggie Wayne* 3.00
119 *Dan Alexander* 1.00
120 *Alge Crumpler* 1.00
121 *Robert Ferguson* 1.50
122 *Rod Gardner* 3.00
123 *Mike McMahon* 1.25
124 *Kevan Barlow* 3.00
125 *Marvin "Snoop" Minnis* 2.00
126 *Sage Rosenfels* 1.50
127 *Jesse Palmer* 1.25
128 *Michael Bennett* 4.00
129 *Rudi Johnson* 3.00
130 *Deuce McAllister* 6.00
131 *Santana Moss* 3.00
132 *Josh Heupel* 2.00
133 *Quincy Morgan* 2.00
134 *Quincy Carter* 3.00
135 *Anthony Thomas* 3.00
136 *James Jackson* 1.75
137 *Kevin Kasper* 1.25
138 *Alex Bannister* 1.25
139 *David Terrell* 2.00
140 *Chad Johnson* 2.00
141 Walter Payton .15
142 Bart Starr .15
143 Sonny Jurgensen .15
144 Jim Brown .15
145A Joe Namath HTA 6.00
145B Joe Namath RETAIL 20.00
NNO Joe Namath BUCKS 5.00

2001 Topps Gallery Autographs

NM/M
Common Player: 15.00
Inserted 1:84
MA Mike Anderson 30.00
AB Aaron Brooks 25.00
TB Tim Brown 25.00
WC Wayne Chrebet 15.00
DC Daunte Culpepper 50.00
TD Tim Dwight 15.00
JG Jeff Garcia 25.00
EG Eddie George 45.00
JL Jamal Lewis 30.00

2001 Topps Gallery Gallery Heritage

NM/M
Complete Set (9): 20.00
Common Player: 1.50
Inserted 1:12
GH1 Johnny Unitas 4.00
GH2 Bart Starr 4.00
GH3 Y.A. Tittle 2.00
GH4 Chuck Bednarik 1.50
GH5 Randy Moss 4.00
GH6 Jerry Rice 2.50
GH7 Peyton Manning 4.00
GH8 Brett Favre 5.00
GH9 Marshall Faulk 1.75

2001 Topps Gallery Gallery Heritage Autographed Relics

Too uncommon to price
GRA BF Brett Favre
GRA FG Frank Gifford
GRA RM Randy Moss
GRA JR Jerry Rice
GRA BS Bart Starr

2001 Topps Gallery Gallery Heritage Relics

NM/M
Common Player: 25.00
Inserted 1:211
GR BF Brett Favre 45.00
GR FG Frank Gifford 25.00
GR RM Randy Moss 40.00
GR JR Jerry Rice 30.00
GR BS Bart Starr 30.00

2001 Topps Gallery Originals

NM/M
Complete Set (10): 140.00
Common Player: 12.00
Inserted 1:50
GO DA Dan Alexander 12.00
GO KB Kevan Barlow 12.00
GO CC Cris Carter 25.00
GO RC Rashard Casey 12.00
GO CD Corey Dillon 20.00
GO RG Rod Gardner 20.00
GO CJ Chad Johnson 12.00
GO PM Peyton Manning 45.00
GO WS Warren Sapp 12.00
GO KW Kurt Warner 40.00

2001 Topps Gallery Star Gallery

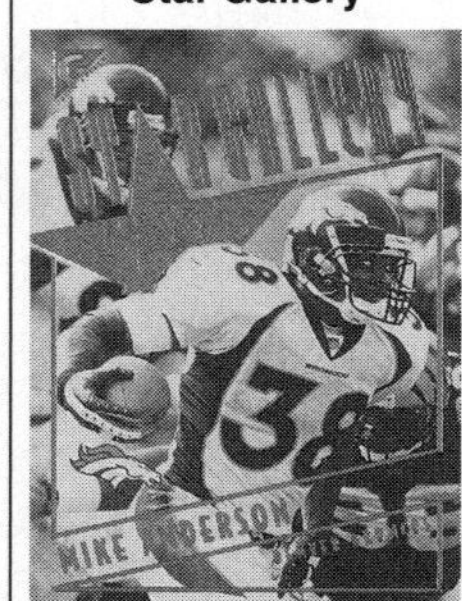

NM/M
Complete Set (10): 12.00
Common Player: 1.00
Inserted 1:8
SG1 Daunte Culpepper 2.00
SG2 Jamal Lewis 2.00
SG3 Peyton Manning 3.00
SG4 Edgerrin James 2.50
SG5 Randy Moss 3.00
SG6 Marshall Faulk 2.00
SG7 Mike Anderson 1.00
SG8 Eddie George 1.25
SG9 Donovan McNabb 1.50
SG10 Cris Carter 1.00

2001 Topps Gallery Team Topps Legends Autographs

NM/M
TTR13 Jim Brown 100.00
TTF3 John Riggins 25.00
TTR9 Otis Sistrunk 25.00
TTF18 Fred Biletnikoff 25.00
TTF2 Dick Butkus 75.00

2001 Topps Hall of Fame Class of 2001

NM/M
Common Player: 2.00
1 Nick Buoniconti 3.00
2 Deacon Jones 4.00
3 Marv Levy 3.00
4 Mike Munchak 2.00
5 Jackie Slater 3.00
6 Ron Yary 2.00
7 Jack Youngblood 4.00

2001 Topps Heritage

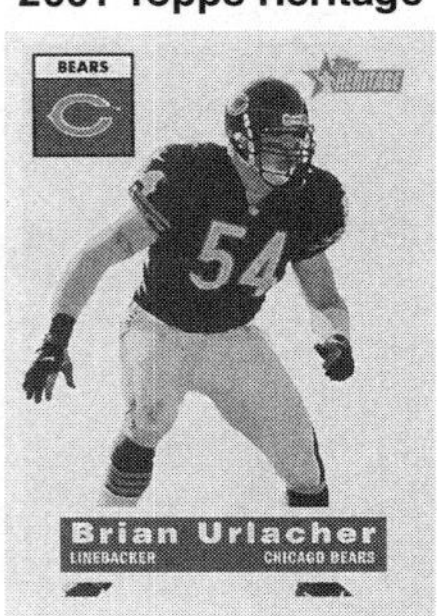

NM/M
Complete Set (146): 275.00
Common Player: .30
Minor Stars: .60
Common Rookie: 2.00
Inserted 1:23
Production 1,956 Sets
Pack (8): 3.00
Wax Box (24): 65.00
1 Ray Lewis .60
2 Peter Warrick 1.50
3 James Stewart .60
4 Junior Seau .60
5 Jeff George .60
6 Amani Toomer .30
7 Elvis Grbac .60
8 David Boston .75
9 Jimmy Smith .60
10 Warrick Dunn .75
11 Hines Ward .60
12 Joe Horn .60
13 Stephen Davis .75
14 Tyrone Wheatley .75
15 Brian Urlacher 1.50
16 Fred Taylor 1.00
17 Jerry Rice 1.75
18 Keyshawn Johnson .75
19 Jay Fiedler .60
20 Jamal Anderson .75
21 Emmitt Smith 2.00
22 Tiki Barber .75
23 Daunte Culpepper 1.50
24 Torry Holt .75
25 Peyton Manning 2.50
26 Eddie George 1.00
27 Jamal Lewis 2.50
28 Ricky Williams 1.00
29 Ahman Green .60
30 Ed McCaffrey .60
31 Curtis Martin .75
32 Isaac Bruce .75
33 Doug Flutie 1.00
34 Steve McNair .75
35 Donovan McNabb 1.25
36 Keenan McCardell .60
37 Charlie Batch .75
38 Cade McNown .75
39 Terrell Owens .75
40 Brad Johnson .75
41 Robert Smith .75
42 Muhsin Muhammad .60
43 Kurt Warner 2.50
44 Lamar Smith .75
45 Brian Griese .75
46 Trent Dilfer .60
47 Jeff Garcia .75
48 Derrick Mason .60
49 Drew Bledsoe 1.00
50 Marshall Faulk 1.00
51 Corey Dillon .75
52 Tony Gonzalez .60
53 Chad Lewis .60
54 Shaun Alexander .75
55 Edgerrin James 2.50
56 Eric Moulds .75
57 Aaron Brooks .75
58 Zach Thomas .60
59 Jerome Bettis .75
60 Shannon Sharpe .60
61 Kerry Collins .60
62 Ricky Watters .60
63 Tim Couch 1.00
64 Marvin Harrison .75
65 Tim Brown .75
66 Mark Brunell 1.00
67 Wayne Chrebet .60
68 Terry Glenn .75
69 Mike Anderson 2.50
70 Randy Moss 2.50
71 Freddie Jones .60
72 Ike Hilliard .60
73 Derrick Alexander .30
74 Travis Prentice .75
75 Brett Favre 3.00
76 Rod Smith .60
77 Troy Aikman 1.50
78 Cris Carter .75
79 Rich Gannon .60
80 Charlie Garner .60
81 Michael Pittman .60
82 Jeff Graham .30
83 Albert Connell .60
84 Bill Schroeder .60
85 Jeff Blake .60
86 Jon Kitna .60
87 Qadry Ismail .30
88 Joey Galloway .75
89 Charles Johnson .30
90 Troy Brown .30
91 Johnnie Morton .60
92 Chris Chandler .60
93 Donald Hayes .60
94 Shaun King .75
95 Vinny Testaverde .60
96 James Allen .75
97 Jake Plummer .75
98 Antonio Freeman .60
99 Sean Dawkins .30
100 Ron Dayne 1.50
101 Rob Johnson .60
102 Kordell Stewart .75
103 Akili Smith .75
104 Shawn Jefferson .30
105 Germane Crowell .60
106 Kevin Johnson .75
107 Steve Beuerlein .60
108 Marcus Robinson .75
109 Peerless Price .60
110 Jerome Pathon .30
111 *Sage Rosenfels* 6.00
112 *Quincy Morgan* 10.00
113 *Chad Johnson* 15.00
114 *Josh Heupel* 10.00
115 *Anthony Thomas* 12.00
116 *Drew Brees* 15.00
117 *Kevan Barlow* 12.00
118 *Chris Chambers* 15.00
119 *Mike McMahon* 6.00
120 *Todd Heap* 5.00
121 *Leonard Davis* 4.00
122 *Richard Seymour* 4.00
123 *Robert Ferguson* 7.00
124 *Andre Carter* 4.00
125 *Jesse Palmer* 5.00
126 *Travis Minor* 7.00
127 *Rudi Johnson* 12.00
128 *Rod Gardner* 12.00
129 *Marvin "Snoop" Minnis* 8.00
130 *Koren Robinson* 8.00
131 *Chris Weinke* 10.00
132 *James Jackson* 7.00
133 *Michael Vick* 50.00
134 *Marques Tuiasosopo* 10.00
135 *Michael Bennett* 15.00
136 *LaDainian Tomlinson* 25.00
137 *Freddie Mitchell* 10.00
138 *Deuce McAllister* 20.00
139 *Quincy Carter* 10.00
140 *Santana Moss* 12.00
141 *David Terrell* 10.00
142 *Reggie Wayne* 12.00
143 *Justin Smith* 2.00
144 *Gerard Warren* 5.00
145 *Travis Henry* 10.00
146 *Dan Morgan* 7.00

2001 Topps Heritage Chrome

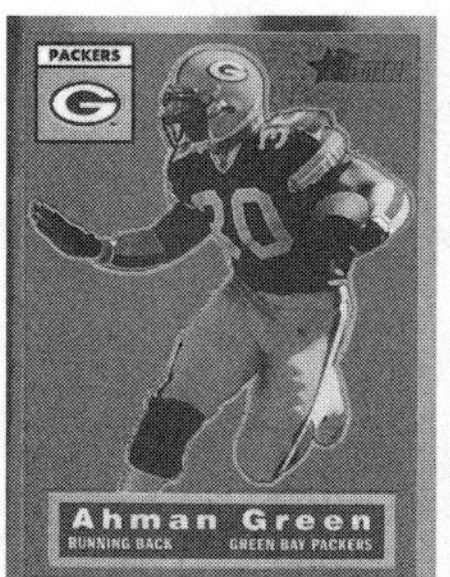

Chrome Cards: 3X-5X
Chrome Rookies: 1X
Inserted 1:27
Production 556 Sets

2001 Topps Heritage Classic Renditions

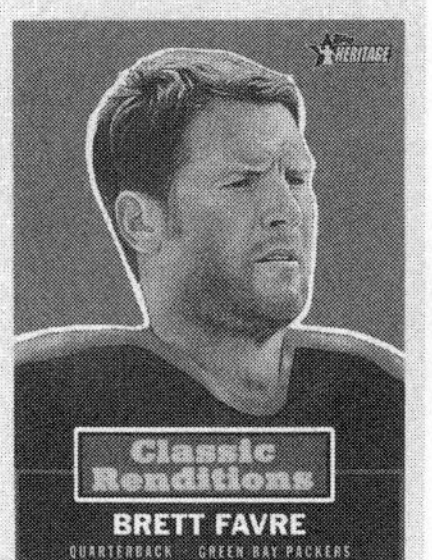

NM/M
Complete Set (10): 15.00
Common Player: .50
Inserted 1:8
CR1 Donovan McNabb 2.00
CR2 Brett Favre 6.00
CR3 Edgerrin James 3.00
CR4 Peyton Manning 4.00
CR5 Marvin Harrison .50
CR6 Kurt Warner 3.00
CR7 Marshall Faulk 2.00
CR8 Brian Urlacher 2.00
CR9 Jeff Garcia 1.00
CR10 Terrell Owens .50

2001 Topps Heritage Classic Renditions Autographs

NM/M
Common Player: 150.00
CRA BF Brett Favre 200.00
CRA EJ Edgerrin James 150.00
CRA BU Brian Urlacher 150.00

2001 Topps Heritage Gridiron Collection Relics

NM/M
Common Player: 15.00
GC1 Daunte Culpepper 25.00
GC2 Eddie George 25.00
GC3 Edgerrin James 40.00
GC4 Tony Gonzalez 15.00
GC5 Marvin Harrison 20.00
GC6 Jimmy Smith 15.00
GC7 Sam Cowart 15.00
GC9 Rod Woodson 20.00
GC10 Mo Lewis 15.00
GC11 Charles Woodson 20.00
GC12 Derrick Brooks 15.00

2001 Topps Heritage New Age Performers

NM/M
Complete Set (15): 15.00
Common Player: .75
Minor Stars: 1.50
Inserted 1:8
NA1 Marshall Faulk 2.00
NA2 Jerry Rice 2.50
NA3 Marvin Harrison 1.50
NA4 Peyton Manning 4.00
NA5 Torry Holt .75
NA6 Isaac Bruce 1.50
NA7 Eddie George 1.75
NA8 Daunte Culpepper 2.00
NA9 Edgerrin James 3.00
NA10 Randy Moss 4.00
NA11 Jeff Garcia 1.50
NA12 Mike Anderson 2.00
NA13 Terrell Owens 1.50
NA14 Rod Smith .75
NA15 Cris Carter 1.50

2001 Topps Heritage Real One Autographs

NM/M
Common Player: 20.00
Red sigs 2X
THRO EJ Edgerrin James 30.00
THRO MA Mike Anderson 20.00
THRO EM Eric Moulds 20.00
THRO RW Ricky Williams 30.00
THRO MH Marvin Harrison 30.00
THRO DC Daunte Culpepper 40.00
THRO WC Wayne Chrebet 20.00
THRO JS Jimmy Smith 20.00
THRO BU Brian Urlacher 50.00
THRO SD Stephen Davis 20.00
THRO JL Jamal Lewis 30.00
THRO TO Terrell Owens 20.00
THRO AB Aaron Brooks 25.00
101 Roosevelt Grier 25.00
58 Ollie Matson 20.00
60 Lenny Moore 20.00
41 Roosevelt Brown 25.00
78 Elroy "Crazy Legs" Hirsch 25.00
28 Chuck Bednarik 25.00
86 Y.A. Tittle 25.00
44 Joe Schmidt 20.00

2001 Topps Heritage Souvenir Seating Relics

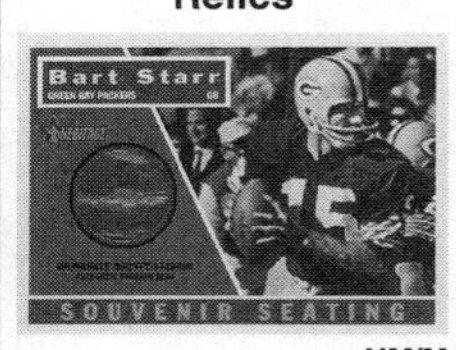

NM/M
Common Player: 10.00
S3 Bart Starr 25.00
S5 Johnny Unitas 25.00
S6 Raymond Berry 10.00
S7 Lenny Moore 10.00
S8 Jim Brown 25.00
S9 10.00
S10 Chuck Bednarik 10.00

2001 Topps Heritage Team Topps Legends Autographs

NM/M
Common Player: 20.00
TTR17 Johnny Unitas 40.00
TTR4 Tommy McDonald 20.00
TTR19 Paul Hornung 40.00
TTF10 Chuck Foreman 20.00
TTF16 Cliff Branch 20.00
TTF20 Tom Dempsey 20.00
TTF12 Don Maynard 20.00
TTR12 Don Maynard 20.00
TTR21 Billy Kilmer 20.00
TTF21 Billy Kilmer 20.00
TTF5 John Hannah 20.00
TTR6 Terry Metcalf 20.00
TTF9 Otis Sistrunk 20.00

2001 Topps Heritage Then and Now

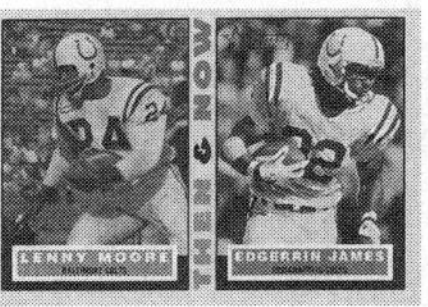

NM/M
Complete Set (3): 2.50
Common Player: .50
Inserted 1:8
TN-BL Chuck Bednarik, Ray Lewis .50
TN-MJ Lenny Moore, Edgerrin James 2.00
TN-TG Y.A. Tittle, Jeff Garcia .50

2001 Topps Heritage 1956 Players

Autographs too uncommon to price.

NM/M
Common Player: 2.00
THRO AA Alan Ameche 2.00
THRO CB Chuck Bednarik 3.00
THRO RB Roosevelt Brown 2.00
THRO CC Charley Conerly 2.00
THRO AD Art Donovan 2.00
THRO TF Tom Fears 2.00
THRO FG Frank Gifford 3.00
THRO RG Roosevelt Grier 2.00
THRO EH Elroy "Crazy Legs" Hirsch 4.00
THRO BH Bill Howton 2.00
THRO BL Bobby Layne 2.00
THRO LM Lenny Moore 2.00
THRO YT Y.A. Tittle 3.00
THRO ET Emlen Tunnell 3.00
THRO NV Norm Van Brocklin 3.00

2001 Topps Heritage 1956 Topps All-Stars

NM/M
Complete Set (3): 2.00
Common Player: .75
Inserted 1:12
HA-CB Chuck Bednarik .75
HA-LM Lenny Moore .75
HA-YT Y.A. Tittle .75

2001 Topps Pro Bowl Promos

NM/M
Common Player: .25
1 Peyton Manning 1.50
2 Donovan McNabb 1.00
3 Marshall Faulk 1.00
4 Randy Moss 1.00
5 Edgerrin James 1.00
6 Daunte Culpepper .75
7 Jamal Lewis .75
8 Jeff Garcia .75
9 Warren Sapp .25

2001 Topps Reserve

NM/M
Complete Set (150): 275.00
Common Player: .30
Minor Stars: .60
Common Rookie: 5.00
Inserted 1:5
Wax Box (10): 125.00
1 Jeff Garcia 1.50
2 Joe Horn .30
3 Jeff George .30
4 Ed McCaffrey .60
5 Keenan McCardell .60
6 Jerome Bettis 1.00
7 Jake Plummer .60
8 Doug Flutie 1.50

NM/M
9 Wayne Chrebet .60
10 Brett Favre 5.00
11 Emmitt Smith 3.00
12 Derrick Mason .60
13 Lamar Smith .60
14 Brian Urlacher 2.50
15 Kurt Warner 4.00
16 Jerry Rice 3.00
17 Tony Gonzalez .60
18 Jeff Blake .60
19 Warrick Dunn 1.00
20 Vinny Testaverde .60
21 Peyton Manning 4.00
22 Drew Bledsoe 1.50
23 Tim Dwight .30
24 Brad Johnson 1.00
25 Peter Warrick 1.00
26 Steve McNair 1.00
27 James Thrash .30
28 Kordell Stewart 1.00
29 Randy Moss 4.00
30 Brian Griese 1.50
31 Curtis Martin 1.00
32 Ike Hilliard .30
33 Torry Holt 1.00
34 James Allen .30
35 Jay Fiedler .60
36 Junior Seau .60
37 Troy Brown .30
38 Ricky Williams 1.00
39 Charlie Garner .60
40 Eddie George 1.50
41 Stephen Davis .60
42 Tim Couch 1.50
43 Jimmy Smith .60
44 Trent Green .60
45 Rod Smith .60
46 Isaac Bruce 1.00
47 Oronde Gadsden .30
48 Keyshawn Johnson 1.00
49 Jeff Graham .30
50 Mark Brunell 1.50
51 Cade McNown .60
52 Terry Glenn .60
53 Derrick Alexander .60
54 Ron Dayne 1.00
55 Shaun Alexander 2.00
56 Chris Chandler .30
57 Rob Johnson .60
58 Germane Crowell .60
59 Cris Carter 1.00
60 Ahman Green 1.00
61 Marshall Faulk 1.50
62 Darrell Jackson .30
63 Duce Staley .60
64 Kevin Johnson .60
65 Muhsin Muhammad .60
66 Elvis Grbac .60
67 Fred Taylor 1.50
68 Marcus Robinson 1.00
69 Edgerrin James 3.00
70 Kerry Collins .60
71 Daunte Culpepper 2.50
72 Matt Hasselbeck .60
73 Akili Smith .30
74 Aaron Brooks 1.50
75 Tim Biakabutuka .30
76 Ray Lewis 1.00
77 David Boston 1.00
78 Donovan McNabb 2.50
79 Marvin Harrison 1.00
80 Rich Gannon 1.00
81 Tony Richardson .30
82 Peerless Price .30
83 Jamal Anderson .60
84 Mike Anderson 2.00
85 Terrell Owens 1.00
86 Antonio Freeman .60
87 Charlie Batch .60
88 Jamal Lewis 2.50
89 Jon Kitna .30
90 Joey Galloway .60
91 Tyrone Wheatley .60
92 Jeff Lewis .30
93 Eric Moulds .60
94 Shawn Jefferson .30
95 Tiki Barber .60
96 Tim Brown 1.00
97 Corey Dillon 1.00
98 Tony Banks .60
99 James Stewart .60
100 Amani Toomer .60
101 *Freddie Mitchell* 8.00
102 *James Jackson* 6.00
103 *Michael Bennett* 15.00
104 *LaDainian Tomlinson* 25.00
105 *Gerard Warren* 5.00
106 *Dan Morgan* 5.00
107 *Alge Crumpler* 5.00
108 *Mike McMahon* 8.00
109 *Justin Smith* 5.00
110 *Chris Weinke* 8.00
111 *Rudi Johnson* 12.00
112 *Rod Gardner* 12.00
113 *Koren Robinson* 8.00
114 *Andre Carter* 5.00
115 *Kevan Barlow* 12.00
116 *Jesse Palmer* 6.00
117 *Anthony Thomas* 12.00
118 *Michael Vick* 35.00
119 *Sage Rosenfels* 6.00
120 *Chad Johnson* 15.00
121 *Robert Ferguson* 5.00
122 *Quincy Carter* 10.00
123 *Travis Minor* 6.00
124 *Travis Henry* 10.00
125 *Reggie Wayne* 12.00
126 *David Terrell* 10.00
127 *Josh Heupel* 6.00
128 *Deuce McAllister* 20.00
129 *Todd Heap* 5.00
130 *Drew Brees* 15.00
131 *Marvin "Snoop" Minnis* 8.00
132 *Marques Tuiasosopo* 10.00
133 *Santana Moss* 12.00
134 *Quincy Morgan* 6.00
135 *Chris Chambers* 15.00
136 *Richard Seymour* 5.00
137 *LaMont Jordan* 5.00
138 *Eddie Berlin* 5.00
139 *Correll Buckhalter* 8.00
140 *Justin McCareins* 10.00
141 *Vinny Sutherland* 5.00
142 *Chris Taylor* 5.00
143 *Scotty Anderson* 5.00
144 *Nate Clements* 5.00
145 *Darnerian McCants* 5.00
146 *Dan Alexander* 5.00
147 *A.J. Feeley* 5.00
148 *Chris Barnes* 5.00
149 *Dee Brown* 5.00
150 *Milton Wynn* 5.00

2001 Topps Reserve Autographs

NM/M
Common Player: 10.00
Inserted 1:9 H; 1:37 R
TR-MA Mike Anderson 25.00
TR-KB Kevan Barlow 15.00
TR-MB Michael Bennett 25.00
TR-JB Josh Booty 10.00
TR-DB Drew Brees 50.00
TR-AB Aaron Brooks 20.00
TR-CC Chris Chambers 25.00
TR-DC Daunte Culpepper 40.00
TR-RG Rod Gardner 20.00
TR-DH Donald Hayes 10.00
TR-TH Travis Henry 15.00
TR-JH Joe Horn 10.00
TR-JJ James Jackson 15.00
TR-WJ Willie Jackson 10.00
TR-CJ Chad Johnson 15.00
TR-JL Jamal Lewis 20.00
TR-DM Derrick Mason 10.00
TR-DMO Dan Morgan 10.00
TR-QM Quincy Morgan 15.00
TR-SMO Sammy Morris 10.00
TR-SM Santana Moss 20.00
TR-EM Eric Moulds 15.00
TR-JP Jesse Palmer 15.00
TR-KR Koren Robinson 20.00
TR-BS Bill Schroeder 10.00
TR-JS Jimmy Smith 15.00
TR-LS Lamar Smith 10.00
TR-TS Tai Streets 10.00
TR-DT David Terrell 25.00
TR-JT James Thrash 10.00
TR-LT LaDainian Tomlinson 40.00
TR-MV Michael Vick 150.00
TR-RWA Reggie Wayne 20.00
TR-CW Chris Weinke 25.00
TR-RW Ricky Williams 25.00

2001 Topps Reserve Autographed Mini-Helmets

NM/M
Common Player: 20.00
Dan Alexander 20.00
Kevan Barlow 20.00
Michael Bennett 40.00
Josh Booty 20.00
Drew Brees 60.00
Quincy Carter 25.00
Chris Chambers 50.00
Rod Gardner 40.00
Travis Henry 20.00
Josh Heupel 20.00
James Jackson 20.00
Chad Johnson 20.00
LaMont Jordan 20.00
Deuce McAllister 60.00
Justin McCareins 20.00
Travis Minor 20.00
Dan Morgan 20.00
Quincy Morgan 20.00
Santana Moss 20.00
Bobby Newcombe 20.00
Jesse Palmer 20.00
Ken-Yon Rambo 20.00
Koren Robinson 20.00
Steve Smith 20.00
Vinny Sutherland 20.00
David Terrell 50.00
Anthony Thomas 45.00
LaDainian Tomlinson 50.00
Michael Vick 125.00
Gerard Warr 20.00
Reggie Wayne 20.00
Chris Weinke 25.00

2001 Topps Reserve Jersey Relics

NM/M
Common Player: 10.00
TRR-SA Sam Adams 10.00
TRR-MA Mike Alstott 10.00
TRR-BB Blaine Bishop 10.00
TRR-DB Derrick Brooks 12.00
TRR-MB Mark Brunell 10.00
TRR-TH Torry Holt 10.00
TRR-ML Mo Lewis 10.00
TRR-SM Sam Madison 12.00
TRR-SR Samari Rolle 10.00
TRR-SS Shannon Sharpe 10.00
TRR-DS Darren Sharper 12.00
TRR-KW Kurt Warner 10.00
TRR-SW Steve Wisniewski 10.00
TRR-CW Charles Woodson 15.00
TRR-FW Frank Wycheck 10.00

2001 Topps Reserve Rookie Premiere Jersey Relics

NM/M
Common Player: 10.00
Inserted 1:23 H; 1:66 R
TRR-JJ James Jackson 12.00
TRR-RJ Rudi Johnson 10.00
TRR-MMC Mike McMahon 15.00
TRR-MM Marvin "Snoop" Minnis 10.00
TRR-TM Travis Minor 12.00
TRR-DM Dan Morgan 10.00
TRR-QM Quincy Morgan 12.00
TRR-MT Marques Tuiasosopo 10.00

2001 Topps Reserve Veteran Game-Worn Relics

NM/M
Common Player: 20.00
TRR-MA Mike Alstott 20.00
TRR-MB Mark Brunell 20.00
TRR-TH Torry Holt 20.00
TRR-SS Shannon Sharpe 20.00

2001 Topps Super Bowl XXV Card Show

NM/M
Common Player: 3.00
1 Peyton Manning 8.00
2 Donovan McNabb 6.00
3 Marshall Faulk 6.00
4 Jeff Garcia 5.00
5 Randy Moss 8.00
6 Fred Taylor 5.00
7 Robert Smith 3.00
8 Mike Anderson 8.00
9 Edgerrin James 6.00
10 Warren Sapp 3.00
11 Daunte Culpepper 5.00
12 Jamal Lewis 8.00

2001 Topps XFL

NM/M
Complete Set (100): 25.00
Common Player: .20
Minor Stars: .40
Pack (8): 2.00
Wax Box (24): 35.00
1 Mike Pawlawski 1.50
2 Todd Doxzon .20
3 James Bostic .75
4 Jim Druckenmiller 1.00
5 Mario Bailey .20
6 Mike Cawley .20
7 Dino Philyaw .40
8 Aaron Bailey .20
9 Juan Johnson .50
10 Kaipo McGuire .20
11 Toya Jones .20
12 Todd Floyd .20
13 Jaimie Baisley .20
14 Brian Shay .50
15 Eric England .20
16 Curtis Alexander .20
17 Tim Lester .75
18 Dialleo Burks .40
19 Charles Puleri .75
20 Zechariah Lord .20
21 Chrys Chukwuma .20
22 Rickey Brady .20
23 Rashaan Salaam 1.50
24 Jermaine Copeland 1.00
25 Butler B'ynote .20
26 Tommy Maddox 1.75
27 Mike Furrey .20
28 Ed Smith .20
29 Pat Barnes 1.00
30 James Hundon .20
31 John Avery 1.75
32 James Willis .20
33 Larry Ryans .20
34 Vaughn Dunbar .40
35 John Williams .20
36 Casey Weldon 1.00
37 Roell Preston .50
38 Jeff Brohm 1.00
39 Rashaan Shehee .40
40 Kevin Swayne .20
41 Ben Snell .20
42 James Williams .20
43 Corte McGuffey .20
44 Charles Jordan .40
45 Frank Leatherwood .20
46 Dwayne Sabb .20
47 Shannon Culver .20
48 Brent Moss .40
49 Zola Davis .20
50 Ryan Clement .50
51 Tyji Armstrong .40
52 Paul Failla .20
53 Michael Blair .20
54 Corey Ivey .20
55 Darryl Hobbs .20
56 Paul Lacoste .20
57 Damon Gourdine .20
58 Wendell Davis .20
59 Joe Cummings .20
60 Stephen Fisher .20
61 Stepfret Williams .75
62 Brandon Sanders .20
63 Michael Black .20
64 Scott Milanovich .75
65 Brian Roche .20
66 Darnell McDonald .75
67 Marcus Hinton .20
68 Quincy Jackson .20
69 Roosevelt Potts .40
70 Rod Smart 2.00
71 Keith Elias .20
72 Latario Rachel .20
73 Mike Sutton .20
74 Kirby Dar Dar .40
75 Derrick Clark .20
76 Antonio Edwards .20
77 Marcus Crandell .20
78 Jerry Crafts .20
79 Brian Roberson .20
80 Las Vegas vs. New York .20
81 Orlando vs. Chicago .20
82 San Francisco vs. Los Angeles .40
83 Memphis vs. Birmingham .20
Kat .20
Rose .20
Dana .20
Lisa Michelle .20
Kiushin .20
Youn .20
Sunni .20
Cicely .20
Tanisha .20
Krissy .20
TK .20
Jensi .20
Jenny .20
Karla .20
Jenny .20
Susanne .20
100 Checklist .20

2001 Topps XFL Endzone Autographs

NM/M
Complete Set (18): 175.00
Common Player: 10.00
Inserted 1:28 Hobby
Mike Archie 12.00
Michael Black 12.00
Rickey Brady 12.00
Chris Brantley 10.00
Chrys Chukwuma 12.00
Jeremaine Copeland 25.00
Todd Doxzon 10.00
Keith Elias 10.00
Paul Failla 10.00
Mike Furrey 12.00
LeShon Johnson 15.00
Tim Lester 15.00
Tommy Maddox 25.00
Ken Oxendine 12.00
Dino Philyaw 12.00
Roell Preston 15.00
Wally Richardson 18.00
Rashaan Shehee 15.00

2001 Topps XFL Football Relics

NM/M
Common Player: 5.00
Inserted 1:34
John Avery 10.00
Pat Barnes 5.00
James Bostic 5.00
Jeff Brohm 5.00
Chuck Clements 5.00
Scott Milanovich 5.00
Charles Puleri 5.00
Rashaan Salaam 10.00

2001 Topps XFL Jersey Relics

NM/M
Common Player: 5.00
Inserted 1:34
John Avery 10.00
Pat Barnes 5.00
James Bostic 5.00
Jeff Brohm 5.00
Chuck Clements 5.00
Scott Milanovich 5.00
Charles Puleri 5.00
Rashaan Salaam 10.00

2001 Topps XFL Loaded Cannon

NM/M
Complete Set (8): 8.00
Common Player: 1.00
Inserted 1:8
1 Tommy Maddox 5.00
2 Casey Weldon 1.00
3 Marcus Crandell 1.00
4 Jeff Brohm 1.00
5 Ryan Clement 1.00
6 Mike Pawlawski 1.00
7 Charles Puleri 1.00
8 Tim Lester 1.00

2001 Topps XFL Stickers

NM/M
Complete Set (10): 5.00
Common Sticker: .50
Inserted 1:2

2001 Topps eTopps

NM/M
1 Ray Lewis $6.50/649
2 Peter Warrick $6.50/281
3 James Stewart $3.50/465
4 Junior Seau $6.50/389
6 Amani Toomer $3.50/538
7 Elvis Grbac $6.50/230
8 David Boston $3.50/560
9 Jimmy Smith $6.50/354
10 Warrick Dunn $3.50/571
11 James Thrash $3.50/431
12 Joe Horn $3.50/606
13 Stephen Davis $6.50/236
14 Tyrone Wheatley $6.50/237
15 Brian Urlacher $3.50/1146
16 Fred Taylor $6.50/283
17 Jerry Rice $6.50/93318
Keyshawn Johnson $6.50/254
19 Jay Fiedler $3.50/478
20 Jamal Anderson $6.50/274
21 Emmitt Smith $6.50/1975
22 Tiki Barber $3.50/861
23 Daunte Culpepper $9.50/457
24 Torry Holt $6.50/553
25 Peyton Manning $9.50/1104
26 Eddie George $9.50/292
27 Jamal Lewis $9.50/237
28 Ricky Williams $6.50/683
29 Ahman Green $3.50/1105
30 Ed McCaffrey $3.50/330
31 Curtis Martin $6.50/404
32 Isaac Bruce $6.50/772
33 Doug Flutie $3.50/684
34 Steve McNair $6.50/341
35 Donovan McNabb $6.50/987
36 Keenan McCardell $3.50/243
37 Charlie Batch $3.50/322
38 Cade McNown $3.50/333
39 Terrell Owens $6.50/528
40 Brad Johnson $3.50/231
41 Tim Dwight $3.50/586
42 Muhsin Muhammad $3.50/270
43 Kurt Warner $9.50/785
44 Lamar Smith $6.50/371
45 Brian Griese $6.50/505
46 Matthew Hatchette $3.50/317
47 Jeff Garcia $6.50/585
48 Derrick Mason $6.50/207
49 Drew Bledsoe $6.50/372
50 Marshall Faulk $6.50/2742
51 Corey Dillon $6.50/726
52 Tony Gonzalez $6.50/950
53 Chad Lewis $3.50/313
54 Shaun Alexander $6.50/1442
55 Edgerrin James $6.50/473
56 Eric Moulds $6.50/217
57 Aaron Brooks $6.50/434
58 Zach Thomas $6.50/380
59 Jerome Bettis $6.50/826
60 Shannon Sharpe $6.50/302
61 Kerry Collins $3.50/355
62 Ricky Watters $3.50/384
63 Tim Couch $6.50/677
64 Marvin Harrison $6.50/391
65 Tim Brown $6.50/377
66 Mark Brunell $6.50/299
67 Wayne Chrebet $3.50/387
68 Terry Glenn $6.50/260
69 Mike Anderson $6.50/352
70 Randy Moss $6.50/881
71 Freddie Jones $3.50/339
72 Ike Hilliard $6.50/280
73 Derrick Alexander $3.50/349
74 Travis Prentice $3.50/443
75 Brett Favre $9.50/1066
76 Rod Smith $6.50/521
77 Todd Pinkston $3.50/1005
78 Cris Carter $6.50/540
79 Rich Gannon $6.50/327
80 Charlie Garner $3.50/518
81 Michael Pittman $3.50/338
82 Jeff Graham $3.50/425
83 Albert Connell $3.50/275
84 Bill Schroeder $3.50/673
85 Jeff Blake $3.50/361
86 Jon Kitna $3.50/537
87 Qadry Ismail $3.50/431
88 Joey Galloway $6.50/413
89 Duce Staley $6.50/688
90 Troy Brown $3.50/559
91 Johnnie Morton $6.50/231
92 Chris Chandle $6.50/307
93 Donald Hayes $3.50/291
94 Mike Alstott $3.50/999
95 Vinny Testaverde $3.50/459
96 James Allen $3.50/467
97 Jake Plummer $3.50/600
98 Antonio Freeman $6.50/348
99 Darrell Jackson $6.50/502
100 Ron Dayne $6.50/257
101 Rob Johnson $3.50/389

#	Player	Price
102	Kordell Stewart	$6.50/346
103	Akili Smith	$6.50/202
104	Shawn Jefferson	$3.50/226
105	Germane Crowell	$3.50/281
106	Kevin Johnson	$3.50/478
108	Marcus Robinson	$3.50/662
109	Priest Holmes	$3.50/418
111	Kevin Lockett	$3.50/319
112	Tony Banks	$6.50/186
113	Terrell Davis	$6.50/269
114	Trent Green	$6.50/313
115	Sylvester Morris	$3.50/299
116	J.R. Redmond	$3.50/272
117	Willie Jackson	$6.50/282
118	Chad Pennington	$6.50/507
119	Tai Streets	$6.50/462
120	Matt Hasselbeck	$6.50/237
121	LaMont Jordan	$3.50/678
122	Quincy Morgan	$3.50/811
123	Chad Johnson	$6.50/331
124	Anthony Thomas	$9.50/2186
125	Drew Brees	$6.50/1290
126	Kevan Barlow	$3.50/1724
127	Chris Chambers	$3.50/1715
128	Mike McMahon	$3.50/1697
129	Todd Heap	$3.50/755
130	Robert Ferguson	$6.50/315
131	Dan Morgan	$3.50/645
132	Jesse Palmer	$3.50/521
133	Travis Minor	$3.50/637
134	Rudi Johnson	$3.50/532
135	Rod Gardner	$6.50/510
136	Marvin "Snoop" Minnis	$3.50/837
137	Koren Robinson	$6.50/482
138	Chris Weinke	$6.50/875
139	James Jackson	$3.50/1053
140	Michael Vick	$9.50/5721
141	Marques Tuiasosopo	$6.50/616
142	Michael Bennett	$6.50/658
143	LaDainian Tomlinson	$9.50/1536
144	Freddie Mitchell	$3.50/634
145	Deuce McAllister	$6.50/597
146	Quincy Carter	$6.50/923
147	Santana Moss	$6.50/620
148	David Terrell	$6.50/638
149	Reggie Wayne	$6.50/595
150	Travis Henry	$3.50/1117

2002 Topps

	NM/M
Complete Set (385):	80.00
Common Player:	.15
Unlisted Stars:	.75
Minor Stars	.40
Common Rookie	.50
Pack (10):	2.00
oax Box (36):	55.00

#	Player	Price
1	Kurt Warner	3.00
2	Jeff Graham	.15
3	Todd Bouman	.15
4	Duce Staley	.30
5	Jon Kitna	.15
6	Shannon Sharpe	.30
7	Darrell Jackson	.15
8	Michael Pittman	.15
9	Tony Gonzalez	.30
10	Wayne Chrebet	.30
11	Jevon Kearse	.30
12	Bill Schroeder	.15
13	Jeremy McDaniel	.15
14	Todd Pinkston	.15
15	Maurice Smith	.15
16	Charlie Batch	.15
17	Olandis Gary	.15
18	Ron Dugans	.15
19	Brian Urlacher	2.50
20	Amani Toomer	.40
21	Tim Couch	1.25
22	Derrick Brooks	.15
23	Frank Sanders	.15
24	James Williams	.30
25	Lamar Smith	.15
26	Darrick Vaughn	.15
27	Cris Carter	.30
28	Roland Williams	.15
29	Bobby Shaw	.15
30	Jerome Pathon	.15
31	Rod Woodson	.30
32	Ronney Jenkins	.15
33	Chris Chandler	.30
34	Dez White	.15
35	Rod Smith	.30
36	Troy Brown	.60
37	JaJuan Dawson	.15
38	Reidel Anthony	.15
39	Mike Green	.15
40	Steve Smith	.15
41	Willie Jackson	.30
42	MarTay Jenkins	.30
43	Reggie Germany	.15
44	Desmond Howard	.15
45	Fred Taylor	.30
46	Scotty Anderson	.15
47	John Lynch	.15
48	Amos Zereoue	.15
49	Darnay Scott	.15
50	Anthony Thomas	2.50
51	Jeff Garcia	.60
52	Charlie Garner	.30
53	Drew Bledsoe	2.00
54	Donnie Edwards	.15
55	Corey Bradford	.15
56	Desmond Clark	.15
57	Courtney Brown	.30
58	Wesley Walls	.15
59	Chad Brown	.15
60	Shawn Jefferson	.15
61	Corey Dillon	.60
62	Johnnie Morton	.15
63	Marcus Pollard	.15
64	Jason Taylor	.30
65	Kevin Faulk	.15
66	Shane Matthews	.15
67	Hines Ward	.30
68	Garrison Hearst	.40
69	Trung Canidate	.15
70	Tony Banks	.15
71	Matt Hasselbeck	.15
72	Correll Buckhalter	.30
73	Ron Dayne	.40
74	Zach Thomas	.30
75	Emmitt Smith	3.00
76	Peter Warrick	.60
77	Rob Johnson	.15
78	Michael Strahan	.40
79	Ray Lewis	.40
80	Jamir Miller	.15
81	Brian Griese	.60
82	Stacey Mack	.15
83	Michael Bennett	.60
84	Ricky Williams	2.00
85	Jamal Lewis	1.25
86	Doug Flutie	.60
87	Jonathan Quinn	.30
88	Mike Alstott	.30
89	Samari Rolle	.15
90	LaMont Jordan	.15
91	Dominic Rhodes	.15
92	Quincy Carter	2.00
93	Marcus Robinson	.30
94	Travis Henry	.50
95	Jason Brookins	.15
96	Nick Goings	.15
97	Brian Finneran	.15
98	Dorsey Levens	.15
99	Reggie Swinton	.15
100	Chris Chambers	.75
101	Kordell Stewart	.40
102	Tai Streets	.15
103	Chris Redman	.15
104	Jacquez Green	.15
105	Rod Gardner	.50
106	Kevin Kasper	.15
107	Anthony Henry	.15
108	Dan Morgan	.15
109	Ronald McKinnon	.15
110	Qadry Ismail	.15
111	Chad Johnson	.15
112	James Stewart	.15
113	Terrence Wilkins	.15
114	Joey Galloway	.15
115	Deuce McAllister	1.25
116	Joe Jurevicius	.15
117	Tyrone Wheatley	.15
118	Jason Gildon	.15
119	LaDainian Tomlinson	2.50
120	Grant Wistrom	.15
121	Eddie George	.75
122	Laveranues Coles	.30
123	Antowain Smith	.15
124	Larry Parker	.15
125	Bubba Franks	.15
126	Troy Hambrick	.15
127	Jamal Reynolds	.15
128	Doug Chapman	.15
129	Freddie Mitchell	.50
130	Tim Dwight	.15
131	Erron Kinney	.15
132	James Allen	.15
133	Eric Moulds	.15
134	Keenan McCardell	.15
135	David Sloan	.15
136	Dennis Northcutt	.15
137	Kevan Barlow	1.00
138	Bobby Engram	.15
139	Champ Bailey	.30
140	Donald Hayes	.15
141	Brandon Bennett	.15
142	Deltha O'Neal	.15
143	James Jackson	.50
144	Shaun Rogers	.15
145	Joe Johnson	.30
146	Ricky Watters	.30
147	Warrick Dunn	.30
148	Steve McNair	.60
149	Marvin Harrison	.60
150	Kendrell Bell	.15
151	Jim Miller	.15
152	Terry Allen	.15
153	Jake Plummer	.30
154	James McKnight	.30
155	Curtis Martin	.30
156	Keyshawn Johnson	.30
157	Kevin Lockett	.15
158	Jeremiah Trotter	.15
159	Derrick Alexander	.40
160	Brandon Stokley	.15
161	J.J. Stokes	.15
162	Drew Bennett	.15
163	Drew Brees	2.50
164	Tim Brown	.60
165	Daunte Culpepper	2.00
166	Raghib Ismail	.15
167	Alex Van Pelt	.15
168	Arnold Jackson	.15
169	Oronde Gadsden	.30
170	Isaac Bruce	.60
171	Warren Sapp	.30
172	Michael Westbrook	.15
173	John Abraham	.15
174	Jessie Armstead	.15
175	Brock Marion	.15
176	Brett Favre	4.00
177	Ben Gay	.15
178	Muhsin Muhammad	.15
179	Reggie Wayne	.50
180	Kailee Wong	.15
181	Rich Gannon	.50
182	Chris Fuamatu-Ma'afala	.15
183	Shaun Alexander	.60
184	Kevin Dyson	.15
185	Kwamie Lassiter	.15
186	Elvis Joseph	.15
187	Trent Dilfer	.30
188	Marty Booker	.40
189	Travis Taylor	.30
190	Michael Vick	3.00
191	Mike McMahon	.60
192	Jay Fiedler	.15
193	Zack Bronson	.15
194	Derrick Mason	.15
195	Anthony Becht	.15
196	Ahman Green	.60
197	Alge Crumpler	.60
198	Thomas Jones	.60
199	Tiki Barber	.60
200	Donovan McNabb	2.00
201	Andre Carter	.15
202	Stephen Davis	.30
203	Troy Edwards	.15
204	Lawyer Milloy	.15
205	Peyton Manning	3.00
206	James Farrior	.15
207	Gerard Warren	.15
208	Peerless Price	.60
209	Avion Black	.15
210	Marcellus Wiley	.15
211	Torry Holt	.15
212	A.J. Feeley	.15
213	Travis Minor	.30
214	Darren Sharper	.30
215	Jerry Porter	.30
216	Randall Cunningham	.30
217	Chris Weinke	.15
218	Mike Anderson	1.25
219	Marvin "Snoop" Minnis	.50
220	David Martin	.30
221	Vinny Sutherland	.15
222	Ki-Jana Carter	.30
223	Kevin Swayne	.15
224	Mark Brunell	.60
225	Quincy Morgan	.50
226	David Terrell	.75
227	Terance Mathis	.15
228	Frank Wycheck	.15
229	Az-Zahir Hakim	.15
230	Freddie Jones	.15
231	Jerry Rice	3.00
232	Ike Hilliard	.15
233	Terrell Davis	1.25
234	Shawn Bryson	.15
235	David Boston	.60
236	Edgerrin James	2.50
237	Trent Green	.30
238	Charlie Rogers	.15
239	Vinny Testaverde	.15
240	Koren Robinson	.60
241	Ronde Barber	.15
242	Dwayne Carswell	.15
243	Dedric Ward	.15
244	Richard Huntley	.15
245	Jamal Anderson	.30
246	Ryan Leaf	.30
247	Priest Holmes	.60
248	Tom Brady	3.00
249	Charles Woodson	.30
250	Jerome Bettis	.60
251	Tommy Polley	.15
252	Anthony Wright	.15
253	Chad Pennington	.60
254	David Patten	.15
255	Antonio Freeman	.15
256	Jamel White	.15
257	Jermaine Lewis	.30
258	Aaron Brooks	1.25
259	Ron Dixon	.15
260	James Thrash	.15
261	Junior Seau	.60
262	Byron Chamberlain	.15
263	Ed McCaffrey	.15
264	Nate Clements	.15
265	Tony Martin	.15
266	Germane Crowell	.15
267	Terrell Owens	.60
268	Marshall Faulk	2.00
269	Dat Nguyen	.15
270	Elvis Grbac	.30
271	Dante Hall	.15
272	Sylvester Morris	.60
273	Mike Brown	.15
274	Kevin Johnson	.15
275	Jimmy Smith	.30
276	Randy Moss	3.00
277	Kerry Collins	.30
278	Santana Moss	.60
279	Plaxico Burress	.75
280	Brad Johnson	.30
281	Curtis Conway	.40
282	Eric Johnson	.15
283	Joe Horn	.40
284	Peter Boulware	.15
285	Larry Foster	.15
286	Nate Jacquet	.15
287	Terry Glenn	.60
288	Jarious Jackson	.15
289	Hugh Douglas	.15
290	Chad Lewis	.15
291	Ahman Green	.60
292	Peyton Manning	3.00
293	Kurt Warner	3.00
294	Daunte Culpepper	2.00
295	Tom Brady	3.00
296	Rod Gardner	.50
297	Corey Dillon	.60
298	Priest Holmes	.75
299	Shaun Alexander	.60
300	Randy Moss	3.00
301	Eric Moulds	.40
302	Brett Favre	4.00
303	Todd Bouman	.15
304	Dominic Rhodes	.15
305	Marvin Harrison	.60
306	Torry Holt	.30
307	Derrick Mason	.15
308	Jerry Rice	3.00
309	Donovan McNabb	2.00
310	Marshall Faulk	2.00
311	*David Carr*	5.00
312	*Quentin Jammer*	1.25
313	*Mike Williams*	1.00
314	*Rocky Calmus*	1.25
315	*Travis Fisher*	.50
316	*Dwight Freeney*	.50
317	*Jeremy Shockey*	3.00
318	*Marquise Walker*	1.25
319	*Eric Crouch*	1.50
320	*DeShaun Foster*	1.50
321	*Roy Williams*	2.50
322	*Andre Davis*	1.50
323	*Alex Brown*	.50
324	*Michael Lewis*	1.00
325	*Terry Charles*	.50
326	*Clinton Portis*	5.00
327	*Dennis Johnson*	.50
328	*Lito Sheppard*	1.00
329	*Ryan Sims*	.75
330	*Raonall Smith*	.50
331	*Albert Haynesworth*	.50
332	*Eddie Freeman*	.50
333	*Alex Brown*	.50
334	*Josh McCown*	1.25
335	*Cliff Russell*	.50
336	*Maurice Morris*	1.50
337	*Antwann Randle El*	2.00
338	*Ladell Betts*	1.25
339	*Daniel Graham*	1.25
340	*David Garrard*	.75
341	*Antonio Bryant*	2.00
342	*Patrick Ramsey*	2.00
343	*Kelly Campbell*	.50
344	*Will Overstreet*	1.00
345	*Ryan Denney*	.50
346	*John Henderson*	.75
347	*Freddie Milons*	.50
348	*Tim Carter*	.50
349	*Kurt Kittner*	1.25
350	*Joey Harrington*	4.00
351	*Ricky Williams*	.50
352	*Bryant McKinnie*	1.00
353	*Edward Reed*	.50
354	*Josh Reed*	1.50
355	*Seth Burford*	.50
356	*Javon Walker*	2.50
357	*Jamar Martin*	.50
358	*Leonard Henry*	.75
359	*Julius Peppers*	2.00
360	*Jabar Gaffney*	1.50
361	*Kalimba Edwards*	.50
362	*Napoleon Harris*	.50
363	*Ashley Lelie*	2.00
364	*Anthony Weaver*	.50
365	*Bryan Thomas*	.50
366	*Wendell Bryant*	.75
367	*Damien Anderson*	.75
368	*Travis Stephens*	1.25
369	*Rohan Davey*	1.50
370	*Mike Pearson*	.50
371	*Marc Colombo*	.50
372	*Phillip Buchanon*	1.25
373	*T.J. Duckett*	2.00
374	*Ron Johnson*	1.00
375	*Larry Tripplett*	.75
376	*Randy Fasani*	.50
377	*Keyuo Craver*	.50
378	*Marquand Manuel*	.50
379	*Jonathan Wells*	1.50
380	*Reche Caldwell*	1.50
381	*Luke Staley*	1.25
382	*Donte Stallworth*	2.00
383	*Levar Fisher*	.50
384	*Lamar Gordon*	1.25
385	*William Green*	2.00

2002 Topps MVP Promotion

Stars:	10X-20X
Rookies:	5X-10X

Inserted 1:112 Hobby

2002 Topps Collection

Stars:	.5X-1X
Rookies:	1X

2002 Topps Autographs

		NM/M
Common Player:		8.00
Inserted 1:300		
TA-CC	Chris Chambers	50.00
TA-WJ	Willie Jackson	12.00
TA-RL	Ray Lewis	12.00
TA-DM	Derrick Mason	8.00
TA-QM	Quincy Morgan	20.00
TA-AT	Anthony Thomas	60.00
TA-JT	James Thrash	8.00
TA-LT	LaDainian Tomlinson	50.00

2002 Topps Hobby Masters

		NM/M
Complete Set (10):		40.00
Common Player:		2.00
Inserted 1:9		
HM1	Kurt Warner	6.00
HM2	Tom Brady	5.00
HM3	Marshall Faulk	4.00
HM4	Marvin Harrison	2.00
HM5	Randy Moss	6.00
HM6	Jerome Bettis	2.00
HM7	Jerry Rice	5.00
HM8	Brett Favre	8.00
HM9	Donovan McNabb	2.00
HM10	Curtis Martin	2.00

2002 Topps King of Kings Super Bowl MVP's

Inserted 1:4069

Too uncommon to price at this time

K-ME	Joe Montana, John Elway
K-MJ	Joe Montana, Jerry Rice
K-YR	Steve Young, Jerry Rice
K-DA	Terrell Davis, Marcus Allen

2002 Topps Own The Game

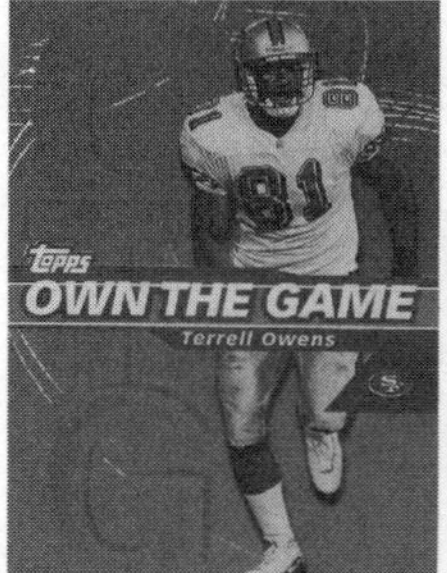

		NM/M
Complete Set (30):		50.00
Common Player:		1.50
Inserted 1:12		
OG1	Kurt Warner	4.00
OG2	Peyton Manning	4.00
OG3	Jeff Garcia	1.50
OG4	Brett Favre	5.00
OG5	Donovan McNabb	2.00
OG6	Rich Gannon	1.50
OG7	Tom Brady	3.00
OG8	Aaron Brooks	1.50
OG9	Priest Holmes	1.50
OG10	Curtis Martin	1.50
OG11	Stephen Davis	1.50
OG12	Ahman Green	2.00
OG13	Marshall Faulk	2.50
OG14	Shaun Alexander	2.50
OG15	Corey Dillon	1.50
OG16	Ricky Williams	1.50
OG17	David Boston	1.50
OG18	Marvin Harrison	1.50
OG19	Terrell Owens	1.50
OG20	Jimmy Smith	1.50
OG21	Torry Holt	1.50
OG22	Rod Smith	1.50
OG23	Keyshawn Johnson	1.50
OG24	Troy Brown	1.50
OG25	Michael Strahan	1.50
OG26	Ronald McKinnon	1.50
OG27	Ray Lewis	1.50
OG28	Zach Thomas	1.50
OG29	Ronde Barber	1.50
OG30	Anthony Henry	1.50

2002 Topps Pro Bowl Jerseys

		NM/M
Common Player:		10.00
Inserted 1:399		
AP-TB	Tom Brady	30.00
AP-TBR	Troy Brown	10.00
AP-JE	Jason Elam	20.00
AP-PH	Priest Holmes	10.00
AP-TH	Torry Holt	10.00
AP-TL	Ty Law	20.00
AP-JL	Jermaine Lewis	10.00
AP-RL	Ray Lewis	15.00
AP-RS	Rod Smith	10.00
AP-AT	Adam Timmerman	10.00

2002 Topps Ring of Honor

		NM/M
Complete Set (36):		75.00
Common Player:		1.00
Inserted 1:9		
BS1	Bart Starr	10.00
BS2	Bart Starr	6.00
JN3	Joe Namath	6.00
LD4	Len Dawson	1.00
CH5	Chuck Howley	1.00
RS6	Roger Staubach	4.00
FH9	Franco Harris	4.00
FB11	Fred Biletnikoff	1.00
RW12	Randy White	1.00
TB13	Terry Bradshaw	5.00
TB14	Terry Bradshaw	5.00
JP15	Jim Plunkett	2.00
JM16	Joe Montana	8.00
JR17	John Riggins	5.00
JM19	Joe Montana	8.00
RD20	Richard Dent	1.00
PS21	Phil Simms	2.00
JR23	Jerry Rice	5.00
JM24	Joe Montana	5.00
OA25	Ottis Anderson	1.00
MR26	Mark Rypien	1.00
TA27	Troy Aikman	4.00
ES28	Emmitt Smith	5.00
SY29	Steve Young	2.00
DH31	Desmond Howard	3.00
TD32	Terrell Davis	2.00
JE33	John Elway	5.00
KW34	Kurt Warner	4.00
RL35	Ray Lewis	1.00
tb36	Tom Brady	5.00

2002 Topps Ring of Honor Autographs

		NM/M
Common Player:		25.00
Inserted 1:598		
RH-TA	Troy Aikman	100.00
RH-OA	Ottis Anderson	40.00
RH-FB	Fred Biletnikoff	50.00
RH-TB	Terry Bradshaw	75.00
RH-TB2	Terry Bradshaw	75.00
RH-TD	Terrell Davis	75.00

Post-1980 cards in Near Mint condition will generally sell for about 75% of the quoted Mint value. Excellent-condition cards bring no more than 40%.

RH-RD	Richard Dent	40.00
RH-RD2	Richard Dent	25.00
RH-JE	John Elway	200.00
RH-FH	Franco Harris	100.00
RH-DH	Desmond Howard	25.00
RH-CH	Chuck Howley	25.00
RH-RL	Ray Lewis	75.00
RH-JM	Joe Montana	200.00
RH-JM2	Joe Montana	200.00
RH-JM3	Joe Montana	200.00
RH-JN	Joe Namath	100.00
RH-JP	Jim Plunkett	40.00
RH-JR	Jerry Rice	175.00
RH-JRI	John Riggins	75.00
RH-MR	Mark Rypien	50.00
RH-PS	Phil Simms	50.00
RH-ES	Emmitt Smith	225.00
RH-BS	Bart Starr	150.00
RH-BS2	Bart Starr	150.00
RH-RS	Roger Staubach	100.00
RH-KW	Kurt Warner	75.00
RH-RW	Randy White	25.00
RH-SY	Steve Young	75.00

2002 Topps Rookie Premier Autographs

		NM/M
Common Player:		30.00
Minor Stars:		40.00
RPLB	Ladell Betts	50.00
PRAB	Antonio Bryant	60.00
RPRC	Reche Caldwell	40.00
RPDC	David Carr	
RPDCH	David Carr, Joey Harrington	
RPTC	Tim Carter	30.00
RPEC	Eric Crouch	60.00
RPRD	Rohan Davey	50.00
RPAD	Andre Davis	50.00
RPTJD	T.J. Duckett	80.00
RPDF	DeShaun Foster	50.00
RPJG	Jabar Gaffney	50.00
RPDGA	David Garrard	40.00
RPDG	Daniel Graham	40.00
RPWG	William Green	80.00
RPDGD	William Green, T.J. Duckett	125.00
RPJH	Joey Harrington	150.00
RPQJ	Quentin Jammer	40.00
RPRJ	Ron Johnson	30.00
RPAL	Ashley Lelie	100.00
RPJM	Josh McCown	80.00
RPMM	Maurice Morris	50.00
RPJP	Julius Peppers	125.00
RPCP	Clinton Portis	200.00
RPPR	Patrick Ramsey	100.00
RPAR	Antwann Randle El	100.00
RPJR	Josh Reed	80.00
RPCR	Cliff Russell	30.00
RPJS	Jeremy Shockey	100.00
RPDS	Donte Stallworth	100.00
RPDSL	Donte Stallworth, Ashley Lelie	150.00
RPTS	Travis Stephens	30.00
RPJW	Javon Walker	100.00
RPMW	Marquise Walker	30.00
RPMWI	Mike Williams	30.00
RPRW	Roy Williams	100.00

2002 Topps Super Bowl Goal Posts

		NM/M
Common Player:		20.00
Inserted 1:410		
Vinateiri Auto Inserted 1:1621		
SBG1	Tom Brady	50.00
SBG2	Kurt Warner	30.00
SBG3	Antowain Smith	20.00
SBG4	Marshall Faulk	20.00
SBG5	Troy Brown	30.00
SBG6	Adam Vinatieri	50.00
SBG7	David Patten	30.00
SBG8	Torry Holt	20.00
SBG9	Ty Law	20.00
SBG10	Isaac Bruce	20.00
SBGAV	Adam Vinitieri Auto	150.00

2002 Topps Super Tix Relics

		NM/M
Common Player:		20.00
Inserted 1:929		
SBT1	Tom Brady	30.00
SBT2	Kurt Warner	30.00
SBT3	Antowain Smith	20.00
SBT4	Marshall Faulk	20.00
SBT5	Troy Brown	20.00
SBT6	Adam Vinatieri	20.00
SBT7	David Patten	20.00
SBT8	Torry Holt	20.00
SBT9	Ty Law	20.00
SBT10	Isaac Bruce	20.00

2002 Topps Terry Bradshaw Reprints

		NM/M
Complete Set (14):		35.00
Common Player:		3.00
Inserted 1:9		
1	Terry Bradshaw	5.00
2	Terry Bradshaw	3.00
3	Terry Bradshaw	3.00
4	Terry Bradshaw	3.00
5	Terry Bradshaw	3.00
6	Terry Bradshaw	3.00
7	Terry Bradshaw	3.00
8	Terry Bradshaw	3.00
9	Terry Bradshaw	3.00
10	Terry Bradshaw	3.00
11	Terry Bradshaw	3.00
12	Terry Bradshaw	3.00
13	Terry Bradshaw	3.00
14	Terry Bradshaw	3.00
1AU	Terry Bradshaw Auto	125.00

2002 Topps Debut

		NM/M
Common Player:		.25
Unlisted Stars:		.75
Minor Stars:		.50
Common Rookie (161-200):		2.00
Inserted 1:3		
Box:		55.00
1	Kurt Warner	2.50
2	James Thrash	.25
3	Aaron Brooks	1.00
4	Mark Brunell	.50
5	Mike Anderson	1.00
6	Benjamin Gay	.25
7	Marvin Harrison	.50
8	Randy Moss	2.50
9	Ron Dayne	.50
10	Tim Brown	.50
11	Vinny Testaverde	.25
12	Mike Alstott	.25
13	Tony Banks	.25
14	Plaxico Burress	.75
15	Chris Chambers	.75
16	Brett Favre	3.00
17	Quincy Carter	1.50
18	Brian Urlacher	2.00
19	Byron Chamberlain	.25
20	Tony Gonzalez	.40
21	Troy Brown	.60
22	Drew Brees	2.00
23	Koren Robinson	.25
24	Donald Hayes	.25
25	Michael Vick	2.50
26	Travis Taylor	.50
27	Peerless Price	.40
28	Chad Johnson	.25
29	Tim Couch	1.00
30	Edgerrin James	2.00
31	Willie Jackson	.25
32	Hines Ward	.25
33	Terrell Owens	.75
34	Eddie George	.75
35	Michael Westbrook	.25
36	Kerry Collins	.50
37	Terrell Davis	1.00
38	Marcus Robinson	.50
39	Charlie Batch	.25
40	Jake Plummer	.50
41	Qadry Ismail	.25
42	Marvin "Snoop" Minnis	.50
43	Jimmy Smith	.25
44	Charlie Garner	.50
45	Jeff Graham	.25
46	Torry Holt	.50
47	Kevin Dyson	.50
48	Maurice Smith	.25
49	Muhsin Muhammad	.25
50	Curtis Martin	.50
51	Todd Pinkston	.25
52	Matt Hasselbeck	.25
53	Corey Dillon	.75
54	Michael Pittman	.25
55	Antonio Freeman	.25
56	Oronde Gadsden	.25
57	Tiki Barber	.25
58	Isaac Bruce	.75
59	Rod Gardner	.50
60	Derrick Mason	.25
61	Joe Horn	.50
62	Antowain Smith	.25
63	Johnnie Morton	.25
64	Kevin Johnson	.25
65	Nick Goings	.25
66	Jason Brookins	.25
67	Travis Henry	.50
68	Brian Griese	.75
69	Priest Holmes	.75
70	Daunte Culpepper	1.50
71	Amani Toomer	.25
72	Rich Gannon	.75
73	Correll Buckhalter	.50
74	Kevan Barlow	.50
75	Stephen Davis	.50
76	Keenan McCardell	.25
77	Jon Kitna	.25
78	Eric Moulds	.50
79	Dez White	.25
80	Raghib Ismail	.25
81	Dominic Rhodes	.25
82	Lamar Smith	.75
83	David Patten	.25
84	Duce Staley	.75
85	Curtis Conway	.25
86	Kordell Stewart	.50
87	Brad Johnson	.50
88	Wayne Chrebet	.25
89	Michael Bennett	.75
90	Quincy Morgan	.75
91	Steve Smith	.25
92	David Boston	.50
93	Shannon Sharpe	.50
94	Mike McMahon	.75
95	Stacey Mack	.25
96	Santana Moss	.50
97	Jeff Garcia	.75
98	Keyshawn Johnson	.50
99	Rod Smith	.50
100	Jerome Bettis	.50
101	LaDainian Tomlinson	2.00
102	Warrick Dunn	.50
103	Ray Lewis	.50
104	Chris Chandler	.25
105	Jim Miller	.25
106	Ahman Green	.75
107	Jay Fiedler	.25
108	Tom Brady	2.50
109	Michael Strahan	.25
110	James Jackson	.50
111	Rob Johnson	.25
112	Elvis Grbac	.25
113	Troy Hambrick	.25
114	Corey Bradford	.25
115	Trent Green	.50
116	Cris Carter	.50
117	Chris Fuamatu-Ma'afala	.25
118	Chris Weinke	.60
119	MarTay Jenkins	.50
120	Laveranues Coles	.25
121	Donovan McNabb	1.50
122	Jerry Rice	2.50
123	Garrison Hearst	.40
124	Steve McNair	.75
125	Trung Canidate	.25
126	Doug Flutie	.75
127	Ricky Williams	.25
128	Peyton Manning	2.50
129	Kevin Kasper	.25
130	Emmitt Smith	2.50
131	Peter Warrick	.50
132	Anthony Thomas	2.00
133	Ike Hilliard	.25
134	Kendrell Bell	.40
135	Shaun Alexander	.75
136	Wesley Walls	.25
137	Gerard Warren	.25
138	James Stewart	.50
139	Drew Bledsoe	1.50
140	Fred Taylor	.50
141	Marshall Faulk	1.50
142	Marcus Pollard	.25
143	Bill Schroeder	.25
144	Marty Booker	.40
145	Amos Zereoue	.25
146	Darrell Jackson	.25
147	Brian Finneran	.25
148	Alex Van Pelt	.25
149	Andre Carter	.25
150	Joey Galloway	.25
151	*Joey Harrington Auto*	50.00
152	*Andre Davis Auto*	25.00
153	*Eric Crouch Auto*	15.00
154	*Kelly Campbell Auto*	12.00
155	*Ron Johnson Auto*	12.00
156	*David Carr JSY*	50.00
157	*Kurt Kittner JSY*	10.00
158	*Javon Walker JSY*	25.00
159	*DeShaun Foster JSY*	12.00
160	*Lamar Gordon JSY*	10.00
161	*Antwann Randle El*	8.00
162	*Clinton Portis*	15.00
163	*Luke Staley*	3.00
164	*Daniel Graham*	3.00
165	*Ashley Lelie*	8.00
166	*Ladell Betts*	4.00
167	*Rocky Calmus*	2.00
168	*Ryan Sims*	2.00
169	*Jeremy Shockey*	10.00
170	*Damien Anderson*	2.00
171	*Bryant McKinnie*	2.00
172	*Kahlil Hill*	2.00
173	*John Henderson*	2.00
174	*Donte Stallworth*	6.00
175	*Kalimba Edwards*	2.00
176	*Freddie Milons*	2.00
177	*Antonio Bryant*	5.00
178	*Cliff Russell*	2.00
179	*T.J. Duckett*	5.00
180	*Roy Williams*	8.00
181	*Patrick Ramsey*	6.00
182	*Josh Reed*	4.00
183	*Wendell Bryant*	2.00
184	*Jabar Gaffney*	4.00
185	*Napoleon Harris*	2.00
186	*Adrian Peterson*	3.00
187	*David Garrard*	4.00
188	*Levar Fisher*	2.00
189	*Quentin Jammer*	3.00
190	*Anthony Weaver*	2.00
191	*Dwight Freeney*	4.00
192	*Donald Reche Caldwell*	3.00
193	*Larry Tripplett*	2.00
194	*Rohan Davey*	5.00
195	*Marquise Walker*	2.00
196	*William Green*	5.00
197	*Tracey Wistrom*	2.00
198	*Alan Harper*	2.00
199	*Lito Sheppard*	2.00
200	*Albert Haynesworth*	2.00

2002 Topps Debut Red

Stars:	3X-6X
151-155 Rookie Autos:	1X-2X

156-160 Rookie JSY:	1X-2X
161-200 Rookies:	1.5X-3X
Production 199 Sets	

2002 Topps Debut All-Star Material

		NM/M
Common Player:		5.00
Inserted 1:14		
Gold Production 25 Sets		
		NM/M
AM-AA	Akin Ayodele	10.00
AM-RC	Rocky Calmus	10.00
AM-KC	Kenyon Coleman	10.00
AM-RD	Rohan Davey	10.00
AM-AD	Andra Davis	10.00
AM-BF	Bryan Fletcher	
AM-DG	David Garrard	10.00
AM-DGR	Daniel Graham	12.00
AM-NH	Napoleon Harris	10.00
AM-CH	Chris Hope	10.00
AM-RJ	Ron Johnson	10.00
AM-JMC	Jason McAddley	10.00
AM-FM	Freddie Milons	12.00
AM-AP	Adrian Peterson	15.00
AM-PR	Patrick Ramsey	20.00
AM-AR	Antwann Randle El	30.00
AM-CR	Cliff Russell	10.00
AM-RS	Ryan Sims	10.00
AM-BT	Bryan Thomas	10.00
AM-MW	Marquise Walker	15.00
AM-AW	Anthony Weaver	10.00
AM-BW	Brian Westbrook	15.00
AM-TW	Tracey Wistrom	12.00

2002 Topps Debut Collegiate Classics

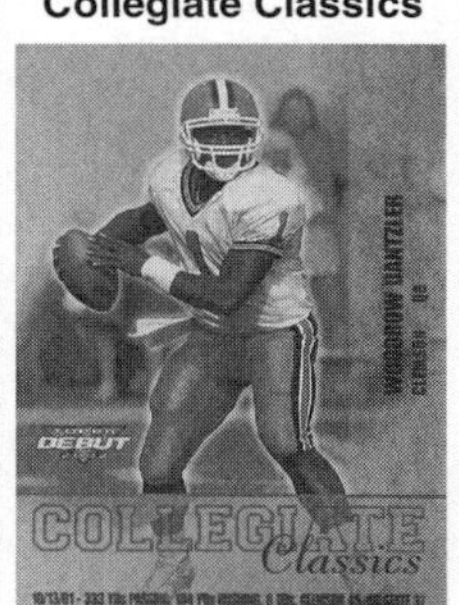

		NM/M
Common Player:		2.00
Inserted 1:12		
CC1	*Randy Moss*	5.00
CC2	Antonio Bryant	4.00
CC3	David Carr	8.00
CC4	William Green	6.00
CC5	Eric Crouch	7.00
CC6	Jabar Gaffney	3.00
CC7	Andre Davis	3.00
CC8	Joey Harrington	7.00
CC9	T.J. Duckett	6.00
CC10	Josh Reed	4.00
CC11	DeShaun Foster	4.00
CC12	Kurt Kittner	3.00
CC13	Marquise Walker	3.00
CC14	Clinton Portis	3.00
CC15	Woodrow Dantzler III	2.00
CC16	David Boston	3.00
CC17	Donovan McNabb	3.00
CC18	Peyton Manning	4.00
CC19	Keyshawn Johnson	2.00

2002 Topps Debut Dynamite Debuts

		NM/M
Common Player:		1.00
Inserted 1:8		
DD1	Anthony Thomas	5.00
DD2	Kendrell Bell	1.00
DD3	LaDainian Tomlinson	4.00
DD4	Chris Chambers	4.00
DD5	Travis Henry	1.00
DD6	Chris Weinke	2.00
DD7	Koren Robinson	1.00
DD8	James Jackson	1.00
DD9	Dominic Rhodes	1.00
DD10	Michael Bennett	4.00
DD11	Correll Buckhalter	2.00
DD12	Rod Gardner	2.00
DD13	Kevan Barlow	1.00
DD14	Michael Vick	4.00
DD15	Mike Anderson	1.00
DD16	Brian Urlacher	3.00
DD17	Jamal Lewis	2.00
DD18	Ron Dayne	1.50
DD19	Darrell Jackson	1.00
DD20	Sylvester Morris	1.00

2002 Topps Debut Heads of Class

		NM/M
Common Player:		20.00
Inserted 1:319		
Gold/25:		1.5X-3X
HC-DO	Stephen Davis, Terrell Owens	30.00
HC-FD	Antonio Freeman, Terrell Davis	30.00
HC-JT	Keyshawn Johnson, Zach Thomas	25.00
HC-SD	Warren Sapp, Terrell Davis	20.00
HC-TB	LaDainian Tomlinson, Drew Brees	40.00

2002 Topps Heritage

		NM/M
Complete Set (194):		250.00
Common Player:		.20
Unlisted Stars:		.50
Minor Stars:		.30
Common Rookie (155-194):		2.00
Minor Rookie Stars:		3.00
28 cards have a variation-black football		
Black football variation:		2X to4X
Pack (8):		4.00
Wax Box (24):		70.00
1	Jerome Bettis	.50
2	Jeff Blake SP	.20
3	Rod Smith	.40
4	Eric Moulds	.20
5	Michael Vick	4.00
6	Randy Moss	4.00
7	Todd Pinkston	.20
8	Trung Canidate SP	.20
9	Steve McNair	1.00
10	J.J. Stokes SP	.20
11	Ricky Williams	2.50
12	Germane Crowell SP	.20
13	Muhsin Muhammad SP	.50
14	Michael Pittman SP	.20
15	James Jackson SP	.40
16	Dominic Rhodes	.20
17	Jay Fiedler	.50
18	Marcus Robinson	.40
19	Qadry Ismail SP	.20
20	Michael Strahan	.40
21	Koren Robinson	.40
22	James Allen SP	.20
23	Chad Pennington	.50
24	Fred Taylor	.60
25	Corey Dillon	1.00
26	Thomas Jones SP	.20
27	Anthony Thomas	3.00
28	Priest Holmes	1.00
29	Troy Brown	1.00
30	Jerry Rice	4.00
31	Correll Buckhalter	.20
32	Drew Brees	3.00
33	Isaac Bruce	.40
34	Warrick Dunn SP	.40
35	Chris Chambers	1.00
36	Antonio Freeman	.20
37	Joey Galloway SP	.50
38	Rob Johnson SP	.50
39	Reggie Wayne	.75
40	Santana Moss	.40
41	Plaxico Burress	1.00
42	Frank Wycheck SP	.20
43	Johnnie Morton	.20
44	Chris Weinke	1.00
45	Raghib Ismail SP	.20
46	Daunte Culpepper	2.50
47	Deuce McAllister SP	2.00
48	Terrell Owens	1.00
49	Michael Westbrook	.20
50	Tom Brady	4.00
51	Mike Anderson	2.00
52	Jake Plummer	.50
53	Travis Taylor SP	.50
54	Marcus Pollard SP	.40
55	Zach Thomas	.40
56	Duce Staley	.60
57	Trent Dilfer	.20
58	Keyshawn Johnson	.40
59	Amani Toomer SP	.20
60	David Terrell	1.00
61	Robert Ferguson SP	.20
62	Jeff Garcia	1.00
63	Eddie George	1.00
64	Marshall Faulk	2.00
65	Travis Henry	.75
66	Tim Couch	2.00
67	Mike McMahon	1.00
68	John Abraham SP	.20
69	James Thrash	.20
70	Shaun Alexander	1.00
71	Ike Hilliard SP	.20
72	Brian Griese	1.00
73	Ray Lewis	.50
74	Jon Kitna	.20
75	Az-Zahir Hakim SP	.60
76	Oronde Gadsden SP	.20
77	Joe Horn	.20
78	Tim Brown	.60
79	Kendrell Bell	.20
80	LaDainian Tomlinson	3.00
81	Brad Johnson	.50
82	Tony Gonzalez	.50
83	Bill Schroeder	.20
84	Quincy Carter	2.50
85	Donald Hayes SP	.20
86	Peyton Manning	4.00
87	Drew Bledsoe	2.50
88	Darrell Jackson	.20
89	Rod Gardner	.20
90	Derrick Mason	.50
91	Byron Chamberlain SP	.20
92	James McKnight SP	.20
93	Kevin Johnson	.20
94	Terry Glenn	.60
95	Marty Booker SP	.20
96	Terrell Davis	2.00
97	Vinny Testaverde	.20
98	Hines Ward	.40
99	Chad Lewis SP	.20
100	Kurt Warner	3.00
101	Michael Bennett	1.00
102	Edgerrin James	3.00
103	Corey Bradford SP	.20
104	Chad Johnson SP	.20
105	Alex Van Pelt	.20
106	Antowain Smith	.20
107	Rich Gannon	.60
108	Kevan Barlow SP	.20
109	Mike Alstott SP	.40
110	Kerry Collins SP	.40
111	Jimmy Smith	.20
112	Jermaine Lewis SP	.20
113	Quincy Morgan SP	.40
114	Maurice Smith SP	.20
115	Willie Jackson	.20
116	Doug Flutie	1.00
117	Matt Hasselbeck	.20
118	Amos Zereoue SP	.20
119	Lamar Smith	.60
120	Marvin "Snoop" Minnis	.50
121	Troy Hambrick SP	.20
122	Shannon Sharpe SP	.50
123	Laveranues Coles	.50
124	Freddie Mitchell	.50
125	Kevin Dyson SP	.20
126	Torry Holt	.20
127	James Stewart SP	.50
128	Brian Urlacher	3.00
129	David Boston	.60
130	Ron Dayne	.40
131	Garrison Hearst	.40
132	Stephen Davis	.75
133	Donovan McNabb	2.50
134	David Patten	.20
135	Travis Minor SP	.40
136	Peerless Price SP	.60
137	Chris Redman SP	.20
138	Ahman Green	1.00
139	Mark Brunell	1.00
140	Charlie Garner	.20
141	Curtis Conway	.20
142	Wayne Chrebet	.20
143	Kordell Stewart	.40
144	Peter Warrick	.40
145	Emmitt Smith	4.00
146	Jim Miller SP	.20
147	Trent Green	.40
148	Cris Carter	.40
149	Aaron Brooks	2.00
150	Curtis Martin	.40
151	Tiki Barber SP	.20
152	Marvin Harrison	.60
153	Tyrone Wheatley SP	.40
154	Brett Favre	5.00
155	*David Carr*	15.00
156	*Quentin Jammer*	4.00
157	*Julius Peppers*	5.00
158	*Mike Williams*	2.00
159	*Antwann Randle El*	5.00
160	*Joey Harrington*	12.00
161	*Ashley Lelie*	6.00
162	*Marquise Walker*	4.00
163	*Rohan Davey*	5.00
164	*Patrick Ramsey*	6.00
165	*T.J. Duckett*	6.00
166	*DeShaun Foster*	6.00
167	*Donte Stallworth*	6.00
168	*William Green*	5.00
169	*Ron Johnson*	3.00
170	*Maurice Morris*	5.00
171	*Travis Stephens*	4.00
172	*Eric Crouch*	4.00
173	*David Garrard*	2.00
174	*Daniel Graham*	4.00
175	*Roy Williams*	8.00
176	*Jeremy Shockey*	10.00
177	*Josh McCown*	4.00
178	*Josh Reed*	5.00
179	*Andre Davis*	5.00
180	*Antonio Bryant*	6.00
181	*Clinton Portis*	15.00
182	*Javon Walker*	8.00
183	*Jabar Gaffney*	5.00
184	*Ladell Betts*	4.00
185	*Tim Carter*	2.00
186	*Donald Reche Caldwell*	4.00
187	*Cliff Russell*	2.00
188	*Brian Westbrook SP*	8.00
189	*Freddie Milons*	2.00
190	*Phillip Buchanon*	4.00
191	*Lamar Gordon*	4.00
192	*Luke Staley*	4.00
193	*Albert Haynesworth*	3.00
194	*Kurt Kittner*	4.00

2002 Topps Heritage Retrofractors

Stars:	3X-6X
SPs:	2X-4X
Production 557 Sets	

2002 Topps Heritage Classic Renditions

		NM/M
Complete Set (10):		25.00
Common Player:		3.00
Inserted 1:6		
CR-KB	Kendrell Bell	3.00
CR-DB	David Boston	4.00
CR-MF	Marshall Faulk	5.00
CR-TH	Torry Holt	3.00
CR-EJ	Edgerrin James	4.00
CR-PM	Peyton Manning	5.00
CR-KS	Kordell Stewart	3.00
CR-MS	Michael Strahan	3.00
CR-AT	Anthony Thomas	5.00
CR-KW	Kurt Warner	5.00

2002 Topps Heritage Classic Renditions Autographs

Production 25 sets
CRA-KB Kendrell Bell
CRA-AT Anthony Thomas
CRA-KW Kurt Warner

2002 Topps Heritage Hall of Fame Autographs

		NM/M
Inserted 1:8337 Hobby		
HOF-DC	Dave Casper	50.00
HOF-DH	Dan Hampton	100.00
HOF-JK	Jim Kelly	150.00
HOF-JS	John Stallworth	50.00

2002 Topps Heritage Gridiron Collection

		NM/M
Common Player:		10.00
Inserted 1:64		
Foil Production 25 Sets		
GC-JA	John Abraham	10.00
GC-RB	Ronde Barber	10.00
GC-TC	Tim Couch	20.00
GC-GC	Bubba Franks	20.00
GC-EG	Eddie George	15.00
GC-KJ	Keyshawn Johnson	12.00
GC-JK	Jevon Kearse	12.00
GC-OK	Olin Kreutz	10.00
GC-CM	Curtis Martin	20.00
GC-JN	Joe Namath	75.00
GC-TO	Terrell Owens	12.00
GC-ES	Emmitt Smith	50.00
GC-JT	Jeremiah Trottier	10.00

2002 Topps Heritage New Age Performers

		NM/M
Complete Set (15):		45.00
Common Player:		3.00
Inserted 1:8		
NAP1	Donovan McNabb	3.00
NAP2	Kurt Warner	6.00
NAP3	Brett Favre	10.00
NAP4	Peyton Manning	6.00
NAP5	Stephen Davis	4.00
NAP6	Terrell Owens	3.00
NAP7	Anthony Thomas	6.00
NAP8	Jeff Garcia	3.00
NAP9	Marshall Faulk	4.00
NAP10	Edgerrin James	5.00
NAP11	David Boston	3.00
NAP12	Tim Couch	3.00
NAP13	Chris Chambers	5.00
NAP14	Marvin Harrison	3.00
NAP15	Curtis Martin	3.00

2002 Topps Heritage 1957 Topps Reprints

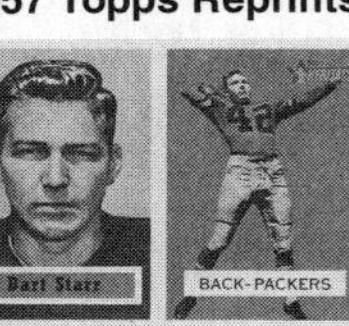

		NM/M
Complete Set (10):		35.00
Common Player:		4.00
Inserted 1:6		
R-CB	Chuck Bednarik	4.00
R-RB	Raymond Berry	4.00
R-GB	George Blanda	4.00
R-AD	Art Donovan	4.00
R-PH	Paul Hornung	8.00
R-GM	Gino Marchetti	4.00
R-TM	Tommy McDonald	4.00
R-BS	Bart Starr	10.00
R-PS	Pat Summerall	8.00
R-YT	Y.A. Tittle	5.00

2002 Topps Heritage Real One Autographs

		NM/M
Common Player:		20.00
Inserted 1:199		
Real One special		
Production 57 sets		
HR-JA	John Abraham	20.00
HR-CB	Chuck Bednarik	
HR-KB	Kendrell Bell	20.00
HR-PB	Raymond Berry	20.00
HR-GB	George Blanda	
HR-MB	Marty Booker	20.00
HR-DB	David Boston	20.00
HR-TB	Tom Brady	50.00
HR-AD	Art Donovan	30.00
HR-GH	Garrison Hearst	20.00
HR-PHO	Priest Holmes	20.00
HR-PH	Paul Hornung	75.00
HR-GM	Gino Marchetti	
HR-TM	Tommy McDonald	20.00
HR-DR	Dominic Rhodes	20.00
HR-BS	Bart Starr	175.00
HR-PS	Pat Summerall	
HR-AT	Anthony Thomas	40.00
HR-YT	Y.A. Tittle	25.00
HR-HW	Hines Ward	20.00

2002 Topps Chrome

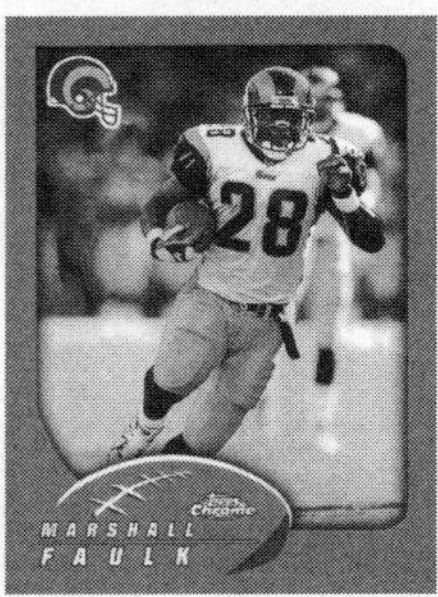

		NM/M
Complete Set (265):		550.00
Common Player:		.25
Unlisted Stars:		.75
Minor Stars:		.50
Minor Rookie Star (166-265):		3.00
All Rookies Feature Refractor Fronts		
Pack (4):		4.75
Wax Box (24):		80.00
1	Anthony Thomas	2.50
2	Jake Plummer	.50
3	Maurice Smith	.25
4	Jamal Lewis	.25
5	Ray Lewis	.40
6	Alex Van Pelt	.25
7	Chris Weinke	.75
8	Corey Dillon	.25
9	Quincy Morgan	.40
10	Raghib Ismail	.25
11	Brian Griese	.75
12	Johnnie Morton	.25
13	Edgerrin James	2.50
14	Keenan McCardell	.25
15	Travis Minor	.25
16	Sylvester Morris	.25
17	Randy Moss	3.00
18	Drew Bledsoe	2.00
19	Willie Jackson	.25
20	Michael Strahan	.25
21	Santana Moss	.25
22	Duce Staley	.50
23	Kendrell Bell	.25
24	LaDainian Tomlinson	2.50
25	Terrell Owens	.60
26	Shaun Alexander	.60
27	Trung Canidate	.25
28	Mike Alstott	.40
29	Kevin Dyson	.25
30	Rod Gardner	.40
31	David Boston	.60
32	Michael Vick	3.00
33	Qadry Ismail	.25
34	Peerless Price	.40
35	Rob Johnson	.40
36	Marcus Robinson	.40
37	Peter Warrick	.60
38	Kevin Johnson	.25
39	Ed McCaffrey	.40
40	Shaun Rogers	.25
41	Marvin Harrison	.75
42	Priest Holmes	.75
43	Oronde Gadsden	.25
44	Terry Glenn	.40
45	Ike Hilliard	.25
46	Charles Woodson	.40
47	Freddie Mitchell	.50
48	Drew Brees	2.50
49	Jeff Garcia	.75
50	Kurt Warner	2.00
51	Keyshawn Johnson	.60
52	Jevon Kearse	.25
53	Stephen Davis	.50
54	Shannon Sharpe	.40
55	Eric Moulds	.40
56	Muhsin Muhammad	.25
57	Brian Urlacher	2.50
58	Chad Johnson	.25
59	Tim Couch	1.25
60	Mike Anderson	1.25
61	James Stewart	.50
62	Corey Bradford	.60
63	Reggie Wayne	.50
64	Mark Brunell	.75
65	Trent Green	.50
66	Zach Thomas	.40
67	Michael Bennett	.75
68	Troy Brown	.25
69	Amani Toomer	.25
70	Curtis Martin	.50
71	Tim Brown	.75
72	Correll Buckhalter	.25
73	Kordell Stewart	.50
74	Junior Seau	.40
75	Kevan Barlow	.25
76	Matt Hasselbeck	.25
77	Marshall Faulk	2.00
78	Warren Sapp	.40
79	Frank Wycheck	.25
80	Michael Westbrook	.25
81	Travis Henry	.50
82	David Terrell	.75
83	Jon Kitna	.25
84	James Jackson	.40
85	Joey Galloway	.40
86	Rod Smith	.40
87	Germane Crowell	.25
88	Bill Schroeder	.25
89	Dominic Rhodes	.25
90	Fred Taylor	.40
91	Marvin "Snoop" Minnis	.40
92	Chris Chambers	.25
93	Daunte Culpepper	2.00
94	Deuce McAllister	1.25
95	Kerry Collins	.40
96	John Abraham	.25
97	Rich Gannon	.40
98	Tiki Barber	.40
99	Hines Ward	.40
100	Tom Brady	3.00
101	Tim Dwight	.25
102	Garrison Hearst	.40
103	Darrell Jackson	.25
104	Isaac Bruce	.40
105	Brad Johnson	.40
106	Steve McNair	.75
107	Champ Bailey	.40
108	Emmitt Smith	3.00
109	Mike McMahon	.75
110	Terrell Davis	.60
111	Antonio Freeman	.25
112	Jimmy Smith	.40
113	Tony Gonzalez	.40
114	Jay Fiedler	.50
115	Cris Carter	.40
116	David Patten	.40
117	Joe Horn	.25
118	Laveranues Coles	.40
119	Charlie Garner	.40
120	Donovan McNabb	2.00
121	Jerome Bettis	.50
122	Curtis Conway	.40
123	Az-Zahir Hakim	.40
124	Warrick Dunn	.40
125	Eddie George	.75
126	Quincy Carter	2.00
127	Ahman Green	.75
128	Peyton Manning	3.00
129	James McKnight	.25
130	Antowain Smith	.25
131	Ricky Williams	2.00
132	Chad Pennington	.75
133	Jerry Rice	3.00
134	Todd Pinkston	.25
135	Plaxico Burress	.75
136	Doug Flutie	.75
137	Koren Robinson	.40
138	Torry Holt	.40
139	Aaron Brooks	1.25
140	Ron Dayne	.40
141	Vinny Testaverde	.40
142	Brett Favre	4.00
143	James Thrash	.25
144	Wayne Chrebet	.25
145	Derrick Mason	.25
146	Ahman Green	.75
147	Peyton Manning	3.00
148	Kurt Warner	3.00
149	Daunte Culpepper	1.50
150	Tom Brady	3.00
151	Rod Gardner	.40
152	Corey Dillon	.40
153	Priest Holmes	.75
154	Shaun Alexander	.75
155	Randy Moss	3.00
156	Eric Moulds	.40
157	Brett Favre	4.00
158	Todd Bouman	.40
159	Dominic Rhodes	.50
160	Marvin Harrison	.50
161	Torry Holt	.40
162	Derrick Mason	.40
163	Jerry Rice	3.00
164	Donovan McNabb	2.00
165	Marshall Faulk	1.50
166	*David Carr*	40.00
167	*Quentin Jammer*	6.00
168	*Mike Williams*	3.00
169	*Rocky Calmus*	5.00
170	*Travis Fisher*	4.00
171	*Dwight Freeney*	10.00
172	*Jeremy Shockey*	25.00
173	*Marquise Walker*	8.00
174	*Eric Crouch*	10.00
175	*DeShaun Foster*	12.00
176	*Roy Williams*	20.00
177	*Andre Davis*	10.00
178	*Alex Brown*	4.00
179	*Michael Lewis*	3.00
180	*Terry Charles*	3.00
181	*Clinton Portis*	40.00
182	*Dennis Johnson*	3.00
183	*Lito Sheppard*	5.00
184	*Ryan Sims*	5.00
185	*Raonall Smith*	3.00
186	*Albert Haynesworth*	3.00
187	*Eddie Freeman*	3.00
188	*Levi Jones*	3.00
189	*Josh McCown*	12.00
190	*Cliff Russell*	3.00
191	*Maurice Morris*	10.00
192	*Antwann Randle El*	8.00
193	*Ladell Betts*	8.00
194	*Daniel Graham*	8.00
195	*David Garrard*	6.00
196	*Antonio Bryant*	12.00
197	*Patrick Ramsey*	15.00
198	*Kelly Campbell*	6.00
199	*Will Overstreet*	4.00
200	*Ryan Denney*	4.00
201	*John Henderson*	4.00
202	*Freddie Milons*	5.00
203	*Tim Carter*	4.00
204	*Kurt Kittner*	8.00
205	*Joey Harrington*	30.00
206	*Ricky Williams*	5.00
207	*Bryant McKinnie*	5.00
208	*Edward Reed*	10.00
209	*Josh Reed*	10.00
210	*Seth Burford*	3.00
211	*Javon Walker*	20.00
212	*Jamar Martin*	3.00
213	*Leonard Henry*	3.00
214	*Julius Peppers*	12.00
215	*Jabar Gaffney*	10.00
216	*Kalimba Edwards*	3.00
217	*Napoleon Harris*	3.00
218	*Ashley Lelie*	15.00
219	*Anthony Weaver*	3.00
220	*Bryan Thomas*	3.00
221	*Wendell Bryant*	4.00
222	*Damien Anderson*	3.00
223	*Travis Stephens*	8.00
224	*Rohan Davey*	10.00
225	*Mike Pearson*	3.00
226	*Marc Colombo*	3.00
227	*Phillip Buchanon*	8.00
228	*T.J. Duckett*	15.00
229	*Ron Johnson*	5.00
230	*Larry Tripplett*	3.00
231	*Randy Fasani*	5.00
232	*Keyuo Craver*	3.00
233	*Marquand Manuel*	3.00
234	*Jonathan Wells*	8.00
235	*Reche Caldwell*	8.00
236	*Luke Staley*	8.00
237	*Donte Stallworth*	15.00
238	*Levar Fisher*	3.00
239	*Lamar Gordon*	8.00
240	*William Green*	15.00
241	*Dusty Bonner*	3.00
242	*Craig Nall*	8.00
243	*Eric McCoo*	3.00
244	*David Thornton*	3.00
245	*Terry Jones*	3.00
246	*Lee Mays*	3.00
247	*Bryan Fletcher*	3.00
248	*Verron Haynes*	5.00
249	*Zak Kustok*	5.00
250	*Chad Hutchinson*	5.00
251	*Andra Davis*	3.00
252	*Wes Pate*	5.00
253	*Jon McGraw*	3.00
254	*Howard Green*	3.00
255	*Daryl Jones*	3.00
256	*David Priestly*	3.00
257	*Marques Anderson*	3.00
258	*Roosevelt Williams*	3.00
259	*Major Applewhite*	5.00
260	*Ronald Curry*	10.00
261	*Adrian Peterson*	8.00
262	*Tellis Redmon*	3.00
263	*Chester Taylor*	3.00
264	*Deion Branch*	20.00
265	*Tank Williams*	4.00

2002 Topps Chrome Refractors

Stars:	3X-6X
Rookies:	1.5X-3X
1-165 Production 599 Sets	
166-265 Production 100 Sets	

2002 Topps Chrome Gridiron Badges

		NM/M
Common Player:		25.00
Inserted 1:392		
GB-DB	David Boston/200	15.00
GB-TB	Tom Brady/200	40.00
GB-TBR	Tim Brown/100	40.00
GB-DC	David Carr/50	200.00
GB-MF	MarshallFaulk/50	50.00
GB-BF	Brett Favre/200	100.00
GB-DF	Doug Flutie/100	20.00
GB-DFO	DeShaun Foster/100	40.00
GB-JG	Jeff Garcia/100	15.00
GB-MH	Marvin Harrison/200	10.00
GB-RL	Ray Lewis/200	15.00
GB-DM	Dan Marino/200	100.00
GB-CM	Curtis Martin/200	35.00
GB-TO	Terrell Owens/100	30.00
GB-JR	Jerry Rice/150	40.00
GB-ES	Emmitt Smith/10	
GB-KS	Kordell Stewart/100	20.00
GB-MS	MichaelStrahan/200	15.00
GB-LT	LaDainian Tomlinson/50	25.00
GB-MW	Marquise Walker/50	25.00
GB-KW	Kurt Warner/200	40.00
GB-SY	Steve Young/100	40.00

2002 Topps Chrome King of Kings Super Bowl MVP's

		NM/M
Inserted 1:3643		
K-MR	Joe Montana, John Elway/50	225.00
K-MJ	Joe Montana, Jerry Rice/50	400.00
K-YR	Steve Young, Jerry Rice/100	125.00
K-DA	Terrell Davis, Marcus Allen	40.00

2002 Topps Chrome Pro Bowl Jerseys

		NM/M
Common Player:		8.00
Insereted 1:109		
PP-RB	Ruben Brown	8.00
PP-LC	Larry Centers	8.00
PP-BD	Brian Dawkins	8.00
PP-LG	La'Roi Glover	8.00
PP-RH	Rodney Harrison	8.00
PP-SK	Sammy Knight	10.00
PP-JM	Jamir Miller	8.00
PP-DO	Deltha O'Neal	8.00
PP-RP	Robert Porcher	8.00
PP-AW	Aeneas Williams	12.00

2002 Topps Chrome Own The Game

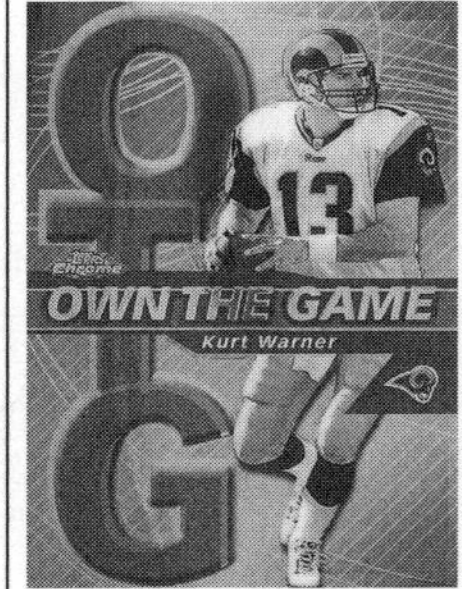

		NM/M
Common Player:		1.00
Inserted 1:8		
Refractors		1.5X-3X
Production 100 sets		
OG1	Kurt Warner	2.00
OG2	Peyton Manning	2.00
OG3	Jeff Garcia	1.00
OG4	Brett Favre	3.00
OG5	Donovan McNabb	1.00
OG6	Rich Gannon	1.00
OG7	Tom Brady	3.00
OG8	Aaron Brooks	1.00
OG9	Priest Holmes	1.00
OG10	Curtis Martin	1.00
OG11	Stephen Davis	1.00
OG12	Ahman Green	1.00
OG13	Marshall Faulk	2.00
OG14	Shaun Alexander	1.00
OG15	Corey Dillon	1.00
OG16	Ricky Williams	1.00
OG17	David Boston	1.00
OG18	Marvin Harrison	1.00
OG19	Terrell Owens	1.00
OG20	Jimmy Smith	1.00
OG21	Torry Holt	1.00
OG22	Rod Smith	1.00
OG23	Keyshawn Johnson	1.00
OG24	Troy Brown	1.00
OG25	Michael Strahan	1.00
OG26	Ronald McKinnon	1.00
OG27	Ray Lewis	1.00
OG28	Zach Thomas	1.00
OG29	Ronde Barber	1.00
OG30	Anthony Henry	1.00

A card number in parenthese ( ) indicates the set is unnumbered.

2002 Topps Chrome Ring of Honor

		NM/M
Common Player:		2.00
Inserted 1:8		
Refractors		1.5X-3X
Production 100 Sets		
BS1	Bart Starr	3.00
BS2	Bart Starr	3.00
JN3	Joe Namath	3.00
LD4	Len Dawson	2.00
CH5	Chuck Howley	2.00
RS6	Roger Staubach	2.00
JS7	Jake Scott	2.00
LC8	Larry Csonka	2.00
FH9	Franco Harris	2.00
FB11	Fred Biletnikoff	2.00
RW12	Randy White	2.00
TB13	Terry Bradshaw	3.00
TB14	Terry Bradshaw	3.00
JP15	Jim Plunkett	2.00
JM16	Joe Montana	5.00
JR17	John Riggins	2.00
MA18	Marcus Allen	2.00
JM19	Joe Montana	4.00
RD20	Richard Dent	2.00
PS21	Phil Simms	2.00
DW22	Doug Williams	2.00
JR23	Jerry Rice	2.00
JM24	Joe Montana	4.00
OA25	Ottis Anderson	2.00
MR26	Mark Rypien	2.00
TA27	Troy Aikman	2.00
ES28	Emmitt Smith	2.00
SY29	Steve Young	2.00
LB30	Larry Brown	2.00
DH31	Desmond Howard	2.00
TD32	Terrell Davis	2.00
JE33	John Elway	4.00
KW34	Kurt Warner	2.00
RL35	Ray Lewis	2.00
TB36	Tom Brady	3.00

2002 Topps Chrome Super Bowl Goal Posts

		NM/M
Common Player:		
Inserted 1:437		
SBG1	Tom Brady	35.00
SBG2	Kurt Warner	35.00
SBG3	Antowain Smith	20.00
SBG4	Marshall Faulk	25.00
SBG5	Troy Brown	20.00
SBG6	Adam Vinatieri	35.00
SBG7	David Patten	25.00
SBG8	Torry Holt	15.00
SBG9	Ty Law	25.00
SBG10	Isaac Bruce	20.00

2002 Topps Chrome Terry Bradshaw Reprints

		NM/M
Common Player:		3.00
Refractor		1.5X-3X
Production 100 Sets		
Black Bordered Refractor		5X-10X
Production 25 Sets		
1	Terry Bradshaw	5.00
2	Terry Bradshaw	3.00
3	Terry Bradshaw	3.00
4	Terry Bradshaw	3.00
5	Terry Bradshaw	3.00
6	Terry Bradshaw	3.00
7	Terry Bradshaw	3.00
8	Terry Bradshaw	3.00
9	Terry Bradshaw	3.00
10	Terry Bradshaw	3.00
11	Terry Bradshaw	3.00
12	Terry Bradshaw	3.00
13	Terry Bradshaw	3.00
14	Terry Bradshaw	3.00

2002 Topps Gallery

NM/M
Complete Set (200): 100.00
Common Player: .20
Unlisted Stars: .75
Minor Stars: .50
Rookie variation 1:12 1X to 3X
Common Rookie (151-200): 1.00
Minor Rookie Stars: 1.50
Pack (6): 2.75
Wax Box (24): 45.00
1 Marshall Faulk 1.50
2 Mark Brunell .75
3 Jeff Garcia .75
4 David Terrell .75
5 Curtis Martin .50
6 Terrell Davis 1.00
7 Jake Plummer .40
8 Eric Moulds .40
9 Peyton Manning 2.50
10 Hines Ward .40
11 Koren Robinson .20
12 Eddie George .75
13 Shane Matthews .20
14 Trent Green .50
15 Marcus Robinson .20
16 Michael Vick 2.50
17 Muhsin Muhammad .40
18 Raghib Ismail .20
19 Quincy Morgan .50
20 Mike McMahon .75
21 Randy Moss 2.50
22 Willie Jackson .20
23 Freddie Mitchell .50
24 LaDainian Tomlinson 2.00
25 Warrick Dunn .40
26 Zach Thomas .40
27 Bill Schroeder .20
28 Jon Kitna .20
29 Rob Johnson .20
30 Drew Bledsoe 1.50
31 Ron Dayne .40
32 Tim Brown .75
33 Michael Westbrook .20
34 Terrell Owens .75
35 Santana Moss .20
36 Edgerrin James 2.00
37 Ray Lewis .50
38 Chris Weinke .60
39 Brian Griese .75
40 Trent Dilfer .50
41 Jay Fiedler .20
42 Joe Horn .20
43 Chad Johnson .20
44 Plaxico Burress .75
45 Trung Canidate .20
46 Steve McNair .75
47 Curtis Conway .20
48 James Stewart .40
49 James Jackson .50
50 Tom Brady 2.50
51 Emmitt Smith 2.50
52 Michael Pittman .20
53 Tony Gonzalez .50
54 Daunte Culpepper 1.50
55 Michael Strahan .50
56 Keyshawn Johnson .50
57 Marvin Harrison .75
58 Brian Urlacher 2.00
59 Jeff Blake .20
60 Chris Redman .50
61 James McKnight .20
62 Jerome Bettis .20
63 Shaun Alexander .75
64 Rod Gardner .50
65 Jimmy Smith .20
66 Thomas Jones .20
67 Peter Warrick .50
68 Mike Anderson 1.25
69 Ahman Green .75
70 Amani Toomer .20
71 Rich Gannon .50
72 Vinny Testaverde .40
73 Isaac Bruce .75
74 Derrick Mason .40
75 John Abraham .20
76 Shannon Sharpe .50
77 Quincy Carter 1.50
78 Todd Pinkston .20
79 Drew Brees 2.00
80 Brad Johnson .20
81 Garrison Hearst .20
82 Anthony Thomas 2.00
83 Brett Favre 3.00
84 Troy Brown .50
85 Charlie Garner .50
86 Kendrell Bell .20
87 Darrell Jackson .20
88 Ricky Williams 1.50
89 Duce Staley .50
90 Stephen Davis .75
91 Dominic Rhodes .20
92 Travis Henry .50
93 David Boston .75
94 Deuce McAllister 1.25
95 Ike Hilliard .20
96 Doug Flutie .75
97 Torry Holt .20
98 Keenan McCardell .20
99 Rod Smith .50
100 Donovan McNabb 1.50
101 Corey Bradford .20
102 Germane Crowell .20
103 Michael Bennett .75
104 Wayne Chrebet .20
105 Mike Alstott .50
106 Kevin Dyson .20
107 Tim Couch 1.25
108 Donald Hayes .20
109 Maurice Smith .20
110 Marvin "Snoop" Minnis .50
111 Antowain Smith .50
112 Kordell Stewart .75
113 Kurt Warner 2.50
114 Jerry Rice 2.50
115 Aaron Brooks 1.25
116 Tiki Barber .20
117 Marty Booker .20
118 Qadry Ismail .20
119 Peerless Price .40
120 Marcus Pollard .20
121 James Allen .20
122 Junior Seau .75
123 Fred Taylor .50
124 Corey Dillon .75
125 Lamar Smith .20
126 Laveranues Coles .40
127 James Thrash .50
128 Kevan Barlow .40
129 Matt Hasselbeck .20
130 David Patten .20
131 Antonio Freeman .40
132 Johnnie Morton .40
133 Priest Holmes .75
134 Cris Carter .40
135 Kevin Johnson .20
136 Jim Miller .40
137 Kerry Collins .50
138 Joey Galloway .40
139 Correll Buckhalter .20
140 Chris Chambers .75
141 Travis Taylor .50
142 Ed McCaffrey .20
143 J.J. Stokes .20
144 Reggie Wayne .20
145 Az-Zahir Hakim .50
146 Tim Dwight .20
147 Jevon Kearse .50
148 Jamal Lewis 1.25
149 Warren Sapp .50
150 Jermaine Lewis .20
151 *William Green* 4.00
152 *Roy Williams* 5.00
153 *Kurt Kittner* 2.00
154 *Daniel Graham* 2.00
155 *Andre Davis* 3.00
156 *Donte Stallworth* 4.00
157 *Josh Reed* 3.00
158 *Rohan Davey* 3.00
159 *Wendell Bryant* 1.00
160 *Lito Sheppard* 1.00
161 *Najeh Davenport* 2.00
162 *Freddie Milons* 1.00
163 *Patrick Ramsey* 4.00
164 *Luke Staley* 2.00
165 *Maurice Morris* 3.00
166 *Dwight Freeney* 2.50
167 *Jeremy Shockey* 6.00
168 *Jabar Gaffney* 3.00
169 *DeShaun Foster* 3.00
170 *Chad Hutchinson* 1.00
171 *Tim Carter* 1.00
172 *Napoleon Harris* 1.00
173 *Kahlil Hill* 1.00
174 *Josh McCown* 2.00
175 *Ron Johnson* 1.00
176 *Marquise Walker* 2.00
177 *Joey Harrington* 8.00
178 *Travis Stephens* 2.00
179 *Julius Peppers* 4.00
180 *Ryan Sims* 1.00
181 *Albert Haynesworth* 1.00
182 *Phillip Buchanon* 2.00
183 *Jonathan Wells* 2.50
184 *Chester Taylor* 1.00
185 *Antonio Bryant* 4.00
186 *Adrian Peterson* 2.00
187 *Clinton Portis* 10.00
188 *Lamar Gordon* 2.00
189 *Reche Caldwell* 2.00
190 *Ashley Lelie* 4.00
191 *T.J. Duckett* 4.00
192 *Eric Crouch* 2.50
193 *David Garrard* 1.00
194 *Quentin Jammer* 2.00
195 *Ladell Betts* 2.00
196 *Antwaan Randle El* 3.00
197 *Cliff Russell* 1.00
198 *Javon Walker* 5.00
199 *John Henderson* 1.00
200 *David Carr* 10.00

2002 Topps Gallery Autographs

NM/M
Common Player: 10.00
Group A inserted 1:3281
Group B inserted 1:155
Artist Proofs: 2X
Production 100 Sets
G-JA John Abraham 10.00
G-KB Kendrell Bell 30.00
G-MB Marty Booker 25.00
G-TB Tom Brady 50.00
G-AB Aaron Brooks 25.00
G-CC Chris Chambers 20.00
G-DS Duce Staley 10.00
G-AT Anthony Thomas 25.00
G-HW Hines Ward 15.00

2002 Topps Gallery Heritage

NM/M
Common Player: 2.00
Inserted 1:12
GH-TB Terry Bradshaw 5.00
GH-TBR Tom Brady 4.00
GH-DC Daunte Culpepper 2.00
GH-CD Corey Dillon 2.00
GH-MF Marshall Faulk 3.00
GH-BF Brett Favre 5.00
GH-EJ Edgerrin James 3.00
GH-JL Jamal Lewis 2.00
GH-PM Peyton Manning 3.00
GH-DM Dan Marino 6.00
GH-DMC Donovan McNabb 2.00
GH-JM Joe Montana 10.00
GH-RM Randy Moss 3.00
GH-JN Joe Namath 10.00
GH-JR Jerry Rice 5.00
GH-ES Emmitt Smith 5.00
GH-MV Michael Vick 4.00
GH-KW Kurt Warner 3.00

2002 Topps Gallery Heritage Relics

NM/M
Common Player: 10.00
Inserted 1:198
GHR-CD Corey Dillon 10.00
GHR-MF Marshall Faulk 12.00
GHR-BF Brett Favre 50.00
GHR-EJ Edgerrin James 15.00
GHR-DM Dan Marino 50.00
GHR-JM Joe Montana 75.00
GHR-JN Joe Namath 75.00
GHR-JR Jerry Rice 30.00
GHR-ES Emmitt Smith 50.00
GHR-KW Kurt Warner 20.00

2002 Topps Gallery Heritage Autographs

Inserted 1:18701
GHA-JN Joe Namath

2002 Topps Gallery Originals

NM/M
Common Player: 10.00
Group A inserted 1:66
Group B inserted 1:82
GO-DB Drew Brees 12.00
GO-TB Tim Brown 15.00
GO-DC David Carr 40.00
GO-CC Cris Carter 15.00
GO-CCH Chris Chambers 15.00
GO-RD Rohan Davey 10.00
GO-SD Stephen Davis 10.00
GO-JG Jeff Garcia 10.00
GO-EG Eddie George 10.00
GO-KJ Keyshawn Johnson 10.00
GO-RJ Ron Johnson 10.00
GO-AL Ashley Lelie 15.00
GO-SM Steve McNair 15.00
GO-TO Terrell Owens 10.00
GO-WS Warren Sapp 10.00
GO-JS Jimmy Smith 10.00
GO-TS Travis Stephens 10.00
GO-FT Fred Taylor 10.00
GO-LT LaDainian Tomlinson 10.00
GO-BU Brian Urlacher 18.00

2002 Topps Reserve

NM/M
Common Player: .40
Unlisted Stars: .75
Minor Stars: .60
Common Rookie (101-150): 3.00
Minor Rookie Stars: 5.00
Production 999 sets
Pack (5): 20.00
Wax Box (10): 145.00
1 Michael Vick 2.50
2 Chris Chambers .75
3 Laveranues Coles .60
4 Koren Robinson .60
5 Rod Gardner .60
6 James Thrash .40
7 Michael Bennett .75
8 Raghib Ismail .40
9 Peter Warrick .60
10 Drew Bledsoe 1.50
11 Marcus Robinson .60
12 Tiki Barber .60
13 LaDainian Tomlinson 2.00
14 Eddie George .75
15 Mike McMahon .75
16 Joe Horn .40
17 Tom Brady 2.50
18 Edgerrin James 2.00
19 Mike Anderson 1.25
20 Lamar Smith .40
21 Chris Redman .60
22 David Boston .75
23 Ike Hilliard .40
24 Jeff Garcia .75
25 Michael Pittman .40
26 Torry Holt .60
27 Priest Holmes .75
28 Germane Crowell .40
29 David Terrell .75
30 Tim Couch 1.25
31 Terry Glenn .60
32 Qadry Ismail .40
33 Aaron Brooks 1.25
34 Donovan McNabb 1.50
35 Jerome Bettis .60
36 Stephen Davis .60
37 Trent Green .60
38 Chris Weinke .75
39 Derrick Alexander .60
40 Ahman Green .75
41 Antowain Smith .60
42 Garrison Hearst .60
43 Keyshawn Johnson .60
44 Plaxico Burress .75
45 Marvin Harrison .60
46 Ray Lewis .60
47 Jake Plummer .60
48 Daunte Culpepper 1.50
49 Troy Brown .60
50 Emmitt Smith 2.50
51 Jerry Rice 2.50
52 Duce Staley .60
53 Kurt Warner 2.50
54 Derrick Mason .60
55 Brad Johnson .60
56 Fred Taylor .60
57 Jimmy Smith .40
58 Sylvester Morris .40
59 Quincy Morgan .60
60 Jamal Lewis 1.25
61 Warrick Dunn .60
62 Rod Smith .60
63 Deuce McAllister 1.25
64 Hines Ward .60
65 Steve McNair .75
66 Ricky Williams 1.50
67 Anthony Thomas 2.00
68 Eric Moulds .60
69 Travis Taylor .40
70 Tim Brown .75
71 Kordell Stewart .60
72 Shaun Alexander .75
73 Peyton Manning 2.50
74 Marty Booker .40
75 Brett Favre 3.00
76 Santana Moss .60
77 James Allen .40
78 Tony Gonzalez .60
79 Mark Brunell .75
80 Randy Moss 2.50
81 Jay Fiedler .60
82 Muhsin Muhammad .60
83 Travis Henry .60
84 Amani Toomer .60
85 Freddie Mitchell .60
86 Terrell Owens .75
87 Drew Brees 2.00
88 Darrell Jackson .40
89 Curtis Martin .60
90 Marvin "Snoop" Minnis .60
91 Quincy Carter 1.50
92 Corey Dillon .75
93 Rich Gannon .60
94 Vinny Testaverde .60
95 Jim Miller .60
96 Kevin Johnson .40
97 Brian Griese .75
98 Kerry Collins .60
99 Brian Urlacher 2.00
100 Marshall Faulk 1.50
101 *David Carr* 25.00
102 *Donte Stallworth* 10.00
103 *Marquise Walker* 5.00
104 *Eric Crouch* 8.00
105 *Jake Schifino* 2.00
106 *Rohan Davey* 8.00
107 *David Garrard* 5.00
108 *Julius Peppers* 8.00
109 *DeShaun Foster* 8.00
110 *Roy Williams* 12.00
111 *Javon Walker* 12.00
112 *Matt Schobel* 2.00
113 *Clinton Portis* 25.00
114 *Albert Haynesworth* 3.00
115 *Jeremy Shockey* 15.00
116 *Antwann Randle El* 8.00
117 *Maurice Morris* 8.00
118 *Andre Davis* 8.00
119 *Chad Hutchinson* 3.00
120 *Lito Sheppard* 3.00
121 *Daniel Graham* 5.00
122 *Jabar Gaffney* 8.00
123 *Josh McCown* 5.00
124 *Randy Fasani* 3.00
125 *Patrick Ramsey* 10.00
126 *Tim Carter* 3.00
127 *Ladell Betts* 5.00
128 *Jonathan Wells* 8.00
129 *Jason McAddley* 2.00
130 *Kurt Kittner* 5.00
131 *Josh Reed* 8.00
132 *T.J. Duckett* 10.00
133 *John Henderson* 3.00
134 *Travis Stephens* 5.00
135 *William Green* 8.00
136 *Freddie Milons* 3.00
137 *Ashley Lelie* 10.00
138 *Brian Westbrook* 8.00
139 *Antonio Bryant* 10.00
140 *Cliff Russell* 3.00
141 *Donald Reche Caldwell* 6.00
142 *Aaron Lockett* 2.00
143 *Mike Williams* 2.00
144 *Ron Johnson* 3.00
145 *Herb Haygood* 2.00
146 *Dwight Freeney* 6.00
147 *Josh Scobey* 2.00
148 *Luke Staley* 5.00
149 *Jerramy Stevens* 3.00
150 *Joey Harrington* 20.00
NNO Joe Namath Auto 150.00

2002 Topps Reserve Autographs

NM/M
Common Player: 10.00
Inserted 1:10
RA-CC Chris Chambers 25.00
RA-RD Richard Dent 15.00
RA-BF Brett Favre 150.00
RA-JG Jeff Garcia 20.00
RA-WJ Willie Jackson 10.00
RA-LJ LaMont Jordan 10.00
RA-DM Derrick Mason 10.00
RA-DMC Deuce McAllister
RA-SM Sammy Morris 10.00
RA-JR Jerry Rice 60.00
RA-MR Marcus Robinson 10.00
RA-BS Bill Schroeder 15.00
RA-LS Lamar Smith 10.00
RA-TS Tai Streets 10.00
RA-DT David Terrell 15.00
RA-AT Anthony Thomas 15.00
RA-LT LaDainian Tomlinson 30.00
RA-BU Brian Urlacher 50.00

2002 Topps Reserve Jerseys

NM/M
Common Player: 8.00
Inserted 1:10
RR-MAL Mike Alstott 10.00
RR-DB Drew Brees 10.00
RR-MB Mark Brunell 10.00
RR-SC Sam Cowart 8.00
RR-DC Daunte Culpepper 10.00
RR-CD Corey Dillon 10.00
RR-RG Rich Gannon 10.00
RR-CG Charlie Garner 8.00
RR-EG Eddie George 10.00
RR-TG Tony Gonzalez
RR-EJ Edgerrin James
RR-KJ Keyshawn Johnson 10.00
RR-PM Peyton Manning
RR-DM Dan Marino 35.00
RR-SM Steve McNair 10.00
RR-TM Travis Minor 8.00
RR-EM Eric Moulds
RR-JN Joe Namath 35.00
RR-TO Terrell Owens 10.00
RR-JS Jimmy Smith 8.00
RR-DS Duce Staley 8.00
RR-FT Fred Taylor 10.00

2002 Topps Reserve Mini-Helmet Autos

NM/M
Inserted 1 per box
Shaun Alexander/32 45.00
Marcus Allen
Mike Anderson/250 50.00
Ottis Anderson
Kevan Barlow/80 35.00
Chuck Bednarik/9 150.00
Michael Bennett
Drew Brees 60.00
Jim Brown
Tim Carter 35.00
Dave Casper 40.00
Mark Clayton 35.00
Laveranues Coles/229 35.00
Tim Couch
Roger Craig/65 40.00
Daunte Culpepper
Stephen Davis
Eric Dickerson
John Elway
Rod Gardner/70 40.00
Tony Gonzalez
Roosevelt Grier 35.00
Jack Ham
Rodney Hampton 35.00
Lester Hayes/35 45.00
Mike Haynes
Travis Henry/160 45.00
Torry Holt
Darrell Jackson 35.00
James Jackson 30.00
Edgerrin James/2 150.00
Kevin Johnson
Bert Jones
Deacon Jones 40.00
Ed Jones
Mo Lewis
Dan Marino
Don Maynard/55 50.00
Justin McCareins 25.00
Tommy McDonald 30.00
Donovan McNabb/543 40.00
Terry Metcalf
Travis Minor 30.00
Joe Montana
Dan Morgan 25.00
Santana Moss/48 45.00
Joe Namath/31 160.00
Christian Okoye/189 40.00
Jesse Palmer/154 25.00
Drew Pearson 25.00
Jim Plunkett
Peerless Price
John Randle/9 30.00
Koren Robinson
Gale Sayers 65.00
Jason Sehorn
Mike Singletary
Otis Sistrunk 30.00
Steve Smith 25.00
Michael Strahan
Lawrence Taylor
Al Toon
Brian Urlacher
Michael Vick
Peter Warrick
Chris Weinke/178 40.00
Doug Williams 35.00

2002 Topps Pristine

NM/M
Common Player: .50
Common Rookie (51-170): 1.00
Common U Rookie: 2.00
Uncommon Production 999 sets
Common R Rookie: 4.00
Rare Production 499 sets
Pack (8): 25.00
Wax Box (5): 90.00
1 Peyton Manning 2.00
2 Darrell Jackson .50

NM/M
3 Donovan McNabb 1.25
4 Rod Smith .50
5 Daunte Culpepper 1.25
6 Drew Brees 1.50
7 Stephen Davis .50
8 Kurt Warner 2.00
9 Eric Moulds .60
10 Jake Plummer .60
11 Chris Weinke .50
12 Brian Griese .75
13 Corey Bradford .50
14 Trent Green .60
15 Tom Brady 2.00
16 Jeff Garcia .75
17 Tiki Barber .50
18 Eddie George .75
19 Jamal Lewis 1.00
20 Troy Brown .60
21 Priest Holmes 1.00
22 Jimmy Smith .50
23 Tim Brown .75
24 Plaxico Burress .75
25 Aaron Brooks 1.00
26 Marshall Faulk 1.25
27 Steve McNair .75
28 Curtis Martin .60
29 Corey Dillon .75
30 Tim Couch 1.00
31 Michael Vick 2.00
32 David Boston .75
33 Kordell Stewart .60
34 Jerome Bettis .60
35 Keyshawn Johnson .60
36 Torry Holt .75
37 Shaun Alexander .75
38 Brett Favre 2.50
39 Marvin Harrison .75
40 Randy Moss 2.00
41 Jerry Rice 2.00
42 LaDainian Tomlinson 1.50
43 Terrell Owens .75
44 Edgerrin James 1.50
45 Anthony Thomas 1.25
46 Drew Bledsoe 1.25
47 Ahman Green .75
48 Ricky Williams 1.25
49 Tony Gonzalez .50
50 Emmitt Smith 2.00
51 *Joey Harrington/C* 8.00
52 *Joey Harrington/U* 8.00
53 *Joey Harrington/R* 15.00
54 *Josh McCown/C* 5.00
55 *Josh McCown/U* 5.00
56 *Josh McCown/R* 10.00
57 *Antwaan Randle El/C* 4.00
58 *Antwaan Randle El/U* 4.00
59 *Antwaan Randle El/R* 8.00
60 *Donald Reche Caldwell/C* 4.00
61 *Donald Reche Caldwell/U* 4.00
62 *Donald Reche Caldwell/R* 8.00
63 *Jason McAddley/C* 2.00
64 *Jason McAddley/U* 2.00
65 *Jason McAddley/R* 5.00
66 *Ashley Lelie/C* 5.00
67 *Ashley Lelie/U* 5.00
68 *Ashley Lelie/R* 10.00
69 *Travis Stephens/C* 2.00
70 *Travis Stephens/U* 2.00
71 *Travis Stephens/R* 4.00
72 *Chad Hutchinson/C* 3.00
73 *Chad Hutchinson/U* 3.00
74 *Chad Hutchinson/R* 6.00
75 *Quentin Jammer/C* 3.00
76 *Quentin Jammer/U* 3.00
77 *Quentin Jammer/R* 6.00
78 *Tim Carter/C* 2.00
79 *Tim Carter/U* 2.00
80 *Tim Carter/R* 4.00
81 *Antonio Bryant/C* 4.00
82 *Antonio Bryant/U* 4.00
83 *Antonio Bryant/R* 8.00
84 *Cliff Russell/C* 2.00
85 *Cliff Russell/U* 2.00
86 *Cliff Russell/R* 4.00
87 *Rohan Davey/C* 4.00
88 *Rohan Davey/U* 4.00
89 *Rohan Davey/R* 8.00
90 *Javon Walker/C* 5.00
91 *Javon Walker/U* 5.00
92 *Javon Walker/R* 10.00
93 *T.J. Duckett/C* 4.00
94 *T.J. Duckett/U* 4.00
95 *T.J. Duckett/R* 8.00
96 *Donte Stallworth/C* 4.00
97 *Donte Stallworth/U* 4.00
98 *Donte Stallworth/R* 8.00
99 *Andre Davis/C* 3.00
100 *Andre Davis/U* 3.00
101 *Andre Davis/R* 6.00
102 *Mike Williams/C* 2.00
103 *Mike Williams/U* 2.00
104 *Mike Williams/R* 4.00
105 *Freddie Milons/C* 2.00
106 *Freddie Milons/U* 2.00
107 *Freddie Milons/R* 4.00
108 *John Henderson/C* 2.00

109 *John Henderson/U* 2.00
110 *John Henderson/R* 4.00
111 *DeShaun Foster/C* 3.00
112 *DeShaun Foster/U* 3.00
113 *DeShaun Foster/R* 6.00
114 *Josh Reed/C* 3.00
115 *Josh Reed/U* 3.00
116 *Josh Reed/R* 6.00
117 *Jabar Gaffney/C* 3.00
118 *Jabar Gaffney/U* 3.00
119 *Jabar Gaffney/R* 6.00
120 *Clinton Portis/C* 10.00
121 *Clinton Portis/U* 10.00
122 *Clinton Portis/R* 20.00
123 *Jeremy Shockey/C* 8.00
124 *Jeremy Shockey/U* 8.00
125 *Jeremy Shockey/R* 15.00
126 *Dwight Freeney/C* 3.00
127 *Dwight Freeney/U* 3.00
128 *Dwight Freeney/R* 6.00
129 *Brian Westbrook/C* 3.00
130 *Brian Westbrook/U* 3.00
131 *Brian Westbrook/R* 6.00
132 *Randy Fasani/C* 2.00
133 *Randy Fasani/U* 2.00
134 *Randy Fasani/R* 4.00
135 *Julius Peppers/C* 2.50
136 *Julius Peppers/U* 2.50
137 *Julius Peppers/R* 5.00
138 *Patrick Ramsey/C* 3.00
139 *Patrick Ramsey/U* 3.00
140 *Patrick Ramsey/R* 6.00
141 *William Green/C* 3.00
142 *William Green/U* 3.00
143 *William Green/R* 6.00
144 *Daniel Graham/C* 2.50
145 *Daniel Graham/U* 2.50
146 *Daniel Graham/R* 5.00
147 *Ron Johnson/C* 2.00
148 *Ron Johnson/U* 2.00
149 *Ron Johnson/R* 4.00
150 *Maurice Morris/C* 2.50
151 *Maurice Morris/U* 2.50
152 *Maurice Morris/R* 5.00
153 *Eric Crouch/C* 2.50
154 *Eric Crouch/U* 2.50
155 *Eric Crouch/R* 5.00
156 *Roy Williams/C* 4.00
157 *Roy Williams/U* 4.00
158 *Roy Williams/R* 8.00
159 *Ladell Betts/C* 2.50
160 *Ladell Betts/U* 2.50
161 *Ladell Betts/R* 5.00
162 *David Garrard/C* 2.50
163 *David Garrard/U* 2.50
164 *David Garrard/R* 5.00
165 *Marquise Walker/C* 2.00
166 *Marquise Walker/U* 2.00
167 *Marquise Walker/R* 4.00
168 *David Carr/C* 10.00
169 *David Carr/U* 10.00
170 *David Carr/R* 20.00
ESA1 Emmitt Smith Auto 250.00
ESJ1 Emmitt Smith JSY 40.00

2002 Topps Pristine Refractors

Stars: 2X-4X
1-50 Production 349 Sets
C Cards (51-170): 1.5X-3X
Common Production 999 Sets
U Cards (51-170): 1X-2X
Uncommon Production 499 Sets
R Cards (51-170): 1.5X-3X
Rare Production 199 Sets

2002 Topps Pristine Gold Refractors

Stars: 3X-6X
C Cards (51-170): 3X-6X
U Cards (51-170): 2X-4X
R Cards (51-170): 1.5X-3X
Production 79 Sets

2002 Topps Pristine All-Rookie Team Jerseys

NM/M
Common Player: 10.00
TRR-JG Jabar Gaffney 10.00
TRR-AL Ashley Lelie 20.00
TRR-CP Clinton Portis 30.00
TRR-JP Julius Peppers 15.00
TRR-MW Mike Williams 10.00

2002 Topps Pristine Driving Force Relics

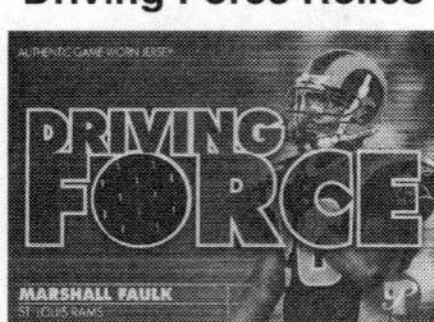

NM/M
Common Player: 10.00
DF-AB Aaron Brooks 10.00
DF-MB Mark Brunell 10.00
DF-SD Stephen Davis 10.00
DF-MF Marshall Faulk 15.00
DF-BF Brett Favre 35.00
DF-DF Doug Flutie 12.00
DF-CM Curtis Martin 10.00
DF-AT Anthony Thomas 15.00
DF-LT LaDainian Tomlinson 15.00
DF-KW Kurt Warner 15.00

A player's name in *italic* type indicates a rookie card.

2002 Topps Pristine Patches

NM/M
Common Player: 15.00
PP-DB Drew Brees
PP-AB Aaron Brooks 30.00
PP-MB Mark Brunell 15.00
PP-SD Stephen Davis 15.00
PP-MF Marshall Faulk 25.00
PP-BF Brett Favre 60.00
PP-DF Doug Flutie 20.00
PP-EG Eddie George 15.00
PP-DG Darrell Green 15.00
PP-BG Brian Griese 25.00
PP-CM Curtis Martin 20.00
PP-TO Terrell Owens 25.00
PP-JR Jerry Rice 30.00
PP-ES Emmitt Smith 60.00
PP-AT Anthony Thomas 25.00
PP-LT LaDainian Tomlinson 25.00
PP-KW Kurt Warner 25.00

2002 Topps Pristine Personal Endorsements

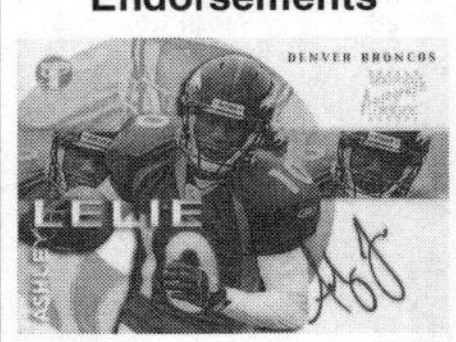

NM/M
Common Player: 10.00
P-DRC Donald Reche Caldwell 15.00
P-KC Kelly Campbell 10.00
P-DC David Carr 80.00
P-RD Rohan Davey 12.00
P-AD Andre Davis 20.00
P-TJD T.J. Duckett 30.00
P-BF Brett Favre 175.00
P-DF DeShaun Foster 20.00
P-DG David Garrard 15.00
P-WG William Green 30.00
P-JH Joey Harrington 80.00
P-RJ Ron Johnson 10.00
P-KK Kurt Kittner 12.00
P-AL Ashley Lelie 30.00
P-JM Josh McCown 15.00
P-BM Bryant McKinnie 15.00
P-PR Patrick Ramsey 25.00
P-JR Josh Reed 20.00
P-CR Cliff Russell 12.00
P-TS Travis Stephens 15.00
P-JW Javon Walker 25.00
P-MW Marquise Walker

2002 Topps Pristine Portions

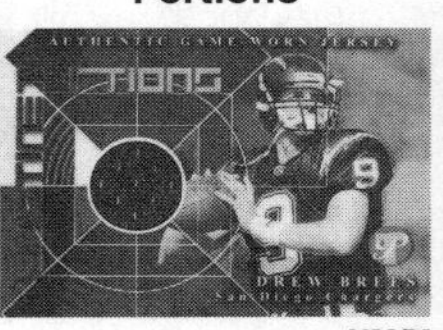

NM/M
Common Player: 10.00
PPR-DB Drew Brees 25.00
PPR-EG Eddie George 10.00
PPR-DG Darrell Green 10.00
PPR-BG Brian Griese 10.00
PPR-TO Terrell Owens 20.00
PPR-JR Jerry Rice 25.00
PPR-ES Emmitt Smith 40.00

2002 Topps Pristine Nickel Package Relics

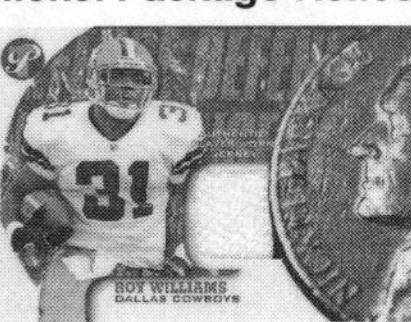

NM/M
Common Player: 10.00
NP-JK Jevon Kearse 10.00
NP-JP Julius Peppers 20.00
NP-JS Justin Smith 12.00
NP-TV Troy Vincent 10.00
NP-RW Roy Williams 25.00

2002 Topps Pristine Rookie Premiere Jerseys

NM/M
Common Player: 10.00
RPR-AB Antonio Bryant 20.00
RPR-EC Eric Crouch 10.00
RPR-AD Andre Davis 10.00
RPR-TD T.J. Duckett 20.00
RPR-DF DeShaun Foster 12.00
RPR-JG Jabar Gaffney 10.00
RPR-WG William Green 20.00
RPR-JH Joey Harrington 40.00
RPR-JM Josh McCown 10.00
RPR-CP Clinton Portis 30.00
RPR-PR Patrick Ramsey 15.00
RPR-JR Josh Reed 15.00
RPR-JS Jeremy Shockey 20.00
RPR-DS Donte Stallworth 20.00
RPR-JW Javon Walker 20.00

2002 Topps Pristine Team Legends Autographs

NM/M
Common Player: 12.00
Cliff Branch 12.00
John Hannah 12.00
Barry Sanders 70.00
Mike Singletary 12.00

2002 Topps Super Bowl XXXVII Card Show

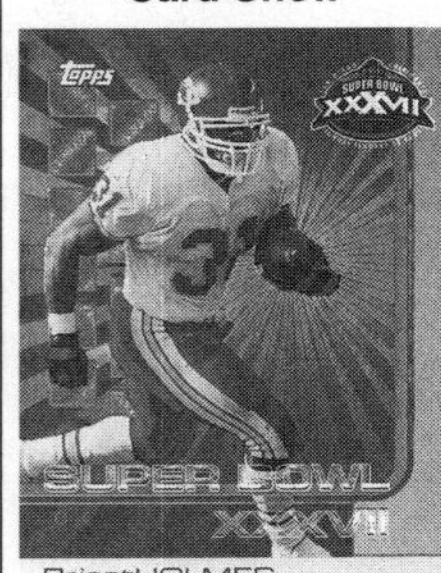

NM/M
Complete Set (18): 20.00
Common Player: 1.00
1 Brett Favre 3.00
2 Clinton Portis 3.00
3 David Carr 3.00
4 Deuce McAllister 1.00
5 Donovan McNabb 1.00
6 Donte Stallworth 1.00
7 Drew Bledsoe 1.00
8 Drew Brees 1.00
9 Edgerrin James 1.00
10 Emmitt Smith 2.00
11 Joey Harrington 3.00
12 LaDainian Tomlinson 1.00
13 Marshall Faulk 1.00
14 Michael Vick 3.00
15 Peyton Manning 2.00
16 Priest Holmes 1.00
17 Ricky Williams 1.50
18 Tom Brady 1.00

2002 Topps e-Topps

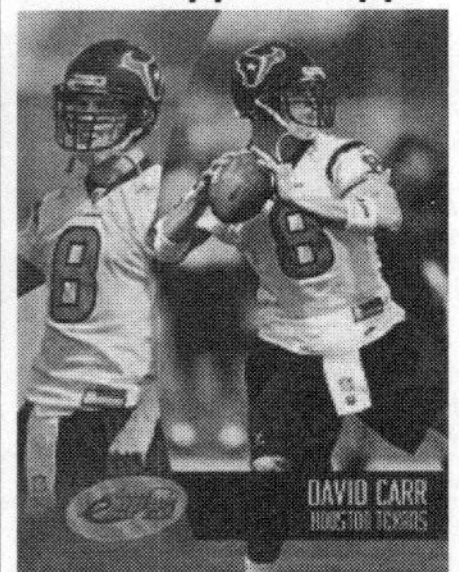

NM/M
1 Tom Brady $9.50/5000
2 Jeff Garcia $6.50/1724
3 Rod Smith $4.00/4000
4 Anthony Thomas $6.50/6000
5 Chris Chambers $6.50/4000
6 Kendrell Bell $6.50/5000
6 Emmitt Smith Rushes Into.$8.00/7184
6 Jerry Rice Grabs 200th TD $8.00/3579
7 Curtis Martin $6.50/1311
8 Eddie George $9.50/3169
8a Marvin Harrison Rec. Record $8.00/952
9 Stephen Davis $6.50/3961
10 Edgerrin James $6.50/3773
11 Michael Vick $9.50/6000
12 Peter Warrick $6.50/1533
13 Priest Holmes $6.50/5000
14 Jake Plummer $6.50/2000
15 Jimmy Smith $6.50/16.92
16 Jerry Rice $9.50/2000
17 LaDainian Tomlinson $9.50/5000
18 Keyshawn Johnson $6.50/1492
19 Shaun Alexander $6.50/2986
20 Terrell Owens $9.50/5000
21 Rod Gardner $6.50/1757
22 Donovan McNabb $9.50/5000
23 Randy Moss $9.50/3000
24 Brian Griese $6.50/2909
25 Marcus Robinson $4.00/2000
26 Jamal Lewis $6.50/3528
27 Peyton Manning $9.50/2336
28 Mike McMahon $4.00/2790
29 Rich Gannon $6.50/3166
30 Jerome Bettis $6.50/2017
31 Matt Hasselbeck $6.50/3000
32 Marshall Faulk $9.50/3554
33 Plaxico Burress $6.50/3000
34 Ricky Williams $9.50/4000
35 Jay Fiedler $6.50/4000
36 Ahman Green $6.50/3730
37 Chris Weinke $4.00/2168
38 David Boston $6.50/2000
39 Troy Brown $4.00/3410
40 Tim Brown $6.50/1739
41 Darrell Jackson $6.50/4000
42 Steve McNair $6.50/2000
43 Torry Holt $6.50/4000
44 Tiki Barber $6.50/2000
45 Brett Favre $9.50/3466
46 Corey Dillon $6.50/4000
47 Emmitt Smith $9.50/2000
48 Marvin Harrison $6.50/4000
49 Daunte Culpepper $6.50/1508
50 Kurt Warner $9.50/1114
51 Tim Couch $6.50/5735
52 Eric Moulds $4.00/2000
53 Vinny Testaverde $6.50/3000
54 Trent Green $4.00/2000
55 Kordell Stewart $4.00/1538
56 Drew Brees $6.50/5000
57 Aaron Brooks $6.50/5000
58 Mark Brunell $4.00/4000
59 Tony Gonzalez $6.50/3274
60 Doug Flutie $4.00/1000
61 David Carr $6.50/6000
62 Travis Stephens $4.00/4000
63 Patrick Ramsey $6.50/5000
64 T.J. Duckett $6.50/6000
65 Javon Walker $6.50/5000
66 DeShaun Foster $6.50/3000
67 William Green $6.50/3000
68 Ashley Lelie $6.50/5000
69 Jabar Gaffney $6.50/5000
70 Ron Johnson $4.00/4000
71 Donald Reche Caldwell $6.50/5000
72 Daniel Graham $6.50/4000
73 Josh Reed $6.50/3765
74 Andre Davis $6.50/2000
75 Joey Harrington $6.50/8000
77 Donte Stallworth $6.50/5000
78 Rohan Davey $6.50/3000
79 Maurice Morris $6.50/4000
80 Antwann Randle El $6.50/4000
81 Cliff Russell $4.00/3000
82 Jeremy Shockey $6.50/7000
83 Julius Peppers $6.50/6000
84 Antonio Bryant $6.50/5000
85 Clinton Portis $6.50/6000
86 Ladell Betts $6.50/2302
87 Josh McCown $6.50/2175
88 Roy Williams $6.50/5000
89 Tim Carter $6.50/3000
90 Marquise Walker $4.00/2000
91 Chad Hutchinson $4.00/5000
92 Deion Branch $4.00/5000
93 Brian Westbrook $4.00/5000
94 Jonathan Wells $4.00/5000
95 Tommy Maddox $6.50/3397
96 Deuce McAllister $6.50/2822
97 Drew Bledsoe $6.50/2000
98 Brian Urlacher $6.50/2000
99 Donald Driver $6.50/2788
100 Peerless Price $6.50/2298
101 Chad Pennington $6.50/3000
102 Randy McMichael $6.50/2220
103 Marty Booker $6.50/1309
104 Hines Ward $6.50/2112
105 Warren Sapp $6.50/1621
106 Marc Bulger $6.50/3000

2002 Topps etopps Classics

NM/M
1 Barry Sanders $12.50/3000
2 Ray Nitschke $12.50/983
3 Dan Marino $12.50/3000
4 Chuck Bednarik $12.50/1291
5 Sammy Baugh $12.50/1259
6 Frank Gifford $12.50/1270
7 Kellen Winslow $12.50/777
7 Terry Bradshaw $12.50/3000
8 Jim Brown $12.50/3000
9 Jim Kelly $12.50/985
10 Y.A. Tittle $12.50/1064
11 Deacon Jones $12.50/865
11 Fran Tarkenton $12.50/1106
12 Joe Montana $12.50/3000
13 Joe Namath $12.50/3000
14 Elroy 'Crazy Legs" Hirsch $12.50/906
14 John Elway $12.50/2422
15 Norm Van Brocklin $12.50/975
19 Bubba Smith $12.50/805
20 Dan Fouts $12.50/843

2002 eTopps Event Series

ES6A Emmitt Smith/7184
ES6B Jerry Rice/3579
ES8 Marvin Harrison/952

2003 Topps

NM/M
Common Player: .15
Unlisted Star: .60
Minor Star: .50
Unlisted Rookie Star: 1.00
Minor Rookie Star: .75
Gold parallel 1X-2X
Production 499 sets
Black parallel 1X-4X
Production 150 sets
Pack(10): 1.50
Wax Box(36): 40.00
1 Michael Vick 2.00
2 Wesley Walls .15
3 Josh Reed .25
4 Josh McCown .40
5 James Stewart .15
6 Deltha O'Neal .15
7 Quincy Morgan .15
8 Tony Fisher .20
9 Corey Bradford .40
10 Byron Chamberlain .15
11 James McKnight .15
12 Fred Taylor .40
13 David Patten .15
14 Jerome Bettis .40
15 Jerry Porter .40
16 Anthony Becht .15
17 Steve McNair .50
18 Stephen Davis .40
19 Terrence Wilkins .15
20 Jamie Martin .15
21 Tai Streets .15
22 Frank Wycheck .15
23 Sammy Knight .15
24 Marcus Pollard .15
25 Jamie Sharper .15
26 T.J. Houshmandzadeh .15
27 Javin Hunter .15
28 Alge Crumpler .15
29 Chris Weinke .15
30 David Terrell .30
31 Troy Hambrick .15
32 Bubba Franks .15
33 Todd Bouman .15
34 Trent Green .40
35 Mark Brunell .50
36 James Thrash .15
37 Donnie Edwards .15
38 Mike Alstott .50
39 Bobby Engram .15
40 Deuce McAllister .75
41 Santana Moss .15
42 Kordell Stewart .50
43 Jason Taylor .30
44 Corey Dillon .50
45 Damien Anderson .15
46 Rodney Peete .15
47 Jeff Blake .15
48 Mike McMahon .40
49 Ed McCaffrey .50
50 Priest Holmes .75
51 Moe Williams .15
52 Brian Dawkins .15
53 Tim Brown .60
54 Curtis Martin .50
55 Charles Stackhouse .15
56 Derrius Thompson .15
57 John Simon .15
58 Joe Jurevicius .15
59 Jonathan Wells .40
60 William Green .60
61 Ken-Yon Rambo .15
62 Frank Sanders .15
63 Chester Taylor .15
64 Keith Brooking .15
65 Bill Schroeder .15
66 Travis Minor .15
67 Eric Parker .15
68 Phillip Buchanon .40
69 Amos Zereoue .15
70 Warren Sapp .40
71 Ladell Betts .40
72 Lamar Gordon .15
73 Koren Robinson .40
74 Ron Dayne .30
75 Donovan McNabb 1.00
76 Edgerrin James 1.00
77 Stacey Mack .15
78 Justin Smith .15
79 Kelly Holcomb .15
80 Thomas Jones .15
81 Randy McMichael .15
82 Daunte Culpepper 1.00
83 Tommy Maddox .50
84 Tyrone Wheatley .15
85 Kevin Dyson .40
86 Rod Gardner .40
87 Wayne Chrebet .40
88 Marc Boerigter .40
89 Darnay Scott .15
90 T.J. Duckett .50
91 Marcel Shipp .15
92 Ross Tucker .15
93 Drew Bledsoe 1.00
94 Scotty Anderson .15
95 Rod Smith .40
96 Jim Kleinsasser .15
97 Peyton Manning 1.50
98 Junior Seau .40
99 Darrell Jackson .15
100 Brett Favre 2.00
101 Ashley Lelie .75
102 JaJuan Dawson .15
103 Kyle Brady .15
104 Kevin Faulk .15
105 Jeremy Shockey 1.50
106 Hines Ward .50
107 Jeff Garcia .50
108 Shane Matthews .15
109 Jevon Kearse .40
110 Eddie Kennison .15
111 Quincy Carter .50
112 Brian Urlacher 1.25
113 Charlie Rogers .40
114 Robert Ferguson .15
115 Christian Fauria .15
116 Brian Westbrook .15
117 Antwann Randle El 1.00
118 Eddie George .15
119 Derrick Brooks .40
120 Isaac Bruce .40

121	Joe Horn	.40
122	Jermaine Lewis	.15
123	Jon Kitna	.15
124	David Boston	.60
125	Todd Heap	.30
126	Lamar Smith	.15
127	Marcus Robinson	.15
128	Germane Crowell	.15
129	Kevin Johnson	.30
130	Cris Carter	.40
131	Drew Brees	1.00
132	Champ Bailey	.15
133	Brian Finneran	.15
134	Mike Anderson	.40
135	Derek Ross	.15
136	Javon Walker	.40
137	D'Wayne Bates	.15
138	Chad Lewis	.15
139	Charlie Garner	.40
140	Laveranues Coles	.40
141	Ron Dixon	.15
142	Rob Johnson	.20
143	Shaun Alexander	.60
144	Kevan Barlow	.15
145	Aaron Brooks	.75
146	Jay Foreman	.15
147	Mike Peterson	.15
148	Brandon Bennett	.15
149	Jake Plummer	.50
150	Emmitt Smith	1.50
151	Mikhael Ricks	.15
152	Terry Glenn	.15
153	Michael Bennett	.60
154	Deion Branch	.60
155	Justin McCareins	.15
156	Keyshawn Johnson	.50
157	Marc Bulger	.60
158	Matt Hasselbeck	.30
159	Garrison Hearst	.30
160	Jamel White	.15
161	Doug Johnson	.15
162	Larry Centers	.15
163	Dee Brown	.15
164	Dez White	.15
165	Brian Griese	.50
166	Johnnie Morton	.15
167	Oronde Gadsden	.15
168	Chad Morton	.15
169	Rod Woodson	.40
170	Ricky Proehl	.15
171	Tim Dwight	.40
172	Patrick Ramsey	.60
173	Donald Driver	.50
174	Joey Harrington	1.25
175	Ricky Williams	1.00
176	David Givens	.15
177	Antonio Freeman	.30
178	Dwight Freeney	.15
179	Jabar Gaffney	.40
180	Leon Johnson	.15
181	Freddie Jones	.15
182	Ron Johnson	.15
183	Duce Staley	.15
184	Charles Woodson	.30
185	Trung Canidate	.40
186	Jerome Pathon	.15
187	Jimmy Smith	.40
188	Reggie Wayne	.15
189	Chad Johnson	.40
190	Steve Beuerlein	.15
191	Joey Galloway	.30
192	Chris Walsh	.15
193	Ty Law	.15
194	Ike Hilliard	.15
195	Curtis Conway	.40
196	Kenny Watson	.15
197	Brad Johnson	.50
198	Shawn Jefferson	.15
199	Jamal Lewis	.40
200	Terrell Owens	.60
201	Todd Pinkston	.15
202	Maurice Morris	.50
203	Dante Hall	.15
204	Jeremiah Trotter	.15
205	Keenan McCardell	.40
206	Antonio Bryant	.60
207	Trevor Gaylor	.15
208	Eric Moulds	.30
209	Jim Miller	.15
210	Kabeer Gbaja-Biamila	.15
211	James Mungro	.40
212	Troy Brown	.40
213	J.J. Stokes	.40
214	Rich Gannon	.50
215	Chad Pennington	.75
216	Michael Strahan	.30
217	David Garrard	.15
218	Chris Chambers	.40
219	Antowain Smith	.15
220	Olandis Gary	.15
221	Jason McAddley	.15
222	Brandon Stokley	.15
223	Derrick Alexander	.15
224	Hugh Douglas	.15
225	Danny Wuerffel	.15
226	Derrick Mason	.40
227	Michael Pittman	.15
228	Torry Holt	.40
229	Bobby Shaw	.15
230	Tony Gonzalez	.50
231	Eddie Hartwell	.15
232	Kris Mangum	.15
233	MarTay Jenkins	.15
234	Marty Booker	.40
235	London Fletcher	.15
236	Shannon Sharpe	.40
237	Zach Thomas	.40
238	Plaxico Burress	.60
239	Trent Dilfer	.15
240	Kurt Warner	1.25
241	Vinny Testaverde	.30
242	Al Wilson	.15
243	Chris Redman	.50
244	Warrick Dunn	.40
245	Jay Fiedler	.40
246	A.J. Feeley	.15
247	LaMont Jordan	.15
248	Kerry Collins	.50
249	Michael Lewis	.15
250	Jerry Rice	1.50
251	Simeon Rice	.30
252	Donald Reche Caldwell	.50
253	Randy Moss	1.50
254	Az-Zahir Hakim	.40
255	Nate Wayne	.15
256	James Allen	.15
257	Qadry Ismail	.15
258	Tom Brady	1.00
259	Brian Kelly	.15
260	Ray Lucas	.15
261	Amani Toomer	.40
262	Travis Henry	.40
263	Chris Chandler	.30
264	Peter Warrick	.20
265	Ray Lewis	.40
266	Sam Cowart	.15
267	Donte Stallworth	.75
268	David Carr	1.25
269	Andre Davis	.60
270	Jake Delhomme	.15
271	Travis Taylor	.15
272	Steve Smith	.15
273	Tiki Barber	.40
274	Chad Hutchinson	.40
275	Marshall Faulk	1.00
276	Chris Claiborne	.15
277	Billy Miller	.15
278	Peerless Price	.60
279	Edward Reed	.15
280	Ahman Green	.60
281	Roy Williams	.60
282	Dennis Northcutt	.15
283	Julius Peppers	.50
284	John Davis	.15
285	LaDainian Tomlinson	1.25
286	Muhsin Muhammad	.40
287	Tim Couch	.75
288	Clinton Portis	1.50
289	Anthony Thomas	.40
290	Marvin Harrison	.60
291	Priest Holmes	.75
292	Drew Bledsoe	1.00
293	Tom Brady	.75
294	Shaun Alexander	.60
295	Brett Favre	1.25
296	Travis Henry	.40
297	Marshall Faulk	.75
298	Terrell Owens	.40
299	Jeff Garcia	.40
300	Plaxico Burress	.40
301	Donovan McNabb	1.00
302	Ricky Williams	1.00
303	Michael Vick	1.50
304	Steve Smith	.30
305	Marvin Harrison	.40
306	Chad Pennington	.50
307	Jeremy Shockey	1.00
308	Tommy Maddox	.50
309	Steve McNair	.30
310	Rich Gannon	.40
311	*Carson Palmer*	4.00
312	*Keenan Howry*	.50
313	*Michael Haynes*	1.00
314	*Terrell Suggs*	1.50
315	*Rashean Mathis*	.50
316	*Chris Kelsay*	.50
317	*Brad Banks*	1.00
318	*Jordan Gross*	.50
319	*Lee Suggs*	1.50
320	*Kliff Kingsbury*	1.00
321	*William Joseph*	1.00
322	*Kelley Washington*	1.00
323	*Jerome McDougle*	1.00
324	*Osi Umenyiora*	.50
325	*Chris Simms*	1.50
326	*Alonzo Jackson*	.50
327	*L.J. Smith*	.50
328	*Mike Doss*	.50
329	*Bobby Wade*	.50
330	*Ken Hamlin*	.50
331	*Brandon Lloyd*	1.00
332	*Justin Fargas*	1.00
333	*Dewayne Robertson*	1.00
334	*Bryant Johnson*	1.50
335	*Boss Bailey*	1.00
336	*Onterrio Smith*	1.50
337	*Doug Gabriel*	.50
338	*Jimmy Kennedy*	.75
339	*B.J. Askew*	.50
340	*Taylor Jacobs*	1.00
341	*Dallas Clark*	.75
342	*Dewayne White*	.50
343	*Arnaz Battle*	.75
344	*Kareem Kelly*	.50
345	*Terry Pierce*	.50
346	*Billy McMullen*	.50
347	*Talman Gardner*	.75
348	*Anquan Boldin*	1.00
349	*Travis Anglin*	.50
350	*Byron Leftwich*	4.00
351	*Marcus Trufant*	1.00
352	*Sam Aiken*	.75
353	*LaBrandon Toefield*	.75
354	*J.R. Tolver*	.50
355	*Charles Rogers*	3.00
356	*Chaun Thompson*	.50
357	*Chris Brown*	1.00
358	*Justin Gage*	.75
359	*Kevin Williams*	.50
360	*Willis McGahee*	3.00
361	*Victor Hobson*	.50
362	*Brian St. Pierre*	.75
363	*Nate Burleson*	.50
364	*Calvin Pace*	.75
365	*Larry Johnson*	3.00
366	*Andre Woolfolk*	.50
367	*Tyrone Calico*	.75
368	*Seneca Wallace*	1.00
369	*Domanick Davis*	1.00
370	*Rex Grossman*	2.50
371	*Artose Pinner*	.75
372	*Jason Witten*	.75
373	*Bennie Joppru*	1.00
374	*Bethel Johnson*	.50
375	*Kyle Boller*	2.50
376	*Shaun McDonald*	.50
377	*Musa Smith*	.75
378	*Ken Dorsey*	1.50
379	*Johnathan Sullivan*	.75
380	*Andre Johnson*	2.50
381	*Nick Barnett*	.50
382	*Teyo Johnson*	.75
383	*Terence Newman*	1.50
384	*Kevin Curtis*	.50
385	*Dave Ragone*	1.50

2003 Topps Black

Production 125 sets 1X-4X

2003 Topps Gold

Production 499 sets 1V-2X

2003 Topps Hall of Fame Autographs

		NM/M
HOF-MA	Marcus Allen	45.00
HOF-EB	Elvin Bethea	55.00
HOF-JD	Joe DeLamielleure	
HOF-JL	James Lofton	
HOF-HS	Hank Stram	

2003 Topps Hobby Masters

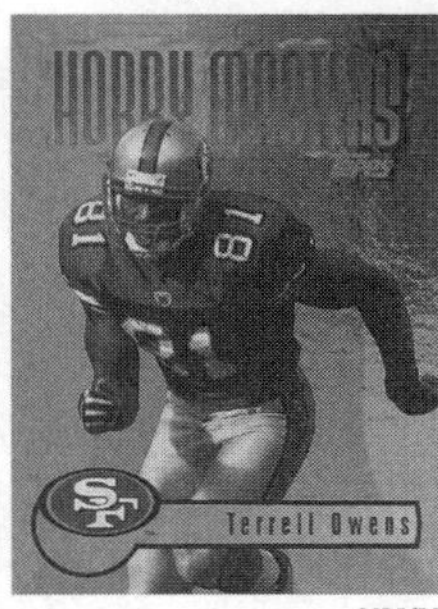

		NM/M
Complete Set (10):		15.00
Common Player:		1.00
Inserted 1:18		
HM1	Michael Vick	4.00
HM2	Priest Holmes	1.50
HM3	Brett Favre	4.00
HM4	LaDainian Tomlinson	1.50
HM5	Terrell Owens	1.00
HM6	Marshall Faulk	1.50
HM7	Donovan McNabb	1.50
HM8	Peyton Manning	2.00
HM9	Deuce McAllister	1.50
HM10	David Carr	2.50

2003 Topps Own The Game

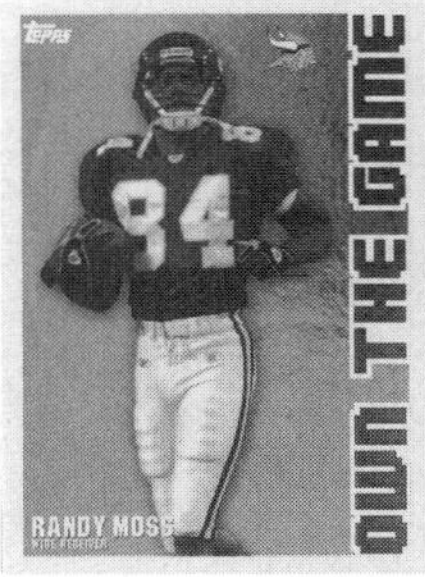

		NM/M
Common Player:		.75
Inserted 1:12		
OTG1	Brett Favre	3.00
OTG2	Rich Gannon	1.00
OTG3	Drew Bledsoe	1.50
OTG4	Michael Vick	3.00
OTG5	Steve McNair	.75
OTG6	Tom Brady	1.00
OTG7	Chad Pennington	1.00
OTG8	Peyton Manning	2.00
OTG9	Donovan McNabb	1.50
OTG10	Ricky Williams	1.50
OTG11	LaDainian Tomlinson	1.00
OTG12	Priest Holmes	1.00
OTG13	Clinton Portis	1.50
OTG14	Travis Henry	.75
OTG15	Deuce McAllister	.75
OTG16	Marshall Faulk	.75
OTG17	Jamal Lewis	.75
OTG18	Marvin Harrison	.75
OTG19	Randy Moss	2.00
OTG20	Amani Toomer	.75
OTG21	Hines Ward	.75
OTG22	Plaxico Burress	.75
OTG23	Terrell Owens	1.00
OTG24	Eric Moulds	.75
OTG25	Jerry Rice	2.00
OTG26	Jason Taylor	.75
OTG27	Simeon Rice	.75
OTG28	Zach Thomas	.75
OTG29	Brian Urlacher	1.50
OTG30	Rod Woodson	.75

2003 Topps Pro Bowl Relics

		NM/M
Common Player:		7.00
Inserted 1:200		
AP-MA	Mike Alstott	10.00
AP-BF	Bubba Franks	7.00
AP-RG	Rich Gannon	8.00
AP-JG	Jeff Garcia	7.00
AP-MH	Marvin Harrison	8.00
AP-THE	Todd Heap	7.00
AP-JH	Joe Horn	7.00
AP-ML	Michael Lewis	7.00
AP-JP	Joey Porter	15.00
AP-JR	Jerry Rice	15.00
AP-MS	Michael Strahan	7.00
AP-LT	LaDainian Tomlinson	10.00
AP-BU	Brian Urlacher	15.00
AP-HW	Hines Ward	12.00
AP-RW	Ricky Williams	15.00

2003 Topps Record Breakers

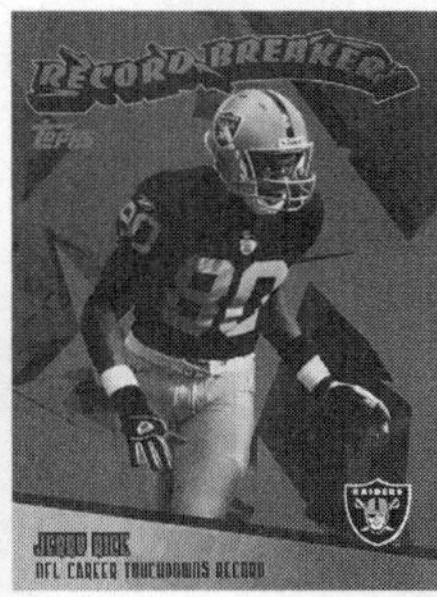

		NM/M
Complete Set (29):		45.00
Common Player:		.75
Inserted 1:6		
RB1	Barry Sanders	2.00
RB2	Brett Favre	3.00
RB3	Brian Mitchell	.75
RB4	Bruce Matthews	.75
RB5	Clinton Portis	2.00
RB6	Corey Dillon	.75
RB7	Dan Marino	2.50
RB8	Derrick Mason	.75
RB9	Emmitt Smith	2.50
RB10	Jason Elam	.75
RB11	Jason Taylor	.75
RB12	Jerry Rice	2.00
RB13	Jimmy Smith	.75
RB14	Terrell Owens	.75
RB15	John Elway	2.00
RB16	LaDainian Tomlinson	.75
RB17	Lawrence Taylor	1.00
RB18	Randy Moss	2.00
RB19	Marshall Faulk	1.00
RB20	Marvin Harrison	.75
RB21	Michael Strahan	.75
RB22	Peyton Manning	2.00
RB23	Priest Holmes	1.00
RB24	Rich Gannon	1.00
RB25	Ricky Williams	1.50
RB26	Rod Woodson	.75
RB27	Jevon Kearse	.75
RB28	Tim Brown	1.00
29	Chris McAlister	.75

2003 Topps Record Breaker Autographs

		NM/M
Common Player:		10.00
Inserted in varying quantities		
RB-JE	John Elway	160.00
RB-BF	Brett Favre	175.00
RB-MH	Marvin Harrison	25.00
RB-PH	Priest Holmes	25.00
RB-DM	Dan Marino	150.00
RB-DMA	Derrick Mason	12.00
RB-CP	Clinton Portis	125.00
RB-BS	Barry Sanders	
RB-JS	Jimmy Smith	10.00
RB-MS	Michael Strahan	
RB-JT	Jason Taylor	25.00
RB-LTO	LaDainian Tomlinson	
RB-SY	Steve Young	60.00

2003 Topps Record Breaker Dual Autographs

		NM/M
Production to varying quantities		
RBD-EM	John Elway, Dan Marino	250.00
RBD-TP	LaDainian Tomlinson, Clinton Portis	125.00
RBD-MS	Derrick Mason, Jimmy Smith	
RBD-ST	Michael Strahan, Jason Taylor	
RBD-SS	Barry Sanders, Emmitt Smith	

2003 Topps Record Breaker Relics

		NM/M
Common Player:		12.00
Production to varying quantities		
RBR-JE	John Elway	65.00
RBR-MF	Marshall Faulk	15.00
RBR-DM	Dan Marino	100.00
RBR-WP	Walter Payton	75.00
RBR-JR	Jerry Rice	20.00
RBR-BS	Barry Sanders	60.00
RBR-ES	Emmitt Smith	40.00
RBR-LT	LaDainian Tomlinson	12.00
RBR-KW	Kurt Warner	15.00
RBR-RW	Ricky Williams	25.00
RBR-SY	Steve Young	25.00

2003 Topps Record Breaker Dual Relics

		NM/M
Production to varying quantities		
RDR-SR	Emmitt Smith, Jerry Rice	175.00
RDR-FW	Marshall Faulk, Ricky Williams	
RDR-DT	Corey Dillon, LaDainian Tomlinson	35.00
RDR-SS	Barry Sanders, Emmitt Smith	75.00
RDR-ME	Dan Marino, John Elway	175.00
RDR-YE	Steve Young, John Elway	95.00
RDR-PS	Walter Payton, Emmitt Smith	275.00
RDR-SP	Barry Sanders, Walter Payton	250.00

2003 Topps Ring of Honor

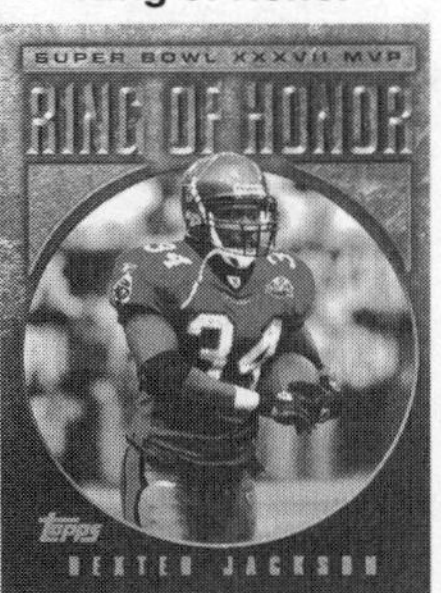

		NM/M
Complete Set (1):		2.00
DJ37	Dexter Jackson	2.00

2003 Topps Split the Uprights

		NM/M
Common Player:		25.00
SU1	Martin Gramatica	40.00
SU2	Sebastian Janikowski	25.00

2003 Topps Super Bowl MVP

		NM/M
Complete Set (1):		50.00
SBMVP37	Dexter Jackson	50.00

2003 Topps Super Tix Relics

		NM/M
Common Player:		10.00
Inserted 1:614		
ST1	Brad Johnson	25.00
ST2	Rich Gannon	20.00
ST3	Keyshawn Johnson	15.00
ST4	Jerry Rice	30.00
ST5	Michael Pittman	10.00
ST6	Charlie Garner	10.00
ST7	Derrick Brooks	20.00
ST8	Jerry Porter	15.00
ST9	Warren Sapp	20.00
ST10	Tim Brown	18.00

2003 Topps Topps Autographs

		NM/M
Common Player:		10.00
Production to varying quantities		
T-LC	Laveranues Coles	12.00
T-AD	Andre Davis	15.00
T-DD	Donald Driver	20.00
T-TH	Travis Henry	15.00
T-LJ	Larry Johnson	40.00
T-RL	Reshard Lee	12.00
T-BL	Byron Leftwich	75.00
T-TM	Tommy Maddox	35.00
T-DM	Derrick Mason	10.00
T-JM	James Mungro	20.00
T-DN	Dennis Northcutt	10.00
T-CPA	Carson Palmer	
T-JPE	Julian Peterson	12.00
T-JP	Jerry Porter	20.00
T-CR	Charles Rogers	55.00
T-MS	Marcel Shipp	10.00
T-SS	Steve Smith	10.00
T-JT	Jason Taylor	

2003 Topps Team Topps Autographs

		NM/M
Complete Set (1):		85.00
	Jim Brown	85.00

2003 Topps All American

		NM/M
Complete Set (150):		65.00
Common Player:		.15
Unlisted Star:		.75
Minor Star:		.50
Common Rookie (101-150):		1.50
Unlisted Rookie Star:		2.00
Rookies Inserted 1:4		
Pack(6):		4.00
Wax Box(20):		60.00
1	Marvin Harrison	.60
2	Tiki Barber	.40
3	Jamal Lewis	.60
4	Tim Couch	1.00
5	Michael Bennett	.60
6	Brad Johnson	.40
7	Garrison Hearst	.40
8	Plaxico Burress	.60
9	Rod Gardner	.40
10	Charlie Garner	.40
11	Chad Pennington	1.00
12	Brian Griese	.60
13	Julius Peppers	.50
14	David Boston	.60
15	Anthony Thomas	.60
16	Ahman Green	.60
17	Fred Taylor	.60
18	Joe Horn	.40
19	Joey Galloway	.40
20	Eddie George	.60
21	Jeff Garcia	.60
22	Hines Ward	.40
23	Kurt Warner	1.50
24	Marty Booker	.40
25	Joey Harrington	2.00
26	Jay Fiedler	.40
27	Troy Brown	.15
28	David Carr	2.00
29	Eric Moulds	.40
30	Michael Vick	2.25
31	Keyshawn Johnson	.60
32	Torry Holt	.60
33	LaDainian Tomlinson	1.50
34	Duce Staley	.40
35	Curtis Martin	.60
36	Stephen Davis	.40
37	Jim Miller	.15
38	Travis Taylor	.15
39	Jimmy Smith	.15
40	Trent Green	.40
41	Tom Brady	2.00
42	Randy Moss	2.00
43	Clinton Portis	2.00
44	Emmitt Smith	2.00
45	Steve McNair	.60
46	Shaun Alexander	.60
47	Jerome Bettis	.40
48	Rich Gannon	.40
49	William Green	.60
50	Priest Holmes	1.00
51	James Stewart	.40
52	Warrick Dunn	.40
53	Jake Plummer	.40
54	Antowain Smith	.15
55	Peyton Manning	2.00
56	Deuce McAllister	1.00
57	Jeremy Shockey	1.50
58	Darrell Jackson	.15
59	Derrick Mason	.40
60	Terrell Owens	.60
61	Laveranues Coles	.40
62	Amani Toomer	.40
63	Tony Gonzalez	.40
64	Corey Bradford	.15
65	Donald Driver	.40
66	Rod Smith	.40
67	Chad Johnson	.15
68	Travis Henry	.40
69	Mark Brunell	.60
70	Edgerrin James	1.50
71	Jerry Rice	2.00
72	Aaron Brooks	1.00
73	Marshall Faulk	1.25
74	Curtis Conway	.40
75	Tommy Maddox	.50
76	Isaac Bruce	.50
77	Matt Hasselbeck	.15
78	Muhsin Muhammad	.40
79	Drew Bledsoe	1.25
80	Ricky Williams	1.25
81	Daunte Culpepper	1.25
82	Chad Hutchinson	.60
83	Brian Urlacher	1.50
84	Drew Brees	1.50
85	Corey Dillon	.60
86	Chris Chambers	.60
87	Peerless Price	.60
88	Kerry Collins	.40
89	Donovan McNabb	1.25
90	Brett Favre	2.50
91	Patrick Ramsey	.60
92	T.J. Duckett	.60
93	Derrick Brooks	.15
94	Jon Kitna	.15
95	Jerry Porter	.60
96	Todd Pinkston	.15
97	Tai Streets	.15
98	Ray Lewis	.40
99	Michael Pittman	.15
100	Brian Finneran	.15
101	*Carson Palmer SP*	7.00
102	*Terrell Suggs SP*	3.00
103	*Boss Bailey*	1.50
104	*Justin Gage*	1.00
105	*Bobby Wade*	1.00
106	*Larry Johnson SP*	3.00
107	*Ken Dorsey SP*	3.00
108	*Quentin Griffin*	2.00
109	*Musa Smith*	1.25
110	*Chris Simms SP*	3.00
111	*Michael Haynes*	1.50
112	*Charles Rogers SP*	5.00
113	*Kliff Kingsbury*	1.50
114	*Jerome McDougle*	1.00
115	*Reshard Lee*	1.00
116	*Chris Brown SP*	4.00
117	*Bryant Johnson SP*	3.00
118	*Teyo Johnson*	1.00
119	*Talman Gardner SP*	1.50
120	*Brian St. Pierre*	1.00
121	*Onterrio Smith SP*	2.00

122 *Marcus Trufant* 1.50
123 *Earnest Graham* 1.00
124 *Kareem Kelly* 1.00
125 *Jason Witten* 1.00
126 *Brandon Lloyd SP* 1.50
127 *Anquan Boldin* 1.00
128 *Lee Suggs* 2.50
129 *Terry Pierce* 1.00
130 *Dallas Clark* 1.00
131 *Kelley Washington SP* 2.00
132 *Seneca Wallace* 1.50
133 *Domanick Davis* 2.00
134 *Terrence Edwards* 1.00
135 *Dave Ragone SP* 2.00
136 *Andre Johnson SP* 4.00
137 *Taylor Jacobs SP* 2.00
138 *Kyle Boller SP* 4.00
139 *Willis McGahee SP* 5.00
140 *Byron Leftwich SP* 7.00
141 *Sam Aiken* 1.00
142 *Bennie Joppru* 1.50
143 *Justin Fargas SP* 1.50
144 *Avon Cobourne* 1.50
145 *Rex Grossman SP* 3.50
146 *LaBrandon Toefield* 1.00
147 *Tyrone Calico* 1.00
148 *Brad Banks* 1.50
149 *Terence Newman* 2.75
150 *Jimmy Kennedy* 1.00

2003 Topps All American Foil

Inserted 1:1 1X-3X

2003 Topps All American Gold

Production 55 sets 3X-15X

2003 Topps All American All American Autographs

NM/M
Common Player: 8.00
Production to varying quantities
AA-BBA Brad Banks 15.00
AA-KB Kyle Boller 35.00
AA-CB Chris Brown 25.00
AA-TC Tyrone Calico/Redem 15.00
AA-AC Avon Cobourne 15.00
AA-KD Ken Dorsey 35.00
AA-JF Justin Fargas 15.00
AA-TG Talman Gardner 8.00
AA-EG Earnest Graham 15.00
AA-QG Quentin Griffin 25.00
AA-RG Rex Grossman
AA-TJ Taylor Jacobs 15.00
AA-AJ Andre Johnson 35.00
AA-BJ Bryant Johnson 20.00
AA-LJ Larry Johnson 60.00
AA-KKE Kareem Kelly 10.00
AA-BL Byron Leftwich 85.00
AA-WM Willis McGahee 50.00
AA-BM Billy McMullen 10.00
AA-CP Carson Palmer 85.00
AA-CR Charles Rogers/ Redem 60.00
AA-CS Chris Simms
AA-OS Onterrio Smith 25.00
AA-LS Lee Suggs
AA-JT Jason Thomas 12.00
AA-LT LaBrandon Toefield 8.00
AA-SW Seneca Wallace 15.00
AA-KW Kelley Washington 15.00

2003 Topps All American Campus Connection Autographs

NM/M
Common Player: 35.00
Production 100 sets
CC-PD Clinton Portis, Ken Dorsey 50.00
CC-HS Priest Holmes, Chris Simms 45.00
CC-MR Derrick Mason, Charles Rogers
CC-ZC Amos Zereoue, Avon Cobourne 40.00
CC-MD Ken Dorsey, Santana Moss 35.00

2003 Topps All American Conference Call Autographs

NM/M
Common Player: 35.00
Production 100 sets
CCA-SM Willis McGahee, Lee Suggs/Redem 60.00
CCA-CM Willis McGahee, Avon Cobourne 50.00
CCA-BP Carson Palmer, Kyle Boller/ Redem 100.00
CCA-RJ Bryant Johnson, Charles Rogers
CCA-GB Chris Brown, Quentin Griffin 50.00

A player's name in *italic* type indicates a rookie card.

2003 Topps All American Fabric of America Relics

NM/M
Common Player: 6.00
Inserted 1:10
FA-SA Sam Aiken 8.00
FA-TBC Tully Banta-Cain 6.00
FA-JB Julian Battle 6.00
FA-TC Tyrone Calico 8.00
FA-AC Angelo Crowell 6.00
FA-DD Domanick Davis 12.00
FA-DG Doug Gabriel 6.00
FA-TG Talman Gardner 6.00
FA-KG Kevin Garrett 8.00
FA-EG Earnest Graham 6.00
FA-JGR Justin Griffith 6.00
FA-JG DeJuan Groce 8.00
FA-MH Michael Haynes 8.00
FA-VH Victor Hobson 8.00
FA-TJ Taylor Jacobs 8.00
FA-BJA Bradie James 6.00
FA-JJ Jarret Johnson 8.00
FA-BJO Bennie Joppru 12.00
FA-CK Chris Kelsay 6.00
FA-KK Kliff Kingsbury 8.00
FA-VM Vincent Manuwai 6.00
FA-RM Rashean Mathis 6.00
FA-JM Jerome McDougle 8.00
FA-BN Bruce Nelson 6.00
FA-CP Carson Palmer 22.00
FA-AP Artose Pinner 8.00
FA-DR Dave Ragone 8.00
FA-CS Chris Simms 12.00
FA-ES Eric Steinbach 8.00
FA-JS Jon Stinchcomb 6.00
FA-MT Marcus Trufant 8.00
FA-AWA Aaron Walker 6.00
FA-TW Ty Warren 8.00
FA-MW Matt Wilhelm 8.00
FA-BW Brett Williams 6.00
FA-KW Kevin Williams 8.00
FA-AW Andre Woolfolk 8.00

2003 Topps All American Jersey Backs Relics

NM/M
Common Player:
Production 25 sets
JB-JF Justin Fargas 35.00
JB-TG Talman Gardner
JB-TJ Taylor Jacobs 50.00
JB-BJ Bryant Johnson
JB-LJ Larry Johnson 75.00
JB-KK Kliff Kingsbury
JB-CP Carson Palmer
JB-DR Dave Ragone
JB-CS Chris Simms

2003 Topps Chrome

NM/M
Complete Set (275): 500.00
Common Player (1-165): .40
Minor Stars: .75
Unlisted Stars: 1.00
Common Rookie (166-275): 4.00
Minor Rookies: 5.00
Unlisted Rookies: 6.00
Pack (4): 3.25
Box (24): 55.00
1 Michael Vick 4.00
2 Josh Reed .75
3 James Stewart .75
4 Quincy Morgan .75
5 Corey Bradford .40
6 Fred Taylor 1.00
7 David Patten .40
8 Jerome Bettis .75
9 Jerry Porter .75
10 Steve McNair 1.00
11 Stephen Davis .75
12 Frank Wycheck .40
13 Marcus Pollard .40
14 David Terrell .75
15 Bubba Franks .75
16 Trent Green .75
17 Mark Brunell .75
18 James Thrash .75
19 Mike Alstott .75
20 Deuce McAllister 1.00
21 Santana Moss .75
22 Jason Taylor .75
23 Corey Dillon 1.00
24 Jeff Blake .75
25 Ed McCaffrey .75
26 Priest Holmes 1.00
27 Tim Brown 1.00
28 Curtis Martin 1.00
29 Derrius Thompson .40
30 Jonathan Wells .40
31 William Green 1.00
32 Bill Schroeder .40
33 Amos Zereoue .75
34 Warren Sapp .75
35 Koren Robinson .75
36 Donovan McNabb 1.50
37 Edgerrin James 1.50
38 Kelly Holcomb .75
39 Daunte Culpepper 1.00
40 Tommy Maddox .75
41 Rod Gardner .75
42 T.J. Duckett 1.00
43 Drew Bledsoe 1.50
44 Rod Smith .75
45 Peyton Manning 2.00
46 Darrell Jackson .75
47 Brett Favre 4.00
48 Ashley Lelie 1.00
49 Jeremy Shockey 2.50
50 Hines Ward .25
51 Jeff Garcia 1.00
52 Eddie Kennison .75
53 Brian Urlacher 2.00
54 Antwann Randle El 1.00
55 Eddie George 1.00
56 Derrick Brooks .75
57 Isaac Bruce .75
58 Joe Horn .75
59 Jon Kitna .75
60 David Boston 1.00
61 Todd Heap .40
62 Lamar Smith .75
63 Germane Crowell .75
64 Kevin Johnson .75
65 Drew Brees 1.50
66 Chad Lewis .40
67 Charlie Garner .75
68 Laveranues Coles .75
69 Shaun Alexander 1.00
70 Kevan Barlow .75
71 Aaron Brooks 1.00
72 Jake Plummer .75
73 Emmitt Smith 3.00
74 Terry Glenn .75
75 Michael Bennett 1.00
76 Deion Branch .75
77 Keyshawn Johnson .75
78 Marc Bulger 1.00
79 Matt Hasselbeck .75
80 Garrison Hearst .75
81 Brian Griese 1.00
82 Johnnie Morton .75
83 Patrick Ramsey 1.00
84 Donald Driver .75
85 Joey Harrington 2.50
86 Ricky Williams 1.00
87 Jabar Gaffney .75
88 Duce Staley .75
89 Jimmy Smith .75
90 Reggie Wayne .75
91 Chad Johnson .75
92 Steve Beuerlein .75
93 Joey Galloway .75
94 Curtis Conway .75
95 Brad Johnson .75
96 Jamal Lewis 1.00
97 Terrell Owens 1.00
98 Todd Pinkston .75
99 Keenan McCardell .75
100 Antonio Bryant .75
101 Eric Moulds .75
102 Jim Miller .75
103 Troy Brown .75
104 Rich Gannon .75
105 Chad Pennington 1.50
106 Michael Strahan .75
107 Chris Chambers 1.00
108 Antowain Smith .75
109 Derrick Mason .75
110 Michael Pittman .75
111 Torry Holt 1.00
112 Tony Gonzalez .75
113 Marty Booker .75
114 Shannon Sharpe 1.00
115 Zach Thomas .75
116 Plaxico Burress 1.00
117 Kurt Warner 2.00
118 Warrick Dunn .75
119 Jay Fiedler .75
120 LaMont Jordan .75
121 Kerry Collins .75
122 Jerry Rice 3.00
123 Randy Moss 2.00
124 Tom Brady 2.00
125 Amani Toomer .75
126 Travis Henry .75
127 Chris Chandler .75
128 Ray Lewis .75
129 Donte Stallworth .75
130 David Carr 2.50
131 Andre Davis .75
132 Travis Taylor .75
133 Steve Smith .75
134 Tiki Barber 1.00
135 Chad Hutchinson 1.00
136 Marshall Faulk 1.50
137 Peerless Price .75
138 Ahman Green 1.00
139 Julius Peppers .75
140 LaDainian Tomlinson 1.50
141 Muhsin Muhammad .75
142 Tim Couch 1.00
143 Clinton Portis 3.00
144 Anthony Thomas 1.00
145 Marvin Harrison 1.00
146 Priest Holmes 1.00
147 Drew Bledsoe 1.00
148 Tom Brady 1.00
149 Shaun Alexander .75
150 Brett Favre 2.50
151 Travis Henry .40
152 Marshall Faulk 1.00
153 Terrell Owens .75
154 Jeff Garcia .75
155 Plaxico Burress .75
156 Donovan McNabb 1.00
157 Ricky Williams 1.50
158 Michael Vick 2.50
159 Steve Smith .40
160 Marvin Harrison .75
161 Chad Pennington 1.00
162 Jeremy Shockey 1.25
163 Tommy Maddox .75
164 Steve McNair .75
165 Rich Gannon .40
166 *Carson Palmer* 30.00
167 *J.R. Tolver* 5.00
168 *Michael Haynes* 5.00
169 *Terrell Suggs* 8.00
170 *Rashean Mathis* 4.00
171 *Chris Kelsay* 5.00
172 *Brad Banks* 6.00
173 *Jordan Gross* 5.00
174 *Lee Suggs* 8.00
175 *Kliff Kingsbury* 6.00
176 *William Joseph* 6.00
177 *Kelley Washington* 8.00
178 *Jerome McDougle* 6.00
179 *Keenan Howry* 6.00
180 *Chris Simms* 12.00
181 *Alonzo Jackson* 6.00
182 *L.J. Smith* 5.00
183 *Mike Doss* 5.00
184 *Bobby Wade* 5.00
185 *Ken Hamlin* 5.00
186 *Brandon Lloyd* 8.00
187 *Justin Fargas* 8.00
188 *Dewayne Robertson* 6.00
189 *Bryant Johnson* 8.00
190 *Boss Bailey* 6.00
191 *Onterrio Smith* 10.00
192 *Doug Gabriel* 5.00
193 *Jimmy Kennedy* 5.00
194 *B.J. Askew* 6.00
195 *Taylor Jacobs* 8.00
196 *Dallas Clark* 8.00
197 *Dewayne White* 4.00
198 *Arnaz Battle* 5.00
199 *Kareem Kelly* 5.00
200 *Talman Gardner* 6.00
201 *Billy McMullen* 6.00
202 *Travis Anglin* 5.00
203 *Anquan Boldin* 12.00
204 *Osi Umenyiora* 4.00
205 *Byron Leftwich* 30.00
206 *Marcus Trufant* 6.00
207 *Sam Aiken* 5.00
208 *LaBrandon Toefield* 6.00
209 *Terry Pierce* 4.00
210 *Charles Rogers* 20.00
211 *Chaun Thompson* 4.00
212 *Chris Brown* 8.00
213 *Justin Gage* 5.00
214 *Kevin Williams* 6.00
215 *Willis McGahee* 20.00
216 *Victor Hobson* 5.00
217 *Brian St. Pierre* 6.00
218 *Nate Burleson* 6.00
219 *Calvin Pace* 4.00
220 *Larry Johnson* 15.00
221 *Andre Woolfolk* 5.00
222 *Tyrone Calico* 6.00
223 *Seneca Wallace* 8.00
224 *Domanick Davis* 10.00
225 *Rex Grossman* 25.00
226 *Artose Pinner* 6.00
227 *Jason Witten* 6.00
228 *Bennie Joppru* 5.00
229 *Bethel Johnson* 6.00
230 *Kyle Boller* 20.00
231 *Shaun McDonald* 5.00
232 *Musa Smith* 8.00
233 *Ken Dorsey* 10.00
234 *Johnathan Sullivan* 4.00
235 *Andre Johnson* 20.00
236 *Nick Barnett* 5.00
237 *Teyo Johnson* 8.00
238 *Terence Newman* 10.00
239 *Kevin Curtis* 6.00
240 *Dave Ragone* 8.00
241 *Ty Warren* 5.00
242 *Walter Young* 4.00
243 *Kevin Walter* 4.00
244 *Carl Ford* 4.00
245 *Cecil Sapp* 6.00
246 *Sultan McCullough* 5.00
247 *Eugene Wilson* 5.00
248 *Ricky Manning* 5.00
249 *Andrew Williams* 5.00
250 *Juston Wood* 4.00
251 *Corey Redding* 4.00
252 *Charles Tillman* 4.00
253 *Terrence Edwards* 5.00
254 *Adrian Madise* 5.00
255 *David Kircus* 5.00
256 *Zuriel Smith* 5.00
257 *Earnest Graham* 5.00
258 *Ronald Bellamy* 5.00
259 *John Anderson* 4.00
260 *David Tyree* 4.00
261 *Malaefou MacKenzie* 4.00
262 *Ahmaad Galloway* 4.00
263 *Brooks Bollinger* 5.00
264 *Gibran Hamdan* 5.00
265 *Taco Wallace* 5.00
266 *LaTarence Dunbar* 4.00
267 *Justin Griffith* 4.00
268 *Bradie James* 5.00
269 *Dan Curley* 4.00
270 *Kenny Peterson* 4.00
271 *DeAndrew Rubin* 4.00
272 *Ryan Hoag* 4.00
273 *Rien Long* 4.00
274 *Troy Polamalu* 8.00
275 *Terrence Holt* 4.00

2003 Topps Chrome Refractors

Stars: 2X-4X
Production 599 Sets
Rookies: 2X-4X
Production 100 Sets
Cards Have Black Borders

2003 Topps Chrome Xfractors

Stars: 5X-10X
Rookies: 2X-4X
Production 101 Sets
Cards Have Gold Borders

2003 Topps Chrome Gridiron Badges

NM/M
Common Player: 12.00
Production 75 Sets
GB-JA John Abraham 12.00
GB-CB Champ Bailey 15.00
GB-DB Drew Bledsoe 20.00
GB-CD Corey Dillon 15.00
GB-MF Marshall Faulk 20.00
GB-BF Bubba Franks 15.00
GB-RG Rich Gannon 15.00
GB-JG Jeff Garcia 15.00
GB-MH Marvin Harrison 20.00
GB-THE Todd Heap 12.00
GB-JH Joe Horn 12.00
GB-JL John Lynch 15.00
GB-PM Peyton Manning 30.00
GB-EM Eric Moulds 15.00
GB-TO Terrell Owens 15.00
GB-JR Jerry Rice 50.00
GB-JS Jeremy Shockey 20.00
GB-ES Emmitt Smith 50.00
GB-MS Michael Strahan 12.00
GB-JT Jason Taylor 12.00
GB-BU Brian Urlacher 30.00
GB-HW Hines Ward 15.00
GB-RW Ricky Williams 30.00
GB-RWO Rod Woodson 12.00

2003 Topps Chrome Pro Bowl Jerseys

NM/M
Common Player: 10.00
Inserted 1:84
PB-CB Champ Bailey 10.00
PB-DB Drew Bledsoe 15.00
PB-MF Marshall Faulk 15.00
PB-LG La'Roi Glover 10.00
PB-TL Ty Law
PB-JL John Lynch 10.00
PB-PM Peyton Manning 15.00
PB-BM Brock Marion
PB-LM Lawyer Milloy
PB-EM Eric Moulds 12.00
PB-JP Julian Peterson 10.00
PB-DS Darren Sharper
PB-JS Jeremy Shockey 15.00
PB-JT Jason Taylor 10.00
PB-RW Rod Woodson 10.00

2003 Topps Chrome Record Breakers

NM/M
Complete Set (29): 60.00
Common Player: 1.00
Refractors: 2X-4X
Production 100 Sets
RB1 Barry Sanders 6.00
RB2 Brett Favre 8.00
RB3 Brian Mitchell 1.00
RB4 Bruce Matthews 1.00
RB5 Clinton Portis 5.00
RB6 Corey Dillon 2.50
RB7 Dan Marino 10.00
RB8 Derrick Mason 1.00

RB9 Emmitt Smith 8.00
NM/M
RB10 Jason Elam 1.00
RB11 Jason Taylor 1.00
RB12 Jerry Rice 6.00
RB13 Jimmy Smith 1.00
RB14 Terrell Owens 2.50
RB15 John Elway 10.00
RB16 LaDainian Tomlinson 2.50
RB17 Lawrence Taylor 2.50
RB18 Randy Moss 5.00
RB19 Marshall Faulk 4.00
RB20 Marvin Harrison 2.50
RB21 Michael Strahan 1.00
RB22 Peyton Manning 5.00
RB23 Priest Holmes 2.50
RB24 Rich Gannon 1.00
RB25 Ricky Williams 4.00
RB26 Rod Woodson 1.00
RB27 Jevon Kearse 1.00
RB28 Tim Brown 2.50
RB29 Chris McAllister 1.00

2003 Topps Chrome Record Breakers Relics

NM/M
Common Player: 20.00
Production 75 Sets
RBR-JE John Elway 75.00
RBR-MF Marshall Faulk 25.00
RBR-DM Dan Marino 75.00
RBR-WP Walter Payton 100.00
RBR-JR Jerry Rice 30.00
RBR-BS Barry Sanders 30.00
RBR-ES Emmitt Smith 50.00
RBR-LT LaDainian Tomlinson 20.00
RBR-KW Kurt Warner 20.00
RBR-RW Ricky Williams 25.00
RBR-SY Steve Young 30.00

2003 Topps Chrome Record Breakers Dual Relics

Production 25 Sets
RDR-SR Emmitt Smith, Jerry Rice
RDR-FW Marshall Faulk, Ricky Williams
RDR-DT Corey Dillon, LaDainian Tomlinson
RDR-SS Barry Sanders, Emmitt Smith
RDR-ME Dan Marino, John Elway
RDR-YE Steve Young, John Elway
RDR-PS Walter Payton, Emmitt Smith

2003 Topps Chrome Rookie Premiere Autographs

RP-AB Anquan Boldin
RP-KB Kyle Boller
RP-CB Chris Brown
RP-NB Nate Burleson
RP-TC Tyrone Calico
RP-DC Dallas Clark
RP-KC Kevin Curtis
RP-JF Justin Fargas
RP-RG Rex Grossman
RP-BL Byron Leftwich
RP-TJ Taylor Jacobs
RP-AJ Andre Johnson
RP-BJO Bethel Johnson
RP-BJ Bryant Johnson
RP-LJ Larry Johnson
RP-TJO Teyo Johnson
RP-KK Kliff Kingsbury
RP-WM Willis McGahee
RP-TN Terence Newman
RP-CP Carson Palmer
RP-AP Artose Pinner
RP-DR Dave Ragone
RP-DRO Dewayne Robertson
RP-BS Brian St. Pierre
RP-MS Musa Smith
RP-OS Onterrio Smith
RP-TS Terrell Suggs
RP-MT Marcus Trufant
RP-SW Seneca Wallace
RP-KW Kelley Washington

2003 Topps Draft Picks & Prospects

NM/M
Common Player: .20
Unlisted Stars: .40
Minor Stars: .60
Chrome Version 1X-3X
Chrome Refractor Version 2X-5X
Overall Autograph/ Relic Inserted 1:12
Pack(5): 3.00
Wax Box(24): 55.00

NM/M
1 Priest Holmes 1.00
2 Tommy Maddox .50
3 Donald Driver .50
4 Drew Bledsoe 1.25
5 Tiki Barber .40
6 Terrell Owens .60
7 Rich Gannon .60
8 Isaac Bruce .60
9 Stephen Davis .40
10 Peyton Manning 2.00
11 Tony Gonzalez .40
12 Marty Booker .40
13 Warrick Dunn .40
14 Jimmy Smith .20
15 Troy Brown .20
16 Jerry Rice 2.00
17 Curtis Conway .40
18 Kurt Warner 1.50
19 Steve McNair .60
20 Edgerrin James 1.50
21 Aaron Brooks 1.00
22 Joey Galloway .40
23 Peerless Price .60
24 Torry Holt .60
25 Derrick Mason .40
26 Curtis Martin .60
27 Daunte Culpepper 1.25
28 Ahman Green .60
29 Tim Couch 1.00
30 Ricky Williams 1.25
31 Darrell Jackson .20
32 Keyshawn Johnson .60
33 Jeff Garcia .60
34 Charlie Garner .40
35 Randy Moss 2.00
36 Rod Smith .40
37 Jamal Lewis .60
38 Corey Dillon .60
39 Marvin Harrison .60
40 Joe Horn .20
41 Laveranues Coles .40
42 Hines Ward .40
43 Brad Johnson .40
44 Eddie George .60
45 Donovan McNabb 1.25
46 Marshall Faulk 1.25
47 Amani Toomer .40
48 Trent Green .40
49 Emmitt Smith 2.00
50 Brett Favre 2.50
51 Brian Griese .60
52 Eric Moulds .40
53 Plaxico Burress .60
54 Fred Taylor .60
55 Tom Brady 2.00
56 Michael Vick 2.25
57 Andre Davis .40
58 Chris Chambers .60
59 Javon Walker .60
60 Marc Bulger .60
61 LaDainian Tomlinson 1.50
62 Chad Pennington 1.00
63 Marc Boerigter .20
64 Rod Gardner .20
65 DeShaun Foster .40
66 Chris Redman .40
67 Chad Hutchinson .60
68 Deion Branch .60
69 Jeremy Shockey 1.50
70 Shaun Alexander .60
71 Derrius Thompson .20
72 A.J. Feeley .20
73 Reggie Wayne .20
74 William Green .60
75 Julius Peppers .60
76 Travis Henry .40
77 Marcel Shipp .20
78 Michael Bennett .60
79 Maurice Morris .40
80 Josh Reed .40
81 David Terrell .40
82 Drew Brees 1.50
83 Jonathan Wells .60
84 Anthony Thomas .60
85 Quincy Morgan .40
86 Jerry Porter .40
87 Ron Johnson .20
88 Najeh Davenport .40
89 Lamar Gordon .40
90 Joey Harrington 1.50
91 Donte Stallworth 1.00
92 Kenny Watson .20
93 LaMont Jordan .20
94 Antonio Bryant .60
95 Steve Smith .20
96 T.J. Duckett .60
97 Patrick Ramsey .60
98 Santana Moss .40
99 Chad Johnson .20
100 Clinton Portis 2.00
101 Donald Reche Caldwell .60
102 Kevan Barlow .40
103 Deuce McAllister 1.00
104 Koren Robinson .40
105 Todd Heap .40
106 Jabar Gaffney .40
107 Randy McMichael .20
108 Dwight Freeney .20
109 Antwann Randle El 1.25
110 David Carr 1.50
111 *Carson Palmer* 8.00
112 *Dahrran Diedrick* 1.50
113 *Kyle Boller* 6.00
114 *Terrell Suggs* 3.50
115 *Rien Long* 1.00
116 *Justin Gage* 1.00
117 *William Joseph* 2.50
118 *Chris Simms* 3.50
119 *Avon Cobourne* 1.50
120 *Victor Hobson* 1.00
121 *Jason Gesser* 1.50
122 *Ronald Bellamy* 1.50
123 *Terence Newman* 3.50
124 *Terrence Edwards* 1.00
125 *Sultan McCullough* 1.00
126 *Kareem Kelly* 1.00
127 *Jason Witten* 1.50
128 *Mike Doss* 1.00
129 *Seneca Wallace* 2.50
130 *Chris Brown* 1.50
131 *Larry Johnson* 3.50
132 *Taylor Jacobs* 2.50
133 *Jerome McDougle* 1.50
134 *Kelley Washington* 1.50
135 *Brad Banks* 2.50
136 *Dewayne White* 1.00
137 *LaBrandon Toefield* 1.00
138 *Brian St. Pierre* 1.50
139 *Kindal Moorehead* 1.00
140 *Willis McGahee* 6.00
141 *Jimmy Kennedy* 1.50
142 *Talman Gardner* 1.50
143 *Chris Kelsay* 1.00
144 *Corey Redding* 1.00
145 *Dave Ragone* 2.50
146 *Earnest Graham* 1.50
147 *Andre Johnson* 6.00
148 *Boss Bailey* 2.50
149 *Sam Aiken* 1.00
150 *Byron Leftwich* 8.00
151 *Teyo Johnson* 1.50
152 *Quentin Griffin* 3.00
153 *Justin Fargas* 1.50
154 *Bradie James* 1.00
155 *Andre Woolfolk* 1.50
156 *Marcus Trufant* 2.00
157 *Ken Dorsey* 3.50
158 *Onterrio Smith* 1.50
159 *Bryant Johnson* 3.50
160 *Charles Rogers* 6.00
161 *Kliff Kingsbury* 1.50
162 *Michael Haynes* 1.50
163 *Bennie Joppru* 1.50
164 *Brandon Lloyd* 1.50
165 *Jarret Johnson* 1.00

2003 Topps Draft Picks & Prospects Class Marks Auto.

NM/M
Common Player: 10.00
Production to varying quantities
Foilboard Version 1X-3X
Inserted 1:272
CM-MB Marquel Blackwell 12.00
CM-KB Kyle Boller/Redem 45.00
CM-CB Chris Brown 12.00
CM-AC Avon Cobourne 15.00
CM-KD Ken Dorsey 25.00
CM-TG Talman Gardner 15.00
CM-QG Quentin Griffin 12.00
CM-TJ Taylor Jacobs 20.00
CM-AJ Andre Johnson 45.00
CM-BJ Bryant Johnson 25.00
CM-LJ Larry Johnson 25.00
CM-KKE Kareem Kelly 10.00
CM-BL Byron Leftwich 65.00
CM-WM Willis McGahee/ Redem 45.00
CM-CP Carson Palmer 65.00
CM-CR Charles Rogers/ Redem 45.00
CM-CS Chris Simms
CM-OS Onterrio Smith/ Redem 15.00
CM-LS Lee Suggs/Redem 20.00
CM-JT Jason Thomas 10.00
CM-LT LaBrandon Toefield 10.00
CM-SW Seneca Wallace 20.00
CM-KW Kelley Washington 15.00

2003 Topps Draft P & P Classmate Cuts Dual Relics

NM/M
Common Player: 15.00
Inserted 1:1951 Production 75 sets
Foilboard Version 2X-4X
Inserted 1:5854 Production 25 sets
CCD-RB Dave Ragone, Kyle Boller 30.00
CCD-FJ Justin Fargas, Larry Johnson
CCD-JL Bryant Johnson, Brandon Lloyd
CCD-DG Ken Dorsey, Jason Gesser 25.00
CCD-CW Kevin Curtis, Kelley Washington 15.00

2003 Topps Draft P & P Collegiate Prep Patch Relics

NM/M
Common Player: 15.00
Inserted 1:427 Production 75 sets
Foilboard Version 2X-4X
Inserted 1:1273
CC-KB Kyle Boller
CC-TC Tyrone Calico
CC-DC Dallas Clark 20.00
CC-KC Kevin Curtis
CC-KD Ken Dorsey
CC-TE Terrence Edwards
CC-JF Justin Fargas 20.00
CC-JG Justin Gage
CC-JGE Jason Gesser 20.00
CC-AJ Andre Johnson
CC-BJ Bryant Johnson
CC-JJ Jarret Johnson
CC-LJ Larry Johnson 50.00
CC-KK Kliff Kingsbury 15.00
CC-RL Reshard Lee 15.00
CC-BLL Brandon Lloyd
CC-WM Willis McGahee 60.00
CC-KM Kindal Moorehead
CC-DR Dave Ragone
CC-TS Terrell Suggs 30.00
CC-SW Seneca Wallace 35.00
CC-KW Kelley Washington 25.00
CC-JW Jason Witten

2003 Topps Draft Picks/Prospects Collegiate Cuts Relics

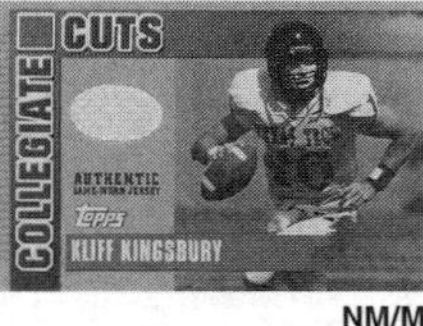

NM/M
Common Player: 8.00
Production to varying quantities
Foilboard Version 1X-2X
Inserted 1:96
CP-KB Kyle Boller 15.00
CPPTC Tyrone Calico 8.00
CP-DC Dallas Clark 8.00
CP-KC Kevin Curtis 8.00
CP-KD Ken Dorsey 12.00
CP-TE Terrence Edwards 8.00
CP-JF Justin Fargas 10.00
CP-JG Justin Gage 8.00
CP-JGE Jason Gesser 10.00
CP-AJ Andre Johnson 15.00
CP-BJ Bryant Johnson 12.00
CP-JJ Jarret Johnson 8.00
CP-LJ Larry Johnson 12.00
CP-KK Kliff Kingsbury 10.00
CP-RL Reshard Lee 8.00
CP-BLL Brandon Lloyd 8.00
CP-WM Willis McGahee 15.00
CP-KM Kindal Moorehead 8.00
CP-DR Dave Ragone 10.00
CP-TS Terrell Suggs 12.00
CP-SW Seneca Wallace 10.00
CP-KW Kelley Washington 10.00
CP-JW Jason Witten 10.00

2003 Topps Draft Picks & Prospects Pen Pals Dual Autos.

NM/M
Common Player: 50.00
Inserted 1:1979 Production 75 sets
Foilboard Version 2X-4X
Inserted 1:6180
PP-LP Byron Leftwich, Carson Palmer 300.00
PP-SS Lee Suggs, Onterrio Smith 50.00
PP-DS Ken Dorsey, Chris Simms 60.00
PP-RJ Charles Rogers, Andre Johnson 125.00
PP-JM Larry Johnson, Willis McGahee 125.00

2003 Topps Hall of Fame Class of 2003

NM/M
Common Player: 2.00
1 Marcus Allen 5.00
2 Elvin Bethea 2.00
3 Joe DeLamielleure 2.00
4 James Lofton 3.00
5 Hank Stram 3.00

2003 Topps Pristine

NM/M
Common Player: 1.00
Minor Stars: 1.50
Unlisted Stars: 2.00
Common Rookies (51-149): 2.50
Minor Rookies: 3.00
Unlisted Rookies: 4.00
Common Uncommon RC: 2.50
Production 1499 Sets
Common Rare RC: 5.00
Production 499 Sets
Pack (8): 25.00
Box (5): 85.00
1 Brett Favre 5.00
2 Rich Gannon 1.00
3 Randy Moss 2.50
4 Travis Henry 1.00
5 Troy Brown 1.00
6 Darrell Jackson 1.00
7 Steve McNair 1.50
8 Plaxico Burress 1.50
9 Jerry Rice 4.00
10 Donovan McNabb 2.00
11 Marty Booker 1.00
12 Joey Galloway 1.00
13 Peerless Price 1.00
14 Emmitt Smith 4.00
15 David Carr 3.00
16 Priest Holmes 1.50
17 LaDainian Tomlinson 2.00
18 Hines Ward 1.00
19 Tiki Barber 1.00
20 Fred Taylor 1.50
21 Marvin Harrison 1.50
22 Marshall Faulk 2.00
23 Terrell Owens 1.50
24 Patrick Ramsey 1.50
25 Michael Vick 4.00
26 Tom Brady 2.00
27 Shaun Alexander 1.50
28 Derrick Mason 1.00
29 Keyshawn Johnson 1.00
30 Ricky Williams 2.50
31 Ahman Green 1.50
32 Joey Harrington 3.00
33 Corey Dillon 1.50
34 Jamal Lewis 1.50
35 Drew Bledsoe 2.00
36 Tommy Maddox 1.50
37 Kurt Warner 2.00
38 Deuce McAllister 1.50
39 Curtis Martin 1.50
40 Chad Pennington 2.00
41 Trent Green 1.00
42 Edgerrin James 2.00
43 Clinton Portis 4.00
44 Eric Moulds 1.00
45 Peyton Manning 2.50
46 Jeff Garcia 1.00
47 Daunte Culpepper 1.50
48 Tim Couch 1.50
49 Drew Brees 2.00
50 Aaron Brooks 1.50
51 *Anquan Boldin* 5.00
52 Anquan Boldin U 5.00
53 Anquan Boldin R 10.00
54 *Andre Johnson* 6.00
55 Andre Johnson U 6.00
56 Andre Johnson R 12.00
57 *Artose Pinner* 2.50
58 Artose Pinner U 2.50
59 Artose Pinner R 5.00
60 *Bryant Johnson* 4.00
61 Bryant Johnson U 4.00
62 Bryant Johnson R 8.00
63 *Bethel Johnson* 3.00
64 Bethel Johnson U 3.00
65 Bethel Johnson R 6.00
66 *Byron Leftwich* 15.00
67 Byron Leftwich U 10.00
68 Byron Leftwich R 20.00
69 *Brian St. Pierre* 3.00
70 Brian St. Pierre U 3.00
71 Brian St. Pierre R 6.00
72 *Chris Brown* 3.00
73 Chris Brown U 3.00
74 Chris Brown R 6.00
75 *Carson Palmer* 8.00
76 Carson Palmer 8.00
77 Carson Palmer 15.00
78 *Charles Rogers* 6.00
79 Charles Rogers U 6.00
80 Charles Rogers R 12.00
81 *Chris Simms* 5.00
82 Chris Simms U 5.00
83 Chris Simms R 10.00
84 *Dallas Clark* 3.00
85 Dallas Clark U 3.00
86 Dallas Clark R 6.00
87 *Dave Ragone* 3.00
88 Dave Ragone U 3.00
89 Dave Ragone R 6.00
90 *Dewayne Robertson* 2.50
91 Dewayne Robertson U 2.50
92 Dewayne Robertson R 5.00
93 *Justin Fargas* 4.00
94 Justin Fargas U 4.00
95 Justin Fargas R 8.00
96 *Kyle Boller* 6.00
97 Kyle Boller U 6.00
98 Kyle Boller R 12.00
99 *Kevin Curtis* 3.00
100 Kevin Curtis U 3.00
101 Kevin Curtis R 6.00
102 *Ken Dorsey* 5.00
103 Ken Dorsey U 5.00
104 Ken Dorsey R 10.00
105 *Kelley Washington* 4.00
106 Kelley Washington U 4.00
107 Kelley Washington R 8.00
108 *Kliff Kingsbury* 3.00
109 Kliff Kingsbury U 3.00
110 Kliff Kingsbury R 6.00
111 *Larry Johnson* 6.00
112 Larry Johnson U 6.00
113 Larry Johnson R 12.00
114 *Musa Smith* 3.00
115 Musa Smith U 3.00
116 Musa Smith R 6.00
117 *Marcus Trufant* 2.50
118 Marcus Trufant U 2.50
119 Marcus Trufant R 5.00
120 *Nate Burleson* 3.00
121 Nate Burleson U 3.00
122 Nate Burleson R 6.00
123 *Onterrio Smith* 4.00
124 Onterrio Smith U 5.00
125 Onterrio Smith R 8.00
126 *Rex Grossman* 10.00
127 Rex Grossman U 6.00
128 Rex Grossman R 12.00
129 *Seneca Wallace* 3.00
130 Seneca Wallace U 3.00
131 Seneca Wallace R 6.00
132 *Tyrone Calico* 4.00
133 Tyrone Calico U 4.00
134 Tyrone Calico R 8.00
135 *Taylor Jacobs* 3.00
136 Taylor Jacobs U 3.00
137 Taylor Jacobs R 6.00
138 *Teyo Johnson* 3.00
139 Teyo Johnson U 3.00
140 Teyo Johnson R 6.00
141 *Terence Newman* 5.00
142 Terence Newman U 5.00
143 Terence Newman R 10.00
144 *Terrell Suggs* 4.00
145 Terrell Suggs U 4.00
146 Terrell Suggs R 8.00
147 *Willis McGahee* 6.00
148 Willis McGahee U 6.00
149 Willis McGahee R 12.00

2003 Topps Pristine Refractors

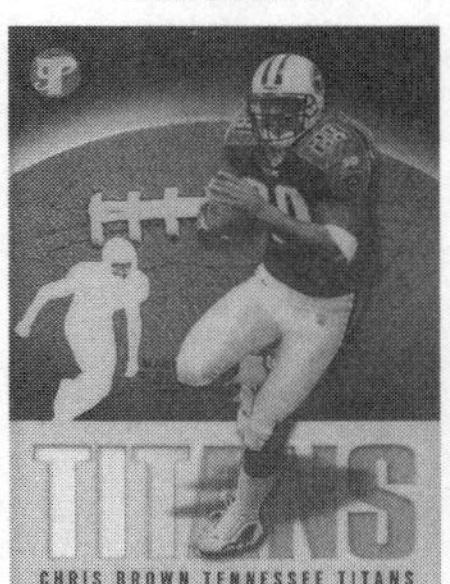

Cards 1-50: 2x-4x
Production 99 Sets
Common Rookies 51-149: 1.5x
Common Production 1499 Sets
Uncommon Rookies 51-149: 1.5x
Unc Production 499 Sets
Rare Rookies 51-149: 2x
Rare Production 99 Sets

2003 Topps Pristine Gold Refractors

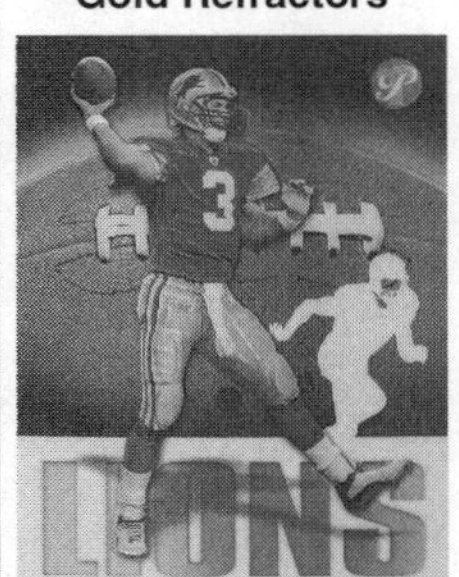

Stars 1-50: 2x-4x
Production 150 Sets
Common Rookies 51-149: 2x-4x
Common Production 75 Sets
Unc Rookies 51-149: 2x-4x
Unc Production 50 Sets
Rare Rookies 51-149: 3x-6x
Rare Production 25 Sets

2003 Topps Pristine Minis

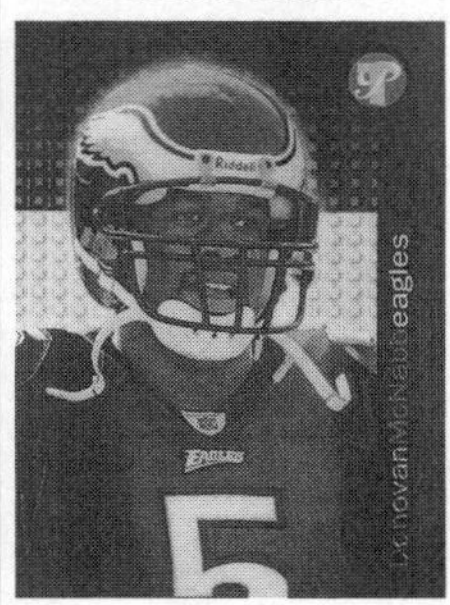

NM/M
Common Player: 1.50
Inserted 1:Box
PM1 Michael Vick 5.00
PM2 Brett Favre 5.00
PM3 Marvin Harrison 1.50
PM4 Chad Pennington 2.00
PM5 Priest Holmes 1.50
PM6 LaDainian Tomlinson 2.00
PM7 Drew Bledsoe 2.00
PM8 Ricky Williams 2.50
PM9 Randy Moss 2.50
PM10 Donovan McNabb 2.00
PM11 Peyton Manning 2.50
PM12 Deuce McAllister 1.50
PM13 Steve McNair 1.50
PM14 Clinton Portis 4.00
PM15 Jerry Rice 4.00
PM16 Terrell Owens 1.50
PM17 Marshall Faulk 2.00
PM18 Rich Gannon 1.00
PM19 Tom Brady 2.00
PM20 Jamal Lewis 1.50
PM21 Carson Palmer 6.00
PM22 Andre Johnson 5.00
PM23 Willis McGahee 5.00
PM24 Bryant Johnson 2.50
PM25 Byron Leftwich 8.00
PM26 Justin Fargas 3.00
PM27 Anquan Boldin 4.00
PM28 Rex Grossman 5.00
PM29 Larry Johnson 4.00
PM30 Taylor Jacobs 2.00
PM31 Kyle Boller 5.00
PM32 Tyrone Calico 3.00
PM33 Bethel Johnson 2.00
PM34 Charles Rogers 5.00
PM35 Teyo Johnson 2.50
PM36 Musa Smith 2.00
PM37 Kelley Washington 2.50
PM38 Chris Brown 2.00
PM39 Dallas Clark 2.00
PM40 Chris Simms 4.00
NNO Jerry Rice Auto 150.00

2003 Topps Pristine All Rookie Team Relics

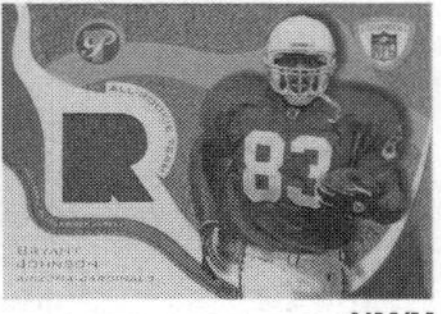

NM/M
Common Player: 10.00
Refractor Production 25 Sets
ARTKB Kyle Boller 12.00
ARTRG Rex Grossman 12.00
ARTAJ Andre Johnson 12.00
ARTBJ Bryant Johnson 10.00
ARTLJ Larry Johnson 12.00
ARTBL Byron Leftwich 20.00
ARTWM Willis McGahee 12.00
ARTCP Carson Palmer 15.00
ARTCR Charles Rogers 12.00

2003 Topps Pristine All Star Endorsements

NM/M
Common Player: 12.00
ASEMB Marty Booker 15.00
ASETG Tony Gonzalez 25.00
ASELK Lincoln Kennedy 12.00
ASEOK Olin Kreutz 12.00
ASEDM Deuce McAllister 30.00
ASEJO Jonathan Ogden 12.00
ASEWR Willie Roaf 12.00
ASEBY Bryant Young 12.00

2003 Topps Pristine Gems

		NM/M
Common Player:		10.00
PGDC	David Carr	20.00
PGJH	Joey Harrington	12.00
PGAJK	Jevon Kearse	10.00
PGADM	Deuce McAllister	12.00
PGATO	Terrell Owens	12.00
PGCP	Chad Pennington	12.00
PGACP	Clinton Portis	20.00
PGAJS	Jeremy Shockey	12.00
PGADS	Duce Staley	10.00
PGAJT	Jason Taylor	10.00
PGATH	Anthony Thomas	10.00
PGAZT	Zach Thomas	10.00
PGAT	Amani Toomer	10.00
PGABU	Brian Urlacher	15.00
PGARW	Ricky Williams	10.00

2003 Topps Pristine Igniters

		NM/M
Common Player:		6.00
Refractor Production 25 Sets		
PIJH	Joey Harrington	12.00
PITO	Terrell Owens	10.00
PICP	Chad Pennington	12.00
PIJS	Jeremy Shockey	12.00
PIJT	Jason Taylor	6.00

2003 Topps Pristine Performance

		NM/M
Common Player:		6.00
Refractor Production 25 Sets		
PPDC	David Carr	15.00
PPJK	Jevon Kearse	8.00
PPDM	Deuce McAllister	10.00
PPCP	Clinton Portis	15.00
PPDS	Duce Staley	6.00
PPATH	Anthony Thomas	8.00
PPZT	Zach Thomas	8.00
PPAT	Amani Toomer	8.00
PPBU	Brian Urlacher	12.00
PPRW	Ricky Williams	8.00

2003 Topps Pristine Personal Endorsements Autos

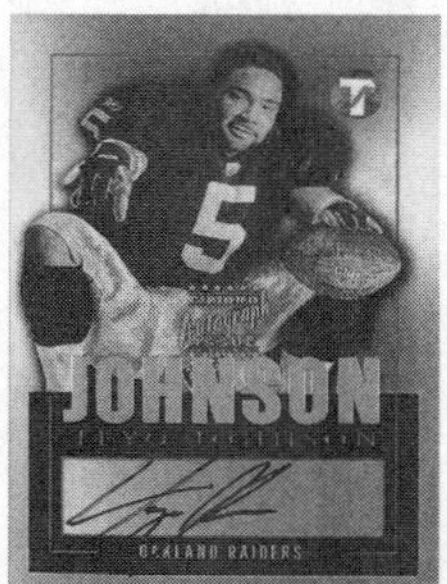

		NM/M
Common Player:		10.00
Gold Production 25 Sets		
PEKB	Kyle Boller	30.00
PECB	Chris Brown	10.00
PETC	Tyrone Calico	15.00
PEJF	Justin Fargas	15.00
PERG	Rex Grossman	40.00
PETJ	Taylor Jacobs	10.00
PEBJ	Bryant Johnson	12.00
PELJ	Larry Johnson	20.00
PETJ	Teyo Johnson	12.00
PEBL	Byron Leftwich	60.00
PEDM	Dan Marino	200.00
PEJR	Jerry Rice	150.00
PEBS	Barry Sanders	100.00
PECS	Chris Simms	20.00
PETS	Terrell Suggs	12.00
PEKW	Kelley Washington	12.00

2003 Topps Pristine Rookie Premiere Relics

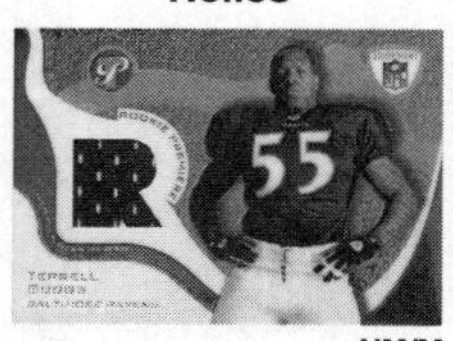

		NM/M
Common Player:		6.00
Refractor Production 25 Sets		
RPRKB	Kyle Boller	12.00
RPRNB	Nate Burleson	8.00
RPRTC	Tyrone Calico	10.00
RPRDC	Dallas Clark	8.00
RPRKC	Kevin Curtis	6.00
RPRKD	Ken Dorsey	10.00
RPRAJ	Andre Johnson	12.00
RPRBJ	Bethel Johnson	8.00
RPRLJ	Larry Johnson	12.00
RPRKK	Kliff Kingsbury	6.00
RPRBL	Byron Leftwich	20.00
RPRTN	Terence Newman	10.00
RPRAP	Artose Pinner	6.00
RPRDR	Dewayne Robertson	6.00
RPRCR	Charles Rogers	12.00
RPRMS	Musa Smith	8.00
RPRTS	Terrell Suggs	8.00
RPRMT	Marcus Trufant	6.00
RPRSW	Seneca Wallace	8.00
RPRKW	Kelley Washington	8.00

2003 Topps Pro Bowl Card Show

		NM/M
Common Player:		1.50
Gold:		3X-5X
1	Brett Favre	5.00
2	Clinton Portis	4.00
3	David Carr	5.00
4	Deuce McAllister	2.00
5	Donovan McNabb	3.00
6	Donte Stallworth	2.00
7	Edgerrin James	3.00
8	Emmitt Smith	4.00
9	Joey Harrington	3.00
10	LaDainian Tomlinson	3.00
11	Marshall Faulk	3.00
12	Peyton Manning	4.00
13	Priest Holmes	3.00
14	Ricky Williams	2.00
15	Tom Brady	4.00
16	Jeff Ulbrich	1.50
17	Ashley Lelie	3.00
18	Chris Fuamatu-Ma'afala	1.50

2003 Topps Pro Bowl Card Show Jumbos

		NM/M
Common Player:		5.00
1	Brett Favre	10.00
2	David Carr	10.00
3	LaDainian Tomlinson	5.00
4	Marshall Faulk	5.00
5	Priest Holmes	5.00
6	Tom Brady	8.00

2003 Topps Super Bowl XXXVII Card Show

		NM/M
Common Player:		2.00
Gold:		4X-6X
1	Brett Favre	5.00
2	Clinton Portis	4.00
3	David Carr	5.00
4	Deuce McAllister	2.00
5	Donovan McNabb	3.00
6	Donte Stallworth	2.00
7	Drew Bledsoe	2.00
8	Drew Brees	2.00
9	Edgerrin James	3.00
10	Emmitt Smith	4.00
11	Joey Harrington	3.00
12	LaDainian Tomlinson	3.00
13	Marshall Faulk	3.00
14	Michael Vick	4.00
15	Peyton Manning	4.00
16	Priest Holmes	3.00
17	Ricky Williams	2.00
18	Tom Brady	4.00

2003 Topps Total

		NM/M
Complete Set (550):		100.00
Common Player (1-440):		.30
Minor Stars:		.60
Unlisted Stars:		.75
Common Rookie (441-550):		.50
Minor Rookies:		.75
Unlisted Rookies:		1.00
Pack (10):		1.50
Box (36):		40.00
1	Rich Gannon	.60
2	Travis Henry	.60
3	Brian Finneran	.30
4	Ed Hartwell	.30
5	Az-Zahir Hakim	.30
6	Rodney Peete	.60
7	David Terrell	.60
8	Matt Schobel	.30
9	Andre Davis	.60
10	Dexter Coakley	.30
11	Rod Smith	.60
12	Darnerian McCants	.30
13	Robert Ferguson	.60
14	Kailee Wong	.30
15	James Mungro	.30
16	Fred Taylor	.75
17	Tony Gonzalez	.75
18	Randall Godfrey	.30
19	Robert Thomas	.30
20	Rohan Davey	.60
21	Terrell Owens	.75
22	Ron Dayne	.60
23	Charlie Batch	.60
24	Brian Westbrook	.30
25	Plaxico Burress	.75
26	Donald Reche Caldwell	.60
27	Fred Beasley	.30
28	Anthony Simmons	.30
29	Rod Woodson	.60
30	Derrick Brooks	.60
31	Shaun Ellis	.30
32	Ladell Betts	.60
33	Russell Davis	.30
34	Warrick Dunn	.60
35	Jeremy Shockey	2.00
36	Alex Van Pelt	.60
37	Todd Bouman	.60
38	Kelly Campbell	.60
39	Justin Smith	.60
40	Jamel White	.60
41	La'Roi Glover	.30
42	Ian Gold	.30
43	Robert Porcher	.30
44	Jermaine Lewis	.60
45	Marvin Harrison	.75
46	Darren Sharper	.60
47	Jamie Sharper	.30
48	Tony Richardson	.60
49	Moe Williams	.60
50	Ricky Williams	1.50
51	Ty Law	.30
52	Donte Stallworth	.75
53	Shannon Sharpe	.75
54	Santana Moss	.60
55	Charlie Garner	.60
56	Brian Dawkins	.30
57	Dan Campbell	.30
58	William Green	.75
59	Ron Dugans	.60
60	Darrell Jackson	.60
61	Marc Bulger	.75
62	Joe Jurevicius	.60
63	Erron Kinney	.30
64	Champ Bailey	.60
65	Peerless Price	.60
66	Gary Baxter	.30
67	Chris Redman	.60
68	London Fletcher	.30
69	Dee Brown	.30
70	Anthony Thomas	.75
71	Jake Delhomme	.60
72	Dorsey Levens	.60
73	Roy Williams	.75
74	Ashley Lelie	.75
75	Joey Harrington	2.00
76	William Henderson	.60
77	Corey Bradford	.60
78	Reggie Wayne	.60
79	Kyle Brady	.30
80	Trent Green	.60
81	Bill Romanowski	.30
82	Chike Okeafor	.30
83	David Patten	.30
84	Terrelle Smith	.30
85	Kerry Collins	.75
86	Derrick Mason	.60
87	Trung Canidate	.60
88	A.J. Feeley	.60
89	Jason Gildon	.30
90	Doug Flutie	.60
91	Tai Streets	.60
92	Keith Newman	.30
93	Adam Archuleta	.30
94	Simeon Rice	.60
95	Eddie George	.75
96	Frank Sanders	.60
97	Freddie Jones	.30
98	Charles Johnson	.60
99	Keith Traylor	.30
100	Drew Bledsoe	1.00
101	Muhsin Muhammad	.60
102	Marques Anderson	.30
103	Donald Hayes	.60
104	Quincy Morgan	.60
105	Chad Hutchinson	.75
106	Mike Anderson	.60
107	Randy McMichael	.60
108	Vonnie Holliday	.30
109	Marcus Coleman	.30
110	Edgerrin James	1.00
111	Michael Lewis	.30
112	Wayne Chrebet	.75
113	Antwann Randle El	.75
114	Byron Chamberlain	.30
115	Jeff Garcia	.75
116	Kim Herring	.30
117	Kenny Holmes	.30
118	John Lynch	.30
119	Doug Jolley	.60
120	Duce Staley	.60
121	Kordell Stewart	.60
122	Stephen Alexander	.30
123	Andre Carter	.30
124	Bobby Engram	.30
125	Marshall Faulk	1.00
126	Peter Sirmon	.30
127	Alge Crumpler	.30
128	Kenny Watson	.30
129	Duane Starks	.30
130	Jeff Blake	.60
131	Todd Heap	.30
132	Bobby Shaw	.30
133	Ricky Proehl	.60
134	John Abraham	.30
135	T.J. Houshmandzadeh	.60
136	Brian Urlacher	1.50
137	Darren Woodson	.30
138	Steve Beuerlein	.60
139	Cory Schlesinger	.30
140	Ahman Green	.75
141	Jabar Gaffney	.60
142	Eddie Drummond	.30
143	Stacey Mack	.60
144	Johnnie Morton	.60
145	Chris Chambers	.75
146	Jim Kleinsasser	.60
147	Tebucky Jones	.30
148	Marcus Pollard	.60
149	Tony Brackens	.30
150	Chad Pennington	1.00
151	Kevin Faulk	.60
152	Michael Lewis	.30
153	Mark Bruener	.30
154	Tim Dwight	.60
155	Jerry Rice	2.50
156	Trent Dilfer	.60
157	Jon Ritchie	.30
158	Michael Pittman	.60
159	Lamar Gordon	.60
160	Rod Gardner	.60
161	Ken Dilger	.30
162	Doug Johnson	.60
163	Peter Boulware	.30
164	Jevon Kearse	.60
165	Julius Peppers	.60
166	Chris Chandler	.60
167	Lorenzo Neal	.30
168	Kevin Johnson	.60
169	Kevin Hardy	.30
170	KaRon Coleman	.30
171	James Stewart	.60
172	Tony Fisher	.60
173	Billy Miller	.30
174	Phillip Crosby	.30
175	Priest Holmes	.75
176	Elvis Joseph	.30
177	Bryan Gilmore	.30
178	D'Wayne Bates	.60
179	Quincy Carter	.75
180	Joe Horn	.60
181	Anthony Henry	.30
182	Anthony Becht	.30
183	Mike Peterson	.30
184	James Thrash	.60
185	Jerome Bettis	.60
186	Marcellus Wiley	.30
187	Tim Rattay	.60
188	Maurice Morris	.60
189	Jason Taylor	.30
190	Keyshawn Johnson	.60
191	John Simon	.30
192	Fred Smoot	.30
193	Wendell Bryant	.30
194	Brandon Stokley	.60
195	Kurt Warner	1.50
196	Steve Smith	.30
197	Dez White	.60
198	Jim Miller	.60
199	Robert Griffith	.30
200	Michael Vick	3.00
201	Antonio Bryant	.60
202	Laveranues Coles	.60
203	Kalimba Edwards	.30
204	Bubba Franks	.60
205	David Carr	2.00
206	Dwight Freeney	.30
207	Eric Johnson	.30
208	Reggie Tongue	.30
209	Cameron Cleeland	.30
210	Michael Bennett	.75
211	Antowain Smith	.60
212	Warren Sapp	.60
213	Ike Hilliard	.60
214	Olandis Gary	.60
215	Tim Brown	.75
216	Kevin Dyson	.60
217	Eddie Kennison	.60
218	Junior Seau	.60
219	Donnie Edwards	.30
220	Shaun Alexander	.75
221	Terrence Wilkins	.30
222	Garrison Hearst	.60
223	Keith Bulluck	.30
224	Zeron Flemister	.30
225	Jake Plummer	.60
226	Chad Johnson	.60
227	Travis Taylor	.60
228	Josh Reed	.60
229	James Farrior	.30
230	Marty Booker	.60
231	Todd Pinkston	.60
232	Dennis Northcutt	.60
233	Troy Hambrick	.60
234	Roland Williams	.30
235	Bill Schroeder	.30
236	Javon Walker	.60
237	Kevin Swayne	.30
238	Dominic Rhodes	.60
239	David Garrard	.30
240	Mike Maslowski	.30
241	Travis Minor	.60
242	Terry Glenn	.60
243	Deion Branch	.60
244	Adrian Peterson	.30
245	Tiki Barber	.75
246	Ray Lewis	.60
247	Marques Tuiasosopo	.60
248	Chad Lewis	.30
249	Takeo Spikes	.30
250	LaDainian Tomlinson	1.00
251	Stephen Davis	.60
252	Koren Robinson	.60
253	Daylon McCutcheon	.30
254	Rob Johnson	.60
255	Donovan McNabb	1.00
256	Derrius Thompson	.30
257	Marcel Shipp	.60
258	Keith Brooking	.30
259	Chris McAlister	.30
260	Eric Moulds	.60
261	Amos Zereoue	.60
262	Drew Brees	.75
263	Jon Kitna	.60
264	Brad Johnson	.60
265	Emmitt Smith	2.50
266	Trevor Pryce	.30
267	Mike McMahon	.60
268	Patrick Ramsey	.75
269	Jonathan Wells	.60
270	Mark Brunell	.60
271	Marc Boerigter	.60
272	Rob Konrad	.30
273	Derrick Alexander	.60
274	Joey Galloway	.60
275	Peyton Manning	1.50
276	Najeh Davenport	.60
277	Jesse Palmer	.60
278	LaMont Jordan	.60
279	Ernie Conwell	.30
280	Hines Ward	.60
281	Freddie Mitchell	.60
282	Curtis Conway	.60
283	Cedrick Wilson	.60
284	Troy Brown	.60
285	Torry Holt	.75
286	Mike Alstott	.60
287	Frank Wycheck	.30
288	Jeremiah Trotter	.30
289	Tyrone Wheatley	.60
290	David Boston	.75
291	Jay Fiedler	.60
292	Troy Walters	.30
293	Warrick Holdman	.30
294	Peter Warrick	.60
295	Tim Couch	.75
296	Aaron Glenn	.30
297	Deuce McAllister	.75
298	Michael Strahan	.60
299	Tom Brady	2.00
300	Brett Favre	3.00
301	Isaac Bruce	.75
302	Jimmy Smith	.60
303	Dante Hall	.60
304	James McKnight	.30
305	Daunte Culpepper	.75
306	Lawyer Milloy	.30
307	Jerome Pathon	.30
308	Steve McNair	.75
309	Vinny Testaverde	.60
310	Tommy Maddox	.75
311	Amani Toomer	.60
312	Aaron Brooks	.75
313	Gus Frerotte	.60
314	Kevan Barlow	.60
315	Matt Hasselbeck	.60
316	Clinton Portis	2.50
317	Keenan McCardell	.30
318	Zach Thomas	.30
319	Curtis Martin	.75
320	Jamal Lewis	.75
321	T.J. Duckett	.60
322	Jerry Porter	.60
323	Randy Moss	1.50
324	Rosevelt Colvin	.30
325	Corey Dillon	.75
326	Kelly Holcomb	.60
327	Josh McCown	.60
328	Ed McCaffrey	.60
329	Mikhael Ricks	.30
330	Donald Driver	.60
331	James Darling, Ray Thompson, Ronald McKinnon	.30
332	Corey Hall, Keion Carpenter, Ray Buchanon	.30
333	Adalius Thomas, Anthony Weaver, Kelly Gregg	.30
334	Antoine Winfield, Coy Wire, Nate Clements	.30
335	Dan Morgan, Mark Fields, Will Witherspoon	.30
336	Alex Brown, Bryan Robinson, Phillip Daniels	.30
337	Carl Powell, John Thornton, Tony Williams	.30
338	Ben Taylor, Earl Little, Kevin Bentley	.30
339	Ebenezer Ekuban, Greg Ellis, Michael Myers	.30
340	Daryl Gardener, Lional Dalton, Bertrand Berry	.30
341	Barrett Green, Donte Curry, Earl Holmes	.30
342	Cletidus Hunt, Kabeer Gbaja-Biamila, Rod Walker	.30
343	Gary Walker, Jerry DeLoach, Seth Payne	.30
344	Chad Bratzke, Marcus Washington, Rob Morris	.30
345	John Henderson, Marco Coleman, Marcus Stroud	.30
346	Eric Hicks, John Browning, Ryan Sims	.30
347	Adewale Ogunleye, Larry Chester, Tim Bowens	.30
348	Fred Robbins, Kenny Mixon, Lance Johnstone	.30
349	Roman Phifer, Ted Johnson, Tedy Bruschi	.30
350	Charles Grant, Martin Chase, Darren Howard	.30
351	Brandon Short, Dhani Jones, Micheal Barrow	.30
352	Marvin Jones, Mo Lewis, Sam Cowart	.30
353	Eric Barton, John Parrella, Napoleon Harris	.30
354	Brandon Whiting, Corey Simon, Darwin Walker	.30
355	Aaron Smith, Casey Hampton, Kimo Von Oelhoffen	.30
356	Jamal Williams, Jason Fisk, Raylee Johnson	.30
357	Derek Smith, Jeff Ulbrich, Julian Peterson	.30
358	Antonio Cochran, Chad Eaton, John Randle	.30
359	Damione Lewis, Grant Wistrom, Leonard Little	.30
360	Dwayne Rudd, Greg Spires, Shelton Quarles	.30
361	Albert Haynesworth, Kevin Carter, Robaire Smith	.30
362	Bruce Smith, Jessie Armstead, Regan Upshaw	.30
363	Adrian Wilson, Dexter Jackson	.30
364	Fred Wakefield, Kyle Vanden Bosch	.30
365	Kevin Kasper, Jason McAddley	.30
366	Brady Smith, Patrick Kerney	.30
367	MarTay Jenkins, Trevor Gaylor	.30
368	Chris Draft, Matt Stewart	.30
369	Javin Hunter, Ron Johnson	.30
370	Corey Fuller, Ed Reed	.30
371	Aaron Schobel, Jeff Posey	.30
372	Pat Williams, Sam Adams	.30
373	Deon Grant, Mike Minter	.30
374	Brentson Buckner, Kris Jenkins	.30
375	Reggie Howard, Terry Cousin	.30
376	Mike Brown, Mike Green	.30
377	Jerry Azumah, R.W. McQuarters	.30
378	Brian Simmons, Steve Foley	.30
379	Artrell Hawkins, Jeff Burris	.30
380	JoJuan Armour, Marquand Manuel	.30
381	Gerard Warren, Orpheus Roye	.30
382	Courtney Brown, Kenard Lang	.30
383	Derek Ross, Mario Edwards	.30
384	Al Singleton, Dat Nguyen	.30
385	Al Wilson, John Mobley	.30
386	Deltha O'Neal, Kenoy Kennedy	.30
387	Luther Elliss, Shaun Rogers	.30
388	Chris Cash, Dre' Bly	.30
389	Brian Walker, Corey Harris	.30
390	Hannibal Navies, Na'il Diggs	.30
391	Al Harris, Mike McKenzie	.30
392	Charlie Clemons, Jay Foreman	.30
393	Eric Brown, Matt Stevens	.30
394	Brad Scioli, Larry Tripplett	.30
395	David Macklin, Walt Harris	.30
396	Akin Ayodele, Hugh Douglas	.30
397	Fernando Bryant, Jason Craft	.30
398	Donovin Darius, Marlon McCree	.30
399	Scott Fujita, Shawn Barber	.30
400	Eric Warfield, William Bartee	.30
401	Greg Wesley, Jerome Woods	.30
402	Patrick Surtain, Sam Madison	.30
403	Brock Marion, Sammy Knight	.30
404	Greg Biekert, Henri Crockett	.30
405	Chris Claiborne, Chris Hovan	.20
406	Corey Chavous, Ken Irvin	.30
407	Christian Fauria, Daniel Graham	.30
408	Otis Smith, Rodney Harrison	.30
409	Anthony Pleasant, Richard Seymour	.30
410	Darrin Smith, Sedrick Hodge	.30
411	Ashley Ambrose, Dale Carter	.30
412	Mel Mitchell, Derrick Rodgers	.30
413	Will Allen, Will Peterson	.30
414	Cornelius Griffin, Keith Hamilton	.30
415	Omar Stoutmire, Shaun Williams	.30
416	Aaron Beasley, Donnie Abraham	.30
417	Jon McGraw, Sam Garnes	.30
418	Charles Woodson, Phillip Buchanon	.30
419	Tony Bryant, Trace Armstrong	.30
420	Bobby Taylor, Troy Vincent	.20
421	Carlos Emmons, Nate Wayne	.30
422	Brent Alexander, Chris Hope	.30
423	Joey Porter, Kendrell Bell	.40
424	Chad Scott, DeWayne Washington	.30
425	Ben Leber, Ryan McNeil	.30

426 Quentin Jammer, Tay Cody .30
427 Ahmed Plummer, Jason Webster .30
428 Tony Parrish, Zack Bronson .30
429 Itula Mili, Jerramy Stevens .30
430 Ken Lucas, Shawn Springs .30
431 Chad Brown, Orlando Huff .30
432 Jamie Duncan, Tommy Polley .30
433 Aeneas Williams, Travis Fisher .30
434 Brian Kelly, Ronde Barber .30
435 Aaron Stecker, Karl Williams .30
436 Drew Bennett, Justin McCareins .30
437 Lance Schulters, Tank Williams .30
438 Andre Dyson, Samari Rolle .30
439 Ifeanyi Ohalete, Matt Bowen .30
440 Brandon Noble, Dan Wilkinson .30
441 *Charles Rogers* 4.00
442 *Jimmy Kennedy* 1.00
443 *Kelley Washington* 1.50
444 *Trent Smith* 1.00
445 *Rashean Mathis* .50
446 *Brian St. Pierre* 1.00
447 *Bethel Johnson* .75
448 *Alonzo Jackson* .75
449 *Arnaz Battle* .75
450 *Carson Palmer* 5.00
451 *Michael Haynes* 1.00
452 *LaBrandon Toefield* 1.00
453 *Earnest Graham* 1.00
454 *Walter Young* .50
455 *Terry Pierce* .75
456 *Talman Gardner* 1.00
457 *J.T. Wall* 1.00
458 *Dewayne Robertson* 1.00
459 *Bradie James* .75
460 *Andre Johnson* 3.00
461 *Bobby Wade* 1.00
462 *Chris Davis* .75
463 *Kliff Kingsbury* 1.00
464 *Osi Umenyiora* .75
465 *Domanick Davis* 1.50
466 *Sam Aiken* 1.00
467 *Ty Warren* 1.00
468 *Terence Newman* 2.50
469 *Zuriel Smith* 1.00
470 *Willis McGahee* 4.00
471 *David Kircus* .75
472 *Billy McMullen* 1.00
473 *Antwoine Sanders* .75
474 *Adrian Madise* .75
475 *Byron Leftwich* 5.00
476 *Justin Gage* .75
477 *Jason Witten* 1.00
478 *Lee Suggs* 1.50
479 *Kareem Kelly* 1.00
480 *Rex Grossman* 4.00
481 *Nate Burleson* 1.00
482 *Chris Brown* 1.00
483 *Julian Battle* 1.00
484 *Carl Ford* 1.00
485 *Angelo Crowell* 1.00
486 *Bennie Joppru* .75
487 *Aaron Walker* .50
488 *Brandon Green* .75
489 *L.J. Smith* .75
490 *Ken Dorsey* 2.00
491 *Eugene Wilson* .75
492 *Chaun Thompson* .50
493 *Kevin Curtis* 1.00
494 *Marcus Trufant* 1.00
495 *Andrew Williams* 1.00
496 *Visanthe Shiancoe* 1.00
497 *Terrence Edwards* 1.00
498 *Rien Long* .75
499 *Nick Barnett* 1.00
500 *Larry Johnson* 4.00
501 *Ken Hamlin* .75
502 *Johnathan Sullivan* .75
503 *Jeremi Johnson* .75
504 *William Joseph* 1.00
505 *Boss Bailey* 1.00
506 *Anquan Boldin* 1.50
507 *Dave Ragone* 1.50
508 *DeJuan Groce* .75
509 *Rashad Moore* .75
510 *Mike Doss* 1.00
511 *Kenny Peterson* .75
512 *Justin Griffith* .75
513 *Jordan Gross* .50
514 *Terrence Holt* .50
515 *Seneca Wallace* 1.00
516 *Ovie Mughelli* .50
517 *Jerome McDougle* 1.00
518 *Kevin Williams* 1.00
519 *Musa Smith* 1.00
520 *Teyo Johnson* 1.00
521 *Victor Hobson* .75
522 *Corey Redding* .75
523 *Cecil Sapp* 1.00
524 *Brandon Lloyd* 1.00
525 *Chris Simms* 2.50
526 *Artose Pinner* 1.00
527 *Dewayne White* .75
528 *Doug Gabriel* .50
529 *Calvin Pace* .50
530 *Onterrio Smith* 2.50
531 *Terrell Suggs* 1.50
532 *Ronald Bellamy* 1.00
533 *Jimmy Wilkerson* .75
534 *Travis Anglin* .75
535 *Tyrone Calico* .75
536 *Keenan Howry* 1.00
537 *Gibran Hamdan* 1.00
538 *Bryant Johnson* 1.50
539 *Brad Banks* 1.00
540 *Justin Fargas* 1.50
541 *B.J. Askew* 1.00
542 *J.R. Tolver* 1.00
543 *Tully Banta-Cain* .75
544 *Shaun McDonald* .75
545 *Taylor Jacobs* 1.00
546 *Ricky Manning* 1.00
547 *Dallas Clark* 1.00
548 *Juston Wood* .75
549 *Andre Woolfolk* 1.00
550 *Kyle Boller* 3.00

2003 Topps Total Silver

Silver: 1X-2X
Inserted 1:1

2003 Topps Total Team Checklists

NM/M
Complete Set (32): 20.00
Common Player: .60
TC1 Emmitt Smith 2.50
TC2 Michael Vick 3.00
TC3 Ray Lewis .60
TC4 Drew Bledsoe .75
TC5 Stephen Davis .75
TC6 Brian Urlacher 1.50
TC7 Corey Dillon .75
TC8 Tim Couch .75
TC9 Chad Hutchinson .75
TC10 Clinton Portis 2.50
TC11 Joey Harrington 2.00
TC12 Brett Favre 3.00
TC13 David Carr 2.00
TC14 Peyton Manning 1.50
TC15 Jimmy Smith .60
TC16 Priest Holmes .75
TC17 Ricky Williams 1.50
TC18 Randy Moss 1.50
TC19 Tom Brady 1.00
TC20 Deuce McAllister .75
TC21 Jeremy Shockey 2.00
TC22 Chad Pennington 1.00
TC23 Rich Gannon .75
TC24 Donovan McNabb 1.00
TC25 Hines Ward .75
TC26 LaDainian Tomlinson 1.00
TC27 Terrell Owens .75
TC28 Shaun Alexander .75
TC29 Marshall Faulk 1.00
TC30 Warren Sapp .60
TC31 Steve McNair .75
TC32 Patrick Ramsey .75

2003 Topps Total 2002 Award Winners

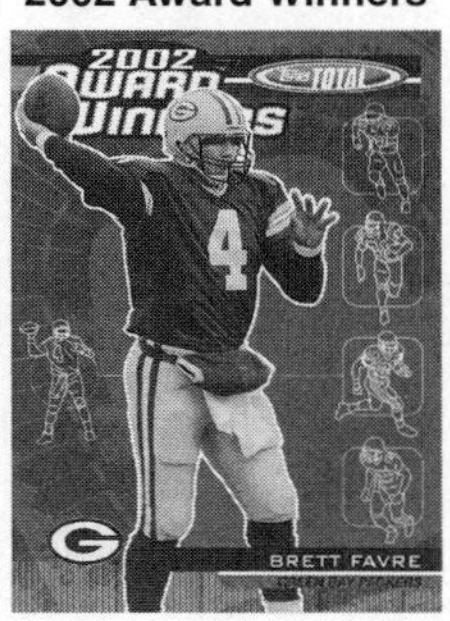

NM/M
Complete Set (20): 20.00
Common Player: .75
Inserted 1:6
AW1 Rich Gannon 1.00
AW2 Derrick Brooks 1.00
AW3 Clinton Portis 4.00
AW4 Julius Peppers 1.00
AW5 Priest Holmes 1.50
AW6 Kerry Collins 1.50
AW7 Tom Brady 1.50
AW8 Brett Favre 5.00
AW9 Chad Pennington 2.00
AW10 Ricky Williams 2.50
AW11 Deuce McAllister 1.50
AW12 Shaun Alexander 1.50
AW13 Marvin Harrison 1.50
AW14 Randy Moss 2.50
AW15 Terrell Owens 1.50
AW16 Hines Ward 1.50
AW17 Jason Taylor .75
AW18 Brian Urlacher 2.50
AW19 Rod Woodson .75
AW20 Brian Kelly .75

2003 Topps Total Total Production

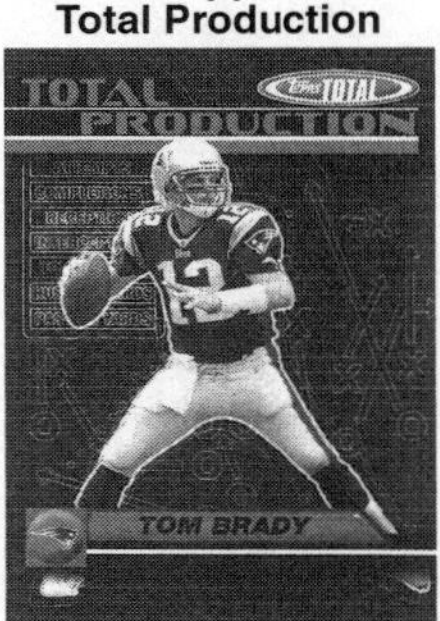

NM/M
Complete Set (10): 12.00
Common Player: 1.00
Inserted 1:12
TP1 Tom Brady 1.00
TP2 Peyton Manning 2.00
TP3 Brett Favre 4.00
TP4 Priest Holmes 1.00
TP5 Shaun Alexander 1.00
TP6 Ricky Williams 1.50
TP7 Clinton Portis 3.00
TP8 Terrell Owens 1.00
TP9 Hines Ward 1.00
TP10 Marvin Harrison 1.00

2003 Topps Total Total Signatures

NM/M
Common Player: 12.00
Inserted 1:185
TS-LB Ladell Betts 20.00
TS-MBO Marc Boerigter 30.00
TS-TB Todd Bouman 25.00
TS-CJ Chad Johnson 15.00
TS-JJ Joe Jurevicius 12.00
TS-DN Dennis Northcutt 12.00
TS-JT Jason Taylor 40.00

2003 Topps Total Total Topps

NM/M
Complete Set (20): 25.00
Common Player: .75
Inserted 1:6
TT1 Rich Gannon 1.00
TT2 Peyton Manning 2.50
TT3 Brett Favre 5.00
TT4 Steve McNair 1.50
TT5 Chad Pennington 2.00
TT6 Michael Vick 5.00
TT7 Ricky Williams 2.50
TT8 Priest Holmes 1.50
TT9 LaDainian Tomlinson 2.00
TT10 Clinton Portis 4.00
TT11 Travis Henry 1.00
TT12 Deuce McAllister 1.50
TT13 Marvin Harrison 1.50
TT14 Jerry Rice 4.00
TT15 Randy Moss 2.50
TT16 Hines Ward 1.50
TT17 Terrell Owens 1.50
TT18 Derrick Brooks 1.00
TT19 Brian Urlacher 2.50
TT20 Jason Taylor .75

2003 eTopps

1 Aaron Brooks/638
2 Ahman Green/917
3 Amani Toomer/706
4 Brett Favre/1197
5 Brian Urlacher/1000
6 Brian Finneran/577
7 Chad Pennington/910
8 Clinton Portis/1495
9 Corey Dillon/1193
10 Curtis Martin/806
11 Darrell Jackson/1000
12 Jake Delhomme/1158
13 David Carr/1490
14 Derrick Mason/488
15 Deuce McAllister/772
16 Donald Driver/899
17 Donovan McNabb/812
18 Drew Bledsoe/647
19 Drew Brees/647
20 Kelly Holcomb/2565
21 Edgerrin James/920
22 Jamel White/1063
23 Hugh Douglas/578
24 Hines Ward/778
25 Jason Taylor/1012
26 Jeff Garcia/773
27 Jeremy Shockey/1763
28 Jerry Rice/1416
29 Jimmy Smith/785
30 Joe Horn/815
31 Joey Harrington/881
32 Kerry Collins/740
33 Keyshawn Johnson/1500
34 Kurt Warner/840
35 LaDainian Tomlinson/842
36 Marshall Faulk/634
37 Marty Booker/693
38 Marvin Harrison/1939
39 Michael Vick/1512
40 Peerless Price/724
41 Trent Green/1111
42 Troy Brown/1000
43 Priest Holmes/1033
44 Randy Moss/1050
45 Ray Lewis/1074
46 Rich Gannon/818
47 Ricky Williams/1052
48 Laveranues Coles/819
49 Rod Smith/951
50 Shaun Alexander/840
51 Steve McNair/1712
52 Terrell Owens/1003
53 Tiki Barber/1338
54 Champ Bailey/1072
55 Tom Brady/665
55AU Tom Brady AU
56 Tommy Maddox/772
57 Torry Holt/1069
58 Travis Henry/600
59 Dewayne Robertson/1197
60 Jerome McDougle/838
61 Andre Johnson/2551
62 Anquan Boldin/3500
63 Artose Pinner/1166
64 Bethel Johnson/1949
65 Brian St. Pierre/1511
66 Bryant Johnson/822
67 Byron Leftwich/5000
68 Carson Palmer/6000
69 Charles Rogers/2500
70 Chris Brown/1568
71 Chris Simms/1852
72 Dallas Clark/2829
73 Dave Ragone/842
74 Justin Fargas/2000
75 Kelley Washington/704
76 Kevin Curtis/785
77 Kliff Kingsbury/1000
78 Kyle Boller/3189
79 Larry Johnson/1858
80 Musa Smith/757
81 Nate Burleson/1491
82 Onterrio Smith/2000
83 Rex Grossman/3287
84 Seneca Wallace/1159
85 Taylor Jacobs/845
86 Terence Newman/1369
87 Terrell Suggs/1855
88 Teyo Johnson/1076
89 Tyrone Calico/1690
90 Willis McGahee/2000
91 Jerry Porter/1148
92 Dante Hall/2000
93 Trung Canidate/614
94 Curtis Conway/586
95 Kevin Faulk/689
96 Troy Hambrick/992
97 Domanick Davis/2000
98 Nick Barnett/955
99 Tim Rattay/880
100 Moe Williams/924
101 Correll Buckhalter/953
102 Steve Smith/765

2003 eTopps Classic

21 Lawrence Taylor/702
22 Gale Sayers/947
23 Johnny Unitas/661
24 Bo Jackson/1000
25 Walter Payton/1500
26 Phil Simms/781
27 Tony Dorsett/788
28 Steve Largent/639
29 Steve Young/592
30 Marcus Allen/722
31 Mike Singletary/953
32 Eric Dickerson/774
33 Otto Graham/547
34 Troy Aikman/587
35 Fred Biletnikoff/450
36 Jim Thorpe/785
37 Ronnie Lott/711
38 Jack Lambert/754
39 Raymond Berry/477
40 Earl Campbell/523

2003 eTopps Event Series

ES12 Jamal Lewis/938

2004 Topps

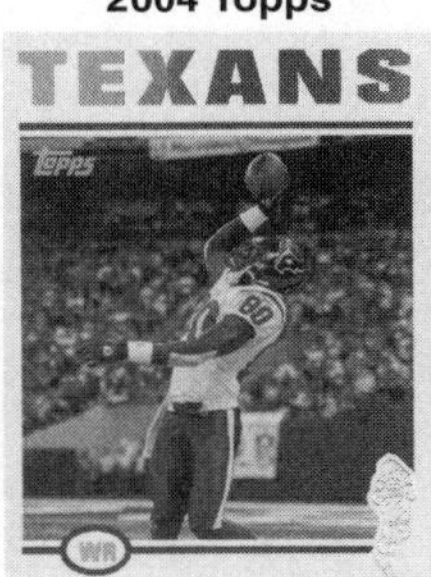

NM/M
Complete Set (385): 60.00
Common Player (1-310): .25
Minor Stars: .40
Unlisted Stars: .75
Common Rookie (311-385): .75
Minor Rookies: 1.00
Unlisted Rookies: 1.25
Pack (10): 3.00
Box (36): 75.00
1 Peyton Manning 1.25
2 Curtis Conway .40
3 Tim Brown .75
4 David Givens .25
5 Dorsey Levens .25
6 Jamal Robertson .25
7 Doug Flutie .40
8 Lamar Gordon .25
9 Leonard Little .25
10 Patrick Ramsey .40
11 Justin McCareins .40
12 Charles Lee .25
13 Matt Hasselbeck .40
14 Chris Chambers .75
15 Derrick Blaylock .25
16 Shannon Sharpe .40
17 Bubba Franks .40
18 London Fletcher .25
19 Eric Moulds .40
20 Anquan Boldin .75
21 Brian Urlacher .75
22 Stephen Davis .40
23 Mikhael Ricks .25
24 Jason Taylor .25
25 Michael Vick 1.50
26 Dante Hall .75
27 Marcus Pollard .25
28 Rick Mirer .25
29 David Tyree .25
30 Chad Pennington 1.00
31 Kevan Barlow .40
32 James Farrior .25
33 James Thrash .25
34 Darnerian McCants .25
35 L.J. Smith .25
36 Tommy Maddox .40
37 Tedy Bruschi .25
38 Moe Williams .25
39 Todd Bouman .25
40 Domanick Davis .75
41 Dwight Freeney .40
42 Kyle Brady .25
43 LaVar Arrington .75
44 Troy Hambrick .40
45 Jake Plummer .40
46 Freddie Jones .25
47 Chester Taylor .25
48 Willis McGahee .75
49 Bobby Wade .40
50 Steve McNair .75
51 Joe Jurevicius .25
52 Ladell Betts .40
53 LaMont Jordan .40
54 Kerry Collins .40
55 Hines Ward .40
56 Scott Fujita .25
57 Kevin Johnson .25
58 Troy Brown .40
59 Jerome Pathon .25
60 Andre Johnson .75
61 DeShaun Foster .40
62 Terrell Suggs .40
63 Marcel Shipp .40
64 Allen Rossum .25
65 Kyle Boller .40
66 Terence Newman .75
67 Javon Walker .40
68 Shawn Bryson .25
69 Travis Minor .25
70 Terrell Owens .75
71 Kassim Osgood .25
72 Bobby Engram .25
73 Drew Bennett .40
74 Rock Cartwright .25
75 Ahman Green .75
76 Steve Beuerlein .25
77 Takeo Spikes .25
78 Dez White .40
79 Tim Couch .40
80 Travis Henry .40
81 T.J. Duckett .40
82 LaBrandon Toefield .40
83 Randy McMichael .25
84 Jonathan Carter .25
85 Jerry Rice 1.50
86 Maurice Morris .40
87 Kurt Warner .40
88 Josh Scobey .40
89 Travis Taylor .40
90 Fred Taylor .75
91 Zach Thomas .40
92 Kelly Campbell .25
93 Tim Carter .25
94 Marques Tuiasosopo .40
95 Laveranues Coles .40
96 Chris Brown .40
97 Thomas Jones .40
98 Dane Looker .25
99 Ross Tucker .25
100 Priest Holmes 1.00
101 Troy Walters .25
102 Jamie Sharper .25
103 Quincy Morgan .40
104 Aveion Cason .25
105 Joey Galloway .40
106 Bill Schroeder .25
107 Tony Fisher .25
108 Adewale Ogunleye .25
109 Justin Fargas .40
110 Daunte Culpepper .75
111 Donnie Edwards .25
112 Jed Weaver .25
113 Arlen Harris .40
114 Keenan McCardell .40
115 Chad Johnson .40
116 Marty Booker .40
117 Anthony Wright .25
118 Brian Finneran .25
119 Robert Ferguson .40
120 Ricky Williams 1.00
121 Shaun Ellis .25
122 Brian Westbrook .40
123 Sam Cowart .25
124 Tim Rattay .40
125 LaDainian Tomlinson 1.00
126 Simeon Rice .25
127 Jason Witten .25
128 Lee Suggs .75
129 Keith Brooking .25
130 Rex Grossman .75
131 Kelley Washington .40
132 Antonio Bryant .40
133 Dallas Clark .40
134 Stacey Mack .25
135 Charles Rogers .75
136 Donte Stallworth .40
137 Deion Branch .40
138 Nate Burleson .40
139 Ike Hilliard .40
140 Randy Moss 1.25
141 Michael Strahan .40
142 John Abraham .25
143 Tim Dwight .40
144 Isaac Bruce .40
145 Brad Johnson .40
146 Trung Canidate .25
147 Warrick Dunn .40
148 Josh McCown .40
149 Muhsin Muhammad .40
150 Donovan McNabb 1.00
151 Tai Streets .40
152 Antonio Gates .40
153 Antwaan Randle .40
154 Doug Jolley .25
155 Shaun Alexander .75
156 William Green .40
157 Carson Palmer 1.00
158 Quentin Griffin .40
159 Az-Zahir Hakim .40
160 Edgerrin James 1.00
161 Gus Frerotte .25
162 Brandon Lloyd .40
163 Brian Griese .40
164 Eddie "Boo" Williams .25
165 Santana Moss .40
166 Tyrone Wheatley .40
167 Eric Parker .25
168 Amos Zereoue .25
169 Itula Mili .25
170 Marshall Faulk 1.00
171 Tyrone Calico .40
172 Tim Hasselbeck .25
173 Anthony Becht .25
174 Larry Johnson .40
175 Marvin Harrison .75
176 Tony Gonzalez .40
177 Wayne Chrebet .40
178 Micheal Barrow .25
179 Bethel Johnson .40
180 Deuce McAllister .75
181 Drew Brees .40
182 Teyo Johnson .40
183 Garrison Hearst .40
184 Todd Pinkston .40
185 Jeff Garcia .40
186 Darrell Jackson .40
187 Billy Volek .25
188 Ray Lewis .40
189 Ricky Proehl .25
190 Rudi Johnson .40
191 Emmitt Smith 1.50
192 Cedrick Wilson .40
193 Julius Peppers .40
194 Peter Warrick .40
195 Trent Green .40
196 Derrius Thompson .25
197 Onterrio Smith .40
198 Jerome Bettis .40
199 Keyshawn Johnson .40
200 Jamal Lewis .75
201 Alge Crumpler .25
202 Justin Gage .40
203 Mike Rucker .25
204 Michael Bennett .75
205 Jimmy Smith .40
206 Ricky Williams .40
207 Corey Bradford .40
208 Jerry Porter .40
209 Erron Kinney .25
210 Marc Bulger .75
211 Jeff Blake .40
212 Terry Jones .25
213 Kordell Stewart .40
214 Andra Davis .25
215 David Carr 1.00
216 Nick Barnett .40
217 Mark Brunell .40
218 Daniel Graham .40
219 Jim Kleinsasser .25
220 Aaron Brooks .75
221 Plaxico Burress .75
222 Correll Buckhalter .40
223 Jevon Kearse .40
224 Michael Pittman .40
225 Clinton Portis 1.25
226 Corey Dillon .40
227 Steve Smith .40
228 David Thornton .25
229 Eddie Kennison .40
230 Amani Toomer .40
231 Artose Pinner .40
232 Kelly Holcomb .25
233 Jay Fiedler .40
234 Ernie Conwell .25
235 Torry Holt .75
236 Eddie George .40
237 Jeremy Shockey .75
238 Troy Edwards .25
239 Antowain Smith .40
240 Jon Kitna .40
241 Bryan Johnson .40
242 Todd Heap .40
243 Doug Johnson .25
244 Ashley Lelie .40
245 Byron Leftwich 1.25
246 Shawn Barber .25
247 Duce Staley .40
248 Rod Gardner .40
249 Warren Sapp .40
250 Brett Favre 2.00
251 Olandis Gary .40
252 Reggie Wayne .40
253 Billy Miller .25
254 Johnnie Morton .40
255 Joe Horn .40
256 Curtis Martin .75
257 Freddie Mitchell .25
258 Charlie Garner .40
259 Marcus Robinson .40
260 Derrick Mason .40
261 Bobby Shaw .25
262 Desmond Clark .25
263 James Jackson .40
264 Josh Reed .40
265 David Boston .40
266 Drew Bledsoe .75
267 Brock Forsey .25
268 Dat Nguyen .25
269 Mike Anderson .25
270 Anthony Thomas .40
271 Najeh Davenport .40

272 Jabar Gaffney .40
273 Tiki Barber .40
274 Rich Gannon .40
275 Tom Brady 1.25
276 Terry Glenn .40
277 Dennis Northcutt .25
278 A.J. Feeley .40
279 Peerless Price .40
280 Jake Delhomme .75
281 Kevin Faulk .40
282 Quincy Carter .40
283 Andre Davis .40
284 Tony Hollings .25
285 Joey Harrington .75
286 Richie Anderson .25
287 Donald Driver .40
288 Koren Robinson .40
289 Tony Banks .25
290 Rod Smith .40
291 Anquan Boldin .40
292 Jamal Lewis .40
293 Priest Holmes .50
294 Peyton Manning .60
295 Marvin Harrison .40
296 Steve McNair .40
297 Travis Henry .25
298 Torry Holt .40
299 Tom Brady .60
300 Ahman Green .40
301 Donovan McNabb .50
302 Deuce McAllister .40
303 Domanick Davis .40
304 Clinton Portis .60
305 Rudi Johnson .25
306 Brett Favre 1.00
307 LaDainian Tomlinson .50
308 Steve Smith .25
309 Edgerrin James .50
310 Ty Law .25
311 *Ben Roethlisberger* 8.00
312 *Ahmad Carroll* 1.00
313 *Johnnie Morant* 1.00
314 *Greg Jones* 1.25
315 *Michael Clayton* 2.00
316 *Josh Harris* .75
317 *Tatum Bell* 2.00
318 *Robert Gallery* 1.50
319 *B.J. Symons* 1.00
320 *Roy Williams* 3.00
321 *DeAngelo Hall* 1.50
322 *Jeff Smoker* 1.25
323 *Lee Evans* 2.00
324 *Michael Jenkins* 2.00
325 *Steven Jackson* 2.50
326 *Will Smith* 1.00
327 *Vince Wilfork* 1.25
328 *Ben Troupe* 1.00
329 *Chris Gamble* 1.00
330 *Kevin Jones* 2.50
331 *Jonathan Vilma* 1.25
332 *Dontarrious Thomas* .75
333 *Michael Boulware* 1.00
334 *Mewelde Moore* 1.00
335 *Drew Henson* 2.00
336 *D.J. Williams* 1.25
337 *Ernest Wilford* 1.00
338 *John Navarre* 1.25
339 *Jerricho Cotchery* 1.00
340 *Derrick Hamilton* 1.00
341 *Carlos Francis* .75
342 *Ben Watson* 1.00
343 *Reggie Williams* 2.00
344 *Devard Darling* 1.25
345 *Chris Perry* 1.50
346 *Derrick Strait* 1.25
347 *Sean Taylor* 2.50
348 *Michael Turner* 2.00
349 *Keary Colbert* 1.50
350 *Eli Manning* 6.00
351 *Julius Jones* 2.50
352 *Jason Babin* 1.25
353 *Cody Pickett* 1.00
354 *Kenechi Udeze* 1.50
355 *Rashaun Woods* 2.00
356 *Matt Schaub* 2.00
357 *Tommie Harris* 1.25
358 *Dwan Edwards* .75
359 *Shawn Andrews* 1.00
360 *Larry Fitzgerald* 3.00
361 *P.K. Sam* 1.25
362 *Teddy Lehman* 1.00
363 *Darius Watts* 1.25
364 *D.J. Hackett* .75
365 *Cedric Cobbs* 1.00
366 *Antwan Odom* 1.00
367 *Marquise Hill* .75
368 *Luke McCown* 1.00
369 *Triandos Luke* .75
370 *Kellen Winslow Jr.* 2.50
371 *Derek Abney* 1.00
372 *Chris Cooley* .75
373 *Dunta Robinson* 1.00
374 *Sean Jones* 1.00
375 *Philip Rivers* 4.00
376 *Craig Krenzel* 1.00
377 *Daryl Smith* 1.00
378 *Samie Parker* .75
379 *Ben Hartsock* .75
380 *J.P. Losman* 2.00
381 *Karlos Dansby* 1.00
382 *Ricardo Colclough* 1.00
383 *Bernard Berrian* 1.25
384 *Junior Siavii* .75
385 *Devery Henderson* 1.00
RH38 *Tom Brady* 5.00
RH38A *Tom Brady Auto* 350.00
SBMVP *Tom Brady Auto/FB/99* 500.00

Post-1980 cards in Near Mint condition will generally sell for about 75% of the quoted Mint value. Excellent-condition cards bring no more than 40%.

2004 Topps Black

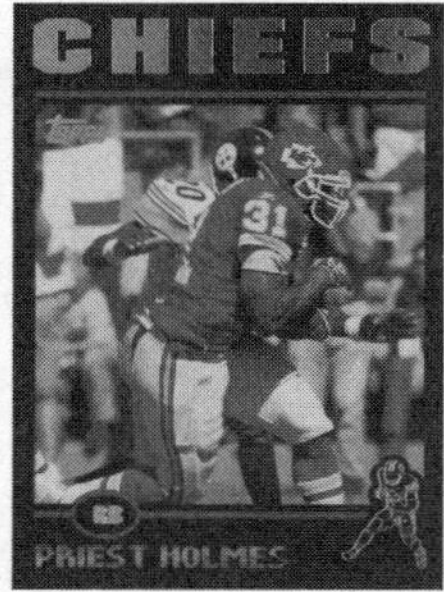

Stars: 5X-10X
Rookies: 4X-8X
Production 150 Sets

2004 Topps Gold

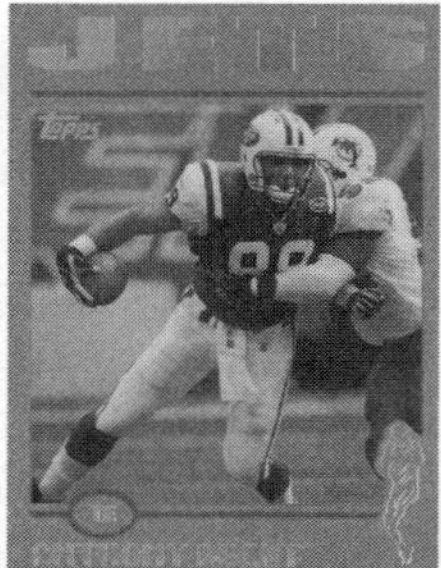

Stars: 2X-4X
Rookies: 1.5X-3X
Production 499 Sets

2004 Topps Autographs

NM/M
Common Player: 12.00
T-KB Kevan Barlow 20.00
T-MC Michael Clayton 25.00
T-DD Domanick Davis 20.00
T-LE Lee Evans 25.00
T-AG Ahman Green 50.00
T-DH Dante Hall 25.00
T-SJ Steven Jackson 80.00
T-GJ Greg Jones 20.00
T-KJ Kevin Jones 40.00
T-EM Eli Manning 150.00
T-PM Peyton Manning 80.00
T-CP Chad Pennington 40.00
T-CPE Chris Perry 40.00
T-CPI Cody Pickett 15.00
T-BR Ben Roethlisberger 150.00
T-MS Matt Schaub 25.00
T-BS Brandon Stokley 12.00
T-RWI Reggie Williams 20.00
T-RW Roy Williams 50.00
T-RWO Rashaun Woods

2004 Topps First Edition

Stars: 1X-2X
Rookies: 1.5X

2004 Topps Game Breakers

NM/M
Inserted 1:7035 Hobby
GB1 Deion Branch 40.00
GB2 Tom Brady 80.00
GB3 Steve Smith 40.00
GB4 Jake Delhomme 50.00
GB5 David Givens 30.00
GB6 Antowain Smith 30.00
GB7 DeShaun Foster 40.00
GB8 Muhsin Muhammad 30.00
GB9 Mike Vrabel 30.00
GB10 Ricky Proehl 40.00

2004 Topps Hall Of Fame Autographs

NM/M
Inserted 1:17.513 Hobby
HOF-BB Bob Brown 125.00
HOF-CE Carl Eller 125.00
HOF-JE John Elway 500.00
HOF-BS Barry Sanders 500.00

2004 Topps Hobby Masters

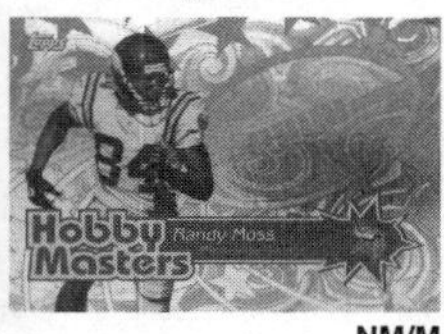

NM/M
Inserted 1:18
HM1 Peyton Manning 3.00
HM2 Michael Vick 4.00
HM3 Steve McNair 1.50
HM4 Ricky Williams 2.00
HM5 Priest Holmes 2.00
HM6 Brett Favre 5.00
HM7 Clinton Portis 3.00
HM8 Donovan McNabb 2.00
HM9 Randy Moss 3.00
HM10 LaDainian Tomlinson 2.00

2004 Topps League Leaders Relics

NM/M
Inserted 1:538
LLR-TH Torry Holt 10.00
LLR-JL Jamal Lewis 10.00
LLR-RL Ray Lewis 10.00
LLR-PM Peyton Manning 15.00
LLR-MS Michael Strahan 10.00

2004 Topps Own The Game

NM/M
Inserted 1:12
OTG1 Brett Favre 5.00
OTG2 Donovan McNabb 2.00
OTG3 Trent Green 1.00
OTG4 Peyton Manning 3.00
OTG5 Matt Hasselbeck 1.00
OTG6 Jon Kitna 1.00
OTG7 Steve McNair 1.50
OTG8 Tom Brady 3.00
OTG9 Marc Bulger 1.25
OTG10 Jamal Lewis 1.25
OTG11 Deuce McAllister 1.25
OTG12 Ahman Green 1.25
OTG13 Stephen Davis 1.00
OTG14 Clinton Portis 3.00
OTG15 Priest Holmes 2.00
OTG16 LaDainian Tomlinson 2.00
OTG17 Fred Taylor 1.25
OTG18 Shaun Alexander 1.25
OTG19 Torry Holt 1.25
OTG20 Randy Moss 3.00
OTG21 Chad Johnson 1.00
OTG22 Anquan Boldin 1.25
OTG23 Laveranues Coles 1.00
OTG24 Derrick Mason 1.00
OTG25 Hines Ward 1.00
OTG26 Marvin Harrison 1.25
OTG27 Santana Moss 1.00
OTG28 Michael Strahan 1.00
OTG29 Ray Lewis 1.00
OTG30 Jamie Sharper 1.00

2004 Topps Premiere Prospects

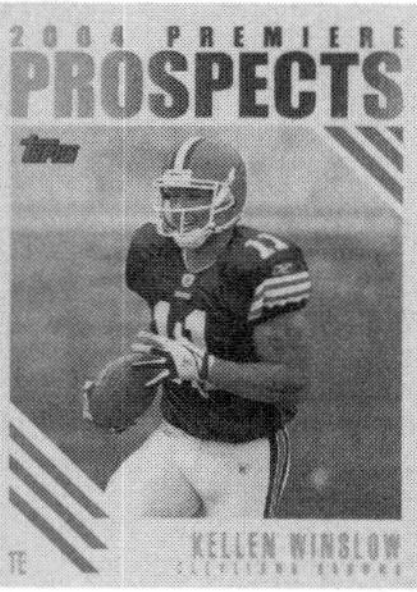

NM/M
Inserted 1:6
PP1 Ben Roethlisberger 4.00
PP2 Chris Perry 1.50
PP3 Darius Watts 1.25
PP4 Devery Henderson 1.25
PP5 Eli Manning 6.00
PP6 Greg Jones 1.50
PP7 J.P. Losman 2.00
PP8 Julius Jones 2.00
PP9 Kellen Winslow Jr. 2.50
PP10 Kevin Jones 2.50
PP11 Larry Fitzgerald 3.00
PP12 Lee Evans 2.00
PP13 Michael Clayton 2.00
PP14 Michael Jenkins 2.00
PP15 Philip Rivers 4.00
PP16 Rashaun Woods 2.00
PP17 Reggie Williams 2.00
PP18 Roy Williams 3.00
PP19 Steven Jackson 2.50
PP20 Tatum Bell 2.00

2004 Topps Premiere Prospects Autographs

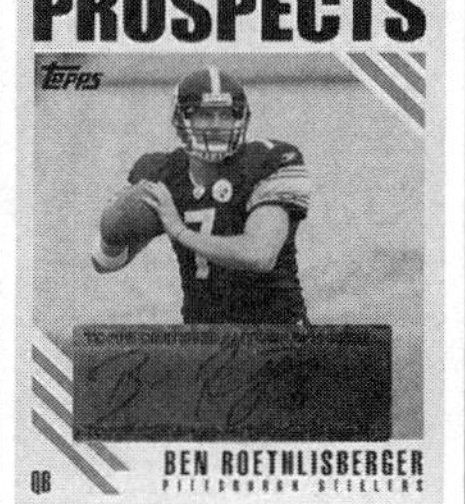

NM/M
Single Auto Production 100 Sets
Dual Auto Production 50 Sets
PP-LE Lee Evans 80.00
PP-SJ Steven Jackson 125.00
PP-GJ Greg Jones 60.00
PP-KJ Kevin Jones 125.00
PP-EM Eli Manning 250.00
PP-CP Chris Perry 80.00
PP-BR Ben Roethlisberger 400.00
PP-RWI Reggie Williams 60.00
PP-RW Roy Williams 125.00
PP-RWO Rashaun Woods 100.00
PPD-FW Larry Fitzgerald, Roy Williams 250.00
PPD-MR Eli Manning, Ben Roethlisberger 600.00
PPD-JJ Steven Jackson, Kevin Jones 200.00
PPD-WW Reggie Williams, Rashaun Woods 125.00
PPD-PJ Chris Perry, Greg Jones 100.00

2004 Topps Pro Bowl Relics

NM/M
Inserted 1:204
PB-LA LaVar Arrington 25.00
PB-CB Champ Bailey 10.00
PB-KB Keith Brooking 8.00
PB-TGO Tony Gonzalez 10.00
PB-AG Ahman Green 12.00
PB-TG Trent Green 8.00
PB-MH Marvin Harrison 10.00
PB-PH Priest Holmes 15.00
PB-TH Torry Holt 10.00
PB-DJ Chad Johnson 8.00
PB-PM Peyton Manning 15.00
PB-SM Steve McNair 10.00
PB-MS Michael Strahan 8.00
PB-BU Brian Urlacher 12.00
PB-HW Hines Ward 10.00

2004 Topps Ring Of Honor Coaches Edition

CRH-BB Bill Belichick
CRH-BB2 Bill Belichick
CRH-BB1 Brian Billick
CRH-MD Mike Ditka
CRH-WE Weeb Ewbank
CRH-TF Tom Flores
CRH-TF2 Tom Flores
CRH-JG Joe Gibbs
CRH-JG2 Joe Gibbs
CRH-JG3 Joe Gibbs
CRH-JGR Jon Gruden
CRH-MH Mike Holmgren
CRH-JJ Jimmy Johnson
CRH-JJ2 Jimmy Johnson
CRH-TL Tom Landry
CRH-TL2 Tom Landry
CRH-VL Vince Lombardi
CRH-VL2 Vince Lombardi
CRH-JM John Madden
CRH-DM Don McCafferty
CRH-CN Chuck Noll
CRH-CN2 Chuck Noll
CRH-CN3 Chuck Noll
CRH-CN4 Chuck Noll
CRH-BP Bill Parcells
CRH-BP2 Bill Parcells
CRH-GS George Seifert
CRH-GS2 George Seifert
CRH-MS Mike Shanahan
CRH-MS2 Mike Shanahan
CRH-DS Don Shula
CRH-DS2 Don Shula
CRH-HS Hank Stram
CRH-BS Barry Switzer
CRH-DV Dick Vermeil
CRH-BW Bill Walsh
CRH-BW2 Bill Walsh
CRH-BW3 Bill Walsh

2004 Topps Rookie Premiere Autographs

NM/M
RP-TB Tatum Bell 150.00
RP-BB Bernard Berrian 80.00
RP-MC Michael Clayton 150.00
RP-CC Cedric Cobbs 80.00
RP-KC Keary Colbert 100.00
RP-DD Devard Darling 80.00
RP-LE Lee Evans 120.00
RP-LF Larry Fitzgerald 250.00
RP-FW Larry Fitzgerald, Roy Williams 350.00
RP-RG Robert Gallery 150.00
RP-DEH DeAngelo Hall 100.00
RP-DHA Derrick Hamilton 60.00
RP-DHE Devery Henderson 80.00
RP-SJ Steven Jackson 250.00
RP-JJ Steven Jackson, Kevin Jones 350.00
RP-MJ Michael Jenkins 100.00
RP-GJ Greg Jones 100.00
RP-JJ Julius Jones 200.00
RP-KJ Kevin Jones 150.00
RP-JPL J.P. Losman 120.00
RP-EM Eli Manning 550.00
RP-MR Eli Manning, Philip Rivers 600.00
RP-LM Luke McCown 100.00
RP-MM Mewelde Moore 100.00
RP-CP Chris Perry 120.00
RP-PR Philip Rivers 250.00
RP-DR Dunta Robinson 80.00
RP-BR Ben Roethlisberger 600.00
RP-MS Matt Schaub 120.00
RP-BT Ben Troupe 80.00
RP-BW Ben Watson 80.00
RP-DW Darius Watts 100.00
RP-RW Roy Williams 250.00
RP-RWI Reggie Williams 150.00
RP-KW Kellen Winslow Jr. 225.00
RP-RWO Rashaun Woods 200.00

2004 Topps Super Tix

NM/M
Inserted 1:696
ST1 Tom Brady 50.00
ST2 Jake Delhomme 25.00
ST3 Antowain Smith 15.00
ST4 Stephen Davis 15.00
ST5 Deion Branch 15.00
ST6 Steve Smith 15.00
ST7 Troy Brown 15.00
ST8 Muhsin Muhammad 15.00
ST9 Ty Law 20.00
ST10 Julius Peppers 15.00

2004 Topps Bazooka

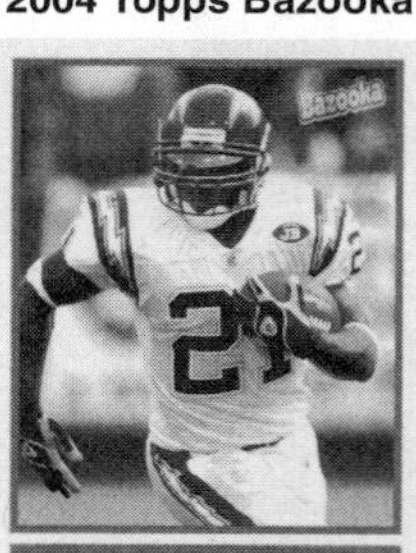

NM/M
Common Player (1-165): .25
Minor Stars: .40
Unlisted Stars: .75
Common Rookie (166-220): 1.00
Minor Rookie: 1.50
Unlisted Rookie: 2.00
Pack (8): 3.75
Box (24): 65.00
1 Peyton Manning 1.25
2 Rod Gardner .40
3 Marc Bulger .75
4 Champ Bailey .40
5 Moe Williams .25
6 Andre Davis .40
7 Corey Dillon .40
8 Trent Green .40
9 Daunte Culpepper .75
10 Chad Pennington 1.00
11 Hines Ward .40
12 Tim Brown .40
13 Jerome Pathon .25
14 Drew Brees .40
15 Eddie George .40
16 Duce Staley .40
17 Marques Tuiasosopo .40
18 Willis McGahee .75
19 T.J. Duckett .40
20 Brian Urlacher .75
21 Ashley Lelie .40
22 Robert Ferguson .40
23 Tai Streets .40
24 Junior Seau .40
25 Priest Holmes 1.00
26 Ty Law .40
27 Correll Buckhalter .40
28 Plaxico Burress .40
29 Brad Johnson .40
30 Shaun Alexander .75
31 Mark Brunell .40
32 Julian Peterson .25
33 Marcel Shipp .40
34 Kyle Boller .75
35 Rudi Johnson .40
36 Quincy Carter .40
37 Jabar Gaffney .40
38 Reggie Wayne .40
39 Deion Branch .40
40 Terrell Owens .75
41 Chris Brown .40
42 Bobby Engram .40
43 Josh Reed .40
44 Thomas Jones .40
45 Stephen Davis .40
46 Mike Anderson .40
47 Javon Walker .40
48 Edgerrin James 1.00
49 Randy McMichael .40
50 Deuce McAllister .75
51 Nate Burleson .40
52 Jevon Kearse .40
53 Jay Fiedler .40
54 Patrick Ramsey .40
55 Brian Westbrook .40
56 Tyrone Calico .40
57 Alge Crumpler .40
58 Josh McCown .40
59 Quincy Morgan .40
60 Jeff Garcia .40
61 Garrison Hearst .40
62 Chad Johnson .40
63 Byron Leftwich 1.25
64 Donald Driver .40
65 Ricky Williams .75
66 Todd Pinkston .40
67 Amani Toomer .40
68 David Givens .40
69 Jerome Bettis .40
70 Derrick Mason .40
71 Darrell Jackson .40
72 Kassim Osgood .25
73 Todd Heap .40
74 Warrick Dunn .40
75 Brett Favre 2.00
76 Chris Chambers .75
77 Fred Taylor .75
78 Charles Rogers .75
79 Onterrio Smith .40
80 Joe Horn .40
81 Justin McCareins .40
82 Ike Hilliard .40
83 Kevan Barlow .40
84 Charlie Garner .40
85 Anquan Boldin .75
86 Anthony Thomas .40
87 Julius Peppers .40
88 Dat Nguyen .40
89 Peerless Price .40
90 Randy Moss 1.25
91 Jamie Sharper .25
92 Travis Henry .40
93 Terrell Suggs .40
94 Joey Galloway .40
95 Torry Holt .75
96 Freddie Mitchell .40
97 Jerry Porter .40
98 Dwight Freeney .40
99 Joey Harrington .75
100 Michael Vick 1.50
101 Kelley Washington .40
102 Marty Booker .40
103 Tim Rattay .40
104 Derrick Brooks .40
105 Laveranues Coles .40
106 Ray Lewis .75
107 Jon Kitna .40
108 Terry Glenn .40
109 Steve Smith .40
110 Ahman Green .75
111 Andre Johnson .75
112 Dallas Clark .40
113 Kevin Faulk .40
114 Michael Bennett .75
115 Tony Gonzalez .40
116 Michael Strahan .40
117 Tommy Maddox .40
118 Isaac Bruce .40
119 Brandon Lloyd .40
120 Steve McNair .75
121 Keith Brooking .40
122 Drew Bledsoe .75
123 Peter Warrick .40
124 Antonio Bryant .40
125 Clinton Portis 1.25
126 Kelly Holcomb .40
127 Jake Delhomme .75
128 Rod Smith .40
129 Lee Suggs .75
130 Domanick Davis .75
131 Carson Palmer 1.00
132 Kerry Collins .40
133 Teyo Johnson .25
134 Curtis Martin .75
135 Matt Hasselbeck .40
136 Cedrick Wilson .40
137 Eric Moulds .40
138 Keyshawn Johnson .40
139 Dante Hall .75
140 Jamal Lewis .75
141 Kelly Campbell .40
142 Jeremy Shockey .75

143 Jerry Rice 1.50
144 Kurt Warner .40
145 Jake Plummer .40
146 Keenan McCardell .40
147 Jimmy Smith .40
148 Zach Thomas .40
149 Eddie Kennison .40
150 Tom Brady 1.25
151 Donte Stallworth .40
152 John Abraham .25
153 Koren Robinson .40
154 Rex Grossman .75
155 Donovan McNabb 1.00
156 David Carr 1.00
157 David Boston .40
158 Tiki Barber .40
159 Santana Moss .40
160 LaDainian Tomlinson 1.00
161 Justin Fargas .40
162 Troy Brown .40
163 Marshall Faulk 1.00
164 Aaron Brooks .40
165 Marvin Harrison .75
166 *Kevin Jones* 3.00
167 *Michael Clayton* 2.50
168 *Bernard Berrian* 1.50
169 *Ben Watson* 1.50
170 *Philip Rivers* 4.00
171 *Vince Wilfork* 1.50
172 *Jason Babin* 2.00
173 *Marcus Tubbs* 1.00
174 *Sean Taylor* 3.00
175 *Larry Fitzgerald* 4.00
176 *Craig Krenzel* 1.50
177 *Cedric Cobbs* 2.00
178 *Lee Evans* 2.50
179 *Johnnie Morant* 1.50
180 *Kellen Winslow Jr.* 3.00
181 *Mewelde Moore* 2.00
182 *Carlos Francis* 1.00
183 *Josh Harris* 1.00
184 *Julius Jones* 3.00
185 *Reggie Williams* 2.00
186 *DeAngelo Hall* 2.50
187 *D.J. Williams* 1.50
188 *Cody Pickett* 1.50
189 *Dunta Robinson* 1.50
190 *J.P. Losman* 2.00
191 *Jonathan Vilma* 1.50
192 *Jerricho Cotchery* 1.50
193 *Keary Colbert* 2.00
194 *Ben Troupe* 1.50
195 *Drew Henson* 3.00
196 *Chris Gamble* 1.50
197 *Samie Parker* 1.50
198 *Tatum Bell* 2.50
199 *Robert Gallery* 2.00
200 *Eli Manning* 6.00
201 *Ahmad Carroll* 1.50
202 *Devery Henderson* 1.50
203 *Matt Schaub* 2.50
204 *Greg Jones* 2.00
205 *Roy Williams* 4.00
206 *Tommie Harris* 1.50
207 *Jeff Smoker* 2.00
208 *Kenechi Udeze* 1.50
209 *Derrick Hamilton* 1.00
210 *Ben Roethlisberger* 10.00
211 *Darius Watts* 2.00
212 *John Navarre* 2.00
213 *Ernest Wilford* 2.00
214 *Rashaun Woods* 2.50
215 *Steven Jackson* 3.00
216 *Michael Jenkins* 2.00
217 *Will Smith* 1.50
218 *Devard Darling* 1.50
219 *Chris Perry* 2.50
220 *Luke McCown* 1.50

2004 Topps Bazooka Mini

Stars: 1X-1.5X
Rookies: 1X
Inserted 1:1

2004 Topps Bazooka Gold

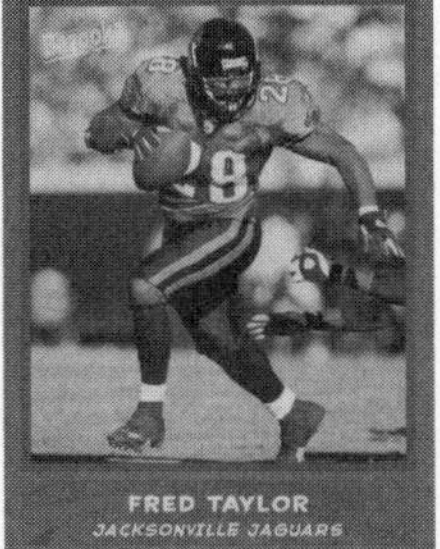

Stars: 1X-2X
Rookies: 1X-1.5X
Inserted 1:1

2004 Topps Bazooka All-Stars Jerseys

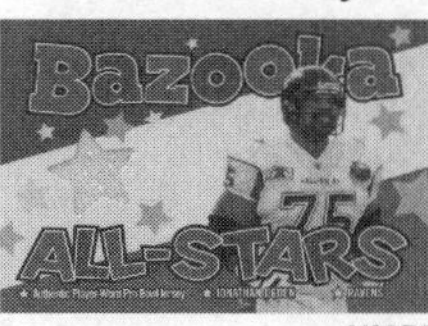

NM/M
Common Player: 5.00
Inserted 1:17
BASFA Flozell Adams 5.00
BASJA Jerry Azumah 5.00
BASAB Alex Bannister 5.00
BASFB Fred Beasley 5.00
BASDB Dre' Bly 5.00
BASRB Ruben Brown 5.00
BASKBU Keith Bulluck 5.00
BASCC Corey Chavous 5.00
BASAC Alge Crumpler 5.00
BASSE Shaun Ellis 5.00
BASLG La'Roi Glover 5.00
BASCH Casey Hampton 5.00
BASKJ Kris Jenkins 5.00
BASWJ Walter Jones 5.00
BASLL Leonard Little 5.00
BASBM Brock Marion 5.00
BASDM Derrick Mason 6.00
BASKM Kevin Mawae 5.00
BASCM Chris McAlister 5.00
BASJO Jonathan Ogden 5.00
BASOP Orlando Pace 6.00
BASJP Julian Peterson 5.00
BASER Ed Reed 6.00
BASTR Tony Richardson 5.00
BASMR Marco Rivera 6.00
BASRS Richard Seymour 5.00
BASWS Will Shields 5.00
BASTS Takeo Spikes 5.00
BASPS Patrick Surtain 5.00
BASMV Mike Vanderjagt 6.00
BASTV Troy Vincent 6.00
BASJW Jeff Wilkins 5.00
BASAW Aeneas Williams 5.00
BASJWO Jerome Woods 5.00

2004 Topps Bazooka College Collection Jerseys

NM/M
Common Player: 6.00
Inserted 1:115
BCCDA Derek Abney 6.00
BCCAB Anquan Boldin 10.00
BCCLD Lane Danielsen 6.00
BCCDD Devard Darling 8.00
BCCCP Carson Palmer 15.00
BCCCPI Cody Pickett 8.00
BCCMS Matt Schaub 10.00
BCCJRT J.R. Tolver 8.00
BCCWW Wes Welker 8.00

2004 Topps Bazooka Comics

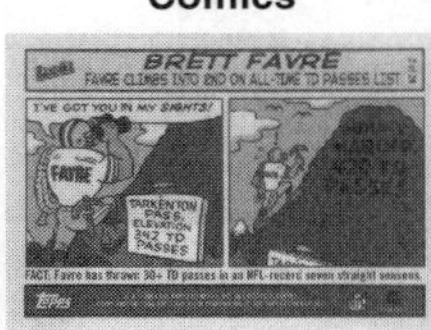

NM/M
Common Player: 1.00
Inserted 1:4
1 Anquan Boldin 1.50
2 Brett Favre 5.00
3 Bruce Smith 1.00
4 Clinton Portis 3.00
5 Dante Hall 1.50
6 Domanick Davis 1.50
7 Jamal Lewis 1.50
8 Jerry Rice 4.00
9 LaDainian Tomlinson 2.00
10 Marvin Harrison 1.50
11 Mike Vanderjagt 1.00
12 New England Patriots 1.50
13 Peyton Manning 3.00
14 Priest Holmes 2.00
15 Randy Moss 3.00
16 Shannon Sharpe 1.50
17 Steve McNair 1.50
18 Terrell Suggs 1.00
19 Tom Brady 3.00
20 Tony Gonzalez 1.00
21 Torry Holt 1.50
22 Michael Vick 4.00
23 Ricky Williams 2.00
24 Jake Delhomme 1.50

2004 Topps Bazooka Originals Jerseys

NM/M
Common Player: 6.00
Inserted 1:21
BOTB Tatum Bell 8.00
BOBB Bernard Berrian 6.00
BOMC Michael Clayton 8.00
BOCC Cedric Cobbs 8.00
BOKC Keary Colbert 8.00
BODD Devard Darling 6.00
BOLE Lee Evans 8.00
BOLF Larry Fitzgerald 12.00

NM/M
BORG Robert Gallery 6.00
BODH DeAngelo Hall 6.00
BODHA Derrick Hamilton 6.00
BODHE Devery Henderson 6.00
BOSJ Steven Jackson 10.00
BOMJ Michael Jenkins 6.00
BOGJ Greg Jones 8.00
BOJJ Julius Jones 8.00
BOKJ Kevin Jones 10.00
BOJPL J.P. Losman 6.00
BOEM Eli Manning 20.00
BOLM Luke McCown 6.00
BOMM Mewelde Moore 6.00
BOCP Chris Perry 8.00
BOPR Philip Rivers 12.00
BODR Dunta Robinson 6.00
BOBR Ben Roethlisberger 20.00
BOMS Matt Schaub 8.00
BOBT Ben Troupe 6.00
BOBW Ben Watson 6.00
BODW Darius Watts 6.00
BORWI Reggie Williams 6.00
BORWO Roy Williams 12.00
BOKW Kellen Winslow Jr. 12.00
BORWO Rashaun Woods 8.00

2004 Topps Bazooka Rookie Roudnup Jerseys

NM/M
Common Player: 6.00
Inserted 1:115
RRTA Tim Anderson 8.00
RRRC Ricardo Colclough 8.00
RRRG Robert Gallery 12.00
RRKR Keiwan Ratliff 6.00
RRPR Philip Rivers 15.00
RRDR Dunta Robinson 6.00
RRKS Keith Smith 6.00
RRJT Joey Thomas 6.00
RRBT Ben Troupe 8.00

2004 Topps Bazooka Stickers

NM/M
Common Player: 1.00
Inserted 1:4
1 Champ Bailey, Ty Law, DeAngelo Hall, Dunta Robinson 1.00
2 Jevon Kearse, Julius Peppers, Dwight Freeney, Michael Strahan 1.00
3 John Abraham, Brian Urlacher, Junior Seau, Jonathan Vilma 2.00
4 Julian Peterson, Dat Nguyen, Jamie Sharper, Terrell Suggs 1.00
5 Derrick Brooks, Ray Lewis, Keith Brooking, Zach Thomas 1.00
6 Peyton Manning, Brett Favre, Donovan McNabb, Michael Vick 5.00
7 Chad Pennington, Daunte Culpepper, Tom Brady, Steve McNair 3.00
8 Mark Brunell, Jeff Garcia, Kurt Warner, Kerry Collins 1.00
9 Kyle Boller, Carson Palmer, Rex Grossman, Byron Leftwich 3.00
10 Trent Green, Marc Bulger, Matt Hasselbeck, Jake Delhomme 1.00
11 Jon Kitna, Drew Brees, Jay Fiedler, Kelly Holcomb 1.00
12 Tim Rattay, Josh McCown, Marques Tuiasosopo, Quincy Carter 1.00
13 Brad Johnson, Tommy Maddox, Drew Bledsoe, Jake Plummer 1.00
14 David Carr, Aaron Brooks, Joey Harrington, Patrick Ramsey 2.00
15 Corey Dillon, Duce Staley, Charlie Garner, Garrison Hearst 1.00
16 Eddie George, Stephen Davis, Jerome Bettis, Curtis Martin 1.50
17 Deuce McAllister, Clinton Portis, LaDainian Tomlinson, Ahman Green 3.00
18 Priest Holmes, Jamal Lewis, Ricky Williams, Marshall Faulk 2.00
19 Rudi Johnson, Lee Suggs, Domanick Davis, Brian Westbrook 1.50
20 Justin Fargas, Chris Brown, Willis McGahee, Onterrio Smith 2.00
21 Fred Taylor, Shaun Alexander, Edgerrin James, Travis Henry 1.50
22 Mike Anderson, Correll Buckhalter, Kevin Faulk, Moe Williams 1.00
23 Warrick Dunn, Tiki Barber, Michael Bennett, Thomas Jones 1.00
24 Marcel Shipp, Kevan Barlow, T.J. Duckett, Anthony Thomas 1.00
25 Randy McMichael, Alge Crumpler, Dallas Clark, Teyo Johnson 1.00
26 Tony Gonzalez, Jeremy Shockey, Todd Heap, Dante Hall 1.50
27 Amani Toomer, Joe Horn, Jimmy Smith, Eric Moulds 1.00
28 Isaac Bruce, Keenan McCardell, Donald Driver, Tim Brown 1.00
29 Anquan Boldin, Andre Johnson, Charles Rogers, Tyrone Calico 1.50
30 Jerry Rice, Rod Smith, Troy Brown, Terry Glenn 3.00
31 Derrick Mason, Hines Ward, Laveranues Coles, Darrell Jackson 1.50
32 Santana Moss, Steve Smith, Jerry Porter, Chris Chambers 1.50
33 Kelly Campbell, Kassim Osgood, Brandon Lloyd, Robert Ferguson 1.00
34 David Boston, Terrell Owens, Joey Galloway, Keyshawn Johnson 1.50
35 Randy Moss, Chad Johnson, Marvin Harrison, Torry Holt 3.00
36 Rod Gardner, Reggie Wayne, Justin McCareins, Quincy Morgan 1.00
37 Plaxico Burress, Ashley Lelie, Koren Robinson, Donte Stallworth 1.00
38 Peerless Price, Marty Booker, Eddie Kennison, Todd Pinkston 1.00
39 Ike Hilliard, Jerome Pathon, Tai Streets, Bobby Engram 1.00
40 Andre Davis, Josh Reed, Jabar Gaffney, Antonio Bryant 1.00
41 Nate Burleson, Deion Branch, Kelley Washington, Javon Walker 1.00
42 Cedrick Wilson, David Givens, Peter Warrick, Freddie Mitchell 1.00
43 Vince Wilfork, Tommie Harris, Teddy Lehman, D.J. Williams 1.50
44 Will Smith, Kenechi Udeze, Jason Babin, Robert Gallery 1.50
45 Eli Manning, Philip Rivers, Ben Roethlisberger, J.P. Losman 6.00
46 Steven Jackson, Chris Perry, Kevin Jones, Tatum Bell 3.00
47 Darius Watts, Keary Colbert, Derrick Hamilton, Bernard Berrian 1.50
48 Kellen Winslow Jr., Ben Watson, Ben Troupe, Devard Darling 2.50
49 Josh Harris, Jeff Smoker, John Navarre, Cody Pickett 1.50
50 Larry Fitzgerald, Roy Williams, Reggie Williams, Lee Evans 3.00
51 Matt Schaub, Luke McCown, Craig Krenzel, Drew Henson 3.00
52 Carlos Francis, Samie Parker, Jerricho Cotchery, Ernest Wilford 1.00
53 Sean Taylor, Ahmad Carroll, Chris Gamble, Johnnie Morant 2.00
54 Julius Jones, Greg Jones, Mewelde Moore, Cedric Cobbs 2.00
55 Michael Clayton, Michael Jenkins, Rashaun Woods, Devery Henderson 1.50

2004 Topps Bazooka Tattoos

NM/M
Common Tattoo: .75
Inserted 1:6

2004 Topps Chrome

NM/M
Common Player (1-165): .30
Minor Stars: .60
Unlisted Stars: 1.00
Common Rookie (166-275): 4.00
Minor Rookie: 5.00
Unlisted Rookie: 6.00
Pack (4): 6.00
Box (24): 100.00
1 Peyton Manning 2.00
2 Patrick Ramsey .60
3 Justin McCareins .60
4 Matt Hasselbeck .60
5 Chris Chambers 1.00
6 Bubba Franks .60
7 Eric Moulds .60
8 Anquan Boldin 1.00
9 Brian Urlacher 1.00
10 Stephen Davis .60
11 Michael Vick 2.50
12 Dante Hall 1.00
13 Chad Pennington 1.50
14 Kevan Barlow .60
15 Tommy Maddox .60
16 Domanick Davis 1.00
17 Dwight Freeney .30
18 LaVar Arrington 1.00
19 Troy Hambrick .60
20 Jake Plummer .60
21 Willis McGahee 1.00
22 Steve McNair 1.00
23 Kerry Collins .60
24 Hines Ward 1.00
25 Terrell Owens 1.00
26 Jerome Pathon .30
27 Andre Johnson 1.00
28 DeShaun Foster .60
29 Terrell Suggs .60
30 Marcel Shipp .60
31 Kyle Boller 1.00
32 Javon Walker .60
33 Ahman Green 1.00
34 Travis Henry .60
35 Randy McMichael .30
36 Jerry Rice 2.50
37 Travis Taylor .60
38 Fred Taylor 1.00
39 Zach Thomas .60
40 Marques Tuiasosopo .60
41 Laveranues Coles .60
42 Thomas Jones .60
43 Jamie Sharper .30
44 Quincy Morgan .60
45 Troy Brown .60
46 Joey Galloway .60
47 Justin Fargas .60
48 Daunte Culpepper 1.00
49 Keenan McCardell .60
50 Priest Holmes 1.50
51 Chad Johnson .60
52 Marty Booker .60
53 Tim Rattay .60
54 Brian Westbrook .60
55 Ricky Williams 1.00
56 Lee Suggs 1.00
57 Keith Brooking .30
58 Rex Grossman 1.00
59 Dallas Clark .60
60 Charles Rogers 1.00
61 Donte Stallworth .60
62 Deion Branch .60
63 Ike Hilliard .60
64 Michael Strahan .60
65 Randy Moss 2.00
66 Isaac Bruce .60
67 Brad Johnson .60
68 Warrick Dunn .60
69 Josh McCown .60
70 Donovan McNabb 1.50
71 Shaun Alexander 1.00
72 William Green .60
73 Carson Palmer 1.50
74 Quentin Griffin 1.00
75 LaDainian Tomlinson 1.50
76 Edgerrin James 1.50
77 Santana Moss .60
78 Marshall Faulk 1.50
79 Tyrone Calico .60
80 Marvin Harrison 1.00
81 Tony Gonzalez .60
82 Deuce McAllister 1.00
83 Drew Brees .60
84 Todd Pinkston .60
85 Jeff Garcia .60
86 Darrell Jackson .60
87 Ray Lewis .60
88 Billy Volek .30
89 Rudi Johnson .60
90 Julius Peppers .60
91 Peter Warrick .60
92 Trent Green .60
93 Onterrio Smith .60
94 Jerome Bettis .60
95 Keyshawn Johnson .60
96 Jamal Lewis 1.00
97 Alge Crumpler .30
98 Michael Bennett 1.00
99 Jimmy Smith .60
100 Brett Favre 3.00
101 Joey Porter .30
102 Marc Bulger 1.00
103 David Carr 1.50
104 Mark Brunell .60
105 Aaron Brooks 1.00
106 Plaxico Burress .60
107 Correll Buckhalter .60
108 Jevon Kearse .60
109 Michael Pittman .60
110 Clinton Portis 2.00
111 Corey Dillon .60
112 Steve Smith .60
113 Eddie Kennison .60
114 Amani Toomer .60
115 Kelly Holcomb .60
116 Torry Holt 1.00
117 Eddie George .60
118 Jeremy Shockey 1.00
119 Jon Kitna .60
120 Todd Heap .30
121 Ashley Lelie .60
122 Byron Leftwich 2.00
123 Duce Staley .60
124 Rod Gardner .60
125 Tom Brady 2.00
126 Reggie Wayne .60
127 Joe Horn .60
128 Curtis Martin 1.00
129 Charlie Garner .60
130 Derrick Mason .60
131 Marcus Robinson .60
132 David Boston .60
133 Drew Bledsoe 1.00
134 Anthony Thomas .60
135 Tiki Barber .60
136 Terry Glenn .60
137 A.J. Feeley .60
138 Peerless Price .60
139 Jake Delhomme 1.00
140 Kevin Faulk .60
141 Quincy Carter .60
142 Joey Harrington 1.00
143 Donald Driver .60
144 Koren Robinson .60
145 Rod Smith .60
146 Anquan Boldin WW .50
147 Jamal Lewis WW .50
148 Priest Holmes WW .60
149 Peyton Manning WW 1.00
150 Marvin Harrison WW .50
151 Steve McNair WW .50
152 Travis Henry WW .30
153 Torry Holt WW .50
154 Tom Brady WW 1.00
155 Ahman Green WW .50
156 Donovan McNabb WW .60
157 Deuce McAllister WW .50
158 Domanick Davis WW .50
159 Clinton Portis WW 1.00
160 Rudi Johnson WW .30
161 Brett Favre WW 1.50
162 LaDainian Tomlinson WW .60
163 Steve Smith WW .30
164 Edgerrin James WW .50
165 Ty Law WW .30
166 *Ben Roethlisberger* 50.00
167 *Ahmad Carroll* 6.00
168 *Johnnie Morant* 5.00
169 *Greg Jones* 8.00
170 *Michael Clayton* 10.00
171 *Josh Harris* 4.00
172 *Tatum Bell* 10.00
173 *Robert Gallery* 6.00
174 *B.J. Symons* 6.00
175 *Roy Williams* 15.00
176 *DeAngelo Hall* 6.00
177 *Jeff Smoker* 6.00
178 *Lee Evans* 10.00
179 *Michael Jenkins* 8.00
180 *Steven Jackson* 12.00
181 *Will Smith* 6.00
182 *Vince Wilfork* 6.00
183 *Ben Troupe* 5.00
184 *Chris Gamble* 6.00
185 *Kevin Jones* 12.00
186 *Jonathan Vilma* 6.00
187 *Dontarrious Thomas* 4.00
188 *Michael Boulware* 5.00
189 *Mewelde Moore* 6.00
190 *Drew Henson* 12.00
191 *D.J. Williams* 6.00
192 *Ernest Wilford* 6.00
193 *John Navarre* 6.00
194 *Jerricho Cotchery* 5.00
195 *Derrick Hamilton* 4.00
196 *Carlos Francis* 4.00
197 *Ben Watson* 5.00
198 *Reggie Williams* 8.00

199 *Devard Darling* 5.00
200 *Chris Perry* 10.00
201 *Derrick Strait* 6.00
202 *Sean Taylor* 12.00
203 *Michael Turner* 4.00
204 *Keary Colbert* 8.00
205 *Eli Manning* 30.00
206 *Julius Jones* 12.00
207 *Jason Babin* 6.00
208 *Cody Pickett* 5.00
209 *Kenechi Udeze* 5.00
210 *Rashaun Woods* 10.00
211 *Matt Schaub* 10.00
212 *Tommie Harris* 6.00
213 *Dwan Edwards* 4.00
214 *Shawn Andrews* 4.00
215 *Larry Fitzgerald* 15.00
216 *P.K. Sam* 5.00
217 *Teddy Lehman* 5.00
218 *Darius Watts* 6.00
219 *D.J. Hackett* 5.00
220 *Cedric Cobbs* 6.00
221 *Antwan Odom* 5.00
222 *Marquise Hill* 5.00
223 *Luke McCown* 5.00
224 *Triandos Luke* 4.00
225 *Kellen Winslow Jr.* 10.00
226 *Derek Abney* 4.00
227 *Chris Cooley* 4.00
228 *Dunta Robinson* 6.00
229 *Sean Jones* 5.00
230 *Philip Rivers* 15.00
231 *Craig Krenzel* 5.00
232 *Daryl Smith* 4.00
233 *Samie Parker* 5.00
234 *Ben Hartsock* 5.00
235 *J.P. Losman* 8.00
236 *Karlos Dansby* 5.00
237 *Ricardo Colclough* 4.00
238 *Bernard Berrian* 5.00
239 *Junior Siavii* 4.00
240 *Devery Henderson* 5.00
241 *Adimchinobe Echemandu* 4.00
242 *Patrick Crayton* 4.00
243 *Marcus Tubbs* 4.00
244 *Jamaar Taylor* 4.00
245 *Andy Hall* 4.00
246 *Darnell Dockett* 5.00
247 *Darrion Scott* 4.00
248 *Jim Sorgi* 5.00
249 *Jeff Dugan* 4.00
250 *Ryan Krause* 4.00
251 *Nate Lawrie* 4.00
252 *Casey Bramlet* 4.00
253 *Donnell Washington* 4.00
254 *Jonathan Smith* 4.00
255 *Tank Johnson* 5.00
256 *Keith Smith* 4.00
257 *Brandon Miree* 4.00
258 *Michael Gaines* 4.00
259 *Keiwan Ratliff* 4.00
260 *Stuart Schweigert* 4.00
261 *Derrick Ward* 4.00
262 *Matt Ware* 5.00
263 *Tim Anderson* 4.00
264 *Bradlee Van Pelt* 5.00
265 *Shawntae Spencer* 4.00
266 *Joey Thomas* 4.00
267 *Maurice Mann* 4.00
268 *Tim Euhus* 4.00
269 *Matt Mauck* 5.00
270 *Sloan Thomas* 4.00
271 *Jeris McIntyre* 4.00
272 *Randy Starks* 4.00
273 *Clarence Moore* 4.00
274 *Drew Carter* 4.00
275 *Sean Ryan* 4.00
RH38 Tom Brady Ref/100 60.00

2004 Topps Chrome Refractors

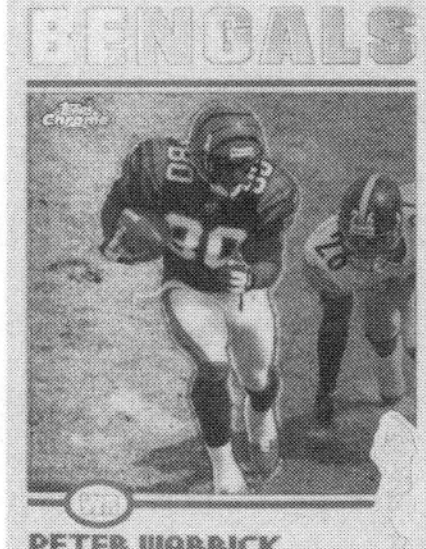

Stars: 2X-4X
Rookies: 1X-2X
Inserted 1:6

2004 Topps Chrome Black Refractors

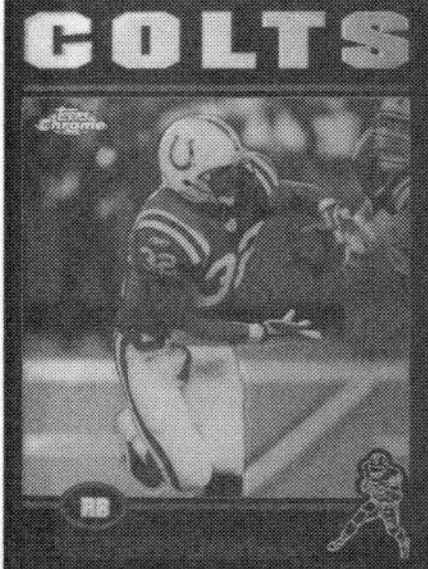

Stars: 4X-8X
Rookies: 3X-6X
Production 100 Sets

2004 Topps Chrome Xfractors

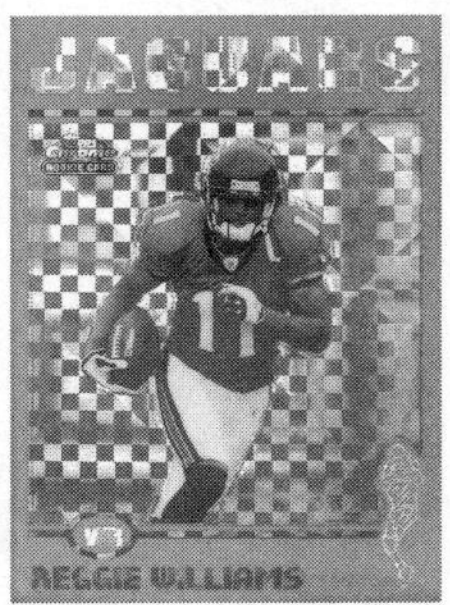

NM/M
Rookies: 1.5X-3X
Production 279 Sets
170 Michael Clayton Auto/250 60.00
172 Tatum Bell Auto/250 60.00
186 Jonathan Vilma Auto/250 30.00
203 Michael Turner Auto/250 30.00
216 P.K. Sam Auto/250 30.00

2004 Topps Chrome Gridiron Badges

NM/M
Common Player: 20.00
Production 50 Sets
GBLA LaVar Arrington
GBAB Anquan Boldin 20.00
GBTG Tony Gonzalez 20.00
GBAG Ahman Green 40.00
GBMH Marvin Harrison 30.00
GBPH Priest Holmes 40.00
GBTH Torry Holt 30.00
GBCJ Chad Johnson 20.00
GBJL Jamal Lewis 30.00
GBRL Ray Lewis 30.00
GBPM Peyton Manning 60.00
GBSM Steve McNair
GBMS Michael Strahan 20.00
GBBU Brian Urlacher 40.00
GBHW Hines Ward 30.00

2004 Topps Chrome Premiere Prospects

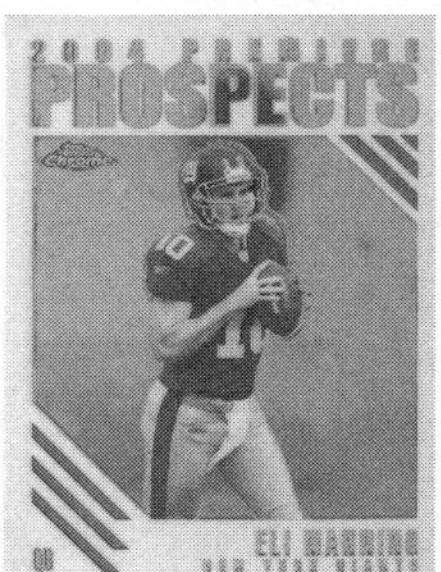

NM/M
Common Player: 2.00
Inserted 1:6.
Refractors: 4X-8X.
Production 100 Sets.
PP1 Ben Roethlisberger. 10.00
PP2 Chris Perry. 3.00
PP3 Darius Watts 2.00
PP4 Devery Henderson 2.00
PP5 Eli Manning 10.00
PP6 Greg Jones 2.00
PP7 J.P. Losman 2.50
PP8 Julius Jones 3.00
PP9 Kellen Winslow Jr. 4.00
PP10 Kevin Jones 4.00
PP11 Larry Fitzgerald 5.00
PP12 Lee Evans 3.00
PP13 Michael Clayton 3.00
PP14 Michael Jenkins 2.50
PP15 Philip Rivers 4.00
PP16 Rashaun Woods 3.00
PP17 Reggie Williams 2.50
PP18 Roy Williams 5.00
PP19 Steven Jackson 4.00
PP20 Tatum Bell 3.00

2004 Topps Chrome Premium Performers Autograph Jerseys

NM/M
PPEM Eli Manning/100 250.00
PPPM Peyton Manning/100 80.00
PPCP Chad Pennington/50
PPMV Michael Vick/100 100.00
PPRW Roy Williams/100 150.00

2004 Topps Chrome Pro Bowl Jerseys

NM/M
Common Player: 6.00
CB Champ Bailey 8.00

NM/M
AB Anquan Boldin 8.00
KB Keith Brooking 6.00
SD Stephen Davis 8.00
SE Shaun Ellis 6.00
DF Dwight Freeney 6.00
DH Dante Hall 8.00
TH Todd Heap 6.00
TL Ty Law 8.00
JL Jamal Lewis 10.00
RL Ray Lewis 8.00
LL Leonard Little 6.00
AO Adewale Ogunleye 6.00
ZT Zach Thomas 6.00

2004 Topps DP & Prospects

NM/M
Common Player (1-110): .30
Minor Stars: .50
Unlisted Stars: .75
Common Rookie (111-165): .60
Minor Rookies: 1.00
Unlisted Rookies: 1.25
Inserted 1:1
Pack (5): 6.00
Box (24): 100.00
1 Steve McNair .75
2 Stephen Davis .50
3 Chris Chambers .75
4 Curtis Martin .75
5 Shaun Alexander .75
6 Jon Kitna .50
7 Jimmy Smith .50
8 Travis Henry .50
9 Torry Holt .75
10 Jamal Lewis .75
11 Clinton Portis 1.25
12 Aaron Brooks .75
13 Plaxico Burress .75
14 Trent Green .50
15 Chad Johnson .50
16 Jake Delhomme .75
17 David Boston .50
18 Joe Horn .50
19 Ahman Green .75
20 Fred Taylor .75
21 Terrell Owens .75
22 Brad Johnson .50
23 Laveranues Coles .50
24 Ricky Williams 1.00
25 Peyton Manning 1.25
26 Hines Ward .50
27 Matt Hasselbeck .50
28 Marshall Faulk 1.00
29 Tony Gonzalez .50
30 Marvin Harrison .75
31 Eric Moulds .50
32 Chad Pennington 1.00
33 Jerry Porter .50
34 Jeff Garcia .75
35 Derrick Mason .50
36 Anthony Thomas .50
37 Drew Bledsoe .75
38 Jake Plummer .50
39 Tiki Barber .50
40 Brett Favre 2.00
41 Joey Harrington .75
42 Daunte Culpepper .75
43 LaVar Arrington .75
44 Santana Moss .50
45 David Carr 1.00
46 Randy Moss 1.25
47 LaDainian Tomlinson 1.00
48 Deuce McAllister .75
49 Amani Toomer .50
50 Donovan McNabb 1.00
51 Priest Holmes 1.00
52 Corey Dillon .50
53 Tom Brady 1.25
54 Edgerrin James 1.00
55 Michael Vick 1.50
56 Anquan Boldin .75
57 Robert Ferguson .50
58 Onterrio Smith .50
59 Marques Tuiasosopo .50
60 Rudi Johnson .50
61 Alge Crumpler .30
62 Antonio Bryant .50
63 LaMont Jordan .50
64 Lamar Gordon .30
65 Tim Rattay .50
66 Antwaan Randle El .50
67 Ladell Betts .50
68 LaBrandon Toefield .30
69 Ashley Lelie .50
70 Marc Bulger .50
71 Reggie Wayne .50
72 William Green .50
73 Josh Reed .50
74 T.J. Duckett .50
75 Andre Johnson .75
76 Deion Branch .50
77 Tyrone Calico .50
78 Jeremy Shockey .75
79 Najeh Davenport .50
80 Byron Leftwich 1.25
81 Correll Buckhalter .50
82 Justin McCareins .50
83 Carson Palmer 1.00
84 Bryant Johnson .50
85 Patrick Ramsey .50
86 Justin Fargas .50
87 Dallas Clark .30
88 Kelly Campbell .30
89 DeShaun Foster .50
90 Charles Rogers .75
91 Donte Stallworth .50
92 Dante Hall .50
93 Randy McMichael .30
94 Marcel Shipp .30
95 Kyle Boller .75
96 Steve Smith .50
97 Brian Westbrook .50
98 Kevan Barlow .50
99 Darnerian McCants .50
100 Domanick Davis .75
101 Andre Davis .50
102 Nate Burleson .50
103 Larry Johnson .50
104 Drew Brees .50
105 Koren Robinson .50
106 Quincy Carter .75
107 Javon Walker .50
108 Willis McGahee .75
109 Chris Simms .50
110 Rex Grossman .75
111 *Steven Jackson* 3.00
112 *Greg Jones* 1.50
113 *Brandon Everage* 1.00
114 *DeAngelo Hall* 2.00
115 *Tatum Bell* 2.00
116 *B.J. Symons* 1.00
117 *Michael Clayton* 2.50
118 *Jared Lorenzen* .60
119 *Josh Harris* 1.00
120 *Roy Williams* 4.00
121 *Mewelde Moore* 1.00
122 *Jeff Smoker* 1.50
123 *Lee Evans* 2.50
124 *Michael Jenkins* 2.00
125 *Drew Henson* 2.50
126 *Ben Watson* 1.00
127 *Jerricho Cotchery* 1.00
128 *Ben Troupe* 1.00
129 *Chris Gamble* 1.25
130 *Kevin Jones* 2.50
131 *Cody Pickett* 1.25
132 *J.P. Losman* 2.50
133 *Michael Boulware* 1.00
134 *Julius Jones* 2.50
135 *Keary Colbert* 1.25
136 *Vince Wilfork* 1.50
137 *Ernest Wilford* 1.25
138 *John Navarre* 1.50
139 *D. Williams* 1.50
140 *Larry Fitzgerald* 4.00
141 *Quincy Wilson* 1.50
142 *James Newson* .60
143 *Reggie Williams* 2.50
144 *Devard Darling* 1.50
145 *Chris Perry* 2.00
146 *Derrick Strait* 1.25
147 *Teddy Lehman* 1.25
148 *Michael Turner* .75
149 *Will Smith* 1.25
150 *Eli Manning* 6.00
151 *Cedric Cobbs* 1.25
152 *Eli Roberson* 1.50
153 *Matt Schaub* 1.25
154 *Derrick Knight* .60
155 *Rashaun Woods* 2.50
156 *Jonathan Vilma* 1.50
157 *Tommie Harris* 1.50
158 *Dwan Edwards* 1.00
159 *Will Poole* 1.00
160 *Mike Williams* 5.00
161 *Philip Rivers* 5.00
162 *Sean Taylor* 4.00
163 *Darius Watts* 1.25
164 *Casey Clausen* 1.25
165 *Ben Roethlisberger* 10.00

2004 Topps DP & Prospects Chrome

Stars: 1X-2X
Rookies: 1.5X-3X
Inserted 1:1

A player's name in *italic* type indicates a rookie card.

2004 Topps DP & Prospects Chrome Gold Refractors

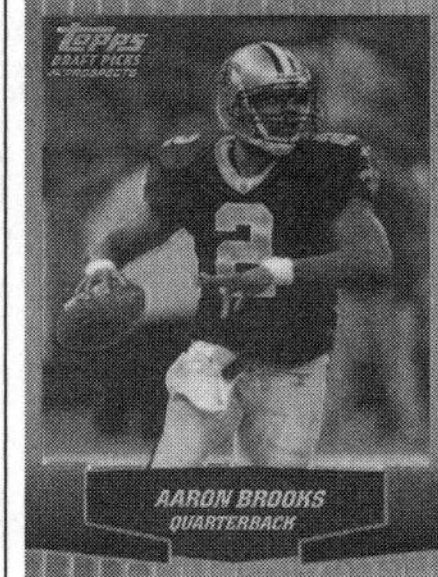

NM/M
Stars: 3X-6X
Rookies: 5X-10X
Inserted 1:12

2004 Topps DP & Prospects Big Dog Relics

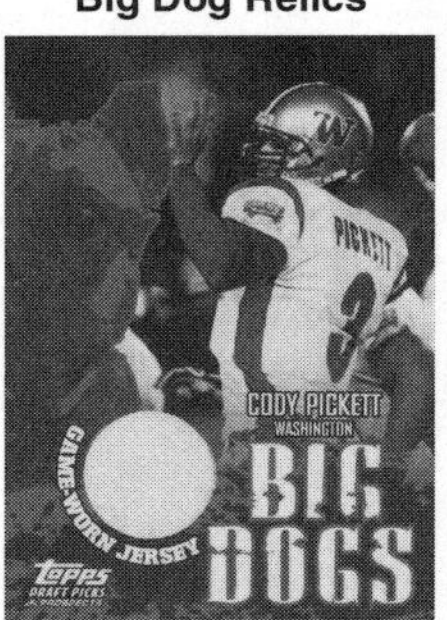

NM/M
Common Player: 6.00
Silver: 1X-2X
Silver Production 100 Sets
BDTB Tatum Bell 12.00
BDMB Michael Boulware 6.00
BDMBR Maurice Brown 6.00
BDDC Darrell Campbell 6.00
BDCC Cedric Cobbs 8.00
BDKC Keary Colbert 6.00
BDCCO Cris Cooley 6.00
BDJC Jerricho Cotchery 6.00
BDDE Dwan Edwards 6.00
BDBE Brandon Everage 6.00
BDKF Keyaron Fox 6.00
BDJH Josh Harris 6.00
BDDH Devery Henderson 6.00
BDBH Bryan Hickman 6.00
BDMJ Michael Jenkins 10.00
BDGJ Greg Jones 10.00
BDJJ Julius Jones 20.00
BDNK Niko Koutouvides 6.00
BDTL Teddy Lehman 8.00
BDRL Rodney Leisle 6.00
BDJPL J.P. Losman 15.00
BDTLU Triandos Luke 6.00
BDBM Bobby McCray 6.00
BDDM DeMarco McNeil 6.00
BDMM Mewelde Moore 6.00
BDJM Johnnie Morant 6.00
BDJN John Navarre 8.00
BDJNE James Newson 6.00
BDCP Cody Pickett 8.00
BDPR Philip Rivers 20.00
BDMS Matt Schaub 8.00
BDAS Antonio Smith 6.00
BDDSM Daryl Smith 6.00
BDDS Derrick Strait 8.00
BDDT Dontarrious Thomas 6.00
BDMT Michael Turner 10.00
BDBW Ben Watson 8.00
BDCW Courtney Watson 6.00
BDEW Ernest Wilford 6.00
BDDW Demorrio Williams 6.00
BDKW Kris Wilson 6.00

2004 Topps DP & Prospects Big Dog Relics Silver Patches

Inserted 1:574
BDPCC Cedric Cobbs
BDPKC Keary Colbert
BDPJC Jerricho Cotchery
BDPJH Josh Harris
BDPMJ Michael Jenkins
BDPGJ Greg Jones
BDPJJ Julius Jones
BDPJPL J.P. Losman
BDPMM Mewelde Moore
BDPJN John Navarre
BDPCP Cody Pickett
BDPPR Philip Rivers
BDPMS Matt Schaub
BDPEW Ernest Wilford

2004 Topps DP & Prospects Class Marks Autographs

NM/M
Common Player: 12.00

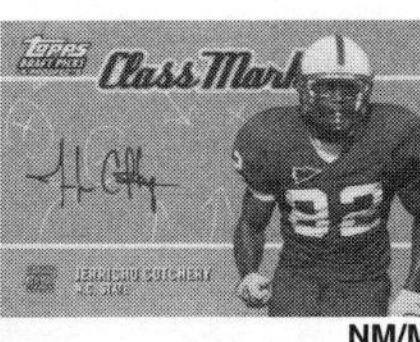

NM/M
Silver: 1X-2X
Silver Production 50 Sets
CMTB Tatum Bell 25.00
CMMC Michael Clayton 20.00
CMCC Cedric Cobbs 15.00
CMJC Jerricho Cotchery 12.00
CMLE Lee Evans 20.00
CMLF Larry Fitzgerald 100.00
CMSJ Steven Jackson
CMMJ Michael Jenkins 20.00
CMGJ Greg Jones 15.00
CMKJ Kevin Jones 50.00
CMEM Eli Manning
CMCP Chris Perry 25.00
CMCPI Cody Pickett 15.00
CMPR Philip Rivers 60.00
CMBR Ben Roethlisberger 200.00
CMMS Matt Schaub 12.00
CMEW Ernest Wilford 12.00
CMRW Roy Williams 50.00
CMRWI Reggie Williams 20.00
CMRWO Rashaun Woods 20.00

2004 Topps DP & Prospects Old School Dual Relics

NM/M
Common Player: 15.00
Production 199 Sets
OSBJ Anquan Boldin, Greg Jones 25.00
OSDP Corey Dillon, Cody Pickett 25.00
OSDW Andre Davis, Ernest Wilford 15.00
OSGJ Eddie George, Michael Jenkins 25.00
OSHR Torry Holt, Philip Rivers 40.00

2004 Topps DP & Prospects QB Legacy Autographs

NM/M
QBG Archie Manning/Gold/1, Peyton Manning/Gold/1, Eli Manning/Gold/1
QBS Archie Manning, Peyton Manning, Eli Manning Silver/50 600.00
QBAM Archie Manning/100 40.00
QBEM Eli Manning/100 200.00
QBPM Peyton Manning/100 80.00

2004 Topps Fan Favorites

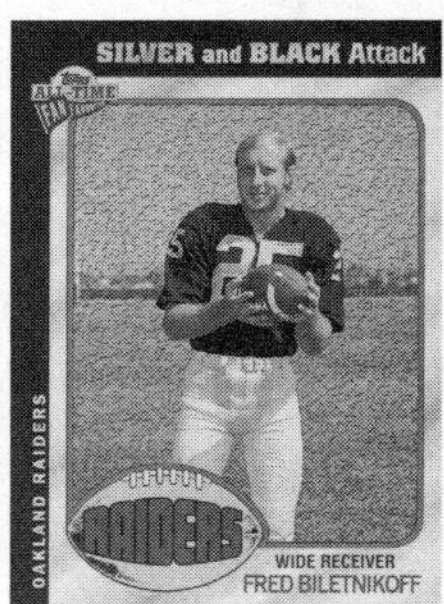

NM/M
Common Player (1-85): 1.00
Minor Stars: 1.25
Unlisted Stars: 1.50
Pack (6): 4.00
Box (24): 75.00
1 Alan Page 1.25
2 Abdul Salaam 1.00
3 Bob Baumhower 1.00
4 Bob Brudzinski 1.00
5 Billy Johnson 1.25
6 Cliff Branch 1.25
7 Carl Banks 1.00
8 Charles Bowser 1.00
9 Clint Didier 1.00
10 Carl Eller 1.00
11 Charlie Joiner 1.25
12 Dick Anderson 1.00
13 Doug Betters 1.00
14 Dave Casper 1.00
15 Dwight Clark 1.25
16 Dan Fouts 1.50
17 Dave Foley 1.00
18 Donnie Green 1.00
19 Deacon Jones 1.25
20 Don Maynard 1.25
21 Dan Pastorini 1.00
22 Drew Pearson 1.25
23 Dwight White 1.00
24 Emerson Boozer 1.00
25 Earl Campbell 1.50
26 Ernie Holmes 1.25
27 Fred Biletnikoff 1.50
28 Glenn Blackwood 1.00
29 Gary Larsen 1.00

30 Greg Lloyd 1.00
31 George Martin 1.00
32 Gene Upshaw 1.00
33 Harry Carson 1.00
34 Harold Jackson 1.00
35 Hugh McElhenny 1.00
36 Jeff Bostic 1.00
37 Jim Burt 1.00
38 Joe Greene 1.50
39 John Hannah 1.00
40 John Henry Johnson 1.00
41 Joe Jacoby 1.00
42 Jim Kiick 1.00
43 Joe Klecko 1.00
44 Joe DeLamielleure 1.00
45 Joe Montana 5.00
46 Jim Marshall 1.00
47 Joe Namath 3.00
48 Jake Scott 1.00
49 John Taylor 1.00
50 Kim Bokamper 1.00
51 Kevin Greene 1.00
52 Karl Mecklenburg 1.00
53 Ken Stabler 2.50
54 Kellen Winslow Jr. 1.50
55 Lyle Blackwood 1.00
56 Larry Csonka 1.50
57 L.C. Greenwood 1.25
58 Lamar Lundy 1.00
59 Leonard Marshall 1.00
60 Lawrence Taylor 1.50
61 Mark Clayton 1.00
62 Mark Duper 1.00
63 Manny Fernandez 1.00
64 Mark Gastineau 1.00
65 Marty Lyons 1.00
66 Mark May 1.00
67 Mike Montler 1.00
68 Merlin Olsen 1.25
69 Matt Snell 1.00
70 Ozzie Newsome 1.25
71 Otis Sistrunk 1.00
72 Phil Villapiano 1.00
73 Roger Craig 1.25
74 Richard Dent 1.25
75 Randy Gradishar 1.00
76 Russ Grimm 1.00
77 Reggie McKenzie 1.00
78 Roosevelt Grier 1.00
79 Roger Staubach 3.00
80 Steve Grogan 1.00
81 Stanley Morgan 1.00
82 Tony Dorsett 1.50
83 Ted Hendricks 1.00
84 Tony Hill 1.00
85 Y.A. Tittle 1.50

2004 Topps Fan Favorites Chrome

Stars: 3X-6X
Production 499 Sets

2004 Topps Fan Favorites Chrome Refractors

Stars: 5X-10X
Production 99 Sets

2004 Topps Fan Favorites Autographs

NM/M
Common Player: 12.00
DA Dick Anderson 20.00
CBA Carl Banks 25.00
BB Bob Baumhower 30.00
DB Doug Betters 20.00
FB Fred Biletnikoff/90 125.00
GB Glenn Blackwood 20.00
LB Lyle Blackwood 20.00
KB Kim Bokamper 20.00
EB Emerson Boozer 20.00
JB Jeff Bostic 20.00
CBO Charles Bowser 20.00
CB Cliff Branch 15.00
CBR Charlie Brown 15.00
BBR Bob Brudzinski 20.00
JBU Jim Burt 30.00
EC Earl Campbell 100.00
HC Harry Carson 40.00
DC Dave Casper 60.00
DCL Dwight Clark 20.00
MC Mark Clayton 30.00
RC Roger Craig 25.00
LCO Larry Csonka 80.00
JL Joe DeLamielleure 30.00
RD Richard Dent 20.00
CD Clint Didier 15.00
TDO Tony Dorsett 100.00
MD Mark Duper 20.00
CE Carl Eller 30.00
GF Gary Fencik 15.00
MF Manny Fernandez 30.00
DFO Dave Foley 20.00
DF Dan Fouts 30.00
MG Mark Gastineau 25.00
RG Randy Gradishar 20.00
DG Donnie Green 15.00
JG Joe Greene 125.00
KG Kevin Greene 60.00
LCG L.C. Greenwood 40.00
ROG Roosevelt Grier 30.00
RGRO Russ Grimm 15.00
SG Steve Grogan 20.00
DH Dan Hampton 30.00
JH John Hannah 20.00
TH Ted Hendricks 30.00
THI Tony Hill 15.00
EH Ernie Holmes 60.00
HJ Harold Jackson 12.00
MJ Mark Jackson 20.00
JJ Joe Jacoby 20.00
BJ Billy Johnson 15.00
JHJ John Henry Johnson 40.00
VJ Vance Johnson 12.00
CJ Charlie Joiner 15.00
DJ Deacon Jones 50.00
JKI Jim Kiick 30.00
JKL Joe Klecko 20.00
GL Gary Larsen 15.00
GLL Greg Lloyd 50.00
LL Lamar Lundy 20.00
ML Marty Lyons 15.00
JMA Jim Marshall 30.00
LM Leonard Marshall 20.00
GM George Martin 20.00
MM Mark May 30.00
DM Don Maynard 30.00
HM Hugh McElhenny 30.00
RM Reggie McKenzie 30.00
KM Karl Mecklenburg 15.00
JM Joe Montana 250.00
MMO Mike Montler 20.00
SM Stanley Morgan 20.00
JN Joe Namath 200.00
RN Ricky Nattiel 20.00
ON Ozzie Newsome 60.00
MO Merlin Olsen 40.00
AP Alan Page 30.00
DP Dan Pastorini 15.00
DPE Drew Pearson 15.00
WP William Perry 50.00
AS Abdul Salaam 12.00
JS Jake Scott 125.00
OS Otis Sistrunk 15.00
MS Matt Snell 20.00
KS Ken Stabler 50.00
RS Roger Staubach 175.00
JT John Taylor 20.00
LT Lawrence Taylor 80.00
YAT Y.A. Tittle 80.00
GU Gene Upshaw 30.00
PV Phil Villapiano 20.00
DW Dwight White 80.00
KW Kellen Winslow Jr. 25.00

2004 Topps Fan Favorites Buy Back Autographs

NM/M
Inserted 1:4692
FB Fred Biletnikoff
LC Larry Csonka
JG Joe Greene 100.00
DM Don Maynard 125.00
HM1 Hugh McElhenny
HM2 Hugh McElhenny
JN Joe Namath
AP Alan Page
KS Ken Stabler
YT Y.A. Tittle

2004 Topps Fan Favorites Co-Signers

NM/M
Common Player: 100.00
Inserted 1:2288
CODC Mark Duper, Mark Clayton 100.00
COFW Dan Fouts, Kellen Winslow Jr. 125.00
COKG Joe Klecko, Mark Gastineau 100.00
CONM Joe Namath, Don Maynard 200.00
COPE Alan Page, Carl Eller 100.00
COSD Roger Staubach, Tony Dorsett 200.00

2004 Topps Fan Favorites Jumbos

NM/M
Common Player: 5.00
1 Charlie Joiner, Dan Fouts, Kellen Winslow Jr. 8.00
2 Drew Pearson, Roger Staubach, Tony Dorsett, Drew Hill 12.00
3 Deacon Jones, Lamar Lundy, Merlin Olsen, Roosevelt Grier 8.00
4 Mark Clayton, Mark Duper 5.00
5 Hugh McElhenny, John Henry Johnson, Y.A. Tittle 8.00
6 Abdul Salaam, Joe Klecko, Mark Gastineau, Marty Lyons 5.00
7 Alan Page, Carl Eller, Gary Larsen, Jim Marshall 8.00
8 Cliff Branch, Dave Casper, Fred Biletnikoff, Ken Stabler 10.00
9 Don Maynard, Joe Namath, Emerson Boozer, Matt Snell 12.00
10 Dwight White, Ernie Holmes, L.C. Greenwood, Joe Greene 10.00

2004 Topps Pristine

NM/M
Common Player (1-50): .40
Minor Stars: .75
Unlisted Stars: 1.50
Common Rookie (51-149): 2.50
Common U/999 Rookie: 2.50
Common R/499 Rookie: 4.00
Pro Plates Production 1 Set
Pack (8): 45.00
Box (5): 160.00
1 Michael Vick 4.00
2 Tony Gonzalez .75
3 Terrell Owens 1.50
4 Brett Favre 5.00
5 Jamal Lewis 1.50
6 Tim Rattay .75
7 Ricky Williams 1.50
8 Edgerrin James 2.00

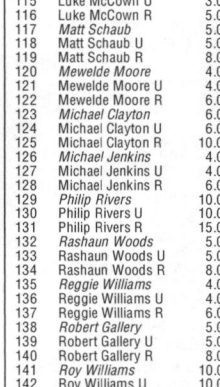

NM/M
9 Torry Holt 1.50
10 Randy Moss 3.00
11 Derrick Mason .75
12 Joe Horn .75
13 Marvin Harrison 1.50
14 Carson Palmer 2.00
15 Anquan Boldin 1.50
16 Quincy Carter .75
17 Byron Leftwich 3.00
18 Eric Moulds .75
19 Marc Bulger 1.50
20 Ahman Green 1.50
21 Jeff Garcia .75
22 Laveranues Coles .75
23 Hines Ward .75
24 Santana Moss .75
25 LaDainian Tomlinson 2.00
26 Domanick Davis 1.50
27 Stephen Davis .75
28 Tiki Barber 1.50
29 Chris Chambers 1.50
30 Priest Holmes 2.00
31 Chad Pennington 2.00
32 Shaun Alexander 1.50
33 Brad Johnson .40
34 Marshall Faulk 2.00
35 Peyton Manning 3.00
36 Jake Plummer .75
37 Clinton Portis 3.00
38 Matt Hasselbeck .75
39 Amani Toomer .75
40 Steve McNair 1.50
41 Daunte Culpepper 1.50
42 Fred Taylor 1.50
43 Joey Harrington 1.50
44 Jake Delhomme 1.50
45 Deuce McAllister 1.50
46 Chad Johnson .75
47 Travis Henry .40
48 Corey Dillon 1.50
49 Tom Brady 3.00
50 Donovan McNabb 2.00
51 *Ben Roethlisberger* 30.00
52 Ben Roethlisberger U 30.00
53 Ben Roethlisberger R 50.00
54 *Ben Troupe* 2.50
55 Ben Troupe U 2.50
56 Ben Troupe R 4.00
57 *Ben Watson* 2.50
58 Ben Watson U 2.50
59 Ben Watson R 4.00
60 *Bernard Berrian* 3.00
61 Bernard Berrian U 3.00
62 Bernard Berrian R 5.00
63 *Cedric Cobbs* 3.00
64 Cedric Cobbs U 3.00
65 Cedric Cobbs R 5.00
66 *Chris Perry* 6.00
67 Chris Perry U 6.00
68 Chris Perry R 10.00
69 *Darius Watts* 3.00
70 Darius Watts U 3.00
71 Darius Watts R 5.00
72 *DeAngelo Hall* 4.00
73 DeAngelo Hall U 4.00
74 DeAngelo Hall R 6.00
75 *Derrick Hamilton* 2.50
76 Derrick Hamilton U 2.50
77 Derrick Hamilton R 4.00
78 *Devard Darling* 3.00
79 Devard Darling U 3.00
80 Devard Darling R 5.00
81 *Devery Henderson* 3.00
82 Devery Henderson U 3.00
83 Devery Henderson R 5.00
84 *Dunta Robinson* 3.00
85 Dunta Robinson U 3.00
86 Dunta Robinson R 5.00
87 *Eli Manning* 15.00
88 Eli Manning U 15.00
89 Eli Manning R 25.00
90 *Greg Jones* 4.00
91 Greg Jones U 4.00
92 Greg Jones R 6.00
93 *J.P. Losman* 6.00
94 J.P. Losman U 5.00
95 J.P. Losman R 8.00
96 *Julius Jones* 8.00
97 Julius Jones U 8.00
98 Julius Jones R 12.00
99 *Keary Colbert* 4.00
100 Keary Colbert U 4.00
101 Keary Colbert R 6.00
102 *Kellen Winslow Jr.* 6.00
103 Kellen Winslow Jr. U 8.00
104 Kellen Winslow Jr. R 12.00
105 *Kevin Jones* 8.00
106 Kevin Jones U 8.00
107 Kevin Jones R 12.00
108 *Larry Fitzgerald* 10.00
109 Larry Fitzgerald U 10.00
110 Larry Fitzgerald R 15.00
111 *Lee Evans* 6.00
112 Lee Evans U 6.00
113 Lee Evans R 10.00
114 *Luke McCown* 3.00
115 Luke McCown U 3.00
116 Luke McCown R 5.00
117 *Matt Schaub* 5.00
118 Matt Schaub U 5.00
119 Matt Schaub R 8.00
120 *Mewelde Moore* 4.00
121 Mewelde Moore U 4.00
122 Mewelde Moore R 6.00
123 *Michael Clayton* 6.00
124 Michael Clayton U 6.00
125 Michael Clayton R 10.00
126 *Michael Jenkins* 4.00
127 Michael Jenkins U 4.00
128 Michael Jenkins R 6.00
129 *Philip Rivers* 10.00
130 Philip Rivers U 10.00
131 Philip Rivers R 15.00
132 *Rashaun Woods* 5.00
133 Rashaun Woods U 5.00
134 Rashaun Woods R 8.00
135 *Reggie Williams* 4.00
136 Reggie Williams U 4.00
137 Reggie Williams R 6.00
138 *Robert Gallery* 5.00
139 Robert Gallery U 5.00
140 Robert Gallery R 8.00
141 *Roy Williams* 10.00
142 Roy Williams U 10.00
143 Roy Williams R 15.00
144 *Steven Jackson* 8.00
145 Steven Jackson U 8.00
146 Steven Jackson R 12.00
147 *Tatum Bell* 6.00
148 Tatum Bell U 6.00
149 Tatum Bell R 10.00

2004 Topps Pristine Refractors

Stars: 1.5X-3X
1-50 Production 99 Sets
Rookies (51-149): 1X-2X
51-149 C Production 1099 Sets
51-149 Uncommon: 1X-2X
51-149 U Production 499 Sets
51-149 Rare: 1.5X-3X
51-149 R Production 99 Sets

2004 Topps Pristine Gold Refractors

Stars: 1.5X-3X
Rookies C (51-149): 2X-4X
Stars/C Rookies Production 99 Sets
Uncommon Rookies: 4X-8X
U Rookie Production 25 Sets
R Rookie Production 10 Sets

2004 Topps Pristine All Pro Endorsement Jersey Autos

NM/M
Common Player: 15.00
APEAC Alge Crumpler 15.00
APEDF Dwight Freeney 15.00
APEDH Dante Hall 20.00
APEPM Peyton Manning 100.00
APESE Shaun Ellis 15.00

2004 Topps Pristine Clutch Performers Jersey

NM/M
Refractors: 2X-4X
Refractor Production 25 Sets
CPAB Aaron Brooks 5.00
CPDB Deion Branch 5.00
CPDH Dante Hall 6.00
CPJH Joey Harrington 8.00
CPTL Ty Law 6.00

2004 Topps Pristine Fantasy Favorites Jersey

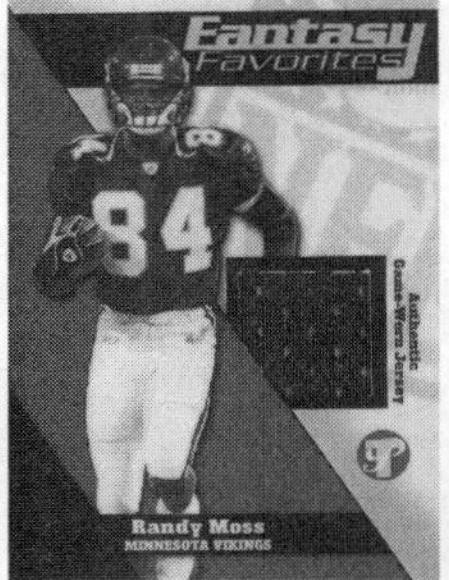

NM/M
Common Player: 5.00
Refractors: 2X-4X
Refractor Production 10 Sets
FFCM Curtis Martin 6.00
FFDM Donovan McNabb 8.00
FFJW Javon Walker 6.00
FFMF Marshall Faulk 6.00
FFMV Michael Vick 12.00
FFPB Plaxico Burress 6.00
FFPM Peyton Manning 12.00
FFRJ Rudi Johnson 5.00
FFRM Randy Moss 8.00
FFSM Santana Moss 5.00

2004 Topps Pristine Gems Jersey

NM/M
Common Player: 8.00
PGAB Aaron Brooks 8.00
PGDM Donovan McNabb 12.00
PGJPL J.P. Losman 10.00
PGKJ Kevin Jones 15.00
PGLF Larry Fitzgerald 20.00
PGMF Marshall Faulk 10.00
PGMV Michael Vick 20.00
PGPM Peyton Manning 20.00
PGRJ Rudi Johnson 8.00
PGRM Randy Moss 15.00
PGRW Roy Williams 20.00
PGSM Santana Moss 8.00

2004 Topps Pristine Minis

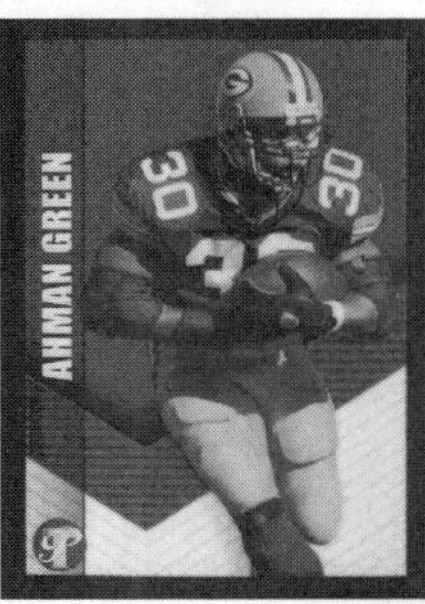

NM/M
Common Player: 3.00
Inserted 1:6
PM1 Michael Vick 8.00
PM2 Randy Moss 8.00
PM3 Marshall Faulk 4.00
PM4 Deuce McAllister 3.00
PM5 Peyton Manning 8.00
PM6 Donovan McNabb 4.00
PM7 Jamal Lewis 3.00
PM8 Tom Brady 8.00
PM9 Torry Holt 3.00
PM10 Priest Holmes 4.00
PM11 Clinton Portis 5.00
PM12 Terrell Owens 3.00
PM13 Anquan Boldin 3.00
PM14 Ahman Green 3.00
PM15 Brett Favre 10.00
PM16 Chris Perry 6.00
PM17 Greg Jones 4.00
PM18 Derrick Hamilton 3.00
PM19 Keary Colbert 4.00
PM20 Reggie Williams 3.00
PM21 Philip Rivers 8.00
PM22 Steven Jackson 8.00
PM23 Kevin Jones 3.00
PM24 Kevin Jones 8.00
PM25 Darius Watts 4.00
PM26 Eli Manning 15.00
PM27 Michael Jenkins 3.00
PM28 Lee Evans 6.00
PM29 Julius Jones 8.00
PM30 Matt Schaub 5.00
PM31 Roy Williams 10.00
PM32 Tatum Bell 6.00
PM33 Rashaun Woods 4.00
PM34 Michael Clayton 6.00
PM35 Devery Henderson 3.00
PM36 Larry Fitzgerald 10.00
PM37 J.P. Losman 5.00
PM38 Kellen Winslow Jr. 8.00
PM39 Ben Roethlisberger 40.00
PMAMV Michael Vick Auto 80.00

2004 Topps Pristine Minis Jersey

NM/M
Common Player: 15.00
Inserted 1:312
PMRBR Ben Roethlisberger 75.00
PMRDM Donovan McNabb 20.00
gMREM Eli Manning 30.00
PMRMF Marshall Faulk 12.00
PMRMV Michael Vick 30.00
PMRPM Peyton Manning 30.00
PMRRM Randy Moss 15.00
PMRRW Roy Williams 20.00
PMRSJ Steven Jackson 15.00

2004 Topps Pristine Personal Endorsement Autos

NM/M
Common Player: 8.00
Gold: 1.5X-3X
Gold Production 25 Sets
PEBB Bernard Berrian 10.00
PECPE Chris Perry 15.00
PEDFO Dwight Freeney 10.00
PEDHA Derrick Hamilton 8.00
PEDHE Devery Henderson 10.00
PEDRH Drew Henson 20.00
PEEM Eli Manning 120.00
PEGJ Greg Jones 10.00
PEJC Jerricho Cotchery 10.00
PEJPL J.P. Losman 20.00
PEJV Jonathan Vilma 12.00
PEKJO Kevin Jones 30.00
PEMJ Michael Jenkins 10.00
PEMV Michael Vick 80.00
PEPKS P.K. Sam 10.00
PEPM Peyton Manning 80.00
PEPR Philip Rivers 40.00
PERW Roy Williams 60.00
PESE Shaun Ellis 8.00
PETB Tatum Bell 15.00

2004 Topps Pristine Real Deal Jersey

NM/M
Refractors: 1.5X-2X
Refractor Production 25 Sets
RDEL Eli Manning, J.P. Losman 25.00
RDFW Larry Fitzgerald, Roy Williams 20.00
RDMR Eli Manning, Ben Roethlisberger 60.00
RDPJ Chris Perry, Kevin Jones 15.00
RDRC Philip Rivers, Michael Clayton 20.00

2004 Topps Pristine Rookie Revolution Jersey

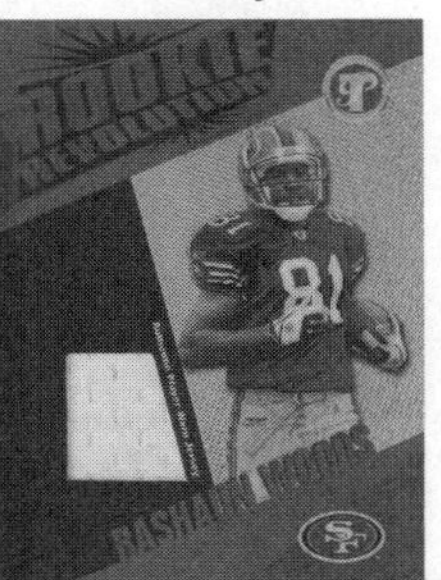

NM/M
Common Player: 5.00
Refractors: 2X-4X
Refractor Production 25 Sets
RRBB Bernard Berrian 5.00
RRBR Ben Roethlisberger 50.00
RRBW Ben Watson 5.00
RRCC Cedric Cobbs 6.00
RRCP Chris Perry 8.00

RRDD Devard Darling 5.00
RRDHA Derrick Hamilton 5.00
RRDHE Devery Henderson 5.00
RRDR Dunta Robinson 5.00
RRDW Darius Watts 6.00
RREM Eli Manning 20.00
RRGJ Greg Jones 6.00
RRJJ Julius Jones 10.00
RRJPL J.P. Losman 6.00
RRKC Keary Colbert 6.00
RRKJ Kevin Jones 10.00
RRLF Larry Fitzgerald 10.00
RRMC Michael Clayton 8.00
RRMM Mewelde Moore 6.00
RRMS Matt Schaub 6.00
RRRG Robert Gallery 6.00
RRRW Roy Williams 10.00
RRRWO Rashaun Woods 6.00

2004 Topps Signature

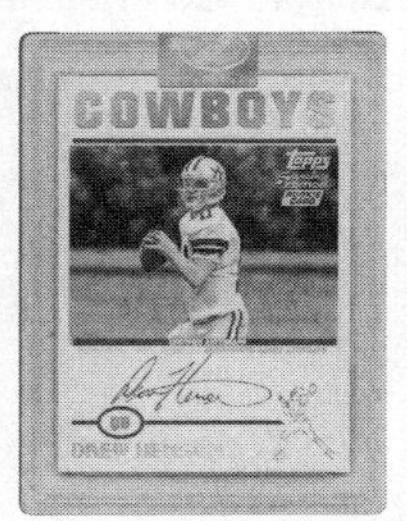

NM/M
Common Player (1-55): .75
Minor Stars: 1.00
Unlisted Stars: 1.50
Common Rookie (56-75): 5.00
56-75 Production 499 Sets
Pack (5): 45.00
Box (4): 150.00
1 Tom Brady 3.00
2 Chad Johnson 1.00
3 Amani Toomer 1.00
4 Shaun Alexander 1.50
5 Terrell Owens 1.50
6 Jake Delhomme 1.50
7 Eric Moulds 1.00
8 Fred Taylor 1.50
9 Mark Brunell 1.00
10 Priest Holmes 2.00
11 Marvin Harrison 1.50
12 Jeff Garcia 1.00
13 Brad Johnson 1.00
14 Laveranues Coles 1.00
15 LaDainian Tomlinson 2.00
16 Anquan Boldin 1.50
17 Curtis Martin 1.50
18 Joe Horn .75
19 Domanick Davis 1.00
20 Jamal Lewis 1.50
21 Steve Smith .75
22 Aaron Brooks 1.50
23 Hines Ward 1.00
24 Marc Bulger 1.50
25 Randy Moss 3.00
26 Jerry Rice 4.00
27 Tiki Barber 1.50
28 Jake Plummer 1.00
29 Travis Henry 1.00
30 Michael Vick 4.00
31 Matt Hasselbeck 1.00
32 Santana Moss 1.00
33 Corey Dillon 1.50
34 Byron Leftwich 3.00
35 Clinton Portis 2.00
36 Derrick Mason .75
37 Tim Rattay 1.00
38 Chris Chambers 1.50
39 Joey Harrington 1.50
40 Deuce McAllister 1.50
41 Tony Gonzalez 1.00
42 Kurt Warner 1.00
43 Carson Palmer 2.00
44 Marshall Faulk 2.00
45 Peyton Manning 3.00
46 Ahman Green 1.50
47 Torry Holt 1.50
48 Chad Pennington 2.00
49 Trent Green 1.00
50 Brett Favre 5.00
51 Stephen Davis 1.00
52 Steve McNair 1.50
53 Daunte Culpepper 1.50
54 Edgerrin James 2.00
55 Donovan McNabb 2.00
56 *Sean Taylor* 6.00
57 *Darius Watts* 6.00
58 *Ben Troupe* 5.00
59 *Josh Harris* 5.00
60 *Jeff Smoker* 8.00
61 *Mewelde Moore* 6.00
62 *Reggie Williams* 6.00
63 *Ben Watson* 5.00
64 *Rashaun Woods* 6.00
65 *Kellen Winslow Jr.* 8.00
66 *Robert Gallery* 8.00
67 *Steven Jackson* 12.00
68 *Craig Krenzel* 5.00
69 *DeAngelo Hall* 8.00
70 *Devard Darling* 5.00
71 *Julius Jones* 15.00
72 *Derrick Hamilton* 5.00
73 *Devery Henderson* 5.00
74 *Dunta Robinson* 5.00
75 *Larry Fitzgerald* 15.00
76 *Chris Perry Auto/999* 20.00
77 *J.P. Losman Auto/1099* 30.00
78 *Lee Evans Auto/1099* 25.00
79 *Cedric Cobbs Auto/1499* 12.00
80 *Philip Rivers Auto/299* 60.00
81 *Greg Jones Auto/1499* 15.00
82 *Michael Clayton Auto/1099* 30.00
83 *Jonathan Vilma Auto/1499* 20.00
84 *Jerricho Cotchery Auto/1499* 15.00
85 *Roy Williams Auto/299* 80.00
86 *Keary Colbert Auto/1499* 20.00
87 *Luke McCown Auto/1499* 12.00
88 *Bernard Berrian Auto/1499* 12.00
89 *Michael Jenkins Auto/1499* 15.00
90 *Eli Manning Auto/299* 200.00
91 *Matt Schaub Auto/1499* 20.00
92 *Tatum Bell Auto/1099* 30.00
93 *Ben Roethlisberger Auto/299* 400.00
94 *Kevin Jones Auto/1099* 50.00
95 *Cody Pickett Auto/999* 15.00
96 *Drew Henson Auto/299* 50.00

2004 Topps Signature Blue

NM/M
Stars (1-55): 2X-4X
Rookies (56-75): 1X-1.5X
1-75 Production 50 Sets
Rookie Auto/1499: 1.5X-3X
Rookie Auto/1099: 1X-2X
Rookie Auto/999: 1X-2X
Rookie Auto/299: 1.5X

2004 Topps Signature Autographs Green

NM/M
Common Player: 12.00
Blue Autos: 1.5X
Blue Production 50 Sets
AKB Kevan Barlow 12.00
ACB Chris Brown 20.00
ADD Domanick Davis 15.00
AJE John Elway 200.00
AJM Justin McCareins 12.00
ASS Steve Smith 12.00
AMV Michael Vick 100.00

2004 Topps Signature Buy Back Autographs

NM/M
Inserted 1:813
JE1 John Elway 87T 250.00
JE2 John Elway 88T 250.00
DF Dan Fouts 60.00
JM Joe Montana 300.00
JN Joe Namath
BS Bart Starr
RS Roger Staubach 200.00

2004 Topps Signature Canton Cuts Autographs

CCGA George Allen
CCLA Lance Alworth
CCCBA Cliff Battles
CCSB Sammy Baugh
CCCB Chuck Bednarik
CCBBE Bert Bell
CCRB Raymond Berry
CCGB George Blanda
CCJB Jim Brown
CCPB Paul Brown
CCBB Buck Buchanan
CCJC Jack Christiansen
CCAD Art Donovan
CCWE Weeb Ewbank
CCTF Tom Fears
CCFG Frank Gifford
CCOG Otto Graham
CCHG Harold "Red" Grange
CCLG Lou Groza
CCGH George Halas
CCEH Elroy Hirsch
CCDH Don Hutson
CCCL Curly Lambeau
CCTL Tom Landry
CCDL Dick "Night Train" Lane
CCBL Bobby Layne
CCVL Vince Lombardi
CCSL Sid Luckman
CCGM Gino Marchetti
CCJM Johnny "Blood" McNally
CCMM Marion Motley
CCBN Bronko Nagurski
CCJN Joe Namath
CCENE Earle "Greasy" Neale
CCEN Ernie Nevers
CCRN Ray Nitschke
CCWP Walter Payton
CCAR Art Rooney
CCPR Pete Rozelle
CCGS Gale Sayers
CCTS Tex Schramm
CCOJS O.J. Simpson
CCYAT Y.A. Tittle
CCCT Clyde "Bulldog" Turner
CCJU Johnny Unitas
CCNVB Norm Van Brocklin
CCSVB Steve Van Buren
CCDW Doak Walker

2004 Topps Super Bowl XXXVIII Card Show

NM/M
Common Player: 1.00
Gold: 3X-5X
1 David Carr 2.00
2 Priest Holmes 2.00
3 Jamal Lewis 1.50
4 Steve McNair 1.50
5 Ricky Williams 1.50
6 Ahman Green 1.50
7 LaDainian Tomlinson 1.50
8 Clinton Portis 2.50
9 Peyton Manning 2.00
10 Michael Vick 4.00
11 Terrell Owens 1.00
12 Daunte Culpepper 1.00
13 Andre Johnson 2.00
14 Byron Leftwich 4.00
15 Anquan Boldin 2.00
16 Domanick Davis 2.00

2004 Topps Super Bowl XXXVIII Card Show Jumbos

NM/M
Common Player: 5.00
1 Priest Holmes 6.00
2 Peyton Manning 8.00
3 Michael Vick 10.00
4 Byron Leftwich 8.00
5 Andre Johnson 5.00

2004 Topps Total

NM/M
Complete Set (440): 75.00
Common Player: .15
Minor Stars: .30
Unlisted Stars: .50
Common Rookie: .50
Minor Rookie: 1.00
Unlisted Rookie: 1.25
Pack (10): 1.25
Box (36): 35.00
1 Donovan McNabb .60
2 Zach Thomas .30
3 Randy Moss .75
4 Kerry Collins .30
5 Hines Ward .50
6 Tyrone Calico .50
7 Patrick Ramsey .50
8 Jeff Garcia .50
9 Aveion Cason .15
10 Stephen Davis .30
11 Marcel Shipp .30
12 T.J. Duckett .30
13 Chris McAllister .15
14 Peter Warrick .30
15 Ahman Green .50
16 Deion Branch .30
17 David Boston .30
18 Wayne Chrebet .30
19 Michael Strahan .30
20 Arnaz Battle .15
21 Darrell Jackson .30
22 Chris Chandler .30
23 Charlie Garner .30
24 James Thrash .30
25 LaDainian Tomlinson .60
26 Jerry Porter .30
27 Jerome Pathon .15
28 Jerome Bettis .30
29 Eddie George .30
30 Jamal Lewis .50
31 Ricky Proehl .30
32 Josh Reed .30
33 David Terrell .30
34 Antonio Bryant .30
35 Domanick Davis .50
36 Artose Pinner .30
37 Jed Weaver .15
38 Johnnie Morton .30
39 Troy Edwards .15
40 Marvin Harrison .50
41 Chris Hovan .15
42 Eddie "Boo" Williams .15
43 Ike Hilliard .30
44 Sam Cowart .15
45 Shaun Alexander .50
46 Freddie Mitchell .30
47 Garrison Hearst .30
48 Joe Jurevicius .30
49 Freddie Jones .15
50 Michael Vick 1.00
51 Mike Rucker .15
52 Carson Palmer .60
53 Az-Zahir Hakim .30
54 Bobby Miller .30
55 Chad Pennington .60
56 Charles Woodson .30
57 Andre Carter .15
58 Maurice Morris .30
59 Leonard Little .15
60 Travis Henry .30
61 Thomas Jones .30
62 Dennis Northcutt .30
63 Quentin Griffin .30
64 Joey Harrington .50
65 Edgerrin James .60
66 Cortez Hankton .15
67 Jason Taylor .30
68 Eddie Kennison .30
69 Ty Law .30
70 Aaron Brooks .50
71 Antonio Gates .30
72 Antwann Randle El .30
73 Kevan Barlow .30
74 Chris Brown .30
75 Clinton Portis .75
76 Rod Gardner .30
77 Isaac Bruce .30
78 Mike Alstott .30
79 Brian Westbrook .30
80 Amani Toomer .30
81 Justin Fargas .30
82 Michael Bennett .50
83 Dante Hall .50
84 Marcus Pollard .30
85 Fred Taylor .50
86 Tai Streets .30
87 Robert Ferguson .30
88 Roy Williams .50
89 Lee Suggs .50
90 Chad Johnson .50
91 DeShaun Foster .30
92 Alge Crumpler .30
93 Travis Taylor .30
94 London Fletcher .15
95 Priest Holmes .60
96 A.J. Feeley .30
97 Kevin Faulk .30
98 Shaun Ellis .15
99 Tim Dwight .30
100 Peyton Manning .75
101 Dane Looker .30
102 Mark Brunell .30
103 Bryant Johnson .30
104 Kelley Washington .30
105 Rex Grossman .50
106 William Green .30
107 Keyshawn Johnson .30
108 Trevor Pryce .15
109 Donald Driver .30
110 David Carr .60
111 Marcus Robinson .30
112 Justin McCareins .30
113 Tim Brown .50
114 James Farrior .15
115 Deuce McAllister .50
116 Simeon Rice .15
117 Koren Robinson .30
118 Kassim Osgood .15
119 Tim Rattay .30
120 Laveranues Coles .30
121 Brian Finneran .30
122 Todd Heap .30
123 Bobby Shaw .15
124 Anthony Thomas .30
125 Brett Favre 2.00
126 Dwight Freeney .30
127 Randy McMichael .15
128 David Givens .30
129 Rich Gannon .30
130 Tiki Barber .30
131 Terrell Owens .50
132 Drew Bennett .30
133 Shawn Bryson .15
134 Jabar Gaffney .30
135 Jake Delhomme .50
136 Warrick Dunn .30
137 Brandon Lloyd .30
138 Brad Johnson .30
139 Jon Kitna .30
140 Marshall Faulk .60
141 Javon Walker .30
142 Nate Burleson .30
143 Jimmy Smith .30
144 Adewale Ogunleye .15
145 Trent Green .30
146 Richard Seymour .15
147 Donte Stallworth .30
148 Curtis Martin .50
149 Todd Pinkston .30
150 Steve McNair .50
151 Josh McCown .30
152 Ray Lewis .50
153 Muhsin Muhammad .30
154 Quincy Morgan .30
155 Jake Plummer .30
156 Jason Witten .30
157 Dallas Clark .30
158 Onterrio Smith .30
159 Jeremy Shockey .50
160 Ricky Williams .50
161 Jevon Kearse .30
162 Plaxico Burress .30
163 Drew Brees .30
164 Bobby Engram .30
165 Torry Holt .50
166 Ladell Betts .30
167 Kelly Holcomb .30
168 Vinny Testaverde .30
169 Marty Booker .30
170 Rudi Johnson .30
171 Andra Davis .15
172 Kurt Warner .30
173 Troy Brown .30
174 Jerry Rice 1.00
175 Daunte Culpepper .50
176 Darren Sharper .30
177 Charles Rogers .50
178 Ashley Lelie .30
179 Correll Buckhalter .30
180 Anquan Boldin .50
181 Terrell Suggs .30
182 Reggie Wayne .30
183 Duce Staley .30
184 Donnie Edwards .15
185 Joe Horn .30
186 LaVar Arrington .50
187 Keenan McCardell .30
188 Cedrick Wilson .30
189 Bubba Franks .30
190 Santana Moss .30
191 Peerless Price .30
192 Kyle Boller .50
193 Julius Peppers .30
194 Drew Bledsoe .30
195 Marc Bulger .50
196 Brian Urlacher .50
197 Andre Davis .30
198 Terry Glenn .30
199 Champ Bailey .30
200 Tom Brady .75
201 Chris Chambers .30
202 Tommy Maddox .30
203 Derrick Brooks .30
204 Corey Dillon .30
205 Matt Hasselbeck .30
206 Keith Brooking .15
207 Steve Smith .30
208 Tony Gonzalez .50
209 Joey Galloway .30
210 Derrick Mason .30
211 Quincy Carter .30
212 Rod Smith .30
213 Andre Johnson .50
214 Rod Woodson .30
215 Byron Leftwich .75
216 Kevin Dyson .30
217 Keith Bulluck .15
218 Eric Moulds .30
219 Jamie Sharper .15
220 Takeo Spikes .15
221 Calvin Pace, Fred Wakefield .15
222 B. Smith, Patrick Kerney .15
223 Ed Reed, Gary Baxter .15
224 Aaron Schobel, Jeff Posey .15
225 K. Jenkins, Brentson Buckner .15
226 J. Smith, Duane Clemons .15
227 Michael Haynes, Bryan Robinson .15
228 C. Brown, Gerard Warren .15
229 Terence Newman, Darren Woodson .30
230 R. Johnson, Mario Fatafehi .15
231 Robert Porcher, J. Hall .30
232 Kabeer Gbaja-Biamila, Cletidus Hunt .15
233 Aaron Glenn, M. Coleman .15
234 N. Harper, Joseph Jefferson .15
235 Hugh Douglas, Tony Brackens .15
236 Vonnie Holliday, Eric Hicks .15
237 Sammy Knight, Arturo Freeman .15
238 Steve Martin, Nick Rogers .15
239 Rosevelt Colvin, Willie McGinest .15
240 Omar Stoutmire, S. Williams .15
241 Eric Barton, Victor Hobson .15
242 Warren Sapp, T. Washington .30
243 Corey Simon, D. Walker .15
244 Troy Polamalu, Mike Logan .15
245 J. Williams, Adrian Dingle .30
246 B. Young, Brandon Whiting .15
247 Ken Hamlin, D. Robinson .30
248 D. Lewis, Ryan Pickett .15
249 Anthony McFarland, Greg Spires .15
250 Albert Haynesworth, Rien Long .15
251 Ifeanyi Ohalete, Matt Bowen .15
252 Bert Berry, Kenny King .15
253 E. Johnson, Ed Jasper .15
254 Charles Tillman, Jerry Azumah .15
255 Marcellus Wiley, La'Roi Glover .15
256 S. Rogers, Dan Wilkinson .15
257 G. Walker, R. Smith .15
258 Mike Doss, Idrees Bashir .15
259 Marcus Stroud, J. Henderson .15
260 Ryan Sims, John Browning .15
261 Junior Seau, Morlon Greenwood .30
262 K. Williams, Kenny Mixon .15
263 Ty Warren, Keith Traylor .15
264 Will Allen, Will Peterson .15
265 David Barrett, Reggie Tongue .15
266 Phillip Buchanon, Derrick Gibson .15
267 Lito Sheppard, Sheldon Brown .15
268 B. Taylor, Marcus Trufant .15
269 Marcus Washington, Micheal Barrow .15
270 Chris Draft, Matt Stewart .15
271 M. Brown, Michael Green .15
272 Eric Brown, Marlon McCree .15
273 Patrick Surtain, Sam Madison .30
274 Brian Dawkins, M. Lewis .15
275 Shawn Springs, Fred Smoot .15
276 Ronald McKinnon, Fisher, Thompson .15
277 Webster, Tod McBride, Scott .15
278 Boulware, Edgerton Hartwell, Thomas .15
279 Troy Vincent, Lawyer Milloy, Nate Clements .15
280 Will Witherspoon, Morgan, Fields .15
281 Simmons, Kevin Hardy, Webster .15
282 Antwan Odom, Brown, Lance Briggs .50
283 Warrick Holdman, Thompson, Kenard Lang .15
284 Dat Nguyen, Dexter Coakley, Alshermond Singleton .15
285 Wilson, Donnie Spragan, Holland .15
286 Holmes, J. Davis, Bailey .15
287 Barnett, Na'il Diggs, Hannibal Navies .15
288 Jay Foreman, Antwan Peek, Wong .15
289 Raheem Brock, Montae Reagor, Larry Tripplett .15
290 Akin Ayodele, Greg Favors, Peterson .15
291 Barber, Mike Maslowski, Scott Fujita .15
292 Chris Claiborne, Henderson, Michael Nattiel .15
293 Tedy Bruschi, Roman Phifer, Mike Vrabel .15
294 Grant, Howard, Sullivan .15
295 Fred Robbins, Joseph, Osi Umenyiora .15
296 Abraham, Robertson, Ferguson .50
297 Harris, Rudd, Tyler Brayton .15
298 Mark Simoneau, Wayne, Jones .15
299 Porter, Bell, Clark Haggans .15
300 Quentin Jammer, Davis, Drayton Florence .15
301 Peterson, Jeff Ulbrich, Smith .15
302 Simmons, Orlando Huff, Brown .15
303 Pisa Tinoisamoa, Tommy Polley, Thomas .15
304 Shelton Quarles, Ellis Wyms, Ryan Nece .15
305 Carter, Hall, Peter Sirmon .15
306 Griffin, Phillip Daniels, Wynn .15
307 Jackson, Wilson, David Macklin .15
308 Kelly Gregg, Douglas, Tony Weaver .15
309 Williams, Ryan Denney, Adams .15
310 Hawkins, Mike Minter, Manning .15
311 James, Kim Herring, Rogers Beckett .15
312 Griffith, Little, Henry .15
313 Lynch, Ferguson, Herndon .15
314 Dre' Bly, Brock Marion, Bryant .15
315 Harris, Mark Roman, Kareem McKenzie .15
316 Thornton, Morris, Brackett .15
317 Mathis, Darius, Bolden .15
318 Warfield, Wesley, Woods .15
319 Winfield, Russell, Corey Chavous .15
320 Harrison, Wilson, Poole .15
321 Rogers, Ruff, Hodge .15
322 Green, Greisen, Emmons .15
323 Kimo Von Oelhoffen, Smith, Hampton .15
324 Godfrey, Foley, Ben Leber .15
325 Plummer, Parrish, Mike Rumph .15
326 Chike Okeafor, Grant Wilstrom, Moore .15
327 Adam Archuleta, Williams, Butler .15
328 Barber, Smith, Phillips .15
329 Andre Dyson, Lance Schulters, Williams .15
330 Thomas, Jay Bellamy, Jones .15
331 *Philip Rivers* 5.00
332 *Dwan Edwards* .50
333 *Ben Watson* 1.00
334 *Karlos Dansby* 1.00
335 *Cedric Cobbs* 1.25
336 *Chris Perry* 2.00
337 *Darius Watts* 2.00
338 *Ricardo Colclough* 1.00
339 *Derrick Hamilton* 1.00
340 *Devard Darling* 1.25

341 *Daryl Smith* 1.00
342 *Luke McCown* 1.25
343 *Dunta Robinson* 1.25
344 *Keith Smith* 1.00
345 *Ben Hartsock* 1.00
346 *J.P. Losman* 2.50
347 *Chris Cooley* .50
348 *Keary Colbert* 2.00
349 *Tommie Harris* 1.25
350 *Eli Manning* 8.00
351 *Kevin Jones* 3.00
352 *Lee Evans* 2.50
353 *D.J. Williams* 1.25
354 *Ben Troupe* 1.25
355 *Mewelde Moore* 1.25
356 *Michael Clayton* 2.50
357 *Michael Jenkins* 2.50
358 *Adimchinobe Echemandu* .50
359 *Rashaun Woods* 2.50
360 *Bernard Berrian* 1.50
361 *Carlos Francis* .50
362 *Roy Williams* 4.00
363 *Sean Taylor* 3.00
364 *Steven Jackson* 3.00
365 *Tatum Bell* 2.50
366 *Jonathan Vilma* 1.50
367 *Derrick Strait* 1.50
368 *Andy Hall* .50
369 *Jason Babin* 1.50
370 *Will Smith* 1.50
371 *Kenechi Udeze* 1.50
372 *Vince Wilfork* 1.50
373 *Ahmad Carroll* 1.25
374 *Marquise Hill* 1.00
375 *Ben Roethlisberger* 12.00
376 *Chris Gamble* 1.50
377 *Junior Siavii* 1.00
378 *Teddy Lehman* 1.00
379 *Antwan Odom* 1.25
380 *DeAngelo Hall* 2.00
381 *Nathan Vasher* .50
382 *B.J. Symons* 1.50
383 *Reggie Williams* 2.50
384 *Michael Boulware* 1.25
385 *Matt Schaub* 2.50
386 *Sean Jones* 1.00
387 *Courtney Watson* 1.00
388 *Nathaniel Adibi* 1.00
389 *Devery Henderson* 1.25
390 *Greg Jones* 1.50
391 *Joey Thomas* 1.25
392 *Drew Carter* 1.00
393 *Julius Jones* 3.00
394 *Keyaron Fox* .50
395 *Darrion Scott* .50
396 *Rich Gardner* .50
397 *Jeff Smoker* 1.50
398 *Will Poole* 1.25
399 *Samie Parker* .50
400 *Larry Fitzgerald* 4.00
401 *Jerricho Cotchery* 1.00
402 *Ernest Wilford* 1.25
403 *Johnnie Morant* 1.25
404 *Craig Krenzel* 1.25
405 *Michael Turner* .50
406 *D.J. Hackett* .50
407 *P.K. Sam* 1.25
408 *Triandos Luke* 1.00
409 *Josh Harris* 1.00
410 *Drew Henson* 3.00
411 *John Navarre* 1.50
412 *Cody Pickett* 1.50
413 *Clarence Moore* 1.00
414 *Michael Gaines* .50
415 *Derek Abney* 1.00
416 *Dontarrious Thomas* .50
417 *Reggie Torbor* .50
418 *Ryan Krause* .50
419 *Travis LaBoy* .50
420 *Kellen Winslow Jr.* 3.00
421 *Keiwan Ratliff* .50
422 *Gilbert Gardner* .50
423 *Jamaar Taylor* .50
424 *Matt Ware* 1.00
425 *Stuart Schweigert* 1.00
426 *Marcus Tubbs* 1.00
427 *Brandon Chillar* .50
428 *Shawntae Spencer* .50
429 *Marquis Cooper* .50
430 *Derrick Ward* .50
431 *Tim Euhus* .50
432 *Patrick Crayton* .50
433 *Caleb Miller* .50
434 *Donnell Washington* .50
435 *Thomas Tapeh* .50
436 *Randy Starks* .50
437 *Sloan Thomas* .50
438 *Maurice Mann* .50
439 *Jim Sorgi* .50
440 *Nate Lawrie* .50

2004 Topps Total First Edition

Stars: 1X-2X
Rookies: 1.5X

2004 Topps Total Silver

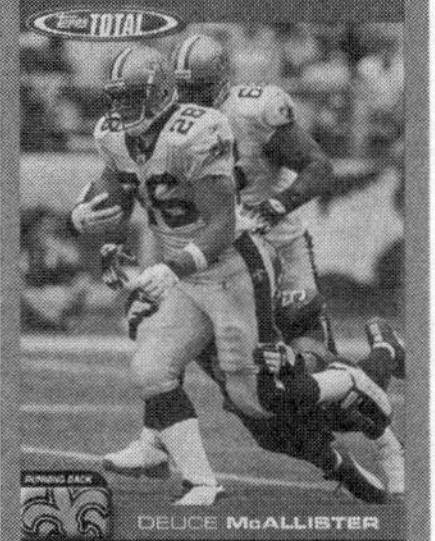

Stars: 1.5X-3X
Rookies: 1X-2X
Inserted 1:1

2004 Topps Total Award Winners

NM/M
Common Player: 1.50
Inserted 1:9
AW1 Jamal Lewis 2.00
AW2 Ahman Green 2.00
AW3 Priest Holmes 2.50
AW4 Torry Holt 2.00
AW5 Randy Moss 3.00
AW6 Chris Chambers 2.00
AW7 LaDainian Tomlinson 2.50
AW8 Peyton Manning 3.00
AW9 Marc Bulger 2.00
AW10 Brett Favre 5.00
AW11 Steve McNair 2.00
AW12 Daunte Culpepper 2.00
AW13 Michael Strahan 2.00
AW14 Adewale Ogunleye 1.50
AW15 Jamie Sharper 1.50
AW16 Micheal Barrow 1.50
AW17 Mike Vanderjagt 1.50
AW18 Anquan Boldin 2.00
AW19 Terrell Suggs 1.50
AW20 Tom Brady 3.00

2004 Topps Total Team Checklists

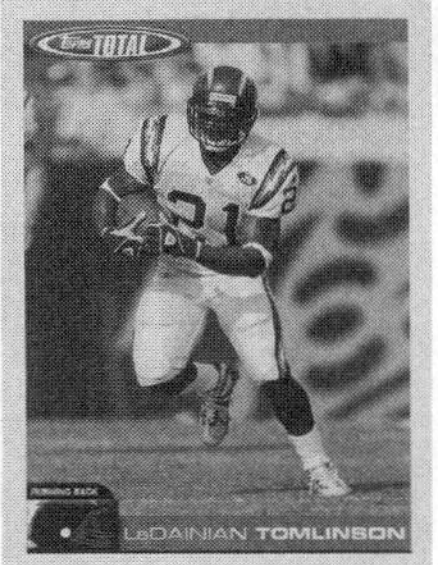

NM/M
Common Player: 1.00
TTC1 Anquan Boldin 1.25
TTC2 Michael Vick 2.50
TTC3 Jamal Lewis 1.25
TTC4 Travis Henry 1.00
TTC5 Jake Delhomme 1.25
TTC6 Brian Urlacher 1.25
TTC7 Chad Johnson 1.00
TTC8 Jeff Garcia 1.25
TTC9 Keyshawn Johnson 1.00
TTC10 Jake Plummer 1.00
TTC11 Joey Harrington 1.25
TTC12 Brett Favre 3.00
TTC13 Domanick Davis 1.25
TTC14 Peyton Manning 2.00
TTC15 Byron Leftwich 2.00
TTC16 Priest Holmes 1.50
TTC17 Ricky Williams 1.50
TTC18 Randy Moss 2.00
TTC19 Tom Brady 2.00
TTC20 Deuce McAllister 1.25
TTC21 Amani Toomer 1.00
TTC22 Chad Pennington 1.50
TTC23 Jerry Rice 2.50
TTC24 Donovan McNabb 1.50
TTC25 Hines Ward 1.25
TTC26 LaDainian Tomlinson 1.50
TTC27 Kevan Barlow 1.00
TTC28 Matt Hasselbeck 1.00
TTC29 Torry Holt 1.25
TTC30 Keenan McCardell 1.00
TTC31 Steve McNair 1.25
TTC32 Clinton Portis 2.00

2004 Topps Total Total Production

NM/M
Common Player: 1.50
Inserted 1:18
TP1 Brett Favre 6.00
TP2 Peyton Manning 4.00
TP3 Priest Holmes 3.00
TP4 Jon Kitna 1.50
TP5 Matt Hasselbeck 2.00
TP6 Daunte Culpepper 2.50
TP7 Ahman Green 2.50
TP8 LaDainian Tomlinson 3.00
TP9 Randy Moss 4.00
TP10 Shaun Alexander 2.50

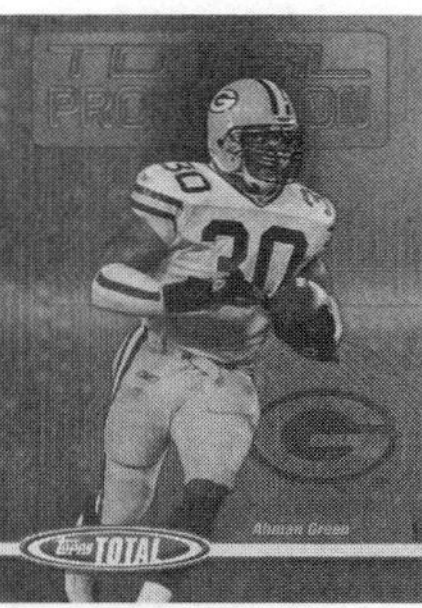

2004 Topps Total Total Signatures

NM/M
Common Player: 10.00
Inserted 1:327
TSNB Nate Burleson 20.00
TSMCL Michael Clayton 20.00
TSCC Cedric Cobbs 25.00
TSKC Keary Colbert 25.00
TSDD Domanick Davis 25.00
TSCP Chad Pennington 60.00
TSBS Brandon Stokley 10.00

2004 Topps Total Total Topps

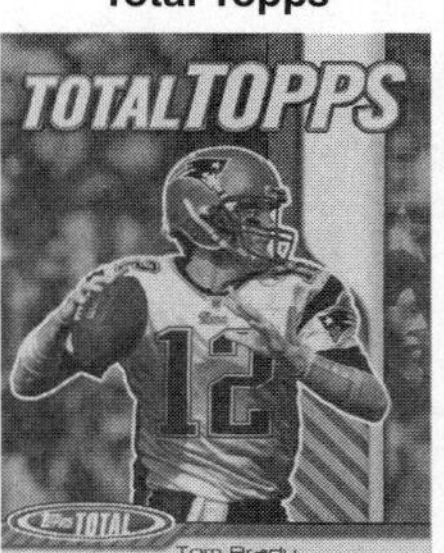

NM/M
Common Player: 1.25
Inserted 1:9
TT1 Peyton Manning 3.00
TT2 Steve McNair 2.00
TT3 Torry Holt 2.00
TT4 Brett Favre 5.00
TT5 Jamal Lewis 2.00
TT6 Deuce McAllister 2.00
TT7 Randy Moss 3.00
TT8 Marvin Harrison 2.00
TT9 Ahman Green 2.00
TT10 Tom Brady 3.00
TT11 Shaun Alexander 2.00
TT12 LaDainian Tomlinson 2.50
TT13 Daunte Culpepper 2.00
TT14 Hines Ward 2.00
TT15 Anquan Boldin 2.00
TT16 Priest Holmes 2.50
TT17 Derrick Mason 1.25
TT18 Donovan McNabb 2.50
TT19 Clinton Portis 3.00
TT20 Terrell Owens 2.00

2004 eTopps

1 Green Bay Packers/2500
2 Chicago Bears/1495
3 New England Patriots/2500
4 Cleveland Browns/1239
5 Carolina Panthers/1668
6 New York Jets/1510
7 Baltimore Ravens/1404
8 Detroit Lions/1192
9 Buffalo Bills/952
10 Washington Redskins/1283
11 Philadelphia Eagles/1750
12 Pittsburgh Steelers/1320
13 Seattle Seahawks/1632
14 New York Giants/981
15 Houston Texans/839
16 Minnesota Vikings/1123
17 Denver Broncos/777
18 Cincinnati Bengals/751
19 Jacksonville Jaguars/908
20 Tennessee Titans/685
21 Atlanta Falcons/1750
22 Tampa Bay Buccaneers/595
23 St. Louis Rams/758
24 Arizona Cardinals/584
25 Kansas City Chiefs/826
26 Indianapolis Colts/1750
27 Oakland Raiders/663
28 Dallas Cowboys/812
29 Miami Dolphins/672
30 New Orleans Saints/591
31 San Francisco 49ers/750
32 San Diego Chargers/900
33 Rashaun Woods/1250
34 Kellen Winslow Jr./3750
35 Ben Roethlisberger/2500
35AU Ben Roethlisberger AU/150
36 Marvin Harrison/1250
37 Terrell Owens/1562
38 Stephen Davis/1250
39 Daunte Culpepper/1250
40 Roy Williams WR/2500
41 Brian Westbrook/1250
42 Julius Jones/1750
43 J.P. Losman/2500
44 Eli Manning/3750
45 Reggie Williams/2276
46 Tatum Bell/1750
47 Philip Rivers/2500
48 Matt Schaub/1750
49 LaDainian Tomlinson/1250
50 Rudi Johnson/1250
51 Robert Gallery/1750
52 Keary Colbert/1669
53 Greg Jones/1481
54 Priest Holmes/1738
55 Peyton Manning/1750
56 Deuce McAllister/1211
57 Larry Fitzgerald/2500
58 Steven Jackson/1750
59 Lee Evans/1540
60 Chad Pennington/1091
61 Chad Johnson/1573
62 Randy Moss/1250
63 Michael Clayton/1446
64 Kevin Jones/1750
65 Ben Watson/1113
66 Clinton Portis/1028
67 Hines Ward/871
68 Quentin Griffin/1750
69 Eddie "Boo" Williams/703
70 Tom Brady/1750
71 Adam Vinatieri/1250
72 Lee Suggs/1250
73 Chris Brown/1046
74 Drew Henson/1559
75 Michael Jenkins/995
76 Darius Watts/1042
77 Chris Perry/1133
78 Donovan McNabb/1418
79 Mike Vanderjagt/688
80 Tiki Barber/839
81 Takeo Spikes/710
82 Deion Sanders/1099
83 Mewelde Moore/1250
84 Brett Favre/900
85 LaVar Arrington/900
86 Jason Elam/900
87A Reuben Droughns/1282
87B Matt Hasselbeck/900
88 Antonio Gates/1000
89 Craig Krenzel/1000

2004 eTopps Event Series

ES14 Peyton Manning/2844

2004 eTopps Event Series Playoffs

ES1 Marc Bulger/727
ES2 Chad Pennington/843
ES3 Peyton Manning, Reggie Wayne/1500
ES4 Daunte Culpepper/830
ES5 Jerome Bettis, Duce Staley/1029
ES6 Michael Vick/990
ES7 Donovan McNabb/892
ES8 Tom Brady, Tedy Bruschi/1207
ES9 Brian Westbrook, Brian Dawkins/923
ES10 Corey Dillon/1083
ES11 Rodney Harrison/987
ES12 Deion Branch/963

2004 eTopps National Promos

3 Bernie Kosar/984

2005 Topps DP & Prospects

NM/M
Common Player (1-100): .25
Minor Stars: .40
Unlisted Stars: .75
Common Rookie (111-170): 1.50
Pack (5): 4.00
Box (24): 70.00
1 Marvin Harrison .75
2 Rudi Johnson .75
3 Matt Hasselbeck .75
4 Plaxico Burress .75
5 Chad Pennington 1.00
6 Jamal Lewis .75
7 Terrell Owens .75
8 LaDainian Tomlinson 1.00
9 Tiki Barber .75
10 Dante Hall .75
11 Peyton Manning 1.25
12 Marshall Faulk 1.00
13 Donovan McNabb 1.00
14 Randy Moss 1.25
15 Muhsin Muhammad .40
16 Deuce McAllister .75
17 Fred Taylor .75
18 Jake Plummer .40
19 Javon Walker .75
20 Tony Gonzalez .75
21 Michael Vick 1.50
22 Brett Favre 2.00
23 Joe Horn .40
24 Jeremy Shockey .75
25 Laveranues Coles .40
26 Trent Green .40
27 Alge Crumpler .40
28 Curtis Martin .75
29 Torry Holt .75
30 Daunte Culpepper .75
31 Aaron Brooks .75
32 Priest Holmes 1.00
33 Eric Moulds .40
34 Jerome Bettis .40
35 David Carr 1.00
36 Chad Johnson .40
37 Ahman Green .75
38 Clinton Portis 1.00
39 Drew Brees .75
40 Darrell Jackson .40
41 Corey Dillon .75
42 Reggie Wayne .40
43 Shaun Alexander .75
44 Hines Ward .75
45 Tom Brady 1.25
46 Isaac Bruce .40
47 Byron Leftwich 1.25
48 Chris Chambers .75
49 Marc Bulger .40
50 Edgerrin James 1.00
51 Jake Delhomme .75
52 Koren Robinson .25
53 Brian Westbrook .40
54 Reuben Droughns .40
55 Joey Harrington .40
56 Eli Manning 1.50
57 Julius Jones 1.25
58 Nick Goings .25
59 T.J. Houshmandzadeh .25
60 Ben Roethlisberger 2.00
61 Charles Rogers .75
62 Billy Volek .25
63 Drew Henson .75
64 Andre Johnson .75
65 Carson Palmer 1.00
66 Anquan Boldin .75
67 Lee Suggs .40
68 Jerry Porter .40
69 J.P. Losman .40
70 Nate Burleson .25
71 Lee Evans .40
72 Tatum Bell .40
73 Chester Taylor .25
74 Philip Rivers .75
75 Rex Grossman .40
76 Willis McGahee .75
77 Antonio Gates .40
78 Steven Jackson .75
79 Roy Williams WR .75
80 Chris Simms .40
81 Najeh Davenport .40
82 Kevin Jones .75
83 Jason Witten .40
84 Brandon Lloyd .40
85 Larry Johnson .40
86 Ronald Curry .40
87 Chris Brown .40
88 Kyle Boller .40
89 Chris Perry .40
90 Keary Colbert .40
91 Sean Taylor .40
92 Greg Jones .25
93 Larry Fitzgerald 1.00
94 Michael Clayton .75
95 Mewelde Moore .40
96 Drew Bennett .40
97 Reggie Williams .25
98 Quentin Griffin .25
99 Josh McCown .25
100 Santana Moss .40
101 Kellen Winslow Jr. .40
102 Michael Jenkins .40
103 Dunta Robinson .25
104 Luke McCown .25
105 Brandon Stokley .40
106 Derrick Blaylock .25
107 Ernest Wilford .25
108 Domanick Davis .75
109 Jonathan Vilma .40
110 Dwight Freeney .40
111 *Alex Smith Auto* 250.00
112 *Derrick Johnson Auto* 150.00
113 *Charlie Frye Auto* 120.00
114 *Ronnie Brown Auto* 180.00
115 Mike Williams Auto 180.00
116 *Erasmus James* 3.00
117 *Alex Smith TE* 3.00
118 *Dan Orlovsky* 3.00
119 *Eric Shelton* 2.00
120 *Reggie Brown* 2.00
121 *Carlos Rogers* 3.00
122 *Dan Cody* 3.00
123 *J.J. Arrington* 4.00
124 *Travis Johnson* 1.50
125 *Antrel Rolle* 4.00
126 *Andrew Walter* 3.00
127 *Craphonso Thorpe* 2.00
128 *Bryan Randall* 1.50
129 *Anttaj Hawthorne* 1.50
130 *David Pollack* 4.00
131 *Heath Miller* 4.00
132 *Charles Frederick* 1.50
133 *Anthony Davis* 2.00
134 *Chris Rix* 2.00
135 *T.A. McLendon* 2.00
136 *David Greene* 3.00
137 *Timmy Chang* 2.00
138 *Marcus Spears* 2.00
139 *Airese Currie* 1.50
140 *Chris Henry* 2.00
141 *Josh Davis* 1.50
142 *Jason Campbell* 6.00
143 *Barrett Ruud* 2.00
144 *Courtney Roby* 1.50
145 *Mike Patterson* 2.00
146 *Jason White* 4.00
147 *Fred Gibson* 3.00
148 *Marion Barber* 2.00
149 *Braylon Edwards* 6.00
150 *Carnell Williams* 6.00
151 *Kyle Orton* 4.00
152 *Aaron Rodgers* 8.00
153 *Alvin Pearman* 1.50
154 *Stefan LeFors* 3.00
155 *Marlin Jackson* 2.00
156 *Taylor Stubblefield* 2.00
157 *Ciatrick Fason* 3.00
158 *Kay-Jay Harris* 2.00
159 *Frank Gore* 3.00
160 *Vernand Morency* 2.00
161 *Adam Jones* 4.00
162 *Troy Williamson* 5.00
163 *Roddy White* 3.00
164 *Thomas Davis* 3.00
165 *Mark Clayton* 4.00
166 *Craig Bragg* 1.50
167 *Noah Herron* 1.50
168 *Darren Sproles* 3.00
169 *Terrence Murphy* 2.00
170 *Walter Reyes* 1.50

2005 Topps DP & Prospects Chrome

NM/M
Stars (1-110): 1X-2X
Rookies (116-190): 1X-1.5X
Inserted 2:1
111 Alex Smith 15.00

2005 Topps DP & Prospects Chrome Refractor

NM/M
Stars (1-110): 4X-8X
Rookies (116-170): 3X-6X
Production 199 Sets
Black Border Production 25 Sets
111 Alex Smith 75.00

2005 Topps DP & Prospects Class Marks Autographs

NM/M
Common Player: 10.00
CMJA J.J. Arrington 25.00
CMMB Marion Barber 12.00
CMCB Cedric Benson 150.00
CMRBR Reggie Brown 20.00
CMJC Jason Campbell 50.00
CMMC Mark Clayton 40.00
CMDC Dan Cody 25.00
CMAD Anthony Davis 12.00
CMBE Braylon Edwards 125.00
CMCF Charles Frederick 10.00
CMFG Fred Gibson 20.00
CMDG David Greene 40.00
CMCH Chris Henry 15.00
CMCHO Cedric Houston 12.00
CMMJ Marlin Jackson 12.00
CMTAM T.A. McLendon 10.00
CMKO Kyle Orton 25.00
CMWR Walter Reyes 10.00
CMCR Chris Rix 12.00
CMAR Aaron Rodgers 100.00
CMES Eric Shelton 12.00
CMCT Craphonso Thorpe 15.00
CMAW Andrew Walter 30.00
CMJW Jason White 40.00
CMCW Carnell Williams 100.00

2005 Topps DP & Prospects Double Feature Dual Autograph

NM/M
DFBW Cedric Benson, Carnell Williams 400.00
DFEC Braylon Edwards, Michael Clayton 200.00
DFEW Braylon Edwards, Mike Williams 400.00
DFSR Alex Smith QB, Aaron Rodgers 450.00
DFWB Carnell Williams, Ronnie Brown 300.00

2005 Topps DP & Prospects Senior Standout Jersey

NM/M
Common Player: 8.00
Silver: 2X-4X
Silver Production 50 Sets
Gold Production 10 Sets
SSJA J.J. Arrington 12.00
SSRB Reggie Brown 8.00
SSRBR Ronnie Brown 15.00
SSJC Jason Campbell 12.00
SSMC Mark Clayton 10.00
SSSC Shaun Cody 8.00
SSSC Sonny Cumbie 8.00
SSCF Charlie Frye 12.00
SSFG Fred Gibson 8.00
SSFGO Frank Gore 10.00
SSDG David Greene 10.00
SSCH Cedric Houston 8.00
SSMJ Marlin Jackson 8.00
SSVJ Vincent Jackson 8.00
SSBJ Brandon Jones 8.00
SSKO Kyle Orton 10.00
SSCR Carlos Rogers 8.00
SSCR2 Carlos Rogers 8.00
SSAR Antrel Rolle 8.00
SSAR2 Antrel Rolle 8.00
SSBR Barrett Ruud 10.00
SSMSC Morgan Scalley 8.00
SSAS Alex Smith TE 8.00
SSMS Marcus Spears 8.00
SSMS2 Marcus Spears 8.00
SSDS Darren Sproles 8.00
SSTS Taylor Stubblefield 8.00
SSCT Craphonso Thorpe 8.00
SSCW Carnell Williams 15.00
SSCW2 Carnell Williams 15.00

2005 Topps DP & Prospects Senior Standout Jersy Autos.

NM/M
Production 50 Sets
SSAJA J.J. Arrington 80.00
SSARB Reggie Brown 50.00
SSARBR Ronnie Brown 150.00
SSAJC Jason Campbell 60.00
SSAMC Mark Clayton
SSACF Charlie Frye 80.00

SSADG David Greene
SSAKO Kyle Orton 60.00
SSAAR Antrel Rolle 80.00
SSATS Taylor Stubblefield
SSACW Carnell Williams 150.00

1977 Touchdown Club

These 50 black-and-white cards were issued as a set in 1977 to honor several Hall-of-Fame caliber retired players. Each front has photo of the player in uniform, with his name below the photo. A black frame borders the photo and his name. The card back has the player's name and number at the top, with his position listed just below them. A brief career summary, listing the player's main honors and accomplishments, is also given. "Touchdown, 1977" is written at the bottom. All of the information on the back is contained within a black box. The set was designed for collectors who wanted the players' autographs; a list of their home addresses was included with the set.

NM/M
Complete Set (50): 50.00
Common Player: .75
1 Harold "Red" Grange 5.00
2 George Halas 2.00
3 Benny Friedman .75
4 Cliff Battles 1.00
5 Mike Michalske .75
6 George McAfee 1.00
7 Beattie Feathers 1.25
8 Ernie Caddel .75
9 George Musso 1.00
10 Sid Luckman 2.25
11 Cecil Isbell .75
12 Bronko Nagurski 3.00
13 Hunk Anderson .80
14 Dick Farman .80
15 Aldo Forte .90
16 Ki Aldrich .80
17 Jim Lee Howell .75
18 Ray Flaherty .75
19 Hampton Pool .80
20 Alex Wojchiechowicz 1.00
21 Bill Osmanski .75
22 Hank Soar .75
23 Dutch Clark 1.00
24 Joe Muha .75
25 Don Hutson 1.50
26 Jim Poole .85
27 Charley Malone .75
28 Charlie Trippi 1.25
29 Andy Farkas .75
30 Clarke Hinkle 1.00
31 Gary Famiglietti .75
32 Bulldog Turner 1.25
33 Sammy Baugh 3.00
34 Pat Harder .75
35 Tuffy Leemans 1.00
36 Ken Strong 1.00
37 Barney Poole .75
38 Bruiser Kinard 1.00
39 Buford Ray .75
40 Ace Parker 1.25
41 Buddy Parker .75
42 Mel Hein 1.00
43 Ed Danowski .75
44 Bill Dudley 1.25
45 Paul Stenn .80
46 George Connor 1.00
47 George Connor .75
48 Armand Niccolai .75
49 Tony Canadeo 1.25
50 Bill Willis 1.50

1989 TV-4NFL Quarterbacks

The 20-card, 2-7/16" x 3-1/8" set features borderless portrait drawings by artist J.C. Ford. The card backs contain career highlights. The set was issued by a television station in Great Britain and were distributed to promote American football in the U.K.

NM/M
Complete Set (20): 25.00
Common Player: .75
1 Dutch Clark .75
2 Sammy Baugh 1.50
3 Bob Waterfield .75
4 Sid Luckman .75
5 Otto Graham 1.00
6 Bobby Layne .75
7 Norm Van Brocklin .75
8 George Blanda .75
9 Y.A. Tittle 1.00
10 Johnny Unitas 3.00
11 Bart Starr 1.25
12 Sonny Jurgensen 1.25
13 Joe Namath 2.50
14 Fran Tarkenton 1.50
15 Roger Staubach 2.50
16 Terry Bradshaw 3.00
17 Dan Fouts 1.25
18 Joe Montana 5.00
19 John Elway 2.00
20 Dan Marino 5.00

A card number in parenthese ( ) indicates the set is unnumbered.

U

1992 Ultimate WLAF

The 200-card, WLAF set features color photos with another color action photo on the card back, along with stats, bio information and a highlight. Each nine-pack of cards contained a game card in which the collector who spelled W-O-R-L-D won one million dollars. The final 20 cards are subsets which deal with playing the game (180-192) and collecting cards (193-200).

NM/M
Complete Set (200): 5.00
Common Player: .05
1 Thomas Woods Barcelona Dragons '91 Team Statistics .10
2 Demetrius Davis .15
3 Tim Egerton .05
4 Scott Erney .05
5 Tony Baker '91 Rushing Attempt Leader .15
6 Anthony Greene .05
7 Mike Hinnant (UER) (No position on front) .05
8 Erik Naposki .05
9 Paul Palmer .15
10 Gene Taylor .05
11 Thomas Woods .05
12 Tony Rice .25
13 Terry O'Shea .05
14 Brett Wiese .05
15 Phillip Alexander Kicking Leader .05
16 Eric Wilkerson Rushing/Scoring Leader .10
17 Barcelona Dragons Team Picture .05
18 Barcelona Dragons Checklist .05
19 Birmingham Fire '91 Team Statistics .05
20 Eric Jones .05
21 Steve Avery .05
22 Willie Bouyer .05
23 Anthony Parker '91 Interception Leader .20
24 Elroy Harris .05
25 James Henry .05
26 Johnny Holland .10
27 Mark Hopkins .05
28 Arthur Hunter .05
29 Danny Lockett '91 Sacking Leader .10
30 Kirk Maggio .05
31 John Miller .05
32 Ricky Shaw .05
33 Phil Ross .05
34 Mike Norseth .05
35 Birmingham Fire Checklist .05
36 Frankfurt Galaxy '91 Team Statistics .05
37 Anthony Wallace .05
38 Lew Barnes .05
39 Richard Buchanan .05
40 Yepi Pau'u .05
41 Pat McGuirk (UER) (Played for Raleigh-Durham in 1991) .05
42 Tony Baker .15
43 1992 TV Schedule 1 .05
44 Tim Broady .05
45 Lonnie Finch .05
46 Chad Fortune .05
47 Harry Jackson .05
48 Jason Johnson .05
49 Pat Moorer .05
50 Mike Perez .15
51 Mark Seals .05
52 Cedric Stallworth .05
53 Tom Whelihan .05
54 Joe Johnson .30
55 Frankfurt Galaxy Checklist .05
56 Stan Gelbaugh London Monarchs '91 Team Statistics .10
57 Stan Gelbaugh .35
58 Jeff Alexander .05
59 Dana Brinson .05
60 Marlon Brown .05
61 Dedrick Dodge .05
62 Judd Garrett .10
63 Greg Horne .05
64 Jon Horton .05
65 Danny Lockett .10
66 Andre Riley .05
67 Charlie Young .10
68 David Smith .05
69 Irvin Smith .05
70 Rickey Williams .05
71 Roland Smith .05
72 William Kirksey .05
73 Phillip Alexander .05
74 London Monarchs Team Picture .10
75 London Monarchs Checklist .05
76 Montreal Machine '91 Team Statistics .05
77 Rollin Putzier .05
78 Adam Bob .05
79 K.D. Dunn .05
80 Darryl Holmes .05
81 Ricky Johnson .05
82 Michael Finn .05
83 Chris Mohr .15
84 Don Murray .05
85 Bjorn Nittmo .10
86 Michael Proctor .10
87 Broderick Sargent .05
88 Richard Shelton .05
89 Emanuel King .10
90 Pete Mandley .15
91 Kris McCall .05
92 1992 TV Schedule 2 .05
93 Montreal Machine Checklist .05
94 NY/NJ Knights '91 Team Statistics .05
95 Andre Alexander .05
96 Pat Marlatt .05
97 Cecil Fletcher .05
98 Lonnie Turner .05
99 Monty Gilbreath .05
100 Tony Jones (UER) (Should be DB, not WR) .05
101 Kip Lewis .05
102 Bob Lilljedahl .05
103 Mark Moore .05
104 Falanda Newton .05
105 Anthony Parker (UER) (Played for Chiefs in 1991, not Bears; was released by the Bears) .20
106 Kendall Trainor .10
107 Eric Wilkerson .05
108 Tony Woods .20
109 Reggie Slack .10
110 Joey Banes .05
111 Ron Sancho .10
112 Mike Husar .05
113 NY/NJ Knights Checklist .05
114 Orlando Thunder '91 Team Statistics .05
115 Byron Williams (UER) (Waived by Orlando and picked up by NY-NJ) .05
116 Charlie Baumann .15
117 Kevin Bell .10
118 Rodney Lossow .05
119 Myron Jones .05
120 Bruce Lasane .05
121 Eric Mitchel .10
122 Billy Owens .05
123 1992 TV Schedule 3 .05
124 Chris Roscoe .05
125 Tommie Stowers .05
126 Wayne Dickson (UER) (Not a rookie, he played for Orlando in 1991) .05
127 Scott Mitchell 1.25
128 Karl Dunbar .05
129 Dana Brinson '91 Punt Return Leader .05
130 Orlando Thunder Checklist .05
131 Sacramento Surge Team Statistics .05
132 1992 TV Schedule 4 .05
133 Mike Adams .05
134 Greg Coauette .05
135 Mel Farr Jr. (Should be TE, not FB) .10
136 Victor Floyd .05
137 Paul Frazier .05
138 Tom Gerhart .05
139 Pete Najarian .05
140 John Nies .05
141 Carl Parker .05
142 Saute Sapolu .05
143 George Bethune .05
144 David Archer .35
145 John Buddenberg .05
146 Jon Horton '91 Receiving Yardage Leader (UER) (Incorrect stats on back) .05
147 Sacramento Surge Checklist .05
148 San Antonio Riders '91 Team Statistics .05
149 Ricky Blake .10
150 Jim Gallery .05
151 Jason Garrett .75
152 John Garrett .10
153 Broderick Graves .05
154 Bill Hess .05
155 Mike Johnson .05
156 Lee Morris .05
157 Dwight Pickens .05
158 Kent Sullivan .05
159 Ken Watson .05
160 Ronnie Williams .05
161 Titus Dixon .05
162 Mike Kiselak .05
163 Greg Lee .05
164 Judd Garrett '91 Receiving Leader (Had 71 receptions in 1991, not 18; game high was 12, not 13) .10
165 San Antonio Riders Checklist .05
166 Tenth Week Summaries .05
167 Randy Bethel .05
168 Melvin Patterson .05
169 Eric Harmon .05
170 Patrick Jackson .05
171 Tim James .05
172 George Koonce .15
173 Babe Laufenberg .25
174 Amir Rasul .05
175 Stan Gelbaugh '91 Passing Leader .25
176 Jason Wallace .05
177 Walter Wilson .05
178 Power Meter Info .15
179 Ohio Glory Checklist .05
180 Jim Kelly The Football Field .20
181 Jim Kelly Moving the Ball .20
182 Lawrence Taylor Safeties .20
183 Lawrence Taylor Defense/Linebackers .20
184 Lawrence Taylor Tackles and Ends .20
185 Jim Kelly Guards, Tackles and Tight Ends .05
186 Lawrence Taylor Offense/Receivers .20
187 Jim Kelly Offense/ Running Backs .20
188 Jim Kelly Offensive/Quarterback .20
189 Special Teams .10
190 differ from NFL 1990 Rules .05
191 and Extra Points .05
192 Goals and Safeties .05
193 Lawrence Taylor How to Collect - What is a Set .20
194 Lawrence Taylor How to Collect - What is a Wax Pack .20
195 Lawrence Taylor How to Collect - Premier Editions .20
196 Lawrence Taylor How to Collect - What Creates Value .20
197 Jim Kelly How to Collect - Rookie Cards .20
198 Jim Kelly How to Collect - Grading Your Cards .20
199 Jim Kelly How to Collect - Storing Your Cards .20
200 Jim Kelly How to Collect - Trading Your Cards .20

A player's name in *italic* type indicates a rookie card.

1992 Ultimate WLAF Logo Holograms

The 10-card, standard-size set features holograms of each of the WLAF teams, which were randomly inserted in Ultimate packs.

NM/M
Complete Set (10): 5.00
Common Player: 1.00
1 Barcelona Dragons 1.00
2 Birmingham Fire 1.00
3 Frankfurt Galaxy 1.00
4 London Monarchs 1.00
5 Montreal Machine 1.00
6 NY/NJ Knights 1.00
7 Ohio Glory 1.00
8 Orlando Thunder 1.00
9 Sacramento Surge 1.00
10 San Antonio Riders 1.00

1991 Ultra

This 300-card set features cards with color action photos with silver borders above and below the photo. The player's name, team and position is in white at the bottom. Backs have silver borders at the top and bottom, with a yellow-to-orange-to-green background. A mug shot is positioned between two smaller action photos on the back. A Rookie Prospect subset was also included; cards are numbered from 279-298. Two 10-card insert sets were also created - Ultra All-Stars and Ultra Performances. The All-Star cards were randomly inserted in 1991 packs which were sold in black boxes; the Performances cards were inserts in packs in green boxes.

NM/M
Complete Set (300): 12.00
Common Player: .05
Minor Stars: .10
Pack (15): .50
Wax Box (36): 10.00
1 Don Beebe .05
2 Shane Conlan .05
3 Pete Metzelaars .05
4 Jamie Mueller .05
5 Scott Norwood .05
6 Andre Reed .10
7 Leon Seals .05
8 Bruce Smith .05
9 Leonard Smith .05
10 Thurman Thomas .25
11 Lewis Billups .05
12 Jim Breech .05
13 James Brooks .05
14 Eddie Brown .05
15 Boomer Esiason .10
16 David Fulcher .05
17 Rodney Holman .05
18 Bruce Kozerski .05
19 Tim Krumrie .05
20 Tim McGee .05
21 Anthony Munoz .05
22 Leon White .05
23 Ickey Woods .05
24 Carl Zander .05
25 Brian Brennan .05
26 Thane Gash .05
27 Leroy Hoard .05
28 Mike Johnson .05
29 Reggie Langhorne .05
30 Kevin Mack .05
31 Clay Matthews .05
32 Eric Metcalf .05
33 Steve Atwater .05
34 Melvin Bratton .05
35 John Elway .40
36 Bobby Humphrey .05
37 Mark Jackson .05
38 Vance Johnson .05
39 Ricky Nattiel .05
40 Steve Sewell .05
41 Dennis Smith .05
42 David Treadwell .05
43 Mike Young .05
44 Ray Childress .05
45 Cris Dishman .05
46 William Fuller .05
47 Ernest Givins .05
48 John Grimsley .05
49 Drew Hill .05
50 Haywood Jeffires .05
51 Sean Jones .05
52 Johnny Meads .05
53 Warren Moon .10
54 Al Smith .05
55 Lorenzo White .05
56 Albert Bentley .05
57 Duane Bickett .05
58 Bill Brooks .05
59 Jeff George .30
60 Mike Prior .05
61 Rohn Stark .05
62 Jack Trudeau .05
63 Clarence Verdin .05
64 Steve DeBerg .05
65 Emile Harry .05
66 Albert Lewis .05
67 Nick Lowery .05
68 Todd McNair .05
69 Christian Okoye .05
70 Stephone Paige .05
71 Kevin Porter .05
72 Derrick Thomas .10
73 Robb Thomas .05
74 Barry Word .05
75 Marcus Allen .10
76 Eddie Anderson .05
77 Tim Brown .10
78 Mervyn Fernandez .05
79 Willie Gault .05
80 Ethan Horton .05
81 Howie Long .05
82 Vance Mueller .05
83 Jay Schroeder .05
84 Steve Smith .05
85 Greg Townsend .05
86 Mark Clayton .05
87 Jim C. Jensen .05
88 Dan Marino 1.00
89 Tim McKyer .05
90 John Offerdahl .05
91 Louis Oliver .05
92 Reggie Roby .05
93 Sammie Smith .05
94 Hart Lee Dykes .05
95 Irving Fryar .05
96 Tommy Hodson .05
97 Maurice Hurst .05
98 John Stephens .05
99 Andre Tippett .05
100 Mark Boyer .05
101 Kyle Clifton .05
102 James Hasty .05
103 Erik McMillan .05
104 Rob Moore .05
105 Joe Mott .05
106 Ken O'Brien .05
107 Ron Stallworth .05
108 Al Toon .05
109 Gary Anderson .05
110 Bubby Brister .05
111 Thomas Everett .05
112 Merril Hoge .05
113 Louis Lipps .05
114 Greg Lloyd .05
115 Hardy Nickerson .05
116 Dwight Stone .05
117 Rod Woodson .10
118 Tim Worley .05
119 Rod Bernstine .05
120 Marion Butts .05
121 Gill Byrd .05
122 Arthur Cox .05
123 Burt Grossman .05
124 Ronnie Harmon .05
125 Anthony Miller .05
126 Leslie O'Neal .05
127 Gary Plummer .05
128 Sam Seale .05
129 Junior Seau .30
130 Broderick Thompson .05
131 Billy Joe Tolliver .05
132 Brian Blades .05
133 Jeff Bryant .05
134 Derrick Fenner .05
135 Jacob Green .05
136 Andy Heck .05
137 Patrick Hunter .05
138 Norm Johnson .05
139 Tommy Kane .05
140 Dave Krieg .05
141 John L. Williams .05
142 Terry Wooden .05
143 Steve Broussard .05
144 Keith Jones .05
145 Brian Jordan .05
146 Chris Miller .05
147 John Rade .05
148 Andre Rison .10
149 Mike Rozier .05
150 Deion Sanders .40
151 Neal Anderson .05
152 Trace Armstrong .05
153 Kevin Butler .05
154 Mark Carrier .05
155 Richard Dent .05
156 Dennis Gentry .05
157 Jim Harbaugh .10
158 Brad Muster .05
159 William Perry .05
160 Mike Singletary .05
161 Lemuel Stinson .05
162 Troy Aikman 1.00
163 Michael Irvin .30
164 Mike Saxon .05
165 Emmitt Smith 2.00
166 Jerry Ball .05
167 Michael Cofer .05
168 Rodney Peete .10
169 Barry Sanders 1.25
170 Robert Brown .05
171 Anthony Dilweg .05
172 Tim Harris .05
173 Johnny Holland .05
174 Perry Kemp .05
175 Don Majkowski .05
176 Brian Noble .05
177 Jeff Query .05
178 Sterling Sharpe .10
179 Charles Wilson .05
180 Keith Woodside .05
181 Flipper Anderson .05
182 Bern Brostek .05
183 Pat Carter .05
184 Aaron Cox .05
185 Henry Ellard .05
186 Jim Everett .05
187 Cleveland Gary .05
188 Jerry Gray .05
189 Kevin Greene .05
190 Mike Wilcher .05
191 Alfred Anderson .05
192 Joey Browner .05
193 Anthony Carter .05
194 Chris Doleman .05
195 Rick Fenney .05
196 Darrell Fullington .05
197 Rich Gannon .05
198 Hassan Jones .05
199 Steve Jordan .05
200 Mike Merriweather .05
201 Al Noga .05
202 Herschel Walker .05
203 Wade Wilson .05
204 Morten Andersen .05
205 Gene Atkins .05
206 Toi Cook .05
207 Craig Heyward .05
208 Dalton Hilliard .05
209 Vaughan Johnson .05
210 Eric Martin .05
211 Brett Perriman .10
212 Pat Swilling .05
213 Steve Walsh .05
214 Ottis Anderson .05
215 Carl Banks .05
216 Maurice Carthon .05
217 Mark Collins .05
218 Rodney Hampton .25
219 Erik Howard .05
220 Mark Ingram .05
221 Pepper Johnson .05
222 Dave Meggett .05
223 Phil Simms .05
224 Lawrence Taylor .10
225 Lewis Tillman .05
226 Everson Walls .05
227 Fred Barnett .05
228 Jerome Brown .05
229 Keith Byars .05
230 Randall Cunningham .10
231 Byron Evans .05
232 Wes Hopkins .05
233 Keith Jackson .05
234 Heath Sherman .05
235 Anthony Toney .05
236 Reggie White .10
237 Rich Camarillo .05
238 Ken Harvey .05
239 Eric Hill .05
240 Johnny Johnson .05
241 Ernie Jones .05
242 Tim McDonald .05
243 Timm Rosenbach .05
244 Jay Taylor .05
245 Dexter Carter .05
246 Mike Cofer .05
247 Kevin Fagan .05

248 Don Griffin .05
249 Charles Haley .05
250 Brent Jones .05
251 Joe Montana 1.00
252 Darryl Pollard .05
253 Tom Rathman .05
254 Jerry Rice 1.00
255 John Taylor .05
256 Steve Young 1.00
257 Gary Anderson .05
258 Mark Carrier .05
259 Chris Chandler .05
260 Reggie Cobb .05
261 Reuben Davis .05
262 Willie Drewrey .05
263 Ron Hall .05
264 Eugene Marve .05
265 Winston Moss .05
266 Vinny Testaverde .05
267 Broderick Thomas .05
268 Jeff Bostic .05
269 Earnest Byner .05
270 Gary Clark .05
271 Darrell Green .05
272 Jim Lachey .05
273 Wilber Marshall .05
274 Art Monk .10
275 Gerald Riggs .05
276 Mark Rypien .05
277 Ricky Sanders .05
278 Alvin Walton .05
279 *Nick Bell* .05
280 *Eric Bieniemy* .10
281 *Jarrod Bunch* .05
282 *Mike Croel* .10
283 *Brett Favre* 10.00
284 *Moe Gardner* .10
285 *Pat Harlow* .05
286 *Randal Hill* .25
287 *Todd Marinovich* .10
288 *Russell Maryland* .10
289 *Dan McGwire* .10
290 *Ernie Mills* .10
291 *Herman Moore* 2.00
292 *Godfrey Myles* .05
293 *Browning Nagle* .05
294 *Mike Pritchard* .30
295 *Esera Tuaolo* .05
296 *Mark Vander Poel* .05
297 *Ricky Watters* 2.00
298 *Chris Zorich* .20
299 Randall Cunningham, Emmitt Smith Checklist Card .10
300 Randall Cunningham, Emmitt Smith Checklist Card .10

1991 Ultra All-Stars

These cards, random inserts in 1991 Fleer Ultra packs, feature 10 top NFL players. Each card front has a shield with a head shot of the player, plus two smaller action photos against a gold background. A green stripe at the bottom contains the player's name, team and position. Each back has a career summary in a white box, bordered with a gold frame. Cards, which are numbered 1 of 10, etc., were randomly inserted in packs that were sold in black boxes.

NM/M

Complete Set (10): 12.00
Common Player: .50
Minor Stars: 1.00
1 Barry Sanders 5.00
2 Keith Jackson .50
3 Bruce Smith .50
4 Randall Cunningham 1.00
5 Dan Marino 6.00
6 Charles Haley .50
7 John L. Williams .50
8 Darrell Green .50
9 Stephone Paige .50
10 Kevin Greene 1.00

1991 Ultra Performances

Each card in this 10-card set features a color action photo on the front, with silver stripes as borders at the top and bottom. The player is pictured against a washed-out background with other players in it. The back has a player profile inside a black-and-silver border, plus a card number (1 of 10, etc.). These cards were random inserts in Fleer Ultra packs sold in green boxes.

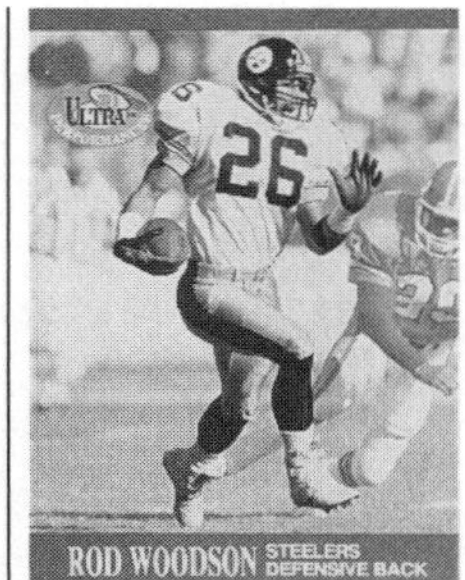

NM/M

Complete Set (10): 15.00
Common Player: .50
Minor Stars: 1.00
1 Emmitt Smith 5.00
2 Andre Rison 1.00
3 Derrick Thomas 1.00
4 Joe Montana 5.00
5 Warren Moon 1.00
6 Mike Singletary .50
7 Thurman Thomas 1.00
8 Rod Woodson .50
9 Jerry Rice 4.00
10 Reggie White 1.00

1991 Ultra Update

This 100-card set features top rookies and players who were traded during the 1991 season. Cards backs are numbered with a U prefix and have a mug shot of the player in a shield, surrounded by two smaller action shots. Fronts have an "Ultra Rookie" logo for the rookies.

NM/M

Complete Set (100): 42.00
Common Player: .10
Minor Stars: .20
1 Brett Favre 35.00
2 Moe Gardner .10
3 Tim McKyer .10
4 *Bruce Pickens* .10
5 Mike Pritchard .30
6 Cornelius Bennett .10
7 *Phil Hansen* .10
8 *Henry Jones* .10
9 Mark Kelso .10
10 James Lofton .10
11 *Anthony Morgan* .20
12 Stan Thomas .10
13 Chris Zorich .30
14 Reggie Rembert .10
15 *Alfred Williams* .10
16 *Michael Jackson* 1.00
17 *Ed King* .10
18 Joe Morris .10
19 Vince Newsome .10
20 Tony Casillas .10
21 Russell Maryland .20
22 Jay Novacek .20
23 Mike Croel .10
24 Gaston Green .10
25 *Kenny Walker* .10
26 *Melvin Jenkins* .10
27 Herman Moore 5.00
28 *Kelvin Pritchett* .10
29 Chris Spielman .10
30 Vinnie Clark .10
31 Allen Rice .10
32 Vai Sikahema .10
33 Esera Tuaolo .10
34 *Mike Dumas* .10
35 *John Flannery* .10
36 Allen Pinkett .10
37 *Tim Barnett* .20
38 Dan Saleaumua .10
39 *Harvey Williams* 1.00
40 Nick Bell .10
41 Roger Craig .10
42 Ronnie Lott .10
43 Todd Marinovich .10
44 Robert Delpino .10
45 *Todd Lyght* .20
46 Robert Young .10
47 *Aaron Craver* .20
48 *Mark Higgs* .20
49 Vestee Jackson .10
50 Carl Lee .10
51 Felix Wright .10
52 Darrell Fullington .10
53 Pat Harlow .10
54 Eugene Lockhart .10
55 *Hugh Millen* .20
56 *Leonard Russell* .25
57 *Jon Vaughn* .10
58 Quinn Early .10
59 Bobby Hebert .10
60 Rickey Jackson .10
61 Sam Mills .10
62 Jarrod Bunch .10
63 John Elliott .10
64 Jeff Hostetler .20
65 *Ed McCaffrey* 12.00
66 *Kanavis McGhee* .10
67 *Mo Lewis* .10
68 Browning Nagle .10
69 Blair Thomas .10
70 *Antone Davis* .10
71 *Brad Goebel* .10
72 Jim McMahon .10
73 Clyde Simmons .10
74 Randal Hill .25
75 *Eric Swann* .50
76 Tom Tupa .10
77 *Jeff Graham* 1.50
78 Eric Green .10
79 *Neil O'Donnell* 2.00
80 Huey Richardson .10
81 Eric Bieniemy .10
82 John Friesz .10
83 *Eric Moten* .10
84 *Stanley Richard* .20
85 Todd Bowles .10
86 *Merton Hanks* .75
87 Tim Harris .10
88 Pierce Holt .10
89 *Ted Washington* .10
90 *John Kasay* .10
91 Dan McGwire .10
92 *Lawrence Dawsey* .20
93 *Charles McRae* .10
94 Jesse Solomon .10
95 Robert Wilson .10
96 *Ricky Ervins* .20
97 Charles Mann .10
98 *Bobby Wilson* .10
99 Jerry Rice PV (PV) 2.00
100 Checklist .10

1992 Ultra

This 450-card set features full-bleed color action photos on the card fronts. The player's name is below a gold-foil stripe at the bottom, along with his team's name and position in bars color-coded according to his team's colors. The back is horizontal and shows a close-up and action shot of the player against a color-coded football field design. Statistics and the player's name are superimposed onto the card. A green marbleized area contains the player's team logo and biography. Subsets include Draft Picks (#s 417-446) and checklists (#s 447-450). Insert sets include Award Winners (10 cards, randomly in foil packs), and Signature Series sets for Chris Miller (10, in foil packs) and Reggie White (10, in foil packs).

NM/M

Complete Set (450): 20.00
Common Player: .05
Pack (15): .50
Wax Box (36): 15.00
1 Steve Broussard .05
2 Rick Bryan .05
3 Scott Case .05
4 Darrion Conner .05
5 Bill Fralic .05
6 Moe Gardner .05
7 Tim Green .05
8 Michael Haynes .40
9 Chris Hinton .05
10 Mike Kenn .05
11 Tim McKyer .05
12 Chris Miller .05
13 Erric Pegram .15
14 Mike Pritchard .20
15 Andre Rison .30
16 Jessie Tuggle .05
17 *Carlton Bailey* .25
18 Howard Ballard .05
19 Cornelius Bennett .05
20 Shane Conlan .05
21 Kenneth Davis .05
22 Kent Hull .05
23 Mark Kelso .05
24 James Lofton .05
25 Keith McKeller .05
26 Nate Odomes .05
27 Jim Ritcher .05
28 Leon Seals .05
29 Darryl Talley .05
30 Steve Tasker .05
31 Thurman Thomas .50
32 Will Wolford .05
33 Jeff Wright .05
34 Neal Anderson .20
35 Trace Armstrong .05
36 Mark Carrier .05
37 Wendell Davis .05
38 Richard Dent .05
39 Shaun Gayle .05
40 Jim Harbaugh .05
41 Jay Hilgenberg .05
42 Darren Lewis .05
43 Steve McMichael .05
44 Anthony Morgan .05
45 Brad Muster .05
46 William Perry .05
47 John Roper .05
48 Lemuel Stinson .05
49 Tom Waddle .15
50 Donnell Woolford .05
51 *Leo Barker* .10
52 Eddie Brown .05
53 James Francis .05
54 David Fulcher .05
55 David Grant .05
56 Harold Green .05
57 Rodney Holman .05
58 Lee Johnson .05
59 Tim Krumrie .05
60 Tim McGee .05
61 *Alonzo Mitz* .10
62 Anthony Munoz .05
63 Alfred Williams .05
64 Stephen Braggs .05
65 *Richard Brown* .10
66 *Randy Hilliard* .10
67 Leroy Hoard .05
68 Michael Jackson .15
69 Mike Johnson .05
70 James Jones .05
71 Tony Jones .05
72 Ed King .05
73 Kevin Mack .05
74 Clay Matthews .05
75 Eric Metcalf .05
76 Vince Newsome .05
77 Steve Beuerlein .20
78 Larry Brown .05
79 Tony Casillas .05
80 Alvin Harper .50
81 Issiac Holt .05
82 Ray Horton .05
83 Michael Irvin .40
84 Daryl Johnston .05
85 Kelvin Martin .05
86 Ken Norton .05
87 Jay Novacek .20
88 Emmitt Smith 5.00
89 *Vinson Smith* .15
90 Mark Stepnoski .05
91 Tony Tolbert .05
92 Alexander Wright .05
93 Steve Atwater .05
94 Tyrone Braxton .05
95 Michael Brooks .05
96 Mike Croel .05
97 John Elway .75
98 Simon Fletcher .05
99 Gaston Green .05
100 Mark Jackson .05
101 Keith Kartz .05
102 Greg Kragen .05
103 Greg Lewis .05
104 Karl Mecklenburg .05
105 Derek Russell .25
106 Steve Sewell .05
107 Dennis Smith .05
108 David Treadwell .05
109 Kenny Walker .05
110 Michael Young .05
111 Jerry Ball .05
112 Bennie Blades .05
113 Lomas Brown .05
114 *Scott Conover* .15
115 Mel Gray .05
116 Willie Green .15
117 Erik Kramer .05
118 Dan Owens .05
119 Rodney Peete .05
120 Brett Perriman .05
121 Barry Sanders 3.00
122 Chris Spielman .05
123 Marc Spindler .05
124 Willie White .05
125 Tony Bennett .05
126 Matt Brock .05
127 Leroy Butler .05
128 Chuck Cecil .05
129 Johnny Holland .05
130 Perry Kemp .05
131 Don Majkowski .05
132 Tony Mandarich .05
133 Brian Noble .05
134 Bryce Paup .05
135 Sterling Sharpe .30
136 Darrell Thompson .05
137 Mike Tomczak .05
138 Vince Workman .05
139 Ray Childress .05
140 Cris Dishman .05
141 Curtis Duncan .05
142 William Fuller .05
143 Ernest Givins .05
144 Haywood Jeffires .15
145 Sean Jones .05
146 Lamar Lathon .05
147 Bruce Matthews .05
148 Bubba McDowell .05
149 Johnny Meads .05
150 Warren Moon .40
151 Mike Munchak .05
152 *Bo Orlando* .30
153 Al Smith .05
154 Doug Smith .05
155 Lorenzo White .05
156 Chip Banks .05
157 Duane Bickett .05
158 Bill Brooks .05
159 Jon Hand .05
160 Jeff Herrod .05
161 Jessie Hester .05
162 Scott Radecic .05
163 Rohn Stark .05
164 Clarence Verdin .05
165 Eugene Daniel .05
166 John Alt .05
167 Tim Barnett .05
168 Tim Grunhard .05
169 Dino Hackett .05
170 Jonathan Hayes .05
171 Bill Maas .05
172 Chris Martin .05
173 Christian Okoye .05
174 Stephone Paige .05
175 *Jayice Pearson* .10
176 Kevin Porter .05
177 Kevin Ross .05
178 Dan Saleaumua .05
179 Tracy Simien .05
180 Neil Smith .05
181 Derrick Thomas .35
182 Robb Thomas .05
183 Barry Wood .15
184 Marcus Allen .08
185 Eddie Anderson .05
186 Nick Bell .15
187 Tim Brown .30
188 Mervyn Fernandez .05
189 Jeff Gossett .05
190 Ethan Horton .05
191 Jeff Jaeger .05
192 Howie Long .05
193 Ronnie Lott .05
194 Todd Marinovich .15
195 Don Mosebar .05
196 Jay Schroeder .05
197 Anthony Smith .05
198 Greg Townsend .05
199 Lionel Washington .05
200 Steve Wisniewski .05
201 Willie Anderson .05
202 Robert Delpino .05
203 Henry Ellard .05
204 Jim Everett .05
205 Kevin Greene .05
206 Darryl Henley .05
207 Damone Johnson .05
208 Larry Kelm .05
209 Todd Lyght .05
210 Jackie Slater .05
211 Michael Stewart .05
212 Pat Terrell .05
213 Robert Young .05
214 Mark Clayton .05
215 Bryan Cox .05
216 Jeff Cross .05
217 Mark Duper .05
218 Harry Galbreath .05
219 David Griggs .05
220 Mark Higgs .10
221 John Offerdahl .05
222 Louis Oliver .05
223 Tony Paige .05
224 Reggie Roby .05
225 Pete Stoyanovich .05
226 Richmond Webb .05
227 Terry Allen .60
228 Ray Berry .05
229 Anthony Carter .05
230 Cris Carter .05
231 Chris Doleman .05
232 Rich Gannon .10
233 Steve Jordan .05
234 Carl Lee .05
235 Randall McDaniel .05
236 Mike Merriweather .05
237 Harry Newsome .05
238 John Randle .05
239 Henry Thomas .05
240 Bruce Armstrong .05
241 Vincent Brown .05
242 Marv Cook .05
243 Irving Fryar .05
244 Pat Harlow .05
245 Maurice Hurst .05
246 Eugene Lockhart .05
247 Greg McMurtry .05
248 Hugh Millen .05
249 Leonard Russell .35
250 Chris Singleton .05
251 Andre Tippett .05
252 Jon Vaughn .10
253 Morten Andersen .05
254 Gene Atkins .05
255 Wesley Carroll .05
256 Jim Dombrowski .05
257 Quinn Early .05
258 Bobby Hebert .05
259 Joel Hilgenberg .05
260 Rickey Jackson .05
261 Vaughan Johnson .05
262 Eric Martin .05
263 Brett Maxie .05
264 *Fred McAfee* .20
265 Sam Mills .05
266 Pat Swilling .05
267 Floyd Turner .05
268 Steve Walsh .05
269 Stephen Baker .05
270 Jarrod Bunch .05
271 Mark Collins .05
272 John Elliott .05
273 Myron Guyton .05
274 Rodney Hampton .50
275 Jeff Hostetler .25
276 Mark Ingram .05
277 Pepper Johnson .05
278 Sean Landeta .05
279 Leonard Marshall .05
280 Kanavis McGhee .05
281 Dave Meggett .05
282 Bart Oates .05
283 Phil Simms .10
284 Reyna Thompson .05
285 Lewis Tillman .05
286 Brad Baxter .05
287 *Mike Brim* .10
288 Chris Burkett .05
289 Kyle Clifton .05
290 James Hasty .05
291 Joe Kelly .05
292 Jeff Lageman .05
293 Mo Lewis .05
294 Erik McMillan .05
295 Scott Mersereau .05
296 Rob Moore .05
297 Tony Stargell .05
298 Jim Sweeney .05
299 Marvin Washington .05
300 Lonnie Young .05
301 Eric Allen .05
302 Fred Barnett .15
303 Keith Byars .05
304 Byron Evans .05
305 Wes Hopkins .05
306 Keith Jackson .15
307 James Joseph .05
308 Seth Joyner .05
309 Roger Ruzek .05
310 Clyde Simmons .05
311 William Thomas .05
312 Reggie White .35
313 Calvin Williams .15
314 Rich Camarillo .05
315 Jeff Faulkner .05
316 Ken Harvey .05
317 Eric Hill .05
318 Johnny Johnson .10
319 Ernie Jones .05
320 Tim McDonald .05
321 Freddie Joe Nunn .05
322 Luis Sharpe .05
323 Eric Swann .05
324 Aeneas Williams .05
325 *Mike Zordich* .15
326 Gary Anderson .05
327 Bubby Brister .05
328 Barry Foster .50
329 Eric Green .05
330 Bryan Hinkle .05
331 Tunch Ilkin .05
332 Carnell Lake .05
333 Louis Lipps .05
334 David Little .05
335 Greg Lloyd .05
336 Neil O'Donnell .60
337 Rod Woodson .08
338 Rod Bernstine .05
339 Marion Butts .08
340 Gill Byrd .05
341 John Friesz .05
342 Burt Grossman .05
343 Courtney Hall .05
344 Ronnie Harmon .05
345 Shawn Jefferson .05
346 Nate Lewis .08
347 *Craig McEwen* .10
348 Eric Moten .05
349 Gary Plummer .05
350 Henry Rolling .05
351 Broderick Thompson .05
352 Derrick Walker .05
353 Harris Barton .05
354 *Steve Bono* .75
355 Todd Bowles .05
356 Dexter Carter .05
357 Michael Carter .05
358 Keith DeLong .05
359 Charles Haley .05
360 Merton Hanks .05
361 Tim Harris .05
362 Brent Jones .05
363 Guy McIntyre .05
364 Tom Rathman .05
365 Bill Romanowski .05
366 Jesse Sapolu .05
367 John Taylor .05
368 Steve Young 2.00
369 Robert Blackmon .05
370 Brian Blades .05
371 Jacob Green .05
372 Dwayne Harper .05
373 Andy Heck .05
374 Tommy Kane .05
375 John Kassay .05
376 Cortez Kennedy .25
377 Bryan Millard .05
378 Rufus Porter .05
379 Eugene Robinson .05
380 John L. Williams .05
381 Terry Wooden .05
382 Gary Anderson .05
383 Ian Beckles .05
384 Mark Carrier .05
385 Reggie Cobb .10
386 Tony Covington .05
387 Lawrence Dawsey .05
388 Ron Hall .05
389 Keith McCants .05
390 Charles McRae .05
391 Tim Newton .05
392 Jesse Solomon .05
393 Vinny Testaverde .05
394 Broderick Thomas .05
395 Robert Wilson .05
396 Earnest Byner .05
397 Gary Clark .05
398 Andre Collins .05
399 Brad Edwards .05
400 Kurt Gouveia .05
401 Darrell Green .05
402 Joe Jacoby .05
403 Chip Lohmiller .05
404 Charles Mann .05
405 Wilber Marshall .05
406 Brian Mitchell .05
407 Art Monk .05
408 Mark Rypien .15
409 Ricky Sanders .05
410 *Mark Schlereth* .15
411 Fred Stokes .05

416	Bobby Wilson	.05
417	*Corey Barlow*	.15
418	*Edgar Bennett*	.50
419	*Eddie Blake*	.15
420	*Terrell Buckley*	.30
421	*Willie Clay*	.15
422	*Rodney Culver*	.25
423	*Ed Cunningham*	.15
424	*Mark D'Onofrio*	.15
425	*Matt Darby*	.10
426	*Charles Davenport*	.10
427	*Will Furrer*	.20
428	*Keith Goganious*	.10
429	*Mario Bailey*	.10
430	*Chris Hakel*	.10
431	*Keith Hamilton*	.25
432	*Aaron Pierce*	.10
433	*Amp Lee*	.35
434	*Scott Lockwood*	.15
435	*Ricardo McDonald*	.15
436	*Dexter McNabb*	.15
437	*Chris Mims*	.40
438	*Mike Mooney*	.15
439	*Ray Roberts*	.15
440	*Patrick Rowe*	.15
441	*Leon Searcy*	.15
442	*Siran Stacy*	.20
443	*Kevin Turner*	.30
444	*Tommy Vardell*	.25
445	*Bob Whitfield*	.20
446	*Darryl Williams*	.25
447	Checklists	.05
448	Checklists	.05
449	Checklists	.05
450	Checklists	.05

1992 Ultra Award Winners

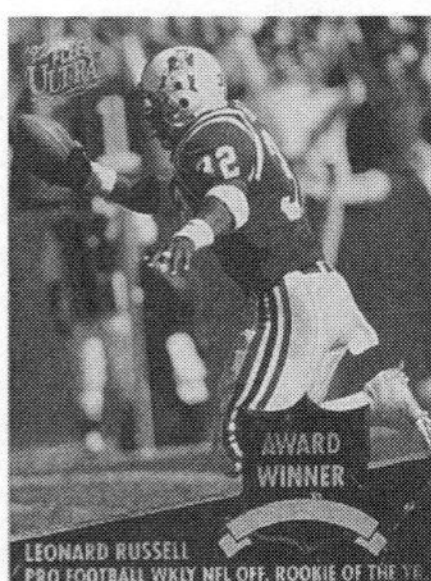

Each of the 10 players in this insert set had award-winning performances during the 1991 season. The front has a full-bleed photo of the player, along with a black marble-like strip at the bottom which contains the player's name and the award he won in gold foil. A black "Award Winner" logo is also superimposed in the lower right corner. The card back has a portrait of the player inside a shield, with his name in a banner above a career summary. Cards were randomly inserted in 1992 Fleer Ultra foil packs and are numbered 1 of 10, etc.

		NM/M
Complete Set (10):		10.00
Common Player:		.50
1	Mark Rypien	1.00
2	Cornelius Bennett	.50
3	Pat Swilling	.50
4	Lawrence Dawsey	.50
5	Thurman Thomas	2.00
6	Michael Irvin	2.00
7	Mike Croel	.50
8	Barry Sanders	4.00
9	Anthony Munoz	.50
10	Leonard Russell	.50

1992 Ultra Chris Miller

These 10 cards were randomly inserted in 1992 Fleer Ultra foil packs as part of Fleer's signature series. Each card front has a player action photo inside an inner black and outer maroon marbleized border. Miller's name and "Performance Highlights" are in gold foil letters at the bottom. The back has a player portrait shot and career summary against a rose-colored background, plus a card number. Cards 11-12 were available only through a mail-in offer from Fleer; 10 1992 Fleer Ultra wrappers and $2 were required. In addition, Miller signed more than 2,000 cards.

	NM/M
Complete Set (10):	2.00
Common Miller:	.20
Autograph:	25.00

1992 Ultra Reggie White

These cards, part of Fleer's signature series, were random inserts in 1992 Fleer Ultra foil packs. Each card front has a color action photo bordered by green and gray marble frames. White's name and "Career Highlights" are in gold foil at the bottom. The back has a career summary and head shot against a gray marble-like background, plus a card number. Cards 11-12 were availble only through a mail-in program to Fleer for 10 1992 Fleer Ultra wrappers and $2. These cards have rose-colored backs. White signed more than 2,000 randomly-inserted cards.

	NM/M
Complete Set (10):	10.00
Common White:	1.00
Autograph:	75.00

1993 Ultra

Fleer's 1993 Ultra set consists of 500 cards featuring UV coating and action photos. Insert sets include NFL Award Winners (10 cards), NFL League Leaders (10), All-Rookie Series (10), Stars (10), Touchdown Kings (10) and a Michael Irvin "Performance Highlights" set (10).

		NM/M
Complete Set (500):		25.00
Common Player:		.05
Minor Stars:		.20
Pack (15):		1.25
Wax Box (36):		35.00
1	Vinnie Clark	.05
2	Darion Connor	.05
3	Eric Dickerson	.20
4	Moe Gardner	.05
5	Tim Green	.05
6	*Roger Harper*	.05
7	Michael Haynes	.05
8	Bobby Hebert	.05
9	Chris Hinton	.05
10	Pierce Holt	.05
11	Mike Kenn	.05
12	*Lincoln Kennedy*	.20
13	Chris Miller	.05
14	Mike Pritchard	.05
15	Andre Rison	.20
16	Deion Sanders	1.50
17	Tony Smith	.05
18	Jessie Tuggle	.05
19	Howard Ballard	.05
20	Don Beebe	.05
21	Cornelius Bennett	.05
22	Bill Brooks	.05
23	Kenneth Davis	.05
24	Phil Hansen	.05
25	Henry Jones	.05
26	Jim Kelly	.50
27	Nate Odomes	.05
28	*John Parrella*	.05
29	Andre Reed	.20
30	Frank Reich	.05
31	Jim Ritcher	.05
32	Bruce Smith	.05
33	*Thomas Smith*	.20
34	Darryl Talley	.05
35	Steve Tasker	.05
36	Thurman Thomas	.50
37	Jeff Wright	.05
38	Neal Anderson	.05
39	Trace Armstrong	.05
40	Mark Carrier	.05
41	*Curtis Conway*	1.50
42	Wendell Davis	.05
43	Richard Dent	.05
44	Shaun Gayle	.05
45	Jim Harbaugh	.05
46	Craig Heyward	.05
47	Darren Lewis	.05
48	Steve McMichael	.05
49	William Perry	.05
50	*Carl Simpson*	.05
51	Alonzo Spellman	.05
52	Keith Van Horne	.05
53	Tom Waddle	.05
54	Donnell Woolford	.05
55	*John Copeland*	.50
56	Derrick Fenner	.05
57	James Francis	.05
58	Harold Green	.05
59	David Klingler	.05
60	Tim Krumrie	.05
61	Ricardo McDonald	.05
62	*Tony McGee*	.75
63	Carl Pickens	1.50
64	Lamar Rogers	.05
65	Jay Schroeder	.05
66	Daniel Stubbs	.05
67	*Steve Tovar*	.05
68	Alfred Williams	.05
69	Darryl Williams	.05
70	Jerry Ball	.05
71	David Brandon	.05
72	Rob Burnett	.05
73	Mark Carrier	.05
74	*Steve Everett*	.20
75	*Dan Footman*	.05
76	Leroy Hoard	.05
77	Michael Jackson	.05
78	Mike Johnson	.05
79	Bernie Kosar	.20
80	Clay Mathews	.05
81	Eric Metcalf	.05
82	Michael Dean Perry	.05
83	Vinny Testaverde	.20
84	Tommy Vardell	.05
85	Troy Aikman	3.00
86	Larry Brown	.05
87	Tony Casillas	.05
88	Thomas Everett	.05
89	Charles Haley	.05
90	Alvin Harper	.20
91	Michael Irvin	.50
92	Jim Jeffcoat	.05
93	Daryl Johnston	.05
94	Robert Jones	.05
95	*Leon Lett*	.50
96	Russell Maryland	.05
97	Nate Newton	.05
98	Ken Norton	.05
99	Jay Novacek	.05
100	*Darrin Smith*	.50
101	Emmitt Smith	5.00
102	Kevin Smith	.05
103	Mark Stepnoski	.05
104	Tony Tolbert	.05
105	*Kevin Williams*	.30
106	Steve Atwater	.05
107	Rod Bernstine	.05
108	Mike Croel	.05
109	Robert Delpino	.05
110	Shane Dronett	.05
111	John Elway	1.50
112	Simon Fletcher	.05
113	Greg Kragen	.05
114	Tommy Maddox	.05
115	*Arthur Marshall*	.20
116	Karl Mecklenburg	.05
117	*Glyn Milburn*	1.00
118	*Reggie Rivers*	.05
119	Shannon Sharpe	.20
120	Dennis Smith	.05
121	Kenny Walker	.05
122	*Dan Williams*	.05
123	Bennie Blades	.05
124	Lomas Brown	.05
125	Bill Fralic	.05
126	Mel Gray	.05
127	Willie Green	.05
128	Jason Hanson	.05
129	*Antonio London*	.05
130	*Ryan McNeil*	.05
131	Herman Moore	2.00
132	Rodney Peete	.05
133	Brett Perriman	.05
134	Kelvin Pritchett	.05
135	Barry Sanders	3.00
136	Tracy Scroggins	.05
137	Chris Spielman	.05
138	Pat Swilling	.05
139	Andre Ware	.05
140	Edgar Bennett	1.00
141	Tony Bennett	.05
142	Matt Brock	.05
143	Terrell Buckley	.05
144	LeRoy Butler	.05
145	Mark Clayton	.05
146	Brett Favre	5.00
147	Jackie Harris	.20
148	Johnny Holland	.05
149	Bill Maas	.05
150	Brian Noble	.05
151	Bryce Paup	.05
152	Ken Ruettgers	.05
153	Sterling Sharpe	.20
154	*Wayne Simmons*	.05
155	John Stephens	.05
156	*George Teague*	.50
157	Reggie White	.20
158	*Micheal Barrow*	.05
159	Cody Carlson	.05
160	Ray Childress	.05
161	Cris Duncan	.05
162	Curtis Duncan	.05
163	William Fuller	.05
164	Ernest Givins	.05
165	*Brad Hopkins*	.05
166	Haywood Jeffires	.05
167	Lamar Lathon	.05
168	Wilber Marshall	.05
169	Bruce Matthews	.05
170	Bubba McDowell	.05
171	Warren Moon	.20
172	Mike Munchak	.05
173	Eddie Robinson	.05
174	Al Smith	.05
175	Lorenzo White	.05
176	Lee Williams	.05
177	Chip Banks	.05
178	John Baylor	.05
179	Duane Bickett	.05
180	Kerry Cash	.05
181	Quentin Coryatt	.05
182	Rodney Culver	.05
183	Steve Emtman	.05
184	Jeff George	.50
185	Jeff Herrod	.05
186	Jessie Hester	.05
187	Anthony Jackson	.05
188	Reggie Langhorne	.05
189	*Roosevelt Potts*	.20
190	Rohn Stark	.05
191	Clarence Verdin	.05
192	Will Wolford	.05
193	Marcus Allen	.20
194	John Alt	.05
195	Tim Barnett	.05
196	J.J. Birden	.05
197	Dale Carter	.05
198	Willie Davis	.05
199	*Jamie Fields*	.05
200	Dave Krieg	.05
201	Nick Lowery	.05
202	*Charles Mincy*	.05
203	Joe Montana	3.00
204	Christian Okoye	.05
205	Dan Saleaumua	.05
206	*Will Shields*	.05
207	Tracy Simien	.05
208	Neil Smith	.05
209	Derrick Thomas	.20
210	Harvey Williams	.05
211	Barry Word	.05
212	Eddie Anderson	.05
213	*Patrick Bates*	.20
214	Nick Bell	.05
215	Tim Brown	.20
216	Willie Gault	.05
217	Gaston Green	.05
218	*Billy Jo Hobert*	.75
219	Ethan Horton	.05
220	Jeff Hostetler	.20
221	James Lofton	.05
222	Howie Long	.05
223	Todd Marinovich	.05
224	Terry McDaniel	.05
225	Winston Moss	.05
226	Anthony Smith	.05
227	Greg Townsend	.05
228	Aaron Wallace	.05
229	Lionel Washington	.05
230	Steve Wisniewski	.05
231	Willie Anderson	.05
232	*Jerome Bettis*	2.00
234	Shane Conlan	.05
235	*Troy Drayton*	.50
236	Henry Ellard	.05
237	Jim Everett	.05
238	Cleveland Gary	.05
239	Sean Gilbert	.05
240	Darryl Henley	.05
241	David Lang	.05
242	Todd Lyght	.05
243	*Anthony Newman*	.05
244	Roman Phiefer	.05
245	Gerald Robinson	.05
246	Henry Rolling	.05
247	Jackie Slater	.05
248	Keith Byars	.05
249	Marco Coleman	.05
250	Bryan Cox	.05
251	Jeff Cross	.05
252	Irving Fryar	.05
253	Mark Higgs	.05
254	*Dwight Hollier*	.05
255	Mark Ingram	.05
256	Keith Jackson	.05
257	*Terry Kirby*	1.00
258	Dan Marino	5.00
259	*O.J. McDuffie*	1.50
260	John Offerdahl	.05
261	Louis Oliver	.05
262	Pete Stoyanovich	.05
263	Troy Vincent	.05
264	Richmond Webb	.05
265	Jarvis Williams	.05
266	Terry Allen	.05
267	Anthony Carter	.05
268	Cris Carter	.20
269	Roger Craig	.05
270	Jack Del Rio	.05
271	Chris Doleman	.05
272	*Qadry Ismail*	1.00
273	Steve Jordan	.05
274	Randall McDaniel	.05
275	Audray McMillian	.05
276	John Randle	.05
277	Sean Salisbury	.05
278	Todd Scott	.05
279	*Robert Smith*	2.50
280	Henry Thomas	.05
281	Ray Agnew	.05
282	Bruce Armstrong	.05
283	*Drew Bledsoe*	6.00
284	*Vincent Brisby*	.50
285	Vincent Brown	.05
286	Eugene Chung	.05
287	Marv Cook	.05
288	Pat Harlow	.05
289	Jerome Henderson	.05
290	Greg McMurty	.05
291	Leonard Russell	.05
292	Chris Singleton	.05
293	*Chris Slade*	.20
294	Andre Tippett	.05
295	Brent Williams	.05
296	Scott Zolak	.05
297	Morten Andersen	.05
298	Gene Atkins	.05
299	Mike Buck	.05
300	Toi Cook	.05
301	Jim Dombrowski	.05
302	Vaughn Dunbar	.05
303	Quinn Early	.05
304	Joel Hilgenberg	.05
305	Dalton Hilliard	.05
306	Ricky Jackson	.05
307	Vaughan Johnson	.05
308	Reginald Jones	.05
309	Eric Martin	.05
310	Wayne Martin	.05
311	Sam Mills	.05
312	Brad Muster	.05
313	*Willie Roaf*	.20
314	*Irv Smith*	.20
315	Wade Wilson	.05
316	Carlton Bailey	.05
317	Michael Brooks	.05
318	Derek Brown	.05
319	*Marcus Buckley*	.05
320	Jarrod Bunch	.05
321	Mark Collins	.05
322	Eric Dorsey	.05
323	Rodney Hampton	.20
324	Mark Jackson	.05
325	Pepper Johnson	.05
326	Ed McCaffrey	.05
327	Dave Meggett	.05
328	Bart Oates	.05
329	Mike Sherrard	.05
330	Phil Simms	.05
331	*Michael Strahan*	.05
332	Lawrence Taylor	.20
333	Brad Baxter	.05
334	Chris Burkett	.05
335	Kyle Clifton	.05
336	Boomer Esiason	.05
337	James Hasty	.05
338	Johnny Johnson	.05
339	*Marvin Jones*	.20
340	Jeff Lageman	.05
341	Mo Lewis	.05
342	Ronnie Lott	.05
343	Leonard Marshall	.05
344	Johnny Mitchell	.05
345	Rob Moore	.05
346	Browning Nagle	.05
347	*Coleman Rudolph*	.05
348	Blair Thomas	.05
349	Eric Thomas	.05
350	Brian Washington	.05
351	Marvin Washington	.05
352	Eric Allen	.05
353	*Victor Bailey*	.20
354	Fred Barnett	.05
355	Mark Bavaro	.05
356	Randall Cunningham	.20
357	Byron Evans	.05
358	*Andy Harmon*	.05
359	Tim Harris	.05
360	*Lester Holmes*	.05
361	Seth Joyner	.05
362	Keith Millard	.05
363	*Leonard Renfro*	.05
364	Heath Sherman	.05
365	Vai Sikahema	.05
366	Clyde Simmons	.05
367	William Thomas	.05
368	Herschel Walker	.05
369	Andre Waters	.05
370	Calvin Williams	.05
371	Johnny Bailey	.05
372	Steve Beuerlein	.05
373	Rich Camarillo	.05
374	Chuck Cecil	.05
375	Chris Chandler	.05
376	Gary Clark	.05
377	*Ben Coleman*	.05
378	*Earnest Dye*	.05
379	Ken Harvey	.05
380	*Garrison Hearst*	1.75
381	Randal Hill	.05
382	Robert Massey	.05
383	Freddie Joe Nunn	.05
384	Ricky Proehl	.05
385	Luis Sharpe	.05
386	Tyronne Stowe	.05
387	Eric Swann	.05
388	Aeneas Williams	.05
389	*Chad Brown*	.50
390	Dermontti Dawson	.05
391	Donald Evans	.05
392	*Deon Figures*	.50
393	Barry Foster	.20
394	Jeff Graham	.05
395	Eric Green	.05
396	Kevin Greene	.05
397	Carlton Haselrig	.05
398	*Andre Hastings*	.75
399	D.J. Johnson	.05
400	Carnell Lake	.05
401	Greg Lloyd	.05
402	Neil O'Donnell	.40
403	Darren Perry	.05
404	Mike Tomczak	.05
405	Rod Woodson	.20
406	Eric Bieniemy	.05
407	Marion Butts	.05
408	Gill Byrd	.05
409	*Darren Carrington*	.20
410	*Darrien Gordon*	.75
411	Burt Grossman	.05
412	Courtney Hall	.05
413	Ronnie Harmon	.05
414	Stan Humphries	.20
415	Nate Lewis	.05
416	*Natrone Means*	1.25
417	Anthony Miller	.05
418	Chris Mims	.05
419	Leslie O'Neal	.05
420	Gary Plummer	.05
421	Stanley Richard	.05
422	Junior Seau	.20
423	Harry Swayne	.05
424	Jerrol Williams	.05
425	Harris Barton	.05
426	Steve Bono	1.00
427	Kevin Fagan	.05
428	Don Griffin	.05
429	Dana Hall	.05
430	*Adrian Hardy*	.05
431	Brent Jones	.05
432	*Todd Kelly*	.05
433	Amp Lee	.05
434	Tim McDonald	.05
435	Guy McIntyre	.05
436	Tom Rathman	.05
437	Jerry Rice	3.00
438	Bill Romanowski	.05
439	*Dana Stubblefield*	1.00
440	John Taylor	.05
441	Steve Wallace	.05
442	Mike Walter	.05
443	Ricky Watters	.50
444	Steve Young	3.00
445	Robert Blackmon	.05
446	Brian Blades	.05
447	Jeff Bryant	.05
448	Ferrell Edmunds	.05
449	*Carlton Gray*	.20
450	Dwayne Harper	.05
451	Andy Heck	.05
452	Tommy Kane	.05
453	Cortez Kennedy	.20
454	Kelvin Martin	.05
455	Dan McGwire	.05
456	*Rick Mirer*	.50
457	Rufus Porter	.05
458	Ray Roberts	.05
459	Eugene Robinson	.05
460	Chris Warren	1.00
461	John L. Williams	.05
462	Gary Anderson	.05
463	Tyji Armstrong	.05
464	Reggie Cobb	.05
465	*Eric Curry*	.50
466	Lawrence Dawsey	.05
467	Steve DeBerg	.05
468	Santana Dotson	.05
469	*Demetrius DuBose*	.20
470	Paul Gruber	.05
471	Ron Hall	.05
472	Courtney Hawkins	.05
473	Hardy Nickerson	.05
474	Ricky Reynolds	.05
475	Broderick Thomas	.05
476	Mark Wheeler	.05
477	Jimmy Williams	.05
478	Carl Banks	.05
479	*Reggie Brooks*	.75
480	Earnest Byner	.05
481	*Tom Carter*	.20
482	Andre Collins	.05
483	Brad Edwards	.05
484	Ricky Ervins	.05
485	Kurt Gouveia	.05
486	Darrell Green	.05
487	Desmond Howard	.20
488	Jim Lachey	.05
489	Chip Lohmiller	.05
490	Charles Mann	.05
491	Tim McGee	.05
492	Brian Mitchell	.05
493	Art Monk	.05
494	Mark Rypien	.05
495	Ricky Sanders	.05
496	Checklist	.05
497	Checklist	.05
498	Checklist	.05
499	Checklist	.05
500	Checklist	.05

1993 Ultra All-Rookies

Ten first-year players are featured on these cards, which were random inserts in 1993 Fleer Ultra 14- and 19-card packs. Each front has a color action photo against an orange background. The player's name and set title are stamped in gold foil at the bottom. The back, in a horizontal format, has a close-up shot of the player, plus career highlights, all against an orange-to-yellow background. Card backs are numbered 1 of 10, etc..

#	Player	NM/M
	Complete Set (10):	35.00
	Common Player:	.50
	Minor Stars:	1.00
1	Patrick Bates	.50
2	Jerome Bettis	10.00
3	Drew Bledsoe	20.00
4	Curtis Conway	5.00
5	Garrison Hearst	5.00
6	Qadry Ismail	1.00
7	Marvin Jones	.50
8	Glyn Milburn	1.00
9	Rick Mirer	1.00
10	Kevin Williams	1.00

1993 Ultra Award Winners

These cards were randomly inserted in 1993 Fleer Ultra 14- and 19-card foil packs. The players who are featured delivered award-winning performances during the 1992 season, such as MVP and Rookie of the Year. Fronts have full-bleed photos on a borderless, gold metallic background. The set's name is at the top, while the player's name is at the bottom. The back has a gold metallic background, with sun rays radiating towards the sides. The player's name and award he won are stamped in silver foil on the back, which also includes his career highlighs and another photo, plus a card number (1 of 10 etc.).

#	Player	NM/M
	Complete Set (10):	20.00
	Common Player:	1.00
	Minor Stars:	2.00
1	Troy Aikman	6.00
2	Dale Carter	1.00
3	Chris Doleman	1.00
4	Santana Dotson	1.00
5	Barry Foster	2.00
6	Jason Hanson	1.00
7	Cortez Kennedy	1.00
8	Carl Pickens	2.00
9	Steve Tasker	1.00
10	Steve Young	5.00

1993 Ultra Michael Irvin

This "Performance Highlights" set features 10 cards devoted to Dallas Cowboys wide receiver Michael Irvin. Each borderless card front features a color action photo and a black marble-like stripe which contains the set subtitle and logo in silver foil. Each back has a color photo, plus career highlights in silver foil letters on a blue-screeen panel with a silver foil frame. A black marble-like stripe creates a border at the card bottom. Cards are numbered 1 of 10, etc., and were random inserts in 1993 Fleer Ultra packs.

	NM/M
Complete Set (10):	5.00
Common Irvin:	.50
Autograph Irvin:	45.00
Mail-In Irvin (11-12):	1.50

A player's name in *italic* type indicates a rookie card.

1993 Ultra League Leaders

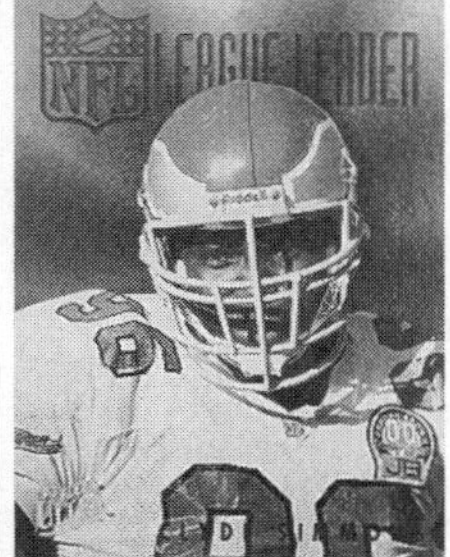

Players who led the league in certain statistical categories are featured on these cards, which were random inserts in 1993 Fleer Ultra 14- and 19-card packs. The card fronts are borderless and have an action shot against a silver metallic background. The player's name is at the bottom; the set title is at the top. The back has a silver metallic background with rays radiating toward the sides. The player's name and set title are stamped in silver foil at the top. The category the player led the league in, and a career summary, follow. The cards are numbered 1 of 10, etc.

#	Player	NM/M
	Complete Set (10):	20.00
	Common Player:	1.00
	Minor Stars:	2.00
1	Haywood Jeffires	1.00
2	Henry Jones	1.00
3	Audray McMillian	1.00
4	Warren Moon	2.00
5	Leslie O'Neal	1.00
6	Deion Sanders	4.00
7	Sterling Sharpe	2.00
8	Clyde Simmons	1.00
9	Emmitt Smith	6.00
10	Thurman Thomas	3.00

1993 Ultra Ultra Stars

Ten of the NFL's premiere players are featured on these cards, which were randomly inserted in 1993 Fleer Ultra 19-card foil packs only. Each front has an action shot of the player superimposed against a ghosted U.S. flag. A grey marble stripe appears at the bottom, along with the player's name, set title and spiraling football, which are stamped in gold foil. Each back has a close-up shot of the player on one side, plus career highlights on the other. The cards are numbered 1 of 10, etc..

#	Player	NM/M
	Complete Set (10):	25.00
	Common Player:	1.00
	Minor Stars:	2.00
1	Brett Favre	10.00
2	Barry Foster	1.00
3	Michael Irvin	2.00
4	Cortez Kennedy	1.00
5	Deion Sanders	4.00
6	Junior Seau	2.00
7	Derrick Thomas	1.00
8	Ricky Watters	2.00
9	Reggie White	2.00
10	Steve Young	6.00

1993 Ultra Touchdown Kings

Ten of the NFL's top offensive players are featured on these cards, which were random inserts in 1993 Fleer Ultra 14-card foil packs only. Each front has an action photo of the player superimposed against a ghosted football field and diagrammed plays. The player's name and set title are stamped in gold foil at the bottom, which has a green marble-like border. Each back is white with a player photo and stats against a background of play diagrams. The cards are numbered 1 of 10, etc..

#	Player	NM/M
	Complete Set (10):	25.00
	Common Player:	1.00
	Minor Stars:	2.00
1	Rodney Hampton	1.00
2	Dan Marino	6.00
3	Art Monk	1.00
4	Joe Montana	5.00
5	Jerry Rice	4.00
6	Andre Rison	2.00
7	Barry Sanders	5.00
8	Sterling Sharpe	2.00
9	Emmitt Smith	5.00
10	Thurman Thomas	2.00

1994 Ultra

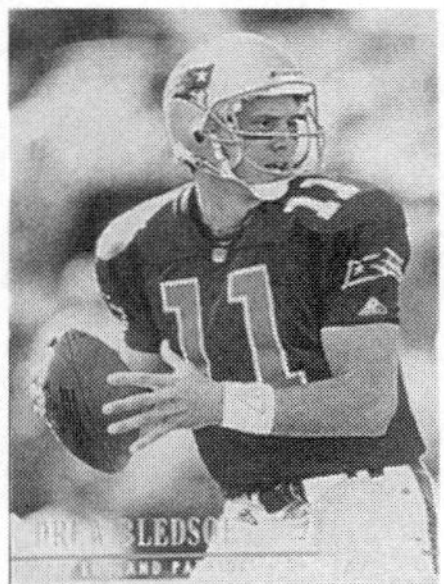

Fleer Ultra Football contains 525 cards using a new design and includes loads of inserts. The first series had six new insert sets, plus a 10-card Rick Mirer highlight set. It also had new enhancements, like gold foil stamping on both sides and four different photos per card. The Series I inserts included: Award Winners (5); Second Year Standouts (15); First Rounders (20), with the cream of the 1994 Draft; Ultra Achievements (10), honoring veteran stars; Touchdown Kings (9) and Ultra Stars (9). Series II inserts included Hot Numbers (15), Scoring Power (6), and Wave of the Future (6).

#	Player	NM/M
	Complete Set (525):	30.00
	Complete Series 1 (325):	20.00
	Complete Series 2 (200):	15.00
	Common Player:	.05
	Minor Stars:	.20
	Series 1 Pack (12):	1.00
	Series 1 Wax Box (36):	20.00
	Series 2 Pack (12):	1.00
	Series 2 Wax Box (36):	20.00
1	Steve Beuerlein	.05
2	Gary Clark	.05
3	Randal Hill	.05
4	Seth Joyner	.05
5	*Jamir Miller*	.20
6	Ron Moore	.20
7	Luis Sharpe	.05
8	Clyde Simmons	.05
9	Eric Swann	.05
10	Aeneas Williams	.05
11	Chris Doleman	.05
12	*Bert Emanuel*	.75
13	Moe Gardner	.05
14	Jeff George	.20
15	Roger Harper	.05
16	Pierce Holt	.05
17	Lincoln Kennedy	.05
18	Erric Pegram	.05
19	Andre Rison	.20
20	Deion Sanders	.75
21	Jessie Tuggle	.05
22	Cornelius Bennett	.05
23	Bill Brooks	.05
24	*Jeff Burris*	.20
25	Kent Hull	.05
26	Henry Jones	.05
27	Jim Kelly	.20
28	Marcus Patton	.05
29	Andre Reed	.15
30	Bruce Smith	.05
31	Thomas Smith	.05
32	Thurman Thomas	.20
33	Jeff Wright	.05
34	Trace Armstrong	.05
35	Mark Carrier	.05
36	Dante Jones	.05
37	Erik Kramer	.05
38	Terry Obee	.05
39	Alonzo Spellman	.05
40	*John Thierry*	.20
41	Tom Waddle	.05
42	Donnell Woolford	.05
43	Tim Worley	.05
44	Chris Zorich	.05
45	John Copeland	.05
46	Harold Green	.05
47	David Klingler	.05
48	Ricardo McDonald	.05
49	Tony McGee	.05
50	Louis Oliver	.05
51	Carl Pickens	.75
52	*Darnay Scott*	.75
53	Steve Tovar	.05
54	*Dan Wilkinson*	.20
55	Darryl Williams	.05
56	*Derrick Alexander*	.50
57	Michael Jackson	.05
58	Tony Jones	.05
59	*Antonio Langham*	.20
60	Eric Metcalf	.05
61	Stevon Moore	.05
62	Michael Dean Perry	.05
63	Anthony Pleasant	.05
64	Vinny Testaverde	.05
65	Eric Turner	.05
66	Tommy Vardell	.05
67	Troy Aikman	1.50
68	Larry Brown	.05
69	*Shante Carver*	.20
70	Charles Haley	.05
71	Michael Irvin	.20
72	Leon Lett	.05
73	Nate Newton	.05
74	Jay Novacek	.05
75	Darrin Smith	.05
76	Emmitt Smith	3.00
77	Tony Tolbert	.05
78	Eric Williams	.05
79	Kevin Williams	.60
80	Steve Atwater	.05
81	Rod Bernstine	.05
82	Ray Crockett	.05
83	Mike Croel	.05
84	Shane Dronett	.05
85	Jason Elam	.05
86	John Elway	.50
87	Simon Fletcher	.05
88	Glyn Milburn	.05
89	Anthony Miller	.05
90	Shannon Sharpe	.05
91	Gary Zimmerman	.05
92	Bennie Blades	.05
93	Lomas Brown	.05
94	Mel Gray	.05
95	Jason Hanson	.05
96	Ryan McNeil	.05
97	Scott Mitchell	.15
98	Herman Moore	.75
99	*Johnnie Morton*	.50
100	Robert Porcher	.05
101	Barry Sanders	2.00
102	Chris Spielman	.05
103	Pat Swilling	.05
104	Edgar Bennett	.05
105	Terrell Buckley	.05
106	Reggie Cobb	.05
107	Brett Favre	4.00
108	Sean Jones	.05
109	Ken Ruettgers	.05
110	Sterling Sharpe	.20
111	Wayne Simmons	.05
112	*Aaron Taylor*	.15
113	George Teague	.05
114	Reggie White	.20
115	Micheal Barrow	.05
116	Gary Brown	.05
117	Cody Carlson	.05
118	Ray Childress	.05
119	Cris Dishman	.05
120	*Henry Ford*	.15
121	Haywood Jeffires	.05
122	Bruce Matthews	.05
123	Bubba McDowell	.05
124	Marcus Robertson	.05
125	Eddie Robinson	.05
126	Webster Slaughter	.05
127	*Trev Alberts*	.20
128	Tony Bennett	.05
129	Ray Buchanan	.05
130	Quentin Coryatt	.05
131	Eugene Daniel	.05
132	Steve Emtman	.05
133	*Marshall Faulk*	5.00
134	Jim Harbaugh	.05
135	Roosevelt Potts	.05
136	Rohn Stark	.05
137	Marcus Allen	.20
138	*Donnell Bennett*	.20
139	Dale Carter	.05
140	Tony Casillas	.05
141	Mark Collins	.05
142	Willie Davis	.05
143	Tim Grunhard	.05
144	*Greg Hill*	.75
145	Joe Montana	2.50
146	Tracy Simien	.05
147	Neil Smith	.05
148	Derrick Thomas	.20
149	Tim Brown	.20
150	*James Folston*	.15
151	*Rob Fredrickson*	.20
152	Jeff Hostetler	.15
153	Raghib Ismail	.15
154	James Jett	.15
155	Terry McDaniel	.05
156	Winston Moss	.05
157	Greg Robinson	.05
158	Anthony Smith	.05
159	Steve Wisniewski	.05
160	Willie Anderson	.05
161	Jerome Bettis	.75
162	*Isaac Bruce*	4.00
163	Shane Conlan	.05
164	*Wayne Gandy*	.05
165	Sean Gilbert	.05
166	Todd Lyght	.05
167	Chris Miller	.05
168	Anthony Newman	.05
169	Roman Phifer	.05
170	Jackie Slater	.05
171	Gene Atkins	.05
172	*Aubrey Beavers*	.20
173	*Tim Bowens*	.20
174	J.B. Brown	.05
175	Marco Coleman	.05
176	Bryan Cox	.05
177	Irving Fryar	.05
178	Terry Kirby	.20
179	Dan Marino	3.00
180	Troy Vincent	.05
181	Richmond Webb	.05
182	Terry Allen	.05
183	Cris Carter	.20
184	Jack Del Rio	.05
185	Vencie Glenn	.05
186	Randall McDaniel	.05
187	Warren Moon	.20
188	*David Palmer*	.50
189	John Randle	.05
190	Todd Scott	.05
191	*Todd Steussie*	.20
192	Henry Thomas	.05
193	*DeWayne Washington*	.20
194	Bruce Armstrong	.05
195	Harlon Barnett	.05
196	Drew Bledsoe	2.00
197	Vincent Brisby	.20
198	Vincent Brown	.05
199	Marion Butts	.05
200	Ben Coates	.50
201	Todd Collins	.05
202	Maurice Hurst	.05
203	*Willie McGinest*	.40
204	Ricky Reynolds	.05
205	Chris Slade	.05
206	*Mario Bates*	.30
207	Derek Brown	.05
208	Vince Buck	.05
209	Quinn Early	.05
210	Jim Everett	.05
211	Michael Haynes	.05
212	Tyrone Hughes	.05
213	*Joe Johnson*	.20
214	Vaughan Johnson	.05
215	William Roaf	.05
216	Renaldo Turnbull	.05
217	Michael Brooks	.05
218	Dave Brown	.20
219	Howard Cross	.05
220	Stacey Dillard	.05
221	John Elliott	.05
222	Keith Hamilton	.05
223	Rodney Hampton	.20
224	*Thomas Lewis*	.20
225	David Meggett	.05
226	Corey Miller	.05
227	*Thomas Randolph*	.20
228	Michael Sherrard	.05
229	Kyle Clifton	.05
230	Boomer Esiason	.15
231	*Aaron Glenn*	.20
232	James Hasty	.05
233	Bobby Houston	.05
234	Johnny Johnson	.05
235	Mo Lewis	.05
236	Ronnie Lott	.15
237	Rob Moore	.05
238	Marvin Washington	.05
239	*Ryan Yarborough*	.20
240	Eric Allen	.05
241	Victor Bailey	.05
242	Fred Barnett	.05
243	Mark Bavaro	.05
244	Randall Cunningham	.20
245	Byron Evans	.05
246	William Fuller	.05
247	Andy Harmon	.05
248	William Perry	.05
249	Herschel Walker	.20
250	*Bernard Williams*	.20
251	Dermontti Dawson	.05
252	Deon Figures	.05
253	Barry Foster	.20
254	Kevin Greene	.05
255	*Charles Johnson*	1.00
256	Levon Kirkland	.05
257	Greg Lloyd	.05
258	Neil O'Donnell	.20
259	Darren Perry	.05
260	Dwight Stone	.05
261	Rod Woodson	.20
262	John Carney	.05
263	*Isaac Davis*	.20
264	Courtney Hall	.05
265	Ronnie Harmon	.05
266	Stan Humphries	.20
267	Vance Johnson	.05
268	Natrone Means	.50
269	Chris Mims	.05
270	Leslie O'Neal	.05
271	Stanley Richard	.05
272	Junior Seau	.20
273	Harris Barton	.05
274	Dennis Brown	.05
275	Eric Davis	.05
276	*William Floyd*	.50
277	John Johnson	.05
278	Tim McDonald	.05
279	Ken Norton	.05
280	Jerry Rice	2.00
281	Jesse Sapolu	.05
282	Dana Stubblefield	.05
283	Ricky Watters	.20
284	*Bryant Young*	.75
285	Steve Young	1.50
286	*Sam Adams*	.20
287	Brian Blades	.05
288	Ferrell Edmunds	.05
289	Patrick Hunter	.05
290	Cortez Kennedy	.20
291	Rick Mirer	.75
292	Nate Odomes	.05
293	Ray Roberts	.05
294	Eugene Robinson	.05
295	Rod Stephens	.05
296	Chris Warren	.20
297	Marty Carter	.05
298	Horace Copeland	.05
299	Eric Curry	.05
300	Santana Dotson	.05
301	Craig Erickson	.20
302	Paul Gruber	.05
303	Courtney Hawkins	.05
304	Martin Mayhew	.05
305	Hardy Nickerson	.05
306	*Errict Rhett*	1.00
307	Vince Workman	.05
308	Reggie Brooks	.05
309	Tom Carter	.05
310	Andre Collins	.05
311	Brad Edwards	.05
312	Kurt Gouveia	.05
313	Darrell Green	.05
314	Ethan Horton	.05
315	Desmond Howard	.05
316	*Tre Johnson*	.20
317	Sterling Palmer	.05
318	*Heath Shuler*	.50
319	Tyronne Stowe	.05
320	NFL 75th Anniversary	.05
321	Checklist	.05
322	Checklist	.05
323	Checklist	.05
324	Checklist	.05
325	Checklist	.05
326	Garrison Hearst	1.00
327	Eric Hill	.05
328	Seth Joyner	.05
329	Jim McMahon	.05
330	Jamir Miller	.05
331	Ricky Proehl	.05
332	Clyde Simmons	.05
333	Chris Doleman	.05
334	Bert Emanuel	.40
335	Jeff George	.20
336	D.J. Johnson	.05
337	Terance Mathis	.05
338	Clay Matthews	.05
339	Tony Smith	.05
340	Don Beebe	.05
341	*Bucky Brooks*	.20
342	Jeff Burris	.20
343	Kenneth Davis	.05
344	Phil Hansen	.05
345	Pete Metzelaars	.05
346	Darryl Talley	.05
347	Joe Cain	.05
348	Curtis Conway	.60
349	Shaun Gayle	.05
350	Chris Gedney	.05
351	Erik Kramer	.05
352	Vinson Smith	.05
353	John Thierry	.05
354	Lewis Tillman	.05
355	Mike Brim	.05
356	Derrick Fenner	.05
357	James Francis	.05
358	Louis Oliver	.05
359	Darnay Scott	1.00
360	Dan Wilkinson	.20
361	Alfred Williams	.05
362	Derrick Alexander	.20
363	Rob Burnett	.05
364	Mark Carrier	.05
365	Steve Everitt	.05
366	Leroy Hoard	.05
367	Pepper Johnson	.05
368	Antonio Langham	.20
369	Shante Carver	.05
370	Alvin Harper	.20
371	Daryl Johnston	.05
372	Russell Maryland	.05
373	Kevin Smith	.05
374	Mark Stepnoski	.05
375	Darren Woodson	.05
376	Allen Aldridge	.05
377	Ray Crockett	.05
378	Karl Mecklenburg	.05
379	Anthony Miller	.05
380	Mike Pritchard	.05
381	Leonard Russell	.05
382	Dennis Smith	.05
383	Anthony Carter	.05
384	Van Malone	.05
385	Robert Massey	.05
386	Scott Mitchell	.05
387	Johnnie Morton	.40
388	Brett Perriman	.05
389	Tracy Scroggins	.05
390	Robert Brooks	.30
391	LeRoy Butler	.05
392	Reggie Cobb	.05
393	Sean Jones	.05
394	George Koonce	.05
395	Steve McMichael	.05
396	Bryce Paup	.05
397	Aaron Taylor	.05
398	Henry Ford	.05
399	Ernest Givins	.05
400	*Jeremy Nunley*	.15
401	Bo Orlando	.05
402	Al Smith	.05
403	*Barron Wortham*	.15
404	Trev Alberts	.20
405	Tony Bennett	.05
406	Kerry Cash	.05
407	*Sean Dawkins*	1.00
408	Marshall Faulk	3.00
409	Jim Harbaugh	.05
410	Jeff Herrod	.05
411	Kimble Anders	.05
412	Donnell Bennett	.05
413	J.J. Birden	.05
414	Mark Collins	.05
415	Lake Dawson	.30
416	Greg Hill	.75
417	Charles Mincy	.05
418	Greg Biekert	.05
419	Rob Fredrickson	.05
420	Nolan Harrison	.05
421	Jeff Jaeger	.05
422	Albert Lewis	.05
423	Chester McGlockton	.05
424	Tom Rathman	.05
425	Harvey Williams	.05
426	Isaac Bruce	2.00
427	Troy Drayton	.05
428	Wayne Gandy	.05
429	Fred Stokes	.05
430	Robert Young	.05
431	Gene Atkins	.05
432	Aubrey Beavers	.05
433	Tim Bowens	.05

434	Keith Byars	.05
435	Jeff Cross	.05
436	Mark Ingram	.05
437	Keith Jackson	.05
438	Michael Stewart	.05
439	Chris Hinton	.05
440	Qadry Ismail	.15
441	Carlos Jenkins	.05
442	Warren Moon	.20
443	David Palmer	.20
444	Jake Reed	.05
445	Robert Smith	.40
446	Todd Steussie	.05
447	DeWayne Washington	.05
448	Marion Butts	.05
449	Tim Goad	.05
450	Myron Guyton	.05
451	*Kevin Lee*	.20
452	Willie McGinest	.20
453	Ricky Reynolds	.05
454	Michael Timpson	.05
455	Morten Andersen	.05
456	Jim Everett	.05
457	Michael Haynes	.05
458	Joe Johnson	.05
459	Wayne Martin	.05
460	Sam Mills	.05
461	Irv Smith	.05
462	Carlton Bailey	.05
463	Chris Calloway	.05
464	Mark Jackson	.05
465	Thomas Lewis	.20
466	Thomas Randolph	.05
467	*Stevie Anderson*	.15
468	Brad Baxter	.05
469	Aaron Glenn	.05
470	Jeff Lageman	.05
471	Johnny Mitchell	.05
472	Art Monk	.15
473	William Fuller	.05
474	*Charlie Garner*	2.50
475	Vaughn Hebron	.05
476	Bill Romanowski	.05
477	William Thomas	.05
478	Greg Townsend	.05
479	Bernard Williams	.05
480	Calvin Williams	.05
481	Eric Green	.05
482	Charles Johnson	.50
483	Carnell Lake	.05
484	*Bam Morris*	.50
485	John L. Williams	.05
486	Darren Carrington	.05
487	*Andre Coleman*	.20
488	Isaac Davis	.05
489	Dwane Harper	.05
490	Tony Martin	.05
491	Mark Seay	.40
492	Richard Dent	.05
493	William Floyd	.75
494	Rickey Jackson	.05
495	Brent Jones	.05
496	Ken Norton	.05
497	Gary Plummer	.05
498	Deion Sanders	1.50
499	John Taylor	.20
500	*Lee Woodall*	.20
501	Bryant Young	.30
502	Sam Adams	.20
503	Howard Ballard	.05
504	Michael Bates	.05
505	Trev Alberts, Robert Blackmon	.05
506	John Kasay	.05
507	Kelvin Martin	.05
508	Kevin Mawae	.05
509	Rufus Porter	.05
510	Lawrence Dawsey	.05
511	*Trent Dilfer*	2.00
512	Thomas Everett	.05
513	Jackie Harris	.05
514	Errict Rhett	1.50
515	Henry Ellard	.05
516	John Friesz	.05
517	Ken Harvey	.05
518	Ethan Horton	.05
519	Tre Johnson	.05
520	Jim Lachey	.05
521	Heath Shuler	1.50
522	Tony Woods	.05
523	Checklist	.05
524	Checklist	.05
525	Checklist	.05

1994 Ultra Achievement Awards

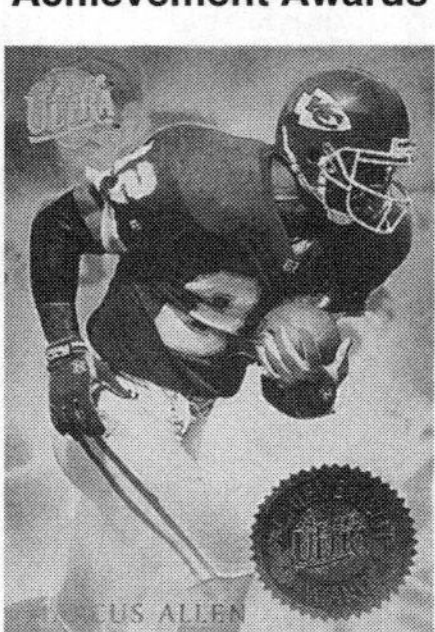

Ultra Achievement Awards featured NFL veteran stars with long records of significant accomplishments. Sterling Sharpe's record breaking reception record is an example of the achievements captured in this 10-card set.

		NM/M
Complete Set (10):		10.00
Common Player:		.50
1	Marcus Allen	.50
2	John Elway	1.00
3	Dan Marino	4.00
4	Joe Montana	3.00
5	Jerry Rice	2.00
6	Barry Sanders	2.00
7	Sterling Sharpe	.50
8	Emmitt Smith	4.00
9	Thurman Thomas	.50
10	Reggie White	.50

1994 Ultra Award Winners

Award Winners were found in random packs of 1994 Ultra Football. It showcases the AFC/NFC Offensive Rookies of the Year, Super Bowl MVP, Defensive Player of the Year, and the NFL Defensive Rookie of the Year. Each card shows the player on a three-photo background.

		NM/M
Complete Set (5):		6.00
Common Player:		.50
1	Jerome Bettis	1.00
2	Rick Mirer	.50
3	Emmitt Smith	4.00
4	Dana Stubblefield	.50
5	Rod Woodson	.50

1994 Ultra First Rounders

First Rounders could be found in 14, 17 and 20-card foil packs of Fleer Ultra Football. This 20-card set features the top selections in the '94 draft cast onto a cobweb- looking background, with a First Rounder stamp in the bottom left corner.

		NM/M
Complete Set (20):		8.00
Common Player:		.20
1	Sam Adams	.20
2	Trev Alberts	.20
3	Shante Carver	.20
4	Marshall Faulk	3.00
5	William Floyd	2.00
6	Rob Fredrickson	.20
7	Wayne Gandy	.20
8	Aaron Glenn	.20
9	Charles Johnson	.20
10	Joe Johnson	.20
11	Antonio Langham	.20
12	Willie McGinest	.20
13	Jamir Miller	.20
14	Johnnie Morton	.20
15	Heath Shuler	1.00
16	John Thierry	.20
17	DeWayne Washington	.20
18	Dan Wilkinson	.20
19	Bernard Williams	.20
20	Bryant Young	1.00

1994 Ultra Flair Hot Numbers

These cards feature the super premium quality of Fleer Flair, including double-thick card stock, polyester lamination and six- color printing. The Hot Number inserts, randomly included in Fleer Ultra Series II packs, showcase 15 running backs, quarterbacks and receivers who pile up yardage. Each card front has an action shot over a team-colored, swirling background. Different dates and numbers that are important to the pictured player appear within the background. Player names are written across the bottom in gold foil, with the Flair logo in the upper right corner. In the bottom right corner a large box, outlined in black, displays "Hot Numbers," with the player's uniform number inside the box. Card backs, numbered 1 of 15, etc., have another photo and career summary.

		NM/M
Complete Set (15):		18.00
Common Player:		.25
1	Troy Aikman	3.00
2	Jerome Bettis	1.00
3	Tim Brown	1.00
4	John Elway	2.00
5	Rodney Hampton	.25
6	Michael Irvin	.75
7	Dan Marino	4.00
8	Joe Montana	4.00
9	Jerry Rice	3.00
10	Andre Rison	.25
11	Barry Sanders	3.00
12	Sterling Sharpe	.25
13	Emmitt Smith	4.00
14	Thurman Thomas	.75
15	Steve Young	3.00

1994 Ultra Flair Scoring Power

Each of these six insert cards contains a football background with the words "Scoring Power" running up and down opposite sides of the card. A black strip across the bottom of each card contains the player's name, and the words "Scoring Power." The inserts, randomly included in 1994 Fleer Ultra Series II packs, feature highly productive quarterbacks, running backs and wide receivers. The Fleer Flair logo is on each card front. Card backs have gold foil stamping, a photo, a career summary and a card number (1 of 6, etc.).

		NM/M
Complete Set (6):		10.00
Common Player:		.50
1	Marcus Allen	1.00
2	Natrone Means	.50
3	Jerry Rice	3.00
4	Andre Rison	.50
5	Emmitt Smith	4.00
6	Ricky Watters	1.00

1994 Ultra Flair Wave of the Future

These 1994 Fleer Ultra Series II inserts, randomly included in packs, feature six top rookies from the 1994 season. Players are pictured in their NFL uniforms over an iridescent, swirling background. The player's name, Flair logo and set logo are stamped in gold foil on the card front. The card back has a photo, career summary and a number (1 of 6, etc.).

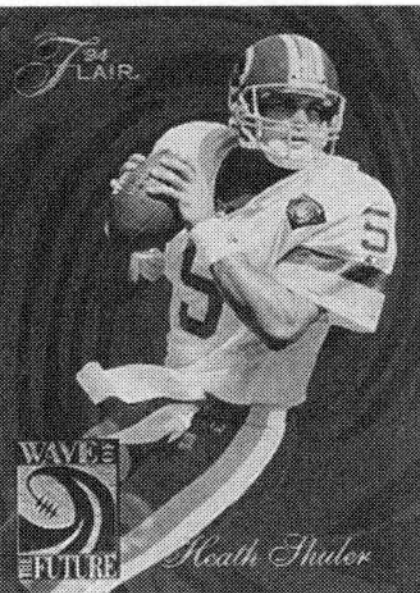

		NM/M
Complete Set (6):		5.00
Common Player:		.50
1	Trent Dilfer	1.50
2	Marshall Faulk	3.00
3	Greg Hill	.50
4	Charles Johnson	.50
5	Heath Shuler	.50
6	Dan Wilkinson	.50

1994 Ultra Rick Mirer

Rick Mirer "Rookie of the Year" is a 10-card set inserted into Ultra packs. It highlights his rookie season and gives a brief history of Mirer.

	NM/M
Complete Set (10):	2.00
Common Mirer:	.20
Mirer Auto:	25.00

1994 Ultra Second Year Standouts

Second Year Standouts highlight high-profile 1993 rookies starting their second season. This 15-card set was inserted into foil packs of Ultra Football. Each card displays the second year standout with fireworks going off in the background.

		NM/M
Complete Set (15):		7.00
Common Player:		.50
1	Jerome Bettis	1.50
2	Drew Bledsoe	5.00
3	Reggie Brooks	.50
4	Tom Carter	.50
5	Eric Curry	.50
6	Jason Elam	.50
7	Tyrone Hughes	.50
8	James Jett	.50
9	Terry Kirby	.50
10	Natrone Means	.50
11	Rick Mirer	.50
12	Ron Moore	.50
13	William Roaf	.50
14	Chris Slade	.50
15	Dana Stubblefield	.50

1994 Ultra Ultra Stars

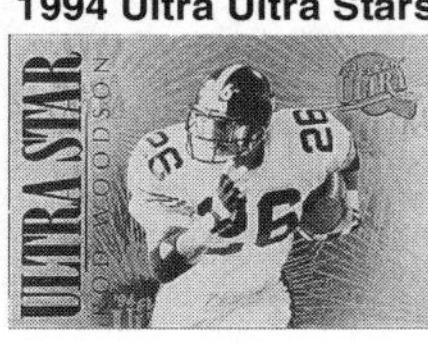

This nine-card set was found in only 17-card packs of Ultra Football. It includes some of the brightest stars in the NFL. Ultra Stars are also quite scarce and are printed on 100% etched-foil.

		NM/M
Complete Set (9):		35.00
Common Player:		1.00
1	Troy Aikman	5.00
2	Jerome Bettis	3.00
3	Tim Brown	1.00
4	Michael Irvin	1.00
5	Rick Mirer	1.00
6	Jerry Rice	6.00
7	Barry Sanders	6.00
8	Emmitt Smith	6.00
9	Rod Woodson	1.00

1994 Ultra Touchdown Kings

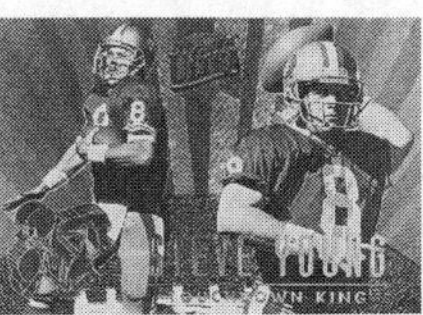

Touchdown Kings are a 100% foil-etched shot of a nine players who have proven scoring ability. Since they were randomly inserted exclusively into 14 and 20-card packs of Ultra Football, they are the rarest insert set. Each card shows two shots of the featured player on a horizontal background

		NM/M
Complete Set (9):		15.00
Common Player:		.50
Minor Stars:		1.00
1	Marcus Allen	1.00
2	Dan Marino	5.00
3	Joe Montana	5.00
4	Jerry Rice	3.00
5	Andre Rison	.50
6	Sterling Sharpe	1.00
7	Emmitt Smith	5.00
8	Ricky Watters	1.00
9	Steve Young	3.00

1995 Ultra

Fleer released its 550-card 1995 Ultra set in two series - a 350-card Series I, plus a 200-card Ultra Extra set. Card fronts have a full-bleed color action photo, with the player name stamped in a square at the bottom, with a mountain range design. The card back has a number in the upper left corner and features two smaller color photos and a ghosted image on a horizontal background. The player's name and position are stamped in gold. A team helmet and 1994 and career statistic lines are also given. All regular and insert cards are on 40-percent thicker stock. A Gold Medallion parallel set, featuring 100-percent gold-foil embossed backgrounds, was also created for each regular and insert card. Cards were include one per pack. Ultra Extra is composed of subsets: 60 Rookies, 60 Player Updates, 60 Extra Stars, six Rollout cards and 12 Extra Effort cards. Series I insert sets include: Award Winners (1 in 5 packs), First Rounders (1 in 7), Touchdown Kings (1 in 7 12-card packs), Rising Stars (1 in 37), Ultra Stars (1 in 7 17-card packs), Ultra Achievement (1 in 7) and Second Year Standouts (1 in 5). Ultra Extra inserts include: 30 Ultrabilties cards (10 each for Guns, Bolts and Blasts; 1 in 5 packs), Big Finish (1 in 20, hobby exclusive packs), Ultra Magna Force (1 in 20, retail exclusive), and All-Rookie Team (1 in 55). Also found in Ultra Extra are Gold Medallion Hot Packs (1 in 72), which contain all Gold Medallion cards, and All-Rookie Team Hot Packs (1 per 360), which contain a complete set of All-Rookie Team inserts.

		NM/M
Complete Set (550):		60.00
Comp. Series 1 (350):		35.00
Comp. Series 2 (200):		35.00
Common Player:		.10
Minor Stars:		.20
Comp. Gold Med. Set (550):		350.00
Comp. Gold Med. Series 1 (350):		200.00
Comp. Gold Med. Series 2 (200):		150.00
Gold Medallion Cards:		3X-6X
Series 1 Pack (12):		1.00
Series 1 Wax Box (36):		25.00
Series 2 Pack (12):		1.25
Series 2 Wax Box (36):		35.00
1	Michael Bankston	.10
2	Larry Centers	.10
3	Garrison Hearst	.20
4	Eric Hill	.10
5	Seth Joyner	.10
6	Lorenzo Lynch	.10
7	Jamir Miller	.20
8	Clyde Simmons	.10
9	Eric Swann	.10
10	Aeneas Williams	.10
11	Devin Bush	.20
12	Ron Davis	.10
13	Chris Doleman	.10
14	Bert Emanuel	.40
15	Jeff George	.20
16	Roger Harper	.10
17	Craig Heyward	.10
18	Pierce Holt	.10
19	D.J. Johnson	.10
20	Terance Mathis	.10
21	Chuck Smith	.10
22	Jessie Tuggle	.10
23	Cornelius Bennett	.10
24	Reuben Brown	.20
25	Jeff Burris	.10
26	Matt Darby	.10
27	Phil Hansen	.10
28	Henry Jones	.10
29	Jim Kelly	.20
30	Mark Maddox	.20
31	Andre Reed	.20
32	Bruce Smith	.10
33	Don Beebe	.10
34	*Kerry Collins*	2.00
35	Darion Conner	.10
36	Pete Metzelaars	.10
37	Sam Mills	.10
38	Tyrone Poole	.20
39	Joe Cain	.10
40	Mark Carrier	.10
41	Curtis Conway	.10
42	Jeff Graham	.10
43	Raymont Harris	.10
44	Erik Kramer	.10
45	*Rashaan Salaam*	.50
46	Lewis Tillman	.10
47	Donnell Woolford	.10
48	Chris Zorich	.10
49	*Jeff Blake*	.50
50	Mike Brim	.10
51	*Ki-Jana Carter*	1.50
52	James Francis	.10
53	Carl Pickens	.20
54	Darnay Scott	.75
55	Steve Tovar	.10
56	Dan Wilkinson	.10
57	Alfred Williams	.10
58	Darryl Williams	.10
59	Derrick Alexander	.20
60	Rob Burnett	.10
61	Steve Everitt	.10
62	Leroy Hoard	.10
63	Michael Jackson	.10
64	Pepper Johnson	.10
65	Tony Jones	.10
66	Antonio Langham	.10
67	Anthony Pleasant	.10
68	Craig Powell	.20
69	Vinny Testaverde	.20
70	Eric Turner	.10
71	Troy Aikman	1.50
72	Charles Haley	.10
73	Michael Irvin	.20
74	Daryl Johnston	.10
75	Robert Jones	.10
76	Leon Lett	.10
77	Russell Maryland	.10
78	Jay Novacek	.10
79	Darrin Smith	.10
80	Emmitt Smith	3.00
81	Kevin Smith	.10
82	Eric Williams	.10
83	Kevin Williams	.10
84	*Sherman Williams*	.20
85	Darren Woodson	.10
86	Elijah Alexander	.20
87	Steve Atwater	.10
88	Ray Crockett	.10
89	Shane Dronett	.10
90	Jason Elam	.10
91	John Elway	.60
92	Simon Fletcher	.10
93	Glyn Milburn	.10
94	Anthony Miller	.10
95	Leonard Russell	.10
96	Shannon Sharpe	.20
97	Bennie Blades	.10
98	Lomas Brown	.10
99	Willie Clay	.10
100	Luther Elliss	.20
101	Mike Johnson	.10
102	Robert Massey	.10
103	Scott Mitchell	.10
104	Herman Moore	.50
105	Brett Perriman	.10

No.	Player	Price
106	Robert Porcher	.10
107	Barry Sanders	2.50
108	Chris Spielman	.10
109	Edgar Bennett	.10
110	Robert Brooks	.10
111	LeRoy Butler	.10
112	Brett Favre	3.00
113	Sean Jones	.10
114	John Jurkovic	.10
115	George Koonce	.10
116	Wayne Simmons	.10
117	George Teague	.10
118	Reggie White	.20
119	Micheal Barrow	.10
120	Gary Brown	.10
121	Cody Carlson	.10
122	Ray Childress	.10
123	Cris Dishman	.10
124	Bruce Matthews	.10
125	*Steve McNair*	4.00
126	Marcus Robertson	.10
127	Webster Slaughter	.10
128	Al Smith	.10
129	Tony Bennett	.10
130	Ray Buchanan	.10
131	Quentin Coryatt	.10
132	Sean Dawkins	.10
133	Marshall Faulk	1.00
134	Stephen Grant	.10
135	Jim Harbaugh	.10
136	Jeff Herrod	.10
137	Ellis Johnson	.20
138	Tony Siragusa	.10
139	Steve Beuerlein	.10
140	*Tony Boselli*	.20
141	Darren Carrington	.10
142	Reggie Cobb	.10
143	Kelvin Martin	.10
144	Kelvin Pritchett	.10
145	Joel Smeenge	.10
146	*James Stewart*	2.50
147	Marcus Allen	.20
148	Kimble Anders	.10
149	Dale Carter	.10
150	Mark Collins	.10
151	Willie Davis	.10
152	Lake Dawson	.20
153	Greg Hill	.20
154	Trezelle Jenkins	.10
155	Darren Mickell	.10
156	Tracy Simien	.10
157	Neil Smith	.10
158	William White	.10
159	Joe Aska	.20
160	Greg Biekert	.10
161	Tim Brown	.20
162	Rob Fredrickson	.10
163	*Andrew Glover*	.20
164	Jeff Hostetler	.20
165	Raghib Ismail	.10
166	*Napoleon Kaufman*	1.00
167	Terry McDaniel	.10
168	Chester McGlockton	.10
169	Anthony Smith	.10
170	Harvey Williams	.10
171	Steve Wisniewski	.10
172	Gene Atkins	.10
173	Aubrey Beavers	.10
174	Tim Bowens	.10
175	Bryan Cox	.10
176	Jeff Cross	.10
177	Irving Fryar	.10
178	Dan Marino	3.00
179	O.J. McDuffie	.10
180	Billy Milner	.10
181	Bernie Parmalee	.20
182	Troy Vincent	.10
183	Richmond Webb	.10
184	Derrick Alexander	.20
185	Cris Carter	.20
186	Jack Del Rio	.10
187	Qadry Ismail	.10
188	Ed McDaniel	.10
189	Randall McDaniel	.10
190	Warren Moon	.20
191	John Randle	.10
192	Jake Reed	.10
193	Fuad Reveiz	.10
194	Korey Stringer	.20
195	DeWayne Washington	.10
196	Bruce Armstrong	.10
197	Drew Bledsoe	1.50
198	Vincent Brisby	.10
199	Vincent Brown	.10
200	Marion Butts	.10
201	Ben Coates	.10
202	Myron Guyton	.10
203	Maurice Hurst	.10
204	Mike Jones	.10
205	Ty Law	.20
206	Willie McGinest	.10
207	Chris Slade	.10
208	Mario Bates	.40
209	Quinn Early	.10
210	Jim Everett	.20
211	Mark Fields	.10
212	Michael Haynes	.10
213	Tyrone Hughes	.10
214	Joe Johnson	.10
215	Wayne Martin	.10
216	William Roaf	.10
217	Irv Smith	.10
218	Jimmy Spencer	.10
219	Winfred Tubbs	.10
220	Renaldo Turnbull	.10
221	Michael Brooks	.10
222	Dave Brown	.10
223	Chris Calloway	.10
224	Howard Cross	.10
225	John Elliott	.10
226	Keith Hamilton	.10
227	Rodney Hampton	.20
228	Thomas Lewis	.10
229	Thomas Randolph	.10
230	Mike Sherrard	.10
231	Michael Strahan	.10
232	*Tyrone Wheatley*	1.50
233	Brad Baxter	.10
234	*Kyle Brady*	.50
235	Kyle Clifton	.10
236	*Hugh Douglas*	.20
237	Boomer Esiason	.20
238	Aaron Glenn	.10
239	Bobby Houston	.10
240	Johnny Johnson	.10
241	Mo Lewis	.10
242	Johnny Mitchell	.10
243	Marvin Washington	.10
244	Fred Barnett	.10
245	Randall Cunningham	.20
246	William Fuller	.10
247	Charlie Garner	.10
248	Andy Harmon	.10
249	Greg Jackson	.10
250	*Mike Mamula*	.20
251	Bill Romanowski	.10
252	Bobby Taylor	.20
253	William Thomas	.10
254	Calvin Williams	.10
255	Michael Zordich	.10
256	Chad Brown	.10
257	*Mark Bruener*	.50
258	Dermontti Dawson	.10
259	Barry Foster	.10
260	Kevin Greene	.10
261	Charles Johnson	.40
262	Carnell Lake	.10
263	Greg Lloyd	.10
264	Bam Morris	.20
265	Neil O'Donnell	.20
266	Darren Perry	.10
267	Ray Seals	.10
268	*Kordell Stewart*	3.00
269	John L. Williams	.10
270	Rod Woodson	.20
271	Jerome Bettis	.20
272	Isaac Bruce	1.00
273	*Kevin Carter*	.20
274	Shane Conlan	.10
275	Troy Drayton	.10
276	Sean Gilbert	.10
277	Todd Lyght	.10
278	Chris Miller	.10
279	Anthony Newman	.10
280	Roman Phifer	.10
281	Robert Young	.10
282	John Carney	.10
283	Andre Coleman	.10
284	Courtney Hall	.10
285	Ronnie Harmon	.10
286	Dwayne Harper	.10
287	Stan Humphries	.20
288	Shawn Jefferson	.10
289	Tony Martin	.10
290	Natrone Means	.20
291	Chris Mims	.10
292	Leslie O'Neal	.10
293	Junior Seau	.20
294	Mark Seay	.10
295	Eric Davis	.10
296	William Floyd	.20
297	Merton Hanks	.10
298	Brent Jones	.10
299	Ken Norton	.10
300	Gary Plummer	.10
301	Jerry Rice	1.50
302	Deion Sanders	.75
303	Jesse Sapolu	.10
304	*J.J. Stokes*	2.00
305	Dana Stubblefield	.10
306	John Taylor	.10
307	Steve Wallace	.10
308	Lee Woodall	.10
309	Bryant Young	.10
310	Steve Young	1.50
311	Sam Adams	.10
312	Howard Ballard	.10
313	Robert Blackman	.10
314	Brian Blades	.10
315	*Joey Galloway*	2.50
316	Carlton Gray	.10
317	Cortez Kennedy	.10
318	Rick Mirer	.20
319	Eugene Robinson	.10
320	Chris Warren	.20
321	Terry Wooden	.10
322	Derrick Brooks	.20
323	Lawrence Dawsey	.10
324	Trent Dilfer	.75
325	Santana Dotson	.10
326	Thomas Everett	.10
327	Paul Gruber	.10
328	Jackie Harris	.10
329	Courtney Hawkins	.10
330	Martin Mayhew	.10
331	Hardy Nickerson	.10
332	Errict Rhett	1.50
333	*Warren Sapp*	1.00
334	Charles Wilson	.10
335	Reggie Brooks	.10
336	Tom Carter	.10
337	Henry Ellard	.10
338	Ricky Ervins	.10
339	Darrell Green	.10
340	Ken Harvey	.10
341	Brian Mitchell	.10
342	Cory Raymer	.20
343	Heath Shuler	1.00
344	*Michael Westbrook*	1.50
345	Tony Woods	.10
346	Checklist	.10
347	Checklist	.10
348	Checklist	.10
349	Checklist	.10
350	Checklist	.10
351	Checklist	.10
352	Checklist	.10
353	Dave Krieg	.10
354	Rob Moore	.10
355	J.J. Birden	.10
356	Eric Metcalf	.10
357	Bryce Paup	.10
358	Willie Green	.10
359	Derrick Moore	.10
360	Michael Timpson	.10
361	Eric Bieniemy	.10
362	Keenan McCardell	.10
363	Andre Rison	.20
364	Lorenzo White	.10
365	Deion Sanders	1.00
366	Wade Wilson	.10
367	Aaron Craver	.10
368	Michael Dean Perry	.10
369	*Rod Smith*	12.00
370	Henry Thomas	.10
371	Mark Ingram	.10
372	Chris Chandler	.10
373	Mel Gray	.10
374	Flipper Anderson	.10
375	Craig Erickson	.10
376	Mark Brunell	1.50
377	Ernest Givens	.10
378	Randy Jordan	.10
379	Webster Slaughter	.10
380	*Tamarick Vanover*	1.50
381	Gary Clark	.10
382	Steve Emtman	.10
383	Eric Green	.10
384	Louis Oliver	.10
385	Robert Smith	.10
386	David Meggett	.10
387	Eric Allen	.10
388	Wesley Walls	.10
389	Herschel Walker	.10
390	Ronald Moore	.10
391	Adrian Murrell	.20
392	Charles Wilson	.10
393	Derrick Fenner	.10
394	Pat Swilling	.10
395	Kelvin Martin	.10
396	Rodney Peete	.10
397	Ricky Watters	.20
398	Erric Pegram	.10
399	Leonard Russell	.10
400	Alexander Wright	.10
401	Darrien Gordon	.10
402	Alfred Pupunu	.10
403	Elvis Grbac	.10
404	Derek Loville	.20
405	Steve Broussard	.10
406	Ricky Proehl	.10
407	Bobby Joe Edmonds	.10
408	Alvin Harper	.10
409	Dave Moore	.10
410	Terry Allen	.10
411	Gus Frerotte	.50
412	*Leslie Shepherd*	.20
413	*Stoney Case*	.75
414	*Frank Sanders*	1.50
415	*Roell Preston*	.20
416	*Lorenzo Styles*	.20
417	*Justin Armour*	.20
418	*Todd Collins*	.20
419	*Darick Holmes*	1.50
420	Kerry Collins	1.00
421	*Tyrone Poole*	.20
422	Rashaan Salaam	.30
423	*Todd Sauerbrun*	.20
424	Ki-Jana Carter	1.50
425	*David Dunn*	.20
426	*Earnest Hunter*	.20
427	*Eric Zeier*	1.00
428	*Eric Bjorson*	.20
429	*Sherman Williams*	.20
430	*Terrell Davis*	7.00
431	*Luther Elliss*	.20
432	*Kez McCorvey*	.20
433	*Antonio Freeman*	2.00
434	*Craig Newsome*	.20
435	Steve McNair	2.00
436	*Chris Sanders*	1.50
437	*Zack Crockett*	.20
438	*Ellis Johnson*	.20
439	*Tony Boselli*	.20
440	James Stewart	.30
441	*J.J. Smith*	.20
442	Tamarick Vanover	1.50
443	*Derrick Alexander*	.20
444	*Chad May*	.20
445	*James Stewart*	.50
446	*Ty Law*	.20
447	*Curtis Martin*	4.00
448	*Will Moore*	.20
449	*Mark Fields*	.20
450	*Ray Zellars*	.20
451	*Charles Way*	.20
452	Tyrone Wheatley	1.00
453	*Kyle Brady*	.20
454	*Wayne Chrebet*	1.00
455	Hugh Douglas	.20
456	*Chris Jones*	1.00
457	*Mike Mamula*	.20
458	*Fred McCrary*	.20
459	*Bobby Taylor*	.20
460	Mark Bruener	.40
461	Kordell Stewart	2.00
462	*Kevin Carter*	.20
463	*Lovell Pinckney*	.20
464	*Johnny Thomas*	.20
465	*Terrell Fletcher*	.50
466	*Jimmy Oliver*	.20
467	J.J. Stokes	1.00
468	*Christian Fauria*	.20
469	Joey Galloway	2.00
470	*Derrick Brooks*	.20
471	Warren Sapp	.20
472	Michael Westbrook	.75
473	Garrison Hearst	.20
474	Jeff George	.20
475	Terance Mathis	.10
476	Andre Reed	.10
477	Bruce Smith	.10
478	Lamar Lathon	.10
479	Curtis Conway	.20
480	Jeff Blake	1.50
481	Carl Pickens	.20
482	Eric Turner	.10
483	Troy Aikman	.75
484	Michael Irvin	.20
485	Emmitt Smith	1.50
486	John Elway	.20
487	Shannon Sharpe	.10
488	Herman Moore	.20
489	Barry Sanders	1.00
490	Brett Favre	1.00
491	Reggie White	.20
492	Haywood Jeffires	.10
493	Sean Dawkins	.10
494	Marshall Faulk	1.00
495	Desmond Howard	.10
496	Steve Bono	.20
497	Derrick Thomas	.20
498	Irving Fryar	.10
499	Terry Kirby	.10
500	Dan Marino	1.75
501	O.J. McDuffie	.10
502	Cris Carter	.20
503	Warren Moon	.20
504	Jake Reed	.10
505	Drew Bledsoe	.75
506	Ben Coates	.10
507	Jim Everett	.10
508	Rodney Hampton	.10
509	Mo Lewis	.10
510	Tim Brown	.20
511	Jeff Hostetler	.20
512	Raghib Ismail	.10
513	Chester McGlockton	.10
514	Fred Barnett	.10
515	Greg Lloyd	.10
516	Bam Morris	.20
517	Rod Woodson	.10
518	Jerome Bettis	.20
519	Isaac Bruce	.75
520	Stan Humphries	.20
521	Natrone Means	.20
522	Junior Seau	.20
523	William Floyd	.20
524	Jerry Rice	.75
525	Steve Young	.75
526	Cortez Kennedy	.10
527	Rick Mirer	.20
528	Chris Warren	.20
529	Trent Dilfer	.20
530	Errict Rhett	.75
531	Darrell Green	.10
532	Heath Shuler	.50
533	Stoney Case	.10
534	Eric Zeier	.50
535	Kerry Collins	1.00
536	Steve McNair	1.50
537	Kordell Stewart	2.00
538	*Rob Johnson*	3.00
539	Eric Ball	.10
540	Darrick Brownlow	.10
541	Paul Butcher	.10
542	Carlester Crumpler	.10
543	Maurice Douglas	.10
544	Keith Elias	.10
545	Kenneth Gant	.10
546	Corey Harris	.10
547	Andre Hastings	.10
548	Thomas Holmco	.10
549	Lenny McGill	.10
550	Mark Pike	.10

1995 Ultra Gold Medallion

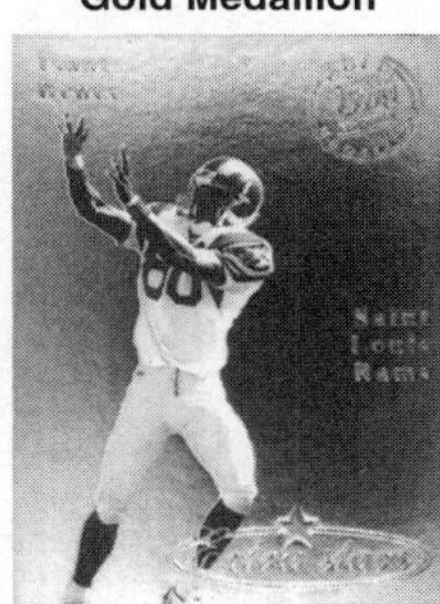

Ultra Gold Medallions paralleled the regular-issue set with the same photo, but a gold foil background. Gold Medallions were found at a rate of one per pack.

Gold Medallion Cards: 2X-4X

1995 Ultra Achievements

These 1995 Fleer Ultra Series I inserts feature 10 of the league's top performers. Cards were randomly included one per every seven packs. The card front has a color action photo, with the player's name and Ultra Achievement and Ultra logos stamped in gold. Running inside the card format are the player's achievements from the 1994 season. The card back, numbered 1 of 10, etc., has another color photo, with a box superimposed over the photo to provide a summary of the player's season recap. The achievements listed along the front borders repeat on the back.

		NM/M
Complete Set (10):		5.00
Common Player:		.25
Comp. Gold Set (10):		10.00
Gold Cards:		1X-2X
1	Drew Bledsoe	2.00
2	Cris Carter	.25
3	Ben Coates	.25
4	Mel Gray	.25
5	Jerry Rice	2.00
6	Barry Sanders	3.00
7	Deion Sanders	1.50
8	Herschel Walker	.50
9	DeWayne Washington	.25
10	Steve Young	2.00

1995 Ultra All-Rookie Team

These 1995 Fleer Ultra Extra inserts are the rarest of the series; they can be found one in every 55 packs. The cards are acetate and feature the top 10 rookies from the 1995 season. "Rookies" is written along one border of the card.

		NM/M
Complete Set (10):		20.00
Common Player:		1.00
Hot Pack Cards Half Price		
1	Michael Westbrook	2.00
2	Terrell Davis	6.00
3	Curtis Martin	4.00
4	Joey Galloway	3.00
5	Rashaan Salaam	1.00
6	J.J. Stokes	2.00
7	Napoleon Kaufman	1.00
8	Mike Mamula	1.00
9	Kyle Brady	1.00
10	Hugh Douglas	1.00

1995 Ultra Award Winners

These 1995 Fleer Ultra Series I inserts could be found one per every five packs. They feature six players who captured postseason awards after the 1994 season ended. The card front has a color photo of the player superimposed over a collage of the award he won. His name and the Ultra and Award Winner logos are stamped in gold. The player's name is also in gold on the back, which is numbered 1 of 6, etc. The back has a player photo on one half of the card, with a recap of why he won the specific award. The award trophy collage is again used for the background.

		NM/M
Complete Set (6):		5.00
Common Player:		.50
Comp. Gold Set (6):		10.00
Gold Cards:		1X-2X
1	Tim Bowens	.50
2	Marshall Faulk	1.00
3	Dan Marino	3.00
4	Barry Sanders	2.00
5	Deion Sanders	1.00
6	Steve Young	1.25

A player's name in *italic* type indicates a rookie card.

1995 Ultra First Rounders

These 1995 Fleer Ultra Series I inserts feature 20 of the top selections from the 1995 draft. The cards could be found one per every seven packs. The card front uses gold stamping for the Fleer Ultra and insert set logos, plus the player's name. A player photo is superimposed against a background collage of his team's logo. The back, numbered 1 of 20, etc., has the same collage as a background, plus a smaller player photo and a draft analysis of the player. His name also appears in gold at the top of the card.

		NM/M
Complete Set (20):		10.00
Common Player:		.25
Comp. Gold Set (20):		20.00
Gold Cards:		1X-2X
1	Derrick Alexander	.25
2	Tony Boselli	.50
3	Kyle Brady	.50
4	Mark Bruener	.25
5	Devin Bush	.25
6	Kevin Carter	.25
7	Ki-Jana Carter	1.00
8	Kerry Collins	2.00
9	Mark Fields	.25
10	Joe Galloway	2.00
11	Napoleon Kaufman	.50
12	Ty Law	.25
13	Mike Mamula	.25
14	Steve McNair	6.00
15	Rashaan Salaam	.50
16	Warren Sapp	1.00
17	James Stewart	1.00
18	J.J. Stokes	2.00
19	Michael Westbrook	1.00
20	Tyrone Wheatley	.50

1995 Ultra Magna Force

These 1995 Fleer Ultra Extra inserts feature 20 top NFL stars and were random inserts in retail packs only, one every 20 packs.

		NM/M
Complete Set (20):		40.00
Common Player:		.50
1	Emmitt Smith	8.00
2	Jerry Rice	6.00
3	Drew Bledsoe	5.00
4	Marshall Faulk	4.00
5	Heath Shuler	1.00
6	Carl Pickens	1.00
7	Ben Coates	.50
8	Terry Allen	.50
9	Terance Mathis	.50
10	Fred Barnett	.50
11	O.J. McDuffie	.50
12	Garrison Hearst	2.00
13	Deion Sanders	2.00
14	Reggie White	2.00
15	Herman Moore	2.00
16	Brett Favre	8.00
17	William Floyd	1.00
18	Curtis Martin	5.00
19	Joey Galloway	2.00
20	Tyrone Wheatley	1.00

1995 Ultra Overdrive

These insert cards were exclusive to 1995 Fleer Ultra Extra hobby packs, one per every 20 packs. The card fronts have a metallic shine to them, with a color action photo in the center. Ultra Overdrive appears along the right border. The player's name and position are in the lower left corner. The card back, numbered one of twenty, etc., features a ghosted image of an action photo, with a square around the player's head, which is in color. A brief player profile is also given.

		NM/M
Complete Set (20):		20.00
Common Player:		.50
1	Barry Sanders	4.00
2	Troy Aikman	3.00
3	Natrone Means	.50
4	Steve Young	3.00
5	Errict Rhett	.50
6	Terrell Davis	4.00
7	Michael Westbrook	.50
8	Michael Irvin	1.00
9	Chris Warren	.50
10	Tim Brown	.50
11	Jerome Bettis	1.00
12	Ricky Watters	.50
13	Derrick Thomas	.50
14	Bruce Smith	.50
15	Rashaan Salaam	.50
16	Jeff Blake	.50
17	Alvin Harper	.50
18	Shannon Sharpe	.50
19	Eric Swann	.50
20	Andre Rison	.50

1995 Ultra Rising Stars

These inserts were randomly included one in every 37 packs, making them the scarcest of the 1995 Fleer Ultra Series I inserts. These nine cards, numbered 1 of 9, etc., are printed on acetate with an "ultra crystal" planetary design. The front has a color photo, with the player, set and insert set names in gold foil. The back, numbered 1 of 9, etc., also uses gold for the player name. He is pictured again as the background, with a brief career summary superimposed over it.

		NM/M
Complete Set (9):		20.00
Common Player:		1.00
Comp. Gold Set (9):		40.00
Gold Cards:		1X-2X
1	Jerome Bettis	2.00
2	Jeff Blake	1.00
3	Drew Bledsoe	4.00
4	Ben Coates	1.00
5	Marshall Faulk	4.00
6	Brett Favre	6.00
7	Natrone Means	1.00
8	Bam Morris	1.00
9	Eric Turner	1.00

1995 Ultra Second Year Standouts

This horizontally-designed insert set was featured in 1995 Fleer Ultra Series I packs, one per every five packs. The front uses gold stamping for the set and insert set logos, plus the name of the player, who is pictured twice. A team helmet collage is used for the background. The back, also horizontal, is numbered 1 of 15, etc., and features one of the players chosen as a top sophomore in the NFL. A color photo and brief recap of the player's rookie season accomplishments are also on the back. His name is in gold. The background says "2nd Year Standout" in a repeated pattern.

		NM/M
Complete Set (15):		4.00
Common Player:		.25
Comp. Gold Set (15):		8.00
Gold Cards:		1X-2X
1	Derrick Alexander	.50
2	Mario Bates	.50
3	Tim Bowens	.50
4	Bert Emanuel	.50
5	Marshall Faulk	3.00
6	William Floyd	.50
7	Rob Fredrickson	.50
8	Antonio Langham	.50
9	Bam Morris	.50
10	Errict Rhett	.75
11	Darnay Scott	.50
12	Heath Shuler	.50
13	DeWayne Washington	.50
14	Dan Wilkinson	.50
15	Bryant Young	.50

1995 Ultra Ultra Stars

These 1995 Fleer Ultra Series I inserts were included one per every seven 17-card packs. They feature 10 of the NFL's top players. The horizontal card front has a larger photo of the player, against a collage of the same photo in different sizes and color patterns. Silver stamping is used for the player's name and set and insert set logos. The back, numbered 1 of 10, etc., uses silver foil and a horizontal format. A color photo is on one half of the card; a brief career summary comprises the other.

		NM/M
Complete Set (10):		10.00
Common Player:		.25
Comp. Gold Med. Set (10):		10.00
Gold Med. Cards:		1X-2X
1	Tim Brown	.50
2	Marshall Faulk	2.00
3	Irving Fryar	.50
4	Dan Marino	3.00
5	Natrone Means	.50
6	Jerry Rice	2.00
7	Barry Sanders	2.00
8	Deion Sanders	1.50
9	Emmitt Smith	3.00
10	Rod Woodson	.50

1995 Ultra Touchdown Kings

These 1995 Fleer Ultra Series I inserts feature 10 of the NFL's top touchdown scorers from 1994. The cards were random inserts, one every seventh 12-card packs. The front uses gold stamping for the player's name and insert and set logos. A TD with a crown on top of it appears in the lower right corner. A color player photo is superimposed against a crystal-like "TD"/football background. The card back, numbered 1 of 10, etc., has a color photo on one side; a recap of the player's scoring accomplishments from 1994 are on the other. Gold foil stamping is used for the number and player's name.

		NM/M
Complete Set (10):		10.00
Common Player:		.50
Comp. Gold Set (10):		20.00
Gold Cards:		1X-2X
1	Marshall Faulk	2.00
2	Terance Mathis	.50
3	Natrone Means	.50
4	Herman Moore	.50
5	Carl Pickens	1.00
6	Jerry Rice	2.00
7	Andre Rison	.50
8	Emmitt Smith	3.00
9	Chris Warren	.50
10	Steve Young	2.00

1995 Ultra Ultrabilities

These 1995 Fleer Ultra Extra inserts could be found one per every five packs. The 30 cards are broken into three subsets of 10 cards each - Guns (quarterbacks), Bolts (receivers and running backs) and Blasts (hard-hitting defensive players and running backs). The respective subset name is on the card front in gold foil, along with the word Ultrabilities. The background is orange; the player's name is in white in a colored panel at the bottom. Each card back is numbered 1 of 30, etc., and includes a mug shot of the player, plus a ghosted image of him in action. A brief player profile is also provided. Near a team logo in the upper left corner is the player's name, in his team's primary uniform color. A word describing a key element of the player's skills is written along the right side of the card.

		NM/M
Complete Set (30):		20.00
Common Player:		.25
1	Dan Marino (Guns)	4.00
2	Steve Young (Guns)	2.00
3	Drew Bledsoe (Guns)	2.00
4	Jeff Blake (Guns)	.50
5	Troy Aikman (Guns)	2.00
6	John Elway (Guns)	2.00
7	Trent Dilfer (Guns)	1.00
8	Steve Bono (Guns)	.50
9	Brett Favre (Guns)	5.00
10	Kerry Collins (Guns)	1.00
11	Barry Sanders (Bolts)	4.00
12	Errict Rhett (Bolts)	.25
13	Emmitt Smith (Bolts)	4.00
14	Chris Warren (Bolts)	.30
15	Irving Fryar (Bolts)	.25
16	Charlie Garner (Bolts)	.25
17	Joey Galloway (Bolts)	1.00
18	Eric Metcalf (Bolts)	.25
19	Herman Moore (Bolts)	.50
20	Robert Smith (Bolts)	.25
21	Natrone Means (Blasts)	.25
22	Derrick Thomas (Blasts)	.25
23	Bruce Smith (Blasts)	.25
24	Hugh Douglas (Blasts)	.25
25	Mike Mamula (Blasts)	.25
26	Jerome Bettis (Blasts)	1.00
27	Bam Morris (Blasts)	.50
28	Tim Bowens (Blasts)	.25
29	William Floyd (Blasts)	.50
30	Daryl Johnston (Blasts)	.25

1996 Ultra

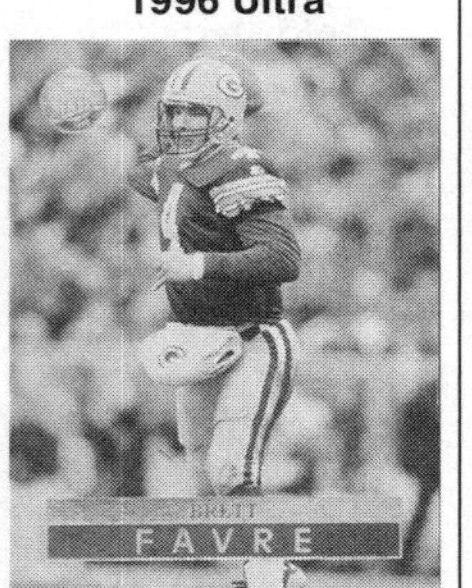

Fleer's 1996 Ultra football set is packed with rookies - 55 in all - featured as cards in a subset and two insert sets. The 15-card subset has the rookies in their college uniforms, with their new NFL team logos. Insert sets featuring rookies include a 30-card Ultra Rookies set and a 10-card All-Rookie Team set. Two other subsets were also produced for the 200-card set - First Impressions and Secret Weapons. The other insert card sets are Mr. Momentum, Sledgehammer, and Pulsating. Similar to last year's format, both NFC and AFC cards feature unique designs, with NFC players' last names printed against a blue background while a red background is used for AFC stars. 1995 Pro Bowl player cards have a special Pro Bowl designation. Each regular card has a full-bleed color action photo on the front. The back also has a color action photo, plus a ghosted image which has a recap of the player's 1995 season. Above the recap and along the top are 1995 and career totals; the player's name, team logo and biographical information are below. A card number is in the upper left corner of the horizontally-designed card back.

		NM/M
Complete Set (200):		30.00
Common Player:		.10
Minor Stars:		.20
Pack (12):		2.00
Wax Box (24):		40.00
1	Larry Centers	.10
2	Garrison Hearst	.20
3	Rob Moore	.20
4	Eric Swann	.10
5	Aeneas Williams	.10
6	Bert Emanuel	.10
7	Jeff George	.20
8	Craig Heyward	.10
9	Terance Mathis	.10
10	Eric Metcalf	.10
11	Cornelius Bennett	.10
12	Darick Holmes	.20
13	Jim Kelly	.50
14	Bryce Paup	.10
15	Bruce Smith	.20
16	Mark Carrier	.10
17	Kerry Collins	.50
18	Lamar Lathon	.10
19	Derrick Moore	.10
20	Tyrone Poole	.10
21	Curtis Conway	.20
22	Jeff Graham	.10
23	Raymont Harris	.10
24	Erik Kramer	.10
25	Rashaan Salaam	.50
26	Jeff Blake	.50
27	Ki-Jana Carter	.20
28	Carl Pickens	.20
29	Darnay Scott	.20
30	Dan Wilkinson	.10
31	Leroy Hoard	.10
32	Michael Jackson	.10
33	Andre Rison	.20
34	Vinny Testaverde	.50
35	Eric Turner	.10
36	Troy Aikman	1.50
37	Charles Haley	.10
38	Michael Irvin	.20
39	Daryl Johnston	.10
40	Jay Novacek	.10
41	Deion Sanders	.75
42	Emmitt Smith	2.00
43	Steve Atwater	.10
44	Terrell Davis	4.00
45	John Elway	2.00
46	Anthony Miller	.10
47	Shannon Sharpe	.50
48	Scott Mitchell	.20
49	Herman Moore	.50
50	Johnnie Morton	.10
51	Brett Perriman	.10
52	Barry Sanders	3.00
53	Chris Spielman	.10
54	Edgar Bennett	.10
55	Robert Brooks	.20
56	Mark Chmura	.20
57	Brett Favre	3.00
58	Reggie White	.50
59	Mel Gray	.10
60	Haywood Jeffires	.10
61	Steve McNair	1.25
62	Chris Sanders	.20
63	Rodney Thomas	.20
64	Quentin Coryatt	.10
65	Sean Dawkins	.10
66	Ken Dilger	.10
67	Marshall Faulk	.50
68	Jim Harbaugh	.20
69	Tony Boselli	.10
70	Mark Brunell	1.50
71	Desmond Howard	.10
72	Jimmy Smith	.50
73	James Stewart	.10
74	Marcus Allen	.50
75	Steve Bono	.20
76	Lake Dawson	.10
77	Neil Smith	.10
78	Derrick Thomas	.20
79	Tamarick Vanover	.20
80	Bryan Cox	.10
81	Irving Fryar	.10
82	Eric Green	.10
83	Dan Marino	2.00
84	O.J. McDuffie	.20
85	Bernie Parmalee	.10
86	Cris Carter	.50
87	Qadry Ismail	.10
88	Warren Moon	.20
89	Jake Reed	.20
90	Robert Smith	.50
91	Drew Bledsoe	1.50
92	Vincent Brisby	.10
93	Ben Coates	.50
94	Curtis Martin	1.25
95	Willie McGinest	.10
96	David Meggett	.10
97	Mario Bates	.20
98	Quinn Early	.10
99	Jim Everett	.20
100	Michael Haynes	.10
101	Renaldo Turnbull	.10
102	Dave Brown	.10
103	Rodney Hampton	.20
104	Mike Sherrard	.10
105	Phillippi Sparks	.10
106	Tyrone Wheatley	.20
107	Hugh Douglas	.10
108	Boomer Esiason	.20
109	Aaron Glenn	.10
110	Mo Lewis	.10
111	Johnny Mitchell	.10
112	Tim Brown	.50
113	Jeff Hostetler	.10
114	Raghib Ismail	.10
115	Chester McGlockton	.10
116	Harvey Williams	.10
117	Fred Barnett	.10
118	William Fuller	.10
119	Charlie Garner	.20
120	Ricky Watters	.50
121	Calvin Williams	.10
122	Kevin Greene	.10
123	Greg Lloyd	.10
124	Bam Morris	.20
125	Neil O'Donnell	.20
126	Erric Pegram	.10
127	Kordell Stewart	2.00
128	Yancey Thigpen	.50
129	Rod Woodson	.10
130	Jerome Bettis	.50
131	Isaac Bruce	.50
132	Troy Drayton	.10
133	Sean Gilbert	.10
134	Chris Miller	.10
135	Andre Coleman	.10
136	Ronnie Harmon	.10
137	Aaron Hayden	.20
138	Stan Humphries	.20
139	Natrone Means	.50
140	Junior Seau	.20
141	William Floyd	.10
142	Merton Hanks	.10
143	Brent Jones	.10
144	Derek Loville	.10
145	Jerry Rice	1.50
146	J.J. Stokes	.50
147	Steve Young	1.25
148	Brian Blades	.10
149	Joey Galloway	1.00
150	Cortez Kennedy	.10
151	Rick Mirer	.20
152	Chris Warren	.20
153	Derrick Brooks	.10
154	Trent Dilfer	.50
155	Alvin Harper	.10
156	Jackie Harris	.10
157	Hardy Nickerson	.10
158	Errict Rhett	.20
159	Terry Allen	.20
160	Henry Ellard	.10
161	Brian Mitchell	.10
162	Heath Shuler	.20
163	Michael Westbrook	.20
164	*Tim Biakabutuka*	1.25
165	*Tony Brackens*	.20
166	*Rickey Dudley*	.75
167	*Bobby Engram*	.30
168	*Daryl Gardener*	.10
169	*Eddie George*	4.00
170	*Terry Glenn*	2.00
171	*Kevin Hardy*	.20
172	*Keyshawn Johnson*	2.50
173	*Cedric Jones*	.10
174	*Leeland McElroy*	.30
175	*Jonathan Ogden*	.20
176	*Lawrence Phillips*	.75
177	*Simeon Rice*	.20
178	*Regan Upshaw*	.10
179	Justin Armour (First Impressions)	.10
180	Kyle Brady (First Impressions)	.10
181	Devin Bush (First Impressions)	.10
182	Kevin Carter (First Impressions)	.10
183	Wayne Chrebet (First Impressions)	.50
184	Napoleon Kaufman (First Impressions)	.75
185	Frank Sanders (First Impressions)	.20
186	Warren Sapp (First Impressions)	.10
187	Eric Zeier (First Impressions)	.10
188	Ray Zellars (First Impressions)	.10
189	Bill Brooks (Secret Weapons)	.10
190	Chris Calloway (Secret Weapons)	.10
191	Zack Crockett (Secret Weapons)	.10
192	Antonio Freeman (Secret Weapons)	1.00
193	Tyrone Hughes (Secret Weapons)	.10
194	Daryl Johnston (Secret Weapons)	.10
195	Tony Martin (Secret Weapons)	.10
196	Keenan McCardell (Secret Weapons)	.10
197	Glyn Milburn (Secret Weapons)	.10
198	David Palmer (Secret Weapons)	.10
199	Checklist	.10
200	Checklist	.10

1996 Ultra All-Rookie Die Cuts

These 10 cards feature the top picks in the 1996 NFL Draft. The cards, which use a die-cut design, show the player in his college uniform. Red-foil stamping is used for "All Rookies," which is written along the left side of the card, below the player's name and foil-stamped Ultra logo. The card back has a ghosted player action photo on one side, with a smaller color action photo on the other. The player's name is at the top, next to a card number (1 of 10, etc.). Below the photo is a recap of the skills the player showed while he was in college. "All Rookies" is also stamped in red foil on the back. Cards were randomly inserted in 1996 Fleer Ultra packs, one every 180 packs.

		NM/M
Complete Set (10):		40.00
Common Player:		1.00
Minor Stars:		2.00
Inserted 1:180		
1	Bobby Engram	2.00
2	Daryl Gardener	1.00
3	Eddie George	15.00
4	Terry Glenn	4.00
5	Kevin Hardy	1.00
6	Keyshawn Johnson	6.00
7	Cedric Jones	1.00
8	Leeland McElroy	1.00
9	Jonathan Ogden	1.00
10	Simeon Rice	4.00

1996 Ultra Mr. Momentum

These 1996 Fleer Ultra inserts, seeded one per every 10 packs, use a holographic foil background to showcase players who jump start their teams. Gold foil stamping is used for the player's name, position, brand logo and "Mr. Momentum." The card back has a color photo in the background, with a card number (1 of 20, etc.) in the upper left corner. The player's name, team name and team logo are underneath. In the middle of the card is a recap of the player's 1995 season, and how he can sway the outcome of a game.

		NM/M
Complete Set (20):		20.00
Common Player:		.50
Minor Stars:		1.00
Inserted 1:10		
1	Robert Brooks	.50
2	Isaac Bruce	1.00
3	Terrell Davis	3.00
4	John Elway	4.00
5	Marshall Faulk	2.00
6	Brett Favre	6.00
7	Joey Galloway	1.00
8	Dan Marino	6.00
9	Curtis Martin	3.00
10	Herman Moore	1.00
11	Carl Pickens	.50
12	Jerry Rice	4.00
13	Barry Sanders	5.00
14	Chris Sanders	.50
15	Deion Sanders	1.00
16	Kordell Stewart	1.00
17	Tamarick Vanover	.50
18	Chris Warren	.50
19	Ricky Watters	1.00
20	Steve Young	2.00

1996 Ultra Pulsating

These 1996 Fleer Ultra inserts feature 10 of the NFL's most thrilling players. The special foil-enhanced cards were seeded one per every 20 packs. Gold foil stamping is used on the card front for the player's name, brand logo and a gold bar at the bottom, which has the word "Pulsating" etched into it.

The back has a wavy pattern to it, similar to the foil design on the front. A color photo is in the card's center, with a wavy-lined recap of the player's 1995 season below. Gold foil is used for the player's name at the top, next to a card number (1 of 10, etc.).

		NM/M
Complete Set (10):		15.00
Common Player:		.50
Minor Stars:		1.00
Inserted 1:20		
1	Isaac Bruce	1.00
2	Brett Favre	4.00
3	Joey Galloway	1.00
4	Curtis Martin	2.00
5	Rashaan Salaam	.50
6	Barry Sanders	3.00
7	Deion Sanders	1.00
8	Emmitt Smith	3.00
9	Kordell Stewart	1.00
10	Chris Warren	.50

1996 Ultra Rookies

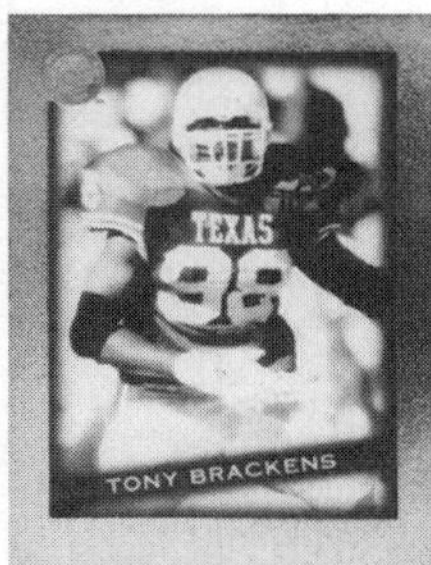

Thirty of the NFL's top 1996 draft picks are featured on these 1996 Fleer Ultra inserts. The cards, seeded one per every three packs, have gold foil borders around a color action photo on the front. The Ultra logo and "Ultra Rookies" are incorporated into the border. A color stripe at the bottom has the player's name inside. The back has a square in the center containing another color photo, with biographical information below. Ultra Rookies is written at the top of the card, with the player's name and card number (1 of 30, etc.) in a color band below.

		NM/M
Complete Set (30):		20.00
Common Player:		.50
Minor Stars:		1.00
Inserted 1:3		
1	Karim Abdul-Jabbar	1.00
2	Mike Alstott	3.00
3	Marco Battaglia	.50
4	Tim Biakabutuka	1.00
5	Sean Boyd	.50
6	Tony Brackens	.50
7	Duane Clemons	.50
8	Bobby Engram	1.00
9	Daryl Gardener	.50
10	Eddie George	5.00
11	Terry Glenn	2.00
12	Kevin Hardy	.50
13	Marvin Harrison	3.00
14	Dietrich Jells	.50
15	Keyshawn Johnson	2.00
16	Lance Johnstone	.50
17	Cedric Jones	.50
18	Marcus Jones	.50
19	Danny Kanell	.50
20	Markco Maddox	.50
21	Derrick Mayes	.50
22	Leeland McElroy	.50
23	Dell McGee	.50
24	Alex Molden	.50
25	Eric Moulds	3.00
26	Jonathan Ogden	.50
27	Lawrence Phillips	.50
28	Simeon Rice	.50
29	Regan Upshaw	.50
30	Jerome Woods	.50

1996 Ultra Sledgehammer

These embossed cards, seeded one per every 15th 1996 Fleer Ultra hobby packs, feature the NFL's power players on both sides of the ball. The embossed front has a raised color action photo on it, with Sledgehammer written along the left side of the card. A logo appears in the lower left corner, framed in gold foil. The player's name is near the bottom in a white stripe; the brand logo is in the upper right corner. The card back has another color photo, with a colored square on it that summarizes the player's skills. The player's team name is written in his team's colors at the top, opposite a card number (1 of 10, etc.). The player's name appears toward the bottom of the card.

		NM/M
Complete Set (10):		15.00
Common Player:		.50
Minor Stars:		1.00
Inserted 1:15 Hobby		
1	Jeff Blake	1.00
2	Terrell Davis	4.00
3	Hugh Douglas	.50
4	Marshall Faulk	3.00
5	Michael Irvin	1.00
6	Steve McNair	3.00
7	Natrone Means	1.00
8	Errict Rhett	.50
9	Emmitt Smith	4.00
10	Rodney Thomas	.50

1996 Ultra Sensations

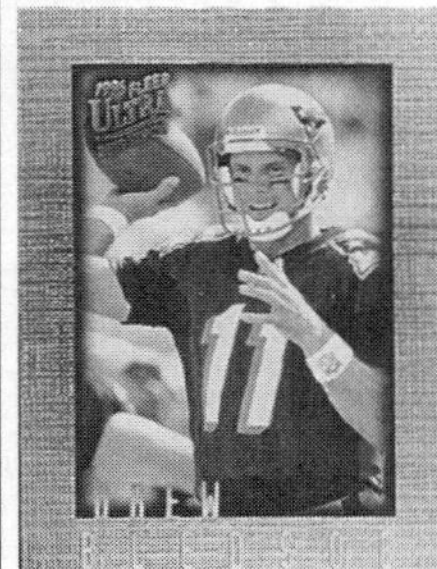

Ultra Sensations was a Series II product, but didn't resemble the Series I release. Instead it went a new direction with 100 cards that appeared in five different versions. Forty percent of the print run had gold borders, 30 percent blue, 20 percent marbleized gold, nine percent pewter and one percent holographic gold foil. The only differentiation between any of the versions was a thick border around the entire card. Ultra Sensations included two inserts: Creative Chaos and Random Rookies.

		NM/M
Complete Gold Set (100):		20.00
Common Player:		.10
Minor Stars:		.20
Blue Cards:		1.5X
Marbleized Gold Cards:		2X
Pewter Cards:		4X
Holographic Gold Cards:		8X
Pack (10):		2.00
Wax Box (24):		40.00
1	*Leeland McElroy*	.30
2	Frank Sanders	.10
3	Eric Swann	.10
4	Jeff George	.10
5	Terrance Mathis	.10
6	Eric Metcalf	.10
7	Michael Jackson	.10
8	Eric Turner	.10
9	Jim Kelly	.10
10	Bryce Paup	.10
11	Bruce Smith	.10
12	Thurman Thomas	.20
13	*Tim Biakabutuka*	1.00
14	Kerry Collins	.30
15	*Muhsin Muhammad*	1.00
16	Winslow Oliver	.10
17	Curtis Conway	.10
18	Bryan Cox	.10
19	*Bobby Engram*	1.00
20	Erik Kramer	.10
21	Rashaan Salaam	.30
22	Jeff Blake	.30
23	Ki-Jana Carter	.20
24	Carl Pickens	.10
25	Troy Aikman	1.25
26	Michael Irvin	.20
27	Daryl Johnston	.10
28	Deion Sanders	.75
29	Emmitt Smith	2.50
30	Terrell Davis	1.75
31	John Elway	1.00
32	Anthony Miller	.10
33	John Mobley	.10
34	Scott Mitchell	.10
35	Herman Moore	.20
36	Barry Sanders	1.25
37	Edgar Bennett	.10
38	Robert Brooks	.10
39	Brett Favre	2.50
40	Reggie White	.20
41	*Eddie George*	3.00
42	Steve McNair	.75
43	Chris Sanders	.10
44	Quentin Coryatt	.10
45	Marshall Faulk	.30
46	Jim Harbaugh	.10
47	*Marvin Harrison*	3.00
48	Mark Brunell	1.00
49	Natrone Means	.10
50	Andre Rison	.10
51	Marcus Allen	.20
52	Steve Bono	.10
53	Greg Hill	.10
54	Tamarick Vanover	.30
55	*Karim Abdul-Jabbar*	.50
56	Dan Marino	2.50
57	O.J. McDuffie	.10
58	*Zach Thomas*	1.00
59	Cris Carter	.10
60	Warren Moon	.10
61	Jake Reed	.10
62	Drew Bledsoe	1.25
63	Ben Coates	.10
64	*Terry Glenn*	1.50
65	Curtis Martin	.75
66	Mario Bates	.10
67	Michael Haynes	.10
68	Dave Brown	.10
69	Rodney Hampton	.10
70	Amani Toomer	.10
71	Tyrone Wheatley	.10
72	*Keyshawn Johnson*	2.00
73	Neil O'Donnell	.10
74	Tim Brown	.10
75	*Rickey Dudley*	.30
76	Napoleon Kaufman	.10
77	Chester McGlockton	.10
78	Charlie Garner	.10
79	Chris T. Jones	.10
80	Ricky Watters	.20
81	Jerome Bettis	.20
82	Kordell Stewart	1.25
83	Rod Woodson	.10
84	Aaron Hayden	.10
85	Stan Humphries	.10
86	Junior Seau	.10
87	*Tony Banks*	1.00
88	Isaac Bruce	.50
89	*Lawrence Phillips*	.50
90	Derek Loville	.10
91	Jerry Rice	1.25
92	J.J. Stokes	.40
93	Steve Young	1.00
94	Joey Galloway	1.00
95	Rick Mirer	.10
96	Chris Warren	.10
97	Trent Dilfer	.10
98	Errict Rhett	.30
99	Terry Allen	.10
100	Michael Westbrook	.20

1996 Ultra Sensations Creative Chaos

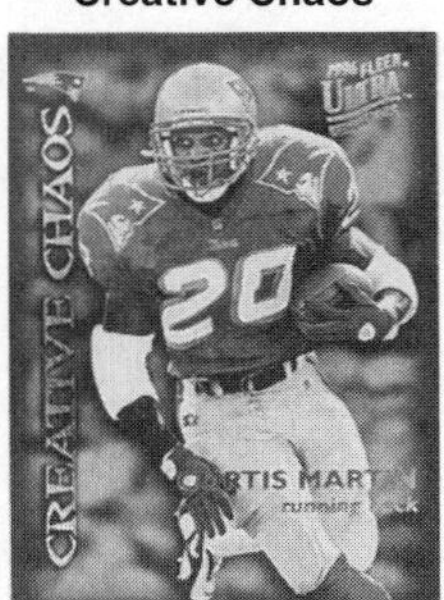

Creative Chaos featured 10 players on double-sided cards that matched each player, resulting in 100 total cards. These inserts were included in every 12 packs.

		NM/M
Complete Set (100):		400.00
Common Player:		1.00
Minor Stars:		2.00
1	Emmitt Smith, Emmitt Smith	12.00
1	Emmitt Smith, Brett Favre	10.00
1	Emmitt Smith, Curtis Martin	8.00
1	Emmitt Smith, Chris Warren	6.00
1	Emmitt Smith, Deion Sanders	8.00
1	Emmitt Smith, Steve Young	8.00
1	Emmitt Smith, Jerry Rice	10.00
1	Emmitt Smith, Terrell Davis	8.00
1	Emmitt Smith, Carl Pickens	6.00
1	Emmitt Smith, Marshall Faulk	8.00
2	Brett Favre, Emmitt Smith	12.00
2	Brett Favre, Brett Favre	12.00
2	Brett Favre, Curtis Martin	10.00
2	Brett Favre, Chris Warren	8.00
2	Brett Favre, Deion Sanders	8.00
2	Brett Favre, Steve Young	8.00
2	Brett Favre, Jerry Rice	8.00
2	Brett Favre, Terrell Davis	8.00
2	Brett Favre, Carl Pickens	6.00
2	Brett Favre, Marshall Faulk	8.00
3	Curtis Martin, Emmitt Smith	10.00
3	Curtis Martin, Brett Favre	10.00
3	Curtis Martin, Curtis Martin	5.00
3	Curtis Martin, Chris Warren	2.00
3	Curtis Martin, Deion Sanders	3.00
3	Curtis Martin, Steve Young	5.00
3	Curtis Martin, Jerry Rice	6.00
3	Curtis Martin, Terrell Davis	6.00
3	Curtis Martin, Carl Pickens	2.00
3	Curtis Martin, Marshall Faulk	5.00
4	Chris Warren, Emmitt Smith	5.00
4	Chris Warren, Brett Favre	5.00
4	Chris Warren, Curtis Martin	2.00
4	Chris Warren, Chris Warren	1.00
4	Chris Warren, Deion Sanders	3.00
4	Chris Warren, Steve Young	3.00
4	Chris Warren, Jerry Rice	2.00
4	Chris Warren, Terrell Davis	2.00
4	Chris Warren, Carl Pickens	1.00
4	Chris Warren, Marshall Faulk	1.00
5	Deion Sanders, Emmitt Smith	7.00
5	Deion Sanders, Brett Favre	7.00
5	Deion Sanders, Curtis Martin	4.00
5	Deion Sanders, Chris Warren	1.00
5	Deion Sanders, Deion Sanders	2.00
5	Deion Sanders, Steve Young	2.00
5	Deion Sanders, Jerry Rice	2.00
5	Deion Sanders, Terrell Davis	2.00
5	Deion Sanders, Carl Pickens	1.00
5	Deion Sanders, Marshall Faulk	2.00
6	Steve Young, Emmitt Smith	8.00
6	Steve Young, Brett Favre	8.00
6	Steve Young, Curtis Martin	6.00
6	Steve Young, Chris Warren	3.00
6	Steve Young, Deion Sanders	3.00
6	Steve Young, Steve Young	5.00
6	Steve Young, Jerry Rice	5.00
6	Steve Young, Terrell Davis	5.00
6	Steve Young, Carl Pickens	3.00
6	Steve Young, Marshall Faulk	3.00
7	Jerry Rice, Emmitt Smith	10.00
7	Jerry Rice, Brett Favre	10.00
7	Jerry Rice, Curtis Martin	8.00
7	Jerry Rice, Chris Warren	3.00
7	Jerry Rice, Deion Sanders	5.00
7	Jerry Rice, Steve Young	6.00
7	Jerry Rice, Jerry Rice	8.00
7	Jerry Rice, Terrell Davis	8.00
7	Jerry Rice, Carl Pickens	2.00
7	Jerry Rice, Marshall Faulk	4.00
8	Terrell Davis, Emmitt Smith	10.00
8	Terrell Davis, Brett Favre	10.00
8	Terrell Davis, Curtis Martin	8.00
8	Terrell Davis, Chris Warren	3.00
8	Terrell Davis, Deion Sanders	3.00
8	Terrell Davis, Steve Young	5.00
8	Terrell Davis, Jerry Rice	8.00
8	Terrell Davis, Terrell Davis	6.00
8	Terrell Davis, Carl Pickens	3.00
8	Terrell Davis, Marshall Faulk	3.00
9	Carl Pickens, Emmitt Smith	6.00
9	Carl Pickens, Brett Favre	6.00
9	Carl Pickens, Curtis Martin	2.00
9	Carl Pickens, Chris Warren	1.00
9	Carl Pickens, Deion Sanders	1.00
9	Carl Pickens, Steve Young	1.00
9	Carl Pickens, Jerry Rice	2.00
9	Carl Pickens, Terrell Davis	2.00
9	Carl Pickens, Carl Pickens	1.00
9	Carl Pickens, Marshall Faulk	2.00
10	Marshall Faulk, Emmitt Smith	10.00
10	Marshall Faulk, Brett Favre	10.00
10	Marshall Faulk, Curtis Martin	6.00
10	Marshall Faulk, Chris Warren	3.00
10	Marshall Faulk, Deion Sanders	3.00
10	Marshall Faulk, Steve Young	4.00
10	Marshall Faulk, Jerry Rice	4.00
10	Marshall Faulk, Terrell Davis	3.00
10	Marshall Faulk, Carl Pickens	1.00
10	Marshall Faulk, Marshall Faulk	3.00

1996 Ultra Sensations Random Rookies

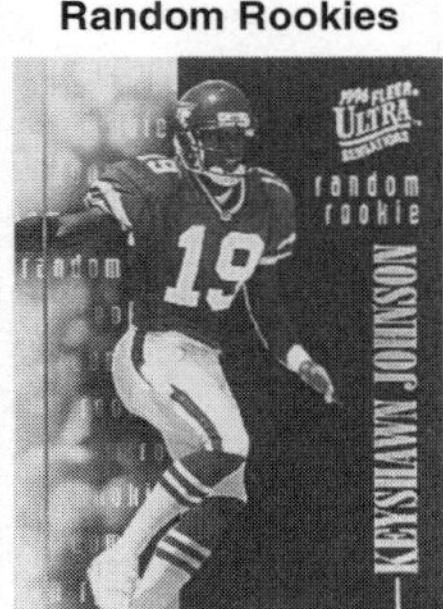

Random Rookies arrived with 80 percent of the print run in silver foil and 20 percent in gold foil. The set included 10 cards, with the first five in hobby and the second five in retail packs. Random Rookies were seeded one every 48 packs.

		NM/M
Complete Set (10):		40.00
Common Player:		1.00
Gold Cards:		2X-3X
1	Keyshawn Johnson	5.00
2	Eddie George	12.00
3	Leeland McElroy	1.00
4	Eric Moulds	3.00
5	Lawrence Phillips	1.00
6	Marvin Harrison	10.00
7	Tim Biakabutuka	1.00
8	Terry Glenn	5.00
9	Rickey Dudley	2.00
10	Tony Banks	2.00

1997 Ultra

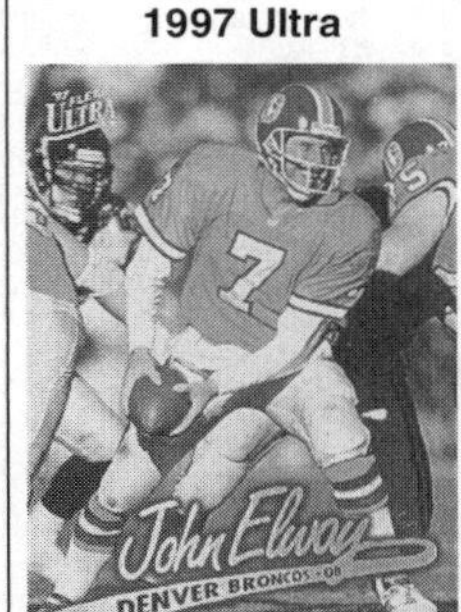

The 350-card set featured 346 cards and four checklists. The fronts showcase a full-bleed photo with the Ultra logo in the upper left. The player's name is written in script at the bottom center, while the team and his position are printed beneath the name. The backs include two photos, with his name, bio and stats beginning in the center and continuing to the bottom. The Gold Medallion parallel cards were inserted one per pack, while the Platinum Medallion parallel cards were exclusive in hobby packs and found 1:100 packs. Inserts in Series I include Blitzkrieg, Play of the Game, Rookies, Starring Role, Sunday School and Talent Show. Inserts in Series II include First Rounders, Rising Stars, Specialists, Comeback Kids, The Main Event, Ultra All-Rookie Team, Ultra Specialists, Ultra Stars, Million Dollar Moments, Memorabilia Offer Card, Lucky 13 Redemption Cards and REEBOK Chase Promotion.

		NM/M
Complete Set (350):		90.00
Complete Series 1 (200):		30.00
Complete Series 2 (150):		60.00
Common Player:		.10
Minor Stars:		.20
Gold Cards:		2X-4X
Platinum Stars:		15X-40X
Platinum Rookies:		5X-10X
Ser. 1, 2 Pack (10):		2.50
Ser. 1, 2 Wax Box (24):		45.00
1	Brett Favre	2.50
2	Ricky Watters	.20
3	Dan Marino	2.00
4	Bryan Still	.10
5	Chester McGlockton	.10
6	Tim Biakabutuka	.20
7	Dave Brown	.10
8	Mike Alstott	.20
9	O.J. McDuffie	.10
10	Mark Brunell	1.25
11	Michael Bates	.10
12	Tyrone Wheatley	.10
13	Eddie George	1.50
14	Kevin Greene	.10
15	Jerris McPhail	.10
16	Harvey Williams	.10
17	Eric Swann	.10
18	Carl Pickens	.10
19	Darrell Davis	.10
20	Charles Way	.10
21	Jamie Asher	.10
22	Qadry Ismail	.10
23	Lawrence Phillips	.20
24	John Friez	.10
25	Dorsey Levens	.20
26	Willie McGinest	.10
27	Chris T. Jones	.10
28	Cortez Kennedy	.10
29	Raymont Harris	.10
30	William Roaf	.10
31	Ted Johnson	.10
32	Tony Martin	.10
33	Jim Everett	.10
34	Ray Zellars	.10
35	Derrick Alexander	.10
36	Leonard Russell	.10
37	William Thomas	.10
38	Karim Abdul-Jabbar	.50
39	Kevin Turner	.10
40	Robert Brooks	.10
41	Kent Graham	.10
42	Tony Brackens	.10
43	Rodney Hampton	.10
44	Drew Bledsoe	1.25
45	Barry Sanders	1.50
46	Tim Brown	.10
47	Reggie White	.20
48	Terry Allen	.10
49	Jim Harbaugh	.10
50	John Elway	.75
51	William Floyd	.10
52	Michael Jackson	.10
53	Larry Centers	.10
54	Emmitt Smith	2.00
55	Bruce Smith	.10
56	Terrell Owens	.50
57	Deion Sanders	.50
58	Neil O'Donnell	.10
59	Kordell Stewart	1.00
60	Bobby Engram	.10
61	Keenan McCardell	.10
62	Ben Coates	.10
63	Curtis Martin	1.75
64	Hugh Douglas	.10
65	Eric Moulds	.20
66	Derrick Thomas	.20
67	Bam Morris	.10
68	Bryan Cox	.10
69	Rob Moore	.10
70	Michael Haynes	.10
71	Brian Mitchell	.10
72	Alex Molden	.10
73	Steve Young	.75
74	Andre Reed	.10
75	Michael Westbrook	.20
76	Eric Metcalf	.10
77	Tony Banks	.30
78	Ken Dilger	.10
79	John Henry Mills	.10
80	Ashley Ambrose	.10
81	Jason Dunn	.10
82	Trent Dilfer	.20
83	Wayne Chrebet	.10
84	Ty Detmer	.10
85	Aeneas Williams	.10
86	Frank Wycheck	.10
87	Jessie Tuggle	.10
88	Steve McNair	1.00
89	Chris Slade	.10
90	Anthony Johnson	.10
91	Simeon Rice	.10
92	Mike Tomczak	.10
93	Sean Jones	.10
94	Wesley Walls	.10
95	Thurman Thomas	.20
96	Scott Mitchell	.10
97	Desmond Howard	.10
98	Chris Warren	.10
99	Glyn Milburn (RB)	.10
100	Vinny Testaverde	.10

No.	Player	Value
101	James Stewart	.10
102	Iheanyi Uwaezuoke	.10
103	Stan Humphries	.10
104	Terance Mathis	.10
105	Thomas Lewis	.10
106	Eddie Kennison	.40
107	Rashaan Salaam	.20
108	Curtis Conway	.10
109	Chris Sanders	.10
110	Marcus Allen	.20
111	Gilbert Brown	.10
112	Jason Sehorn	.10
113	Zach Thomas	.20
114	Bobby Hebert	.10
115	Herman Moore	.20
116	Ray Lewis	.10
117	Darnay Scott	.10
118	Jamal Anderson	.20
119	Keyshawn Johnson	.40
120	Adrian Murrell	.10
121	Sam Mills	.10
122	Irving Fryar	.10
123	Ki-Jana Carter	.10
124	Gus Frerotte	.10
125	Terry Glenn	.50
126	Quentin Coryatt	.10
127	Robert Smith	.10
128	Jeff Blake	.20
129	Natrone Means	.20
130	Isaac Bruce	.30
131	Lamar Lathon	.10
132	Johnnie Morton	.10
133	Jerry Rice	1.25
134	Errict Rhett	.20
135	Junior Seau	.20
136	Joey Galloway	.40
137	Napoleon Kaufman	.10
138	Troy Aikman	1.25
139	Kevin Hardy	.10
140	Jimmy Smith	.10
141	Edgar Bennett	.10
142	Hardy Nickerson	.10
143	Greg Lloyd	.10
144	Dale Carter (WR)	.10
145	Jake Reed	.10
146	Cris Carter	.10
147	Todd Collins	.10
148	Mel Gray	.10
149	Lawyer Milloy	.10
150	Kimble Anders	.10
151	Darick Holmes	.10
152	Bert Emanuel	.10
153	Marshall Faulk	.20
154	Frank Sanders	.10
155	Leeland McElroy	.20
156	Rickey Dudley	.20
157	Tamarick Vanover	.20
158	Kerry Collins	.40
159	Jeff Graham	.10
160	Jerome Bettis	.20
161	Greg Hill	.10
162	John Mobley	.10
163	Michael Irvin	.20
164	Marvin Harrison	.40
165	Jim Schwantz	.10
166	Jermaine Lewis	.10
167	Levon Kirkland	.10
168	Nilo Silvan	.10
169	Ken Norton	.10
170	Yancey Thigpen	.10
171	Antonio Freeman	.20
172	Terry Kirby	.10
173	Brad Johnson	.10
174	*Reidel Anthony*	1.50
175	*Tiki Barber*	3.00
176	*Pat Barnes*	.50
177	*Michael Booker*	.20
178	*Peter Boulware*	.20
179	*Rae Carruth*	1.00
180	*Troy Davis*	.50
181	*Corey Dillon*	5.00
182	*Jim Druckenmiller*	1.00
183	*Warrick Dunn*	2.00
184	*James Farrior*	.20
185	*Yatil Green*	.50
186	*Walter Jones*	.20
187	*Tom Knight*	.20
188	*Sam Madison*	.20
189	*Tyrus McCloud*	.20
190	*Orlando Pace*	.50
191	*Jake Plummer*	2.00
192	*Dwayne Rudd*	.20
193	*Darrell Russell*	.20
194	*Sedrick Shaw*	.50
195	*Shawn Springs*	.50
196	*Bryant Westbrook*	.50
197	*Danny Wuerffel*	.75
198	*Reinard Wilson*	.20
199	Checklist	.10
200	Checklist	.10
201	Rick Mirer	.10
202	Torrance Small	.10
203	Ricky Proehl	.10
204	Will Blackwell	.30
205	Warrick Dunn	.50
206	Rob Johnson	.20
207	Jim Schwantz	.10
208	*Ike Hilliard*	1.00
209	Chris Canty	.10
210	Chris Boniol	.10
211	Jim Druckenmiller	.75
212	*Tony Gonzalez*	1.00
213	Scottie Graham	.10
214	*Byron Hanspard*	.50
215	Gary Brown	.10
216	Darrell Russell	.10
217	Sedrick Shaw	.50
218	Boomer Esiason	.10
219	Peter Boulware	.10
220	Willie Green	.10
221	Dietrich Jells	.10
222	Freddie Jones	.30
223	Eric Metcalf	.10
224	John Henry Mills	.10
225	Michael Timpson	.10
226	Danny Wuerffel	.50
227	Daimon Shelton	.10
228	Henry Ellard	.10
229	Flipper Anderson	.10
230	Hunter Goodwin	.10
231	Jay Graham	.50
232	*Duce Staley*	12.00
233	Lamar Thomas	.10
234	Rod Woodson	.10
235	Zack Crockett	.10
236	Ernie Mills	.10
237	Kyle Brady	.10
238	Jesse Campbell	.10
239	Anthony Miller	.10
240	Michael Haynes	.10
241	Qadry Ismail	.10
242	Tom Knight	.10
243	Brian Manning	.10
244	Derrick Mayes	.10
245	Jamie Sharper	.10
246	Sherman Williams	.10
247	Yatil Green	.30
248	Howard Griffith	.10
249	Brian Blades	.10
250	Mark Chmura	.20
251	Chris Darkins	.10
252	Willie Davis	.10
253	Quinn Early	.10
254	Marc Edwards	.10
255	Charlie Jones	.10
256	Jake Plummer	2.00
257	Heath Shuler	.10
258	Fred Barnett	.10
259	Koy Detmer	.20
260	Michael Booker	.10
261	Chad Brown	.10
262	Garrison Hearst	.20
263	Leon Johnson	.10
264	*Antowain Smith*	2.00
265	*Darnell Autry*	.40
266	Craig Heyward	.10
267	Walter Jones	.10
268	Dexter Coakley	.30
269	Mercury Hayes	.10
270	Brett Perriman	.10
271	Chris Spielman	.10
272	Kevin Greene	.10
273	Kevin Lockett	.10
274	Troy Davis	.30
275	Brent Jones	.10
276	Chris Chandler	.10
277	Bryant Westbrook	.20
278	Desmond Howard	.10
279	Tyrone Hughes	.10
280	Kez McCorvey	.10
281	Stephen Davis	.10
282	Steve Everitt	.10
283	Andre Hastings	.10
284	*Marcus Robinson*	10.00
285	Donnell Woolford	.10
286	Mario Bates	.10
287	Corey Dillon	1.25
288	Jackie Harris	.10
289	Lorenzo Neal	.10
290	Anthony Pleasant	.10
291	Andre Rison	.10
292	Amani Toomer	.10
293	Eric Turner	.10
294	Elvis Grbac	.10
295	Cris Dishman	.10
296	Tom Carter	.10
297	Mark Carrier	.10
298	Orlando Pace	.20
299	Jay Riemersma	.10
300	Daryl Johnston	.10
301	Joey Kent	.30
302	Ronnie Harmon	.10
303	Raghib Ismail	.10
304	Terrell Davis	1.25
305	Sean Dawkins	.10
306	Jeff George	.20
307	David Palmer	.10
308	Dwayne Rudd	.10
309	J.J. Stokes	.20
310	James Farrior	.10
311	William Fuller	.10
312	George Jones	.20
313	John Allred	.10
314	Tony Graziani	.10
315	Jeff Hostetler	.10
316	Keith Poole	.10
317	Neil Smith	.10
318	Steve Tasker	.10
319	Mike Vrabel	.10
320	Pat Barnes	.30
321	James Hundon	.10
322	O.J. Santiago	.10
323	Billy Davis	.10
324	Shawn Springs	.20
325	Reinard Wilson	.10
326	Charles Johnson	.10
327	Micheal Barrow	.10
328	*Derrick Mason*	3.00
329	Muhsin Muhammad	.10
330	*David LaFleur*	.50
331	Reidel Anthony	.75
332	Tiki Barber	1.00
333	Ray Buchanan	.10
334	John Elway	.75
335	Alvin Harper	.10
336	Damon Jones	.10
337	*Dedric Ward*	3.00
338	Jim Everett	.10
339	Jon Harris	.10
340	Warren Moon	.10
341	Rae Carruth	.50
342	John Mobley	.10
343	Tyrone Poole	.10
344	Mike Cherry	.10
345	Horace Copeland	.10
346	Deon Figures	.10
347	Antowuan Wyatt	.10
348	Tommy Vardell	.10
349	Checklist	.10
350	Checklist	.10

A card number in parenthese ( ) indicates the set is unnumbered.

1997 Ultra Gold

Gold Medallions ran parallel to the Ultra Football set, and included 198 cards from Series I and 148 cards from Series II (the two checklist cards in each series were not issued in Gold Medallion versions). The foil on the front of the card was printed in gold versus the silver foil used on regular-issue cards. In addition, the words "Gold Medallion Edition" were printed across the front bottom right of the cards, while card backs carried a "G" prefix on the card number. Gold Medallion parallels were issued at a rate of one per pack in both Series.

Gold Stars:	2X-4X
Gold Rookies:	2X

1997 Ultra Platinum

Platinum Medallions were a parallel set to the Ultra Football set and included 198 cards from Series I and 148 from Series II (the two checklist cards in each series were not issued in Platinum Medallion versions). A prismatic foil is used on the front of the card versus the silver foil used on regular-issue cards. In addition, the words "Platinum Medallion Edition" were printed across the front bottom right of the cards, while card backs carried a "P" prefix on the card number. Platinum Medallion parallels were issued at a rate of one per 100 hobby packs in both Series.

	NM/M
Platinum Stars:	15X-40X
Platinum Rookies:	5X-10X

1997 Ultra All-Rookie Team

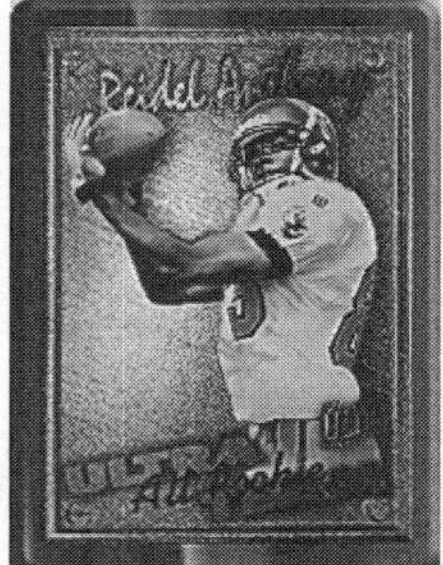

This 12-card insert features the top rookies of 1997. An action shot of the players is set on a golden plaque. The cards were inserted once per 18 packs in Series II.

		NM/M
Complete Set (12):		20.00
Common Player:		.50
Minor Stars:		1.00
1	Antowain Smith	2.00
2	Jay Graham	.50
3	Ike Hilliard	2.00
4	Warrick Dunn	5.00
5	Tony Gonzalez	.50
6	David LaFleur	.50
7	Reidel Anthony	1.00
8	Rae Carruth	1.00
9	Byron Hanspard	.50
10	Joey Kent	.50
11	Kevin Lockett	.50
12	Jake Plummer	4.00

1997 Ultra Blitzkrieg

Inserted 1:6 packs, the 18-card set featured "Blitzkrieg" printed along the left border of the card. The player's photo is superimposed over a multiple-photo background. The player's name is printed vertically along the upper right border. The Ultra logo is in the lower right. The backs have the player's photo on the left, with his name in the upper right. His highlights appear to the right of the photo. The card number, which is labeled "of 18," is printed in the lower right. The Ultra Blitzkrieg die-cut parallel set was inserted 1:36 packs. The die-cut was featured on the left border. This insert was only available in Series I.

		NM/M
Complete Set (18):		25.00
Common Player:		.50
Die-Cut Cards:		2X-3X
1	Eddie George	2.00
2	Terry Glenn	2.00
3	Karim Abdul-Jabbar	1.00
4	Emmitt Smith	3.00
5	Dan Marino	4.00
6	Brett Favre	4.00
7	Keyshawn Johnson	.50
8	Curtis Martin	2.00
9	Marvin Harrison	2.00
10	Barry Sanders	3.00
11	Jerry Rice	3.00
12	Terrell Davis	2.00
13	Troy Aikman	3.00
14	Drew Bledsoe	3.00
15	John Elway	3.00
16	Kordell Stewart	1.00
17	Kerry Collins	1.00
18	Steve Young	2.00

1997 Ultra Comeback Kids

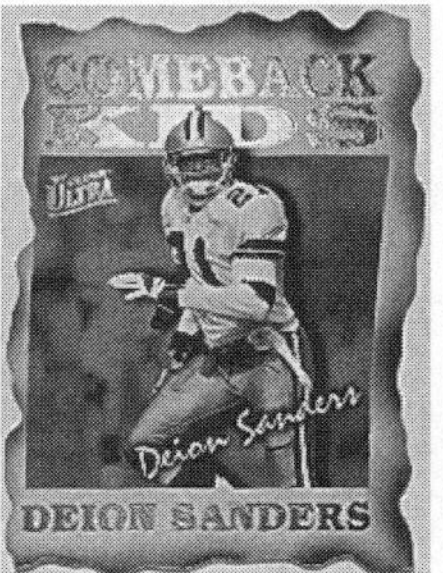

Comeback Kids contains 10 cards featuring the NFL's top go-to players. The cards are designed as die-cut wanted posters. They were inserted 1:8 in Series II.

		NM/M
Complete Set (10):		15.00
Common Player:		.50
1	Dan Marino	5.00
2	Barry Sanders	4.00
3	Jerry Rice	4.00
4	John Elway	4.00
5	Steve Young	3.00
6	Deion Sanders	1.00
7	Mark Brunell	1.00
8	Tim Biakabutuka	.50
9	Tony Banks	.50
10	Terry Allen	.50

1997 Ultra First Rounders

This 12-card insert features first-round draft picks who made an immediate impression in 1997. The card fronts feature an action shot of the player against a gridiron background. The insertion rate was 1:4 in Series II.

		NM/M
Complete Set (12):		6.00
Common Player:		.25
Minor Stars:		.50
1	Antowain Smith	1.00
2	Rae Carruth	.25
3	Peter Boulware	.25
4	Shawn Springs	.50
5	Bryant Westbrook	.25
6	Orlando Pace	.50
7	Jim Druckenmiller	.50
8	Yatil Green	1.00
9	Reidel Anthony	1.00
10	Ike Hilliard	2.00
11	Darrell Russell	.25
12	Warrick Dunn	4.00

1997 Ultra Play of the Game

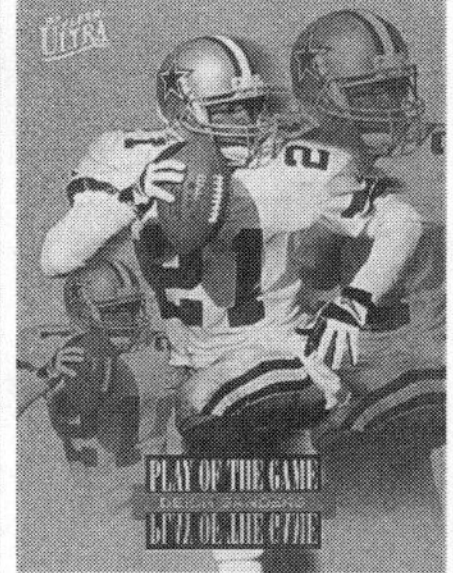

The 10-card set was inserted 1:8 packs in Series I. The front features three player photos. The back has information on a specific game that the player excelled in.

		NM/M
Complete Set (10):		10.00
Common Player:		1.00
1	Deion Sanders	1.00
2	Jerry Rice	3.00
3	Michael Westbrook	1.00
4	Steve McNair	3.00
5	Marshall Faulk	2.00
6	Terrell Davis	3.00
7	Mark Brunell	2.00
8	Isaac Bruce	2.00
9	Tony Banks	1.00
10	Jamal Anderson	1.00

1997 Ultra Reebok Bronze

The Reebok Chase Promotion consisted of parallel versions of 15 basic cards. The parallels featured a Reebok logo on the back and came in three tiers of scarcity (bronze, silver , and gold). The cards were inserted one per pack in Series II.

		NM/M
Complete Bronze Set (15):		3.00
Common Bronze Player:		.20
Gold Cards:		3X
Green Cards:		5X-10x
Red Cards:		3X-5X
Silver Cards:		1X
	Torrance Small	.20
	Jim Schwantz	.20
	Chris Boniol	.20
	Eric Metcalf	.20
	Jesse Campbell	.20
	Qadry Ismail	.20
	Brett Perriman	.20
	Chris Spielman	.20
	Desmond Howard	.20
	Steve Everitt	.20
	Lorenzo Neal	.20
	Neil Smith	.20
	Steve Tasker	.20
	John Elway	.75
	Tyrone Poole	.20

1997 Ultra Rising Stars

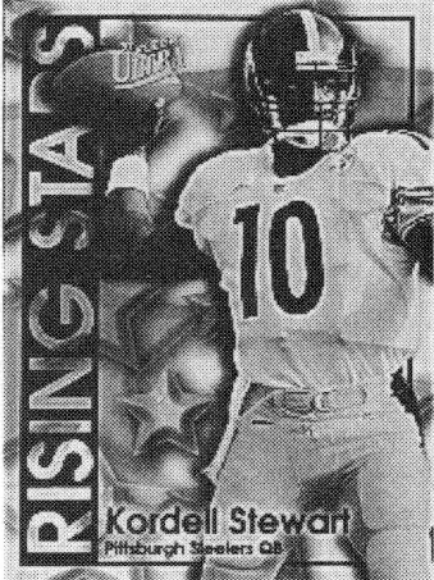

Rising Stars were inserted 1:4 in Series II. The 10 cards feature a soon-to-be star player. The front has an action shot with a star-filled background.

		NM/M
Complete Set (10):		6.00
Common Player:		.50
Minor Stars:		1.00
1	Keyshawn Johnson	1.00
2	Terrell Davis	2.00
3	Kordell Stewart	1.00
4	Kerry Collins	1.00
5	Joey Galloway	1.00
6	Steve McNair	2.00
7	Jamal Anderson	.50
8	Michael Westbrook	.50
9	Marshall Faulk	2.00
10	Isaac Bruce	1.00

1997 Ultra Rookies

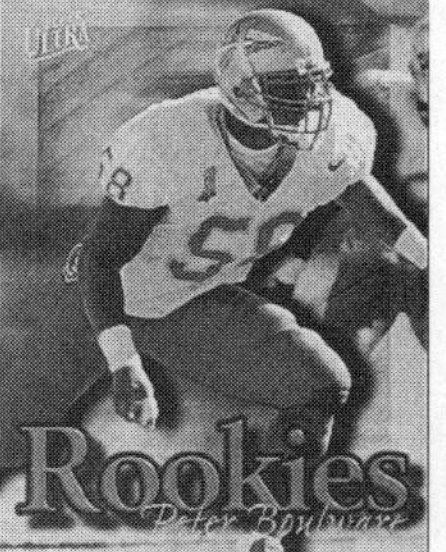

The 12-card set was inserted 1:4 packs. The player is featured in his college photo on the front and superimposed over a purple and blue background. "Rookies" is printed in green at the bottom, with his name in silver foil in the lower right. The backs, which are numbered "of 12," features "Rookies" in the upper left and his highlights below. His photo and name are printed along the right side. The Ultra Rookies parallel version was seeded 1:18 packs. The parallel cards feature a sculpted-embossed player image over a matte finish background. Rookies were only available in Series I.

		NM/M
Complete Set (12):		6.00
Common Player:		.50
Gold Embossed:		1X-2X
1	Darnell Autry	1.00
2	Orlando Pace	1.50
3	Peter Boulware	.50
4	Shawn Springs	.50
5	Bryant Westbrook	.50
6	Rae Carruth	.50
7	Jim Druckenmiller	.50
8	Yatil Green	1.00
9	James Farrior	.50
10	Dwayne Rudd	.50
11	Darrell Russell	.50
12	Warrick Dunn	3.00

1997 Ultra Specialists

This 18-card insert features top players on a die-cut card that looks like a manilla file folder. The cards were inserted 1:6 in Series II. Ultra Specialists parallels the regular insert. Inserted 1:36, the die-cut folders open up to reveal an oversized photo. Ultra Specialists also appeared only in Series II.

		NM/M
Complete Set (18):		40.00
Common Player:		1.00
Ultra Specialists:		3X
1	Eddie George	3.00
2	Terry Glenn	3.00
3	Karim Abdul-Jabbar	1.00
4	Emmitt Smith	5.00
5	Brett Favre	6.00
6	Mark Brunell	2.00
7	Curtis Martin	3.00
8	Kerry Collins	1.00
9	Marvin Harrison	2.00
10	Jerry Rice	4.00
11	Tony Martin	1.00
12	Terrell Davis	4.00
13	Troy Aikman	4.00
14	Drew Bledsoe	4.00
15	John Elway	4.00
16	Kordell Stewart	2.00
17	Keyshawn Johnson	1.00
18	Steve Young	3.00

1997 Ultra Starring Role

The 10-card set was inserted 1:288 packs. The acrylic die-cut cards feature a silver-foil stamp on the front. The insert was featured in Series I.

		NM/M
Complete Set (10):		60.00
Common Player:		2.00
1	Emmitt Smith	10.00
2	Barry Sanders	10.00
3	Curtis Martin	6.00
4	Dan Marino	12.00
5	Keyshawn Johnson	2.00
6	Marvin Harrison	4.00
7	Terry Glenn	3.00
8	Eddie George	6.00
9	Brett Favre	12.00
10	Karim Abdul-Jabbar	2.00

1997 Ultra Stars

This 10-card set features top players on a pattern holofoil background. Inserted 1:288 and found in Series II.

		NM/M
Complete Set (10):		50.00
Common Player:		3.00
1	Emmitt Smith	8.00
2	Barry Sanders	8.00
3	Curtis Martin	6.00
4	Dan Marino	10.00
5	Mark Brunell	3.00
6	Marvin Harrison	3.00
7	Terry Glenn	3.00
8	Eddie George	5.00
9	Brett Favre	10.00
10	Karim Abdul-Jabbar	3.00

1997 Ultra Sunday School

Inserted 1:8 packs, the 10-card chase set features a player photo superimposed over a black background on the left side of the card. Also included in the background is a play diagramed in silver foil. The player's name is printed in silver foil in the lower left, while the Sunday School logo is printed vertically along the right border. The backs, numbered "of 10," have the player's photo on the left side, with his name, highlights and card number to the right of it. Only in Series I.

		NM/M
Complete Set (10):		10.00
Common Player:		.50
1	Marvin Harrison	2.00
2	Barry Sanders	4.00
3	Troy Aikman	3.00
4	Drew Bledsoe	3.00
5	John Elway	4.00
6	Kordell Stewart	1.00
7	Kerry Collins	1.00
8	Steve Young	3.00
9	Deion Sanders	1.00
10	Joey Galloway	.50

1997 Ultra Talent Show

Inserted 1:4 packs, this 10-card set features the player photo superimposed over a multicolored background. The Talent Show logo appears in gold in the lower left, with the player's name in the lower right. The back, numbered "of 10," features a full-bleed photo of the player. Printed along the left border inside a box is the player's name, his highlights and card number. This insert appeared in Series I.

		NM/M
Complete Set (10):		6.00
Common Player:		.50
1	Joey Galloway	1.00
2	Steve McNair	2.00
3	Marshall Faulk	2.00
4	Isaac Bruce	1.50
5	Michael Westbrook	.75
6	Zach Thomas	1.25
7	Jamal Anderson	.75
8	Mike Alstott	.75
9	Mark Brunell	2.00
10	Eddie Kennison	1.00

1997 Ultra The Main Event

This 10-card insert features headline making players. The cards are printed on canvas stock and resemble a top view of a boxing ring. The Main Event was inserted 1:8 in Series II.

		NM/M
Complete Set (10):		15.00
Common Player:		1.00
1	Dan Marino	4.00
2	Barry Sanders	3.00
3	Jerry Rice	2.00
4	Drew Bledsoe	3.00
5	John Elway	3.00
6	Troy Aikman	3.00
7	Deion Sanders	1.00
8	Joey Galloway	1.00
9	Steve McNair	1.00
10	Marshall Faulk	2.00

1998 Ultra

Ultra Football was released in two series in 1998 and contained a total of 425 cards. Series I had 197 veterans, three checklists and a 25-card 1998 Rookies subset seeded one per three packs. Series II had 132 player cards, 25 '98 Greats, three checklists and 40 rookies seeded one per three packs. Cards featured a full color shot of the player, with his name embossed foil writing in the lower right corner. Every card appears in three different parallels - Gold Medallion, Platinum Medallion and Masterpieces. Inserts in Series I include: Canton Classics, Flair Showcase Preview, Next Century, Sensational Sixty, Shots and Touchdown Kings. Inserts in Series II include: Rush Hour, Damage, Inc., Caught in the Draft, Indefensible and Exclamation Points.

		NM/M
Complete Set (425):		175.00
Complete Series 1 (225):		125.00
Complete Series 2 (200):		60.00
Common Player:		.15
Minor Stars:		.30
Common Rookie (201-225):		2.00
Common Rookie (386-425):		1.00
Inserted 1:3		
Gold Cards:		2X-4X
Inserted 1:1 Hobby		
Gold Rookies:		1.5X
Inserted 1:24 Hobby		
Platinum Cards:		40X-80X
Production 98 Sets		
Platinum Rookies:		4X-8X
Production 66 Sets		
Series 1 Pack (10):		6.00
Series 1 Wax Box (24):		100.00
Series 2 Pack (10):		3.00
Series 2 Wax Box (24):		45.00
1	Barry Sanders	2.00
2	Brett Favre	2.50
3	Napoleon Kaufman	.50
4	Robert Smith	.30
5	Terry Allen	.15
6	Vinny Testaverde	.15
7	William Floyd	.15
8	Carl Pickens	.15
9	Antonio Freeman	.30
10	Ben Coates	.15
11	Elvis Grbac	.15
12	Kerry Collins	.30
13	Orlando Pace	.15
14	Steve Broussard	.15
15	Terance Mathis	.15
16	Tiki Barber	.30
17	Cris Carter	.15
18	Derrick Alexander	.15
19	Eric Metcalf	.15
20	Jeff George	.30
21	Leslie Shepherd	.15
22	Natrone Means	.30
23	Scott Mitchell	.15
24	Adrian Murrell	.15
25	Gilbert Brown	.15
26	Jimmy Smith	.15
27	Mark Bruener	.15
28	Troy Aikman	1.00
29	Warrick Dunn	1.50
30	Jay Graham	.15
31	Craig Whelihan	.15
32	Ed McCaffrey	.15
33	Jamie Asher	.15
34	John Randle	.15
35	Michael Jackson	.15
36	Rickey Dudley	.15
37	Sean Dawkins	.15
38	Andre Rison	.15
39	Bert Emanuel	.15
40	Jeff Blake	.30
41	Curtis Conway	.15
42	Eddie Kennison	.30
43	James McKnight	.15
44	Rae Carruth	.15
45	Tito Wooten	.15
46	Cris Dishman	.15
47	Ernie Conwell	.15
48	Fred Lane	.15
49	Jamal Anderson	.15
50	Lake Dawson	.15
51	Michael Strahan	.15
52	Reggie White	.30
53	Trent Dilfer	.30
54	Troy Brown	.15
55	Wesley Walls	.15
56	Chidi Ahanotu	.15
57	Dwayne Rudd	.15
58	Jerry Rice	1.25
59	Johnnie Morton	.15
60	Sherman Williams	.15
61	Steve McNair	.75
62	Yancey Thigpen	.15
63	Chris Chandler	.15
64	Dexter Coakley	.15
65	Horace Copeland	.15
66	Jerald Moore	.15
67	Leon Johnson	.15
68	Mark Chmura	.30
69	Micheal Barrow	.15
70	Muhsin Muhammad	.15
71	Terry Glenn	.30
72	Tony Brackens	.15
73	Chad Scott	.15
74	Glenn Foley	.15
75	Keenan McCardell	.15
76	Peter Boulware	.15
77	Reidel Anthony	.30
78	William Henderson	.15
79	Tony Martin	.15
80	Tony Gonzalez	.15
81	Charlie Jones	.15
82	Chris Gedney	.15
83	Chris Calloway	.15
84	Dale Carter	.15
85	Ki-Jana Carter	.15
86	Shawn Springs	.15
87	Antowain Smith	.75
88	Eric Turner	.15
89	John Mobley	.15
90	Ken Dilger	.15
91	Bobby Hoying	.15
92	Curtis Martin	1.00
93	Drew Bledsoe	1.00
94	Gary Brown	.15
95	Marvin Harrison	.30
96	Todd Collins	.15
97	Chris Warren	.15
98	Danny Kanell	.15
99	Tony McGee	.15
100	Rod Smith	.15
101	Frank Sanders	.15
102	Irving Fryar	.15
103	Marcus Allen	.30
104	Marshall Faulk	.30
105	Bruce Smith	.15
106	Charlie Garner	.15
107	Jim Harbaugh	.30
108	Randal Hill	.15
109	Ricky Proehl	.15
110	Rob Moore	.15
111	Shannon Sharpe	.15
112	Warren Moon	.15
113	Zach Thomas	.15
114	Dan Marino	2.00
115	Duce Staley	.15
116	Eric Swann	.15
117	Kenny Holmes	.15
118	Merton Hanks	.15
119	Raymont Harris	.15
120	Terrell Davis	1.00
121	Thurman Thomas	.30
122	Wayne Martin	.15
123	Charles Way	.15
124	Chuck Smith	.15
125	Corey Dillon	1.00
126	Darnell Autry	.15
127	Isaac Bruce	.30
128	Joey Galloway	.30
129	Kimble Anders	.15
130	Aeneas Williams	.15
131	Andre Hastings	.15
132	Chad Lewis	.15
133	J.J. Stokes	.15
134	John Elway	1.00
135	Karim Abdul-Jabbar	.30
136	Ken Harvey	.15
137	Robert Brooks	.15
138	Rodney Thomas	.15
139	James Stewart	.15
140	Billy Joe Hobert	.15
141	Frank Wycheck	.15
142	Jake Plummer	1.50
143	Jerris McPhail	.15
144	Kordell Stewart	1.25
145	Terrell Owens	.30
146	Willie Green	.15
147	Anthony Miller	.15
148	Courtney Hawkins	.15
149	Larry Centers	.15
150	Gus Frerotte	.15
151	O.J. McDuffie	.15
152	Ray Zellars	.15
153	Terry Kirby	.15
154	Tommy Vardell	.15
155	Willie Davis	.15
156	Chris Canty	.15
157	Byron Hanspard	.15
158	Chris Penn	.15
159	Damon Jones	.15
160	Derrick Mayes	.15
161	Emmitt Smith	2.00
162	Keyshawn Johnson	.15
163	Mike Alstott	.50
164	Tom Carter	.15
165	Tony Banks	.30
166	Bryant Westbrook	.15
167	Chris Sanders	.15
168	Deion Sanders	.50
169	Garrison Hearst	.15
170	Jason Taylor	.15
171	Jerome Bettis	.30
172	John Lynch	.15
173	Troy Davis	.15
174	Freddie Jones	.15
175	Herman Moore	.30
176	Jake Reed	.15
177	Mark Brunell	1.00
178	Ray Lewis	.15
179	Stephen Davis	.15
180	Tim Brown	.15
181	Willie McGinest	.15
182	Andre Reed	.15
183	Darrien Gordon	.15
184	David Palmer	.15
185	James Jett	.15
186	Junior Seau	.15
187	Zack Crockett	.15
188	Brad Johnson	.30
189	Charles Johnson	.15
190	Eddie George	1.25
191	Jermaine Lewis	.15
192	Michael Irvin	.30
193	Reggie Brown	.15
194	Steve Young	.50
195	Warren Sapp	.15
196	Wayne Chrebet	.15
197	David Dunn	.15
198	Dorsey Levens CL	.15
199	Troy Aikman CL	.30
200	John Elway CL	.30
201	*Peyton Manning*	20.00
202	*Ryan Leaf*	4.00
203	*Charles Woodson*	5.00
204	*Andre Wadsworth*	3.00
205	*Brian Simmons*	3.00
206	*Curtis Enis*	4.00
207	*Randy Moss*	15.00
208	*Germane Crowell*	4.00
209	*Greg Ellis*	2.00
210	*Kevin Dyson*	4.00
211	*Skip Hicks*	4.00
212	*Alonzo Mayes*	2.00
213	*Robert Edwards*	4.00
214	*Fred Taylor*	6.00
215	*Robert Holcombe*	3.00
216	*John Dutton*	2.00
217	*Vonnie Holliday*	3.00
218	*Tim Dwight*	4.00
219	*Tavian Banks*	3.00
220	*Marcus Nash*	3.00
221	*Jason Peter*	2.00
222	*Michael Myers*	2.00
223	*Takeo Spikes*	2.00
224	*Kivuusama Mays*	2.00
225	*Jacquez Green*	4.00
226	Doug Flutie	2.50
227	Ike Hillard	.15
228	Craig Heyward	.15
229	Kevin Hardy	.15
230	Jason Dunn	.15
231	Billy Davis	.15
232	Chester McGlockton	.15
233	Sean Gilbert	.15
234	Bert Emanuel	.15
235	Keith Byars	.15
236	Tyrone Wheatley	.15
237	Ricky Proehl	.15
238	Michael Bates	.15
239	Derrick Alexander	.15
240	Harvey Williams	.15
241	Mike Pritchard	.15
242	Paul Justin	.15
243	Jeff Hostetler	.15
244	Eric Moulds	.30
245	Jeff Burris	.15
246	Gary Brown	.15
247	Antwuan Wyatt	.15
248	Dan Wilkinson	.15
249	Chris Warren	.15
250	Lawrence Phillips	.15
251	Eric Metcalf	.15
252	Pat Swilling	.15
253	Lamar Smith	.15
254	Quinn Early	.15
255	Carlester Crumpler	.15
256	Eric Bieniemy	.15
257	Aaron Bailey	.15
258	Gabe Wilkins	.15
259	Rod Woodson	.15
260	Ricky Whittle	.15
261	Iheanyi Uwaezuoke	.15
262	Heath Shuler	.15
263	Darren Sharper	.15
264	John Henry Mills	.15
265	Marco Battaglia	.15
266	Yancey Thigpen	.15
267	Irv Smith	.15
268	Jamie Sharper	.15
269	Marcus Robinson	5.00
270	Dorsey Levens	.30
271	Qadry Ismail	.15
272	Desmond Howard	.15
273	Webster Slaughter	.15
274	Eugene Robinson	.15
275	Bill Romanowski	.15
276	Vincent Brisby	.15
277	Errict Rhett	.15
278	Albert Connell	.15
279	Thomas Lewis	.15
280	John Farquhar	.15
281	Marc Edwards	.15
282	Tyrone Davis	.50
283	Eric Allen	.15
284	Aaron Glenn	.15
285	Roosevelt Potts	.15
286	Kez McCorvey	.15
287	Joey Kent	.15
288	Jim Druckenmiller	.30
289	Sean Dawkins	.15
290	Edgar Bennett	.15
291	Vinny Testaverde	.30
292	Chris Slade	.15
293	Lamar Lathon	.15
294	Jackie Harris	.15
295	Jim Harbaugh	.30
296	Rob Fredrickson	.15
297	Ty Detmer	.15
298	Karl Williams	.15
299	Troy Drayton	.15
300	Curtis Martin	.75
301	Tamarick Vanover	.15
302	Lorenzo Neal	.15
303	John Hall	.15
304	Kevin Greene	.15
305	Bryan Still	.15
306	Neil Smith	.15
307	Mark Rypien	.15
308	Shawn Jefferson	.15
309	Aaron Taylor	.15
310	Sedrick Shaw	.15
311	O.J. Santiago	.15
312	Kevin Abrams	.15
313	Dana Stubblefield	.15
314	Daryl Johnston	.15
315	Yatil Green	.15
316	Jeff Graham	.15
317	Mario Bates	.15
318	Adrian Murrell	.30
319	Larry Brown	.15
320	Jahine Arnold	.15
321	Justin Armour	.15
322	Ricky Watters	.30
323	Lamont Warren	.15
324	Mack Strong	.15
325	Darnay Scott	.15
326	Brian Mitchell	.15
327	Rob Johnson	.30
328	Kent Graham	.15
329	Hugh Douglas	.15
330	Simeon Rice	.15
331	Corey Holliday	.15
332	Randall Cunningham	.75
333	Steve Atwater	.15
334	Latario Rachel	.15
335	Tony Martin	.15
336	Leroy Hoard	.15
337	Howard Griffith	.15
338	Kevin Lockett	.15
339	William Floyd	.15
340	Jerry Ellison	.15
341	Kyle Brady	.15
342	Michael Westbrook	.15
343	Kevin Turner	.15
344	David LaFleur	.15
345	Robert Jones	.15
346	Dave Brown	.15
347	Kevin Williams	.15
348	Amani Toomer	.15
349	Amp Lee	.15
350	Bryce Paup	.15
351	DeWayne Washington	.15
352	Mercury Hayes	.15
353	Scottie Graham	.15
354	Ray Crockett	.15
355	Ted Washington	.15
356	Pete Mitchell	.15
357	Billy Jenkins	.15
358	Troy Aikman CL	.50
359	Drew Bledsoe CL	.50
360	Steve Young CL	.40
361	Antonio Freeman	.30
362	Antowain Smith	.50
363	Barry Sanders	3.00
364	Bobby Hoying	.15
365	Brett Favre	3.00
366	Corey Dillon	.75
367	Dan Marino	2.00
368	Drew Bledsoe	1.50
369	Eddie George	1.25
370	Emmitt Smith	2.00
371	Herman Moore	.30
372	Jake Plummer	1.00
373	Jerome Bettis	.30
374	Jerry Rice	1.50
375	Joey Galloway	.30
376	John Elway	1.50
377	Kordell Stewart	1.00
378	Mark Brunell	1.00
379	Keyshawn Johnson	.15
380	Steve Young	1.00
381	Steve McNair	.75
382	Terrell Davis	2.00
383	Tim Brown	.15
384	Troy Aikman	1.50
385	Warrick Dunn	1.00
386	Ryan Leaf	2.00
387	*Tony Simmons*	3.00
388	*Chris Howard*	1.00
389	*John Avery*	2.00
390	*Shaun Williams*	1.00
391	*Anthony Simmons*	2.00
392	*Rashaan Shehee*	2.00
393	Robert Holcombe	1.50
394	*Larry Shannon*	1.00
395	Skip Hicks	2.00
396	*Rod Rutledge*	1.00
397	*Donald Hayes*	2.00
398	Curtis Enis	4.00
399	*Mikhael Ricks*	3.00
400	*Brian Griese*	10.00
401	*Michael Pittman*	3.00
402	Jacquez Green	3.00
403	*Jerome Pathon*	3.00
404	*Ahman Green*	15.00
405	Marcus Nash	1.50
406	Randy Moss	10.00
407	*Terry Fair*	3.00
408	*Jammi German*	2.00
409	*Stephen Alexander*	3.00
410	*Grant Wistrom*	1.00
411	*Charlie Batch*	2.00
412	Fred Taylor	4.00
413	*Patrick Johnson*	2.00
414	Robert Edwards	2.00
415	*Keith Brooking*	2.00
416	Peyton Manning	12.00
417	*Duane Starks*	2.00
418	Andre Wadsworth	2.00
419	*Brian Alford*	2.00
420	*Brian Kelly*	1.00
421	*Joe Jurevicius*	2.00
422	*Tebucky Jones*	1.00
423	*R.W. McQuarters*	2.00
424	Kevin Dyson	3.00
425	Charles Woodson	2.00

1998 Ultra Gold Medallion

All 425 cards in Ultra Series I and II were paralleled in Gold Medallion versions. The cards featured a gold tint to the front and were numbered with a "G" suffix. Throughout both series, they were inserted in hobby packs only at a rate of one per pack, except for the rookie subsets in both series which were seeded one per 24 packs.

Gold Medallion Cards:	2X-4X
Gold Medallion Rookies:	1.5X

1998 Ultra Platinum Medallion

All 425 cards in Ultra Series I and II were also available in Platinum Medallion versions. These cards added a platinum tint to the background, showed the player image in black and white and added silver prismatic writing to the player's name. All cards were hobby-only with cards all regular cards sequentially numbered to 98, while the 25-card rookie subset in Series I and the 40-card rookie subset in Series II are numbered to only 66.

Platinum Medallion Cards:	10X-30X
Platinum Medallion Rookies:	3X-6X

1998 Ultra Canton Classics

Canton Classics features 10 future Hall of Famers on cards enhanced with 23 karat gold coating and embossing, with an etched border. Backs are numbered with a "CC" suffix and feature an off-color shot of the player again along with some career highlights. These were inserted one per 288 packs.

		NM/M
Complete Set (10):		100.00
Common Player:		5.00
1	Terrell Davis	10.00
2	Brett Favre	15.00
3	John Elway	10.00
4	Barry Sanders	12.00
5	Eddie George	6.00
6	Jerry Rice	10.00
7	Emmitt Smith	12.00
8	Dan Marino	15.00
9	Troy Aikman	10.00
10	Marcus Allen	5.00

1998 Ultra Caught in the Draft

Caught in the Draft singles were found in Series II packs and inserted 1:24. Only rookies who made an impact in '98 were included.

		NM/M
Complete Set (15):		35.00
Common Player:		1.00
Inserted 1:24		
1	Andre Wadsworth	1.00
2	Curtis Enis	1.00
3	Germane Crowell	1.00
4	Peyton Manning	10.00
5	Tavian Banks	1.00
6	Fred Taylor	5.00
7	John Avery	1.00
8	Randy Moss	10.00
9	Robert Edwards	2.00
10	Charles Woodson	3.00
11	Ryan Leaf	1.00
12	Ahman Green	7.00
13	Robert Holcombe	1.00
14	Jacquez Green	1.00
15	Skip Hicks	1.00

1998 Ultra Damage Inc.

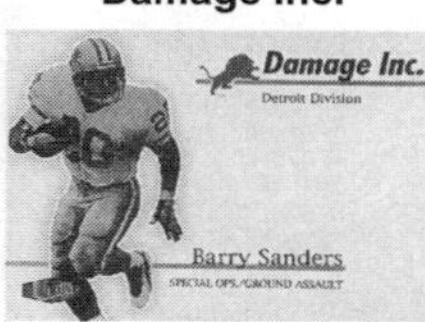

Each single in this set has a business card look to it. Singles were found in Series II packs at 1:72.

		NM/M
Complete Set (15):		40.00
Common Player:		1.00
Inserted 1:72		
1	Terrell Davis	5.00
2	Joey Galloway	2.00
3	Kordell Stewart	2.00
4	Troy Aikman	5.00
5	Barry Sanders	6.00
6	Ryan Leaf	1.00
7	Antonio Freeman	1.00
8	Keyshawn Johnson	2.00
9	Eddie George	4.00
10	Warrick Dunn	3.00
11	Drew Bledsoe	4.00
12	Peyton Manning	5.00
13	Antowain Smith	1.00
14	Brett Favre	6.00
15	Emmitt Smith	5.00

1998 Ultra Exclamation Points

Exclamation Point cards can be found in Series II packs at 1:288. Each single in this 15-card set is printed on plastic and has a pattern holofoil front.

		NM/M
Complete Set (15):		125.00
Common Player:		2.00
Inserted 1:288		
1	Terrell Davis	10.00
2	Brett Favre	15.00
3	John Elway	10.00
4	Barry Sanders	10.00
5	Peyton Manning	10.00
6	Jerry Rice	8.00
7	Emmitt Smith	12.00
8	Dan Marino	12.00
9	Kordell Stewart	3.00
10	Mark Brunell	2.00
11	Ryan Leaf	1.00
12	Corey Dillon	3.00
13	Antowain Smith	2.00
14	Curtis Martin	4.00
15	Deion Sanders	2.00

1998 Ultra Flair Showcase Preview

This 10-card insert previewed the upcoming Flair Showcase set. Cards featured the designs of 1998 Flair Showcase and included the logo. They were inserted one per 144 packs of Series I.

		NM/M
Complete Set (10):		60.00
Common Player:		2.00
1	Kordell Stewart	5.00
2	Mark Brunell	5.00
3	Terrell Davis	8.00
4	Brett Favre	10.00
5	Steve McNair	5.00
6	Curtis Martin	5.00
7	Warrick Dunn	3.00
8	Emmitt Smith	8.00
9	Dan Marino	8.00
10	Corey Dillon	5.00

1998 Ultra Indefensible

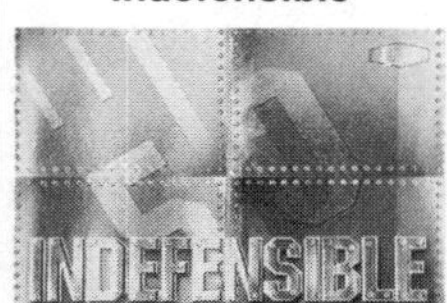

Each card in this 10-card set folds out from its original size and has embossed graphics on the front. Singles were inserted 1:144 packs.

		NM/M
Complete Set (10):		40.00
Common Player:		2.00
Inserted 1:144		
1	Jake Plummer	3.00
2	Mark Brunell	3.00
3	Terrell Davis	5.00
4	Jerry Rice	6.00
5	Barry Sanders	7.00
6	Curtis Martin	3.00
7	Warrick Dunn	3.00
8	Emmitt Smith	7.00
9	Dan Marino	8.00
10	Corey Dillon	4.00

1998 Ultra Next Century

This 15-card insert featured top rookies from 1998 on cards printed on 100 percent gold foil and sculpture embossing. Next Century inserts were numbered with a "NC" suffix and inserted one per 72 packs.

		NM/M
Complete Set (15):		40.00
Common Player:		1.00
1	Ryan Leaf	1.00
2	Peyton Manning	8.00
3	Charles Woodson	4.00
4	Randy Moss	8.00
5	Curtis Enis	1.00
6	Ahman Green	6.00
7	Peter Warrick	1.00
8	Andre Wadsworth	2.00
9	Germane Crowell	1.00
10	Robert Edwards	3.00
11	Tavian Banks	2.00
12	Takeo Spikes	3.00
13	Jacquez Green	4.00
14	Brian Simmons	1.00
15	Alonzo Mayes	1.00

1998 Ultra Rush Hour

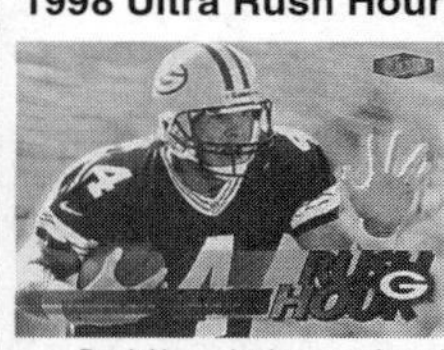

Rush Hour singles were found in Series II packs at a rate of 1:6. Fleer included both veterans and rookies from '98 in this 20-card set.

		NM/M
Complete Set (20):		20.00
Common Player:		.50
Minor Stars:		1.00
Inserted 1:6		
1	Robert Edwards	1.00
2	John Elway	4.00
3	Mike Alstott	1.00
4	Robert Holcombe	1.00
5	Mark Brunell	2.00
6	Deion Sanders	1.00
7	Curtis Martin	2.50
8	Curtis Enis	1.00
9	Dorsey Levens	.50
10	Fred Taylor	2.00
11	John Avery	1.00
12	Eddie George	2.00
13	Jake Plummer	2.00
14	Andre Wadsworth	.50
15	Fred Lane	.50
16	Corey Dillon	2.50
17	Brett Favre	6.00
18	Kordell Stewart	2.00
19	Steve McNair	3.00
20	Warrick Dunn	3.00

1998 Ultra Sensational Sixty

This 60-card insert was available only in retail packs at a rate of one per pack. These were numbered with a "SS" suffix and found in Series I.

		NM/M
Complete Set (60):		20.00
Common Player:		.25
Minor Stars:		.50
Inserted 1:1 Retail		
1	Karim Abdul-Jabbar	.50
2	Troy Aikman	2.00
3	Terry Allen	.25
4	Mike Alstott	.50
5	Tony Banks	.50
6	Jerome Bettis	.50
7	Drew Bledsoe	1.50
8	Peter Boulware	.25
9	Robert Brooks	.25
10	Tim Brown	.25
11	Isaac Bruce	.50
12	Mark Brunell	1.00
13	Cris Carter	.50
14	Kerry Collins	.50
15	Curtis Conway	.25
16	Terrell Davis	3.00
17	Troy Davis	.25
18	Trent Dilfer	.50
19	Corey Dillon	1.25
20	Warrick Dunn	1.50
21	John Elway	2.00
22	Bert Emanuel	.25
23	Brett Favre	4.00
24	Antonio Freeman	.50
25	Gus Frerotte	.25
26	Joey Galloway	.50
27	Eddie George	1.50
28	Jeff George	.50
29	Elvis Grbac	.25
30	Marvin Harrison	.50
31	Bobby Hoying	.25
32	Michael Irvin	.50
33	Brad Johnson	.50
34	Keyshawn Johnson	.50
35	Dan Marino	3.00
36	Curtis Martin	.50
37	Tony Martin	.25
38	Keenan McCardell	.25
39	Steve McNair	.50
40	Warren Moon	.50
41	Herman Moore	.50
42	Johnnie Morton	.25
43	Terrell Owens	.50
44	Carl Pickens	.50
45	Jake Plummer	1.50
46	Jerry Rice	2.00
47	Andre Rison	.25
48	Barry Sanders	3.00
49	Deion Sanders	.50
50	Junior Seau	.25
51	Shannon Sharpe	.50
52	Antowain Smith	.50
53	Emmitt Smith	3.00
54	Jimmy Smith	.25
55	Robert Smith	.50
56	Kordell Stewart	1.50
57	Jeff Blake	.25
58	Charles Way	.25
59	Reggie White	.50
60	Steve Young	1.25

A player's name in *italic* type indicates a rookie card.

1998 Ultra Shots

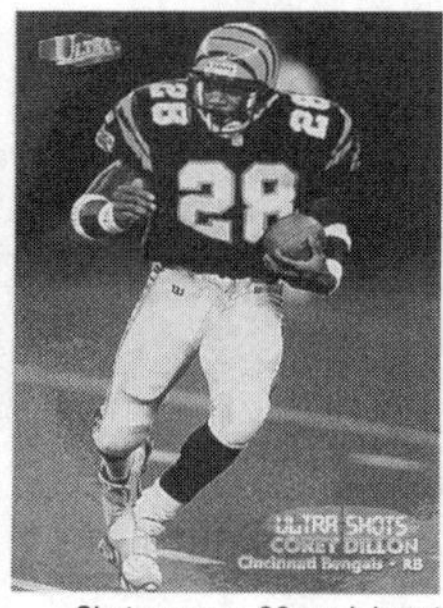

Shots was a 20-card insert that allowed photographers to discuss the shot that is captured on the card front. These were numbered with a "US" suffix and inserted one per six packs of Series I.

		NM/M
Complete Set (20):		15.00
Common Player:		.50
Minor Stars:		1.00
1	Deion Sanders	1.00
2	Corey Dillon	3.00
3	Mike Alstott	1.00
4	Jake Plummer	2.00
5	Antowain Smith	1.00
6	Kordell Stewart	2.00
7	Curtis Martin	2.00
8	Bobby Hoying	.50
9	Kerry Collins	1.00
10	Herman Moore	1.00
11	Terry Glenn	1.00
12	Eddie George	2.00
13	Drew Bledsoe	4.00
14	Steve McNair	1.00
15	Jerry Rice	4.00
16	Trent Dilfer	.50
17	Joey Galloway	1.00
18	Dan Marino	5.00
19	Barry Sanders	5.00
20	Warrick Dunn	2.00

1998 Ultra Top 30

This retail exclusive insert could be found in Retail Series II packs at a rate of 1:1.

		NM/M
Complete Set (30):		12.00
Common Player:		.25
1	Warrick Dunn	.75
2	Troy Aikman	2.00
3	Trent Dilfer	.50
4	Tony Banks	.50
5	Tim Brown	.50
6	Terrell Davis	3.00
7	Steve McNair	.75
8	Steve Young	1.50
9	Mark Brunell	1.00
10	Kordell Stewart	1.00
11	Keyshawn Johnson	.75
12	John Elway	2.00
13	Joey Galloway	.50
14	Jerry Rice	2.00
15	Jerome Bettis	.50
16	Jake Plummer	1.50
17	Emmitt Smith	3.00
18	Eddie George	.75
19	Drew Bledsoe	1.50
20	Dan Marino	3.00
21	Curtis Martin	1.00
22	Curtis Conway	.25
23	Cris Carter	.50
24	Corey Dillon	.75
25	Carl Pickens	.25
26	Brett Favre	4.00
27	Bobby Hoying	.25
28	Barry Sanders	3.00
29	Antowain Smith	.50
30	Antonio Freeman	.50

1998 Ultra Touchdown Kings

This die-cut insert showcased 15 players on an embossed design. Cards were numbered on the back with a "TK" suffix and inserted one per 24 packs of Series I.

		NM/M
Complete Set (15):		35.00
Common Player:		1.00
Minor Stars:		2.00
1	Terrell Davis	4.00
2	Joey Galloway	2.00
3	Kordell Stewart	2.00
4	Corey Dillon	3.00
5	Barry Sanders	5.00
6	Cris Carter	1.00
7	Antonio Freeman	1.00
8	Mike Alstott	1.00
9	Eddie George	2.00
10	Warrick Dunn	2.00
11	Drew Bledsoe	4.00
12	Karim Abdul-Jabbar	1.00
13	Mark Brunell	2.00
14	Brett Favre	5.00
15	Emmitt Smith	4.00

1999 Ultra

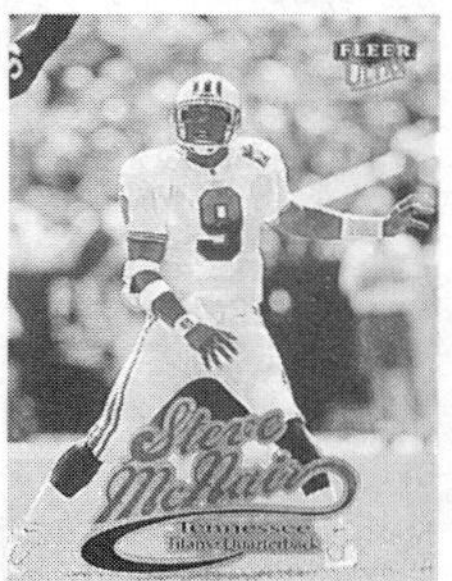

Ultra Football is a 300-card set with 50 short-printed cards. The short prints are 40 Rookies (1:4) and 10 Super Bowl XXXIII (1:8). Ultra has two parallel sets with Gold and Platinum Medallions. Other inserts include: As Good As It Gets, Caught in the Draft, Counterparts, Damage Inc. and Over the Top.

		NM/M
Complete Set (300):		200.00
Common Player:		.15
Minor Stars:		.30
Common Rookie (261-300):		1.50
Inserted 1:4		
Common Back 2 Back:		3.00
Inserted 1:8		
Pack (10):		2.25
Wax Box (24):		40.00
1	Terrell Davis	1.50
2	Courtney Hawkins	.15
3	Cris Carter	.50
4	Darnay Scott	.15
5	Darrell Green	.15
6	Jimmy Smith	.30
7	Doug Flutie	.75
8	Michael Jackson	.15
9	Warren Sapp	.15
10	Greg Hill	.15
11	Karim Abdul	.50
12	Greg Ellis	.15
13	Dan Marino	2.00
14	Napoleon Kaufman	.50
15	Peyton Manning	2.50
16	Simeon Rice	.15
17	Tony Simmons	.30
18	Carlester Crumpler	.15
19	Charles Johnson	.15
20	Derrick Alexander	.15
21	Kent Graham	.15
22	Randall Cunningham	.50
23	Trent Green	.50
24	Chris Spielman	.15
25	Carl Pickens	.30
26	Bill Romanowski	.15
27	Jermaine Lewis	.15
28	Ahman Green	.30
29	Bryan Still	.15
30	Dorsey Levens	.50
31	Frank Wycheck	.15
32	Jerome Bettis	.50
33	Reidel Anthony	.30
34	Robert Jones	.15
35	Terry Glenn	.50
36	Tim Brown	.50
37	Eric Metcalf	.15
38	Kevin Greene	.15
39	Takeo Spikes	.15
40	Brian Mitchell	.15
41	Duane Starks	.15
42	Eddie George	1.00
43	Joe Jurevicius	.15

#	Player	Price
44	Kimble Anders	.15
45	Kordell Stewart	1.00
46	Leroy Hoard	.15
47	Rod Smith	.30
48	Terrell Owens	.75
49	Tony McGee	.15
50	Charles Woodson	.50
51	Andre Rison	.15
52	Chris Slade	.15
53	Frank Sanders	.30
54	Michael Irvin	.30
55	Jerome Pathon	.15
56	Desmond Howard	.15
57	Billy Davis	.15
58	Anthony Simmons	.15
59	James Jett	.15
60	Jake Plummer	1.50
61	John Avery	.30
62	Marvin Harrison	.50
63	Merton Hanks	.15
64	Ricky Proehl	.15
65	Steve Beuerlein	.15
66	Willie McGinest	.15
67	Bryce Paup	.15
68	Brett Favre	3.00
69	Brian Griese	1.00
70	Curtis Martin	.75
71	Drew Bledsoe	1.25
72	Jim Harbaugh	.30
73	Joey Galloway	.50
74	Natrone Means	.50
75	O.J. McDuffie	.15
76	Tiki Barber	.15
77	Wesley Walls	.15
78	Will Blackwell	.15
79	Bert Emanuel	.15
80	J.J. Stokes	.30
81	Steve McNair	1.00
82	Adrian Murrell	.15
83	Dexter Coakley	.15
84	Jeff George	.30
85	Marshall Faulk	.50
86	Tim Biakabutuka	.30
87	Troy Drayton	.15
88	Ty Law	.15
89	Brian Simmons	.15
90	Eric Allen	.15
91	Jon Kitna	.75
92	Junior Seau	.30
93	Kevin Turner	.15
94	Larry Centers	.15
95	Robert Edwards	.50
96	Rocket Ismail	.15
97	Sam Madison	.15
98	Stephen Alexander	.15
99	Trent Dilfer	.30
100	Vonnie Holliday	.30
101	Charlie Garner	.15
102	Deion Sanders	.75
103	Jamal Anderson	.75
104	Mike Vanderjagt	.15
105	Aeneas Williams	.15
106	Daryl Johnston	.15
107	Hugh Douglas	.15
108	Torrance Small	.15
109	Amani Toomer	.15
110	Amp Lee	.15
111	Germane Crowell	.30
112	Marco Battaglia	.15
113	Michael Westbrook	.15
114	Randy Moss	4.00
115	Ricky Watters	.50
116	Rob Johnson	.30
117	Tony Gonzalez	.30
118	Charles Way	.15
119	Chris Penn	.15
120	Eddie Kennison	.15
121	Elvis Grbac	.15
122	Eric Moulds	.50
123	Terry Fair	.15
124	Tony Banks	.30
125	Chris Chandler	.30
126	Emmitt Smith	2.00
127	Herman Moore	.50
128	Irv Smith	.15
129	Kyle Brady	.15
130	Lamont Warren	.15
131	Troy Davis	.15
132	Andre Reed	.30
133	Justin Armour	.15
134	James Hasty	.15
135	Johnnie Morton	.15
136	Reggie Barlow	.15
137	Robert Holcombe	.30
138	Sean Dawkins	.15
139	Steve Atwater	.15
140	Tim Dwight	.50
141	Wayne Chrebet	.50
142	Alonzo Mayes	.15
143	Mark Brunell	1.25
144	Antowain Smith	.50
145	Bam Morris	.15
146	Isaac Bruce	.50
147	Bryan Cox	.15
148	Bryant Westbrook	.15
149	Duce Staley	.15
150	Barry Sanders	2.00
151	La'Roi Glover	.15
152	Ray Crockett	.15
153	Tony Brackens	.15
154	Roy Barker	.15
155	Kerry Collins	.30
156	Andre Wadsworth	.30
157	Cameron Cleeland	.30
158	Koy Detmer	.15
159	Marcus Pollard	.15
160	*Patrick Jeffers*	6.00
161	Aaron Glenn	.15
162	Andre Hastings	.15
163	Bruce Smith	.15
164	David Palmer	.15
165	Erik Kramer	.15
166	Orlando Pace	.15
167	Robert Brooks	.30
168	Shawn Springs	.15
169	Terance Mathis	.15
170	Chris Calloway	.15
171	Gilbert Brown	.15
172	Charlie Jones	.15
173	Curtis Enis	.75
174	Eugene Robinson	.15
175	Garrison Hearst	.50
176	Jason Elam	.15
177	John Randle	.15
178	Keith Poole	.15
179	Kevin Hardy	.15
180	Keyshawn Johnson	.75
181	O.J. Santiago	.15
182	Jacquez Green	.30
183	Bobby Engram	.15
184	Damon Jones	.15
185	Freddie Jones	.15
186	Jake Reed	.15
187	Jerry Rice	1.50
188	Joey Kent	.15
189	Lamar Smith	.15
190	John Elway	2.00
191	Leon Johnson	.15
192	Mark Chmura	.30
193	Peter Boulware	.15
194	Zach Thomas	.30
195	Marc Edwards	.15
196	Mike Alstott	.75
197	Yancey Thigpen	.30
198	Oronde Gadsden	.30
199	Rae Carruth	.15
200	Troy Aikman	1.50
201	Shawn Jefferson	.15
202	Rob Moore	.30
203	Rickey Dudley	.15
204	Jason Taylor	.15
205	Curtis Conway	.30
206	Darrien Gordon	.15
207	Eric Green	.15
208	Jesse Armstead	.15
209	Keenan McCardell	.30
210	Robert Smith	.50
211	Mo Lewis	.15
212	Ryan Leaf	1.00
213	Steve Young	1.00
214	Tyrone Davis	.15
215	Chad Brown	.15
216	Ike Hilliard	.15
217	Jimmy Hitchcock	.15
218	Kevin Dyson	.30
219	Levon Kirkland	.15
220	Neil O'Donnell	.15
221	Ray Lewis	.15
222	Shannon Sharpe	.50
223	Skip Hicks	.50
224	Brad Johnson	.50
225	Charlie Batch	1.00
226	Corey Dillon	.75
227	Dale Carter	.15
228	John Mobley	.15
229	Hines Ward	.30
230	Leslie Shepherd	.15
231	Michael Strahan	.15
232	R.W. McQuarters	.15
233	Mike Pritchard	.15
234	Antonio Freeman	.75
235	Ben Coates	.50
236	Michael Bates	.15
237	Ed McCaffrey	.50
238	Gary Brown	.15
239	Mark Bruener	.15
240	Mikhael Ricks	.15
241	Muhsin Muhammad	.15
242	Priest Holmes	.75
243	Stephen Davis	.15
244	Vinny Testaverde	.50
245	Warrick Dunn	1.00
246	Derrick Mayes	.15
247	Fred Taylor	1.50
248	Drew Bledsoe CL	.50
249	Eddie George CL	.50
250	Steve Young CL	.50
251	Back-2-Back - Super Bowl XXXIII	3.00
252	Back-2-Back - Super Bowl XXXIII	3.00
253	Back-2-Back - Super Bowl XXXIII	3.00
254	Back-2-Back - Super Bowl XXXIII	3.00
255	Back-2-Back - Super Bowl XXXIII	3.00
256	Back-2-Back - Super Bowl XXXIII	3.00
257	Back-2-Back - Super Bowl XXXIII	3.00
258	Back-2-Back - Super Bowl XXXIII	3.00
259	Back-2-Back - Super Bowl XXXIII	3.00
260	Back-2-Back - Super Bowl XXXIII	3.00
261	*Ricky Williams*	10.00
262	*Tim Couch*	3.00
263	*Chris Claiborne*	3.00
264	*Champ Bailey*	4.00
265	*Torry Holt*	6.00
266	*Donovan McNabb*	12.00
267	*David Boston*	6.00
268	*Chris McAlister*	3.00
269	*Brock Huard*	4.00
270	*Daunte Culpepper*	12.00
271	*Matt Stinchcomb*	1.50
272	*Edgerrin James*	12.00
273	*Jevon Kearse*	4.00
274	*Ebenezer Ekuban*	1.50
275	*Kris Farris*	1.50
276	*Chris Terry*	1.50
277	*Jerame Tuman*	1.50
278	*Akili Smith*	4.00
279	*Aaron Gibson*	3.00
280	*Rahim Abdullah*	1.50
281	*Peerless Price*	5.00
282	*Antoine Winfield*	3.00
283	*Antwan Edwards*	3.00
284	*Rob Konrad*	3.00
285	*Troy Edwards*	4.00
286	*John Thornton*	1.50
287	*James Johnson*	2.00
288	*Gary Stills*	1.50
289	*Mike Peterson*	1.50
290	*Kevin Faulk*	2.00
291	*Jared DeVries*	1.50
292	*Martin Gramatica*	3.00
293	*Montae Reagor*	1.50
294	*Andy Katzenmoyer*	3.00
295	*Sedrick Irvin*	3.00
296	*D'Wayne Bates*	3.00
297	*Amos Zereoue*	3.00
298	*Dre' Bly*	1.50
299	*Kevin Johnson*	4.00
300	*Cade McNown*	3.00

1999 Ultra Gold Medallion

This is a 300-card parallel to the base and is the same except for each card is printed on gold foil and stamped Gold Medallion Edition on the back. Veterans were inserted 1:1, Rookies 1:25 and Super Bowl singles at 1:50.

	NM/M
Gold Cards:	2X-4X
Inserted 1:1	
Gold Rookies:	1.5X
Inserted 1:25	
Gold Back 2 Back:	3X-5X
Inserted 1:50	

1999 Ultra Platinum Medallion

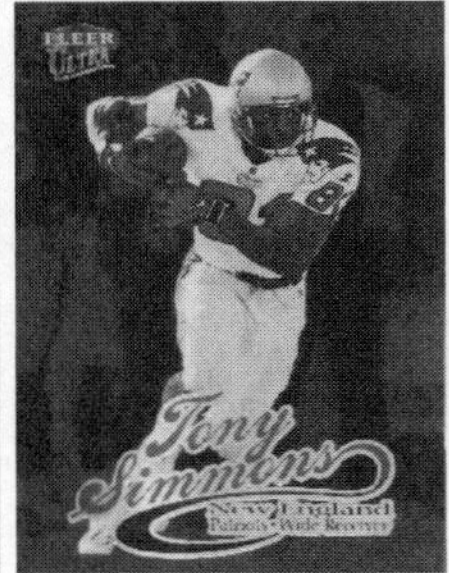

This is a parallel to the base and is the same except for each card is printed on a silver stock and on the backs are sequentially numbered and have a Platinum Medallion stamp. Veterans are numbered to 99, Rookies to 65 and Super Bowl singles to 40.

	NM/M
Platinum Cards:	10X-25X
Production 99 Sets	
Platinum Rookies:	2X-4X
Production 65 Sets	
Platinum Back 2 Back:	5X-10X
Production 40 Sets	

1999 Ultra As Good As It Gets

Each of the 15 players in this set are the best in the NFL. Each is on a die-cut felt stock with silver and gold holofoil. Singles were inserted 1:288 packs.

		NM/M
	Complete Set (15):	75.00
	Common Player:	2.00
	Inserted 1:288	
1	Warrick Dunn	2.00
2	Terrell Davis	6.00
3	Robert Edwards	2.00
4	Randy Moss	8.00
5	Peyton Manning	8.00
6	Mark Brunell	3.00
7	John Elway	6.00
8	Jerry Rice	5.00
9	Jake Plummer	3.00
10	Fred Taylor	3.00
11	Emmitt Smith	7.00
12	Dan Marino	8.00
13	Charlie Batch	2.00
14	Brett Favre	8.00
15	Barry Sanders	6.00

1999 Ultra Caught In The Draft

This 15-card set includes the top rookies from 1999 and captures them on a silver pattern holofoil card. They were inserted 1:18 packs.

		NM/M
	Complete Set (15):	40.00
	Common Player:	.50
	Minor Stars:	1.00
	Inserted 1:18	
1	Ricky Williams	6.00
2	Tim Couch	4.00
3	Chris Claiborne	1.00
4	Champ Bailey	2.00
5	Torry Holt	3.00
6	Donovan McNabb	5.00
7	David Boston	3.00
8	Andy Katzenmoyer	.50
9	Daunte Culpepper	5.00
10	Edgerrin James	5.00
11	Cade McNown	2.00
12	Troy Edwards	2.00
13	Akili Smith	2.00
14	Peerless Price	3.00
15	Amos Zereoue	1.00

1999 Ultra Counterparts

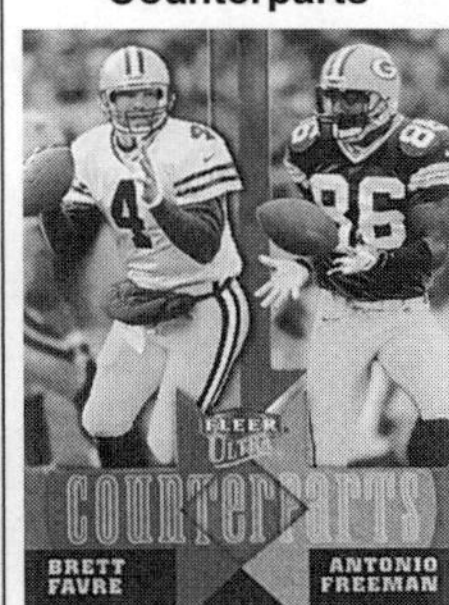

Each card in this 15-card set highlights two players from the same team and puts them on an embossed silver holofoil card. Singles were found 1:36 packs.

		NM/M
	Complete Set (15):	40.00
	Common Player:	1.00
	Inserted 1:36	
1	Troy Aikman, Michael Irvin	4.00
2	Drew Bledsoe, Ben Coates	4.00
3	Terrell Davis, Howard Griffith	4.00
4	Warrick Dunn, Mike Alstott	2.00
5	Brett Favre, Antonio Freeman	6.00
6	Jake Plummer, Frank Sanders	2.00
7	Randy Moss, Randall Cunningham	5.00
8	Eddie George, Steve McNair	3.00
9	Keyshawn Johnson, Wayne Chrebet	1.00
10	Ryan Leaf, Mikhael Ricks	1.00
11	Peyton Manning, Marshall Faulk	5.00
12	Barry Sanders, Tommy Vardell	5.00
13	Charlie Batch, Herman Moore	1.00
14	Emmitt Smith, Daryl Johnston	5.00
15	Kordell Stewart, Jerome Bettis	2.00

1999 Ultra Damage Inc.

This 15-card set includes the top players in the league and showcases them on a sculpted special silver foil card. Singles were found 1:72 packs.

		NM/M
	Complete Set (15):	50.00
	Common Player:	1.00
	Inserted 1:72	
1	Brett Favre	6.00
2	Dan Marino	6.00
3	John Elway	4.00
4	Mark Brunell	3.00
5	Peyton Manning	5.00
6	Robert Edwards	1.00
7	Terrell Davis	4.00
8	Troy Aikman	4.00
9	Randy Moss	5.00
10	Kordell Stewart	3.00
11	Jerry Rice	5.00
12	Fred Taylor	3.00
13	Emmitt Smith	5.00
14	Charlie Batch	1.00
15	Barry Sanders	5.00

1999 Ultra Over The Top

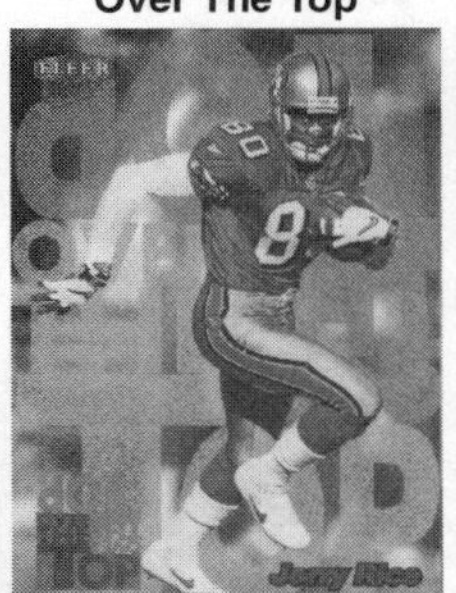

This was a 20-card set that included gold foil stamping and was inserted 1:6 packs.

		NM/M
	Complete Set (20):	20.00
	Common Player:	.50
	Minor Stars:	1.00
	Inserted 1:6	
1	Troy Aikman	3.00
2	Drew Bledsoe	3.00
3	Mark Brunell	2.00
4	Randall Cunningham	1.00
5	Jamal Anderson	1.00
6	Warrick Dunn	1.00
7	Robert Edwards	1.00
8	John Elway	4.00
9	Eddie George	2.00
10	Eric Moulds	.50
11	Keyshawn Johnson	1.00
12	Ryan Leaf	.50
13	Dan Marino	4.00
14	Steve McNair	2.00
15	Jake Plummer	2.00
16	Jerry Rice	3.00
17	Deion Sanders	1.00
18	Kordell Stewart	1.00
19	Fred Taylor	1.00
20	Steve Young	2.00

2000 Ultra

		NM/M
	Complete Set (249):	100.00
	Common Player:	.15
	Minor Stars:	.30
	Common Rookie:	1.25
	Inserted 1:4	
	Pack (10):	3.25
	Wax Box (24):	55.00
1	Kurt Warner	2.00
2	Derrick Alexander	.15
3	Aaron Craver	.15
4	Kevin Faulk	.30
5	Marcus Robinson	.30
6	Tony Banks	.30
7	Jon Ritchie	.15
8	Torry Holt	.50
9	Joe Horn	.15
10	Eddie George	.60
11	Michael Westbrook	.30
12	Gus Frerotte	.15
13	Tim Brown	.30
14	Tamarick Vanover	.15
15	David Sloan	.15
16	Darnay Scott	.30
17	Junior Seau	.30
18	Warren Sapp	.30
19	Priest Holmes	.50
20	Jerry Rice	1.25
21	Cade McNown	.75
22	Johnnie Morton	.15
23	Vinny Testaverde	.30
24	James Jett	.15
25	Tony Gonzalez	.30
26	Charlie Batch	.50
27	Tony Simmons	.15
28	James Stewart	.30
29	Corey Dillon	.50
30	Ricky Williams	1.25
31	Ryan Leaf	.50
32	Terry Allen	.30
33	Freddie Jones	.15
34	Terry Kirby	.15
35	Charles Johnson	.15
36	William Henderson	.15
37	Stephen Alexander	.15
38	Moe Williams	.15
39	David Boston	.50
40	Emmitt Smith	1.75
41	Ken Oxendine	.15
42	Byron Hanspard	.15
43	Dwight Stone	.15
44	Jim Harbaugh	.30
45	Curtis Enis	.30
46	Peerless Price	.30
47	Terance Mathis	.15
48	Mike Alstott	.50
49	Rod Smith	.30
50	Marshall Faulk	.50
51	Derrick Mayes	.30
52	Keenan McCardell	.30
53	Curtis Martin	.50
54	Bobby Engram	.15
55	Carl Pickens	.30
56	Robert Smith	.50
57	Ike Hilliard	.30
58	Reidel Anthony	.30
59	Jeff Graham	.15
60	Mark Brunell	1.00
61	Joe Montgomery	.15
62	Ed McCaffrey	.30
63	Kenny Bynum	.15
64	Curtis Conway	.30
65	Trent Dilfer	.30
66	Jake Reed	.15
67	Jake Plummer	.75
68	Tony Martin	.15
69	Yatil Green	.15
70	Keyshawn Johnson	.50
71	Leroy Hoard	.15
72	Skip Hicks	.15
73	Marvin Harrison	.50
74	Steve Beuerlein	.30
75	Will Blackwell	.15
76	Derek Loville	.15
77	Warrick Dunn	.50
78	Amos Zereoue	.30
79	Ray Lucas	.50
80	Randy Moss	2.50
81	Wesley Walls	.30
82	Jimmy Smith	.50
83	Kordell Stewart	.50
84	Brian Griese	.50
85	Martin Gramatica	.15
86	Chris Chandler	.30
87	Reggie Barlow	.15
88	Jeff George	.30
89	Tavian Banks	.15
90	Muhsin Muhammad	.30
91	Steve McNair	.60
92	Hines Ward	.30
93	Brian Mitchell	.15
94	Daunte Culpepper	.75
95	Tim Dwight	.50
96	Terrence Wilkins	.30
97	Fred Lane	.15
98	Brett Favre	2.50
99	Richie Anderson	.15
100	Jamal Anderson	.50
101	Doug Flutie	.75
102	Charles Woodson	.50
103	Jacquez Green	.30
104	Olandis Gary	.50
105	Steve Young	.75
106	Wayne Chrebet	.50
107	Karim Abdul	.30
108	Andre Rison	.30
109	Eddie Kennison	.30
110	Jevon Kearse	.60
111	Tony Richardson	.15
112	*Jake Delhomme*	3.00
113	Errict Rhett	.30
114	Akili Smith	.75
115	Tyrone Wheatley	.30
116	Corey Bradford	.30
117	J.J. Stokes	.30
118	Simeon Rice	.15
119	Brad Johnson	.50
120	Edgerrin James	2.50
121	Amani Toomer	.30
122	O.J. McDuffie	.30
123	Az-Zahir Hakim	.30
124	Troy Edwards	.50
125	Tim Biakabutuka	.30
126	Jason Tucker	.50
127	Charles Way	.15
128	Terrell Davis	1.00
129	Garrison Hearst	.30
130	Fred Taylor	.75
131	Robert Holcombe	.15
132	Frank Sanders	.15
133	Morten Andersen	.15
134	Cris Carter	.50
135	Patrick Jeffers	.50
136	Antonio Freeman	.50
137	Jonathon Linton	.30
138	Rashaan Shehee	.15

139 Luther Broughton .15
140 Tim Couch 1.25
141 Keith Poole .15
142 Champ Bailey .50
143 Yancey Thigpen .30
144 Joey Galloway .50
145 Mac Cody .15
146 Damon Huard .30
147 Dorsey Levens .50
148 Donovan McNabb .75
149 Jamie Asher .15
150 Peyton Manning 2.00
151 Leslie Shepherd .15
152 Charlie Rogers .15
153 Tony Horne .15
154 Jim Miller .15
155 Richard Huntley .15
156 Germane Crowell .30
157 Natrone Means .30
158 Justin Armour .15
159 Drew Bledsoe .75
160 Dedric Ward .15
161 Allen Rossum .15
162 Ricky Watters .30
163 Kerry Collins .30
164 J.J. Johnson .30
165 Elvis Grbac .30
166 Larry Centers .15
167 Rob Moore .30
168 Jay Riemersma .15
169 Bill Schroeder .15
170 Deion Sanders .50
171 Jerome Bettis .50
172 Dan Marino 1.75
173 Terrell Owens .50
174 Kevin Carter .15
175 Lamar Smith .15
176 Ken Dilger .15
177 Napoleon Kaufman .30
178 Kevin Williams .15
179 Tremain Mack .15
180 Troy Aikman 1.25
181 Glyn Milburn .15
182 Pete Mitchell .15
183 Cameron Cleeland .30
184 Qadry Ismail .15
185 Michael Pittman .15
186 Kevin Dyson .30
187 Matt Hasselbeck .30
188 Kevin Johnson .50
189 Rich Gannon .30
190 Stephen Davis .50
191 Frank Wycheck .15
192 Eric Moulds .50
193 Jon Kitna .50
194 Mario Bates .15
195 Na Brown .15
196 Jeff Blake .30
197 Charles Evans .15
198 Oronde Gadsden .15
199 Donell Bennett .15
200 Isaac Bruce .50
201 Olindo Mare .15
202 Darnell McDonald .30
203 Charlie Garner .30
204 Shawn Jefferson .15
205 Adrian Murrell .30
206 Peter Boulware .15
207 LeShon Johnson .15
208 Herman Moore .30
209 Duce Staley .50
210 Sean Dawkins .15
211 Antowain Smith .30
212 Albert Connell .30
213 Jeff Garcia .50
214 Kimble Anders .15
215 Shaun King .75
216 Raghib Ismail .15
217 Andrew Glover .15
218 Rickey Dudley .15
219 Michael Basnight .15
220 Terry Glenn .30
221 *Peter Warrick* 4.00
222 *Ron Dayne* 2.00
223 *Thomas Jones* 3.00
224 *Joe Hamilton* 2.50
225 *Tim Rattay* 3.00
226 *Chad Pennington* 12.00
227 *Dennis Northcutt* 2.50
228 *Troy Walters* 1.25
229 *Travis Prentice* 3.00
230 *Shaun Alexander* 8.00
231 *J.R. Redmond* 3.00
232 *Chris Redman* 3.00
233 *Tee Martin* 2.50
234 *Tom Brady* 20.00
235 *Travis Taylor* 3.00
236 *R. Jay Soward* 2.50
237 *Jamal Lewis* 8.00
238 *Giovanni Carmazzi* 2.50
239 *Dez White* 2.50
240 *LaVar Arrington* 125.00
241 *Laveranues Coles* 4.00
242 *Sherrod Gideon* 1.25
243 *Trung Canidate* 2.50
244 *Michael Wiley* 2.50
245 *Anthony Lucas* 1.25
246 *Darrell Jackson* 4.00
247 *Plaxico Burress* 6.00
248 *Reuben Droughns* 4.00
249 *Marc Bulger* 6.00
250 *Danny Farmer* 2.50

Values quoted in this guide reflect the retail price of a card—the price a collector can expect to pay when buying a card from a dealer. The wholesale price—that which a collector can expect to receive from a dealer when selling cards—will be significantly lower, depending on desirability and condition.

2000 Ultra Gold Medallion

NM/M
Gold Cards: 2X-4X
Inserted 1:1
Gold Rookies: 1.5X
Inserted 1:24

2000 Ultra Masterpiece

Production 1 Set

2000 Ultra Platinum Medallion

NM/M
Platinum Cards: 15X-30X
Production 50 Sets
Platinum Rookies: 4X-8X
Production 25 Sets

2000 Ultra Autographics

NM/M
Common Player: 10.00
Minor Stars: 20.00
Inserted 1:72
Troy Aikman 10.00
Jamal Anderson 10.00
Jerome Bettis 20.00
Tim Biakabutuka 10.00
David Boston 20.00
Peter Boulware 10.00
Tom Brady 50.00
Isaac Bruce 20.00
Mark Brunell 45.00
Cris Carter 30.00
Germane Crowell 20.00
Terrell Davis 10.00
Ron Dayne 40.00
Tim Dwight 30.00
Deon Dyer 10.00
Kevin Dyson 10.00
Troy Edwards 10.00
Marshall Faulk 30.00
Christian Fauria 10.00
Jermaine Fazande 10.00
Rich Gannon 10.00
Jeff Garcia 25.00
Charlie Garner 10.00
Jeff Graham 10.00
Damon Griffin 10.00
Marvin Harrison 25.00
Tony Horne 20.00
Damon Huard 30.00
Darrell Jackson 20.00
Edgerrin James 75.00
Patrick Jeffers 20.00
Brad Johnson 25.00
Kevin Johnson 30.00
Rob Johnson 10.00
Terry Kirby 10.00
Jon Kitna 25.00
O.J. McDuffie 20.00
Rondell Mealey 20.00
Joe Montgomery 10.00
Herman Moore 20.00
Sylvester Morris 40.00
Eric Moulds 20.00
Muhsin Muhammad 20.00
Chad Pennington 100.00
Travis Prentice 35.00
Tim Rattay 20.00
Jon Ritchie 10.00
Antowain Smith 10.00
Kurt Warner 60.00
Chris Watson 10.00

2000 Ultra Dream Team

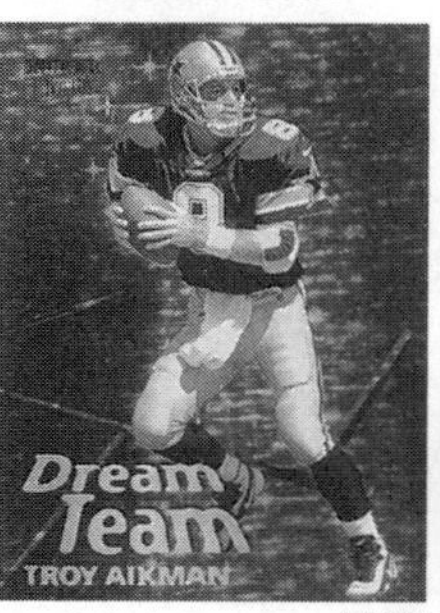

NM/M
Complete Set (10): 30.00
Common Player: 1.00
Inserted 1:24
1 Terrell Davis 4.00
2 Brett Favre 6.00
3 Troy Aikman 4.00
4 Keyshawn Johnson 1.00
5 Edgerrin James 4.00
6 Randy Moss 5.00
7 Marvin Harrison 2.00
8 Kurt Warner 3.00
9 Fred Taylor 3.00
10 Ricky Williams 5.00

2000 Ultra Fast Lane

NM/M
Complete Set (15): 12.00
Common Player: .50
Minor Stars: 1.00
Inserted 1:3
1 Jimmy Smith 1.00
2 Cris Carter 1.00
3 Marvin Harrison 1.00
4 Tim Brown 1.00
5 Muhsin Muhammad 1.00
6 Isaac Bruce 1.00
7 Bobby Engram .50
8 Terance Mathis .50
9 Randy Moss 3.00
10 Raghib Ismail .50
11 Keyshawn Johnson 1.00
12 Terry Glenn 1.00
13 Jerry Rice 2.00
14 Marcus Robinson 1.50
15 Antonio Freeman 1.00

2000 Ultra Feel the Game

NM/M
Common Player: 10.00
Inserted 1:144
Gold Cards: 2X
Production 50 Sets
Karim Abdul 10.00
Mark Brunell 35.00
Chris Chandler 10.00
Tim Couch 35.00
Curtis Enis 10.00
Doug Flutie 15.00
Terry Glenn 15.00
Trent Green 10.00
Brian Griese 25.00
Az-Zahir Hakim 10.00
Terry Kirby 10.00
Dorsey Levens 15.00
Rob Moore 10.00
Jake Plummer 25.00
Frank Sanders 10.00
Emmitt Smith 75.00
Jimmy Smith 15.00
J.J. Stokes 10.00
Amani Toomer 10.00
Kurt Warner 50.00
Charles Woodson 12.00

2000 Ultra Head of the Class

NM/M
Complete Set (10): 10.00
Common Player: .75
Inserted 1:6
1 Peter Warrick 1.00
2 Ron Dayne 1.00
3 Thomas Jones 2.00
4 Chad Pennington 5.00
5 Joe Hamilton .75
6 Shaun Alexander 2.00
7 J.R. Redmond 1.25
8 Troy Walters .75
9 Travis Prentice 1.25
10 Chris Redman 1.50

2000 Ultra Instant 3 Play

NM/M
Complete Set (15): 12.00
Common Player: .50
Minor Stars: 1.00
1 Peyton Manning 3.00
2 Curtis Enis .50
3 Charlie Batch .50
4 Fred Taylor 1.50
5 Az-Zahir Hakim .50
6 Randy Moss 3.00
7 Jacquez Green .50
8 Kevin Dyson .50
9 Brian Griese 1.25
10 Rashaan Shehee .50
11 Tony Simmons .50
12 Charles Woodson 1.00
13 Hines Ward 1.00
14 Skip Hicks .50
15 Tim Dwight 1.00

2000 Ultra Millenium Monsters

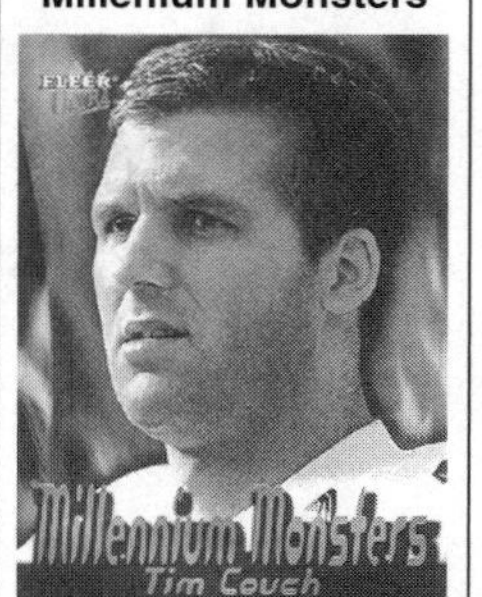

NM/M
Complete Set (10): 20.00
Common Player: 1.00
Inserted 1:12
1 Tim Couch 2.00
2 Eddie George 1.00
3 Brian Griese 1.00
4 Keyshawn Johnson 1.00
5 Peyton Manning 4.00
6 Randy Moss 4.00
7 Ricky Williams 4.00
8 Edgerrin James 3.00
9 Cade McNown 1.00
10 Donovan McNabb 2.50

2000 Ultra Season Pass

NM/M
Complete Set (6): 20.00
Common Player: 2.00
1 Tim Couch 4.00
2 Troy Aikman 4.00
3 Mark Brunell 2.00
4 Drew Bledsoe 4.00
5 Chad Pennington 8.00
6 Chris Redman 2.00

2000 Ultra Won by One

NM/M
Complete Set (10): 40.00
Common Player: 1.00
Inserted 1:72
1 Peyton Manning 8.00
2 Randy Moss 8.00
3 Brett Favre 10.00
4 Terrell Davis 6.00
5 Dan Marino 10.00
6 Jake Plummer 3.00
7 Tim Couch 3.00
8 Eddie George 1.00
9 Brian Griese 1.00
10 Kurt Warner 5.00

2001 Ultra

NM/M
Complete Set (300): 225.00
Common Player: .15
Minor Stars: .30
Common Rookie: 2.00
Production 2,499 Sets
Pack (10): 3.00
Wax Box (24): 60.00
1 Daunte Culpepper 1.25
2 Kurt Warner 2.00
3 Emmitt Smith 1.50
4 Eddie George .75
5 Ron Dayne 1.25
6 Zach Thomas .30
7 Itula Mili .15
8 Jake Reed .30

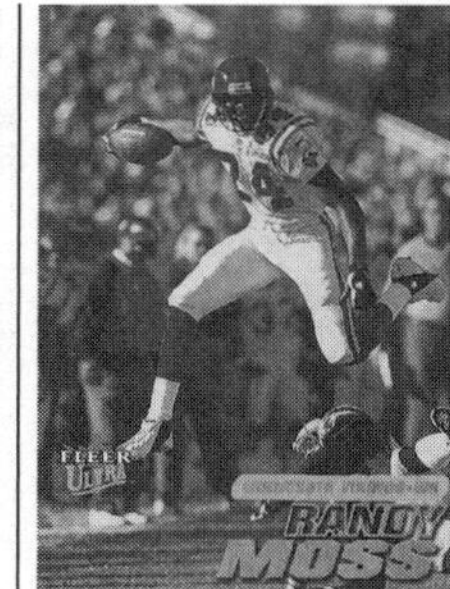

NM/M
9 James Stewart .50
10 Terrence Wilkins .30
11 Jeff Blake .30
12 Kerry Collins .50
13 Christian Fauria .15
14 Jackie Harris .15
15 Kevin Johnson .50
16 Tony Martin .15
17 Joey Galloway .50
18 Junior Seau .30
19 Jason Tucker .30
20 Steve Beuerlein .30
21 Mike Cloud .15
22 Kevin Faulk .30
23 Az-Zahir Hakim .30
24 Charles Johnson .15
25 Curtis Martin .50
26 Eric Moulds .50
27 Bill Schroeder .30
28 Amani Toomer .30
29 Obafemi Ayanbadejo .15
30 Aaron Shea .15
31 Ken Dilger .15
32 Terry Glenn .50
33 Raghib Ismail .30
34 Dorsey Levens .50
35 Brian Mitchell .15
36 Tony Richardson .30
37 Sam Madison .15
38 Darren Sharper .15
39 Derrick Alexander .30
40 Aaron Brooks .75
41 Casey Crawford .15
42 Terrell Fletcher .15
43 William Henderson .15
44 Thomas Jones .50
45 Keenan McCardell .30
46 Chad Pennington 1.25
47 Akili Smith .50
48 Hines Ward .30
49 Champ Bailey .30
50 Cris Carter .50
51 Corey Dillon .50
52 Tony Gonzalez .30
53 Darrell Jackson .30
54 Chad Lewis .30
55 Dave Moore .15
56 Jay Riemersma .30
57 J.J. Stokes .30
58 Frank Wycheck .30
59 Tiki Barber .30
60 Tony Carter .15
61 Rickey Dudley .15
62 John Lynch .15
63 Larry Foster .15
64 Willie Jackson .15
65 Jamal Lewis 1.75
66 Herman Moore .30
67 Andre Rison .30
68 Michael Strahan .15
69 Charlie Batch .50
70 Larry Centers .15
71 Ron Dugans .15
72 Jeff Graham .15
73 Edgerrin James 1.75
74 Jermaine Lewis .30
75 Charles Woodson .30
76 Chris Redman .75
77 Jon Ritchie .15
78 Fred Taylor .75
79 Jamal Anderson .50
80 Isaac Bruce .50
81 Terrell Davis 1.50
82 Rich Gannon .30
83 Joe Horn .30
84 Eddie Kennison .15
85 Steve McNair .50
86 Travis Prentice .50
87 Rod Smith .50
88 Ricky Watters .30
89 Michael Bates .15
90 Byron Chamberlain .15
91 Warrick Dunn .50
92 Elvis Grbac .30
93 Patrick Jeffers .50
94 Ray Lewis .30
95 Sammy Morris .50
96 Marcus Robinson .50
97 Travis Taylor .50
98 Fred Beasley .15
99 Chris Chandler .30
100 Tim Dwight .50
101 Ahman Green .50
102 Shawn Jefferson .15
103 Jeremy McDaniel .15
104 Sylvester Morris .50
105 John Randle .30
106 Vinny Testaverde .50
107 Anthony Becht .15
108 Wayne Chrebet .50
109 Stephen Boyd .15
110 Jacquez Green .15
111 Mar Tay Jenkins .15
112 Jason Gildon .15
113 Chad Morton .15
114 Deion Sanders .50
115 Yancey Thigpen .30
116 Marty Booker .15
117 Curtis Conway .30
118 Jermaine Fazande .30
119 Matthew Hatchette .30
120 Pat Johnson .15
121 Terance Mathis .15
122 Terrell Owens .50
123 Corey Simon .30
124 Darrick Vaughn .15
125 Drew Bledsoe .75
126 Albert Connell .30
127 Brett Favre 2.50
128 Marvin Harrison .50
129 Keyshawn Johnson .50
130 Derrick Mason .50
131 Dennis Northcutt .30
132 Shannon Sharpe .30
133 Brian Urlacher 1.25
134 Mike Anderson 1.75
135 Mark Bruener .15
136 Sean Dawkins .15
137 Jeff Garcia .50
138 Tony Horne .15
139 Shaun King .50
140 Cade McNown .50
141 Peerless Price .30
142 R. Jay Soward .30
143 Tyrone Wheatley .50
144 Richie Anderson .15
145 Mark Brunell .75
146 JaJuan Dawson .30
147 Charlie Garner .30
148 Desmond Howard .15
149 Jon Kitna .30
150 Duane Starks .15
151 J.R. Redmond .50
152 Duce Staley .50
153 Dez White .30
154 David Boston .50
155 Tim Couch .75
156 Jay Fiedler .30
157 Jessie Armstead .15
158 Rob Johnson .30
159 Brad Johnson .50
160 Derrick Mayes .30
161 Jerome Pathon .15
162 David Sloan .15
163 Wesley Walls .15
164 Shaun Alexander .50
165 Derrick Brooks .15
166 Germane Crowell .50
167 Doug Flutie .50
168 Ike Hilliard .15
169 Hugh Douglas .15
170 Wane McGarity .15
171 Michael Pittman .15
172 Shawn Bryson .15
173 Richard Huntley .15
174 Darnell Autry .15
175 Plaxico Burress .50
176 Trent Dilfer .30
177 Jeff George .30
178 Qadry Ismail .15
179 Ryan Leaf .50
180 Jim Miller .15
181 Jerry Rice 1.25
182 Kordell Stewart .50
183 Ricky Williams 1.00
184 James Allen .50
185 Courtney Brown .50
186 Reidel Anthony .15
187 Bubba Franks .50
188 Priest Holmes .50
189 Napoleon Kaufman .30
190 Trevor Pryce .15
191 Jake Plummer .50
192 Jimmy Smith .50
193 Michael Wiley .30
194 Brock Huard .30
195 Troy Brown .15
196 Stephen Davis .50
197 Oronde Gadsden .30
198 Brad Hoover .50
199 La'Roi Glover .15
200 Donovan McNabb 1.00
201 Jerry Porter .30
202 Robert Smith .30
203 J.D. Watson .15
204 Tim Biakabutuka .30
205 Laveranues Coles .50
206 Marshall Faulk .75
207 Jim Harbaugh .30
208 Doug Johnson .30
209 Tee Martin .30
210 Muhsin Muhammad .30
211 Darnay Scott .30
212 Jeremiah Trotter .15
213 Troy Aikman 1.25
214 Kyle Brady .15
215 Sam Cowart .15
216 Darren Howard .15
217 Donald Hayes .30
218 Freddie Jones .30
219 Ed McCaffrey .50
220 David Patten .15
221 Brian Griese .75
222 Dedric Ward .15
223 Jerome Bettis .50
224 Greg Clark .15
225 Bobby Engram .15
226 Matt Hasselbeck .50
227 James Jett .15
228 Peyton Manning 1.75
229 Randy Moss 1.75
230 Warren Sapp .30
231 James Thrash .30
232 Mike Alstott .50
233 Tim Brown .30
234 Randall Cunningham .30
235 Antonio Freeman .50
236 Torry Holt .50
237 Jevon Kearse .50
238 James McKnight .15
239 Marcus Pollard .15
240 Lamar Smith .50
241 Peter Warrick 1.25

242	Donnell Bennett	.15
243	Joe Johnson	.15
244	Troy Edwards	.30
245	Trent Green	.50
246	Jason Taylor	.15
247	Aeneas Williams	.15
248	Johnnie Morton	.30
249	Frank Sanders	.30
250	Jason Sehorn	.15
251	*Chris Weinke*	8.00
252	*Bobby Newcombe*	4.00
253	*LaDainian Tomlinson*	25.00
254	*Chad Johnson*	12.00
255	*Derrick Gibson*	2.00
256	*Sage Rosenfels*	6.00
257	*LaMont Jordan*	6.00
258	*Mike McMahon*	6.00
259	*Vinny Sutherland*	4.00
260	*Drew Brees*	12.00
261	*Deuce McAllister*	20.00
262	*Kevan Barlow*	10.00
263	*Jamar Fletcher*	4.00
264	*Gerard Warren*	2.00
265	*Todd Heap*	6.00
266	*Travis Henry*	10.00
267	*Quincy Morgan*	6.00
268	*Anthony Thomas*	10.00
269	*Andre Carter*	2.00
270	*Freddie Mitchell*	8.00
271	*Richard Seymour*	2.00
272	*Josh Booty*	4.00
273	*Robert Ferguson*	6.00
274	*Marques Tuiasosopo*	8.00
275	*Reggie Wayne*	10.00
276	*Jabari Holloway*	4.00
277	*Rudi Johnson*	10.00
278	*Michael Bennett*	15.00
279	*Marvin "Snoop" Minnis*	2.00
280	*Dan Morgan*	2.00
281	*Rod Gardner*	10.00
282	*Jesse Palmer*	4.00
283	*Michael Vick*	50.00
284	*Chris Chambers*	12.00
285	*James Jackson*	8.00
286	*David Terrell*	8.00
287	*Koren Robinson*	6.00
288	*Travis Minor*	8.00
289	*Santana Moss*	8.00
290	*Josh Heupel*	4.00
291	*Jamal Reynolds*	2.00
292	*Ken-Yon Rambo*	4.00
293	*Cedrick Wilson*	2.00
294	*Alge Crumpler*	4.00
295	*Fred Smoot*	4.00
296	*Dan Alexander*	2.00
297	*Tim Hasselbeck*	5.00
298	*Will Allen*	2.00
299	*Keith Adams*	2.00
300	*Heath Evans*	2.00

2001 Ultra Gold Medallion

Gold Cards:	8X-16X
Production 250 Sets	
Gold Rookies:	2X-4X
Production 100 Sets	

2001 Ultra Platinum Medallion

Platinum Cards:	10X-30X
Production 50 Sets	
Platinum Rookies:	4X-8X
Production 25 Sets	

2001 Ultra Ball Hawks

	NM/M
Common Player:	6.00
Inserted 1:144	
Troy Aikman	10.00
Derrick Alexander	6.00
Jamal Anderson	8.00
Charlie Batch	8.00
Courtney Brown	8.00
Mark Brunell	8.00
Tim Couch	12.00
Eddie George	8.00
Tony Gonzalez	6.00
Elvis Grbac	6.00
Marvin Harrison	8.00
Edgerrin James	15.00
Kevin Johnson	8.00
Jevon Kearse	8.00
Peyton Manning	15.00
Donovan McNabb	15.00
Steve McNair	8.00
Cade McNown	8.00
Herman Moore	6.00
Travis Prentice	8.00
Marcus Robinson	8.00
Emmitt Smith	20.00
Jimmy Smith	6.00
Duce Staley	8.00
Brian Urlacher	20.00

2001 Ultra Ground Command

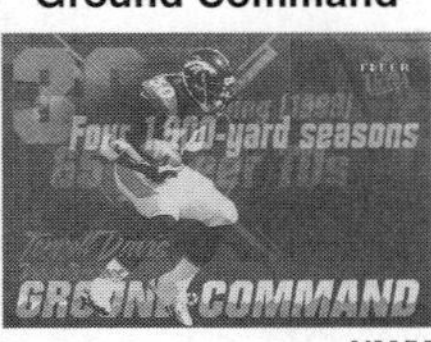

		NM/M
Complete Set (10):		25.00
Common Player:		1.50
Inserted 1:22		
Gold Cards:		2X-4X
Production 250 Sets		
Platinum Cards:		3X-5X
Production 50 Sets		
1GC	Emmitt Smith	4.00
2GC	Edgerrin James	3.00
3GC	Marshall Faulk	2.00
4GC	Jamal Lewis	2.00
5GC	Mike Anderson	2.00
6GC	Duce Staley	1.50
7GC	Jamal Anderson	1.50
8GC	Ricky Williams	4.00
9GC	Corey Dillon	1.50
10GC	Terrell Davis	4.00

2001 Ultra Head of the Class

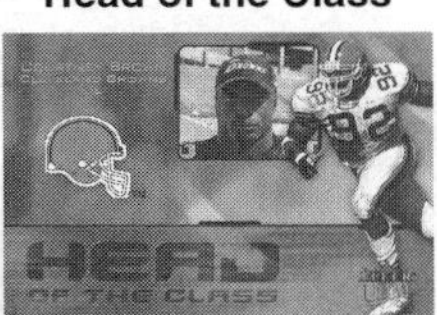

		NM/M
Complete Set (25):		40.00
Common Player:		1.00
Minor Stars:		2.00
Inserted 1:22		
1HC	Trung Canidate	1.00
2HC	Thomas Jones	2.00
3HC	Curtis Keaton	1.00
4HC	Courtney Brown	2.00
5HC	Chris Redman	2.00
6HC	Dennis Northcutt	1.00
7HC	Sylvester Morris	2.00
8HC	Shaun Alexander	5.00
9HC	Dez White	1.00
10HC	Laveranues Coles	4.00
11HC	R. Jay Soward	2.00
12HC	Jamal Lewis	6.00
13HC	J.R. Redmond	2.00
14HC	Travis Taylor	4.00
15HC	Plaxico Burress	5.00
16HC	Peter Warrick	2.00
17HC	Joe Hamilton	2.00
18HC	Ron Dugans	1.00
19HC	Tee Martin	2.00
20HC	Brian Urlacher	6.00
21HC	Ron Dayne	1.00
22HC	Travis Prentice	4.00
23HC	Chad Pennington	8.00
24HC	Corey Simon	1.00
25HC	Mike Anderson	4.00

2001 Ultra Quick Strike

	NM/M
Complete Set (20):	40.00
Common Player:	1.00
Minor stars:	2.00
Inserted 1:22	
Gold Cards:	2X-4X
Production 250 Sets	
Platinum Cards:	3X-5X
Production 50 Sets	

1QS	Kurt Warner	4.00
2QS	Mark Brunell	3.00
3QS	Fred Taylor	3.00
4QS	Emmitt Smith	5.00
5QS	Jerry Rice	4.00
6QS	Eddie George	2.00
7QS	Cade McNown	1.00
8QS	Randy Moss	4.00
9QS	Donovan McNabb	3.00
10QS	Peyton Manning	4.00
11QS	Edgerrin James	4.00
12QS	Shaun King	1.00
13QS	Troy Aikman	4.00
14QS	Tim Couch	2.00
15QS	Jamal Lewis	2.00
16QS	Daunte Culpepper	3.00
17QS	Brett Favre	5.00
18QS	Drew Bledsoe	3.00
19QS	Terrell Davis	3.00
20QS	Marshall Faulk	3.00

2001 Ultra Head of the Class Hats

		NM/M
Common Player:		10.00
Production 100 Sets		
1HC	Trung Canidate	10.00
2HC	Thomas Jones	15.00
3HC	Curtis Keaton	10.00
4HC	Courtney Brown	10.00
5HC	Chris Redman	15.00
6HC	Dennis Northcutt	10.00
7HC	Sylvester Morris	20.00
8HC	Shaun Alexander	30.00
9HC	Dez White	10.00
10HC	Laveranues Coles	35.00
11HC	R. Jay Soward	10.00
12HC	Jamal Lewis	45.00
13HC	J.R. Redmond	25.00
14HC	Travis Taylor	25.00
15HC	Plaxico Burress	35.00
16HC	Peter Warrick	15.00
17HC	Joe Hamilton	10.00
18HC	Ron Dugans	10.00
19HC	Tee Martin	15.00
20HC	Brian Urlacher	50.00
21HC	Ron Dayne	20.00
22HC	Travis Prentice	35.00
23HC	Chad Pennington	60.00
24HC	Corey Simon	10.00
25HC	Mike Anderson	35.00

2001 Ultra Sunday's Best

	NM/M
Common Player:	6.00
Inserted 1:63	
Jamal Anderson	6.00
Jerome Bettis	6.00
Drew Bledsoe	12.00
Isaac Bruce	12.00
Mark Brunell	12.00
Trung Canidate	6.00
Tim Couch	15.00
Stephen Davis	12.00
Ron Dayne	6.00
Warrick Dunn	8.00
Marshall Faulk	15.00
Doug Flutie	12.00
Antonio Freeman	6.00
Brian Griese	12.00
Kevin Johnson	6.00
Thomas Jones	6.00
Napoleon Kaufman	6.00
Curtis Martin	12.00
Keenan McCardell	6.00
Terrell Owens	12.00
Jake Plummer	12.00
Jerry Rice	20.00
Jimmy Smith	6.00
Rod Smith	6.00
R. Jay Soward	6.00
Fred Taylor	10.00
Brian Urlacher	20.00
Kurt Warner	20.00

2001 Ultra Two Minute Thrill

		NM/M
Complete Set (20):		30.00
Common Player:		1.00
Inserted 1:22		
Gold Cards:		2X-4X
Production 250 Sets		
Platinum Cards:		3X-5X
Production 50 Sets		
1TT	Troy Aikman	3.00
2TT	Terrell Davis	3.00
3TT	Keyshawn Johnson	1.00
4TT	Peyton Manning	3.00
5TT	Donovan McNabb	3.00
6TT	Steve McNair	1.00
7TT	Cade McNown	1.00
8TT	Ricky Williams	4.00
9TT	Brett Favre	5.00
10TT	Edgerrin James	3.00
11TT	Tim Couch	2.50
12TT	Fred Taylor	2.00
13TT	Rich Gannon	1.00
14TT	Kurt Warner	3.00
15TT	Randy Moss	4.00
16TT	Peter Warrick	1.00
17TT	Ron Dayne	1.00
18TT	Mark Brunell	2.00
19TT	Daunte Culpepper	3.00
20TT	Marshall Faulk	3.00

2002 Ultra

		NM/M
Complete Set (240):		200.00
Common Player:		.15
Unlisted Stars:		.60
Minor Stars:		.40
Common Rookie (201-240):		1.00
Minor Rookies:		2.00
Pack (10):		3.00
Wax Box (24):		50.00
1	Donovan McNabb	1.50
2	Chad Pennington	1.00
3	Shaun Alexander	.60
4	Corey Dillon	.50
5	Kurt Warner	2.50
6	Ed McCaffrey	.40
7	Hugh Douglas	.15
8	Tony Gonzalez	.40
9	Travis Taylor	.40
10	Tony Boselli	.15
11	Chad Scott	.15
12	Ernie Conwell	.15
13	Brad Johnson	.40
14	Donald Hayes	.15
15	Emmitt Smith	2.50
16	Jimmy Smith	.15
17	Anthony Becht	.15
18	Rod Gardner	.40
19	Muhsin Muhammad	.40
20	Troy Hambrick	.15
21	Keenan McCardell	.15
22	Laveranues Coles	.40
23	Kevin Dyson	.40
24	Grant Wistrom	.15
25	Eric Moulds	.15
26	Nate Clements	.15
27	Terrell Davis	1.25
28	Aaron Glenn	.15
29	Eric Hicks	.15
30	Tiki Barber	.40
31	Jake Plummer	.50
32	Junior Seau	.50
33	Marshall Faulk	1.50
34	Warrick Dunn	.50
35	Bill Gramatica	.15
36	Tim Couch	1.25
37	Kabeer Gbaja-Biamila	.40
38	Kailee Wong	.15
39	David Patten	.15
40	Correll Buckhalter	.40
41	Troy Brown	.60
42	Drew Bledsoe	1.50
43	Travis Henry	.40
44	Jim Miller	.40
45	Rod Smith	.40
46	Tai Streets	.15
47	Marvin "Snoop" Minnis	.50
48	Ron Dayne	.50
49	Tyrone Wheatley	.15
50	LaDainian Tomlinson	2.00
51	Akili Smith	.40
52	Warren Sapp	.40
53	Adam Archuleta	.15
54	Chris Fuamatu-Ma'afala	.15
55	Marty Booker	.40
56	Trevor Pryce	.15
57	Peyton Manning	2.50
58	Lamar Smith	.50
59	Amani Toomer	.40
60	Greg Biekert	.15
61	Marcellus Wiley	.15
62	Ahmed Plummer	.40
63	Mike Alstott	.40
64	Gary Walker	.15
65	Champ Bailey	.40
66	Chris Redman	.40
67	David Terrell	.60
68	Mike McMahon	.60
69	Marvin Harrison	.50
70	Jay Fiedler	.50
71	JaJuan Dawson	.15
72	Charlie Garner	.50
73	Curtis Conway	.40
74	J.J. Stokes	.40
75	Ronde Barber	.15
76	Alge Crumpler	.40
77	Jamir Miller	.15
78	Brett Favre	3.00
79	Randy Moss	2.50
80	Joe Horn	.40
81	Hines Ward	.40
82	Lawyer Milloy	.15
83	Aeneas Williams	.15
84	Chris McAlister	.15
85	Anthony Thomas	2.00
86	Johnnie Morton	.15
87	Edgerrin James	2.00
88	Chris Chambers	.60
89	Michael Strahan	.40
90	Charles Woodson	.50
91	Tim Dwight	.40
92	Kevan Barlow	.15
93	Donnie Abraham	.15
94	Peter Boulware	.15
95	Marcus Robinson	.15
96	Shaun Rogers	.15
97	Dominic Rhodes	.15
98	Zach Thomas	.40
99	Kerry Collins	.50
100	Tim Brown	.60
101	Garrison Hearst	.50
102	Steve McNair	.60
103	Fred Smoot	.15
104	Isaac Bruce	.50
105	Jamal Lewis	1.25
106	Brian Urlacher	2.00
107	Takeo Spikes	.15
108	Marcus Pollard	.15
109	Jason Taylor	.40
110	Deuce McAllister	1.25
111	Jerry Rice	2.50
112	Terrell Owens	.60
113	Eddie George	.60
114	Rob Morris	.15
115	Mike Brown	.15
116	Joey Galloway	.40
117	Fred Taylor	.50
118	Rich Gannon	.50
119	Chris Chandler	.40
120	Koren Robinson	.15
121	Dan Morgan	.40
122	Raghib Ismail	.15
123	Mark Brunell	.60
124	John Abraham	.15
125	Stephen Davis	.50
126	Patrick Kerney	.15
127	Anthony Henry	.50
128	Scotty Anderson	.15
129	Oronde Gadsden	.15
130	Willie Jackson	.15
131	Kendrell Bell	.40
132	Ray Lewis	.50
133	Quincy Carter	1.50
134	James Stewart	.75
135	Travis Minor	.50
136	Kyle Turley	.15
137	Jason Gildon	.15
138	David Boston	.60
139	Justin Smith	.15
140	Jamie Sharper	.15
141	Antowain Smith	.50
142	Freddie Mitchell	.40
143	Frank Sanders	.15
144	Kevin Johnson	.15
145	Darren Sharper	.15
146	Eric Johnson	.15
147	Ty Law	.15
148	James Thrash	.15
149	Matt Hasselbeck	.50
150	Peerless Price	.40
151	T.J. Houshmandzadeh	.15
152	Mike Anderson	1.25
153	Jermaine Lewis	.15
154	Trent Green	.50
155	Ron Dixon	.15
156	Duce Staley	.50
157	Drew Brees	2.00
158	Torry Holt	.50
159	Keyshawn Johnson	.50
160	Michael Vick	2.50
161	Ben Gay	.15
162	Bill Schroeder	.50
163	Byron Chamberlain	.15
164	Tedy Bruschi	.15
165	Kordell Stewart	.50
166	Deltha O'Neal	.15
167	Quincy Morgan	.40
168	Bubba Franks	.40
169	Daunte Culpepper	1.50
170	Ricky Williams	1.50
171	Plaxico Burress	.75
172	Trent Dilfer	.50
173	Steve Smith	.15
174	Greg Ellis	.15
175	Tony Brackens	.15
176	Santana Moss	.50
177	Frank Wycheck	.15
178	Michael Pittman	.15
179	Peter Warrick	.50
180	Antonio Freeman	.40
181	Tom Brady	2.50
182	Bobby Taylor	.15
183	Jeff Garcia	.60
184	Darrell Jackson	.15
185	Chris Weinke	.50
186	Darren Woodson	.50
187	Hardy Nickerson	.15
188	Wayne Chrebet	.50
189	Samari Rolle	.15
190	Jamal Anderson	.15
191	James Jackson	.50
192	Ahman Green	.60
193	Michael Bennett	.60
194	Aaron Brooks	1.25
195	Jerome Bettis	.50
196	Jay Riemersma	.15
197	Brian Griese	.60
198	Priest Holmes	.60
199	Curtis Martin	.50
200	Derrick Mason	.15
201	Antonio Bryant	6.00
202	David Carr	15.00
203	Eric Crouch	8.00
204	Freddie Milons	3.00
205	Najeh Davenport	3.00
206	Rohan Davey	5.00
207	T.J. Duckett	8.00
208	DeShaun Foster	4.00
209	Jabar Gaffney	8.00
210	William Green	6.00
211	Joey Harrington	12.00
212	Travis Stephens	3.00
213	Julius Peppers	8.00
214	Adrian Peterson	3.00
215	Josh Reed	6.00
216	Mike Williams	2.00
217	Javon Walker	10.00
218	Marquise Walker	3.00
219	Patrick Ramsey	10.00
220	Lamar Gordon	3.00
221	David Garrard	3.00
222	Major Applewhite	4.00
223	Andre Davis	4.00
224	Roy Williams	10.00
225	Tim Carter	3.00
226	Ron Johnson	3.00
227	Randy Fasani	3.00
228	Ashley Lelie	10.00
229	Ladell Betts	3.00
230	Antwann Randle El	8.00
231	Jonathan Wells	4.00
232	Brian Westbrook	8.00
233	Clinton Portis	15.00
234	Luke Staley	3.00
235	Cliff Russell	3.00
236	Jeremy Shockey	10.00
237	Donte Stallworth	10.00
238	Daniel Graham	3.00
239	Donald Reche Caldwell	3.00
240	Ryan Sims	2.00

2002 Ultra Gold Medallion

Stars:	2X-4X
Rookies:	1.5X-3X
Overall Inserted 1:1	
Rookie Production 100 Sets	

2002 Ultra League Leaders

		NM/M
Common Player:		1.00
Inserted 1:6		
1LL	Brett Favre	5.00
2LL	Kurt Warner	3.00
3LL	Marshall Faulk	2.00
4LL	Daunte Culpepper	1.00
5LL	LaDainian Tomlinson	1.00
6LL	Jeff Garcia	1.00
7LL	Terrell Owens	1.00
8LL	Zach Thomas	1.00
9LL	Brian Urlacher	3.00
10LL	Corey Dillon	1.00
11LL	David Boston	1.00
12LL	Donovan McNabb	1.00
13LL	Anthony Thomas	2.00
14LL	Priest Holmes	1.00
15LL	Torry Holt	1.00
16LL	Marvin Harrison	1.00
17LL	Stephen Davis	1.00
18LL	Michael Strahan	1.00
19LL	Rod Smith	1.00
20LL	Ray Lewis	1.00
21LL	Curtis Martin	1.00
22LL	Aaron Brooks	1.00
23LL	Antowain Smith	1.00
24LL	Eddie George	1.00
25LL	Emmitt Smith	3.00
26LL	Laveranues Coles	1.00
27LL	Ricky Williams	2.00

2002 Ultra League Leaders Memorabilia

	NM/M
Common Player:	5.00
Inserted 1:20	
Platinum Cards:	2X to4X
Production 25 sets	
Aaron Brooks	5.00
Laveranues Coles	5.00
Daunte Culpepper	10.00
Stephen Davis	5.00
Marshall Faulk	10.00
Jeff Garcia	5.00
Eddie George	5.00
Torry Holt	5.00
Curtis Martin	5.00
Donovan McNabb	10.00
Terrell Owens	5.00
Antowain Smith	5.00
Emmitt Smith	20.00
Anthony Thomas	10.00
LaDainian Tomlinson	5.00
Brian Urlacher	15.00
Kurt Warner	12.00
Ricky Williams	8.00

2002 Ultra LOGO Rhythm

		NM/M
Common Player:		1.50
Inserted 1:12		
1LR	Brett Favre	5.00
2LR	Kurt Warner	4.00
3LR	Marshall Faulk	3.00
4LR	Daunte Culpepper	2.00
5LR	LaDainian Tomlinson	2.00
6LR	Jeff Garcia	1.50
7LR	Terrell Owens	1.50
8LR	Zach Thomas	1.50
9LR	Brian Urlacher	3.00
10LR	Drew Brees	1.50
11LR	Rich Gannon	1.50
12LR	Germane Crowell	1.50
13LR	Brian Griese	1.50
14LR	Mark Brunell	1.50
15LR	Ron Dayne	1.50
16LR	Jake Plummer	1.50
17LR	Ray Lewis	1.50
18LR	Corey Dillon	1.50
19LR	Kordell Stewart	1.50
20LR	Donovan McNabb	2.00
21LR	Michael Vick	4.00
22LR	Chad Pennington	1.50

2002 Ultra LOGO Rhythm Memorabilia

	NM/M
Common Player:	10.00
Inserted 1:96	
Germane Crowell	10.00
Daunte Culpepper	15.00
Marshall Faulk	15.00
Jeff Garcia	10.00
Brian Griese	15.00
Donovan McNabb	15.00
Terrell Owens	10.00
Chad Pennington	10.00
LaDainian Tomlinson	10.00

Brian Urlacher 25.00
Michael Vick 25.00
Kurt Warner 20.00

2002 Ultra San Diego Bound

NM/M
Common Player: 1.50
Inserted 1:72
1SB Brett Favre 5.00
2SB Kurt Warner 3.00
3SB Marshall Faulk 2.50
4SB Daunte Culpepper 2.00
5SB LaDainian Tomlinson 2.00
6SB Jeff Garcia 1.50
7SB Terrell Owens 1.50
8SB Zach Thomas 1.50
9SB Brian Urlacher 4.00
10SB Drew Brees 2.00
11SB Donovan McNabb 2.00
12SB Brian Griese 2.00
13SB Marvin Harrison 1.50
14SB Tim Couch 1.50
15SB Anthony Thomas 2.50
16SB Tom Brady 4.00
17SB Michael Vick 5.00
18SB Fred Taylor 1.50
19SB Chad Pennington 1.50
20SB Trung Canidate 1.50

2002 Ultra San Diego Bound Memorabilia

NM/M
Common Player: 8.00
Inserted 1:48
Platinum Cards: 2X to 4X
Production 25 sets
Tom Brady 15.00
Tim Couch 8.00
Daunte Culpepper 10.00
Marshall Faulk 12.00
Jeff Garcia 8.00
Brian Griese 8.00
Donovan McNabb 8.00
Terrell Owens 8.00
Chad Pennington 10.00
Fred Taylor 8.00
Anthony Thomas 12.00
LaDainian Tomlinson 8.00
Brian Urlacher 20.00
Michael Vick 20.00
Kurt Warner 15.00

2003 Ultra

NM/M
Common Player (1-160): .15
Unlisted Star: .40
Minor Star: .50
Common Rookie (161-198): 2.00
Inserted 1:4
Common Rookie (U199-U218): 3.00
Inserted 1:4
Pack (8): 2.00
Wax Box (24): 35.00
1 Rich Gannon .50
2 Warren Sapp .40
3 Steve McNair .60
4 Donovan McNabb 1.25
5 Chad Pennington 1.00
6 Michael Vick 2.25
7 Hines Ward .50
8 Terrell Owens .60
9 Brett Favre 2.50
10 Jeremy Shockey 1.50
11 William Green .60
12 Marvin Harrison .60
13 Mark Brunell .60
14 Todd Heap .50
15 Tim Couch 1.00
16 Javon Walker .60
17 Zach Thomas .40
18 Brian Westbrook .40
19 Matt Hasselbeck .15
20 Jevon Kearse .15
21 David Boston .60
22 Michael Bennett .60
23 James Mungro .15
24 Antowain Smith .40
25 Laveranues Coles .50
26 Curtis Conway .40
27 Peerless Price .60
28 Michael Strahan .40
29 Tommy Maddox .50
30 Dennis Northcutt .15
31 Rod Gardner .40
32 Marcel Shipp .15
33 Quincy Morgan .40
34 Reggie Wayne .40
35 Troy Brown .50
36 John Abraham .15
37 Tim Dwight .15
38 Jamal Lewis .60
39 Chad Hutchinson .40
40 Jerramy Stevens .15
41 Deion Branch .40
42 Jake Plummer .60
43 Junior Seau .40
44 T.J. Duckett .60
45 Emmitt Smith 2.00
46 Edgerrin James 1.50
47 David Patten .15
48 Charlie Garner .40
49 Quentin Jammer .40
50 Corey Dillon .60
51 Rod Smith .40
52 Marc Boerigter .50
53 Michael Lewis .15
54 Kendrell Bell .40
55 Isaac Bruce .60
56 Warrick Dunn .40
57 Antonio Bryant .60
58 Peyton Manning 2.00
59 Ty Law .15
60 Jerry Rice 2.00
61 Jeff Garcia .60
62 Joey Galloway .40
63 Aaron Glenn .15
64 Aaron Brooks 1.00
65 Tim Brown .60
66 David Terrell .40
67 Fred Smoot .15
68 Brian Finneran .15
69 Roy Williams .60
70 Corey Bradford .15
71 Deuce McAllister 1.00
72 Jerry Porter .40
73 Kevan Barlow .40
74 Keith Brooking .15
75 Brian Urlacher 1.50
76 Jabar Gaffney .40
77 Randy Moss 2.00
78 Charles Woodson .40
79 Darrell Jackson .15
80 John Lynch .15
81 Chester Taylor .15
82 Anthony Thomas .60
83 Jonathan Wells .60
84 Daunte Culpepper 1.25
85 Phillip Buchanon .40
86 Koren Robinson .15
87 Ronde Barber .15
88 Julius Peppers .40
89 Clinton Portis 2.00
90 Jay Fiedler .40
91 Donte Stallworth 1.00
92 Marc Bulger .60
93 Joe Jurevicius .15
94 Jon Kitna .15
95 Ricky Williams 1.25
96 Joe Horn .40
97 Jerome Bettis .40
98 Kurt Warner 1.50
99 Travis Henry .40
100 Ahman Green .60
101 Jimmy Smith .15
102 Curtis Martin .60
103 Simeon Rice .15
104 Patrick Ramsey .60
105 Josh Reed .60
106 James Stewart .40
107 Trent Green .40
108 Randy McMichael .15
109 Amos Zereoue .40
110 Keyshawn Johnson .60
111 DeShaun Foster .40
112 Kevin Johnson .40
113 Dwight Freeney .15
114 Tom Brady 1.25
115 Santana Moss .40
116 LaDainian Tomlinson 1.50
117 Joey Harrington 1.50
118 Priest Holmes 1.00
119 Amani Toomer .40
120 Plaxico Burress .60
121 Brad Johnson .40
122 Champ Bailey .15
123 Muhsin Muhammad .50
124 Ashley Lelie 1.00
125 Tony Gonzalez .40
126 Kerry Collins .40
127 Antwann Randle El 1.25
128 Torry Holt .60
129 Ladell Betts .40
130 Travis Taylor .40
131 Marty Booker .15
132 Patrick Surtain .15
133 Duce Staley .40
134 Shaun Alexander .60
135 Eddie George .60
136 Eric Moulds .40
137 David Carr 1.50
138 Fred Taylor .60
139 Wayne Chrebet .15
140 Bobby Taylor .40
141 Derrick Brooks .15
142 Stephen Davis .40
143 Ray Lewis .40
144 Kelly Holcomb .40
145 Terry Glenn .40
146 Jason Taylor .15
147 Todd Pinkston .15
148 Derrick Mason .40
149 Chad Johnson .15
150 Ed McCaffrey .15
151 Tiki Barber .40
152 Drew Brees 1.50
153 Marshall Faulk 1.25
154 Drew Bledsoe 1.25
155 Andre Davis .60
156 Donald Driver .40
157 Chris Chambers .60
158 Brian Dawkins .15
159 Garrison Hearst .40
160 Frank Wycheck .15
161 *Carson Palmer* 10.00
162 *Byron Leftwich* 10.00
163 *Charles Rogers* 6.00
164 *Andre Johnson* 10.00
165 *Chris Simms* 6.00
166 *Rex Grossman* 8.00
167 *Brandon Lloyd* 4.00
168 *Lee Suggs* 8.00
169 *Larry Johnson* 6.00
170 *Onterrio Smith* 6.00
171 *Dave Ragone* 4.00
172 *Taylor Jacobs* 2.00
173 *Kelley Washington* 4.00
174 *Bryant Johnson* 4.00
175 *Kyle Boller* 8.00
176 *Ken Dorsey* 6.00
177 *Kliff Kingsbury* 2.00
178 *Jason Gesser* 3.00
179 *Brian St. Pierre* 3.00
180 *Brad Banks* 2.00
181 *Seneca Wallace* 3.00
182 *Tony Romo* 2.00
183 *Terrell Suggs* 3.00
184 *Terence Newman* 5.00
185 *Willis McGahee* 10.00
186 *Justin Fargas* 4.00
187 *Musa Smith* 4.00
188 *Earnest Graham* 2.00
189 *Chris Brown* 8.00
190 *LaBrandon Toefield* 3.00
191 *Bennie Joppru* 2.00
192 *Jason Witten* 6.00
193 *Anquan Boldin* 8.00
194 *Talman Gardner* 2.00
195 *Justin Gage* 4.00
196 *Sam Aiken* 2.00
197 *Kevin Curtis* 2.00
198 *Terrence Edwards* 2.00
U199 *Dewayne Robertson* 2.00
U200 *Kevin Williams* 2.00
U201 *Marcus Trufant* 3.00
U202 *Jimmy Kennedy* 3.00
U203 *Ty Warren* 3.00
U204 *Michael Haynes* 3.00
U205 *Jerome McDougle* 3.00
U206 *Dallas Clark* 6.00
U207 *William Joseph* 3.00
U208 *Andre Woolfolk* 3.00
U209 *Bethel Johnson* 5.00
U210 *Teyo Johnson* 4.00
U211 *Tyrone Calico* 6.00
U212 *L.J. Smith* 3.00
U213 *Nate Burleson* 4.00
U214 *B.J. Askew* 4.00
U215 *Billy McMullen* 3.00
U216 *Domanick Davis* 8.00
U217 *Doug Gabriel* 3.00
U218 *Quentin Griffin* 8.00

2003 Ultra Gold Medallion

Stars: 1.5X-3X
Rookies: .5X-1X
Inserted 1:1

2003 Ultra Platinum Medallion

Stars: 5X-10X
Rookies: 2X-4X
Production 100 Sets

2003 Ultra Award Winners

NM/M
Common Player: 1.00
Inserted 1:12
1AW Priest Holmes 2.00
2AW Clinton Portis 3.00
3AW Rich Gannon 1.00
4AW Derrick Brooks 1.00
5AW Michael Vick 4.00
6AW Jeremy Shockey 3.00
7AW Ricky Williams 2.00
8AW Marvin Harrison 1.00
9AW Chad Pennington 3.00
10AW Tommy Maddox 1.00

2003 Ultra Award Winners Game-Used

NM/M
Common Player: 6.00
Inserted 1:25
1AWG Priest Holmes 12.00
2AWG Clinton Portis 18.00
3AWG Rich Gannon 12.00
4AWG Derrick Brooks 6.00
5AWG Michael Vick 20.00
6AWG Jeremy Shockey 15.00
7AWG Ricky Williams 15.00
8AWG Marvin Harrison 8.00
9AWG Chad Pennington 15.00
10AWG Deuce McAllister 6.00
11AWG Marshall Faulk 12.00
12AWG Terrell Owens 10.00
13AWG LaDainian Tomlinson 8.00
14AWG Travis Henry 6.00

2003 Ultra Award Winners UltraSwatch

NM/M
Common Player: 15.00
AWDB Derrick Brooks/55 20.00
AWMF Marshall Faulk/28 40.00
AWRG Rich Gannon/12
AWMH Marvin Harrison/88 15.00
AWTH Travis Henry/20 20.00
AWPH Priest Holmes/31 40.00
AWDM Deuce McAllister/26 40.00
AWTO Terrell Owens/81 20.00
AWCP2 Chad Pennington/10
AWCP Clinton Portis/26 50.00
AWJS Jeremy Shockey/80 20.00
AWLT LaDainian Tomlinson/21 50.00
AWMV Michael Vick/7
AWRW Ricky Williams/34 50.00

2003 Ultra Autographs

NM/M
UAJ Andre Johnson/300 75.00
ULJ Larry Johnson/350 30.00
UBL Byron Leftwich/300 100.00
UCP Carson Palmer/300 75.00

2003 Ultra Head of the Class

NM/M
Common Player: 3.00
Production 599 sets
1HC Carson Palmer 10.00
2HC Byron Leftwich 10.00
3HC Charles Rogers 8.00
4HC Andre Johnson 8.00
5HC Chris Simms 6.00
6HC Rex Grossman 7.00
7HC Brandon Lloyd 4.00
8HC Lee Suggs 6.00
9HC Larry Johnson 8.00
10HC Onterrio Smith 3.00
11HC Dave Ragone 4.00
12HC Taylor Jacobs 4.00
13HC Kelley Washington 4.00
14HC Bryant Johnson 6.00
15HC Willis McGahee 8.00

2003 Ultra Touchdown Kings

NM/M
Common Player: 2.00
Inserted 1:24
1TD Jerry Rice 4.00
2TD Peyton Manning 3.00
3TD Randy Moss 3.00
4TD Tom Brady 3.00
5TD Brett Favre 5.00
6TD Drew Bledsoe 3.00
7TD Steve McNair 2.00
8TD Emmitt Smith 5.00
9TD Priest Holmes 3.00
10TD Michael Vick 5.00
11TD Chad Pennington 4.00
12TD Donovan McNabb 3.00
13TD Shaun Alexander 2.00
14TD Ricky Williams 4.00
15TD Clinton Portis 4.00

2003 Ultra Touchdown Kings Career

NM/M
Common Player: 15.00
TKSA Shaun Alexander/36 20.00
TKDB Drew Bledsoe/194 15.00
TKTB Tom Brady/47 25.00
TKBF Brett Favre/326 25.00
TKPH Priest Holmes/45 25.00
TKPM Peyton Manning/147 25.00
TKDM Donovan McNabb/85 20.00
TKSM Steve McNair/103 15.00
TKRM Randy Moss/60 30.00
TKCP2 Chad Pennington/26 40.00
TKCP Clinton Portis/17
TKJR Jerry Rice/202 20.00
TKES Emmitt Smith/164 30.00
TKRW Ricky Williams/35 30.00
TKMV Michael Vick/27 50.00

2003 Ultra Touchdown Kings Memorabilia

NM/M
Common Player: 8.00
Inserted 1:26
1TD Jerry Rice 15.00
2TD Peyton Manning 15.00
3TD Randy Moss 15.00
4TD Tom Brady 12.00
5TD Brett Favre 25.00
6TD Drew Bledsoe 12.00
7TD Steve McNair 8.00
8TD Emmitt Smith 25.00
9TD Priest Holmes 15.00
10TD Michael Vick 20.00
11TD Chad Pennington 12.00
12TD Donovan McNabb 12.00
13TD Shaun Alexander 8.00
14TD Ricky Williams 10.00
15TD Clinton Portis 15.00

2003 Ultra Touchdown Kings Ultraswatch

NM/M
TKSA Shaun Alexander/37 25.00
TKDB Drew Bledsoe/11
TKTB Tom Brady/12
TKBF Brett Favre/4
TKPH Priest Holmes/31 30.00
TKPM Peyton Manning/18
TKDM Donovan McNabb/5
TKSM Steve McNair/9
TKRM Randy Moss/2
TKCP2 Chad Pennington/10
TKCP Clinton Portis/26 50.00
TKJR Jerry Rice/12
TKES Emmitt Smith/22
TKMV Michael Vick/7
TKRW Ricky Williams/34 40.00

2004 Ultra

NM/M
Common Player (1-200): .25
Minor Stars: .50
Unlisted Stars: .75
Common Rookie (201-213): 25.00
Production 500 Sets
Common Rookie (214-232): 1.00
Common Rookie Update (U234-U253): 3.00
Inserted 2:1 Tradition Hot Pack
Inserted 1:4
Pack (8): 5.00
Box (24): 85.00
1 Michael Vick 2.25
2 Kelley Washington .25
3 Rex Grossman .75
4 Boss Bailey .25
5 Johnnie Morton .25
6 Michael Strahan .25
7 Joey Porter .25
8 Keenan McCardell .25
9 Quincy Carter .75
10 Travis Henry .25
11 Bert Berry .25
12 Marvin Harrison .75
13 Ty Law .25
14 Phillip Buchanon .25
15 Kevan Barlow .25
16 Eddie George .75
17 Drew Bledsoe .75
18 Antonio Bryant .50
19 Marcus Pollard .25
20 *Brian Russell* .25
21 Santana Moss .25
22 Julian Peterson .25
23 Justin McCareins .25
24 Ed Reed .25
25 Charles Tillman .25
26 Dat Nguyen .25
27 Ricky Manning .25
28 Dwight Freeney .25
29 Zach Thomas .25
30 Tiki Barber .25
31 Jay Riemersma .25
32 Joe Jurevicius .25
33 Marcel Shipp .25
34 Justin Gage .25
35 Charles Rogers .75
36 Eddie Kennison .25
37 Deion Branch .25
38 Matt Hasselbeck .50
39 L.J. Smith .25
40 Jamal Lewis .75
41 Muhsin Muhammad .50
42 Terence Newman .50
43 Jabar Gaffney .25
44 Junior Seau .50
45 Jeremy Shockey .75
46 Hines Ward .50
47 Brad Johnson .25
48 Kyle Boller .75
49 Steve Smith .25
50 Quincy Morgan .25
51 Corey Bradford .25
52 Ricky Williams 1.00
53 Amani Toomer .50
54 Plaxico Burress .75
55 Derrick Brooks .25
56 Dre' Bly .25
57 Terrell Suggs .25
58 DeShaun Foster .25
59 Andre Davis .50
60 Rod Smith .25
61 Andre Johnson .75
62 Randy McMichael .25
63 Ike Hilliard .25
64 Antwann Randle El .50
65 Warren Sapp .25
66 LaBrandon Toefield .25
67 Chad Johnson .50
68 Javon Walker .50
69 Jimmy Smith .25
70 Donte Stallworth .50
71 Brian Dawkins .25
72 Leonard Little .25
73 Ladell Betts .25
74 Ray Lewis .50
75 Stephen Davis .50
76 Dennis Northcutt .25
77 Ashley Lelie .50
78 Billy Miller .25
79 Chris Chambers .75
80 John Abraham .25
81 Quentin Jammer .50
82 Isaac Bruce .50
83 Peerless Price .50
84 Jake Delhomme .75
85 Lee Suggs .50
86 Shannon Sharpe .50
87 Domanick Davis .75
88 Daunte Culpepper .75
89 Shaun Ellis .25
90 Drew Brees .75
91 Torry Holt .75
92 Alge Crumpler .25
93 Mike Rucker .25
94 Tim Couch .25
95 Quentin Griffin .25
96 David Carr 1.00
97 Moe Williams .25
98 Chad Pennington 1.00
99 LaDainian Tomlinson 1.00
100 Adam Archuleta .25
101 Julius Peppers .25
102 Clinton Portis 1.50
103 Marcus Stroud .25
104 Tom Brady 1.50
105 Teyo Johnson .75
106 Terrell Owens .75
107 Keith Bulluck .25
108 Eric Moulds .25
109 Jake Plummer .50
110 Reggie Wayne .50
111 Tedy Bruschi .25
112 Rich Gannon .50
113 Tony Parrish .25
114 Steve McNair .75
115 T.J. Duckett .50
116 Peter Warrick .50
117 Donald Driver .50
118 Fred Taylor .75
119 Joe Horn .25
120 Jerry Porter .25
121 Marc Bulger .25
122 Trung Canidate .25
123 Warrick Dunn .25
124 Kelly Holcomb .25
125 Robert Ferguson .25
126 Byron Leftwich 1.50
127 Michael Lewis .25
128 Jerry Rice 2.00
129 Marshall Faulk 1.00
130 Patrick Ramsey .50
131 Josh McCown .25
132 Anthony Thomas .50
133 Joey Harrington .75
134 Dante Hall .25
135 Daniel Graham .25
136 Richard Seymour .25
137 Brandon Lloyd .25
138 Anquan Boldin .75
139 Jon Kitna .25
140 Nick Barnett .25
141 Priest Holmes 1.00
142 Bethel Johnson .25
143 Shaun Alexander .75
144 Todd Heap .50
145 Brian Urlacher .75
146 Peyton Manning 1.50
147 Jason Taylor .25
148 Kerry Collins .25
149 Tommy Maddox .50
150 Charles Lee .25
151 Tim Rattay .25
152 Carson Palmer 1.00
153 Brett Favre 2.50
154 Trent Green .25
155 Aaron Brooks .75
156 Brian Westbrook .25
157 Itula Mili .25
158 Keith Brooking .25
159 Rudi Johnson .50
160 Najeh Davenport .25
161 Kevin Johnson .25
162 Eddie "Boo" Williams .25
163 Corey Simon .25
164 Darrell Jackson .25
165 Darnerian McCants .25
166 Willis McGahee .75
167 Terry Glenn .25
168 Dallas Clark .25
169 Randy Moss 1.50
170 Charles Woodson .25
171 Jeff Garcia .75
172 Chris Brown .25
173 Emmitt Smith 2.00
174 Marty Booker .25
175 Artose Pinner .25
176 Tony Gonzalez .50
177 Troy Brown .25
178 Freddie Mitchell .25
179 Marcus Trufant .25
180 London Fletcher .25
181 Roy Williams .25
182 Edgerrin James 1.00
183 Michael Bennett .75
184 Jerald Sowell .25
185 David Boston .50
186 Derrick Mason .25
187 Bryant Johnson .25
188 Corey Dillon .50
189 Ahman Green .75
190 Vonnie Holliday .25
191 Deuce McAllister .75
192 Donovan McNabb 1.00
193 Koren Robinson .25
194 Laveranues Coles .50
195 Takeo Spikes .25
196 Richie Anderson .25
197 Onterrio Smith .25
198 Curtis Martin .75
199 Antonio Gates .25
200 Champ Bailey .25
201 *Eli Manning* 80.00
202 *Philip Rivers* 40.00
203 *Roy Williams* 40.00
204 *Drew Henson* 30.00
205 *Chris Perry* 25.00
206 *Larry Fitzgerald* 40.00
207 *Rashaun Woods* 25.00
208 *Reggie Williams* 25.00
209 *Mike Williams* 60.00
210 *Kellen Winslow* 25.00
211 *Steven Jackson* 30.00
212 *Kevin Jones* 30.00
213 *Ben Roethlisberger* 125.00
214 *Michael Turner* 1.00
215 *Tatum Bell* 3.00
216 *Quincy Wilson* 1.00
217 *Devery Henderson* 1.00
218 *Ernest Wilford* 1.50
219 *Cody Pickett* 2.00
220 *Ryan Dinwiddie* 1.00
221 *J.P. Losman* 4.00
222 *Derrick Knight* 1.00
223 *Michael Jenkins* 1.50
224 *Greg Jones* 4.00
225 *Cedric Cobbs* 2.00
226 *Will Poole* 1.50
227 *Michael Clayton* 4.00
228 *Sean Taylor* 4.00
229 *Will Smith* 2.00
230 *Jonathan Vilma* 2.50
231 *Lee Evans* 4.00
232 *Julius Jones* 5.00
U234 *D.J. Williams* 4.00
U235 *Mewelde Moore* 3.00
U236 *Ben Watson* 3.00
U237 *Robert Gallery* 6.00
U238 *DeAngelo Hall* 6.00
U239 *Luke McCown* 3.00
U240 *Ben Troupe* 3.00
U241 *Keary Colbert* 3.00
U242 *Matt Schaub* 3.00
U243 *Kenechi Udeze* 3.00
U244 *Jeff Smoker* 6.00
U245 *Derrick Hamilton* 3.00
U246 *Bernard Berrian* 3.00
U247 *Devard Darling* 3.00
U248 *Johnnie Morant* 3.00
U249 *Vince Wilfork* 4.00
U250 *Jericho Cotchery* 3.00
U251 *Darius Watts* 3.00
U252 *Carlos Francis* 3.00
U253 *P.K. Sam* 4.00

2004 Ultra Gold Medallion

Stars (1-200): 1X-2X
Rookies (201-213): .25X-.5X
Rookies (214-232): 1X-2X

2004 Ultra Platinum Medallion

Stars (1-200): 5X-15X
Production 66 Sets
Rookies (201-213): No Pricing
Production 13 Sets
Rookies (214-232): 2X-5X
Production 66 Sets

2004 Ultra Gridiron Producers

NM/M
Common Player: 3.00
Inserted 1:44
Copper: 1X-1.5X
Gold: 1.5X-2.5X
Gold Production 77 Sets
Platinum Production 9 Sets
1GP Donovan McNabb 8.00
2GP Charles Rogers 5.00
3GP Daunte Culpepper 5.00
4GP Matt Hasselbeck 3.00
5GP Jerry Rice 12.00
6GP Tom Brady 10.00
7GP Byron Leftwich 10.00
8GP Ahman Green 5.00
9GP Stephen Davis 3.00
10GP LaDainian Tomlinson 8.00

2004 Ultra Gridiron Producers Ultraswatch

NM/M
1 Donovan McNabb/5
2 Charles Rogers/80
3 Daunte Culpepper/11
4 Matt Hasselbeck/8
5 Jerry Rice/80
6 Tom Brady/12
7 Byron Leftwich/7
8 Ahman Green/30
9 Stephen Davis/48
10 LaDainian Tomlinson/21

2004 Ultra Passing Kings

NM/M
Common Player: 3.00
Inserted 1:96
Gold: 1X-2.5X
Production 50 Sets
1 3.00
1PA Brett Favre 15.00
2PA Donovan McNabb 8.00
3PA Peyton Manning 10.00
4PA Steve McNair 5.00
5PA Daunte Culpepper 5.00
6PA Tom Brady 10.00
7PA Byron Leftwich 10.00
8PA Joey Harrington 8.00
9PA Matt Hasselbeck 3.00
10PA Marc Bulger 10.00
NNO Manning AU/50 500.00

2004 Ultra Performers

NM/M
Common Player: 1.00
Inserted 1:6
Copper: 1X-2X
Gold: 2X-5X
Gold Production 88 Sets
Platinum: No Pricing
Platinum Production 19 Sets
1UP Tom Brady 2.00
2UP Clinton Portis 2.00

NM/M
3UP Priest Holmes 1.50
4UP Marshall Faulk 1.50
5UP Randy Moss 2.00
6UP Marvin Harrison 1.25
7UP Donovan McNabb 1.50
8UP Ricky Williams 1.50
9UP Brett Favre 3.00
10UP Steve McNair 1.25
11UP Peyton Manning 2.00
12UP Shaun Alexander 1.25
13UP Edgerrin James 1.50
14UP Chad Johnson 1.00
15UP Torry Holt 1.25

2004 Ultra Performers Ultraswatch

1 Tom Brady/12
2 Clinton Portis/26
3 Priest Holmes/31
4 Marshall Faulk/28
5 Randy Moss/84
6 Marvin Harrison/88
7 Donovan McNabb/5
8 Ricky Williams/34
9 Brett Favre/4
10 Steve McNair/9
11 Peyton Manning/18
12 Shaun Alexander/37
13 Edgerrin James/32
14 Chad Johnson/80
15 Torry Holt/88

2004 Ultra Receiving Kings

NM/M
Common Player: 3.00
Inserted 1:96
Gold: 1X-2X
Gold Production 50 Sets
1RE Randy Moss 10.00
2RE Torry Holt 8.00
3RE Anquan Boldin 8.00
4RE Chad Johnson 5.00
5RE Derrick Mason 3.00
6RE Marvin Harrison 8.00
7RE Laveranues Coles 5.00
8RE Terrell Owens 8.00
9RE Charles Rogers 5.00
10RE Jerry Rice 12.00

2004 Ultra Rushing Kings

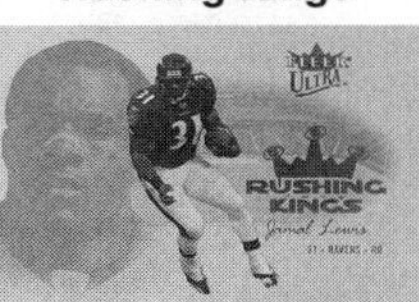

NM/M
Common Player: 2.00
Inserted 1:24
Gold: 1X-2X
Gold Production 50 Sets
1RU Clinton Portis 6.00
2RU Priest Holmes 5.00
3RU Stephen Davis 2.00
4RU Marshall Faulk 5.00
5RU LaDainian Tomlinson 5.00
6RU Shaun Alexander 3.00
7RU Deuce McAllister 3.00
8RU Ricky Williams 5.00
9RU Jamal Lewis 5.00
10RU Ahman Green 3.00

2004 Ultra Season Crowns Autographs

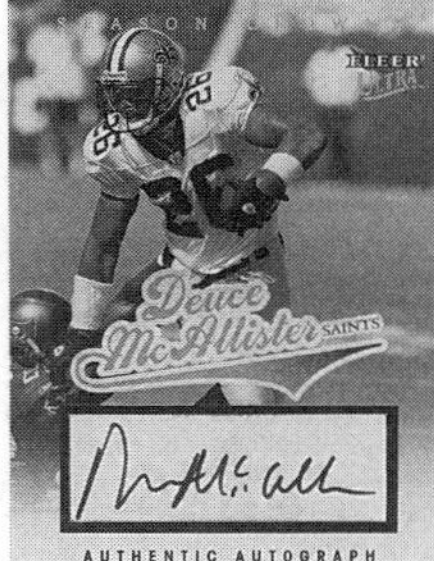

NM/M
Common Player: 15.00
Production 150 Sets
Gold Production 25 Sets
1 Kyle Boller 20.00
2 Plaxico Burress 15.00
3 David Carr 30.00
4 LaDainian Tomlinson 30.00
5 Chad Pennington 30.00
6 Donovan McNabb/25
7 Matt Hasselbeck/75 50.00
8 Philip Rivers 60.00
9 Roy Williams 60.00
10 Eli Manning 150.00
11 Dante Hall 25.00
12 Brian Westbrook 15.00
13 Jake Delhomme 40.00
14 Kelley Washington 15.00
15 Joe Jurevicius 15.00
16 Byron Leftwich 50.00
17 Shaun Alexander 25.00
18 Drew Henson 75.00
19 Deuce McAllister 30.00
20 Mike Williams 120.00
21 Steven Jackson 50.00
22 Will Poole 15.00

2004 Ultra Season Crowns Game Used Copper

NM/M
Common Player: 5.00
Production 349 Sets
Silver: .75X-1.5X
Silver Production 149 Sets
Gold: 1.5X-2.5X
Gold Production 99 Sets
Platinum: 3X-5X
Platinum Production 29 Sets
1 Rex Grossman 8.00
2 Julius Peppers 5.00
3 Antwann Randle El 8.00
4 Charles Rogers 8.00
5 Brian Urlacher 10.00
6 Carson Palmer 10.00
7 Priest Holmes 10.00
8 Travis Henry 5.00
9 Andre Johnson 6.00
10 Marvin Harrison 6.00
11 Randy Moss 10.00
12 Corey Dillon 5.00
13 Ray Lewis 8.00
14 Ricky Williams 10.00
15 Peyton Manning Pants 12.00
16 Michael Bennett 6.00
17 Torry Holt 6.00
18 Deuce McAllister 8.00
19 Deion Branch 5.00
20 DeShaun Foster 5.00
21 Edgerrin James 8.00
22 Steve McNair 6.00
23 Brett Favre 25.00
24 Chad Pennington 8.00
25 Brad Johnson 5.00
26 Fred Taylor 6.00
27 Michael Vick 20.00
28 Derrick Brooks 5.00
29 LaDainian Tomlinson 8.00
30 Warren Sapp 5.00
31 Byron Leftwich 8.00
32 Donovan McNabb 10.00
33 Ahman Green 10.00
34 Emmitt Smith 20.00
35 Tommy Maddox 5.00
36 Shaun Alexander 6.00
37 Joey Harrington 8.00
38 Marshall Faulk 8.00
39 Jerry Rice 15.00
40 T.J. Duckett 5.00
41 Eric Moulds 5.00
42 Tom Brady 12.00
43 David Carr 10.00
44 Daunte Culpepper 6.00
45 Isaac Bruce 5.00
46 Chad Johnson 6.00
47 Jeremy Shockey 8.00
48 Eddie George 5.00
49 Quincy Carter 6.00
50 Aaron Brooks 6.00

2004 Ultra Three Kings Game Used

NM/M
Common Card: 30.00
Production 33 Sets
1 Marvin Harrison, Randy Moss, Jerry Rice 80.00
2 Steve McNair, Donovan McNabb, Daunte Culpepper 60.00
3 Priest Holmes, Ricky Williams, Marshall Faulk 80.00
4 Chad Johnson, Charles Rogers, Anquan Boldin 30.00
5 Peyton Manning, Tom Brady, Brett Favre 120.00
6 Matt Hasselbeck, Joey Harrington, Byron Leftwich 50.00
7 Jamal Lewis, Shaun Alexander, Stephen Davis 40.00
8 Terrell Owens, Jerry Rice, Randy Moss 80.00
9 Ahman Green, Deuce McAllister, LaDainian Tomlinson 60.00
10 Marshall Faulk, Torry Holt, Marc Bulger 60.00

1991 Upper Deck Promos

These two promo card preview Upper Deck's 1991 debut football set. The design is similar to that which was used for the regular set, but the photos and card numbers for the two players' corresponding cards are different. Cards were also available through 900-number promotion by Upper Deck. The Montana card is $4; the Sanders card is $2.50.

NM/M
Complete Set (2): 12.00
Common Player: 7.00
1 Joe Montana 7.00
500 Barry Sanders 8.00

1991 Upper Deck

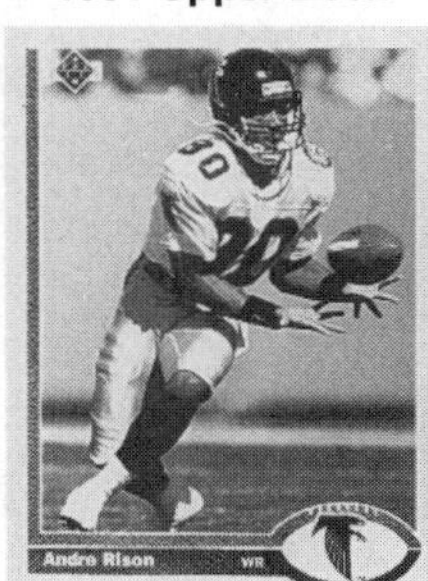

Issued in August, Upper Deck's premier football set was issued on foil packs. Upper Deck also randomly issued 2,500 autographed Joe Montana Heroes of Football cards. The set includes many of the elements from the baseball and hockey sets, including a "Star Rookies" subset. (Key: SR - star rookie, SL - season leader)

NM/M
Complete Set (700): 15.00
Complete Lo Series (500): 10.00
Complete Hi Series (200): 5.00
Complete Factory Set (700): 20.00
Common Player: .05
Low or High Pack (12): .50
Low or High Wax Box (36): 15.00
1 Star Rookie Checklist .10
2 *Eric Bieniemy* (SR) .15
3 Mike Dumas (SR) .05
4 *Mike Croel* (SR) .15
5 *Russell Maryland* (SR) .50
6 *Charles McRae* (SR) .10
7 *Dan McGwire* (SR) .10
8 *Mike Pritchard* (SR) .35
9 *Ricky Watters* (SR) 1.75
10 *Chris Zorich* (SR) .30
11 *Browning Nagle* (SR) .20
12 *Wesley Carroll* (SR) .10
13 *Brett Favre* (SR) 15.00
14 *Rob Carpenter* (SR) .15
15 *Eric Swann* (SR) .25
16 *Stanley Richard* .35
17 *Herman Moore* (SR) 2.00
18 *Todd Marinovich* (SR) .10
19 Aaron Craver (SR) .10
20 Chuck Webb (SR) .05
21 *Todd Lyght* (SR) .10
22 *Greg Lewis* (SR) .10
23 *Eric Turner* (SR) .20
24 *Alvin Harper* (SR) .30
25 *Jarrod Bunch* (SR) .10
26 *Bruce Pickens* (SR) .10
27 *Harvey Williams* (SR) .50
28 *Randal Hill* (SR) .40
29 *Nick Bell* (SR) .15
30 Jim Everett, Henry Ellard .05
31 Randall Cunningham, Keith Jackson .10
32 Steve DeBerg, Stephone Paige .05
33 Warren Moon, Drew Hill .10
34 Dan Marino, Mark Clayton .20
35 Montana, Rice .40
36 Percy Snow .05
37 Kelvin Martin .05
38 Scott Case .05
39 *John Gesek* .10
40 *Barry Word* .15
41 Cornelius Bennett .05
42 Mike Kenn .05
43 Andre Reed .15
44 Bobby Hebert .05
45 William Perry .05
46 Dennis Byrd .05
47 Martin Mayhew .05
48 Issiac Holt .05
49 William White .05
50 JoJo Townsell .05
51 Jarvis Williams .05
52 Joey Browner .05
53 Pat Terrell .05
54 Joe Montana 1.00
55 Jeff Jerrod .05
56 Cris Carter .05
57 Jerry Rice .75
58 Brett Perriman .05
59 Kevin Fagen .05
60 Wayne Haddix .05
61 Tommy Kane .05
62 Pat Beach .05
63 Jeff Lageman .05
64 Hassan Jones .05
65 Bennie Blades .05
66 Tim McGee .05
67 Robert Blackmon .05
68 *Fred Stokes* .20
69 *Barney Bussey* .10
70 Eric Metcalf .05
71 Mark Kelso .05
72 Neal Anderson Bears Checklist .05
73 Boomer Esiason Bengals Checklist .05
74 Thurman Thomas Bills Checklist .25
75 John Elway Broncos Checklist .15
76 Eric Metcalf Browns Checklist .05
77 Vinny Testaverde Buccaneers Checklist .05
78 Johnny Johnson Cardinals Checklist .10
79 Anthony Miller Chargers Checklist .05
80 Derrick Thomas Chiefs Checklist .12
81 Jeff George Colts Checklist .12
82 Troy Aikman Cowboys Checklist .65
83 Dan Marino Dolphins Checklist .30
84 Randall Cunningham Eagles Checklist .10
85 Deion Sanders Falcons Checklist .12
86 Jerry Rice 49ers Checklist .40
87 Lawrence Taylor Giants Checklist .08
88 Al Toon Jets Checklist .05
89 Barry Sanders Lions Checklist .50
90 Warren Moon Oilers Checklist .10
91 Sterling Sharpe Packers Checklist .20
92 Andre Tippett Patriots Checklist .05
93 Jim Everett Rams Checklist .05
94 Bo Jackson Raiders Checklist .25
95 Art Monk Redskins Checklist .05
96 Morten Andersen Saints Checklist .05
97 John L. Williams Seahawks Checklist .05
98 Rod Woodson Steelers Checklist .05
99 Herschel Walker Vikings Checklist .05
100 Checklist .05
101 Steve Young .75
102 Jim Lachey .05
103 Tom Rathman .05
104 Earnest Byner .05
105 Karl Mecklenburg .05
106 Wes Hopkins .05
107 Michael Irvin .20
108 Burt Grossman .05
109 Jay Novacek .25
110 Ben Smith .05
111 Rod Woodson .05
112 Ernie Jones .05
113 Bryan Hinkle .05
114 Vai Sikahema .05
115 Bubby Brister .05
116 Brian Blades .05
117 Don Majkowski .05
118 Rod Bernstine .05
119 Brian Noble .05
120 Eugene Robinson .05
121 John Taylor .12
122 Vance Johnson .05
123 Art Monk .05
124 John Elway .35
125 Dexter Carter .05
126 Anthony Miller .05
127 Keith Jackson .15
128 Albert Lewis .05
129 Bill Ray Smith .05
130 Clyde Simmons .05
131 Merril Hoge .05
132 Ricky Proehl .12
133 Tim McDonald .05
134 Louis Lipps .05
135 Ken Harvey .05
136 Sterling Sharpe .20
137 Gill Byrd .05
138 Tim Harris .05
139 Derrick Fenner .10
140 Johnny Holland .05
141 Ricky Sanders .05
142 Bobby Humphrey .05
143 Roger Craig .05
144 Steve Atwater .05
145 Ickey Woods .05
146 Randall Cunningham .15
147 Marion Butts .05
148 Reggie White .15
149 Ronnie Harmon .05
150 Mike Saxon .05
151 Greg Townsend .05
152 Troy Aikman 1.00
153 Shane Conlan .05
154 Deion Sanders .25
155 Bo Jackson .35
156 Jeff Hostetler .20
157 Albert Bentley .05
158 James Williams .05
159 Bill Brooks .05
160 Nick Lowery .05
161 Ottis Anderson .05
162 Kevin Greene .05
163 Neil Smith .05
164 Jim Everett .05
165 Derrick Thomas .25
166 John L. Williams .05
167 Timm Rosenbach .05
168 Leslie O'Neal .05
169 Clarence Verdin .05
170 Dave Krieg .05
171 Steve Broussard .05
172 Emmitt Smith 2.00
173 Andre Rison .25
174 Bruce Smith .05
175 Mark Clayton .05
176 Christian Okoye .05
177 Duane Bickett .05
178 Stephone Paige .05
179 Fredd Young .05
180 Mervyn Fernandez .05
181 Phil Simms .10
182 Pete Holohan .05
183 Pepper Johnson .05
184 Jackie Slater .05
185 Stephen Baker .05
186 Frank Cornish .05
187 Dave Waymer .05
188 Terance Mathis .10
189 Darryl Talley .05
190 James Hasty .05
191 Jay Schroeder .05
192 Kenneth Davis .05
193 Chris Miller .05
194 Scott Davis .05
195 Tim Green .05
196 Dan Saleaumua .05
197 Rohn Stark .05
198 John Alt .05
199 Steve Tasker .05
200 Checklist .05
201 Freddie Joe Nunn .05
202 Jim Breech .05
203 Roy Green .05
204 Gary Anderson (T.B.) .05
205 Rich Camarillo .05
206 Mark Bortz .05
207 Eddie Brown .05
208 Brad Muster .05
209 Anthony Munoz .05
210 Dalton Hilliard .05
211 Erik McMillan .05
212 Perry Kemp .05
213 Jim Thornton .05
214 Anthony Dilweg .05
215 Cleveland Gary .05
216 Leo Goeas .05
217 Mike Merriweather .05
218 Courtney Hall .05
219 Wade Wilson .05
220 Billy Joe Tolliver .05
221 Harold Green .10
222 Al Baker .05
223 Carl Zander .05
224 Thane Gash .05
225 Kevin Mack .05
226 Morten Andersen .05
227 Dennis Gentry .05
228 Vince Buck .05
229 Mike Singletary .05
230 Rueben Mayes .05
231 Mark Carrier (T.B.) .05
232 Tony Mandarich .05
233 Al Toon .05
234 Renaldo Turnbull .05
235 Broderick Thomas .05
236 Anthony Carter .05
237 Flipper Anderson .05
238 Jerry Robinson .05
239 Vince Newsome .05
240 Keith Millard .05
241 Reggie Langhorne .05
242 James Francis .05
243 Felix Wright .05
244 Neal Anderson .10
245 Boomer Esiason .15
246 Pat Swilling .05
247 Richard Dent .05
248 Craig Heyward .05
249 Ron Morris .05
250 Eric Mann .05
251 Jim Jensen .05
252 Anthony Toney .05
253 Sammie Smith .05
254 Calvin Williams .20
255 Dan Marino .75
256 Warren Moon .20
257 Tommie Agee .05
258 Haywood Jeffires .25
259 Eugene Lockhart .05
260 Drew Hill .05
261 Vinny Testaverde .10
262 Jim Arnold .05
263 Steve Christie .05
264 Chris Spielman .05
265 Reggie Cobb .25
266 John Stephens .05
267 Jay Hilgenberg .05

268 Brent Williams .05
269 Rodney Hampton .75
270 Irving Fryar .05
271 Terry McDaniel .05
272 Reggie Roby .05
273 Allen Pinkett .05
274 Tim McKyer .05
275 Bob Golic .05
276 Wilber Marshall .05
277 Ray Childress .05
278 Charles Mann .05
279 *Cris Dishman* .15
280 Mark Rypien .15
281 Michael Cofer (Det.) .05
282 Keith Byars .05
283 Mike Rozier .05
284 Seth Joyner .05
285 Jessie Tuggle .05
286 Mark Bavaro .05
287 Eddie Anderson .05
288 Sean Landeta .05
289 Howie Long .12
290 Reyna Thompson .05
291 Ferrell Edmunds .05
292 Willie Gault .05
293 John Offerdahl .05
294 Tim Brown .12
296 Kevin Ross .05
297 Lorenzo White .10
298 Dino Hackett .05
299 Curtis Duncan .05
300 Checklist .05
301 Andre Ware .12
302 David Little .05
303 Jerry Ball .05
304 Dwight Stone .05
305 Rodney Peete .05
306 Mike Baab .05
307 Tim Worley .05
308 Paul Farren .05
309 Carnell Lake .05
310 Clay Matthews .05
311 Alton Montgomery .05
312 Ernest Givins .05
313 Mike Horan .05
314 Sean Jones .05
315 Leonard Smith .05
316 Carl Banks .05
317 Jerome Brown .05
318 Everson Walls .05
319 Ron Heller .05
320 Mark Collins .05
321 Eddie Murray .05
322 Jim Harbaugh .10
323 Mel Gray .05
324 Keith Van Horne .05
325 Lomas Brown .05
326 Carl Lee .05
327 Ken O'Brien .05
328 Dermontti Dawson .05
329 Brad Baxter .15
330 Chris Doleman .05
331 Louis Oliver .05
332 Frank Stams .05
333 Mike Munchak .05
334 Fred Strickland .05
335 Mark Duper .05
336 Jacob Green .05
337 Tony Paige .05
338 Jeff Bryant .05
339 Lemuel Stinson .05
340 David Wyman .05
341 Lee Williams .05
342 Trace Armstrong .05
343 Junior Seau .30
344 John Roper .05
345 Jeff George .30
346 Herschel Walker .05
347 Sam Clancy .05
348 Steve Jordan .05
349 Nate Odomes .05
350 Martin Bayless .05
351 Brent Jones .05
352 Ray Agnew .05
353 Charles Haley .05
354 Andre Tippett .05
355 Ronnie Lott .10
356 Thurman Thomas .50
357 Fred Barnett .15
358 James Lofton .05
359 *William Frizzell* .10
360 Keith McKeller .05
361 Rodney Holman .05
362 Henry Ellard .05
363 David Fulcher .05
364 Jerry Gray .05
365 James Brooks .05
366 Tony Stargell .05
367 Keith McCants .05
368 Lewis Billups .05
369 Ervin Randle .05
370 Pat Leahy .05
371 Bruce Armstrong .05
372 Steve DeBerg .05
373 Guy McIntyre .05
374 Deron Cherry .05
375 Fred Marion .05
376 Michael Haddix .05
377 Kent Hull .05
378 Jerry Holmes .05
379 Jim Richter .05
380 Ed West .05
381 Richmond Webb .05
382 Mark Jackson .05
383 Tom Newberry .05
384 Ricky Nattiel .05
385 Keith Sims .05
386 Ron Hall .05
387 Ken Norton .05
388 Paul Gruber .05
389 Danny Stubbs .05
390 Ian Beckles .05
391 Hoby Brenner .05
392 Tory Epps .05
393 Sam Mills .05
394 Chris Hinton .05
395 Steve Walsh .05
396 Simon Fletcher .05
397 Tony Bennett .05
398 Aundray Bruce .05
399 Mark Murphy .05
400 Checklist .05
401 Barry Sanders (SL) .50
402 Jerry Rice (SL) .35
403 Warren Moon (SL) .10
404 Derrick Thomas (SL) .12
405 Nick Lowery (SL) .05
406 Mark Carrier (Chi.) (SL) .05
407 Michael Carter .05
408 Chris Singleton .05
409 Matt Millen .05
410 Ronnie Lippett .05
411 E.J. Junior .05
412 Ray Donaldson .05
413 Keith Willis .05
414 Jessie Hester .05
415 Jeff Cross .05
416 Greg Jackson .10
417 Alvin Walton .05
418 Bart Oates .05
419 Chip Lohmiller .05
420 John Elliot .05
421 Randall McDaniel .05
422 Richard Johnson .05
423 Al Noga .05
424 Lamar Lathon .05
425 Ricky Fenney .05
426 Jack Del Rio .05
427 Don Mosebar .05
428 Luis Sharpe .05
429 Steve Wisniewski .05
430 Jimmie Jones .05
431 Freeman McNeil .05
432 Ron Rivera .05
433 Hart Lee Dykes .05
434 Mark Carrier (Chi.) .05
435 Rob Moore .15
436 Gary Clark .12
437 Heath Sherman .10
438 Darrell Greem .05
439 Jessie Small .05
440 Monte Coleman .05
441 Leonard Marshall .05
442 Richard Johnson .05
443 Dave Meggett .05
444 Barry Sanders 1.25
445 Lawrence Taylor .10
446 Marcus Allen .05
447 Johnny Johnson .25
448 Aaron Wallace .05
449 Anthony Thompson .05
450 Gary Lewis .05
451 Andre Rison (MVP) .12
452 Thurman Thomas (MVP) .25
453 Neal Anderson (MVP) .05
454 Boomer Esiason (MVP) .05
455 Eric Metcalf (MVP) .05
456 Emmitt Smith (MVP) 1.00
457 Bobby Humphrey (MVP) .05
458 Barry Sanders (MVP) .50
459 Sterling Sharpe (MVP) .20
460 Warren Moon (MVP) .10
461 Albert Bentley (MVP) .05
462 Steve DeBerg (MVP) .05
463 Greg Townsend (MVP) .05
464 Henry Ellard (MVP) .05
465 Dan Marino (MVP) .40
466 Anthony Carter (MVP) .05
467 John Stephens (MVP) .05
468 Pat Swilling (MVP) .05
469 Ottis Anderson (MVP) .05
470 Dennis Byrd (MVP) .05
471 Randall Cunningham (MVP) .10
472 Johnny Johnson (MVP) .10
473 Rod Woodson (MVP) .05
474 Anthony Miller (MVP) .05
475 Jerry Rice (MVP) .35
476 John L. Williams (MVP) .05
477 Wayne Haddix (MVP) .05
478 Earnest Byner (MVP) .05
479 Doug Widell .05
480 Tommy Hodson .05
481 Shawn Collins .05
482 Rickey Jackson .05
483 Tony Casillas .05
484 Vaughan Johnson .05
485 Floyd Dixon .05
486 Eric Green .12
487 Harry Hamilton .05
488 Gary Anderson (Pit.) .05
489 Bruce Hill .05
490 Gerald Williams .05
491 Cortez Kennedy .30
492 Chet Brooks .05
493 Dwayne Harper .15
494 Don Griffin .05
495 Andy Heck .05
496 David Treadwell .05
497 Irv Pankey .05
498 Dennis Smith .05
499 Marcus Dupree .05
500 Checklist .05
501 Wendell Davis .05
502 Matt Bahr .05
503 *Rob Burnett* .12
504 Maurice Carthon .05
505 Donnell Woolford .05
506 Howard Ballard .05
507 Mark Boyer .05
508 Eugene Marve .05
509 Joe Kelly .05
510 Will Wolford .05
511 Robert Clark .05
512 *Matt Brock* .12
513 Chris Warren .50
514 Ken Willis .05
515 *George Jamison* .12
516 Rufus Porter .05
517 *Mark Higgs* .25
518 Thomas Everett .05
519 Robert Brown .05
520 Gene Atkins .05
521 Hardy Nickerson .05
522 Johnny Bailey .05
523 William Fryar .05
524 Steve McMichael .05
525 Kevin Porter .05
526 Carwell Gardner .05
527 Eugene Daniel .05
528 Vestee Jackson .05
529 Chris Goode .05
530 Leon Seals .05
531 Darion Conner .05
532 Stan Brock .05
533 *Kirby Jackson* .10
534 Marv Cook .05
535 Bill Fralic .05
536 Keith Woodside .05
537 Hugh Green .05
538 Grant Feasel .05
539 Bubba McDowell .05
540 Vai Sikahema .05
541 Aaron Cox .05
542 Roger Craig .05
543 Robb Thomas .05
544 Ronnie Lott .10
545 Robert Delpino .05
546 Greg McMurtry .05
547 *Jim Morrissey* .10
548 Johnny Rembert .05
549 *Markus Paul* .12
550 *Karl Wilson* .12
551 Gaston Green .05
552 Willie Drewrey .05
553 Michael Young .05
554 Tom Tupa .05
555 John Friesz .15
556 *Cody Carlson* .35
557 Eric Allen .05
558 Tom Bensen .05
559 *Scott Mersereau* .10
560 Lionel Washington .05
561 Brian Brennan .05
562 Jim Jeffcoat .05
563 Jeff Jaeger .05
564 David Johnson .05
565 Danny Villa .05
566 Don Beebe .05
567 Michael Haynes .30
568 Brett Faryniarz .05
569 Mike Prior .05
570 *John Davis* .12
571 *Vernon Turner* .12
572 Michael Brooks .05
573 Mike Gann .05
574 Ron Holmes .05
575 Gary Plummer .05
576 Bill Romanowski .05
577 Chris Jacke .05
578 Gary Reasons .05
579 *Tim Jorden* .08
580 Tim McKyer .05
581 Johnny Jackson .05
582 Ethan Horton .05
583 Pete Stoyanovich .05
584 Jeff Query .05
585 Frank Reich .05
586 Riki Ellison .05
587 Eric Hill .05
588 Anthony Shelton .05
589 Steve Smith .05
590 *Garth Jax* .08
591 *Greg Davis* .10
592 Bill Maas .05
593 *Henry Rolling* .10
594 Keith Jones .05
595 Tootie Robbins .05
596 *Brian Jordan* .25
597 *Derrick Walker* .12
598 Jonathan Hayes .05
599 *Nate Lewis* .25
600 Checklist 501-600 .05
601 Greg Lewis, Keith Traylor, Kenny Walker, Denver Broncos AFC Checklist RF .15
602 *James Jones* .15
603 *Tim Barnett* .15
604 *Ed King* .10
605 Shane Curry .05
606 Mike Croel .20
607 *Bryan Cox* .50
608 *Shawn Jefferson* .12
609 *Kenny Walker* .25
610 *Michael Jackson* .75
611 *Jon Vaughn* .20
612 Greg Lewis .05
613 Joe Valerio .05
614 *Pat Harlow* .10
615 *Henry Jones* .20
616 *Jeff Graham* .75
617 *Darryll Lewis* .12
618 *Keith Traylor* .10
619 Scott Miller .05
620 Nick Bell .10
621 *John Flannery* .12
622 *Leonard Russell* .50
623 *Alfred Williams* .10
624 Browning Nagle .15
625 Harvey Williams .10
626 Dan McGwire .10
627 Brett Favre, Moe Gardner, Erric Pegram, Bruce Pickens, Mike Pritchard (CL) .50
628 *William Thomas* .10
629 *Lawrence Dawsey* .15
630 *Aeneas Williams* .10
631 Stan Thomas .05
632 Randal Hill .15
633 *Moe Gardner* .10
634 Alvin Harper .25
635 *Esera Tuaolo* .08
636 Russell Maryland .20
637 Anthony Morgan .15
638 *Erric Pegram* .40
639 Herman Moore .75
640 *Ricky Ervins* .20
641 *Kelvin Pritchett* .10
642 *Roman Phifer* .10
643 *Antone Davis* .10
644 Mike Pritchard .40
645 *Vinnie Clark* .10
646 *Jake Reed* 1.00
647 Brett Favre 3.00
648 Todd Lyght .10
649 Bruce Pickens .05
650 *Darren Lewis* .25
651 Wesley Carroll .10
652 *James Joseph* .25
653 Robert Delpino .05
654 Vencie Glenn .05
655 Jerry Rice .20
656 Barry Sanders .50
657 Ken Tippins .05
658 Christian Okoye .05
659 Rich Gannon .05
660 Johnny Meads .05
661 *J.J. Birden* .10
662 Bruce Kozerski .05
663 Felix Wright .05
664 Al Smith .05
665 Stan Humphries .30
666 Alfred Anderson .05
667 Nate Newton .05
668 *Vince Workman* .10
669 Ricky Reynolds .05
670 *Bryce Paup* .75
671 Gill Generty .05
672 Darrell Thompson .20
673 Anthony Smith .05
674 *Darryl Henley* .08
675 Brett Maxie .05
676 Craig Taylor .05
677 Steve Wallace .05
678 *Jeff Feagles* .08
679 *James Washington* .10
680 Tim Harris .05
681 Dennis Gibson .05
682 *Toi Cook* .10
683 Lorenzo Lynch .05
684 *Brad Edwards* .10
685 *Ray Crockett* .10
686 Harris Barton .05
687 Byron Evans .05
688 Eric Thomas .05
689 Jeff Criswell .05
690 Eric Ball .05
691 Brian Mitchell .20
692 Quinn Early .05
693 Aaron Jones .05
694 Jim Dombrowski .05
695 Jeff Bostic .05
696 Tony Casillas .05
697 Ken Lanier .05
698 Henry Thomas .05
699 Steve Beuerlein .20
700 Checklist 601-700 .05
SP1 Darrell Green .50
SP2 Don Shula 1.00

1991 Upper Deck Game Breaker Holograms

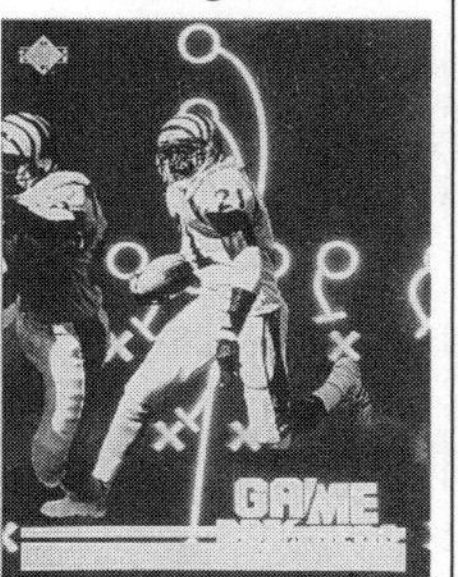

Nine top running backs are featured on these insert cards, which were randomly included in 1991 Upper Deck packs. Series I packs contained cards 1-6; Series II packs had cards 7-9. Each card front has an action hologram against a background with a diagramed football play. "Gamebreakers" is in the bottom right corner, next to a stripe which has the player's name in it. The card backs are numbered with a "GB" prefix and contain the player's team logo and a career summary.

NM/M
Complete Set (9): 8.00
Common Player: .60
1 Barry Sanders 4.00
2 Thurman Thomas 1.25
3 Bobby Humphrey .60
4 Earnest Byner .60
5 Emmitt Smith 4.50
6 Neal Anderson .60
7 Marion Butts .60
8 James Brooks .60
9 Marcus Allen .75

1991 Upper Deck Joe Montana Heroes

This is the first set of Upper Deck's Football Heroes series. These 10 cards are devoted to 49er quarterback Joe Montana. Each card front has an oval framed with white and blue borders. A color photo is inside the oval. The card is two-toned - it shades from mustard to brown, and has the set logo in the bottom left corner. The card back is designed like a football field and includes a career summary and card number (1 of 9, etc.). Cards were random inserts in 1991 Upper Deck Series I packs. Montana autographed 2,500 of the cards. The tenth card is an unnumbered header card. A title appears on each card, too.

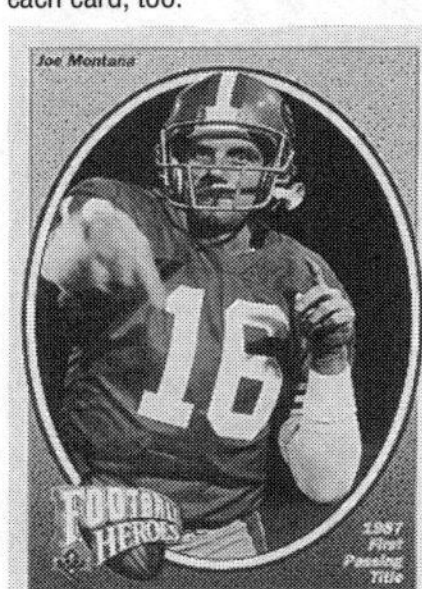

NM/M
Complete Set (10): 15.00
Common Player: 1.50
Montana Header SP (NNO): 6.00
Montana Auto/2500: 200.00
1 Joe Montana 1974-78 College Years 1.50
2 Joe Montana 1981 A Star is Born 1.50
3 Joe Montana 1984 Super Bowl MVP 1.50
4 Joe Montana 1987 1st Passing Title 1.50
5 Joe Montana 1988 Rematch 1.50
6 Joe Montana 1989 NFL's MVP 1.50
7 Joe Montana 1989 Back-to-Back 1.50
8 Joe Montana 1990 Career Highs 1.50
9 Joe Montana Checklist Heroes 1-9 (Vernon Wells potrait of Montana) 1.50
---- Joe Montana Title/Header card SP (Unnumbered) 6.00

1991 Upper Deck Heroes Montana Box Bottoms

This eight-card set is identical to the Montana Heroes insert except they have blank backs and are oversized. Cards measure 5-1/4" x 7-1/4" and were found on the bottom of 1991 Upper Deck low series wax boxes.

NM/M
Complete Set (8): 5.00
Common Player: 1.00
1 1974-78 College Years 1.00
2 1981 A Star is Born 1.00
3 1984 Super Bowl MVP 1.00
4 1987 1st Passing Title 1.00
5 1988 Rematch 1.00
6 1989 NFL's MVP 1.00
7 1989 Back-to-Back 1.00
8 1990 Career Highs 1.00

1991 Upper Deck Joe Namath Heroes

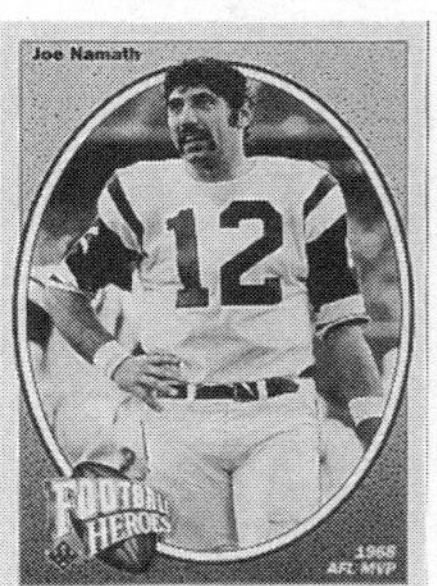

Hall of Fame quarterback Joe Namath is featured in this Football Heroes set which starts where the similar Joe Montana set ended. Cards are numbered 10-18 and were randomly inserted in 1991 Upper Deck Series II packs. The front has an oval with a picture in it, bordered with a white and blue frame. The player's name is in the bottom right corner, along with a title. A "Football Heroes" logo is in the lower left corner. The back has a football field design and includes a career summary and card number. Namath autographed 2,500 cards; he autographed every 100th card "Broadway Joe."

NM/M
Complete Set (10): 15.00
Common Player: 1.50
Namath Header SP (NNO): 6.00
Namath Auto/2500: 200.00
10 Joe Namath 1962-65 Crimson Tide 1.50
11 Joe Namath 1965 Broadway Joe 1.50
12 Joe Namath 1967 4,000 Yards Passing 1.50
13 Joe Namath 1968 AFL MVP 1.50
14 Joe Namath 1969 Super Bowl III 1.50
15 Joe Namath 1969 All-Pro 1.50
16 Joe Namath 1972 400 Yards 1.50
17 Joe Namath 1985 Hall of Fame 1.50
18 Joe Namath Checklist Heroes 10-18 1.50
---- Joe Namath Title/Header Card SP (Unnumbered) 6.00

1991 Upper Deck Heroes Namath Box Bottoms

This eight-card set has identical photos to the Namath Heroes insert, but has blank backs and printed on an oversized format. The cards measure 5-1/4" x 7-1/4" and are found on the bottom of 1991 Upper Deck high series football wax boxes.

NM/M
Complete Set (8): 5.00
Common Player: 1.00
10 1962-65 Crimson Tide 1.00
11 1965 Broadway Joe 1.00
12 1967 4,000 Yards Passing 1.00
13 1968 AFL MVP 1.00
14 1969 Super Bowl III 1.00
15 1969 All-Pro 1.00
16 1972 400 Yards 1.00
17 1985 Hall of Fame 1.00

1991 Upper Deck Sheets

Upper Deck offered two 8-1/2" x 11" sheets, with one commemorating the New York Giants Super Bowl XXV Champions and the second commemorating the 40th anniversay of the 1951 Rams championship team. The Giants sheet has the issue date, production run and issue number in the lower right hand corner. The Rams sheet was limited to 60,000.

NM/M
Complete Set (2): 10.00
Common Player: 5.00
1 October 1991 (60,000) 5.00
2 Rodney Hampton, Lawrence Taylor, Dave Meggett, Jeff Hostetler, Mark Collins, Ottis Anderson October 27, 1991 (SB XXV Champions) (72,000) 5.00

1992 Upper Deck

Upper Deck's 1992 set was issued in two series - 440 and 220 cards each. The card front has an action photo with a shadowed border framed by a white border. The player's name is at the bottom left; his position and team logo are on the right. Both are encompassed by a granite bar with a team color-coded bar accent. The back has another photo, plus stats and a biography. Subsets include Star Rookies, All-Rookies, Team Checklists, Season Leaders, Team MVP, Rookie Force and NFL Scrapbook. Insert sets include a Gold set of 50 (each card has a gold hologram); Pro Bowlers; Game Breakers; Walter Payton; Football Heroes (Dan Marino); NFL Fanimation and Coach's Report, which features comments from former Pittsburgh Steelers coach Chuck Noll about top rookies and second-year players.

		NM/M
Complete Set (620):		17.00
Complete Series 1 (400):		10.00
Complete Series 2 (220):		7.00
Common Player:		.05
Series 1 or 2 Pack (15):		1.00
Series 1 or 2 Wax Box (36):		20.00
1	Star Rookie CL	.25
2	*Edgar Bennett*	.50
3	*Eddie Blake*	.08
4	*Brian Bollinger*	.08
5	*Joe Bowden*	.08
6	*Terrell Buckley*	.25
7	*Willie Clay*	.10
8	*Ed Cunningham*	.10
9	*Matt Darby*	.10
10	*Will Furrer*	.20
11	*Chris Hakel*	.10
12	*Carlos Huerta*	.10
13	*Amp Lee*	.30
14	*Ricardo McDonald*	.10
15	*Dexter McNabb*	.10
16	*Chris Mims*	.30
17	*Derrick Moore*	.50
18	*Robert Porcher*	.05
19	*Patrick Rowe*	.08
20	*Leon Searcy*	.08
21	*Torrance Small*	.08
22	*Jimmy Smith*	2.00
23	*Tony Smith*	.08
24	*Siran Stacy*	.08
25	*Kevin Turner*	.08
26	*Tommy Vardell*	.20
27	*Bob Whitfield*	.10
28	*Darryl Williams*	.10
29	*Jeff Sydner*	.10
30	All-Rookie Checklist	.10
31	Todd Marinovich	.10
33	Nick Bell	.10
34	Alvin Harper	.30
35	Mike Pritchard	.15
36	Lawrence Dawsey	.10
37	Tim Barnett	.05
38	John Flannery	.05
39	Stan Thomas	.05
40	Ed King	.05
41	Charles McRae	.08
42	Eric Moten	.08
43	Moe Gardner	.08
44	Kenny Walker	.08
45	Esera Tuaolo	.08
46	Alfred Williams	.10
47	Bryan Cox	.15
48	Mo Lewis	.05
49	Mike Croel	.08
50	Stanley Richard	.08
51	Tony Covington	.05
52	Larry Brown	.05
53	Aeneas Williams	.05
54	John Kasay	.05
55	Jon Vaughn	.08
56	David Fulcher	.05
57	Barry Foster	.40
58	Terry Wooden	.05
59	Gary Anderson	.05
60	Alfred Williams	.05
61	Robert Blackmon	.05
62	Brian Noble	.05
63	Terry Allen	.40
64	Darrell Green	.05
65	Darren Comeaux	.05
66	Rob Burnett	.05
67	Jerrod Bunch	.05
68	Michael Jackson	.15
69	Greg Lloyd	.05
70	Richard Brown	.05
71	Harold Green	.05
72	William Fuller	.05
73	Mark Carrier (TC)	.05
74	David Fulcher (TC)	.05
75	Cornelius Bennett (TC)	.05
76	Steve Atwater (TC)	.05
77	Kevin Mack (TC)	.05
78	Mark Carrier (TC)	.05
79	Tim McDonald (TC)	.05
80	Marion Butts (TC)	.05
81	Christian Okoye (TC)	.05
82	Jeff Herrod (TC)	.05
83	Emmitt Smith (TC)	1.00
84	Mark Duper (TC)	.05
85	Keith Jackson (TC)	.05
86	Andre Rison (TC)	.10
87	John Taylor (TC)	.05
88	Rodney Hampton (TC)	.10
89	Rob Moore (TC)	.05
90	Chris Spielman (TC)	.05
91	Haywood Jeffires (TC)	.05
92	Sterling Sharpe (TC)	.15
93	Irving Fryar (TC)	.05
94	Marcus Allen (TC)	.05
95	Henry Ellard (TC)	.05
96	Mark Rypien (TC)	.05
97	Pat Swilling (TC)	.05
98	Brian Blades (TC)	.05
99	Eric Green (TC)	.05
100	Anthony Carter (TC)	.05
101	Burt Grossman	.05
102	Gary Anderson	.05
103	Neil Smith	.05
104	Jeff Feagles	.05
105	Shane Conlon	.05
106	Jay Novacek	.05
107	Billy Brooks	.05
108	Mark Ingram	.05
109	Anthony Munoz	.05
110	Wendell Davis	.05
111	Jim Everett	.05
112	Bruce Matthews	.05
113	Mark Higgs	.20
114	Chris Warren	.10
115	Brad Baxter	.05
116	Greg Townsend	.05
117	Al Smith	.05
118	Jeff Cross	.05
119	Terry McDaniel	.05
120	Ernest Givins	.05
121	Fred Barnett	.05
122	Flipper Anderson	.05
123	Floyd Turner	.05
124	Stephen Baker	.05
125	Tim Johnson	.05
126	Brent Jones	.05
127	Leonard Marshall	.05
128	Jim Price	.05
129	Jessie Hester	.05
130	Mark Carrier	.05
131	Bubba McDowell	.05
132	Andre Tippett	.05
133	James Hasty	.05
134	Mel Gray	.05
135	Christian Okoye	.05
136	Earnest Byner	.05
137	Ferrell Edmunds	.05
138	Henry Ellard	.05
140	Brian Jordan	.05
141	Clarence Verdin	.05
142	Cornelius Bennett	.05
143	John Taylor	.05
144	Derrick Thomas	.05
145	Thurman Thomas	.50
146	Warren Moon	.25
147	Vinny Testaverde	.05
148	*Steve Bono*	.50
149	Robb Thomas	.05
150	John Friesz	.05
151	Richard Dent	.05
152	Eddie Anderson	.05
153	Kevin Greene	.05
154	Marion Butts	.05
155	Barry Sanders	1.25
156	Andre Rison	.25
157	Ronnie Lott	.10
158	Eric Allen	.05
159	Mark Clayton	.05
160	Terance Mathis	.05
161	Darryl Talley	.05
162	Eric Metcalf	.05
163	Reggie Cobb	.10
164	Ernie Jones	.05
165	David Griggs	.05
166	Tom Rathman	.05
167	Bubby Brister	.05
168	Broderick Thomas	.05
169	Chris Doleman	.05
170	Charles Haley	.05
171	Michael Haynes	.30
172	Rodney Hampton	.35
173	Nick Bell	.10
174	Gene Atkins	.05
175	Mike Merriweather	.05
176	Reggie Roby	.05
177	Bennie Blades	.05
178	John L. Williams	.05
179	Rodney Peete	.05
180	Greg Montgomery	.15
181	Vince Newsome	.05
182	Andre Collins	.05
183	Erik Kramer	.05
184	Bryan Hinkle	.05
185	Reggie White	.20
186	Bruce Armstrong	.05
187	Anthony Carter	.05
188	Pat Swilling	.05
189	Robert Delpino	.05
190	Brent Williams	.05
191	Johnny Johnson	.05
192	Aaron Craver	.05
193	Vincent Brown	.05
194	Herschel Walker	.10
195	Tim McDonald	.05
196	Gaston Green	.05
197	Brian Blades	.05
198	Rod Bernstine	.05
199	Brett Perriman	.05
200	John Elway	.40
201	Michael Carter	.05
202	Mark Carrier	.05
203	Cris Carter	.05
204	Kyle Clifton	.05
205	Alvin Wright	.10
206	Andre Ware	.05
207	Dave Waymer	.05
208	Darren Lewis	.05
209	Joey Browner	.05
210	Rich Miano	.05
211	Marcus Allen	.05
212	Steve Broussard	.05
213	Joel Hilgenberg	.05
214	*Bo Orlando*	.05
215	Clay Matthews	.05
216	Chris Hinton	.05
217	Al Edwards	.05
218	Tim Brown	.05
219	Sam Mills	.05
220	Don Majkowski	.05
221	James Francis	.05
222	Steve Hendrickson	.05
223	James Thornton	.05
224	Byron Evans	.05
225	Pepper Johnson	.05
226	Darryl Henley	.05
227	Simon Fletcher	.05
228	Hugh Millen	.05
229	Tim McGee	.05
230	Richmond Webb	.05
231	Tony Bennett	.05
232	Nate Odomes	.05
233	Scott Case	.05
234	Dalton Hilliard	.05
235	Paul Gruber	.05
236	Jeff Lageman	.05
237	Tony Mandarich	.05
238	Cris Dishman	.05
239	Steve Walsh	.05
240	Moe Gardner	.05
241	Bill Romanowski	.05
242	Chris Zorich	.05
243	Stephone Paige	.05
244	Mike Croel	.05
245	Leonard Russell	.30
246	Mark Rypien	.10
247	Aeneas Williams	.05
248	Steve Atwater	.05
249	Michael Stewart	.05
250	Pierce Holt	.05
251	Kevin Mack	.05
252	Sterling Sharpe	.10
253	Lawrence Dawsey	.05
254	Emmitt Smith	2.00
255	Todd Marinovich	.05
256	Neal Anderson	.05
257	Mo Lewis	.05
258	Vance Johnson	.05
259	Rickey Jackson	.05
260	Esera Tuaolo	.05
261	Wilber Marshall	.05
262	Keith Henderson	.05
263	William Thomas	.05
264	Rickey Dixon	.05
265	Dave Meggett	.05
266	Gerald Riggs	.05
267	Tim Harris	.05
268	Ken Harvey	.05
269	Clyde Simmons	.05
270	Irving Fryar	.05
271	Darion Conner	.05
272	Vince Workman	.05
273	Jim Harbaugh	.05
274	Lorenzo White	.05
275	Bobby Hebert	.05
276	Duane Bickett	.05
277	Jeff Bryant	.05
278	Scott Stephen	.05
279	Bob Golic	.05
280	Steve McMichael	.05
281	Jeff Graham	.05
282	Keith Jackson	.05
283	Howard Ballard	.05
284	Michael Brooks	.05
285	Freeman McNeil	.05
286	Rodney Holman	.05
287	Eric Bieniemy	.05
288	Seth Joyner	.05
289	Carwell Gardner	.05
290	Brian Mitchell	.05
291	Chris Miller	.05
292	Ray Berry	.05
293	Matt Brock	.05
294	Eric Thomas	.05
295	John Kasay	.05
296	Jay Hilgenberg	.05
297	Darrell Thompson	.05
298	Rich Gannon	.05
299	Steve Young	1.00
300	Mike Kenn	.05
301	Emmitt Smith (SL)	1.00
302	Haywood Jeffires (SL)	.05
303	Michael Irvin (SL)	.25
304	Warren Moon (SL)	.15
305	Chip Lohmiller (SL)	.05
306	Barry Sanders (SL)	.50
307	Ronnie Lott (SL)	.05
308	Pat Swilling (SL)	.05
309	Thurman Thomas (SL)	.25
310	Reggie Roby (SL)	.05
311	Season Leader Checklist	.05
312	Jacob Green	.05
313	Stephen Braggs	.05
314	Haywood Jeffires	.15
315	Freddie Joe Nunn	.05
316	Gary Clark	.05
317	Tim Barnett	.05
318	Mark Duper	.05
319	Eric Green	.05
320	Robert Wilson	.05
321	Michael Ball	.05
322	Eric Martin	.05
323	Alexander Wright	.05
324	Jessie Tuggle	.05
325	Ronnie Harmon	.05
326	Jeff Hostetler	.05
327	Eugene Daniel	.05
328	Ken Norton	.05
329	Reyna Thompson	.05
330	Jerry Ball	.05
331	Leroy Hoard	.05
332	Chris Martin	.05
333	Keith McKeller	.05
334	Brian Washington	.05
335	Eugene Robinson	.05
336	Maurice Hurst	.05
337	Dan Saleaumua	.05
338	Neil O'Donnell	.40
339	Dexter Davis	.05
340	Keith McCants	.05
341	Steve Beuerlein	.10
342	Roman Phifer	.05
343	Bryan Cox	.05
344	Art Monk	.05
345	Michael Irvin	.25
346	Vaughn Johnson	.05
347	Jeff Herrod	.05
348	Stanley Richard	.05
349	Michael Young	.05
350	Team MVP Checklist	.05
351	Jim Harbaugh (MVP)	.05
352	David Fulcher (MVP)	.05
353	Thurman Thomas	.25
354	Gaston Green (MVP)	.05
355	Leroy Hoard (MVP)	.05
356	Reggie Cobb (MVP)	.05
357	Tim McDonald (MVP)	.05
358	Ronnie Harmon (MVP)	.05
359	Derrick Thomas (MVP)	.15
360	Jeff Herrod (MVP)	.05
361	Michael Irvin (MVP)	.25
362	Mark Higgs (MVP)	.10
363	Reggie White (MVP)	.10
364	Chris Miller (MVP)	.05
365	Steve Young (MVP)	.50
366	Rodney Hampton (MVP)	.10
367	Jeff Lageman (MVP)	.05
368	Barry Sanders (MVP)	.50
369	Haywood Jeffires (MVP)	.10
370	Tony Bennett	.05
371	Leonard Russell	.05
372	Jeff Jaeger	.05
373	Robert Delpino	.05
374	Mark Rypien	.05
375	Pat Swilling	.05
376	Cortez Kennedy	.05
377	Eric Green	.05
378	Cris Carter	.05
379	John Roper	.05
380	Barry Word	.05
381	Shawn Jefferson	.05
382	Tony Casillas	.05
383	*John Baylor*	.10
384	Al Noga	.05
385	Charles Mann	.05
386	Gil Byrd	.05
387	Chris Singleton	.05
388	James Joseph	.05
389	Larry Brown	.05
390	Chris Spielman	.05
391	Anthony Thompson	.05
392	Karl Mecklenburg	.05
393	Joe Kelly	.05
394	Kanavis McGhee	.05
395	Bill Maas	.05
396	Marv Cook	.05
397	Louis Lipps	.05
398	*Marty Carter*	.25
399	Louis Oliver	.05
400	Eric Swann	.05
401	*Troy Auzenne*	.10
402	Kurt Barber	.05
403	*Mark Boutte*	.10
404	*Dale Carter*	.10
405	*Marco Coleman*	.25
406	Quentin Coryatt	.40
407	*Shane Dronett*	.20
408	Vaughn Dunbar	.20
409	Steve Emtman	.15
410	*Dana Hall*	.10
411	*Jason Hansen*	.10
412	*Courtney Hawkins*	.30
413	Terrell Buckley	.10
414	*Robert Jones*	.10
415	David Klingler	.20
416	Tommy Maddox	2.75
417	*Johnny Mitchell*	.50
418	Carl Pickens	.50
419	Tracy Scroggins	.10
420	*Tony Sacca*	.15
421	Kevin Smith	.10
422	Alonzo Spellman	.10
423	*Troy Vincent*	.15
424	*Sean Gilbert*	.40
425	*Larry Webster*	.10
426	Rookie Force Checklist	.20
427	Bill Fralic	.05
428	Kevin Murphy	.05
429	Lemuel Stinson	.10
430	Harris Barton	.05
431	Dino Hackett	.10
432	John Stephens	.05
433	*Keith Jennings*	.10
434	Derrick Fenner	.05
435	*Kenneth Gant*	.25
436	Willie Gault	.05
437	Steve Jordan	.05
438	Charles Haley	.05
439	Keith Kartz	.05
440	Nate Lewis	.05
441	Doug Widell	.05
442	William White	.05
443	Eric Hill	.05
444	Melvin Jenkins	.05
445	David Wyman	.05
446	Ed West	.05
447	Brad Muster	.05
448	Ray Childress	.05
449	Kevin Ross	.05
450	Johnnie Jackson	.05
451	Tracy Simien	.05
452	Don Mosebar	.05
453	Jay Hilgenberg	.05
454	Wes Hopkins	.05
455	Jay Shcoreder	.05
456	Jeff Bostic	.05
457	Bryce Paup	.05
458	Dave Waymer	.05
459	Toi Cook	.05
460	Anthony Smith	.05
461	Don Griffin	.05
462	Bill Hawkins	.05
463	Courtney Hall	.05
464	Jeff Ulenhake	.05
465	Mike Sherrard	.05
466	James Jones	.05
467	Jerrol Williams	.05
468	Eric Ball	.05
469	Randall McDaniel	.05
470	Alvin Harper	.40
471	Tom Waddle	.10
472	Tony Woods	.05
473	Kelvin Martin	.05
474	Jon Vaughn	.10
475	Gil Fenerty	.05
476	Aundray Bruce	.05
477	Morton Anderson	.05
478	Lamar Lathon	.05
479	Steve DeOssie	.05
480	Marvin Washington	.05
481	Herschel Walker	.05
482	Howie Long	.05
483	Calvin Williams	.10
484	Brett Favre	2.00
485	Johnny Bailey	.05
486	Jeff Gossett	.05
487	Carnell Lake	.05
488	*Michael Zordich*	.10
489	Henry Rolling	.05
490	Steve Smith	.05
491	Vestee Jackson	.05
492	Ray Crockett	.05
493	Dexter Carter	.05
494	Nick Lowery	.05
495	Cortez Kennedy	.15
496	Cleveland Gary	.05
497	Kelly Stouffer	.05
498	Carl Carter	.05
499	Shannon Sharpe	.30
500	Roger Craig	.05
501	Willie Drewrey	.05
502	Mark Schlereth	.05
503	Tony Martin	.05
504	Tom Newberry	.05
505	Ron Hall	.05
506	Scott Miller	.05
507	Donnell Woolford	.05
508	Dave Krieg	.05
509	Erric Pegram	.50
510	Checklist	.05
511	Barry Sanders (ScpBk)	.50
512	Thurman Thomas (ScpBk)	.25
513	Warren Moon (ScpBk)	.10
514	John Elway (ScpBk)	.20
515	Ronnie Lott (ScpBk)	.10
516	Emmitt Smith (ScpBk)	1.00
517	Andre Rison (ScpBk)	.20
518	Steve Atwater (ScpBk)	.05
519	Steve Young (ScpBk)	.20
520	Mark Rypien (ScpBk)	.05
521	Rich Camarillo	.05
522	Mark Bavaro	.05
523	Brad Edwards	.05
524	*Chad Hennings*	.05
525	Tony Paige	.05
526	Shawn Moore	.05
527	*Sidney Johnson*	.05
528	*Sanjay Beach*	.05
529	Kelvin Pritchett	.05
530	Jerry Holmes	.05
531	Al Del Greco	.05
532	Bob Gagliano	.05
533	Drew Hill	.05
534	*Donald Frank*	.05
535	*Pio Sagapolutele*	.05
536	Donald Hollas	.05
537	Vernon Turner	.05
538	Bobby Humphrey	.05
539	Audray McMillen	.05
540	*Gary Brown*	.25
541	Wesley Carroll	.05
542	Nate Newton	.05
543	Vai Sikahema	.05
544	Chris Chandler	.05
545	*Nolan Harrison*	.10
546	Mark Green	.05
547	Ricky Watters	.50
548	J.J. Birden	.05
549	Cody Carlson	.05
550	Tim Green	.05
551	Mark Jackson	.05
552	Vince Buck	.05
553	George Jamison	.05
554	Anthony Pleasant	.05
555	Reggie Johnson	.05
556	John Jackson	.05
557	Ian Beckles	.05
558	Buford McGee	.05
559	Fuad Reveiz	.05
560	Joe Montana	1.00
561	Phil Simms	.05
562	Greg McMurtry	.05
563	Gerald Williams	.05
564	Dave Cadigan	.05
565	Rufus Porter	.05
566	Jim Kelly	.25
567	Deion Sanders	.50
568	Mike Singletary	.05
569	Boomer Esiason	.10
570	Andre Reed	.15
571	James Washington	.05
572	Jack Del Rio	.05
573	Gerald Perry	.05
574	Vinnie Clark	.05
575	Mike Piel	.05
576	Michael Dean Perry	.05
577	Ricky Proehl	.05
578	Leslie O'Neal	.05
579	Russell Maryland	.15
580	Eric Dickerson	.05
581	Fred Strickland	.05
582	Nick Lowery	.05
583	*Joe Milinichik*	.06
584	Mark Vlasic	.05
585	James Lofton	.05
586	Bruce Smith	.15
587	Harvey Williams	.15
588	Bernie Kosar	.05
589	Carl Banks	.05
590	Jeff George	.05
591	*Fred Jones*	.10
592	Todd Scott	.05
593	Keith Jones	.05
594	Tootie Robbins	.05
595	*Todd Philcox*	.25
596	Browning Nagle	.05
597	Troy Aikman	1.25
598	Dan Marino	1.50
599	Lawrence Taylor	.15
600	Webster Slaughter	.05
601	Aaron Cox	.05
602	Matt Stover	.05
603	Keith Sims	.05
604	Dennis Smith	.05
605	Kevin Porter	.05
606	Anthony Miller	.10
607	Ken O'Brien	.05
608	Randall Cunningham	.20
609	Timm Rosenbach	.05
610	Junior Seau	.15
611	Johnny Rembert	.05
612	Rick Tuten	.05
613	Willie Green	.15
614	*Sean Salisbury*	.40
615	Martin Bayless	.05
616	Jerry Rice	.75
617	Randal Hill	.10
618	Dan McGwire	.05
619	Merril Hoge	.05
620	Checklist	.05

1992 Upper Deck Gold

These inserts, numbered with a G prefix, feature cards from three subsets - NFL Top Prospects (1-20), Quarterback Club (21- 25) and veterans (26-50). Each 1992 Upper Deck Series I foil box contained a 15-card foil pack of these cards. Jerry Rice and Andre Reed Game Breaker holograms were also randomly included in these packs. All players were licensed by NFL Properties. Each card front has a color action photo with a white border. The player's name and position are at the bottom for cards 1-20 and 26-50; Quarterback Club cards have the player's name printed along the left side in a black stripe. The backs have a closeup photo, statistics, biography or profile, except for the Prospects cards, which only have a summary of the player's career. The NFL Properties logo is on the back of the card, along with a gold Upper Deck hologram football, instead of the usual silver design.

		NM/M
Complete Set (50):		15.00
Common Player:		.10
1	*Steve Emtman*	.25
2	*Carl Pickens*	1.00
3	*Dale Carter*	.60
4	*Greg Skrepenak*	.10
5	*Kevin Smith*	.50
6	*Marco Coleman*	.50
7	*David Klingler*	.50
8	*Phillippi Sparks*	.10
9	*Tommy Maddox*	.40
10	*Quentin Coryatt*	.50
11	Ty Detmer	.25
12	*Vaughn Dunbar*	.40
13	Ashley Ambrose	.10
14	Kurt Barber	.10
15	Chester McGlockton	.10
16	*Todd Collins*	.35
17	*Steve Israel*	.10
18	*Marquez Pope*	.25
19	*Alonzo Spellman*	.50
20	*Tracy Scroggins*	.60
21	Jim Kelly	.50
22	Troy Aikman	1.00
23	Randall Cunningham	.50
24	Bernie Kosar	.10
25	Dan Marino	2.00
26	Andre Reed	.35
27	Deion Sanders	.50
28	Randall Hill	.40
29	Eric Dickerson	.10
30	Jim Kelly	.75
31	Bernie Kosar	.10
32	Mike Singletary	.10
33	Anthony Miller	.10
34	Harvey Williams	.10
35	Randall Cunningham	.50
36	Joe Montana	1.00
37	Dan McGwire	.10
38	Al Toon	.10
39	Carl Banks	.10
40	Troy Aikman	1.00
41	Junior Seau	.50
42	Jeff George	.50
43	Michael Dean Perry	.10
44	Lawrence Taylor	.30
45	Dan Marino	2.00
46	Jerry Rice	1.00
47	Boomer Esiason	.10
48	Bruce Smith	.10
49	Leslie O'Neal	.10
50	Form Checklist	.10

1992 Upper Deck Coach's Report

Top rookies and second-year players are analyzed by former Pittsburgh Steelers Coach Chuck Noll for this 20-card insert set. The set's logo is on the card front, along with a color full-bleed action photo and the player's name and position, which are printed on a pencil at the bottom of the card. The card back has a spiral notebook on top of a chalkboard and wooden desk. "From the desk of Chuck Noll" is written at the top; Noll's evaluation is on the notebook paper. The card number uses a "CR" prefix and appears at the top of the card in a white bar. Cards were randomly inserted in 1992 Upper Deck Series II hobby foil packs only.

		NM/M
Complete Set (20):		25.00
Common Player:		1.00
1	Mike Pritchard	.40
2	Will Furrer	.40
3	Alfred Williams	.40
4	Tommy Vardell	.40
5	Brett Favre	10.00
6	Alvin Harper	1.00
7	Mike Croel	1.00
8	Herman Moore	3.00
9	Edgar Bennett	2.00
10	Todd Marinovich	1.00
11	Aeneas Williams	1.00
12	Ricky Watters	4.00
13	Amp Lee	1.00
14	Terrell Buckley	1.00
15	Tim Barnett	.40
16	Nick Bell	.40
17	Leonard Russell	.40
18	Lawrence Dawsey	.40
19	Robert Porcher	1.00
20	Ricky Watters (CL)	2.00

1992 Upper Deck Fanimation

The artwork of artists Jim Lee and Rob Liefeld are featured on these 10 insert cards, available in 1992 Upper Deck Series II retail packs. Each card front features a color cartoon portraying the player, plus a "Fanimation" logo at the bottom. The back has a mug shot, biography and analysis of the player's strengths. The background has shades of red, orange and yellow. A card number, using an "F" for a prefix, also appears.

		NM/M
Complete Set (10):		10.00
Common Player:		.50
1	Jim Kelly	1.00
2	Dan Marino	4.00
3	Lawrence Taylor	.50
4	Deion Sanders	1.00
5	Troy Aikman	3.00
6	Junior Seau	.50
7	Mike Singletary	.50
8	Eric Dickerson	.50
9	Jerry Rice	3.00
10	Checklist	.50

1992 Upper Deck Game Breaker Holograms

Some of the NFL's top wide receivers are featured in this nine-card hologram set. The front has a hologram image against a football field background. The player's name is at the bottom, along with the Upper Deck logo. The back has a marble-like tablet which contains career highlights. The player's name and "Game Breakers" are at the top of the card. Each card back is also numbered, using a "GB" prefix. Cards 1, 3, 4, 6, 8 and 9 were random inserts in 1992 Upper Deck Series I packs; cards 2, 5, and 7 were in Series II packs.

		NM/M
Complete Set (9):		15.00
Common Player:		1.50
1	Art Monk	1.50
2	Drew Hill	1.50
3	Haywood Jeffires	1.00
4	Andre Rison	1.50
5	Mark Clayton	1.50
6	Jerry Rice	5.00
7	Michael Haynes	1.50
8	Andre Reed	1.50
9	Michael Irvin	2.00

1992 Upper Deck Dan Marino Heroes

These 10 cards are a continuation of Upper Deck's Football Heroes set and starts with number 28, where the Walter Payton set left off. Cards, random inserts in 1992 Upper Deck Series II foil packs, have an oval picture on the front, featuring Dan Marino in a different stage in his career. The card's title is in the bottom right corner. The back has a marble-like background with career highlights, plus an Upper Deck hologram and card number. There is a checklist card in the set which is unnumbered.

		NM/M
Complete Set (10):		35.00
Common Marino:		3.50
Marino Header (NNO):		6.00
28	Dan Marino College Years	3.50
29	Dan Marino Rookie of the Year	3.50
30	Dan Marino 5,000 Yards Passing	3.50
31	Dan Marino Super Bowl XIX	3.50
32	Dan Marino 4,000 Yards Passing	3.50
33	Dan Marino 200th Touchdown	3.50
34	Dan Marino 30,000 Yards	3.50
35	Dan Marino Still Counting	3.50
36	Dan Marino Checklist	3.50

1992 Upper Deck Walter Payton Heroes

These insert cards feature Hall of Fame running back Walter Payton and continue with card 19, where the Joe Namath Football Heroes series ended. Cards were random inserts in 1992 Upper Deck football Series II foil packs. Each card front has an oval with a picture of Payton in it during a different point in his career. The picture is bordered by a marble-like frame. The card title appears in the lower right corner. Each card back has a career summary on a marble background with dark gray borders. The back is numbered and includes an Upper Deck hologram football. An unnumbered header card was also made.

		NM/M
Complete Set (10):		30.00
Common Payton:		3.00
Payton Header (NNO):		6.00
19	Walter Payton College Years	3.00
20	Walter Payton Sweetness	3.00
21	Walter Payton Career Year	3.00
22	Walter Payton NFL Rushing Record	3.00
23	Walter Payton 2,000 Yard Seasons	3.00
24	Walter Payton Super Bowl XX	3.00
25	Walter Payton Walter Payton Day	3.00
26	Walter Payton Hall of Fame Bound	3.00
27	Walter Payton Checklist	3.00

1992 Upper Deck Heroes Payton Box Bottoms

Much like the Montana and Namath Heroes inserts were printed on a 5-1/4" x 7-1/4" format in 1991, Walter Payton Heroes were printed on the bottoms of 1992 Upper Deck Series I boxes. All box bottoms are blank on the back and feature identical fronts to the Payton Heroes insert.

		NM/M
Complete Set (8):		5.00
Common Payton:		1.00
19	College Years 1971-74	1.00
20	Sweetness 1975	1.00
21	Career Year 1977	1.00
22	NFL Rushing Record 1984	1.00
23	2,000 Yard Seasons 1983-85	1.00
24	Super Bowl XX 1986	1.00
25	Walter Payton Day 1987	1.00
26	Hall of Fame Bound 1992	1.00

1992 Upper Deck Pro Bowl

Players from the 1992 Pro Bowl are featured on these insert cards randomly included in 1992 Upper Deck Series I foil packs. The front is horizontally designed and features pictures of two different players; the AFC player is on the left, while the NFC player appears on the right. "Pro Bowl" is written in silver foil on a rainbow colored panel which separates the two photos. The rainbow colored band creates a prism-like effect when held under a light. The players' names are at the bottom of the card in silver foil. Each back is in a horizontal format and includes a summary paragraph about each player. Cards are numbered with a PB prefix and include an Upper Deck hologram football.

		NM/M
Complete Set (16):		12.00
Common Player:		.50
1	Jeffires, Irvin	.50
2	Mark Clayton, Gary Clark	1.00
3	Anthony Munoz, Jim Lachey	.50
4	Moon, Rypien	2.00
5	Thomas, Sanders	5.00
6	Butts, Smith	3.00
7	Townsend, White	2.00
8	Cornelius Bennett, Seth Joyner	.50
9	Thomas, Swilling	.50
10	Darryl Talley, Chris Spielman	.50
11	Ronnie Lott, Mark Carrier	.50
12	Steve Atwater, Shaun Gayle	.50
13	Rod Woodson, Darrell Green	.50
14	Jeff Gossett, Chip Lohmiller	.50
15	Tim Brown, Mel Gray	.50
16	Checklist	3.00

1992 Upper Deck NFL Sheets

Upper Deck produced four different NFL Sheets in 1992. They commemorated the AFC Championship, NFC Championship, Super Bowl XXVI and Comic Ball IV, with each having a blank back. The AFC and NFC Championship sheets were given away at Upper Deck's Super Bowl Card Show III and at the NFL Experience in Minneapolis. The Super Bowl XXVI sheet was given away at various locations in the Minneapolis area during the week of the Super Bowl.

		NM/M
Complete Set (4):		30.00
Common Player:		5.00
1	Thurman Thomas, Cornelius Bennett, Andre Reed, John Elway, Steve Atwater, Gaston Green Jan 12, 1992 (30,000)	5.00
2	Mark Rypien, Ricky Ervins, Charles Mann, Barry Sanders, Chris Spielman, Mel Gray Jan. 12, 1992 (30,000)	5.00
3	Mark Rypien, Ricky Ervins, Charles Mann, Gary Clark, Darrell Green, Earnest Byner Jan. 26, 1992 (15,000)	10.00
4	Lawrence Taylor, Jerry Rice, Thurman Thomas, Dan Marino Looney Tunes Characters (15,000)	12.00

1992 Upper Deck SCD Sheets

This eight-card set of 8-1/2" x 11" sheets was produced by Upper Deck and included in the Sept. 18, 1992 issue of Sports Collector's Digest at a rate of one per issue. Each sheet contained six cards and sheets were numbered 1-8. Sheet backs were covered with the repeated phrase "Upper Deck Limited Edition Commemorative Sheet."

		NM/M
Complete Set (8):		75.00
Common Player:		8.00
1	Randall Cunningham, David Klingler, Dan Marino, Troy Aikman, Jim Kelly, Bernie Kosar	15.00
2	Phillippi Sparks, Dale Carter, Steve Emtman, Kevin Smith, Marco Coleman, Carl Pickens	8.00
3	Quentin Coryatt, Greg Skrepenak, Chester McGlockton, Kurt Barber, Vaughn Dunbar, Ashley Ambrose	8.00
4	Ty Detmer, Steve Israel, Tracy Scroggins, Todd Collins, Alonzo Spellman, Marquez Pope	8.00
5	Eric Dickerson, Randal Hill, Jim Kelly, Bernie Kosar, Deion Sanders, Andre Reed	10.00
6	Joe Montana, Mike Singletary, Randall Cunningham, Anthony Miller, Dan McGwire, Harvey Williams	10.00
7	Al Toon, Michael Dean Perry, Troy Aikman, Jeff George, Carl Banks, Junior Seau	10.00
8	Dan Marino, Tommy Maddox, Bruce Smith, Leslie O'Neal, Lawrence Taylor, Jerry Rice	15.00

1992-93 Upper Deck NFL Experience

This 50-card set was distributed during the NFL Experience/ Super Bowl Card Show held during the Super Bowl XXVII week Pasadena, Calif. Two designs are used for the card fronts. Cards 1-20 have color photos bordered by different colored stripes on the left and bottom sides. Cards 21-50 have the photos slanted to the left, edged by a ghosted background. Each card back has another photo of the player close up, plus a quote, profile or game summary. The cards, which have a Super Bowl theme, are numbered on the back and include the NFL Experience logo. Some cards were stamped with silver foil; others were stamped in gold. The gold foils are about five times more valuable.

		NM/M
Complete Set (50):		13.00
Common Player:		.20
1	Joe Montana	1.25
2	Roger Staubach	.25
3	Bart Starr	.25
4	Len Dawson	.20
5	Fred Biletnikoff	.20
6	Jim Plunkett	.20
7	Terry Bradshaw	.25
8	Jerry Rice	.75
9	Doug Williams	.20
10	Dan Marino	.85
11	David Klingler	.60
12	Steve Emtman	.20
13	Dale Carter	.20
14	Quentin Coryatt	.25
15	Tommy Maddox	.50
16	Vaughn Dunbar	.20
17	Marco Coleman	.30
18	Carl Pickens	.50
19	Sean Gilbert	.50
20	Tony Smith	.20
21	Jim Kelly	.80
22	Dan Marino	1.00
23	Boomer Esiason	.35
24	Bernie Kosar	.25
25	Ken O'Brien	.20
26	Deion Sanders	.30
27	Mike Singletary	.20
28	Andre Reed	.35
29	Michael Dean Perry	.20
30	Ricky Proehl	.30
31	Leslie O'Neal	.25
32	Jerry Rice	1.00
33	Eric Dickerson	.20
34	Troy Aikman	2.00
35	Bruce Smith	.45
36	Browning Nagle	.20
37	Carl Banks	.20
38	Harvey Williams	.20
39	Jeff George	.20
40	Lawrence Taylor	.25
41	Webster Slaughter	.20
42	Anthony Miller	.30
43	Randall Cunningham	.35
44	Timm Rosenbach	.20
45	Russell Maryland	.40
46	Randal Hill	.20
47	Dan McGwire	.20
48	Merril Hoge	.20
49	Kevin Fagan	.20
50	Junior Seau	.50

1993 Upper Deck

Upper Deck issued its 530-card 1993 set in one series. Each standard-size card has an action photo on the front, with two team color-coded stripes at the bottom with the player's name and position. His team name runs along the left side using team colors. The card back has a hologram, close-up photo, statistics and biographical information. Subsets include Star Rookies, All Rookie Team, NFL Hitmen, Team Checklist, Season Leaders and Berman's Best. Insert sets include America's Team, Future Heroes, Pro Bowlers and Team MVPs.

		NM/M
Complete Set (530):		25.00
Common Player:		.05
Minor Stars:		.10
Pack (12):		.75
Wax Box (36):		15.00
1	Star Rookie Checklist	.25
2	*Eric Curry* (SR)	.10
3	*Rick Mirer* (SR)	.30
4	*Dan Williams* (SR)	.10
5	*Marvin Jones* (SR)	.10
6	*Willie Roaf* (SR)	.10
7	*Reggie Brooks* (SR)	.10
8	*Horace Copeland* (SR)	.50
9	*Lincoln Kennedy* (SR)	.10
10	*Curtis Conway* (SR)	1.00
11	*Drew Bledsoe* (SR)	3.00
12	*Patrick Bates* (SR)	.10
13	*Wayne Simmons* (SR)	.10
14	*Irv Smith* (SR)	.10
15	*Robert Smith* (SR)	1.50
16	*O.J. McDuffie* (SR)	1.00
17	*Darrien Gordon* (SR)	.10
18	*John Copeland* (SR)	.10
19	*Derek Brown* (SR)	.10
20	*Jerome Bettis* (SR)	1.50
21	*Deion Figures* (SR)	.20
22	*Glyn Milburn* (SR)	.50
23	*Garrison Hearst* (SR)	1.00
24	*Qadry Ismail* (SR)	.50
25	*Terry Kirby* (SR)	.50
26	*Lamar Thomas* (SR)	.10
27	*Tom Carter* (SR)	.10
28	*Andre Hastings* (SR)	.25
29	*George Teague* (SR)	.20
30	All Rookie Checklist	.10
31	David Klingler (ART)	.05
32	Tommy Maddox (ART)	.05
33	Vaughn Dunbar (ART)	.05
34	Rodney Culver (ART)	.05
35	Carl Pickens (ART)	.05
36	Courtney Hawkins (ART)	.05
37	Tyji Armstrong (ART)	.05
38	Ray Roberts (ART)	.05
39	Troy Auzenne (ART)	.05
40	Shane Dronett (ART)	.05
41	Chris Mims (ART)	.05
42	Sean Gilbert (ART)	.05
43	Steve Emtman (ART)	.05
44	Robert Jones (ART)	.05
45	Marco Coleman (ART)	.05
46	Ricardo McDonald (ART)	.05
47	Quentin Coryatt (ART)	.05
48	Dana Hall (ART)	.05
49	Derren Perry (ART)	.05
50	Darryl Williams (ART)	.05
51	Kevin Smith (ART)	.05
52	Terrell Buckley (ART)	.05
53	Troy Vincent (ART)	.05
54	Lin Elliot (ART)	.05
55	Dale Carter (ART)	.05
56	Steve Atwater (NFL)	.05
57	Junior Seau (NFL)	.10
58	Ronnie Lott (NFL)	.05
59	Louis Oliver (NFL)	.05
60	Cortez Kennedy (NFL)	.05
61	Pat Swilling	.05
62	NFL Hitmen Checklist	.05
63	Curtis Conway (TC)	.05
64	Alfred Williams (TC)	.05
65	Jim Kelly (TC)	.10
66	Simon Fletcher (TC)	.05
67	Eric Metcalf (TC)	.05
68	Lawrence Dawsey (TC)	.05
69	Garrison Hearst (TC)	.40
70	Anthony Miller (TC)	.05
71	Neil Smith (TC)	.05
72	Jeff George (TC)	.05
73	Emmitt Smith (TC)	1.00
74	Dan Marino (TC)	1.00
75	Clyde Simmons (TC)	.05
76	Deion Sanders (TC)	.25
77	Ricky Watters (TC)	.10
78	Rodney Hampton (TC)	.05
79	Brad Baxter (TC)	.05
80	Barry Sanders (TC)	.50
81	Warren Moon (TC)	.10
82	Brett Favre (TC)	.50
83	Drew Bledsoe (TC)	1.00
84	Eric Dickerson (TC)	.05
85	Cleveland Gary (TC)	.05
86	Earnest Byner (TC)	.05
87	Wayne Martin (TC)	.05
88	Rick Mirer (TC)	.50
89	Barry Foster (TC)	.05
90	Terry Allen (TC)	.05
91	Vinnie Clark	.05
92	Howard Ballard	.05
93	Eric Ball	.05
94	Marc Boutte	.05
95	*Larry Centers*	.25
96	Gary Brown	.05
97	Hugh Millen	.05
98	*Anthony Newman*	.05
99	Darrell Thompson	.05
100	George Jamison	.05
101	James Francis	.05
102	Leonard Harris	.05
103	Lomas Brown	.05
104	James Lofton	.05
105	Jamie Dukes	.05
106	Quinn Early	.05
107	Ernie Jones	.05
108	Torrance Small	.05
109	Michael Carter	.05
110	Aeneas Williams	.05
111	Renaldo Turnbull	.05
112	Al Smith	.05
113	Troy Auzenne	.05
114	Stephen Baker	.05

115 Daniel Stubbs .05
116 Dana Hall .05
117 Lawrence Taylor .10
118 Ron Hall .05
119 Derrick Fenner .05
120 Martin Mayhew .05
121 Jay Schroeder .05
122 Michael Zordich .05
123 Ed McCaffery .05
124 John Stephens .05
125 Brad Edwards .05
126 Don Griffin .05
127 Broderick Thomas .05
128 Ted Washington .05
129 Haywood Jeffires .05
130 Gary Plummer .05
131 Mark Wheeler .05
132 Ty Detmer .50
133 Derrick Walker .05
134 Henry Ellard .05
135 Neal Anderson .05
136 Bruce Smith .05
137 Cris Carter .10
138 Vaughn Dunbar .05
139 Dan Marino 2.00
140 Troy Aikman .75
141 Randall Cunningham .10
142 Darryl Johnston .05
143 Mark Clayton .05
144 Rich Gannon .05
145 Nate Newton .05
146 Willie Gault .05
147 Brian Washington .05
148 Fred Barnett .05
149 Gill Byrd .05
150 Art Monk .05
151 Stan Humphries .10
152 Charles Mann .05
153 Greg Lloyd .05
154 Marvin Washington .05
155 Bernie Kosar .05
156 Pete Metzelaars .05
157 Chris Hinton .05
158 Jim Harbaugh .05
159 Willie Davis .05
160 Leroy Thompson .05
161 Scott Miller .05
162 Eugene Robinson .05
163 David Little .05
164 Pierce Holt .05
165 James Hasty .05
166 Dave Krieg .05
167 Gerald Williams .05
168 Kyle Clifton .05
169 Bill Brooks .05
170 Vance Johnson .05
171 Greg Townsend .05
172 Jason Belser .05
173 Brett Perriman .05
174 Steve Jordan .05
175 Kelvin Martin .05
176 Greg Kragen .05
177 Kerry Cash .05
178 Chester McGlockton .05
179 Jim Kelly .10
180 Todd McNair .05
181 Leroy Hoard .05
182 Seth Joyner .05
183 *Sam Gash* .05
184 Joe Nash .05
185 *Lin Elliott* .05
186 Robert Porcher .05
187 Tom Hodson .05
188 Greg Lewis .05
189 Dan Saleaumua .05
190 Chris Goode .05
191 Henry Thomas .05
192 Bobby Hebert .05
193 Clay Matthews .05
194 Mark Carrier .05
195 Anthony Pleasant .05
196 Eric Dorsey .05
197 Clarence Verdin .05
198 Marc Spindler .05
199 Tommy Maddox .05
200 Wendell Davis .05
201 John Fina .05
202 Alonzo Spellman .05
203 Darryl Williams .05
204 Mike Croel .05
205 Ken Norton .05
206 Mel Gray .05
207 Chuck Cecil .05
208 John Flannery .05
209 Chip Banks .05
210 Chris Martin .05
211 Dennis Brown .05
212 Vinny Testaverde .05
213 Nick Bell .05
214 Robert Delpino .05
215 Mark Higgs .05
216 Al Noga .05
217 Andre Tippett .05
218 Pat Swilling .05
219 Phil Simms .05
220 Ricky Proehl .05
221 William Thomas .05
222 Jeff Graham .05
223 Darion Conner .05
224 Mark Carrier .05
225 Willie Green .05
226 *Reggie Rivers* .05
227 Andre Reed .10
228 Deion Sanders .40
229 Chris Doleman .05
230 Jerry Ball .05
231 Eric Dickerson .05
232 Carlos Jenkins .05
233 Mike Johnson .05
234 Marco Coleman .05
235 Leslie O'Neal .05
236 Browning Nagle .05
237 Carl Pickens .10
238 Steve Emtman .05
239 Alvin Harper .10
240 Keith Jackson .05
241 Jerry Rice .75
242 Cortez Kennedy .10
243 Tyji Armstrong .05
244 Troy Vincent .05
245 Randal Hill .05
246 Robert Blackmon .05
247 Junior Seau .10
248 Sterling Sharpe .10
249 Thurman Thomas .10
250 David Klingler .05
251 Jeff George .20
252 Anthony Miller .05
253 Earnest Byner .05
254 Eric Swann .05
255 Jeff Herrod .05
256 Eddie Robinson .05
257 Eric Allen .05
258 John Taylor .05
259 Sean Gilbert .05
260 Ray Childress .05
261 Michael Haynes .05
262 Greg McMurtry .05
263 Bill Romanowski .05
264 Todd Lyght .05
265 Clyde Simmons .05
266 Webster Slaughter .05
267 J.J. Birden .05
268 Aaron Wallace .05
269 Carl Banks .05
270 Richardo McDonald .05
271 Michael Brooks .05
272 Dale Carter .05
273 Mike Pritchard .05
274 Derek Brown .05
275 Burt Grossman .05
276 Mark Schlereth .05
277 Karl Mecklenburg .05
278 Ricky Jackson .05
279 Ricky Ervins .05
280 Jeff Bryant .05
281 Eric Martin .05
282 Eric Martin .05
283 Kevin Mack .05
284 Brad Muster .05
285 Kelvin Pritchett .05
286 Courtney Hawkins .05
287 Levon Kirkland .05
288 Steve DeBerg .05
289 Edgar Bennett .10
290 Michael Dean Perry .05
291 Richard Dent .05
292 Howie Long .05
293 Chris Mims .05
294 Kurt Barber .05
295 Wilber Marshall .05
296 Ethan Horton .05
297 Tony Bennett .05
298 Johnny Johnson .05
299 Craig Heyward .05
300 Steve Isreal .05
301 Kenneth Gant .05
302 Eugene Chung .05
303 Harvey Williams .05
304 Jerrod Bunch .05
305 Darren Perry .05
306 Steve Christie .05
307 John Randle .05
308 Warren Moon .10
309 Charles Haley .05
310 Tony Smith .05
311 Steve Broussard .05
312 Alfred Williams .05
313 Terrell Buckley .05
314 Trace Armstrong .05
315 Brian Mitchell .05
316 Steve Atwater .05
317 Nate Lewis .05
318 Richard Brown .05
319 Rufus Porter .05
320 Pat Harlow .05
321 Anthony Smith .05
322 Jack Del Rio .05
323 Darryl Talley .05
324 Sam Mills .05
325 Chris Miller .05
326 Ken Harvey .05
327 Rod Woodson .10
328 Tony Tolbert .05
329 Todd Kinchen .05
330 *Brian Noble* .05
331 David Meggett .05
332 Chris Spielman .05
333 Barry Word .05
334 Jessie Hester .05
335 Michael Jackson .05
336 Mitchell Price .05
337 Michael Irvin .10
338 Simon Fletcher .05
339 Keith Jennings .05
340 Vai Sikahema .05
341 Roger Craig .05
342 Ricky Watters .10
343 Reggie Cobb .05
344 Kanavis McGhee .05
345 Barry Foster .10
346 Marion Butts .05
347 Bryan Cox .05
348 Wayne Martin .05
349 Jim Everett .10
350 Nate Odomes .05
351 Anthony Johnson .05
352 Rodney Hampton .10
353 Terry Allen .05
354 Derrick Thomas .10
355 Calvin Williams .05
356 Pepper Johnson .05
357 John Elway .30
358 Steve Young .75
359 Emmitt Smith 2.00
360 Brett Favre 2.00
361 Cody Carlson .05
362 Vincent Brown .05
363 Gary Anderson .05
364 Jon Vaughn .05
365 Todd Marinovich .05
366 Carnell Lake .05
367 Kurt Gouveia .05
368 Lawrence Dawsey .05
369 Neil O'Donnell .15
370 Duane Bickett .05
371 Ronnie Harmon .05
372 Rodney Peete .05
373 Cornelius Bennett .05
374 Brad Baxter .05
375 Ernest Givins .05
376 Keith Byars .05
377 Eric Bieniemy .05
378 Mike Brim .05
379 Darren Lewis .05
380 Heath Sherman .05
381 Leonard Russell .05
382 Brent Jones .05
383 David Whitmore .05
384 Ray Roberts .05
385 John Offerdahl .05
386 Keith McCants .05
387 John Baylor .05
388 Amp Lee .05
389 Chris Warren .20
390 Herman Moore .50
391 Johnny Bailey .05
392 Tim Johnson .05
393 Eric Metcalf .05
394 Chris Chandler .05
395 Mark Rypien .05
396 Christian Okoye .05
397 Shannon Sharpe .10
398 Eric Hill .05
399 David Lang .05
400 Bruce Matthews .05
401 Harold Green .05
402 Moe Lewis .05
403 Terry McDaniel .05
404 Wesley Carroll .05
405 Richmond Webb .05
406 Andre Rison .10
407 Lonnie Young .05
408 Tommy Vardell .05
409 Gene Atkins .05
410 Sean Salisbury .05
411 Kenneth Davis .05
412 John L. Williams .05
413 Roman Phifer .05
414 Bennie Blades .05
415 Tim Brown .10
416 Lorenzo White .05
417 Tony Casillas .05
418 Tom Waddle .05
419 David Fulcher .05
420 Jessie Tuggle .05
421 Emmitt Smith (SL) .75
422 Clyde Simmons (SL) .05
423 Sterling Sharpe (SL) .10
424 Sterling Sharpe (SL) .10
425 Emmitt Smith (SL) .75
426 Dan Marino (SL) .75
427 Jones, McMillan (SL) .05
428 Thurman Thomas (SL) .10
429 Greg Montgomery (SL) .05
430 Pete Stoyanovich (SL) .05
431 Emmitt Smith (CL) .50
432 Steve Young (BB) .50
433 Jerry Rice (BB) .40
434 Ricky Watters (BB) .10
435 Barry Foster (BB) .10
436 Cortez Kennedy (BB) .10
437 Warren Moon (BB) .10
438 Thurman Thomas (BB) .10
439 Brett Favre (BB) .50
440 Andre Rison (BB) .10
441 Barry Sanders (BB) .50
442 Chris Berman (CL) .05
443 Moe Gardner .05
444 Robert Jones .05
445 Reggie Langhorne .05
446 Willie Anderson .05
447 James Washington .05
448 Aaron Craver .05
449 Jack Trudeau .05
450 Neil Smith .05
451 Chris Burkett .05
452 Darren Woodson .05
453 Drew Hill .05
454 Barry Sanders 1.25
455 Jeff Cross .05
456 Bennie Thompson .05
457 Marcus Allen .10
458 Tracy Scroggins .05
459 Leroy Butler .05
460 Joe Montana 1.25
461 Eddie Anderson .05
462 Tim McDonald .05
463 Ronnie Lott .05
464 Gaston Green .05
465 Shane Conlan .05
466 Leonard Marshall .05
467 Melvin Jenkins .05
468 Don Beebe .05
469 Johnny Mitchell .05
470 Darryl Henley .05
471 Boomer Esiason .10
472 Mark Kelso .05
473 John Booty .05
474 Pete Stoyanovich .05
475 *Thomas Smith* .10
476 *Carlton Gray* .10
477 *Dana Stubblefield* .50
478 *Ryan McNeil* .10
479 *Natrone Means* 1.00
480 *Carl Simpson* .10
481 *Robert O'Neal* .10
482 *Demetrius Dubose* .10
483 *Darrin Smith* .20
484 *Micheal Barrow* .10
485 *Chris Slade* .40
486 *Steve Tovar* .10
487 *Ron George* .10
488 Steve Tasker .05
489 Will Furrer .05
490 Reggie White .10
491 Sean Jones .05
492 Gary Clark .05
493 Donnell Woolford .05
494 Steve Beuerlein .05
495 Anthony Carter .05
496 Louis Oliver .05
497 Chris Zorich .05
498 Bubba McDowell .05
500 Adrian Cooper .05
501 Bill Johnson .05
502 Shawn Jefferson .05
503 Siran Stacy .05
504 James Jones .05
505 Tom Rathman .05
506 Vince Buck .05
507 *Kent Graham* .30
508 *Darren Carrington* .10
509 Ricky Dixon .05
510 Toi Cook .05
511 Steve Smith .05
512 Ostell Miles .05
513 Phil Sparks .05
514 Lee Williams .05
515 Gary Reason .05
516 Shane Dronett .05
517 Jay Novacek .05
518 Kevin Greene .05
519 Derek Russell .05
520 Quentin Coryatt .10
521 Santana Dotson .05
522 Donald Frank .05
523 Mike Prior .05
524 *Dwight Hollier* .05
525 Eric Davis .05
526 Dalton Hilliard .05
527 Rodney Culver .05
528 Jeff Hostetler .10
529 Ernie Mills .05
530 Craig Erickson .05

1993 Upper Deck America's Team

This 15-card insert set is devoted to the players from Super Bowl Championship Dallas Cowboys teams. Cards 1-6 feature Cowboys from Super Bowl XXVII; players from Super Bowl XXVIII are featured on cards 7-13. The front has a color action photo, plus the player's name and team stamped in silver foil along the left side of the card. An "America's Team" logo is also on the front. The back has this logo as a background, with a paragraph devoted to the player's accomplishments in the Super Bowl game. Cards are numbered with an "AT" prefix and were random inserts in 1993 Upper Deck hobby foil packs. There is also an unnumbered title card which features Emmitt Smith.

		NM/M
Complete Set (15):		20.00
Common Player:		1.00
E. Smith Header:		5.00
1	Roger Staubach	3.00
2	Chuck Howley	1.00
3	Harvey Martin	1.00
4	Randy White	1.00
5	Bob Lilly	1.00
6	Drew Pearson	1.00
7	Emmitt Smith	5.00
8	Troy Aikman	4.00
9	Ken Norton	1.00
10	Robert Jones	1.00
11	Russell Maryland	1.00
12	Jay Novacek	1.00
13	Michael Irvin	2.00
14	Troy Aikman (CL)	3.00

1993 Upper Deck Future Heroes

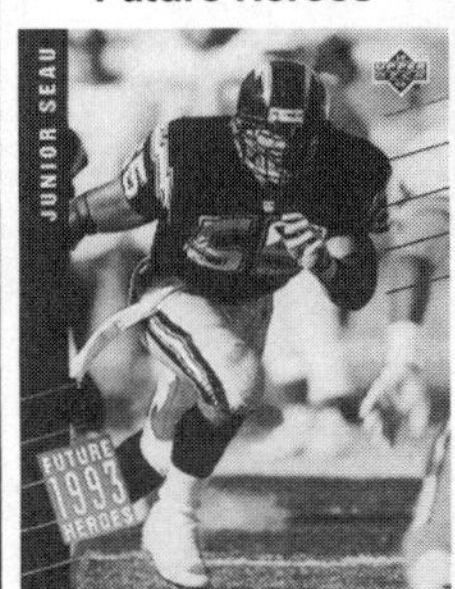

These cards feature color action photos on the front, along with the team color-coded stripe on the left which contains the player's name. A 1993 "Future Heroes" logo is in gold foil in the bottom left corner, too. The back has another small color photo and player profile against a team color-coded background. The player's name and card number are at the top of the card. Numbering begins with #37, where the Upper Deck Football Series ended. These inserts, which were randomly included in all types of packs, also include an unnumbered title card which features Ricky Watters.

		NM/M
Complete Set (10):		8.00
Common Player:		.50
37	Barry Foster	.50
38	Junior Seau	.50
39	Emmitt Smith	4.00
40	Troy Aikman	3.00
41	David Klingler	.50
42	Ricky Watters	1.50
43	Barry Sanders	4.00
44	Brett Favre	5.00
45	Checklist	2.00

1993 Upper Deck Pro Bowl

These glossy cards feature two photos on the horizontally-designed front - a color photo on the left with holographic borders on the left and bottom, and a second photo on the right. Each player was a Pro Bowl selection; the Pro Bowl logo is on the front in the lower left corner. The card back has a blue- and-white background with a career profile on it. A card number, using a "PB" prefix, also appears. Cards were random inserts in retail foil packs.

		NM/M
Complete Set (20):		40.00
Common Player:		1.00
1	Andre Reed	1.00
2	Dan Marino	5.00
3	Warren Moon	1.00
4	Anthony Miller	1.00
5	Barry Foster	1.00
6	Steve Atwater	1.00
7	Cortez Kennedy	1.00
8	Junior Seau	1.00
9	Jerry Rice	4.00
10	Michael Irvin	1.00
11	Sterling Sharpe	1.00
12	Steve Young	4.00
13	Troy Aikman	4.00
14	Brett Favre	6.00
15	Emmitt Smith	5.00
16	Rodney Hampton	1.00
17	Barry Sanders	5.00
18	Ricky Watters	1.00
19	Pat Swilling	1.00
20	Checklist	1.00

1993 Upper Deck Rookie Exchange

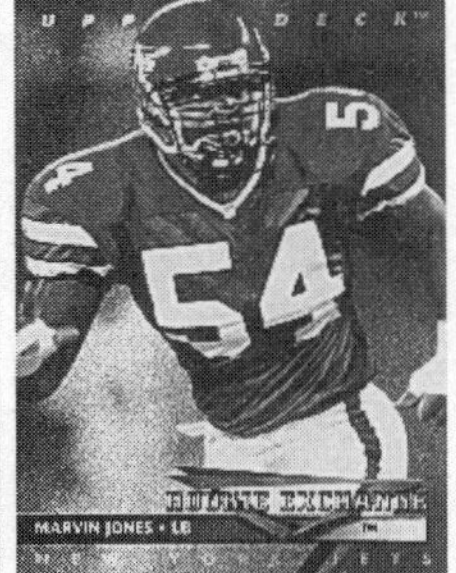

This set could be obtained by redeeming a "Trade Upper Deck" card, available randomly in every 72nd pack of Upper Deck football card packs. The card front uses Upper Deck's Electric printing, which gives it a metallic quality. A player photo is featured on the front, along with the player's name and position in a team color-coded bar at the bottom. His team name is also given, in silver letters. The back has another color photo on the left, plus a recap of the player's previous season. The background is in team colors. The player's name, position and card number, using an "RE" prefix, also appears on the card back.

		NM/M
Complete Set (7):		8.00
Common Player:		.50
1	Rookie Trade Card	.50
2	Drew Bledsoe	4.00
3	Rick Mirer	.50
4	Garrison Hearst	2.00
5	Marvin Jones	.50
6	Curtis Conway	1.50
7	Jerome Bettis	2.00

1993 Upper Deck Team MVPs

The Most Valuable Player on each of the 28 NFL teams is represented in this 29-card insert set. Each card front has a full-bleed color action photo, plus two team color-coded stripes at the bottom which contain the player's name and team. A Team MVP logo is also at the bottom of the card. Team color-coded stripes are also used on the back, which features another player photo and career highlights. A card number, using a "TM" prefix, is also given. Cards were random inserts in jumbo foil packs.

		NM/M
Complete Set (29):		15.00
Common Player:		.50
Minor Stars:		1.00
1	Neal Anderson	.50
2	Harold Green	.50
3	Thurman Thomas	1.00
4	John Elway	2.00
5	Eric Metcalf	.50
6	Reggie Cobb	.50
7	Johnny Bailey	.50
8	Junior Seau	1.00
9	Derrick Thomas	1.00
10	Steve Emtman	.50
11	Troy Aikman	3.00
12	Dan Marino	4.00
13	Clyde Simmons	.50
14	Andre Rison	1.00
15	Steve Young	2.00
16	Rodney Hampton	1.00
17	Rob Moore	.50
18	Barry Sanders	3.00
19	Warren Moon	1.00
20	Sterling Sharpe	1.00
21	Jon Vaughn	.50
22	Tim Brown	1.00
23	Jim Everett	.50
24	Gary Clark	.50
25	Wayne Martin	.50
26	Cortez Kennedy	1.00
27	Barry Foster	1.00
28	Terry Allen	.50
29	Checklist	.50

1993 Upper Deck Kansas City Chiefs

This 25-card team set is devoted to the Kansas City Chiefs. The cards use the same design format as Upper Deck's main 1993 issue. However, the cards, which are standard size, are numbered on the back using a "KC" prefix. The photos used on both sides are identical to those used for the regular set.

		NM/M
Complete Set (25):		8.00
Common Player:		.20
1	Nick Lowery	.25
2	Lonnie Marts	.20
3	Marcus Allen	1.00
4	Bennie Thompson	.20
5	Bryan Barker	.20
6	Christian Okoye	.25
7	Dale Carter	.25
8	Dan Saleaumua	.25
9	Dave Krieg	.25
10	Derrick Thomas	1.00
11	Doug Terry	.20
12	Fred Jones	.20
13	Harvey Williams	.60
14	J.J. Birden	.25
15	Joe Montana	3.00
16	John Alt	.25
17	Leonard Griffin	.20
18	Matt Blundin	.30
19	Neil Smith	.35

20 Tim Barnett .25
21 Tim Grunhard .20
22 Todd McNair .25
23 Tracy Simien .20
24 Willie Davis .35
25 Joe Montana (Checklist back) 2.00

1993 Upper Deck Dallas Cowboys

This 25-card team set is devoted to the Dallas Cowboys. The cards are standard size and use the same design as Upper Deck's regular 1993 set. These cards, however, are numbered on the back using a "D" prefix. But the photos on both sides are the same as those used for the regular set.

NM/M
Complete Set (25): 10.00
Common Player: .25
1 Alvin Harper 1.00
2 Charles Haley .50
3 Jimmy Smith .25
4 Darrin Smith .25
5 Jim Jeffcoat .25
6 Darryl Johnston .75
7 Dixon Edwards .25
8 Emmitt Smith 3.00
9 James Washington .25
10 Jay Novacek .40
11 Ken Norton .40
12 Kenneth Gant .25
13 Larry Brown .25
14 Leon Lett .35
15 Lin Elliott .25
16 Mark Tuinei .25
17 Michael Irvin 1.50
18 Nate Newton .25
19 Robert Jones .25
20 Thomas Everett .25
21 Tony Casillas .25
22 Tony Tolbert .25
23 Troy Aikman 3.00
24 Russell Maryland .50
25 Troy Aikman (Checklist back) 2.00

1993 Upper Deck San Francisco 49ers

The San Francisco 49ers are represented in this 25-card team set from Upper Deck. The cards are standard size and follow the design format used in Upper Deck's regular 1993 issue. However, the card backs are numbered using an "SF" prefix. This set uses the same photos on each side as those which were used for the regular issue.

NM/M
Complete Set (25): 8.00
Common Player: .20
1 Amp Lee .40
2 Bill Romanowski .25
3 Brent Jones .50
4 Dana Hall .25
5 Dana Stubblefield .40
6 Dennis Brown .20
7 Dexter Carter .25
8 Don Griffin .20
9 Eric Davis .25
10 Guy McIntyte .20
11 Jamie Williams .20
12 Jerry Rice 2.00
13 John Taylor .35
14 Keith DeLong .25
15 Marc Logan .25
16 Michael Walters .20
17 Mike Cofer .20
18 Odessa Turner .20
19 Ricky Watters .75
20 Steve Bono .50
21 Steve Young 2.00
22 Ted Washington .25
23 Tom Rathman .35
24 Jesse Sapolu .20
25 Steve Young (Checklist back) 1.00

1993 Upper Deck Authenticated Classic Confrontations

The 3-1/2" x 5" card features Montana and Marino. "Classic Confrontations XIX" is printed on the right side of the card. The card back is sequentially numbered as "x of 20,000."

NM/M
Complete Set (1): 20.00
Common Player: 20.00
1 Joe Montana, Dan Marino Classic Confrontation 20.00

1993-94 Upper Deck Miller Lite SB

The five-card, 5" x 3-1/2" set was sponsored by Miller and Tombstone Pizza. One card was issued in each 12-pack of Miller Lite. The set was available through mail-in UPC offers. All entries received were entered in a drawing for 1,000 Montana autographed sheets. The card fronts feature two quarterbacks from a past Super Bowl on a horizontal design. The backs include highlight info over a ghosted Super Bowl logo.

NM/M
Complete Set (5): 20.00
Common Player: 2.50
1 Troy Aikman, Jim Kelly Super Bowl XXVII 5.00
2 Jim Kelly, Mark Rypien Super Bowl XXVI 2.50
3 John Elway, Joe Montana Super Bowl XXIV 7.00
4 John Elway, Phil Simms Super Bowl XXI 3.00
5 Joe Montana, Dan Marino Super Bowl XIX 8.00

1994 Upper Deck Pro Bowl Samples

The six-card, standard-size set was distributed at the National Convention in Houston. The cards are very similar to the basic insert issue, except that the card backs have "Sample Card" printed diagonally.

NM/M
Complete Set (6): 25.00
Common Player: 2.50
1 Jerome Bettis 2.50
2 Brett Favre 6.00
3 John Elway 4.00
4 Thurman Thomas 2.50
5 Jerry Rice 4.00
6 Steve Young 4.00

1994 Upper Deck

The Upper Deck Co. kicked off its 1994 football campaign, with a 330-card, single series issue. Upper Deck also introduced an upgraded card design and an interactive 50-card insert set, called Predictor Series. Two parallel Electric Field sets were also available. All 330 regular-issue cards will also be printed using gold and silver foil. These sets-within-a-set are called Silver Electric and Gold Electric, respectively. There are two other insert sets, called Then and Now and Pro Bowl Holoview.

NM/M
Complete Set (330): 30.00
Common Player: .10
Minor Stars: .20
Silver Cards: 3X
Silver Rookies: 2X
Inserted 1:1
Gold Cards: 4X-6X
Gold Rookies: 2X-5X
Inserted 1:35
Pack (12): 1.25
Wax Box (36): 35.00
1 *Dan Wilkinson* .20
2 *Antonio Langham* .20
3 *Derrick Alexander* .50
4 *Charles Johnson* .50
5 *Bucky Brooks* .20
6 *Trev Alberts* .20
7 *Marshall Faulk* 5.00
8 *Willie McGinest* .50
9 *Aaron Glenn* .20
10 *Ryan Yarborough* .20
11 *Greg Hill* .50
12 *Sam Adams* .20
13 John Thierry .20
14 *Johnnie Morton* .50
15 *LeShon Johnson* .20
16 *David Palmer* .20
17 *Trent Dilfer* 2.00
18 *Jamir Miller* .20
19 *Thomas Lewis* .20
20 *Heath Shuler* .50
21 *Wayne Gandy* .20
22 *Isaac Bruce* 3.00
23 *Joe Johnson* .20
24 *Mario Bates* .30
25 *Bryant Young* .50
26 *William Floyd* .50
27 *Errict Rhett* .75
28 *Chuck Levy* .20
29 *Darnay Scott* .75
30 *Rob Fredrickson* .20
31 Jamir Miller .10
32 Thomas Lewis .25
33 John Thierry .10
34 Sam Adams .25
35 Joe Johnson .10
36 Bryant Young .25
37 Wayne Gandy .10
38 LaShon Johnson .25
39 Mario Bates .50
40 Greg Hill .75
41 Andy Heck .10
42 Warren Moon .40
43 Jim Everett .10
44 Bill Romanowski .10
45 Michael Haynes .10
46 Chris Doleman .10
47 Merril Hoge .10
48 Chris Miller .10
49 Clyde Simmons .10
50 Jeff George .20
51 Jeff Burris .20
52 Ethan Horton .10
53 Scott Mitchell .20
54 Howard Ballard .10
55 Lawyer Tillman .10
56 Marion Butts .10
57 Erik Kramer .10
58 Ken Norton .10
59 Anthony Miller .20
60 Chris Hinton .10
61 Ricky Proehl .10
62 Craig Heyward .10
63 Darryl Talley .10
64 Tim Worley .10
65 Derrick Fenner .10
66 Jerry Ball .10
67 Darren Woodson .10
68 Mike Croel .10
69 Ray Crockett .10
70 Tony Bennett .10
71 Webster Slaughter .10
72 Anthony Johnson .10
73 Charles Mincy .10
74 *Calvin Jones* .40
75 Henry Ellard .10
76 Troy Vincent .10
77 Sean Salisbury .10
78 Pat Harlow .10
79 James Williams .10
80 Derek Brown .20
81 Marvin Jones .10
82 Seth Joyner .10
83 Deion Figures .10
84 Stanley Richards .10
85 Tom Rathman .10
86 Rod Stephens .10
87 Ray Seals .10
88 Andre Collins .10
89 Cornelius Bennett .10
90 Richard Dent .10
91 Louis Oliver .10
92 Rodney Peete .10
93 Jackie Harris .10
94 Tracy Simien .10
95 Greg Townsend .10
96 Michael Stewert .10
97 Irving Fryar .10
98 Todd Collins .10
99 Irv Smith .10
100 Chris Calloway .10
101 Kevin Greene .10
102 John Friesz .10
103 Steve Bono .10
104 Brian Blades .10
105 Reggie Cobb .10
106 Eric Swann .10
107 Mike Pritchard .10
108 Bill Brooks .10
109 Jim Harbaugh .10
110 David Whitmore .10
111 Eddie Anderson .10
112 Ray Crittenden .25
113 Mark Collins .10
114 Brian Washington .10
115 Barry Foster .25
116 Gary Plummer .10
117 Marc Logan .10
118 John L. Williams .20
119 Marty Carter .10
120 Marvin Jones .10
121 Ron Moore .25
122 Pierce Holt .10
123 Henry Jones .10
124 Donnell Woolford .10
125 Steve Tovar .10
126 Anthony Pleasant .10
127 Jay Novacek .10
128 Dan Williams .10
129 Barry Sanders 2.00
130 Robert Brooks .10
131 Lorenzo White .10
132 Kerry Cash .10
133 Joe Montana 2.00
134 Jeff Hostetler .10
135 Jerome Bettis .75
136 Dan Marino 3.00
137 Vencie Glenn .10
138 Vincent Brown .10
139 Ricky Jackson .10
140 Carlton Bailey .10
141 Jeff Lageman .10
142 William Thomas .10
143 Neil O'Donnell .20
144 Shawn Jefferson .10
145 Steve Young 1.00
146 Chris Warren .10
147 Courtney Hawkins .10
148 Brad Edwards .10
149 O.J. McDuffie .25
150 David Lang .10
151 Chuck Cecil .10
152 Norm Johnson .10
153 Pete Metzelaars .10
154 Shaun Gayle .10
155 Alfred Williams .10
156 Eric Turner .10
157 Emmitt Smith 3.00
158 Steve Atwater .10
159 Robert Porcher .10
160 Edgar Bennett .10
161 Bubba McDowell .10
162 Jeff Herrod .10
163 Keith Cash .10
164 Patrick Bates .10
165 Todd Lyght .10
166 Mark Higgs, Rob Burnett .10
167 Carlos Jenkins .10
168 Drew Bledsoe 2.00
169 Wayne Martin .10
170 Mike Sherrard .10
171 Ronnie Lott .10
172 Fred Barnett .10
173 Eric Green .10
174 Leslie O'Neal .10
175 Brent Jones .10
176 John Vaughn .10
177 Vince Workman .10
178 Ron Middleton .10
179 Terry McDaniel .10
180 Willie Davis .10
181 Gary Clark .10
182 Bobby Hebert .10
183 Russell Copeland .10
184 Chris Gadney .10
185 Tony McGhee .10
187 Charles Haley .10
188 Shannon Sharpe .20
189 Mel Gray .10
190 George Teague .10
191 Ernest Givins .10
192 Ray Buchannan .10
193 J.J. Birden .10
194 Tim Brown .20
195 Tim Lester .10
196 Marco Coleman .10
197 Randall McDaniel .10
198 Bruce Armstrong .10
199 Willie Roaf .10
200 Greg Jackson .10
201 Johnny Mitchell .10
202 Calvin Williams .10
203 Jeff Graham .10
204 Darren Carrington .10
205 Jerry Rice 1.00
206 Cortez Kennedy .20
207 Charles Wilson .10
208 James Jenkins .10
209 Ray Childress .10
210 Leroy Butler .10
211 Randal Hill .10
212 Lincoln Kennedy .10
213 Kenneth Davis .10
214 Terry Obee .10
215 Richardo McDonald .10
216 Pepper Johnson .10
217 Alvin Harper .20
218 John Elway .50
219 Derrick Moore .10
220 Terrell Buckley .10
221 Haywood Jeffires .10
222 Jessie Hester .10
223 Kimble Anders .10
224 Raghib Ismail .10
225 Roman Phifer .10
226 Bryan Cox .10
227 Cris Carter .20
228 Sam Gash .10
229 Renaldo Turnbull .10
230 Rodney Hampton .20
231 Johnny Johnson .10
232 Tim Harris .10
233 Leroy Thompson .10
234 Junior Seau .20
235 Tim McDonald .10
236 Eugene Robinson .10
237 Lawrence Dawsey .10
238 Tim Johnson .10
239 Jason Elam .10
240 Willie Green .10
241 Larry Centers .10
242 Erric Pegram .15
243 Bruce Smith .10
244 Alonzo Spellman .10
245 Carl Pickens .30
246 Michael Jackson .10
247 Kevin Williams .25
248 Glyn Milburn .15
249 Herman Moore .50
250 Brett Favre 3.00
251 Al Smith .10
252 Roosevelt Potts .10
253 Marcus Allen .20
254 Anthony Smith .10
255 Sean Gilbert .10
256 Keith Byars .10
257 *Scottie Graham* .50
258 Leonard Russell .10
259 Eric Martin .10
260 Jerrod Bunch .10
261 Rob Moore .10
262 Herschel Walker .10
263 Levon Kirkland .10
264 Chris Mims .10
265 Ricky Watters .25
266 Rick Mirer .75
267 Santana Dotson .10
268 Reggie Brooks .15
269 Garrison Hearst .50
270 Thurman Thomas .25
271 Johnny Bailey .10
272 Andre Rison .20
273 Jim Kelly .25
274 Mark Carrier .10
275 David Klingler .10
276 Eric Metcalf .10
277 Troy Aikman 1.25
278 Simon Fletcher .10
279 Pat Swilling .10
280 Sterling Sharpe .25
281 Cody Carlson .10
282 Steve Emtman .10
283 Neil Smith .10
284 James Jett .10
285 Shane Conlan .10
286 Keith Jackson .10
287 Qadry Ismail .15
288 Chris Slade .15
289 Derek Brown .10
290 Phil Simms .10
291 Boomer Esiason .10
292 Eric Allen .10
293 Rod Woodson .20
294 Ronnie Harmon .10
295 John Taylor .20
296 Ferrell Edmunds .10
297 Craig Erickson .15
298 Brian Mitchell .10
299 Dante Jones .10
300 John Copeland .10
301 Steve Beuerlein .10
302 Deion Sanders .75
303 Andre Reed .20
304 Curtis Conway .20
305 Harold Green .10
306 Vinny Testaverde .10
307 Michael Irvin .50
308 Rod Bernstine .10
309 Chris Spielman .10
310 Reggie White .20
311 Gary Brown .10
312 Quentin Coryatt .10
313 Derrick Thomas .20
314 Greg Robinson .10
315 Troy Drayton .10
316 Terry Kirby .15
317 John Randle .10
318 Ben Coates .50
319 Tyrone Hughes .10
320 Corey Miller .10
321 Brad Baxter .10
322 Randall Cunningham .25
323 Greg Lloyd .10
324 Stan Humphries .20
325 Dana Stubblefield .20
326 Kelvin Martin .10
327 Hardy Nickerson .10
328 Desmond Howard .10
329 Mark Carrier .10
330 Darryl Johnston .10

1994 Upper Deck Electric Silver

The 330-card, standard-size set was a parallel to the basic Upper Deck set. The cards differ from the gold versions by the logo that was produced with a foil finish instead of prismatic finish.

NM/M
Common Player: .25
Veteran Stars: 2X-4X
Young Stars: 1.5X-3X
RCs: 1.25X-2.5X

1994 Upper Deck Electric Gold

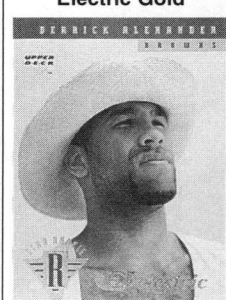

The Upper Deck Co. kicked off its 1994 football campaign, with a 330-card, single series issue. Upper Deck also introduced an upgraded card design and an interactive 50-card insert set, called Predictor Series. Two parallel Electric Field sets were also available. All 330 regular-issue cards will also be printed using gold and silver foil. These sets-within-a-set are called Silver Electric and Gold Electric, respectively. There are two other insert sets, called Then and Now and Pro Bowl Holoview.

NM/M
Common Player: .50
Minor Stars: 1.00
Unlisted Stars: 4X-6X

A card number in parenthese ( ) indicates the set is unnumbered.

1994 Upper Deck Predictor Award Winners

Hobby Predictor cards predicted what player would win the 1994 Most Valuable Player and Rookie of the Year. Each category included nine players and a longshot card. If the player pictured won that category, the card was redeemable for a gold foil set of Hobby Predictors. If the the pictured player finished second in his category, the card could be redeemed for a 10-card, gold foil set of his specific category.

NM/M
Complete Set (20): 20.00
Common Player: .50
Minor Stars: 1.00
Inserted 1:20 Hobby
1 Emmitt Smith 4.00
2 Barry Sanders 4.00
3 Jerome Bettis 1.00
4 Joe Montana 4.00
5 Dan Marino 4.00
6 Marshall Faulk 1.00
7 Dan Wilkinson .50
8 Sterling Sharpe 1.00
9 Thurman Thomas 1.00
10 The Longshot 1.00
11 Marshall Faulk 3.00
12 Trent Dilfer 1.00
13 Heath Shuler .50
14 David Palmer .50
15 Charles Johnson .50
16 Greg Hill .50
17 Johnnie Morton .50
18 Errict Rhett .50
19 Darney Scott .50
20 The Longshot .50

1994 Upper Deck Predictor League Leaders

The 30-card Retail Predictor insert set predicted the winner for 1994 rushing yardage, passing yardage and receiving yardage. As with the Hobby Predictors, a winner could be exchanged for the entire Retail Predictor set, while a second place finisher could be redeemed for his specific category 10-card set.

NM/M
Complete Set (30): 25.00
Common Player: .50
Minor Stars: 1.00
Inserted 1:20 Retail
1 Troy Aikman 4.00
2 Steve Young 4.00
3 John Elway 4.00
4 Joe Montana 5.00
5 Brett Favre 5.00
6 Heath Shuler .50
7 Dan Marino 5.00
8 Rick Mirer .50
9 Drew Bledsoe 2.00
10 The Longshot .50
11 Emmitt Smith 4.00
12 Barry Sanders 4.00
13 Jerome Bettis 1.00
14 Rodney Hampton .50
15 Thurman Thomas 1.00
16 Marshall Faulk 1.00
17 Barry Foster .50
18 Reggie Brooks .50
19 Ricky Watters 1.00

20 The Longshot .50
21 Jerry Rice 3.00
22 Sterling Sharpe 1.00
23 Andre Rison 1.00
24 Michael Irvin 1.00
25 Tim Brown 1.00
26 Shannon Sharpe 1.00
27 Andre Reed .50
28 Irving Fryar .50
29 Charles Johnson .50
30 The Longshot 1.00

1994 Upper Deck Pro Bowl

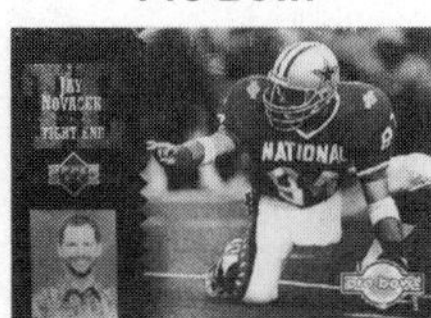

The Upper Deck Pro Bowl insert set was randomly inserted into hobby and retail packs of 1994 Upper Deck football. It marked the debut of Holoview cards, which feature a three-dimensional image.

NM/M

Complete Set (20): 30.00
Common Player: 1.00
Minor Stars: 2.00
Inserted 1:20
1 Jerome Bettis 2.00
2 Jay Novacek 1.00
3 Shannon Sharpe 1.00
4 Brent Jones 1.00
5 Andre Rison 1.00
6 Tim Brown 2.00
7 Anthony Miller 1.00
8 Jerry Rice 4.00
9 Brett Favre 5.00
10 Emmitt Smith 4.00
11 Steve Young 3.00
12 John Elway 3.00
13 Warren Moon 1.00
14 Thurman Thomas 1.00
15 Ricky Watters 1.00
16 Rod Woodson 1.00
17 Reggie White 1.00
18 Tyrone Hughes 1.00
19 Derrick Thomas 1.00
20 Checklist 1.00

1994 Upper Deck 24K Gold

The eight-card, standard-size set has horizontal fronts with player facsimile autographs on the left and an etched portrait on the right. Even though the cards are numbered on the back out of 2,500, reportedly just 1,500 of each card was produced.

NM/M

Complete Set (8): 110.00
Common Player: 5.00
1 Troy Aikman 15.00
2 Drew Bledsoe 15.00
3 Dan Marino 25.00
4 Rick Mirer 5.00
5 Joe Montana 25.00
6 Emmitt Smith 20.00
7 Thurman Thomas 10.00
8 Steve Young 15.00

1994-95 Upper Deck Sheets

The four-sheet, 8-1/2" x 11" set was issued at the Super Bowl Card Show VI in 1995.

NM/M

Complete Set (4): 30.00
Common Sheet: 4.00
NNO Rookie Class 1994 8.00
NNO Jan. 26-29, 1995 4.00
NNO Sean Gilbert, Kevin Carter, Isaac Bruce, Jerome Bettis, Chris Miller, Shane Conlan Upper Deck Salutes / St. Louis Rams (Undated numbered of 30,000) 8.00
NNO Dan Marino 1995 Record Breaker (Numbered of 30,000) 12.00

1995 Upper Deck

This 300-card 1995 Upper Deck football set contains 270 regular cards and 30 Star Rookies. In addition, retail packs have each card featured in an Electric (one per pack) and Electric Gold (one per box) parallel sets. Each regular card front has a full-bleed color photo, with the Upper Deck logo in the upper left corner and the player's name at the bottom stamped in gold foil. The player's team name and his position are in white letters, below his name. The card back has an action photo, with statistics and a brief recap of his 1994 season underneath. A black panel along the left side of the card has a card number, with a team logo under it. The player's name and biographical information are also included in the panel. A set-within-a-set, Special Edition, was also created. These cards, featuring photos by Walter Iooss Jr., have a different design from the base brand and were found in hobby packs only, one per pack. Gold versions were also created for the Special Edition cards; they were available one per box. Continued from Collector's Choice are the Joe Montana Trilogy cards, numbers MT9-16, plus a header card. Pro Bowl and Hobby and Retail Predictors also return. In addition, one in 144 packs is a Predictor Pack, which contain certain types of insert cards, depending on if the pack is retail or hobby.

NM/M

Complete Set (300): 30.00
Common Player: .10
Minor Stars: .20
Comp. Elec. Gold Set (300): 600.00
Electric Gold Cards: 3X-6X
Comp. Elec. Silv. Set (300): 120.00
Electric Silver Cards: 2X-4X
Pack (12): 1.00
Wax Box (36): 25.00
1 *Ki-Jana Carter* .50
2 *Tony Boselli* .20
3 *Steve McNair* 3.00
4 *Michael Westbrook* 1.50
5 *Kerry Collins* 2.00
6 *Kevin Carter* .20
7 *James Stewart* .20
8 *Joey Galloway* 2.00
9 *Kyle Brady* .50
10 *J.J. Stokes* 1.50
11 *Derrick Alexander* .20
12 *Warren Sapp* 1.00
13 *Mark Fields* .10
14 *Tyrone Wheatley* 1.00
15 *Napoleon Kaufman* 1.00
16 *James Stewart* 1.50
17 *Luther Elliss* .10
18 *Rashaan Salaam* .50
19 *Ty Law* .20
20 *Mark Bruener* .50
21 *Derrick Brooks* 2.00
22 *Christian Fauria* .20
23 *Ray Zellars* .20
24 *Todd Collins* .20
25 *Sherman Williams* .20
26 *Frank Sanders* .30
27 *Rodney Thomas* .20
28 *Rob Johnson* 1.00
29 *Steve Stenstrom* .20
30 *Curtis Martin* 3.00
31 Gary Clark .10
32 Troy Aikman 1.00
33 Mike Sherrard .10
34 Fred Barnett .10
35 Henry Ellard .10
36 Terry Allen .10
37 Jeff Graham .10
38 Herman Moore .40
39 Brett Favre 3.00
40 Trent Dilfer .20
41 Derek Brown .10
42 Andre Rison .10
43 Willie Anderson .10
44 Jerry Rice 1.25
45 Andre Reed .10
46 Sean Dawkins .10
47 Irving Fryar .10
48 Vincent Brisby .10
49 Rob Moore .10
50 Carl Pickens .20
51 Vinny Testaverde .10
52 Ray Childress .10
53 Eric Green .10
54 Anthony Miller .10
55 Lake Dawson .20
56 Tim Brown .20
57 Stan Humphries .10
58 Rick Mirer .20
59 Randal Hill .10
60 Charles Haley .10
61 Chris Calloway .10
62 Calvin Williams .10
63 Ethan Horton .10
64 Cris Carter .20
65 Curtis Conway .20
66 Scott Mitchell .10
67 Edgar Bennett .10
68 Craig Erickson .10
69 Jim Everett .10
70 Terance Mathis .10
71 Robert Young .10
72 Brent Jones .10
73 Thurman Thomas .20
74 Marshall Faulk 1.50
75 O.J. McDuffie .10
76 Ben Coates .10
77 Johnny Mitchell .10
78 Darnay Scott .50
79 Derrick Alexander .10
80 Lorenzo White .10
81 Charles Johnson .20
82 John Elway .40
83 Willie Davis .10
84 James Jett .10
85 Mark Seay .10
86 Brian Blades .10
87 Ronald Moore .10
88 Alvin Harper .10
89 Dave Brown .10
90 Randall Cunningham .10
91 Heath Shuler .75
92 Jake Reed .10
93 Donnell Woolford .10
94 Barry Sanders 2.00
95 Reggie White .20
96 Lawrence Dawsey .10
97 Michael Haynes .10
98 Bert Emanuel .40
99 Troy Drayton .10
100 Steve Young 1.25
101 Bruce Smith .10
102 Roosevelt Potts .10
103 Dan Marino 3.00
104 Michael Timpson .10
105 Boomer Esiason .10
106 David Klingler .10
107 Eric Metcalf .10
108 Gary Brown .10
109 Neil O'Donnell .20
110 Shannon Sharpe .10
111 Joe Montana 1.25
112 Jeff Hostetler .10
113 Ronnie Harmon .10
114 Chris Warren .20
115 Larry Centers .10
116 Michael Irvin .20
117 Rodney Hampton .10
118 Herschel Walker .10
119 Reggie Brooks .10
120 Qadry Ismail .10
121 Chris Zorich .10
122 Chris Spielman .10
123 Sean Jones .10
124 Errict Rhett .20
125 Tyrone Hughes .10
126 Jeff George .20
127 Chris Miller .10
128 Ricky Watters .20
129 Jim Kelly .20
130 Tony Bennett .10
131 Terry Kirby .10
132 Drew Bledsoe 1.25
133 Johnny Johnson .10
134 Dan Wilkinson .10
135 Leroy Hoard .10
136 Darryl Lewis .10
137 Barry Foster .10
138 Shane Dronett .10
139 Marcus Allen .10
140 Harvey Williams .10
141 Tony Martin .10
142 Rod Stephens .10
143 Eric Swann .10
144 Daryl Johnston .10
145 Dave Meggett .10
146 Charlie Garner .10
147 Ken Harvey .10
148 Warren Moon .20
149 Steve Walsh .10
150 Pat Swilling .10
151 Terrell Buckley .10
152 Courtney Hawkins .10
153 Willie Roaf .10
154 Chris Doleman .10
155 Jerome Bettis .20
156 Dana Stubblefield .10
157 Cornelius Bennett .10
158 Quentin Coryatt .10
159 Bryan Cox .10
160 Marion Butts .10
161 Aaron Glenn .10
162 Louis Oliver .10
163 Eric Turner .10
164 Cris Dishman .10
165 John L. Williams .10
166 Simon Fletcher .10
167 Neil Smith .10
168 Chester McGlockton .10
169 Natrone Means .20
170 Sam Adams .10
171 Clyde Simmons .10
172 Jay Novacek .10
173 Keith Hamilton .10
174 William Fuller .10
175 Tom Carter .10
176 John Randle .10
177 Lewis Tillman .10
178 Mel Gray .10
179 George Teague .10
180 Hardy Nickerson .10
181 Mario Bates .40
182 D.J. Johnson .10
183 Sean Gilbert .10
184 Bryant Young .10
185 Jeff Burris .10
186 Floyd Turner .10
187 Troy Vincent .10
188 Willie McGinest .10
189 James Hasty .10
190 *Jeff Blake* .50
191 Stevon Moore .10
192 Ernest Givins .10
193 Bam Morris .20
194 Ray Crockett .10
195 Dale Carter .10
196 Terry McDaniels .10
197 Leslie O'Neal .10
198 Cortez Kennedy .10
199 Seth Joyner .10
200 Emmitt Smith 3.00
201 Thomas Lewis .10
202 Andy Harmon .10
203 Ricky Ervins .10
204 Fuad Reveiz .10
205 John Thierry .10
206 Johnnie Morton .10
207 LeShon Johnson .10
208 Charles Wilson .10
209 Joe Johnson .10
210 Charles Smith .10
211 Roman Phifer .10
212 Ken Norton .10
213 Bucky Brooks .10
214 Ray Buchanan .10
215 Tim Bowens .10
216 Vincent Brown .10
217 Marcus Turner .10
218 Derrick Fenner .10
219 Antonio Langham .10
220 Cody Carlson .10
221 Greg Lloyd .10
222 Steve Atwater .10
223 Donnell Bennett .10
224 Raghib Ismail .10
225 John Carney .10
226 Eugene Robinson .10
227 Aeneas Williams .10
228 Darrin Smith .10
229 Phillipi Sparks .10
230 Eric Allen .10
231 Brian Mitchell .10
232 David Palmer .10
233 Mark Carrier .10
234 Dave Krieg .10
235 Robert Brooks .10
236 Eric Curry .10
237 Wayne Martin .10
238 Craig Heyward .10
239 Isaac Bruce 1.00
240 Deion Sanders 1.00
241 Steve Tasker .10
242 Jim Harbaugh .10
243 Aubrey Beavers .10
244 Chris Slade .10
245 Mo Lewis .10
246 Alfred Williams .10
247 Michael Dean Perry .10
248 Marcus Robertson .10
249 Kevin Greene .10
250 Leonard Russell .10
251 Greg Hill .20
252 Rob Fredrickson .10
253 Junior Seau .20
254 Rick Tuten .10
255 Garrison Hearst .30
256 Russell Maryland .10
257 Michael Brooks .10
258 Bernard Williams .10
259 Reggie Roby .10
260 DeWayne Washington .10
261 Raymont Harris .10
262 Brett Perriman .10
263 LeRoy Butler .10
264 Santana Dotson .10
265 Irv Smith .10
266 Ron George .10
267 Marquez Pope .10
268 William Floyd .20
269 Matt Darby .10
270 Jeff Herrod .10
271 Bernie Parmalee .20
272 Leroy Thompson .10
274 Marvin Jones .10
275 Michael Jackson .10
276 Al Smith .10
277 Rod Woodson .10
278 Glyn Milburn .10
279 Kimble Anders .10
280 Anthony Smith .10
281 Andre Coleman .10
282 Terry Wooden .10
283 Ernest Givins .10
284 Steve Beuerlein .10
285 Mark Brunell 1.50
286 Keith Goganious .10
287 Desmond Howard .10
288 Darren Carrington .10
289 Derek Brown .10
290 Reggie Cobb .10
291 Jeff Lageman .10
292 Lamar Lathon .10
293 Sam Mills .10
294 Carlton Bailey .10
295 Mark Carrier .10
296 Willie Green .10
297 Frank Reich .10
298 Don Beebe .10
299 Tim McKyer .10
300 Pete Metzelaars .10

1995 Upper Deck Electric Silver

The 300-card, standard-size parallel set was inserted every pack and features a silver-foil "Electric" stamp on the card front.

NM/M

Common Player: .20
Veteran Stars: 2X-4X
Young Stars: 1.5X-3X
RCs: 1.25X-2.5X

1995 Upper Deck Electric Gold

The 300-card, standard-size set was a parallel to the base set and was inserted every 35 packs. The card fronts have a gold-foil "Electric" logo.

Veteran Stars: 3X-6X
Young Stars: 3X-5X
RCs: 2X-5X

1995 Upper Deck Montana Trilogy

Continued from Upper Deck's 1995 Collector's Choice football are eight more Joe Montana Trilogy cards, seeded one per 12 packs. These cards, numbered 9-16 with an "MT" prefix, feature a metallic-like front background, with gold foil for the brand logo and a panel at the bottom of the card which describes the card's title. The title is listed above in a black strip. The Montana Trilogy logo also appears on the front. The card back has a player photo and a recap of the play being depicted on the front.

NM/M

Complete Set (9): 40.00
Common Player: 6.00
Header Card: 6.00
9 The Drive 6.00
10 Super Bowl XXII 6.00
11 1989 - Dream Season 6.00
12 NFL MVP Back-to-Back 6.00
13 Super Bowl XXIV 6.00
14 Super Bowl XXIV MVP 6.00
15 Back-to-Back Super Bowls 6.00
16 The Comeback 6.00
UDH Trilogy Header 6.00

1995 Upper Deck Hobby Predictor

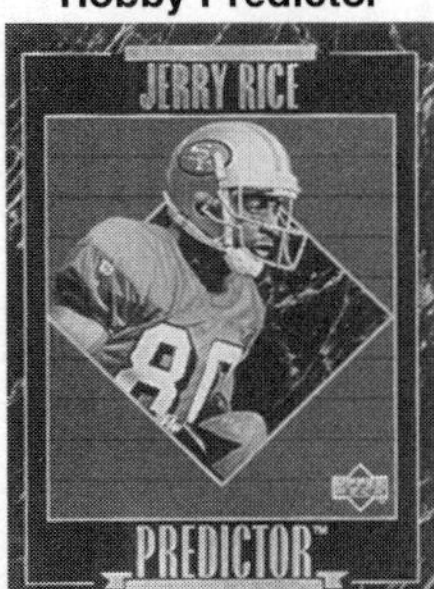

These 20 cards, random inserts in 1995 Upper Deck hobby packs, feature 18 players who were potential MVP and Rookie of the Year Award winners. Two longshot cards were also made. Cards were in one per every 30 packs. If the player featured won the category, or finished second in the voting, collectors could redeem the cards for prizes. Card backs, numbered using an "HP" prefix, explained the rules of the game.

NM/M

Complete Set (20): 30.00
Common Player: 1.00
1 Dan Marino 5.00
2 Steve Young 3.00
3 Drew Bledsoe 3.00
4 Troy Aikman 3.00
5 Barry Sanders 5.00
6 Emmitt Smith 5.00
7 Jerry Rice 3.00
8 Ki-Jana Carter 1.00
9 John Elway 3.00
10 The Longshot 1.00
11 Ki-Jana Carter 1.00
12 Steve McNair 2.00
13 Michael Westbrook 1.00
14 Kerry Collins 1.00
15 Joey Galloway 2.00
16 Kyle Brady 1.00
17 Napoleon Kaufman 1.00
18 Tyrone Wheatley 1.00
19 Rashaan Salaam 1.00
20 The Longshot 1.00

1995 Upper Deck Retail Predictor

These 30 1995 Upper Deck football cards feature 28 players with the potential to win either the rushing yardage, passing efficiency and receiving yardage categories. Cards were randomly inserted one per every 30 retail packs. The card back, numbered using an "RP" prefix, explained the rules for if a player finished first or second in a category, and what prizes collectors could receive if they redeemed a winning card.

NM/M

Complete Set (30): 40.00
Common Player: .50
Minor Stars: 1.00
Inserted 1:30 Retail
1 Dan Marino 7.50
2 Steve Young 4.00
3 Drew Bledsoe 5.00
4 Troy Aikman 5.00
5 John Elway 7.50
6 Brett Favre 5.00
7 Stan Humphries .50
8 Jeff George 1.00
9 Kerry Collins 1.00
10 Longshot .50
11 Barry Sanders 4.00
12 Chris Warren .50
13 Emmitt Smith 4.00
14 Natrone Means 1.00
15 Rodney Hampton .50
16 Marshall Faulk 3.00
17 Errict Rhett .50
18 Napoleon Kaufman .50
19 Ki-Jana Carter .50
20 Longshot .50
21 Jerry Rice 3.00
22 Ben Coates .50
23 Cris Carter 1.00
24 Andre Reed .50
25 Andre Rison .50
26 Tim Brown .50
27 Michael Irvin 1.00
28 Irving Fryar .50
29 Michael Westbrook 1.00
30 Longshot .50

1995 Upper Deck Pro Bowl

These 25 cards, random inserts one per every 35 packs of 1995 Upper Deck football, use the Holoview process. Top players from the 1995 Pro Bowl are included. In addition to the hologram front, which shows the player against a Hawaiian setting with palm trees, the Pro Bowl logo is in the upper right corner. The player's name, team, position and Upper Deck logo are along the bottom of the card, which uses a horizontal format for the front. The horizontal back has a photo of the player in his Pro Bowl uniform, against a ghosted action photo as a background. A recap of the player's 1994 season is also included, as is a card number, which uses a "PB" prefix.

		NM/M
Complete Set (25):		30.00
Common Player:		.50
1	Barry Sanders	4.00
2	Brent Jones	.50
3	Cris Carter	.50
4	Emmitt Smith	4.00
5	Jay Novacek	.50
6	Jerome Bettis	.50
7	Jerry Rice	3.00
8	Michael Irvin	1.00
9	Ricky Watters	.50
10	Steve Young	3.00
11	Troy Aikman	3.00
12	Warren Moon	.50
13	Terance Mathis	.50
14	Ben Coates	.50
15	Chris Warren	.50
16	Dan Marino	5.00
17	Drew Bledsoe	3.00
18	Irving Fryar	.50
19	Jeff Hostetler	.50
20	John Elway	3.00
21	Leroy Hoard	.50
22	Marshall Faulk	3.00
23	Natrone Means	.50
24	Tim Brown	.50
25	Checklist	.50

1995 Upper Deck Special Edition

This set-within-a-set features the photography of Walter Iooss Jr. The cards, random inserts one per every 1995 Upper Deck hobby pack, use a different design from the base brand. Each card front has a full-bleed color action photo on it, with Special Edition written at the top of the card. The player's name is at the bottom of the card. Card backs are numbered using an "SE" prefix. Special Edition Gold versions were also created for each card in the set; these cards were seeded one per every box.

		NM/M
Complete Set (90):		15.00
Common Player:		.10
Minor Stars:		.40
Unlisted Gold Stars:		3X-5X
1	Terry Kirby	.10
2	Marcus Allen	.50
3	Bernie Parmalee	.50
4	Vernon Turner	.10
5	Dolphins Defense	.10
6	Kevin Turner	.10
7	Henry Thomas	.10
8	Barry Sanders	3.00
9	Marshall Faulk	2.00
10	Bill Bates	.10
11	Stan Humphries	.50
12	Barry Foster	.10
13	Shannon Sharpe	.50
14	Joe Montana	2.00
15	Bryan Cox	.10
16	Dale Carter	.10
17	Drew Bledsoe	2.00
18	Dan Marino	4.00
19	Ricky Watters	.50
20	Alvin Harper	.50
21	49ers Offensive Line	.10
22	Dan Marino	4.00
23	Ronnie Harmon	.10
24	Michael Irvin	.50
25	Emmitt Smith	3.00
26	Jeff Christie	.10
27	Terry Allen	.10
28	Randall Cunningham	.50
29	Todd Steussie	.10
30	Warren Moon	.50
31	Vikings Defense	.10
32	Tony Tolbert	.10
33	William Fuller	.10
34	Bernard Williams	.10
35	Charlie Garner	.10
36	Troy Aikman	2.00
37	Alvin Harper	.50
38	Kenneth Gant	.10
39	Daryl Johnston	.10
40	Ben Coates	.10
41	Rickey Jackson	.10
42	O.J. McDuffie	.10
43	Marion Butts	.10
44	NFL Offenses	.10
45	Kimble Anders	.10
46	Natrone Means	.50
47	Richmond Webb	.10
48	Carlos Jenkins	.10
49	James Harris	.10
50	Dexter Carter	.10
51	Qadry Ismail	.10
52	Jeff Herrod	.10
53	Sean Jones	.10
54	Keith Sims	.10
55	William Floyd	.50
56	Don Majkowski	.10
57	Charger Defense	.10
58	Byron Evans	.10
59	Chad Hennings	.10
60	Eric Allen	.10
61	Curtis Martin	3.00
62	Napoleon Kaufman	1.00
63	Kevin Carter	.50
64	Luther Elliss	.10
65	Frank Sanders	2.00
66	Rob Johnson	1.00
67	Christian Fauria	.10
68	Kyle Brady	.50
69	Michael Westbrook	1.50
70	James A. Stewart	.50
71	Ty Law	.10
72	Rodney Thomas	.10
73	Jimmy Oliver	.10
74	James O. Stewart	.50
75	Dave Barr	.10
76	Kordell Stewart	2.00
77	Michael Westbrook	1.50
78	Bobby Taylor	.10
79	Mark Fields	.10
80	Kerry Collins	1.00
81	Natrone Means	.50
82	Chargers Offense	.10
83	Deion Sanders	1.50
84	Dana Stubblefield	.10
85	49ers Defense	.10
86	Alfred Pupunu	.10
87	Tim Harris	.10
88	Jerry Rice	2.00
89	Steve Young	2.00
90	Super Bowl XXIX Champs.	2.00

1995 Upper Deck GTE Phone Cards AFC

The 15-card, 3-3/8" x 2-1/8" prepaid set has rounded corners and color action photos on the fronts. The card backs have instructions for usage on the five-unit cards.

		NM/M
Complete Set (15):		20.00
Common Player:		1.00
1	Marcus Allen	2.00
2	Drew Bledsoe	3.00
3	Gary Brown	1.00
4	Tim Brown	2.00
5	John Elway	3.00
6	Marshall Faulk	3.00
7	Barry Foster	1.00
8	Jim Kelly	2.00
9	Ronnie Lott	1.00
10	Dan Marino	4.00
11	Rick Mirer	1.00
12	Carl Pickens	1.00
13	Junior Seau	2.00
14	Vinny Testaverde	1.00
15	Title Card	1.00

1995 Upper Deck GTE Phone Cards NFC

The 15-card, 3-3/8" x 2-1/8" set is identical to the AFC set in design, but with NFC players. The card backs feature card usage instructions.

		NM/M
Complete Set (15):		20.00
Common Player:		1.00
1	Jerome Bettis	2.00
2	Gary Clark	1.00
3	Curtis Conway	1.00
4	Randall Cunningham	1.00
5	Rodney Hampton	1.00
6	Michael Haynes	1.00
7	Michael Irvin	1.00
8	Warren Moon	1.00
9	Hardy Nickerson	1.00
10	Jerry Rice	3.00
11	Andre Rison	1.00
12	Barry Sanders	4.00
13	Sterling Sharpe	1.00
14	Heath Shuler	1.00
15	Title Card	1.00

1995 Upper Deck Joe Montana Box Set

The 45-card, over-sized set highlights Montana's career from childhood through the pros. The card fronts feature gold foil with commentary text on the backs. The set was limited to 38,000 sets.

		NM/M
Complete Set (45):		20.00
Common Player:		.60
1	A Star Is Born	.60
2	Quarterback State	.60
3	Making Of A Hero	.60
4	National Champion	.60
5	Never-Say-Die	.60
6	The Protege	.60
7	New Orleans - The First Victim	.60
8	The Catch	.60
9	Super Bowl Fever	.60
10	Super Bowl XVI	.60
11	Emergence Of A/ Record-Breaker	.60
12	Career-Year	.60
13	Heroic Comeback	.60
14	Super Bowl XIX	.60
15	Repeat Performance	.60
16	First Passing Crown	.60
17	Super Bowl XXIII	.60
18	Super Leader	.60
19	Best Of The Best	.60
20	Super Bowl XXIV	.60
21	Four-Time Champs	.60
22	Team Of The 80's	.60
23	Back-To-Back MVP's	.60
24	Down, But Far From Out	.60
25	Farewell Performance	.60
26	The Trade	.60
27	First K.C. Comeback	.60
28	Playoff Magic	.60
29	Dueling Quaterbacks	.60
30	Another Milestone Falls	.60
31	39 300-Yard Games	.60
32	273 Touchdowns	.60
33	112.4 Pass Efficiency Rating	.60
34	92.3 Pass Efficiency Rating	.60
35	117 Wins	.60
36	31 Comeback Victories	.60
37	5,391 Attempts	.60
38	3 Super Bowl MVP's	.60
39	3,409 Completions	.60
40	40,551 Yards	.60
41	Bill Walsh	.60
42	Russ Francis	.60
43	Roger Craig	.60
44	Jerry Rice	.60
45	Dwight Clark	.60
NNO	Super Bowl XIX / Quarterbabck Duel (Numbered of 38,000)	5.00
JM16	Joe Montana (Promo)	2.00

1995 Upper Deck Authenticated Joe Montana Jumbos

The four-card, 5" x 3-1/2" set was offered to collectors through UDA's catalog. Each card shows Montana playing in a different Super Bowl. The card backs feature regular and post season statistics.

		NM/M
Complete Set (4):		35.00
Common Player:		10.00
1	Joe Montana Super Bowl XVI	10.00
2	Joe Montana Super Bowl XIX	10.00
3	Joe Montana Super Bowl XXIII	10.00
4	Joe Montana Super Bowl XXIV	10.00

1996 Upper Deck

Upper Deck's Series I football has 300 cards in it, with more than 90 percent of them highlighting the actual game date of the photo on the card front. Silver foil stamping is used for an Upper Deck logo, team logo and the player's last name, which appears between two parallel foiled stripes. The back has a close-up shot of the player, statistics, a recap of the featured game and season highlights. Series I inserts include Game Jersey, Hobby and Retail Predictor cards, Team Trio, Hot Properties and Meet the Stars promotional scratch-off cards. These trivia cards give collectors a chance to meet Dan Marino and win Upper Deck merchandise. Cards were seeded one per every four packs.

		NM/M
Complete Set (300):		35.00
Common Player:		.10
Minor Stars:		.20
Pack (12):		2.00
Wax Box (24):		35.00
1	*Keyshawn Johnson*	2.50
2	*Kevin Hardy*	.20
3	*Simeon Rice*	.20
4	*Jonathan Ogden*	.10
5	*Cedric Jones*	.10
6	*Lawrence Phillips*	.75
7	*Tim Biakabutuka*	1.00
8	*Terry Glenn*	2.00
9	*Rickey Dudley*	.75
10	*Willie Anderson*	.10
11	*Alex Molden*	.10
12	*Regan Upshaw*	.10
13	*Walt Harris*	.20
14	*Eddie George*	3.00
15	*John Mobley*	.10
16	*Duane Clemons*	.10
17	*Eddie Kennison*	.30
18	*Marvin Harrison*	3.00
19	*Daryl Gardener*	.10
20	*Leeland McElroy*	.30
21	*Eric Moulds*	2.00
22	*Alex Van Dyke*	.20
23	*Mike Alstott*	1.50
24	*Jeff Lewis*	.75
25	*Bobby Engram*	.30
26	*Derrick Mayes*	.50
27	*Karim Abdul-Jabbar*	.75
28	*Bobby Hoying*	.75
29	*Stepfret Williams*	.10
30	*Chris Darkins*	.20
31	*Stephen Davis*	2.00
32	*Danny Kanell*	.75
33	*Tony Brackens*	.40
34	Leslie O'Neal	.10
35	Chris Doleman	.10
36	Larry Brown	.10
37	Ronnie Harmon	.10
38	Chris Spielman	.10
39	John Jurkovic	.10
40	Shawn Jefferson	.10
41	Tommy Vardell	.10
42	Eric Davis	.10
43	Willie Clay	.10
44	Marco Coleman	.10
45	Lorenzo White	.10
46	Neil O'Donnell	.20
47	Natrone Means	.20
48	Cornelius Bennett	.10
49	Steve Walsh	.10
50	Jerome Bettis	.10
51	Boomer Esiason	.10
52	Glyn Milburn	.10
53	Kevin Greene	.10
54	Seth Joyner	.10
55	Jeff Harrod	.10
56	Darren Woodson	.10
57	Dale Carter	.10
58	Lorenzo Lynch	.10
59	Tim Brown	.10
60	Jerry Rice	1.50
61	Garrison Hearst	.20
62	Eric Metcalf	.10
63	Leroy Hoard	.10
64	Thurman Thomas	.20
65	Sam Mills	.10
66	Curtis Conway	.20
67	Carl Pickens	.20
68	Deion Sanders	.75
69	Shannon Sharpe	.10
70	Herman Moore	.40
71	Robert Brooks	.20
72	Rodney Thomas	.20
73	Ken Dilger	.10
74	Mark Brunell	1.00
75	Marcus Allen	.20
76	Dan Marino	3.00
77	Robert Smith	.10
78	Drew Bledsoe	1.25
79	Jim Everett	.10
80	Rodney Hampton	.10
81	Adrien Murrell	.10
82	Daryl Hobbs	.10
83	Ricky Watters	.20
84	Yancey Thigpen	.50
85	Roman Phifer	.10
86	Tony Martin	.10
87	Dana Stubblefield	.10
88	Joey Galloway	1.00
89	Errict Rhett	.75
90	Terry Allen	.10
91	Aeneas Williams	.10
92	Craig Heyward	.10
93	Vinny Testaverde	.10
94	Bryce Paup	.10
95	Kerry Collins	.30
96	Rashaan Salaam	.30
97	Dan Wilkinson	.10
98	Jay Novacek	.10
99	John Elway	.30
100	Bennie Blades	.10
101	Edgar Bennett	.10
102	Darryll Lewis	.10
103	Marshall Faulk	.50
104	Bryan Schwartz	.10
105	Tamarick Vanover	.75
106	Terry Kirby	.10
107	John Randle	.10
108	Ted Johnson	.10
109	Mario Bates	.10
110	Philippi Sparks	.10
111	Marvin Washington	.10
112	Terry McDaniel	.10
113	Bobby Taylor	.10
114	Carnell Lake	.10
115	Troy Drayton	.10
116	Darren Bennett	.10
117	J.J. Stokes	.30
118	Rick Mirer	.20
119	Jackie Harris	.10
120	Ken Harvey	.10
121	Rob Moore	.10
122	Jeff George	.20
123	Andre Rison	.10
124	Darick Holmes	.20
125	Tim McKyer	.10
126	Alonzo Spellman	.10
127	Jeff Blake	.75
128	Kevin Williams	.10
129	Anthony Miller	.10
130	Barry Sanders	1.75
131	Brett Favre	3.00
132	Steve McNair	1.00
133	Jim Harbaugh	.20
134	Desmond Howard	.10
135	Steve Bono	.10
136	Bernie Parmalee	.10
137	Warren Moon	.10
138	Curtis Martin	2.00
139	Irv Smith	.10
140	Thomas Lewis	.10
141	Kyle Brady	.10
142	Napoleon Kaufman	.10
143	Mike Mamula	.10
144	Erric Pegram	.10
145	Isaac Bruce	1.00
146	Andre Coleman	.10
147	Merton Hanks	.10
148	Brian Blades	.10
149	Hardy Nickerson	.10
150	Michael Westbrook	.20
151	Larry Centers	.10
152	Morten Andersen	.10
153	Michael Jackson	.10
154	Bruce Smith	.10
155	Derrick Moore	.10
156	Mark Carrier	.10
157	John Copeland	.10
158	Emmitt Smith	3.00
159	Jason Elam	.10
160	Scott Mitchell	.10
161	Mark Chmura	.30
162	Blaine Bishop	.10
163	Tony Bennett	.10
164	Pete Mitchell	.10
165	Dan Saleaumua	.10
166	Pete Stoyanovich	.10
167	Cris Carter	.10
168	Vincent Brisby	.10
169	Wayne Martin	.10
170	Tyrone Wheatley	.10
171	Mo Lewis	.10
172	Harvey Williams	.10
173	Calvin Williams	.10
174	Norm Johnson	.10
175	Mark Rypien	.10
176	Stan Humphries	.10
177	Derek Loville	.10
178	Christian Fauria	.10
179	Warren Sapp	.10
180	Henry Ellard	.10
181	Jamir Miller	.10
182	Jessie Tuggle	.10
183	Stevon Moore	.10
184	Jim Kelly	.20
185	Mark Carrier	.10
186	Chris Zorich	.10
187	Harold Green	.10
188	Chris Boniol	.10
189	Allen Aldridge	.10
190	Brett Perriman	.10
191	Chris Jackie (Jacke)	.10
192	Todd McNair	.10
193	Floyd Turner	.10
194	Jeff Lageman	.10
195	Derrick Thomas	.10
196	Eric Green	.10
197	Orlanda Thomas	.10
198	Ben Coates	.10
199	Tyrone Hughes	.10
200	Dave Brown	.10
201	Brad Baxter	.10
202	Chester McGlockton	.10
203	Rodney Peete	.10
204	Willie Williams	.10
205	Kevin Carter	.10
206	Aaron Hayden	.20
207	Steve Young	1.00
208	Chris Warren	.20
209	Eric Curry	.10
210	Brian Mitchell	.10
211	Frank Sanders	.10
212	Terance Mathis	.10
213	Eric Turner	.10
214	Bill Brooks	.10
215	John Kasay	.10
216	Erik Kramer	.10
217	Darnay Scott	.20
218	Charles Haley	.10
219	Steve Atwater	.10
220	Jason Hanson	.10
221	LeRoy Butler	.10
222	Cris Dishman	.10
223	Sean Dawkins	.10
224	James O. Stewart	.10
225	Greg Hill	.10
226	Jeff Cross	.10
227	Qadry Ismail	.10
228	Dave Meggett	.10
229	Eric Allen	.10
230	Chris Calloway	.10
231	Wayne Chrebet	.10
232	Jeff Hostetler	.10
233	Andy Harmon	.10
234	Greg Lloyd	.10
235	Toby Wright	.10
236	Junior Seau	.10
237	Bryant Young	.10
238	Robert Blackmon	.10
239	Trent Dilfer	.10
240	Leslie Shepherd	.10
241	Eric Swann	.10
242	Bert Emanuel	.10
243	Antonio Langham	.10
244	Steve Christie	.10
245	Tyrone Poole	.10
246	Jim Flanigan	.10
247	Tony McGee	.10
248	Michael Irvin	.20
249	Bam Morris	.10
250	Terrell Davis	1.50
251	Johnnie Morton	.10
252	Sean Jones	.10
253	Chris Sanders	.30
254	Quentin Coryatt	.10
255	Willie Jackson	.10
256	Mark Collins	.10
257	Randal Hill	.10
258	David Palmer	.10
259	Will Moore	.10
260	Michael Haynes	.10
261	Mike Sherrard	.10
262	William Thomas	.10
263	Kordell Stewart	.75
264	D'Marco Farr	.10
265	Terrell Fletcher	.10
266	Lee Woodall	.10
267	Eugene Robinson	.10
268	Alvin Harper	.10
269	Gus Frerotte	.10
270	Antonio Freeman	.10
271	Clyde Simmons	.10
272	Chuck Smith	.10
273	Steve Tasker	.10
274	Kevin Butler	.10
275	Steve Tovar	.10
276	Troy Aikman	1.00
277	Aaron Craver	.10
278	Henry Thomas	.10
279	Craig Newsome	.10
280	Brent Jones	.10
281	Micheal Barrow	.10
282	Ray Buchanan	.10
283	Jimmy Smith	.10
284	Neil Smith	.10
285	O.J. McDuffie	.10
286	Jake Reed	.10
287	Ty Law	.10
288	Torrance Small	.10
289	Hugh Douglas	.10
290	Pat Swilling	.10
291	Charlie Garner	.10
292	Ernie Mills	.10
293	John Carney	.10
294	Ken Norton	.10
295	Cortez Kennedy	.10
296	Derrick Brooks	.10
297	Heath Shuler	.20
298	Reggie White	.10
299	Kimble Anders	.10
300	Willie McGinest	.10

1996 Upper Deck Game Jersey

Each of these 1996 Upper Deck insert cards features an actual piece of a player's game-worn uniform. Cards, seeded one per every 2,500 Series I packs, are numbered using a "GJ" prefix. There are two different cards of Jerry Rice and Dan Marino.

		NM/M
Complete Set (10):		4,000
Common Player:		150.00
1	Dan Marino	350.00
2	Jerry Rice	300.00
3	Joe Montana	350.00
4	Jerry Rice	300.00
5	Rashaan Salaam	60.00
6	Marshall Faulk	275.00
7	Dan Marino	350.00
8	Steve Young	200.00
9	Barry Sanders	275.00
10	Mark Brunell	75.00

1996 Upper Deck Predictor

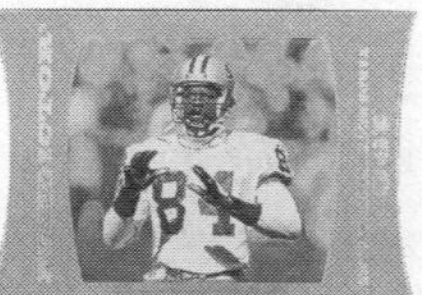

All new die-cut F/X designs grace the fronts of these 1996 Upper Deck Series I inserts, which are now based on personal goals. For example, if Dan Marino passes for 450 or more yards in a game, a collector can mail in the Marino card for a special TV-CEL redemption card. The player's goal and the word "Predictor" are stamped in silver foil along the sides of the card. The back of the card explains the rules for the promotion. A maximum of 500 of each player's winning TV-CEL cards will be randomly inserted in packs. The same 20 players are represented in both retail and hobby versions, but the personal goals are different. The cards also use the corresponding "PH" or "PR" prefix for the card number.

		NM/M
Comp. Hobby Set (20):		30.00
Comp. Retail Set (20):		30.00
Common Player:		.50
PH1	Dan Marino	5.00
PH2	Steve Young	3.00
PH3	Brett Favre	5.00
PH4	Drew Bledsoe	3.00
PH5	Jeff George	.50
PH6	John Elway	3.00
PH7	Barry Sanders	4.00
PH8	Curtis Martin	3.00
PH9	Marshall Faulk	3.00
PH10	Emmitt Smith	4.00
PH11	Terrell Davis	3.00
PH12	Errict Rhett	1.00
PH13	Lawrence Phillips	.50
PH14	Jerry Rice	3.00
PH15	Michael Irvin	1.00
PH16	Joey Galloway	1.00
PH17	Herman Moore	1.00
PH18	Isaac Bruce	1.00
PH19	Carl Pickens	1.00
PH20	Keyshawn Johnson	2.00
PR1	Dan Marino	5.00
PR2	Steve Young	4.00
PR3	Brett Favre	5.00
PR4	Drew Bledsoe	4.00
PR5	Jeff George	.50
PR6	John Elway	4.00
PR7	Barry Sanders	4.00
PR8	Curtis Martin	4.00
PR9	Marshall Faulk	4.00
PR10	Emmitt Smith	5.00
PR11	Terrell Davis	4.00
PR12	Errict Rhett	.50
PR13	Lawrence Phillips	.50
PR14	Jerry Rice	4.00
PR15	Michael Irvin	1.00
PR16	Joey Galloway	1.00
PR17	Herman Moore	1.00
PR18	Isaac Bruce	2.00
PR19	Carl Pickens	1.00
PR20	Keyshawn Johnson	2.00

1996 Upper Deck Pro Bowl

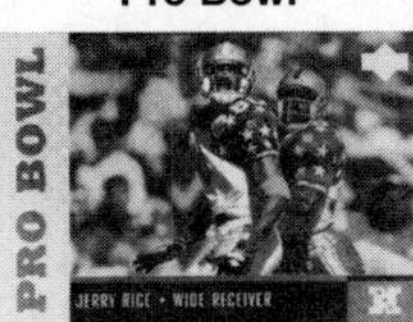

The 20-card Pro Bowl set was inserted every 33 packs of Upper Deck's Series One football. Cards are numbered and carry a "PB" prefix.

		NM/M
Complete Set (20):		35.00
Common Player:		1.00
1	Warren Moon	1.00
2	Brett Favre	5.00
3	Steve Young	3.00
4	Barry Sanders	4.00
5	Emmitt Smith	4.00
6	Jerry Rice	3.00
7	Herman Moore	1.00
8	Michael Irvin	1.00
9	Mark Chmura	1.00
10	Reggie White	1.00
11	Jim Harbaugh	1.00
12	Jeff Blake	1.00
13	Curtis Martin	3.00
14	Marshall Faulk	3.00
15	Chris Warren	1.00
16	Bryan Cox	1.00
17	Junior Seau	2.00
18	Carl Pickens	1.00
19	Yancey Thigpen	1.00
20	Ben Coates	1.00

1996 Upper Deck Proview

One Proview card was inserted in each Upper Deck Tech retail pack. The cards feature a cel window with a player close up. The fronts include another photo and the backs have basic player information. Silver (1:35) and Gold (1:143) parallel versions were also created.

		NM/M
Complete Set (40):		50.00
Common Player:		.50
Minor Stars:		1.00
1	Warren Moon	.50
2	Jerry Rice	3.00
3	Brett Favre	5.00
4	Jim Harbaugh	.50
5	Junior Seau	.50
6	Jeff Blake	1.00
7	John Elway	3.00
8	Troy Aikman	3.00
9	Steve Young	3.00
10	Kordell Stewart	2.00
11	Drew Bledsoe	3.00
12	Jim Kelly	1.00
13	Dan Marino	5.00
14	Kerry Collins	1.00
15	Jeff Hostetler	.50
16	Terry Allen	.50
17	Carl Pickens	.50
18	Mark Brunell	2.00
19	Keyshawn Johnson	2.00
20	Barry Sanders	4.00
21	Deion Sanders	2.00
22	Emmitt Smith	4.00
23	Curtis Conway	.50
24	Herman Moore	1.00
25	Joey Galloway	1.00
26	Robert Smith	.50
27	Eddie George	2.00
28	Curtis Martin	3.00
29	Marshall Faulk	3.00
30	Terrell Davis	3.00
31	Rashaan Salaam	.50
32	Jamal Anderson	1.00
33	Karim Abdul-Jabbar	1.00
34	Edgar Bennett	.50
35	Thurman Thomas	1.00
36	Jerome Bettis	1.00
37	Tim Brown	.50
38	Chris Sanders	.50
39	Eddie Kennison	1.00
40	Shannon Sharpe	.50

1996 Upper Deck Hot Properties

Each of these 1996 Upper Deck Series I inserts features a different player on each side. The card design features a color action photo (outlined with a red glow) against a silver metallic background. Red foil is used for the Upper Deck logo and the word "Hot" in the set's logo. The card number, using an "HT" prefix, is on one side, above an Upper Deck football-shaped hologram. Cards were seeded one per every 11 Series I packs.

		NM/M
Complete Set (20):		40.00
Common Player:		.50
Gold Cards:		1.5X-3X
1	Dan Marino, Drew Bledsoe	6.00
2	Jerry Rice, J.J. Stokes	4.00
3	Kordell Stewart, Deion Sanders	2.00
4	Brett Favre, Rick Mirer	5.00
5	Jeff Blake, Steve McNair	2.00
6	Emmitt Smith, Errict Rhett	5.00
7	John Elway, Warren Moon	3.00
8	Steve Young, Mark Brunell	3.00
9	Troy Aikman, Kerry Collins	3.00
10	Joey Galloway, Chris Sanders	2.00
11	Herman Moore, Cris Carter	.50
12	Rodney Hampton, Terrell Davis	3.00
13	Carl Pickens, Isaac Bruce	2.00
14	Rashaan Salaam, Michael Westbrook	1.00
15	Marshall Faulk, Curtis Martin	4.00
16	Tamarick Vanover, Eric Metcalf	1.00
17	Keyshawn Johnson, Terry Glenn	1.00
18	Lawrence Phillips, Tim Biakabutuka	1.00
19	Kevin Hardy, Simeon Rice	.50
20	Barry Sanders, Thurman Thomas	5.00

1996 Upper Deck Game Face

Game Face inserts were only found in special retail packs, and were numbered GF1-GF10. They included a close-up shot of the player, who had his intense, "game face" on.

		NM/M
Complete Set (10):		6.00
Common Player:		.50
1	Dan Marino	3.00
2	Barry Sanders	2.00
3	Jerry Rice	2.00
4	Stan Humphries	.50
5	Drew Bledsoe	2.00
6	Greg Lloyd	.50
7	Jim Harbaugh	.50
8	Rashaan Salaam	.50
9	Jeff Blake	.50
10	Reggie White	.50

1996 Upper Deck TV Cels

TV Cels were available by redeeming winner Predictor cards. They include a television-like frame with cel technology inside, which reveals the player's image when held to light. Cards are numbered and carry a "PH" prefix.

		NM/M
Complete Set (20):		125.00
Common Player:		2.00
1	Dan Marino	15.00
2	Steve Young	10.00
3	Brett Favre	15.00
4	Drew Bledsoe	10.00
5	Jeff George	2.00
6	John Elway	10.00
7	Barry Sanders	12.00
8	Curtis Martin	6.00
9	Marshall Faulk	6.00
10	Emmitt Smith	12.00
11	Terrell Davis	8.00
12	Errict Rhett	2.00
13	Lawrence Phillips	2.00
14	Jerry Rice	10.00
15	Michael Irvin	2.00
16	Joey Galloway	4.00
17	Herman Moore	2.00
18	Isaac Bruce	2.00
19	Carl Pickens	2.00
20	Keyshawn Johnson	4.00

1996 Upper Deck Silver

Upper Deck's 1996 premium Silver Collection contains 210 regular cards of the top stars and rookies in the NFL, printed on silver paper stock. Silver foil is used for the player's name, team name, position and brand logo on the front, which has a full-bleed color action photo. The back has a black strip along the left side, with the player's name, position and biographical information in it, plus a team logo and card number toward the top. A color action photo is at the top of the card, with statistics underneath. Subset cards are devoted to top players in certain offensive and defensive statistical leaders from the 1995 NFL season. Insert sets include All-NFL Team, All-Rookie Team, team helmet cards, Dan Marino Record Season, and a Rookie Draft Trade card, which is redeemable for 20-card Light F/X Rookie Redemption set from the 1996 NFL Draft. Cards were seeded one per every 103 packs.

		NM/M
Complete Set (225):		30.00
Common Player:		.10
Minor Stars:		.20
Pack (10):		1.00
Wax Box (28):		22.00
1	Larry Centers	.10
2	Terance Mathis	.10
3	Justin Armour	.10
4	Kerry Collins	.30
5	Mike Flanagan	.10
6	Dan Wilkinson	.10
7	Eric Zeier	.75
8	Deion Sanders	.75
9	Steve Atwater	.10
10	Johnnie Morton	.10
11	Craig Newsome	.10
12	Denver Broncos Offensive Line	.10
13	Ken Dilger	.10
14	Mark Brunell	.50
15	Tamarick Vanover	.50
16	Bernie Parmalee	.10
17	Orlanda Thomas	.10
18	Will Moore	.10
19	Mark Fields	.10
20	Tyrone Wheatley	.20
21	Kyle Brady	.10
22	Napoleon Kaufman	.50
23	Mike Mamula	.10
24	Erric Pegram	.10
25	Brent Jones	.10
26	*Aaron Hayden*	.50
27	Christian Fauria	.10
28	Dallas Cowboys Offensive Lines	.10
29	Derrick Brooks	.10
30	Brian Mitchell	.10
31	Garrison Hearst	.20
32	Devin Bush	.10
33	Andre Reed	.10
34	Derrick Moore	.10
35	Erik Kramer	.10
36	Jeff Blake	.75
37	Andre Rison	.10
38	Troy Aikman	1.50
39	Anthony Miller	.10
40	Scott Mitchell	.10
41	Reggie White	.20
42	Chris Sanders	.40
43	Ellis Johnson	.10
44	Willie Jackson	.10
45	Steve Bono	.20
46	Terry Kirby	.10
47	Jake Reed	.10
48	Vincent Brisby	.10
49	Quinn Early	.10
50	Thomas Lewis	.10
51	Wayne Chrebet	.10
52	Pat Swilling	.10
53	Bobby Taylor	.10
54	Mark Bruener	.10
55	Jerry Rice	1.50
56	Natrone Means	.25
57	Rick Mirer	.10
58	Kevin Carter	.10
59	Hardy Nickerson	.10
60	Detroit Lions Offensive Lines	.10
61	Eric Swann	.10
62	Eric Metcalf	.10
63	Russell Copeland	.10
64	Pete Metzelaars	.10
65	Curtis Conway	.10
66	Darnay Scott	.20
67	Leroy Hoard	.10
68	Darren Woodson	.10
69	John Elway	.50
70	Brett Perriman	.10
71	Mark Chmura	.10
72	Chris Chandler	.10
73	Marshall Faulk	1.00
74	Pete Mitchell	.10
75	Willie Davis	.10
76	Irving Fryar	.10
77	Robert Smith	.10
78	Drew Bledsoe	1.00
79	Mario Bates	.30
80	Chris Calloway	.10
81	Boomer Esiason	.10
82	Harvey Williams	.10
83	Fred Barnett	.10
84	Neil O'Donnell	.20
85	Lee Woodall	.10
86	Junior Seau	.20
87	Brian Blades	.10
88	Chris Miller	.10
89	Warren Sapp	.10
90	Terry Allen	.10
91	Dave Krieg	.10
92	Bert Emanuel	.10
93	Jim Kelly	.20
94	Mark Carrier	.10
95	Jeff Graham	.10
96	Tony McGee	.10
97	Vinny Testaverde	.10
98	Michael Irvin	.30
99	Shannon Sharpe	.10
100	Chris Spielman	.10
101	Edgar Bennett	.10
102	Haywood Jeffires	.10
103	Quentin Coryatt	.10
104	Jeff Lageman	.10
105	Neil Smith	.10
106	O.J. McDuffie	.10
107	Warren Moon	.10
108	Ben Coates	.10
109	Michael Haynes	.10
110	Mike Sherrard	.10
111	Adrian Murrell	.10
112	Jeff Hostetler	.10
113	Charlie Garner	.10
114	Yancey Thigpen	.10
115	Steve Young	1.50
116	Tony Martin	.10
117	San Francisco Offensive Lines	.10
118	Jerome Bettis	.10
119	Alvin Harper	.10
120	Heath Shuler	.40
121	Rob Moore	.10
122	Chris Doleman	.10
123	Bruce Smith	.10
124	Sam Mills	.10
125	Donnell Woolford	.10
126	Harold Green	.10
127	Antonio Langham	.10
128	Charles Haley	.10
129	Aaron Craver	.10
130	Barry Sanders	1.50
131	Sean Jones	.10
132	Steve McNair	1.00
133	Tony Bennett	.10
134	Miami Dolphins Offensive Lines	.10
135	Greg Hill	.10
136	Eric Green	.10
137	John Randle	.10
138	Dave Meggett	.10
139	Irv Smith	.10
140	Dave Brown	.10
141	Oakland Raiders Offensive Lines	.10
142	Raghib Ismail	.10
143	Rodney Peete	.10
144	Kevin Greene	.10
145	Derek Loville	.10
146	Leslie O'Neal	.10
147	Cortez Kennedy	.10
148	Sean Gilbert	.10
149	Jackie Harris	.10
150	Henry Ellard	.10
151	Frank Sanders	.30
152	Jeff George	.20
153	Darick Holmes	.75
154	Tyrone Poole	.10
155	Rashaan Salaam	.75
156	Carl Pickens	.20
157	Eric Turner	.10
158	Jay Novacek	.10
159	Terrell Davis	1.50
160	Herman Moore	.40
161	Robert Brooks	.10
162	Rodney Thomas	.40
163	Sean Dawkins	.10
164	James O. Stewart	.10
165	Marcus Allen	.10
166	Dan Marino	3.00
167	Cris Carter	.20
168	Curtis Martin	3.00
169	Tyrone Hughes	.10
170	Rodney Hampton	.10
171	Hugh Douglas	.10
172	Tim Brown	.10
173	Ricky Watters	.10
174	Kordell Stewart	2.00
175	J.J. Stokes	.75
176	Stan Humphries	.10
177	Joey Galloway	.50
178	Isaac Bruce	.75
179	Errict Rhett	.50
180	Michael Westbrook	.75
181	Pittsburgh Steelers Offensive Lines	.10
182	Craig Heyward	.10
183	Bryce Paup	.10
184	Brett Maxie	.10
185	Kevin Butler	.10
186	John Copeland	.10
187	Keenan McCardell	.10
188	Emmitt Smith	3.00
189	Glyn Milburn	.10
190	Jason Hanson	.10
191	Brett Favre	3.00
192	Darryll Lewis	.10
193	Jim Harbaugh	.10
194	Desmond Howard	.10
195	Derrick Thomas	.10
196	Bryan Cox	.10
197	Amp Lee	.10
198	Ty Law	.10
199	Jim Everett	.10
200	Vencie Glenn	.10
201	Charles Wilson	.10
202	Terry McDaniel	.10
203	Calvin Williams	.10
204	Greg Lloyd	.10
205	Merton Hanks	.10
206	Andre Coleman	.10
207	Chris Warren	.20
208	D'Marco Farr	.10
209	Trent Dilfer	.20
210	Ken Harvey	.10
211	Jim Harbaugh	.10
212	Brett Favre SL	1.00
213	Curtis Martin SL	1.50
214	Carl Pickens	.10
215	Norm Johnson	.10
216	Bryce Paup	.10
217	Herman Moore	.10
218	Jerry Rice SL	.75
219	Orlanda Thomas	.10
220	Emmitt Smith SL	1.50
221	Tyrone Hughes	.10
222	Tamarick Vanover	.30
223	Rick Tuten	.10
224	San Francisco 49ers	.10
225	Detroit Lions	.10
NNO	Draft Trade Card	20.00

1996 Upper Deck Silver All-NFL

Top NFL stars have been selected for this 1996 Upper Deck Silver insert set. The 20 cards, seeded one per every five packs, are produced as a special Light F/X die-cut card. The front of the card has a gold foil border, with a photo in the center framed by a silver foil oval. The player's name is in a team color-coded bar below the photo. The Upper Deck logo and a team logo are stamped in silver foil on the front too, with All NFL Team written at the top. The back has a border which looks like a pigskin football. A square in the center has a color action photo in the top half, with the player's name and position given below. Then, a recap of the player's 1995 season and "All NFL Team" and a team logo follow. A card number, using an "AN" prefix, is in the upper left corner of the card.

		NM/M
Complete Set (20):		20.00
Common Player:		1.00
1	Herman Moore	1.00
2	Isaac Bruce	2.00
3	Jerry Rice	4.00
4	Michael Irvin	1.00
5	Eric Metcalf	1.00
6	Ben Coates	1.00
7	Brett Favre	5.00
8	Jim Harbaugh	1.00
9	Emmitt Smith	4.00
10	Barry Sanders	4.00
11	Chris Warren	1.00
12	Curtis Martin	3.00
13	Hugh Douglas	1.00
14	Neil Smith	1.00
15	Reggie White	1.00
16	Bryce Paup	1.00
17	Greg Lloyd	1.00
18	Carnell Lake	1.00
19	Merton Hanks	1.00
20	Tamarick Vanover	1.00

1996 Upper Deck Silver All-Rookie Team

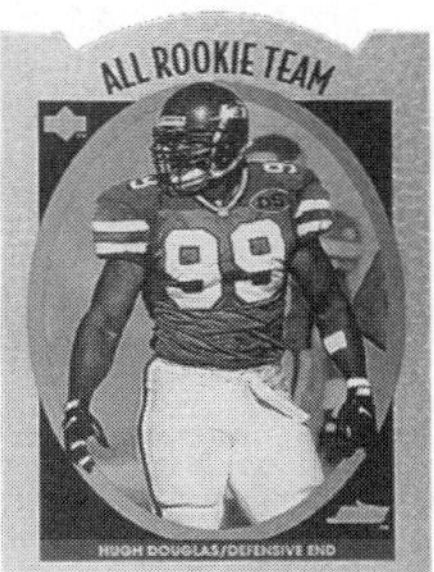

These 1996 Upper Deck Silver Collection insert cards, seeded one per every 18 packs, feature 20 of the top rookies selected to Upper Deck's "All-Rookie Team." The die-cut cards use Upper Deck's Light F/X technology. Cards are numbered and carry an "AR" prefix.

		NM/M
Complete Set (20):		35.00
Common Player:		1.00
1	Joey Galloway	2.00
2	Chris Sanders	1.00
3	J.J. Stokes	2.00
4	Ken Dilger	1.00
5	Pete Mitchell	1.00
6	Kordell Stewart	5.00
7	Kerry Collins	6.00
8	Tony Boselli	1.00
9	Terrell Davis	10.00
10	Rodney Thomas	1.00
11	Rashaan Salaam	1.00
12	Curtis Martin	10.00
13	Napoleon Kaufman	1.00
14	Hugh Douglas	1.00
15	Ellis Johnson	1.00
16	Kevin Carter	1.00
17	Derrick Brooks	1.00
18	Craig Newsome	1.00
19	Orlanda Thomas	1.00
20	Tamarick Vanover	1.00

1996 Upper Deck Silver Dan Marino

These four 1996 Upper Deck Silver Collection cards honor the record-setting 1995 season by future Hall of Famer Dan Marino. The cards, numbered with an "RS" prefix, were seeded one per every 81 packs.

		NM/M
Complete Set (4):		60.00
Common Player:		15.00
1	All-Time Completions 3,686	15.00
2	All-Time Passing Yards 47,003	15.00
3	All-Time Touchdown Pts. 342	15.00
4	300-Yards Passing Games 52	15.00

A player's name in *italic* type indicates a rookie card.

1996 Upper Deck Silver Helmet Cards

These 1996 Upper Deck Silver Collection insert cards were seeded one per every 23 packs. The cards, the first to use double-sided Light F/X technology, have a team helmet on one side, bordered on either side by a team color-coordinated panel which lists the team name or respective conference. A card number, using an "AC" or "NC" prefix, is also on this side. The opposite side has two action photos of teammates from that team, with their names below the photos in color-coded strips.

		NM/M
Complete Set (30):		45.00
Common Player:		.50
NE1	Garrison Hearst, Frank Sanders Arizona Cardinals	.50
NW1	Jeff George, Devin Bush Atlanta Falcons	.50
NW2	Sam Mills, Kerry Collins Carolina Panthers	2.00
NC1	Erik Kramer, Rashaan Salaam Chicago Bears	1.00
AC1	Jeff Blake, David Dunn Cincinnati Bengals	1.00
AC2	Vinny Testaverde, Eric Zeier Cleveland Browns	.50
NC2	Herman Moore, Luther Elliss Detroit Lions	1.00
AC3	Rodney Thomas, Chris Sanders Houston Oilers	1.00
AE1	Marshall Faulk, Ken Dilger Indianapolis Colts	3.00
AC4	Mark Brunell, James O. Stewart Jacksonville Jaguars	3.00
AW1	Steve Bono, Tamarick Vanover Kansas City Chiefs	.50
NC3	Cris Carter, Orlanda Thomas Minnesota Vikings	.50
NW3	Mario Bates, Mark Fields New Orleans Saints	.50
NE2	Rodney Hampton, Tyrone Wheatley New York Giants	.50
AE2	Wayne Chrebet, Hugh Douglas New York Jets	.50
NE3	Ricky Watters, Mike Mamula Philadelphia Eagles	.50
AW2	Chris Warren, Joey Galloway Seattle Seahawks	1.00
NW4	Isaac Bruce, Kevin Carter St. Louis Rams	1.00
NC4	Errict Rhett, Derrick Brooks Tampa Bay Buccaneers	1.00
NE4	Terry Allen, Michael Westbrook Washington Redskins	1.00
AC5	Greg Lloyd, Kordell Stewart Pittsburgh Steelers	2.00
AW4	Natrone Means, Terrance Shaw San Diego Chargers	1.00
NW5	Jerry Rice, J.J. Stokes San Francisco 49ers	4.00
AW4	Tim Brown, Napoleon Kaufman Oakland Raiders	2.00
AE3	Dan Marino, Billy Milner Miami Dolphins	4.00
NE5	Emmitt Smith, Sherman Williams Dallas Cowboys	4.00
AE4	Jim Kelly, Darick Holmes Buffalo Bills	2.00
NC5	Robert Brooks, Craig Newsome Green Bay Packers	1.00
AW5	John Elway, Terrell Davis Denver Broncos	6.00
AE5	Drew Bledsoe, Curtis Martin New England Patriots	6.00

1996 Upper Deck Silver Prime Choice Rookies

This 20-card set was available via redemption of a special trade card inserted in 1996 Upper Deck Silver. The card fronts feature a foil-accented photo and an inset photo of the player. The backs contain another player photo and biographical information.

		NM/M
Complete Set (20):		30.00
Common Player:		.50
Minor Stars:		1.00
1	Keyshawn Johnson	4.00
2	Kevin Hardy	.50
3	Simeon Rice	.50
4	Tim Biakabutuka	.75
5	Terry Glenn	2.00
6	Rickey Dudley	1.00
7	Alex Molden	.50
8	Regan Upshaw	.50
9	Eddie George	6.00
10	John Mobley	.50
11	Eddie Kennison	1.00
12	Marvin Harrison	10.00
13	Leeland McElroy	1.00
14	Eric Moulds	6.00
15	Mike Alstott	5.00
16	Bobby Engram	1.00
17	Derrick Mayes	1.00
18	Karim Abdul-Jabbar	2.00
19	Stepfret Williams	.50
20	Jeff Lewis	.50
NNO	Redemption Card Expired	1.00

1997 Upper Deck

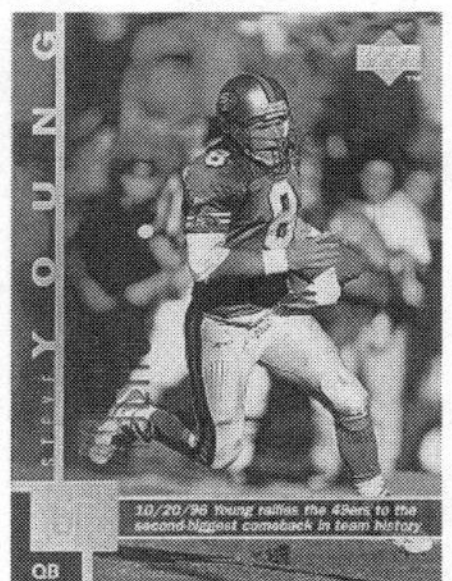

The 300-card set includes subsets of Star Rookies (35 cards), Star Rookie Flashback (10 cards) and Game Dated Moments (30 cards). The base cards have the player's name printed vertically along the left border, with the Upper Deck logo and player's position in the lower left corner. The team's name is to the right of the Upper Deck logo on the card front.

		NM/M
Complete Set (300):		40.00
Common Player:		.10
Minor Stars:		.20
Game Dated Foils:		10X-20X
Inserted 1:1,500		
Pack (12):		3.00
Wax Box (24):		50.00
1	*Orlando Pace*	.50
2	*Darrell Russell*	.10
3	*Shawn Springs*	.75
4	*Bryant Westbrook*	.30
5	*Ike Hilliard*	1.50
6	*Peter Boulware*	.10
7	*Tom Knight*	.10
8	*Yatil Green*	.50
9	*Tony Gonzalez*	1.00
10	*Reidel Anthony*	1.00
11	*Warrick Dunn*	2.00
12	*Kenny Holmes*	.10
13	*Jim Druckenmiller*	.50
14	*James Farrior*	.10
15	*David LaFleur*	.50
16	*Antowain Smith*	2.00
17	*Rae Carruth*	.50
18	*Dwayne Rudd*	.10
19	*Jake Plummer*	2.00
20	*Reinard Wilson*	.10
21	*Byron Hanspard*	1.25
22	*Will Blackwell*	.50
23	*Troy Davis*	.50
24	*Corey Dillon*	3.00
25	*Joey Kent*	.75
26	*Renaldo Wynn*	.10
27	*Pat Barnes*	.50
28	*Kevin Lockett*	.10
29	*Darnell Autry*	.50
30	*Walter Jones*	.10
31	Trevor Pryce	.10
32	Dan Marino SRF	2.00
33	Steve Young SRF	1.00
34	John Elway SRF	1.00
35	Jerry Rice SRF	1.00
36	Tim Brown SRF	.10
37	Deion Sanders SRF	.50
38	Troy Aikman SRF	1.00
39	Barry Sanders SRF	1.00
40	Emmitt Smith SRF	2.00
41	Junior Seau SRF	.10
42	Neil Smith	.10
43	Brett Perriman	.10
44	Jim Everett	.10
45	Qadry Ismail	.10
46	Dana Stubblefield	.10
47	Bryant Young	.10
48	Ken Norton Jr.	.10
49	Terrell Owens	.75
50	Jerry Rice	1.50
51	Steve Young	.75
52	Terry Kirby	.10
53	Chris Doleman	.10
54	Lee Woddall	.10
55	Merton Hanks	.10
56	Garrison Hearst	.10
57	Rashaan Salaam	.20
58	Raymont Harris	.10
59	Curtis Conway	.10
60	Bobby Engram	.10
61	Bryan Cox	.10
62	Walt Harris	.10
63	Tyrone Hughes	.10
64	Rick Mirer	.10
65	Jeff Blake	.20
66	Carl Pickens	.10
67	Darnay Scott	.10
68	Tony McGee	.10
69	Ki-Jana Carter	.10
70	Ashley Ambrose	.10
71	Dan Wilkinson	.10
72	Chris Spielman	.10
73	Todd Collins	.10
74	Andre Reed	.10
75	Quinn Early	.10
76	Eric Moulds	.10
77	Darrick Holmes	.10
78	Thurman Thomas	.20
79	Bruce Smith	.10
80	Bryce Paup	.10
81	John Elway	2.00
82	Terrell Davis	1.00
83	Anthony Miller	.10
84	Shannon Sharpe	.10
85	Alfred Williams	.10
86	John Mobley	.10
87	Tory James	.10
88	Steve Atwater	.10
89	Darrien Gordon	.10
90	Mike Alstott	.10
91	Errict Rhett	.20
92	Trent Dilfer	.10
93	Courtney Hawkins	.10
94	Warren Sapp	.10
95	Regan Upshaw	.10
96	Hardy Nickerson	.10
97	Donnie Abraham	.10
98	Larry Centers	.10
99	Aeneas Williams	.10
100	Kent Graham	.10
101	Rob Moore	.10
102	Frank Sanders	.10
103	Leeland McElroy	.10
104	Eric Swann	.10
105	Simeon Rice	.10
106	Seth Joyner	.10
107	Stan Humphries	.10
108	Tony Martin	.10
109	Charlie Jones	.10
110	Andre Coleman ERR.#103	.10
111	Terrell Fletcher	.10
112	Junior Seau	.20
113	Eric Metcalf	.10
114	Chris Penn	.10
115	Marcus Allen	.20
116	Greg Hill	.10
117	Tamarick Vanover	.10
118	Lake Dawson	.10
119	Derrick Thomas	.10
120	Dale Carter	.10
121	Elvis Grbac	.10
122	Aaron Bailey	.10
123	Jim Harbaugh	.10
124	Marshall Faulk	.20
125	Sean Dawkins	.10
126	Marvin Harrison	.50
127	Ken Dilger	.10
128	Tony Bennett	.10
129	Jeff Herrod	.10
130	Chris Gardocki	.10
131	Cary Blanchard	.10
132	Troy Aikman	1.50
133	Emmitt Smith	2.00
134	Sherman Williams	.10
135	Michael Irvin	.20
136	Eric Bjornson	.10
137	Herschel Walker	.10
138	Tony Tolbert	.10
139	Deion Sanders	.50
140	Daryl Johnston	.10
141	Dan Marino	2.00
142	O.J. McDuffie	.10
143	Troy Drayton	.10
144	Karim Abdul-Jabbar	.75
145	Stanley Pritchett	.10
146	Fred Barnett	.10
147	Zach Thomas	.20
148	Sean Wooden	.10
149	Ty Detmer	.10
150	Derrick Witherspoon	.10
151	Ricky Watters	.20
152	Charlie Garner	.10
153	Chris T. Jones	.10
154	Irving Fryar	.10
155	Mike Mamula	.10
156	Troy Vincent	.10
157	Bobby Taylor	.10
158	Chris Boniol	.10
159	Devin Bush	.10
160	Bert Emanuel	.10
161	Jamal Anderson	.20
162	Terance Mathis	.10
163	Cornelius Bennett	.10
164	Ray Buchanan	.10
165	Chris Chandler	.10
166	Dave Brown	.10
167	Danny Kanell	.10
168	Rodney Hampton	.10
169	Tyrone Wheatley	.10
170	Amani Toomer	.10
171	Chris Calloway	.10
172	Thomas Lewis	.10
173	Phillipi Sparks	.10
174	Mark Brunell	.60
175	Keenan McCardell	.10
176	Willie Jackson	.10
177	Jimmy Smith	.10
178	Pete Mitchell	.10
179	Natrone Means	.20
180	Kevin Hardy	.10
181	Tony Brackens	.10
182	James O. Stewart	.10
183	Wayne Chrebet	.10
184	Keyshawn Johnson	.50
185	Adrian Murrell	.10
186	Neil O'Donnell	.10
187	Hugh Douglas	.10
188	Mo Lewis	.10
189	Marvin Washington	.10
190	Aaron Glenn	.10
191	Barry Sanders	3.00
192	Scott Mitchell	.10
193	Herman Moore	.20
194	Johnnie Morton	.10
195	Glyn Milburn	.10
196	Reggie Brown	.10
197	Jason Hanson	.10
198	Steve McNair	.75
199	Eddie George	1.25
200	Ronnie Harmon	.10
201	Chris Sanders	.10
202	Willie Davis	.10
203	Frank Wycheck	.10
204	Darryll Lewis	.10
205	Blaine Bishop	.10
206	Robert Brooks	.10
207	Brett Favre	3.00
208	Edgar Bennett	.10
209	Dorsey Levens	.20
210	Derrick Mayes	.10
211	Antonio Freeman	.30
212	Mark Chmura	.10
213	Reggie White	.20
214	Gilbert Brown	.10
215	LeRoy Butler	.10
216	Craig Newsome	.10
217	Kerry Collins	1.00
218	Wesley Walls	.10
219	Muhsin Muhammad	.10
220	Anthony Johnson	.10
221	Tshimanga Biakabutuka	.20
222	Kevin Greene	.10
223	Sam Mills	.10
224	John Kasay	.10
225	Micheal Barrow	.10
226	Drew Bledsoe	1.25
227	Curtis Martin	.75
228	Terry Glenn	.50
229	Ben Coates	.10
230	Shawn Jefferson	.10
231	Willie McGinest	.10
232	Ted Johnson	.10
233	Lawyer Milloy	.10
234	Ty Law	.10
235	Willie Clay	.10
236	Tim Brown	.10
237	Rickey Dudley	.10
238	Napoleon Kaufman	.10
239	Chester McGlockton	.10
240	Rob Fredrickson	.10
241	Terry McDaniel	.10
242	Desmond Howard	.10
243	Jeff George	.10
244	Isaac Bruce	.20
245	Tony Banks	.50
246	Lawrence Phillips ERR.#247	.20
247	Kevin Carter	.10
248	Roman Phifer	.10
249	Keith Lyle	.10
250	Eddie Kennison	.50
251	Craig Heyward	.10
252	Vinny Testaverde	.10
253	Derrick Alexander	.10
254	Michael Jackson	.10
255	Bam Morris	.10
256	Eric Green	.10
257	Ray Lewis	.10
258	Antonio Langham	.10
259	Michael McCreary	.10
260	Gus Frerotte	.10
261	Terry Allen	.10
262	Brian Mitchell	.10
263	Michael Westbrook	.10
264	Sean Gilbert	.10
265	Rich Owens	.10
266	Ken Harvey	.10
267	Jeff Hostetler	.10
268	Michael Haynes	.10
269	Mario Bates	.10
270	Eric Allen ERR.#273	.10
271	Ray Zellars	.10
272	Joe Johnson	.10
273	Renaldo Turnbull	.10
274	Heath Shuler	.10
275	Daryl Hobbs	.10
276	John Friesz	.10
277	Brian Blades	.10
278	Joey Galloway	.30
279	Chris Warren	.10
280	Lamar Smith	.10
281	Cortez Kennedy	.10
282	Chad Brown	.10
283	Warren Moon	.10
284	Jerome Bettis	.20
285	Charles Johnson	.10
286	Kordell Stewart	1.00
287	Erric Pegram	.10
288	Norm Johnson	.10
289	Levon Kirkland	.10
290	Greg Lloyd	.10
291	Carnell Lake	.10
292	Brad Johnson	.10
293	Cris Carter	.10
294	Jake Reed	.10
295	Robert Smith	.10
296	Derrick Alexander	.10
297	John Randle	.10
298	Dixon Edwards	.10
299	Orlanda Thomas	.10
300	DeWayne Washington	.10

1997 Upper Deck Game Jersey

The 10-card set includes a piece of the player's jersey. The cards were inserted 1:2,500 packs. Cards are numbered with a "GM" prefix.

		NM/M
Complete Set (10):		3,000
Common Player:		150.00
1	Warren Moon	75.00
2	Joey Galloway	75.00
3	Terrell Davis	125.00
4	Brett Favre	225.00
5	Brett Favre	225.00
6	Reggie White	75.00
7	John Elway	175.00
8	Troy Aikman	100.00
9	Carl Pickens	40.00
10	Herman Moore	40.00

1997 Upper Deck MVP

The 20-card set featured the players on gold Light F/X Cel Chrome cards. Upper Deck produced 100 of each card. Cards are numbered with a "MP" prefix.

		NM/M
Common Player:		10.00
Minor Stars:		25.00
1	Jerry Rice	60.00
2	Carl Pickens	20.00
3	Terrell Davis	60.00
4	Mike Alstott	10.00
5	Vinny Testaverde	10.00
6	Junior Seau	10.00
7	Marcus Allen	25.00
8	Troy Aikman	60.00
9	Dan Marino	75.00
10	Ricky Watters	10.00
11	Mark Brunell	15.00
12	Barry Sanders	65.00
13	Eddie George	35.00
14	Brett Favre	75.00
15	Kerry Collins	15.00
16	Drew Bledsoe	35.00
17	Napoleon Kaufman	10.00
18	Isaac Bruce	25.00
19	Terry Allen	10.00
20	Jerome Bettis	10.00

1997 Upper Deck Star Crossed

The 27-card set was inserted 1:27 packs. The player's photo is superimposed over an etched-foil starry background on the Light F/X cards. The cards are numbered on the back with an "SC" prefix.

		NM/M
Complete Set (30):		20.00
Common Player:		.25
Minor Stars:		.50
1	Dan Marino	4.00
2	Mark Brunell	1.00
3	Kerry Collins	.50
4	Jerry Rice	3.00
5	Kevin Greene	.25
6	Curtis Martin	2.00
7	Isaac Bruce	.50
8	Eddie George	2.00
9	Deion Sanders	1.00
10	Troy Aikman	3.00
11	John Elway	3.00
12	Steve Young	3.00
13	Barry Sanders	4.00
14	Jerome Bettis	.50
15	Herman Moore	.50
16	Keyshawn Johnson	.50
17	Simeon Rice	.25
18	Bruce Smith	.25
19	Drew Bledsoe	3.00
20	Kordell Stewart	1.00
21	Brett Favre	4.00
22	Emmitt Smith	4.00
23	Terrell Davis	2.00
24	Carl Pickens	.25
25	Terry Glenn	.50
26	Reggie White	.50
27	Rod Woodson	.25

1997 Upper Deck Team Mates

The 60-card set was inserted 1:4 packs. The die-cut cards feature the player's photo superimposed over a silver etched foil background. The die-cut cards fit together to show the two teammates from each team. The player's name, team, position and Upper Deck logo are printed in gold foil at the bottom. The cards are numbered on the back with a "TM" prefix.

		NM/M
Complete Set (60):		18.00
Common Player:		.10
Minor Stars:		.25
1	Simeon Rice	.10
2	Eric Swann	.10
3	Jamal Anderson	.25
4	Terance Mathis	.10
5	Vinny Testaverde	.10
6	Michael Jackson	.10
7	Thurman Thomas	.25
8	Bruce Smith	.10
9	Kerry Collins	.25
10	Anthony Johnson	.10
11	Bobby Engram	.10
12	Rashaan Salaam	.25
13	Carl Pickens	.10
14	Jeff Blake	.25
15	Troy Aikman	2.00
16	Emmitt Smith	3.00
17	John Elway	2.00
18	Terrell Davis	2.00
19	Herman Moore	.25
20	Barry Sanders	2.00
21	Brett Favre	3.00
22	Reggie White	.25
23	Eddie George	1.00
24	Steve McNair	1.00
25	Marshall Faulk	.25
26	Jim Harbaugh	.10
27	Mark Brunell	.50
28	Keenan McCardell	.10
29	Marcus Allen	.25
30	Derrick Thomas	.10
31	Dan Marino	3.00
32	Karim Abdul-Jabbar	.75
33	Cris Carter	.75
34	Jake Reed	.10
35	Curtis Martin	1.00
36	Drew Bledsoe	1.00
37	Mario Bates	.10
38	Ray Zellars	.10
39	Keyshawn Johnson	.25
40	Adrian Murrell	.10
41	Tyrone Wheatley	.10
42	Rodney Hampton	.10
43	Napoleon Kaufman	.10
44	Tim Brown	.10
45	Ricky Watters	.25
46	Chris T. Jones	.10
47	Kordell Stewart	.50
48	Jerome Bettis	.25
49	Junior Seau	.25
50	Tony Martin	.10
51	Steve Young	1.25
52	Jerry Rice	2.00
53	Joey Galloway	.25
54	Chris Warren	.10
55	Eddie Kennison	.75
56	Tony Banks	.75
57	Mike Alstott	.10
58	Errict Rhett	.25
59	Terry Allen	.10
60	Gus Frerotte	.10

1997 Upper Deck Crash the Game Super Bowl XXXI

Upper Deck produced this special You Crash the Game set for Super Bowl XXXI. The cards were inserted in issues of Sports Collectors Digest. If the player pictured on the card scored a touchdown in the Super Bowl, collectors could redeem the card for a complete parallel set printed on foil stock. The game cards feature a player photo on a purple background with the Super Bowl date printed in gold foil.

		NM/M
Complete Set (8):		7.00
Common Player:		.25
Comp. Foil Prize Set (9):		5.00
Common Foil Prize:		.25
A1	Drew Bledsoe	1.50
A2	Curtis Martin	1.50
A3	Ben Coates	.25
A4	Terry Glenn	.50
N1	Brett Favre	3.00

N2 Edgar Bennett .25
N3 Don Beebe .25
N4 Antonio Freeman .50

1997 Upper Deck Black Diamond

The 180-card, regular-sized set was released in six-card packs. The set was tiered in three levels: 90 single diamond, 60 double diamonds (1:4) and 30 triple diamonds (1:30). A parallel gold version was issued for each card: single diamond (1:15), double diamonds (1:46) and triple diamonds (limited to a production of 50). One insert set was included, Title Quest.

	NM/M
Complete Set (180):	275.00
Comp. Single Diamond (90):	20.00
Comp. Double Diamond (60):	80.00
Comp. Triple Diamond (30):	320.00
Common Diamond(1-90):	.10
Common Double Diamond (91-150):	.75
Common Triple Diamond (151-180):	4.00
Gold Diamond(1-90):	4X-8X
Gold Double Diamond (91-150):	2X-4X
Gold Triple Diamond (151-180):	5X-10X
Pack (6):	2.25
Wax Box (36):	60.00

1 Alfred Williams .10
2 Alvin Harper .10
3 Andre Hastings .10
4 Andre Reed .10
5 Anthony Johnson .10
6 Anthony Miller .10
7 Bam Morris .10
8 Bobby Hebert .10
9 Bobby Taylor .10
10 Boomer Esiason .10
11 Brett Perriman .10
12 Brian Blades .10
13 Bryan Cox .10
14 Bryant Young .10
15 Bryce Paup .10
16 Carnell Lake .10
17 Cedric Jones .10
18 Chad Brown .10
19 Charlie Garner .10
20 Chris Chandler .10
21 Cornelius Bennett .10
22 Cortez Kennedy .10
23 Cris Carter .10
24 Dale Carter .10
25 Daryl Gardner .10
26 Derrick Alexander .10
27 Derrick Mayes .10
28 Don Beebe .10
29 Eric Allen .10
30 Eric Moulds .10
31 Errict Rhett .20
32 Frank Sanders .10
33 Glyn Milburn .10
34 Henry Ellard .10
35 Jamal Anderson .75
36 James O. Stewart .10
37 Jason Dunn .10
38 Jerry Rice 2.00
39 Jim Everett .10
40 Jim Kelly .10
41 Joey Galloway 1.00
42 John Carney .10
43 John Elway 1.50
44 John Randle .10
45 Karim Abdul-Jabbar .50
46 Keenan McCardell .10
47 Ken Dilger .10
48 Ken Norton .10
49 Ki-Jana Carter .10
50 Kordell Stewart 1.00
51 Lawrence Phillips .10
52 Leslie O'Neal .10
53 Mark Chmura .10
54 Marshall Faulk .25
55 Michael Haynes .10
56 Michael Irvin .20
57 Michael Jackson .10
58 Michael Westbrook .10
59 Mike Tomczak .10
60 Napoleon Kaufman .50
61 Neil O'Donnell .10
62 Neil Smith .10
63 O.J. McDuffie .10
64 Orlanda Thomas .10
65 Rashaan Salaam .20
66 Regan Upshaw .10
67 Rick Mirer .10
68 Rob Moore .10
69 Ronnie Harmon .10
70 Sam Mills .10
71 Sean Dawkins .10
72 Shawn Jefferson .10
73 Stan Humphries .10
74 Stepfret Williams .10
75 Stephen Davis .10
76 Steve Atwater .10
77 Terance Mathis .10
78 Terrell Fletcher .10
79 Terry Glenn 1.00
80 Terry McDaniel .10
81 Tony McGee .10
82 Trent Dilfer .10
83 Troy Drayton .10
84 Ty Detmer .10
85 Tyrone Hughes .10
86 Walt Harris .10
87 Wayne Chrebet .10
88 Wesley Walls .10
89 Willie Davis .10
90 Willie McGinest .10
91 Adrian Murrell .75
92 Alex Molden .75
93 Alex Van Dyke .75
94 Andre Coleman .75
95 Ben Coates .75
96 Bobby Engram .75
97 Bruce Smith .75
98 Charles Johnson .75
99 Chris Sanders .75
100 Chris T. Jones .75
101 Chris Warren .75
102 Darnay Scott .75
103 Dave Brown .75
104 Derrick Thomas .75
105 Drew Bledsoe 7.00
106 Edgar Bennett .75
107 Emmitt Smith 14.00
108 Eric Bjornson .75
109 Eric Metcalf .75
110 Garrison Hearst .75
111 Gus Frerotte .75
112 Hardy Nickerson .75
113 Herman Moore 1.50
114 Hugh Douglas .75
115 Irving Fryar .75
116 J.J. Stokes .75
117 Jake Reed .75
118 Jeff Hostetler .75
119 Jeff Lewis .75
120 Jim Harbaugh .75
121 Johnnie Morton .75
122 Jonathan Ogden .75
123 Kevin Carter .75
124 Kevin Greene .75
125 Kevin Hardy .75
126 Leeland McElroy .75
127 Mike Alstott 1.50
128 Muhsin Muhammad 2.50
129 Natrone Means .75
130 Quentin Coryatt .75
131 Ray Lewis .75
132 Ray Zellars .75
133 Rickey Dudley .75
134 Ricky Watters .75
135 Robert Smith .75
136 Scott Mitchell .75
137 Sean Gilbert .75
138 Shannon Sharpe .75
139 Simeon Rice .75
140 Stanley Pritchett .75
141 Steve McNair 4.00
142 Steve Young 5.00
143 Tamarick Vanover 1.50
144 Terry Allen .75
145 Thurman Thomas .75
146 Tony Banks 3.00
147 Tony Martin .75
148 Tyrone Wheatley .75
149 Vinny Testaverde .75
150 Zach Thomas 4.00
151 Amani Toomer 4.00
152 Barry Sanders 30.00
153 Bobby Hoying 4.00
154 Brett Favre 35.00
155 Carl Pickens 4.00
156 Curtis Conway 4.00
157 Curtis Martin 15.00
158 Dan Marino 35.00
159 Deion Sanders 5.00
160 Eddie George 15.00
161 Eddie Kennison 5.00
162 Elvis Grbac 4.00
163 Isaac Bruce 6.00
164 Jeff Blake 8.00
165 Jerome Bettis 4.00
166 Junior Seau 4.00
167 Kerry Collins 8.00
168 Keyshawn Johnson 10.00
169 Larry Centers 4.00
170 Marcus Allen 4.00
171 Mark Brunell 10.00
172 Marvin Harrison 10.00
173 Reggie White 4.00
174 Rodney Hampton 4.00
175 Terrell Davis 15.00
176 Tim Brown 4.00
177 Todd Collins 4.00
178 Troy Aikman 15.00
179 Tim Biakabutuka 4.00
180 Warren Moon 4.00

1997 Upper Deck Black Diamond Gold

Gold parallel cards were available for all 180 cards in the 1997 Black Diamond set. The only difference between regular and gold versions is that the silver foil that is used on regular-issue cards is replaced by gold foil. Gold version of Single Black Diamond cards (1-90) were seeded one per 15 packs, while gold versions of Double Black Diamond cards (91-150) were inserted every 46 packs and gold Triple Black Diamond cards (151-180) were limited to 50 each.

Gold Single Diamonds:	4X-8X
Gold Double Diamonds:	2X-4X
Gold Triple Diamonds:	5X-10X

1997 Upper Deck Black Diamond Title Quest

The 20-card, regular-sized, die-cut set was inserted into packs of 1997 Black Diamond football and was limited to a production of 100. The card fronts feature a square color action shot with a gold border.

	NM/M
Common Player:	10.00
Minor Stars:	25.00

1 Dan Marino 125.00
2 Jerry Rice 100.00
3 Drew Bledsoe 40.00
4 Emmitt Smith 100.00
5 Troy Aikman 40.00
6 Steve Young 40.00
7 Brett Favre 150.00
8 John Elway 100.00
9 Barry Sanders 100.00
10 Jerome Bettis 25.00
11 Deion Sanders 25.00
12 Karim Abdul-Jabbar 10.00
13 Terrell Davis 60.00
14 Marshall Faulk 40.00
15 Curtis Martin 60.00
16 Eddie George 25.00
17 Steve McNair 25.00
18 Terry Glenn 15.00
19 Joey Galloway 10.00
20 Keyshawn Johnson 25.00

1997 Upper Deck Legends

Legends is a 208-card set featuring the greatest players from the NFL's past. Besides the 168 regular cards, a 30-card Super Bowl Memories by Walter Iooss, Jr. subset and a 10-card Legendary Leaders subset were added. A parallel of the 168 regular cards featuring player autographs was inserted 1:5. The insert sets are Sign of the Times, Big Game Hunters and Marquee Matchups.

	NM/M
Complete Set (208):	35.00
Common Player:	.10
Minor Stars:	.20
Pack (10):	12.00
Wax Box (20):	175.00

1 Bart Starr 1.50
2 Jim Brown 2.50
3 Joe Namath 2.50
4 Walter Payton 2.50
5 Terry Bradshaw 2.50
6 Franco Harris .50
7 Dan Fouts .20
8 Steve Largent .20
9 Johnny Unitas 1.50
10 Gale Sayers 1.00
11 Roger Staubach 2.50
12 Tony Dorsett .50
13 Fran Tarkenton 1.00
14 Charley Taylor .10
15 Ray Nitschke .20
16 Jim Ringo .10
17 Dick Butkus 1.00
18 Fred Biletnikoff .20
19 Lenny Moore .10
20 Len Dawson .10
21 Lance Alworth .10
22 Chuck Bednarik .10
23 Raymond Berry .10
24 Donnie Shell .10
25 Mel Blount .10
26 Willie Brown .10
27 Ken Houston .10
28 Larry Csonka .50
29 Mike Ditka .75
30 Art Donovan .50
31 Sam Huff .10
32 Lem Barney .10
33 Hugh McElhenny .10
34 Otto Graham .75
35 Joe Greene .50
36 Mike Rozier .10
37 Lou Groza .10
38 Ted Hendricks .10
39 Elroy Hirsch .10
40 Paul Hornung .75
41 Charlie Joiner .10
42 Deacon Jones .20
43 Bill Bradley .10
44 Floyd Little .10
45 Willie Lanier .10
46 Bob Lilly .10
47 Sid Luckman .10
48 John Mackey .10
49 Don Maynard .10
50 Mike McCormack .10
51 Bobby Mitchell .10
52 Ron Mix .10
53 Marion Motley .10
54 Leo Nomellini .10
55 Mark Duper .10
56 Mel Renfro .10
57 Jim Otto .10
58 Alan Page .10
59 Joe Perry .10
60 Andy Robustelli .10
61 Lee Roy Selmon .10
62 Jackie Smith .10
63 Art Shell .10
64 Jan Stenerud .10
65 Gene Upshaw .10
66 Y.A. Tittle .10
67 Paul Warfield .10
68 Kellen Winslow .20
69 Randy White .10
70 Larry Wilson .10
71 Willie Wood .10
72 Jack Ham .10
73 Jack Youngblood .10
74 Dan Abramowicz .10
75 Dick Anderson .10
76 Ken Anderson .10
77 Steve Bartkowski .10
78 Bill Bergey .10
79 Rocky Bleier .10
80 Cliff Branch .10
81 John Brodie .10
90 Bobby Bell .10
83 Billy Cannon .10
84 Gino Capelletti .10
85 Harold Carmichael .10
86 Dave Casper .10
87 Wes Chandler .10
88 Todd Christensen .10
89 Dwight Clark .10
90 Mark Clayton .10
91 Cris Collinsworth .10
92 Roger Craig .10
93 Randy Cross .10
94 Isaac Curtis .10
95 Mike Curtis .10
96 Ben Davidson .10
97 Fred Dean .10
98 Tom Dempsey .10
99 Eric Dickerson .10
100 Lynn Dickey .10
101 John McKay .10
102 Carl Eller .10
103 Chuck Foreman .10
104 Russ Francis .10
105 Joe Gibbs .10
106 Gary Garrison .10
107 Randy Gradishar .10
108 L.C. Greenwood .10
109 Roosevelt Grier .10
110 Steve Grogan .10
111 Ray Guy .10
112 John Hadl .10
113 Jim Hart .10
114 George Halas .10
115 Mike Haynes .10
116 Charlie Hennigan .10
117 Chuck Howley .10
118 Harold Jackson .10
119 Tom Jackson .10
120 Ron Jaworski .10
121 John Jefferson .10
122 Billy Johnson .10
123 Ed "Too Tall" Jones .10
124 Jack Kemp 1.50
125 Jim Kiick .10
126 Billy Kilmer .10
127 Jerry Kramer .10
128 Paul Krause .10
129 Daryle Lamonica .10
130 Bill Walsh .10
131 James Lofton .10
132 Hank Stram .10
133 Archie Manning .10
134 Jim Marshall .10
135 Harvey Martin .10
136 Tommy McDonald .10
137 Max McGee .10
138 Reggie McKenzie .10
139 Karl Mecklenburg .10
140 Tom Landry .20
141 Terry Metcalf .10
142 Matt Millen .10
143 Earl Morrall .10
144 Mercury Morris .10
145 Chuck Noll .10
146 Joe Morris .10
147 Mark Moseley .10
148 Haven Moses .10
149 Chuck Muncie .10
150 Anthony Munoz .10
151 Tommy Nobis .10
152 Babe Parilli .10
153 Drew Pearson .10
154 Ozzie Newsome .10
155 Jim Plunkett .20
156 William Perry .10
157 Johnny Robinson .10
158 Ahmad Rashad .30
159 George Rogers .10
160 Sterling Sharpe .10
161 Billy Sims .10
162 Sid Gillman .10
163 Mike Singletary .10
164 Charlie Sanders .10
165 Bubba Smith .10
166 Ken Stabler 1.50
167 Freddie Soloman .10
168 John Stallworth .10
169 Dwight Stephenson .10
170 Vince Lombardi .30
171 Weeb Ewbank .10
172 Lionel Taylor .10
173 Otis Taylor .10
174 Joe Theismann .20
175 Bob Trumpy .10
176 Mike Webster .10
177 Jim Zorn .10
178 Joe Montana 3.00
179 Packer Defense .10
180 Bart Starr .75
181 Max McGee .10
182 Joe Namath 1.25
183 Johnny Unitas .75
184 Len Dawson .10
185 Chuck Howley .10
186 Roger Staubach .75
187 Paul Warfield .10
188 Larry Csonka .20
189 Fran Tarkenton .20
190 Joe Green .10
191 Ken Stabler .10
192 Fred Biletnikoff .10
193 Dick Anderson .10
194 Harvey Martin .10
195 Tony Dorsett .20
196 Terry Bradshaw 1.00
197 John Stallworth .10
198 Franco Harris .20
199 Ken Anderson .10
200 Joe Theismann .10
201 Jim Plunkett .10
202 Roger Craig .10
203 William Perry .10
204 Joe Morris .10
205 Karl Mecklenberg .10
206 Joe Montana 1.50
207 Joe Montana 1.50
208 Joe Montana 1.50

1997 Upper Deck Legends Big Game Hunters

This 20-card insert features the top 20 clutch QBs on a die-cut card. They were inserted 1:75. Cards are numbered with the "BG" prefix.

	NM/M
Complete Set (20):	125.00
Common Player:	5.00
Minor Stars:	10.00

1 Joe Montana 18.00
2 Bart Starr 15.00
3 Roger Staubach 12.00
4 Johnny Unitas 15.00
5 Terry Bradshaw 12.00
6 Ken Stabler 5.00
7 Jim Plunkett 5.00
8 Len Dawson 5.00
9 Fran Tarkenton 10.00
10 Dan Fouts 5.00
11 Daryle Lamonica 5.00
12 Y.A. Tittle 5.00
13 Joe Namath 15.00
14 Kenny Anderson 5.00
15 John Brodie 5.00
16 Billy Kilmer 5.00
17 Earl Morrall 5.00
18 Jack Kemp 10.00
19 Steve Grogan 5.00
20 Joe Theismann 10.00

1997 Upper Deck Legends Marquee Matchups

This 30-card insert features two of the NFL's greatest and creates a classic matchup. The cards use Light F/X technology and were inserted 1:17. Cards are numbered with a "MM" prefix.

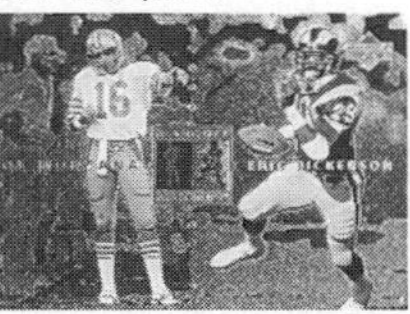

	NM/M
Complete Set (30):	70.00
Common Player:	1.00
Minor Stars:	4.00

1 Joe Namath, Dan Fouts 6.00
2 Johnny Unitas, Joe Namath 6.00
3 Len Dawson, Bart Starr 4.00
4 Roger Staubach, Fran Tarkenton 5.00
5 Terry Bradshaw, Ken Stabler 5.00
6 Joe Montana, Kenny Anderson 5.00
7 Bart Starr, Johnny Unitas 6.00
8 Joe Greene, Jim Kiick 1.00
9 Franco Harris, Walter Payton 5.00
10 Ken Stabler, Dan Fouts 4.00
11 Charlie Joiner, Steve Largent 4.00
12 James Lofton, Drew Pearson 1.00
13 John Brodie, Deacon Jones 1.00
14 Fred Biletnikoff, Don Maynard 1.00
15 Jim Brown, Chuck Bednarik 5.00
16 Ray Nitschke, Gale Sayers 5.00
17 Paul Hornung, Dick Butkus 4.00
18 Joe Montana, Eric Dickerson 5.00
19 Tony Dorsett, Mike Singletary 4.00
20 Billy Sims, Chuck Foreman 1.00
21 Len Dawson, Willie Brown 1.00
22 Johnny Robinson, Larry Wilson 1.00
23 Marion Motley, Raymond Berry 1.00
24 Ron Mix, Jim Otto 1.00
25 Roger Staubach, Terry Bradshaw 5.00
26 Bob Lilly, Billy Kilmer 1.00
27 Ted Hendricks, Russ Francis 1.00
28 Babe Parilli, Jack Kemp 2.00
29 Deacon Jones, Alan Page 1.00
30 Dick Butkus, Ray Nitschke 5.00

1997 Upper Deck Legends Sign of the Times

This 10-card insert features autographs from some of the greatest players ever. The set was limited to less than 1,000 total cards. Cards were numbered with a "ST" prefix.

	NM/M
Complete Set (10):	2,500
Common Player:	125.00

1 Joe Montana 400.00
2 Fran Tarkenton 150.00
3 Johnny Unitas 200.00
4 Joe Namath 300.00
5 Terry Bradshaw 175.00
6 Jim Brown 200.00
7 Franco Harris 125.00
8 Walter Payton 300.00
9 Steve Largent 125.00
10 Bart Starr 225.00

1997 Upper Deck UD3

UD3 consists of a 90-card base set made up of three unique subsets. The first 30 cards are Prime Choice Rookies. The rookies are all featured with Light F/X technology. Cards 31-60 are Eye of a Champion. This subset features Cel-Chrome technology. The final subset is Pigskin Heroes. These cards feature two player shots on the front with an embossed, pigskin feel to the card. The inserts for UD3 are Generation eXcitement, Marquee Attraction and Signature Performers.

		NM/M
Complete Set (90):		40.00
Common Player:		.20
Minor Stars:		.40
Pack (3):		4.00
Wax Box (24):		80.00
1	*Orlando Pace*	.50
2	*Walter Jones*	.20
3	*Tony Gonzalez*	1.00
4	*David LaFleur*	.50
5	*Jim Druckenmiller*	.50
6	*Jake Plummer*	3.00
7	*Pat Barnes*	.50
8	*Ike Hilliard*	1.50
9	*Reidel Anthony*	1.00
10	*Rae Carruth*	.75
11	*Yatil Green*	.50
12	*Joey Kent*	.50
13	*Will Blackwell*	.50
14	*Kevin Lockett*	.50
15	*Warrick Dunn*	2.00
16	*Antowain Smith*	3.00
17	*Troy Davis*	.50
18	*Byron Hanspard*	.50
19	*Corey Dillon*	5.00
20	*Darnell Autry*	1.00
21	*Peter Boulware*	.20
22	*Darrell Russell*	.20
23	*Kenny Holmes*	.20
24	*Reinard Wilson*	.20
25	*Renaldo Wynn*	.20
26	*Dwayne Rudd*	.20
27	*James Farrior*	.20
28	*Shawn Springs*	.40
29	*Bryant Westbrook*	.20
30	*Tom Knight*	.20
31	Barry Sanders	4.00
32	Brett Favre	5.00
33	Brian Mitchell	.20
34	Curtis Martin	2.00
35	Dan Marino	4.00
36	Deion Sanders	1.50
37	Drew Bledsoe	2.00
38	Eddie George	2.00
39	Edgar Bennett	.20
40	Emmitt Smith	4.00
41	Isaac Bruce	.40
42	Jerome Bettis	.40
43	Jerry Rice	4.00
44	John Elway	3.00
45	Junior Seau	.20
46	Karim Abdul-Jabbar	.50
47	Kerry Collins	.50
48	Marshall Faulk	.50
49	Marvin Harrison	.50
50	Michael Irvin	.40
51	Natrone Means	.40
52	Reggie White	.40
53	Ricky Watters	.40
54	Stan Humphries	.20
55	Steve Young	2.00
56	Terry Glenn	.50
57	Thurman Thomas	.40
58	Tony Martin	.20
59	Troy Aikman	3.00
60	Vinny Testaverde	.20
61	Anthony Johnson	.20
62	Bobby Engram	.20
63	Carl Pickens	.20
64	Cris Carter	.20
65	Derrick Witherspoon	.20
66	Eddie Kennison	.50
67	Eric Swann	.20
68	Gus Frerotte	.20
69	Herman Moore	.40
70	Irving Fryar	.20
71	Jamal Anderson	.40
72	Jeff Blake	.40
73	Jim Harbaugh	.20
74	Joey Galloway	.40
75	Keenan McCardell	.20
76	Kevin Greene	.20
77	Keyshawn Johnson	.50
78	Kordell Stewart	1.00
79	Marcus Allen	.40
80	Mario Bates	.20
81	Mark Brunell	1.00
82	Michael Jackson	.20
83	Mike Alstott	.40
84	Scott Mitchell	.20
85	Shannon Sharpe	.20
86	Steve McNair	2.00
87	Terrell Davis	2.00
88	Tim Brown	.20
89	Ty Detmer	.20
90	Tyrone Wheatley	.20

1997 Upper Deck UD3 Generation Excitement

This 15-card insert features the NFL's most spectacular players. Each card has a die-cut, Light F/X design and features two action shots of the player on the front. The cards were inserted 1:11. Cards are numbered with a "GE" prefix.

		NM/M
Complete Set (15):		35.00
Common Player:		.50
1	Jerry Rice	4.00
2	Carl Pickens	.50
3	Curtis Conway	.50
4	John Elway	4.00
5	Ike Hilliard	1.00
6	Marvin Harrison	2.00
7	Emmitt Smith	5.00
8	Barry Sanders	5.00
9	Deion Sanders	1.00
10	Rae Carruth	.50
11	Curtis Martin	3.00
12	Terry Glenn	1.00
13	Napoleon Kaufman	.50
14	Kordell Stewart	1.00
15	Jake Plummer	1.00

1997 Upper Deck UD3 Marquee Attraction

Marquee Attraction features the most collectible NFL players in a 15-card insert set. The cards are die-cut and feature Cel-Chrome technology. They were inserted 1:144 in UD3. Cards were numbered with a "MA" prefix.

		NM/M
Complete Set (15):		60.00
Common Player:		1.00
Minor Stars:		3.00
Inserted 1:144		
1	Steve Young	7.00
2	Troy Aikman	7.00
3	Keyshawn Johnson	2.00
4	Marcus Allen	2.00
5	Dan Marino	12.00
6	Mark Brunell	2.00
7	Eddie George	3.00
8	Brett Favre	12.00
9	Drew Bledsoe	7.00
10	Eddie Kennison	1.00
11	Terrell Davis	7.00
12	Warrick Dunn	3.00
13	Yatil Green	1.00
14	Troy Davis	1.00
15	Shawn Springs	1.00

1997 Upper Deck UD3 Signature Performers

Signature Performers is a four-card insert featuring special electric technology. The cards were autographed by the players in the set: Curtis Martin, Troy Aikman, Marcus Allen and Eddie George. The cards were inserted 1:1,500. Cards are numbered with a "PF" prefix.

		NM/M
Complete Set (4):		
Common Player:		40.00
1	Curtis Martin	50.00
2	Troy Aikman	100.00
3	Marcus Allen	40.00
4	Eddie George	50.00

1998 UD3

UD Cubed Football consists of a 270-card base set built from three 30-card subsets. Each subset is printed on three different technologies. Future Shock features rookies, Next Wave has young stars and Upper Realm highlights the established stars. Future Shock Embossed cards are inserted 1:6, Light F/X is seeded 1:12 and Rainbow Foil cards are found 1:1.33. Next Wave Embossed are seeded 1:4, Light F/X are found 1:1.5 and Rainbow Foil cards are inserted 1:12. Upper Realm Embossed cards are seeded 1:1.25, Light F/X are found 1:6 and Rainbow Foil cards are inserted 1:24. Die-cut versions of each card were also produced.

		NM/M
Complete Set (270):		750.00
Common Player (1-30):		2.50
#1-30 Inserted 1:6		
Common Player (31-60):		1.25
#31-60 Inserted 1:4		
Common Player (61-90):		.50
#61-90 Inserted 1:1.25		
Common Player (91-120):		5.00
#91-120 Inserted 1:12		
Common Player (121-150):		.50
#121-150 Inserted 1:1.5		
Common Player (151-180):		2.50
#151-180 Inserted 1:6		
Common Player (181-210):		.75
#181-210 Inserted 1:1.33		
Common Player (211-240):		5.00
#211-240 Inserted 1:12		
Common Player (241-270):		7.00
#241-270 Inserted 1:24		
Pack (3):		4.00
Wax Box (24):		90.00
1	Peyton Manning	25.00
2	Ryan Leaf	3.00
3	Andre Wadsworth	3.00
4	Charles Woodson	7.00
5	Curtis Enis	3.00
6	Grant Wistrom	2.50
7	Greg Ellis	2.50
8	Fred Taylor	6.00
9	Duane Starks	5.00
10	Keith Brooking	2.50
11	Takeo Spikes	5.00
12	Jason Peter	5.00
13	Anthony Simmons	2.00
14	Kevin Dyson	8.00
15	Brian Simmons	2.00
16	Robert Edwards	4.00
17	Randy Moss	20.00
18	John Avery	2.00
19	Marcus Nash	3.00
20	Jerome Pathon	5.00
21	Jacquez Green	3.00
22	Robert Holcombe	3.00
23	Patrick Johnson	3.00
24	Germane Crowell	3.00
25	Joe Jurevicius	5.00
26	Skip Hicks	3.00
27	Ahman Green	8.00
28	Brian Griese	8.00
29	Hines Ward	8.00
30	Tavian Banks	3.00
31	Warrick Dunn	4.00
32	Jake Plummer	2.00
33	Derrick Mayes	1.25
34	Napoleon Kaufman	1.00
35	Jamal Anderson	1.25
36	Marvin Harrison	1.25
37	Jermaine Lewis	.75
38	Corey Dillon	3.00
39	Keyshawn Johnson	2.50
40	Mike Alstott	2.50
41	Bobby Hoying	1.00
42	Keenan McCardell	1.25
43	Will Blackwell	1.00
44	Peter Boulware	1.00
45	Tony Banks	1.00
46	Rod Smith	1.25
47	Tony Gonzalez	1.25
48	Antowain Smith	2.00
49	Rae Carruth	1.00
50	J.J. Stokes	1.25
51	Brad Johnson	2.50
52	Shawn Springs	1.00
53	Elvis Grbac	1.00
54	Jimmy Smith	1.00
55	Terry Glenn	2.00
56	Tiki Barber	1.25
57	Gus Frerotte	1.25
58	Danny Wuerffel	1.25
59	Fred Lane	2.50
60	Todd Collins	1.25
61	Barry Sanders	8.00
62	Troy Aikman	4.00
63	Dan Marino	6.00
64	Drew Bledsoe	4.00
65	Dorsey Levens	1.00
66	Jerome Bettis	1.00
67	John Elway	6.00
68	Steve Young	3.00
69	Terrell Davis	2.00
70	Kordell Stewart	1.00
71	Jeff George	1.00
72	Emmitt Smith	6.00
73	Irving Fryar	.50
74	Brett Favre	8.00
75	Eddie George	3.00
76	Terry Allen	.50
77	Warren Moon	1.00
78	Mark Brunell	2.00
79	Robert Smith	1.00
80	Jerry Rice	5.00
81	Tim Brown	2.00
82	Carl Pickens	1.00
83	Joey Galloway	1.00
84	Herman Moore	1.00
85	Adrian Murrell	1.00
86	Thurman Thomas	1.00
87	Robert Brooks	.50
88	Michael Irvin	1.00
89	Andre Rison	1.00
90	Marshall Faulk	2.00
91	Peyton Manning	30.00
92	Ryan Leaf	3.00
93	Andre Wadsworth	3.00
94	Charles Woodson	8.00
95	Curtis Enis	3.00
96	Grant Wistrom	5.00
97	Greg Ellis	5.00
98	Fred Taylor	8.00
99	Duane Starks	3.00
100	Keith Brooking	4.00
101	Takeo Spikes	6.00
102	Jason Peter	4.00
103	Anthony Simmons	4.00
104	Kevin Dyson	10.00
105	Brian Simmons	4.00
106	Robert Edwards	8.00
107	Randy Moss	25.00
108	John Avery	4.00
109	Marcus Nash	5.00
110	Jerome Pathon	8.00
111	Jacquez Green	6.00
112	Robert Holcombe	6.00
113	Patrick Johnson	4.00
114	Germane Crowell	4.00
115	Joe Jurevicius	8.00
116	Skip Hicks	5.00
117	Ahman Green	15.00
118	Brian Griese	15.00
119	Hines Ward	12.00
120	Tavian Banks	6.00
121	Warrick Dunn	2.00
122	Jake Plummer	1.00
123	Derrick Mayes	.50
124	Napoleon Kaufman	1.00
125	Jamal Anderson	1.00
126	Marvin Harrison	1.00
127	Jermaine Lewis	.50
128	Corey Dillon	2.00
129	Keyshawn Johnson	1.00
130	Mike Alstott	1.00
131	Bobby Hoying	.50
132	Keenan McCardell	.50
133	Will Blackwell	.50
134	Peter Boulware	.50
135	Tony Banks	.50
136	Rod Smith	.50
137	Tony Gonzalez	.50
138	Antowain Smith	1.00
139	Rae Carruth	.50
140	J.J. Stokes	.50
141	Brad Johnson	1.00
142	Shawn Springs	.50
143	Elvis Grbac	.50
144	Jimmy Smith	1.00
145	Terry Glenn	1.00
146	Tiki Barber	1.00
147	Gus Frerotte	.50
148	Danny Wuerffel	.50
149	Fred Lane	.50
150	Todd Collins	.50
151	Barry Sanders	15.00
152	Troy Aikman	10.00
153	Dan Marino	15.00
154	Drew Bledsoe	10.00
155	Dorsey Levens	5.00
156	Jerome Bettis	5.00
157	John Elway	10.00
158	Steve Young	8.00
159	Terrell Davis	6.00
160	Kordell Stewart	4.00
161	Jeff George	2.00
162	Emmitt Smith	12.00
163	Irving Fryar	2.50
164	Brett Favre	15.00
165	Eddie George	6.00
166	Terry Allen	2.50
167	Warren Moon	3.00
168	Mark Brunell	4.00
169	Robert Smith	4.00
170	Jerry Rice	10.00
171	Tim Brown	6.00
172	Carl Pickens	3.00
173	Joey Galloway	3.00
174	Herman Moore	3.00
175	Adrian Murrell	2.00
176	Thurman Thomas	3.00
177	Robert Brooks	2.50
178	Michael Irvin	3.00
179	Andre Rison	2.50
180	Marshall Faulk	6.00
181	*Peyton Manning*	15.00
182	*Ryan Leaf*	2.00
183	*Andre Wadsworth*	1.50
184	*Charles Woodson*	4.00
185	*Curtis Enis*	2.00
186	*Grant Wistrom*	.75
187	*Greg Ellis*	1.50
188	*Fred Taylor*	5.00
189	*Duane Starks*	1.50
190	*Keith Brooking*	1.50
191	*Takeo Spikes*	2.00
192	*Jason Peter*	1.50
193	*Anthony Simmons*	1.50
194	*Kevin Dyson*	3.00
195	*Brian Simmons*	1.00
196	*Robert Edwards*	4.00
197	*Randy Moss*	10.00
198	*John Avery*	3.00
199	*Marcus Nash*	2.00
200	*Jerome Pathon*	3.00
201	*Jacquez Green*	2.00
202	*Robert Holcombe*	2.00
203	*Patrick Johnson*	1.50
204	*Germane Crowell*	2.00
205	*Joe Jurevicius*	3.00
206	*Skip Hicks*	1.50
207	*Ahman Green*	12.00
208	*Brian Griese*	6.00
209	*Hines Ward*	3.00
210	*Tavian Banks*	2.00
211	Warrick Dunn	10.00
212	Jake Plummer	6.00
213	Derrick Mayes	4.00
214	Napoleon Kaufman	4.00
215	Jamal Anderson	6.00
216	Marvin Harrison	6.00
217	Jermaine Lewis	4.00
218	Corey Dillon	8.00
219	Keyshawn Johnson	6.00
220	Mike Alstott	6.00
221	Bobby Hoying	6.00
222	Keenan McCardell	4.00
223	Will Blackwell	4.00
224	Peter Boulware	4.00
225	Tony Banks	6.00
226	Rod Smith	6.00
227	Tony Gonzalez	4.00
228	Antowain Smith	6.00
229	Rae Carruth	4.00
230	J.J. Stokes	4.00
231	Brad Johnson	6.00
232	Shawn Springs	4.00
233	Elvis Grbac	4.00
234	Jimmy Smith	6.00
235	Terry Glenn	6.00
236	Tiki Barber	6.00
237	Gus Frerotte	4.00
238	Danny Wuerffel	4.00
239	Fred Lane	6.00
240	Todd Collins	4.00
241	Barry Sanders	30.00
242	Troy Aikman	25.00
243	Dan Marino	30.00
244	Drew Bledsoe	20.00
245	Dorsey Levens	10.00
246	Jerome Bettis	10.00
247	John Elway	20.00
248	Steve Young	15.00
249	Terrell Davis	15.00
250	Kordell Stewart	8.00
251	Jeff George	4.00
252	Emmitt Smith	25.00
253	Irving Fryar	4.00
254	Brett Favre	30.00
255	Eddie George	12.00
256	Terry Allen	4.00
257	Warren Moon	5.00
258	Mark Brunell	8.00
259	Robert Smith	5.00
260	Jerry Rice	20.00
261	Tim Brown	10.00
262	Carl Pickens	4.00
263	Joey Galloway	5.00
264	Herman Moore	5.00
265	Adrian Murrell	3.00
266	Thurman Thomas	4.00
267	Robert Brooks	4.00
268	Michael Irvin	5.00
269	Andre Rison	3.00
270	Marshall Faulk	10.00

1998 UD3 Die Cuts

Die-cut versions were produced of each UD Cubed base card. The Embossed Die-Cut parallel is numbered to 2,000, Light F/X Die-Cut parallel cards are numbered to 1,000 and Rainbow Foil Die-Cuts are numbered to 100.

Die-Cuts	2X-5X

1998 UD Choice Preview

Upper Deck released a 55-card UD Choice Preview set at retail outlets. The set consists of cards from the regular 1998 UD Choice set.

		NM/M
Complete Set (55):		10.00
Common Player:		.10
Minor Stars:		.20
Wax Box:		10.00
2	Rob Moore	.10
4	Larry Centers	.10
7	Jamal Anderson	.50
12	Byron Hanspard	.10
15	Jermaine Lewis	.10
20	Eric Moulds	.20
22	Bruce Smith	.10
26	Rae Carruth	.10
28	Winslow Oliver	.10
32	Bryan Cox	.10
35	Curtis Conway	.20
39	Jeff Blake	.10
40	Carl Pickens	.10
49	Deion Sanders	.30
53	Ed McCaffrey	.20
55	John Mobley	.10
58	Scott Mitchell	.10
62	Bryant Westbrook	.10
67	Reggie White	.20
70	LeRoy Butler	.10
72	Marshall Faulk	.50
76	Quentin Coryatt	.10
77	Keenan McCardell	.10
80	Jimmy Smith	.20
84	Andre Rison	.10
86	Tony Gonzalez	.10
92	Yatil Green	.10
96	Brad Johnson	.30
98	Jake Reed	.10
103	Troy Davis	.10
104	Andre Hastings	.10
110	Terry Glenn	.20
111	Ben Coates	.20
115	Danny Kanell	.10
119	Tiki Barber	.20
122	Glenn Foley	.20
124	Adrian Murrell	.20
129	Jeff George	.20
131	Darrell Russell	.10
136	Irving Fryar	.10
137	Mike Mamula	.10
143	Levon Kirkland	.10
147	Greg Lloyd	.10
150	Orlando Pace	.20
151	Isaac Bruce	.20
155	Eric Metcalf	.10
157	Tony Martin	.10
161	Merton Hanks	.10
165	J.J. Stokes	.20
168	Chad Brown	.10
173	Trent Dilfer	.30
175	Warren Sapp	.10
180	Steve McNair	.50
186	Gus Frerotte	.10
191	Chris Dishman	.10

1998 UD Choice

UD Choice was released in two series. Series One consists of a 255-card base set. The set has 165 regular cards featuring white borders and 27 full-bleed regular cards. Subsets include 30 Rookie Class cards and 30 Draw Your Own Trading Card contest winners. Three checklists round out the set. The base set is paralleled in Choice Reserve and Prime Choice Reserve. Inserts include StarQuest and Mini Bobbing Head cards. A Draw Your Own Trading Card entry was inserted in each pack. UD Choice Series Two consists of a 183-card base set, featuring the 30-card Domination Next subset (1:4). Series Two also has Choice Reserve and Prime Choice Reserve parallels. Inserts include NFL GameDay '99, StarQuest-RookQuest and Domination Next SE.

		NM/M
Complete Set (438):		60.00
Complete Series 1 (255):		35.00
Complete Series 2 (183):		35.00
Common Player:		.10
Minor Stars:		.20
Common Domination Next:		.75
Inserted 1:4		
Domination Next SE:		3X
Production 2,000 Sets		
Choice Reserve Stars:		5X-10X
Choice Reserve Rookies:		3X
Inserted 1:6		
PC Reserve Stars:		40X-80X
PC Reserve Rookies:		12X-25X
Production 100 Sets		
Pack (12):		1.40
Wax Box (36):		50.00
1	Jake Plummer	.40
2	Rob Moore	.10
3	Simeon Rice	.10
4	Larry Centers	.10
5	Aeneas Williams	.10
6	Chris Gedney	.10
7	Jamal Anderson	.20
8	Michael Booker	.10
9	Ronnie Bradford	.10
10	Cornelius Bennett	.10
11	Terance Mathis	.10
12	Byron Hanspard	.20
13	Peter Boulware	.10
14	Jonathan Ogden	.10
15	Jermaine Lewis	.10
16	Tony Siragusa	.10
17	Brian Kinchen	.10
18	Michael Jackson	.10
19	Doug Flutie	.50
20	Eric Moulds	.10
21	Antowain Smith	.40
22	Bruce Smith	.10
23	Jay Riemersma	.10
24	Ruben Brown	.10
25	Fred Lane	.20
26	Rae Carruth	.10
27	Wesley Walls	.10
28	Winslow Oliver	.10
29	Tyrone Poole	.10
30	Lamar Lathon	.10
31	Anthony Johnson	.10
32	Erik Kramer	.10
33	Darnell Autry	.20
34	Bobby Engram	.10
35	Curtis Conway	.20
36	Jeff Jaeger	.10
37	Chris Penn	.10
38	Corey Dillon	.50
39	Jeff Blake	.20
40	Carl Pickens	.10
41	Ki-Jana Carter	.10
42	Reinard Wilson	.10
43	Tremain Mack	.10
44	Troy Aikman	1.00
45	Larry Allen	.10
46	Darren Woodson	.10
47	Anthony Miller	.10
48	Eric Williams	.10
49	Deion Sanders	.50
50	Rick Cunningham	.10
51	John Elway	1.00
52	Steve Atwater	.10
53	Ed McCaffrey	.10
54	Maa Tanuvasa	.10
55	John Mobley	.10
56	Bill Romanowski	.10
57	Shannon Sharpe	.20
58	Scott Mitchell	.10
59	Jason Hansen	.10
60	Herman Moore	.20
61	Luther Elliss	.10
62	Bryant Westbrook	.10
63	Kevin Abrams	.10
64	Brett Favre	2.00
65	Gilbert Brown	.10
66	Antonio Freeman	.20
67	Reggie White	.20
68	Mark Chmura	.10
69	Seth Joyner	.10
70	LeRoy Butler	.10
71	Marvin Harrison	.20
72	Marshall Faulk	.20
73	Ken Dilger	.10
74	Steve Morrison	.10
75	Zack Crockett	.10
76	Quentin Coryatt	.10
77	Keenan McCardell	.10
78	Mark Brunell	.75
79	Renaldo Wynn	.10

80 Jimmy Smith .10
81 James O. Stewart .10
82 Kevin Hardy .10
83 Marcus Allen .20
84 Andre Rison .10
85 Pete Stoyanovich .10
86 Tony Gonzalez .20
87 Derrick Thomas .10
88 Rich Gannon .10
89 Elvis Grbac .10
90 Dan Marino 1.50
91 Lawrence Phillips .10
92 Yatil Green .20
93 Zach Thomas .10
94 Olindo Mare .10
95 Charles Jordan .10
96 Brad Johnson .20
97 Cris Carter .20
98 Jake Reed .10
99 Ed McDaniel .10
100 Dwayne Rudd .10
101 Leroy Hoard .10
102 Danny Wuerffel .10
103 Troy Davis .10
104 Andre Hastings .10
105 Nicky Savoie .10
106 Willie Roaf .10
107 Ray Zellars .10
108 Tedy Bruschi .10
109 Drew Bledsoe 1.00
110 Terry Glenn .20
111 Ben Coates .10
112 Willie Clay .10
113 Chris Slade .10
114 Larry Whigham .10
115 Danny Kanell .10
116 Jessie Armstead .10
117 Phillipi Sparks .10
118 Michael Strahan .10
119 Tiki Barber .20
120 Charles Way .10
121 Chris Calloway .10
122 Glenn Foley .10
123 Wayne Chrebet .10
124 Kyle Brady .10
125 Keyshawn Johnson .20
126 Aaron Glenn .10
127 James Farrior .10
128 Victor Green .10
129 Jeff George .20
130 Rickey Dudley .10
131 Darrell Russell .10
132 Tim Brown .10
133 James Trapp .10
134 Napoleon Kaufman .40
135 Bobby Hoying .10
136 Irving Fryar .10
137 Mike Mamula .10
138 Troy Vincent .10
139 Bobby Taylor .10
140 Chris Boniol .10
141 Jerome Bettis .20
142 Charles Johnson .10
143 Levon Kirkland .10
144 Carnell Lake .10
145 Will Blackwell .10
146 Tim Lester .10
147 Greg Lloyd .10
148 Tony Banks .20
149 Ryan McNeil .10
150 Orlando Pace .10
151 Isaac Bruce .20
152 Eddie Kennison .20
153 Leslie O'Neal .10
154 Darren Bennett .10
155 Natrone Means .20
156 Junior Seau .20
157 Tony Martin .10
158 Rodney Harrison .10
159 Freddie Jones .10
160 Terrell Owens .20
161 Merton Hanks .10
162 Chris Doleman .10
163 Steve Young .50
164 Chuck Levy .10
165 J.J. Stokes .20
166 Ken Norton .10
167 Bennie Blades .10
168 Chad Brown .10
169 Warren Moon .20
170 Cortez Kennedy .10
171 Darryl Williams .10
172 Michael Sinclair .10
173 Trent Dilfer .20
174 Mike Alstott .40
175 Warren Sapp .10
176 Reidel Anthony .20
177 Derrick Brooks .10
178 Horace Copeland .10
179 Hardy Nickerson .10
180 Steve McNair .50
181 Anthony Dorsett .10
182 Chris Sanders .10
183 Derrick Mason .10
184 Eddie George 1.00
185 Blaine Bishop .10
186 Gus Frerotte .10
187 Terry Allen .10
188 Darrell Green .10
189 Ken Harvey .10
190 Matt Turk .10
191 Chris Dishman .10
192 Keith Thibodeaux .10
193 *Peyton Manning* 8.00
194 *Ryan Leaf* 1.00
195 *Charles Woodson* 2.00
196 *Andre Wadsworth* .30
197 *Keith Brooking* .10
198 *Jason Peter* .30
199 *Curtis Enis* 1.00
200 *Randy Moss* 6.00
201 *Tre Thomas* .10
202 *Robert Edwards* 1.00
203 *Kevin Dyson* 1.00
204 *Fred Taylor* 4.00
205 *Corey Chavous* .10
206 *Grant Wistrom* .10
207 *Vonnie Holliday* .40
208 *Brian Simmons* .50
209 *Jeremy Staat* .10
210 *Alonzo Mayes* .10
211 *Anthony Simmons* .10
212 *Sam Cowart* .10
213 *Flozell Adams* .10
214 *Terry Fair* .10
215 *Germane Crowell* 1.50
216 *Robert Holcombe* 1.00
217 *Jacquez Green* 1.00
218 *Skip Hicks* .50
219 *Takeo Spikes* .40
220 *Az-Zahir Hakim* 1.00
221 *Ahman Green* 6.00
222 *Chris Fuamatu-Ma'afala* .75
223 Darnell Autry .10
224 John Randle .10
225 Scott Mitchell .10
226 Troy Aikman .30
227 Terrell Davis .30
228 Kordell Stewart .30
229 Warrick Dunn .20
230 Craig Newsome .10
231 Brett Favre .60
232 Kordell Stewart .30
233 Barry Sanders .50
234 Dan Marino .50
235 Dan Marino .50
236 Tamarick Vanover .10
237 Warrick Dunn .20
238 Andre Rison .10
239 Dan Marino .50
240 Reggie White .10
241 Tim Brown .10
242 Joe Montana .30
243 Robert Brooks .10
244 Danny Kanell .10
245 Emmitt Smith .50
246 Barry Sanders .50
247 Brett Favre .60
248 Brett Favre .60
249 Jerome Bettis .10
250 Kordell Stewart .30
251 Terrell Davis .30
252 Drew Bledsoe .30
253 Troy Aikman .30
254 Dan Marino .50
255 Warrick Dunn .30
256 Peyton Manning 4.00
257 Ryan Leaf 1.00
258 Andre Wadsworth 1.00
259 Charles Woodson 3.00
260 Curtis Enis 1.00
261 Grant Wistrom .75
262 Greg Ellis .75
263 Fred Taylor 3.00
264 Duane Starks 1.00
265 Keith Brooking .75
266 Takeo Spikes .75
267 Anthony Simmons .75
268 Kevin Dyson 2.00
269 Robert Edwards 1.25
270 Randy Moss 3.00
271 *John Avery* 1.50
272 *Marcus Nash* 1.50
273 *Jerome Pathon* 1.50
274 Jacquez Green 1.00
275 Robert Holcombe 1.00
276 *Patrick Johnson* .75
277 *Germane Crowell* 2.00
278 *Tony Simmons* 1.50
279 *Joe Jurevicius* 1.00
280 Skip Hicks .50
281 Sam Cowart .50
282 *Rashaan Shehee* .50
283 *Brian Griese* 4.00
284 *Tim Dwight* 2.00
285 Ahman Green 2.00
286 Adrian Murrell .20
287 Corey Chavous .10
288 Eric Swann .10
289 Frank Sanders .10
290 Eric Metcalf .10
291 *Jammi German* .50
292 Eugene Robinson .10
293 Chris Chandler .10
294 Tony Martin .10
295 Jessie Tuggle .10
296 Errict Rhett .10
297 Jim Harbaugh .10
298 Eric Green .10
299 Ray Lewis .10
300 Jamie Sharper .10
301 *Fred Coleman* .30
302 Rob Johnson .20
303 Quinn Early .10
304 Thurman Thomas .20
305 Andre Reed .10
306 Sean Gilbert .10
307 Kerry Collins .20
308 Jason Peter .10
309 Michael Bates .10
310 William Floyd .10
311 *Alonzo Mayes* .30
312 *Tony Parrish* .30
313 Walt Harris .10
314 Edgar Bennett .10
315 Jeff Jaeger .10
316 Brian Simmons .20
317 David Dunn .10
318 Ashley Ambrose .10
319 Darnay Scott .10
320 Neil O'Donnell .10
321 Flozell Adams .10
322 Stepfret Williams .10
323 Emmitt Smith 2.00
324 Michael Irvin .20
325 Chris Warren .10
326 *Eric Brown* .20
327 Rod Smith .20
328 Terrell Davis 1.00
329 Neil Smith .10
330 Darrien Gordon .10
331 *Curtis Alexander* .20
332 Barry Sanders 2.00
333 David Sloan .10
334 Johnnie Morton .10
335 Robert Porcher .10
336 Tommy Vardell .10
337 Vonnie Holliday .20
338 Dorsey Levens .20
339 Derrick Mayes .10
340 Robert Brooks .10
341 Raymont Harris .10
342 *E.G. Green* .75
343 Torrance Small .10
344 Carlton Gray .10
345 Aaron Bailey .10
346 Jeff Burris .10
347 *Donovin Darius* .20
348 *Tavian Banks* .75
349 *Aaron Beasley* .20
350 Tony Brackens .10
351 Bryce Paup .10
352 Chester McGlockton .10
353 Leslie O'Neal .10
354 Derrick Alexander .10
355 Kimble Anders .10
356 Tamarick Vanover .10
357 Brock Marion .10
358 *Larry Shannon* .20
359 Karim Abdul-Jabbar .30
360 Troy Drayton .10
361 O.J. McDuffie .10
362 John Randle .10
363 David Palmer .10
364 Robert Smith .20
365 *Kailee Wong* .20
366 Duane Clemons .10
367 *Kyle Turley* .20
368 Sean Dawkins .10
369 Lamar Smith .10
370 *Cameron Cleeland* .50
371 Keith Poole .10
372 *Tebucky Jones* .20
373 Willie McGinest .10
374 Ty Law .10
375 Lawyer Milloy .10
376 Tony Carter .10
377 *Shaun Williams* .20
378 *Brian Alford* .20
379 Tyrone Wheatley .10
380 Jason Sehorn .10
381 *David Patten* .20
382 *Scott Frost* .20
383 Mo Lewis .10
384 Kevin Williams .10
385 Curtis Martin .30
386 Vinny Testaverde .20
387 *Mo Collins* .20
388 James Jett .10
389 Eric Allen .10
390 *Jon Ritchie* .20
391 Harvey Williams .10
392 Tre Thomas .10
393 Rodney Peete .10
394 Hugh Douglas .10
395 Charlie Garner .10
396 *Karl Hankton* .20
397 Kordell Stewart .75
398 George Jones .10
399 Earl Holmes .10
400 *Hines Ward* .75
401 Jason Gildon .10
402 Ricky Proehl .10
403 Az-Zahir Hakim .20
404 Amp Lee .10
405 Eric Hill .10
406 *Leonard Little* .20
407 Charlie Jones .10
408 Craig Whelihan .10
409 Terrell Fletcher .10
410 *Kenny Bynum* .20
411 *Mikhael Ricks* .75
412 *R.W. McQuarters* .50
413 Jerry Rice 1.00
414 Garrison Hearst .20
415 Ty Detmer .10
416 Gabe Wilkins .10
417 *Michael Black* .20
418 James McKnight .10
419 Darrin Smith .10
420 Joey Galloway .20
421 Ricky Watters .20
422 Warrick Dunn .75
423 Brian Kelly .10
424 Bert Emanuel .10
425 John Lynch .10
426 Regan Upshaw .10
427 Yancey Thigpen .10
428 Kenny Holmes .10
429 Frank Wycheck .10
430 *Samari Rolle* .20
431 Brian Mitchell .10
432 Stephen Alexander .10
433 Jamie Asher .10
434 Michael Westbrook .10
435 Dana Stubblefield .10
436 Dan Wilkinson .10
437 Dan Marino Checklist .75
438 Jerry Rice Checklist .50

1998 UD Choice Choice Reserve

Choice Reserve is a parallel of the entire 438-card UD Choice set (255 cards from Series One and 183 from Series Two). The parallel was inserted one per six packs in each series.

Choice Reserve Cards: 2X-6X
Choice Reserve Rookies: 3X

1998 UD Choice Prime Choice Reserve

Prime Choice Reserve is a parallel of the complete 438-card UD Choice base set (255 cards from Series One and 183 from Series Two). This hobby-only set has "Prime Choice Reserve" foil-stamped on the card fronts and is numbered to 100.

NM/M

PC Reserve Cards: 20X-40X
PC Reserve Rookies: 8X-15X

1998 UD Choice Mini Bobbing Head

Mini Bobbing Head cards were an insert in Series One. The 30-card set consists of cards that can be folded into a stand-up figure with a removable bobbing head. The cards were inserted one per four packs.

NM/M

Complete Set (30): 15.00
Common Player: .25
Minor Stars: .50
M1 Jake Plummer 1.00
M2 Jamal Anderson .25
M3 Michael Jackson .25
M4 Bruce Smith .25
M5 Rae Carruth .25
M6 Curtis Conway .25
M7 Jeff Blake .50
M8 Troy Aikman 1.50
M9 Michael Irvin .50
M10 Terrell Davis 1.50
M11 Barry Sanders 3.00
M12 Herman Moore .50
M13 Reggie White .50
M14 Dorsey Levens .50
M15 Marvin Harrison .25
M16 Keenan McCardell .25
M17 Andre Rison .25
M18 Dan Marino 3.00
M19 Curtis Martin 1.00
M20 Keyshawn Johnson .25
M21 Tim Brown .25
M22 Kordell Stewart 1.50
M23 Greg Lloyd .25
M24 Junior Seau .25
M25 Jerry Rice 1.00
M26 Merton Hanks .25
M27 Joey Galloway .50
M28 Warrick Dunn 1.00
M29 Warren Sapp .25
M30 Darrell Green .25

1998 UD Choice Starquest Blue

StarQuest is a 30-card, four-tiered insert in UD Choice Series One. Each tier has a different insertion rate and foil color. StarQuest 1-Star cards were seeded 1:1, 2-Star cards were found 1:7, 3-Stars were inserted 1:23 and 4-Star cards are numbered to 100.

NM/M

Complete Set (30): 15.00
Common Player: .25
Minor Stars: .50
Green Cards: 1X-3X
Red Cards: 2X-5X
Gold Cards: 10X-25X
W1 Warren Moon .25
W2 Jerry Rice 1.00
W3 Jeff George .25
W4 Brett Favre 2.00
W5 Junior Seau .25
W6 Cris Carter .25
W7 John Elway 1.00
W8 Troy Aikman 1.00
W9 Steve Young .75
W10 Kordell Stewart .50
W11 Drew Bledsoe 1.00
W12 Dorsey Levens .50
W13 Dan Marino 1.75
W14 Joey Galloway .50
W15 Antonio Freeman .50
W16 Jake Plummer .50
W17 Corey Dillon .75
W18 Mark Brunell .75
W19 Andre Rison .25
W20 Barry Sanders 1.50
W21 Deion Sanders .60
W22 Emmitt Smith 1.75
W23 Antowain Smith .60
W24 Herman Moore .50
W25 Napoleon Kaufman .60
W26 Jerome Bettis .50
W27 Eddie George 1.00
W28 Warrick Dunn 1.00
W29 Adrian Murrell .25
W30 Terrell Davis 1.00

1998 Upper Deck

Upper Deck Series One Football consists of a 255-card base set. The base cards have a color photo bordered on three sides, with the player's name, team and position printed at the bottom. The set consists of 210 regular cards, 42 Star Rookie subset cards (1:4) and three checklists. The set is paralleled in UD Exclusives. Inserts include SuperPowers, Constant Threat, Define the Game (each with a tiered Quantum parallel), Game Jerseys and Hobby-Exclusive Game Jerseys.

NM/M

Complete Set (255): 175.00
Common Player: .15
Minor Stars: .30
Common Rookie (1-42): 2.50
Bronze Cards: 15X-50X
Bronze Rookies: 2X-4X
Pack (10): 7.00
Wax Box (24): 125.00
1 *Peyton Manning* 30.00
2 *Ryan Leaf* 3.00
3 *Andre Wadsworth* 3.00
4 *Charles Woodson* 6.00
5 *Curtis Enis* 3.00
6 *Grant Wistrom* 2.50
7 *Greg Ellis* 2.50
8 *Fred Taylor* 8.00
9 *Duane Starks* 2.50
10 *Keith Brooking* 2.50
11 *Takeo Spikes* 4.00
12 *Jason Peter* 2.50
13 *Anthony Simmons* 2.50
14 *Kevin Dyson* 5.00
15 *Brian Simmons* 2.50
16 *Robert Edwards* 5.00
17 *Randy Moss* 20.00
18 *John Avery* 4.00
19 *Marcus Nash* 4.00
20 *Jerome Pathon* 4.00
21 *Jacquez Green* 4.00
22 *Robert Holcombe* 5.00
23 *Patrick Johnson* 2.50
24 *Germane Crowell* 4.00
25 *Joe Jurevicius* 4.00
26 *Skip Hicks* 4.00
27 *Ahman Green* 25.00
28 *Brian Griese* 15.00
29 *Hines Ward* 10.00
30 *Tavian Banks* 4.00
31 *Tony Simmons* 4.00
32 *Victor Riley* 2.50
33 *Rashaan Shehee* 4.00
34 *R.W. McQuarters* 2.50
35 *Flozell Adams* 2.50
36 *Tre Thomas* 2.50
37 *Greg Favors* 2.50
38 *Jon Ritchie* 2.50
39 *Jessie Haynes* 2.50
40 *Ryan Sutter* 2.50
41 *Mo Collins* 2.50
42 *Tim Dwight* 5.00
43 Chris Chandler .15
44 Byron Hanspard .15
45 Jessie Tuggle .15
46 Jamal Anderson .30
47 Terance Mathis .15
48 Morten Andersen .15
49 Jake Plummer .75
50 Mario Bates .15
51 Frank Sanders .15
52 Adrian Murrell .30
53 Simeon Rice .15
54 Aeneas Williams .15
55 Eric Swann .15
56 Jim Harbaugh .15
57 Michael Jackson .15
58 Peter Boulware .15
59 Errict Rhett .15
60 Jermaine Lewis .15
61 Eric Zeier .15
62 Rod Woodson .15
63 Rob Johnson .30
64 Antowain Smith 1.00
65 Bruce Smith .15
66 Eric Moulds .15
67 Andre Reed .15
68 Thurman Thomas .30
69 Lonnie Johnson .15
70 Kerry Collins .50
71 Kevin Greene .15
72 Fred Lane .30
73 Rae Carruth .15
74 Michael Bates .15
75 William Floyd .15
76 Sean Gilbert .15
77 Erik Kramer .15
78 Edgar Bennett .15
79 Curtis Conway .30
80 Darnell Autry .15
81 Ryan Wetnight .15
82 Walt Harris .15
83 Bobby Engram .15
84 Jeff Blake .30
85 Carl Pickens .30
86 Darnay Scott .15
87 Corey Dillon 1.25
88 Reinard Wilson .15
89 Ashley Ambrose .15
90 Troy Aikman 1.50
91 Michael Irvin .30
92 Emmitt Smith 2.50
93 Deion Sanders .50
94 David LaFleur .15
95 Chris Warren .15
96 Darren Woodson .15
97 John Elway 1.50
98 Terrell Davis 1.00
99 Rod Smith .30
100 Shannon Sharpe .30
101 Ed McCaffrey .15
102 Steve Atwater .15
103 John Mobley .15
104 Darrian Gordon .15
105 Barry Sanders 3.00
106 Scott Mitchell .15
107 Herman Moore .30
108 Johnnie Morton .15
109 Robert Porcher .15
110 Bryant Westbrook .15
111 Tommy Vardell .15
112 Brett Favre 3.00
113 Dorsey Levens .30
114 Reggie White .30
115 Antonio Freeman .30
116 Robert Brooks .15
117 Mark Chmura .30
118 Derrick Mayes .15
119 Gilbert Brown .15
120 Marshall Faulk .30
121 Torrance Small .15
122 Marvin Harrison .30
123 Quentin Coryatt .15
124 Ken Dilger .15
125 Zack Crockett .15
126 Mark Brunell .75
127 Bryce Paup .15
128 Tony Brackens .15
129 Renaldo Wynn .15
130 Keenan McCardell .15
131 Jimmy Smith .30
132 Kevin Hardy .15
133 Elvis Grbac .15
134 Tamarick Vanover .15
135 Chester McGlockton .15
136 Andre Rison .15
137 Derrick Alexander .15
138 Tony Gonzalez .15
139 Derrick Thomas .15
140 Dan Marino 2.50
141 Karim Abdul-Jabbar .30
142 O.J. McDuffie .15
143 Yatil Green .15
144 Charles Jordan .15
145 Brock Marion .15
146 Zach Thomas .15
147 Brad Johnson .30
148 Cris Carter .30
149 Jake Reed .15
150 Robert Smith .30
151 John Randle .15
152 Dwayne Rudd .15
153 Randall Cunningham .15
154 Drew Bledsoe 1.25
155 Terry Glenn .30
156 Ben Coates .15
157 Willie Clay .15
158 Chris Slade .15
159 Derrick Cullors .15
160 Ty Law .15
161 Danny Wuerffel .30
162 Andre Hastings .15
163 Troy Davis .30
164 Billy Joe Hobert .15
165 Eric Guliford .15
166 Mark Fields .15
167 Alex Molden .15
168 Danny Kanell .15
169 Tiki Barber .30
170 Charles Way .15
171 Amani Toomer .15
172 Michael Strahan .15
173 Jesse Armstead .15
174 Jason Sehorn .15
175 Glenn Foley .30
176 Curtis Martin 1.00
177 Aaron Glenn .15

178	Keyshawn Johnson	.30
179	James Farrior	.15
180	Wayne Chrebet	.15
181	Keith Byars	.15
182	Jeff George	.30
183	Napoleon Kaufman	.50
184	Tim Brown	.30
185	Darrell Russell	.15
186	Rickey Dudley	.15
187	James Jett	.15
188	Desmond Howard	.15
189	Bobby Hoying	.15
190	Charlie Garner	.15
191	Irving Fryar	.15
192	Chris T. Jones	.15
193	Mike Mamula	.15
194	Troy Vincent	.15
195	Kordell Stewart	.75
196	Jerome Bettis	.30
197	Will Blackwell	.15
198	Levon Kirkland	.15
199	Carnell Lake	.15
200	Charles Johnson	.15
201	Greg Lloyd	.15
202	Donnell Woolford	.15
203	Tony Banks	.30
204	Amp Lee	.15
205	Isaac Bruce	.30
206	Eddie Kennison	.30
207	Ryan McNeil	.15
208	Craig Heyward	.15
209	Ernie Conwell	.15
210	Natrone Means	.30
211	Junior Seau	.30
212	Tony Martin	.15
213	Freddie Jones	.15
214	Bryan Still	.15
215	Rodney Harrison	.15
216	Steve Young	1.00
217	Jerry Rice	2.50
218	Garrison Hearst	.15
219	J.J. Stokes	.15
220	Ken Norton	.15
221	Greg Clark	.15
222	Bryant Young	.15
223	Gabe Wilkins	.15
224	Warren Moon	.30
225	Jon Kitna	.15
226	Ricky Watters	.30
227	Chad Brown	.15
228	Joey Galloway	.30
229	Shawn Springs	.15
230	Cortez Kennedy	.15
231	Trent Dilfer	.30
232	Warrick Dunn	1.00
233	Mike Alstott	.30
234	Warren Sapp	.15
235	Bert Emanuel	.15
236	Reidel Anthony	.15
237	Hardy Nickerson	.15
238	Derrick Brooks	.15
239	Steve McNair	1.25
240	Yancey Thigpen	.15
241	Anthony Dorsett	.15
242	Blaine Bishop	.15
243	Kenny Holmes	.15
244	Eddie George	1.25
245	Chris Sanders	.15
246	Gus Frerotte	.15
247	Terry Allen	.15
248	Dana Stubblefield	.15
249	Michael Westbrook	.15
250	Darrell Green	.15
251	Brian Mitchell	.15
252	Ken Harvey	.15
253	Troy Aikman Checklist A	.75
254	Dan Marino Checklist B	1.25
255	Herman Moore Checklist C	.15

1998 Upper Deck Bronze

The UD Exclusives set parallels the Upper Deck Series One base set. One level is numbered to 100 and the other is a 1-of-1 set.

Bronze Cards:	15X-50X
Bronze Rookies:	2X-4X

1998 Upper Deck Constant Threat

Constant Threat is a 30-card insert seeded one per 12 packs. The cards have a horizontal layout and two player photos. The color player photo is on the left and a negative exposure is on the right. The cards also feature blue foil highlights. Cards are numbered with a "CT" prefix.

		NM/M
Complete Set (30):		25.00
Common Player:		.50
Minor Stars:		1.00
Bronze Cards:		3X-5X
Silver Cards:		2X
1	Dan Marino	5.00
2	Peyton Manning	4.00
3	Randy Moss	4.00
4	Brett Favre	5.00
5	Mark Brunell	1.00
6	Keyshawn Johnson	.50
7	John Elway	3.00
8	Troy Aikman	3.00
9	Steve Young	3.00
10	Kordell Stewart	1.00
11	Drew Bledsoe	3.00
12	Joey Galloway	1.00
13	Elvis Grbac	.50
14	Marvin Harrison	1.00
15	Napoleon Kaufman	.50
16	Ryan Leaf	.50
17	Jake Plummer	1.00
18	Terrell Davis	3.00
19	Steve McNair	3.00
20	Barry Sanders	4.00
21	Deion Sanders	1.00
22	Emmitt Smith	4.00
23	Antowain Smith	1.00
24	Herman Moore	1.00
25	Curtis Martin	3.00
26	Jerry Rice	4.00
27	Eddie George	2.00
28	Warrick Dunn	1.00
29	Curtis Enis	.50
30	Michael Irvin	1.00

1998 Upper Deck Constant Threat Bronze/Silver

The Constant Threat insert has a three-tiered Quantum parallel. The cards are die-cut and sequentially numbered. Tier One features silver foil and is numbered to 1,000, Tier Two has bronze foil and numbering to 25 and Tier Three has gold foil and is a 1-of-1 set.

Bronze Cards:	3X-5X
Silver Cards:	2X-4X

1998 Upper Deck Define the Game

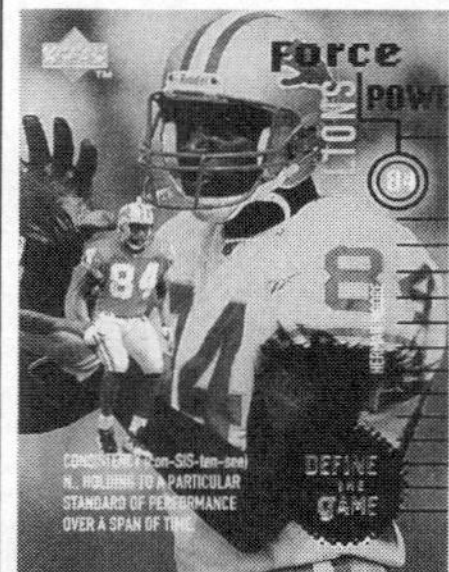

Define the Game is a 30-card insert seeded one per eight packs. The cards feature a small color photo of the player with a larger black-and-white photo in the background. The front of each card has a word that describes the player and the definition. Cards are numbered with a "DG" prefix.

		NM/M
Complete Set (30):		30.00
Common Player:		.50
Minor Stars:		1.00
Bronze Cards:		3X-5X
Silver Cards:		2X
1	Dan Marino	5.00
2	Curtis Enis	.50
3	Dorsey Levens	.50
4	Charles Woodson	1.00
5	Junior Seau	.50
6	Tiki Barber	.50
7	Randy Moss	4.00
8	Troy Aikman	3.00
9	Jake Plummer	1.00
10	Corey Dillon	1.00
11	Jerry Rice	4.00
12	Emmitt Smith	4.00
13	Herman Moore	1.00
14	Brad Johnson	.50
15	Gus Frerotte	.50
16	Ryan Leaf	.50
17	Shannon Sharpe	.50
18	Jermaine Lewis	.50
19	Jerome Bettis	1.00
20	Barry Sanders	4.00
21	Terry Allen	.50
22	Reidel Anthony	.50
23	Isaac Bruce	1.00
24	Mike Alstott	1.00
25	Rae Carruth	.50
26	Tamarick Vanover	.50
27	Eddie George	2.00
28	Warrick Dunn	1.00
29	Tony Gonzalez	.50
30	Keenan McCardell	.50

1998 Upper Deck Define the Game Bronze/Silver

Define the Game has a three-tiered Quantum parallel. The cards are die-cut and sequentially numbered. Tier One is numbered to 1,500, Tier Two to 50 and Tier Three to 1.

Bronze Cards:	15X-30X
Silver Cards:	2X

1998 Upper Deck Game Jersey

The Game Jersey insert features 10 cards inserted 1:2,500. The set contains both veterans and rookies. The veteran cards feature a piece of game-used jersey and the rookie cards have a piece of jersey worn during the NFL rookie photo shoot. Dan Marino signed 13 of his cards. Cards are numbered with "GJ" prefix.

		NM/M
Common Player:		40.00
1	Brett Favre	150.00
2	Reggie White	75.00
3	Barry Sanders	150.00
4	John Elway	150.00
5	Mark Brunell	50.00
6	Mike Alstott	50.00
7	Ryan Leaf	40.00
8	Andre Wadsworth	40.00
9	Robert Edwards	50.00
10	Kevin Dyson	50.00

1998 Upper Deck Hobby Exclusive Game Jerseys

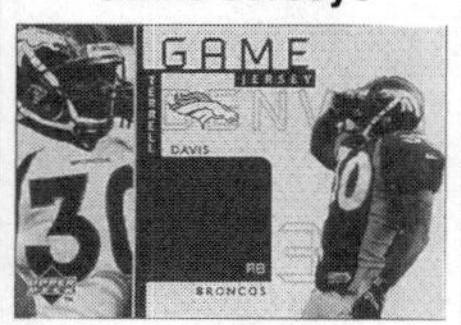

The Hobby-Exclusive Game Jersey insert features 10-cards inserted 1:288. The set features veterans and rookies. The veteran cards have a piece of game-worn jersey and the rookie cards have a piece of jersey from the NFL rookie photo shoot. Cards are numbered with "GJ" prefix.

		NM/M
Complete Set (10):		25.00
Common Player:		25.00
11	Dan Marino	175.00
12	Deion Sanders	75.00
13	Steve Young	100.00
14	Terrell Davis	75.00
15	Tim Brown	60.00
16	Peyton Manning	125.00
17	Takeo Spikes	25.00
18	Curtis Enis	25.00
19	Fred Taylor	50.00
20	John Avery	25.00

1998 Upper Deck SuperPowers

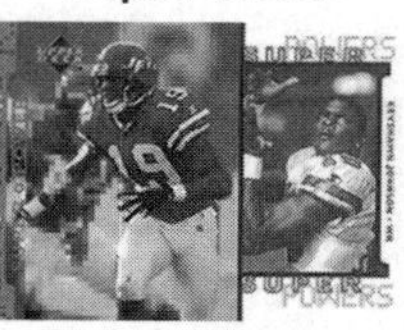

SuperPowers is a 30-card insert seeded one per four packs. The cards have a horizontal layout and feature a color photo on the left with a black-and-white photo on the right.

		NM/M
Complete Set (30):		25.00
Common Player:		.25
Minor Stars:		.50
Bronze Cards:		3X-5X
Silver Cards:		2X
S1	Dan Marino	4.00
S2	Jerry Rice	3.00
S3	Napoleon Kaufman	.50
S4	Brett Favre	4.00
S5	Andre Rison	.25
S6	Jerome Bettis	.50
S7	John Elway	2.00
S8	Troy Aikman	2.00
S9	Steve Young	1.50
S10	Kordell Stewart	.50
S11	Drew Bledsoe	2.00
S12	Antonio Freeman	.50
S13	Mark Brunell	.50
S14	Shannon Sharpe	.25
S15	Trent Dilfer	.50
S16	Peyton Manning	2.00
S17	Cris Carter	.25
S18	Michael Irvin	.50
S19	Terry Glenn	.50
S20	Keyshawn Johnson	.50
S21	Deion Sanders	1.50
S22	Emmitt Smith	3.00
S23	Marcus Allen	.50
S24	Dorsey Levens	.50
S25	Jake Plummer	.50
S26	Eddie George	1.00
S27	Tim Brown	.25
S28	Warrick Dunn	.50
S29	Reggie White	.50
S30	Terrell Davis	2.00

1998 Upper Deck SuperPowers Bronze/Silver

The SuperPowers insert has a three-tiered Quantum parallel. The cards are die-cut and sequentially numbered. Tier One is numbered to 2,000, Tier Two to 100 and Tier Three is a 1-of-1 set.

Bronze Cards:	3X-5X
Silver Cards:	2X

1998 Upper Deck Black Diamond

The Black Diamond Football base set consists of 150 cards designated by the Black Diamond logo and a single Black Diamond in the lower right corner. Three parallel versions were produced. Double Black Diamond cards (inserted 1:1) have two diamonds and red Light F/X backgrounds. Triple Black Diamonds (1:5) have gold Light F/X backgrounds and Quadruple Black Diamonds (50 total sets) have black Light F/X backgrounds. The Premium Cuts insert (30 cards) features the same four diamond levels of scarcity and a special die-cut. Single Diamond (1:7), Double Diamond (1:15), Triple Diamond (1:30) and Quadruple Diamond (1:180) versions were created. Upper Deck also included a hobby-only "Mystery Premium Cut" insert in Black Diamond. The 30 cards feature Black Light F/X backgrounds, embossing and a horizontal die-cut design. The cards in the "Mystery" insert have different insertion rates.

		NM/M
Complete Set (150):		40.00
Common Player:		.25
Minor Stars:		.50
Doubles:		2X
Triples:		3X-6X
Quadruples:		10X-25X
Pack (6):		2.50
Wax Box (30):		55.00
1	Kent Graham	.25
2	Darrell Russell	.25
3	Jim Harbaugh	.25
4	Cornelius Bennett	.25
5	Troy Vincent	.25
6	Natrone Means	.50
7	Michael Jackson	.25
8	Will Blackwell	.25
9	Greg Hill	.25
10	Andre Reed	.25
11	Darren Bennett	.25
12	Dan Marino	5.00
13	Tshimanga Biakabutuka	.25
14	Terrell Owens	.75
15	Cris Carter	.25
16	Darnell Autry	.50
17	Joey Galloway	.50
18	Terry Glenn	1.00
19	Ki-Jana Carter	.25
20	Isaac Bruce	.50
21	Shawn Jefferson	.25
22	Michael Irvin	.50
23	Warren Sapp	.25
24	Dave Brown	.25
25	Terrell Davis	2.00
26	Frank Wycheck	.25
27	Neil O'Donnell	.25
28	Scott Mitchell	.25
29	Michael Westbrook	.25
30	Tim Brown	.50
31	Antonio Freeman	.75
32	Jake Plummer	.75
33	Irving Fryar	.25
34	Quentin Coryatt	.25
35	Jamal Anderson	.50
36	Jerome Bettis	.50
37	Keenan McCardell	.25
38	Derrick Alexander	.25
39	Stan Humphries	.25
40	Andre Rison	.25
41	Bruce Smith	.25
42	Garrison Hearst	.25
43	Zach Thomas	.50
44	Rae Carruth	.50
45	Kevin Greene	.25
46	Robert Smith	.25
47	Curtis Conway	.50
48	Christian Fauria	.25
49	Curtis Martin	2.00
50	Dan Wilkinson	.25
51	Eddie Kennison	.75
52	Mark Fields	.25
53	Anthony Miller	.25
54	Mike Alstott	1.00
55	Tiki Barber	.75
56	Neil Smith	.25
57	Gus Frerotte	.25
58	Adrian Murrell	.50
59	Johnnie Morton	.25
60	O.J. McDuffie	.25
61	Napoleon Kaufman	.50
62	Robert Brooks	.25
63	Byron Hanspard	.75
64	Ty Detmer	.25
65	Mark Brunell	1.00
66	Bam Morris	.25
67	Kordell Stewart	1.00
68	Elvis Grbac	.25
69	Antowain Smith	1.50
70	Junior Seau	.50
71	Tony Gonzalez	.50
72	Anthony Johnson	.25
73	Steve Young	1.50
74	Brian Manning	.25
75	Rick Mirer	.25
76	Warren Moon	.50
77	Torrian Gray	.25
78	Carl Pickens	.25
79	Tony Banks	.50
80	Willie McGinest	.25
81	Deion Sanders	1.25
82	Warrick Dunn	1.00
83	Danny Wuerffel	.75
84	Rod Smith	.25
85	Steve McNair	1.75
86	Danny Kanell	.25
87	Herman Moore	.50
88	Brian Mitchell	.25
89	James Farrior	.25
90	Reggie White	.50
91	Simeon Rice	.25
92	James Jett	.25
93	Marshall Faulk	.50
94	Chris Chandler	.25
95	Mike Mamula	.25
96	Jimmy Smith	.25
97	Jamie Sharper	.25
98	Carnell Lake	.25
99	Marcus Allen	.50
100	Thurman Thomas	.50
101	Freddie Jones	.25
102	Karim Abdul-Jabbar	1.00
103	Kerry Collins	.50
104	Jerry Rice	2.50
105	Brad Johnson	.50
106	Raymont Harris	.25
107	Lamar Smith	.25
108	Drew Bledsoe	2.00
109	Corey Dillon	2.00
110	Lawrence Phillips	.25
111	Heath Shuler	.25
112	Emmitt Smith	4.00
113	Reidel Anthony	1.00
114	Ike Hilliard	.75
115	Shannon Sharpe	.25
116	Chris Sanders	.25
117	Keyshawn Johnson	.75
118	Barry Sanders	3.00
119	Cris Dishman	.25
120	Jeff George	.50
121	Dorsey Levens	.50
122	Rob Moore	.25
123	Ricky Watters	.50
124	Marvin Harrison	.75
125	Vinny Testaverde	.25
126	Charles Johnson	.25
127	Renaldo Wynn	.25
128	Todd Collins	.25
129	Tony Martin	.25
130	Derrick Thomas	.25
131	Wesley Walls	.25
132	Rod Woodson	.25
133	Troy Drayton	.25
134	Bryan Cox	.25
135	Shawn Springs	.25
136	Jake Reed	.25
137	Jeff Blake	.50
138	Craig Heyward	.25
139	Ben Coates	.25
140	Troy Aikman	2.50
141	Trent Dilfer	1.00
142	Troy Davis	.75
143	John Elway	3.00
144	Eddie George	1.50
145	Rodney Hampton	.25
146	Ed McCaffrey	.25
147	Terry Allen	.25
148	Wayne Chrebet	.25
149	Brett Favre	5.00
150	Daryl Johnston	.25

1998 Upper Deck Black Diamond Premium Cut

Premium Cut is a 30-card insert with four diamond versions. The cards have a special die-cut and Light F/X technology. Single Diamond (inserted 1:7), Double Diamond (1:15), Triple Diamond (1:30) and Quadruple Diamond (1:180) versions were produced. Cards are numbered with a "PC" prefix.

		NM/M
Common Player:		3.00
Minor Stars:		6.00
Doubles:		2X
Triples:		2X-4X
Quad Horizontals:		2X-4X
Quad Verticals:		5X-10X
1	Karim Abdul-Jabbar	6.00
2	Troy Aikman	12.00
3	Kerry Collins	6.00
4	Drew Bledsoe	12.00
5	Barry Sanders	20.00
6	Marcus Allen	6.00
7	John Elway	12.00
8	Adrian Murrell	3.00
9	Junior Seau	3.00
10	Eddie George	12.00
11	Antowain Smith	8.00
12	Reggie White	6.00
13	Dan Marino	24.00
14	Joey Galloway	6.00
15	Kordell Stewart	12.00
16	Terry Allen	3.00
17	Napoleon Kaufman	6.00
18	Curtis Martin	12.00
19	Steve Young	10.00
20	Rod Smith	3.00
21	Mark Brunell	12.00
22	Emmitt Smith	24.00
23	Rae Carruth	6.00
24	Brett Favre	30.00
25	Jeff George	6.00
26	Terry Glenn	6.00
27	Warrick Dunn	12.00
28	Herman Moore	6.00
29	Cris Carter	3.00
30	Terrell Davis	12.00

1998 Upper Deck Black Diamond Rookies

This 120-card set includes 90 regular player cards (all possessing Light F/X foil treatment) with each card sporting a Single Black Diamond, along with a 30-card, short-printed "Rookie Single Black Diamond" subset (1:4 packs). The parallel Double Black Diamond singles feature red Light F/X technology with veterans numbered to 3,000 and rookies to 2,500. The Triple Black Diamond parallel set has veterans numbered to 1,500 and rookies to 1,000. The Quadruple Black Diamond set has veterans numbered to 150 and rookies to 100.

		NM/M
Complete Set (120):		100.00
Common Player:		.15
Minor Stars:		.30
Common Rookie (91-120):		1.00
Inserted 1:4		
Double Cards:		2X-4X
Production 3,000 Sets		
Double Rookies:		1X
Production 2,500 Sets		
Triple Cards:		4X-8X
Production 1,500 Sets		
Triple Rookies:		2X
Production 1,000 Sets		
Quad. Cards:		5X-15X
Production 150 Sets		
Quad. Rookies:		3X-6X
Production 100 Sets		
Pack (6):		3.00
Wax Box (30):		60.00
1	Jake Plummer	.50
2	Adrian Murrell	.15
3	Frank Sanders	.15
4	Jamal Anderson	.75
5	Chris Chandler	.30
6	Tony Martin	.15
7	Jim Harbaugh	.30
8	Errict Rhett	.15
9	Michael Jackson	.15
10	Rob Johnson	.30
11	Antowain Smith	.50
12	Thurman Thomas	.30
13	Fred Lane	.15
14	Kerry Collins	.30
15	Rae Carruth	.15
16	Erik Kramer	.15
17	Edgar Bennett	.15
18	Curtis Conway	.30
19	Corey Dillon	.75
20	Neil O'Donnell	.15
21	Carl Pickens	.30
22	Troy Aikman	1.50
23	Emmitt Smith	2.00
24	Deion Sanders	.50
25	John Elway	1.50
26	Terrell Davis	1.25
27	Rod Smith	.30
28	Barry Sanders	3.00
29	Johnnie Morton	.15
30	Herman Moore	.30
31	Brett Favre	3.00
32	Antonio Freeman	.50
33	Dorsey Levens	.30
34	Marshall Faulk	.50
35	Marvin Harrison	.30
36	Zack Crockett	.15
37	Mark Brunell	.75
38	Jimmy Smith	.30
39	Keenan McCardell	.30
40	Elvis Grbac	.30
41	Andre Rison	.30
42	Derrick Alexander	.15
43	Dan Marino	2.00
44	Karim Abdul-Jabbar	.30
45	Zach Thomas	.30
46	Brad Johnson	.50
47	Cris Carter	.50
48	Robert Smith	.50
49	Drew Bledsoe	1.25
50	Terry Glenn	.30
51	Ben Coates	.30
52	Danny Wuerffel	.30
53	Lamar Smith	.15
54	Sean Dawkins	.15
55	Danny Kanell	.15
56	Tiki Barber	.15
57	Ike Hilliard	.15
58	Curtis Martin	.50
59	Vinny Testaverde	.30
60	Keyshawn Johnson	.50
61	Napoleon Kaufman	.50
62	Jeff George	.30
63	Tim Brown	.30
64	Bobby Hoying	.30
65	Charlie Garner	.15
66	Duce Staley	.30
67	Kordell Stewart	.75
68	Jerome Bettis	.50
69	Charles Johnson	.30
70	Tony Banks	.30
71	Isaac Bruce	.30
72	Eddie Kennison	.30
73	Natrone Means	.30
74	Bryan Still	.15
75	Junior Seau	.30
76	Steve Young	1.00
77	Jerry Rice	2.50
78	Garrison Hearst	.50
79	Ricky Watters	.30
80	Joey Galloway	.50
81	Warren Moon	.30
82	Warrick Dunn	1.00
83	Trent Dilfer	.30
84	Bert Emanuel	.15
85	Steve McNair	.75
86	Eddie George	1.25
87	Yancey Thigpen	.15
88	Leslie Shepherd	.15
89	Terry Allen	.30
90	Michael Westbrook	.15
91	*Peyton Manning*	15.00
92	*Jacquez Green*	3.00
93	*Fred Taylor*	5.00
94	*Terry Fair*	3.00
95	*Patrick Johnson*	3.00
96	*Corey Chavous*	2.00
97	*Randy Moss*	12.00
98	*Curtis Enis*	3.00
99	*Rashaan Shehee*	3.00
100	*Kevin Dyson*	4.00
101	*Shaun Williams*	1.00
102	*Grant Wistrom*	2.00
103	*John Avery*	4.00
104	*Brian Griese*	8.00
105	*Ryan Leaf*	4.00
106	*Jerome Pathon*	3.00
107	*Sam Cowart*	1.00
108	*Germane Crowell*	4.00
109	*Ahman Green*	12.00
110	*Greg Ellis*	1.00
111	*Robert Holcombe*	3.00
112	*Marcus Nash*	3.00
113	*Duane Starks*	3.00
114	*Andre Wadsworth*	3.00
115	*Takeo Spikes*	3.00
116	*Eric Brown*	1.00
117	*Robert Edwards*	3.00
118	*Charlie Batch*	3.00
119	*Mikhael Ricks*	2.50
120	*Charles Woodson*	4.00

1998 Upper Deck Black Diamond Rookies Sheer Brilliance

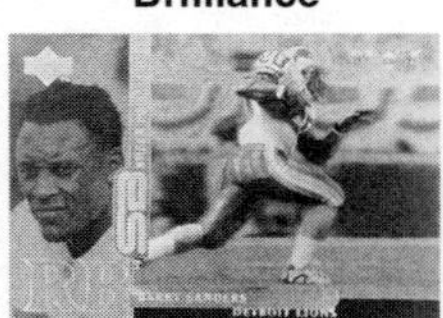

Each of these hobby-only singles has the Quadruple Black Diamond stamp on the front and each is sequentially numbered to the player's uniform number multiplied by 100. Cards are numbered with a "B" prefix.

		NM/M
Complete Set (30):		75.00
Common Player:		1.00
Hobby Only		
1	Dan Marino(1300)	5.00
2	Troy Aikman(800)	4.00
3	Brett Favre(400)	10.00
4	Ryan Leaf(1600)	1.00
5	Peyton Manning(1800)	5.00
6	Barry Sanders(2000)	6.00
7	Emmitt Smith(2200)	5.00
8	John Elway(700)	7.00
9	Steve Young(800)	5.00
10	Steve McNair(900)	3.00
11	Antowain Smith(2300)	1.00
12	Corey Dillon(2800)	2.00
13	Terrell Davis(3000)	3.00
14	Mark Brunell(800)	2.00
15	Charles Woodson (2400)	1.00
16	Brian Griese(1400)	2.00
17	Curtis Martin(2800)	1.00
18	Keyshawn Johnson (1900)	1.00
19	Kordell Stewart(1000)	3.00
20	Eddie George(2700)	2.00
21	Drew Bledsoe(1100)	3.00
22	Jake Plummer(1600)	2.00
23	Warren Moon(100)	3.00
24	Curtis Enis(3900)	1.00
25	John Avery(2000)	1.00
26	Randy Moss(1800)	4.00
27	Rob Johnson(1100)	1.00
28	Warrick Dunn(2800)	1.00
29	Terry Allen(2100)	1.00
30	Robert Smith(2600)	1.00

1998 Upper Deck Black Diamond Rookies White Onyx

This insert incorporates a new design with Pearl Light F/X treatment and also has the Quadruple Black Diamond logo. Each is sequentially numbered to 2,250. Cards have an "ON" prefix.

		NM/M
Complete Set (30):		75.00
Common Player:		.50
Minor Stars:		1.00
Production 2,250 Sets		
1	Peyton Manning	4.00
2	Corey Dillon	1.00
3	Jerome Bettis	1.00
4	Brett Favre	5.00
5	Napoleon Kaufman	1.00
6	Joey Galloway	1.00
7	John Elway	3.00
8	Troy Aikman	3.00
9	Robert Smith	.50
10	Kordell Stewart	1.00
11	Garrison Hearst	1.00
12	Curtis Enis	1.00
13	Dan Marino	5.00
14	Jimmy Smith	.50
15	Steve Young	3.00
16	Ryan Leaf	.50
17	Steve McNair	1.00
18	Randy Moss	4.00
19	Curtis Martin	1.00
20	Barry Sanders	4.00
21	Rob Johnson	1.00
22	Emmitt Smith	4.00
23	Jake Plummer	1.00
24	Antonio Freeman	.50
25	Mark Brunell	1.00
26	Warrick Dunn	1.00
27	Eddie George	2.00
28	Jerry Rice	4.00
29	Drew Bledsoe	3.00
30	Terrell Davis	3.00

1998 Upper Deck Encore

Encore was a fine-tuned version of Upper Deck's 1998 NFL Series I product that utilized a special rainbow-foil treatment on 150 of the earlier set's 255 cards (120 regular player cards and 30 Star Rookie subset cards). The rookies could be found 1:4 packs. The F/X set is a direct parallel of the entire Encore set. The differentiation comes in a color shift with a special "Encore F/X" call-out featured on the card fronts and backs. Singles are sequentially numbered to 125.

		NM/M
Complete Set (150):		175.00
Common Player:		.20
Minor Stars:		.40
Common Rookie:		2.00
Inserted 1:4		
F/X Gold Cards:		8X-20X
F/X Gold Rookies:		2X-4X
Production 125 Sets		
Pack (6):		4.75
Wax Box (24):		80.00
1	*Peyton Manning*	25.00
2	*Ryan Leaf*	3.00
3	*Andre Wadsworth*	3.00
4	*Charles Woodson*	5.00
5	*Curtis Enis*	3.00
6	*Fred Taylor*	6.00
7	*Duane Starks*	3.00
8	*Keith Brooking*	3.00
9	*Takeo Spikes*	4.00
10	*Kevin Dyson*	4.00
11	*Robert Edwards*	4.00
12	*Randy Moss*	20.00
13	*John Avery*	4.00
14	*Marcus Nash*	4.00
15	*Jerome Pathon*	4.00
16	*Jacquez Green*	4.00
17	*Robert Holcombe*	4.00
18	*Pat Johnson*	4.00
19	*Skip Hicks*	4.00
20	*Ahman Green*	20.00
21	*Brian Griese*	12.00
22	*Hines Ward*	8.00
23	*Tavian Banks*	3.00
24	*Tony Simmons*	2.00
25	*Rashaan Shehee*	2.00
26	*R.W. McQuarters*	3.00
27	*Jon Ritchie*	2.00
28	*Ryan Sutter*	2.00
29	*Tim Dwight*	4.00
30	*Charlie Batch*	4.00
31	Chris Chandler	.40
32	Jamal Anderson	1.00
33	Terance Mathis	.20
34	Jake Plummer	.75
35	Mario Bates	.20
36	Frank Sanders	.20
37	Adrian Murrell	.20
38	Jim Harbaugh	.40
39	Michael Jackson	.20
40	Jermaine Lewis	.20
41	Doug Flutie	.75
42	Rob Johnson	.40
43	Antowain Smith	1.00
44	Eric Moulds	1.00
45	Thurman Thomas	.40
46	Kevin Greene	.20
47	Fred Lane	.40
48	Rae Carruth	.20
49	William Floyd	.20
50	Erik Kramer	.20
51	Edgar Bennett	.20
52	Curtis Conway	.20
53	Bobby Engram	.20
54	Jeff Blake	.40
55	Carl Pickens	.75
56	Darnay Scott	.20
57	Corey Dillon	1.50
58	Troy Aikman	2.50
59	Michael Irvin	.40
60	Emmitt Smith	3.50
61	Deion Sanders	1.00
62	John Elway	3.00
63	Terrell Davis	2.00
64	Rod Smith	.40
65	Shannon Sharpe	.40
66	Ed McCaffrey	.75
67	Barry Sanders	5.00
68	Scott Mitchell	.40
69	Herman Moore	.75
70	Johnnie Morton	.20
71	Brett Favre	5.00
72	Dorsey Levens	.40
73	Reggie White	.50
74	Antonio Freeman	.50
75	Robert Brooks	.20
76	Marshall Faulk	2.00
77	Marvin Harrison	.40
78	Mark Brunell	1.00
79	Keenan McCardell	.40
80	Jimmy Smith	.75
81	Elvis Grbac	.20
82	Andre Rison	.40
83	Tony Gonzalez	.20
84	Derrick Thomas	.20
85	Dan Marino	3.50
86	Karim Abdul	1.00
87	O.J. McDuffie	.40
88	Zach Thomas	.40
89	Brad Johnson	1.00
90	Cris Carter	1.00
91	Jake Reed	.20
92	Robert Smith	.40
93	John Randle	.20
94	Randall Cunningham	1.00
95	Drew Bledsoe	2.00
96	Terry Glenn	1.00
97	Ben Coates	.40
98	Danny Wuerffel	.20
99	Andre Hastings	.20
100	Troy Davis	.20
101	Danny Kanell	.20
102	Tiki Barber	.20
103	Amani Toomer	.20
104	Vinny Testaverde	.40
105	Glenn Foley	.40
106	Curtis Martin	1.00
107	Keyshawn Johnson	1.00
108	Wayne Chrebet	.75
109	Jeff George	.40
110	Napoleon Kaufman	.50
111	Tim Brown	.40
112	James Jett	.20
113	Bobby Hoying	.20
114	Charlie Garner	.20
115	Irving Fryar	.20
116	Kordell Stewart	1.00
117	Jerome Bettis	1.00
118	Will Blackwell	.20
119	Charles Johnson	.20
120	Tony Banks	.40
121	Amp Lee	.20
122	Isaac Bruce	.40
123	Eddie Kennison	.40
124	Natrone Means	.75
125	Junior Seau	.40
126	Bryan Still	.20
127	Steve Young	1.50
128	Jerry Rice	4.00
129	Garrison Hearst	.75
130	J.J. Stokes	.40
131	Terrell Owens	1.00
132	Warren Moon	.40
133	Jon Kitna	.40
134	Ricky Watters	.40
135	Joey Galloway	1.00
136	Trent Dilfer	.40
137	Warrick Dunn	1.00
138	Mike Alstott	1.00
139	Bert Emanuel	.20
140	Reidel Anthony	.20
141	Steve McNair	2.00
142	Yancey Thigpen	.20
143	Eddie George	1.50
144	Chris Sanders	.20
145	Gus Frerotte	.20
146	Terry Allen	.40
147	Michael Westbrook	.20
148	Troy Aikman CL	1.25
149	Dan Marino CL	1.50
150	Randy Moss CL	5.00

1998 Upper Deck Encore Constant Threat

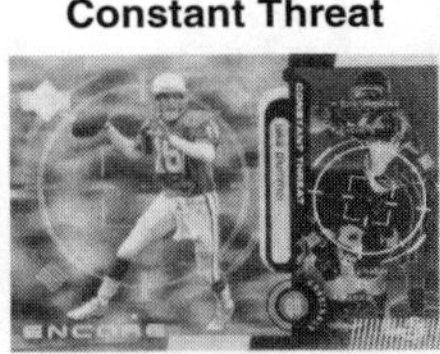

This lineup showcases high-impact players who could affect the outcome of a game in the blink of an eye. Singles have the prefix "CT" before the card number and were inserted 1:11 packs.

		NM/M
Complete Set (15):		25.00
Common Player:		1.00
Inserted 1:11		
1	Dan Marino	4.00
2	Peyton Manning	4.00
3	Randy Moss	4.00
4	Brett Favre	5.00
5	Mark Brunell	1.00
6	John Elway	3.00
7	Ryan Leaf	1.00
8	Jake Plummer	1.00
9	Terrell Davis	2.00
10	Barry Sanders	4.00
11	Emmitt Smith	4.00
12	Curtis Martin	2.00
13	Eddie George	2.00
14	Warrick Dunn	1.00
15	Curtis Enis	1.00

1998 Upper Deck Encore Driving Forces

This insert consists of 14 NFL superstars, including top QB's, running backs and wide receivers. Singles have the prefix "F" before the card number and were inserted 1:23. The parallel F/X Golds are in gold foil and were sequentially numbered to 1,500.

		NM/M
Complete Set (14):		35.00
Common Player:		1.00
Inserted 1:23		
F/X Golds:		2X
Production 1,500 Cards		
1	Terrell Davis	3.00
2	Barry Sanders	4.00
3	Doug Flutie	1.00
4	Mark Brunell	1.00
5	Garrison Hearst	1.00
6	Jamal Anderson	4.00
7	Jerry Rice	4.00
8	John Elway	3.00
9	Robert Smith	1.00
10	Kordell Stewart	1.00
11	Eddie George	2.00
12	Antonio Freeman	1.00
13	Dan Marino	5.00
14	Steve Young	3.00

1998 Upper Deck Encore Milestones

This collection includes cards that will boast special "UD Milestones" stamps. Designated sequential numbering for each gold-foil card signifies a remarkable milestone reached by that player for the '98 season. For example, Dan Marino (400th touchdown pass thrown on 11/28/98) will be crash-numbered to 400.

		NM/M
Common Player:		50.00
1	Peyton Manning/26	175.00
12	Randy Moss/17	300.00
60	Emmitt Smith/124	100.00
62	John Elway/50	150.00
63	Terrell Davis/30	125.00
67	Barry Sanders/100	125.00
85	Dan Marino/400	60.00
128	Jerry Rice/184	50.00

1998 Upper Deck Encore Rookie Encore

The 1998 season produced a host of solid first-year players and this lineup captures the best of the best. Each card has the prefix "RE" before the number and were found 1:23 packs. The FX Gold parallel singles are in gold foil and are sequentially numbered to 500.

		NM/M
Complete Set (10):		35.00
Common Player:		1.00
Inserted 1:23		
F/X Golds:		2X-4X
Production 500 Sets		
1	Randy Moss	12.00
2	Peyton Manning	12.00
3	Charlie Batch	2.00
4	Fred Taylor	4.00
5	Robert Edwards	2.00
6	Curtis Enis	1.00
7	Robert Holcombe	1.00
8	Ryan Leaf	1.00
9	John Avery	1.00
10	Tim Dwight	2.00

1998 Upper Deck Encore Super Powers

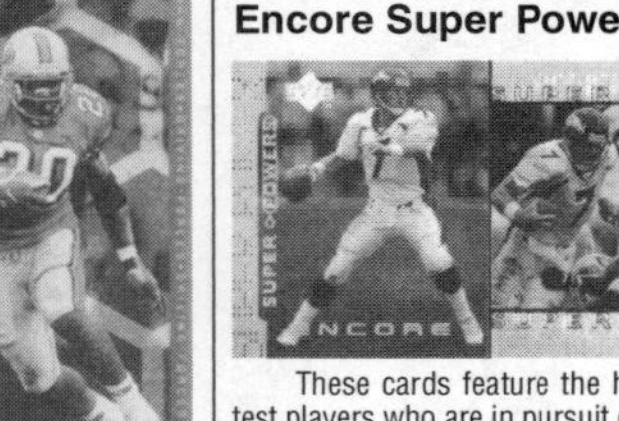

These cards feature the hottest players who are in pursuit of a Super Bowl ring. Singles are on rainbow-foil stock and were inserted 1:11 packs. Cards are numbered with a "S" prefix.

		NM/M
Complete Set (15):		35.00
Common Player:		1.00
Inserted 1:11		
1	Dan Marino	5.00
2	Napoleon Kaufman	1.00
3	Brett Favre	5.00
4	John Elway	3.00
5	Randy Moss	4.00
6	Kordell Stewart	1.00
7	Mark Brunell	1.00
8	Peyton Manning	4.00
9	Emmitt Smith	4.00
10	Jake Plummer	1.00
11	Eddie George	1.00
12	Warrick Dunn	1.00
13	Jerome Bettis	1.00
14	Terrell Davis	3.00
15	Fred Taylor	2.00

1998 Upper Deck Encore Superstar Encore

This insert includes the top six players in the league including rookie Randy Moss. Each single has the prefix "RR" before the card number and were inserted 1:23 packs. The F/X Gold parallel singles were limited to only 25 of each.

		NM/M
Complete Set (6):		20.00
Common Player:		1.00
Inserted 1:23		
F/X Gold Cards:		8X-20X
F/X Gold Rookies:		5X-10X
Production 25 Sets		
1	Brett Favre	5.00
2	Barry Sanders	4.00
3	Mark Brunell	1.00
4	Emmitt Smith	4.00
5	Randy Moss	5.00
6	Terrell Davis	3.00

1998 Upper Deck Encore UD Authentics

This collection includes autographed cards of five NFL superstars: Mark Brunell, Dan Marino, Randy Moss, Terrell Davis and Joe Montana. Singles were inserted 1:288 packs.

		NM/M
Complete Set (5):		750.00
Common Player:		75.00
Inserted 1:288		
MB	Mark Brunell	40.00
DM	Dan Marino	175.00
RM	Randy Moss	175.00
TD	Terrell Davis	75.00
JM	Joe Montana	125.00

1999 UD Ionix

UD Ionix is a 90-card set with 30 seeded rookies found 1:4 packs. Each card is super thick, double laminated and metalized. Inserts include: Reciprocal, Astronomix, Electric Forces, HoloGrFX, Power F/X, UD Authentics and Warp Zone.

	NM/M
Complete Set (90):	125.00
Common Player:	.25
Minor Stars:	.50
Common Rookie:	1.50
Inserted 1:4	
Pack (4):	2.00
Wax Box (20):	30.00
1 Jake Plummer	1.00
2 Adrian Murrell	.25
3 Jamal Anderson	1.00
4 Chris Chandler	.50
5 Priest Holmes	2.00
6 Michael Jackson	.50
7 Antowain Smith	1.00
8 Doug Flutie	1.00
9 Tshimanga Biakabutuka	.25
10 Muhsin Muhammad	.25
11 Erik Kramer	.25
12 Curtis Enis	.50
13 Corey Dillon	1.00
14 Ty Detmer	.50
15 Justin Armour	.25
16 Troy Aikman	2.00
17 Emmitt Smith	3.00
18 John Elway	3.00
19 Terrell Davis	1.50
20 Barry Sanders	3.00
21 Charlie Batch	.50
22 Brett Favre	4.00
23 Dorsey Levens	1.00
24 Marshall Faulk	1.00
25 Peyton Manning	3.00
26 Mark Brunell	1.00
27 Fred Taylor	1.00
28 Elvis Grbac	.50
29 Andre Rison	.50
30 Dan Marino	3.00
31 Karim Abdul	.75
32 Randall Cunningham	.75
33 Randy Moss	3.00
34 Drew Bledsoe	1.50
35 Terry Glenn	.75
36 Danny Wuerffel	.25
37 Kent Graham	.25
38 Gary Brown	.25
39 Vinny Testaverde	.50
40 Keyshawn Johnson	.75
41 Napoleon Kaufman	.75
42 Tim Brown	.50
43 Koy Detmer	.25
44 Duce Staley	.25
45 Kordell Stewart	1.00
46 Jerome Bettis	1.00
47 Isaac Bruce	.75
48 Robert Holcombe	.25
49 Jim Harbaugh	.50
50 Natrone Means	.75
51 Steve Young	1.50
52 Jerry Rice	3.00
53 Jon Kitna	.75
54 Joey Galloway	.75
55 Warrick Dunn	1.00
56 Trent Dilfer	.75
57 Steve McNair	1.25
58 Eddie George	1.25
59 Skip Hicks	.50
60 Michael Westbrook	.50
61 *Tim Couch*	3.00
62 *Ricky Williams*	5.00
63 *Daunte Culpepper*	10.00
64 *Akili Smith*	3.00
65 *Donovan McNabb*	10.00
66 *Michael Bishop*	3.00
67 *Brock Huard*	3.00
68 *Torry Holt*	5.00
69 *Cade McNown*	3.00
70 *Shaun King*	3.00
71 *Champ Bailey*	3.00
72 *Chris Claiborne*	2.00
73 *Jevon Kearse*	3.00
74 *D'Wayne Bates*	2.50
75 *David Boston*	5.00
76 *Edgerrin James*	10.00
77 *Sedrick Irvin*	2.50
78 *Dameane Douglas*	2.50
79 *Troy Edwards*	3.00
80 *Ebenezer Ekuban*	1.50
81 *Kevin Faulk*	3.00
82 *Joe Germaine*	2.50
83 *Kevin Johnson*	3.00
84 *Andy Katzenmoyer*	2.50
85 *Rob Konrad*	1.50
86 *Chris McAlister*	2.50
87 *Peerless Price*	4.00
88 *Tai Streets*	2.50
89 *Autry Denson*	2.50
90 *Amos Zereoue*	2.50

1999 UD Ionix Reciprocal

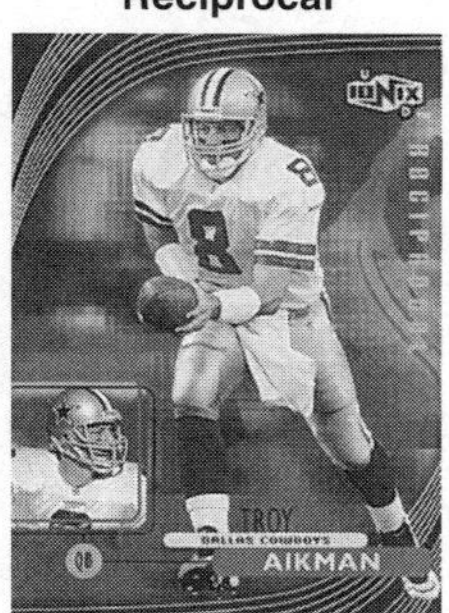

This is a parallel to the base and has the prefix R before the card number. Cards #1-60 were found 1:6 packs and the rookies #61-90 were inserted 1:19 packs. The word "Reciprocal" is printed on the fronts of each card.

Reciprocal Cards:	2X-4X
Inserted 1:6	
Reciprocal Rookies:	2X
Inserted 1:19	

1999 UD Ionix Astronomix

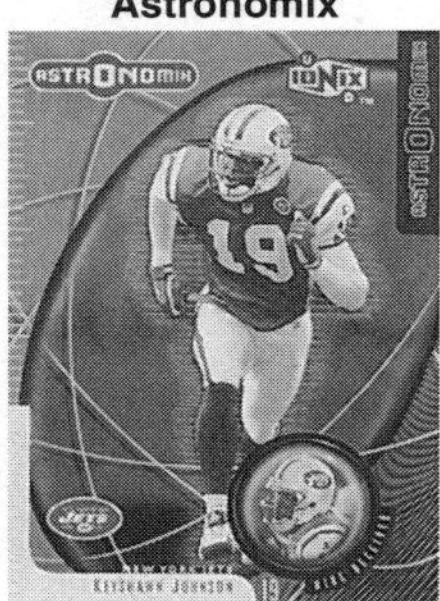

Each card in this 25-card set highlights a statistical achievement by that particular player. Singles were inserted 1:23 packs.

	NM/M
Complete Set (25):	55.00
Common Player:	1.00
Inserted 1:23	
1 Keyshawn Johnson	1.00
2 Emmitt Smith	4.00
3 Eddie George	2.00
4 Fred Taylor	2.00
5 Peyton Manning	4.00
6 John Elway	4.00
7 Brett Favre	5.00
8 Terrell Davis	3.00
9 Mark Brunell	2.00
10 Dan Marino	5.00
11 Randall Cunningham	1.00
12 Steve McNair	1.00
13 Jamal Anderson	1.00
14 Barry Sanders	4.00
15 Jake Plummer	2.00
16 Drew Bledsoe	4.00
17 Jerome Bettis	1.00
18 Jerry Rice	4.00
19 Warrick Dunn	1.00
20 Steve Young	3.00
21 Terrell Owens	1.00
22 Ricky Williams	5.00
23 Akili Smith	1.00
24 Cade McNown	1.00
25 David Boston	2.00

1999 UD Ionix Electric Forces

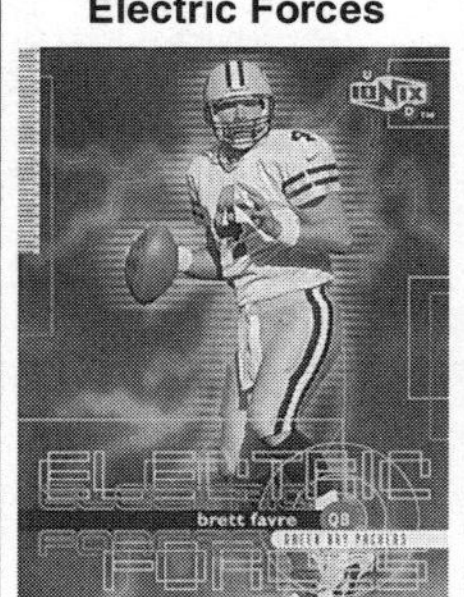

This 20-card set includes the most collectible NFL stars of today. Singles were inserted 1:6 packs.

	NM/M
Complete Set (20):	30.00
Common Player:	1.00
Inserted 1:6	
1 Ricky Williams	5.00
2 Tim Couch	3.00
3 Daunte Culpepper	4.00
4 Akili Smith	1.00
5 Cade McNown	1.00
6 Donovan McNabb	4.00
7 Brock Huard	1.00
8 Michael Bishop	1.00
9 Torry Holt	3.00
10 Peerless Price	3.00
11 Peyton Manning	4.00
12 Jake Plummer	1.00
13 John Elway	4.00
14 Mark Brunell	1.00
15 Steve Young	2.50
16 Jamal Anderson	1.00
17 Kordell Stewart	1.00
18 Eddie George	1.00
19 Fred Taylor	2.00
20 Brett Favre	4.00

A card number in parenthese ( ) indicates the set is unnumbered.

1999 UD Ionix HoloGrFX

The top NFL stars and rookies are included in this 10-card set. Singles were issued at 1:1,500 packs.

	NM/M
Common Player:	50.00
Inserted 1:1,500	
1 Ricky Williams	75.00
2 Tim Couch	45.00
3 Cade McNown	40.00
4 Peyton Manning	60.00
5 Jake Plummer	40.00
6 Randy Moss	60.00
7 Barry Sanders	100.00
8 Jamal Anderson	40.00
9 Terrell Davis	50.00
10 Brett Favre	125.00

1999 UD Ionix Power F/X

The game's most impressive talents, with a mix of rookies and veterans are highlighted in this 9-card set. Singles were inserted 1:11 packs.

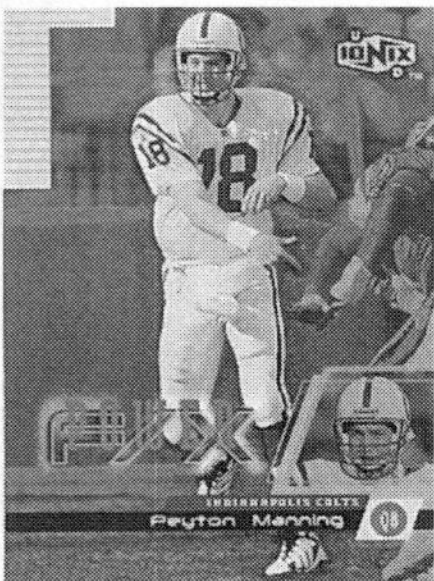

	NM/M
Complete Set (9):	20.00
Common Player:	1.00
Inserted 1:11	
1 Peyton Manning	4.00
2 Randy Moss	4.00
3 Terrell Davis	3.00
4 Steve Young	3.00
5 Dan Marino	5.00
6 Warrick Dunn	1.00
7 Keyshawn Johnson	1.00
8 Barry Sanders	4.00
9 Tim Couch	3.00

1999 UD Ionix UD Authentics

This 10-card set includes autographs from the top rookies from the 1999 draft. Each player signed 100 cards each except for Ricky Williams who signed only 50.

	NM/M
Common Player:	40.00
Production 100 Sets	
Ricky Williams Only Signed 50	
MB Michael Bishop	40.00
TC Tim Couch	75.00
DC Daunte Culpepper	100.00
TH Torry Holt	40.00
BH Brock Huard	25.00
SK Shaun King	25.00
DM Donovan McNabb	115.00
CM Cade McNown	40.00
AS Akili Smith	40.00
RW Ricky Williams	275.00

1999 UD Ionix Warp Zone

A mix of stars and rookies from the NFL make up this 15-card set that was inserted 1:108 packs.

	NM/M
Complete Set (15):	375.00
Common Player:	10.00
Inserted 1:108	
1 Ricky Williams	60.00
2 Tim Couch	50.00
3 Cade McNown	25.00
4 Daunte Culpepper	50.00
5 Akili Smith	10.00
6 Brock Huard	10.00
7 Donovan McNabb	40.00
8 Jake Plummer	10.00
9 Jamal Anderson	10.00
10 John Elway	40.00
11 Randy Moss	50.00
12 Terrell Davis	30.00
13 Troy Aikman	25.00
14 Barry Sanders	50.00
15 Fred Taylor	15.00

1999 Upper Deck

Upper Deck is a 270-card set that includes 45 seeded rookies found 1:4 packs. Each base card has a parallel Exclusive Silver and Exclusive Gold. Other inserts include: 21 TD Salute, Game Jersey, Game Jersey Patch, Highlight Zone, Livewires, PowerDeck, Quarterback Class and Strike Force.

	NM/M
Complete Set (270):	110.00
Common Player:	.15
Minor Stars:	.30
Common Rookie:	1.25
Inserted 1:4	
Pack (10):	2.50
Wax Box (24):	40.00
1 Jake Plummer	.50
2 Adrian Murrell	.15
3 Rob Moore	.30
4 Larry Centers	.15
5 Simeon Rice	.15
6 Andre Wadsworth	.15
7 Frank Sanders	.30
8 Tim Dwight	.50
9 Ray Buchanan	.15
10 Chris Chandler	.30
11 Jamal Anderson	.50
12 O.J. Santiago	.15
13 Danny Kanell	.15
14 Terance Mathis	.15
15 Priest Holmes	.50
16 Tony Banks	.30
17 Ray Lewis	.15
18 Patrick Johnson	.15
19 Michael Jackson	.15
20 Michael McCrary	.15
21 Jermaine Lewis	.30
22 Eric Moulds	.50
23 Doug Flutie	.50
24 Antowain Smith	.50
25 Rob Johnson	.30
26 Bruce Smith	.15
27 Andre Reed	.15
28 Thurman Thomas	.15
29 Fred Lane	.15
30 Wesley Walls	.15
31 Tshimanga Biakabutuka	.15
32 Kevin Greene	.15
33 Steve Beuerlein	.15
34 Muhsin Muhammad	.15
35 Rae Carruth	.15
36 Bobby Engram	.15
37 Curtis Enis	.30
38 Edgar Bennett	.15
39 Erik Kramer	.15
40 Steve Stenstrom	.15
41 Alonzo Mayes	.15
42 Curtis Conway	.30
43 Tony McGee	.15
44 Darnay Scott	.15
45 Jeff Blake	.30
46 Corey Dillon	.50
47 Ki-Jana Carter	.15
48 Takeo Spikes	.15
49 Carl Pickens	.30
50 Ty Detmer	.15
51 Leslie Shepherd	.15
52 Terry Kirby	.15
53 Marquez Pope	.15
54 Antonio Langham	.15
55 Jamir Miller	.15
56 Derrick Alexander	.15
57 Troy Aikman	1.25
58 Raghib Ismail	.15
59 Emmitt Smith	2.00
60 Michael Irvin	.30
61 David LaFleur	.15
62 Chris Warren	.15
63 Deion Sanders	.50
64 Greg Ellis	.15
65 John Elway	2.00
66 Bubby Brister	.30
67 Terrell Davis	1.00
68 Ed McCaffrey	.30
69 John Mobley	.15
70 Bill Romanowski	.15
71 Rod Smith	.30
72 Shannon Sharpe	.30
73 Charlie Batch	.75
74 Germane Crowell	.30
75 Johnnie Morton	.15
76 Barry Sanders	2.00
77 Robert Porcher	.15
78 Stephen Boyd	.15
79 Herman Moore	.50
80 Brett Favre	2.50
81 Mark Chmura	.30
82 Antonio Freeman	.50
83 Robert Brooks	.15
84 Vonnie Holliday	.15
85 Bill Schroeder	.15
86 Dorsey Levens	.50
87 Santana Dotson	.15
88 Peyton Manning	2.00
89 Jerome Pathon	.15
90 Marvin Harrison	.30
91 Ellis Johnson	.15
92 Ken Dilger	.15
93 E.G. Green	.15
94 Jeff Burris	.15
95 Mark Brunell	.50
96 Fred Taylor	.50
97 Jimmy Smith	.30
98 James Stewart	.15
99 Kyle Brady	.15
100 Dave Thomas	.15
101 Keenan McCardell	.15
102 Elvis Grbac	.30
103 Tony Gonzalez	.30
104 Andre Rison	.30
105 Donnell Bennett	.15
106 Derrick Thomas	.15
107 Warren Moon	.30
108 Derrick Alexander	.15
109 Dan Marino	2.00
110 O.J. McDuffie	.30
111 Karim Abdul	.30
112 John Avery	.30
113 Sam Madison	.15
114 Jason Taylor	.15
115 Zach Thomas	.30
116 Randall Cunningham	.50
117 Randy Moss	2.00
118 Cris Carter	.50
119 Jake Reed	.15
120 Matthew Hatchette	.15
121 John Randle	.15
122 Robert Smith	.30
123 Drew Bledsoe	1.00
124 Ben Coates	.30
125 Terry Glenn	.30
126 Ty Law	.15
127 Tony Simmons	.30
128 Ted Johnson	.15
129 Tony Carter	.15
130 Willie McGinest	.15
131 Danny Wuerffel	.15
132 Cameron Cleeland	.15
133 Eddie Kennison	.15
134 Joe Johnson	.15
135 Andre Hastings	.15
136 La'Roi Glover	.15
137 Kent Graham	.15
138 Tiki Barber	.15
139 Gary Brown	.15
140 Ike Hilliard	.15
141 Jason Sehorn	.15
142 Michael Strahan	.15
143 Amani Toomer	.15
144 Kerry Collins	.30
145 Vinny Testaverde	.30
146 Wayne Chrebet	.30
147 Curtis Martin	.50
148 Mo Lewis	.15
149 Aaron Glenn	.15
150 Steve Atwater	.15
151 Keyshawn Johnson	.50
152 James Farrior	.15
153 Rich Gannon	.15
154 Tim Brown	.30
155 Darrell Russell	.15
156 Rickey Dudley	.15
157 Charles Woodson	.50
158 James Jett	.15
159 Napoleon Kaufman	.50
160 Duce Staley	.30
161 Doug Pederson	.15
162 Bobby Hoying	.15
163 Koy Detmer	.15
164 Kevin Turner	.15
165 Charles Johnson	.15
166 Mike Mamula	.15
167 Jerome Bettis	.50
168 Courtney Hawkins	.15
169 Will Blackwell	.15
170 Kordell Stewart	.75
171 Richard Huntley	.15
172 Levon Kirkland	.15
173 Hines Ward	.30
174 Trent Green	.30
175 Marshall Faulk	.50
176 Az-Zahir Hakim	.15
177 Amp Lee	.15
178 Robert Holcombe	.30
179 Isaac Bruce	.30
180 Kevin Carter	.15
181 Jim Harbaugh	.30
182 Junior Seau	.30
183 Natrone Means	.50
184 Ryan Leaf	.50
185 Charlie Jones	.15
186 Rodney Harrison	.15
187 Mikhael Ricks	.15
188 Steve Young	.75
189 Terrell Owens	.50
190 Jerry Rice	2.00
191 J.J. Stokes	.30
192 Irv Smith	.15
193 Bryant Young	.15
194 Garrison Hearst	.30
195 Jon Kitna	.75
196 Ahman Green	.30
197 Joey Galloway	.50
198 Ricky Watters	.30
199 Chad Brown	.15
200 Shawn Springs	.15
201 Mike Pritchard	.15
202 Trent Dilfer	.30
203 Reidel Anthony	.30
204 Bert Emanuel	.15
205 Warrick Dunn	.50
206 Jacquez Green	.30
207 Hardy Nickerson	.15
208 Mike Alstott	.50
209 Eddie George	.75
210 Steve McNair	.75
211 Kevin Dyson	.30
212 Frank Wycheck	.15
213 Jackie Harris	.15
214 Blaine Bishop	.15
215 Yancey Thigpen	.15
216 Brad Johnson	.50
217 Rodney Peete	.15
218 Michael Westbrook	.30
219 Skip Hicks	.50
220 Brian Mitchell	.15
221 Dan Wilkinson	.15
222 Dana Stubblefield	.15
223 Set Checklist #1	.15
224 Checklist #2	.15
225 Checklist #3	.15
226 *Champ Bailey*	4.00
227 *Chris McAlister*	2.50
228 *Jevon Kearse*	4.00
229 *Ebenezer Ekuban*	1.25
230 *Chris Claiborne*	2.50
231 *Andy Katzenmoyer*	2.50
232 *Tim Couch*	4.00
233 *Daunte Culpepper*	12.00
234 *Akili Smith*	3.00
235 *Donovan McNabb*	12.00
236 *Sean Bennett*	2.50
237 *Brock Huard*	3.00
238 *Cade McNown*	3.00
239 *Shaun King*	3.00
240 *Joe Germaine*	2.50
241 *Ricky Williams*	5.00
242 *Edgerrin James*	12.00
243 *Sedrick Irvin*	2.50
244 *Kevin Faulk*	3.00
245 *Rob Konrad*	2.50
246 *James Johnson*	2.50
247 *Amos Zereoue*	2.50
248 *Torry Holt*	6.00
249 *D'Wayne Bates*	2.50
250 *David Boston*	6.00
251 *Dameane Douglas*	1.25
252 *Troy Edwards*	3.00
253 *Kevin Johnson*	3.00
254 *Peerless Price*	5.00
255 *Antoine Winfield*	2.50
256 *Michael Cloud*	2.50
257 *Joe Montgomery*	2.50
258 *Jermaine Fazande*	2.50
259 *Scott Covington*	1.25
260 *Aaron Brooks*	12.00
261 *Patrick Kerney*	1.25
262 *Cecil Collins*	2.50
263 *Chris Greisen*	1.25
264 *Craig Yeast*	1.25
265 *Karsten Bailey*	1.25
266 *Reginald Kelly*	1.25
267 *Travis McGriff*	1.25
268 *Jeff Paulk*	1.25
269 *Jim Kleinsasser*	2.50
270 *Darrin Chiaverini*	2.50

1999 Upper Deck Exclusives Silver

This is a parallel to the base set and is the same card except for on the bottom of the card the words "UD Exclusives" are printed on it along with the sequential numbering to 100 on gold foil.

UDE Cards:	10X-30X
UDE Rookies:	3X
Production 100 Sets	

1999 Upper Deck Exclusives Gold

This is a parallel to the base set with each single sequentially numbered to only 1.

Production 1 Set

1999 Upper Deck 21 TD Salute

This 10-card insert is a salute to Denver running back Terrell Davis for becoming the fourth NFL player in history to run for more than 2,000 yards in a single season. He also set a Broncos' franchise record with 21 rushing touchdowns. Singles were found 1:23 packs. A parallel Silver set was made and sequentially numbered to 100 and a Gold limited to only one.

		NM/M
Complete Set (10):		30.00
Common Player:		3.00
Inserted 1:23		
Quantum Silver:		3X-5X
Production 100 Sets		
Quantum Gold		
Production 1 Set		
1	Terrell Davis	3.00
2	Terrell Davis	3.00
3	Terrell Davis	3.00
4	Terrell Davis	3.00
5	Terrell Davis	3.00
6	Terrell Davis	3.00
7	Terrell Davis	3.00
8	Terrell Davis	3.00
9	Terrell Davis	3.00
10	Terrell Davis	3.00

1999 Upper Deck Game Jersey

Singles from this 11-card set were inserted in both hobby and retail product at 1:2,500 packs. Each single has a piece of actual game-used (or rookie photo shoot-used) jersey on the fronts of the cards. Both Terrell Davis and Cade McNown signed cards to their jersey numbers of 30 and 8.

		NM/M
Common Player:		40.00
Inserted 1:2,500		
JA	Jamal Anderson	40.00
DB	Drew Bledsoe	40.00
TC	Tim Couch	75.00
TC-A	Tim Couch Auto.	40.00
TD	Terrell Davis	75.00
TD-A	Terrell Davis Auto.	225.00
DF	Doug Flutie	40.00
EJ	Edgerrin James	75.00
KJ	Keyshawn Johnson	40.00
DM	Dan Marino	125.00
RM	Randy Moss	100.00
AS	Akili Smith	40.00
SY	Steve Young	40.00

1999 Upper Deck Game Jersey Hobby

This 12-card insert could only be found in hobby product at 1:288 packs. Each single includes a piece of game-used (or rookie photo shoot-used) jersey on the fronts of the cards. Both Tim Couch and Brock Huard signed cards to their jersey number of 2 and 5.

		NM/M
Common Player:		40.00
Inserted 1:288		
TA	Troy Aikman	150.00
DV	David Boston	75.00
DC	Daunte Culpepper	100.00
JE	John Elway	150.00
BH	Brock Huard	30.00
BH-A	Brock Huard Auto.	40.00
PM	Peyton Manning	150.00
MC	Donovan McNabb	100.00
CM	Cade McNown	40.00
CM-A	Cade McNown Auto.	40.00
EM	Eric Moulds	40.00
JP	Jake Plummer	50.00
JR	Jerry Rice	150.00
BS	Barry Sanders	175.00

1999 Upper Deck Game Jersey Patch

Each single in this 20-card set has a piece of the team logo from the jersey on the card. Singles were inserted 1:7,500 packs.

		NM/M
Common Player:		75.00
Inserted 1:7,500		
TA	Troy Aikman	275.00
JA	Jamal Anderson	75.00
DB	Drew Bledsoe	200.00
DV	David Boston	100.00
TC	Tim Couch	250.00
DC	Daunte Culpepper	225.00
TD	Terrell Davis	175.00
JE	John Elway	275.00
DF	Doug Flutie	75.00
BH	Brock Huard	50.00
EJ	Edgerrin James	225.00
PM	Peyton Manning	225.00
DM	Dan Marino	250.00
DV	Donovan McNabb	175.00
CM	Cade McNown	50.00
RM	Randy Moss	225.00
JR	Jerry Rice	225.00
BS	Barry Sanders	250.00
AS	Akili Smith	50.00
SY	Steve Young	200.00

Values quoted in this guide reflect the retail price of a card—the price a collector can expect to pay when buying a card from a dealer. The wholesale price—that which a collector can expect to receive from a dealer when selling cards—will be significantly lower, depending on desirability and condition.

1999 Upper Deck Highlight Zone

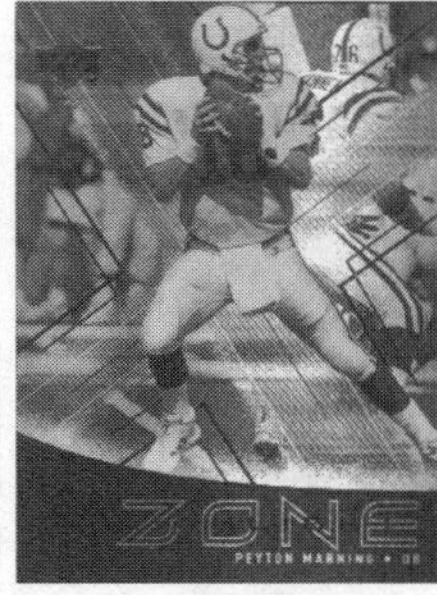

This 20-card insert spotlights the top players in the NFL. Singles were printed on a foil board and found 1:23 packs. A Silver parallel was printed and sequentially numbered to 100, along with a Gold numbered to only 1.

		NM/M
Complete Set (20):		60.00
Common Player:		1.00
Minor Stars:		2.00
Inserted 1:23		
Quantum Silver:		3X-5X
Production 100 Sets		
Quantum Gold		
Production 1 Set		
1	Terrell Davis	3.00
2	Ricky Williams	5.00
3	Akili Smith	1.00
4	Charlie Batch	1.00
5	Jake Plummer	2.00
6	Emmitt Smith	4.00
7	Dan Marino	5.00
8	Tim Couch	3.00
9	Randy Moss	4.00
10	Troy Aikman	4.00
11	Barry Sanders	4.00
12	Jerry Rice	4.00
13	Mark Brunell	2.00
14	Jamal Anderson	1.00
15	Peyton Manning	5.00
16	Jerome Bettis	1.00
17	Donovan McNabb	4.00
18	Steve Young	3.00
19	Keyshawn Johnson	2.00
20	Brett Favre	6.00

1999 Upper Deck Livewires

Each card in this 15-card set has actual printed transcripts of statements made by big-name players during games. Singles were inserted 1:10 packs. A Silver parallel was produced and numbered to 100, along with a Gold that was limited to only one set.

		NM/M
Complete Set (15):		25.00
Common Player:		.50
Minor Stars:		1.00
Inserted 1:10		
Quantum Silver:		3X-5X
Production 100 Sets		
Quantum Gold:		
Production 1 Set		
1	Jake Plummer	1.00
2	Jamal Anderson	.50
3	Emmitt Smith	4.00
4	John Elway	3.00
5	Barry Sanders	4.00
6	Brett Favre	5.00
7	Mark Brunell	.50
8	Fred Taylor	.50
9	Randy Moss	4.00
10	Drew Bledsoe	3.00
11	Keyshawn Johnson	1.00
12	Jerome Bettis	1.00
13	Kordell Stewart	1.00
14	Terrell Owens	1.00
15	Eddie George	1.00

1999 Upper Deck PowerDeck I

Each of these singles are an interactive card that comes to life with game-action footage, sound, photos and career highlights of the featured player. Singles were found 1:288 packs.

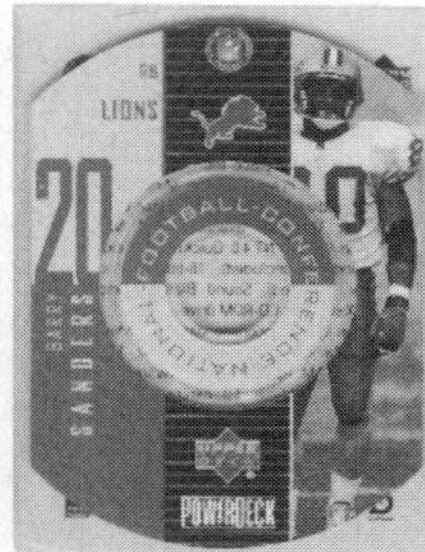

		NM/M
Complete Set (8):		75.00
Common Player:		5.00
Inserted 1:288		
TC-PD	Tim Couch	15.00
DC-PD	Daunte Culpepper	15.00
JE-PD	John Elway	25.00
PM-PD	Peyton Manning	25.00
DM-PD	Dan Marino	30.00
CM-PD	Cade McNown	5.00
BS-PD	Barry Sanders	25.00
AS-PD	Akili Smith	5.00

1999 Upper Deck PowerDeck II

Each single in this set is a interactive card with game-action footage, sound, photos and career highlights of that featured player. Singles were found 1:24 packs.

		NM/M
Complete Set (8):		25.00
Common Player:		1.00
Inserted 1:24		
TA-PD	Troy Aikman	4.00
TD-PD	Terrell Davis	4.00
JG-PD	Joe Germaine	1.00
BH-PD	Brock Huard	1.00
SK-PD	Shaun King	1.00
Mc-PD	Donovan McNabb	4.00
JM-PD	Joe Montana	5.00
RM-PD	Randy Moss	4.00

1999 Upper Deck Quarterback Class

This 15-card insert includes the top QB's in the NFL along with rookies from 1999. Singles were found 1:10 packs. A parallel Silver was numbered to 100 and a parallel Gold was limited to only one set.

		NM/M
Complete Set (15):		30.00
Common Player:		.50
Minor Stars:		1.00
Inserted 1:10		
Quantum Silver:		3X-5X
Production 100 Sets		
Quantum Gold		
Production 1 Set		
1	Tim Couch	3.00
2	Akili Smith	1.00
3	Daunte Culpepper	4.00
4	Cade McNown	1.00
5	Donovan McNabb	4.00
6	Brock Huard	.50
7	John Elway	3.00
8	Dan Marino	4.00
9	Brett Favre	4.00
10	Charlie Batch	1.00
11	Steve Young	2.50
12	Jake Plummer	1.00
13	Peyton Manning	3.00
14	Mark Brunell	1.00
15	Troy Aikman	3.00

1999 Upper Deck Strike Force

This 30-card set includes the top scoring threats in the NFL and brings them to life on a silver-foil board card. Singles were inserted 1:4 packs. A parallel Silver was sequentially numbered to 100 and a Gold parallel was issued with only one set made.

		NM/M
Complete Set (30):		20.00
Common Player:		.25
Minor Stars:		1.00
Inserted 1:4		
1	Jamal Anderson	.25
2	Keyshawn Johnson	.50
3	Eddie George	1.00
4	Steve Young	2.50
5	Emmitt Smith	4.00
6	Karim Abdul	.25
7	Kordell Stewart	2.00
8	Cade McNown	.50
9	Tim Couch	3.00
10	Corey Dillon	1.00
11	Peyton Manning	4.00
12	Curtis Martin	1.00
13	Jerome Bettis	1.00
14	Jon Kitna	1.00
15	Dan Marino	4.00
16	Eric Moulds	1.00
17	Charlie Batch	.50
18	Ricky Williams	5.00
19	Terrell Owens	1.00
20	Ty Detmer	.25
21	Curtis Enis	1.00
22	Doug Flutie	1.00
23	Randall Cunningham	1.00
24	Donovan McNabb	3.50
25	Steve McNair	2.00
26	Terrell Davis	3.00
27	Daunte Culpepper	3.50
28	Warrick Dunn	1.00
29	Akili Smith	1.00
30	Barry Sanders	4.00

1999 Upper Deck Black Diamond

This was a 150-card set that included 40 rookies that were inserted 1:4 packs. Each single has a parallel Diamond Cut card with veterans inserted 1:7 packs and rookies inserted 1:12. Each also has a parallel Final Cut single with veterans numbered to 100 and rookies numbered to 50. Other insert sets included: A Piece of History, Diamonation, Gallery, Might, Myriad, Skills and the Walter Payton Autograph Game Jersey card. SRP was $3.99 for six-card packs.

		NM/M
Complete Set (150):		100.00
Common Player:		.20
Minor Stars:		.40
Common Rookie:		1.50
Inserted 1:4		
Pack (6):		2.00
Wax Box (30):		40.00
1	Adrian Murrell	.20
2	Jake Plummer	.50
3	Rob Moore	.40
4	Frank Sanders	.40
5	Jamal Anderson	.75
6	Terance Mathis	.20
7	Chris Chandler	.40
8	Tim Dwight	.75
9	Jermaine Lewis	.20
10	Priest Holmes	.75
11	Peter Boulware	.20
12	Doug Flutie	.75
13	Antowain Smith	.75
14	Eric Moulds	.75
15	Bruce Smith	.20
16	Rae Carruth	.20
17	Muhsin Muhammad	.40
18	Wesley Walls	.40
19	Tshimanga Biakabutuka	.40
20	Curtis Enis	.50
21	Curtis Conway	.40
22	Bobby Engram	.20
23	Darnay Scott	.40
24	Corey Dillon	.75
25	Jeff Blake	.40
26	Ty Detmer	.20
27	Terry Kirby	.20
28	Leslie Shepherd	.20
29	Emmitt Smith	3.00
30	Troy Aikman	2.00
31	Michael Irvin	.40
32	Raghib Ismail	.20
33	Brian Griese	1.50
34	Terrell Davis	1.50
35	Shannon Sharpe	.40
36	Rod Smith	.50
37	Barry Sanders	3.00
38	Herman Moore	.75
39	Charlie Batch	.50
40	Johnnie Morton	.20
41	Brett Favre	4.00
42	Dorsey Levens	.75
43	Antonio Freeman	.75
44	Mark Chmura	.40
45	Peyton Manning	3.00
46	Jerome Pathon	.20
47	Marvin Harrison	.75
48	Fred Taylor	.75
49	Mark Brunell	.75
50	Jimmy Smith	.75
51	Keenan McCardell	.40
52	Andre Rison	.40
53	Elvis Grbac	.40
54	Derrick Alexander	.20
55	Tony Gonzalez	.40
56	Dan Marino	3.00
57	Oronde Gadsden	.40
58	O.J. McDuffie	.40
59	Randy Moss	3.00
60	Randall Cunningham	.75
61	Cris Carter	.75
62	Robert Smith	.75
63	Drew Bledsoe	1.50
64	Terry Glenn	.75
65	Ben Coates	.40
66	Billy Joe Hobert	.20
67	Eddie Kennison	.20
68	Cam Cleeland	.40
69	Gary Brown	.20
70	Ike Hilliard	.40
71	Amani Toomer	.40
72	Vinny Testaverde	.40
73	Keyshawn Johnson	.75
74	Curtis Martin	.75
75	Wayne Chrebet	.75
76	Tim Brown	.50
77	Rickey Dudley	.40
78	Napoleon Kaufman	.75
79	Charles Woodson	.75
80	Duce Staley	.75
81	Doug Pederson	.20
82	Charles Johnson	.20
83	Kordell Stewart	.75
84	Jerome Bettis	.75
85	Courtney Hawkins	.20
86	Isaac Bruce	.75
87	Marshall Faulk	.75
88	Trent Green	.50
89	Jim Harbaugh	.40
90	Junior Seau	.40
91	Natrone Means	.50
92	Lawrence Phillips	.40
93	Steve Young	1.25
94	Terrell Owens	.75
95	Jerry Rice	3.00
96	Jon Kitna	.50
97	Ricky Watters	.50
98	Joey Galloway	.75
99	Shawn Springs	.20
100	Warrick Dunn	.75
101	Trent Dilfer	.40
102	Reidel Anthony	.40
103	Mike Alstott	.75
104	Steve McNair	1.25
105	Eddie George	1.00
106	Kevin Dyson	.40
107	Yancey Thigpen	.40
108	Michael Westbrook	.40
109	Brad Johnson	.75
110	Skip Hicks	.40
111	*Tim Couch*	5.00
112	*Akili Smith*	4.00
113	*Ricky Williams*	10.00
114	*Donovan McNabb*	15.00
115	*Edgerrin James*	15.00
116	*Cade McNown*	3.00
117	*Daunte Culpepper*	15.00
118	*Shaun King*	3.00
119	*Brock Huard*	3.00
120	*Joe Germaine*	3.00
121	*Troy Edwards*	3.00
122	*Champ Bailey*	5.00
123	*Kevin Faulk*	4.00
124	*David Boston*	8.00
125	*Kevin Johnson*	3.00
126	*Torry Holt*	8.00
127	*James Johnson*	3.00
128	*Peerless Price*	6.00
129	*D'Wayne Bates*	3.00
130	*Cecil Collins*	3.00
131	*Na Brown*	1.50
132	*Rob Konrad*	3.00
133	*Joel Makovicka*	1.50
134	*Dameane Douglas*	1.50
135	*Scott Covington*	1.50
136	*Daylon McCutcheon*	1.50
137	*Chris Claiborne*	3.00
138	*Karsten Bailey*	3.00
139	*Mike Cloud*	3.00
140	*Sean Bennett*	3.00
141	*Jermaine Fazande*	3.00
142	*Chris McAlister*	3.00
143	*Ebenezer Ekuban*	1.50
144	*Jeff Paulk*	1.50
145	*Jim Kleinsasser*	3.00
146	*Bobby Collins*	1.50
147	*Andy Katzenmoyer*	3.00
148	*Jevon Kearse*	4.00
149	*Amos Zereoue*	3.00
150	*Sedrick Irvin*	3.00

1999 Upper Deck Black Diamond Diamond Cut

This was a 150-card parallel to the base set. Each of these singles was printed on a die-cut card with a rainbow foil design. Veterans were inserted 1:7 packs and rookies were found 1:12.

Diamond Cut Cards:	2X-4X
Inserted 1:7	
Diamond Cut Rookies:	1.5X
Inserted 1:12	

1999 Upper Deck Black Diamond Final Cut

This was a 150-card parallel to the base set. Each single was printed with gold foil and sequentially numbered. Veterans were numbered to 100 and rookies to 50.

	NM/M
Final Cut Cards:	8X-20X
Production 100 Sets	
Final Cut Rookies:	4X-8X
Production 50 Sets	

1999 Upper Deck Black Diamond A Piece of History

This was a 30-card insert set that displayed a single piece of a game-used football. Some singles were only found in hobby product and were inserted 1:179 packs. Others were inserted in both hobby and retail and they were found 1:359 packs. Each single had a parallel Double Diamond single that featured two pieces of a game-used football. Hobby singles were found 1:1,079 and hobby/retail singles were also inserted 1:1,079.

		NM/M
Common Player:		25.00
H Inserted 1:179		
HR Inserted 1:359		
Double Diamond Cards:		2X
H Inserted 1:1,079		
HR Inserted 1:1,079		
TA	Troy Aikman	60.00
CB	Charlie Batch	35.00
DBl	Drew Bledsoe	45.00
DBo	David Boston	35.00
TB	Tim Brown	25.00
TC	Tim Couch	40.00
DC	Daunte Culpepper	60.00
TD	Terrell Davis	40.00
WD	Warrick Dunn	25.00
BF	Brett Favre	75.00
DF	Doug Flutie	35.00
BG	Brian Griese	45.00
TH	Torry Holt	35.00
BH	Brock Huard	35.00
EJ	Edgerrin James	60.00
KJ	Keyshawn Johnson	25.00
PM	Peyton Manning	75.00
DM	Dan Marino	75.00
CMa	Curtis Martin	25.00
DMc	Donovan McNabb	60.00
CM	Cade McNown	20.00
HM	Herman Moore	25.00
RM	Randy Moss	60.00

JP	Jake Plummer	20.00
JR	Jerry Rice	60.00
DS	Deion Sanders	25.00
AS	Akili Smith	20.00
ES	Emmitt Smith	75.00
RW	Ricky Williams	50.00
SY	Steve Young	50.00

1999 Upper Deck Black Diamond Diamonation

This was a 20-card insert set that included the most dominant players in the game. Singles were inserted 1:6 packs.

		NM/M
Complete Set (20):		25.00
Common Player:		.50
Inserted 1:6		
1	Brett Favre	4.00
2	Eddie George	2.00
3	Terrell Davis	3.00
4	Jerome Bettis	.50
5	Randall Cunningham	.50
6	Jon Kitna	.50
7	Troy Aikman	3.00
8	Marshall Faulk	2.00
9	Steve Young	3.00
10	Warrick Dunn	.50
11	Jake Plummer	1.00
12	Fred Taylor	2.00
13	Antonio Freeman	.50
14	Peyton Manning	3.00
15	Randy Moss	3.00
16	Steve McNair	2.00
17	Emmitt Smith	4.00
18	Terrell Owens	.50
19	Kordell Stewart	.50
20	Ricky Williams	4.00

1999 Upper Deck Black Diamond Gallery

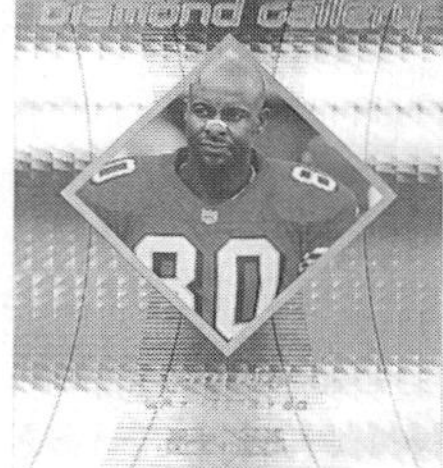

This was a 10-card insert set that featured candid gallery, portrait-style photography of the most collectible players in the NFL. Singles were inserted 1:14 packs.

		NM/M
Complete Set (10):		20.00
Common Player:		1.00
Inserted 1:14		
1	Akili Smith	1.00
2	Barry Sanders	4.00
3	Curtis Martin	1.00
4	Drew Bledsoe	3.00
5	Emmitt Smith	4.00
6	Keyshawn Johnson	1.00
7	Jerry Rice	3.00
8	Tim Couch	2.00
9	Terrell Owens	1.00
10	Troy Aikman	3.00

1999 Upper Deck Black Diamond Might

This was a 10-card insert set that included ten powerhouse players. Singles were inserted 1:12 packs.

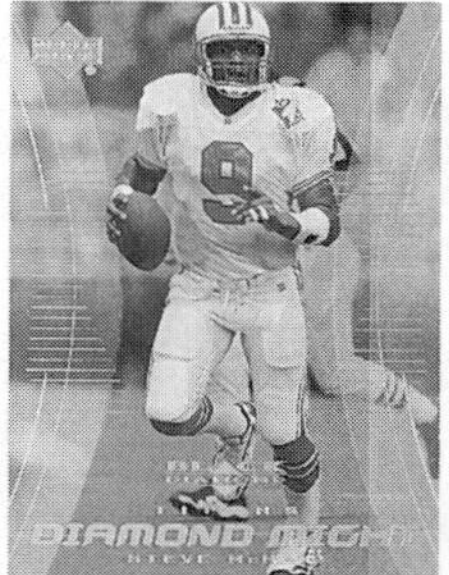

		NM/M
Complete Set (10):		15.00
Common Player:		1.00
Inserted 1:12		
1	Antowain Smith	1.00
2	Steve McNair	2.00
3	Corey Dillon	2.00
4	Dan Marino	4.00
5	Eddie George	2.00
6	Jerome Bettis	1.00
7	Jerry Rice	3.00
8	Randall Cunningham	1.00
9	Brian Griese	2.00
10	Joey Galloway	1.00

1999 Upper Deck Black Diamond Myriad

This was a 10-card insert set that captured the electrifying exploits of NFL standouts in action. Singles were inserted 1:29 packs.

		NM/M
Complete Set (10):		25.00
Common Player:		1.00
Inserted 1:29		
1	Barry Sanders	4.00
2	Randy Moss	4.00
3	Terrell Davis	3.00
4	Brett Favre	5.00
5	Jamal Anderson	1.00
6	Mark Brunell	1.00
7	Edgerrin James	3.00
8	Steve Young	3.00
9	Ricky Williams	4.00
10	Warrick Dunn	1.00

1999 Upper Deck Black Diamond Skills

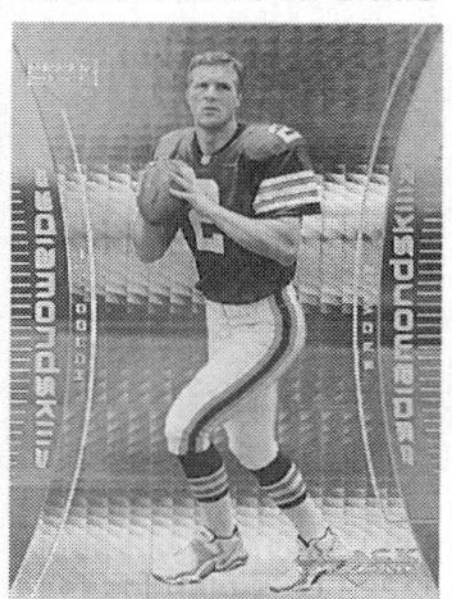

This was a 10-card insert set that included the most versatile and skilled athletes in the game. Singles were found 1:29 packs.

		NM/M
Complete Set (10):		25.00
Common Player:		1.00
Inserted 1:29		
1	Drew Bledsoe	3.00
2	Fred Taylor	1.00
3	Dan Marino	5.00
4	Jake Plummer	1.00
5	Kurt Warner	4.00
6	Marshall Faulk	2.00
7	Randy Moss	4.00
8	Peyton Manning	4.00
9	Keyshawn Johnson	1.00
10	Tim Couch	3.00

1999 Upper Deck Black Diamond W. Payton Jersey Auto.

Walter Payton signed 34 of these singles that included a piece of a game-used jersey. Singles were randomly inserted.

		NM/M
WPA	Walter Payton 34	1,500

1999 Upper Deck Century Legends

This was a 173-card set that included both past and present NFL players. Cards #4,6,14, 26,31,38 and 43 were never produced. Each single has a parallel Century Collection die-cut that was numbered to 100. Other insert sets included: 20th Century Superstars, Epic Milestones, Epic Signatures, Jerseys of the Century, Tour de France and Walter Payton signed cards. SRP was $4.99 for 12-card packs.

		NM/M
Complete Set (173):		55.00
Common Player:		.15
Minor Stars:		.30
Common Rookie:		.50
#4,6,14,26,31,38 & 43 never produced		
Pack (5):		4.50
Wax Box (24):		75.00
1	Jim Brown	2.00
2	Jerry Rice	1.00
3	Joe Montana	3.00
5	Johnny Unitas	1.00
7	Otto Graham	.30
8	Walter Payton	3.00
9	Dick Butkus	1.00
10	Bob Lilly	.15
11	Sammy Baugh	.30
12	Barry Sanders	2.00
13	Deacon Jones	.50
15	Gino Marchetti	.15
16	John Elway	1.50
17	Anthony Munoz	.15
18	Ray Nitschke	.30
19	Dick "Night Train" Lane	.15
20	John Hannah	.15
21	Gale Sayers	1.00
22	Reggie White	.30
23	Ronnie Lott	.30
24	Jim Parker	.15
25	Merlin Olsen	.30
27	Dan Marino	1.50
28	Forrest Gregg	.15
29	Roger Staubach	1.50
30	Jack Lambert	.15
32	Marion Motley	.15
33	Earl Campbell	.50
34	Alan Page	.15
35	Bronko Nagurski	.30
36	Mel Blount	.15
37	Deion Sanders	.30
39	Sid Luckman	.15
40	Raymond Berry	.15
41	Bart Starr	1.00
42	Willie Lanier	.15
44	Terry Bradshaw	1.50
45	Herb Adderley	.30
46	Steve Largent	.30
47	Jack Ham	.15
48	John Mackey	.15
49	Bill George	.15
50	Willie Brown	.15
51	Jerry Rice	1.00
52	Barry Sanders	2.00
53	John Elway	1.50
54	Reggie White	.30
55	Dan Marino	1.50
56	Deion Sanders	.30
57	Bruce Smith	.15
58	Steve Young	.75
59	Emmitt Smith	1.50
60	Brett Favre	2.00
61	Rod Woodson	.15
62	Troy Aikman	1.00
63	Terrell Davis	1.50
64	Michael Irvin	.30
65	Andre Rison	.15
66	Warren Moon	.30
67	Thurman Thomas	.30
68	Randall Cunningham	.30
69	Jerome Bettis	.50
70	Junior Seau	.30
71	Drew Bledsoe	.75
72	Andre Reed	.15
73	Tim Brown	.30
74	Derrick Thomas	.15
75	Jake Plummer	.75
76	Kordell Stewart	.50
77	Herman Moore	.50
78	Shannon Sharpe	.30
79	Antonio Freeman	.50
80	Ricky Watters	.30
81	Warrick Dunn	.50
82	Mark Brunell	.75
83	Randy Moss	2.00
84	Fred Taylor	1.00
85	Curtis Martin	.50
86	Keyshawn Johnson	.50
87	Eddie George	.60
88	Marshall Faulk	.50
89	Joey Galloway	.50
90	Vinny Testaverde	.30
91	Garrison Hearst	.30
92	Jimmy Smith	.50
93	Doug Flutie	.75
94	Napoleon Kaufman	.50
95	Natrone Means	.30
96	Peyton Manning	1.50
97	Steve McNair	.60
98	Corey Dillon	.50
99	Terrell Owens	.50
100	Charlie Batch	.75
101	Brett Favre	2.00
102	Terrell Davis	1.50
103	Roger Staubach	1.00
104	Terry Bradshaw	1.00
105	Fran Tarkenton	.50
106	Walter Payton	3.00
107	Mark Brunell	.75
108	Jim Brown	1.50
109	Kordell Stewart	.50
110	Bart Starr	1.00
111	Steve Largent	.30
112	Raymond Berry	.15
113	Emmitt Smith	1.50
114	Forrest Gregg	.15
115	Drew Bledsoe	.75
116	Dick Butkus	.50
117	Johnny Unitas	1.00
118	Joe Montana	3.00
119	Deacon Jones	.30
120	Steve Young	.75
121	Bob Lilly	.15
122	Troy Aikman	1.00
123	Alan Page	.15
124	Earl Campbell	.50
125	Deion Sanders	.30
126	Ronnie Lott	.30
127	Reggie White	.30
128	Marshall Faulk	.50
129	Gale Sayers	1.00
130	Dick "Night Train" Lane	.15
131	*Ricky Williams*	5.00
132	*Tim Couch*	2.00
133	*Donovan McNabb*	6.00
134	*Daunte Culpepper*	6.00
135	*Edgerrin James*	6.00
136	*Cade McNown*	2.00
137	*Torry Holt*	3.00
138	*David Boston*	3.00
139	*Champ Bailey*	1.75
140	*Peerless Price*	2.00
141	*D'Wayne Bates*	.75
142	*Joe Germaine*	.75
143	*Brock Huard*	1.25
144	*Chris Claiborne*	.75
145	*Jevon Kearse*	2.00
146	*Troy Edwards*	2.00
147	*Amos Zereoue*	.75
148	*Aaron Brooks*	6.00
149	*Andy Katzenmoyer*	.75
150	*Kevin Faulk*	1.00
151	*Shaun King*	2.00
152	*Kevin Johnson*	2.00
153	*Dameane Douglas*	.50
154	*Mike Cloud*	.50
155	*Sedrick Irvin*	1.50
156	*Akili Smith*	2.00
157	*Rob Konrad*	.50
158	*Scott Covington*	.50
159	*Jeff Paulk*	.50
160	*Shawn Bryson*	.50
161	Joe Montana	3.00
162	John Elway	1.50
163	Joe Namath	1.50
164	Jerry Rice	1.00
165	Terry Bradshaw	1.00
166	Jim Brown	2.00
167	Paul Warfield	.30
168	Herman Moore	.50
169	Walter Payton	3.00
170	Roger Staubach	1.00
171	Ken Stabler	1.00
172	Steve Young	.75
173	Troy Aikman	1.00
174	Fran Tarkenton	.50
175	Doug Williams	.15
176	Steve Largent	.30
177	Marcus Allen	.30
178	Mike Singletary	.30
179	Earl Campbell	.30
180	Dan Fouts	.30

1999 Upper Deck Century Legends Century Collection

This was a 173-card parallel to the base set. Each single was die-cut and sequentially numbered to 100.

	NM/M
Century Cards:	8X-15X
Century Rookies:	5X-10X
Production 100 Sets	

1999 Upper Deck Century Legends 20th Century Superstars

This 10-card insert set focused on the NFL's most-talked about players. Singles were inserted 1:11 packs.

		NM/M
Complete Set (10):		25.00
Common Player:		1.00
Inserted 1:11		
1	Tim Couch	3.00
2	Ricky Williams	5.00
3	Akili Smith	1.00
4	Donovan McNabb	4.00
5	Jake Plummer	2.00
6	Brett Favre	6.00
7	Steve Young	3.00
8	Randy Moss	4.00
9	Kordell Stewart	1.00
10	Peyton Manning	3.00

1999 Upper Deck Century Legends Epic Milestones

This was a 10-card insert set that pinpointed ten of the most impressive NFL milestones ever reached. Singles were inserted 1:11 packs.

		NM/M
Complete Set (10):		25.00
Common Player:		1.00
Inserted 1:11		
1	John Elway	4.00
2	Joe Montana	5.00
3	Randy Moss	4.00
4	Terrell Davis	3.00
5	Dan Marino	5.00
6	Jamal Anderson	1.00
7	Jerry Rice	3.00
8	Barry Sanders	4.00
9	Emmitt Smith	4.00
10	Walter Payton	4.00

1999 Upper Deck Century Legends Epic Signatures

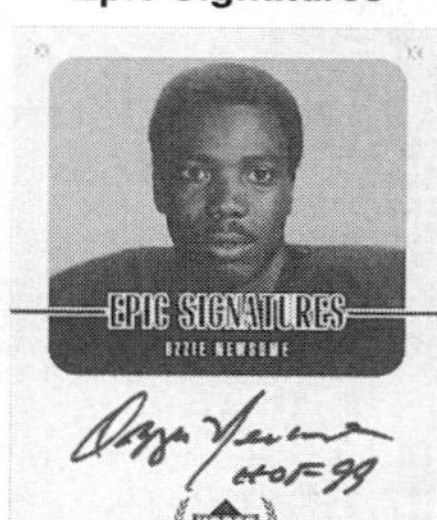

This 30-card insert set included autographs of both past and present stars. Singles were inserted 1:23 packs. A parallel Gold version was also released for every player except for Johnny Unitas. Each of those singles were numbered to 100.

		NM/M
Common Player:		10.00
Minor Stars:		20.00
Inserted 1:23		
Century Gold Cards:		2X
Unitas never produced		
Production 100 Sets		
TA	Troy Aikman	75.00
RB	Raymond Berry	10.00
TB	Terry Bradshaw	125.00
DB	Dick Butkus	75.00
EC	Earl Campbell	50.00
HC	Harold Carmichael	20.00
CC	Cris Carter	20.00
TD	Terrell Davis	85.00
LD	Len Dawson	20.00
DF	Dan Fouts	20.00
CJ	Charlie Joiner	20.00
SL	Steve Largent	25.00
FL	Floyd Little	10.00
DM	Dan Marino	180.00
MY	Don Maynard	20.00
AM	Art Monk	20.00
JM	Joe Montana	250.00
RM	Randy Moss	175.00
JN	Joe Namath	250.00
ON	Ozzie Newsome	10.00
DR	Dan Reeves	20.00
JR	Jerry Rice	250.00
GS	Gale Sayers	30.00
MS	Michael Singletary	10.00
RS	Roger Staubach	100.00
FT	Fran Tarkenton	65.00
JU	Johnny Unitas	125.00
PW	Paul Warfield	10.00
DW	Doug Williams	20.00
JY	Jack Youngblood	10.00

1999 Upper Deck Century Legends Jerseys of the Century

This nine-card insert set included swatches of game jerseys from both past and present NFL stars. Singles were inserted 1:418 packs.

		NM/M
Common Player:		75.00
#9 never produced		
Inserted 1:418		
1	Jerry Rice	175.00
2	Roger Staubach	150.00
3	Warren Moon	75.00
4	Ken Stabler	125.00
5	Reggie White	75.00
6	Dan Marino	275.00
7	Doug Flutie	75.00
8	Bob Lilly	75.00
9	Jim Brown	250.00

1999 Upper Deck Century Legends Tour de Force

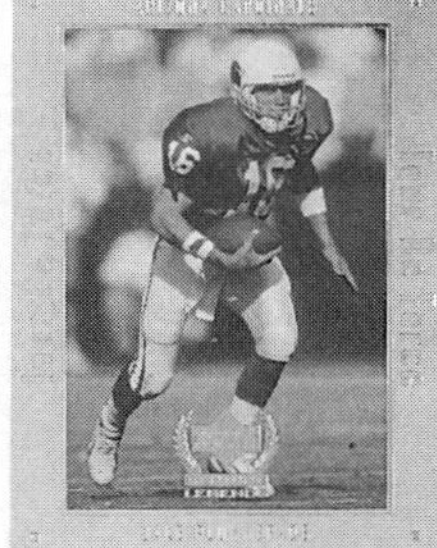

This was a 10-card insert set that highlighted the ten most important players in the NFL. Singles were inserted 1:23 packs.

		NM/M
Complete Set (10):		25.00
Common Player:		1.00
Inserted 1:23		
1	Tim Couch	3.00
2	Ricky Williams	5.00
3	Peyton Manning	4.00
4	Troy Aikman	4.00
5	Jake Plummer	2.00
6	Jamal Anderson	1.00
7	Terrell Davis	3.00
8	Barry Sanders	5.00
9	Fred Taylor	2.00
10	Keyshawn Johnson	1.00

1999 Upper Deck Century Legends Walter Payton

Walter Payton signed 50 UD Authentic cards and 34 Game-Used Jersey cards. Singles were randomly inserted.

		NM/M
WPAC	W.Payton AUTO/50	650.00
WPCL	W.Payton Jersey AUTO/34	1,500

1999 Upper Deck Encore

This was a 225-card set that included 45 rookies found 1:8 packs. Parallel sets included F/X and F/X Gold. Other insert sets included: Electric Currents, Game Used Helmets, Live Wires, Seize the Game, UD Authentics, Upper Realm and the Walter Payton Game Jersey card. SRP was $3.99 for six-card packs.

		NM/M
Complete Set (225):		225.00
Common Player:		.20
Minor Stars:		.40
Common Rookie:		2.00
Inserted 1:8		
Pack (6):		4.00
Wax Box (24):		65.00
1	Jake Plummer	.50
2	Adrian Murrell	.20
3	Rob Moore	.40
4	Simeon Rice	.20
5	Andre Wadsworth	.20
6	Frank Sanders	.20
7	Tim Dwight	.75
8	Chris Chandler	.40
9	Jamal Anderson	.75
10	O.J. Santiago	.20
11	Tony Graziani	.20
12	Terance Mathis	.20
13	Priest Holmes	1.00
14	Stoney Case	.40
15	Ray Lewis	.20
16	Peter Boulware	.20
17	Scott Mitchell	.20
18	Jermaine Lewis	.20
19	Eric Moulds	.75
20	Doug Flutie	.50
21	Antowain Smith	.75
22	Rob Johnson	.40
23	Bruce Smith	.20
24	Andre Reed	.40
25	Wesley Walls	.40
26	Tshimanga Biakabutuka	.40
27	Fred Lane	.20
28	Steve Beurlein	.40
29	Muhsin Muhammad	.40
30	Rae Carruth	.20
31	Bobby Engram	.20
32	Curtis Enis	.50
33	Edgar Bennett	.20
34	Curtis Conway	.40
35	Shane Matthews	.40
36	Tony McGee	.20
37	Darnay Scott	.40
38	Jeff Blake	.40
39	Corey Dillon	.75
40	Ki-Jana Carter	.20
41	Ty Detmer	.20
42	Leslie Shepherd	.20
43	Terry Kirby	.20
44	Antonio Langham	.20
45	Jamir Miller	.20
46	Marc Edwards	.20
47	Troy Aikman	1.50
48	Raghib Ismail	.20
49	Emmitt Smith	2.00
50	Michael Irvin	.40
51	Deion Sanders	.75
52	Greg Ellis	.20
53	Bubby Brister	.40
54	Terrell Davis	1.25
55	Ed McCaffrey	.75
56	Rod Smith	.75
57	Shannon Sharpe	.40
58	Brian Griese	1.25
59	Charlie Batch	.50
60	Germane Crowell	.40
61	Johnnie Morton	.20
62	Robert Porcher	.20
63	Ron Rivers	.20
64	Herman Moore	.75
65	Brett Favre	3.00
66	Bill Schroeder	.40
67	Antonio Freeman	.75
68	Dorsey Levens	.75
69	Desmond Howard	.20
70	Vonnie Holliday	.20
71	Peyton Manning	2.00
72	Jerome Pathon	.20
73	Marvin Harrison	.75
74	Ken Dilger	.20
75	E.G. Green	.20
76	Cornelius Bennett	.20
77	Mark Brunell	.75
78	Fred Taylor	.75
79	Jimmy Smith	.75
80	James Stewart	.75
81	Keenan McCardell	.40
82	Carnell Lake	.20
83	Elvis Grbac	.40
84	Tony Gonzalez	.40
85	Andre Rison	.40
86	Derrick Thomas	.40
87	Warren Moon	.40
88	Derrick Alexander	.20
89	Dan Marino	2.00
90	O.J. McDuffie	.40
91	Karim Abdul	.40
92	Sam Madison	.20
93	Zach Thomas	.40
94	Tony Martin	.20
95	Randall Cunningham	.75
96	Randy Moss	2.00
97	Cris Carter	.75
98	Jake Reed	.40
99	John Randle	.40
100	Robert Smith	.75
101	Drew Bledsoe	1.25
102	Ben Coates	.40
103	Terry Glenn	.75
104	Tony Simmons	.40
105	Terry Allen	.40
106	Danny Wuerffel	.40
107	Cameron Cleeland	.40
108	Eddie Kennison	.20
109	Billy Joe Hobert	.20
110	Andre Hastings	.20
111	Kent Graham	.20
112	Tiki Barber	.40
113	Gary Brown	.20
114	Ike Hilliard	.40
115	Jason Sehorn	.20
116	Kerry Collins	.40
117	Vinny Testaverde	.40
118	Wayne Chrebet	.75
119	Curtis Martin	.75
120	Rick Mirer	.20
121	Aaron Glenn	.20
122	Keyshawn Johnson	.75
123	Rich Gannon	.40
124	Tim Brown	.40
125	Darrell Russell	.20
126	Tyrone Wheatley	.40
127	Charles Woodson	.75
128	Napoleon Kaufman	.75
129	Duce Staley	.75
130	Doug Pederson	.20
131	Kevin Turner	.20
132	Charles Johnson	.20
133	Jerome Bettis	.75
134	Courtney Hawkins	.20
135	Kordell Stewart	.75
136	Richard Huntley	.40
137	Levon Kirkland	.20
138	Hines Ward	.40
139	*Kurt Warner*	10.00
140	Marshall Faulk	.75
141	Az Hakim	.40
142	Amp Lee	.20
143	Isaac Bruce	.75
144	Kevin Carter	.20
145	Jim Harbaugh	.40
146	Junior Seau	.40
147	Natrone Means	.40
148	Rodney Harrison	.20
149	Mikhael Ricks	.20
150	Erik Kramer	.20
151	Steve Young	1.00
152	Terrell Owens	.75
153	Jerry Rice	2.00
154	J.J. Stokes	.40
155	*Jeff Garcia*	10.00
156	Lawrence Phillips	.40
157	Jon Kitna	.50
158	Derrick Mayes	.40
159	Ricky Watters	.40
160	Chad Brown	.20
161	Shawn Springs	.20
162	Sean Dawkins	.20
163	Trent Dilfer	.40
164	Reidel Anthony	.40
165	Bert Emanuel	.20
166	Warrick Dunn	.75
167	Jacquez Green	.40
168	Mike Alstott	.75
169	Eddie George	1.00
170	Steve McNair	1.00
171	Kevin Dyson	.40
172	Frank Wycheck	.20
173	Blaine Bishop	.20
174	Yancey Thigpen	.40
175	Brad Johnson	.75
176	Michael Westbrook	.40
177	Skip Hicks	.20
178	Brian Mitchell	.20
179	Dana Stubblefield	.20
180	Stephen Davis	.75
181	*Champ Bailey*	4.00
182	*Chris McAlister*	3.00
183	*Jevon Kearse*	4.00
184	*Ebenezer Ekuban*	3.00
185	*Chris Claiborne*	2.00
186	*Andy Katzenmoyer*	2.00
187	*Tim Couch*	3.00
188	*Daunte Culpepper*	12.00
189	*Akili Smith*	3.00
190	*Donovan McNabb*	12.00
191	*Sean Bennett*	2.00
192	*Brock Huard*	3.00
193	*Cade McNown*	3.00
194	*Shaun King*	3.00
195	*Joe Germaine*	2.00
196	*Ricky Williams*	10.00
197	*Edgerrin James*	12.00
198	*Sedrick Irvin*	2.00
199	*Kevin Faulk*	3.00
200	*Rob Konrad*	2.00
201	*James Johnson*	3.00
202	*Amos Zereoue*	3.00
203	*Torry Holt*	6.00
204	*D'Wayne Bates*	3.00
205	*David Boston*	6.00
206	*Dameane Douglas*	2.00
207	*Troy Edwards*	3.00
208	*Kevin Johnson*	4.00
209	*Peerless Price*	5.00
210	*Antoine Winfield*	2.00
211	*Michael Cloud*	2.00
212	*Joe Montgomery*	2.00
213	*Jermaine Fazande*	2.00
214	*Scott Covington*	2.00
215	*Aaron Brooks*	12.00
216	*Terry Jackson*	2.00
217	*Cecil Collins*	3.00
218	*Olandis Gary*	3.00
219	*Craig Yeast*	2.00
220	*Karsten Bailey*	2.00
221	*Reginald Kelly*	2.00
222	*Travis McGriff*	2.00
223	*Jeff Paulk*	2.00
224	*Jim Kleinsasser*	3.00
225	*Jason Tucker*	2.00

1999 Upper Deck Encore F/X

This was a 225-card parallel to the base set. Each single from this set was numbered to 100.

F/X Cards: 8X-15X
F/X Rookies: 2X-4X
Production 100 Sets
F/X Gold Cards:
Production 1 Set

1999 Upper Deck Encore F/X Gold

This was a 225-card parallel to the base set. Only one of each card was produced.

F/X Gold Cards:
Production 1 Set

1999 Upper Deck Encore Electric Currents

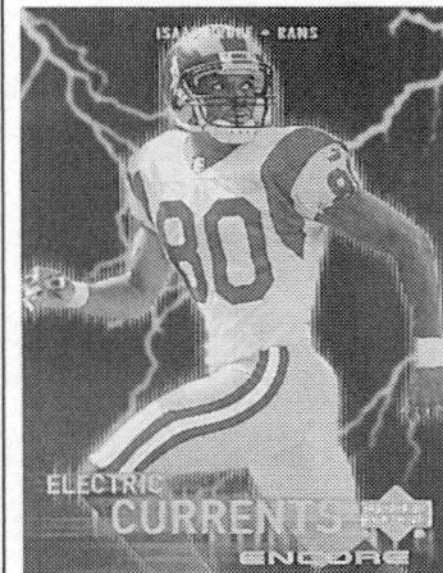

This was a 20-card insert set that featured the NFL's premier offensive stars. Singles were inserted 1:6 packs.

		NM/M
Complete Set (20):		15.00
Common Player:		.50
Minor Stars:		1.00
Inserted 1:6		
1	Steve Young	2.00
2	Doug Flutie	1.00
3	Jon Kitna	.50
4	Randall Cunningham	1.00
5	Curtis Enis	.50
6	Jerry Rice	3.00
7	Antonio Freeman	.50
8	Keyshawn Johnson	1.00
9	Steve McNair	1.00
10	Kordell Stewart	1.00
11	Drew Bledsoe	2.00
12	Corey Dillon	1.00
13	Vinny Testaverde	.50
14	Tim Brown	1.00
15	Antowain Smith	1.00
16	Charlie Batch	.50
17	Stephen Davis	.50
18	Isaac Bruce	1.00
19	Curtis Martin	1.00
20	Ricky Watters	1.00

1999 Upper Deck Encore Game-Used Helmets

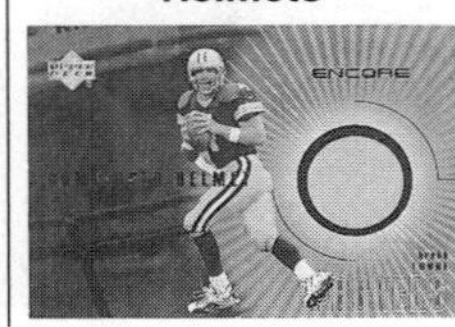

This was a six-card insert set that included a piece of a game-used helmet of that respected player. Singles were inserted 1:575 packs.

		NM/M
Common Player:		30.00
Inserted 1:575		
MB	Mark Brunell	40.00
TD	Terrell Davis	60.00
MF	Marshall Faulk	60.00
BF	Brett Favre	150.00
DM	Dan Marino	120.00
JR	Jerry Rice	100.00

1999 Upper Deck Encore Game-Used Rookie Helmets

This 15-card insert set included pieces of helmets used in NFL Rookie Shoot. Singles were inserted 1:575 packs.

		NM/M
Common Player:		30.00
Inserted 1:575		
CB	Champ Bailey	40.00
DW	D'Wayne Bates	30.00
DB	David Boston	50.00
CC	Cecil Collins	40.00
TC	Tim Couch	75.00
DC	Daunte Culpepper	100.00
TE	Troy Edwards	50.00
KF	Kevin Faulk	40.00
TH	Torry Holt	60.00
BH	Brock Huard	30.00
EJ	Edgerrin James	125.00
KJ	Kevin Johnson	40.00
Mc	Donovan McNabb	100.00
CM	Cade McNown	30.00
AS	Akili Smith	40.00

1999 Upper Deck Encore Live Wires

This 15-card insert set included the top stars in the NFL and inserted them 1:11 packs.

		NM/M
Complete Set (15):		25.00
Common Player:		1.00
Inserted 1:11		
1	Jake Plummer	1.00
2	Jamal Anderson	1.00
3	Emmitt Smith	4.00
4	John Elway	3.00
5	Barry Sanders	4.00
6	Brett Favre	5.00
7	Mark Brunell	1.00
8	Fred Taylor	1.00
9	Randy Moss	3.00
10	Drew Bledsoe	3.00
11	Keyshawn Johnson	1.00
12	Jerome Bettis	1.00
13	Kordell Stewart	1.00
14	Terrell Owens	1.00
15	Eddie George	2.00

1999 Upper Deck Encore Seize the Game

This 30-card insert set included the game's biggest game-breakers. Cards #1-#20 were inserted 1:20 packs and cards #21-#30 were inserted 1:23 packs. Each single also has a parallel Gold version and each was numbered to 250.

		NM/M
Complete Set (30):		60.00
Common Player (1-20):		1.00
Inserted 1:20		
Common Player (21-30):		2.00
Inserted 1:23		
F/X Gold Cards:		3X
Production 250 Sets		
1	Donovan McNabb	3.00
2	Keyshawn Johnson	1.00
3	Eddie George	1.00
4	Randall Cunningham	1.00
5	Charlie Batch	1.00
6	Curtis Martin	1.00
7	Edgerrin James	4.00
8	Jake Plummer	2.00
9	Drew Bledsoe	3.00
10	Marshall Faulk	1.00
11	Fred Taylor	1.00
12	Terrell Owens	1.00
13	Jerome Bettis	1.00
14	Antonio Freeman	1.00
15	Corey Dillon	1.00
16	Jerry Rice	4.00
17	Curtis Enis	1.00
18	Warrick Dunn	1.00
19	Kordell Stewart	1.00
20	Jamal Anderson	1.00
21	Terrell Davis	3.00
22	Randy Moss	4.00
23	Troy Aikman	4.00
24	Dan Marino	6.00
25	Ricky Williams	6.00
26	Peyton Manning	4.00
27	Steve Young	2.00
28	Tim Couch	2.00
29	Emmitt Smith	4.00
30	Brett Favre	5.00

1999 Upper Deck Encore UD Authentics

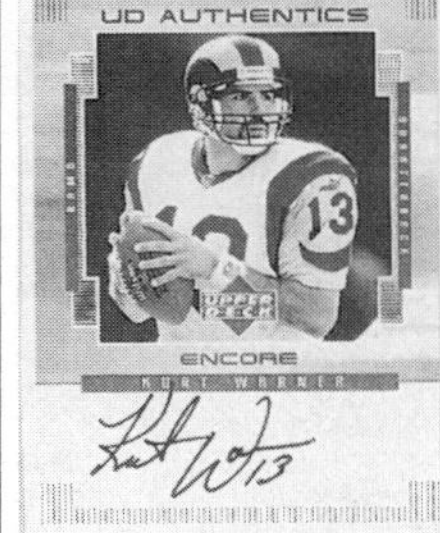

This 15-card insert set included autographs of the top current NFL stars. Singles were inserted 1:144 packs.

		NM/M
Common Player:		25.00
Inserted 1:144		
TA	Troy Aikman	85.00
DB	David Boston	40.00
MB	Mark Brunell	40.00
TC	Tim Couch	75.00
TE	Troy Edwards	40.00
KF	Kevin Faulk	25.00
TH	Torry Holt	40.00
BH	Brock Huard	25.00
EJ	Edgerrin James	90.00
SK	Shaun King	20.00
PM	Peyton Manning	100.00
CM	Cade McNown	20.00
RM	Randy Moss	100.00
JN	Joe Namath	125.00
KW	Kurt Warner	75.00

1999 Upper Deck Encore Upper Realm

This 10-card insert set pays tribute to ten of the NFL's current elite stars. Singles were inserted 1:12 packs.

		NM/M
Complete Set (10):		15.00
Common Player:		.50
Minor Stars:		1.00
Inserted 1:12		
1	Randy Moss	4.00
2	Warrick Dunn	1.00
3	Stephen Davis	1.00
4	Peyton Manning	3.00
5	Tim Biakabutuka	.50
6	Steve Young	2.50
7	Kurt Warner	3.00
8	Steve McNair	1.00
9	Dan Marino	4.00
10	Jake Plummer	1.00

1999 Upper Deck Encore Walter Payton

Walter Payton signed 34 Game Jersey cards. Each single included a swatch of a game-used jersey and his signature. Singles were randomly inserted into the product.

		NM/M
WPE	W.Payton Jersey AUTO/34	1,500

A card number in parenthese ( ) indicates the set is unnumbered.

1999 Upper Deck HoloGrFX

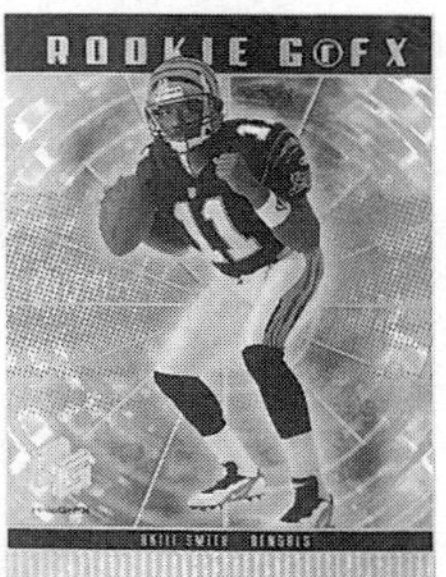

This was a 90-card set that included 30 rookies found 1:2 packs. Each single had an Ausome parallel with veterans inserted 1:8 packs and rookies inserted 1:17. Other insert sets included: 24/7, Future Fame, Star View and UD Authentics. SRP was $1.99 for three-card packs.

		NM/M
Complete Set (90):		40.00
Common Player:		.20
Minor Stars:		.40
Common Rookies:		.75
Pack (3):		1.75
Wax Box (36):		40.00
1	Jake Plummer	.50
2	Jamal Anderson	.75
3	Priest Holmes	1.50
4	Antowain Smith	.75
5	Doug Flutie	.75
6	Tshimanga Biakabutuka	.40
7	Curtis Enis	.75
8	Corey Dillon	.75
9	Darnay Scott	.40
10	Leslie Shepherd	.20
11	Troy Aikman	1.50
12	Emmitt Smith	2.00
13	Michael Irvin	.40
14	Terrell Davis	1.25
15	Shannon Sharpe	.40
16	Rod Smith	.75
17	Barry Sanders	3.00
18	Charlie Batch	.50
19	Herman Moore	.75
20	Brett Favre	3.00
21	Dorsey Levens	.75
22	Antonio Freeman	.75
23	Peyton Manning	2.00
24	Mark Brunell	.75
25	Fred Taylor	.75
26	Jimmy Smith	.75
27	Andre Rison	.40
28	Tony Gonzalez	.40
29	Dan Marino	2.00
30	Karim Abdul	.40
31	Randy Moss	2.00
32	Randall Cunningham	.75
33	Drew Bledsoe	1.25
34	Terry Glenn	.75
35	Cameron Cleeland	.40
36	Andre Hastings	.20
37	Amani Toomer	.20
38	Kent Graham	.20
39	Curtis Martin	.75
40	Keyshawn Johnson	.75
41	Vinny Testaverde	.40
42	Napoleon Kaufman	.75
43	Tim Brown	.40
44	Duce Staley	.75
45	Kordell Stewart	.75
46	Jerome Bettis	.75
47	Marshall Faulk	.75
48	Natrone Means	.50
49	Ryan Leaf	.75
50	Steve Young	1.00
51	Jerry Rice	2.00
52	Terrell Owens	.75
53	Joey Galloway	.75
54	Ricky Watters	.40
55	Jon Kitna	.75
56	Warrick Dunn	.75
57	Trent Dilfer	.40
58	Steve McNair	.75
59	Eddie George	.75
60	Brad Johnson	.75
61	*Tim Couch*	3.00
62	*Donovan McNabb*	6.00
63	*Akili Smith*	2.00
64	*Edgerrin James*	6.00
65	*Ricky Williams*	6.00
66	*Torry Holt*	3.00
67	*Champ Bailey*	1.50
68	*David Boston*	3.00
69	*Daunte Culpepper*	6.00
70	*Cade McNown*	1.50
71	*Troy Edwards*	1.50
72	*Kevin Johnson*	1.50
73	*James Johnson*	1.00
74	*Rob Konrad*	.75
75	*Kevin Faulk*	1.00
76	*Shaun King*	2.00
77	*Peerless Price*	2.50
78	*Michael Cloud*	.75
79	*Jermaine Fazande*	1.25
80	*D'Wayne Bates*	.75
81	*Brock Huard*	1.50
82	*Marty Booker*	.75
83	*Karsten Bailey*	.75
84	*Al Wilson*	.75

85	*Joe Germaine*	1.00
86	*Dameane Douglas*	.75
87	*Sedrick Irvin*	1.50
88	*Aaron Brooks*	6.00
89	*Cecil Collins*	1.75
90	*Michael Bishop*	1.50

1999 Upper Deck HoloGrFX Ausome

This was a 90-card parallel to the base set. Each single had gold foil added to the background. Veterans were inserted 1:8 packs and rookies were found 1:17.

	NM/M
Ausome Cards:	2X-4X
Inserted 1:8	
Ausome Rookies:	2X
Inserted 1:17	

1999 Upper Deck HoloGrFX 24/7

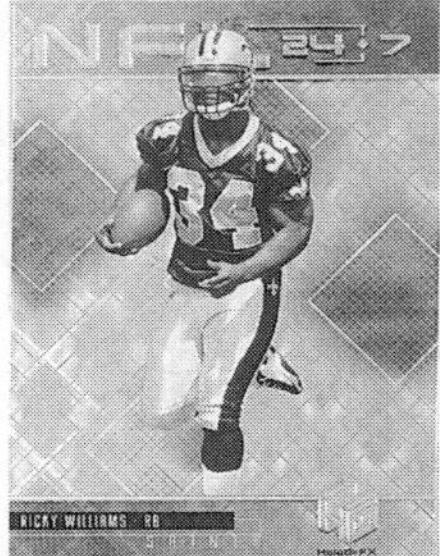

This was a 15-card insert set that captured the most exciting players in the NFL today. Singles were inserted 1:3 packs. A parallel Gold version was also made and singles were inserted 1:105 packs.

		NM/M
Complete Set (15):		20.00
Common Player:		.50
Inserted 1:3		
Gold Cards:		2X-4X
Inserted 1:105		
1	Jake Plummer	.50
2	Emmitt Smith	3.00
3	Terrell Davis	2.00
4	Peyton Manning	2.00
5	Drew Bledsoe	2.00
6	Troy Aikman	2.00
7	Ricky Williams	3.00
8	Keyshawn Johnson	.50
9	Akili Smith	.50
10	Eddie George	.50
11	Edgerrin James	2.00
12	David Boston	1.50
13	Cade McNown	.50
14	Jerome Bettis	.50
15	Herman Moore	.50

1999 Upper Deck HoloGrFX Future Fame

This was a six-card insert set that included the most impressive talents in the NFL. Singles were inserted 1:34 packs. A parallel Gold version was also released and inserted 1:431 packs.

		NM/M
Complete Set (6):		20.00
Common Player:		1.00
Inserted 1:34		
Gold Cards:		3X
Inserted 1:431		
1	John Elway	4.00
2	Dan Marino	5.00
3	Emmitt Smith	4.00
4	Randy Moss	3.00
5	Tim Brown	1.00
6	Barry Sanders	4.00

1999 Upper Deck HoloGrFX Star View

This was a nine-card insert set that focused on the NFL's marquee players. Singles were found 1:17 packs. A parallel Gold version was also released with singles inserted 1:210 packs.

		NM/M
Complete Set (9):		20.00
Common Player:		1.00
Inserted 1:17		
Gold Cards:		3X
Inserted 1:210		
1	Dan Marino	5.00
2	Brett Favre	5.00
3	Barry Sanders	4.00
4	Terrell Davis	3.00
5	Mark Brunell	2.00
6	Eddie George	1.00
7	Fred Taylor	2.00
8	Tim Couch	2.00
9	Randy Moss	3.00

1999 Upper Deck HoloGrFX UD Authentics

This was a 19-card insert set that included autographs of the top standouts in the league. Singles were inserted 1:144 packs.

		NM/M
Common Player:		25.00
Inserted 1:432		
TA	Troy Aikman	100.00
JA	Jamal Anderson	25.00
TC	Tim Couch	100.00
DC	Daunte Culpepper	100.00
TD	Terrell Davis	60.00
EG	Eddie George	60.00
TH	Torry Holt	50.00
BH	Brock Huard	25.00
EJ	Edgerrin James	125.00
SK	Shaun King	30.00
PM	Peyton Manning	125.00
DM	Donovan McNabb	70.00
CM	Cade McNown	40.00
EM	Eric Moulds	25.00
JP	Jake Plummer	40.00
JR	Jerry Rice	125.00
AS	Akili Smith	30.00
RW	Ricky Williams	125.00
SY	Steve Young	75.00

1999 Upper Deck MVP

MVP Football is a 220-card set that includes 20 unseeded rookie cards. Three different parallel sets were made with Gold Script, Silver Script and Super Script. Other inserts include: Draw Your Own Card, Drive Time, Dynamics, Game Used Souvenirs, Power Surge, Strictly Business and Theatre.

		NM/M
Complete Set (220):		30.00
Common Player:		.10
Minor Stars:		.20
Hobby Pack (10):		1.50
Hobby Wax Box (28):.		35.00
1	Jake Plummer	.40
2	Adrian Murrell	.10
3	Larry Centers	.10
4	Frank Sanders	.10
5	Andre Wadsworth	.20
6	Rob Moore	.20
7	Simeon Rice	.10
8	Jamal Anderson	.50
9	Chris Chandler	.20
10	Chuck Smith	.10
11	Terance Mathis	.10
12	Tim Dwight	.50
13	Ray Buchanan	.10
14	O.J. Santiago	.10
15	Eric Zeier	.10
16	Priest Holmes	.50
17	Michael Jackson	.10
18	Jermaine Lewis	.20
19	Michael McCrary	.10
20	Rob Johnson	.20
21	Antowain Smith	.50
22	Thurman Thomas	.20
23	Doug Flutie	.75
24	Eric Moulds	.30
25	Bruce Smith	.10
26	Andre Reed	.20
27	Fred Lane	.10
28	Tshimanga Biakabutuka	.20
29	Rae Carruth	.10
30	Wesley Walls	.10
31	Steve Beuerlein	.10
32	Muhsin Muhammad	.10
33	Erik Kramer	.10
34	Edgar Bennett	.10
35	Curtis Conway	.20
36	Curtis Enis	.50
37	Bobby Engram	.10
38	Alonzo Mayes	.10
39	Corey Dillon	.50
40	Jeff Blake	.20
41	Carl Pickens	.20
42	Darnay Scott	.10
43	Tony McGee	.10
44	Ki-Jana Carter	.20
45	Ty Detmer	.20
46	Terry Kirby	.10
47	Justin Armour	.10
48	Freddie Solomon	.10
49	Marquez Pope	.10
50	Antonio Langham	.10
51	Troy Aikman	1.00
52	Emmitt Smith	1.50
53	Deion Sanders	.50
54	Raghib Ismail	.10
55	Michael Irvin	.20
56	Chris Warren	.20
57	Greg Ellis	.10
58	John Elway	1.50
59	Terrell Davis	.75
60	Rod Smith	.20
61	Shannon Sharpe	.20
62	Ed McCaffrey	.20
63	John Mobley	.10
64	Bill Romanowski	.10
65	Barry Sanders	2.00
66	Johnnie Morton	.10
67	Herman Moore	.50
68	Charlie Batch	.75
69	Germane Crowell	.20
70	Robert Porcher	.10
71	Brett Favre	2.00
72	Antonio Freeman	.50
73	Dorsey Levens	.50
74	Mark Chmura	.20
75	Vonnie Holliday	.20
76	Bill Schroeder	.10
77	Marshall Faulk	.50
78	Marvin Harrison	.20
79	Peyton Manning	1.50
80	Jerome Pathon	.10
81	E.G. Green	.10
82	Ellis Johnson	.10
83	Mark Brunell	.75
84	Jimmy Smith	.20
85	Keenan McCardell	.10
86	Fred Taylor	.50
87	James Stewart	.10
88	Kevin Hardy	.10
89	Elvis Grbac	.10
90	Andre Rison	.20
91	Derrick Alexander	.10
92	Tony Gonzalez	.20
93	Donnell Bennett	.10
94	Derrick Thomas	.20
95	Tamarick Vanover	.10
96	Dan Marino	1.50
97	Karim Abdul	.50
98	Zach Thomas	.20
99	O.J. McDuffie	.20
100	John Avery	.20
101	Sam Madison	.10
102	Randall Cunningham	.50
103	Cris Carter	.50
104	Robert Smith	.50
105	Randy Moss	1.50
106	Jake Reed	.10
107	Matthew Hatchette	.10
108	John Randle	.20
109	Drew Bledsoe	.75
110	Terry Glenn	.50
111	Ben Coates	.20
112	Ty Law	.10
113	Tony Simmons	.20
114	Ted Johnson	.10
115	Danny Wuerffel	.20
116	Lamar Smith	.10
117	Sean Dawkins	.10
118	Cameron Cleeland	.20
119	Joe Johnson	.10
120	Andre Hastings	.10
121	Kent Graham	.10
122	Gary Brown	.10
123	Amani Toomer	.10
124	Tiki Barber	.20
125	Ike Hilliard	.20
126	Jason Sehorn	.10
127	Vinny Testaverde	.20
128	Curtis Martin	.50
129	Keyshawn Johnson	.50
130	Wayne Chrebet	.50
131	Mo Lewis	.10
132	Steve Atwater	.10
133	Donald Hollas	.10
134	Napoleon Kaufman	.50
135	Tim Brown	.20
136	Darrell Russell	.10
137	Rickey Dudley	.20
138	Charles Woodson	.50
139	Koy Detmer	.10
140	Duce Staley	.10
141	Charlie Garner	.10
142	Doug Pederson	.10
143	Jeff Graham	.10
144	Charles Johnson	.10
145	Kordell Stewart	.75
146	Jerome Bettis	.50
147	Hines Ward	.20
148	Courtney Hawkins	.10
149	Will Blackwell	.10
150	Richard Huntley	.10
151	Levon Kirkland	.10
152	Trent Green	.30
153	Tony Banks	.10
154	Isaac Bruce	.30
155	Eddie Kennison	.20
156	Az-Zahir Hakim	.20
157	Amp Lee	.10
158	Robert Holcombe	.20
159	Ryan Leaf	.75
160	Natrone Means	.50
161	Jim Harbaugh	.20
162	Junior Seau	.20
163	Charlie Jones	.10
164	Rodney Harrison	.10
165	Steve Young	.75
166	Jerry Rice	1.50
167	Garrison Hearst	.30
168	Terrell Owens	.50
169	J.J. Stokes	.20
170	Bryant Young	.10
171	Ricky Watters	.30
172	Joey Galloway	.50
173	Jon Kitna	.50
174	Ahman Green	.20
175	Mike Pritchard	.10
176	Chad Brown	.10
177	Warrick Dunn	.75
178	Trent Dilfer	.20
179	Mike Alstott	.50
180	Reidel Anthony	.20
181	Bert Emanuel	.10
182	Jacquez Green	.20
183	Hardy Nickerson	.10
184	Steve McNair	.50
185	Eddie George	.75
186	Yancey Thigpen	.20
187	Frank Wycheck	.10
188	Kevin Dyson	.20
189	Jackie Harris	.10
190	Blaine Bishop	.10
191	Skip Hicks	.20
192	Michael Westbrook	.20
193	Stephen Alexander	.10
194	Leslie Shepherd	.10
195	Casey Weldon	.10
196	Brian Mitchell	.10
197	Dan Wilkinson	.10
198	Terrell Davis CL Checklist Card #1	.50
199	Troy Aikman CL Checklist Car #2	.30
200	Tim Couch CL Checklist Card #3	1.00
201	*Ricky Williams*	5.00
202	*Tim Couch*	2.50
203	*Akili Smith*	1.00
204	*Daunte Culpepper*	5.00
205	*Torry Holt*	2.50
206	*Edgerrin James*	5.00
207	*David Boston*	2.50
208	*Peerless Price*	2.00
209	*Chris Claiborne*	1.00
210	*Champ Bailey*	1.25
211	*Cade McNown*	1.00
212	*Jevon Kearse*	2.00
213	*Joe Germaine*	1.00
214	*D'Wayne Bates*	.75
215	*Dameane Douglas*	.75
216	*Troy Edwards*	1.50
217	*Sedrick Irvin*	1.25
218	*Brock Huard*	1.00
219	*Amos Zereoue*	1.75
220	*Donovan McNabb*	5.00

1999 Upper Deck MVP Gold Script

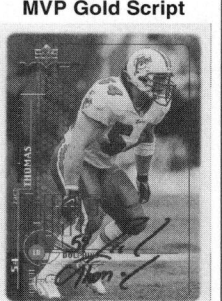

This is a parallel to the base set and is the same except for the players facsimile signature on the front in gold foil along with all the other foil in gold too. On the back the hologram is in gold foil and each single is sequentially numbered to 100.

Gold Cards:	8X-20X
Gold Rookies:	5X-10X
Production 100 Sets	

1999 Upper Deck MVP Silver Script

This is a parallel to the base and is the same except for the players facsimile autograph on the front in silver foil and the words Silver Script on the back. Singles were inserted 1:2 packs.

Silver Cards:	4X
Silver Rookies:	2X
Inserted 1:2	

1999 Upper Deck MVP Super Script

This is a parallel to the base set and each single has a holo foil facsimile signature of the player on the front and each is sequentially numbered to 25.

Super Cards:	20X-50X
Super Rookies:	10X-25X
Production 25 Sets	

1999 Upper Deck MVP Draw Your Own

Each single from this 30-card set is a drawing from a young collector from a previous contest winner. Singles were inserted 1:6 packs.

		NM/M
Complete Set (30):		18.00
Common Player:		.20
Minor Stars:		.40
Inserted 1:6		
1	Brett Favre	2.00
2	Emmitt Smith	1.50
3	John Elway	1.50
4	Emmitt Smith	1.50
5	Randy Moss	1.50
6	Terrell Davis	1.00
7	Steve Young	.75
8	Drew Bledsoe	.75
9	Troy Aikman	1.00
10	Terry Allen	.20
11	Warrick Dunn	.75
12	Kimble Anders	.20
13	Joey Galloway	.40
14	Barry Sanders	2.00
15	Mark Brunell	.75
16	Bruce Smith	.20
17	Randy Moss	2.00
18	Jerome Bettis	.40
19	John Elway	1.50
20	Jerome Bettis	.40
21	Brett Favre	2.00
22	Troy Aikman	1.00
23	Cris Carter	.75
24	Jason Gildon	.20
25	Randall Cunningham	.75
26	Thurman Thomas	.40
27	Jerry Rice	1.00
28	Jerome Bettis	.40
29	Steve Young	.75
30	Reggie White	.40

1999 Upper Deck MVP Drive Time

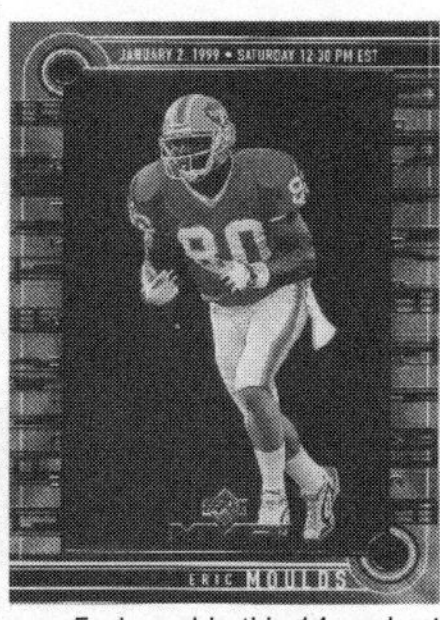

Each card in this 14-card set pays tribute to a star player who led the best offensive drive during the 1998 season. Singles were found 1:6 packs.

		NM/M
Complete Set (14):		10.00
Common Player:		.50
Minor Stars:		1.00
Inserted 1:6		
1	Steve Young	1.50
2	Kordell Stewart	1.00
3	Eric Moulds	1.00
4	Corey Dillon	1.00
5	Doug Flutie	1.00
6	Charlie Batch	.75
7	Curtis Martin	1.00
8	Marshall Faulk	1.00
9	Terrell Owens	1.25
10	Antowain Smith	1.00
11	Troy Aikman	2.50
12	Drew Bledsoe	1.50
13	Keyshawn Johnson	1.00
14	Steve McNair	1.25

1999 Upper Deck MVP Dynamics

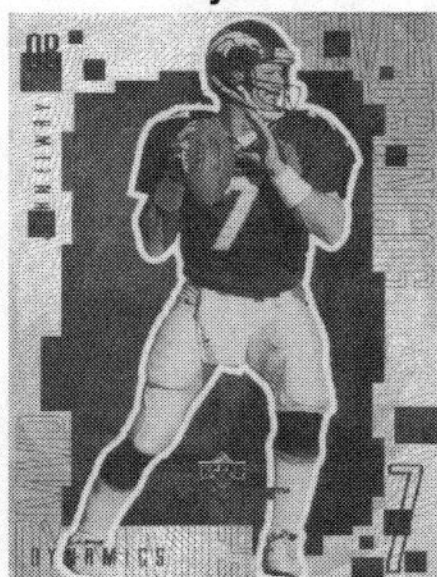

This 15-card set includes the top players in the NFL and puts them on a holo foil card. Singles were inserted 1:28 packs.

		NM/M
Complete Set (15):		25.00
Common Player:		1.00
Minor Stars:		2.00
Inserted 1:28		
1	John Elway	4.00
2	Steve Young	4.00
3	Jake Plummer	2.00
4	Fred Taylor	2.00
5	Mark Brunell	2.00
6	Joey Galloway	1.00
7	Terrell Davis	3.00
8	Randy Moss	4.00
9	Charlie Batch	1.00
10	Peyton Manning	4.00
11	Barry Sanders	5.00
12	Eddie George	2.00
13	Warrick Dunn	1.00
14	Jamal Anderson	1.00
15	Brett Favre	5.00

1999 Upper Deck MVP Game-Used Souvenirs

Each card in this 21-card set includes a piece of a game-used football by that player pictured on the card. Singles were inserted 1:130 packs.

		NM/M
Common Player:		20.00
Inserted 1:130		
BS	Barry Sanders	75.00
ES	Emmitt Smith	75.00
DF	Doug Flutie	40.00

KJ	Keyshawn Johnson	40.00
JP	Jake Plummer	30.00
JE	John Elway	75.00
PM	Peyton Manning	75.00
RM	Randy Moss	75.00
TD	Terrell Davis	20.00
JA	Jamal Anderson	40.00
MC	Donovan McNabb	75.00
AS	Akili Smith	30.00
EJ	Edgerrin James	75.00
BH	Brock Huard	25.00
TH	Torry Holt	35.00
CB	Champ Bailey	25.00
DB	David Boston	40.00
DC	Daunte Culpepper	75.00
CM	Cade McNown	35.00
DM	Dan Marino	100.00

1999 Upper Deck MVP Power Surge

The game's most impressive talents are highlighted in this 15-card set. Each foil card was inserted 1:9 packs.

		NM/M
Complete Set (15):		15.00
Common Player		.50
Minor Stars:		1.00
Inserted 1:9		
1	Jerome Bettis	1.00
2	Eddie George	1.00
3	Karim Abdul	.50
4	Curtis Martin	1.00
5	Antowain Smith	1.75
6	Kordell Stewart	1.00
7	Curtis Enis	.50
8	Joey Galloway	1.00
9	Mark Brunell	1.00
10	Peyton Manning	3.00
11	Antonio Freeman	1.00
12	Jerry Rice	3.00
13	Eric Moulds	1.00
14	Drew Bledsoe	2.00
15	Fred Taylor	1.25

1999 Upper Deck MVP Strictly Business

Only the top players in the game were included in this 13-card insert. Singles were found 1:14 packs.

		NM/M
Complete Set (15):		25.00
Common Player:		1.00
Inserted 1:14		
1	Eddie George	2.00
2	Curtis Martin	2.00
3	Fred Taylor	1.00
4	Steve Young	3.00
5	Kordell Stewart	1.00
6	Corey Dillon	1.00
7	Dan Marino	5.00
8	Jake Plummer	1.00
9	Jerry Rice	4.00
10	Warrick Dunn	2.00
11	Jerome Bettis	1.00
12	John Elway	4.00
13	Randy Moss	4.00
14	Troy Aikman	3.00
15	Brett Favre	5.00

1999 Upper Deck MVP Theatre

Each card in this 15-card set pictures a star player in action. Singles were inserted 1:9 packs.

		NM/M
Complete Set (15):		15.00
Common Player:		.50
Minor Stars:		1.00

		NM/M
Inserted 1:9		
1	Terrell Davis	3.00
2	Corey Dillon	1.00
3	Brett Favre	4.00
4	Jerry Rice	3.00
5	Emmitt Smith	3.00
6	Dan Marino	4.00
7	Jerome Bettis	.50
8	Napoleon Kaufman	1.00
9	Keyshawn Johnson	1.00
10	Warrick Dunn	1.00
11	Barry Sanders	3.00
12	Troy Aikman	2.00
13	Jamal Anderson	1.00
14	Randall Cunningham	.50
15	Doug Flutie	1.75

1999 Upper Deck Ovation

This was a 90-card set that included 30 rookies found 1:4 packs. Each single had a parallel Standing Ovation that was sequentially numbered to 50. Other insert sets included: A Piece of History, Center Stage, Curtain Calls, Spotlight, Star Performers, Super Signatures Silver and the Walter Payton Autographed Game Jersey. SRP was $3.99 for five-card packs.

		NM/M
Complete Set (90):		125.00
Common Player:		.25
Minor Stars:		.50
Common Rookie:		1.50
Inserted 1:4		
Pack (5):		3.50
Wax Box (20):		50.00
1	Jake Plummer	.50
2	Adrian Murrell	.25
3	Jamal Anderson	.75
4	Chris Chandler	.50
5	Tony Banks	.50
6	Antowain Smith	.50
7	Doug Flutie	.75
8	Tshimanga Biakabutuka	.50
9	Steve Beuerlein	.25
10	Curtis Conway	.50
11	Curtis Enis	.75
12	Corey Dillon	.75
13	Jeff Blake	.50
14	Ty Detmer	.25
15	Troy Aikman	1.50
16	Emmitt Smith	2.00
17	Terrell Davis	1.25
18	Bubby Brister	.50
19	Barry Sanders	2.50
20	Charlie Batch	.50
21	Brett Favre	3.00
22	Dorsey Levens	.50
23	Peyton Manning	2.00
24	Marvin Harrison	.75
25	Mark Brunell	.75
26	Fred Taylor	.75
27	Elvis Grbac	.25
28	Andre Rison	.25
29	Dan Marino	2.00
30	Karim Abdul	.50
31	Randall Cunningham	.75
32	Randy Moss	2.50
33	Drew Bledsoe	1.25
34	Terry Glenn	.75
35	Danny Wuerffel	.50
36	Cameron Cleeland	.50
37	Kerry Collins	.50
38	Amani Toomer	.25
39	Curtis Martin	.75
40	Keyshawn Johnson	.75
41	Napoleon Kaufman	.75
42	Tim Brown	.50
43	Doug Pederson	.25
44	Charles Johnson	.25
45	Kordell Stewart	.75
46	Jerome Bettis	.75
47	Trent Green	.50
48	Marshall Faulk	.75
49	Natrone Means	.75
50	Jim Harbaugh	.50
51	Steve Young	1.00
52	Jerry Rice	2.50
53	Joey Galloway	.75
54	Jon Kitna	.75
55	Warrick Dunn	.75
56	Trent Dilfer	.50
57	Steve McNair	.75
58	Eddie George	.75
59	Brad Johnson	.50
60	Skip Hicks	.50
61	*Tim Couch*	3.00
62	*Donovan McNabb*	10.00
63	*Akili Smith*	2.00
64	*Edgerrin James*	10.00
65	*Ricky Williams*	5.00
66	*Torry Holt*	5.00
67	*Champ Bailey*	2.00
68	*David Boston*	5.00
69	*Daunte Culpepper*	10.00
70	*Cade McNown*	2.00
71	*Troy Edwards*	2.00
72	*Kevin Johnson*	3.00
73	*James Johnson*	2.00
74	*Rob Konrad*	2.00
75	*Kevin Faulk*	2.00
76	*Shaun King*	2.00
77	*Peerless Price*	4.00
78	*Michael Cloud*	2.00
79	*Jermaine Fazande*	2.00
80	*D'Wayne Bates*	2.00
81	*Brock Huard*	2.00
82	*Marty Booker*	3.00
83	*Karsten Bailey*	1.50
84	*Al Wilson*	2.00
85	*Joe Germaine*	2.00
86	*Dameane Douglas*	1.50
87	*Sedrick Irvin*	2.00
88	*Amos Zereoue*	3.00
89	*Cecil Collins*	2.00
90	*Ebenezer Ekuban*	1.50

1999 Upper Deck Ovation Standing Ovation

This was a 90-card parallel to the base set. Each single was sequentially numbered to 50.

Standing Ovation Cards:	20X-40X
Standing Ovation Rookies:	5X-10X
Production 50 Sets	

1999 Upper Deck Ovation A Piece of History

This 13-card insert set included pieces of game-used footballs. A total of 4,560 cards were produced and randomly inserted.

		NM/M
Complete Set (13):		1,250
Common Player:		50.00
Production 4,560 Total Cards		
DC	Daunte Culpepper	60.00
BF	Brett Favre	100.00
JG	Joe Germaine	20.00
TH	Torry Holt	40.00
BH	Brock Huard	20.00
EJ	Edgerrin James	75.00
DM	Dan Marino	100.00
MC	Donovan McNabb	60.00
CM	Cade McNown	20.00
JR	Jerry Rice	75.00
AS	Akili Smith	20.00
RW	Ricky Williams	100.00
SY	Steve Young	60.00

1999 Upper Deck Ovation Center Stage

This 24-card insert set was a three-tiered collection focusing on eight great running backs from the NFL's past to present. Cards #1-#8 were inserted 1:9, cards #9-#16 were found 1:25 and cards #17-#24 were pulled 1:99 packs.

		NM/M
Complete Set (24):		100.00
Common Player #1-8:		1.00
Inserted 1:9		
Common Player #9-16:		2.00
Inserted 1:25		
Common Player #17-24:		3.00

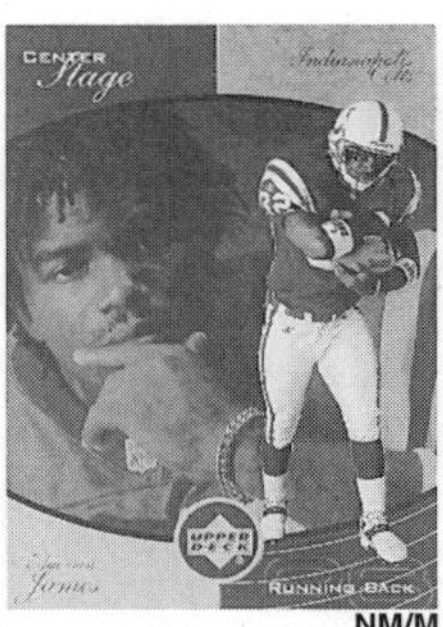

		NM/M
Inserted 1:99		
1	Walter Payton	2.00
2	Barry Sanders	2.00
3	Emmitt Smith	2.00
4	Terrell Davis	1.50
5	Jamal Anderson	1.00
6	Fred Taylor	1.00
7	Ricky Williams	4.00
8	Edgerrin James	2.00
9	Walter Payton	3.00
10	Barry Sanders	3.00
11	Emmitt Smith	3.00
12	Terrell Davis	2.00
13	Jamal Anderson	2.00
14	Fred Taylor	2.00
15	Ricky Williams	10.00
16	Edgerrin James	8.00
17	Walter Payton	10.00
18	Barry Sanders	10.00
19	Emmitt Smith	10.00
20	Terrell Davis	8.00
21	Jamal Anderson	3.00
22	Fred Taylor	3.00
23	Ricky Williams	15.00
24	Edgerrin James	12.00

1999 Upper Deck Ovation Curtain Calls

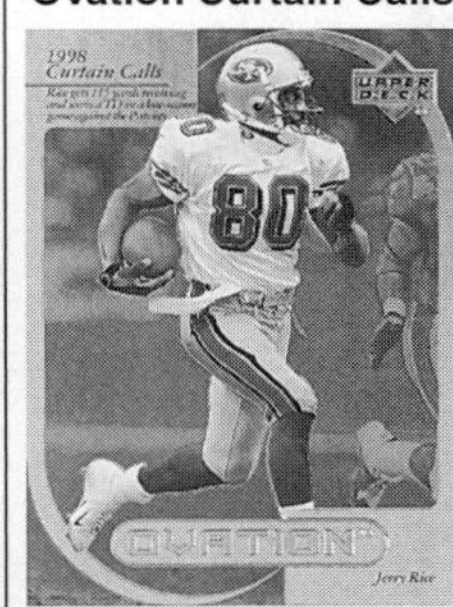

This 30-card insert set focused on some of the most memorable accomplishments posted during the 1998 NFL season. Inserted 1:4 packs.

		NM/M
Complete Set (30):		35.00
Common Player:		.50
Minor Stars:		1.00
Inserted 1:4		
1	Peyton Manning	4.00
2	Fred Taylor	2.00
3	Randy Moss	4.00
4	Cris Carter	1.00
5	Troy Aikman	3.00
6	Randall Cunningham	1.00
7	Mark Brunell	1.00
8	Jon Kitna	1.00
9	Steve McNair	1.00
10	Jake Plummer	1.00
11	Jerry Rice	4.00
12	Kordell Stewart	1.00
13	Warrick Dunn	1.00
14	Emmitt Smith	5.00
15	Jerome Bettis	1.00
16	Terrell Owens	1.00
17	Antonio Freeman	1.00
18	Joey Galloway	1.00
19	Curtis Martin	1.00
20	Tim Brown	1.00
21	Charlie Batch	1.00
22	Doug Flutie	1.00
23	Barry Sanders	5.00
24	Drew Bledsoe	3.00
25	Corey Dillon	1.00
26	Eddie George	1.00
27	Keyshawn Johnson	1.00
28	Steve Young	3.00
29	Brett Favre	6.00
30	Terrell Davis	3.00

1999 Upper Deck Ovation Spotlight

This was a 15-card insert set that featured the top players from the 1999 NFL Draft. Singles were inserted 1:9 packs.

		NM/M
Complete Set (15):		20.00
Common Player:		.50
Inserted 1:9		
1	Tim Couch	3.00
2	Donovan McNabb	4.00
3	Akili Smith	.50

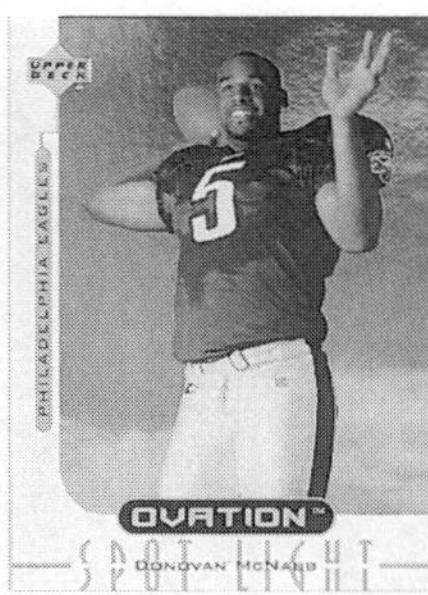

		NM/M
4	Edgerrin James	5.00
5	Ricky Williams	6.00
6	Torry Holt	3.00
7	Champ Bailey	.50
8	David Boston	3.00
9	Daunte Culpepper	4.00
10	Cade McNown	.50
11	Troy Edwards	2.00
12	Kevin Johnson	1.00
13	Joe Germaine	.50
14	Brock Huard	.50
15	Kevin Faulk	.50

1999 Upper Deck Ovation Star Performers

This was a 15-card insert set that included some of the top names in the NFL. Singles were inserted 1:39 packs.

		NM/M
Complete Set (15):		35.00
Common Player:		1.00
Inserted 1:39		
1	Terrell Davis	3.00
2	Peyton Manning	3.00
3	Brett Favre	5.00
4	Dan Marino	5.00
5	Barry Sanders	4.00
6	Jamal Anderson	1.00
7	Mark Brunell	1.00
8	Jerome Bettis	1.00
9	Charlie Batch	1.00
10	Antowain Smith	1.00
11	Jake Plummer	1.00
12	Joey Galloway	1.00
13	Randy Moss	4.00
14	Steve Young	3.00
15	Warrick Dunn	1.00

1999 Upper Deck Ovation Super Signatures

This was a three-card insert set that included autographs from three retired NFL superstars. Each single was sequentially numbered to 300. A parallel Gold version was also released and each of those were numbered to 150. A parallel Rainbow version was made and each was sequentially numbered to 10.

		NM/M
Common Player:		200.00
Production 300 Sets		
Gold Cards:		1.5X
Production 150 Sets		
Rainbow Cards:		
Production 10 Sets		
NA	Joe Namath	175.00
MN	Joe Montana	200.00
WP	Walter Payton	200.00

1999 Upper Deck Ovation Walter Payton Auto. Jersey

Walter Payton signed a total of 34 Game Jersey cards. Each came with a swatch of a game-used jersey and were sequentially numbered to 34. Singles were randomly inserted.

		NM/M
WPJ	Walter Payton	1,500

1999 Upper Deck PowerDeck

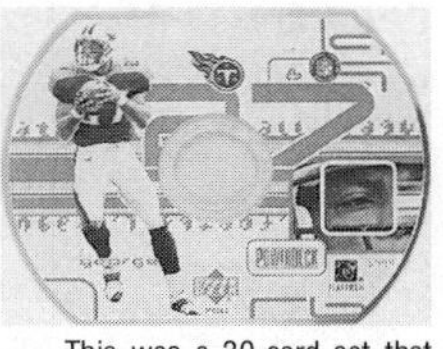

This was a 30-card set that pictured each player on a digital trading card. Each card was to be used on a CD-Rom and contained complete stats, bios, 20 to 30 images, music, audio clips and game highlights. Each single also had a parallel Auxiliary single. The CD singles were issued one-per-pack and the Auxiliary cards were issued two-per-pack. Other insert sets included: Autographs, Most Valuable Performances, Powerful Moments, Time Capsule and Walter Payton Autograph Game Jersey. SRP was $4.99 for three-card packs.

		NM/M
Complete Set (30):		50.00
Common Player:		1.00
Inserted 1:1		
Pack (3):		5.00
Wax Box (24):		90.00
1	Troy Aikman	3.00
2	Drew Bledsoe	1.00
3	Randy Moss	3.00
4	Barry Sanders	4.00
5	Brett Favre	5.00
6	Terrell Davis	3.00
7	Peyton Manning	3.00
8	Emmitt Smith	4.00
9	Dan Marino	5.00
10	Jake Plummer	1.00
11	Eddie George	1.00
12	Jerry Rice	3.00
13	Steve Young	3.00
14	Mark Brunell	1.00
15	Kordell Stewart	1.00
16	Keyshawn Johnson	1.00
17	Fred Taylor	1.00
18	Jamal Anderson	1.00
19	*Cecil Collins*	1.00
20	*Ricky Williams*	8.00
21	*Tim Couch*	4.00
22	*Donovan McNabb*	8.00
23	*Akili Smith*	2.00
24	*Edgerrin James*	8.00
25	*Daunte Culpepper*	8.00
26	*Brock Huard*	2.00
27	*Torry Holt*	4.00
28	*David Boston*	4.00
29	*Cade McNown*	2.00
30	*Champ Bailey*	2.00

1999 Upper Deck PowerDeck Auxiliary

Each card in this 30-card set was printed on regular cardboard stock. Singles were issued two-per-pack. Each single had a parallel one-of-one Gold card.

		NM/M
Complete Set (30):		15.00
Common Player:		.25
1	Troy Aikman	1.00
2	Drew Bledsoe	.75
3	Randy Moss	2.00
4	Barry Sanders	2.00
5	Brett Favre	2.00
6	Terrell Davis	1.50
7	Peyton Manning	1.50
8	Emmitt Smith	1.50
9	Dan Marino	1.50
10	Jake Plummer	.75
11	Eddie George	.25
12	Jerry Rice	1.00
13	Steve Young	.75
14	Mark Brunell	.75
15	Kordell Stewart	.25
16	Keyshawn Johnson	.25
17	Fred Taylor	1.00
18	Jamal Anderson	.25
19	Cecil Collins	1.50
20	Ricky Williams	4.00
21	Tim Couch	2.00
22	Donovan McNabb	3.00
23	Akili Smith	3.00
24	Edgerrin James	3.50
25	Daunte Culpepper	3.00
26	Brock Huard	1.50
27	Torry Holt	2.00
28	David Boston	2.00
29	Cade McNown	1.00
30	Champ Bailey	1.00

A player's name in *italic* type indicates a rookie card.

1999 Upper Deck PowerDeck Autographed Cards

This was a 12-card insert set that included autographs from both veterans and prospects. Each single was sequentially numbered to 50.

		NM/M
Complete Set (12):		1,250
Common Player:		75.00
Production 50 Sets		
TA	Troy Aikman	175.00
CB	Champ Bailey	40.00
DB	David Boston	75.00
TC	Tim Couch	150.00
DC	Daunte Culpepper	125.00
TH	Torry Holt	75.00
BH	Brock Huard	75.00
EJ	Edgerrin James	200.00
DM	Dan Marino	250.00
CM	Cade McNown	60.00
JP	Jake Plummer	50.00
AS	Akili Smith	50.00

1999 Upper Deck PowerDeck Most Valuable Performances

This seven-card insert set highlighted historic performances in the Super Bowl and other notable games. Singles were inserted 1:287 packs. Each card also had a parallel Auxiliary single and they were also issued 1:287.

		NM/M
Complete Set (7):		300.00
Common Player:		15.00
Inserted 1:287		
Auxiliary Cards:		1x
Inserted 1:287		
1	Joe Montana	75.00
2	John Elway	45.00
3	Emmitt Smith	45.00
4	Jamal Anderson	15.00
5	Randy Moss	45.00
6	Brett Favre	75.00
7	Terrell Davis	35.00

1999 Upper Deck PowerDeck Powerful Moments

This six-card insert set showcased some of the most significant games in pro football history. Singles were inserted 1:23 packs. Each card had an Auxiliary single that was also issued 1:23 packs.

		NM/M
Complete Set (6):		60.00
Common Player:		8.00
Inserted 1:23		
Auxiliary Cards:		1x
Inserted 1:23		
1	Joe Montana	12.00
2	Terrell Davis	6.00
3	John Elway	10.00
4	Randy Moss	10.00
5	Dan Marino	10.00
6	Emmitt Smith	10.00

1999 Upper Deck PowerDeck Time Capsule

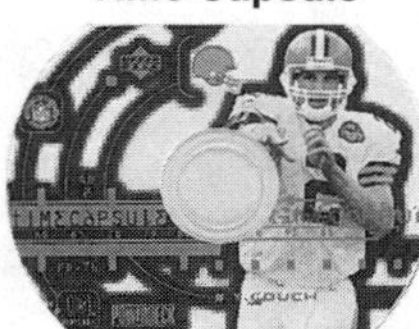

This was a six-card insert set that included flashbacks of the greatest superstars' rookie seasons. Singles were found 1:7 packs. Each single had a parallel Auxiliary card that was also inserted 1:7 packs.

		NM/M
Complete Set (6):		20.00
Common Player:		2.00
Inserted 1:7		
Auxiliary Cards:		1x
Inserted 1:7		
1	Edgerrin James	4.00
2	Barry Sanders	4.00
3	Terrell Davis	2.00
4	Emmitt Smith	5.00
5	Dan Marino	6.00
6	Tim Couch	2.00

1999 Upper Deck Retro

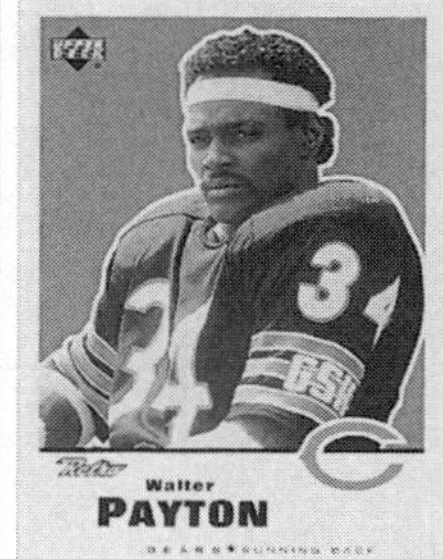

This was a 165-card set that pictured both past and present NFL stars. Each card had a classic old-time look and feel. Each single had a parallel Gold card that was numbered to 175. Other insert sets included: Inkredible, Legends of the Fall, Old School/New School, Smashmouth and Throwback Attack.The packaging was unique in that each of the 24 packs were inserted into an actual lunch box. SRP was $4.99 for six-card packs.

		NM/M
Complete Set (165):		60.00
Common Player:		.15
Minor Stars:		.30
Common Rookie:		.75
Pack (6):		3.25
Wax Box (24):		55.00
1	Jake Plummer	.50
2	Adrian Murrell	.15
3	Rob Moore	.30
4	Frank Sanders	.15
5	*David Boston*	2.50
6	Tim Dwight	.75
7	Chris Chandler	.30
8	Jamal Anderson	.75
9	O.J. Santiago	.15
10	Terance Mathis	.30
11	Priest Holmes	1.50
12	Tony Banks	.30
13	Patrick Johnson	.15
14	Scott Mitchell	.15
15	Jermaine Lewis	.15
16	Eric Moulds	.75
17	Doug Flutie	.75
18	Antowain Smith	.50
19	Thurman Thomas	.30
20	*Peerless Price*	2.00
21	Fred Lane	.15
22	Tshimanga Biakabutuka	.30
23	Steve Beurlein	.30
24	Muhsin Muhammad	.50
25	Rae Carruth	.15
26	Curtis Enis	.75
27	Walter Payton	5.00
28	Bobby Engram	.15
29	*Cade McNown*	1.50
30	Curtis Conway	.30
31	Darnay Scott	.30
32	Jeff Blake	.30
33	Corey Dillon	.75
34	*Akili Smith*	1.50
35	Carl Pickens	.30
36	*Tim Couch*	1.50
37	Ty Detmer	.15
38	Jim Brown	3.00
39	*Kevin Johnson*	1.50
40	Ozzie Newsome	.30
41	Troy Aikman	1.50
42	Raghib Ismail	.15
43	Emmitt Smith	2.00
44	Michael Irvin	.30
45	Deion Sanders	.50
46	Roger Staubach	2.00
47	John Elway	2.00
48	Bubby Brister	.30
49	Terrell Davis	1.00
50	Ed McCaffrey	.50
51	Rod Smith	.50
52	Shannon Sharpe	.30
53	Charlie Batch	.50
54	Johnnie Morton	.15
55	Barry Sanders	3.00
56	*Sedrick Irvin*	1.00
57	Herman Moore	.50
58	Brett Favre	3.00
59	Mark Chmura	.30
60	Antonio Freeman	.75
61	Robert Brooks	.15
62	Dorsey Levens	.75
63	Peyton Manning	2.00
64	Jerome Pathon	.15
65	Marvin Harrison	.75
66	*Edgerrin James*	5.00
67	Ken Dilger	.15
68	Mark Brunell	.75
69	Fred Taylor	.75
70	Jimmy Smith	.75
71	James Stewart	.50
72	Keenan McCardell	.30
73	Elvis Grbac	.30
74	*Michael Cloud*	.75
75	Andre Rison	.30
76	Tony Gonzalez	.30
77	Warren Moon	.30
78	Derrick Alexander	.15
79	Dan Marino	2.00
80	O.J. McDuffie	.30
81	*James Johnson*	1.00
82	Paul Warfield	.30
83	*Cecil Collins*	1.00
84	Randall Cunningham	.75
85	Randy Moss	2.00
86	Cris Carter	.75
87	Fran Tarkenton	1.00
88	*Daunte Culpepper*	5.00
89	Robert Smith	.75
90	Drew Bledsoe	1.25
91	Terry Glenn	.75
92	*Kevin Faulk*	1.00
93	Tony Simmons	.30
94	Ben Coates	.30
95	Billy Joe Hobert	.15
96	Cameron Cleeland	.30
97	Eddie Kennison	.15
98	Andre Hastings	.15
99	*Ricky Williams*	5.00
100	Kerry Collins	.30
101	*Joe Montgomery*	.75
102	Gary Brown	.15
103	Ike Hilliard	.15
104	Amani Toomer	.15
105	Vinny Testaverde	.30
106	Wayne Chrebet	.75
107	Curtis Martin	.75
108	Joe Namath	2.50
109	Keyshawn Johnson	.75
110	Don Maynard	.50
111	Rich Gannon	.30
112	Tim Brown	.30
113	Charles Woodson	.75
114	Rickey Dudley	.15
115	Darrell Russell	.15
116	Napoleon Kaufman	.75
117	*Donovan McNabb*	5.00
118	Doug Pederson	.15
119	Duce Staley	.75
120	Torrance Small	.15
121	Charles Johnson	.15
122	Jerome Bettis	.75
123	Courtney Hawkins	.15
124	Kordell Stewart	.75
125	*Troy Edwards*	1.50
126	*Amos Zereoue*	.75
127	Trent Green	.50
128	Marshall Faulk	.75
129	Az Hakim	.30
130	*Joe Germaine*	.75
131	*Torry Holt*	2.50
132	Isaac Bruce	.75
133	Jim Harbaugh	.30
134	Junior Seau	.30
135	Natrone Means	.30
136	Ryan Leaf	.50
137	Dan Fouts	.50
138	Mikhael Ricks	.15
139	Steve Young	1.00
140	Terrell Owens	.75
141	Jerry Rice	1.50
142	J.J. Stokes	.30
143	Lawrence Phillips	.30
144	Joe Montana	3.50
145	Jon Kitna	.75
146	Ahman Green	.30
147	Joey Galloway	.75
148	Ricky Watters	.30
149	*Brock Huard*	1.50
150	Steve Largent	.75
151	Trent Dilfer	.50
152	Reidel Anthony	.30
153	Warrick Dunn	.75
154	Mike Alstott	.75
155	*Shaun King*	1.00
156	Eddie George	1.00
157	Steve McNair	1.00
158	Kevin Dyson	.30
159	Frank Wycheck	.15
160	Yancey Thigpen	.30
161	Brad Johnson	.75
162	Rodney Peete	.15
163	Michael Westbrook	.50
164	Skip Hicks	.30
165	*Champ Bailey*	1.00

1999 Upper Deck Retro Gold

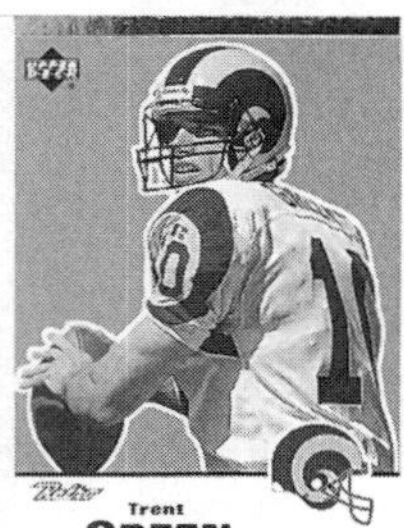

This was a 165-card parallel to the base set. Each card included gold foil and was sequentially numbered to 175.

	NM/M
Gold Cards:	4X-8X
Gold Rookies:	3X-6X
Production 175 Sets	

A card number in parenthese ( ) indicates the set is unnumbered.

1999 Upper Deck Retro Inkredible

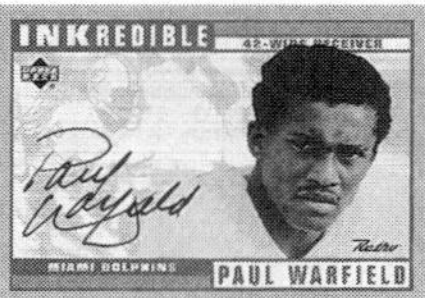

This was a 30-card insert set that featured authentic autograph cards of past and present NFL stars. Singles were inserted 1:23 packs. Each single also had a parallel Gold version that was sequentially numbered to the player's jersey number.

		NM/M
Complete Set (30):		1,500
Common Player:		10.00
Minor Stars:		20.00
1:Box		
Gold numbered to jersey number		1X to 4X
DB	David Boston	35.00
CC	Cris Carter	30.00
WC	Wayne Chrebet	20.00
TC	Tim Couch	75.00
DC	Daunte Culpepper	45.00
TD	Terrell Davis	60.00
DF	Dan Fouts	20.00
GH	Garrison Hearst	10.00
TH	Torry Holt	35.00
BH	Brock Huard	20.00
SK	Shaun King	20.00
JK	Jon Kitna	20.00
SL	Steve Largent	20.00
DL	Dorsey Levens	20.00
MC	Donovan McNabb	45.00
CM	Cade McNown	45.00
JM	Joe Montana	180.00
RM	Randy Moss	150.00
AM	Adrian Murrell	10.00
JN	Joe Namath	150.00
OZ	Ozzie Newsome	10.00
TO	Terrell Owens	40.00
WP	Walter Payton	275.00
AK	Akili Smith	25.00
AS	Antowain Smith	20.00
RS	Rod Smith	20.00
RG	Roger Staubach	100.00
FT	Fran Tarkenton	50.00
PW	Paul Warfield	10.00
RW	Ricky Williams	120.00

1999 Upper Deck Retro Legends of the Fall

This was a 30-card insert set that focused on both current and former NFL stars who transcended their eras. Singles were inserted 1:11 packs. Each card had a parallel Silver version that was sequentially numbered to 75.

		NM/M
Complete Set (30):		25.00
Common Player:		.50
Minor Stars:		1.00
Inserted 1:11		
Silver Cards:		10X-20X
Production 75 Sets		
1	Jake Plummer	1.00
2	Corey Dillon	1.00
3	Curtis Martin	1.00
4	Vinny Testaverde	.50
5	Brett Favre	4.00
6	Randy Moss	2.00
7	John Elway	3.00
8	Jerry Rice	3.00
9	Troy Aikman	2.00
10	Ricky Watters	.50
11	Keyshawn Johnson	1.00
12	Mark Brunell	1.00
13	Dorsey Levens	.50
14	Steve McNair	1.00
15	Emmitt Smith	3.00
16	Marshall Faulk	1.00
17	Priest Holmes	2.00
18	Steve Young	2.00
19	Skip Hicks	.50
20	Eddie George	1.00
21	Garrison Hearst	.50
22	Drew Bledsoe	2.50
23	Warrick Dunn	1.00
24	Eric Moulds	1.00
25	Joey Galloway	1.00
26	Tim Brown	.50
27	Chris Chandler	.50
28	Peyton Manning	3.00
29	Antonio Freeman	1.00
30	Deion Sanders	1.00

1999 Upper Deck Retro Lunch Boxes

This was a 16-box set that was used for the packing of the packs. Each box was a usable lunch box that featured a player or players on both sides. Dual player boxes were inserted one-per-case.

	NM/M
Complete Set (16):	70.00
Common Player:	4.00
One dual box per case	
Joe Montana	10.00
Ricky Williams	8.00
Randy Moss	6.00
Barry Sanders	8.00
John Elway	6.00
Terrell Davis	4.00
Dan Marino	8.00
Joe Namath	8.00
Joe Montana, John Elway	10.00
Joe Montana, Dan Marino	10.00
John Elway, Dan Marino	10.00
Joe Montana, Joe Namath	10.00
Ricky Williams, Tim Couch	8.00
Joe Namath, Dan Marino	10.00
Tim Couch, Joe Montana	8.00
Barry Sanders, Terrell Davis	8.00

1999 Upper Deck Retro Old School/New School

This was a 30-card insert set that focused on the NFL's top stars of yesterday and today and paired one of each player on one card. Each of these singles were sequentially numbered to 1,000. A parallel Level 2 was issued and each was numbered to 50.

		NM/M
Complete Set (30):		70.00
Common Player:		.50
Minor Stars:		1.00
Production 1,000 Sets		
Level 2 Cards:		3X-5X
Production 50 Sets		
1	Terrell Davis, Ricky Williams	5.00
2	Joe Montana, Jake Plummer	4.00
3	Cris Carter, Randy Moss	4.00
4	Randall Cunningham, Daunte Culpepper	3.00
5	Brett Favre, Jon Kitna	5.00
6	Emmitt Smith, Fred Taylor	4.00
7	Mark Brunell, Brock Huard	2.00
8	John Elway, Peyton Manning	4.00
9	Steve Young, Cade McNown	3.00
10	Don Maynard, Keyshawn Johnson	1.00
11	Dan Marino, Tim Couch	4.00
12	Jerry Rice, Terrell Owens	4.00
13	Marshall Faulk, Edgerrin James	4.00
14	Dan Fouts, Akili Smith	2.00
15	Barry Sanders, Jamal Anderson	3.00
16	Terry Glenn, David Boston	1.00
17	Deion Sanders, Champ Bailey	1.00
18	Andre Reed, Eric Moulds	.50
19	Junior Seau, Chris Claiborne	.50
20	Steve Largent, Joey Galloway	1.00
21	Kordell Stewart, Shaun King	1.00
22	Ricky Watters, Kevin Faulk	1.00
23	Thurman Thomas, Warrick Dunn	.50
24	Tim Brown, Troy Edwards	1.00
25	Jerome Bettis, Cecil Collins	1.00
26	Isaac Bruce, Torry Holt	1.00
27	Fran Tarkenton, Donovan McNabb	3.00
28	Warren Moon, Charlie Batch	2.00
29	Herman Moore, D'Wayne Bates	.50
30	Roger Staubach, Troy Aikman	5.00

1999 Upper Deck Retro Smashmouth

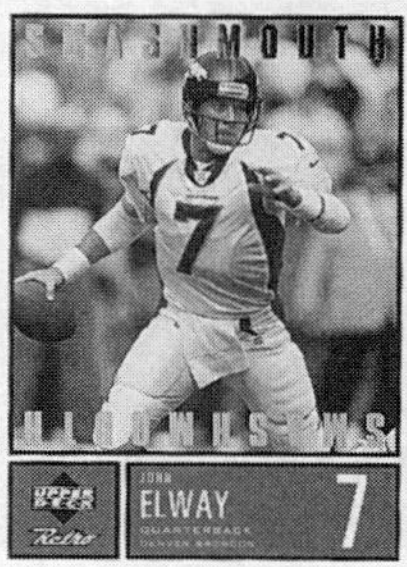

This was a 15-card insert set that took a look at 15 of the game's most aggressive players. Singles were inserted 1:8 packs. A parallel Level 2 was also released and each was sequentially numbered to 100.

		NM/M
Complete Set (15):		20.00
Common Player:		.75
Minor Stars:		1.50
Inserted 1:8		
Level 2 Cards:		3X-5X
Production 100 Sets		
1	Fred Taylor	1.00
2	Jamal Anderson	1.50
3	John Elway	4.00
4	Brock Huard	1.00
5	Daunte Culpepper	3.00
6	Charlie Batch	1.00
7	Steve McNair	1.50
8	Corey Dillon	1.50
9	Natrone Means	.75
10	Randall Cunningham	.75
11	Drew Bledsoe	2.00
12	Jerome Bettis	1.50
13	Antowain Smith	.75
14	Steve Young	2.00
15	Eddie George	1.50

1999 Upper Deck Retro Throwback Attack

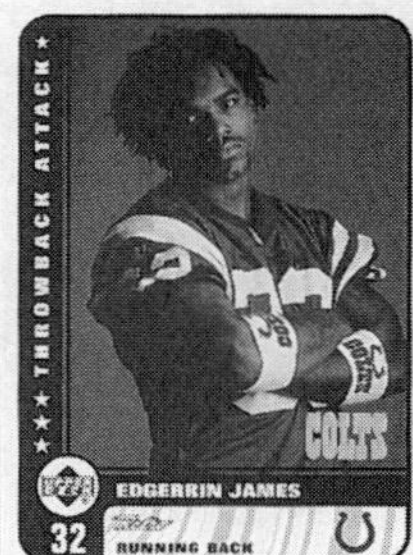

THROWBACK ATTACK
EDGERRIN JAMES
32
RUNNING BACK
COLTS

This was a 15-card insert set that showcased collectible, modern players with playing styles of the bygone era of football. Singles were inserted 1:5 packs. Each card had a parallel Gold single that was sequentially numbered to 500.

		NM/M
Complete Set (15):		25.00
Common Player:		.75
Minor Stars:		1.50
Inserted 1:5		
Gold Cards:		3X-5X
Production 500 Sets		
1	Brett Favre	4.00
2	Herman Moore	.75
3	Troy Aikman	2.50
4	Eric Moulds	1.50
5	Tim Couch	3.00
6	Terrell Owens	1.50
7	Champ Bailey	1.00
8	Kordell Stewart	1.00
9	Mark Brunell	1.00
10	Curtis Martin	1.50
11	Torry Holt	1.75
12	David Boston	1.75
13	Doug Flutie	1.75

14 Edgerrin James 5.00
15 Akili Smith 1.00

1999 Upper Deck Retro Walter Payton

Walter Payton signed 200 UD Authentic cards and each was sequentially numbered.

NM/M
WP1 W.Payton AUTO 300.00

1999 Victory

This was the premiere edition of Victory Football. The 440-card set included 60 rookie cards found one-per-pack. This was a retail-only release that didn't include any inserts. Subsets included: All-Victory, Season Leaders, Victory Parade, Rookie Flashback and '99 Rookie Class.

NM/M
Complete Set (440): 70.00
Common Player: .10
Minor Stars: .20
Common Rookie: .50
Inserted 1:1
Pack (12): 1.00
Wax Box (36): 20.00
1 Arizona Cardinals visit .10
2 Jake Plummer .40
3 Adrian Murrell .10
4 Michael Pittman .10
5 Frank Sanders .20
6 Andre Wadsworth .10
7 Rob Moore .20
8 Simeon Rice .10
9 Kwamie Lassiter .10
10 Mario Bates .10
11 Atlanta Falcons visit .10
12 Jamal Anderson .30
13 Chris Chandler .20
14 Chuck Smith .10
15 Terance Mathis .10
16 Tim Dwight .30
17 Ray Buchanan .10
18 O.J. Santiago .10
19 Lester Archambeau .10
20 Baltimore Ravens visit .10
21 Tony Banks .20
22 Priest Holmes .30
23 Michael Jackson .10
24 Jermaine Lewis .20
25 Michael McCrary .10
26 Rod Woodson .10
27 Buffalo Bills visit .10
28 Rob Johnson .20
29 Antowain Smith .30
30 Thurman Thomas .20
31 Doug Flutie .50
32 Eric Moulds .30
33 Bruce Smith .10
34 Andre Reed .20
35 Phil Hansen .10
36 Carolina Panthers visit .10
37 Fred Lane .10
38 Tshimanga Biakabutuka .10
39 Rae Carruth .10
40 Wesley Walls .10
41 Steve Beuerlein .10
42 Muhsin Muhammad .10
43 Kevin Greene .10
44 Chicago Bears visit .10
45 Erik Kramer .10
46 Edgar Bennett .10
47 Curtis Conway .20
48 Curtis Enis .30
49 Bobby Engram .10
50 Alonzo Mayes .10
51 Tony Parrish .10
52 Glyn Milburn .10
53 Cincinnati Bengals visit .10
54 Corey Dillon .30
55 Jeff Blake .20
56 Carl Pickens .20
57 Darnay Scott .10
58 Tony McGee .10
59 Ki-Jana Carter .10
60 Takeo Spikes .10
61 Cleveland Browns visit .10
62 Ty Detmer .10
63 Terry Kirby .10
64 Derrick Alexander .10
65 Leslie Shepherd .10
66 Marquez Pope .10
67 Antonio Langham .10
68 Marc Edwards .10
69 Dallas Cowboys visit .10
70 Troy Aikman 1.00
71 Emmitt Smith 1.50
72 Deion Sanders .30
73 Raghib Ismail .10
74 Michael Irvin .20
75 Chris Warren .10
76 Greg Ellis .10
77 Kavika Pittman .10
78 David LaFleur .10
79 Denver Broncos visit .10
80 John Elway 1.50
81 Terrell Davis 1.00
82 Rod Smith .20
83 Shannon Sharpe .20
84 Ed McCaffrey .20
85 John Mobley .10
86 Bill Romanowski .10
87 Jason Elam .10
88 Howard Griffith .10
89 Detroit Lions visit .10
90 Barry Sanders 2.00
91 Johnnie Morton .10
92 Herman Moore .30
93 Charlie Batch .50
94 Germane Crowell .20
95 Robert Porcher .10
96 Stephen Boyd .10
97 Green Bay Packers visit .10
98 Brett Favre 2.00
99 Antonio Freeman .30
100 Dorsey Levens .30
101 Mark Chmura .20
102 Vonnie Holliday .20
103 Bill Schroeder .10
104 LeRoy Butler .10
105 William Henderson .10
106 Indianapolis Colts visit .10
107 Peyton Manning 1.50
108 Marvin Harrison .30
109 Ken Dilger .10
110 Jerome Pathon .10
111 E.G. Green .10
112 Ellis Johnson .10
113 Jeff Burris .10
114 Jacksonville Jaguars visit .10
115 Mark Brunell .75
116 Jimmy Smith .20
117 Keenan McCardell .10
118 Fred Taylor 1.00
119 James Stewart .10
120 Dave Thomas .10
121 Kyle Brady .10
122 Bryce Paup .10
123 Kansas City Chiefs visit .10
124 Elvis Grbac .20
125 Andre Rison .20
126 Derrick Alexander .10
127 Tony Gonzalez .20
128 Donnell Bennett .10
129 Derrick Thomas .20
130 Tamarick Vanover .10
131 Donnie Edwards .10
132 Miami Dolphins visit .10
133 Dan Marino 1.50
134 Karim Abdul .30
135 Zach Thomas .20
136 O.J. McDuffie .20
137 John Avery .20
138 Sam Madison .10
139 Terrell Buckley .10
140 Jason Taylor .10
141 Oronde Gadsden .20
142 Minnesota Vikings visit .10
143 Randall Cunningham .30
144 Cris Carter .30
145 Robert Smith .20
146 Randy Moss 1.50
147 Jake Reed .10
148 Leroy Hoard .10
149 Matthew Hatchette .10
150 John Randle .10
151 Gary Anderson .10
152 New England Patriots visit .10
153 Drew Bledsoe .75
154 Terry Glenn .30
155 Ben Coates .20
156 Ty Law .10
157 Tony Simmons .20
158 Ted Johnson .10
159 Willie McGinest .10
160 Tony Carter .10
161 Shawn Jefferson .10
162 New Orleans Saints visit .10
163 Danny Wuerffel .20
164 Lamar Smith .10
165 Keith Poole .10
166 Cameron Cleeland .20
167 Joe Johnson .10
168 Andre Hastings .10
169 La'Roi Glover .10
170 Aaron Craver .10
171 New York Giants visit .10
172 Kent Graham .20
173 Gary Brown .20
174 Amani Toomer .10
175 Tiki Barber .10
176 Ike Hilliard .10
177 Jason Sehorn .10
178 Michael Strahan .10
179 Charles Way .10
180 New York Jets visit .10
181 Vinny Testaverde .20
182 Curtis Martin .30
183 Keyshawn Johnson .30
184 Wayne Chrebet .30
185 Mo Lewis .10
186 Steve Atwater .10
187 Leon Johnson .10
188 Bryan Cox .10
189 Oakland Raiders visit .10
190 Rich Gannon .10
191 Napoleon Kaufman .30
192 Tim Brown .30
193 Darrell Russell .10
194 Rickey Dudley .10
195 Charles Woodson .30
196 Harvey Williams .10
197 James Jett .10
198 Philadelphia Eagles visit .10
199 Koy Detmer .10
200 Duce Staley .20
201 Bobby Taylor .10
202 Doug Pederson .10
203 Karl Hankton .10
204 Charles Johnson .10
205 Kevin Turner .10
206 Hugh Douglas .10
207 Pittsburgh Steelers visit .10
208 Kordell Stewart .50
209 Jerome Bettis .30
210 Hines Ward .20
211 Courtney Hawkins .10
212 Will Blackwell .10
213 Richard Huntley .10
214 Levon Kirkland .10
215 Jason Gildon .10
216 St. Louis Rams visit .10
217 Trent Green .30
218 Isaac Bruce .20
219 Az Hakim .20
220 Amp Lee .10
221 Robert Holcombe .20
222 Ricky Proehl .10
223 Kevin Carter .10
224 Marshall Faulk .30
225 San Diego Chargers visit .10
226 Ryan Leaf .30
227 Natrone Means .30
228 Jim Harbaugh .20
229 Junior Seau .20
230 Charlie Jones .10
231 Rodney Harrison .10
232 Terrell Fletcher .10
233 Tremayne Stephens .10
234 San Francisco 49ers visit .10
235 Steve Young .75
236 Jerry Rice 1.50
237 Garrison Hearst .30
238 Terrell Owens .30
239 J.J. Stokes .20
240 Bryant Young .10
241 Tim McDonald .10
242 Merton Hanks .10
243 Travis Jervey .10
244 Seattle Seahawks visit .10
245 Ricky Watters .20
246 Joey Galloway .30
247 Jon Kitna .30
248 Ahman Green .20
249 Mike Pritchard .10
250 Chad Brown .10
251 Christian Fauria .10
252 Michael Sinclair .10
253 Tampa Bay Bucs visit .10
254 Warrick Dunn .30
255 Trent Dilfer .20
256 Mike Alstott .30
257 Reidel Anthony .20
258 Bert Emanuel .10
259 Jacquez Green .20
260 Hardy Nickerson .10
261 Derrick Brooks .10
262 Dave Moore .10
263 Tennessee Titans visit .10
264 Steve McNair .30
265 Eddie George .50
266 Yancey Thigpen .20
267 Frank Wycheck .10
268 Kevin Dyson .20
269 Jackie Harris .10
270 Blaine Bishop .10
271 Willie Davis .10
272 Washington 'Skins visit .10
273 Skip Hicks .20
274 Michael Westbrook .20
275 Stephen Alexander .10
276 Dana Stubblefield .10
277 Brad Johnson .30
278 Brian Mitchell .10
279 Dan Wilkinson .10
280 Stephen Davis .20
281 John Elway (All-Victory Team) .50
282 Dan Marino (All-Victory Team) .50
283 Troy Aikman (All-Victory Team) .30
284 Vinny Testaverde (All-Victory Team) .10
285 Corey Dillon (All-Victory Team) .10
286 Steve Young (All-Victory Team) .20
287 Randy Moss (All-Victory Team) .75
288 Drew Bledsoe (All-Victory Team) .30
289 Jerome Bettis (All-Victory Team) .10
290 Antonio Freeman (All-Victory Team) .10
291 Fred Taylor (All-Victory Team) .30
292 Doug Flutie (All-Victory Team) .10
293 Jerry Rice (All-Victory Team) .30
294 Peyton Manning (All-Victory Team) .50
295 Brett Favre (All-Victory Team) .50
296 Barry Sanders (All-Victory Team) .50
297 Keyshawn Johnson (All-Victory Team) .10
298 Mark Brunell (All-Victory Team) .20
299 Jamal Anderson (All-Victory Team) .10
300 Terrell Davis (All-Victory Team) .50
301 Randall Cunningham (All-Victory Team) .10
302 Kordell Stewart (All-Victory Team) .10
303 Warrick Dunn (All-Victory Team) .10
304 Jake Plummer (All-Victory Team) .20
305 Junior Seau (All-Victory Team) .10
306 Antowain Smith (All-Victory Team) .10
307 Charlie Batch (All-Victory Team) .20
308 Eddie George (All-Victory Team) .20
309 Michael Irvin (All-Victory Team) .10
310 Joey Galloway (All-Victory Team) .10
311 Randall Cunningham (Season Leaders) .10
312 Vinny Testaverde (Season Leaders) .10
313 Steve Young (Season Leaders) .20
314 Chris Chandler (Season Leaders) .10
315 John Elway (Season Leaders) .50
316 Steve Young (Season Leaders) .20
317 Randall Cunningham (Season Leaders) .10
318 Brett Favre (Season Leaders) .50
319 Vinny Testaverde (Season Leaders) .10
320 Peyton Manning (Season Leaders) .50
321 Terrell Davis (Season Leaders) .50
322 Jamal Anderson (Season Leaders) .10
323 Garrison Hearst (Season Leaders) .10
324 Barry Sanders (Season Leaders) .50
325 Emmitt Smith (Season Leaders) .30
326 Terrell Davis (Season Leaders) .50
327 Fred Taylor (Season Leaders) .30
328 Jamal Anderson (Season Leaders) .10
329 Emmitt Smith (Season Leaders) .30
330 Ricky Watters (Season Leaders) .10
331 O.J. McDuffie (Season Leaders) .10
332 Frank Sanders (Season Leaders) .10
333 Rod Smith (Season Leaders) .10
334 Marshall Faulk (Season Leaders) .10
335 Antonio Freeman (Season Leaders) .10
336 Randy Moss (Season Leaders) .75
337 Antonio Freeman (Season Leaders) .10
338 Terrell Owens (Season Leaders) .10
339 Cris Carter (Season Leaders) .10
340 Terance Mathis (Season Leaders) .10
341 Jake Plummer (Victory Parade) .20
342 Steve McNair (Victory Parade) .10
343 Randy Moss (Victory Parade) .75
344 Peyton Manning (Victory Parade) .50
345 Mark Brunell (Victory Parade) .20
346 Terrell Owens (Victory Parade) .10
347 Antowain Smith (Victory Parade) .10
348 Jerry Rice (Victory Parade) .30
349 Troy Aikman (Victory Parade) .30
350 Fred Taylor (Victory Parade) .30
351 Charlie Batch (Victory Parade) .10
352 Dan Marino (Victory Parade) .50
353 Eddie George (Victory Parade) .20
354 Drew Bledsoe (Victory Parade) .20
355 Kordell Stewart (Victory Parade) .10
356 Doug Flutie (Victory Parade) .10
357 Deion Sanders (Victory Parade) .10
358 Keyshawn Johnson (Victory Parade) .10
359 Jerome Bettis (Victory Parade) .10
360 Warrick Dunn (Victory Parade) .10
361 John Elway (Rookie Flashback) .50
362 Dan Marino (Rookie Flashback) .50
363 Brett Favre (Rookie Flashback) .50
364 Andre Rison (Rookie Flashback) .10
365 Rod Woodson (Rookie Flashback) .10
366 Jerry Rice (Rookie Flashback) .30
367 Barry Sanders (Rookie Flashback) .50
368 Thurman Thomas (Rookie Flashback) .10
369 Troy Aikman (Rookie Flashback) .30
370 Ricky Watters (Rookie Flashback) .10
371 Jerome Bettis (Rookie Flashback) .10
372 Reggie White (Rookie Flashback) .10
373 Junior Seau (Rookie Flashback) .10
374 Deion Sanders (Rookie Flashback) .10
375 Chris Chandler (Rookie Flashback) .10
376 Curtis Martin (Rookie Flashback) .10
377 Kordell Stewart (Rookie Flashback) .10
378 Mark Brunell (Rookie Flashback) .20
379 Cris Carter (Rookie Flashback) .10
380 Emmitt Smith (Rookie Flashback) .30
381 *Tim Couch* 2.00
382 *Donovan McNabb* 6.00
383 *Akili Smith* 2.00
384 *Edgerrin James* 6.00
385 *Ricky Williams* 5.00
386 *Torry Holt* 3.00
387 *Champ Bailey* 2.00
388 *David Boston* 3.00
389 *Chris Claiborne* 1.00
390 *Chris McAlister* 1.00
391 *Daunte Culpepper* 6.00
392 *Cade McNown* 2.00
393 *Troy Edwards* 2.00
394 *John Tait* .50
395 *Anthony McFarland* 1.00
396 *Jevon Kearse* 2.00
397 *Damien Woody* .50
398 *Matt Stinchcomb* .50
399 *Luke Petitgout* .50
400 *Ebenezer Ekuban* 1.00
401 *L.J. Shelton* .50
402 *Marty Booker* .50
403 *Antoine Winfield* 1.00
404 *Scott Covington* 1.00
405 *Antwan Edwards* 1.00
406 *Fernando Bryant* .50
407 *Aaron Gibson* .50
408 *Andy Katzenmoyer* 1.00
409 *Dimitrius Underwood* 1.00
410 *Patrick Kerney* .50
411 *Al Wilson* .50
412 *Kevin Johnson* 3.00
413 *Joel Makovicka* 1.00
414 *Reginald Kelly* .50
415 *Jeff Paulk* 1.00
416 *Brandon Stokley* 1.00
417 *Peerless Price* 2.50
418 *D'Wayne Bates* 1.50
419 *Travis McGriff* 1.00
420 *Sedrick Irvin* 1.50
421 *Aaron Brooks* 6.00
422 *Michael Cloud* 1.00
423 *Joe Montgomery* 1.50
424 *Shaun King* 2.00
425 *Dameane Douglas* 1.00
426 *Joe Germaine* 1.50
427 *James Johnson* 2.00
428 *Michael Bishop* 2.00
429 *Karsten Bailey* 1.00
430 *Craig Yeast* 1.00
431 *Jim Kleinsasser* 1.00
432 *Martin Gramatica* 1.00
433 *Jermaine Fazande* 1.00
434 *Dre' Bly* 1.00
435 *Brock Huard* 1.50
436 *Rob Konrad* 1.00
437 *Tony Bryant* 1.00
438 *Sean Bennett* 1.50
439 *Kevin Faulk* 2.00
440 *Amos Zereoue* 1.00

2000 Upper Deck Super Bowl XXXIV Special Moments

NM/M
Complete Set (10): 20.00
Common Player: 1.00
1 Jerry Rice 2.50
2 Terrell Davis 2.50
3 Brett Favre 4.00
4 Joe Namath 2.50
5 Jamal Anderson 1.50
6 Chris Chandler 1.00
7 Steve Young 2.00
8 Joe Montana 4.00
9 Antonio Freeman 1.50
10 Emmitt Smith 3.00

2000 UD Graded

NM/M
Common Player (1-90): 1.50
Minor Stars (1-90): 3.00
Production 1,500 Sets
Common Rookie (91-135): 5.00
Production 1,325 Sets
Common Rookie Auto (136-155): 15.00
Production 500 Sets
Common Rookie Auto (156-165): 25.00
Production 250 Sets
Cards 138,139,147,148 & 163 never issued
Pack (3+SGC): 40.00
Wax Box (6): 175.00
1 Jake Plummer 3.00
2 David Boston 3.00
3 Jamal Anderson 3.00
4 Shawn Jefferson 1.50
5 Qadry Ismail 1.50
6 Tony Banks 1.50
7 Priest Holmes 5.00
8 Rob Johnson 1.50
9 Eric Moulds 3.00
10 Steve Beuerlein 1.50
11 Muhsin Muhammad 1.50
12 Donald Hayes 1.50
13 Tim Biakabutuka 1.50
14 Cade McNown 2.00
15 Marcus Robinson 3.00
16 James Allen 3.00
17 Akili Smith 2.00
18 Corey Dillon 3.00
19 Tim Couch 5.00
20 Kevin Johnson 3.00
21 Troy Aikman 7.00
22 Emmitt Smith 8.00
23 Raghib Ismail 1.50
24 Terrell Davis 5.00
25 Rod Smith 3.00
26 Brian Griese 4.00
27 Charlie Batch 2.00
28 James O. Stewart 1.50
29 Germane Crowell 3.00
30 Brett Favre 12.00
31 Antonio Freeman 3.00
32 Dorsey Levens 3.00
33 Peyton Manning 10.00
34 Edgerrin James 8.00
35 Marvin Harrison 3.00
36 Mark Brunell 5.00
37 Jimmy Smith 3.00
38 Fred Taylor 5.00
39 Elvis Grbac 1.50
40 Tony Gonzalez 3.00
41 Lamar Smith 3.00
42 Jay Fiedler 3.00
43 Randy Moss 10.00
44 Daunte Culpepper 6.00
45 Robert Smith 3.00
46 Cris Carter 3.00
47 Drew Bledsoe 5.00
48 Kevin Faulk 3.00
49 Terry Glenn 3.00
50 Ricky Williams 5.00
51 Jeff Blake 3.00
52 Joe Horn 3.00
53 Kerry Collins 3.00
54 Amani Toomer 1.50
55 Tiki Barber 3.00
56 Wayne Chrebet 3.00
57 Curtis Martin 3.00
58 Vinny Testaverde 3.00
59 Tyrone Wheatley 3.00
60 Tim Brown 3.00
61 Rich Gannon 1.50
62 Duce Staley 3.00
63 Charles Johnson 1.50
64 Donovan McNabb 4.50
65 *Bobby Shaw* 4.00
66 Kordell Stewart 3.00
67 Jerome Bettis 3.00
68 Marshall Faulk 4.00
69 Isaac Bruce 3.00
70 Torry Holt 3.00
71 Kurt Warner 10.00
72 Neil Smith 1.50
73 Ryan Leaf 2.00
74 Curtis Conway 1.50
75 Jeff Garcia 3.00
76 Charlie Garner 1.50
77 Jerry Rice 10.00
78 Ricky Watters 3.00
79 Brock Huard 3.00
80 Jon Kitna 3.00
81 Keyshawn Johnson 3.00
82 Jacquez Green 1.50
83 Mike Alstott 3.00
84 Shaun King 4.00
85 Eddie George 4.00
86 Kevin Dyson 1.50
87 Steve McNair 3.00
88 Brad Johnson 3.00
89 Stephen Davis 3.00
90 Jeff George 3.00
91 *Ronald Dixon* 5.00
92 *Avion Black* 5.00
93 *Hank Poteat* 5.00
94 *Doug Chapman* 5.00
95 *Drew Haddad* 5.00
96 *Rondell Mealey* 5.00
97 *Spergon Wynn* 5.00
98 *Keith Bulluck* 5.00
99 *John Abraham* 5.00
100 *Rob Morris* 5.00
101 *Jerry Porter* 12.00
102 *Laveranues Coles* 12.00
103 *Jarious Jackson* 6.00
104 *Tom Brady* 75.00
105 *Jonas Lewis* 5.00
106 *Todd Husak* 7.00
107 *Shyrone Stith* 5.00
108 *Sammy Morris* 8.00
109 *Corey Simon* 8.00
110 *Chad Morton* 8.00
111 *Brian Urlacher* 25.00
112 *Anthony Becht* 5.00

113 *Chris Cole* 5.00
114 *Anthony Lucas* 5.00
115 *Charles Lee* 5.00
116 *JaJuan Dawson* 5.00
117 *Darrell Jackson* 15.00
118 *Gari Scott* 5.00
119 *Windrell Hayes* 5.00
120 *Paul Smith* 5.00
121 *Mareno Philyaw* 5.00
122 *Trevor Gaylor* 5.00
123 *Muneer Moore* 5.00
124 *Michael Wiley* 5.00
125 *Ronney Jenkins* 5.00
126 *Frank Moreau* 5.00
127 *Dante Hall* 20.00
128 *Darren Howard* 5.00
129 *Todd Pinkston* 12.00
130 *Mike Anderson* 10.00
131 *Doug Johnson* 8.00
132 *Shaun Ellis* 5.00
133 *James Williams* 5.00
134 *Ron Dugans* 5.00
135 *Frank Murphy* 5.00
136 *Dez White* 10.00
137 *Danny Farmer* 8.00
140 *Reuben Droughns* 30.00
141 *Jamal Lewis* 100.00
142 *J.R. Redmond* 20.00
143 *Tee Martin* 20.00
144 *Giovanni Carmazzi* 20.00
145 *Tim Rattay* 60.00
146 *Trung Canidate* 30.00
149 *Chris Coleman* 15.00
150 *Corey Moore* 15.00
151 *Troy Walters* 15.00
152 *Joe Hamilton* 20.00
153 *Kwame Cavil* 15.00
154 *Dennis Northcutt* 20.00
155 *Travis Taylor* 30.00
156 *Curtis Keaton* 15.00
157 *Shaun Alexander* 125.00
158 *Chad Pennington* 250.00
159 *Sylvester Morris* 30.00
160 *Plaxico Burress* 100.00
161 *Ron Dayne* 40.00
162 *Courtney Brown* 30.00
164 *Peter Warrick* 60.00
165 *Chris Redman* 30.00

2000 UD Graded SGC Blue Labels

#'s 1-90 1x of base set
Cards Graded 92 1X
Cards Graded 96 1X to 3X
Cards Graded 98 3X to 10X

2000 UD Graded Jerseys

NM/M
Common Player: 10.00
TA Troy Aikman 25.00
DB Drew Bledsoe 20.00
IB Isaac Bruce 20.00
MB Mark Brunell 20.00
CC Cris Carter 15.00
RD Ron Dayne 20.00
BF Brett Favre 50.00
TH Torry Holt 10.00
EJ Edgerrin James 40.00
KJ Keyshawn Johnson 20.00
RJ Rob Johnson 10.00
TJ Thomas Jones 10.00
SK Shaun King 10.00
PM Peyton Manning 40.00
DM Dan Marino 50.00
SM Steve McNair 20.00
RM Randy Moss 40.00
JR Jerry Rice 40.00
ES Emmitt Smith 50.00
KW Kurt Warner 40.00
PW Peter Warrick 10.00

2000 UD Graded Jerseys SGC Blue Labels

Cards Graded 921X of base Jersey set
Cards Graded 961X to 5X base Jersey set

2000 UD Ionix

NM/M
Complete Set (120): 400.00
Common Player: .15
Minor Stars: .30
Common Rookie: 3.00
Production 2,000 Sets
Pack (4): 2.75
Wax Box (24): 45.00
1 Jake Plummer .50
2 Jamal Anderson .50
3 Qadry Ismail .15
4 Rob Johnson .30
5 Eric Moulds .50
6 Muhsin Muhammad .30
7 Patrick Jeffers .50
8 Cade McNown .30
9 Marcus Robinson .50
10 Akili Smith .60
11 Corey Dillon .50
12 Tim Couch 1.00
13 Kevin Johnson .50
14 Troy Aikman 1.00
15 Emmitt Smith 1.25
16 Raghib Ismail .15
17 Terrell Davis 1.00
18 Olandis Gary .60
19 Charlie Batch .50
20 James O. Stewart .50
21 Brett Favre 1.75
22 Antonio Freeman .50
23 Peyton Manning 1.50
24 Edgerrin James 1.00
25 Marvin Harrison .50
26 Mark Brunell .60
27 Fred Taylor .75
28 Elvis Grbac .30
29 Tony Gonzalez .30
30 O.J. McDuffie .15
31 Damon Huard .30
32 Randy Moss 1.50
33 Cris Carter .50
34 Drew Bledsoe .60
35 Terry Glenn .50
36 Ricky Williams 1.00
37 Kerry Collins .30
38 Amani Toomer .30
39 Keyshawn Johnson .50
40 Vinny Testaverde .50
41 Tim Brown .30
42 Rich Gannon .30
43 Duce Staley .50
44 Donovan McNabb .75
45 Troy Edwards .50
46 Jerome Bettis .30
47 Marshall Faulk .50
48 Kurt Warner 1.50
49 Junior Seau .30
50 Jeff Graham .15
51 Charlie Garner .30
52 Jerry Rice 1.50
53 Ricky Watters .30
54 Jon Kitna .50
55 Mike Alstott .50
56 Shaun King .50
57 Eddie George .60
58 Steve McNair .60
59 Brad Johnson .50
60 Stephen Davis .50
61 *Ahmed Plummer* 3.00
62 *Courtney Brown* 6.00
63 *Delthea O'Neal* 3.00
64 *Chad Morton* 3.00
65 *Corey Simon* 3.00
66 *Hank Poteat* 3.00
67 *Raynoch Thompson* 3.00
68 *Darren Howard* 3.00
69 *Rondell Mealey* 3.00
70 *Marcus Knight* 3.00
71 *Keith Bulluck* 3.00
72 *John Abraham* 3.00
73 *Rob Morris* 3.00
74 *Chris Redman* 8.00
75 *Joe Hamilton* 4.00
76 *Jarious Jackson* 4.00
77 *Tom Brady* 40.00
78 *Chad Pennington* 30.00
79 *Tee Martin* 6.00
80 *Giovanni Carmazzi* 4.00
81 *Tim Rattay* 12.00
82 *Marc Bulger* 15.00
83 *Todd Husak* 3.00
84 *Curtis Keaton* 3.00
85 *Ron Dayne* 8.00
86 *Shaun Alexander* 20.00
87 *Thomas Jones* 10.00
88 *Reuben Droughns* 12.00
89 *Jamal Lewis* 20.00
90 *J.R. Redmond* 5.00
91 *Travis Prentice* 6.00
92 *Shyrone Stith* 3.00
93 *Chris Hovan* 4.00
94 *Michael Wiley* 3.00
95 *Trung Canidate* 10.00
96 *Sebastian Janikowski* 6.00
97 *Brian Urlacher* 15.00
98 *Bubba Franks* 10.00
99 *Anthony Becht* 4.00
100 *Chris Cole* 3.00
101 *R. Jay Soward* 3.00
102 *Peter Warrick* 12.00
103 *Plaxico Burress* 15.00
104 *Sylvester Morris* 6.00
105 *Dez White* 6.00
106 *Travis Taylor* 10.00
107 *Trevor Gaylor* 3.00
108 *Anthony Lucas* 3.00
109 *Sherrod Gideon* 3.00
110 *Todd Pinkston* 10.00
111 *Dennis Northcutt* 3.00
112 *Jerry Porter* 12.00
113 *Ron Dugans* 3.00
114 *Laveranues Coles* 12.00
115 *Darrell Jackson* 12.00
116 *Danny Farmer* 4.00
117 *Gari Scott* 3.00
118 *JaJuan Dawson* 3.00
119 *Troy Walters* 3.00
120 *Quinton Spotwood* 3.00

2000 UD Ionix Game Jersey Greats

NM/M
Production 375 Sets
DM Dan Marino AUTO 250.00

2000 UD Ionix High Voltage

NM/M
Complete Set (15): 8.00
Common Player: .50
Minor Stars: 1.00
Inserted 1:4
NM/M
HV1 Fred Taylor 1.00
HV2 Michael Westbrook .50
HV3 James O. Stewart .50
HV4 Keyshawn Johnson 1.00
HV5 Marcus Robinson 1.00
HV6 Charlie Batch .50
HV7 Marvin Harrison 1.00
HV8 Olandis Gary .50
HV9 Curtis Martin .50
HV10 Isaac Bruce 1.00
HV11 Jake Plummer 1.00
HV12 Shaun King .50
HV13 Jimmy Smith 1.00
HV14 Muhsin Muhammad .50
HV15 Raghib Ismail .50

2000 UD Ionix Majestix

NM/M
Complete Set (15): 20.00
Common Player: .75
Minor Stars: 1.50
Inserted 1:11
M1 Steve Young 2.00
M2 Jerry Rice 3.50
M3 Troy Aikman 3.50
M4 Emmitt Smith 3.50
M5 Vinny Testaverde .75
M6 Cris Carter 1.50
M7 Brett Favre 5.00
M8 Eddie George 1.75
M9 Herman Moore .75
M10 Drew Bledsoe 2.50
M11 Tim Brown .75
M12 Steve Beuerlein .75
M13 Brad Johnson 1.50
M14 Mark Brunell 1.50
M15 Randy Moss 3.50

2000 UD Ionix Rookie Xtreme

NM/M
Complete Set (15): 30.00
Common Player: 1.00
Inserted 1:11
RX1 Trung Canidate 1.00
RX2 Peter Warrick 2.00
RX3 Plaxico Burress 4.50
RX4 Jamal Lewis 2.00
RX5 Thomas Jones 2.00
RX6 Chad Pennington 4.50
RX7 Chris Redman 2.00
RX8 Ron Dayne 2.00
RX9 Courtney Brown 2.00
RX10 Corey Simon 1.00
RX11 Shaun Alexander 3.50
RX12 Dez White 1.00
RX13 J.R. Redmond 2.00
RX14 Shyrone Stith 1.00
RX15 Travis Taylor 2.00

2000 UD Ionix Sunday Best

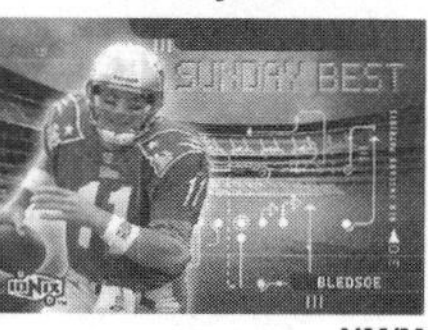

NM/M
Complete Set (15): 20.00
Common Player: 1.00
Minor Stars: 2.00
Inserted 1:23
SB1 Stephen Davis 2.00
SB2 Brian Griese 2.50
SB3 Corey Dillon 2.00
SB4 Muhsin Muhammad 1.00
SB5 Charlie Batch 1.00
SB6 Shaun King 1.00
SB7 Germane Crowell 1.00
SB8 Drew Bledsoe 3.50
SB9 Jake Plummer 2.00
SB10 Torry Holt 1.00
SB11 Marcus Robinson 2.00
SB12 Ricky Williams 4.50
SB13 Tim Couch 4.50
SB14 Kevin Johnson 2.00
SB15 Warrick Dunn 2.00

2000 UD Ionix Super Trio

NM/M
Complete Set (15): 30.00
Common Player: 1.00
Minor Stars: 2.00
Inserted 1:23
ST1 Peyton Manning 6.00
ST2 Edgerrin James 4.00
ST3 Marvin Harrison 2.00
ST4 Kurt Warner 6.00
ST5 Marshall Faulk 2.00
ST6 Isaac Bruce 2.00
ST7 Mark Brunell 2.00
ST8 Fred Taylor 2.00
ST9 Jimmy Smith 2.00
ST10 Troy Aikman 4.00
ST11 Emmitt Smith 6.00
ST12 Raghib Ismail 1.00
ST13 Brad Johnson 2.00
ST14 Stephen Davis 2.00
ST15 Michael Westbrook 1.00

2000 UD Ionix UD Authentics Blue

NM/M
Common Player: 10.00
Minor Stars: 20.00
Production 300 Sets
SA Shaun Alexander 50.00
CA Champ Bailey 20.00
CB Charlie Batch 25.00
DA David Boston 25.00
TB Tim Brown 25.00
IB Isaac Bruce 25.00
CC Cris Carter 25.00
WC Wayne Chrebet 20.00
CN Chris Coleman 10.00
DF Danny Farmer 20.00
KF Kevin Faulk 25.00
FR Bubba Franks 30.00
OG Olandis Gary 25.00
SG Sherrod Gideon 10.00
BG Brian Griese 30.00
JH Joe Hamilton 20.00
TH Torry Holt 25.00
RJ Rob Johnson 20.00
RL Ray Lucas 25.00
TM Tee Martin 25.00
DN Dennis Northcutt 25.00
TO Terrell Owens 25.00
TP Travis Prentice 30.00
TR Tim Rattay 30.00
RS R. Jay Soward 25.00
BU Brian Urlacher 25.00
TW Troy Walters 10.00
MW Michael Wiley 25.00

2000 UD Ionix UD Authentics Gold

NM/M
Common Player: 20.00
Minor Stars: 40.00
Production 100 Sets
TA Troy Aikman 85.00
MB Mark Brunell 60.00
TC Tim Couch 85.00
TD Terrell Davis 75.00
RD Ron Dayne 50.00
MF Marshall Faulk 50.00
AF Antonio Freeman 20.00
MH Marvin Harrison 40.00
EJ Edgerrin James 100.00
BJ Brad Johnson 40.00
KJ Keyshawn Johnson 40.00
TJ Thomas Jones 50.00
DL Dorsey Levens 20.00
JL Jamal Lewis 50.00
PM Peyton Manning 125.00
MC Cade McNown 60.00
SL Sylvester Morris 50.00
RM Randy Moss 100.00
EM Eric Moulds 40.00
CP Chad Pennington 125.00
JP Jake Plummer 40.00
CR Chris Redman 65.00
KW Kurt Warner 125.00
PW Peter Warrick 50.00

A player's name in *italic* type indicates a rookie card.

2000 UD Ionix Warp Zone

NM/M
Complete Set (15): 200.00
Common Player: 10.00
Inserted 1:239
WZ1 Marshall Faulk 10.00
WZ2 Kurt Warner 30.00
WZ3 Peyton Manning 30.00
WZ4 Edgerrin James 20.00
WZ5 Brett Favre 40.00
WZ6 Tim Couch 20.00
WZ7 Ricky Williams 20.00
WZ8 Mark Brunell 15.00
WZ9 Fred Taylor 15.00
WZ10 Terrell Davis 20.00
WZ11 Dan Marino 30.00
WZ12 Randy Moss 30.00
WZ13 Emmitt Smith 30.00
WZ14 Eddie George 12.00
WZ15 Steve McNair 10.00

2000 Upper Deck

NM/M
Complete Set (270): 100.00
Common Player: .15
Minor Stars: .30
Common Rookie: 2.00
Inserted 1:4
Pack (10): 3.75
Wax Box (24): 65.00
1 Jake Plummer .50
2 Michael Pittman .15
3 Rob Moore .30
4 David Boston .50
5 Frank Sanders .30
6 Aeneas Williams .15
7 Kwamie Lassiter .15
8 Rob Fredrickson .15
9 Tim Dwight .50
10 Chris Chandler .30
11 Jamal Anderson .50
12 Shawn Jefferson .15
13 Ken Oxendine .15
14 Terance Mathis .15
15 Bob Christian .15
16 Qadry Ismail .15
17 Jermaine Lewis .15
18 Rod Woodson .15
19 Michael McCrary .15
20 Tony Banks .30
21 Peter Boulware .15
22 Shannon Sharpe .30
23 Peerless Price .30
24 Rob Johnson .30
25 Eric Moulds .50
26 Doug Flutie .75
27 Jay Riemersma .15
28 Antowain Smith .30
29 Jonathon Linton .15
30 Muhsin Muhammad .30
31 Patrick Jeffers .50
32 Steve Beuerlein .30
33 Natrone Means .15
34 Tim Biakabutuka .15
35 Michael Bates .15
36 Chuck Smith .15
37 Wesley Walls .30
38 Cade McNown .50
39 Curtis Enis .50
40 Marcus Robinson .50
41 Eddie Kennison .15
42 Bobby Engram .15
43 Glyn Milburn .15
44 Marty Booker .50
45 Akili Smith .75
46 Corey Dillon .50
47 Darnay Scott .30
48 Tremain Mack .15
49 Damon Griffin .15
50 Takeo Spikes .15
51 Tony McGee .15
52 Tim Couch 1.50
53 Kevin Johnson .30
54 Darrin Chiaverini .15
55 Jamir Miller .15
56 Errict Rhett .15
57 Terry Kirby .15
58 Marc Edwards .15
59 Troy Aikman 1.25
60 Emmitt Smith 1.75
61 Raghib Ismail .15
62 Jason Tucker .15
63 Dexter Coakley .15
64 Joey Galloway .50
65 Wane McGarity .15
66 Terrell Davis 1.00
67 Olandis Gary .50
68 Brian Griese .75
69 Gus Frerotte .15
70 Byron Chamberlain .15
71 Ed McCaffrey .30
72 Rod Smith .50
73 Al Wilson .15
74 Charlie Batch .50
75 Germane Crowell .50
76 Sedrick Irvin .15
77 Johnnie Morton .30
78 Robert Porcher .15
79 Herman Moore .50
80 James O. Stewart .50
81 Brett Favre 2.50
82 Antonio Freeman .50
83 Bill Schroeder .15
84 Dorsey Levens .50
85 Corey Bradford .15
86 Demond Parker .15
87 Vonnie Holliday .15
88 Peyton Manning 2.00
89 Edgerrin James 2.00
90 Marvin Harrison .50
91 Ken Dilger .15
92 Terrence Wilkins .30
93 Marcus Pollard .15
94 Fred Lane .15
95 Mark Brunell .75
96 Fred Taylor .75
97 Jimmy Smith .50
98 Keenan McCardell .30
99 Carnell Lake .15
100 Tavian Banks .15
101 Kyle Brady .15
102 Hardy Nickerson .15
103 Elvis Grbac .30
104 Tony Gonzalez .30
105 Derrick S. Alexander .15
106 Donnell Bennett .15
107 Mike Cloud .15
108 Donnie Edwards .15
109 Jay Fiedler .30
110 James Johnson .30
111 Tony Martin .15
112 Damon Huard .30
113 O.J. McDuffie .30
114 Thurman Thomas .30
115 Zach Thomas .30
116 Oronde Gadsden .15
117 Randy Moss 2.00
118 Robert Smith .50
119 Cris Carter .50
120 Matthew Hatchette .15
121 Daunte Culpepper 1.00
122 Leroy Hoard .15
123 Drew Bledsoe 1.00
124 Terry Glenn .50
125 Troy Brown .15
126 Kevin Faulk .30
127 Lawyer Milloy .15
128 Ricky Williams 1.00
129 Keith Poole .15
130 Jake Reed .15
131 Cameron Cleeland .30
132 Jeff Blake .30
133 Andrew Glover .15
134 Kerry Collins .50
135 Amani Toomer .30
136 Joe Montgomery .15
137 Ike Hilliard .30
138 Tiki Barber .30
139 Pete Mitchell .15
140 Ray Lucas .15
141 Mo Lewis .15
142 Curtis Martin .50
143 Vinny Testaverde .50
144 Wayne Chrebet .30
145 Dedric Ward .15
146 Tim Brown .30
147 Rich Gannon .75
148 Tyrone Wheatley .30
149 Napoleon Kaufman .50
150 Charles Woodson .50
151 Darrell Russell .15
152 James Jett .15
153 Rickey Dudley .15
154 Jon Ritchie .15
155 Duce Staley .50
156 Donovan McNabb 1.00
157 Torrance Small .15
158 Allen Rossum .15
159 Mike Mamula .15
160 Na Brown .15
161 Charles Johnson .15
162 Kent Graham .15
163 Troy Edwards .50
164 Jerome Bettis .50
165 Hines Ward .30
166 Kordell Stewart .50
167 Levon Kirkland .15
168 Richard Huntley .15
169 Marshall Faulk .50
170 Kurt Warner 2.00
171 Torry Holt .50
172 Isaac Bruce .50
173 Kevin Carter .15
174 Az-Zahir Hakim .30
175 Ricky Proehl .15
176 Jermaine Fazande .30
177 Curtis Conway .30
178 Freddie Jones .30
179 Junior Seau .30
180 Jeff Graham .15
181 Jim Harbaugh .15
182 Rodney Harrison .15
183 Steve Young 1.00
184 Jerry Rice 2.00
185 Charlie Garner .50
186 Terrell Owens .50
187 Jeff Garcia .50
188 Fred Beasley .15
189 J.J. Stokes .30
190 Ricky Watters .30
191 Jon Kitna .50
192 Derrick Mayes .15
193 Sean Dawkins .15
194 Charlie Rogers .15
195 Mike Pritchard .15
196 Cortez Kennedy .15
197 Christian Fauria .15
198 Warrick Dunn .50
199 Shaun King .50
200 Mike Alstott .50
201 Warren Sapp .30
202 Jacquez Green .30

203 Reidel Anthony .30
204 Dave Moore .15
205 Keyshawn Johnson .50
206 Eddie George .75
207 Steve McNair .60
208 Kevin Dyson .30
209 Jevon Kearse .60
210 Yancey Thigpen .15
211 Frank Wycheck .15
212 Isaac Byrd .15
213 Neil O'Donnell .15
214 Brad Johnson .50
215 Stephen Davis .50
216 Michael Westbrook .30
217 Albert Connell .15
218 Brian Mitchell .15
219 Bruce Smith .15
220 Stephen Alexander .15
221 Jeff George .50
222 Adrian Murrell .15
223 *Courtney Brown* 3.00
224 *John Engleberger* 2.00
225 *Deltha O'Neal* 2.00
226 *Corey Simon* 3.00
227 *R. Jay Soward* 3.00
228 *Marc Bulger* 10.00
229 *Raynoch Thompson* 2.00
230 *Deon Grant* 2.00
231 *Darrell Jackson* 6.00
232 *Chris Cole* 2.00
233 *Trevor Gaylor* 2.00
234 *John Abraham* 2.00
235 *Chris Redman* 3.00
236 *Joe Hamilton* 3.00
237 *Chad Pennington* 20.00
238 *Tee Martin* 3.00
239 *Giovanni Carmazzi* 3.00
240 *Tim Rattay* 6.00
241 *Ron Dayne* 4.00
242 *Shaun Alexander* 12.00
243 *Thomas Jones* 5.00
244 *Reuben Droughns* 3.00
245 *Jamal Lewis* 12.00
246 *Michael Wiley* 2.00
247 *J.R. Redmond* 3.00
248 *Travis Prentice* 4.00
249 *Todd Husak* 2.00
250 *Trung Canidate* 4.00
251 *Brian Urlacher* 10.00
252 *Anthony Becht* 2.00
253 *Bubba Franks* 5.00
254 *Tom Brady* 25.00
255 *Peter Warrick* 6.00
256 *Plaxico Burress* 10.00
257 *Sylvester Morris* 4.00
258 *Dez White* 5.00
259 *Travis Taylor* 4.00
260 *Todd Pinkston* 3.00
261 *Dennis Northcutt* 3.00
262 *Jerry Porter* 6.00
263 *Laveranues Coles* 6.00
264 *Danny Farmer* 2.00
265 *Curtis Keaton* 2.00
266 *Sherrod Gideon* 2.00
267 *Ron Dugans* 2.00
268 Steve McNair Checklist .30
269 Jake Plummer Checklist .30
270 Antonio Freeman Checklist .15

2000 Upper Deck Exclusives Gold

Gold Cards: 20X-40X
Gold Rookies: 6X-12X
Production 25 Sets

2000 Upper Deck Exclusives Silver

Silver Cards: 10X-20X
Silver Rookies: 3X-6X
Production 100 Sets

2000 Upper Deck e-Card

NM/M
Complete Set (6): 25.00
Common Player: 2.50
Inserted 2:Box
SA Shaun Alexander 6.00
TJ Thomas Jones 6.00
JL Jamal Lewis 6.00
CP Chad Pennington 10.00
CR Chris Redman 2.50
TT Travis Taylor 4.00

2000 Upper Deck Game Jersey

NM/M
Common Player: 20.00
Minor Stars: 40.00
Inserted 1:287
MA Mike Alstott 30.00
JA Jamal Anderson 25.00
BO David Boston 25.00
CB Courtney Brown 25.00
TB Tim Brown 35.00
PB Plaxico Burress 40.00
DC Daunte Culpepper 40.00
BF Brett Favre 75.00
FR Bubba Franks 25.00
AF Antonio Freeman 20.00
OG Olandis Gary 20.00
BG Brian Griese 40.00
TH Torry Holt 30.00
TJ Thomas Jones 20.00
SK Shaun King 20.00
DL Dorsey Levens 20.00
JL Jamal Lewis 40.00
RL Ray Lucas 20.00
CM Curtis Martin 40.00
TM Tee Martin 20.00
DO Donovan McNabb 40.00
SM Steve McNair 40.00
HM Herman Moore 20.00
SL Sylvester Morris 20.00
EM Eric Moulds 25.00
TO Terrell Owens 30.00
CR Chris Redman 20.00
JR Jerry Rice 75.00
ES Emmitt Smith 75.00
RJ R. Jay Soward 20.00
JJ J.J. Stokes 20.00
TT Travis Taylor 20.00
RW Ricky Williams 30.00
SY Steve Young 40.00

2000 Upper Deck Game Jersey Autographs

NM/M
Common Player: 80.00
Inserted 1:287 Hobby
TA Troy Aikman 125.00
JA Jamal Anderson 80.00
DB Drew Bledsoe 125.00
BO David Boston 80.00
TB Tim Brown 80.00
IB Isaac Bruce 100.00
MB Mark Brunell 75.00
TC Tim Couch 75.00
TD Terrell Davis 75.00
RD-A Ron Dayne 50.00
MF Marshall Faulk 120.00
AF Antonio Freeman 40.00
OG Olandis Gary 40.00
EG Eddie George 75.00
BG Brian Griese 75.00
MH Marvin Harrison 75.00
TH Torry Holt 50.00
EJ Edgerrin James 100.00
JO Kevin Johnson 40.00
KJ Keyshawn Johnson 50.00
DL Dorsey Levens 40.00
RL Ray Lucas 40.00
PM Peyton Manning 150.00
DM Dan Marino 225.00
MC Cade McNown 40.00
RM Randy Moss 150.00
CP-A Chad Pennington 200.00
KW Kurt Warner 125.00
SY Steve Young 100.00

2000 Upper Deck Game Jersey-Hobby Autographs

NM/M
Common Player: 80.00
TA Troy Aikman 125.00
SA Shaun Alexander 100.00
DB Drew Bledsoe 125.00
CB Courtney Brown 80.00
IB Isaac Bruce 75.00
MB Mark Brunell 75.00
TC Tim Couch 125.00
TD Terrell Davis 100.00
RD Ron Dayne 75.00
FA Danny Farmer 50.00
MF Marshall Faulk 125.00
EG Eddie George 125.00
MH Marvin Harrison 80.00
EJ Edgerrin James 150.00
JO Kevin Johnson 50.00
KJ Keyshawn Johnson 80.00
TJ Thomas Jones 50.00
PM Peyton Manning 150.00
DM Dan Marino 200.00
MC Cade McNown 50.00
RM Randy Moss 200.00
CP Chad Pennington 150.00
CR Chris Redman 50.00
KW Kurt Warner 200.00
PW Peter Warrick 50.00

2000 Upper Deck Game Jersey Greats

NM/M
Production 200 Sets
BS Bart Starr AUTO 225.00

2000 Upper Deck Game Jersey Patch

NM/M
Common Player: 100.00
Inserted 1:7,500
JA Jamal Anderson 100.00
DB Drew Bledsoe 175.00
BO David Boston 100.00
TB Tim Brown 100.00
MB Mark Brunell 100.00
TC Tim Couch 125.00
DA Daunte Culpepper 150.00
TD Terrell Davis 150.00
BF Brett Favre 375.00
AF Antonio Freeman 100.00
MF Marshall Faulk 225.00
OG Olandis Gary 60.00
EG Eddie George 125.00
BG Brian Griese 100.00
MH Marvin Harrison 100.00
TH Torry Holt 60.00
EJ Edgerrin James 225.00
JO Kevin Johnson 60.00
KJ Keyshawn Johnson 100.00
SK Shaun King 60.00
DL Dorsey Levens 60.00
RL Ray Lucas 60.00
PM Peyton Manning 325.00
DM Dan Marino 400.00
CM Curtis Martin 100.00
MC Cade McNown 60.00
RM Randy Moss 275.00
TO Terrell Owens 100.00
ES Emmitt Smith 300.00
FT Fred Taylor 60.00

2000 Upper Deck Game Jersey Patch Autographs

NM/M
Complete Set (6):
Common Player:
TC Tim Couch 200.00
MF Marshall Faulk 250.00
EG Eddie George 200.00
EJ Edgerrin James 250.00
RM Randy Moss 300.00
KW Kurt Warner 300.00

2000 Upper Deck Headline Heroes

NM/M
Complete Set (15): 25.00
Common Player: 1.00
Minor Stars: 2.00
Inserted 1:23
HH1 Mark Brunell 2.00
HH2 Damon Huard 2.00
HH3 Ricky Williams 5.00
HH4 Jevon Kearse 2.50
HH5 Keyshawn Johnson 2.00
HH6 Ricky Watters 1.00
HH7 Michael Westbrook 2.00
HH8 Charlie Batch 1.00
HH9 Warren Sapp 1.00
HH10 Muhsin Muhammad 1.00
HH11 Brett Favre 8.00
HH12 Jeff George 1.00
HH13 Germane Crowell 2.00
HH14 Troy Aikman 5.00
HH15 Jimmy Smith 2.00

2000 Upper Deck Highlight Zone

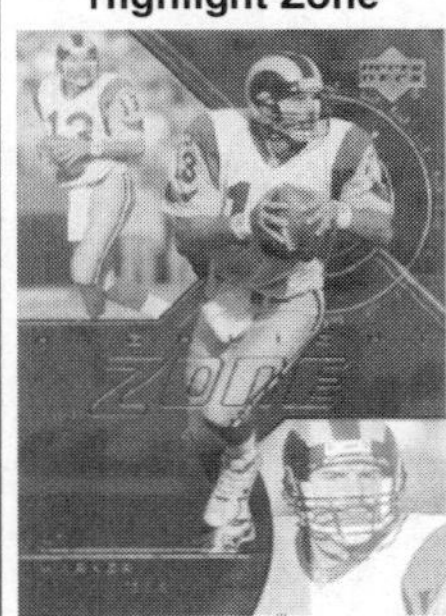

NM/M
Complete Set (10): 10.00
Common Player: .50
Minor Stars: 1.00
Inserted 1:11
HZ1 Eddie George 1.50
HZ2 Steve McNair 1.25
HZ3 Kevin Dyson .50
HZ4 Kurt Warner 3.00
HZ5 Emmitt Smith 3.00
HZ6 Brad Johnson 1.00
HZ7 Curtis Martin 1.00
HZ8 Ray Lucas .50
HZ9 Akili Smith 1.00
HZ10 Jake Plummer 1.00

2000 Upper Deck New Guard

NM/M
Complete Set (15): 35.00
Common Player: 1.25
Minor Stars: 2.50
Inserted 1:23
NG1 Tim Couch 4.00
NG2 Ricky Williams 5.00
NG3 Shaun King 1.00

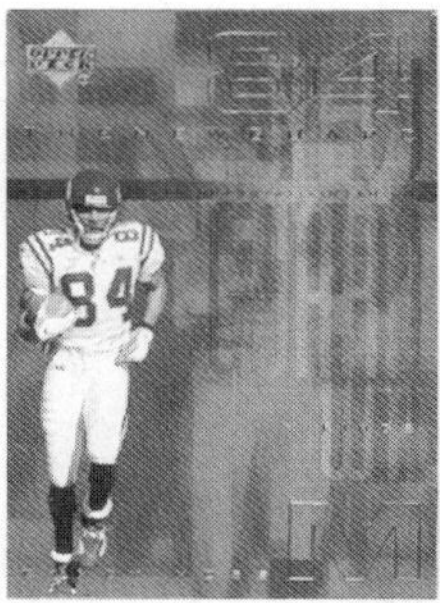

NM/M
NG4 Brian Griese 2.50
NG5 Rob Johnson 1.00
NG6 Marcus Robinson 2.50
NG7 Troy Edwards 1.25
NG8 Kevin Johnson 1.25
NG9 Cade McNown 1.00
NG10 Jon Kitna 1.00
NG11 Peyton Manning 10.00
NG12 Edgerrin James 8.00
NG13 Akili Smith 1.00
NG14 Donovan McNabb 3.00
NG15 Randy Moss 10.00

2000 Upper Deck Proving Ground

NM/M
Complete Set (10): 7.00
Common Player: .50
Minor Stars: 1.00
Inserted 1:11
PG1 Marcus Robinson 1.00
PG2 Stephen Davis 1.00
PG3 Daunte Culpepper 2.00
PG4 Jevon Kearse 1.00
PG5 Marshall Faulk 1.00
PG6 Marvin Harrison 1.00
PG7 Germane Crowell .50
PG8 Darnay Scott .50
PG9 Duce Staley .50
PT10 Warrick Dunn 1.00

2000 Upper Deck Strike Force

NM/M
Complete Set (15): 5.00
Common Player: .30
Minor Stars: .60
Inserted 1:4
SF1 Fred Taylor 1.00
SF2 Muhsin Muhammad .60
SF3 Tony Gonzalez .30
SF4 Marcus Robinson .60
SF5 Charlie Garner .30
SF6 Torry Holt .60
SF7 Germane Crowell .60
SF8 Amani Toomer .30
SF9 Patrick Jeffers .30
SF10 Albert Connell .30
SF11 Olandis Gary .60
SF12 Robert Smith .60
SF13 Napoleon Kaufman .30
SF14 Tim Biakabutuka .30
SF15 Priest Holmes .30

2000 Upper Deck Wired

NM/M
Complete Set (15): 12.00
Common Player: .75
Minor Stars: 1.50
Inserted 1:8
W1 Charlie Batch 1.50

NM/M
W2 Terrell Davis 2.00
W3 Jake Plummer 1.50
W4 Cris Carter 1.50
W5 James O. Stewart 1.50
W6 Corey Dillon 1.50
W7 Ricky Watters .75
W8 Curtis Enis 1.00
W9 Errict Rhett .75
W10 Stephen Davis 1.50
W11 Mike Alstott 1.50
W12 Steve Beuerlein .75
W13 Michael Westbrook .75
W14 Terry Glenn 1.50
W15 Bill Schroeder .75

2000 Upper Deck Black Diamond

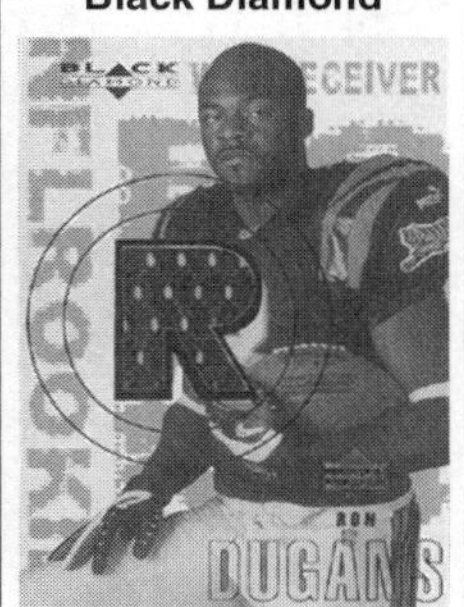

NM/M
Common Player: .15
Minor Stars: .30
Common Rookie (121-150): 1.50
Inserted 1:8
Common Rookie Jersey (151-180): 12.00
Inserted 1:23
Pack (6): 3.00
Wax Box (24): 50.00
1 Jake Plummer .50
2 David Boston .50
3 Frank Sanders .30
4 Tim Dwight .50
5 Chris Chandler .30
6 Jamal Anderson .50
7 Shawn Jefferson .15
8 Terance Mathis .15
9 Qadry Ismail .15
10 Tony Banks .30
11 Shannon Sharpe .30
12 Peerless Price .30
13 Rob Johnson .30
14 Eric Moulds .50
15 Antowain Smith .30
16 Muhsin Muhammad .30
17 Patrick Jeffers .30
18 Steve Beuerlein .30
19 Tim Biakabutuka .30
20 Cade McNown .50
21 Marcus Robinson .50
22 Eddie Kennison .15
23 Bobby Engram .15
24 Akili Smith .50
25 Corey Dillon .50
26 Darnay Scott .30
27 Tim Couch 1.25
28 Kevin Johnson .50
29 Errict Rhett .30
30 Troy Aikman 1.25
31 Emmitt Smith 1.75
32 Raghib Ismail .15
33 Joey Galloway .50
34 Terrell Davis 1.00
35 Olandis Gary .60
36 Brian Griese .60
37 Ed McCaffrey .50
38 Rod Smith .50
39 Charlie Batch .50
40 Germane Crowell .50
41 Johnnie Morton .30
42 James O. Stewart .50
43 Brett Favre 2.50
44 Antonio Freeman .50
45 Dorsey Levens .50
46 Peyton Manning 2.00
47 Edgerrin James 1.50
48 Marvin Harrison .50
49 Terrence Wilkins .50
50 Mark Brunell .75
51 Fred Taylor .75
52 Jimmy Smith .50
53 Keenan McCardell .30
54 Elvis Grbac .30
55 Tony Gonzalez .30
56 Derrick S. Alexander .15
57 James Johnson .30
58 Tony Martin .15
59 Damon Huard .50
60 Oronde Gadsden .30
61 Randy Moss 2.00
62 Robert Smith .50
63 Cris Carter .50
64 Daunte Culpepper 1.50
65 Drew Bledsoe 1.00
66 Terry Glenn .75
67 Sean Morey .15
68 Ricky Williams 1.50
69 Keith Poole .15
70 Jake Reed .30
71 Jeff Blake .30
72 Kerry Collins .30
73 Amani Toomer .30
74 Joe Montgomery .15
75 Ike Hilliard .30
76 Ray Lucas .50
77 Curtis Martin .50
78 Vinny Testaverde .50
79 Wayne Chrebet .50
80 Tim Brown .50
81 Rich Gannon .30
82 Tyrone Wheatley .30
83 Rickey Dudley .30
84 Napoleon Kaufman .50
85 Duce Staley .50
86 Donovan McNabb 1.00
87 Torrance Small .15
88 Charles Johnson .30
89 Kent Graham .15
90 Troy Edwards .50
91 Jerome Bettis .50
92 Kordell Stewart .60
93 Marshall Faulk .50
94 Kurt Warner 2.00
95 Torry Holt .50
96 Isaac Bruce .50
97 Jermaine Fazande .30
98 Ryan Leaf .50
99 Jeff Graham .15
100 Moses Moreno .30
101 Jerry Rice 2.00
102 Terrell Owens .50
103 Jeff Garcia .50
104 Ricky Watters .30
105 Jon Kitna .50
106 Derrick Mayes .30
107 Charlie Rogers .15
108 Warrick Dunn .50
109 Shaun King .50
110 Mike Alstott .50
111 Keyshawn Johnson .50
112 Eddie George .75
113 Steve McNair .60
114 Kevin Dyson .30
115 Kevin Daft .15
116 Jevon Kearse .50
117 Brad Johnson .50
118 Stephen Davis .50
119 Michael Westbrook .30
120 Jeff George .50
121 *Kwame Cavil* 1.50
122 *Corey Moore* 1.50
123 *Sebastian Janikowski* 4.00
124 *Troy Walters* 3.00
125 *Mike Anderson* 4.00
126 *Tom Brady* 12.00
127 *Spergon Wynn* 4.00
128 *Tim Rattay* 3.00
129 *Giovanni Carmazzi* 3.00
130 *Chris Cole* 1.50
131 *Demario Brown* 1.50
132 *Chris Coleman* 1.50
133 *Michael Wiley* 3.00
134 *JaJuan Dawson* 3.00
135 *Deon Dyer* 3.00
136 *Trevor Gaylor* 3.00
137 *Todd Husak* 4.00
138 *Darrell Jackson* 4.00
139 *Erron Kinney* 3.00
140 *Anthony Lucas* 1.50
141 *Rondell Mealey* 3.00
142 *Chad Morton* 2.00
143 *Leon Murray* 1.50
144 *Mareno Philyaw* 1.50
145 *Gari Scott* 2.00
146 *Paul Smith* 1.50
147 *Terrelle Smith* 1.50
148 *Shyrone Stith* 2.00
149 *Bashir Yamini* 1.50
150 *Windrell Hayes* 1.50
151 *Courtney Brown* 15.00
152 *Corey Simon* 15.00
153 *R. Jay Soward* 15.00
154 *Chris Redman* 10.00
155 *Joe Hamilton* 10.00
156 *Chad Pennington* 40.00
157 *Tee Martin* 10.00
158 *Ron Dayne* 10.00
159 *Shaun Alexander* 25.00
160 *Thomas Jones* 12.00
161 *Reuben Droughns* 20.00
162 *Jamal Lewis* 25.00
163 *J.R. Redmond* 10.00
164 *Travis Prentice* 10.00
165 *Trung Canidate* 12.00
166 *Brian Urlacher* 30.00
167 *Anthony Becht* 10.00
168 *Bubba Franks* 12.00
169 *Peter Warrick* 15.00
170 *Plaxico Burress* 20.00
171 *Sylvester Morris* 10.00
172 *Dez White* 12.00
173 *Travis Taylor* 10.00
174 *Todd Pinkston* 12.00
175 *Dennis Northcutt* 10.00
176 *Jerry Porter* 15.00
177 *Laveranues Coles* 15.00
178 *Danny Farmer* 10.00
179 *Curtis Keaton* 10.00
180 *Ron Dugans* 10.00

2000 Upper Deck Black Diamond Gold

Gold Cards: 4X
#1-120 Production 1,000 Sets

Gold Rookies: 1.5X
#121-150 Production 500 Sets
Gold Rookie Jersey: 2X
#151-180 Production 100 Sets

2000 Upper Deck Black Diamond Diamonation

NM/M
Complete Set (10): 8.00
Common Player: .50
Minor Stars: 1.00
Inserted 1:8
D1 Marshall Faulk 1.00
D2 Marcus Robinson 1.00
D3 Eddie George 1.25
D4 Kurt Warner 2.00
D5 Amani Toomer .50
D6 Muhsin Muhammad .50
D7 Jevon Kearse 1.00
D8 Jon Kitna 1.00
D9 Terrell Davis 1.50
D10 Tony Gonzalez .50

2000 Upper Deck Black Diamond Might

NM/M
Complete Set (15): 25.00
Common Player: 1.00
Inserted 1:11
DM1 Fred Taylor 1.00
DM2 Edgerrin James 3.00
DM3 Cade McNown 1.00
DM4 Randy Moss 4.00
DM5 Shaun King 1.00
DM6 Keyshawn Johnson 2.00
DM7 Jamal Anderson 1.00
DM8 Ricky Williams 3.00
DM9 Jerry Rice 4.00
DM10 Isaac Bruce 1.00
DM11 Peyton Manning 4.00
DM12 Mark Brunell 1.00
DM13 Tim Couch 3.00
DM14 Akili Smith 1.00
DM15 Emmitt Smith 4.00

2000 Upper Deck Black Diamond Skills

NM/M
Complete Set (15): 25.00
Common Player: 1.00
Inserted 1:11
DS1 Eddie George 1.50
DS2 Brett Favre 4.00
DS3 Marshall Faulk 1.00
DS4 Rob Johnson 1.00
DS5 Kevin Johnson 1.00
DS6 Randy Moss 3.00
DS7 Peyton Manning 3.00
DS8 Kurt Warner 3.00
DS9 Jake Plummer 1.50
DS10 Troy Aikman 3.00
DS11 Daunte Culpepper 2.50
DS12 Drew Bledsoe 2.00
DS13 Vinny Testaverde 1.00
DS14 Marvin Harrison 1.00
DS15 Charlie Batch 1.00

2000 Upper Deck Black Diamond Super Bowl

NM/M
Complete Set (14): 60.00
Common Player: 3.00
CB Champ Bailey 3.00
DB David Boston 3.00
CC Cecil Collins 3.00
TC Tim Couch 10.00
DC Daunte Culpepper 10.00
TH Torry Holt 3.00
EJ Edgerrin James 10.00
JJ James Johnson 3.00
JK Jevon Kearse 3.00
DM Donovan McNabb 5.00
CM Cade McNown 3.00
PP Peerless Price 3.00
AS Akili Smith 3.00
RW Ricky Williams 5.00

2000 Upper Deck Encore

NM/M
Complete Set (270): 125.00
Common Player: .15
Minor Stars: .30
Common Rookie: 1.00
Inserted 1:6
Pack (5): 3.50
Wax Box (24): 60.00
Common Player (271-283): 2.00
Production 2,000 Sets
1 Jake Plummer .50
2 Michael Pittman .30
3 Rob Moore .30
4 David Boston .50
5 Frank Sanders .30
6 Aeneas Williams .15
7 Kwamie Lassiter .15
8 Rob Fredrickson .15
9 Tim Dwight .50
10 Chris Chandler .30
11 Jamal Anderson .50
12 Shawn Jefferson .15
13 Brian Finneran .15
14 Terance Mathis .15
15 Bob Christian .15
16 Qadry Ismail .15
17 Jermaine Lewis .15
18 Rod Woodson .15
19 Michael McCrary .15
20 Tony Banks .30
21 Peter Boulware .15
22 Shannon Sharpe .30
23 Peerless Price .50
24 Rob Johnson .30
25 Eric Moulds .50
26 Doug Flutie .75
27 Jeremy McDaniel .15
28 Antowain Smith .30
29 Shawn Bryson .15
30 Muhsin Muhammad .30
31 Donald Hayes .30
32 Steve Beuerlein .30
33 Reggie White .30
34 Tshimanga Biakabutuka .30
35 Michael Bates .15
36 Chuck Smith .30
37 Wesley Walls .30
38 Cade McNown .30
39 Curtis Enis .30
40 Marcus Robinson .50
41 Eddie Kennison .15
42 Bobby Engram .15
43 Glyn Milburn .15
44 Marty Booker .50
45 Akili Smith .30
46 Corey Dillon .50
47 James Allen .30
48 Tremain Mack .15
49 Damon Griffin .15
50 Takeo Spikes .15
51 Tony McGee .15
52 Tim Couch 1.00
53 Kevin Johnson .50
54 Darrin Chiaverini .15
55 Jamir Miller .15
56 Errict Rhett .30
57 Aaron Shea .15
58 Kevin Thompson .15
59 Troy Aikman 1.25
60 Emmitt Smith 1.50
61 Raghib Ismail .15
62 Jason Tucker .30
63 Chris Brazzell .15
64 Joey Galloway .50
65 Wane McGarity .15
66 Terrell Davis 1.00
67 Olandis Gary .50
68 Brian Griese .75
69 Gus Frerotte .30
70 Byron Chamberlain .15
71 Ed McCaffrey .30
72 Rod Smith .50
73 Al Wilson .15
74 Charlie Batch .30
75 Germane Crowell .50
76 Sedrick Irvin .15
77 Johnnie Morton .30
78 Robert Porcher .15
79 Herman Moore .50
80 James O. Stewart .30
81 Brett Favre 2.50
82 Antonio Freeman .50
83 Bill Schroeder .30
84 Dorsey Levens .50
85 Herbert Goodman .15
86 Ahman Green .30
87 Matt Hasselbeck .30
88 Peyton Manning 2.00
89 Edgerrin James 1.50
90 Marvin Harrison .50
91 Basil Mitchell .15
92 Terrence Wilkins .30
93 Kareem Abdul Jabbar .15
94 Ken Dilger .15
95 Mark Brunell .75
96 Fred Taylor .75
97 Jimmy Smith .50
98 Keenan McCardell .30
99 Stacey Mack .15
100 Jonathan Quinn .15
101 Kyle Brady .15
102 Hardy Nickerson .15
103 Elvis Grbac .30
104 Tony Gonzalez .30
105 Derrick S. Alexander .15
106 Tony Richardson .15
107 Michael Cloud .15
108 Donnie Edwards .15
109 Jay Fiedler .30
110 James Johnson .30
111 Tony Martin .15
112 Damon Huard .30
113 Lamar Smith .30
114 Thurman Thomas .30
115 Mike Quinn .15
116 Oronde Gadsden .30
117 Randy Moss 2.00
118 Robert Smith .50
119 Cris Carter .50
120 Matthew Hatchette .30
121 Daunte Culpepper 1.00
122 Moe Williams .15
123 Drew Bledsoe .75
124 Terry Glenn .50
125 Troy Brown .15
126 Kevin Faulk .30
127 Lawyer Milloy .15
128 Ricky Williams 1.00
129 Keith Poole .15
130 Jake Reed .30
131 *Jake Delhomme* 5.00
132 Jeff Blake .30
133 Andrew Glover .15
134 Kerry Collins .30
135 Amani Toomer .30
136 Joe Montgomery .15
137 Ike Hilliard .30
138 Tiki Barber .30
139 Pete Mitchell .15
140 Ray Lucas .30
141 Mo Lewis .15
142 Curtis Martin .50
143 Vinny Testaverde .30
144 Wayne Chrebet .50
145 Dedric Ward .30
146 Tim Brown .50
147 Rich Gannon .30
148 Tyrone Wheatley .30
149 Napoleon Kaufman .50
150 Charles Woodson .50
151 Darrell Russell .15
152 James Jett .30
153 Rickey Dudley .15
154 Jon Ritchie .15
155 Duce Staley .50
156 Donovan McNabb .75
157 Torrance Small .15
158 Ron Powlus .50
159 Mike Mamula .15
160 Dameane Douglas .15
161 Charles Johnson .30
162 Kent Graham .15
163 Troy Edwards .30
164 Jerome Bettis .50
165 Hines Ward .30
166 Kordell Stewart .50
167 Levon Kirkland .15
168 *Bobby Shaw* .75
169 Marshall Faulk .50
170 Kurt Warner 2.00
171 Torry Holt .50
172 Isaac Bruce .50
173 Kevin Carter .15
174 Az-Zahir Hakim .30
175 Ricky Proehl .15
176 Robert Chancey .15
177 Curtis Conway .30
178 Freddie Jones .30
179 Junior Seau .30
180 Jeff Graham .15
181 Reggie Jones .50
182 Rodney Harrison .15
183 Rick Mirer .30
184 Jerry Rice 2.00
185 Charlie Garner .30
186 Terrell Owens .50
187 Jeff Garcia .50
188 Fred Beasley .15
189 J.J. Stokes .30
190 Ricky Watters .50
191 Jon Kitna .50
192 Derrick Mayes .30
193 Sean Dawkins .15
194 Charlie Rogers .15
195 Brock Huard .50
196 Cortez Kennedy .15
197 Christian Fauria .15
198 Warrick Dunn .50
199 Shaun King .50
200 Mike Alstott .50
201 Warren Sapp .30
202 Jacquez Green .30
203 Reidel Anthony .30
204 Dave Moore .15
205 Keyshawn Johnson .50
206 Eddie George .75
207 Steve McNair .50
208 *Billy Volek* .50
209 Jevon Kearse .50
210 Yancey Thigpen .30
211 Frank Wycheck .30
212 Carl Pickens .30
213 Neil O'Donnell .30
214 Brad Johnson .30
215 Stephen Davis .50
216 Michael Westbrook .30
217 Albert Connell .30
218 *Aaron Stecker* .50
219 Bruce Smith .15
220 Stephen Alexander .15
221 Jeff George .30
222 Adrian Murrell .30
223 *Courtney Brown* 2.00
224 *John Engleberger* 1.00
225 *Deltha O'Neal* 1.00
226 *Corey Simon* 2.00
227 *R. Jay Soward* 2.00
228 *Chris Samuels* 1.00
229 *Avion Black* 1.00
230 *Doug Chapman* 1.00
231 *Darrell Jackson* 5.00
232 *Chris Cole* 1.00
233 *Trevor Gaylor* 2.00
234 *Chad Morton* 2.00
235 *Chris Redman* 4.00
236 *Joe Hamilton* 2.00
237 *Chad Pennington* 12.00
238 *Tee Martin* 2.00
239 *Giovanni Carmazzi* 2.00
240 *Tim Rattay* 4.00
241 *Ron Dayne* 4.00
242 *Shaun Alexander* 8.00
243 *Thomas Jones* 4.00
244 *Reuben Droughns* 5.00
245 *Jamal Lewis* 8.00
246 *Michael Wiley* 2.00
247 *J.R. Redmond* 3.00
248 *Travis Prentice* 3.50
249 *Todd Husak* 2.00
250 *Trung Canidate* 3.00
251 *Brian Urlacher* 6.00
252 *Anthony Becht* 2.00
253 *Bubba Franks* 2.00
254 *Tom Brady* 20.00
255 *Peter Warrick* 5.00
256 *Plaxico Burress* 6.00
257 *Sylvester Morris* 3.00
258 *Dez White* 2.00
259 *Travis Taylor* 4.00
260 *Todd Pinkston* 2.00
261 *Dennis Northcutt* 2.00
262 *Jerry Porter* 5.00
263 *Laveranues Coles* 5.00
264 *Danny Farmer* 2.00
265 *Curtis Keaton* 1.00
266 *Windrell Hayes* 1.00
267 *Ron Dugans* 2.00
268 Steve McNair CL .30
269 Jake Plummer CL .30
270 Antonio Freeman CL .30
271 *Brad Hoover* 2.00
272 *Charles Lee* 2.00
273 *Deon Dyer* 2.00
274 *Doug Johnson* 4.00
275 *JaJuan Dawson* 3.00
276 *Jarious Jackson* 3.00
277 *Larry Foster* 3.00
278 *Mike Anderson* 4.00
279 *Ron Dixon* 4.00
280 *Sammy Morris* 3.00
281 *Shyrone Stith* 2.00
282 *Spergon Wynn* 3.00
283 *Troy Walters* 2.00

2000 Upper Deck Encore SGC Blue Label Rookies

NM/M
Common SGC 98: 15.00
SGC 96: 30%
SGC 92: 20%
Inserted 1:Box
223 Courtney Brown 20.00
224 John Engleberger 20.00
225 Deltha O'Neal 15.00
226 Corey Simon 20.00
227 R. Jay Soward 15.00
228 Chris Samuels 20.00
229 Avion Black 15.00
230 Doug Chapman 15.00
231 Darrell Jackson 30.00
232 Chris Cole 15.00
233 Trevor Gaylor 20.00
234 Chad Morton 20.00
235 Chris Redman 20.00
236 Joe Hamilton 20.00
237 Chad Pennington 50.00
238 Tee Martin 25.00
239 Giovanni Carmazzi 20.00
240 Tim Rattay 20.00
241 Ron Dayne 30.00
242 Shaun Alexander 50.00
243 Thomas Jones 25.00
244 Reuben Droughns 25.00
245 Jamal Lewis 50.00
246 Michael Wiley 20.00
247 J.R. Redmond 25.00
248 Travis Prentice 25.00
249 Todd Husak 25.00
250 Trung Canidate 20.00
251 Brian Urlacher 55.00
252 Anthony Becht 25.00
253 Bubba Franks 30.00
254 Tom Brady 20.00
255 Peter Warrick 30.00
256 Plaxico Burress 35.00
257 Sylvester Morris 25.00
258 Dez White 20.00
259 Travis Taylor 20.00
260 Todd Pinkston 30.00
261 Dennis Northcutt 20.00
262 Jerry Porter 30.00
263 Laveranues Coles 25.00
264 Danny Farmer 15.00
265 Curtis Keaton 20.00
266 Windrell Hayes 20.00
267 Ron Dugans 20.00

2000 Upper Deck Encore Highlight Zone

NM/M
Complete Set (10): 7.00
Common Player: .50
Minor Stars: 1.00
Inserted 1:7
HZ1 Eddie George 1.50
HZ2 Steve McNair 1.00
HZ3 Kevin Dyson .50
HZ4 Kurt Warner 3.00
HZ5 Emmitt Smith 3.00
HZ6 Brad Johnson .50
HZ7 Curtis Martin 1.00
HZ8 Ray Lucas .50
HZ9 Akili Smith 1.00
HZ10 Jake Plummer 1.00

2000 Upper Deck Encore Proving Ground

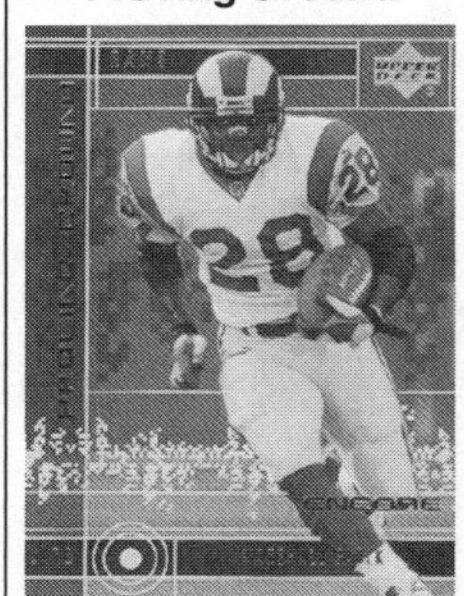

NM/M
Complete Set (10): 5.00
Common Player: .50
Minor Stars: 1.00
Inserted 1:7
PG1 Marcus Robinson 1.00
PG2 Stephen Davis 1.00
PG3 Daunte Culpepper 2.00
PG4 Jevon Kearse 1.00
PG5 Marshall Faulk 1.00
PG6 Marvin Harrison 1.00
PG7 Germane Crowell 1.00
PG8 Darnay Scott .50
PG9 Duce Staley 1.00
PG10 Warrick Dunn 1.00

2000 Upper Deck Encore Rookie Combo Jerseys

NM/M
Complete Set (9): 450.00
Common Player: 25.00
Inserted 1:287
RC1 Dez White, Brian Urlacher 75.00
RC2 Tee Martin, Plaxico Burress 45.00
RC3 Jerry Porter, Sylvester Morris 30.00
RC4 Peter Warrick, Courtney Brown 30.00
RC5 Peter Warrick, Curtis Keaton 30.00
RC6 Travis Prentice, Dennis Northcutt 25.00
RC7 Travis Taylor, Jamal Lewis, Chris Redman 75.00
RC8 Ron Dayne, Thomas Jones, Shaun Alexander 75.00
RC9 Chad Pennington, Laveranues Coles, Anthony Becht 100.00

2000 Upper Deck Encore Rookie Helmets

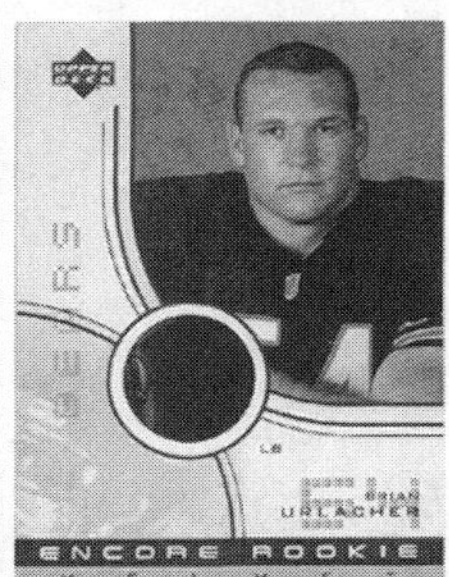

NM/M
Complete Set (28): 700.00
Common Player: 15.00
Inserted 1:287
Autographed Cards: 3X
Production 25 Sets
HSA Shaun Alexander 50.00
HTW Anthony Becht 15.00
HCB Courtney Brown 20.00
HPB Plaxico Burress 40.00
HLC Laveranues Coles 25.00
HRD Ron Dayne 30.00
HDR Reuben Droughns 20.00
HDU Ron Dugans 20.00
HDF Danny Farmer 20.00
HBF Bubba Franks 20.00
HTJ Thomas Jones 25.00
HCK Curtis Keaton 20.00
HJL Jamal Lewis 50.00
HTM Tee Martin 20.00
HSM Sylvester Morris 20.00
HDN Dennis Northcutt 20.00
HCP Chad Pennington 100.00
HPI Todd Pinkston 20.00
HJP Jerry Porter 30.00
HTP Travis Prentice 30.00
HCR Chris Redman 25.00
HJR J.R. Redmond 25.00
HCS Corey Simon 20.00
HRJ R. Jay Soward 20.00
HTT Travis Taylor 25.00
HBU Brian Urlacher 75.00
HPW Peter Warrick 25.00
HDW Dez White 20.00

2000 Upper Deck Encore Signed Rookie Helmets

NM/M
Common Player: 50.00
SA Shaun Alexander 150.00
CB Courtney Brown 40.00
PB Plaxico Burress 50.00
LC Laveranues Coles 50.00
RD Ron Dayne 40.00
DU Ron Dugans 25.00
DF Danny Farmer 25.00
TM Tee Martin 50.00
SM Sylvester Morris 50.00
DN Dennis Northcutt 50.00
CP Chad Pennington 200.00
TP Travis Prentice 50.00
CR Chris Redman 50.00
BU Brian Urlacher 275.00
DW Dez White 50.00

2000 Upper Deck Encore UD Authentics

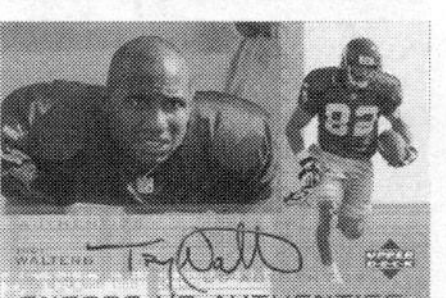

NM/M
Complete Set (28): 375.00
Common Player: 10.00
Inserted 1:23
SA Shaun Alexander 30.00
MA Mike Anderson 35.00
CB Courtney Brown 15.00
PB Plaxico Burress 25.00
TC Trung Canidate 10.00
KC Kwame Cavil 10.00
CC Chris Coleman 10.00
LC Laveranues Coles 15.00
RD Ron Dayne 20.00
DX Ron Dixon 15.00
DU Ron Dugans 10.00
DF Danny Farmer 10.00
TG Trevor Gaylor 10.00
SG Sherrod Gideon 10.00
DJ. Darrell Jackson 15.00
JO Doug Johnson 15.00
TM Tee Martin 15.00
CM Corey Moore 10.00
SM Sylvester Morris 15.00
DN Dennis Northcutt 15.00
CP Chad Pennington 75.00
TP Travis Prentice 20.00
TR Tim Rattay 15.00
CR Chris Redman 25.00
BU Brian Urlacher 50.00
TW Troy Walters 10.00
DW Dez White 10.00
MW Michael Wiley 10.00

2000 Upper Deck Gold Reserve

		NM/M
Complete Set (222):		150.00
Common Player:		.15
Minor Stars:		.30
Common Rookie:		2.00
Production 2,500 Sets		
Pack (10):		2.25
Wax Box (24):		40.00
1	Jake Plummer	.50
2	Rob Moore	.30
3	David Boston	.50
4	Frank Sanders	.30
5	Chris Chandler	.30
6	Jamal Anderson	.50
7	Shawn Jefferson	.15
8	Terance Mathis	.15
9	Qadry Ismail	.15
10	Jermaine Lewis	.15
11	Tony Banks	.30
12	Peter Boulware	.15
13	Shannon Sharpe	.30
14	Peerless Price	.30
15	Rob Johnson	.30
16	Eric Moulds	.50
17	Doug Flutie	.75
18	Antowain Smith	.30
19	Muhsin Muhammad	.30
20	Patrick Jeffers	.30
21	Steve Beuerlein	.30
22	Natrone Means	.30
23	Tshimanga Biakabutuka	.30
24	Wesley Walls	.15
25	Cade McNown	.50
26	Curtis Enis	.30
27	Marcus Robinson	.50
28	Eddie Kennison	.15
29	Bobby Engram	.15
30	Akili Smith	.50
31	Corey Dillon	.50
32	Damon Griffin	.15
33	Takeo Spikes	.15
34	Tony McGee	.15
35	Tim Couch	1.25
36	Kevin Johnson	.30
37	Darrin Chiaverini	.15
38	Errict Rhett	.30
39	Troy Aikman	1.25
40	Emmitt Smith	1.75
41	Raghib Ismail	.15
42	Jason Tucker	.15
43	Joey Galloway	.50
44	Wane McGarity	.15
45	Terrell Davis	1.00
46	Olandis Gary	.50
47	Brian Griese	.75
48	Gus Frerotte	.15
49	Ed McCaffrey	.30
50	Rod Smith	.30
51	Charlie Batch	.50
52	Germane Crowell	.15
53	Johnnie Morton	.30
54	Robert Porcher	.15
55	Herman Moore	.50
56	James O. Stewart	.30
57	Brett Favre	2.50
58	Antonio Freeman	.50
59	Bill Schroeder	.15
60	Dorsey Levens	.50
61	Corey Bradford	.15
62	Vonnie Holliday	.15
63	Peyton Manning	2.00
64	Edgerrin James	1.50
65	Marvin Harrison	.50
66	Ken Dilger	.15
67	Terrence Wilkins	.30
68	Marcus Pollard	.15
69	Mark Brunell	.75
70	Fred Taylor	.75
71	Jimmy Smith	.50
72	Keenan McCardell	.30
73	Carnell Lake	.15
74	Kyle Brady	.15
75	Hardy Nickerson	.15
76	Elvis Grbac	.30
77	Tony Gonzalez	.30
78	Derrick S. Alexander	.15
79	Donnell Bennett	.15
80	Mike Cloud	.15
81	Donnie Edwards	.15
82	Jay Fiedler	.50
83	James Johnson	.15
84	Tony Martin	.15
85	Damon Huard	.50
86	O.J. McDuffie	.30
87	Thurman Thomas	.30
88	Oronde Gadsden	.30
89	Randy Moss	2.00
90	Robert Smith	.50
91	Cris Carter	.50
92	Daunte Culpepper	1.25
93	Matthew Hatchette	.30
94	Drew Bledsoe	1.00
95	Terry Glenn	.50
96	Troy Brown	.15
97	Kevin Faulk	.30
98	Lawyer Milloy	.15
99	Ricky Williams	1.00
100	Keith Poole	.15
101	Jake Reed	.30
102	Jeff Blake	.30
103	Andrew Glover	.15
104	Kerry Collins	.30
105	Amani Toomer	.30
106	Joe Montgomery	.15
107	Ike Hilliard	.30
108	Tiki Barber	.30
109	Ray Lucas	.50
110	Mo Lewis	.15
111	Curtis Martin	.50
112	Vinny Testaverde	.30
113	Wayne Chrebet	.50
114	Dedric Ward	.30
115	Tim Brown	.75
116	Rich Gannon	.30
117	Tyrone Wheatley	.30
118	Napoleon Kaufman	.50
119	Charles Woodson	.30
120	James Jett	.15
121	Rickey Dudley	.30
122	Duce Staley	.50
123	Donovan McNabb	1.00
124	Torrance Small	.15
125	Allen Rossum	.15
126	Na Brown	.15
127	Charles Johnson	.30
128	Kent Graham	.15
129	Troy Edwards	.30
130	Jerome Bettis	.50
131	Hines Ward	.30
132	Kordell Stewart	.60
133	Richard Huntley	.15
134	Marshall Faulk	.50
135	Kurt Warner	2.00
136	Torry Holt	.50
137	Isaac Bruce	.50
138	Kevin Carter	.15
139	Az-Zahir Hakim	.30
140	Jermaine Fazande	.15
141	Curtis Conway	.30
142	Freddie Jones	.30
143	Junior Seau	.30
144	Jeff Graham	.15
145	Jim Harbaugh	.30
146	Jerry Rice	2.00
147	Charlie Garner	.30
148	Terrell Owens	.50
149	Jeff Garcia	.50
150	J.J. Stokes	.30
151	Ricky Watters	.30
152	Jon Kitna	.50
153	Derrick Mayes	.30
154	Sean Dawkins	.15
155	Charlie Rogers	.15
156	Cortez Kennedy	.15
157	Warrick Dunn	.50
158	Shaun King	.50
159	Mike Alstott	.50
160	Warren Sapp	.30
161	Jacquez Green	.15
162	Reidel Anthony	.15
163	Keyshawn Johnson	.50
164	Eddie George	.75
165	Steve McNair	.50
166	Kevin Dyson	.30
167	Jevon Kearse	.50
168	Yancey Thigpen	.15
169	Isaac Byrd	.15
170	Neil O'Donnell	.15
171	Brad Johnson	.30
172	Stephen Davis	.50
173	Michael Westbrook	.30
174	Albert Connell	.15
175	Bruce Smith	.15
176	Stephen Alexander	.15
177	Jeff George	.30
178	*Bubba Franks*	6.00
179	*Brian Urlacher*	10.00
180	*Chad Pennington*	20.00
181	*Tim Rattay*	8.00
182	*Chris Redman*	3.00
183	*Corey Simon*	2.50
184	*Courtney Brown*	3.00
185	*Curtis Keaton*	2.00
186	*Danny Farmer*	2.00
187	*Erron Kinney*	2.00
188	*Deltha O'Neal*	2.00
189	*Dennis Northcutt*	4.00
190	*Dez White*	4.00
191	*Frank Murphy*	2.00
192	*Gari Scott*	2.00
193	*Giovanni Carmazzi*	2.00
194	*J.R. Redmond*	3.00
195	*JaJuan Dawson*	2.00
196	*Jamal Lewis*	12.00
197	*Jerry Porter*	8.00
198	*Joe Hamilton*	3.00
199	*Laveranues Coles*	8.00
200	*Michael Wiley*	2.00
201	*Peter Warrick*	8.00
202	*Plaxico Burress*	10.00
203	*R. Jay Soward*	2.00
204	*Reuben Droughns*	8.00
205	*Rob Morris*	4.00
206	*Ron Dayne*	4.00
207	*Ron Dugans*	2.00
208	*Sebastian Janikowski*	2.50
209	*Shaun Alexander*	12.00
210	*Sylvester Morris*	4.00
211	*Tee Martin*	3.00
212	*Thomas Jones*	8.00
213	*Todd Husak*	2.00
214	*Todd Pinkston*	5.00
215	*Tom Brady*	30.00
216	*Travis Prentice*	3.00
217	*Travis Taylor*	5.00
218	*Trevor Gaylor*	2.00
219	*Trung Canidate*	4.00
223	Peyton Manning CL	1.00
224	Randy Moss CL	1.00
225	Kurt Warner CL	1.50

2000 Upper Deck Gold Reserve Face Masks

		NM/M
Complete Set (15):		650.00
Common Player:		20.00
Production 100 Sets		
Gold Cards:		2X
Production 25 Sets		
FMSA	Shaun Alexander	60.00
FMCB	Courtney Brown	20.00
FMPB	Plaxico Burress	45.00
FMRD	Ron Dayne	30.00
FMDR	Reuben Droughns	20.00
FMTJ	Thomas Jones	40.00
FMCK	Curtis Keaton	20.00
FMJL	Jamal Lewis	75.00
FMSM	Sylvester Morris	45.00
FMCP	Chad Pennington	100.00
FMCR	Chris Redman	40.00
FMJR	J.R. Redmond	25.00
FMRJ	R. Jay Soward	20.00
FMTT	Travis Taylor	25.00
FMPW	Peter Warrick	40.00

2000 Upper Deck Gold Reserve Face Masks Gold

		NM/M
Common Player:		50.00
PB	Plaxico Burress	60.00
RD	Ron Dayne	75.00
TJ	Thomas Jones	50.00
JL	Jamal Lewis	100.00
CP	Chad Pennington	200.00
PW	Peter Warrick	75.00
		50.00

2000 Upper Deck Gold Reserve Gold Mine

		NM/M
Complete Set (12):		15.00
Common Player:		1.50
Inserted 1:12		
GM1	Dez White	1.50
GM2	Peter Warrick	2.00
GM3	Plaxico Burress	2.50
GM4	Bubba Franks	1.50
GM5	Jamal Lewis	3.00
GM6	Travis Taylor	2.00
GM7	Chris Redman	2.25
GM8	Sylvester Morris	2.00
GM9	Courtney Brown	1.50
GM10	Shaun Alexander	3.00
GM11	Trung Canidate	1.50
GM12	J.R. Redmond	1.75

2000 Upper Deck Gold Reserve Gold Strike

		NM/M
Complete Set (12):		15.00
Common Player:		1.50
Inserted 1:12		
GS1	Eddie George	1.75
GS2	Edgerrin James	3.00
GS3	Terrell Davis	2.00
GS4	Jamal Anderson	1.50
GS5	Ricky Williams	2.50
GS6	Marshall Faulk	1.50
GS7	Keyshawn Johnson	1.50
GS8	Brett Favre	5.00
GS9	Cade McNown	1.50
GS10	Emmitt Smith	4.00
GS11	Peyton Manning	4.00
GS12	Kurt Warner	4.00

2000 Upper Deck Gold Reserve Setting the Standard

		NM/M
Complete Set (12):		15.00
Common Player:		1.50
Inserted 1:12		
SS1	Randy Moss	5.00
SS2	Peyton Manning	5.00
SS3	Stephen Davis	1.50
SS4	Cris Carter	1.50
SS5	Jevon Kearse	1.50
SS6	Jerry Rice	5.00
SS7	Troy Aikman	3.00
SS8	Edgerrin James	3.00
SS9	Daunte Culpepper	2.50
SS10	Shaun King	1.00
SS11	Mark Brunell	1.50
SS12	Fred Taylor	1.00

2000 Upper Deck Gold Reserve Solid Gold Gallery

		NM/M
Complete Set (6):		20.00
Common Player:		3.00
Inserted 1:23		
SG1	Jamal Lewis	3.00
SG2	Peter Warrick	3.00
SG3	Ron Dayne	3.00
SG4	Chad Pennington	6.00
SG5	Thomas Jones	3.00
SG6	Plaxico Burress	4.00

2000 Upper Deck Gold Reserve UD Authentics

		NM/M
Common Player:		10.00
Inserted 1:160		
Gold Cards:		4X
Production 25 Sets		
TA	Troy Aikman	50.00
SA	Shaun Alexander	40.00
KC	Kwame Cavil	10.00
CC	Chris Coleman	10.00
RD	Ron Dayne	25.00
DU	Ron Dugans	10.00
FA	Danny Farmer	10.00
DF	Doug Flutie	25.00
SG	Sherrod Gideon	10.00
JH	Joe Hamilton	10.00
BJ	Brad Johnson	20.00
TJ	Thomas Jones	10.00
TM	Tee Martin	10.00
CP	Chad Pennington	60.00
TR	Tim Rattay	10.00
CR	Chris Redman	10.00
TW	Troy Walters	10.00
DW	Dez White	15.00
MW	Michael Wiley	10.00

2000 Upper Deck Legends

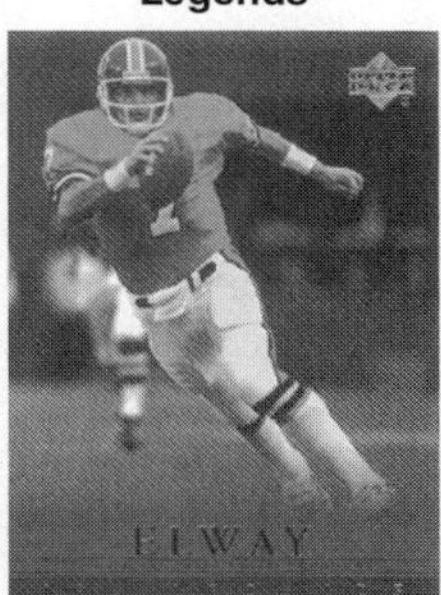

		NM/M
Complete Set (132):		350.00
Common Player:		.15
Minor Stars:		.30
Common 20th Century:		8.00
Production 2,500 Sets		
Common Rookie:		5.00
Production 2,000 Sets		
Pack (5):		5.50
Wax Box (24):		95.00
1	Jake Plummer	.50
2	Jamal Anderson	.50
3	Doug Flutie	.75
4	Jim Kelly	.50
5	Dick Butkus	.75
6	Mike Singletary	.30
7	Gale Sayers	.75
8	Boomer Esiason	.30
9	Anthony Munoz	.15
10	Otto Graham	.50
11	Jim Brown	1.00
12	Ozzie Newsome	.30
13	Bob Lilly	.30
14	Troy Aikman	1.25
15	Emmitt Smith	1.50
16	Roger Staubach	1.25
17	Deion Sanders	.50
18	Tony Dorsett	.50
19	Terrell Davis	1.00
20	John Elway	1.50
21	Charlie Batch	.50
22	Brett Favre	2.50
23	Bart Starr	1.50
24	Reggie White	.30
25	Earl Campbell	.50
26	Peyton Manning	2.00
27	Edgerrin James	2.00
28	Johnny Unitas	1.25
29	Marvin Harrison	.50
30	Mark Brunell	.75
31	Fred Taylor	.75
32	Len Dawson	.50
33	Dan Marino	2.00
34	Bob Griese	.50
35	Mark Duper	.15
36	Thurman Thomas	.30
37	Fran Tarkenton	.75
38	Randy Moss	2.00
39	Cris Carter	.50
40	Gary Anderson	.15
41	John Randle	.15
42	Drew Bledsoe	.75
43	Archie Manning	.30
44	Ricky Williams	1.25
45	Frank Gifford	.50
46	Kerry Collins	.30
47	Phil Simms	.30
48	Vinny Testaverde	.30
49	Curtis Martin	.50
50	Keyshawn Johnson	.50
51	Joe Namath	2.00
52	Marcus Allen	.50
53	Bruce Smith	.15
54	Ken Stabler	.75
55	Fred Biletnikoff	.15
56	Howie Long	.50
57	Ron Jaworski	.50
58	Harold Carmichael	.30
59	Kordell Stewart	.50
60	Levon Kirkland	.15
61	Mel Blount	.15
62	Jerome Bettis	.50
63	John Stallworth	.30
64	Franco Harris	.50
65	Jim Harbaugh	.30
66	Kellen Winslow	.30
67	Charlie Joiner	.30
68	Junior Seau	.30
69	Jerry Rice	1.25
70	Steve Young	.75
71	Joe Montana	2.50
72	Roger Craig	.30
73	Ronnie Lott	.30
74	Jon Kitna	.50
75	Steve Largent	.50
76	Ricky Watters	.30
77	Kurt Warner	2.00
78	Marshall Faulk	.50
79	Isaac Bruce	.50
80	Merlin Olsen	.50
81	Lee Roy Selmon	.15
82	Tim Brown	.50
83	Tim Couch	1.25
84	Mike Alstott	.50
85	Eddie George	.60
86	Steve McNair	.50
87	Brad Johnson	.50
88	Sonny Jurgensen	.50
89	Art Monk	.50
90	Joe Theismann	.50
91	Ray Nitschke TCL	8.00
92	Doak Walker TCL	8.00
93	Thurman Thomas TCL	8.00
94	Jim Brown TCL	10.00
95	Sammy Baugh TCL	10.00
96	Reggie White TCL	8.00
97	Eric Dickerson TCL	8.00
98	Paul Hornung TCL	8.00
99	Deion Sanders TCL	10.00
100	Bronko Nagurski TCL	8.00
101	Walter Payton TCL	25.00
102	Jim Thorpe TCL	10.00
103	*Ron Dayne*	5.00
104	*Tim Rattay*	8.00
105	*Brian Urlacher*	10.00
106	*Bubba Franks*	6.00
107	*Chad Pennington*	20.00
108	*Chris Cole*	5.00
109	*Chris Redman*	6.00
110	*Courtney Brown*	6.00
111	*Curtis Keaton*	5.00
112	*Dennis Northcutt*	6.00
113	*Dez White*	6.00
114	*Giovanni Carmazzi*	6.00
115	*J.R. Redmond*	6.00
116	*JaJuan Dawson*	6.00
117	*Jamal Lewis*	10.00
118	*Jerry Porter*	8.00
119	*Laveranues Coles*	8.00
120	*Peter Warrick*	8.00
121	*Plaxico Burress*	10.00
122	*R. Jay Soward*	6.00
123	*Reuben Droughns*	8.00
124	*Ron Dixon*	6.00
125	*Ron Dugans*	6.00
126	*Shaun Alexander*	12.00
127	*Sylvester Morris*	6.00
128	*Thomas Jones*	6.00
129	*Todd Pinkston*	6.00
130	*Travis Prentice*	6.00
131	*Travis Taylor*	6.00
132	*Trung Canidate*	6.00

2000 Upper Deck Legends Autographs

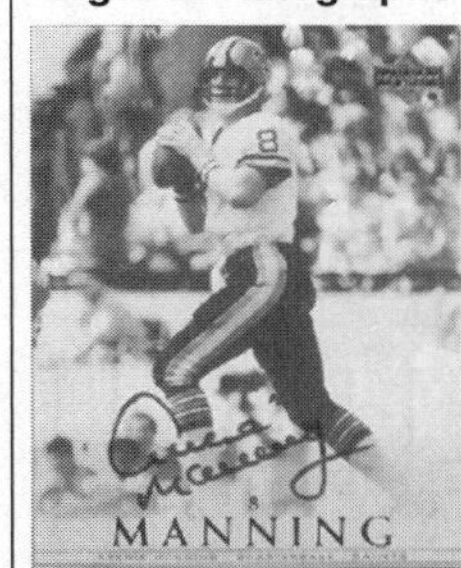

		NM/M
Common Player:		10.00
Minor Stars:		20.00
Inserted 1:47		
Gold Cards:		3X
Production 25 Sets		
TA	Troy Aikman	60.00
MA	Marcus Allen	35.00
JA	Jamal Anderson	30.00
BU	Jerome Bettis	40.00
FB	Fred Biletnikoff	30.00
DR	Drew Bledsoe	50.00
MB	Mel Blount	20.00
JB	Jim Brown	75.00
TB	Tim Brown	30.00
IB	Isaac Bruce	30.00
BR	Mark Brunell	45.00
DB	Dick Butkus	75.00
EC	Earl Campbell	30.00
HC	Harold Carmichael	10.00
CC	Cris Carter	40.00
TC	Tim Couch	60.00
RC	Roger Craig	10.00
DA	Terrell Davis	50.00
LD	Len Dawson	25.00
TD	Tony Dorsett	50.00
MD	Mark Duper	10.00
BE	Boomer Esiason	30.00
FL	Doug Flutie	25.00
EG	Eddie George	40.00
FG	Frank Gifford	100.00
OG	Otto Graham	20.00
BG	Bob Griese	40.00
FH	Franco Harris	50.00
MH	Marvin Harrison	30.00
EJ	Edgerrin James	50.00
RJ	Ron Jaworski	25.00
BJ	Brad Johnson	25.00
KJ	Keyshawn Johnson	30.00
CJ	Charlie Joiner	10.00
SJ	Sonny Jurgensen	40.00
JK	Jim Kelly	50.00
KI	Jon Kitna	20.00
SL	Steve Largent	20.00
BL	Bob Lilly	25.00
HL	Howie Long	50.00
RL	Ronnie Lott	50.00
AM	Archie Manning	20.00
PM	Peyton Manning	125.00
DM	Dan Marino	175.00
RG	Art Monk	25.00
JM	Joe Montana	175.00
RM	Randy Moss	125.00
AZ	Anthony Munoz	20.00
JN	Joe Namath	100.00
ON	Ozzie Newsome	10.00
JP	Jake Plummer	20.00
GS	Gale Sayers	50.00
LR	Lee Roy Selmon	10.00
PS	Phil Simms	20.00
MS	Mike Singletary	20.00
KS	Ken Stabler	40.00
JS	John Stallworth	20.00
ST	Bart Starr	150.00
RS	Roger Staubach	75.00
FT	Fran Tarkenton	50.00
VT	Vinny Testaverde	20.00
JT	Joe Theismann	30.00
JU	Johnny Unitas	175.00
WA	Kurt Warner	75.00
RI	Ricky Watters	20.00
KW	Kellen Winslow	20.00
SY	Steve Young	50.00

2000 Upper Deck Legends Canton Calling

		NM/M
Complete Set (6):		15.00
Common Player:		1.50
Inserted 1:18		
CC1	Peyton Manning	5.00
CC2	Steve Young	3.00
CC3	Jerry Rice	5.00
CC4	Randy Moss	5.00
CC5	Cris Carter	1.50
CC6	Emmitt Smith	5.00

2000 Upper Deck Legends Defining Moments

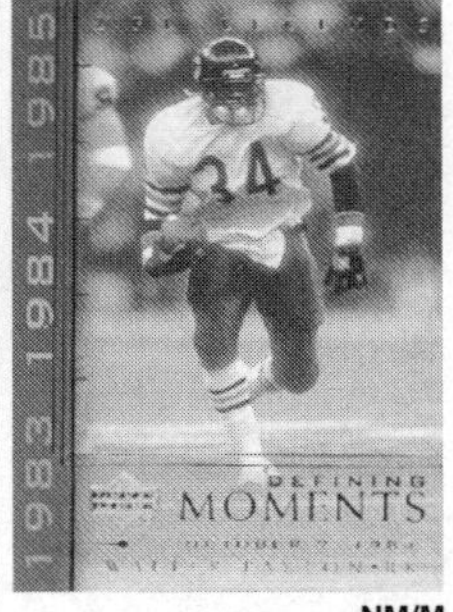

		NM/M
Complete Set (10):		25.00
Common Player:		1.50
Inserted 1:9		
DM1	Terrell Davis	3.00
DM2	Troy Aikman	3.00
DM3	Jerry Rice	4.00
DM4	Walter Payton	7.00
DM5	Joe Namath	4.00
DM6	Emmitt Smith	4.00
DM7	Steve Young	1.50
DM8	Franco Harris	1.50
DM9	Kurt Warner	3.00
DM10	Brett Favre	6.00

2000 Upper Deck Legends Game Jersey Greats

		NM/M
Production 400 Sets		
RS	Roger Staubach 400	175.00

2000 Upper Deck Legends Legendary Jerseys

		NM/M
Common Player:		20.00
Inserted 1:23		
LJTA	Troy Aikman	40.00
LJLJ-MA	Marcus Allen	20.00
LJSE-MA	Marcus Allen	20.00

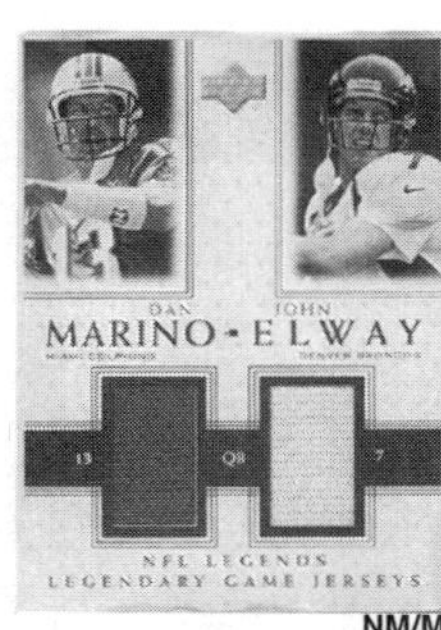

NM/M
LJJA Jamal Anderson 20.00
LJFB Fred Biletnikoff 25.00
LJDB Drew Bledsoe 25.00
LJCB Cliff Branch 20.00
LJJB John Brodie 20.00
LJMB Mark Brunell 20.00
LJTC Todd Christensen 20.00
LJTD Terrell Davis 40.00
LJED Eric Dickerson 25.00
LJJE John Elway 60.00
LJEM John Elway, Dan Marino 325.00
LJMF Marshall Faulk 40.00
LJBF Brett Favre 75.00
LJDF Doug Flutie 30.00
LJCH Charles Haley 20.00
LJLJ-TH Ted Hendricks 20.00
LJSE-TH Ted Hendricks 20.00
LJMI Michael Irvin 30.00
LJDJ Daryl Johnston 20.00
LJBL Bob Lilly 30.00
LJHL Howie Long 40.00
LJRL Ronnie Lott 40.00
LJPM Peyton Manning 60.00
LJDM Dan Marino 60.00
LJJM Joe Montana 75.00
LJWM Warren Moon 30.00
LJRM Randy Moss 50.00
LJJN Joe Namath 75.00
LJKN Ken Norton Jr. 20.00
LJNO Jay Novacek 20.00
LJWP Walter Payton 100.00
LJLJ-JP Jim Plunkett 25.00
LJSE-JP Jim Plunkett 25.00
LJJR Jerry Rice 60.00
LJDS Deion Sanders 40.00
LJOS Otis Sistrunk 20.00
LJSM Bruce Smith 20.00
LJES Emmitt Smith 60.00
LJKS Ken Stabler 30.00
LJRS Roger Staubach 50.00
LJFT Fran Tarkenton 30.00
LJGU Gene Upshaw 20.00
LJVE Mark Van Eeghen 20.00
LJHW Herschel Walker 35.00
LJKW Kurt Warner 50.00
LJRW Reggie White 30.00
LJSY Steve Young 40.00

2000 Upper Deck Legends Millennium QBs

NM/M
Complete Set (10): 10.00
Common Player: .50
Inserted 1:5
M1 Joe Montana 3.00
M2 Dan Marino 2.50
M3 John Elway 2.50
M4 Fran Tarkenton 1.00
M5 Sammy Baugh 1.00
M6 Joe Namath 2.50
M7 Warren Moon .50
M8 Mark Brunell .75
M9 Brett Favre 2.50
M10 Drew Bledsoe .75

2000 Upper Deck Legends Reflections in Time

NM/M
Complete Set (10): 15.00
Common Player: 1.50
Inserted 1:11
R1 Earl Campbell, Eddie George 2.00
R2 Mike Singletary, Junior Seau 1.50
R3 Doak Walker, Ricky Williams 3.00
R4 Archie Manning, Peyton Manning 6.00

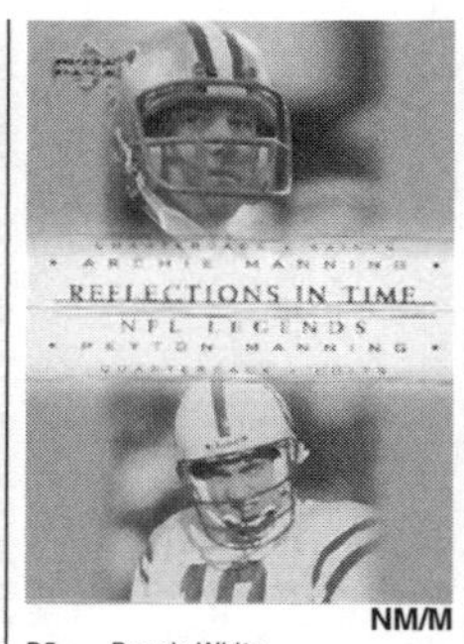

NM/M
R5 Reggie White, Jevon Kearse 1.50
R6 Harold Carmichael, Randy Moss 6.00
R7 Gale Sayers, Edgerrin James 4.00
R8 Warren Moon, Daunte Culpepper 2.50
R9 Roger Staubach, Troy Aikman 4.00
R10 Thurman Thomas, Marshall Faulk 1.50

2000 Upper Deck Legends Rookie Gallery

NM/M
Complete Set (10): 45.00
Common Player: 3.00
Inserted 1:21
RG1 Peter Warrick 3.00
RG2 Chris Redman 3.00
RG3 Courtney Brown 3.00
RG4 Thomas Jones 3.00
RG5 Chad Pennington 8.00
RG6 Jamal Lewis 4.00
RG7 Plaxico Burress 6.00
RG8 Ron Dayne 3.00
RG9 Sylvester Morris 3.00
RG10 Shaun Alexander 6.00

2000 Upper Deck MVP

NM/M
Complete Set (218): 25.00
Common Player: .10
Minor Stars: .20
Common Rookie: .30
Pack (10): 1.75
Wax Box (28): 35.00
1 Jake Plummer .40
2 Michael Pittman .10
3 Rob Moore .20
4 David Boston .40
5 Frank Sanders .20
6 Aeneas Williams .10
7 Kwamie Lassiter .10
8 Tim Dwight .40
9 Chris Chandler .20
10 Jamal Anderson .40
11 Shawn Jefferson .10
12 Qadry Ismail .10
13 Jermaine Lewis .20
14 Rod Woodson .10
15 Michael McCrary .10
16 Tony Banks .20
17 Peter Boulware .10
18 Shannon Sharpe .20
19 Peerless Price .40
20 Rob Johnson .20
21 Eric Moulds .40
22 Doug Flutie .50
23 Muhsin Muhammad .20
24 Patrick Jeffers .30
25 Steve Beuerlein .20
26 Tshimanga Biakabutuka .20
27 Michael Bates .10
28 Cade McNown .30
29 Curtis Enis .30
30 Marcus Robinson .40
31 Shane Matthews .10
32 Bobby Engram .10
33 Glyn Milburn .10
34 Akili Smith .30
35 Corey Dillon .40
36 Darnay Scott .20
37 Tremain Mack .10
38 Tim Couch 1.00
39 Kevin Johnson .40
40 Darrin Chiaverini .10
41 Jamir Miller .10
42 Errict Rhett .20
43 Troy Aikman 1.00
44 Emmitt Smith 1.25
45 Raghib Ismail .10
46 Jason Tucker .30
47 Dexter Coakley .10
48 Joey Galloway .40
49 Greg Ellis .10
50 Terrell Davis 1.00
51 Olandis Gary .50
52 Brian Griese .50
53 Ed McCaffrey .30
54 Rod Smith .30
55 Trevor Pryce .10
56 Charlie Batch .40
57 Germane Crowell .20
58 Johnnie Morton .10
59 Robert Porcher .10
60 Luther Ellis .10
61 James O. Stewart .20
62 Brett Favre 1.50
63 Antonio Freeman .40
64 Bill Schroeder .10
65 Dorsey Levens .40
66 Peyton Manning 1.25
67 Edgerrin James 1.00
68 Marvin Harrison .40
69 Ken Dilger .10
70 Terrence Wilkins .20
71 Mark Brunell .60
72 Fred Taylor .60
73 Jimmy Smith .30
74 Keenan McCardell .20
75 Carnell Lake .10
76 Tony Brackens .10
77 Kevin Hardy .10
78 Hardy Nickerson .10
79 Elvis Grbac .20
80 Tony Gonzalez .20
81 Derrick Alexander .10
82 Donnell Bennett .10
83 James Hasty .10
84 Jay Fiedler .20
85 James Johnson .20
86 Tony Martin .20
87 Damon Huard .40
88 O.J. McDuffie .20
89 Oronde Gadsden .20
90 Zach Thomas .20
91 Sam Madison .10
92 Jeff George .30
93 Randy Moss 1.50
94 Robert Smith .30
95 Cris Carter .40
96 Matthew Hatchette .10
97 Drew Bledsoe .60
98 Terry Glenn .40
99 Troy Brown .10
100 Kevin Faulk .30
101 Lawyer Milloy .10
102 Ricky Williams 1.00
103 Keith Poole .10
104 Jake Reed .10
105 Cameron Cleeland .20
106 Jeff Blake .20
107 Andrew Glover .10
108 Kerry Collins .20
109 Amani Toomer .20
110 Joe Montgomery .20
111 Ike Hilliard .20
112 Michael Strahan .10
113 Jessie Armstead .10
114 Ray Lucas .30
115 Keyshawn Johnson .40
116 Curtis Martin .40
117 Vinny Testaverde .30
118 Wayne Chrebet .40
119 Dedric Ward .10
120 Tim Brown .30
121 Rich Gannon .20
122 Tyrone Wheatley .20
123 Napoleon Kaufman .30
124 Charles Woodson .30
125 Darrell Russell .10
126 Duce Staley .30
127 Donovan McNabb .60
128 Torrance Small .10
129 Allen Rossum .10
130 Brian Dawkins .10
131 Troy Vincent .10
132 Troy Edwards .40
133 Jerome Bettis .30
134 Hines Ward .20
135 Kordell Stewart .40
136 Levon Kirkland .10
137 Kent Graham .10
138 Marshall Faulk .75
139 Kurt Warner 1.25
140 Torry Holt .40
141 Isaac Bruce .40
142 Kevin Carter .10
143 Az-Zahir Hakim .30
144 Todd Lyght .10
145 Jermaine Fazande .20
146 Curtis Conway .20
147 Freddie Jones .20
148 Junior Seau .30
149 Jeff Graham .10
150 Ryan Leaf .40
151 Rodney Harrison .10
152 Steve Young .60
153 Jerry Rice 1.00
154 Charlie Garner .20
155 Terrell Owens .40
156 Jeff Garcia .30
157 Bryant Young .10
158 Lance Schulters .10
159 Ricky Watters .30
160 Jon Kitna .40
161 Derrick Mayes .20
162 Sean Dawkins .10
163 Cortez Kennedy .10
164 Chad Brown .10
165 Warrick Dunn .40
166 Shaun King .60
167 Mike Alstott .40
168 Warren Sapp .20
169 Jacquez Green .20
170 Derrick Brooks .10
171 John Lynch .10
172 Donnie Abraham .10
173 Eddie George .50
174 Steve McNair .50
175 Kevin Dyson .20
176 Jevon Kearse .40
177 Yancey Thigpen .20
178 Frank Wycheck .10
179 Eddie Robinson .10
180 Samari Rolle .10
181 Brad Johnson .40
182 Stephen Davis .40
183 Michael Westbrook .30
184 Albert Connell .20
185 Brian Mitchell .10
186 Bruce Smith .10
187 Stephen Alexander .10
188 *Peter Warrick* 1.00
189 *LaVar Arrington cutout* 25.00
190 *Chris Redman* 1.00
191 *Courtney Brown* .50
192 *Brian Urlacher* 1.25
193 *Plaxico Burress* 1.25
194 *Corey Simon* .50
195 *Bubba Franks* .75
196 *Deon Grant* .30
197 *Michael Wiley* .50
198 *Tim Rattay* 1.00
199 *Ron Dayne* 1.00
200 *Sylvester Morris* .75
201 *Shaun Alexander* 1.50
202 *Dez White* .50
203 *Thomas Jones* .75
204 *Reuben Droughns* .50
205 *Travis Taylor* .75
206 *Trevor Gaylor* .30
207 *Jamal Lewis* 1.50
208 *Chad Pennington* 2.50
209 *J.R. Redmond* .75
210 *Laveranues Coles* 1.00
211 *Travis Prentice* .75
212 *R. Jay Soward* .50
213 *Todd Pinkston* .75
214 *Dennis Northcutt* .50
215 *Shyrone Stith* .30
216 *Tee Martin* .50
217 *Giovanni Carmazzi* .50
218 Drew Bledsoe CL .30
219 Steve Young CL .20
220 Donovan McNabb CL SP 25.00

2000 Upper Deck MVP Gold Script

Gold Script Cards: 8X-15X
Gold Script Rookies: 5X-10X
Production 100 Sets

2000 Upper Deck MVP Silver Script

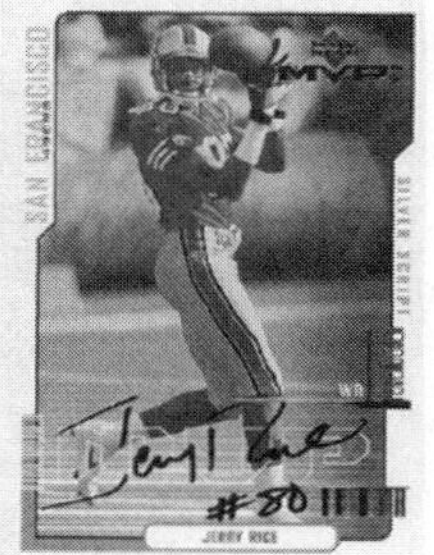

NM/M
Complete Set (218): 75.00
Silver Script Cards: 3X
Silver Script Rookies: 2X
Inserted 1:2

2000 Upper Deck MVP Super Script

Super Script Cards: 25X-50X
Super Script Rookies: 15X-30X
Production 25 Sets

2000 Upper Deck MVP Air Show

NM/M
Complete Set (10): 10.00
Common Player: .75
Minor Stars: 1.50
Inserted 1:14
AS1 Brian Griese 2.00
AS2 Drew Bledsoe 2.50
AS3 Rob Johnson .75
AS4 Jeff Garcia 1.50
AS5 Ray Lucas 1.00
AS6 Jon Kitna 1.00
AS7 Jeff George 1.00
AS8 Shaun King 1.00
AS9 Troy Aikman 4.00
AS10 Steve Beuerlein .75

2000 Upper Deck MVP Game-Jersey Greats

NM/M
JM Joe Montana 350.00

2000 Upper Deck MVP Game-Used Souvenirs

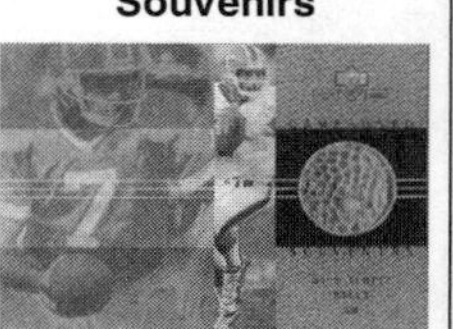

NM/M
Common Player: 20.00
Inserted 1:229 Hobby
TA Troy Aikman 40.00
MA Mike Alstott 20.00
CB Charlie Batch 15.00
MB Mark Brunell 20.00
CC Cris Carter 30.00
TC Tim Couch 25.00
SD Stephen Davis 15.00
TD Terrell Davis 20.00
MF Marshall Faulk 30.00
BF Brett Favre 50.00
DF Doug Flutie 25.00
EG Eddie George SB/40 100.00
BG Brian Griese 20.00
EJ Edgerrin James 30.00
BJ Brad Johnson 20.00
KJ Kevin Johnson 20.00
KE Keyshawn Johnson 25.00
SK Shaun King 15.00
JK Jon Kitna 15.00
PM Peyton Manning 40.00
DM Dan Marino 50.00
DM Donovan McNabb 25.00
CM Cade McNown 15.00
RM Randy Moss 40.00
JP Jake Plummer 15.00
JR Jerry Rice 40.00
AS Akili Smith 15.00
ES Emmitt Smith 50.00
FT Fred Taylor 20.00
KW Kurt Warner SB/40 200.00
RW Ricky Williams 25.00

2000 Upper Deck MVP Game-Used Souvenirs Autographs

NM/M
Common Player: 100.00
Production 25 Sets
TA Troy Aikman 250.00
CB Charlie Batch 75.00
MB Mark Brunell 100.00
CC Cris Carter 75.00
TC Tim Couch 150.00
SD Stephen Davis 75.00
TD Terrell Davis 150.00
MF Marshall Faulk 150.00
DF Doug Flutie 100.00
BG Brian Griese 100.00
EJ Edgerrin James 175.00
BJ Brad Johnson 100.00
KJ Kevin Johnson 75.00
KE Keyshawn Johnson 125.00
JK Jon Kitna 75.00
PM Peyton Manning 300.00
DM Dan Marino 350.00
RM Randy Moss 300.00
JP Jake Plummer 75.00
AS Akili Smith 75.00
KW Kurt Warner 300.00
RW Ricky Williams 200.00

2000 Upper Deck MVP Headliners

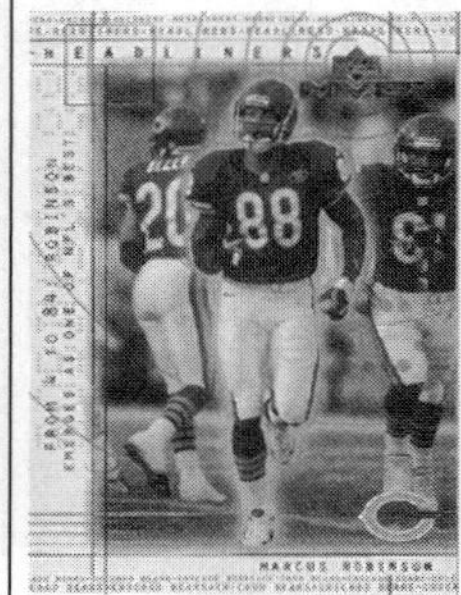

NM/M
Complete Set (10): 7.00
Common Player: .50
Minor Stars: 1.00
Inserted 1:6
H1 Isaac Bruce 1.00
H2 Michael Westbrook .50
H3 James O. Stewart .50
H4 Keyshawn Johnson 1.00
H5 Marcus Robinson 1.00
H6 Charlie Batch .50
H7 Marvin Harrison 1.00
H8 Olandis Gary .50
H9 Curtis Martin 1.00
H10 Jevon Kearse .50

2000 Upper Deck MVP Highlight Reel

NM/M
Complete Set (7): 15.00
Common Player: 1.50
Inserted 1:28
HR1 Marvin Harrison 2.50
HR2 Isaac Bruce 2.50
HR3 Cris Carter 2.50
HR4 Ray Lucas 1.00
HR5 Muhsin Muhammad 1.50
HR6 Eddie George 3.00
HR7 Ricky Williams 5.00

2000 Upper Deck MVP Prolifics

NM/M
Complete Set (7): 30.00
Common Player: 2.00
Inserted 1:28
P1 Brett Favre 7.00
P2 Marshall Faulk 3.00
P3 Edgerrin James 4.00
P4 Peyton Manning 5.00
P5 Tim Couch 3.00
P6 Dan Marino 6.00
P7 Kurt Warner 5.00

2000 Upper Deck MVP ProSign

		NM/M
Common Player:		25.00
Inserted 1:215 Retail		
Gold Cards:		4X
Production 25 Sets		
SA	Shaun Alexander	40.00
CB	Charlie Batch	15.00
IB	Isaac Bruce	25.00
MB	Mark Brunell	25.00
KC	Kwame Cavil	15.00
TC	Tim Couch	40.00
HT	Ron Dayne	35.00
RD	Ron Dugans	15.00
MF	Marshall Faulk	40.00
BG	Brian Griese	35.00
TH	Torry Holt	25.00
EJ	Edgerrin James	50.00
KJ	Keyshawn Johnson	30.00
TJ	Thomas Jones	20.00
JK	Jon Kitna	20.00
JL	Jamal Lewis	50.00
PM	Peyton Manning	85.00
DM	Dan Marino Gold	350.00
TM	Tee Martin	20.00
RM	Randy Moss	85.00
CP	Chad Pennington	75.00
JP	Jake Plummer	20.00
CR	Chris Redman	20.00
TT	Travis Taylor	20.00
KW	Kurt Warner	125.00
PW	Peter Warrick	40.00
DW	Dez White	30.00
RW	Ricky Williams	50.00

2000 Upper Deck MVP Theatre

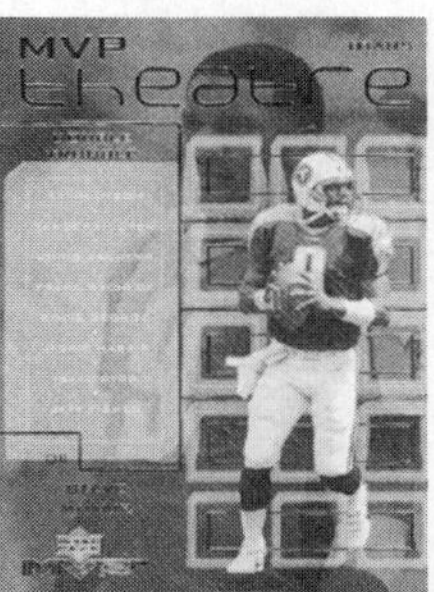

		NM/M
Complete Set (10):		7.00
Common Player:		.50
Minor Stars:		1.00
Inserted 1:6		
M1	Troy Edwards	1.00
M2	Ed McCaffrey	.50
M3	Stephen Davis	1.00
M4	Corey Dillon	1.00
M5	Steve McNair	1.00
M6	Jimmy Smith	.50
M7	Fred Taylor	1.00
M8	Terrell Davis	2.00
M9	Jon Kitna	1.00
M10	Germane Crowell	.50

2000 Upper Deck Ovation

		NM/M
Complete Set (90):		220.00
Common Player:		.15
Minor Stars:		.30
Common Rookie:		4.00
Production 2,500 Sets		
Pack (5):		3.00
Wax Box (20):		40.00
1	Jake Plummer	.50
2	Frank Sanders	.30
3	Chris Chandler	.30
4	Jamal Anderson	.50
5	Qadry Ismail	.15
6	Eric Moulds	.50
7	Muhsin Muhammad	.30
8	Steve Beuerlein	.30
9	Cade McNown	.30
10	Marcus Robinson	.50
11	Akili Smith	.30
12	Corey Dillon	.50
13	Tim Couch	1.25
14	Kevin Johnson	.30
15	Troy Aikman	1.00
16	Emmitt Smith	1.50
17	Terrell Davis	1.00
18	Olandis Gary	.60
19	Charlie Batch	.50
20	Germane Crowell	.50
21	Brett Favre	2.00
22	Antonio Freeman	.50
23	Peyton Manning	1.75
24	Edgerrin James	1.50
25	Mark Brunell	.75
26	Fred Taylor	.75
27	Elvis Grbac	.30
28	Tony Gonzalez	.30
29	Tony Martin	.15
30	Damon Huard	.50
31	Randy Moss	1.50
32	Daunte Culpepper	1.00
33	Drew Bledsoe	.75
34	Terry Glenn	.50
35	Ricky Williams	1.00
36	Jeff Blake	.30
37	Kerry Collins	.30
38	Amani Toomer	.15
39	Curtis Martin	.50
40	Vinny Testaverde	.30
41	Tim Brown	.30
42	Rickey Dudley	.15
43	Duce Staley	.50
44	Donovan McNabb	.75
45	Troy Edwards	.50
46	Jerome Bettis	.50
47	Marshall Faulk	.50
48	Kurt Warner	1.50
49	Freddie Jones	.30
50	Junior Seau	.30
51	Jerry Rice	1.50
52	Steve Young	.75
53	Ricky Watters	.30
54	Jon Kitna	.50
55	Shaun King	.50
56	Keyshawn Johnson	.50
57	Eddie George	.60
58	Steve McNair	.50
59	Brad Johnson	.50
60	Stephen Davis	.50
61	*Courtney Brown*	4.00
62	*Corey Simon*	5.00
63	*R. Jay Soward*	4.00
64	*Anthony Becht*	4.00
65	*Chris Redman*	6.00
66	*Chad Pennington*	20.00
67	*Tee Martin*	5.00
68	*Giovanni Carmazzi*	5.00
69	*Ron Dayne*	5.00
70	*Shaun Alexander*	12.00
71	*Thomas Jones*	8.00
72	*Reuben Droughns*	8.00
73	*Jamal Lewis*	12.00
74	*J.R. Redmond*	5.00
75	*Travis Prentice*	5.00
76	*Trung Canidate*	5.00
77	*Brian Urlacher*	10.00
78	*Bubba Franks*	6.00
79	*Peter Warrick*	8.00
80	*Plaxico Burress*	10.00
81	*Sylvester Morris*	4.00
82	*Dez White*	5.00
83	*Travis Taylor*	6.00
84	*Todd Pinkston*	5.00
85	*Dennis Northcutt*	4.00
86	*Jerry Porter*	8.00
87	*Laveranues Coles*	8.00
88	*Danny Farmer*	4.00
89	*Curtis Keaton*	4.00
90	*Ron Dugans*	4.00

2000 Upper Deck Ovation Standing Ovation

Standing Cards:	10X-25X
Standing Rookies:	2X-4X
Production 50 Sets	

2000 Upper Deck Ovation A Piece of History

		NM/M
Production 4,800 total cards		
IB	Isaac Bruce Helmet	30.00
TC	Tim Couch	40.00
DC	Daunte Culpepper	40.00
RD	Ron Dayne Helmet	40.00
RD	Ron Dayne	30.00
BF	Brett Favre	70.00
EJ	Edgerrin James	50.00
TJ	Thomas Jones	20.00
SK	Shaun King Helmet	30.00
PM	Peyton Manning	50.00
DM	Dan Marino	70.00
RM	Randy Moss	50.00
CP	Chad Pennington	50.00
CR	Chris Redman	20.00
JR	Jerry Rice	60.00
KW	Kurt Warner Helmet	150.00
PW	Peter Warrick Helmet	40.00
PW	Peter Warrick	30.00

2000 Upper Deck Ovation A Piece of History Autographs

		NM/M
MB	Mark Brunell	100.00
RD	Ron Dayne	100.00
TJ	Thomas Jones	100.00
PM	Peyton Manning	300.00
RM	Randy Moss	200.00
CP	Chad Pennington	150.00
CR	Chris Redman	100.00
PW	Peter Warrick	100.00

2000 Upper Deck Ovation Center Stage

		NM/M
Complete Set (10):		35.00
Common Player:		3.00
Inserted 1:19		
Act 2 Cards:		3X
Inserted 1:79		
Act 3 Cards:		4X-8X
Production 50 Sets		
CS1	Tim Couch	3.00
CS2	Fred Taylor	2.00
CS3	Kurt Warner	5.00
CS4	Edgerrin James	4.00
CS5	Ron Dayne	3.00
CS6	Jamal Lewis	3.00
CS7	Thomas Jones	2.00
CS8	Peter Warrick	3.00
CS9	Plaxico Burress	4.50
CS10	Chad Pennington	7.00

2000 Upper Deck Ovation Curtain Calls

		NM/M
Complete Set (15):		8.00
Common Player:		.50
Minor Stars:		1.00
Inserted 1:3		
CC1	Eddie George	1.25
CC2	Muhsin Muhammad	.50
CC3	Marvin Harrison	1.00
CC4	Marcus Robinson	1.00
CC5	Duce Staley	1.00
CC6	Isaac Bruce	1.00
CC7	Germane Crowell	.75
CC8	Amani Toomer	.75
CC9	Fred Taylor	1.00
CC10	Michael Westbrook	.50
CC11	Olandis Gary	.75
CC12	Stephen Davis	1.00
CC13	Cade McNown	.75
CC14	Priest Holmes	1.00
CC15	Corey Dillon	1.00

2000 Upper Deck Ovation Game-Jersey Greats

		NM/M
Production 175 Cards		
1	Joe Namath 175	300.00

2000 Upper Deck Ovation Spotlight

		NM/M
Complete Set (15):		15.00
Common Player:		.75
Minor Stars:		1.50
Inserted 1:9		
OS1	Edgerrin James	4.00
OS2	Rob Johnson	.75
OS3	Jake Plummer	1.50
OS4	Jamal Anderson	1.50
OS5	James O. Stewart	.75
OS6	Shaun King	1.00
OS7	Jon Kitna	1.50
OS8	Ricky Williams	3.50
OS9	Errict Rhett	.75
OS10	Stephen Davis	1.50
OS11	Daunte Culpepper	2.50
OS12	Donovan McNabb	2.00
OS13	Kevin Johnson	1.50
OS14	Akili Smith	1.00
OS15	Cade McNown	1.00

2000 Upper Deck Ovation Star Performers

		NM/M
Complete Set (15):		25.00
Common Player:		.75
Minor Stars:		1.50
Inserted 1:9		
SP1	Mark Brunell	1.00
SP2	Eddie George	2.00
SP3	Brad Johnson	1.50
SP4	Vinny Testaverde	.75
SP5	Marshall Faulk	1.50
SP6	Tim Couch	2.00
SP7	Brett Favre	6.00
SP8	Ricky Williams	3.50
SP9	Peyton Manning	5.00
SP10	Keyshawn Johnson	1.50
SP11	Emmitt Smith	5.00
SP12	Jerry Rice	5.00
SP13	Tim Brown	1.50
SP14	Randy Moss	5.00
SP15	Jamal Anderson	1.50

2000 Upper Deck Ovation Super Signatures

		NM/M
Production 100 Sets		
Gold Cards:		1.5X
Production 50 Sets		
Rainbow Cards:		
Production 10 Sets		
JB	Jim Brown	125.00
MB	Mark Brunell	50.00
TD	Terrell Davis	85.00
MF	Marshall Faulk	50.00
EG	Eddie George	50.00
PM	Peyton Manning	150.00
RM	Randy Moss	125.00
JN	Joe Namath	150.00

2000 Upper Deck Pros & Prospects

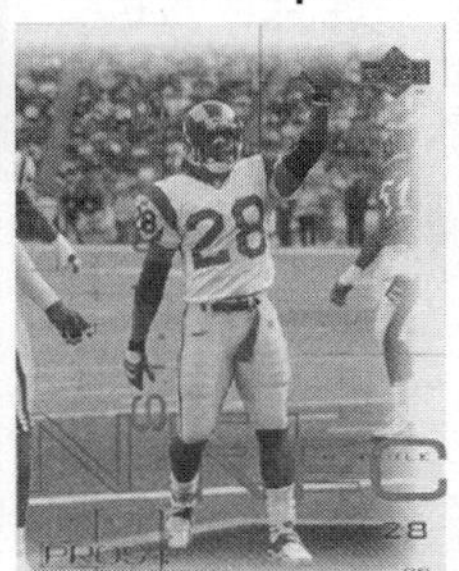

		NM/M
Complete Set (126):		900.00
Common Player:		.15
Minor Stars:		.30
Common Rookie:		8.00
Production 1,000 Sets		
Pack (5):		4.75
Wax Box (24):		80.00
Common Rookie (127-152):		5.00
Production 1,000 Sets		
1	Jake Plummer	.50
2	Michael Pittman	.15
3	Tim Dwight	.30
4	Chris Chandler	.30
5	Qadry Ismail	.15
6	Shannon Sharpe	.30
7	Peerless Price	.50
8	Rob Johnson	.30
9	Eric Moulds	.50
10	Muhsin Muhammad	.30
11	Patrick Jeffers	.30
12	Steve Beuerlein	.30
13	Cade McNown	.50
14	Curtis Enis	.30
15	Marcus Robinson	.50
16	Akili Smith	.50
17	Corey Dillon	.30
18	Tim Couch	1.00
19	Kevin Johnson	.50
20	Errict Rhett	.30
21	Troy Aikman	1.00
22	Emmitt Smith	1.25
23	Raghib Ismail	.15
24	Terrell Davis	1.00
25	Olandis Gary	.50
26	Brian Griese	.50
27	Ed McCaffrey	.30
28	Charlie Batch	.50
29	Germane Crowell	.30
30	James O. Stewart	.30
31	Brett Favre	1.50
32	Antonio Freeman	.30
33	Dorsey Levens	.30
34	Peyton Manning	1.25
35	Edgerrin James	1.00
36	Marvin Harrison	.50
37	Mark Brunell	.75
38	Fred Taylor	.75
39	Jimmy Smith	.30
40	Elvis Grbac	.30
41	Tony Gonzalez	.30
42	Damon Huard	.50
43	James Johnson	.30
44	Jay Fiedler	.30
45	Randy Moss	1.25
46	Robert Smith	.30
47	Cris Carter	.50
48	Drew Bledsoe	.75
49	Terry Glenn	.30
50	Ricky Williams	1.00
51	Jeff Blake	.30
52	Keith Poole	.15
53	Kerry Collins	.30
54	Amani Toomer	.30
55	Vinny Testaverde	.30
56	Keyshawn Johnson	.50
57	Curtis Martin	.50
58	Tim Brown	.30
59	Rich Gannon	.30
60	Tyrone Wheatley	.30
61	Duce Staley	.50
62	Donovan McNabb	.75
63	Troy Edwards	.50
64	Jerome Bettis	.30
65	Marshall Faulk	.50
66	Kurt Warner	1.25
67	Torry Holt	.50
68	Isaac Bruce	.50
69	Junior Seau	.30
70	Jeff Graham	.15
71	Steve Young	.75
72	Jerry Rice	1.25
73	Charlie Garner	.30
74	Ricky Watters	.30
75	Jon Kitna	.50
76	Warrick Dunn	.50
77	Shaun King	.75
78	Mike Alstott	.50
79	Eddie George	.50
80	Steve McNair	.50
81	Kevin Dyson	.30
82	Brad Johnson	.30
83	Stephen Davis	.50
84	Michael Westbrook	.30
85	*Peter Warrick*	20.00
86	*LaVar Arrington*	50.00
87	*Chris Redman*	15.00
88	*Courtney Brown*	12.00
89	*Plaxico Burress*	20.00
90	*Corey Simon*	10.00
91	*Bubba Franks*	15.00
92	*Deon Grant*	10.00
93	*Brian Urlacher*	25.00
94	*Ron Dayne*	12.00
95	*Sylvester Morris*	10.00
96	*Shaun Alexander*	30.00
97	*Dez White*	15.00
98	*Thomas Jones*	20.00
99	*Travis Taylor*	15.00
100	*Kwame Cavil*	10.00
101	*Jamal Lewis*	30.00
102	*Chad Pennington*	50.00
103	*J.R. Redmond*	12.00
104	*Sebastian Janikowski*	12.00
105	*Anthony Lucas*	10.00
106	*Travis Prentice*	12.00
107	*Danny Farmer*	10.00
108	*Sherrod Gideon*	10.00
109	*Todd Pinkston*	15.00
110	*Dennis Northcutt*	15.00
111	*Tim Rattay*	20.00
112	*Troy Walters*	12.00
113	*Michael Wiley*	10.00
114	*R. Jay Soward*	10.00
115	*Trung Canidate*	15.00
116	*Reuben Droughns*	20.00
117	*Rondell Mealey*	10.00
118	*Chris Coleman*	10.00
119	*Giovanni Carmazzi*	12.00
120	*Trevor Insley*	10.00
121	*Shyrone Stith*	10.00
122	*Gari Scott*	10.00
123	*Tee Martin*	12.00
124	*Tom Brady*	110.00
125	*Marcus Knight*	10.00
126	*Jerry Porter*	20.00
127	*Brad Hoover*	10.00
128	*Chad Morton*	12.00
129	*Charles Lee*	8.00
130	*Damon Hodge*	8.00
131	*Darrell Jackson*	20.00
132	*Doug Johnson*	10.00
133	*Frank Moreau*	12.00
134	*JaJuan Dawson*	10.00
135	*Jake Delhomme*	25.00
136	*Jarious Jackson*	10.00
137	*Joe Hamilton*	10.00
138	*Larry Foster*	10.00
139	*Laveranues Coles*	20.00
140	*Aaron Shea*	8.00
141	*Matt Lytle*	12.00
142	*Mike Anderson*	15.00
143	*Ron Dixon*	10.00
144	*Ronney Jenkins*	8.00
145	*Sammy Morris*	12.00
146	*Shockmain Davis*	8.00
147	*Spergon Wynn*	10.00
148	*Todd Husak*	10.00
149	*Trevor Gaylor*	10.00
150	*Tywan Mitchell*	8.00
151	*Windrell Hayes*	8.00
152	*Bobby Shaw*	10.00

2000 Upper Deck Pros & Prospects Future Fame

		NM/M
Complete Set (10):		25.00
Common Player:		2.00
Inserted 1:6		
FF1	Peter Warrick	1.00
FF2	Lavar Arrington	1.00
FF3	Courtney Brown	2.00
FF4	Travis Taylor	3.00
FF5	Plaxico Burress	4.00
FF6	Ron Dayne	2.00
FF7	Jamal Lewis	4.00
FF8	Thomas Jones	3.00
FF9	Chad Pennington	6.00
FF10	Chris Redman	2.00

2000 Upper Deck Pros & Prospects Elway Autograph Jersey

		NM/M
JE	John Elway	250.00

2000 Upper Deck Pros & Prospects Mirror Image

		NM/M
Complete Set (10):		25.00
Common Player:		2.00
Inserted 1:12		
M1	Thomas Jones, Fred Taylor	3.00
M2	Ron Dayne, Jerome Bettis	3.00
M3	Plaxico Burress, Randy Moss	6.00
M4	Peter Warrick, Marvin Harrison	3.00
M5	Tee Martin, Peyton Manning	5.00
M6	Chris Redman, Brett Favre	5.00
M7	Lavar Arrington, Junior Seau	4.00
M8	Dez White, Jimmy Smith	2.00
M9	Chad Pennington, Kurt Warner	8.00
M10	Shaun Alexander, Marshall Faulk	3.00

2000 Upper Deck Pros & Prospects ProMotion

		NM/M
Complete Set (10):		12.00
Common Player:		1.00
Inserted 1:6		
P1	Kurt Warner	3.00
P2	Eddie George	1.50
P3	Marshall Faulk	1.00
P4	Keyshawn Johnson	1.00
P5	Emmitt Smith	3.00
P6	Randy Moss	3.00
P7	Marvin Harrison	1.00
P8	Mark Brunell	2.00
P9	Curtis Martin	1.00
P10	Brett Favre	4.00

2000 Upper Deck Pros & Prospects Report Card

		NM/M
Complete Set (12):		18.00
Common Player:		1.00
Inserted 1:12		
RC1	Edgerrin James	3.00
RC2	Tim Couch	3.00
RC3	Cade McNown	1.00
RC4	Champ Bailey	1.00
RC5	Donovan McNabb	2.50

RC6 Kevin Johnson 2.00
RC7 Shaun King 1.00
RC8 Peerless Price 2.00
RC9 David Boston 1.00
RC10 Ricky Williams 3.00
RC11 Akili Smith 1.00
RC12 Jevon Kearse 2.00

2000 Upper Deck Pros & Prospects Signature Piece 1

NM/M
Complete Set (23): 2,300
Common Player: 30.00
Inserted 1:96
SPCB Champ Bailey 40.00
SPDB Drew Bledsoe 100.00
SPIB Isaac Bruce 60.00
SPMB Mark Brunell 60.00
SPCC Chris Claiborne 30.00
SPRD Ron Dayne 60.00
SPDF Danny Farmer 60.00
SPMF Marshall Faulk 60.00
SPOG Olandis Gary 40.00
SPBG Brian Griese 70.00
SPMH Marvin Harrison 60.00
SPTH Torry Holt 50.00
SPEG Edgerrin James 125.00
SPWR Kevin Johnson 70.00
SPDL Dorsey Levens 45.00
SPRL Ray Lucas 45.00
SPRM Randy Moss 150.00
SPTO Terrell Owens 60.00
SPKW Kurt Warner 225.00
SPTA Troy Aikman 150.00
SPKJ Keyshawn Johnson 70.00
SPPM Peyton Manning 200.00
SPDM Dan Marino 275.00

2000 Upper Deck Pros & Prospects Signature Piece 2

Too uncommon to price.

NM/M
IB Isaac Bruce
MB Mark Brunell
CC Chris Claiborne
RD Ron Dayne
DF Danny Farmer
MF Marshall Faulk 225.00
OG Olandis Gary
BG Brian Griese
MH Marvin Harrison
TH Torry Holt
EG Edgerrin James 325.00
WR Kevin Johnson
RL Ray Lucas
RM Randy Moss 275.00
TO Terrell Owens
KW Kurt Warner
TA Troy Aikman
KJ Keyshawn Johnson
PM Peyton Manning
DM Dan Marino

2000 Upper Deck Ultimate Victory

NM/M
Complete Set (150): 325.00
Common Player: .15
Minor Stars: .30
Common Rookie: 2.50
Production 2,000 Sets
Pack (5): 3.00
Wax Box (24): 45.00
1 Jake Plummer .50
2 David Boston .50
3 Frank Sanders .30
4 Chris Chandler .30
5 Jamal Anderson .50
6 Shawn Jefferson .15
7 Qadry Ismail .15
8 Tony Banks .30
9 Shannon Sharpe .15
10 Peerless Price .30
11 Rob Johnson .30
12 Eric Moulds .50
13 Muhsin Muhammad .30
14 Steve Beuerlein .30
15 Tshimanga Biakabutuka .30
16 Cade McNown .30
17 Curtis Enis .30
18 Marcus Robinson .50
19 Akili Smith .30
20 Corey Dillon .50
21 Darnay Scott .30
22 Tim Couch 1.00
23 Kevin Johnson .30
24 Errict Rhett .15
25 Troy Aikman 1.00
26 Emmitt Smith 1.25
27 Raghib Ismail .15
28 Joey Galloway .50
29 Terrell Davis 1.00
30 Olandis Gary .60
31 Ed McCaffrey .30
32 Charlie Batch .50
33 Germane Crowell .50
34 James O. Stewart .30
35 Brett Favre 1.50
36 Antonio Freeman .50
37 Dorsey Levens .50
38 Peyton Manning 1.25
39 Edgerrin James 1.00
40 Marvin Harrison .50
41 Mark Brunell .75
42 Fred Taylor .75
43 Jimmy Smith .50
44 Elvis Grbac .30
45 Tony Gonzalez .30
46 Derrick Alexander .15
47 Tony Martin .15
48 Damon Huard .30
49 O.J. McDuffie .30
50 Randy Moss 1.25
51 Robert Smith .50
52 Daunte Culpepper 1.00
53 Drew Bledsoe .75
54 Terry Glenn .50
55 Ricky Williams 1.00
56 Jake Reed .30
57 Jeff Blake .30
58 Kerry Collins .30
59 Amani Toomer .15
60 Ike Hilliard .15
61 Ray Lucas .30
62 Curtis Martin .50
63 Vinny Testaverde .30
64 Tim Brown .30
65 Rich Gannon .30
66 Tyrone Wheatley .30
67 Duce Staley .50
68 Donovan McNabb .75
69 Troy Edwards .50
70 Jerome Bettis .50
71 Marshall Faulk .50
72 Kurt Warner 1.25
73 Isaac Bruce .50
74 Curtis Conway .30
75 Freddie Jones .30
76 Jeff Graham .15
77 Jeff Garcia .50
78 Jerry Rice 1.25
79 Ricky Watters .30
80 Jon Kitna .50
81 Derrick Mayes .30
82 Keyshawn Johnson .50
83 Shaun King .75
84 Mike Alstott .50
85 Eddie George .60
86 Steve McNair .50
87 Jevon Kearse .50
88 Brad Johnson .50
89 Stephen Davis .50
90 Michael Westbrook .30
91 *Anthony Becht* 2.50
92 *Anthony Lucas* 2.50
93 *Bashir Yamini* 2.50
94 *Brian Urlacher* 10.00
95 *Chad Morton* 4.00
96 *Chad Pennington* 20.00
97 *Chris Cole* 2.50
98 *Chris Hovan* 3.00
99 *Tim Rattay* 3.00
100 *Chris Redman* 4.00
101 *Chris Samuels* 3.00
102 *Corey Simon* 3.00
103 *Courtney Brown* 3.00
104 *Curtis Keaton* 2.50
105 *Danny Farmer* 3.50
106 *Erron Kinney* 2.50
107 *Darren Howard* 2.50
108 *Deltha O'Neal* 2.50
109 *Dennis Northcutt* 3.00
110 *Demario Brown* 2.50
111 *Dez White* 3.50
112 *Frank Murphy* 2.50
113 *Gari Scott* 2.50
114 *Giovanni Carmazzi* 3.00
115 *J.R. Redmond* 3.00
116 *JaJuan Dawson* 3.00
117 *Jamal Lewis* 12.00
118 *Leon Murray* 2.50
119 *Jerry Porter* 8.00
120 *Joe Hamilton* 3.00
121 *John Abraham* 2.50
122 *John Engleberger* 2.50
123 *Keith Bulluck* 2.50
124 *Kwame Cavil* 2.50
125 *Laveranues Coles* 8.00
126 *Marc Bulger* 10.00
127 *Marcus Knight* 2.50
128 *Mareno Philyaw* 2.50
129 *Michael Wiley* 3.00
130 *Na'il Diggs* 2.50
131 *Peter Warrick* 8.00
132 *Plaxico Burress* 10.00
133 *Raynoch Thompson* 2.50
134 *Reuben Droughns* 8.00
135 *Rob Morris* 2.50
136 *Ron Dayne* 5.00
137 *Ron Dugans* 3.50
138 *Sebastian Janikowski* 4.00
139 *Shaun Alexander* 12.00
140 *Sherrod Gideon* 2.50
141 *Sylvester Morris* 4.00
142 *Tee Martin* 5.00
143 *Thomas Jones* 8.00
144 *Todd Husak* 3.50
145 *Todd Pinkston* 6.00
146 *Tom Brady* 30.00
147 *Travis Prentice* 3.00
148 *Travis Taylor* 6.00
149 *Trevor Gaylor* 3.50
150 *Trung Canidate* 6.00

2000 Upper Deck Ultimate Victory Collection

Collection Cards: 2X-6X
Inserted 1:11
Collection Rookies: 1X
Inserted 1:23

2000 Upper Deck Ultimate Victory Collection 100

Collection 100 Cards: 8X-20X
Collection 100 Rookies: 3X
Production 100 Sets

2000 Upper Deck Ultimate Victory Collection 25

Collection 25 Cards: 20X-40X
Collection 25 Rookies: 3X-6X
Production 25 Sets

2000 Upper Deck Ultimate Victory Battle Ground

NM/M
Complete Set (10): 20.00
Common Player: 1.00
Inserted 1:11
BG1 Eddie George 1.50
BG2 Edgerrin James 3.00
BG3 Terrell Davis 2.00
BG4 Jamal Anderson 1.00
BG5 Ricky Williams 3.00
BG6 Thomas Jones 2.00
BG7 Jamal Lewis 2.00
BG8 Ron Dayne 2.00
BG9 Shaun Alexander 4.00
BG10 Trung Canidate 1.00

2000 Upper Deck Ultimate Victory Competitors

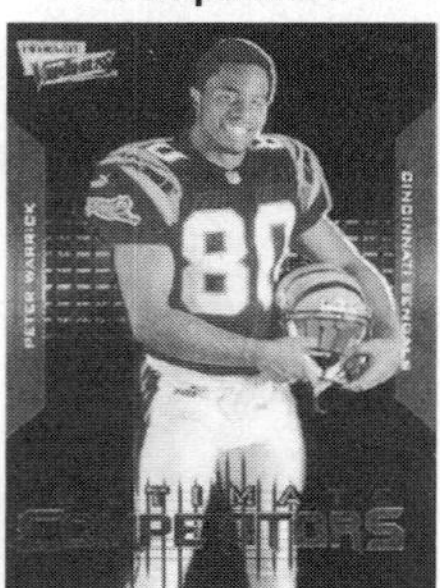

NM/M
Complete Set (10): 15.00
Common Player: 1.00
Inserted 1:11
UC1 Randy Moss 5.00
UC2 Peyton Manning 5.00
UC3 Stephen Davis 1.00
UC4 Cris Carter 1.00
UC5 Jevon Kearse 1.00
UC6 Peter Warrick 2.00
UC7 Plaxico Burress 3.50
UC8 Travis Taylor 2.50
UC9 Sylvester Morris 2.00
UC10 R. Jay Soward 1.00

2000 Upper Deck Ultimate Victory Crowning Glory

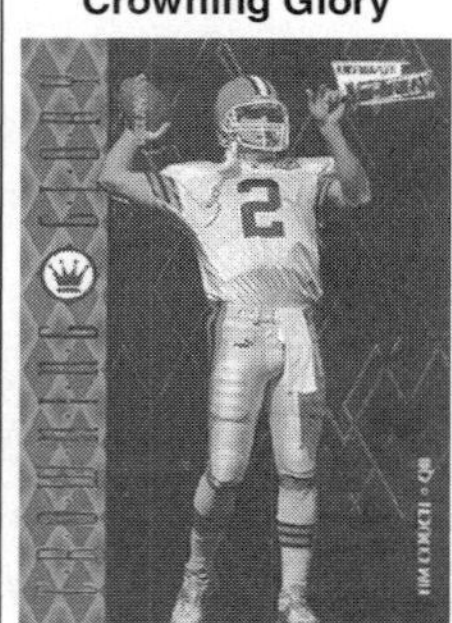

NM/M
Complete Set (10): 30.00
Common Player: 2.00
Inserted 1:23
CG1 Peyton Manning 8.00
CG2 Edgerrin James 5.00
CG3 Randy Moss 8.00
CG4 Tim Couch 5.00
CG5 Eddie George 2.50
CG6 Terrell Davis 4.00
CG7 Marcus Robinson 2.00
CG8 Marvin Harrison 2.00
CG9 Charlie Batch 2.00
CG10 Shaun King 3.00

2000 Upper Deck Ultimate Victory Fabric

NM/M
Common Player: 20.00
Inserted 1:239
IB Isaac Bruce 20.00
KC Kevin Carter 15.00
MF Marshall Faulk 30.00
MF-KW Marshall Faulk, Kurt Warner 50 175.00
AZ Az Hakim 20.00
TH Torry Holt 20.00
TH-IB Torry Holt, Isaac Bruce 100 85.00
RAMS Torry Holt, Isaac Bruce, Marshall Faulk, Kurt Warner 10
KW Kurt Warner 100.00

2000 Upper Deck Ultimate Victory Legendary Fabrics

NM/M
Common Player: 75.00
HL Howie Long 250 75.00
RL Ronnie Lott 250 75.00
JM Joe Montana 250 200.00
HoF Joe Montana, Ronnie Lott, Howie Long 100 300.00

2000 Upper Deck Vintage Preview

NM/M
Complete Set (90): 350.00
Common Player: .75
Minor Stars: 1.50
Common Rookie (#1-10): 15.00
Production 500 Sets
Common Rookie (#11-20): 6.00
Production 1,000 Sets
Common Rookie (#21-40): 4.00
Production 1,500 Sets
1 *Jamal Lewis* 25.00
2 *Sammy Morris* 5.00
3 *Peter Warrick* 10.00
4 *Travis Prentice* 5.00
5 *Mike Anderson* 12.00
6 *Sylvester Morris* 5.00
7 *Ron Dayne* 12.00
8 *Chad Pennington* 60.00
9 *Plaxico Burress* 25.00
10 *Laveranues Coles* 10.00
11 *Spergon Wynn, Dennis Northcutt* 8.00
12 *Courtney Brown, JaJuan Dawson* 8.00
13 *Raynoch Thompson, Thomas Jones* 10.00
14 *Tom Brady, J.R. Redmond* 30.00
15 *John Abraham, Windrell Hayes* 6.00
16 *Todd Husak, Chris Samuels* 7.00
17 *Giovanni Carmazzi, Tim Rattay* 8.00
18 *Shaun Alexander, Darrell Jackson* 15.00
19 *Rob Morris, Kevin McDougal* 6.00
20 *Brian Urlacher, Dez White* 25.00
21 *Doug Johnson, Darrick Vaughn, Mark Simoneau* 6.00
22 *Chris Redman, John Jones, Travis Taylor* 15.00
23 *Kwame Cavil, Corey Moore, Erik Flowers* 4.00
24 *Ray Green, Lester Towns, Brad Hoover* 8.00
25 *Curtis Keaton, Danny Farmer, Ron Dugans* 6.00
26 *Scottie Montgomery, KaRon Coleman, Deltha O'Neal* 4.00
27 *Bubba Franks, Na'il Diggs, Charles Lee* 8.00
28 *Troy Walters, Chris Hovan, Doug Chapman* 8.00
29 *Chad Morton, Darren Howard, Terrelle Smith* 6.00
30 *Gari Scott, Todd Pinkston, Corey Simon* 8.00
31 *Chris Coleman, Keith Bulluck, Erron Kinney* 4.00
32 *Peter Sirmon, Billy Volek, Bashir Yamini* 4.00
33 *Jason Webster, Ahmed Plummer, Julian Peterson* 6.00
34 *Shockmain D, Antwan Harris* 4.00
35 *R. Jay Soward, Shyrone Stith, T.J. Slaughter* 8.00
36 *Trevor Gaylor, Ronney Jenkins, Rogers Beckett* 6.00
37 *Tee Martin, Joe Hamilton, Jarious Jackson* 10.00
38 *Chris Cole, Ron Dixon, James Williams* 8.00
39 *Reuben Droughns, Trung Canidate, Frank Moreau* 15.00
40 *Mike Brown, Jerry Porter, Michael Wiley* 8.00
41 Jake Plummer 1.50
42 Jamal Anderson 1.50
43 Qadry Ismail .75
44 Doug Flutie 2.00
45 Rob Johnson 1.50
46 Steve Beuerlein .75
47 Marcus Robinson 1.50
48 Cade McNown 1.50
49 Tim Couch 4.00
50 Corey Dillon 1.50
51 Troy Aikman 5.00
52 Emmitt Smith 7.00
53 Charlie Batch 1.50
54 Brian Griese 3.00
55 Terrell Davis 4.00
56 Brett Favre 10.00
57 Antonio Freeman 1.50
58 Peyton Manning 8.00
59 Edgerrin James 8.00
60 Marvin Harrison 1.50
61 Mark Brunell 3.50
62 Fred Taylor 3.50
63 Elvis Grbac 1.50
64 Derrick Alexander .75
65 Lamar Smith 2.00
66 Daunte Culpepper 5.00
67 Randy Moss 8.00
68 Drew Bledsoe 3.50
69 Vinny Testaverde 1.50
70 Curtis Martin 1.50
71 Kerry Collins 1.50
72 Amani Toomer .75
73 Jeff Blake 1.50
74 Ricky Williams 3.00
75 Rich Gannon 1.50
76 Tim Brown 1.50
77 Jerome Bettis 1.50
78 Kurt Warner 8.00
79 Marshall Faulk 2.00
80 Junior Seau 1.50
81 Jeff Garcia 1.50
82 Terrell Owens 1.50
83 Jerry Rice 8.00
84 Ricky Watters 1.50
85 Shaun King 2.00
86 Keyshawn Johnson 1.50
87 Steve McNair 1.50
88 Eddie George 3.00
89 Stephen Davis 1.50
90 Brad Johnson 1.50

2000 Victory

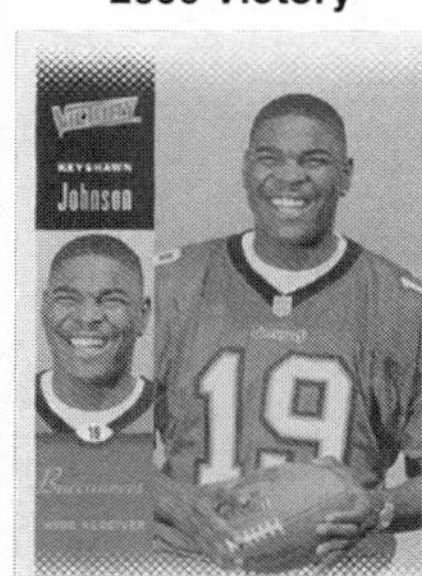

NM/M
Complete Set (330): 45.00
Common Player: .10
Minor Stars: .20
Common Rookie: .30
Inserted 1:1
Pack (12): 1.25
Wax Box (36): 25.00
1 Jake Plummer .30
2 Michael Pittman .10
3 Rob Moore .20
4 David Boston .30
5 Frank Sanders .10
6 Aeneas Williams .10
7 Tim Dwight .30
8 Chris Chandler .20
9 Jamal Anderson .30
10 Shawn Jefferson .10
11 Ken Oxendine .10
12 Terance Mathis .10
13 Qadry Ismail .10
14 Jermaine Lewis .10
15 Rod Woodson .10
16 Michael McCrary .10
17 Tony Banks .20
18 Peter Boulware .10
19 Shannon Sharpe .20
20 Peerless Price .30
21 Rob Johnson .20
22 Eric Moulds .30
23 Doug Flutie .30
24 Jay Riemersma .10
25 Antowain Smith .30
26 Sam Cowart .10
27 Muhsin Muhammad .20
28 Patrick Jeffers .30
29 Steve Beuerlein .20
30 Natrone Means .20
31 Tim Biakabutuka .10
32 Michael Bates .10
33 Wesley Walls .20
34 Cade McNown .50
35 Curtis Enis .30
36 Marcus Robinson .30
37 Bobby Engram .10
38 Glyn Milburn .10
39 Marty Booker .10
40 Akili Smith .20
41 Corey Dillon .30
42 Darnay Scott .20
43 Tremain Mack .10
44 Michael Bankston .10
45 Tony McGee .10
46 Tim Couch .75
47 Kevin Johnson .30
48 Darrin Chiaverini .10
49 Jamir Miller .10
50 Errict Rhett .10
51 Ty Detmer .10
52 Terry Kirby .10
53 Troy Aikman .60
54 Emmitt Smith 1.00
55 Raghib Ismail .10
56 Chris Warren .10
57 Joey Galloway .30
58 Terrell Davis .75
59 Olandis Gary .40
60 Brian Griese .40
61 Gus Frerotte .10
62 Glenn Cadrez .10
63 Ed McCaffrey .20
64 Rod Smith .20
65 Charlie Batch .30
66 Germane Crowell .20
67 Stephen Boyd .10
68 Johnnie Morton .10
69 Robert Porcher .10
70 James O. Stewart .20
71 Brett Favre 1.25
72 Antonio Freeman .30
73 Bill Schroeder .10
74 Dorsey Levens .30
75 Darren Sharper .10
76 Peyton Manning 1.00
77 Edgerrin James .75
78 Marvin Harrison .30
79 Ken Dilger .10
80 Terrence Wilkins .20
81 Cornelius Bennett .10
82 E.G. Green .10
83 Mark Brunell .50
84 Fred Taylor .50
85 Jimmy Smith .30
86 Keenan McCardell .20
87 Carnell Lake .10
88 Kevin Hardy .10
89 Elvis Grbac .20
90 Tony Gonzalez .20
91 Derrick S. Alexander .10
92 Donnell Bennett .10
93 James Hasty .10
94 Kevin Lockett .10
95 Trace Armstrong .10
96 Terrell Buckley .10
97 Tony Martin .10
98 Damon Huard .20
99 O.J. McDuffie .20
100 Brock Marion .10
101 Zach Thomas .20
102 Randy Moss 1.00
103 Robert Smith .30
104 Cris Carter .30
105 Bubby Brister .10
106 Daunte Culpepper .50
107 John Randle .10
108 Drew Bledsoe .50
109 Terry Glenn .30
110 Willie McGinest .10
111 Kevin Faulk .20
112 Tedy Bruschi .10
113 Ricky Williams .75
114 Keith Poole .10
115 Jake Reed .10
116 Mark Fields .10
117 Jeff Blake .20
118 Andrew Glover .10
119 Kerry Collins .20
120 Amani Toomer .10
121 Jesse Armstead .10
122 Ike Hilliard .10
123 Ray Lucas .30
124 Curtis Martin .20
125 Vinny Testaverde .20
126 Wayne Chrebet .20
127 Dedric Ward .10
128 Tim Brown .20
129 Rich Gannon .20
130 Tyrone Wheatley .10
131 Napoleon Kaufman .30
132 Charles Woodson .20
133 Greg Biekert .10
134 Rickey Dudley .10
135 Duce Staley .30
136 Donovan McNabb .50
137 Torrance Small .10
138 Mike Mamula .10
139 Brian Dawkins .10
140 Troy Vincent .10
141 Kent Graham .10
142 Troy Edwards .30
143 Jerome Bettis .30
144 Hines Ward .20
145 Kordell Stewart .30
146 Levon Kirkland .10
147 Richard Huntley .20
148 Marshall Faulk .30
149 Kurt Warner 1.00
150 Torry Holt .30
151 Isaac Bruce .30
152 Kevin Carter .10

153 Az-Zahir Hakim .20
154 Todd Lyght .10
155 Jermaine Fazande .20
156 Curtis Conway .10
157 Freddie Jones .10
158 Junior Seau .20
159 Jeff Graham .10
160 Moses Moreno .10
161 Rodney Harrison .10
162 Steve Young .50
163 Jerry Rice 1.00
164 Ken Norton .10
165 Terrell Owens .30
166 Jeff Garcia .20
167 Ricky Watters .20
168 Jon Kitna .30
169 Derrick Mayes .20
170 Sean Dawkins .10
171 Chad Brown .10
172 Warrick Dunn .30
173 Keyshawn Johnson .30
174 Shaun King .50
175 Mike Alstott .30
176 Warren Sapp .10
177 Jacquez Green .20
178 Derrick Brooks .10
179 John Lynch .10
180 Eddie George .40
181 Steve McNair .30
182 Kevin Dyson .20
183 Jevon Kearse .30
184 Yancey Thigpen .10
185 Frank Wycheck .10
186 Eddie Robinson .10
187 Jeff George .20
188 Brad Johnson .30
189 Stephen Davis .30
190 Michael Westbrook .20
191 Albert Connell .20
192 Brian Mitchell .10
193 Bruce Smith .10
194 Champ Bailey .20
195 Sam Shade .10
196 Marvin Harrison .20
197 Jimmy Smith .20
198 Randy Moss .50
199 Marcus Robinson .20
200 Tim Brown .50
201 Jimmy Smith .20
202 Marvin Harrison .20
203 Muhsin Muhammad .10
204 Tim Brown .10
205 Cris Carter .20
206 Edgerrin James .50
207 Curtis Martin .20
208 Stephen Davis .20
209 Emmitt Smith .40
210 Marshall Faulk .20
211 Kurt Warner .60
212 Steve Beuerlein .10
213 Jeff George .10
214 Peyton Manning .50
215 Brad Johnson .10
216 Kurt Warner .50
217 Peyton Manning .50
218 Edgerrin James .50
219 Marshall Faulk .20
220 Randy Moss .50
221 Jimmy Smith .20
222 Tony Gonzalez .10
223 Tony Boselli .10
224 Orlando Pace .10
225 Larry Allen .10
226 Randall McDaniel .10
227 Tom Nalen .10
228 Kevin Carter .10
229 Jevon Kearse .20
230 Warren Sapp .10
231 Darrell Russell .10
232 Derrick Brooks .10
233 Peter Boulware .10
234 Junior Seau .10
235 Sam Madison .10
236 Charles Woodson .10
237 John Lynch .10
238 Carnell Lake .10
239 Mitch Berger .10
240 Jason Hanson .10
241 Randy Moss .50
242 Kurt Warner .50
243 Peyton Manning .50
244 Marshall Faulk .20
245 Edgerrin James .40
246 Eddie George .20
247 Stephen Davis .20
248 Keyshawn Johnson .20
249 Brad Johnson .20
250 Ricky Williams .40
251 Jimmy Smith .20
252 Isaac Bruce .20
253 Muhsin Muhammad .10
254 Marcus Robinson .20
255 Kevin Johnson .10
256 Tim Couch .10
257 Curtis Martin .20
258 Charlie Batch .20
259 Tim Brown .10
260 Jerry Rice .50
261 Drew Bledsoe .25
262 Brett Favre .60
263 Mark Brunell .25
264 Fred Taylor .25
265 Troy Edwards .20
266 Marvin Harrison .20
267 Germane Crowell .10
268 Terry Glenn .20
269 Qadry Ismail .10
270 Jake Plummer .10
271 *Anthony Becht* .30
272 *Anthony Lucas* .30
273 *Bashir Yamini* .30
274 *Brian Urlacher* 1.50
275 *Chad Morton* .50
276 *Chad Pennington* 2.50
277 *Chris Cole* .30
278 *Chris Hovan* .50
279 *Tim Rattay* 1.25
280 *Chris Redman* 1.00
281 *Chris Samuels* .50
282 *Corey Simon* .50
283 *Courtney Brown* .50
284 *Curtis Keaton* .30
285 *Danny Farmer* .50
286 *Erron Kinney* .30
287 *Darren Howard* .30
288 *Deltha O'Neal* .30
289 *Dennis Northcutt* .50
290 *Demario Brown* .30
291 *Dez White* .50
292 *Frank Murphy* .30
293 *Gari Scott* .30
294 *Giovanni Carmazzi* .50
295 *J.R. Redmond* .75
296 *JaJuan Dawson* .30
297 *Jamal Lewis* 2.00
298 *Leon Murray* .30
299 *Jerry Porter* 1.25
300 *Joe Hamilton* .50
301 *John Abraham* .30
302 *John Engleberger* .50
303 *Keith Bulluck* .30
304 *Kwame Cavil* .30
305 *Laveranues Coles* 1.25
306 *Marc Bulger* 1.50
307 *Marcus Knight* .30
308 *Mareno Philyaw* .30
309 *Michael Wiley* .50
310 *Na'il Diggs* .30
311 *Peter Warrick* 1.25
312 *Plaxico Burress* 1.50
313 *Raynoch Thompson* .30
314 *Reuben Droughns* 1.50
315 *Rob Morris* .30
316 *Ron Dayne* 1.00
317 *Ron Dugans* .50
318 *Sebastian Janikowski* .50
319 *Shaun Alexander* 2.00
320 *Sherrod Gideon* .30
321 *Sylvester Morris* 1.00
322 *Tee Martin* .50
323 *Thomas Jones* 1.50
324 *Todd Husak* .50
325 *Todd Pinkston* .50
326 *Tom Brady* 3.00
327 *Travis Prentice* 1.00
328 *Travis Taylor* 1.00
329 *Trevor Gaylor* .50
330 *Trung Canidate* 1.00

2001 UD Game Gear

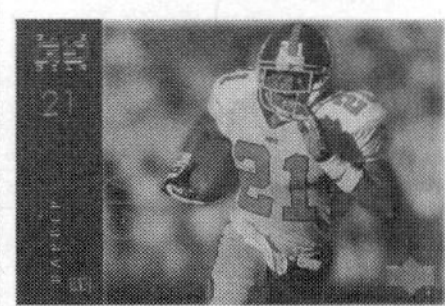

NM/M

Complete Set (110): 250.00
Common Player: .25
Minor Stars: .50
Common Rookie (91-100): 7.00
Production 1,000 Sets
Common Rookie (101-110): 10.00
Production 500 Sets
Pack (4): 8.00
Wax Box (18): 100.00
1 Jake Plummer 1.00
2 David Boston 1.00
3 Jamal Anderson 1.00
4 Shawn Jefferson .25
5 Jamal Lewis 2.50
6 Elvis Grbac .50
7 Ray Lewis .50
8 Rob Johnson .50
9 Shawn Bryson .25
10 Muhsin Muhammad .50
11 Jeff Lewis .50
12 Marcus Robinson 1.00
13 James Allen .75
14 Brian Urlacher 2.00
15 Cade McNown 1.00
16 Peter Warrick 2.50
17 Akili Smith 1.00
18 Corey Dillon 1.00
19 Tim Couch 1.25
20 Kevin Johnson 1.00
21 Emmitt Smith 2.50
22 Raghib Ismail .50
23 Joey Galloway 1.00
24 Terrell Davis 2.50
25 Brian Griese 1.25
26 Ed McCaffrey 1.00
27 Mike Anderson 2.50
28 Charlie Batch 1.00
29 Germane Crowell 1.00
30 James O. Stewart .75
31 Brett Favre 4.00
32 Dorsey Levens .75
33 Ahman Green .75
34 Peyton Manning 3.00
35 Edgerrin James 2.50
36 Marvin Harrison 1.50
37 Mark Brunell 1.25
38 Jimmy Smith 1.00
39 Fred Taylor 1.25
40 Tony Gonzalez .75
41 Derrick Alexander .50
42 Trent Green 1.00
43 Lamar Smith 1.00
44 Oronde Gadsden .50
45 Zach Thomas .50
46 Randy Moss 3.00
47 Daunte Culpepper 2.00
48 Doug Chapman .50
49 Cris Carter 1.00
50 Drew Bledsoe 1.25
51 Terry Glenn 1.00
52 Troy Brown .50
53 Ricky Williams 1.50
54 Jeff Blake .50
55 Aaron Brooks 1.25
56 Joe Horn .75
57 Kerry Collins .75
58 Ron Dayne 1.50
59 Amani Toomer .50
60 Tiki Barber .75
61 Vinny Testaverde .75
62 Curtis Martin 1.00
63 Wayne Chrebet .75
64 Rich Gannon .75
65 Jerry Rice 2.00
66 Tim Brown 1.00
67 Duce Staley 1.00
68 Donovan McNabb 1.50
69 Jerome Bettis 1.00
70 Kordell Stewart 1.00
71 Marshall Faulk 1.25
72 Kurt Warner 3.00
73 Torry Holt 1.00
74 Isaac Bruce 1.00
75 Doug Flutie 1.25
76 Junior Seau .75
77 Jeff Garcia 1.00
78 Terrell Owens 1.00
79 Matt Hasselbeck 1.00
80 Shaun Alexander 1.00
81 Ricky Watters .75
82 Keyshawn Johnson 1.00
83 Brad Johnson .75
84 Warrick Dunn 1.00
85 Mike Alstott 1.00
86 Eddie George 1.25
87 Steve McNair 1.00
88 Jeff George .75
89 Michael Westbrook .75
90 Stephen Davis 1.00
91 *Mike McMahon* 6.00
92 *James Jackson* 6.00
93 *Quincy Morgan* 8.00
94 *Travis Minor* 6.00
95 *Chris Chambers* 12.00
96 *Jesse Palmer* 6.00
97 *Santana Moss* 10.00
98 *Marques Tuiasosopo* 8.00
99 *Freddie Mitchell* 6.00
100 *Kevan Barlow* 10.00
101 *Michael Vick* 60.00
102 *Chris Weinke* 12.00
103 *Reggie Wayne* 15.00
104 *Robert Ferguson* 12.00
105 *Michael Bennett* 20.00
106 *Deuce McAllister* 25.00
107 *Drew Brees* 20.00
108 *LaDainian Tomlinson* 30.00
109 *Koren Robinson* 10.00
110 *Rod Gardner* 15.00

2001 UD Game Gear Autographs

NM/M

Common Player: 10.00
Inserted 1:18
MB-GS Michael Bennett 50.00
DB-GS Drew Brees 75.00
JB-GS Jim Brown 295 75.00
CC-GS Chris Chambers 20.00
TD-GS Terrell Davis 95 40.00
RD-GS Ron Dayne 25.00
GA-GS Rich Gannon 360 20.00
JG-GS Jeff Garcia 25.00
RG-GS Rod Gardner 150 40.00
AZ-GS Az-Zahir Hakim 10.00
CJ-GS Chad Johnson 15.00
JL-GS Jamal Lewis 295 35.00
PM-GS Peyton Manning 60.00
DU-GS Deuce McAllister 25.00
DM-GS Dan Morgan 15.00
RM-GS Randy Moss 95 150.00
SM-GS Santana Moss 25.00
JN-GS Joe Namath 295 100.00
KY-GS Ken-Yon Rambo 15.00
JR-GS John Riggins 395 85.00
KR-GS Koren Robinson 25.00
DT-GS David Terrell 25.00
AT-GS Anthony Thomas 20.00
LT-GS LaDainian Tomlinson 85.00
MV-GS Michael Vick 195 100.00
GW-GS Gerard Warren 15.00
PW-GS Peter Warrick 20.00
RW-GS Reggie Wayne 25.00
CW-GS Chris Weinke 390 50.00

2001 UD Game Gear Jerseys

NM/M

Common Player: 10.00
Inserted 1:18
TA-J Troy Aikman 30.00
DB-J Drew Bledsoe 20.00
MB-J Mark Brunell 20.00
WC-J Wayne Chrebet 10.00
TC-J Tim Couch 25.00
RD-J Ron Dayne 15.00
WD-J Warrick Dunn 10.00
MF-J Marshall Faulk 20.00
BF-J Brett Favre 45.00
RG-J Rich Gannon 15.00
EG-J Eddie George 20.00
TG-J Terry Glenn 10.00
AH-J Az-Zahir Hakim 10.00
PM-J Peyton Manning 40.00
SM-J Steve McNair 20.00
JR-J Jerry Rice 25.00
ES-J Emmitt Smith 35.00
RW-J Ricky Williams 20.00

2001 UD Game Gear Helmets

NM/M

Common Player: 18.00
Inserted 1:108
TA-H Troy Aikman 50.00
TB-H Tiki Barber 18.00
KB-H Kevan Barlow 25.00
MBe-H Michael Bennett 60.00
DBo-H David Boston 18.00
DBr-H Drew Brees 75.00
IB-H Isaac Bruce 25.00
MBr-H Mark Brunell 30.00
CD-H Corey Dillon 25.00
MF-H Marshall Faulk 30.00
RG-H Rod Gardner 30.00
TJ-H Thomas Jones 18.00
PM-H Peyton Manning 85.00
DM-H Deuce McAllister 50.00
KM-H Keenan McCardell 18.00
SM-H Santana Moss 45.00
JR-H Jerry Rice 60.00
KR-H Koren Robinson 30.00
JS-H Jason Sehorn 18.00
AS-H Akili Smith 18.00
ES-H Emmitt Smith 75.00
FT-H Fred Taylor 30.00
DT-H David Terrell 30.00
LT-H LaDainian Tomlinson 65.00
AT-H Amani Toomer 18.00
MV-H Michael Vick 125.00
KW-H Kurt Warner 75.00
PW-H Peter Warrick 25.00
RW-H Reggie Wayne 10.00
CW-H Chris Weinke 30.00

2001 UD Game Gear Uniforms

NM/M

Common Player: 10.00
Inserted 1:18
JA-U Jesse Armstead 10.00
CB-U Courtney Brown 10.00
JB-U Jim Brown 50.00
KC-U Kerry Collins 15.00
RD-U Ron Dayne 15.00
TH-U Torry Holt 15.00
JL-U Jamal Lewis 25.00
RL-U Ray Lewis 15.00
DM-U Dan Marino SP 60.00
FM-U Freddie Mitchell 20.00
RM-U Randy Moss 45.00
WP-U Walter Payton 85.00
JP-U Jim Plunkett 15.00

2001 UD Graded

NM/M

Complete Set (90): 500.00
Common Player: .50
Minor Stars: 1.00
Common Rookie: 5.00
Production 900 Sets
Pack (4 + BGS): 55.00
Wax Box (6): 250.00
1 Jake Plummer 2.00
2 Jamal Anderson 2.00
3 Jamal Lewis 5.00
4 Rob Johnson 1.00
5 Muhsin Muhammad 1.00
6 Marcus Robinson 2.00
7 Peter Warrick 2.50
8 Corey Dillon 2.00
9 Tim Couch 2.50
10 Emmitt Smith 5.00
11 Terrell Davis 4.00
12 Brian Griese 2.50
13 Charlie Batch 2.00
14 Brett Favre 8.00
15 Peyton Manning 7.00
16 Edgerrin James 6.00
17 Mark Brunell 2.50
18 Fred Taylor 2.50
19 Tony Gonzalez 1.00
20 Trent Green 2.00
21 Lamar Smith 1.00
22 Randy Moss 7.00
23 Daunte Culpepper 4.00
24 Drew Bledsoe 2.50
25 Ricky Williams 3.00
26 Kerry Collins 1.00
27 Ron Dayne 3.00
28 Vinny Testaverde 1.00
29 Curtis Martin 2.00
30 Rich Gannon 1.00
31 Charlie Garner 1.00
32 Duce Staley 2.00
33 Donovan McNabb 3.00
34 Jerome Bettis 2.00
35 Marshall Faulk 2.50
36 Kurt Warner 5.00
37 Doug Flutie 2.50
38 Jeff Garcia 2.00
39 Terrell Owens 2.00
40 Matt Hasselbeck 2.00
41 Keyshawn Johnson 2.00
42 Mike Alstott 2.00
43 Eddie George 2.50
44 Steve McNair 2.00
45 Stephen Davis 2.00
46 *Michael Bennett* 25.00
47 *Drew Brees* 25.00
48 *Chad Johnson* 25.00
49 *Deuce McAllister* 50.00
50 *Santana Moss* 20.00
51 *Koren Robinson* 12.00
52 *David Terrell* 15.00
53 *LaDainian Tomlinson* 50.00
54 *Michael Vick* 100.00
55 *Chris Weinke* 15.00
56 *Reggie Wayne* 20.00
57 *Anthony Thomas* 25.00
58 *Sage Rosenfels* 10.00
59 *Rod Gardner* 20.00
60 *Quincy Morgan* 12.00
61 *Freddie Mitchell* 12.00
62 *Gerard Warren* 10.00
63 *James Jackson* 12.00
64 *Travis Henry* 15.00
65 *Chris Chambers* 20.00
66 *Vinny Sutherland* 5.00
67 *Todd Heap* 8.00
68 *Dan Morgan* 5.00
69 *Rudi Johnson* 15.00
70 *Quincy Carter* 12.00
71 *Kevin Kasper* 8.00
72 *Scotty Anderson* 5.00
73 *Mike McMahon* 8.00
74 *Robert Ferguson* 8.00
75 *Marvin "Snoop" Minnis* 8.00
76 *Josh Heupel* 8.00
77 *Travis Minor* 12.00
78 *Justin Smith* 8.00
79 *Jesse Palmer* 12.00
80 *Marques Tuiasosopo* 12.00
81 *A.J. Freely* 15.00
82 *Correll Buckhalter* 12.00
83 *Kevan Barlow* 20.00
84 *Alex Bannister* 8.00
85 *Josh Booty* 8.00
86 *Eddie Berlin* 10.00
87 *Andre Carter* 8.00
88 *LaMont Jordan* 10.00
89 *Ken-Yon Rambo* 8.00
90 *Alge Crumpler* 8.00

2001 UD Graded Jerseys

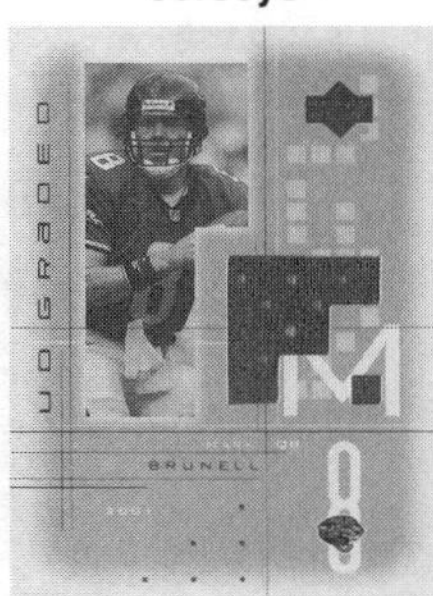

NM/M

Common Player: 10.00
Inserted 1:2
Blue Cards: 1.5X
Production 125 Sets
TB Tiki Barber 10.00
CB Charlie Batch 10.00
DB David Boston 10.00
MB Mark Brunell 15.00
CC Cris Carter 15.00
CH Chris Chandler 10.00
DC Daunte Culpepper 25.00
RD Ron Dayne 15.00
MF Marshall Faulk 20.00
BF Brett Favre 45.00
TH Torry Holt BLUE 30.00
KJ Keyshawn Johnson 15.00
JL Jamal Lewis 25.00
PM Peyton Manning 40.00
KM Keenan McCardell 10.00
RM Randy Moss 40.00
JR Jerry Rice 25.00
SS Shannon Sharpe 10.00
JS Jimmy Smith 10.00
KW Kurt Warner 35.00
PW Peter Warrick 15.00

2001 UD Graded Rookie Autographs

NM/M

Common Player: 20.00
46 Michael Bennett 125.00
47 Drew Brees 175.00
48 Chad Johnson 30.00
49 Deuce McAllister 65.00
50 Santana Moss 50.00
51 Koren Robinson 50.00
52 David Terrell 50.00
53 LaDainian Tomlinson 175.00
54 Michael Vick 200.00
55 Chris Weinke 100.00
56 Reggie Wayne 25.00
57 Anthony Thomas 30.00
58 Sage Rosenfels 20.00
59 Rod Gardner 30.00
60 Quincy Morgan 30.00
61 Freddie Mitchell 35.00
62 Gerard Warren 20.00
63 James Jackson 40.00
64 Travis Henry 40.00
65 Chris Chambers 35.00

2001 UD Graded Rookie Jerseys

NM/M

Common Player: 15.00
46 Michael Bennett 60.00
47 Drew Brees 80.00
48 Chad Johnson 20.00
49 Deuce McAllister 30.00
50 Santana Moss 25.00
51 Koren Robinson 20.00
52 David Terrell 40.00
53 LaDainian Tomlinson 80.00
54 Michael Vick 100.00
55 Chris Weinke 50.00
56 Reggie Wayne 25.00
57 Anthony Thomas 25.00
58 Sage Rosenfels 15.00
59 Rod Gardner 25.00
60 Quincy Morgan 20.00
61 Freddie Mitchell 25.00
62 Gerard Warren 15.00
63 James Jackson 30.00
64 Travis Henry 25.00
65 Chris Chambers 20.00

2001 UD Graded Rookie Series

NM/M

Common Player: 10.00
46A Michael Bennett A Gem Mt 150.00
46A Michael Bennett A Mt 50.00
46P Michael Bennett P Gem Mt 200.00
46P Michael Bennett P Mt 60.00
47A Drew Brees A Gem Mt 200.00
47A Drew Brees A Mt 60.00
47P Drew Brees P Gem Mt 200.00
47P Drew Brees P Mt 60.00
48A Chad Johnson A Gem Mt 30.00
48A Chad Johnson A Mt 10.00
48P Chad Johnson P Gem Mt 30.00
48P Chad Johnson P Mt 10.00
49A Deuce McAllister A Gem Mt 80.00
49A Deuce McAllister A Mt 30.00
49P Deuce McAllister P Gem Mt 80.00
49P Deuce McAllister P Mt 30.00
50A Santana Moss A Gem Mt 60.00
50A Santana Moss A Mt 30.00
50P Santana Moss P Mt 30.00
51A Koren Robinson A Gem Mt 60.00
51A Koren Robinson A Mt 30.00
51P Koren Robinson P Gem Mt 60.00
51P Koren Robinson P Mt 30.00
52A David Terrell A Gem Mt 80.00
52A David Terrell A Mt 30.00
52P David Terrell P Gem Mt 80.00
52P David Terrell P Mt 30.00
53A LaDainian Tomlinson A Gem Mt 250.00
53A LaDainian Tomlinson A Mt 100.00
53P LaDainian Tomlinson P Gem Mt 250.00
53P LaDainian Tomlinson P Mt 100.00
54A Michael Vick A Gem Mt 275.00
54A Michael Vick A Mt 110.00
54P Michael Vick P Gem Mt 300.00
54P Michael Vick P Mt 120.00
55A Chris Weinke A Gem Mt 225.00
55A Chris Weinke A Mt 60.00
55P Chris Weinke P Gem Mt 175.00
55P Chris Weinke P Mt 50.00
56A Reggie Wayne A Mt 10.00
56P Reggie Wayne P Gem Mt 40.00
56P Reggie Wayne P Mt 10.00
57A Anthony Thomas A Gem Mt 50.00
57A Anthony Thomas A Mt 20.00
57P Anthony Thomas P Gem Mt 50.00
57P Anthony Thomas P Mt 20.00
58A Sage Rosenfels A Gem Mt 30.00
58A Sage Rosenfels A Mt 10.00
58P Sage Rosenfels P Gem Mt 30.00
58P Sage Rosenfels P Mt 10.00
59A Rod Gardner A Gem Mt 50.00
59A Rod Gardner A Mt 20.00
59P Rod Gardner P Gem Mt 50.00
59P Rod Gardner P Mt 20.00
60A Quincy Morgan A Gem Mt 30.00
60A Quincy Morgan A Mt 15.00
60P Quincy Morgan P Gem Mt 30.00
60P Quincy Morgan P Mt 15.00
61A Freddie Mitchell A Gem Mt 40.00
61A Freddie Mitchell A Mt 20.00
61P Freddie Mitchell P Gem Mt 40.00
61P Freddie Mitchell P Mt 20.00
62A Gerard Warren A Gem Mt 20.00
62A Gerard Warren A Mt 10.00
62P Gerard Warren P Gem Mt 20.00
62P Gerard Warren P Mt 10.00

63A James Jackson A Gem Mt 40.00
63A James Jackson A Mt 15.00
63P James Jackson P Gem Mt 40.00
63P James Jackson P Mt 15.00
64A Travis Henry A Gem Mt 60.00
64A Travis Henry A Mt 25.00
64P Travis Henry P Gem Mt 60.00
64P Travis Henry P Mt 25.00
65A Chris Chambers A Gem Mt 40.00
65A Chris Chambers A Mt 20.00
65P Chris Chambers P Gem Mt 40.00
65P Chris Chambers P Mt 20.00
66A Vinny Sutherland A Gem Mt 20.00
66A Vinny Sutherland A Mt 10.00
66P Vinny Sutherland P Gem Mt 20.00
66P Vinny Sutherland P Mt 10.00
67A Todd Heap A Gem Mt 25.00
67A Todd Heap A Mt 10.00
67P Todd Heap P Gem Mt 25.00
67P Todd Heap P Mt 10.00
68A Dan Morgan A Gem Mt 20.00
68A Dan Morgan A Mt 10.00
68P Dan Morgan P Gem Mt 20.00
68P Dan Morgan P Mt 10.00
69A Rudi Johnson A Gem Mt 20.00
69A Rudi Johnson A Mt 10.00
69P Rudi Johnson P Gem Mt 20.00
69P Rudi Johnson P Mt 10.00
70A Quincy Carter A Gem Mt 60.00
70A Quincy Carter A Mt 25.00
70P Quincy Carter P Gem Mt 80.00
70P Quincy Carter P Mt 30.00
70P Quincy Carter P NmMt+ 20.00
71A Kevin Kasper A Gem Mt 20.00
71A Kevin Kasper A Mt 10.00
71P Kevin Kasper P Gem Mt 20.00
71P Kevin Kasper P Mt 10.00
72A Scotty Anderson A Gem Mt 20.00
72A Scotty Anderson A Mt 10.00
72P Scotty Anderson P Gem Mt 20.00
72P Scotty Anderson P Mt 10.00
73A Mike McMahon A Gem Mt 25.00
73A Mike McMahon A Mt 12.00
73P Mike McMahon P Gem Mt 25.00
73P Mike McMahon P Mt 12.00
74A Robert Ferguson A Gem Mt 20.00
74A Robert Ferguson A Mt 10.00
74P Robert Ferguson P Gem Mt 20.00
74P Robert Ferguson P Mt 10.00
75A Marvin "Snoop" Minnis A Gem Mt 40.00
75A Marvin "Snoop" Minnis A Mt 20.00
75P Marvin "Snoop" Minnis P Gem Mt 40.00
75P Marvin "Snoop" Minnis P Mt 20.00
76A Josh Heupel A Gem Mt 35.00
76A Josh Heupel A Mt 15.00
76P Josh Heupel P Gem Mt 35.00
76P Josh Heupel P Mt 15.00
77A Travis Minor A Gem Mt 30.00
77A Travis Minor A Mt 12.00
77P Travis Minor P Gem Mt 30.00
77P Travis Minor P Mt 12.00
78A Justin Smith A Gem Mt 20.00
78A Justin Smith A Mt 10.00
78P Justin Smith P Gem Mt 20.00
78P Justin Smith P Mt 10.00
79A Jesse Palmer A Gem Mt 30.00
79A Jesse Palmer A Mt 12.00
79P Jesse Palmer P Gem Mt 30.00
79P Jesse Palmer P Mt 12.00
80A Marques Tuiasosopo A Gem Mt 40.00
80A Marques Tuiasosopo A Mt 20.00
80P Marques Tuiasosopo P Gem Mt 40.00
80P Marques Tuiasosopo P Mt 20.00
81A A.J. Feeley A Gem Mt 20.00
81A A.J. Feeley A Mt 10.00
81P A.J. Feeley P Gem Mt 20.00
81P A.J. Feeley P Mt 10.00
82A Correll Buckhalter A Gem Mt 30.00
82A Correll Buckhalter A Mt 15.00
82P Correll Buckhalter P Gem Mt 30.00
82P Correll Buckhalter P Mt 15.00
83A Kevan Barlow A Gem Mt 40.00
83A Kevan Barlow A Mt 20.00
83P Kevan Barlow P Gem Mt 40.00
83P Kevan Barlow P Mt 20.00
84A Alex Bannister A Gem Mt 20.00
84A Alex Bannister A Mt 10.00
84P Alex Bannister P Gem Mt 20.00
84P Alex Bannister P Mt 10.00
85A Josh Booty A Gem Mt 20.00
85A Josh Booty A Mt 10.00
85P Josh Booty P Gem Mt 20.00
85P Josh Booty P Mt 10.00
86A Eddie Berlin A Gem Mt 20.00
86A Eddie Berlin A Mt 10.00
86P Eddie Berlin P Gem Mt 20.00
86P Eddie Berlin P Mt 10.00
87A Andre Carter A Gem Mt 20.00
87A Andre Carter A Mt 10.00
87P Andre Carter P Gem Mt 20.00
87P Andre Carter P Mt 10.00
88A LaMont Jordan A Gem Mt 25.00
88A LaMont Jordan A Mt 12.00
88P LaMont Jordan P Gem Mt 25.00
88P LaMont Jordan P Mt 12.00
89A Ken-Yon Rambo A Gem Mt 20.00
89A Ken-Yon Rambo A Mt 10.00
89P Ken-Yon Rambo P Gem Mt 20.00
89P Ken-Yon Rambo P Mt 10.00
90A Alge Crumpler A Gem Mt 20.00
90A Alge Crumpler A Mt 10.00
90P Alge Crumpler P Gem Mt 20.00
90P Alge Crumpler P Mt 10.00

2001 UD Graded Rookie Series Autographs Graded

NM/M
Common Player: 20.00
46 Michael Bennett Mt 180.00
46 Michael Bennett NmMt+ 120.00
47 Drew Brees Mt 200.00
47 Drew Brees NmMt+ 150.00
48 Chad Johnson Mt 40.00
48 Chad Johnson NmMt+ 30.00
49 Deuce McAllister Mt 80.00
49 Deuce McAllister NmMt+ 60.00
50 Santana Moss Mt 60.00
50 Santana Moss NmMt+ 50.00
51 Koren Robinson Mt 50.00
51 Koren Robinson NmMt+ 40.00
52 David Terrell Mt 60.00
52 David Terrell NmMt+ 50.00
53 LaDainian Tomlinson Mt 200.00
53 LaDainian Tomlinson NmMt+ 150.00
54 Michael Vick Mt 300.00
54 Michael Vick NmMt+ 200.00
55 Chris Weinke Mt 125.00
55 Chris Weinke NmMt+ 100.00
56 Reggie Wayne Gem Mt 100.00
56 Reggie Wayne Mt 40.00
56 Reggie Wayne NmMt+ 25.00
57 Anthony Thomas Mt 50.00
57 Anthony Thomas NmMt+ 30.00
58 Sage Rosenfels Mt 35.00
58 Sage Rosenfels NmMt+ 25.00
59 Rod Gardner Mt 40.00
59 Rod Gardner NmMt+ 30.00
60 Quincy Morgan Mt 40.00
60 Quincy Morgan NmMt+ 30.00
61 Freddie Mitchell Mt 50.00
61 Freddie Mitchell NmMt+ 40.00
62 Gerard Warren Mt 25.00
62 Gerard Warren NmMt+ 20.00
63 James Jackson Mt 50.00
63 James Jackson NmMt+ 40.00
64 Travis Henry Mt 50.00
64 Travis Henry NmMt+ 40.00
65 Chris Chambers Mt 40.00
65 Chris Chambers NmMt+ 30.00

2001 UD Graded Rookie Series Jerseys Graded

NM/M
Common Player: 15.00
46 Michael Bennett Mt 100.00
46 Michael Bennett NmMt+ 60.00
47 Drew Brees Gem Mt 275.00
47 Drew Brees Mt 130.00
47 Drew Brees NmMt+ 70.00
48 Chad Johnson Mt 25.00
48 Chad Johnson NmMt+ 20.00
49 Deuce McAllister Gem Mt 100.00
49 Deuce McAllister Mt 40.00
49 Deuce McAllister NmMt+ 30.00
50 Santana Moss Gem Mt 80.00
50 Santana Moss Mt 30.00
50 Santana Moss NmMt+ 25.00
51 Koren Robinson Gem Mt 100.00
51 Koren Robinson Mt 40.00
51 Koren Robinson NmMt+ 30.00
53 LaDainian Tomlinson Gem Mt 275.00
53 LaDainian Tomlinson Mt 130.00
53 LaDainian Tomlinson NmMt+ 70.00
54 Michael Vick Gem Mt 300.00
54 Michael Vick Mt 150.00
54 Michael Vick NmMt+ 100.00
55 Chris Weinke Gem Mt 180.00
55 Chris Weinke Mt 70.00
55 Chris Weinke NmMt+ 50.00
56 Reggie Wayne Gem Mt 60.00
56 Reggie Wayne Mt 30.00
56 Reggie Wayne NmMt+ 25.00
58 Sage Rosenfels Mt 25.00
58 Sage Rosenfels NmMt+ 15.00
59 Rod Gardner Gem Mt 80.00
59 Rod Gardner Mt 30.00
59 Rod Gardner NmMt+ 25.00
60 Quincy Morgan Mt 25.00
60 Quincy Morgan NmMt+ 20.00
61 Freddie Mitchell Gem Mt 70.00
61 Freddie Mitchell Mt 25.00
61 Freddie Mitchell NmMt+ 20.00
62 Gerard Warren Gem Mt 40.00
62 Gerard Warren Mt 25.00
62 Gerard Warren NmMt+ 15.00
63 James Jackson Mt 40.00
63 James Jackson NmMt+ 30.00
64 Travis Henry Mt 30.00
64 Travis Henry NmMt+ 25.00
65 Chris Chambers Gem Mt 60.00
65 Chris Chambers Mt 25.00
65 Chris Chambers NmMt+ 20.00

2001 UD Top Tier

NM/M
Complete Set (280): 350.00
Common Player: .25
Minor Stars: .50
Common Rookie: 2.00
Pack (5): 2.00
Wax Box (24): 40.00
1 Jake Plummer .75
2 David Boston .75
3 Thomas Jones .50
4 Frank Sanders .50
5 Tony Martin .25
6 Jamal Anderson .75
7 Chris Chandler .50
8 Shawn Jefferson .25
9 Jammi German .25
10 Terance Mathis .25
11 Jamal Lewis 2.00
12 Shannon Sharpe .50
13 Elvis Grbac .50
14 Ray Lewis .75
15 Qadry Ismail .25
16 Sam Gash .25
17 Rob Johnson .50
18 Eric Moulds .50
19 Sammy Morris .50
20 Shawn Bryson .25
21 Jeremy McDaniel .25
22 Muhsin Muhammad .50
23 Brad Hoover .50
24 Tim Biakabutuka .25
25 Donald Hayes .25
26 Dameyune Craig .25
27 Wesley Walls .50
28 Cade McNown .75
29 James Allen .50
30 Marcus Robinson .75
31 Brian Urlacher 1.50
32 Bobby Engram .25
33 Shane Matthews .50
34 Peter Warrick 1.00
35 Corey Dillon .75
36 Akili Smith .75
37 Scott Mitchell .50
38 Jon Kitna .50
39 Tim Couch 1.00
40 Kevin Johnson .75
41 Travis Prentice .50
42 Spergon Wynn .25
43 Jamel White .25
44 JaJuan Dawson .50
45 Courtney Brown .50
46 Tony Banks .50
47 Emmitt Smith 2.00
48 Joey Galloway .75
49 Raghib Ismail .25
50 Anthony Wright .50
51 Darren Woodson .25
52 Terrell Davis 1.50
53 Mike Anderson 2.00
54 Brian Griese 1.00
55 Rod Smith .75
56 Ed McCaffrey .50
57 Eddie Kennison .25
58 Olandis Gary .75
59 Charlie Batch .75
60 Germane Crowell .75
61 James O. Stewart .50
62 Johnnie Morton .50
63 Desmond Howard .25
64 Brett Favre 3.00
65 Antonio Freeman .75
66 Dorsey Levens .50
67 Ahman Green .75
68 Bill Schroeder .50
69 Bubba Franks .25
70 Peyton Manning 2.50
71 Edgerrin James 2.00
72 Marvin Harrison .75
73 Jerome Pathon .25
74 Lennox Gordon .25
75 Terrence Wilkins .25
76 Mark Brunell 1.00
77 Fred Taylor 1.00
78 Jimmy Smith .75
79 Keenan McCardell .50
80 Kevin Hardy .25
81 Stacey Mack .25
82 Tony Gonzalez .75
83 Derrick Alexander .50
84 Priest Holmes .50
85 Trent Green .75
86 Tony Horne .25
87 Oronde Gadsden .50
88 Lamar Smith .75
89 Jay Fiedler .75
90 Zach Thomas .50
91 Ray Lucas .50
92 O.J. McDuffie .50
93 Randy Moss 2.50
94 Cris Carter .75
95 Daunte Culpepper 1.50
96 Robert Griffith .25
97 Jake Reed .50
98 Drew Bledsoe 1.00
99 Terry Glenn .50
100 Kevin Faulk .25
101 Michael Bishop .50
102 Troy Brown .25
103 Ricky Williams 1.25
104 Jeff Blake .50
105 Joe Horn .50
106 Willie Jackson .25
107 Aaron Brooks 1.00
108 Albert Connell .50
109 Kerry Collins .50
110 Amani Toomer .50
111 Ron Dayne 1.25
112 Tiki Barber .50
113 Ike Hilliard .50
114 Ron Dixon .25
115 Michael Strahan .50
116 Vinny Testaverde .50
117 Wayne Chrebet .50
118 Curtis Martin .75
119 Richie Anderson .25
120 Laveranues Coles .50
121 Chad Pennington 1.50
122 Tim Brown .75
123 Rich Gannon .50
124 Tyrone Wheatley .25
125 Charlie Garner .50
126 Jerry Rice 1.75
127 Charles Woodson .75
128 Duce Staley .75
129 Donovan McNabb 1.25
130 Todd Pinkston .50
131 Chad Lewis .25
132 Brian Mitchell .25
133 Kordell Stewart .75
134 Jerome Bettis .75
135 Plaxico Burress .75
136 Bobby Shaw .25
137 Hines Ward .50
138 Marshall Faulk 1.00
139 Kurt Warner 2.75
140 Isaac Bruce .75
141 Torry Holt .75
142 Justin Watson .25
143 Az-Zahir Hakim .50
144 Junior Seau .50
145 Curtis Conway .50
146 Doug Flutie 1.00
147 Jeff Graham .25
148 Freddie Jones .50
149 Rodney Harrison .25
150 Jeff Garcia .75
151 Tai Streets .50
152 Terrell Owens .75
153 J.J. Stokes .50
154 Garrison Hearst .50
155 Paul Smith .50
156 Ricky Watters .50
157 Shaun Alexander 1.00
158 Matt Hasselbeck .75
159 Brock Huard .50
160 Darrell Jackson .75
161 Karsten Bailey .25
162 Warrick Dunn .75
163 Shaun King .50
164 Reidel Anthony .25
165 Mike Alstott .75
166 Jacquez Green .25
167 Brad Johnson .50
168 Keyshawn Johnson .75
169 Eddie George 1.00
170 Steve McNair .75
171 Neil O'Donnell .25
172 Derrick Mason .50
173 Frank Wycheck .25
174 Chris Sanders .25
175 Jevon Kearse .75
176 Jeff George .50
177 Stephen Davis .75
178 Kevin Lockett .25
179 Michael Westbrook .50
180 Stephen Alexander .25
181 *Arnold Jackson 2,000* 3.00
182 *Bobby Newcombe 2,000* 5.00
183 *Vinny Sutherland 2,000* 5.00
184 *Michael Vick 1,500* 50.00
185 *Quentin McCord 2,500* 2.00
186 *Todd Heap 1,500* 8.00
187 *Chris Barnes 2,000* 4.00
188 *Travis Henry 1,500* 10.00
189 *Reggie Germany 2,500* 4.00
190 *Tim Hasselbeck 2,000* 5.00
191 *Dan Morgan 2,500* 3.00
192 *Dadrian "Dee" Brown 2,000* 3.00
193 *Chris Weinke 2,000* 8.00
194 *David Terrell 1,500* 8.00
195 *Anthony Thomas 1,500* 12.00
196 *Rudi Johnson 2,500* 12.00
197 *Chad Johnson 1,500* 15.00
198 *Quincy Morgan 2,500* 8.00
199 *James Jackson 1,500* 8.00
200 *Quincy Carter 2,000* 10.00
201 *Kevin Kasper 2,500* 5.00
202 *Scotty Anderson 2,000* 3.00
203 *Mike McMahon 1,500* 8.00
204 *Robert Ferguson 1,500* 6.00
205 *David Martin 2,000* 3.00
206 *Reggie Wayne 2,000* 12.00
207 *Kabeer Gbaja-Biamila 2,500* 10.00
208 *Marvin "Snoop" Minnis 2,000* 8.00
209 *Derrick Blaylock 1,500* 6.00
210 *Josh Heupel 2,500* 5.00
211 *Travis Minor 2,000* 5.00
212 *Chris Chambers 2,000* 12.00
213 *Michael Bennett 1,500* 12.00
214 *Justin Smith 1,500* 5.00
215 *Deuce McAllister 2,000* 20.00
216 *Moran Norris 2,500* 2.00
217 *Onomo Ojo 2,500* 3.00
218 *Jesse Palmer 1,500* 5.00
219 *Santana Moss 2,000* 10.00
220 *LaMont Jordan 2,000* 5.00
221 *Marques Tuiasosopo 2,000* 8.00
222 *A.J. Feeley 1,500* 10.00
223 *Correll Buckhalter 1,500* 8.00
224 *Freddie Mitchell 2,000* 8.00
225 *Chris Taylor 2,500* 2.00
226 *Drew Brees 1,500* 12.00
227 *LaDainian Tomlinson 1,500* 25.00
228 *Dave Dickenson 2,000* 6.00
229 *Kevan Barlow 2,000* 10.00
230 *Andre Carter 2,000* 6.00
231 *Cedrick Wilson 2,000* 5.00
232 *David Allen 2,500* 3.00
233 *Alex Bannister 1,500* 5.00
234 *Josh Booty 2,000* 5.00
235 *Koren Robinson 2,500* 10.00
236 *Damione Lewis 2,000* 4.00
237 *Eddie Berlin 2,500* 4.00
238 *Darnerian McCants 1,500* 4.00
239 *Sage Rosenfels 2,500* 5.00
240 *Rod Gardner 1,500* 12.00
241 *Billy Baber 2,500* 2.00
242 *Dan Alexander 2,000* 5.00
243 *Reggie White 2,500* 3.00
244 *Adam Archuleta 2,000* 6.00
245 *Derrick Gibson 2,500* 2.00
246 *Hakim Akbar 2,000* 2.00
247 *Brandon Manumaleuna 2,500* 3.00
248 *Andre King 2,500* 2.00
249 *Corey Alston 2,500* 2.00
250 *Fred Smoot 1,500* 6.00
251 *Kyle Vanden Bosch 2,500* 4.00
252 *Richard Seymour 1,500* 5.00
253 *Derek Combs 2,000* 4.00
254 *Ken-Yon Rambo 2,500* 5.00
255 *Joey Getherall 2,000* 4.00
256 *Jonathan Carter 1,500* 4.00
257 *Gerard Warren 1,500* 6.00
258 *Carlos Polk 2,000* 3.00
259 *Milton Wynn 2,500* 3.00
260 *Ronney Daniels 2,000* 3.00
261 *Edgerton Hartwell 1,500* 4.00
262 *Steve Smith 2,000* 8.00
263 *T.J. Houshmandzadeh 1,500* 4.00
264 *Alge Crumpler 2,000* 5.00
265 *Torrance Marshall 1,500* 5.00
266 *Tommy Polley 2,000* 3.00
267 *Sedrick Hodge 2,000* 3.00
268 *Kendrell Bell 2,500* 8.00
269 *Jamie Winborn 1,500* 4.00
270 *Brian Allen 2,000* 2.00
271 *Brandon Spoon 1,500* 5.00
272 *Paul Toviessa 2,000* 2.00
273 *Aaron Schobel 2,500* 2.00
274 *Will Allen 2,500* 5.00
275 *Jamar Fletcher 1,500* 5.00
276 *Andre Dyson 2,000* 2.00
277 *Nate Clements 2,500* 3.00
278 *Willie Middlebrooks 2,500* 2.00
279 *Ken Lucas 2,500* 2.00
280 *Jamal Reynolds 2,000* 5.00

2001 UD Top Tier Home/Away Jerseys

NM/M
Common Player: 15.00
Inserted 1:239
HA-KB Kevan Barlow 20.00
HA-MB Michael Bennett 30.00
HA-DB Drew Brees 40.00
HA-CC Chris Chambers 20.00
HA-RF Robert Ferguson 15.00
HA-RG Rod Gardner 20.00
HA-TH Travis Henry 20.00
HA-JH Josh Heupel 15.00
HA-JJ James Jackson 20.00
HA-RJ Rudi Johnson 15.00
HA-MC Deuce McAllister 25.00
HA-MM Mike McMahon 18.00
HA-TM Travis Minor 15.00
HA-FM Freddie Mitchell 20.00
HA-DM Dan Morgan 15.00
HA-QM Quincy Morgan 18.00
HA-SM Santana Moss 20.00
HA-JP Jesse Palmer 15.00
HA-KR Koren Robinson 20.00
HA-LT LaDainian Tomlinson 50.00
HA-MT Marques Tuiasosopo 18.00
HA-MV Michael Vick 50.00
HA-RW Reggie Wayne 18.00

2001 UD Top Tier Rookie Duos

NM/M
Common Player: 15.00
Inserted 1:239
RD-BT Drew Brees, LaDainian Tomlinson 45.00
RD-HC Josh Heupel, Chris Chambers 18.00
RD-TT David Terrell, Anthony Thomas 30.00
RD-WM Chris Weinke, Dan Morgan 20.00
RD-JJ Chad Johnson, Rudi Johnson 15.00
RD-RG Sage Rosenfels, Rod Gardner 20.00
RD-MJ Quincy Morgan, James Jackson 20.00
RD-VB Michael Vick, Drew Brees 45.00
RD-GR Koren Robinson, Rod Gardner 20.00
RD-MW Reggie Wayne, Santana Moss 20.00

2001 UD Top Tier Then and Now Jerseys

NM/M
Common Player: 15.00
Inserted 1:239
TN-TA Troy Aikman 50.00
TN-RD Ron Dayne 30.00
TN-KJ Keyshawn Johnson 15.00
TN-DM Deuce McAllister 20.00
TN-FM Freddie Mitchell 20.00
TN-JS Junior Seau 15.00
TN-JJ J.J. Stokes 15.00

2001 UD Top Tier Two of a Kind

NM/M
Common Player: 15.00
Inserted 1:239
2K-UM Brian Urlacher, Dan Morgan 20.00
2K-DB Ron Dayne, Michael Bennett 20.00
2K-NO Ricky Williams, Deuce McAllister 20.00
2K-MT Randy Moss, David Terrell 30.00
2K-CV Daunte Culpepper, Michael Vick 35.00
2K-WM Peter Warrick, Marvin "Snoop" Minnis 15.00
2K-FF Brett Favre, Robert Ferguson 35.00
2K-JT Edgerrin James, LaDainian Tomlinson 35.00
2K-JJ Keyshawn Johnson, Chad Johnson 15.00

2001 UD Top Tier Tri-Stars

NM/M
Common Player: 20.00
Inserted 1:239
3S-SF Jeff Garcia, Terrell Owens, J.J. Stokes 20.00
3S-CH Cade McNown, Brian Urlacher, David Terrell 30.00
3S-IC Edgerrin James, Peyton Manning, Marvin Harrison 40.00
3S-MV Daunte Culpepper, Randy Moss, Cris Carter 40.00
3S-MD Josh Heupel, Travis Minor, Chris Chambers 25.00
3S-NO Aaron Brooks, Ricky Williams, Joe Horn 25.00
3S-GB Brett Favre, Ahman Green, Antonio Freeman 50.00
3S-TB Warrick Dunn, Mike Alstott, Keyshawn Johnson 20.00

2001 UD Vintage

NM/M
Complete Set (290): 50.00
Common Player: .10
Minor Stars: .20
Common Rookies: .50
Pack (10): 1.75
Wax Box (24): 30.00
1 Jake Plummer .50
2 David Boston .50
3 Thomas Jones .30
4 Frank Sanders .20
5 Bob Christian .10
6 Jamal Anderson .50

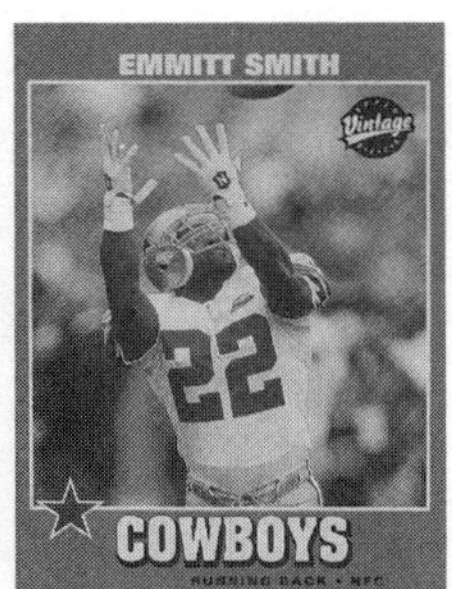

		NM/M
7	Chris Chandler	.20
8	Shawn Jefferson	.10
9	Brian Finneran	.10
10	Terance Mathis	.20
11	Jamal Lewis	1.00
12	Shannon Sharpe	.30
13	Elvis Grbac	.30
14	Ray Lewis	.50
15	Qadry Ismail	.30
16	Brandon Stokely	.30
17	Rob Johnson	.50
18	Eric Moulds	.50
19	Sammy Morris	.30
20	Shawn Bryson	.30
21	Jeremy McDaniel	.10
22	Muhsin Muhammad	.30
23	Brad Hoover	.50
24	Tim Biakabutuka	.30
25	Donald Hayes	.30
26	Jeff Lewis	.30
27	Wesley Walls	.30
28	Cade McNown	.50
29	James Allen	.50
30	Marcus Robinson	.50
31	Brian Urlacher	1.50
32	Jim Miller	.30
33	Peter Warrick	1.50
34	Corey Dillon	.50
35	Akili Smith	.50
36	Danny Farmer	.30
37	Ron Dugans	.30
38	Jon Kitna	.50
39	Tim Couch	.75
40	Kevin Johnson	.50
41	Travis Prentice	.50
42	Spergon Wynn	.30
43	Errict Rhett	.30
44	Dennis Northcutt	.30
45	Courtney Brown	.30
46	Tony Banks	.30
47	Emmitt Smith	1.00
48	Joey Galloway	.50
49	Raghib Ismail	.30
50	Anthony Wright	.30
51	Jackie Harris	.10
52	Terrell Davis	1.00
53	Mike Anderson	1.00
54	Brian Griese	.60
55	Rod Smith	.50
56	Ed McCaffrey	.50
57	Howard Griffith	.10
58	Olandis Gary	.30
59	Charlie Batch	.50
60	Germane Crowell	.30
61	James O. Stewart	.30
62	Johnnie Morton	.30
63	Desmond Howard	.10
64	Brett Favre	1.50
65	Antonio Freeman	.50
66	Dorsey Levens	.30
67	Ahman Green	.30
68	Bill Schroeder	.30
69	Bubba Franks	.30
70	Peyton Manning	1.25
71	Edgerrin James	1.25
72	Marvin Harrison	.50
73	Jerome Pathon	.10
74	Ken Dilger	.10
75	Terrence Wilkins	.30
76	Mark Brunell	.60
77	Fred Taylor	.60
78	Jimmy Smith	.30
79	Keenan McCardell	.20
80	R. Jay Soward	.20
81	Todd Collins	.10
82	Tony Gonzalez	.30
83	Derrick Alexander	.20
84	Trent Green	.40
85	Sylvester Morris	.40
86	Oronde Gadsden	.30
87	Lamar Smith	.40
88	Jay Fiedler	.50
89	Zach Thomas	.30
90	Ray Lucas	.30
91	O.J. McDuffie	.30
92	Randy Moss	1.25
93	Cris Carter	.50
94	Daunte Culpepper	.75
95	Robert Griffith	.10
96	Jake Reed	.20
97	Drew Bledsoe	.60
98	Terry Glenn	.30
99	Kevin Faulk	.30
100	Michael Bishop	.30
101	Troy Brown	.10
102	Ricky Williams	.75
103	Jeff Blake	.30
104	Joe Horn	.30
105	Willie Jackson	.20
106	Aaron Brooks	.50
107	Keith Poole	.10
108	Kerry Collins	.30
109	Amani Toomer	.20
110	Ron Dayne	.75
111	Tiki Barber	.30
112	Ike Hilliard	.20
113	Ron Dixon	.20
114	Michael Strahan	.10
115	Vinny Testaverde	.30
116	Wayne Chrebet	.30
117	Curtis Martin	.50
118	Richie Anderson	.10
119	Laveranues Coles	.50
120	Chad Pennington	.75
121	Tim Brown	.40
122	Rich Gannon	.30
123	Tyrone Wheatley	.30
124	Charlie Garner	.30
125	Andre Rison	.30
126	Charles Woodson	.30
127	Jon Ritchie	.10
128	Duce Staley	.50
129	Donovan McNabb	.60
130	Darnell Autry	.20
131	Chad Lewis	.20
132	Brian Mitchell	.10
133	Kordell Stewart	.40
134	Jerome Bettis	.40
135	Plaxico Burress	.40
136	Bobby Shaw	.20
137	Hines Ward	.20
138	Marshall Faulk	.60
139	Kurt Warner	1.50
140	Isaac Bruce	.50
141	Torry Holt	.50
142	Justin Watson	.10
143	Az-Zahir Hakim	.20
144	Junior Seau	.30
145	Curtis Conway	.20
146	Doug Flutie	.50
147	Jeff Graham	.10
148	Freddie Jones	.30
149	Rodney Harrison	.10
150	Jeff Garcia	.50
151	Jerry Rice	1.00
152	Jonas Lewis	.10
153	Terrell Owens	.50
154	J.J. Stokes	.20
155	Garrison Hearst	.30
156	Ricky Watters	.30
157	Shaun Alexander	.50
158	Matt Hasselbeck	.50
159	Brock Huard	.30
160	Darrell Jackson	.50
161	Itula Mili	.10
162	Warrick Dunn	.50
163	Shaun King	.40
164	Reidel Anthony	.20
165	Mike Alstott	.50
166	Jacquez Green	.20
167	Brad Johnson	.40
168	Keyshawn Johnson	.50
169	Eddie George	.60
170	Steve McNair	.50
171	Neil O'Donnell	.20
172	Derrick Mason	.40
173	Frank Wycheck	.10
174	Chris Sanders	.10
175	Jevon Kearse	.50
176	Jeff George	.30
177	Stephen Davis	.50
178	Skip Hicks	.30
179	Michael Westbrook	.30
180	Stephen Alexander	.10
181	Vinny Testaverde	.10
182	Trent Green	.20
183	Brian Griese	.30
184	Kerry Collins	.20
185	Aaron Brooks	.25
186	Jamal Lewis	.50
187	Jeff Garcia	.20
188	Warrick Dunn	.20
189	Mike Anderson	.50
190	Lamar Smith	.20
191	Daunte Culpepper	.40
192	Darren Sharper	.10
193	Marvin Harrison	.20
194	Torry Holt	.20
195	Trent Green	.20
196	Peyton Manning	.50
197	Muhsin Muhammad	.20
198	La'Roi Glover	.10
199	Brian Griese	.30
200	Darrick Vaughn	.10
201	*Bobby Newcombe*	1.00
202	*Leonard Davis*	.50
203	*Alge Crumpler*	1.00
204	*Michael Vick*	8.00
205	*Vinny Sutherland*	1.00
206	*Chris Barnes*	1.00
207	*Todd Heap*	1.00
208	*Travis Henry*	2.50
209	*Tim Hasselbeck*	1.00
210	*Nate Clements*	.50
211	*Chris Weinke*	2.00
212	*Dan Morgan*	1.00
213	*Anthony Thomas*	3.00
214	*David Terrell*	2.00
215	*Chad Johnson*	3.00
216	*Justin Smith*	1.00
217	*Rudi Johnson*	2.50
218	*T.J. Houshmandzadeh*	.50
219	*Gerard Warren*	1.00
220	*James Jackson*	1.25
221	*Quincy Morgan*	1.25
222	*Quincy Carter*	2.00
223	*Tony Dixon*	.50
224	*Kevin Kasper*	.75
225	*Willie Middlebrooks*	.75
226	*Mike McMahon*	1.25
227	*Shaun Rogers*	.50
228	*Jamal Reynolds*	.75
229	*Robert Ferguson*	1.25
230	*Reggie Wayne*	2.00
231	*Marcus Stroud*	.75
232	*Dustin McClintock*	.75
233	*Marvin "Snoop" Minnis*	1.75
234	*Chris Chambers*	3.00
235	*Josh Heupel*	1.50
236	*Travis Minor*	1.25
237	*Michael Bennett*	3.00
238	*Richard Seymour*	.75
239	*Hakim Akbar*	.50
240	*Deuce McAllister*	4.00
241	*Moran Norris*	.50
242	*Jesse Palmer*	1.00
243	*Will Allen*	.75
244	*LaMont Jordan*	1.25
245	*Santana Moss*	2.50
246	*Marques Tuiasosopo*	2.00
247	*Correll Buckhalter*	1.50
248	*Freddie Mitchell*	2.00
249	*A.J. Feeley*	2.00
250	*Dave Dickenson*	1.00
251	*Drew Brees*	3.00
252	*LaDainian Tomlinson*	4.00
253	*David Allen*	.75
254	*Andre Carter*	1.00
255	*Kevan Barlow*	2.50
256	*Josh Booty*	1.00
257	*Koren Robinson*	2.00
258	*Adam Archuleta*	1.00
259	*Rod Gardner*	2.50
260	*Sage Rosenfels*	1.25
261	*Reggie Germany, Ken-Yon Rambo*	2.00
262	*Edgerton Hartwell, Gary Baxter*	.75
263	*Aaron Schobel, Brandon Spoon*	.75
264	*John Capel, Karon Riley*	.75
265	*Billy Baber, Derrick Blaylock*	.75
266	*Jamar Fletcher, Morlon Greenwood*	1.00
267	*Andre King, Ronney Daniels*	.75
268	*Arthur Love, Jabari Holloway*	.75
269	*Jonas Jennings, Kenyatta Walker*	.50
270	*Ben Hamilton, Paul Toviessa*	.50
271	*Chris Taylor, Joey Getherall*	1.00
272	*Casey Hampton, Kendrell Bell*	.75
273	*Cedrick Wilson, Jamie Winborn*	.75
274	*Alex Bannister, Heath Evans*	1.25
275	*Damione Lewis, Ryan Pickett*	1.00
276	*Tommy Polley, Brian Allen*	.75
277	*Jamie Henderson, Reggie White*	1.00
278	*Eddie Berlin, Justin McCareins*	2.00
279	*Andre Dyson, Dan Alexander*	1.00
280	*Quentin McCord, Robert Garza*	.75
281	*Scotty Anderson, Eric Kelly, Willie Howard*	.75
282	*Bhawoh Jue, David Martin, Torrance Marshall*	1.00
283	*Stevonne Smith, Dee Brown, Jarrod Cooper*	1.00
284	*DeLawrence Grant, Derek Combs, Derrick Gibson*	1.00
285	*Carlos Polk, Tay Cody, Zeke Moreno*	.75
286	*David Rivers, Francis St. Paul, Milton Wynn*	.50
287	*Ennis Davis, Kenny Smith, Sedrick Hodge*	.50
288	*Ken Lucas, Orlando Huff, Steve Hutchinson*	.75
289	*Marcellus Rivers, Derrick Burgess, Tony Driver*	.75
290	*Darnerian McCants, Fred Smoot, Mike Cerimele*	1.00

2001 UD Vintage Franchise Players

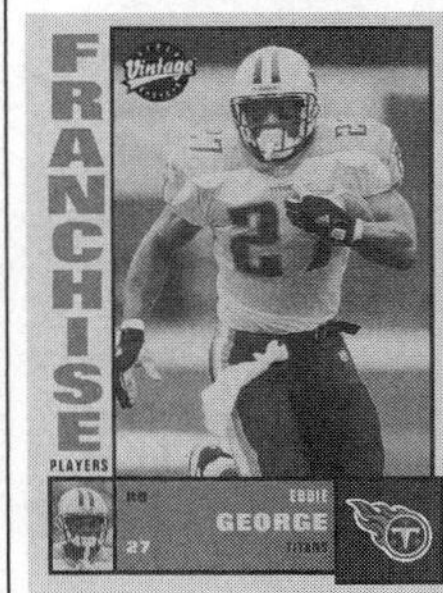

		NM/M
Complete Set (7):		18.00
Common Player:		1.50
Inserted 1:24		
FP1	Charlie Batch	1.50
FP2	Ricky Williams	3.50
FP3	Brett Favre	10.00
FP4	Emmitt Smith	6.00
FP5	Terrell Davis	5.00
FP6	Jerome Bettis	1.50
FP7	Eddie George	2.00

2001 UD Vintage Matinee Idols

		NM/M
Complete Set (10):		18.00
Common Player:		1.00
Inserted 1:18		

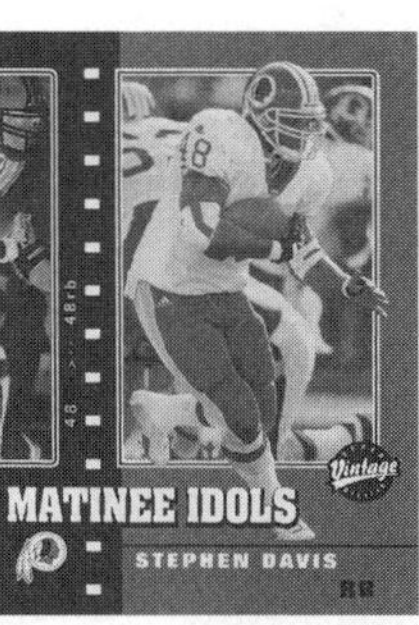

		NM/M
M1	Stephen Davis	2.00
M2	Mike Alstott	2.00
M3	Ricky Williams	3.00
M4	Ricky Watters	1.00
M5	Donovan McNabb	3.50
M6	Charlie Batch	1.00
M7	Jamal Lewis	5.00
M8	Drew Bledsoe	2.50
M9	Aaron Brooks	2.50
M10	Vinny Testaverde	1.00

2001 UD Vintage Old School Attitude

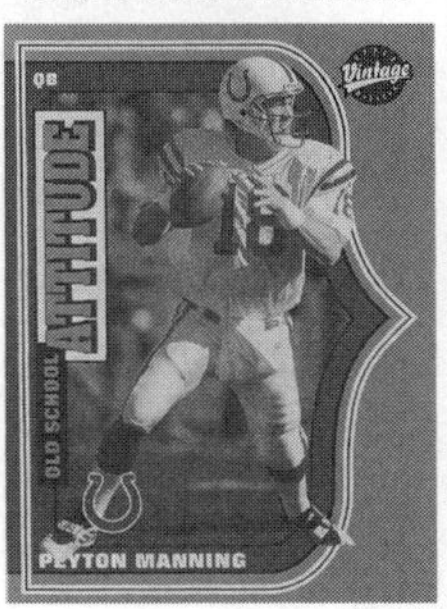

		NM/M
Complete Set (10):		18.00
Common Player:		1.00
Inserted 1:18		
OS1	Tim Brown	1.00
OS2	Peyton Manning	7.00
OS3	Jamal Anderson	1.00
OS4	Doug Flutie	2.50
OS5	Emmitt Smith	5.00
OS6	Cris Carter	1.00
OS7	Ed McCaffrey	1.00
OS8	Fred Taylor	2.50
OS9	Curtis Martin	1.00
OS10	Tim Couch	3.00

2001 UD Vintage Rookie Vintage Threads

		NM/M
Common Player:		10.00
KB-VT	Kevan Barlow	12.00
BE-VT	Michael Bennett	45.00
DR-VT	Drew Brees	50.00
RG-VT	Rod Gardner	25.00
JJ-VT	James Jackson	12.00
CJ-VT	Chad Johnson	10.00
DM-VT	Deuce McAllister	30.00
FM-VT	Freddie Mitchell	20.00
QM-VT	Quincy Morgan	12.00
SM-VT	Santana Moss	20.00
KR-VT	Koren Robinson	20.00
LT-VT	LaDainian Tomlinson	50.00
MV-VT	Michael Vick	70.00
RW-VT	Reggie Wayne	20.00
CW-VT	Chris Weinke	30.00

2001 UD Vintage Signed Vintage Threads

		NM/M
Common Player:		50.00
Production 100 Sets		
TA-SVT	Troy Aikman	100.00
MA-SVT	Mike Alstott	50.00
DB-SVT	Drew Bledsoe	60.00
MB-SVT	Mark Brunell	60.00
TC-SVT	Tim Couch	60.00
DC-SVT	Daunte Culpepper	85.00
SD-SVT	Stephen Davis	50.00
CD-SVT	Corey Dillon	50.00
JG-SVT	Jeff Garcia	50.00
PM-SVT	Peyton Manning	150.00
JM-SVT	Joe Montana	300.00
RM-SVT	Randy Moss	150.00
JR-SVT	Jerry Rice	125.00
KW-SVT	Kurt Warner	150.00

2001 UD Vintage Smashmouth

		NM/M
Complete Set (15):		12.00
Common Player:		.75
Inserted 1:12		
S1	Ray Lewis	1.50
S2	Junior Seau	.75
S3	Eddie George	2.50
S4	Jerome Bettis	1.50

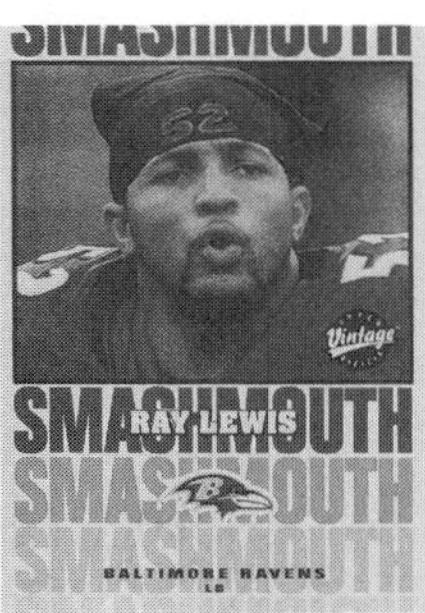

		NM/M
S5	Ricky Williams	3.00
S6	Terrell Owens	1.50
S7	Warren Sapp	.75
S8	John Lynch	.75
S9	Brian Urlacher	3.00
S10	Zach Thomas	.75
S11	Tyrone Wheatley	.75
S12	Stephen Davis	1.50
S13	Mike Alstott	1.50
S14	Fred Taylor	2.00
S15	Cris Carter	1.50

2001 UD Vintage Vintage Signatures

		NM/M
Common Player:		12.00
Inserted 1:144		
MA-VS	Mike Anderson	35.00
CB-VS	Charlie Batch	18.00
NO-VS	Jeff Blake	12.00
TB-VS	Terry Bradshaw	100.00
AB-VS	Aaron Brooks	30.00
JB-VS	Jim Brown	125.00
IB-VS	Isaac Bruce	20.00
MB-VS	Mark Brunell	20.00
TC-VS	Tim Couch	30.00
WC-VS	Wayne Chrebet	12.00
TD-VS	Terrell Davis	35.00
DI-VS	Trent Dilfer	18.00
CD-VS	Corey Dillon	18.00
DF-VS	Doug Flutie	20.00
MF-VS	Marshall Faulk	30.00
TG-VS	Tony Gonzalez	20.00
PH-VS	Paul Hornung	30.00
EJ-VS	Edgerrin James	30.00
PM-VS	Peyton Manning	60.00
JN-VS	Joe Namath	175.00
JR-VS	John Riggins	175.00
MR-VS	Marcus Robinson	15.00
JS-VS	Junior Seau	20.00
VT-TS	Vinny Testaverde	12.00

2001 UD Vintage Vintage Threads

		NM/M
Common Player:		10.00
Inserted 1:144		
TA-VT	Troy Aikman	30.00
MB-VT	Mark Brunell	20.00
RD-VT	Ron Dayne	20.00
CD-VT	Corey Dillon	12.00
BF-VT	Brett Favre	50.00
JG-VT	Jeff Garcia	20.00
IH-VT	Ike Hilliard	10.00
RL-VT	Ray Lewis	20.00
RM-VT	Randy Moss	40.00
JR-VT	Jerry Rice	30.00
WS-VT	Warren Sapp	12.00
AS-VT	Akili Smith	10.00
ZT-VT	Zach Thomas	20.00
KW-VT	Kurt Warner	40.00
PW-VT	Peter Warrick	20.00

2001 UD Vintage Vintage Threads Combos

		NM/M
Common Player:		50.00
Production 50 Sets		
AM-VTC	Troy Aikman, Cade McNown	60.00
BF-VTC	Mark Brunell, Brett Favre	100.00
DB-VTC	Ron Dayne, Michael Bennett	85.00
FM-VTC	Marshall Faulk, Deuce McAllister	50.00
MJ-VTC	Peyton Manning, Edgerrin James	125.00

2001 Upper Deck

		NM/M
Complete Set (280):		325.00
Common Player:		.15
Minor Stars:		.30
Common Rookie:		1.50
Inserted 1:4		
Pack (8):		5.00
Wax Box (24):		85.00
1	Jake Plummer	.50
2	David Boston	.50
3	Thomas Jones	.15
4	Frank Sanders	.15
5	Eric Zeier	.15
6	Jamal Anderson	.50
7	Chris Chandler	.15
8	Shawn Jefferson	.15
9	Darrick Vaughn	.15
10	Terance Mathis	.15
11	Jamal Lewis	1.50
12	Shannon Sharpe	.15
13	Elvis Grbac	.15
14	Ray Lewis	.50
15	Qadry Ismail	.15
16	Chris Redman	.15
17	Rob Johnson	.50
18	Eric Moulds	.15
19	Sammy Morris	.15
20	Shawn Bryson	.15
21	Jeremy McDaniel	.15
22	Muhsin Muhammad	.15
23	Brad Hoover	.50
24	Tim Biakabutuka	.15
25	Steve Beuerlein	.15
26	Jeff Lewis	.15
27	Wesley Walls	.15
28	Cade McNown	.50
29	James Allen	.15
30	Marcus Robinson	.50
31	Brian Urlacher	1.25
32	Bobby Engram	.15
33	Peter Warrick	1.25
34	Corey Dillon	.50
35	Akili Smith	.50
36	Danny Farmer	.50
37	Ron Dugans	.15
38	Jon Kitna	.15
39	Tim Couch	.75
40	Kevin Johnson	.50
41	Travis Prentice	.15
42	Spergon Wynn	.15
43	Errict Rhett	.15
44	Dennis Northcutt	.15
45	Courtney Brown	.15
46	Tony Banks	.15
47	Emmitt Smith	1.75
48	Joey Galloway	.50
49	Raghib Ismail	.15
50	Randall Cunningham	.30
51	James McKnight	.15
52	Terrell Davis	1.50
53	Mike Anderson	1.50
54	Brian Griese	.75
55	Rod Smith	.15
56	Ed McCaffrey	.50
57	Eddie Kennison	.15
58	Olandis Gary	.15
59	Charlie Batch	.50
60	Germane Crowell	.15
61	James O. Stewart	.15
62	Johnnie Morton	.15
63	Brett Favre	2.50
64	Antonio Freeman	.50
65	Dorsey Levens	.15
66	Ahman Green	.15
67	Bill Schroeder	.15
68	Peyton Manning	2.00
69	Edgerrin James	1.75
70	Marvin Harrison	.50
71	Jerome Pathon	.15
72	Ken Dilger	.15
73	Mark Brunell	.75
74	Fred Taylor	.75
75	Jimmy Smith	.15
76	Keenan McCardell	.15
77	R. Jay Soward	.15
78	Todd Collins	.15
79	Tony Gonzalez	.15
80	Derrick Alexander	.15
81	Tony Richardson	.15
82	Sylvester Morris	.15
83	Oronde Gadsden	.15
84	Lamar Smith	.15
85	Jay Fiedler	.50
86	Jason Taylor	.15
87	Ray Lucas	.15
88	O.J. McDuffie	.15
89	Randy Moss	2.00
90	Cris Carter	.50
91	Daunte Culpepper	1.25
92	Moe Williams	.15
93	Troy Walters	.15
94	Drew Bledsoe	.75
95	Terry Glenn	.15
96	Kevin Faulk	.15
97	J.R. Redmond	.15
98	Troy Brown	.15
99	Ricky Williams	1.00
100	Jeff Blake	.15
101	Joe Horn	.15
102	Albert Connell	.15
103	Aaron Brooks	.75
104	Chad Morton	.15
105	Kerry Collins	.15
106	Amani Toomer	.15
107	Ron Dayne	1.25
108	Tiki Barber	.15
109	Ike Hilliard	.15
110	Ron Dixon	.15
111	Jason Sehorn	.15
112	Vinny Testaverde	.15
113	Wayne Chrebet	.15
114	Curtis Martin	.50
115	Dedric Ward	.15
116	Laveranues Coles	.50
117	Windrell Hayes	.15
118	Tim Brown	.50
119	Rich Gannon	.15
120	Tyrone Wheatley	.15

121 Charlie Garner .15
122 Andre Rison .15
123 Charles Woodson .15
124 Trace Armstrong .15
125 Duce Staley .50
126 Donovan McNabb 1.00
127 Darnell Autry .15
128 Charles Johnson .15
129 Torrance Small .15
130 Kordell Stewart .50
131 Jerome Bettis .50
132 Plaxico Burress .50
133 Bobby Shaw .15
134 Troy Edwards .15
135 Marshall Faulk .75
136 Kurt Warner 2.00
137 Isaac Bruce .50
138 Torry Holt .50
139 Trent Green .15
140 Az-Zahir Hakim .15
141 Junior Seau .15
142 Curtis Conway .15
143 Doug Flutie .75
144 Jeff Graham .15
145 Freddie Jones .15
146 Marcellus Wiley .15
147 Jeff Garcia .50
148 Jerry Rice 1.50
149 Fred Beasley .15
150 Terrell Owens .50
151 J.J. Stokes .15
152 Garrison Hearst .15
153 Ricky Watters .15
154 Shaun Alexander .75
155 Matt Hasselbeck .15
156 Brock Huard .15
157 Darrell Jackson .50
158 John Randle .15
159 Warrick Dunn .50
160 Shaun King .30
161 Ryan Leaf .50
162 Mike Alstott .50
163 Jacquez Green .15
164 Brad Johnson .50
165 Keyshawn Johnson .50
166 Eddie George .75
167 Steve McNair .50
168 Neil O'Donnell .15
169 Derrick Mason .15
170 Frank Wycheck .15
171 Kevin Dyson .15
172 Jevon Kearse .30
173 Jeff George .15
174 Stephen Davis .30
175 Larry Centers .15
176 Michael Westbrook .15
177 Stephen Alexander .15
178 Ron Dayne 1.25
179 Donovan McNabb 1.00
180 Jimmy Smith .15
181 *Adam Archuleta* 3.00
182 *A.J. Feeley* 1.50
183 *Alex Bannister* 4.00
184 *Alge Crumpler* 3.00
185 *Andre Carter* 3.00
186 *Andre Dyson* 1.50
187 *Anthony Thomas* 10.00
188 *Arthur Love* 1.50
189 *Bobby Newcombe* 3.00
190 *Brandon Spoon* 3.00
191 *Carlos Polk* 1.50
192 *Casey Hampton* 1.50
193 *Cedrick Wilson* 3.00
194 *Chad Johnson* 12.00
195 *Chris Chambers* 12.00
196 *Chris Taylor* 3.00
197 *Chris Weinke* 8.00
198 *Correll Buckhalter* 4.00
199 *Damione Lewis* 3.00
200 *Dan Alexander* 3.00
201 *Dan Morgan* 4.00
202 *Willie Middlebrooks* 1.50
203 *David Terrell* 8.00
204 *Derrick Gibson* 1.50
205 *Deuce McAllister* 15.00
206 *Drew Brees* 12.00
207 *Edgerton Hartwell* 1.50
208 *Fred Smoot* 3.00
209 *Freddie Mitchell* 8.00
210 *Gary Baxter* 1.50
211 *Gerard Warren* 3.00
212 *Hakim Akbar* 1.50
213 *Heath Evans* 1.50
214 *Jabari Holloway* 1.50
215 *Jamal Reynolds* 3.00
216 *Jamar Fletcher* 3.00
217 *James Jackson* 5.00
218 *Jamie Winborn* 1.50
219 *Jesse Palmer* 4.00
220 *Josh Booty* 4.00
221 *Josh Heupel* 8.00
222 *Justin Smith* 4.00
223 *Karon Riley* 1.50
224 *Ken Lucas* 1.50
225 *Kenyatta Walker* 1.50
226 *Ken-Yon Rambo* 3.00
227 *Kevan Barlow* 10.00
228 *Kevin Kasper* 4.00
229 *Koren Robinson* 8.00
230 *LaDainian Tomlinson* 15.00
231 *LaMont Jordan* 5.00
232 *Leonard Davis* 1.50
233 *Marcus Stroud* 3.00
234 *Marques Tuiasosopo* 8.00
235 *Marvin "Snoop" Minnis* 6.00
236 *Michael Bennett* 12.00
237 *Michael Stone* 1.50
238 *Mike McMahon* 5.00
239 *Michael Vick* 30.00
240 *Moran Norris* 1.50
241 *Morlon Greenwood* 1.50
242 *Nate Clements* 3.00
243 *Orlando Huff* 1.50
244 *Quincy Morgan* 6.00
245 *Reggie Wayne* 10.00
246 *Richard Seymour* 3.00
247 *Robert Ferguson* 6.00
248 *Rod Gardner* 10.00
249 *Rudi Johnson* 10.00
250 *Sage Rosenfels* 5.00
251 *Santana Moss* 10.00
252 *Scotty Anderson* 1.50
253 *Sedrick Hodge* 1.30
254 *Shaun Rogers* 1.30
255 *Steve Hutchinson* 3.00
256 *T.J. Houshmandzadeh* 3.00
257 *Tay Cody* 1.50
258 *George Layne* 1.50
259 *Todd Heap* 4.00
260 *Tommy Polley* 1.50
261 *Tony Dixon* 1.50
262 *Brian Allen* 1.50
263 *Torrance Marshall* 3.00
264 *Travis Henry* 10.00
265 *Travis Minor* 8.00
266 *Vinny Sutherland* 3.00
267 *Will Allen* 3.00
268 *Derrick Blaylock* 1.50
269 *Zeke Moreno* 1.50
270 *Chris Barnes* 1.50
271 Dee Brown 3.00
272 *Reggie White* 4.00
273 *Derek Combs* 3.00
274 *Steve Smith* 10.00
275 *Milton Wynn* 3.00
276 *Justin McCareins* 10.00
277 *Darnerian McCants* 3.00
278 *Eddie Berlin* 6.00
279 *Francis St. Paul* 3.00
280 *Quincy Carter* 8.00

2001 Upper Deck Gold

Gold Stars: 5X-10X
Production 100 Sets
Gold Rookies: 2X-4X
Production 50 Sets

2001 Upper Deck Championship Threads

NM/M
Common Player: 10.00
Inserted 1:144
CT-IB Isaac Bruce 15.00
CT-TD Terrell Davis 30.00
CT-DI Trent Dilfer 15.00
CT-MF Marshall Faulk 25.00
CT-BF Brett Favre 60.00
CT-AF Antonio Freeman 15.00
CT-TH Torry Holt 15.00
CT-DL Dorsey Levens 15.00
CT-JL Jamal Lewis 35.00
CT-RL Ray Lewis 20.00
CT-EM Ed McCaffrey 15.00
CT-JR Jerry Rice 40.00
CT-SS Shannon Sharpe 10.00
CT-RS Rod Smith 10.00
CT-KW Kurt Warner 50.00

2001 Upper Deck Classic Drafts-Jersey

NM/M
Common Player: 20.00
Inserted 1:288
DB-CD Drew Bledsoe 35.00
MB-CD Mark Brunell 25.00
TC-CD Tim Couch 30.00
DC-CD Daunte Culpepper 50.00
JE-CD John Elway 100.00
BG-CD Brian Griese 30.00
KE-CD Jevon Kearse 20.00
JK-CD Jim Kelly 60.00
DM-CD Dan Marino 100.00
FT-CD Fred Taylor 25.00

2001 Upper Deck Constant Threat

NM/M
Complete Set (10): 12.00
Common Player: 2.00
Inserted 1:36
CT1 Aaron Brooks 3.00
CT2 Charlie Batch 2.00
CT3 Donovan McNabb 3.50
CT4 Mark Brunell 3.00
CT5 Akili Smith 2.00
CT6 Ray Lucas 1.00
CT7 Jake Plummer 2.00
CT8 Steve McNair 2.00
CT9 Trent Green 1.00
CT10 Doug Flutie 2.50

2001 Upper Deck Game Jersey Autographs

NM/M
Common Player: 40.00
Inserted 1:288
MA-AJ Mike Alstott 40.00
IB-AJ Isaac Bruce 40.00
DC-AJ Daunte Culpepper 125.00
JG-AJ Jeff Garcia 50.00
BJ-AJ Brad Johnson 40.00
JL-AJ Jamal Lewis 85.00
PM-AJ Peyton Manning 150.00
RM-AJ Randy Moss 150.00
JP-AJ Jake Plummer 40.00

2001 Upper Deck Power Surge

NM/M
Complete Set (10): 20.00
Common Player: 2.00
Inserted 1:36
PS1 Eddie George 2.50
PS2 Cris Carter 2.00
PS3 Curtis Martin 2.00
PS4 Jerry Rice 5.00
PS5 Jamal Anderson 2.00
PS6 Keyshawn Johnson 2.00
PS7 Ricky Williams 3.00
PS8 Randy Moss 7.00
PS9 Marvin Harrison 2.00
PS10 Corey Dillon 2.00

2001 Upper Deck Proving Ground

NM/M
Complete Set (20): 15.00
Common Player: .50
Inserted 1:9
PG1 Mike Anderson 2.50
PG2 Tim Couch 1.75
PG3 Donovan McNabb 2.00
PG4 Aaron Brooks 1.50
PG5 Trent Dilfer .50
PG6 Brian Griese 1.50
PG7 Kevin Johnson 1.00
PG8 Ahman Green .50
PG9 Sylvester Morris .50
PG10 Peter Warrick 2.00
PG11 Tiki Barber .50
PG12 Torry Holt 1.25
PG13 Trent Green .50
PG14 Ed McCaffrey 1.25
PG15 Joe Horn .50
PG16 Muhsin Muhammad .50
PG17 Kerry Collins .50
PG18 Edgerrin James 4.00
PG19 Brad Hoover 1.25
PG20 Ron Dayne 2.00

2001 Upper Deck Rookie Threads

NM/M
Common Player: 20.00
Inserted 1:144
RT-KB Kevan Barlow 20.00
RT-MB Michael Bennett 50.00
RT-DB Drew Brees 60.00
RT-CC Chris Chambers 20.00
RT-RF Robert Ferguson 20.00
RT-RG Rod Gardner 30.00
RT-TH Travis Henry 20.00
RT-CJ Chad Johnson 102 25.00
RT-DM Deuce McAllister 50.00
RT-FM Freddie Mitchell 25.00
RT-KR Koren Robinson 30.00
RT-LT LaDainian Tomlinson 50 100.00
RT-MV Michael Vick 100.00
RT-RW Reggie Wayne 25.00
RT-CW Chris Weinke 40.00

2001 Upper Deck Running Wild

NM/M
Complete Set (15): 25.00
Common Player: 1.00
Inserted 1:24
RW1 Eddie George 2.50
RW2 Corey Dillon 2.00
RW3 Edgerrin James 6.00
RW4 Charlie Garner 1.00
RW5 Jamal Anderson 2.00
RW6 Emmitt Smith 6.00
RW7 Terrell Davis 5.00
RW8 Mike Anderson 5.00
RW9 James O. Stewart 1.00
RW10 Ricky Watters 1.00
RW11 Lamar Smith 1.00
RW12 Curtis Martin 2.00
RW13 Ricky Williams 3.00
RW14 Stephen Davis 2.00
RW15 Jerome Bettis 2.00

2001 Upper Deck Starstruck

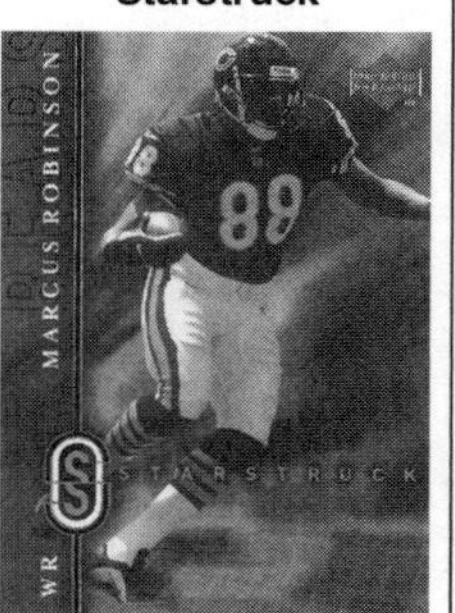

NM/M
Complete Set (15): 20.00
Common Player: 1.00
Inserted 1:24
S1 Curtis Martin 2.00
S2 Keyshawn Johnson 2.00
S3 Tim Brown 2.00
S4 Terrell Owens 2.00
S5 Duce Staley 2.00
S6 Rich Gannon 1.00
S7 Mike Anderson 5.00
S8 Stephen Davis 2.00
S9 Emmitt Smith 6.00
S10 Steve McNair 2.00
S11 Ricky Williams 3.00
S12 Marcus Robinson 2.00
S13 Vinny Testaverde 1.00
S14 Rod Smith 1.00
S15 Drew Bledsoe 2.50

2001 Upper Deck Teammates-Jersey

NM/M
Common Player: 20.00
Inserted 1:144
CM-T Daunte Culpepper, Randy Moss 85.00
KJ-T Shaun King, Keyshawn Johnson 20.00
MJ-T Peyton Manning, Edgerrin James 100.00
MH-T Peyton Manning, Marvin Harrison 75.00
FS-T Brett Favre, Dorsey Levens 60.00
AS-T Troy Aikman, Emmitt Smith 125.00
WF-T Kurt Warner, Marshall Faulk 80.00
BM-T Charlie Batch, Herman Moore 25.00
GO-T Jeff Garcia, Terrell Owens 25.00
DB-T Ron Dayne, Tiki Barber 30.00

2001 Upper Deck UD Lettermen Patches

NM/M
Complete Set (9):
Common Player: 75.00
MB-LP Michael Bennett 125.00
DB-LP Drew Brees 150.00
DM-LP Deuce McAllister 125.00
FM-LP Freddie Mitchell 75.00
AT-LP Anthony Thomas 225.00
LT-LP LaDainian Tomlinson 125.00
MT-LP Marques Tuiasosopo 75.00
MV-LP Michael Vick 225.00
CW-LP Chris Weinke 125.00

2001 Upper Deck UD Premium Patch Cards

NM/M
Common Player: 25.00
TA-PP Troy Aikman 75.00
AF-PP Drew Bledsoe 50.00
IB-PP Isaac Bruce 40.00
MB-PP Mark Brunell 50.00
TC-PP Tim Couch 75.00
TDa-PP Terrell Davis 50.00
MF-PP Marshall Faulk 100.00
BF-PP Brett Favre 225.00
EG-PP Eddie George 75.00
BG-PP Brian Griese 50.00
TH-PP Torry Holt 25.00
DL-PP Dorsey Levens 25.00
JL-PP Jamal Lewis 100.00
EM-PP Ed McCaffrey 25.00
SM-PP Steve McNair 25.00
JR-PP Jerry Rice 125.00
SS-PP Shannon Sharpe 25.00
RS-PP Rod Smith 25.00
FT-PP Fred Taylor 40.00
KW-PP Kurt Warner 125.00

2001 Upper Deck E-card

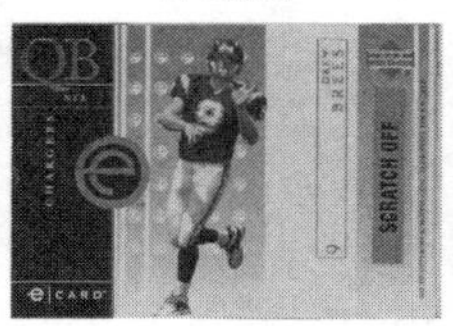

NM/M
Complete Set (6): 30.00
Common Player: 4.00
Inserted 1:12
E-MB Michael Bennett 7.00
E-DB Drew Brees 10.00
E-FM Freddie Mitchell 4.00
E-LT LaDainian Tomlinson 10.00
E-MV Michael Vick 12.00
E-CW Chris Weinke 5.00

2001 Upper Deck E-card-Autographed

NM/M
EA-MB Michael Bennett 75.00
EA-DB Drew Brees 75.00
EA-FM Freddie Mitchell 50.00
EA-LT LaDainian Tomlinson 75.00
EA-MV Michael Vick 75.00
EA-CW Chris Weinke 50.00

2001 Upper Deck E-card-Graded Rookie Watch

NM/M
EA-MB Michael Bennett 40.00
EA-DB Drew Brees 40.00
EA-FM Freddie Mitchell 30.00
EA-LT LaDainian Tomlinson 40.00
EA-MV Michael Vick 40.00
EA-CW Chris Weinke 30.00

2001 Upper Deck E-card-Jersey

NM/M
EJ-MB Michael Bennett 50.00
EJ-DB Drew Brees 50.00
EJ-FM Freddie Mitchell 40.00
EJ-LT LaDainian Tomlinson 60.00
EJ-MV Michael Vick 50.00
EJ-CW Chris Weinke 40.00

2001 Upper Deck Legends

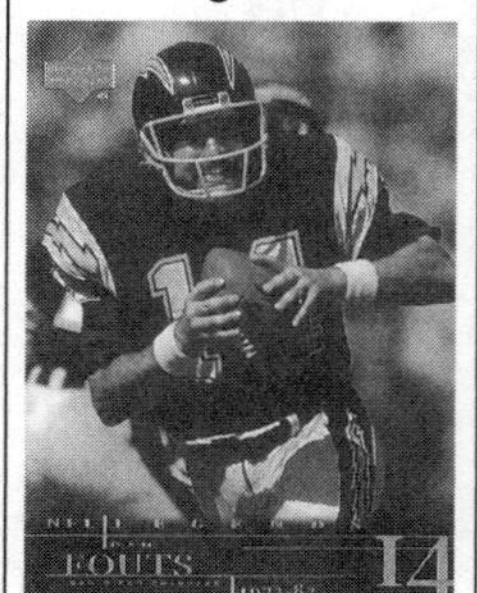

NM/M
Complete Set (180): 275.00
Common Player: .25
Minor Stars: .50
Common Rookie: 2.50
Production 750 Sets
Pack (5): 5.50
Wax Box (18): 70.00
1 Jake Plummer .50
2 Jamal Anderson .50
3 Ray Lewis .50
4 Johnny Unitas 1.50
5 Jamal Lewis 1.50
6 Andre Reed .50
7 Jim Kelly .75
8 Thurman Thomas .50
9 Rob Johnson .25
10 Brian Urlacher 1.50
11 Dick Butkus 1.00
12 Gale Sayers 1.25
13 James Allen .25
14 Corey Dillon .50
15 Jim Brown 2.00
16 Tim Couch 1.00
17 Joey Galloway .50
18 Emmitt Smith 2.00
19 Randy White .25
20 Roger Staubach 2.00
21 Troy Aikman 1.50
22 Tony Dorsett .75
23 Brian Griese 1.00
24 Floyd Little .25
25 John Elway 3.00
26 Mike Anderson 1.25
27 Terrell Davis 1.50
28 Barry Sanders 2.50
29 Charlie Batch .25
30 Bart Starr 2.00
31 Paul Hornung 1.00
32 Reggie White .75
33 Warren Moon .50
34 Edgerrin James 2.00
35 Peyton Manning 2.50
36 Mark Brunell .50
37 Tony Gonzalez .50
38 Eric Dickerson .75
39 Jack Youngblood .25
40 Jay Fiedler .50
41 Lamar Smith .25
42 Dan Marino 3.00
43 Oronde Gadsden .25
44 Cris Carter .75
45 Fran Tarkenton 1.00
46 Daunte Culpepper 1.50
47 Randy Moss 2.50
48 Robert Smith .25
49 Drew Bledsoe 1.00
50 Archie Manning .50
51 Jeff Blake .25
52 Ricky Williams 1.25
53 Kerry Collins .50
54 Ron Dayne .50
55 Lawrence Taylor .75
56 Wayne Chrebet .50
57 Vinny Testaverde .50
58 Joe Namath 2.00
59 Jim Plunkett .50
60 George Blanda .75
61 Tim Brown .75
62 Jerry Rice 2.00
63 Ken Stabler .50
64 Marcus Allen .75
65 Donovan McNabb 1.50
66 Harold Carmichael .50
67 Franco Harris .75
68 Jerome Bettis .50
69 Terry Bradshaw 2.00
70 Doug Flutie 1.00
71 Lance Alworth .50
72 Junior Seau .50
73 Kellen Winslow .75
74 Dan Fouts .75
75 Joe Montana 5.00
76 Terrell Owens .75
77 Jeff Garcia 1.00
78 Steve Young 1.00
79 Matt Hasselbeck .25
80 Kurt Warner 2.50
81 Marshall Faulk 1.00
82 Brad Johnson .50
83 Eddie George 1.00
84 Charlie Taylor .50
85 Stephen Davis .50
86 Jeff George .25
87 John Riggins .75
88 Joe Theismann .75
89 Michael Westbrook .50
90 Sonny Jurgensen .75
91 *Andre Carter* 3.00
92 *Cedrick Wilson* 3.00
93 *Kevan Barlow* 10.00
94 *Anthony Thomas* 30.00
95 *David Terrell* 20.00
96 *Chad Johnson* 10.00
97 *Justin Smith* 5.00
98 *Rudi Johnson* 10.00
99 *T.J. Houshmandzadeh* 3.00
100 *Brandon Spoon* 3.00
101 *Nate Clements* 3.00
102 *Travis Henry* 10.00
103 *Kevin Kasper* 8.00
104 *Willie Middlebrooks* 3.00
105 *Gerard Warren* 5.00
106 *James Jackson* 8.00
107 *Quincy Morgan* 8.00
108 *Bobby Newcombe* 5.00
109 *Arnold Jackson* 3.00
110 *Carlos Polk* 3.00
111 *Drew Brees* 25.00
112 *LaDainian Tomlinson* 30.00
113 *Tay Cody* 3.00
114 *Zeke Moreno* 3.00
115 *Marvin "Snoop" Minnis* 10.00
116 *George Layne* 3.00
117 *Derrick Blaylock* 3.00
118 *Reggie Wayne* 12.00
119 *Tony Dixon* 3.00
120 *Quincy Carter* 15.00

121 *Chris Chambers* 15.00
122 *Jamar Fletcher* 3.00
123 *Josh Heupel* 8.00
124 *Travis Minor* 8.00
125 *A.J. Feeley* 6.00
126 *Correll Buckhalter* 10.00
127 *Freddie Mitchell* 12.00
128 *Alge Crumpler* 5.00
129 *Michael Vick* 40.00
130 *Vinny Sutherland* 5.00
131 *Marcus Stroud* 3.00
132 *Mike McMahon* 12.00
133 *Scotty Anderson* 3.00
134 *Shaun Rogers* 3.00
135 *Jesse Palmer* 8.00
136 *Will Allen* 3.00
137 *Lamont Jordon* 6.00
138 *Santana Moss* 12.00
139 *Reggie White* 3.00
140 *Jamal Reynolds* 3.00
141 *Robert Ferguson* 5.00
142 *Torrance Marshall* 3.00
143 *Chris Weinke* 12.00
144 *Dan Morgan* 3.00
145 *Steve Smith* 5.00
146 *Dee Brown* 3.00
147 *Arther Love* 3.00
148 *Hakim Akbar* 3.00
149 *Jabari Holloway* 3.00
150 *Derek Combs* 3.00
151 *Derrick Gibson* 3.00
152 *Ken-Yon Rambo* 5.00
153 *Marques Tuiasosopo* 12.00
154 *Adam Archuleta* 5.00
155 *Tommy Polley* 6.00
156 *Brian Allen* 3.00
157 *Milton Wynn* 3.00
158 *Francis St. Paul* 3.00
159 *Edgerton Hartwell* 3.00
160 *Gary Baxter* 3.00
161 *Todd Heap* 5.00
162 *Chris Barnes* 3.00
163 *Fred Smoot* 3.00
164 *Rob Gardner* 12.00
165 *Sage Rosenfels* 8.00
166 *Darnerian McCants* 3.00
167 *Deuce McAllister* 15.00
168 *Moran Norris* 3.00
169 *Sedrick Hodge* 5.00
170 *Alex Bannister* 5.00
171 *Heath Evans* 3.00
172 *Josh Booty* 5.00
173 *Ken Lucas* 3.00
174 *Koren Robinson* 8.00
175 *Chris Taylor* 3.00
176 *Andre Dyson* 3.00
177 *Dan Alexander* 5.00
178 *Justin McCareins* 3.00
179 *Eddie Berlin* 3.00
180 *Michael Bennett* 15.00

2001 Upper Deck Legends Legendary Artwork

NM/M
Complete Set (15): 70.00
Common Player: 3.00
Inserted 1:18
LA1 Jim Thorpe 4.00
LA2 Jerry Rice 6.00
LA3 Bart Starr 6.00
LA4 Fran Tarkenton 3.00
LA5 Barry Sanders 6.00
LA6 Jim Brown 6.00
LA7 Joe Montana 12.00
LA8 Joe Namath 7.00
LA9 John Elway 8.00
LA10 Johnny Unitas 6.00
LA11 Roger Staubach 5.00
LA12 Terry Bradshaw 5.00
LA13 Walter Payton 12.00
LA14 Dan Marino 8.00
LA15 Dick Butkus 3.00

2001 Upper Deck Legends Legendary Autographs

NM/M
Common Player: 10.00
Inserted 1:54
Some are SP's runs of 50 or 100
TA Troy Aikman 50.00
MA Marcus Allen 25.00
LA Lance Alworth 50.00
JB Jeff Blake 10.00
TB Terry Bradshaw 50.00
JB Jim Brown 200.00
TB Tim Brown 25.00
DB Dick Butkus 50.00
HC Harold Carmichael 10.00
WC Wayne Chrebet 10.00
DC Daunte Culpepper 75.00
ED Eric Dickerson 25.00
TD Tony Dorsett 25.00
JE John Elway 75.00
DF Doug Flutie 50.00
DF Dan Fouts 25.00
JG Jeff Garcia 10.00
JG Jeff George 10.00
FH Franco Harris 50.00
PH Paul Hornung 50.00
EJ Ed Jones 10.00
JK Jim Kelly 50.00
AM Archie Manning 25.00
PM Peyton Manning 50.00
DM Dan Marino 100.00
CM Cade McNown 25.00
JM Joe Montana 125.00
WM Warren Moon 25.00
RM Randy Moss 125.00
JN Joe Namath 75.00
JP Jake Plummer 25.00
JP Jim Plunkett 10.00
AR Andre Reed 10.00
JR John Riggins 75.00
BS Barry Sanders 100.00
GS Gale Sayers 50.00
KS Ken Stabler 50.00
BS Bart Starr 100.00
RS Roger Staubach 50.00
FT Fran Tarkenton 50.00
CT Charlie Taylor 10.00
LT Lawrence Taylor 75.00
VT Vinny Testaverde 50.00
JT Joe Theismann 10.00
TT Thurman Thomas 25.00
JU Johnny Unitas 75.00
BU Brian Urlacher 50.00
KW Kurt Warner 50.00
RW Ricky Williams 75.00
KW Kellen Winslow 10.00
SY Steve Young 100.00
JY Jack Youngblood 10.00

2001 Upper Deck Legends Legendary Cuts

LC-RB Red Badgro
LC-WE Weeb Ewbank 10
LC-TF Tom Fears 6
LC-RG Harold "Red" Grange 10
LC-GH George Halas
LC-TL Tom Landry 8
LC-BL Bobby Layne 10
LC-VL Vince Lombardi 5
LC-SL Sid Luckman 9
LC-MM Marion Motley 6
LC-BN Bronko Nagurski 28
LC-EN Ernie Nevers 63
LC-RN Ray Nitschke 10
LC-PR Pete Rozelle 3
LC-JT Jim Thorpe 1
LC-ET Emlen Tunnell 22
LC-VB Norm Van Brocklin 3

2001 Upper Deck Legends Memorable Materials

NM/M
Common Player: 12.00
Inserted 1:36
MM-CB Charlie Batch 12.00
MM-DB Drew Bledsoe 15.00
MM-IB Isaac Bruce 15.00
MM-MB Mark Brunell 12.00
MM-ED Eric Dickerson/150 25.00
MM-JE John Elway 40.00
MM-MF Marshall Faulk 30.00
MM-DF Doug Flutie 20.00
MM-DM Dan Marino 60.00
MM-SM Steve McNair 12.00
MM-WP Walter Payton/150 125.00
MM-BS Barry Sanders 30.00

2001 Upper Deck Legends Past Patterns

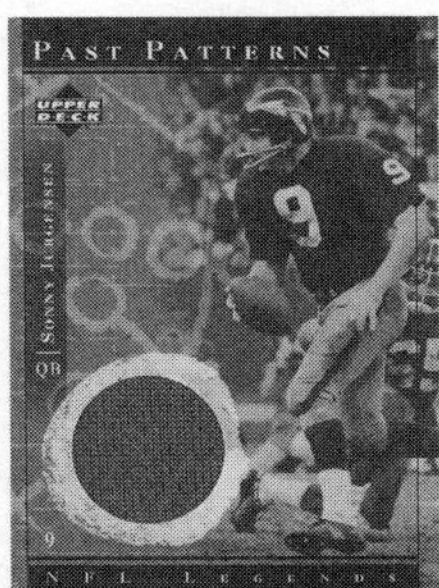

NM/M
Common Player: 10.00
Inserted 1:18
PP-TA Troy Aikman 25.00
PP-MA Mike Alstott 12.00
PP-GB George Blanda 15.00
PP-TB Terry Bradshaw/150 60.00
PP-CC Cris Carter 12.00
PP-KC Kerry Collins 12.00
PP-TC Tim Couch 15.00
PP-SD Stephen Davis 10.00
PP-WD Warrick Dunn 12.00
PP-BF Brett Favre 40.00
PP-DF Doug Flutie 20.00
PP-JG Jeff George 10.00
PP-PH Paul Hornung 25.00
PP-SJ Sonny Jurgensen 20.00
PP-JK Jim Kelly 20.00
PP-SK Shaun King 10.00
PP-AM Archie Manning 20.00
PP-PM Peyton Manning 30.00
PP-DM Dan Marino 50.00
PP-JM Joe Montana/150 100.00
PP-WM Warren Moon 15.00
PP-JN Joe Namath/150 60.00
PP-KN Ken Norton 10.00
PP-JP Jim Plunkett 15.00
PP-AR Andre Reed 12.00
PP-JR Jerry Rice 30.00
PP-JS Junior Seau 12.00
PP-SS Shannon Sharpe 15.00
PP-ES Emmitt Smith 40.00
PP-RSm Robert Smith 10.00
PP-RS Roger Staubach/95 60.00
PP-FT Fred Taylor 12.00
PP-JTa John Taylor 10.00
PP-LT Lawrence Taylor 20.00
PP-RW Reggie White 15.00
PP-RW Rod Woodson 15.00
PP-SY Steve Young 20.00

2001 Upper Deck Legends Timeless Tributes

NM/M
Common Player: 12.00
Inserted 1:6
TT-JB Jerome Bettis 12.00
TT-DG Darrell Green 15.00
TT-HM Harvey Martin 20.00
TT-JM Joe Montana 75.00
TT-KN Ken Norton Jr. 12.00
TT-WS Warren Sapp 12.00
TT-BS Bruce Smith 15.00
TT-LT Derrick Thomas 25.00
TT-TT Thurman Thomas 12.00
TT-RW Randy White 12.00

2001 Upper Deck MVP

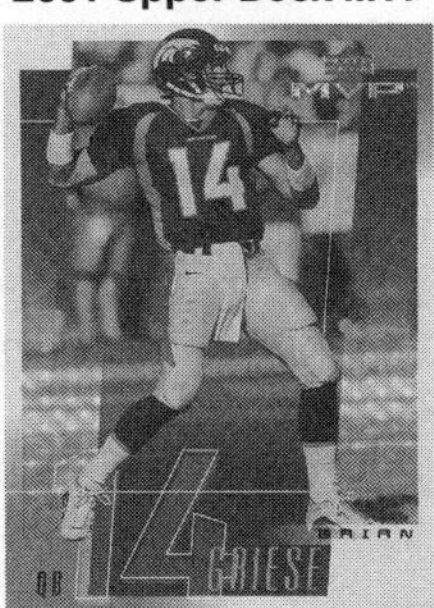

NM/M
Complete Set (330): 35.00
Common Player: .10
Minor Stars: .20
Common Rookie: .30
Pack (8): 2.00
Wax Box (24): 35.00
1 Jake Plummer .40
2 David Boston .20
3 Thomas Jones .40
4 Michael Pittman .20
5 Frank Sanders .20
6 Mar Tay Jenkins .10
7 Pat Tilman .10
8 Tywan Mitchell .10
9 Jamal Anderson .40
10 Doug Johnson .20
11 Ephraim Salaam .10
12 Chris Chandler .20
13 Shawn Jefferson .10
14 Tim Dwight .20
15 Terance Mathis .10
16 Jamal Lewis 1.25
17 Shannon Sharpe .20
18 Trent Dilfer .20
19 Ray Lewis .20
20 Qadry Ismail .10
21 Travis Taylor .40
22 Chris Redman .40
23 Priest Holmes .20
24 Rod Woodson .10
25 Jamie Sharper .10
26 Doug Flutie .50
27 Rob Johnson .20
28 Eric Moulds .40
29 Sammy Morris .20
30 Shawn Bryson .10
31 Antowain Smith .20
32 Jeremy McDaniel .10
33 Sam Cowart .10
34 Muhsin Muhammad .20
35 Brad Hoover .40
36 Tim Biakabutuka .20
37 Steve Beuerlein .20
38 Donald Hayes .20
39 Jeff Lewis .20
40 Dameyune Craig .20
41 Wesley Walls .20
42 Isaac Byrd .10
43 Cade McNown .40
44 James Allen .40
45 Marcus Robinson .40
46 Brian Urlacher .75
47 Jim Miller .10
48 Curtis Enis .20
49 Eddie Kennison .20
50 Marty Booker .10
51 Bobby Engram .10
52 Peter Warrick .75
53 Corey Dillon .40
54 Akili Smith .40
55 Danny Farmer .20
56 Brandon Bennett .10
57 Curtis Keaton .10
58 Ron Dugans .20
59 Takeo Spikes .10
60 Scott Mitchell .20
61 Tim Couch .50
62 Kevin Johnson .20
63 Travis Prentice .40
64 Spergon Wynn .10
65 Errict Rhett .10
66 David Patten .10
67 Dennis Northcutt .20
68 Aaron Shea .10
69 Courtney Brown .20
70 Troy Aikman .75
71 Emmitt Smith 1.25
72 Joey Galloway .40
73 Raghib Ismail .10
74 Randall Cunningham .20
75 Anthony Wright .10
76 James McKnight .10
77 Dexter Coakley .10
78 Terrell Davis 1.25
79 Mike Anderson 1.25
80 Brian Griese .50
81 Rod Smith .20
82 Ed McCaffrey .20
83 Olandis Gary .40
84 Trevor Pryce .10
85 John Mobley .10
86 Charlie Batch .40
87 Germane Crowell .30
88 James O. Stewart .30
89 Johnnie Morton .20
90 Herman Moore .30
91 Mario Bates .10
92 Desmond Howard .10
93 Stephen Boyd .10
94 Chris Claiborne .10
95 Kurt Schulz .10
96 Brett Favre 1.75
97 Antonio Freeman .30
98 Dorsey Levens .30
99 Ahman Green .30
100 Matt Hasselbeck .40
101 De'Mond Parker .20
102 Bill Schroeder .20
103 Bubba Franks .10
104 Donald Driver .10
105 Darren Sharper .10
106 Peyton Manning 1.25
107 Edgerrin James 1.25
108 Marvin Harrison .40
109 Jerome Pathon .10
110 Terrence Wilkins .20
111 Ken Dilger .10
112 Marcus Pollard .10
113 Brad Scioli .10
114 Mark Brunell .50
115 Fred Taylor .50
116 Jimmy Smith .30
117 Jamie Martin .10
118 Keenan McCardell .20
119 Kyle Brady .10
120 R. Jay Soward .20
121 Alvis Whitted .10
122 Brant Boyer .10
123 Elvis Grbac .30
124 Tony Gonzalez .30
125 Derrick Alexander .20
126 Tony Richardson .20
127 Frank Moreau .10
128 Sylvester Morris .40
129 Kevin Lockett .10
130 Donnie Edwards .10
131 Oronde Gadsden .20
132 Lamar Smith .40
133 Jay Fiedler .40
134 J.J. Johnson .10
135 Thurman Thomas .30
136 Leslie Shepherd .10
137 Tony Martin .10
138 O.J. McDuffie .20
139 Zach Thomas .30
140 Randy Moss 1.50
141 Bubby Brister .20
142 Cris Carter .40
143 Daunte Culpepper .75
144 Moe Williams .10
145 Troy Walters .10
146 Chris Walsh .10
147 Matthew Hatchette .10
148 Kailee Wong .10
149 Robert Griffith .10
150 Drew Bledsoe .50
151 Terry Glenn .30
152 Kevin Faulk .20
153 J.R. Redmond .30
154 Tony Carter .10
155 Patrick Pass .20
156 Troy Brown .10
157 Tony Simmons .10
158 Michael Bishop .30
159 Lawyer Milloy .10
160 Ricky Williams .60
161 Jeff Blake .20
162 Joe Horn .20
163 Aaron Brooks .40
164 La'Roi Glover .10
165 Chad Morton .10
166 Keith Mitchell .10
167 Willie Jackson .10
168 Robert Wilson .10
169 Jake Reed .20
170 Kerry Collins .30
171 Amani Toomer .20
172 Ron Dayne .75
173 Tiki Barber .30
174 Greg Comella .10
175 Ike Hilliard .20
176 Joe Jurevicius .10
177 Ron Dixon .20
178 Jason Sehorn .10
179 Michael Strahan .10
180 Vinny Testaverde .30
181 Wayne Chrebet .30
182 Curtis Martin .40
183 Richie Anderson .10
184 Dedric Ward .20
185 Laveranues Coles .40
186 Windrell Hayes .10
187 Chad Pennington .75
188 Tim Brown .30
189 Rich Gannon .30
190 Tyrone Wheatley .30
191 Napoleon Kaufman .20
192 Jon Ritchie .10
193 James Jett .10
194 Rickey Dudley .10
195 Andre Rison .20
196 Eric Allen .10
197 Charles Woodson .20
198 Duce Staley .40
199 Donovan McNabb .50
200 Darnell Autry .10
201 Chad Lewis .10
202 Charles Johnson .10
203 Torrance Small .10
204 Todd Pinkston .20
205 Brian Mitchell .10
206 Hugh Douglas .10
207 David Akers .10
208 Kordell Stewart .40
209 Jerome Bettis .40
210 Bobby Shaw .10
211 Hines Ward .30
212 Plaxico Burress .40
213 Courtney Hawkins .10
214 Troy Edwards .20
215 Earl Holmes .10
216 Richard Huntley .10
217 Marshall Faulk .50
218 Kurt Warner 1.75
219 Isaac Bruce .40
220 Torry Holt .40
221 Trent Green .30
222 Justin Watson .10
223 Trung Canidate .20
224 Az-Zahir Hakim .20
225 Ricky Proehl .10
226 Dexter McCleon .10
227 London Fletcher .10
228 Junior Seau .20
229 Curtis Conway .20
230 Rodney Harrison .10
231 Jeff Graham .10
232 Freddie Jones .20
233 Reggie Jones .20
234 Ronney Jenkins .10
235 Trevor Gaylor .10
236 Jeff Garcia .40
237 Jerry Rice 1.00
238 Charlie Garner .30
239 Terrell Owens .40
240 J.J. Stokes .20
241 Fred Beasley .10
242 Tim Rattay .30
243 Garrison Hearst .30
244 Ricky Watters .30
245 Shaun Alexander .50
246 Jon Kitna .30
247 Brock Huard .30
248 Darrell Jackson .20
249 James Williams .10
250 Sean Dawkins .10
251 John Hilliard .10
252 Warrick Dunn .30
253 Shaun King .40
254 Ryan Leaf .40
255 Mike Alstott .40
256 Jacquez Green .20
257 Reidel Anthony .20
258 Derrick Brooks .10
259 John Lynch .20
260 Warren Sapp .30
261 Eddie George .50
262 Steve McNair .40
263 Rodney Thomas .10
264 Derrick Mason .25
265 Yancey Thigpen .20
266 Frank Wycheck .10
267 Chris Sanders .10
268 Carl Pickens .20
269 Kevin Dyson .20
270 Jevon Kearse .40
271 Jeff George .30
272 Stephen Davis .40
273 Brad Johnson .30
274 Albert Connell .20
275 James Thrash .25
276 Michael Westbrook .30
277 Stephen Alexander .10
278 Deion Sanders .40
279 Champ Bailey .30
280 Todd Husak .20
281 *Dan Morgan* .30
282 *Josh Booty* .30
283 *Michael Vick* 6.00
284 *Mike McMahon* .75
285 *Reggie White* .30
286 *Chris Weinke* 1.50
287 *Drew Brees* 3.00
288 *Sage Rosenfels* .75
289 *Marques Tuiasosopo* 1.50
290 *Josh Heupel* 1.50
291 *David Rivers* .30
292 *Kevin Kasper* .30
293 *Jesse Palmer* .50
294 *LaDainian Tomlinson* 4.00
295 *Deuce McAllister* 4.00
296 *Kevan Barlow* 2.50
297 *LaMont Jordan* 1.00
298 *James Jackson* 1.00
299 *Anthony Thomas* 2.50
300 *Correll Buckhalter* .30
301 *Travis Henry* 1.50
302 *Dan Alexander* .30
303 *Travis Minor* 1.00
304 *Derrick Gibson* .50
305 *Rudi Johnson* 2.00
306 *Michael Bennett* 3.00
307 *Alge Crumpler* .30
308 *Todd Heap* .50
309 *Marvin "Snoop" Minnis* 1.00
310 *Santana Moss* 2.50
311 *Reggie Wayne* 2.00
312 *Koren Robinson* 2.00
313 *Chris Chambers* 3.00
314 *David Terrell* 1.50
315 *Rod Gardner* 2.25
316 *Quincy Morgan* 1.00
317 *Ken-Yon Rambo* .50
318 *Vinny Sutherland* .50
319 *David Allen* .30
320 *Bobby Newcombe* .50
321 *Ronney Daniels* .30
322 *T.J. Houshmandzadeh* .50
323 *Chad Johnson* 3.00
324 *Freddie Mitchell* 1.25
325 *Moran Norris* .30
326 Ron Dayne .30
327 Mike Anderson .50
328 Jamal Lewis .50
329 Brian Urlacher .40
330 Darren Howard .10

2001 Upper Deck MVP Campus Classics

NM/M
Common Player: 15.00
Multi-Color Swatches: 1.5X
Inserted 1:144
Autographs: 2.5X
Production 25 Sets
CC-TA Troy Aikman 50.00
CC-MB Michael Bennett 35.00
CC-DB Drew Brees 60.00
CC-RD Ron Dayne 35.00
CC-MF Marshall Faulk 35.00
CC-JF Jamar Fletcher 20.00
CC-KJ Keyshawn Johnson 15.00
CC-PM Peyton Manning 85.00
CC-DM Deuce McAllister 35.00
CC-CM Cade McNown 15.00
CC-FM Freddie Mitchell 25.00
CC-AT Anthony Thomas 50.00
CC-LT LaDainian Tomlinson 85.00
CC-MT Marques Tuiasosopo 20.00
CC-MV Michael Vick 85.00
CC-CW Chris Weinke 40.00

2001 Upper Deck MVP Souvenirs

NM/M
Common Player: 8.00
Inserted 1:48
Autographs: 5X
Production 25 Sets
CB-S Charlie Batch 8.00
AB-S Aaron Brooks 12.00
BW-S Aaron Brooks, Kurt Warner 35.00
DC-S Daunte Culpepper 20.00
CM-S Daunte Culpepper, Randy Moss 40.00
SD-S Stephen Davis 8.00
RD-S Ron Dayne 15.00
BF-S Brett Favre 30.00
FM-S Brett Favre, Donovan McNabb 35.00
GB-S Rich Gannon, Tim Brown 15.00
GR-S Jeff Garcia, Jerry Rice 30.00
GD-S Jeff George, Stephen Davis 10.00
EJ-S Edgerrin James 30.00
KJ-S Keyshawn Johnson 8.00
TJ-S Thomas Jones 8.00
TB-S Shaun King, Keyshawn Johnson 10.00
JL-S Jamal Lewis 25.00
PM-S Peyton Manning 30.00
MJ-S Peyton Manning, Edgerrin James 45.00
DM-S Donovan McNabb 15.00
MC-S Donovan McNabb, Daunte Culpepper 40.00
MR-S Cade McNown, Marcus Robinson 10.00
RM-S Randy Moss 30.00
RE-S J.R. Redmond 8.00
JR-S Jerry Rice 20.00
TM-S Vinny Testaverde, Curtis Martin 10.00
BU-S Brian Urlacher 18.00
KW-S Kurt Warner 25.00
WF-S Kurt Warner, Marshall Faulk 40.00
PW-S Peter Warrick 15.00

2001 Upper Deck MVP Team MVP

NM/M
Complete Set (20): 15.00
Common Player: .50
Minor Stars: 1.00
Inserted 1:6
MVP1 Brian Griese 1.25
MVP2 Rich Gannon .50
MVP3 Marshall Faulk 1.25
MVP4 Edgerrin James 6.00
MVP5 Eddie George 1.25
MVP6 Mike Anderson 3.00
MVP7 Ed McCaffrey .50
MVP8 Marvin Harrison 1.00
MVP9 Isaac Bruce 1.00
MVP10 Eric Moulds 1.00
MVP11 Tony Gonzalez .50
MVP12 Mike Alstott 1.00
MVP13 Ray Lewis .50
MVP14 Junior Seau 1.00
MVP15 Warren Sapp 1.00
MVP16 La'Roi Glover .50
MVP17 Derrick Brooks .50
MVP18 Charles Woodson 1.00
MVP19 Champ Bailey 1.00
MVP20 John Lynch .50

2001 Upper Deck MVP Top 10 Performers

NM/M
Complete Set (10): 18.00
Common Player: .75

NM/M
Minor Stars: 1.50
Inserted 1:13
TOP1 Mike Anderson 5.00
TOP2 Vinny Testaverde 1.50
TOP3 Terrell Owens 1.50
TOP4 Aaron Brooks 1.50
TOP5 Jamal Lewis 6.00
TOP6 Fred Taylor 2.50
TOP7 Randy Moss 6.00
TOP8 Ricky Williams 3.00
TOP9 Jason Sehorn .75
TOP10 Shannon Sharpe .75

2001 Upper Deck NFL Rookie FX

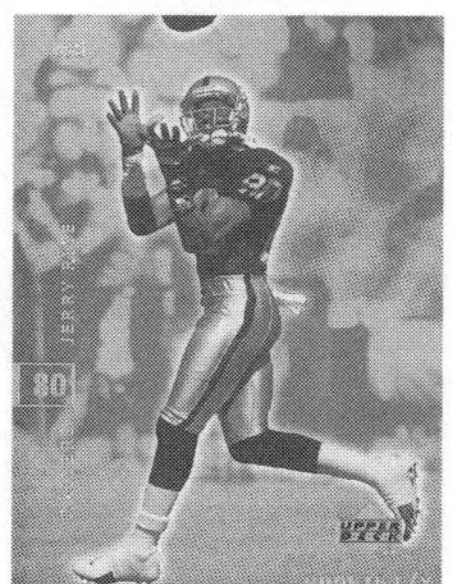

NM/M
Complete Set (225): 35.00
Common Player: .20
Minor Stars: .40
Common Player (226-338): 1.00
Common F/X (226-338): 3.00
Production 750 Sets
Only F/X Cards Are Rookies
Pack (5): 3.00
Box (24): 70.00
1 Jake Plummer .40
2 Thomas Jones .20
3 David Boston .60
4 Jamal Anderson .40
5 Chris Chandler .20
6 Tony Martin .20
7 Jamal Lewis 1.25
8 Elvis Grbac .40
9 Ray Lewis .50
10 Rob Johnson .40
11 Eric Moulds .50
12 Muhsin Muhammad .40
13 Tim Biakabutuka .40
14 James Allen .20
15 Marcus Robinson .50
16 Brian Urlacher 1.25
17 Jon Kitna .20
18 Peter Warrick .60
19 Corey Dillon .50
20 Kevin Johnson .40
21 Dennis Northcutt .20
22 Tim Couch .75
23 Raghib Ismail .20
24 Emmitt Smith 1.50
25 Joey Galloway .40
26 Terrell Davis 1.25
27 Rod Smith .40
28 Brian Griese .75
29 Mike Anderson 1.00
30 Charlie Batch .40
31 James O. Stewart .40
32 Germane Crowell .40
33 Brett Favre 2.50
34 Antonio Freeman .50
35 Ahman Green .60
36 Peyton Manning 2.00
37 Edgerrin James 1.50
38 Marvin Harrison .60
39 Jerome Pathon .20
40 Mark Brunell .60
41 Fred Taylor .75
42 Jimmy Smith .40
43 Tony Gonzalez .50
44 Priest Holmes .40
45 Trent Green .40
46 Oronde Gadsden .20
47 Jay Fiedler .40
48 Lamar Smith .40
49 Randy Moss 2.00
50 Cris Carter .50
51 Daunte Culpepper 1.25
52 Drew Bledsoe .75
53 Antowain Smith .20
54 Tom Brady 5.00
55 Ricky Williams 1.00
56 Joe Horn .20
57 Aaron Brooks .75
58 Kerry Collins .40
59 Tiki Barber .40
60 Ron Dayne .40
61 Vinny Testaverde .50
62 Wayne Chrebet .40
63 Curtis Martin .50
64 Tyrone Wheatley .20
65 Rich Gannon .40
66 Jerry Rice 1.50
67 Duce Staley .40
68 Donovan McNabb 1.25
69 Kordell Stewart .60
70 Jerome Bettis .40
71 Marshall Faulk .75
72 Kurt Warner 2.00
73 Torry Holt .60
74 Doug Flutie .75
75 Freddie Jones .20
76 Jeff Garcia .50
77 Garrison Hearst .40
78 Terrell Owens .50
79 Tai Streets .40
80 Ricky Watters .40
81 Matt Hasselbeck .40
82 Darrell Jackson .20
83 Brad Johnson .40
84 Warrick Dunn .40
85 Keyshawn Johnson .50
86 Eddie George .75
87 Steve McNair .50
88 Tony Banks .40
89 Michael Westbrook .40
90 Stephen Davis .60
91 Bob Christian .20
92 Brian Finneran .20
93 Brandon Stokely .20
94 Jeremy McDaniel .20
95 Brad Hoover .20
96 Donald Hayes .20
97 Jim Miller .40
98 Danny Farmer .20
99 Anthony Wright .40
100 Jackie Harris .20
101 Howard Griffith .20
102 Desmond Howard .20
103 Bill Schroeder .40
104 Terrence Wilkins .20
105 Todd Collins .20
106 Sylvester Morris .40
107 Zach Thomas .20
108 Robert Griffith .20
109 Kevin Faulk .40
110 Willie Jackson .20
111 Ron Dixon .20
112 Michael Strahan .20
113 Richie Anderson .20
114 Chad Pennington 1.00
115 Charles Woodson .40
116 Chad Lewis .20
117 Az-Zahir Hakim .40
118 Rodney Harrison .20
119 Mike Alstott .50
120 Jevon Kearse .50
121 MarTay Jenkins .20
122 Pat Tillman .20
123 Rod Woodson .40
124 Marty Booker .20
125 Scott Mitchell .20
126 John Mobley .20
127 Stephen Boyd .20
128 Kurt Schultz .20
129 Kyle Brady .20
130 Donnie Edwards .20
131 J.J. Johnson .20
132 Chris Walsh .20
133 J.R. Redmond .20
134 Keith Mitchell .20
135 Joe Jurivicius .20
136 Eric Allen .20
137 Todd Pinkston .20
138 Bobby Shaw .20
139 Hines Ward .40
140 Ricky Proehl .20
141 London Fletcher .20
142 Jeff Graham .20
143 Tim Rattay .20
144 Fred Beasley .20
145 James Williams .20
146 Derrick Brooks .20
147 Warren Sapp .40
148 Derrick Mason .40
149 Kevin Dyson .40
150 Champ Bailey .20
151 Michael Pittman .20
152 Kwamie Lassiter .20
153 Maurice Smith .20
154 Keith Brooking .20
155 Travis Taylor .40
156 Tony Siragusa .20
157 Alex Van Pelt .20
158 Shane Matthews .20
159 Darnay Scott .40
160 Aaron Shea .20
161 JaJuan Dawson .20
162 Clint Stoerner .50
163 Dat Nguyen .20
164 Bill Romanowski .20
165 Robert Porcher .20
166 Bubba Franks .20
167 Rob Morris .20
168 Stacey Mack .20
169 Chris Hovan .20
170 Lawyer Milloy .20
171 La'Roi Glover .20
172 Jessie Armstead .20
173 Mo Lewis .20
174 Jon Ritchie .20
175 James Thrash .40
176 Trung Canidate .40
177 Grant Wistrom .20
178 Curtis Conway .40
179 Ronney Jenkins .20
180 John Lynch .20
181 Frank Sanders .40
182 Shawn Jefferson .20
183 Darrick Vaughn .20
184 Terance Mathis .20
185 Shannon Sharpe .40
186 Qadry Ismail .40
187 Sammy Morris .20
188 Shawn Bryson .20
189 Wesley Walls .20
190 Akili Smith .50
191 Ron Dugans .20
192 Travis Prentice .40
193 Courtney Brown .20
194 Ed McCaffrey .50
195 Olandis Gary .40
196 Johnnie Morton .40
197 Dorsey Levens .40
198 Ken Dilger .20
199 Keenan McCardell .40
200 Derrick Alexander .40
201 Tony Richardson .20
202 Jason Taylor .20
203 O.J. McDuffie .20
204 Troy Walters .20
205 Troy Brown .40
206 Jeff Blake .40
207 Albert Connell .40
208 Amani Toomer .40
209 Ike Hilliard .20
210 Jason Sehorn .20
211 Laveranues Coles .40
212 Tim Brown .60
213 Charlie Garner .40
214 Plaxico Burress .60
215 Troy Edwards .40
216 Isaac Bruce .60
217 Junior Seau .40
218 Marcellus Wiley .20
219 J.J. Stokes .40
220 Shaun Alexander 1.00
221 John Randle .20
222 Jacquez Green .40
223 Neil O'Donnell .20
224 Frank Wycheck .20
225 Stephen Alexander .20

UD Star Rookies
226 A.J. Feeley 2.50
227 Adam Archuleta 2.00
228 Willie Middlebrooks 2.00
229 Alex Bannister 2.50
230 Alge Crumpler 2.00
231 Andre Carter 1.00
232 Andre Dyson 1.00
233 Anthony Thomas 10.00
234 Arthur Love 1.00
235 Bobby Newcombe 2.00
236 Zeke Moreno 2.00
237 Brandon Spoon 1.00
238 Brian Allen 1.00
239 Carlos Polk 1.00
240 Casey Hampton 1.00
241 Cedrick Wilson 1.00
242 Chad Johnson 2.50
243 Chris Barnes 1.00
244 Chris Chambers 6.00
245 Chris Taylor 1.00
246 Chris Weinke 5.00
247 Correll Buckhalter 4.00
248 Damione Lewis 1.00
249 Dan Alexander 2.00
250 Dan Morgan 1.00
251 Darnerian McCants 1.00
255 David Terrell 6.00
256 Dee Brown 1.00
257 Derek Combs 1.00
258 Derrick Blaylock 1.00
259 Derrick Gibson 1.00
260 Deuce McAllister 5.00
263 Drew Brees 8.00
265 Eddie Berlin 1.00
266 Edgerton Hartwell 1.00
267 Francis St. Paul 1.00
268 Fred Smoot 2.00
269 Freddie Mitchell 5.00
270 Gary Baxter 1.00
271 George Layne 1.00
272 Gerard Warren 1.00
273 Hakim Akbar 1.00
274 Heath Evans 1.00
275 Jabari Holloway 1.00
276 Jamal Reynolds 2.00
277 Jamar Fletcher 2.00
278 James Jackson 3.00
279 Jamie Winborn 1.00
280 Jesse Palmer 3.00
281 John Capel 2.00
282 Josh Booty 2.50
283 Josh Heupel 3.00
284 Justin McCareins 1.00
285 Justin Smith 2.00
286 Karon Riley 1.00
287 Ken Lucas 1.00
288 Ken-Yon Rambo 2.00
289 Kenyatta Walker 1.00
290 Kevan Barlow 4.00
291 Kevin Kasper 2.00
292 Koren Robinson 5.00
293 LaDainian Tomlinson 8.00
294 Lamont Jordan 2.50
295 Leonard Davis 1.00
296 Marcus Stroud 1.00
297 Marques Tuiasosopo 5.00
298 Marvin "Snoop" Minnis 4.00
299 Michael Bennett 6.00
300 Michael Stone 1.00
301 Michael Vick 10.00
302 Mike McMahon 5.00
303 Moran Norris 1.00
304 Morlon Greenwood 1.00
305 Nate Clements 1.00
307 Orlando Huff 1.00
308 Quincy Carter 6.00
309 Quincy Morgan 3.00
310 Reggie Wayne 5.00
311 Reggie White 1.00
312 Richard Seymour 1.00
313 Robert Ferguson 2.50
314 Rod Gardner 5.00
316 Rudi Johnson 2.50
317 Sage Rosenfels 3.00
318 Santana Moss 5.00
319 Scotty Anderson 1.00
320 Sedrick Hodge 2.00
321 Shaun Rogers 1.00
322 Steve Hutchinson 1.00
323 Stevonne Smith 1.00
324 T.J. Houshmandzadeh 1.00
325 Tay Cody 1.00
327 Todd Heap 2.00
328 Tommy Polley 3.00
329 Tony Dixon 1.00
330 Torrance Marshall 1.00
331 Travis Henry 4.00
332 Travis Minor 3.00
333 Vinny Sutherland 2.50
334 Will Allen 2.00

MVP
230 Alge Crumpler 2.00
233 Anthony Thomas 10.00
235 Bobby Newcombe 2.00
242 Chad Johnson 2.50
244 Chris Chambers 6.00
246 Chris Weinke 5.00
247 Correll Buckhalter 4.00
249 Dan Alexander 2.00
250 Dan Morgan 1.00
253 David Allen 1.00
254 David Rivers 1.00
255 David Terrell 6.00
259 Derrick Gibson 1.00
260 Deuce McAllister 5.00
263 Drew Brees 8.00
269 Freddie Mitchell 5.00
278 James Jackson 3.00
280 Jesse Palmer 3.00
282 Josh Booty 2.50
283 Josh Heupel 3.00
288 Ken-Yon Rambo 2.00
290 Kevan Barlow 4.00
291 Kevin Kasper 2.00
292 Koren Robinson 5.00
293 LaDainian Tomlinson 8.00
294 LaMont Jordan 2.50
297 Marques Tuiasosopo 5.00
298 Marvin "Snoop" Minnis 4.00
299 Michael Bennett 6.00
301 Michael Vick 10.00
302 Mike McMahon 5.00
303 Moran Norris 1.00
309 Quincy Morgan 3.00
310 Reggie Wayne 5.00
311 Reggie White 1.00
314 Rod Gardner 5.00
315 Ronney Daniels 1.00
316 Rudi Johnson 2.50
317 Sage Rosenfels 3.00
318 Santana Moss 5.00
324 T.J. Houshmandzadeh 1.00
327 Todd Heap 2.00
331 Travis Henry 4.00
332 Travis Minor 3.00
333 Vinny Sutherland 2.50

Rookie F/X
226 *A.J. Feeley* 4.00
233 *Anthony Thomas* 15.00
241 *Cedrick Wilson* 3.00
242 *Chad Johnson* 4.00
244 *Chris Chambers* 10.00
246 *Chris Weinke* 8.00
247 *Correll Buckhalter* 6.00
250 *Dan Morgan* 3.00
255 *David Terrell* 10.00
260 *Deuce McAllister* 8.00
261 *Dominic Rhodes* 10.00
262 *Drew Bennett* 6.00
263 *Drew Brees* 12.00
269 *Freddie Mitchell* 8.00
278 *James Jackson* 5.00
280 *Jesse Palmer* 5.00
282 *Josh Booty* 4.00
284 *Justin McCareins* 3.00
290 *Kevan Barlow* 6.00
291 *Kevin Kasper* 4.00
292 *Koren Robinson* 8.00
293 *LaDainian Tomlinson* 12.00
294 *LaMont Jordan* 4.00
297 *Marques Tuiasosopo* 8.00
298 *Marvin "Snoop" Minnis* 6.00
299 *Michael Bennett* 10.00
301 *Michael Vick* 15.00
302 *Mike McMahon* 8.00
306 *Nick Goings* 3.00
308 *Quincy Carter* 10.00
309 *Quincy Morgan* 5.00
310 *Reggie Wayne* 8.00
313 *Robert Ferguson* 4.00
314 *Rod Gardner* 8.00
316 *Rudi Johnson* 4.00
318 *Santana Moss* 8.00
323 *Steve Smith* 3.00
327 *Todd Heap* 3.00
331 *Travis Henry* 6.00
332 *Travis Minor* 5.00

Victory
227 Adam Archuleta 2.00
229 Alex Bannister 2.50
230 Alge Crumpler 2.00
233 Anthony Thomas 10.00
235 Bobby Newcombe 2.00
241 Cedrick Wilson 1.00
242 Chad Johnson 2.50
243 Chris Barnes 1.00
244 Chris Chambers 6.00
246 Chris Weinke 5.00
247 Correll Buckhalter 4.00
249 Dan Alexander 2.00
250 Dan Morgan 1.00
255 David Terrell 6.00
259 Derrick Gibson 1.00
260 Deuce McAllister 5.00
263 Drew Brees 8.00
265 Eddie Berlin 1.00
269 Freddie Mitchell 5.00
270 Gary Baxter 1.00
272 Gerard Warren 1.00
274 Heath Evans 1.00
275 Jabari Holloway 1.00
276 Jamal Reynolds 2.00
277 Jamar Fletcher 2.00
278 James Jackson 3.00
280 Jesse Palmer 3.00
282 Josh Booty 2.50
283 Josh Heupel 3.00
285 Justin Smith 2.00
288 Ken-Yon Rambo 2.00
290 Kevan Barlow 4.00
291 Kevin Kasper 2.00
292 Koren Robinson 5.00
293 LaDainian Tomlinson 8.00
294 LaMont Jordan 2.50
297 Marques Tuiasosopo 5.00
298 Marvin "Snoop" Minnis 4.00
299 Michael Bennett 6.00
302 Mike McMahon 5.00
303 Moran Norris 1.00
305 Nate Clements 1.00
308 Quincy Carter 6.00
309 Quincy Morgan 3.00
310 Reggie Wayne 5.00
313 Robert Ferguson 2.50
314 Rod Gardner 5.00
316 Rudi Johnson 2.50
317 Sage Rosenfels 3.00
318 Santana Moss 5.00
319 Scotty Anderson 1.00
323 Steve Smith 2.00
324 T.J. Houshmandzadeh 1.00
326 Tim Hasselbeck 2.00
327 Todd Heap 2.00
331 Travis Henry 4.00
332 Travis Minor 3.00
333 Vinny Sutherland 2.50
334 Will Allen 1.00
338 Troy Hambrick 12.00

Vintage Rookies-Singles
226 A.J. Feeley 2.50
227 Adam Archuleta 2.00
228 Willie Middlebrooks 2.00
230 Alge Crumpler 2.00
231 Andre Carter 1.00
233 Anthony Thomas 10.00
235 Bobby Newcombe 2.00
242 Chad Johnson 2.50
243 Chris Barnes 1.00
244 Chris Chambers 6.00
246 Chris Weinke 5.00
247 Correll Buckhalter 4.00
250 Dan Morgan 1.00
252 Dave Dickenson 3.00
253 David Allen 1.00
255 David Terrell 6.00
260 Deuce McAllister 5.00
263 Drew Brees 8.00
264 Dustin McClintock 1.00
269 Freddie Mitchell 5.00
272 Gerard Warren 1.00
273 Hakim Akbar 1.00
276 Jamal Reynolds 2.00
278 James Jackson 3.00
280 Jesse Palmer 3.00
282 Josh Booty 2.50
283 Josh Heupel 3.00
285 Justin Smith 2.00
290 Kevan Barlow 4.00
291 Kevin Kasper 2.00
292 Koren Robinson 5.00
293 LaDainian Tomlinson 8.00
294 LaMont Jordan 2.50
295 Leonard Davis 1.00
296 Marcus Stroud 1.00
297 Marques Tuiasosopo 5.00
298 Marvin "Snoop" Minnis 4.00
299 Michael Bennett 6.00
301 Michael Vick 10.00
302 Mike McMahon 5.00
303 Moran Norris 1.00
305 Nate Clements 1.00
308 Quincy Carter 6.00
309 Quincy Morgan 3.00
310 Reggie Wayne 5.00
312 Richard Seymour 1.00
313 Robert Ferguson 2.50
314 Rod Gardner 5.00
316 Rudi Johnson 2.50
317 Sage Rosenfels 3.00
318 Santana Moss 5.00
321 Shaun Rogers 1.00
324 T.J. Houshmandzadeh 1.00
326 Tim Hasselbeck 2.00
327 Todd Heap 2.00
329 Tony Dixon 1.00
331 Travis Henry 4.00
332 Travis Minor 3.00
333 Vinny Sutherland 2.50
334 Will Allen 1.00
335 Jason Brookins 3.00
336 Dominic Rhodes 10.00
337 Benjamin Gay 5.00
338 Troy Hambrick 12.00

2001 Upper Deck NFL Rookie FX Heroes of Football

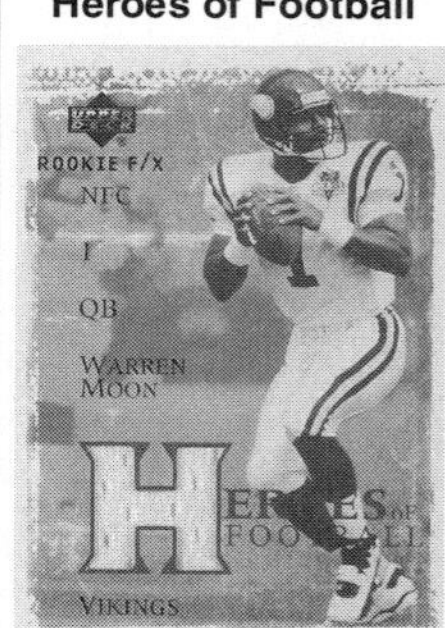

NM/M
Common Player: 15.00
Inserted 1:48
HF-HA Herb Adderley 15.00
HF-JE John Elway 40.00
HF-JK Jim Kelly 20.00
HF-RL Ronnie Lott 15.00
HF-TM Tom Mack 15.00
HF-DM Dan Marino 50.00
HF-MA Jim Marshall 15.00
HF-WM Warren Moon 15.00
HF-ON Ozzie Newsome 15.00
HF-JR John Riggins 40.00
HF-JT Jim Taylor 25.00
HF-TT Thurman Thomas 15.00
HF-DW Danny White 15.00
HF-RW Reggie White 15.00
HF-SY Steve Young 25.00

2001 Upper Deck NFL Rookie FX Legendary Combos

NM/M
Common Player: 25.00
Production 100 Sets
LC-FG Brett Favre, Ahman Green 75.00
LC-GM Brian Griese, Ed McCaffrey 25.00
LC-WF Kurt Warner, Marshall Faulk 75.00
LC-TB LaDainian Tomlinson, Drew Brees 75.00
LC-MH Peyton Manning, Marvin Harrison 50.00
LC-DB Ron Dayne, Tiki Barber 25.00
LC-YR Steve Young, Jerry Rice 60.00

2001 Upper Deck NFL Rookie FX Legends in the Making

NM/M
Common Player: 10.00
Inserted 1:48
LM-JA Jamal Anderson 10.00
LM-DB Drew Bledsoe 15.00
LM-DBr Drew Brees 25.00
LM-TB Tim Brown 10.00
LM-KC Kerry Collins 10.00
LM-TC Tim Couch 10.00
LM-TD Terrell Davis 20.00
LM-BF Brett Favre 40.00
LM-EG Eddie George 15.00
LM-EG Elvis Grbac 10.00
LM-PM Peyton Manning 30.00
LM-JR Jerry Rice 30.00
LM-WS Warren Sapp 10.00
LM-JrS Junior Seau 12.00
LM-JS Jimmy Smith 10.00
LM-LT LaDainian Tomlinson 20.00

2001 Upper Deck Ovation

NM/M
Complete Set (150): 450.00
Common Player: .15
Minor Stars: .30
Common Rookie: 3.00
Black & White Rookie: 80%
Embossed Rookie: 1X
Pack (5): 3.25
Wax Box (20): 45.00
1 Jake Plummer .50
2 Thomas Jones .30
3 Frank Sanders .30
4 Jamal Anderson .50
5 Chris Chandler .15
6 Terance Mathis .15
7 Jamal Lewis 1.25
8 Elvis Grbac .30
9 Travis Taylor .50
10 Shawn Bryson .15
11 Rob Johnson .30
12 Eric Moulds .50
13 Muhsin Muhammad .30
14 Donald Hayes .30
15 Tim Biakabutuka .30
16 Cade McNown .50
17 Marcus Robinson .30
18 Brian Urlacher 1.00
19 Akili Smith .50
20 Peter Warrick .60
21 Corey Dillon .50
22 Kevin Johnson .50
23 Spergon Wynn .15
24 Tim Couch .60
25 Tony Banks .30
26 Emmitt Smith 1.25
27 Anthony Wright .30
28 Terrell Davis 1.00
29 Mike Anderson 1.25
30 Brian Griese .60
31 Ed McCaffrey .50
32 Charlie Batch .50
33 Germane Crowell .50

34 Johnnie Morton .30
35 Brett Favre 2.00
36 Antonio Freeman .50
37 Dorsey Levens .30
38 Ahman Green .50
39 Peyton Manning 1.50
40 Edgerrin James 1.25
41 Marvin Harrison .50
42 Mark Brunell .60
43 Fred Taylor .60
44 Jimmy Smith .50
45 Tony Gonzalez .30
46 Trent Green .50
47 Derrick Alexander .30
48 Oronde Gadsden .30
49 Tony Martin .15
50 Lamar Smith .50
51 Randy Moss 1.50
52 Cris Carter .50
53 Daunte Culpepper 1.00
54 Drew Bledsoe .60
55 Terry Glenn .30
56 Ricky Williams .75
57 Jeff Blake .30
58 Aaron Brooks .60
59 Kerry Collins .30
60 Tiki Barber .50
61 Ron Dayne .75
62 Vinny Testaverde .30
63 Wayne Chrebet .50
64 Curtis Martin .50
65 Tim Brown .30
66 Rich Gannon .30
67 Jerry Rice 1.00
68 Duce Staley .50
69 Donovan McNabb .75
70 Kordell Stewart .50
71 Jerome Bettis .50
72 Marshall Faulk .60
73 Kurt Warner 1.50
74 Isaac Bruce .50
75 Doug Flutie .60
76 Junior Seau .30
77 Jeff Garcia .50
78 Garrison Hearst .30
79 Terrell Owens .50
80 Ricky Watters .30
81 Matt Hasselbeck .50
82 Keyshawn Johnson .50
83 Warrick Dunn .50
84 Mike Alstott .50
85 Kevin Dyson .30
86 Eddie George .60
87 Steve McNair .50
88 Jeff George .30
89 Michael Westbrook .30
90 Stephen Davis .50
91 *Milton Wynn* 4.00
92 *Dan Alexander* 6.00
93 *Rudi Johnson* 15.00
94 *Ken-Yon Rambo* 7.00
95 *Alex Bannister* 6.00
96 *Adam Archuleta* 8.00
97 *Andre Dyson* 3.00
98 *Cedrick Wilson* 6.00
99 *Chris Taylor* 5.00
100 *Eddie Berlin* 5.00
101 *Gary Baxter* 5.00
102 *Heath Evans* 5.00
103 *Jabari Holloway* 6.00
104 *Jamal Reynolds* 5.00
105 *Jamar Fletcher* 6.00
106 *Justin Smith* 4.00
107 *Kevin Kasper* 10.00
108 *Moran Norris* 3.00
109 *Nate Clements* 5.00
110 *Scotty Anderson* 5.00
111 *T.J. Houshmandzadeh* 5.00
112 *Travis Minor* 8.00
113 *Vinny Sutherland* 7.00
114 *Will Allen* 5.00
115 *Derrick Gibson* 3.00
116 *Kevan Barlow* 15.00
117 *LaMont Jordan* 12.00
118 *Todd Heap* 10.00
119 *Quincy Morgan* 12.00
120 *Dan Morgan* 10.00
121 *Gerard Warren* 10.00
122 *Mike McMahon* 10.00
123 *Sage Rosenfels* 12.00
124 *Marques Tuiasosopo* 12.00
125 *Josh Heupel* 10.00
126 *Jesse Palmer* 10.00
127 *Quincy Carter* 12.00
128 *Josh Booty* 10.00
129 *Correll Buckhalter* 10.00
130 *Travis Henry* 15.00
131 *Alge Crumpler* 10.00
132 *Marvin "Snoop" Minnis* 10.00
133 *Bobby Newcombe* 7.00
134 *Robert Ferguson* 8.00
135 *James Jackson* 10.00
136 *Michael Bennett* 20.00
137 *Drew Brees* 20.00
138 *Chris Chambers* 20.00
139 *Rod Gardner* 30.00
140 *Chad Johnson* 20.00
141 *Freddie Mitchell* 12.00
142 *Deuce McAllister* 30.00
143 *Santana Moss* 15.00
144 *Koren Robinson* 15.00
145 *David Terrell* 12.00
146 *LaDainian Tomlinson* 30.00
147 *Anthony Thomas* 20.00
148 *Reggie Wayne* 15.00
149 *Michael Vick* 60.00
150 *Chris Weinke* 12.00

2001 Upper Deck Ovation Rookie Gear

NM/M
Common Player: 12.00
Inserted 1:20
R-KB Kevan Barlow 20.00
R-MB Michael Bennett 30.00
R-DB Drew Brees 40.00
R-MM Chris Chambers 15.00
R-RF Robert Ferguson 12.00
R-RG Rod Gardner 20.00
R-JJ James Jackson 15.00
R-DM Deuce McAllister 25.00
R-QM Quincy Morgan 15.00
R-SM Santana Moss 20.00
R-KR Koren Robinson 15.00
R-MV Michael Vick 50.00
R-CW Chris Weinke 30.00

2001 Upper Deck Ovation Train for the Game

NM/M
Common Player: 15.00
Inserted 1:120
TG-JA Jesse Armstead 15.00
TG-MB Mark Brunell 20.00
TG-BF Brett Favre 65.00
TG-DF Doug Flutie 30.00
TG-JS Junior Seau 20.00

2001 Upper Deck Ovation Training Gear

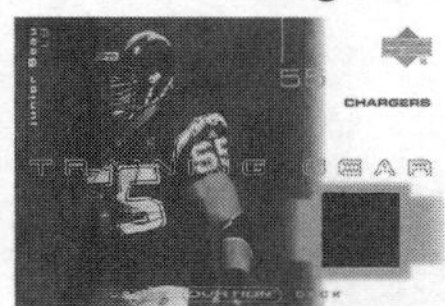

NM/M
Common Player: 10.00
Inserted 1:20
T-TB Tiki Barber 10.00
T-BO David Boston 15.00
T-DB Drew Brees 40.00
T-MB Mark Brunell 15.00
T-CC Curtis Conway 10.00
T-TC Tim Couch 20.00
T-RD Ron Dayne 15.00
T-CD Corey Dillon 15.00
T-BF Brett Favre 45.00
T-RG Rich Gannon 15.00
T-JG Jeff Garcia 15.00
T-CG Charlie Garner 10.00
T-EG Elvis Grbac 15.00
T-JH Jim Harbaugh 10.00
T-TJ Thomas Jones 15.00
T-CK Curtis Keaton 10.00
T-KM Keenan McCardell 10.00
T-TO Terrell Owens 15.00
T-MP Michael Pittman 10.00
T-JP Jake Plummer 15.00
T-JR Jerry Rice 30.00
T-FS Frank Sanders 10.00
T-JrS Junior Seau 15.00
T-JS Jason Sehorn 15.00
T-AS Akili Smith 15.00
T-JJ J.J. Stokes 10.00
T-FT Fred Taylor 20.00
T-PW Peter Warrick 15.00
T-TW Tyrone Wheatley 10.00
T-CW Charles Woodson 15.00

2001 Upper Deck Ovation Training Gear Trios

NM/M
Common Player: 25.00
Inserted 1:240
TT-J Mark Brunell, Fred Taylor, Keenan McCardell 45.00
TT-C Akili Smith, Corey Dillon, Peter Warrick 40.00
TT-A Jake Plummer, Thomas Jones, David Boston 25.00
TT-NY Jesse Armstead, Tiki Barber, Ron Dayne 30.00
TT-SD Junior Seau, Drew Brees, Doug Flutie 85.00
TT-GB Jeff Garcia, Terrell Owens, J.J. Stokes 40.00
TT-O Rich Gannon, Tyrone Wheatley, Jerry Rice 60.00

2001 Upper Deck Pros & Prospects

NM/M
Complete Set (140): 1,250
Common Player: .15
Minor Stars: .30
Common Rookie: 12.00
Production 1,000 Sets
Pack (5): 4.75
Wax Box (24): 80.00
1 Jake Plummer .50
2 David Boston .50
3 Jamal Anderson .50
4 Doug Johnson .50
5 Maurice Smith .15
6 Jamal Lewis 1.50
7 Shannon Sharpe .30
8 Trent Dilfer .30
9 Doug Flutie .75
10 Rob Johnson .30
11 Eric Moulds .50
12 Muhsin Muhammad .30
13 Brad Hoover .50
14 Tim Biakabutuka .30
15 Cade McNown .50
16 James Allen .30
17 Marcus Robinson .50
18 Brian Urlacher 1.00
19 Peter Warrick 1.00
20 Corey Dillon .50
21 Tim Couch .75
22 Kevin Johnson .30
23 Travis Prentice .50
24 Troy Aikman 1.00
25 Emmitt Smith 1.25
26 Terrell Davis 1.25
27 Mike Anderson 1.25
28 Brian Griese .50
29 Charlie Batch .30
30 Germane Crowell .30
31 James O. Stewart .30
32 Brett Favre 2.00
33 Antonio Freeman .30
34 Dorsey Levens .30
35 Ahman Green .30
36 Peyton Manning 1.50
37 Edgerrin James 1.50
38 Marvin Harrison .50
39 Mark Brunell .75
40 Fred Taylor .50
41 Jimmy Smith .30
42 Elvis Grbac .30
43 Tony Gonzalez .30
44 Derrick Alexander .15
45 Oronde Gadsden .15
46 Lamar Smith .50
47 Jay Fiedler .30
48 Randy Moss 1.50
49 Moe Williams .15
50 Cris Carter .50
51 Daunte Culpepper 1.00
52 Drew Bledsoe .75
53 Terry Glenn .50
54 Ricky Williams .75
55 Jeff Blake .30
56 Joe Horn .30
57 Aaron Brooks .50
58 La'Roi Glover .15
59 Kerry Collins .30
60 Amani Toomer .30
61 Ron Dayne 1.00
62 Vinny Testaverde .30
63 Wayne Chrebet .30
64 Curtis Martin .50
65 Tim Brown .30
66 Rich Gannon .30
67 Tyrone Wheatley .30
68 Duce Staley .50
69 Donovan McNabb .75
70 Kordell Stewart .50
71 Jerome Bettis .50
72 Marshall Faulk .50
73 Kurt Warner 1.50
74 Isaac Bruce .50
75 Junior Seau .30
76 Curtis Conway .30
77 Jeff Garcia .50
78 Jerry Rice 1.00
79 Charlie Garner .30
80 Terrell Owens .50
81 Ricky Watters .30
82 Shaun Alexander .50
83 Warrick Dunn .30
84 Shaun King .30
85 Derrick Brooks .15
86 Eddie George .50
87 Steve McNair .50
88 Brad Johnson .30
89 Jeff George .30
90 Stephen Davis .50
91 *Jamal Reynolds* 12.00
92 *Justin Smith* 12.00
93 *Dan Morgan* 12.00
94 *Deuce McAllister* 50.00
95 *Drew Brees* 30.00
96 *Josh Booty* 15.00
97 *Mike McMahon* 15.00
98 *Sage Rosenfels* 15.00
99 *Marques Tuiasosopo* 15.00
100 *Josh Heupel* 15.00
101 *Heath Evans* 12.00
102 *Reggie White* 12.00
103 *Tim Hasselbeck* 15.00
104 *LaDainian Tomlinson* 60.00
105 *Kevan Barlow* 20.00
106 *LaMont Jordan* 20.00
107 *James Jackson* 12.00
108 *Anthony Thomas* 25.00
109 *Correll Buckhalter* 12.00
110 *Travis Henry* 20.00
111 *Dan Alexander* 12.00
112 *Travis Minor* 12.00
113 *Rudi Johnson* 25.00
114 *Michael Bennett* 30.00
115 *Todd Heap* 12.00
116 *Marvin "Snoop" Minnis* 12.00
117 *Santana Moss* 25.00
118 *Reggie Wayne* 25.00
119 *Koren Robinson* 20.00
120 *Chris Chambers* 30.00
121 *David Terrell* 15.00
122 *Rod Gardner* 25.00
123 *Quincy Morgan* 15.00
124 *Ken-Yon Rambo* 12.00
125 *Ronney Daniels* 12.00
126 *Ja'Mar Toombs* 12.00
127 *Bobby Newcombe* 12.00
128 *Cedrick Wilson* 12.00
129 *Chad Johnson* 30.00
130 *Shaun Rogers* 12.00
131 *Robert Ferguson* 15.00
132 *Kevin Kasper* 12.00
133 *Chris Weinke JERSEY* 20.00
134 *Freddie Mitchell JERSEY* 20.00
135 *Michael Vick JERSEY* 150.00
136 *Chris Taylor* 12.00
137 *Vinny Sutherland* 15.00
138 *Gerard Warren* 12.00
139 *Torrance Marshall* 12.00
140 *Jesse Palmer* 12.00

2001 Upper Deck Pros & Prospects Centerpiece

NM/M
Complete Set (6): 25.00
Common Player: 2.00
Inserted 1:22
C1 Randy Moss 7.00
C2 Donovan McNabb 3.00
C3 Kurt Warner 8.00
C4 Jamal Lewis 6.00
C5 Eddie George 2.00
C6 Mike Anderson 3.50

2001 Upper Deck Pros & Prospects Combo Jersey

NM/M
Common Player: 200.00
Production 25 Sets
SU-C Bart Starr, Johnny Unitas 250.00
SB-C Terry Bradshaw, Roger Staubach 250.00
MY-C Joe Montana, Steve Young 300.00
AS-C Troy Aikman, Emmitt Smith 250.00
JM-C Edgerrin James, Peyton Manning 250.00
MC-C Daunte Culpepper, Randy Moss 225.00
FW-C Marshall Faulk, Kurt Warner 200.00

2001 Upper Deck Pros & Prospects Future Fame

NM/M
Complete Set (6): 25.00
Common Player: 3.00
Inserted 1:22
F1 Michael Vick 12.00
F2 Deuce McAllister 6.00
F3 Drew Brees 10.00
F4 LaDainian Tomlinson 7.00
F5 Chris Weinke 4.00
F6 Santana Moss 3.00

2001 Upper Deck Pros & Prospects Game-Worn Jersey

NM/M
Common Player: 15.00
Inserted 1:23
Parallel Cards: 2X
Production 50 Sets
TA-J Troy Aikman 30.00
MA-J Marcus Allen 25.00
AN-J Mike Anderson
BA-J Tiki Barber 15.00
TB-J Terry Bradshaw 70.00
MB-J Mark Brunell 20.00
KC-J Kerry Collins 25.00
DC-J Daunte Culpepper 40.00
RD-J Ron Dayne 25.00
CD-J Corey Dillon 25.00
WD-J Warrick Dunn 20.00
JE-J John Elway 85.00
MF-J Marshall Faulk 35.00
BF-J Brett Favre 50.00
JG-J Jeff Garcia 35.00
TH-J Torry Holt 25.00
PH-J Paul Hornung 75.00
EJ-J Edgerrin James 45.00
KJ-J Keyshawn Johnson 15.00
TJ-J Thomas Jones 20.00
SK-J Shaun King 15.00
DL-J Dorsey Levens 15.00
PM-J Peyton Manning 45.00
KM-J Keenan McCardell 15.00
JM-J Joe Montana 100.00
RM-J Randy Moss 45.00
JN-J Joe Namath 100.00
WP-J Walter Payton 150.00
JP-J Jake Plummer 15.00
PL-J Jim Plunkett 25.00
JR-J Jerry Rice 35.00
JS-J Junior Seau 15.00
PS-J Phil Simms 20.00
ES-J Emmitt Smith 40.00
KS-J Kordell Stewart 15.00
FT-J Fred Taylor 20.00
KW-J Kurt Warner 70.00

2001 Upper Deck Pros & Prospects ProActive

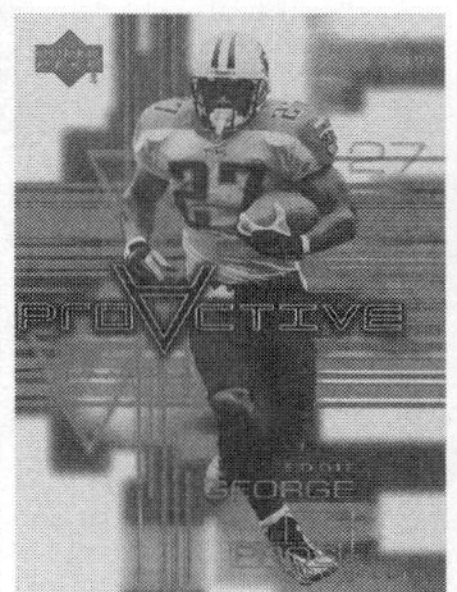

NM/M
Complete Set (9): 20.00
Common Player: 1.00
Minor Stars: 2.00
Inserted 1:15
PA1 Kurt Warner 6.00
PA2 Eddie George 2.00
PA3 Marshall Faulk 2.00
PA4 Corey Dillon 2.00
PA5 Emmitt Smith 5.00
PA6 Randy Moss 5.00
PA7 Marvin Harrison 2.00
PA8 Rich Gannon 1.00
PA9 Brett Favre 7.00

2001 Upper Deck Pros & Prospects ProMotion

NM/M
Complete Set (9): 25.00
Common Player: 1.00
Inserted 1:15
PM1 Michael Vick 10.00
PM2 Michael Bennett 4.00
PM3 Reggie Wayne 2.00
PM4 Chad Johnson 2.00
PM5 Chris Chambers 2.00
PM6 David Terrell 5.00
PM7 Marvin "Snoop" Minnis 1.00
PM8 Koren Robinson 4.00
PM9 Rod Gardner 4.00

2001 Upper Deck Pros & Prospects Signed Jersey

NM/M
Common Player: 25.00
Inserted 1:192
Parallel Cards: 2X
Production 50 Sets
JK-AJ Jim Kelly 125.00
AM-AJ Art Monk
BS-AJ Bart Starr 150.00
RS-AJ Roger Staubach 100.00
FT-AJ Fran Tarkenton 75.00
CT-AJ Charlie Taylor 25.00
JT-AJ Joe Theismann 45.00
JU-AJ Johnny Unitas 125.00
SY-AJ Steve Young SP 150.00
JY-AJ Jack Youngblood 25.00

2001 Upper Deck Super Bowl XXXV Black Diamond

NM/M
Common Player: 5.00
1 Courtney Brown 5.00
2 Ron Dayne 10.00
3 Shaun Alexander 15.00
4 Thomas Jones 12.00
5 Jamal Lewis 15.00
6 J.R. Redmond 5.00
7 Peter Warrick 12.00
8 Plaxico Burress 12.00
9 Sylvester Morris 5.00
10 Laveranues Coles 10.00

2001 Upper Deck Super Bowl XXXV Special Moments

NM/M
Common Player: 2.00
TA Troy Aikman 4.00
JA Jamal Anderson 2.00
TD Terrell Davis 3.00
MF Marshall Faulk 3.00
BF Brett Favre 5.00
EG Eddie George 2.00

2001 Upper Deck Victory

NM/M
Complete Set (440): 70.00
Common Player: .10
Minor Stars: .20
Common Rookie: .25
Pack (10): 1.00
Wax Box (36): 25.00
1 Jake Plummer .40
2 David Boston .40
3 Thomas Jones .30
4 Michael Pittman .20
5 Frank Sanders .20
6 Joel Makovicka .10
7 Corey Chavous .10
8 Kwamie Lassiter .10
9 Rob Moore .20
10 Jamal Anderson .40
11 Tony Martin .20
12 Travis Jervey .10
13 Chris Chandler .20
14 Shawn Jefferson .10
15 Rodney Thomas .10
16 Terance Mathis .10
17 Jessie Tuggle .10
18 Ashley Ambrose .10
19 Brian Finneran .10
20 Maurice Smith .40
21 Keith Brooking .10
22 Jamal Lewis 1.00
23 Shannon Sharpe .20
24 Brandon Stokley .20
25 Ray Lewis .40
26 Qadry Ismail .20
27 Travis Taylor .40
28 Chris Redman .10
29 Rod Woodson .20
30 Patrick Johnson .10
31 Jermaine Lewis .20
32 Elvis Grbac .30
33 Tony Siragusa .10
34 Larry Centers .10
35 Rob Johnson .30
36 Eric Moulds .40
37 Sammy Morris .20
38 Shawn Bryson .10
39 Alex Van Pelt .10
40 Jeremy McDaniel .10
41 Sam Cowart .10
42 Peerless Price .30
43 Avion Black .10
44 Phil Hansen .10
45 Muhsin Muhammad .30
46 Brad Hoover .20
47 Tim Biakabutuka .30
48 Wesley Walls .20
49 Donald Hayes .20
50 Jeff Lewis .10
51 Dameyune Craig .20
52 Mike Minter .10
53 Isaac Byrd .10
54 Patrick Jeffers .20
55 Cade McNown .40
56 James Allen .40
57 Marcus Robinson .40
58 Brian Urlacher .75

59	Shane Matthews	.20
60	Glyn Milburn	.10
61	Scott Dragos	.10
62	Marty Booker	.20
63	Bobby Engram	.20
64	Kaseem Sinceno	.10
65	Ted Washington	.10
66	Peter Warrick	.50
67	Corey Dillon	.40
68	Akili Smith	.40
69	Danny Farmer	.20
70	Scott Mitchell	.20
71	Darryl Williams	.10
72	Ron Dugans	.20
73	Takeo Spikes	.10
74	Jon Kitna	.30
75	Darnay Scott	.20
76	Tony McGee	.10
77	Tim Couch	.75
78	Kevin Johnson	.40
79	Travis Prentice	.30
80	Spergon Wynn	.20
81	Errict Rhett	.20
82	Ty Detmer	.20
83	Dennis Northcutt	.30
84	Aaron Shea	.10
85	Courtney Brown	.30
86	JaJuan Dawson	.10
87	Rickey Dudley	.10
88	Jamir Miller	.10
89	Clint Stoerner	.40
90	Emmitt Smith	.75
91	Joey Galloway	.40
92	Raghib Ismail	.20
93	Ebenezer Ekuban	.10
94	Anthony Wright	.20
95	David LaFleur	.10
96	Dexter Coakley	.10
97	Jackie Harris	.10
98	Michael Wiley	.20
99	Wane McGarity	.10
100	Dat Nguyen	.10
101	Terrell Davis	.75
102	Mike Anderson	1.00
103	Brian Griese	.50
104	Rod Smith	.40
105	Ed McCaffrey	.30
106	Olandis Gary	.40
107	Kavika Pittman	.10
108	Bill Romanowski	.10
109	Gus Frerotte	.10
110	Howard Griffith	.10
111	Eddie Kennison	.20
112	Charlie Batch	.40
113	Germane Crowell	.30
114	James O. Stewart	.30
115	Johnnie Morton	.20
116	Herman Moore	.30
117	Larry Foster	.10
118	Desmond Howard	.10
119	Cory Schlesinger	.10
120	Robert Porcher	.10
121	Sedrick Irvin	.10
122	David Sloan	.10
123	Jim Harbaugh	.20
124	Brett Favre	1.50
125	Antonio Freeman	.40
126	Dorsey Levens	.30
127	Ahman Green	.30
128	Leroy Butler	.10
129	De'Mond Parker	.10
130	Bill Schroeder	.20
131	Bubba Franks	.20
132	Donald Driver	.10
133	Darren Sharper	.10
134	Corey Bradford	.10
135	Charles Lee	.10
136	Peyton Manning	1.25
137	Edgerrin James	1.00
138	Marvin Harrison	.40
139	E.G. Green	.20
140	Terrence Wilkins	.30
141	Ken Dilger	.10
142	Jerome Pathon	.10
143	Rob Morris	.10
144	Lennox Gordon	.10
145	Chad Bratzke	.10
146	Mark Brunell	.50
147	Fred Taylor	.50
148	Jimmy Smith	.30
149	Jamie Martin	.10
150	Keenan McCardell	.20
151	Kyle Brady	.10
152	R. Jay Soward	.20
153	Alvis Whitted	.10
154	Stacey Mack	.10
155	Damon Jones	.10
156	Carnell Lake	.10
157	Kevin Hardy	.10
158	Trent Green	.40
159	Tony Gonzalez	.40
160	Derrick Alexander	.10
161	Tony Richardson	.10
162	Frank Moreau	.10
163	Sylvester Morris	.40
164	Priest Holmes	.30
165	Donnie Edwards	.10
166	Marvcus Patton	.10
167	Larry Parker	.10
168	Tony Horne	.10
169	Bubby Brister	.20
170	Oronde Gadsden	.20
171	Lamar Smith	.40
172	Jay Fiedler	.40
173	J.J. Johnson	.20
174	Rob Konrad	.10
175	James McKnight	.10
176	Dedric Ward	.10
177	O.J. McDuffie	.20
178	Zach Thomas	.30
179	Ray Lucas	.30
180	Sam Madison	.10
181	Randy Moss	1.25
182	Jake Reed	.20
183	Cris Carter	.40
184	Daunte Culpepper	.75
185	Moe Williams	.10
186	Troy Walters	.10
187	Todd Bouman	.10
188	Jim Kleinsasser	.20
189	Ed McDaniel	.10
190	Robert Griffith	.10
191	Byron Chamberlain	.10
192	Chris Hovan	.20
193	Drew Bledsoe	.50
194	Terry Glenn	.40
195	Kevin Faulk	.30
196	J.R. Redmond	.30
197	Antowain Smith	.20
198	Bert Emanuel	.10
199	Troy Brown	.10
200	Tony Simmons	.10
201	Michael Bishop	.20
202	Lawyer Milloy	.10
203	Torrence Small	.10
204	Ty Law	.10
205	Charles Johnson	.10
206	Willie McGinest	.10
207	Ricky Williams	.60
208	Jeff Blake	.20
209	Joe Horn	.30
210	Aaron Brooks	.60
211	La'Roi Glover	.10
212	Chad Morton	.10
213	Keith Mitchell	.10
214	Willie Jackson	.20
215	Robert Wilson	.10
216	Norman Hand	.10
217	Albert Connell	.20
218	Joe Johnson	.20
219	Kerry Collins	.40
220	Amani Toomer	.20
221	Ron Dayne	.75
222	Tiki Barber	.40
223	Greg Comella	.10
224	Ike Hilliard	.20
225	Joe Jurevicius	.10
226	Ron Dixon	.10
227	Jason Sehorn	.10
228	Michael Strahan	.30
229	Jessie Armstead	.10
230	Mike Barrowman	.10
231	Jason Garrett	.10
232	Vinny Testaverde	.30
233	Wayne Chrebet	.40
234	Curtis Martin	.40
235	Richie Anderson	.10
236	Mo Lewis	.10
237	Laveranues Coles	.30
238	Windrell Hayes	.60
239	Chad Pennington	.40
240	Matthew Hatchette	.10
241	Anthony Becht	.10
242	Marvin Jones	.10
243	Tim Brown	.40
244	Rich Gannon	.30
245	Tyrone Wheatley	.20
246	Charlie Garner	.20
247	Jon Ritchie	.10
248	James Jett	.10
249	Roland Williams	.10
250	Jerry Porter	.20
251	Darrell Russell	.10
252	Charles Woodson	.30
253	Jerry Rice	1.00
254	Greg Biekert	.10
255	Duce Staley	.40
256	Donovan McNabb	.60
257	Darnell Autry	.20
258	Chad Lewis	.20
259	Na Brown	.10
260	Koy Detmer	.10
261	Todd Pinkston	.30
262	Brian Mitchell	.10
263	Hugh Douglas	.10
264	James Thrash	.20
265	Ron Powlus	.10
266	Corey Simon	.10
267	Kordell Stewart	.40
268	Jerome Bettis	.40
269	Bobby Shaw	.10
270	Hines Ward	.30
271	Plaxico Burress	.40
272	Courtney Hawkins	.10
273	Troy Edwards	.10
274	Earl Holmes	.10
275	Richard Huntley	.10
276	Kent Graham	.10
277	Tee Martin	.30
278	Jon Witman	.10
279	Marshall Faulk	.50
280	Kurt Warner	1.25
281	Isaac Bruce	.40
282	Torry Holt	.40
283	Joe Germaine	.20
284	Ernie Conwell	.10
285	Trung Canidate	.30
286	Az-Zahir Hakim	.20
287	Ricky Proehl	.10
288	Grant Wistrom	.10
289	London Fletcher	.10
290	Paul Justin	.10
291	Robert Holcombe	.10
292	Junior Seau	.30
293	Curtis Conway	.20
294	Rodney Harrison	.10
295	Jeff Graham	.10
296	Freddie Jones	.20
297	Reggie Jones	.20
298	Ronney Jenkins	.10
299	Robert Gaylor	.10
300	Tim Dwight	.20
301	Fred McCrary	.10
302	Terrell Fletcher	.10
303	Doug Flutie	.50
304	Dave Dickenson	.40
305	Marcellus Wiley	.10
306	Jeff Garcia	.40
307	Jonas Lewis	.10
308	Tai Streets	.20
309	Terrell Owens	.40
310	J.J. Stokes	.20
311	Fred Beasley	.10
312	Tim Rattay	.20
313	Garrison Hearst	.30
314	Giovanni Carmazzi	.30
315	Bryant Young	.10
316	Ricky Watters	.30
317	Shaun Alexander	.40
318	Matt Hasselbeck	.40
319	Brock Huard	.20
320	Darrell Jackson	.20
321	James Williams	.10
322	Charlie Rogers	.10
323	Christian Fauria	.10
324	Karsten Bailey	.10
325	Travis Brown	.10
326	Chad Brown	.10
327	John Randle	.20
328	Warrick Dunn	.40
329	Shaun King	.40
330	Rahib Abdullah	.10
331	Mike Alstott	.40
332	Jacquez Green	.20
333	Reidel Anthony	.20
334	Derrick Brooks	.10
335	John Lynch	.20
336	Warren Sapp	.30
337	Brad Johnson	.30
338	Keyshawn Johnson	.40
339	Mark Royals	.10
340	Dave Moore	.10
341	Simeon Rice	.10
342	Ronde Barber	.10
343	Eddie George	.50
344	Steve McNair	.40
345	Samari Rolle	.10
346	Derrick Mason	.30
347	Randall Godfrey	.10
348	Frank Wycheck	.10
349	Chris Sanders	.10
350	Neil O'Donnell	.20
351	Kevin Dyson	.20
352	Jevon Kearse	.40
353	Chris Coleman	.10
354	Mike Green	.10
355	Blaine Bishop	.10
356	Eddie Robinson	.10
357	Jeff George	.20
358	Stephen Davis	.40
359	Donnell Bennett	.10
360	Kevin Lockett	.10
361	Derrius Thompson	.10
362	Michael Westbrook	.30
363	Stephen Alexander	.20
364	Ki-Jana Carter	.20
365	Champ Bailey	.30
366	Todd Husak	.20
367	Dan Wilkinson	.10
368	Darrell Green	.20
369	Sam Shade	.10
370	Bruce Smith	.20
371	*Bobby Newcombe*	.40
372	*Vinny Sutherland*	.40
373	*Alge Crumpler*	.50
374	*Michael Vick*	5.00
375	*Gary Baxter*	.50
376	*Todd Heap*	.50
377	*Nate Clements*	.50
378	*Travis Henry*	1.50
379	*Dan Morgan*	.50
380	*Chris Weinke*	1.50
381	*David Terrell*	1.50
382	*Anthony Thomas*	2.00
383	*Rudi Johnson*	2.00
384	*Justin Smith*	.50
385	*T.J. Houshmandzadeh*	.50
386	*Chad Johnson*	3.00
387	*Quincy Morgan*	1.25
388	*Gerard Warren*	.75
389	*James Jackson*	1.00
390	*Quincy Carter*	1.50
391	*Kevin Kasper*	.75
392	*Scotty Anderson*	.75
393	*Mike McMahon*	.75
394	*Jamal Reynolds*	.50
395	*Robert Ferguson*	.60
396	*Reggie Wayne*	2.00
397	*Marvin "Snoop" Minnis*	1.00
398	*Chris Chambers*	3.00
399	*Jamar Fletcher*	.50
400	*Travis Minor*	.75
401	*Josh Heupel*	1.00
402	*Michael Bennett*	2.50
403	*Jabari Holloway*	.50
404	*Moran Norris*	.25
405	*Deuce McAllister*	3.00
406	*Will Allen*	.50
407	*Jesse Palmer*	.50
408	*LaMont Jordan*	1.50
409	*Santana Moss*	2.50
410	*Ken-Yon Rambo*	.50
411	*Derrick Gibson*	.25
412	*Marques Tuiasosopo*	1.25
413	*Correll Buckhalter*	1.25
414	*Freddie Mitchell*	1.25
415	*Drew Brees*	2.50
416	*LaDainian Tomlinson*	3.00
417	*Cedrick Wilson*	.50
418	*Kevan Barlow*	2.00
419	*Alex Bannister*	.50
420	*Heath Evans*	.50
421	*Josh Booty*	.50
422	*Koren Robinson*	2.00
423	*Adam Archuleta*	.75
424	*Dan Alexander*	.50
425	*Eddie Berlin*	1.00
426	*Rod Gardner*	2.00
427	*Sage Rosenfels*	.75
428	*Steve Smith*	1.50
429	*Chris Barnes*	.60
430	*Tim Hasselbeck*	.60
431	Peyton Manning	.50
432	Mike Anderson	.50
433	Jamal Lewis	.50
434	Randy Moss	.50
435	Donovan McNabb	.30
436	Daunte Culpepper	.30
437	Kurt Warner	.50
438	Eddie George	.30
439	Marshall Faulk	.30
440	Brett Favre	.75

2001 Upper Deck Victory Gold

Gold Cards:	2X-4X
Gold Rookies:	3X
Inserted 1:2	

2002 Upper Deck

		NM/M
	Common Player:	.15
	Unlisted Stars:	.75
	Minor Stars:	.40
	Common Rookie (181-210):	2.00
	Minor Rookies:	3.00
	Pack (8):	4.00
	Wax Box (24):	65.00
1	Jake Plummer	.40
2	Marcel Shipp	.15
3	David Boston	.60
4	Arnold Jackson	.15
5	Frank Sanders	.15
6	Freddie Jones	.15
7	Michael Vick	2.00
8	Jamal Anderson	.40
9	Warrick Dunn	.40
10	Maurice Smith	.15
11	Shawn Jefferson	.15
12	Chris Redman	.40
13	Jeff Blake	.40
14	Jamal Lewis	1.00
15	Travis Taylor	.75
16	Ray Lewis	.40
17	Chris McAlister	.15
18	Drew Bledsoe	1.50
19	Travis Henry	.50
20	Larry Centers	.15
21	Eric Moulds	.40
22	Reggie Germany	.15
23	Peerless Price	.40
24	Chris Weinke	.60
25	Lamar Smith	.40
26	Nick Goings	.15
27	Muhsin Muhammad	.40
28	Isaac Byrd	.15
29	Wesley Walls	.15
30	Jim Miller	.60
31	Anthony Thomas	2.00
32	Dez White	.40
33	David Terrell	.75
34	Marty Booker	.40
35	Brian Urlacher	2.00
36	Jon Kitna	.40
37	Corey Dillon	.60
38	Peter Warrick	.40
39	Darnay Scott	.15
40	Chad Johnson	.15
41	Tim Couch	1.00
42	James Jackson	.75
43	JaJuan Dawson	.15
44	Kevin Johnson	.40
45	Quincy Morgan	.75
46	Courtney Brown	.15
47	Quincy Carter	1.50
48	Emmitt Smith	2.50
49	Joey Galloway	.40
50	Raghib Ismail	.15
51	Ken-Yon Rambo	.15
52	Brian Griese	.75
53	Terrell Davis	.50
54	Mike Anderson	1.00
55	Shannon Sharpe	.50
56	Ed McCaffrey	.40
57	Rod Smith	.40
58	Mike McMahon	.75
59	James Stewart	.40
60	Az-Zahir Hakim	.40
61	Desmond Howard	.15
62	Germane Crowell	.15
63	Brett Favre	3.00
64	Ahman Green	.75
65	Antonio Freeman	.40
66	Terry Glenn	.40
67	Kabeer Gbaja-Biamila	.15
68	Alex Graham	.40
69	James Allen	.15
70	Corey Bradford	.40
71	Jermaine Lewis	.15
72	Jamie Sharper	.15
73	Peyton Manning	2.50
74	Edgerrin James	1.50
75	Dominic Rhodes	.15
76	Marvin Harrison	.60
77	Qadry Ismail	.15
78	Mark Brunell	.75
79	Fred Taylor	.50
80	Stacey Mack	.15
81	Jimmy Smith	.40
82	Keenan McCardell	.15
83	Trent Green	.75
84	Priest Holmes	.75
85	Derrick Alexander	.15
86	Johnnie Morton	.40
87	Marvin "Snoop" Minnis	.40
88	Tony Gonzalez	.40
89	Jay Fiedler	.75
90	Ricky Williams	1.50
91	Chris Chambers	.75
92	Oronde Gadsden	.15
93	Zach Thomas	.40
94	Daunte Culpepper	1.50
95	Michael Bennett	.75
96	Randy Moss	2.50
97	Sean Dawkins	.15
98	Tom Brady	2.50
99	Antowain Smith	.50
100	David Patten	.40
101	Troy Brown	.40
102	Adam Vinatieri	.40
103	Aaron Brooks	1.00
104	Deuce McAllister	1.00
105	Jake Reed	.15
106	Jerome Pathon	.40
107	Joe Horn	.15
108	Kyle Turley	.15
109	Kerry Collins	.40
110	Ron Dayne	.40
111	Tiki Barber	.40
112	Amani Toomer	.40
113	Ike Hilliard	.40
114	Michael Strahan	.40
115	Vinny Testaverde	.40
116	Chad Pennington	.50
117	Curtis Martin	.50
118	Santana Moss	.40
119	Laveranues Coles	.40
120	Wayne Chrebet	.40
121	Rich Gannon	.75
122	Charlie Garner	.40
123	Jerry Rice	2.50
124	Tim Brown	.75
125	Charles Woodson	.40
126	Donovan McNabb	1.50
127	Duce Staley	.40
128	Correll Buckhalter	.40
129	Freddie Mitchell	.50
130	James Thrash	.15
131	Todd Pinkston	.15
132	Kordell Stewart	.50
133	Jerome Bettis	.40
134	Chris Fuamatu-Ma'afala	.15
135	Hines Ward	.40
136	Plaxico Burress	.75
137	Kendrell Bell	.15
138	Doug Flutie	.75
139	Drew Brees	2.00
140	LaDainian Tomlinson	2.00
141	Curtis Conway	.40
142	Tim Dwight	.15
143	Junior Seau	.40
144	Jeff Garcia	.75
145	Garrison Hearst	.40
146	Kevan Barlow	.15
147	Terrell Owens	.60
148	J.J. Stokes	.15
149	Trent Dilfer	.60
150	Shaun Alexander	.75
151	Ricky Watters	.40
152	Bobby Engram	.15
153	Koren Robinson	.40
154	Kurt Warner	2.50
155	Marshall Faulk	1.50
156	Isaac Bruce	.60
157	Ricky Proehl	.15
158	Terrence Wilkins	.15
159	Torry Holt	.40
160	Brad Johnson	.75
161	Shaun King	.15
162	Rob Johnson	.15
163	Mike Alstott	.40
164	Michael Pittman	.15
165	Keyshawn Johnson	.40
166	Steve McNair	.75
167	Eddie George	.75
168	Derrick Mason	.15
169	Kevin Dyson	.40
170	Frank Wycheck	.15
171	Jevon Kearse	.15
172	Danny Wuerffel	.15
173	Stephen Davis	.40
174	Michael Westbrook	.40
175	Rod Gardner	.40
176	Champ Bailey	.40
177	Darrell Green	.40
178	Kurt Warner	2.00
179	Brett Favre	3.00
180	Randy Moss	2.00
181	David Boston	.75
182	Jake Plummer	.40
183	Michael Vick	2.00
184	Drew Bledsoe	1.00
185	Anthony Thomas	1.00
186	Tim Couch	.75
187	Emmitt Smith	2.00
188	Ahman Green	.75
189	Brett Favre	3.00
190	Edgerrin James	2.00
191	Peyton Manning	2.00
192	Mark Brunell	.75
193	Daunte Culpepper	1.50
194	Randy Moss	2.00
195	Tom Brady	2.00
196	Aaron Brooks	.60
197	Ricky Williams	.75
198	Curtis Martin	.40
199	Jerry Rice	2.00
200	Donovan McNabb	1.00
201	Jerome Bettis	.60
202	Kordell Stewart	.60
203	LaDainian Tomlinson	1.00
204	Jeff Garcia	.40
205	Terrell Owens	.60
206	Shaun Alexander	1.00
207	Kurt Warner	2.00
208	Marshall Faulk	1.00
209	Keyshawn Johnson	.40
210	Steve McNair	.60
211	*Damien Anderson*	4.00
212	*Jason McAddley*	2.00
213	*Josh McCown*	10.00
214	*Josh Scobey*	4.00
215	*Preston Parson*	2.00
216	*Dusty Bonner*	2.00
217	*Kahlil Hill*	2.00
218	*Kurt Kittner*	4.00
219	*T.J. Duckett*	10.00
220	*Chester Taylor*	2.00
221	*Kalimba Edwards*	3.00
222	*Edward Reed*	2.00
223	*Ron Johnson*	2.00
224	*Tellis Redmon*	4.00
225	*Wes Pate*	3.00
226	*David Priestley*	3.00
227	*Josh Reed*	6.00
228	*Mike Williams*	3.00
229	*Ryan Denney*	3.00
230	*DeShaun Foster*	8.00
231	*Julius Peppers*	8.00
232	*Randy Fasani*	3.00
233	*Adrian Peterson*	6.00
234	*Alex Brown*	1.00
235	*Gavin Hoffman*	1.00
236	*Levi Jones*	1.00
237	*Andra Davis*	1.00
238	*Andre Davis*	10.00
239	*William Green*	8.00
240	*Antonio Bryant*	10.00
241	*Chad Hutchinson*	3.00
242	*Roy Williams*	12.00
243	*Woodrow Dantzler III*	3.00
244	*Ashley Lelie*	10.00
245	*Clinton Portis*	25.00
246	*Lamont Thompson*	3.00
247	*James Mungro*	3.00
248	*Joey Harrington*	20.00
249	*Luke Staley*	4.00
250	*Craig Nall*	6.00
251	*Javon Walker*	12.00
252	*Najeh Davenport*	6.00
253	*David Carr*	25.00
254	*Saleem Rasheed*	3.00
255	*Mike Rumph*	3.00
256	*Jabar Gaffney*	5.00
257	*Jonathan Wells*	6.00
258	*Dwight Freeney*	6.00
259	*Larry Tripplett*	3.00
260	*David Garrard*	3.00
261	*John Henderson*	3.00
262	*Ryan Sims*	3.00
263	*Leonard Henry*	2.00
264	*Brian Allen*	2.00
265	*Atrews Bell*	2.00
266	*Bryant McKinnie*	3.00
267	*Kelly Campbell*	3.00
268	*Raonall Smith*	3.00
269	*Antwoine Womack*	3.00
270	*Daniel Graham*	6.00
271	*Deion Branch*	12.00
272	*Sam Simmons*	2.00
273	*Rohan Davey*	8.00
274	*Charles Grant*	2.00
275	Derrick Lewis	2.00
276	*Donte Stallworth*	10.00
277	*J.T. O'Sullivan*	2.00
278	*Keyuo Craver*	2.00
279	*Ricky Williams*	2.00
280	*Bryan Thomas*	2.00
281	*Jeremy Shockey*	15.00
282	*Tim Carter*	2.00
283	*Larry Ned*	2.00
284	*Napoleon Harris*	3.00
285	*Phillip Buchanon*	4.00
286	*Ronald Curry*	8.00
287	*Brian Westbrook*	10.00
288	*Freddie Milons*	3.00
289	*Lito Sheppard*	3.00
290	*Antwann Randle El*	8.00
291	*Lee Mays*	2.00
292	*Daryl Jones*	2.00
293	*Justin Peelle*	2.00
294	*Quentin Jammer*	4.00
295	*Reche Caldwell*	6.00
296	*Seth Burford*	2.00
297	*Terry Charles*	2.00
298	*Brandon Doman*	2.00
299	*Maurice Morris*	8.00
300	*Eric Crouch*	5.00
301	*Lamar Gordon*	4.00
302	*Marquise Walker*	3.00
303	*Tracey Wistrom*	2.00
304	*Travis Stephens*	4.00
305	*Herb Haygood*	2.00
306	*Albert Haynesworth*	3.00
307	*Rocky Calmus*	4.00
308	*Cliff Russell*	3.00
309	*Ladell Betts*	4.00
310	Patrick Ramsey	10.00

2002 Upper Deck Battle-Worn Jerseys

		NM/M
	Common Player:	8.00
	Inserted 1:144	
BW-TB	Tiki Barber	8.00
BW-TD	Terrell Davis	12.00
BW-BG	Brian Griese/SP	20.00
BW-RH	Rodney Harrison	10.00
BW-JK	Jevon Kearse	8.00
BW-RL	Ray Lewis	8.00
BW-JS	Junior Seau	12.00
BW-MS	Michael Strahan	8.00
BW-AT	Anthony Thomas/SP	20.00
BW-BU	Brian Urlacher	25.00

2002 Upper Deck Blitz Brigade

		NM/M
	Common Player:	2.00
	Inserted 1:12	
BB-1	Ray Lewis	3.00
BB-2	Brian Urlacher	6.00
BB-3	Kabeer Gbaja-Biamila	2.00
BB-4	Zach Thomas	2.00
BB-5	Michael Strahan	2.00
BB-6	Charles Woodson	2.00
BB-7	Kendrell Bell	2.00
BB-8	Junior Seau	2.00
BB-9	Rodney Harrison	2.00
BB-10	Levon Kirkland	2.00
BB-11	Warren Sapp	3.00
BB-12	Jevon Kearse	2.00
BB-13	Bruce Smith	2.00
BB-14	Champ Bailey	2.00

2002 Upper Deck Buybacks

NM/M
Production maximum 25 sets
UDB-DB David Boston
UDB-AB Aaron Brooks
UDB-TC Tim Couch
UDB-JE John Elway
UDB-RG Rich Gannon
UDB-JG Jeff Garcia
UDB-TG Tony Gonzalez
UDB-EG Elvis Grbac
UDB-AG Ahman Green
UDB-BJ Brad Johnson 20.00
UDB-AM Archie Manning
UDB-PM Peyton Manning 75.00
UDB-JR John Riggins
UDB-AS Antowain Smith
UDB-KS Kordell Stewart

2002 Upper Deck Collectors Club

NM/M
Complete Set (20): 20.00
Common Player: .50
NFL1 Peyton Manning 2.00
NFL2 Aaron Brooks .50
NFL3 Brett Favre 3.00
NFL4 Daunte Culpepper 2.00
NFL5 Donovan McNabb 2.00
NFL6 Eddie George 1.00
NFL7 Edgerrin James 2.00
NFL8 Emmitt Smith 3.00
NFL9 Jerome Bettis .50
NFL10 Jerry Rice 2.00
NFL11 Kerry Collins .50
NFL12 Kurt Warner 1.00
NFL13 LaDainian Tomlinson 2.00
NFL14 Marshall Faulk 1.00
NFL15 Michael Vick 3.00
NFL16 Ahman Green 1.00
NFL17 Randy Moss 2.00
NFL18 Ricky Williams 1.00
NFL19 Shaun Alexander .50
NFL20 Terrell Davis 1.00

2002 Upper Deck First Team Fabrics

NM/M
Common Player: 8.00
Inserted 1:144
FT-DB David Boston 12.00
FT-TB Tom Brady 25.00
FT-TC Tim Couch 12.00
FT-CD Corey Dillon 8.00
FT-MH Marvin Harrison 8.00
FT-KJ Keyshawn Johnson 8.00
FT-JP Jake Plummer 8.00
FT-ES Emmitt Smith 25.00
FT-JS Jimmy Smith 8.00
FT-RS Rod Smith 8.00

2002 Upper Deck Flight Suit Jerseys

NM/M
Common Player: 12.00
Inserted 1:288
FS-TB Tom Brady 25.00
FS-DC Daunte Culpepper 15.00
FS-BF Brett Favre 25.00
FS-DM Donovan McNabb 12.00
FS-KS Kordell Stewart 12.00
FS-MV Michael Vick 20.00

2002 Upper Deck Fourth Quarter Fabrics

NM/M
Common Player: 12.00
Inserted 1:288
FQ-MF Marshall Faulk/SP 25.00
FQ-BF Brett Favre 30.00
FQ-BG Brian Griese 15.00
FQ-PM Peyton Manning 20.00
FQ-RM Randy Moss 20.00
FQ-JR Jerry Rice/SP 30.00
FQ-KW Kurt Warner 20.00

2002 Upper Deck Ground Shakers Jerseys

NM/M
Common Player: 10.00
Inserted 1:288
GS-TD Terrell Davis 15.00
GS-CM Curtis Martin 10.00
GS-ES Emmitt Smith/SP 30.00
GS-AT Anthony Thomas 15.00
GS-LT LaDainian Tomlinson 15.00

2002 Upper Deck Kick-Off Classics Jerseys

NM/M
Common Player: 12.00
Inserted 1:288
KO-CC Chris Chambers 15.00
KO-BF Brett Favre 30.00
KO-EJ Edgerrin James 15.00
KO-DM Donovan McNabb 12.00
KO-LT LaDainian Tomlinson 12.00

2002 Upper Deck NFL Patches

Common Player:
Production 1 Set
NP-DC Daunte Culpepper
NP-MF Marshall Faulk
NP-BF Brett Favre
NP-EJ Edgerrin James
NP-PM Peyton Manning
NP-DM Donovan McNabb
NP-RM Randy Moss
NP-ES Emmitt Smith
NP-MV Michael Vick
NP-KW Kurt Warner

2002 Upper Deck Pigskin Patches

NM/M
Inserted 1:2500
PP-JB Jerome Bettis
PP-AB Aaron Brooks
PP-BF Brett Favre
PP-JG Jeff Garcia
PP-EJ Edgerrin James
PP-PM Peyton Manning 100.00
PP-RM Randy Moss 100.00
PP-JR Jerry Rice
PP-ES Emmitt Smith
PP-KW Kurt Warner

2002 Upper Deck Pigskin Patches - Hobby

NM/M
Inserted 1:2500
PP-TB Tom Brady
PP-DC Daunte Culpepper
PP-MF Marshall Faulk
PP-DF Doug Flutie
PP-RG Rich Gannon
PP-DM Donovan McNabb 125.00
PP-AT Anthony Thomas
PP-LT LaDainian Tomlinson
PP-MV Michael Vick
PP-RW Ricky Williams 75.00

2002 Upper Deck Playbooks Jerseys

NM/M
Inserted 1:100
PB-JB Jerome Bettis
PB-BO David Boston
PB-TB Tom Brady
PB-AB Aaron Brooks 100.00
PB-DC Daunte Culpepper
PB-MF Marshall Faulk
PB-BF Brett Favre 200.00
PB-AG Ahman Green
PB-PM Peyton Manning
PB-CM Curtis Martin 150.00
PB-DM Donovan McNabb
PB-RS Rod Smith 75.00
PB-AT Anthony Thomas 150.00
PB-LT LaDainian Tomlinson
PB-KW Kurt Warner

2002 Upper Deck Power Surge

NM/M
Common Player: 3.00
Inserted 1:12
PS-1 Michael Vick 4.00
PS-2 Anthony Thomas 3.00
PS-3 Emmitt Smith 4.00
PS-4 Terrell Davis 3.00
PS-5 Brett Favre 5.00
PS-6 Edgerrin James 3.00
PS-7 Peyton Manning 4.00
PS-8 Ricky Williams 3.00
PS-9 Curtis Martin 3.00
PS-10 Jerome Bettis 3.00
PS-11 LaDainian Tomlinson 3.00
PS-12 Shaun Alexander 3.00
PS-13 Kurt Warner 4.00
PS-14 Marshall Faulk 3.00

2002 Upper Deck Rookie Futures Jerseys

Inserted 1:72
RF-DC David Carr
RF-DF DeShaun Foster
RF-WG William Green
RF-JH Joey Harrington
RF-AL Ashley Lelie
RF-CP Clinton Portis
RF-PR Patrick Ramsey
RF-EL Antwaan Randle El
RF-JR Josh Reed
RF-DS Donte Stallworth

2002 Upper Deck Stadium Swatches

NM/M
Common Player: 10.00
Inserted 1:144
SS-MB Michael Bennett 15.00
SS-MB Mark Brunell/SP 15.00
SS-QC Quincy Carter/SP 20.00
SS-DF Doug Flutie 15.00
SS-EG Eddie George 15.00
SS-PW Peter Warrick 10.00

Values quoted in this guide reflect the retail price of a card—the price a collector can expect to pay when buying a card from a dealer. The wholesale price—that which a collector can expect to receive from a dealer when selling cards—will be significantly lower, depending on desirability and condition.

2002 Upper Deck Super Bowl XXXVII Card Show

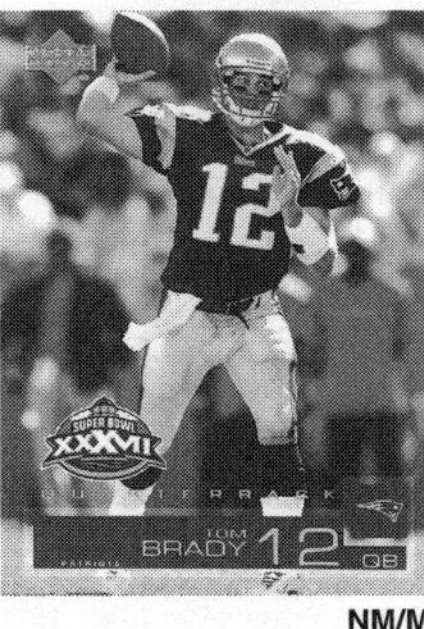

NM/M
Complete Set (10): 15.00
Common Player: 1.00
1 Tom Brady 2.00
2 Kurt Warner 2.00
3 Brett Favre 4.00
4 Drew Bledsoe 3.00
5 Joey Harrington 4.00
6 Jeff Garcia 1.00
7 Michael Vick 4.00
8 Peyton Manning 3.00
9 Donovan McNabb 2.00
10 David Carr 4.00

2002 Upper Deck Synchronicity

NM/M
Common Player: 3.00
Inserted 1:12
SY-1 Jake Plummer, David Boston 3.00
SY-2 Michael Vick, Warrick Dunn 4.00
SY-3 Drew Bledsoe, Josh Reed 4.00
SY-4 Tim Couch, Andre Davis 3.00
SY-5 Brett Favre, Javon Walker 10.00
SY-6 Peyton Manning, Marvin Harrison 6.00
SY-7 Mark Brunell, Jimmy Smith 3.00
SY-8 Daunte Culpepper, Randy Moss 6.00
SY-9 Tom Brady, Troy Brown 4.00
SY-10 Aaron Brooks, Donte Stallworth 6.00
SY-11 Kurt Warner, Isaac Bruce 5.00
SY-12 Donovan McNabb, Freddie Mitchell 3.00
SY-13 Kordell Stewart, Plaxico Burress 4.00
SY-14 Jeff Garcia, Terrell Owens 3.00

2002 Upper Deck Uniforms

NM/M
Common Player: 8.00
Inserted 1:72
UDU-DB Drew Brees 10.00
UDU-TB Tim Brown 15.00
UDU-IB Isaac Bruce 10.00
UDU-MB Mark Brunell 8.00
UDU-CC Chris Chambers 10.00
UDU-RD Ron Dayne 8.00
UGU-JG Jeff Garcia 10.00
UDU-BG Brian Griese 15.00
UDU-TH Travis Henry 15.00
UDU-BJ Brad Johnson 8.00
UDU-PM Peyton Manning 25.00
UDU-QM Quincy Morgan 10.00
UDU-JP Jerome Pathon 8.00
UDU-SS Shannon Sharpe 12.00
UDU-FT Fred Taylor 8.00

2002 Upper Deck Wildcards Jerseys

Inserted 1:144
Golds: 1.5X
Gold Production 150 Sets
WC-MB Michael Bennett
WC-IB Isaac Bruce
WC-CD Corey Dillon
WC-AG Ahman Green
WC-RM Randy Moss
WC-TO Terrell Owens
WC-JP Jerome Pathon
WC-DT David Terrell
WC-MV Michael Vick
WC-PW Peter Warrick

2002 UD Authentics

NM/M
Common Player: .20
Unlisted Stars: .75
Minor Stars: .40
Production 1000 sets
1989 Missing Rookies (141-144):
Production 1989 sets
1990 Missing Rookies (145-148):
Production to 1990 sets
Pack (5): 6.00
Wax Box (18): 75.00
1 Jake Plummer .40
2 David Boston .60
3 Thomas Jones .20
4 Michael Vick 2.00
5 Warrick Dunn .40
6 Jamal Lewis 1.00
7 Chris Redman .40
8 Travis Taylor .40
9 Drew Bledsoe 1.25
10 Eric Moulds .40
11 Travis Henry .40
12 Chris Weinke .60
13 Muhsin Muhammad .40
14 Anthony Thomas 1.50
15 Jim Miller .40
16 Marty Booker .40
17 Corey Dillon .40
18 Jon Kitna .20
19 Peter Warrick .40
20 Tim Couch 1.00
21 Emmitt Smith 2.00
22 Joey Galloway .40
23 Quincy Carter 1.50
24 Brian Griese .60
25 Terrell Davis 1.00
26 Shannon Sharpe .40
27 Germane Crowell .20
28 James Stewart .20
29 Az-Zahir Hakim .40
30 Brett Favre 2.50
31 Ahman Green .60
32 Terry Glenn .40
33 Jermaine Lewis .20
34 James Allen .20
35 Corey Bradford .20
36 Edgerrin James 1.50
37 Marvin Harrison .60
38 Peyton Manning 2.00
39 Jimmy Smith .40
40 Mark Brunell .60
41 Trent Green .20
42 Johnnie Morton .20
43 Priest Holmes .60
44 Ricky Williams 1.25
45 Chris Chambers .75
46 Jay Fiedler .20
47 Daunte Culpepper 1.25
48 Randy Moss 2.00
49 Michael Bennett .75
50 Troy Brown .60
51 Antowain Smith .40
52 Tom Brady 2.00
53 Aaron Brooks 1.00
54 Deuce McAllister 1.00
55 Joe Horn .40
56 Amani Toomer .40
57 Kerry Collins .40
58 Ron Dayne .40
59 Chad Pennington .50
60 Curtis Martin .40
61 Vinny Testaverde .40
62 Jerry Rice 2.00
63 Rich Gannon .60
64 Tim Brown .75
65 Donovan McNabb 1.25
66 Duce Staley .40
67 James Thrash .20
68 Plaxico Burress .75
69 Jerome Bettis .60
70 Kordell Stewart .60
71 Doug Flutie .75
72 Drew Brees 1.50
73 LaDainian Tomlinson 1.50
74 Garrison Hearst .40
75 Jeff Garcia .60
76 Terrell Owens .60
77 Ricky Watters .40
78 Shaun Alexander .75
79 Trent Dilfer .20
80 Isaac Bruce .60
81 Kurt Warner 2.00
82 Marshall Faulk 1.25
83 Keyshawn Johnson .40
84 Michael Pittman .20
85 Brad Johnson .40
86 Eddie George .60
87 Jevon Kearse .40
88 Steve McNair .60
89 Shane Matthews .20
90 Stephen Davis .60
91 *Josh McCown* 8.00
92 *Kurt Kittner* 8.00
93 *T.J. Duckett* 10.00
94 *Wes Pate* 5.00
95 *Chester Taylor* 5.00
96 *Ron Johnson* 6.00
97 *Lamont Brightful* 5.00
98 *Josh Reed* 8.00
99 *Randy Fasani* 5.00
100 *DeShaun Foster* 8.00
101 *Julius Peppers* 8.00
102 *William Green* 8.00
103 *Andre Davis* 10.00
104 *Chad Hutchinson* 6.00
105 *Antonio Bryant* 10.00
106 *Roy Williams* 12.00
107 *Clinton Portis* 25.00
108 *Herb Haygood* 5.00
109 *Ashley Lelie* 10.00
110 *Joey Harrington* 20.00
111 *Luke Staley* 6.00
112 *Javon Walker* 12.00
113 *David Carr* 25.00
114 *Jonathan Wells* 8.00
115 *Jabar Gaffney* 8.00
116 *Brian Allen* 5.00
117 *David Garrard* 6.00
118 *Leonard Henry* 5.00
119 *Rohan Davey* 8.00
120 *Deion Branch* 12.00
121 *J.T. O'Sullivan* 5.00
122 *Donte Stallworth* 10.00
123 *Tim Carter* 8.00
124 *Daryl Jones* 5.00
125 *Ronald Curry* 8.00
126 *Napoleon Harris* 5.00
127 *Brian Westbrook* 10.00
128 *Antwaan Randle El* 8.00
129 *Reche Caldwell* 8.00
130 *Quentin Jammer* 8.00
131 *Brandon Doman* 5.00
132 *Maurice Morris* 8.00
133 *Eric Crouch* 6.00
134 *Lamar Gordon* 8.00
135 *Travis Stephens* 8.00
136 *Marquise Walker* 8.00
137 *Jake Schifino* 5.00
138 *Patrick Ramsey* 10.00
139 *Ladell Betts* 8.00
140 *Cliff Russell* 5.00
141 Chris Chandler 2.00
142 Tim Brown 3.00
143 Wesley Walls 2.00
144 Rod Woodson 2.00
145 Rich Gannon 2.00
146 Emmitt Smith 6.00
147 Junior Seau 3.00
148 Shannon Sharpe 3.00

2002 UD Authentics Gold

Production 25 Sets

2002 UD Authentics All Star Authentics

NM/M
Common Player: 5.00
Inserted 1:18
Gold Production 25 Sets
AA-BL Drew Bledsoe 15.00
AA-BO David Boston 8.00
AA-CB Courtney Brown 5.00
AA-TC Tim Couch 10.00
AA-SD Stephen Davis 5.00
AA-DF Doug Flutie 8.00
AA-RG Rod Gardner 5.00
AA-PH Priest Holmes 8.00
AA-EJ Edgerrin James 15.00
AA-TJ Thomas Jones 5.00
AA-CM Curtis Martin 8.00
AA-SM Steve McNair 5.00
AA-EM Eric Moulds 5.00
AA-JP Jake Plummer 5.00
AA-PP Peerless Price 5.00
AA-JS Junior Seau 6.00
AA-CS Corey Simon 5.00
AA-TW Terrence Wilkins 5.00
AA-DW Darren Woodson 10.00

2002 UD Authentics American Authentics

NM/M
Inserted 1:216
Gold Production 15 Sets
Level 2 Production 25 Sets
Level 2 Gold Production 5 Sets
ST1-DC Daunte Culpepper/56 35.00
ST1-TG Tony Gonzalez/56 30.00
ST1-PM Peyton Manning 40.00
ST1-AT Anthony Thomas 20.00
ST1-LT LaDainian Tomlinson 30.00

2002 UD Authentics Glory Bound Jersey

NM/M
Common Player: 5.00
Inserted 1:18
Gold Production 25 Sets
GBJ-LB Ladell Betts 5.00
GBJ-AB Antonio Bryant 12.00
GBJ-DC David Carr 30.00
GBJ-RD Rohan Davey 10.00
GBJ-TD T.J. Duckett 15.00
GBJ-DF DeShaun Foster 10.00
GBJ-JG Jabar Gaffney 10.00
GBJ-DG David Garrard 5.00
GBJ-WG William Green 12.00
GBJ-JH Joey Harrington 25.00
GBJ-RJ Ron Johnson 5.00
GBJ-AL Ashley Lelie 15.00
GBJ-JM osh McCown 8.00
GBJ-MM Maurice Morris 10.00
GBJ-JP Julius Peppers 12.00
GBJ-CP Patrick Ramsey 10.00
GBJ-JR Josh Reed 8.00
GBJ-DS Donte Stallworth 15.00
GBJ-TS Travis Stephens 8.00
GBJ-JW Javon Walker 12.00
GBJ-MW Marquise Walker 8.00
GBJ-RW Roy Williams 12.00

2002 UD Authentics Rumble Backs

NM/M
Common Player: 2.00
Inserted 1:18
RB-1 Emmitt Smith 4.00
RB-2 Marshall Faulk 2.00
RB-3 Edgerrin James 3.00
RB-4 Terrell Davis 2.00
RB-5 Anthony Thomas 2.00
RB-6 LaDainian Tomlinson 3.00
RB-7 Curtis Martin 2.00
RB-8 Jerome Bettis 2.00
RB-9 Ricky Watters 2.00
RB-10 Ricky Williams 3.00
RB-11 Eddie George 2.00
RB-12 Jamal Lewis 2.00
RB-13 Corey Dillon 2.00
RB-14 Warrick Dunn 2.00
RB-15 Ahman Green 3.00
RB-16 Priest Holmes 3.00
RB-17 Duce Staley 2.00
RB-18 Michael Bennett 2.00
RB-19 Deuce McAllister 2.00
RB-20 Ron Dayne 2.00

2002 UD Authentics UDA Redemption

NM/M
Inserted 1:108
All items autographed/item/production
1 Brad Johnson 8X10/50
2 Brad Johnson 16X20/43 30.00
3 Brad Johnson Football/125 65.00
4 Brad Johnson Replica Mini-Helmet/53 60.00
5 Joe Montana, Roger Craig, Dwight Clark Football/2
6 Joe Montana, Roger Craig, Dwight Clark, Jerry Rice /Football/16
7 Dan Marino Embroidered Jersey/60 325.00
8 Dan Marino Dolphins Jersey/1
9 Dan Marino Super Bowl 19 Football/9
10 Dan Marino Football/106 175.00
11 Dan Marino Mini Football/4
12 Dan Marino Football w/Collector's Logo/2
13 Dan Marino 343 TD Card/3
14 Dan Marino 300 TD Card/44 100.00
15 Dan Marino Dan the Man Football/62
16 Dan Marino 16X20/1
17 Dan Marino 8X10/2
18 Dan Marino Lithograph/1
19 Dan Marino Replica Mini-Helmet/2
20 Dan Marino Replica Mini new design/14
21 Eddie George Football/86 115.00
22 Jim Brown 8X10/340 65.00
23 Jim Brown 16X20/127 110.00
24 Jim Brown Jersey/89 300.00
25 Jim Brown Mini-Helmet/127 90.00
26 Jim Brown Old Mask Mini-Helmet/44
27 Jim Brown Helmet/28 125.00
28 Jim Brown Football/107 175.00
29 Jerry Rice 49ers Helmet w/ Sticker/1
30 Jerry Rice 49ers Helmet/12
31 Jerry Rice Breakaway Filmstrip/113
32 Jerry Rice #3 Filmstrip/94 150.00
33 Jerry Rice 16X20/1
34 Jerry Rice Football/11 200.00
35 Jerry Rice Photo on Canvas/30 225.00
36 Jerry Rice Gallery Photo/79 120.00
37 Joe Montana SF Replica Mini-Helmet/11 115.00
38 Joe Montana ND Mini-Helmet/2
39 Joe Montana Super Joe Mini-Helmet/1
40 Joe Montana Notre Dame Football/241
Joe Montana Super Joe Football/1 200.00
42 Joe Montana Football/17 175.00
43 Joe Montana Super Bowl 24 Football/2
04 Joe Montana 16X20/7 150.00
45 Joe Montana Kansas City 8X10/12
46 Joe Montana 1st Championship 8X10/86
47 Joe Montana SF Chronicle Pape/7
48 Joe Montana Sports Illustrated Cover/1
49 Joe Montana 1993 Commemorative Card/14
50 Joe Montana 95 All-Pro Card/6
51 Joe Montana Commemorative Sheet/13 150.00
52 Joe Montana Filmstrip/195 150.00
53 Kurt Warner 16X20/103
54 Kurt Warner SB MVP Football/93 160.00
55 Dan Marino/ Joe Montana 8X10/1
56 Dan Marino, Joe Montana Commemorative Card/7 300.00
57 Mark Brunell Replica Mini-Helmet/11
58 Mark Brunell Mini-Helmet/44 90.00
59 Mark Brunell Helmet/130 175.00
60 Mark Brunell Football/176 75.00
61 Mark Brunell Filmstrip/3
62 Mark Brunell 16X20/182 40.00
63 Peyton Manning Embroidered Jersey/44
64 Peyton Manning Blue Jersey/271 280.00
65 Peyton Manning Jersey Numbers Piece/75 240.00
66 Peyton Manning 16X20/125

67 Peyton Manning 16X20 Card Blow Up/93
68 Peyton Manning 16X20 Background Image/9
69 Peyton Manning 8X10/50
70 Peyton Manning Football/100 160.00
71 Peyton Manning Rookie Record Football/60
72 Peyton Manning Helmet/75
73 Peyton Manning Tennessee Helmet/78
74 Peyton Manning Mini-Helmet/50
75 Randy Moss Football/48
76 Randy Moss Puma Jersey w/Patch/140 250.00
77 Randy Moss Jersey w/ROY Patch/36 450.00
78 Randy Moss Embroidered Jersey/19
79 Randy Moss Jersey w/ #4 Patch/129 200.00
80 Randy Moss Rookie Starter Jersey/3
81 Randy Moss 16X20 Trading Card/25 150.00
82 Randy Moss 16X20 Card Blow Up/67
83 Randy Moss 16X20 w/Foil Stamp/142
84 Ron Dayne Football/246 65.00
85 Ron Dayne Jersey/144
86 Ron Dayne Helmet/36 175.00
87 Ron Dayne Mini-Helmet/23
88 Ron Dayne Chromed Mini-Helmet/113
89 Ron Dayne 16X20/118 75.00
90 Ron Dayne 8X10/111
91 Roger Staubach, Troy Aikman Football/3
92 Tim Couch Football/42 170.00
93 Terrell Davis #66 Trading Card/129
94 Terrell Davis #17 Trading Card/129
95 Terrell Davis #19 Trading Card/144 40.00
96 Terrell Davis 8X10/128 90.00
97 Terrell Davis 16X20 Blow Up Card/127
98 Terrell Davis 16X20/50
99 Terrell Davis 16X20 Super Bowl/17
100 Terrell Davis 16X20 in Toploader/50
101 Terrell Davis Mini-Helmet/17
102 Terrell Davis Helmet/5
103 Terrell Davis Filmstrip/223 75.00
104 Terrell Davis Nike Jersey 2008 Yards/15
105 Terrell Davis Jersey/25
106 Terrell Davis Super Bowl Football/46 145.00
107 Terry Bradshaw Football/6
108 Terry Bradshaw 16X20/230 150.00
109 Tim Couch Embroidered Jersey/25 225.00
110 Tim Couch Jersey/145
111 Tim Couch Mini-Helmet/50
112 Tim Couch Helmet/10
113 Tim Couch 16X20/92
114 Tim Couch 8X10/160 45.00
115 Troy Aikman #43 Trading Card/78 50.00
116 Troy Aikman #21 Trading Card/66 50.00
117 Troy Aikman #58 Trading Card/216
118 Troy Aikman Steel Mini-Helmet/5
119 Troy Aikman Replica Mini-Helmet/25
120 Troy Aikman 8X10/86 50.00
121 Troy Aikman 16X20 The Run/67 120.00
122 Troy Aikman 16X20 Star Quarterback/51
123 Troy Aikman 16X20 Passing Follow.../118 120.00
124 Troy Aikman 16X20 Charging/49 120.00
125 Troy Aikman Filmstrip w/Foil/104 120.00
126 Troy Aikman Sports Illustrated/100
127 Troy Aikman White Jersey/2
128 Troy Aikman Blue Jersey/7 280.00
129 Joe Montana, Jerry Rice Helmet/10

2002 UD Graded

NM/M
Common Player: .50
Common Rookie (91-150): 4.00
Production 700 sets
Common Rookie Auto (151-200): 10.00
151-180 Production 550 sets
181-200 Production 250 sets
Pack (5): 32.00
Wax Box(6): 140.00

1 David Boston 1.00
2 Frank Sanders .50
3 Jake Plummer .75
4 Shawn Jefferson .50
5 Michael Vick 3.00
6 Warrick Dunn .75
7 Chris Redman .75
8 Ray Lewis .75
9 Travis Taylor .75
10 Drew Bledsoe 2.00
11 Eric Moulds .75
12 Travis Henry .75
13 Chris Weinke 1.00
14 Muhsin Muhammad .75
15 Anthony Thomas 2.50
16 Brian Urlacher 2.50
17 Jim Miller .75
18 Corey Dillon 1.00
19 Jon Kitna .75
20 Peter Warrick .75
21 James Jackson .75
22 Kevin Johnson .50
23 Tim Couch 1.50
24 Emmitt Smith 3.00
25 Joey Galloway .75
26 Quincy Carter 2.00
27 Brian Griese 1.00
28 Shannon Sharpe .75
29 Terrell Davis 1.50
30 Az-Zahir Hakim .75
31 Germane Crowell .50
32 Mike McMahon 1.00
33 Ahman Green 1.00
34 Brett Favre 4.00
35 Terry Glenn .75
36 Jermaine Lewis .50
37 James Allen .50
38 Edgerrin James 2.50
39 Marvin Harrison .75
40 Peyton Manning 3.00
41 Fred Taylor .75
42 Jimmy Smith .50
43 Mark Brunell 1.00
44 Priest Holmes 1.00
45 Trent Green .75
46 Chris Chambers 1.00
47 Jay Fiedler .75
48 Ricky Williams 2.00
49 Daunte Culpepper 2.00
50 Michael Bennett 1.00
51 Randy Moss 3.00
52 Antowain Smith .75
53 Tom Brady 3.00
54 Troy Brown 1.00
55 Aaron Brooks 1.50
56 Deuce McAllister 1.50
57 Joe Horn .50
58 Kerry Collins .75
59 Ron Dayne .75
60 Chad Pennington .75
61 Curtis Martin .75
62 Vinny Testaverde .75
63 Jerry Rice 3.00
64 Rich Gannon .75
65 Tim Brown 1.00
66 Donovan McNabb 2.00
67 Duce Staley .75
68 Freddie Mitchell .75
69 Hines Ward .75
70 Jerome Bettis .75
71 Kordell Stewart .75
72 Doug Flutie 1.00
73 Drew Brees 2.50
74 LaDainian Tomlinson 2.50
75 Garrison Hearst .75
76 Jeff Garcia 1.00
77 Terrell Owens 1.00
78 Koren Robinson .75
79 Shaun Alexander 1.00
80 Trent Dilfer .75
81 Isaac Bruce .75
82 Kurt Warner 2.00
83 Marshall Faulk 2.00
84 Brad Johnson .75
85 Keyshawn Johnson .75
86 Rob Johnson .75
87 Eddie George 1.00
88 Steve McNair 1.00
89 Rod Gardner .75
90 Stephen Davis .75
91 *Daniel Graham* 6.00
92 *Josh McCown* 10.00
93 *Josh Scobey* 4.00
94 *T.J. Duckett* 10.00
95 *Ronald Curry* 8.00
96 *Kalimba Edwards* 4.00
97 *Chester Taylor* 6.00
98 *Randy Fasani* 5.00
99 *Adrian Peterson* 6.00
100 *Chad Hutchinson* 5.00
101 *Javon Walker* 12.00
102 *Jonathan Wells* 8.00
103 *David Garrard* 8.00
104 *Leonard Henry* 4.00
105 *Dusty Bonner* 4.00
106 *Donte Stallworth* 10.00
107 *J.T. O'Sullivan* 4.00
108 *Mike Williams* 4.00
109 *Tim Carter* 6.00
110 *Larry Ned* 4.00
111 *Brian Westbrook* 10.00
112 *Freddie Milons* 5.00
113 *Ed Reed* 8.00
114 *Antwann Randle El* 10.00
115 *Julius Peppers* 8.00
116 *Quentin Jammer* 6.00
117 *John Henderson* 5.00
118 *Travis Stephens* 5.00
119 *Ladell Betts* 8.00
120 *Cliff Russell* 5.00
121 *Daniel Graham* 6.00
122 *Josh McCown* 10.00
123 *Josh Scobey* 5.00
124 *T.J. Duckett* 10.00
125 *Ronald Curry* 8.00
126 *Kalimba Edwards* 4.00
127 *Chester Taylor* 6.00
128 *Randy Fasani* 4.00
129 *Adrian Peterson* 6.00
130 *Chad Hutchinson* 5.00
131 *Javon Walker* 10.00
132 *Jonathan Wells* 6.00
133 *David Garrard* 5.00
134 *Leonard Henry* 4.00
135 *Dusty Bonner* 4.00
136 *Donte Stallworth* 10.00
137 *J.T. O'Sullivan* 4.00
138 *Mike Williams* 4.00
139 *Tim Carter* 6.00
140 *Larry Ned* 4.00
141 *Brian Westbrook* 10.00
142 *Freddie Milons* 5.00
143 *Ed Reed* 8.00
144 *Antwann Randle El* 10.00
145 *Julius Peppers* 8.00
146 *Quentin Jammer* 8.00
147 *John Henderson* 4.00
148 *Travis Stephens* 5.00
149 *Ladell Betts* 6.00
150 *Cliff Russell* 5.00
151 *Ron Johnson Auto* 10.00
152 *Josh Reed Auto* 15.00
153 *DeShaun Foster Auto* 20.00
154 *Andre Davis Auto* 20.00
155 *Antonio Bryant Auto* 20.00
156 *Roy Williams Auto* 40.00
157 *Woodrow Dantzler Auto* 12.00
158 *Luke Staley Auto* 12.00
159 *Jabar Gaffney Auto* 15.00
160 *Rohan Davey Auto* 20.00
161 *Brandon Doman Auto* 10.00
162 *Napoleon Harris Auto* 10.00
163 *Reche Caldwell Auto* 15.00
164 *Kelly Campbell Auto* 15.00
165 *Eric Crouch Auto* 20.00
166 *Ron Johnson Auto* 10.00
167 *Josh Reed Auto* 15.00
168 *DeShaun Foster Auto* 20.00
169 *Andre Davis Auto* 20.00
170 *Antonio Bryant Auto* 20.00
171 *Roy Williams Auto* 40.00
172 *Woodrow Dantzler Auto* 15.00
173 *Luke Staley Auto* 12.00
174 *Jabar Gaffney Auto* 15.00
175 *Rohan Davey Auto* 20.00
176 *Brandon Doman Auto* 10.00
177 *Napoleon Harris Auto* 10.00
178 *Reche Caldwell Auto* 15.00
179 *Kelly Campbell Auto* 15.00
180 *Eric Crouch Auto* 20.00
181 *Kurt Kittner Auto* 25.00
182 *Jeremy Shockey Auto* 80.00
183 *William Green Auto* 30.00
184 *Clinton Portis Auto* 100.00
185 *Ashley Lelie Auto* 40.00
186 *Joey Harrington Auto* 80.00
187 *David Carr Auto* 100.00
188 *Maurice Morris Auto* 25.00
189 *Marquise Walker Auto* 20.00
190 *Patrick Ramsey Auto* 40.00
191 *Kurt Kittner Auto* 25.00
192 *Jeremy Shockey Auto* 80.00
193 *William Green Auto* 40.00
194 *Clinton Portis Auto* 100.00
195 *Ashley Lelie Auto* 40.00
196 *Joey Harrington Auto* 80.00
197 *David Carr Auto* 100.00
198 *Maurice Morris Auto* 25.00
199 *Marquise Walker Auto* 20.00
200 *Patrick Ramsey Auto* 40.00

2002 UD Graded Dual Game Jerseys

NM/M
Common Player: 10.00
Production 100 sets
PB-100 Jake Plummer, David Boston 10.00
FS-100 Junior Seau, Doug Flutie 20.00
TB-100 Anthony Thomas, Marty Booker 25.00
JC-100 Tim Couch, Kevin Johnson 15.00
WF-100 Brett Favre, Kurt Warner 45.00
MJ-100 Peyton Manning, Edgerrin James 30.00
BS-100 Mark Brunell, Jimmy Smith 10.00
FC-100 Jay Fiedler, Chris Chambers 20.00
CM-100 Daunte Culpepper, Randy Moss
BP-100 Drew Bledsoe, Peerless Price 25.00
MT-100 Curtis Martin, Vinny Testaverde
GR-100 Rich Gannon, Jerry Rice 20.00
SS-100 Corey Simon, Duce Staley 15.00
SB-100 Kordell Stewart, Kendrell Bell 20.00
BT-100 Drew Brees, LaDainian Tomlinson 40.00
WH-100 Kurt Warner, Torry Holt 25.00
JP-100 Michael Pittman, Keyshawn Johnson 10.00

2002 UD Graded Game Jerseys

NM/M
Common Player: 10.00
Gold Not Priced Due to Scarcity
G1-MA Mike Alstott/200 12.00
G1-AN Mike Anderson/200 12.00
G1-BL Drew Bledsoe/200 20.00
G1-BO David Boston/200 10.00
G1-BR Drew Brees/200 12.00
G1-MB Mark Brunell/200 10.00
G1-SD Stephen Davis/200 10.00
G1-RA Ron Dayne/200 10.00
G1-MF Marshall Faulk/200 15.00
G1-DF Doug Flutie/200 10.00
G1-RG Rod Gardner/200 10.00
G1-EG Eddie George/200 10.00
G1-TG Trent Green/200 10.00
G1-PH Priest Holmes/200 15.00
G1-BA Brad Johnson/200 10.00
G1-KJ Keyshawn Johnson/200 10.00
G1-PM Peyton Manning/200 20.00
G1-CM Curtis Martin/200 10.00
G1-SM Steve McNair/200 10.00
G1-MO Johnnie Morton/200 10.00
G1-RM Randy Moss/200 25.00
G1-CP Chad Pennington/200 12.00
G1-JS Junior Seau/200 10.00
G1-SE Junior Seau/200 10.00
G1-JJ J.J. Stokes/200 10.00
G1-MS Michael Strahan/200 10.00
G1-VT Vinny Testaverde/200 10.00
G1-LT LaDainian Tomlinson/200 15.00
G1-BU Brian Urlacher/200 25.00
G1-CW Chris Weinke/200 10.00
G1-WE Chris Weinke/200 10.00
G1-DB Drew Bledsoe/200 15.00
G1-TC Tim Couch/200 15.00
G1-TD Terrell Davis/200 15.00
G1-RD Ron Dayne/200 10.00
G1-RG Rich Gannon/200 10.00
G1-EJ Edgerrin James/200 15.00
G1-TJ Thomas Jones/200 10.00
G1-MN Peyton Manning/200 20.00
G1-TO Terrell Owens/200 10.00
G1-TT Travis Taylor/200 10.00
G1-KW Kurt Warner/200 15.00
G2-DB Drew Bledsoe/100 15.00
G2-TC Tim Couch/100 15.00
G2-SD Stephen Davis/100 10.00
G2-EJ Edgerrin James/100 12.00
G2-SM Steve McNair/100 10.00
G2-RM Randy Moss/100 30.00
G2-TO Terrell Owens/100 15.00
G2-JP Jake Plummer/100 10.00
G2-JR Jerry Rice/100 30.00
G2-KW Kurt Warner/100 15.00
G3-CB Champ Bailey/50 15.00
G3-BO David Boston/50 15.00
G3-BN Courtney Brown/50 10.00
G3-TB Tim Brown/50 20.00
G3-IB Isaac Bruce/50 15.00
G3-MB Mark Brunell/50 10.00
G3-CA David Carr/50 80.00
G3-TC Tim Couch/50 15.00
G3-TD Terrell Davis/50 25.00
G3-RD Ron Dayne/50 10.00
G3-RG Rich Gannon/50 15.00
G3-EG Eddie George/50 10.00
G3-MH Marvin Harrison/50 10.00
G3-EJ Edgerrin James/50 25.00
G3-PM Peyton Manning/50 30.00
G3-CM Curtis Martin/50 15.00
G3-SM Steve McNair/50 10.00
G3-RM Randy Moss/50 60.00
G3-TO Terrell Owens/50 25.00
G3-DS Duce Staley/50 15.00
G3-KS Kordell Stewart/50 15.00
G3-KW Kurt Warner/50 15.00
G4-DB Drew Bledsoe/75 25.00
G4-BO David Boston/75 15.00
G4-BR Drew Brees/75 20.00
G4-IB Isaac Bruce/75 10.00
G4-MB Mark Brunell/75 10.00
G4-DC Daunte Culpepper/75 25.00
G4-SD Stephen Davis/75 10.00
G4-JE John Elway/75 80.00
G4-BF Brett Favre/75 80.00
G4-DF Doug Flutie/75 20.00
G4-FO DeShaun Foster/75 15.00
G4-RG Rich Gannon/75 10.00
G4-JH Joey Harrington/75 70.00
G4-MH Marvin Harrison/75 10.00
G4-TH Torry Holt/75 15.00
G4-EJ Edgerrin James/75 15.00
G4-PM Peyton Manning/75 40.00
G4-DM Dan Marino/75 90.00
G4-CM Curtis Martin/75 10.00
G4-SM Steve McNair/75 15.00
G4-EM Eric Moulds/75 10.00
G4-JP Jake Plummer/75 10.00
G4-PR Patrick Ramsey/75 25.00
G4-JR Jerry Rice/75 50.00
G4-WS Warren Sapp/75 15.00
G4-DS Duce Staley/75 15.00
G4-JS James Stewart/75 10.00
G4-KS Kordell Stewart/75 15.00
G4-AT Anthony Thomas/75 12.00
G4-KW Kurt Warner/75 20.00
G5-BO David Boston/75 15.00
G5-MB Mark Brunell/75 15.00
G5-CA David Carr/75 65.00
G5-DC Daunte Culpepper/75 20.00
G5-WD Warrick Dunn/75 10.00
G5-BF Brett Favre/75 80.00
G5-DF Doug Flutie/75 20.00
G5-JH Joey Harrington/75 70.00
G5-KJ Keyshawn Johnson/75 10.00
G5-JL Jamal Lewis/75 10.00
G5-RL Ray Lewis/75 10.00
G5-PM Peyton Manning/75 25.00
G5-CM Curtis Martin/75 10.00
G5-EM Eric Moulds/75 15.00
G5-CP ChadPennington/75 20.00
G5-JP Jake Plummer/75 10.00
G5-JR Jerry Rice/75 25.00
G5-JS James Stewart/75 10.00
G5-AT Anthony Thomas/75 15.00
G5-LT LaDainian Tomlinson/75 25.00
G5-BU Brian Urlacher/75 30.00
G5-KW Kurt Warner/75 10.00
G6-BO David Boston/50 20.00
G6-DC David Carr/50 75.00
G6-BF Brett Favre/50 80.00
G6-DF Doug Flutie/50 20.00
G6-CG Charlie Gardner/50 10.00
G6-TJ Thomas Jones/50 10.00
G6-JR Jerry Rice/50 50.00
G6-AT Anthony Thomas/50 45.00
G6-LT LaDainian Tomlinson/50 40.00
G6-KW Kurt Warner/50 30.00

2002 UD Graded Rookie Game Jerseys

NM/M
Common Player: 10.00
Production 350 Sets
Gold/125: 1.5X
LB-500 Ladell Betts 10.00
AB-500 Antonio Bryant 20.00
RC-500 Reche Caldwell 10.00
DC-500 David Carr 40.00
TC-500 Tim Carter 10.00
EC-500 Eric Crouch 15.00
RD-500 Rohan Davey 12.00
AD-500 Andre Davis 10.00
TJ-500 T.J. Duckett 25.00
DF-500 DeShaun Foster 12.00
JG-500 Jabar Gaffney 10.00
DG-500 Daniel Graham 10.00
WG-500 William Green 15.00
RJ-500 Ron Johnson 10.00
AL-500 Ashley Lelie 25.00
JM-500 Josh McCown 10.00
MM-500 Maurice Morris 10.00
JP-500 Julius Peppers 15.00
CP-500 Clinton Portis 25.00
PR-500 Patrick Ramsey 12.00
EL-500 Antwann Randle El 20.00
JR-500 Josh Reed 10.00
CR-500 Cliff Russell 10.00
JS-500 Jeremy Shockey 15.00
DS-500 Donte Stallworth 25.00
TS-500 Travis Stephens 10.00
WA-500 Javon Walker 15.00
MW-500 Marquise Walker 10.00
RW-500 Roy Williams 15.00
JH-500 Joey Harrington/50 50.00
RGDC David Carr/50 80.00
RGDS Donte Stallworth/50 40.00
RGJP Julius Peppers/50 25.00
RGWG William Green/50 30.00

2002 UD Honor Roll

NM/M
Common Player (1-90): .25
Unlisted Stars: .60
Minor Stars: .50
Common Rookie (91-180): 1.50
Minor Rookie: 2.00
Unlisted Rookie: 3.00
Production 1375 sets
Pack (5): 2.00
Wax Box (24): 35.00

1 Jake Plummer .50
2 David Boston .60
3 Michael Vick 2.00
4 Warrick Dunn .50
5 Jamal Lewis 1.00
6 Chris Redman .50
7 Drew Bledsoe 1.25
8 Travis Henry .50
9 Chris Weinke .60
10 Anthony Thomas 1.50
11 Marty Booker .60
12 Corey Dillon .60
13 Michael Westbrook .50
14 Tim Couch 1.00
15 Emmitt Smith 2.00
16 Quincy Carter 1.25
17 Brian Griese .60
18 Terrell Davis 1.00
19 Az-Zahir Hakim .50
20 Brett Favre 2.50
21 Ahman Green .60
22 Corey Bradford .25
23 Edgerrin James 1.50
24 Peyton Manning 2.00
25 Stacey Mack .25
26 Mark Brunell .60
27 Trent Green .60
28 Priest Holmes .60
29 Ricky Williams 1.25
30 Jay Fiedler .50
31 Daunte Culpepper 1.25
32 Randy Moss 2.00
33 Antowain Smith .50
34 Tom Brady 2.00
35 Aaron Brooks 1.00
36 Deuce McAllister 1.00
37 Kerry Collins .50
38 Ron Dayne .50
39 Curtis Martin .50
40 Vinny Testaverde .50
41 Jerry Rice 2.00
42 Rich Gannon .50
43 Donovan McNabb 1.25
44 Duce Staley .50
45 Jerome Bettis .50
46 Kordell Stewart .50
47 Doug Flutie .60
48 LaDainian Tomlinson 1.50
49 Jeff Garcia .60
50 Terrell Owens .60
51 Darrell Jackson .25
52 Shaun Alexander .60
53 Kurt Warner 2.00
54 Marshall Faulk 1.25
55 Keyshawn Johnson .50
56 Brad Johnson .50
57 Eddie George .60
58 Steve McNair .60
59 Stephen Davis .50
60 Rod Gardner .50
61 Jake Plummer, Thomas Jones, David Boston .50
62 Michael Vick, Warrick Dunn, Shawn Jefferson 1.00
63 Chris Redman, Jamal Lewis, Travis Taylor .50
64 Drew Bledsoe, Travis Henry, Peerless Price 1.00
65 Jim Miller, Anthony Thomas, Marty Booker .75
66 Jon Kitna, Corey Dillon, Peter Warrick .50
67 Tim Couch, Jamel White, Kevin Johnson .50
68 Quincy Carter, Emmitt Smith, Raghib Ismail 2.00
69 Brian Griese, Terrell Davis, Rod Smith 1.00
70 Mike McMahon, James Stewart, Az-Zahir Hakim .50
71 Brett Favre, Ahman Green, Terry Glenn 2.50
72 Peyton Manning, Edgerrin James, Marvin Harrison 2.00
73 Mark Brunell, Fred Taylor, Jimmy Smith .50
74 Trent Green, Priest Holmes, Johnnie Morton .50
75 Jay Fiedler, Ricky Williams, Chris Chambers 1.00
76 Daunte Culpepper, Michael Bennett, Randy Moss 2.00
77 Tom Brady, Antowain Smith, Troy Brown 2.00
78 Aaron Brooks, Deuce McAllister, Joe Horn 1.00
79 Kerry Collins, Ron Dayne, Amani Toomer .50
80 Vinny Testaverde, Curtis Martin, Laveranues Coles .50
81 Rich Gannon, Tim Brown, Jerry Rice 2.00
82 Donovan McNabb, Duce Staley, James Thrash 1.00
83 Kordell Stewart, Jerome Bettis, Hines Ward 1.00
84 Drew Brees, LaDainian Tomlinson, Curtis Conway 1.50
85 Jeff Garcia, Garrison Hearst, Terrell Owens 1.00
86 Trent Dilfer, Shaun Alexander, Darrell Jackson .50
87 Kurt Warner, Marshall Faulk, Isaac Bruce 2.00
88 Brad Johnson, Michael Pittman, Keyshawn Johnson .50
89 Steve McNair, Eddie George, Derrick Mason .50
90 Shane Matthews, Stephen Davis, Rod Gardner .50
91 *Adrian Peterson* 2.00
92 *Albert Haynesworth* 2.00
93 *Alex Brown* 1.50
94 *Andre Davis* 3.00
95 *Antwoine Womack* 1.50
96 *Antonio Bryant* 4.00
97 *Antwaan Randle El* 3.00
98 *Ashley Lelie* 4.00
99 *Ed Reed* 3.00
100 *Brandon Doman* 1.50
101 *Brian Allen* 1.50
102 *Najeh Davenport* 3.00
103 *Brian Westbrook* 4.00
104 *Chad Hutchinson* 2.00
105 *Chester Taylor* 2.50
106 *Cliff Russell* 2.00
107 *Clinton Portis* 10.00
108 *Craig Nall* 3.00
109 *Javin Hunter* 1.50
110 *Bryan Thomas* 2.00
111 *Daniel Graham* 2.50
112 *Daryl Jones* 1.50
113 *David Carr* 10.00
114 *David Garrard* 2.50
115 *Shaun Hill* 1.50
116 *Deion Branch* 5.00
117 *Derrick Lewis* 1.50
118 *DeShaun Foster* 3.00
119 *Jeff Kelly* 1.50
120 *Donte Stallworth* 4.00
121 *Levi Jones* 1.50
122 *Dwight Freeney* 3.00
123 *Eric Crouch* 2.00
124 *Freddie Milons* 2.00
125 *Jamin Elliott* 1.50
126 *Herb Haygood* 1.50
127 *J.T. O'Sullivan* 1.50
128 *Jabar Gaffney* 3.00
129 *Jake Schifino* 1.50
130 *Jason McAddley* 1.50
131 *Javon Walker* 5.00
132 *Jeremy Shockey* 6.00
133 *Jerramy Stevens* 2.00
134 *Joey Harrington* 8.00
135 *John Henderson* 2.00
136 *Jonathan Wells* 3.00
137 *Josh McCown* 4.00
138 *Josh Reed* 3.00
139 *Josh Scobey* 1.50
140 *Julius Peppers* 3.00
141 *Kalimba Edwards* 1.50
142 *Kelly Campbell* 3.00
143 *Keyuo Craver* 1.50
144 *Kurt Kittner* 3.00
145 *Ladell Betts* 3.00
146 *Lamar Gordon* 2.50
147 *Larry Ned* 1.50
148 *Lee Mays* 1.50
149 *Leonard Henry* 1.50
150 *Lito Sheppard* 2.00
151 *Luke Staley* 2.50
152 *Marquise Walker* 2.50

153 *Maurice Morris* 3.00
154 *Darrell Hill* 1.50
155 *Napoleon Harris* 1.50
156 *Patrick Ramsey* 4.00
157 *Kevin Curtis* 1.50
158 *Phillip Buchanon* 2.50
159 *Kendall Newson* 1.50
160 *Quentin Jammer* 2.50
161 *Randy Fasani* 2.00
162 *Reche Caldwell* 3.00
163 *Ricky Williams* 2.00
164 *Rocky Calmus* 2.50
165 *Rohan Davey* 3.00
166 *Ron Johnson* 2.50
167 *Ronald Curry* 3.00
168 *Roy Williams* 5.00
169 *Ryan Sims* 2.00
170 *Sam Simmons* 1.50
171 *Seth Burford* 1.50
172 *T.J. Duckett* 4.00
173 *Tellis Redmon* 2.00
174 *Tim Carter* 2.50
175 *Travis Stephens* 2.50
176 *Wendell Bryant* 2.00
177 *Lamont Thompson* 1.50
178 *William Green* 4.00
179 *Dennis Johnson* 1.50
180 *Michael Lewis* 1.50

2002 UD Honor Roll Gold

Gold Production 25 Sets

2002 UD Honor Roll Dean's List

NM/M
Common Player: 1.00
Inserted 1:24
Gold Production 25 Sets
DLQ-1 Jake Plummer 1.00
DLQ-2 Donovan McNabb 2.00
DLQ-3 Kurt Warner 3.00
DLQ-4 Brett Favre 5.00
DLQ-5 Peyton Manning 3.00
DLQ-6 Rich Gannon 1.00
DLQ-7 Daunte Culpepper 2.00
DLQ-8 Drew Bledsoe 2.00
DLQ-9 Vinny Testaverde 1.00
DLQ-10 Jeff Garcia 1.00
DLR-1 Marshall Faulk 2.00
DLR-2 Edgerrin James 3.00
DLR-3 Curtis Martin 1.00
DLR-4 Stephen Davis 1.00
DLR-5 Eddie George 1.00
DLR-6 Ricky Williams 2.00
DLR-7 Jerome Bettis 2.00
DLR-8 Terrell Davis 1.00
DLR-9 Emmitt Smith 5.00
DLR-10 Warrick Dunn 1.00
DLW-1 Randy Moss 3.00
DLW-2 Wayne Chrebet 1.00
DLW-3 Marvin Harrison 1.00
DLW-4 Jimmy Smith 1.00
DLW-5 Jerry Rice 3.00
DLW-6 Tim Brown 2.00
DLW-7 Keyshawn Johnson 1.00
DLW-8 David Boston 1.00
DLW-9 Terrell Owens 2.00
DLW-10 Isaac Bruce 1.00

2002 UD Honor Roll Students of the Game

NM/M
Common Player: 2.00
Inserted 1:24
Gold Production 25 Sets
SGQ-1 David Carr 6.00
SGQ-2 Joey Harrington 6.00
SGQ-3 Patrick Ramsey 3.00
SGQ-4 Josh McCown 2.00
SGQ-5 Kurt Kittner 2.00
SGQ-6 Randy Fasani 2.00
SGQ-7 J.T. O'Sullivan 2.00
SGQ-8 Rohan Davey 2.00
SGQ-9 Chad Hutchinson 3.00
SGQ-10 David Garrard 2.00
SGR-1 William Green 2.00
SGR-2 T.J. Duckett 4.00
SGR-3 DeShaun Foster 2.00
SGR-4 Clinton Portis 4.00
SGR-5 Maurice Morris 1.00
SGR-6 Travis Stephens 2.00
SGR-7 Jonathan Wells 2.00
SGR-8 Lamar Gordon 1.00
SGR-9 Ladell Betts 1.00
SGR-10 Brian Westbrook 2.00
SGW-1 Ashley Lelie 4.00
SGW-2 Donte Stallworth 4.00
SGW-3 Javon Walker 3.00
SGW-4 Josh Reed 2.00
SGW-5 Jabar Gaffney 2.00
SGW-6 Reche Caldwell 2.00
SGW-7 Antonio Bryant 3.00
SGW-8 Tim Carter 2.00
SGW-9 Marquise Walker 2.00
SGW-10 Ron Johnson 2.00

2002 UD Honor Roll Sophmore Standouts

NM/M
Common Player: 1.00
Inserted 1:24
Gold Production 25 Sets
SSQ-1 Michael Vick 3.00
SSQ-2 Tom Brady 3.00
SSQ-3 Chris Redman 1.00
SSQ-4 Quincy Carter 2.00
SSQ-5 Mike McMahon 1.00
SSQ-6 Chris Weinke 1.00
SSQ-7 Aaron Brooks 2.00
SSQ-8 Drew Brees 2.00
SSQ-9 Chad Pennington 2.00
SSQ-10 Sage Rosenfels 1.00
SSR-1 LaDainian Tomlinson 2.00
SSR-2 Anthony Thomas 2.00
SSR-3 Shaun Alexander 1.00
SSR-4 James Jackson 1.00
SSR-5 Dominic Rhodes 1.00
SSR-6 Thomas Jones 1.00
SSR-7 Michael Bennett 1.00
SSR-8 Elvis Joseph 1.00
SSR-9 Travis Henry 1.00
SSR-10 Kevan Barlow 1.00
SSW-1 Chris Chambers 2.00
SSW-2 Marvin "Snoop" Minnis 1.00
SSW-3 Plaxico Burress 2.00
SSW-4 Quincy Morgan 1.00
SSW-5 Robert Ferguson 1.00
SSW-6 Travis Taylor 1.00
SSW-7 Santana Moss 1.00
SSW-8 Rod Gardner 1.00
SSW-9 David Terrell 2.00
SSW-10 Freddie Mitchell 1.00

2002 UD Honor Roll Clutch Performers

NM/M
Common Player: 10.00
Inserted 1:72
CP-BO David Boston 10.00
CP-CC Cris Carter 15.00
CP-CD Corey Dillon 10.00
CP-MH Marvin Harrison 10.00
CP-EJ Edgerrin James 10.00
CP-PM Peyton Manning 20.00
CP-RM Randy Moss 25.00
CP-JP Jake Plummer 10.00
CP-VT Vinny Testaverde 10.00

2002 UD Honor Roll Rookie Honor Roll

NM/M
Common Player: 10.00
Inserted 1:72
RHR-DC David Carr 25.00
RHR-RD Rohan Davey 10.00
RHR-DG David Garrard 10.00
RHR-JH Joey Harrington 25.00
RHR-AL Ashley Lelie 15.00
RHR-JM Josh McCown 10.00
RHR-PR Patrick Ramsey 10.00
RHR-EL Antwann Randle El 15.00
RHR-DS Donte Stallworth 15.00

2002 UD Honor Roll Up and Coming

NM/M
Common Player: 8.00
Inserted 1:72
UC-BO David Boston 8.00
UC-BR Drew Brees 8.00
UC-LC Laveranues Coles
UC-TC Tim Couch 8.00
UC-RD Ron Dayne 8.00
UC-TJ Thomas Jones 8.00
UC-RM Randy Moss 20.00
UC-SM Santana Moss 8.00

2002 UD Honor Roll Great Connections

NM/M
Common Player: 10.00
Inserted 1:240
GC-CJ LaMont Jordan, Wayne Chrebet 10.00
GC-GM Johnnie Morton, Trent Green 10.00
GC-RB Ladell Betts, Patrick Ramsey 10.00
GC-BF Doug Flutie, Drew Brees 15.00
GC-SF Doug Flutie, Junior Seau

2002 UD Honor Roll Offensive Threats

NM/M
Common Player: 15.00
Inserted 1:240
OT-CF Curtis Conway, Doug Flutie 15.00
OT-MB Mark Brunell, Peyton Manning 25.00
OT-GS J.J. Stokes, Jeff Garcia 15.00
OT-BF Brett Favre, Mark Brunell 40.00
OT-WR Charles Woodson, Jerry Rice 25.00

2002 UD Honor Roll Field Generals

NM/M
Common Player: 10.00
Inserted 1:240
FG-HR Joey Harrington, Patrick Ramsey 20.00
FG-MG Josh McCown, David Garrard 10.00
FG-DC Rohan Davey, David Carr 25.00
FG-CH David Carr, Joey Harrington 75.00
FG-HM Joey Harrington, Josh McCown 25.00

2002 UD Honor Roll Lettermen Autographs

NM/M
Common Player: 20.00
Inserted 1:480
HRL-BR Drew Brees
HRL-RC Rosevelt Colvin 40.00
HRL-PM Peyton Manning 40.00
HRL-AT Anthony Thomas
HRL-LT LaDainian Tomlinson/SP
HRL-MV Michael Vick 60.00
HRL-CW Chris Weinke 20.00

2002 Upper Deck MVP

NM/M
Common Player: .15
Unlisted Stars: .75
Minor Stars: .40
Common Rookie (251-300): 1.00
Minor Rookies: 1.50
Unlisted Rookies: 2.00
Pack (8): 2.00
Wax Box (24): 45.00
1 Arnold Jackson .15
2 Dave Brown .15
3 David Boston .60
4 Frank Sanders .15
5 Jake Plummer .25
6 MarTay Jenkins .15
7 Freddie Jones .25
8 Jamal Anderson .50
9 Keith Brooking .15
10 Michael Vick 2.50
11 Rodney Thomas .15
12 Shawn Jefferson .25
13 Tony Martin .25
14 Warrick Dunn .50
15 Brandon Stokley .15
16 Chris McAlister .15
17 Chris Redman .50
18 Ray Lewis .50
19 Sam Gash .15
20 Travis Taylor .50
21 Terry Allen .15
22 Drew Bledsoe 1.50
23 Alex Van Pelt .15
24 Eric Moulds .50
25 Kenyatta Wright .15
26 Larry Centers .15
27 Peerless Price .50
28 Shawn Bryson .15
29 Travis Henry .50
30 Chris Weinke .60
31 Lamar Smith .40
32 Isaac Byrd .15
33 Muhsin Muhammad .40
34 Nick Goings .15
35 Richard Huntley .15
36 Tim Biakabutuka .15
37 Wesley Walls .15
38 Anthony Thomas 2.00
39 Brian Urlacher 2.00
40 David Terrell .60
41 Dez White .15
42 Jim Miller .40
43 Larry Whigham .15
44 Marty Booker .40
45 Chris Chandler .15
46 Corey Dillon .60
47 Darnay Scott .15
48 Jon Kitna .15
49 Peter Warrick .40
50 Ron Dugans .15
51 Scott Mitchell .15
52 Chad Johnson .15
53 Courtney Brown .50
54 JaJuan Dawson .15
55 James Jackson 1.00
56 Kevin Johnson .15
57 Quincy Morgan .75
58 Rickey Dudley .15
59 Tim Couch 1.00
60 Chris Sanders .15
61 Emmitt Smith 2.50
62 Joey Galloway .40
63 Ken-Yon Rambo .15
64 La'Roi Glover .15
65 Quincy Carter 1.50
66 Raghib Ismail .15
67 Darren Woodson .15
68 Ryan Leaf .15
69 Chester McGlockton .15
70 Brian Griese .75
71 Shannon Sharpe .50
72 Kevin Kasper .15
73 Mike Anderson 1.00
74 Olandis Gary .15
75 Rod Smith .50
76 Terrell Davis .50
77 Antonio Carter .15
78 Az-Zahir Hakim .40
79 Charlie Batch .15
80 Chris Claiborne .15
81 Cory Schlesinger .15
82 Desmond Howard .15
83 Germane Crowell .15
84 James Stewart .75
85 Mike McMahon .60
86 Bill Schroeder .50
87 Ahman Green .75
88 Brett Favre 3.00
89 Bubba Franks .15
90 Antonio Freeman .15
91 Donald Driver .15
92 Kabeer Gbaja-Biamila .50
93 William Henderson .15
94 Corey Bradford .50
95 Jamie Sharper .15
96 Jermaine Lewis .15
97 Kailee Wong .15
98 Matt Stevens .15
99 Tony Boselli .15
100 James Allen .15
101 Aaron Glenn .15
102 Edgerrin James 2.00
103 Dominic Rhodes .15
104 Marcus Pollard .15
105 Marvin Harrison .50
106 Peyton Manning 2.50
107 Qadry Ismail .15
108 Reggie Wayne .15
109 Stacey Mack .15
110 Elvis Joseph .15
111 Fred Taylor .50
112 Jimmy Smith .15
113 Jonathan Quinn .15
114 Keenan McCardell .15
115 Mark Brunell .75
116 Trent Green .50
117 Derrick Alexander .15
118 Johnnie Morton .15
119 Marvin "Snoop" Minnis .40
120 Mike Cloud .15
121 Priest Holmes .75
122 Tony Gonzalez .50
123 Tony Richardson .15
124 Ricky Williams .75
125 Chris Chambers .75
126 James McKnight .15
127 Jay Fiedler .50
128 Zach Thomas .40
129 Oronde Gadsden .15
130 Ray Lucas .15
131 Randy Moss 2.50
132 Spergon Wynn .15
133 Cris Carter .25
134 Daunte Culpepper 1.50
135 Doug Chapman .15
136 Michael Bennett .75
137 Tom Brady 2.50
138 Troy Brown .15
139 Adam Vinatieri .25
140 Antowain Smith .15
141 David Patten .15
142 Donald Hayes .15
143 J.R. Redmond .75
144 Willie Jackson .50
145 Jerome Pathon .15
146 Jake Reed .15
147 Aaron Brooks 1.00
148 John Carney .15
149 Deuce McAllister 1.00
150 Joe Horn .15
151 Kyle Turley .15
152 Robert Wilson .15
153 Tiki Barber .40
154 Amani Toomer .40
155 Ike Hilliard .15
156 Jason Sehorn .15
157 Joe Jurevicius .15
158 Kerry Collins .40
159 Michael Strahan .25
160 Ron Dayne .50
161 Wayne Chrebet .15
162 Chad Pennington .50
163 Curtis Martin .50
164 LaMont Jordan .50
165 Laveranues Coles .50
166 Marvin Jones .15
167 Santana Moss .50
168 Vinny Testaverde .25
169 Tyrone Wheatley .15
170 Charles Woodson .50
171 Charlie Garner .75
172 Jerry Rice 2.50
173 John Parrella .15
174 Jon Ritchie .15
175 Rich Gannon .50
176 Tim Brown .75
177 Todd Pinkston .15
178 Correll Buckhalter .50
179 Donovan McNabb 1.50
180 Duce Staley .50
181 Freddie Mitchell .50
182 Hugh Douglas .15
183 James Thrash .15
184 Koy Detmer .15
185 Troy Edwards .15
186 Chris Fuamatu-Ma'afala .15
187 Hines Ward .50
188 Jerome Bettis .50
189 Kendrell Bell .50
190 Kordell Stewart .75
191 Mark Bruener .15
192 Plaxico Burress .75
193 Tim Dwight .50
194 Curtis Conway .15
195 Doug Flutie .75
196 Drew Brees 2.00
197 Junior Seau .50
198 LaDainian Tomlinson 2.00
199 Marcellus Wiley .15
200 Rodney Harrison .15
201 Stephen Alexander .40
202 Terrell Owens .75
203 Andre Carter .15
204 Cedrick Wilson .15
205 Fred Beasley .15
206 Garrison Hearst .25
207 J.J. Stokes .25
208 Jeff Garcia .75
209 Kevan Barlow .15
210 Tai Streets .15
211 Doug Evans .15
212 Bobby Engram .15
213 Darrell Jackson .15
214 James Williams .15
215 John Randle .15
216 Koren Robinson .50
217 Matt Hasselbeck .15
218 Shaun Alexander .75
219 Trent Dilfer .25
220 Aeneas Williams .15
221 Isaac Bruce .50
222 Kurt Warner 2.50
223 Marshall Faulk 1.50
224 Ricky Proehl .15
225 Torry Holt .40
226 Trung Canidate .15
227 Terrence Wilkins .15
228 John Lynch .15
229 Keyshawn Johnson .50
230 Michael Pittman .15
231 Mike Alstott .50
232 Rob Johnson .50
233 Shaun King .15
234 Warren Sapp .50
235 Brad Johnson .50
236 Derrick Mason .15
237 Eddie George .75
238 Frank Wycheck .15
239 Jevon Kearse .25
240 Kevin Dyson .15
241 Steve McNair .75
242 Chris Coleman .15
243 Darrell Green .25
244 Jacquez Green .15
245 Ki-Jana Carter .25
246 Michael Westbrook .50
247 Rod Gardner .50
248 Stephen Davis .50
249 Tony Banks .25
250 Champ Bailey .50
251 *David Carr* 8.00
252 *DeShaun Foster* 2.00
253 *Antonio Bryant* 3.00
254 *Joey Harrington* 6.00
255 *William Green* 3.00
256 *Josh Reed* 2.00
257 *Patrick Ramsey* 3.00
258 *Clinton Portis* 8.00
259 *Jabar Gaffney* 2.00
260 *Rohan Davey* 2.00
261 *T.J. Duckett* 3.00
262 *Ashley Lelie* 3.00
263 *Kurt Kittner* 1.50
264 *Luke Staley* 1.50
265 *Ron Johnson* 1.00
266 *Antwann Randle El* 2.00
267 *Travis Stephens* 1.50
268 *Marquise Walker* 1.50
269 *Julius Peppers* 2.00
270 *Chad Hutchinson* 1.00
271 *Maurice Morris* 2.00
272 *Donald Reche Caldwell* 1.50
273 *Randy Fasani* 1.00
274 *Lamar Gordon* 1.50
275 *Donte Stallworth* 3.00
276 *Brandon Doman* 1.00
277 *Damien Anderson* 1.00
278 *Roy Williams* 4.00
279 *J.T. O'Sullivan* 1.00
280 *Leonard Henry* 1.00
281 *Javon Walker* 4.00
282 *David Garrard* 1.00
283 *Chester Taylor* 1.00
284 *Andre Davis* 2.00
285 *Josh McCown* 1.50
286 *Adrian Peterson* 1.50
287 *Seth Burford* 1.00
288 *Deion Branch* 4.00
289 *Jonathan Wells* 2.00
290 *Ladell Betts* 1.50
291 *Cliff Russell* 1.00
292 *Eric Crouch* 2.00
293 *Dusty Bonner* 1.00
294 *Tim Carter* 1.00
295 *Brian Westbrook* 3.00
296 *Quentin Jammer* 1.50
297 *Brian Poli-Dixon* 1.00
298 Donovan McNabb Checklist .25
299 Curtis Martin Checklist .25
300 Tom Brady Checklist 1.00

2002 Upper Deck MVP Gold

Stars: 20X-40X
Rookies: 10X-20X
Production 25 Sets

2002 Upper Deck MVP Silver

Stars: 6X-12X
Rookies: 2X-4X
Production 100 Sets

2002 Upper Deck MVP Prosign

NM/M
Common Player: 20.00
Production 127 sets
PS-DB Drew Brees 35.00
PS-CC Chris Chambers 35.00
PS-EC Eric Crouch 75.00
PS-WG William Green 75.00
PS-RJ Ron Johnson 25.00
PS-PM Peyton Manning 75.00
PS-MMc Mike McMahon 60.00
PS-FM Freddie Mitchell 60.00
PS-QM Quincy Morgan 35.00
PS-JR Josh Reed 60.00
PS-AT Anthony Thomas 60.00
PS-MW Marquise Walker 40.00
PS-CW Chris Weinke 30.00

2002 Upper Deck MVP Souvenir Singles

NM/M
Common Player: 10.00
Inserted 1:40
SS-JA Jesse Armstead 10.00
SS-CB Champ Bailey 10.00
SS-AB Anthony Becht 10.00
SS-DB Drew Brees 15.00
SS-MB Mark Brunell 15.00
SS-CC Curtis Conway 10.00
SS-SD Stephen Davis 15.00
SS-BF Brett Favre 40.00
SS-DF Doug Flutie 15.00
SS-JG Jeff Garcia 15.00
SS-RG Rod Gardner 10.00
SS-EM Eric Moulds 10.00
SS-CP Chad Pennington 15.00
SS-FS Frank Sanders 10.00
SS-JS Junior Seau 15.00
SS-DS Duce Staley 15.00
SS-JJ J.J. Stokes 10.00
SS-FT Fred Taylor 10.00
SS-DT David Terrell 25.00
SS-AT Anthony Thomas 30.00
SS-CW Charles Woodsen 15.00

2002 Upper Deck MVP Souvenir Doubles

NM/M
Common Player: 20.00
Inserted 1:48
SD-PS Jake Plummer, Frank Sanders 20.00
SD-TT Anthony Thomas, LaDainian Tomlinson 40.00
SD-US Brian Urlacher, Junior Seau 35.00
SD-MT Jim Miller, David Terrell 30.00
SD-MJ Quincy Morgan, James Jackson 20.00
SD-CJ Tim Couch, Kevin Johnson 20.00
SD-LS Jermaine Lewis, Jamie Sharper 20.00
SD-MH Peyton Manning, Marvin Harrison 25.00
SD-BB Mark Brunell Packers, Mark Brunell Jaguars 20.00
SD-CM Daunte Culpepper, Randy Moss 30.00
SD-CH Kerry Collins, Ike Hilliard 20.00
SD-TM Vinny Testaverde, Curtis Martin 20.00
SD-BT Drew Brees, LaDainian Tomlinson 30.00
SD-JF Freddie Jones, Doug Flutie 25.00
SD-GF Jeff Garcia, Doug Flutie 30.00
SD-RR Jerry Rice Raiders, Jerry Rice 49ers 50.00
SD-DA Warrick Dunn, Mike Alstott 20.00
SD-BG Champ Bailey, Darrell Green 20.00
SD-SM Duce Staley, Donovan McNabb 25.00
SD-PJ Lamont Jordan, Chad Pennington 25.00

2002 Upper Deck MVP Team MVP

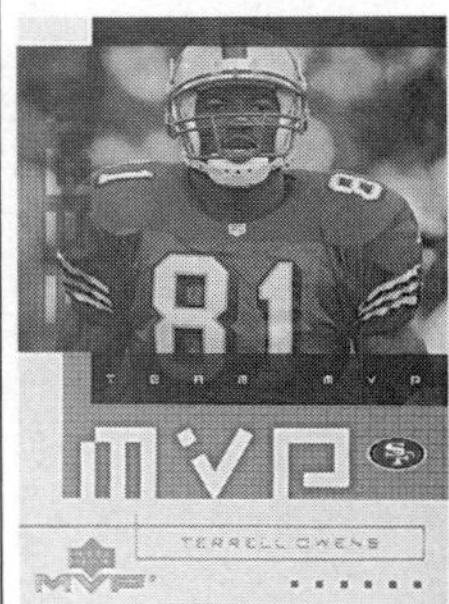

NM/M
Common Player: 2.00
Inserted 1:6
TM-1 Jake Plummer 1.00
TM-2 Michael Vick 3.00
TM-3 Corey Dillon 2.00
TM-4 Tim Couch 2.00
TM-5 Rod Smith 1.00
TM-6 Brett Favre 5.00
TM-7 Peyton Manning 3.00
TM-8 Mark Brunell 1.00
TM-9 Randy Moss 2.00
TM-10 Ricky Williams 1.00
TM-11 Curtis Martin 1.00
TM-12 Donovan McNabb 1.00
TM-13 Kordell Stewart 2.00
TM-14 LaDainian Tomlinson 3.00
TM-15 Jeff Garcia 2.00
TM-16 Terrell Owens 2.00
TM-17 Shaun Alexander 3.00
TM-18 Isaac Bruce 2.00
TM-19 Keyshawn Johnson 2.00
TM-20 Eddie George 2.00

2002 Upper Deck MVP Top-10

NM/M
Common Player: 3.00
Inserted 1:12

		NM/M
TT-1	Anthony Thomas	4.00
TT-2	Priest Holmes	3.00
TT-3	Tom Brady	5.00
TT-4	Michael Strahan	3.00
TT-5	Jerry Rice	4.00
TT-6	Rich Gannon	3.00
TT-7	Emmitt Smith	4.00
TT-8	Jerome Bettis	3.00
TT-9	Kurt Warner	4.00
TT-10	Marshall Faulk	3.00

2002 Upper Deck Ovation

NM/M
Common Player: .20
Unlisted Stars: .75
Minor Stars: .40
Common Rookie (91-120): 4.00
Minor Rookies: 5.00
Unlisted Rookies: 6.00
Pack (5): 1.75
Wax Box (24): 30.00

		NM/M
1	David Boston	.60
2	Jake Plummer	.40
3	Warrick Dunn	.40
4	Michael Vick	2.50
5	Jamal Anderson	.20
6	Travis Taylor	.20
7	Ray Lewis	.40
8	Alex Van Pelt	.20
9	Travis Henry	.40
10	Drew Bledsoe	1.50
11	Muhsin Muhammad	.40
12	Chris Weinke	.60
13	Lamar Smith	.50
14	Marty Booker	.40
15	Jim Miller	.40
16	Anthony Thomas	2.00
17	Peter Warrick	.50
18	Jon Kitna	.20
19	Corey Dillon	.60
20	Quincy Morgan	.50
21	Tim Couch	1.00
22	Raghib Ismail	.20
23	Quincy Carter	1.50
24	Emmitt Smith	2.50
25	Shannon Sharpe	.20
26	Brian Griese	.75
27	Terrell Davis	1.00
28	Mike McMahon	.60
29	James Stewart	.50
30	Az-Zahir Hakim	.50
31	Terry Glenn	.50
32	Brett Favre	3.00
33	Ahman Green	.75
34	James Allen	.20
35	Jermaine Lewis	.20
36	Marvin Harrison	.50
37	Peyton Manning	2.50
38	Edgerrin James	2.00
39	Jimmy Smith	.50
40	Mark Brunell	.60
41	Johnnie Morton	.40
42	Trent Green	.40
43	Priest Holmes	.60
44	Jay Fiedler	.40
45	Chris Chambers	.75
46	Ricky Williams	1.50
47	Randy Moss	2.50
48	Michael Bennett	.75
49	Daunte Culpepper	1.50
50	Troy Brown	.75
51	Tom Brady	2.50
52	Antowain Smith	.40
53	Joe Horn	.40
54	Aaron Brooks	1.00
55	Deuce McAllister	1.00
56	Amani Toomer	.40
57	Kerry Collins	.40
58	Ron Dayne	.40
59	Vinny Testaverde	.40
60	Curtis Martin	.50
61	Santana Moss	.40
62	Tim Brown	.75
63	Jerry Rice	2.50
64	Rich Gannon	.40
65	Donovan McNabb	1.50
66	Duce Staley	.50
67	Freddie Mitchell	.40
68	Plaxico Burress	.75
69	Kordell Stewart	.40
70	Jerome Bettis	.40
71	Doug Flutie	.60
72	LaDainian Tomlinson	2.00
73	Drew Brees	2.00
74	Terrell Owens	.75
75	Jeff Garcia	.75
76	Garrison Hearst	.20
77	Shaun Alexander	.75
78	Trent Dilfer	.40
79	Kurt Warner	2.50
80	Marshall Faulk	1.50
81	Isaac Bruce	.40
82	Keyshawn Johnson	.40
83	Brad Johnson	.40
84	Mike Alstott	.40
85	Rob Johnson	.40
86	Steve McNair	.40
87	Eddie George	.75
88	Jessie Armstead	.20
89	Rod Gardner	.40
90	Stephen Davis	.50
91	*Andre Davis*	10.00
92	*Antonio Bryant*	10.00
93	*Antwann Randle El*	8.00
94	*Ashley Lelie*	10.00
95	*Cliff Russell*	3.00
96	*Clinton Portis*	25.00
97	*Daniel Graham*	6.00
98	*David Carr*	25.00
99	*David Garrard*	4.00
100	*DeShaun Foster*	8.00
101	*Reche Caldwell*	6.00
102	*Donte Stallworth*	10.00
103	*Jabar Gaffney*	8.00
104	*Javon Walker*	12.00
105	*Jeremy Shockey*	15.00
106	*Joey Harrington*	20.00
107	*Josh McCown*	10.00
108	*Josh Reed*	8.00
109	*Julius Peppers*	8.00
110	*Marquise Walker*	4.00
111	*Maurice Morris*	8.00
112	*Patrick Ramsey*	10.00
113	*Quentin Jammer*	5.00
114	*Rohan Davey*	8.00
115	*Ron Johnson*	4.00
116	*Roy Williams*	12.00
117	*T.J. Duckett*	10.00
118	*Tim Carter*	4.00
119	*Travis Stephens*	4.00
120	*William Green*	10.00

2002 Upper Deck Ovation Gold

Stars: 20X-40X
Production 25 Sets

2002 Upper Deck Ovation Silver

Stars: 6X-12X
Production 100 Sets

2002 Upper Deck Ovation Bound for Glory Jersey

NM/M
Common Player: 10.00
Inserted 1:72
Gold Production 25 Sets

		NM/M
BG-TBa	Tiki Barber	10.00
BG-MB	Michael Bennett	20.00
BG-TBr	Tom Brady	40.00
BG-RD	Ron Dayne	10.00
BG-RG	Rod Gardner	10.00
BG-JH	Joey Harrington	30.00
BG-TH	Travis Henry	15.00
BG-JJ	James Jackson	10.00
BG-QM	Quincy Morgan	10.00
BG-PP	Peerless Price	10.00
BG-DS	Duce Staley	10.00
BG-DT	David Terrell	20.00
BG-LT	LaDainian Tomlinson	20.00
BG-CW	Charles Woodson	20.00

2002 Upper Deck Ovation Jerseys

NM/M
Common Player: 10.00
Inserted 1:72
Gold Production 25 Sets

		NM/M
OJ-AB	Aaron Brooks	10.00
OJ-IB	Isaac Bruce	10.00
OJ-MB	Mark Brunell	10.00
OJ-TC	Tim Couch	15.00
OJ-DC	Daunte Culpepper	20.00
OJ-MF	Marshall Faulk	25.00
OJ-JF	Jay Fiedler	10.00
OJ-DF	DeShaun Foster	25.00
OJ-PM	Peyton Manning	35.00
OJ-DM	Donovan McNabb	10.00
OJ-WS	Warren Sapp	10.00
OJ-ES	Emmitt Smith	40.00
OJ-RW	Ricky Williams	10.00

2002 Upper Deck Ovation Lead Performers

NM/M
Common Player: 1.00
Inserted 1:12

		NM/M
LP-1	Jake Plummer	1.00
LP-2	Warrick Dunn	1.00
LP-3	Michael Vick	3.00
LP-4	Travis Henry	2.00
LP-5	David Terrell	2.00
LP-6	Brian Urlacher	2.00
LP-7	Tim Couch	1.00
LP-8	Brett Favre	5.00
LP-9	Peyton Manning	3.00
LP-10	Jimmy Smith	1.00
LP-11	Mark Brunell	1.00
LP-12	Trent Green	1.00
LP-13	Chris Chambers	2.00
LP-14	Jay Fiedler	1.00
LP-15	Ricky Williams	1.00
LP-16	Daunte Culpepper	2.00
LP-17	Michael Bennett	2.00
LP-18	Randy Moss	3.00
LP-19	Antowain Smith	1.00
LP-20	Tom Brady	5.00
LP-21	Aaron Brooks	1.00
LP-22	Deuce McAllister	2.00
LP-23	Kerry Collins	1.00
LP-24	Ron Dayne	1.00
LP-25	Duce Staley	1.00
LP-26	Kordell Stewart	1.00
LP-27	Jerome Bettis	1.00
LP-28	Drew Brees	1.00
LP-29	Isaac Bruce	1.00
LP-30	Steve McNair	1.00

2002 Upper Deck Ovation Milestones

NM/M
Common Player: 1.00
Inserted 1:12

		NM/M
OM-1	David Boston	1.00
OM-2	Jamal Anderson	1.00
OM-3	Tony Martin	1.00
OM-4	Ray Lewis	1.00
OM-5	Anthony Thomas	2.00
OM-6	Corey Dillon	1.00
OM-7	Emmitt Smith	3.00
OM-8	Terrell Davis	1.00
OM-9	Brett Favre	5.00
OM-10	Edgerrin James	2.00
OM-11	Peyton Manning	3.00
OM-12	James Stewart	1.00
OM-13	Mark Brunell	1.00
OM-14	Priest Holmes	1.00
OM-15	Randy Moss	3.00
OM-16	Tom Brady	5.00
OM-17	Drew Bledsoe	1.00
OM-18	Curtis Martin	1.00
OM-19	Michael Strahan	1.00
OM-20	Vinny Testaverde	1.00
OM-21	Jerry Rice	3.00
OM-22	Rich Gannon	1.00
OM-23	Tim Brown	1.00
OM-24	Jerome Bettis	1.00
OM-25	Kendrell Bell	1.00
OM-26	Terrell Owens	1.00
OM-27	Kurt Warner	3.00
OM-28	Marshall Faulk	2.00
OM-29	Eddie George	1.00
OM-30	Darrell Green	1.00

2002 Upper Deck Ovation Standing O

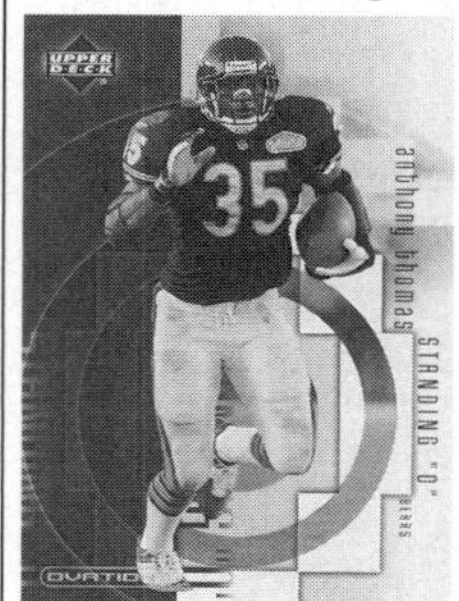

NM/M
Common Player: 1.00
Inserted 1:12

		NM/M
SO-1	David Boston	1.00
SO-2	Michael Vick	3.00
SO-3	Jamal Lewis	1.00
SO-4	Chris Weinke	1.00
SO-5	Anthony Thomas	2.00
SO-6	Jim Miller	1.00
SO-7	Marty Booker	1.00
SO-8	Peter Warrick	1.00
SO-9	Emmitt Smith	3.00
SO-10	Quincy Carter	1.00
SO-11	Brian Griese	1.00
SO-12	Mike Anderson	1.00
SO-13	Rod Smith	1.00
SO-14	Mike McMahon	2.00
SO-15	Ahman Green	1.00
SO-16	Edgerrin James	2.00
SO-17	Marvin Harrison	1.00
SO-18	Peyton Manning	3.00
SO-19	Donovan McNabb	1.00
SO-20	Donovan McNabb	1.00
SO-21	Jerome Bettis	1.00
SO-22	Plaxico Burress	2.00
SO-23	Doug Flutie	1.00
SO-24	LaDainian Tomlinson	2.00
SO-25	Garrison Hearst	1.00
SO-26	Jeff Garcia	1.00
SO-27	Terrell Owens	1.00
SO-28	Shaun Alexander	2.00
SO-29	Keyshawn Johnson	1.00
SO-30	Rod Gardner	1.00

2002 Upper Deck Ovation Tried and True Jerseys

NM/M
Common Player: 10.00
Inserted 1:72
Gold Production 25 Sets

		NM/M
TT-JB	Jerome Bettis	10.00
TT-CD	Corey Dillon	10.00
TT-JE	John Elway	50.00
TT-BF	Brett Favre	40.00
TT-MH	Marvin Harrison	10.00
TT-TH	Torry Holt	10.00
TT-EJ	Edgerrin James	25.00
TT-DM	Dan Marino	50.00
TT-RM	Randy Moss	35.00
TT-JR	Jerry Rice	35.00
TT-BS	Bruce Smith	10.00
TT-AT	Amani Toomer	10.00
TT-KW	Kurt Warner	35.00
TT-MW	Michael Westbrook	10.00

2002 UD Piece of History

NM/M
Common Player: .20
Unlisted Stars: .75
Minor Stars: .40
Common Rookie (101-140): 2.00
Rookies Tier 1 Production 2002 Sets
Rookies Tier 2 Production 500 Sets
Common Rookie JSY (141-162): 10.00
Rookie JSY Tier 1 Production 1500 Sets
Rookie JSY Tier 2 Production 500 Sets
Pack (5): 2.25
Wax Box (24): 35.00

		NM/M
1	David Boston	.60
2	Jake Plummer	.40
3	Chris Chandler	.20
4	Jamal Anderson	.40
5	Michael Vick	2.50
6	Elvis Grbac	.20
7	Qadry Ismail	.20
8	Ray Lewis	.50
9	Eric Moulds	.20
10	Rob Johnson	.40
11	Travis Henry	.20
12	Chris Weinke	.60
13	Donald Hayes	.20
14	Muhsin Muhammad	.20
15	Anthony Thomas	2.00
16	Brian Urlacher	2.00
17	David Terrell	.75
18	Jim Miller	.20
19	Marty Booker	.20
20	Corey Dillon	.75
21	Jon Kitna	.20
22	Peter Warrick	.40
23	James Jackson	.20
24	Kevin Johnson	.20
25	Tim Couch	1.00
26	Emmitt Smith	2.50
27	Quincy Carter	1.50
28	Raghib Ismail	.20
29	Brian Griese	.75
30	Ed McCaffrey	.40
31	Rod Smith	.50
32	Terrell Davis	1.00
33	Charlie Batch	.20
34	James Stewart	.50
35	Mike McMahon	.60
36	Ahman Green	.75
37	Antonio Freeman	.40
38	Bill Schroeder	.20
39	Brett Favre	3.00
40	Dominic Rhodes	.20
41	Edgerrin James	2.00
42	Marvin Harrison	.75
43	Peyton Manning	2.50
44	Jimmy Smith	.20
45	Mark Brunell	.75
46	Priest Holmes	.50
47	Tony Gonzalez	.50
48	Trent Green	.20
49	Chris Chambers	.75
50	Jay Fiedler	.50
51	Lamar Smith	.50
52	Oronde Gadsden	.20
53	Daunte Culpepper	1.50
54	Michael Bennett	.75
55	Randy Moss	2.50
56	Antowain Smith	.50
57	Drew Bledsoe	1.50
58	Tom Brady	2.50
59	Troy Brown	.60
60	Aaron Brooks	1.00
61	Joe Horn	.40
62	Michael Strahan	.50
63	Kerry Collins	.50
64	Ron Dayne	.50
65	Tiki Barber	.40
66	Curtis Martin	.50
67	Laveranues Coles	.20
68	Santana Moss	.50
69	Vinny Testaverde	.20
70	Jerry Rice	2.50
71	Rich Gannon	.50
72	Tim Brown	.75
73	Donovan McNabb	1.50
74	Duce Staley	.50
75	Freddie Mitchell	.50
76	James Thrash	.20
77	Jerome Bettis	.50
78	Kendrell Bell	.50
79	Kordell Stewart	.50
80	Doug Flutie	.75
81	Junior Seau	.50
82	LaDainian Tomlinson	2.00
83	Garrison Hearst	.20
84	Jeff Garcia	.75
85	Terrell Owens	.50
86	Matt Hasselbeck	.20
87	Ricky Watters	.20
88	Shaun Alexander	.75
89	Isaac Bruce	.50
90	Kurt Warner	2.50
91	Marshall Faulk	1.50
92	Torry Holt	.40
93	Brad Johnson	.40
94	Keyshawn Johnson	.50
95	Mike Alstott	.50
96	Warrick Dunn	.50
97	Eddie George	.75
98	Steve McNair	.75
99	Stephen Davis	.50
100	Tony Banks	.20
101	*Antonio Bryant*	10.00
102	*Adrian Peterson*	6.00
103	*Brian Poli-Dixon*	2.00
104	*Kyle Johnson*	2.00
105	*Clinton Portis*	30.00
106	*David Carr/500*	50.00
107	*Rocky Calmus*	6.00
108	*Eric Crouch*	8.00
109	*Jeremy Shockey*	20.00
110	*Jabar Gaffney*	10.00
111	*Damien Anderson*	4.00
112	*Josh Reed*	10.00
113	*Lamar Gordon*	6.00
114	*Julius Peppers/500*	20.00
115	*Kelly Campbell*	6.00
116	*Leonard Henry*	3.00
117	*Chad Hutchinson/500*	15.00
118	*Luke Staley*	6.00
119	*Josh Scobey*	3.00
120	*Marquise Walker*	6.00
121	*Roy Williams*	15.00
122	*Patrick Ramsey*	12.00
123	*Ashley Lelie/500*	25.00
124	*Rohan Davey*	10.00
125	*Ron Johnson*	4.00
126	*T.J. Duckett*	12.00
127	*Cliff Russell*	4.00
128	*William Green/500*	20.00
129	*Donald Reche Caldwell*	8.00
130	*Donte Stallworth*	12.00
131	*Javon Walker*	15.00
132	*David Garrard*	6.00
133	*Quentin Jammer*	6.00
134	*Ladell Betts*	6.00
135	*Freddie Milons*	4.00
136	*Brian Westbrook*	12.00
137	*John Henderson*	3.00
138	*Kalimba Edwards*	3.00
139	*Daniel Graham*	6.00
140	*Josh McCown*	10.00
141	*Joey Harrington JSY/500*	40.00
142	*Phillip Buchanon JSY/500*	15.00
143	*Maurice Morris JSY/1500*	10.00
144	*George Godsey JSY/1500*	6.00
145	*J.T. O'Sullivan JSY/1500*	8.00
146	*Kurt Kittner JSY/500*	15.00
147	*DeShaun Foster JSY/500*	20.00
148	*Antwann Randle El JSY/1500*	15.00
149	*Woodrow Dantzler JSY/1500*	10.00
150	*Randy Fasani JSY/1500*	8.00
151	*Kahlil Hill JSY/1500*	10.00
152	*Atrews Bell JSY/1500*	10.00
153	*Eric McCoo JSY/1500*	6.00
154	*Ricky Williams JSY/1500*	8.00
155	*Albert Haynesworth JSY/500*	10.00
156	*Lamont Thompson JSY/1500*	8.00
157	*Andre Davis JSY/1500*	12.00
158	*Travis Stevens JSY/500*	12.00
159	*Delvon Flowers JSY/1500*	8.00
160	*Robert Thomas JSY/1500*	10.00
161	*Marques Anderson JSY/1500*	8.00
162	*Kenyon Coleman JSY/1500*	8.00

2002 UD Piece of History The Big Game

NM/M
Common Player: 1.00
Inserted 1:10

		NM/M
BG-1	Chris Chandler	1.00
BG-2	Trent Dilfer	1.00
BG-3	Darren Sharper	1.00
BG-4	Jamal Lewis	2.00
BG-5	Ray Lewis	2.00
BG-6	Rod Woodson	2.00
BG-7	Bruce Smith	1.00
BG-8	Emmitt Smith	5.00
BG-9	Larry Allen	1.00
BG-10	Ed McCaffrey	1.00
BG-11	Rod Smith	2.00
BG-12	Terrell Davis	2.00
BG-13	John Elway	6.00
BG-14	Brett Favre	8.00
BG-15	Antonio Freeman	1.00
BG-16	Dorsey Levens	1.00
BG-17	Drew Bledsoe	2.00
BG-18	Tom Brady	6.00
BG-19	Troy Brown	1.00
BG-20	Michael Strahan	2.00
BG-21	Jessie Armstead	1.00
BG-22	Junior Seau	2.00
BG-23	Jerry Rice	5.00
BG-24	Ricky Watters	1.00
BG-25	Kurt Warner	6.00
BG-26	Marshall Faulk	4.00
BG-27	London Fletcher	1.00
BG-28	Isaac Bruce	2.00
BG-29	Steve McNair	2.00
BG-30	Darrell Green	1.00

2002 UD Piece of History The Big Game Jerseys

NM/M
Common Player: 5.00
Inserted 1:48
Patch Production 25 Sets

		NM/M
BGJ-LA	Larry Allen	5.00
BGJ-JA	Jessie Armstead	5.00
BGJ-DB	Drew Bledsoe	10.00
BGJ-IB	Isaac Bruce	10.00
BGJ-CC	Chris Chandler	5.00
BGJ-RD	Ron Dayne	5.00
BGJ-TD	Trent Dilfer	10.00
BGJ-JE	John Elway	40.00
BGJ-MF	Marshall Faulk	20.00
BGJ-BF	Brett Favre	40.00
BGJ-LF	London Fletcher	5.00
BGJ-DG	Darrell Green	5.00
BGJ-JK	Jim Kelly	15.00
BGJ-JL	Jamal Lewis	10.00
BGJ-RL	Ray Lewis	10.00
BGJ-DM	Dan Marino	40.00
BGJ-CM	Curtis Martin	15.00
BGJ-SM	Steve McNair	15.00
BGJ-OP	Orlando Pace	5.00
BGJ-JR	Jerry Rice	25.00
BGJ-JS	Junior Seau	15.00
BGJ-BS	Bruce Smith	5.00
BGJ-MS	Michael Strahan	10.00
BGJ-TT	Travis Taylor	5.00
BGJ-KW	Kurt Warner	30.00
BGJ-RW	Rod Woodson	10.00
BGJ-SY	Steve Young	15.00

2002 UD Piece of History Hitmakers

NM/M
Common Player: 2.00
Inserted 1:50

		NM/M
HM-1	Dan Morgan	3.00
HM-2	Chris Claiborne	3.00
HM-3	Marvin Jones	3.00
HM-4	Andy Katzenmoyer	5.00
HM-5	Rocky Calmus	8.00
HM-6	Kevin Hardy	3.00

2002 UD Piece of History Hitmakers Jerseys

NM/M
Common Player: 12.00
Inserted 1:336

		NM/M
HMJ-CC	Chris Claiborne	12.00
HMJ-RH	Rodney Harrison	12.00
HMJ-RL	Ray Lewis	25.00
HMJ-DM	Dan Morgan	12.00
HMJ-JSJ	unior Seau	25.00
HMJ-BU	Brian Urlacher	60.00

2002 UD Piece of History National Honors

NM/M
Common Player: 3.00
Inserted 1:10

		NM/M
NH-1	Doug Flutie	4.00
NH-2	Chris Weinke	5.00
NH-3	Desmond Howard	3.00
NH-4	Ty Detmer	3.00
NH-5	Eric Crouch	10.00
NH-6	Ricky Williams	4.00
NH-7	Ron Dayne	3.00
NH-8	Vinny Testaverde	3.00
NH-9	Charles Woodson	3.00
NH-10	Tim Brown	4.00
NH-11	Eddie George	5.00

A card number in parenthese ( ) indicates the set is unnumbered.

2002 UD Piece of History National Honors Jerseys

NM/M
Common Player: 10.00
Inserted 1:168
NHJ-MA Marcus Allen 10.00
NHJ-TB Tim Brown 12.00
NHJ-RD Ron Dayne 25.00
NHJ-DF Doug Flutie 20.00
NHJ-EG Eddie George 12.00
NHJ-DH Desmond Howard 10.00
NHJ-VT Vinny Testaverde 10.00
NHJ-CW Chris Weinke 20.00
NHJ-RW Ricky Williams 10.00
NHJ-CW Charles Woodson 12.00

2002 UD Piece of History Rookie Glory

NM/M
Common Player: 2.00
Inserted 1:13
RG-1 Brian Urlacher 5.00
RG-2 Anthony Thomas 7.00
RG-3 Emmitt Smith 7.00
RG-4 Mike Anderson 2.00
RG-5 Edgerrin James 4.00
RG-6 Randy Moss 5.00
RG-7 Curtis Martin 3.00
RG-8 Charles Woodson 2.00
RG-9 Hugh Douglas 2.00
RG-10 Jerome Bettis 2.00
RG-11 Kendrell Bell 2.00
RG-12 Warrick Dunn 2.00
RG-13 Jevon Kearse 2.00

2002 UD Piece of History Rookie Glory Jerseys

NM/M
Common Player: 10.00
Inserted 1:108
RGJ-MB Michael Bennett 25.00
RGJ-DC Daunte Culpepper 20.00
RGJ-HD Hugh Douglas 10.00
RGJ-WD Warrick Dunn 10.00
RGJ-EJ Edgerrin James 25.00
RGJ-JK Jevon Kearse 10.00
RGJ-PM Peyton Manning 30.00
RGJ-CM Curtis Martin 15.00
RGJ-RM Randy Moss 30.00
RGJ-AT Anthony Thomas 30.00
RGJ-LT LaDainian Tomlinson 20.00
RGJ-BU Brian Urlacher 30.00
RGJ-CW Charles Woodson 25.00

2002 UD Piece of History Run to History

NM/M
Common Player: 4.00
Inserted 1:30
RH-1 Luke Staley 4.00
RH-2 Ricky Williams 5.00
RH-3 Ron Dayne 4.00
RH-4 LaDainian Tomlinson 7.00
RH-5 Garrison Hearst 4.00
RH-6 Eddie George 5.00

2002 UD Piece of History Run to History Jerseys

NM/M
Common Player: 10.00
RHJ-RD Ron Dayne 10.00
RHJ-EG Eddie George 12.00
RHJ-EJ Edgerrin James 20.00
RHJ-JL Jamal Lewis 10.00
RHJ-LT LaDainian Tomlinson 25.00
RHJ-RW Ricky Williams 12.00

2002 Upper Deck Sweet Spot

NM/M
Common Player: .25
Common Rookie (91-150): 1.00
91-150 Production 1050 Sets
Common Rookie Auto (151-166): 12.00
Pack (4): 9.00
Wax Box (12): 110.00
1 Aaron Brooks 1.25
2 Tim Couch 1.25
3 Jon Kitna .25
4 Brett Favre 3.00
5 Donovan McNabb 1.50
6 Jeff Garcia .75
7 Michael Vick 2.50
8 Mark Brunell .75
9 Steve McNair .75
10 Kordell Stewart .50
11 Drew Bledsoe 1.50
12 Tom Brady 2.50
13 Kurt Warner 2.50
14 Brian Griese .75
15 Jim Miller .25
16 Jake Plummer .50
17 Quincy Carter 1.25
18 Peyton Manning 2.50
19 Keyshawn Johnson .75
20 Travis Henry .50
21 LaDainian Tomlinson 2.00
22 Emmitt Smith 2.50
23 Michael Bennett .75
24 Duce Staley .50
25 Thomas Jones .25
26 Deuce McAllister 1.25
27 Eddie George .75
28 Marshall Faulk 1.50
29 Curtis Martin .75
30 Ahman Green .75
31 Priest Holmes 1.25
32 Edgerrin James 2.00
33 Antowain Smith .50
34 Ricky Williams 1.50
35 Anthony Thomas 1.50
36 Jerome Bettis .50
37 Shaun Alexander .75
38 Kerry Collins .50
39 Drew Brees 2.00
40 Chris Redman .50
41 Marc Bulger 1.25
42 Jay Fiedler .50
43 Trent Green .75
44 Daunte Culpepper 1.50
45 Rich Gannon .75
46 Rodney Peete .25
47 Vinny Testaverde .25
48 Stephen Davis .50
49 James Allen .25
50 Tiki Barber .50
51 Ron Dayne .50
52 Ray Lewis .50
53 Corey Dillon .75
54 Brian Urlacher 2.00
55 Junior Seau .50
56 Warrick Dunn .50
57 Fred Taylor .50
58 Jamal Lewis 1.25
59 Trent Dilfer .50
60 James Stewart .50
61 David Patten .25
62 Eric Moulds .50
63 Isaac Bruce .50
64 Troy Brown .50
65 Terrell Owens .75
66 Moe Williams .25
67 Joe Horn .50
68 Az-Zahir Hakim .50
69 Jimmy Smith .25
70 Michael Westbrook .25
71 Olandis Gary .25
72 Chris Chambers .25
73 Kevin Johnson .25
74 Joey Galloway .50
75 Hines Ward .50
76 Garrison Hearst .50
77 Wayne Chrebet .50
78 Muhsin Muhammad .50
79 Rod Gardner .50
80 Jerry Rice 2.50
81 Tim Brown .75
82 Shannon Sharpe .50
83 Terry Glenn .50
84 Randy Moss 2.50
85 Corey Bradford .25
86 Marty Booker .50
87 Keenan McCardell .50
88 Marvin Harrison .75
89 David Boston .75
90 Eddie Kennison .25
91 *Tim Carter* 6.00
92 *Joey Harrington* 15.00
93 *Patrick Ramsey* 10.00
94 *David Garrard* 6.00
95 *Donte Stallworth* 10.00
96 *Reche Caldwell* 6.00
97 *William Green* 10.00
98 *Josh Reed* 6.00
99 *DeShaun Foster* 8.00
100 *Jeremy Shockey* 15.00
101 *Mike Williams* 5.00
102 *Daniel Graham* 6.00
103 *Josh McCown* 10.00
104 *Javon Walker* 15.00
105 *Travis Stephens* 5.00
106 *Marquise Walker* 5.00
107 *T.J. Duckett* 10.00
108 *Damien Anderson* 5.00
109 *Quentin Jammer* 6.00
110 *Bryan Thomas* 5.00
111 *Chad Hutchinson* 6.00
112 *Brian Westbrook* 10.00
113 *Lamar Gordon* 6.00
114 *Deion Branch* 15.00
115 *Ed Reed* 8.00
116 *Jonathan Wells* 6.00
117 *Phillip Buchanon* 6.00
118 *Wendell Bryant* 5.00
119 *Kurt Kittner* 6.00
120 *Randy McMichael* 8.00
121 *Brandon Doman* 5.00
122 *Adrian Peterson* 6.00
123 *Ricky Williams* 6.00
124 *Seth Burford* 5.00
125 *Shaun Hill* 5.00
126 *Anthony Weaver* 5.00
127 *Freddie Milons* 5.00
128 *Darrell Hill* 5.00
129 *Daryl Jones* 5.00
130 *Chester Taylor* 6.00
131 *Najeh Davenport* 8.00
132 *Jason McAddley* 5.00
133 *Preston Parsons* 5.00
134 *Michael Lewis* 5.00
135 *Mike Rumph* 5.00
136 *Lamont Thompson* 5.00
137 *Dwight Freeney* 8.00
138 *Napoleon Harris* 5.00
139 *Tank Williams* 5.00
140 *Lee Mays* 5.00
141 *Robert Thomas* 5.00
142 *Tellis Redmon* 5.00
143 *Alex Brown* 5.00
144 *Ryan Sims* 5.00
145 *Larry Tripplett* 5.00
146 *Quinn Gray* 5.00
147 *Jesse Chatman* 6.00
148 *Jamin Elliott* 5.00
149 *Ben Leber* 5.00
150 *Lito Sheppard* 5.00
151 *Antonio Bryant Auto/550* 30.00
152 *Rohan Davey Auto/550* 20.00
153 *Randy Fasani Auto/550* 15.00
154 *J.T. O'Sullivan Auto/550* 15.00
155 *Ron Johnson Auto/550* 15.00
156 *Maurice Morris Auto/550* 25.00
157 *Kahlil Hill Auto/550* 15.00
158 *Antwann Randle El Auto/550* 25.00
159 *Cliff Russell Auto/550* 12.00
160 *Ladell Betts Auto/550* 20.00
161 *David Carr Auto/125* 150.00
162 *Andre Davis Auto/125* 30.00
163 *Julius Peppers Auto/125* 60.00
164 *Ashley Lelie Auto/125* 75.00
165 *Jabar Gaffney Auto/125* 30.00
166 *Clinton Portis Auto/125* 200.00

2002 Upper Deck Sweet Spot Gold

Production 25 Sets

2002 Upper Deck Sweet Spot Hot Spots

NM/M
Production to varying quantities
HS-SA Shaun Alexander/44 30.00
HS-DB Drew Brees/41 40.00
HS-AB Antonio Bryant/18 65.00
HS-QC Quincy Carter/29 30.00
HS-DC Daunte Culpepper/44 40.00
HS-SD Stephen Davis
HS-RD Ron Dayne/21 40.00
HS-BF Brett Favre/15 225.00
HS-DF DeShaun Foster/18 40.00
HS-JG Jabar Gaffney
HS-AG Ahman Green/21 50.00
HS-WG William Green
HS-JH Joey Harrington/18 125.00
HS-EJ Edgerrin James/49 50.00
HS-KJ Keyshawn Johnson/12 30.00
HS-TJ Thomas Jones
HS-AL Ashley Lelie/18 40.00
HS-PM Peyton Manning/74 60.00
HS-MC Deuce McAllister/35 60.00
HS-DM Donovan McNabb/41 100.00
HS-MM Maurice Morris/18 25.00
HS-RM Randy Moss/23 125.00
HS-SM Santana Moss
HS-CP Chad Pennington/23 60.00
HS-PO Clinton Portis/18 100.00
HS-PR Patrick Ramsey/18 70.00
HS-CR Chris Redman/32 25.00
HS-JR Jerry Rice
HS-CS Corey Simon/58 20.00
HS-DS Donte Stallworth/18 35.00
HS-TS Travis Stephens/18 40.00
HS-AT Anthony Thomas/12 60.00
HS-LT LaDainian Tomlinson/32 40.00
HS-BU Brian Urlacher/41 50.00
HS-MV Michael Vick/21 100.00
HS-JW Javon Walker/18 50.00
HW-MW Marquise Walker
HS-KW Kurt Warner
HS-PW Peter Warrick/23 25.00
HS-RO Roy Williams/18 50.00

2002 Upper Deck Sweet Spot Patches

NM/M
Common Player: 10.00
Inserted 1:12 Box Topper
SWP-SA Shaun Alexander 15.00
SWP-TB Tiki Barber 10.00
SWP-JB Jerome Bettis 15.00
SWP-DB Drew Bledsoe 20.00
SWP-BO David Boston 10.00
SWP-BR Tom Brady 20.00
SWP-DR Drew Brees 12.00
SWP-AB Aaron Brooks 12.00
SWP-MB Mark Brunell 10.00
SWP-CA David Carr 40.00
SWP-TC Tim Couch 10.00
SWP-DC Daunte Culpepper 12.00
SWP-SD Stephen Davis 10.00
SWP-CD Corey Dillon 10.00
SWP-WD Warrick Dunn 10.00
SWP-MF Marshall Faulk 15.00
SWP-BF Brett Favre 40.00
SWP-AF Antonio Freeman 10.00
SWP-RG Rich Gannon 15.00
SWP-JG Jeff Garcia 12.00
SWP-EG Eddie George 10.00
SWP-AG Ahman Green 12.00
SWP-WG William Green 25.00
SWP-BG Brian Griese 12.00
SWP-JH Joey Harrington 40.00
SWP-EJ Edgerrin James 15.00
SWP-BJ Brad Johnson 10.00
SWP-KJ Keyshawn Johnson 12.00
SWP-PM Peyton Manning 25.00
SWP-CM Curtis Martin 10.00
SWP-DE Deuce McAllister 15.00
SWP-DM Donovan McNabb 15.00
SWP-SM Steve McNair 10.00
SWP-RM Randy Moss 15.00
SWP-TO Terrell Owens 15.00
SWP-PE Julius Peppers 15.00
SWP-JP Jake Plummer 10.00
SWP-PR Patrick Ramsey
SWP-JR Jerry Rice 30.00
SWP-SS Shannon Sharpe 10.00
SWP-JS Jeremy Shockey 30.00
SWP-ES Emmitt Smith 30.00
SWP-KS Kordell Stewart 10.00
SWP-VT Vinny Testaverde 10.00
SWP-AT Anthony Thomas 10.00
SWP-LT LaDainian Tomlinson 15.00
SWP-BU Brian Urlacher 35.00
SWP-MV Michael Vick 35.00
SWP-KW Kurt Warner 15.00
SWP-RM Ricky Williams 20.00

2002 Upper Deck Sweet Spot Rookie Gallery Jersey

NM/M
Common Player: 8.00
Inserted 1:8
Gold/100: 1.5X
Gold/50: 2X
RG-AB Antonio Bryant 10.00
RG-RC Reche Caldwell 8.00
RG-DC David Carr/350 40.00
RG-TC Tim Carter 8.00
RG-EC Eric Crouch 20.00
RG-RD Rohan Davey 8.00
RG-TJ T.J. Duckett 12.00
RG-DF DeShaun Foster 8.00
RG-JG Jabar Gaffney/350 8.00
RG-WG William Green 12.00
RG-JH Joey Harrington/350 40.00
RG-AL Ashley Lelie 15.00
RG-JM Josh McCown 8.00
RG-MM Maurice Morris 8.00
RG-CP Clinton Portis 30.00
RG-PR Patrick Ramsey/350 8.00
RG-EL Antwann Randle El 8.00
RG-JR Josh Reed 8.00
RG-DS Donte Stallworth/350 8.00
RG-TS Travis Stephens 8.00
RG-JW Javon Walker 8.00
RG-MW Marquise Walker 8.00

2002 Upper Deck Sweet Spot Sunday Stars Jerseys

NM/M
Common Player: 10.00
Level 1 Production 250 sets
Gold Production 25 Sets
Level 2 Production 150 sets
Gold Production 10 Sets
SS-JB Jerome Bettis/250 10.00
SS-TB Tom Brady/250 20.00
SS-TC Tim Couch/250 10.00
SS-DC Daunte Culpepper/150 15.00
SS-MF Marshall Faulk/150 15.00
SS-BF Brett Favre/150 40.00
SS-AG Ahman Green/250 15.00
SS-EJ Edgerrin James/150 15.00
SS-KJ Keyshawn Johnson/250 12.00
SS-PM Peyton Manning/250 20.00
SS-DM Donovan McNabb/150 20.00
SS-RM Randy Moss/150 25.00
SS-JP Jake Plummer/250 10.00
SS-JR Jerry Rice/250 30.00
SS-ES Emmitt Smith/150 30.00
SS-AT Anthony Thomas/250 10.00
SS-LT LaDainian Tomlinson/250 15.00
SS-MV Michael Vick/150 25.00
SS-KW Kurt Warner/150 15.00
SS-RW Ricky Williams/250 15.00

2002 Upper Deck Sweet Spot Sweet Impressions

NM/M
Common Player: 15.00
Gold Production 25 Sets
SI-MB Michael Bennett/450 30.00
SI-JB Jerome Bettis/450 35.00
SI-DB Drew Bledsoe/450 50.00
SI-BR Drew Brees/50 60.00
SI-AB Aaron Brooks/75 60.00
SI-TC Tim Carter/450 15.00
SI-DC Daunte Culpepper/50 50.00
SI-JF Jay Fiedler/Redem 20.00
SI-TG Tony Gonzalez/100 25.00
SI-GH Garrison Hearst/450 15.00
SI-PM1 Peyton Manning/450 60.00
SI-PM2 Peyton Manning/450
SI-PM3 Peyton Manning/450
SI-PM4 Peyton Manning/450
SI-JM Jim Miller/450 15.00
SI-FM Freddie Mitchell/450 15.00
SI-QM Quincy Morgan/Redem 15.00
SI-SM Santana Moss/450 20.00
SI-JP Jake Plummer/75 25.00
SI-ER Ed Reed/450 15.00
SI-SR Sage Rosenfels/450 15.00
SI-AS Antowain Smith/100 20.00
SI-MW Mike Williams/Redem 15.00

2002 Upper Deck XL

NM/M
Common Player: .15
Unlisted Stars: .75
Minor Stars: .50
Common Rookie (501-600): .75
Minor Rookie Stars: 1.00
Pack (10): 2.50
Wax Box (24): 50.00
1 David Boston .60
2 Dave Brown .15
3 Frank Sanders .15
4 Jake Plummer .40
5 Joel Makovicka .15
6 Kwamie Lassiter .15
7 MarTay Jenkins .15
8 Michael Pittman .15
9 Raynoch Thompson .15
10 Rob Fredrickson .15
11 Ronald McKinnon .15
12 Steve Bush .15
13 Thomas Jones .15
14 Tywan Mitchell .15
15 Alvis Whitted .15
16 Ashley Ambrose .15
17 Bob Christian .15
18 Brady Smith .15
19 Brian Finneran .15
20 Chris Chandler .15
21 Chris Draft .15
22 Darrien Gordon .15
23 Doug Johnson .15
24 Ephraim Salaam .15
25 Jamal Anderson .40
26 Keith Brooking .15
27 Maurice Smith .15
28 Michael Vick 2.50
29 Ray Buchanan .15
30 Shawn Jefferson .15
31 Terance Mathis .15
32 Tony Martin .15
33 Brandon Stokley .15
34 Chris McAlister .15
35 Chris Redman .50
36 Elvis Grbac .25
37 Jonathan Ogden .15
38 Moe Williams .15
39 Obafemi Ayanbadejo .15
40 Peter Boulware .15
41 Qadry Ismail .15
42 Randall Cunningham .25
43 Ray Lewis .50
44 Rod Woodson .50
45 Sam Adams .15
46 Shannon Sharpe .40
47 Terry Allen .15
48 Todd Heap .15
49 Tony Siragusa .15
50 Travis Taylor .15
51 Alex Van Pelt .15
52 Antoine Winfield .15
53 Eric Moulds .40
54 Jay Foreman .15
55 Jay Riemersma .15
56 Jeremy McDaniel .15
57 Keith Newman .15
58 Kenyatta Wright .15
59 Larry Centers .15
60 Peerless Price .50
61 Rob Johnson .40
62 Ruben Brown .15
63 Shawn Bryson .15
64 Travis Brown .15
65 Travis Henry .75
66 Brad Hoover .15
67 Brentson Buckner .15
68 Chris Weinke .60
69 Dameyune Craig .15
70 Deon Grant .15
71 Donald Hayes .15
72 Doug Evans .15
73 Isaac Byrd .15
74 Jay Williams .15
75 Lester Towns .15
76 Muhsin Muhammad .40
77 Richard Huntley .15
78 Steve Smith .15
79 Tim Biakabutuka .15
80 Todd Sauerbrun .15
81 Wesley Walls .15
82 Anthony Thomas 2.00
83 Brian Urlacher 2.00
84 Daimon Shelton .15
85 David Terrell .60
86 Dez White .50
87 Fred Baxter .15
88 James Allen .15
89 James Williams .15
90 Jim Miller .40
91 Keith Traylor .15
92 Larry Whigham .15
93 Marcus Robinson .40
94 Marty Booker .40
95 Mike Brown .15
96 Olin Kruetz .15
97 R.W. McQuarters .15
98 Rosevelt Colvin .15
99 Shane Matthews .15
100 Ted Washington .15
101 Akili Smith .25
102 Brandon Bennett .15
103 Brian Simmons .15
104 Chad Johnson .15
105 Corey Dillon .60
106 Darnay Scott .15
107 Jon Kitna .25
108 Lorenzo Neal .15
109 Peter Warrick .50
110 Ron Dugans .15
111 Scott Mitchell .15
112 Takeo Spikes .15
113 Tony McGee .15
114 Brant Boyer .15
115 Corey Fuller .15
116 Courtney Brown .25
117 Dwayne Rudd .15
118 JaJuan Dawson .15
119 Jamel White .15
120 James Jackson .50
121 Jamir Miller .15
122 Josh Booty .15
123 Kelly Holcomb .15
124 Kevin Johnson .15
125 Lenoy Jones .15
126 Quincy Morgan .50
127 Raymond Jackson .15
128 Rickey Dudley .15
129 Tim Couch 1.00
130 Darren Woodson .15
131 Dat Nguyen .25
132 Dexter Coakley .15
133 Duane Hawthorne .15
134 Emmitt Smith 2.50
135 Jackie Harris .15
136 Joey Galloway .25
137 Ken-Yon Rambo .15
138 Larry Allen .15
139 Mike Lucky .15
140 Quincy Carter 1.25
141 Raghib Ismail .15
142 Reginald Swinton .15
143 Robert Thomas .15
144 Ryan Leaf .15
145 Troy Hambrick .15
146 Al Wilson .15
147 Bill Romanowski .15
148 Brian Griese .75
149 Chester McGlockton .15
150 Chris Cole .15
151 Deltha O'Neal .15
152 Desmond Clark .15
153 Dwayne Carswell .15
154 Ian Gold .15
155 Jarious Jackson .15
156 Jason Elam .15
157 Keith Burns .15
158 Mike Anderson 1.00
159 Olandis Gary .15
160 Rod Smith .50
161 Scottie Montgomery .15
162 Terrell Davis 1.00
163 Trevor Pryce .15
164 Charlie Batch .15
165 Chris Claiborne .15
166 Cory Schlesinger .15
167 David Sloan .15
168 Desmond Howard .15
169 Germane Crowell .15
170 James Stewart .50
171 Johnnie Morton .15
172 Lamont Warren .15
173 Larry Foster .15
174 Mike McMahon .60
175 Robert Porcher .15
176 Shaun Rogers .15
177 Todd Lyght .15
178 Ty Detmer .15
179 Ahman Green .75
180 Antonio Freeman .15
181 Bhawoh Jue .15
182 Bill Schroeder .15
183 Brett Favre 3.00
184 Bubba Franks .15
185 Corey Bradford .15
186 Darren Sharper .15
187 Donald Driver .15
188 Dorsey Levens .15
189 Doug Pederson .15
190 Kabeer Gbaja-Biamila .25
191 William Henderson .15
192 Aaron Glenn .15
193 Danny Wuerffel .15
194 Gary Walker .15
195 Jamie Sharper .15
196 Jermaine Lewis .15
197 Matt Stevens .15
198 Seth Payne .15
199 Tony Boselli .15
200 Dominic Rhodes .15
201 Edgerrin James 2.00
202 Jerome Pathon .15
203 Ken Dilger .15
204 Kevin McDougal .15
205 Marcus Pollard .15
206 Mark Rypien .15
207 Marvin Harrison .75
208 Peyton Manning 2.50
209 Reggie Wayne .15
210 Terrence Wilkins .15
211 Donovin Darius .15
212 Elvis Joseph .15
213 Fred Taylor .40
214 Hardy Nickerson .15
215 Jimmy Smith .25
216 Jonathan Quinn .15
217 Keenan McCardell .50
218 Kevin Hardy .15
219 Kyle Brady .15
220 Mark Brunell .75
221 Patrick Washington .15

222 Sean Dawkins .15
223 Stacey Mack .15
224 Tony Brackens .15
225 Derrick Alexander .15
226 Donnie Edwards .15
227 Eric Hicks .15
228 Kendall Gammon .15
229 Marvin "Snoop" Minnis .50
230 Michael Cloud .15
231 Priest Holmes .50
232 Todd Collins .15
233 Tony Gonzalez .25
234 Tony Richardson .15
235 Trent Green .25
236 Will Shields .15
237 Brock Marion .15
238 Chris Chambers .75
239 Dedric Ward .15
240 Hunter Goodwin .15
241 James McKnight .15
242 Jay Fiedler .40
243 Kenny Mixon .15
244 Lamar Smith .25
245 Oronde Gadsden .15
246 Patrick Surtain .15
247 Ray Lucas .15
248 Sam Madison .15
249 Travis Minor .15
250 Zach Thomas .40
251 Byron Chamberlain .15
252 Chris Walsh .15
253 Cris Carter .40
254 Daunte Culpepper 1.50
255 Doug Chapman .15
256 Gary Anderson .15
257 Jake Reed .15
258 Jim Kleinsasser .15
259 Kailee Wong .15
260 Matt Birk .15
261 Michael Bennett .75
262 Randy Moss 2.50
263 Robert Tate .15
264 Spergon Wynn .15
265 Antowain Smith .15
266 Bryan Cox .15
267 David Patten .15
268 Drew Bledsoe 1.50
269 Adam Vinatieri .25
270 J.R. Redmond .50
271 Jermaine Wiggins .15
272 Kevin Faulk .15
273 Lawyer Milloy .15
274 Marc Edwards .15
275 Tedy Bruschi .15
276 Tom Brady 2.50
277 Troy Brown .60
278 Ty Law .15
279 Willie McGinest .15
280 Aaron Brooks .50
281 Albert Connell .15
282 Eddie "Boo" Williams .15
283 Charlie Clemons .15
284 Deuce McAllister 1.00
285 Jay Bellamy .15
286 Jeff Blake .15
287 Joe Horn .40
288 John Carney .15
289 Kyle Turley .15
290 La'Roi Glover .15
291 Norman Hand .15
292 Ricky Williams 1.50
293 Robert Wilson .15
294 Sammy Knight .15
295 Terrelle Smith .15
296 Willie Jackson .15
297 Amani Toomer .40
298 Anthony Becht .15
299 Chad Pennington .50
300 Curtis Martin .50
301 Dan Campbell .15
302 Dave Thomas .15
303 Greg Comella .15
304 Ike Hilliard .40
305 James Farrior .15
306 Jason Garrett .15
307 Jason Sehorn .15
308 Jessie Armstead .15
309 Joe Jurevicius .15
310 John Abraham .15
311 Kerry Collins .40
312 Kevin Mawae .15
313 LaMont Jordan .40
314 Laveranues Coles .40
315 Marvin Jones .15
316 Matthew Hatchette .15
317 Michael Strahan .40
318 Mike Barrowman .15
319 Morten Andersen .15
320 Richie Anderson .15
321 Ron Dayne .25
322 Ron Dixon .15
323 Ron Stone .15
324 Santana Moss .50
325 Tiki Barber .40
326 Vinny Testaverde .40
327 Wayne Chrebet .40
328 Anthony Dorsett .15
329 Charles Woodson .50
330 Charlie Garner .40
331 Regan Upshaw .15
332 Jerry Porter .15
333 Jerry Rice 2.50
334 Jon Ritchie .15
335 Lincoln Kennedy .15
336 Marques Tuiasosopo .50
337 Rich Gannon .50
338 Roland Williams .15
339 Sebastian Janikowski .15
340 Barry Sims .15
341 Terry Kirby .15
342 Tim Brown .75
343 Tyrone Wheatley .15
344 Zack Crockett .15
345 A.J. Feeley .15
346 Brian Dawkins .15
347 Cecil Martin .15
348 Chad Lewis .15
349 Corey Simon .15
350 Correll Buckhalter .15
351 David Akers .15
352 Donovan McNabb 1.50
353 Duce Staley .50
354 Freddie Mitchell .50
355 Hugh Douglas .15
356 James Thrash .15
357 Brian Mitchell .15
358 Koy Detmer .15
359 Todd Pinkston .15
360 Tra Thomas .15
361 Troy Vincent .25
362 Alan Faneca .15
363 Amos Zereoue .25
364 Bobby Shaw .15
365 Chris Fuamatu-Ma'afala .15
366 Dan Kreider .15
367 Hines Ward .50
368 Jason Gildon .15
369 Jerome Bettis .50
370 Jon Witman .15
371 Kendrell Bell .15
372 Kordell Stewart .50
373 Mark Bruener .15
374 Plaxico Burress .75
375 Tommy Maddox .15
376 Troy Edwards .15
377 Curtis Conway .15
378 Darren Bennett .15
379 Doug Flutie .75
380 Drew Brees 2.00
381 Fred McCrary .15
382 Freddie Jones .15
383 Jeff Graham .15
384 John Parrella .15
385 Junior Seau .40
386 LaDainian Tomlinson 2.00
387 Marcellus Wiley .15
388 Tay Cody .15
389 Raylee Johnson .15
390 Rodney Harrison .15
391 Ronney Jenkins .15
392 Ryan McNeil .15
393 Orlando Ruff .15
394 Terrell Fletcher .15
395 Tim Dwight .15
396 Ahmed Plummer .15
397 Andre Carter .15
398 Bryant Young .15
399 Dana Stubblefield .15
400 Eric Johnson .15
401 Fred Beasley .15
402 Garrison Hearst .40
403 J.J. Stokes .15
404 Jeff Garcia .60
405 Jeremy Newberry .15
406 Junior Bryant .15
407 Justin Swift .15
408 Kevan Barlow .15
409 Ray Brown .15
410 Tai Streets .15
411 Terrell Owens .75
412 Terry Jackson .15
413 Tim Rattay .15
414 Bobby Engram .15
415 Chad Brown .15
416 Christian Fauria .15
417 Darrell Jackson .15
418 James Williams .15
419 John Randle .15
420 Koren Robinson .50
421 Levon Kirkland .15
422 Mack Strong .15
423 Matt Hasselbeck .15
424 Ricky Watters .40
425 Shaun Alexander .75
426 Shawn Springs .15
427 Trent Dilfer .40
428 Walter Jones .15
429 Adam Timmerman .15
430 Aeneas Williams .15
431 Az-Zahir Hakim .40
432 Dre' Bly .15
433 Ernie Conwell .15
434 Isaac Bruce .75
435 James Hodgins .15
436 Jamie Martin .15
437 Kurt Warner 2.50
438 Leonard Little .15
439 London Fletcher .15
440 Marshall Faulk 1.50
441 O.J. Brigance .15
442 Orlando Pace .15
443 Ricky Proehl .15
444 Torry Holt .40
445 Trung Canidate .15
446 Aaron Stecker .15
447 Brad Johnson .40
448 Dave Moore .15
449 Derrick Brooks .15
450 Jacquez Green .15
451 John Lynch .15
452 Karl Williams .15
453 Kenyatta Walker .15
454 Keyshawn Johnson .40
455 Mark Royals .15
456 Mike Alstott .40
457 Rabih Abdullah .15
458 Reidel Anthony .40
459 Ronde Barber .15
460 Shaun King .15
461 Simeon Rice .15
462 Warren Sapp .40
463 Warrick Dunn .40
464 Bruce Matthews .25
465 Chris Sanders .15
466 Derrick Mason .40
467 Eddie George .75
468 Erron Kinney .15
469 Frank Wycheck .15
470 Jevon Kearse .40
471 Kevin Dyson .15
472 Mike Green .15
473 Neil O'Donnell .15
474 Perry Phenix .15
475 Skip Hicks .15
476 Steve McNair .75
477 Champ Bailey .40
478 Chris Samuels .15
479 Dan Wilkinson .15
480 Darrell Green .25
481 Donnell Bennett .15
482 Donovan Greer .15
483 Ethan Albright .15
484 Fred Smoot .15
485 Kent Graham .15
486 Kevin Lockett .15
487 Ki-Jana Carter .25
488 Michael Bates .15
489 Michael Westbrook .40
490 Rod Gardner .50
491 Shawn Barber .15
492 Stephen Alexander .40
493 Stephen Davis .50
494 Tony Banks .25
495 Jeremiah Trotter .15
496 Jerome Bettis .50
497 Kurt Warner 2.50
498 Marshall Faulk 1.50
499 Randy Moss 2.50
500 Tom Brady 2.50
501 *Joey Harrington* 10.00
502 *David Carr* 10.00
503 *Rohan Davey* 3.00
504 *Brandon Doman* .75
505 *Woodrow Danztler* .75
506 *Kurt Kittner* 2.50
507 *Donte Stallworth* 5.00
508 *Major Applewhite* 5.00
509 *Eric Crouch* 3.00
510 *Justin Peelle* .75
511 *J.T. O'Sullivan* .75
512 *Jason McAddley* .75
513 *Patrick Ramsey* 3.00
514 *Randy Fasani* .75
515 *Antwann Randle El* 4.00
516 *DeShaun Foster* 3.00
517 *T.J. Duckett* 5.00
518 *William Green* .60
519 *Travis Stephens* 2.50
520 *Luke Staley* 2.50
521 *Leonard Henry* 1.00
522 *Najeh Davenport* 1.00
523 *Ricky Williams* .75
524 *Maurice Morris* 3.00
525 *Anthony Weaver* .75
526 *Jeremy Allen* .75
527 *Chester Taylor* .75
528 *Clinton Portis* 8.00
529 *Damien Anderson* 1.00
530 *Larry Ned* .75
531 *Jonathan Wells* 3.00
532 *Antoine Womack* .75
533 *Adrian Peterson* 2.50
534 *Lamar Gordon* 1.00
535 *Chad Hutchinson* 1.00
536 *Antonio Bryant* 4.00
537 *Josh Reed* 3.00
538 *Jabar Gaffney* 3.00
539 *Ashley Lelie* 5.00
540 *Ron Johnson* 1.00
541 *Marquise Walker* 2.50
542 *Kelly Campbell* 1.00
543 *Andre Davis* 3.00
544 *Deion Branch* 2.50
545 *James Mungro* .75
546 *Brian Poli-Dixon* 1.00
547 *Kahlil Hill* .75
548 *Donald Reche Caldwell* 2.50
549 *Jeremy Shockey* 4.00
550 *Julius Peppers* 4.00
551 *Wendell Bryant* 1.00
552 *John Henderson* 1.00
553 *Quentin Jammer* 2.50
554 *Roy Williams* 4.00
555 *Daniel Graham* 2.50
556 *Charles Grant* .75
557 *Verron Haynes* .75
558 *Edward Reed* .75
559 *Pete Rebstock* .75
560 *Tellis Redmon* .75
561 *Javon Walker* 4.00
562 *Larry Triplett* 1.00
563 *Cliff Russell* .75
564 *Rocky Calmus* 2.50
565 *Tim Carter* .75
566 *Josh Scobey* .75
567 *Kyle Johnson* .75
568 *Brian Westbrook* 2.50
569 *Zak Kustok* 1.00
570 *Ronald Curry* 2.50
571 *Atrews Bell* .75
572 *Levar Fisher* .75
573 *Dicenzo Miller* .75
574 *Phillip Buchanon* 2.50
575 *Freddie Milons* .75
576 *Kalimba Edwards* 1.00
577 *Raonall Smith* .75
578 *Dameon Hunter* .75
579 *Lee Mays* .75
580 *Mike Rumph* .75
581 *Josh McCown* 2.50
582 *Napoleon Harris* .75
583 *David Garrard* 1.00
584 *Wes Pate* .75
585 *Lito Sheppard* 1.50
586 *Gavin Hoffman* .75
587 *David Priestley* .75
588 *Dwight Freeney* .75
589 *Dusty Bonner* .75
590 *Eric McCoo* .75
591 *Robert Thomas* .75
592 *Delvon Flowers* .75
593 *Ladell Betts* 2.50
594 *Jamar Martin* .75
595 *Seth Burford* .75
596 *Mike Williams* 1.00
597 *Bryant McKinnie* 1.00
598 *Ryan Sims* 1.00
599 *Albert Haynesworth* 1.00
600 *Craig Nall* 2.00

2002 Upper Deck XL Holofoil

Stars: 10X-20X
Rookies: 4X-8X
Production 65 Sets

2002 Upper Deck XL Big Time Jersey

NM/M
Common Player: 10.00
Tier 1 Production 500 Sets
Tier 2 Production 250 Sets
Parallel Cards: 1.5X
BTJA Jamal Anderson 10.00
BTDB Drew Brees 15.00
BTCA Cris Carter 10.00
BTKC Kerry Collins 10.00
BTCC Curtis Conway 10.00
BTJD JaJuan Dawson 10.00
BTMF Marshall Faulk 20.00
BTJF Jay Fiedler 10.00
BTRG Rich Gannon 15.00
BTGA Rod Gardner 10.00
BTJG Jeff Graham 10.00
BTDG Darrell Green 10.00
BTBG Brian Griese 15.00
BTJH Joey Harrington 60.00
BTIK Ike Hillard 10.00
BTBJ Brad Johnson 10.00
BTFJ Freddie Jones 10.00
BTKK Kurt Kittner 30.00
BTPM Peyton Manning 30.00
BTDM Donovan McNabb 20.00
BTSM Santana Moss 10.00
BTEM Eric Moulds 10.00
BTMP Michael Pittman 10.00
BTWS Warren Sapp 10.00
BTDS Duce Staley 10.00
BTDT David Terrell 20.00
BTZT Zach Thomas 25.00
BTKW Kurt Warner 40.00
BTPW Peter Warrick 10.00
BTRW Ricky Williams 10.00

2002 Upper Deck XL Super Swatch Jersey

NM/M
Common Player: 10.00
Tier 1 Production 800 Sets
Tier 2 Production 75 Sets
Parallel Cards/400: 1X
Parallel Cards/25: 1.5X
SSSA Stephen Alexander 20.00
SSMA Mike Alstott 15.00
SSTB Tony Banks 10.00
SSAB Anthony Becht 10.00
SSDB Drew Bledsoe 25.00
SSMB Marty Booker 10.00
SSDR Drew Brees 40.00
SSBR Mark Brunell 20.00
SSTC Tim Couch 20.00
SSWC Wayne Chrebet 10.00
SSDC Daunte Culpepper 20.00
SSSD Stephen Davis 15.00
SSRD Ron Dayne 15.00
SSDF Doug Flutie 20.00
SSDS DeShaun Foster 10.00
SSTH Travis Henry 10.00
SSJJ James Jackson 15.00
SSJO Kevin Johnson 10.00
SSKJ Keyshawn Johnson 15.00
SSPM Peyton Manning 40.00
SSCM Curtis Martin 25.00
SSMM Maurice Morris 15.00
SSRM Randy Moss 40.00
SSEM Eric Moulds 10.00
SSJP Jake Plummer 10.00
SSAR Antwann Randle El 25.00
SSJR Jerry Rice 50.00
SSJS Junior Seau 15.00
SSAT Anthony Thomas 50.00
SSLT LaDainian Tomlinson 40.00

2003 Upper Deck

NM/M
Common Player (1-210): .30
Minor Stars: .60
Unlisted Stars: .75
Common Rookie (211-285): 2.00
Minor Rookies: 3.00
Unlisted Rookies: 4.00
181-210 Inserted 1:12
211-240 Inserted 1:4
241-255 Inserted 1:24
256-285 Inserted 1:8 Hobby
Pack (8): 2.00
Box (24): 40.00
1 Brad Johnson .60
2 Derrick Brooks .60
3 Simeon Rice .30
4 Warren Sapp .60
5 Thomas Jones .60
6 Mike Alstott .60
7 Michael Pittman .30
8 Tim Brown .75
9 Rich Gannon .60
10 Charlie Garner .60
11 Jerry Porter .60
12 Phillip Buchanon .30
13 Charles Woodson .60
14 James Thrash .60
15 Duce Staley .60
16 Brian Westbrook .30
17 Correll Buckhalter .30
18 Koy Detmer .60
19 Brian Dawkins .30
20 Jon Ritchie .30
21 Ahman Green .75
22 Donald Driver .60
23 Bubba Franks .60
24 Javon Walker .60
25 Kabeer Gbaja-Biamila .30
26 Robert Ferguson .60
27 Eddie George .75
28 Jevon Kearse .60
29 Billy Volek .30
30 Frank Wycheck .30
31 Derrick Mason .60
32 Tommy Maddox .75
33 Jerome Bettis .60
34 Antwann Randle El .75
35 Amos Zereoue .60
36 Hines Ward .60
37 Jeff Garcia .75
38 Terrell Owens .75
39 Tim Rattay .60
40 Brandon Doman .30
41 Tai Streets .60
42 Garrison Hearst .60
43 Kerry Collins .60
44 Tiki Barber .60
45 Amani Toomer .60
46 Jesse Palmer .60
47 Tim Carter .30
48 Michael Strahan .30
49 Ike Hilliard .60
50 Marvin Harrison .75
51 Peyton Manning 1.50
52 Marcus Pollard .30
53 James Mungro .30
54 Reggie Wayne .60
55 Peerless Price .60
56 Warrick Dunn .60
57 T.J. Duckett .60
58 Keith Brooking .30
59 Doug Johnson .30
60 Brian Finneran .30
61 Chad Pennington 1.00
62 Curtis Martin .75
63 Marvin Jones .30
64 Wayne Chrebet .60
65 LaMont Jordan .60
66 Curtis Conway .60
67 Vinny Testaverde .60
68 Tim Couch .75
69 William Green .75
70 Andre Davis .60
71 Quincy Morgan .60
72 Dennis Northcutt .60
73 Kelly Holcomb .60
74 Jake Plummer .60
75 Mike Anderson .60
76 Ashley Lelie .75
77 Ed McCaffrey .60
78 Shannon Sharpe .75
79 Rod Smith .60
80 Terrell Davis .75
81 Antowain Smith .60
82 Kevin Faulk .60
83 David Patten .30
84 Deion Branch .30
85 Troy Brown .30
86 Rohan Davey .30
87 Jay Fiedler .60
88 Randy McMichael .30
89 Derrius Thompson .30
90 Jason Taylor .30
91 Zach Thomas .30
92 Ricky Williams 1.50
93 Deuce McAllister .75
94 Donte Stallworth .75
95 Jerome Pathon .30
96 Michael Lewis .30
97 Joe Horn .60
98 Priest Holmes .75
99 Johnnie Morton .60
100 Eddie Kennison .60
101 Dante Hall .30
102 Tony Gonzalez .60
103 Marc Boerigter .60
104 Drew Brees 1.00
105 David Boston .75
106 Reche Caldwell .60
107 Tim Dwight .60
108 Doug Flutie .60
109 Drew Bledsoe 1.00
110 Eric Moulds .75
111 Alex Van Pelt .30
112 Charles Johnson .30
113 Takeo Spikes .30
114 Josh Reed .60
115 Ladell Betts .30
116 Laveranues Coles .60
117 Champ Bailey .60
118 Trung Canidate .60
119 Kenny Watson .30
120 Rod Gardner .60
121 Kurt Warner 1.50
122 Lamar Gordon .30
123 *Shaun McDonald* .75
124 Marc Bulger .75
125 Isaac Bruce .75
126 Torry Holt .75
127 Matt Hasselbeck .60
128 Maurice Morris .60
129 Bobby Engram .30
130 Darrell Jackson .60
131 Koren Robinson .60
132 Chris Redman .60
133 Todd Heap .30
134 Travis Taylor .60
135 Ron Johnson .30
136 Ray Lewis .60
137 Jake Delhomme .60
138 Muhsin Muhammad .30
139 Stephen Davis .60
140 Julius Peppers .60
141 Rodney Peete .60
142 Mark Brunell .60
143 Jimmy Smith .60
144 Kyle Brady .30
145 Kevin Lockett .30
146 David Garrard .60
147 Fred Taylor .75
148 Michael Bennett .75
149 *Ronald Bellamy* .75
150 Randy Moss 1.50
151 D'Wayne Bates .60
152 Josh McCown .60
153 Marquise Walker .30
154 Jeff Blake .60
155 Freddie Jones .30
156 Marcel Shipp .60
157 Troy Hambrick .60
158 Joey Galloway .60
159 Terry Glenn .60
160 Roy Williams .60
161 Antonio Bryant .60
162 Quincy Carter .75
163 Anthony Thomas .75
164 Marty Booker .60
165 Dez White .60
166 Adrian Peterson .60
167 Kordell Stewart .60
168 David Terrell .60
169 Jabar Gaffney .60
170 *Bennie Joppru* .75
171 Corey Bradford .30
172 David Carr 2.00
173 James Stewart .60
174 Ty Detmer .60
175 Az-Zahir Hakim .30
176 Bill Schroeder .30
177 Jon Kitna .60
178 Chad Johnson .60
179 Ron Dugans .30
180 Peter Warrick .60
181 Brett Favre 8.00
182 Emmitt Smith 6.00
183 LaDainian Tomlinson 3.00
184 Joey Harrington 5.00
185 Brian Urlacher 4.00
186 Daunte Culpepper 2.00
187 Jamal Lewis 2.00
188 Shaun Alexander 2.00
189 Marshall Faulk 3.00
190 Travis Henry 1.50
191 Trent Green 1.50
192 Aaron Brooks 2.00
193 Chris Chambers 2.00
194 Tom Brady 3.00
195 Clinton Portis 6.00
196 Kevin Johnson 1.50
197 Santana Moss 1.50
198 Michael Vick 8.00
199 Edgerrin James 3.00
200 Jeremy Shockey 5.00
201 Kevan Barlow 1.50
202 Plaxico Burress 2.00
203 Steve McNair 2.00
204 Donovan McNabb 3.00
205 Jerry Rice 6.00
206 Keyshawn Johnson 2.00
207 Patrick Ramsey 2.00
208 Stephen Davis 1.50
209 Corey Dillon 2.00
210 Chad Hutchinson 2.00
211 *Brad Banks* 4.00
212 *Kliff Kingsbury* 5.00
213 *Jason Gesser* 4.00
214 *Jason Johnson* 2.00
215 *Brian St. Pierre* 4.00
216 *Ken Dorsey* 6.00
217 *Seneca Wallace* 5.00
218 *Brooks Bollinger* 4.00
219 *Chris Brown* 4.00
220 *B.J. Askew* 4.00
221 *Earnest Graham Jr.* 4.00
222 *Quentin Griffin* 10.00
223 *Musa Smith* 5.00
224 *Artose Pinner* 4.00
225 *Domanick Davis* 5.00
226 *Anquan Boldin* 8.00
227 *Talman Gardner* 4.00
228 *Brandon Lloyd* 5.00
229 *Bryant Johnson* 6.00
230 *Kareem Kelly* 2.00
231 *Arnaz Battle* 2.00
232 *Keenan Howry* 4.00
233 *Justin Gage* 3.00
234 *Tyrone Calico* 3.00
235 *Teyo Johnson* 4.00
236 *Malaefou MacKenzie* 2.00
237 *Terence Newman* 6.00
238 *Marcus Trufant* 3.00
239 *Mike Doss* 3.00
240 *Terrell Suggs* 5.00
241 *Carson Palmer* 30.00
242 *Byron Leftwich* 30.00
243 *Rex Grossman* 25.00
244 *Kyle Boller* 20.00
245 *Dave Ragone* 8.00
246 *Chris Simms* 15.00
247 *Larry Johnson* 20.00
248 *Lee Suggs* 10.00
249 *Justin Fargas* 10.00
250 *Onterrio Smith* 12.00
251 *Willis McGahee* 25.00
252 *Charles Rogers* 25.00
253 *Andre Johnson* 20.00
254 *Taylor Jacobs* 8.00
255 *Kelley Washington* 10.00
256 *Tony Romo* 8.00
257 *Jerel Myers* 4.00
258 *Kirk Farmer* 4.00

259 Kevin Walter 4.00
260 Gibran Hamdan 5.00
261 Juston Wood 5.00
262 Travis Anglin 4.00
263 Marquel Blackwell 4.00
264 Jason Thomas 5.00
265 Carl Ford 6.00
266 Walter Young 4.00
267 Sultan McCullough 5.00
268 Dahrran Diedrick 5.00
269 Cecil Sapp 6.00
270 Doug Gabriel 5.00
271 LaBrandon Toefield 6.00
272 Adrian Madise 5.00
273 J.R. Tolver 5.00
274 Kevin Curtis 6.00
275 Bobby Wade 5.00
276 Sam Aiken 4.00
277 Mike Bush 4.00
278 Billy McMullen 5.00
279 Bethel Johnson 5.00
280 David Kircus 5.00
281 Zuriel Smith 5.00
282 LaTarence Dunbar 4.00
283 Nate Burleson 6.00
284 Antwone Savage 4.00
285 Terrence Edwards 5.00

2003 Upper Deck Gold

Stars (1-180): 10X-20X
181-240: 2X-4X
241-255: 2X
256-285: 1.5X-3X
Production 50 Sets

2003 Upper Deck Game Jerseys

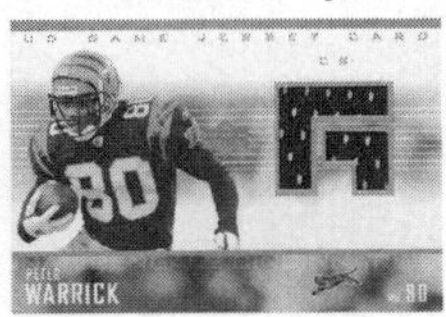

NM/M
Common Player: 8.00
Gold: 2X
Production 99 Sets
GJ-MA Mike Alstott 8.00
GJ-CB Champ Bailey 10.00
GJ-JB Jerome Bettis 10.00
GJ-AB Aaron Brooks 10.00
GJ-MB Mark Brunell 10.00
GJ-BR Antonio Bryant 8.00
GJ-CB Correll Buckhalter 8.00
GJ-DC David Carr 15.00
GJ-WC Wayne Chrebet 8.00
GJ-MF Marshall Faulk 15.00
GJ-BF Brett Favre 25.00
GJ-RG Rich Gannon 10.00
GJ-OG Olandis Gary 8.00
GJ-BG Brian Griese 10.00
GJ-TH Torry Holt 10.00
GJ-QJ Quentin Jammer 8.00
GJ-BJ Brad Johnson 10.00
GJ-CJ Chad Johnson 10.00
GJ-KJ Kevin Johnson 8.00
GJ-JK Jevon Kearse 10.00
GJ-AL Ashley Lelie 10.00
GJ-JL Jamal Lewis 12.00
GJ-RL Ray Lewis 10.00
GJ-PM Peyton Manning 15.00
GJ-SM Steve McNair 10.00
GJ-RM Randy Moss 15.00
GJ-EM Eric Moulds 10.00
GJ-CP Clinton Portis 15.00
GJ-WS Warren Sapp 10.00
GJ-SE Junior Seau 8.00
GJ-JS Jeremy Shockey 12.00
GJ-DS Duce Staley 8.00
GJ-KS Kordell Stewart 10.00
GJ-MS Michael Strahan 10.00
GJ-ZT Zach Thomas 10.00
GJ-AT Amani Toomer 8.00
GJ-MV Michael Vick 25.00
GJ-KW Kurt Warner 12.00
GJ-PW Peter Warrick 8.00
GJ-RW Roy Williams 12.00
GJ-CW Charles Woodson 8.00

2003 Upper Deck Game Jersey Autographs

NM/M
Common Player: 30.00
Production 99 Sets
GJA-AB Antonio Bryant/99 60.00
GJA-DC David Carr/99 75.00
GJA-WD Woodrow Dantzler/99 30.00
GJA-DF DeShaun Foster/99 30.00
GJA-KK Kurt Kittner/45
GJA-AL Ashley Lelie/99 60.00
GJA-PM Peyton Manning/18
GJA-DM Donovan McNabb/5
GJA-CP Clinton Portis/26 200.00
GJA-JS Jeremy Shockey/99 100.00
GJA-MV Michael Vick/7
GJA-RW Roy Williams/99 75.00

2003 Upper Deck Game Jersey Dual

NM/M
Common Player: 12.00
Inserted 1:144
Gold: 1.5X
Production 99 Sets
DGJ-CS Kerry Collins, Jeremy Shockey 15.00
DGJ-PC Chad Pennington, Wayne Chrebet 15.00
DGJ-CR David Carr, Dave Ragone 15.00
DGJ-FG Brett Favre, Ahman Green 40.00
DGJ-WH Kurt Warner, Torry Holt 12.00
DGJ-FC Jay Fiedler, Chris Chambers 15.00
DGJ-KJ Keyshawn Johnson 12.00
DGJ-DM Daunte Culpepper, Randy Moss 25.00
DGJ-MC Peyton Manning, Dallas Clark 20.00
DGJ-CJ Tim Couch, Kevin Johnson 12.00
DGJ-BM Drew Bledsoe, Willis McGahee 25.00
DGJ-JG Taylor Jacobs, Rod Gardner 12.00
DGJ-GR Rich Gannon, Jerry Rice 20.00
DGJ-BT Drew Brees, LaDainian Tomlinson 15.00
DGJ-BS Nate Burleson, Onterrio Smith 20.00
DGJ-CW Carson Palmer, Kelley Washington 20.00
DGJ-JB Bryant Johnson, Anquan Boldin 20.00

2003 Upper Deck Game Jersey Patch Logos

Inserted 1:5000
PLO-DC David Carr/4
PLO-MF Marshall Faulk
PLO-JG Jeff Garcia
PLO-LT LaDainian Tomlinson
PLO-RW Ricky Williams/24

2003 Upper Deck Game Jersey Patch Names

Inserted 1:7500
PNA-TB Tom Brady
PNA-BF Brett Favre
PNA-EJ Edgerrin James/18
PNA-DeM Deuce McAllister
PNA-DoM Donovan McNabb
PNA-RM Randy Moss
PNA-TO Terrell Owens
PNA-CP Chad Pennington
PNA-MV Michael Vick/11
PNA-KW Kurt Warner

2003 Upper Deck Game Jersey Patch Numbers

Inserted 1:2500
PNU-JB Jerome Bettis
PNU-DB Drew Bledsoe
PNU-BR Drew Brees
PNU-TC Tim Couch
PNU-DC Daunte Culpepper
PNU-EG Eddie George
PNU-AG Ahman Green
PNU-MH Marvin Harrison
PNU-CP Clinton Portis
PNU-JS Jeremy Shockey

2003 Upper Deck Power Surge

NM/M
Complete Set (18): 15.00
Common Player: .75
Inserted 1:8
PS-1 Marshall Faulk 1.50
PS-2 LaDainian Tomlinson 1.50
PS-3 Ricky Williams 2.00
PS-4 Edgerrin James 1.50
PS-5 Deuce McAllister 1.00
PS-6 Jerome Bettis .75
PS-7 Ahman Green 1.00
PS-8 Jeremy Shockey 2.50
PS-9 Steve McNair 1.00
PS-10 William Green 1.00
PS-11 Daunte Culpepper 1.00
PS-12 Terrell Owens 1.00
PS-13 Jerry Rice 3.00
PS-14 Brad Johnson .75
PS-15 Priest Holmes .75
PS-16 Clinton Portis 3.00
PS-17 Brian Urlacher 2.00
PS-18 Rod Gardner .75

2003 Upper Deck Rookie Premiere

NM/M
Complete Set (30): 40.00
Common Player: 1.00
Inserted 1:1 Retail
RP-1 Carson Palmer 5.00
RP-2 Byron Leftwich 5.00
RP-3 Kyle Boller 3.00
RP-4 Rex Grossman 4.00
RP-5 Dave Ragone 1.00
RP-6 Kliff Kingsbury 1.00
RP-7 Seneca Wallace 1.00
RP-8 Brian St. Pierre 1.00
RP-9 Dallas Clark 1.00
RP-10 Willis McGahee 4.00
RP-11 Larry Johnson 3.00
RP-12 Musa Smith 1.00
RP-13 Chris Brown 1.00
RP-14 Justin Fargas 2.00
RP-15 Artose Pinner 1.00
RP-16 Onterrio Smith 2.50
RP-17 Nate Burleson 1.00
RP-18 Andre Johnson 3.00
RP-19 Bryant Johnson 1.50
RP-20 Taylor Jacobs 1.00
RP-21 Bethel Johnson 1.00
RP-22 Anquan Boldin 2.50
RP-23 Tyrone Calico 1.00
RP-24 Teyo Johnson 1.00
RP-25 Kelley Washington 1.50
RP-26 Kevin Curtis 1.00
RP-27 Terence Newman 2.00
RP-28 Marcus Trufant 1.00
RP-29 Terrell Suggs 1.50
RP-30 Dewayne Robertson 1.00

2003 Upper Deck Rookie Futures Jerseys

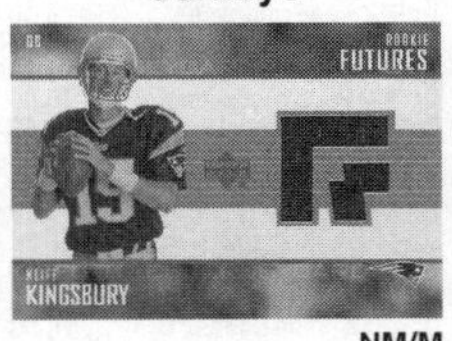

NM/M
Common Player: 8.00
Inserted 1:24
Golds: 3X
Production 99 Sets
RF-AB Anquan Boldin 15.00
RF-KB Kyle Boller 20.00
RF-CB Chris Brown 8.00
RF-NB Nate Burleson 8.00
RF-TG Tyrone Calico 8.00
RF-DC Dallas Clark 8.00
RF-KC Kevin Curtis 8.00
RF-JF Justin Fargas 15.00
RF-RG Rex Grossman 25.00
RF-TJ Taylor Jacobs 10.00
RF-AJ Andre Johnson 20.00
RF-BE Bethel Johnson 8.00
RF-BJ Bryant Johnson 10.00
RF-LJ Larry Johnson 20.00
RF-TE Teyo Johnson 10.00
RF-KK Kliff Kingsbury 10.00
RF-BL Byron Leftwich 30.00
RF-RM Ricky Manning Jr. 8.00
RF-WM Willis McGahee 25.00
RF-TN Terence Newman 12.00
RF-CP Carson Palmer 30.00
RF-WP Willie Pile 8.00
RF-AP Artose Pinner 8.00
RF-DR Dave Ragone 8.00
RF-RO Dewayne Robertson 8.00
RF-BS Brian St. Pierre 8.00
RF-MS Musa Smith 8.00
RF-OS Onterrio Smith 15.00
RF-TS Terrell Suggs 10.00
RF-KC Marcus Trufant 8.00
RF-SW Seneca Wallace 10.00
RF-KW Kelley Washington 10.00

2003 Upper Deck Rookie Futures Jersey Autographs

RFA-KB Kyle Boller/8
RFA-JF Justin Fargas/20
RFA-RG Rex Grossman/8
RFA-LJ Larry Johnson/34
RFA-KK Kliff Kingsbury/115
RFA-BL Byron Leftwich/7
RFA-CP Carson Palmer/9
RFA-DR Dave Ragone/4
RFA-RO Dewayne Robertson/63
RFA-KW Kelley Washington/87

2003 Upper Deck Super Powers

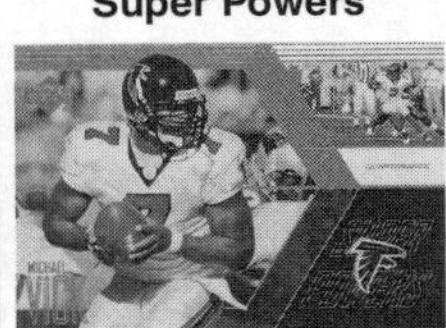

NM/M
Complete Set (12): 25.00
Common Player: 1.50
Inserted 1:12
SP-1 Kurt Warner 2.50
SP-2 Aaron Brooks 1.50
SP-3 Joey Harrington 3.00
SP-4 Brett Favre 5.00
SP-5 Donovan McNabb 2.00
SP-6 Emmitt Smith 4.00
SP-7 Michael Vick 5.00
SP-8 David Carr 3.00
SP-9 Drew Brees 2.00
SP-10 Chad Pennington 2.00
SP-11 Drew Bledsoe 2.00
SP-12 Tom Brady 2.00

2003 Upper Deck Finite

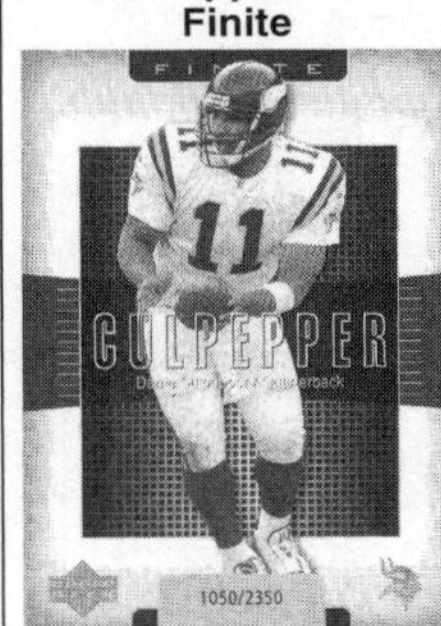

NM/M
Common Player (1-100): .40
Minor Stars: .75
Unlisted Stars: 1.00
1-100 Production 2,350 Sets
Common Player (101-160): 1.50
Common Rookie (101-160): 2.00
101-160 Production 750 Sets
Common Player (161-185): 1.50
161-185 Production 500 Sets
Common Player (186-200): 5.00
186-200 Production 100 Sets
Common Rookie (201-250): 2.00
201-250 Production 999 Sets
Common Rookie (251-285): 2.50
251-285 Production 500 Sets
Common Rookie (286-300): 15.00
286-300 Production 100 Sets
Pack (3): 8.50
Box (10): 60.00
1 Peyton Manning 2.00
2 Aaron Brooks 1.00
3 Joey Harrington 2.00
4 Brett Favre 4.00
5 Donovan McNabb 1.50
6 Steve McNair 1.50
7 Michael Vick 4.00
8 David Carr 2.50
9 Drew Brees 1.00
10 Chad Pennington 1.50
11 Daunte Culpepper 1.00
12 Tom Brady 2.00
13 Kurt Warner 1.00
14 Brad Johnson .75
15 Drew Bledsoe 1.50
16 Jake Plummer .75
17 Jeff Garcia .75
18 Mark Brunell .75
19 Josh McCown .40
20 Travis Henry .75
21 LaDainian Tomlinson 1.50
22 Emmitt Smith 3.00
23 Michael Bennett 1.00
24 Brian Westbrook .75
25 Curtis Martin 1.00
26 Clinton Portis 3.00
27 Eddie George 1.00
28 Marshall Faulk 1.50
29 Deuce McAllister 1.00
30 Ahman Green 1.00
31 LaMont Jordan .75
32 Edgerrin James 1.50
33 Jamel White .40
34 Ricky Williams 2.00
35 Anthony Thomas 1.00
36 Amos Zereoue .75
37 Ladell Betts .40
38 Stephen Davis .75
39 T.J. Duckett 1.00
40 Troy Hambrick .75
41 Maurice Morris .75
42 James Jackson .75
43 Correll Buckhalter .75
44 Keith Brooking .40
45 Michael Strahan .75
46 Jason Taylor .75
47 Kendrell Bell .75
48 Jevon Kearse .75
49 Chris Horn .75
50 Quentin Jammer .75
51 Phillip Buchanon .40
52 Charles Woodson .75
53 Rod Woodson .75
54 Simeon Rice .75
55 Derrick Brooks .75
56 Warren Sapp .75
57 John Lynch .75
58 Champ Bailey .75
59 Reggie Wayne .75
60 Darrell Jackson .75
61 Derrick Mason .75
62 Travis Minor .40
63 Eric Parker .40
64 Ron Johnson .40
65 Dante Hall 1.00
66 David Terrell .75
67 Daniel Graham .40
68 Randy McMichael .40
69 Jeremy Shockey 2.50
70 J.J. Stokes .75
71 Johnnie Morton .75
72 Dennis Northcutt .75
73 Peter Warrick 1.00
74 Rod Smith .75
75 Javon Walker .75
76 Tim Carter .40
77 Wayne Chrebet .75
78 Corey Bradford .40
79 Deion Branch .40
80 Jerry Rice 3.00
81 Terrell Owens 1.00
82 Josh Reed .75
83 Ed McCaffrey .40
84 Randy Moss 2.00
85 Chad Johnson .75
86 Hines Ward 1.00
87 Rod Gardner .75
88 Tony Gonzalez .75
89 David Boston 1.00
90 Jerry Porter .75
91 Kevin Johnson .75
92 Rohan Davey .75
93 Tim Rattay .75
94 Jon Kitna .75
95 Jay Fiedler .75
96 Doug Flutie 1.00
97 Quincy Carter 1.00
98 Vinny Testaverde .75
99 Kelly Holcomb .75
100 Marc Bulger 1.00
101 Patrick Ramsey 3.00
102 Tim Couch 3.00
103 Tommy Maddox 3.00
104 Chad Hutchinson 2.00
105 Trent Green 2.00
106 Kerry Collins 2.00
107 Will Heller 3.00
108 Brian Griese 2.00
109 Kordell Stewart 2.00
110 Jake Delhomme 2.00
111 Chris Redman 1.50
112 Mike Anderson 2.00
113 Olandis Gary 2.00
114 Antonio Gates 6.00
115 Garrison Hearst 2.00
116 Fred Taylor 3.00
117 Casey Fitzsimmons 4.00
118 Tiki Barber 3.00
119 Mike Alstott 2.00
120 Kevan Barlow 2.00
121 Jamal Lewis 3.00
122 Mike Banks 2.00
123 Jimmy Farris 4.00
124 Warrick Dunn 2.00
125 Jerome Bettis 2.00
126 Antonio Chatman 6.00
127 Bubba Franks 2.00
128 Todd Heap 2.00
129 Shannon Sharpe 2.00
130 Donald Driver 2.00
131 Antonio Freeman 2.00
132 Joey Galloway 2.00
133 Marc Boerigter 1.50
134 Torry Holt 3.00
135 Amani Toomer 2.00
136 Marty Booker 2.00
137 Santana Moss 2.00
138 Jimmy Smith 2.00
139 Jabar Gaffney 2.00
140 Isaac Bruce 2.00
141 Laveranues Coles 2.00
142 Quincy Morgan 2.00
143 Peerless Price 2.00
144 Eric Moulds 2.00
145 Troy Brown 2.00
146 Plaxico Burress 3.00
147 Chris Chambers 3.00
148 Tim Brown 3.00
149 Antonio Brown 4.00
150 Koren Robinson 2.00
151 David Boston 3.00
152 C.J. Jones 2.00
153 Marvin Harrison 3.00
154 Keyshawn Johnson 2.00
155 J.J. Moses 3.00
156 Antwann Randle El 3.00
157 Ashley Lelie 2.00
158 Andre Davis 2.00
159 Donte Stallworth 2.00
160 Antonio Bryant 2.00
161 Tom Brady 8.00
162 Drew Bledsoe 5.00
163 Rich Gannon 4.00
164 David Carr 8.00
165 Drew Brees 4.00
166 Aaron Brooks 4.00
167 Joey Harrington 6.00
168 Matt Hasselbeck 2.00
169 Jake Plummer 2.00
170 Edgerrin James 5.00
171 Ahman Green 4.00
172 Deuce McAllister 4.00
173 Priest Holmes 5.00
174 Travis Henry 2.00
175 William Green 3.00
176 Corey Dillon 3.00
177 Shaun Alexander 4.00
178 Jeremy Shockey 6.00
179 Brian Dawkins 1.50
180 Roy Williams 3.00
181 Julius Peppers 3.00
182 Ray Lewis 3.00
183 Junior Seau 2.00
184 Zach Thomas 2.00
185 Brian Urlacher 6.00
186 Michael Vick 15.00
187 Jeff Garcia 5.00
188 Daunte Culpepper 8.00
189 Steve McNair 8.00
190 Chad Pennington 8.00
191 LaDainian Tomlinson 8.00
192 Clinton Portis 10.00
193 Ricky Williams 10.00
194 Donovan McNabb 8.00
195 Peyton Manning 10.00
196 Marshall Faulk 8.00
197 Kurt Warner 6.00
198 Emmitt Smith 15.00
199 Jerry Rice 12.00
200 Brett Favre 15.00
201 Carson Palmer 10.00
202 Kyle Boller 8.00
203 Kliff Kingsbury 3.00
204 Brooks Bollinger 3.00
205 Mike Doss 2.50
206 Dewayne White 2.00
207 Roderick Babers 2.00
208 Seneca Wallace 2.50
209 Nate Hybl 2.00
210 Jason Gesser 2.50
211 Willis McGahee 8.00
212 George Wrighster 2.00
213 Drayton Florence 2.00
214 L.J. Smith 2.50
215 B.J. Askew 3.00
216 Adewale Ogunleye 3.00
217 Ahmaad Galloway 2.50
218 Dwone Hicks 2.00
219 Travaris Robinson 2.00
220 William Joseph 2.00
221 Terrence Kiel 2.00
222 Marcus Trufant 2.50
223 Terence Newman 5.00
224 Nnamdi Asomugha 2.00
225 Troy Polamalu 4.00
226 Terrell Suggs 4.00
227 Boss Bailey 4.00
228 Dan Klecko 4.00
229 Jerome McDougle 2.00
230 Johnathan Sullivan 2.00
231 Mike Seidman 2.00
232 Dallas Clark 2.50
233 Tony Romo 2.50
234 Reggie Newhouse 2.00
235 David Tyree 2.50
236 Andre Woolfolk 2.50
237 Domanick Davis 6.00
238 Zuriel Smith 2.50
239 Tommy Jones 2.00
240 Arnaz Battle 2.50
241 Kassim Osgood 2.50
242 Gerald Hayes 2.00
243 Keenan Howry 3.00
244 Bobby Wade 3.00
245 Brock Forsey 5.00
246 Walter Young 3.00
247 Shaun McDonald 2.50
248 Nate Burleson 4.00
249 Anquan Boldin 8.00
250 Taylor Jacobs 3.00
251 Chris Simms 8.00
252 Rex Grossman 12.00
253 Arlen Harris 6.00
254 Dave Ragone 4.00
255 Chris Brown 6.00
256 Musa Smith 4.00
257 Artose Pinner 4.00
258 Sammy Davis 2.50
259 Dewayne Robertson 3.00
260 Tony Hollings 4.00
261 LaBrandon Toefield 4.00
262 Cortez Hankton 2.50
263 Justin Griffith 3.00
264 Jeremi Johnson 2.50
265 E.J. Henderson 3.00
266 Casey Moore 2.50
267 Ken Hamlin 4.00
268 Nick Barnett 6.00
269 Visanthe Shiancoe 2.50
270 Aaron Walker 2.50
271 Bennie Joppru 3.00
272 Terrence Edwards 4.00
273 Willie Ponder 2.50
274 Pisa Tinoisamoa 5.00
275 Doug Gabriel 3.00
276 Kerry Carter 2.50
277 Avon Cobourne 5.00
278 Sam Aiken 2.50
279 Brandon Lloyd 5.00
280 LaTarence Dunbar 3.00
281 J.R. Tolver 3.00
282 Kevin Curtis 3.00
283 Tyrone Calico 8.00
284 Bryant Johnson 5.00
285 Charles Rogers 10.00
286 Teyo Johnson 25.00
287 Jason Witten 25.00
288 Kelley Washington 25.00
289 Billy McMullen 20.00
290 Adrian Madise 15.00
291 Justin Gage 30.00
292 Andre Johnson 80.00
293 Bethel Johnson 30.00
294 Lee Suggs 50.00
295 Larry Johnson 60.00
296 Justin Fargas 30.00
297 Onterrio Smith 50.00
298 Ken Dorsey 30.00
299 Brian St. Pierre 20.00
300 Byron Leftwich 100.00

2003 Upper Deck Finite Gold

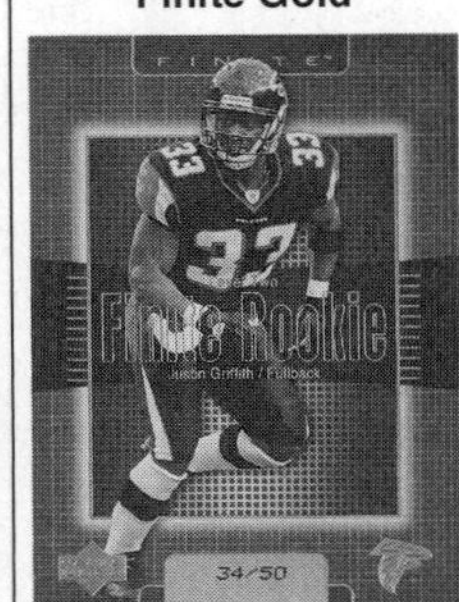
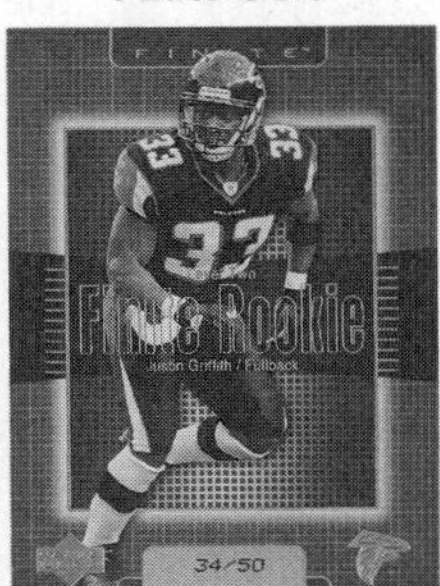

Stars 1-100: 3X-6X
Stars 101-160: 2X-4X
Stars 161-185: 1X-2X
Stars 186-200: 1.5X
Rookies 201-250: 1.5X-3X
Rookies 251-285: 1X-2X
Rookies 286-300: 1X-1.5X
Production 50 Sets

2003 Upper Deck Finite Autographs

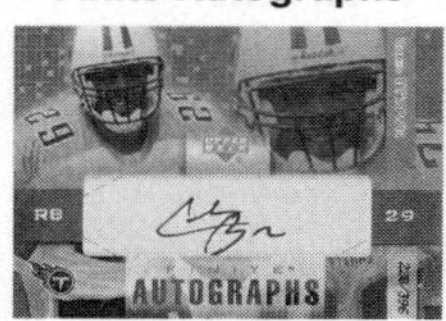

NM/M
Common Player: 8.00
Inserted 1:10
Gold Production 25 Sets
AL Mike Alstott/175 30.00
BB Brad Banks/1000 10.00
KB Kevan Barlow/107 20.00
JB Jeff Blake/35 15.00
AQ Anquan Boldin/396 50.00
CB Chris Brown/396 20.00
AB Antonio Bryant/100 15.00
MB Marc Bulger/35 40.00
NB Nate Burleson/396 15.00
RC Reche Caldwell/261 8.00
KC Kelly Campbell/262 8.00
DC Dallas Clark/396 15.00
EC Eric Crouch/263 30.00
KC Kevin Curtis/396 10.00
WD Woodrow Dantzler III/207 12.00
RD Rohan Davey/262 10.00
AD Andre Davis/263 12.00
BD Brandon Doman/262 8.00
JF Justin Fargas/396 20.00
DF DeShaun Foster/207 15.00
DF2 DeShaun Foster/647 12.00
JG Jabar Gaffney/260 10.00
TG Tony Gonzalez/46 25.00
EG Earnest Graham/800 10.00
QG Quentin Griffin/447 60.00
AZ Az-Zahir Hakim/186 10.00
NH Napoleon Harris/262 8.00
TH Todd Heap/63 20.00
JJ James Jackson/300 8.00
TA Taylor Jacobs/409 REDEMP 8.00
BR Bryant Johnson/396 12.00
CJ Chad Johnson/815 12.00
JA Jason Johnson/205 8.00
LJ Larry Johnson/396 15.00
RJ Ron Johnson/263 8.00
KA Kareem Kelly/1300 8.00
KL Kliff Kingsbury/396 10.00
KK Kurt Kittner/55 20.00
PM1 Peyton Manning/1280 40.00
PM2 Peyton Manning/1250 40.00
KM Keenan McCardell/30 15.00
TM Travis Minor/364 10.00
AP Artose Pinner/396 12.00
CP Clinton Portis/70 80.00
PR Patrick Ramsey/190 20.00
DR Dewayne Robertson/20 REDEMP 15.00
BS Brian St. Pierre/720 12.00
JS Jeremy Shockey/93 50.00
CS Chris Simms/80 40.00
MS Musa Smith/396 10.00
LS Luke Staley/263 8.00
SU Lee Suggs/30 80.00
TS Terrell Suggs/950 12.00
VT Vinny Testaverde/212 15.00
MT Marcus Trufant/396 10.00
SW Seneca Wallace/414 10.00
KW Kelley Washington/1058 12.00
RW Roy Williams/151 50.00

2003 Upper Deck Finite Jerseys

NM/M
Common Player: 6.00
Inserted 1:4
Black Jerseys: 1X-2X
Production 99 Sets
Gold Production 25 Sets
FJ-AB Anquan Boldin 12.00
FJ-KB Kyle Boller 10.00
FJ-CB Chris Brown 8.00
FJ-NB Nate Burleson 6.00
FJ-TC Tyrone Calico 8.00
FJ-DC David Carr 10.00
FJ-DA Dallas Clark 6.00
FJ-CU Daunte Culpepper 8.00
FJ-KC Kevin Curtis 6.00
FJ-JF Justin Fargas 8.00
FJ-BF Brett Favre 25.00
FJ-GA Rich Gannon 6.00
FJ-AG Ahman Green 10.00
FJ-RG Rex Grossman 12.00
FJ-PH Priest Holmes 12.00
FJ-TA Taylor Jacobs 6.00
FJ-AJ Andre Johnson 12.00
FJ-BE Bethel Johnson 8.00
FJ-BJ Bryant Johnson 8.00
FJ-LJ Larry Johnson 10.00
FJ-TJ Teyo Johnson 6.00
FJ-KK Kliff Kingsbury 6.00
FJ-BL Byron Leftwich 20.00
FJ-PM Peyton Manning 15.00
FJ-WM Willis McGahee 10.00
FJ-MC Donovan McNabb 10.00
FJ-TN Terence Newman 10.00
FJ-CP Carson Palmer 15.00
FJ-PE Chad Pennington 10.00
FJ-AP Artose Pinner 6.00
FJ-PO Clinton Portis 12.00
FJ-DR Dave Ragone 6.00
FJ-DR Dewayne Robertson 6.00
FJ-BS Brian St. Pierre 6.00
FJ-ES Emmitt Smith 20.00
FJ-MS Musa Smith 6.00
FJ-OS Onterrio Smith 10.00
FJ-TS Terrell Suggs 8.00
FJ-MT Marcus Trufant 6.00
FJ-MV Michael Vick SP 25.00
FJ-SW Seneca Wallace 6.00
FJ-KW Kelley Washington 8.00

2003 UD Honor Roll

NM/M
Complete Set (190): 200.00
Common Player (1-100): .20
Minor Stars: .40
Unlisted Stars: .60
Common Rookie (1-100): 1.00
Minor Rookies: 1.50
Unlisted Rookies: 2.00
Common SP (101-130): 1.50
Inserted 1:6
Common Rookie (131-190): 2.00
Minor Rookie: 2.50
Unlisted Rookie: 3.00
Production 2003 Sets
Pack (5): 1.75
Box (24): 30.00
1 Corey Dillon .60
2 *Kelley Washington* 2.00
3 Peter Warrick .40
4 Joey Harrington 1.25
5 Az-Zahir Hakim .40
6 *David Kircus* 1.50
7 Jabar Gaffney .40
8 *Domanick Davis* 4.00
9 *Dave Ragone* 1.50
10 Kordell Stewart .40
11 *Justin Gage* 1.50
12 *Bobby Wade* 1.50
13 Anthony Thomas .60
14 Chad Hutchinson .40
15 Antonio Bryant .40
16 *Bradie James* 1.50
17 Josh McCown .40
18 Jeff Blake .40
19 *Kenny King* 1.00
20 Daunte Culpepper .60
21 Michael Bennett .60
22 Randy Moss 1.00
23 *Onterrio Smith* 3.00
24 Mark Brunell .40
25 *George Wrighster* 1.00
26 Fred Taylor .60
27 Jake Delhomme .40
28 *Mike Seidman* 1.00
29 *Walter Young* 1.00
30 Chris Redman .40
31 Jamal Lewis .60
32 *Ovie Mughelli* 1.00
33 Koren Robinson .40
34 Shaun Alexander .60
35 *Taco Wallace* 1.00
36 Kurt Warner .75
37 *Kevin Curtis* 1.00
38 Torry Holt .60
39 Patrick Ramsey .60
40 Laveranues Coles .40
41 *Gibran Hamdan* 1.00
42 Drew Bledsoe .60
43 *Jerel Myers* 1.00
44 Eric Moulds .40
45 Drew Brees .75
46 David Boston .60
47 LaDainian Tomlinson .75
48 Reche Caldwell .40
49 Priest Holmes .60
50 Tony Gonzalez .40
51 *Mike Pinkard* 1.00
52 Aaron Brooks .60
53 Deuce McAllister .60
54 *Montrae Holland* 1.00
55 Jay Fiedler .40
56 Junior Seau .40
57 Chris Chambers .60
58 Ricky Williams 1.00
59 Tom Brady .75
60 Troy Brown .40
61 Antowain Smith .40
62 Jake Plummer .40
63 *Cecil Sapp* 1.50
64 *Adrian Madise* 1.00
65 Tim Couch .60
66 William Green .60
67 Kelly Holcomb .20
68 Chad Pennington .75
69 Santana Moss .40
70 Curtis Martin .60
71 Michael Vick 2.00
72 *LaTarence Dunbar* 1.00
73 Peerless Price .40
74 Marvin Harrison .60
75 Peyton Manning 1.00
76 Edgerrin James .75
77 Jeremy Shockey 1.00
78 Tiki Barber .60
79 *Kevin Walter* 1.00
80 Jeff Garcia .60
81 Terrell Owens .60
82 *Andrew Williams* 1.00
83 Tommy Maddox .60
84 Plaxico Burress .60
85 *Brian St. Pierre* 1.50
86 Steve McNair .60
87 Eddie George .60
88 Derrick Mason .40
89 Brett Favre 2.00
90 Ahman Green .60
91 Donald Driver .40
92 Donovan McNabb .75
93 Brian Dawkins .20
94 *Norman LeJune* 1.00
95 Jerry Rice 1.50
96 Rich Gannon .40
97 *Siddeeq Shabazz* 1.00
98 *Dewayne White* 1.00
99 Brad Johnson .40
100 Keyshawn Johnson .40
101 Chad Johnson 1.50
102 *Artose Pinner* 3.00
103 David Carr 5.00
104 Brian Urlacher 4.00
105 *Jason Witten* 3.00
106 Emmitt Smith 6.00
107 *Nate Burleson* 3.00
108 *LaBrandon Toefield* 3.00
109 Julius Peppers 1.50
110 *Musa Smith* 3.00
111 *Seneca Wallace* 3.00
112 Marshall Faulk 3.00
113 *Brad Banks* 3.00
114 Travis Henry 1.50
115 *Mike Scifres* 1.50
116 *J.R. Tolver* 2.00
117 *Kliff Kingsbury* 3.00
118 Clinton Portis 6.00
119 Kevin Johnson 1.50
120 *Brooks Bollinger* 3.00
121 *Terrence Edwards* 3.00
122 *Steve Sciullo* 1.50
123 *Ken Dorsey* 4.00
124 Jerome Bettis 1.50
125 *Chris Brown* 3.00
126 *Carl Ford* 3.00
127 *Billy McMullen* 2.00
128 *Doug Gabriel* 3.00
129 *Earnest Graham* 3.00
130 *Chris Simms* 5.00
131 *Carson Palmer* 12.00
132 *Charles Rogers* 10.00
133 *Andre Johnson* 8.00
134 *Dewayne Robertson* 2.00
135 *Terence Newman* 5.00
136 *Johnathan Sullivan* 2.00
137 *Byron Leftwich* 12.00
138 *Jordan Gross* 2.50
139 *Kevin Williams* 2.00
140 *Terrell Suggs* 4.00
141 *Marcus Trufant* 3.00
142 *Jimmy Kennedy* 2.50
143 *Ty Warren* 2.00
144 *Michael Haynes* 2.50
145 *Jerome McDougle* 2.50
146 *J.T. Wall* 2.00
147 *Bryant Johnson* 4.00
148 *Calvin Pace* 2.00
149 *Kyle Boller* 8.00
150 *Quentin Griffin* 6.00
151 *Lee Suggs* 8.00
152 *Rex Grossman* 10.00
153 *Willis McGahee* 10.00
154 *Dallas Clark* 4.00
155 *William Joseph* 2.50
156 *Kwame Harris* 2.00
157 *Larry Johnson* 8.00
158 *Andre Woolfolk* 2.50
159 *Nick Barnett* 3.00
160 *Dahrran Diedrick* 3.00
161 *Teyo Johnson* 4.00
162 *Justin Fargas* 5.00
163 *Eric Steinbach* 2.50
164 *Boss Bailey* 4.00
165 *Charles Tillman* 3.00
166 *Eugene Wilson* 2.00
167 *Jonathan Stinchcomb* 2.00
168 *Al Johnson* 2.00
169 *Rashean Mathis* 2.00
170 *Keenan Howry* 3.00
171 *Bennie Joppru* 2.50
172 *Rashad Moore* 2.00
173 *Shaun McDonald* 2.00
174 *Taylor Jacobs* 3.00
175 *Bethel Johnson* 3.00
176 *Matt Wilhelm* 2.50
177 *Kawicka Mitchell* 2.00
178 *Chris Kelsay* 2.00
179 *Lon Sheriff* 2.00
180 *Ricky Manning Jr.* 2.00
181 *Terry Pierce* 2.00
182 *Chaun Thompson* 2.00
183 *Victor Hobson* 2.00
184 *Anquan Boldin* 6.00
185 *Justin Griffith* 2.00
186 *Osi Umenyiora* 2.00
187 *Brandon Lloyd* 3.00
188 *Mike Doss* 2.50
189 *Alonzo Jackson* 2.50
190 *Tyrone Calico* 5.00

2003 UD Honor Roll Silver

Silver 1-100: 3X-6X
Silver Rookies 1-100: 2X-3X
Silver 101-190: 1.5X
Production 200 Sets

A player's name in *italic* type indicates a rookie card.

2003 UD Honor Roll Dean's List

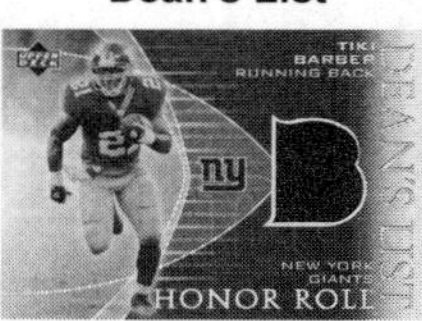

NM/M
Common Player: 5.00
Inserted 1:13
Silver Cards: 1.5X
Production 200 Sets
Gold Production 25 Sets
DL-SA Shaun Alexander 8.00
DL-MA Mike Alstott 6.00
DL-AN Mike Anderson 6.00
DL-CB Champ Bailey 8.00
DL-TB Tiki Barber 8.00
DL-KB Kendrell Bell 10.00
DL-BO Kyle Boller 12.00
DL-MB Marty Booker 6.00
DL-JB Josh Booty 5.00
DL-PB Plaxico Burress 8.00
DL-DC Dallas Clark 6.00
DL-KC Kerry Collins 6.00
DL-OG Olandis Gary 6.00
DL-RG Rex Grossman 12.00
DL-TH Torry Holt 8.00
DL-QJ Quentin Jammer 6.00
DL-CJ Chad Johnson 6.00
DL-JK Jevon Kearse 6.00
DL-BL Byron Leftwich 20.00
DL-PM Peyton Manning 15.00
DL-CU Curtis Martin 8.00
DL-CM Chris McAllister 5.00
DL-DM Darnerian McCants 6.00
DL-MM Michael McCrary 5.00
DL-MC Donovan McNabb 12.00
DL-SM Sammy Morris 5.00
DL-OP Orlando Pace 5.00
DL-SC Carson Palmer 15.00
DL-DR Dave Ragone 6.00
DL-RO Dewayne Robertson 5.00
DL-MR Marcus Robinson 6.00
DL-CS Chris Samuels 5.00
DL-SH Jeremy Shockey 12.00
DL-SI Corey Simon 5.00
DL-BS Brandon Stokley 5.00
DL-ZT Zach Thomas 6.00
DL-MV Michael Vick 20.00
DL-KW Kevin Ware 5.00
DL-RW Reggie Wayne 6.00
DL-DW Dez White 5.00

2003 UD Honor Roll Letterman Autographs

NM/M
Common Player: 10.00
Inserted 1:240
Gold Production 25 Sets
HRL-KB Kevan Barlow 15.00
HRL-TH Todd Heap 10.00
HRL-HE Travis Henry 12.00
HRL-JJ James Jackson 10.00
HRL-CJ Chad Johnson 15.00
HRL-RJ Rudi Johnson 12.00
HRL-PM Peyton Manning 40.00
HRL-DM Deuce McAllister 20.00
HRL-MM Marvin "Snoop" Minnis 10.00
HRL-TM Travis Minor 10.00

2003 Upper Deck MVP

NM/M
Common Player: .10
Silver parallel 1X-3X
Pack(8): 2.00
Wax Box(24): 40.00
1 Brad Johnson .20
2 Dexter Jackson .10
3 Derrick Brooks .20
4 Simeon Rice .10
5 Warren Sapp .20
6 John Lynch .10
7 Joe Jurevicius .10
8 Ronde Barber .10
9 Mike Alstott .40
10 Michael Pittman .10
11 Keyshawn Johnson .40
12 Jerry Rice 1.25
13 Tim Brown .40
14 Rich Gannon .40
15 Charlie Garner .30
16 Jerry Porter .30
17 Sebastian Janikowski .10
18 Zack Crockett .10
19 Tyrone Wheatley .10
20 Bill Romanowski .10
21 Charles Woodson .30
22 Rod Woodson .30
23 Donovan McNabb .75
24 James Thrash .10
25 Duce Staley .10
26 Brian Westbrook .10
27 A.J. Feeley .10
28 Koy Detmer .10
29 Brian Dawkins .10
30 Dorsey Levens .10
31 Jon Ritchie .10
32 Todd Pinkston .10
33 Chad Lewis .10
34 Brett Favre 1.50
35 Ahman Green .50
36 Donald Driver .40
37 Bubba Franks .10
38 Javon Walker .30
39 Kabeer Gbaja-Biamila .10
40 Robert Ferguson .10
41 Tony Fisher .10
42 Marques Anderson .10
43 Ryan Longwell .10
44 Craig Nall .30
45 Steve McNair .40
46 Eddie George .40
47 Jevon Kearse .30
48 Kevin Carter .10
49 Samari Rolle .10
50 Keith Bulluck .10
51 Joe Nedney .10
52 Robert Holcombe .10
53 Drew Bennett .10
54 Frank Wycheck .10
55 Derrick Mason .30
56 Tommy Maddox .40
57 Jerome Bettis .40
58 Plaxico Burress .40
59 Antwaan Randle El .75
60 Amos Zereoue .20
61 Chris Fuamatu-Ma'afala .10
62 Jason Gildon .10
63 Kendrell Bell .20
64 DeWayne Washington .10
65 Jeff Reed .10
66 Hines Ward .40
67 Jeff Garcia .40
68 Terrell Owens .40
69 Andre Carter .10
70 Tai Streets .10
71 Tim Rattay .10
72 Eric Johnson .10
73 Cedrick Wilson .10
74 Brandon Doman .10
75 Kevan Barlow .10
76 Bryant Young .10
77 Garrison Hearst .10
78 Kerry Collins .30
79 Daryl Jones .10
80 Tiki Barber .30
81 Amani Toomer .40
82 Tim Carter .10
83 Michael Strahan .40
84 Ike Hilliard .10
85 Brian Mitchell .10
86 Ron Dixon .10
87 Jeremy Shockey 1.00
88 Marvin Harrison .40
89 Peyton Manning 1.25
90 Edgerrin James .75
91 Dominic Rhodes .30
92 Brock Huard .10
93 Marcus Pollard .10
94 James Mungro .10
95 Dwight Freeney .30
96 Reggie Wayne .30
97 Rob Morris .10
98 Michael Vick 1.50
99 Warrick Dunn .20
100 T.J. Duckett .40
101 Keith Brooking .10
102 Ray Buchanan .10
103 Alge Crumpler .10
104 Quentin McCord .10
105 Doug Johnson .10
106 Brian Finneran .10
107 Peerless Price .40
108 Chad Pennington .60
109 Curtis Martin .40
110 Laveranues Coles .30
111 Wayne Chrebet .10
112 LaMont Jordan .10
113 Anthony Becht .10
114 Marvin Jones .10
115 Mo Lewis .10
116 Sam Cowart .10
117 Vinny Testaverde .10
118 Santana Moss .10
119 Tim Couch .60
120 William Green .40
121 Andre Davis .30
122 Quincy Morgan .30
123 Kevin Johnson .10
124 James Jackson .10
125 Jamel White .10
126 Robert Griffith .10
127 Dennis Northcutt .10
128 Josh Booty .10
129 Kelly Holcomb .40
130 Jake Plummer .40
131 Olandis Gary .10
132 Clinton Portis 1.25
133 Mike Anderson .40
134 Ashley Lelie .60
135 Ed McCaffrey .30
136 Shannon Sharpe .10
137 Rod Smith .30
138 John Mobley .10
139 Jason Elam .10
140 Terrell Davis .40
141 Tom Brady .75
142 Christian Fauria .10
143 Antowain Smith .30
144 Kevin Faulk .10
145 Ty Law .10
146 Lawyer Milloy .10
147 David Patten .10
148 Deion Branch .30
149 Troy Brown .30
150 Rohan Davey .10
151 Adam Vinatieri .10
152 Jay Fiedler .40
153 Chris Chambers .40
154 Randy McMichael .10
155 Rob Konrad .10
156 Morlon Greenwood .10
157 Derrius Thompson .10
158 Travis Minor .10
159 Olindo Mare .10
160 Jason Taylor .10
161 Zach Thomas .40
162 Ricky Williams .75
163 Aaron Brooks .60
164 Deuce McAllister .60
165 Donte Stallworth .60
166 Jerome Pathon .10
167 J.T. O'Sullivan .10
168 Darrin Smith .10
169 Michael Lewis .10
170 John Carney .10
171 Kyle Turley .10
172 Joe Horn .30
173 Trent Green .30
174 Priest Holmes .60
175 Johnnie Morton .10
176 Eddie Kennison .10
177 Marvcus Patton .10
178 Omar Easy .10
179 Derrick Blaylock .10
180 Marvin "Snoop" Minnis .10
181 Dante Hall .10
182 Tony Gonzalez .30
183 Marc Boerigter .30
184 Drew Brees .10
185 David Boston .10
186 Stephen Alexander .30
187 Quentin Jammer .10
188 Donnie Edwards .10
189 LaDainian Tomlinson 1.00
190 Junior Seau .40
191 Reche Caldwell .30
192 Lorenzo Neal .10
193 Tim Dwight .30
194 Doug Flutie .30
195 Drew Bledsoe .75
196 Travis Henry .40
197 Eric Moulds .40
198 Alex Van Pelt .10
199 Charles Johnson .10
200 Nate Clements .10
201 Takeo Spikes .10
202 Bobby Shaw .10
203 London Fletcher .10
204 Sammy Morris .10
205 Josh Reed .10
206 Patrick Ramsey .40
207 Ladell Betts .30
208 Chad Morton .10
209 Trung Canidate .30
210 Kenny Watson .10
211 Jessie Armstead .10
212 Fred Smoot .10
213 Champ Bailey .10
214 Bruce Smith .10
215 Rod Gardner .30
216 Kurt Warner 1.00
217 Troy Edwards .10
218 Adam Archuleta .10
219 Grant Wistrom .10
220 Marshall Faulk .75
221 Jeff Wilkins .10
222 Aeneas Williams .10
223 Lamar Gordon .30
224 Marc Bulger .40
225 Isaac Bruce .40
226 Torry Holt .40
227 Matt Hasselbeck .30
228 Maurice Morris .30
229 Bobby Engram .10
230 Darrell Jackson .10
231 James Williams .40
232 Chad Brown .10
233 Anthony Simmons .10
234 Shaun Alexander .40
235 Koren Robinson .30
236 Chris Redman .10
237 Jamal Lewis .30
238 Brandon Stokley .10
239 Peter Boulware .10
240 Randy Hymes .10
241 Todd Heap .30
242 Travis Taylor .30
243 Ron Johnson .10
244 Ray Lewis .20
245 Jake Delhomme .10
246 DeShaun Foster .30
247 Dee Brown .10
248 Steve Smith .10
249 Kevin Dyson .10
250 Muhsin Muhammad .30
251 Stephen Davis .40
252 Julius Peppers .40
253 Rodney Peete .10
254 Mark Brunell .40
255 Jimmy Smith .20
256 Kyle Brady .10
257 Kevin Lockett .10
258 Quinn Gray .10
259 Tony Brackens .10
260 Marco Coleman .10
261 David Garrard .20
262 Fred Taylor .10
263 Daunte Culpepper .75
264 Michael Bennett .40
265 D'Wayne Bates .10
266 Cedric James .10
267 Kelly Campbell .10
268 Derrick Alexander .10
269 Byron Chamberlain .10
270 Shaun Hill .10
271 Randy Moss 1.25
272 Josh McCown .10

#	Player	NM/M
273	Thomas Jones	.10
274	Wendell Bryant	.10
275	Kevin Kasper	.10
276	Jason McAddley	.10
277	Emmitt Smith	1.25
278	Preston Parsons	.10
279	Freddie Jones	.10
280	Marcel Shipp	.30
281	Chad Hutchinson	.30
282	Troy Hambrick	.30
283	Dat Nguyen	.10
284	Michael Wiley	.10
285	Joey Galloway	.30
286	Terry Glenn	.10
287	La'Roi Glover	.10
288	Roy Williams	.40
289	Antonio Bryant	.40
290	Quincy Carter	.30
291	Anthony Thomas	.30
292	Marty Booker	.10
293	Dez White	.10
294	Marcus Robinson	.30
295	Kordell Stewart	.40
296	David Terrell	.30
297	John Davis	.10
298	Mike Brown	.10
299	Brian Urlacher	1.00
300	Jabar Gaffney	.30
301	Jonathan Wells	.40
302	JaJuan Dawson	.10
303	Corey Bradford	.10
304	Frank Murphy	.10
305	Billy Miller	.10
306	Aaron Glenn	.10
307	Avion Black	.10
308	David Carr	1.00
309	Joey Harrington	1.00
310	James Stewart	.10
311	Ty Detmer	.10
312	Jason Hanson	.10
313	Bill Schroeder	.10
314	Mikhael Ricks	.10
315	Scotty Anderson	.10
316	Robert Porcher	.10
317	Az-Zahir Hakim	.30
318	Jon Kitna	.30
319	Ron Dugans	.10
320	Chad Johnson	.40
321	Brandon Bennett	.10
322	T.J. Houshmandzadeh	.10
323	Rudi Johnson	.10
324	Kevin Hardy	.10
325	Corey Dillon	.40
326	Peter Warrick	.20
327	*Carson Palmer*	3.00
328	*Byron Leftwich*	3.00
329	*Rex Grossman*	1.75
330	*Kyle Boller*	1.75
331	*Dave Ragone*	1.25
332	*Chris Simms*	1.25
333	*Brad Banks*	.75
334	*Kliff Kingsbury*	.50
335	*Jason Gesser*	.50
336	*Jason Johnson*	.50
337	*Brian St. Pierre*	.50
338	*Ken Dorsey*	1.25
339	*Seneca Wallace*	.75
340	*Seth Marler*	.50
341	*Tony Romo*	.75
342	*J.T. Wall*	.40
343	*Kirk Farmer*	.40
344	*Ricky Manning Jr.*	.40
345	*B.J. Askew*	.40
346	*Juston Wood*	.40
347	*Jeremi Johnson*	.40
348	*Tom Lopienski*	.40
349	*Justin Griffith*	.50
350	*Ovie Mughelli*	.40
351	*Bradie James*	.40
352	*Larry Johnson*	2.25
353	*Lee Suggs*	1.25
354	*Justin Fargas*	.75
355	*Chris Brown*	.75
356	*Onterrio Smith*	1.25
357	*Willis McGahee*	2.25
358	*Claude Diggs*	.50
359	*Lance Briggs*	.50
360	*Earnest Graham*	.50
361	*Quentin Griffin*	1.00
362	*Michael Haynes*	.75
363	*Musa Smith*	.50
364	*Artose Pinner*	.50
365	*Domanick Davis*	.75
366	*LaBrandon Toefield*	.40
367	*Bethel Johnson*	.40
368	*Sultan McCullough*	.40
369	*Dahrran Diedrick*	.40
370	*Solomon Bates*	.40
371	*Andrew Pinnock*	.40
372	*Charles Rogers*	2.25
373	*Andre Johnson*	1.75
374	*Taylor Jacobs*	.75
375	*Anquan Boldin*	.50
376	*Talman Gardner*	.50
377	*Brandon Lloyd*	.75
378	*Bryant Johnson*	1.25
379	*Kelley Washington*	.75
380	*Kareem Kelly*	.50
381	*Arnaz Battle*	.50
382	*Billy McMullen*	.50
383	*Keenan Howry*	.50
384	*Nate Burleson*	.50
385	*Doug Gabriel*	.50
386	*J.R. Tolver*	.50
387	*Wayne Hunter*	.50
388	*Teyo Johnson*	.50
389	*Eric Steinbach*	.40
390	*Kevin Curtis*	.40
391	*Bobby Wade*	.40
392	*Sam Aiken*	.50
393	*Willie Pile*	.40
394	*Jerel Myers*	.40
395	*Tyrone Calico*	.50
396	*Terrence Edwards*	.40
397	*Travis Anglin*	.40
398	*Antwone Savage*	.40
399	*Cato June*	.40
400	*Charles Drake*	.40
401	*Ronald Bellamy*	.40
402	*Justin Gage*	.40
403	*Mat McBriar*	.40
404	*Kevin Garrett*	.40
405	*Kenny Peterson*	.50
406	*L.J. Smith*	.40
407	*Jason Witten*	.50
408	*Dallas Clark*	.50
409	*Dewayne White*	.50
410	*Mike Seidman*	.40
411	*Aaron Walker*	.40
412	*Bennie Joppru*	.75
413	*Mike Pinkard*	.50
414	*Danny Curley*	.40
415	*Trent Smith*	.40
416	*George Wrighster*	.40
417	*Terrell Suggs*	1.25
418	*Tully Banta-Cain*	.50
419	*Jerome McDougle*	.60
420	*William Joseph*	.75
421	*Dewayne Robertson*	.60
422	*Jimmy Kennedy*	.60
423	*Chris Kelsay*	.40
424	*Kevin Williams*	.40
425	*Boss Bailey*	.75
426	*Terry Pierce*	.40
427	*Terence Newman*	1.25
428	*Marcus Trufant*	.75
429	*Mike Doss*	.60
430	*Dennis Weathersby*	.50
431	*Matt Wilhelm*	.50
432	*Andre Woolfolk*	.50
433	*Shane Walton*	.40
434	*DeJuan Groce*	.40
435	*Antwoine Sanders*	.40
436	*Julian Battle*	.40
437	Brett Favre Checklist	.50
438	Chad Pennington Checklist	.30
439	David Carr Checklist	.40
440	Drew Brees Checklist	.30

2003 Upper Deck MVP Future MVP Rookie RB

		NM/M
Common Player:		.75
Inserted 1:12		
RB-1	Larry Johnson	2.00
RB-2	Lee Suggs	1.25
RB-3	Onterrio Smith	1.25
RB-4	Willis McGahee	2.00
RB-5	Justin Fargas	.75
RB-6	Chris Brown	1.00
RB-7	Domanick Davis	1.00
RB-8	LaBrandon Toefield	.75
RB-9	Earnest Graham	.75
RB-10	Musa Smith	.75
RB-11	Artose Pinner	.75
RB-12	Sultan McCullough	.75
RB-13	Dahrran Diedrick	.75
RB-14	Quentin Griffin	.75

2003 Upper Deck MVP Future MVP Rookie QB

		NM/M
Common Player:		.75
Inserted 1:12		
QB-1	Carson Palmer	3.00
QB-2	Byron Leftwich	3.00
QB-3	Dave Ragone	1.50
QB-4	Kyle Boller	2.00
QB-5	Chris Simms	2.00
QB-6	Kliff Kingsbury	1.00
QB-7	Jason Gesser	.75
QB-8	Brad Banks	.75
QB-9	Ken Dorsey	1.50
QB-10	Rex Grossman	2.00
QB-11	Jason Johnson	.75
QB-12	Tony Romo	.75
QB-13	Brian St. Pierre	.75
QB-14	Seneca Wallace	1.00

2003 Upper Deck MVP Future MVP Rookie WR

		NM/M
Common Player:		.75
Inserted 1:12		
WR-1	Charles Rogers	2.50
WR-2	Andre Johnson	2.00
WR-3	Taylor Jacobs	1.00
WR-4	Anquan Boldin	.75
WR-5	Brandon Lloyd	1.00
WR-6	Bryant Johnson	1.50
WR-7	Kelley Washington	1.00
WR-8	Kareem Kelly	.75
WR-9	Talman Gardner	.75
WR-10	Arnaz Battle	.75
WR-11	Tyrone Calico	.75
WR-12	Billy McMullen	.75
WR-13	Keenan Howry	.75
WR-14	Teyo Johnson	.75

2003 Upper Deck MVP MVP Pro Sign Autograph

		NM/M
Inserted 1:480		
PS-KB	Kyle Boller	
PS-RC	Reche Caldwell	8.00
PS-KD	Ken Dorsey	
PS-RF	Randy Fasani	8.00
PS-EL	Elvis Grbac	
PS-RG	Rex Grossman	
PS-LJ	Larry Johnson	
PS-RJ	Ron Johnson	5.00
PS-KL	Kliff Kingsbury	
PS-KK	Kurt Kittner	
PS-BL	Byron Leftwich	75.00
PS-PM	Peyton Manning	30.00
PS-WM	Willis McGahee	
PS-JM	Jim Miller	8.00
PS-QM	Quincy Morgan	15.00
PS-JT	J.T. O'Sullivan	10.00
PS-CP	Carson Palmer	
PS-LP	Luke Petitgout	
PS-CS	Chris Simms	

2003 Upper Deck MVP Souvenirs - Game Ball Cards

		NM/M
Common Player:		5.00
Inserted 1:96		
GB-SA	Shaun Alexander	8.00
GB-KB	Kevan Barlow	
GB-MB	Michael Bennett	10.00
GB-TB	Tom Brady	10.00
GB-DB	Drew Brees	8.00
GB-TB	Tim Brown	10.00
GB-PB	Plaxico Burress	8.00
GB-DA	David Carr	12.00
GB-LC	Laveranues Coles	
GB-TC	Tim Couch	10.00
GB-DC	Daunte Culpepper	
GB-SD	Stephen Davis	5.00
GB-BF	Brett Favre	15.00
GB-RG	Rich Gannon	5.00
GB-AG	Ahman Green	8.00
GB-JH	Joey Harrington	12.00
GB-TH	Travis Henry	5.00
GB-EJ	Edgerrin James	6.00
GB-KJ	Keyshawn Johnson	
GB-JL	Jamal Lewis	5.00
GB-PM	Peyton Manning	12.00
GB-DM	Deuce McAllister	6.00
GB-MC	Donovan McNabb	10.00
GB-SM	Steve McNair	10.00
GB-RM	Randy Moss	12.00
GB-MO	Santana Moss	5.00
GB-TO	Terrell Owens	8.00
GB-CP	Chad Pennington	8.00
GB-PO	Clinton Portis	12.00
GB-CR	Chris Redman	5.00
GB-JR	Jerry Rice	12.00
GB-LT	LaDainian Tomlinson	5.00
GB-BU	Brian Urlacher	12.00
GB-MV	Michael Vick	15.00
GB-KW	Kurt Warner	

2003 Upper Deck MVP Talk of the Town

		NM/M
Common Player:		.25
Inserted 1:3		
TT-1	Peyton Manning	2.00
TT-2	Aaron Brooks	1.00
TT-3	Joey Harrington	1.50
TT-4	Brett Favre	2.50
TT-5	Donovan McNabb	1.25
TT-6	Tim Couch	1.00
TT-7	Michael Vick	2.50
TT-8	David Carr	1.50
TT-9	Drew Brees	1.25
TT-10	Chad Pennington	1.00
TT-11	Daunte Culpepper	1.25
TT-12	Tom Brady	1.25
TT-13	Kurt Warner	1.50
TT-14	Brad Johnson	.25
TT-15	Rich Gannon	.50
TT-16	Jake Plummer	.25
TT-17	Jeff Garcia	.50
TT-18	Drew Bledsoe	1.25
TT-19	Steve McNair	.50
TT-20	Mark Brunell	.50
TT-21	Dave Ragone	.50
TT-22	Kordell Stewart	.25
TT-23	Jay Fiedler	.25
TT-24	Tommy Maddox	.50
TT-25	Chris Redman	.25
TT-26	Jon Kitna	.25
TT-27	Trent Green	.25
TT-28	Kerry Collins	.50
TT-29	Patrick Ramsey	.75
TT-30	Chad Hutchinson	.25
TT-31	Rodney Peete	.25
TT-32	Josh McCown	.25
TT-33	Matt Hasselbeck	.25
TT-34	Kelly Holcomb	.25
TT-35	Marc Bulger	.75
TT-36	Carson Palmer	3.00
TT-37	Byron Leftwich	3.00
TT-38	Kyle Boller	2.00
TT-39	Chris Simms	2.00
TT-40	Rex Grossman	2.00
TT-41	Marshall Faulk	1.00
TT-42	LaDainian Tomlinson	1.50
TT-43	Emmitt Smith	2.00
TT-44	Ricky Williams	1.25
TT-45	Edgerrin James	1.25
TT-46	Deuce McAllister	1.00
TT-47	Eddie George	.50
TT-48	Ahman Green	.75
TT-49	Clinton Portis	2.00
TT-50	Anthony Thomas	.50
TT-51	Priest Holmes	1.00
TT-52	Curtis Martin	.50
TT-53	Michael Bennett	.40
TT-54	Shaun Alexander	.50
TT-55	Jerome Bettis	.50
TT-56	Fred Taylor	.25
TT-57	Travis Henry	.25
TT-58	Garrison Hearst	.25
TT-59	Charlie Garner	.25
TT-60	Kevan Barlow	.25
TT-61	Corey Dillon	.25
TT-62	Duce Staley	.25
TT-63	Jamal Lewis	.25
TT-64	William Green	.50
TT-65	Jerry Rice	2.00
TT-66	Terrell Owens	.50
TT-67	Randy Moss	2.00
TT-68	David Boston	.40
TT-69	Marvin Harrison	.75
TT-70	Isaac Bruce	.25
TT-71	Torry Holt	.50
TT-72	Plaxico Burress	.50
TT-73	Keyshawn Johnson	.25
TT-74	Chris Chambers	.50
TT-75	Rod Smith	.25
TT-76	Tim Brown	.50
TT-77	Rod Gardner	.25
TT-78	Peerless Price	.75
TT-79	Jabar Gaffney	.25
TT-80	Antonio Bryant	.75
TT-81	Troy Brown	.25
TT-82	Jimmy Smith	.25
TT-83	Donald Driver	.60
TT-84	Eric Moulds	.25
TT-85	Kevin Johnson	.25
TT-86	Charles Rogers	2.50
TT-87	Andre Johnson	2.00
TT-88	Taylor Jacobs	1.50
TT-89	Tony Gonzalez	.25
TT-90	Jeremy Shockey	1.50

2003 UD Patch Collection

		NM/M
Common Player (1-90):		.30
Minor Stars:		.60
Unlisted Stars:		.75
Rookies (91-120):		1.50
Minor Rookies:		2.00
Unlisted Rookies:		2.50
Inserted 1:4		
Common Rookie (121-132):		2.50
Inserted 1:20		
Common Rookie (133-147):		3.00
Inserted 1:40		
Common All-Pro (148-162):		3.00
Inserted 1:40		
Pack (5):		3.50
Box (20):		50.00
1	Peyton Manning	1.50
2	Aaron Brooks	.75
3	Joey Harrington	2.00
4	Brett Favre	3.00
5	Donovan McNabb	1.00
6	Jeff Garcia	.75
7	Michael Vick	3.00
8	David Carr	2.00
9	Drew Brees	1.00
10	Chad Pennington	1.00
11	Daunte Culpepper	.75
12	Tom Brady	1.00
13	Kurt Warner	1.00
14	Brad Johnson	.60
15	Josh McCown	.60
16	Drew Bledsoe	1.00
17	Rich Gannon	.60
18	Tim Couch	.60
19	Keyshawn Johnson	.60
20	Travis Henry	.60
21	LaDainian Tomlinson	1.00
22	Emmitt Smith	2.50
23	Michael Bennett	.75
24	Mark Brunell	.60
25	Steve McNair	.75
26	Clinton Portis	2.50
27	Eddie George	.75
28	Marshall Faulk	1.00
29	Curtis Martin	.75
30	Ahman Green	.75
31	Priest Holmes	.75
32	Edgerrin James	1.00
33	Deuce McAllister	.75
34	Ricky Williams	1.50
35	Anthony Thomas	.75
36	Jerome Bettis	.60
37	Shaun Alexander	.75
38	Jake Plummer	.60
39	Patrick Ramsey	.75
40	Laveranues Coles	.60
41	David Boston	.75
42	Jay Fiedler	.60
43	Garrison Hearst	.60
44	Corey Dillon	.75
45	Charlie Garner	.60
46	Fred Taylor	.75
47	Chad Hutchinson	.60
48	Quincy Carter	.75
49	Kevan Barlow	.60
50	Tommy Maddox	.75
51	Kordell Stewart	.60
52	Chris Redman	.60
53	Jamal Lewis	.75
54	Zach Thomas	.60
55	Junior Seau	.60
56	Chris Chambers	.75
57	Matt Hasselbeck	.75
58	Marc Bulger	.75
59	Isaac Bruce	.60
60	Torry Holt	.75
61	Kelly Holcomb	.60
62	Plaxico Burress	.75
63	Ray Lewis	.60
64	Brian Urlacher	1.50
65	Tim Brown	.60
66	William Green	.75
67	Kevin Johnson	.30
68	Trent Green	.60
69	Santana Moss	.60
70	Tony Gonzalez	.60
71	Rod Smith	.60
72	Ashley Lelie	.75
73	Peerless Price	.60
74	Antonio Bryant	.60
75	Duce Staley	.60
76	Darrell Jackson	.60
77	Jeremy Shockey	1.50
78	Kerry Collins	.60
79	Koren Robinson	.60
80	Jerry Rice	2.50
81	Terrell Owens	.75
82	Antwann Randle El	.60
83	Donte Stallworth	.60
84	Randy Moss	1.50
85	Chad Johnson	.60
86	Hines Ward	.60
87	Rod Gardner	.60
88	Marvin Harrison	.75
89	Eric Moulds	.60
90	Julius Peppers	.60
91	*Nate Hybl*	2.00
92	*Lon Sheriff*	1.50
93	*Gerald Hayes*	1.50
94	*B.J. Askew*	2.50
95	*Artose Pinner*	2.00
96	*Domanick Davis*	5.00
97	*LaBrandon Toefield*	2.50
98	*Lee Suggs*	3.00
99	*Cecil Sapp*	2.50
100	*Kelley Washington*	3.00
101	*Kevin Curtis*	2.50
102	*Zuriel Smith*	2.00
103	*Carl Ford*	2.50
104	*Travis Anglin*	1.50
105	*Terrence Edwards*	2.50
106	*Troy Polamalu*	4.00
107	*Nate Burleson*	2.50
108	*Cecil Moore*	1.50
109	*Kassim Osgood*	1.50
110	*Teyo Johnson*	3.00
111	*Jason Witten*	3.00
112	*Visanthe Shiancoe*	2.00
113	*Kevin Ware*	2.00
114	*Mike Pinkard*	2.00
115	*Donald Lee*	2.00
116	*Justin Gage*	3.00
117	*Adrian Madise*	1.50
118	*Anthony Adams*	1.50
119	*Dan Curley*	1.50
120	*Dallas Clark*	3.00
121	*Kyle Boller*	8.00
122	*Chris Simms*	6.00
123	*Dave Ragone*	3.00
124	*Kliff Kingsbury*	3.00
125	*Brad Banks*	3.00
126	*Gibran Hamdan*	2.50
127	*Ken Dorsey*	5.00
128	*Seneca Wallace*	3.00
129	*Brian St. Pierre*	3.00
130	*Rex Grossman*	10.00
131	*Brooks Bollinger*	3.00
132	*Jason Gesser*	3.00
133	*Carson Palmer*	12.00
134	*Byron Leftwich*	15.00
135	*Charles Rogers*	10.00
136	*Andre Johnson*	10.00
137	*Willis McGahee*	10.00
138	*Larry Johnson*	8.00
139	*Musa Smith*	3.00
140	*Chris Brown*	4.00
141	*Onterrio Smith*	5.00
142	*Justin Fargas*	5.00
143	*Bryant Johnson*	4.00
144	*Taylor Jacobs*	3.00
145	*Bethel Johnson*	3.00
146	*Tyrone Calico*	5.00
147	*Anquan Boldin*	8.00
148	Michael Vick	10.00
149	Brett Favre	10.00
150	Chad Pennington	4.00
151	Kurt Warner	3.00
152	David Carr	6.00
153	Donovan McNabb	5.00
154	LaDainian Tomlinson	3.00
155	Marshall Faulk	4.00
156	Emmitt Smith	10.00
157	Jerry Rice	8.00
158	Terrell Owens	3.00
159	Brian Urlacher	5.00
160	Randy Moss	5.00
161	Ricky Williams	5.00
162	Peyton Manning	6.00

2003 UD Patch Collection All-Upper Deck Patches

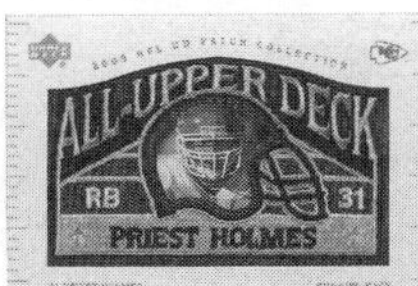

		NM/M
Common Player:		5.00
Inserted 1:22		
Gold Production 25 Sets		
UD1	Edgerrin James	8.00
UD2	Aaron Brooks	5.00
UD3	Steve McNair	6.00
UD4	Tim Couch	5.00
UD5	Tom Brady	10.00
UD6	Joey Harrington	10.00
UD7	Jeremy Shockey	10.00
UD8	Daunte Culpepper	6.00
UD9	Jeff Garcia	5.00
UD10	David Boston	5.00
UD11	Deuce McAllister	6.00
UD12	Ahman Green	6.00
UD13	Tim Brown	5.00
UD14	Shaun Alexander	6.00
UD15	Laveranues Coles	5.00
UD16	Priest Holmes	10.00
UD17	Clinton Portis	10.00
UD18	Marvin Harrison	6.00
UD19	Drew Bledsoe	6.00
UD20	Corey Dillon	5.00
UD21	Drew Brees	6.00

2003 UD Patch Collection Jumbo Patch Box Toppers

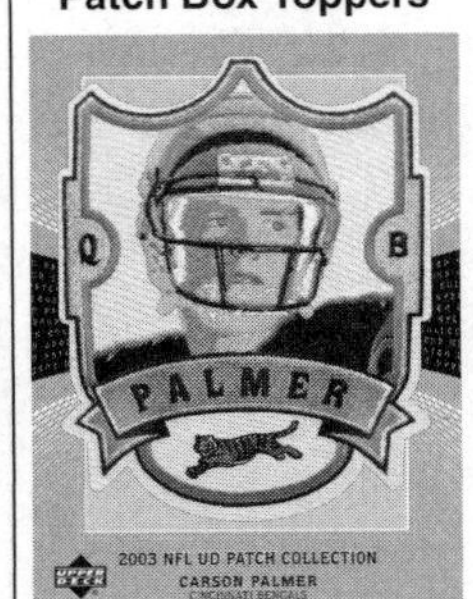

		NM/M
Common Player:		8.00
Inserted 1:Box		
Gold Production 25 Sets		
KB	Kyle Boller	10.00
DB	Drew Brees	10.00
DC	David Carr	12.00
MF	Marshall Faulk	10.00
BF	Brett Favre	20.00
JH	Joey Harrington	10.00

AJ Andre Johnson 12.00
LJ Larry Johnson 10.00
BL Byron Leftwich 15.00
PM Peyton Manning 15.00
MC Deuce McAllister 8.00
DM Donovan McNabb 10.00
RM Randy Moss 12.00
TO Terrell Owens 8.00
SC Carson Palmer 15.00
CP Chad Pennington 10.00
PO Clinton Portis 15.00
JR Jerry Rice 15.00
JS Jeremy Shockey 12.00
ES Emmitt Smith 20.00
LT LaDainian Tomlinson 8.00
BU Brian Urlacher 12.00
MV Michael Vick 20.00
RW Ricky Williams 10.00

2003 UD Patch Collection Jumbo Patch Box Topper Autos

NM/M
PM Peyton Manning 100.00
TO Terrell Owens 40.00

2003 UD Patch Collection Signature Patches

NM/M
Common Player: 10.00
Inserted 1:410
Gold Production 25 Sets
SP-KB Kevan Barlow 15.00
SP-DB Drew Brees 30.00
SP-AB Aaron Brooks 20.00
SP-JG Jeff Garcia 30.00
SP-RG Rod Gardner 20.00
SP-TH Todd Heap 20.00
SP-JJ James Jackson 10.00
SP-CJ Chad Johnson 20.00
SP-RJ Rudi Johnson 20.00
SP-BL Byron Leftwich 100.00
SP-PM Peyton Manning 80.00
SP-WM Willis McGahee 80.00
SP-CP Carson Palmer 100.00
SP-CH Chad Pennington 60.00
SP-RW Reggie Wayne 20.00

2003 Upper Deck Pros & Prospects

NM/M
Common Player: .15
Unlisted Star: .60
Minor Star: .40
Common Rookie: 1.00
Unlisted Rookie Star: 3.00
Minor Rookie Star: 2.00
Cards 91-120 are SP's
Common SP: .50
Cards 121-190 are dual cards
Production from 250-2000 sets
Non-Autographed production 1800
Rookie Autographed production 2000
Veteran Autograph production 500
Dual Autograph production 250
Gold Parallel (121-190): 2X-5X
Production 50 sets
Pack (5): 3.00
Wax Box (24): 50.00
1 Jake Plummer .40
2 David Boston .60
3 Warrick Dunn .40
4 T.J. Duckett .60
5 Chris Redman .40
6 Jamal Lewis .60
7 Drew Bledsoe 1.00
8 Travis Henry .40
9 Eric Moulds .40
10 Peerless Price .40
11 Rodney Peete .15
12 Julius Peppers .40
13 Anthony Thomas .60
14 Brian Urlacher 1.25
15 Marty Booker .40
16 David Terrell .40
17 Corey Dillon .60
18 Peter Warrick .40
19 Jon Kitna .15
20 Tim Couch .75
21 Andre Davis .60
22 Quincy Morgan .40
23 Dennis Northcutt .15
24 Roy Williams .60
25 Emmitt Smith 1.50
26 Joey Galloway .40
27 Antonio Bryant .60
28 Brian Griese .60
29 Clinton Portis 1.50
30 Shannon Sharpe .40
31 Joey Harrington 1.25
32 Az-Zahir Hakim .60
33 Brett Favre 2.00
34 Robert Ferguson .15
35 Donald Driver .40
36 David Carr 1.25
37 Jabar Gaffney .40
38 Edgerrin James 1.25
39 Marvin Harrison .60
40 Reggie Wayne .40
41 Mark Brunell .60
42 Fred Taylor .40
43 Priest Holmes .75
44 Trent Green .40
45 Marc Boerigter .40
46 Jay Fiedler .40
47 Chris Chambers .60
48 Randy McMichael .15
49 Randy Moss 1.50
50 Daunte Culpepper 1.00
51 Michael Bennett .60
52 Antowain Smith .40
53 David Patten .15
54 Troy Brown .40
55 Aaron Brooks .75
56 Joe Horn .40
57 Donte Stallworth .75
58 Amani Toomer .40
59 Kerry Collins .40
60 Tiki Barber .40
61 Santana Moss .40
62 Curtis Martin .60
63 Wayne Chrebet .15
64 Rich Gannon .60
65 Charlie Garner .40
66 Tim Brown .60
67 Donovan McNabb 1.00
68 Duce Staley .40
69 Hines Ward .40
70 Antwaan Randle El 1.00
71 Plaxico Burress .60
72 Jerome Bettis .40
73 Junior Seau .40
74 LaDainian Tomlinson 1.25
75 Tai Streets .15
76 Kevan Barlow .40
77 Garrison Hearst .40
78 Jeff Garcia .60
79 Shaun Alexander .60
80 Matt Hasselbeck .15
81 Marshall Faulk 1.00
82 Marc Bulger .60
83 Torry Holt .60
84 Isaac Bruce .60
85 Brad Johnson .40
86 Keyshawn Johnson .60
87 Steve McNair .60
88 Kevin Dyson .40
89 Patrick Ramsey .60
90 Ladell Betts .40
91 Marcel Shipp SP .25
92 Michael Vick SP 2.50
93 Ray Lewis SP .25
94 Josh Reed SP 1.00
95 Josh McCown SP 1.00
96 Kelly Holcomb SP .60
97 William Green SP 1.00
98 Chad Hutchinson SP .75
99 Rod Smith SP .50
100 James Stewart SP .25
101 Ahman Green SP 1.00
102 Peyton Manning SP 2.00
103 Jimmy Smith SP .50
104 Tony Gonzalez SP .50
105 Ricky Williams SP 1.75
106 Jason Taylor SP .75
107 Tom Brady SP 1.50
108 Deuce McAllister SP 1.25
109 Jeremy Shockey SP 2.00
110 Chad Pennington SP 1.25
111 Jerry Rice SP 2.00
112 A.J. Feeley SP .50
113 Tommy Maddox SP .75
114 Drew Brees SP 1.75
115 Terrell Owens SP 1.00
116 Maurice Morris SP .75
117 Kurt Warner SP 1.50
118 Derrick Brooks SP .75
119 Eddie George SP 1.00
120 Rod Gardner SP .75
121 Chad Pennington, Byron Leftwich 250 200.00
122 Ken Dorsey, Vinny Testaverde 2000 25.00
123 Peyton Manning, Carson Palmer 250 185.00
124 Mark Brunell, Chris Simms 250 55.00
125 Andre Johnson, Santana Moss 1800 5.00
126 Brad Banks, Aaron Brooks 250 45.00
127 J.R. Tolver, Az-Zahir Hakim 1800 3.00
128 Josh Reed, Jerel Myers 1800 1.00
129 Amani Toomer, Ronald Bellamy 1800 3.00
130 Drew Bledsoe, Jason Gesser 1800 3.00
131 Kliff Kingsbury, Sammy Baugh 2000 12.00
132 Drew Brees, Kyle Boller 500 20.00
133 Anthony Thomas, Larry Johnson 500 50.00
134 Johnnie Morton, Kareem Kelly 2000 10.00
135 Rod Gardner, Bryant Johnson 500 12.00
136 Tim Couch, Jason Johnson 500 15.00
137 Leo Nomellini, Terrell Suggs 2000 25.00
138 Dave Ragone, Mark Brunell 500 15.00
139 Musa Smith, Charley Trippi 1800 3.00
140 Joey Harrington, Juston Wood 1800 3.00
141 Michael Vick, Jason Thomas 1800 3.00
142 Emmitt Smith, Earnest Graham 2000 15.00
143 Edgerrin James, Willis McGahee 2000 45.00
144 Rashard Lee, Shaun Alexander 500 15.00
145 Javon Walker, Anquan Boldin 1800 3.00
146 Reche Caldwell, Taylor Jacobs 250 25.00
147 Laveranues Coles, Talman Gardner 1800 2.00
148 Dennis Northcutt, Bobby Wade 1800 1.00
149 Billy McMullen, Isaac Bruce 500 15.00
150 Avon Cobourne, Amos Zereoue 1800 4.00
151 Bradie James, Frank "Bruiser" Kinard 1800 1.00
152 Peerless Price, Kelley Washington 2000 15.00
153 Jim Parker, Eric Steinbach 1800 1.00
154 Jimmy Kennedy, Ernie Stautner 1800 1.00
155 Rien Long, Arnie Weinmeister 1800 1.00
156 Mike Anderson, Chris Brown 2000 12.00
157 Teyo Johnson, Tony Gonzalez 1800 1.00
158 Onterrio Smith, Maurice Morris 1800 3.00
159 Clinton Portis, Justin Fargas 2000 15.00
160 Seneca Wallace, Antwaan Randle El 1800 3.00
161 Peyton Manning, Brian St. Pierre 500 25.00
162 LaDainian Tomlinson, LaBrandon Toefield 500 18.00
163 Marquel Blackwell, Daunte Culpepper 1800 1.00
164 Keenan Howry, A.J. Feeley 1800 2.00
165 Justin Gage, Kirk Farmer 1800 4.00
166 Andre Davis, Shawn Witten 1800 2.00
167 Dennis Weathersby, Aeneas Williams 1800 1.00
168 Boss Bailey, Champ Bailey 1800 4.00
169 Kurt Kittner, Brandon Lloyd 1800 3.00
170 Chris Chambers, Doug Gabriel 1800 2.00
171 Akbar Gbaja-Biamila, Kabeer Gbaja-Biamila 1800 3.00
172 Dahrran Diedrick, Ahman Green 1800 3.00
173 Kevin Curtis, Kevin Dyson 1800 3.00
174 Deuce McAllister, Sultan McCullough 500 15.00
175 Marcus Trufant, Mike Bush 1800 4.00
176 Sam Aiken, Zach Hilton 1800 2.00
177 Andre Woolfolk, Terence Newman 1800 6.00
178 Tyrone Calico, Kelly Holcomb 1800 2.00
179 J.T. Wall, Terrence Edwards 1800 3.00
180 Cory Paus, Mike Seidman 1800 3.00
181 Marco Battaglia, L.J. Smith 1800 2.00
182 Antwone Savage, Quentin Griffin 2000 20.00
183 Michael Vick, Lee Suggs 1800 15.00
184 B.J. Askew, Bennie Joppru 1800 4.00
185 Todd Heap, Mike Pinkard 1800 3.00
186 Arnaz Battle, Tim Brown 1800 3.00
187 Charles Rogers, Plaxico Burress 1800 8.00
188 Duce Staley, Andrew Pinnock 1800 1.00
189 Peyton Manning, Rex Grossman 500 40.00
190 Justin Peelle, George Wrighster 1800 1.00
CL Checklist .15

2003 UD Pros & Prospects Gold NFL Dual Signed Rookie

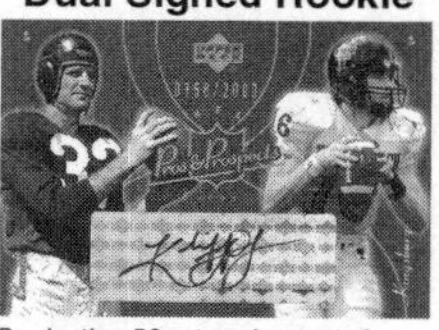

Production 50 sets unless noted
121 Byron Leftwich, Chad Pennington
122 Ken Dorsey, Vinny Testaverde
123 Carson Palmer, Peyton Manning
124 Chris Simms, Mark Brunell
125 Andre Johnson, Santana Moss
126 Brad Banks, Aaron Brooks
127 J.R. Tolver, Az-Zahir Hakim
128 Jerel Myers, Josh Reed
129 Ronald Bellamy, Amani Toomer
130 Jason Gesser, Drew Bledsoe
131 Kliff Kingsbury, Sammy Baugh
132 Kyle Boller, Drew Brees
133 Larry Johnson, Anthony Thomas
134 Kareem Kelly, Johnnie Morton
135 Bryant Johnson, Rod Gardner
136 Jason Johnson, Tim Couch
137 Terrell Suggs, Leo Nomellini
138 Dave Ragone, Mark Brunell
139 Musa Smith, Charley Trippi
140 Juston Wood, Joey Harrington
141 Jason Thomas, Michael Vick
142 Earnest Graham, Emmitt Smith
143 Willis McGahee, Edgerrin James
144 Rashard Lee, Shaun Alexander
145 Anquan Boldin, Javon Walker
146 Taylor Jacobs, Reche Caldwell
147 Talman Gardner, Laveranues Coles
148 Bobby Wade, Dennis Northcutt
149 Billy McMullen, Isaac Bruce
150 Avon Cobourne, Amos Zereoue
151 Bradie James, Frank "Bruiser" Kinard
152 Kelley Washington, Peerless Price
153 Eric Steinbach, Jim Parker
154 Jimmy Kennedy, Ernie Stautner
155 Rien Long, Arnie Weinmeister
156 Chris Brown, Mike Anderson
157 Teyo Johnson, Tony Gonzalez
158 Onterrio Smith, Maurice Morris
159 Justin Fargas, Clinton Portis
160 Seneca Wallace, Antwaan Randle El
161 Brian St. Pierre, Peyton Manning
162 LaBrandon Toefield, LaDainian Tomlinson
163 Marquel Blackwell, Daunte Culpepper
164 Keenan Howry, A.J. Feeley
165 Justin Gage, Kirk Farmer
166 Shawn Witten, Andre Davis
167 Dennis Weathersby, Aeneas Williams
168 Boss Bailey, Champ Bailey
169 Brandon Lloyd, Kurt Kittner
170 Doug Gabriel, Chris Chambers
171 Akbar Gbaja-Biamila, Kabeer Gbaja-Biamila
172 Dahrran Diedrick, Ahman Green
173 Kevin Curtis, Kevin Dyson
174 Deuce McAllister, Sultan McCullough
175 Marcus Trufant, Mike Bush
176 Sam Aiken, Zach Hilton
177 Andre Woolfolk, Terence Newman
178 Tyrone Calico, Kelly Holcomb
179 J.T. Wall, Terrence Edwards
180 Cory Paus, Mike Seidman
181 Marco Battaglia, L.J. Smith
182 Antwone Savage, Quentin Griffin
183 Michael Vick, Lee Suggs
184 B.J. Askew, Bennie Joppru
185 Todd Heap, Mike Pinkard
186 Arnaz Battle, Tim Brown
187 Charles Rogers, Plaxico Burress
188 Duce Staley, Andrew Pinnock
189 Peyton Manning, Rex Grossman
190 Justin Peelle, George Wrighster
KB/BF Kyle Boller, Brett Favre 25
RG/BF Rex Grossman, Brett Favre 25 400.00

2003 Upper Deck Pros & Prospects Game Day Jersey

NM/M
Common Player: 5.00
Production 350 sets
JC-RB Ronald Bellamy 10.00
JC-AC Avon Cobourne 12.00
JC-KD Ken Dorsey 15.00
JC-MD Mike Doss 10.00
JC-MF Marshall Faulk 15.00
JC-JGa Justin Gage 5.00
JC-JG Jason Gesser 12.00
JC-AG Antonio Gilbert 6.00
JC-ZH Zach Hilton 6.00
JC-KH Keenan Howry 8.00
JC-JJ Jason Johnson 5.00
JC-KJ Keyshawn Johnson 8.00
JC-KK Kareem Kelly 6.00
JC-KL Kliff Kingsbury 10.00
JC-BL Byron Leftwich 35.00
JC-PM Peyton Manning 15.00
JC-SM Sultan McCullough 6.00
JC-CP Carson Palmer 35.00
JC-AP Andrew Pinnock 8.00
JC-DR Dave Ragone 10.00
JC-BS Brian St. Pierre 10.00
JC-JS Jeremy Shockey 15.00
JC-ST J.J. Stokes 5.00
JC-LS Lee Suggs 18.00
JC-TS Terrell Suggs 15.00
JC-JTh Jason Thomas 5.00
JC-JT J.R. Tolver 8.00
JC-SW Seneca Wallace 10.00
JC-JW Juston Wood 8.00

2003 Upper Deck Pros & Prospects Game Day Jersey Black

Production 75 sets 1X-3X

2003 Upper Deck Pros & Prospects Game Day Jersey Gold

Production 50 sets 1X-4X

2003 Upper Deck Pros & Prospects Game Day Dual Jersey

NM/M
Common Player: 6.00
Production 350 sets
DJC-BT Anthony Thomas, Ronald Bellamy 10.00
DJC-CD Ken Dorsey, Carson Palmer 30.00
DJC-DS Jeremy Shockey, Ken Dorsey 25.00
DJC-DT Ken Dorsey, Vinny Testaverde 15.00
DJC-GB Drew Bledsoe, Jason Gesser 15.00
DJC-HH Keenan Howry, Joey Harrington
DJC-JF J.J. Stokes, DeShaun Foster 6.00
DJC-JT Jason Thomas, Jason Johnson 6.00
DJC-KG Jason Gesser, Ken Dorsey 12.00
DJC-KM Kareem Kelly, Sultan McCullough 10.00
DJC-LD Ken Dorsey, Byron Leftwich 40.00
DJC-LP Chad Pennington, Byron Leftwich 75.00
DJC-PJ Keyshawn Johnson, Carson Palmer 25.00
DJC-PK Carson Palmer, Kareem Kelly 20.00
DJC-PL Byron Leftwich, Carson Palmer 60.00
DJC-PW Brian St. Pierre, Juston Wood 6.00
DJC-RK Dave Ragone, Kliff Kingsbury 15.00
DJC-RU Dave Ragone, Johnny Unitas 50.00
DJC-SB Wendell Bryant, Terrell Suggs 10.00
DJC-SF Doug Flutie, Brian St. Pierre 10.00
DJC-SS Warren Sapp, Terrell Suggs 6.00
DJC-SV Michael Vick, Lee Suggs 40.00
DJC-TD Mike Doss, Marcus Trufant 15.00
DJC-TF J.R. Tolver, Marshall Faulk 6.00
DJC-WJ Juston Wood, Jason Johnson 6.00
DJC-WR Seneca Wallace, Antwaan Randle El 15.00

2003 UD Pros & Prospects Game Day Dual Jersey Black

Production 75 sets 1X-3X

2003 UD Pros & Prospects Game Day Dual Jersey Gold

Production 50 sets 1X-4X

2003 UD Pros & Prospects The Power & The Potential

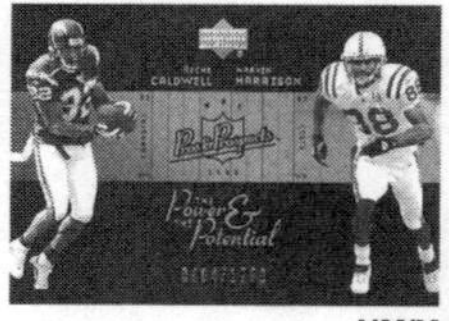

NM/M
Complete Set (30): 25.00
Common Player: .50
Production 1700 sets
PP-1 Tom Brady, David Carr 2.00
PP-2 Brett Favre, Joey Harrington 3.00
PP-3 Tim Couch, Patrick Ramsey 1.00
PP-4 David Garrard, Steve McNair .50
PP-5 Peyton Manning, Kurt Kittner 2.00
PP-6 Josh McCown, Drew Bledsoe 1.00
PP-7 Rohan Davey, Daunte Culpepper 1.00
PP-8 Clinton Portis, Edgerrin James 2.00
PP-9 Garrison Hearst, William Green 1.00
PP-10 T.J. Duckett, Jerome Bettis .50
PP-11 Maurice Morris, Shaun Alexander .50
PP-12 Jonathan Wells, Eddie George .50
PP-13 Lamar Gordon, Marshall Faulk .50
PP-14 Mike Alstott, Ladell Betts .50
PP-15 Brian Westbrook, Duce Staley .50
PP-16 Donte Stallworth, Joe Horn .50
PP-17 Antwaan Randle El, Plaxico Burress 2.00
PP-18 Ashley Lelie, Rod Smith 1.00
PP-19 Donald Driver, Javon Walker 1.00
PP-20 Eric Moulds, Josh Reed .50
PP-21 Jimmy Smith, Jabar Gaffney .50
PP-22 Reche Caldwell, Marvin Harrison .50
PP-23 Antonio Bryant, Joey Galloway 1.00
PP-24 Deion Branch, Troy Brown .50
PP-25 Keyshawn Johnson, Marquise Walker .50
PP-26 Cliff Russell, Rod Gardner .50
PP-27 Chad Hutchinson, Chad Pennington 1.50
PP-28 Warren Sapp, Julius Peppers .50
PP-29 Andre Davis, Quincy Morgan .50
PP-30 Tony Gonzalez, Jeremy Shockey 1.50

2003 UD Standing O

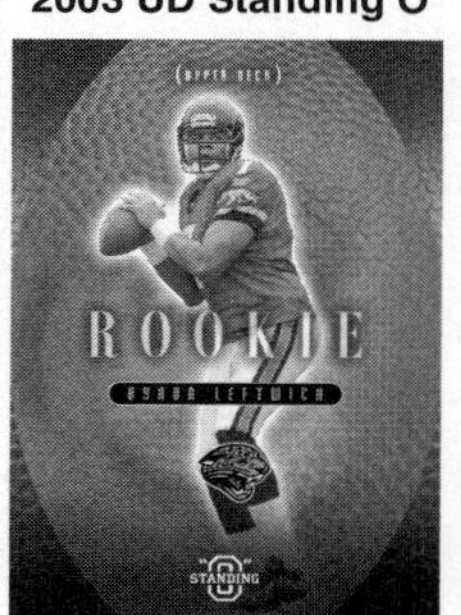

NM/M
Complete Set (84): 25.00
Common Player (1-84): .15
Minor Stars: .25
Unlisted Stars: .40
Pack (4): 2.75
Box (24): 45.00
1 Michael Vick 1.50
2 Tim Couch .50
3 Joey Harrington 1.00
4 Brett Favre 1.50
5 Donovan McNabb .60
6 Jeff Garcia .50
7 Chris Redman .15
8 David Carr 1.00
9 Steve McNair .50
10 Chad Pennington .60
11 Daunte Culpepper .50
12 Tom Brady .60
13 Kurt Warner .60
14 Brad Johnson .30
15 Aaron Brooks .50
16 Mark Brunell .30
17 Drew Brees .60
18 Peyton Manning .75
19 Drew Bledsoe .60
20 Rich Gannon .30
21 Kordell Stewart .30
22 Josh McCown .30
23 Chad Hutchinson .30
24 Jake Delhomme .30
25 Patrick Ramsey .50
26 Jay Fiedler .30
27 Trent Green .30
28 Jake Plummer .30
29 Tommy Maddox .50
30 Matt Hasselbeck .30
31 Kerry Collins .30
32 Marshall Faulk .60
33 Edgerrin James .60
34 Ricky Williams .75
35 Emmitt Smith 1.25
36 Deuce McAllister .50
37 Ahman Green .50
38 LaDainian Tomlinson .60
39 Priest Holmes .50
40 Curtis Martin .50
41 Travis Henry .50
42 Anthony Thomas .50
43 Fred Taylor .50
44 Jamal Lewis .50
45 Michael Bennett .50
46 Shaun Alexander .50
47 Garrison Hearst .30
48 Kevan Barlow .30
49 Charlie Garner .30
50 Clinton Portis 1.25
51 Eddie George .50
52 Corey Dillon .50
53 Jerome Bettis .30
54 Jeremy Shockey .75
55 Tony Gonzalez .50
56 Jerry Rice 1.25
57 Tim Brown .50
58 Terrell Owens .50
59 Randy Moss .75
60 Keyshawn Johnson .50
61 Marvin Harrison .50

62 Peerless Price .30
63 Chris Chambers .50
64 David Boston .50
65 Laveranues Coles .30
66 Rod Gardner .30
67 Isaac Bruce .30
68 Torry Holt .50
69 Troy Brown .30
70 Antonio Bryant .30
71 Plaxico Burress .50
72 Antwann Randle El .30
73 Rod Smith .30
74 Ashley Lelie .50
75 Eric Moulds .30
76 Chad Johnson .30
77 Kevin Johnson .30
78 Jevon Kearse .30
79 Zach Thomas .30
80 Roy Williams .50
81 Julius Peppers .30
82 Junior Seau .30
83 Ray Lewis .30
84 Brian Urlacher .75

2003 UD Standing O Die-Cut

NM/M
Cards: 1X-2X

2003 UD Standing O Rookie Ovation

NM/M
Common Player: 2.50
Inserted 1:4
Embossed: 1X-2X
Inserted 1:24
1 Carson Palmer 10.00
2 Byron Leftwich 10.00
3 Kyle Boller 6.00
4 Rex Grossman 8.00
5 Dave Ragone 3.00
6 Chris Simms 5.00
7 Seneca Wallace 3.00
8 Brian St. Pierre 3.00
9 Brooks Bollinger 3.00
10 Kliff Kingsbury 3.00
11 Gibran Hamdan 3.00
12 Ken Dorsey 4.00
13 Willis McGahee 8.00
14 Larry Johnson 6.00
15 Musa Smith 3.00
16 B.J. Askew 3.00
17 Chris Brown 3.00
18 Justin Fargas 4.00
19 Artose Pinner 3.00
20 Domanick Davis 5.00
21 Onterrio Smith 5.00
22 Quentin Griffin 4.00
23 Charles Rogers 8.00
24 Andre Johnson 6.00
25 Bryant Johnson 4.00
26 Taylor Jacobs 3.00
27 Bethel Johnson 3.00
28 Anquan Boldin 5.00
29 Tyrone Calico 4.00
30 Teyo Johnson 3.00
31 Kelley Washington 3.00
32 Nate Burleson 3.00
33 Kevin Curtis 2.50
34 Billy McMullen 2.50
35 Dallas Clark 3.00
36 Bennie Joppru 2.50
37 L.J. Smith 3.00
38 Dewayne Robertson 3.00
39 Marcus Trufant 2.50
40 Boss Bailey 3.00
41 Troy Polamalu 4.00
42 Terence Newman 4.00

2003 UD Standing O Signatures

NM/M
Common Player: 10.00
Inserted 1:480
SI-AB Antonio Bryant/164 20.00
SI-RC Reche Caldwell/141 15.00
SI-KC Kelly Campbell/141 15.00
SI-DC David Carr/86 50.00
SI-EC Eric Crouch/141 20.00
SI-WD Woodrow Dantzler III/95 15.00
SI-RD Rohan Davey/141 25.00
SI-AD Andre Davis/141 20.00
SI-BD Brandon Doman/141 10.00
SI-DF DeShaun Foster/95 30.00
SI-JG Jabar Gaffney/141 25.00
SI-NH Napoleon Harris/141 15.00
SI-RJ Ron Johnson/141 15.00
SI-KK Kurt Kittner/86 25.00
SI-AL Ashley Lelie/86 25.00
SI-AM Archie Manning/95 25.00
SI-PM Peyton Manning/95 100.00
SI-MM Maurice Morris/86 25.00
SI-LS Luke Staley/85 15.00
SI-MW Marquise Walker/109 10.00
SI-RW Roy Williams/149 40.00

2003 UD Standing O Swatches

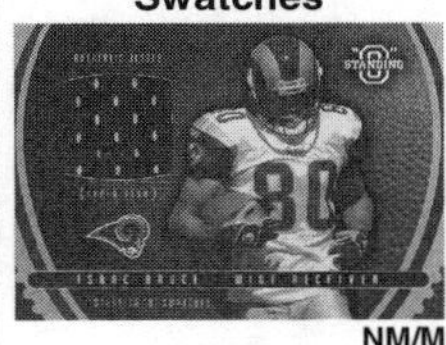

NM/M
Common Player: 8.00
Inserted 1:72
SW-JB Jeff Blake 8.00
SW-TB Tom Brady 15.00
SW-IB Isaac Bruce 10.00
SW-MB Mark Brunell 8.00
SW-BU Marc Bulger 15.00
SW-AB Antonio Bryant 8.00
SW-AD Andre Davis 8.00
SW-JG Jeff Garcia 10.00
SW-JH Joey Harrington 10.00
SW-MH Matt Hasselbeck 10.00
SW-BJ Brad Johnson 8.00
SW-KM Keenan McCardell 8.00
SW-JM Josh McCown 8.00
SW-PE Julius Peppers 8.00
SW-JP Jerry Porter 8.00
SW-CP Clinton Portis 15.00
SW-PR Patrick Ramsey 10.00
SW-AR Antwann Randle El 8.00
SW-JS Jeremy Shockey 12.00
SW-RS Rod Smith 8.00
SM-MV Michael Vick 25.00

2003 Upper Deck Star Rookie Sportsfest

NM/M
Common Player: 2.00
KB Kyle Boller 2.00
RG Rex Grossman 4.00
AJ Andre Johnson 2.00
BL Byron Leftwich 5.00
WM Willis McGahee 4.00
CP Carson Palmer 5.00

2003 Upper Deck Super Bowl Card Show

NM/M
Common Player: 1.00
1 Tom Brady 3.00
2 Kurt Warner 2.00
3 Brett Favre 4.00
4 Drew Bledsoe 1.00
5 Joey Harrington 3.00
6 Jeff Garcia 1.00
7 Michael Vick 3.00
8 Peyton Manning 3.00
9 Donovan McNabb 2.00
10 David Carr 4.00

2003 UD Sweet Spot

NM/M
Common Player (1-90): .40
Minor Stars: .75
Unlisted Stars: 1.00
Common Rookie (91-120): 1.00
Production 1,500 Sets
Common SS (121-135): 6.00
Production 100 Sets
Common Rookie (136-185): 2.00
Production 675 Sets
Common Rookie (186-210): 3.00
Production 300 Sets
Common Rookie (211-225): 6.00
Production 100 Sets
Common Rookie Auto (226-231): 40.00
Production 250 Sets
Pack (4): 8.00
Box (12): 65.00
1 Chad Pennington 1.50
2 Aaron Brooks 1.00
3 Joey Harrington 2.50
4 Brett Favre 4.00
5 Donovan McNabb 1.50
6 Jeff Garcia 1.00
7 Michael Vick 4.00
8 David Carr 2.50
9 Drew Brees 1.50
10 Trent Green .75
11 Patrick Ramsey 1.00
12 Tom Brady 1.50
13 Kurt Warner 1.50
14 Brad Johnson .75
15 Brian Griese .75
16 Jake Plummer .75
17 Drew Bledsoe 1.50
18 Peyton Manning 2.00
19 Tim Couch 1.00
20 Kordell Stewart 1.00
21 Jay Fiedler .75
22 Rich Gannon .75
23 Josh McCown .75
24 Matt Hasselbeck .75
25 Tommy Maddox .75
26 Rodney Peete .40
27 Jake Delhomme .75
28 Chris Redman .75
29 Mark Brunell .75
30 Marc Bulger .75
31 Kelly Holcomb .40
32 Chad Hutchinson .75
33 Quincy Carter 1.00
34 Steve McNair 1.00
35 Marshall Faulk 1.50
36 Deuce McAllister 1.00
37 Emmitt Smith 3.00
38 LaDainian Tomlinson 1.50
39 Kevan Barlow .75
40 Michael Bennett 1.00
41 Shaun Alexander 1.00
42 Edgerrin James 1.50
43 Ricky Williams 2.00
44 Priest Holmes 1.00
45 Ahman Green 1.00
46 Curtis Martin 1.00
47 Anthony Thomas 1.00
48 Travis Henry .75
49 Jerome Bettis .75
50 Fred Taylor 1.00
51 Corey Dillon .75
52 Jamal Lewis 1.00
53 William Green 1.00
54 Brian Urlacher 1.50
55 Junior Seau .75
56 Ray Lewis .75
57 Julius Peppers .75
58 Terrell Owens 1.00
59 David Boston .75
60 Isaac Bruce .75
61 Marvin Harrison 1.00
62 Chris Chambers .75
63 Chad Johnson .75
64 Peter Warrick .75
65 Peerless Price .75
66 Antonio Bryant .75
67 Laveranues Coles .75
68 Rod Gardner .75
69 Hines Ward .75
70 Plaxico Burress 1.00
71 Keyshawn Johnson .75
72 Jabar Gaffney .40
73 Eric Moulds .75
74 Santana Moss .75
75 Koren Robinson .75
76 Jimmy Smith .40
77 Donte Stallworth .75
78 Kevin Johnson .40
79 Quincy Morgan .75
80 Jerry Rice 3.00
81 Tim Brown .75
82 Rod Smith .75
83 Ashley Lelie .75
84 Randy Moss 2.00
85 Torry Holt 1.00
86 Troy Brown .75
87 Donald Driver .75
88 Todd Heap .75
89 Tony Gonzalez .75
90 Jeremy Shockey 2.00
91 Casey Moore 2.00
92 Chris Crocker 1.00
93 Pisa Tinoisamoa 5.00
94 Nnamdi Asomugha 2.00
95 Tyler Brayton 3.00
96 Eddie Moore 2.00
97 Terrence Kiel 2.00
98 Casey Fitzsimmons 3.00
99 George Foster 1.00
100 J.J. Moses 2.00
101 Dan Klecko 5.00
102 Terry Pierce 1.00
103 Brad Pyatt 2.00
104 Boss Bailey 5.00
105 Michael Haynes 2.00
106 Jimmy Kennedy 2.00
107 Jerome McDougle 3.00
108 William Joseph 3.00
109 Visanthe Shiancoe 1.00
110 L.J. Smith 3.00
111 Avon Cobourne 5.00
112 Bennie Joppru 3.00
113 Ken Hamlin 3.00
114 Jeremi Johnson 2.00
115 Justin Griffith 1.00
116 Joffrey Reynolds 1.00
117 Kassim Osgood 2.00
118 Donald Lee 2.00
119 Denero Marriott 1.00
120 Jamal Burke 1.00
121 Michael Vick SS 20.00
122 Donovan McNabb SS 12.00
123 Jerry Rice SS 15.00
124 Brett Favre SS 20.00
125 Kurt Warner SS 6.00
126 Marshall Faulk SS 10.00
127 Ricky Williams SS 12.00
128 Emmitt Smith SS 20.00
129 Tom Brady SS 12.00
130 Randy Moss SS 12.00
131 LaDainian Tomlinson SS 8.00
132 Jeff Garcia SS 6.00
133 Brian Urlacher SS 10.00
134 Drew Bledsoe SS 6.00
135 Peyton Manning SS 15.00
136 Dave Ragone 4.00
137 Brian St. Pierre 4.00
138 Kliff Kingsbury 4.00
139 Marquel Blackwell 2.00
140 Brett Engemann 3.00
141 Kirk Farmer 2.00
142 Andrew Pinnock 3.00
143 Tony Romo 5.00
144 Nate Hybl 4.00
145 Ken Dorsey 8.00
146 Brock Forsey 8.00
147 Musa Smith 4.00
148 Domanick Davis 10.00
149 LaBrandon Toefield 5.00
150 B.J. Askew 5.00
151 Quentin Griffin 8.00
152 Ahmaad Galloway 3.00
153 Cecil Sapp 4.00
154 Justin Fargas 8.00
155 Sultan McCullough 3.00
156 Malaefou MacKenzie 2.00
157 Tom Lopienski 2.00
158 Lee Suggs 8.00
159 Richard Angulo 3.00
160 Dwone Hicks 3.00
161 Nate Burleson 5.00
162 Billy McMullen 3.00
163 David Tyree 3.00
164 Gerald Hayes 2.00
165 Anthony Adams 2.00
166 George Wrighster 2.00
167 Tyrone Calico 8.00
168 Shaun McDonald 3.00
169 Bobby Wade 4.00
170 Larry Johnson 10.00
171 Ryan Hoag 3.00
172 Doug Gabriel 4.00
173 Antonio Gates 4.00
174 Brandon Lloyd 6.00
175 Arnaz Battle 3.00
176 Kelley Washington 6.00
177 Antwone Savage 3.00
178 Keenan Howry 5.00
179 Adrian Madise 3.00
180 LaTarence Dunbar 3.00
181 Walter Young 3.00
182 Travaris Robinson 2.00
183 DeAndrew Rubin 3.00
184 Carl Ford 5.00
185 Zuriel Smith 4.00
186 Willie Ponder 3.00
187 Gibran Hamdan 5.00
188 Aaron Moorehead 3.00
189 Nick Barnett 8.00
190 Chris Brown 6.00
191 Reshard Lee 3.00
192 Anquan Boldin 12.00
193 Kevin Curtis 5.00
194 Taylor Jacobs 5.00
195 Sam Aiken 4.00
196 Aaron Walker 3.00
197 Mike Seidman 3.00
198 Jason Witten 8.00
199 Dallas Clark 6.00
200 Rashean Mathis 3.00
201 Dewayne Robertson 4.00
202 Johnathan Sullivan 4.00
203 Drayton Florence 3.00
204 Sammy Davis 4.00
205 Andre Woolfolk 5.00
206 Terence Newman 10.00
207 Mike Doss 5.00
208 Troy Polamalu 5.00
209 Terrell Suggs 6.00
210 Marcus Trufant 5.00
211 Seneca Wallace 8.00
212 Brooks Bollinger 8.00
213 Jason Gesser 8.00
214 Onterrio Smith 12.00
215 Artose Pinner 8.00
216 J.R. Tolver 6.00
217 Kerry Carter 6.00
218 Tony Hollings 8.00
219 Teyo Johnson 8.00
220 Bethel Johnson 12.00
221 Rex Grossman 30.00
222 Andre Johnson 40.00
223 Terrence Edwards 8.00
224 Willis McGahee 25.00
225 Charles Rogers 15.00
226 Chris Simms 50.00
227 Bryant Johnson 40.00
228 Byron Leftwich 100.00
229 Carson Palmer 80.00
230 Justin Gage 40.00
231 Kyle Boller 50.00

2003 UD Sweet Spot Gold

Production 25 Sets

2003 UD Sweet Spot By the Letters

AB Anquan Boldin/43
KB Kyle Boller/40
DB Drew Brees/9
CB Chris Brown/43
NB Nate Burleson/43
TC Tyrone Calico/44
DA David Carr/8
DC Dallas Clark/43
KC Kevin Curtis/39
JF Justin Fargas/42
RG Rex Grossman/43
TJ Taylor Jacobs/43
AJ Andre Johnson/49
BJ Bethel Johnson/43
BR Bryant Johnson/43
LJ Larry Johnson/47
TE Teyo Johnson/43
KK Kliff Kingsbury/43
BL Byron Leftwich/43
PM Peyton Manning/18
WM Willis McGahee/43
DM Donovan McNabb/5
TN Terence Newman/43
CP Carson Palmer/43
PE Chad Pennington/10
AP Artose Pinner/43
DR Dave Ragone/43
RO Dewayne Robertson/24
OS Onterrio Smith/43
MS Musa Smith/43
SP Brian St. Pierre/45
TS Terrell Suggs/43
MT Marcus Trufant/43
SW Seneca Wallace/43
KW Kelley Washington/43

2003 UD Sweet Spot Rookie Gallery Jerseys

NM/M
Common Player: 5.00
Production 300 Sets
Gold Production 25 Sets
RG-CA Curt Anes 5.00
RG-AB Anquan Boldin 15.00
RG-KB Kyle Boller 12.00
RG-CB Chris Brown 8.00
RG-NB Nate Burleson 8.00
RG-TC Tyrone Calico 10.00
TG-DC Dallas Clark 8.00
RG-KC Kevin Curtis 5.00
RG-JF Justin Fargas 10.00
RG-JG Justin Gage 8.00
RG-RG Rex Grossman 15.00
RG-AJ Andre Johnson 15.00
RG-BE Bethel Johnson 10.00
RG-BJ Bryant Johnson 8.00
RG-LJ Larry Johnson 12.00
RG-TE Teyo Johnson 8.00
RG-KK Kliff Kingsbury 6.00
RG-BL Byron Leftwich 20.00
RG-WM Willis McGahee 15.00
RG-CM Carl Morris 5.00
RG-TN Terence Newman 10.00
RG-KO Kassim Osgood 6.00
RG-CP Carson Palmer 15.00
RG-AP Artose Pinner 6.00
RG-TP Troy Polamalu 8.00
RG-DR Dave Ragone 5.00
RG-RO Dewayne Robertson 5.00
RG-SP Brian St. Pierre 6.00
RG-MS Musa Smith 6.00
RG-OS Onterrio Smith 10.00
RG-TS Terrell Suggs 8.00
RG-MT Marcus Trufant 6.00
RG-SW Seneca Wallace 6.00
RG-KW Kelley Washington 8.00
RG-WY Walter Young 6.00

2003 UD Sweet Spot Signatures

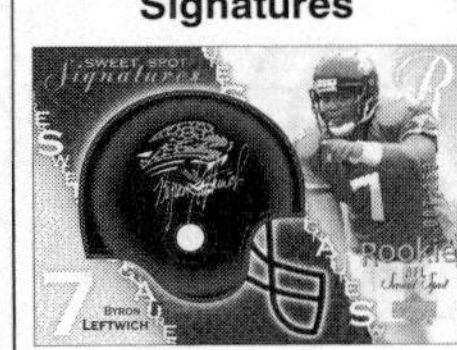

NM/M
Common Player: 10.00
Gold Production 25 Sets
SS-TA Troy Aikman 100.00
SS-BB Boss Bailey 20.00
SS-BL Drew Bledsoe 30.00
SS-AN Anquan Boldin/100 80.00
SS-TB Terry Bradshaw/65 60.00
SS-DB Drew Brees 20.00
SS-AB Aaron Brooks 30.00
SS-JB Jim Brown/75 120.00
SS-TB Tim Brown/75 60.00
SS-TC Tyrone Calico 25.00
SS-DC David Carr 40.00
SS-LD LaTarence Dunbar 10.00
SS-JG Jeff Garcia 30.00
SS-TG Trent Green 40.00
SS-MH Matt Hasselbeck 60.00
SS-DH Dwone Hicks 10.00
SS-PH Priest Holmes 60.00
SS-CJ Chad Johnson 30.00
SS-PM Peyton Manning 80.00
SS-DE Deuce McAllister/75 60.00
SS-DM Donovan McNabb/99 80.00
SS-JM Joe Montana/60 200.00
SS-RM Randy Moss/15
SS-TO Terrell Owens 30.00
SS-CP Chad Pennington 60.00
SS-PO Clinton Portis 60.00
SS-JR Jerry Rice/20
SS-RI John Riggins/75 80.00
SS-MS Musa Smith 12.00
SS-OS Onterrio Smith 40.00
SS-LS Lynn Swann 100.00
SS-BU Brian Urlacher 50.00
SS-SW Seneca Wallace 15.00
SS-RW Ricky Williams/75 60.00

2003 UD Sweet Spot Sweet Spot Jerseys

NM/M
Common Player: 8.00
Production 300 Sets
Gold Production 25 Sets
JC-BO David Boston 8.00
JC-TB Tom Brady 15.00
JC-DB Drew Brees 8.00
JC-AB Aaron Brooks 10.00
JC-TI Tim Brown 8.00
JC-DC David Carr 12.00
JC-LC Laveranues Coles 8.00
JC-KC Kerry Collins 8.00
JC-WD Warrick Dunn 8.00
JC-BF Brett Favre 25.00
JC-JF Jay Fiedler 8.00
JC-RG Rich Gannon 8.00
JC-JG Jeff Garcia 8.00
JC-EG Eddie George 10.00
JC-BG Brian Griese 8.00
JC-EJ Edgerrin James 12.00
JC-RL Ray Lewis 10.00
JC-PM Peyton Manning 20.00
JC-DM Donovan McNabb 12.00
JC-SM Steve McNair 10.00
JC-RM Randy Moss 15.00
JC-TO Terrell Owens 10.00
JC-CP Chad Pennington 12.00
JC-JP Jake Plummer 8.00
JC-PO Clinton Portis 15.00
JC-JR Jerry Rice 20.00
JC-JS Jeremy Shockey 10.00
JC-ES Emmitt Smith 20.00
JC-KS Kordell Stewart 10.00
JC-LT LaDainian Tomlinson 10.00
JC-BU Brian Urlacher 15.00
JC-MV Michael Vick 20.00
JC-KW Kurt Warner 8.00

2003 UD Sweet Spot Team Patch Logo

NM/M
Common Player: 6.00
Inserted 1:4
Numbers: 1X-2X
Production 100 Sets
Gold Production 25 Sets
P-DB Drew Bledsoe 6.00
P-KB Kyle Boller 10.00
P-TB Tom Brady 12.00
P-BR Drew Brees 5.00
P-AB Aaron Brooks 6.00
P-DC David Carr 10.00
P-CU Daunte Culpepper 8.00
P-MF Marshall Faulk 8.00
P-BF Brett Favre 20.00
P-JG Jeff Garcia 6.00
P-EG Eddie George 6.00
P-AG Ahman Green 8.00
P-RG Rex Grossman 12.00
P-JH Joey Harrington 8.00
P-PH Priest Holmes 10.00
P-TJ Taylor Jacobs 5.00
P-EJ Edgerrin James 10.00
P-AJ Andre Johnson 12.00
P-BE Bethel Johnson 8.00
P-BJ Brad Johnson 5.00
P-JO Bryant Johnson 6.00
P-LJ Larry Johnson 8.00
P-BL Byron Leftwich 20.00
P-PM Peyton Manning 12.00
P-DU Deuce McAllister 8.00
P-WM Willis McGahee 12.00
P-DM Donovan McNabb 10.00
P-RM Randy Moss 12.00
P-TO Terrell Owens 8.00
P-SC Carson Palmer 15.00
P-CP Chad Pennington 10.00
P-PO Clinton Portis 12.00
P-JR Jerry Rice 12.00
P-CR Charles Rogers 10.00
P-JS Jeremy Shockey 10.00
P-CS Chris Simms 8.00
P-ES Emmitt Smith 15.00
P-LT LaDainian Tomlinson 8.00
P-BU Brian Urlacher 10.00
P-MV Michael Vick 20.00
P-KW Kurt Warner 5.00
P-RW Ricky Williams 12.00

2003 UD Ultimate Collection

NM/M
Common Player (1-55): 2.00
Minor Stars: 3.00
Unlisted Stars: 4.00
Common Rookie (56-107): 5.00
Minor Rookies: 6.00
Unlisted Rookies: 8.00
Pack (4): 110.00
Box (4): 310.00
1 Peyton Manning 5.00
2 Aaron Brooks 3.00
3 Joey Harrington 6.00
4 Brett Favre 10.00
5 Donovan McNabb 4.00
6 Jeff Garcia 3.00
7 Michael Vick 10.00
8 David Carr 6.00
9 Drew Brees 4.00
10 Chad Pennington 4.00
11 Drew Bledsoe 4.00
12 Tom Brady 4.00
13 Kurt Warner 4.00
14 Brad Johnson 2.00
15 Jay Fiedler 2.00
16 Tim Couch 3.00
17 Trent Green 2.00
18 Daunte Culpepper 3.00
19 Keyshawn Johnson 3.00
20 Garrison Hearst 2.00
21 LaDainian Tomlinson 4.00
22 Emmitt Smith 8.00
23 Steve McNair 3.00
24 Chris Redman 2.00
25 Chad Hutchinson 2.00
26 Deuce McAllister 3.00
27 Eddie George 3.00
28 Marshall Faulk 4.00
29 Julius Peppers 2.00
30 Ahman Green 3.00
31 Priest Holmes 3.00
32 Edgerrin James 4.00
33 Jerry Rice 8.00
34 Ricky Williams 5.00
35 Anthony Thomas 3.00
36 Jerome Bettis 2.00
37 Shaun Alexander 3.00
38 Randy Moss 5.00
39 Jeremy Shockey 5.00
40 Patrick Ramsey 3.00
41 Clinton Portis 8.00
42 Terrell Owens 3.00
43 Corey Dillon 3.00
44 Mark Brunell 2.00
45 Rich Gannon 2.00
46 Curtis Martin 3.00
47 Josh McCown 2.00
48 Kerry Collins 2.00
49 Peerless Price 2.00
50 David Boston 3.00
51 Plaxico Burress 3.00
52 Marvin Harrison 3.00
53 Travis Henry 2.00
54 Brian Urlacher 5.00
55 Jake Plummer 2.00
56 Dave Ragone/750 8.00
57 Brian St. Pierre/250 AU 5.00
58 Tony Romo/750 8.00
59 Dallas Clark/750 8.00
60 Kirk Farmer/750 5.00
61 Juston Wood/750 5.00
62 Justin Gage/750 6.00
63 Sam Aiken/750 6.00
64 LaBrandon Toefield/750 8.00
65 L.J. Smith/750 6.00
66 Domanick Davis/750 25.00
67 Artose Pinner/750 6.00
68 Dahrran Diedrick/750 6.00
69 Lee Suggs/750 8.00
70 Bethel Johnson/750 6.00
71 Tyrone Calico/750 8.00
72 Kevin Curtis/750 6.00
73 Bobby Wade/750 6.00
74 Brandon Lloyd/750 8.00
75 Bryant Johnson/750 10.00
76 J.R. Tolver/750 6.00
77 Billy McMullen/750 6.00
78 Nate Burleson/750 6.00
79 Jason Johnson/250 AU 15.00
80 Talman Gardner/250 10.00
81 Anquan Boldin/250 50.00
82 Musa Smith/250 15.00
83 Teyo Johnson/250 20.00
84 Kyle Boller/250 AU 125.00
85 Carson Palmer/250 AU 250.00
86 Byron Leftwich/250 AU 300.00
87 Earnest Graham/250 AU 25.00
88 Chris Brown/250 AU 50.00
89 Chris Simms/250 AU 75.00
90 Kliff Kingsbury/250 AU 30.00
91 Jason Gesser/750 8.00
92 Brad Banks/250 AU 25.00
93 Ken Dorsey/250 AU 50.00
94 Rex Grossman/250 AU 100.00
95 Willis McGahee/250 AU 125.00
96 Larry Johnson/250 AU 75.00
97 Quentin Griffin/250 AU 80.00
98 Onterrio Smith/250 AU 60.00
99 Justin Fargas/250 AU 60.00
100 Kareem Kelly/250 AU 25.00
101 Arnaz Battle/250 AU 30.00
102 Kelley Washington/250 AU 40.00
103 Seneca Wallace/250 AU 40.00
104 Taylor Jacobs/250 AU 40.00
105 Andre Johnson/750 40.00
106 Charles Rogers/250 60.00
107 Terrell Suggs/250 AU 40.00

2003 UD Ultimate Collection Gold

Stars: 1.5X-3X
Rookies/75: 1X-2X
Rookies/25: 1.5X-3X

2003 UD Ultimate Collection Dual Game Jersey Patch

DGP-MG Joe Montana, Jeff Garcia/25
DGP-SF Bart Starr, Brett Favre/10
DGP-PT Walter Payton, Anthony Thomas/25
DGP-AM Troy Aikman, Peyton Manning/25
DGP-BW Terry Bradshaw, Kurt Warner/25
DGP-VM Michael Vick, Donovan McNabb/25
DGP-RM Jerry Rice, Randy Moss/25
DGP-MF Dan Marino, Jay Fiedler/25
DGP-JM Edgerrin James, Willis McGahee/25
DGP-BR Mark Brunell, Dave Ragone/25
DGP-MC Randy Moss, Daunte Culpepper/25
DGP-RO Jerry Rice, Terrell Owens/25

2003 UD Ultimate Collection Game Jersey

NM/M
Common Player: 10.00
Production 250 Sets
Gold versions to 25
UJ-TA Troy Aikman/99 25.00
UJ-MA Marcus Allen 20.00
UJ-DB Drew Bledsoe 12.00
UJ-BA Tom Brady 12.00
UJ-BR Drew Brees 10.00
UJ-AB Aaron Brooks 10.00
UJ-TC Tim Couch 10.00
UJ-DC Daunte Culpepper 12.00
UJ-JE John Elway/99 50.00
UJ-MF Marshall Faulk 15.00
UJ-BF Brett Favre 30.00
UJ-JG Jeff Garcia 10.00
UJ-AG Ahman Green 12.00
UJ-PH Priest Holmes 20.00
UJ-EJ Edgerrin James 15.00
UJ-KJ Keyshawn Johnson 10.00
UJ-JK Jim Kelly/99 20.00
UJ-PM Peyton Manning 20.00
UJ-DA Dan Marino/99 60.00
UJ-MC Deuce McAllister 12.00
UJ-DM Donovan McNabb 15.00
UJ-JM Joe Montana/99 60.00
UJ-RM Randy Moss 20.00
UJ-JN Joe Namath/99 40.00
UJ-TO Terrell Owens 10.00
UJ-WP Walter Payton/99 80.00
UJ-CP Chad Pennington 15.00
UJ-CP Clinton Portis 20.00
UJ-JR Jerry Rice 25.00
UJ-BS Barry Sanders/99 40.00
UJ-ST Bart Starr/99 60.00
UJ-FT Fran Tarkenton/99 30.00
UJ-LT LaDainian Tomlinson 10.00
UJ-BU Brian Urlacher 15.00
UJ-MV Michael Vick 30.00
UJ-KW Kurt Warner 10.00
UJ-RW Ricky Williams 20.00
UJ-SY Steve Young/99 25.00

2003 UD Ultimate Collection Game Jersey Autographs

UJS-PM Peyton Manning
UJS-DM Dan Marino
UJS-SM Joe Montana
UJS-JN Joe Namath
UJS-BS Bart Starr
UJS-MV Michael Vick

2003 UD Ultimate Collection Game Jersey Duals

NM/M
Common Player: 15.00
Production 250 Sets
Gold versions 25 Sets
UDJ-MV Donovan McNabb, Michael Vick 30.00
UDJ-PM Chad Pennington, Randy Moss 25.00
UDJ-KB Jim Kelly, Drew Bledsoe 30.00
UDJ-RO Jerry Rice, Terrell Owens 25.00
UDJ-PT Walter Payton, Anthony Thomas 50.00
UDJ-FR Brett Favre, Jerry Rice 50.00
UDJ-PD Clinton Portis, Terrell Davis 25.00
UDJ-HB Joey Harrington, Drew Brees 20.00
UDJ-CB David Carr, Tom Brady 20.00
UDJ-MS Deuce McAllister, Barry Sanders/100 40.00
UDJ-HW Priest Holmes, Ricky Williams 30.00
UDJ-BC Aaron Brooks, Tim Couch 15.00
UDJ-MG Donovan McNabb, Jeff Garcia 20.00
UDJ-FM Marshall Faulk, Curtis Martin 20.00
UDJ-MG Joe Montana, Jeff Garcia/99 60.00
UDJ-NP Joe Namath, Chad Pennington/99 50.00
UDJ-ST Barry Sanders, LaDainian Tomlinson/50 50.00
UDJ-PW Walter Payton, Ricky Williams/99 60.00
UDJ-SF Bart Starr, Brett Favre/99 80.00
UDJ-MC Dan Marino, David Carr/99 60.00
UDJ-TC Fran Tarkenton, Daunte Culpepper/99 40.00
UDJ-AM Troy Aikman, Peyton Manning/99 40.00
UDJ-PF Walter Payton, Marshall Faulk/99 60.00
UDJ-YV Steve Young, Michael Vick/99 60.00

2003 UD Ultimate Collection Game Jersey Dual Autographs

DJS-SF Bart Starr, Brett Favre
DJS-YV Steve Young, Michael Vick
DJS-NP Joe Namath, Chad Pennington
DJS-VM Michael Vick, Donovan McNabb
DJS-MM Dan Marino, Peyton Manning
DJS-EM John Elway, Donovan McNabb

2003 UD Ultimate Collection Game Jersey Patches

NM/M
Common Player: 15.00
Production 175 Sets
GJP-TA Troy Aikman/99 40.00
GJP-DB Drew Bledsoe 25.00
GJP-TB Terry Bradshaw/25
GJP-DB Drew Brees/99 25.00
GJP-AB Aaron Brooks 15.00
GJP-TB Tom Brady 25.00
GJP-CA David Carr 35.00
GJP-TC Tim Couch 15.00
GJP-DC Daunte Culpepper 25.00
GJP-JE John Elway/99 60.00
GJP-MF Marshall Faulk 25.00
GJP-BF Brett Favre/99 80.00
GJP-JG Jeff Garcia 20.00
GJP-EG Eddie George 20.00
GJP-AG Ahman Green 20.00
GJP-PH Priest Holmes 35.00
GJP-EJ Edgerrin James/99 30.00
GJP-KJ Keyshawn Johnson 20.00
GJP-PM Peyton Manning 35.00
GJP-DM Dan Marino/25
GJP-DM Deuce McAllister 20.00
GJP-DM Donovan McNabb/99 40.00
GJP-JM Joe Montana/25
GJP-RM Randy Moss 40.00
GJP-JN Joe Namath/25
GJP-TO Terrell Owens 25.00
GJP-WP Walter Payton/25
GJP-CP Chad Pennington/99 25.00
GJP-CP Clinton Portis/141 30.00
GJP-JR Jerry Rice 40.00
GJP-BA Barry Sanders/25
GJP-ES Emmitt Smith 50.00
GJP-BS Bart Starr/25
GJP-FT Fran Tarkenton/99 40.00
GJP-LT LaDainian Tomlinson 20.00
GJP-BU Brian Urlacher 35.00
GJP-MV Michael Vick/99 80.00
GJP-KW Kurt Warner/99 25.00
GJP-RW Ricky Williams/99 50.00
GJP-SY Steve Young/25

2003 UD Ultimate Collection Signatures

NM/M
Common Player: 20.00
US-TA Troy Aikman/25
US-MA Marcus Allen 30.00
US-BB Brad Banks 20.00
US-TB Terry Bradshaw/25
US-DB Drew Brees 25.00
US-AB Aaron Brooks 25.00
US-DC David Carr/25
US-TC Tim Couch 25.00
US-JE John Elway/25
US-JF Justin Fargas 30.00
US-BF Brett Favre/25
US-RG Rex Grossman 50.00
US-JK Jim Kelly 40.00
US-KK Kliff Kingsbury 20.00
US-BL Byron Leftwich 100.00
US-PM Peyton Manning 50.00
US-DM Dan Marino/25
US-DE Deuce McAllister 30.00
US-SU Donovan McNabb 50.00
US-JM Joe Montana/25
US-RM Randy Moss 60.00
US-JN Joe Namath/25
US-CP Carson Palmer 80.00
US-CH Chad Pennington 40.00
US-JR Jerry Rice/25
US-BA Barry Sanders 100.00
US-CS Chris Simms 40.00
US-KS Ken Stabler 40.00
US-BS Bart Starr/25
US-FT Fran Tarkenton/25
US-LT LaDainian Tomlinson 30.00
US-SY Steve Young/25

2003 UD Ultimate Collection Signatures Dual

Common Player:
Production 50 Sets
DS-BT Drew Brees, LaDainian Tomlinson
DS-PL Carson Palmer, Byron Leftwich
DS-MM Peyton Manning, Archie Manning
DS-SS Phil Simms, Chris Simms
DS-MP Peyton Manning, Carson Palmer
DS-MY Joe Montana, Steve Young
DS-NP Joe Namath, Chad Pennington
DS-SF Bart Starr, Brett Favre
DS-MF Dan Marino, Jay Fiedler
DS-GM Jeff Garcia, Joe Montana
DS-GY Jeff Garcia, Steve Young

2004 Upper Deck

NM/M
Common Player (1-200): .25
Minor Stars: .40
Unlisted Stars: .75
Common Rookie (201-225): 5.00
Inserted 1:8
Common Rookie (226-275): 2.00
Inserted 1:1
Pack (8): 5.00
Box (24): 85.00
1 Anquan Boldin .75
2 Josh McCown .40
3 Emmitt Smith 2.00
4 Freddie Jones .25
5 Marcel Shipp .40
6 Shaun King .40
7 Michael Vick 1.50
8 T.J. Duckett .40
9 Peerless Price .40
10 Warrick Dunn .40
11 Keith Brooking .25
12 Brian Finneran .25
13 Anthony Wright .25
14 Kyle Boller .75
15 Jamal Lewis .75
16 Todd Heap .40
17 Ray Lewis .40
18 Terrell Suggs .40
19 Travis Taylor .40
20 Drew Bledsoe .75
21 Willis McGahee .75
22 Eric Moulds .40
23 Travis Henry .40
24 Takeo Spikes .25
25 Josh Reed .40
26 Lawyer Milloy .25
27 Stephen Davis .40
28 Jake Delhomme .75
29 Steve Smith .40
30 DeShaun Foster .40
31 Dan Morgan .25
32 Julius Peppers .40
33 Rod Smart .40
34 Rex Grossman .75
35 Thomas Jones .40
36 Marty Booker .40
37 Anthony Thomas .40
38 Brian Urlacher .75
39 Justin Gage .40
40 Chad Johnson .40
41 Carson Palmer 1.00
42 Peter Warrick .40
43 Jon Kitna .40
44 Kelley Washington .40
45 Rudi Johnson .40
46 Jeff Garcia .40
47 Dennis Northcutt .25
48 Lee Suggs .75
49 Andre Davis .40
50 Quincy Morgan .40
51 Kelly Holcomb .40
52 Keyshawn Johnson .40
53 Quincy Carter .40
54 Antonio Bryant .40
55 Terry Glenn .40
56 Terence Newman .40
57 Roy Williams .75
58 Champ Bailey .40
59 Jake Plummer .40
60 Quentin Griffin .40
61 John Lynch .40
62 Rod Smith .40
63 Ashley Lelie .40
64 Joey Harrington .75
65 Az-Zahir Hakim .40
66 Charles Rogers .75
67 Tai Streets .40
68 Shawn Bryson .40
69 Artose Pinner .40
70 Brett Favre 2.00
71 Nick Barnett .40
72 Ahman Green .75
73 Kabeer Gbaja-Biamila .40
74 Javon Walker .40
75 Donald Driver .40
76 Tim Couch .40
77 David Carr 1.00
78 Corey Bradford .40
79 J.J. Moses .25
80 Domanick Davis .75
81 Jabar Gaffney .40
82 Andre Johnson .75
83 Marvin Harrison .75
84 Peyton Manning 1.25
85 Dallas Clark .40
86 Edgerrin James 1.00
87 Reggie Wayne .40
88 Dwight Freeney .40
89 Byron Leftwich 1.25
90 LaBrandon Toefield .40
91 Fred Taylor .75
92 Troy Edwards .40
93 Jimmy Smith .40
94 Kyle Brady .40
95 Trent Green .40
96 Tony Gonzalez .40
97 Dante Hall .75
98 Priest Holmes 1.00
99 Eddie Kennison .40
100 Johnnie Morton .40
101 Jay Fiedler .40
102 Junior Seau .40
103 Ricky Williams 1.00
104 Chris Chambers .75
105 Zach Thomas .40
106 David Boston .40
107 A.J. Feeley .40
108 Daunte Culpepper .75
109 Onterrio Smith .40
110 Randy Moss 1.25
111 Moe Williams .40
112 Michael Bennett .75
113 Jim Kleinsasser .40
114 Tom Brady 1.25
115 Kevin Faulk .40
116 Deion Branch .40
117 Corey Dillon .40
118 Troy Brown .40
119 Adam Vinatieri .40
120 Tedy Bruschi .25
121 Aaron Brooks .75
122 Deuce McAllister .75
123 Donte Stallworth .40
124 Joe Horn .40
125 Jerome Pathon .40
126 Eddie "Boo" Williams .25
127 Jeremy Shockey .75
128 Kurt Warner .40
129 Amani Toomer .40
130 Tiki Barber .40
131 Ike Hilliard .40
132 Michael Strahan .40
133 Chad Pennington 1.00
134 Santana Moss .40
135 Wayne Chrebet .40
136 Curtis Martin .75
137 LaMont Jordan .40
138 Justin McCareins .40
139 Jerry Rice 1.50
140 Rich Gannon .40
141 Tim Brown .40
142 Jerry Porter .40
143 Warren Sapp .40
144 Charles Woodson .40
145 Donovan McNabb 1.00
146 Brian Westbrook .40
147 Todd Pinkston .40
148 Jevon Kearse .40
149 Freddie Mitchell .40
150 Correll Buckhalter .40
151 Terrell Owens .75
152 Tommy Maddox .40
153 Duce Staley .40
154 Plaxico Burress .40
155 Ward Hines .40
156 Antwann Randle El .40
157 Jerome Bettis .40
158 Kendrell Bell .40
159 LaDainian Tomlinson 1.00
160 Doug Flutie .40
161 Quentin Jammer .40
162 Drew Brees .40
163 Reche Caldwell .40
164 Tim Dwight .40
165 Tim Rattay .40
166 Kevan Barlow .40
167 Brandon Lloyd .40
168 Cedrick Wilson .40
169 Julian Peterson .25
170 Ahmed Plummer .25
171 Matt Hasselbeck .40
172 Koren Robinson .40
173 Shaun Alexander .75
174 Darrell Jackson .40
175 Marcus Trufant .25
176 Bobby Engram .40
177 Marc Bulger .75
178 Torry Holt .75
179 Marshall Faulk 1.00
180 Orlando Pace .40
181 Isaac Bruce .40
182 Kyle Turley .25
183 Brad Johnson .40
184 Charlie Garner .40
185 Keenan McCardell .40
186 Mike Alstott .40
187 Derrick Brooks .40
188 Brian Griese .40
189 Steve McNair .75
190 Chris Brown .75
191 Eddie George .40
192 Tyrone Calico .40
193 Derrick Mason .40
194 Drew Bennett .40
195 Mark Brunell .40
196 LaVar Arrington .75
197 Clinton Portis 1.25
198 Laveranues Coles .40
199 Patrick Ramsey .40
200 Rod Gardner .40
201 Eli Manning 30.00
202 Larry Fitzgerald 15.00
203 Michael Jenkins 8.00
204 Ben Roethlisberger 40.00
205 Philip Rivers 15.00
206 Kellen Winslow Jr. 10.00
207 Kevin Jones 12.00
208 Steven Jackson 12.00
209 Reggie Williams 8.00
210 Chris Perry 10.00
211 Roy Williams 15.00
212 Rashaun Woods 10.00
213 Chris Gamble 6.00
214 Sean Taylor 12.00
215 Robert Gallery 8.00
216 Ben Troupe 5.00
217 Lee Evans 10.00
218 Michael Clayton 10.00
219 J.P. Losman 10.00
220 Devery Henderson 5.00
221 Drew Henson 12.00
222 DeAngelo Hall 8.00
223 Julius Jones 12.00
224 Ben Watson 5.00
225 Greg Jones 8.00
226 D.J. Williams 4.00
227 Tommie Harris 3.00
228 Shawn Andrews 2.50
229 Vince Wilfork 4.00
230 Dunta Robinson 3.00
231 Will Smith 3.00
232 Jonathan Vilma 4.00
233 Ricardo Colclough 2.00
234 Ahmad Carroll 3.00
235 Karlos Dansby 3.00
236 Matt Ware 3.00
237 Jim Sorgi 2.50
238 Will Poole 3.00
239 Derrick Strait 3.00
240 Andrew Hall 2.00
241 Nathan Vasher 2.50
242 D.J. Hackett 3.00
243 Jason Babin 4.00
244 Derrick Hamilton 2.00
245 Michael Boulware 2.50
246 Michael Turner 2.00
247 Sean Jones 2.00
248 Ernest Wilford 3.00
249 Cedric Cobbs 4.00
250 Tatum Bell 6.00
251 Bernard Berrian 2.50
252 Vernon Carey 2.00
253 Kenechi Udeze 2.50
254 P.K. Sam 3.00
255 Ben Hartsock 2.50
256 Chris Cooley 2.00
257 Josh Harris 2.00
258 Cody Pickett 3.00
259 Carlos Francis 2.00
260 Devard Darling 2.50
261 Johnnie Morant 2.50
262 John Navarre 4.00
263 Kris Wilson 2.00
264 Jerricho Cotchery 2.00
265 Darius Watts 3.00
266 Quincy Wilson 3.00
267 Maurice Mann 2.50
268 Samie Parker 2.50
269 B.J. Symons 3.00
270 Matt Schaub 6.00
271 Jeff Smoker 4.00
272 Craig Krenzel 3.00
273 Luke McCown 3.00
274 Mewelde Moore 5.00
275 Keary Colbert 4.00

2004 Upper Deck Game Jerseys

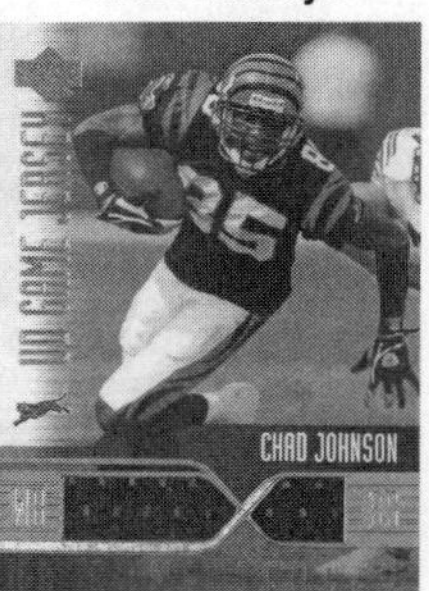

NM/M
Common Player: 6.00
Inserted 1:32
SA-GJ Shaun Alexander 8.00
AB-GJ Anquan Boldin 8.00
KB-GJ Kyle Boller 8.00
TB-GJ Tom Brady 15.00
DC-GJ Daunte Culpepper 10.00
DD-GJ Domanick Davis 8.00
JD-GJ Jake Delhomme 10.00
CD-GJ Corey Dillon 6.00
BF-GJ Brett Favre 25.00
PH-GJ Priest Holmes 10.00
AJ-GJ Andre Johnson 8.00
CJ-GJ Chad Johnson 6.00

PM-GJ Peyton Manning 15.00
DM-GJ Deuce McAllister 8.00
DO-GJ Donovan McNabb 12.00
SM-GJ Steve McNair 8.00
RM-GJ Randy Moss 12.00
CP-GJ Clinton Portis 10.00
TS-GJ Terrell Suggs 6.00
LT-GJ LaDainian Tomlinson 10.00
MV-GJ Michael Vick 20.00

2004 Upper Deck Game Jerseys Dual

NM/M
Common Player: 15.00
Inserted 1:288
BD-2J Tom Brady, Jake Delhomme 20.00
FM-2J Brett Favre, Peyton Manning 40.00
HF-2J Priest Holmes, Marshall Faulk 20.00
MH-2J Randy Moss, Marvin Harrison 20.00
SR-2J Emmitt Smith, Jerry Rice 40.00
TP-2J LaDainian Tomlinson, Clinton Portis 20.00
US-2J Brian Urlacher, Junior Seau 15.00
VM-2J Michael Vick, Donovan McNabb 25.00

2004 Upper Deck Game Jersey Patch Logos

NM/M
Common Player: 20.00
Inserted 1:2500
PLO-DC David Carr 60.00
PLO-MF Marshall Faulk 50.00
PLO-AG Ahman Green 50.00
PLO-MH Marvin Harrison 30.00
PLO-TH Todd Heap 20.00
PLO-PH Priest Holmes 60.00
PLO-JH Joe Horn 20.00
PLO-BL Byron Leftwich 75.00
PLO-RM Randy Moss 100.00
PLO-CP Chad Pennington 60.00
PLO-CL Clinton Portis 75.00
PLO-BU Brian Urlacher 50.00
PLO-MV Michael Vick 125.00
PLO-HW Hines Ward 30.00

2004 Upper Deck Game Jersey Patch Names

NM/M
Common Player: 30.00
Inserted 1:5000
PNA-AB Anquan Boldin 60.00
PNA-TB Tom Brady 150.00
PNA-DD Domanick Davis 40.00
PNA-GO Tony Gonzalez 40.00
PNA-TG Trent Green 30.00
PNA-TH Torry Holt 60.00
PNA-EJ Edgerrin James 75.00
PNA-DM Donovan McNabb 100.00
PNA-SM Steve McNair 60.00
PNA-SA Santana Moss 40.00
PNA-TO Terrell Owens 75.00
PNA-MS Michael Strahan 30.00
PNA-LT LaDainian Tomlinson 75.00
PNA-RW Ricky Williams 75.00

2004 Upper Deck Game Jersey Patch Numbers

NM/M
Common Player: 15.00
Inserted 1:1500
PNU-MB Marc Bulger 20.00
PNU-CC Chris Chambers 15.00
PNU-DC Daunte Culpepper 25.00
PNU-BF Brett Favre 100.00
PNU-RG Rex Grossman 20.00
PNU-DH Dante Hall 15.00
PNU-CJ Chad Johnson 15.00
PNU-JK Jevon Kearse 15.00
PNU-JL Jamal Lewis 20.00
PNU-PM Peyton Manning 60.00
PNU-DM Deuce McAllister 20.00
PNU-CP Clinton Portis 40.00
PNU-JR Jerry Rice 60.00
PNU-JS Jeremy Shockey 20.00

2004 Upper Deck Rewind to 1997 Jerseys

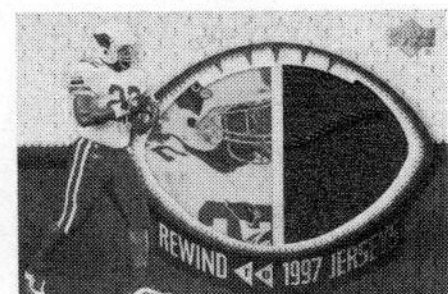

NM/M
Common Player: 12.00
Inserted 1:288
97-JB Jerome Bettis 12.00
97-TB Tim Brown SP 12.00
97-CD Corey Dillon 12.00
97-WD Warrick Dunn 12.00
97-MF Marshall Faulk 15.00
97-BF Brett Favre 40.00
97-DF Doug Flutie 12.00
97-TG Tony Gonzalez 12.00
97-CM Curtis Martin 15.00
97-EM Eric Moulds 12.00
97-JP Jake Plummer 12.00
97-JR Jerry Rice SP 25.00
97-JS Junior Seau 12.00
97-ES Emmitt Smith SP 30.00

2004 Upper Deck Rookie Future Jerseys

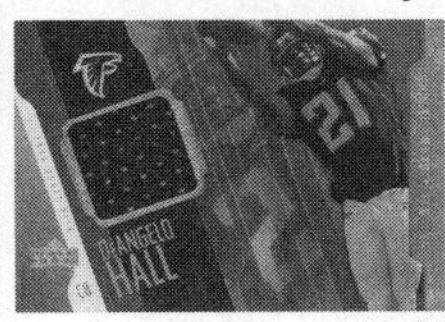

NM/M
Common Player: 8.00
Inserted 1:24
RF-TB Tatum Bell 12.00
RF-BB Bernard Berrian 8.00
RF-MI Michael Clayton 12.00
RF-CC Cedric Cobbs 10.00
RF-KC Keary Colbert 10.00
RF-DD Devard Darling 8.00
RF-LE Lee Evans 12.00
RF-LF Larry Fitzgerald 20.00
RF-RG Robert Gallery 12.00
RF-HA DeAngelo Hall 10.00
RF-DK Derrick Hamilton 8.00
RF-DE Devery Henderson 8.00
RF-SJ Steven Jackson 15.00
RF-MJ Michael Jenkins 10.00
RF-GJ Greg Jones 10.00
RF-JJ Julius Jones 12.00
RF-KJ Kevin Jones 15.00
RF-JP J.P. Losman 12.00
RF-EM Eli Manning 30.00
RF-LM Luke McCown 8.00
RF-MM Mewelde Moore 10.00
RF-CP Chris Perry 12.00
RF-PR Philip Rivers 15.00
RF-DR Dunta Robinson 8.00
RF-BR Ben Roethlisberger 30.00
RF-MS Matt Schaub 12.00
RF-BT Ben Troupe 8.00
RF-BW Ben Watson 8.00
RF-DW Darius Watts 10.00
RF-RW Reggie Williams 10.00
RF-RO Roy Williams 20.00
RF-KW Kellen Winslow Jr. 10.00
RF-RA Rashaun Woods 12.00

2004 Upper Deck Rookie Prospects

NM/M
Common Player: 1.50
Inserted 1:24
RP-TB Tatum Bell 2.50
RP-MI Michael Clayton 2.50
RP-CC Cedric Cobbs 2.00
RP-KC Keary Colbert 2.00
RP-DD Devard Darling 1.50
RP-LE Lee Evans 2.50
RP-LF Larry Fitzgerald 4.00
RP-DH Derrick Hamilton 1.50
RP-DE Devery Henderson 1.50
RP-DR Drew Henson 3.00
RP-SJ Steven Jackson 3.00
RP-MJ Michael Jenkins 2.00
RP-GJ Greg Jones 2.00
RP-JJ Julius Jones 2.50
RP-KJ Kevin Jones 3.00
RP-JP J.P. Losman 2.00
RP-EM Eli Manning 6.00
RP-LM Luke McCown 2.00
RP-MM Mewelde Moore 2.00
RP-CP Chris Perry 2.50
RP-PR Philip Rivers 4.00
RP-BR Ben Roethlisberger 5.00
RP-MS Matt Schaub 2.50
RP-BT Ben Troupe 1.50
RP-BW Ben Watson 1.50
RP-DW Darius Watts 2.00
RP-RW Reggie Williams 2.00
RP-RO Roy Williams 4.00
RP-KW Kellen Winslow Jr. 3.00
RP-RA Rashaun Woods 2.50

2004 Upper Deck Rookie Review Jerseys

NM/M
Common Player: 8.00
Inserted 1:288
RR-AB Anquan Boldin 20.00
RR-KB Kyle Boller 15.00
RR-CB Chris Brown 15.00
RR-TC Tyrone Calico 12.00
RR-DC Dallas Clark 8.00
RR-JF Justin Fargas 12.00
RR-RG Rex Grossman 20.00
RR-AJ Andre Johnson 20.00
RR-BJ Bethel Johnson 8.00
RR-LJ Larry Johnson 12.00
RR-TJ Teyo Johnson 8.00
RR-BL Byron Leftwich 30.00
RR-WM Willis McGahee 15.00
RR-TN Terence Newman 12.00
RR-CP Carson Palmer 25.00
RR-AP Artose Pinner 8.00
RR-OS Onterrio Smith 15.00
RR-TS Terrell Suggs 10.00
RR-MT Marcus Trufant 8.00
RR-KW Kelley Washington 8.00

2004 Upper Deck Signature Sensations

NM/M
SS-TA Tatum Bell/26 80.00
SS-KB Kyle Boller/8
SS-TB Tom Brady/12
SS-DC David Carr/8
SS-MI Michael Clayton/80 50.00
SS-CC Cedric Cobbs/34 30.00
SS-KC Keary Colbert/85 40.00
SS-DA Daunte Culpepper/11
SS-DE Devard Darling/11
SS-DD Domanick Davis/37 30.00
SS-JE John Elway/7
SS-LE Lee Evans/83 50.00
SS-BF Brett Favre/4
SS-LF Larry Fitzgerald/11
SS-RG Robert Gallery/74 50.00
SS-TG Tony Gonzalez/88 25.00
SS-JG Jon Gruden/30 30.00
SS-HA Dante Hall/82 30.00
SS-DH DeAngelo Hall/21 50.00
SS-HE Todd Heap/86 30.00
SS-DV Devery Henderson/19
SS-TH Travis Henry/20 20.00
SS-DR Drew Henson/11
SS-JH Joe Horn/87 10.00
SS-SJ Steven Jackson/39 125.00
SS-MJ Michael Jenkins/12
SS-JJ Jimmy Johnson/60 40.00
SS-RJ Rudi Johnson/32 30.00
SS-GJ Greg Jones/33 40.00
SS-JU Julius Jones/21
SS-KJ Kevin Jones/34 125.00
SS-BL Brandon Lloyd/85 20.00
SS-JP J.P. Losman/7
SS-EM Eli Manning/10
SS-PM Peyton Manning/18
SS-DM Deuce McAllister/26 30.00
SS-JM Josh McCown/12
SS-LM Luke McCown/12 12.00
SS-WM Willis McGahee/21 21.00
SS-JO Joe Montana/16
SS-JN John Navarre/16 50.00
SS-BP Bill Parcells/10
SS-CP Chris Perry/26 50.00
SS-PR Philip Rivers/17 150.00
SS-BR Ben Roethlisberger/7
SS-BS Barry Sanders/20 150.00
SS-MS Matt Schaub/8
SS-FT Fran Tarkenton/10
SS-ST Sean Taylor/26
SS-JT Joe Theismann/7
SS-LT LaDainian Tomlinson/21
SS-BT Ben Troupe/86 20.00
SS-MV Michael Vick/7
SS-BE Ben Watson/84 20.00
SS-BW Brian Westbrook/36 36.00
SS-RO Roy Williams/11
SS-RW Roy Williams/31 40.00
SS-KW Kellen Winslow Jr./81 60.00
SS-WI Kellen Winslow Sr./80 50.00
SS-RA Rashaun Woods/81 50.00

2004 Upper Deck UD Exclusives

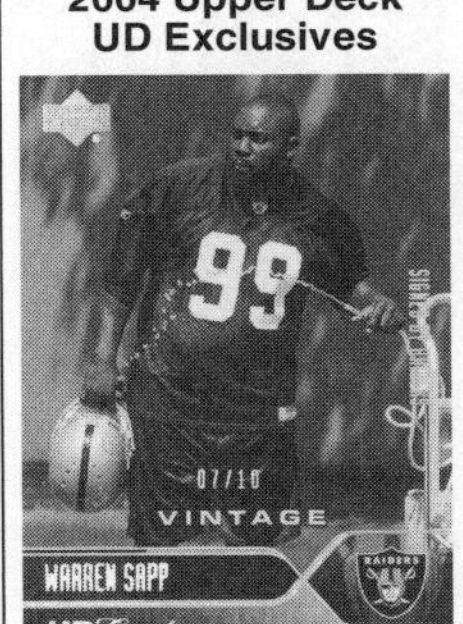

Stars: 8X-12X
SP Rookies: 2X
Rookies: 1.5X-3X
UD Exclusive Vintage Production 10 Sets
Master Player Print Production 1 Set

2004 UD Diamond AS

NM/M
Complete Set (120): 60.00
Common Player (1-90): .15
Minor Stars: .30
Unlisted Stars: .50
Common Rookie (91-120): 2.00
Minor Rookie: 2.50
Inserted 1:6
Pack (6): 3.25
Box (24): 55.00
1 Michael Vick 1.00
2 Julius Peppers .30
3 Roy Williams .50
4 Ahman Green .50
5 Trent Green .30
6 Tom Brady .75
7 Rich Gannon .30
8 Drew Brees .30
9 Brad Johnson .30
10 Todd Heap .30
11 Chad Johnson .30
12 Ashley Lelie .30
13 Marvin Harrison .50
14 Daunte Culpepper .50
15 Amani Toomer .30
16 Terrell Owens .50
17 Shaun Alexander .50
18 Mark Brunell .30
19 Drew Bledsoe .30
20 Rudi Johnson .30
21 Charles Rogers .50
22 Edgerrin James .60
23 Randy Moss .75
24 Tiki Barber .50
25 Hines Ward .50
26 Koren Robinson .30
27 Laveranues Coles .30
28 Travis Henry .30
29 Carson Palmer .60
30 Joey Harrington .50
31 Byron Leftwich .75
32 Moe Williams .30
33 Chad Pennington .60
34 Duce Staley .30
35 Marshall Faulk .60
36 Clinton Portis .75
37 Marcel Shipp .30
38 Eric Moulds .30
39 Andre Davis .30
40 Brett Favre 1.50
41 Fred Taylor .50
42 Ty Law .30
43 Santana Moss .30
44 Tommy Maddox .30
45 Torry Holt .50
46 Peerless Price .30
47 Stephen Davis .30
48 Quincy Carter .30
49 David Carr .60
50 Dante Hall .50
51 Deuce McAllister .50
52 Jerry Rice 1.00
53 Tim Rattay .30
54 Derrick Brooks .30
55 Warrick Dunn .30
56 Anthony Thomas .15
57 Keyshawn Johnson .30
58 Domanick Davis .50
59 Ricky Williams .50
60 Aaron Brooks .50
61 Tim Brown .50
62 Brandon Lloyd .30
63 Steve McNair .50
64 Kyle Boller .50
65 Brian Urlacher .50
66 Jake Plummer .30
67 Peyton Manning .75
68 Chris Chambers .30
69 Jeremy Shockey .30
70 Brian Westbrook .30
71 Matt Hasselbeck .30
72 Derrick Mason .30
73 Anquan Boldin .50
74 Jake Delhomme .50
75 Jeff Garcia .30
76 Donald Driver .30
77 Priest Holmes .60
78 Corey Dillon .30
79 Curtis Martin .50
80 LaDainian Tomlinson .60
81 Marc Bulger .50
82 Jamal Lewis .50
83 Marty Booker .30
84 Quentin Griffin .30
85 Andre Johnson .50
86 Junior Seau .30
87 Joe Horn .30
88 Donovan McNabb .60
89 Kevan Barlow .30
90 Eddie George .30
91 *Eli Manning* 8.00
92 *Larry Fitzgerald* 5.00
93 *Ben Roethlisberger* 10.00
94 *Roy Williams* 5.00
95 *Derrick Hamilton* 2.00
96 *Kellen Winslow Jr.* 3.00
97 *Bernard Berrian* 2.00
98 *Steven Jackson* 4.00
99 *DeAngelo Hall* 2.50
100 *Kevin Jones* 4.00
101 *Reggie Williams* 3.00
102 *Michael Clayton* 3.00
103 *Rashaun Woods* 3.00
104 *Devery Henderson* 2.00
105 *Ben Troupe* 2.00
106 *Cedric Cobbs* 2.00
107 *Lee Evans* 3.00
108 *Luke McCown* 2.00
109 *Chris Perry* 2.50
110 *J.P. Losman* 3.00
111 *Philip Rivers* 5.00
112 *Michael Jenkins* 3.00
113 *Greg Jones* 2.50
114 *Darius Watts* 2.00
115 *Tatum Bell* 3.00
116 *Ben Watson* 2.00
117 *Drew Henson* 4.00
118 *Keary Colbert* 2.50
119 *Matt Schaub* 3.00
120 *Julius Jones* 4.00

2004 UD Diamond AS Dean's List Jerseys

NM/M
Inserted 1:24:
DL-TB Tom Brady 15.00
DL-DC Daunte Culpepper 8.00
DL-BF Brett Favre 20.00
DL-AG Ahman Green 8.00
DL-MH Marvin Harrison 8.00
DL-PH Priest Holmes 10.00
DL-TH Torry Holt 6.00
DL-PM Peyton Manning 12.00
DL-DM Donovan McNabb 10.00
DL-SM Steve McNair 6.00
DL-RM Randy Moss 10.00
DL-CP Clinton Portis 10.00
DL-LT LaDainian Tomlinson 8.00
DL-BU Brian Urlacher 10.00
DL-MV Michael Vick 15.00
DL-RW Ricky Williams 8.00

2004 UD Diamond AS Future Gems Jerseys

NM/M
Inserted 1:24
FG-AB Anquan Boldin 8.00
FG-KB Kyle Boller 8.00
FG-CS Chris Brown 6.00
FG-TC Tyrone Calico 6.00
FG-DC Dallas Clark 5.00
FG-DD Domanick Davis 8.00
FG-JF Justin Fargas 6.00
FG-RG Rex Grossman 10.00
FG-AJ Andre Johnson 8.00
FG-BJ Bethel Johnson 5.00
FG-LJ Larry Johnson 6.00
FG-BL Byron Leftwich 12.00
FG-WM Willis McGahee 8.00
FG-TN Terence Newman 6.00
FG-CP Carson Palmer 10.00
FG-CR Charles Rogers 8.00
FG-OS Onterrio Smith 6.00
FG-LS Lee Suggs 8.00
FG-TS Terrell Suggs 5.00
FG-KW Kelley Washington 5.00

2004 UD Diamond AS Premium Stars

NM/M
Inserted 1:24
PS1 Michael Vick 5.00
PS2 Brett Favre 6.00
PS3 Peyton Manning 4.00
PS4 Randy Moss 4.00
PS5 Clinton Portis 4.00
PS6 Donovan McNabb 3.00
PS7 LaDainian Tomlinson 3.00
PS8 Jerry Rice 5.00
PS9 Ricky Williams 2.50
PS10 Chad Pennington 3.00
PS11 Priest Holmes 3.00
PS12 Tom Brady 5.00
PS13 Deuce McAllister 2.50
PS14 Michael Strahan 2.00
PS15 Steve McNair 2.50

2004 UD Diamond AS Stars of 2004 Autos

NM/M
Production 100 Sets
CC Chris Chambers 15.00
DD Domanick Davis 25.00
TG Tony Gonzalez 20.00
DH Dante Hall 25.00
CJ Chad Johnson 15.00
BL Brandon Lloyd 20.00

2004 UD Finite

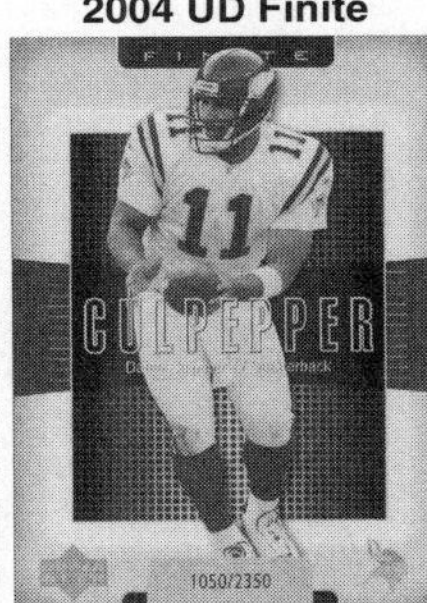

NM/M
Common Player (1-100): .30
Minor Stars: .60
Unlisted Stars: 1.00
Common Rookie (101-265): 5.00
101-265 Production 275 Sets
Common Rookie (266-278): 15.00
266-278 Production 99 Sets
Pack (3): 10.00
Box (10): 70.00
1 Emmitt Smith 2.50
2 Anquan Boldin 1.00
3 Josh McCown .60
4 Michael Vick 2.50
5 Peerless Price .60
6 Warrick Dunn .60
7 Todd Heap .60
8 Jamal Lewis 1.00
9 Kyle Boller .60
10 Drew Bledsoe 1.00
11 Travis Henry .60
12 Eric Moulds .60
13 Jake Delhomme 1.00
14 Steve Smith .60
15 Stephen Davis .60
16 Rex Grossman 1.00
17 Brian Urlacher 1.00
18 Thomas Jones .60
19 Rudi Johnson .60
20 Carson Palmer 1.50
21 Chad Johnson .60
22 Jeff Garcia .60
23 Andre Davis .60
24 Lee Suggs 1.00
25 Keyshawn Johnson .60
26 Eddie George .60
27 Vinny Testaverde .60
28 Quentin Griffin .60
29 Champ Bailey .60
30 Jake Plummer .60
31 Az-Zahir Hakim .30
32 Joey Harrington 1.00
33 Charles Rogers 1.00
34 Javon Walker 1.00
35 Ahman Green 1.00
36 Brett Favre 3.00
37 Domanick Davis 1.00
38 David Carr 1.50
39 Andre Johnson 1.00
40 Edgerrin James 1.50
41 Marvin Harrison 1.00
42 Reggie Wayne .60
43 Peyton Manning 2.00
44 Fred Taylor 1.00
45 Jimmy Smith .60
46 Byron Leftwich 2.00
47 Dante Hall .60
48 Tony Gonzalez .60
49 Trent Green .60
50 Priest Holmes 1.50
51 Zach Thomas .60
52 A.J. Feeley .60
53 Chris Chambers 1.00
54 Randy McMichael .30
55 Randy Moss 2.00
56 Onterrio Smith .60
57 Daunte Culpepper 1.00
58 Tom Brady 2.00
59 Deion Branch .60
60 Corey Dillon 1.00
61 Donte Stallworth .60
62 Deuce McAllister 1.00
63 Aaron Brooks 1.00
64 Amani Toomer .60
65 Jeremy Shockey 1.00
66 Kurt Warner .60
67 Curtis Martin 1.00
68 Chad Pennington 1.50
69 Santana Moss .60
70 Jerry Porter .60
71 Jerry Rice 2.50
72 Rich Gannon .60
73 Justin Fargas .60
74 Terrell Owens 1.00
75 Brian Westbrook .60
76 Donovan McNabb 1.50
77 Tommy Maddox .60
78 Hines Ward .60
79 Plaxico Burress 1.00
80 Antonio Gates .60
81 LaDainian Tomlinson 1.50
82 Drew Brees 1.00
83 Brandon Lloyd .60
84 Tim Rattay .60
85 Kevan Barlow .60
86 Koren Robinson .60
87 Shaun Alexander 1.00
88 Matt Hasselbeck .60
89 Torry Holt 1.00
90 Marc Bulger 1.00
91 Marshall Faulk 1.50
92 Chris Simms .60
93 Keenan McCardell .60
94 Derrick Brooks .60
95 Steve McNair 1.00
96 Chris Brown .60
97 Derrick Mason .60
98 Mark Brunell .60
99 Laveranues Coles .60
100 Clinton Portis 2.00
101 *Michael Jenkins* 10.00
102 *Ryan Krause* 6.00
103 *Darnell Dockett* 8.00
104 *Quincy Wilson* 8.00
105 *Nate Lawrie* 6.00
106 *Joey Thomas* 8.00
107 *Junior Siavii* 8.00
108 *Landon Johnson* 5.00
109 *Michael Waddell* 5.00
110 *Lee Evans* 15.00
111 *Jason David* 6.00
112 *Chris Collins* 6.00
113 *Troy Fleming* 6.00
114 *Tim Euhus* 8.00
115 *Sean Jones* 8.00
116 *Jason Babin* 12.00
117 *Jorge Cordova* 5.00
118 *Josh Scobey* 5.00
119 *Luke McCown* 8.00
120 *Darius Watts* 10.00
121 *Clarence Moore* 8.00
122 *Randy Starks* 5.00
123 *Brandon Miree* 8.00
124 *Gibril Wilson* 6.00
125 *Jeremy LeSueur* 6.00
126 *Dwan Edwards* 5.00
127 *Richard Seigler* 6.00
128 *Stanford Samuels* 6.00
129 *Casey Clausen* 10.00
130 *Erik Coleman* 5.00
131 *Donnell Washington* 8.00
132 *Jammal Lord* 8.00
133 *Chris Cooley* 8.00
134 *Shawntae Spencer* 8.00
135 *Marcus Tubbs* 8.00
136 *Caleb Miller* 6.00
137 *Jeff Shoate* 5.00
138 *Bradlee Van Pelt* 8.00
139 *D.J. Hackett* 6.00
140 *Greg Brooks* 5.00
141 *Thomas Tapeh* 6.00
142 *Ben Hartsock* 8.00
143 *Madieu Williams* 6.00
144 *Vince Wilfork* 10.00
145 *Marquis Cooper* 6.00
146 *Nate Kaeding* 8.00
147 *B.J. Symons* 10.00
148 *Maurice Mann* 6.00
149 *Tim Anderson* 8.00
150 *Michael Turner* 6.00
151 *Kris Wilson* 8.00
152 *Keiwan Ratliff* 6.00
153 *Kenechi Udeze* 8.00
154 *Courtney Watson* 8.00
155 *Stacy Andrews* 5.00
156 *Jeff Smoker* 15.00
157 *Carlos Francis* 6.00

158 Derek Abney 8.00
159 Dexter Wynn 6.00
160 Jason Wright 6.00
161 Dunta Robinson 8.00
162 Nathan Vasher 8.00
163 Karlos Dansby 8.00
164 Jake Grove 5.00
165 Matt Mauck 10.00
166 Johnnie Morant 8.00
167 Justin Jenkins 6.00
168 Cedric Cobbs 8.00
169 Ben Troupe 8.00
170 Bob Sanders 8.00
171 Will Smith 8.00
172 Michael Boulware 8.00
173 Nat Dorsey 5.00
174 Casey Bramlet 5.00
175 Ernest Wilford 8.00
176 Kendrick Starling 5.00
177 Mewelde Moore 12.00
178 Ben Watson 8.00
179 Ricardo Colclough 8.00
180 Tommie Harris 8.00
181 Dontarrious Thomas 8.00
182 Keith Lewis 5.00
183 John Navarre 10.00
184 Samie Parker 10.00
185 B.J. Johnson 8.00
186 Tatum Bell 15.00
187 Mike Karney 5.00
188 Ahmad Carroll 8.00
189 Will Allen 8.00
190 Teddy Lehman 8.00
191 Justin Smiley 6.00
192 Cody Pickett 8.00
193 Jerricho Cotchery 8.00
194 Tramon Douglas 5.00
195 Greg Jones 10.00
196 Kellen Winslow Jr. 12.00
197 Chris Gamble 10.00
198 Dexter Reid 5.00
199 Daryl Smith 8.00
200 Max Starks 5.00
201 J.P. Losman 15.00
202 Rashaun Woods 10.00
203 Triandos Luke 8.00
204 Rashad Washington 6.00
205 Derrick Ward 5.00
206 Matt Kranchick 8.00
207 Keith Smith 6.00
208 Travis LaBoy 6.00
209 Demorrio Williams 8.00
210 Jason Shivers 5.00
211 Craig Krenzel 8.00
212 Keary Colbert 10.00
213 Mark Jones 5.00
214 Shawn Johnson 6.00
215 Jarrett Payton 8.00
216 Michael Gaines 5.00
217 Matt Ware 8.00
218 Antwan Odom 8.00
219 Brandon Chillar 6.00
220 Michael Clayton 15.00
221 Jamaar Taylor 8.00
222 George Wilson 5.00
223 Tony Hargrove 5.00
224 Sean Ryan 6.00
225 Stuart Schweigert 6.00
226 Igor Olshansky 8.00
227 Keyaron Fox 5.00
228 Glenn Earl 5.00
229 Bruce Thornton 5.00
230 Derrick Hamilton 5.00
231 Sloan Thomas 6.00
232 Matthias Askew 6.00
233 Ran Carthon 6.00
234 Ben Utecht 5.00
235 Kendyll Pope 5.00
236 Marquise Hill 6.00
237 Shawn Andrews 6.00
238 Jim Sorgi 6.00
239 Devard Darling 8.00
240 Patrick Crayton 8.00
241 Ryan McGuffey 5.00
242 Darrion Scott 6.00
243 DeAngelo Hall 10.00
244 Alex Lewis 8.00
245 D.J. Williams 8.00
246 Chris Snee 5.00
247 Matt Schaub 15.00
248 Devery Henderson 8.00
249 Jeris McIntyre 8.00
250 Wes Welker 8.00
251 Bruce Perry 8.00
252 Jeff Dugan 5.00
253 Derrick Strait 8.00
254 Terry Johnson 5.00
255 Niko Koutouvides 6.00
256 Tahaya Hutchins 6.00
257 Josh Harris 6.00
258 Bernard Berrian 8.00
259 Rogerick Green 6.00
260 Romar Crenshaw 5.00
261 Jacob Rogers 10.00
262 Sean Taylor 12.00
263 J.R. Reed 8.00
264 Jonathan Vilma 10.00
265 Stephen Peterman 25.00
266 Eli Manning/99 60.00
267 Philip Rivers/99 30.00
268 Larry Fitzgerald/99 40.00
269 Ben Roethlisberger/99 120.00
270 Kevin Jones/99 30.00
271 Steven Jackson/99 30.00
272 Roy Williams/99 40.00
273 Julius Jones/99 40.00
274 Reggie Williams/99 15.00
275 Chris Perry/99 20.00
276 Robert Gallery/99 15.00
277 Kellen Winslow Jr./99 25.00
278 Drew Henson/99 30.00

Post-1980 cards in Near Mint condition will generally sell for about 75% of the quoted Mint value. Excellent-condition cards bring no more than 40%.

2004 UD Finite Radiance

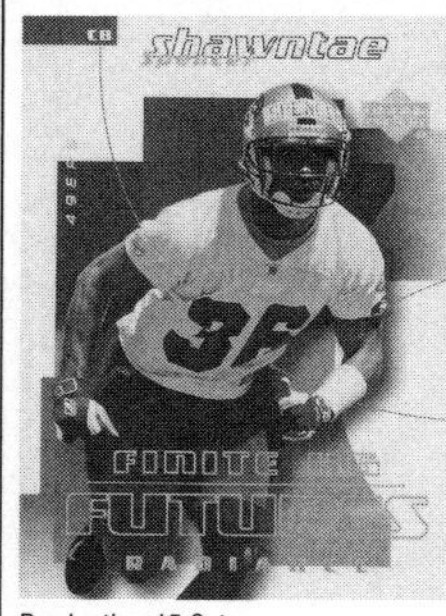

Production 15 Sets

2004 UD Finite Fabrics

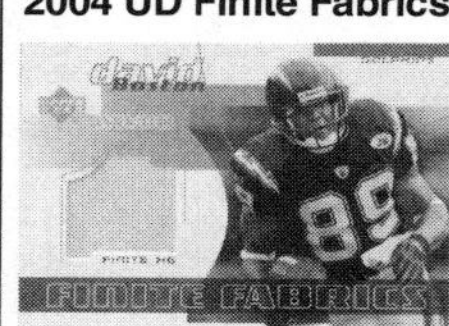

NM/M
Common Player: 6.00
Inserted 1:10
Radiance: 1.5X-3X
Radiance Production 25 Sets
FF-TA Troy Aikman SP 20.00
FF-LA LaVar Arrington 10.00
FF-JB Jerome Bettis 8.00
FF-DB Drew Bledsoe 8.00
FF-DA David Boston 6.00
FF-TB Tom Brady 15.00
FF-IB Isaac Bruce 6.00
FF-MA Mark Brunell 6.00
FF-MB Marc Bulger 8.00
FF-KC Kerry Collins 6.00
FF-DC Daunte Culpepper 10.00
FF-LD Len Dawson SP 20.00
FF-JE John Elway 25.00
FF-BF Brett Favre 20.00
FF-TG Tony Gonzalez 8.00
FF-JK Jevon Kearse 6.00
FF-TM Tommy Maddox 6.00
FF-PM Peyton Manning 15.00
FF-DM Dan Marino SP 40.00
FF-DE Deuce McAllister 8.00
FF-ST Steve McNair 8.00
FF-JM Joe Montana SP 50.00
FF-RM Randy Moss 12.00
FF-SM Santana Moss 6.00
FF-EM Eric Moulds 6.00
FF-TO Terrell Owens 10.00
FF-JP Jake Plummer 6.00
FF-CP Clinton Portis 10.00
FF-CR Charles Rogers 8.00
FF-BA Barry Sanders SP 40.00
FF-WS Warren Sapp 6.00
FF-ES Emmitt Smith 15.00
FF-RS Roger Staubach SP 20.00
FF-FT Fred Taylor 8.00
FF-ZT Zach Thomas 8.00
FF-LT LaDainian Tomlinson 10.00
FF-JU Johnny Unitas 30.00
FF-BU Brian Urlacher 10.00
FF-MV Michael Vick 15.00
FF-KW Kurt Warner 6.00
FF-KE Kellen Winslow Jr. SP 15.00
FF-CW Charles Woodson 8.00

2004 UD Finite Fabrics Dual

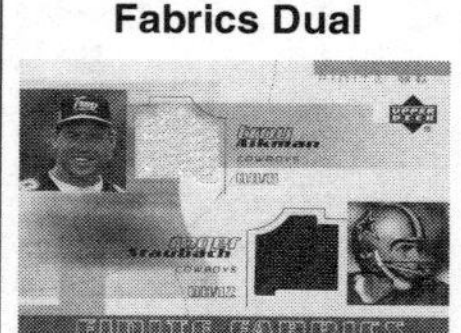

NM/M
Common Player: 10.00
Inserted 1:30
FF2-BB Marc Bulger, Isaac Bruce 10.00
FF2-BM David Boston, Eric Moulds 10.00
FF2-BP Mark Brunell, Clinton Portis 12.00
FF2-BW Tom Brady, Kurt Warner 15.00
FF2-EM John Elway, Dan Marino SP 80.00
FF2-FW Larry Fitzgerald, Roy Williams 20.00
FF2-JJ Julius Jones, Kevin Jones 30.00
FF2-UD Johnny Unitas, Len Dawson SP 50.00
FF2-LR J.P. Losman, Ben Roethlisberger 30.00
FF2-MB Tommy Maddox, Jerome Bettis 10.00
FF2-PA Clinton Portis, LaVar Arrington 15.00
FF2-AS Troy Aikman, Roger Staubach SP 40.00
FF2-RM Philip Rivers, Eli Manning 30.00
FF2-MM Peyton Manning, Steve McNair 15.00
FF2-WS Charles Woodson, Warren Sapp 10.00

2004 UD Finite Fabrics Triple

NM/M
Common Player: 15.00
Inserted 1:40
FF3-USE Johnny Unitas, Roger Staubach, John Elway SP 80.00
FF3-BRB Isaac Bruce, Charles Rogers, David Boston 15.00
FF3-BVB Marc Bulger, Michael Vick, Mark Brunell 20.00
FF3-JJJ Julius Jones, Greg Jones, Kevin Jones 40.00
FF3-MMF Eli Manning, Joe Montana, Brett Favre 80.00
FF3-MRR Eli Manning, Philip Rivers, Ben Roethlisberger 80.00
FF3-NAM Joe Namath, Troy Aikman, Dan Marino SP 80.00
FF3-OMM Terrell Owens, Randy Moss, Santana Moss SP 20.00
FF3-PBM Jake Plummer, Drew Bledsoe, Steve McNair 15.00
FF3-SPT Barry Sanders, Chris Perry, LaDainian Tomlinson 30.00
FF3-PST Clinton Portis, Emmitt Smith, LaDainian Tomlinson 30.00
FF3-WMF Reggie Williams, Randy Moss, Larry Fitzgerald 20.00
FF3-UAT Brian Urlacher, LaVar Arrington, Zach Thomas 20.00
FF3-WWG Kellen Winslow Jr., Kellen Winslow Sr., Tony Gonzalez 15.00
FF3-WFW Roy Williams, Larry Fitzgerald, Kellen Winslow Jr. 30.00

2004 UD Finite Fabrics Rookies

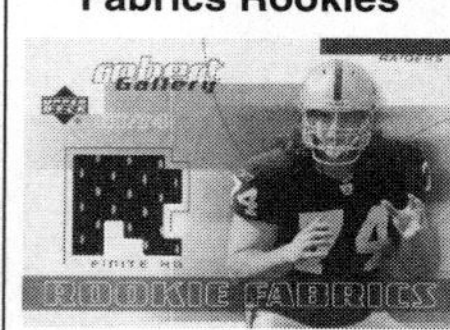

NM/M
Common Player: 6.00
Inserted 1:10
FFR-TB Tatum Bell 12.00
FFR-BB Bernard Berrian 6.00
FFR-MC Michael Clayton 10.00
FFR-KC Keary Colbert 8.00
FFR-RG Robert Gallery 8.00
FFR-DH Devery Henderson 6.00
FFR-LE Lee Evans 10.00
FFR-LF Larry Fitzgerald 15.00
FFR-SJ Steven Jackson 15.00
FFR-MJ Michael Jenkins 8.00
FFR-GJ Greg Jones 8.00
FFR-JJ Julius Jones 15.00
FFR-KJ Kevin Jones 15.00
FFR-JP J.P. Losman 10.00
FFR-EM Eli Manning 20.00
FFR-LM Luke McCown 8.00
FFR-CP Chris Perry 10.00
FFR-PR Philip Rivers 15.00
FFR-BR Ben Roethlisberger 50.00
FFR-BT Ben Troupe 6.00
FFR-DW Darius Watts 8.00
FFR-RE Reggie Williams 8.00
FFR-RW Roy Williams 15.00
FFR-KW Kellen Winslow Jr. 12.00
FFR-RA Rashaun Woods 8.00

2004 UD Finite Signatures

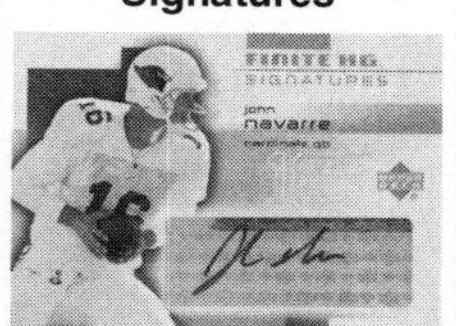

NM/M
Inserted 1:10
Radiance: 1X-2X
Radiance Production 25 Sets
FS-TB Tatum Bell 20.00
FS-DB Drew Bledsoe SP
FS-BC Brandon Chillar 8.00
FS-CC Casey Clausen 12.00
FS-CE Cedric Cobbs 10.00
FS-KC Keary Colbert 12.00
FS-JC Jerricho Cotchery 10.00
FS-DD Devard Darling 10.00
FS-LE Lee Evans 15.00
FS-JU Justin Fargas 12.00
FS-CF Clarence Farmer 8.00
FS-JF John Fox SP
FS-GA Robert Gallery 15.00
FS-JG Joey Galloway 10.00
FS-RG Rex Grossman 15.00
FS-GR Jon Gruden SP
FS-HA DeAngelo Hall 15.00
FS-TH Tommie Harris 12.00
FS-BH Ben Hartsock 8.00
FS-DH Devery Henderson 8.00
FS-TR Travis Henry 8.00
FS-DR Drew Henson SP 40.00
FS-SJ Steven Jackson 40.00
FS-MJ Michael Jenkins 15.00
FS-RJ Rudi Johnson 15.00
FS-JJ Julius Jones 60.00
FS-KJ Kevin Jones 40.00
FS-BL Brandon Lloyd 10.00
FS-JP J.P. Losman 20.00
FS-EM Eli Manning 100.00
FS-PM Peyton Manning SP 100.00
FS-DE Deuce McAllister 15.00
FS-JS Josh McCown
FS-WM Willis McGahee 15.00
FS-JO Joe Montana SP
FS-JM Johnnie Morant 8.00
FS-NA Joe Namath 80.00
FS-JN John Navarre 12.00
FS-SP Samie Parker 10.00
FS-CP Chad Pennington 25.00
FS-CO Cody Pickett 10.00
FS-AR Antwann Randle El 15.00
FS-AN Andy Reid SP
FS-PR Philip Rivers 40.00
FS-BR Ben Roethlisberger SP
FS-BS Barry Sanders SP
FS-MS Matt Schaub 15.00
FS-JT Joe Theismann SP 25.00
FS-BT Ben Troupe 12.00
FS-MV Michael Vick SP 100.00
FS-JV Jonathan Vilma 20.00
FS-JW Javon Walker
FS-KE Kelley Washington 10.00
FS-BE Ben Watson 12.00
FS-DW Darius Watts 12.00
FS-BW Brian Westbrook 15.00
FS-RE Reggie Williams 15.00
FS-RW Roy Williams 40.00
FS-QW Quincy Wilson 8.00

2004 UD Foundations

NM/M
Common Player (1-100): .25
Minor Stars: .40
Unlisted Stars: .75
Common Rookie (101-240): 3.00
Minor Rookies: 5.00
Unlisted Rookies: 6.00
101-240 Production 350 Sets
Common Rookie Jsy (241-263): 6.00
241-257 Production 1299 Sets
258-263 Production 499 Sets
Box: 70.00
1 Josh McCown .40
2 Emmitt Smith 1.50
3 Anquan Boldin .75
4 T.J. Duckett .40
5 Peerless Price .40
6 Michael Vick 1.50
7 Todd Heap .40
8 Kyle Boller .75
9 Jamal Lewis .75
10 Travis Henry .40
11 Eric Moulds .40
12 Drew Bledsoe .75
13 Steve Smith .40
14 Steve Davis .40
15 Jake Delhomme .75
16 Rex Grossman .75
17 Brian Urlacher .75
18 Anthony Thomas .40
19 Rudi Johnson .40
20 Chad Johnson .40
21 Carson Palmer 1.00
22 Quincy Morgan .40
23 Jeff Garcia .40
24 Andre Davis .40
25 Roy Williams .75
26 Eddie George .40
27 Keyshawn Johnson .40
28 Jake Plummer .40
29 Champ Bailey .40
30 Ashley Lelie .40
31 Joey Harrington .75
32 Charles Rogers .75
33 Az-Zahir Hakim .25
34 Javon Walker .40
35 Brett Favre 2.00
36 Ahman Green .75
37 Domanick Davis .75
38 David Carr 1.00
39 Andre Johnson .75
40 Peyton Manning 1.25
41 Marvin Harrison .75
42 Edgerrin James 1.00
43 Jimmy Smith .40
44 Fred Taylor .75
45 Byron Leftwich 1.25
46 Trent Green .40
47 Tony Gonzalez .40
48 Priest Holmes 1.00
49 Dante Hall .40
50 Ricky Williams .75
51 David Boston .40
52 Chris Chambers .75
53 A.J. Feeley .40
54 Randy Moss 1.25
55 Michael Bennett .75
56 Daunte Culpepper .75
57 Troy Brown .25
58 Tom Brady 1.25
59 Corey Dillon .40
60 Donte Stallworth .40
61 Deuce McAllister .75
62 Aaron Brooks .75
63 Kurt Warner .40
64 Jeremy Shockey .75
65 Santana Moss .40
66 Curtis Martin .75
67 Chad Pennington 1.00
68 Amani Toomer .40
69 Tim Brown .40
70 Rich Gannon .40
71 Jerry Rice 1.50
72 Jerry Porter .40
73 Terrell Owens .75
74 Jevon Kearse .40
75 Donovan McNabb 1.00
76 Tommy Maddox .40
77 Plaxico Burress .75
78 Hines Ward .40
79 Duce Staley .40
80 LaDainian Tomlinson 1.00
81 Drew Brees .75
82 Donnie Edwards .25
83 Tim Rattay .40
84 Kevan Barlow .40
85 Brandon Lloyd .40
86 Shaun Alexander .75
87 Matt Hasselbeck .40
88 Koren Robinson .40
89 Torry Holt .75
90 Marshall Faulk 1.00
91 Marc Bulger .75
92 Keenan McCardell .40
93 Derrick Brooks .40
94 Brad Johnson .40
95 Steve McNair .75
96 Derrick Mason .40
97 Chris Brown .40
98 Mark Brunell .40
99 LaVar Arrington .40
100 Clinton Portis 1.25
101 Brandon Chillar 5.00
102 Mike Karney 5.00
103 Jamaar Taylor 5.00
104 Casey Clausen 5.00
105 Drew Carter 6.00
106 Travis LaBoy 3.00
107 Jonathan Vilma 6.00
108 Tramon Douglas 3.00
109 Bob Sanders 5.00
110 Mewelde Moore 8.00
111 Randy Starks 5.00
112 Tank Johnson 5.00
113 Triandos Luke 6.00
114 Dexter Reid 3.00
115 Cedric Cobbs 6.00
116 Darius Watts 6.00
117 Ryan Krause 5.00
118 Igor Olshansky 5.00
119 Joe Echemandu 5.00
120 Jason Fife 5.00
121 Justin Smiley 5.00
122 Marcus Tubbs 6.00
123 Nathan Vasher 3.00
124 Troy Fleming 3.00
125 Ben Troupe 5.00
126 Jammal Lord 5.00
127 Jared Lorenzen 5.00
128 Shawntae Spencer 5.00
129 Darnell Dockett 5.00
130 Derrick Strait 6.00
131 Clarence Moore 6.00
132 Jason Babin 6.00
133 Jerricho Cotchery 6.00
134 Karlos Dansby 5.00
135 Marquise Hill 5.00
136 Niko Koutouvides 5.00
137 Andrew Hall 3.00
138 Teddy Lehman 6.00
139 Will Smith 6.00
140 Bernard Berrian 6.00
141 Chris Cooley 5.00
142 Landon Johnson 3.00
143 Devard Darling 6.00
144 Mark Jones 5.00
145 Jake Grove 3.00
146 John Navarre 6.00
147 Keary Colbert 8.00
148 Gilbert Gardner 5.00
149 P.K. Sam 6.00
150 Richard Seigler 3.00
151 Marquis Cooper 5.00
152 Tommie Harris 6.00
153 Thomas Tapeh 3.00
154 Ben Utecht 3.00
155 Chris Gamble 6.00
156 Daryl Smith 5.00
157 Sean Taylor 10.00
158 Caleb Miller 5.00
159 Johnnie Morant 6.00
160 Keith Smith 5.00
161 Matt Mauck 6.00
162 Matt Ware 6.00
163 Quincy Wilson 6.00
164 Samie Parker 5.00
165 Kendrick Starling 3.00
166 Antwan Odom 6.00
167 Brandon Miree 5.00
168 Casey Bramlet 5.00
169 Cody Pickett 6.00
170 Demorrio Williams 5.00
171 Dunta Robinson 6.00
172 D.J. Hackett 5.00
173 Josh Harris 5.00
174 Kenechi Udeze 6.00
175 Michael Boulware 6.00
176 Ricardo Colclough 5.00
177 Shawn Andrews 5.00
178 Jeris McIntyre 3.00
179 Jim Sorgi 5.00
180 Clarence Farmer 3.00
181 Courtney Watson 5.00
182 Derek Abney 5.00
183 Dwan Edwards 3.00
184 Ryan Dinwiddie 3.00
185 B.J. Johnson 5.00
186 Ben Watson 5.00
187 Kris Wilson 5.00
188 Michael Turner 5.00
189 Derrick Ward 3.00
190 Jonathan Smith 3.00
191 Vernon Carey 5.00
192 Ben Hartsock 6.00
193 Rich Gardner 3.00
194 D.J. Williams 8.00
195 Derrick Hamilton 6.00
196 Drew Henson 12.00
197 Jeff Smoker 8.00
198 Joey Thomas 6.00
199 Keyaron Fox 5.00
200 Nate Lawrie 5.00
201 Sloan Thomas 3.00
202 Justin Jenkins 5.00
203 Stuart Schweigert 5.00
204 Ran Carthon 5.00
205 Ahmad Carroll 6.00
206 Bradlee Van Pelt 6.00
207 Patrick Crayton 5.00
208 Chris Snee 5.00
209 Fred Russell 6.00
210 Dontarrious Thomas 5.00
211 Will Poole 6.00
212 Jarrett Payton 6.00
213 Keiwan Ratliff 5.00
214 Nate Kaeding 6.00
215 Tim Euhus 5.00
216 Sean Jones 5.00
217 Will Allen 5.00
218 B.J. Symons 6.00
219 Carlos Francis 5.00
220 Craig Krenzel 5.00
221 Andrae Thurman 3.00
222 Ernest Wilford 6.00
223 Glenn Earl 3.00
224 Jeremy LeSueur 5.00
225 Junior Siavii 5.00
226 Maurice Mann 5.00
227 Michael Waddell 3.00
228 Jason Wright 5.00
229 Sean Ryan 5.00
230 Vince Wilfork 6.00
231 Matt Kegel 5.00
232 Chris Collins 5.00
233 Jonathan Smith 5.00
234 Renaldo Works 5.00
235 Matt Kranchick 6.00
236 J.R. Reed 3.00
237 Jason Shivers 5.00
238 Donnell Washington 5.00
239 Jorge Cordova 3.00
240 Wes Welker 5.00
241 Robert Gallery Jsy 8.00
242 Luke McCown Jsy 6.00
243 Roy Williams Jsy 15.00
244 Julius Jones Jsy 15.00
245 Tatum Bell Jsy 10.00
246 Steven Jackson Jsy 12.00
247 Reggie Williams Jsy 8.00
248 Devery Henderson Jsy 6.00
249 DeAngelo Hall Jsy 8.00
250 Rashaun Woods Jsy 10.00
251 Chris Perry Jsy 10.00
252 Matt Schaub Jsy 8.00
253 Lee Evans Jsy 10.00
254 Michael Jenkins Jsy 8.00
255 J.P. Losman Jsy 8.00
256 Kevin Jones Jsy 12.00
257 Michael Clayton Jsy 10.00
258 Eli Manning Jsy 30.00
259 Ben Roethlisberger Jsy 40.00
260 Larry Fitzgerald Jsy 15.00
261 Philip Rivers Jsy 15.00
262 Greg Jones Jsy 8.00
263 Kellen Winslow Jr. Jsy 10.00

2004 UD Foundations Dual Endorsements

NM/M
Common Player: 30.00
Inserted 1:96
DE-FW Reggie Williams, Roy Williams 60.00
DE-MR Eli Manning, Ben Roethlisberger 500.00
DE-RR Ben Roethlisberger, Philip Rivers 300.00
DE-JJ Kevin Jones, Steven Jackson 125.00
DE-JH Julius Jones, Drew Henson SP 100.00
DE-BH Tom Brady, Drew Henson SP 125.00
DE-HJ DeAngelo Hall, Michael Jenkins 30.00
DE-JW Greg Jones, Reggie Williams 30.00
DE-EW Lee Evans, J.P. Losman 60.00
DE-BW Tatum Bell, Darius Watts 30.00
DE-CH Michael Clayton, Devery Henderson 30.00
DE-WW Kellen Winslow Sr., Kellen Winslow Jr. SP
DE-BL Drew Bledsoe, J.P. Losman
DE-MM Peyton Manning, Eli Manning 200.00

DE-BR Kyle Boller, Philip Rivers 60.00
DE-VM Michael Vick, Eli Manning SP
DE-WJ Roy Williams, Kevin Jones 150.00
DE-HW Joe Horn, Roy Williams 60.00
DE-RS Roy Williams, Sean Taylor
DE-MP Deuce McAllister, Chris Perry SP 40.00

2004 UD Foundations Exclusive Gold

Stars: 4X-8X
Rookies (101-240): 1X-1.5X
Production 100 Sets
Rainbow Production 10 Sets

2004 UD Foundations Foundations Patches

NM/M
Common Player: 15.00
Production 50 Sets
FP-CB Champ Bailey 25.00
FP-TB Tiki Barber 20.00
FP-KB Kyle Boller 20.00
FP-DB David Boston 15.00
FP-TI Tim Brown 20.00
FP-IB Isaac Bruce 20.00
FP-MB Mark Brunell 20.00
FP-AB Antonio Bryant 15.00
FP-CC Chris Chambers 20.00
FP-DC Daunte Culpepper 25.00
FP-CD Corey Dillon 20.00
FP-WD Warrick Dunn 15.00
FP-MF Marshall Faulk 25.00
FP-BF Brett Favre 50.00
FP-JG Jeff Garcia 20.00
FP-JH Joey Harrington 25.00
FP-MH Marvin Harrison 25.00
FP-TH Travis Henry 15.00
FP-CJ Chad Johnson 20.00
FP-KJ Keyshawn Johnson 20.00
FP-JK Jevon Kearse 20.00
FP-BL Byron Leftwich 30.00
FP-AL Ashley Lelie 20.00
FP-JL Jamal Lewis 25.00
FP-RL Ray Lewis 20.00
FP-CM Curtis Martin 25.00
FP-KM Keenan McCardell 15.00
FP-RM Randy Moss 30.00
FP-EM Eric Moulds 20.00
FP-TO Terrell Owens 25.00
FP-PP Peerless Price 15.00
FP-JR Jerry Rice 40.00
FP-WS Warren Sapp 20.00
FP-JS Junior Seau 20.00
FP-DS Duce Staley 15.00
FP-FT Fred Taylor 20.00
FP-AN Anthony Thomas 15.00
FP-ZT Zach Thomas 20.00
FP-LT LaDainian Tomlinson 25.00
FP-AT Amani Toomer 15.00
FP-RW Ricky Williams 25.00
FP-CW Charles Woodson 15.00

2004 UD Foundations Rookie Foundations Patches

NM/M
Common Player: 20.00
Production 25 Sets
241-P Robert Gallery 30.00
242-P Luke McCown 25.00
243-P Roy Williams 60.00
244-P Julius Jones 40.00
245-P Tatum Bell 40.00
246-P Steven Jackson 50.00
247-P Reggie Williams 25.00
248-P Devery Henderson 20.00
249-P DeAngelo Hall 40.00
250-P Rashaun Woods 40.00
251-P Chris Perry 40.00
252-P Matt Schaub 30.00
253-P Lee Evans 40.00
254-P Michael Jenkins 30.00
255-P J.P. Losman 30.00
256-P Kevin Jones 50.00
257-P Michael Clayton 40.00
258-P Eli Manning 100.00
259-P Ben Roethlisberger 150.00
260-P Larry Fitzgerald 60.00
261-P Philip Rivers 60.00
262-P Greg Jones 25.00
263-P Kellen Winslow Jr. 40.00

2004 UD Foundations Rookie Foundations Patches Autos

NM/M
Common Player: 80.00
Production 25 Sets
241-P Robert Gallery 100.00
242-P Luke McCown 80.00
243-P Roy Williams 250.00
244-P Julius Jones 200.00
245-P Tatum Bell 150.00
246-P Steven Jackson 200.00
247-P Reggie Williams 125.00
248-P Devery Henderson 80.00
249-P DeAngelo Hall 100.00
250-P Rashaun Woods 150.00
251-P Chris Perry 150.00
252-P Matt Schaub 100.00
253-P Lee Evans 150.00
254-P Michael Jenkins 100.00
255-P J.P. Losman 100.00
256-P Kevin Jones 200.00
257-P Michael Clayton 150.00
258-P Eli Manning 600.00
259-P Ben Roethlisberger 750.00
260-P Larry Fitzgerald 250.00
261-P Philip Rivers 250.00
262-P Greg Jones 125.00
263-P Kellen Winslow Jr. 175.00

2004 UD Foundations Signature Foundations

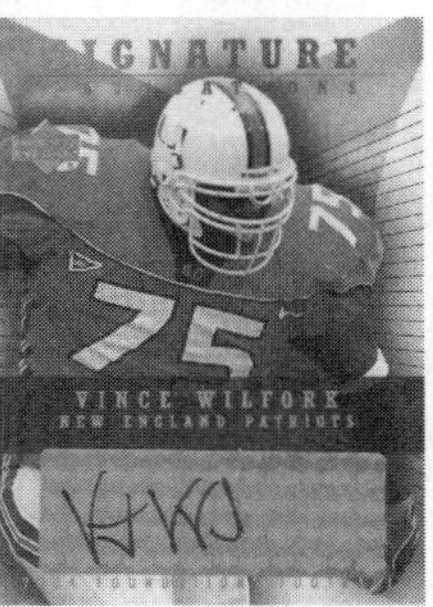

NM/M
Common Player: 10.00
Inserted 1:12
SF-BB Bernard Berrian 12.00
SF-BC Brandon Chillar 10.00
SF-CC Casey Clausen 15.00
SF-MI Michael Clayton 20.00
SF-KC Keary Colbert 20.00
SF-JC Jerricho Cotchery 10.00
SF-DA Devard Darling 10.00
SF-LE Lee Evans 20.00
SF-RG Robert Gallery 15.00
SF-DH Dante Hall SP 20.00
SF-DE DeAngelo Hall 15.00
SF-BH Ben Hartsock SP 12.00
SF-DV Devery Henderson 10.00
SF-DR Drew Henson SP 40.00
SF-MJ Michael Jenkins 15.00
SF-GJ Greg Jones 12.00
SF-JJ Julius Jones 25.00
SF-KJ Kevin Jones SP 30.00
SF-JP J.P. Losman 20.00
SF-EM Eli Manning SP 100.00
SF-PM Peyton Manning 50.00
SF-LM Luke McCown 12.00
SF-JO Johnnie Morant 10.00
SF-JN John Navarre 12.00
SF-CP Chris Perry 20.00
SF-CO Cody Pickett 12.00
SF-PR Philip Rivers 50.00
SF-BR Ben Roethlisberger SP 250.00
SF-MS Matt Schaub 15.00
SF-JS Jeff Smoker 15.00
SF-BJ B.J. Symons 10.00
SF-LT LaDainian Tomlinson SP 25.00
SF-KU Kenechi Udeze 12.00
SF-MV Michael Vick SP 60.00
SF-JV Jonathan Vilma 12.00
SF-BW Ben Watson 12.00
SF-DW Darius Watts 15.00
SF-EW Ernest Wilford 12.00
SF-RE Reggie Williams 15.00
SF-RO Roy Williams 60.00
SF-QW Quincy Wilson 10.00
SF-KE Kellen Winslow Jr. SP 30.00

2004 UD Legends

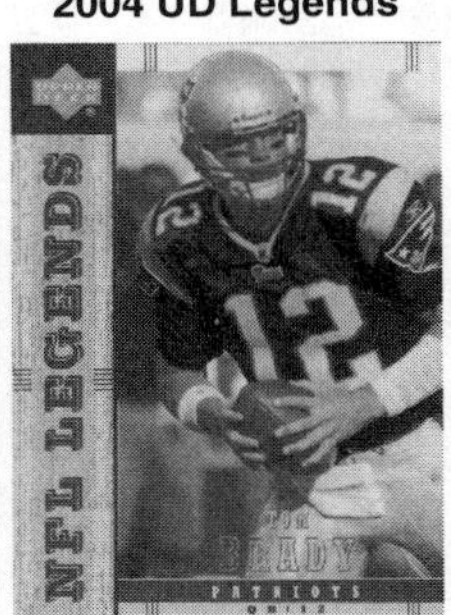

NM/M
Common Player (1-90): .40
Minor Stars: .75
Unlisted Stars: 1.00
Common Legend (91-110): 4.00
Legend Production 1,250 Sets
Common Rookie (111-190): 3.00
111-190 Production 650 Sets
Pack (5): 5.00
Box (24): 100.00
1 Josh McCown .40
2 Emmitt Smith 1.50
3 Michael Vick 1.50
4 Peerless Price .40
5 Ray Lewis .40
6 Kyle Boller .75
7 Deion Sanders .75
8 Drew Bledsoe .75
9 Travis Henry .40
10 Eric Moulds .40
11 Steve Smith .40
12 Stephen Davis .40
13 Jake Delhomme .75
14 Rex Grossman .75
15 Brian Urlacher .75
16 Thomas Jones .40
17 Chad Johnson .40
18 Rudi Johnson .40
19 Carson Palmer 1.00
20 William Green .40
21 Andre Davis .40
22 Jeff Garcia .40
23 Roy Williams .75
24 Eddie George .75
25 Keyshawn Johnson .40
26 Reuben Droughns .40
27 Jake Plummer .40
28 Champ Bailey .40
29 Charles Rogers .75
30 Joey Harrington .75
31 Ahman Green .75
32 Brett Favre 2.00
33 Javon Walker .75
34 David Carr 1.00
35 Domanick Davis .40
36 Andre Johnson .75
37 Marvin Harrison .75
38 Edgerrin James 1.00
39 Peyton Manning 1.25
40 Byron Leftwich 1.25
41 Fred Taylor .75
42 Trent Green .40
43 Tony Gonzalez .40
44 Priest Holmes 1.00
45 Zach Thomas .40
46 Chris Chambers .75
47 Jay Fiedler .75
48 Daunte Culpepper .75
49 Randy Moss 1.25
50 Ozzie Smith .40
51 Tom Brady 1.25
52 Deion Branch .40
53 Corey Dillon .75
54 Deuce McAllister .75
55 Aaron Brooks .75
56 Joe Horn .40
57 Tiki Barber .75
58 Kurt Warner .40
59 Jeremy Shockey .75
60 Chad Pennington 1.00
61 Santana Moss .40
62 Curtis Martin .75
63 Kerry Collins .40
64 Jerry Rice 1.50
65 Jerry Porter .40
66 Terrell Owens .75
67 Jevon Kearse .40
68 Donovan McNabb 1.00
69 Hines Ward .40
70 Plaxico Burress .75
71 Duce Staley .40
72 Drew Brees .75
73 LaDainian Tomlinson 1.00
74 Tim Rattay .40
75 Brandon Lloyd .25
76 Kevan Barlow .40
77 Shaun Alexander .75
78 Koren Robinson .40
79 Matt Hasselbeck .40
80 Marshall Faulk 1.00
81 Torry Holt .75
82 Marc Bulger .75
83 Brian Griese .40
84 Derrick Brooks .40
85 Steve McNair .75
86 Derrick Mason .40
87 Chris Brown .40
88 Mark Brunell .40
89 Laveranues Coles .40
90 Clinton Portis 1.00
91 Dick Butkus 5.00
92 Gale Sayers 5.00
93 Mike Ditka 5.00
94 Jim Brown 6.00
95 Roger Staubach 6.00
96 Troy Aikman 6.00
97 John Elway 8.00
98 Barry Sanders 8.00
99 Bart Starr 6.00
100 Paul Hornung 5.00
101 Len Dawson 4.00
102 Dan Marino 10.00
103 Fran Tarkenton 4.00
104 Archie Manning 4.00
105 Joe Namath 6.00
106 Ken Stabler 5.00
107 Lynn Swann 5.00
108 Terry Bradshaw 8.00
109 Joe Montana 10.00
110 Joe Theismann 5.00
111 *Bernard Berrian* 5.00
112 *Ben Hartsock* 5.00
113 *Karlos Dansby* 5.00
114 *Thomas Tapeh* 3.00
115 *Keary Colbert* 8.00
116 *Ben Troupe* 5.00
117 *Jonathan Vilma* 6.00
118 *Jamaar Taylor* 4.00
119 *Ben Roethlisberger* 50.00
120 *Samie Parker* 5.00
121 *Dunta Robinson* 5.00
122 *Dontarrious Thomas* 5.00
123 *Joe Echema* 3.00
124 *Darius Watts* 6.00
125 *Ben Watson* 5.00
126 *Terry Johnson* 3.00
127 *D.J. Hackett* 4.00
128 *Devery Henderson* 5.00
129 *Kellen Winslow Jr.* 8.00
130 *Travis LaBoy* 3.00
131 *Maurice Mann* 3.00
132 *Rashaun Woods* 6.00
133 *Michael Turner* 3.00
134 *Junior Siavii* 4.00
135 *Johnnie Morant* 5.00
136 *Larry Fitzgerald* 15.00
137 *Kevin Jones* 15.00
138 *Will Smith* 5.00
139 *Robert Gallery* 6.00
140 *Michael Jenkins* 5.00
141 *Cedric Cobbs* 5.00
142 *Igor Olshansky* 4.00
143 *Josh Harris* 4.00
144 *Michael Clayton* 10.00
145 *Mewelde Moore* 6.00
146 *Jason Babin* 6.00
147 *Cody Pickett* 5.00
148 *Lee Evans* 8.00
149 *Greg Jones* 5.00
150 *Marcus Tubbs* 5.00
151 *Craig Krenzel* 5.00
152 *Roy Williams* 15.00
153 *Tatum Bell* 8.00
154 *Kenechi Udeze* 5.00
155 *Shawn Andrews* 4.00
156 Reggie Williams 5.00
157 *Julius Jones* 20.00
158 *Vince Wilfork* 5.00
159 *Vernon Carey* 4.00
160 *Eli Manning* 30.00
161 *Devard Darling* 5.00
162 *Sean Taylor* 6.00
163 *Teddy Lehman* 5.00
164 *Jammal Lord* 5.00
165 *J.P. Losman* 10.00
166 *Jerricho Cotchery* 5.00
167 *Ahmad Carroll* 5.00
168 *Michael Boulware* 5.00
169 *Quincy Wilson* 4.00
170 *Derrick Hamilton* 3.00
171 *Kris Wilson* 5.00
172 *D.J. Williams* 6.00
173 *P.K. Sam* 4.00
174 *Matt Schaub* 8.00
175 *Ernest Wilford* 5.00
176 *Chris Gamble* 5.00
177 *Courtney Watson* 3.00
178 *Drew Henson* 10.00
179 *Chris Perry* 10.00
180 *Tommie Harris* 6.00
181 *Marquis Cooper* 3.00
182 *Philip Rivers* 15.00
183 *Carlos Francis* 3.00
184 *DeAngelo Hall* 6.00
185 *Daryl Smith* 5.00
186 *Troy Fleming* 3.00
187 *Luke McCown* 5.00
188 *Steven Jackson* 12.00
189 *Ricardo Colclough* 5.00
190 *Gilbert Gardner* 4.00

2004 UD Legends Gold

Stars (1-90): 8X-16X
Legends (91-110): 1.5X-3X
Rookies (111-190): 2X-4X
Gold Production 25 Sets

2004 UD Legends Future Legends Jerseys

NM/M
Common Player: 6.00
Inserted 1:24
FL-TB Tatum Bell 8.00
FL-MC Michael Clayton 10.00
FL-LE Lee Evans 10.00
FL-LF Larry Fitzgerald 15.00
FL-RG Robert Gallery 6.00
FL-SJ Steven Jackson 12.00
FL-MJ Michael Jenkins 6.00
FL-GJ Greg Jones 6.00
FL-JJ Julius Jones 20.00
FL-KJ Kevin Jones 15.00
FL-JP J.P. Losman 10.00
FL-EM Eli Manning 25.00
FL-CP Chris Perry 10.00
FL-PR Philip Rivers 15.00
FL-BR Ben Roethlisberger 50.00
FL-RE Reggie Williams 6.00
FL-RW Roy Williams 15.00
FL-KW Kellen Winslow Jr. 12.00

2004 UD Legends Future Legends Throwbback Jerseys

NM/M
Common Player: 8.00
Inserted 1:192
FLT-TB Tatum Bell 15.00
FLT-BB Bernard Berrian 10.00
FLT-MC Michael Clayton 20.00
FLT-CC Cedric Cobbs 10.00
FLT-KC Keary Colbert 12.00
FLT-LE Lee Evans 15.00
FLT-LF Larry Fitzgerald 25.00
FLT-RG Robert Gallery 12.00
FLT-DH DeAngelo Hall 10.00
FLT-HA Derrick Hamilton 8.00
FLT-DE Devery Henderson 8.00
FLT-SJ Steven Jackson 20.00
FLT-MJ Michael Jenkins 12.00
FLT-GJ Greg Jones 10.00
FLT-JJ Julius Jones 30.00
FLT-KJ Kevin Jones 25.00
FLT-JP J.P. Losman 15.00
FLT-EM Eli Manning 50.00
FLT-LM Luke McCown 10.00
FLT-CP Chris Perry 15.00
FLT-PR Philip Rivers 25.00
FLT-BR Ben Roethlisberger 100.00
FLT-MS Matt Schaub 12.00
FLT-BT Ben Troupe 8.00
FLT-BW Ben Watson 8.00
FLT-DW Darius Watts 10.00
FLT-RE Reggie Williams 12.00
FLT-RW Roy Williams 25.00
FLT-KW Kellen Winslow Jr. 20.00
FLT-RA Rashaun Woods 12.00

2004 UD Legends Immortal Inscriptions

NM/M
Common Player: 30.00
Production 45 Sets
II-TA Troy Aikman 75.00
II-TB Terry Bradshaw 100.00
II-JB Jim Brown 120.00
II-DB Dick Butkus 100.00
II-JE John Elway 200.00
II-FH Franco Harris 75.00
II-PH Paul Hornung
II-HL Howie Long 75.00
II-AM Archie Manning 50.00
II-DM Dan Marino 200.00
II-JM Joe Montana 250.00
II-JN Joe Namath 120.00
II-BS Barry Sanders 150.00
II-GS Gale Sayers 60.00
II-KS Ken Stabler 60.00
II-RS Roger Staubach 100.00
II-FT Fran Tarkenton 60.00
II-LT Lawrence Taylor
II-JT Joe Theismann 50.00
II-KW Kellen Winslow Jr. 30.00

2004 UD Legends Legendary Jerseys

NM/M
Common Player: 20.00
Production 99 Sets
LJ-TA Troy Aikman 40.00
LJ-TB Terry Bradshaw 40.00
LJ-LD Len Dawson 20.00
LJ-JE John Elway 60.00
LJ-HL Howie Long 30.00
LJ-AM Archie Manning 25.00
LJ-DM Dan Marino 60.00
LJ-JM Joe Montana 80.00
LJ-JN Joe Namath 50.00
LJ-ON Ozzie Newsome 20.00
LJ-WP Walter Payton 80.00
LJ-JR John Riggins
LJ-BS Barry Sanders 60.00
LJ-GS Gale Sayers 40.00
LJ-KS Ken Stabler 30.00
LJ-RS Roger Staubach 40.00
LJ-LS Lynn Swann 40.00
LJ-FT Fran Tarkenton 30.00
LJ-JT Joe Theismann 25.00
LJ-JU Johnny Unitas 60.00
LJ-KW Kellen Winslow Jr. 20.00

2004 UD Legends Legendary Lines of Defense

NM/M
Common Player: 50.00
Production 75 Sets
LLD-PEM Alan Page, Carl Eller, Jim Marshall 100.00
LLD-HGL Jack Ham, Joe Greene, Jack Lambert 200.00
LLD-SHD Mike Singletary, Dan Hampton, Richard Dent 100.00
LLD-JGW Tom Jackson, Randy Gradishar, Louis Wright 50.00
LLD-YYJ Jim Youngblood, Jack Youngblood, Deacon Jones 60.00
LLD-AFB Dick Anderson, Manny Fernandez, Nick Buoniconti 50.00

2004 UD Legends Legendary Signatures

NM/M
Common Player: 10.00
Inserted 1:8
LS-TA Troy Aikman 80.00
LS-DI Dick Anderson 12.00
LS-KA Kenny Anderson 15.00
LS-DA Doug Atkins 15.00
LS-SB Steve Bartkowski 12.00
LS-BB Bill Bergey 10.00
LS-BE Raymond Berry 15.00
LS-TB Terry Bradshaw SP
LS-CB Cliff Branch 12.00
LS-RB Robert Brazile 10.00
LS-JB Jim Brown 100.00
LS-WB Willie Brown 15.00
LS-NB Nick Buoniconti
LS-DB Dick Butkus 60.00
LS-EC Earl Campbell 40.00
LS-HC Harold Carmichael 12.00
LS-DC Dave Casper 15.00
LS-MC Mark Clayton 15.00
LS-RC Roger Craig 15.00
LS-IC Isaac Curtis 10.00
LS-MI Mike Curtis 10.00
LS-LD Len Dawson 60.00
LS-RD Richard Dent 20.00
LS-ED Eric Dickerson 50.00
LS-MD Mike Ditka 60.00
LS-TD Tony Dorsett SP 50.00
LS-MA Mark Duper 15.00
LS-CE Carl Eller 15.00
LS-JE John Elway SP
LS-MF Manny Fernandez 10.00
LS-CF Chuck Foreman 10.00
LS-DF Dan Fouts 30.00
LS-GA Roman Gabriel 15.00
LS-FG Frank Gifford 60.00
LS-VG Vencie Glenn 10.00
LS-RG Randy Gradishar 10.00
LS-JG Joe Greene SP
LS-LC L.C. Greenwood 50.00
LS-BG Bob Griese 25.00
LS-RA Ray Guy 20.00
LS-JH Jack Ham
LS-DH Dan Hampton 20.00
LS-HA Chris Hanburger 10.00
LS-HN John Hannah 12.00
LS-FH Franco Harris
LS-HT Jim Hart 10.00
LS-PH Paul Hornung SP
LS-SH Sam Huff 20.00
LS-TJ Tom Jackson
LS-RJ Ron Jaworski 20.00
LS-BY Billy Johnson 15.00
LS-CJ Charlie Joiner 15.00
LS-BJ Bert Jones 15.00
LS-DJ Deacon Jones 20.00
LS-EJ Ed "Too Tall" Jones 20.00
LS-SJ Sonny Jurgensen 30.00
LS-AK Alex Karras 15.00
LS-BK Billy Kilmer 15.00
LS-KI Jim Klick 15.00
LS-JK Jerry Kramer 20.00
LS-PK Paul Krause 12.00
LS-JL Jack Lambert 100.00
LS-DL Daryle Lamonica 15.00
LS-BL Bob Lilly 20.00
LS-HL Howie Long 100.00
LS-AM Archie Manning 50.00
LS-DM Dan Marino 150.00
LS-JI Jim Marshall 20.00
LS-OM Ollie Matson 20.00
LS-DO Don Maynard 12.00
LS-JM Joe Montana SP
LS-WM Wilbert Montgomery 20.00
LS-MM Mercury Morris 12.00
LS-CM Craig Morton 15.00
LS-MU Anthony Munoz 15.00
LS-JN Joe Namath
LS-ON Ozzie Newsome 15.00
LS-AP Alan Page 20.00
LS-DP Drew Pearson 15.00
LS-JP Jim Plunkett 15.00
LS-MR Mel Renfro 15.00
LS-AN Andy Russell 15.00
LS-BS Barry Sanders 125.00
LS-GS Gale Sayers SP 75.00
LS-BI Billy Sims 15.00
LS-MS Mike Singletary 60.00
LS-SS Steve Spurrier 40.00
LS-KS Ken Stabler 60.00
LS-RS Roger Staubach
LS-FT Fran Tarkenton 50.00
LS-CT Charley Taylor 12.00
LS-JO John Taylor 15.00
LS-LT Lawrence Taylor
LS-JT Joe Theismann 40.00
LS-YO Jack Youngblood 15.00
LS-JY Jim Youngblood 12.00
LS-RO Roger Wehrli 10.00
LS-RW Randy White 20.00
LS-KW Kellen Winslow Jr. 30.00
LS-LW Louis Wright 10.00

2004 UD Legends Link to the Future

LF-BL Drew Bledsoe, J.P. Losman/50
LF-GB Ahman Green, Tatum Bell/50
LF-HT Todd Heap, Ben Troupe/50
LF-JW Chad Johnson, Reggie Williams/50
LF-HH Joe Horn, Devery Henderson/50
LF-GW Tony Gonzalez, Kellen Winslow Jr./50
LF-JP Rudi Johnson, Chris Perry/50
LF-RJ Roy Williams, Julius Jones/50
LF-HE Dante Hall, Lee Evans/50
LF-MW Derrick Mason, Roy Williams/50
LF-GC Joey Galloway, Michael Clayton/50
LF-TV Zach Thomas, Jonathan Vilma/50
LF-WJ Brian Westbrook, Greg Jones/50
LF-BM Kyle Boller, Luke McCown/50
LF-PS Chad Pennington, Matt Schaub/50
LF-CC Chris Chambers, Keary Colbert/25
LF-MM Peyton Manning, Eli Manning/25
LF-VR Michael Vick, Ben Roethlisberger/25
LF-DK Deuce McAllister, Kevin Jones/25
LF-TJ LaDainian Tomlinson, Julius Jones/25
LF-TE Tom Brady, Eli Manning/25
LF-BR Drew Bledsoe, Philip Rivers/25
LF-MJ Deuce McAllister, Steven Jackson/25

2004 UD Legends Link to the Past

LP-BS Mark Brunell, Ken Stabler/50
LP-CC Chris Chambers, Mark Clayton/50
LP-CT Daunte Culpepper, Fran Tarkenton/50
LP-DC Domanick Davis, Earl Campbell/50
LP-GT Rex Grossman, Joe Theismann/50
LP-HH Tommie Harris, Dan Hampton/50
LP-JD Julius Jones, Tony Dorsett/50

LP-JE Steven Jackson, Eric Dickerson/50
LP-MM Eli Manning, Archie Manning/50
LP-RF Philip Rivers, Dan Fouts/50
LP-UE Kenechi Udeze, Carl Eller/50
LP-VA Michael Vick, Troy Aikman/50
LP-JH Greg Jones, Franco Harris/50
LP-MJ Donovan McNabb, Ron Jaworski/50
LP-WW Kellen Winslow Jr., Kellen Winslow Sr./50
LP-BM Tom Brady, Joe Montana/25
LP-DP Dan Marino, Peyton Manning/25
LP-FT Larry Fitzgerald, Charley Taylor/25
LP-HS Drew Henson, Roger Staubach/25
LP-JS Kevin Jones, Barry Sanders/25
LP-PA Peyton Manning, Archie Manning/25
LP-PN Chad Pennington, Joe Namath/25
LP-RB Ben Roethlisberger, Terry Bradshaw/25

2004 UD Power Up

NM/M
Complete Set (100): 12.00
Common Player: .15
Unlisted Stars: .50
Pack (9): 1.75
Box (24): 30.00

1 Emmitt Smith 1.00
2 Anquan Boldin .50
3 Josh McCown .30
4 Michael Vick 1.00
5 Peerless Price .30
6 Warrick Dunn .30
7 Jamal Lewis .50
8 Kyle Boller .50
9 Ray Lewis .30
10 Drew Bledsoe .30
11 Travis Henry .30
12 Eric Moulds .30
13 Jake Delhomme .50
14 Steve Smith .30
15 Stephen Davis .30
16 Anthony Thomas .30
17 Marty Booker .30
18 Rex Grossman .50
19 Chad Johnson .30
20 Rudi Johnson .30
21 Jon Kitna .30
22 Andre Davis .30
23 Jeff Garcia .50
24 Willie Green .30
25 Antonio Bryant .30
26 Quincy Carter .30
27 Keyshawn Johnson .30
28 Champ Bailey .30
29 Jake Plummer .30
30 Ashley Lelie .30
31 Charles Rogers .50
32 Joey Harrington .50
33 Az-Zahir Hakim .30
34 Brett Favre 1.50
35 Javon Walker .30
36 Ahman Green .50
37 David Carr .60
38 Domanick Davis .50
39 Andre Johnson .50
40 Peyton Manning .75
41 Marvin Harrison .50
42 Edgerrin James .60
43 Byron Leftwich .75
44 Fred Taylor .50
45 Jimmy Smith .30
46 Priest Holmes .60
47 Trent Green .30
48 Dante Hall .50
49 Tony Gonzalez .30
50 Ricky Williams .50
51 Jay Fiedler .30
52 Chris Chambers .30
53 Daunte Culpepper .50
54 Randy Moss .75
55 Onterrio Smith .30
56 Troy Brown .30
57 Deion Branch .30
58 Tom Brady .75
59 Deuce McAllister .50
60 Aaron Brooks .50
61 Joe Horn .30
62 Jeremy Shockey .50
63 Amani Toomer .30
64 Tiki Barber .30
65 Chad Pennington .60
66 Santana Moss .30
67 Curtis Martin .50
68 Rich Gannon .30
69 Jerry Rice 1.00
70 Tim Brown .30
71 Jerry Porter .30
72 Donovan McNabb .60
73 Terrell Owens .50
74 Jevon Kearse .30
75 Hines Ward .50
76 Jerome Bettis .30
77 Tommy Maddox .30
78 Plaxico Burress .30
79 LaDainian Tomlinson .60
80 Antonio Gates .30
81 Drew Brees .30
82 Tim Rattay .30
83 Brandon Lloyd .30
84 Kevan Barlow .30
85 Matt Hasselbeck .30
86 Shaun Alexander .50
87 Koren Robinson .30
88 Marshall Faulk .60
89 Torry Holt .50
90 Marc Bulger .50
91 Isaac Bruce .30
92 Brad Johnson .30
93 Charlie Garner .30
94 Keenan McCardell .30
95 Steve McNair .30
96 Eddie George .30
97 Derrick Mason .30
98 Mark Brunell .30
99 Laveranues Coles .30
100 Clinton Portis .75

2004 UD Power Up Shining Through

NM/M
Inserted 1:1

ST-1 Anquan Boldin .75
ST-2 Michael Vick 1.50
ST-3 Jamal Lewis .75
ST-4 Aaron Brooks .75
ST-5 DeShaun Foster .50
ST-6 Rex Grossman .75
ST-7 Rudi Johnson .50
ST-8 Andre Davis .50
ST-9 Antonio Bryant .50
ST-10 Clinton Portis 1.25
ST-11 Brett Favre 2.00
ST-12 David Carr 1.00
ST-13 Marvin Harrison .75
ST-14 Byron Leftwich 1.25
ST-15 Priest Holmes 1.00
ST-16 Dante Hall .75
ST-17 Chris Chambers .60
ST-18 Daunte Culpepper .75
ST-19 Tom Brady 1.25
ST-20 Deuce McAllister .75
ST-21 Jeremy Shockey .75
ST-22 Santana Moss .50
ST-23 Jerry Rice 1.50
ST-24 Donovan McNabb 1.00
ST-25 Plaxico Burress .60
ST-26 LaDainian Tomlinson 1.00
ST-27 Koren Robinson .50
ST-28 Ahman Green .75
ST-29 Steve McNair .75
ST-30 Laveranues Coles .60

2004 UD Power Up Stickers

NM/M
Inserted 1:6

PU-1 Emmitt Smith 4.00
PU-2 Michael Vick 4.00
PU-3 Kyle Boller 2.00
PU-4 Drew Bledsoe 1.50
PU-5 Jake Delhomme 2.00
PU-6 Brian Urlacher 2.00
PU-7 Carson Palmer 2.50
PU-8 Quincy Carter 1.50
PU-9 Jake Plummer 1.50
PU-10 Joey Harrington 2.00
PU-11 Brett Favre 5.00
PU-12 David Carr 2.50
PU-13 Peyton Manning 3.00
PU-14 Byron Leftwich 3.00
PU-15 Priest Holmes 2.50
PU-16 Ricky Williams 2.00
PU-17 Randy Moss 3.00
PU-18 Tom Brady 3.00
PU-19 Deuce McAllister 2.00
PU-20 Chad Pennington 2.50
PU-21 Jeremy Shockey 1.50
PU-22 Jerry Rice 4.00
PU-23 Donovan McNabb 2.50
PU-24 Hines Ward 2.00
PU-25 LaDainian Tomlinson 2.50
PU-26 Kevan Barlow 1.50
PU-27 Matt Hasselbeck 1.50
PU-28 Marshall Faulk 2.50
PU-29 Steve McNair 2.00
PU-30 Clinton Portis 3.00

2004 UD Pro Sigs

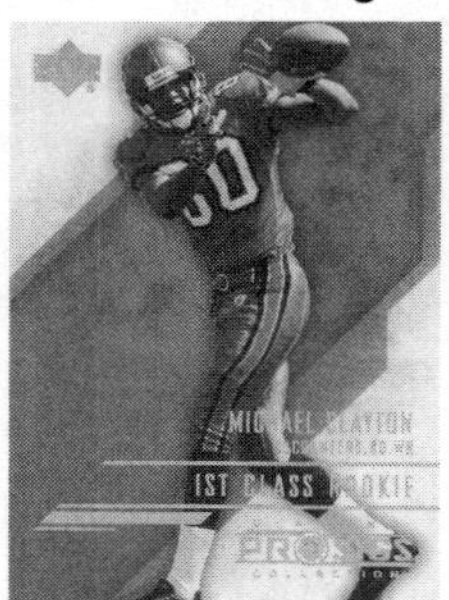

NM/M
Common Player (1-90): .15
Minor Stars: .30
Unlisted Stars: .60
Common Rookie (91-140): 2.00
91-140 Inserted 1:6
Pack (6): 2.50
Box (24): 40.00

1 Marcel Shipp .15
2 Anquan Boldin .60
3 Michael Vick 1.25
4 Peerless Price .30
5 Warrick Dunn .30
6 Todd Heap .30
7 Kyle Boller .60
8 Jamal Lewis .60
9 Drew Bledsoe .60
10 Travis Henry .30
11 Eric Moulds .30
12 Julius Peppers .30
13 Stephen Davis .30
14 Jake Delhomme .60
15 Anthony Thomas .30
16 Brian Urlacher .60
17 Marty Booker .15
18 Chad Johnson .30
19 Rudi Johnson .30
20 Carson Palmer .75
21 Andre Davis .30
22 Jeff Garcia .30
23 Eddie George .30
24 Vinny Testaverde .30
25 Keyshawn Johnson .30
26 Ashley Lelie .30
27 Jake Plummer .30
28 Quentin Griffin .30
29 Charles Rogers .60
30 Joey Harrington .60
31 Ahman Green .60
32 Brett Favre 1.50
33 Donald Driver .30
34 David Carr .75
35 Domanick Davis .60
36 Andre Johnson .60
37 Marvin Harrison .60
38 Edgerrin James .75
39 Peyton Manning 1.00
40 Byron Leftwich 1.00
41 Fred Taylor .60
42 Trent Green .30
43 Dante Hall .30
44 Priest Holmes .75
45 Ricky Williams .60
46 Chris Chambers .60
47 Junior Seau .30
48 Daunte Culpepper .60
49 Randy Moss 1.00
50 Moe Williams .15
51 Tom Brady 1.25
52 Deion Branch .30
53 Corey Dillon .30
54 Deuce McAllister .60
55 Aaron Brooks .60
56 Joe Horn .30
57 Michael Strahan .30
58 Tiki Barber .60
59 Jeremy Shockey .60
60 Chad Pennington .75
61 Santana Moss .30
62 Curtis Martin .60
63 Rich Gannon .30
64 Jerry Rice 1.25
65 Jerry Porter .30
66 Terrell Owens .60
67 Brian Westbrook .30
68 Donovan McNabb .75
69 Hines Ward .30
70 Duce Staley .30
71 Tommy Maddox .15
72 Drew Brees .60
73 LaDainian Tomlinson .75
74 Tim Rattay .30
75 Brandon Lloyd .30
76 Kevan Barlow .30
77 Shaun Alexander .60
78 Koren Robinson .30
79 Matt Hasselbeck .30
80 Marshall Faulk .75
81 Torry Holt .60
82 Marc Bulger .60
83 Brad Johnson .30
84 Derrick Brooks .30
85 Steve McNair .60
86 Derrick Mason .30
87 Chris Brown .30
88 Mark Brunell .30
89 Laveranues Coles .30
90 Clinton Portis 1.00
91 Eli Manning 15.00
92 Larry Fitzgerald 10.00
93 Ben Roethlisberger 20.00
94 Roy Williams 10.00
95 Sean Taylor 5.00
96 Kellen Winslow Jr. 6.00
97 Chris Gamble 3.00
98 Steven Jackson 8.00
99 DeAngelo Hall 4.00
100 Kevin Jones 8.00
101 Reggie Williams 4.00
102 Michael Clayton 6.00
103 Rashaun Woods 6.00
104 D.J. Williams 3.00
105 Ben Troupe 2.00
106 Mewelde Moore 4.00
107 Lee Evans 6.00
108 Jonathan Vilma 3.00
109 Chris Perry 6.00
110 J.P. Losman 4.00
111 Philip Rivers 10.00
112 Michael Jenkins 4.00
113 Greg Jones 4.00
114 John Navarre 4.00
115 Jerricho Cotchery 3.00
116 Michael Turner 2.00
117 Drew Henson 8.00
118 Keary Colbert 4.00
119 Matt Schaub 4.00
120 Cody Pickett 3.00
121 Luke McCown 3.00
122 P.K. Sam 3.00
123 Ernest Wilford 3.00
124 Will Smith 3.00
125 Bernard Berrian 3.00
126 Robert Gallery 4.00
127 Ben Watson 2.00
128 Devery Henderson 3.00
129 Jeff Smoker 4.00
130 Josh Harris 2.00
131 Julius Jones 8.00
132 Dunta Robinson 3.00
133 Tatum Bell 5.00
134 Cedric Cobbs 3.00
135 Devard Darling 3.00
136 Johnnie Morant 3.00
137 Derrick Hamilton 2.00
138 Darius Watts 4.00
139 Tommie Harris 3.00
140 B.J. Symons 3.00

2004 UD Pro Sigs Gold Rookies

Rookies: 1X-2X
Production 349 Sets

2004 UD Pro Sigs Signature Collection

NM/M
Common Player: 8.00
Inserted 1:24
Gold Production 25 Sets

SC-BB Bernard Berrian 12.00
SC-CB Chris Brown SP 20.00
SC-BC Brandon Chillar 8.00
SC-CL Casey Clausen 15.00
SC-MC Michael Clayton 25.00
SC-CC Cedric Cobbs 12.00
SC-KC Keary Colbert 15.00
SC-JC Jerricho Cotchery 12.00
SC-DD Devard Darling 15.00
SC-LE Lee Evans SP 20.00
SC-CF Clarence Farmer 8.00
SC-BF Brett Favre SP
SC-RG Robert Gallery 15.00
SC-JG Joey Galloway SP 12.00
SC-DA Dante Hall SP 15.00
SC-DH DeAngelo Hall 15.00
SC-TH Tommie Harris 12.00
SC-BH Ben Hartsock SP 10.00
SC-HE Todd Heap SP 12.00
SC-DV Devery Henderson SP 15.00
SC-TR Travis Henry 12.00
SC-SJ Steven Jackson 40.00
SC-MJ Michael Jenkins 15.00
SC-CJ Chad Johnson SP 20.00
SC-RJ Rudi Johnson SP 12.00
SC-GJ Greg Jones 15.00
SC-KJ Kevin Jones 40.00
SC-BL Brandon Lloyd 8.00
SC-JP J.P. Losman 25.00
SC-EM Eli Manning 100.00
SC-PM Peyton Manning SP 60.00
SC-DE Derrick Mason SP 15.00
SC-LM Luke McCown 15.00
SC-WM Willis McGahee SP 20.00
SC-JM Johnnie Morant 8.00
SC-JN John Navarre 15.00
SC-JE Jesse Palmer SP 10.00
SC-SP Samie Parker 15.00
SC-PE Chris Perry 15.00
SC-CP Cody Pickett 15.00
SC-AR Antwann Randle El 12.00
SC-BR Ben Roethlisberger SP 300.00
SC-MS Matt Schaub 15.00
SC-WS Will Smith 10.00
SC-JS Jeff Smoker 12.00
SC-BJ B.J. Symons 10.00
SC-ST Sean Taylor 20.00
SC-ZT Zach Thomas SP 15.00
SC-BT Ben Troupe 8.00
SC-KU Kenechi Udeze 12.00
SC-JV Jonathan Vilma 12.00
SC-JW Javon Walker 20.00
SC-BW Ben Watson 12.00
SC-DW Darius Watts SP 15.00
SC-EW Ernest Wilford 12.00
SC-VW Vince Wilfork 12.00
SC-RE Reggie Williams 15.00
SC-RW Roy Williams SP 60.00
SC-QW Quincy Wilson 8.00
SC-RA Rashaun Woods 15.00

2004 UD Reflections

NM/M
Common Player (1-100): .50
Minor Stars: .75
Unlisted Stars: 1.25
Common Rookie (101-200): 2.00
Production 750 Sets
Common Rookie (201-300): 2.00
Production 1150 Sets
Pack (4): 15.00
Box (8): 85.00

1 Emmitt Smith 4.00
2 Anquan Boldin 1.50
3 Josh McCown .75
4 Michael Vick 4.00
5 Peerless Price .75
6 T.J. Duckett .75
7 Todd Heap .50
8 Jamal Lewis 1.50
9 Kyle Boller 1.50
10 Drew Bledsoe 1.50
11 Travis Henry .75
12 Eric Moulds .75
13 Jake Delhomme 1.50
14 Steve Smith .75
15 Stephen Davis .75
16 Rex Grossman 1.50
17 Brian Urlacher 1.50
18 Anthony Thomas .50
19 Rudi Johnson .75
20 Carson Palmer 2.00
21 Chad Johnson .75
22 Jeff Garcia 1.50
23 Andre Davis .75
24 Quincy Morgan .75
25 Keyshawn Johnson .75
26 Roy Williams 1.50
27 Quincy Carter .75
28 Ashley Lelie .75
29 Champ Bailey .75
30 Jake Plummer .75
31 Az-Zahir Hakim .50
32 Joey Harrington 1.50
33 Charles Rogers 1.50
34 Javon Walker .75
35 Ahman Green 1.50
36 Brett Favre 5.00
37 Domanick Davis 1.50
38 David Carr 2.00
39 Andre Johnson 1.50
40 Edgerrin James 2.00
41 Marvin Harrison 1.50
42 Dwight Freeney .50
43 Peyton Manning 3.00
44 Fred Taylor 1.50
45 Jimmy Smith .75
46 Byron Leftwich 3.00
47 Dante Hall 1.50
48 Tony Gonzalez .75
49 Trent Green .75
50 Priest Holmes 2.00
51 Zach Thomas .75
52 A.J. Feeley .75
53 Chris Chambers 1.50
54 Ricky Williams 1.50
55 Randy Moss 3.00
56 Onterrio Smith .75
57 Daunte Culpepper 1.50
58 Tom Brady 3.00
59 Troy Brown .75
60 Corey Dillon .75
61 Donte Stallworth .75
62 Deuce McAllister 1.50
63 Aaron Brooks 1.50
64 Amani Toomer .75
65 Jeremy Shockey 1.50
66 Michael Strahan .75
67 Curtis Martin 1.50
68 Chad Pennington 2.00
69 Santana Moss .75
70 Jerry Porter .75
71 Jerry Rice 4.00
72 Rich Gannon .75
73 Tim Brown .75
74 Terrell Owens 1.50
75 Brian Westbrook .75
76 Donovan McNabb 2.00
77 Tommy Maddox .75
78 Hines Ward 1.50
79 Duce Staley .75
80 Donnie Edwards .50
81 LaDainian Tomlinson 2.00
82 Drew Brees 1.50
83 Brandon Lloyd .75
84 Tim Rattay .75
85 Kevan Barlow .75
86 Koren Robinson .75
87 Shaun Alexander 1.50
88 Matt Hasselbeck 1.50
89 Torry Holt 1.50
90 Marc Bulger 1.50
91 Marshall Faulk 2.00
92 Brad Johnson .75
93 Keenan McCardell .50
94 Charlie Garner .75
95 Steve McNair 1.50
96 Chris Brown .75
97 Eddie George .75
98 Mark Brunell .75
99 Laveranues Coles .75
100 Clinton Portis 3.00
101 Kris Wilson 4.00
102 Carlos Francis 4.00
103 D.J. Williams 5.00
104 Devery Henderson/450 6.00
105 Craig Krenzel 4.00
106 Jonathan Vilma 5.00
107 Luke McCown 4.00
108 Michael Turner 4.00
109 Richard Seigler 2.00
110 Stuart Schweigert 4.00
111 Ben Watson 4.00
112 Chris Perry/450 12.00
113 Jason Fife 4.00
114 Eli Manning/450 40.00
115 Matt Kegel 4.00
116 Kellen Winslow Jr./450 12.00
117 Chris Cooley 3.00
118 Quincy Wilson 4.00
119 Samie Parker 4.00
120 Vince Wilfork 5.00
121 Bernard Berrian 4.00
122 Ahmad Carroll 5.00
123 Derrick Hamilton 3.00
124 Rich Gardner 3.00
125 Jeff Smoker 6.00
126 Kenechi Udeze 5.00
127 Mewelde Moore 4.00
128 Keyaron Fox 3.00
129 Sean Jones 3.00
130 Will Poole 4.00
131 Travelle Wharton 3.00
132 Demorrio Williams 5.00
133 Jason Babin 5.00
134 Ernest Wilford 4.00
135 Jerricho Cotchery 4.00
136 Kevin Jones/450 15.00
137 Michael Boulware 4.00
138 D.J. Hackett 4.00
139 Sean Taylor/450 15.00
140 Will Smith 4.00
141 John Standeford 3.00
142 Max Starks 3.00
143 Cody Pickett 4.00
144 Derrick Strait 5.00
145 Greg Jones/450 8.00
146 John Navarre 5.00
147 Larry Fitzgerald/450 20.00
148 Michael Clayton/450 10.00
149 Rashaun Woods/450 10.00
150 Shawn Andrews 3.00
151 B.J. Symons 4.00
152 Cedric Cobbs/450 8.00
153 Darius Watts 5.00
154 B.J. Johnson 4.00
155 Ricardo Colclough 3.00
156 Josh Harris 4.00
157 Derek Abney 4.00
158 Kendrick Starling 2.00
159 Robert Gallery/450 10.00
160 Tatum Bell/450 12.00
161 Ben Hartsock 3.00
162 Dwan Edwards 2.00
163 Darnell Dockett 3.00
164 Igor Olshansky 3.00
165 Justin Smiley 4.00
166 Julius Jones/450 18.00
167 Matt Mauck 5.00
168 Derek McCoy 2.00
169 Chris Pittman 3.00
170 Teddy Lehman 5.00
171 Ben Troupe/450 6.00
172 Chris Gamble 5.00
173 DeAngelo Hall 6.00
174 Dunta Robinson 4.00
175 Jason Shivers 3.00
176 Keary Colbert/450 8.00
177 Jared Lorenzen 4.00
178 Philip Rivers/450 25.00
179 Roy Williams/450 20.00
180 Bob Sanders 4.00
181 Antwan Odom 4.00
182 Josh Davis 2.00
183 Courtney Watson 3.00
184 Devard Darling 4.00
185 J.P. Losman/450 10.00
186 Johnnie Morant 4.00
187 Lee Evans/450 10.00
188 Michael Jenkins/450 8.00
189 Reggie Williams/450 8.00
190 Steven Jackson/450 15.00
191 Ben Roethlisberger/450 50.00
192 P.K. Sam 4.00
193 Derrick Knight 3.00
194 Drew Henson/450 12.00
195 Marquise Hill 3.00
196 Karlos Dansby 4.00
197 Matt Schaub 6.00
198 Ben Utecht 2.00
199 Darrion Scott 2.00
200 Tommie Harris 5.00
201 Andrae Thurman 2.00
202 Matt Kranchick 5.00
203 Shaun Phillips 3.00
204 Landon Johnson 2.00
205 Jeff Dugan 2.00
206 Wes Welker 3.00
207 Michael Gaines 3.00
208 Jamaar Taylor 2.00
209 Brandon Chillar 2.00
210 Jermaine Green 2.00
211 Triandos Luke 3.00
212 Brandon Miree 3.00
213 Dexter Reid 2.00
214 Isaac Hilton 3.00
215 Adrian Jones 2.00
216 Grant Wiley 2.00
217 Matt Cherry 2.00
218 Courtney Anderson 2.00
219 Antonio Smith 2.00
220 Sean Tufts 2.00
221 Johnny Lamar 3.00
222 Shawn Johnson 2.00
223 Jason Peters 3.00
224 Rodney Leisle 2.00
225 Lane Danielsen 2.00
226 Zack Abron 2.00
227 Romar Crenshaw 2.00
228 Keiwan Ratliff 3.00
229 Chad Lavalais 2.00
230 Jason Wright 2.00
231 Rayshun Reed 2.00
232 Patrick Crayton 2.00
233 Casey Bramlet 2.00
234 Nathaniel Adibi 2.00
235 Dontarrious Thomas 2.00
236 B.J. Sander 2.00
237 Ryan McGuffey 2.00
238 Shawntae Spencer 2.00
239 Amon Gordon 2.00
240 Vernon Carey 2.00
241 Stanford Samuels 2.00
242 Thomas Tapeh 2.00
243 Keith Smith 2.00
244 Casey Clausen 5.00
245 Jake Grove 2.00
246 Omar Nazel 2.00
247 Jammal Lord 4.00
248 Jeremy LeSueur 2.00
249 Daryl Smith 3.00
250 Nat Dorsey 2.00
251 Tim Anderson 3.00
252 Chris Snee 2.00
253 Sean Ryan 2.00
254 Terry Johnson 2.00
255 Marquis Cooper 2.00
256 Josh Scobey 2.00
257 Justin Jenkins 2.00

258 *Nate Lawrie* 2.00
259 *Randy Starks* 2.00
260 *Caleb Miller* 2.00
261 *A.J. Ricker* 2.00
262 *Andrew Hall* 2.00
263 *Troy Fleming* 2.00
264 *Matt Ware* 4.00
265 *Christian Ferrara* 2.00
266 *Stacy Andrews* 2.00
267 *Reggie Torbor* 2.00
268 *Jeris McIntyre* 2.00
269 *Jarrett Payton* 5.00
270 *Ronald Jones* 2.00
271 *Kelly Butler* 2.00
272 *Bryan Hickman* 2.00
273 *Chris Collins* 2.00
274 *Ryan Dinwiddie* 2.00
275 *Robert Geathers* 2.00
276 *Niko Koutouvides* 2.00
277 *Clarence Farmer* 2.00
278 *Jim Sorgi* 2.00
279 *Ran Carthon* 3.00
280 *Michael Waddell* 2.00
281 *Andrew Strojny* 2.00
282 *Sloan Thomas* 2.00
283 *Tim Euhus* 2.00
284 *Lawrence Richardson* 3.00
285 *Nate Kaeding* 4.00
286 *Ryan Krause* 2.00
287 *Derrick Ward* 2.00
288 *Nathan Vasher* 2.00
289 *Bobby McCray* 2.00
290 *Scott Rislov* 2.00
291 *Ryan Boschetti* 2.00
292 *Fred Russell* 4.00
293 *Von Hutchins* 3.00
294 *Derrick Crawford* 2.00

2004 UD Reflections Green

Stars (1-100): 3X-6X
Rookies/450: 1X-2X
Rookies/750/1150: 1.5X-3X
Production 50 Sets

2004 UD Reflections Red

Stars (1-100): 2X-4X
Rookies/450: .5X-1X
Rookies/750/1150: 1X-1.5X
Production 100 Sets

2004 UD Reflections Blue

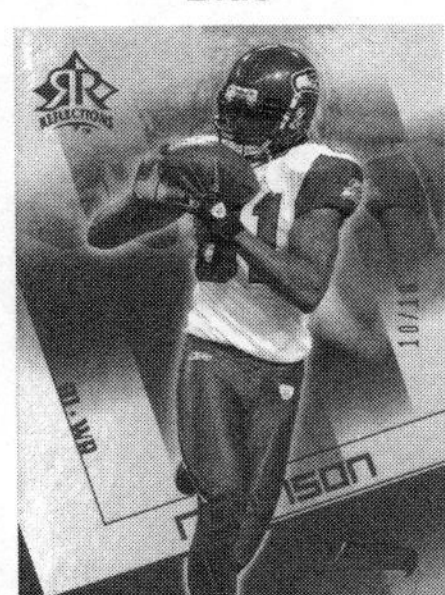

Production 10 Sets
Black Production 1 Set

2004 UD Reflections Fantasy Fabrics

NM/M
Common Player: 8.00
Production 99 Sets
Rainbow Production 15 Sets
LTD Patches: 2X-4X
Patch Production 21 Sets
FF-SA Shaun Alexander 10.00
FF-JB Jerome Bettis 8.00
FF-AB Anquan Boldin 10.00
FF-TB Tom Brady 20.00
FF-DA David Carr 12.00
FF-CC Chris Chambers 8.00
FF-LC Laveranues Coles 8.00
FF-DC Daunte Culpepper 12.00
FF-DD Domanick Davis 10.00
FF-SD Stephen Davis 8.00
FF-MF Marshall Faulk 12.00
FF-BF Brett Favre 30.00
FF-TG Tony Gonzalez 8.00
FF-AG Ahman Green 12.00
FF-GR Trent Green 8.00
FF-MH Marvin Harrison 10.00
FF-TR Travis Henry 8.00
FF-PH Priest Holmes 15.00
FF-TH Torry Holt 10.00
FF-EJ Edgerrin James 12.00
FF-CJ Chad Johnson 8.00
FF-RJ Rudi Johnson 8.00
FF-JL Jamal Lewis 10.00
FF-PM Peyton Manning 20.00
FF-CM Curtis Martin 12.00
FF-MA Derrick Mason 8.00
FF-DE Deuce McAllister 10.00
FF-DM Donovan McNabb 15.00
FF-SM Steve McNair 12.00
FF-RM Randy Moss 15.00
FF-MO Santana Moss 8.00
FF-CH Chad Pennington 15.00
FF-CP Clinton Portis 15.00
FF-PP Peerless Price 8.00
FF-PR Patrick Ramsey 8.00
FF-AR Antwann Randle El 8.00
FF-KR Koren Robinson 8.00
FF-LT LaDainian Tomlinson 12.00
FF-MV Michael Vick 20.00
FF-JW Javon Walker 8.00
FF-HW Hines Ward 10.00
FF-RW Ricky Williams 12.00

2004 UD Reflections Focus on the Future Jerseys

NM/M
Common Player: 5.00
Gold Inserted 1:3
Rainbow: 1X-2X
Rainbow Production 85 Sets
FO-TB Tatum Bell 10.00
FO-AB Anquan Boldin 6.00
FO-KB Kyle Boller 5.00
FO-CB Chris Brown 6.00
FO-MB Marc Bulger 6.00
FO-PB Plaxico Burress 6.00
FO-TC Tyrone Calico 5.00
FO-DC David Carr 8.00
FO-CC Chris Chambers 6.00
FO-LC Laveranues Coles SP 6.00
FO-DD Domanick Davis 6.00
FO-LF Larry Fitzgerald 12.00
FO-RG Rex Grossman 6.00
FO-DH Dante Hall 6.00
FO-JH Joey Harrington 6.00
FO-TH Todd Heap 5.00
FO-SJ Steven Jackson 10.00
FO-AJ Andre Johnson 6.00
FO-BJ Bethel Johnson 5.00
FO-RJ Rudi Johnson 5.00
FO-JJ Julius Jones 10.00
FO-KJ Kevin Jones 10.00
FO-BL Byron Leftwich 10.00
FO-AL Ashley Lelie 5.00
FO-JP J.P. Losman 8.00
FO-EM Eli Manning 20.00
FO-CP Carson Palmer 8.00
FO-CH Chris Perry 10.00
FO-PA Patrick Ramsey SP 6.00
FO-PR Philip Rivers 15.00
FO-KR Koren Robinson 5.00
FO-BR Ben Roethlisberger 20.00
FO-CR Charles Rogers 6.00
FO-JS Jeremy Shockey 6.00
FO-OS Onterrio Smith 6.00
FO-DS Donte Stallworth 6.00
FO-LS Lee Suggs SP 8.00
FO-TS Terrell Suggs 5.00
FO-RE Reggie Williams 6.00
FO-RO Roy Williams 10.00
FO-RW Roy Williams 6.00
FO-KW Kellen Winslow Jr. 10.00

2004 UD Reflections Offensive Threads

NM/M
Common Player: 8.00
Production 99 Sets
Rainbow Production 15 Sets
LTD Patches: 2X-4X
Patch Production 21 Sets
OT-SA Shaun Alexander 10.00
OT-DR Drew Bledsoe 10.00
OT-DB David Boston 8.00
OT-TB Tom Brady 20.00
OT-AB Aaron Brooks 8.00
OT-TR Troy Brown 8.00
OT-MB Marc Bulger 10.00
OT-PB Plaxico Burress 8.00
OT-QC Quincy Carter 8.00
OT-DC Daunte Culpepper 12.00
OT-SD Stephen Davis 8.00
OT-CD Corey Dillon 8.00
OT-MF Marshall Faulk 12.00
OT-BF Brett Favre 30.00
OT-AG Ahman Green 12.00
OT-DH Dante Hall 10.00
OT-JH Joey Harrington 10.00
OT-MH Marvin Harrison 10.00
OT-HA Matt Hasselbeck 10.00
OT-PH Priest Holmes 15.00
OT-TH Torry Holt 10.00
OT-EJ Edgerrin James 12.00
OT-AJ Andre Johnson 10.00
OT-BJ Brad Johnson 8.00
OT-BL Byron Leftwich 15.00
OT-JL Jamal Lewis 10.00
OT-PM Peyton Manning 20.00
OT-MA Derrick Mason 8.00
OT-DE Deuce McAllister 10.00
OT-DM Donovan McNabb 15.00
OT-SM Steve McNair 12.00
OT-RM Randy Moss 15.00
OT-TO Terrell Owens 12.00
OT-CP Chad Pennington 15.00
OT-JP Jake Plummer 8.00
OT-CL Clinton Portis 15.00
OT-JR Jerry Rice 25.00
OT-CR Charles Rogers 10.00
OT-JS Jeremy Shockey 10.00
OT-LT LaDainian Tomlinson 12.00
OT-MV Michael Vick 20.00
OT-RW Ricky Williams 12.00

2004 UD Reflections Pro Cuts Jerseys

NM/M
Common Player: 6.00
Inserted 1:6
Silver: 1X-1.5X
Silver Production 85 Sets
PC-LA LaVar Arrington SP 10.00
PC-TI Tiki Barber 6.00
PC-TB Tom Brady 12.00
PC-AB Aaron Brooks 6.00
PC-BR Tim Brown 8.00
PC-DC Daunte Culpepper 10.00
PC-JD Jake Delhomme SP 10.00
PC-MF Marshall Faulk SP 10.00
PC-BF Brett Favre 20.00
PC-EG Eddie George 6.00
PC-TG Tony Gonzalez 6.00
PC-AG Ahman Green 10.00
PC-MH Marvin Harrison 8.00
PC-PH Priest Holmes 10.00
PC-TH Torry Holt 8.00
PC-JH Joe Horn 6.00
PC-EJ Edgerrin James 10.00
PC-CJ Chad Johnson 6.00
PC-KJ Keyshawn Johnson 6.00
PC-JL Jamal Lewis 8.00
PC-RL Ray Lewis 10.00
PC-PM Peyton Manning 12.00
PC-CM Curtis Martin 8.00
PC-DM Deuce McAllister 8.00
PC-DO Donovan McNabb 12.00
PC-ST Steve McNair 8.00
PC-RM Randy Moss 12.00
PC-SM Santana Moss 6.00
PC-TO Terrell Owens 10.00
PC-CH Chad Pennington 10.00
PC-CP Clinton Portis 10.00
PC-JR Jerry Rice 12.00
PC-WS Warren Sapp 6.00
PC-JS Junior Seau 6.00
PC-ES Emmitt Smith 15.00
PC-MS Michael Strahan 6.00
PC-LT LaDainian Tomlinson 10.00
PC-BU Brian Urlacher 10.00
PC-MV Michael Vick 15.00
PC-RI Ricky Williams 10.00
PC-RW Roy Williams 10.00

2004 UD Reflections Select Swatches

NM/M
Common Player: 8.00
Production 99 Sets
Rainbow Production 15 Sets
LTD Patches: 2X-4X
Patch Production 21 Sets
SS-SA Shaun Alexander 10.00
SS-LA LaVar Arrington 20.00
SS-AN Anquan Boldin 10.00
SS-TB Tom Brady 20.00
SS-AB Aaron Brooks 8.00
SS-MB Marc Bulger 10.00
SS-DA David Carr 12.00
SS-LC Laveranues Coles 8.00
SS-DC Daunte Culpepper 12.00
SS-DD Domanick Davis 10.00
SS-MF Marshall Faulk 12.00
SS-BF Brett Favre 30.00
SS-TG Tony Gonzalez 8.00
SS-AG Ahman Green 12.00
SS-DH Dante Hall 10.00
SS-MH Marvin Harrison 10.00
SS-MA Matt Hasselbeck 10.00
SS-PH Priest Holmes 15.00
SS-TH Torry Holt 10.00
SS-EJ Edgerrin James 12.00
SS-CJ Chad Johnson 8.00
SS-JL Jamal Lewis 10.00
SS-RL Ray Lewis 12.00
SS-PM Peyton Manning 20.00
SS-DE Deuce McAllister 10.00
SS-DM Donovan McNabb 15.00
SS-SM Steve McNair 12.00
SS-RM Randy Moss 15.00
SS-TO Terrell Owens 12.00
SS-CP Chad Pennington 15.00
SS-CL Clinton Portis 15.00
SS-JR Jerry Rice 25.00
SS-KR Koren Robinson 8.00
SS-JS Jeremy Shockey 10.00
SS-MS Michael Strahan 8.00
SS-ZT Zach Thomas 10.00
SS-LT LaDainian Tomlinson 12.00
SS-BU Brian Urlacher 15.00
SS-MV Michael Vick 20.00
SS-HW Hines Ward 10.00
SS-RW Ricky Williams 12.00
SS-WI Roy Williams 12.00

2004 UD Reflections Signature Reflections

NM/M
Common Player: 12.00
Inserted 1:28
SR-TR Troy Aikman SP 80.00
SR-BB Bernard Berrian 15.00
SR-TB Tom Brady SP 80.00
SR-MC Michael Clayton 20.00
SR-KC Keary Colbert 25.00
SR-DC Daunte Culpepper 40.00
SR-LE Lee Evans 25.00
SR-BF Brett Favre 200.00
SR-LF Larry Fitzgerald SP
SR-JF John Fox 12.00
SR-RO Robert Gallery 30.00
SR-RG Rex Grossman 20.00
SR-GR Jon Gruden SP 25.00
SR-DE DeAngelo Hall 30.00
SR-DV Devery Henderson 12.00
SR-TH Travis Henry SP 20.00
SR-DH Drew Henson 50.00
SR-SJ Steven Jackson 50.00
SR-MJ Michael Jenkins 15.00
SR-GJ Greg Jones 15.00
SR-KJ Kevin Jones 50.00
SR-JP J.P. Losman 30.00
SR-EM Eli Manning 125.00
SR-PM Peyton Manning 40.00
SR-LM Luke McCown 20.00
SR-DM Donovan McNabb SP
SR-JO Joe Montana SP
SR-BP Bill Parcells 30.00
SR-CP Chris Perry 30.00
SR-AR Andy Reid 15.00
SR-PR Philip Rivers 60.00
SR-BR Ben Roethlisberger SP 150.00
SR-MS Matt Schaub 25.00
SR-ST Sean Taylor 40.00
SR-BT Ben Troupe 12.00
SR-MV Michael Vick 125.00
SR-DW Darius Watts 30.00
SR-RE Reggie Williams 15.00
SR-RW Ricky Williams 30.00
SR-WI Roy Williams 75.00
SR-KW Kellen Winslow Jr. 40.00
SR-WO Rashaun Woods 40.00

2004 UD Reflections Signature Threads

NM/M
Common Player: 20.00
Production 99 Sets
Rainbow Production 15 Sets
LTD Patches: 1.5X-3X
Patch Production 21 Sets
ST-DB Drew Bledsoe 40.00
ST-KB Kyle Boller 30.00
ST-TB Tom Brady 125.00
ST-CB Chris Brown 50.00
ST-MA Mark Brunell 25.00
ST-DC David Carr 50.00
ST-DD Domanick Davis 30.00
ST-LE Lee Evans 50.00
ST-BF Brett Favre 200.00
ST-GA Robert Gallery 60.00
ST-JG Joey Galloway 20.00
ST-TG Tony Gonzalez 25.00
ST-RG Rex Grossman 30.00
ST-DH Dante Hall 30.00
ST-TH Todd Heap 20.00
ST-TR Travis Henry 25.00
ST-CJ Chad Johnson 30.00
ST-RJ Rudi Johnson 30.00
ST-KJ Kevin Jones 100.00
ST-BL Byron Leftwich 50.00
ST-LO J.P. Losman 50.00
ST-EM Eli Manning 250.00
ST-PM Peyton Manning 75.00
ST-MC Deuce McAllister 30.00
ST-JM Josh McCown 20.00
ST-WM Willis McGahee 30.00
ST-DM Donovan McNabb 75.00
ST-SM Steve McNair 40.00
ST-JP Jesse Palmer 20.00
ST-CP Chad Pennington 50.00
ST-CH Chris Perry 50.00
ST-PR Philip Rivers 100.00
ST-BR Ben Roethlisberger 150.00
ST-JT Joe Theismann 40.00
ST-ZT Zach Thomas 40.00
ST-LT LaDainian Tomlinson 40.00
ST-MV Michael Vick 150.00
ST-KW Kelley Washington 20.00
ST-RW Ricky Williams 40.00
ST-RO Roy Williams 40.00
ST-WI Roy Williams 125.00
ST-KE Kellen Winslow Jr. 40.00

2004 UD Rookie Premiere

NM/M
Common Player (1-30): .50
Minor Stars: 1.00
Unlisted Stars: 1.50
1 Eli Manning 6.00
2 Ben Roethlisberger 12.00
3 Philip Rivers 3.00
4 Roy Williams WR 3.00
5 Larry Fitzgerald 3.00
6 Tatum Bell 2.00
7 J.P. Losman 2.00
8 Steven Jackson 3.00
9 Ben Watson .50
10 Devery Henderson .50
11 Kevin Jones 3.00
12 Chris Perry 2.00
13 Kellen Winslow Jr. 2.50
14 Lee Evans 2.00
15 Reggie Williams 1.50
16 Ben Troupe .50
17 Michael Clayton 2.00
18 Michael Jenkins 1.00
19 Rashaun Woods 1.50
20 DeAngelo Hall 1.50
21 Cedric Cobbs 1.00
22 Luke McCown 1.00
23 Robert Gallery 1.50
24 Julius Jones 4.00
25 Matt Schaub 1.50
26 Keary Colbert 1.50
27 Bernard Berrian 1.00
28 Greg Jones 1.50
29 Darius Watts 1.00
30 Checklist Card .50

2004 UD Rookie Premiere Gold

Gold: 1X-2X
Inserted 1:Set

2004 UD Rookie Premiere Autographs

NM/M
Common Player: 25.00
Minor Stars: 30.00
Unlisted Stars: 40.00
BB Bernard Berrian 40.00
MC Michael Clayton 80.00
CC Cedric Cobbs 30.00
KC Keary Colbert 50.00
DD Devard Darling 25.00
LE Lee Evans 60.00
LF Larry Fitzgerald 125.00
RG Robert Gallery 60.00
DH DeAngelo Hall 50.00
DH2 Devery Henderson 25.00
MJ Michael Jenkins 30.00
GJ Greg Jones 40.00
JJ Julius Jones 150.00
KJ Kevin Jones 125.00
EM Eli Manning 200.00
LM Luke McCown 30.00
CP Chris Perry 50.00
PR Philip Rivers 125.00
BR Ben Roethlisberger 300.00
MS Matt Schaub 40.00
BT Ben Troupe 30.00
BW Ben Watson 30.00
DW Darius Watts 40.00
RW2 Reggie Williams 40.00
RW Rashaun Woods 50.00
RW3 Roy Williams WR 125.00

2004 Upper Deck Sportsfest

NM/M
Common Player: 2.00
SF11 Tom Brady 2.00
SF12 Eli Manning 8.00

2004 UD Sweet Spot

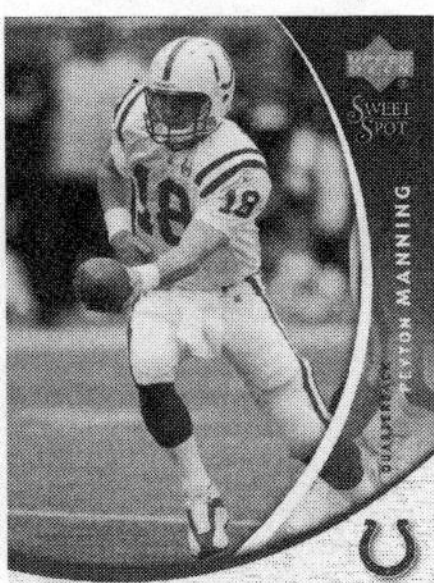

NM/M
Common Player (1-100): .30
Minor Stars: .60
Unlisted Stars: 1.00
Common Legend (101-112): 5.00
101-112 Production 2,499 Sets
Common Rookie (113-175): 3.00
113-175 Production 1,299 Sets
Common Rookie (176-210): 4.00
176-210 Production 999 Sets
Common Rookie (211-230): 6.00
211-230 Production 499 Sets
Pack (4): 12.00
Box (12): 140.00
1 Anquan Boldin 1.00
2 Emmitt Smith 2.50
3 Josh McCown .60
4 Michael Vick 2.50
5 Warrick Dunn .60
6 Peerless Price .60
7 Jamal Lewis 1.00
8 Deion Sanders 1.00
9 Kyle Boller .60
10 Drew Bledsoe .60
11 Travis Henry .60
12 Eric Moulds .60
13 Jake Delhomme 1.00
14 Stephen Davis .60
15 Julius Peppers .60
16 Thomas Jones .60
17 Rex Grossman 1.00
18 Brian Urlacher 1.00
19 Carson Palmer 1.50
20 Chad Johnson .60
21 Rudi Johnson .60
22 Jeff Garcia .60
23 William Green .60
24 Andre Davis .60
25 Vinny Testaverde .60
26 Eddie George .60
27 Keyshawn Johnson .60
28 Reuben Droughns .60
29 Jake Plummer .60
30 Ashley Lelie .60
31 Rod Smith .60
32 Joey Harrington 1.00
33 Artose Pinner .30
34 Az-Zahir Hakim .30
35 Brett Favre 3.00
36 Javon Walker 1.00
37 Ahman Green 1.00
38 Andre Johnson 1.00
39 David Carr 1.50
40 Domanick Davis .60
41 Peyton Manning 2.00
42 Edgerrin James 1.50
43 Marvin Harrison 1.00
44 Byron Leftwich 2.00
45 Fred Taylor 1.00
46 Jimmy Smith .60
47 Priest Holmes 1.50
48 Trent Green .60
49 Dante Hall .60
50 Tony Gonzalez .60
51 Randy McMichael .60
52 Jay Fiedler .60
53 Chris Chambers 1.00
54 Randy Moss 2.00
55 Daunte Culpepper 1.00
56 Onterrio Smith .60
57 Tom Brady 2.00
58 Deion Branch .60
59 Corey Dillon 1.00
60 Deuce McAllister 1.00
61 Aaron Brooks 1.00
62 Joe Horn .60
63 Jeremy Shockey .60
64 Tiki Barber 1.00
65 Michael Strahan .60
66 Curtis Martin 1.00
67 Chad Pennington 1.50
68 Santana Moss .60
69 Charles Woodson .60
70 Kerry Collins .60
71 Warren Sapp .60
72 Donovan McNabb 1.50
73 Brian Westbrook .60
74 Terrell Owens 1.00
75 Hines Ward .60
76 Plaxico Burress 1.00

77 Duce Staley .60
78 LaDainian Tomlinson 1.50
79 Antonio Gates .60
80 Drew Brees 1.00
81 Eric Johnson .30
82 Kevan Barlow .60
83 Tim Rattay .60
84 Matt Hasselbeck .60
85 Shaun Alexander 1.00
86 Jerry Rice 2.50
87 Marc Bulger 1.00
88 Torry Holt 1.00
89 Marshall Faulk 1.50
90 Isaac Bruce .60
91 Brad Johnson .60
92 Derrick Brooks .60
93 Joey Galloway .60
94 Steve McNair 1.00
95 Derrick Mason .60
96 Chris Brown .60
97 Clinton Portis 1.50
98 Mark Brunell .60
99 Laveranues Coles .60
100 LaVar Arrington 1.00
101 Roger Staubach 5.00
102 Troy Aikman 5.00
103 John Elway 8.00
104 Barry Sanders 8.00
105 Fran Tarkenton 5.00
106 Archie Manning 5.00
107 Joe Namath 6.00
108 Ken Stabler 5.00
109 Howie Long 5.00
110 Kellen Winslow Sr. 5.00
111 Joe Montana 10.00
112 Joe Theismann 5.00
113 *Darnell Dockett* 5.00
114 *Randy Starks* 4.00
115 *Rashad Baker* 5.00
116 *Tim Anderson* 5.00
117 *Darrion Scott* 5.00
118 *Courtney Watson* 5.00
119 *Gilbert Gardner* 4.00
120 *Marquis Cooper* 4.00
121 *Caleb Miller* 3.00
122 *Jeff Shoate* 3.00
123 *Keyaron Fox* 5.00
124 *Landon Johnson* 3.00
125 *Reggie Torbor* 4.00
126 *Demorrio Williams* 5.00
127 *Niko Koutouvides* 5.00
128 *Richard Seigler* 4.00
129 *Brandon Chillar* 4.00
130 *Nate Kaeding* 5.00
131 *Dave Ball* 3.00
132 *Josh Thomas* 5.00
133 *Josh Scobey* 3.00
134 *Wes Welker* 4.00
135 *Darrell McClover* 4.00
136 *Ben Utecht* 3.00
137 *Chris Snee* 3.00
138 *Jake Grove* 3.00
139 *Justin Smiley* 4.00
140 *Max Starks* 3.00
141 *Randall Gay* 15.00
142 *Charlie Anderson* 3.00
143 *Alain Kashama* 5.00
144 *Eric Edwards* 12.00
145 *Jacques Reeves* 4.00
146 *Jarrett Payton* 8.00
147 *Curtis Deloatch* 3.00
148 *Michael Gaines* 3.00
149 *Erik Jensen* 4.00
150 *Courtney Anderson* 4.00
151 *Bruce Thornton* 3.00
152 *Glenn Earl* 3.00
153 *Michael Waddell* 3.00
154 *J.R. Reed* 6.00
155 *Dwight Anderson* 5.00
156 *Von Hutchins* 4.00
157 *Travis LaBoy* 4.00
158 *Terry Johnson* 3.00
159 *Dwan Edwards* 3.00
160 *Colby Bockwoldt* 3.00
161 *Madieu Williams* 4.00
162 *Will Poole* 6.00
163 *Igor Olshansky* 5.00
164 *Michael Boulware* 5.00
165 *Shaun Phillips* 3.00
166 *Keith Smith* 4.00
167 *Will Smith* 6.00
168 *D.J. Williams* 8.00
169 *Derrick Strait* 6.00
170 Karlos Dansby 6.00
171 *Ricardo Colclough* 6.00
172 *Chad Lavalais* 4.00
173 *Teddy Lehman* 6.00
174 *Jim Sorgi* 6.00
175 *Bob Sanders* 6.00
176 *Sean Taylor* 10.00
177 *Marcus Tubbs* 8.00
178 *Daryl Smith* 8.00
179 *Bradlee Van Pelt* 8.00
180 *Shawntae Spencer* 6.00
181 *Nathan Vasher* 8.00
182 *Jared Allen* 6.00
183 *Rod Davis* 4.00
184 *Brian Jones* 6.00
185 *Will Allen* 8.00
186 *Antwan Odom* 8.00
187 *Vernon Carey* 5.00
188 *Mike Karney* 5.00
189 *Joey Thomas* 6.00
190 *Casey Bramlet* 5.00
191 *Keiwan Ratliff* 6.00
192 *Rich Gardner* 5.00
193 *Jason Babin* 10.00
194 *Dontarrious Thomas* 8.00
195 *Dexter Reid* 4.00
196 *Marquise Hill* 6.00
197 *Jonathan Smith* 6.00
198 *Larry Croom* 5.00
199 *Gibril Wilson* 8.00
200 *Erik Coleman* 4.00
201 *B.J. Sams* 8.00
202 *Bruce Perry* 5.00
203 *Brock Lesnar* 15.00
204 *Brandon Miree* 6.00
205 *Clarence Moore* 8.00
206 *Mark Jones* 5.00
207 *Patrick Crayton* 8.00
208 *Jeff Dugan* 4.00
209 *Sean Ryan* 6.00
210 *Sloan Thomas* 6.00
211 *Triandos Luke* 10.00
212 *Dexter Wynn* 8.00
213 *Matt Kranchick* 10.00
214 *Tim Euhus* 10.00
215 *Ryan Krause* 8.00
216 *Junior Siavii* 8.00
217 *Ran Carthon* 8.00
218 *Derrick Pope* 8.00
219 *Alex Lewis* 10.00
220 *Chris Cooley* 10.00
221 *Jamaar Taylor* 10.00
222 *Stuart Schweigert* 8.00
223 *Jason David* 8.00
224 *Maurice Mann* 8.00
225 *Robert Geathers* 8.00
226 *Matt Mauck* 10.00
227 *Jammal Lord* 10.00
228 *Travelle Wharton* 6.00
229 *D.J. Hackett* 8.00
230 *Thomas Tapeh* 8.00
231 *Dunta Robinson*
Auto/699 20.00
232 *Ahmad Carroll*
Auto/699 20.00
233 *Kenechi Udeze*
Auto/699 15.00
234 *Tommie Harris*
Auto/699 15.00
235 *Jonathan Vilma*
Auto/699 30.00
236 *Vince Wilfork*
Auto/699 20.00
237 *B.J. Symons*
Auto/699 15.00
238 *B.J. Johnson*
Auto/699 12.00
239 *Kris Wilson*
Auto/699 15.00
240 *Josh Harris*
Auto/699 15.00
241 *Troy Fleming*
Auto/699 12.00
242 *Johnnie Morant*
Auto/699 15.00
243 *Craig Krenzel*
Auto/699 15.00
244 *Quincy Wilson*
Auto/699 15.00
245 *P.K. Sam Auto/699* 12.00
246 *Michael Turner*
Auto/699 12.00
247 *Carlos Francis*
Auto/699 15.00
248 *Jared Lorenzen*
Auto/699 12.00
249 *John Navarre*
Auto/675 15.00
250 *Jeff Smoker*
Auto/699 30.00
251 *Ernest Wilford*
Auto/559 20.00
252 *Mewelde Moore*
Auto/699 25.00
253 *Chris Gamble*
Auto/699 25.00
254 *Jericho Cotchery*
Auto/699 15.00
255 *Derrick Hamilton*
Auto/699 15.00
256 *Samie Parker*
Auto/699 20.00
257 *Cody Pickett*
Auto/699 20.00
258 Does not exist
259 *Ben Hartsock*
Auto/699 20.00
260 *Cedric Cobbs*
Auto/699 20.00
261 *Matt Schaub*
Auto/699 25.00
262 *Bernard Berrian*
Auto/699 20.00
263 *Devard Darling*
Auto/699 20.00
264 *Ben Watson*
Auto/699 15.00
265 *Darius Watts*
Auto/699 25.00
266 *DeAngelo Hall*
Auto/399 25.00
267 *Ben Troupe*
Auto/699 15.00
268 *Michael Jenkins*
Auto/399 25.00
269 *Keary Colbert*
Auto/699 30.00
270 *Robert Gallery*
Auto/699 25.00
271 *Greg Jones*
Auto/650 20.00
272 *Michael Clayton*
Auto/699 40.00
273 *Luke McCown*
Auto/699 20.00
274 *Rashaun Woods*
Auto/699 20.00
275 *Reggie Williams*
Auto/699 20.00
276 *Devery Henderson*
Auto/699 20.00
277 *Tatum Bell*
Auto/699 40.00
278 *Lee Evans Auto/350* 50.00
279 *J.P. Losman*
Auto/199 60.00
280 *Drew Henson*
Auto/199 60.00
281 *Kellen Winslow Jr.*
Auto/125 80.00
282 *Chris Perry*
Auto/199 50.00
283 *Julius Jones*
Auto/199 175.00
284 *Steven Jackson*
Auto/199 125.00
285 *Kevin Jones*
Auto/199 125.00
286 *Roy Williams*
Auto/149 125.00
287 *Ben Roethlisberger*
Auto/199 300.00
288 *Philip Rivers*
Auto/199 80.00
289 *Larry Fitzgerald*
Auto/150 125.00
290 *Eli Manning*
Auto/150 200.00

2004 UD Sweet Spot Gold

Stars (1-100): 4X-8X
Legends (101-112): 1.5X-3X
Rookies (113-175): 1X-2X
Rookies (176-210): 1X-2X
Rookies (211-230): 1X-1.5X
Production 50 Sets

2004 UD Sweet Spot Silver

Stars (1-100): 2X-4X
Legends (101-112): 1.5X
Rookies (113-175): 1X-1.5X
Rookies (176-210): 1X-1.2X
Rookies (211-230): 1X
Production 100 Sets

2004 UD Sweet Spot Gold Rookie Autographs

NM/M

Golds: 1X-1.5X
Production 100 Sets
266 DeAngelo Hall 40.00
268 Michael Jenkins 40.00
278 Lee Evans 50.00
279 J.P. Losman 60.00
280 Drew Henson 60.00
281 Kellen Winslow Jr./50 125.00
282 Chris Perry 50.00
283 Julius Jones 175.00
284 Steven Jackson 125.00
285 Kevin Jones 125.00
286 Roy Williams 125.00
287 Ben Roethlisberger 300.00
288 Philip Rivers 100.00
289 Larry Fitzgerald/35 175.00
290 Eli Manning/50 300.00

2004 UD Sweet Spot Signatures

NM/M

Common Player: 20.00
Inserted 1:24
Gold: 1X-1.2X
Gold Production 100 Sets
SSTA Troy Aikman 100.00
SSKA Ken Anderson 20.00
SSCB Chris Brown 20.00
SSDA Dave Casper 20.00
SSMC Mark Clayton 25.00
SSDD Domanick Davis 20.00
SSLD Len Dawson 40.00
SSJE John Elway SP 200.00
SSBF Brett Favre 250.00
SSDF Dan Fouts 50.00
SSAG Ahman Green 50.00
SSBG Bob Griese 40.00
SSRG Rex Grossman 25.00
SSJG Jon Gruden 25.00
SSJA Jack Ham 40.00
SSPHO Paul Hornung SP 80.00
SSCJ Chad Johnson 20.00
SSJJ Jimmy Johnson 50.00
SSRJ Rudi Johnson 20.00
SSCH Charlie Joiner 20.00
SSHL Howie Long 40.00
SSPM Peyton Manning SP 120.00
SSMA Dan Marino SP 225.00
SSDM Donovan McNabb 80.00
SSJO Joe Montana SP 250.00
SSJN Joe Namath SP 125.00
SSAP Alan Page 30.00
SSBP Bill Parcells 50.00
SSDP Drew Pearson 30.00
SSCP Chad Pennington 40.00
SSBS Barry Sanders SP 200.00
SSKS Ken Stabler 50.00
SSRS Roger Staubach SP 100.00
SSFT Fran Tarkenton 60.00
SSJT Joe Theismann SP 60.00
SSLT LaDainian Tomlinson 50.00
SSMV Michael Vick SP 120.00
SSBW Brian Westbrook 30.00
SSRW Randy White 20.00
SSRO Roy Williams 40.00
SSKE Kellen Winslow Sr. 40.00

2004 UD Sweet Spot Sweet Panel Signatures

NM/M

Common Player: 25.00
Production 100 Sets
Gold: 1.5X
Gold Production 25 Sets
SPTA Tatum Bell 40.00
SPDD Domanick Davis 25.00
SPRO Roman Gabriel 40.00
SPPH Paul Hornung 60.00
SPRJ Rudi Johnson 25.00
SPKJ Kevin Jones 80.00
SPBL Byron Leftwich 40.00
SPHL Howie Long 60.00
SPJP J.P. Losman 60.00
SPEM Eli Manning 200.00
SPPM Peyton Manning 120.00
SPCP Chad Pennington 40.00
SPCHO Chris Perry 30.00
SPPR Philip Rivers 80.00
SPBR Ben Roethlisberger 300.00
SPBS Bart Starr/80 150.00
SPFT Fran Tarkenton 40.00
SPJT Joe Theismann 60.00
SPZT Zach Thomas 30.00
SPMV Michael Vick 100.00
SPKW Kellen Winslow Jr. 50.00

2004 UD Sweet Spot Sweet Swatches

NM/M

Common Player: 6.00
Inserted 1:12
SWTB Tatum Bell 10.00
SWMC Michael Clayton 12.00
SWCC Cedric Cobbs 6.00
SWKC Keary Colbert 8.00
SWDD Devard Darling 6.00
SWLE Lee Evans 12.00
SWLF Larry Fitzgerald 15.00
SWRG Robert Gallery 8.00
SWDH DeAngelo Hall 8.00
SWHA Derrick Hamilton 6.00
SWDE Devery Henderson 6.00
SWSJ Steven Jackson 15.00
SWMJ Michael Jenkins 6.00
SWGJ Greg Jones 8.00
SWJJ Julius Jones 20.00
SWKJ Kevin Jones SP 15.00
SWJP J.P. Losman 10.00
SWEM Eli Manning 30.00
SWLM Luke McCown 6.00
SWCP Chris Perry 8.00
SWPR Philip Rivers 15.00
SWBR Ben Roethlisberger 75.00
SWMS Matt Schaub 8.00
SWBT Ben Troupe 6.00
SWBW Ben Watson 6.00
SWDW Darius Watts 6.00
SWRW Reggie Williams SP 8.00
SWRO Roy Williams 15.00
SWKW Kellen Winslow Jr. 12.00
SWRA Rashaun Woods 8.00

1993 U.S. Playing Cards Ditka's Picks

The 56-card, standard-size set, with rounded corners, are actually playing cards. The fronts have a borderless action shot with each card having the same generic back. "Ditka's Picks," "NFL," and other logos appear on the backs.

NM/M

Complete Set (56): 5.00
Common Player: .05
1C Steve Young .30
1D Joe Montana .50
1H Dan Marino .50
1S Troy Aikman .50
2C Jim Lachey .05
2D Richmond Webb .05
2H Wilber Marshall .05
2S Ronnie Lott .10
3C Sean Gilbert .10
3D Clay Matthews .10
3H Jeff Lageman .05
3S Audray McMillian .05
4C Morten Andersen .05
4D Pete Stoyanovich .05
4H Rohn Stark .05
4S Sean Landeta .05
5C Broderick Thomas .05
5D James Francis .05
5H Derrick Thomas .20
5S Tony Bennett .05
6C Seth Joyner .10
6D Percy Snow .05
6H Junior Seau .20
6S Chris Spielman .10
7C Pierce Holt .05
7D Rod Woodson .20
7H Ray Childress .10
7S Deion Sanders .40
8C Jay Novacek .20
8D Eric Green .05
8H Marv Cook .05
8S Brent Jones .10
9C Randall McDaniel .05
9D Mike Munchak .05
9H Bruce Matthews .05
9S Mark Stepnoski .05
10C Harris Barton .05
10D Steve Atwater .05
10H Henry Jones .05
10S Chuck Cecil .05
11C Sterling Sharpe .20
11D Anthony Miller .10
11H Haywood Jeffires .10
11S Jerry Rice .50
12C Reggie White .20
12D Howie Long .10
12H Cortez Kennedy .10
12S Chris Doleman .10
13C Emmitt Smith .05
13D Thurman Thomas .20
13H Barry Foster .10
13S Barry Sanders 1.00
WILD Tom Waddle .05
WILD Steve Wisniewski .05
NNO Ditka's AFC Picks .10
NNO Ditka's NFC Picks .10

1994 U.S. Playing Cards Ditka's Picks

The U.S. Playing Card Co. released a 56-card deck of playing cards, featuring a cast of NFL stars, as well as rookies expected to shine in the 1994 season. Each card in the four-color deck contains an action shot of the player with the denomination in the upper left and lower right hand corners.

NM/M

Complete Set (56): 5.00
Common Player: .05
1C Sterling Sharpe .20
1D Rickey Jackson .05
1H Emmitt Smith 1.00
1S Rod Woodson .20
2C Marcus Robertson .05
2D Rohn Stark .05
2H Dave Cadigan .05
2S Kevin Williams .20
3C John Kasay .05
3D Carlton Haselrig .05
3H Donnell Woolford .05
3S Dan Wilkinson .20
4C Marshall Faulk 1.00
4D Greg Montgomery .05
4H Leslie O'Neal .10
4S Eric Curry .10
5C Eric Turner .10
5D Rick Mirer .25
5H Kevin Smith .10
5S Troy Vincent .10
6C Cornelius Bennett .10
6D Seth Joyner .10
6H Gary Zimmerman .05
6S LeRoy Butler .05
7C Tommy Vardell .05
7D Richmond Webb .05
7H Ben Coates .20
7S Steve Everitt .05
8C Tom Rathman .05
8D Ray Childress .05
8H Tim Brown .20
8S Mark Bavaro .05
9C Bennie Blades .05
9D John "Jumbo" Elliott .05
9H Jim Lachey .05
9S Neil Smith .20
10C Sean Gilbert .10
10D Steve Tasker .10
10H Chris Zorich .10
10S Haywood Jeffires .10
11C Troy Aikman .50
11D Jeff Hostetler .10
11H Junior Seau .20
11S Mark Stepnoski .05
12C Chris Spielman .10
12D Marcus Allen .20
12H Reggie White .20
12S Harris Barton .05
13C Andre Rison .20
13D Randall McDaniel .05
13H Cortez Kennedy .10
13S Norm Johnson .05
WILD Heath Shuler .60
WILD Shannon Sharpe .10
NNO Ditka's AFC Picks .10
NNO Ditka's NFC Picks .10

1995 U.S. Playing Cards Ditka's Picks

The 56-card, standard-size set, with rounded edges, is similar in design to the 1994 set, with color photos on the card fronts and a generic card back.

NM/M

Complete Set (56): 5.00
Common Player: .05
1C Randall McDaniel .05
1D Dan Marino 1.00
1H Drew Bledsoe .40
1S Steve Young .50
2C Renaldo Turnbull .05
2D Tony Boselli .10
2H Ki-Jana Carter .20
2S Todd Sauerbrun .05
3C Aeneas Williams .05
3D Bruce Smith .20
3H Shawn Jefferson .10
3S Andy Harmon .05
4C Donnell Woolford .05
4D Ronnie Lott .20
4H Tim Brown .20
4S Charles Haley .10
5C Merton Hanks .05
5D Eric Turner .10
5H Ben Coates .20
5S Brian Williams .05
6C Eric Metcalf .20
6D Dave Meggett .10
6H Neil Smith .10
6S Ian Beckles .05
7C Herman Moore .20
7D Mel Gray .05
7H Ray Childress .05
7S Jim Lachey .05
8C Bennie Blades .05
8D Kevin Greene .10
8H Gary Zimmerman .05
8S Willie Roaf .10
9C Bryant Young .10
9D Bruce Matthews .05
9H Richmond Webb .05
9S Howard Cross .05
10C Seth Joyner .05
10D Marshall Faulk .50
10H Jeff Dellenbach .05
10S Cris Carter .20
11C Sean Gilbert .10
11D John Carney .05
11H Rohn Stark .05
11S Jerry Rice .50
12C Reggie White .20
12D Terry McDaniel .05
12H Rod Woodson .20
12S Daryl Johnston .10
13C Norm Johnson .05
13D Cortez Kennedy .10
13H Cornelius Bennett .10
13S Barry Sanders 1.00
WILD Junior Seau .20
WILD Chris Spielman .10
NNO Ditka's NFC Picks .10
NNO Ditka's AFC Picks .10

1967-68 Vikings

The 29-card, 8" x 10" set features black-and-white photos with blank backs.

NM/M

Complete Set (29): 120.00
Common Player: 4.00
1 Grady Alderman (Tackle) 4.00
2 Grady Alderman (Offensive lineman) 4.00
3 John Beasley 4.00
4 Bob Berry 4.00
5 Larry Bowie 4.00
6 Gary Cuozzo 5.00
7 Doug Davis 4.00
8 Paul Dickinson 4.00
9 Paul Flatley 5.00
10 Bob Grim 5.00
11 Dale Hackbart 4.00
12 Don Hansen 4.00
13 Jim Hargrove 4.00
14 Clint Jones 5.00
15 Jeff Jordan 4.00
16 Joe Kapp 8.00
17 John Kirby 4.00
18 Gary Larsen 5.00
19 Earsell Mackbee 4.00
20 Marlin McKeever 5.00
21 Milt Sunde 5.00
22 David Tobey 4.00
23 Ron Vanderkelen 5.00
24 Jim Vellone 4.00
25 Bobby Walden 4.00
26 Lonnie Warwick 4.00
27 Gene Washington (Wide receiver) 5.00
28 Gene Washington (End) 5.00
29 Roy Winston 5.00

1969 Vikings Team Issue

The 27-card, 5" x 6-7/8" set features black-and-white borderless player portraits with blank backs.

NM/M

Complete Set (27): 75.00
Common Player: 3.00
1 Bookie Bolin 3.00
2 Bobby Bryant 4.00
3 John Beasley 3.00
4 Gary Cuozzo 4.00
5 Doug Davis 3.00
6 Paul Dickson 3.00
7 Bob Grim 4.00
8 Dale Hackbart 3.00
9 Jim Hargrove 3.00
10 John Henderson 3.00
11 Wally Hilgenberg 4.00
12 Clinton Jones 4.00
13 Karl Kassulke 4.00
14 Kent Kramer 3.00
15 Gary Larsen 4.00
16 Bob Lee 3.00
17 Jim Lindsey 3.00
18 Earsell Mackbee 3.00
19 Mike McGill 3.00
20 Oscar Reed 3.00
21 Ed Sharockman 3.00
22 Steve Smith 3.00
23 Milt Sunde 3.00
24 Jim Vellone 3.00
25 Lonnie Warwick 3.00
26 Gene Washington 5.00
27 Charlie West 4.00

1971 Vikings Photos

The 52-card, 5" x 7-7/16" set consists of color close-up shots with blank backs. The player's name, position, and team name appear on the bottom border.

NM/M

Complete Set (52): 125.00
Common Player: 2.00
1 Grady Alderman 2.00
2 Neil Armstrong (CO) 2.00
3 John Beasley 2.00
4 Bill Brown 4.00
5 Bob Brown 2.00
6 Bobby Bryant 3.00
7 Jerry Burns (CO) 3.00

8 Fred Cox 3.00
9 Gary Cuozzo 3.00
10 Doug Davis 2.00
11 Al Denson 2.00
12 Paul Dickson 2.00
13 Carl Eller 10.00
14 Bud Grant (CO) 12.00
15 Bob Grim 3.00
16 Leo Hayden 2.00
17 John Henderson 2.00
18 Wally Hilgenberg 3.00
19 Noel Jenke 2.00
20 Clint Jones 3.00
21 Karl Kassulke 3.00
22 Paul Krause 5.00
23 Gary Larsen 2.00
24 Bob Lee 2.00
25 Jim Lindsey 2.00
26 Jim Marshall 10.00
27 Bus Mertes (CO) 2.00
28 John Michels (CO) 2.00
29 Jocko Nelson (CO) 2.00
30 Dave Osborn 4.00
31 Alan Page 12.00
32 Jack Patera (CO) 3.00
33 Jerry Patton 2.00
34 Pete Perreault 2.00
35 Oscar Reed 2.00
36 Ed Sharockman 2.00
37 Norm Snead 6.00
38 Milt Sunde 3.00
39 Doug Sutherland 2.00
40 Mick Tingelhoff 4.00
41 Stu Voigt 4.00
42 John Ward 2.00
43 Lonnie Warwick 2.00
44 Gene Washington 6.00
45 Charlie West 2.00
46 Ed White 4.00
47 Carl Winfrey 2.00
48 Roy Winston 3.00
49 Jeff Wright 2.00
50 Nate Wright 2.00
51 Ron Yary 4.00
52 Godfrey Zaunbrecher 2.00

1971 Vikings Postcards

The 19-card, 5" x 7-7/16" set features color posed close-ups with the backs containing a typical postcard layout. Bio information appears in the upper left corner of the horizontal backs. The set was issued during the season.

NM/M
Complete Set (19): 45.00
Common Player: 2.00
1 Grady Alderman 2.00
2 Neil Armstrong (CO) 2.00
3 John Beasley 2.00
4 Paul Dickson 2.00
5 Bud Grant (CO) 12.00
6 Wally Hilgenburg 2.00
7 Noel Jenke 2.00
8 Paul Krause 5.00
9 Gary Larsen 2.00
10 Dave Osborn 4.00
11 Alan Page 12.00
12 Jerry Patton 2.00
13 Doug Sutherland 2.50
14 Mick Tingelhoff 4.00
15 Lonnie Warwick 2.00
16 Charlie West 2.00
17 Jeff Wright 2.00
18 Nate Wright 2.00
19 Godfrey Zaunbrecher 2.00

1978 Vikings Country Kitchen

The seven-card, 5" x 7" set features a black-and-white player headshot with bio and stat information on the backs. The card fronts have a white border with the player's name and "Minnesota Vikings" printed.

NM/M
Complete Set (7): 35.00
Common Player: 4.00
1 Bobby Bryant 4.00
2 Tommy Kramer 6.00
3 Paul Krause 6.00
4 Ahmad Rashad 12.00
5 Jeff Siemon 4.00
6 Mick Tingelhoff 5.00
7 Sammie White 6.00

1983 Vikings Police

The 17-card, 2-5/8" x 4-1/8" set was sponsored by Green Giant, Burger King, Pillsbury and Minnesota Crime Prevention Officers Association. The fronts contain an action photo with the back including bio and stat information.

NM/M
Complete Set (17): 10.00
Common Player: .50
1 Checklist Card .75
2 Tommy Kramer 1.00
3 Ted Brown .50
4 Joe Senser .50
5 Sammie White 1.00
6 Doug Martin .50
7 Matt Blair 1.00
8 Bud Grant (CO) 2.00
9 Scott Studwell .75
10 Greg Coleman .50
11 John Turner .50

NM/M
12 Jim Hough .50
13 Joey Browner 1.00
14 Dennis Swilley .50
15 Darrin Nelson .75
16 Mark Mullaney .50
17 Fran Tarkenton (All-Time Great) 3.00

1984 Vikings Police

The 18-card, 2-5/8" x 4-1/8" set, sponsored by Pillsbury, Burger King, the Minnesota Crime Prevention Officers Association and Green Giant, features an action shot on the card front with a crime prevention tip on the back.

NM/M
Complete Set (18): 8.00
Common Player: .40
1 Checklist Card .50
2 Keith Nord .40
3 Joe Senser .40
4 Tommy Kramer 1.25
5 Darrin Nelson .50
6 Tim Irwin .40
7 Mark Mullaney .40
8 Les Steckel (CO) .40
9 Greg Coleman .40
10 Tommy Hannon .40
11 Curtis Rouse .40
12 Scott Studwell .50
13 Steve Jordan 1.00
14 Willie Teal .40
15 Ted Brown .40
16 Sammie White 1.00
17 Matt Blair .40
18 Jim Marshall (All-Time Great) 2.50

1985 Vikings Police

The 16-card, 2-5/8" x 4-1/8" set was sponsored by Frito- Lay, Pepsi-Cola, KS95-FM and local law enforcement. The cards are similar in design to previous Police sets, with crime prevention tips on the backs.

NM/M
Complete Set (16): 8.00
Common Player: .40
1 Checklist Card .50
2 Bud Grant (CO) 1.50
3 Matt Blair .50
4 Alfred Anderson .50
5 Fred McNeill .40
6 Tommy Kramer .75
7 Jan Stenerud 1.25
8 Sammie White .75
9 Doug Martin .40
10 Greg Coleman .40
11 Steve Riley .40
12 Walker Lee Ashley .40
13 Tim Irwin .40
14 Scott Studwell .50
15 Darrin Nelson .50
16 Mick Tingelhoff (All-Time Great) .75

1986 Vikings Police

The 14-card, 2-5/8" x 4-1/8" set is similar to Police sets from previous years with a "Crime Prevention Tip" on the card back.

NM/M
Complete Set (14): 8.00
Common Player: .40
1 Jerry Burns (CO) (Checklist back) .50
2 Darrin Nelson .50
3 Tommy Kramer .75
4 Anthony Carter 1.50
5 Scott Studwell .50
6 Chris Doleman 1.50
7 Joey Browner .75
8 Steve Jordan .50
9 David Howard .40
10 Tim Newton .40
11 Leo Lewis .40
12 Keith Millard 1.00
13 Doug Martin .40
14 Bill Brown (All-Time Great) .75

1987 Vikings Police

The 14-card, 2-5/8" x 4-1/8" set features a color action shot on the front with a "Crime Prevention Tip" on the back. Card No. 1, Purple Power '87, is a Vikings montage by artist Cliff Spohn. Over 2 million sets were distributed over a 14-week period by the Vikings, Campbell's Soup, Frito-Lay, KSTP-FM and the Minnesota Crime Prevention Association.

NM/M
Complete Set (14): 8.00
Common Player: .40
1 Purple Power '87 (checklist back) .50
2 Jerry Burns (CO) .50
3 Scott Studwell .50
4 Tommy Kramer .75
5 Gerald Robinson .40
6 Wade Wilson 1.75
7 Anthony Carter 1.00
8 Terry Tausch .40
9 Leo Lewis .40
10 Keith Millard .75
11 Carl Lee .50
12 Steve Jordan .50
13 D.J. Dozier .75
14 Alan Page (ATG) 1.75

1988 Vikings Police

The 12-card, 2-5/8" x 4-1/8" set featured nine current players, one offense card, one defense card and one all-time great card (Paul Krause). The cards are similar in design to previous Police issues.

NM/M
Complete Set (12): 5.00
Common Player: .40
1 Vikings Offense (Checklist on back) .50
2 Jesse Solomon .50
3 Kirk Lowdermilk .40
4 Darrin Nelson .50
5 Chris Doleman 1.00
6 D.J. Dozier .50
7 Gary Zimmerman .75
8 Allen Rice .40
9 Joey Browner .75
10 Anthony Carter 1.00
11 Vikings Defense .50
12 Paul Krause (All-Time Great) 1.00

1989 Vikings Police

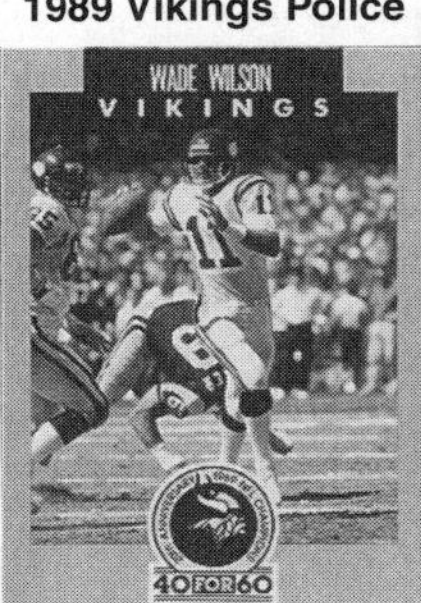

The 10-card, standard-size set features color photos on the gray-border fronts. The card backs are horizontal and contain safety tips, bio information and career highlights. Production was limited to 175,000 for each card.

NM/M
Complete Set (10): 5.00
Common Player: .50
1 Team Card (schedule on back) .75
2 Henry Thomas 1.00
3 Rick Fenney .50
4 Chuck Nelson .50
5 Jim Gustafson .50
6 Wade Wilson 1.00
7 Randall McDaniel .75
8 Jesse Solomon .50
9 Anthony Carter 1.00
10 Joe Kapp (All-Time Great) 1.00

1989 Vikings Taystee Discs

The 12-disc, 2-3/4" in diameter set, features Minnesota players in closeups on the fronts with bio and stat information on the backs. Each disc was issued with a Taystee product in the Minnesota area.

NM/M
Complete Set (12): 5.00
Common Player: .50
1 Anthony Carter 1.00
2 Chris Doleman 1.00
3 Joey Browner .75
4 Steve Jordan .75
5 Scott Studwell .50
6 Wade Wilson 1.00
7 Kirk Lowdermilk .50
8 Tommy Kramer .75
9 Keith Millard .75
10 Rick Fenney .50
11 Gary Zimmerman .50
12 Darrin Nelson .75

A card number in parenthese ( ) indicates the set is unnumbered.

1990 Vikings Police

The 10-card, standard-size set was sponsored by Gatorade, WCCO Radio and local law enforcement and contained a crime prevention tip on the card backs.

NM/M
Complete Set (10): 5.00
Common Player: .50
1 Raymond Berry .50
2 Anthony Carter 1.00
3 Chris Doleman .75
4 Rick Fenney .50
5 Hassan Jones .75
6 Carl Lee .50
7 Mike Merriweather .50
8 Scott Studwell .50
9 Herschel Walker 1.50
10 Wade Wilson 1.00

1991 Vikings Police

The 10-card, standard-size set was sponsored by KFAN Radio, Gatorade, K102 Radio and Super Bowl XXVI. The cards were distributed on a weekly basis by area police departments in the order listed below.

NM/M
Complete Set (10): 5.00
Common Player: .40
1 Rick Fenney .40
2 Wade Wilson .75
3 Mike Merriweather .40
4 Hassan Jones .40
5 Rich Gannon 1.00
6 Mark Dusbabek .40
7 Sean Salisbury .75
8 Reggie Rutland .40
9 Tim Irwin .40
10 Chris Doleman .75

1992 Vikings Gatorade

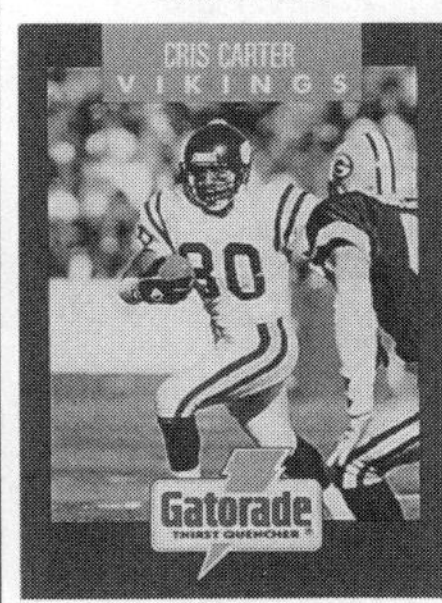

Gatorade and the Minnesota Vikings teamed up to produce this 10-card team set.

NM/M
Complete Set (10): 8.00
Common Player: .50
1 Dennis Green .75
2 John Randle .75
3 Todd Scott .50
4 Anthony Carter .50
5 Steve Jordan .50
6 Terry Allen 2.00
7 Brian Habib .50
8 Fuad Reveiz .50
9 Roger Craig 1.00
10 Cris Carter 2.00

1992 Vikings Police

The 10-card, standard-size set was sponsored by Gatorade, KFAN Radio, K102 Radio and local law enforcement. The card fronts have a color action shot framed by a purple border with the Gatorade logo centered on the card front bottom edge. The card backs have a black and white headshot and other sponsor logos.

NM/M
Complete Set (10): 5.00
Common Player: .40
1 Dennis Green (CO) (Schedule on back) .75
2 John Randle .75
3 Todd Scott .40
4 Anthony Carter 1.00
5 Steve Jordan .40
6 Terry Allen 2.00
7 Brian Habib .40
8 Fuad Reveiz .40
9 Roger Craig 1.00
10 Cris Carter 1.50

1993 Vikings Police

The 10-card, standard-size set is similar in design to the 1992 Police set, complete with the Gatorade logo on the card fronts and a black and white headshot on the horizontal card back.

NM/M
Complete Set (10): 5.00
Common Player: .40
1 Dennis Green (CO) (CL/Schedule on back) .60
2 Henry Thomas .60
3 Todd Scott .40
4 Jack Del Rio .60
5 Vencie Glenn .40
6 Fuad Reveiz .40
7 Cris Carter 1.25
8 Terry Allen 1.50
9 Roger Craig .60
10 Carlos Jenkins .40

1995 Vikings Police

The 10-card, standard-size set features a purple border on the card front with the Gatorade logo appearing in the left lower corner. The Vikings 35th anniversary logo is printed in the lower right corner of the card front, with the player's name and "Vikings" appearing centered along the top edge in a gray box. The card backs feature a black and white headshot with brief bio information.

NM/M
Complete Set (10): 5.00
Common Player: .40
1 Warren Moon (CL/Schedule on the back) 1.00
2 Randall McDaniel .40
3 Jake Reed .75
4 Jack Del Rio .60
5 Cris Carter .75
6 Fuad Reveiz .40
7 Amp Lee .40
8 John Randle .60
9 Andrew Jordan .40
10 DeWayne Washington .60

1997 Vikings Police

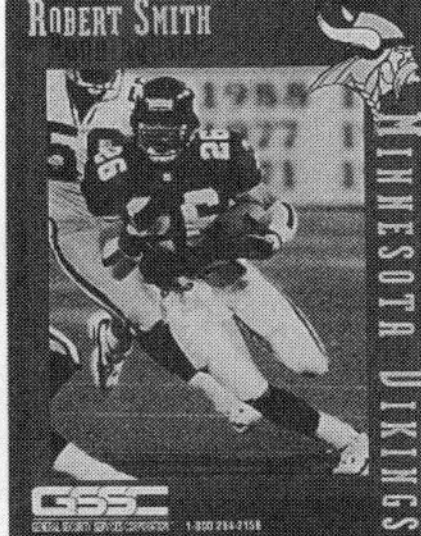

The Minnesota Vikings were featured in this eight-card set, which was bordered in purple, with the Vikings logo in the upper right and the words "Minnesota Vikings" printed down the right side. Fronts also feature a color shot of the player with a General Security Services Corp. logo and a toll free number in the bottom left corner. Card backs feature a head shot of the player, stats and Vikadontis Rex and McGruff the Crime Dog logos along with The Minnesota Crime Prevention Association logo. Card No. 1 features a set checklist and 1997 team schedule.

NM/M
Complete Set (8): 5.00
Common Player: .40
1 Cris Carter, Jake Reed 1.00
2 Robert Smith 1.00
3 Jeff Brady .40
4 Brad Johnson 1.50
5 Robert Griffith .40
6 Randall McDaniel .40
7 Leroy Hoard .40
8 John Randle .50

1998 Vikings Police

NM/M
Complete Set (8): 4.00
Common Player: .50
Cris Carter 1.00
Stalin Colinet .50
Randall Cunningham 1.00
Brad Johnson .50
John Randle .50
Dwayne Ruud .50
Robert Smith .50
Todd Steussie .50

1999 Vikings Police

NM/M
Complete Set (8): 6.00
Common Player: .50
Gary Anderson .50
Cris Carter 1.00
Jeff Christy .50
Randall Cunningham 1.00
Robert Griffith .50
Randy Moss 3.00
John Randle .50
Robert Smith .50

2000 Vikings Police

NM/M
Complete Set (8): 8.00
Common Player: .50
Mitch Berger .50
Cris Carter 1.00
Daunte Culpepper 2.00
Ed McDaniel .50
Randy Moss 3.00
John Randle .50
Dwayne Ruud .50
Robert Smith .50

2001 Vikings Police

NM/M
Complete Set (9): 10.00
Common Player: .50
Michael Bennett 4.00
Mitch Berger .50
Matt Birk .50
Cris Carter 1.00
Daunte Culpepper 2.00
Robert Griffith .50
Randy Moss 3.00
Jake Reed .50
Kailee Wong .50

2002 Vikings Police

NM/M
Complete Set (8): 8.00
Common Player: .50
Michael Bennett 2.00
Matt Birk .50
Byron Chamberlain .50
Daunte Culpepper 2.00
Chris Hovan .50
Jim Kleinsasser .50
Randy Moss 3.00
Mike Tice .50

1986 Waddingtons Game

Produced in England, this NFL card game consists of 40 cards measuring 3-1/2" x 5-11/16". The card fronts feature color illustrations of NFL teams. Five different teams are portrayed on seven cards each. The other five cards in the set are interception cards, which have the NFL logo on the front. The backs of all the cards feature the NFL logo.

NM/M
Complete Set (40): 60.00
Common Player: .50
1 Walter Payton Bears 10 3.00
2 Walter Payton Bears 20 3.00
3 Walter Payton Bears 40 3.00
4 Walter Payton Bears 50 3.00
5 Walter Payton Bears First Down 3.00
6 Walter Payton Bears Punt 3.00
7 Walter Payton Bears Touchdown 3.00
8 Danny White, Tony Dorsett Cowboys 10 1.00
9 Danny White, Tony Dorsett Cowboys 20 1.00
10 Danny White, Tony Dorsett Cowboys 40 1.00
11 Danny White, Tony Dorsett Cowboys 50 1.00
12 Danny White, Tony Dorsett Cowboys First Down 1.00
13 Danny White, Tony Dorsett Cowboys Punt 1.00
14 Danny White, Tony Dorsett Cowboys Touchdown 1.00
15 Lorenzo Hampton, Eric Laakso Dolphins 10 .50
16 Lorenzo Hampton, Eric Laakso Dolphins 20 .50
17 Lorenzo Hampton, Eric Laakso Dolphins 40 .50
18 Lorenzo Hampton, Eric Laakso Dolphins 50 .50
19 Lorenzo Hampton, Eric Laakso Dolphins First Down .50
20 Lorenzo Hampton, Eric Laakso Dolphins Punt .50
21 Lorenzo Hampton, Eric Laakso Dolphins Touchdown .50
22 John Riggins, Joe Theismann Redskins 10 1.00
23 John Riggins, Joe Theismann Redskins 20 1.00
24 John Riggins, Joe Theismann Redskins 40 1.00

25 John Riggins, Joe Theismann Redskins 50 1.00
26 John Riggins, Joe Theismann Redskins First Down 1.00
27 John Riggins, Joe Theismann Redskins Punt 1.00
28 John Riggins, Joe Theismann Redskins Touchdown 1.00
29 Terry Bradshaw, Lynn Swann Steelers 10 2.00
30 Terry Bradshaw, Lynn Swann Steelers 20 2.00
31 Terry Bradshaw, Lynn Swann Steelers 40 2.00
32 Terry Bradshaw, Lynn Swann Steelers 50 2.00
33 Terry Bradshaw, Lynn Swann Steelers First Down 2.00
34 Terry Bradshaw, Lynn Swann Steelers Punt 2.00
35 Terry Bradshaw, Lynn Swann Steelers Touchdown 2.00
36 Interception Card .50
37 Interception Card .50
38 Interception Card .50
39 Interception Card .50
40 Interception Card .50

1988 Wagon Wheel

The eight-card, 6-5/16" x 4-5/16" set was issued in the United Kingdom by Burtons and each card was included in boxes of Chocolate Biscuits. Players are not specifically identified as the purpose of the set was to explain American football to the British by giving examples of positions.

NM/M
Complete Set (8): 60.00
Common Player: 6.00
1 Defensive Back (Todd Bowles covering Mark Bavaro) 6.00
2 Ed "Too Tall" Jones, Neil Lomax Defensive Lineman 8.00
3 Kevin Butler Kicker 6.00
4 Bob Brudzinski Linebacker 6.00
5 Offensive Lineman (Keith Van Horne leading Walter Payton) 15.00
6 John Elway Quarterback 20.00
7 Receiver (Steve Largent between Vann McElroy and Mike Haynes) 10.00
8 Running Back (Rodney Carter of the Steelers) 6.00

1964 Wheaties Stamps

These unnumbered stamps, which measure 2-1/2" x 2-3/4", were created to be stored in an accompanying stamp album titled "Pro Bowl Football Player Stamp Album." Each stamp has a color photo of the player, plus his facsimile signature, bordered by a white frame. The stamps were in panels of 12 inside the album and were perforated so they could be put on the corresponding spot within the album. Two stickers were attached to the inside front cover. Four team logo stamps and 70 players are represented on the stamps, but there were no spots in the album for the logo stamps or those for Y.A. Tittle or Joe Schmidt.

NM/M
Complete Set (74): 250.00
Common Player: 2.00
(1) Herb Adderley 6.00
(2) Grady Alderman 2.00
(3) Doug Atkins 4.00
(4) Sam Baker 2.00
(5) Erich Barnes 2.00
(6) Terry Barr 2.00
(7) Dick Bass 2.00
(8) Maxie Baughan 3.00
(9) Raymond Berry 6.00
(10) Charley Bradshaw 2.50
(11) Jim Brown 35.00
(12) Roger Brown 2.50
(13) Timmy Brown 3.00
(14) Gail Cogdill 2.00
(15) Tommy Davis 2.00
(16) Willie Davis 6.00
(17) Bob DeMarco 2.00
(18) Darrell Dess 2.00
(19) Buddy Dial 3.00
(20) Mike Ditka 18.00
(21) Galen Fiss 2.00
(22) Lee Folkins 2.00
(23) Joe Fortunato 2.00
(24) Bill Glass 3.00
(25) John Gordy 2.00
(26) Ken Gray 2.50
(27) Forrest Gregg 5.00
(28) Rip Hawkins 2.00
(29) Charlie Johnson 3.00
(30) John Henry Johnson 5.00
(31) Henry Jordan 3.00
(32) Jim Katcavage 2.00
(33) Jerry Kramer 5.00
(34) Joe Krupa 2.00
(35) John LoVetere 2.00
(36) Dick Lynch 3.00
(37) Gino Marchetti 5.00
(38) Joe Marconi 2.00
(39) Tommy Mason 3.00
(40) Dale Meinert 2.00
(41) Lou Michaels 2.00
(42) Minnesota Vikings Emblem 3.00
(43) Bobby Mitchell 6.00
(44) John Morrow 2.00
(45) New York Giants Emblem 3.00
(46) Merlin Olsen 10.00
(47) Jack Pardee 4.00
(48) Jim Parker 4.00
(49) Bernie Parrish 2.00
(50) Don Perkins 3.00
(51) Richie Petitbon 2.00
(52) Vince Promuto 2.00
(53) Myron Pottios 2.00
(54) Mike Pyle 2.00
(55) Pete Retzlaff 3.00
(56) Jim Ringo 5.00
(57) Joe Rutgens 2.00
(58) St. Louis Cardinals Emblem 3.00
(59) San Francisco 49ers Emblem 3.00
(60) Dick Schafrath 2.00
(61) Joe Schmidt 6.00
(62) Del Shofner 3.00
(63) Norm Snead 3.00
(64) Bart Starr 15.00
(65) Jim Taylor 6.00
(66) Roosevelt Taylor 2.00
(67) Clendon Thomas 2.00
(68) Y.A. Tittle 12.50
(69) John Unitas 18.00
(70) Bill Wade 3.00
(71) Wayne Walker 2.00
(72) Jesse Whittenton 2.00
(73) Larry Wilson 5.00
(74) Abe Woodson 2.00
--- Album 25.00

1987 Wheaties

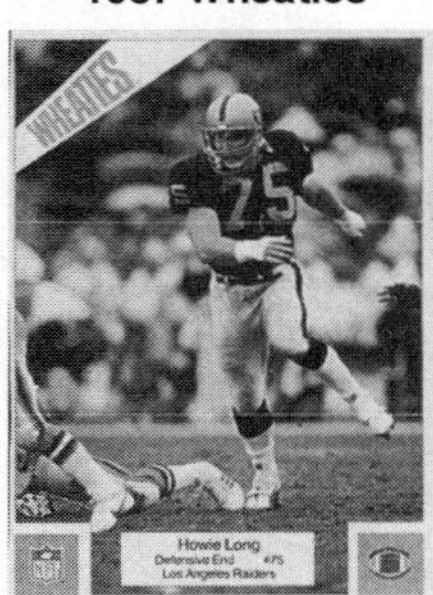

Specially-marked boxes of Wheaties cereal each contained one of these 5" x 7" posters. The posters, which were wrapped in cellophane, were produced by Starline Inc. with the cooperation of the NFLPA and organizational efforts of Michael Schechter Associates. Each front has a color action photo, with the player's name, team, position and uniform number listed in a white box at the bottom. "Wheaties" is written in a banner in the upper left corner. The poster back is numbered and includes biographical information and career summary notes. Bernie Kosar's card was not listed in the set on the checklist Wheaties provided on the box. It is assumed Kosar was pulled from the set at some point - his card is listed as a short print.

NM/M
Complete Set (26): 130.00
Common Player: 2.50
1 Tony Dorsett 5.00
2 Herschel Walker 5.00
3 Marcus Allen 5.00
4 Eric Dickerson 6.00
5 Walter Payton 12.00
6 Phil Simms 4.00
7 Tommy Kramer 2.50
8 Joe Morris 2.50
9 Roger Craig 4.00
10 Curt Warner 3.50
11 Andre Tippett 2.50
12 Joe Montana 20.00
13 Jim McMahon 3.00
14 Bernie Kosar 25.00
15 Jay Schroeder 2.50
16 Al Toon 2.50
17 Mark Gastineau 2.50
18 Kenny Easley 2.50
19 Howie Long 2.50
20 Dan Marino 15.00
21 Karl Mecklenburg 3.25
22 John Elway 10.00
23 Boomer Esiason 5.00
24 Dan Fouts 4.00
25 Jim Kelly 10.00
26 Louis Lipps 3.00

1991 Wild Card National Promos

This three-card set was given away as a promo at the 12th Annual National Covention in Anaheim. The cards are numbered on the back, starting with the Dan McGwire card as "Prototype-2". Striped versions of the cards with a hologram in the upper left corner were also issued.

NM/M
Complete Set (3): 12.00
Common Player: 2.50
2 Dan McGwire 6.00
3 Randal Hill 2.50
4 Todd Marinovich 6.00

1991 Wild Card College Draft Picks

Each of these cards features a glossy color action photo of a player in his college uniform. The card is black with an orange frame, which has different denominations running on top and down the right side. A circle with "1st Edition" appears in the lower left corner. The purple back has statistics, biographical information and a color photo. Striped, limited-edition Wild Card random inserts of each card were also produced (1 out of every 100 is wild). These cards had denominations of 5, 10, 20, 50, 100 and 1,000; the higher numbers were made in scarcer numbers. The finder was able to redeem the card for a like amount of the player's regular card.

NM/M
Complete Set (160): 15.00
Common Player: .05
1 Todd Lyght Wild Card 1 .60
2 Kelvin Pritchett .20
3 Robert Young .05
4 Reggie Johnson .05
5 Eric Turner .50
6 Pat Tyrance .10
7 Curvin Richards .20
8 Calvin Stephens .10
9 Corey Miller .10
10 Michael Jackson .30
11 Simmie Carter .05
12 Roland Smith .10
13 Pat O'Hara .20
14 Scott Conover .05
15 Russell Maryland Wild Card 2 .75
16 Greg Amsier .10
17 Moe Gardner .30
18 Howard Griffith .20
19 David Daniels .10
20 Henry Jones .10
21 Don Davey .10
22 Raghib (Rocket) Ismail Wild Card 3 1.00
23 Richie Andrews .05
24 Shawn Moore .25
25 Anthony Moss .10
26 Vince Moore .05
27 Leroy Thompson .15
28 Darrick Brownlow .20
29 Mel Agee .10
30 Darryll Lewis .25
31 Hyland Hickson .05
32 Leonard Russell 1.00
33 Floyd Fields .05
34 Esera Tuaolo .15
35 Todd Marinovich 1.25
36 Gary Wellman .10
37 Ricky Ervins 2.50
38 Pat Harlow .20
39 Mo Lewis .25
40 John Kasay .30
41 Phil Hansen .10
42 Kevin Donnalley .10
43 Dexter Davis .10
44 Vance Hammond .05
45 Chris Gardocki .10
46 Bruce Pickens .20
47 Godfrey Myles .15
48 Ernie Mills .25
49 Derek Russell .35
50 Chris Zorich .50
51 Alfred Williams .25
52 Jon Vaughn .45
53 Adrian Cooper .25
54 Eric Bieniemy .05
55 Robert Bailey .05
56 Ricky Watters .25
57 Mark Vander Poel .10
58 James Joseph .50
59 Darren Lewis .45
60 Wesley Carroll .40
61 Dave Key .10
62 Mike Pritchard .75
63 Craig Erickson .40
64 Browning Nagle .75
65 Mike Dumas .20
66 Andre Jones .05
67 Herman Moore .75
68 Greg Lewis .60
69 James Goode .05
70 Stan Thomas .10
71 Jerome Henderson .10
72 Doug Thomas .10
73 Tony Covington .10
74 Charles Mincy .10
75 Kanavis McGhee .20
76 Tom Backes .05
77 Fernandus Vinson .05
78 Marcus Robertson .05
79 Eric Harmon .05
80 Rob Selby .10
81 Ed King .20
82 William Thomas .10
83 Mike Jones .10
84 Paul Justin .20
85 Robert Wilson .20
86 Jesse Campbell .10
87 Hayward Haynes .05
88 Mike Croel .75
89 Jeff Graham .20
90 Vinnie Clark .25
91 Keith Cash .20
92 Tim Ryan .10
93 Jarrod Bunch .20
94 Stanley Richard .30
95 Alvin Harper .60
96 Bob Dahl .10
97 Mark Gunn .05
98 Frank Blevins .05
99 Harvey Williams 1.00
100 Dixon Edwards .20
101 Blake Miller .05
102 Bobby Wilson .25
103 Chuck Webb .25
104 Randal Hill .75
105 Shane Curry .05
106 Barry Sanders .75
107 Richard Fain .15
108 Joe Garten .05
109 Dean Dingham .05
110 Mark Tucker .05
111 Dan McGwire 1.00
112 Paul Glonek .05
113 Tom Dohring .05
114 Joe Sims .05
115 Bryan Cox .30
116 Bobby Olive .05
117 Blaise Bryant .15
118 Charles Johnson .15
119 Brett Favre 2.00
120 Luis Cristobal .05
121 Don Gibson .05
122 Scott Ross .05
123 Huey Richardson .15
124 Chris Smith .10
125 Duane Young .05
126 Eric Swann .30
127 Jeff Fite .05
128 Eugene Williams .05
129 Harlan Davis .05
130 James Bradley .05
131 Rob Carpenter .20
132 Dennis Ransom .05
133 Mike Arthur .05
134 Chuck Weatherspoon .30
135 Darrell Malone .05
136 George Thornton .10
137 Lamar McGriggs .05
138 Alex Johnson .05
139 Eric Moten .10
140 Joe Valerio .10
141 Jake Reed .20
142 Ernie Thompson .10
143 Roland Poles .05
144 Randy Bethel .05
145 Terry Bagsby .05
146 Tim James .05
147 Kenny Walker .60
148 Nolan Harrison .05
149 Keith Traylor .20
150 Nick Subis .05
151 Scott Zolak .25
152 Pio Sagapolutele .15
153 James Jones .10
154 Mike Sullivan .05
155 Joe Johnson .05
156 Todd Scott .10
157 Checklist 1 .05
158 Checklist 2 .05
159 Checklist 3 .05
160 Checklist 4 .05

1991 Wild Card NFL Prototypes

The six-card set promoted Wild Card's upcoming 1991 NFL set. The card fronts showcase an action photo bordered in black with different colored numbers around the top and right border. The Wild Card logo is in the upper left, with "NFL Premier Edition" printed inside a football in the lower left. The player's name and position are in the lower right. The card backs, numbered by a prefix of "prototype," have a photo of the player, his name, position and bio at the top. The player's stats are included inside a box at the bottom.

NM/M
Complete Set (6): 40.00
Common Player: 5.00
1 Troy Aikman 9.00
2 Barry Sanders 10.00
3 Thurman Thomas 9.00
4 Emmitt Smith 12.50
5 Jerry Rice 7.50
6 Lawrence Taylor 5.00

1991 Wild Card NFL

These cards, similar in design to Wild Cards' collegiate draft picks set, have a full-color glossy action photo on the front, with a black and yellow border. Multi-color numbers appear in the upper right corner and along the right side of the card. The player's name and position are in the lower right corner, opposite a football with the words "NFL Premier Edition" inside. The card back has a mug shot, statisitics, a card number and biographical information. Striped "Wild Cards," printed in limited editions, were also created for each card, in denominations of 10, 20, 50, 100 and 1,000. The card could be redeemed for a similar amount of the player's regular card, according to the denomination number in the stripe. A surprise Wild Card, #126, was also created; finders could redeem it for a 10-card NFL Experience subset which featured players from the Buffalo Bills and Washington Redskins. Also created were three bonus cards, which enabled finders to redeem them for the item pictured - either a case of cards, a box of cards, or a Wild Card cap.

NM/M
Complete Set (160): 10.00
Common Player: .03
Wax Box: 6.00
1 Jeff George .35
2 Sean Jones .03
3 Duane Bickett .03
4 John Elway .15
5 Christian Okoye .08
6 Steve Atwater .06
7 Anthony Munoz .08
8 Dave Krieg .08
9 Nick Lowery .06
10 Albert Bentley .06
11 Mark Jackson .06
12 Jeff Bryant .03
13 Johnny Hector .03
14 John L. Williams .08
15 Jim Everett .15
16 Mark Duper .06
17 Drew Hill .08
18 Randal Hill .60
19 Ernest Givins .10
20 Ken O'Brien .08
21 Blair Thomas .40
22 Derrick Thomas .15
23 Harvey Williams .75
24 Simon Fletcher .03
25 Stephone Paige .06
26 Barry Wood .25
27 Warren Moon .20
28 Derrick Fenner .12
29 Shane Conlan .06
30 Karl Mecklenburg .06
31 Gary Anderson .06
32 Sammie Smith .08
33 Steve DeBerg .08
34 Dan McGwire 1.25
35 Roger Craig .10
36 Tom Tupa .10
37 Rod Woodson .08
38 Junior Seau .08
39 Bruce Pickens .20
40 Greg Townsend .03
41 Gary Clark .12
42 Broderick Thomas .06
43 Charles Mann .06
44 Browning Nagle .75
45 James Joseph .45
46 Emmitt Smith 2.00
47 Cornelius Bennett .08
48 Maurice Hurst .03
49 Art Monk .10
50 Louis Lipps .06
51 Mark Rypien .20
52 Bubby Brister .08
53 John Stephens .06
54 Merril Hoge .03
55 Kevin Mack .06
56 Al Toon .08
57 Ronnie Lott .10
58 Eric Metcalf .06
59 Vinny Testaverde .08
60 Darrell Green .10
61 Randall Cunningham .15
62 Charles Haley .06
63 Mark Carrier .08
64 Jim Harbaugh .10
65 Richard Dent .08
66 Stan Thomas .08
67 Neal Anderson .15
68 Troy Aikman 1.25
69 *Mike Pritchard* .40
70 Deion Sanders .20
71 Andre Rison .15
72 Keith Millard .06
73 Jerry Rice .85
74 Johnny Johnson .25
75 Tim McDonald .06
76 *Leonard Russell* 1.25
77 Keith Jackson .08
78 Keith Byars .06
79 Ricky Proehl .10
80 Dexter Carter .08
81 *Alvin Harper* .75
82 Irving Fryar .06
83 Marion Butts .10
84 Alfred Williams .15
85 Timm Rosenbach .10
86 Steve Young .60
87 Albert Lewis .06
88 Rodney Peete .08
89 Barry Sanders .85
90 Bennie Blades .06
91 Chris Spielman .06
92 John Friesz .35
93 Jerome Brown .06
94 Reggie White .08
95 Michael Irvin .20
96 Keith McCants .08
97 Vinnie Clark .10
98 Louis Oliver .03
99 Mark Clayton .08
100 John Offerdahl .03
101 Michael Carter .06
102 John Taylor .12
103 William Perry .08
104 Gill Byrd .06
105 Burt Grossman .03
106 *Herman Moore* 1.50
107 Howie Long .06
108 Bo Jackson .35
109 Kelvin Pritchett .12
110 Jacob Green .06
111 Chris Doleman .06
112 Herschel Walker .12
113 Russell Maryland .45
114 Anthony Carter .08
115 Joey Browner .06
116 Tony Mandarich .06
117 Don Majkowski .08
118 Ricky Ervins 1.50
119 Sterling Sharpe .75
120 Tim Harris .06
121 Hugh Millen .75
122 Mike Rozier .06
123 Chris Miller .15
124 Morten Andersen .06
125 *Neil O'Donnell* 1.50
126 Surprise Wild Card .25
127 Eddie Brown .06
128 James Francis .08
129 James Brookss .08
130 David Fulcher .03
131 *Michael Jackson* .75
132 Clay Matthews .03
133 Scott Norwood .03
134 Wesley Carroll .40
135 Thurman Thomas .40
136 Mark Ingram .03
137 Bobby Hebert .08
138 Bobby Wilson .08
139 Craig Heyward .08
140 Dalton Hilliard .06
141 Jeff Hostetler .20
142 Dave Meggett .10
143 Cris Dishman .20
144 Lawrence Taylor .10
145 Leonard Marshall .06
146 Pepper Johnson .06
147 Todd Marinovich 1.25
148 Mike Croel .75
149 Erik McMillan .06
150 Flipper Anderson .06
151 Cleveland Gary .06
152 Henry Ellard .08
153 Kevin Greene .06
154 Michael Cofer .03
155 Todd Lyght .40
156 Bruce Smith .08
157 Checklist 1 .06
158 Checklist 2 .06
159 Checklist 3 .06
160 Checklist 4 .06

1991 Wild Card NFL Redemption Cards

This surprise Wild Card, #126, inserted randomly in 1991 Wild Card NFL packs, could be redeemed for the 10-card NFL Experience subset which is listed below. The cards feature members of the Buffalo Bills and Washington Redskins.

NM/M
Complete Set (10): 3.50
Common Player: .12
126A Mark Rypien .60
126B Ricky Ervins 1.50
126C Darrell Green .25
126D Charles Mann .12
126E Art Monk .30
126F Thurman Thomas .90
126G Bruce Smith .30
126H Cornelius Bennett .25
126I Scott Norwood .12
126J Shane Conlan .18

1991 Wild Card NFL Super Bowl Promos

Super Bowl XXVI is honored on this 10-card set, which spotlights five players from each team. The cards were handed out to attendees at the Super Bowl Card Show. The card fronts have an action photo borded in black, with different colored numbers on the top and right borders. The NFL Experience logo is in the lower left. The player's name and position are located in the lower right. The card backs showcase a player photo, his name, position and bio at the top of the card. A text box at the bottom of the card explains that Wild Card was a corporate sponsor of the Super Bowl Card Show III.

NM/M
Complete Set (10): 30.00
Common Player: 1.00
1 Mark Rypien 5.00
2 Ricky Ervins 10.00
3 Darrell Green 2.00

4	Charles Mann	1.00
5	Art Monk	2.50
6	Thurman Thomas	7.50
7	Bruce Smith	2.50
8	Cornelius Bennett	2.00
9	Scott Norwood	1.00
10	Shane Conlan	1.50

1991-92 Wild Card Redemption Prototypes

The six-card, standard-size set was available to collectors via a redemption mail-in offer. In exchange for three Collegiate Football Surprise wild cards before April 30, 1992, collectors also received the set, which is similar to the 1992 Wild Card NFL set. The cards are numbered with the "P" prefix.

		NM/M
Complete Set (6):		2.00
Common Player:		.20
1	Edgar Bennett (Florida State)	1.00
2	Jimmy Smith (Jackson State)	.75
3	Will Furrer (Virginia Tech)	.20
4	Terrell Buckley (Florida State)	.30
5	Tommy Vardell (Stanford)	.30
6	Amp Lee (Florida State)	.30

1992 Wild Card Prototypes

Picking up where the 1991 Wild Card Prototypes left off, this 12-card set begins with card No. P7. The card fronts include a color photo, bordered with colored numbers on the top and right border. The Wild Card logo is in the upper left, with the player's team name along the left side. His name and position are in the lower right. The team's helmet is printed in the lower left of the photo. The backs have the player's name, picture and bio on the right side of the card. The player's stats are located inside a box on the left side. The cards are numbered with the "P" prefix.

		NM/M
Complete Set (12):		25.00
Common Player:		1.00
7	Barry Sanders	4.00
8	John Taylor	2.00
9	John Elway	3.00
10	Erik Kramer	2.00
11	Christian Okoye	1.00
12	Leonard Russell	1.00
13	Barry Sanders	4.00
14	Earnest Byner	1.00
15	Warren Moon	2.50
16	Ronnie Lott	2.00
17	Michael Irvin	2.50
18	Haywood Jeffires	2.00

1992 Wild Card

This 460-card set showcased a color photo on the front, with the Wild Card logo in the upper left, the team name along the left border, team helmet in the lower left of the photo and player's name and position in the lower right. The border of the card front changes from white to gray to black. The card backs have the card number in the upper right, with the player's name, bio and photo along the right side. His stats are located in a box along the left border. Reportedly, Wild Card produced 30,000 10-box cases of the 250-card Series I product. Overall, 100 case cards and 1,000 box cards were seeded in foil packs. A numbered stripe on the front of the cards would carry denominations of 5, 10, 20, 50, 100 and 1,000. The Surprise Cards could be redeemed for a four-card set which included a P1 Barry Sanders (with Surprise Card No. 1) or P2 Emmitt Smith Stat Smasher card (with Series II Surprise Card No. 251), Red-Hot rookie card, Field Force card and a silver or gold Field Force card. In addition, a Barry Sanders promo card was handed out at the 1992 National Convention. It featured the National logo and had value stripes of 5, 10, 20, 50 and 100.

		NM/M
Complete Set (460):		15.00
Complete Series 1 (250):		7.50
Complete Series 2 (210):		7.50
Common Player:		.05
Minor Stars:		.10
Series 1/2 Wax Box:		8.00
1	Surprise Card	.10
2	Marcus Dupree	.05
3	Jackie Slater	.05
4	Robert Delpino	.05
5	Jerry Gray	.05
6	Jim Everett	.05
7	Roman Phifer	.05
8	Alvin Wright	.05
9	Todd Lyght	.05
10	Reggie White	.20
11	Randal Hill	.05
12	Keith Byars	.05
13	Clyde Simmons	.05
14	Keith Jackson	.05
15	Seth Joyner	.05
16	James Joseph	.05
17	Eric Allen	.05
18	Sammie Smith	.05
19	Mark Clayton	.05
20	Aaron Craver	.05
21	Hugh Green	.05
22	John Offerdahl	.05
23	Jeff Cross	.05
24	Ferrell Edmunds	.05
25	Mark Duper	.05
26	Ronnie Harmon	.05
27	Derrick Walker	.05
28	Gary Plummer	.05
29	Rod Bernstine	.05
30	Burt Grossman	.05
31	Donnie Elder	.05
32	John Friesz	.10
33	Bill Ray Smith	.05
34	Luis Sharpe	.05
35	Aeneas Williams	.10
36	Ken Harvey	.05
37	Johnny Johnson	.05
38	Eric Swann	.05
39	Tom Tupa	.05
40	Anthony Thompson	.05
41	Broderick Thomas	.05
42	Vinny Testaverde	.20
43	Mark Carrier	.05
44	Gary Anderson	.05
45	Keith McCants	.05
46	Reggie Cobb	.05
47	Lawrence Dawsey	.05
48	Kevin Murphy	.05
49	Keith Woodside	.05
50	Darrell Thompson	.05
51	Vinnie Clark	.05
52	Sterling Sharpe	.20
53	Mike Tomczak	.05
54A	Dan Majikowski (err)	.05
54B	Don Majikowski (cor)	.05
55	Tony Mandarich	.05
56	Mark Murphy	.05
57	Dexter McNabb	.05
58	Rick Fenney	.05
59	Cris Carter	.30
60	Wade Wilson	.05
61	Mike Merriweather	.05
62	Rich Gannon	.05
63	Herschel Walker	.05
64	Chris Doleman	.05
65	Al Noga UER (On front, he's a DE; on back, he's a DT)	.05
66	*Chris Mims*	.10
67	Ed Cunningham	.05
68	Marcus Allen	.20
69	*Kevin Turner*	.10
70	Howie Long	.10
71	Tim Brown	.20
72	Nick Bell	.05
73	Todd Marinovich	.05
74	Jay Schroeder	.05
75	Mervyn Fernandez	.05
76	Tony Smith	.05
77	John Alt	.05
78	Christian Okoye	.05
79	Nick Lowery	.05
80	Derrick Thomas	.10
81	Bill Maas	.05
82	Dino Hackett	.05
83	Deron Cherry	.05
84	Barry Word	.05
85	Mike Mooney	.05
86	Cris Dishman	.05
87	Bruce Matthews	.05
88	Tony Jones	.05
89	William Fuller	.05
90	Ray Childress	.05
91	Warren Moon	.10
92	Lorenzo White	.05
93	Joe Bowden	.05
94	Tom Rathman	.05
95	Keith Henderson	.05
96	Jesse Sapolu	.05
97	Charles Haley	.05
98	Steve Young	.50
99	John Taylor	.05
100	Tim Harris	.05
101	Scott Davis	.05
102	*Steve Bono*	.30
103	Mike Kenn	.05
104	Mike Farr	.05
105	Rodney Peete	.05
106	Jerry Ball	.05
107	Chris Spielman	.05
108	Barry Sanders	1.50
109	Bennie Blades	.05
110	Herman Moore	.50
111	Erik Kramer	.05
112	Vance Johnson	.05
113	Mike Croel	.05
114	Mark Jackson	.05
115	Steve Atwater	.05
116	Gaston Green	.05
117	John Elway	1.00
118	Simon Fletcher	.05
119	Karl Mecklenburg	.05
120	Hart Lee Dykes	.05
121	Jerome Henderson	.05
122	Chris Singleton	.05
123	Marv Cook	.05
124	Leonard Russell	.05
125	Hugh Millen	.05
126	Pat Harlow	.05
127	Andre Tippett	.05
128	Bruce Armstrong	.05
129	Gary Clark	.05
130	Art Monk	.10
131	Darrell Green	.05
132	Wilber Marshall	.05
133	Jim Lachey	.05
134	Earnest Byner	.05
135	Chip Lohmiller	.05
136	Mark Rypien	.10
137	Ricky Sanders	.05
138	Stan Thomas	.05
139	Neal Anderson	.05
140	Trace Armstrong	.05
141	Kevin Butler	.05
142	Mark Carrier	.05
143	Dennis Gentry	.05
144	Jim Harbaugh	.10
145	Richard Dent	.10
146	Andre Rison	.20
147	Bruce Pickens	.05
148	Chris Hinton UER (Dealt to Falcons in 1990, not 1989)	.05
149	Brian Jordan	.10
150	Chris Miller	.05
151	Moe Gardner	.05
152	Bill Fralic	.05
153	Michael Haynes	.10
154	Mike Pritchard	.10
155	Dean Biasucci	.05
156	Clarence Verdin	.05
157	Donnell Thompson	.05
158	Duane Bickett	.05
159	Jon Hand	.05
160	Sam Graddy	.05
161	Emmitt Smith	1.50
162	Michael Irvin	.20
163	Danny Noonan	.05
164	Jack Del Rio	.05
165	Jim Jeffcoat	.05
166	Alexander Wright	.05
167	Frank Minnifield	.05
168	Ed King	.05
169	Reggie Langhorne	.05
170	Mike Baab	.05
171	Eric Metcalf	.05
172	Clay Matthews	.05
173	Kevin Mack	.05
174	Mike Johnson	.05
175	Jeff Lageman	.05
176	Freeman McNeil	.05
177	Erik McMillan	.05
178	James Hasty	.05
179	Kyle Clifton	.05
180	Joe Kelly	.05
181	Phil Simms	.10
182	Everson Walls	.05
183	Jeff Hostetler	.10
184	Dave Meggett	.05
185	Matt Bahr	.05
186	Mark Ingram	.05
187	Rodney Hampton	.10
188	Kanavis McGhee	.05
189	Tim McGee	.05
190	Eddie Brown	.05
191	Rodney Holman	.05
192	Harold Green	.05
193	James Francis	.05
194	Anthony Munoz	.05
195	David Fulcher	.05
196	Tim Krumrie	.05
197	Bubby Brister	.05
198	Rod Woodson	.05
199	Louis Lipps	.05
200	Carnell Lake	.05
201	Don Beebe	.05
202	Thurman Thomas	.20
203	Cornelius Bennett	.05
204	Mark Kelso	.05
205	James Lofton	.10
206	Darryl Talley	.05
207	Morten Andersen	.05
208	Vince Buck	.05
209	Wesley Carroll	.05
210	Bobby Hebert	.05
211	Craig Heyward	.05
212	Dalton Hilliard	.05
213	Rickey Jackson	.05
214	Eric Martin	.05
215	Pat Swilling	.05
216	Steve Walsh	.05
217	Torrance Small	.05
218	Jacob Green	.05
219	Cortez Kennedy	.05
220	John L. Williams	.05
221	Terry Wooden	.05
222	Grant Feasel	.05
223	Siran Stacy	.05
224	Chris Hakel	.05
225	Todd Harrison	.05
226	Bob Whitfield	.05
227	Eddie Blake	.05
228	*Keith Hamilton*	.10
229	*Darryl Williams*	.10
230	Ricardo McDonald	.05
231	Alan Haller	.05
232	Leon Searcy	.05
233	Patrick Rowe	.05
234	*Edgar Bennett*	.30
235	*Terrell Buckley*	.30
236	Will Furrer	.05
237	*Amp Lee*	.05
238	*Jimmy Smith*	2.00
239	*Tommy Vardell*	.20
240	Leonard Russell	.05
241	Mike Croel	.05
242	Warren Moon	.10
243	Mark Rypien	.05
244	Thurman Thomas	.10
245	Emmitt Smith	.75
246	Checklist 1	.05
247	Checklist 2	.05
248	Checklist 3	.05
249	Checklist 4	.05
250	Checklist 5	.05
251	Surprise Card	.10
252	Erric Pegram	.10
253	Anthony Carter	.05
254	Roger Craig	.10
255	Hassan Jones	.05
256	Steve Jordan	.05
257	Randall McDaniel	.05
258	Henry Thomas	.05
259	Carl Lee	.05
260	Ray Agnew	.05
261	Irving Fryar	.05
262	Tom Waddle	.05
263	Greg McMurtry	.05
264	Stephen Baker	.05
265	Mark Collins	.05
266	Howard Cross	.05
267	Pepper Johnson	.05
268	Fred Barnett	.05
269	Heath Sherman	.05
270	William Thomas	.05
271	Bill Bates	.05
272	Issiac Holt	.05
273	Emmitt Smith	3.00
274	Eric Bieniemy	.05
275	Marion Butts	.05
276	Gill Byrd	.05
277	Robert Blackmon	.05
278	Brian Blades	.05
279	Joe Nash	.05
280	Bill Brooks	.05
281	Mel Gray	.05
282	Andre Ware	.05
283	Steve McMichael	.05
284	Brad Muster	.05
285	Ron Rivera	.05
286	Chris Zorich	.05
287	Chris Burkett	.05
288	Irv Eatman	.05
289	Rob Moore	.20
290	Joe Mott	.05
291	Brian Washington	.05
292	Michael Carter	.05
293	Dexter Carter	.05
294	Don Griffin	.05
295	John Taylor	.05
296	Ted Washington	.05
297	Monte Coleman	.05
298	Andre Collins	.05
299	Charles Mann	.05
300	Shane Conlon	.05
301	Keith McKeller	.05
302	Nate Odomes	.05
303	Riki Ellison	.05
304	Willie Gault	.05
305	Bob Golic	.05
306	Ethan Horton	.05
307	Ronnie Lott	.10
308	Don Mosebar	.05
309	Aaron Wallace	.05
310	Wymon Henderson	.05
311	Vance Johnson	.05
312	Ken Lanier	.05
313	Steve Sewell	.05
314	Dennis Smith	.05
315	Kenny Walker	.05
316	Chris Martin	.05
317	Albert Lewis	.05
318	Todd McNair	.05
319	*Tracy Simien*	.05
320	Percy Snow	.05
321	Mark Rypien	.05
322	Bryan Hinkle	.05
323	David Little	.05
324	Dwight Stone	.05
325	*Van Waiters*	.05
326	*Pio Sagapolutele*	.05
327	Michael Jackson	.10
328	Vestee Jackson	.05
329	Tony Paige	.05
330	Reggie Roby	.05
331	Haywood Jeffires	.10
332	Lamar Lathon	.05
333	Bubba McDowell	.05
334	Doug Smith	.05
335	Dean Steinkuhler	.05
336	Jessie Tuggle	.05
337	Freddie Joe Nunn	.05
338	Pat Terrell	.05
339	Tom McHale	.05
340	Sam Mills	.05
341	John Tice	.05
342	Brent Jones	.05
343	*Robert Porcher*	.20
344	*Mark D'Onofrio*	.05
345	David Tate	.05
346	*Courtney Hawkins*	.10
347	Ricky Watters	.20
348	Amp Lee	.10
349	Steve Young	.50
350	Natu Tuatagaloa	.05
351	Alfred Williams	.05
352	*Derek Brown*	.10
353	*Marco Coleman*	.10
354	*Tommy Maddox*	.10
355	Siran Stacy	.05
356	Greg Lewis	.05
357	Paul Gruber	.05
358	*Troy Vincent*	.10
359	Robert Wilson	.05
360	Jessie Hester	.05
361	Shaun Gayle	.05
362	Deron Cherry	.05
363	Wendell Davis	.05
364	*David Klingler*	.20
365	*Jason Hanson*	.10
366	*Marquez Pope*	.10
367	*Robert Williams*	.05
368	Kelvin Pritchett	.05
369	Dana Hall	.05
370	*David Brandon*	.05
371	Tim McKyer	.05
372	Darion Conner	.05
373	Derrick Fenner	.05
374	Hugh Millen	.05
375	Bill Jones	.05
376	J.J. Birden	.05
377	Ty Detmer	.10
378	*Alonzo Spellman*	.20
379	Sammie Smith	.05
380	Al Smith	.05
381	*Louis Clark*	.05
382	*Vernice Smith*	.05
383	Tony Martin	.20
384	Willie Green	.05
385	*Sean Gilbert*	.20
386	*Eugene Chung*	.05
387	Toi Cook	.05
388	Brett Maxie	.05
389	Steve Israel	.05
390	Mike Mularkey	.05
391	Barry Foster	.05
392	Hardy Nickerson	.05
393	*Johnny Mitchell*	.10
394	Thurman Thomas	.20
395	*Tony Smith*	.10
396	*Keith Goganious*	.05
397	*Matt Darby*	.05
398	*Nate Turner*	.05
399	*Keith Jennings*	.05
400	*Mitchell Benson*	.05
401	*Kurt Barber*	.05
402	*Tony Sacca*	.05
403	*Steve Hendrickson*	.05
404	Johnny Johnson	.05
405	Lorenzo Lynch	.05
406	Luis Sharpe	.05
407	Jim Everett	.05
408	Neal Anderson	.05
409	*Ashley Ambrose*	.10
410	*George Williams*	.05
411	Clarence Kay	.05
412	Dave Krieg	.05
413	Terrell Buckley	.10
414	Ricardo McDonald	.05
415	Kelly Stouffer	.05
416	Barney Bussey	.05
417	Ray Roberts	.05
418	*Fred McAfee*	.05
419	Fred Banks	.05
420	Tim McDonald	.05
421	*Darryl Williams*	.05
422	*Bobby Abrams*	.05
423	Tommy Vardell	.10
424	William White	.05
425	Billy Ray Smith	.05
426	Lemuel Stinson	.05
427	*Brad Johnson*	15.00
428	Herschel Walker	.20
429	Eric Thomas	.05
430	Anthony Thompson	.05
431	Ed West	.05
432	Edgar Bennett	.10
433	Warren Powers	.05
434	Byron Evans	.05
435	Rodney Culver	.05
436	Ray Horton	.05
437	Richmond Webb	.05
438	*Mark McMillian*	.05
439	Subset checklist	.05
440	*Lawrence Pete*	.05
441	*Rodney Smith*	.05
442	*Mark Rodenhauser*	.05
443	*Scott Lockwood*	.05
444	*Charles Davenport*	.05
445	Terry McDaniel	.05
446	*Darren Perry*	.10
447	*Darrick Owens*	.10
448	Alvin Wright	.05
449	Frank Stams	.05
450	*Santana Dotson*	.20
451	Mark Carrier	.05
452	Kevin Murphy	.05
453	Jeff Bryant	.05
454	Eric Allen	.05
455	*Brian Bollinger*	.05
456	Elston Ridgle	.05
457	Jim Riggs	.05
458	Series II, checklist #6	.05
459	Series II, checklist #7	.05
460	Series II, checklist #8	.05

1992 Wild Card Class Back Attack

Inserted in 1992 Wild Card WLAF foil packs, the five-card set showcases a color action photo on the front. A green and black border surrounds the photo, with different colored numbers running along the right side of the card. In a football in the lower left is printed "Class Back Attack" or "Red Hot Rookie." The player's name and team are listed in the lower right. The card backs, numbered with an "SP" prefix, feature the player's photo and bio at the top. A text box at the bottom invites collectors to collect all singles and then continue to collect sets of the different value denominations.

		NM/M
Complete Set (5):		16.00
Common Player:		1.25
1	Vaughn Dunbar	1.25
2	Barry Sanders	4.00
3	Emmitt Smith	7.50
4	Thurman Thomas	2.00
5	David Klingler (Red Hot Rookie; Surprise Card Redemption)	2.00

1992 Wild Card Field Force

Randomly seeded in 1992 Wild Card Series II foil packs, the 30-card set was also issued in both gold and silver foil versions. Each card front includes a photo which is bordered by a dark purple border on the left. It changes to purple and light purple as it runs to the right side of the card. The dark purple area on the left features gold or silver horizontal lines which run the length of the card. The Field Force logo is in the lower left, with the player's name and position in the lower right. The card back includes a photo on the left side and the player's stats on the right. The card number is located in the upper right.

		NM/M
Complete Set (30):		18.00
Common Player:		.25
1	Joe Montana	3.00
2	Quentin Coryatt	.75
3	Tommy Vardell	.50
4	Jim Kelly	1.00
5	John Elway	1.25
6	Ricky Watters	1.50
7	Vinny Testaverde	.25
8	Randal Hill	.25
9	Amp Lee	.50
10	Vaughn Dunbar	.25
11	Troy Aikman	3.50
12	Deion Sanders	.50
13	Rodney Hampton	1.50
14	Brett Favre	2.00
15	Warren Moon	.75
16	Browning Nagle	.25
17	Terrell Buckley	.30
18	Barry Sanders	3.00
19	Dan Marino	2.50
20	Carl Pickens	.60
21	Herschel Walker	.25
22	Ronnie Lott	.25
23	Steve Emtman	.30
24	Mark Rypien	.25
25	Bobby Hebert	.25
26	Dan McGwire	.25
27	Neil O'Donnell	1.00
28	Cris Carter	.25
29	Randall Cunningham	.60
30	Jerry Rice	2.00

1992 Wild Card Pro Picks

Randomly seeded in 1992 Wild Card Series II foil packs, the 30-card chase set includes a Red Hot Rookies' logo inside a football in the lower left corner. Different colored numbers border the top and right of the photo. The player's name and position are at the lower right. The backs, numbered "of 30," have the player's name, bio and photo on the right, with his highlights in a box on the left. Gold and silver editions were inserted one per jumbo pack.

		NM/M
Complete Set (8):		10.00
Common Player:		.30
1	Emmitt Smith	4.00
2	Mark Rypien	.30
3	Warren Moon	.50
4	Leonard Russell	.30
5	Thurman Thomas	.50
6	John Elway	1.00
7	Barry Sanders	2.00
8	Steve Young	1.50

1992 Wild Card Red Hot Rookies

This 30-card set is identified by a flaming football with the words "Red Hot Rookies" in the lower right corner. The set was inserted into Series II packs of Wild Card, with gold and silver versions also available one per jumbo pack. Red Hot Rookies were also available in 5, 10, 20, 50, 100 and 1,000 stripe varieties, with the stripe placed in the upper right hand corner of the photo.

		NM/M
Complete Set (30):		15.00
Complete Series 1 (10):		5.00
Complete Series 2 (20):		10.00
Common Player:		.50
1	Darryl Williams	.50
2	Amp Lee	.75
3	Will Furrer	.50
4	Edgar Bennett	1.50
5	Terrell Buckley	.50
6	Bob Whitfield	.50
7	Siran Stacy	.50
8	Jimmy Smith	1.00
9	Kevin Turner	.50
10	Tommy Vardell	.75
11	Surprise Card	1.00
12	Derek Brown	.50

13 Marco Coleman 1.00
14 Quentin Coryatt 1.00
15 Rodney Culver .50
16 Ty Detmer .50
17 Vaughn Dunbar .50
18 Steve Emtman .50
19 Sean Gilbert 1.00
20 Courtney Hawkins 1.25
21 David Klingler 1.00
22 Amp Lee .90
23 Tommy Maddox .50
24 Johnny Mitchell 1.25
25 Darren Perry .50
26 Carl Pickens 1.00
27 Robert Porcher .50
28 Tony Smith .50
29 Alonzo Spellman .50
30 Troy Vincent .50

1992 Wild Card Running Wild Silver

Inserted one per 1992 Wild Card Series II jumbo pack, the 40-card set showcased the Running Wild logo inside an arrow which overlapped the photo. Arrows also ran the length of the card from the top to the Running Wild logo. The player's name and team are located in the lower right. The card backs have a player photo on the left side, with his stats in a box on the right.

NM/M
Complete Set (40): 18.00
Common Player: .30
1 Terry Allen .75
2 Neal Anderson .50
3 Eric Ball .30
4 Nick Bell .30
5 Edgar Bennett .75
6 Rod Bernstine .30
7 Marion Butts .50
8 Keith Byars .30
9 Earnest Byner .30
10 Reggie Cobb .30
11 Roger Craig .50
12 Rodney Culver .50
13 Barry Foster .50
14 Cleveland Gary .30
15 Harold Green .50
16 Gaston Green .30
17 Rodney Hampton .75
18 Mark Higgs .30
19 Dalton Hilliard .30
20 Bobby Humphrey (UER) (Misspelled Humphries) .30
21 Amp Lee .50
22 Kevin Mack .30
23 Eric Metcalf .75
24 Brad Muster .30
25 Christian Okoye .50
26 Tom Rathman .30
27 Leonard Russell .50
28 Barry Sanders 2.50
29 Heath Sherman .30
30 Emmitt Smith 4.00
31 Blair Thomas .30
32 Thurman Thomas .75
33 Tommy Vardell .50
34 Herschel Walker .50
35 Chris Warren .75
36 Ricky Watters .75
37 Lorenzo White .50
38 John L. Williams .30
39 Barry Word .30
40 Vince Workman .50

1992 Wild Card Stat Smashers

Card Nos. 1-16 were randomly seeded in Series II foil packs, while card Nos. 17-52 were found one per pack in Series II jumbo packs. The card fronts have the Stat Smashers' logo in the upper right, while the player's name, team and position are in stripes near the bottom. A photo of the player is placed over a foil background. The card backs, numbered with a prefix of "SS," include the player's name, bio and photo on the left, while a highlights box appears on the right. A Barry Sanders card could be received in exchange for a Surprise Card in Series I. A Series II Surprise Card could be redeemed for an Emmitt Smith card.

NM/M
Complete Set (52): 55.00
Complete Series 1 (16): 30.00
Complete Series 2 (36): 25.00
Common Player (1-16): 1.25
Common Player (17-52): .45
1 Barry Sanders 6.00
2 Leonard Russell 2.00
3 Thurman Thomas 3.00
4 John Elway 4.00
5 Steve Young 4.00
6 Warren Moon 2.00
7 Terrell Buckley 1.25
8 Randall Cunningham 2.00
9 Steve Emtman 1.25
10 Dan Marino 10.00
11 Joe Montana 8.00
12 Carl Pickens 1.25
13 Jerry Rice 6.00
14 Deion Sanders 2.50
15 Tommy Vardell 2.00
16 Ricky Watters 3.00
17 Troy Aikman 6.00
18 Dale Carter .60
19 Quentin Coryatt .75
20 Vaughn Dunbar .50
21 Mark Duper .45
22 Eric Metcalf .45
23 Brett Favre 10.00
24 Barry Foster 2.25
25 Jeff George .75
26 Sean Gilbert 1.00
27 Jim Harbaugh .45
28 Courtney Hawkins 1.25
29 Charles Haley .45
30 Bobby Hebert .50
31 Stan Humphries .55
32 Michael Irvin 2.50
33 Jim Kelly 1.50
34 David Klingler 1.50
35 Ronnie Lott .45
36 Tommy Maddox 1.00
37 Todd Marinovich .45
38 Hugh Millen .60
39 Art Monk .60
40 Browning Nagle .65
41 Neil O'Donnell 1.00
42 Tom Rathman .50
43 Andre Rison 1.00
44 Mike Singletary .50
45 Tony Smith .45
46 Emmitt Smith 10.00
47 Pete Stoyanovich .45
48 John Taylor .65
49 Troy Vincent .60
50 Herschel Walker .60
51 Lorenzo White .80
52 Rodney Culver 1.00

1992 Wild Card NASDAM

Produced for and handed out at the 1992 NASDAM trade show in Orlando, this five card set features a color action photo on a white-bordered card front. Different colored numbers surround the photo on the top and right borders. The NASDAM logo appears in the lower left of the photo, while the player's name and position are in the lower right. The player's team's nickname is printed along the left border. The backs feature a photo of the player, along with his name, bio and stats.

NM/M
Complete Set (5): 3.00
Common Player: .40
1 Edgar Bennett 1.50
2 Amp Lee .60
3 Terrell Buckley .60
4 Tony Smith .40
5 Will Furrer (UER) (Misspelled Furer) .40

1992 Wild Card NASDAM/SCAI Miami

Produced and handed out at the 1992 NASDAM/SCAI conference in Miami, the six-card set showcases only Miami Dolphins. The card fronts feature a color action photo, with the NASDAM/SCAI logo in the lower left of the photo. "Dolphins" is printed along the left side of the photo. The top and right borders of the photo include different colored numbers. The player's name and position are located in the lower right. The card backs feature the player's name, bio and photo inside a football shape on the right side of the card. His stats are listed inside a box on the left side.

NM/M
Complete Set (6): 4.00
Common Player: .75
1 Mark Clayton 1.50
2 Aaron Craver .75
3 Tony Paige .75
4 Mark Duper 1.25
5 Tony Martin 1.25
6 Reggie Roby .75

1992 Wild Card Sacramento CardFest

This six-card San Francisco 49ers set was given out at Sacramento CardFest in 1992, and contains the logo for the event in the lower left hand corner. The design is consistent with other 1992 Wild Card designs, with a white framed background that includes multi-colored trim on the top and right edge.

NM/M
Complete Set (6): 3.00
Common Player: .40
1 Tom Rathman .40
2 Steve Young 1.00
3 Steve Bono 1.00
4 Brett Jones .40
5 Ricky Watters .60
6 Amp Lee .40

1992 Wild Card WLAF

With a reported press run of 6,000 10-box cases, this 150-card set featured players from the World League of American Football. Card fronts featured a color photo surrounded by black, gray and white. The city the player performed in is printed like a postmark on the left, while the team's logo is located in the lower left. The World League logo is included with the Wild Card logo inside a stamp in the upper right. The player's name and team are in the lower right. The card backs have the player's name printed under the photo, while his bio and card number are to the right of his photo. His highlights are listed in a box near the bottom of the card.

NM/M
Complete Set (150): 9.00
Common Player: .05
1 World Bowl Champs .10
2 Pete Mandley .10
3 Steve Williams .05
4 Dee Thomas .05
5 Emanuel King .10
6 Anthony Dilweg .25
7 Ben Brown .05
8 Darryl Harris .05
9 Aaron Emanuel .20
10 Andre Brown .10
11 Reggie McKenzie .10
12 Darryl Holmes .05
13 Michael Proctor .05
14 Ricky Johnson .05
15 Ray Savage .05
16 George Searcy .05
17 Titus Dixon .05
18 Willie Fears .10
19 Terrence Cooks .05
20 Ivory Lee Brown .20
21 Mike Johnson .05
22 Doug Williams .10
23 Brad Goebel .20
24 Tony Boles .15
25 Cisco Richard .05
26 Robb White .05
27 Darrell Colbert .05
28 Wayne Walker .10
29 Ronnie Williams .05
30 Erik Norgard .05
31 Darren Willis .05
32 Kent Wells .05
33 Phil Logan .05
34 Pat O'Hara .05
35 Melvin Patterson .05
36 Amir Rasul .05
37 Tom Rouen .10
38 Chris Cochrane .05
39 Randy Bethel .05
40 Eric Harmon .05
41 Archie Herring .05
42 Tim James .05
43 Babe Laufenberg .15
44 Herb Welch .05
45 Stefon Adams .05
46 Tony Burse .10
47 Carl Parker .05
48 Mike Prugle .05
49 Michael Jones .05
50 David Archer .25
51 Corian Freeman .05
52 Eddie Brown .15
53 Paul Green .05
54 Basil Proctor .05
55 Mike Sinclair .05
56 Louis Riddick .05
57 Roman Matuez .05
58 Darryl Clack .10
59 Willie Davis .05
60 Glen Rodgers .05
61 Grantis Bell .05
62 Joe Howard-Johnson .15
63 Rocen Keeton .05
64 Dean Witkowski .05
65 Stacey Simmons .10
66 Roger Vick .10
67 Scott Mitchell .20
68 Todd Krumm .05
69 Kerwin Bell .15
70 Richard Carey .05
71 Kip Lewis .05
72 Andre Alexander .05
73 Reggie Slack .20
74 Falanda Newton .10
75 Tony Woods .10
76 Chris McLemore .05
77 Eric Wilkerson .10
78 Cornell Burbage .10
79 Doug Pederson .05
80 Brent Pease .15
81 Monty Gilbreath .05
82 Wes Pritchett .05
83 Byron Williams .05
84 Ron Sancho .10
85 Tony Jones .10
86 Anthony Wallace .05
87 Mike Perez .15
88 Steve Bartalo .05
89 Teddy Garcia .05
90 Joe Greenwood .05
91 Tony Baker .05
92 Glenn Cobb .05
93 Mark Tucker .05
94 Lyneil Mayo .05
95 Alex Espinoza .05
96 Mike Norseth .15
97 Steve Avery .05
98 John Brantley .05
99 Eddie Britton .05
100 Philip Doyle .05
101 Elroy Harris .05
102 John R. Holland .10
103 Mark Hopkins .05
104 Arthur Hunter .05
105 Paul McGowan .05
106 John Miller .05
107 Shawn Moore .05
108 Phil Ross .05
109 Eugene Rowell .05
110 Joe Valerio .10
111 Harvey Wilson .05
112 Irvin Smith .05
113 Tony Sargent .05
114 Ricky Shaw .05
115 Curtis Moore .05
116 Fred McNair .05
117 Danny Lockett .10
118 William Kirksey .05
119 Stan Gelbaugh .25
120 Judd Garrett .15
121 Dedrick Dodge .05
122 Dan Crossman .05
123 Jeff Alexander .05
124 Lew Barnes .05
125 Willie Don Wright .05
126 Johnny Thomas .05
127 Richard Buchanan .05
128 Chad Fortune .05
129 Eric Lindstrom .05
130 Ron Goetz .05
131 Bruce Clark .10
132 Anthony Greene .10
133 Demetrius Davis .10
134 Mike Roth .05
135 Tony Moss .05
136 Scott Erney .10
137 Brad Henke .05
138 Malcolm Frank .05
139 Sean Foster .05
140 Michael Titley .05
141 Rickey Williams .05
142 Karl Dunbar .05
143 Carl Bax .05
144 Willie Bouyer .05
145 Howard Feggins .05
146 David Smith .05
147 Bernard Ford .10
148 Checklist 1 .05
149 Checklist 2 .05
150 Checklist 3 .05

1992-93 Wild Card San Francisco

Originally produced for the Sports Collectors Card Expo in San Francisco in 1992, the six-card set focused solely on 49ers. The set was later reissued with a different logo for the 1993 Spring National Sports Collectors Convention in San Francisco. The 1993 set also had different card numbers and two different players. The card fronts have the show's logo in the lower left of the photo. The usual Wild Card denominations are printed along the top and right borders of the photo. The player's name and position are listed in the lower right. The card backs, numbered "of 6," have the player's name, bio and photo on the right, with stats listed in a box on the left. Cards listed below with an "A" are from the 1992 set, while those with a "B" are from the 1993 set.

NM/M
Complete Set (6): 4.00
Common Player: .30
1A John Taylor .30
1B Tom Rathman .30
2A Amp Lee .30
2B Steve Young .75
3A Steve Bono .60
3B Steve Bono .60
4A Steve Young .75
4B Brent Jones .30
5A Tom Rathman .30
5B Ricky Watters .50
6A Don Griffin .30
6B Amp Lee .30

1993 Wild Card Prototypes

Produced for the 1993 National Sports Collectors Convention, the six-card set showcases a full-bleed color photo. The Wild Card logo is printed in the upper left, with the player's name, team and position printed inside a gold 3-D band at the bottom. "NFL players" is printed on the right side of the band. The card backs have a photo of the player on the right side, with his name, bio and stats printed over a photo of the team's city skyline. The card numbers are prefixed by a "P." The numbers begin at P19, which is where the 1992 Wild Card promos ended.

NM/M
Complete Set (6): 5.00
Common Player: .50
19 Emmitt Smith 2.00
20 Ricky Watters .50
21 Drew Bledsoe 1.50
22 Garrison Hearst .50
23 Barry Foster .50
24 Rick Mirer .75

1993 Wild Card Superchrome Promos

The six-card foil set features the same design as the 1993 Wild Card Prototypes, except the card fronts are printed in chrome. The card backs are also designed the same as the 1993 Prototypes, except the card numbers carry an "SCP" prefix.

NM/M
Complete Set (6): 7.00
Common Player: .50
1 Emmitt Smith 3.00
2 Ricky Watters .75
3 Drew Bledsoe 2.50
4 Garrison Hearst .50
5 Barry Foster .50
6 Rick Mirer 1.00

1993 Wild Card

The 260-card set features full-bleed photos, with the Wild Card logo in the upper left and the player's name, team and position printed in a gold 3-D band at the bottom. The card backs have a photo on the right side. The player's name, bio and stats are located to the left of the player photo and printed over a skyline of the team's city. Series I boasted Field Force, Red Hot Rookies and Stat Smashers chase cards. In 1994, Wild Card changed its packages by adding Superchrome cards to packs. The Superchrome parallel cards were seeded in Superchrome 15-card low-series packs and 13-card high-series hobby packs. They are valued at four to nine times the value of the regular cards. In addition, denomination striped cards were randomly seeded into packs. Denominations fell between 5-1,000.

NM/M
Complete Set (260): 10.00
Complete Series 1 (200): 6.00
Complete Series 2 (60): 4.00
Common Player: .05
Minor Stars: .10
Stripes 5/10/20: 2X-4X
Stripes 50/100: 5X-10X
Stripes 1000: 10X-35X
Superchrome 1 Set (200): 20.00
Superchrome 2 Set (60): 15.00
Superchromes: 1.5X-3X
Wax Box: 10.00
1 Surprise card .05
2 Steve Young .50
3 John Taylor .05
4 Jerry Rice .75
5 Brent Jones .05
6 Ricky Watters .20
7 *Elvis Grbac* 1.00
8 Amp Lee .05
9 Steve Bono .20
10 Wendell Davis .05
11 Mark Carrier .05
12 Jim Harbaugh .05
13 *Curtis Conway* .40
14 Neal Anderson .05
15 Tom Waddle .05
16 Jeff Query .05
17 David Klingler .10
18 Eric Ball .05
19 Derrick Fenner .05
20 Steve Tovar .05
21 Carl Pickens .20
22 Ricardo McDonald .05
23 Harold Green .05
24 Keith McKeller .05
25 Steve Christie .05
26 Andre Reed .10
27 Kenneth Davis .05
28 Frank Reich .05
29 Jim Kelly .15
30 Bruce Smith .05
31 Thurman Thomas .20
32 *Glyn Milburn* .30
33 John Elway .40
34 Vance Johnson .05
35 Greg Lewis .05
36 Steve Atwater .05
37 Shannon Sharpe .05
38 Mike Croel .05
39 Kevin Mack .05
40 Lawyer Tillman .05
41 Tommy Vardell .05
42 Bernie Kosar .05
43 Eric Metcalf .05
44 Clay Matthews .05
45 Keith McCants .05
46 Broderick Thomas .05
47 Lawrence Dawsey .05
48 Reggie Cobb .05
49 *Lamar Thomas* .10
50 Courtney Hawkins .05
51 *Ivory Lee Brown* .05
52 Ernie Jones .05
53 Freddie Joe Nunn .05
54 Chris Chandler .05
55 Randal Hill .05
56 Lorenzo Lynch .05
57 *Garrison Hearst* 1.00
58 Marion Butts .05
59 Anthony Miller .05
60 Eric Bieneimy .05
61 Ronnie Harmon .05
62 Junior Seau .15
63 Gill Byrd .05
64 Stan Humphries .15
65 John Friesz .05
66 J.J. Birden .05
67 Joe Montana 1.00
68 Christian Okoye .05
69 Dale Carter .05
70 Barry Wood .05
71 Derrick Thomas .10
72 Todd McNair .05
73 Harvey Williams .05
74 Jack Trudeau .05
75 Rodney Culver .05
76 Anthony Johnson .05
77 Steve Emtman .05
78 Quentin Coryatt .05
79 Keith Cash .05
80 Jeff George .10
81 *Darrin Smith* .10
82 Jay Novacek .05
83 Michael Irvin .30
84 Alvin Harper .20
85 *Kevin Williams* .50
86 Troy Aikman .60
87 Emmitt Smith 1.25
88 *O.J. McDuffie* .50
89 *Mike Williams* .05
90 Dan Marino 1.25
91 Aaron Craver .05
92 Troy Vincent .05
93 Keith Jackson .05
94 Marco Coleman .05
95 Mark Higgs .05
96 Fred Barnett .05
97 Wes Hopkins .05
98 Randall Cunningham .10
99 Heath Sherman .05
100 Vai Sikahema .05
101 Tony Smith .05
102 Andre Rison .10
103 Chris Miller .05
104 Deion Sanders .30
105 Mike Pritchard .05
106 Steve Broussard .05
107 Stephen Baker .05
108 Carl Banks .05
109 Jarrod Bunch .05
110 Phil Simms .05
111 Rodney Hampton .15
112 Dave Meggett .05
113 Pepper Johnson .05
114 *Coleman Rudolph* .05
115 Boomer Esiason .10
116 Browning Nagle .05
117 Rob Moore .05
118 *Marvin Jones* .10
119 Herman Moore .25
120 Bennie Blades .05
121 Erik Kramer .05
122 Mel Gray .05
123 Rodney Peete .05
124 Barry Sanders .75
125 Chris Spielman .05
126 Lamar Lathon .05
127 Ernest Givins .05
128 Lorenzo White .05
129 *Micheal Barrow* .05
130 Warren Moon .10
131 Cody Carlson .05
132 Reggie White .10

133 Terrell Buckley .05
134 Ed West .05
135 *Mark Brunell* 2.00
136 Brett Favre 1.25
137 Edgar Bennett .10
138 Sterling Sharpe .10
139 *George Teague* .10
140 Leonard Russell .05
141 *Drew Bledsoe* 2.00
142 Eugene Chung .05
143 Walter Stanley .05
144 Scott Zolak .05
145 Jon Vaughn .05
146 Andre Tippet .05
147 Alexander Wright .05
148 *Billy Joe Hobert* .20
149 Terry McDaniel .05
150 Tim Brown .10
151 Willie Gault .05
152 Howie Long .05
153 Todd Marinovich .05
154 Jim Everett .05
155 David Lang .05
156 Henry Ellard .05
157 Cleveland Gary .05
158 Steve Israel .05
159 *Jerome Bettis* 1.00
160 Jackie Slater .05
161 Art Monk .10
162 Ricky Sanders .05
163 Brian Mitchell .05
164 *Reggie Brooks* .15
165 Mark Rypien .05
166 Earnest Byner .05
167 Andre Collins .05
168 Quinn Early .05
169 Fred McAfee .05
170 Wesley Carroll .05
171 Gene Atkins .05
172 *Derek Brown* .15
173 Vaughn Dunbar .05
174 Ricky Jackson .05
175 John L. Williams .05
176 *Carlton Gray* .10
177 Cortez Kennedy .10
178 Kelly Stouffer .05
179 *Rick Mirer* .50
180 Dan McGwire .05
181 Chris Warren .15
182 Barry Foster .05
183 Merril Hoge .05
184 Darren Perry .05
185 *Deon Figures* .10
186 Jeff Graham .15
187 Dwight Stone .05
188 Neil O'Donnell .10
189 Rod Woodson .05
190 *Alex Van Pelt* .05
191 Steve Jordan .05
192 Roger Craig .05
193 *Qadry Ismail* .40
194 *Robert Smith* .50
195 *Gino Torretta* .10
196 Anthony Carter .05
197 Terry Allen .05
198 Rich Gannon .05
199 Checklist #1 .05
200 Checklist #2 .05
201 *Victor Bailey* .15
202 *Micheal Barrow* .05
203 *Patrick Bates* .05
204 Jerome Bettis .30
205 Drew Bledsoe .75
206 *Vincent Brisby* .75
207 Reggie Brooks .10
208 *Derek Brown* .10
209 Keith Byars .05
210 *Tom Carter* .15
211 Curtis Conway .20
212 *Russell Copeland* .10
213 *John Copeland* .10
214 *Eric Curry* .10
215 *Troy Drayton* .30
216 *Jason Elam* .10
217 *Steve Everitt* .10
218 Deon Figures .05
219 Irving Fryar .05
220 Darrien Gordon .20
221 Carlton Gray .05
222 Kevin Greene .05
223 *Andre Hastings* .20
224 Michael Haynes .05
225 Garrison Hearst .40
226 Bobby Hebert .05
227 Lester Holmes .05
228 Jeff Hostetler .10
229 Desmond Howard .05
230 *Tyrone Hughes* .20
231 Quadry Ismail .20
232 Rocket Ismail .10
233 *James Jett* .20
234 Marvin Jones .05
235 *Todd Kelly* .10
236 *Lincoln Kennedy* .10
237 *Terry Kirby* .40
238 Bernie Kosar .05
239 *Derrick Lassic* .10
240 Wilber Marshall .05
241 O.J. McDuffie .30
242 *Ryan McNeil* .05
243 *Natrone Means* 1.00
244 Glyn Milburn .10
245 Rick Mirer .40
246 Scott Mitchell .10
247 *Ron Moore* .30
248 *Lorenzo Neal* .20
249 Eric Pegram .20
250 *Roosevelt Potts* .20
251 *Leonard Renfro* .10
252 *Greg Robinson* .10
253 Wayne Simmons .10
254 *Chris Slade* .25
255 *Irv Smith* .20
256 Robert Smith .25
257 *Dana Stubblefield* .40
258 George Teague .10
259 Kevin Williams .20
260 Checklist .05

1993 Wild Card Bomb Squad

According to reports, 10,000 of these 30-card sets were produced. They were seeded in high-number (201-260) packs. The chromium fronts feature an action shot of a wide receiver inside a football shape. "Bomb Squad" is printed on the left side of the football. The player's name, team and position are printed in a rectangle at the bottom of the card. The orange-colored backs showcase the player's name, team and position at the top. His stats are listed horizontally along the left side of the card, while a player photo is on the right.

	NM/M
Complete Set (30):	12.00
Common Player:	.30
1 Jerry Rice	2.00
2 John Taylor	.50
3 J.J. Birden	.50
4 Stephen Baker	.30
5 Victor Bailey	.50
6 O.J. McDuffie	.50
7 Haywood Jeffires	.50
8 Eric Green	.30
9 Johnny Mitchell	.50
10 Art Monk	.50
11 Quinn Early	.50
12 Troy Drayton	.50
13 Vincent Brisby	.50
14 Courtney Hawkins	.50
15 Tom Waddle	.30
16 Curtis Conway	.50
17 Andre Reed	.50
18 Carl Pickens	.50
19 Sterling Sharpe	.50
20 Shannon Sharpe	.50
21 Qadry Ismail	.50
22 Rocket Ismail	.50
23 Andre Rison	.50
24 Michael Haynes	.50
25 Alvin Harper	.50
26 Michael Irvin	.50
27 Michael Jackson	.50
28 Herman Moore	.75
29 Anthony Miller	.50
30 Gary Clark	.50

1993 Wild Card Bomb Squad B/B

This 15-card set is a double-front version of the Bomb Squad chase set. The same design is featured for each player on the front and back. Inserted one per 20-pack box of the 1993 Wild Card high-number jumbo packs, the cards were part of the 1,000 sets which were reportedly produced.

	NM/M
Complete Set (15):	20.00
Common Player:	1.25
1 Jerry Rice, John Taylor	4.00
2 Tom Waddle, Curtis Conway	1.25
3 Andre Reed, Carl Pickens	2.00
4 Sterling Sharpe, Shannon Sharpe	2.00
5 Qadry Ismail, Rocket Ismail	2.00
6 Andre Rison, Michael Haynes	2.00
7 Alvin Harper, Michael Irwin	2.00
8 Michael Jackson, Herman Moore	1.25
9 Anthony Miller, Gary Clark	1.25
10 J.J. Birden, Stephen Baker	1.25
11 Victor Bailey, O.J. McDuffie	1.25
12 Haywood Jeffires, Eric Green	1.25
13 Johnny Mitchell, Art Monk	1.25
14 Quinn Early, Troy Drayton	1.25
15 Vincent Brisby, Courtney Hawkins	2.00

1993 Wild Card Field Force

The 90-card chase set was randomly seeded into packs, however, it was released in three 30-card series based on Divisional alignment. The Field Force logo appears at the bottom left of the card fronts, while the player's name and position are located in the lower right. The Wild Card logo is in the upper left. The left border has black and blue jagged lines, while the rest of the card is blue and white. The card backs, numbered with either a "WFF," "EFF" or "CFF," depending on divisions, have a photo on the left and stats on the right. The card number is at the top right.

	NM/M
Complete Set (90):	30.00
Complete West Series (30):	10.00
Complete East Series (30):	10.00
Complete Cent. Series (30):	10.00
Common Player:	.25
Minor Stars:	.50
Stripes 5/10/20:	1.5X-3X
Stripes 50/100:	8X-16X
Stripes 1000:	70X-140X
Silver Cards:	1X-1.5X
Gold Cards:	1X-2X
Superchrome Set (10):	20.00
Superchrome Cards:	1X-2X
31 Jerry Rice	2.00
32 Ricky Watters	.50
33 Steve Bono	1.00
34 Amp Lee	.25
35 Steve Young	2.00
36 Tommy Maddox	.25
37 Cleveland Gary	.25
38 John Elway	1.00
39 Glyn Milburn	.50
40 Stan Humphries	.75
41 Junior Seau	.75
42 Natrone Means	2.00
43 Dale Carter	.25
44 Joe Montana	2.00
45 Christian Okoye	.25
46 Deion Sanders	1.00
47 Roger Harper	.25
48 Steve Broussard	.25
49 Todd Marinovich	.25
50 BIlly Joe Hobert	.50
51 Patrick Bates	.25
52 Jerome Bettis	1.00
53 Willie Anderson	.25
54 Irv Smith	.25
55 Quinn Early	.25
56 Vaughn Dunbar	.25
57 Rick Mirer	2.00
58 Carlton Gary	.25
59 Chris Warren	.50
60 Dan McGwire	.25
61 Pete Metzelaars	.25
62 Kenneth Davis	.25
63 Thurman Thomas	.75
64 Chris Chandler	.50
65 Garrison Hearst	1.25
66 Ricky Proehl	.25
67 Steven Emtman	.25
68 Jeff George	.75
69 Clarence Verdin	.25
70 Troy Aikman	1.50
71 Emmitt Smith	2.50
72 Alvin Harper	.50
73 Michael Irvin	1.00
74 O.J. McDuffie	.50
75 Troy Vincent	.25
76 Keith Jackson	.25
77 Dan Marino	2.50
78 Leonard Renfro	.25
79 Heath Sherman	.25
80 Derek Brown	.25
81 Rodney Hampton	.50
82 James Hasty	.25
83 Johnny Mitchell	.25
84 Brad Baxter	.25
85 Leonard Russell	.25
86 Marv Cook	.25
87 Drew Bledsoe	5.00
88 Ricky Ervins	.25
89 Art Monk	.50
90 Earnest Byner	.25
91 Tom Waddle	.25
92 Neal Anderson	.25
93 Curtis Conway	.75
94 Harold Green	.25
95 Jeff Query	.25
96 Carl Pickens	1.00
97 David Klingler	.50
98 Michael Jackson	.25
99 Eric Metcalf	.25
100 Courtney Hawkins	.25
101 Eric Curry	.25
102 Reggie Cobb	.25
103 Mel Gray	.25
104 Barry Sanders	1.75
105 Rodney Peete	.25
106 Haywood Jeffires	.25
107 Cody Carlson	.25
108 Curtis Duncan	.25
109 Edgar Bennett	.50
110 George Teague	.25
111 Terrell Buckley	.25
112 Brett Favre	2.50
113 Deon Figures	.25
114 Rod Woodson	.25
115 Neil O'Donnell	.50
116 Barry Foster	.50
117 Cris Carter	.75
118 Gino Torretta	.25
119 Terry Allen	.25
120 Qadry Iamail	.25

A card number in parenthese ( ) indicates the set is unnumbered.

1993 Wild Card Field Force Superchrome

A 10-card partial parallel set to the Field Force chase set, this featured the same design as the regular Field Force, except this set had chromium fronts. The card backs have a photo on the left, with stats on the right. The card number is printed in the upper right, prefixed by "SCF."

	NM/M
Complete Set (10):	12.00
Common Player:	.40
1 Jerry Rice	1.50
2 Glyn Milburn	.40
3 Joe Montana	1.50
4 Rick Mirer	.75
5 Troy Aikman	1.50
6 Emmitt Smith	3.00
7 Dan Marino	3.00
8 Drew Bledsoe	2.00
9 Barry Sanders	1.50
10 Brett Favre	3.00

1993 Wild Card Red Hot Rookies

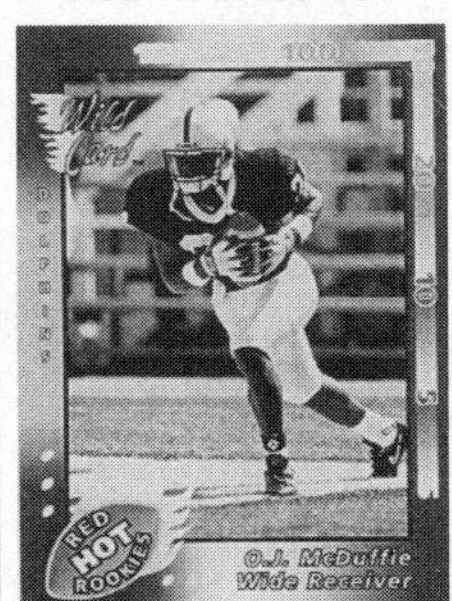

Randomly seeded into packs, the 30-card set was divided into three 10-card sets based on NFL divisions. The card fronts have the Red Hot Rookies logo in the lower left, with the Wild Card logo in the upper left. Various colored numbers border the photo on the top and right. The player's name and position are printed at the bottom. The backs -- numbered with a prefix of "WRHR," "ERHR" and "CRHR," depending on divisions -- have stats on the left. The player's name, bio and headshot are along the right side.

	NM/M
Complete Set (30):	18.00
Complete West Series (10):	8.00
Complete East Series (10):	5.00
Comp. Central Series (10):	5.00
Common Player (31-60):	.25
31 Dana Stubblefield	.60
32 Todd Kelly	.25
33 Dan Williams	.25
34 Glyn Milburn	.60
35 Natrone Means	1.00
36 Lincoln Kennedy	.25
37 Patrick Bates	.25
38 Jerome Bettis	1.00
39 Irv Smith	.60
40 Rick Mirer	1.00
41 Garrison Hearst	1.50
42 Kevin Williams	1.25
43 Terry Kirby	.60
44 O.J. McDuffie	.60
45 Leonard Renfro	.25
46 Victor Bailey	.40
47 Marvin Jones	.40
48 Drew Bledsoe	3.00
49 Reggie Brooks (UER) (Missing career college stats)	.40
50 Tom Carter	.40
51 Curtis Conway	1.25
52 Dan Footman	.25
53 Lamar Thomas	.40
54 Eric Curry	.60
55 Ryan McNeil	.40
56 Micheal Barrow	.40
57 Wayne Simmons	.40
58 George Teague	.40
59 Robert Smith	1.25
60 Qadry Ismail	.60

1993 Wild Card Red Hot Rookies Superchrome

This 10-card partial parallel set of Red Hot Rookies has the same design as the regular set, except it is done in chromium. The card backs are numbered with the "SCR" prefix. In addition, 20 high-number Superchrome Red Hot Rookies could be received by sending $29.95 to the company. Reportedly, 10,000 sets were produced.

	NM/M
Complete Set (10):	20.00
Common Player:	1.00
1 Dana Stubblefield	1.25
2 Glyn Milburn	1.00
3 Jerome Bettis	5.00
4 Rick Mirer	2.50
5 Garrison Hearst	3.00
6 Terry Kirby	1.50
7 Victor Bailey	1.00
8 Drew Bledsoe	6.00
9 Reggie Brooks	1.00
10 Qadry Ismail	1.25

1993 Wild Card Stat Smashers

This 20-card set features a silver foil front, with the Stat Smashers' logo in the upper right. The player's name, team and position are located in stripes at the bottom. The card backs, numbered with a "CSS" prefix, have the player's name, bio, headshot and highlights. The backs are black-bordered. In addition, a gold version was also randomly inserted. This set features players who play with teams in the AFC and NFC Central Divisions.

	NM/M
Complete Set (60):	60.00
Complete West Series (20):	20.00
Complete East Series (20):	20.00
Complete Central Series (20):	20.00
Common Player:	.50
Gold Cards:	.75X-1.25X
53 Ricky Watters	1.00
54 Jerry Rice	3.00
55 Steve Young	2.50
56 Shannon Sharpe	1.00
57 John Elway	1.50
58 Glyn Milburn	1.00
59 Marion Butts	.75
60 Junior Seau	1.00
61 Natrone Means	1.50
62 Joe Montana	4.00
63 J.J. Birden	.50
64 Michael Haynes	.75
65 Deion Sanders	2.00
66 Billy Joe Hobert	1.00
67 Nick Bell	.50
68 Jerome Bettis	1.50
69 Vaughn Dunbar	.50
70 Quinn Early	.75
71 Dan McGwire	.50
72 Rick Mirer	1.50
73 Kenneth Davis	.50
74 Thurman Thomas	1.00
75 Garrison Hearst	2.00
76 Ricky Proehl	.50
77 Jeff George	1.00
78 Rodney Culver	.50
79 Troy Aikman	3.00
80 Emmitt Smith	6.00
81 Rick Mirer	1.00
82 O.J. McDuffie	1.00
83 Keith Jackson	.75
84 Dan Marino	6.00
85 Heath Sherman	.50
86 Fred Barnett	.75
87 Rodney Hampton	1.00
88 Marvin Jones	.75
89 Brad Baxter	.50
90 Drew Bledsoe	5.00
91 Ricky Ervins	.50
92 Art Monk	.75
93 Neal Anderson	.75
94 Curtis Conway	1.75
95 John Copeland	1.00
96 Carl Pickens	1.00
97 David Klingler	.75
98 Michael Jackson	.75
99 Kevin Mack	.50
100 Eric Curry	1.00
101 Reggie Cobb	.50
102 Willie Green	.50
103 Barry Sanders	3.00
104 Haywood Jeffires	.75
105 Lorenzo White	.75
106 Sterling Sharpe	1.00
107 Brett Favre	3.00
108 Neil O'Donnell	1.00
109 Barry Foster	.75
110 Rich Gannon	.75
111 Robert Smith	1.75
112 Qadry Ismail	1.00

1993 Wild Card Stat Smashers Rookies

Produced in gold and silver foil versions, the 52-card set was randomly seeded one per jumbo pack. The designs of the card fronts and backs resemble the other Stat Smasher set.

	NM/M
Complete Set (52):	15.00
Common Player:	.25
Complete Gold Set (52):	25.00
Gold Cards:	.75X-1.5X
1 Todd Kelly	.25
2 Dana Stubblefield	.60
3 Curtis Conway	.60
4 John Copeland	.60
5 Russell Copeland	.40
6 Thomas Smith	.40
7 Glyn Milburn	.60
8 Jason Elam	.40
9 Steve Everitt	.40
10 Eric Curry	.60
11 Horace Copeland	.40
12 Ronald Moore	.60
13 Garrison Hearst	1.50
14 Natrone Means	1.00
15 Darrien Gordon	.40
16 Roosevelt Potts	.40
17 Kevin Williams	1.25
18 Derrick Lassic	.40
19 O.J. McDuffie	.60
20 Terry Kirby	.60
21 Scott Mitchell	.60
22 Victor Bailey	.40
23 Vaughn Hebron	.40
24 Lincoln Kennedy	.25
25 Michael Strahan	.25
26 Marvin Jones	.40
27 Tony McGee	.60
28 Ryan McNeil	.40
29 Micheal Barrow	.40
30 Wayne Simmons	.40
31 George Teague	.40
32 Vincent Brisby	.60
33 Drew Bledsoe	3.00
34 Rocket Ismail	.40
35 Patrick Bates	.25
36 James Jett	.40
37 Jerome Bettis	.60
38 Troy Drayton	.60
39 Tom Carter	.40
40 Reggie Brooks	.40
41 Lorenzo Neal	.40
42 Derek Brown (BB)	.60
43 Tyrone Hughes	.60
44 Rick Mirer	1.00
45 Carlton Gray	.25
46 Andre Hastings	.60
47 Deon Figures	.60
48 Qadry Ismail	.60
49 Robert Smith	.60
50 Irv Smith	.60
51 Chris Slade	.60
52 Willie Roaf	.60

1993 Wild Card Superchrome FF/RHR B/B

Wild Card doubled up card fronts from the Red Hot Rookies and Field Force on these back-to-back cards. The designs of both card fronts resemble the regular chase set design. This 10-card set was randomly seeded in Superchrome Series II packs. The cards are unnumbered.

	NM/M
Complete Set (10):	25.00
Common Player:	1.25
1 Troy Aikman, Dana Stubblefield	2.50
2 Drew Bledsoe, Drew Bledsoe	3.00
3 Brett Favre, Terry Kirby	5.00
4 Dan Marino, Reggie Brooks	5.00
5 Glyn Milburn, Rick Mirer	1.25
6 Rick Mirer, Glyn Milburn	1.25
7 Joe Montana, Jerome Bettis	3.00
8 Jerry Rice, Garrison Hearst	2.50
9 Barry Sanders, Victor Bailey	2.50
10 Emmitt Smith, Qadry Ismail (UER) (Misspelled Quadry)	5.00

1993 Wild Card Superchrome Rookies Promos

This five-card set featured purple chromium borders with the player photos inside a gold chrome oval. "Superchrome" is printed at the top, while "Rookies" is printed at the bottom. The player's name, team and position are printed within the gold oval at the top. In addition, "Wild Card sample" is printed on the card front. The card backs, numbered with a prefix of "P," are bordered in black and purple. The player's name, bio and highlights are included on the left, with a player photo on the right.

	NM/M
Complete Set (5):	6.00
Common Player:	.75
1 Rick Mirer	1.25
2 Reggie Brooks	.75
3 Glyn Milburn	.75
4 Drew Bledsoe	3.00
5 Jerome Bettis	1.25

1993 Wild Card Superchrome Rookies

This 50-card set, released in early 1994, was inserted six cards per Superchrome Rookies 15-card foil pack. The other nine cards were 1993 Wild Card cards. The chromium fronts showcase "Superchrome" at the top and "Rookies" at the bottom. A photo is located inside a gold oval, with the player's name, team and position printed inside. The card backs include a player photo on the right, while his name, bio and stats are listed on the left.

		NM/M
Complete Set (50):		20.00
Common Player:		.20
1	Dana Stubblefield	.50
2	Todd Kelly	.20
3	Curtis Conway	1.00
4	John Copeland	.50
5	Tony McGee	.50
6	Russell Copeland	.30
7	Thomas Smith	.30
8	Jason Elam	.30
9	Glyn Milburn	.50
10	Steve Everitt	.30
11	Demetrius DuBose	.20
12	Eric Curry	.50
13	Garrison Hearst	1.25
14	Ronald Moore	.50
15	Darrien Gordon	.30
16	Natrone Means	.75
17	Roosevelt Potts	.30
18	Derrick Lassic	.30
19	Kevin Williams	1.00
20	Scott Mitchell (UER) (Text indicates drafted in '91; should be '90)	1.00
21	O.J. McDuffie	.75
22	Terry Kirby	.50
23	Vaughn Hebron	.30
24	Victor Bailey	.30
25	Lincoln Kennedy	.20
26	Michael Strahan	.20
27	Marvin Jones	.30
28	Will Shields	.20
29	Ryan McNeil	.30
30	Micheal Barrow	.30
31	George Teague	.30
32	Wayne Simmons	.30
33	Vincent Brisby	.50
34	Drew Bledsoe	3.00
35	Patrick Bates	.20
36	James Jett	.30
37	Rocket Ismail	.30
38	Troy Drayton	.50
39	Jerome Bettis	.75
40	Tom Carter	.30
41	Reggie Brooks	.30
42	Tyrone Hughes	.50
43	Derek Brown	.50
44	Willie Roaf	.50
45	Carlton Gray	.20
46	Rick Mirer	.75
47	Andre Hastings	.50
48	Deon Figures	.50
49	Qadry Ismail	.50
50	Robert Smith	.50

1993 Wild Card Superchrome Rookies B/B

These 25 double-fronted back-to-back cards were randomly seeded in Superchrome Rookies foil packs. The unnumbered cards carry the same design as the regular Superchrome Rookies cards.

		NM/M
Complete Set (25):		30.00
Common Player:		.75
1	Victor Bailey, Vaughn Hebron	.75
2	Micheal Barrow, Ryan McNeil	.75
3	Patrick Bates, Vincent Brisby	.75
4	Jerome Bettis, Natrone Means	2.00
5	Drew Bledsoe, Rick Mirer	5.00
6	Reggie Brooks, Glyn Milburn	.75
7	Derek Brown RB, Tyrone Hughes	1.25
8	Tom Carter, Jason Elam	.75
9	Curtis Conway, Steve Everitt	2.50
10	John Copeland, Tony McGee	1.25
11	Russell Copeland, Thomas Smith	.75
12	Eric Curry, Demetrius DuBose	1.25
13	Troy Drayton, Darrien Gordon	1.25
14	Deon Figures, Andre Hastings	1.25
15	Carlton Gray, Willie Roaf	.75
16	Garrison Hearst, Ronald Moore	2.50
17	Qadry Ismail, Rocket Ismail	1.25
18	James Jett, Robert Smith	2.00
19	Marvin Jones, Will Shields	.75
20	Todd Kelly, Dana Stubblefield	1.25
21	Lincoln Kennedy, Michael Strahan	.75
22	Terry Kirby, O.J. McDuffie	2.00
23	Derrick Lassic, Kevin Williams	2.00
24	Scott Mitchell, Roosevelt Potts	2.00
25	Wayne Simmons, George Teague	.75

1967 Williams Portraits

Measuring 8" x 10", these 512 charcoal portraits of NFL players were a Kraft Cheese promotion. Sold in eight-portrait sets for $1 and a proof of purchase from various Kraft Cheese products, the set was broken down into four eight-portrait groups for each of the 16 NFL teams. In addition, an album which held 32 portraits was available for $2. The unnumbered portraits featured the player's name and position under the player portrait. The backs of the portraits were blank. An 8" x 10" checklist sheet was also issued, but it is not considered a card.

		NM/M
Complete Set (512):		5,000
Common Player:		6.00
1	Taz Anderson	10.00
2	Gary Barnes	10.00
3	Lee Calland	10.00
4	Junior Coffey	12.00
5	Ed Cook	10.00
6	Perry Lee Dunn	10.00
7	Dan Grimm	10.00
8	Alex Hawkins	15.00
9	Randy Johnson	12.00
10	Lou Kirouac	10.00
11	Errol Linden	10.00
12	Billy Lothridge	10.00
13	Frank Marchlewski	10.00
14	Richard Marshall	10.00
15	Billy Martin	10.00
16	Tom Moore	12.00
17	Tommy Nobis	20.00
18	Jim Norton	10.00
19	Nick Rassas	10.00
20	Ken Reaves	10.00
21	Bobby Richards	10.00
22	Jerry Richardson	15.00
23	Bob Riggle	10.00
24	Karl Rubke	10.00
25	Marion Rushing	10.00
26	Chuck Sieminski	10.00
27	Steve Sloan	12.00
28	Ron Smith	10.00
29	Don Talbert	10.00
30	Ernie Wheelwright	12.00
31	Sam Williams	10.00
32	Jim Wilson	10.00
33	Sam Ball	10.00
34	Raymond Berry	30.00
35	Bob Boyd	12.00
36	Ordell Braase	10.00
37	Barry Brown	10.00
38	Bill Curry	12.00
39	Mike Curtis	15.00
40	Alvin Haymond	10.00
41	Jerry Hill	10.00
42	David Lee	10.00
43	Jerry Logan	10.00
44	Tony Lorick	10.00
45	Lenny Lyles	10.00
46	John Mackey	18.00
47	Tom Matte	15.00
48	Lou Michaels	12.00
49	Fred Miller	10.00
50	Lenny Moore	30.00
51	Jimmy Orr	12.00
52	Jim Parker	18.00
53	Glenn Ressler	10.00
54	Willie Richardson	12.00
55	Don Shinnick	10.00
56	Billy Ray Smith	12.00
57	Bubba Smith	20.00
58	Dan Sullivan	10.00
59	Dick Szymanski	10.00
60	Johnny Unitas	50.00
61	Bob Vogel	10.00
62	Rick Volk	10.00
63	Jim Welch	10.00
64	Butch Wilson	10.00
65	Charlie Bivins	10.00
66	Charlie Brown	10.00
67	Doug Buffone	12.00
68	Rudy Bukich	12.00
69	Ron Bull	12.00
70	Dick Butkus	50.00
71	Jim Cadile	10.00
72	Jack Concannon	12.00
73	Frank Cornish	10.00
74	Don Croftcheck	10.00
75	Dick Evey	10.00
76	Joe Fortunato	12.00
77	Curtis Gentry	10.00
78	Bobby Joe Green	10.00
79	John Henry Johnson	15.00
80	Bob Jones	10.00
81	Jimmy Jones	10.00
82	Ralph Kurek	10.00
83	Roger LeClerc	10.00
84	Andy Livingston	10.00
85	Bennie McRae	10.00
86	Johnny Morris	12.00
87	Richie Petitbon	12.00
88	Loyd Phillips	10.00
89	Brian Piccolo	45.00
90	Jim Purnell	10.00
91	Mike Pyle	10.00
92	Mike Reilly	10.00
93	Gale Sayers	50.00
94	George Seals	10.00
95	Roosevelt Taylor	12.00
96	Bob Wetoska	10.00
97	Erich Barnes	12.00
98	Johnny Brewer	10.00
99	Monte Clark	10.00
100	Gary Collins	15.00
101	Larry Conjar	10.00
102	Vince Costello	10.00
103	Ross Fichtner	10.00
104	Bill Glass	12.00
105	Ernie Green	15.00
106	Jack Gregory	10.00
107	Charlie Harraway	12.00
108	Gene Hickerson	12.00
109	Fred Hoaglin	10.00
110	Jim Houston	12.00
111	Mike Howell	10.00
112	Joe Bob Isbell	10.00
113	Walter Johnson	12.00
114	Jim Kanicki	10.00
115	Ernie Kellerman	12.00
116	Leroy Kelly	20.00
117	Dale Lindsey	10.00
118	Clifton McNeil	12.00
119	Milt Morin	12.00
120	Nick Pietrosante	12.00
121	Frank Ryan	15.00
122	Dick Schafrath	12.00
123	Randy Schultz	10.00
124	Ralph Smith	10.00
125	Carl Ward	10.00
126	Paul Warfield	20.00
127	Paul Wiggin	12.00
128	John Wooten	12.00
129	George Andrie	10.00
130	Jim Boeke	10.00
131	Frank Clarke	12.00
132	Mike Connelly	10.00
133	Buddy Dial	12.00
134	Leon Donohue	10.00
135	Dave Edwards	12.00
136	Mike Gaechter	10.00
137	Walt Garrison	15.00
138	Pete Gent	12.00
139	Cornell Green	15.00
140	Bob Hayes	20.00
141	Chuck Howley	15.00
142	Lee Roy Jordan	18.00
143	Bob Lilly	30.00
144	Tony Liscio	10.00
145	Warren Livingston	10.00
146	Dave Manders	10.00
147	Don Meredith	30.00
148	Ralph Neely	12.00
149	John Niland	10.00
150	Pettis Norman	12.00
151	Don Perkins	15.00
152	Jethro Pugh	12.00
153	Dan Reeves	30.00
154	Mel Renfro	18.00
155	Jerry Rhome	15.00
156	Les Shy	10.00
157	J.D. Smith	10.00
158	Willie Townes	10.00
159	Danny Villanueva	10.00
160	John Wilbur	10.00
161	Mike Alford	10.00
162	Lem Barney	18.00
163	Charley Bradshaw	10.00
164	Roger Brown	12.00
165	Ernie Clark	10.00
166	Gail Cogdill	12.00
167	Nick Eddy	12.00
168	Mel Farr	12.00
169	Bobby Felts	10.00
170	Ed Flanagan	10.00
171	Jim Gibbons	12.00
172	John Gordy	12.00
173	Larry Hand	10.00
174	Wally Hilgenberg	10.00
175	Alex Karras	20.00
176	Bob Kowalkowski	10.00
177	Ron Kramer	12.00
178	Mike Lucci	15.00
179	Bruce Maher	10.00
180	Amos Marsh	10.00
181	Darris McCord	10.00
182	Tom Nowatzke	10.00
183	Milt Plum	15.00
184	Wayne Rasmussen	10.00
185	Roger Shoals	10.00
186	Pat Studstill	12.00
187	Karl Sweetan	10.00
188	Bobby Thompson	10.00
189	Doug Van Horn	12.00
190	Wayne Walker	12.00
191	Tommy Watkins	10.00
192	Garo Yepremian	15.00
193	Herb Adderley	12.00
194	Lionel Aldridge	6.00
195	Donny Anderson	8.00
196	Ken Bowman	6.00
197	Zeke Bratkowski	8.00
198	Bob Brown (DT)	6.00
199	Tom Brown	6.00
200	Lee Roy Caffey	6.00
201	Don Chandler	7.00
202	Tommy Crutcher	6.00
203	Carroll Dale	8.00
204	Willie Davis	15.00
205	Boyd Dowler	8.00
206	Marv Fleming	7.00
207	Gale Gillingham	6.00
208	Jim Grabowski	6.00
209	Forrest Gregg	15.00
210	Doug Hart	6.00
211	Bob Jeter	6.00
212	Hank Jordan	12.00
213	Ron Kostelnik	6.00
214	Jerry Kramer	15.00
215	Bob Long	6.00
216	Max McGee	8.00
217	Ray Nitschke	18.00
218	Elijah Pitts	7.00
219	Dave Robinson	7.00
220	Bob Skoronski	7.00
221	Bart Starr	25.00
222	Fred Thurston	7.00
223	Willie Wood	18.00
224	Steve Wright	6.00
225	Dick Bass	15.00
226	Maxie Baughan	12.00
227	Joe Carollo	10.00
228	Bernie Casey	15.00
229	Don Chuy	10.00
230	Charlie Cowan	10.00
231	Irv Cross	12.00
232	Willie Ellison	12.00
233	Roman Gabriel	18.00
234	Bruce Gossett	10.00
235	Roosevelt Grier	18.00
236	Anthony Guillory	10.00
237	Ken Iman	10.00
238	Deacon Jones	20.00
239	Les Josephson	12.00
240	Jon Kilgore	10.00
241	Chuck Lamson	10.00
242	Lamar Lundy	12.00
243	Tom Mack	15.00
244	Tommy Mason	12.00
245	Tommy McDonald	15.00
246	Ed Meador	12.00
247	Bill Munson	15.00
248	Bob Nichols	10.00
249	Merlin Olsen	25.00
250	Jack Pardee	15.00
251	Bucky Pope	10.00
252	Joe Scibelli	10.00
253	Jack Snow	15.00
254	Billy Truax	12.00
255	Clancy Williams	10.00
256	Doug Woodlief	10.00
257	Grady Alderman	12.00
258	John Beasley	10.00
259	Bob Berry	12.00
260	Larry Bowie	10.00
261	Bill Brown	15.00
262	Fred Cox	12.00
263	Doug Davis	10.00
264	Paul Dickson	10.00
265	Carl Eller	18.00
266	Paul Flatley	12.00
267	Dale Hackbart	10.00
268	Don Hansen	10.00
269	Clint Jones	10.00
270	Jeff Jordan	10.00
271	Karl Kassulke	12.00
272	John Kirby	10.00
273	Gary Larsen	12.00
274	Jim Lindsey	10.00
275	Earsell Mackbee	10.00
276	Jim Marshall	18.00
277	Marlin McKeever	10.00
278	Dave Osborn	15.00
279	Jim Phillips	10.00
280	Ed Sharockman	10.00
281	Jerry Shay	10.00
282	Milt Sunde	12.00
283	Archie Sutton	10.00
284	Mick Tingelhoff	15.00
285	Ron Vanderkelen	10.00
286	Jim Vellone	10.00
287	Lonnie Warwick	10.00
288	Roy Winston	12.00
289	Doug Atkins	20.00
290	Vern Burke	10.00
291	Bruce Cortez	10.00
292	Gary Cuozzo	12.00
293	Ted Davis	10.00
294	John Douglas	10.00
295	Jim Garcia	10.00
296	Tom Hall	10.00
297	Jim Heidel	10.00
298	Leslie Kelley	10.00
299	Billy Kilmer	18.00
300	Kent Kramer	10.00
301	Jake Kupp	10.00
302	Earl Leggett	10.00
303	Obert Logan	10.00
304	Tom McNeill	10.00
305	John Morrow	10.00
306	Ray Ogden	10.00
307	Ray Rissmiller	10.00
308	George Rose	10.00
309	David Rowe	10.00
310	Brian Schweda	10.00
311	Dave Simmons	10.00
312	Jerry Simmons	10.00
313	Steve Stonebreaker	12.00
314	Jim Taylor	20.00
315	Mike Tilleman	10.00
316	Phil Vandersea	10.00
317	Joe Wendryhoski	10.00
318	Dave Whitsell	12.00
319	Fred Whittingham	10.00
320	Gary Wood	10.00
321	Ken Avery	10.00
322	Bookie Bolin	10.00
323	Henry Carr	12.00
324	Pete Case	10.00
325	Clarence Childs	10.00
326	Mike Ciccolella	10.00
327	Glen Condren	10.00
328	Bob Crespino	10.00
329	Don Davis	10.00
330	Tucker Frederickson	15.00
331	Charlie Harper	10.00
332	Phil Harris	10.00
333	Allen Jacobs	10.00
334	Homer Jones	12.00
335	Jim Katcavage	12.00
336	Tom Kennedy	10.00
337	Ernie Koy	12.00
338	Greg Larson	12.00
339	Spider Lockhart	12.00
340	Chuck Mercein	12.00
341	Jim Moran	10.00
342	Earl Morrall	15.00
343	Joe Morrison	12.00
344	Francis Peay	10.00
345	Del Shofner	12.00
346	Jeff Smith	10.00
347	Fran Tarkenton	40.00
348	Aaron Thomas	12.00
349	Larry Vargo	10.00
350	Freeman White	10.00
351	Sidney Williams	10.00
352	Willie Young	10.00
353	Sam Baker	10.00
354	Gary Ballman	10.00
355	Randy Beisler	10.00
356	Bob Brown (OT)	12.00
357	Timmy Brown	15.00
358	Mike Ditka	45.00
359	Dave Graham	10.00
360	Ben Hawkins	10.00
361	Fred Hill	10.00
362	King Hill	12.00
363	Lynn Hoyem	10.00
364	Don Hultz	10.00
365	Dwight Kelley	10.00
366	Israel Lang	10.00
367	Dave Lloyd	10.00
368	Aaron Martin	10.00
369	Ron Medved	10.00
370	John Meyers	10.00
371	Mike Morgan	10.00
372	Al Nelson	10.00
373	Jim Nettles	10.00
374	Floyd Peters	12.00
375	Gary Pettigrew	10.00
376	Ray Poage	10.00
377	Nate Ramsey	10.00
378	Dave Recher	10.00
379	Jim Ringo	15.00
380	Joe Scarpati	10.00
381	Jim Skaggs	10.00
382	Norm Snead	18.00
383	Harold Wells	10.00
384	Tom Woodeshick	12.00
385	Bill Asbury	10.00
386	John Baker	10.00
387	Jim Bradshaw	10.00
388	Rod Breedlove	10.00
389	John Brown	10.00
390	Amos Bullocks	10.00
391	Jim Butler	10.00
392	John Campbell	10.00
393	Mike Clark	10.00
394	Larry Gagner	10.00
395	Earl Gros	12.00
396	John Hilton	10.00
397	Dick Hoak	12.00
398	Roy Jefferson	12.00
399	Tony Jeter	10.00
400	Brady Keys	10.00
401	Ken Kortas	10.00
402	Ray Mansfield	10.00
403	Paul Martha	10.00
404	Ben McGee	10.00
405	Bill Nelsen	15.00
406	Kent Nix	10.00
407	Fran O'Brien	10.00
408	Andy Russell	15.00
409	Bill Saul	10.00
410	Don Shy	10.00
411	Clendon Thomas	12.00
412	Bruce Van Dyke	10.00
413	Lloyd Voss	10.00
414	Ralph Wenzel	10.00
415	J.R. Wilburn	10.00
416	Marv Woodson	10.00
417	Jim Bakken	12.00
418	Don Brumm	10.00
419	Vidal Carlin	10.00
420	Bobby Joe Conrad	12.00
421	Willis Crenshaw	10.00
422	Bob DeMarco	10.00
423	Pat Fischer	12.00
424	Billy Gambrell	10.00
425	Prentice Gault	12.00
426	Ken Gray	10.00
427	Jerry Hillebrand	10.00
428	Charlie Johnson	15.00
429	Bill Koman	10.00
430	Dave Long	10.00
431	Ernie McMillan	10.00
432	Dave Meggysey	12.00
433	Dale Meinert	10.00
434	Mike Melinkovich	10.00
435	Dave O'Brien	10.00
436	Sonny Randle	12.00
437	Bob Reynolds	10.00
438	Joe Robb	10.00
439	Johnny Roland	12.00
440	Roy Shivers	10.00
441	Sam Silas	10.00
442	Jackie Smith	18.00
443	Rick Sortun	10.00
444	Jerry Stovall	10.00
445	Chuck Walker	10.00
446	Bobby Williams	10.00
447	Dave Williams	12.00
448	Larry Wilson	18.00
449	Kermit Alexander	10.00
450	Cas Banaszek	10.00
451	Bruce Bosley	10.00
452	John Brodie	20.00
453	Joe Cerne	10.00
454	John David Crow	12.00
455	Tommy Davis	12.00
456	Bob Harrison	10.00
457	Matt Hazeltine	10.00
458	Stan Hindman	10.00
459	Charlie Johnson	10.00
460	Jim Johnson	18.00
461	Dave Kopay	10.00
462	Charlie Krueger	12.00
463	Roland Lakes	10.00
464	Gary Lewis	10.00
465	Dave McCormick	10.00
466	Kay McFarland	10.00
467	Clark Miller	10.00
468	George Mira	12.00
469	Howard Mudd	10.00
470	Frank Nunley	10.00
471	Dave Parks	12.00
472	Walt Rock	10.00
473	Len Rohde	10.00
474	Steve Spurrier	35.00
475	Monty Stickles	10.00
476	John Thomas	10.00
477	Bill Tucker	10.00
478	Dave Wilcox	10.00
479	Ken Willard	12.00
480	Dick Witcher	10.00
481	Willie Adams	6.00
482	Walt Barnes	6.00
483	Jim Carroll	6.00
484	Dave Crossan	6.00
485	Charlie Gogolak	7.00
486	Tom Goosby	6.00
487	Chris Hanburger	8.00
488	Rickie Harris	6.00
489	Len Hauss	7.00
490	Sam Huff	18.00
491	Steve Jackson	6.00
492	Mitch Johnson	6.00
493	Sonny Jurgensen	18.00
494	Carl Kammerer	6.00
495	Paul Krause	12.00
496	Joe Don Looney	12.00
497	Ray McDonald	6.00
498	Bobby Mitchell	15.00
499	Jim Ninowski	7.00
500	Brig Owens	6.00
501	Vince Promuto	6.00
502	Pat Richter	7.00
503	Joe Rutgens	6.00
504	Lonnie Sanders	6.00
505	Ray Schoenke	6.00
506	Jim Shorter	6.00
507	Jerry Smith	8.00
508	Ron Snidow	6.00
509	Jim Snowden	6.00
510	Charley Taylor	18.00
511	Steve Thurlow	6.00
512	A.D. Whitfield	6.00

1994 Ted Williams Card Co. NFL Football

The Ted Williams Card Co., associated with the famous baseball Hall of Famer, followed up its debut baseball set with a 90-card set devoted to NFL greats from the past. Football Hall of Famer Roger Staubach lends his name to the set - the "Roger Staubach's NFL Football '94" set. The cards are numbered and grouped by teams first, followed by the set's three subsets - Chalkboard Legends (famous coaches), Golden Arms (great quarterbacks) and Dawning of a Legacy (two active quarterbacks). Cards were sold in packs of 10, or jumbo packs of 18. The set is limited to 5,000 numbered cases, meaning perhaps 200,000 of each card was made. There were also random inserts from six different sets available - Path to Greatness; Etched in Stone; the Walter Payton Collection; the Auckland Collection; Instant Replays; and limited print cards for Charles Barkley, Fred Dryer and Ted Williams throwing a football. Roger Staubach and Terry Bradshaw promo cards were also issued to preview the 1994 set. Also produced for the set were 18 different POG cards, which were inserted one per pack. Each case of cards also included a "Trade For Roger" card, which enabled collectors to obtain a 9-card Roger Staubach set available only through the mail.

		NM/M
Complete Set (90):		15.00
Common Player:		.10
Wax Box:		15.00
1	Roger Staubach	1.75
2	Tony Dorsett	.50
3	Bob Lilly	.35
4	Art Donovan	.25
5	Bert Jones	.30
6	Johnny Unitas	1.25
7	Jack Kemp	1.25
8	O.J. Simpson	1.75
9	Dick Butkus	.60
10	Gale Sayers	1.00
11	Mike Singletary	.25
12	Bronko Nagurski	.35
13	Ken Anderson	.25
14	Otto Graham	.35
15	Louis Groza	.25
16	Marion Motley	.30
17	Floyd Little	.15
18	Haven Moses	.10
19	Lem Barney	.25
20	Dick "Night Train"Lane	.25
21	Bobby Layne	.40
22	Ray Nitschke	.25
23	Willie Wood	.25
24	White Shoes Johnson	.20
25	Mike Bell	.10
26	Buck Buchanan	.30
27	Len Dawson	.35
28	Roman Gabriel	.20
29	Leroy Irvin	.10
30	Deacon Jones	.30
31	Bob Waterfield	.35
32	Bob Griese	1.00
33	Carl Eller	.25
34	Fran Tarkenton	1.00
35	John Hannah	.25
36	Jim Plunkett	.20
37	Tom Dempsey	.15
38	Archie Manning	.25
39	Charlie Conerly	.25
40	Sam Huff	.25
41	Andy Robustelli	.25
42	Don Maynard	.25
43	Matt Snell	.15
44	Wesley Walker	.15
45	George Blanda	.40
46	Ben Davidson	.15
47	Jim Otto	.25
48	Norm Van Brocklin	.35
49	Harold Carmichael	.20
50	Joe Greene	.30
51	L.C. Greenwood	.15
52	Jack Lambert	.35
53	Lance Alworth	.35
54	Dan Fouts	.45
55	John Brodie	.30
56	Steve Largent	.35
57	Jim Zorn	.15
58	Jim Hart	.15
59	Mel Gray	.15
60	Lee Roy Selmon	.15
61	Sammy Baugh	.30
62	Sonny Jurgensen	.60
63	Checklist	.10
64	George Allen	.15
65	George Halas	.40
66	Tom Landry	.60
67	Vince Lombardi	.60
68	John Madden	.40
69	Chuck Noll	.20
70	Don Shula	.30
71	Hank Stram	.15
72	Checklist	.10
73	Terry Bradshaw	.85
74	Len Dawson	.35
75	Dan Fouts	.35
76	Bart Starr	.50
77	Roger Staubach	1.50
78	Fran Tarkenton	.75
79	Y.A. Tittle	.35
80	Johnny Unitas	1.25
81	Checklist	.10
82	Brett Favre	.50
83	Brett Favre	.65
84	Brett Favre	.65
85	Brett Favre	.65
86	Neil O'Donnell	.20
87	Neil O'Donnell	.20
88	Neil O'Donnell	.20
89	Neil O'Donnell	.20
90	Checklist	.10

1994 Ted Williams Card Co. Auckland Collection

The Auckland Collection of insert cards features artwork by sports artist Jim Auckland. The cards have a special paper stock. The color illustration on each front is framed by a white border. The card back, numbered using an "AC" prefix, has a collage of ghosted player illustrations, plus a player profile, all bordered with a red and white frame. Cards were random inserts.

		NM/M
Complete Set (9):		30.00
Common Player:		3.00
1	Brett Favre	6.00
2	Vince Lombardi	7.00
3	Walter Payton	8.00
4	Phil Simms	5.00
5	Bart Starr	7.00
6	Roger Staubach	8.00
7	Jim Thorpe	6.00
8	Johnny Unitas	7.00
9	Checklist	3.00

1994 Ted Williams Card Co. Charles Barkley

These limited-edition inserts, devoted to NBA star Charles Barkley, were randomly included in Roger Staubach's NFL Football '94 packs. The cards are numbered with a "CB" prefix.

		NM/M
Complete Set (1):		5.00
1	Charles Barkley (LP)	5.00

1994 Ted Williams Card Co. Etched in Stone

This 9-card insert set highlights the Hall of Fame career of quarterback Johnny Unitas. Each card front has either a color action photo or sepia-toned photo against a full-bleed background. However, gold triangles are located in the upper left corner, with the set logo in it, and the lower right corner, where Unitas' name is located. Each card back is numbered with a "ES" prefix and presents text which traces Unitas' career. The brick red background of the cards form a puzzle which says "Etched in Stone" and shows a chisel and gold star.

		NM/M
Complete Set (9):		20.00
Common Unitas:		2.50
1	Johnny Unitas (1970 Championship Game)	2.50
2	Johnny Unitas (Super Bowl V)	2.50
3	Johnny Unitas (Memories)	2.50
4	Johnny Unitas (Injuries)	2.50
5	Johnny Unitas (1959 Rematch)	2.50
6	Johnny Unitas (College Days)	2.50
7	Johnny Unitas (1972)	2.50
8	Johnny Unitas (Greatest Game Ever)	2.50
9	Checklist	2.50

1994 Ted Williams Card Co. Instant Replays

Four great teams from the NFL's past are featured on these inserts, which were randomly included in Roger Staubach's NFL Football '94 packs. The cards, available in hobby stores on a regional basis, feature players from the New York Giants, Green Bay Packers, Pittsburgh Steelers and Raiders. Each card front has either a sepia-toned or color photo, with gold filmstrip borders on the right and left side. The set logo is in the lower left corner, next to the player's name, which is in a filmstrip at the bottom. The orange back, numbered using an "IR" prefix, has the player's name at the top in a gold banner. A ghosted roll of film is in the background. Cards were random inserts in hobby packs only.

		NM/M
Complete Set (17):		40.00
Common Player:		1.50
1	Phil Simms	2.50
2	Y.A. Tittle	3.00
3	Sam Huff	2.00
4	Brad Van Pelt	1.50
5	Brett Favre	4.00
6	Bart Starr	6.00
7	Paul Hornung	4.00
8	Ray Nitschke	3.00
9	Neil O'Donnell	2.00
10	Terry Bradshaw	6.00
11	Joe Greene	3.00
12	Jack Lambert	3.00
13	Jeff Hostetler	2.00
14	Lyle Alzado	1.50
15	Dave Casper	1.50
16	Ken Stabler	3.00
17	Replays Checklist	1.50

1994 Ted Williams Card Co. Path to Greatness

This 9-card Roger Staubach NFL Football '94 insert set is devoted to collegiate coaches and players who went on to star in the NFL. Each card front has a gold framed border along the top and left side of the photo, which is either sepia toned or in color. The player's name is stamped in gold foil in a white banner at the bottom of the card, next to the set's logo. The backs, numbered using a "PG" prefix, have a summary of the player's collegiate accomplishments.

		NM/M
Complete Set (9):		35.00
Common Player:		1.25
1	Tony Dorsett	5.00
2	Harold "Red" Grange	3.00
3	Bob Griese	4.00
4	Jeff Hostetler	2.00
5	Neil O'Donnell	1.75
6	Jim Plunkett	2.50
7	O.J. Simpson	12.00
8	Roger Staubach	8.00
9	Checklist	1.25

1994 Ted Williams Card Co. Sweetness - Walter Payton

These insert cards, devoted to "Sweetness," Walter Payton, were random inserts in jumbo packs only. Each card front has a full-bleed color photo of Payton, with the set logos appearing in the corners on the right side of the card. The card back, numbered using a "WP" prefix, is blue. It includes an explanation about the card's title, which covers a specific point in the Hall of Famer's career.

		NM/M
Complete Set (9):		15.00
Common Player:		2.00
1	Walter Payton Ditka On Payton	2.00
2	Walter Payton Winning It All	2.00
3	Walter Payton Rookie	2.00
4	Walter Payton 1977	2.00
5	Walter Payton College	2.00
6	Walter Payton Payton vs. O.J.	4.00
7	Walter Payton Sweetness	2.00
8	Walter Payton The Records	2.00
9	Checklist Card	2.00

1994 Ted Williams Card Co. POG Cards

Each of these cards contains two POGs, measuring 1-5/8" in diameter. The POGs were intended to be punched out of the blue card, which is standard size. Each POG has a closeup shot of the player on the front, in either black-and-white or color, plus his name. A card number also appears on the front; the backs are blank. Each pack of 1994 Ted Williams Roger Staubach football cards contained one of these POG cards.

		NM/M
Complete Set (18):		5.00
Common Player:		.20
1	Roger Staubach, Brett Favre	.75
2	Roman Gabriel, Lee Roy Jordan	.25
3	Dan Fouts, John Brodie	.35
4	Terry Bradshaw, Bart Starr	.75
5	O.J. Simpson, Floyd Little	1.00
6	Pete Pihos, Larry Csonka	.25
7	Dick "Night Train" Lane, Carl Eller	.35
8	Sam Huff, Ben Davidson	.35
9	Jack Lambert, Jethro Pugh	.30
10	Mike Singletary, Harold Carmichael	.25
11	Chuck Noll, Bud Grant	.20
12	John Madden, Lyle Alzado	.20
13	Walter Payton, Gale Sayers	1.00
14	Fred Dryer, Ron Mix	.25
15	Bob Griese, Doug Williams	.30
16	Tony Dorsett, Harold "Red" Grange	.50
17	Sonny Jurgensen, Jeff Hostetler	.30
18	Checklist Card	.20

1994 Ted Williams Card Co. Trade for Staubach

A "Trade for Roger" redemption card was randomly seeded one per case in the 5,000 cases. The redemption card, along with $3, entitled the collector to receive a nine-card set. The redemption card was returned to collectors with a validation stamp on it. Card fronts include borderless color or black-and-white photos, with the Roger Staubach NFL Football logo at the top right and the Ted Williams Card Co. logo in the lower left. Staubach's name is printed in foil along the right border. The card backs include a write-up of various highlights of Staubach's life. Cards are numbered with a "TR" prefix.

		NM/M
Complete Set (10):		30.00
Common Player:		3.00
1	Roger Staubach The Dodger	3.00
2	Roger Staubach College Years	3.00
3	Roger Staubach The Heisman Trophy	3.00
4	Roger Staubach The Draft	3.00
5	Roger Staubach Coach's Decision	3.00
6	Roger Staubach A Leader	3.00
7	Roger Staubach MVP Year	3.00
8	Roger Staubach Hall of Fame	3.00
9	Checklist	3.00
10	Trade for Roger Redemption Card	3.00

1974 Wonder Bread

Topps printed these 30 cards to be randomly included inside packages of Wonder Bread. Players from 18 NFL teams are represented on the cards, which have a closeup shot of the player and either a bright yellow or red border. The card back has biographical and statistical information about the player, plus a description and photograph illustrating a particular football play.

		NM/M
Complete Set (30):		25.00
Common Player:		.40
1	Jim Bakken	.45
2	Forrest Blue	.40
3	Bill Bradley	.40
4	Willie Brown	1.50
5	Larry Csonka	4.00
6	Ken Ellis	.40
7	Bruce Gossett	.40
8	Bob Griese	4.00
9	Chris Hanburger	.75
10	Winston Hill	.40
11	Jim Johnson	1.25
12	Paul Krause	1.00
13	Ted Kwalick	.85
14	Willie Lanier	1.50
15	Tom Mack	1.00
16	Jim Otto	1.50
17	Alan Page	1.75
18	Frank Pitts	.40
19	Jim Plunkett	1.50
20	Mike Reid	1.00
21	Paul Smith	.40
22	Bob Tucker	.75
23	Jim Tryer	.75
24	Eugene Upshaw	1.50
25	Phil Villapiano	1.00
26	Paul Warfield	2.00
27	Dwight White	.50
28	Steve Owens	.75
29	Jerrel Wilson	.40
30	Ron Yary	.75

1975 Wonder Bread

Once again, Topps produced this set for Wonder Bread to include the cards in specially-marked loaves of bread. The card front has a closeup shot of the player, with either a red or blue border surrounding it. The card back has statistics and biographical information about the player, plus questions and answers about the player and the game of football. The answers were written upside down.

		NM/M
Complete Set (24):		25.00
Common Player:		.35
1	Alan Page	1.50
2	Emmitt Thomas	.40
3	John Mendenhall	.35
4	Ken Houston	1.25
5	Jack Ham	1.25
6	L.C. Greenwood	.75
7	Tom Mack	.75
8	Winston Hill	.35
9	Isaac Curtis	.50
10	Terry Owens	.50
11	Drew Pearson	.60
12	Don Cockroft	.35
13	Bob Griese	2.50
14	Riley Odoms	.50
15	Chuck Foreman	.75
16	Forrest Blue	.35
17	Franco Harris	3.50
18	Larry Little	1.00
19	Bill Bergey	.60
20	Ray Guy	.90
21	Ted Hendricks	1.25
22	Levi Johnson	.35
23	Jack Mildren	.50
24	Mel Tom	.35

1976 Wonder Bread

These 24 cards use two different frames for the card front; red frames are used for defensive players, while blue frames are used for the offensive players in the set. A close-up shot of the player is featured prominently on the front. Each back has biographical information about the player, plus a diagram of a favorite play of coach Hank Stram. The corresponding text indicates the offensive players' assignments for that particular play. Topps produced the cards for Wonder Bread to insert into loaves of bread.

		NM/M
Complete Set (24):		5.00
Common Player:		.20
1	Craig Morton	.35
2	Chuck Foreman	.35
3	Franco Harris	1.00
4	Mel Gray	.35
5	Charley Taylor	.60
6	Rich Caster	.20
7	George Kunz	.20
8	Rayfield Wright	.20
9	Gene Upshaw	.75
10	Tom Mack	.50
11	Len Hauss	.35
12	Garo Yepremian	.20
13	Cedrick Hardman	.20
14	Jack Youngblood	1.00
15	Wally Chambers	.20
16	Jerry Sherk	.20
17	Bill Bergey	.35
18	Jack Ham	.75
19	Fred Carr	.20
20	Jack Tatum	.35
21	Cliff Harris	.35
22	Emmitt Thomas	.20
23	Ken Riley	.20
24	Ray Guy	1.00

1984 Wranglers Carl's Jr.

The 10-card, 2-1/2" x 3-5/8" set was sponsored by Carl's Jr. restaurants and the Tempe Police Department in Arizona and featured top players from the USFL Arizona Wranglers football team. Included in the set is coach George Allen and former longtime NFL quarterback Greg Landry. The card fronts have a black and white posed photo with bio information appearing on the back.

		NM/M
Complete Set (10):		30.00
Common Player:		2.50
1	George Allen (CO)	8.00
2	Luther Bradley (27)	3.50
3	Trumaine Johnson (2)	3.50
4	Greg Landry (11)	6.00
5	Kit Lathrop (70)	2.50
6	John Lee (64)	2.50
7	Keith Long (33)	2.50
8	Alan Risher (7)	2.50
9	Tim Spencer (46)	3.50
10	Lenny Willis (89)	2.50

1984 Wranglers 8x10 Arizona

The eight-sheet, 8" x 10" set features two rows of four black and white cards, with the player's name printed below each card. The sheets are numbered.

		NM/M
Complete Set (8):		40.00
Common Panel:		5.00
1	Edward Diethrich PRES, Bill Harris VP, George Allen CO, G. Bruce Allen GM, Robert Barnes, Dennis Bishop, Mack Boatner, Luther Bradley	8.00

2	Clay Brown, Eddie Brown, Wamon Buggs, Bob Clasby, Frank Corral, Doug Cozen, Doug Dennison, Robert Dillon	6.00
3	Larry Douglas, Joe Ehrmann, Nick Eyre, Jim Fahnhorst, Doak Field, Bruce Gheesling, Frank Giddens, Alfondia Hill	5.00
4	David Huffman, Hubert Hurst, Donnie Johnson, Randy Johnson, Trumaine Johnson, Jeff Kiewel, Bruce Laird, Greg Landry	7.00
5	Kit Lathrop, John Lee, Alva Liles, Dan Lloyd, Kevin Long, Karl Lorch, Andy Melontree, Frank Minnifield	5.00
6	Tom Piette, Tom Porras, Paul Ricker, Alan Risher, Don Schwartz, Bobby Scott, Lance Shields, Ed Smith	5.00
7	Robert Smith, Tim Spencer, John Stadnik, Mark Stevenson, Dave Steif, Gerry Sullivan, Ted Sutton, Motrandy Taylor	5.00
8	Rob Taylor, Tom Thayer, Todd Thomas, Ted Walton, Stan White, Lenny Willis, Tim Wrightman, Wilbur Young	5.00

Z

1995 Zenith Promos

The four-card, standard-size set was issued to promote the 1995 Pinnacle Zenith set. "Promo" is printed across the card back but otherwise they are similar to the regular-issue cards.

		NM/M
Complete Set (4):		25.00
Common Player:		1.00
1	Emmitt Smith	10.00
94	Steve Young	5.00
97	Dan Marino	10.00
NNO	Title Card	1.00

1995 Zenith

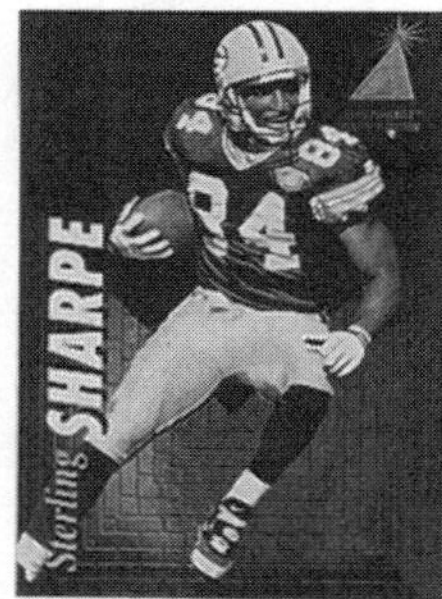

This 1995 Pinnacle Football Series II-Zenith Edition is a super-premium set that was the most limited of all Pinnacle football releases. All 150 cards in the set are printed on gold foil and noticeably thicker card stock. Each card front has a player action photo, with the set logo in the upper right corner. The player's first name is stamped in gold along the right side, next to his last name in white letters. The card back is horizontal and includes another action photo and analysis/breakdown of where the player makes his yardage or other types of plays. The cards are numbered using a Z prefix. Three types of inserts were randomly included in packs - Second Season, Rookie Roll Call and Z-Team.

		NM/M
Complete Set (150):		25.00
Common Player:		.10
Minor Stars:		.25
Pack (6):		2.00
Wax Box (24):		35.00
1	Emmitt Smith	4.00
2	Mark Carrier	.10
3	Johnny Mitchell	.10
4	Boomer Esiason	.40
5	Jackie Harris	.10
6	Warren Moon	.40
7	Harvey Williams	.10
8	Steve Walsh	.10
9	Cris Carter	.40
10	Natrone Means	.40
11	Art Monk	.40
12	Johnny Johnson	.10
13	Adrian Murrell	.10
14	John Elway	3.00
15	Larry Centers	.10
16	Ricky Ervins	.10
17	Jeff Graham	.10
18	Ricky Watters	.40
19	Eric Green	.10
20	Curtis Conway	.10
21	Jake Reed	.10
22	Michael Timpson	.10
23	Marcus Allen	.50
24	Andre Rison	.40
25	Terry Kirby	.10
26	Reggie White	.40
27	Randall Cunningham	.40
28	Jim Kelly	1.00
29	Robert Brooks	.75
30	Terance Mathis	.10
31	Anthony Miller	.40
32	Neil O'Donnell	.50
33	Jeff Hostetler	.10
34	Drew Bledsoe	3.00
35	Irving Spikes	.50
36	Keith Byars	.10
37	Rod Woodson	.10
38	Rob Moore	.50
39	Scott Mitchell	.10
40	Cody Carlson	.10
41	Alvin Harper	.75
42	Chris Warren	.50
43	Ben Coates	.75
44	Jim Everett	.10
45	Vinny Testaverde	.10
46	Glyn Milburn	.10
47	Calvin Williams	.10
48	Fred Barnett	.10
49	Tim Brown	1.00
50	Lorenzo White	.10
51	Brent Jones	.10
52	Henry Ellard	.10
53	Rick Mirer	.50
54	Junior Seau	1.00
55	Jeff Blake	.50
56	Desmond Howard	.10
57	Jerry Rice	3.00
58	Lewis Tillman	.10
59	Roosevelt Potts	.10
60	Raghib Ismail	.50
61	Eric Hill	.10
62	Brett Favre	4.00
63	Haywood Jeffires	.10
64	Barry Foster	.40
65	Willie Anderson	.10
66	Troy Aikman	3.00
67	Herschel Walker	1.00
68	Sean Dawkins	.50
69	Erric Pegram	.10
70	Irving Fryar	.10
71	Thurman Thomas	1.00
72	Eric Metcalf	.10
73	John Taylor	.10
74	Jeff George	.60
75	Courtney Hawkins	.10
76	Carl Pickens	.10
77	Mike Sherrard	.10
78	Rodney Hampton	.10
79	Joe Montana	4.00
80	Willie Davis	.10
81	Chris Penn	.10
82	Dave Brown	.10
83	Gary Brown	.10
84	Andre Reed	.50
85	Michael Irvin	1.00
86	Vincent Brisby	.10
87	Barry Sanders	4.00
88	Qadry Ismail	1.00
89	Reggie Brooks	.10
90	Bruce Smith	.10
91	David Klingler	.10
92	Michael Haynes	.10
93	Derek Russell	.10
94	Steve Young	3.00
95	Terry Allen	.10
96	Mark Seay	.10
97	Dan Marino	4.00
98	Jerry Rice All-Time TD Record	3.00
99	Cris Carter Single-Season Recp.	1.00
100	Art Monk Consecutive Games	1.00
101	Cortez Kennedy	.40
102	Stan Humphries	.50
103	Herman Moore	.50
104	Ron Moore	.40
105	Chris Miller	.10
106	Jerome Bettis	.50
107	Craig Erickson	.10
108	Keith Jackson	.10
109	Sterling Sharpe	.60
110	Ronnie Harmon	.10
111	Deion Sanders	2.00
112	Steve Beuerlein	.10
113	Bernie Parmalee	.50
114	Leroy Hoard	.10
115	O.J. McDuffie	.50
116	Garrison Hearst	1.00
117	Reggie Cobb	.10
118	Derek Brown	.10
119	David Palmer	.75
120	Gus Frerotte	.50
121	Dan Wilkinson	.50
122	Chuck Levy	.10
123	Derrick Alexander	.50
124	Aaron Bailey	.10
125	Thomas Lewis	.10
126	Antonio Langham	.10
127	Bryan Reeves	.10
128	William Floyd	.75
129	Lake Dawson	.50
130	Bert Emanuel	.50
131	Marshall Faulk	2.00
132	Heath Shuler	.50
133	Mark Brunell	2.00
134	Willie McGinest	.50
135	Mario Bates	.50
136	Byron Morris	.75
137	Tim Bowens	.10
138	Errict Rhett	.50
139	Charlie Garner	1.00
140	Darnay Scott	.75
141	Greg Hill	.50
142	LeShon Johnson	.10
143	Charles Johnson	.50
144	Trent Dilfer	1.00
145	Gus Frerotte	.40
146	Johnnie Morton	.50
147	Glenn Foley	.20
148	Perry Klein	.10
149	Ryan Yarborough	.10
150	Tydus Winans	.10

1995 Zenith Rookie Roll Call

These cards were randomly inserted in 1995 Pinnacle Series II-Zenith Edition packs, one per 72 packs. The 18-card set features some of the league's top rookies on an all-foil Dufex design. The front has an action photo, plus a second photo in a rectangle at the bottom with the insert set's starry logo in its upper left corner. Card backs are numbered using an "RC" prefix.

		NM/M
Complete Set (18):		100.00
Common Player:		4.00
Minor Stars:		8.00
Inserted 1:72		
1	Marshall Faulk	50.00
2	Charlie Garner	15.00
3	Derrick Alexander	4.00
4	Heath Shuler	5.00
5	Glenn Foley	4.00
6	Trent Dilfer	10.00
7	David Palmer	4.00
8	Gus Frerotte	5.00
9	Byron Morris	4.00
10	Mario Bates	4.00
11	Greg Hill	5.00
12	Errict Rhett	8.00
13	Darnay Scott	5.00
14	Lake Dawson	4.00
15	Bert Emanuel	8.00
16	LeShon Johnson	4.00
17	William Floyd	4.00
18	Charles Johnson	4.00

1995 Zenith Z-Team

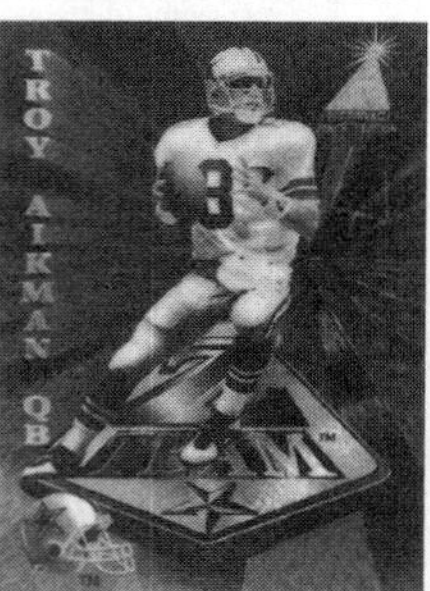

Z-Team inserts in 1995 Pinnacle Series II-Zenith packs could be found one per every 24 packs. The cards feature 18 of today's legends, utilizing an all-new 3D Dufex printing technology. The card front has a photo of the player standing on the Z Team logo, with his name and position running down the left side of the card. A team helmet is in the lower left corner; the Zenith logo is in the upper right. The card back is numbered using a "ZT" prefix.

		NM/M
Complete Set (18):		150.00
Common Player:		5.00
1	Dan Marino	25.00
2	Troy Aikman	20.00
3	Emmitt Smith	25.00
4	Barry Sanders	25.00
5	Joe Montana	25.00
6	Jerry Rice	20.00
7	John Elway	20.00
8	Marshall Faulk	15.00
9	Brett Favre	25.00
10	Steve Young	15.00
11	Sterling Sharpe	5.00
12	Drew Bledsoe	15.00
13	Ricky Watters	5.00
14	Cris Carter	5.00
15	Warren Moon	5.00
16	Natrone Means	5.00
17	Michael Irvin	5.00
18	Chris Warren	5.00

1995 Zenith Second Season

These Pinnacle Series II-Zenith Edition inserts pay tribute to the greatest moments from the 1994 post season, and the 25 players who made the plays happen. Included among the cards is one devoted to Joe Montana's final game. The front has the names of the teams and players involved in a game at the top; the insert set logo appears in the bottom left corner, opposite the Pinnacle logo. Card backs are numbered using an "SS" prefix. Cards were inserted one per six packs.

		NM/M
Complete Set (25):		60.00
Common Player:		1.00
Minor Stars:		2.00
1	Brett Favre	10.00
2	Dan Marino	10.00
3	Marcus Allen	3.00
4	Joe Montana	10.00
5	Vinny Testaverde	1.00
6	Emmitt Smith	10.00
7	Troy Aikman	6.00
8	Steve Young	6.00
9	William Floyd	1.00
10	Yancey Thigpen	2.00
11	Barry Foster	1.00
12	Natrone Means	1.00
13	Mark Seay	1.00
14	Stan Humphries	1.00
15	Tony Martin	1.00
16	Jerry Rice	8.00
17	Deion Sanders	3.00
18	Steve Young	6.00
19	Steve Young	6.00
20	Emmitt Smith	10.00
21	Troy Aikman	6.00
22	Jerry Rice (Super Bowl)	8.00
23	Ricky Watters (Super Bowl)	1.00
24	Steve Young (Super Bowl)	6.00
25	Jerry Rice, Steve Young (Super Bowl)	8.00

1996 Zenith Promos

The four-card, standard-size set was issued to promote the 1996 Zenith release. The cards are basically identical to the regular-issue cards, except for "Promo" which is printed on the card backs.

		NM/M
Complete Set (4):		30.00
Common Player:		.50
4	Emmitt Smith Z-Team	25.00
32	Jerry Rice	4.00
36	John Elway	2.00
NNO	Title Card	.50

1996 Zenith

This 1996 Pinnacle Zenith set includes a 35-card Rookies subset, 15 Proof Positive cards, three checklists and one Triple Trouble card featuring Troy Aikman, Emmitt Smith and Michael Irvin. Each regular card has extra-thick stock. The front has a color action photo of the player against a foil football with a silver glow around it. The player's name is in gold foil in the lower right corner; the brand logo is in gold foil in the upper left corner. The card back has a photo on the right side, with the player's name, position and team underneath. A card number, using a "Z" prefix, is in the upper left corner. A football field grid appears on the left, containing statistical achievement breakdowns by yardage increments. Each card in the regular set is also printed as part of an Artist's Proof parallel set. These cards use rainbow holographic gold foil stamping in the design and are seeded one per 23 packs. There were also three insert sets available: Noteworthy '95, Rookie Rising and Z Team.

		NM/M
Complete Set (150):		25.00
Common Player:		.10
Minor Stars:		.30
Artist Proof Cards:		3X-5X
Inserted 1:23		
Pack (6):		3.00
Wax Box (24):		50.00
1	Dan Marino	3.00
2	Yancey Thigpen	.50
3	Marcus Allen	.50
4	Curtis Conway	.50
5	Troy Aikman	2.50
6	William Floyd	.10
7	Ricky Watters	.50
8	Herman Moore	.75
9	Jim Harbaugh	.10
10	Isaac Bruce	.50
11	Drew Bledsoe	2.50
12	Jeff Blake	.50
13	Tim Brown	.50
14	Deion Sanders	1.50
15	Greg Hill	.10
16	Ben Coates	.10
17	Errict Rhett	.10
18	Barry Sanders	3.00
19	Erik Kramer	.10
20	Emmitt Smith	3.00
21	Brett Favre	4.00
22	Jerome Bettis	.75
23	Garrison Hearst	.50
24	Michael Irvin	.50
25	Chris Warren	.10
26	Steve Young	2.00
27	Cris Carter	.75
28	Carl Pickens	.50
29	Lake Dawson	.10
30	Marshall Faulk	.75
31	Vincent Brisby	.10
32	Jerry Rice	2.50
33	Eric Metcalf	.10
34	Natrone Means	.50
35	Steve Bono	.10
36	John Elway	3.00
37	Jeff Hostetler	.10
38	Scott Mitchell	.10
39	Andre Rison	.50
40	Daryl Johnston	.10
41	Mark Brunell	1.00
42	Jeff George	.50
43	Mario Bates	.10
44	Erric Pegram	.10
45	Brent Jones	.10
46	Trent Dilfer	.75
47	Larry Centers	.10
48	Anthony Miller	.10
49	Reggie White	.75
50	Bill Brooks	.10
51	Chris Zorich	.10
52	Jim Kelly	.75
53	Junior Seau	.50
54	Chris Miller	.10
55	Gus Frerotte	.50
56	Andre Reed	.50
57	Darnay Scott	.50
58	Brett Perriman	.10
59	Edgar Bennett	.10
60	Warren Moon	.50
61	Neil O'Donnell	.50
62	Jay Novacek	.10
63	Bam Morris	.10
64	Jim Everett	.10
65	Ken Norton Jr.	.10
66	Tony Martin	.50
67	Steve Atwater	.10
68	Henry Ellard	.10
69	Rodney Hampton	.10
70	Derrick Thomas	.10
71	Stan Humphries	.10
72	Harvey Williams	.10
73	Greg Lloyd	.10
74	Jake Reed	.10
75	Charles Haley	.10
76	Quinn Early	.10
77	Rodney Peete	.10
78	Brian Blades	.10
79	Robert Brooks	.10
80	Terry Allen	.50
81	Dave Brown	.10
82	Derrick Alexander	.10
83	Terance Mathis	.10
84	Rick Mirer	.50
85	Herschel Walker	.10
86	Charlie Garner	.50
87	Jeff Graham	.10
88	Bruce Smith	.10
89	Terry Kirby	.10
90	Craig Heyward	.10
91	Bernie Parmalee	.10
92	Adrian Murrell	.50
93	Derek Loville	.10
94	Heath Shuler	.50
95	Shannon Sharpe	.50
96	Bert Emanuel	.50
97	Hugh Douglas	.10
98	Lovell Pinkney	.10
99	Sherman Williams	.10
100	Tony Boselli	.10
101	Wayne Chrebet	.75
102	Orlanda Thomas	.10
103	Darick Holmes	.50
104	Tyrone Wheatley	.50
105	Christian Fauria	.10
106	Frank Sanders	.50
107	Chad May	.10
108	James Stewart	.50
109	Ken Dilger	.10
110	Kyle Brady	.10
111	Todd Collins	.50
112	Terrell Fletcher	.50
113	Eric Bjornson	.10
114	Justin Armour	.10
115	Rob Johnson	.75
116	Terrell Davis	3.00
117	J.J. Stokes	.75
118	Rashaan Salaam	.50
119	Chris Sanders	.50
120	Kerry Collins	.75
121	Michael Westbrook	.50
122	Eric Zeier	.50
123	Curtis Martin	3.00
124	Rodney Thomas	.10
125	Kordell Stewart	1.00
126	Joey Galloway	1.00
127	Steve McNair	1.50
128	Napoleon Kaufman	.40
129	Tamarick Vanover	.50
130	Stoney Case	.10
131	James Stewart	.10
132	Carl Pickens	.10
133	Jim Harbaugh	.10
134	Yancey Thigpen PP	.10
135	Ricky Watters	.10
136	Isaac Bruce PP	.10
137	Kordell Stewart PP	1.00
138	Jeff Blake PP	.10
139	Terrell Davis PP	3.00
140	Scott Mitchell	.10
141	Rodney Thomas	.10
142	Robert Brooks	.10
143	Joey Galloway PP	.50
144	Brett Favre PP	2.50
145	Kerry Collins PP	.10
146	Herman Moore	.10
147	Michael Irvin, Emmitt Smith, Troy Aikman	2.00
148	Dan Marino CL	1.00
149	Jerry Rice CL	.50
150	Emmitt Smith CL	.75

1996 Zenith Artist's Proofs

Each card in Pinnacle's 1996 Zenith football has a parallel Artist's Proof version. The cards, seeded one per 23 packs, use a rainbow holographic gold foil stamping in the design.

	NM/M
Common Player:	5.00
Minor Stars:	10.00
Artist's Proof Cards:	3X-5X

1996 Zenith Noteworthy '95

This 18-card insert set recaps some of the top events from the 1995 season. Each card front has a closeup photo of the player on the top half, against a silver-foiled background which says Noteworthy '95. The brand logo is in the upper right corner. The bottom half of the card has gold foil to show an action photo. The player's name and accomplishment are in silver foil above it. The card back is horizontal and is numbered in the upper left corner. A player photo appears on the card's left side, between two parallel gold bars. A recap of the player's 1995 season is on the right side. The player's name and team name are in the top gold bar; his accomplishment is in the lower bar. Cards were random inserts, one per 12 packs of 1996 Pinnacle Zenith football.

		NM/M
Complete Set (18):		40.00
Common Player:		1.00
Minor Stars:		2.00
Inserted 1:12		
1	Dan Marino	4.00
2	Jerry Rice	3.00
3	Michael Irvin	1.00
4	Emmitt Smith	4.00
5	Michael Irvin, Emmitt Smith	4.00
6	Herman Moore	1.00
7	Brett Favre	5.00
8	Barry Sanders	4.00
9	Marcus Allen	2.00
10	Steve Young	2.00
11	John Elway	3.00
12	Warren Moon	1.00
13	Jim Kelly	2.00
14	Jim Everett	1.00
15	Charles Haley	1.00
16	Emmitt Smith	4.00
17	Troy Aikman	3.00
18	Larry Brown	1.00

1996 Zenith Rookie Rising

Pinnacle's 1996 version of Rookie Roll Call is its 18-card Rookie Rising set. The cards, randomly inserted one per 24 packs of 1996 Pinnacle Zenith football, feature players from the 1995 rookie class. The cards use a double-sided Dufex process, which gives each card a 3-D look. The front has an action photo of the player on top of a football. An official is on the horizon, signalling a touchdown. The player's name along the left side is stamped in gold foil, as are the brand logo in the upper left corner and the insert set name, in a colored panel at the bottom. The horizontal back has a closeup shot of the player, along with his team's helmet. A card number is in the upper right corner in a black rectangle.

		NM/M
Complete Set (18):		40.00
Common Player:		1.00
Minor Stars:		2.00
Inserted 1:24		
1	Sherman Williams	1.00
2	Curtis Martin	4.00
3	Michael Westbrook	2.00
4	Darick Holmes	2.00
5	James Stewart	3.00
6	Eric Zeier	1.00
7	Tamarick Vanover	2.00
8	J.J. Stokes	3.00
9	Kordell Stewart	5.00
10	Rodney Thomas	1.00
11	Kerry Collins	3.00
12	Terrell Davis	15.00
13	Steve McNair	12.00
14	Rashaan Salaam	2.00
15	Joey Galloway	3.00
16	Wayne Chrebet	3.00
17	Chris Sanders	2.00
18	Frank Sanders	2.00

1996 Zenith Z-Team

These 1996 Pinnacle inserts, using clear plastic for the card design, have a see-through design that includes gold foil-stamping and etched highlights. The card front has a black Z running through it, with an action player photo on it. See-through etched action photos appear on each side of the Z. Gold foil is used for the brand logo, which appears in the upper right corner, and the set icon, which is in the lower left corner, next to the gold foil-stamped player's name. The back repeats the photo design from the front, except the Z cuts through the main photo and has a brief career summary inside it. A card number is in the upper left corner.

		NM/M
Complete Set (18):		200.00
Common Player:		2.00
Minor Stars:		4.00
Inserted 1:72		
1	Troy Aikman	10.00
2	Drew Bledsoe	10.00
3	Errict Rhett	2.00
4	Emmitt Smith	15.00
5	Jerry Rice	12.00
6	Cris Carter	6.00
7	Curtis Martin	12.00
8	Deion Sanders	6.00
9	Brett Favre	15.00
10	Michael Irvin	6.00
11	Chris Warren	2.00
12	Dan Marino	15.00
13	Steve Young	12.00
14	Marshall Faulk	12.00
15	Barry Sanders	15.00
16	John Elway	12.00
17	Isaac Bruce	6.00
18	Carl Pickens	2.00

1997 Zenith

The 150-card, regular-sized set included Season Highlights (15), Awesome Foursome (1) and Rookies (35) subsets and was available in six-card packs. The base cards feature the player's image over a gold foil circle. The player's name is also printed in gold foil on the card face bottom. The card backs feature another photo with in-depth statistical information. Insert sets include Rookie Rising, V2, Z Team, Gold Mirror Mylar Z Team and the base-set parallel Artist's Proof.

		NM/M
Complete Set (150):		50.00
Common Player:		.15
Minor Stars:		.30
Artist's Proof Cards:		5X-10X
Pack (6):		2.75
Wax Box (24):		45.00
1	Brett Favre	4.00
2	Jerry Rice	2.00
3	Shannon Sharpe	.15
4	Dan Marino	4.00
5	James Stewart	.15
6	Warren Moon	.15
7	Emmitt Smith	4.00
8	Kordell Stewart	2.00
9	Kerry Collins	.40
10	Ricky Watters	.15
11	Gus Frerotte	.15
12	Barry Sanders	3.00
13	Joey Galloway	.75
14	Marshall Faulk	.40
15	Todd Collins	.15
16	Steve McNair	.50
17	Tyrone Wheatley	.15
18	Isaac Bruce	.50
19	Troy Aikman	2.00
20	Larry Centers	.15
21	Alvin Harper	.15
22	Rashaan Salaam	.15
23	Eric Metcalf	.15
24	Jim Everett	.15
25	Ken Dilger	.15
26	Curtis Martin	3.00
27	Neil O'Donnell	.15
28	Thurman Thomas	.15
29	Andre Rison	.15
30	Steve Bono	.15
31	Garrison Hearst	.15
32	Junior Seau	.15
33	Napoleon Kaufman	.15
34	Jerome Bettis	.15
35	Frank Wycheck	.15
36	Lamar Smith	.15
37	Derrick Alexander	.15
38	Steve Young	1.50
39	Cris Carter	.15
40	O.J. McDuffie	.15
41	Deion Sanders	1.25
42	Robert Brooks	.15
43	Jeff Blake	.50
44	Marcus Allen	.15
45	Herman Moore	.15
46	Ray Zellars	.15
47	Tim Brown	.15
48	John Elway	1.50
49	Charles Johnson	.15
50	Rodney Peete	.15
51	Curtis Conway	.15
52	Kevin Greene	.15
53	Andre Reed	.15
54	Mark Brunell	2.00
55	Tony Martin	.15
56	Elvis Grbac	.15
57	Wayne Chrebet	.15
58	Vinny Testaverde	.15
59	Terry Allen	.15
60	Dave Brown	.15
61	LaShon Johnson	.15
62	Trent Dilfer	.15
63	Chris Warren	.15
64	Chris Sanders	.15
65	Kevin Carter	.15
66	Jim Harbaugh	.15
67	Terance Mathis	.15
68	Ben Coates	.15
69	Robert Smith	.15
70	Drew Bledsoe	2.00
71	Henry Ellard	.15
72	Scott Mitchell	.15
73	Andre Hastings	.15
74	Rodney Hampton	.15
75	Michael Jackson	.15
76	Jeff Hostetler	.15
77	Reggie White	.15
78	Kent Graham	.15
79	Adrian Murrell	.15
80	Carl Pickens	.15
81	Erik Kramer	.15
82	Terrell Davis	2.50
83	Sean Dawkins	.15
84	Jamal Anderson	.50
85	Stan Humphries	.15
86	Chris T. Jones	.15
87	Hardy Nickerson	.15
88	Anthony Johnson	.15
89	Michael Haynes	.15
90	Irving Spikes	.15
91	Bruce Smith	.15
92	Keenan McCardell	.15
93	Chris Chandler	.15
94	Tamarick Vanover	.15
95	Cortez Kennedy	.15
96	Roman Phifer	.15
97	Michael Irvin	.15
98	Tim Biakabutuka	.50
99	Stepfret Williams	.15
100	Eddie George	3.00
101	Karim Abdul-Jabbar	.50
102	Amani Toomer	.15
103	Tony Banks	.30
104	Regan Upshaw	.15
105	Leeland McElroy	.15
106	Jason Dunn	.15
107	Keyshawn Johnson	.40
108	Winslow Oliver	.15
109	Walt Harris	.15
110	Stanley Pritchett	.15
111	Eddie Kennison	.30
112	Terrell Owens	1.75
113	Duane Clemons	.15
114	John Mobley	.15
115	Simeon Rice	.15
116	Ernie Conwell	.15
117	Eric Moulds	.30
118	Marvin Harrison	.40
119	Rickey Dudley	.30
120	Mike Alstott	.30
121	Terry Glenn	.50
122	Brian Dawkins	.15
123	Kevin Hardy	.15
124	Bobby Engram	.30
125	Alex Van Dyke	.15
126	Zach Thomas	.75
127	Bryan Still	.15
128	Detron Smith	.15
129	Jerome Woods	.15
130	Muhsin Muhammad	.50
131	Lawrence Phillips	.30
132	Alex Molden	.15
133	Steve Young	.75
134	Troy Aikman	1.00
135	Junior Seau	.15
136	John Elway	.75
137	Dan Marino	2.00
138	Lawrence Phillips	.15
139	Brett Favre	2.00
140	Jerry Rice	1.00
141	Kerry Collins	.40
142	Barry Sanders	1.50
143	Mark Brunell	1.00
144	Drew Bledsoe	1.00
145	Eddie Kennison	.50
146	Marvin Harrison	.50
147	Emmitt Smith	2.00
148	Eddie George, Terry Glenn, Rickey Dudley, Bobby Hoying	2.00
149	Emmitt Smith	2.00
150	Dan Marino	2.00

1997 Zenith Artist's Proofs

Artist's Proofs parallel all 150 cards in the regular-issue set. The cards are distinguished by a holographic foil Artist's Proof stamp, and are inserted every 47 packs.

	NM/M
Complete Set (150):	1,500
Artist's Proof Cards:	15X-30X

1997 Zenith V2

The 18-card, regular-sized set features full-motion lenticular printing along with a conventional player photo. Inserted every 23 packs, the die-cut cards have "V2" printed underneath a motion picture with the player's name and team on the top and bottom of the horizontal card, respectively. The card backs are numbered with the "V" prefix and contain 1996 statistics and a brief highlight.

		NM/M
Complete Set (18):		125.00
Common Player:		2.00
1	Troy Aikman	10.00
2	John Elway	12.00
3	Jim Harbaugh	2.00
4	Barry Sanders	15.00
5	Deion Sanders	6.00
6	Drew Bledsoe	12.00
7	Dan Marino	15.00
8	Terrell Davis	10.00
9	Isaac Bruce	4.00
10	Jerome Bettis	2.00
11	Emmitt Smith	15.00
12	Brett Favre	15.00
13	Steve Young	10.00
14	Mark Brunell	6.00
15	Joey Galloway	2.00
16	Kordell Stewart	5.00
17	Jerry Rice	12.00
18	Curtis Martin	12.00

1997 Zenith Rookie Rising

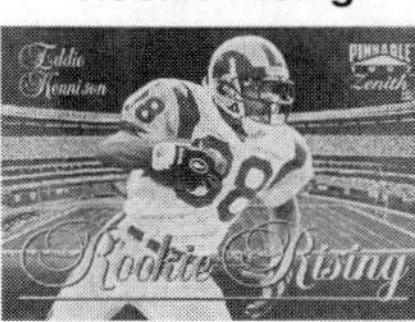

The 24-card, regular-sized set was inserted every 23 packs of Pinnacle Zenith. The cards are individually numbered and feature the rookie on the card face in Dufex printing over a common stadium. The horizontal cards have "Rookie Rising" printed in gold script on the front with the player's name written in script in the upper left corner. The backs feature a player shot over a football.

		NM/M
Complete Set (24):		60.00
Common Player:		1.00
1	Eddie Kennison	2.00
2	Marvin Harrison	8.00
3	Keyshawn Johnson	5.00
4	Leeland McElroy	1.00
5	Terrell Owens	12.00
6	Terry Glenn	4.00
7	Bobby Engram	1.00
8	Karim Abdul-Jabbar	2.00
9	Lawrence Phillips	1.00
10	Amani Toomer	4.00
11	Eric Moulds	4.00
12	Jason Dunn	1.00
13	Stanley Pritchett	1.00
14	Eddie George	12.00
15	Muhsin Muhammad	5.00
16	Rickey Dudley	1.00
17	Tony Banks	3.00
18	Bryan Still	1.00
19	Tim Biakabutuka	1.00
20	Simeon Rice	3.00
21	Zach Thomas	5.00
22	Kevin Hardy	1.00
23	Jerris McPhail	1.00
24	Mike Alstott	6.00

1997 Zenith Z-Team

The 18-card, regular-sized set was inserted every 71 packs of Pinnacle Zenith while the parallel Gold Mirror Mylar Z Team set was found every 191 packs. The standard Z Team cards feature the player's image on a horizontal card with a "Z" printed on the left side over a large football backdrop. The card backs are numbered with the "Z" prefix and feature another player shot over a large football. A large black "Z" with a highlight text insert is on the left side. The Gold Mirror Mylar Z Team inserts are distinguishable by the reflective gold background on the card fronts. The card backs are essentially the same, with the exception of the words "Mirror Gold" printed along the left border.

		NM/M
Complete Set (18):		250.00
Common Player:		10.00
Mirror Gold Cards:		2X-3X
1	Emmitt Smith	30.00
2	Dan Marino	30.00
3	Jerry Rice	25.00
4	John Elway	25.00
5	Curtis Martin	20.00
6	Deion Sanders	15.00
7	Tony Banks	10.00
8	Jim Harbaugh	10.00
9	Joey Galloway	10.00
10	Troy Aikman	25.00
11	Brett Favre	30.00
12	Keyshawn Johnson	10.00
13	Eddie George	15.00
14	Barry Sanders	30.00
15	Kordell Stewart	10.00
16	Steve Young	20.00
17	Terrell Davis	15.00
18	Drew Bledsoe	15.00

1997 Zenith Z-Team Mirror Golds

Z-Team Mirror Golds feature all 18 cards in the regular Z-Team set, but these inserts feature a Mirror Gold finish, and are inserted every 191 packs.

Mirror Golds:	2X-3X

COLLEGE

1971 Alabama Team Sheets

		NM/M
Complete Set (6):		45.00
Common Player:		6.00
1	Mike Raines, Pat Raines, Terry Rowell, Gary Rutledge, Bubba Sawyer, Bill Sexton, Wayne Wheeler, Jack White, Steve Williams, Dexter Wood	8.00
2	Johnny Musso, Lanny Norris, Robin Parkhouse, Jim Patterson, Steve Root, Jimmy Rosser, Jeff Rouzie, Robby Rowan, Chuck Strickland, Tom Surlas, Steve Wade, David Watkins	10.00
3	Fred Marshall, Noah Miller, John Mitchell, Randy Moore, Gary Reynolds, Benny Rippetoe, Ronny Robertson, John Rogers, Jim Simmons, Paul Spivey, Steve Sprayberry, Rod Steakley	6.00
4	Richard Bryan, Chip Burke, Jerry Cash, Don Cokely, Greg Gantt, Jim Grammer, Wayne Hall, John Hannah, Rand Lambert, Tom Lusk, Bobby McKinney, David McMakin	8.00
5	Ellis Beck, Steve Bisceglia, Jeff Blitz, Buddy Brown, Steve Dean, Mike Denson, Joe Doughty, Mike Eckenrod, Pat Keever, David Knapp, Jim Krapf, Joe LaBue	6.00
6	Wayne Adkinson, David Bailey, Marvin Barron, Jeff Beard, Andy Cross, John Croyle, Bill Davis, Terry Davis, Steve Higginbotham, Ed Hines, Jimmy Horton, Wilbur Jackson	7.00

1972 Alabama

		NM/M
Complete Set (54):		95.00
Common Player:		1.50
1C	Skip Kubelius	1.50
1D	Terry Davis	2.50
1H	Robert Fraley	1.50
1S	Paul "Bear" Bryant (CO)	25.00
2C	David Watkins	1.50
2D	Bobby McKinney	1.50
2H	Dexter Wood	1.50
2S	Chuck Strickland	1.50
3C	John Hannah	15.00
3D	Tom Lusk	1.50
3H	Jim Krapf	1.50
3S	Warren Dyar	1.50
4C	Greg Gantt	2.50
4D	Johnny Sharpless	1.50
4H	Steve Wade	1.50
4S	John Rogers	1.50
5C	Doug Faust	1.50
5D	Jeff Rouzie	1.50
5H	Buddy Brown	1.50
5S	Randy Moore	1.50
6C	David Knapp	2.50
6D	Lanny Norris	1.50
6H	Paul Spivey	1.50
6S	Pat Raines	1.50
7C	Pete Pappas	1.50
7D	Ed Hines	1.50
7H	Mike Washington	1.50
7S	David McMakin	2.50
8C	Steve Dean	1.50
8D	Joe LaBue	1.50
8H	John Croyle	1.50
8S	Noah Miller	1.50
9C	Bobby Stanford	1.50
9D	Sylvester Croom	2.50
9H	Wilbur Jackson	6.00
9S	Ellis Beck	1.50
10C	Steve Bisceglia	1.50
10D	Andy Cross	1.50
10H	John Mitchell	2.50
10S	Bill Davis	1.50
11C	Gary Rutledge	2.50
11D	Randy Billingsley	1.50
11H	Randy Hall	1.50
11S	Ralph Stokes	1.50
12C	Jeff Blitz	1.50
12D	Robby Rowan	1.50
12H	Mike Raines	1.50
12S	Wayne Wheeler	1.50
13C	Steve Sprayberry	1.50
13D	Wayne Hall	2.50
13H	Morris Hunt	1.50
13S	Butch Norman	1.50
JK	Denny Stadium	1.50
JK	Memorial Coliseum	1.50

1973 Alabama

		NM/M
Complete Set (54):		80.00
Common Player:		1.50
1C	Skip Kubelius	1.50
1D	Mark Prudhomme	1.50
1H	Robert Fraley	1.50
1S	Paul "Bear" Bryant (CO)	20.00
2C	David Watkins	1.50
2D	Richard Todd	12.00
2H	Buddy Pope	1.50
2S	Chuck Strickland	1.50
3C	Bob Bryan	1.50
3D	Gary Hanrahan	1.50
3H	Greg Montgomery	1.50
3S	Warren Dyar	1.50
4C	Greg Gantt	2.50
4D	Johnny Sharpless	1.50
4H	Rick Watson	1.50
4S	John Rogers	1.50
5C	George Pugh	2.50
5D	Jeff Rouzie	1.50
5H	Buddy Brown	1.50
5S	Randy Moore	1.50
6C	Ray Maxwell	1.50
6D	Alan Pizzitola	1.50
6H	Paul Spivey	1.50
6S	Ron Robertson	1.50
7C	Pete Pappas	1.50
7D	Steve Kulback	1.50
7H	Mike Washington	1.50
7S	David McMakin	2.50
8C	Steve Dean	1.50
8D	Jerry Brown	1.50
8H	John Croyle	1.50
8S	Noah Miller	1.50
9C	Leroy Cook	1.50
9D	Sylvester Croom	2.50
9H	Wilbur Jackson	6.00
9S	Ellis Beck	1.50
10C	Tyrone King	1.50
10D	Mike Stock	1.50
10H	Mike Dubose	1.50
10S	Bill Davis	1.50
11C	Gary Rutledge	2.50
11D	Randy Billingsley	1.50
11H	Randy Hall	1.50
11S	Ralph Stokes	1.50
12C	Woodrow Lowe	6.00
12D	Marvin Barron	1.50
12H	Mike Raines	1.50
12S	Wayne Wheeler	1.50
13C	Steve Sprayberry	1.50
13D	Wayne Hall	2.50
13H	Morris Hunt	1.50
13S	Butch Norman	1.50
JKO	Denny Stadium	1.50
JKO	Memorial Coliseum	1.50

1988 Alabama Winners

		NM/M
Complete Set (73):		10.00
Common Player:		.15
1	Title Card (Schedule on back)	.25
2	Charlie Abrams	.15
3	Sam Atkins	.15
4	Marco Battle	.15
5	George Bethune	.15
6	Scott Bolt	.15
7	Tommy Bowden	.25
8	Danny Cash	.15
9	John Cassimus	.15
10	David Casteal	.15
11	Terrill Chatman	.15
12	Andy Christoff	.15
13	Tommy Cole	.15
14	Tony Cox	.15
15	Howard Cross	.75
16	Bill Curry (CO)	.25
17	Johnny Davis	.25
18	Vantreise Davis	.15
19	Joe Demos	.15
20	Philip Doyle	.15
21	Jeff Dunn	.15
22	John Fruhmorgen	.15
23	Jim Fuller	.15
24	Greg Gilbert	.15
25	Pierre Goode	.25
26	John Guy	.15
27	Spencer Hammond	.15
28	Stacy Harrison	.15
29	Murry Hill	.15
30	Byron Holdbrooks	.15
31	Ben Holt	.15
32	Bobby Humphrey	.75
33	Gene Jelks	.50
34	Kermit Kendrick	.15
35	William Kent	.15
36	David Lenoir	.15
37	Butch Lewis	.15
38	Don Lindsey	.15
39	John Mangum	.50
40	Tim Matheny	.15
41	Mac McWhorter	.25
42	Chris Mohr	.25
43	Larry New	.15
44	Gene Newberry	.15
45	Lee Ozmint	.15
46	Trent Patterson	.15
47	Greg Payne	.15
48	Thomas Rayam	.15
49	Chris Robinette	.15
50	Larry Rose	.15
51	Derrick Rushton	.15
52	Lamonde Russell	.15
53	Craig Sanderson	.15
54	Wayne Shaw	.15
55	Willie Shepherd	.15
56	Roger Shultz	.15
57	David Smith	.15
58	Homer Smith	.15
59	Mike Smith	.15
60	Byron Sneed	.15
61	Robert Stewart	.15
62	Vince Strickland	.15
63	Brian Stutson	.15
64	Vince Sutton	.15
65	Derrick Thomas	5.00
66	Steve Turner	.15
67	Alan Ward	.15
68	Lorenzo Ward	.15
69	Steve Webb	.15
70	Woody Wilson	.15
71	Chip Wisdom	.15
72	Willie Wyatt	.15
73	Mike Zuga	.15

1989 Alabama Coke 20

		NM/M
Complete Set (20):		10.00
Common Player:		.35
C1	Paul "Bear" Bryant (CO)	1.50
C2	John Hannah	.75
C3	Fred Sington	.35
C4	Derrick Thomas	1.50
C5	Dwight Stephenson	.75
C6	Cornelius Bennett	1.00
C7	Ozzie Newsome	1.00
C8	Joe Namath (Art)	2.00
C9	Steve Sloan	.60
C10	Bill Curry (CO)	.35
C11	Paul "Bear" Bryant (CO)	1.50
C12	Big Al (Mascot)	.35
C13	Scott Hunter	.50
C14	Lee Roy Jordan	.75
C15	Walter Lewis	.35
C16	Bobby Humphrey	.35
C17	John Mitchell	.35
C18	Johnny Musso	.75
C19	Pat Trammell	.35
C20	Ray Perkins (CO)	.60

1989 Alabama Coke 580

		NM/M
Complete Set (580):		35.00
Common Player:		.08
1	Paul "Bear" Bryant (CO)	.75
2	W.T. Van De Graff	.08
3	A.T.S. Hubert	.08
4	Bill Buckler	.08
5	Hoyt (Wu) Winslett	.08
6	Tony Holm	.08
7	Fred Sington Sr.	.15
8	John Suther	.08
9	Johnny Cain	.08
10	Tom Hupke	.15
11	Millard Howell	.25
12	Steve Wright	.08
13	Bill Searcey	.08
14	Riley Smith	.08
15	Arthur "Tarzan" White	.08
16	Joe Kilgrow	.08
17	Leroy Monsky	.08
18	James Ryba	.08
19	Carey Cox	.08
20	Holt Rast	.08
21	Joe Domnanovich	.08
22	Don Whitmire	.15
23	Harry Gilmer	.25
24	Vaughn Mancha	.08
25	Ed Salem	.08
26	Bobby Marlow	.30
27	George Mason	.08
28	Billy Neighbors	.25
29	Lee Roy Jordan	.50
30	Wayne Freeman	.08
31	Dan Kearley	.08
32	Joe Namath	1.00
33	David Ray	.15
34	Paul Crane	.08
35	Steve Sloan	.25
36	Richard Cole	.08
37	Cecil Dowdy	.15
38	Bobby Johns	.08
39	Ray Perkins	.30
40	Dennis Homan	.25
41	Ken Stabler	.60
42	Robert W. Boylston	.08
43	Mike Hall	.08
44	Alvin Samples	.08
45	Johnny Musso	.25
46	Bryant-Denny Stadium	.08
47	Tom Surlas	.08
48	John Hannah	.30
49	Jim Krapf	.08
50	John Mitchell	.15
51	Buddy Brown	.08
52	Woodrow Lowe	.15
53	Wayne Wheeler	.08
54	Leroy Cook	.08
55	Sylvester Croom	.15
56	Mike Washington	.08
57	Ozzie Newsome	.50
58	Barry Krauss	.15
59	Marty Lyons	.25
60	Jim Bunch	.08
61	Don McNeal	.15
62	Dwight Stephenson	.30
63	Bill Davis	.08
64	E.J. Junior	.15
65	Tommy Wilcox	.15
66	Jeremiah Castille	.15
67	Bobby Swafford	.08
68	Cornelius Bennett	.50
69	David Knapp	.15
70	Bobby Humphrey	.30
71	Van Tiffin	.08
72	Sid Smith	.08
73	Pat Trammell	.25
74	Mickey Andrews	.08
75	Steve Bowman	.08
76	Bob Baumhower	.25
77	Bob Cryder	.08
78	Bryon Braggs	.15
79	Warren Lyles	.08
80	Steve Mott	.08
81	Walter Lewis	.15
82	Ricky Moore	.08
83	Wes Neighbors	.08
84	Derrick Thomas	.75
85	Kermit Kendrick	.08
86	Larry Rose	.08
87	Charlie Marr	.08
88	James Whatley	.08
89	Erin Warren	.08
90	Charlie Holm	.08
91	Fred Davis	.08
92	John Wyhonic	.08
93	Jimmy Nelson	.08
94	Roy Steiner	.15
95	Tom Whitley	.08
96	John Wozniak	.08
97	Ed Holdnak	.08
98	Al Lary	.08
99	Mike Mizerany	.08
100	Pat O'Sullivan	.08
101	Jerry Watford	.08
102	Cecil Ingram	.15
103	Mike Fracchia	.08
104	Benny Nelson	.08
105	Tommy Tolleson	.08
106	Creed Gilmer	.08
107	John Calvert	.08
108	Derrick Slaughter	.08
109	Mike Ford	.08
110	Bruce Stephens	.08
111	Danny Ford	.25
112	Jimmy Grammer	.08
113	Steve Higginbotham	.08
114	David Bailey	.08
115	Greg Gantt	.25
116	Terry Davis	.15
117	Chuck Strickland	.08
118	Bobby McKinney	.08
119	Wilbur Jackson	.25
120	Mike Raines	.08
121	Steve Sprayberry	.08
122	David McMakin	.15
123	Ben Smith	.08
124	Steadman Shealy	.25
125	John Rogers	.08
126	Ricky Davis	.15
127	Conley Duncan	.08
128	Wayne Rhodes	.08
129	Buddy Seay	.08
130	Alan Pizzitola	.08
131	Richard Todd	.25
132	Charlie Ferguson	.08
133	Charley Hannah	.15
134	Wiley Barnes	.08
135	Mike Brock	.08
136	Murray Legg	.08
137	Wayne Hamilton	.08
138	David Hannah	.08
139	Jim Bob Harris	.08
140	Bart Krout	.08
141	Bob Cayavec	.08
142	Joe Beazley	.08
143	Mike Adcock	.08
144	Albert Bell	.08
145	Mike Shula	.40
146	Curt Jarvis	.08
147	Freddie Robinson	.08
148	Bill Condon	.08
149	Howard Cross	.30
150	Joe Demyanovich	.08
151	Major Ogilvie	.25
152	Perron Shoemaker	.08
153	Ralph Jones	.08
154	Vic Bradford	.08
155	Ed Hickerson	.08
156	Mitchell Olenski	.08
157	George Hecht	.08
158	Russ Craft	.08
159	Joey Jones	.25
160	Jack Green	.08
161	Lowell Tew	.15
162	Lamar Moye	.08
163	Jesse Richardson	.15
164	Harold Lutz	.08
165	Travis Hunt	.08
166	Ed Culpepper	.08
167	Nick Germanos	.08
168	Billy Rains	.08
169	Don Cochran	.08
170	Cotton Clark	.08
171	Gaylon McCollogh	.08
172	Tim Bates	.08
173	Wayne Cook	.08
174	Jerry Duncan	.08
175	Steve Davis	.08
176	Donnie Sutton	.08
177	Randy Barron	.08
178	Frank Mann	.08
179	Jeff Rouzie	.08
180	John Croyle	.08
181	Skip Kubelius	.08
182	Steve Bisceglia	.08
183	Gary Rutledge	.15
184	Mike Dubose	.08
185	Johnny Davis	.25
186	K.J. Lazenby	.08
187	Jeff Rutledge	.25
188	Mike Tucker	.08
189	Tony Nathan	.25
190	Buddy Aydelette	.08
191	Steve Whitman	.08
192	Ricky Tucker	.08
193	Randy Scott	.08
194	Warren Averitte	.08
195	Doug Vickers	.08
196	Jackie Cline	.08
197	Wayne Davis	.08
198	Hardy Walker	.08
199	Paul Ott Carruth	.15
200	Paul "Bear" Bryant (CO)	.75
201	Randy Rockwell	.08
202	Chris Mohr	.15
203	Walter Merrill	.08
204	Johnny Sullivan	.08
205	Harold Newman	.08
206	Erskine Walker	.08
207	Ted Cook	.08
208	Charles Compton	.08
209	Bill Cadenhead	.08
210	Butch Avinger	.08
211	Bobby Wilson	.08
212	Sid Youngelman	.25
213	Leon Fuller	.08
214	Tommy Brooker	.15
215	Richard Williamson	.25
216	Riggs Stephenson	.25
217	Al Clemens	.08
218	Grant Gillis	.08
219	Johnny Mack Brown	.40
220	Major Ogilvie	.25
221	Fred Pickhard	.08
222	Herschel Caldwell	.08
223	Emile Barnes	.08
224	Mike McQueen	.08
225	Ray Abruzzese	.15
226	Jesse Bendross	.25
227	Lew Bostick	.08
228	Jimmy Bowdoin	.08
229	Dave Brown	.08
230	Tom Calvin	.08
231	Ken Emerson	.08
232	Calvin Frey	.08
233	Thornton Chandler	.15
234	George Weeks	.08
235	Randy Edwards	.08
236	Phillip Brown	.08
237	Clay Whitehurst	.08
238	Chris Goode	.08
239	Preston Gothard	.08
240	Herb Hannah	.08
241	John M. Snoderly	.08
242	Scott Hunter	.25
243	Bobby Jackson	.08
244	Bruce Jones	.08
245	Robbie Jones	.08
246	Terry Jones	.08
247	Leslie Kelley	.08
248	Larry Lauer	.08
249	Tommy Brooker, Pat Trammell, Lee Roy Jordan, Paul "Bear" Bryant, Mike Fracchia, Billy Neighbors '61 National Champs	.25
250	Bobby Luna	.08
251	Keith Pugh	.08
252	Alan McElroy	.08
253	'25 National Champs (Team Photo)	.15
254	Curtis McGriff	.25
255	Norman Mosley	.08
256	Herky Mosley	.08
257	Ray Ogden	.15
258	Pete Jilleba	.08
259	Benny Perrin	.08
260	Claude Perry	.08
261	Tommy Cole	.08
262	Ed Versprille	.08
263	'30 National Champs (Team Photo)	.15
264	Don Jacobs	.08
265	Robert Skelton	.08
266	Joe Curtis	.08
267	Bart Starr	.75
268	Young Boozer	.08
269	Tommy Lewis	.15
270	Woody Umphrey	.08
271	Carney Laslie	.08
272	Russ Wood	.08
273	David Smith	.08
274	Paul Spivey	.08
275	Linnie Patrick	.08
276	Ron Durby	.08
277	'26 National Champs (Team Photo)	.15
278	Robert Higginbotham	.08
279	William Oliver	.08
280	Stan Moss	.08
281	Eddie Propst	.08
282	Laurien Stapp	.08
283	Clem Gryska	.08
284	Clark Pearce	.08
285	Pete Cavan	.08
286	Tom Newton	.08
287	Rich Wingo	.15
288	Rickey Gilliland	.08
289	Conrad Fowler	.08
290	Rick Neal	.08
291	James Blevins	.08
292	Dick Flowers	.08
293	Marshall Brown	.08
294	Jeff Beard	.08
295	Pete Moore	.08
296	Vince Boothe	.08

297 Charley Boswell .08
298 Van Marcus .08
299 Randy Billingsley .15
300 Paul "Bear" Bryant (CO) .75
301 Gene Blackwell .08
302 Johnny Mosley .08
303 Ray Perkins (CO) .25
304 Harold Drew (CO) .08
305 Frank Thomas (CO) (Not the Frank Thomas that went to Auburn) .25
306 Wallace Wade .15
307 Newton Godfree .08
308 Steve Williams .08
309 Al Lewis .08
310 Fred Grant .08
311 Jerry Brown .08
312 Mal Moore .15
313 Tilden Campbell .08
314 Jack Smalley .08
315 Paul "Bear" Bryant (CO) .75
316 C.B. Clements .08
317 Billy Piper .08
318 Robert Lee Hamner .08
319 Donnie Faust .08
320 Gary Bramblett .08
321 Peter Kim .08
322 Fred Berrey .08
323 Paul "Bear" Bryant (CO) .75
324 John Fruhmorgen .08
325 Jim Fuller .08
326 Doug Allen .08
327 Russ Mosley .08
328 Ricky Thomas .08
329 Vince Sutton .08
330 Larry Roberts .15
331 Rick McLain .08
332 Charles Eckerly .08
333 '34 National Champs (Team Photo) .15
334 Eddie McCombs .08
335 Scott Allison .08
336 Vince Cowell .08
337 David Watkins .08
338 Jim Duke .08
339 Don Harris .08
340 Lanny Norris .08
341 Thad Flanagan .08
342 Albert Elmore .08
343 Alan Gray .08
344 David Gilmer .08
345 Hal Self .08
346 Ben McLeod .08
347 Clell (Butch) Hobson .50
348 Jimmy Carroll .08
349 Frank Canterbury .08
350 John Byrd Williams .08
351 Marvin Barron .08
352 William Stone .08
353 Barry Smith .15
354 Jerrill Sprinkle .08
355 Hank Crisp (CO) .08
356 Bobby Smith .08
357 Charles Gray .08
358 Marlin Dyess .08
359 '41 National Champs (Team Photo) .15
360 Robert Moore .08
361 Billy Neighbors, Pat Trammell, Darwin Holt 1961 National Champs (Team Photo) .15
362 Tommy White .08
363 Earl Wesley .08
364 John O'Linger .08
365 Bill Battle .08
366 Butch Wilson .08
367 Tim Davis .08
368 Larry Wall .08
369 Hudson Harris .08
370 Mike Hopper .08
371 Jackie Sherrill .40
372 Tom Somerville .08
373 David Chatwood .08
374 George Ranager .08
375 Tommy Wade .25
376 Joe Namath '64 National Champs .60
377 Reid Drinkard .08
378 Mike Hand .08
379 Ed White .25
380 Angelo Stafford .08
381 Ellis Beck .08
382 Wayne Hall .15
383 Randy Lee Hall .08
384 Jack O'Rear .08
385 Colenzo Hubbard .08
386 Gus White .08
387 Rich Watson .08
388 Steve Allen .08
389 John David Crow Jr. .15
390 Britton Cooper .08
391 Mike Rodriguez .08
392 Steve Wade .08
393 William J. Rice .08
394 Greg Richardson .08
395 Joe Jones .15
396 Todd Richardson .08
397 Anthony Smiley .08
398 Duff Morrison .08
399 Jay Grogan .08
400 Steve Booker .08
401 Larry Abney .08
402 Bill Abston .08
403 Wayne Adkinson .08
404 Charles Allen .08
405 Phil Allman .08
406 1965 National Champs (1965 Seniors) .25
407 James Angelich .08
408 Troy Barker .08
409 George Bethune .08
410 Bill Blair .08
411 Clark Boler .08
412 Duffy Boles .08
413 Ray Bolden .08
414 Bruce Bolton .08
415 Alvin Davis .08
416 Baxter Booth .08
417 Paul Boschung .08
418 1979 National Champs (Team Photo) .25
419 Richard Brewer .08
420 Jack Brown .08
421 Larry Brown .08
422 David Brungard .08
423 Jim Burkett .08
424 Auxford Burks .08
425 Jim Cain .08
426 Dick Turpin .08
427 Neil Callaway .08
428 David Casteal .08
429 Phil Chaffin .08
430 Howard Chappell .08
431 Bob Childs .08
432 Knute Rockne Christian .08
433 Richard Ciemny .08
434 J.B. Whitworth .08
435 Mike Clements .08
436 1973 National Champs (Coaching Staff) .08
437 Rocky Colburn .08
438 Danny Collins .08
439 James Taylor .08
440 Joe Compton .08
441 Bob Conway .08
442 Charlie Stephens .08
443 Kerry Goode .15
444 Joe LaBue .08
445 Allen Crumbley .08
446 Bill Curry (CO) .15
447 David Bedwell .08
448 Jim Davis .08
449 Mike Dean .08
450 Steve Dean .08
451 Vince DeLaurentis .08
452 Gary Deniro .08
453 Jim Dildy .08
454 Joe Dildy .08
455 Jimmy Dill .08
456 Jamie Dismuke .08
457 Junior Davis .08
458 Warren Dyar .08
459 Hugh Morrow .08
460 Grady Elmore .08
461 Jeff Rutledge, Tony Nathan, Barry Krauss, Marty Lyons, Rich Wingo 1978 National Champs .25
462 Ed Hines .08
463 D. Joe Gambrell .08
464 Kavanaugh (Kay) Francis .08
465 Robert Fraley .08
466 Milton Frank .08
467 Jim Franko .08
468 Buddy French .08
469 Wayne Rhoads .08
470 Ralph Gandy .08
471 Danny Gilbert .08
472 Greg Gilbert .08
473 Joe Godwin .08
474 Richard Grammer .08
475 Louis Green .08
476 Gary Martin .08
477 Bill Hannah .08
478 Allen Harpole .08
479 Neb Hayden .08
480 Butch Henry .08
481 Norwood Hodges .08
482 Earl Smith .08
483 Darwin Holt .08
484 Scott Homan .08
485 Nathan Rustin .08
486 Gene Raburn .08
487 Ellis Houston .08
488 Frank Howard .08
489 Larry Hughes .08
490 Joe Kelley .08
491 Charlie Harris .08
492 Legion Field .08
493 Tim Hurst .08
494 Hunter Husband .08
495 Lou Ikner .08
496 Craig Epps .08
497 Jug Jenkins .08
498 Billy Johnson .08
499 David Johnson .08
500 Jon Hand .25
501 Max Kelley .08
502 Terry Killgore .08
503 Eddie Lowe .08
504 Noah Langdale .08
505 Ed Lary .08
506 Foy Leach .08
507 Harry Lee .08
508 Jim Loftin .08
509 Curtis Lynch .08
510 John Mauro .08
511 Ray Maxwell .08
512 Frank McClendon .08
513 Tom McCrary .08
514 Sonny McGahey .08
515 John McIntosh .08
516 David McIntyre .08
517 Wes Thompson .08
518 James Melton .08
519 John Miller .08
520 Fred Mims .08
521 Dewey Mitchell .08
522 Lydell Mitchell (Linebacker) .08
523 Greg Montgomery .15
524 Jimmie Moore .08
525 Randy Moore .08
526 Ed Morgan .08
527 Norris Hamer .08
528 Frank Mosely .08
529 Sidney Neighbors .08
530 Rod Nelson .08
531 James Nisbet .08
532 Mark Nix .08
533 L.W. Noonan .08
534 Louis Thompson .08
535 William Oliver .08
536 Gary Otten .08
537 Wayne Owen .08
538 Steve Patterson .08
539 Charley Pell .25
540 Bob Pettee .08
541 Gordon Pettus .08
542 Gary Phillips .08
543 Clay Walls .08
544 Douglas Potts .08
545 Mike Stock .08
546 John Mark Prudhomme .08
547 George Pugh .15
548 Pat Raines .08
549 Joe Riley .08
550 Wayne Trimble .08
551 Darryl White .08
552 Bill Richardson .08
553 Ray Richeson .08
554 Danny Ridgeway .08
555 Terry Sanders .08
556 Kenneth Roberts .08
557 Jimmy Watts .08
558 Ronald Robertson .08
559 Norbie Ronsonet .08
560 Jimmy Lynn Rosser .08
561 Terry Rowell .08
562 Larry Joe Ruffin .08
563 Jack Rutledge .08
564 Al Sabo .08
565 David Sadler .08
566 Donald Sanford .08
567 Hayward Sanford .08
568 Paul Tripoli .08
569 Lou Scales .08
570 Kurt Schmissrauter .08
571 Willard Scissum .08
572 Joe Sewell .15
573 Jimmy Sharpe .08
574 Willie Shepherd .08
575 Jack Smalley Jr. .08
576 Jim Simmons (Tight End) .08
577 Jim Simmons (Tackle) .08
578 Malcolm Simmons .08
579 Dave Sington .08
580 Fred Sington Jr. .15

1992 Alabama Greats Hoby

NM/M
Complete Set (42): 12.00
Common Player: .25
1 Bob Baumhower .50
2 Cornelius Bennett .75
3 Buddy Brown .25
4 Paul "Bear" Bryant (CO) .75
5 Johnny Cain .25
6 Jeremiah Castille .35
7 Leroy Cook .25
8 Paul Crane .35
9 Philip Doyle .25
10 Harry Gilmer .35
11 Jon Hand .50
12 Herb Hannah .25
13 John Hannah .75
14 Dennis Homan .35
15 Dixie Howell .35
16 Bobby Humphrey .35
17 Don Hutson .75
18 Curt Jarvis .35
19 Lee Roy Jordan .75
20 Barry Krauss .35
21 Woodrow Lowe .35
22 Marty Lyons .35
23 Vaughn Mancha .25
24 John Mangum .35
25 Bobby Marlow .35
26 Don McNeal .35
27 Chris Mohr .35
28 Johnny Musso .50
29 Billy Neighbors .25
30 Ozzie Newsome .75
31 Ray Perkins .50
32 Fred Sington .25
33 Ken Stabler .75
34 Siran Stacy .35
35 Dwight Stephenson .50
36 Robert Stewart .25
37 Derrick Thomas 1.00
38 Van Tiffin .25
39 Mike Washington .25
40 Arthur "Tarzan" White .25
41 Tommy Wilcox .25
42 Willie Wyatt .25

1980 Arizona Police

NM/M
Complete Set (24): 90.00
Common Player: 3.00
1 Brian Clifford 3.00
2 Mark Fulcher 3.00
3 Bob Gareeb 3.00
4 Marcellus Green 4.00
5 Drew Hardville 3.00
6 Neal Harris 3.00
7 Richard Hersey 3.00
8 Alfondia Hill 3.00
9 Tim Holmes 3.00
10 Jack Housley 3.00
11 Glenn Hutchinson 3.00
12 Bill Jensen 3.00
13 Frank Kalil 3.00
14 Dave Liggins 3.00
15 Tom Manno 3.00
16 Bill Nettling 3.00
17 Hubert Oliver 6.00
18 Glenn Perkins 3.00
19 John Ramseyer 3.00
20 Mike Robinson 3.00
21 Chris Schultz 4.00
22 Larry Smith (CO) 4.00
23 Reggie Ware (SP) 30.00
24 Bill Zivic 3.00

1981 Arizona Police

NM/M
Complete Set (27): 30.00
Common Player: 1.50
1 Moe Ankney (ACO) 2.25
2 Van Brandon 1.50
3 Bob Carter 1.50
4 Brian Christiansen 1.50
5 Mark Fulcher 1.50
6 Bob Gareeb 1.50
7 Gary Gibson 1.50
8 Mark Gobel 1.50
9 Alfred Gross 1.50
10 Kevin Hardcastle 1.50
11 Neal Harris 1.50
12 Brian Holland 1.50
13 Ricky Hunley 3.00
14 Frank Kalil 1.50
15 Jeff Kiewel 1.50
16 Chris Knudsen 1.50
17 Ivan Lesnik 1.50
18 Tony Neely 1.50
19 Glenn Perkins 1.50
20 Randy Robbins 1.50
21 Gerald Roper 1.50
22 Chris Schultz 2.25
23 Gary Shaw 1.50
24 Larry Smith (CO) 2.25
25 Tom Tunnicliffe 2.25
26 Sergio Vega 1.50
27 Brett Weber 2.25

1982 Arizona Police

NM/M
Complete Set (26): 35.00
Common Player: 1.50
1 Brad Anderson 1.50
2 Steve Boadway 1.50
3 Bruce Bush 1.50
4 Mike Freeman 1.50
5 Marsharne Graves 1.50
6 Courtney Griffin 1.50
7 Al Gross 2.00
8 Julius Holt 1.50
9 Lamonte Hunley 2.00
10 Ricky Hunley 2.50
11 Vance Johnson 5.00
12 Chris Kaesman 1.50
13 John Kaiser 1.50
14 Mark Keel 1.50
15 Jeff Kiewell 1.50
16 Ivan Lesnik 1.50
17 Glenn McCormick 1.50
18 Ray Moret 1.50
19 Tony Neely 1.50
20 Byron Nelson 2.00
21 Glenn Perkins 1.50
22 Randy Robbins 1.50
23 Larry Smith (CO) 2.00
24 Tom Tunnicliffe 2.00
25 Kevin Ward 1.50
26 David Wood 1.50

1983 Arizona Police

NM/M
Complete Set (24): 35.00
Common Player: 1.50
1 John Barthalt 1.50
2 Steve Boadway 1.50
3 Chris Brewer 1.50
4 Lynnden Brown 1.50
5 Charlie Dickey 1.50
6 Jay Dobins 1.50
7 Joe Drake 1.50
8 Allan Durden 2.00
9 Byron Evans 5.00
10 Nils Fox 1.50
11 Mike Freeman 1.50
12 Marsharne Graves 1.50
13 Lamonte Hunley 2.00
14 Vance Johnson 4.00
15 John Kaiser 1.50
16 Ivan Lesnik 1.50
17 Byron Nelson 2.00
18 Randy Robbins 1.50
19 Craig Schiller 1.50
20 Larry Smith (CO) 2.00
21 Tom Tunnicliffe 2.00
22 Mark Walczak 1.50
23 David Wood 1.50
24 Max Zendejas 2.00

1984 Arizona Police

NM/M
Complete Set (25): 15.00
Common Player: .75
1 Alfred Jenkins 2.00
8 John Connor 1.00
13 Max Zendejas 1.00
15 Gordon Bunch .75
19 Allen Durden 1.00
23 Lynnden Brown .75
25 Vance Johnson 2.00
28 Tom Bayse .75
35 Brent Wood .75
40 Greg Turner .75
47 Steve Boadway .75
52 Nils Fox .75
54 Craig Vesling .75
62 David Connor .75
67 Charlie Dickey .75
71 Brian Denton .75
78 John DuBose .75
79 Joe Drake .75
82 Joy Dobyns .75
85 Mark Walczak .75
86 Jon Horton .75
92 David Wood .75
98 Lamonte Hunley 1.00
99 John Barthalt .75
NNO Larry Smith (CO) 1.00

1985 Arizona Police

NM/M
Complete Set (23): 15.00
Common Player: .75
1 Alfred Jenkins 1.50
2 David Adams .75
6 Chuck Cecil 2.00
13 Max Zendejas 1.00
15 Gordon Bunch .75
18 Jeff Fairholm 1.00
19 Allen Durden 1.00
29 Don Be'ans .75
32 Joe Prior .75
42 Blake Custer .75
44 Boomer Gibson .75
48 Byron Evans 3.00
50 Val Bichekas .75
52 Joe Tofflemire 1.00
54 Craig Vesling .75
59 Jim Birmingham .75
72 Curt DiGiacomo .75
73 Lee Brunelli .75
78 John DuBose .75
83 Gary Parrish .75
95 Cliff Thorpe .75
96 Glenn Howell .75
NNO Larry Smith (CO) 1.00

1986 Arizona Police

NM/M
Complete Set (24): 15.00
Common Player: .75
1 David Adams .75
2 Frank Arriola .75
3 Val Biehekas .75
4 Jim Birmingham .75
5 Chuck Cecil 1.50
6 James Debow .75
7 Brian Denton .75
8 Byron Evans 2.00
9 Jeff Fairholm 1.00
10 Boomer Gibson .75
11 Eugene Hardy .75
12 Derek Hill 1.50
13 Jon Horton .75
14 Alfred Jenkins 1.25
15 Danny Lockett 1.00
16 Stan Mataele .75
17 Chris McLemore .75
18 Jeff Rinehart .75
19 Ruben Rodriguez 1.00
20 Martin Rudolph .75
21 Larry Smith (CO) 1.00
22 Joe Tofflemire 1.00
23 Dana Wells .75
24 Brent Wood .75

1987 Arizona Police

NM/M
Complete Set (23): 15.00
Common Player: .75
2 Bobby Watters 1.00
3 Doug Pfaff .75
6 Chuck Cecil 1.50
11 Gary Coston .75
18 Jeff Fairholm 1.00
22 Eugene Hardy .75
26 Troy Cephers .75
34 Charles Webb .75
38 James Debow .75
40 Art Greathouse .75
43 Jerry Beasley .75
44 Boomer Gibson .75
47 Gallen Allen .75
52 Joe Tofflemire 1.00
60 Jeff Rinehart .75
64 Kevin McKinney .75
68 Tom Lynch .75
82 Derek Hill 1.25
84 Kevin Singleton 1.00
87 Chris Singleton 3.00
97 George Hinkle .75
99 Dana Wells .75
NNO Dick Tomey (CO) 1.25

1988 Arizona Police

NM/M
Complete Set (25): 15.00
Common Player: .75
2 Bobby Watters 1.00
4 Darryl Lewis 2.00
5 Durrell Jones .75
8 Reggie McGill .75
10 Ronald Veal 1.00
15 Jeff Hammerschmidt .75
22 Scott Geyer .75
24 R. Groppenbacher .75
25 David Eldridge .75
35 Mario Hampton .75
38 James Debow .75
40 Art Greathouse .75
50 Darren Case .75
51 Doug Penner .75
52 Joe Tofflemire 1.00
63 John Brandom .75
65 Ken Hakes .75
74 Glenn Parker 1.25
78 Rob Woods .75
82 Derek Hill 1.25
84 Kevin Singleton 1.00
87 Chris Singleton 2.00
96 Brad Henke .75
99 Dana Wells .75
NNO Dick Tomey (CO) 1.00

1989 Arizona Police

NM/M
Complete Set (26): 12.00
Common Player: .60
1 Zeno Alexander .60
2 John Brandom .60
3 Todd Burden .60
4 Darren Case .60
5 David Eldridge .60
6 Nick Fineanganofo .60
7 Scott Geyer .60
8 Art Greathouse .60
9 Richard Griffith .60
10 Ken Hakes .60
11 Jeff Hammerschmidt .60
12 Mario Hampton .60
13 Darryl Lewis 1.50
14 Kip Lewis .60
15 George Malauulu .75
16 Reggie McGill .60
17 John Nies .60
18 Glenn Parker 1.00
19 Mike Parker .60
20 Doug Pfaff .60
21 David Roney .60
22 Pete Russell .60
23 Chris Singleton 1.50
24 Paul Tofflemire .60
25 Dick Tomey (CO) .75
26 Ronald Veal .75

1992 Arizona Police

NM/M
Complete Set (21): 10.00
Common Player: .50
1 Tony Bouie 1.00
2 Heath Bray .50
3 Charlie Camp .50
4 Ontiwaun Carter .60
5 Richard Griffith .50
6 Sean Harris .75
7 Mike Heemsbergen .50
8 Jimmy Hopkins .50
9 Billy Johnson .50
10 Keshon Johnson .50
11 Chuck Levy 1.25
12 Richard Maddox .50
13 George Malauulu .60
14 Darryl Morrison .75
15 Mani Ott .50
16 Ty Parten .50
17 Mike Scurlock .60
18 Warner Smith .50
19 Dick Tomey (CO) .60
20 Terry Vaughn .50
21 Rob Waldrop .75

1993 Army Smokey

NM/M
Complete Set (15): 12.00
Common Player: .75
1 Paul Andrzejewski .75
2 Kevin Czarnecki .75
3 Chad Davis .75
4 Glenn Davis 3.00
5 Mark Escobedo .75
6 Gary Graves .75
7 Leamon Hall 1.00
8 Jason Miller 1.00
9 Mike Plaia .75
10 Rick Roper 1.00
11 Jim Slomka .75
12 Bob Sutton (CO) .75
13 Jason Sutton .75
14 Pat Zelley .75
15 Army Mule (Mascot) .75

1972 Auburn Tigers

NM/M
Complete Set (54): 70.00
Common Player: 1.50
1C Ken Calleja 1.50
1D James Owens 1.50
1H Mac Lorendo 1.50
1S Ralph (Shug) Jordan (CO) 6.00
2C Rick Neel 1.50
2D Ted Smith 1.50
2H Eddie Welch 1.50
2S Mike Neel 1.50
3C Larry Taylor 1.50
3D Rett Davis 1.50
3H Rusty Fuller 1.50
3S Lee Gross 1.50
4C Bruce Evans 1.50
4D Rusty Deen 1.50
4H Johnny Simmons 1.50
4S Bill Newton 1.50
5C David Beverly 2.00
5D Dave Lyon 1.50
5H Mike Fuller 3.00
5S Bill Luka 1.50
6C Ken Bernich 1.50
6D Andy Steele 1.50
6H Wade Whatley 1.50
6S Bob Newton 2.00
7C Benny Sivley 2.00
7D Gardner Jett 2.00
7H Rob Spivey 2.00
7S Jay Casey 1.50
8C David Langner 1.50
8D Terry Henley 1.50
8H Thomas Gossom 1.50
8S Joe Tanory 1.50
9C Chris Linderman 1.50
9D Harry Unger 1.50
9H Kenny Burks 1.50
9S Sandy Cannon 1.50
10C Roger Mitchell 1.50
10D Jim McKinney 1.50
10H Gaines Lanier 1.50
10S Dave Beck 1.50
11C Bob Farrior 1.50
11D Miles Jones 1.50
11H Tres Rogers 1.50
11S David Hughes 1.50
12C Sherman Moon 1.50
12D Danny Sanspree 1.50
12H Steve Taylor 1.50
12S Randy Walls 1.50
13C Steve Wilson 1.50
13D Bobby Davis 1.50
13H Hamlin Caldwell 1.50
13S Dan Nugent 1.50
JK Joker - Auburn Memorial Coliseum 1.50
JK Joker - Cliff Hare Stadium 1.50

1973 Auburn Tigers

NM/M
Complete Set (54): 60.00
Common Player: 1.50
1C Ken Calleja 1.50
1D Chris Wilson 1.50
1H Lee Hayley 1.50
1S Ralph (Shug) Jordan (CO) 5.00
2C Rick Neel 1.50

2D Johnny Sumner 1.50
2H Mitzi Jackson 1.50
2S Jim Pitts 1.50
3C Steve Stanaland 1.50
3D Rett Davis 1.50
3H Rusty Fuller 1.50
3S Lee Gross 1.50
4C Bruce Evans 1.50
4D Rusty Deen 1.50
4H Liston Eddins 1.50
4S Bill Newton 1.50
5C Jimmy Sirmans 1.50
5D Harry Ward 1.50
5H Mike Fuller 2.50
5S Bill Luka 1.50
6C Ken Bernich 1.50
6D Andy Steele 1.50
6H Wade Whatley 1.50
6S Bob Newton 2.00
7C Benny Sivley 2.00
7D Rick Telhiard 2.00
7H Rob Spivey 2.00
7S David Williams 1.50
8C David Langner 1.50
8D Chuck Fletcher 1.50
8H Thomas Gossom 1.50
8S Holley Caldwell 1.50
9C Chris Linderman 1.50
9D Ed Butler 1.50
9H Kenny Burks 1.50
9S Mike Flynn 1.50
10C Roger Mitchell 1.50
10D Jim McKinney 1.50
10H Gaines Lanier 1.50
10S Carl Hubbard 1.50
11C Bob Farrior 1.50
11D Ronnie Jones 1.50
11H Billy Woods 1.50
11S David Hughes 1.50
12C Sherman Moon 1.50
12D Mike Gates 1.50
12H Steve Taylor 1.50
12S Randy Walls 1.50
13C Roger Pruett 1.50
13D Bobby Davis 1.50
13H Hamlin Caldwell 1.50
13S Dan Nugent 1.50
JK Joker - Auburn Memorial Coliseum 1.50
JK Joker - Cliff Hare Stadium 1.50

1989 Auburn Coke 20

NM/M
Complete Set (20): 8.00
Common Player: .35
C1 Pat Dye (CO) .50
C2 Zane Smith .35
C3 War Eagle (Mascot) .50
C4 Tucker Frederickson .50
C5 John Heisman .50
C6 Ralph (Shug) Jordan (CO) .50
C7 Pat Sullivan .50
C8 Terry Beasley .35
C9 Ralph (Shug) Jordan, Paul "Bear" Bryant Punt Bama Punt .50
C10 Pat Sullivan, Terry Beasley Retired Jerseys .50
C11 Bo Jackson 2.00
C12 Lawyer Tillman .75
C13 Gregg Carr .35
C14 Lionel James .35
C15 Joe Cribbs .60
C16 Pat Sullivan, Bo Jackson, Pat Dye CO Heisman Winners 1.00
C17 Aundray Bruce .50
C18 Aubie (Mascot) .35
C19 Tracy Rocker .35
C20 James Brooks 1.00

1989 Auburn Coke 580

NM/M
Complete Set (580): 30.00
Common Player: .07
1 Pat Dye (CO) (His First Game) .25
2 Auburn's First Team (1892 Team Photo) .15
3 Pat Sullivan .25
4 Bo Jackson Over The Top .75
5 Jimmy Hitchcock .07
6 Walter Gilbert .07
7 Monk Gafford .07
8 Frank D'Agostino .07
9 Joe Childress .15
10 Jim Pyburn .15
11 Tex Warrington .07
12 Travis Tidwell .15
13 Fob James .07
14 Jim Phillips .15
15 Zeke Smith .07
16 Mike Fuller .15
17 Ed Dyas .07
18 Jack Thornton .07
19 Ken Rice .07
20 Freddie Hyatt .07
21 Jackie Burkett .15
22 Jimmy Sidle .15
23 Buddy McClinton .07
24 Larry Willingham .15
25 Bob Harris .07
26 Bill Cody .07
27 Lewis Colbert .07
28 Brent Fullwood .25
29 Tracy Rocker .15
30 Kurt Grain .07
31 Walter Reeves .15
32 Jordan-Hare Stadium .07
33 Ben Tamburello .07
34 Benji Roland .07
35 Chris Knapp .07
36 Dowe Aughtman .07
37 Auburn Tigers Logo .07
38 Tommie Agee .15
39 Bo Jackson .75
40 Freddy Weygand .15
41 Rodney Garner .07
42 Brian Shulman .07
43 Jim Thompson .07
44 Shan Morris .07
45 Ralph (Shug) Jordan (CO) .15
46 Stacy Searels .07
47 1957 Champs (Team Photo) .15
48 Mike Kolen .15
49 Pat Dye A Challenge Met .15
50 Mark Dorminey .07
51 Greg Staples .07
52 Randy Campbell .07
53 Duke Donaldson .07
54 Yann Cowart .07
55 Second Blocked Punt (vs. Alabama 1972) .15
56 Keith Uecker .15
57 David Jordan .07
58 Tim Drinkard .07
59 Connie Frederick .07
60 Pat Arrington .07
61 Willie Howell .07
62 Terry Page .07
63 Ben Thomas .07
64 Ron Stallworth .15
65 Charlie Trotman .07
66 Ed West .15
67 James Brooks .50
68 Doug Barfield, Ralph (Shug) Jordan Changing of the Guard .15
69 Ken Bernich .07
70 Chris Woods .07
71 Ralph (Shug) Jordan (CO) .15
72 Steve Dennis (CO) .07
73 Reggie Herring (CO) .07
74 Al Del Greco .15
75 Wayne Hall (CO) .07
76 Langdon Hall .07
77 Donnie Humphrey .07
78 Jeff Burger .15
79 Vernon Blackard .07
80 Larry Blakeney (CO) .07
81 Doug Smith .07
82 Ralph (Shug) Jordan, Vince Dooley Two Eras Meet .15
83 Kyle Collins .07
84 Bobby Freeman .07
85 Pat Sullivan (CO) .25
86 Neil Callaway (CO) .07
87 William Andrews .25
88 Curtis Kuykendall .07
89 David Campbell .07
90 Seniors of '83 .25
91 Bud Casey (CO) .07
92 Jay Jacobs (CO) .07
93 Al Del Greco .15
94 Pate Mote .07
95 Rob Shuler .07
96 Jerry Beasley .07
97 Pat Washington .07
98 Ed Graham .07
99 Leon Myers .07
100 Paul Davis (CO) .07
101 Tom Banks Jr. .15
102 Mike Simmons .07
103 Alex Bowden .07
104 Jim Bone .07
105 Wincent Harris .07
106 James Daniel .07
107 Jimmy Carter .07
108 Pat Sullivan Leading Passers .25
109 Alvin Mitchell .07
110 Mark Clement .07
111 Bob Brown .07
112 Shot Senn .07
113 Loran Carter .07
114 Pat Dye's First Team (Team Photo) .15
115 Bob Hix .07
116 Bo Russell .07
117 Mike Mann .07
118 Mike Shirey .07
119 Pat Dye (CO) .15
120 Kevin Greene .25
121 Auburn Creed .07
122 Ralph (Shug) Jordan, Tucker Frederickson, Jimmy Sidle Jordan's All-Americans .15
123 Dave Blanks .07
124 Scott Bolton .07
125 Vince Dooley .15
126 Tim Jessie .07
127 Joe Davis .07
128 Clayton Beauford .07
129 Wilbur Hutsell (AD) .15
130 Joe Whit (CO) .07
131 Gary Kelley .15
132 Bo Jackson .75
133 Aundray Bruce .25
134 Ronny Bellew .07
135 Hindman Wall .07
136 Frank Warren .07
137 Abb Chrietzberg .07
138 Collis Campbell .07
139 Randy Stokes .07
140 Teedy Faulk .07
141 Reese McCall .15
142 Jeff Jackson .07
143 Bill Burgess .07
144 Willie Huntley .07
145 Doug Huntley .07
146 Walter Gilbert Bacardi Bowl .07
147 Russ Carreker .07
148 Joe Moon .07
149 Pat Dye A Look Ahead (CO) .15
150 Joe Sullivan .07
151 Scott Riley .07
152 Larry Ellis .07
153 Jeff Parks .07
154 Gerald Williams .07
155 Mike Griffith .07
156 First Blocked Punt (vs. Alabama 1972) .15
157 Bill Beckwith (ADMIN) .07
158 Celebration (1957 Action Photo) .15
159 Tommy Carroll .15
160 John Dailey .07
161 George Stephenson .07
162 Danny Arnold .07
163 Mike Edwards .07
164 1894 Auburn-Alabama Trophy .15
165 Don Anderson .07
166 Alvin Briggs .07
167 Herb Waldrop (CO) .07
168 Jim Skuthan .07
169 Alan Hardin .07
170 Pat Sullivan, Bobby Freeman Coaching Generations .25
171 Georgia Celebration (1971 Locker Room) .07
172 Auburn 17, Alabama 16 (1972) .15
173 Nat Ceasar .07
174 Billy Hitchcock .15
175 SEC Championship Trophy .15
176 Dr. James E. Martin (PRES) .07
177 Ricky Westbrook .15
178 Fob James .15
179 Stacy Dunn .07
180 Tracy Turner .07
181 Pat Dye (CO) .15
182 Terry Beasley In the Record Book .07
183 Ed "Foots" Bauer .07
184 1984 Sugar Bowl Scoreboard .07
185 Mark Robbins .07
186 Paul White (CO) .07
187 Hindman Wall (AD) .07
188 David Beverly .15
189 Sugar Bowl Trophy .07
190 Edmund Nelson .07
191 Edmund Nelson .07
192 Cliff Hare .07
193 Byron Franklin .15
194 Richard Manry .07
195 Malcolm McCary .07
196 Patrick Waters (ADMIN) .07
197 Chester Willis .07
198 Alex Dudchock .07
199 Pat Sullivan In the Record Book .25
200 Pat Dye Victory Ride (CO) .15
201 Dr. George Petrie (CO) .07
202 D.M. Balliet (CO) .07
203 G.H. Harvey (CO) .07
204 F.M. Hall (CO) .07
205 John Heisman (CO) .25
206 Billy Watkins (CO) .07
207 J.R. Kent (CO) .07
208 Mike Harvey (CO) .07
209 Billy Bates (CO) .07
210 Mike Donahue (CO) .07
211 W.S. Kienholz (CO) .07
212 Mike Donahue (CO) .07
213 Boozer Pitts (CO) .07
214 David Morey (CO) .07
215 George Bohler (CO) .07
216 John Floyd (CO) .07
217 Chet Wynne (CO) .07
218 Jack Meagher (CO) .07
219 Carl Voyles (CO) .07
220 Earl Brown (CO) .07
221 Ralph (Shug) Jordan (CO) .15
222 Doug Barfield (CO) .15
223 Bo Jackson Most Career Points .35
224 Sonny Ferguson .07
225 Ronnie Ross .07
226 Gardner Jett .15
227 Jerry Wilson .07
228 Dick Schmatz .07
229 Morris Savage .07
230 James Owens .07
231 Eddie Welch .07
232 Lee Hayley .07
233 Dick Hayley .07
234 Jeff McCollum .07
235 Rick Freeman .07
236 Bobby Freeman (CO) .07
237 Auburn 32, Alabama 22 (Trophy) .15
238 Chip Powell .07
239 Nick Ardillo .07
240 Don Bristow .07
241 Bucky Waid .07
242 Greg Robert .07
243 Ray Rollins .07
244 Tommy Hicks .07
245 Steve Wallace .15
246 David Hughes .07
247 Chuck Hurston .07
248 Jimmy Long .07
249 John Cochran (AD) .07
250 Bobby Davis .07
251 G.W. Clapp .07
252 Jere Colley .07
253 Tim James .07
254 Joe Dolan .07
255 Jerry Gordon .07
256 Billy Edge .07
257 Lawyer Tillman .25
258 John McAfee .07
259 Scotty Long .07
260 Billy Austin .07
261 Tracy Rocker .15
262 Mickey Sutton .07
263 Tommy Traylor .07
264 Billy Van Dyke .07
265 Sam McClurkin .07
266 Mike Flynn .07
267 Jim Sirmans .07
268 Reggie Ware .15
269 Bill Luke .07
270 Don Machen .07
271 Bill Grisham .07
272 Bruce Evans .07
273 Hank Hall .07
274 Tommy Lunceford .07
275 Pat Thomas .07
276 Marvin Trott .07
277 Brad Everett .07
278 Frank Reeves .07
279 Bishop Reeves .07
280 Carver Reeves .07
281 Billy Haas .07
282 Pat Dye Dye's First AU Bowl (CO) .15
283 Nate Hill .07
284 Bucky Howard .07
285 Tim Christian .07
286 Tim Christian (CO) .07
287 Tom Nettleman .07
288 Carl Hubbard .07
289 Auburn's Biggest Wins (Chart) .07
290 Jay Jacobs .07
291 Jimmy Pettus .07
292 Cliff Hare Stadium .07
293 Richard Wood .15
294 Sandy Cannon .07
295 Bill Braswell .07
296 Foy Thompson .07
297 Robert Margeson .07
298 Pipeline to the Pros (Seven Pro Players) .25
299 Bill Evans .07
300 Marvin Tucker .07
301 Jack Locklear .07
302 Mike Locklear .07
303 Harry Unger .07
304 Lee Marke Sellers .07
305 Ted Foret .07
306 Bobby Foret .07
307 Mike Neel .07
308 Rick Neel .07
309 Mike Alford .07
310 Mac Crawford .07
311 Bill Cunningham .07
312 Pat Sullivan, Jeff Burger Legends .25
313 Frank LaRussa .07
314 Chris Vacarella .07
315 Gerald Robinson .15
316 Ronnie Baynes .07
317 Dave Edwards .07
318 Steve Taylor .07
319 Phillip Gilchrist .07
320 Ben McCurdy .07
321 Dave Hill .07
322 Jimmy Reynolds .07
323 Chuck Fletcher .07
324 Bogue Miller .07
325 Dave Beck .07
326 Johnny Simmons .07
327 Howard Simpson .07
328 Benny Sivley .15
329 1987 SEC Champions (Team Photo) .15
330 Frank Cox .07
331 Phil Gargis .07
332 Don Webb .07
333 Dan Presley .07
334 Al Giffin .07
335 Don Lewis .07
336 Eric Floyd .15
337 Ralph (Shug) Jordan Stadium .15
338 Terry Hendly .07
339 Billy Atkins .07
340 Tony Long .07
341 Jimmy Clemmer .07
342 John Valentine .07
343 Bruce Bylsma .07
344 Merrill Shirley .07
345 Kenny Howard (CO) .07
346 Hal Hamrick .07
347 Greg Zipp .07
348 Mac Champion .07
349 Kurt Crain Most Tackles in One Game .07
350 Bo Jackson Leading Career Rushers .35
351 Homer Williams .07
352 Mike Gates .07
353 Rusty Fuller .07
354 Rusty Deen .07
355 Bob Harris, Mark Dorminey Stalwart Defenders .07
356 Ralph (Shug) Jordan, Jerry Elliott, Frank Reeves Heroes of '56 .15
357 Road to the Top (Cartoon) .15
358 Cleve Wester .07
359 Jackie Burkett, Zeke Smith Line Stars .15
360 Bob Scarbrough .07
361 Jimmy Speigner .07
362 Danny Speigner .07
363 Alvin Bresler .07
364 Wade Whatley .07
365 Lance Hill .07
366 Andy Steele .07
367 John Whatley .07
368 Alton Shell .07
369 Larry Blakeney .07
370 Mickey Zofko .07
371 Gene Lorendo (CO) .07
372 Mac Lorendo .07
373 Buddy Davidson (CO) .07
374 Dave Woodward .07
375 Richard Guthrie .07
376 George Rose .07
377 Alan Bollinger .07
378 Danny Sanspree .07
379 Winky Giddens .07
380 Franklin Fuller .07
381 Charles Collins .07
382 Auburn, 23-22 (Scoreboard) .07
383 Jeff Weekley .07
384 Larry Haynie .07
385 Miles Jones .07
386 Bobby Wilson .15
387 Bobby Lauder .07
388 Charlie Glenn .07
389 Claude Saia .07
390 Tom Bryan .07
391 Lee Gross .07
392 Jerry Popwell .07
393 Tommy Groat .07
394 Neal Dettmering .07
395 Dr. W.S. Bailey (ADMIN) .07
396 Jim Pitts .07
397 College Football History (Cliff Hare Stadium) .07
398 Doc Griffith .07
399 Liston Eddins .07
400 Woody Woodall .07
401 Auburn Helmet .07
402 Skip Johnston .07
403 Trey Gainous .07
404 Randy Walls .07
405 Jimmy Partin .07
406 Dick Ingwerson .07
407 David Shelby .07
408 Harry Ward .07
409 Thomas Gossom .07
410 Sanford T. Gower .07
411 Jeff Beard, Ralph (Shug) Jordan Architects of the Future .15
412 Ed Butler .07
413 Bob Butler .07
414 Ben Strickland .07
415 Jeff Lott .07
416 Harris Rabren .07
417 Mike McQuaig .07
418 Steve Wilson .07
419 Jorge Portela .07
420 Dave Middleton .15
421 Tommy Yearout .07
422 Gusty Yearout .07
423 The Auburn Stadium .07
424 Cliff Hare Stadium .07
425 Oscar Burford .07
426 Cliff Hare Stadium .07
427 Cliff Hare Stadium .07
428 Jordan-Hare Stadium .07
429 Jack Meagher (CO) .07
430 Jeff Beard (AD) .07
431 Frank Young (ADMIN) .07
432 Frank Riley .07
433 Ernie Warren .07
434 Brian Atkins .07
435 George Atkins .07
436 Ricky Sanders .35
437 George Kenmore .07
438 Don Heller .07
439 Pat Meagher .07
440 Tim Davis .07
441 Tiger Meat (Cooks) .07
442 Joe Connally (CO) .07
443 Bob Newton .15
444 Bill Newton .07
445 David Langner .07
446 Charlie Langner .07
447 Brownie Flournoy (ADMIN) .07
448 Mike Hicks .07
449 Larry Hill .07
450 Tim Baker .07
451 Danny Bentley .07
452 Tommy Lowry .07
453 Jim Price .07
454 Lloyd Nix .07
455 Kenny Burks .07
456 Rusty Deen, Sallie Deen (ADMIN) .07
457 Johnny Sumner .07
458 Scott Blackmon .07
459 Chuck Maxime .07
460 Big SEC Wins (Chart) .07
461 Bo Davis .07
462 George Rose .07
463 Bob Bradley .07
464 Steve Osburne .07
465 George Gross .07
466 Andy Gross .07
467 M.L. Brackett .07
468 Herman Wilkes .07
469 Roger Mitchell .07
470 Bobby Beaird .07
471 Sammy Oates .07
472 Jimmy Ricketts .07
473 Bucky Ayters .07
474 Bill James .07
475 Johnny Wallis .07
476 Chris Jornson .07
477 Joe Overton .07
478 Tommy Lorino .07
479 James Warren .07
480 Lynn Johnson .07
481 Sam Mitchell .07
482 Sedrick McIntyre .07
483 Mike Holtzclaw .07
484 Dave Ostrowski .07
485 Jim Walsh .07
486 Mike Henley .07
487 Roy Tatum .07
488 Al Parks .07
489 Billy Wilson .15
490 Ken Luke .07
491 Phillip Hall .07
492 Bruce Yates .07
493 Dan Hataway .07
494 Joe Leichtnam .07
495 Danny Fulford .07
496 Ken Hardy .07
497 Rob Spivey .07
498 Rick Telhiard .07
499 Ron Yarbrough .07
500 Leo Sexton .07
501 Dick McGowen (CO) .07
502 Lee Kidd .07
503 Rex McKissick .07
504 Fagen Canzoneri, Zach Jenkins .07
505 Jim Bouchillon .07
506 Forrest Blue .25
507 Mike Helms .07
508 Bobby Hunt .15
509 John Liptak .07
510 James McKinney .07
511 Ed Baker .07
512 Heisman Trophies .25
513 Eddy Jackson .07
514 Jimmy Powell .07
515 Jerry Elliott .07
516 Jimmy Jones .07
517 Jimmy Laster .07
518 Larry Laster .07
519 Jerry Sansom .07
520 Don Downs .07
521 Danny Skutack .07
522 Keith Green .07
523 Spence McCracken .07
524 Lloyd Cheattom .07
525 Mike Shows .07
526 Spec Kelley .07
527 Dick McGowen .07
528 Jon Kilgore .07
529 Frank Gatski .25
530 Joel Eaves .07
531 John Adcock .07
532 Jimmy Fenton .07
533 Mike McCartney .07
534 Harrison McCraw .07
535 Mailon Kent .07
536 Dickie Flournoy .07
537 Coker Barton .07
538 Scotty Elam .07
539 Tim Wood .07
540 Terry Fuller .07
541 Johnny Kern .07
542 Mike Currier .07
543 Richard Cheek .07
544 Dan Dickerson .07
545 Arnold Fagen .07
546 John "Rat" Riley .07
547 Jimmy Burson .15
548 Bob Fleming .07
549 Mike Fitzhugh .07
550 Jim Patton .25
551 Bryant Harvard .07
552 Leon Cochran .07
553 Wayne Frazier .07
554 Phillip Dembowski .07
555 Alex Spurlin, Ed Spurlin .07
556 Bill Kilpatrick .07
557 Gaines Lanier .07
558 Johnny McDonald .07
559 Ray Powell .07
560 Jimmy Putman .07
561 Bobby Wasden .07
562 Roger Pruett .07
563 Don Braswell .07
564 Jim Jeffery .07
565 Pat Dye Auburn - A TV Favorite (CO) .15
566 Lamar Rawson .07
567 Larry Rawson .07
568 David Rawson .07
569 Hal Herring (CO) .07
570 Pat Sullivan .25
571 John Cochran .07
572 Jerry Gulledge .07
573 Steve Stanaland .15
574 Greg Zipp .07
575 John Trotman .07
576 Clyde Baumgartner .07
577 Jay Casey .07
578 Ralph O'Gwynne .07
579 Sid Scarborough .07
580 Tom Banks Sr. .15

1991 Auburn Hoby

NM/M
Complete Set (42): 9.00
Common Player: .25
523 Thomas Bailey .25
524 Corey Barlow .35
525 Reggie Barlow .35
526 Fred Baxter .35
527 Eddie Blake .35
528 Herbert Casey .25
529 Pedro Cherry .25
530 Darrel Crawford .35
531 Tim Cromartie .35
532 Juan Crum .25
533 Karekin Cunningham .25
534 Alonzo Etheridge .25
535 Joe Frazier .25
536 Pat Dye (AD/CO) .35
537 Thery George .25
538 Chris Gray .35
539 Victor Hall .25
540 Randy Hart .25
541 Chris Holland .25
542 Chuckie Johnson .25
543 Anthony Judge .25
544 Corey Lewis .25
545 Reid McMillion .25
546 Bob Meeks .25
547 Dale Overton .25
548 Mike Pelton .35
549 Bennie Pierce .25
550 Mike Pina .25
551 Anthony Redmon .25
552 Tony Richardson .25

553	Richard Shea	.25
554	Fred Smith	.35
555	Otis Mounds	.25
556	Ricky Sutton	.25
557	Alex Thomas	.25
558	Greg Thompson	.25
559	Tim Tillman	.25
560	Jim Von Wyl	.25
561	Stan White	.50
562	Darrell Williams	.25
563	James Willis	.25
564	Jon Wilson	.25

B

1984 BYU All-Time Greats

		NM/M
Complete Set (15):		18.00
Common Player:		.50
1	Steve Young	10.00
2	Eldon Fortie	.50
3	Bart Oates	1.50
4	Pete Van Valkenburg	.60
5	Mike Mees	.50
6	Wayne Baker	.50
7	Gordon Gravelle	.60
8	Gordon Hudson	.60
9	Kurt Gunther	.50
10	Todd Shell	.60
11	Chris Farasopoulos	1.00
12	Paul Howard	.50
13	Dave Atkinson	.50
14	Paul Linford	.50
15	Phil Odle	.60

1984-85 BYU National Champions

		NM/M
Complete Set (15):		25.00
Common Player:		1.50
1	Mark Allen	1.50
2	Adam Hysbert	1.50
3	Larry Hamilton	1.50
4	Jim Hermann	1.50
5	Kyle Morrell	2.00
6	Lee Johnson	1.50
7	David Mills	1.50
8	Garrick Wright, Matich Wright, Anae Wright, Louis Wong	3.00
9	Jim Hermann, Larry Hamilton	2.00
10	Louis Wong	1.50
11	Robbie Bosco Bosco in Holiday Bowl	5.00
12	BYU Cougar Stadium	1.50
13	UPI Final Top 20	1.50
14	BYU National Championship Roster	1.50
15	Schedule and Scores For 1984	1.50

1990 BYU Safety

		NM/M
Complete Set (12):		15.00
Common Player:		1.00
1	Rocky Beigel	1.00
2	Matt Bellini	1.50
3	Tony Crutchfield	1.00
4	Ty Detmer	6.00
5	Norm Dixon	1.00
6	Earl Kauffman	1.00
7	Rich Kaufusi	1.50
8	Bryan May	1.00
9	Brent Nyberg	1.00
10	Chris Smith	1.50
11	Mark Smith	1.00
12	Robert Stephens	1.00

1991 BYU Safety

		NM/M
Complete Set (16):		10.00
Common Player:		.75
1	Josh Arnold	.75
2	Rocky Biegel	.75
3	Scott Charlton	.75
4	Tony Crutchfield	.75
5	Ty Detmer	3.00
6	LaVell Edwards (CO)	1.50
7	Scott Giles	.75
8	Derwin Gray	1.00
9	Shad Hansen	.75
10	Brad Hunter	.75
11	Earl Kauffman	.75
12	Jared Leavitt	.75
13	Micah Matsuzaki	.75
14	Bryan May	.75
15	Peter Tuipulotu	.75
16	Matt Zundel	.75

1992 BYU Safety

		NM/M
Complete Set (16):		10.00
Common Player:		.60
1	Tyler Anderson	.60
2	Randy Brock	.60
3	Brad Clark	.60
4	Eric Drage	1.00
5	LaVell Edwards (CO)	1.00
6	Mike Empey	.60
7	Lenny Gomes	.60
8	Derwin Gray	1.00
9	Shad Hansen	.60
10	Eli Herring	.75
11	Micah Matsuzaki	.60
12	Patrick Mitchell	.75
13	Garry Pay	.60
14	Greg Pitts	.60
15	Byron Rex	.75
16	Jamal Willis	1.00

1993 BYU

		NM/M
Complete Set (20):		12.00
Common Player:		.60
1	Tyler Anderson	.60
2	Randy Brock	.75
3	Frank Christianson	.60
4	Eric Drage	1.00
5	LaVell Edwards	.75
6	Mike Empey	.60
7	Lenny Gomes	.75
8	Kalin Hall	.60
9	Nathan Hall	.60
10	Hema Heimuli	.75
11	Todd Herget	.60
12	Eli Herring	.75
13	Micah Matsuzaki	.60
14	Casey Mazzota	.60
15	Patrick Mitchell	.60
16	Evan Pilgrim	1.00
17	Greg Pitts	.60
18	Vic Tarleton	.60
19	John Walsh	3.00
20	Jamal Willis	1.00

C

1988 California Smokey

		NM/M
Complete Set (12):		12.00
Common Player:		1.25
1	Rob Bimson	1.25
2	Joel Dickson	1.25
3	Robert DosRemedios	1.25
4	Mike Ford	1.25
5	Darryl Ingram	1.25
6	David Ortega	1.25
7	Chris Richards	1.25
8	Bruce Snyder (CO)	1.50
9	Troy Taylor	2.00
10	Natu Tuatagaloa	2.00
11	Majett Whiteside	1.25
12	Dave Zawatson	1.25

1989 California Smokey

		NM/M
Complete Set (16):		12.00
Common Player:		1.00
1	John Hardy	1.00
2	Mike Ford	1.00
10	Robbie Keen	1.00
11	Troy Taylor	1.25
20	Dwayne Jones	1.00
21	Travis Oliver	1.00
34	Darrin Greer	1.00
40	David Ortega	1.00
41	Dan Slevin	1.00
52	Troy Auzenne	3.00
69	Tony Smith	1.00
80	Junior Tagaloa	1.00
83	Michael Smith	1.00
95	DeWayne Odom	1.00
99	Joel Dickson	1.00
NNO	Bruce Snyder (CO)	1.25

1990 California Smokey

		NM/M
Complete Set (16):		10.00
Common Player:		.75
1	Troy Auzenne (52)	2.00
2	John Belli (61)	.75
3	Joel Dickson (99)	.75
4	Ron English (42)	.75
5	Rhett Hall (57)	2.00
6	John Hardy (1)	.75
7	Robbie Keen (10)	.75
8	DeWayne Odom (95)	.75
9	Mike Pawlawski (9)	1.50
10	Castle Redmond (37)	.75
11	James Richards (64)	.75
12	Ernie Rogers (68)	.75
13	Bruce Snyder (CO)	1.00
14	Brian Treggs (3)	1.00
15	Anthony Wallace (6)	.75
16	Greg Zomalt (28)	.75

1991 California Smokey

		NM/M
Complete Set (16):		14.00
Common Player:		.75
1	Troy Auzenne	1.50
2	Chris Cannon	.75
3	Cornell Collier	.75
4	Sean Dawkins	3.00
5	Steve Gordon	.75
6	Mike Pawlawski	1.25
7	Bruce Snyder (CO)	1.00
8	Todd Steussie	2.00
9	Mack Travis	.75
10	Brian Treggs	1.00
11	Russell White	2.00
12	Jason Wilborn	.75
13	David Wilson	.75
14	Brent Woodall	.75
15	Eric Zomalt	1.25
16	Greg Zomalt	.75

1992 California Smokey

		NM/M
Complete Set (16):		10.00
Common Player:		.60
1	Chidi Ahanotu	.60
2	Wolf Barber	.60
3	Mick Barsala	.60
4	Doug Brien	1.50
5	Al Casner	.60
6	Lindsey Chapman	.60
7	Sean Dawkins	2.50
8	Keith Gilbertson (CO)	.75
9	Eric Mahlum	1.00
10	Chris Noonan	.60
11	Todd Steussie	1.50
12	Mack Travis	.60
13	Russell White	1.50
14	Jerrott Willard	1.00
15	Eric Zomalt	1.00
16	Greg Zomalt	.60

1993 California Smokey

		NM/M
Complete Set (16):		10.00
Common Player:		.60
1	Dave Barr	2.00
2	Doug Brien	1.25
3	Mike Caldwell	.60
4	Lindsey Chapman	.60
5	Jerod Cherry	1.00
6	Michael Davis	.60
7	Tyrone Edwards	.60
8	Keith Gilbertson (CO)	.60
9	Jody Graham	.60
10	Marty Holly	.60
11	Paul Joiner	.60
12	Eric Mahlum	.75
13	Damien Semien	.60
14	Todd Steussie	1.25
15	Jerrott Willard	.75
16	Eric Zomalt	.75

1995 California Smokey

		NM/M
Complete Set (16):		8.00
Common Player:		.50
1	Pat Barnes	.50
2	Nai'il Benjamin	.60
3	Sean Bullard	.50
4	Je'Rod Cherry	.75
5	Duane Clemons	1.00
6	Dante Depaola	.50
7	Kevin Devine	.50
8	Keith Gilbertson (CO)	.60
9	Andy Jacobs	.50
10	Ryan Longwell	.50
11	Ben Lynch	.50
12	Reynard Rutherford	.50
13	James Stallworth	.50
14	Regan Upshaw	2.00
15	Iheanyi Uwaezuoke	.75
16	Brandon Whiting	.50

1989 Clemson

		NM/M
Complete Set (32):		20.00
Common Player:		.75
1	Wally Ake (CO)	.75
2	Larry Beckman (CO)	.75
3	Mitch Belton (32)	.75
4	Scott Beville (61)	.75
5	Doug Brewster (92)	.75
6	Larry Brinson (CO)	1.00
7	Reggie Demps (30)	.75
8	Robin Eaves (44)	.75
9	Barney Farrar (CO)	.75
10	Stacy Fields (46)	.75
11	Vance Hammond (90)	.75
12	Eric Harmon (76)	.75
13	Ken Hatfield (CO)	1.50
14	Jerome Henderson (36)	1.50
15	Les Herrin (CO)	.75
16	Roger Hinshaw (CO)	.75
17	John Johnson (12)	1.50
18	Reggie Lawrence (34)	.75
19	Stacy Long (67)	.75
20	Eric Mader (82)	.75
21	Arlington Nunn (39)	.75
22	David Puckett (68)	.75
23	Danny Sizer (54)	.75
24	Robbie Spector (2)	.75
25	Rick Stockstill (CO)	1.00
26	Bruce Taylor (6)	.75
27	Doug Thomas (41)	.75
28	The Tiger (Mascot)	.75
29	Tiger Paw Title Card	.75
30	Bob Trott (CO)	.75
31	Larry Van Der Heyden (CO)	.75
32	Richard Wilson (CO)	.75

1950 C.O.P. Betsy Ross

		NM/M
Complete Set (6):		75.00
Common Player:		8.00
1	Don Campora	8.00
2	Don Hardey	8.00
3	Robert Klein	8.00
4	Eddie LeBaron	35.00
5	Eddie Macon	15.00
6	John Rohde	8.00

1990 Colorado Smokey

		NM/M
Complete Set (16):		16.00
Common Player:		.75
1	Eric Bieniemy	2.50
2	Joe Garten	1.00
3	Darian Hagan	2.00
4	George Hemingway	.75
5	Garry Howe	.75
6	Tim James	.75
7	Charles Johnson	2.50
8	Bill McCartney (CO)	2.00
9	Dave McCloughan	1.00
10	Kanavis McGhee	1.00
11	Mike Pritchard	5.00
12	Tom Rouen	1.00
13	Michael Simmons	.75
14	Mark Vander Poel	1.00
15	Alfred Williams	2.50
16	Ralphie (Mascot)	.75

1992 Colorado Pepsi

		NM/M
Complete Set (12):		15.00
Common Player:		1.00
1	Greg Biekert	2.00
2	Pat Blottiaux	1.00
3	Ronnie Bradford	1.50
4	Chad Brown	2.50
5	Marcellous Elder	1.50
6	Deon Figures	2.50
7	Jim Hansen	1.00
8	Jack Keys	1.00
9	Bill McCartney (CO)	2.00
10	Clint Moles	1.00
11	Jason Perkins	1.00
12	Scott Starr	1.00

1993 Colorado Smokey

		NM/M
Complete Set (16):		15.00
Common Player:		1.00
1	Craig Anderson	1.00
2	Mitch Berger	1.50
3	Jeff Brunner	1.00
4	Dennis Collier	1.00
5	Dwayne Davis	1.00
6	Brian Dyet	1.00
7	Sean Embree	1.00
8	Garrett Ford	1.00
9	James Hill	1.00
10	Charles Johnson	3.00
11	Greg Lindsey	1.00
12	Sam Rogers	1.00
13	Mark Smith	1.00
14	Duke Tobin	1.00
15	Ron Woolfork	1.50
16	Derek Agnew	1.00

1994 Colorado Smokey

		NM/M
Complete Set (16):		18.00
Common Player:		.75
1	Blake Anderson	.75
2	Norm Barnett	.75
3	Tony Berti	1.00
4	Ken Browne	.75
5	Christian Fauria	2.00
6	Darius Holland	1.50
7	Chris Hudson	1.00
8	Ted Johnson	1.50
9	Vance Joseph	.75
10	Jon Knutson	.75
11	Bill McCartney (CO)	1.50
12	Erik Mitchell	.75
13	Kordell Stewart	8.00
14	Derek West	.75
15	Michael Westbrook	4.00
16	Team Logo	.75

1973 Colorado State

		NM/M
Complete Set (8):		75.00
Common Player:		6.00
1	Wes Cerveny	6.00
2	Mark Driscoll	6.00
3	Jim Kennedy	6.00
4	Greg Kuhn	6.00
5	Willie Miller	20.00
6	Al Simpson (SP)	12.00
7	Jan Stuebbe (SP)	12.00
8	Tom Wallace	6.00

D

1987 Duke Police

		NM/M
Complete Set (16):		25.00
Common Player:		1.50
1	Andy Andreasik (60)	1.50
2	Brian Bernard (93)	1.50
3	Bob Calamari (31)	1.50
4	Jason Cooper (22)	1.50
5	Dave Demore (92)	1.50
6	Mike Dimitrio (21)	1.50
7	Jim Godfrey (56)	1.50
8	Doug Green (5)	1.50
9	Stanley Monk (24)	1.50
10	Chris Port (73)	2.00
11	Steve Ryan (63)	1.50
12	Steve Slayden (7)	2.00
13	Steve Spurrier (CO)	9.00
14	Dewayne Terry (27)	1.50
15	Fonda Williams (19)	1.50
16	Blue Devil (Mascot)	2.00

F

1988 Florida Burger King

		NM/M
Complete Set (16):		60.00
Common Player:		.75
1	Florida Gators Team	5.00
2	Emmitt Smith (22)	45.00
3	David Williams (73)	1.25
4	Jeff Roth (96)	.75
5	Rhondy Weston (68)	1.00
6	Stacey Simmons (25)	1.00
7	Huey Richardson (90)	1.25
8	Wayne Williams (23)	1.00
9	Charlie Wright (79)	.75
10	Tracy Daniels (63)	.75
11	Ernie Mills (14)	3.00
12	Willie McGrady (38)	.75
13	Chris Bromley (52)	.75
14	Louis Oliver (18)	2.00
15	Galen Hall (CO)	1.25
16	Albert the Alligator (Mascot)	.75

1989 Florida

		NM/M
Complete Set (22):		16.00
Common Player:		.50
1	Dale Van Sickle	.50
2	Cris Collinsworth	1.00
3	Wilber Marshall	1.50
4	Jack Youngblood	1.00
5	Steve Spurrier	4.00
6	David Little	.75
7	Bruce Bennett	.50
8	Charlie LaPradd	.50
9	John L. Williams	1.50
10	Steve Tannen	.75
11	Neal Anderson	1.50
12	Larry Dupree	.50
13	Guy Dennis	.50
14	Jarvis Williams	.75
15	Bill Carr	.50
16	Clifford Charlton	.50
17	Wes Chandler	1.00
18	David Galloway	.50
19	Carlos Alvarez	.50
20	Lomas Brown	1.00
21	Larry Smith	.50
22	Ricky Nattiel	.75

1989 Florida Smokey

		NM/M
Complete Set (16):		35.00
Common Player:		1.00
1	Chris Bromley (52)	1.00
2	Richard Fain (28)	1.25
3	John David Francis (7)	1.00
4	Galen Hall (CO) (SP)	7.00
5	Tony Lomack (20)	1.00
6	Willie McClendon (5)	1.00
7	Pat Moorer (45)	1.00
8	Kyle Morris (1)	1.00
9	Huey Richardson (90)	1.25
10	Stacey Simmons (25)	1.00
11	Emmitt Smith (22)	25.00
12	Richard Starowesky (75)	1.00
13	Kerry Watkins (4)	1.00
14	Albert (Mascot)	1.00
15	Cheerleaders	1.25
16	Gator Helmet	1.00

1990 Florida Smokey

		NM/M
Complete Set (12):		15.00
Common Player:		1.00
1	Terence Barber (3)	1.00
2	Chris Bromley (52)	1.00
3	Richard Fain (28)	1.25
4	Willie McClendon (5)	1.25
5	Dexter McNabb (21)	1.25
6	Ernie Mills (14)	2.50
7	Mark Murray (54)	1.00
8	Jerry Odom	1.00
9	Huey Richardson (90)	1.25
10	Steve Spurrier (CO)	4.00
11	Albert and Alberta (Mascots)	1.00
12	Mr. Two-Birts (Fan)	1.00

1991 Florida Smokey

		NM/M
Complete Set (12):		12.00
Common Player:		1.00
1	Ephesians Bartley	1.25
2	Mike Brandon	1.00
3	Brad Culpepper	1.50
4	Arden Czyzewski	1.00
5	Cal Dixon	1.25
6	Tre Everett	1.00
7	Hesham Ismail	1.00
8	Shane Matthews	2.50
9	Steve Spurrier (CO)	4.00
10	Mark White	1.00
11	Will White	1.00
12	Albert and Alberta (Mascots)	1.00

1993 Florida State

		NM/M
Complete Set (6):		85.00
Common Player:		6.00
1	Bobby Bowden (CO)	15.00
2	Derrick Brooks	15.00
3	Corey Sawyer	10.00
4	Tamarick Vanover	30.00
5	Charlie Ward	25.00
6	Chief Osceola (Mascot)	6.00

1996 Florida State

		NM/M
Complete Set (12):		10.00
Common Player:		.50
1	Chad Bates, Todd Fordham	.50
2	Scott Bentley	1.00
3	Byron Capers	.75
4	James Colzie	.75
5	Andre Cooper	1.00
6	Henri Crockett	1.00
7	Warrick Dunn	5.00
8	Sean Hamlet	.75
9	Sean Liss	.75
10	Wayne Messam	1.00
11	Connell Spain	1.00
12	Reinard Wilson	2.00

1987 Fresno State Burger King

		NM/M
Complete Set (16):		25.00
Common Player:		1.50
1	Gene Taylor	1.50
5	Michael Stewart	3.00
9	Kevin Sweeney	3.00
12	Eric Buechele	1.50
19	Rod Webster	1.50
26	Kelly Skipper	1.50
27	Barry Belli	1.50
32	Kelly Brooks	1.50
45	David Grayson	2.00
67	Jethro Franklin	1.50
71	Jeff Truschel	1.50
80	John O'Leary	1.50
81	Stephen Baker	3.00
83	Henry Ellard	6.00
86	Stephone Paige	4.00
NNO	Jim Sweeney (CO)	2.00

1989 Fresno State Smokey

		NM/M
Complete Set (16):		15.00
Common Player:		1.00
1	Mark Barsotti	1.00
2	Rich Bartlewski	1.00
3	Ron Cox	2.50
4	Myron Jones	1.00
5	Steve Loop	1.00
6	Fil Lujan	1.00
7	Darrel Martin	1.00
8	Lance Oberparleiter	1.00
9	Dwight Pickens	1.00
10	Marquez Pope	3.00
11	Nick Ruggeroli	1.00
12	Jim Sweeney CO	1.50
13	Jeff Thiesen	1.00
14	Paul Vial	1.00
15	James Williams	1.00
16	Bulldog Stadium	1.00

1990 Fresno State Smokey

		NM/M
Complete Set (16):		15.00
Common Player:		1.00
1	Mark Barsotti	1.25
2	Ron Cox	1.50
3	Aaron Craver	1.50
4	DeVonne Edwards	1.00
5	Courtney Griffin	1.00
6	Jesse Hardwick	1.00
7	Melvin Johnson	1.00
8	Brian Lasho	1.00
9	Kelvin Means	1.00
10	Marquez Pope	2.50
11	Zack Rix	1.00
12	Nick Ruggeroli	1.00
13	Jim Sweeney (CO)	1.25
14	Erick Tanuvasa	1.00
15	Jeff Thiesen	1.00
16	James Williams	1.50

G

1988 Georgia McDag

		NM/M
Complete Set (16):		65.00
Common Player:		1.00
1	UGA IV (Mascot)	1.00
2	Vince Dooley (AD/CO)	3.00
3	Steve Crumley	1.00
4	Aaron Chubb	1.00
5	Keith Henderson	2.00
6	Steve Harmon	1.00
7	Terrie Webster	1.00
8	John Kasay	4.00
9	Wayne Johnson	1.00

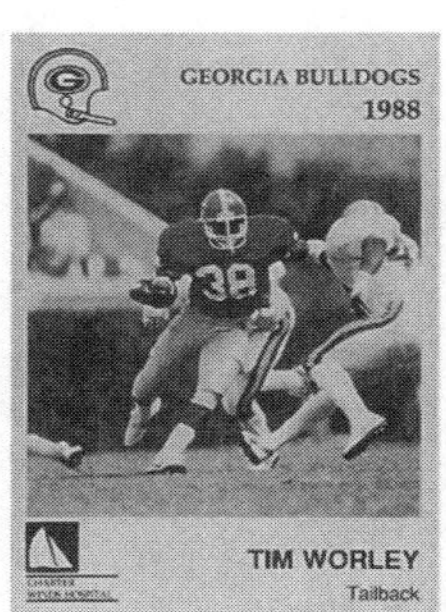

		NM/M
10	Tim Worley	2.00
11	Wycliffe Lovelace	1.00
12	Brent Collins	1.00
13	Vince Guthrie	1.00
14	Todd Wheeler	1.00
15	Bill Goldberg	50.00
16	Rodney Hampton	7.00

1989 Georgia 200

		NM/M
Complete Set (200):		18.00
Common Player:		.10
1	Vince Dooley (AD)	.20
2	Ivy M. Shiver	.10
3	Vince Dooley (CO)	.20
4	Vince Dooley (CO)	.20
5	Ray Goff (CO)	.20
6	Ray Goff (CO)	.20
7	Wally Butts (CO)	.20
8	Wally Butts (CO)	.20
9	Herschel Walker	.75
10	Frank Sinkwich	.20
11	Bob McWhorter	.10
12	Joe Bennett	.10
13	Dan Edwards	.10
14	Tom A. Nash	.10
15	Herb Maffett	.10
16	Ralph Maddox	.10
17	Vernon Smith	.10
18	Bill Hartman Jr.	.10
19	Frank Sinkwich	.20
20	Joe O'Malley	.10
21	Mike Castronis	.10
22	Aschel M. Day	.10
23	Herb St. John	.10
24	Craig Hertwig	.10
25	Johnny Rauch	.20
26	Harry Babcock	.10
27	Bruce Kemp	.10
28	Pat Dye	.20
29	Fran Tarkenton	1.00
30	Larry Kohn	.10
31	Ray Rissmiller	.10
32	George Patton	.20
33	Mixon Robinson	.10
34	Lynn Hughes	.10
35	Bill Stanfill	.20
36	Robert Dicks	.10
37	Lynn Hunnicutt	.10
38	Tommy Lyons	.10
39	Royce Smith	.10
40	Steve Greer	.10
41	Randy Johnson	.20
42	Mike Wilson	.10
43	Joel Parrish	.10
44	Ben Zambiasi	.20
45	Allan Leavitt	.10
46	George Collins	.10
47	Rex Robinson	.10
48	Scott Woerner	.10
49	Herschel Walker	.75
50	Bob Burns	.10
51	Jimmy Payne	.10
52	Fred Brown	.10
53	Kevin Butler	.20
54	Don Porterfield	.10
55	Mac McWhorter	.10
56	John Little	.10
57	Marion Campbell	.20
58	Zeke Bratkowski	.30
59	Buck Belue	.20
60	Duward Pennington	.10
61	Lamar Davis	.10
62	Steve Wilson	.10
63	Leman L. Rosenberg	.10
64	Dennis Hughes	.10
65	Wayne Radloff	.10
66	Lindsay Scott	.20
67	Wayne Swinford	.10
68	Kim Stephens	.10
69	Willie McClendon	.20
70	Ron Jenkins	.10
71	Jeff Lewis	.10
72	Larry Rakestraw	.10
73	Spike Jones	.20
74	Tom Nash Jr.	.10
75	Vassa Cate	.10
76	Theron Sapp	.20
77	Claude Hipps	.20
78	Charley Trippi	.30
79	Mike Weaver	.10
80	Anderson Johnson	.10
81	Matt Robinson	.20
82	Bill Krug	.10
83	Todd Wheeler	.10
84	Mack Guest	.10
85	Frank Ros	.10
86	Jeff Hipp	.10
87	Milton Leathers	.10
88	George Morton	.10
89	Jim Broadway	.10
90	Tim Morrison	.10
91	Homer Key	.10
92	Richard Tardits	.20
93	Tommy Thurson	.10
94	Bob Kelley	.10
95	Bob McWhorter	.10
96	Vernon Smith	.10
97	Eddie Weaver	.10
98	Bill Stanfill	.20
99	Scott Williams	.10
100	Checklist Card	.10
101	Len Hauss	.20
102	Jim Griffith	.10
103	Nat Dye	.10
104	Quinton Lumpkin	.10
105	Mike Garrett	.10
106	Glynn Harrison	.10
107	Aaron Chubb	.10
108	John Brantley	.10
109	Pat Hodgson	.10
110	Guy McIntyre	.30
111	Keith Harris	.10
112	Mike Cavan	.10
113	Kevin Jackson	.10
114	Jim Cagle	.10
115	Charles Whittemore	.10
116	Graham Batchelor	.10
117	Art DeCarlo	.20
118	Kendall Keith	.10
119	Jeff Pyburn	.20
120	James Ray	.10
121	Mack Burroughs	.10
122	Jimmy Vickers	.10
123	Charley Britt	.10
124	Matt Braswell	.10
125	Jake Richardson	.10
126	Ronnie Stewart	.10
127	Tim Crowe	.10
128	Troy Sadowski	.10
129	Robert Honeycutt	.10
130	Warren Gray	.10
131	David Guthrie	.10
132	John Lastinger	.20
133	Chip Wisdom	.10
134	Butch Box	.10
135	Tony Cushenberry	.10
136	Vince Guthrie	.10
137	Floyd Reid	.20
138	Mark Hodge	.10
139	Joe Happe	.10
140	Al Bodine	.10
141	Gene Chandler	.10
142	Tommy Lawhorne	.10
143	Bobby Walden	.20
144	Douglas McFalls	.10
145	Jim Milo	.10
146	Billy Payne	.75
147	Paul Holmes	.10
148	Bob Clemens	.10
149	Kenneth Sims	.10
150	Reid Moseley Jr.	.10
151	Tim Callaway	.10
152	Rusty Russell	.10
153	Jim McCollough	.10
154	Wally Williamson	.10
155	John Bond	.10
156	Charley Trippi	.30
157	Lindsay Scott The Play	.20
158	Joe Boland	.10
159	Michael Babb	.10
160	Jimmy Poulos	.10
161	Chris McCarthy	.10
162	Billy Mixon	.10
163	Dicky Clark	.10
164	David Rholetter	.10
165	Chuck Heard	.10
166	Pat Field	.10
167	Preston Ridlehuber	.10
168	Heyward Allen	.10
169	Kirby Moore	.10
170	Chris Welton	.10
171	Bill McKenny	.10
172	Steve Boswell	.10
173	Bob Towns	.10
174	Anthony Towns	.10
175	Porter Payne	.10
176	Bobby Garrard	.10
177	Jack Griffith	.10
178	Herschel Walker	.75
179	Andy Perhach	.10
180	Dr. Charles Herty (CO)	.10
181	Kent Lawrence	.20
182	David McKnight	.10
183	Joe Tereshinski	.10
184	Cicero Lucas	.10
185	Glenn "Pop" Warner (CO)	.20
186	Tony Flack	.10
187	Kevin Butler	.20
188	Bill Mitchell	.10
189	Jimmy Poulos Poulos vs. Tech	.10
190	Pete Case	.20
191	Pete Tinsley	.10
192	Joe Tereshinski	.20
193	Jimmy Harper	.10
194	Don Leebern	.10
195	Harry Mehre (CO)	.10
196	Herschel Walker, Theron Sapp, Charley Trippi, Frank Sinkwich Retired Jerseys	.30
197	Terrie Webster	.10
198	George Woodruff (CO)	.10
199	First Georgia Team (1892 Team Photo)	.10
200	Checklist Card	.10

1989 Georgia Police

		NM/M
Complete Set (16):		60.00
Common Player:		.75
1	Hiawatha Berry (58)	.75
2	Brian Cleveland (37)	.75
3	Demetrius Douglas (53)	.75
4	Alphonso Ellis (33)	.75
5	Ray Goff (CO)	1.00
6	Bill Goldberg (95)	50.00
7	Rodney Hampton (7)	6.00
8	David Hargett (25)	.75
9	Joey Hester (1)	.75
10	John Kasay (3)	3.00
11	Mo Lewis	3.00
12	Arthur Marshall (12)	1.50
13	Curt Mull (50)	.75
14	Ben Smith (26)	1.50
15	Greg Talley (11)	.75
16	Kirk Warner (83)	.75

1990 Georgia Police

		NM/M
Complete Set (14):		10.00
Common Player:		.75
1	John Allen (44)	.75
2	Brian Cleveland (37)	.75
3	Norman Cowins (59)	.75
4	Alphonso Ellis (33)	.75
5	Ray Goff (CO)	1.00
6	David Hargett (25)	.75
7	Sean Hunnings (6)	.75
8	Preston Jones (14)	1.00
9	John Kasay (3)	1.50
10	Arthur Marshall (12)	1.50
11	Jack Swan (76)	.75
12	Greg Talley (11)	.75
13	Lemonte Tellis (77)	.75
14	Chris Wilson (16)	.75

1991 Georgia Police

		NM/M
Complete Set (16):		15.00
Common Player:		.75
1	John Allen	.75
2	Chuck Carswell	.75
3	Russell DeFoor	.75
4	Ray Goff (CO)	1.00
5	David Hargett	.75
6	Andre Hastings	2.50
7	Garrison Hearst	6.00
8	Arthur Marshall	1.25
9	Kevin Maxwell	.75
10	DeWayne Simmons	.75
11	Jack Swan	.75
12	Greg Talley	.75
13	Lemonte Tellis	.75
14	Chris Wilson	.75
15	George Wynn	.75
16	UGA V (Mascot)	.75

1992 Georgia Police

		NM/M
Complete Set (15):		12.00
Common Player:		.50
1	Mitch Davis	.60
2	Damon Evans	.50
3	Torrey Evans	.50
4	Ray Goff (CO)	.60
5	Andre Hastings	2.00
6	Garrison Hearst	5.00
7	Donnie Maib	.50
8	Alec Millen	.50
9	Shannon Mitchell	.50
10	Mack Strong	1.00
11	Jack Swan	.50
12	UGA (Mascot)	.50
13	Bernard Williams	.60
14	Chris Wilson	.50
15	Eric Zeier	6.00

1993 Georgia Police

		NM/M
Complete Set (16):		18.00
Common Player:		.50
1	Scott Armstrong	.50
2	Brian Bohannon	.50
3	Carlo Butler	.50
4	Charlie Clemons	.50
5	Mitch Davis	.60
6	Terrell Davis	12.00
7	Randall Godfrey	.75
8	Ray Goff (CO)	.60
9	Frank Harvey	.50
10	Travis Jones	.50
11	Shannon Mitchell	.50
12	Greg Tremble	.50
13	Bernard Williams	.60
14	Chad Wilson	.50
15	Eric Zeier	3.00
16	UGA (Mascot)	.50

H

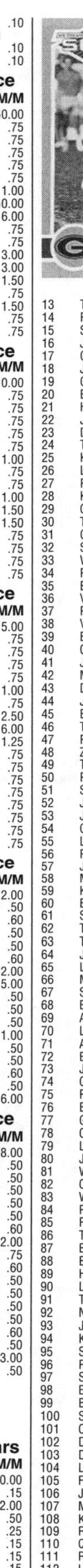

1991 Hoby SEC Stars

		NM/M
Complete Set (396):		50.00
Common Player:		.15
1	Paul "Bear" Bryant (CO)	2.00
2	Johnny Musso	.50
3	Keith McCants	.25
4	Cecil Dowdy	.15
5	Thomas Rayam	.15
6	Van Tiffin	.15
7	Efrum Thomas	.15
8	Jon Hand	.25
9	David Smith	.15
10	Larry Rose	.15
11	Lamonde Russell	.15
12	Mike Washington	.15
13	Tommy Cole	.15
14	Roger Shultz	.15
15	Spencer Hammond	.15
16	John Fruhmorgen	.15
17	Gene Jelks	.25
18	John Mangum	.25
19	George Thornton	.15
20	Billy Neighbors	.25
21	Howard Cross	.40
22	Jeremiah Castille	.25
23	Derrick Thomas	1.00
24	Terrill Chatman	.15
25	Ken Stabler	1.25
26	Lee Ozmint	.15
27	Philip Doyle	.15
28	Kermit Kendrick	.15
29	Chris Mohr	.15
30	Tommy Wilcox	.15
31	Gary Hollingsworth	.15
32	Sylvester Croom	.25
33	Willie Wyatt	.15
34	Pooley Hubert	.15
35	Bobby Humphrey	.25
36	Vaughn Mancha	.15
37	Reggie Slack	.40
38	Vince Dooley (CO)	.40
39	Ed King	.25
40	Connie Frederick	.15
41	Jeff Burger	.25
42	Monk Gafford	.15
43	David Rocker	.25
44	Jim Pyburn	.15
45	Bob Harris	.15
46	Travis Tidwell	.15
47	Ralph (Shug) Jordan (CO)	.40
48	Zeke Smith	.25
49	Terry Beasley	.25
50	Pat Sullivan	.40
51	Stacy Danley	.15
52	Jimmy Hitchcock	.15
53	John Wiley	.15
54	Greg Taylor	.15
55	Lamar Rogers	.25
56	Rob Selby	.15
57	James Joseph	.25
58	Mike Kolen	.15
59	Kevin Greene	.50
60	Ben Thomas	.15
61	Shayne Wasden	.15
62	Tex Warrington	.15
63	Tommie Agee	.25
64	Jim Phillips	.25
65	Lawyer Tillman	.40
66	Mark Dorminey	.15
67	Steve Wallace	.25
68	Ed Dyas	.15
69	Alexander Wright	.25
70	Lionel James	.25
71	Aundray Bruce	.25
72	Edmund Nelson	.25
73	Jack Youngblood	.50
74	Carlos Alvarez	.25
75	Ricky Nattiel	.25
76	Bill Carr	.15
77	Guy Dennis	.15
78	Charles Casey	.15
79	Louis Oliver	.40
80	John Reaves	.25
81	Wayne Peace	.25
82	Charlie LaPradd	.15
83	Wes Chandler	.40
84	Richard Trapp	.15
85	Ralph Ortega	.15
86	Tommy Durrance	.15
87	Burton Lawless	.25
88	Bruce Bennett	.15
89	Huey Richardson	.25
90	Larry Smith	.15
91	Trace Armstrong	.40
92	Nat Moore	.40
93	James Jones	.40
94	Kay Stephenson	.25
95	Scot Brantley	.25
96	Ray Criswell	.15
97	Steve Tannen	.25
98	Ernie Mills	.40
99	Bruce Vaughn	.15
100	Steve Spurrier	2.50
101	Crawford Ker	.25
102	David Galloway	.25
103	David Williams	.25
104	Lomas Brown	.40
105	Fernando Jackson	.15
106	Jeff Roth	.15
107	Mark Murray	.15
108	Kirk Kirkpatrick	.15
109	Ray Goff (CO)	.25
110	Quinton Lumpkin	.15
111	Royce Smith	.15
112	Larry Rakestraw	.25
113	Kevin Butler	.25
114	Aschel M. Day	.25
115	Scott Woerner	.25
116	Herb St. John	.15
117	Ray Rissmiller	.15
118	Buck Belue	.25
119	George Collins	.15
120	Joel Parrish	.15
121	Terry Hoage	.25
122	Frank Sinkwich	.40
123	Billy Payne	.50
124	Zeke Bratkowski	.25
125	Herschel Walker	1.00
126	Pat Dye (CO)	.40
127	Vernon Smith	.15
128	Rex Robinson	.15
129	Mike Castronis	.15
130	Pop Warner (CO)	.40
131	George Patton	.25
132	Harry Babcock	.15
133	Lindsay Scott	.25
134	Bill Stanfill	.25
135	Bill Hartman Jr.	.15
136	Eddie Weaver	.15
137	Tim Worley	.40
138	Ben Zambiasi	.40
139	Bob McWhorter	.15
140	Rodney Hampton	1.00
141	Len Hauss	.25
142	Wallace Butts	.25
143	Andy Johnson	.25
144	I.M. Shiver Jr.	.15
145	Clyde Johnson	.15
146	Steve Meilinger	.15
147	Howard Schnellenberger (CO)	.50
148	Irv Goode	.25
149	Sam Ball	.15
150	Babe Parilli	.40
151	Rick Norton	.25
152	Warren Bryant	.25
153	Mike Pfeifer	.15
154	Sonny Collins	.15
155	Mark Higgs	.40
156	Randy Holleran	.15
157	Bill Ransdell	.15
158	Joey Worley	.15
159	Jim Kovach	.25
160	Joe Federspiel	.15
161	Larry Seiple	.25
162	Darryl Bishop	.15
163	George Blanda	1.00
164	Oliver Barnett	.15
165	Paul Calhoun	.15
166	Dicky Lyons	.25
167	Tom Hutchinson	.25
168	George Adams	.25
169	Derrick Ramsey	.25
170	Rick Kestner	.15
171	Art Still	.40
172	Rick Nuzum	.15
173	Richard Jaffe	.15
174	Rodger Bird	.15
175	Jeff Van Note	.40
176	Herschel Turner	.15
177	Lou Michaels	.25
178	Ray Correll	.15
179	Doug Moseley	.15
180	Bob Gain	.25
181	Tommy Casanova	.40
182	Mike Anderson	.15
183	Craig Burns	.15
184	A.J. Duhe	.25
185	Lyman White	.15
186	Paul Dietzel (CO)	.40
187	Paul Lyons	.15
188	Eddie Ray	.15
189	Roy Winston	.25
190	Brad Davis	.15
191	Mike Williams	.15
192	Karl Wilson	.25
193	Ronnie Estay	.15
194	Malcolm Scott	.15
195	Greg Jackson	.15
196	Willie Teal	.25
197	Eddie Fuller	.15
198	Ralph Norwood	.15
199	Bert Jones	.40
200	Y.A. Tittle	.50
201	Jerry Stovall	.40
202	Henry Thomas	.40
203	Lance Smith	.15
204	Doug Moreau	.25
205	Tyler LaFauci	.15
206	George Bevan	.15
207	Robert Dugas	.15
208	Carlos Carson	.15
209	Andy Hamilton	.25
210	James Britt	.15
211	Wendell Davis	.40
212	Ron Sancho	.15
213	Johnny Robinson	.40
214	Eric Martin	.40
215	Michael Brooks	.15
216	Toby Caston	.25
217	Jesse Anderson	.15
218	Jimmy Webb	.15
219	Mardye McDole	.15
220	David Smith	.15
221	Dana Moore	.15
222	Cedric Corse	.15
223	Louis Clark	.15
224	Walter Packer	.15
225	George Wonsley	.25
226	Billy Jackson	.25
227	Bruce Plummer	.15
228	Aaron Pearson	.15
229	Glen Collins	.15
230	Paul Davis (CO)	.15
231	Wayne Jones	.15
232	John Bond	.15
233	Johnnie Cooks	.25
234	Robert Young	.15
235	Don Smith	.15
236	Kent Hull	.40
237	Tony Shell	.15
238	Steve Freeman	.25
239	James Williams	.15
240	Tom Goode	.25
241	Stan Black	.15
242	Bo Russell	.15
243	Ricky Byrd	.15
244	Frank Dowsing	.15
245	Wayne Harris	.40
246	Richard Keys	.15
247	Artie Cosby	.15
248	Dave Marler	.15
249	Michael Haddix	.25
250	Jerry Clower	.25
251	Bill Bell	.15
252	Jerry Bouldin	.15
253	Parker Hall	.15
254	Allen Brown	.15
255	Bill Smith	.15
256	Freddie Joe Nunn	.25
257	John Vaught (CO)	.25
258	Buford McGee	.25
259	Kenny Dill	.15
260	Jim Miller	.15
261	Doug Jacobs	.15
262	John Dottley	.25
263	Willie Green	.40
264	Tony Bennett	.40
265	Stan Hindman	.15
266	Charles Childers	.15
267	Harry Harrison	.15
268	Todd Sandroni	.15
269	Glynn Griffing	.15
270	Chris Mitchell	.15
271	Shawn Cobb	.15
272	Doug Elmore	.15
273	Dawson Pruett	.15
274	Warner Alford	.15
275	Archie Manning	1.00
276	Kelvin Pritchett	.25
277	Pat Coleman	.15
278	Stevon Moore	.25
279	John Darnell	.15
280	Wesley Walls	.25
281	Billy Brewer	.25
282	Mark Young	.15
283	Andre Townsend	.25
284	Billy Ray Adams	.15
285	Jim Dunaway	.25
286	Paige Cothren	.25
287	Jake Gibbs	.40
288	Jim Urbanek	.15
289	Tony Thompson	.15
300	Johnny Majors (CO)	.40
301	Roland Poles	.15
302	Alvin Harper	.50
303	Doug Baird	.15
304	Greg Burke	.15
305	Sterling Henton	.15
306	Preston Warren	.15
307	Stanley Morgan	.50
308	Bobby Scott	.25
309	Doug Atkins	.40
310	Bill Young	.15
311	Bob Garmon	.15
312	Herman Weaver	.15
313	Dewey Warren	.15
314	John Boynton	.25
315	Bob Davis	.15
316	Pat Ryan	.15
317	Keith DeLong	.25
318	Bobby Dodd (CO)	.25
319	Ricky Townsend	.15
320	Eddie Brown	.25
321	Herman Hickman (CO)	.25
322	Nathan Dougherty	.15
323	Mickey Marvin	.15
324	Reggie Cobb	.40
325A	Condredge Holloway	.50
325B	Josh Cody	.15
326A	Anthony Hancock	.40
326B	Jack Jenkins	.15
327A	Steve Kiner	.15
327B	Bob Goodridge	.15
328A	Mike Mauck	.15
328B	Chris Gaines	.15
329A	Bill Bates	.40
329B	Willie Geny	.15
330A	Austin Denney	.25
330B	Bob Laws	.15
331A	Robert Nevland (CO)	.40
331B	Rob Monaco	.15
332A	Bob Suffridge	.15
332B	Chuck Scott	.15
333A	Abe Shires	.15
333B	Hek Wakefield	.15
334A	Robert Shaw	.40
334B	Ken Stone	.15
335	Mark Adams	.15
336	Ed Smith	.15
337	Dan McGugin (CO)	.15
338	Doug Mathews	.15
339	Whit Taylor	.40
340	Gene Moshier	.15
341	Christine Hauck	.15
342	Lee Nalley	.15
343	Wamon Buggs	.15
344	Jim Arnold	.25
345	Buford Ray	.25
346	Will Wolford	.25
347	Steve Bearden	.15
348	Frank Mordica	.15
349	Barry Burton	.15
350	Bill Wade	.40
351	Tommy Woodroof	.15
352	Steve Wade	.15
353	Preston Brown	.15
354	Ben Roderick	.15
355	Charles Horton	.15
356	DeMond Winston	.15
357	John North	.15
358	Don Orr	.15
359	Art Demmas	.15
360	Mark Johnson	.15
361	Hootie Ingram (AD)	.25
362	Gene Stallings (CO)	.50
363	Alabama Checklist	.15
364	Pat Dye (CO)	.25
365	Auburn Checklist	.15
366	Vince Dooley (AD)	.25
367	Ray Goff (CO)	.25
368	Georgia Checklist	.15
369	C.M. Newton (AD)	.25
370	Bill Curry (CO)	.25
371	Kentucky Checklist	.15
372	Joe Dean (AD)	.15
373	Curley Hallman (CO)	.25

374 LSU Checklist .15
375 Warner Alford (AD) .15
376 Billy Brewer (CO) .25
377 Ole Miss Checklist .15
378 Larry Templeton (AD) .15
379 Jackie Sherrill (CO) .40
380 Mississippi State Checklist .15
381 Bill Arnsparger (AD) .25
382 Steve Spurrier (CO) 1.25
383 Florida Checklist .15
384 Doug Dickey (AD) .15
385 Johnny Majors (CO) .25
386 Tennessee Checklist .15
387 Paul Hoolahan (AD) .15
388 Gerry DiNardo (CO) .25
389 Vanderbilt Checklist .15
390 The Iron Bowl - Alabama vs. Auburn .40
391 Florida vs. Georgia .15
392 Mississippi State vs. Ole Miss .15
393 The Beer Barrel - Kentucky vs. Tennessee .15
394 Drama on Halloween - LSU vs. Ole Miss .15
395 Tennessee vs. Vanderbilt .15
396 Roy Kramer (COMM) .15

1991 Hoby SEC Stars Signature

NM/M
Complete Set (10): 375.00
Common Player: 15.00
1 Carlos Alvarez 15.00
2 Zeke Bratkowski 25.00
3 Jerry Clower 15.00
4 Condredge Holloway 25.00
5 Bert Jones 50.00
6 Archie Manning 75.00
7 Ken Stabler 100.00
8 Pat Sullivan 50.00
9 Jeff Van Note 20.00
10 Bill Wade 25.00

1992 Houston Motion Sports

NM/M
Complete Set (66): 30.00
Common Player: .50
1 Freddie Gilbert .60
2 Lorenzo Dickson .50
3 Sherman Smith 1.00
4 Brad Whigham .50
5 Allen Aldridge 1.00
6 Truett Akin .50
7 Nahala Johnson .60
8 Terald Clark 1980 Garden State Bowl .50
9 1977 Cotton Bowl .60
10 Tyrone Davis .50
11 Kevin Bleier .50
12 Nigel Ventress .50
13 Darren Woods .50
14 Linton Weatherspoon .50
15 John R. Morris .50
16 Kevin Batiste .60
17 Kelvin McKnight .50
18 Stewart Carpenter .50
19 Ron Peters .50
20 Stephen Dixon .60
21 Chandler Evans .50
22 Tyler Mucho .50
23 Kevin Labay .50
24 Steve Clarke .50
25 Keith Jack .50
26 Steve Matejka .50
27 The Astrodome .50
28 Roman Anderson .50
29 Andre Ware, David Klingler Quarterback U 1.50
30 Andre Ware, David Klingler Cougar Pride 1.50
31 Bayou Bucket (Annual Houston vs. Rice game) .50
32 Jeff Tait .50
33 Donald Douglas .50
34 Victor Mamich .50
35 John W. Brown .50
36 Zach Chatman .50
37 Jason Youngblood .50
38 David Klingler 2.00
39 John H. Brown .50
40 Tommy Guy .50
41 1980 Cotton Bowl (Game action) .60
42 1973 Bluebonnet Bowl (Game action) .60
43 Chris Pezman .50
44 Tracy Good .50
45 Stephen Harris .50
46 Ryan McCoy .60
47 Michael Newhouse .50
48 Jimmy Klingler 1.50
49 Joe Wheeler .50
50 Eric Harrison .50
51 Craig Hall .50
52 Shasta (Mascot) .50
53 NCAA Records (Passing and Receiving) .60
54 Darrell Clapp .60
55 Eric Blount .50
56 Tiandre Sanders .50
57 Kyle Allen .50
58 Brisket Howard .50
59 Greg Thornburgh .50
60 Wilson Whitley 1.00
61 Andre Ware 2.00
62 John Jenkins (CO) .60
NNO Ad Card Motion Sports .50
NNO Front Card .50
NNO Back Card .50
NNO Checklist .50

I

1989 Idaho

NM/M
Complete Set (12): 12.00
Common Player: .75
3 Brian Smith .75
11 Tim S. Johnson .75
16 Lee Allen .75
17 John Friesz 5.00
20 Todd Hoiness .75
25 David Jackson .75
53 Steve Unger .75
58 John Rust .75
63 Troy Wright .75
67 Todd Neu .75
83 Michael Davis .75
93 Mike Zeller .75

1990 Illinois Centennial

NM/M
Complete Set (45): 25.00
Common Player: .35
1 Harold "Red" Grange 3.00
2 Dick Butkus 2.50
3 Ray Nitschke 1.50
4 Jim Grabowski .50
5 Alex Agase .50
6 Claude Young .50
7 Scott Studwell .50
8 Tony Eason .50
9 John Mackovic .75
10 Jack Trudeau .75
11 Jeff George 2.00
12 Ray Eliot, Pete Elliott, Mike White Rose Bowl Coaches .35
13 George Huff .35
14 David Williams .35
15 Bob Zuppke .50
16 George Halas 2.00
17 Dike Eddleman .35
18 Dave Wilson .35
19 Tab Bennett .35
20 Jim Juriga .35
21 John Karras .35
22 Bobby Mitchell 1.00
23 Dan Beaver .35
24 Joe Rutgens .50
25 Bill Burrell .35
26 J.C. Caroline .50
27 Al Brosky .35
28 Don Thorp .35
29 First Football Team .35
30 Harold "Red" Grange (Retired) 1.00
31 Memorial Stadium .35
32 Chris White .35
33 Ralph Chapman, Perry Graves, Bart Macomber Early Stars .35
34 John Depler, Jim McMillen Early Stars .35
35 Burt Ingwerson, Butch Nowack, Bernie Shively Early Stars .35
36 Fred Custardo, Mike Wells, Tom O'Connell Great Quarterbacks .35
37 Thomas Rooks, Abe Woodson, Keith Jones Great Running Backs .50
38 Mike Bellamy, Doug Dieken, John Wright Great Receivers .50
39 Forrest Van Hook, Larry McCarren, Chris Babyar Great Offensive .35
40 Craig Swope, George Donnelly, Mike Gower Great Defensive Backs .35
41 Charles Boerlo, Don Hansen, John Sullivan Great Linebackers .35
42 Archie Sutton, Chuck Studley, Scott Davis Defensive Linemen .35
43 Mike Bass K, Bill Brown, Frosty Peters Great Kickers .35
44 Dick Butkus Retired Numbers 1.50
45 Football Centennial Logo .35

1992 Illinois

NM/M
Complete Set (48): 18.00
Common Player: .35
1 Derek Allen .35
2 Jeff Arneson .35
3 Randy Bierman .35
4 Darren Boyer .35
5 Rod Boykin .35
6 Mike Cole .35
7 Chad Copher .35
8 Fred Cox .50
9 Robert Crumpton .50
10 Ken Dilger 2.00
11 Jason Edwards .35
12 Greg Engel .35
13 Steve Feagin .35
14 Erik Foggey .35
15 Kevin Hardy 3.00
16 Jeff Hasenstab .35
17 John Holecek .50
18 Brad Hopkins .75
19 John Horn .35
20 Dana Howard 1.00
21 Filmel Johnson .35
22 Jon Kerr .35
23 Jeff Kinney .50
24 Jim Klein .35
25 Todd Leach .35
26 Wagner Lester .35
27 Lashon Ludington .35
28 Clinton Lynch .35
29 Tim McCloud .35
30 David Olson .35
31 Antwoine Patton .50
32 Jim Pesek .35
33 Alfred Pierce .35
34 Mark Qualls .35
35 Phil Rathke .35
36 Chris Richardson .50
37 Derrick Rucker .35
38 Aaron Shelby .35
39 John Sidari .35
40 J.J. Strong .35
41 Mike Suarez .35
42 Lou Tepper (CO) .50
43 Scott Turner .35
44 Jason Verduzco 1.00
45 Tyrone Washington .35
46 Forry Wells .35
47 Pat Wendt .35
48 John Wright .35

1982 Indiana State Police

NM/M
Complete Set (64): 175.00
Common Player: 3.00
1 David Allen 3.00
2 Doug Arnold 3.00
3 James Banks 3.00
4 Scott Bartel 3.00
5 Kurt Bell 3.00
6 Terry Bell 3.00
7 Steve Bidwell 3.00
8 Keith Bonney 3.00
9 Mark Boster 3.00
10 Bobby Boyce 3.00
11 Steve Brickey (CO) 3.00
12 Mark Bryson 3.00
13 Steve Buxton 3.00
14 Ed Campbell 3.00
15 Jeff Campbell 5.00
16 Tom Chapman 3.00
17 Cheerleaders (Ruth Ann Medworth DIR) 4.00
18 Darrold Clardy 3.00
19 Wayne Davis 3.00
20 Herbert Dawson 3.00
21 Richard Dawson 4.00
22 Chris Delaplaine 3.00
23 Max Dillon 3.00
24 Rick Dwenger 3.00
25 Ed Foggs 3.00
26 Allen Hartwig 3.00
27 Pat Henderson (CO) 3.00
28 Don Hitz 3.00
29 Pete Hoener (CO) 3.00
30 Bob Hopkins 3.00
31 Kris Huber (Baton Twirler) 4.00
32 Leroy Irvin 20.00
33 Mike Johannes 3.00
34 Anthony Kimball 3.00
35 Gregg Kimbrough 3.00
36 Bob Koehne 3.00
37 Jerry Lasko (CO) 3.00
38 Kevin Lynch 3.00
39 Dan Maher 3.00
40 Ed Martin 3.00
41 Regis Mason 3.00
42 Rob McIntyre 3.00
43 Quintin Mikell 3.00
44 Jeff Miller 3.00
45 Mark Miller 3.00
46 Mike Osborne 3.00
47 Max Payne (CO) 3.00
48 Scott Piercy 3.00
49 Dennis Raetz (CO) 3.00
50 Kevin Ramsey 3.00
51 Dean Reader 3.00
52 Eric Robinson 3.00
53 Walter Seaphus 3.00
54 Sparkettes (Marthann Markler DIR) 4.00
55 John Spradley 3.00
56 Manual Studway 3.00
57 Sam Suggs 3.00
58 Larry Swart 3.00
59 Bob Tyree 3.00
60 Bob Turner (CO) 3.00
61 Brad Verdun 3.00
62 Keith Ward 3.00
63 Sean Whiten 3.00
64 Perry Willett 3.00

1971 Iowa Team Photos

NM/M
Complete Set (4): 25.00
Common Sheet: 6.00
1 Geoff Mickelson, Craig Clemons, Frank Holmes, Levi Mitchell, Charles Podolak, Lorin Lynch, Steve Penney, Larry Horton 8.00
2 Alan Schaefer, Dave Triplett, John Muller, Jim Kaiser, Wendell Bell, Clark Malmer, Rich Solomon, Kelly Disser 6.00
3 Bill Schoonover, Frank Sunderman, Craig Darling, Tom Cabalka, Dave Simms, Bill Rose, Buster Hoinkes, Charles Cross 6.00
4 Kyle Skogman, Jerry Reardon, Dave Harris, Rob Fick, Mike Dillner, Ike White, Mark Nelson, Harry Kokolus 6.00

1984 Iowa

NM/M
Complete Set (60): 50.00
Common Player: .75
1 Kevin Angel .75
2 Kerry Burt .75
3 Fred Bush .75
4 Craig Clark .75
5 Zane Corbin .75
6 Nate Creer .75
7 Dave Croston .75
8 George Davis .75
9 Jeff Drost .75
10 Quinn Early 4.00
11 Mike Flagg .75
12 Hayden Fry (CO) 2.50
13 Bruce Gear .75
14 Owen Gill 2.00
15 Bill Glass 1.00
16 Mike Haight 1.50
17 Bill Happel .75
18 Kevin Harmon 1.00
19 Ronnie Harmon 4.00
20 Craig Hartman .75
21 Jon Hayes 2.00
22 Erric Hedgeman .75
23 Scott Helverson .75
24 Mike Hooks .75
25 Paul Hufford .75
26 Keith Hunter .75
27 George Little .75
28 Chuck Long 2.00
29 J.C. Love-Jordan .75
30 George Millett .75
31 Devon Mitchell 1.00
32 Tom Nichol .75
33 Kelly O'Brien .75
34 Hap Peterson .75
35 Joe Schuster 1.00
36 Tim Sennott .75
37 Ken Sims .75
38 Mark Sindlinger .75
39 Robert Smith .75
40 Kevin Spitzig .75
41 Larry Station .75
42 Mike Stoops .75
43 Dave Strobel .75
44 Mark Vlasic 2.00
45 Jon Vrieze .75
46 Tony Wancket .75
47 Herb Webster .75
48 Coaching Staff 1.00
49 Captains 1.50
50 Bowl Players 1.00
51 Kevin Harmon, Ronnie Harmon Harmon Brothers 1.50
52 Cheerleaders 1.00
53 Pompons 1.00
54 Kinnick Stadium .75
55 Herky the Hawk (Mascot) .75
56 Rose Bowl Ring .75
57 Peach Bowl Trophy .75
58 Gator Bowl Stadium .75
59 Floyd of Rosedale (Trophy) .75
60 Checklist Card .75

1987 Iowa

NM/M
Complete Set (63): 40.00
Common Player: .60
1 Mark Adams .60
2 Dave Alexander 1.00
3 Bill Anderson .60
4 Tim Anderson .60
5 Rick Bayless .60
6 Jeff Beard .60
7 Mike Burke .60
8 Kerry Burt .60
9 Malcolm Christie .60
10 Craig Clark .60
11 Marv Cook 2.00
12 Jeff Croston .60
13 Greg Divis .60
14 Quinn Early 2.50
15 Greg Fedders .60
16 Mike Flagg .60
17 Melvin Foster .60
18 Hayden Fry (CO) 2.00
19 Grant Goodman .60
20 Dave Haight 1.00
21 Merton Hanks 3.00
22 Deven Harberts .60
23 Kevin Harmon .75
24 Chuck Hartlieb 1.25
25 Tork Hook .60
26 Rob Houghtlin .60
27 David Hudson .60
28 Myron Keppy .60
29 Jeff Koeppel .60
30 Bob Kratch 1.50
31 Peter Marciano .60
32 Jim Mauro .60
33 Marc Mazzeri .60
34 Dan McGwire 2.00
35 Mike Miller .60
36 Joe Mott .60
37 James Pipkins .60
38 Tom Poholsky .75
39 Jim Poynton .60
40 J.J. Puk .75
41 Brad Quast .60
42 Jim Reilly .60
43 Matt Ruhland .60
44 Bob Schmitt .60
45 Joe Schuster .75
46 Dwight Sistrunk .75
47 Mark Stoops .60
48 Steve Thomas .60
49 Kent Thompson .60
50 Travis Watkins .60
51 Herb Wester .60
52 Anthony Wright .60
53 Ring and Rose Bowl Ring .60
54 Cheerleaders .75
55 Floyd of Rosedale (Trophy) .60
56 Freedom Bowl (Game Action Photo) .75
57 Herky the Hawk (Mascot) .60
58 Holiday Bowl (Game Action Photo) .75
59 Indoor Practice Facility .60
60 Iowa Team Captains (Quinn Early and five others) 1.50
61 Kinnick Stadium .60
62 Peach Bowl (Game Action Photo) .60
63 Pom Pons (Cheerleaders) 1.00

1988 Iowa

NM/M
Complete Set (64): 30.00
Common Player: .50
2 Travis Watkins .60
4 James Pipkins .75
5 Mike Burke .50
8 Chuck Hartlieb 1.00
10 Anthony Wright .50
14 Tom Poholsky .60
16 Deven Harberts .50
18 Leroy Smith .50
20 David Hudson .50
21 Tony Stewart .50
22 Sean Smith .50
23 Richard Bass .50
26 Peter Marciano .50
29 Greg Brown .50
30 Grant Goodman .50
31 John Derby .50
32 Mike Saunders 1.00
35 Brad Quast .50
38 Chet Davis .50
40 Marc Mazzeri .50
41 Mark Stoops .50
42 Tork Hook .50
44 Keaton Smiley .50
45 Merton Hanks 2.00
48 Tyrone Berrie .50
50 Bill Anderson .50
51 Jeff Koeppel .50
53 Greg Fedders .50
57 Matt Ruhland .50
58 Greg Davis .50
60 Bob Schmitt .50
61 Dave Turner .50
64 Dave Haight .75
66 Melvin Foster .50
67 Jim Poynton .50
68 Tim Anderson .50
70 Bob Kratch 1.00
71 Jim Johnson .50
74 George Hawthorne .50
75 Greg Aegerter .50
77 Paul Glonek .50
80 Steve Green .50
81 Brian Wise .50
82 Jon Filloon .50
84 Marv Cook 1.50
85 John Palmer .60
87 Jeff Skillett .50
88 Tom Ward .50
95 Jim Reilly .50
96 Ron Geater .50
97 Joe Mott .75
99 Moses Santos .50
NNO Team Captains (Marv Crook and four others) 1.00
NNO Hayden Fry (CO) 1.00
NNO Hayden Fry Holiday Bowl 1987 (CO) .75
NNO Peach Bowl (Game Action Photo) .60
NNO Holiday Bowl 1986 (Game Action Photo) .60
NNO Herky the Hawk (Mascot) .50
NNO Cheerleaders .60
NNO Kinnick Stadium .50
NNO Pom Pons (Cheerleaders) .60
NNO Championship Rings .50
NNO Indoor Practice Facility .50
NNO Symbolic Tiger Hawk (Helmet) .50

1989 Iowa

NM/M
Complete Set (90): 30.00
Common Player: .40
1 Greg Aegerter .40
2 Kevin Allendorf .40
3 Bill Anderson .40
4 Richard Bass .40
5 Rob Baxley .40
6 Nick Bell 1.50
7 Phil Bradley .40
8 Greg Brown .40
9 Doug Buch .40
10 Gary Clark .40
11 Roderick Davis .40
12 Scott Davis 1.00
13 John Derby .50
14 Mike Devlin .40
15 Jason Dumont .40
16 Mike Ertz .40
17 Ted Faley .40
18 Greg Fedders .40
19 Mike Ferroni .50
20 Jon Filloon .40
21 Melvin Foster .50
22 Hayden Fry (CO) 1.00
23 Ron Geater .40
24 Ed Gochenour .40
25 Merton Hanks 2.00
26 Jim Hartlieb .50
27 George Hawthorne .40
28 Tork Hook .40
29 Danan Hughes 1.00
30 Jim Johnson .40
31 Jeff Koeppel .40
32 Marvin Lampkin .40
33 Peter Marciano .40
34 Ed Marshall .40
35 Kirk McGowan .40
36 Mike Miller .40
37 Lew Montgomery .40
38 George Murphy .40
39 John Palmer .50
40 James Pipkins .40
41 Tom Poholsky .50
42 Eddie Polly .40
43 Jim Poyton .40
44 Brad Quast .40
45 Matt Rodgers .75
46 Matt Ruhland .40
47 Ron Ryan .40
48 Moses Santos .40
49 Mike Saunders .75
50 Doug Scott .40
51 Jeff Skillett .40
52 Leroy Smith .40
53 Sean Smith .40
54 Sean Snyder .40
55 Tony Stewart .40
56 Mark Stoops .40
57 Dave Turner .40
58 Darin Vande Zande .40
59 Ted Velicer .40
60 Travis Watkins .40
61 Dusty Weiland .40
62 Ladd Wessles .40
63 Matt Whitaker .40
64 Brian Wise .40
65 Anthony Wright .40
66 100 Years of Iowa Football (Logo) .40
67 The Tigerhawk (School Logo) .40
68 Herky the Hawk (Mascot) .40
69 Kinnick Stadium .40
70 Hawkeye Fans .40
71 NFL Tradition (Logo) .40
72 1982 Beach Bowl (Logo) .40
73 1982 Rose Bowl (Logo) .40
74 1983 Gator Bowl (Logo) .40
75 1984 Freedom Bowl (Logo) .40
76 1986 Holiday Bowl (Logo) .40
77 1986 Rose Bowl (Logo) .40
78 1987 Holiday Bowl (Logo) .40
79 1988 Beach Bowl (Logo) .40
80 Big Ten Conference (Logo) .40
81 Iowa Marching Band .40
82 Indoor Practice Facility .40
83 Iowa Locker Rooms .40
84 Iowa Weight Room .40
85 Iowa Class Rooms .40
86 Players' Lounge .40
87 Floyd of Rosedale (Trophy) .40
88 Medical Facilities .40
89 Media Coverage .40
90 Television Coverage (Camera) .40

1993 Iowa

NM/M
Complete Set (64): 25.00
Common Player: .40
1 Ryan Abraham .50
2 Greg Allen .40
3 Jeff Andrews .40
4 Jeff Anttila .40
5 Jefferson Bates .40
6 George Bennett .40
7 Lloyd Bickham .40
8 Larry Blue .40
9 Pat Boone .40
10 Tyrone Boudreaux .40
11 Paul Burmeister .75
12 Tyler Casey .40
13 Billy Coats .40
14 Maurea Crain .40
15 Ernest Crank .50
16 Mike Dailey .40
17 Anthony Dean .50
18 Bobby Diaco .40
19 Mike Duprey .40
20 Billy Ennis-Inge .40
21 Matt Eyde .40
22 Fritz Fequiere .75
23 Hayden Fry (CO) 1.00
24 Willie Guy .40
25 John Hartlieb .50
26 Jason Henlon .40
27 Matt Hilliard .40
28 Mike Hornaday .40
29 Rob Huber .40
30 Chris Jackson .40
31 Harold Jasper .75
32 Jamar Jones .40
33 Kent Kahl .40
34 Cliff King .40
35 John Kline .40
36 Tom Knight .40
37 Aaron Kooiker .40
38 Andy Kreider .40
39 Bill Lange .40
40 Doug Laufenberg .40
41 Hal Mady .50
42 Brian McCullouch .40
43 Jason Olejniczak .40
44 Chris Palmer .40
45 Scott Plate .50

46 Marquis Porter .50
47 Matt Purdy .40
48 Matt Quest .40
49 Damien Robinson .50
50 Todd Romano .40
51 Mark Roussell .40
52 Ted Serama .40
53 Scott Sether .40
54 Sedrick Shaw .50
55 Scott Slutzker .50
56 Ryan Terry .50
57 Mike Wells .40
58 Casey Wiegmann .40
59 Parker Wildeman .40
60 Big Ten Conference (Logo card) .40
61 Hawkeyes Schedule .40
62 Herky (Mascot) .40
63 Indoor Practice Facility .40
64 Kinnick Stadium .40

1997 Iowa

NM/M
Complete Set (19): 30.00
Common Player: 1.50
1 Brett Chambers 1.50
2 Billy Coats 1.50
3 Ryan Driscoll 2.00
4 Bill Ennis-Inge 2.50
5 Rodney Flier 1.50
6 Hayden Fry 2.50
7 Nick Gallery 1.50
8 Aaron Granquist 1.50
9 Brion Hurley 1.50
10 Tom Knight 3.00
11 Mark Mitchell 1.50
12 Demo Odems 1.50
13 Jon Ortlieb 1.50
14 Bill Reardon 1.50
15 Damien Robinson 2.00
16 Ted Serama 1.50
17 Ross Verba 3.00
18 Hawk Watch (1996 Seniors Iowa Hawkeyes Football) 2.00
19 Hawkeyes Logo 1.50

1989 Kansas

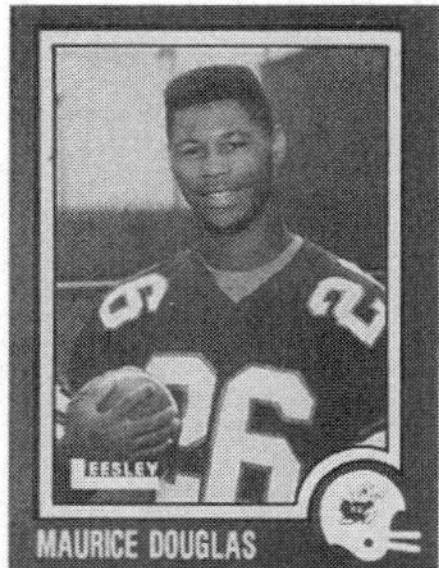

NM/M
Complete Set (40): 12.00
Common Player: .35
1 Kelly Donohoe .75
2 Roger Robben .35
3 Tony Sands .35
4 Paul Zaffaroni .35
5 Lance Flachsbarth .35
6 Brad Fleeman .35
7 Chip Budde .35
8 Bill Hundelt .35
9 Dan Newbrough .35
10 Gary Oatis .35
11 B.J. Lohsen .50
12 John Fritch .35
13 Russ Bowen .35
14 Smith Holland .35
15 Jason Priest .50
16 Scott McCabe .35
17 Jason Tyrer .35
18 Mongo Allen .35
19 Glen Mason (CO) 1.00
20 Deral Boykin .35
21 Quintin Smith .35
22 Mark Koncz .50
23 John Baker .50
24 Football Staff (schedule on back) .50
25 Maurice Hooks .35
26 Frank Hatchett .35
27 Paul Friday .35
28 Doug Terry .35
29 Kenny Drayton .35
30 Jim New .35
31 Chris Perez .35
32 Maurice Douglas 1.25
33 Curtis Moore .35
34 David Gordon .35
35 Matt Nolen .35
36 Dave Walton .35
37 King Dixon .50
38 Memorial Stadium .35
39 Kelly Donohoe Jayhawks in Action .50
40 John Baker Jayhawks in Action (OL) .50
NNO Title Card .75

1992 Kansas

NM/M
Complete Set (52): 20.00
Common Player: .40
1 Mark Allison .40
2 Hassan Bailey .50
3 Greg Ballard .40
4 Martin Blakeney .40
5 Kristopher Booth .40
6 Charley Bowen .40
7 Gilbert Brown 1.00
8 Dwayne Chandler .40
9 Brian Christian .40
10 David Converse .40
11 Monte Cozzens .40
12 Don Davis .40
13 Maurice Douglas 1.00
14 Dan Eichloff .50
15 Chad Fette .40
16 Matt Gay .40
17 Harold Harris .40
18 Rodney Harris .50
19 Steve Harvey .40
20 Hessley Hempstead .40
21 Chip Hilleary 1.00
22 Dick Holt .40
23 Guy Howard .40
24 Chaka Johnson .40
25 John Jones .40
26 Rod Jones .40
27 Kwamie Lassiter .50
28 Rob Licursi .40
29 Trace Liggett .40
30 Keith Loneker .40
31 Dave Marcum .40
32 Glen Mason (CO) .75
33 Chris Maumalanga 1.00
34 Gerald McBurrows .40
35 Robert Mitchell .40
36 Ty Moeder .40
37 Kyle Moore .40
38 Ron Page .40
39 Chris Powell .40
40 Dan Schmidt .40
41 Ashaundai Smith .40
42 Mike Steele .40
43 Dana Stubblefield 4.00
44 Wes Swinford .40
45 Larry Thiel .40
46 Frederick Thomas .50
47 Pete Vang .40
48 Robert Vaughn .40
49 George White .50
50 Sylvester Wright .40
NNO Schedule Card .40
NNO Coaching Staff .40

1982 Kentucky Schedules

NM/M
Complete Set (19): 45.00
Common Player: 3.00
1 Richard Abraham 3.00
2 Glenn Amerson 3.00
3 Effley Brooks 3.00
4 Shawn Donigan 3.00
5 Rod Francis 3.00
6 Terry Henry 3.00
7 Ben Johnson 3.00
8 Dave Lyons 3.00
9 John Maddox 3.00
10 Rob Mangas 4.00
11 David "Buzz" Meers 3.00
12 Andy Molls 3.00
13 Tom Petty 3.00
14 Don Roe 3.00
15 Todd Shadowen 3.00
16 Gerald Smyth 3.00
17 Pete Venable 3.00
18 Allan Watson 3.00
19 Steve Williams 3.00

1986 Kentucky Schedules

NM/M
Complete Set (4): 15.00
Common Player: 4.00
1 Jerry Claiborne (CO) 4.00
2 Mark Higgs 7.50
3 Marc Logan 6.00
4 Bill Ransdell 4.00

L

1981 Louisville Police

NM/M
Complete Set (64): 94.00
Common Player: .70
1 Title Card SP (Catch That Cardinal Spirit) 37.00
2 Bob Weber (CO) .70
3 Assistant Coaches .70
4 Jay Trautwein .70
5 Darrell Wimberly .70
6 Jeff Van Camp .70
7 Joe Welch .70
8 Fred Blackmon .70
9 Lamar "Toot" Evans .70
10 Tom Blair .70
11 Joe Kader .70
12 Mike Trainor .70
13 Richard Tharpe .70
14 Gene Hagan .70
15 Greg Jones .70
16 Leon Williams .70
17 Ellsworth Larkins .70
18 Sebastian Curry .70
19 Frank Minnifield 4.50
20 Roger Clay .70
21 Mark Blasinsky .70
22 Mike Cruz .70
23 David Arthur .70
24 Johnny Unitas (In front background, list of Cardinals who played pro ball) 11.00
25 John DeMarco .70
26 Eric Rollins .70
27 Jack Pok .70
28 Pete McCartney .70
29 Mark Clayton 11.00
30 Jeff Hortert .70
31 Pete Bowen .70
32 Robert Niece .70
33 Todd McMahan .70
34 John Wall .70
35 Kelly Stickrod .70
36 Jim Miller .70
37 Tom Moore .70
38 Kurt Knop .70
39 Mark Musgrave .70
40 Tony Campbell .70
41 Mark Wilson .70
42 Robert Mitchell .70
43 Courtney Jeter .70
44 Wayne Taylor .70
45 Jeff Speedy .70
46 Donald Craft .70
47 Glenn Hunter .70
48 1981 Louisville Schedule .70
49 Greg Hickman .70
50 Nate Dozier .70
51 Pat Patterson .70
52 Scott Gannon .70
53 Dean May .70
54 David Hatfield .70
55 Mike Nuzzolese .70
56 John Ayers .70
57 Lamar Cummins .70
58 Bill Olsen (AD) .70
59 Tailgating .70
60 Football Complex .70
61 Marching Band .70
62 Cheerleaders .70
63 Administration Bldg. .70
64 Cardinal Bird .70

1990 Louisville Smokey

NM/M
Complete Set (16): 25.00
Common Player: 1.25
1 Greg Brohm 1.25
2 Jeff Brohm 1.50
3 Pete Burkey 1.25
4 Mike Flores 1.25
5 Dan Gangwer 1.25
6 Reggie Johnson 1.50
7 Scott McAllister 1.25
8 Ken McKay 1.25
9 Browning Nagle 4.00
10 Ed Reynolds 1.25
11 Mark Sander 1.25
12 Howard Schnellenberger (CO) 5.00
13 Ted Washington 2.50
14 Klaus Wilmsmeyer 2.00
15 Cardinal Bird (Mascot) 1.25
16 Cardinal Stadium 1.25

1992 Louisville Kraft

NM/M
Complete Set (30): 15.00
Common Player: .60
1 Jamie Asher 1.50
2 Xzavia Atkins .60
3 Kevin Blumeier .60
4 Greg Brohm .75
5 Jeff Brohm .75
6 Brandon Brookfield .60
7 Ray Buchanan 2.00
8 Rawle Bynoe .60
9 Tom Cavallo .60
10 Kevin Cook .60
11 Andy Culley .60
12 Ralph Dawkins .75
13 Dave Debold .60
14 Chris Fitzpatrick .60
15 Kevin Gaines .60
16 Jose Gonzalez .60
17 Jim Hanna .60
18 Ken Harnden .60
19 Ivey Henderson .60
20 Joe Johnson 1.50
21 Robert Knuutila .60
22 Marty Lowe 1.00
23 Roman Oben 1.25
24 Garin Patrick .60
25 Leonard Ray .60
26 Shawn Rodriguez .60
27 Anthony Shelman 1.00
28 Brevin Smith .60
29 Jason Stinson .75
30 Ben Sumpter .75

1993 Louisville Kraft

NM/M
Complete Set (30): 15.00
Common Player: .60
1 Jamie Asher 1.25
2 Aaron Bailey .60
3 Zoe Barney .60
4 Anthony Bridges .60
5 Jeff Brohm .75
6 Brandon Brookfield .60
7 Kendall Brown .60
8 Tom Carrol .60
9 Tom Cavallo .60
10 Kevin Cook .60
11 Ralph Dawkins .75
12 Dave Debold .60
13 Reggie Ferguson .60
14 Chris Fitzpatrick .60
15 Johnny Frost .60
16 Jim Hanna .60
17 Ivey Henderson .60
18 Marcus Hill .60
19 Shawn Jackson .60
20 Joe Johnson 1.25
21 Marty Lowe .75
22 Vertis McKinney .60
23 Greg Minnis .60
24 Roman Oben 1.00
25 Garin Patrick .60
26 Terry Quinn .75
27 Leonard Ray .60
28 Anthony Shelman .75
29 Jason Stinson .60
30 Ben Sumpter .60

1983 LSU Sunbeam

NM/M
Complete Set (100): 12.00
Common Player: .10
1 1958 LSU National Championship Team .20
2 Abe Mickal .10
3 Carlos Carson .20
4 Charles Alexander .20
5 Steve Ensminger .10
6 Ken Kavanaugh Sr. .20
7 Bert Jones .50
8 David Woodley .20
9 Jerry Marchand .10
10 Clyde Lindsey .10
11 James Britt .10
12 Warren Rabb .20
13 Mike Hillman .10
14 Nelson Stokley .10
15 Abner Wimberly .10
16 Terry Robiskie .20
17 Steve Van Buren .30
18 Doug Moreau .20
19 George Tarasovic .10
20 Billy Cannon .30
21 Jerry Stovall .20
22 Joe Labruzzo .10
23 Mickey Mangham .10
24 Craig Burns .10
25 Y.A. Tittle .75
26 Wendell Harris .20
27 Leroy Labat .10
28 Hokie Gajan .20
29 Mike Williams .10
30 Sammy Grezaffi .20
31 Clinton Burrell .10
32 Orlando McDaniel .10
33 George Bevan .10
34 Johnny Robinson .20
35 Billy Masters .10
36 J.W. Brodnax .10
37 Tommy Casanova .20
38 Fred Miller .10
39 George Rice .10
40 Earl Gros .20
41 Lynn LeBlanc .10
42 Jim Taylor .40
43 Joe Tumenello .10
44 Tommy Davis .20
45 Alvin Dark .30
46 Richard Picou .10
47 Challie Percy .10
48 John Garlington .20
49 Mike Morgan .10
50 Charles "Bo" Strange .10
51 Max Fugler .30
52 Don Schwab .10
53 Dennis Gaubatz .20
54 Jimmy Field .10
55 Warren Capone .10
56 Albert Richardson .10
57 Charley Cusiman .10
58 Brad Davis .10
59 Gaynell "Gus" Kinchen .10
60 Roy "Moonie" Winston .20
61 Mike Anderson .10
62 Jesse Fatherree .10
63 Gene "Red" Knight .10
64 Tyler LaFauci .10
65 Emile Fournet .10
66 Gaynell "Gus" Tinsley .20
67 Remi Prudhomme .20
68 Marvin "Moose" Stewart .10
69 Jerry Guillot .10
70 Steve Cassidy .10
71 Bo Harris .20
72 Robert Dugas .10
73 Malcolm Scott .10
74 Charles "Pinky" Rohm .10
75 Gerald Keigley .10
76 Don Alexander .10
77 A.J. Duhe .20
78 Ronnie Estay .10
79 John Wood .10
80 Andy Hamilton .20
81 Jay Michaelson .10
82 Kenny Konz .20
83 Tracy Porter .10
84 Billy Truax .20
85 Alan Risher .10
86 John Adams .10
87 Tommy Neck .10
88 Brad Boyd .10
89 Greg LaFluer .10
90 Bill Elko .10
91 Binks Miciotto .10
92 Lew Sibley .10
93 Willie Teal .10
94 Lyman White .10
95 Chris Williams .10
96 Sid Fournet .10
97 Leonard Marshall .20
98 Ramsey Dardar .10
99 Kenny Bordelon .10
100 Fred "Skinny" Hall .10

1985 LSU Police

NM/M
Complete Set (16): 8.00
Common Player: .50
1 Mitch Andrews .50
2 Bill Arnsparger (CO) .75
3 Roland Barbay .50
4 Michael Brooks 1.00
5 Shawn Burks .50
6 Tommy Clapp .50
7 Matt DeFrank .50
8 Kevin Guidry .50
9 Dalton Hilliard 1.50
10 Garry James .75
11 Norman Jefferson .50
12 Rogie Magee .50
13 Mike the Tiger (Mascot) .50
14 Craig Rathjen .50
15 Jeff Wickersham .75
16 Karl Wilson .75

1986 LSU Police

NM/M
Complete Set (16): 8.00
Common Player: .50
1 Nacho Albergamo .50
2 Eric Andolsek 1.00
3 Bill Arnsparger (CO) .75
4 Roland Barbay .50
5 Michael Brooks 1.00
6 Chris Carrier .50
7 Toby Caston 1.00
8 Wendell Davis 1.50
9 Kevin Guidry .50
10 John Hazard .50
11 Oliver Lawrence .50
12 Rogie Magee .50
13 Sam Martin .75
14 Darrell Phillips .50
15 Steve Rehage .50
16 Ron Sancho .75

1987 LSU Police

NM/M
Complete Set (16): 10.00
Common Player: .50
1 Nacho Albergamo .50
2 Eric Andolsek .75
3 Mike Archer (CO) .75
4 David Browndyke .50
5 Chris Carrier .50
6 Wendell Davis 1.00
7 Matt DeFrank .50
8 Nicky Hazard .50
9 Eric Hill 1.00
10 Tommy Hodson 1.50
11 Greg Jackson 1.00
12 Brian Kinchen 1.00
13 Darren Malbrough .50
14 Sam Martin .50
15 Ron Sancho .50
16 Harvey Williams 3.50

1988 LSU Police

NM/M
Complete Set (16): 8.00
Common Player: .50
1 Mike the Tiger (Mascot) .50
2 Mike Archer (CO) .75
3 Tommy Hodson 1.50
4 Harvey Williams 2.50
5 David Browndyke .50
6 Karl Dunbar .50
7 Eddie Fuller .50
8 Mickey Guidry .50
9 Greg Jackson .75
10 Clint James .50
11 Victor Jones .50
12 Tony Moss .50
13 Ralph Norwood .50
14 Darrell Phillips .50
15 Ruffin Rodrigue .50
16 Ron Sancho .50

1989 LSU Police

NM/M
Complete Set (16): 8.00
Common Player: .50
1 Mike the Tiger (Mascot) .50
2 David Browndyke .50
3 Mike Archer (CO) .75
4 Ruffin Rodrigue (68) .50
5 Marc Boutte (95) 1.00
6 Clint James (70) .50
7 Jimmy Young (5) .50
8 Alvin Lee (26) .50
9 Eddie Fuller (33) .50
10 Tiger Stadium .50
11 Harvey Williams (22) 2.00
12 Verge Ausberry (98) .50
13 Karl Dunbar (63) .50
14 Tommy Hodson (13) 1.25
15 Tony Moss (6) .50
16 The Golden Girls (Cheerleaders) .75

1992 LSU McDag

NM/M
Complete Set (16): 6.00
Common Player: .50
1 Curley Hallman (CO) .75
2 Ray Adams .50
3 Chad Loup .75
4 Odell Beckham .50
5 Wesley Jacob .50
6 Kevin Mawae 1.00
7 Clayton Mouton .50
8 Roovelroe Swan .50
9 Ricardo Washington .50
10 David Walkup .50
11 Jessie Daigle .50
12 Carlton Buckles .50
13 Anthony Williams .50
14 Darron Landry .50
15 Frank Godfrey .50
16 Pedro Suarez .50

M

1969 Maryland Team Sheets

NM/M
Complete Set (6): 25.00
Common Panel: 6.00
1 Bill Backus, Lou Bracken, Sonny Demczuk, Roland Merritt, Rich Slaninka, Ralph Sonntag, Mike Stubljar, Jim Stull 6.00
2 Bill Bell CO, George Boutselis CO, Albert Ferguson CO, James Kehoe CO, Roy Lester CO, Dim Montero CO, Lee Royer CO 6.00
3 Pat Burke, John Dyer, Craig Gienger, Tony Greene, Bob MacBride, Bill Meister, Russ Nolan, Ray Soporowski 6.00
4 Steve Ciambor, Kenny Dutton, Dan Kecman, Bob Mahnic, Len Santacroce, David Seifert, Len Spicer, Rick Stoll 6.00
5 Bob Colbert, John Dill, Henry Gareis, Bill Grant, Glenn Kubany, Bill Reilly, Wally Stalnaker, Gary Vansickler 6.00
6 Paul Fitzpatrick, Larry Marshall, Tom Miller, Will Morris, Dennis O'Hara, Scott Shank, Jeff Shugars, Al Thomas 6.00

1988 McNeese State McDag/Police

NM/M
Complete Set (16): 6.00
Common Player: .50
1 Sonny Jackson (CO) .50
2 Lance Wiley .50
3 Brian McZeal .50
4 Berwick Davenport .50
5 Gary Irvin .50
6 Glenn Koch .50
7 Chad Habetz .50
8 Pete Sinclair .50
9 Tony Citizen .50
10 Scott Dieterich .50
11 Hud Jackson .50
12 Darrin Andrus .50
13 Jeff Mathews .50
14 Devin Babineaux .50
15 Jeff Delhomme .50
16 Eric LeBlanc, Mike Pierce .50

1989 McNeese State McDag/Police

NM/M
Complete Set (16): 6.00
Common Player: .50
1 Marc Stampley .50
2 Mark LeBlanc .50
3 Kip Texada .50
4 Brian Champagne .50
5 Ronald Scott .50
6 Jimmy Poirier .50
7 Cliff Buckner .50
8 Jericho Loupe .50
9 Vaughn Calbert .50
10 Rodney Burks .50
11 Troy Jones .50
12 Chris Andrus .50
13 Robbie Vizier .50
14 Kenneth Pierce .50
15 Bobby Smith .50
16 Trent Lee .50

1990 McNeese State McDag/Police

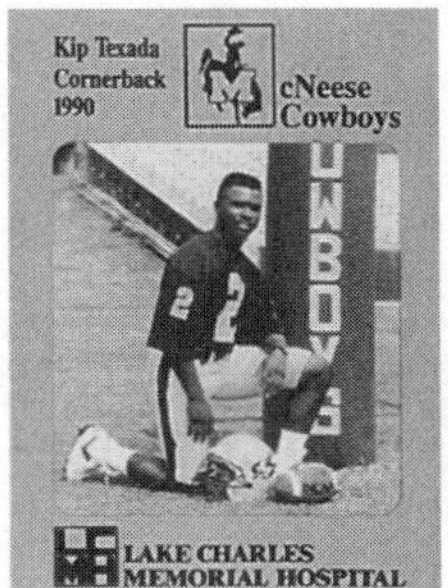

Kip Texada
Cornerback
1990
cNeese
Cowboys
LAKE CHARLES
MEMORIAL HOSPITAL

NM/M
Complete Set (16): 6.00
Common Player: .50
1 Hud Jackson .50
2 Wes Watts .50
3 Mark LeBlanc .50
4 Jeff Delhomme .50
5 Mike Reed .50
6 Chuck Esponge .50
7 Ronald Scott .50
8 Ken Naquin .50
9 Steve Aultman .50
10 Sean Judge .50
11 Greg Rayson .50
12 Kip Texada .50
13 Mike Pierce .50
14 Jimmy Poirier .50
15 Ronald Solomon .50
16 Eric Foster .50

1991 McNeese State McDag/Police

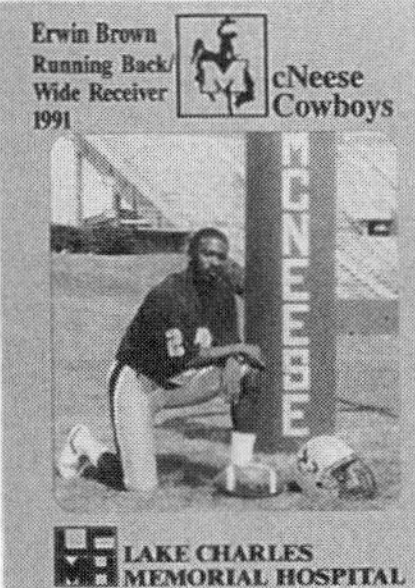

NM/M
Complete Set (16): 6.00
Common Player: .50
1 Eric Roberts .50
2 Irwin Brown .50
3 Marcus Bowie .50
4 Wes Watts .50
5 Brian Brumfield .50
6 Marc Stampley .50
7 Sean Judge .50
8 Joey Bernard .50
9 Ken Naquin .50
10 Bobby Smith .50
11 Sam Breaux .50
12 Ronald Scott .50
13 Edward Dyer .50
14 Blayne Rush .50
15 Ronald Solomon .50
16 Steve Aultman .50

1992 McNeese State McDag/Police

NM/M
Complete Set (16): 6.00
Common Player: .50
1 Eric Acheson .50
2 Pat Neck .50
3 Marcus Bowie .50
4 Marty Posey .50
5 Brian Brumfield .50
6 Terry Irving .75
7 Eric Fleming .50
8 Lance Guidry .50
9 Ken Naquin .50
10 Chris Fontenette .50
11 Sam Breaux .50

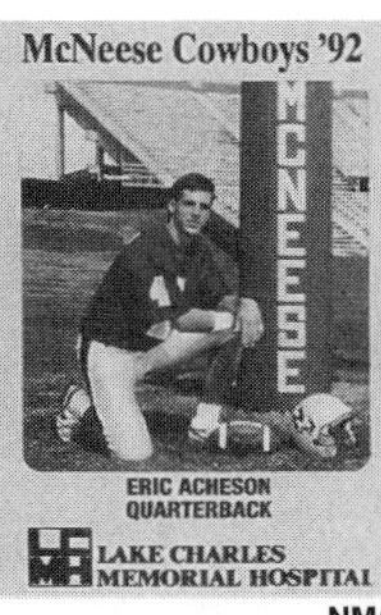

NM/M
12 Dana Scott .50
13 Edward Dyer .50
14 Blayne Rush .50
15 Ronald Solomon .50
16 Steve Aultman .50

1990 Miami Smokey

NM/M
Complete Set (16): 18.00
Common Player: .75
1 Randy Bethel (93) .75
2 Wesley Carroll (81) 2.00
3 Rob Chudzinski (84) .75
4 Leonard Conley (28) 1.50
5 Luis Cristobal (59) .75
6 Maurice Crum (49) .75
7 Shane Curry (44) 1.50
8 Craig Erickson (7) 4.00
9 Dennis Erickson (CO) 2.00
10 Darren Handy (66) .75
11 Randal Hill (3) 4.00
12 Carlos Huerta (27) 1.50
13 Russell Maryland (67) 3.00
14 Stephen McGuire (30) 1.50
15 Roland Smith (16) .75
16 Mike Sullivan (79) .75

1991 Miami Police

NM/M
Complete Set (16): 15.00
Common Player: 1.00
1 Jessie Armstead 1.50
2 Micheal Barrow 2.00
3 Hurlie Brown 1.00
4 Dennis Erickson (CO) 2.00
5 Anthony Hamlet 1.00
6 Carlos Huerta 1.50
7 Herbert James 1.00
8 Claude Jones 1.00
9 Stephen McGuire 1.50
10 Eric Miller 1.00
11 Joe Moore 1.00
12 Charles Pharms 1.00
13 Leon Searcy 2.00
14 Darrin Smith 2.00
15 Lamar Thomas 1.50
16 Gino Torretta 2.00

1992 Miami Police

NM/M
Complete Set (16): 15.00
Common Player: .75
1 Jessie Armstead 1.00
2 Micheal Barrow 1.50
3 Coleman Bell .75
4 Mark Caesar .75
5 Horace Copeland (UER) (Name misspelled Horrace on front) 2.00
6 Mario Cristobal .75
7 Dennis Erickson (CO) 1.50
8 Casey Greer .75
9 Stephen McGuire 1.00
10 Ryan McNeil 1.50
11 Rusty Medearis .75
12 Darrin Smith 1.50
13 Darryl Spencer .75
14 Lamar Thomas 2.00
15 Gino Torretta 2.00
16 Kevin Williams (WR) 3.00

1993 Miami Bumble Bee

NM/M
Complete Set (16): 12.00
Common Player: .60
1 Rudy Barber .60
2 Robert Bass .60
3 Donnell Bennett 2.00
4 Jason Budroni .60
5 Marcus Carey .60
6 Ryan Collins 1.00
7 Frank Costa 1.00
8 Dennis Erickson (CO) 1.00
9 Terris Harris .60
10 Chris T. Jones 2.00
11 Larry Jones 1.50
12 Darren Krein 1.00
13 Kenny Lopez .60
14 Kevin Patrick .60
15 Dexter Seigler .60
16 Paul White .60

1907 Michigan Postcards

NM/M
Complete Set (15): 600.00
Common Player: 30.00
1 Dave Allerdice 40.00
2 William Casey 30.00
3 William Embs 30.00
4 Keene Fitzpatrick (TR) 30.00
5 Flanagan 30.00
6 Walter Graham 30.00
7 H.S. Hammond 30.00
8 John Loell 30.00
9 Paul Magoffin 40.00
10 James Miller 30.00
11 Walter Rheinschild 30.00
12 Mason Rumney 30.00
13 Adolph "Germany" Schultz 125.00
14 William Wasmund 30.00
15 Fielding Yost (CO) 125.00

1977 Michigan

NM/M
Complete Set (21): 25.00
Common Player: .75
1 John Anderson 1.25
2 Russell Davis 1.25
3 Mark Donahue .75
4 Walt Downing .75
5 Bill Dufek 1.25
6 Jon Giesler (SP) 2.00
7 Steve Graves .75
8 Curtis Greer 2.00
9 Dwight Hicks 2.50
10 Derek Howard .75
11 Harlan Huckleby 2.50
12 Gene Johnson .75
13 Dale Keitz .75
14 Mike Kenn 2.50
15 Rick Leach 2.50
16 Mark Schmerge .75
17 Ron Simpkins 1.25
18 Curt Stephenson (SP) 2.00
19 Gerry Szara (SP) 2.00
20 Rick White .75
21 Gregg Willner .75

1989 Michigan

NM/M
Complete Set (22): 12.00
Common Player: .50
1 H.O. "Fritz" Crisler (CO) .60
2 Anthony Carter 1.50
3 Willie Heston .50
4 Reggie McKenzie .50
5 Bo Schembechler (CO) 1.50
6 Dan Dierdorf 1.50
7 Jim Harbaugh 1.50
8 Bennie Oosterbaan .50
9 Jamie Morris .60
10 Gerald R. Ford 1.50
11 Curtis Greer .60
12 Ron Kramer .60
13 Calvin O'Neal .50
14 Bob Chappuis .50
15 Fielding Yost (CO) .60
16 Dennis Franklin .50
17 Benny Friedman .60
18 Jim Mandich .60
19 Rob Lytle .60
20 Bump Elliott .60
21 Harry Kipke .50
22 Dave Brown .60

2002 Michigan Football

NM/M
Complete Set (34): 15.00
Common Player: .25
L1 Tom Harmon 1.00
L2 Forest Evashevski .25
L3 Ed Frutig .25
L4 Albert Wistert .25
L5 Francis Wistert .25
L6 Alvin Wistert .25
L7 Robert "Al" Wahl .25
L8 Bob Chappuis .25
L9 Pete Elliott .25
L10 Chalmers "Bump" Elliott .25
L11 Chuck Ortmann .25
L12 Don Dufek Sr. .25
L13 Bill Putich .25
L14 Don Lund .25
L15 Don Lund .25
L16 Bob Timberlake .25
L17 Don Moorhead .25
L18 Jim Mandich .25
L19 Reggie McKenzie .25
L20 Dan Dierdorf 3.00
L21 Jim Brandstaater .25
L22 Don Dufek Jr. .25
L23 Bill Dufek .25
L24 Rob Lytle .25
L25 Rick Leach 1.00
L26 Harlan Huckleby .25
L27 Gerald Ford 4.00
L28 Tom Slade .25
L29 Aaron Shea .25
L30 Tai Streets 1.00
L31 Bennie Oosterbaan .25
L32 Jack Weisenburger .25
L33 Jamie Morris .25
L34 Mike Kenn .25

2002 Michigan Football Broadcaster

NM/M
Complete Set (1): 1.00
B1 Bob Ufer 1.00

2002 Michigan Football Coaches

NM/M
Complete Set (2): 2.00
Common Player: 1.00
C1 H.O. "Fritz" Crisler 1.00
C2 Bo Schembechler 1.00

2002 Michigan Football Promo Cards

NM/M
Complete Set (3): 5.00
Common Player: 2.00
P48 Gerald Ford 3.00
P1 Bo Schembechler 3.00
Tom Harmon, Forest Evashevski Checklist 2.00

2002 Michigan Football M Go Blue! Signature

NM/M
Complete Set (25):
Common Player: 15.00
A1 Ed Frutig 15.00
A2 Robert "Al" Wahl 15.00
A3 Reggie McKenzie 15.00
A4 Dan Dierdorf 25.00
A5 Don Lund 15.00
A6 Rob Lytle 20.00
A7 Jim Mandich 15.00
A8 Don Dufek Jr. 15.00
A9 Bill Dufek 15.00
A10 Ron Kramer 15.00
A11 Chalmers "Bump" Elliott 15.00
A12 Chuck Ortmann 15.00
A13 Alvin Wistert 15.00
A14 Aaron Shea 25.00
A15 Tai Streets 15.00
A16 Bill Putich 15.00
A17 Bob Timberlake 15.00
A18 Don Canham 15.00
A19 Don Moorhead 15.00
A20 Jim Brandstaater 15.00
A21 Harlan Huckleby 15.00
A22 Jack Weisenburger 15.00
A23 Jamie Morris 15.00
A24 Mike Kenn 15.00
A25 Bo Schembechler 45.00

2002 Michigan Football Michigan M-Mates

NM/M
Complete Set (10):
Common Player: 20.00
MM1 Rick Leach, Rob Lytle 25.00
MM2 Pete Elliott, Chalmers "Bump" Elliott 20.00
MM3 Forest Evashevski, Rick Leach 20.00
MM4 Jim Mandich, Don Moorhead 20.00
MM5 Bob Chappuis, Alvin Wistert 20.00
MM6 Jamie Morris, Rob Lytle 20.00
MM7 Aaron Shea, Tai Streets 30.00
MM8 Bo Schembechler, Rick Leach 50.00
MM9 Reggie McKenzie, Bo Schembechler, Dan Dierdorf 75.00
MM10 The Dufek Family 35.00

2002 Michigan Football QB Club

NM/M
Complete Set (7):
Common Player: 15.00
QB1 Rick Leach 20.00
QB2 Bob Timberlake 15.00
QB3 Forest Evashevski 15.00
QB4 Pete Elliott 15.00
QB5 Bill Putich 15.00
QB6 Don Moorhead 15.00
QB7 Tom Slade 15.00

2002 Michigan Football Victors

NM/M
Complete Set (10):
Common Player: 20.00
1947A Chalmers "Bump" Elliott 20.00
1947B Bob Chappuis 20.00
1947C Alvin Wistert 25.00
1947D Jack Weisenburger 20.00
1948A Pete Elliott 20.00
1948B Robert "Al" Wahl 20.00
1948C Chuck Ortmann 20.00
1948D Don Dufek Sr. 20.00
1997A Tai Streets 20.00
1997B Aaron Shea 20.00

2002 Michigan Football M Sketch

NM/M
Complete Set (6): 15.00
Common Player: 2.00
S1 Tom Harmon throwing 4.00
S2 Tom Harmon candid 4.00
S3 Gerald Ford head shot 5.00
S4 Gerald Ford hiking 5.00
S5 Rick Leach candid 3.00
S6 Modern Michigan helmet 3.00

2002 Michigan Football Retired Numbers

NM/M
Complete Set (7): 5.00
Common Player: 1.00
RN1 Ron Kramer 1.00
RN2 Albert Wistert 1.00
RN3 Alvin Wistert 1.00
RN4 Francis Wistert 1.00
RN5 Tom Harmon 2.00
RN6 Bennie Oosterbaan 1.00
RN7 Gerald Ford 3.00

2002 Michigan Football Case Card

NM/M
Complete Set (1): 1.00
UM98 Tom Harmon 1.00

2002 Michigan Football Jersey Card

NM/M
Complete Set (2): 60.00
Common Player: 15.00
J1 Aaron Shea 15.00
J2 Aaron Shea autograph 45.00

1988 Mississippi McDag

NM/M
Complete Set (2): 4.00
Common Player: 2.00
15 Mark Young 2.00
16 Bryan Owen 2.00

1991 Mississippi Hoby

NM/M
Complete Set (42): 9.00
Common Player: .25
439 Gary Abide .25
440 Dwayne Amos .25
441 Tyji Armstrong 1.00
442 Tyrone Ashley .25
443 Darron Billings .25
444 Danny Boyd .25
445 Billy Brewer (CO) .35
446 Chad Brown .35
447 Tony Brown .25
448 Vincent Brownlee .25
449 Jeff Carter .35
450 Richard Chisolm .25
451 Clint Conlee .25
452 Marvin Courtney .25
453 Cliff Dew .25
454 Johnny Dixon .25
455 Artis Ford .25
456 Chauncey Godwin .25
457 Brian Harper .25
458 David Harris .25
459 Pete Harris .25
460 David Herring .25
461 James Holcombe .25
462 Kevin Ingram .25
463 Phillip Kent .35
464 Derrick King .25
465 Brian Lee .25
466 Jim Lentz .25
467 Everett Lindsay .25
468 Tom Luke .25
469 Thomas McLeish .25
470 Wesley Melton .25
471 Tyrone Montgomery .75
472 Deano Orr .25
473 Darrick Owens .35
474 Lynn Ross .25
475 Russ Shows .25
476 Eddie Small .35
477 Trea Southerland .25
478 Gerald Vaughn .25
479 Abner White .25
480 Sebastian Williams .25

1991 Mississippi State Hoby

NM/M
Complete Set (42): 9.00
Common Player: .25
481 Lance Aldridge .25
482 Treddis Anderson .25
483 Shea Bell .25
484 Chris Bosarge .25
485 Daniel Boyd .25
486 Jerome Brown .25
487 Torrance Brown .25
488 Keith Carr .25
489 Herman Carroll .25
490 Keo Coleman .35
491 Michael Davis .25
492 Trenell Edwards .25
493 Chris Firle .25
494 Lee Ford .25
495 Tay Galloway .25
496 Chris Gardner .25
497 Arleye Gibson .25
498 Tony Harris .25
499 Willie Harris .25
500 Kevin Henry .35
501 Jackie Sherrill (CO) .50
502 John James .25
503 Tony James .25
504 Todd Jordan .25
505 Keith Joseph .25
506 Kelvin Knight .25
507 Lee Lipscomb .25
508 Juan Long .25
509 Kyle McCoy .25
510 Tommy Morrell .25
511 Kelly Ray .25
512 Mike Riley .25
513 Kenny Roberts .25
514 William Robinson .25
515 Bill Sartin .25
516 Kenny Stewart .25
517 Rodney Stowers .50
518 Anthony Thames .25
519 Edward Williams .25
520 Nate Williams .25
521 Karl Williamson .25
522 Marc Woodard .25

1992 Mobil Cotton Bowl

NM/M
Complete Set (24): 35.00
Common Player: 1.00
1 The Cotton Bowl 1.00
2 Sammy Baugh 2.50
3 Doak Walker 2.00
4 Dicky Moegle 1.00
5 Bobby Layne 2.50
6 Curtis Sanford (Founder) 1.00
7 John Kimbrough 1.00
8 Ernie Davis 5.00
9 Lance Alworth 2.00
10 James Street, Darrell Royal CO 1.50
11 Mike Singletary 1.50
12 Roger Staubach 4.00
13 Earl Campbell 3.50
14 Wilson Whitley 1.00
15 Jim Swink 1.00
16 Martin Ruby 1.00
17 Davey O'Brien 1.50
18 Gene Stallings, Paul "Bear" Bryant (CO) 2.50
19 Bo Jackson 2.00
20 Joe Theismann 1.50
21 Field Scovell Mr. Cotton Bowl 1.00
22 Ken Hatfield 1.00
23 Joe Montana 5.00
24 Mobil Cotton Bowl Classic CL 1.00

N

1974 Nebraska

NM/M
Complete Set (54): 65.00
Common Player: 1.00
1 Tom Osborne (CO) 20.00
2 Terry Rogers 1.00
3 Tom Ruud 1.50
4 Jeff Schneider 1.00
5 Mark Heydorff 1.00
6 Dean Gissler 1.00
7 Jim Burrow 1.00
8 Al Eveland 1.00
9 Chuck Jones 1.00
10 Brad Jenkins 1.00
11 Dave Butterfield 1.00
12 Rich Duda 1.50
13 Steve Hoins 1.00
14 Ron Pruitt 1.00
15 Tony Davis 1.50
16 Mike Fultz 1.00
17 Chad Leonardi 1.00
18 John Starkebaum 1.00
19 Marvin Crenshaw 1.50
20 Larry Mushinskie 1.00
21 Tom Pate 1.00
22 David Humm 4.00
23 Willie Thornton 1.50
24 Dave Redding 1.00
25 Dave Shamblin 1.00
26 Earl Everett 1.00
27 Rik Bonness 1.50
28 Mark Doak 1.00
29 John Lee 1.00
30 Mike Coyle 1.00
31 George Kyros 1.00
32 Gary Higgs 1.00
33 Dennis Pavelka 1.00
34 Jeff Moran 1.00
35 John O'Leary 1.00
36 Percy Eichelberger 1.00
37 Greg Jorgensen 1.00
38 George Mills 1.00
39 Terry Luck 1.00
40 Don Westbrook 1.00
41 Mike Offner 1.00
42 Stan Waldemore 1.00
43 Stan Hegener 1.00
44 Bobby Thomas 1.00
45 Bob Martin 1.00
46 Ritch Bahe 1.00
47 Tom Heiser 1.00
48 Steve Wieser 1.00
49 Ardell Johnson 1.00
50 Chuck Malito 1.00
51 Bob Lingenfelter 1.00
52 Wonder Monds 1.50
53 Bob Nelson 1.50
54 Memorial Stadium 1.50

1977 Nebraska

NM/M
Complete Set (54): 65.00

Common Player: 1.00
1 Tom Osborne (CO) 15.00
2 Tom Alward 1.00
3 Dan Anderson 1.00
4 Frosty Anderson 1.00
5 Al Austin 1.00
6 Ritch Bahe 1.00
7 John Bell 1.00
8 Rik Bonness 1.50
9 Randy Borg 1.00
10 Rich Costanzo 1.00
11 Maury Damkroger 1.50
12 Tony Davis 1.50
13 Mark Doak 1.00
14 Richard Duda 1.50
15 John Dutton 3.00
16 Pat Fischer 3.00
17 Marvin Crenshaw 1.50
18 Dean Gissler 1.00
19 Dave Goeller 1.00
20 Percy Eichelberger 1.00
21 Stan Hegener 1.00
22 Dave Humm 2.50
23 Ardell Johnson 1.00
24 Doug Johnson 1.00
25 Chuck Jones 1.00
26 Wonder Monds 1.50
27 Terry Rogers 1.00
28 Bob Revelle 1.00
29 Tom Pate 1.00
30 Mike O'Holleran 1.00
31 Ron Pruitt 1.00
32 Bob Nelson 1.50
33 Larry Mushinskie 1.00
34 Jeff Moran 1.00
35 Bob Martin 1.00
36 Ralph Powell 1.00
37 Steve Manstedt 1.00
38 Brent Longwell 1.00
39 George Kyros 1.00
40 Zaven Yaralian 1.00
41 Bob Wolfe 1.00
42 Steve Wieser 1.00
43 Daryl White 1.00
44 Bob Thornton 1.00
45 John Starkebaum 1.00
46 Dave Shamblin 1.00
47 Don Westbrook 1.50
48 Bob Schmit 1.50
49 Rich Sanger 1.00
50 Willie Thornton 1.50
51 Tom Ruud 1.50
52 Steve Runty 1.00
53 Stadium (Red) 1.50
54 Stadium (Black) 1.50

1989 Nebraska 100

NM/M

Complete Set (100): 40.00
Common Player: .35
1 Tony Davis .50
2 Keith Jones .35
3 Turner Gill 1.25
4 Dave Butterfield .35
5 Wonder Monds .50
6 Dave Rimington .75
7 John Dutton .75
8 Irving Fryar 3.00
9 Dean Steinkuhler .75
10 Mike Rozier 1.25
11 Jarvis Redwine .75
12 Randy Schleusener .35
13 Junior Miller .50
14 Broderick Thomas 1.25
15 Steve Taylor .50
16 Neil Smith 2.00
17 John McCormick .35
18 Danny Noonan .50
19 Mike Fultz .35
20 Vince Ferragamo 1.00
21 Jerry Tagge .75
22 Jeff Kinney .50
23 Rich Glover .50
24 Johnny Rodgers 1.25
25 Rik Bonness .50
26 Dave Humm .50
27 Mark Traynowicz .50
28 Harry Grimminger .35
29 Bill Lewis .50
30 Jim Skow .50
31 Larry Kramer .35
32 Tony Jeter .50
33 Robert Brown .35
34 Larry Wachholtz .35
35 Wayne Meylan .50
36 Bob Newton .35
37 Willie Harper .50
38 Bob Martin .35
39 Jerry Murtaugh .50
40 Daryl White .35
41 Larry Jacobson .35
42 Joe Armstrong .35
43 Laverne Allers .35
44 Freeman White .50
45 Marvin Crenshaw .50
46 Forrest Behm .35
47 Jerry Minnick .35
48 Tom Davis .35
49 Kelvin Clark .50
50 Tom Rathman 1.25
51 Sam Francis .35
52 Joe Orduna .50
53 Ed Weir .35
54 Bill Thornton .35
55 Bob Devaney (CO) .75
56 Bret Clark .35
57 Frank Solich .35
58 Tim Smith .35
59 George Andrews .35
60 Rick Berns .50
61 Monte Johnson .50
62 Walt Barnes .35
63 Jim McFarland .35
64 Jimmy Williams .35
65 Vic Halligan .35
66 Guy Chamberlin .35
67 Hugh Rhea .35
68 George Sauer .50
69 E.O. Stiehm (CO) .35
70 Walter G. Booth (CO) .35
71 First Night Game (Memorial Stadium) .35
72 Memorial Stadium .35
73 M-Stadium Expansions .35
74 Andra Franklin .75
75 Ron McDole .50
76 Pat Fischer .50
77 Dan McMullen .35
78 Charles Brock .35
79 Verne Lewellen .35
80 Bob Nelson .50
81 Roger Craig 3.00
82 Fred Shirey .35
83 Tom Novak .35
84 Ray Richards .35
85 Warren Alfson .35
86 Lawrence Ely .35
87 Mike Rozier 1.25
88 Dean Steinkuhler .75
89 John Dutton .75
90 Dave Rimington .75
91 Johnny Rodgers 1.25
92 Herbie Husker (Mascot) .35
93 Tom Osborne (CO) 1.25
94 Broderick Thomas 1.25
95 Bob Reynolds .35
96 Mike Tingelhoff (UER) (Name misspelled Tinglehoff) .75
97 Lloyd Cardwell .35
98 Johnny Rodgers 1.25
99 '70 National Champs (Team Photo) .50
100 '71 National Champs (Team Photo) .50
NNO Title Card (Contest on back) .50

1993 Nebraska

NM/M

Complete Set (25): 15.00
Common Player: .50
1 Trev Alberts 2.00
2 Mike Anderson .75
3 Ernie Beler .75
4 Byron Bennett .75
5 Troy Bromawn (Men's baseball) .50
6 NaFeesah Brown (Women's basketball) .50
7 Jed Dalton (Men's baseball) .50
8 Sumner Darling (Men's gymnastics) .50
9 Corey Dixon .75
10 Troy Dumas .75
11 Nicole Duval (Women's gymnastics) .50
12 Mike Eierman (Wrestling) .50
13 Amy Erlenbusch (Women's softball) .50
14 Dennis Harrison (Men's gymnastics) .50
15 Jamar Johnson (Men's basketball) 1.00
16 Calvin Jones 1.50
17 Laura Luther (Women's volleyball) .50
18 Denise McMillen (Women's softball) .50
19 Bruce Moore .75
20 David Noonan 1.00
21 Lori Phillips (Women's gymnastics) .50
22 Eric Piatkowski (Men's basketball) 2.00
23 Nikki Stricker (Women's volleyball) .50
24 Frank Velazquez (Wrestling) .50
25 Meggan Yedsena (Women's basketball) .50

1994 Nebraska

NM/M

Complete Set (21): 12.00
Common Player: .50
1 Kelly Aspergren (Women's volleyball) .50
2 Jaron Boone (Men's basketball) 1.00
3 Terry Connealy .75
4 Jed Dalton (Men's basketball) .50
5 Troy Dumas .75
6 Cody Dusenberry (Women's softball) .50
7 Nicole Duval (Women's gymnastics) .50
8 Richard Grace (Men's gymnastics) .50
9 Donta Jones 1.50
10 Rick Kieffer (Men's gymnastics) .50
11 Barron Miles 1.00
12 Darin Petersen (Men's baseball) .50
13 Cory Schlesinger 2.00
14 Ed Stewart .75
15 Erick Strickland (Men's basketball) .75
16 Joy Taylor (Women's gymnastics) .50
17 Emily Thompson (Women's basketball) .50
18 Tanya Upthegrove (Women's basketball) .50
19 Zach Wiegert 1.50
20 Billie Winsett (Women's volleyball) .50
21 Rob Zatechka 1.50

A card number in parenthese ( ) indicates the set is unnumbered.

1996 Nebraska

NM/M

Complete Set (22): 30.00
Common Player: 1.00
1 Jacques Allen 1.00
2 Reggie Baul 1.50
3 Brook Berringer 3.00
4 Clinton Childs 2.00
5 Doug Colman 1.00
6 Phil Ellis 1.00
7 Tommie Frazier 5.00
8 Mark Gilman 1.00
9 Aaron Graham 1.50
10 Luther Hardin 1.00
11 Jason Jenkins 1.00
12 Chester Johnson 1.00
13 Jeff Makovicka 1.50
14 Brian Nunns 1.00
15 Steve Ott 1.00
16 Aaron Penland 1.00
17 Christian Peter 1.50
18 Darren Schmadeke 1.50
19 Tony Veland 1.00
20 Steve Volin 1.00
21 Tyrone Williams 1.00
22 Checklist Card Team Logo 1.00

1979 North Carolina Schedules

NM/M

Complete Set (4): 12.00
Common Player: 3.00
1 Ricky Barden 3.00
2 Steve Junkman 3.00
3 Matt Kupec 5.00
4 Doug Paschal 3.00

1982 North Carolina Schedules

NM/M

Complete Set (8): 25.00
Common Player: 3.00
1 Kelvin Bryant 7.50
2 Alan Burrus 3.00
3 David Drechsler 3.00
4 Rod Elkins 4.00
5 Jack Parry 3.00
6 Greg Poole 3.00
7 Ron Spruill 3.00
8 Mike Wilcher 4.00

1986 North Carolina Schedules

NM/M

Complete Set (4): 15.00
Common Player: 3.00
1 Walter Bailey 3.00
2 Harris Barton 6.00
3 C.A. Brooks 3.00
4 Eric Streater 4.00

1988 North Carolina

NM/M

Complete Set (16): 15.00
Common Player: 1.00
1 Mack Brown (CO) 1.50
2 Pat Crowley 1.00
3 Torin Dorn 2.00
4 Jeff Garnica 1.00
5 Antonio Goss 1.25
6 Jonathan Hall 1.25
7 Darrell Hamilton 1.00
8 Creighton Incorminias 1.00
9 John Keller 1.00
10 Randy Marriott 1.00
11 Deems May 1.00
12 John Reed 1.00
13 James Thompson 1.25
14 Steve Steinbacher 1.00
15 Dan Vooletich 1.00
16 Mitch Wike 1.00

1991 North Carolina Schedules

NM/M

Complete Set (3): 7.00
Common Player: 2.00
1 Eric Gash 2.00
2 Dwight Hollier 4.00
3 Tommy Thigpen 2.00

1993 North Carolina State

NM/M

Complete Set (56): 25.00
Common Player: .50
1 John Akins .75
2 Darryl Beard .50
3 Ricky Bell .50
4 Geoff Bender .50
5 Chuck Browning .50
6 Chuck Cole .50
7 Chris Cotton .50
8 Eric Counts .50
9 Damien Covington 1.00
10 Dallas Dickerson .50
11 Gary Downs .50
12 Brian Fitzgerald .50
13 Ed Gallon .50
14 Ledel George .50
15 Walt Gerard .50
16 Gregg Giannamore .50
17 Eddie Goines 1.00
18 Ray Griffis .50
19 Mike Harrison .50
20 Terry Harvey .50
21 George Hegamin 1.00
22 Chris Hennie-Roed .50
23 Adrian Hill .50
24 Robert Hinton .50
25 David Inman .50
26 Dave Janik .50
27 Shawn Johnson .50
28 Tyler Lawrence .50
29 Miller Lawson .50
30 Sean Maguire .50
31 Drea Major .50
32 Mike Moore .50
33 James Newsome .50
34 Mike O'Cain (CO) .50
35 Loren Pinkney .50
36 Carlos Pruitt .50
37 Carl Reeves 1.00
38 Jon Rissler .50
39 Chad Robinson .50
40 Ryan Schultz .75
41 William Strong .75
42 Jimmy Sziksai .50
43 Eric Taylor .50
44 Pat Threatt .50
45 Steve Videtich .75
46 James Walker .75
47 Todd Ward .75
48 DeWayne Washington 2.00
49 Heath Woods .50
50 Scott Woods .50
51 Buddy Green, Kent Briggs, Ken Pettus, Jeff Snipes, Henry Trevathan Defensive Coaches .50
52 Ted Cain, Robbie Caldwell, Jimmy Kiser, Brette Simmons, Dick Portee Offensive Coaches .50
53 John Akins, Todd Ward, DeWayne Washington Tri-Captains .50
54 Carter-Finley Stadium .50
55 Checklist .50
56 Title Card .75

1989 North Texas McDag

NM/M

Complete Set (16): 7.00
Common Player: .50
1 Clay Bode .50
2 Scott Bowles .50
3 Keith Chapman .50
4 Darrin Collins .50
5 Tony Cook .50
6 Scott Davis 1.00
7 Byron Gross .50
8 Larry Green .50
9 Major Greene 1.00
10 Carl Brewer .50
11 J.D. Martinez .50
12 Charles Monroe .50
13 Kregg Sanders .50
14 Lou Smith .50
15 Jeff Tutson .50
16 Trent Touchstone .50

1992 Northwestern Louisiana State

NM/M

Complete Set (16): 7.00
Common Player: .50
1 Darius Adams .50
2 Paul Arevalo .50
3 Brad Brown .50
4 Steve Brown .60
5 J.J. Eldridge .50
6 Sam Goodwin (CO) .60
7 Adrian Hardy .60
8 Guy Hedrick .60
9 Brad Laird .60
10 Lawann Latson .60
11 Deon Ridgell .50
12 Bryan Roussell .50
13 Brannon Rowlett .50
14 Marcus Spears .60
15 Carlos Treadway .60
16 Vic (Team Mascot) .50

1930 Notre Dame Postcards

NM/M

Complete Set (25): 800.00
Common Player: 30.00
1 Marty Brill 35.00
2 Frank Carideo 35.00
3 Tom Conley 30.00
4 Al Culver (October 25) 30.00
5 Dick Donaghue (October 18) 30.00
6 Nordy Hoffmann 30.00
7 Al Howard (November 15) 30.00
8 Chuck Jaskwich (November 22) 30.00
9 Clarence Kaplan (October 18) 30.00
10 Tom Kassis 30.00
11 Ed Koska (November 22) 30.00
12 Joe Kurth 35.00
13 Bernie Leahy 50.00
14 Bernie Leahy 125.00
15 Dick Mahoney (November 8) 30.00
16 Art McManmon (November 1) 30.00
17 Bert Metzger 30.00
18 Larry "Moon" Mullins 50.00
19 John O'Brien 30.00
20 Bucky O'Connor 30.00
21 Joe Savoldi 35.00
22 Marchmont Schwartz 35.00
23 Robert Terlaak (November 8) 30.00
24 George Vik (October 25) 30.00
25 Tom Yarr 35.00

1988 Notre Dame

NM/M

Complete Set (60): 20.00
Common Player: .25
1 Golden Dome .50
2 Lou Holtz (CO) 2.00
3 Mark Green .50
4 Andy Heck .75
5 Ned Bolcar .50
6 Anthony Johnson .50
7 Flash Gordon .25
8 Pat Ellers .25
9 Raghib Ismail 5.00
10 Ted FitzGerald .25
11 Ted Healy .25
12 Braxston Banks .50
13 Steve Belles .25
14 Steve Alaniz .25
15 Chris Zorich 2.00
16 Kent Graham 1.00
17 Mike Brennan .25
18 Marty Lippincott .25
19 Rod West .25
20 Dean Brown .25
21 Tom Gorman .25
22 Tony Rice 1.50
23 Steve Roddy .25
24 Reggie Ho .50
25 Pat Terrell .75
26 Joe Jarosz .25
27 Mike Stonebreaker 1.00
28 David Jandric .25
29 Jeff Alm .75
30 Pete Graham .25
31 Corny Southall .25
32 Joe Allen .25
33 Jim Sexton .25
34 Michael Crounse .25
35 Walt Zackrison .25
36 Stan Smagala .50
37 Mike Heidt .25
38 Frank Stams .75
39 D'Juan Francisco .50
40 Tim Ryan .50
41 Arnold Ale .25
42 Andre Jones .25
43 Wes Pritchett .25
44 Tim Grunhard .75
45 Chuck Killian .25
46 Scott Kowalkowski .50
47 George Streeter .25
48 Donn Grimm .25
49 Ricky Watters 6.00
50 Ryan Mihalko .25
51 Tony Brooks .75
52 Todd Lyght 1.00
53 Winston Sandri .25
54 Aaron Robb .25
55 Derek Brown (TE) 1.00
56 Bryan Flannery .25
57 Kevin McShane .25
58 Billy Hackett .25
59 George Williams .25
60 Frank Jacobs .25

1988 Notre Dame Smokey

NM/M

Complete Set (14): 30.00
Common Player (1-10): 1.50
Common Sport (11-14): 1.50
1 Braxston Banks (39) 2.00
2 Ned Bolcar (47) 2.00
3 Tom Gorman (87) 1.50
4 Mark Green (24) 2.00
5 Andy Heck (66) 2.00
6 Lou Holtz (CO) 3.50
7 Anthony Johnson (22) 2.00
8 Wes Pritchett (34) 1.50
9 George Streeter (27) 1.50
10 Ricky Watters (12) 9.00
11 Men's Soccer 1.50
12 Volleyball 1.50
13 Women's Basketball 1.50
14 Women's Tennis 1.50

1989 Notre Dame 1903-32

NM/M

Complete Set (22): 7.00
Common Player: .35
1 Hunk Anderson .50
2 Bert Metzger .35
3 Roger Kiley .35
4 Nordy Hoffman .35
5 Knute Rockne (CO) 2.00
6 Elmer Layden .75
7 Gus Dorais .50
8 Ray Eichenlaub .35
9 Don Miller .50
10 Moose Krause .75
11 Jesse Harper .35
12 Jack Cannon .35
13 Eddie Anderson .35
14 Louis Salmon .35
15 John Smith .35
16 Harry Stuhldreher .75
17 Joe Kurth .35
18 Frank Carideo .35
19 Marchy Schwartz .35
20 Adam Walsh .35
21 George Gipp 2.00
22 Jim Crowley .75

1989 Notre Dame 1935-59

NM/M

Complete Set (22): 7.00
Common Player: .35
1 Frank Leahy (CO) .75
2 John Lattner .75
3 Jim Martin .50
4 Joe Heap .35
5 Paul Hornung 1.25
6 Bill Shakespeare .75
7 Bob Dove .35
8 Bob Williams .35
9 Al Ecuyer .35
10 George Connor .75
11 Leon Hart .75
12 Joe Beinor .35
13 Bill Fischer .35
14 Angelo Bertelli .75
15 Ralph Guglielmi .50
16 Pat Filley .35
17 Emil (Red) Sitko .50
18 Don Schaefer .35
19 Monty Stickles .50
20 Creighton Miller .35
21 Chuck Sweeney .35
22 John Lujack 1.00

1989 Notre Dame 1964-87

NM/M

Complete Set (22): 7.00
Common Player: .35
1 Dan Devine (CO) .50
2 Joe Theismann 1.00
3 Tom Gatewood .50
4 Timmy Brown 1.25
5 Ara Parseghian (CO) .75
6 Jim Lynch .50
7 Luther Bradley .35
8 Ross Browner .50
9 John Huarte 1.00
10 Bob Crable .50
11 Ken MacAfee .50
12 Alan Page .75
13 Vagas Ferguson .50
14 Dick Arrington .35
15 Bob Golic .50
16 Mike Townsend .35
17 Walt Patulski .50
18 Allen Pinkett .50
19 Terry Hanratty .75
20 Dave Casper .75
21 Jack Snow .75
22 Nick Eddy .50

1990 Notre Dame Promos

NM/M

Complete Set (10): 7.00
Common Player: .50
1 Knute Rockne (CO) 1.00
2 Joe Theismann 1.00
3 Joe Montana 4.00
4 George Gipp 1.00
5 Notre Dame Stadium .50
6 Ara Parseghian (CO) .75
7 Frank Leahy (CO) .50
8 Lou Holtz (CO) .75
9 Tony Rice .50
10 Rocky Bleier .75

1990 Notre Dame 200

NM/M

Complete Set (200): 18.00
Common Player: .10
1 Joe Montana 1.25
2 Tim Brown .50
3 Reggie Barnett .20
4 Joe Theismann .50
5 Bob Clasby .10
6 Dave Casper .20
7 George Kunz .20
8 Vince Phelan .10
9 Tom Gibbons .10
10 Tom Thayer .10
11 Notre Dame Helmet .10
12 John Scully .10
13 Lou Holtz (CO) .30
14 Larry Dinardo .20
15 Greg Marx .10
16 Greg Dingens .10
17 Jim Seymour .20
18 1979 Cotton Bowl (Program) .10
19 Mike Kadish .20
20 Bob Crable .20
21 Tony Rice .20
22 Phil Carter .10
23 Ken MacAfee .20
24 Nick Eddy .20
25 1988 National Champs (Trophies) .20
26 Clarence Ellis .10
27 Joe Restic .10
28 Dan Devine (CO) .20
29 John K. Carney .10
30 Stacey Toran .20
31 47th Sugar Bowl (Program) .10
32 J. Heavens .10
33 Mike Fanning .10
34 Dave Vinson .10
35 Ralph Gugliemi .10
36 Reggie Ho .10
37 Allen Pinkett .20
38 Jim Browner .20
39 Blair Kiel .20
40 Joe Montana 1.25
41 Rocky Bleier .30

42 Terry Hanratty .20
43 Tom Regner .20
44 Pete Holohan .10
45 Greg Bell .20
46 Dave Duerson .20
47 Frank Varrichione .20
48 1988 Championship (Team Photo) .20
49 Ted Burgmeier .10
50 Ara Parseghian (CO) .30
51 Mike Townsend .10
52 Liberty Bowl 1983 (Program) .10
53 Tony Furjanic .10
54 Luther Bradley .20
55 Steve Niehaus .20
56 56th Orange Bowl (Program) .10
57 32nd Gator Bowl (Program) .10
58 40th Sugar Bowl (Program) .10
59 52nd Cotton Bowl (Program) .10
60 1975 Orange Bowl (Program) .10
61 Wayne Bullock .10
62 Larry Moriarty .10
63 Jim Lynch .20
64 Mike McCoy .20
65 Tony Hunter .20
66 1984 Aloha Bowl (Program) .10
67 Dave Huffman .10
68 John Lattner .20
69 Tom Gatewood .20
70 Knute Rockne (CO) .35
71 Phil Pozderac .10
72 Ross Browner .20
73 Pete Demmerle .10
74 Sunkist Fiesta Bowl (Program) .10
75 Walt Patulski .20
76 George Gipp .50
77 LeRoy Leopold .10
78 John Huarte .30
79 Tony Yelovich (CO) .10
80 John Lujack .30
81 Cotton Bowl Classic (Program) .10
82 Tim Huffman .10
83 Bob Golic .20
84 Tom Clements .20
85 39th Orange Bowl (Program) .10
86 James J. White (ADMIN) .10
87 Frank Carideo .10
88 Vinny Cerrato .10
89 Louis Salmon .10
90 Bob Burger .10
91 Gerry Dinardo .20
92 Mike Creaney .10
93 John Krimm .10
94 Vagas Ferguson .10
95 Kris Haines .10
96 Gus Dorais .20
97 Tom Schoen .10
98 Jack Robinson .10
99 Joe Heap .10
100 Checklist 1-99 .10
101 Gary Darnell (CO) .10
102 Peter Vaas (CO) .10
103 1924 National Champs (Team Photo) .20
104 Wayne Millner .20
105 Moose Krause .20
106 Jack Cannon .10
107 Christy Flanagan .10
108 Bob Lehmann .10
109 1947 Champions (Team Photo) .20
110 Joe Kurth .10
111 Tommy Yarr .10
112 Nick Buoniconti .30
113 Jim Smithberger .10
114 Joe Beinor .10
115 Pete Cordelli (CO) .10
116 Daryle Lamonica .30
117 Kevin Hardy .10
118 Creighton Miller .20
119 Bob Gladieux .20
120 Fred Miller (Later Miller Brewing) .20
121 Gary Potempa .10
122 Bob Kuechenberg .20
123 Jesse Harper (CO) .10
124 1929 National Champs (Team Photo) .20
125 Alan Page .30
126 Don Miller .20
127 1943 National Champs (Team Photo) .20
128 Bob Wetoska .10
129 Skip Holtz (CO) .10
130 Hunk Anderson (CO) .10
131 Bob Williams .10
132 1966 National Champs (Team Photo) .10
133 Jim Reilly .10
134 Earl "Curly" Lambeau .20
135 Ernie Hughes .10
136 Dick Bumpas (CO) .10
137 Jay Haynes (CO) .10
138 Harry Stuhldreher .20
139 1971 Cotton Bowl (Game Photo) .20
140 1930 National Champs (Team Photo) .20
141 Larry Conjar .20
142 1977 National Champs (Team Photo) .20
143 Pete Duranko .20
144 Heisman Winners (Seven Trophy Winners) .30
145 Bill Fisher .10
146 Marchy Schwartz .10
147 Chuck Heater (CO) .10
148 Bert Metzger .10
149 Bill Shakespeare .20
150 Adam Walsh .10
151 Nordy Hoffman .10
152 Ted Gradel .10
153 Monty Stickles .20
154 Neil Worden .10
155 Pat Filley .10
156 Angelo Bertelli .20
157 Nick Pietrosante .20
158 Art Hunter .10
159 Ziggy Czarobski .10
160 1925 Rose Bowl (Program) .10
161 Al Ecuyer .10
162 1949 Notre Dame Champs (Team Photo) .10
163 Elmer Layden .20
164 Joe Moore (CO) .10
165 1946 National Champs (Team Photo) .10
166 Frank Rydzewski .10
167 Bud Boeringer .10
168 Jerry Groom .10
169 Jack Snow .20
170 Joe Montana 1.25
171 John Smith .10
172 Frank Leahy (CO) .30
173 Emil "Red" Sitko .20
174 Dick Arrington .10
175 Eddie Anderson .10
176 1928 Army (Logo and score) .10
177 1913 Army (Logo and score) .10
178 1935 Ohio State (Logo and game score) .10
179 1946 Army (Logo and game score) .10
180 1953 Georgia Tech (Logo and game score) .10
181 Don Schaefer .10
182 1973 Football Team (Team Photo) .20
183 Bob Dove .10
184 Dick Szymanski .10
185 Jim Martin .20
186 1957 Oklahoma (Logo and game score) .10
187 1966 Michigan State (Logo and game score) .10
188 1973 USC (Logo and game score) .10
189 1980 Michigan (Logo and game score) .10
190 1982 Michigan (Logo and game score) .10
191 Chuck Sweeney .10
192 Notre Dame Stadium .10
193 Roger Kiley .10
194 Ray Eichenlaub .10
195 George Connor .20
196 1982 Pittsburgh (Logo and game score) .10
197 1986 USC (Logo and game score) .10
198 1988 Miami (Logo and game score) .10
199 1988 USC (Logo and game score) .10
200 Checklist 101-199 .10

1990 Notre Dame 60

NM/M
Complete Set (60): 25.00
Common Player: .35
1 Joe Allen .35
2 William Pollard .35
3 Tony Smith .35
4 Tony Brooks .75
5 Kenny Spears .35
6 Mike Heldt .35
7 Derek Brown (TE) .75
8 Rodney Culver .75
9 Ricky Watters 3.00
10 Raghib Ismail 2.50
11 Lou Holtz (CO) .75
12 Chris Zorich 1.00
13 Erik Simien .35
14 Shawn Davis .35
15 Greg Davis .35
16 Walter Boyd .35
17 Tim Ryan .50
18 Lindsay Knapp .35
19 Junior Bryant .35
20 Mike Stonebreaker .50
21 Randy Scianna .35
22 Rick Mirer 6.00
23 Ryan Mihalko .35
24 Todd Lyght .75
25 Andre Jones .35
26 Rod Smith (DB) .50
27 Winston Sandri .35
28 Bob Dahl .50
29 Stuart Tyner .35
30 Brian Shannon .35
31 Shawn Smith .35
32 Jim Sexton .35
33 Dorsey Levens 1.00
34 Lance Johnson .35
35 George Poorman .35
36 Irv Smith 1.00
37 George Williams .35
38 George Marshall .50
39 Reggie Brooks 2.00
40 Scott Kowalkowski .50
41 Jerry Bodine .35
42 Karmeeleyah McGill .35
43 Donn Grimm .35
44 Billy Hackett .35
45 Jordan Halter .35
46 Mirko Jurkovic .75
47 Mike Callan .35
48 Justin Hall .35
49 Nick Smith .35
50 Brian Ratigan .35
51 Eric Jones .35
52 Todd Norman .35
53 Devon McDonald .50
54 Marc deManigold .35
55 Bret Hankins .35
56 Adrian Jarrell .35
57 Craig Hentrich .50
58 Demetrius DuBose .75
59 Gene McGuire .75
60 Ray Griggs .35

1990 Notre Dame Greats

NM/M
Complete Set (22): 8.00
Common Player: .35
1 Clarence Ellis .50
2 Rocky Bleier .75
3 Tom Regner .50
4 Jim Seymour .35
5 Joe Montana 3.00
6 Art Hunter .50
7 Mike McCoy .50
8 Bud Boeringer .35
9 Greg Marx .35
10 Nick Buoniconti .75
11 Pete Demmerle .35
12 Fred Miller .35
13 Tommy Yarr .35
14 Frank Rydzewski .35
15 Dave Duerson .50
16 Ziggy Czarobski .35
17 Jim White .50
18 Larry DiNardo .50
19 George Kunz .50
20 Jack Robinson .35
21 Steve Niehaus .50
22 John Scully .50

1992 Notre Dame

NM/M
Complete Set (59): 25.00
Common Player: .35
1 Lou Holtz (CO) 1.00
2 Rick Mirer 4.00
3 Demetrius DuBose .75
4 Lee Becton 1.25
5 Pete Bercich .50
6 Jerome Bettis 4.00
7 Reggie Brooks 1.50
8 Junior Bryant .35
9 Jeff Burris 1.25
10 Tom Carter 1.00
11 Willie Clark .35
12 John Covington .50
13 Travis Davis .35
14 Lake Dawson 1.50
15 Mark Zataveski .35
16 Paul Failla .75
17 Jim Flanigan .75
18 Oliver Gibson .35
19 Justin Goheen .50
20 Tracy Graham .35
21 Ray Griggs .35
22 Justin Hall .35
23 Jordan Halter .35
24 Brian Hamilton .50
25 Craig Hentrich .50
26 Germaine Holden .35
27 Adrian Jarrell .50
28 Clint Johnson .50
29 Lance Johnson .35
30 Lindsay Knapp .50
31 Ryan Leahy (Not alphabetical order) .50
32 Greg Lane .50
33 Dean Lytle .35
34 Bernard Mannelly .35
35 Oscar McBride .35
36 Devon McDonald .50
37 Kevin McDougal 1.00
38 Karl McGill .35
39 Mike McGlinn .35
40 Mike Miller .75
41 Jeremy Nau .35
42 Todd Norman .50
43 Tim Ruddy (Not alphabetical order) .50
44 William Pollard .35
45 Brian Ratigan .35
46 Leshane Saddler .35
47 Jeremy Sample .35
48 Irv Smith 1.00
49 Laron Moore (Not alphabetical order) .35
50 Anthony Peterson (No alphabetical order) .50
51 Charles Stafford .35
52 Nick Smith .35
53 Greg Stec .35
54 John Taliaferro .35
55 Aaron Taylor 1.00
56 Stuart Tyner .35
57 Ray Zellars (Not alphabetical order) 1.50
58 Tyler Young (Not alphabetical order) .35
59 Bryant Young 1.50

1993 Notre Dame

NM/M
Complete Set (72): 20.00
Common Player: .25
1 Jeremy Akers .35
2 Joe Babey .25
3 Huntley Bakich .25
4 Jason Beckwith .25
5 Lee Becton .75
6 Pete Bercich .35
7 Jeff Burris 1.25
8 Pete Chryplewicz .25
9 Willie Clark .25
10 John Covington .35
11 Travis Davis .25
12 Lake Dawson 1.25
13 Paul Failla .50
14 Jim Flanigan .50
15 Reggie Fleurima .25
16 Ben Foos .25
17 Herbert Gibson .25
18 Oliver Gibson .50
19 Justin Goheen .35
20 Tracy Graham .25
21 Paul Grasmanis .35
22 Jordan Halter .25
23 Brian Hamilton .35
24 Germaine Holden .25
25 Lou Holtz (CO) 1.00
26 Robert Hughes .25
27 Adrian Jarrell .35
28 Clint Johnson .35
29 Lance Johnson .25
30 Thomas Knight .35
31 Jim Kordas .25
32 Greg Lane .35
33 Ryan Leahy .35
34 Will Lyell .35
35 Dean Lytle .25
36 Brian Magee .25
37 Alton Malden .25
38 Derrick Mayes 1.50
39 Oscar McBride .35
40 Mike McCullough .50
41 Kevin McDougal .50
42 Mike McGlinn .25
43 Brian Meter .25
44 Mike Miller .50
45 Steve Misetic .25
46 Jeremy Nau .25
47 Todd Norman .35
48 Kevin Pendergast .35
49 Anthony Peterson .25
50 David Quist .25
51 Jeff Riney .25
52 Tim Ruddy .35
53 Leshane Saddler .25
54 Jeremy Sample .25
55 Charles Stafford .25
56 Greg Stec .25
57 Cliff Stroud .25
58 John Taliaferro .25
59 Aaron Taylor 1.00
60 Bobby Taylor 1.25
61 Bill Wagasy .25
62 Leon Wallace .25
63 Shawn Wooden .25
64 Renaldo Wynn .35
65 Bryant Young 1.25
66 Mark Zataveski .35
67 Dusty Zeigler .35
68 Ray Zellars 1.25
69 Blue Roster Checklist .25
70 Gold Roster Checklist .25
71 Green Roster Checklist .25
72 White Roster Checklist .25

1961 Nu-Card

NM/M
Complete Set (80): 175.00
Common Player: 2.00
101 Bob Ferguson 5.00
102 Ron Snidow 3.00
103 Steve Barnett 2.00
104 Greg Mather 2.00
105 Vern Von Sydow 2.00
106 John Hewitt 2.00
107 Eddie Johns 2.00
108 Walt Rappold 2.00
109 Roy Winston 4.00
110 Bob Boyda 2.00
111 Bill Neighbors 5.00
112 Don Purcell 2.00
113 Ken Byers 2.00
114 Ed Pine 2.00
115 Fred Oblak 2.00
116 Bobby Iles 2.00
117 John Hadl 18.00
118 Charlie Mitchell 2.00
119 Bill Swinford 2.00
120 Bill King 2.00
121 Mike Lucci 5.00
122 Dave Sarette 2.00
123 Alex Kroll 3.00
124 Steve Bauwens 2.00
125 Jimmy Saxton 3.00
126 Steve Simms 2.00
127 Andy Timura 2.00
128 Gary Collins 6.00
129 Ron Taylor 2.00
130 Bobby Dodd 8.00
131 Curtis McClinton 6.00
132 Ray Poage 3.00
133 Gus Gonzales 2.00
134 Dick Locke 2.00
135 Larry Libertore 2.00
136 Stan Sczurek 2.00
137 Pete Case 3.00
138 Jesse Bradford 2.00
139 Coolidge Hunt 2.00
140 Walter Doleschal 2.00
141 Bill Williamson 2.00
142 Pat Trammell 6.00
143 Ernie Davis 65.00
144 Chuck Lamson 2.00
145 Bobby Plummer 3.00
146 Sonny Gibbs 3.00
147 Joe Ellers 2.00
148 Roger Kochman 2.00
149 Norman Beal 2.00
150 Sherwyn Torson 2.00
151 Russ Hepner 2.00
152 Joe Romig 2.00
153 Larry Thompson 2.00
154 Tom Perdue 2.00
155 Ken Bolin 2.00
156 Art Perkins 2.00
157 Jim Sanderson 2.00
158 Bob Asack 2.00
159 Dan Celoni 2.00
160 Bill McGuirt 2.00
161 Dave Hoppmann 2.00
162 Gary Barnes 2.00
163 Don Lisbon 3.00
164 Jerry Cross 2.00
165 George Pierovich 2.00
166 Roman Gabriel 25.00
167 Billy White 2.00
168 Gale Weidner 2.00
169 Charles Rieves 2.00
170 Jim Furlong 2.00
171 Tom Hutchinson 3.00
172 Galen Hall 8.00
173 Wilburn Hollis 2.00
174 Don Kasso 2.00
175 Bill Miller 3.00
176 Ron Miller 2.00
177 Joe Williams 2.00
178 Mel Mellin 2.00
179 Tom Vassell 2.00
180 Mike Cotton 3.00

O

1991 Oberlin College Heisman Club

NM/M
Complete Set (5): 5.00
Common Player: 1.00
1 C.W. "Doc" Savage, J.H. Nichols 50 Years, Two Careers (Athletic Directors) 1.00
2 John W. Heisman (CO) 2.00
3 Oberline's 1892 Team 1.00
4 Doc Edgar Fauver, Doc Edwin Fauver Oberlin's Fauver Twins 1.00
5 Carl Semple, Carl Williams, H.K. Regal, C.W. "Doc" Savage Oberlin's Four Horsemen 1.00

1979 Ohio State Greats

NM/M
Complete Set (53): 35.00
Common Player: .75
1C Chris Ward .75
1D Jan White 1.00
1H Ernest R. Godfrey (ACO) .75
1S Ray Pryor .75
2C Ray Griffin 1.00
2D Tom Deleone 1.00
2H Francis A. Schmidt (CO) .75
2S Dave Foley 1.00
3C Tom Cousineau 1.25
3D Randy Gradishar 2.00
3H Jim Parker 2.00
3S Rufus Mayes 1.00
4C Aaron Brown 1.00
4D John Hicks 1.25
4H Vic Janowicz 1.50
4S Rex Kern 1.50
5C Chris Ward .75
5D Van Decree .75
5H Les Horvath 1.50
5S Jim Otis 1.50
6C Tom Skladany 1.25
6D Randy Gradishar 2.00
6H Bill Willis 1.25
6S Ted Provost .75
7C Bob Brudzinski 1.00
7D Archie Griffin 2.50
7H James Daniell .75
7S Jim Stillwagon 1.25
8C Ted Smith .75
8D John Hicks 1.25
8H Gust Zarnas .75
8S Jack Tatum 1.50
9C Tom Skladany 1.25
9D Neal Colzie 1.00
9H Gomer Jones .75
9S Tim Anderson .75
10C Archie Griffin 2.50
10D Pete Cusick .75
10H Wes Fesler 1.00
10S John Brockington 1.50
11C Tim Fox 1.00
11D Van Decree .75
11H Gaylord Stinchcomb .75
11S Mike Sensibaugh 1.00
12C Tom Skladany 1.25
12D Archie Griffin 2.50
12H Chic Harley .75
12S Jim Stillwagon 1.25
13C Kurt Schumacher 1.00
13D Steve Meyers 1.00
13H Tom Cousineau 1.25
13S Jack Tatum 1.50
JK Howard Jones (CO) 1.00

1988 Ohio State

NM/M
Complete Set (22): 40.00
Common Player: .40
1 Bob Brudzinski .50
2 Keith Byars 1.50
3 Hopalong Cassady 1.00
4 Arnold Chonko .50
5 Wes Fesler .40
6 Randy Gradishar 1.00
7 Archie Griffin 1.50
8 Chic Harley .40
9 Woody Hayes (CO) 1.00
10 John Hicks .50
11 Les Horvath 1.00
12 Jim Houston .75
13 Vic Janowicz 1.00
14 Pepper Johnson .75
15 Ike Kelley .40
16 Rex Kern .75
17 Jim Lachey .75
18 Jim Parker 1.00
19 Tom Skladany .40
20 Chris Spielman 1.00
21 Jim Stillwagon .75
22 Jack Tatum 1.00

1989 Ohio State

NM/M
Complete Set (22): 8.00
Common Player: .40
1 Mike Tomczak 1.00
2 Paul Warfield 1.50
3 Kirk Lowdermilk .50
4 Bob Ferguson .50
5 Jack Graf .40
6 Tim Fox .50
7 Eric Kumerow .50
8 Neal Colzie .50
9 Jim Otis .75
10 John Brockington 1.00
11 Cornelius Greene .40
12 Jim Marshall 1.00
13 Tim Spencer .50
14 Don Scott .40
15 Chris Ward .50
16 Marcus Marek .50
17 Dave Foley .50
18 Bill Willis .75
19 John Frank .75
20 Rufus Mayes .50
21 Tom Tupa .75
22 Jan White .50

1990 Ohio State

NM/M
Complete Set (22): 8.00
Common Player: .35
1 Jeff Uhlenhake .50
2 Ray Ellis .35
3 Todd Bell .50
4 Jeff Logan .35
5 Pete Johnson .75
6 Van DeCree .35
7 Ted Provost .35
8 Mike Lanese .35
9 Aaron Brown .50
10 Pete Cusick .35
11 Vlade Janakievski .35
12 Steve Myers .35
13 Ted Smith .35
14 Doug Donley .50
15 Ron Springs .50
16 Ken Fritz .35
17 Jeff Davidson .35
18 Art Schlichter .75
19 Tom Cousineau .75
20 Call Murray .35
21 Brian Baschnagel .50
22 Joe Staysniak .35

1992 Ohio State

NM/M
Complete Set (59): 20.00
Common Player: .25
1 John Cooper (CO) .75
2 Kirk Herbstreit .50
3 Steve Tovar 1.00
4 Chico Nelson .25
5 Tim Patillo .25
6 Tito Paul .50
7 Jim Borchers .25
8 Craig Powell .75
9 Deron Brown .25
10 Alex Rodriguez .25
11 Chris Sanders 1.50
12 Cedric Saunders .25
13 Walter Taylor .40
14 Jack Thrush .25
15 Brian Stablein .50
16 Tim Walton .25
17 Rod Smith .50
18 Brad Pope .25
19 William Houston .25
20 Dan Wilkinson 1.50
21 Jason Winrow .40
22 Mark Williams .25
23 Jason Simmons .50
24 Luke Fickell .50
25 Tim Williams .25
26 Raymont Harris 1.50
27 Preston Harrison .25
28 Len Hartman .25
29 Eddie George 3.00
30 Jayson Gwinn .50
31 Korey Stringer 1.00
32 Tom Lease .25
33 Randall Brown .25
34 DeWayne Carter .25
35 Bryan Cook .25
36 Allen DeGraffenreid .50
37 Brian Stoughton .25
38 Derrick Foster .25
39 Butler By'not'e .75
40 Jeff Cothran .75
41 Robert Davis .25
42 Joey Galloway 5.00
43 Roger Harper .75
44 Bobby Hoying 1.50
45 C.J. Kelly .25
46 Brent Johnson .25
47 Paul Long .25
48 Joe Metzger .25
49 Jason Louis .25
50 Dave Monnot .25
51 Greg Beatty .25

No.	Player	NM/M
52	Pete Beckman	.25
53	Matt Bonhaus	.25
54	Marlon Kerner	.50
55	Alan Kline	.25
56	Greg Kuszmaul	.25
57	Jim Otis Buckeye Flashback - October 12, 1968	.40
58	Buckeye Flashback - September 30, 1972	.40
NNO	Title Card (CL)	.40

1997 Ohio State

		NM/M
	Complete Set (24):	25.00
	Common Player:	1.00
1	Greg Bellisari	1.50
2	Matt Calhoun	1.00
3	Shane Clark	1.00
4	Dan Colson	1.00
5	John Cooper CO	1.50
6	LeShun Daniels	1.00
7	Luke Fickell	1.00
8	Matt Finkes	2.00
9	Anthony Gwinn	1.50
10	Bob Houser	1.00
11	Ty Howard	1.50
12	Josh Jackson	1.00
13	D.J. Jones	1.00
14	Rob Kelly	1.50
15	Heath Knisely	1.00
16	Ryan Miller	1.00
17	Juan Porter	1.00
18	Chad Pulliam	1.00
19	Dimitrious Stanley	1.50
20	Buster Tillman	1.50
21	Mike Vrabel	2.00
22	American Marketing Associates	1.00
23	1997 Senior Rose Bowl Champions	1.50
24	Team Logo	1.00
25	Sponsor card	1.00

2001 Ohio State Buckeyes

		NM/M
	Complete Set (31):	20.00
	Common Player:	.50
	Brian Baschnagel	.50
	Paul Brown	.50
	Bob Brudzinski	.50
	Keith Byars	.50
	Cris Carter	.50
	Howard "Hopalong" Cassady	.50
	John Cooper	.50
	Wes Fesler	.50
	David Foley	.50
	Tim Fox	.50
	Joey Galloway	1.00
	Eddie George	2.00
	Terry Glenn	.50
	Randy Gradishar	.50
	Cornelius Greene	.50
	Archie Griffin	1.00
	Chic Harley	.50
	Woody Hayes	1.00
	Les Horvath	.50
	Vic Janowicz	.50
	Pete Johnson	.50
	Ike Kelley	.50
	Rex Kern	.50
	Rufus Mayes	.50
	Orlando Pace	.50
	Tom Skladany	.50
	Chris Spielman	.50
	Shawn Springs	.50
	Jim Stillwagon	.50
	Jack Tatum	.50
	Bill Willis	.50

1982 Oklahoma Playing Cards

		NM/M
	Complete Set (56):	40.00
	Common Player:	.50
C1	Joe Washington Action Shot	1.00
C2	Coaches 1895-1934	.50
C3	Buddy Burris All-Americans 1946-48	1.00
C4	Buck McPhail, J.D. Roberts, Max Boydston, Kurt Burris All-Americans 1953-54	1.00
C5	Ralph Neely, Carl McAdams, Bob Kalsu, Steve Owens All-Americans 1963-69	1.00
C6	Kyle Davis, Tinker Owens, Dewey Selmon, Lee Roy Selmon All-Americans 1974-75	1.00
C7	Jim Weatherall 1951	1.00
C8	Billy Vessels 1952	1.00
C9	NCAA Champions 1955	1.00
C10	Uwe Von Schamann Action Shot	.50
C11	Tony DiRienzo Action Shot	.50
C12	Joe Washington Action Shot	1.00
C13	Tinker Owens Action Shot	.50
D1	Joe Washington Action Shot	1.00
D2	Coaches 1935-1982	.50
D3	Jimmy Owens, Darrell Royal All-Americans 1949	1.00
D4	Bo Bolinger, Ed Gray, Jerry Tubbs, Terry McDonald All-Americans 1955-56	1.00
D5	Granville Liggins, Steve Zabel, Ken Mendenhall, Jack Mildren All-Americans 1966-71	1.00
D6	Terry Webb, Billy Brooks, Jimbo Elrod, Mike Vaughan All-Americans 1975-76	1.00
D7	J.D. Roberts 1953	1.00
D8	Steve Owens 1969	1.50
D9	NCAA Champions 1956	1.00
D10	Barry Switzer (CO)	.50
D11	Lucius Selmon Action Shot	.50
D12	Elvis Peacock Action Shot	.50
D13	Billy Sims Action Shot	1.00
H1	Jimbo Elrod Action Shot	.50
H2	All-Americans 1913-37	1.00
H3	Jim Weatherall All-Americans 1949-51	1.00
H4	Bill Krisher, Clendon Thomas, Bob Harrison, Jerry Thompson All-Americans 1957-59	1.00
H5	Greg Pruitt, Tom Brahaney, Derland Moore, Rod Shoate All-Americans 1971-74	1.00
H6	Zac Henderson, Greg Roberts, Daryl Hunt, George Cumby All-Americans 1976-78	1.00
H7	Lee Roy Selmon 1975	1.50
H8	Billy Sims 1978	1.50
H9	NCAA Champions 1974	1.00
H10	Lee Roy Selmon Action Shot	1.00
H11	Tinker Owens Action Shot	.50
H12	Action Shot	.50
H13	Lee Roy Selmon Action Shot	1.00
S1	Horace Ivory Action Shot	.50
S2	All-Americans 1938-46	1.00
S3	Tom Catlin, Billy Vessels, Eddie Crowder All-Americans 1951-52	1.00
S4	Leon Cross, Wayne Lee, Jim Grisham, Joe Don Looney All-Americans 1962-63	1.00
S5	Lucius Selmon, Eddie Foster, John Roush, Joe Washington All-Americans 1973-75	1.00
S6	Reggie Kinlaw, Billy Sims, Louis Oubre, Terry Crouch All-Americans 1978-81	1.00
S7	Greg Roberts 1978	1.00
S8	NCAA Champions 1950	1.00
S9	NCAA Champions 1975	1.00
S10	Bobby Proctor Action Shot (CO)	.50
S11	Steve Davis Action Shot	.50
S12	Greg Pruitt Action Shot	1.00
S13	Elvis Peacock Action Shot	.50
JK1	Sooner Schooner	.50
JK2	Sooner Schooner	.50
NNO	Mail Order Card	.50
NNO	Mail Order Card	.50

1986 Oklahoma

		NM/M
	Complete Set (16):	8.00
	Common Player:	.35
1	Championship Ring - 1985 National Champs	.50
2	Orange Bowl (In Bowl Play)	.35
3	On The Road To Record	.35
4	Graduation Record	.35
5	Lawrence G. Rawl President of Exxon	.35
6	Barry Switzer (Winners)	1.50
7	Win Streaks Hold Records	.35
8	Brian Bosworth	1.00
9	Billy Vessels 1952, Steve Owens 1969, Billy Sims 1978 Heisman Trophy	.75
10	Tony Casillas All-America Sooners	.75
11	Jamelle Holieway	.50
12	Sooner Strength	.35
13	Sooner Support	.35
14	Go Sonners (Crimson and Cream)	.35
15	Border Battle (Oklahoma vs. Texas)	.50
16	Barry Switzer (CO) (SP) (Caricature; "I Want You..."; '86 OU football schedule on back)	2.50

1986 Oklahoma McDag

		NM/M
	Complete Set (16):	20.00
	Common Player:	1.00
1	Brian Bosworth	3.00
2	Sonny Brown	1.00
3	Steve Bryan	1.00
4	Lydell Carr	1.50
5	Patrick Collins	1.50
6	Jamelle Holieway	2.00
7	Mark Hutson	1.00
8	Keith Jackson	6.00
9	Troy Johnson	1.00
10	Dante Jones	3.00
11	Tim Lashar	1.00
12	Paul Migliazzo	1.00
13	Anthony Phillips	1.00
14	Darrell Reed	1.00
15	Derrick Shepard	1.50
16	Spencer Tillman	1.50

1987 Oklahoma Police

		NM/M
	Complete Set (16):	18.00
	Common Player:	.75
1	Eric Mitchel	1.25
4	Jamelle Holieway	2.00
10	David Vickers	.75
25	Anthony Stafford	1.25
29	Rickey Dixon	2.00
33	Patrick Collins	1.25
40	Darrell Reed	.75
45	Lydell Carr	1.25
50	Dante Jones	2.00
66	Jon Phillips	.75
68	Anthony Phillips	.75
75	Greg Johnson	.75
79	Mark Hutson	.75
80	Troy Johnson	.75
88	Keith Jackson	6.00
98	Dante Williams	.75
NNO	Barry Switzer (CO)	3.00

1988 Oklahoma Greats

		NM/M
	Complete Set (30):	7.00
	Common Player:	.20
1	Jerry Anderson	.20
2	Dee Andros	.30
3	Dean Blevins	.20
4	Rick Bryan	.50
5	Paul (Buddy) Burris	.20
6	Eddie Crowder	.30
7	Jack Ging	.20
8	Jim Grisham	.30
9	Jimmy Harris	.30
10	Scott Hill	.20
11	Eddie Hinton	.30
12	Earl Johnson	.20
13	Don Key	.20
14	Tim Lashar	.20
15	Granville Liggins	.50
16	Thomas Lott	.30
17	Carl McAdams	.30
18	Jack Mitchell	.30
19	Billy Pricer	.20
20	John Roush	.20
21	Darrell Royal	.50
22	Lucius Selmon	.30
23	Ron Shotts	.20
24	Jerry Tubbs	.30
25	Bob Warmack	.30
26	Joe Washington	.50
27	Jim Weatherall	.30
28	'86 Sooner Great Game	.20
29	'75 Sooners	.20
30	Checklist Card	.30

1988 Oklahoma Police

		NM/M
	Complete Set (16):	18.00
	Common Player:	1.00
1	Rotnei Anderson	2.00
2	Eric Bross	1.00
3	Mike Gaddis	2.50
4	Scott Garl	1.00
5	James Goode	1.00
6	Jamelle Holieway	2.00
7	Bob Latham	1.00
8	Ken McMichel	1.00
9	Eric Mitchel	1.50
10	Leon Perry	1.50
11	Anthony Phillips	1.00
12	Anthony Stafford	1.50
13	Barry Switzer (CO)	4.00
14	Mark Vankeirsbilck	1.00
15	Curtice Williams	1.00
16	Dante Williams	1.00

1989 Oklahoma Police

		NM/M
	Complete Set (16):	15.00
	Common Player:	1.00
1	Tom Backes	1.00
2	Frank Blevins	1.00
3	Eric Bross	1.00
4	Adrian Cooper	3.00
5	Scott Evans	1.00
6	Mike Gaddis	2.00
7	Gary Gibbs (CO)	1.50
8	James Goode	1.00
9	Ken McMichel	1.00
10	Leon Perry	1.50
11	Mike Sawatzky	1.00
12	Don Smitherman	1.00
13	Kevin Thompson	1.00
14	Mark VanKeirsbilck	1.00
15	Mike Wise	1.00
16	Dante Williams	1.00

1991 Oklahoma Police

		NM/M
	Complete Set (16):	15.00
	Common Player:	1.00
1	Gary Gibbs (CO)	1.50
2	Cale Gundy	2.00
3	Charles Franks	1.00
4	Mike Gaddis	1.50
5	Brad Reddell	1.00
6	Brandon Houston	1.00
7	Chris Wilson	1.00
8	Darnell Walker	1.00
9	Mike McKinley	1.00
10	Kenyon Rasheed	2.00
11	Joe Bowden	2.00
12	Jason Belser	2.00
13	Steve Collins	1.00
14	Reggie Barnes	1.00
15	Randy Wallace	1.00
16	Proctor Land	1.00

1953 Oregon

		NM/M
	Complete Set (20):	340.00
	Common Player:	15.00
1	Farrell Albright	20.00
2	Ted Anderson	15.00
3	Len Berrie	15.00
4	Tom Elliott	15.00
5	Tim Flaherty	15.00
6	Cecil Hodges	15.00
7	Barney Holland	15.00
8	Dick James	25.00
9	Harry Johnson	15.00
10	Dave Lowe	15.00
11	Jack Patera	35.00
12	Ron Pheister	20.00
13	John Reed	15.00
14	Hal Reeve	20.00
15	Larry Rose	15.00
16	George Shaw	25.00
17	Lon Stiner Jr.	15.00
18	Ken Sweitzer	15.00
19	Keith Tucker	15.00
20	Dean Van Leuven	15.00

1956 Oregon

		NM/M
	Complete Set (19):	285.00
	Common Player:	15.00
1	Bruce Brenn	15.00
2	Jack Brown	15.00
3	Reanous Cochran	15.00
4	Jack Crabtree	20.00
5	Tom Crabtree	15.00
6	Tom Hale	15.00
7	Spike Hillstrom	15.00
8	Jim Linden	15.00
9	Hank Loumena	15.00
10	Nick Markulis	15.00
11	Phil McHugh	15.00
13	Harry Mondale	15.00
14	Leroy Phelps	15.00
15	Jack Pocock	15.00
16	John Roventos	15.00
17	Jim Shanley	15.00
18	Ron Stover	20.00
19	J.C. Wheeler	15.00

1958 Oregon

		NM/M
	Complete Set (20):	260.00
	Common Player:	15.00
1	Greg Altenhofen	15.00
2	Darrel Aschbacher	20.00
3	Dave Fish	15.00
4	Sandy Fraser	15.00
5	Dave Grosz	20.00
6	Bob Grottkau	20.00
7	Marlan Holland	15.00
8	Tom Keele	15.00
9	Alden Kimbrough	15.00
10	Don Laudenslager	15.00
11	Riley Mattson	25.00
12	Bob Peterson	15.00
13	Dave Powell	15.00
14	Len Read	15.00
15	Will Reeve	15.00
16	Joe Schaffeld	15.00
17	Charlie Tourville	15.00
18	Dave Urell	15.00
19	Pete Welch	15.00
20	Willie West	25.00

1991 Oregon Smokey

		NM/M
	Complete Set (12):	12.00
	Common Player:	1.00
1	Bud Bowie	1.00
2	Rich Brooks (CO)	3.00
3	Sean Burwell	1.00
4	Eric Castle	1.50
5	Andy Conner	1.00
6	Joe Farwell	1.00
7	Matt LaBounty	1.50
8	Gregg McCallum	1.00
9	Daryle Smith	1.00
10	Jeff Thomason	1.50
11	Tommy Thompson	1.00
12	Marcus Woods	1.50

1988 Oregon State Smokey

		NM/M
	Complete Set (12):	12.00
	Common Player:	1.25
1	Troy Bussanich	1.25
2	Andre Harris	1.25
3	Teddy Johnson	1.25
4	Jason Kent	1.25
5	Dave Kragthorpe (CO)	1.25
6	Mike Matthews	1.25
7	Phil Ross	1.25
8	Brian Taylor	1.25
9	Robb Thomas	2.50
10	Esera Tuaolo	2.50
11	Erik Wilhelm	2.50
12	Dowell Williams	1.25

1990 Oregon State Smokey

		NM/M
	Complete Set (16):	10.00
	Common Player:	1.00
1	Brian Beck	1.00
2	Martin Billings	1.00
3	Matt Booher	1.00
4	George Breland	1.00
5	Brad D'Ancona	1.00
6	Dennis Edwards	1.00
7	Brent Huff	1.00
8	James Jones	1.00
9	Dave Kragthorpe (CO)	1.00
10	Todd McKinney	1.00
11	Torey Overstreet	1.00
12	Reggie Pitchford	1.00
13	Todd Sahlfeld	1.00
14	Scott Thompson	1.00
15	Esera Tuaolo	2.00
16	Maurice Wilson	1.00

1991 Oregon State Smokey

		NM/M
	Complete Set (12):	10.00
	Common Player:	1.00
1	Adam Albaugh	1.00
2	Jamie Burke	1.00
3	Chad de Sully	1.00
4	Dennis Edwards	1.00
5	James Jones	1.00
6	Fletcher Keister	1.00
7	Tom Nordquist	1.00
8	Tony O'Billovich	1.00
9	Jerry Pettibone (CO)	1.25
10	Mark Price	1.00
11	Todd Sahlfeld	1.00
12	Earl Zackery	1.00

1992 Oregon State Smokey

		NM/M
	Complete Set (12):	9.00
	Common Player:	.75
1	Zechariah Davis	.75
2	Chad De Sully	.75
3	Michael Hale	.75
4	Fletcher Keister	.75
5	Chad Paulson	.75
6	Rico Petrini	.75
7	Jerry Pettibone (CO)	1.00
8	Sailusi Poulivaati	.75
9	Tony O'Billovich	.75
10	Dwayne Owens	.75
11	J.J. Young	1.50
12	Maurice Wilson	.75

1994 Oregon State Smokey

		NM/M
	Complete Set (12):	8.00
	Common Player:	.75
1	William Ephraim	.75
2	Johnny Feinga	.75
3	John Garrett	.75
4	Michael Hale	.75
5	Tom Holmes	.75
6	Cory Huot	.75
7	Rico Petrini	.75
8	Cameron Reynolds	.75
9	Kane Rogers	.75
10	Don Shanklin	1.00
11	Reggie Tongue	.75
12	J.J. Young	1.00

P

1988 Penn State Police

		NM/M
	Complete Set (12):	25.00
	Common Player:	1.25
5	Michael Timpson	4.00
20	John Greene	1.25
28	Brian Chizmar	1.25
31	Andre Collins	4.00
32	Blair Thomas	4.00
39	Eddie Johnson	1.25
66	Steve Wisniewski	4.00
75	Rich Schonewolf	1.25
78	Roger Duffy	1.25
84	Keith Karpinski	1.25
NNO	Joe Paterno (CO)	5.00
NNO	Penn State Mascot - The Nittany Lion	1.50

1989 Penn State Police

		NM/M
	Complete Set (15):	20.00
	Common Player:	1.00
1	Brian Chizmar	1.00
2	Andre Collins	2.50
3	David Daniels	2.50
4	Roger Duffy	1.00
5	Tim Freeman	1.00
6	Scott Gob	1.00
7	David Jakob	1.00
8	Geoff Japchen	1.00
9	Joe Paterno (CO)	4.00
10	Sherrod Rainge	1.00
11	Rich Schonewolf	1.00
12	Dave Szott	2.50
13	Blair Thomas	2.50
14	Leroy Thompson	4.00
15	Nittany Lion (Mascot)	1.00

1990 Penn State Police

		NM/M
	Complete Set (16):	15.00
	Common Player:	.75
1	Gerry Collins	.75
2	David Daniels	1.25
3	Jim Deter	.75
4	Mark D'Onofrio	1.25
5	Sam Gash	2.00
6	Frank Giannetti	.75
7	Keith Goganious	1.25
8	Doug Helkowski	.75
9	Hernon Henderson	.75
10	Matt McCartin	.75
11	Joe Paterno (CO)	3.00
12	Darren Perry	2.00
13	Tony Sacca	2.00
14	Terry Smith	.75
15	Willie Thomas	.75
16	Leroy Thompson	2.50

1991-92 Penn State Legends

		NM/M
	Complete Set (51):	15.00
	Common Player:	.35
1	Joe Paterno (CO)	2.00
2	Kurt Allerman	.35
3	Chris Bahr	.50
4	Matt Bahr	.50
5	Bruce Bannon	.35
6	Greg Buttle	.50
7	John Capelletti	.75
8	Bruce Clark	.35
9	Andre Collins	.75
10	Shane Conlan	.75
11	Chris Conlin	.35
12	Randy Crowder	.35
13	Keith Dorney	.50
14	D.J. Dozier	.75
15	Bill Dugan	.35
16	Chuck Fusina	.50
17	Leon Gajecki	.35
18	Jack Ham	1.25
19	Bob Higgins	.35
20	John Hufnagel	.75
21	Kenny Jackson	.50
22	Tim Johnson	.35
23	Dave Joyner	.35
24	Roger Kochman	.35
25	Ted Kwalick	.50
26	Richie Lucas	.75
27	Matt Millen	.75
28	Lydell Mitchell	.75
29	Bob Mitinger	.35
30	John Nessel	.35
31	Ed O'Neil	.50
32	Dennis Onkotz	.35
33	Darren Perry	.50
34	Charlie Pittman	.50
35A	Tom Rafferty (ERR) (Photo actually T. Quinn)	5.00
35B	Tom Rafferty (COR)	1.25
36	Mike Reid (UER) (Reversed negative)	1.25
37	Glenn Ressler	.50
38	Dave Robinson	.50
39	Mark Robinson	.35
40	Randy Sidler	.35
41	John Skorupan	.50
42	Neal Smith	.35
43	Steve Suhey	.50
44	Sam Tamburo	.35
45	Blair Thomas	1.25
46	Curt Warner	1.50
47	Steve Wisniewski	.75
48	Charlie Zapiec	.35
49	Michael Zordich	.50
50	Harry Wilson, Joe Bedenk	.35
P1	Joe Paterno (CO) (Promo)	4.00
P10	Shane Conlan (Promo)	2.00
P18	Jack Ham (Promo)	2.50
NNO	Checklist Card	.35

1992 Penn State Police

		NM/M
	Complete Set (16):	20.00
	Common Player:	.60
1	Richie Anderson	2.00
2	Lou Benfatti	1.00
3	Derek Bochna	.60
4	Kyle Brady	4.00
5	Kerry Collins	8.00
6	Troy Drayton	2.00
7	John Gerak	1.00
8	Reggie Givens	1.00
9	Shelly Hammonds	.60
10	Greg Huntington	.60
11	Tyoka Jackson	1.00
12	O.J. McDuffie	4.00
13	Lee Rubin	.60
14	E.J. Sandusky	.60
15	Tisen Thomas	.60
16	Brett Wright	.60

1993 Penn State

		NM/M
	Complete Set (25):	18.00
	Common Player:	.50
1	Mike Archie, Ki-Jana Carter, Stephen Pitts	5.00
2	Lou Benfatti	.75
3	Derek Bochna	.50
4	Kyle Brady	3.00

5 Kerry Collins 5.00
6 Criag Fayak .50
7 Marlon Forbes .50
8 Brian Gelzheiser 1.00
9 Bucky Greeley .50
10 Ryan Grube .75
11 Shelly Hammonds .75
12 Jeff Hartings .75
13 Rob Holmberg 1.00
14 Tyoka Jackson .75
15 Mike Malinoski .75
16 Brian Monaghan .50
17 Brian O'Neal .75
18 Jeff Perry .50
19 Derick Pickett .50
20 Tony Pittman .50
21 Eric Ravotti .75
22 Lee Rubin .50
23 Vin Stewart .50
24 Tisen Thomas .50
25 Phil Yeboah-Kodie .75

1989 Pittsburgh

NM/M
Complete Set (22): 10.00
Common Player: .30
1 Tony Dorsett 2.00
2 Pop Warner (CO) .40
3 Hugh Green .60
4 Matt Cavanaugh .50
5 Mike Gottfried .40
6 Jimbo Covert .50
7 Bob Peck .30
8 Gibby Welch .30
9 Bill Daddio .40
10 Jock Sutherland (CO) .40
11 Joe Walton .40
12 Dan Marino 4.00
13 Russ Grimm .40
14 Mike Ditka 2.00
15 Marshall Goldberg .50
16 Bill Fralic .40
17 Paul Martha .40
18 Joe Schmidt .75
19 Rickey Jackson .60
20 Ave Daniell .30
21 Bill Maas .40
22 Mark May .40

1990 Pitt Foodland

NM/M
Complete Set (12): 8.00
Common Player: .50
1 Curtis Bray .50
2 Craig Gob .50
3 Paul Hackett (CO) .50
4 Keith Hamilton 1.50
5 Ricardo McDonald 1.50
6 Ronald Redmon .50
7 Curvin Richards .50
8 Louis Riddick 1.50
9 Chris Sestili .50
10 Olanda Truitt 1.50
11 Alex Van Pelt 1.50
12 Nelson Walker .50

1991 Pitt Foodland

NM/M
Complete Set (12): 7.00
Common Player: .75
1 Richard Allen .75
2 Curtis Bray .75
3 Jeff Christy .75
4 Steve Israel 1.00
5 Scott Kaplan .75
6 Ricardo McDonald 1.00
7 Dave Moore .75
8 Eric Seaman .75
9 Chris Sestili .75
10 Alex Van Pelt 1.50
11 Nelson Walker .75
12 Kevin Williams (HB) .75

1991 Pitt State

NM/M
Complete Set (18): 12.00
Common Player: .60
1 Chuck Broyles (CO) .60
2 Darren Dawson .60
3 Kendall Gammon .60
4 Jamie Goodson .60
5 Brian Hoover .60
6 James Jenkins .60
7 Ky Kiger .60
8 Phil McCoy .60
9 Kline Minniefield .60
10 Ron Moore 4.00
11 Jeff Mundhenke .60
12 Brian Pinamonti .60
13 Michael Rose .60
14 Shane Tafoya .60
15 Ronnie West 1.25
16 Michael Wilber .60
17 Troy Wilson 1.50
18 Team Photo 1.25

1992 Pitt State

NM/M
Complete Set (18): 10.00
Common Player: .60
1 Ron Moore 2.00
2 Craig Jordan .60
3 Joel Thornton .60
4 Don Tolar .60
5 Andy Kesinger .60
6 Mike Brockel .60
7 Troy Wilson 1.25
8 Brian Hutchins .60
9 Chris Hanna .60
10 Coaching Staff .60
11 Gus Gorilla (Mascot) .60
12 Lance Gosch .60
13 Jerry Boone, Chad Watskey .60
14 Jeff Moreland, Scott Lutz .60
15 Ronnie Fuller, Mickey Beagle .60
16 Todd Hafner, Kevin Duncan .60
17 Duke Palmer, Eric Perks .60
18 Kris Mengarelli .60

1989 Purdue Legends Smokey

NM/M
Complete Set (16): 25.00
Common Player: 1.25
1 Fred Akers (CO) 1.50
2 Jim Everett (LEG) 4.00
3 Bob Griese (LEG) 6.00
4 Mark Herrmann (LEG) 2.00
5 Bill Hitchcock 1.25
6 Steve Jackson 1.50
7 Derrick Kelson 1.25
8 Leroy Keyes (LEG) 2.00
9 Shawn McCarthy 1.50
10 Dwayne O'Connor 1.25
11 Mike Phipps (LEG) 2.00
12 Darren Trieb 1.25
13 Tony Vinson 1.25
14 Calvin Williams 3.00
15 Rod Woodson (LEG) 5.00
16 Dave Young (LEG) 1.25

S

1990 San Jose State Smokey

NM/M
Complete Set (15): 10.00
Common Player: .75
1 Bob Bleisch (90) .75
2 Sheldon Canley (20) .75
3 Paul Franklin (37) .75
4 Anthony Gallegos (72) .75
5 Steve Hieber (48) .75
6 Everett Lampkins (43) .75
7 Kelly Liebengood (21) .75
8 Ralph Martini (9) .75
9 Lyneil Mayo (62) .75
10 Mike Powers (57) .75
11 Mike Scialabba (46) .75
12 Terry Shea (CO) .75
13 Freddie Smith (4) .75
14 Eddie Thomas (26) .75
15 Brian Woods (64) .75

1992 San Jose State

NM/M
Complete Set (20): 10.00
Common Player: .60
1 Maceo Barbosa .60
2 Bobby Blackmon .60
3 David Blakes .60
4 Walter Brooks Jr. .60
5 Greg Bruggeman .60
6 Bryce Burnett .60
7 Doug Calcagno .60
8 Gary Charlton .60
9 Chris Clarke .60
10 Hesh Colar .60
11 Jeff Greeney .60
12 Leon Hawthorne .60
13 Peni Iosefa .60
14 Byron Jackson .60
15 Robbie Miller .60
16 Freddie Smith .60
17 Spencer Smith .60
18 Simon Vaoifi .60
19 Matt Veatch .60
20 Blair Zerr .60

1969 South Carolina Team Sheets

NM/M
Complete Set (6): 45.00
Common Player: 6.00
1 Tim Bice, Candler Boyd, Don Buckner, Ronald Bunch, Bob Cole, Carl Cowart, Don Dunning, Mike Fair, Tony Fusaro, Benny Galloway 6.00
2 Allen Brown, Don Somma, Billy Tharp, Scott Townsend, Pat Watson, Bob Wehmeyer, Bob White, Curtis Williams, Tom Wingard, Fred Zeigler 6.00
3 Andy Chavous, Wally Orrel, Ronnie Palmer, Hyrum Pierce, Jimmy Poole, Roy Don Reeves, Larry Royal, Gene Schwarting, Fletcher Spigner, Frank Tetterton 6.00
4 Paul Dietzel CO, Larry Jones CO, Johnny Menger CO, Pride Ratterree CO, Bill Rowe CO, Bill Shalosky CO, Lou Holtz CO, Don Purvis CO, Jack Powers CO, Dick Weldon CO 15.00
5 Ben Garnto, Gordon Gibson, Johnny Glass, Jimmy Gobble, Dave Grant, Johnny Gregory, Bob Harris, Rudy Holloman, Earl Hunter, Jack James 6.00
6 Jimmy Killen, Joe Komoroski, Dave Lucas, Bob Mauro, George McCarthy, Toy McCord, Wally Medlin, Bob Morris, Warren Muir, Jim Mulvihill 6.00

1974 Southern Cal Discs

NM/M
Complete Set (30): 75.00
Common Player: 2.00
1 Bill Bain 2.50
2 Otha Bradley 2.50
3 Kevin Bruce 2.00
4 Mario Celotto 2.00
5 Marvin Cobb 4.00
6 Anthony Davis 8.00
7 Joe Davis 2.00
8 Shelton Diggs 2.50
9 Dave Farmer 2.50
10 Pat Haden 10.00
11 Donnie Hickman 2.00
12 Doug Hogan 2.00
13 Mike Howell 2.00
14 Gary Jeter 4.00
15 Steve Knutson 2.00
16 Chris Limahelu 2.50
17 Bob McCaffrey 2.00
18 J.K. McKay 4.00
19 John McKay (CO) 5.00
20 Jim O'Bradovich 4.00
21 Charles Phillips 2.50
22 Ed Powell 2.00
23 Marvin Powell 4.00
24 Danny Reece 2.50
25 Art Riley 2.00
26 Richard Sako Traveller II 2.50
27 Tommy Trojan Trojan Statue 2.50
28 USC Song Girls 2.50
29 USC Song Girls 2.50
30 Richard Wood 4.00
--- Holder 25.00

1988 Southern Cal Smokey

NM/M
Complete Set (17): 12.00
Common Player: .75
1 Erik Affholter 1.25
2 Gene Arrington .75
3 Scott Brennan .75
4 Jeff Brown .75
5 Tracy Butts .75
6 Martin Chesley .75
7 Paul Green .75
8 John Guerrero .75
9 Chris Hale .75
10 Rodney Peete 4.00
11 Dave Powroznik .75
12 Mark Sager .75
13 Mike Serpa .75
14 Larry Smith (CO) 1.25
15 Chris Sperle .75
16 Joe Walshe .75
17 Steven Webster .75

1988 Southern Cal Winners

NM/M
Complete Set (73): 15.00
Common Player: .15
1 Title Card (schedule on back) .25
2 George Achica .25
3 Marcus Allen 2.00
4 Jon Arnett .35
5 Johnny Baker .15
6 Damon Bame .15
7 Chip Banks .35
8 Mike Battle .25
9 Hal Bedsole .25
10 Ricky Bell .35
11 Jeff Bregel .15
12 Tay Brown .15
13 Brad Budde .25
14 Dave Cadigan .25
15 Pat Cannamela .15
16 Paul Cleary .15
17 Sam Cunningham .35
18 Anthony Davis .50
19 Clarence Davis .25
20 Morley Drury .15
21 John Ferraro .15
22 Bill Fisk .15
23 Roy Foster .25
24 Mike Garrett .35
25 Frank Gifford 1.25
26 Ralph Heywood .15
27 Pat Howell .15
28 Gary Jeter .25
29 Dennis Johnson .15
30 Mort Kaer .15
31 Grenny Lansdell .15
32 Ronnie Lott 1.25
33 Paul McDonald .25
34 Tim McDonald .35
35 Ron Mix .35
36 Don Mosebar .35
37 Artimus Parker .25
38 Charles Phillips .15
39 Erny Pinckert .15
40 Marvin Powell .25
41 Aaron Rosenberg .15
42 Tim Rossovich .25
43 Jim Sears .15
44 Gus Shaver .15
45 Nate Shaw .15
46 O.J. Simpson 5.00
47 Ernie Smith .15
48 Harry Smith .15
49 Larry Stevens .15
50 Lynn Swann 1.00
51 Brice Taylor .15
52 Dennis Thurman .25
53 Keith Van Horne .25
54 Cotton Warburton .15
55 Charles White .50
56 Elmer Willhoite .15
57 Richard Wood .25
58 Ron Yary .35
59 Adrian Young .15
60 Charles Young (UER) (listed as Adrian Young on card front) .25
61 Pete Adams, John Grant .15
62 Bill Bain, Jim O'Bradovich .25
63 Nate Barrager, Francis Tappan .15
64 Booker Brown, Steve Riley .15
65 Al Cowlings, Jimmy Gunn, Charles Weaver 1.00
66 Jack Del Rio, Duane Bickett .50
67 Clay Matthews, Bruce Matthews .50
68 Marlin McKeever, Mike McKeever .35
69 Orv Mohler, Garrett Arbelbide .15
70 Sid Smith, Marv Montgomery .15
71 John Vella, Willie Hall .25
72 Don Williams, Jesse Hibbs .15
73 Stan Williamson, Tony Slaton .15

1989 Southern Cal Smokey

NM/M
Complete Set (23): 10.00
Common Player: .60
1 Dan Barnes .60
2 Dwight Carner .60
3 Delmar Chesley .60
4 Cleveland Colter .60
5 Aaron Emanuel 1.25
6 Scott Galbraith 1.25
7 Leroy Holt .75
8 Randy Hord .60
9 John Jackson 1.50
10 Brad Leggett .60
11 Marching Band .60
12 Dan Owens 1.50
13 Brent Parkinson .60
14 Tim Ryan 1.50
15 Bill Schultz .60
16 Larry Smith (CO) .75
17 Ernest Spears .60
18 J.P. Sullivan .60
19 Cordell Sweeney .60
20 Traveler (Horse Mascot) .60
21 Marlon Washington .60
22 Michael Williams .60
23 Yell Leaders and Song Girls .75

1991 Southern Cal College Classics

NM/M
Complete Set (100): 30.00
Common Player: .25
1 Charles White .75
2 Anthony Davis .75
3 Clay Matthews .75
4 Hoby Brenner .35
5 Mike Garrett .50
6 Bill Sharman (Basketball) 1.25
7 Bob Seagren (Track) .35
8 Mike McKeever .35
9 Celso Kalache (Volleyball) .25
10 John Williams (CO) (Water Polo) .25
11 John Naber (Swimming) .50
12 Brad Budde .35
13 Tim Ryan .35
14 Mark Tucker .25
15 Rodney Peete 1.00
16 Art Mazmanian (Baseball) .25
17 Red Badgro (Baseball) .35
18 Sue Habernigg (Women's Swimming) .25
19 Craig Fertig .25
20 John Block (Basketball) .50
21 Jen-Kai Liu (Volleyball) .25
22 Kim Ruddins (Women's Volleyball) .25
23 Al Cowlings 1.00
24 Ronnie Lott 1.00
25 Adam Johnson (Volleyball) 1.50
26 Fred Lynn (Baseball) .50
27 Rick Leach (Tennis) .35
28 Tim Rossovich .50
29 Marvin Powell .35
30 Ron Yary .50
31 Ken Ruettgers .50
32 Bob Yoder (CO) (Men's Volleyball) .25
33 Megan McCallister (Women's Volleyball) .25
34 Dave Cadigan .25
35 Jeff Bregel .25
36 Michael Wayman (Tennis) .25
37 Sippy Woodhead-Kantzer (Women's Swimming) .50
38 Tim Hovland (Volleyball) 1.00
39 Steve Busby (Baseball) .50
40 Tom Seaver (Baseball) 2.00
41 Anthony Colorito .25
42 Wayne Carlander (Basketball) .35
43 Erik Affholter .35
44 Jim Obradovich .35
45 Duane Bickett .50
46 Leslie Daland (Women's Swimming) .25
47 Ole Oleson (Track) .25
48 Ed Putnam (Baseball) .25
49 Stan Smith (Tennis) .75
50 Jeff Hart (Golf) .25
51 Jack Del Rio .50
52 Bob Boyd (CO) (Basketball) .35
53 Pat Haden 1.00
54 John Lambert (Basketball) .35
55 Pete Beathard .75
56 Anna-Maria Fernandez (Women's Tennis) .50
57 Marta Figueras-Dotti (Women's Golf) .35
58 Don Mosebar .35
59 Don Doll .35
60 Dave Stockton (Golf) .75
61 Trisha Laux (Women's Tennis) .25
62 Roy Foster .35
63 Bruce Matthews .35
64 Steve Sogge .35
65 Tracy Nakamura (Women's Golf) .35
66 Marv Montgomery .25
67 Jack Tingley (Swimming) .25
68 Larry Stevens .25
69 Harry Smith .25
70 Bill Bain .25
71 Mark McGwire (Baseball) 3.00
72 Brad Brink (Baseball) .25
73 Richard Wood .35
74 Rod Dedeaux (CO) (Baseball) .50
75 Paul Westphal (Basketball) 1.25
76 Al Krueger .25
77 James McConica (Swimming) .25
78 Rod Martin .35
79 Bill Yardley (Volleyball) .25
80 Bill Stetson (Volleyball) .25
81 Ray Looze (Swimming) .25
82 Dan Jorgensen (Swimming) .25
83 Anna-Lucia Fernandez (Women's Tennis) .50
84 Terri O'Loughlin (Women's Swimming) .25
85 John Grant .25
86 Chris Lewis (Tennis) .25
87 Steve Timmons (Volleyball) 2.00
88 Dr. Dallas Long (Track) .35
89 John McKay (CO) .50
90 Joe Bottom (Swimming) .25
91 John Jackson .35
92 Paul McDonald .35
93 Jimmy Gunn .25
94 Rod Sherman .35
95 Cecilia Fernandez (Women's Tennis) .25
96 Doug Adler (Tennis) .25
97 Ron Orr (Swimming) .25
98 Debbie Landreth Brown (Women's Volleyball) .25
99 Debbie Green (Women's Volleyball) .25
100 Pat Harrison (Baseball) .25

1991 Southern Cal Smokey

NM/M
Complete Set (16): 8.00
Common Player: .60
1 Kurt Barber 1.25
2 Ron Dale .60
3 Derrick Deese 1.00
4 Michael Gaytan .60
5 Matt Gee .60
6 Calvin Holmes 1.00
7 Scott Lockwood 1.00
8 Michael Moody .60
9 Marvin Pollard .60
10 Mark Raab .60
11 Larry Smith (CO) .75
12 Raoul Spears .60
13 Matt Willig .60
14 Alan Wilson .60
15 James Wilson .60
16 Traveler (The Trojan Horse) .60

1992 Southern Cal Smokey

NM/M
Complete Set (16): 8.00
Common Player: .60
1 Wes Bender .60
2 Estrus Crayton .60
3 Eric Dixon .60
4 Travis Hannah 1.50
5 Zuri Hector .60
6 Lamont Hollinquest .60
7 Yonnie Jackson .60
8 Bruce Luizzi .60
9 Mike Mooney .60
10 Stephon Pace .60
11 Joel Scott .60
12 DeNail Sparks .60
13 Titus Tuiasosopo .60
14 Larry Wallace .60
15 David Webb .60
16 Title Card ART .60

A card number in parenthese ( ) indicates the set is unnumbered.

1991 Stanford All-Century

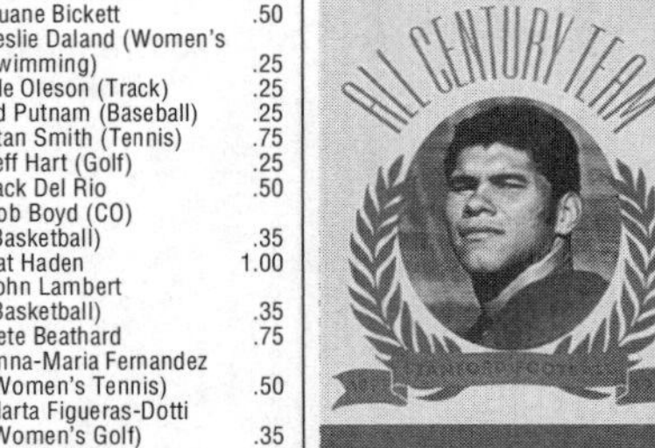

NM/M
Complete Set (100): 100.00
Common Player: .75
1 Frankie Albert 1.25
2 Lester Archambeau 1.00
3 Bruno Banducci .75
4 Benny Barnes 1.00
5 Guy Benjamin 2.00
6 Mike Boryla 1.25
7 Marty Brill .75
8 John Brodie 6.00
9 Jackie Brown .75
10 George Buehler 1.00
11 Don Bunce 1.25
12 Chris Burford 1.25
13 Walter Camp (CO) 2.50
14 Gordy Ceresino .75
15 Jack Chapple .75
16 Toi Cook 2.00
17 Bill Corbus .75
18 Steve Dils 2.50
19 Pat Donovan 1.25
20 John Elway 20.00
21 Chuck Evans .75
22 Skip Face .75
23 Hugh Gallarneau .75
24 Rod Garcia .75
25 Bob Garrett .75
26 Rick Gervais .75
27 John Gillory .75
28 Bobby Grayson 1.00
29 Bones Hamilton 1.00
30 Ray Handley 2.00
31 Mark Harmon .75
32 Marv Harris .75
33 Emile Harry 1.25
34 Tony Hill 2.50
35 Brian Holloway 1.25
36 John Hopkins .75
37 Dick Horn .75
38 Jeff James 1.00
39 Gary Kerkorian .75
40 Gordon King 1.00
41 Younger Klippert .75
42 Pete Kmetovic .75
43 Jim Lawson .75
44 Pete Lazetich .75
45 Dave Lewis 1.00
46 Vic Lindskog .75
47 James Lofton 6.00
48 Ken Margerum 1.25
49 Ed McCaffrey 2.00
50 Charles McCloud .75
51 Bill McColl 1.00
52 Duncan McColl .75
53 Milt McColl .75
54 Jim Merlo 1.00
55 Phil Moffatt .75
56 Bob Moore 1.00
57 Sam Morley .75
58 Monk Moscrip .75
59 Brad Muster 2.50
60 Ken Naber .75
61 Darrin Nelson 2.00
62 Ernie Nevers 3.00
63 Dick Norman .75
64 Blaine Nye 1.25
65 Don Parish .75
66 John Paye 2.00
67 Gary Pettigrew 1.00
68 Jim Plunkett 6.00
69 Randy Poltl .75
70 Seraphim Post .75
71 John Ralston (CO) 1.25
72 Bob Reynolds .75
73 Don Robesky .75
74 Doug Robison .75
75 Greg Sampson .75
76 John Sande .75
77 Turk Schonert 2.00
78 Jack Schultz .75
79 Clark Shaughnessy (CO) 1.25
80 Ted Shipkey .75
81 Jeff Siemon 2.00
82 Andy Sinclair .75
83 Malcolm Snider 1.00
84 Norm Standlee 1.00
85 Roger Stillwell .75
86 Chuck Taylor (CO) .75
87 Dink Templeton .75
88 Tiny Thornhill (CO) .75
89 Dave Tipton .75
90 Keith Topping .75
91 Randy Vataha .75
92 Garin Veris 1.25
93 Jon Volpe 2.50
94 Bill Walsh (CO) 5.00
95 Pop Warner (CO) 2.00
96 Gene Washington 2.00
97 Vincent White .75
98 Paul Wiggin 1.25
99 John Wilbur 1.00
100 Dave Wyman 1.25

1992 Stanford

NM/M
Complete Set (35): 15.00
Common Player: .35
1 Seyon Albert .35
2 Estevan Avila .50
3 Tyler Batson .35
4 Guy Benjamin (ACO) .60
5 David Calomese .35
6 Mike Cook .50
7 Chris Dalman .50
8 Dave Garnett .35
9 Ron George 1.00
10 Darrien Gordon 2.00
11 Tom Holmoe (ACO) .60
12 Derron Klafter .35
13 J.J. Lasley .50
14 John Lynch .60
15 Glyn Milburn 4.00
16 Fernando Montes (ACO) .50
17 Vince Otoupal .35
18 Rick Pallow .35
19 Ron Redell .35
20 Aaron Rembisz .35
21 Bill Ring (ACO) .50
22 Ellery Roberts .60
23 Scott Schuhmann (ACO) .35
24 Terry Shea (ACO) .35
25 Bill Singler (ACO) .35
26 Paul Stonehouse .35
27 Dave Tipton (ACO) .35
28 Keena Turner (ACO) .75
29 Fred von Appen (ACO) .35
30 Bill Walsh (CO) 3.00
31 Ryan Wetnight 2.00
32 Tom Williams .35
33 Mike Wilson (ACO) .50
34 Billy Wittman .35
35 J.J. Lasley Checklist Card .50

1993 Stanford

NM/M
Complete Set (18): 10.00
Common Player: .50
1 Jeff Bailey .50
2 Parker Bailey .50
3 Roger Boden .50
4 Hartwell Brown .50
5 Vaughn Bryant .60
6 Brian Cassidy .50
7 Glen Cavanaugh .50
8 Kevin Garnett .50
9 Mark Hatzenbuhler .50
10 Steve Hoyem .60
11 Mike Jerich .50
12 Paul Nickel .50
13 Toby Norwood .60
14 Tyrone Parker .60
15 Ellery Roberts .60
16 David Shaw .50
17 Bill Walsh (CO) 2.50
18 Josh Wright .50

1989 Syracuse Burger King

NM/M
Complete Set (15): 15.00
Common Player: 1.00
1 David Bavaro 1.50
2 Blake Bednars 1.00
3 Alban Brown 1.00
4 Dan Burey 1.00
5 Rob Burnett 2.50
6 Fred DeRiggi 1.00
7 John Flannery 2.00
8 Duane Kinnon 1.00
9 Dick MacPherson (CO) 2.00
10 Rob Moore 5.00
11 Michael Owens 1.50
12 Bill Scharr 1.00
13 Turnell Sims 1.00
14 Sean Whiteman 1.00
15 Terry Wooden 2.50

1991 Syracuse Program Cards

NM/M
Complete Set (36): 30.00
Common Player: .75
1 George Rooks .75
2 Marvin Graves 4.00
3 Andrew Dees .75
4 Glen Young 1.00
5 Chris Gedney 2.00
6 Paul Pasqualoni 1.00
7 Terrence Wisdom .75
8 John Biskup .75
9 Mark McDonald .75
10 Dan Conley 1.00
11 Kevin Mitchell .75
12 Qadry Ismail 6.00
13 John Lusardi .75
14 David Walker .75
15 John Capachione .75
16 Shelby Hill 1.25
17 Dwayne Joseph .75
18 Greg Walker .75
19 Jerry Sharp .75
20 Tim Sandquist .75
21 Chuck Bull .75
22 Jo Jo Wooden .75
23 Terry Richardson .75
24 Doug Womack .75
25 Reggie Terry .75
26 Garland Hawkins .75
27 Tony Montemorra .75
28 Chip Todd .75
29 Pat O'Neill 1.00
30 Kevin Barker .75
31 John Reagan .75
32 Pat O'Rourke .75
33 Jim Wentworth .75
34 Ernie Brown .75
35 John Nilsen .75
36 Al Wooten .75

T

1980 Tennessee Police

NM/M
Complete Set (19): 37.00
Common Player: 1.50
1 Bill Bates 1.50
2 James Berry 1.50
3 Chris Bolton 1.50
4 Mike L. Cofer 1.50
5 Glenn Ford 1.50
6 Anthony Hancock 1.50
7 Brian Ingram 1.50
8 Tim Irwin 1.50
9 Kenny Jones 1.50
10 Wilbert Jones 1.50
11 Johnny Majors (CO) 1.50
12 Bill Marren 1.50
13 Danny Martin 1.50
14 Jim Noonan 1.50
15 Lee North 1.50
16 Hubert Simpson 1.50
17 Danny Spradlin 1.50
18 John Warren 1.50
19 Brad White 1.50

1990 Tennessee Centennial

NM/M
Complete Set (294): 30.00
Common Player: .10
1 Vince Moore .20
2 Steve Matthews .10
3 Joey Chapman .10
4 Terence Cleveland .10
5 Thomas Wood .10
6 J.J. McCleskey .10
7 Jason Julian .10
8 Andy Kelly .20
9 Derrick Folsom .10
10 Chip McCallum .10
11 Lloyd Kerr .10
12 Cory Fleming .30
13 Kevin Zurcher .10
14 Lee England .10
15 Carl Pickens 2.00
16 Sterling Henton .10
17 Lee Wood .10
18 Kent Elmore .10
19 Craig Faulkner .10
20 Keith Denson .10
21 Preston Warren .10
22 Floyd Miley .10
23 Earnest Fields .10
24 Tony Thompson .10
25 Jeremy Lincoln .30
26 David Bennett .10
27 Greg Burke .10
28 Tavio Henson .10
29 Kevin Wendelboe .10
30 Cedric Kline .10
31 Keith Jeter .10
32 Chris Russ .10
33 DeWayne Dotson .10
34 Mike Rapien .10
35 Clemons McCroskey .10
36 Mark Fletcher .10
37 Chuck Smith .20
38 Jeff Tullis .10
39 Kelly Days .10
40 Shazzon Bradley .10
41 Reggie Ingram .10
42 Roland Poles .10
43 Tracy Smith .10
44 Chuck Webb .30
45 Shon Walker .20
46 Eric Riffer .10
47 Greg Amsler .10
48 J.J. Surlas .10
49 Brian Bradley .10
50 Tom Myslinski .20
51 John Fisher .10
52 Craig Martin .10
53 Carey Bailey .10
54 Houston Thomas .10
55 Ryan Patterson .10
56 Chad Goodin .10
57 Brian Spivey .10
58 Todd Kelly .10
59 Mike Stowell .10
60 Jim Fenwick .10
61 Marc Jones .10
62 Chris Ragan .10
63 Rodney Gordon .10
64 Mark Needham .10
65 Patrick Lenoir .10
66 Martin Williams .10
67 Brad Seiber .10
68 Larry Smith .10
69 Jerry Teel .10
70 Charles McRae .30
71 Rex Hargrove .10
72 James Wilson .10
73 Doug Baird .10
74 Mark Moore .10
75 Lance Nelson .10
76 Robert Todd .10
77 Greg Gerardi .10
78 Antone Davis .30
79 Eric Still .10
80 Anthony Morgan .75
81 Alvin Harper 1.00
82 Charles Longmire .10
83 Mark Adams .10
84 Chris Benson .10
85 Horace Morris .10
86 Harlan Davis .10
87 Darryl Hardy .10
88 Tracy Hayworth .20
89 Von Reeves .10
90 Marion Hobby .10
91 John Ward (ANN) .10
92 Roderick Lewis .10
93 Orion McCants .10
94 James Warren .10
95 Mario Brunson .10
96 Joe Davis .10
97 Shawn Truss .10
98 Keith Steed .10
99 Kacy Rodgers .10
100 Johnny Majors (CO) .30
101 Phillip Fulmer (CO) .30
102 Larry Lacewell (CO) .20
103 Charlie Coe (CO) .10
104 Tommy West (CO) .10
105 David Cutcliffe (CO) .10
106 Jack Sells (CO) .10
107 Rex Norris (CO) .10
108 John Chavis (CO) .10
109 Tim Keane (CO) .10
110 Tim Mingey Recruiter .10
111 Bill Higdon Sr. Admin. Asst. .10
112 Tim Kerin (TR) .10
113 Bruno Pauletto (CO) .10
114 Chuck Webb Vols 17, Co. State 14 .20
115 Chuck Webb Vols 24, UCLA 6 .20
116 Vols 28, Duke 6 (Game Action Photo) .10
117 Vols 21, Auburn 14 (Game Action Photo) .10
118 Jason Julian Vols 17, Georgia 14 .10
119 Roland Poles Vols 30, Alabama 47 .10
120 Charles McRae Vols 45, LSU 39 .20
121 Brian Spivey Vols 52, Akron 9 .10
122 Alvin Harper Vols 33, Ole Miss 21 .30
123 Kelly Days Vols 31, Kentucky 10 .10
124 Vols 17, Vanderbilt 10 (Game Action Photo) .10
125 Jason Julian '90 Mobil Cotton Bowl 1 .10
126 Andy Kelly '90 Mobil Cotton Bowl 2 .10
127 Chuck Webb '90 Mobil Cotton Bowl 3 .20
128 '90 Mobil Cotton Bowl 4 (Scoreboard) .10
129 Eric Still .10
130 Chris Benson .10
131 Preston Warren .10
132 Lee England .10
133 Kent Elmore .10
134 Eric Still .10
135 Chuck Webb .30
136 Marion Hobby .10
137 Kent Elmore .10
138 Antone Davis .30
139 Thomas Woods .10
140 Charles McRae .30
141 Preston Warren .10
142 Darryl Hardy .10
143 Carl Pickens Offense or Defense 1.00
144 Carl Pickens 2.00
145 Chuck Webb .30
146 Thomas Woods .10
147 Andy Kelly Total Offense Game .10
148 The TVA (Offensive Line) .10
149 Smokey (Mascot) .10
150 Doug Dickey Director of Athletics .10
151 Neyland Stadium .10
152 Neyland-Thompson Ctr .10
153 Gibbs Hall (Dormitory) .10
154 Carmen Tegano Asst. AD (Academics and Athletics) .10
155 Gene McEver (HOF) .10
156 Beattie Feathers (HOF) .30
157 Robert Neyland (HOF) (CO) .50
158 Herman Hickman (HOF) .20
159 Bowden Wyatt (HOF) .20
160 Hank Lauricella (HOF) .10
161 Doug Atkins (HOF) .30
162 Johnny Majors (HOF) .30
163 Bobby Dodd (HOF) .30
164 Bob Suffridge (HOF) .10
165 Nathan Dougherty (HOF) .10
166 George Cafego (HOF) .10
167 Bob Johnson (HOF) .20
168 Ed Molinski (HOF) .10
169 Reggie White 2.00
170 Willie Gault .60
171 Doug Atkins .30
172 Keith DeLong .30
173 Ron Widby .20
174 Bill Johnson .20
175 Jack Reynolds .30
176 Tim McGee .50
177 Harry Galbreath .20
178 Roland James .20
179 Abe Shires .10
180 Ted Daffer .10
181 Bob Foxx .10
182 Richmond Flowers .30
183 Beattie Feathers .30
184 Condredge Holloway .50
185 Larry Sievers .20
186 Johnnie Jones .10
187 Carl Zander .20
188 Dale Jones .10
189 Bruce Wilkerson .20
190 Terry McDaniel .30
191 Craig Colquitt .20
192 Stanley Morgan .75
193 Curt Watson .10
194 Bobby Majors .10
195 Steve Kiner .20
196 Paul Naumoff .20
197 Bud Sherrod .10
198 Murray Warmath .20
199 Steve DeLong .20
200 Bill Pearman .10
201 Bobby Gordon .10
202 John Michels .10
203 Bill Mayo .10
204 Andy Kozar .10
205 1892 Volunteers (Team Photo) .10
206 1900 Volunteers (Team Photo) .10
207 1905 Volunteers (Team Photo) .10
208 1907 Volunteers (Individual player photos) .10
209 1916 Volunteers (Team Photo) .10
210 1914 Volunteers (Team Photo) .10
211 1896 Volunteers (Team Photo) .10
212 1908 Volunteers (Team Photo) .10
213 1926 Volunteers (Team Photo) .10
214 1930 Volunteers (Team Photo) .10
215 1934 Volunteers (Team Photo) .10
216 1938 Volunteers (Team Photo) .10
217 1940 Volunteers (Team Photo) .10
218 1944 Volunteers (Team Photo) .10
219 1945 Volunteers (Team Photo) .10
220 1954 Volunteers (Team Photo) .10
221 1969 Volunteers (Team Photo) .10
222 1962 Volunteers (Team Photo) .10
223 1976 Volunteers (Team Photo) .10
224 1985 Volunteers (Team Photo) .10
225 1978 Volunteers (Team Photo) .10
226 1980 Volunteers (Team Photo) .10
227 1984 Volunteers (Team Photo) .10
228 1988 Volunteers (Team Photo) .10
229 James Baird .10
230 Condredge Holloway .50
231 J.G. Lowe .10
232 E.A. McLean .10
233 Lemont Holt Jeffers .10
234 Howard Johnson .10
235 Malcolm Aiken .10
236 Toby Palmer .10
237 Sam Bartholomew .10
238 Ray Graves .10
239 Billy Bevis .10
240 Bert Rechichar .20
241 Jim Beutel .10
242 Mike Lucci .30
243 Hal Wantland .10
244 Jackie Walker .10
245 Ron McCartney .10
246 Robert Shaw .10
247 Lee North .10
248 James Berry .10
249 Carl Zander .20
250 Chris White .10
251 Timmy Sims .10
252 Tim McGee .50
253 Keith DeLong .30
254 1931 NY Charity Game (Program) .10
255 1941 Super Bowl (Program) .10
256 1945 Rose Bowl (Program) .10
257 1957 Gator Bowl (Program) .10
258 1968 Orange Bowl (Program) .10
259 1972 Bluebonnet Bowl (Program) .10
260 1981 Graden State Bowl (Program) .10
261 1968 Sugar Bowl (Program) .10
262 Checklist 1-76 .10
263 Checklist 77-152 .10
264 Checklist 153-228 .10
265 Checklist 229-294 .10
266 Chris White .10
267 Kelsey Finch .10
268 Johnnie Jones .10
269 Johnnie Jones .10
270 Curt Watson .10
271 William Howard .10
272 Bubba Wyche .10
273 Tony Robinson .30
274 Daryl Dickey .30
275 Alan Cockrell, Willie Gault .30
276 Alan Cockrell .30
277 Bobby Scott .30
278 Tony Robinson .30
279 Jeff Francis .20
280 Alvin Harper 1.00
281 Johnny Mills .10
282 Thomas Woods .10
283 Bob Lund .10
284 Gene McEver .10
285 Stanley Morgan .75
286 Fuad Reveiz .30
287 Kent Elmore .10
288 Jimmy Colquitt .10
289 Willie Gault .60
290 Reggie White 100 Years Celebration .75
291 The 100 Years Kickoff (Group Photo) .10
292 Keith DeLong, Steve DeLong Like Father, Like Son .30
293 Raleigh McKenzie, Reggie McKenzie Offense and Defense .20
294 It's Football Time (1990 schedule on back) .20

1991 Tennessee Hoby

NM/M
Complete Set (42): 25.00
Common Player: .25
397 Mark Adams .25
398 Carey Bailey .25
399 David Bennett .25
400 Shazzon Bradley .25
401 Kenneth Campbell .25
402 Dale Carter 1.50
403 Joey Chapman .25
404 Jerry Colquitt .50
405 Bernard Daffney .50
406 Craig Faulkner .25
407 Earnest Fields .25
408 John Fisher .25
409 Cory Fleming .75
410 Mark Fletcher .25
411 Tom Fuhler .25
412 Johnny Majors (CO) .50
413 Darryl Hardy .25
414 Aaron Hayden 3.00
415 Tavio Henson .25
416 Reggie Ingram .25
417 Andy Kelly .50
418 Todd Kelly .75
419 Patrick Lenoir .25
420 Roderick Lewis .25
421 Jeremy Lincoln 1.50
422 J.J. McCleskey .35
423 Floyd Miley .25
424 Chris Mims 1.50
425 Tom Myslinski .35
426 Carl Pickens 5.00
427 Roc Powe .25
428 Von Reeves .25
429 Eric Riffer .25
430 Kacy Rodgers .25
431 Steve Session .25
432 Heath Shuler 6.00
433 Chuck Smith .35
434 James O. Stewart 3.00
435 Mike Stowell .25
436 J.J. Surlas .25
437 Shon Walker .35
438 James Wilson .25

1993 Texas Taco Bell

NM/M
Complete Set (50): 25.00
Common Player: .50
1 Mike Adams 2.00
2 Thomas Baskin .50
3 Tony Brackens 2.00
4 Steve Bradley .50
5 Blake Brockermeyer (Wearing home jersey) 1.50
6 Blake Brockermeyer (Wearing away jersey) 1.50
7 Phil Brown .50
8 Chris Carter .50
9 Stonie Clark .75
10 Gerald Crawford .50
12 Trent Elliot .50
13 Joey Ellis .75
14 John Elmore .75
15 Jon Feick .50
16 Victor Frazier .50
17 Jimmy Hakes .50
18 Anthony Holmes .50
19 Brian Howard .50
20 Jon Hunter .50
21 Curtis Jackson .75
22 Eric Jackson .50
23 Bryan Johnson .75
24 James Lane .50
25 Doug Livingston .50
26 Chad Lucas .50
27 John Mackovic (CO) 1.00
28 Van Malone 1.25
29 Justin McLemore .75
30 Shea Morenz 2.50
31 Dan Neil .75
32 Cosmo Palmieri .50
33 Joe Phillips .50
34 Lovell Pinkney 2.50
35 Chris Rapp .50
36 Robert Reed .50
37 Jason Reeves .50
38 Troy Riemer .50
39 Scott Szeredy .50
40 Tre Thomas .75
41 Winfred Tubbs 1.50
42 Duane Vacek .75
43 Brian Vasek .75
44 Rodrick Walker 1.00
45 Norman Watkins .50
46 Kevin Watler .50
47 Pascal Watty .50
48 Bryant Westbrook .75
49 Longhorns Band .50
50 schedule .50

1992 Texas A and M

NM/M
Complete Set (65): 25.00
Common Player: .35
1 Matt Miller .50
2 Steve Emerson .35
3 Brad Cooper .35
4 Mike Hendricks .50
5 Dexter Wesley .35
6 Darrell Reed .35
7 Antonio Shorter 1.00
8 Larry Wallace .35
9 Kefa Chatham .35
10 Billy Mitchell .35
11 Patrick Bates 2.00
12 Greg Hill 5.00
13 Tommy Preston .35
14 Ryan Mathews .35
15 Steve Kenney .35
16 John Richard .35
17 John Ellisor .35
18 Ryan Kern .35
19 Jeff Jones .35
20 Chris Sanders .35
21 Reggie Graham .35
22 David Davis .35
23 Tony Harrison .50
24 Jason Mathews .50
25 Otis Nealy .35
26 Kent Petty .35
27 Rodney Thomas 5.00
28 Sam Adams 2.00
29 Clif Groce .35
30 Tyler Harrison .35
31 Eric England .35
32 Jason Atkinson .50
33 Lance Teichelman .35
34 Marcus Buckley 2.00
35 Steve Solari .35
36 Aggie Coaches .50
37 Derrick Frazier .50
38 James McKeehan .50
39 Doug Carter .35
40 Larry Jackson .35
41 Brian Mitchell .75
42 Greg Schorp .50
43 Greg Cook .35
44 Kyle Maxfield .35
45 Todd Mathison .35
46 Chris Dausin .35
47 Junior White .35
48 Wilbert Biggens .35
49 Terry Venetoulias .35
50 Jessie Cox .35
51 R.C. Slocum (CO) 1.00
52 Bob Davie, Kirk Doll, Bill Johnson, Trent Walters Defensive Coaches .35
53 Mike Sherman, Shawn Slocum, Bob Toledo, Gary Kubiak, David Culley Offensive Coaches .50
54 Tim Cassidy Recruiting Coordinator .35
55 Steve Scanlon, Adin Pfeuffer, Tim Isgitt, Ronnie McDonald, Mark Rollins Yell Leaders .35
56 A and M Band .35
57 Reveille V Mascot .35
58 Twelfth Man Statue .50
59 Bonfire .35
60 Training Facility .35
61 Kyle Field .35
62 Texas A and M Campus .35
NNO Front Card (Texas A and M Logo) .35
NNO Back Card .35
NNO Checklist Card .35

U

2002 UCLA

NM/M
Complete Set (11): 6.00
Common Player: .50
Bryce Bohlander .50
Nate Fikse .50
Joe Hunter .50
Ricky Manning Jr. .50
Steve Morgan .50
Cory Paus 2.00
Sean Phillips .50
Marcus Reese .50
Mike Saffer .50
Mike Seidman .50
Rusty Williams .50

V

1990 Virginia

NM/M
Complete Set (16): 25.00
Common Player: 1.25
1 Chris Borsari 1.25
2 Ron Carey 1.25
3 Paul Collins 1.25
4 Tony Covington 3.00
5 Derek Dooley 1.25
6 Joe Hall 1.25
7 Myron Martin 1.25
8 Bruce McGonnigal 1.50
9 Jake McInerney 1.25
10 Keith McMeans 1.25
11 Herman Moore 12.00

12 Shawn Moore 4.00
13 Trevor Ryals 1.25
14 Chris Stearns 1.25
15 Jason Wallace 1.25
16 George Welsh (CO) 1.50

1992 Virginia Coca-Cola

NM/M
Complete Set (16): 15.00
Common Player: 1.00
1 Bobby Goodman 1.25
2 Michael Husted 2.00
3 Greg Jeffries 2.00
4 Charles Keiningham 1.00
5 Terry Kirby 5.00
6 Kenneth Miles 1.00
7 Tim Samec 1.00
8 Chris Slade 3.50
9 Alvin Snead 1.00
10 Gary Steele 1.00
11 Jeff Tomlin 1.00
12 Terrence Tomlin 1.00
13 David Ware 1.00
14 George Welsh (CO) 1.25
15 Virginia 20, Clemson 7; Sept. 8, 1990 1.00
16 Virginia 20, N.Carolina 17; Nov 14, 1987 1.00

1993 Virginia Coca-Cola

NM/M
Complet Set (16): 15.00
Common Player: 1.00
1 Tom Burns 1.00
2 Peter Collins 1.00
3 Bill Curry 1.00
4 Mark Dixon 1.00
5 Bill Edwards 1.00
6 P.J. Killian 1.00
7 Keith Lyle 1.00
8 Greg McClellan 1.00
9 Matt Mikeska 1.00
10 Aaron Mundy 1.00
11 Jim Reid 1.00
12 Josh Schrader 1.00
13 Jerrod Washington 1.00
14 George Welsh (CO) 1.25
15 Cavalier Spirit (Cheerleaders) 1.00
16 Cavalier Mascot 1.00

1973 Washington KFC

NM/M
Complete Set (30): 350.00
Common Player: 12.00
1 Jim Anderson 12.00
2 Jim Andrilenas 12.00
3 Glen Bonner 18.00
4 Bob Boustead 12.00
5 Skip Boyd 18.00
6 Gordie Bronson 12.00
7 Reggie Brown 12.00
8 Dan Celoni 12.00
9 Brian Daheny 12.00
10 Fred Dean 12.00
11 Pete Elswick 12.00
12 Dennis Fitzpatrick 12.00
13 Bob Graves 12.00
14 Pedro Hawkins 12.00
15 Rick Hayes 12.00
16 Barry Houlihan 12.00
17 Roberto Jourdan 12.00
18 Washington Keenan 12.00
19 Eddie King 12.00
20 Jim Kristoff 12.00
21 Murphy McFarland 12.00
22 Walter Oldes 12.00
23 Louis Quinn 12.00
24 Frank Reed 18.00
25 Dain Rodwell 12.00
26 Ron Stanley 12.00
27 Joe Tabor 12.00
28 Pete Taggares 12.00
29 John Whitacre 12.00
30 Hans Woldseth 12.00
NNO Color Team Photo (Large 8x10) 18.00
NNO Coaches Photo (Large 8x10) 25.00

1988 Washington Smokey

NM/M
Complete Set (16): 15.00
Common Player: 1.00
1 Ricky Andrews 1.00
2 Bern Brostek 2.00
3 Dennis Brown 2.00
4 Cary Conklin 2.00
5 Tony Covington 1.00
6 Darryl Hall 1.00
7 Martin Harrison 2.00
8 Don James (CO) 2.00
9 Aaron Jenkins 1.00
10 Le-Lo Lang 2.00
11 Art Malone 1.00
12 Andre Riley 1.00
13 Brian Slater 1.00
14 Vince Weathersby 1.00
15 Brett Wiese 1.00
16 Mike Zandofsky 1.50

1990 Washington Smokey

NM/M
Complete Set (16): 15.00
Common Player (1-12): .75
Common Player (13-16): .75
1 Eric Briscoe (28) .75
2 Mark Brunell (11) 6.00
3 James Clifford (53) .75
4 John Cook (93) .75
5 Ed Cunningham (79) 2.00
6 Dana Hall (5) 2.50
7 Don James (CO) 1.50
8 Donald Jones (48) .75
9 Dean Kirkland (51) .75
10 Greg Lewis (20) 2.00
11 Orlando McKay (4) .75
12 Travis Richardson (58) .75
13 Kelley Larsen (Women's Volleyball) .75
14 Michelle Reid (Women's Volleyball) .75
15 Ashleigh Robertson (Women's Volleyball) .75
16 Gail Thorpe (Women's Volleyball) .75

1991 Washington Smokey

NM/M
Complete Set (16): 15.00
Common Player (1-12): .75
Common Player (13-16): .75
1 Mario Bailey 1.50
2 Beno Bryant 1.50
3 Brett Collins .75
4 Ed Cunningham 1.50
5 Steve Emtman 2.00
6 Dana Hall 2.00
7 Billy Joe Hobert 4.00
8 Dave Hoffmann .75
9 Don James (CO) 1.25
10 Donald Jones .75
11 Siupeli Malamala 1.50
12 Orlando McKay .75
13 Diane Flick (Women's Volleyball) .75
14 Kelley Larsen (Women's Volleyball) .75
15 Ashleigh Robertson (Women's Volleyball) .75
16 Dana Thompson (Women's Volleyball) .75

1992 Washington Greats/Pacific

NM/M
Complete Set (110): 15.00
Common Player: .15
1 Don James (CO) .50
2 Cary Conklin .50
3 Tom Cowan .15
4 Thane Cleland .15
5 Steve Pelluer .50
6 Sonny Sixkiller .50
7 Koll Hagen .15
8 Danny Greene .15
9 George Black .15
10 Mike Baldassin .15
11 Bill Douglas .15
12 Tom Flick .25
13 Brian Slater .15
14 Dick Sprague .15
15 Bob Schloredt .35
16 Bill Smith .15
17 Marv Bergmann .15
18 Sam Mitchell .25
19 Bill Earley .15
20 Clarence Dirks .15
21 Jimmie Cain .15
22 Don Heinrich .35
23 Paul (Socko) Sulkosky .15
24 By Haines .15
25 Joe Steele .15
26 Bob Monroe .15
27 Roy McKasson .15
28 Charlie Mitchell .25
29 Ernie Steele .15
30 Kyle Heinrich .25
31 Travis Richardson .1
32 Hugh McElhenny 1.00
33 George Wildcat Wilson .15
34 Merle Hufford .15
35 Steve Thompson .15
36 Jim Krieg .15
37 Chuck Olson .15
38 Charley Russell .15
39 Duane Wardlow .15
40 Jay MacDowell .15
41 Alf Hemstad .15
42 Max Starcevich .15
43 Ray Mansfield .25
44 Brooks Biddle .15
45 Toussaint Tyler .35
46 Randy Van Diver .15
47 John Cook .15
48 Paul Skansi .25
49 Tim Meamber .15
50 Milt Bohart .15
51 Curt Marsh .25
52 Antowaine Richardson .15
53 Jim Rodgers .15
54 Mike Rohrbach .15
55 Dan Agen .15
56 Tom Turnure .15
57 Ron Medved .25
58 Vick Markov .15
59 Carl (Bud) Ericksen .15
60 Bill Kinnune .15
61 Karsten (Corky) Lewis .15
62 Sam Robinson .25
63 Dave Nisbet .15
64 Barry Bullard .15
65 Norm Dicks .15
66 Rick Redman .25
67 Mark Jerue .25
68 Jeff Toews .15
69 Fletcher Jenkins .15
70 Ray Horton .25
71 Tom Erlandson .15
72 Steve Alvord .15
73 Dean Browning .15
74 Scott Greenwood .15
75 Bo Yates .15
76 Jake Kupp .25
77 Jim Owens (CO) .15
78 Don McKeta .15
79 Ben Davidson .50
80 Tim Bullard .15
81 Bill Albrecht .15
82 Jim Cope .15
83 Earl Monlux .15
84 Paul Schwegler .15
85 Steve Bramwell .15
86 Ted Holzknecht .15
87 Larry Hatch .15
88 John Brady .15
89 Bob Hivner .15
90 Chuck Nelson .25
91 Jeff Jaeger .25
92 Rich Camarillo .25
93 Jim Houston .25
94 Jim Skaggs .25
95 John Cherberg (CO) .15
96 Bo Cornell .25
97 Bill Cahill .15
98 Dean McAdams .15
99 Gil Dobie (CO) .25
100 Walter Shiel .15
101 Enoch Bagshaw (CO) .15
102 Ray Eckmann .15
103 Luther Carr .15
104 Jimmy Bryan .15
105 Darrell Royal .35
106 Ray Frankowski .15
107 Ray Pinney .25
108 Skip Boyd .15
109 Al Burleson .15
110 Dennis Fitzpatrick .25
NNO Checklist Card 3.00
AU32 Hugh McElhenny (Certified Autograph, serially numbered of 1000) 50.00

1992 Washington Pay Less

NM/M
Complete Set (16): 15.00
Common Player: .75
1 Walter Bailey .75
2 Jay Barry .75
3 Mark Brunell 5.00
4 Beno Bryant 1.00
5 James Clifford .75
6 Jaime Fields .75
7 Travis Hanson .75
8 Billy Joe Hobert (SP) 4.00
9 Dave Hoffmann .75
10 Matt Jones .75
11 Lincoln Kennedy 2.00
12 Andy Mason .75
13 Shane Pahukoa .75
14 Tommie Smith .75
15 Darius Turner .75
16 Team Photo (Schedule) .75

1993 Washington Safeway

NM/M
Complete Set (16): 10.00
Common Player: .75
1 Beno Bryant 1.00
2 Hillary Butler .75
3 D'Marco Farr 1.50
4 Jamal Fountaine .75
5 Tom Gallagher .75
6 Travis Hanson .75
7 Damon Huard 1.50
8 Matt Jones .75
9 Pete Kaligis .75
10 Napoleon Kaufman 5.00
11 Joe Kralik .75
12 Andy Mason .75
13 Jim Nevelle .75
14 Pete Pierson .75
15 Steve Springstead .75
16 John Werdel .75

1994 Washington

NM/M
Complete Set (12): 12.00
Common Player: .60
1 Eric Bjornson 2.00
2 Mark Bruener 3.00
3 Richie Chambers 1.00
4 Frank Garcia 1.00
5 Russell Hairston .60
6 Damon Huard 1.25
7 Napoleon Kaufman 3.50
8 David Killpatrick .60
9 Lamar Lyons .60
10 Andrew Peterson 1.00
11 Donovan Schmidt .60
12 Richard Thomas .60

1995 Washington

NM/M
Complete Set (16): 8.00
Common Player: .50
1 Ink Aleaga .75
2 Eric Battle .75
3 Ernie Conwell .50
4 Deke Devers .50
5 Mike Ewaliko .50
6 Scott Greenlaw .50
7 Trevor Highfield .50
8 Stephen Hoffmann .50
9 Damon Huard 1.00
10 Dave Janoski .50
11 Patrick Kesi .50
12 Jim Lambright (CO) .75
13 Lawyer Milloy 1.50
14 Leon Neal .50
15 Reggie Reser .50
16 Richard Thomas .50

1988 Washington State Smokey

NM/M
Complete Set (12): 12.00
Common Player: 1.00
3 Timm Rosenbach 2.00
18 Shawn Landrum 1.00
19 Artie Holmes 1.00
31 Steve Broussard 2.00
42 Ron Lee 1.00
55 Tuineau Alipate 1.00
60 Mike Utley 4.00
68 Chris Dyko 1.00
74 Jim Michalczik 1.00
75 Tony Savage 1.00
76 Ivan Cook 1.00
82 Doug Wellsandt 1.00

1990 Washington State Smokey

NM/M
Complete Set (16): 8.00
Common Player: .75
1 Lewis Bush (48) .75
2 Carrie Couturier (Women's Volleyball) .75
3 Steve Cromer (70) .75
4 C.J. Davis (1) .75
5 John Diggs (22) .75
6 Alvin Dunn (27) .75
7 Aaron Garcia (9) .75
8 Bob Garman (74) .75
9 Brad Gossen (12) 1.00
10 Calvin Griggs (5) .75
11 Kelly Hankins (Women's Volleyball) .75
12 Jason Hanson (4) 2.50
13 Kristen Hovde (Women's Volleyball) .75
14 Keri Killebrew (Women's Volleyball) .75
15 Chris Moton (6) .75
16 Ron Ricard (26) .75

1991 Washington State Smokey

NM/M
Complete Set (16): 9.00
Common Player (1-12): .75
Common Player (13-16): .75
1 Lewis Bush .75
2 Chad Cushing .75
3 C.J. Davis .75
4 Bob Garman .75
5 Jason Hanson 2.00
6 Gabriel Oladipo .75
7 Anthony Prior 1.50
8 Jay Reyna .75
9 Lee Tilleman .75
10 Kirk Westerfield .75
11 Butch Williams .75
12 Michael Wright .75
13 Carrie Couturier (Women's Volleyball) .75
14 Kelly Hankins (Women's Volleyball) .75
15 Kristen Hovde (Women's Volleyball) .75
16 Keri Killebrew (Women's Volleyball) .75

1992 Washington State Smokey

NM/M
Complete Set (20): 20.00
Common Player (1-12): .50
Common Player (13-20): .50
1 Drew Bledsoe 12.00
2 Phillip Bobo .75
3 Lewis Bush .50
4 C.J. Davis .50
5 Shaumbe Wright-Fair .75
6 Bob Garman .50
7 Ray Hall .50
8 Torey Hunter .75
9 Kurt Loertscher .50
10 Anthony McClanahan .50
11 John Rushing .50
12 Clarence Williams .75
13 Betty Bartram (Women's Volleyball) .50
14 Krista Beightol (Women's Volleyball) .50
15 Carrie Gilley (Women's Volleyball) .50
16 Shannan Griffin (Women's Volleyball) .50
17 Becky Howlett (Women's Volleyball) .50
18 Kristen Hovde (Women's Volleyball) .50
19 Keri Killebrew (Women's Volleyball) .50
20 Cindy Fredrick CO, M. Farokhmanesh ACO, Gweyn Leabo ACO (Women's Volleyball) .50

1974 West Virginia

NM/M
Complete Set (53): 80.00
Common Player: 1.00
1C Stu Wolpert 1.00
1D Mountaineer Coaches 4.00
1H Leland Byrd (AD) 1.00
1S Bobby Bowden (CO) 25.00
2C Jay Sheehan 1.00
2D Tom Brandner 1.00
2H Tom Bowden 1.00
2S Chuck Smith 1.00
3C Ray Marshall 1.00
3D Randy Swinson 1.00
3H Tom Loadman 1.00
3S Bob Kaminski 1.00
4C Ron Lee 3.00
4D Kirk Lewis 1.00
4H Greg Dorn 1.00
4S Emil Ros 1.00
5C Mark Burke 1.00
5D Rory Fields 1.00
5H Gary Lombard 1.00
5S Brian Gates 1.00
6C John Schell 1.00
6D Paul Jordan 1.00
6H Mike Hubbard 1.00
6S Chuck Kelly 1.00
7C Rick Pennypacker 2.00
7D Heywood Smith 1.00
7H Jack Eastwood 1.00
7S Andy Peters 1.00
8C Steve Dunlap 1.00
8D Dave Wilcher 2.00
8H Greg Anderson 1.00
8S Ken Culbertson 1.00
9C David Van Halanger 1.00
9D Rick Shaffer 1.00
9H Rich Lukowski 1.00
9S Al Gluchoski 1.00
10C Dwayne Woods 1.00
10D Ben Williams 2.00
10H John Adams 1.00
10S Tom Florence 1.00
11C Marcus Mauney 1.00
11D John Spraggins 1.00
11H Bruce Huffman 1.00
11S Bernie Kirchner 1.00
12C Artie Owens 2.00
12D Charlie Miller 1.00
12H 1974 Cheerleaders 1.00
12S Eddie Russell 1.00
13C Danny Buggs 4.00
13D Marshall Mills 1.00
13H John Everly 1.00
13S Jeff Merrow 4.00
JK Student Foundation 1.00

1988 West Virginia

NM/M
Complete Set (16): 20.00
Common Player: 1.00
1 Charlie Baumann 1.50
2 Anthony Brown 1.00
3 Willie Edwards 1.00
4 Theron Ellis 1.50
5 Chris Haering 1.00
6 Major Harris 4.00
7 Undra Johnson 1.50
8 Kevin Koken 1.00
9 Pat Marlatt 1.00
10 Eugene Napoleon 1.00
11 Don Nehlen (CO) 2.00
12 Bo Orlando 3.00
13 Chris Parker 1.00
14 Robert Pickett 1.00
15 Brian Smider 1.00
16 John Stroia 1.00

1990 West Virigina Program Cards

NM/M
Complete Set (49): 35.00
Common Player: .75
1 Tarris Alexander .75
2 Leroy Axem .75
3 Michael Beasley .75
4 Calvin Bell .75
5 Matt Bland .75
6 John Brown 1.25
7 Brad Carroll .75
8 Mike Collins .75
9 Mike Compton 1.25
10 Cecil Doggette .75
11 Rick Dolly .75
12 Theron Ellis 1.25
13 Charlie Fedorco .75
14 Garrett Ford .75
15 Scott Gaskins .75
16 Boris Graham .75
17 Keith Graley .75
18 Chris Gray .75
19 Greg Hertzog .75
20 Ed Hill .75
21 Verne Howard .75
22 James Jett 4.00
23 Greg Jones .75
24 Jon James .75
25 Ted Kester .75
26 Darroll Mitchell .75
27 John Murphy .75
28 Don Nehlen (CO) 2.50
29 Tim Newsom .75
30 Joe Pabian .75
31 John Ray .75
32 Steve Redd .75
33 Joe Ruth .75
34 Alex Shook .75
35 Jeff Sniffen .75
36 Ray Staten .75
37 Rick Stead .75
38 Darren Studstill 2.00
39 Lorenzo Styles 2.00
40 Gary Tillis .75
41 Rico Tyler .75
42 Darrell Whitmore 2.00
43 E.J. Wheeler .75
44 Darrick Wiley .75
45 Tim Williams .75
46 Sam Wilson .75
47 Dale Wolfley .75
48 Rob Yachini .75
49 Mountaineer Field .75

1991 West Virginia ATG

NM/M
Complete Set (50): 15.00
Common Player: .35
1 Jeff Hostetler 2.50
2 Tom Allman .35
3 Russ Bailey .35
4 Paul Bischoff .35
5 Bruce Bosley .50
6 Jim Braxton .50
7 Danny Buggs .50
8 Harry Clarke .35
9 Ken Culbertson .35
10 Willie Drewrey .50
11 Steve Dunlap .35
12 Garrett Ford .35
13 Dennis Fowlkes .35
14 Bob Gresham .50
15 Chris Haering .50
16 Major Harris 1.00
17 Steve Hathaway .35
18 Rick Hollins .35
19 Chuck Howley 1.00
20 Sam Huff 1.25
21 Brian Jozwiak .50
22 Gene Lamone .35
23 Oliver Luck .75
24 Kerry Marbury .35
25 Joe Marconi .50
26 Jeff Merrow .50
27 Steve Newberry .35
28 Bob Orders .35
29 Artie Owens .50
30 Tom Pridemore .50
31 Mark Raugh .35
32 Reggie Rembert .50
33 Ira Rodgers .35
34 Mike Sherwood .35
35 Joe Stydahar .50
36 Renaldo Turnbull 1.25
37 Paul Woodside .35
38 Fred Wyant .35
39 Carl Leatherwood .35
40 Darryl Talley 1.00
41 David Grant .50
42 Bobby Bowden (CO) 1.00
43 Jim Carlen (CO) .35
44 Frank Cignetti (CO) .35
45 Gene Corum (CO) .35
46 Art Lewis (CO) .35
47 Don Nehlen (CO) .50
48 New Mountaineer Field .35
49 Old Mountaineer Field .35
50 Lambert Trophy .50

1991 West Virginia Program Cards

NM/M
Complete Set (42): 25.00
Common Player: .75
1 Tarris Alexander .75
2 Johnathan Allen .75
3 Leroy Axem .75
4 Joe Ayuso .75
5 Michael Beasley .75
6 Rich Braham 1.00
7 Tom Briggs .75
8 John Cappa .75
9 Mike Collins 1.00
10 Mike Compton 1.00
11 Doug Cooley .75
12 Cecil Doggette .75
13 Rick Dolly .75
14 Garrett Ford .75
15 Scott Gaskins 1.00
16 Boris Graham .75
17 Keith Graley .75
18 Chris Gray .75
19 Barry Hawkins .75
20 Ed Hill 1.00
21 James Jett 3.00
22 Jon Jones .75
23 Jim LeBlanc 1.00
24 David Mayfield 1.00
25 Adrian Murrell 3.00
26 Sam Mustipher .75
27 Tim Newsom .75
28 Tommy Orr .75
29 Joe Pabian .75
30 John Ray .75
31 Wes Richardson 1.00
32 Nate Rine .75
33 Joe Ruth .75
34 Alex Shook .75
35 Kwame Smith .75
36 Darren Studstill 2.00
37 Lorenzo Styles 1.50
38 Gary Tillis .75

39 Ron Weaver .75
40 Darrell Whitmore 2.50
41 Darrick Wiley .75
42 Rodney Woodard .75

1992 West Virginia Program Cards

NM/M

Complete Set (49): 25.00
Common Player: .75
1 Tarris Alexander .75
2 Joe Avila .75
3 Leroy Axem .75
4 Mike Baker .75
5 Sean Biser .75
6 Mike Booth .75
7 Rich Braham 1.00
8 Tom Briggs .75
9 Tim Brown .75
10 Darius Burwell .75
11 John Cappa .75
12 Matt Ceglie .75
13 Mike Collins .75
14 Mike Compton 1.00
15 Rick Dolly .75
16 Garrett Ford .75
17 Scott Gaskins 1.00
18 Boris Graham .75
19 Dan Harless .75
20 Barry Hawkins .75
21 Ed Hill 1.00
22 James Jett 3.00
23 Mark Johnson .75
24 Jon Jones .75
25 Jake Kelchner 2.50
26 Harold Kidd .75
27 Jim LeBlanc 1.00
28 David Mayfield 1.00
29 Brian Moore .75
30 Adrian Murrell 2.50
31 Robert Nelson .75
32 Tommy Orr .75
33 Joe Pabian .75
34 Brett Parise .75
35 Steve Perkins .75
36 Steve Redd .75
37 Wes Richardson 1.00
38 Nate Rine .75
39 Tom Robsock .75
40 Kwame Smith .75
41 Darren Studstill 1.50
42 Lorenzo Styles 1.50
43 Matt Taffoni .75
44 Mark Ulmer .75
45 Mike Vanderjagt .75
46 Darrick Wiley .75
47 Dale Williams .75
48 Rodney Woodard .75
49 James Wright .75

1993 West Virginia

NM/M

Complete Set (49): 20.00
Common Player: .50
1 Zach Abraham .50
2 Tarris Alexander .50
3 Mike Baker .50
4 Aaron Beasley .50
5 Derrick Bell .50
6 Mike Booth .50
7 Rich Braham .75
8 Tim Brown .50
9 Mike Collins .75
10 Doug Costin .50
11 Calvin Edwards .50
12 Jim Freeman .50
13A Big East Trophy 1.50
13B Daymeian Gallimore 1.50
14 Jimmy Gary .50
15 Scott Gaskins .75
16 Buddy Hager .50
17 Dan Harless .50
18 John Harper .50
19 Barry Hawkins .75
20 Ed Hill .75
21 Jon Jones .50
22 Jay Kearney .50
23 Jake Kelchner 2.00
24 Harold Kidd .50
25 Chris Klick .50
26 Jim LeBlanc .75
27 Chris Ling .50
28 David Mayfield .75
29 Keith Morris .50
30 Tommy Orr .50
31 Joe Pabian .50
32 Ken Painter .50
33 Steve Perkins .50
34 Maurice Richards .50
35 Wes Richardson .75
36 Nate Rine .50
37 Tom Robsock .50
38 Todd Sauerbrun 1.50
39 Darren Studstill 1.50
40 Matt Taffoni .50
41 Keith Taparausky .50
42 Mark Ulmer .50
43 Robert Walker 1.25
44 Charles Washington .50
45 Darrick Wiley .50
46 Dale Williams .50
47 James (Puppy) Wright .50
48 Don Nehlen (CO) 1.00
49 Mountaineer Field .50

1992 Wisconsin Program Cards

NM/M

Complete Set (27): 20.00
Common Player: .75
1 Troy Vincent 2.50
2 Tim Krumrie 1.25
3 Barry Alvarez (CO) 1.50
4 Pat Richter 1.25
5 Nate Odomes 1.25
6 Ron Vander Kelen 1.50
7 Don Davey 1.25
8 Alan Ameche 2.00
9 Randy Wright 1.25
10 Ken Bowman 1.00
11 Chuck Belin .75
12 Elroy Hirsch 2.00
13 Paul Gruber 1.25
14 Al Toon 1.50
15 Richard Johnson 1.00
16 Pat Harder 1.00
17 Gary Casper .75
18 Rufus Ferguson .75
19 Pat O'Donahue .75
20 Dennis Lick .75
21 Jeff Dellenbach 1.00
22 Jim Bakken 1.00
23 Milt Bruhn (CO) .75
24 Mike Webster 1.50
25 Dave McClain (CO) .75
26 Bill Marek .75
27 Rick Graf .75

CANADIAN

1991 All-World CFL

NM/M
Complete Set (110): 3.00
Common Player: .04
1 Raghib (Rocket) Ismail .25
2 Bruce McNall (owner) .04
3 Ray Alexander .08
4 Matt Clark .08
5 Bobby Jurasin .08
6 Dieter Brock (LEG) .08
7 Doug Flutie .75
8 Stewart Hill .04
9 James Mills .08
10 Raghib (Rocket) Ismail, With Bruce McNall .25
11 Tom Clements (LEG) .15
12 Lui Passaglia .20
13 Ian Sinclair .08
14 Chris Skinner .08
15 Joe Theismann (LEG) .15
16 Jon Volpe .30
17 Deatrich Wise .04
18 Danny Barrett .08
19 Warren Moon (LEG) .25
20 Leo Blanchard .04
21 Derrick Crawford .08
22 Lloyd Fairbanks .08
23 David Beckman (CO) .04
24 Matt Finlay .04
25 Darryl Hall .04
26 Ron Hopkins .08
27 Wally Buono (CO) .04
28 Kenton Leonard .08
29 Brent Matich .04
30 Greg Peterson .04
31 Steve Goldman (CO) .04
32 Allen Pitts .25
33 Raghib (Rocket) Ismail .25
34 Danny Bass .08
35 John Gregory (CO) .04
36 Rod Connop .04
37 Craig Ellis .08
38 Raghib (Rocket) Ismail (Rookie) .25
39 Ron Lancaster (CO) .08
40 Tracy Ham .25
41 Ray Macoritti .08
42 Willie Pless .08
43 Bob O'Billovich (CO) .04
44 Michael Soles .08
45 Reggie Taylor .15
46 Henry Williams .20
47 Adam Rita (CO) .04
48 Larry Wruck .08
49 Grover Covington .08
50 Rocky DePietro .08
51 Darryl Rogers (CO) .04
52 Pete Giftopoulus .08
53 Herman Heard .08
54 Mike Kerrigan .08
55 Reggie Barnes (AS) .08
56 Derrick McAdoo .08
57 Paul Osbaldiston .08
58 Earl Winfield .08
59 Greg Battle (AS) .08
60 Damon Allen .08
61 Reggie Barnes .15
62 Bob Molle .04
63 Raghib (Rocket) Ismail .25
64 Irv Daymond .04
65 Andre Francis .04
66 Bart Hull .15
67 Stephen Jones .08
68 Raghib (Rocket) Ismail .25
69 Glenn Kulka .08
70 Loyd Lewis .04
71 Rob Smith .04
72 Roger Aldag .08
73 Kent Austin .25
74 Ray Elgaard .08
75 Mike Clemons (AS) .25
76 Jeff Fairholm .08
77 Richie Hall .04
78 Willis Jacox .08
79 Eddie Lowe .04
80 Ray Elgaard (AS) .08
81 Donald Narcisse .15
82 James Mills (AS) .08
83 Dave Ridgway .08
84 Ted Wahl .08
85 Carl Brazley .08
86 Mike Clemons .35
87 Matt Dunigan .35
88 Grey Cup (Checklist 1) .04
89 Harold Hallman .08
90 Rodney Harding .08
91 Don Moen .08
92 Raghib (Rocket) Ismail .25
93 Reggie Pleasant .08
94 Darrell Smith (UER) (One L on front, two on back) .15
95 Group Shot (Checklist 2) .04
96 Chris Schultz .08
97 Don Wilson .04
98 Greg Battle .08
99 Lyle Bauer .04
100 Less Browne .08
101 Raghib (Rocket) Ismail .25
102 Tom Burgess .15
103 Mike Gray .04
104 Rod Hill .08
105 Warren Hudson .08
106 Tyrone Jones .15
107 Stan Mikawos .04
108 Robert Mimbs .15
109 James West .08
110 Raghib (Rocket) Ismail .25
P1 Rocket Ismail Promo# (numbered P) 1.00
NNO Raghib (Rocket) Ismail (Autographed card/1600) 50.00

1992 All-World CFL

NM/M
Complete Set (180): 10.00
Common Player: .05
1 Checklist 1-90 .05
2 Draft Picks Checklist .05
3 Western Final .05
4 Eastern Final .05
5 79th Grey Cup .05
6 Rocket Ismail Grey Cup Most Outstanding Player .20
7 Memorable Grey Cups 1909 .05
8 Memorable Grey Cups 1969 .05
9 Memorable Grey Cups 1982 .05
10 Memorable Grey Cups 1989 .05
11 Jeff Braswell .05
12 Glenn Kulka .05
13 Will Johnson .20
14 Lance Chomyc .10
15 Stan Mikawos .05
16 Bobby Jurasin .20
17 Terry Baker .05
18 Tracy Ham .50
19 Todd Wiseman .05
20 Rob Crifo .05
21 Chris Morris .20
22 Jon Volpe .50
23 Donald Narcisse .20
24 David Williams .20
25 Paul Clatney .05
26 Willie Pless .20
27 Rickey Foggie .20
28 Denny Chronopoulos .05
29 Darryl Sampson .05
30 Patrick Wayne .05
31 Terrence Jones .20
32 Larry Wruck .10
33 Angelo Snipes .20
34 Tony Champion .20
35 Steve Taylor .20
36 Lorne King .05
37 Roger Aldag .10
38 Damon Allen .30
39 Chris Walby .10
40 Doug Davies .05
41 Dan Rashovich .05
42 Mark Scott .05
43 Reggie Pleasant .10
44 Bob Cameron .05
45 Danny McManus .20
46 Matt Clark .10
47 Bart Hull .10
48 Hank Ilesic .05
49 Pee Wee Smith .30
50 Irv Daymond .05
51 Greg Battle (J.P. McCaffrey Trophy) .10
52 Will Johnson (Norm Fieldgate Trophy) .10
53 Lance Chomyc (Lew Hayman Trophy) .10
54 Jim Mills (DeMarco-Becket Memorial Trophy) .10
55 Jon Volpe (Jackie Parker Trophy) .20
56 Raghib (Rocket) Ismail (Frank M. Gibson Trophy) .30
57 Dave Ridgway (David Dryburgh Memorial Trophy) .10
58 Chris Walby (Leo Dandurand Trophy) .10
59 Doug Flutie (Jeff Nicklin Memorial Trophy) .75
60 Robert Mimbs (Jeff Russell Memorial Trophy) .20
61 Jon Volpe (Eddie James Memorial Trophy) .20
62 Blake Marshall (Dr. Beattie Martin Trophy) .10
63 Eric Streater .10
64 Carl Brazley .05
65 Kent Warnock .05
66 Brian Bonner .05
67 Tom Burgess .20
68 Bob Gordon .05
69 Milson Jones .05
70 Todd Dillon .05
71 Keyvan Jenkins .20
72 Ken Evraire .20
73 Willis Jacox .20
74 Carl Bland .20
75 Daniel Hunter .05
76 Chris Schultz .05
77 Earl Winfield .20
78 Henry Williams .30
79 Matt Dunigan .75
80 Mark McLoughlin .05
81 Craig Ellis .10
82 Rodney Harding .20
83 Scott Douglas .05
84 Ray Elgaard .20
85 Doug Flutie 1.00
86 Gary Lewis .05
87 Rod Hill .10
88 Greg Stumon .10
89 Ray Alexander .05
90 Blake Dermott .05
91 Checklist 91-180 .05
92 Trophy Winners CL .10
93 British Columbia CL .05
94 Calgary CL .05
95 Edmonton CL .05
96 Saskatchewan CL .05
97 Hamilton CL .05
98 Ottawa CL .05
99 Toronto CL .05
100 Winnipeg CL .05
101 James West .20
102 Jeff Fairholm .20
103 Mike Campbell .05
104 Darren Flutie .40
105 Blake Marshall .25
106 Loyd Lewis .05
107 Enis Jackson .05
108 John Motton .20
109 Ken Walcott .05
110 Richie Hall .05
111 Greg Peterson .05
112 Wally Zatylny .05
113 Lui Passaglia .25
114 Darryl Hall .05
115 Michael Soles .10
116 Doug Brewster .05
117 Mike Gray .05
118 Mike Trevathan .05
119 Don Moen .05
120 Chris Armstrong .05
121 Lucius Floyd .05
122 Ken Pettway .05
123 Anthony Drawhorn .20
124 Brian Walling .05
125 Troy Westwood .20
126 Reggie Barnes .20
127 Raghib (Rocket) Ismail .50
128 Rod Connop .10
129 Chris Major .20
130 David Bovell .05
131 Quency Williams .05
132 Michel Bourgeau .05
133 Harold Hallman .10
134 Junior Thurman .20
135 Stewart Hill .05
136 Brent Matich .05
137 Leroy Blugh .05
138 Nick Mazzoli .05
139 Dave Ridgway .20
140 Matt Finlay .05
141 Mike Clemons 1.00
142 Jason Riley .05
143 Stacey Hairston .05
144 Jim Mills .10
145 Paul Randolph .05
146 David Sapunjis .25
147 Charles Gordon .05
148 Chris Tsangaris .05
149 Darrell Smith .20
150 Leo Groenewegen .05
151 Greg Battle .20
152 Bruce Covernton .10
153 Paul Osbaldiston .10
154 Don Wilson .05
155 Kent Austin .30
156 Jamie Morris .20
157 Andre Francis .05
158 O.J. Brigance .20
159 Less Browne .10
160 Alondra Johnson .05
161 Dexter Manley .20
162 Bob Poley .05
163 Ed Berry .05
164 Pete Giftopoulus .05
165 Glen Suitor .05
166 Eddie Thomas .05
167 Danny Barrett .20
168 Robert Mimbs .20
169 Jim Sandusky .20
170 Maurice Smith .05
171 David Conrad .05
172 Larry Willis .05
173 Ian Sinclair .05
174 Allen Pitts .50
175 Don McPherson .20
176 Ray Bernard .05
177 Dale Sanderson .05
178 Dan Ferrone .10
179 Vic Stevenson .05
180 Rob Smith .05
P1 Doug Fluti Promo# (Numbered P) 1.50
P2 Rocket Ismail Promo# (Numbered P) 1.00

1954 Blue Ribbon Tea CFL

NM/M
Complete Set (80): 9,000
Common Player: 100.00
1 Jack Jacobs 250.00
2 Neil Armstrong 150.00
3 Lorne Benson 100.00
4 Tom Casey 125.00
5 Vincent Drake 100.00
6 Tommy Ford 100.00
7 Bud Grant 500.00
8 Dick Huffman 125.00
9 Gerry James 150.00
10 Bud Korchak 100.00
11 Thomas Lumsden 100.00
12 Steve Patrick 100.00
13 Keith Pearce 100.00
14 Jesse Thomas 100.00
15 Buddy Tinsley 125.00
16 Alan Scott Wiley 100.00
17 Winty Young 100.00
18 Joseph Zaleski 100.00
19 Ron Vaccher 100.00
20 John Gramling 100.00
21 Bob Simpson 150.00
22 Bruno Bitkowski 125.00
23 Kaye Vaughan 125.00
24 Don Carter 100.00
25 Gene Roberts 100.00
26 Howie Turner 100.00
27 Avatus Stone 100.00
28 Tom McHugh 100.00
29 Clyde Bennett 100.00
30 Bill Berezowski 100.00
31 Eddie Bevan 100.00
32 Dick Brown 100.00
33 Bernie Custis 125.00
34 Merle Hapes 125.00
35 Tip Logan 100.00
36 Vince Mazza 125.00
37 Pete Neumann 125.00
38 Vince Scott 125.00
39 Ralph Toohy 100.00
40 Frank Anderson 100.00
41 Bob Dean 100.00
42 Leon Manley 100.00
43 Bill Zock 125.00
44 Frank Morris 150.00
45 Jim Quondamatteo 100.00
46 Eagle Keys 150.00
47 Bernie Faloney 400.00
48 Jackie Parker 500.00
49 Ray Willsey 100.00
50 Mike King 100.00
51 Johnny Bright 300.00
52 Gene Brito 125.00
53 Stan Heath 125.00
54 Roy Jenson 100.00
55 Don Loney 100.00
56 Eddie Macon 100.00
57 Peter Maxwell-Muir 100.00
58 Tom Miner 100.00
59 Jim Prewett 100.00
60 Lowell Wagner 100.00
61 Red O'Quinn 125.00
62 Ray Poole 125.00
63 Jim Staton 100.00
64 Alex Webster 200.00
65 Al Dekdebruin 100.00
66 Ed Bradley 100.00
67 Tex Coulter 150.00
68 Sam Etcheverry 500.00
69 Larry Grigg 100.00
70 Tom Hugo 100.00
71 Chuck Hunsinger 100.00
72 Herb Trawick 125.00
73 Virgil Wagner 125.00
74 Phil Adrian 100.00
75 Bruce Coulter 100.00
76 Jim Miller 100.00
77 Jim Mitchener 100.00
78 Tom Moran 100.00
79 Doug McNichol 100.00
80 Joey Pal 100.00
--- Album 500.00

1988 Bootlegger B.C. Lions

NM/M
Complete Set (13): 15.00
Common Player: 1.00
1 Jamie Buis 1.00
2 Jan Carinci 1.00
3 Dwayne Derban 1.00
4 Roy Dewalt 3.00
5 Andre Francis 1.25
6 Rick Klassen 2.00
7 Kevin Konar 1.25
8 Scott Lecky 1.00
9 James Parker 3.00
10 John Ulmer 1.00
11 Peter VandenBos 1.00
12 Todd Wiseman 1.00
13 NNO Title Card (Corporate Sponsors) 1.25

1971 Chevron B.C. Lions

NM/M
Complete Set (50): 225.00
Common Player: 3.00
Common SP: 12.00
1 George Anderson 3.00
2 Josh Ashton 4.00
3 Ross Boice (SP) 12.00
4 Paul Brothers 3.00
5 Tom Cassese 3.00
6 Roy Cavallin 3.00
7 Rusty Clark (SP) 12.00
8 Owen Dejanovich (CO) 3.00
9 Dave Denny 3.00
10 Brian Donnelly 3.00
11 Steve Duich (SP) 12.00
12 Jim Duke 3.00
13 Dave Easley 3.00
14 Trevor Ekdahl 4.00
15 Jim Evenson 4.00
16 Greg Findlay 3.00
17 Ted Gerela 3.00
18 Dave Golinsky 3.00
19 Lefty Hendrickson 3.00
20 Lach Heron 3.00
21 Gerry Herron 3.00
22 Larry Highbaugh (SP) 12.00
23 Wayne Holm 3.00
24 Bob Howes 3.00
25 Max Huber 3.00
26 Garrett Hunsperger 3.00
27 Lawrence James (SP) 12.00
28 Brian Kelsey (SP) 12.00
29 Eagle Keys (CO) 4.00
30 Mike Leveille 3.00
31 John Love 3.00
32 Ray Lychak 3.00
33 Dick Lyons (SP) 12.00
34 Wayne Matherne 3.00
35 Ken McCullough (CO) 3.00
36 Don Moorhead 3.00
37 Peter Palmer 3.00
38 Jackie Parker (GM) 12.00
39 Ken Phillips 3.00
40 Cliff Powell 3.00
41 Gary Robinson 3.00
42 Ken Sugarman 4.00
43 Bruce Taupier 3.00
44 Jim Tomlin (SP) 12.00
45 Bud Tynes (CO) 3.00
46 Carl Weathers (SP) 12.00
47 Jim White 3.00
48 Mike Wilson 3.00
49 Jim Young 8.00
50 Contest Card (For Chevron) 3.00

1971 Chiquita CFL All-Stars

NM/M
Complete Set (13): 200.00
Common Pair: 15.00
1 Bill Baker, 2 Ken Sugarman 20.00
3 Wayne Giardino, 4 Peter Dalla Riva 20.00
5 Leon McQuay, 6 Jim Thorpe 25.00
7 George Reed, 8 Jerry Campbell 20.00
9 Tommy Joe Coffey, 10 Terry Evanshen 25.00
11 Jim Young, 12 Mark Kosmos 20.00
13 Ron Forwick, 14 Jack Abendschan 15.00
15 Don Jonas, 16 Al Marcellin 20.00
17 Joe Theismann, 18 Jim Corrigall (Toronto Argonauts) 50.00
19 Ed George, 20 Dick Dupuis 15.00
21 Ted Dushinski, 22 Bob Swift 15.00
23 John Lagrone, 24 Bill Danychuk 15.00
25 Garney Henley, 26 John Williams 20.00
NNO Yellow Viewer 40.00

1961 CKNW B.C. Lions

NM/M
Complete Set (30): 200.00
Common Player: 6.00
1 By Bailey 15.00
2 Nub Beamer 6.00
3 Bob Belak (Kings Drive-In) 6.00
4 Neil Beaumont 6.00
5 Bill Britton (Nestle's Quik) 6.00
6 Tom Brown (Kings Drive-In) 8.00
7 Mike Cacic 6.00
8 Jim Carphin 6.00
9 Bruce Claridge 6.00
10 Pat Claridge 6.00
11 Steve Cotter 6.00
12 Lonnie Dennis (Nestle's Quik) 6.00
13 Norm Fieldgate 8.00
14 Willie Fleming 18.00
15 George Grant 6.00
16 Sonny Homer (Nestle's Quik) 8.00
17 Bob Jeter 10.00
18 Dick Johnson 6.00
19 Earl Keeley 6.00
20 Vic Kristopatis 6.00
21 Gordie Mitchell 6.00
22 Rae Ross (Nestle's Quik) 6.00
23 Bob Schloredt 8.00
24 Gary Schwertfeger 6.00
25 Mel Semenko (Kings Drive-In) 6.00
26 Ed Sullivan 8.00
27 Barney Therrien (Nestle's Quik) 6.00
28 Ed Vereb 6.00
29 Don Vicic 6.00
30 Ron Watton 6.00

1962 CKNW B.C. Lions

NM/M
Complete Set (32): 200.00
Common Player: 5.00
1 By Bailey 15.00
2 Nub Beamer 5.00
3 Neil Beaumont 5.00
4 Bob Belak 5.00
5 Walt Bilicki 5.00
6 Tom Brown (Shop-Easy) 8.00
7 Mark Burton (Shop-Easy) 8.00
8 Mike Cacic 5.00
9 Jim Carphin 5.00
10 Pat Claridge 5.00
11 Steve Cotter 5.00
12 Lonnie Dennis 5.00
13 Norm Fieldgate 8.00
14 Willie Fleming (Shop-Easy) 18.00

15 Dick Fouts 8.00
16 George Grant 5.00
17 Ian Hagemoen 5.00
18 Tommy Hinton 8.00
19 Sonny Homer 8.00
20 Joe Kapp 25.00
21 Earl Keeley 5.00
22 Vic Kristopatis (Shop-Easy) 5.00
23 Tom Larscheid 5.00
24 Mike Martin 5.00
25 Gordie Mitchell 5.00
26 Baz Nagle 5.00
27 Bob Schloredt 8.00
28 Gary Schwertfeger 5.00
29 Willie Taylor 8.00
30 Barney Therrien 5.00
31 Don Vicic 5.00
32 Tom Walker 5.00

1952 Crown Brand

NM/M

Complete Set (48): 2,000
Common Player: 50.00
1 John Brown 50.00
2 Tom Casey 75.00
3 Tommy Ford 50.00
4 Ian Gibb 50.00
5 Dick Huffman 75.00
6 Jack Jacobs 100.00
7 Thomas Lumsden 50.00
8 George McPhail 50.00
9 Jim McPherson 50.00
10 Buddy Tinsley 75.00
11 Ron Vaccher 50.00
12 Al Wiley 50.00
13 Ken Charlton 75.00
14 Glenn Dobbs 75.00
15 Sully Glasser 50.00
16 Nelson Greene 50.00
17 Bert Iannone 50.00
18 Art McEwan 50.00
19 Jimmy McFaul 50.00
20 Bob Pelling 50.00
21 Chuck Radley 50.00
22 Martin Ruby 100.00
23 Jack Russell 50.00
24 Roy Wright 50.00
25 Paul Alford 50.00
26 Sugarfoot Anderson 50.00
27 Dick Bradley 50.00
28 Bob Bryant 50.00
29 Cliff Cyr 50.00
30 Cal Green 50.00
31 Stan Heath 50.00
32 Stan Kaluznick 50.00
33 Guss Knickerhm 50.00
34 Paul Salata 50.00
35 Murry Sullivan 50.00
36 Dave West 50.00
37 Joe Aquirre 50.00
38 Claude Arnold 50.00
39 Bill Briggs 50.00
40 Mario DeMarco 50.00
41 Mike King 50.00
42 Donald Lord 50.00
43 Frank Morris 75.00
44 Gayle Pace 50.00
45 Rod Pantages 50.00
46 Rollin Prather 50.00
47 Chuck Quilter 50.00
48 Jim Quondamatteo 50.00

1981 JOGO CFL B/W

NM/M

Complete Set (51): 150.00
Common Player: .70
1 Richard Crump 1.50
2 Tony Gabriel 5.75
3 Gerry Organ .70
4A Greg Marshall 2.00
4B J.C. Watts (SP) 30.00
5 Mike Raines .70
6 Larry Brune .70
7 Randy Rhino 2.00
8 Bruce Clark 3.00
9 Condredge Holloway 5.75
10 Dave Newman .70
11 Cedric Minter .70
12 Peter Muller .70
13 Vince Ferragamo 6.00
14 James Scott 1.50
15 Billy Johnson (White Shoes) 4.50
16 David Overstreet 4.50
17 Keith Gary 1.25
18 Tom Clements 11.00
19 Keith Baker .70
20 David Shaw .70
21 Ben Zambiasi 2.25
22 John Priestner .70
23 Warren Moon 75.00
24 Tom Wilkinson 2.25
25 Brian Kelly 4.50
26 Dan Kepley 1.50
27 Larry Highbaugh 2.00
28 David Boone .70
29 John Henry White .70
30 Joe Paopao 2.25
31 Larry Key .70
32 Glen Jackson .70
33 Joe Hollimon .70
34 Dieter Brock 4.50
35 Mike Holmes .70
36 William Miller .70
37 John Helton 2.25
38 Joe Poplawski 1.25
39 Joe Barnes 3.75
40 John Hufnagel 4.50
41 Bobby Thompson .70
42 Steve Stapler .70
43 Tom Cousineau 4.50
44 Bruce Threadgill .70
45 Ed McAleney .70
46 Leif Petterson 1.25
47 Paul Bennett .70
48 James Reed .70
49 Gerry Dattilio 1.25
50 Checklist Card 1.25

1982 JOGO Ottawa

NM/M

Complete Set (24): 8.00
Common Player: .40
1 Jordan Case .50
2 Larry Brune .50
3 Val Belcher .50
4 Greg Marshall .75
5 Mike Raines .40
6 Rick Sowieta .40
7 John Glassford .40
8 Bruce Walker .40
9 Jim Reid .40
10 Kevin Powell .40
11 Jim Piaskoski .40
12 Kelvin Kirk .40
13 Gerry Organ .50
14 Carl Brazley .75
15 William Mitchell .40
16 Billy Hardee .40
17 Jonathan Sutton .40
18 Doug Seymour .40
19 Pat Staub .40
20 Larry Tittley .40
21 Pat Stoqua .40
22 Sam Platt .40
23 Gary Dulin .40
24 John Holland .50

1982 JOGO Ottawa Past

NM/M

Complete Set (16): 25.00
Common Player (1-12): 1.25
Common Player (13-16): 2.00
Common DP: .75
1 Tony Gabriel 3.00
2 Whit Tucker (DP) 1.50
3 Dave Thelen 2.00
4 Ron Stewart (DP) 1.50
5 Russ Jackson (DP) 3.50
6 Kaye Vaughan 2.00
7 Bob Simpson 2.00
8 Ken Lehmann 1.50
9 Lou Bruce 1.25
10 Wayne Giardino (DP) .75
11 Moe Racine 1.25
12 Gary Schreider 1.25
13 Don Sutherin 4.00
14 Mark Kosmos (DP) 1.25
15 Jim Foley (DP) 2.00
16 Jim Conroy .75

1983 JOGO CFL Limited

NM/M

Complete Set (110): 900.00
Common Player: 4.00
1 Steve Ackroyd 4.00
2 Joe Barnes 12.00
3 Bob Bronk 4.00
4 Jan Carinci 4.00
5 Gordon Elser 4.00
6 Dan Ferrone 5.00
7 Terry Greer 12.00
8 Mike Hameluck 4.00
9 Condredge Holloway 15.00
10 Greg Holmes 4.00
11 Hank Llesic 10.00
12 John Malinosky 4.00
13 Cedric Minter 4.00
14 Don Moen 4.00
15 Rick Mohr 4.00
16 Darrell Nicholson 4.00
17 Paul Pearson 5.00
18 Matthew Teague 4.00
19 Geoff Townsend 4.00
20 Tom Trifaux 4.00
21 Darrell Wilson 4.00
22 Earl Wilson 4.00
23 Ricky Barden 4.00
24 Roger Cattelan 4.00
25 Michael Collymore 4.00
26 Charles Cornelius 4.00
27 Mariet Ford 4.00
28 Tyron Gray 5.00
29 Steve Harrison 4.00
30 Tim Hook 4.00
31 Greg Marshall 5.00
32 Ken Miller 4.00
33 Dave Newman 4.00
34 Rudy Phillips 4.00
35 Jim Reid 4.00
36 Junior Robinson 4.00
37 Mark Seale 4.00
38 Rick Sowieta 4.00
39 Pat Stoqua 4.00
40 Skip Walker 10.00
41 Al Washington 4.00
42 J.C. Watts 50.00
43 Keith Baker 4.00
44 Dieter Brock 35.00
45 Rocky DiPietro 20.00
46 Howard Fields 4.00
47 Ron Johnson 6.00
48 John Priestner 4.00
49 Johnny Shepherd 4.00
50 Mike Walker 6.00
51 Ben Zambiasi 12.00
52 Nick Arakgi 5.00
53 Brian DeRoo 4.00
54 Denny Ferdinand 4.00
55 Willie Hampton 4.00
56 Kevin Starkey 4.00
57 Glen Weir 4.00
58 Larry Crawford 6.00
59 Tyrone Crews 4.00
60 James Curry 10.00
61 Roy DeWalt 12.00
62 Mervyn Fernandez 50.00
63 Sammy Green 4.00
64 Glen Jackson 4.00
65 Glenn Leonhard 4.00
66 Nelson Martin 4.00
67 Joe Paopao 8.00
68 Lui Passaglia 10.00
69 Al Wilson 4.00
70 Nick Bastaja 4.00
71 Paul Bennett 4.00
72 John Bonk 4.00
73 Aaron Brown 4.00
74 Bob Cameron 4.00
75 Tom Clements 60.00
76 Rick House 5.00
77 John Hufnagel 15.00
78 Sean Kehoe 4.00
79 James Murphy 12.00
80 Tony Norman 4.00
81 Joe Poplawski 4.00
82 Willard Reaves 15.00
83 Bobby Thompson 4.00
84 Wylie Turner 4.00
85 Dave Fennell 6.00
86 Jim Germany 5.00
87 Larry Highbaugh 6.00
88 Joe Hollimon 4.00
89 Dan Kepley 10.00
90 Neil Lumsden 4.00
91 Warren Moon 500.00
92 James Parker 12.00
93 Dale Potter 4.00
94 Angelo Santucci 4.00
95 Tom Towns 4.00
96 Tom Tuinei 5.00
97 Danny Bass 12.00
98 Ray Crouse 4.00
99 Gerry Dattilio 7.50
100 Tom Forzani 4.00
101 Mike Levenseller 4.00
102 Mike McTague 5.00
103 Bernie Morrison 4.00
104 Darrell Toussaint 4.00
105 Chris DeFrance 4.00
106 Dwight Edwards 5.00
107 Vince Goldsmith 10.00
108 Homer Jordan 4.00
109 Mike Washington 4.00
110A Darrell Moir (Set number on back) 12.00
110B Darrell Moir (Without set number) 50.00

1983 JOGO Quarterbacks

NM/M

Complete Set (9): 75.00
Common Player: 1.50
1 Dieter Brock 5.00
2 Tom Clements 7.50
3 Gerry Dattilio 1.50
4 Roy DeWalt 3.00
5 Johnny Evans 1.50
6 Condredge Holloway 4.00
7 John Hufnagel 4.00
8 Warren Moon 40.00
9 J.C. Watts 25.00

1984 JOGO CFL

NM/M

Complete Set (160): 275.00
Complete Series 1 (110): 150.00
Complete Series 2 (50): 125.00
Common Player (1-110): 1.00
Common Player (111-160): 2.50
1 Mike Hameluck 1.50
2 Bob Bronk 1.00
3 Paul Pearson 1.00
4 Dan Ferrone 1.50
5 Paul Bennett 1.00
6 Joe Barnes 4.00
7 Condredge Holloway 6.00
8 Terry Greer 5.00
9 Vince Goldsmith 3.00
10 Darrell Wilson 1.00
11 Tom Trifaux 1.00
12 Kelvin Pruenster 1.00
13 Earl Wilson 1.00
14 Hank Llesic 2.50
15 Stephen Del Col 1.00
16 Lamont Meacham 1.00
17 Lester Brown 1.00
18 Rob Forbes 1.00
19 Darrell Nicholson 1.00
20 James Curry 2.50
21 Skip Walker 2.50
22 J.C. Watts 25.00
23 Kevin Powell 1.00
24 Dean Dorsey 2.00
25 Tyron Gray 2.00
26 Mike Hudson 1.50
27 Dan Rashovich 1.00
28 Rudy Phillips 1.50
29 Larry Tittley 1.00
30 Ricky Barden (UER) (Number missing) 1.00
31 Mark Seale 1.00
32 Prince McJunkins 1.50
33 Kevin Dalliday 1.00
34 Rick Sowieta 1.00
35 Roger Cattelan 1.00
36 Damir Dupin 1.00
37 Jack Williams 1.00
38 Dave Newman 1.00
39 Maurice Doyle 1.00
40 Tim Hook 1.00
41 Dieter Brock 12.00
42 Rufus Crawford 5.00
43 Steve Kearns 1.00
44 Ross Francis 1.00
45 Henry Waszczuk 1.00
46 Mark Streeter 1.00
47 Mike McIntyre 1.00
48 John Priestner 1.00
49 Paul Palma 1.00
50 Mike Walker 1.50
51 Mike Barker 1.00
52 Todd Brown 1.00
53 Andre Francis 2.00
54 Glenn Keeble 1.00
55 Turner Gill 10.00
56 Eugene Belliveau 1.00
57 Willie Hampton 1.00
58 Ken Ciancone 1.00
59 Preston Young 1.00
60 Stanley Washington 1.00
61 Denny Ferdinand 1.00
62 Steve Smith 1.00
63 Rick Klassen 1.50
64 Larry Crawford 1.50
65 John Henry White 1.00
66 Bernie Glier 1.00
67 Don Taylor 1.00
68 Roy DeWalt 3.00
69 Mervyn Fernandez 25.00
70 John Blain 1.00
71 James Parker 4.00
72 Henry Vereen 1.00
73 Gerald Roper 1.00
74 Jim Sandusky 12.00
75 John Pankratz 1.00
76 Tom Clements 10.00
77 Vernon Pahl 1.00
78 Trevor Kennerd 2.50
79 Stan Mikawos 1.00
80 Ken Hailey 1.00
81 James Murphy 1.50
82 Jeff Boyd 2.00
83 Bob Cameron 1.00
84 Jerome Erdman 1.00
85 Tyrone Jones 2.50
86 John Bonk 1.00
87 John Sturdivant 1.00
88 Dan Huclack 1.00
89 Tony Norman 1.00
90 Kevin Neiles 1.00
91 Dave Kirzinger 1.00
92 Kevin Molle 1.00
93 Jerry DeBrouolny 1.00
94 Larry Hogue 1.00
95 Ken Moore 1.00
96 Jerry Friesen 1.00
97 Mike McTague 1.50
98 Jason Riley 1.00
99 Roger Aldag 2.00
100 Dave Ridgway 4.00
101 Eric Upton 1.00
102 Laurent DesLauriers 1.00
103 Brian Fryer 1.00
104 Brian DeRoo 1.00
105 Neil Lumsden 1.00
106 Hector Pothier 1.00
107 Brian Kelly 12.00
108 Dan Kepley 3.00
109 Danny Bass 5.00
110 Nick Arakgi 1.50
111 Lyle Bauer 2.50
112 Al Washington 3.00
113 Michel Bourgeau 3.00
114 Keith Gooch 2.50
115 Sean Kehoe 2.50
116 Ken Clark 3.00
117 Orlando Flanagan 2.50
118 Greg Vavra 2.50
119 Mark Bragagnolo 2.50
120 Dave Cutler 7.50
121 Nick Hebeler 2.50
122 Harry Skipper 5.00
123 Frank Robinson 3.00
124 DeWayne Jett 3.00
125 Mark Young 2.50
126 Felix Wright 25.00
127 Bob Poley 2.50
128 Leo Ezerins 2.50
129 Johnny Shepherd 3.00
130 Jeff Inglis 2.50
131 Dwaine Wilson 2.50
132 Aaron Hill 2.50
133 Brian Dudley 2.50
134 Ned Armour 2.50
135 Darryl Hall 2.50
136 Vince Phason 2.50
137 Terry Lymon 2.50
138 Jerry Dobrovolny 2.50
139 Richard Nemeth 2.50
140 Matt Dunigan 60.00
141 Rick Mohr 2.50
142 Lawrie Skolrood 2.50
143 Craig Ellis 6.00
144 Steve Johnson 2.50
145 Glen Suitor 3.00
146 Jeff Roberts 2.50
147 Greg Fieger 2.50
148 Sterling Hinds 2.50
149 Willard Reaves 9.00
150 John Pitts 2.50
151 Delbert Fowler 3.00
152 Mark Hopkins 2.50
153 Pat Cantner 2.50
154 Scott Flagel 3.00
155 Don Rose 2.50
156 David Shaw 2.50
157 Mark Moors 2.50
158 Chris Walby 5.00
159 Eugene Belliveau 2.50
160 Trevor Kennerd 10.00

1984 JOGO Ottawa Yesterday's Heroes

NM/M

Complete Set (22): 75.00
Common Player: 3.50
1 Tony Gabriel 5.00
2 Whit Tucker 3.50
3 Dave Thelen 3.50
4 Ron Stewart 3.50
5 Russ Jackson 10.00
6 Kaye Vaughan 3.50
7 Bob Simpson 3.50
8 Ken Lehmann 3.50
9 Lou Bruce 3.50
10 Wayne Giardino 3.50
11 Moe Racine 3.50
12 Gary Schreider 3.50
13 Don Sutherin 5.00
14 Mark Kosmos 3.50
15 Jim Foley 3.50
16 Jim Conroy 3.50
17 George Brancato 5.00
18 Art Green 5.00
19 Rudy Sims 5.00
20 Jim Coode 5.00
21 Jerry Campbell 5.00
22 Jim Piaskoski 5.00

1985 JOGO CFL

NM/M

Complete Set (110): 150.00
Common Player: 1.00
1 Mike Hameluck 1.50
2 Michel Bourgeau 1.50
3 Waymon Alridge 1.00
4 Daric Zeno 1.50
5 J.C. Watts 20.00
6 Kevin Gray 1.00
7 Steve Harrison 1.00
8 Ralph Dixon 1.00
9 Jo Jo Heath 1.00
10 Rick Sowieta 1.00
11 Brad Fawcett 1.00
12 Lamont Meacham 1.00
13 Dean Dorsey 1.50
14 Bernard Quarles 1.00
15 Mike Caterbone 1.00
16 Bob Stephen 1.00
17 Nick Benjamin 1.50
18 Tim McCray 1.50
19 Chris Sigler 1.00
20 Tony Johns 1.00
21 Jason Riley 1.00
22 Ralph Scholz 1.00
23 Ken Hobart 2.50
24 Paul Bennett 1.00
25 Dan Ferrone 1.50
26 Jim Kalafat 1.00
27 William Mitchell 1.00
28 Denny Ferdinand 1.00
29 James Curry 2.50
30 Jeff Inglis 1.00
31 Bob Bronk 1.00
32 Dan Petschenig 1.00
33 Terry Greer 4.00
34 Condredge Holloway 5.00
35 Ian Beckstead 1.00
36 James Parker 3.00
37 Tim Cowan 1.50
38 Roy DeWalt 2.50
39 Mervyn Fernandez 15.00
40 Bernie Glier 1.00
41 Keyvan Jenkins 3.00
42 Melvin Byrd 2.00
43 Ron Robinson 2.00
44 Andre Jones 1.00
45 Jim Sandusky 6.00
46 Darnell Clash 2.50
47 Rick Klassen 2.50
48 Brian Kelly 6.00
49 Rick House 1.50
50 Stewart Hill 3.00
51 Chris Woods 3.00
52 Darryl Hall 1.50
53 Laurent DesLauriers 1.00
54 Larry Cowan 1.00
55 Matt Dunigan 15.00
56 Andre Francis 1.50
57 Roy Kurtz 1.00
58 Steve Raquet 1.00
59 Turner Gill 5.00
60 Sandy Armstrong 1.00
61 Nick Arakgi 1.50
62 Mike McTague 1.50
63 Aaron Hill 1.00
64 Brett Williams 2.00
65 Trevor Bowles 1.50
66 Mark Hopkins 1.00
67 Frank Kosec 1.00
68 Ken Ciancone 1.00
69 Dwaine Wilson 1.00
70 Mark Stevens 1.00
71 George Voelk 1.00
72 Doug Scott 1.00
73 Rob Smith 1.00
74 Alan Reid 1.00
75 Rick Mohr 1.00
76 Dave Ridgway 3.50
77 Homer Jordan 1.00
78 Terry Leschuk 1.00
79 Rick Goltz 1.00
80 Neil Quilter 1.00
81 Joe Paopao 2.50
82 Stephen Jones 2.50
83 Scott Redl 1.00
84 Tony Dennis 1.00
85 Glen Suitor 1.50
86 Mike Anderson 1.00
87 Stewart Fraser 1.00
88 Fran McDermott 1.00
89 Craig Ellis 3.00
90 Eddie Ray Walker 2.00
91 Trevor Kennerd 3.00
92 Pat Cantner 1.00
93 Tom Clements 10.00
94 Glen Steele 1.00
95 Willard Reaves 4.00
96 Tony Norman 1.00
97 Tyrone Jones 2.50
98 Jerome Erdman 1.00
99 Sean Kehoe 1.00
100 Kevin Neiles 1.00
101 Ken Hailey 1.00
102 Scott Flagel 1.50
103 Mark Moors 1.00
104 Gerry McGrath 1.00
105 James Hood 1.00
106 Randy Ambrosie 1.00
107 Terry Irvin 1.00
108 Joe Barnes 3.00
109 Richard Nemeth 1.00
110 Darrell Patterson 1.00

1985 JOGO Ottawa Program Inserts

NM/M

Complete Set (9): 50.00
Common Player: 5.00
1 1960 Grey Cup Team 5.00
2 Russ Jackson 12.00
3 Angelo Mosca 10.00
4 Joe Poirier 5.00
5 Sam Scoccia 5.00
6 Gilles Archambeault 5.00
7 Ron Lancaster 5.00
8 Tom Jones 5.00
9 Gerry Nesbitt 5.00

1986 JOGO CFL

NM/M

Complete Set (169): 135.00
Common Series 1 (110): 75.00
Common Series 2 (59): 60.00
Common Player (1-110): .75
Common Player (111-169): .75
1 Ken Hobart 2.00
2 Tom Porras 1.25
3 Jason Riley .75
4 Ron Ingram .75
5 Steve Stapler 1.25
6 Mike Derks .75
7 Grover Covington 5.00
8 Lance Shields 1.25
9 Mike Robinson .75
10 Mark Napiorkowski .75
11 Romel Andrews .75
12 Ed Gataveckas .75
13 Tony Champion 5.00
14 Dale Sanderson .75
15 Mark Barousse .75
16 Nick Benjamin 1.25
17 Reginal Butts .75
18 Tom Burgess 6.00
19 Todd Dillon 3.00
20 Jim Reid 1.25
21 Robert Reid .75
22 Roger Cattelan .75
23 Kevin Powell .75
24 Randy Fabi .75
25 Gerry Hornett .75
26 Rick Sowieta .75
27 Warren Hudson 1.25
28 Steven Cox .75
29 Dean Dorsey 1.25
30 Michel Bourgeau 1.25
31 Ken Joiner .75
32 Mark Seale .75
33 Condredge Holloway 4.00
34 Bob Bronk .75
35 Jeff Inglis .75
36 Lance Chomyc 1.50
37 Craig Ellis 2.00
38 Marcellus Greene .75
39 David Marshall .75
40 Kerry Parker .75
41 Darrell Wilson .75
42 Walter Lewis 3.50
43 Sandy Armstrong .75
44 Ken Ciancone .75
45 Steve Raquet .75
46 Lemont Jeffers .75
47 Paul Gray .75
48 Jacques Chapdelaine .75
49 Rick Ryan .75
50 Mark Hopkins .75
51 Glenn Keeble .75
52 Roy Kurtz .75
53 Brian Dudley .75
54 Mike Gray .75
55 Tyrone Crews .75
56 Roy DeWalt 2.50
57 Mervyn Fernandez 6.00
58 Bernie Glier .75
59 James Parker 3.00
60 Bruce Barnett .75
61 Keyvan Jenkins 1.50
62 Alan Wilson .75
63 Delbert Fowler 1.25
64 James Jefferson 5.00
65 James West 7.50
66 Laurent DesLauriers .75
67 Damon Allen 10.00
68 Roy Bennett 3.00
69 Hasson Arbubakrr .75
70 Tom Clements 7.50
71 Trevor Kennerd 1.50
72 Perry Tuttle 3.50
73 Pat Cantner .75
74 Mike Hameluck .75
75 Rob Prodanovic .75
76 James Bell 1.25
77 Hector Pothier .75
78 Milson Jones 2.00
79 Craig Shaffer .75
80 Chris Skinner 1.25
81 Matt Dunigan 7.50
82 Tom Dixon .75
83 Brian Pillman 1.25
84 Randy Ambrosie .75
85 Rick Johnson 3.50
86 Larry Hogue .75
87 Garrett Doll .75
88 Stu Laird 1.25
89 Greg Fieger .75
90 Sean McKeown .75
91 Rob Bresciani .75
92 Harold Hallman 2.50
93 Jamie Harris .75
94 Dan Rashovich .75
95 David Conrad .75
96 Glen Suitor 1.25
97 Mike Siroishka .75
98 Michael McGruder 3.00
99 Brad Calip .75
100 Mike Anderson .75
101 Trent Bryant .75
102 Gary Lewis .75
103 Tony Dennis .75
104 Paul Tripoli .75
105 Daric Zeno .75
106 Michael Elarms .75
107 Donohue Grant .75
108 Ray Elgaard 15.00
109 Joe Paopao 2.00
110 Dave Ridgway 2.50
111 Rudy Phillips 1.25
112 Carl Brazley 1.25
113 Andre Francis .75

114 Mitchell Price 1.50
115 Wayne Lee .75
116 Tim McCray 1.50
117 Scott Virkus .75
118 Nick Hebeler .75
119 Eddie Ray Walker 1.25
120 Bobby Johnson .75
121 Mike McTague .75
122 Jeff Inglis .75
123 Joe Fuller .75
124 Steve Crane .75
125 Bill Henry .75
126 Ron Brown .75
127 Henry Taylor .75
128 Greg Holmes .75
129 Steve Harrison .75
130 Paul Osbaldiston 3.00
131 Craig Walls .75
132 Clorindo Grilli .75
133 Marty Palazeti .75
134 Darryl Hall .75
135 David Black .75
136 Bennie Thompson 2.50
137 Darryl Sampson .75
138 James Murphy 2.50
139 Scott Flagel .75
140 Trevor Kennerd 2.00
141 Bob Molle .75
142 Darrell Patterson .75
143 Stan Mikawos .75
144 John Sturdivant .75
145 Tyrone Jones 2.00
146 Jim Zorn 15.00
147 Steve Howlett .75
148 Jeff Volpe .75
149 Jerome Erdman .75
150 Ned Armour .75
151 Rick Klassen 1.25
152 Brett Williams 2.00
153 Richie Hall .75
154 Ray Alexander 2.50
155 Willie Pless 5.00
156 Marion Jones .75
157 Danny Bass 3.50
158 Frank Balkovec .75
159 Less Browne 4.00
160 Paul Osbaldiston 1.50
161 Trevor Bowles .75
162 David Daniels .75
163 Kevin Konar 1.50
164 Gary Allen 2.00
165 Karlton Watson .75
166 Ron Hopkins 1.25
167 Rob Smith .75
168 Garrett Doll .75
169 Rod Skillman 2.00

1987 JOGO CFL

NM/M
Complete Set (110): 90.00
Common Player: .60
1 Jim Reid 2.00
2 Nick Benjamin 1.00
3 Dean Dorsey 1.00
4 Hasson Arbubakrr .60
5 Gerald Alphin 6.00
6 Larry Willis 3.00
7 Rick Wolkensperg .60
8 Roy DeWalt 2.00
9 Michel Bourgeau 1.00
10 Anthony Woodson .60
11 Marv Allemang .60
12 Jerry Dobrovolny .60
13 Larry Mohr .60
14 Kyle Hall .60
15 Irv Daymond .60
16 Ken Ford .60
17 Leo Groenewegen .60
18 Michael Cline .60
19 Gilbert Renfroe 3.00
20 Danny Barrett 6.00
21 Dan Petschenig .60
22 Gill Fenerty (UER) (Misspelled Gil on card front) 10.00
23 Lance Chomyc 1.00
24 Jake Vaughan .60
25 John Congemi 2.00
26 Kelvin Pruenster .60
27 Mike Siroishka .60
28 Dwight Edwards 1.00
29 Darnell Clash 1.50
30 Glenn Kulka 1.50
31 Jim Kardash .60
32 Selwyn Drain .60
33 Ian Sinclair 1.00
34 Pat Cantner .60
35 Trevor Kennerd 2.50
36 Bob Cameron .60
37 Willard Reaves 3.00
38 Jeff Treftlin .60
39 David Black .60
40 Chris Walby 2.00
41 Tom Clements 4.00
42 Mike Gray .60
43 Bennie Thompson 1.50
44 Tyrone Jones 2.00
45 Ken Winey .60
46 Nick Arakgi 1.00
47 James West 2.50
48 Ken Pettway .60
49 James Murphy 2.50
50 Carl Fodor .60
51 Tom Muecke 2.00
52 Alvis Satele .60
53 Grover Covington 2.00
54 Tom Porras 1.00
55 Jason Riley .60
56 Jed Tommy .60
57 Bernie Ruoff 1.00
58 Ed Gataveckas .60
59 Wayne Lee .60
60 Ken Hobart 1.50
61 Frank Robinson 1.00
62 Mike Robinson .60
63 Ben Zambiasi (UER) (No team listed on front of card) 2.00
64 Byron Williams .60
65 Lance Shields 1.00
66 Ralph Scholz .60
67 Earl Winfield 5.00
68 Terry Lehne .60
69 Alvin Bailey .60
70 David Sauve .60
71 Bernie Glier .60
72 Nelson Martin .60
73 Kevin Konar 1.00
74 Greg Peterson .60
75 Harold Hallman 1.50
76 Sandy Armstrong .60
77 Glenn Harper .60
78 Rick Worman 1.50
79 Darrell Toussaint .60
80 Larry Hogue .60
81 Rick Johnson 2.50
82 Richie Hall .60
83 Stu Laird 1.00
84 Mike Emery .60
85 Cliff Toney .60
86 Matt Dunigan 6.00
87 Hector Pothier .60
88 Stewart Hill 1.50
89 Stephen Jones 1.50
90 Dan Huclack .60
91 Mark Napiorkowski .60
92 Mike Derks .60
93 Mike Walker 1.50
94 Michael McGruder 2.00
95 Terry Baker 3.00
96 Bobby Jurasin 4.00
97 James Curry 2.50
98 Tracey Mack .60
99 Tom Burgess 3.50
100 Steve Crane .60
101 Glen Suitor 1.00
102 Walter Bender .60
103 Jeff Bentrim 2.00
104 Eric Florence .60
105 Terry Cochrane .60
106 Tony Dennis .60
107 Dave Albright .60
108 David Sidoo .60
109 Harry Skipper 1.00
110 Dave Ridgway 2.00

1988 JOGO CFL

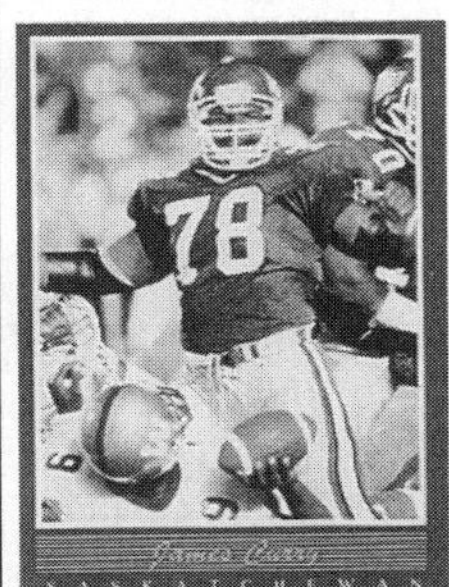

NM/M
Complete Set (110): 110.00
Common Player: .60
1 Roy DeWalt 2.00
2 Jim Reid 1.25
3 Patrick Wayne .60
4 Jerome Erdman .60
5 Tom Dixon .60
6 Brad Fawcett .60
7 Tom Muecke 1.25
8 Mike Hudson .60
9 Orville Lee 1.50
10 Michel Bourgeau 1.00
11 Dan Sellers .60
12 Rob Pavan .60
13 Rae Robirtis .60
14 Rod Brown .60
15 Ken Evraire 1.00
16 Irv Daymond .60
17 Tim Jessie 1.00
18 Jim Sandusky 4.00
19 Blake Dermott 1.00
20 Brian Warren .60
21 Mike Walker 3.00
22 Tom Porras 1.00
23 Less Browne 1.25
24 Paul Osbaldiston 1.00
25 Vernell Quinn .60
26 Mike Derks .60
27 Arnold Grevious .60
28 Jim Lorenz .60
29 Mike Robinson .60
30 Doug Davies .60
31 Earl Winfield 3.00
32 Wally Zatylny 2.00
33 Martin Sartin .60
34 Lee Knight .60
35 Jason Riley .60
36 Darrell Gorbin .60
37 Tony Champion 2.50
38 Steve Stapler 1.00
39 Scott Flagel 1.00
40 Grover Covington 1.50
41 Mark Napiorkowski .60
42 Jacques Chapdelaine .60
43 Lance Shields 1.00
44 Donohue Grant .60
45 Henry Williams 25.00
46 Trevor Bowles 1.00
47 Don Wilson .60
48 Tracy Ham 15.00
49 Richie Hall 1.00
50 Rob Bresciani .60
51 James Curry 1.25
52 Kent Austin 15.00
53 Jeff Bentrim 1.00
54 Dave Ridgway 1.25
55 Terry Baker 1.00
56 Lance Chomyc 1.00
57 Paul Sandor .60
58 Kevin Cummings .60
59 John Congemi 1.25
60 Gilbert Renfroe 1.50
61 Jake Vaughan .60
62 Doran Major .60
63 Dwight Edwards 1.00
64 Bruce Elliott .60
65 Lorenzo Graham .60
66 Jim Kardash .60
67 Reggie Pleasant 1.50
68 Carl Brazley 1.00
69 Gill Fenerty 5.00
70 Selwyn Drain .60
71 Warren Hudson 1.00
72 Willie Fears .60
73 Randy Ambrosie .60
74 George Ganas .60
75 Glenn Kulka 1.00
76 Kelvin Pruenster .60
77 Darrell Smith 1.50
78 Jearld Baylis 1.50
79 Blaine Schmidt .60
80 Tony Visco 1.00
81 Carl Fodor .60
82 Rudy Phillips 1.00
83 Craig Watson 1.00
84 Kent Warnock 1.00
85 Ken Ford .60
86 Blake Marshall 2.00
87 Terry Cochrane .60
88 Shawn Faulkner .60
89 Marshall Toner .60
90 Darren Yewshyn .60
91 Eugene Belliveau .60
92 Jay Christensen .60
93 Anthony Parker 1.25
94 Walter Ballard .60
95 Matt Dunigan 6.00
96 Andre Francis 1.00
97 Rickey Foggie 6.00
98 Delbert Fowler .60
99 Michael Allen .60
100 Greg Battle 6.00
101 Mike Gray .60
102 Dan Wicklum .60
103 Paul Shorten .60
104 Paul Clatney .60
105 Rod Hill 2.00
106 Steve Rodehutskors .60
107 Sean Salisbury 4.00
108 Vernon Pahl .60
109 Trevor Kennerd 1.00
110 David Williams 2.50

1988 JOGO CFL League

NM/M
Complete Set (106): 250.00
Common Player: 1.25
1 Walter Ballard 1.25
2 Jan Carinci 1.25
3 Larry Crawford 1.25
4 Tyrone Crews 1.25
5 Andre Francis 2.00
6 Bernie Glier 1.25
7 Keith Gooch 1.25
8 Kevin Konar 1.25
9 Scott Lecky 1.25
10 James Parker 3.00
11 Jim Sandusky (Traded) 10.00
12 Greg Stumon 1.25
13 Todd Wiseman (Not listed on checklist card) 1.25
14 Gary Allen 2.00
15 Scott Flagel (Traded) 3.00
16 Harold Hallman 1.25
17 Larry Hogue (UER) (Misspelled Hogue) 1.25
18 Ron Hopkins 1.25
19 Stu Laird 2.00
20 Andy McVey 1.25
21 Bernie Morrison 1.25
22 Tim Petros 1.25
23 Bob Poley 1.25
24 Tom Spoletini 1.25
25 Emmanuel Tolbert 4.00
26 Larry Willis 2.00
27 Damon Allen 4.00
28 Danny Bass 4.00
29 Stanley Blair 1.25
30 Marco Cyncar 1.25
31 Tracy Ham 25.00
32 Milson Jones (Traded) 4.00
33 Stephen Jones 3.00
34 Jerry Kauric 3.00
35 Hector Pothier 1.25
36 Tom Richards 3.00
37 Chris Skinner 2.00
38 Henry Williams 40.00
39 Larry Wruck 1.25
40 Pat Brady 1.25
41 Grover Covington 3.00
42 Rocky DiPietro 4.00
43 Howard Fields 1.25
44 Miles Gorrell 1.25
45 Johnnie Jones 1.25
46 Tom Porras 2.00
47 Jason Riley 1.25
48 Dale Sanderson 1.25
49 Ralph Scholz 1.25
50 Lance Shields 2.00
51 Steve Stapler 1.25
52 Mike Walker 3.00
53 Gerald Alphin 4.00
54 Nick Arakgi (SP) (Retired before season) 20.00
55 Nick Benjamin 2.00
56 Tom Dixon 1.25
57 Leo Groenewegen 1.25
58 Will Lewis 2.00
59 Greg Marshall (Injured and retired) 5.00
60 Larry Mohr 1.25
61 Kevin Powell (Traded) 3.00
62 Jim Reid 2.00
63 Art Schlichter 8.00
64 Rick Wolkensperg 1.25
65 Anthony Woodson 1.25
66 Dave Albright 1.25
67 Roger Aldag 1.25
68 Mike Anderson 1.25
69 Kent Austin 25.00
70 Tom Burgess 6.00
71 James Curry 3.00
72 Ray Elgaard 4.00
73 Denny Ferdinand 1.25
74 Bobby Jurasin 6.00
75 Gary Lewis 1.25
76 Dave Ridgway 3.00
77 Harry Skipper 2.00
78 Glen Suitor 2.00
79 Ian Beckstead 1.25
80 Lance Chomyc 2.00
81 John Congemi 3.00
82 Gill Fenerty 8.00
83 Dan Ferrone 2.00
84 Warren Hudson 2.00
85 Hank Llesic 3.50
86 Jim Kardash 1.25
87 Glenn Kulka 2.00
88 Don Moen 1.25
89 Gilbert Renfroe 3.00
90 Chris Schultz 1.25
91 Darrell Smith 3.00
92 Lyle Bauer 1.25
93 Nick Bastaja 1.25
94 David Black 1.25
95 Bob Cameron 1.25
96 Randy Fabi 1.25
97 James Jefferson 6.00
98 Stan Mikawos 1.25
99 James Murphy 3.00
100 Ken Pettway 1.25
101 Willard Reaves (Signed with Redskins) 12.00
102 Darryl Sampson 1.25
103 Chris Walby 4.00
104 James West 5.00
105 Tom Clements (SP) (Retired before season) 20.00
106 Checklist Card SP 6.00

1989 JOGO CFL

NM/M
Complete Set (160): 95.00
Complete Series 1 (110): 60.00
Complete Series 2 (50): 35.00
Common Player (1-160): .50
1 Mike Kerrigan 2.50
2 Ian Beckstead .50
3 Lance Chomyc .75
4 Gill Fenerty 3.50
5 Lee Morris .50
6 Todd Wiseman .50
7 John Congemi .75
8 Harold Hallman .75
9 Jim Kardash .50
10 Kelvin Pruenster .50
11 Blaine Schmidt .50
12 Bruce Holmes .50
13 Ed Berry .50
14 Bobby McAllister 2.50
15 Frank Robinson .75
16 Darrell Corbin .50
17 Jason Riley .50
18 Darrell Patterson .50
19 Darrell Harle .50
20 Mark Napiorkowski .50
21 Derrick McAdoo 2.00
22 Sam Loucks .50
23 Ronnie Glanton .50
24 Lance Shields .75
25 Tony Champion 2.00
26 Floyd Salazar .50
27 Tony Visco .75
28 Glenn Kulka .75
29 Reggie Pleasant .75
30 Rod Skillman .50
31 Grover Covington 1.50
32 Gerald Alphin 2.00
33 Gerald Wilcox .75
34 Daniel Hunter .50
35 Tony Kimbrough .75
36 Willie Fears .50
37 Tyrone Thurman 4.00
38 Dean Dorsey .75
39 Tom Schimmer .50
40 Ken Evraire .75
41 Steve Wiggins .50
42 Donovan Wright .50
43 Tuineau Alipate .50
44 Richie Hall .50
45 Rob Bresciani .50
46 Tom Burgess 1.50
47 Jeff Fairholm 4.00
48 John Hoffman .50
49 Dave Ridgway 1.25
50 Terry Baker .75
51 Mike Hildebrand .75
52 Danny Bass 2.50
53 Jeff Braswell .50
54 Michel Bourgeau .75
55 Ken Ford .50
56 Enis Jackson .50
57 Tony Hunter 1.25
58 Andre Francis .75
59 Larry Wruck .75
60 Pierre Vercheval 1.00
61 Keith Wright .50
62 Andrew McConnell .50
63 Gregg Stumon .75
64 Steve Taylor 3.00
65 Brett Williams .75
66 Tracy Ham 5.00
67 Stewart Hill .75
68 Eugene Belliveau .50
69 Tom Porras .75
70 Jay Christensen .50
71 Michael Soles 1.00
72 John Mandarich 1.25
73 Dan Wicklum .50
74 Shawn Daniels .50
75 Marshall Toner .50
76 Kent Warnock .75
77 Terrence Jones 4.00
78 Damon Allen 2.00
79 Kevin Konar .75
80 Phillip Smith .50
81 Marcus Thomas .50
82 Jamie Taras .50
83 Rob Moretto .50
84 Eugene Mingo .50
85 Matt Dunigan 5.00
86 Jan Carinci .50
87 Anthony Parker 2.00
88 Keith Gooch .50
89 Ron Howard .50
90 David Williams 1.50
91 Less Browne .75
92 Quency Williams .50
93 Tim McCray .75
94 Jeff Croonen .50
95 Greg Battle 2.00
96 Moustafa Ali .50
97 Michael Allen .50
98 David Black .50
99 Paul Randolph .50
100 Trevor Kennerd .75
101 Ken Pettway .50
102 Sean Salisbury 2.50
103 Bob Cameron .50
104 Tim Jessie .75
105 Leon Hatziioannou .50
106 Matt Pearce .50
107 Paul Clatney .50
108 Randy Fabi .50
109 Mike Gray .50
110 James Murphy 2.00
111 Danny Barrett 1.50
112 Wally Zatylny .75
113 Tony Truelove .50
114 Leroy Blugh .50
115 Reggie Taylor 1.50
116 Mark Zeno 2.50
117 Paul Wetmore .50
118 Mark McLoughlin .50
119 Randy Ambrosie .50
120 Will Johnson .75
121 Brock Smith .50
122 Willie Gillus .50
123 Andy McVey .50
124 Wes Cooper .50
125 Tyrone Pope .50
126 Craig Ellis 1.50
127 Darrel Hopper .50
128 Brad Fawcett .50
129 Pat Miller .50
130 Irv Daymond .50
131 Bob Molle .50
132 James Mills 3.00
133 Darrell Wallace .75
134 Jerry Beasley .50
135 Loyd Lewis .50
136 Bernie Glier .50
137 Eric Streater 2.00
138 Gerald Roper .50
139 Brad Tierney .50
140 Patrick Wayne .50
141 Craig Watson .50
142 Doug Landry 3.50
143 Orville Lee 1.50
144 Rocco Romano .50
145 Todd Dillon 1.00
146 Michel Lamy .50
147 Tony Cherry 3.50
148 Flint Fleming .50
149 Kennard Martin .50
150 Lorenzo Graham .50
151 Junior Thurman 1.50
152 Darnell Graham .75
153 Dan Ferrone .75
154 Matt Finlay .50
155 Brent Matich .50
156 Kent Austin 5.00
157 Will Lewis .50
158 Mike Walker 1.50
159 Tim Petros .75
160 Stu Laird 1.50

1990 JOGO CFL

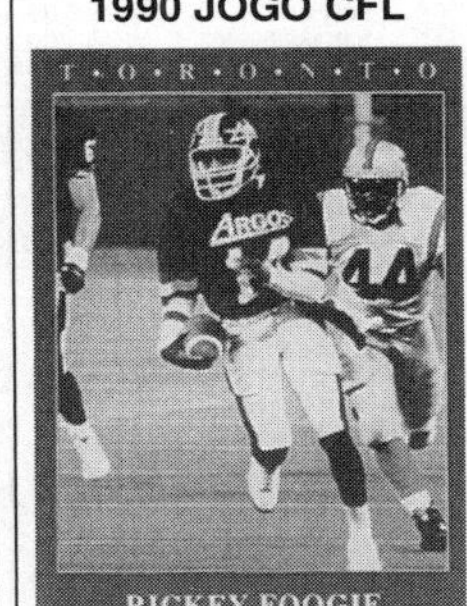

NM/M
Complete Set (220): 60.00
Complete Series 1 (110): 30.00
Complete Series 2 (110): 30.00
Common Player: .25
1 1989 Grey Cup Champs (Saskatchewan) 1.00
2 Kent Austin 2.50
3 James Ellingson .40
4 Vince Goldsmith .40
5 Gary Lewis .25
6 Bobby Jurasin 1.00
7 Tim McCray .40
8 Chuck Klingbeil 1.50
9 Albert Brown .25
10 Dave Ridgway .75
11 Tony Rice 3.00
12 Richie Hall .25
13 Jeff Fairholm 1.00
14 Ray Elgaard 1.25
15 Sonny Gordon .25
16 Peter Giftopoulos .75
17 Mike Kerrigan 1.00
18 Jason Riley .25
19 Wally Zatylny .40
20 Derrick McAdoo .40
21 Dale Sanderson .25
22 Paul Osbaldiston .40
23 Todd Dillon .40
24 Miles Gorrell .25
25 Earl Winfield .75
26 Bill Henry .25
27 Darrell Harle .25
28 Ernie Schramayr .25
29 Greg Peterson .25
30 Marshall Toner .25
31 Danny Barrett 1.50
32 Mike Palumbo .25
33 Ken Ford .25
34 Brock Smith .25
35 Tom Spoletini .25
36 Will Johnson .40
37 Terrence Jones 1.50
38 Darcy Kopp .25
39 Tim Petros .40
40 Mitchell Price .40
41 Junior Thurman 1.00
42 Kent Warnock .40
43 Darrell Smith 1.00
44 Chris Schultz (UER) (No team on back) .40
45 Kelvin Pruenster .25
46 Matt Dunigan 3.00
47 Lance Chomyc .40
48 John Congemi .75
49 Mike Clemons 10.00
50 Glenn Harper .25
51 Branko Vincic .25
52 Tom Porras .40
53 Reggie Pleasant .40
54 Randy Marriott .25
55 James Parker .75
56 Don Moen .40
57 James West 1.00
58 Trevor Kennerd .75
59 Warren Hudson .40
60 Tom Burgess 1.50
61 David Black .25
62 Matt Pearce .25
63 Steve Rodehutskors .40
64 Rod Hill .40
65 Nick Benjamin .40
66 Bob Cameron .25
67 Leon Hatziioannou .25
68 Robert Mimbs 2.50
69 Mike Gray .25
70 Ken Winey .25
71 Mike Hildebrand .25
72 Brett Williams .40
73 Tracy Ham 2.50
74 Danny Bass .75
75 Mark Norman .25
76 Andre Francis .40
77 Todd Storme .25
78 Henry Williams 5.00
79 Kevin Clark .75
80 Enis Jackson .25
81 Leroy Blugh .25
82 Jeff Braswell .40
83 Larry Wruck .40
84A Mike McLean (ERR) (Photo actually 24 Mike Hildebrand) 3.00
84B Mike McLean (COR) (Two players shown) 5.00
85 Leo Groenewegen (UER) (Misspelled Groenewegan on card back) .25
86 Mark Gastineau 1.50
87 Larry Clarkson .25
88 Major Harris 2.50
89 Ray Alexander .40
90 Joe Paopao .40
91 Ian Sinclair .40
92 Tony Visco (UER) (British Columbia on front, correctly has team as Toronto on front) .25
93 Lui Passaglia .75
94 Doug Flutie 20.00
95 Glenn Kulka .40
96 Bruce Holmes .25
97 Stacey Dawsey .25
98 Damon Allen .75
99 Ken Evraire .40
100 David Williams .60
101 Gregg Stumon .40
102 Scott Flagel .40
103 Gerald Roper .25
104 Tony Cherry 1.00
105 Jim Mills .25
106 Dean Dorsey .40
107 Patrick Wayne .25
108 Reggie Barnes 2.00
109 Kari Yli-Renko .25
110 Ken Hobart .75
111 Doug Flutie 15.00
112 Grover Covington .75

113 Michael Allen .25
114 Mike Walker .75
115 Danny McManus 4.00
116 Greg Battle 1.25
117 Quency Williams .25
118 Jeff Croonen .25
119 Paul Randolph .25
120 Rick House .40
121 Rob Smith .40
122 Mark Napiorkowski .25
123 Ed Berry .25
124 Rob Crifo .25
125 Gord Weber .25
126 Jeff Boyd .40
127 Paul McGowan .40
128 Reggie Taylor .75
129 Warren Jones .25
130 Blake Marshall .40
131 Darrell Corbin .25
132 Jim Rockford .40
133 Richard Nurse .25
134 Bryan Illerbrun .25
135 Mark Waterman .25
136 Doug Landry 1.25
137 Ronnie Glanton .25
138 Mark Guy .40
139 Mike Anderson .25
140 Remi Trudel .25
141 Stephen Jones 1.00
142 Mike Derks .25
143 Michel Bourgeau (Edmonton Oilers) .40
144 Jeff Bentrim .40
145 Roger Aldag .40
146 Donald Narcisse 2.50
147 Troy Wilson .25
148 Glen Suitor .40
149 Stewart Hill 1.00
150 Chris Johnstone .25
151 Mark Mathis .25
152 Blaine Schmidt .25
153 Craig Ellis .75
154 John Mandarich .40
155 Steve Zatylny .25
156 Michel Lamy .25
157 Irv Daymond .25
158 Tom Porras .40
159 Rick Worman .40
160 Major Harris 1.50
161 Darryl Hall .40
162 Terry Andrysiak .40
163 Harold Hallman .40
164 Carl Brazley .25
165 Kevin Smellie .25
166 Mark Campbell .40
167 Andy McVey .25
168 Derrick Crawford .40
169 Howard Dell .25
170 Dave Van Belleghem .25
171 Don Wilson .25
172 Robert Smith .40
173 Keith Browner .40
174 Chris Munford .25
175 Gary Wilkerson .25
176 Rickey Foggie (UER) (Misspelled Foogie on card front) 1.25
177 Robin Belanger .25
178 Andrew Murray .25
179 Paul Masotti .40
180 Chris Gaines .25
181 Joe Clausi .25
182 Greg Harris .25
183 David Bovell .25
184 Eric Streater .40
185 Larry Hogue .25
186 Jan Carinci .25
187 Floyd Salazar .25
188 Alondra Johnson .40
189 Jay Christensen (UER) (Misspelled Christenson on card front) .40
190 Rick Ryan .25
191 Willie Pless 1.50
192 Walter Ballard .25
193 Lee Knight .25
194 Ray Macoritti .40
195 Dan Payne .25
196 Dan Sellers .25
197 Rae Robirtis .25
198 Dave Mossman .25
199 Sam Loucks .25
200 Derek MacCready .25
201 Tony Cherry .75
202 Ali Moustafa .25
203 Terry Baker .40
204 Matt Finlay .25
205 Daniel Hunter .25
206 Chris Major 2.00
207 Henry Smith .25
208 David Sapunjis 4.00
209 Darrell Wallace .40
210 Mark Singer .25
211 Tuineau Alipate .25
212 Tony Champion 1.25
213 Mike Lazecki .25
214 Larry Clarkson .25
215 Lorenzo Graham .25
216 Tony Martino .25
217 Ken Watson .25
218 Paul Clatney .25
219 Ken Pettway .25
220 Tyrone Jones 1.00

1991 JOGO CFL

NM/M
Complete Set (220): 6.00
Complete Series 1 (110): 3.00
Complete Series 2 (110): 3.00
Common Player: .04
1 Tracy Ham .35
2 Larry Wruck .08
3 Pierre Vercheval .04
4 Rod Connop .04
5 Michel Bourgeau .04
6 Leroy Blugh .04
7 Mike Walker .04
8 Ray Macoritti .04
9 Michael Soles .04
10 Brett Williams .15
11 Blake Marshall .15
12 David Williams .08
13 Enis Jackson .04
14 Craig Ellis .15
15 Reggie Taylor .15
16 Mike McLean .04
17 Blake Dermott .04
18 Henry Williams .50
19 Jordan Gaertner .04
20 Willie Pless .15
21 Danny Bass .15
22 Trevor Bowles .04
23 Rob Davidson .04
24 Mark Norman .04
25 Ron Lancaster (CO) .10
26 Chris Johnstone .04
27 Randy Ambrosie .04
28 Glenn Kulka .04
29 Gerald Wilcox .15
30 Kari Yli-Renko .04
31 Daniel Hunter .04
32 Bryan Illerbrun .04
33 Terry Baker .04
34 Jeff Braswell .04
35 Andre Francis .04
36 Irv Daymond .04
37 Sean Foudy .04
38 Brad Tierney .04
39 Gregg Stumon .04
40 Scott Flagel .04
41 Gerald Roper .04
42 Charles Wright .04
43 Rob Smith .04
44 James Ellingson .04
45 Damon Allen .08
46 John Congemi .04
47 Reggie Barnes .20
48 Stephen Jones .15
49 Rob Prodanovic .04
50 Steve Goldman .04
51 Patrick Wayne .04
52 David Conrad .04
53 John Krupke .04
54 Loyd Lewis .04
55 Tony Cherry .20
56 Terrence Jones .25
57 Dan Wicklum .04
58 Allen Pitts .50
59 Junior Thurman .04
60 Ron Hopkins .04
61 Andy McVey .04
62 Leo Blanchard .04
63 Mark Singer .04
64 Darryl Hall .04
65 David McCrary .04
66 Mark Guy .04
67 Marshall Toner .04
68 Derrick Crawford .04
69 Danny Barrett .20
70 Kent Warnock .08
71 Brent Matich .04
72 Mark McLoughlin .04
73 Joe Clausi .04
74 Wally Buono (CO) .04
75 Will Johnson .04
76 Walter Ballard .04
77 Matt Finlay .04
78 David Sapunjis .35
79 Greg Peterson .04
80 Paul Clatney .04
81 Lloyd Fairbanks .04
82 Herman Heard .15
83 Richard Nurse .04
84 Dave Richardson .04
85 Ernie Schramayr .04
86 Todd Dillon .04
87 Tuineau Alipate .04
88 Peter Giftopoulos .04
89 Miles Gorrell .04
90 Earl Winfield .20
91 Paul Osbaldiston .04
92 Dale Sanderson .04
93 Jason Riley .04
94 Ken Evraire .04
95 Lee Knight .04
96 Tim Lorenz .04
97 Derrick McAdoo .15
98 Bobby Dawson .04
99 Rickey Royal .04
100 Ronald Veal .20
101 Grover Covington .20
102 Mike Kerrigan .20
103 Rocky DiPietro .20
104 Mark Dennis .04
105 Tony Champion .20
106 Tony Visco .04
107 Darrell Harle .04
108 Wally Zatylny .04
109 David Beckman (CO) .04
110 Checklist 1-110 .04
111 Jeff Fairholm .04
112 Roger Aldag .04
113 Dave Albright .04
114 Gary Lewis .04
115 Dan Rashovich .04
116 Lucius Floyd .04
117 Bob Poley .04
118 Donald Narcisse .20
119 Bobby Jurasin .15
120 Orville Lee .15
121 Stacey Hairston .04
122 Richie Hall .04
123 John Gregory (CO) .04
124 Rick Worman .04
125 Dave Ridgway .15
126 Wayne Drinkwater .04
127 Eddie Lowe .04
128 Mike Hogue .04
129 Larry Hogue .04
130 Milson Jones .15
131 Ray Elgaard .20
132 Dave Pitcher .04
133 Vic Stevenson .04
134 Albert Brown .04
135 Mike Anderson .04
136 Glen Suitor .04
137 Kent Austin .30
138 Mike Gray .04
139 Steve Rodehutskors .04
140 Eric Streater .04
141 David Black .04
142 James West .15
143 Danny McManus .30
144 Darryl Sampson .04
145 Bob Cameron .04
146 Tom Burgess .35
147 Rick House .04
148 Chris Walby .15
149 Michael Allen .04
150 Warren Hudson .04
151 David Bovell .04
152 Rob Crifo .04
153 Lyle Bauer .04
154 Trevor Kennerd .20
155 Troy Johnson .04
156 Less Browne .04
157 Nick Benjamin .04
158 Matt Pearce .04
159 Tyrone Jones .04
160 Rod Hill .04
161 Bob Molle .04
162 Lee Hull .04
163 Greg Battle .20
164 Robert Mimbs .30
165 Giulio Caravatta .04
166 James Mills .15
167 Ian Sinclair .04
168 Robin Belanger .04
169 Deatrich Wise .04
170 Chris Skinner .04
171 Norman Jefferson .04
172 Larry Clarkson .04
173 Chris Major .35
174 Stewart Hill .04
175 Tony Hunter .04
176 Stacey Dawsey .04
177 Doug Flutie 1.00
178 Mike Trevathan .04
179 Jearld Baylis .04
180 Matt Clark .25
181 Ken Pettway .04
182 Lloyd Joseph .04
183 Jon Volpe 1.00
184 Leo Groenewegen .04
185 Carl Coulter .04
186 O.J. Brigance .35
187 Ryan Hanson .04
188 Rocco Romano .04
189 Ray Alexander .04
190 Bob O'Billovich (CO) .04
191 Paul Wetmore .04
192 Harold Hallman .04
193 Ed Berry .04
194 Brian Warren .04
195 Matt Dunigan .40
196 Kelvin Pruenster .04
197 Ian Beckstead .04
198 Carl Brazley .04
199 Trevor Kennerd .15
200 Reggie Pleasant .04
201 Kevin Smellie .04
202 Don Moen .04
203 Blaine Schmidt .04
204 Chris Schultz .04
205 Lance Chomyc .04
206 Darrell Smith .20
207 Dan Ferrone .04
208 Chris Gaines .04
209 Keith Castello .04
210 Chris Munford .04
211 Rodney Harding .20
212 Darryl Ford .04
213 Rickey Foggie .20
214 Don Wilson .04
215 Andrew Murray .04
216 Jim Kardash .04
217 Mike Clemens 1.25
218 Bruce Elliott .04
219 Mike McCarthy .04
220 Checklist .04

1991 JOGO CFL Stamp Card Inserts

NM/M
Complete Set (3): 30.00
Common Player: 10.00
1 Albert H.G. Grey 10.00
2 Trevor Kennerd 10.00
NNO Grey Cup Trophy (Grey Cup Winners listed on card back) 10.00

1992 JOGO CFL Promos

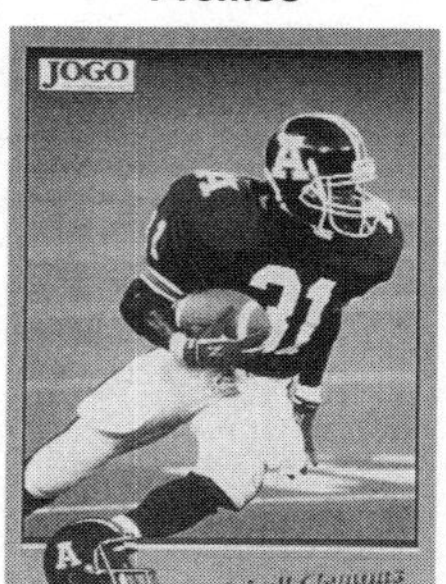

NM/M
Complete Set (7): 12.00
Common Player: .75
A1 Mike Clemons 2.00
A2 Jon Volpe 2.00
A3 Rocket Rat (Cartoon character) .75
P1 Mike Clemons 3.00
P2 Jon Volpe 3.00
CC1 Ken Danby Art Coll. Classic Library .75
CC2 Ken Danby Art Coll. Classic Library .75

1992 JOGO CFL

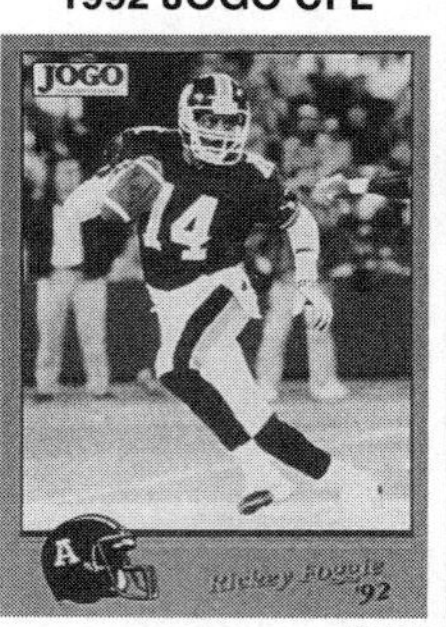

NM/M
Complete Set (220): 20.00
Common Player: .05
1 David Bovell .05
2 Don Moen .10
3 Ian Beckstead .05
4 David Williams .10
5 Hank Ilesic .10
6 Brian Warren .05
7 Paul Massotti .10
8 Kelvin Pruenster .05
9 Mike Clemons 1.00
10 Chris Schultz .10
11 Andrew Murray .05
12 Lance Chomyc .10
13 Ed Berry .05
14 Harold Hallman .10
15 Dave Van Belleghem .05
16 Rodney Harding .10
17 Rickey Foggie .20
18 Darrell Smith .25
19 Bob Skemp .05
20 Carl Brazley .10
21 J.P. Izquierdo .05
22 Mike Campbell .10
23 Reggie Pleasant .05
24 Dan Ferrone .10
25 Kevin Smellie .05
26 Don Wilson .05
27 Adam Rita (CO) .05
28 Greg Peterson .05
29 David Sapunjis .50
30 Srecko Zizakovic .05
31 Carl Bland .05
32 Errol Tucker .05
33 Allen Pitts .30
34 Pee Wee Smith .30
35 Will Johnson .30
36 Kent Warnock .10
37 Brent Matich .05
38 Stu Laird .10
39 Shawn Beals .05
40 Darcy Kopp .05
41 Ken Moore .05
42 Alondra Johnson .10
43 Matt Finlay .05
44 Andy McVey .05
45 Paul Clatney .05
46 Karl Anthony .05
47 Bruce Covernton .35
48 Mark McLoughlin (UER) (Name misspelled several times on the card back) .10
49 Pat Hinds .05
50 Eric Mitchel (UER) (Misspelled Mitchell on both sides) .20
51 Dan Wicklum .05
52 Tim Cofield .25
53 Steve Taylor .35
54 Darryl Hall .10
55 Angelo Snipes .60
56 Shawn Daniels .05
57 Terrence Jones .25
58 Brian Bonner .05
59 Kari Yli-Renko .05
60 Denny Chronopoulos .05
61 Damon Allen .10
62 Reggie Barnes .30
63 Andre Francis (UER) (Misspelled Frances on card front) .10
64 Rob Smith .25
65 Anthony Drawhorn .20
66 David Conrad (UER) (Back text says team is Green Riders) .05
67 Irv Daymond .05
68 Terry Baker .10
69 Daniel Hunter .05
70 Gord Weber .05
71 Tom Burgess .30
72 Charles Gordon .05
73 Bobby Gordon .05
74 Jock Climie .25
75 Patrick Wayne .05
76 Sean Foudy .05
77 James Ellingson .10
78 Gregg Stumon .10
79 John Kropke .10
80 Stephen Jones .25
81 Ron Smeltzer .05
82 Scott Campbell .50
83 Henry Williams 1.00
84 Willie Pless .25
85 Dan Murphy .05
86 Chris Armstrong .05
87 Tracy Ham .50
88 Larry Wruck .10
89 Rod Connop .05
90 Jim Sandusky .25
91 Randy Ambrosie .05
92 Michel Bourgeau .10
93 Bennie Goods (UER) (Misspelled Benny) .10
94 Rob Davidson .05
95 Leroy Blugh .05
96 Brian Walling .05
97 Michael Soles .10
98 Craig Ellis .25
99 Pierre Vercheval .10
100 Matt Dunigan .40
101 Enis Jackson .05
102 Tom Muecke .20
103 Jed Roberts .05
104 Steve Krupey .05
105 Blake Marshall .35
106 Trevor Bowles .10
107 Eddie Thomas .05
108 Rocket Ray (Jogo Mascot) .10
109 Checklist 1-110 (UER) (50 Eric Mitchell 93 Benny Goods) .10
110 Tom Burgess .35
111 Bob Cameron .05
112 James West .20
113 Chris Walby .15
114 David Black .05
115 Nick Benjamin .10
116 Matt Pearce .05
117 Bob Molle .05
118 Rod Hill .10
119 Kyle Hall .05
120 Danny McManus .35
121 Calvin Murphy .15
122 Stan Mikawos .05
123 Bobby Evans .05
124 Larry Willis .10
125 Eric Streater .10
126 Perry Tuttle .20
127 Leon Hatziioannou .05
128 Sammy Garza .05
129 Greg Battle .25
130 Elfrid Payton .25
131 Troy Westwood .20
132 Mike Gray .05
133 Dave Vankoughnett .05
134 Paul Randolph .05
135 Darryl Sampson .05
136 Less Browne .10
137 Quency Williams .05
138 Robert Mimbs .35
139 Matt Dunigan 1.50
140 Dan Rashovich .05
141 Dan Farthing .05
142 Bruce Boyko .05
143 Kim McCloud .05
144 Richie Hall .05
145 Paul Vajda .05
146 Willis Jacox .25
147 Glen Scrivner .05
148 Dave Ridgway .15
149 Lucius Floyd .10
150 James King .05
151 Kent Austin .50
152 Jeff Fairholm .10
153 Roger Aldag .10
154 Albert Brown .05
155 Chris Gioskos .05
156 Stacey Hairston .05
157 Glen Suitor .10
158 Milson Jones .10
159 Vic Stevenson .05
160 Bob Poley .05
161 Bobby Jurasin .20
162 Gary Lewis .05
163 Donald Narcisse .25
164 Mike Anderson .05
165 Nick Mazzoli .05
166 Lance Trumble .05
167 Dale Sanderson .05
168 Todd Wiseman .05
169 Mark Dennis .05
170 Peter Giftopoulos .10
171 Ken Evraire .10
172 Darrell Harle .05
173 Terry Wright .05
174 Jamie Morris .20
175 Corris Ervin .05
176 Don McPherson .30
177 Jason Riley .05
178 Tim Jackson .05
179 Todd Dillon .10
180 Lee Knight .05
181 Scott Douglas .05
182 Dave Richardson .05
183 Wally Zatylny .10
184 Rickey Martin .05
185 John Motton .30
186 Mark Waterman .05
187 Ernie Schramayr .05
188 Miles Gorrell .05
189 Tony Champion .20
190 Earl Winfield .25
191 John Zajdel .05
192 Danny Barrett .30
193 Ian Sinclair .10
194 Norman Jefferson .05
195 Ryan Hanson .05
196 Matt Clark .15
197 Leo Groenewegen .05
198 Ray Alexander .10
199 James Mills .20
200 Jon Volpe .60
201 Doug Hocking .05
202 Tony Kimbrough .05
203 Lui Passaglia .15
204 Bruce Holmes .05
205 Jamie Taras .05
206 Derek MacCready .05
207 Jay Christensen .10
208 O.J. Brigance .30
209 Robin Belanger .05
210 Stewart Hill .10
211 Mike Marasco .05
212 Mike Trevathan .10
213 Chris Major .25
214 Steve Rodehutskors .10
215 Paul Wetmore .05
216 Ken Pettway .05
217 Darren Flutie 1.25
218 Giulio Caravatta .05
219 Murray Pezim .10
220 Checklist 111-220 .10

1992 JOGO CFL Missing Years

NM/M
Complete Set (22): 20.00
Common Player: 1.00
1 Larry Smith 1.50
2 Mike Nelms 1.50
3 John Sciarra 2.00
4 Ed Chalupka 1.00
5 Mike Rae 1.50
6 Terry Metcalf (UER) (His CFL years were 78-80, not 78-90) 2.50
7 Chuck Ealey 5.00
8 Junior Ah-You 1.50
9 Mike Samples 1.00
10 Ray Nettles 1.00
11 Dickie Harris 1.00
12 Willie Burden 3.00
13 Johnny Rodgers 5.00
14 Anthony Davis 3.00
15 Joe Pisarcik (UER) (His CFL years were 74-76, not 74-75) 1.50
16 Jim Washington 1.00
17 Tom Scott (UER) (11 years in CFL, not 10) 1.50
18 Butch Norman 1.00
19 Steve Molnar 1.00
20 Jerry Tagge 2.50
21 Leon Bright (UER) (His CFL years were 77-80, not 77-79) 2.50
22 Waddell Smith 2.00

1992 JOGO CFL Stamp Cards

NM/M
Complete Set (5): 30.00
Common Player: 6.00
1 CFL Hall of Fame Museum and Statue 6.00
2 Toronto Argonauts 1991 Grey Cup Champs 6.00
3 Tom Pate Memorial Trophy 6.00
4 Russ Jackson (MVP) 6.00
5 Oldest Trophy in The Hall of Fame (Montreal Football Challenge Cup) 6.00

1993 JOGO CFL

NM/M
Complete Set (220): 60.00

Complete Series 1 (110): 35.00
Complete Series 2 (110): 25.00
Common Player: .20
1 Stephen Jones .50
2 Chris Gioskos .20
3 Treamelle Taylor .20
4 Irv Daymond .20
5 Gord Weber .20
6 James Ellingson .35
7 Lybrant Robinson .20
8 Michael Allen .75
9 Greg Stumon .35
10 Darren Joseph .35
11 Terry Baker .35
12 Denis Chronopoulos .20
13 Tom Burgess 1.00
14 Wayne Walker .50
15 Brendan Rogers .20
16 Matt Pearce .20
17 Chris Tsangaras .20
18 Leon Hatziioannou .20
19 Bob Cameron 1.00
20 Don Smith .20
21 Michael Richardson 1.00
22 Jayson Dzikowicz .20
23 Matt Dunigan 2.00
24 Steve Grant .20
25 Rob Crifo .20
26 Dave Vankoughnett .20
27 Paul Massotti .35
28 Blaine Schmidt .20
29 Dave Van Belleghem .20
30 Hank Ilesic .20
31 Reggie Pleasant .35
32 Tracy Ham 1.00
33 Mike Clemons 2.00
34 Lance Chomyc .35
35 Ken Benson .20
36 Chris Green .20
37 Mike Campbell .35
38 Chris Schultz .35
39 Reggie Rogers .35
40 John Hood .35
41 Dave Richardson .20
42 Mike Jovanovich .35
43 Joey Jauch .35
44 Lubo Zizokovich .20
45 Don McPherson .35
46 Brett Williams .50
47 Tod Wiseman .20
48 Jim Jauch .20
49 Erus Sanchez .35
50 Scott Walker .20
51 Roger Hennig .20
52 Glen Suitor .35
53 Bobby Jurasin .35
54 Scott Hendrickson .20
55 Venson Donelson .20
56 Dan Rahsovich .20
57 Kent Austin .75
58 Ray Elgaard .35
59 Dave Ridgway .50
60 Byron Williams .20
61 Larry Ryckman (PRES) .20
62 Karl Anthony .20
63 Greg Knox .20
64 Ken Moore .20
65 Allen Pitts .50
66 Matt Finlay .35
67 Tony Martino .20
68 Harold Hasselbach 1.00
69 David Sapunjis 1.00
70 Andy McVey .20
71 Stu Laird .35
72 Derrick Crawford .35
73 Mark McLoughlin .20
74A Will Johnson (ERR) (Eskimo logo) 2.00
74B Will Johnson (COR) (Stampeder logo) .75
75 Don Wilson .20
76 J.P. Izquierdo .20
77 Henry Williams 1.25
78 Larry Wruck .35
79 David Shelton .35
80 Damion Lyons .20
81 Jed Roberts .20
82 Trent Brown .20
83 Michel Bourgeau .35
84 Blake Dermott .35
85 Willie Pless .50
86 Leroy Blugh .20
87 Steve Krupey .20
88 Jim Sandusky .35
89 Danny Barrett .50
90 James West .50
91 Glen Scrivner .20
92 Tyrone Jones .35
93A Jon Volpe (Photo has poor color) 2.00
93B John Volpe (corrected) .75
94 Less Browne .35
95 Matt Clark .35
96 Andre Francis .35
97 Darren Flutie 1.25
98 Ray Alexander .35
99 Rob Smith 1.00
100 Fred Anderson (Managing General Partner) .35
101 Rob White .20
102 Bobby Humphrey .35
103 Willie Bouyer .20
104 Titus Dixon .35
105 John Wiley .20
106 Kerwin Bell 1.00
107 Carl Parker .20
108 Mike Oliphant .75
109 David Archer 2.50
110 Freeman Baysinger .35
111 Gerlad Alphin .35
112 Gerald Wilcox .35
113 Reggie Barnes .50
114 Michel Raby .20
115 Charles Wright .20
116 Brett Young .35
117 Charles Gordon .20
118 Anthony Drawhorn .35
119 Daved Benefield .35
120 Patrick Burke .20
121 Joe Sardo .20
122 Dexter Manley .35
123 Bruce Beaton .20
124 Joe Fuller .20
125 Michel Lamy .20
126 Terrence Jones .50
127 Jeff Croonen .20
128 Leonard Johnson .20
129 Dan Payne .20
130 Carlton Lance .20
131 Errol Brown .20
132 Wayne Drinkwater .20
133 Malvin Hunter .20
134 Maurice Crum .20
135 Brooks Findlay .20
136 Ray Bernard .20
137 Paul Osbaldiston .35
138 Mark Dennis .35
139 Glenn Kulka .35
140 Lee Knight .20
141 Mike O'Shea 1.00
142 Paul Bushey .20
143 Nick Mazzoli .20
144 Earl Winfield .50
145 Gary Wilkerson .20
146 Jason Riley .20
147 Bob MacDonald .35
148 Dale Sanderson .20
149 Bobby Dawson .20
150 Rod Connop .20
151 Tony Woods .35
152 Dan Murphy .20
153 Mike DuMaresq .20
154 Alan Boyko .20
155 Vaughn Booker .75
156 Elfrid Payton .35
157 Mike Kerrigan .50
158 Charles Anthony .20
159 Brent Matich .20
160 Craig Hendrickson .20
161 Dave Pitcher .20
162 Stewart Hill .35
163 Terryl Ulmer .20
164 Paul Cranmer .20
165 Mike Saunders 1.50
166 Doug Flutie 2.00
167 Kelian Matthews .20
168 Kip Texada .20
169 Jonathan Wilson .20
170 Bruce Dickson .20
171 Mike Trevathan .35
172 Vic Stevenson .20
173 Keith Powe .20
174 Eddie Taylor .20
175 Tim Lorenz .20
176 Sesan Millington .35
177 Ryan Hanson .20
178 Ed Berry .20
179 Kent Warnock .35
180 Spencer McLennan .20
181 Brian Walling .35
182 Danny McManus .75
183 Donovan Wright .20
184 Giulio Caravatta .20
185 Derek MacCready .20
186 Greg Eaglin .20
187 Jim Mills .20
188 Tom Europe .20
189 Zock Allen .30
190 Ian Sinclair .35
191 O.J. Brigance 1.00
192 Steve Rodehutskors .35
193 Lou Cafazzo .20
194 Mark Dube .20
195 Srecko Zizakovic .20
196 Alondra Johnson .35
197 Rocco Romano .20
198 Raymond Biggs .20
199 Frank Marof .20
200 Brian Wiggins .35
201 Marvin Pope .20
202 Gerald Vaughn .20
203 Todd Storme .20
204 Blair Zerr .20
205 Eric Johnson .35
206 Mark Pearce .20
207 Will Moore 2.00
208 Bruce Plummer .20
209 Kari Yli-Renko .20
210 Doug Parrish .20
211 Warren Hudson .35
212 Kevin Whitley .20
213 Enis Jackson .20
214 Wally Zatylny .35
215 Bruce Elliott .20
216 Harold Hallman .35
217 Glenn Rogers .20
218 Manny Hazard .50
219 Robert Clark .35
220 Doug Flutie (UER) (Three misspelled Tree on back) 2.00

1993 JOGO CFL Missing Years

NM/M
Complete Set (22): 15.00
Common Player: .60
1B Jim Edwards 1.00
2B Lou Harris .75
3B George Mira 1.25
4B Fred Biletnikoff 3.50
5B Randy Halsall .60
6B Don Sweet .60
7B Jim Coode .60
8B Steve Mazurak .75
9B Wayne Allison .60
10B Paul Williams .60
11B Eric Allen 1.25
12B M.L. Harris .75
13B James Sykes 1.50
14B Chuck Zapiec .75
15B George McGowan .60
16B Bob Macoritti .75
17B Chuck Walton .60
18B Willie Armstead .75
19B Rocky Long .60
20B Gene Mack .60
21B David Green 1.25
22B Don Warrington .75

1994 JOGO CFL Caravan

NM/M
Complete Set (22): 40.00
Common Player: 1.00
1 Glenn Kulka 1.00
2 Jock Climie 2.00
3 Danny Barrett 3.00
4 Stephen Jones 2.00
5 Mike Clemons 4.00
6 Pierre Vercheval 1.50
7 Ken Evraire 1.50
8 Brett Williams (UER) (Misspelled Willians on card front) 1.50
9 Wally Zatylny 1.50
10 Mike O'Shea 2.50
11 Earl Winfield 2.00
12 Mike Oliphant 2.00
13 Matt Dunigan 4.00
14 Chris Walby 2.00
15 Tracy Ham 3.00
16 Darrell Smith 2.00
17 Glen Suitor 1.50
18 Mark McLoughlin 1.00
19 Bruce Covernton 1.50
20 Willie Pless 2.00
21 Henry Williams 4.00
22 Lui Passaglia 1.50

1994 JOGO CFL

NM/M
Complete Set (310): 75.00
Complete Series 1 (110): 20.00
Complete Series 2 (110): 20.00
Complete Series 3 (90): 35.00
Common Player (1-110): .15
Common Player (111-220): .15
Common Player (221-310): .30
1 Danny Barrett .50
2 Remi Trudel .15
3 Terry Baker .15
4 Paul Clatney .15
5 Michael Richardson .75
6 John Kropke .30
7 Glenn Kulka .15
8 Daved Benefield .30
9 Derek MacCready .15
10 Jessie Small .30
11 Chris Gioskos .15
12 Gregg Stumon .30
13 Lee Johnson .30
14 Michael Jefferson Jr. .15
15 Mario Perry .15
16 Joe Mero .15
17 Reggie Barnes .30
18 Mike Stowell .15
19 Tony Moss .15
20 Antoine Worthman .15
21 Joe Fuller .15
22 Daniel Hunter .15
23 Doug Flutie 2.50
24 Douglas Craft .50
25 Lubo Zizakovic .15
26 Srecko Zizakovic .15
27 Stu Laird .30
28 Brian Wiggins .30
29 Will Johnson .50
30 David Sapunjis 1.00
31 Rocco Romano .15
32 Raymond Biggs .15
33 Ken Moore .15
34 Matt Finlay .30
35 Ian Sinclair .30
36 Glen Scrivner .15
37 Less Browne .30
38 Darren Flutie 1.00
39 Freeman Baysinger .15
40 Kent Austin .50
41 Donovan Wright .15
42 Cory Philpot 1.50
43 Tom Europe .15
44 Giulio Caravatta .15
45 Mike Clemons 1.50
46 Leon Hatziioannou .15
47 Blaine Schmidt .15
48 Reggie Pleasant .30
49 Paul Masotti .30
50 Pierre Vercheval .30
51 Duane Forde .15
52 Jeff Fairholm .30
53 Carl Coulter .15
54 Bobby Gordon .15
55 Mike Jovanovich .15
56 Chris Johnstone .15
57 Matt Pearce .15
58 Bob Cameron .75
59 Brett MacNeil .15
60 Blaise Bryant .40
61 Chris Tsangaris .15
62 Dave Vankoughnett .15
63 Gerald Alphin .30
64 Alfred Jackson .30
65 Jayson Dzikowicz .15
66 Bobby Evans .15
67 Dave Ridgway .30
68 Bobby Jurasin .30
69 Dan Payne .15
70 Ray Elgaard .50
71 Dan Farthing .15
72 Glen Suitor .30
73 Mike Saunders 1.00
74 Brent Matich .15
75 Scott Hendrickson .15
76 Dan Rashovich .15
77 Wayne Drinkwater .15
78 Larry Wruck .30
79 J.P. Izquierdo .15
80 Jed Roberts .15
81 Michel Bourgeau .30
82 Malvin Hunter .15
83 Bruce Dickson .15
84 Jim Sandusky .50
85 Mike DuMaresq .15
86 Tracy Gravely .30
87 Tracy Ham 1.00
88 John Congemi .30
89 Darrell Corbin .15
90 Maurice Kelly .30
91 Doug Flutie (MVP) 2.50
92 Alfred Jordan .30
93 Curtis Mayfield .40
94 David Hollis .15
95 James Blake .15
96 Anthony Blue .30
97 Jeffrey Sawyer .15
98 Al Whiting .15
99 Brad LaCombe .15
100 Wally Zatylny .30
101 Bob Torrance .15
102 Jeffery Fields .15
103 John G. Motton Jr. .30
104 Todd Wiseman .15
105 Mike O'Shea .75
106 Scott Douglas .15
107 Dale Sanderson .15
108 David Diaz-Infante .30
109 Mike Kiselak .15
110 Chris Thieneman .15
111 Horace Brooks .30
112 Andre Francis .30
113 Nick Mazzoli .15
114 Irv Daymond .15
115 Alfred Smith .15
116 Stephen Jones .40
117 Bruce Beaton .15
118 Corey Dowden .15
119 Gerald Collins .30
120 Joe Washington .30
121 Irvin Smith .15
122 Harold Nash Jr. .30
123 Ray Savage Jr. .15
124 Billy Scott .15
125 Aaron Kanner .15
126 Ben Williams .40
127 Keith Browner .30
128 Eros Sanchez .30
129 Don Caparotti .15
130 Earnest Fields .15
131 O.J. Brigance .75
132 Walter Wilson .30
133 Allen Pitts .50
134 Tony Stewart .30
135 Marvin Pope .15
136 Tony Martino .15
137 Vince Danielsen .15
138 Pee Wee Smith .50
139 Bruce Covernton .40
140 Greg Knox .15
141 Gerald Vaughn .15
142 Jay McNeil .15
143 Larry Ryckman (OWN) .15
144 Blair Zerr .15
145 Danny McManus .75
146 Jamie Taras .15
147 Kelly Sims .30
148 Denny Chronopoulos .15
149 Enis Jackson .15
150 Virgil Robertson .15
151 Tyrone Chatman .15
152 Brian Forde .15
153 Andrew Stewart .15
154 Ryan Hanson .15
155 Francois Belanger .15
156 Tony O'Billovich .15
157 Erik White .30
158 Kevin Whitley .15
159 Chris Schultz .30
160 Mike Campbell .15
161 Wayne Lammie .15
162 Keith Ballard .15
163 Neil Fort .15
164 Charles Anthony .15
165 John Buddenberg .15
166 Allan Boyko .15
167 Paul Randolph .15
168 Gerald Wilcox .40
169 Brendan Rogers .15
170 Kim Phillips .15
171 David Williams .30
172 James Pruitt .30
173 Kevin O'Brien .15
174 Tre Everett .30
175 Hurlie Brown .15
176 Malcolm Frank .15
177 Sean Brantley .15
178 Aaron Ruffin .15
179 Anthony Drawhorn .30
180 Larry Thompson .75
181 Brooks Findlay .15
182 Dallas Rysavy .15
183 Ray Bernard .15
184 Donald Narcisse .75
185 Warren Jones .30
186 Tom Gerhart .15
187 David Robinson Jr. .30
188 Damon Allen .30
189 Henry Williams 1.00
190 Jay Christensen .30
191 Trent Brown .15
192 Rod Connop .15
193 Michael Soles .30
194 Vance Hammond .15
195 Maurice Miller .15
196 Shar Pourdanesh .50
197 Elfrid Payton .30
198 Ken Benson .15
199 David Maeva .15
200 Carlos Huerta .30
201 Prince Wimbley III .30
202 Anthony Calvillo 2.00
203 Kenny Wilhite .30
204 Peter Shorts .15
205 Willie Fears .30
206 Rod Harris .75
207 Terry Wright .15
208 Stephen Bates .30
209 John Hood .30
210 Steven McKee .15
211 Richard Nurse .30
212 Lee Knight .15
213 Joey Jauch .30
214 Dave Richardson .15
215 Paul Bushey .15
216 Lou Cafazzo .15
217 Don Odegard .15
218 Mark Ledbetter .15
219 Curtis Moore .15
220 CFL Team Helmets (Set number card) .30
221 Patrick Burke .30
222 Dean Noel .60
223 Leonard Johnson .30
224 Darren Joseph .60
225 Adam Rita (CO) .30
226 Fred Ward .60
227 Tony Bailey .30
228 Frank Marof .30
229 Andrew Thomas .60
230 Peter Tuipulotu .60
231 Shawn Beals .30
232 Ken Watson .30
233 Robert Holland .30
234 John Terry .30
235 Michael Philbrick .30
236 Reggie Slack 1.25
237 Gary Wilkerson (UER) (First name misspelled Garry on back) .30
238 Brett Young .30
239 Eric Carter .60
240 Sheldon Canley .60
241 Lester Smith .30
242 Donald Igwebuike .60
243 Keith Ballard .30
244 Roger Reinson .30
245 Dwayne Dmytryshyn .30
246 Marvin Coleman .30
247 Ken Burress .30
248 Jearld Baylis .75
249 Rickey Foggie .75
250 Dave Dinnall .60
251 Darrell Harle .30
252 Peter Martin .60
253 Val St. Germain .30
254 Tim Cofield .75
255 Charles Gordon .30
256 Keilly Rush .30
257 James Pruitt .60
258 Brian McCurdy .60
259 Joe Johnson (UER) (Front says last name is Jackson) .60
260 Joe Burgos .30
261 Tim Jackson .30
262 George Nimako .60
263 Hency Charles .30
264 Eric Drage .60
265 Joe Sardo .30
266 Norm Casola .30
267 Dave Irwin .60
268 Tommy Henry .30
269 Taly Williams .30
270 Swift Burch III .30
271 Keita Crespina .30
272 Michael Brooks .60
273 Chris Armstrong .30
274 Karl Anthony .30
275 David Archer 3.00
276 Kevin Robson .30
277 Jamie Holland .60
278 Don Smith .30
279 Norris Thomas .60
280 Matt Dunigan 1.50
281 Greg Clarke .30
282 Del Lyles .30
283 Alan Wetmore .30
284 Errol Brown .30
285 Ryan Carey .30
286 Rob Davidson .30
287 Ed Kucy .30
288 Tom Burgess 1.00
289 Peter Miller .30
290 Dale Joseph .30
291 Chris Burns .30
292 Nathaniel Bolton .60
293 Byron Williams .15
294 David Harper .30
295 Jason Wallace .30
296 Greg Joelson .15
297 Doug Parrish .30
298 Sean Fleming .30
299 Mike Lee .60
300 Chris Morris .60
301 Eddie Brown .60
302 Blake Dermott .30
303 Brian Walling .60
304 Charles Miles .60
305 Rob Crifo .60
306 Nick Benjamin .60
307 Jim Speros (PR/OWN) .60
308 Robert Presbury .30
309 Mike Pringle 2.50
310 Jon Volpe 1.00

1994 JOGO CFL Hall of Fame C

NM/M
Complete Set (25): 18.00
Common Player: .75
C1 Leo Lewis 2.00
C2 Tom Brown .75
C3 Samuel Berger .75
C4 David Fennell 1.25
C5 Arthur Chipman .75
C6 Tony Gabriel 1.25
C7 Frank Clair .75
C8 Dean Griffing .75
C9 Hec Crighton .75
C10 Eddie James .75
C11 Andrew Currie .75
C12 Ab Box .75
C13 Gord Perry .75
C14 Terry Evanshen 2.00
C15 Syd Halter .75
C16 Don Luzzi 1.25
C17 Norm Kimball .75
C18 Percival Molson .75
C19 Bob Kramer .75
C20 Angelo Mosca 2.50
C21 Ralph Cooper .75
C22 Ken Charlton .75
C23 Jim Young 1.25
C24 Joe Tubman .75
C25 Virgil Wagner 1.25

1994 JOGO CFL Hall of Fame D

NM/M
Complete Set (25): 18.00
Common Player: .75
D1 Teddy Morris .75
D2 John Ferraro .75
D3 Len Back .75
D4 Harold Ballard 1.25
D5 Seppi DuMoulin .75
D6 Herman Harrison 1.25
D7 William Foulds .75
D8 Peter Dalla Riva 1.25
D9 John Metras .75
D10 Don Sutherin 1.25
D11 Ken Preston .75
D12 Ellison Kelly 1.25
D13 Annis Stukus .75
D14 Brian Timmis .75
D15 Ralph Sazio .75
D16 Hugh Stirling .75
D17 Jimmie Simpson .75
D18 Russ Rebholz .75
D19 Seymour Wilson .75
D20 Paul Rowe .75
D21 Jeff Russel .75
D22 Art Stevenson .75
D23 Whit Tucker 1.25
D24 Dave Thelen 1.25
D25 Tom Wilkinson 2.00

1994 JOGO CFL Hall of Fame Inductees

NM/M
Complete Set (5): 5.00
Common Player: .75
1 Bill Baker 1.00
2 Tom Clements 2.50
3 Gene Gaines 1.00
4 Don McNaughton .75
5 Title Card .75

1994 JOGO CFL Missing Years

NM/M
Complete Set (20): 12.00
Common Player: .50
C1 Steve Ferrughelli (UER) (Photo actually John O'Leary) 1.50
C2 Rhome Nixon .75
C3 Don Moorhead .75
C4 Mike Widger .75
C5 Pete Catan .75
C6 Ron Meeks .50
C7 Ezzret Anderson 1.25
C8 Bill Hatanaka .50
C9 Joe Jackson .75
C10 Tom Campana .75
C11 Vernon Perry 1.00
C12 Ian Mofford .75
C13 Walter Highsmith .75
C14 Jake Dunlop .75
C15 Bill Stevenson .50
C16 Pete Lavorato .50
C17 Cyril McFall .50
C18 Maurice Butler .50
C19 Tom Pate 1.25
C20 Eugene Clark 1.25

1995 JOGO CFL

NM/M
Complete Set (399): 145.00
Complete Series 1 (110): 40.00
Complete Series 2 (110): 40.00
Complete Series 3 (110): 40.00
Complete Update Set (69): 25.00
Common Player: .20
1 Doug Flutie 3.00
2 Lubo Zizakovic .20
3 Srecko Zizakovic .20
4 Greg Knox .20
5 Kenny Walker .35
6 Raymond Biggs .20
7 Stu Laird .35
8 Jeff Garcia 10.00
9 Alfred Jordan .35
10 Tracy Gravely .35
11 Tracy Ham .75
12 O.J. Brigance .75
13 Mike Pringle 1.50
14 Nick Subis .20
15 Irvin Smith .20
16 Shar Pourdanesh .35
17 Lester Smith .20
18 Josh Miller .20
19 Jamie Taras .20
20 Darren Flutie 1.00
21 Danny McManus .75
22 Spencer McLennan .20
23 Tony Collier .20
24 Cory Philpot 1.00
25 Ian Sinclair .35
26 Dave Chaytors .20
27 Dave Ritchie (UER) (Richie on front) .20
28 Rob Wallow .20
29 Brad Breedlove .50
30 Adrian Smith .20
31 Stephen Bates .20
32 Don Odegard .20
33 Eric Nelson .20
34 Danton Barto .20
35 Donald Smith .20
36 Gary Morris .20
37 Mike Jovanovich .20
38 Danny Barrett .35
39 Ray Alexander .35
40 John Kropke .35

41 Remi Trudel .20
42 Ray Bernard .20
43 Pat Mahon .20
44 Dan Murphy .20
45 Stefen Reid .20
46 Marcus Gates .20
47 Tom Gerhard .20
48 Mike Kiselak .20
49 David Archer 2.00
50 Tommie Smith .20
51 Roman Anderson .20
52 Tony Burse .20
53 Todd Jordan .20
54 Peter Shorts .20
55 Jimmy Klingler .75
56 Mark Ledbetter .20
57 Thomas Rayam .20
58 Andre Strode .20
59 Eddie Davis .20
60 Jimmie Reed .20
61 Fernando Thomas .20
62 Craig Gibson .20
63 Akaba Delaney .20
64 Mike Clemons 1.25
65 Kent Austin .75
66 Joe Burgos .20
67 John Terry .20
68 Don Wilson .20
69 Eric Blount (DE) .20
70 Reggie Barnes .35
71 Darrick Branch .20
72 P.J. Gleason .20
73 Rod Connop .20
74 J.P. Izquierdo .20
75 Jed Roberts .20
76 Jim Sandusky .20
77 Chris Vargas .20
78 Henry Williams .75
79 Michael Soles .35
80 Robert Holland .20
81 Larry Wruck .35
82 Dale Sanderson .20
83 Anthony Calvillo .75
84 Kalin Hall .20
85 Sam Rogers .20
86 Lee Knight .20
87 Wally Zatylny .35
88 Earl Winfield .35
89 Dave Richardson .20
90 Mike O'Shea .75
91 Bruce Boyko .20
92 Dave Ridgway .35
93 Dave Van Belleghem .20
94 Mike Anderson .20
95 Ray Elgaard .35
96 Dan Rashovich .20
97 Wayne Drinkwalter .20
98 Brent Matich .20
99 Joe Fuller .20
100 Freeman Baysinger .20
101 Billy Joe Tolliver .75
102 Martin Patton .20
103 Wayne Walker .75
104 Bjorn Nittmo .75
105 Alan Wetmore .20
106 K.D. Williams .20
107 Bob Cameron .75
108 Ken Burress .20
109 Chris Johnstone .20
110 Allan Boyko .20
111 David Sapunjis 1.25
112 Matt Finlay .35
113 Jamie Crysdale .20
114 Marvin Pope .20
115 Craig Brenner .20
116 Vince Danielsen .20
117 Will Johnson .35
118 Tony Stewart .20
119 Chris Wright .50
120 Grant Carter .20
121 Karl Anthony .20
122 Elfrid Payton .35
123 Ken Watson .20
124 Cory Mantyka .20
125 Todd Furdyk .20
126 Keithen McCant .20
127 Ryan Hanson .20
128 Glen Scrivner .20
129 Mike Trevathan .35
130 Tom Europe .20
131 Giulio Caravatta .20
132 Eddie Thomas .20
133 Shelton Quarles .20
134 Robert E. Davis II .20
135 Damon Allen .35
136 Derek Brown .20
137 Joe Horn .50
138 John Tweet Martin .20
139 Greg Battle .35
140 Ed Berry .20
141 Irv Daymond .20
142 Jay Christensen .35
143 Michael Richardson .50
144 James Ellingson .35
145 Brett Young .35
146 Kai Bjorn .20
147 James Monroe .20
148 Eric Geter .20
149 Emanuel Martin .20
150 DeWayne Knight .20
151 Mike Saunders 1.00
152 David Harper .20
153 Bobby Humphrey .35
154 Charles Franks .20
155 Jeffrey Sawyer .20
156 John Buddenberg .20
157 Willie Fears .35
158 Jason Wallace .20
159 Robert Gordon .20
160 Scott Player .35
161 York Kurinsky .20
162 Stephen Anderson .20
163 Shonte Peoples .20
164 Angelo Snipes .50
165 Ted Long .20
166 Anthony Drawhorn .35
167 Marvin Graves .20
168 Joe Sardo .20
169 Duane Forde .20
170 P.J. Martin .20
171 Jock Climie .20
172 Jeff Fairholm .35
173 Tommy Henry .20
174 Paul Masotti .35
175 Chris Green .20
176 Bruce Dickson .20
177 Darian Hagan .20
178 Malvin Hunter .20
179 Steve Krupey .20
180 Sean Fleming .20
181 Blake Dermott .35
182 Leroy Blugh .20
183 Steve Taylor .50
184 Eric Carter .35
185 Jessie Small .35
186 Blaine Schmidt .20
187 Lou Cafazzo .20
188 Doug Davies .20
189 Kelvin Means .20
190 Derek R. Grier .20
191 Darren Joseph .35
192 Aaron Ruffin .20
193 Dan Farthing .20
194 Dan Payne .20
195 Brooks Findlay .20
196 Paul Vajda .20
197 Ron Goetz .20
198 Tim Broady .20
199 Terryl Ulmer .20
200 Harold Nash Jr. .35
201 Mike Stowell .20
202 Ben Williams .35
203 Curtis Mayfield .35
204 Reggie Rogers .35
205 Donnell Johnson .20
206 Jon Heidenreich .20
207 Ronald Perry .20
208 Robbie Keen .20
209 Alex Mash Jr. .20
210 Jason Mallett .20
211 Miles Gorrell .20
212 Juran Bolden .75
213 Greg Clark .20
214 Ryan Carey .20
215 Del Lyles .20
216 Brendan Rogers .20
217 Kevin Robson .20
218 Paul Randolph .20
219 Shannon Garrett .20
220 Charlie Clemons .20
221 Matt Dunigan 1.50
222 Jay McNeil .20
223 Denny Chronopoulos .20
224 Bobby Pandelidis .20
225 Bruce Beaton .20
226 Mark Pearce .20
227 Rocco Romano .20
228 Alondra Johnson .35
229 Tony Martino .20
230 John James .20
231 Courtney Griffin .20
232 Robert Davis .20
233 Manny Hazard .35
234 Joe Mero .20
235 Maurice Kelly .35
236 Michael Morreale .20
237 Reggie Slack .50
238 Greg Eaglin .20
239 Noah Cantor .20
240 Shawn Daniels .20
241 Charles Gordon .20
242 Enis Jackson .20
243 Matt Clark .35
244 Dave Lucas .20
245 Roger Hennig .20
246 Leonard Nelson .20
247 George Bethune .20
248 Maurice Miller .20
249 Kenny Walker .35
250 Andre Ware 1.00
251 Jay Macias .20
252 Mark Ricks .20
253 Chris Tsangaris .20
254 Wayne Lammie .20
255 Derek MacCready .20
256 Paul Yatkowski .20
257 Horace Brooks .35
258 Kerry Brown .20
259 Jude St. John .20
260 Mike Schad 1.00
261 Malcolm Frank .20
262 Kenny Wilhite .35
263 Bill Hess .20
264 Grady Cavness .35
265 Roosevelt Collins Jr. .20
266 Darren Muilenberg .20
267 Kitrick Taylor .75
268 Chuck Esty .20
269 Myron M. Wise .20
270 James King .20
271 Jim Kemp 1.00
272 Oscar Giles .35
273 Dave Ritchie (CO) .20
274 Joe Kralik .20
275 Troy Mills .20
276 Mark Stock .20
277 Pierre Vercheval .35
278 Terry Baker .35
279 Scott Douglas .20
280 Leon Hatziioannou .20
281 Jeff Cummins .20
282 Allen Pitts .50
283 Ken Walcott .20
284 Swift Burch III .20
285 Charles Davis .20
286 Leo Groenewegen .20
287 Bennie Goods .35
288 Craig Hendrickson .20
289 John Kalin .20
290 Trent Brown .20
291 Marc Tobert .20
292 Nick Mazzoli .20
293 Singor Mobley .20
294 Dondre Owens .20
295 Kerwin Bell .75
296 Mike Kerrigan .50
297 Hassan Bailey .20
298 Frank Marof .20
299 Derrick McAdoo .35
300 Brian McCurdy .35
301 Larry Thompson .50
302 Errol Brown .20
303 Troy Alexander .20
304 Dave Pitcher .20
305 Joey Jauch .35
306 Gene Makowsky .20
307 Ventson Donelson .20
308 Gary Rogers .20
309 Carl Coulter .20
310 Chris Gioskos .20
311 Mike DuMaresq .20
312 Rob Crifo .20
313 Terry Smith .20
314 Don Robinson .20
315 Uzooma Okeke .20
316 Eldonta Osborne .20
317 Rob Hitchcock .20
318 Ray Savage Jr. .20
319 Terry Beauford .20
320 Cliff Baskerville .20
321 David Gamble .20
322 Darrius Watson .20
323 Tim Daniel .20
324 Len Johnson .20
325 Blaise Bryant .35
326 Doug Hocking .20
327 Sean Graham .20
328 Jamie Holland .35
329 Matt Pearce .20
330 Doug Flutie (C.F.L. MVP) 2.00
331 Donald Narcisse .50
332 Chuck Reed .20
333 Sheldon Benoit .20
334 John Motton .35
335 Franco Grilla .20
336 Brett MacNeil .20
337 Wade Miller .20
338 Steven McKee .20
339 Brad Elberg .20
340 Greg Patrick .20
341 Andrew Grigg .20
342 Kevin McDougal .20
343 Prince Wimbley III .35
344 Sam Hairston .20
345 Curtis Gordon .35
346 Chris Keneally .20
347 Michael Philbrick .20
348 Keith Embray .20
349 Steve Grant .20
350 Taly Williams .20
351 Garry Sawatzky .20
352 Dean Noel .35
353 Mike Armstrong .20
354 David Pool .20
355 Tyrone Edwards .20
356 Tim Cofield 1.00
357 Gerald Vaughn .20
358 Mark McLoughlin .20
359 Robert Dougherty .20
360 Norm Casola .20
361 Shawn Knight .20
362 Kelvin Means .20
363 Reggie Pleasant .35
364 Jim Smyrl .20
365 Fred Montgomery .20
366 Ron Perry .20
367 Jami Anderson .20
368 Jeff Reinebold .20
369 Steve Brannon .20
370 Jimmy Cunningham .50
371 Damion Lyons .20
372 John Tweet Martin .20
373 Mike Campbell .20
374 Jonathan Wilson .20
375 Sandy Annunziata .20
376 Brian Walling .20
377 Eric Blount (RB) .50
378 Tom Gerhart .20
379 Milt Stegall .20
380 Bob Kronenberg .20
381 Barry Rose .20
382 Tim Walton .20
383 Kelvin Harris .20
384 Dwayne Provo .20
385 Jayson Dzikowicz .20
386 Melendez Byrd .20
387 Val St. Germain .20
388 Dave Vankoughnett .20
389 Aaron Kanner .20
390 Nicky Richards .20
391 Rohan Marley .50
392 Chris Burns .20
393 Joe Fuller .20
394 Donovan Gans .20
395 Jermaine Chaney .20
396 Jackie Kellogg .20
397 Ray Savage Jr. .20
398 Oscar Giles .35
399 Jeff Neal .20

1995 JOGO CFL Athletes in Action

NM/M

Complete Set (21): 10.00
Common Player: .40
1 Kelly Sims .60
2 Craig Hendrickson .40
3 Kerwin Bell 1.50
4 Glenn Harper .40
5 Jim Sandusky .60
6 Eldonta Osborne .40
7 Guy Earle .40
8 Charles Anthony .40
9 O.J. Brigance 1.50
10 Junior Thurman .60
11 Erik White .60
12 Henry Newby .40
13 Darryl Sampson .40
14 Tony Woods .40
15 Sean Brantley .40
16 Shalon Baker .40
17 Greg Frers .40
18 Danny Barrett .60
19 John Earle .40
20 Tracy Ham 2.00
21 Jimmy Klingler 1.00

1995 JOGO CFL Missing Years

NM/M

Complete Set (20): 12.00
Common Player: .50
1D Jimmy Jones .75
2D Charlie Brandon .50
3D Erik Kramer (UER) (name spelled Krammer) 3.00
4D Jeff Avery .50
5D Wally Buono .50
6D Mike Strickland .75
7D Bob Toogood .75
8D Joe Hernandez .50
9D Doug Battershill .50
10D Al Brenner .50
11D Tim Anderson .50
12D Ted Provost .50
13D Eugene Goodlow .75
14D Rudy Florio .50
15D Joey Walters .75
16D Bob Viccars .50
17D Tyrone Walls .75
18D John Harvey .75
19D Dick Aldridge .50
20D Grady Cavness .75

1996 JOGO CFL

This 220-card set features players from the Canadian Football League.

NM/M

Complete Set (220): 50.00
Common Player: .20
1 Jeff Garcia .50
2 Jeff Cummins .50
3 Terry Baker .35
4 James Taras .20
5 Eric Blount RB .50
6 Dan Rashovich .20
7 Dale Sanderson .20
8 Paul Masotti .35
9 Giulio Caravatta .20
10 Stefen Reid .20
11 Lee Knight .20
12 Dave Vankoughnett .20
13 Stu Laird .35
14 Todd Storme .20
15 Glenn Rogers Jr. .20
16 Miles Gorrell .20
17 Mike Kiselak .20
18 Mike Trevathan .50
19 Troy Westwood .20
20 Michael Jovanovich .20
21 Alan Wetmore .20
22 Bruce Covernton .35
23 Ryan Carey .20
24 Larry Wruck .35
25 Lou Cafazzo .20
26 Mac Cody 1.00
27 Todd Furdyk .20
28 Shannon Garrett .20
29 Kenny Wilhite .35
30 Bruce Beaton .20
31 Tony Martino .20
32 Brooks Findlay .20
33 Matt Dunigan 1.00
34 Ed Kucy .20
35 Mike Clemons 1.00
36 Cory Philpot 1.00
37 Steve Taylor .50
38 Jackie Kellogg .20
39 Spencer McLennan .20
40 Jason Mallett .20
41 Robert Mimbs .75
42 Doug Davies .20
43 Malvin Hunter .20
44 Wayne Lammle .20
45 David Maeva .20
46 Jay McNeil .20
47 Ed Berry .20
48 Irvin Smith .20
49 Wade Miller .20
50 Dan Farthing .20
51 Tom Gerhart .20
52 Ray Bernard .20
53 Jude St. John .20
54 Terry Vaughn .20
55 Shelton Quarles .20
56 Kelvin Anderson 1.50
57 Mike Withycombe .20
58 Sean Graham .20
59 Errol Brown .20
60 Swift Burch III .20
61 Jed Roberts .20
62 Ted Long .20
63 Mike Morreale .20
64 Tyrone Chatman .20
65 Anthony McClanahan .20
66 David Pitcher .20
67 Shannon Baker .20
68 Fred Childress .20
69 John Terry .20
70 Chris Morris .50
71 Andrew Grigg .20
72 Reggie Givens .50
73 Cory Mantyka .20
74 Alfred Jordan .35
75 Harold Nash Jr. .20
76 Brett MacNeil .20
77 Brent Matich .20
78 Gerry Collins .20
79 Johnson Joseph .20
80 Jimmy Cunningham .50
81 Eddie Davis .20
82 Tom Europe .20
83 Darryl Hall .35
84 Tracy Gravely .20
85 Bob Cameron .50
86 Paul McCallum .20
87 Tyrone Williams .20
88 Maurice Kelly .35
89 Sammie Brennan .20
90 Ken Benson .20
91 Sean Millington .20
92 Greg Knox .20
93 Kevin Robson .20
94 Rod Harris .50
95 Charles Gordon .20
96 Donald Smith .20
97 Joe Mero .20
98 Reggie Slack .50
99 Garry Sawatzky .20
100 Adrion Smith .20
101 Allan Boyko .20
102 Scott Hendrickson .20
103 Eddie Britton .20
104 Will Johnson .50
105 John Raposo .20
106 Chris Tsangaris .20
107 Cooper Harris .20
108 Quinn Magnuson .20
109 Blaine Schmidt .20
110 David Archer 2.00
111 David Sapunjis .75
112 Stephen Anderson .20
113 Raymond Biggs .20
114 Jean-Agnes Charles .20
115 Vince Danielsen .20
116 Wayne Drinkwalter .35
117 Farell Duclair .20
118 Duane Forde .20
119 Rohn Meyer .20
120 Travis Moore .20
121 Kevin Reid .20
122 Roger Reinson .20
123 Gonzalo Floyd .20
124 Dwayne Provo .20
125 Peter Tuipulotu .20
126 Curtis Mayfield .35
127 Ray Elgaard .50
128 John James .20
129 Dave Van Belleghem .20
130 J.P. Izquierdo .20
131 Darren Joseph .35
132 Frank Jagas .20
133 Heath Rylance .20
134 Rick Walters .20
135 Michael Philbrick .20
136 Val St. Germain .20
137 Justin Ring .20
138 Mike Campbell .20
139 Burt Thornton .20
140 Jason Kaiser .20
141 Tim Brown .20
142 Ken Watson .20
143 Tommie Frasier 2.50
144 Tyrone Rodgers .20
145 Craig Hendrickson .20
146 Johnny R. Scott .20
147 Mark Pimiskern .20
148 Frank Pimiskern .20
149 Carl Coulter .20
150 Reggie Carthon .20
151 Ronald Williams .20
152 Ted Alford .20
153 Dave Chaytors .20
154 Robert Gordon .20
155 Jayson Dzikowicz .20
156 Lubo Zizakovic .20
157 Mike Hendricks .20
158 Obie Spanic .20
159 Andre Bolduc .20
160 Robert Drummond .50
161 Chuck Esty .20
162 Tommy Henry .20
163 Nick Richards .20
164 Profail Grier .20
165 Melvin Aldridge .20
166 Uzooma Okeke .20
167 Courtney Griffin .20
168 Leonard Humphries .20
169 Jason Wallace .20
170 Derek MacCready .20
171 Franky West .20
172 Kelvin Means .20
173 David Harper .20
174 Rob Stevenson .20
175 John Kalin .20
176 Nigel Williams .20
177 Chris Armstrong .50
178 Douglas Craft .50
179 Michael Soles .35
180 Mike Saunders 1.00
181 Michel Lamy .20
182 Jock Climie .50
183 Grant Carter .20
184 Hency Charles .20
185 Jason Bryant .20
186 Dexter Dawson .20
187 Glen Scrivener .20
188 K.D. Williams .20
189 Dean Lytle .20
190 Donovan Wright .20
191 Andrew Henry .20
192 Doug Flutie 3.50
193 Brendan Rogers .20
194 Darian Hagan .20
195 Jeff Fairholm .35
196 Marcello Simmons .20
197 Oscar Giles .35
198 Chris Gioskos .20
199 Dan Murphy .20
200 Norm Casola .20
201 Vic Stevenson .20
202 Duane Dmytryshyn .20
203 Christopher Perez .20
204 Noah Cantor .20
205 Mike Vanderjagt .20
206 George Nimako .35
207 Andrew Stewart .20
208 Pierre Vercheval .35
209 Chris Green .20
210 Maurice Miller .20
211 Leroy Blugh .35
212 Jim Sandusky .35
213 Thomas Rayam .20
214 Cody Ledbetter .20
215 Michael Sellers .20
216 Reggie Pleasant .50
217 Errol Martin .20
218 Trent Brown .20
219 Bruce Dickson .20
220 Dan Payne .20

1983 Mohawk B.C. Lions

NM/M

Complete Set (24): 18.00
Common Player: .60
1 John Blain .60
2 Tim Cowan .60
3 Larry Crawford 1.00
4 Tyrone Crews .60
5 James Curry 1.00
6 Roy Dewalt 1.50
7 Mervyn Fernandez 3.00
8 Sammy Greene .60
9 Jo Jo Heath .60
10 Nick Hebeler .60
11 Glen Jackson .60
12 Tim Kearse .60
13 Rick Klassen 1.00
14 Kevin Konar 1.00
15 Glenn Leonhard .60
16 Nelson Martin .60
17 Mack Moore .60
18 John Pankratz .60
19 Joe Paopao 1.25
20 Lui Passaglia 2.00
21 Don Taylor .60
22 Mike Washburn .60
23 John Henry White .60
24 Al Wilson .60

1984 Mohawk B.C. Lions

NM/M

Complete Set (32): 18.00
Common Player: .50
1 Ned Armour .50
2 John Blain .50
3 Melvin Byrd .75
4 Darnell Clash 1.00
5 Tim Cowan .50
6 Larry Crawford .75
7 Tyrone Crews .50
8 Roy DeWalt 1.50
9 Mervyn Fernandez 3.00
10 Bernie Glier .50
11 Dennis Guevin .50
12 Nick Hebeler .50
13 Bryan Illerbrun .50
14 Glen Jackson .50
15 Andre Jones .50
16 Rick Klassen .75
17 Kevin Konar .75
18 Glenn Leonhard .50
19 Nelson Martin .50
20 Billy McBride .50
21 Mack Moore .50
22 John Pankratz .50
23 James Parker 1.25
24 Lui Passaglia 1.50
25 Ryan Potter .50
26 Gerald Roper .50
27 Jim Sandusky 2.00
28 Don Taylor .50
29 John Henry White .50
30 Al Wilson .50
31 Team Card .75
32 Checklist .75

1985 Mohawk B.C. Lions

NM/M

Complete Set (32): 18.00
Common Player: .50
1 John Blain .50
2 Jamie Buis .50
3 Melvin Byrd .75
4 Darnell Clash 1.00
5 Tim Cowan .75
6 Tyrone Crews .50
7 Mark DeBrueys .50
8 Roy Dewalt 1.50
9 Mervyn Fernandez 3.00
10 Bernie Glier .50
11 Keith Gooch .50
12 Dennis Guevin .50
13 Nick Hebeler .50
14 Bryan Illerbrun .50
15 Glen Jackson .50
16 Keyvan Jenkins 1.00
17 Andre Jones .50
18 Rick Klassen .75
19 Kevin Konar .75
20 Glenn Leonhard .50
21 Nelson Martin .50
22 John Pankratz .50
23 James Parker 1.25
24 Lui Passaglia 1.50
25 Ryan Potter .50
26 Ron Robinson .75
27 Gerald Roper .50
28 Jim Sandusky 2.00
29 John Henry White .50
30 Al Wilson .50
31 Team Photo .75
32 Checklist .75

1963 Nalley's Coins

NM/M

Complete Set (160): 2,750
Common Player: 4.00
1 Jackie Parker 20.00
2 Dick Shatto 8.00
3 Dave Mann 5.00
4 Danny Nykoluk 4.00
5 Billy Shipp 4.00
6 Doug McNichol 4.00
7 Jim Rountree 4.00
8 Art Johnson 4.00
9 Walt Radzick 4.00
10 Jim Andreotti 4.00
11 Gerry Philip 20.00

12 Lynn Bottoms 20.00
13 Ron Morris (SP) 100.00
14 Nobby Wirkowski (CO) 20.00
15 John Wydareny 20.00
16 Gerry Wilson 20.00
17 Gerry Patrick (SP) 50.00
18 Aubrey Linne 20.00
19 Norm Stoneburgh 20.00
20 Ken Beck 20.00
21 Russ Jackson 15.00
22 Kaye Vaughan 8.00
23 Dave Thelen 8.00
24 Ron Stewart 8.00
25 Moe Racine 4.00
26 Jim Conroy 4.00
27 Joe Poirier 4.00
28 Mel Seminko 4.00
29 Whit Tucker 8.00
30 Ernie White 4.00
31 Frank Clair (CO) 20.00
32 Marv Bevan 20.00
33 Jerry Selinger 20.00
34 Jim Cain 20.00
35 Mike Snodgrass 20.00
36 Ted Smale 20.00
37 Billy Joe Booth 20.00
38 Len Chandler 20.00
39 Rick Black 20.00
40 Allen Schau 20.00
41 Bernie Faloney 15.00
42 Bobby Kuntz 4.00
43 Joe Zuger 4.00
44 Hal Patterson 12.00
45 Bronko Nagurski 10.00
46 Zeno Karcz 4.00
47 Hardiman Cureton 4.00
48 John Barrow 8.00
49 Tommy Grant 8.00
50 Garney Henley 8.00
51 Dick Easterly 20.00
52 Frank Cosentino 20.00
53 Geno DeNobile 20.00
54 Ralph Goldston 20.00
55 Chet Miksza 20.00
56 Bob Minihane 20.00
57 Don Sutherin 40.00
58 Ralph Sazio (CO) 20.00
59 Dave Viti (SP) 35.00
60 Angelo Mosca (SP) 100.00
61 Sandy Stephens 8.00
62 George Dixon 8.00
63 Don Clark 4.00
64 Don Paquette 4.00
65 Billy Wayte 4.00
66 Ed Nickla 4.00
67 Marv Luster 8.00
68 Joe Stracina 4.00
69 Bobby Jack Oliver 4.00
70 Ted Elsby 4.00
71 Jim Trimble (CO) 20.00
72 Bob Leblanc 20.00
73 Dick Schnell 20.00
74 Milt Crain 20.00
75 Dick Dalatri 20.00
76 Billy Roy 20.00
77 Dave Hoppmann 20.00
78 Billy Ray Locklin 20.00
79 Ed Learn (SP) 125.00
80 Meco Poliziani (SP) 40.00
81 Leo Lewis 8.00
82 Kenny Ploen 8.00
83 Steve Patrick 4.00
84 Farrell Funston 4.00
85 Charlie Shepard 4.00
86 Ronnie Latourelle 4.00
87 Gord Rowland 4.00
88 Frank Rigney 5.00
89 Cornel Piper 4.00
90 Ernie Pitts 4.00
91 Roger Hagberg 30.00
92 Herb Gray 50.00
93 Jack Delveaux 20.00
94 Roger Savoie 20.00
95 Nick Miller 20.00
96 Norm Rauhaus 20.00
97 Cec Luining 20.00
98 Hal Ledyard 20.00
99 Neil Thomas 20.00
100 Bud Grant (CO) 75.00
101 Eagle Keys (CO) 8.00
102 Mike Wicklum 4.00
103 Bill Mitchell 4.00
104 Mike Lashuk 4.00
105 Tommy Joe Coffey 8.00
106 Zeke Smith 4.00
107 Joe Hernandez 4.00
108 Johnny Bright 8.00
109 Don Getty 8.00
110 Nat Dye 4.00
111 James Earl Wright 20.00
112 Mike Volcan (SP) 35.00
113 Jon Rechner 20.00
114 Len Vella 20.00
115 Ted Frechette 20.00
116 Larry Fleisher 20.00
117 Oscar Kruger 20.00
118 Ken Peterson 20.00
119 Bobby Walden 30.00
120 Mickey Ording 20.00
121 Pete Manning 4.00
122 Harvey Wylie 4.00
123 Tony Pajaczkowski 8.00
124 Wayne Harris 10.00
125 Earl Lunsford 8.00
126 Don Luzzi 4.00
127 Ed Buckanan 4.00
128 Lovell Coleman 5.00
129 Hal Krebs 4.00
130 Eagle Day 8.00
131 Bobby Dobbs (CO) 20.00
132 George Hansen 20.00
133 Roy Jokanovich (SP) 75.00
134 Jerry Keeling 30.00
135 Larry Anderson 20.00
136 Bill Crawford 20.00
137 Ron Albright 20.00
138 Bill Britton 20.00
139 Jim Dillard 20.00
140 Jim Furlong 20.00
141 Dave Skrien (CO) 5.00
142 Willie Fleming 10.00
143 Nub Beamer 4.00
144 Norm Fieldgate 8.00
145 Joe Kapp 35.00
146 Tom Hinton 8.00
147 Pat Claridge 4.00
148 Bill Munsey 4.00
149 Mike Martin 4.00
150 Tom Brown 8.00
151 Ian Hagemoen 20.00
152 Jim Carphin 20.00
153 By Bailey 40.00
154 Steve Cotter 20.00
155 Mike Cacic 20.00
156 Neil Beaumont 20.00
157 Lonnie Dennis 20.00
158 Barney Therrien 20.00
159 Sonny Homer 20.00
160 Walt Bilicki 20.00
S1 Toronto Shield 50.00
S2 Ottawa Shield 50.00
S3 Hamilton Shield 50.00
S4 Montreal Shield 50.00
S5 Winnipeg Shield 50.00
S6 Edmonton Shield 50.00
S7 Calgary Shield 50.00
S8 British Columbia Shield 50.00

1964 Nalley's Coins

NM/M
Complete Set (100): 720.00
Common Player: 4.00
1 Joe Kapp 30.00
2 Willie Fleming 10.00
3 Norm Fieldgate 8.00
4 Bill Murray 4.00
5 Tom Brown 10.00
6 Neil Beaumont 4.00
7 Sonny Homer 4.00
8 Lonnie Dennis 4.00
9 Dave Skrien 4.00
10 Dick Fouts (CO) 4.00
11 Paul Seale 4.00
12 Peter Kempf 4.00
13 Steve Shafer 4.00
14 Tom Hinton 8.00
15 Pat Claridge 4.00
16 By Bailey 8.00
17 Nub Beamer 5.00
18 Steve Cotter 4.00
19 Mike Cacic 4.00
20 Mike Martin 4.00
21 Eagle Day 12.00
22 Jim Dillard 4.00
23 Pete Murray 4.00
24 Tony Pajaczkowski 8.00
25 Don Luzzi 4.00
26 Wayne Harris 10.00
27 Harvey Wylie 4.00
28 Bill Crawford 4.00
29 Jim Furlong 4.00
30 Lovell Coleman 5.00
31 Pat Haines 4.00
32 Bob Taylor 4.00
33 Ernie Danjean 4.00
34 Jerry Keeling 8.00
35 Larry Robinson 4.00
36 George Hansen 4.00
37 Ron Albright 4.00
38 Larry Anderson 4.00
39 Bill Miller 4.00
40 Bill Britton 4.00
41 Lynn Amadee 8.00
42 Mike Lashuk 4.00
43 Tommy Joe Coffey 8.00
44 Junior Hawthorne 4.00
45 Nat Dye 4.00
46 Al Ecuyer 4.00
47 Howie Schumm 4.00
48 Zeke Smith 4.00
49 Mike Wicklum 4.00
50 Mike Volcan 4.00
51 E.A. Sims 4.00
52 Bill Mitchell 4.00
53 Ken Reed 4.00
54 Len Vella 4.00
55 Johnny Bright 8.00
56 Don Getty 8.00
57 Oscar Kruger 4.00
58 Ted Frechette 4.00
59 James Earl Wright 4.00
60 Roger Nelson 4.00
61 Ron Lancaster 10.00
62 Bill Clarke 4.00
63 Bob Shaw 4.00
64 Ray Purdin 4.00
65 Ron Atchison 8.00
66 Ted Urness 8.00
67 Bob Ptacek 4.00
68 Neil Habig 4.00
69 Garner Ekstran 4.00
70 Gene Wlasiuk 4.00
71 Jack Gotta 4.00
72 Dick Cohee 4.00
73 Ron Meadmore 4.00
74 Martin Fabi 4.00
75 Bob Good 4.00
76 Len Legault 4.00
77 Al Benecick 4.00
78 Dale West 4.00
79 Reg Whitehouse 4.00
80 George Reed 10.00
81 Kenny Ploen 8.00
82 Leo Lewis 10.00
83 Dick Thornton 5.00
84 Steve Patrick 4.00
85 Frank Rigney 5.00
86 Cornel Piper 4.00
87 Sherwyn Thorson 4.00
88 Ernie Pitts 4.00
89 Roger Hagberg 5.00
90 Bud Grant (CO) 50.00
91 Jack Delveaux 4.00
92 Farrell Funston 4.00
93 Ronnie Latourelle 4.00
94 Roger Hamelin 4.00
95 Gord Rowland 4.00
96 Herb Gray 10.00
97 Nick Miller 4.00
98 Norm Rauhaus 4.00
99 Bill Whisler 4.00
100 Hal Ledyard 4.00
S1 British Columbia Shield 45.00
S2 Calgary Shield 45.00
S3 Edmonton Shield 45.00
S4 Saskatchewan Shield 45.00
S5 Winnipeg Shield 45.00

1976 Nalley's Chips CFL

NM/M
Complete Set (30): 300.00
Common Player: 8.00
1 Bill Baker 20.00
2 Eric Guthrie 8.00
3 Lou Harris 10.00
4 Layne McDowell 8.00
5 Ray Nettles 8.00
6 Lui Passaglia 25.00
7 John Sciarra 15.00
8 Wayne Smith 8.00
9 Michael Strickland 8.00
10 Jim Young 20.00
11 Dave Cutler 15.00
12 Larry Highbaugh 12.00
13 John Koniszewski 8.00
14 Bruce Lemmerman 8.00
15 George McGowan 12.00
16 Dale Potter 8.00
17 Charlie Turner 8.00
18 Tyrone Walls 8.00
19 Don Warrington 8.00
20 Tom Wilkinson 25.00
21 Willie Burden 35.00
22 Larry Cates 8.00
23 Lloyd Fairbanks 12.00
24 Joe Forzani 8.00
25 Tom Forzani 8.00
26 Rick Galbos 8.00
27 John Helton 15.00
28 Harold Holton 8.00
29 Rudy Linterman 12.00
30 Joe Pisarcik 15.00

1968 O-Pee-Chee CFL

NM/M
Complete Set (132): 1,100
Common Player: 6.00
1 Roger Murphy 15.00
2 Charlie Parker 6.00
3 Mike Webster 6.00
4 Carroll Williams 6.00
5 Phil Brady 6.00
6 Dave Lewis 6.00
7 John Baker 6.00
8 Basil Bark 6.00
9 Donnie Davis 6.00
10 Pierre Desjardins 6.00
11 Larry Fairholm 6.00
12 Peter Paquette 6.00
13 Ray Lychak 6.00
14 Ted Collins 6.00
15 Margene Adkins 15.00
16 Ron Stewart 20.00
17 Russ Jackson 35.00
18 Bo Scott 15.00
19 Joe Poirier 6.00
20 Wayne Giardino 6.00
21 Gene Gaines 15.00
22 Billy Joe Booth 6.00
23 Whit Tucker 15.00
24 Rick Black 6.00
25 Ken Lehmann 12.00
26 Bob Brown 6.00
27 Moe Racine 6.00
28 Dick Thornton 8.00
29 Bob Taylor 6.00
30 Mel Profit 12.00
31 Dave Mann 8.00
32 Marv Luster 12.00
33 Ed Buchanan 6.00
34 Ed Harrington 8.00
35 Jim Dillard 6.00
36 Bob Taylor 6.00
37 Ron Arends 6.00
38 Mike Wadsworth 6.00
39 Wally Gabler 12.00
40 Pete Martin 6.00
41 Danny Nykoluk 6.00
42 Bill Frank 6.00
43 Gordon Christian 6.00
44 Tommy Joe Coffey 20.00
45 Ellison Kelly 20.00
46 Angelo Mosca 30.00
47 John Barrow 20.00
48 Bill Danychuk 12.00
49 Jon Hohman 6.00
50 Bill Redell 6.00
51 Joe Zuger 8.00
52 Willie Bethea 12.00
53 Dick Cohee 6.00
54 Tommy Grant 15.00
55 Garney Henley 20.00
56 Ted Page 6.00
57 Bob Krouse 6.00
58 Phil Minnick 6.00
59 Butch Pressley 6.00
60 Dave Raimey 8.00
61 Sherwyn Thorson 6.00
62 Bill Whisler 6.00
63 Roger Hamelin 6.00
64 Chuck Harrison 6.00
65 Ken Nielsen 12.00
66 Ernie Pitts 6.00
67 Mitch Zainasky 6.00
68 John Schneider 6.00
69 Ron Kirkland 6.00
70 Paul Desjardins 6.00
71 Luther Selbo 6.00
72 Don Gilbert 6.00
73 Bob Lueck 6.00
74 Gerry Shaw 6.00
75 Chuck Zickefoose 6.00
76 Frank Andruski 6.00
77 Lanny Boleski 6.00
78 Terry Evanshen 20.00
79 Jim Furlong 6.00
80 Wayne Harris 20.00
81 Jerry Keeling 15.00
82 Roger Kramer 8.00
83 Pete Liske 20.00
84 Dick Suderman 12.00
85 Granville Liggins 20.00
86 George Reed 30.00
87 Ron Lancaster 30.00
88 Alan Ford 6.00
89 Gordon Barwell 6.00
90 Wayne Shaw 6.00
91 Bruce Bennett 15.00
92 Henry Dorsch 6.00
93 Ken Reed 6.00
94 Ron Atchison 15.00
95 Clyde Brock 6.00
96 Alex Benecick 6.00
97 Ted Urness 12.00
98 Wally Dempsey 6.00
99 Don Gerhardt 6.00
100 Ted Dushinski 6.00
101 Ed McQuarters 12.00
102 Bob Kosid 6.00
103 Gary Brandt 6.00
104 John Wydareny 6.00
105 Jim Thomas 6.00
106 Art Perkins 6.00
107 Frank Cosentino 12.00
108 Earl Edwards 8.00
109 Garry Lefebvre 6.00
110 Greg Pipes 8.00
111 Ian MacLeod 6.00
112 Dick Dupuis 6.00
113 Ron Forwick 6.00
114 Jerry Griffin 6.00
115 John LaGrone 12.00
116 E.A. Sims 6.00
117 Greenard Poles 6.00
118 Leroy Sledge 6.00
119 Ken Sugarman 6.00
120 Jim Young 30.00
121 Garner Ekstran 12.00
122 Jim Evenson 12.00
123 Greg Findlay 6.00
124 Ted Gerela 8.00
125 Lach Heron 8.00
126 Mike Martin 6.00
127 Craig Murray 6.00
128 Pete Ohler 6.00
129 Sonny Homer 6.00
130 Bill Lasseter 6.00
131 John McDowell 6.00
132 Checklist Card 60.00

1968 O-Pee-Chee CFL Poster Inserts

NM/M
Complete Set (16): 325.00
Common Player: 15.00
1 Margene Adkins 20.00
2 Tommy Joe Coffey 25.00
3 Frank Cosentino 18.00
4 Terry Evanshen 25.00
5 Larry Fairholm 15.00
6 Wally Gabler 15.00
7 Russ Jackson 35.00
8 Ron Lancaster 30.00
9 Pete Liske 25.00
10 Dave Mann 18.00
11 Ken Nielsen 18.00
12 Dave Raimey 18.00
13 George Reed 30.00
14 Carroll Williams 15.00
15 Jim Young 30.00
16 Joe Zuger 15.00

1970 O-Pee-Chee CFL

NM/M
Complete Set (115): 300.00
Common Player: 2.00
1 Ed Harrington 5.00
2 Danny Nykoluk 2.00
3 Marv Luster 4.00
4 Dave Raimey 3.00
5 Bill Symons 3.00
6 Tom Wilkinson 20.00
7 Mike Wadsworth 2.00
8 Dick Thornton 3.00
9 Jim Tomlin 2.00
10 Mel Profit 3.00
11 Bob Taylor 4.00
12 Dave Mann 3.00
13 Tommy Joe Coffey 5.00
14 Angelo Mosca 15.00
15 Joe Zuger 3.00
16 Garney Henley 10.00
17 Mike Strofolino 2.00
18 Billy Ray Locklin 2.00
19 Ted Page 2.00
20 Bill Danychuk 3.00
21 Bob Krouse 2.00
22 John Reid 2.00
23 Dick Wesolowski 2.00
24 Willie Bethea 3.00
25 Ken Sugarman 3.00
26 Rich Robinson 2.00
27 Dave Tobey 2.00
28 Paul Brothers 2.00
29 Charlie Brown 2.00
30 Jerry Bradley 2.00
31 Ted Gerela 3.00
32 Jim Young 8.00
33 Gary Robinson 2.00
34 Bob Howes 2.00
35 Greg Findlay 2.00
36 Trevor Ekdahl 3.00
37 Ron Stewart 6.00
38 Joe Poirier 3.00
39 Wayne Giardino 2.00
40 Tom Schuette 2.00
41 Roger Perdrix 2.00
42 Jim Mankins 2.00
43 Jay Roberts 2.00
44 Ken Lehmann 3.00
45 Jerry Campbell 3.00
46 Billy Joe Booth 3.00
47 Whit Tucker 5.00
48 Moe Racine 2.00
49 Corey Colehour 3.00
50 Dave Gasser 2.00
51 Jerry Griffin 2.00
52 Greg Pipes 3.00
53 Roy Shatzko 2.00
54 Ron Forwick 2.00
55 Ed Molstad 2.00
56 Ken Ferguson 2.00
57 Terry Swarn 5.00
58 Tom Nettles 2.00
59 John Wydareny 2.00
60 Bayne Norrie 2.00
61 Wally Gabler 3.00
62 Paul Desjardins 2.00
63 Peter Francis 2.00
64 Bill Frank 2.00
65 Chuck Harrison 2.00
66 Gene Lakusiak 2.00
67 Phil Minnick 2.00
68 Doug Strong 2.00
69 Glen Schapansky 2.00
70 Ed Ulmer 2.00
71 Bill Whisler 2.00
72 Ted Collins 2.00
73 Larry DeGraw 2.00
74 Henry Dorsch 2.00
75 Alan Ford 2.00
76 Ron Lancaster 20.00
77 Bob Kosid 2.00
78 Bobby Thompson 2.00
79 Ted Dushinski 2.00
80 Bruce Bennett 4.00
81 George Reed 15.00
82 Wayne Shaw 2.00
83 Cliff Shaw 2.00
84 Jack Abendschan 2.00
85 Ed McQuarters 5.00
86 Jerry Keeling 5.00
87 Gerry Shaw 2.00
88 Basil Bark (UER) (Misspelled Back) 2.00
89 Wayne Harris 6.00
90 Jim Furlong 2.00
91 Larry Robinson 2.00
92 John Helton 10.00
93 Dave Cranmer 2.00
94 Lanny Boleski (UER) (Misspelled Larry) 2.00
95 Herman Harrison 5.00
96 Granville Liggins 5.00
97 Joe Forzani 3.00
98 Terry Evanshen 8.00
99 Sonny Wade 6.00
100 Dennis Duncan 2.00
101 Al Phaneuf 2.00
102 Larry Fairholm 2.00
103 Moses Denson 4.00
104 Gino Baretta 2.00
105 Gene Ceppetelli 2.00
106 Dick Smith 2.00
107 Gordon Judges 2.00
108 Harry Olszewski 2.00
109 Mike Webster 2.00
110 Checklist 1-115 30.00
111 Outstanding Player (list from 1953-1969) 8.00
112 Player of the Year (list from 1954-1969) 8.00
113 Lineman of the Year (list from 1955-1969) 6.00
114 CFL Coaches (listed on card front) 6.00
115 Identifying Player (explanation of uniform numbering system) 15.00

1970 O-Pee-Chee CFL Push-Out Inserts

NM/M
Complete Set (16): 200.00
Common Player: 10.00
1 Ed Harrington 10.00
2 Danny Nykoluk 10.00
3 Tommy Joe Coffey 25.00
4 Angelo Mosca 30.00
5 Ken Sugarman 12.00
6 Jay Roberts 10.00
7 Joe Poirier 12.00
8 Corey Colehour 10.00
9 Dave Gasser 10.00
10 Wally Gabler 15.00
11 Paul Desjardins 10.00
12 Larry DeGraw 10.00
13 Jerry Keeling 20.00
14 Gerry Shaw 10.00
15 Terry Evanshen 25.00
16 Sonny Wade 12.00

1971 O-Pee-Chee CFL

NM/M
Complete Set (132): 250.00
Common Player: 1.00
1 Bill Symons 5.00
2 Mel Profit 1.50
3 Jim Tomlin 1.00
4 Ed Harrington 1.50
5 Jim Corrigall 4.00
6 Chip Barrett 1.00
7 Marv Luster 3.00
8 Ellison Kelly 4.00
9 Charlie Bray 1.00
10 Pete Martin 1.00
11 Tony Moro 1.00
12 Dave Raimey 1.50
13 Joe Theismann 100.00
14 Greg Barton 6.00
15 Leon McQuay 6.00
16 Don Jonas 6.00
17 Doug Strong 1.00
18 Paul Brule 1.00
19 Bill Frank 1.00
20 Joe Critchlow 1.00
21 Chuck Liebrock 1.00
22 Rob McLaren 1.00
23 Bob Swift 1.00
24 Rick Shaw 1.00
25 Ross Richardson 1.00
26 Benji Dial 1.00
27 Jim Heighton 1.00
28 Ed Ulmer 1.00
29 Glen Schapansky 1.00
30 Larry Slagle 1.00
31 Tom Cassese 1.00
32 Ted Gerela 1.00
33 Bob Howes 1.00
34 Ken Sugarman 1.50
35 A.D. Whitfield 1.50
36 Jim Young 6.00
37 Tom Wilkinson 10.00
38 Lefty Hendrickson 1.00
39 Dave Golinsky 1.00
40 Gerry Herron 1.00
41 Jim Evenson 1.50
42 Greg Findlay 1.00
43 Garrett Hunsperger 1.00
44 Jerry Bradley 1.00
45 Trevor Ekdahl 1.50
46 Bayne Norrie 1.00
47 Henry King 1.00
48 Terry Swarn 1.50
49 Jim Thomas 1.50
50 Bob Houmard 1.00
51 Don Trull 3.00
52 Dave Cutler 8.00
53 Mike Law 1.00
54 Dick Dupuis 1.50
55 Dave Gasser 1.00
56 Ron Forwick 1.00
57 John LaGrone 1.50
58 Greg Pipes 1.50
59 Ted Page 1.00
60 John Wydareny 1.50
61 Joe Zuger 1.50
62 Tommy Joe Coffey 6.00
63 Rensi Perdoni 1.00
64 Bob Taylor 2.50
65 Garney Henley 6.00
66 Dick Wesolowski 1.00
67 Dave Fleming 1.00
68 Bill Danychuk 1.50
69 Angelo Mosca 15.00
70 Bob Krouse 1.00
71 Tony Gabriel 18.00
72 Wally Gabler 1.50
73 Bob Steiner 1.00
74 John Reid 1.00
75 Jon Hohman 1.00
76 Barry Ardern 1.00
77 Jerry Campbell 1.50
78 Billy Cooper 1.00
79 Dave Braggins 1.00
80 Tom Schuette 1.00
81 Dennis Duncan 1.00
82 Moe Racine 1.00
83 Rod Woodward 1.00
84 Al Marcelin 1.50
85 Garry Wood 5.00
86 Wayne Giardino 1.00
87 Roger Perdrix 1.00
88 Hugh Oldham 1.00
89 Rick Cassatta 2.50
90 Jack Abendschan 1.50
91 Don Bahnuik 1.00
92 Bill Baker 10.00
93 Gordon Barwell 1.00
94 Gary Brandt 1.00
95 Henry Dorsch 1.00
96 Ted Dushinski 1.00
97 Alan Ford 1.00
98 Ken Frith 1.00
99 Ralph Galloway 1.00
100 Bob Kosid 1.00
101 Ron Lancaster 15.00
102 Silas McKinnie 1.00
103 George Reed 8.00
104 Gene Ceppetelli 1.00
105 Merl Code 1.00
106 Peter Dalla Riva 8.00
107 Moses Denson 2.50
108 Pierre Desjardins 1.00
109 Terry Evanshen 6.00
110 Larry Fairholm 1.50
111 Gene Gaines 5.00
112 Ed George 1.50
113 Gordon Judges 1.00
114 Garry Lefebvre 1.00
115 Al Phaneuf 1.50
116 Steve Smear 5.00
117 Sonny Wade 3.00
118 Frank Andruski 1.00
119 Basil Bark 1.00
120 Lanny Boleski 1.00
121 Joe Forzani 1.50
122 Jim Furlong 1.00
123 Wayne Harris 6.00
124 Herman Harrison 4.00
125 John Helton 4.00
126 Wayne Holm 1.00
127 Fred James 1.00
128 Jerry Keeling 4.00
129 Rudy Linterman 1.50
130 Larry Robinson 1.50
131 Gerry Shaw 1.00
132 Checklist Card 25.00
1.00

1971 O-Pee-Chee CFL Poster Inserts

NM/M
Complete Set (16): 150.00
Common Player: 6.00
1 Tommy Joe Coffey 15.00
2 Herman Harrison 15.00
3 Bill Frank 6.00
4 Ellison Kelly 10.00
5 Charlie Bray 6.00
6 Bill Danychuk 7.50
7 Ron Lancaster Saskatchewan Roughriders 20.00

8	Bill Symons	7.50
9	Steve Smear	10.00
10	Angelo Mosca	20.00
11	Wayne Harris	15.00
12	Greg Findlay	6.00
13	John Wydareny	7.50
14	Garney Henley	15.00
15	Al Phaneuf	7.50
16	Ed Harrington	6.00

1972 O-Pee-Chee CFL

		NM/M
Complete Set (132):		175.00
Common Player:		1.00
1	Bob Krouse	2.50
2	John Williams	1.00
3	Garney Henley	6.00
4	Dick Wesolowski	1.00
5	Paul McKay	1.00
6	Bill Danychuk	1.50
7	Angelo Mosca	10.00
8	Tommy Joe Coffey	5.00
9	Tony Gabriel	10.00
10	Mike Blum	1.00
11	Doug Mitchell	1.00
12	Emery Hicks	1.00
13	Max Anderson	1.00
14	Ed George	1.50
15	Mark Kosmos	1.50
16	Ted Collins	1.00
17	Peter Dalla Riva	5.00
18	Pierre Desjardins	1.00
19	Terry Evanshen	6.00
20	Larry Fairholm	1.50
21	Jim Foley	1.50
22	Gordon Judges	1.00
23	Barry Randall	1.00
24	Brad Upshaw	1.00
25	Jorma Kuisma	1.00
26	Mike Widger	1.00
27	Joe Theismann	50.00
28	Greg Barton	4.00
29	Bill Symons	3.00
30	Leon McQuay	4.00
31	Jim Corrigall	4.00
32	Jim Stillwagon	4.00
33	Dick Thornton	1.50
34	Marv Luster	4.00
35	Paul Desjardins	1.00
36	Mike Eben	1.00
37	Eric Allen	5.00
38	Chip Barrett	1.00
39	Noah Jackson	3.00
40	Jim Young	6.00
41	Trevor Ekdahl	1.50
42	Garrett Hunsperger	1.00
43	Willie Postler	1.00
44	George Anderson	1.00
45	Ron Estay	1.00
46	Johnny Musso	15.00
47	Eric Guthrie	1.00
48	Monroe Eley	1.00
49	Don Bunce	5.00
50	Jim Evenson	1.50
51	Ken Sugarman	1.50
52	Dave Golinsky	1.00
53	Wayne Harris	5.00
54	Jerry Keeling	4.00
55	Herman Harrison	4.00
56	Larry Robinson	1.50
57	John Helton	4.00
58	Gerry Shaw	1.00
59	Frank Andruski	1.00
60	Basil Bark	1.00
61	Joe Forzani	1.50
62	Jim Furlong	1.00
63	Rudy Linterman	1.50
64	Granville Liggins	4.00
65	Lanny Boleski	1.00
66	Hugh Oldham	1.00
67	Dave Braggins	1.00
68	Jerry Campbell	1.50
69	Al Marcelin	1.50
70	Tom Pullen	1.00
71	Rudy Sims	1.00
72	Marshall Shirk	1.00
73	Tom Laputka	1.00
74	Barry Ardern	1.00
75	Billy Cooper	1.00
76	Dan Deever	1.00
77	Wayne Giardino	1.00
78	Terry Wellesley	1.00
79	Ron Lancaster	12.00
80	George Reed	10.00
81	Bobby Thompson	1.00
82	Jack Abendschan	1.00
83	Ed McQuarters	3.00
84	Bruce Bennett	3.00
85	Bill Baker	5.00
86	Don Bahnuik	1.00
87	Gary Brandt	1.00
88	Henry Dorach	1.00
89	Ted Dushinski	1.00
90	Alan Ford	1.00
91	Bob Kosid	1.00
92	Greg Pipes	1.50
93	John LaGrone	1.50
94	Dave Gasser	1.00
95	Bob Taylor	1.50
96	Dave Cutler	5.00
97	Dick Dupuis	1.00
98	Ron Forwick	1.00
99	Bayne Norrie	1.00
100	Jim Henshall	1.00
101	Charlie Turner	1.00
102	Fred Dunn	1.00
103	Sam Scarber	1.00
104	Bruce Lemmerman	5.00
105	Don Jonas	6.00
106	Doug Strong	1.00
107	Ed Williams	1.00
108	Paul Markle	1.00
109	Gene Lakusiak	1.00
110	Bob LaRose	1.00
111	Rob McLaren	1.00
112	Pete Ribbins	1.00
113	Bill Frank	1.00
114	Bob Swift	1.00
115	Chuck Liebrock	1.00
116	Joe Critchlow	1.00
117	Paul Williams	1.00
118	Pro Action	1.00
119	Pro Action	1.00
120	Pro Action	1.00
121	Pro Action	1.00
122	Pro Action	1.00
123	Pro Action	1.00
124	Pro Action	1.00
125	Pro Action	1.00
126	Pro Action	1.00
127	Pro Action	1.00
128	Pro Action	1.00
129	Pro Action	1.00
130	Pro Action	1.00
131	Pro Action	1.00
132	Checklist Card	30.00
		1.00

1972 O-Pee-Chee CFL Trio Sticker Insert

		NM/M
Complete Set (24):		250.00
Common Player:		4.00
1	Johnny Musso, 2 Ron Lancaster, 3 Don Jonas	4.00
4	Jerry Campbell, 5 Bill Symons, 6 Ted Collins	4.00
7	Dave Cutler, 8 Paul McKay, 9 Rudy Sims	4.00
10	Wayne Harris, 11 Greg Pipes, 12 Chuck Ealey	4.00
13	Ron Estay, 14 Jack Abendschan, 15 Paul Markle	4.00
16	Jim Stillwagon, 17 Terry Evanshen, 18 Willie Postler	4.00
19	Hugh Oldham, 20 Joe Theismann, 21 Ed George	4.00
22	Larry Robinson, 23 Bruce Lemmerman, 24 Garney Henley	4.00
25	Bill Baker, 26 Bob LaRose, 27 Frank Andruski	4.00
28	Don Bunce, 29 George Reed, 30 Doug Strong	4.00
31	Al Marcelin, 32 Leon McQuay, 33 Peter Dalla Riva	4.00
34	Dick Dupuis, 35 Bill Danychuk, 36 Marshall Shirk	4.00
37	Jerry Keeling, 38 John LaGrone, 39 Bob Krouse	4.00
40	Jim Young, 41 Ed McQuarters, 42 Gene Lakusiak	4.00
43	Dick Thornton, 44 Larry Fairholm, 45 Garrett Hunsperger	4.00
46	Dave Braggins, 47 Greg Barton, 48 Mark Kosmos	4.00
49	John Helton, 50 Bobby Taylor, 51 Dick Wesolowski	4.00
52	Don Bahnuik, 53 Rob McLaren, 54 Granville Liggins	4.00
55	Monroe Eley, 56 Bob Thompson, 57 Ed Williams	4.00
58	Tom Pullen, 59 Jim Corrigall, 60 Pierre Desjardins	4.00
61	Ron Forwick, 62 Angelo Mosca, 63 Tom Laputka	4.00
64	Herman Harrison, 65 Dave Gasser, 66 John Williams	4.00
67	Trevor Ekdahl, 68 Bruce Bennett, 69 Gerry Shaw	4.00
70	Jim Foley, 71 Pete Ribbins, 72 Marv Luster	4.00

1952 Parkhurst CFL

		NM/M
Complete Set (100):		3,000
Common Player (1-19):		20.00
Common Player (20-100):		30.00
1	Watch The Games	50.00
2	Teamwork	20.00
3	Football Equipment	20.00
4	Hang Onto The Ball	20.00
5	The Head On Tackle	20.00
6	The Football Field	20.00
7	The Lineman's Stance	20.00
8	Centre's Spiral Pass	20.00
9	The Lineman	20.00
10	The Place Kick	20.00
11	The Cross-Body Block	20.00
12	T Formation	20.00
13	Falling On The Ball	20.00
14	The Throw	20.00
15	Breaking From Tackle	20.00
16	How To Catch A Pass	20.00
17	The Punt	20.00
18	Shifting The Ball	20.00
19	Penalty Signals	20.00
20	Leslie Ascott	30.00
21	Robert Marshall	30.00
22	Tom Harpley	30.00
23	Robert McClelland	30.00
24	Rod Smylie	30.00
25	Bill Bass	30.00
26	Fred Black	30.00
27	Jack Carpenter	30.00
28	Bob Hack	30.00
29	Ulysses Curtis	30.00
30	Nobby Wirkowski	50.00
31	George Arnett	30.00
32	Lorne Parkin	30.00
33	Alex Toogood	30.00
34	Marshall Haymes	30.00
35	Shanty McKenzie	30.00
36	Byron Karrys	30.00
37	George Rooks	30.00
38	Red Ettinger	30.00
39	Al Bruno	40.00
40	Stephen Karrys	30.00
41	Herb Trawick	50.00
42	Sam Etcheverry	350.00
43	Marv Melrowitz	30.00
44	John Red O'Quinn	50.00
45	Jim Ostendarp	30.00
46	Tom Tofaute	30.00
47	Joey Pal	30.00
48	Ray Cicia	30.00
49	Bruce Coulter	35.00
50	Jim Mitchener	30.00
51	Lally Lalonde	30.00
52	Jim Staton	30.00
53	Glenn Douglas	30.00
54	Dave Tomlinson	30.00
55	Ed Salem	30.00
56	Virgil Wagner	50.00
57	Dawson Tilley	30.00
58A	Cec Findlay	40.00
58B	Tommy Manastersky	40.00
59	Frank Nable	30.00
60	Chuck Anderson	30.00
61	Charlie Hubbard	30.00
63	Benny MacDonnell	30.00
64	Peter Karpuk	30.00
65	Tom O'Malley	30.00
66	Bill Stanton	30.00
67	Matt Anthony	30.00
68	John Morneau	30.00
69	Howie Turner	30.00
70	Alton Baldwin	30.00
71	John Bovey	30.00
72	Bruno Bitkowski	35.00
73	Gene Roberts	30.00
74	John Wagoner	30.00
75	Ted MacLarty	30.00
76	Jerry Lefebvre	30.00
77	Buck Rogers	30.00
78	Bruce Cummings	30.00
79	Hal Wagner	40.00
80	Joe Shinn	30.00
81	Eddie Bevan	30.00
82	Ralph Sazio	50.00
83	Bob McDonald	30.00
84	Vince Scott	40.00
85	Jack Stewart	30.00
86	Ralph Bartolini	30.00
87	Blake Taylor	30.00
88	Richard Brown	30.00
89	Douglas Gray	30.00
90	Alex Muzyka	30.00
91	Pete Neumann	50.00
92	Jack Rogers	30.00
93	Bernie Custis	40.00
94	Cam Fraser	30.00
95	Vince Mazza	40.00
96	Peter Wooley	30.00
97	Earl Valiquette	30.00
98	Floyd Cooper	30.00
99	Louis DiFrancisco	30.00
100	Robert Simpson	125.00

1956 Parkhurst CFL

		NM/M
Complete Set (50):		3,500
Common Player:		40.00
1	Art Walker	80.00
2	Frank Anderson	40.00
3	Normie Kwong	150.00
4	Johnny Bright	150.00
5	Jackie Parker	500.00
6	Bob Dean	40.00
7	Don Getty	125.00
8	Rollie Miles	100.00
9	Ted Tully	40.00
10	Frank Morris	90.00
11	Martin Ruby	80.00
12	Mel Beckett	80.00
13	Bill Clarke	40.00
14	John Wozniak	40.00
15	Larry Isbell	40.00
16	Ken Carpenter	80.00
17	Sully Glasser	40.00
18	Bobby Marlow	90.00
19	Paul Anderson	40.00
20	Gord Sturtridge	80.00
21	Alex Macklin	40.00
22	Duke Cook	40.00
23	Bill Stevenson	40.00
24	Lynn Bottoms	80.00
25	Aramis Dandoy	40.00
26	Peter Muir	40.00
27	Harvey Wylie	80.00
28	Joe Yamauchi	40.00
29	John Alderton	40.00
30	Bill McKenna	40.00
31	Edward Kotowich	40.00
32	Herb Gray	100.00
33	Calvin Jones	100.00
34	Herman Day	40.00
35	Buddy Leake	40.00
36	Robert McNamara	40.00
37	Bud Grant	300.00
38	Gord Rowland	80.00
39	Glen McWhinney	40.00
40	Lorne Benson	40.00
41	Sam Etcheverry	300.00
42	Joey Pal	40.00
43	Tom Hugo	40.00
44	Tex Coulter	80.00
45	Doug McNichol	40.00
46	Tom Moran	40.00
47	Red O'Quinn	80.00
48	Hal Patterson	200.00
49	Jacques Belec	40.00
50	Pat Abruzzi	100.00

1962 Post Cereal CFL

		NM/M
Complete Set (137):		1,600
Common Player:		7.50
1A	Don Clark (Brown Back)	20.00
1B	Don Clark (SP) (White Back)	60.00
2	Ed Meadows	7.50
3	Meco Poliziani	7.50
4	George Dixon	20.00
5	Bobby Jack Oliver	10.00
6	Ross Buckle	7.50
7	Jack Espenship	7.50
8	Howard Cissell	7.50
9	Ed Nickla	7.50
10	Ed Learn	7.50
11	Billy Ray Locklin	7.50
12	Don Paquette	7.50
13	Milt Crain	7.50
14	Dick Schnell	7.50
15	Dick Cohee	7.50
16	Joe Francis	7.50
17	Gilles Archambeault	7.50
18	Angelo Mosca	25.00
19	Ernie White	7.50
20	George Brancato	7.50
21	Ron Lancaster	35.00
22	Jim Cain	7.50
23	Gerry Nesbitt	7.50
24	Russ Jackson	30.00
25	Bob Simpson	18.00
26	Sam Scoccia	7.50
27	Tom Jones	7.50
28	Kaye Vaughan	15.00
29	Chuck Stanley	7.50
30	Dave Thelen	15.00
31	Gary Schreider	7.50
32	Jim Reynolds	7.50
33	Doug Daigneault	7.50
34	Joe Poirier	10.00
35	Clare Exelby	7.50
36	Art Johnson	7.50
37	Menan Schriewer	7.50
38	Art Darch	7.50
39	Cookie Gilchrist	25.00
40	Brian Aston	7.50
41	Bobby Kuntz (SP)	50.00
42	Gerry Patrick	7.50
43	Norm Stoneburgh	7.50
44	Billy Shipp	7.50
45	Jim Andreotti	15.00
46	Tobin Rote	20.00
47	Dick Shatto	15.00
48	Dave Mann	10.00
49	Ron Morris	7.50
50	Lynn Bottoms	10.00
51	Jim Rountree	7.50
52	Bill Mitchell	7.50
53	Wes Gideon (SP)	50.00
54	Boyd Carter	7.50
55	Ron Howell	10.00
56	John Barrow	15.00
57	Bernie Faloney	30.00
58	Ron Ray	7.50
59	Don Sutherin	15.00
60	Frank Cosentino	10.00
61	Hardiman Cureton	7.50
62	Hal Patterson	20.00
63	Ralph Goldston	7.50
64	Tommy Grant	15.00
65	Larry Hickman	7.50
66	Zeno Karcz	10.00
67	Garney Henley	20.00
68	Gerry McDougall	10.00
69	Vince Scott	12.00
70	Gerry James	15.00
71	Roger Hagberg	10.00
72	Gord Rowland	10.00
73	Ernie Pitts	7.50
74	Frank Rigney	12.00
75	Norm Rauhaus	12.00
76	Leo Lewis	20.00
77	Mike Wright	7.50
78	Jack Delveaux	7.50
79	Steve Patrick	7.50
80	Dave Burkholder	7.50
81	Charlie Shepard	7.50
82	Kenny Ploen	20.00
83	Ronnie Latourelle	7.50
84	Herb Gray	15.00
85	Hal Ledyard	7.50
86	Cornel Piper (SP)	50.00
87	Farrell Funston	7.50
88	Ray Smith	7.50
89	Clair Branch	7.50
90	Fred Burket	7.50
91	Dave Grosz	7.50
92	Bob Golic	10.00
93	Billy Gray	7.50
94	Neil Habig	7.50
95	Reg Whitehouse	7.50
96	Jack Gotta	10.00
97	Bob Ptacek	10.00
98	Jerry Keeling	15.00
99	Ernie Danjean	7.50
100	Don Luzzi	12.00
101	Wayne Harris	20.00
102	Tony Pajaczkowski	15.00
103	Earl Lunsford	12.00
104	Ernie Warlick	12.00
105	Gene Filipski	12.00
106	Eagle Day	15.00
107	Bill Crawford	7.50
108	Oscar Kruger	7.50
109	Gino Fracas	10.00
110	Don Stephenson	7.50
111	Jim Letcavits	7.50
112	Howie Schumm	7.50
113	Jackie Parker	45.00
114	Rollie Miles	15.00
115	Johnny Bright	20.00
116	Don Getty	15.00
117	Bobby Walden	10.00
118	Roger Nelson	15.00
119	Al Ecuyer	7.50
120	Ed Gray	7.50
121	Vic Chapman (SP)	50.00
122	Earl Keeley	7.50
123	Sonny Homer	7.50
124	Bob Jetter	20.00
125	Jim Carphin	7.50
126	By Bailey	15.00
127	Norm Fieldgate	15.00
128	Vic Kristopaitis	7.50
129	Willie Fleming	20.00
130	Don Vicic	7.50
131	Tom Brown (SP)	50.00
132	Tom Hinton (SP)	50.00
133	Pat Claridge	7.50
134	Bill Britton	7.50
135	Neal Beaumont	10.00
136	Nub Beamer (SP)	50.00
137	Joe Kapp	60.00
NNO	Post Album	75.00

1963 Post Cereal CFL

		NM/M
Complete Set (160):		900.00
Common Player:		5.00
1	Larry Hickman	7.50
2	Dick Schnell	5.00
3	Don Clark	7.50
4	Ted Page	5.00
5	Milt Crain	7.50
6	George Dixon	10.00
7	Ed Nickla	5.00
8	Barrie Hansen	5.00
9	Ed Learn	5.00
10	Billy Ray Locklin	5.00
11	Bobby Jack Oliver	7.50
12	Don Paquette	5.00
13	Sandy Stephens	12.00
14	Billy Wayte	5.00
15	Jim Reynolds	5.00
16	Ross Buckle	5.00
17	Bob Geary	5.00
18	Bobby Lee Thompson	5.00
19	Mike Snodgrass	5.00
20	Billy Joe Booth	7.50
21	Jim Cain	5.00
22	Kaye Vaughan	10.00
23	Doug Daigneault	5.00
24	Millard Flemming	5.00
25	Russ Jackson	25.00
26	Joe Poirier	7.50
27	Moe Racine	5.00
28	Norb Roy	5.00
29	Ted Smale	5.00
30	Ernie White	5.00
31	Whit Tucker	10.00
32	Dave Thelen	10.00
33	Len Chandler	5.00
34	Jim Conroy	7.50
35	Jerry Selinger	5.00
36	Ron Stewart	12.00
37	Jim Andreotti	7.50
38	Jackie Parker	25.00
39	Lynn Bottoms	7.50
40	Gerry Patrick	5.00
41	Gerry Philip	5.00
42	Art Johnson	5.00
43	Aubrey Linne	5.00
44	Dave Mann	7.50
45	Marty Martinello	5.00
46	Doug McNichol	5.00
47	Ron Morris	5.00
48	Walt Radzick	5.00
49	Jim Rountree	5.00
50	Dick Shatto	10.00
51	Billy Shipp	5.00
52	Norm Stoneburgh	5.00
53	Gerry Wilson	5.00
54	Danny Nykoluk	5.00
55	John Barrow	10.00
56	Frank Cosentino	7.50
57	Hardiman Cureton	7.50
58	Bobby Kuntz	7.50
59	Bernie Faloney	20.00
60	Garney Henley	12.00
61	Zeno Karcz	7.50
62	Dick Easterly	5.00
63	Bronko Nagurski	12.00
64	Hal Patterson	15.00
65	Ron Ray	5.00
66	Don Sutherin	8.00
67	Dave Viti	5.00
68	Joe Zuger	7.50
69	Angelo Mosca	20.00
70	Ralph Goldston	5.00
71	Tommy Grant	10.00
72	Geno DeNobile	5.00
73	Dave Burkholder	5.00
74	Jack Delveaux	5.00
75	Farrell Funston	5.00
76	Herb Gray	10.00
77	Roger Hagberg	7.50
78	Henry Janzen	7.50
79	Ronnie Latourelle	5.00
80	Leo Lewis	10.00
81	Cornel Piper	5.00
82	Ernie Pitts	5.00
83	Kenny Ploen	10.00
84	Norm Rauhaus	7.50
85	Charlie Shepard	5.00
86	Gar Warren	5.00
87	Dick Thornton	7.50
88	Hal Ledyard	5.00
89	Frank Rigney	7.50
90	Gord Rowland	7.50
91	Don Walsh	5.00
92	Bill Burrell	5.00
93	Ron Atchison	9.00
94	Billy Gray	5.00
95	Neil Habig	5.00
96	Bob Ptacek	7.50
97	Ray Purdin	5.00
98	Ted Urness	8.00
99	Dale West	7.50
100	Reg Whitehouse	5.00
101	Clair Branch	5.00
102	Bill Clarke	5.00
103	Garner Ekstran	7.50
104	Jack Gotta	7.50
105	Len Legault	5.00
106	Larry Dumelie	5.00
107	Bill Britton	5.00
108	Ed Buchanan	5.00
109	Lovell Coleman	7.50
110	Bill Crawford	5.00
111	Ernie Danjean	5.00
112	Eagle Day	9.00
113	Jim Furlong	5.00
114	Wayne Harris	15.00
115	Roy Jakanovich	5.00
116	Phil Lohmann	5.00
117	Earl Lunsford	8.00
118	Don Luzzi	8.00
119	Tony Pajaczkowski	8.00
120	Pete Manning	7.50
121	Harvey Wylie	8.00
122	George Hansen	5.00
123	Pat Holmes	5.00
124	Larry Robinson	7.50
125	Johnny Bright	15.00
126	Jon Rechner	5.00
127	Al Ecuyer	5.00
128	Don Getty	12.00
129	Ed Gray	5.00
130	Oscar Kruger	5.00
131	Jim Letcavits	5.00
132	Mike Lashuk	7.50
133	Don Duncalfe	5.00
134	Bobby Walden	7.50
135	Tommy Joe Coffey	12.00
136	Nat Dye	5.00
137	Roy Stevenson	5.00
138	Howie Schumm	5.00
139	Roger Nelson	8.00
140	Larry Fleisher	7.50
141	Dunc Harvey	5.00
142	James Earl Wright	7.50
143	By Bailey	8.00
144	Nub Beamer	5.00
145	Neal Beaumont	7.50
146	Tom Brown	8.00
147	Pat Claridge	5.00
148	Lonnie Dennis	7.50
149	Norm Fieldgate	8.00
150	Willie Fleming	12.00
151	Dick Fouts	7.50
152	Tom Hinton	8.00
153	Sonny Homer	7.50
154	Joe Kapp	30.00
155	Tom Larscheid	5.00
156	Mike Martin	5.00
157	Mel Mein	5.00
158	Mike Cacic	5.00
159	Walt Bilicki	5.00
160	Earl Keeley	7.50
NNO	Post Album	75.00

1956 Shredded Wheat CFL

		NM/M
Complete Set (105):		9,000
Common Player:		80.00
A1	Peter Muir	80.00
A2	Harry Langford	80.00
A3	Tony Pajaczkowski	150.00
A4	Bob Morgan	80.00
A5	Baz Nagle	80.00
A6	Alex Macklin	80.00
A7	Bob Geary	80.00
A8	Don Klosterman	125.00
A9	Bill McKenna	80.00
A10	Bill Stevenson	80.00
A11	Charles Baillie	80.00
A12	Berdett Hess	80.00
A13	Lynn Bottoms	90.00
A14	Doug Brown	80.00
A15	Jack Hennemier	80.00
B1	Frank Anderson	80.00
B2	Don Barry	80.00
B3	Johnny Bright	200.00
B4	Kurt Burris	80.00
B5	Bob Dean	80.00
B6	Don Getty	150.00
B7	Normie Kwong	200.00
B8	Earl Lindley	80.00
B9	Art Walker	100.00
B10	Rollie Miles	125.00
B11	Frank Morris	125.00
B12	Jackie Parker	300.00
B13	Ted Tully	80.00
B14	Frank Ivy	90.00
B15	Bill Rowekamp	80.00
C1	Al Sherman	80.00
C2	Larry Cabrelli	80.00
C3	Ron Kelly	80.00
C4	Edward Kotowich	80.00
C5	Buddy Leake	100.00
C6	Thomas Lumsden	80.00
C7	Bill Smitiuk	80.00
C8	Buddy Tinsley	125.00
C9	Ron Vaccher	80.00
C10	Eagle Day	125.00
C11	Buddy Allison	80.00
C12	Bob Haas	90.00
C13	Steve Patrick	80.00
C14	Keith Pearce (UER) (Misspelled Pierce on front)	80.00
C15	Lorne Benson	80.00
D1	George Arnett	80.00
D2	Eddie Bevan	80.00
D3	Art Darch	80.00
D4	John Fedosoff	80.00
D5	Cam Fraser	80.00
D6	Ron Howell	90.00
D7	Alex Muzyka	80.00
D8	Chet Miksza	80.00
D9	Walt Nikorak	80.00
D10	Pete Neumann	125.00
D11	Steve Oneschuk	80.00
D12	Vince Scott	125.00
D13	Ralph Toohy	80.00
D14	Ray Truant	80.00
D15	Nobby Wirkowski	100.00
E1	Pete Bennett	80.00
E2	Fred Black	80.00
E3	Jim Copeland	80.00
E4	Al Pfeifer	90.00
E5	Ron Albright	80.00
E6	Tom Dublinski	80.00
E7	Billy Shipp	80.00
E8	Baz Mackie	80.00
E9	Bill McFarlane	80.00

E10 John Sopinka 100.00
E11 Dick Brown 80.00
E12 Gerry Doucette 80.00
E13 Dan Shaw 80.00
E14 Dick Shatto 175.00
E15 Bill Swiacki 100.00
F1 Ray Syrnyk 80.00
F2 Martin Ruby 125.00
F3 Bobby Marlow 125.00
F4 Doug Kiloh 80.00
F5 Gord Sturtridge 90.00
F6 Stan Williams 80.00
F7 Larry Isbell 80.00
F8 Ken Casner 80.00
F9 Mel Becket 100.00
F10 Reg Whitehouse 80.00
F11 Harry Lampman 80.00
F12 Mario DeMarco 90.00
F13 Ken Carpenter 100.00
F14 Frank Filchock 100.00
F15 Frank Tripucka 125.00
G1 Tom Tracy 150.00
G2 Pete Ladygo 80.00
G3 Sam Scoccia 80.00
G4 Joe Upton 80.00
G5 Bob Simpson 150.00
G6 Bruno Bitkowski 90.00
G7 Joe Stracini (UER) (Misspelled Straccini on card front) 80.00
G8 Hal Ledyard 80.00
G9 Milt Graham 80.00
G10 Bill Sowalski 80.00
G11 Avatus Stone 80.00
G12 John Boich 100.00
G13 Don Pinhey (UER) (Misspelled Bob Pinkney on card front) 80.00
G14 Peter Karpuk 80.00
G15 Frank Clair 125.00

1994 Smokey Sacramento

NM/M
Complete Set (18): 30.00
Common Player: 1.25
1 Fred Anderson (GEO) 1.25
2 David Archer 5.00
3 George Bethune 1.25
4 David Diaz-Infante 1.25
5 Willie Fears 1.25
6 Corian Freeman 1.25
7 Pete Gardere 1.50
8 Tom Gerhart 1.25
9 Rod Harris 1.25
10 Bobby Humphery 2.50
11 Mike Kiselak 1.25
12 Mark Ledbetter 1.25
13 Maurice Miller 1.25
14 Troy Mills 1.25
15 Mike Oliphant 2.50
16 James Pruitt 1.25
17 Junior Robinson 1.25
18 Kay Stephenson (CO) 1.25

1993 Sport Chek Calgary Stampeders

NM/M
Complete Set (24): 15.00
Common Player: .60
1 Karl Anthony .60
2 Raymond Biggs .60
3 Douglas Craft .60
4 Doug Davies .60
5 Mark Dube .60
6 Matt Finlay .60
7 Doug Flutie 4.00
8 Fred Gatlin .60
9 Keyvan Jenkins 1.00
10 Alondra Johnson .60
11 Pat Mahon .60
12 Tony Martino .60
13 Mark McLoughlin .60
14 Andy McVey .60
15 Will Moore 2.50
16 Mark Pearce .60
17 Allen Pitts 1.25
18 David Sapunjis 1.25
19 Junior Thurman 1.25
20 Gerald Vaughn .60
21 Ken Watson .60
22 Brian Wiggins 1.00
23 Blair Zerr .60
24 Srecko Zizakovic 1.00

1958 Topps CFL

NM/M
Complete Set (88): 500.00
Common Player: 5.00
1 Paul Anderson 12.00
2 Leigh McMillan 5.00
3 Vic Chapman 5.00
4 Bobby Marlow 12.00
5 Mike Cacic 5.00
6 Ron Pawlowski 5.00
7 Frank Morris 9.00
8 Earl Keeley 6.00
9 Don Walsh 5.00
10 Bryan Engram 5.00
11 Bobby Kuntz 6.00
12 Jerry Janes 5.00
13 Don Bingham 5.00
14 Paul Fedor 5.00
15 Tommy Grant 12.00
16 Don Getty 20.00
17 George Brancato 6.00
18 Jackie Parker 40.00
19 Alan Valdes 5.00
20 Paul Dekker 5.00
21 Frank Tripucka 12.00
22 Gerry McDougall 9.00
23 Duke Dewveall 6.00
24 Ted Smale 5.00
25 Tony Pajaczkowski 12.00
26 Don Pinhey 5.00
27 Buddy Tinsley 12.00
28 Cookie Gilchrist 35.00
29 Larry Isbell 5.00
30 Bob Kelley 5.00
31 Tom "Corky" Tharp 6.00
32 Steve Patrick 5.00
33 Hardiman Cureton 5.00
34 Joe Mobra 5.00
35 Harry Lunn 5.00
36 Gord Rowland 6.00
37 Herb Gray 15.00
38 Bob Simpson 15.00
39 Cam Fraser 5.00
40 Kenny Ploen 18.00
41 Lynn Bottoms 6.00
42 Bill Stevenson 5.00
43 Jerry Selinger 5.00
44 Oscar Kruger 9.00
45 Gerry James 15.00
46 Dave Mann 12.00
47 Tom Dimitroff 5.00
48 Vince Scott 12.00
49 Fran Rogel 6.00
50 Henry Hair 5.00
51 Bob Brady 5.00
52 Gerry Doucette 5.00
53 Ken Carpenter 6.00
54 Bernie Faloney 25.00
55 John Barrow 20.00
56 George Druxman 5.00
57 Rollie Miles 12.00
58 Jerry Cornelison 5.00
59 Harry Langford 5.00
60 Johnny Bright 20.00
61 Ron Clinkscale 5.00
62 Jack Hill 5.00
63 Ron Quillian 5.00
64 Ted Tully 5.00
65 Pete Neft 5.00
66 Arvyd Buntins 5.00
67 Normie Kwong 20.00
68 Matt Phillips 5.00
69 Pete Bennett 5.00
70 Vern Lofstrom 5.00
71 Norm Stoneburgh 5.00
72 Danny Nykoluk 5.00
73 Chuck Dubuque 5.00
74 John Varone 5.00
75 Bob Kimoff 5.00
76 John Pyeatt 5.00
77 Pete Neumann 12.00
78 Ernie Pitts 9.00
79 Steve Oneschuk 5.00
80 Kaye Vaughan 12.00
81 Joe Yamauchi 5.00
82 Harvey Wylie 9.00
83 Berdett Hess 5.00
84 Dick Shatto 20.00
85 Floyd Harrawood 5.00
86 Ron Atchison 12.00
87 Bobby Judd 5.00
88 Keith Pearce 9.00

1959 Topps CFL

NM/M
Complete Set (88): 400.00
Common Player: 4.00
1 Norm Rauhaus 10.00
2 Cornel Piper (UER) (Misspelled Cornell on both sides) 4.00
3 Leo Lewis 20.00
4 Roger Savoie 4.00
5 Jim Van Pelt 10.00
6 Herb Gray 10.00
7 Gerry James 10.00
8 By Bailey 12.00
9 Tom Hinton 8.00
10 Chuck Quilter 4.00
11 Mel Gillett 4.00
12 Ted Hunt 4.00
13 Sonny Homer 5.00
14 Bill Jessup 4.00
15 Al Dorow (Checklist 1-44 back) 20.00
16 Norm Fieldgate 12.00
17 Urban Henry 5.00
18 Paul Cameron 4.00
19 Bruce Claridge 4.00
20 Jim Bakhtiar 4.00
21 Earl Lunsford 12.00
22 Walt Radzick 4.00
23 Ron Albright 4.00
24 Art Scullion 4.00
25 Ernie Warlick 6.00
26 Nobby Wirkowski 5.00
27 Harvey Wylie 9.00
28 Gordon Brown 4.00
29 Don Luzzi 10.00
30 Hal Patterson 20.00
31 Jackie Simpson 15.00
32 Doug McNichol 4.00
33 Bob MacLellan 4.00
34 Ted Elsby 4.00
35 Mike Kovac 4.00
36 Bob Leary 4.00
37 Hal Krebs 4.00
38 Steve Jennings 4.00
39 Don Getty 12.00
40 Normie Kwong 12.00
41 Johnny Bright 15.00
42 Art Walker 5.00
43 Jackie Parker (UER) (Incorrectly listed as Tackle on card front) 35.00
44 Don Barry (Checklist 45-88 back) 20.00
45 Tommy Joe Coffey 25.00
46 Mike Volcan 4.00
47 Stan Renning 4.00
48 Gino Fracas 9.00
49 Ted Smale 4.00
50 Mack Yoho 5.00
51 Bobby Gravens 4.00
52 Milt Graham 4.00
53 Lou Bruce 4.00
54 Bob Simpson 12.00
55 Bill Sowalski 4.00
56 Russ Jackson 40.00
57 Don Clark 4.00
58 Dave Thelen 10.00
59 Larry Cowart 4.00
60 Dave Mann 5.00
61 Norm Stoneburgh (UER) (Misspelled Stoneburg) 4.00
62 Ronnie Knox 9.00
63 Dick Shatto 12.00
64 Bobby Kuntz 5.00
65 Phil Muntz 4.00
66 Gerry Doucette 4.00
67 Sam DeLuca 5.00
68 Boyd Carter 4.00
69 Vic Kristopaitis 9.00
70 Gerry McDougall (UER) (Misspelled Jerry) 5.00
71 Vince Scott 10.00
72 Angelo Mosca 35.00
73 Chet Miksza 4.00
74 Eddie Macon 5.00
75 Harry Lampman 4.00
76 Bill Graham 4.00
77 Ralph Goldston 5.00
78 Cam Fraser 4.00
79 Ron Dundas 4.00
80 Bill Clarke 4.00
81 Len Legault 4.00
82 Reg Whitehouse 4.00
83 Dale Parsons 4.00
84 Doug Kiloh 4.00
85 Tom Whitehouse 4.00
86 Mike Hagler 4.00
87 Paul Anderson 4.00
88 Danny Banda 5.00

1960 Topps CFL

NM/M
Complete Set (88): 500.00
Common Player: 4.00
1 By Bailey 12.00
2 Paul Cameron 4.00
3 Bruce Claridge 4.00
4 Chuck Dubuque 4.00
5 Randy Duncan 12.00
6 Norm Fieldgate 10.00
7 Urban Henry 5.00
8 Ted Hunt 4.00
9 Bill Jessup 4.00
10 Ted Tully 4.00
11 Vic Chapman 4.00
12 Gino Fracas 5.00
13 Don Getty 10.00
14 Ed Gray 4.00
15 Oscar Kruger (Checklist 1-44 back) 20.00
16 Rollie Miles 10.00
17 Jackie Parker 30.00
18 Joe-Bob Smith (UER) (Misspelled Bob-Joe on both sides) 4.00
19 Mike Volcan 4.00
20 Art Walker 5.00
21 Ron Albright 4.00
22 Jim Bakhtiar 4.00
23 Lynn Bottoms 5.00
24 Jack Gotta 8.00
25 Joe Kapp 50.00
26 Earl Lunsford 9.00
27 Don Luzzi 9.00
28 Art Scullion 4.00
29 Hugh Simpson 9.00
30 Ernie Warlick 8.00
31 John Barrow 12.00
32 Paul Dekker 4.00
33 Bernie Faloney 20.00
34 Cam Fraser 4.00
35 Ralph Goldston 5.00
36 Ron Howell 5.00
37 Gerry McDougall (UER) (Misspelled Jerry) 4.00
38 Angelo Mosca 20.00
39 Pete Neumann 8.00
40 Vince Scott 8.00
41 Ted Elsby 4.00
42 Sam Etcheverry 25.00
43 Mike Kovac 4.00
44 Ed Learn 4.00
45 Ivan Livingstone (Checklist 45-88 back) 20.00
46 Hal Patterson 18.00
47 Jackie Simpson 12.00
48 Veryl Switzer 4.00
49 Bill Bewley 9.00
50 Joel Wells 4.00
51 Ron Atchison 9.00
52 Ken Carpenter 5.00
53 Bill Clarke 4.00
54 Ron Dundas 4.00
55 Mike Hagler 4.00
56 Jack Hill 4.00
57 Doug Kiloh 4.00
58 Bobby Marlow 10.00
59 Bob Mulgado 4.00
60 George Brancato 5.00
61 Lou Bruce 4.00
62 Hardiman Cureton 4.00
63 Russ Jackson 25.00
64 Gerry Nesbitt 4.00
65 Bob Simpson 10.00
66 Ted Smale 4.00
67 Dave Thelen 9.00
68 Kaye Vaughan 8.00
69 Pete Bennett 4.00
70 Boyd Carter 4.00
71 Gerry Doucette 4.00
72 Bobby Kuntz 5.00
73 Alex Panton 4.00
74 Tobin Rote 18.00
75 Jim Rountree 5.00
76 Dick Shatto 10.00
77 Norm Stoneburgh 4.00
78 Tom "Corky" Tharp 5.00
79 George Druxman 4.00
80 Herb Gray 10.00
81 Gerry James 10.00
82 Leo Lewis 10.00
83 Ernie Pitts 4.00
84 Kenny Ploen 15.00
85 Norm Rauhaus 4.00
86 Gord Rowland 4.00
87 Charlie Shepard 5.00
88 Don Clark 10.00

1961 Topps CFL

NM/M
Complete Set (132): 900.00
Common Player: 6.00
1 By Bailey 15.00
2 Bruce Claridge 6.00
3 Norm Fieldgate 12.00
4 Willie Fleming 20.00
5 Urban Henry 7.50
6 Bill Herron 6.00
7 Tom Hinton 10.00
8 Sonny Homer 7.50
9 Bob Jeter 15.00
10 Vic Kristopaitis 6.00
11 Baz Nagle 6.00
12 Ron Watton 6.00
13 Joe Yamauchi 6.00
14 Bob Schloredt 15.00
15 B.C. Lions Team 12.00
16 Ron Albright 6.00
17 Gordon Brown 6.00
18 Gerry Doucette 6.00
19 Gene Filipski 12.00
20 Joe Kapp 30.00
21 Earl Lunsford 12.00
22 Don Luzzi 12.00
23 Bill McKenna 6.00
24 Ron Morris 6.00
25 Tony Pajaczkowski 12.00
26 Lorne Reid 6.00
27 Art Scullion 6.00
28 Ernie Warlick 10.00
29 Stampeders Team 12.00
30 Johnny Bright 15.00
31 Vic Chapman 6.00
32 Gino Fracas 7.50
33 Tommy Joe Coffey 18.00
34 Don Getty 15.00
35 Ed Gray 6.00
36 Oscar Kruger 7.50
37 Rollie Miles 12.00
38 Roger Nelson 12.00
39 Jackie Parker 35.00
40 Howie Schumm 6.00
41 Joe-Bob Smith (UER) (Misspelled Bob-Joe on both sides) 6.00
42 Art Walker 7.50
43 Eskimos Team 12.00
44 John Barrow 15.00
45 Paul Dekker 6.00
46 Tom Dublinski 6.00
47 Bernie Faloney 25.00
48 Cam Fraser 6.00
49 Ralph Goldston 7.50
50 Ron Howell 7.50
51 Gerry McDougall 7.50
52 Pete Neumann 12.00
53 Bronko Nagurski 15.00
54 Vince Scott 10.00
55 Steve Oneschuk 7.50
56 Hal Patterson 20.00
57 Jim Taylor 7.50
58 Tiger-Cats Team 12.00
59 Ted Elsby 6.00
60 Don Clark 7.50
61 Dick Cohee 10.00
62 George Dixon 20.00
63 Wes Gideon 6.00
64 Harry Lampman 6.00
65 Meco Poliziani 6.00
66 Charles Baillie 6.00
67 Howard Cissell 6.00
68 Ed Learn 6.00
69 Tom Moran 6.00
70 Jack Simpson 12.00
71 Bill Bewley 7.50
72 Tom Hugo 6.00
73 Alouettes Team 15.00
74 Gilles Archambeault 6.00
75 Lou Bruce 6.00
76 Russ Jackson 30.00
77 Tom Jones 6.00
78 Gerry Nesbitt 6.00
79 Ron Lancaster 40.00
80 Joe Kelly 6.00
81 Joe Poirier 7.50
82 Doug Daigneault 6.00
83 Kaye Vaughan 10.00
84 Dave Thelen 15.00
85 Ron Stewart 25.00
86 Ted Smale 6.00
87 Bob Simpson 15.00
88 Ottawa Rough Riders Team 12.00
89 Don Allard 6.00
90 Ron Atchison 12.00
91 Bill Clarke 6.00
92 Ron Dundas 6.00
93 Jack Gotta 10.00
94 Bob Golic 7.50
95 Jack Hill 6.00
96 Doug Kiloh 7.50
97 Len Legault 6.00
98 Doug McKenzie 6.00
99 Bob Ptacek 6.00
100 Roy Smith 6.00
101 Saskatchewan Roughriders Team 12.00
102 Checklist 1-132 90.00
103 Jim Andreotti 7.50
104 Boyd Carter 6.00
105 Dick Fouts 7.50
106 Cookie Gilchrist 25.00
107 Bobby Kuntz 7.50
108 Jim Rountree 7.50
109 Dick Shatto 15.00
110 Norm Stoneburgh 6.00
111 Dave Mann 10.00
112 Ed Ochiena 6.00
113 Bill Stribling 6.00
114 Tobin Rote 20.00
115 Stan Wallace 6.00
116 Billy Shipp 7.50
117 Argonauts Team 15.00
118 Dave Burkholder 6.00
119 Jack Delveaux 6.00
120 George Druxman 6.00
121 Farrell Funston 7.50
122 Herb Gray 12.00
123 Gerry James 12.00
124 Ronnie Latourelle 6.00
125 Leo Lewis 15.00
126 Steve Patrick 6.00
127 Ernie Pitts 6.00
128 Kenny Ploen 15.00
129 Norm Rauhaus 7.50
130 Gord Rowland 7.50
131 Charlie Shepard 7.50
132 Winnipeg Blue Bombers Team Card 20.00

1961 Topps CFL Transfers

NM/M
Complete Set (24): 700.00
Common Player (1-15): 25.00
Common Team (19-27): 20.00
1 Don Clark 30.00
2 Gene Filipski 30.00
3 Willie Fleming 40.00
4 Cookie Gilchrist 45.00
5 Jack Hill 25.00
6 Bob Jeter 30.00
7 Joe Kapp 65.00
8 Leo Lewis 40.00
9 Gerry McDougall 25.00
10 Jackie Parker 50.00
11 Hal Patterson 40.00
12 Kenny Ploen 40.00
13 Bob Ptacek 25.00
14 Ron Stewart 40.00
15 Dave Thelen 40.00
16 British Columbia Lions Logo/Pennant 20.00
20 Calgary Stampeders Logo/Pennant 20.00
21 Edmonton Eskimos Logo/Pennant 20.00
22 Hamilton Tiger-Cats Logo/Pennant 20.00
23 Montreal Alouettes Logo/Pennant 20.00
24 Ottawa Rough Riders Logo/Pennant 20.00
25 Saskatchewan Roughriders Logo/Pennant 20.00
26 Toronto Argonauts Logo/Pennant 20.00
27 Winnipeg Blue Bombers Logo/Pennant 20.00

1962 Topps CFL

NM/M
Complete Set (169): 500.00
Common Player: 2.00
1 By Bailey 6.00
2 Nub Beamer 2.00
3 Tom Brown 8.00
4 Mack Burton 2.00
5 Mike Cacic 2.00
6 Pat Claridge 2.00
7 Steve Cotter 2.00
8 Lonnie Dennis 2.00
9 Norm Fieldgate 5.00
10 Willie Fleming 10.00
11 Tom Hinton 4.00
12 Sonny Homer 3.00
13 Joe Kapp 14.00
14 Tom Larscheid 2.00
15 Gordie Mitchell 2.00
16 Baz Nagle 2.00
17 Norris Stevenson 2.00
18 Barney Therrien (UER) (Misspelled Therien on card front) 2.00
19 Don Vicic 2.00
20 B.C. Lions Team 8.00
21 Ed Buchanan 2.00
22 Joe Carruthers 2.00
23 Lovell Coleman 4.00
24 Barrie Cyr 2.00
25 Ernie Danjean 3.00
26 Gene Filipski 4.00
27 George Hansen 2.00
28 Earl Lunsford 5.00
29 Don Luzzi 4.00
30 Bill McKenna 2.00
31 Tony Pajaczkowski 4.00
32 Chuck Quilter 2.00
33 Lorne Reid 2.00
34 Art Scullion 2.00
35 Jim Walden 2.00
36 Harvey Wylie 4.00
37 Calgary Stampeders Team Card 8.00
38 Johnny Bright 10.00
39 Vic Chapman 2.00
40 Marion Drew Deese 2.00
41 Al Ecuyer 2.00
42 Gino Fracas 3.00
43 Don Getty 6.00
44 Ed Gray 2.00
45 Urban Henry 3.00
46 Bill Hill 2.00
47 Mike Kmeche 2.00
48 Oscar Kruger 3.00
49 Mike Lashuk 2.00
50 Jim Letcavits 2.00
51 Roger Nelson 4.00
52 Jackie Parker 15.00
53 Howie Schumm 2.00
54 Jim Shipka 2.00
55 Bill Smith 2.00
56 Jo Bob Smith 2.00
57 Art Walker 3.00
58 Edmonton Eskimos Team Card 8.00
59 John Barrow 8.00
60 Hardiman Cureton 2.00
61 Geno DeNobile 2.00
62 Tom Dublinski 2.00
63 Bernie Faloney 12.00
64 Cam Fraser 2.00
65 Ralph Goldston 3.00
66 Tommy Grant 7.00
67 Garney Henley 15.00
68 Ron Howell 3.00
69 Zeno Karcz 3.00
70 Gerry McDougall (UER) (Misspelled Jerry) 3.00
71 Chet Miksza 2.00
72 Bronko Nagurski 6.00
73 Hal Patterson 10.00
74 George Scott 2.00
75 Vince Scott 4.00
76 Hamilton Tiger-Cats Team Card 8.00
77 Ron Brewer 3.00
78 Ron Brooks 2.00
79 Howard Cissell 2.00
80 Don Clark 3.00
81 Dick Cohee 3.00
82 John Conroy 2.00
83 Milt Crain 3.00
84 Ted Elsby 2.00
85 Joe Francis 3.00
86 Gene Gaines 8.00
87 Barrie Hansen 2.00
88 Mike Kovac 2.00
89 Ed Learn 2.00
90 Billy Ray Locklin 2.00
91 Marv Luster 6.00
92 Bobby Jack Oliver 3.00
93 Sandy Stephens 8.00
94 Montreal Alouettes Team Card 10.00
95 Gilles Archambeault 2.00
96 Bruno Bitkowski 3.00
97 Jim Conroy 3.00
98 Doug Daigneault 2.00
99 Dick Desmarais 2.00
100 Russ Jackson 15.00
101 Tom Jones 2.00
102 Ron Lancaster 20.00
103 Angelo Mosca 15.00
104 Gerry Nesbitt 2.00
105 Joe Poirier 3.00
106 Moe Racine 2.00
107 Gary Schreider 2.00
108 Bob Simpson 6.00
109 Ted Smale 2.00
110 Ron Stewart 7.00
111 Dave Thelen 6.00
112 Kaye Vaughan 4.00
113 Ottawa Rough Ridgers Team Card 8.00
114 Ron Atchison (UER) (Misspelled Atcheson on card front) 4.00
115 Danny Banda 2.00
116 Al Benecick 2.00
117 Clair Branch 2.00
118 Fred Burket 2.00
119 Bill Clarke 2.00
120 Jim Copeland 2.00
121 Ron Dundas 2.00
122 Bob Golic 3.00
123 Jack Gotta 4.00
124 Dave Grosz 2.00
125 Neil Habig 3.00
126 Jack Hill 2.00
127 Len Legault 2.00
128 Bob Ptacek 2.00
129 Roy Smith 2.00
130 Saskatchewan Roughriders Team Card 8.00
131 Lynn Bottoms 3.00
132 Dick Fouts 3.00
133 Wes Gideon 2.00
134 Cookie Gilchrist 15.00
135 Art Johnson 2.00
136 Bobby Kuntz 3.00
137 Dave Mann 4.00
138 Marty Martinello 2.00
139 Doug McNichol 2.00
140 Bill Mitchell 2.00
141 Danny Nykoluk 2.00
142 Walt Radzick 2.00
143 Tobin Rote 10.00
144 Jim Rountree 3.00
145 Dick Shatto 8.00
146 Billy Shipp 3.00
147 Norm Stoneburgh 2.00
148 Toronto Argonauts Team Card 10.00
149 Dave Burkholder 2.00
150 Jack Delveaux 2.00
151 George Druxman 2.00
152 Farrell Funston 3.00
153 Herb Gray 5.00
154 Roger Hagberg 3.00
155 Gerry James 6.00
156 Henry Janzen 3.00
157 Ronnie Latourelle 2.00
158 Hal Ledyard 2.00
159 Leo Lewis 6.00
160 Steve Patrick 2.00
161 Cornel Piper 2.00
162 Ernie Pitts 2.00
163 Kenny Ploen 8.00
164 Norm Rauhaus 3.00
165 Frank Rigney 6.00
166 Gord Rowland 3.00
167 Roger Savoie 2.00
168 Charlie Shepard 3.00
169 Winnipeg Blue Bombers Team Card 20.00

1963 Topps CFL

NM/M
Complete Set (88): 300.00
Common Player: 2.50
1 Willie Fleming 12.00
2 Dick Fouts 3.50
3 Joe Kapp 15.00
4 Nub Beamer 2.50

5 By Bailey 6.00
6 Tom Walker 2.50
7 Sonny Homer 3.50
8 Tom Hinton 5.00
9 Lonnie Dennis 2.50
10 British Columbia Lions Team Card 7.50
11 Ed Buchanan 2.50
12 Ernie Danjean 2.50
13 Eagle Day 6.00
14 Earl Lunsford 5.00
15 Don Luzzi 5.00
16 Tony Pajaczkowski 5.00
17 Jerry Keeling 15.00
18 Pat Holmes 2.50
19 Wayne Harris 15.00
20 Calgary Stampeders Team Card 7.50
21 Tommy Joe Coffey 7.50
22 Mike Lashuk 2.50
23 Bobby Walden 5.00
24 Don Getty 8.00
25 Len Vella 2.50
26 Ted Frechette 2.50
27 E.A. Sims 2.50
28 Nat Dye 2.50
29 Edmonton Eskimos Team Card 7.50
30 Bernie Faloney 10.00
31 Hal Patterson 8.00
32 John Barrow 6.00
33 Sam Fernandez 2.50
34 Garney Henley 12.00
35 Joe Zuger 5.00
36 Hardiman Cureton 2.50
37 Zeno Karcz 3.50
38 Bobby Kuntz 3.50
39 Hamilton Tiger-Cats Team Card 7.50
40 George Dixon 6.00
41 Don Clark 3.50
42 Marv Luster 6.00
43 Bobby Jack Oliver 3.50
44 Billy Ray Locklin 2.50
45 Sandy Stephens 6.00
46 Milt Crain 3.50
47 Meco Poliziani 2.50
48 Ted Elsby 2.50
49 Montreal Alouettes Team Card 9.00
50 Russ Jackson 15.00
51 Ron Stewart 8.00
52 Dave Thelen 6.00
53 Kaye Vaughan 5.00
54 Joe Poirier 3.50
55 Moe Racine 2.50
56 Whit Tucker 10.00
57 Ernie White 2.50
58 Ottawa Rough Ridgers Team Card 7.50
59 Bob Ptacek 2.50
60 Ray Purdin 2.50
61 Dale West 3.50
62 Neil Habig 2.50
63 Jack Gotta 3.50
64 Billy Gray 2.50
65 Don Walsh 2.50
66 Bill Clarke 2.50
67 Saskatchewan Roughriders Team Card 7.50
68 Jackie Parker 15.00
69 Dave Mann 5.00
70 Dick Shatto 6.00
71 Norm Stoneburgh (UER) (Misspelled Stoneburg front) 2.50
72 Clare Exelby 2.50
73 Art Johnson 2.50
74 Doug McNichol 2.50
75 Danny Nykoluk 2.50
76 Walt Radzick 2.50
77 Toronto Argonauts Team Card 9.00
78 Leo Lewis 6.00
79 Kenny Ploen 7.00
80 Henry Janzen 3.50
81 Charlie Shepard 3.50
82 Roger Hagberg 3.50
83 Herb Gray 6.00
84 Frank Rigney 5.00
85 Jack Delveaux 2.50
86 Ronnie Latourelle 2.50
87 Winnipeg Blue Bombers Team Card 7.50
88 Checklist Card 50.00

1964 Topps CFL

NM/M
Complete Set (88): 300.00
Common Player: 2.50
1 Willie Fleming 12.00
2 Dick Fouts 3.50
3 Joe Kapp 15.00
4 Nub Beamer 2.50
5 Tom Brown 5.00
6 Tom Walker 2.50
7 Sonny Homer 3.50
8 Tom Hinton 5.00
9 Lonnie Dennis 2.50
10 B.C. Lions Team 7.50
11 Lovell Coleman 4.00
12 Ernie Danjean 2.50
13 Eagle Day 5.00
14 Jim Furlong 2.50
15 Don Luzzi 5.00
16 Tony Pajaczkowski 5.00
17 Jerry Keeling 6.00
18 Pat Holmes 2.50
19 Wayne Harris 7.50
20 Calgary Stampeders Team Card 7.50
21 Tommy Joe Coffey 7.50
22 Al Ecuyer 2.50
23 Checklist Card 35.00
24 Don Getty 6.00
25 Len Vella 2.50
26 Ted Frechette 2.50
27 E.A. Sims 2.50
28 Nat Dye 2.50
29 Edmonton Eskimos Team Card 7.50
30 Bernie Faloney 15.00
31 Hal Patterson 8.00
32 John Barrow 6.00
33 Tommy Grant 6.00
34 Garney Henley 9.00
35 Joe Zuger 3.50
36 Hardiman Cureton 2.50
37 Zeno Karcz 3.50
38 Bobby Kuntz 3.50
39 Hamilton Tiger-Cats Team Card 7.50
40 George Dixon 7.50
41 Dave Hoppmann 2.50
42 Dick Walton 2.50
43 Jim Andreotti 3.50
44 Billy Ray Locklin 2.50
45 Fred Burket 2.50
46 Milt Crane 3.50
47 Meco Poliziani 2.50
48 Ted Elsby 2.50
49 Montreal Alouettes Team Card 9.00
50 Russ Jackson 15.00
51 Ron Stewart 8.00
52 Dave Thelen 5.00
53 Kaye Vaughan 5.00
54 Joe Poirier 3.50
55 Moe Racine 2.50
56 Whit Tucker 6.00
57 Ernie White 2.50
58 Ottawa Roughriders Team Card 7.50
59 Bob Ptacek 2.50
60 Ray Purdin 2.50
61 Dale West 3.50
62 Neil Habig 2.50
63 Jack Gotta 3.50
64 Billy Gray 2.50
65 Don Walsh 2.50
66 Bill Clarke 2.50
67 Saskatchewan Roughriders Team Card 7.50
68 Jackie Parker 15.00
69 Dave Mann 4.00
70 Dick Shatto 6.00
71 Norm Stoneburgh 2.50
72 Clare Exelby 2.50
73 Jim Christopherson 2.50
74 Sherman Lewis 6.00
75 Danny Nykoluk 2.50
76 Walt Radzick 2.50
77 Toronto Argonauts Team Card 9.00
78 Leo Lewis 6.00
79 Kenny Ploen 6.00
80 Henry Janzen 3.50
81 Charlie Shepard 3.50
82 Roger Hagberg 3.50
83 Herb Gray 6.00
84 Frank Rigney 5.00
85 Jack Delveaux 2.50
86 Ronnie Latourelle 2.50
87 Winnipeg Blue Bombers Team Card 7.50
88 Checklist Card 50.00

1965 Topps CFL

NM/M
Complete Set (132): 325.00
Common Player: 2.00
1 Neal Beaumont 6.00
2 Tom Brown 6.00
3 Mike Cacic 2.00
4 Pat Claridge 2.00
5 Steve Cotter 2.00
6 Lonnie Dennis 2.00
7 Norm Fieldgate 4.00
8 Willie Fleming 10.00
9 Dick Fouts 3.00
10 Tom Hinton 4.00
11 Sonny Homer 3.00
12 Joe Kapp 12.00
13 Paul Seale 2.00
14 Steve Shafer 2.00
15 Bob Swift 2.00
16 Larry Anderson 2.00
17 Lu Bain 2.00
18 Lovell Coleman 3.00
19 Eagle Day 4.00
20 Jim Furlong 2.00
21 Wayne Harris 6.00
22 Herman Harrison 12.00
23 Jerry Keeling 5.00
24 Hal Krebs 2.00
25 Don Luzzi 4.00
26 Tony Pajaczkowski 4.00
27 Larry Robinson 4.00
28 Bob Taylor 3.00
29 Ted Woods 2.00
30 Jon Anabo 2.00
31 Jim Battle 2.00
32 Charlie Brown 2.00
33 Tommy Joe Coffey 7.50
34 Marcel Deleeuw 2.00
35 Al Ecuyer 2.00
36 Jim Higgins 2.00
37 Oscar Kruger 3.00
38 Barry Mitchelson 2.00
39 Roger Nelson 4.00
40 Bill Redell 2.00
41 E.A. Sims 2.00
42 Jim Stinnette 2.00
43 Jim Thomas 2.00
44 Terry Wilson 2.00
45 Art Baker 2.00
46 John Barrow 6.00
47 Dick Cohee 3.00
48 Frank Cosentino 4.00
49 Johnny Counts 2.00
50 Tommy Grant 5.00
51 Garney Henley (See also number 57) 9.00
52 Zeno Karcz 3.00
53 Ellison Kelly 12.00
54 Bobby Kuntz 3.00
55 Angelo Mosca 12.00
56 Bronko Nagurski 6.00
57 Don Sutherin (UER) (number 51 on back) 12.00
58 Dave Viti 2.00
59 Joe Zuger 3.00
60 Checklist 1-60 25.00
61 Jim Andreotti 3.00
62 Harold Cooley 2.00
63 Nat Craddock 2.00
64 George Dixon 6.00
65 Ted Elsby 2.00
66 Clare Exelby 2.00
67 Bernie Faloney 12.00
68 Al Irwin 2.00
69 Ed Learn 2.00
70 Moe Levesque 2.00
71 Bob Minihane 2.00
72 Jim Reynolds 2.00
73 Billy Roy 2.00
74 Billy Joe Booth 3.00
75 Jim Cain 2.00
76 Larry DeGraw 2.00
77 Don Estes 2.00
78 Gene Gaines 5.00
79 John Kennerson 2.00
80 Roger Kramer 3.00
81 Ken Lehmann 3.00
82 Bob O'Billovich 2.00
83 Joe Poirier 3.00
84 Bill Quinter 2.00
85 Jerry Selinger 2.00
86 Bill Siekierski 2.00
87 Len Sparks 2.00
88 Whit Tucker 4.00
89 Ron Atchison 4.00
90 Ed Buchanan 2.00
91 Hugh Campbell 10.00
92 Henry Dorsch 2.00
93 Garner Ekstran 3.00
94 Martin Fabi 2.00
95 Bob Good 2.00
96 Ron Lancaster 12.00
97 Bob Ptacek 2.00
98 George Reed 25.00
99 Wayne Shaw 2.00
100 Dale West 3.00
101 Reg Whitehouse 2.00
102 Jim Worden 2.00
103 Ron Brewer 3.00
104 Don Fuell 2.00
105 Ed Harrington 3.00
106 George Hughley 2.00
107 Dave Mann 4.00
108 Marty Martinello 2.00
109 Danny Nykoluk 2.00
110 Jackie Parker 15.00
111 Dave Pivec 2.00
112 Walt Radzick 2.00
113 Lee Sampson 2.00
114 Dick Shatto 5.00
115 Norm Stoneburgh 2.00
116 Jim Vollenweider 2.00
117 John Wydareny 3.00
118 Billy Cooper 2.00
119 Farrell Funston 3.00
120 Herb Gray 5.00
121 Henry Janzen 3.00
122 Leo Lewis 6.00
123 Brian Palmer 2.00
124 Cornel Piper 2.00
125 Ernie Pitts 2.00
126 Kenny Ploen 6.00
127 Norm Rauhaus 3.00
128 Frank Rigney 4.00
129 Roger Savoie 2.00
130 Dick Thornton 4.00
131 Bill Whisler 2.00
132 Checklist 61-132 40.00

1965 Topps CFL Transfers

NM/M
Complete Set (27): 500.00
Common Player: 20.00
1 British Columbia Lions Crest 20.00
2 British Columbia Lions Pennant 20.00
3 Calgary Stampeders Crest 20.00
4 Calgary Stampeders Pennant 20.00
5 Edmonton Eskimos Crest 20.00
6 Edmonton Eskimos Pennant 20.00
7 Hamilton Tiger-Cats Crest 20.00
8 Hamilton Tiger-Cats Pennant 20.00
9 Montreal Alouettes Crest 20.00
10 Montreal Alouettes Pennant 20.00
11 Ottawa Rough Riders Crest 20.00
12 Ottawa Rough Riders Pennant 20.00
13 Saskatchewan Roughriders Crest 20.00
14 Saskatchewan Roughriders Pennant 20.00
15 Toronto Argonauts Crest 20.00
16 Toronto Argonauts Pennant 20.00
17 Winnipeg Blue Bombers Crest 20.00
18 Winnipeg Blue Bombers Pennant 20.00
19 Quebec Provincial Crest 20.00
20 Ontario Provincial Crest 20.00
21 Manitoba Provincial Crest 20.00
22 Saskatchewan Provincial Crest 20.00
23 Alberta Provincial Crest 20.00
24 British Columbia Provincial Crest 20.00
25 Northwest Territories Territorial Crest 20.00
26 Yukon Territory Territorial Crest 20.00
27 Canada 30.00

1988 Vachon CFL

NM/M
Complete Set (160): 135.00
Common Player: .75
1 Dave Albright 1.00
2 Roger Aldag 1.00
3 Marv Allemang .75
4 Damon Allen 2.50
5 Gary Allen 1.00
6 Randy Ambrosie .75
7 Mike Anderson .75
8 Kent Austin 4.00
9 Terry Baker 1.00
10 Danny Bass 3.00
11 Nick Bastaja .75
12 Greg Battle 2.50
13 Lyle Bauer .75
14 Jearld Baylis 2.00
15 Ian Beckstead .75
16 Walter Bender 1.50
17 Nick Benjamin 1.00
18 David Black .75
19 Leo Blanchard .75
20 Trevor Bowles .75
21 Ken Braden .75
22 Rod Brown .75
23 Less Browne 1.00
24 Jamie Buis .75
25 Tom Burgess 3.50
26 Bob Cameron 1.00
27 Jan Carinci .75
28 Tony Champion 2.50
29 Jacques Chapdelaine .75
30 Tony Cherry 2.50
31 Lance Chomyc 1.00
32 John Congemi 2.00
33 Rod Connop .75
34 David Conrad .75
35 Grover Covington 2.00
36 Larry Crawford 1.25
37 James Curry 2.00
38 Marco Cyncar 1.00
39 Gabriel DeLaGarza .75
40 Mike Derks .75
41 Blake Dermott 1.00
42 Roy DeWalt (SP) 4.00
43 Todd Dillon 1.25
44 Rocky DiPietro 2.00
45 Kevin Dixon (SP) 2.00
46 Tom Dixon .75
47 Selwyn Drain .75
48 Matt Dunigan 7.50
49 Ray Elgaard 3.00
50 Jerome Erdman .75
51 Randy Fabi .75
52 Gill Fenerty 2.00
53 Denny Ferdinand 1.00
54 Dan Ferrone 1.00
55 Howard Fields .75
56 Matt Finlay .75
57 Rickey Foggie 2.00
58 Delbert Fowler 1.00
59 Ed Gataveckas .75
60 Keith Gooch .75
61 Miles Gorrell .75
62 Mike Gray .75
63 Leo Groenewegen .75
64 Ken Hailey .75
65 Harold Hallman 1.00
66 Tracy Ham 5.00
67 Rodney Harding 2.00
68 Glenn Harper .75
69 J.T. Hay .75
70 Larry Hogue .75
71 Ron Hopkins (SP) 2.00
72 Hank Llesic 2.00
73 Bryan Illerbrun .75
74 Lemont Jeffers .75
75 James Jefferson 2.00
76 Rick Johnson 2.00
77 Chris Johnstone .75
78 Johnnie Jones .75
79 Milson Jones 1.50
80 Stephen Jones 2.00
81 Bobby Jurasin 2.50
82 Jerry Kauric 1.00
83 Dan Kearns .75
84 Trevor Kennerd 2.00
85 Mike Kerrigan 4.00
86 Rick Klassen 2.00
87 Lee Knight .75
88 Kevin Konar 1.00
89 Glenn Kulka 1.25
90 Doug (Tank) Landry 2.00
91 Scott Lecky .75
92 Orville Lee 1.50
93 Marc Lewis 1.00
94 Eddie Lowe .75
95 Lynn Madsen .75
96 Chris Major 3.00
97 Doran Major .75
98 Tony Martino .75
99 Tim McCray 1.25
100 Michael McGruder 1.25
101 Sean McKeown (SP) 4.00
102 Andy McVey .75
103 Stan Mikawos .75
104 James Mills 2.00
105 Larry Mohr .75
106 Bernie Morrison .75
107 James Murphy 2.00
108 Paul Osbaldiston 1.00
109 Anthony Parker 1.50
110 James Parker 2.00
111 Greg Peterson .75
112 Tim Petros 1.25
113 Reggie Pleasant 1.25
114 Willie Pless 2.00
115 Bob Poley .75
116 Tom Porras 1.50
117 Hector Pothier .75
118 Jim Reid 1.50
119 Robert Reid .75
120 Gilbert Renfroe 2.00
121 Tom Richards 1.25
122 Dave Ridgway 2.00
123 Rae Robirtis .75
124 Gerald Roper .75
125 Darryl Sampson .75
126 Jim Sandusky 2.50
127 David Sauve .75
128 Art Schlichter 2.00
129 Ralph Scholz .75
130 Mark Seale 1.00
131 Dan Sellers .75
132 Lance Shields 1.00
133 Ian Sinclair 1.50
134 Mike Siroishka .75
135 Chris Skinner .75
136 Harry Skipper 1.00
137 Darrell Smith 3.00
138 Tom Spoletini .75
139 Steve Stapler 1.00
140 Bill Stevenson .75
141 Gregg Stumon 1.25
142 Glen Suitor .75
143 Emmanuel Tolbert 2.50
144 Perry Tuttle (SP) 4.00
145 Peter VandenBos .75
146 Jake Vaughan .75
147 Chris Walby 1.50
148 Mike Walker 1.50
149 Patrick Wayne .75
150 James West 2.00
151 Brett Williams 1.50
152 David Williams 2.50
153 Henry Williams 8.00
154 Tommy Williams .75
155 Larry Willis 1.00
156 Don Wilson .75
157 Earl Winfield 2.50
158 Rick Worman 2.00
159 Larry Wruck .75
160 Kari Yli-Renko .75

1989 Vachon CFL

NM/M
Complete Set (160): 125.00
Common Player: .75
1 Tony Williams 1.00
2 Sean Foudy .75
3 Tom Schimmer .75
4 Ken Evraire 1.00
5 Gerald Wilcox 1.00
6 Damon Allen 2.00
7 Tony Kimbrough .75
8 Dean Dorsey 1.00
9 Rocco Romano .75
10 Ken Braden .75
11 Kari Yli-Renko .75
12 Darrel Hopper .75
13 Irv Daymond .75
14 Orville Lee 1.00
15 Steve Howlett .75
16 Kyle Hall .75
17 Reggie Ward .75
18 Gerald Alphin 2.00
19 Troy Wilson .75
20 Patrick Wayne .75
21 Harold Hallman 1.25
22 John Congemi 1.50
23 Doran Major .75
24 Hank Llesic 1.50
25 Gilbert Renfroe 2.00
26 Rodney Harding 1.00
27 Todd Wiseman .75
28 Chris Schultz 1.00
29 Carl Brazley 1.00
30 Darrell Smith 2.50
31 Glenn Kulka 1.00
32 Bob Skemp .75
33 Don Moen 1.00
34 Jearld Baylis 2.00
35 Lorenzo Graham .75
36 Lance Chomyc 1.00
37 Warren Hudson .75
38 Gill Fenerty 2.00
39 Paul Masotti 1.00
40 Reggie Pleasant 1.25
41 Scott Flagel .75
42 Mike Kerrigan 2.50
43 Frank Robinson 1.00
44 Jacques Chapdelaine .75
45 Miles Gorrell .75
46 Mike Walker 1.50
47 Jason Riley .75
48 Grover Covington 1.50
49 Ralph Scholz .75
50 Mike Derks .75
51 Derrick McAdoo 1.50
52 Rocky DiPietro 2.00
53 Lance Shields 1.00
54 Dale Sanderson .75
55 Tim Lorenz .75
56 Rod Skillman .75
57 Jed Tommy .75
58 Paul Osbaldiston 1.00
59 Darrell Corbin .75
60 Tony Champion 1.50
61 Romel Andrews .75
62 Bob Cameron 1.00
63 Greg Battle 2.00
64 Rod Hill 1.00
65 Steve Rodehutskors 1.00
66 Trevor Kennerd 1.50
67 Moustafa Ali 1.00
68 Mike Gray .75
69 Bob Molle .75
70 Tim Jessie 1.00
71 Matt Pearce .75
72 Will Lewis .75
73 Sean Salisbury 2.50
74 Chris Walby 1.00
75 Jeff Croonen .75
76 David Black .75
77 Buster Rhymes 2.00
78 James Murphy 1.50
79 Stan Mikawos .75
80 Lee Saltz 2.00
81 Bryan Illerbrun .75
82 Donald Narcisse 3.00
83 Milson Jones 1.00
84 Dave Ridgway 1.50
85 Glen Suitor .75
86 Terry Baker 1.00
87 James Curry 1.50
88 Harry Skipper 1.00
89 Bobby Jurasin 2.00
90 Gary Lewis .75
91 Roger Aldag 1.00
92 Jeff Fairholm 2.00
93 Dave Albright .75
94 Ray Elgaard 2.50
95 Kent Austin 3.50
96 Tom Burgess 3.00
97 Richie Hall .75
98 Eddie Lowe .75
99 Vince Goldsmith 1.00
100 Tim McCray 1.00
101 Leo Blanchard .75
102 Tom Spoletini .75
103 Dan Ferrone 1.00
104 Doug (Tank) Landry 1.50
105 Chris Major 1.50
106 Mike Palumbo .75
107 Terrence Jones 2.00
108 Larry Willis 1.25
109 Kent Warnock .75
110 Tim Petros 1.00
111 Marshall Toner .75
112 Ken Ford .75
113 Ron Hopkins .75
114 Eric Kramer 7.50
115 Stu Laird .75
116 Vernell Quinn .75
117 Lemont Jeffers .75
118 Derrick Taylor .75
119 Jay Christensen 1.00
120 Mitchell Price .75
121 Rod Connop .75
122 Mark Norman .75
123 Andre Francis 1.00
124 Reggie Taylor 1.50
125 Rick Worman 1.00
126 Marco Cyncar 1.00
127 Blake Dermott .75
128 Jerry Kauric 1.00
129 Steve Taylor 2.00
130 Dave Richardson .75
131 John Mandarich 1.00
132 Gregg Stumon 1.00
133 Tracy Ham 4.00
134 Danny Bass 2.50
135 Blake Marshall 1.50
136 Jeff Braswell 1.00
137 Larry Wruck 1.00
138 Warren Jones .75
139 Stephen Jones 1.50
140 Tom Richards 1.00
141 Tony Cherry 1.50
142 Anthony Parker 1.50
143 Gerald Roper .75
144 Lui Passaglia 2.00
145 Mack Moore .75
146 Jamie Taras .75
147 Rickey Foggie 1.50
148 Matt Dunigan 6.00
149 Anthony Drawhorn 1.00
150 Eric Streater 1.25
151 Marcus Thomas .75
152 Wes Cooper .75
153 James Mills 1.00
154 Peter VandenBos .75
155 Ian Sinclair 1.00
156 James Parker 1.50
157 Andrew Murray .75
158 Larry Crawford 1.25
159 Kevin Konar 1.00
160 David Williams 1.50

1959 Wheaties CFL

NM/M
Complete Set (48): 4,000
Common Player: 60.00
1 Ron Adam 60.00
2 Bill Bewley 75.00
3 Lynn Bottoms 75.00
4 Johnny Bright 150.00
5 Ken Carpenter 75.00
6 Tony Curcillo 60.00
7 Sam Etcheverry 250.00
8 Bernie Faloney 200.00
9 Cam Fraser 75.00
10 Don Getty 125.00
11 Jack Gotta 75.00
12 Milt Graham 60.00
13 Jack Hill 60.00
14 Ron Howell 75.00
15 Russ Jackson 200.00
16 Gerry James 125.00
17 Doug Kiloh 60.00
18 Ronnie Knox 75.00
19 Vic Kristopaitis 60.00
20 Oscar Kruger 60.00
21 Bobby Kuntz 75.00
22 Normie Kwong 175.00
23 Leo Lewis 150.00
24 Harry Lunn 60.00
25 Don Luzzi 100.00
26 Dave Mann 75.00
27 Bobby Marlow 90.00
28 Gerry McDougall 75.00
29 Doug McNichol 60.00
30 Rollie Miles 100.00
31 Red O'Quinn 90.00
32 Jackie Parker 250.00
33 Hal Patterson 150.00
34 Don Pinhey 60.00
35 Kenny Ploen 125.00
36 Gord Rowland 75.00
37 Vince Scott 90.00
38 Art Scullion 60.00
39 Dick Shatto 125.00
40 Bob Simpson 125.00
41 Jackie Simpson (UER) (Misspelled Jacki) 100.00
42 Bill Sowalski 60.00
43 Norm Stoneburgh 60.00
44 Buddy Tinsley 90.00
45 Frank Tripucka 100.00
46 Jim Van Pelt 60.00
47 Ernie Warlick 75.00
48 Nobby Wirkowski 100.00